Peterson's®
Graduate Programs in the Humanities, Arts & Social Sciences

2016

About Peterson's®

Peterson's® is excited to be celebrating 50 years of trusted educational publishing. It's a milestone we're quite proud of, as we continue to provide the most accurate, dependable, high-quality education content in the field, providing you with everything you need to succeed. No matter where you are on your academic or professional path, you can rely on Peterson's publications and its online information at **www.petersons.com** for the most up-to-date education exploration data, expert test-prep tools, and the highest quality career success resources—everything you need to achieve your educational goals.

For more information, contact Peterson's, 3 Columbia Circle, Suite 205, Albany, NY 12203-5158; 800-338-3282 Ext. 54229; or find us online at **www.petersons.com.**

ISSN 1093-8443
ISBN: 978-0-7689-3969-9

Printed in the United States of America

10 9 8 7 6 5 4 3 2 1   18 17 16 15

Fiftieth Edition

By producing this book on recycled paper (10% post-consumer waste) 100 trees were saved.

SUSTAINABLE FORESTRY INITIATIVE

Certified Sourcing
www.sfiprogram.org
SFI-00453

CONTENTS

ACADEMIC AND PROFESSIONAL PROGRAMS IN INTERDISCIPLINARY STUDIES

ACADEMIC AND PROFESSIONAL PROGRAMS IN THE SOCIAL SCIENCES

CONTENTS

A Note from the Peterson's Editors

The six volumes of Peterson's *Graduate and Professional Programs*, the only annually updated reference work of its kind, provide wide-ranging information on the graduate and professional programs offered by accredited colleges and universities in the United States, U.S. territories, and Canada and by those institutions outside the United States that are accredited by U.S. accrediting bodies. More than 44,000 individual academic and professional programs at more than 2,300 institutions are listed. Peterson's *Graduate and Professional Programs* have been used for more than fifty years by prospective graduate and professional students, placement counselors, faculty advisers, and all others interested in postbaccalaureate education.

Graduate & Professional Programs: An Overview contains information on institutions as a whole, while the other books in the series are devoted to specific academic and professional fields:

- *Graduate Programs in the Biological/Biomedical Sciences & Health-Related Medical Professions*

- *Graduate Programs in Business, Education, Information Studies, Law & Social Work*

- *Graduate Programs in Engineering & Applied Sciences*

- *Graduate Programs in the Humanities, Arts & Social Sciences*

- *Graduate Programs in the Physical Sciences, Mathematics, Agricultural Sciences, the Environment & Natural Resources*

The books may be used individually or as a set. For example, if you have chosen a field of study but do not know what institution you want to attend or if you have a college or university in mind but have not chosen an academic field of study, it is best to begin with the Overview guide.

Graduate & Professional Programs: An Overview presents several directories to help you identify programs of study that might interest you; you can then research those programs further in the other books in the series by using the Directory of Graduate and Professional Programs by Field, which lists 500 fields and gives the names of those institutions that offer graduate degree programs in each.

For geographical or financial reasons, you may be interested in attending a particular institution and will want to know what it has to offer. You should turn to the Directory of Institutions and Their Offerings, which lists the degree programs available at each institution. As in the Directory of Graduate and Professional Programs by Field, the level of degrees offered is also indicated.

All books in the series include advice on graduate education, including topics such as admissions tests, financial aid, and accreditation. **The Graduate Adviser** includes two essays and information about accreditation. The first essay, "The Admissions Process," discusses general admission requirements, admission tests, factors to consider when selecting a graduate school or program, when and how to apply, and how admission decisions are made. Special information for international students and tips for minority students are also included. The second essay, "Financial Support," is an overview of the broad range of support available at the graduate level. Fellowships, scholarships, and grants; assistantships and internships; federal and private loan programs, as well as Federal Work-Study; and the GI bill are detailed. This essay concludes with advice on applying for need-based financial aid. "Accreditation and Accrediting Agencies" gives information on accreditation and its purpose and lists institutional accrediting agencies first and then specialized accrediting agencies relevant to each volume's specific fields of study.

With information on more than 40,000 graduate programs in more than 500 disciplines, Peterson's *Graduate and Professional Programs* give you all the information you need about the programs that are of interest to you in three formats: **Profiles** (capsule summaries of basic information), **Displays** (information that an institution or program wants to emphasize), and **Close-Ups** (written by administrators, with more expansive information than the **Profiles**, emphasizing different aspects of the programs). By using these various formats of program information, coupled with **Appendixes** and **Indexes** covering directories and subject areas for all six books, you will find that these guides provide the most comprehensive, accurate, and up-to-date graduate study information available.

Peterson's publishes a full line of resources with information you need to guide you through the graduate admissions process. Peterson's publications can be found at college libraries and career centers and your local bookstore or library—or visit us on the Web at www.petersons.com.

Colleges and universities will be pleased to know that Peterson's helped you in your selection. Admissions staff members are more than happy to answer questions, address specific problems, and help in any way they can. The editors at Peterson's wish you great success in your graduate program search!

NOTICE: Certain portions of or information contained in this book have been submitted and paid for by the educational institution identified, and such institutions take full responsibility for the accuracy, timeliness, completeness and functionality of such contents. Such portions or information include (i) each display ad that comprises a half page of information covering a single educational institution or program and (ii) each two-page description or Close-Up of a graduate school or program that appear in the different sections of this guide. The "Close-Ups and Displays" are listed in various sections throughout the book.

THE GRADUATE ADVISER

The Admissions Process

Generalizations about graduate admissions practices are not always helpful because each institution has its own set of guidelines and procedures. Nevertheless, some broad statements can be made about the admissions process that may help you plan your strategy.

Factors Involved in Selecting a Graduate School or Program

Selecting a graduate school and a specific program of study is a complex matter. Quality of the faculty; program and course offerings; the nature, size, and location of the institution; admission requirements; cost; and the availability of financial assistance are among the many factors that affect one's choice of institution. Other considerations are job placement and achievements of the program's graduates and the institution's resources, such as libraries, laboratories, and computer facilities. If you are to make the best possible choice, you need to learn as much as you can about the schools and programs you are considering before you apply.

The following steps may help you narrow your choices.

- Talk to alumni of the programs or institutions you are considering to get their impressions of how well they were prepared for work in their fields of study.
- Remember that graduate school requirements change, so be sure to get the most up-to-date information possible.
- Talk to department faculty members and the graduate adviser at your undergraduate institution. They often have information about programs of study at other institutions.
- Visit the websites of the graduate schools in which you are interested to request a graduate catalog. Contact the department chair in your chosen field of study for additional information about the department and the field.
- Visit as many campuses as possible. Call ahead for an appointment with the graduate adviser in your field of interest and be sure to check out the facilities and talk to students.

General Requirements

Graduate schools and departments have requirements that applicants for admission must meet. Typically, these requirements include undergraduate transcripts (which provide information about undergraduate grade point average and course work applied toward a major), admission test scores, and letters of recommendation. Most graduate programs also ask for an essay or personal statement that describes your personal reasons for seeking graduate study. In some fields, such as art and music, portfolios or auditions may be required in addition to other evidence of talent. Some institutions require that the applicant have an undergraduate degree in the same subject as the intended graduate major.

Most institutions evaluate each applicant on the basis of the applicant's total record, and the weight accorded any given factor varies widely from institution to institution and from program to program.

The Application Process

You should begin the application process at least one year before you expect to begin your graduate study. Find out the application deadline for each institution (many are provided in the **Profile** section of this guide). Go to the institution's website and find out if you can apply online. If not, request a paper application form. Fill out this form thoroughly and neatly. Assume that the school needs all the information it is requesting and that the admissions officer will be sensitive to the neatness and overall quality of what you submit. Do not supply more information than the school requires.

The institution may ask at least one question that will require a three- or four-paragraph answer. Compose your response on the assumption that the admissions officer is interested in both what you think and how you express yourself. Keep your statement brief and to the point, but, at the same time, include all pertinent information about your past experiences and your educational goals. Individual statements vary greatly in style and content, which helps admissions officers differentiate among applicants. Many graduate departments give considerable weight to the statement in making their admissions decisions, so be sure to take the time to prepare a thoughtful and concise statement.

If recommendations are a part of the admissions requirements, carefully choose the individuals you ask to write them. It is generally best to ask current or former professors to write the recommendations, provided they are able to attest to your intellectual ability and motivation for doing the work required of a graduate student. It is advisable to provide stamped, preaddressed envelopes to people being asked to submit recommendations on your behalf.

Completed applications, including references, transcripts, and admission test scores, should be received at the institution by the specified date.

Be advised that institutions do not usually make admissions decisions until all materials have been received. Enclose a self-addressed postcard with your application, requesting confirmation of receipt. Allow at least ten days for the return of the postcard before making further inquiries.

If you plan to apply for financial support, it is imperative that you file your application early.

ADMISSION TESTS

The major testing program used in graduate admissions is the Graduate Record Examinations (GRE®) testing program, sponsored by the GRE Board and administered by Educational Testing Service, Princeton, New Jersey.

The Graduate Record Examinations testing program consists of a General Test and eight Subject Tests. The General Test measures critical thinking, verbal reasoning, quantitative reasoning, and analytical writing skills. It is offered as an Internet-based test (iBT) in the United States, Canada, and many other countries.

The GRE® revised General Test's questions were designed to reflect the kind of thinking that students need to do in graduate or business school and demonstrate that students are indeed ready for graduate-level work.

- **Verbal Reasoning**—Measures ability to analyze and evaluate written material and synthesize information obtained from it, analyze relationships among component parts of sentences, and recognize relationships among words and concepts.
- **Quantitative Reasoning**—Measures problem-solving ability, focusing on basic concepts of arithmetic, algebra, geometry, and data analysis.
- **Analytical Writing**—Measures critical thinking and analytical writing skills, specifically the ability to articulate and support complex ideas clearly and effectively.

The computer-delivered GRE® revised General Test is offered year-round at Prometric™ test centers and on specific dates at testing locations outside of the Prometric test center network. Appointments are scheduled on a first-come, first-served basis. The GRE® revised General Test is also offered as a paper-based test three times a year in areas where computer-based testing is not available.

You can take the computer-delivered GRE® revised General Test once every twenty-one days, up to five times within any continuous rolling twelve-month period (365 days)—even if you canceled your

scores on a previously taken test. You may take the paper-delivered GRE® revised General Test as often as it is offered.

Three scores are reported on the revised General Test:

1. A **Verbal Reasoning score** is reported on a 130–170 score scale, in 1-point increments.

2. A **Quantitative Reasoning score** is reported on a 130–170 score scale, in 1-point increments.

3. An **Analytical Writing score** is reported on a 0–6 score level, in half-point increments.

The GRE® Subject Tests measure achievement and assume undergraduate majors or extensive background in the following eight disciplines:

- Biochemistry, Cell and Molecular Biology
- Biology
- Chemistry
- Computer Science
- Literature in English
- Mathematics
- Physics
- Psychology

The Subject Tests are available three times per year as paper-based administrations around the world. Testing time is approximately 2 hours and 50 minutes. You can obtain more information about the GRE® by visiting the ETS website at www.ets.org or consulting the *GRE® Information and Registration Bulletin*. The *Bulletin* can be obtained at many undergraduate colleges. You can also download it from the ETS website or obtain it by contacting Graduate Record Examinations, Educational Testing Service, P.O. Box 6000, Princeton, NJ 08541-6000; phone: 609-771-7670.

If you expect to apply for admission to a program that requires any of the GRE® tests, you should select a test date well in advance of the application deadline. Scores on the computer-based General Test are reported within ten to fifteen days; scores on the paper-based Subject Tests are reported within six weeks.

Another testing program, the Miller Analogies Test® (MAT®), is administered at more than 500 Controlled Testing Centers, licensed by Harcourt Assessment, Inc., in the United States, Canada, and other countries. The MAT® computer-based test is now available. Testing time is 60 minutes. The test consists of 120 partial analogies. You can obtain the *Candidate Information Booklet,* which contains a list of test centers and instructions for taking the test, from http://www.milleranalogies.com or by calling 800-328-5999 (toll-free).

Check the specific requirements of the programs to which you are applying.

How Admission Decisions Are Made

The program you apply to is directly involved in the admissions process. Although the final decision is usually made by the graduate dean (or an associate) or the faculty admissions committee, recommendations from faculty members in your intended field are important. At some institutions, an interview is incorporated into the decision process.

A Special Note for International Students

In addition to the steps already described, there are some special considerations for international students who intend to apply for graduate study in the United States. All graduate schools require an indication of competence in English. The purpose of the Test of English as a Foreign Language (TOEFL®) is to evaluate the English proficiency of people who are nonnative speakers of English and want to study at colleges and universities where English is the language of instruction. The TOEFL® is administered by Educational Testing Service (ETS) under the general direction of a policy board established by the College Board and the Graduate Record Examinations Board.

The TOEFL® iBT assesses the four basic language skills: listening, reading, writing, and speaking. It was administered for the first time in September 2005, and ETS continues to introduce the TOEFL® iBT in selected cities. The Internet-based test is administered at secure, official test centers. The testing time is approximately 4 hours. Because the TOEFL® iBT includes a speaking section, the Test of Spoken English (TSE) is no longer needed.

The TOEFL® is also offered in the paper-based format in areas of the world where Internet-based testing is not available. The paper-based TOEFL® consists of three sections—listening comprehension, structure and written expression, and reading comprehension. The testing time is approximately 3 hours. The Test of Written English (TWE®) is also given. The TWE® is a 30-minute essay that measures the examinee's ability to compose in English. Examinees receive a TWE® score separate from their TOEFL® score. The *Information Bulletin* contains information on local fees and registration procedures.

The TOEFL® paper-based test (TOEFL® PBT) began being phased out in mid-2012. For those who may have taken the TOEFL® PBT, scores remain valid for two years after the test date. The Test of Written English (TWE®) is also given. The TWE® is a 30-minute essay that measures the examinee's ability to compose in English. Examinees receive a TWE® score separate from their TOEFL® score. The Information Bulletin contains information on local fees and registration procedures.

Additional information and registration materials are available from TOEFL® Services, Educational Testing Service, P.O. Box 6151, Princeton, New Jersey 08541-6151. Phone: 609-771-7100. Website: www.toefl.org.

International students should apply especially early because of the number of steps required to complete the admissions process. Furthermore, many United States graduate schools have a limited number of spaces for international students, and many more students apply than the schools can accommodate.

International students may find financial assistance from institutions very limited. The U.S. government requires international applicants to submit a certification of support, which is a statement attesting to the applicant's financial resources. In addition, international students *must* have health insurance coverage.

Tips for Minority Students

Indicators of a university's values in terms of diversity are found both in its recruitment programs and its resources directed to student success. Important questions: Does the institution vigorously recruit minorities for its graduate programs? Is there funding available to help with the costs associated with visiting the school? Are minorities represented in the institution's brochures or website or on their faculty rolls? What campus-based resources or services (including assistance in locating housing or career counseling and placement) are available? Is funding available to members of underrepresented groups?

At the program level, it is particularly important for minority students to investigate the "climate" of a program under consideration. How many minority students are enrolled and how many have graduated? What opportunities are there to work with diverse faculty and mentors whose research interests match yours? How are conflicts resolved or concerns addressed? How interested are faculty in building strong and supportive relations with students? "Climate" concerns should be addressed by posing questions to various individuals, including faculty members, current students, and alumni.

Information is also available through various organizations, such as the Hispanic Association of Colleges & Universities (HACU), and publications such as *Diverse Issues in Higher Education* and *Hispanic Outlook* magazine. There are also books devoted to this topic, such as *The Multicultural Student's Guide to Colleges* by Robert Mitchell.

Financial Support

The range of financial support at the graduate level is very broad. The following descriptions will give you a general idea of what you might expect and what will be expected of you as a financial support recipient.

Fellowships, Scholarships, and Grants

These are usually outright awards of a few hundred to many thousands of dollars with no service to the institution required in return. Fellowships and scholarships are usually awarded on the basis of merit and are highly competitive. Grants are made on the basis of financial need or special talent in a field of study. Many fellowships, scholarships, and grants not only cover tuition, fees, and supplies but also include stipends for living expenses with allowances for dependents. However, the terms of each should be examined because some do not permit recipients to supplement their income with outside work. Fellowships, scholarships, and grants may vary in the number of years for which they are awarded.

In addition to the availability of these funds at the university or program level, many excellent fellowship programs are available at the national level and may be applied for before and during enrollment in a graduate program. A listing of many of these programs can be found at the Council of Graduate Schools' website: http://www. cgsnet.org. There is a wealth of information in the "Programs" and "Awards" sections.

Assistantships and Internships

Many graduate students receive financial support through assistantships, particularly involving teaching or research duties. It is important to recognize that such appointments should not be viewed simply as employment relationships but rather should constitute an integral and important part of a student's graduate education. As such, the appointments should be accompanied by strong faculty mentoring and increasingly responsible apprenticeship experiences. The specific nature of these appointments in a given program should be considered in selecting that graduate program.

TEACHING ASSISTANTSHIPS

These usually provide a salary and full or partial tuition remission and may also provide health benefits. Unlike fellowships, scholarships, and grants, which require no service to the institution, teaching assistantships require recipients to provide the institution with a specific amount of undergraduate teaching, ideally related to the student's field of study. Some teaching assistants are limited to grading papers, compiling bibliographies, taking notes, or monitoring laboratories. At some graduate schools, teaching assistants must carry lighter course loads than regular full-time students.

RESEARCH ASSISTANTSHIPS

These are very similar to teaching assistantships in the manner in which financial assistance is provided. The difference is that recipients are given basic research assignments in their disciplines rather than teaching responsibilities. The work required is normally related to the student's field of study; in most instances, the assistantship supports the student's thesis or dissertation research.

ADMINISTRATIVE INTERNSHIPS

These are similar to assistantships in application of financial assistance funds, but the student is given an assignment on a part-time basis, usually as a special assistant with one of the university's administrative offices. The assignment may not necessarily be directly related to the recipient's discipline.

RESIDENCE HALL AND COUNSELING ASSISTANTSHIPS

These assistantships are frequently assigned to graduate students in psychology, counseling, and social work, but they may be offered to students in other disciplines, especially if the student has worked in this capacity during his or her undergraduate years. Duties can vary from being available in a dean's office for a specific number of hours for consultation with undergraduates to living in campus residences and being responsible for both counseling and administrative tasks or advising student activity groups. Residence hall assistantships often include a room and board allowance and, in some cases, tuition assistance and stipends. Contact the Housing and Student Life Office for more information.

Health Insurance

The availability and affordability of health insurance is an important issue and one that should be considered in an applicant's choice of institution and program. While often included with assistantships and fellowships, this is not always the case and, even if provided, the benefits may be limited. It is important to note that the U.S. government requires international students to have health insurance.

The GI Bill

This provides financial assistance for students who are veterans of the United States armed forces. If you are a veteran, contact your local Veterans Administration office to determine your eligibility and to get full details about benefits. There are a number of programs that offer educational benefits to current military enlistees. Some states have tuition assistance programs for members of the National Guard. Contact the VA office at the college for more information.

Federal Work-Study Program (FWS)

Employment is another way some students finance their graduate studies. The federally funded Federal Work-Study Program provides eligible students with employment opportunities, usually in public and private nonprofit organizations. Federal funds pay up to 75 percent of the wages, with the remainder paid by the employing agency. FWS is available to graduate students who demonstrate financial need. Not all schools have these funds, and some only award them to undergraduates. Each school sets its application deadline and workstudy earnings limits. Wages vary and are related to the type of work done. You must file the Free Application for Federal Student Aid (FAFSA) to be eligible for this program.

Loans

Many graduate students borrow to finance their graduate programs when other sources of assistance (which do not have to be repaid) prove insufficient. You should always read and understand the terms of any loan program before submitting your application.

FEDERAL DIRECT LOANS

Federal Direct Stafford Loans. The Federal Direct Stafford Loan Program offers a variable-fixed interest rate loan to graduate students with the Department of Education acting as the lender. Students receive a new rate with each new loan, but that rate is fixed for the life of the loan. Beginning with loans made on or after July 1, 2013, the interest rate for loans made each July 1st to June 30th period are determined based on the last 10-year Treasury note auction prior to June 1st of that year,

plus an added percentage. The interest rate can be no higher than 9.5%.

Beginning July 1, 2012, the Federal Direct Stafford Loan for graduate students is an unsubsidized loan. Under the *unsubsidized* program, the grad borrower pays the interest on the loan from the day proceeds are issued and is responsible for paying interest during all periods. If the borrower chooses not to pay the interest while in school, or during the grace periods, deferment, or forbearance, the interest accrues and will be capitalized.

Graduate students may borrow up to $20,500 per year through the Direct Stafford Loan Program, up to a cumulative maximum of $138,500, including undergraduate borrowing. No more than $65,000 of the $138,500 can be from subsidized loans that the grad borrower may have received for periods of enrollment that began before July 1, 2012, or for prior undergraduate borrowing. You may borrow up to the cost of attendance at the school in which you are enrolled or will attend, minus estimated financial assistance from other federal, state, and private sources, up to a maximum of $20,500. Grad borrowers who reach the aggregate loan limit over the course of their education cannot receive additional loans; however, if they repay some of their loans to bring the outstanding balance below the aggregate limit, they could be eligible to borrow again, up to that limit.

For Unsubsidized loans first disbursed on or after July 1, 2014 and before July 1, 2015, the interest rate was 6.21%. For those first disbursed on or after July 1, 2015 and before July 1, 2016, the interest rate is 5.84%.

A fee is deducted from the loan proceeds upon disbursement. Loans with a first disbursement on or after July 1, 2010 but before July 1, 2012, have a borrower origination fee of 1 percent. For loans disbursed after July 1, 2012, these fee deductions no longer apply. The Budget Control Act of 2011, signed into law on August 2, 2011, eliminated Direct Subsidized Loan eligibility for graduate and professional students for periods of enrollment beginning on or after July 1, 2012 and terminated the authority of the Department of Education to offer most repayment incentives to Direct Loan borrowers for loans disbursed on or after July 1, 2012.

Under the *subsidized* Federal Direct Stafford Loan Program, repayment begins six months after your last date of enrollment on at least a half-time basis. Under the *unsubsidized* program, repayment of interest begins within thirty days from disbursement of the loan proceeds, and repayment of the principal begins six months after your last enrollment on at least a half-time basis. Some borrowers may choose to defer interest payments while they are in school. The accrued interest is added to the loan balance when the borrower begins repayment. There are several repayment options.

Federal Perkins Loans. The Federal Perkins Loan is available to students demonstrating financial need and is administered directly by the school. Not all schools have these funds, and some may award them to undergraduates only. Eligibility is determined from the information you provide on the FAFSA. The school will notify you of your eligibility.

Eligible graduate students may borrow up to $8,000 per year, up to a maximum of $60,000, including undergraduate borrowing (even if your previous Perkins Loans have been repaid). The interest rate for Federal Perkins Loans is 5 percent, and no interest accrues while you remain in school at least half-time. Students who are attending less than half-time need to check with their school to determine the length of their grace period. There are no guarantee, loan, or disbursement fees. Repayment begins nine months after your last date of enrollment on at least a half-time basis and may extend over a maximum of ten years with no prepayment penalty.

Federal Direct Graduate PLUS Loans. Effective July 1, 2006, graduate and professional students are eligible for Graduate PLUS loans. This program allows students to borrow up to the cost of attendance, less any other aid received. These loans have a fixed interest rate, and interest begins to accrue at the time of disbursement. Beginning with loans made on or after July 1, 2013, the interest rate for loans made each July 1st to June 30th period are determined based on the last 10-year Treasury note auction prior to June 1st of that year. The interest rate can be no higher than 10.5%. The PLUS loans do involve a credit check; a PLUS borrower may obtain a loan with a cosigner if his or her credit is not good enough. Grad PLUS loans may be deferred while a student is in school and for the six months following a drop below half-time

enrollment. For more information, you should contact a representative in your college's financial aid office.

Deferring Your Federal Loan Repayments. If you borrowed under the Federal Direct Stafford Loan Program, Federal Direct PLUS Loan Program, or the Federal Perkins Loan Program for previous undergraduate or graduate study, your payments may be deferred when you return to graduate school, depending on when you borrowed and under which program.

There are other deferment options available if you are temporarily unable to repay your loan. Information about these deferments is provided at your entrance and exit interviews. If you believe you are eligible for a deferment of your loan payments, you must contact your lender or loan servicer to request a deferment. The deferment must be filed prior to the time your payment is due, and it must be re-filed when it expires if you remain eligible for deferment at that time.

SUPPLEMENTAL (PRIVATE) LOANS

Many lending institutions offer supplemental loan programs and other financing plans, such as the ones described here, to students seeking additional assistance in meeting their education expenses. Some loan programs target all types of graduate students; others are designed specifically for business, law, or medical students. In addition, you can use private loans not specifically designed for education to help finance your graduate degree.

If you are considering borrowing through a supplemental or private loan program, you should carefully consider the terms and be sure to read the fine print. Check with the program sponsor for the most current terms that will be applicable to the amounts you intend to borrow for graduate study. Most supplemental loan programs for graduate study offer unsubsidized, credit-based loans. In general, a credit-ready borrower is one who has a satisfactory credit history or no credit history at all. A creditworthy borrower generally must pass a credit test to be eligible to borrow or act as a cosigner for the loan funds.

Many supplemental loan programs have minimum and maximum annual loan limits. Some offer amounts equal to the cost of attendance minus any other aid you will receive for graduate study. If you are planning to borrow for several years of graduate study, consider whether there is a cumulative or aggregate limit on the amount you may borrow. Often this cumulative or aggregate limit will include any amounts you borrowed and have not repaid for undergraduate or previous graduate study.

The combination of the annual interest rate, loan fees, and the repayment terms you choose will determine how much you will repay over time. Compare these features in combination before you decide which loan program to use. Some loans offer interest rates that are adjusted monthly, quarterly, or annually. Some offer interest rates that are lower during the in-school, grace, and deferment periods and then increase when you begin repayment. Some programs include a loan origination fee, which is usually deducted from the principal amount you receive when the loan is disbursed and must be repaid along with the interest and other principal when you graduate, withdraw from school, or drop below half-time study. Sometimes the loan fees are reduced if you borrow with a qualified cosigner. Some programs allow you to defer interest and/or principal payments while you are enrolled in graduate school. Many programs allow you to capitalize your interest payments; the interest due on your loan is added to the outstanding balance of your loan, so you don't have to repay immediately, but this increases the amount you owe. Other programs allow you to pay the interest as you go, which reduces the amount you later have to repay. The private loan market is very competitive, and your financial aid office can help you evaluate these programs.

Applying for Need-Based Financial Aid

Schools that award federal and institutional financial assistance based on need will require you to complete the FAFSA and, in some cases, an institutional financial aid application.

If you are applying for federal student assistance, you **must** complete the FAFSA. A service of the U.S. Department of Education, the FAFSA is free to all applicants. Most applicants apply online at www.fafsa.ed.gov. Paper applications are available at the financial aid office of your local college.

After your FAFSA information has been processed, you will receive a Student Aid Report (SAR). If you provided an e-mail address on the FAFSA, this will be sent to you electronically; otherwise, it will be mailed to your home address.

Follow the instructions on the SAR if you need to correct information reported on your original application. If your situation changes after you file your FAFSA, contact your financial aid officer to discuss amending your information. You can also appeal your financial aid award if you have extenuating circumstances.

If you would like more information on federal student financial aid, visit the FAFSA website or download the most recent version of *Funding Education Beyond High School: The Guide to Federal Student Aid* at http://studentaid.ed.gov/students/publications/student_guide/index.html. This guide is also available in Spanish.

The U.S. Department of Education also has a toll-free number for questions concerning federal student aid programs. The number is 1-800-4-FED AID (1-800-433-3243). If you are hearing impaired, call toll-free, 1-800-730-8913.

Summary

Remember that these are generalized statements about financial assistance at the graduate level. Because each institution allots its aid differently, you should communicate directly with the school and the specific department of interest to you. It is not unusual, for example, to find that an endowment vested within a specific department supports one or more fellowships. You may fit its requirements and specifications precisely.

Accreditation and Accrediting Agencies

Colleges and universities in the United States, and their individual academic and professional programs, are accredited by nongovernmental agencies concerned with monitoring the quality of education in this country. Agencies with both regional and national jurisdictions grant accreditation to institutions as a whole, while specialized bodies acting on a nationwide basis—often national professional associations—grant accreditation to departments and programs in specific fields.

Institutional and specialized accrediting agencies share the same basic concerns: the purpose an academic unit—whether university or program—has set for itself and how well it fulfills that purpose, the adequacy of its financial and other resources, the quality of its academic offerings, and the level of services it provides. Agencies that grant institutional accreditation take a broader view, of course, and examine university-wide or college-wide services with which a specialized agency may not concern itself.

Both types of agencies follow the same general procedures when considering an application for accreditation. The academic unit prepares a self-evaluation, focusing on the concerns mentioned above and usually including an assessment of both its strengths and weaknesses; a team of representatives of the accrediting body reviews this evaluation, visits the campus, and makes its own report; and finally, the accrediting body makes a decision on the application. Often, even when accreditation is granted, the agency makes a recommendation regarding how the institution or program can improve. All institutions and programs are also reviewed every few years to determine whether they continue to meet established standards; if they do not, they may lose their accreditation.

Accrediting agencies themselves are reviewed and evaluated periodically by the U.S. Department of Education and the Council for Higher Education Accreditation (CHEA). Recognized agencies adhere to certain standards and practices, and their authority in matters of accreditation is widely accepted in the educational community.

This does not mean, however, that accreditation is a simple matter, either for schools wishing to become accredited or for students deciding where to apply. Indeed, in certain fields the very meaning and methods of accreditation are the subject of a good deal of debate. For their part, those applying to graduate school should be aware of the safeguards provided by regional accreditation, especially in terms of degree acceptance and institutional longevity. Beyond this, applicants should understand the role that specialized accreditation plays in their field, as this varies considerably from one discipline to another. In certain professional fields, it is necessary to have graduated from a program that is accredited in order to be eligible for a license to practice, and in some fields the federal government also makes this a hiring requirement. In other disciplines, however, accreditation is not as essential, and there can be excellent programs that are not accredited. In fact, some programs choose not to seek accreditation, although most do.

Institutions and programs that present themselves for accreditation are sometimes granted the status of candidate for accreditation, or what is known as "preaccreditation." This may happen, for example, when an academic unit is too new to have met all the requirements for accreditation. Such status signifies initial recognition and indicates that the school or program in question is working to fulfill all requirements; it does not, however, guarantee that accreditation will be granted.

Institutional Accrediting Agencies—Regional

MIDDLE STATES ASSOCIATION OF COLLEGES AND SCHOOLS

Accredits institutions in Delaware, District of Columbia, Maryland, New Jersey, New York, Pennsylvania, Puerto Rico, and the Virgin Islands.

Dr. Elizabeth Sibolski, President
Middle States Commission on Higher Education
3624 Market Street, Second Floor West
Philadelphia, Pennsylvania 19104
Phone: 267-284-5000
Fax: 215-662-5501
E-mail: info@msche.org
Website: www.msche.org

NEW ENGLAND ASSOCIATION OF SCHOOLS AND COLLEGES

Accredits institutions in Connecticut, Maine, Massachusetts, New Hampshire, Rhode Island, and Vermont.

Dr. Barbara E. Brittingham, President/Director
Commission on Institutions of Higher Education
3 Burlington Woods Drive, Suite 100
Burlington, Massachusetts 01803-4531
Phone: 855-886-3272 or 781-425-7714
Fax: 781-425-1001
E-mail: cihe@neasc.org
Website: http://cihe.neasc.org

THE HIGHER LEARNING COMMISSION

Accredits institutions in Arizona, Arkansas, Colorado, Illinois, Indiana, Iowa, Kansas, Michigan, Minnesota, Missouri, Nebraska, New Mexico, North Dakota, Ohio, Oklahoma, South Dakota, West Virginia, Wisconsin, and Wyoming.

Dr. Barbara Gellman-Danley, President
The Higher Learning Commission
230 South LaSalle Street, Suite 7-500
Chicago, Illinois 60604-1413
Phone: 800-621-7440 or 312-263-0456
Fax: 312-263-7462
E-mail: info@hlcommission.org
Website: www.hlcommission.org

NORTHWEST COMMISSION ON COLLEGES AND UNIVERSITIES

Accredits institutions in Alaska, Idaho, Montana, Nevada, Oregon, Utah, and Washington.

Dr. Sandra E. Elman, President
8060 165th Avenue, NE, Suite 100
Redmond, Washington 98052
Phone: 425-558-4224
Fax: 425-376-0596
E-mail: selman@nwccu.org
Website: www.nwccu.org

SOUTHERN ASSOCIATION OF COLLEGES AND SCHOOLS

Accredits institutions in Alabama, Florida, Georgia, Kentucky, Louisiana, Mississippi, North Carolina, South Carolina, Tennessee, Texas, and Virginia.

Dr. Belle S. Wheelan, President
Commission on Colleges
1866 Southern Lane
Decatur, Georgia 30033-4097
Phone: 404-679-4500 Ext. 4504
Fax: 404-679-4558
E-mail: questions@sacscoc.org
Website: www.sacscoc.org

WESTERN ASSOCIATION OF SCHOOLS AND COLLEGES

Accredits institutions in California, Guam, and Hawaii.

Dr. Mary Ellen Petrisko, President
Accrediting Commission for Senior Colleges and Universities
985 Atlantic Avenue, Suite 100
Alameda, California 94501
Phone: 510-748-9001
Fax: 510-748-9797
E-mail: wasc@wascsenior.org
Website: http://www.wascsenior.org/

Institutional Accrediting Agencies—Other

ACCREDITING COUNCIL FOR INDEPENDENT COLLEGES AND SCHOOLS
Albert C. Gray, Ph.D., Executive Director and CEO
750 First Street, NE, Suite 980
Washington, DC 20002-4241
Phone: 202-336-6780
Fax: 202-842-2593
E-mail: info@acics.org
Website: www.acics.org

DISTANCE EDUCATION AND ACCREDITING COMMISSION (DEAC)
Accrediting Commission
Leah Matthews, Executive Director
1101 17th Street, NW, Suite 808
Washington, DC 20036-4704
Phone: 202-234-5100
Fax: 202-332-1386
E-mail: info@deac.org
Website: www.deac.org

Specialized Accrediting Agencies

ACUPUNCTURE AND ORIENTAL MEDICINE
Mark S. McKenzie, LAc MsOM DiplOM, Executive Director
Accreditation Commission for Acupuncture and Oriental Medicine
8941 Aztec Drive
Eden Prairie, Minnesota 55347
Phone: 952-212-2434
Fax: 301-313-0912
E-mail: coordinator@acaom.org
Website: www.acaom.org

ART AND DESIGN
Karen P. Moynahan, Executive Director
National Association of Schools of Art and Design (NASAD)
Commission on Accreditation
11250 Roger Bacon Drive, Suite 21
Reston, Virginia 20190-5248
Phone: 703-437-0700
Fax: 703-437-6312
E-mail: info@arts-accredit.org
Website: http://nasad.arts-accredit.org

ATHLETIC TRAINING EDUCATION
Micki Cuppett, Executive Director
Commission on Accreditation of Athletic Training Education (CAATE)
6850 Austin Center Blvd., Suite 100
Austin, Texas 78731-3184
Phone: 512-733-9700
E-mail: micki@caate.net
Website: www.caate.net

AUDIOLOGY EDUCATION
Doris Gordon, Executive Director
Accreditation Commission for Audiology Education (ACAE)
1718 M Street, NW #297
Washington, DC 20036
Phone: 202-986-9550
Fax: 202-986-9500
E-mail: info@acaeaccred.org
Website: www.acaeaccred.org

AVIATION
Gary J. Northam, Executive Director
Aviation Accreditation Board International (AABI)
3410 Skyway Drive
Auburn, Alabama 36830
Phone: 334-844-2431
Fax: 334-844-2432
E-mail: bayenva@auburn.edu
Website: www.aabi.aero

BUSINESS
Robert D. Reid, Executive Vice President and Chief Accreditation Officer
AACSB International—The Association to Advance Collegiate Schools of Business
777 South Harbour Island Boulevard, Suite 750
Tampa, Florida 33602
Phone: 813-769-6500
Fax: 813-769-6559
E-mail: bob@aacsb.edu
Website: www.aacsb.edu

BUSINESS EDUCATION
Dennis N. Gash, President and Chief Accreditation Officer
International Assembly for Collegiate Business Education (IACBE)
11257 Strang Line Road
Lenexa, KS 66215
Phone: 913-631-3009
Fax: 913-631-9154
E-mail:iacbe@iacbe.org
Website: www.iacbe.org

CHIROPRACTIC
Craig S. Little, President
Council on Chiropractic Education (CCE)
Commission on Accreditation
8049 North 85th Way
Scottsdale, Arizona 85258-4321
Phone: 480-443-8877 or 888-443-3506
Fax: 480-483-7333
E-mail: cce@cce-usa.org
Website: www.cce-usa.org

CLINICAL LABORATORY SCIENCES
Dianne M. Cearlock, Ph.D., Chief Executive Officer
National Accrediting Agency for Clinical Laboratory Sciences
5600 North River Road, Suite 720
Rosemont, Illinois 60018-5119
Phone: 773-714-8880 or 847-939-3597
Fax: 773-714-8886
E-mail: info@naacls.org
Website: www.naacls.org

CLINICAL PASTORAL EDUCATION
Trace Haythorn, Executive Director
Association for Clinical Pastoral Education, Inc.
1549 Clairmont Road, Suite 103
Decatur, Georgia 30033-4611
Phone: 404-320-1472
Fax: 404-320-0849
E-mail: acpe@acpe.edu
Website: www.acpe.edu

DANCE
Karen P. Moynahan, Executive Director
National Association of Schools of Dance (NASD)
Commission on Accreditation
11250 Roger Bacon Drive, Suite 21
Reston, Virginia 20190-5248
Phone: 703-437-0700
Fax: 703-437-6312
E-mail: info@arts-accredit.org
Website: http://nasd.arts-accredit.org

DENTISTRY
Dr. Sherin Tooks, Director
Commission on Dental Accreditation
American Dental Association
211 East Chicago Avenue, Suite 1900
Chicago, Illinois 60611
Phone: 312-440-4643 or 800-621-8099
E-mail: accreditation@ada.org
Website: www.ada.org

DIETETICS AND NUTRITION
Mary B. Gregoire, Ph.D., Executive Director; RD, FADA, FAND
Academy of Nutrition and Dietetics
Accreditation Council for Education in Nutrition and Dietetics (ACEND)
120 South Riverside Plaza, Suite 2000
Chicago, Illinois 60606-6995
Phone: 800-877-1600 Ext. 5400 or 312-899-0040
Fax: 312-899-4817
E-mail: acend@eatright.org
Website: www.eatright.org/ACEND

EDUCATION PREPARATION
Christopher Koch, Interim President
Council for the Accreditation of Education Preparation (CAEP)
1140 19th Street NW, Suite 400
Washington, DC 20036
Phone: 202-223-0077
E-mail: christopher.koch@caepnet.org
Website: www.caepnet.org

ENGINEERING
Michael Milligan, Ph.D., PE, Executive Director
Accreditation Board for Engineering and Technology, Inc. (ABET)
415 North Charles Street
Baltimore, Maryland 21201
Phone: 410-347-7700
E-mail: accreditation@abet.org
Website: www.abet.org

FORENSIC SCIENCES
Nancy J. Jackson, Director of Development and Accreditation
American Academy of Forensic Sciences (AAFS)
Forensic Science Education Program Accreditation Commission (FEPAC)
410 North 21st Street
Colorado Springs, Colorado 80904
Phone: 719-636-1100
Fax: 719-636-1993
E-mail: njackson@aafs.org
Website: www.fepac-edu.org

FORESTRY
Carol L. Redelsheimer
Director of Science and Education
Society of American Foresters
5400 Grosvenor Lane
Bethesda, Maryland 20814-2198
Phone: 301-897-8720 or 866-897-8720
Fax: 301-897-3690
E-mail: redelsheimerc@safnet.org
Website: www.safnet.org

HEALTHCARE MANAGEMENT
Commission on Accreditation of Healthcare Management Education (CAHME)
Margaret Schulte, President and CEO
1700 Rockville Pike
Suite 400
Rockville, Maryland 20852
Phone: 301-998-6101
E-mail: info@cahme.org
Website: www.cahme.org

HEALTH INFORMATICS AND HEALTH MANAGEMENT
Claire Dixon-Lee, Executive Director
Commission on Accreditation for Health Informatics and Information Management Education (CAHIIM)
233 North Michigan Avenue, 21st Floor
Chicago, Illinois 60601-5800
Phone: 312-233-1100

Fax: 312-233-1948
E-mail:E-mail: claire.dixon-lee@cahiim.org
Website: www.cahiim.org

HUMAN SERVICE EDUCATION
Dr. Elaine Green, President
Council for Standards in Human Service Education (CSHSE)
3337 Duke Street
Alexandria, VA 22314
Phone: 571-257-3959
E-mail: info@cshse.org
Web: http://www.cshse.org

INTERIOR DESIGN
Holly Mattson, Executive Director
Council for Interior Design Accreditation
206 Grandview Avenue, Suite 350
Grand Rapids, Michigan 49503-4014
Phone: 616-458-0400
Fax: 616-458-0460
E-mail: info@accredit-id.org
Website: www.accredit-id.org

JOURNALISM AND MASS COMMUNICATIONS
Susanne Shaw, Executive Director
Accrediting Council on Education in Journalism and Mass Communications (ACEJMC)
School of Journalism
Stauffer-Flint Hall
University of Kansas
1435 Jayhawk Boulevard
Lawrence, Kansas 66045-7575
Phone: 785-864-3973
Fax: 785-864-5225
E-mail: sshaw@ku.edu
Website: http://www2.ku.edu/~acejmc/

LANDSCAPE ARCHITECTURE
Ronald C. Leighton, Executive Director
Landscape Architectural Accreditation Board (LAAB)
American Society of Landscape Architects (ASLA)
636 Eye Street, NW
Washington, DC 20001-3736
Phone: 202-898-2444 or 888-999-2752
Fax: 202-898-1185
E-mail: info@asla.org
Website: www.asla.org

LAW
Barry Currier, Managing Director of Accreditation & Legal Education
American Bar Association
321 North Clark Street, 21st Floor
Chicago, Illinois 60654
Phone: 312-988-6738
Fax: 312-988-5681
E-mail: legaled@americanbar.org
Website: http://www.americanbar.org/groups/legal_education/resources/accreditation.html

LIBRARY
Karen O'Brien, Director
Office for Accreditation
American Library Association
50 East Huron Street
Chicago, Illinois 60611-2795
Phone: 312-280-2432
Fax: 312-280-2433
E-mail: accred@ala.org
Website: www.ala.org/accreditation/

MARRIAGE AND FAMILY THERAPY
Tanya A. Tamarkin, Director of Educational Affairs
Commission on Accreditation for Marriage and Family Therapy
    Education (COAMFTE)
American Association for Marriage and Family Therapy
112 South Alfred Street
Alexandria, Virginia 22314-3061
Phone: 703-838-9808
Fax: 703-838-9805
E-mail: coa@aamft.org
Website: www.aamft.org

MEDICAL ILLUSTRATION
Kathleen Megivern, Executive Director
Commission on Accreditation of Allied Health Education Programs
    (CAAHEP)
1361 Park Street
Clearwater, Florida 33756
Phone: 727-210-2350
Fax: 727-210-2354
E-mail: mail@caahep.org
Website: www.caahep.org

MEDICINE
Liaison Committee on Medical Education (LCME)
Robert B. Hash, M.D., LCME Secretary
American Medical Association
Council on Medical Education
330 North Wabash Avenue, Suite 39300
Chicago, Illinois 60611-5885
Phone: 312-464-4933
E-mail: lcme@aamc.org
Website: www.ama-assn.org

Liaison Committee on Medical Education (LCME)
Heather Lent, M.A., Director
Accreditation Services
Association of American Medical Colleges
655 K Street, NW
Washington, DC 20001-2399
Phone: 202-828-0596
E-mail: lcme@aamc.org
Website: www.lcme.org

MUSIC
Karen P. Moynahan, Executive Director
National Association of Schools of Music (NASM)
Commission on Accreditation
11250 Roger Bacon Drive, Suite 21
Reston, Virginia 20190-5248
Phone: 703-437-0700
Fax: 703-437-6312
E-mail: info@arts-accredit.org
Website: http://nasm.arts-accredit.org/

NATUROPATHIC MEDICINE
Daniel Seitz, J.D., Ed.D., Executive Director
Council on Naturopathic Medical Education
P.O. Box 178
Great Barrington, Massachusetts 01230
Phone: 413-528-8877
E-mail: www.cnme.org/contact.html
Website: www.cnme.org

NURSE ANESTHESIA
Francis R.Gerbasi, Ph.D., CRNA, COA Executive Director
Council on Accreditation of Nurse Anesthesia Educational Programs
    (CoA-NAEP)
American Association of Nurse Anesthetists
222 South Prospect Avenue, Suite 304
Park Ridge, Illinois 60068-4001
Phone: 847-692-7050, Ext. 1154
Fax: 847-692-7137
E-mail: accreditation@coa.us.com
Website: http://home.coa.us.com

NURSE EDUCATION
Jennifer L. Butlin, Executive Director
Commission on Collegiate Nursing Education (CCNE)
One Dupont Circle, NW, Suite 530
Washington, DC 20036-1120
Phone: 202-887-6791
Fax: 202-887-8476
E-mail: jbutlin@aacn.nche.edu
Website: www.aacn.nche.edu/accreditation

NURSE MIDWIFERY
Heather L. Maurer, M.A., Executive Director
Accreditation Commission for Midwifery Education (ACME)
American College of Nurse-Midwives
8403 Colesville Road, Suite 1550
Silver Spring, Maryland 20910
Phone: 240-485-1800
Fax: 240-485-1818
E-mail: info@acnm.org
Website: www.midwife.org/Program-Accreditation

NURSE PRACTITIONER
Gay Johnson, CEO
National Association of Nurse Practitioners in Women's Health
Council on Accreditation
505 C Street, NE
Washington, DC 20002
Phone: 202-543-9693 Ext. 1
Fax: 202-543-9858
E-mail: info@npwh.org
Website: www.npwh.org

NURSING
Marsal P. Stoll, Chief Executive Director
Accreditation Commission for Education in Nursing (ACEN)
3343 Peachtree Road, NE, Suite 850
Atlanta, Georgia 30326
Phone: 404-975-5000
Fax: 404-975-5020
E-mail: info@acenursing.org
Website: www.acenursing.org

OCCUPATIONAL THERAPY
Heather Stagliano, DHSc, OTR/L, Director of Accreditation
The American Occupational Therapy Association, Inc.
4720 Montgomery Lane, Suite 200
Bethesda, Maryland 20814-3449
Phone: 301-652-6611 Ext. 2914
TDD: 800-377-8555
Fax: 240-762-5150
E-mail: accred@aota.org
Website: www.aoteonline.org

OPTOMETRY
Joyce L. Urbeck, Administrative Director
Accreditation Council on Optometric Education (ACOE)
American Optometric Association
243 North Lindbergh Boulevard
St. Louis, Missouri 63141-7881
Phone: 314-991-4100, Ext. 4246
Fax: 314-991-4101
E-mail: accredit@aoa.org
Website: www.theacoe.org

OSTEOPATHIC MEDICINE
Konrad C. Miskowicz-Retz, Ph.D., CAE
Director, Department of Accreditation
Commission on Osteopathic College Accreditation (COCA)
American Osteopathic Association
142 East Ontario Street
Chicago, Illinois 60611
Phone: 312-202-8097
Fax: 312-202-8397
E-mail: predoc@osteopathic.org
Website: www.osteopathic.org

PHARMACY
Peter H. Vlasses, PharmD, Executive Director
Accreditation Council for Pharmacy Education
135 South LaSalle Street, Suite 4100
Chicago, Illinois 60603-4810
Phone: 312-664-3575
Fax: 312-664-4652
E-mail: csinfo@acpe-accredit.org
Website: www.acpe-accredit.org

PHYSICAL THERAPY
Sandra Wise, Senior Director
Commission on Accreditation in Physical Therapy Education (CAPTE)
American Physical Therapy Association (APTA)
1111 North Fairfax Street
Alexandria, Virginia 22314-1488
Phone: 703-706-3240
Fax: 703-706-3387
E-mail: accreditation@apta.org
Website: www.capteonline.org

PHYSICIAN ASSISTANT STUDIES
John E. McCarty, Executive Director
Accredittion Review Commission on Education for the Physician Assistant, Inc. (ARC-PA)
12000 Findley Road, Suite 150
Johns Creek, Georgia 30097
Phone: 770-476-1224
Fax: 770-476-1738
E-mail: arc-pa@arc-pa.org
Website: www.arc-pa.org

PLANNING
Ms. Shonagh Merits, Executive Director
American Institute of Certified Planners/Association of Collegiate Schools of Planning/American Planning Association
Planning Accreditation Board (PAB)
2334 West Lawrence Avenue, Suite 209
Chicago, Illinois 60625
Phone: 773-334-7200
E-mail: smerits@planningaccreditationboard.org
Website: www.planningaccreditationboard.org

PODIATRIC MEDICINE
Alan R. Tinkleman, M.P.A., Executive Director
Council on Podiatric Medical Education (CPME)
American Podiatric Medical Association (APMA)
9312 Old Georgetown Road
Bethesda, Maryland 20814-1621
Phone: 301-581-9200
Fax: 301-571-4903
Website: www.cpme.org

PSYCHOLOGY AND COUNSELING
Jacqueline Remondet Wall, Director, Office of Program Consultation and Accreditation and Associate Executive Director
Education Directorate
American Psychological Association
750 First Street, NE
Washington, DC 20002-4202
Phone: 202-336-5979 or 800-374-2721
TDD/TTY: 202-336-6123
Fax: 202-336-5978
E-mail: apaaccred@apa.org
Website: www.apa.org/ed/accreditation

Carol L. Bobby, Ph.D., Executive Director
Council for Accreditation of Counseling and Related Educational Programs (CACREP)
1001 North Fairfax Street, Suite 510
Alexandria, Virginia 22314
Phone: 703-535-5990
Fax: 703-739-6209
E-mail: cacrep@cacrep.org
Website: www.cacrep.org

Richard M. McFall, Executive Director
Psychological Clinical Science Accreditation System (PCSAS)
1101 East Tenth Street
IU Psychology Building
Bloomington, Indiana 47405-7007
Phone: 812-856-2570
Fax: 812-322-5545
E-mail: rmmcfall@pcsas.org
Website: www.pcsas.org

PUBLIC HEALTH
Laura Rasar King, M.P.H., MCHES, Executive Director
Council on Education for Public Health
1010 Wayne Avenue, Suite 220
Silver Spring, Maryland 20910
Phone: 202-789-1050
Fax: 202-789-1895
E-mail: Lking@ceph.org
Website: www.ceph.org

PUBLIC POLICY, AFFAIRS AND ADMINISTRATION
Crystal Calarusse, Chief Accreditation Officer
Commission on Peer Review and Accreditation
Network of Schools of Public Policy, Affairs, and Administration (NASPAA-COPRA)
1029 Vermont Avenue, NW, Suite 1100
Washington, DC 20005
Phone: 202-628-8965
Fax: 202-626-4978
E-mail: copra@naspaa.org
Website: www.naspaa.org

REHABILITATION EDUCATION
Frank Lane, Ph.D., Executive Director
Council on Rehabilitation Education (CORE)
Commission on Standards and Accreditation
1699 Woodfield Road, Suite 300
Schaumburg, Illinois 60173
Phone: 847-944-1345
Fax: 847-944-1346
E-mail: flane@core-rehab.org
Website: www.core-rehab.org

RESPIRATORY CARE
Thomas Smalling, Executive Director
Commission on Accreditation for Respiratory Care (CoARC)
1248 Harwood Road
Bedford, TX 76021-4244
Phone: 817-283-2835
Fax: 817-354-8519
E-mail: tom@coarc.com
Website: www.coarc.com

SOCIAL WORK
Jo Ann Regan, Ph.D., Director
Office of Social Work Accreditation
Council on Social Work Education
1701 Duke Street, Suite 200
Alexandria, Virginia 22314
Phone: 703-683-8080
Fax: 703-683-8099
E-mail: info@cswe.org
Website: www.cswe.org

SPEECH-LANGUAGE PATHOLOGY AND AUDIOLOGY
Patrima L. Tice, Director of Accreditation
American Speech-Language-Hearing Association
Council on Academic Accreditation in Audiology and Speech-Language
    Pathology
2200 Research Boulevard
Rockville, Maryland 20850-3289
Phone: 301-296-5796
Fax: 301-296-8750
E-mail: ptice@asha.org
Website: www.asha.org/academic/accreditation/default.htm

TEACHER EDUCATION
Mark LaCelle-Peterson, President
Council for the Accreditation of Educator Preparation
1140 19th Street, NW, Suite 400
Washington, DC 20036
Phone: 202-223-0077
E-mail: caep@caepnet.org
Website: www.teac.org

TECHNOLOGY
Michale S. McComis, Ed.D., Executive Director
Accrediting Commission of Career Schools and Colleges
2101 Wilson Boulevard, Suite 302
Arlington, Virginia 22201
Phone: 703-247-4212
Fax: 703-247-4533
E-mail: mccomis@accsc.org
Website: www.accsc.org

TECHNOLOGY, MANAGEMENT, AND APPLIED ENGINEERING
Michele Anderson, Director of Accreditation
The Association of Technology, Management, and Applied Engineering
(ATMAE)
275 N. York Street, Suite 401
Elmhurst, Illinois 60126
Phone: 630-433-4514
Fax: 630-563-9181
E-mail: Michele@atmae.org
Website: www.atmae.org

THEATER
Karen P. Moynahan, Executive Director
National Association of Schools of Theatre Commission on
    Accreditation
11250 Roger Bacon Drive, Suite 21
Reston, Virginia 20190
Phone: 703-437-0700
Fax: 703-437-6312
E-mail: info@arts-accredit.org
Website: http://nast.arts-accredit.org/

THEOLOGY
Keith Sharfman, Director
Association of Advanced Rabbinical and Talmudic Schools (AARTS)
Accreditation Commission
11 Broadway, Suite 405
New York, New York 10004
Phone: 212-363-1991
Fax: 212-533-5335
E-mail: k.sharfman.aarts@gmail.com

Daniel O. Aleshire, Executive Director
Association of Theological Schools in the United States and Canada
    (ATS)
Commission on Accrediting
10 Summit Park Drive
Pittsburgh, Pennsylvania 15275
Phone: 412-788-6505
Fax: 412-788-6510
E-mail: ats@ats.edu
Website: www.ats.edu

Paul Boatner, President
Transnational Association of Christian Colleges and Schools (TRACS)
Accreditation Commission
15935 Forest Road
Forest, Virginia 24551
Phone: 434-525-9539
Fax: 434-525-9538
E-mail: info@tracs.org
Website: www.tracs.org

VETERINARY MEDICINE
Dr. Karen Brandt, Director of Education and Research
American Veterinary Medical Association (AVMA)
Council on Education
1931 North Meacham Road, Suite 100
Schaumburg, Illinois 60173-4360
Phone: 847-925-8070 Ext. 6674
Fax: 847-285-5732
E-mail: info@avma.org
Website: www.avma.org

How to Use These Guides

As you identify the particular programs and institutions that interest you, you can use both the *Graduate & Professional Programs: An Overview* volume and the specialized volumes in the series to obtain detailed information.

- *Graduate Programs in the Biological/Biomedical Sciences & Health-Related Professions*
- *Graduate Programs in Business, Education, Information Studies, Law & Social Work*
- *Graduate Programs in Engineering & Applied Sciences*
- *Graduate Programs the Humanities, Arts & Social Sciences*
- *Graduate Programs in the Physical Sciences, Mathematics, Agricultural Sciences, the Environment & Natural Resources*

Each of the specialized volumes in the series is divided into sections that contain one or more directories devoted to programs in a particular field. If you do not find a directory devoted to your field of interest in a specific volume, consult "Directories and Subject Areas" (located at the end of each volume). After you have identified the correct volume, consult the "Directories and Subject Areas in This Book" index, which shows (as does the more general directory) what directories cover subjects not specifically named in a directory or section title.

Each of the specialized volumes in the series has a number of general directories. These directories have entries for the largest unit at an institution granting graduate degrees in that field. For example, the general Engineering and Applied Sciences directory in the *Graduate Programs in Engineering & Applied Sciences* volume consists of **Profiles** for colleges, schools, and departments of engineering and applied sciences.

General directories are followed by other directories, or sections, that give more detailed information about programs in particular areas of the general field that has been covered. The general Engineering and Applied Sciences directory, in the previous example, is followed by nineteen sections with directories in specific areas of engineering, such as Chemical Engineering, Industrial/Management Engineering, and Mechanical Engineering.

Because of the broad nature of many fields, any system of organization is bound to involve a certain amount of overlap. Environmental studies, for example, is a field whose various aspects are studied in several types of departments and schools. Readers interested in such studies will find information on relevant programs in the *Graduate Programs in the Biological/Biomedical Sciences & Health-Related Professions* volume under Ecology and Environmental Biology and Environmental and Occupational Health; in the *Graduate Programs in the Physical Sciences, Mathematics, Agricultural Sciences, the Environment & Natural Resources* volume under Environmental Management and Policy and Natural Resources; and in the *Graduate Programs in Engineering & Applied Sciences* volume under Energy Management and Policy and Environmental Engineering. To help you find all of the programs of interest to you, the introduction to each section within the specialized volumes includes, if applicable, a paragraph suggesting other sections and directories with information on related areas of study.

Directory of Institutions with Programs in the Humanities, Arts & Social Sciences

This directory lists institutions in alphabetical order and includes beneath each name the academic fields in which each institution offers graduate programs. The degree level in each field is also indicated, provided that the institution has supplied that information in response to Peterson's Annual Survey of Graduate and Professional Institutions.

An M indicates that a master's degree program is offered; a D indicates that a doctoral degree program is offered; an O signifies that other advanced degrees (e.g., certificates or specialist degrees) are

offered; and an * (asterisk) indicates that a **Close-Up** and/or **Display** is located in this volume. See the index, "Close-Ups and Displays," for the specific page number.

Profiles of Academic and Professional Programs in the Specialized Volumes

Each section of **Profiles** has a table of contents that lists the Program Directories, **Displays**, and **Close-Ups**. Program Directories consist of the **Profiles** of programs in the relevant fields, with **Displays** following if programs have chosen to include them. **Close-Ups,** which are more individualized statements, are also listed for those graduate schools or programs that have chosen to submit them.

The **Profiles** found in the 500 directories in the specialized volumes provide basic data about the graduate units in capsule form for quick reference. To make these directories as useful as possible, **Profiles** are generally listed for an institution's smallest academic unit within a subject area. In other words, if an institution has a College of Liberal Arts that administers many related programs, the **Profile** for the individual program (e.g., Program in History), not the entire College, appears in the directory.

There are some programs that do not fit into any current directory and are not given individual **Profiles**. The directory structure is reviewed annually in order to keep this number to a minimum and to accommodate major trends in graduate education.

The following outline describes the **Profile** information found in the guides and explains how best to use that information. Any item that does not apply to or was not provided by a graduate unit is omitted from its listing. The format of the **Profiles** is constant, making it easy to compare one institution with another and one program with another.

A ★ graphic next to the school's name indicates the institution has additional detailed information in a "Premium Profile" on Petersons.com. After reading their information here, you can learn more about the school by visiting www.petersons.com and searching for that particular college or university's graduate program.

Identifying Information. The institution's name, in boldface type, is followed by a complete listing of the administrative structure for that field of study. (For example, University of Akron, Buchtel College of Arts and Sciences, Department of Theoretical and Applied Mathematics, Program in Mathematics.) The last unit listed is the one to which all information in the **Profile** pertains. The institution's city, state, and zip code follow.

Offerings. Each field of study offered by the unit is listed with all postbaccalaureate degrees awarded. Degrees that are not preceded by a specific concentration are awarded in the general field listed in the unit name. Frequently, fields of study are broken down into subspecializations, and those appear following the degrees awarded; for example, "Offerings in secondary education (M.Ed.), including English education, mathematics education, science education." Students enrolled in the M.Ed. program would be able to specialize in any of the three fields mentioned.

Professional Accreditation. Some **Profiles** indicate whether a program is professionally accredited. Because it is possible for a program to receive or lose professional accreditation at any time, students entering fields in which accreditation is important to a career should verify the status of programs by contacting either the chairperson or the appropriate accrediting association.

Jointly Offered Degrees. Explanatory statements concerning programs that are offered in cooperation with other institutions are included in the list of degrees offered. This occurs most commonly on a regional basis (for example, two state universities offering a cooperative Ph.D. in special education) or where the specialized nature of the institutions encourages joint efforts (a J.D./M.B.A. offered by a law school at an institution with no formal business programs and an institution with

15

a business school but lacking a law school). Only programs that are truly cooperative are listed; those involving only limited course work at another institution are not. Interested students should contact the heads of such units for further information.

Part-Time and Evening/Weekend Programs. When information regarding the availability of part-time or evening/weekend study appears in the **Profile**, it means that students are able to earn a degree exclusively through such study.

Postbaccalaureate Distance Learning Degrees. A postbaccalaureate distance learning degree program signifies that course requirements can be fulfilled with minimal or no on-campus study.

Faculty. Figures on the number of faculty members actively involved with graduate students through teaching or research are separated into full- and part-time as well as men and women whenever the information has been supplied.

Students. Figures for the number of students enrolled in graduate and professional programs pertain to the semester of highest enrollment from the 2014–15 academic year. These figures are broken down into full- and part-time and men and women whenever the data have been supplied. Information on the number of matriculated students enrolled in the unit who are members of a minority group or are international students appears here. The average age of the matriculated students is followed by the number of applicants, the percentage accepted, and the number enrolled for fall 2014.

Degrees Awarded. The number of degrees awarded in the calendar year is listed. Many doctoral programs offer a terminal master's degree if students leave the program after completing only part of the requirements for a doctoral degree; that is indicated here. All degrees are classified into one of four types: master's, doctoral, first professional, and other advanced degrees. A unit may award one or several degrees at a given level; however, the data are only collected by type and may therefore represent several different degree programs.

Degree Requirements. The information in this section is also broken down by type of degree, and all information for a degree level pertains to all degrees of that type unless otherwise specified. Degree requirements are collected in a simplified form to provide some very basic information on the nature of the program and on foreign language, thesis or dissertation, comprehensive exam, and registration requirements. Many units also provide a short list of additional requirements, such as fieldwork or an internship. For complete information on graduation requirements, contact the graduate school or program directly.

Entrance Requirements. Entrance requirements are broken down into the four degree levels of master's, doctoral, first professional, and other advanced degrees. Within each level, information may be provided in two basic categories: entrance exams and other requirements. The entrance exams are identified by the standard acronyms used by the testing agencies, unless they are not well known. Other entrance requirements are quite varied, but they often contain an undergraduate or graduate grade point average (GPA). Unless otherwise stated, the GPA is calculated on a 4.0 scale and is listed as a minimum required for admission. Additional exam requirements/recommendations for international students may be listed here. Application deadlines for domestic and international students, the application fee, and whether electronic applications are accepted may be listed here. Note that the deadline should be used for reference only; these dates are subject to change, and students interested in applying should always contact the graduate unit directly about application procedures and deadlines.

Expenses. The typical cost of study for the 2015–2016 academic year (2014–15 if 2015–16 figures were not available) is given in two basic categories: tuition and fees. Cost of study may be quite complex at a graduate institution. There are often sliding scales for part-time study, a different cost for first-year students, and other variables that make it impossible to completely cover the cost of study for each graduate program. To provide the most usable information, figures are given for full-time study for a full year where available and for part-time study in terms of a per-unit rate (per credit, per semester hour, etc.). Occasionally, variances may be noted in tuition and fees for reasons such as the type of program, whether courses are taken during the day or evening, whether courses are at the master's or doctoral level, or other institution-specific reasons. Respondents were also given the opportunity to provide more specific and detailed tuition and fees information at the unit level. When provided, this information will appear in place of any typical costs entered elsewhere on the university-level survey. Expenses are usually subject to change; for exact costs at any given time, contact your chosen schools and programs directly. Keep in mind that the tuition of Canadian institutions is usually given in Canadian dollars.

Financial Support. This section contains data on the number of awards administered by the institution and given to graduate students during the 2014–15 academic year. The first figure given represents the total number of students receiving financial support enrolled in that unit. If the unit has provided information on graduate appointments, these are broken down into three major categories: fellowships give money to graduate students to cover the cost of study and living expenses and are not based on a work obligation or research commitment, research assistantships provide stipends to graduate students for assistance in a formal research project with a faculty member, and teaching assistantships provide stipends to graduate students for teaching or for assisting faculty members in teaching undergraduate classes. Within each category, figures are given for the total number of awards, the average yearly amount per award, and whether full or partial tuition reimbursements are awarded. In addition to graduate appointments, the availability of several other financial aid sources is covered in this section. Tuition waivers are routinely part of a graduate appointment, but units sometimes waive part or all of a student's tuition even if a graduate appointment is not available. Federal WorkStudy is made available to students who demonstrate need and meet the federal guidelines; this form of aid normally includes 10 or more hours of work per week in an office of the institution. Institutionally sponsored loans are low-interest loans available to graduate students to cover both educational and living expenses. Career-related internships or fieldwork offer money to students who are participating in a formal off-campus research project or practicum. Grants, scholarships, traineeships, unspecified assistantships, and other awards may also be noted. The availability of financial support to part-time students is also indicated here.

Some programs list the financial aid application deadline and the forms that need to be completed for students to be eligible for financial awards. There are two forms: FAFSA, the Free Application for Federal Student Aid, which is required for federal aid, and the CSS PROFILE®.

Faculty Research. Each unit has the opportunity to list several keyword phrases describing the current research involving faculty members and graduate students. Space limitations prevent the unit from listing complete information on all research programs. The total expenditure for funded research from the previous academic year may also be included.

Unit Head and Application Contact. The head of the graduate program for each unit may be listed with academic title, phone and fax numbers, and e-mail address. In addition to the unit head's contact information, many graduate programs also list a separate contact for application and admission information, followed by the graduate school, program, or department's website. If no unit head or application contact is given, you should contact the overall institution for information on graduate admissions.

Displays and Close-Ups

The **Displays** and **Close-Ups** are supplementary insertions submitted by deans, chairs, and other administrators who wish to offer an additional, more individualized statement to readers. A number of graduate school and program administrators have attached a **Display** ad near the **Profile** listing. Here you will find information that an institution or program wants to emphasize. The **Close-Ups** are by their very nature more expansive and flexible than the **Profiles**, and the administrators who have written them may emphasize different aspects of their programs. All of the **Close-Ups** are organized in the same way (with the exception of a few that describe research and training opportunities instead of degree programs), and in each one you will find information on the same basic topics, such as programs of study, research facilities, tuition and fees, financial aid, and application procedures. If an institution or program has submitted a **Close-Up**, a boldface cross-reference appears below its **Profile**. As with the **Displays**, all of the **Close-Ups** in the guides have been submitted by choice; the absence of a **Display** or **Close-Up** does not reflect any

type of editorial judgment on the part of Peterson's, and their presence in the guides should not be taken as an indication of status, quality, or approval. Statements regarding a university's objectives and accomplishments are a reflection of its own beliefs and are not the opinions of the Peterson's editors.

Appendixes

This section contains two appendixes. The first, "Institutional Changes Since the 2015 Edition," lists institutions that have closed, merged, or changed their name or status since the last edition of the guides. The second, "Abbreviations Used in the Guides," gives abbreviations of degree names, along with what those abbreviations stand for. These appendixes are identical in all six volumes of *Peterson's Graduate and Professional Programs*.

Indexes

There are three indexes presented here. The first index, "Close-Ups and Displays," gives page references for all programs that have chosen to place **Close-Ups** and **Displays** in this volume. It is arranged alphabetically by institution; within institutions, the arrangement is alphabetical by subject area. It is not an index to all programs in the book's directories of **Profiles**; readers must refer to the directories themselves for **Profile** information on programs that have not submitted the additional, more individualized statements. The second index, "Directories and Subject Areas in Other Books in This Series", gives book references for the directories in the specialized volumes and also includes cross-references for subject area names not used in the directory structure, for example, "Computing Technology (see Computer Science)." The third index, "Directories and Subject Areas in This Book," gives page references for the directories in this volume and cross-references for subject area names not used in this volume's directory structure.

Data Collection Procedures

The information published in the directories and Profiles of all the books is collected through Peterson's Annual Survey of Graduate and Professional Institutions. The survey is sent each spring to nearly 2,300 institutions offering postbaccalaureate degree programs, including accredited institutions in the United States, U.S. territories, and Canada and those institutions outside the United States that are accredited by U.S. accrediting bodies. Deans and other administrators complete these surveys, providing information on programs in the 500 academic and professional fields covered in the guides as well as overall insti-

tutional information. While every effort has been made to ensure the accuracy and completeness of the data, information is sometimes unavailable or changes occur after publication deadlines. All usable information received in time for publication has been included. The omission of any particular item from a directory or Profile signifies either that the item is not applicable to the institution or program or that information was not available. Profiles of programs scheduled to begin during the 2015–16 academic year cannot, obviously, include statistics on enrollment or, in many cases, the number of faculty members. If no usable data were submitted by an institution, its name, address, and program name appear in order to indicate the availability of graduate work.

Criteria for Inclusion in This Guide

To be included in this guide, an institution must have full accreditation or be a candidate for accreditation (preaccreditation) status by an institutional or specialized accrediting body recognized by the U.S. Department of Education or the Council for Higher Education Accreditation (CHEA). Institutional accrediting bodies, which review each institution as a whole, include the six regional associations of schools and colleges (Middle States, New England, North Central, Northwest, Southern, and Western), each of which is responsible for a specified portion of the United States and its territories. Other institutional accrediting bodies are national in scope and accredit specific kinds of institutions (e.g., Bible colleges, independent colleges, and rabbinical and Talmudic schools). Program registration by the New York State Board of Regents is considered to be the equivalent of institutional accreditation, since the board requires that all programs offered by an institution meet its standards before recognition is granted. A Canadian institution must be chartered and authorized to grant degrees by the provincial government, affiliated with a chartered institution, or accredited by a recognized U.S. accrediting body. This guide also includes institutions outside the United States that are accredited by these U.S. accrediting bodies. There are recognized specialized or professional accrediting bodies in more than fifty different fields, each of which is authorized to accredit institutions or specific programs in its particular field. For specialized institutions that offer programs in one field only, we designate this to be the equivalent of institutional accreditation. A full explanation of the accrediting process and complete information on recognized institutional (regional and national) and specialized accrediting bodies can be found online at www.chea.org or at www.ed.gov/admins/finaid/accred/index.html.

DIRECTORY OF INSTITUTIONS AND THEIR OFFERINGS

ABILENE CHRISTIAN UNIVERSITY
Clinical Psychology M
Communication—General M
Conflict Resolution and Mediation/Peace Studies M,O
Counseling Psychology M
English M
Liberal Studies M
Marriage and Family Therapy M
Missions and Missiology M
Pastoral Ministry and Counseling M,D
Psychology—General M
Religion M
Rhetoric M
School Psychology O
Theology M
Writing M

ACADEMY OF ART UNIVERSITY
Applied Arts and Design—General M
Architecture M
Art History M
Art/Fine Arts M
Arts Journalism M
Clothing and Textiles M
Computer Art and Design M
Film, Television, and Video Production M
Graphic Design M
Illustration M
Industrial Design M
Interior Design M
Internet and Interactive Multimedia M
Landscape Architecture M
Music M
Photography M
Textile Design M
Theater M
Writing M

ACADIA UNIVERSITY
Clinical Psychology M
English M
Geographic Information Systems M
Philosophy M
Political Science M
Psychology—General M
Sociology M
Sustainable Development M
Theology M,D

ADAMS STATE UNIVERSITY
Art/Fine Arts M
History M

ADELPHI UNIVERSITY
Art/Fine Arts M
Clinical Psychology D
Counseling Psychology M
Emergency Management O
Gerontology M,O
Psychology—General M,D*
Public Administration O
School Psychology M
Writing M*

ADLER GRADUATE SCHOOL
Addictions/Substance Abuse Counseling M
Art Therapy M
Clinical Psychology M
Counseling Psychology M
Marriage and Family Therapy M
Psychoanalysis and Psychotherapy M

ADLER UNIVERSITY
Addictions/Substance Abuse Counseling M,D,O
Art Therapy M,D,O
Clinical Psychology M,D,O
Counseling Psychology M,D,O
Criminal Justice and Criminology M,D,O
Emergency Management M,D,O
Forensic Psychology M,D,O
Health Psychology M,D,O
Industrial and Organizational Psychology M,D,O
Marriage and Family Therapy M,D,O
Psychoanalysis and Psychotherapy M,D,O
Psychology—General M,D,O*
Public Administration M,D,O
Public Policy M,D,O
Rehabilitation Counseling M,D,O
Social Psychology M,D,O
Sport Psychology M,D,O

ADRIAN COLLEGE
Criminal Justice and Criminology M

ALABAMA AGRICULTURAL AND MECHANICAL UNIVERSITY
Clinical Psychology M,O
Counseling Psychology M,O
Family and Consumer Sciences-General M,D
Music M
Psychology—General M,O
School Psychology M,O
Urban and Regional Planning M

ALABAMA STATE UNIVERSITY
Forensic Sciences M
Rehabilitation Counseling M

ALASKA PACIFIC UNIVERSITY
Counseling Psychology M
Interdisciplinary Studies M
Liberal Studies M

ALBANY STATE UNIVERSITY
Criminal Justice and Criminology M
Economic Development M
Economics M
Forensic Sciences M
Public Administration M
Public Policy M

ALBERTUS MAGNUS COLLEGE
Art Therapy M
Criminal Justice and Criminology M
Liberal Studies M
Writing M

ALCORN STATE UNIVERSITY
Agricultural Economics and Agribusiness M

ALFRED UNIVERSITY
Applied Arts and Design—General M
Art/Fine Arts M,D
Computer Art and Design M
Counseling Psychology M,D,O
Internet and Interactive Multimedia M
School Psychology M,D,O

ALLIANT INTERNATIONAL UNIVERSITY–FRESNO
Clinical Psychology D
Forensic Psychology D
Industrial and Organizational Psychology M,D
Psychology—General M,D

ALLIANT INTERNATIONAL UNIVERSITY–IRVINE
Forensic Psychology D
Forensic Sciences D
Marriage and Family Therapy M,D
School Psychology M,D,O

ALLIANT INTERNATIONAL UNIVERSITY–LOS ANGELES
Addictions/Substance Abuse Counseling M
Clinical Psychology D
Forensic Psychology D
Gerontology M
Health Psychology D
Industrial and Organizational Psychology M,D
Marriage and Family Therapy M,D
Psychology—General M,D
School Psychology M,D,O
Social Psychology D

ALLIANT INTERNATIONAL UNIVERSITY–MÉXICO CITY
Counseling Psychology M
International Affairs M

ALLIANT INTERNATIONAL UNIVERSITY–SACRAMENTO
Clinical Psychology D
Forensic Psychology D
Marriage and Family Therapy M,D
Psychology—General M,D

ALLIANT INTERNATIONAL UNIVERSITY–SAN DIEGO
Clinical Psychology M,D
Forensic Psychology D
Industrial and Organizational Psychology M,D
Marriage and Family Therapy M,D
Psychology—General M,D
School Psychology M,D,O

ALLIANT INTERNATIONAL UNIVERSITY–SAN FRANCISCO
Clinical Psychology M,D,O
Criminal Justice and Criminology M
Forensic Psychology M,D
Industrial and Organizational Psychology M,D
Psychology—General M,D,O
School Psychology M,D,O

ALVERNIA UNIVERSITY
Liberal Studies M
Social Psychology M

ALVERNO COLLEGE
Social Psychology M

AMBERTON UNIVERSITY
Counseling Psychology M
Interdisciplinary Studies M

AMBROSE UNIVERSITY
Cultural Studies M,O
Pastoral Ministry and Counseling M,O
Religion M,O
Theology M,O

AMERICAN BAPTIST COLLEGE OF AMERICAN BAPTIST THEOLOGICAL SEMINARY
Pastoral Ministry and Counseling M

AMERICAN BAPTIST SEMINARY OF THE WEST
Pastoral Ministry and Counseling M
Theology M

AMERICAN CONSERVATORY THEATER
Theater M,O

AMERICAN FILM INSTITUTE CONSERVATORY
Film, Television, and Video Production M

AMERICAN GRADUATE SCHOOL IN PARIS
International Affairs M,D

AMERICAN INTERCONTINENTAL UNIVERSITY ONLINE
Industrial and Organizational Psychology M

AMERICAN INTERNATIONAL COLLEGE
Clinical Psychology M
Counseling Psychology M
Forensic Psychology M
Psychology—General M

AMERICAN JEWISH UNIVERSITY
Jewish Studies M
Theology M

AMERICAN MUSEUM OF NATURAL HISTORY–RICHARD GILDER GRADUATE SCHOOL
Museum Studies D

AMERICAN PUBLIC UNIVERSITY SYSTEM
American Studies M
Classics M
Conflict Resolution and Mediation/Peace Studies M
Criminal Justice and Criminology M
Emergency Management M
Forensic Sciences M
History M
Homeland Security M
Humanities M
International Affairs M
Military and Defense Studies M
National Security M
Political Science M
Psychology—General M
Public Administration M
Public History M
Public Policy M
School Psychology M
Western European Studies M

AMERICAN UNIVERSITY
American Studies M,D,O
Communication—General M,D
Conflict Resolution and Mediation/Peace Studies M,D,O
Cultural Studies M,D,O
Economics M,D,O
Ethics M,D,O
Film, Television, and Video Production M
Gender Studies O
International Affairs M,D,O
International Development M,D,O
Journalism M
Mass Communication M,D,O
Media Studies M,D
Political Science M,D,O
Public Affairs M
Sustainable Development M,D,O
Western European Studies M,D,O
Women's Studies O

THE AMERICAN UNIVERSITY IN CAIRO
Anthropology M
Communication—General M
Comparative Literature M,O
Demography and Population Studies M,O
Economic Development M,O
Economics M,O
English M,O
Gender Studies M
International Affairs M,O
Journalism M
Near and Middle Eastern Languages M,O
Near and Middle Eastern Studies M,O
Political Science M
Psychology—General M
Public Administration M,O
Public Policy M,O
Sociology M
Women's Studies M

AMERICAN UNIVERSITY OF ARMENIA
Economics M
International Affairs M
Political Science M

AMERICAN UNIVERSITY OF BEIRUT
Agricultural Economics and Agribusiness M
American Studies M,D
Anthropology M,D
Archaeology M,D
Clinical Psychology M,D
Economics M,D
English M,D
History M,D
Media Studies M,D
Near and Middle Eastern Languages M,D
Near and Middle Eastern Studies M,D
Political Science M,D
Psychology—General M,D
Public Administration M,D
Sociology M,D
Urban and Regional Planning M,D
Urban Design M,D

THE AMERICAN UNIVERSITY OF PARIS
Communication—General M
Conflict Resolution and Mediation/Peace Studies M
Cultural Studies M
International Affairs M
Near and Middle Eastern Studies M
Public Policy M

AMERICAN UNIVERSITY OF PUERTO RICO
Criminal Justice and Criminology M

THE AMERICAN UNIVERSITY OF ROME
Historic Preservation M
Religion M

AMERICAN UNIVERSITY OF SHARJAH
Translation and Interpretation M
Urban and Regional Planning M

AMRIDGE UNIVERSITY
Counseling Psychology M,D
Marriage and Family Therapy M,D
Pastoral Ministry and Counseling M,D
Religion M,D
Theology M,D

ANABAPTIST MENNONITE BIBLICAL SEMINARY
Conflict Resolution and Mediation/Peace Studies M,O
Missions and Missiology M,O
Theology M,O

ANDERSON UNIVERSITY (IN)
Missions and Missiology M,D
Theology M,D

ANDERSON UNIVERSITY (SC)
Criminal Justice and Criminology M
Pastoral Ministry and Counseling M

ANDOVER NEWTON THEOLOGICAL SCHOOL
Theology M,D

ANDREWS UNIVERSITY
Architecture M
Clinical Psychology M
Communication—General M
Counseling Psychology M,D
Developmental Psychology M,D
Economics M
English M
International Development M
Missions and Missiology D
Music M
Pastoral Ministry and Counseling M,D,O
Psychology—General M,D,O
School Psychology M,O
Social Psychology M
Theology M,D,O

ANGELO STATE UNIVERSITY
Applied Psychology M
Communication—General M
Counseling Psychology M
English M
Industrial and Organizational Psychology M
Journalism M
National Security M
Psychology—General M

ANNA MARIA COLLEGE
Art/Fine Arts M,O
Counseling Psychology M
Criminal Justice and Criminology M
Emergency Management M,O
Pastoral Ministry and Counseling M
Public Administration M

ANTIOCH UNIVERSITY LOS ANGELES
Clinical Psychology M
Psychology—General M
Sustainable Development M
Writing M,O

ANTIOCH UNIVERSITY MIDWEST
Art/Fine Arts M
Comparative Literature M
Conflict Resolution and Mediation/Peace Studies M
Counseling Psychology M
Liberal Studies M
Psychology—General M
Writing M

ANTIOCH UNIVERSITY NEW ENGLAND
Addictions/Substance Abuse Counseling M
Applied Behavior Analysis M,O
Applied Psychology M,D,O
Clinical Psychology M,D
Counseling Psychology M
Humanities M
Interdisciplinary Studies M
Marriage and Family Therapy M,D,O
Sustainable Development M,O
Therapies—Dance, Drama, and Music M,O

ANTIOCH UNIVERSITY SANTA BARBARA
Clinical Psychology M,D

ANTIOCH UNIVERSITY SEATTLE
Psychology—General M,D

APEX SCHOOL OF THEOLOGY
Theology M,D

APPALACHIAN BIBLE COLLEGE
Pastoral Ministry and Counseling M

APPALACHIAN STATE UNIVERSITY
American Studies M
Child Development M
Clinical Psychology M
Counseling Psychology M
Criminal Justice and Criminology M
Cultural Studies M
English M
Experimental Psychology M
Family and Consumer Sciences-General M
Geographic Information Systems M
Geography M
Gerontology M,O
Health Psychology M
History M
Industrial and Organizational Psychology M
International Affairs M
Marriage and Family Therapy M
Music M
Political Science M
Psychology—General M
Public Administration M
Romance Languages M
School Psychology M
Sociology M,O
Sustainable Development M

Therapies—Dance, Drama, and Music — M

AQUINAS INSTITUTE OF THEOLOGY
Music — M,D,O
Pastoral Ministry and Counseling — M,D,O
Theology — M,D,O

ARCADIA UNIVERSITY
Conflict Resolution and Mediation/Peace Studies — M
English — M
Forensic Sciences — M
Genetic Counseling — M
Humanities — M
International Affairs — M
Psychology—General — M,D,O
School Psychology — M
Social Psychology — M
Theater — M,D,O

ARGOSY UNIVERSITY, ATLANTA
Clinical Psychology — M,D,O
Forensic Psychology — M,D,O
Health Psychology — M,D,O
Industrial and Organizational Psychology — M,D,O
Marriage and Family Therapy — M,D,O
Psychology—General — M,D,O
Social Psychology — M,D,O
Sport Psychology — M,D,O

ARGOSY UNIVERSITY, CHICAGO
Clinical Psychology — M,D
Counseling Psychology — D
Forensic Psychology — D
Health Psychology — D
Human Development — D
Industrial and Organizational Psychology — M,D
Marriage and Family Therapy — D
Psychoanalysis and Psychotherapy — D
Psychology—General — M,D
Public Administration — M,D
Social Psychology — M,D

ARGOSY UNIVERSITY, DALLAS
Clinical Psychology — M,D
Forensic Psychology — M
Industrial and Organizational Psychology — M
Psychology—General — M,D
Public Administration — M,D,O
School Psychology — M,D
Social Psychology — M

ARGOSY UNIVERSITY, DENVER
Clinical Psychology — M,D
Counseling Psychology — M,D
Forensic Psychology — M,D
Industrial and Organizational Psychology — M,D
Marriage and Family Therapy — M,D
Psychology—General — M,D
Public Administration — M,D

ARGOSY UNIVERSITY, HAWAI'I
Addictions/Substance Abuse Counseling — O
Clinical Psychology — M,D,O
Counseling Psychology — D
Forensic Psychology — M
Marriage and Family Therapy — M
Psychology—General — M,D,O
School Psychology — M

ARGOSY UNIVERSITY, INLAND EMPIRE
Clinical Psychology — M,D
Counseling Psychology — M,D
Forensic Psychology — M,D
Industrial and Organizational Psychology — M,D
Marriage and Family Therapy — M,D
Psychology—General — M,D
Public Administration — M,D
Sport Psychology — M,D

ARGOSY UNIVERSITY, LOS ANGELES
Clinical Psychology — M,D
Counseling Psychology — M,D
Forensic Psychology — M,D
Marriage and Family Therapy — M,D
Psychology—General — M,D
Public Administration — M,D

ARGOSY UNIVERSITY, NASHVILLE
Counseling Psychology — M,D
Psychology—General — M,D

ARGOSY UNIVERSITY, ORANGE COUNTY
Clinical Psychology — M,D
Counseling Psychology — M,D
Forensic Psychology — M
Marriage and Family Therapy — M,D
Psychology—General — M,D
Public Administration — M,D,O
Sport Psychology — M,D

ARGOSY UNIVERSITY, PHOENIX
Clinical Psychology — M,D
Counseling Psychology — M,D
Forensic Psychology — M
Industrial and Organizational Psychology — M
Psychology—General — M,D
Public Administration — M,D
School Psychology — M,D
Sport Psychology — M,D

ARGOSY UNIVERSITY, SALT LAKE CITY
Counseling Psychology — M,D
Forensic Psychology — M,D
Marriage and Family Therapy — M,D

Psychology—General — M,D
Public Administration — M,D

ARGOSY UNIVERSITY, SAN DIEGO
Clinical Psychology — M,D
Counseling Psychology — M,D
Forensic Psychology — M,D
Marriage and Family Therapy — M,D
Psychology—General — M,D
Public Administration — M,D

ARGOSY UNIVERSITY, SAN FRANCISCO BAY AREA
Clinical Psychology — M,D
Counseling Psychology — M,D
Forensic Psychology — M
Psychology—General — M,D
Public Administration — M,D
Sport Psychology — M,D

ARGOSY UNIVERSITY, SARASOTA
Counseling Psychology — M,D
Forensic Psychology — M,D
Marriage and Family Therapy — M,D
Pastoral Ministry and Counseling — M,D
Psychology—General — M,D
Public Administration — M,D
School Psychology — M,D,O
Social Psychology — M,D

ARGOSY UNIVERSITY, SCHAUMBURG
Clinical Psychology — M,D
Corporate and Organizational Communication — M,D,O
Counseling Psychology — M,O
Forensic Psychology — M,O
Industrial and Organizational Psychology — M,O
Psychology—General — M,O
Public Administration — M,D,O
Sport Psychology — M,O

ARGOSY UNIVERSITY, SEATTLE
Clinical Psychology — M,D,O
Counseling Psychology — M,D
Psychology—General — M,D,O
Public Administration — M,D

ARGOSY UNIVERSITY, TAMPA
Clinical Psychology — M,D
Counseling Psychology — M,D
Industrial and Organizational Psychology — M,D
Marriage and Family Therapy — M,D
Psychology—General — M,D
Public Administration — M,D

ARGOSY UNIVERSITY, TWIN CITIES
Clinical Psychology — M,D,O
Forensic Psychology — M,D
Health Psychology — M,D,O
Industrial and Organizational Psychology — M,D,O
Marriage and Family Therapy — M,D
Psychology—General — M,D,O
Public Administration — M,D

ARGOSY UNIVERSITY, WASHINGTON DC
Clinical Psychology — M,D
Counseling Psychology — M,D
Forensic Psychology — M,D
Health Psychology — M,D
Marriage and Family Therapy — M,D
Psychology—General — M,D
Public Administration — M,D,O
Social Psychology — M,D

ARIZONA STATE UNIVERSITY AT THE TEMPE CAMPUS
African Studies — M,D,O
Agricultural Economics and Agribusiness — D
Anthropology — M,D,O
Applied Arts and Design—General — M,D
Applied Behavior Analysis — M,D
Applied Psychology — M
Archaeology — M,D,O
Architectural History — D
Architecture — M,D
Art History — M,D
Art/Fine Arts — M,D
Arts Administration — M,D
Building Science — M,D
Child and Family Studies — M,D
Chinese — M,D
Clinical Psychology — M,D
Cognitive Sciences — M,D
Communication—General — M,D
Comparative Literature — M,D,O
Counseling Psychology — D
Criminal Justice and Criminology — M,D
Cultural Studies — M,D
Dance — M
Developmental Psychology — M,D
Economics — D
Emergency Management — M,D
English — M,D,O
Environmental Design — D
Ethics — M,D
Film, Television, and Video Production — M
French — M,D
Gender Studies — M,D,O
Geographic Information Systems — M,D,O
Geography — M,D,O
German — M
Gerontology — M,D,O
History of Science and Technology — M
History — M,D,O
Homeland Security — M,D
Human Development — M,D
Interdisciplinary Studies — M

Japanese — M
Journalism — M,D
Landscape Architecture — M,D
Liberal Studies — M
Linguistics — M,D,O
Marriage and Family Therapy — M,D
Mass Communication — M,D
Media Studies — M,D
Medieval and Renaissance Studies — M,D,O
Museum Studies — M,D,O
Music — M,D
Philosophy — M,D,O
Political Science — M,D
Psychology—General — M,D
Public Administration — M,D
Public Affairs — M,D
Public History — M,D,O
Public Policy — M,D
Publishing — M,D,O
Religion — M,D,O
Rhetoric — M,D,O
Social Psychology — M,D
Sociology — M,D
Spanish — M,D
Sustainable Development — M,D,O
Textile Design — M,D
Theater — M,D
Therapies—Dance, Drama, and Music — M,D
Translation and Interpretation — M,D,O
Urban and Regional Planning — M,D,O
Urban Design — M,D
Urban Studies — M,D,O
Writing — M,D

ARKANSAS STATE UNIVERSITY
Addictions/Substance Abuse Counseling — M,O
Clinical Psychology — M,O
Communication—General — M,O
Counseling Psychology — M,O
Criminal Justice and Criminology — M,O
Emergency Management — M,O
English — M,O
Gerontology — M,D,O
Historic Preservation — M,D
History — M,O
Journalism — M
Media Studies — M
Music — M,O
Political Science — M
Public Administration — M,O
Rehabilitation Counseling — M,O
School Psychology — M,O
Sociology — M,O
Speech and Interpersonal Communication — M,O

ARKANSAS TECH UNIVERSITY
Emergency Management — M
English — M
History — M
Journalism — M
Liberal Studies — M
Psychology—General — M

ARLINGTON BAPTIST COLLEGE
Theology — M

ARMSTRONG STATE UNIVERSITY
American Studies — M
Corporate and Organizational Communication — M,O
Criminal Justice and Criminology — M,O
History — M
Public History — M
Western European Studies — M
Writing — M,O

ART CENTER COLLEGE OF DESIGN
Art/Fine Arts — M
Computer Art and Design — M
Environmental Design — M
Film, Television, and Video Production — M
Industrial Design — M

THE ART INSTITUTE OF CALIFORNIA–SAN FRANCISCO, A CAMPUS OF ARGOSY UNIVERSITY
Computer Art and Design — M
Film, Television, and Video Production — M

THE ART INSTITUTE OF DALLAS, A CAMPUS OF SOUTH UNIVERSITY
Applied Arts and Design—General — M

ASBURY THEOLOGICAL SEMINARY
Missions and Missiology — M,D,O
Pastoral Ministry and Counseling — M,D,O
Theology — M,D,O

ASBURY UNIVERSITY
Child and Family Studies — M
Classics — M
English — M
French — M
Spanish — M
Writing — M

ASHLAND THEOLOGICAL SEMINARY
Counseling Psychology — M,D,O
Missions and Missiology — M,D,O
Pastoral Ministry and Counseling — M,D,O
Theology — M,D,O

ASHLAND UNIVERSITY
History — M
Political Science — M
Writing — M

ASHWORTH COLLEGE
Criminal Justice and Criminology — M

ASSEMBLIES OF GOD THEOLOGICAL SEMINARY
Cultural Studies — M,D
Missions and Missiology — M,D
Pastoral Ministry and Counseling — M,D
Theology — M,D

ASSUMPTION COLLEGE
Child and Family Studies — M,O
Corporate and Organizational Communication — M,O
Counseling Psychology — M,O
Economics — M,O
Psychology—General — M,O
Rehabilitation Counseling — M,O
School Psychology — M,O

ATHABASCA UNIVERSITY
Applied Psychology — M,O
Art Therapy — M,O
Counseling Psychology — M,O
Cultural Studies — M
Interdisciplinary Studies — M
International Development — M

THE ATHENAEUM OF OHIO
Pastoral Ministry and Counseling — M,D
Theology — M,D

ATLANTIC SCHOOL OF THEOLOGY
Pastoral Ministry and Counseling — M,O
Theology — M,O

ATLANTIC UNIVERSITY
Pastoral Ministry and Counseling — O
Psychoanalysis and Psychotherapy — O
Transpersonal and Humanistic Psychology — M

ATLANTIC UNIVERSITY COLLEGE
Graphic Design — M

AUBURN UNIVERSITY
Agricultural Economics and Agribusiness — M
Applied Behavior Analysis — M,D
Applied Economics — D
Architecture — M
Building Science — M
Child and Family Studies — M,D
Clothing and Textiles — M,D
Communication—General — M,O
Economics — M
English — M,D,O
Experimental Psychology — M,D
Geography — M
History — M,D,O
Human Development — M,D
Industrial and Organizational Psychology — M,D
Industrial Design — M
Landscape Architecture — M
Mass Communication — M,O
Political Science — M,D,O
Psychology—General — M,D
Public Administration — M,D,O
Rehabilitation Counseling — M,D
Rural Sociology — M
Sociology — M
Spanish — M
Technical Communication — M,D,O
Urban and Regional Planning — M

AUBURN UNIVERSITY AT MONTGOMERY
Clinical Psychology — M
Criminal Justice and Criminology — M,O
Emergency Management — M,O
Homeland Security — M,O
International Affairs — M,D,O
Liberal Studies — M,D,O
Political Science — M,D,O
Psychology—General — M
Public Administration — M,D,O
Public Policy — M,D,O
Sociology — M,D,O

AURORA UNIVERSITY
Criminal Justice and Criminology — M,D

AUSTIN GRADUATE SCHOOL OF THEOLOGY
Theology — M

AUSTIN PEAY STATE UNIVERSITY
Communication—General — M
Counseling Psychology — M
English — M
Industrial and Organizational Psychology — M
Military and Defense Studies — M
Music — M
Psychology—General — M

AUSTIN PRESBYTERIAN THEOLOGICAL SEMINARY
Pastoral Ministry and Counseling — M,D
Theology — M,D

AVE MARIA UNIVERSITY
Pastoral Ministry and Counseling — M,D
Theology — M,D

AVERETT UNIVERSITY
History — M
Liberal Studies — M
Theater — M

AVILA UNIVERSITY
Counseling Psychology — M
Psychology—General — M

AZUSA PACIFIC UNIVERSITY
Art/Fine Arts — M
Clinical Psychology — M,D
Ethics — M

---

*M—masters degree; D—doctorate; O—other advanced degree; *—Close-Up and/or Display*

International Affairs — M
Marriage and Family Therapy — M,D
Music — M
Pastoral Ministry and Counseling — M
Psychology—General — M,D
Public Administration — M
School Psychology — M
Theology — M,D
Urban Studies — M

BABEL UNIVERSITY PROFESSIONAL SCHOOL OF TRANSLATION
Translation and Interpretation — M

BAKER UNIVERSITY
Liberal Studies — M

BAKKE GRADUATE UNIVERSITY
Pastoral Ministry and Counseling — M,D
Theology — M,D

BALL STATE UNIVERSITY
Anthropology — M
Applied Behavior Analysis — M,D,O
Architecture — M*
Art/Fine Arts — M
Clinical Psychology — M
Cognitive Sciences — M
Communication—General — M
Counseling Psychology — M,D
Criminal Justice and Criminology — M
English — M,D
Family and Consumer
    Sciences-General — M
Geography — M
Gerontology — M
Historic Preservation — M
History — M
Journalism — M
Landscape Architecture — M
Linguistics — M,D
Political Science — M
Psychology—General — M
Public Administration — M
Rhetoric — M
School Psychology — M,D,O
Social Psychology — M
Sociology — M
Speech and Interpersonal
    Communication — M
Urban and Regional Planning — M
Urban Design — M
Writing — M,D

BANK STREET COLLEGE OF EDUCATION
Child and Family Studies — M

BAPTIST BIBLE COLLEGE
Cultural Studies — M
Pastoral Ministry and Counseling — M
Theology — M

THE BAPTIST COLLEGE OF FLORIDA
Music — M
Theology — M

BAPTIST MISSIONARY ASSOCIATION THEOLOGICAL SEMINARY
Theology — M

BAPTIST THEOLOGICAL SEMINARY AT RICHMOND
Conflict Resolution and
    Mediation/Peace Studies — M,D,O
Pastoral Ministry and Counseling — M,D,O
Religion — M,D,O
Theology — M,D,O

BARCLAY COLLEGE
Theology — M

BARD COLLEGE
Art/Fine Arts — M
Economics — M
Museum Studies — M
Music — M,O
Photography — M

BARD GRADUATE CENTER: DECORATIVE ARTS, DESIGN HISTORY, MATERIAL CULTURE
Art History — M,D*
Decorative Arts — M,D

BARRY UNIVERSITY
Art/Fine Arts — M
Clinical Psychology — M,O
Communication—General — M,O
Corporate and Organizational
    Communication — M,O
Liberal Studies — M
Marriage and Family Therapy — M,O
Pastoral Ministry and Counseling — M,D
Photography — M
Psychology—General — M,O
Public Administration — M
Rehabilitation Counseling — M,O
School Psychology — M,O
Sport Psychology — M
Theology — M,D

BARUCH COLLEGE OF THE CITY UNIVERSITY OF NEW YORK
Arts Administration — M
Corporate and Organizational
    Communication — M
Counseling Psychology — M
Economics — M
Industrial and Labor Relations — M
Industrial and Organizational
    Psychology — M,D
Public Administration — M
Public Policy — M

BASTYR UNIVERSITY
Counseling Psychology — M,O
Environmental Design — M,O

Health Psychology — M,O
Landscape Architecture — M,O

BAYAMÓN CENTRAL UNIVERSITY
Industrial and Organizational
    Psychology — M
Marriage and Family Therapy — M,O
Rehabilitation Counseling — M,O

BAYLOR UNIVERSITY
American Studies — M,D
Applied Behavior Analysis — M,D,O
Clinical Psychology — D
Communication—General — M
Criminal Justice and Criminology — D
Cultural Studies — M,D
Economics — M
English — M,D
History — M,D
Interdisciplinary Studies — D
International Affairs — M,D
Journalism — M
Museum Studies — M
Music — M,D
Philosophy — M,D
Political Science — M,D
Psychology—General — M,D
Public Administration — M,D
Public Policy — M,D
Religion — M,D
School Psychology — M,D,O
Sociology — M,D
Spanish — M
Theater — M
Theology — M,D
Western European Studies — M,D

BAY PATH UNIVERSITY
Applied Behavior Analysis — M,O
Clinical Psychology — M
Counseling Psychology — M
Developmental Psychology — M
Forensic Sciences — M
Writing — M

BELHAVEN UNIVERSITY (MS)
Public Administration — M

BELLARMINE UNIVERSITY
Communication—General — M
Religion — M

BELLEVUE UNIVERSITY
Corporate and Organizational
    Communication — M
Criminal Justice and Criminology — M
Military and Defense Studies — M
National Security — M
Public Administration — M

BELMONT UNIVERSITY
English — M
Music — M

BEMIDJI STATE UNIVERSITY
English — M

BENEDICTINE UNIVERSITY
Clinical Psychology — M
Emergency Management — M
Women's Studies — M

BENNINGTON COLLEGE
Dance — M
English — M
French — M
Music — M
Spanish — M
Writing — M

BERKLEE COLLEGE OF MUSIC
Music — M

BETHANY THEOLOGICAL SEMINARY
Conflict Resolution and
    Mediation/Peace Studies — M,O
Pastoral Ministry and Counseling — M,O
Religion — M,O
Theology — M,O

BETHEL COLLEGE
Pastoral Ministry and Counseling — M
Theology — M

BETHEL SEMINARY
Classics — M,D,O
Marriage and Family Therapy — M,D,O
Near and Middle Eastern Languages — M,D,O
Pastoral Ministry and Counseling — M,D,O
Religion — M,D,O
Theology — M,D,O

BETHEL UNIVERSITY (MN)
Communication—General — M,D,O
Counseling Psychology — M,D,O
Gerontology — M,D,O

BETHEL UNIVERSITY (TN)
Conflict Resolution and
    Mediation/Peace Studies — M

BETHESDA UNIVERSITY
Music — M
Religion — M
Theology — M

BETH HAMEDRASH SHAAREI YOSHER INSTITUTE
Theology — M

BETH HATALMUD RABBINICAL COLLEGE
Theology — M

BETH MEDRASH GOVOHA
Theology — M

BETHUNE-COOKMAN UNIVERSITY
Theology — M

BEULAH HEIGHTS UNIVERSITY
Religion — M

BEXLEY HALL EPISCOPAL SEMINARY
Theology — M

BIBLICAL THEOLOGICAL SEMINARY
Missions and Missiology — M,D,O
Pastoral Ministry and Counseling — M,D,O
Theology — M,D,O

BINGHAMTON UNIVERSITY, STATE UNIVERSITY OF NEW YORK
Anthropology — M,D
Art History — M,D
Asian Studies — M,O
Asian-American Studies — M,O
Clinical Psychology — D
Cognitive Sciences — D
Comparative Literature — M,D
Cultural Studies — M,D
Economics — M,D
English — M,D
French — M
Geography — M
History — M,D
Italian — M
Music — M
Philosophy — M,D
Political Science — M,D
Psychology—General — D
Public Administration — M
Sociology — M,D
Spanish — M
Theater — M
Translation and Interpretation — D,O
Writing — M,D

BIOLA UNIVERSITY
Anthropology — M,D,O
Clinical Psychology — D
Cultural Studies — M,D,O
Jewish Studies — M,D,O
Linguistics — M,D,O
Missions and Missiology — M,D,O
Pastoral Ministry and Counseling — M,D,O
Psychology—General — D
Religion — M,D,O
Theology — M,D,O

BOB JONES UNIVERSITY
Art/Fine Arts — M,D,O
English — M,D,O
Film, Television, and Video
    Production — M,D,O
Graphic Design — M,D,O
History — M,D,O
Illustration — M,D,O
Journalism — M,D,O
Media Studies — M,D,O
Music — M,D,O
Pastoral Ministry and Counseling — M,D,O
Religion — M,D,O
Rhetoric — M,D,O
Speech and Interpersonal
    Communication — M,D,O
Theater — M,D,O
Theology — M,D,O

BOISE STATE UNIVERSITY
Anthropology — M
Art/Fine Arts — M
Communication—General — M
Criminal Justice and Criminology — M,O
English — M
History — M
Interdisciplinary Studies — M
Music — M
Public Administration — M,O
Public Policy — M,O
Technical Communication — M
Urban and Regional Planning — M,O
Writing — M

BORICUA COLLEGE
Latin American Studies — M

BOSTON ARCHITECTURAL COLLEGE
Architecture — M
Historic Preservation — M
Interior Design — M
Landscape Architecture — M
Sustainable Development — M

BOSTON COLLEGE
Applied Psychology — M,D
Classics — M
Counseling Psychology — M,D
Developmental Psychology — M,D
East European and Russian Studies — D
Economics — D
English — M,D
French — M
History — M
Italian — M
Linguistics — M
Pastoral Ministry and Counseling — M,D,O
Philosophy — M,D
Political Science — M,D
Psychology—General — M,D
Russian — M
School Psychology — M,D
Sociology — M,D
Spanish — M
Theology — M,D,O
Western European Studies — M,D

THE BOSTON CONSERVATORY
Music — M,O
Theater — M

BOSTON GRADUATE SCHOOL OF PSYCHOANALYSIS
Counseling Psychology — M
Developmental Psychology — O
Psychoanalysis and Psychotherapy — M,D,O
Psychology—General — M

BOSTON UNIVERSITY
African-American Studies — M
American Studies — D

Anthropology — M,D
Archaeology — M,D
Art History — M,D,O
Art/Fine Arts — M
Arts Administration — M,O
Classics — M,D
Communication—General — M,D
Corporate and Organizational
    Communication — M
Counseling Psychology — M
Criminal Justice and Criminology — M,D
Cultural Studies — M,D
Economics — M,D
Emergency Management — M
English — M,D
Film, Television, and Video
    Production — M
Forensic Sciences — M
French — M,D
Genetic Counseling — M
Geographic Information Systems — M,D
Geography — M,D
Graphic Design — M
Health Communication — M
Hispanic and Latin American
    Languages — M,D
Historic Preservation — M
History — M,D
International Affairs — M
Internet and Interactive
    Multimedia — M,O
Journalism — M
Latin American Studies — M
Linguistics — M,D
Mass Communication — M
Media Studies — M,D
Museum Studies — M,D,O
Music — M,D,O
Philosophy — M,D
Political Science — M,D
Psychology—General — M,D
Religion — M,D
Romance Languages — M,D
Sociology — M,D
Theater — M,O
Theology — M,D
Urban and Regional Planning — M
Urban Studies — M
Writing — M,D

BOWIE STATE UNIVERSITY
Corporate and Organizational
    Communication — M,O
Counseling Psychology — M
English — M
Public Administration — M

BOWLING GREEN STATE UNIVERSITY
American Studies — M,D
Applied Arts and Design—
    General — M
Art History — M
Art/Fine Arts — M
Child and Family Studies — M
Clinical Psychology — M,D
Communication—General — M,D
Computer Art and Design — M
Counseling Psychology — M
Criminal Justice and Criminology — M
Demography and Population Studies — M,D
Developmental Psychology — M,D
Economics — M
English — M,D
Experimental Psychology — M,D
Family and Consumer
    Sciences-General — M
Film, Television, and Video
    Production — M,D
French — M
German — M
Graphic Design — M
History — M,D
Human Development — M
Industrial and Organizational
    Psychology — M,D
Interdisciplinary Studies — M,D
Music — M,D
Philosophy — M,D
Political Science — M
Psychology—General — M,D
Public Administration — M
Rehabilitation Counseling — M
Rhetoric — M,D
School Psychology — M,O
Social Psychology — M,D
Sociology — M,D
Spanish — M
Speech and Interpersonal
    Communication — M,D
Technical Communication — M,D
Theater — M,D
Writing — M,D

BRADLEY UNIVERSITY
Art/Fine Arts — M
Clinical Psychology — M
Comparative and Interdisciplinary
    Arts — M
Counseling Psychology — M
English — M
Human Development — M
Photography — M

BRANDEIS UNIVERSITY
Anthropology — M,D
Child and Family Studies — M,D
Classics — M,O
Cognitive Sciences — M,D
Communication—General — M
Conflict Resolution and
    Mediation/Peace Studies — M
Developmental Psychology — M,D
Disability Studies — D
Economics — M,D
English — M,D

Gender Studies	M,D
Genetic Counseling	M
History	M,D
International Affairs	M
Jewish Studies	M,D
Linguistics	M
Music	M,D
Near and Middle Eastern Languages	M,D
Near and Middle Eastern Studies	M,D
Philosophy	M
Political Science	M
Psychology—General	M,D
Public Policy	M
Social Psychology	M,D
Sociology	M,D
Sustainable Development	M
Theater	M
Women's Studies	M,D

BRANDMAN UNIVERSITY

Counseling Psychology	M
Emergency Management	M
Health Communication	M
Marriage and Family Therapy	M
Psychology—General	M
Public Administration	M

BRANDON UNIVERSITY

Music	M
Rural Planning and Studies	M,O

BRENAU UNIVERSITY

Interior Design	M
Psychology—General	M

BRIDGEWATER STATE UNIVERSITY

Criminal Justice and Criminology	M
English	M
Psychology—General	M
Public Administration	M

BRIERCREST SEMINARY

Marriage and Family Therapy	M
Missions and Missiology	M
Pastoral Ministry and Counseling	M
Religion	M
Theology	M

BRIGHAM YOUNG UNIVERSITY

Anthropology	M
Art/Fine Arts	M
Child and Family Studies	M,D
Classics	M
Clinical Psychology	M,D
Communication—General	M
Comparative and Interdisciplinary Arts	M
Comparative Literature	M
Counseling Psychology	M,D,O
English	M
Film, Television, and Video Production	M
French	M
Hispanic and Latin American Languages	M
Human Development	M,D
Humanities	M
Industrial Design	M
Linguistics	M
Marriage and Family Therapy	M,D
Mass Communication	M
Music	M
Political Science	M
Portuguese	M
Psychology—General	M,D
Public Administration	M
Rhetoric	M
School Psychology	M,D,O
Slavic Languages	M,D
Sociology	M
Spanish	M
Theater	M
Writing	M

BROCK UNIVERSITY

Child and Family Studies	M
Classics	M
Comparative Literature	M
Cultural Studies	M
Disability Studies	M,O
Economics	M
English	M
Geography	M
History	M
Human Development	M,D
International Affairs	M
Philosophy	M
Political Science	M
Psychology—General	M,D
Public Policy	M
Social Psychology	M,D
Sociology	M

BROOKLYN COLLEGE OF THE CITY UNIVERSITY OF NEW YORK

Art History	M
Art/Fine Arts	M
Arts Administration	M
Counseling Psychology	M,D,O
Economics	M
English	M
Experimental Psychology	M,D
Film, Television, and Video Production	M
French	M
History	M
Industrial and Organizational Psychology	M,D
International Affairs	M
Internet and Interactive Multimedia	M
Jewish Studies	M
Liberal Studies	M

Media Studies	M
Music	M
Photography	M
Political Science	M
Psychology—General	M,D
Public Policy	M
School Psychology	M,O
Social Psychology	M,D
Sociology	M,D
Spanish	M
Speech and Interpersonal Communication	M,D
Thanatology	M
Theater	M
Urban Studies	M
Writing	M

BROOKS INSTITUTE

Photography	M

BROWN UNIVERSITY

American Studies	M,D
Anthropology	M,D
Archaeology	D
Art History	D
Asian Studies	D
Classics	M,D
Cognitive Sciences	M,D
Comparative Literature	D
East European and Russian Studies	M,D
Economics	D
English	M,D
French	D
German	D
Hispanic Studies	D
History of Science and Technology	D
History	M,D
Italian	D
Latin American Studies	M,D
Linguistics	M,D
Music	D
Near and Middle Eastern Studies	D
Philosophy	D
Political Science	D
Psychology—General	M,D
Public Policy	M
Publishing	M,D
Religion	D
Russian	M,D
Slavic Languages	M,D
Sociology	M,D
Theater	M,D
Western European Studies	M,D
Writing	M

BRYN ATHYN COLLEGE OF THE NEW CHURCH

Religion	M
Theology	M

BRYN MAWR COLLEGE

Archaeology	M,D
Art History	M,D
Classics	M,D

BUCKNELL UNIVERSITY

English	M
Psychology—General	M

BUFFALO STATE COLLEGE, STATE UNIVERSITY OF NEW YORK

Applied Economics	M
Criminal Justice and Criminology	M
Economics	M
English	M
Historic Preservation	M,O
History	M
Interdisciplinary Studies	M

BURLINGTON COLLEGE

Interdisciplinary Studies	M

BUTLER UNIVERSITY

English	M
History	M
Music	M
Writing	M

CAIRN UNIVERSITY

Pastoral Ministry and Counseling	M
Religion	M
Theology	M

CALDWELL UNIVERSITY

Applied Behavior Analysis	M,D,O
Art Therapy	M,O
Counseling Psychology	M,O
School Psychology	M,O

CALIFORNIA BAPTIST UNIVERSITY

Architecture	M
Communication—General	M
Counseling Psychology	M
Disability Studies	M
English	M
Forensic Psychology	M
Music	M
Pastoral Ministry and Counseling	M
Public Administration	M
School Psychology	M

CALIFORNIA COAST UNIVERSITY

Criminal Justice and Criminology	M
Psychology—General	M

CALIFORNIA COLLEGE OF THE ARTS

Applied Arts and Design—General	M
Architecture	M
Art/Fine Arts	M
Computer Art and Design	M
Film, Television, and Video Production	M
Film, Television, and Video Theory and Criticism	M

Graphic Design	M
Industrial Design	M
Interdisciplinary Studies	M
Media Studies	M
Museum Studies	M
Photography	M
Textile Design	M
Writing	M

CALIFORNIA INSTITUTE OF INTEGRAL STUDIES

Art Therapy	M,D
Asian Studies	M,D
Clinical Psychology	M,D
Counseling Psychology	M,D
Cultural Anthropology	M,D
Health Psychology	M,D
Humanities	M,D
Interdisciplinary Studies	M,D
Philosophy	M,D
Psychology—General	M,D
Religion	M,D
Social Psychology	M,D
Theology	M,D
Therapies—Dance, Drama, and Music	M,D
Women's Studies	M,D
Writing	M,D

CALIFORNIA INSTITUTE OF TECHNOLOGY

Social Sciences	M,D

CALIFORNIA INSTITUTE OF THE ARTS

Applied Arts and Design—General	M,O
Art/Fine Arts	M,O
Dance	M,O
Film, Television, and Video Production	M,O
Graphic Design	M,O
Music	M,O
Photography	M,O
Theater	M,O
Writing	M,O

CALIFORNIA LUTHERAN UNIVERSITY

Clinical Psychology	M,D
Economics	M,O
Marriage and Family Therapy	M,D
Psychology—General	M,D
Public Administration	M
Public Policy	M
Theology	M,D,O

CALIFORNIA MARITIME ACADEMY

Emergency Management	M

CALIFORNIA POLYTECHNIC STATE UNIVERSITY, SAN LUIS OBISPO

Agricultural Economics and Agribusiness	M
Architecture	M
English	M
History	M
Political Science	M
Psychology—General	M
Urban and Regional Planning	M

CALIFORNIA STATE POLYTECHNIC UNIVERSITY, POMONA

Architecture	M
Economics	M
English	M
History	M
Interior Design	M
Landscape Architecture	M
Psychology—General	M
Public Administration	M
Urban and Regional Planning	M

CALIFORNIA STATE UNIVERSITY, BAKERSFIELD

Anthropology	M
Counseling Psychology	M
English	M
History	M
Interdisciplinary Studies	M
Public Administration	M
Sociology	M
Spanish	M

CALIFORNIA STATE UNIVERSITY, CHICO

Anthropology	M
Applied Psychology	M
Art History	M
Art/Fine Arts	M
Communication—General	M
English	M
History	M
Marriage and Family Therapy	M
Museum Studies	M
Political Science	M
Psychology—General	M
Public Administration	M
Rural Planning and Studies	M
Social Sciences	M
Urban and Regional Planning	M

CALIFORNIA STATE UNIVERSITY, DOMINGUEZ HILLS

Applied Social Research	M,O
Clinical Psychology	M
Conflict Resolution and Mediation/Peace Studies	M
English	M,O
Humanities	M
Marriage and Family Therapy	M
Psychology—General	M
Public Administration	M
Rhetoric	M,O
Sociology	M,O

CALIFORNIA STATE UNIVERSITY, EAST BAY

Anthropology	M
Child and Family Studies	M
Communication—General	M
Economics	M
English	M
Geography	M
History	M
Interdisciplinary Studies	M
Internet and Interactive Multimedia	M
Marriage and Family Therapy	M
Music	M
Public Administration	M
Public History	M
Public Policy	M
School Psychology	M
Social Psychology	M
Writing	M

CALIFORNIA STATE UNIVERSITY, FRESNO

Applied Arts and Design—General	M
Art/Fine Arts	M
Communication—General	M
Criminal Justice and Criminology	M
English	M
Family and Consumer Sciences-General	M
History	M
International Affairs	M
Journalism	M
Linguistics	M
Marriage and Family Therapy	M
Mass Communication	M
Music	M
Psychology—General	M
Public Administration	M
Rehabilitation Counseling	M
Spanish	M
Sport Psychology	M
Writing	M

CALIFORNIA STATE UNIVERSITY, FULLERTON

American Studies	M
Anthropology	M
Applied Arts and Design—General	M
Art History	M
Art/Fine Arts	M
Clinical Psychology	M
Communication—General	M
Dance	M
Economics	M
English	M
Film, Television, and Video Production	M
French	M
Geography	M
German	M
Gerontology	M
Graphic Design	M
History	M
Illustration	M
Linguistics	M
Mass Communication	M
Museum Studies	M
Music	M
Photography	M
Political Science	M
Psychology—General	M
Public Administration	M
Social Psychology	M
Sociology	M
Spanish	M
Speech and Interpersonal Communication	M
Theater	M

CALIFORNIA STATE UNIVERSITY, LONG BEACH

African Studies	M
American Studies	M
Anthropology	M
Art History	M
Art/Fine Arts	M
Asian Studies	M
Asian-American Studies	M
Communication—General	M
Consumer Economics	M
Criminal Justice and Criminology	M
Dance	M
Economics	M
Emergency Management	M
English	M
Family and Consumer Sciences-General	M
French	M
Geography	M
German	M
Gerontology	M
History	M
Industrial and Organizational Psychology	M
Interdisciplinary Studies	M
Latin American Studies	M
Linguistics	M
Marriage and Family Therapy	M
Medieval and Renaissance Studies	M
Music	M
Near and Middle Eastern Studies	M
Philosophy	M
Political Science	M
Psychology—General	M
Public Administration	M
Public Policy	M
Religion	M
Spanish	M

*M—masters degree; D—doctorate; O—other advanced degree; *—Close-Up and/or Display*

Sport Psychology — M
Theater — M
Western European Studies — M
Writing — M

CALIFORNIA STATE UNIVERSITY, LOS ANGELES
Anthropology — M
Applied Arts and Design—General — M
Art History — M
Art Therapy — M
Art/Fine Arts — M
Child and Family Studies — M
Child Development — M
Communication—General — M
Criminal Justice and Criminology — M
Economics — M
English — M
French — M
Geography — M
Graphic Design — M
Hispanic Studies — M
History — M
Latin American Studies — M
Music — M
Philosophy — M
Photography — M
Political Science — M
Psychology—General — M
Public Administration — M
Rehabilitation Counseling — M,D
School Psychology — M,D
Sociology — M
Spanish — M
Textile Design — M
Theater — M

CALIFORNIA STATE UNIVERSITY, NORTHRIDGE
Anthropology — M
Applied Psychology — M
Archaeology — M
Art History — M
Art/Fine Arts — M
Clinical Psychology — M
Communication—General — M
Comparative Literature — M
English — M
Experimental Psychology — M
Family and Consumer Sciences-General — M
Film, Television, and Video Production — M
Geography — M
Hispanic Studies — M
History — M
Journalism — M
Linguistics — M
Marriage and Family Therapy — M
Mass Communication — M
Music — M
Political Science — M
Psychology—General — M
Public Administration — M,O
Rhetoric — M
School Psychology — M
Sociology — M
Spanish — M
Speech and Interpersonal Communication — M
Theater — M
Writing — M

CALIFORNIA STATE UNIVERSITY, SACRAMENTO
Anthropology — M
Applied Behavior Analysis — M
Art/Fine Arts — M
Communication—General — M
Counseling Psychology — M
Criminal Justice and Criminology — M
English — M
Gender Studies — M
Industrial and Organizational Psychology — M
Marriage and Family Therapy — M
Music — M
Political Science — M
Psychology—General — M
Public Administration — M
Public History — M,D
Public Policy — M
School Psychology — M
Sociology — M
Writing — M

CALIFORNIA STATE UNIVERSITY, SAN BERNARDINO
Art/Fine Arts — M
Child Development — M
Clinical Psychology — M
Communication—General — M
Corporate and Organizational Communication — M
Counseling Psychology — M
Criminal Justice and Criminology — M
English — M
Experimental Psychology — M
Industrial and Organizational Psychology — M
Interdisciplinary Studies — M
Music — M
National Security — M
Psychology—General — M
Public Administration — M
Rehabilitation Counseling — M
Social Sciences — M
Spanish — M
Theater — M
Writing — M

CALIFORNIA STATE UNIVERSITY, SAN MARCOS
Child and Family Studies — M

CALIFORNIA STATE UNIVERSITY, STANISLAUS
Applied Behavior Analysis — M
Counseling Psychology — M
Criminal Justice and Criminology — M
English — M,O
Genetic Counseling — M
History — M
Interdisciplinary Studies — M
International Affairs — M
Psychology—General — M
Public Administration — M
Rhetoric — M,O
Sustainable Development — M
Writing — M,O

CALIFORNIA UNIVERSITY OF MANAGEMENT AND SCIENCES
Economics — M,D

CALIFORNIA UNIVERSITY OF PENNSYLVANIA
Criminal Justice and Criminology — M
School Psychology — M
Social Sciences — M
Sport Psychology — M

CALUMET COLLEGE OF SAINT JOSEPH
Criminal Justice and Criminology — M

CALVARY BIBLE COLLEGE AND THEOLOGICAL SEMINARY
Pastoral Ministry and Counseling — M
Theology — M

CALVIN THEOLOGICAL SEMINARY
Missions and Missiology — M,D
Pastoral Ministry and Counseling — M,D
Religion — M,D
Theology — M,D

CAMBRIDGE COLLEGE
Addictions/Substance Abuse Counseling — M,O
Conflict Resolution and Mediation/Peace Studies — M
Counseling Psychology — M,O
Forensic Psychology — M,O
Interdisciplinary Studies — M,D,O
Marriage and Family Therapy — M,O
Psychology—General — M,O
School Psychology — M,D,O

CAMERON UNIVERSITY
Psychology—General — M

CAMPBELLSVILLE UNIVERSITY
Music — M
Social Sciences — M
Theology — M

CAMPBELL UNIVERSITY
Interdisciplinary Studies — M
Pastoral Ministry and Counseling — M,D
Theology — M,D

CANADIAN SOUTHERN BAPTIST SEMINARY
Pastoral Ministry and Counseling — M
Religion — M
Theology — M

CANISIUS COLLEGE
Anthropology — M
Corporate and Organizational Communication — M
School Psychology — M
Social Psychology — M

CAPELLA UNIVERSITY
Addictions/Substance Abuse Counseling — M,D
Applied Behavior Analysis — M
Child and Family Studies — M
Clinical Psychology — M,D
Counseling Psychology — M
Criminal Justice and Criminology — M,D
Developmental Psychology — M
Emergency Management — M,D
Gerontology — M
Homeland Security — M
Industrial and Organizational Psychology — M,D
Marriage and Family Therapy — M
Psychology—General — M,D
Public Administration — M,D
School Psychology — M
Sport Psychology — M

CAPITAL UNIVERSITY
Music — M

CARDINAL STRITCH UNIVERSITY
Applied Arts and Design—General — M
Clinical Psychology — M
Graphic Design — M
History — M
Liberal Studies — M
Music — M
Pastoral Ministry and Counseling — M
Psychology—General — M
Religion — M

CAREY THEOLOGICAL COLLEGE
Theology — M,D

CARIBBEAN UNIVERSITY
Art History — M,D

Criminal Justice and Criminology — M,D
Museum Studies — M,D

CARLETON UNIVERSITY
Anthropology — M
Architecture — M
Art History — M
Canadian Studies — M,D
Cognitive Sciences — D
Communication—General — M,D
Comparative Literature — D
Conflict Resolution and Mediation/Peace Studies — M,O
East European and Russian Studies — M,O
Economics — M,D
English — M,D
Film, Television, and Video Production — M
French — M
Geography — M,D
History — M,D
Industrial Design — M,D
International Affairs — M,D
Journalism — M,D
Linguistics — M
Music — M
Philosophy — M
Political Science — M,D
Psychology—General — M,D
Public Administration — M,D
Public Policy — M,D
Sociology — M,D
Western European Studies — M,O

CARLOS ALBIZU UNIVERSITY
Clinical Psychology — M,D
Industrial and Organizational Psychology — M,D
Psychology—General — M,D

CARLOS ALBIZU UNIVERSITY, MIAMI CAMPUS
Clinical Psychology — M,D
Counseling Psychology — M,D
Industrial and Organizational Psychology — M,D
Marriage and Family Therapy — M,D
Psychology—General — M,D
School Psychology — M,D

CARLOW UNIVERSITY
Addictions/Substance Abuse Counseling — M,O
Counseling Psychology — M,D,O
Forensic Sciences — M
Writing — M

CARNEGIE MELLON UNIVERSITY
African Studies — D
African-American Studies — D
Applied Arts and Design—General — M,D
Architecture — M,D
Art/Fine Arts — M
Arts Administration — M
Building Science — M,D
Cognitive Sciences — D
Communication—General — M,D
Comparative Literature — M,D
Computer Art and Design — M
Corporate and Organizational Communication — M
Criminal Justice and Criminology — M
Cultural Studies — D
Developmental Psychology — D
Economics — D
English — M,D
Film, Television, and Video Production — M
Gender Studies — D
History of Science and Technology — D
History — D
Industrial and Labor Relations — D
Linguistics — M,D
Media Studies — M
Music — M
Philosophy — M,D
Psychology—General — D
Public Administration — M
Public Policy — M,D
Publishing — M
Rhetoric — M,D
Social Psychology — D
Social Sciences — D
Sustainable Development — M,D
Technical Writing — M
Theater — M
Urban Design — M,D
Women's Studies — D
Writing — M

CAROLINA CHRISTIAN COLLEGE
Pastoral Ministry and Counseling — M

CAROLINA EVANGELICAL DIVINITY SCHOOL
Pastoral Ministry and Counseling — D
Theology — M

CARSON-NEWMAN UNIVERSITY
Pastoral Ministry and Counseling — M
Theology — M

CASE WESTERN RESERVE UNIVERSITY
Anthropology — M,D
Art History — M,D
Clinical Psychology — D
Cognitive Sciences — M
Comparative Literature — M
Dance — M
English — M,D
Experimental Psychology — D
French — M
Genetic Counseling — M
History — M,D
Linguistics — M
Museum Studies — M

Music — M,D
Political Science — M,D
Psychology—General — M,D
Sociology — M,D
Theater — M

CASTLETON STATE COLLEGE
Forensic Psychology — M
Psychology—General — M

CATHOLIC DISTANCE UNIVERSITY
Theology — M

CATHOLIC THEOLOGICAL UNION
Missions and Missiology — M,D,O
Pastoral Ministry and Counseling — M,D,O
Theology — M,D,O

THE CATHOLIC UNIVERSITY OF AMERICA
Anthropology — M
Applied Psychology — M,D
Architecture — M
Classics — M,D,O
Clinical Psychology — M,D
Economic Development — M
Economics — M
English — M,D,O
Experimental Psychology — M,D
History — M,D
International Affairs — M,D
Medieval and Renaissance Studies — M,D
Music — M,D,O
Near and Middle Eastern Languages — M,D
Near and Middle Eastern Studies — M,D
Pastoral Ministry and Counseling — M,D,O
Philosophy — M,D,O
Political Science — M,D
Psychology—General — M,D
Religion — M,D,O
Rhetoric — M,D,O
Sociology — M,D
Spanish — M,D
Theater — M
Theology — M,D,O
Urban and Regional Planning — M
Western European Studies — M,D

CEDAR CREST COLLEGE
Art Therapy — M
Forensic Sciences — M
Writing — M

CENTENARY COLLEGE
Counseling Psychology — M

CENTRAL BAPTIST THEOLOGICAL SEMINARY
Missions and Missiology — M,O
Theology — M,O

CENTRAL CONNECTICUT STATE UNIVERSITY
Communication—General — M,O
Corporate and Organizational Communication — M,O
Criminal Justice and Criminology — M
English — M,O
French — M,O
Geography — M
German — M,O
Health Psychology — M
Hispanic and Latin American Languages — M,O
History — M,O
International Affairs — M
Italian — M,O
Marriage and Family Therapy — M,O
Psychology—General — M
Rehabilitation Counseling — M,O
School Psychology — M,O
Social Psychology — M
Spanish — M,O

CENTRAL EUROPEAN UNIVERSITY
Anthropology — M,D
Cognitive Sciences — D
Economics — M,D
Gender Studies — M,D
History — M,D
International Affairs — M,D
Medieval and Renaissance Studies — M,D
Philosophy — M,D
Political Science — M,D
Public Policy — M,D
Sociology — M,D

CENTRAL MICHIGAN UNIVERSITY
American Indian/Native American Studies — M
American Studies — M,O
Applied Psychology — M,D
Child and Family Studies — M,O
Clinical Psychology — D
Clothing and Textiles — M,O
Communication—General — M
Counseling Psychology — M,D,O
Cultural Studies — M
Economics — M
English — M
Experimental Psychology — M,D
Family and Consumer Sciences-General — M,O
Film, Television, and Video Production — M
Film, Television, and Video Theory and Criticism — M
Gender Studies — M
Geographic Information Systems — M
Gerontology — M,O
Health Psychology — M,D
History — M,O
Human Development — M,O
Humanities — M
Industrial and Organizational Psychology — M,D
International Affairs — M,O

Media Studies — M
Music — M
Political Science — M,O
Psychology—General — M,D,O
Public Administration — M,O
School Psychology — D,O
Spanish — M
Western European Studies — M,O
Writing — M

CENTRAL WASHINGTON UNIVERSITY
Art/Fine Arts — M
Child and Family Studies — M
Counseling Psychology — M
English — M
Experimental Psychology — M
Family and Consumer
 Sciences-General — M
History — M
Interdisciplinary Studies — M
Music — M
Psychology—General — M
School Psychology — M
Theater — M

CENTRAL YESHIVA TOMCHEI TMIMIM-LUBAVITCH
Jewish Studies — M
Theology — M

CENTRO DE ESTUDIOS AVANZADOS DE PUERTO RICO Y EL CARIBE
History — M,D
Latin American Studies — M,D

CHAMINADE UNIVERSITY OF HONOLULU
Child Development — M
Counseling Psychology — M
Criminal Justice and Criminology — M,O
Forensic Sciences — M,O
Homeland Security — M,O
Marriage and Family Therapy — M
Pastoral Ministry and Counseling — M
School Psychology — M
Theology — M

CHAMPLAIN COLLEGE
Conflict Resolution and
 Mediation/Peace Studies — M
Forensic Sciences — M
Media Studies — M

CHAPMAN UNIVERSITY
Cultural Studies — M,D,O
Disability Studies — M,D,O
English — M
Film, Television, and Video
 Production — M
Health Communication — M
Holocaust and Genocide Studies — M
International Affairs — M
Marriage and Family Therapy — M
School Psychology — M,D,O
Writing — M

CHARLESTON SOUTHERN UNIVERSITY
Criminal Justice and Criminology — M

CHARLOTTE CHRISTIAN COLLEGE AND THEOLOGICAL SEMINARY
Cultural Studies — M
Missions and Missiology — M
Music — M
Pastoral Ministry and Counseling — M
Religion — M
Theology — M

CHATHAM UNIVERSITY
Computer Art and Design — M
Counseling Psychology — M,D
Developmental Psychology — M,D
Film, Television, and Video
 Production — M
Health Psychology — M,D
Industrial and Organizational
 Psychology — M,D
Interior Design — M
Landscape Architecture — M
Marriage and Family Therapy — M,D
Sport Psychology — M,D
Women's Studies — M
Writing — M

CHESTNUT HILL COLLEGE
Addictions/Substance Abuse
 Counseling — M,O
Clinical Psychology — M,D,O
Counseling Psychology — M,O
Marriage and Family Therapy — M,D,O
Psychology—General — M,D,O

CHEYNEY UNIVERSITY OF PENNSYLVANIA
Public Administration — M

THE CHICAGO SCHOOL OF PROFESSIONAL PSYCHOLOGY
Applied Behavior Analysis — M,D
Clinical Psychology — D
Forensic Psychology — M,D
Industrial and Organizational
 Psychology — M,D
Psychology—General — M,D
School Psychology — D,O

THE CHICAGO SCHOOL OF PROFESSIONAL PSYCHOLOGY AT DOWNTOWN LOS ANGELES
Applied Behavior Analysis — M,D
Clinical Psychology — M,D
Forensic Psychology — D
Industrial and Organizational
 Psychology — M
Marriage and Family Therapy — M,D

THE CHICAGO SCHOOL OF PROFESSIONAL PSYCHOLOGY AT GRAYSLAKE
Clinical Psychology — M
Counseling Psychology — M
School Psychology — O

THE CHICAGO SCHOOL OF PROFESSIONAL PSYCHOLOGY AT IRVINE
Clinical Psychology — D
Forensic Psychology — D
Marriage and Family Therapy — M,D
Psychology—General — D

THE CHICAGO SCHOOL OF PROFESSIONAL PSYCHOLOGY AT WESTWOOD
Clinical Psychology — M
Marriage and Family Therapy — M,D
Psychology—General — D

THE CHICAGO SCHOOL OF PROFESSIONAL PSYCHOLOGY: ONLINE
Applied Psychology — M,O
Forensic Psychology — M,O
Industrial and Organizational
 Psychology — M,D,O
Psychology—General — M,D

CHICAGO STATE UNIVERSITY
Criminal Justice and Criminology — M
English — M
Geographic Information Systems — M
Geography — M
History — M
Writing — M

CHICAGO THEOLOGICAL SEMINARY
Ethics — M,D
Pastoral Ministry and Counseling — M,D
Religion — M,D
Theology — M,D

CHRISTENDOM COLLEGE
Theology — M

CHRISTIAN BROTHERS UNIVERSITY
Religion — M

CHRISTIAN THEOLOGICAL SEMINARY
Marriage and Family Therapy — M,D
Pastoral Ministry and Counseling — M,D
Religion — M,D
Theology — M,D

CHRISTIE'S EDUCATION
Art History — M
Art/Fine Arts — O
Arts Administration — O
Museum Studies — M

CHRIST THE KING SEMINARY
Pastoral Ministry and Counseling — M
Theology — M

CHURCH DIVINITY SCHOOL OF THE PACIFIC
Theology — M,D,O

CINCINNATI CHRISTIAN UNIVERSITY
Pastoral Ministry and Counseling — M
Religion — M
Theology — M

THE CITADEL, THE MILITARY COLLEGE OF SOUTH CAROLINA
English — M
History — M
Psychology—General — M,O
School Psychology — O
Social Sciences — M

CITY COLLEGE OF THE CITY UNIVERSITY OF NEW YORK
Architecture — M
Art History — M
Art/Fine Arts — M
Clinical Psychology — M,D
Corporate and Organizational
 Communication — M
Counseling Psychology — M
Economics — M
English — M
Experimental Psychology — M,D
Graphic Design — M
History — M
International Affairs — M
Landscape Architecture — M
Media Studies — M
Museum Studies — M
Music — M
Psychology—General — M,D
Public Administration — M,D
Sociology — M
Spanish — M
Sustainable Development — M
Urban Design — M
Writing — M

CITY UNIVERSITY OF SEATTLE
Counseling Psychology — M

CLAREMONT GRADUATE UNIVERSITY
African Studies — M,D,O
American Studies — M,D,O
Art/Fine Arts — M
Arts Administration — M
Cognitive Sciences — M,D,O
Comparative Literature — M,D
Computer Art and Design — M
Cultural Studies — M,D,O
Developmental Psychology — M,D,O
Economic Development — M,D,O

Economics — M,D,O
English — M,D
Ethics — M,D
Film, Television, and Video
 Theory and Criticism — M,D
Health Psychology — M,D,O
History — M,D,O
Human Development — M,D,O
Humanities — M,D,O
Industrial and Organizational
 Psychology — M,D,O
International Affairs — M,D
International Economics — M,D,O
Media Studies — M,D,O
Museum Studies — M,D,O
Music — M,D
Philosophy — M,D
Photography — M
Political Science — M,D
Psychology—General — M,D,O
Public Policy — M,D,O
Religion — M,D
Social Psychology — M,D,O
Theology — M,D
Western European Studies — M,D,O
Women's Studies — M,D
Writing — M,D

CLAREMONT SCHOOL OF THEOLOGY
Ethics — M,D
Pastoral Ministry and Counseling — M,D
Religion — M,D
Theology — M,D

CLARION UNIVERSITY OF PENNSYLVANIA
Communication—General — M

CLARK ATLANTA UNIVERSITY
African-American Studies — M,D
Criminal Justice and Criminology — M
Economics — M,D
English — M,D
History — M
Political Science — M,D
Public Administration — M
Romance Languages — M,D
Sociology — M
Women's Studies — M,D

CLARKSON UNIVERSITY
Interdisciplinary Studies — M,D
Sustainable Development — M,D

CLARK UNIVERSITY
American Studies — M,D
Clinical Psychology — D
Communication—General — M
Developmental Psychology — D
Economics — D
English — M
Geographic Information Systems — M
Geography — M,D
History — M,D,O
Holocaust and Genocide Studies — D
International Development — M
Public Administration — M,O
Social Psychology — D
Sustainable Development — M
Urban and Regional Planning — M

CLAYTON STATE UNIVERSITY
Applied Psychology — M
Clinical Psychology — M
Developmental Psychology — M
Liberal Studies — M
Psychology—General — M

CLEMSON UNIVERSITY
Applied Economics — M,D
Applied Psychology — M
Architecture — M
Art/Fine Arts — M
Communication—General — M,D
Computer Art and Design — M
Counseling Psychology — M
Economics — M,D
English — M
Environmental Design — D
Historic Preservation — M
History — M
Human Development — M
Humanities — D
Industrial and Organizational
 Psychology — D
Landscape Architecture — M
Psychology—General — D
Public Administration — M
Public Affairs — D
Public Policy — D,O
Rhetoric — M
Social Sciences — D
Sociology — M
Urban and Regional Planning — M
Writing — M

CLEVELAND INSTITUTE OF MUSIC
Music — M,D,O

CLEVELAND STATE UNIVERSITY
Addictions/Substance Abuse
 Counseling — M,O
Art History — M
Communication—General — M,D,O
Counseling Psychology — M,D,O
Economic Development — M,O
Economics — M,O
English — M
French — M
Geographic Information Systems — M,O
Health Communication — M,O
Historic Preservation — M,O
History — M
Industrial and Labor Relations — M,D,O

International Affairs — M
International Economics — M
Latin American Studies — M
Linguistics — M
Museum Studies — M
Music — M
Philosophy — M,O
Psychology—General — M,D,O
Public Administration — M,D,O
Public Affairs — D
Public Policy — M,O
Social Psychology — M,O
Sociology — M
Spanish — M
Sport Psychology — M
Sustainable Development — M,O
Urban and Regional Planning — M,O
Urban Studies — M,D,O
Writing — M

COASTAL CAROLINA UNIVERSITY
Writing — M

COLGATE ROCHESTER CROZER DIVINITY SCHOOL
Theology — M,D,O

THE COLLEGE AT BROCKPORT, STATE UNIVERSITY OF NEW YORK
American Studies — M
Art/Fine Arts — M
Arts Administration — M,O
Communication—General — M
Counseling Psychology — M,O
Dance — M
English — M,O
Forensic Sciences — M
Gerontology — M,O
History — M
Liberal Studies — M
Psychology—General — M
Public Administration — M,O
Writing — M,O

COLLÈGE DOMINICAIN DE PHILOSOPHIE ET DE THÉOLOGIE
Philosophy — M,D
Theology — M,D,O

COLLEGE FOR CREATIVE STUDIES
Applied Arts and Design—
 General — M
Art/Fine Arts — M

COLLEGE OF CHARLESTON
Arts Administration — M,O
Communication—General — M
English — M
Historic Preservation — M
History — M
Public Administration — M
Urban and Regional Planning — O

COLLEGE OF EMMANUEL AND ST. CHAD
Theology — M,O

THE COLLEGE OF NEW JERSEY
Addictions/Substance Abuse
 Counseling — M,O
English — M
Gender Studies — O
Marriage and Family Therapy — O

THE COLLEGE OF NEW ROCHELLE
Art Therapy — M
Communication—General — M,O
Counseling Psychology — M,O
Marriage and Family Therapy — M
Public Administration — M
School Psychology — M
Thanatology — M,O

COLLEGE OF SAINT ELIZABETH
Counseling Psychology — M,O
Criminal Justice and Criminology — M
Forensic Psychology — M,O
Psychology—General — M,O
Public Administration — M
Theology — M

COLLEGE OF ST. JOSEPH
Addictions/Substance Abuse
 Counseling — M
Clinical Psychology — M
Counseling Psychology — M
Psychology—General — M
School Psychology — M
Social Psychology — M

THE COLLEGE OF SAINT ROSE
Counseling Psychology — M,O
English — M
History — M
Mass Communication — M
Music — M
Political Science — M
School Psychology — M,O

COLLEGE OF STATEN ISLAND OF THE CITY UNIVERSITY OF NEW YORK
Clinical Psychology — M
Counseling Psychology — M
English — M
Film, Television, and Video
 Theory and Criticism — M
History — M
Liberal Studies — M
Media Studies — M

THE COLLEGE OF WILLIAM AND MARY
American Studies — M,D
Anthropology — M,D
Experimental Psychology — M
Geographic Information Systems — M,D

M—masters degree; D—doctorate; O—other advanced degree; *—Close-Up and/or Display

History M,D
Interdisciplinary Studies M,D
Public Policy M
School Psychology M

COLORADO CHRISTIAN UNIVERSITY
Counseling Psychology M

THE COLORADO COLLEGE
American Studies M
Humanities M
Liberal Studies M

COLORADO SCHOOL OF MINES
International Affairs O
Mineral Economics M,D

COLORADO STATE UNIVERSITY
Agricultural Economics and
  Agribusiness M,D
Anthropology M
Art/Fine Arts M
Child and Family Studies M,D
Consumer Economics M
Economics M,D
English M
History M
Human Development M,D
Landscape Architecture M,D
Mass Communication M,D
Music M
Philosophy M
Political Science M,D
Psychology—General M,D
Sociology M,D
Speech and Interpersonal
  Communication M
Technical Communication M,D
Technical Writing M,D
Writing M

**COLORADO STATE UNIVERSITY–
GLOBAL CAMPUS**
Criminal Justice and Criminology M

**COLORADO TECHNICAL UNIVERSITY
COLORADO SPRINGS**
Conflict Resolution and
  Mediation/Peace Studies M,D
Criminal Justice and Criminology M

**COLORADO TECHNICAL UNIVERSITY
DENVER SOUTH**
Conflict Resolution and
  Mediation/Peace Studies M
Criminal Justice and Criminology M

COLUMBIA COLLEGE (MO)
Criminal Justice and Criminology M
Military and Defense Studies M

COLUMBIA COLLEGE (SC)
Conflict Resolution and
  Mediation/Peace Studies M,O

COLUMBIA COLLEGE CHICAGO
Arts Administration M
Comparative and Interdisciplinary
  Arts M
Film, Television, and Video
  Production M
Journalism M
Music M
Photography M
Therapies—Dance, Drama, and
  Music M,O
Writing M

**COLUMBIA INTERNATIONAL
UNIVERSITY**
Cultural Studies M,D,O
Missions and Missiology M,D,O
Pastoral Ministry and Counseling M,D,O
Theology M,D,O

COLUMBIA SOUTHERN UNIVERSITY
Criminal Justice and Criminology M
Emergency Management M

COLUMBIA THEOLOGICAL SEMINARY
Theology M,D

COLUMBIA UNIVERSITY
African Studies M,D,O
African-American Studies M,D
American Studies M,D
Anthropology M,D
Archaeology M,D
Architecture M,D
Art History M,D
Art/Fine Arts M,D,O
Asian Studies M,D
Classics M,D
Communication—General M,D
Comparative Literature M,D
Conflict Resolution and
  Mediation/Peace Studies M
Corporate and Organizational
  Communication M
East European and Russian Studies M,D,O
Economics M,D
English M,D
Environmental Design M
Ethics M
Film, Television, and Video
  Production M
French M,D
German M,D
Hispanic Studies M,D
Historic Preservation M,O
History M,D
International Affairs M
Italian M,D
Japanese M,D
Jewish Studies M,D
Journalism M,D
Landscape Architecture M
Latin American Studies M,D,O
Medieval and Renaissance Studies M,D

Museum Studies M,D
Music M,D
Near and Middle Eastern Studies M,D,O
Philosophy M,D
Photography M
Political Science M,D
Psychology—General M,D
Public Administration M
Public Policy M
Religion M,D
Romance Languages M,D
Russian M,D
Slavic Languages M,D
Social Sciences M,D
Sociology M,D
Spanish M,D
Sustainable Development M,D
Theater M,D*
Translation and Interpretation M,D
Urban and Regional Planning M,D
Western European Studies M,D,O
Writing M

**COLUMBUS COLLEGE OF ART &
DESIGN**
Art/Fine Arts M

COLUMBUS STATE UNIVERSITY
Counseling Psychology M,D,O
History M
Homeland Security M
Music M,O
Public Administration M
Theater M

CONCORDIA LUTHERAN SEMINARY
Theology M,O

CONCORDIA SEMINARY
Theology M,D,O

CONCORDIA THEOLOGICAL SEMINARY
Theology M,D

CONCORDIA UNIVERSITY (CA)
Applied Social Research M
Cultural Studies M
International Affairs M
Religion M
Theology M

CONCORDIA UNIVERSITY (CANADA)
Anthropology M
Applied Arts and Design—
  General O
Art History M,D
Art Therapy M
Art/Fine Arts M
Child and Family Studies M
Clinical Psychology M,D,O
Communication—General M,D,O
Computer Art and Design O
Cultural Anthropology M
Economic Development O
Economics M,D,O
English M
Film, Television, and Video
  Production M
Film, Television, and Video
  Theory and Criticism M
French M,O
Geography M,D,O
History M,D
Humanities D
Interdisciplinary Studies M,D
Internet and Interactive
  Multimedia M,O
Jewish Studies M
Journalism O
Linguistics M,O
Media Studies M,D,O
Music O
Philosophy M
Political Science M,D
Psychology—General M,D
Public Administration M,D
Public Affairs O
Public Policy M,D
Religion M,D
Sociology M
Theology M
Translation and Interpretation M,O
Urban and Regional Planning O
Urban Studies M,O
Writing M

CONCORDIA UNIVERSITY CHICAGO
Counseling Psychology M
Gerontology M
Liberal Studies M
Music M
Psychology—General M
Religion M

**CONCORDIA UNIVERSITY COLLEGE OF
ALBERTA**
Religion M
Theology M

CONCORDIA UNIVERSITY, NEBRASKA
Pastoral Ministry and Counseling M

CONCORDIA UNIVERSITY, ST. PAUL
Child and Family Studies M,D,O
Corporate and Organizational
  Communication M
Criminal Justice and Criminology M,D,O
Forensic Psychology M,D,O

CONCORDIA UNIVERSITY WISCONSIN
Child and Family Studies M
Corporate and Organizational
  Communication M
Counseling Psychology M
Music M
Psychology—General M
Public Administration M

CONCORD UNIVERSITY
Geography M

CONNECTICUT COLLEGE
Clinical Psychology M
Health Psychology M
Psychology—General M
Social Psychology M

**CONSERVATORIO DE MUSICA DE
PUERTO RICO**
Music O

CONVERSE COLLEGE
English M
History M
Liberal Studies M
Marriage and Family Therapy M
Music M
Political Science M

THE CONWAY SCHOOL
Landscape Architecture M
Sustainable Development M

**COOPER UNION FOR THE
ADVANCEMENT OF SCIENCE AND ART**
Architecture M

COPENHAGEN BUSINESS SCHOOL
Economics M,D
Public Administration M,D

COPPIN STATE UNIVERSITY
Addictions/Substance Abuse
  Counseling M
Criminal Justice and Criminology M
Rehabilitation Counseling M

CORBAN UNIVERSITY
Pastoral Ministry and Counseling M,D,O
Theology M,D,O

CORNELL UNIVERSITY
African Studies M,D
African-American Studies M,D
Agricultural Economics and
  Agribusiness M,D
American Studies M,D
Anthropology D
Applied Economics M,D
Archaeology M,D
Architectural History M,D
Architecture M,D
Art History D
Art/Fine Arts M
Asian Languages M,D
Asian Studies M,D
Child and Family Studies M,D
Classics D
Clothing and Textiles M,D
Cognitive Sciences D
Communication—General M,D
Comparative Literature D
Computer Art and Design M,D
Conflict Resolution and
  Mediation/Peace Studies M,D
Consumer Economics M,D
Corporate and Organizational
  Communication M,D
Cultural Anthropology D
Cultural Studies M,D
Demography and Population Studies M,D
Developmental Psychology M,D
East European and Russian Studies M,D
Economic Development M,D
Economics M,D
English M,D
Environmental Design M
Ethnic Studies M,D
Experimental Psychology D
French D
Gender Studies M,D
German M,D
Health Communication M,D
Hispanic and Latin American
  Languages D
Historic Preservation M,D
History of Science and Technology M,D
History M,D
Human Development M,D
Industrial and Labor Relations M,D
Interior Design M
International Affairs D
Italian D
Jewish Studies M,D
Landscape Architecture M
Latin American Studies M,D
Linguistics M,D
Media Studies M,D
Medieval and Renaissance Studies M,D
Music M,D
Near and Middle Eastern Studies M,D
Philosophy M,D
Photography M,D
Political Science D
Psychology—General M
Public Affairs M
Public Policy M,D
Religion M,D
Romance Languages M,D
Rural Sociology M,D
Scandinavian Languages M,D
Slavic Languages M,D
Social Psychology M,D
Sociology M,D
Spanish D
Sustainable Development M,D
Textile Design M,D
Theater D
Urban and Regional Planning M,D
Urban Design M,D
Western European Studies M,D
Women's Studies M,D
Writing M,D

COVENANT THEOLOGICAL SEMINARY
Pastoral Ministry and Counseling M,D,O
Theology M,D,O

CRANBROOK ACADEMY OF ART
Applied Arts and Design—
  General M
Architecture M
Art/Fine Arts M
Photography M
Textile Design M

CREIGHTON UNIVERSITY
Anthropology M
Asian Studies M
Conflict Resolution and
  Mediation/Peace Studies M,O
English M
International Affairs M
Social Psychology M,D
Theology M
Western European Studies M
Writing M

THE CRISWELL COLLEGE
Jewish Studies M
Pastoral Ministry and Counseling M
Theology M

CROWN COLLEGE
Theology M

CUMBERLAND UNIVERSITY
Public Administration M

**CUNY GRADUATE SCHOOL OF
JOURNALISM**
Journalism M,O

CURRY COLLEGE
Criminal Justice and Criminology M

CURTIS INSTITUTE OF MUSIC
Music M

DAEMEN COLLEGE
Arts Administration M

DALHOUSIE UNIVERSITY
Anthropology M,D
Architecture M
Classics M,D
Clinical Psychology M,D
Economics M,D
English M,D
French M,D
German M
History M,D
Interdisciplinary Studies D
International Development M
Music M
Philosophy M,D
Political Science M,D
Psychology—General M,D
Public Administration M,O
Rural Planning and Studies M
Sociology M,D
Urban and Regional Planning M

DALLAS BAPTIST UNIVERSITY
Asian Studies M
Conflict Resolution and
  Mediation/Peace Studies M
Corporate and Organizational
  Communication M
Counseling Psychology M
Criminal Justice and Criminology M
Experimental Psychology M
Interdisciplinary Studies M
Liberal Studies M
Missions and Missiology M
Music M
Pastoral Ministry and Counseling M,D
Religion M
Theology M

DALLAS THEOLOGICAL SEMINARY
Child and Family Studies M,D,O
Jewish Studies M,D,O
Media Studies M,D,O
Missions and Missiology M,D,O
Pastoral Ministry and Counseling M,D,O
Philosophy M,D,O
Religion M,D,O
Theology M,D,O

DARTMOUTH COLLEGE
Cognitive Sciences D
Comparative Literature M
Liberal Studies M*
Music M
Psychology—General D

DEFIANCE COLLEGE
Criminal Justice and Criminology M

DELAWARE STATE UNIVERSITY
Historic Preservation M

DELAWARE VALLEY UNIVERSITY
Agricultural Economics and
  Agribusiness M
Counseling Psychology M
Developmental Psychology M
Social Psychology M

**DELL'ARTE INTERNATIONAL SCHOOL
OF PHYSICAL THEATRE**
Theater M

DELTA STATE UNIVERSITY
Criminal Justice and Criminology M
Gender Studies M
Liberal Studies M
Philosophy M
Religion M
Urban and Regional Planning M

DENVER SEMINARY
Marriage and Family Therapy M,D,O
Pastoral Ministry and Counseling M,D,O

Religion | M,D,O
Theology | M,D,O

DEPAUL UNIVERSITY
Applied Economics | M
Chinese | M
Clinical Psychology | M,D
Communication—General | M
Computer Art and Design | M,D
Corporate and Organizational
   Communication | M
Counseling Psychology | M,D
Economics | M
English | M
Film, Television, and Video
   Production | M,D
Film, Television, and Video
   Theory and Criticism | M
French | M
German | M
Health Communication | M
History | M
Interdisciplinary Studies | M
International Affairs | M
Internet and Interactive
   Multimedia | M,D
Italian | M
Japanese | M
Journalism | M
Liberal Studies | M
Media Studies | M
Music | M,O
Near and Middle Eastern Languages | M
Psychology—General | M,D
Public Administration | M
Public Policy | M
Publishing | M
Rhetoric | M
School Psychology | M,D
Sociology | M
Spanish | M
Sustainable Development | M
Theater | M
Urban Design | M
Women's Studies | M
Writing | M

DEREE - THE AMERICAN COLLEGE OF GREECE
Applied Psychology | M
Communication—General | M

DESALES UNIVERSITY
Criminal Justice and Criminology | M
Forensic Sciences | M
Interdisciplinary Studies | M

DEVRY UNIVERSITY
Communication—General | M
Public Administration | M

DIGIPEN INSTITUTE OF TECHNOLOGY
Computer Art and Design | M

DIGITAL MEDIA ARTS COLLEGE
Computer Art and Design | M
Graphic Design | M
Media Studies | M

DOMINICAN HOUSE OF STUDIES, PONTIFICAL FACULTY OF THE IMMACULATE CONCEPTION
Theology | M,D,O

DOMINICAN SCHOOL OF PHILOSOPHY AND THEOLOGY
Philosophy | M,O
Theology | M,O

DOMINICAN UNIVERSITY
Conflict Resolution and
   Mediation/Peace Studies | M

DOMINICAN UNIVERSITY OF CALIFORNIA
Art History | M
Counseling Psychology | M
English | M
Gender Studies | M
History | M
Humanities | M
Marriage and Family Therapy | M
Music | M
Philosophy | M
Political Science | M
Religion | M
Women's Studies | M
Writing | M

DRAKE UNIVERSITY
Communication—General | M
Public Administration | M

DREW UNIVERSITY
English | M
French | M
History | M,D
Holocaust and Genocide Studies | M,D,O
Humanities | M,D,O
Interdisciplinary Studies | M,D,O
Italian | M
Spanish | M
Theater | M
Theology | M,D,O
Translation and Interpretation | M
Writing | M

DREXEL UNIVERSITY
Applied Arts and Design—
   General | M
Applied Behavior Analysis | M,D
Art Therapy | M,O
Arts Administration | M
Clinical Psychology | D
Communication—General | M

Computer Art and Design | M
Corporate and Organizational
   Communication | M
Economics | M,D,O
Emergency Management | M
Film, Television, and Video
   Production | M
Forensic Psychology | D
Health Psychology | D
History of Science and Technology | M
Homeland Security | M
Interior Design | M
Journalism | M
Marriage and Family Therapy | M,D
Mass Communication | M
Psychology—General | M,D
Publishing | M
Technical Communication | M
Technical Writing | M
Textile Design | M
Therapies—Dance, Drama, and
   Music | M,O

DRURY UNIVERSITY
Architecture | M
Art/Fine Arts | M
Communication—General | M
Criminal Justice and Criminology | M

DUKE UNIVERSITY
Art History | M,D
Art/Fine Arts | M,D
Asian Studies | M,O
Biological Anthropology | D
Classics | D
Clinical Psychology | D
Cognitive Sciences | D
Comparative Literature | D
Cultural Anthropology | D
Developmental Psychology | D
Economics | M,D
English | D
Ethics | M,O
Experimental Psychology | D
French | D
German | D
Health Psychology | D
History | M,D
Human Development | D
Humanities | M
International Development | M
Italian | D
Latin American Studies | M,D
Liberal Studies | M
Media Studies | M
Music | D
Philosophy | D
Political Science | M,D
Psychology—General | D
Public Policy | M,D
Religion | M,D
Slavic Languages | M,O
Sociology | M,D
Spanish | D
Theology | M,D

DUQUESNE UNIVERSITY
Classics | M
Clinical Psychology | M,D,O
Communication—General | M,D
Conflict Resolution and
   Mediation/Peace Studies | M,O
Counseling Psychology | M,D,O
English | M,D
Forensic Sciences | M
History | M
Internet and Interactive
   Multimedia | M,O
Marriage and Family Therapy | M,D,O
Music | M,O
Philosophy | M,D
Psychology—General | D
Public Administration | M,O
Public History | M
Public Policy | M,O
Rhetoric | M,D
School Psychology | M,D,O
Theology | M,D

EARLHAM SCHOOL OF RELIGION
Religion | M
Theology | M

EAST CAROLINA UNIVERSITY
Addictions/Substance Abuse
   Counseling | M,D,O
American Studies | M
Anthropology | M
Applied Economics | M
Art/Fine Arts | M
Child and Family Studies | M,D
Child Development | M,D
Clinical Psychology | D
Comparative Literature | M,D,O
Criminal Justice and Criminology | M,O
Economic Development | M,O
English | M,D,O
Family and Consumer
   Sciences-General | M,D
Geographic Information Systems | M,O
Geography | M,O
Gerontology | M,O
Graphic Design | M
Health Communication | M
Health Psychology | D
History | M
Illustration | M
Industrial and Organizational
   Psychology | M
International Affairs | M
Linguistics | M,D,O
Marriage and Family Therapy | M,D

Military and Defense Studies | M
Music | M,D,O
Photography | M
Political Science | M,O
Public Administration | M,O
Public History | M
Rehabilitation Counseling | M,D,O
Rhetoric | M,D,O
Rural Planning and Studies | M,O
School Psychology | M
Sociology | M
Technical Communication | M,D,O
Textile Design | M
Therapies—Dance, Drama, and
   Music | M,O
Urban and Regional Planning | M,O
Western European Studies | M
Writing | M,D,O

EAST CENTRAL UNIVERSITY
Criminal Justice and Criminology | M
Psychology—General | M
Rehabilitation Counseling | M

EASTERN ILLINOIS UNIVERSITY
Art/Fine Arts | M
Clinical Psychology | M,O
Economics | M
English | M
Family and Consumer
   Sciences-General | M
Geographic Information Systems | M
Gerontology | M
History | M
Music | M
Political Science | M
Psychology—General | M,O
Public History | M
School Psychology | M,O
Speech and Interpersonal
   Communication | M
Sustainable Development | M

EASTERN KENTUCKY UNIVERSITY
Clinical Psychology | M,O
Criminal Justice and Criminology | M
English | M
History | M
Industrial and Organizational
   Psychology | M,O
Music | M
Political Science | M
Psychology—General | M,O
Public Administration | M
School Psychology | M,O
Urban and Regional Planning | M
Writing | M

EASTERN MENNONITE UNIVERSITY
Conflict Resolution and
   Mediation/Peace Studies | M,O
Pastoral Ministry and Counseling | M,O
Religion | M,O
Theology | M,O

EASTERN MICHIGAN UNIVERSITY
African-American Studies | O
American Studies | M,O
Art/Fine Arts | M
Arts Administration | M
Clinical Psychology | M,D
Clothing and Textiles | M
Communication—General | M
Corporate and Organizational
   Communication | M
Criminal Justice and Criminology | M
Cultural Studies | M,O
Economics | M,O
English | M,O
French | M,O
Gender Studies | M,O
Geographic Information Systems | M,O
Geography | M,O
German | M,O
Gerontology | O
Hispanic and Latin American
   Languages | M,O
Hispanic Studies | M,O
Historic Preservation | M,O
History | M,O
Interior Design | M
Japanese | M,O
Linguistics | M,O
Music | M
Philosophy | M
Psychology—General | M,D
Public Administration | M,O
Public Policy | M,O
Social Sciences | M,O
Sociology | M
Spanish | M,O
Technical Communication | M,O
Theater | M
Urban and Regional Planning | M,O
Urban Studies | M
Women's Studies | M
Writing | M,O

EASTERN NAZARENE COLLEGE
Counseling Psychology | M
Marriage and Family Therapy | M

EASTERN NEW MEXICO UNIVERSITY
Anthropology | M
Communication—General | M
English | M

EASTERN UNIVERSITY
Applied Behavior Analysis | M,O
Communication—General | M,O
Counseling Psychology | M,O
Cultural Anthropology | M
Economic Development | M

French | M,O
International Development | M
Marriage and Family Therapy | M,D
Missions and Missiology | M,D
Pastoral Ministry and Counseling | M,D
Public Policy | M,D
School Psychology | M,O
Spanish | M,O
Theology | M,D
Urban and Regional Planning | M
Urban Studies | M

EASTERN VIRGINIA MEDICAL SCHOOL
Art Therapy | M
Clinical Psychology | D

EASTERN WASHINGTON UNIVERSITY
Applied Psychology | M
Clinical Psychology | M
Communication—General | M
Counseling Psychology | M
English | M
Experimental Psychology | M
History | M
Interdisciplinary Studies | M
Music | M
Psychology—General | M
Public Administration | M
Rhetoric | M
School Psychology | M
Technical Communication | M
Urban and Regional Planning | M
Writing | M

EAST STROUDSBURG UNIVERSITY OF PENNSYLVANIA
History | M
Political Science | M

EAST TENNESSEE STATE UNIVERSITY
Art/Fine Arts | M
Communication—General | M
Computer Art and Design | M,O
Corporate and Organizational
   Communication | M
Criminal Justice and Criminology | M,O
Economic Development | M,O
English | M,O
History | M,O
Human Development | M
Liberal Studies | M,O
Political Science | M,O
Psychology—General | D
Public Administration | M,O
Sociology | M
Urban and Regional Planning | M,O

EAST TEXAS BAPTIST UNIVERSITY
Counseling Psychology | M
Pastoral Ministry and Counseling | M
Religion | M

ECUMENICAL THEOLOGICAL SEMINARY
Pastoral Ministry and Counseling | D
Theology | M

EDEN THEOLOGICAL SEMINARY
Theology | M,D

EDGEWOOD COLLEGE
Marriage and Family Therapy | M

EDINBORO UNIVERSITY OF PENNSYLVANIA
Anthropology | M
Art Therapy | M,O
Art/Fine Arts | M
Clinical Psychology | M,O
Communication—General | M
Counseling Psychology | M,O
History | M
Rehabilitation Counseling | M,O
School Psychology | M,O
Social Sciences | M

ELIZABETH CITY STATE UNIVERSITY
Geographic Information Systems | M

ELMHURST COLLEGE
Geographic Information Systems | M
Industrial and Organizational
   Psychology | M

ELMS COLLEGE
Religion | M

ELON UNIVERSITY
Internet and Interactive
   Multimedia | M

EMBRY-RIDDLE AERONAUTICAL UNIVERSITY–DAYTONA
International Affairs | M

EMBRY-RIDDLE AERONAUTICAL UNIVERSITY–PRESCOTT
Military and Defense Studies | M

EMBRY-RIDDLE AERONAUTICAL UNIVERSITY–WORLDWIDE
International Affairs | M

EMERSON COLLEGE
Broadcast Journalism | M
Communication—General | M
Corporate and Organizational
   Communication | M
Health Communication | M
Journalism | M
Media Studies | M
Publishing | M
Theater | M
Writing | M

---

*M—masters degree; D—doctorate; O—other advanced degree; *—Close-Up and/or Display*

EMILY CARR UNIVERSITY OF ART + DESIGN
Applied Arts and Design—
General — M
Art/Fine Arts — M
Computer Art and Design — M

EMMANUEL CHRISTIAN SEMINARY
Missions and Missiology — M,D
Pastoral Ministry and Counseling — M,D
Religion — M,D
Theology — M,D

EMORY & HENRY COLLEGE
American Studies — M
History — M

EMORY UNIVERSITY
Anthropology — D
Art History — D
Clinical Psychology — D
Cognitive Sciences — D
Comparative Literature — D,O
Developmental Psychology — D
Economics — D
English — D,O
Ethics — M,D
Film, Television, and Video
Theory and Criticism — M,D,O
French — D
Genetic Counseling — M
History — D
Interdisciplinary Studies — D
Music — M
Pastoral Ministry and Counseling — M,D
Philosophy — D,O
Political Science — D
Portuguese — D,O
Psychology—General — D
Religion — D
Sociology — D
Spanish — D,O
Sustainable Development — M
Theology — M,D
Women's Studies — D,O

EMPORIA STATE UNIVERSITY
Art Therapy — M
Clinical Psychology — M
Counseling Psychology — M
English — M
History — M
Industrial and Organizational
Psychology — M
Music — M
Psychology—General — M
Rehabilitation Counseling — M
School Psychology — M,O

ENDICOTT COLLEGE
Applied Behavior Analysis — M,D
Homeland Security — M
Interior Design — M

EPISCOPAL DIVINITY SCHOOL
Theology — M,D,O

ERIKSON INSTITUTE
Child Development — M
Developmental Psychology — M,O
Human Development — M,O

ERSKINE THEOLOGICAL SEMINARY
Theology — M,D

EVANGELICAL SEMINARY
Marriage and Family Therapy — M
Missions and Missiology — M
Pastoral Ministry and Counseling — M
Theology — M

EVANGELICAL SEMINARY OF PUERTO RICO
Theology — M,D

EVANGEL UNIVERSITY
Clinical Psychology — M
Counseling Psychology — M
Music — M
Psychology—General — M
School Psychology — M

EVEREST UNIVERSITY
Criminal Justice and Criminology — M

EVEREST UNIVERSITY
Criminal Justice and Criminology — M

EVEREST UNIVERSITY
Criminal Justice and Criminology — M

THE EVERGREEN STATE COLLEGE
Public Administration — M

EXCELSIOR COLLEGE
Criminal Justice and Criminology — M,O
Emergency Management — M
Homeland Security — M
Internet and Interactive
Multimedia — M,O
Liberal Studies — M
Public Administration — M

FAIRFIELD UNIVERSITY
Addictions/Substance Abuse
Counseling — M,O
American Studies — M
Applied Behavior Analysis — M,O
Applied Psychology — M,O
Child and Family Studies — M,O
Clinical Psychology — M,O
Communication—General — M
Counseling Psychology — M,O
Internet and Interactive
Multimedia — M,O
Marriage and Family Therapy — M,O
Pastoral Ministry and Counseling — M,O
Public Administration — M
School Psychology — M,O
Writing — M

FAIRLEIGH DICKINSON UNIVERSITY, COLLEGE AT FLORHAM
Clinical Psychology — M
Corporate and Organizational
Communication — M
Counseling Psychology — M
Industrial and Organizational
Psychology — M
Psychology—General — M,O
Public Administration — M
Writing — M

FAIRLEIGH DICKINSON UNIVERSITY, METROPOLITAN CAMPUS
Art/Fine Arts — M
Clinical Psychology — M,D
Communication—General — M
Comparative Literature — M
Criminal Justice and Criminology — M
English — M
Experimental Psychology — M,O
Forensic Psychology — M
History — M
Homeland Security — M
International Affairs — M
Media Studies — M
Political Science — M
Psychology—General — M,D,O
Public Administration — M,O
School Psychology — M,D

FAIRMONT STATE UNIVERSITY
Criminal Justice and Criminology — M

FAITH BAPTIST BIBLE COLLEGE AND THEOLOGICAL SEMINARY
Pastoral Ministry and Counseling — M
Religion — M
Theology — M

FAITH EVANGELICAL COLLEGE & SEMINARY
Theology — M,D

FAITH THEOLOGICAL SEMINARY
Theology — M,D

FASHION INSTITUTE OF TECHNOLOGY
Applied Arts and Design—
General — M*
Art History — M*
Arts Administration — M*
Clothing and Textiles — M
Illustration — M*
Interior Design — M*
Museum Studies — M*
Sustainable Development — M

FAULKNER UNIVERSITY
Criminal Justice and Criminology — M
History — M
Liberal Studies — M
Missions and Missiology — M
Pastoral Ministry and Counseling — M
Theology — M

FAYETTEVILLE STATE UNIVERSITY
Criminal Justice and Criminology — M
English — M
History — M
Political Science — M
Psychology—General — M
Sociology — M

FELICIAN COLLEGE
Counseling Psychology — M

FERRIS STATE UNIVERSITY
Applied Arts and Design—
General — M
Art/Fine Arts — M
Criminal Justice and Criminology — M

FIELDING GRADUATE UNIVERSITY
Clinical Psychology — M,D,O
Forensic Psychology — M,D,O
Gerontology — M,D,O
Health Psychology — M,D,O
Human Development — M,D,O
Media Studies — M,D,O
Psychology—General — M,D,O

FISK UNIVERSITY
Clinical Psychology — M
Psychology—General — M

FITCHBURG STATE UNIVERSITY
Communication—General — M,O
Counseling Psychology — M
English — M,O
Health Communication — M,O
History — M,O
Interdisciplinary Studies — O
Technical Writing — M,O

FIVE TOWNS COLLEGE
Music — M,D

FLORIDA AGRICULTURAL AND MECHANICAL UNIVERSITY
Architecture — M
Criminal Justice and Criminology — M
History — M
Journalism — M
Landscape Architecture — M
Political Science — M
Psychology—General — M
Public Administration — M
Social Psychology — M
Social Sciences — M

FLORIDA ATLANTIC UNIVERSITY
Anthropology — M
Applied Arts and Design—
General — M
Art/Fine Arts — M
Communication—General — M,O
Comparative and Interdisciplinary
Arts — D

Comparative Literature — M
Counseling Psychology — M
Criminal Justice and Criminology — M
Economic Development — M,O
Economics — M
English — M
Environmental Design — M,O
Experimental Psychology — M,D
Film, Television, and Video
Production — M,O
Forensic Sciences — M,D
French — M
Geography — M,D
German — M
Graphic Design — M
History — M,O
Liberal Studies — M
Linguistics — M
Marriage and Family Therapy — M,D,O
Media Studies — M,O
Music — M
Political Science — M
Psychology—General — M,D
Public Administration — M,D
Rehabilitation Counseling — M,D,O
Rhetoric — M
Sociology — M
Spanish — M
Sustainable Development — M
Theater — M
Urban and Regional Planning — M,O
Women's Studies — M,O
Writing — M

FLORIDA GULF COAST UNIVERSITY
Criminal Justice and Criminology — M
English — M
Forensic Sciences — M
History — M
Interdisciplinary Studies — M
Public Administration — M

FLORIDA INSTITUTE OF TECHNOLOGY
Applied Behavior Analysis — M,D
Communication—General — M
Emergency Management — M,D
Interdisciplinary Studies — M
Psychology—General — M,D
Public Administration — M,D

FLORIDA INTERNATIONAL UNIVERSITY
African Studies — M
Applied Behavior Analysis — M,D
Architecture — M,O
Art/Fine Arts — M,O
Asian Studies — M
Clinical Psychology — M,D,O
Communication—General — M
Counseling Psychology — M,D,O
Criminal Justice and Criminology — M
Developmental Psychology — M,D
Economics — M
English — M
Forensic Sciences — M,D
History — M,D
Industrial and Organizational
Psychology — M,D
Interior Design — M,O
International Affairs — M,D
Journalism — M
Landscape Architecture — M
Latin American Studies — M
Liberal Studies — M
Linguistics — M
Mass Communication — M
Museum Studies — M,O
Music — M
Political Science — M,D
Psychology—General — M,D
Public Administration — M,D
Public Affairs — M,D
Rehabilitation Counseling — M,D,O
Religion — M
School Psychology — M,D,O
Sociology — M,D
Spanish — M,D
Writing — M

FLORIDA STATE UNIVERSITY
American Studies — M
Applied Behavior Analysis — M
Archaeology — M,D
Art History — M,D,O
Art/Fine Arts — M
Arts Administration — M,D
Asian Studies — M
Child and Family Studies — M,D
Classics — M,D
Clinical Psychology — D
Cognitive Sciences — D
Communication—General — M,D
Corporate and Organizational
Communication — M,D
Counseling Psychology — D
Criminal Justice and Criminology — M,D
Cultural Studies — M,D,O
Dance — M
Demography and Population Studies — M
Developmental Psychology — D
East European and Russian Studies — M
Economics — M,D
English — M,D
Family and Consumer
Sciences-General — M
Film, Television, and Video
Production — M
French — M,D
Geographic Information Systems — M,D
Geography — M,D
German — M
History — M,D
Industrial Design — M
Interior Design — M
International Affairs — M
Italian — M

Marriage and Family Therapy — M,D
Media Studies — M,D
Museum Studies — M,D,O
Music — M,D
Philosophy — M,D
Political Science — M,D
Psychology—General — M,D
Public Administration — M,D,O
Public History — M,D
Public Policy — M,D,O
Religion — M,D
Rhetoric — M,D
School Psychology — D
Slavic Languages — M
Social Psychology — D
Sociology — M,D
Spanish — M,D
Sport Psychology — M,D,O
Theater — M,D
Therapies—Dance, Drama, and
Music — M,D
Urban and Regional Planning — M,D
Writing — M,D

FONTBONNE UNIVERSITY
Art/Fine Arts — M
Family and Consumer
Sciences-General — M
Theater — M

FORDHAM UNIVERSITY
Applied Psychology — M,D
Classics — M,D
Clinical Psychology — D
Corporate and Organizational
Communication — M
Counseling Psychology — M,D,O
Developmental Psychology — D
Economic Development — M,O
Economics — M,D,O
Emergency Management — M
English — M,D
Ethics — M,O
History — M,D
International Affairs — M,O
International Development — M,O
International Economics — M,O
Media Studies — M
Medieval and Renaissance Studies — M
Pastoral Ministry and Counseling — M,D,O
Philosophy — M,D
Political Science — M
Psychology—General — M,D
Religion — M,D,O
School Psychology — M,D,O
Theater — M
Theology — M,D
Urban Studies — M

FORT HAYS STATE UNIVERSITY
Art/Fine Arts — M
Communication—General — M
English — M
Geography — M
History — M
Liberal Studies — M
Psychology—General — M,O
School Psychology — O

FORT VALLEY STATE UNIVERSITY
Counseling Psychology — M
Rehabilitation Counseling — M

FRAMINGHAM STATE UNIVERSITY
Art/Fine Arts — M
Psychology—General — M
Public Administration — M
Spanish — M

FRANCISCAN SCHOOL OF THEOLOGY
Theology — M

FRANCISCAN UNIVERSITY OF STEUBENVILLE
Clinical Psychology — M
Counseling Psychology — M
Philosophy — M
Theology — M

FRANCIS MARION UNIVERSITY
Applied Psychology — M,O
Clinical Psychology — M,O
Counseling Psychology — M,O
Psychology—General — M,O
School Psychology — M,O

FRANKLIN UNIVERSITY
Corporate and Organizational
Communication — M

FRANK LLOYD WRIGHT SCHOOL OF ARCHITECTURE
Architecture — M*

FREDERICK S. PARDEE RAND GRADUATE SCHOOL
Public Policy — M,D

FREED-HARDEMAN UNIVERSITY
Ethics — M
Pastoral Ministry and Counseling — M
Theology — M

FRESNO PACIFIC UNIVERSITY
Conflict Resolution and
Mediation/Peace Studies — M,O
Interdisciplinary Studies — M
Marriage and Family Therapy — M
Missions and Missiology — M
Pastoral Ministry and Counseling — M
School Psychology — M
Theology — M

FRIENDS UNIVERSITY
Marriage and Family Therapy — M
Theology — M

FROSTBURG STATE UNIVERSITY
Counseling Psychology — M

Interdisciplinary Studies — M
Psychology—General — M

FULLER THEOLOGICAL SEMINARY
Clinical Psychology — M,D,O
Marriage and Family Therapy — M,D,O
Missions and Missiology — M,D,O
Music — M,D,O
Pastoral Ministry and Counseling — M,D,O
Theology — M,D,O

FULL SAIL UNIVERSITY
Art/Fine Arts — M
Computer Art and Design — M
Graphic Design — M
Internet and Interactive
    Multimedia — M
Journalism — M
Media Studies — M
Writing — M

FUTURE GENERATIONS GRADUATE SCHOOL
Conflict Resolution and
    Mediation/Peace Studies — M
Social Psychology — M
Sustainable Development — M
Urban and Regional Planning — M

GALLAUDET UNIVERSITY
Clinical Psychology — M,D,O
Counseling Psychology — M,D,O
Linguistics — M,D,O
Public Administration — M,D,O
School Psychology — M,D,O
Translation and Interpretation — M,D,O

GANNON UNIVERSITY
Clinical Psychology — M
Counseling Psychology — M
English — M
Internet and Interactive
    Multimedia — M
Pastoral Ministry and Counseling — M,O
Public Administration — M
Theology — M,O

GARDNER-WEBB UNIVERSITY
Counseling Psychology — M
Cultural Studies — M,D
English — M
Missions and Missiology — M,D
Pastoral Ministry and Counseling — M,D
Psychology—General — M
School Psychology — M
Theology — M,D

GARRETT-EVANGELICAL THEOLOGICAL SEMINARY
Music — M,D
Pastoral Ministry and Counseling — M,D
Theology — M,D

GENERAL THEOLOGICAL SEMINARY
Pastoral Ministry and Counseling — M,D,O
Religion — M,D,O
Theology — M,D,O

GENEVA COLLEGE
Clinical Psychology — M
Counseling Psychology — M
Marriage and Family Therapy — M
Psychology—General — M

GEORGE FOX UNIVERSITY
Clinical Psychology — M,D,O
Counseling Psychology — M,O
Marriage and Family Therapy — M,O
Pastoral Ministry and Counseling — M,D,O
School Psychology — M,O
Theology — M,D,O

GEORGE MASON UNIVERSITY
Anthropology — M,D
Applied Psychology — M,D,O
Art History — M
Art/Fine Arts — M
Arts Administration — M,O
Cognitive Sciences — M,D,O
Communication—General — M,D,O
Conflict Resolution and
    Mediation/Peace Studies — M,D,O
Criminal Justice and Criminology — M,D,O
Cultural Studies — M,D
Developmental Psychology — M,D,O
Economics — M,D,O
Emergency Management — M,D,O
English — M,D,O
Ethics — M
Film, Television, and Video
    Theory and Criticism — M
Folklore — M
Forensic Sciences — M,D,O
French — M
Gender Studies — M
Geographic Information Systems — M,D,O
Geography — M,D,O
Graphic Design — M
History — M,D
Homeland Security — M,D,O
Industrial and Organizational
    Psychology — M,D,O
Interdisciplinary Studies — M
International Affairs — M
Linguistics — M,D,O
Media Studies — M,D
Military and Defense Studies — M
Music — M,D
National Security — M,D
Near and Middle Eastern Studies — M,O
Philosophy — M
Photography — M
Political Science — M,D,O
Psychology—General — M,D,O

Public Administration — M,D,O
Public Affairs — M
Public History — M,D
Public Policy — M,D
Religion — M
Rhetoric — M,D,O
School Psychology — M,O
Social Sciences — D,O
Sociology — M,D
Women's Studies — M
Writing — M

GEORGETOWN UNIVERSITY
American Studies — M,D
Asian Studies — M
Communication—General — M
Comparative Literature — M,D
Conflict Resolution and
    Mediation/Peace Studies — M
East European and Russian Studies — M
Economic Development — D
Economics — D
Emergency Management — M,D
English — M
Ethics — M,D
German — M,D
History — M,D
Human Development — M
Humanities — M,D
Industrial and Labor Relations — D
Interdisciplinary Studies — M,D
International Affairs — M,D
Internet and Interactive
    Multimedia — M
Journalism — M,D
Latin American Studies — M
Liberal Studies — M,D
Linguistics — M,D
Media Studies — M,D
Medieval and Renaissance Studies — M,D
Near and Middle Eastern Languages — M,O
Near and Middle Eastern Studies — M,O
Philosophy — M,D
Political Science — M,D
Psychology—General — D
Public Policy — M,D
Religion — M,D
Spanish — M,D
Theology — D
Urban and Regional Planning — M,D
Western European Studies — M

THE GEORGE WASHINGTON UNIVERSITY
Addictions/Substance Abuse
    Counseling — M
American Studies — M,D
Anthropology — M,D
Applied Psychology — D
Art History — M
Art Therapy — M,O
Art/Fine Arts — M,O
Asian Studies — M
Clinical Psychology — M,D
Cognitive Sciences — D
Communication—General — M
Criminal Justice and Criminology — M,O
Dance — M,O
East European and Russian Studies — M
Economics — M,D
Emergency Management — M,D,O
English — M,D
Folklore — M,D
Forensic Psychology — O
Forensic Sciences — M,O
Gender Studies — O
Geography — M,O
Health Communication — M,D
Historic Preservation — M,D
History — M,D
Human Development — M
Interior Design — M
International Affairs — M,D
International Development — M,D
International Trade Policy — M
Latin American Studies — M
Mass Communication — M,O
Military and Defense Studies — M
Museum Studies — M,D,O
National Security — M,D
Near and Middle Eastern Studies — M
Philosophy — M
Photography — M,O
Political Science — M,D
Psychology—General — M,D,O
Public Administration — M,D
Public Affairs — M,O
Public Policy — M,D
Publishing — M
Rehabilitation Counseling — M
Religion — M
Social Psychology — D
Sociology — M
Theater — M,O
Western European Studies — M
Women's Studies — M,O

GEORGIA CHRISTIAN UNIVERSITY
Missions and Missiology — M,D
Music — M
Pastoral Ministry and Counseling — M,D
Theology — M,D

GEORGIA COLLEGE & STATE UNIVERSITY
American Studies — M
Art Therapy — M
Criminal Justice and Criminology — M
English — M
History — M
Public Administration — M
Public History — M

Therapies—Dance, Drama, and
    Music — M
Western European Studies — M
Writing — M

GEORGIA INSTITUTE OF TECHNOLOGY
Architecture — M,D
Building Science — M,D
Computer Art and Design — M,D
Economic Development — M,D
Economics — M,D
Geographic Information Systems — M,D
History of Science and Technology — M,D
Industrial Design — M
International Affairs — M,D
Internet and Interactive
    Multimedia — M,D
Music — M,D
Psychology—General — M,D
Public Policy — M,D
Urban and Regional Planning — M,D
Urban Design — M,D

GEORGIAN COURT UNIVERSITY
Applied Behavior Analysis — M,O
Clinical Psychology — M,O
Counseling Psychology — M,O
Health Psychology — M,O
Homeland Security — M,O
Pastoral Ministry and Counseling — M,O
School Psychology — M,O
Theology — M,O

GEORGIA REGENTS UNIVERSITY
Medical Illustration — M
Political Science — M
Psychology—General — M

GEORGIA SOUTHERN UNIVERSITY
Applied Economics — M,O
Art/Fine Arts — M
English — M
Graphic Design — M
History — M,O
Music — M
Psychology—General — M,D
Public Administration — M
School Psychology — M,O
Sociology — M
Spanish — M

GEORGIA STATE UNIVERSITY
African-American Studies — M
Anthropology — M
Art History — M
Art/Fine Arts — M
Clinical Psychology — D
Clothing and Textiles — M
Cognitive Sciences — D
Communication—General — M,D
Counseling Psychology — M,O
Criminal Justice and Criminology — M,D,O
Developmental Psychology — D
Economic Development — M,D,O
Economics — M,D
Emergency Management — M,D,O
English — M,D
Film, Television, and Video
    Production — M,D
Forensic Sciences — M,O
French — M,O
Geographic Information Systems — O
Geography — M,D
German — O
Gerontology — M,O
Graphic Design — M
Historic Preservation — M,D
History — M,D
Industrial and Labor Relations — M,D
Interior Design — M
Latin American Studies — M,O
Linguistics — M,D
Mass Communication — M,D
Media Studies — M,D
Music — M,D,O
Philosophy — M
Photography — M,D
Political Science — M,D
Psychology—General — D
Public Administration — M,D
Public History — M,D
Public Policy — M,D,O
Rehabilitation Counseling — M
Religion — M
Rhetoric — M,D
School Psychology — M,D,O
Social Psychology — D
Sociology — M,D
Spanish — M,O
Speech and Interpersonal
    Communication — M,D
Translation and Interpretation — O
Urban and Regional Planning — M,D,O
Women's Studies — M,O
Writing — M,D

GLOBAL UNIVERSITY
Missions and Missiology — M
Theology — M

GODDARD COLLEGE
Comparative and Interdisciplinary
    Arts — M
Counseling Psychology — M
Interdisciplinary Studies — M
Writing — M

GOLDEN GATE BAPTIST THEOLOGICAL SEMINARY
Pastoral Ministry and Counseling — M,D,O
Theology — M,D,O

GOLDEN GATE UNIVERSITY
Corporate and Organizational
    Communication — M,D,O
Forensic Sciences — M,O
Psychology—General — M,D,O
Public Administration — M,D,O

GONZAGA UNIVERSITY
Communication—General — M
Counseling Psychology — M
Philosophy — M

GORDON-CONWELL THEOLOGICAL SEMINARY
Archaeology — M,D
Missions and Missiology — M,D
Pastoral Ministry and Counseling — M,D
Religion — M,D
Theology — M,D

GOUCHER COLLEGE
Arts Administration — M
Computer Art and Design — M
Cultural Studies — M
Historic Preservation — M
Writing — M

GOVERNORS STATE UNIVERSITY
Addictions/Substance Abuse
    Counseling — M
Art/Fine Arts — M
Communication—General — M
Counseling Psychology — M
English — M
Media Studies — M
Political Science — M
Psychology—General — M
Public Administration — M

GRACE COLLEGE
Clinical Psychology — M
Counseling Psychology — M

GRACELAND UNIVERSITY (IA)
Religion — M
Theology — M

GRACE THEOLOGICAL SEMINARY
Cultural Studies — M,D,O
Missions and Missiology — M,D,O
Pastoral Ministry and Counseling — M,D,O
Theology — M,D,O

GRACE UNIVERSITY
Counseling Psychology — M
Pastoral Ministry and Counseling — M
Theology — M

THE GRADUATE CENTER, CITY UNIVERSITY OF NEW YORK
Anthropology — D
Archaeology — D
Architectural History — D
Art History — D
Classics — M,D
Clinical Psychology — D
Cognitive Sciences — D
Comparative Literature — M,D
Criminal Justice and Criminology — D
Cultural Anthropology — D
Developmental Psychology — D
Economics — D
English — D
Experimental Psychology — D
French — D
German — M,D
Hispanic and Latin American
    Languages — D
History — D
Industrial and Organizational
    Psychology — D
Interdisciplinary Studies — M,D
Italian — M,D
Liberal Studies — M
Linguistics — M,D
Medieval and Renaissance Studies — M,D
Music — D
Philosophy — M,D
Political Science — M,D
Psychology—General — D
Public Policy — M,D
Social Psychology — D
Sociology — D
Theater — D
Urban Studies — M,D
Women's Studies — M,D

GRADUATE INSTITUTE OF APPLIED LINGUISTICS
Linguistics — M,O

GRADUATE THEOLOGICAL UNION
Art History — M,D,O
Cultural Studies — M,D,O
Ethics — M,D,O
Jewish Studies — M,D,O
Religion — M,D,O
Social Sciences — M,D,O
Theology — M,D,O

GRAMBLING STATE UNIVERSITY
Criminal Justice and Criminology — M
English — M,D,O
Mass Communication — M
Political Science — M
Public Administration — M

GRAND CANYON UNIVERSITY
Addictions/Substance Abuse
    Counseling — M
Cognitive Sciences — D
Counseling Psychology — M
Emergency Management — M
Industrial and Organizational
    Psychology — D

---

*M—masters degree; D—doctorate; O—other advanced degree; *—Close-Up and/or Display*

Marriage and Family Therapy — M
Psychology—General — D
Public Administration — M

GRAND RAPIDS THEOLOGICAL SEMINARY OF CORNERSTONE UNIVERSITY
Missions and Missiology — M
Pastoral Ministry and Counseling — M
Religion — M
Theology — M

GRAND VALLEY STATE UNIVERSITY
Communication—General — M
Criminal Justice and Criminology — M
English — M
Public Administration — M
School Psychology — M,O

GRATZ COLLEGE
Holocaust and Genocide Studies — M,O
Jewish Studies — M,O

GREENVILLE COLLEGE
Pastoral Ministry and Counseling — M

HAMLINE UNIVERSITY
Liberal Studies — M
Public Administration — M,D
Writing — M

HAMPTON UNIVERSITY
Architecture — M
Pastoral Ministry and Counseling — M,D,O
Psychology—General — M

HARDING SCHOOL OF THEOLOGY
Pastoral Ministry and Counseling — M,D
Religion — M,D
Theology — M,D

HARDING UNIVERSITY
Counseling Psychology — M
Marriage and Family Therapy — M
Pastoral Ministry and Counseling — M

HARDIN-SIMMONS UNIVERSITY
Counseling Psychology — M
English — M
History — M
Marriage and Family Therapy — M
Music — M
Pastoral Ministry and Counseling — M,D
Psychology—General — M
Religion — M
Theology — M,D

HARRISBURG UNIVERSITY OF SCIENCE AND TECHNOLOGY
Public Administration — M

HARRISON MIDDLETON UNIVERSITY
Comparative Literature — M,D
Humanities — M,D
Interdisciplinary Studies — M,D
Philosophy — M,D
Religion — M,D
Social Sciences — M,D

HARTFORD SEMINARY
Pastoral Ministry and Counseling — M,D,O
Religion — M,D,O
Theology — M,D,O

HARVARD UNIVERSITY
African Studies — D
African-American Studies — D
American Studies — D
Anthropology — M,D
Archaeology — M,D
Architectural History — D
Architecture — M,D
Art History — D
Asian Languages — M,D
Asian Studies — M,D
Celtic Languages — D
Chinese — D
Classics — D
Cognitive Sciences — M,D
Communication—General — M,O
Comparative Literature — D
Demography and Population Studies — M,D
Developmental Psychology — D
East European and Russian Studies — M
Economics — D
English — M,D,O
Experimental Psychology — D
French — M,D
German — D
History of Science and Technology — M,D
History — D
Human Development — M
International Affairs — D
International Development — M
Italian — M,D
Japanese — D
Jewish Studies — M,D
Journalism — M,O
Landscape Architecture — M,D
Liberal Studies — M,O
Linguistics — D
Medieval and Renaissance Studies — D
Museum Studies — M,O
Music — M,D
Near and Middle Eastern Languages — M,D
Near and Middle Eastern Studies — M,D
Philosophy — M,D
Political Science — M,D
Portuguese — M,D
Psychology—General — D
Public Administration — M
Public Policy — M,D
Religion — D
Russian — D
Scandinavian Languages — D
Slavic Languages — D
Social Psychology — D
Sociology — D

HAWAI'I PACIFIC UNIVERSITY
Clinical Psychology — M
Communication—General — M
Economics — M
Military and Defense Studies — M
Sustainable Development — M

HAZELDEN GRADUATE SCHOOL OF ADDICTION STUDIES
Addictions/Substance Abuse
  Counseling — M,O

HEBREW COLLEGE
Jewish Studies — M,O
Music — M,O
Theology — M

HEBREW UNION COLLEGE–JEWISH INSTITUTE OF RELIGION (NY)
Jewish Studies — M
Music — M
Near and Middle Eastern Languages — D
Theology — M,D

HEC MONTREAL
Applied Economics — M
Arts Administration — O
Corporate and Organizational
  Communication — O
Sustainable Development — O

HEIDELBERG UNIVERSITY
Counseling Psychology — M
School Psychology — M
Social Psychology — M

HENDERSON STATE UNIVERSITY
Counseling Psychology — M,O
Liberal Studies — M

HENLEY-PUTNAM UNIVERSITY
Conflict Resolution and
  Mediation/Peace Studies — M
Homeland Security — M
Military and Defense Studies — M
National Security — D

HERITAGE CHRISTIAN UNIVERSITY
Classics — M
Pastoral Ministry and Counseling — M
Religion — M

HERITAGE COLLEGE AND SEMINARY
Theology — M,O

HERITAGE UNIVERSITY
English — M

HIGH POINT UNIVERSITY
Corporate and Organizational
  Communication — M
History — M

HILBERT COLLEGE
Criminal Justice and Criminology — M
Public Administration — M

HILLSDALE COLLEGE
Political Science — M,D

HILLSDALE FREE WILL BAPTIST COLLEGE
Pastoral Ministry and Counseling — M

HIRAM COLLEGE
Interdisciplinary Studies — M

HODGES UNIVERSITY
Clinical Psychology — M
Counseling Psychology — M

HOFSTRA UNIVERSITY
Applied Behavior Analysis — M,D,O
Art Therapy — M,O
Art/Fine Arts — M,D,O
Clinical Psychology — M,D
Communication—General — M
Counseling Psychology — M,O
English — M
Film, Television, and Video
  Production — M
French — M,D,O
Human Development — M,D,O
Humanities — M,D,O
Industrial and Organizational
  Psychology — M,D
Journalism — M
Linguistics — M,D,O
Marriage and Family Therapy — M,O
Psychology—General — M,D
Rehabilitation Counseling — M,O
Rhetoric — M
School Psychology — M,D
Social Psychology — M,D
Sustainable Development — M
Urban Design — M
Writing — M

HOLLINS UNIVERSITY
Art/Fine Arts — M,O
Dance — M
English — M
Film, Television, and Video
  Production — M
Film, Television, and Video
  Theory and Criticism — M
Humanities — M,O
Illustration — M
Interdisciplinary Studies — M,O
Liberal Studies — M
Music — M,O
Social Sciences — M,O
Theater — M
Writing — M,O

HOLMES INSTITUTE
Pastoral Ministry and Counseling — M

HOLY APOSTLES COLLEGE AND SEMINARY
Theology — M,O

HOLY CROSS GREEK ORTHODOX SCHOOL OF THEOLOGY
Theology — M

HOLY FAMILY UNIVERSITY
Counseling Psychology — M
Criminal Justice and Criminology — M

HOLY NAMES UNIVERSITY
Counseling Psychology — M,O
Forensic Psychology — M,O
Music — M,O
Pastoral Ministry and Counseling — M,O
Religion — M,O
Writing — M

HOOD COLLEGE
Art/Fine Arts — M,O
Human Development — M,O
Humanities — M,O
Psychology—General — M,O
Public Administration — M
Thanatology — M,O

HOOD THEOLOGICAL SEMINARY
Theology — M,D

HOPE INTERNATIONAL UNIVERSITY
International Development — M
Marriage and Family Therapy — M
Missions and Missiology — M
Music — M
Religion — M

HOUGHTON COLLEGE
Music — M

HOUSTON BAPTIST UNIVERSITY
Art/Fine Arts — M
Counseling Psychology — M
Liberal Studies — M
Pastoral Ministry and Counseling — M
Philosophy — M
Psychology—General — M
Theology — M

HOUSTON GRADUATE SCHOOL OF THEOLOGY
Pastoral Ministry and Counseling — M,D
Theology — M,D

HOWARD PAYNE UNIVERSITY
Pastoral Ministry and Counseling — M
Theology — M

HOWARD UNIVERSITY
African Studies — M,D
Applied Arts and Design—
  General — M
Art History — M
Art/Fine Arts — M
Clinical Psychology — M,D
Communication—General — M,D
Corporate and Organizational
  Communication — M,D
Counseling Psychology — D
Developmental Psychology — M,D
Economics — M,D
English — M,D
Experimental Psychology — M,D
Film, Television, and Video
  Production — M
French — M
History — M,D
Mass Communication — M,D
Media Studies — M
Music — M
Philosophy — M
Photography — M
Political Science — M,D
Psychology—General — M
Public Administration — M
School Psychology — M,D
Social Psychology — M,D
Sociology — M,D
Spanish — M
Theology — M

HULT INTERNATIONAL BUSINESS SCHOOL (UNITED STATES)
Conflict Resolution and
  Mediation/Peace Studies — M
International Affairs — M
National Security — M
Political Science — M

HUMBOLDT STATE UNIVERSITY
Anthropology — M
Counseling Psychology — M
English — M
Psychology—General — M
School Psychology — M
Social Sciences — M
Sociology — M

HUNTER COLLEGE OF THE CITY UNIVERSITY OF NEW YORK
Anthropology — M
Applied Social Research — M
Art History — M
Art/Fine Arts — M
Chinese — M
Classics — M
Economics — M,D
English — M
French — M
Geography — M,O
History — M
Italian — M
Media Studies — M
Music — M
Psychology—General — M

Rehabilitation Counseling — M
Romance Languages — M
Sociology — M
Spanish — M
Theater — M
Urban and Regional Planning — M
Urban Studies — M
Writing — M

HUNTINGTON UNIVERSITY
Missions and Missiology — M,D
Pastoral Ministry and Counseling — M,D

HUSSON UNIVERSITY
Clinical Psychology — M
Counseling Psychology — M
Criminal Justice and Criminology — M
Pastoral Ministry and Counseling — M
School Psychology — M
Social Psychology — M

ICAHN SCHOOL OF MEDICINE AT MOUNT SINAI
Genetic Counseling — M,D

IDAHO STATE UNIVERSITY
Anthropology — M
Art/Fine Arts — M
Clinical Psychology — D
Counseling Psychology — M,D,O
English — M,D,O
Experimental Psychology — D
Geographic Information Systems — M,O
History — M
Interdisciplinary Studies — M
Marriage and Family Therapy — M,D,O
Political Science — M,D
Psychology—General — D
Public Administration — M
Rhetoric — M
School Psychology — M,D,O
Sociology — M
Speech and Interpersonal
  Communication — M
Theater — M

ILIFF SCHOOL OF THEOLOGY
Pastoral Ministry and Counseling — M,D
Religion — M,D
Theology — M,D

ILLINOIS INSTITUTE OF TECHNOLOGY
Applied Arts and Design—
  General — M,D
Architecture — M,D
Clinical Psychology — M,D
Communication—General — M,D
Corporate and Organizational
  Communication — M
Humanities — M,D
Industrial and Organizational
  Psychology — M,D
Landscape Architecture — M,D
Psychology—General — M
Public Administration — M
Rehabilitation Counseling — M,D
Technical Writing — M,D

ILLINOIS STATE UNIVERSITY
Agricultural Economics and
  Agribusiness — M
Archaeology — M
Art History — M
Art/Fine Arts — M
Clinical Psychology — M,D,O
Communication—General — M
Counseling Psychology — M,D,O
Criminal Justice and Criminology — M
Developmental Psychology — M,D,O
Economics — M
English — M
Experimental Psychology — M,D,O
Family and Consumer
  Sciences-General — M
French — M
German — M
Graphic Design — M
History — M
Industrial and Organizational
  Psychology — M,D,O
Music — M
Photography — M
Political Science — M
Psychology—General — M,D,O
School Psychology — D,O
Sociology — M
Spanish — M
Textile Design — M
Theater — M
Writing — M

IMMACULATA UNIVERSITY
Clinical Psychology — M,D,O
Counseling Psychology — M,D,O
Forensic Psychology — M,D,O
Psychoanalysis and Psychotherapy — M,D,O
Psychology—General — M,D,O
School Psychology — M,D,O
Therapies—Dance, Drama, and
  Music — M

INDIANA STATE UNIVERSITY
Art/Fine Arts — M
Clinical Psychology — M,D
Communication—General — M
Comparative Literature — M
Consumer Economics — M
Counseling Psychology — M,D,O
Criminal Justice and Criminology — M
English — M
Family and Consumer
  Sciences-General — M
Geography — M,D
Graphic Design — M
History — M
Linguistics — M,O
Media Studies — M

Music | M
Photography | M
Political Science | M
Psychology—General | M,D
Public Administration | M
School Psychology | M,D,O
Writing | M

INDIANA UNIVERSITY BLOOMINGTON

African Studies | M
African-American Studies | M
Anthropology | M,D
Art History | M,D
Art/Fine Arts | M,D
Arts Administration | M
Asian Languages | M,D
Asian Studies | M
Chinese | M,D
Classics | M,D
Cognitive Sciences | D
Communication—General | M,D
Comparative Literature | M,D
Computer Art and Design | M,D,O
Criminal Justice and Criminology | M,D
Developmental Psychology | D
East European and Russian Studies | M,O
Economic Development | M,D,O
Economics | D
English | M,D
Film, Television, and Video
   Theory and Criticism | M,D
Folklore | M,D
French | M,D
Gender Studies | D
Geography | M,D
German | M,D
Hispanic and Latin American
   Languages | M,D
History of Science and Technology | M,D
History | M,D
International Development | M,D,O
Italian | M,D
Japanese | M,D
Jewish Studies | M
Journalism | M,D
Latin American Studies | M
Linguistics | M,D
Mass Communication | M,D
Media Studies | M,D
Medieval and Renaissance Studies | M,D
Music | M,D,O
Near and Middle Eastern Languages | M,D
Philosophy | M,D
Political Science | M,D
Portuguese | M,D
Psychology—General | D
Public Administration | M,D,O
Public Affairs | M,D,O
Public Policy | M,D,O
Religion | M,D
Rhetoric | M,D
School Psychology | M,D,O
Slavic Languages | M,D
Social Psychology | D
Social Sciences | M,D,O
Sociology | M,D
Spanish | M,D
Speech and Interpersonal
   Communication | M,D
Theater | M,D
Western European Studies | M
Writing | M

INDIANA UNIVERSITY KOKOMO

Public Administration | M,O

INDIANA UNIVERSITY NORTHWEST

Addictions/Substance Abuse
   Counseling | M
Counseling Psychology | M
Criminal Justice and Criminology | M,O
Liberal Studies | M
Public Administration | M,O
Public Affairs | M,O

INDIANA UNIVERSITY OF PENNSYLVANIA

Archaeology | M
Art/Fine Arts | M
Clinical Psychology | M,D
Communication—General | M,D
Criminal Justice and Criminology | M,D
Emergency Management | M
English | M,D
Geographic Information Systems | M,O
Geography | M
Hispanic and Latin American
   Languages | M
History | M
Industrial and Labor Relations | M
Media Studies | D
Music | M
Psychology—General | M,D
Public Affairs | M
Public History | M
School Psychology | D,O
Social Psychology | M
Sociology | M
Urban and Regional Planning | M

INDIANA UNIVERSITY–PURDUE UNIVERSITY FORT WAYNE

Communication—General | M
English | M,O
Liberal Studies | M
Marriage and Family Therapy | M,O
Public Policy | M,O
Sociology | M

INDIANA UNIVERSITY–PURDUE UNIVERSITY INDIANAPOLIS

Addictions/Substance Abuse
   Counseling | M,D

Applied Arts and Design—
   General | M
Art/Fine Arts | M
Child and Family Studies | M
Clinical Psychology | M,D
Communication—General | M,O
Criminal Justice and Criminology | M,O
Economics | M
Emergency Management | M,O
English | M,O
Forensic Sciences | M
Gender Studies | M
Geographic Information Systems | M,O
Health Communication | M,D
History | M
Homeland Security | M,O
Industrial and Organizational
   Psychology | M,D
Internet and Interactive
   Multimedia | M,D
Liberal Studies | M,D,O
Museum Studies | M,O
Music | M
Philanthropic Studies | M,D
Philosophy | M,O
Political Science | M,O
Psychology—General | M,D
Public Administration | M,O
Public Affairs | M,O
Public History | M
Social Sciences | M,D
Sociology | M
Therapies—Dance, Drama, and
   Music |
Writing | M,O

INDIANA UNIVERSITY SOUTH BEND

English | M
Liberal Studies | M
Music | M
Public Affairs | M

INDIANA UNIVERSITY SOUTHEAST

Interdisciplinary Studies | M,O

INDIANA WESLEYAN UNIVERSITY

Addictions/Substance Abuse
   Counseling | M
Counseling Psychology | M
Marriage and Family Therapy | M
Pastoral Ministry and Counseling | M
Social Psychology | M
Theology | M

INSTITUTE FOR CHRISTIAN STUDIES

Philosophy | M,D
Political Science | M,D
Theology | M,D

INSTITUTE FOR CREATION RESEARCH

Theology | M

INSTITUTE FOR DOCTORAL STUDIES IN THE VISUAL ARTS

Art/Fine Arts | D
Philosophy | D

THE INSTITUTE FOR THE PSYCHOLOGICAL SCIENCES

Clinical Psychology | M,D

INSTITUTE OF AMERICAN INDIAN ARTS

Writing | M

INSTITUTE OF PUBLIC ADMINISTRATION

Public Administration | M,O

THE INSTITUTE OF WORLD POLITICS

Military and Defense Studies | M,O
National Security | M,O
Political Science | M,O
Public Affairs | M,O
Public Policy | M,O

INSTITUTO CENTROAMERICANO DE ADMINISTRACIÓN DE EMPRESAS

Agricultural Economics and
   Agribusiness | M
Sustainable Development | M

INSTITUTO TECNOLOGICO DE SANTO DOMINGO

Communication—General | M,O
Counseling Psychology | M,O
Economics | M,O
Gender Studies | M,O
Humanities | M,O
International Affairs | M,O
Linguistics | M,O
Marriage and Family Therapy | M,O
Sustainable Development | M,O

INSTITUTO TECNOLÓGICO Y DE ESTUDIOS SUPERIORES DE MONTERREY, CAMPUS CENTRAL DE VERACRUZ

Humanities | M

INSTITUTO TECNOLÓGICO Y DE ESTUDIOS SUPERIORES DE MONTERREY, CAMPUS CIUDAD DE MÉXICO

Economics | M,D
Humanities | M,D

INSTITUTO TECNOLÓGICO Y DE ESTUDIOS SUPERIORES DE MONTERREY, CAMPUS CIUDAD JUÁREZ

Humanities | M
Public Administration | M

INSTITUTO TECNOLÓGICO Y DE ESTUDIOS SUPERIORES DE MONTERREY, CAMPUS CIUDAD OBREGÓN

Communication—General | M
International Affairs | M

INSTITUTO TECNOLÓGICO Y DE ESTUDIOS SUPERIORES DE MONTERREY, CAMPUS ESTADO DE MÉXICO

Architecture | M,D
Humanities | M,D

INSTITUTO TECNOLÓGICO Y DE ESTUDIOS SUPERIORES DE MONTERREY, CAMPUS IRAPUATO

Architecture | M,D
Humanities | M,D

INSTITUTO TECNOLÓGICO Y DE ESTUDIOS SUPERIORES DE MONTERREY, CAMPUS MONTERREY

Communication—General | M,D

INTER AMERICAN UNIVERSITY OF PUERTO RICO, AGUADILLA CAMPUS

Counseling Psychology | M
Criminal Justice and Criminology | M

INTER AMERICAN UNIVERSITY OF PUERTO RICO, METROPOLITAN CAMPUS

American Studies | M,D
Counseling Psychology | M,D
Criminal Justice and Criminology | M
English | M
History | M,D
Industrial and Labor Relations | M,D
Industrial and Organizational
   Psychology | M,D
Pastoral Ministry and Counseling | D
Psychology—General | M,D
School Psychology | M,D
Spanish | M
Theology | D
Women's Studies | M

INTER AMERICAN UNIVERSITY OF PUERTO RICO, PONCE CAMPUS

Criminal Justice and Criminology | M
Spanish | M

INTER AMERICAN UNIVERSITY OF PUERTO RICO, SAN GERMÁN CAMPUS

Art/Fine Arts | M
Counseling Psychology | M,D
Graphic Design | M
Music | M
Photography | M
Psychology—General | M,D
School Psychology | M,D

INTERDENOMINATIONAL THEOLOGICAL CENTER

Theology | M,D

INTERIOR DESIGNERS INSTITUTE

Interior Design | M

INTERNATIONAL BAPTIST COLLEGE AND SEMINARY

Pastoral Ministry and Counseling | M,D
Theology | M

INTERNATIONAL TECHNOLOGICAL UNIVERSITY

Computer Art and Design | M

IONA COLLEGE

Counseling Psychology | M,O
Criminal Justice and Criminology | M,O
English | M
Experimental Psychology | M,O
Forensic Sciences | M,O
History | M
Industrial and Organizational
   Psychology | M,O
Marriage and Family Therapy | M
Mass Communication | M,O
Psychology—General | M,O
School Psychology | M,O
Spanish | M

IOWA STATE UNIVERSITY OF SCIENCE AND TECHNOLOGY

Agricultural Economics and
   Agribusiness | M,D
Anthropology | M
Architecture | M
Art/Fine Arts | M
Child and Family Studies | M,D
Clothing and Textiles | M,D
Cognitive Sciences | D
Consumer Economics | M,D
Corporate and Organizational
   Communication | M,D
Counseling Psychology | D
Economics | M,D
English | M,D
Family and Consumer
   Sciences-General | M
Graphic Design | M
History of Science and Technology | M,D
History | M,D
Human Development | M
Industrial Design | M
Interdisciplinary Studies | M
Interior Design | M
Journalism | M
Landscape Architecture | M
Linguistics | M,D
Mass Communication | M
Political Science | M

Psychology—General | D
Public Administration | M
Rhetoric | M,D
Rural Planning and Studies | M,D
Rural Sociology | M,D
Social Psychology | D
Sociology | M,D
Sustainable Development | M,D
Urban and Regional Planning | M
Writing | M,D

ITHACA COLLEGE

Communication—General | M
Internet and Interactive
   Multimedia | M
Music | M

JACKSON STATE UNIVERSITY

Clinical Psychology | D
Criminal Justice and Criminology | M
English | M
History | M
Mass Communication | M
Political Science | M
Psychology—General | D*
Public Administration | M,D
Public Affairs | M,D
Public Policy | M,D
Rehabilitation Counseling | M
Sociology | M
Urban and Regional Planning | M,D

JACKSONVILLE STATE UNIVERSITY

Criminal Justice and Criminology | M
Emergency Management | M,D
English | M
History | M
Liberal Studies | M
Music | M
Political Science | M
Psychology—General | M

JACKSONVILLE UNIVERSITY

Dance | M

JAMES MADISON UNIVERSITY

Applied Behavior Analysis | M,D,O
Art History | M
Art/Fine Arts | M
Clinical Psychology | M,D,O
Communication—General | M
Counseling Psychology | M,D,O
English | M
History | M
Music | D
Photography | M
Political Science | M
Psychology—General | M,D,O
Public Administration | M
Rhetoric | M
School Psychology | M,D,O
Technical Writing | M
Writing | M

THE JEWISH THEOLOGICAL SEMINARY

Jewish Studies | M,D
Music | M
Religion | M,D
Theology | M,D,O
Women's Studies | M,D

JOHN BROWN UNIVERSITY

Clinical Psychology | M,O
Counseling Psychology | M,O
International Development | M
Marriage and Family Therapy | M,O

JOHN CARROLL UNIVERSITY

Corporate and Organizational
   Communication | M
Counseling Psychology | M,O
English | M
History | M
Humanities | M
Religion | M

JOHN F. KENNEDY UNIVERSITY

Art/Fine Arts | M
Comparative and Interdisciplinary
   Arts | M
Counseling Psychology | M
Health Psychology | M
Industrial and Organizational
   Psychology | M,O
Museum Studies | M,O
Psychology—General | M,D,O
Sport Psychology | M
Transpersonal and Humanistic
   Psychology | M

JOHN JAY COLLEGE OF CRIMINAL JUSTICE OF THE CITY UNIVERSITY OF NEW YORK

Criminal Justice and Criminology | M,D
Forensic Psychology | M,D
Forensic Sciences | M,D
Public Administration | M
Public Policy | M,D

JOHN PAUL THE GREAT CATHOLIC UNIVERSITY

Theology | M

JOHNS HOPKINS UNIVERSITY

Addictions/Substance Abuse
   Counseling | M,D
Anthropology | D
Applied Behavior Analysis | O
Applied Economics | M
Archaeology | D
Art History | M,D
Asian Studies | M,D,O
Classics | D
Clinical Psychology | M,D
Cognitive Sciences | D

M—masters degree; D—doctorate; O—other advanced degree; *—Close-Up and/or Display

Communication—General M
Comparative Literature D
Counseling Psychology M,O
Demography and Population Studies M,D
Economics D
English D
French D
Genetic Counseling M,D
Geographic Information Systems M,D
Geography M,D
German D
Health Communication M,D
History of Science and Technology M,D
History D
Homeland Security M,O
International Affairs M,D,O
International Development M,D,O
International Economics M,D,O
Italian D
Liberal Studies M,O
Medical Illustration M
Military and Defense Studies M
Museum Studies M,O
Music M,D,O
Near and Middle Eastern Languages D
Near and Middle Eastern Studies D
Philosophy M,D
Political Science M,D,O
Psychology—General D
Public Administration M,O
Public Policy M,D
Romance Languages D
Social Sciences M,D
Sociology M,D
Spanish D
Technical Writing M,O
Writing M,O

JOHNSON & WALES UNIVERSITY
Criminal Justice and Criminology M

JOHNSON STATE COLLEGE
Addictions/Substance Abuse
  Counseling M
Applied Behavior Analysis M
Art/Fine Arts M

JOHNSON UNIVERSITY
Cultural Studies M,D,O
Marriage and Family Therapy M,D,O
Theology M,D,O

THE JUDGE ADVOCATE GENERAL'S SCHOOL, U.S. ARMY
Military and Defense Studies M

JUDSON UNIVERSITY
Architecture M
Pastoral Ministry and Counseling M
Sustainable Development M
Urban Design M

THE JUILLIARD SCHOOL
Music M,D,O

KANSAS STATE UNIVERSITY
Agricultural Economics and
  Agribusiness M,D
Applied Arts and Design—
  General M
Architecture M
Art/Fine Arts M
Child and Family Studies M,D,O
Child Development M,O
Clothing and Textiles M,D
Communication—General M,D
Conflict Resolution and
  Mediation/Peace Studies M,O
Consumer Economics M,D
Economics M,D
English M,O
Environmental Design D
Family and Consumer
  Sciences-General M,D,O
Geography M,D,O
Gerontology M,O
Health Communication M
History M,D
Human Development M,D,O
International Affairs M
Journalism M
Landscape Architecture M
Marriage and Family Therapy M,D,O
Mass Communication M
Music M
National Security M,D
Political Science M
Psychology—General M,D
Public Administration M
Sociology M,D
Theater M
Urban and Regional Planning M
Women's Studies O

KAPLAN UNIVERSITY, DAVENPORT CAMPUS
Criminal Justice and Criminology M
Political Science M,O

KEAN UNIVERSITY
Addictions/Substance Abuse
  Counseling M
Art/Fine Arts M
Clinical Psychology M,D
Communication—General M
Counseling Psychology M
Criminal Justice and Criminology M
Holocaust and Genocide Studies M
Industrial and Organizational
  Psychology M
Marriage and Family Therapy M,O
Psychology—General M
Public Administration M
School Psychology M,D,O
Sociology M
Spanish M
Writing M

KEENE STATE COLLEGE
School Psychology M,O

KEHILATH YAKOV RABBINICAL SEMINARY
Theology

KEISER UNIVERSITY
Criminal Justice and Criminology M
Homeland Security M
Industrial and Organizational
  Psychology M,D
Psychology—General M,D

KENNESAW STATE UNIVERSITY
American Studies M
Communication—General M
Conflict Resolution and
  Mediation/Peace Studies M,D
Criminal Justice and Criminology M
Ethics O
International Affairs M
Public Administration M
Writing M

KENRICK-GLENNON SEMINARY
Theology M

KENT STATE UNIVERSITY
Anthropology M
Architecture M
Art History M
Art/Fine Arts M
Biological Anthropology M,D
Child and Family Studies M
Clinical Psychology M,D
Communication—General M,D
Counseling Psychology M
Economics M
English M,D,O
Environmental Design M
Experimental Psychology M,D
Geography M,D
Graphic Design M
History M,D
Human Development M
Illustration M
Japanese M,D
Journalism M
Liberal Studies M
Mass Communication M
Music M,D,O
Philosophy M
Political Science M,D
Psychology—General M,D
Public Administration M,D
Rehabilitation Counseling M
Rhetoric M,D,O
Russian M
School Psychology M,D,O
Sociology M
Theater M
Translation and Interpretation M,D
Urban Design M
Writing M,D,O

KENTUCKY CHRISTIAN UNIVERSITY
Religion M
Theology M

KENTUCKY STATE UNIVERSITY
International Development M,D
Public Administration M,D

KEUKA COLLEGE
Criminal Justice and Criminology M

KING'S UNIVERSITY
Pastoral Ministry and Counseling M,D,O
Theology M,D,O

KINGSWOOD UNIVERSITY
Pastoral Ministry and Counseling M
Theology M

KNOX COLLEGE
Theology M,D

KNOX THEOLOGICAL SEMINARY
Classics M
Pastoral Ministry and Counseling D
Religion M
Theology M

KUTZTOWN UNIVERSITY OF PENNSYLVANIA
Counseling Psychology M
English M
Internet and Interactive
  Multimedia M
Marriage and Family Therapy M
Media Studies M
Public Administration M

LAGUNA COLLEGE OF ART & DESIGN
Art/Fine Arts M

LAKE FOREST COLLEGE
American Studies M
Art/Fine Arts M
French M
History M
Liberal Studies M
Spanish M
Writing M

LAKEHEAD UNIVERSITY
Clinical Psychology M,D
Economics M
English M
Experimental Psychology M,D
Gerontology M,D
History M
Psychology—General M,D
Sociology M
Women's Studies M,D

LAKELAND COLLEGE
Theology M

LAMAR UNIVERSITY
Clinical Psychology M
Counseling Psychology M
Criminal Justice and Criminology M
English M
Family and Consumer
  Sciences-General M
History M
Industrial and Organizational
  Psychology M
Music M
Political Science M
Psychology—General M
Public Administration M

LANCASTER BIBLE COLLEGE
Counseling Psychology M,D
Marriage and Family Therapy M,D
Pastoral Ministry and Counseling M,D,O
Theology M,D,O

LANCASTER THEOLOGICAL SEMINARY
Art History M,D,O
Ethics M,D,O
Religion M,D,O
Theology M,D,O

LANGSTON UNIVERSITY
Rehabilitation Counseling M

LA SALLE UNIVERSITY
American Studies M,O
Art/Fine Arts M,O
Clinical Psychology M,D
Communication—General M,O
Comparative Literature M,O
Corporate and Organizational
  Communication M,O
Counseling Psychology M
Cultural Studies M,O
Developmental Psychology M,D
East European and Russian Studies M,O
English M,O
Forensic Sciences M,O
Gerontology M,D,O
Health Psychology M,O
Hispanic Studies M,O
History M,O
Latin American Studies M,O
Marriage and Family Therapy M
Media Studies M,O
National Security M,O
Pastoral Ministry and Counseling M,D,O
Psychology—General M,D
Public History M,O
Religion M,D,O
Theology M,D,O
Translation and Interpretation M,O
Western European Studies M,O

LASELL COLLEGE
Communication—General M,O
Corporate and Organizational
  Communication M,O
Health Communication M,O

LA SIERRA UNIVERSITY
Communication—General M
English M
Pastoral Ministry and Counseling M
Religion M
School Psychology M
Writing M

LAURENTIAN UNIVERSITY
Applied Psychology M
Applied Social Research M
Experimental Psychology M
History M
Human Development M
Humanities M
Psychology—General M
Sociology M
Technical Writing O

LAWRENCE TECHNOLOGICAL UNIVERSITY
Architecture M
Interior Design M
Technical Communication M
Urban Design M

LEBANESE AMERICAN UNIVERSITY
International Affairs M

LEE UNIVERSITY
Child Development M
Counseling Psychology M
Marriage and Family Therapy M
Music M
Pastoral Ministry and Counseling M
Religion M
Theology M

LEHIGH UNIVERSITY
American Studies M,D,O
Counseling Psychology M,D,O
Economics M,D
English M,D
History M,D
Interdisciplinary Studies M,D
International Development M,D,O
Political Science M
Psychology—General M,D
Public History M,D
School Psychology D,O
Sociology M

LEHMAN COLLEGE OF THE CITY UNIVERSITY OF NEW YORK
Art/Fine Arts M
English M
History M
Spanish M

LE MOYNE COLLEGE
Urban Studies M,O

LENOIR-RHYNE UNIVERSITY
Addictions/Substance Abuse
  Counseling M
Clinical Psychology M
Counseling Psychology M
School Psychology M
Sustainable Development M
Writing M

LESLEY UNIVERSITY
Art Therapy M,D,O
Art/Fine Arts M,D,O
Clinical Psychology M,D,O
Conflict Resolution and
  Mediation/Peace Studies M,D,O
Counseling Psychology M,D,O
Health Psychology M,D,O
Interdisciplinary Studies M,D,O
International Affairs M,D,O
Photography M
Psychology—General M,D,O
School Psychology M,D,O
Social Psychology M,D,O
Sustainable Development M,D,O
Therapies—Dance, Drama, and
  Music M,D,O
Urban and Regional Planning M,D,O
Women's Studies M,D,O
Writing M,D,O

LETOURNEAU UNIVERSITY
Counseling Psychology M
Marriage and Family Therapy M
Psychology—General M

LEWIS & CLARK COLLEGE
Addictions/Substance Abuse
  Counseling M
Counseling Psychology M
Cultural Studies M,O
Marriage and Family Therapy M
Psychology—General M,O
School Psychology M,O

LEWIS UNIVERSITY
Clinical Psychology M
Counseling Psychology M
Criminal Justice and Criminology M

LEXINGTON THEOLOGICAL SEMINARY
Theology M,D

LIBERTY UNIVERSITY
Addictions/Substance Abuse
  Counseling M,D,O
Art/Fine Arts M
Child and Family Studies M,D,O
Clinical Psychology M,D,O
Communication—General M
Counseling Psychology M,D,O
Criminal Justice and Criminology M,D,O
Emergency Management M,D,O
English M,D,O
History M,D,O
International Affairs M,D,O
Marriage and Family Therapy M,D,O
Military and Defense Studies M,D,O
Missions and Missiology M,D,O
Music M,D
Near and Middle Eastern Studies M
Pastoral Ministry and Counseling M,D,O
Philosophy M
Political Science M
Public Administration M
Public Policy M
Religion M,D,O
Theology M,D,O

LIM COLLEGE
Clothing and Textiles M
Textile Design M

LINCOLN CHRISTIAN SEMINARY
Pastoral Ministry and Counseling M,D
Theology M,D

LINCOLN CHRISTIAN UNIVERSITY
Cultural Studies M
Marriage and Family Therapy M
Theology M

LINCOLN UNIVERSITY (MO)
Criminal Justice and Criminology M,O
History M,O
Public Administration M,O
Public Policy M,O
Sociology M,O

LINDENWOOD UNIVERSITY
Art/Fine Arts M
Communication—General M,O
Counseling Psychology M,D,O
Criminal Justice and Criminology M,O
Gerontology M,O
Internet and Interactive
  Multimedia M
Journalism M
Public Administration M
School Psychology M,D,O
Textile Design M
Theater M
Writing M,O

LINDENWOOD UNIVERSITY–BELLEVILLE
Communication—General M
Computer Art and Design M
Criminal Justice and Criminology M
Internet and Interactive
  Multimedia M
Media Studies M

LINDSEY WILSON COLLEGE
Counseling Psychology M,D
Human Development M,D
Internet and Interactive
  Multimedia M

LIPSCOMB UNIVERSITY

Applied Behavior Analysis	M,D,O
Clinical Psychology	M,O
Conflict Resolution and Mediation/Peace Studies	M,O
Counseling Psychology	M,O
English	M,D,O
Film, Television, and Video Production	M
Marriage and Family Therapy	M,O
Pastoral Ministry and Counseling	M,D,O
Psychology—General	M,O
Sustainable Development	M,O
Theology	M,D,O

LOCK HAVEN UNIVERSITY OF PENNSYLVANIA

Clinical Psychology	M
Counseling Psychology	M
Sport Psychology	M

LOGOS EVANGELICAL SEMINARY

Theology	M,D

LOMA LINDA UNIVERSITY

Child and Family Studies	M,D,O
Pastoral Ministry and Counseling	M,O
Psychology—General	D
Religion	M

LONG ISLAND UNIVERSITY–BRENTWOOD CAMPUS

Criminal Justice and Criminology	M

LONG ISLAND UNIVERSITY–HUDSON AT WESTCHESTER

Counseling Psychology	M,O
School Psychology	M,O

LONG ISLAND UNIVERSITY–LIU BROOKLYN

Applied Behavior Analysis	M,O
Clinical Psychology	M,D,O
Counseling Psychology	M,O
Marriage and Family Therapy	M,O
Public Administration	M

LONG ISLAND UNIVERSITY–LIU POST

Clinical Psychology	M,D,O
Counseling Psychology	M,D,O
Public Administration	M,D,O

LONG ISLAND UNIVERSITY–RIVERHEAD

Homeland Security	M,O

LONGWOOD UNIVERSITY

Criminal Justice and Criminology	M
Public Policy	M

LORAS COLLEGE

Applied Psychology	M
Pastoral Ministry and Counseling	M
Theology	M

LOUISIANA COLLEGE

Pastoral Ministry and Counseling	M
Theology	M

LOUISIANA STATE UNIVERSITY AND AGRICULTURAL & MECHANICAL COLLEGE

Agricultural Economics and Agribusiness	M,D
Anthropology	M,D
Applied Arts and Design—General	M
Architecture	M
Art History	M
Art/Fine Arts	M
Clinical Psychology	M,D
Cognitive Sciences	M,D
Communication—General	M,D
Comparative Literature	M,D
Developmental Psychology	M,D
Economics	M,D
English	M,D
Family and Consumer Sciences-General	M,D
French	M,D
Geography	M,D
Graphic Design	M
Hispanic Studies	M
History	M,D
Landscape Architecture	M
Liberal Studies	M
Mass Communication	M,D
Media Studies	M,D
Music	M,D
Philosophy	M
Photography	M
Political Science	M,D
Psychology—General	M,D
Public Administration	M,D
School Psychology	M,D
Sociology	M,D
Theater	M,D
Writing	M,D

LOUISIANA STATE UNIVERSITY HEALTH SCIENCES CENTER

Rehabilitation Counseling	M

LOUISIANA STATE UNIVERSITY IN SHREVEPORT

Counseling Psychology	M
Liberal Studies	M
School Psychology	O

LOUISIANA TECH UNIVERSITY

Applied Arts and Design—General	M
Architecture	M,D
Art/Fine Arts	M
Counseling Psychology	M,D
Economics	M,D
English	M,O
Family and Consumer Sciences-General	M
Graphic Design	M
History	M
Industrial and Organizational Psychology	M,D
Photography	M
Psychology—General	M,D
Speech and Interpersonal Communication	M,D
Technical Writing	M,O

LOUISVILLE PRESBYTERIAN THEOLOGICAL SEMINARY

Religion	M,D
Theology	M,D

LOURDES UNIVERSITY

Theology	M

LOYOLA MARYMOUNT UNIVERSITY

English	M
Film, Television, and Video Production	M
Marriage and Family Therapy	M
Pastoral Ministry and Counseling	M
Philosophy	M
School Psychology	M
Theology	M
Writing	M

LOYOLA UNIVERSITY CHICAGO

Applied Psychology	M,D
Clinical Psychology	M,D
Corporate and Organizational Communication	M
Counseling Psychology	D
Criminal Justice and Criminology	M
Developmental Psychology	M,D
Economics	M
English	M,D
Ethics	M
History	M,D
Humanities	M
Industrial and Labor Relations	M
Pastoral Ministry and Counseling	M
Philosophy	M,D
Political Science	M,D
Psychology—General	M,D
Public History	M,D
Public Policy	M
School Psychology	D,O
Social Psychology	M,D,O
Sociology	M,D
Spanish	M
Theology	M,D,O
Urban and Regional Planning	M
Urban Studies	M

LOYOLA UNIVERSITY MARYLAND

Clinical Psychology	M,D,O
Counseling Psychology	M,O
Liberal Studies	M
Media Studies	M
Pastoral Ministry and Counseling	M,D,O
Psychology—General	M,D,O
Theology	M,D

LOYOLA UNIVERSITY NEW ORLEANS

Clinical Psychology	M
Criminal Justice and Criminology	M
Music	M
Theology	M,O
Therapies—Dance, Drama, and Music	M

LUBBOCK CHRISTIAN UNIVERSITY

Theology	M

LUTHERAN SCHOOL OF THEOLOGY AT CHICAGO

Pastoral Ministry and Counseling	M,D
Theology	M,D

LUTHERAN THEOLOGICAL SEMINARY AT GETTYSBURG

Pastoral Ministry and Counseling	M,D
Religion	M,D
Theology	M,D

THE LUTHERAN THEOLOGICAL SEMINARY AT PHILADELPHIA

Pastoral Ministry and Counseling	M,D,O
Religion	M,D,O
Theology	M,D,O

LUTHERAN THEOLOGICAL SEMINARY SASKATOON

Ethics	M,D
Pastoral Ministry and Counseling	M,D
Religion	M,D
Theology	M,D

LUTHERAN THEOLOGICAL SOUTHERN SEMINARY

Theology	M,D

LUTHER RICE COLLEGE & SEMINARY

Pastoral Ministry and Counseling	M,D
Religion	M,D
Theology	M,D

LUTHER SEMINARY

Missions and Missiology	M,D
Pastoral Ministry and Counseling	M,D
Theology	M,D

LYNCHBURG COLLEGE

Clinical Psychology	M
Counseling Psychology	M
English	M
History	M
Music	M
School Psychology	M

LYNN UNIVERSITY

Applied Psychology	M
Criminal Justice and Criminology	M
Emergency Management	M
Internet and Interactive Multimedia	M,O
Mass Communication	M,O
Media Studies	M,O
Music	M,O

MACHZIKEI HADATH RABBINICAL COLLEGE

Theology	O

MADONNA UNIVERSITY

Clinical Psychology	M
Criminal Justice and Criminology	M
Liberal Studies	M
Pastoral Ministry and Counseling	M
Psychology—General	M
Theology	M

MAHARISHI UNIVERSITY OF MANAGEMENT

Asian Studies	M,D

MAINE COLLEGE OF ART

Art/Fine Arts	M

MALONE UNIVERSITY

Theology	M

MANHATTAN SCHOOL OF MUSIC

Music	M,D,O

MANHATTANVILLE COLLEGE

Corporate and Organizational Communication	M
Writing	M

MANSFIELD UNIVERSITY OF PENNSYLVANIA

Music	M
Psychology—General	M

MAPLE SPRINGS BAPTIST BIBLE COLLEGE AND SEMINARY

Pastoral Ministry and Counseling	M,D,O
Theology	M,D,O

MARANATHA BAPTIST UNIVERSITY

Cultural Studies	M
Pastoral Ministry and Counseling	M
Religion	M
Theology	M

MARIAN UNIVERSITY (WI)

Criminal Justice and Criminology	M

MARIETTA COLLEGE

Psychology—General	M

MARIST COLLEGE

Communication—General	M
Corporate and Organizational Communication	M
Counseling Psychology	M,O
Museum Studies	M
Psychology—General	M,O
Public Administration	M
School Psychology	M,O

MARLBORO COLLEGE

Internet and Interactive Multimedia	M,O

MARQUETTE UNIVERSITY

Clinical Psychology	M,D
Communication—General	M,O
Conflict Resolution and Mediation/Peace Studies	M,O
Counseling Psychology	M,D
Criminal Justice and Criminology	M,O
Economics	M,O
English	M,D
Ethics	M,D
Health Communication	M,O
History	M,D
Interdisciplinary Studies	D
International Affairs	M,D
Journalism	M,O
Mass Communication	M,O
Philosophy	M,D
Political Science	M
Psychology—General	D
Public Administration	M,O
Social Psychology	M,D
Spanish	M
Speech and Interpersonal Communication	M,O
Theology	M,D

MARSHALL UNIVERSITY

Art/Fine Arts	M
Classics	M,O
Clinical Psychology	M,D,O
Communication—General	M
Criminal Justice and Criminology	M
English	M,O
Forensic Sciences	M
Geography	M,O
History	M,O
Humanities	M,O
Journalism	M
Music	M
Political Science	M
Psychology—General	M,D,O
Public Administration	M
School Psychology	O
Sociology	M
Spanish	M

MARTIN UNIVERSITY

Pastoral Ministry and Counseling	M
Psychology—General	M
Social Psychology	M

MARY BALDWIN COLLEGE

English	M
Theater	M

MARYGROVE COLLEGE

English	M
Translation and Interpretation	O

MARYLAND INSTITUTE COLLEGE OF ART

Applied Arts and Design—General	M
Art/Fine Arts	M,O
Film, Television, and Video Production	M
Graphic Design	M,O
Illustration	M
Media Studies	M
Museum Studies	M
Photography	M

MARYLHURST UNIVERSITY

Art Therapy	M,O
Counseling Psychology	M,O
Interdisciplinary Studies	M
Theology	M

MARYMOUNT CALIFORNIA UNIVERSITY

International Development	M
Social Psychology	M

MARYMOUNT UNIVERSITY

Clinical Psychology	M,O
Counseling Psychology	M,O
English	M
Forensic Psychology	M
Interior Design	M
Pastoral Ministry and Counseling	M,O

MARYVILLE UNIVERSITY OF SAINT LOUIS

Addictions/Substance Abuse Counseling	M
Marriage and Family Therapy	M
Rehabilitation Counseling	M
Therapies—Dance, Drama, and Music	M

MARYWOOD UNIVERSITY

Architecture	M
Art Therapy	M,O
Art/Fine Arts	M
Clinical Psychology	M,D
Communication—General	M
Counseling Psychology	M
Criminal Justice and Criminology	M
Gerontology	M
Graphic Design	M
Human Development	D
Illustration	M
Interdisciplinary Studies	D
Interior Design	M
Photography	M
Psychology—General	M
Public Administration	M

MASSACHUSETTS COLLEGE OF ART AND DESIGN

Applied Arts and Design—General	M,O
Architecture	M
Art/Fine Arts	M,O
Film, Television, and Video Production	M,O
Interdisciplinary Studies	M,O
Media Studies	M,O
Photography	M,O
Textile Design	M,O

MASSACHUSETTS INSTITUTE OF TECHNOLOGY

Archaeology	M,D,O
Architectural History	M,D
Architecture	M,D
Art History	M,D
Cognitive Sciences	D
Economics	M,D
History of Science and Technology	D
Linguistics	D
Media Studies	M,D
Philosophy	D
Political Science	M,D
Social Sciences	D
Technical Writing	M
Urban and Regional Planning	M,D
Urban Studies	M,D
Writing	M

MASSACHUSETTS MARITIME ACADEMY

Emergency Management	M

MASSACHUSETTS SCHOOL OF PROFESSIONAL PSYCHOLOGY

Applied Psychology	M,D,O
Clinical Psychology	M,D,O
Counseling Psychology	M,D,O
Forensic Psychology	M,D,O
Industrial and Organizational Psychology	M,D,O
Psychology—General	M,D,O
School Psychology	M,D,O

THE MASTER'S COLLEGE AND SEMINARY

Pastoral Ministry and Counseling	M,D
Theology	M,D

MCCORMICK THEOLOGICAL SEMINARY

Pastoral Ministry and Counseling	M,D,O
Theology	M,D,O

MCDANIEL COLLEGE

Gerontology	M,O
Liberal Studies	M

*M—masters degree; D—doctorate; O—other advanced degree; *—Close-Up and/or Display*

MCGILL UNIVERSITY
Agricultural Economics and Agribusiness M
Anthropology M,D
Architecture M,D,O
Art History M,D
Asian Studies M,D
Clinical Psychology M,D
Communication—General M,D
Counseling Psychology M,D,O
Developmental Psychology M,D,O
Economics M,D
English M,D
Experimental Psychology M,D
Forensic Sciences M,D,O
French M,D
Genetic Counseling M,D
Geography M,D
German M,D
Hispanic Studies M,D
History of Medicine M,D
History M,D
International Development M,D,O
Italian M,D
Jewish Studies M
Linguistics M,D
Music M,D
Near and Middle Eastern Studies M,D,O
Philosophy M,D
Political Science M,D
Psychology—General M,D
Religion M,D
Russian M,D
School Psychology M,D,O
Sociology M,D,O
Theology M,D
Urban and Regional Planning M,D

MCKENDREE UNIVERSITY
Clinical Psychology M
Counseling Psychology M

MCMASTER UNIVERSITY
Anthropology M,D
Classics M,D
Cultural Studies M,D
Economics M,D
English M,D
French M
Geography M,D
History M,D
Industrial and Labor Relations M
International Affairs M,D
Pastoral Ministry and Counseling M,D,O
Philosophy M,D
Political Science M,D
Psychology—General M,D
Public Administration M,D
Public Affairs M,D
Public Policy M,D
Religion M,D
Sociology M,D
Theology M,D,O

MCNALLY SMITH COLLEGE OF MUSIC
Music M

MCNEESE STATE UNIVERSITY
Addictions/Substance Abuse Counseling M
Applied Behavior Analysis M
Counseling Psychology M
Criminal Justice and Criminology M
English M
Experimental Psychology M
Psychology—General M
School Psychology M
Writing M

MEADVILLE LOMBARD THEOLOGICAL SCHOOL
Pastoral Ministry and Counseling M,D
Theology M,D

MEDAILLE COLLEGE
Clinical Psychology M,D
Counseling Psychology M,D
Marriage and Family Therapy M,D
Psychology—General M,D

MEMORIAL UNIVERSITY OF NEWFOUNDLAND
Anthropology M,D
Archaeology M,D
Classics M
Cultural Anthropology M,D
Economics M
English M,D
Experimental Psychology M,D
Folklore M,D
French M
Gender Studies M,D
Geography M,D
German M
History M,D
Humanities M
Industrial and Labor Relations M
Linguistics M,D
Music M,D
Philosophy M
Political Science M
Psychology—General M,D
Religion M
Social Psychology M,D
Sociology M,D
Sport Psychology M
Women's Studies M

MEMPHIS COLLEGE OF ART
Applied Arts and Design—General M
Art/Fine Arts M

MEMPHIS THEOLOGICAL SEMINARY
Theology M,D

MERCER UNIVERSITY
Clinical Psychology M,D
Music M
Pastoral Ministry and Counseling M,D
Rehabilitation Counseling M,D
School Psychology M,D
Theology M,D

MERCY COLLEGE
Counseling Psychology M,O
English M
Marriage and Family Therapy M,O
Psychology—General M
School Psychology M

MERCYHURST UNIVERSITY
Biological Anthropology M
Criminal Justice and Criminology M,O
Forensic Sciences M

MESIVTA OF EASTERN PARKWAY–YESHIVA ZICHRON MEILECH
Theology

MESIVTA TORAH VODAATH RABBINICAL SEMINARY
Theology

MESIVTHA TIFERETH JERUSALEM OF AMERICA
Theology

MESSIAH COLLEGE
Clinical Psychology M,O
Counseling Psychology M,O
Marriage and Family Therapy M,O
Music M

METHODIST THEOLOGICAL SCHOOL IN OHIO
Theology M,D

METHODIST UNIVERSITY
Criminal Justice and Criminology M

METROPOLITAN COLLEGE OF NEW YORK
Corporate and Organizational Communication M
Media Studies M
Public Administration M

METROPOLITAN STATE UNIVERSITY
Criminal Justice and Criminology M
Liberal Studies M
Psychology—General M,D
Public Administration M,D,O
Technical Writing M

MIAMI INTERNATIONAL UNIVERSITY OF ART & DESIGN
Applied Arts and Design—General M
Film, Television, and Video Production M

MIAMI UNIVERSITY
Architecture M
Art/Fine Arts M
Child and Family Studies M
Demography and Population Studies M,D
Economics M
English M,D
French M
Geography M
Gerontology M,D
History M
Music M
Philosophy M
Political Science M
Psychology—General M,D
Theater M

MICHIGAN SCHOOL OF PROFESSIONAL PSYCHOLOGY
Clinical Psychology M,D
Psychology—General M,D
Transpersonal and Humanistic Psychology M,D

MICHIGAN STATE UNIVERSITY
African Studies M,D
African-American Studies M,D
Agricultural Economics and Agribusiness M,D
American Studies M,D
Anthropology M,D
Art/Fine Arts M
Child and Family Studies M,D
Child Development M,D
Communication—General M,D
Computer Art and Design M
Criminal Justice and Criminology M,D
Economics M,D
English M,D
Environmental Design M,D
Forensic Sciences M,D
French M,D
Geography M,D
German M,D
Health Communication M
Hispanic and Latin American Languages M,D
Hispanic Studies M,D
History M,D
Industrial and Labor Relations M,D
Interior Design M,D
Journalism M
Latin American Studies D
Linguistics M,D
Marriage and Family Therapy M,D
Media Studies M,D
Music M,D
Philosophy M,D
Political Science M,D
Portuguese M,D
Psychology—General M,D
Rehabilitation Counseling M,D,O
Rhetoric M,D
Romance Languages M,D
School Psychology M,D,O
Sociology M,D
Spanish M,D
Theater M
Therapies—Dance, Drama, and Music M,D
Urban and Regional Planning M,D
Writing M,D

MICHIGAN TECHNOLOGICAL UNIVERSITY
Archaeology M,D
Cognitive Sciences M,D
Geographic Information Systems M
Historic Preservation M,D
Interdisciplinary Studies M,D,O
Mineral Economics M
Rhetoric M,D
Technical Communication M,D

MID-AMERICA BAPTIST THEOLOGICAL SEMINARY
Theology M,D

MID-AMERICA BAPTIST THEOLOGICAL SEMINARY NORTHEAST BRANCH
Theology M

MID-AMERICA CHRISTIAN UNIVERSITY
Counseling Psychology M
Marriage and Family Therapy M
Pastoral Ministry and Counseling M
Public Administration M

MIDAMERICA NAZARENE UNIVERSITY
Counseling Psychology M,O

MID-AMERICA REFORMED SEMINARY
Theology M

MIDDLEBURY COLLEGE
Chinese M
English M
French M,D
German M,D
Italian M,D
Near and Middle Eastern Languages M
Russian M,D
Spanish M,D

MIDDLEBURY INSTITUTE OF INTERNATIONAL STUDIES
Conflict Resolution and Mediation/Peace Studies M
International Affairs M
International Development M
Public Administration M
Translation and Interpretation M

MIDDLE TENNESSEE STATE UNIVERSITY
Clinical Psychology M,O
Counseling Psychology M
Criminal Justice and Criminology M
Economics M,D
English M,D
Experimental Psychology M,O
French M
Gender Studies O
German M
Gerontology O
History M
Industrial and Organizational Psychology M,O
International Affairs M
Mass Communication M
Music M
Political Science M
Psychology—General M,O
Public History D
School Psychology M,O
Sociology M
Spanish M
Women's Studies O

MIDWESTERN BAPTIST THEOLOGICAL SEMINARY
Music M,D,O
Pastoral Ministry and Counseling M,D,O
Theology M,D,O

MIDWESTERN STATE UNIVERSITY
Clinical Psychology M
Counseling Psychology M
Criminal Justice and Criminology M,O
English M,D
History M
Philosophy M,D
Political Science M

MIDWESTERN UNIVERSITY, DOWNERS GROVE CAMPUS
Clinical Psychology M,D

MIDWESTERN UNIVERSITY, GLENDALE CAMPUS
Clinical Psychology D

MILLERSVILLE UNIVERSITY OF PENNSYLVANIA
Art/Fine Arts M
Clinical Psychology M
Emergency Management M
English M
French M
Geographic Information Systems M
German M
History M
Psychology—General M
School Psychology M
Spanish M

MILLS COLLEGE
Art/Fine Arts M
Dance M
English M
Illustration M
Interdisciplinary Studies M,O
Music M
Photography M
Public Policy M
Writing M

MINNEAPOLIS COLLEGE OF ART AND DESIGN
Applied Arts and Design—General M
Art/Fine Arts M,O
Computer Art and Design O
Film, Television, and Video Production M
Graphic Design M,O
Illustration M
Photography M
Sustainable Development O

MINNESOTA STATE UNIVERSITY MANKATO
Anthropology M
Art/Fine Arts M
Clinical Psychology M,D
Communication—General M,O
Corporate and Organizational Communication M,O
Counseling Psychology M,D,O
English M,O
Ethnic Studies M,O
French M
Gender Studies M,O
Geographic Information Systems M,O
Geography M,O
Gerontology M,O
History M
Industrial and Organizational Psychology M,D
Interdisciplinary Studies M
Marriage and Family Therapy M,D,O
Music M
Psychology—General M,D
Public Administration M
Rehabilitation Counseling M
School Psychology M,D
Sociology M
Spanish M
Technical Communication M,O
Theater M
Urban and Regional Planning M,O
Urban Studies M,O
Women's Studies M,O
Writing M,O

MINOT STATE UNIVERSITY
School Psychology O

MIRRER YESHIVA
Theology

MISSISSIPPI COLLEGE
Art/Fine Arts M
Communication—General M
Corporate and Organizational Communication M
Counseling Psychology M,O
Criminal Justice and Criminology M,O
English M
History M,O
Liberal Studies M
Marriage and Family Therapy M,O
Music M
Political Science M,O
Social Sciences M,O

MISSISSIPPI STATE UNIVERSITY
Agricultural Economics and Agribusiness M
American Studies M,D
Anthropology M
Applied Economics M,D
Child and Family Studies M,D
Clinical Psychology M,D,O
Cognitive Sciences M,D
Economics M,D
English M
Experimental Psychology M,D
French M
Geography M,D
German M
History M,D
Human Development M,D
Landscape Architecture M
Political Science M,D
Psychology—General M,D
Public Administration M,D
Public Policy M,D
Rehabilitation Counseling M,D,O
School Psychology M,D,O
Sociology M,D
Spanish M
Sustainable Development M,D
Western European Studies M,D

MISSISSIPPI VALLEY STATE UNIVERSITY
Criminal Justice and Criminology M

MISSOURI BAPTIST UNIVERSITY
Pastoral Ministry and Counseling M,O

MISSOURI SOUTHERN STATE UNIVERSITY
Criminal Justice and Criminology M

MISSOURI STATE UNIVERSITY
Anthropology M
Child and Family Studies M
Clinical Psychology M
Communication—General M
Counseling Psychology M
Criminal Justice and Criminology M,O
English M
Experimental Psychology M
Geography M
History M
Homeland Security M,O

International Affairs M
Military and Defense Studies M
Music M
Political Science M,O
Psychology—General M
Public Administration M
Religion M
Theater M
Urban and Regional Planning M

MISSOURI WESTERN STATE UNIVERSITY
Forensic Sciences M,O
Media Studies M
Rhetoric M,O
Technical Communication M
Writing M

MOLLOY COLLEGE
Criminal Justice and Criminology M
Therapies—Dance, Drama, and
　Music M

MONMOUTH UNIVERSITY
Addictions/Substance Abuse
　Counseling M,O
American Studies M
Anthropology M
Applied Behavior Analysis M,O
Communication—General M,O
Corporate and Organizational
　Communication M,O
Counseling Psychology M,O
Criminal Justice and Criminology M,O
English M
History M
Homeland Security M,O
Media Studies M,O
Psychology—General M,O
Public Policy M
Rhetoric M
Western European Studies M
Writing M

MONROE COLLEGE
Criminal Justice and Criminology M

MONTANA STATE UNIVERSITY
American Indian/Native American
　Studies M
Architecture M
Art History M
Art/Fine Arts M
English M
Film, Television, and Video
　Production M
History M,D
Human Development M
Psychology—General M
Public Administration M
School Psychology M,D,O

MONTANA STATE UNIVERSITY BILLINGS
Communication—General M
Counseling Psychology M
Interdisciplinary Studies M
Psychology—General M
Public Administration M
Rehabilitation Counseling M

MONTANA TECH OF THE UNIVERSITY OF MONTANA
Interdisciplinary Studies M
Technical Communication M

MONTCLAIR STATE UNIVERSITY
Addictions/Substance Abuse
　Counseling O
Art/Fine Arts M
Arts Administration M
Child and Family Studies M,D,O
Child Development M,O
Clinical Psychology M
Conflict Resolution and
　Mediation/Peace Studies M,O
Disability Studies M,O
English M
Forensic Psychology O
French M
Geographic Information Systems O
History M,O
Industrial and Organizational
　Psychology M
Linguistics M,O
Music M,O
Political Science M,O
Psychology—General M
Social Sciences M
Spanish M
Sustainable Development M
Theater M
Therapies—Dance, Drama, and
　Music M,O
Translation and Interpretation O
Writing O

MOODY BIBLE INSTITUTE
Pastoral Ministry and Counseling M,O
Theology M,O
Urban Studies M,O

MOODY THEOLOGICAL SEMINARY• MICHIGAN
Counseling Psychology M,O
Religion M,O
Theology M,O

MOORE COLLEGE OF ART & DESIGN
Art/Fine Arts M
Arts Administration M
Communication—General M
Interior Design M

MORAVIAN THEOLOGICAL SEMINARY
Theology M,O

MOREHEAD STATE UNIVERSITY
Art/Fine Arts M
Clinical Psychology M
Communication—General M
Counseling Psychology M
Criminal Justice and Criminology M
English M
Experimental Psychology M
Gerontology M
Graphic Design M
Music M
Psychology—General M
Public Administration M
Public Policy M
Sociology M

MORGAN STATE UNIVERSITY
African-American Studies M,D
Architecture M
Economics M
English M,D
Historic Preservation M,D
History M,D
International Affairs M
Landscape Architecture M
Museum Studies M,D
Music M
Psychology—General M,D
Sociology M
Urban and Regional Planning M

MOUNT ALOYSIUS COLLEGE
Applied Behavior Analysis M
Psychology—General M
Social Psychology M

MOUNT ANGEL SEMINARY
Theology M

MOUNT HOLYOKE COLLEGE
Psychology—General M

MOUNT IDA COLLEGE
Interior Design M

MOUNT MARTY COLLEGE
Pastoral Ministry and Counseling M

MOUNT MARY UNIVERSITY
Art Therapy M,D
Clinical Psychology M,O
Counseling Psychology M,O
English M
Internet and Interactive
　Multimedia M
Writing M

MOUNT MERCY UNIVERSITY
Criminal Justice and Criminology M
Marriage and Family Therapy M

MOUNT ST. JOSEPH UNIVERSITY
Pastoral Ministry and Counseling M,O
Religion M,O
Theology M,O

MOUNT SAINT MARY'S UNIVERSITY (CA)
Counseling Psychology M,D,O
English M,D,O
Film, Television, and Video
　Production M,D,O
Humanities M,D,O
Religion M,D,O
Writing M,D,O

MOUNT ST. MARY'S UNIVERSITY (MD)
Philosophy M
Theology M

MOUNT SAINT VINCENT UNIVERSITY
Child and Family Studies M
Gerontology M
School Psychology M
Women's Studies M

MOUNT VERNON NAZARENE UNIVERSITY
Theology M

MULTNOMAH UNIVERSITY
Theology M,D

MURRAY STATE UNIVERSITY
Clinical Psychology M
Corporate and Organizational
　Communication M
Economics M
English M
History M
Mass Communication M
Music M
Psychology—General M
Public Affairs M
Writing M

NAROPA UNIVERSITY
Art Therapy M
Asian Languages M
Counseling Psychology M
Psychoanalysis and Psychotherapy M
Religion M
Social Psychology M
Theater M
Theology M
Therapies—Dance, Drama, and
　Music M
Transpersonal and Humanistic
　Psychology M
Writing M

NASHOTAH HOUSE
Theology M,D,O

NATIONAL DEFENSE UNIVERSITY
Conflict Resolution and
　Mediation/Peace Studies M
Homeland Security M
Military and Defense Studies M
National Security M

THE NATIONAL GRADUATE SCHOOL OF QUALITY MANAGEMENT
Homeland Security M,D

NATIONAL INTELLIGENCE UNIVERSITY
Military and Defense Studies M

NATIONAL LOUIS UNIVERSITY
Human Development M,D,O
Psychology—General M,D,O
Public Policy M,D,O
School Psychology M,D,O
Writing M,D,O

NATIONAL UNIVERSITY
Applied Behavior Analysis M,O
Clinical Psychology M,O
Corporate and Organizational
　Communication M,O
Counseling Psychology M,O
Criminal Justice and Criminology M,O
Emergency Management M,O
English M,O
Film, Television, and Video
　Production M
Film, Television, and Video
　Theory and Criticism M,O
Forensic Sciences M,O
History M,O
Homeland Security M,O
Internet and Interactive
　Multimedia M,O
Journalism M
Linguistics M,O
Marriage and Family Therapy M,O
Psychology—General M,O
Public Administration M
Rhetoric M,O
School Psychology M,O
Sport Psychology M,O
Writing M,O

NAVAJO TECHNICAL UNIVERSITY
American Indian/Native American
　Studies M

NAVAL POSTGRADUATE SCHOOL
Conflict Resolution and
　Mediation/Peace Studies M,D
Geographic Information Systems M,D,O
Homeland Security M,D
Military and Defense Studies M,D
National Security M,D

NAVAL WAR COLLEGE
National Security M

NAZARENE THEOLOGICAL SEMINARY
Missions and Missiology M,D
Theology M,D

NAZARETH COLLEGE OF ROCHESTER
Art Therapy M
Liberal Studies M
Therapies—Dance, Drama, and
　Music M

NEBRASKA WESLEYAN UNIVERSITY
Forensic Sciences M
History M

NER ISRAEL RABBINICAL COLLEGE
Theology M,D,O

NER ISRAEL YESHIVA COLLEGE OF TORONTO
Theology M

NEUMANN UNIVERSITY
Pastoral Ministry and Counseling M,O

NEW BRUNSWICK THEOLOGICAL SEMINARY
Pastoral Ministry and Counseling M,D
Theology M,D

NEW CHARTER UNIVERSITY
Criminal Justice and Criminology M
Public Administration M

NEW ENGLAND COLLEGE
Counseling Psychology M
International Affairs M
Public Policy M
Writing M

NEW ENGLAND COLLEGE OF BUSINESS AND FINANCE
Ethics M

NEW ENGLAND CONSERVATORY OF MUSIC
Music M,D,O

NEW HAMPSHIRE INSTITUTE OF ART
Art/Fine Arts M
Photography M
Writing M

NEW JERSEY CITY UNIVERSITY
Art/Fine Arts M
Counseling Psychology M
Criminal Justice and Criminology M,D
Music M
National Security M
School Psychology M,O
Urban Studies M

NEW JERSEY INSTITUTE OF TECHNOLOGY
Architecture M,D

Emergency Management M,D
History M,D
Technical Communication M,D
Urban Studies M,D

NEWMAN THEOLOGICAL COLLEGE
Theology M

NEWMAN UNIVERSITY
Theology M

NEW MEXICO HIGHLANDS UNIVERSITY
American Studies M
Anthropology M
Clinical Psychology M
Computer Art and Design M
Counseling Psychology M
English M
History M
Internet and Interactive
　Multimedia M
Media Studies M
Political Science M
Psychology—General M
Public Affairs M
Rhetoric M
Sociology M
Writing M

NEW MEXICO STATE UNIVERSITY
Agricultural Economics and
　Agribusiness M,D
Anthropology M,O
Art History M
Art/Fine Arts M
Cognitive Sciences M,D
Communication—General M
Corporate and Organizational
　Communication M,D
Counseling Psychology M,D,O
Criminal Justice and Criminology M
Dance M,D,O
Economic Development M,D,O
Economics M,D,O
English M,D
Experimental Psychology M,D
Family and Consumer
　Sciences-General M
Geography M
History M
Interdisciplinary Studies M,D
Marriage and Family Therapy M
Museum Studies M,O
Music M
Political Science M
Psychology—General M,D
Rhetoric M,D
School Psychology M,D,O
Social Psychology M,D
Sociology M
Spanish M
Writing M,D

NEW ORLEANS BAPTIST THEOLOGICAL SEMINARY
Music M,D
Pastoral Ministry and Counseling M,D
Theology M,D

NEW SAINT ANDREWS COLLEGE
Religion M,O
Theology M,O

THE NEW SCHOOL
Anthropology M,D
Applied Arts and Design—
　General M
Applied Social Research M,D
Architecture M
Art/Fine Arts M
Clinical Psychology M,D
Cognitive Sciences M
Computer Art and Design M
Decorative Arts M
Developmental Psychology M,D
Economics M,D
History M,D
Interior Design M
International Affairs M
International Economics M,D
Liberal Studies M
Lighting Design M
Media Studies M,O
Music M
Philosophy M,D
Photography M
Political Science M,D
Psychology—General M,D
Public Policy D
Social Sciences M,D
Sociology M,D
Textile Design M
Theater M
Urban Design M
Urban Studies M
Writing M

NEWSCHOOL OF ARCHITECTURE AND DESIGN
Architecture M

NEW YORK ACADEMY OF ART
Art/Fine Arts M

NEW YORK FILM ACADEMY
Film, Television, and Video
　Production M
Photography M

NEW YORK INSTITUTE OF TECHNOLOGY
Addictions/Substance Abuse
　Counseling M,O
Architecture M

Art/Fine Arts M
Communication—General M
Computer Art and Design M
Graphic Design M
Industrial and Labor Relations M,O
Urban Design M

NEW YORK MEDICAL COLLEGE
Emergency Management O

NEW YORK SCHOOL OF INTERIOR DESIGN
Interior Design M
Lighting Design M
Sustainable Development M

NEW YORK STUDIO SCHOOL OF DRAWING, PAINTING AND SCULPTURE
Art/Fine Arts M,O*

NEW YORK THEOLOGICAL SEMINARY
Theology M,D

NEW YORK UNIVERSITY
African Studies M,D,O
American Studies M,D
Anthropology M,D
Applied Arts and Design—General M
Applied Economics M,D,O
Applied Psychology M,D,O
Applied Social Research M
Archaeology M,D
Architectural History M
Art History M,D
Art Therapy M
Art/Fine Arts M,D,O
Arts Administration M
Asian Studies M,D
Chinese M,D,O
Classics M,D,O
Cognitive Sciences M,D,O
Communication—General M,D
Comparative Literature M,D
Computer Art and Design M
Conflict Resolution and Mediation/Peace Studies M,O
Corporate and Organizational Communication M
Counseling Psychology M,D,O
Cultural Studies M,D,O
Dance M,D,O
Demography and Population Studies M,D
Developmental Psychology M,D
Economics M,D,O
English M,D
Film, Television, and Video Production M
French M,D,O
German M,D
Gerontology D
Graphic Design M
Historic Preservation
History M,D,O
Human Development M,D,O
Humanities M,O
Industrial and Organizational Psychology M,D,O
Interdisciplinary Studies M
International Affairs M,D,O
International Development M,D,O
Internet and Interactive Multimedia M,O
Italian M,D,O
Japanese M,D,O
Jewish Studies M,D,O
Journalism M,D,O
Latin American Studies M,O
Linguistics M,D,O
Media Studies M,D,O
Museum Studies M,O
Music M,D,O
National Security M,O
Near and Middle Eastern Languages M,D,O
Near and Middle Eastern Studies M,D,O
Philosophy M,D
Political Science M,D
Portuguese M,D
Psychoanalysis and Psychotherapy M,D,O
Psychology—General M,D,O
Public Administration M,D,O
Public History M,D,O
Public Policy M
Publishing M
Religion M,O
Romance Languages M,D
Russian M
Slavic Languages M
Social Psychology M,D,O
Social Sciences M,D
Sociology M,D
Spanish M,D,O
Speech and Interpersonal Communication M,D
Sustainable Development M
Theater M,D,O
Therapies—Dance, Drama, and Music M
Translation and Interpretation M
Urban and Regional Planning M
Urban Studies M
Western European Studies M
Writing M

NIAGARA UNIVERSITY
Criminal Justice and Criminology M
Interdisciplinary Studies M
School Psychology M,O

NICHOLLS STATE UNIVERSITY
Counseling Psychology M,O
School Psychology M,O

NORFOLK STATE UNIVERSITY
Art/Fine Arts M
Clinical Psychology M
Communication—General M
Criminal Justice and Criminology M
Media Studies M
Music M
Psychology—General M,D
Social Psychology M
Urban Studies M

NORTH CAROLINA AGRICULTURAL AND TECHNICAL STATE UNIVERSITY
African-American Studies M
Agricultural Economics and Agribusiness M
Applied Economics M
Child and Family Studies M
Child Development M
Computer Art and Design M
Consumer Economics M
English M
Graphic Design M

NORTH CAROLINA CENTRAL UNIVERSITY
Criminal Justice and Criminology M
English M
Family and Consumer Sciences-General M
History M
Music M
Psychology—General M
Public Administration M
Social Psychology M
Sociology M

NORTH CAROLINA STATE UNIVERSITY
Agricultural Economics and Agribusiness M
Anthropology M
Applied Arts and Design—General M,D
Architecture M
Clothing and Textiles D
Communication—General M
Computer Art and Design D
Cultural Anthropology M
Developmental Psychology D
Economics M,D
English M
Experimental Psychology D
French M
Geographic Information Systems M,D
Graphic Design M
History M
Industrial and Organizational Psychology D
Industrial Design M
International Affairs M
Landscape Architecture M
Liberal Studies M
Psychology—General D
Public Administration M,D
Public History M
Rhetoric D
School Psychology D
Social Psychology D
Sociology M,D
Spanish M
Technical Communication M
Writing M

NORTH CENTRAL COLLEGE
Cultural Studies M
Ethics M
Internet and Interactive Multimedia M
Liberal Studies M
Publishing M
Technical Communication M
Writing M

NORTHCENTRAL UNIVERSITY
Marriage and Family Therapy M,D,O
Psychology—General M,D,O

NORTH DAKOTA STATE UNIVERSITY
Agricultural Economics and Agribusiness M
Architecture M
Child and Family Studies M,D,O*
Child Development M,D,O
Clinical Psychology M,O
Clothing and Textiles M,O
Cognitive Sciences M,D
Communication—General M,D
Consumer Economics O
Criminal Justice and Criminology M,D
Developmental Psychology D
Emergency Management M,D
English M,D
Family and Consumer Sciences-General M
Gerontology M,O
Health Psychology M,D
History M,D
Human Development M,D
Marriage and Family Therapy M,D,O
Mass Communication M,D
Music M,D
Psychology—General M,D
Rhetoric M,D*
Social Psychology M,D
Social Sciences M,D
Sociology M,D
Speech and Interpersonal Communication M,D
Urban and Regional Planning M
Urban Studies M,D
Writing M,D

NORTHEASTERN ILLINOIS UNIVERSITY
English M
Geography M
Gerontology M
History M
Latin American Studies M
Linguistics M
Marriage and Family Therapy M
Music M
Political Science M
Rehabilitation Counseling M
Social Psychology M
Speech and Interpersonal Communication M
Writing M

NORTHEASTERN SEMINARY AT ROBERTS WESLEYAN COLLEGE
Theology M,D

NORTHEASTERN STATE UNIVERSITY
Addictions/Substance Abuse Counseling M
American Studies M
Communication—General M
Counseling Psychology M
Criminal Justice and Criminology M
English M
Psychology—General M

NORTHEASTERN UNIVERSITY
Applied Arts and Design—General M
Architecture M
Art/Fine Arts M
Corporate and Organizational Communication M
Counseling Psychology M,D,O
Criminal Justice and Criminology M,D
Economic Development M
Economics M,D
English M,D
Experimental Psychology D
Geographic Information Systems M
History M,D
Homeland Security M,D
Interdisciplinary Studies M,D,O
International Affairs M
Internet and Interactive Multimedia M
Journalism M
Political Science M,D
Public Administration M,D
Public History M,D
Public Policy M,D
School Psychology M,D,O
Sociology M,D
Technical Communication M
Urban Studies M,D,O

NORTHERN ARIZONA UNIVERSITY
Anthropology M
Archaeology M
Clinical Psychology M
Communication—General M
Counseling Psychology M,D,O
Criminal Justice and Criminology M
Cultural Anthropology M
English M,D,O
Ethnic Studies O
Gender Studies O
Geographic Information Systems M,O
Geography M,O
History M,D
Human Development O
Liberal Studies M
Linguistics M,D,O
Music M,D
Political Science M,D,O
Psychology—General M
Public Administration M,D,O
Rhetoric M,D,O
School Psychology M,D,O
Sociology M
Spanish M
Sustainable Development M
Urban and Regional Planning M,O
Women's Studies O
Writing M,D,O

NORTHERN BAPTIST THEOLOGICAL SEMINARY
Missions and Missiology M,D
Pastoral Ministry and Counseling M,D
Theology M,D

NORTHERN ILLINOIS UNIVERSITY
Anthropology M
Art/Fine Arts M
Child and Family Studies M
Communication—General M
Dance M
Economics M,D
English M,D
French M
Geography M,D
History M,D
Music M,O
Philosophy M
Political Science M,D
Psychology—General M,D
Public Administration M
Romance Languages M
Sociology M
Spanish M
Theater M

NORTHERN KENTUCKY UNIVERSITY
Clinical Psychology M
Communication—General M,O
Counseling Psychology M
Cultural Studies M,O
English M,O
Geographic Information Systems M,O
Health Psychology M,O
Industrial and Organizational Psychology M,O
Liberal Studies M
Marriage and Family Therapy M,O
Media Studies M,O
Music M,O
Public Administration M,O
Public History M
Rhetoric M,O
Writing M,O

NORTHERN MICHIGAN UNIVERSITY
Applied Behavior Analysis M,O
Criminal Justice and Criminology M
English M,O
Psychology—General M,O
Public Administration M
Theater M,O
Writing M,O

NORTHERN STATE UNIVERSITY
Clinical Psychology M
Counseling Psychology M

NORTH GREENVILLE UNIVERSITY
Pastoral Ministry and Counseling M,D

NORTH PARK THEOLOGICAL SEMINARY
Pastoral Ministry and Counseling M,O
Theology M,D

NORTH PARK UNIVERSITY
Music M

NORTHWEST CHRISTIAN UNIVERSITY
Counseling Psychology M

NORTHWESTERN OKLAHOMA STATE UNIVERSITY
American Studies M
Counseling Psychology M

NORTHWESTERN STATE UNIVERSITY OF LOUISIANA
Art/Fine Arts M
Clinical Psychology M
English M
Homeland Security M
Music M
Psychology—General M

NORTHWESTERN UNIVERSITY
African Studies O
African-American Studies D
American Studies M
Anthropology D
Art History D
Art/Fine Arts M
Arts Administration M
Broadcast Journalism M
Clinical Psychology D
Cognitive Sciences D
Communication—General M,D
Comparative Literature M,D
Corporate and Organizational Communication M,D
Economics D
English M,D
Ethics M
Film, Television, and Video Production M,D
French D,O
Gender Studies O
Genetic Counseling M
German D
History M,D
Human Development D
International Affairs M,D,O
Internet and Interactive Multimedia M
Italian D,O
Journalism M
Liberal Studies M
Linguistics D
Marriage and Family Therapy M
Media Studies M,D
Music M,D
Philosophy D
Political Science D
Portuguese D
Psychology—General D
Public Administration M
Public Policy M,D
Publishing M
Religion M,D
Rhetoric M,D
Slavic Languages D
Social Psychology D
Sociology M,D
Spanish D
Speech and Interpersonal Communication M,D
Theater M,D
Writing M

NORTHWEST INSTITUTE OF LITERARY ARTS
Writing M

NORTHWEST MISSOURI STATE UNIVERSITY
Agricultural Economics and Agribusiness M
English M
Geographic Information Systems M,O
History M,O
Psychology—General M

NORTHWEST NAZARENE UNIVERSITY
Addictions/Substance Abuse Counseling M
Clinical Psychology M
Marriage and Family Therapy M
Missions and Missiology M
Pastoral Ministry and Counseling M
Religion M
School Psychology M
Theology M
Urban and Regional Planning M

NORTHWEST UNIVERSITY
Counseling Psychology M,D
Cultural Studies M
Missions and Missiology M
Pastoral Ministry and Counseling M

Psychology—General M,D
Theology M
Urban and Regional Planning M,D

NORWICH UNIVERSITY
American Studies M
Conflict Resolution and
    Mediation/Peace Studies M
History M
International Affairs M
International Development M
Military and Defense Studies M
Public Administration M
Public Policy M

NOTRE DAME COLLEGE (OH)
Homeland Security M,O

NOTRE DAME DE NAMUR UNIVERSITY
Art Therapy M,D
Clinical Psychology M
English M,O
Marriage and Family Therapy M,D
Music M,O
Psychology—General M
Public Administration M
Public Affairs M

NOTRE DAME OF MARYLAND UNIVERSITY
Communication—General M
Liberal Studies M

NOTRE DAME SEMINARY
Theology M

NOVA SOUTHEASTERN UNIVERSITY
Clinical Psychology M,D,O
Conflict Resolution and
    Mediation/Peace Studies M,D,O
Counseling Psychology M,D,O
Emergency Management M,D,O
Experimental Psychology M
Interdisciplinary Studies M,D,O
Marriage and Family Therapy M,D,O
Psychology—General M,D,O
Public Administration M
School Psychology M,D,O
Writing M

NSCAD UNIVERSITY
Applied Arts and Design—
    General M
Art/Fine Arts M

NYACK COLLEGE
Counseling Psychology M
Marriage and Family Therapy M
Missions and Missiology M,D
Pastoral Ministry and Counseling M,D
Religion M
Theology M,D

OAKLAND CITY UNIVERSITY
Theology M,D

OAKLAND UNIVERSITY
Counseling Psychology M,D,O
Economics O
English M
History M
Liberal Studies M
Linguistics M,O
Music M,D
Public Administration M

OAKWOOD UNIVERSITY
Pastoral Ministry and Counseling M

OBERLIN COLLEGE
Music M,O

OBLATE SCHOOL OF THEOLOGY
African-American Studies M,D,O
Pastoral Ministry and Counseling M,D,O
Religion M,D,O
Theology M,D,O

OCCIDENTAL COLLEGE
Liberal Studies M

OHIO DOMINICAN UNIVERSITY
English M
Public Administration M
Theology M

THE OHIO STATE UNIVERSITY
African Studies M,D
African-American Studies M,D
Agricultural Economics and
    Agribusiness M,D
Anthropology M,D
Architecture M,D
Art History M,D
Art/Fine Arts M
Arts Administration M
Asian Languages M,D
Asian Studies M
Child and Family Studies M,D
Chinese M,D
Classics M,D
Clinical Psychology D
Cognitive Sciences D
Communication—General M,D
Computer Art and Design M
Dance M,D
Developmental Psychology D
East European and Russian Studies M,D
Economics M,D
English M,D
Family and Consumer
    Sciences-General M,D
French M,D
Gender Studies M,D
Geography M,D
German M,D

History M,D
Human Development M,D
Industrial and Labor Relations M,D
Industrial Design M
Interdisciplinary Studies M,D
Interior Design M
Internet and Interactive
    Multimedia M
Italian M,D
Japanese M,D
Landscape Architecture M
Latin American Studies M
Linguistics M,D
Music M,D
Near and Middle Eastern Languages M,D
Philosophy M,D
Political Science D
Portuguese M,D
Psychology—General D
Public Administration M,D
Public Affairs M,D
Public Policy M,D
Rural Sociology M,D
Slavic Languages M,D
Social Psychology D
Social Sciences M,D
Sociology D
Spanish M,D
Theater M,D
Urban and Regional Planning M,D
Women's Studies M,D

OHIO UNIVERSITY
African Studies M
Applied Economics M
Art History M
Art/Fine Arts M
Asian Studies M
Child and Family Studies M
Child Development M
Clinical Psychology M,D
Clothing and Textiles M
Communication—General M,D
Comparative and Interdisciplinary
    Arts D
Consumer Economics M
Corporate and Organizational
    Communication M,D
Economics M
English M,D
Experimental Psychology M,D
Family and Consumer
    Sciences-General M
Film, Television, and Video
    Production M
Film, Television, and Video
    Theory and Criticism M
French M
Geography M
Graphic Design M
Health Communication M,D
History M,D
Industrial and Organizational
    Psychology M,D
International Affairs M
International Development M
Journalism M,D
Latin American Studies M
Linguistics M
Media Studies M,D
Music M,O
Philosophy M
Photography M
Political Science M
Psychology—General M,D
Public Administration M
Rehabilitation Counseling M,D
Rhetoric M,D
Social Sciences M
Sociology M
Spanish M
Speech and Interpersonal
    Communication M,D
Theater M
Therapies—Dance, Drama, and
    Music M,O

OHR HAMEIR THEOLOGICAL SEMINARY
Theology M

OKLAHOMA BAPTIST UNIVERSITY
Marriage and Family Therapy M

OKLAHOMA CHRISTIAN UNIVERSITY
Pastoral Ministry and Counseling M
Theology M

OKLAHOMA CITY UNIVERSITY
Applied Behavior Analysis M
Criminal Justice and Criminology M
Dance M
Liberal Studies M
Music M
Religion M
Sociology M
Theater M

OKLAHOMA STATE UNIVERSITY
Agricultural Economics and
    Agribusiness M,D
Applied Arts and Design—
    General M,D
Applied Behavior Analysis M,D,O
Applied Psychology M,D,O
Child and Family Studies M,D
Clinical Psychology M,D
Clothing and Textiles M,D
Consumer Economics M,D
Economics M,D
Emergency Management M,D
English M,D
Family and Consumer
    Sciences-General M,D

Geography M,D
Health Psychology M,D,O
History M,D
Human Development M,D
International Affairs M,D,O
Landscape Architecture M,D
Marriage and Family Therapy M,D
Mass Communication M
Music M
Philosophy M
Political Science M,D
Psychology—General M,D
Sociology M,D
Theater M
Writing M,D

OKLAHOMA STATE UNIVERSITY CENTER FOR HEALTH SCIENCES
Forensic Psychology M
Forensic Sciences M

OKLAHOMA WESLEYAN UNIVERSITY
Theology M

OLD DOMINION UNIVERSITY
Applied Economics M
Applied Psychology D
Clinical Psychology D
Computer Art and Design M
Conflict Resolution and
    Mediation/Peace Studies M,D
Counseling Psychology M,D,O
Criminal Justice and Criminology D
Cultural Studies M,D
Economics M
English M,D
Experimental Psychology D
History M
Humanities M
International Affairs M,D
International Development M,D
Linguistics M
Psychology—General M,D
Public Administration M,D
Sociology M
Speech and Interpersonal
    Communication M
Urban Studies D
Writing M

OLIVET NAZARENE UNIVERSITY
Religion M
Theology M

ORAL ROBERTS UNIVERSITY
Marriage and Family Therapy M,D
Missions and Missiology M,D
Near and Middle Eastern Languages M,D
Pastoral Ministry and Counseling M,D
Theology M,D

OREGON COLLEGE OF ART & CRAFT
Art/Fine Arts M

OREGON HEALTH & SCIENCE UNIVERSITY
Gerontology M,O

OREGON STATE UNIVERSITY
Anthropology M,D
Child and Family Studies M,D
Clothing and Textiles M,D
Economics M,D
English M
Ethics M
Gender Studies M
Geography M,D
Hispanic Studies M
History of Science and Technology M,D
Human Development M,D
Interdisciplinary Studies M
Public Policy M,D
Sport Psychology M,D
Women's Studies M
Writing M

OREGON STATE UNIVERSITY– CASCADES
School Psychology M
Social Psychology M

OTIS COLLEGE OF ART AND DESIGN
Art/Fine Arts M
Graphic Design M
Photography M
Writing M

OTTAWA UNIVERSITY
Art Therapy M
Counseling Psychology M
Marriage and Family Therapy M
Pastoral Ministry and Counseling M
School Psychology M

OUR LADY OF HOLY CROSS COLLEGE
Marriage and Family Therapy M

OUR LADY OF THE LAKE UNIVERSITY OF SAN ANTONIO
Communication—General M
Counseling Psychology M,D
English M
Human Development M
Marriage and Family Therapy M,D
Psychology—General M,D
School Psychology M,D
Writing M

OXFORD GRADUATE SCHOOL
Child and Family Studies M,D
Religion M,D
Sociology M,D

PACE UNIVERSITY
Addictions/Substance Abuse
    Counseling M,D

Clinical Psychology M,D
Counseling Psychology M,D
Forensic Sciences M
Homeland Security M
Internet and Interactive
    Multimedia M,D,O
Media Studies M
Psychology—General M
Public Administration M
Publishing M,O
School Psychology M,D
Sustainable Development M,D
Theater M

PACIFICA GRADUATE INSTITUTE
Clinical Psychology M,D
Counseling Psychology M,D
Psychology—General M,D

PACIFIC LUTHERAN UNIVERSITY
Marriage and Family Therapy M
Writing M

PACIFIC NORTHWEST COLLEGE OF ART
Applied Arts and Design—
    General M
Art/Fine Arts M
Cultural Studies M

PACIFIC OAKS COLLEGE
Human Development M
Marriage and Family Therapy M

PACIFIC SCHOOL OF RELIGION
Religion M,D,O
Theology M,D,O

PACIFIC UNIVERSITY
Psychology—General M,D
Writing M

PALM BEACH ATLANTIC UNIVERSITY
Addictions/Substance Abuse
    Counseling M
Counseling Psychology M
Marriage and Family Therapy M
Theology M

PALO ALTO UNIVERSITY
Clinical Psychology D
Counseling Psychology M
Psychology—General M,D

PARK UNIVERSITY
Emergency Management M,O
Music M
Public Administration M,O
Public Affairs M,O
Writing M,O

PAYNE THEOLOGICAL SEMINARY
Theology M

PENN STATE HARRISBURG
American Studies M,D,O
Applied Behavior Analysis M,D,O
Applied Psychology M,D,O
Clinical Psychology M,D,O
Communication—General M,D,O
Criminal Justice and Criminology M,D,O
Folklore M,D,O
Historic Preservation M,D,O
Humanities M,D,O
Museum Studies M,D,O
Psychology—General M,D,O
Public Administration M,D,O
Public Affairs M,D,O
Public Policy M,D,O
Social Psychology M,D,O
Writing M,D,O

PENN STATE UNIVERSITY PARK
Agricultural Economics and
    Agribusiness M,D
Anthropology M,D
Architecture M,D
Art History M,D
Art/Fine Arts M,D,O
Child and Family Studies M,D
Communication—General M,D
Comparative Literature M,D
Criminal Justice and Criminology M,D
Economics M,D
English M,D
French M,D
Geography M,D
German M,D
History M,D
Homeland Security M
Human Development M,D
Industrial and Labor Relations M
International Affairs M
Landscape Architecture M,D
Linguistics M,D
Mass Communication M,D
Media Studies M,D
Music M,D,O
Philosophy M,D
Political Science M,D
Psychology—General M,D
Rural Sociology M,D,O
Russian M,D
School Psychology M,D,O
Sociology M,D
Spanish M,D
Sustainable Development M
Theater M
Writing M,D

PENNSYLVANIA ACADEMY OF THE FINE ARTS
Art/Fine Arts M,O

*M—masters degree; D—doctorate; O—other advanced degree; *—Close-Up and/or Display*

PENTECOSTAL THEOLOGICAL SEMINARY
Pastoral Ministry and Counseling M,D
Theology M,D

PEPPERDINE UNIVERSITY
American Studies M
Clinical Psychology M
Communication—General M
Conflict Resolution and Mediation/Peace Studies M
Economics M
Film, Television, and Video Production M
International Affairs M
Marriage and Family Therapy M
Media Studies M
Pastoral Ministry and Counseling M
Political Science M
Psychology—General M,D
Public Administration M
Public Policy M
Religion M
Theology M
Writing M

PERU STATE COLLEGE
Economics M

PFEIFFER UNIVERSITY
Theology M

PHILADELPHIA COLLEGE OF OSTEOPATHIC MEDICINE
Applied Behavior Analysis M,D,O
Clinical Psychology M,D,O
Counseling Psychology M,D,O
Forensic Sciences M
Industrial and Organizational Psychology M,D,O
Psychology—General M,D,O*
School Psychology M,D,O

PHILADELPHIA UNIVERSITY
Architecture M
Art/Fine Arts M
Clothing and Textiles M
Emergency Management M
Geography M
Industrial Design M
Interior Design M
Internet and Interactive Multimedia M
Social Psychology M
Sustainable Development M
Textile Design M
Urban and Regional Planning M

PHILLIPS GRADUATE INSTITUTE
Art Therapy M
Marriage and Family Therapy M

PHILLIPS THEOLOGICAL SEMINARY
Ethics M,D
Missions and Missiology M,D
Music M,D
Pastoral Ministry and Counseling D
Theology M,D

PHOENIX SEMINARY
Counseling Psychology M,D,O
Pastoral Ministry and Counseling M,D,O
Theology M,D,O

PIEDMONT INTERNATIONAL UNIVERSITY
Pastoral Ministry and Counseling M,D
Theology M,D

PITTSBURGH THEOLOGICAL SEMINARY
Pastoral Ministry and Counseling M,D
Theology M,D

PITTSBURG STATE UNIVERSITY
Art/Fine Arts M
Communication—General M
English M
Graphic Design M
History M
Music M
Psychology—General M
School Psychology O
Social Psychology M
Theater M

PLYMOUTH STATE UNIVERSITY
Clinical Psychology M,O
Cultural Studies M
Historic Preservation M
School Psychology M,O

POINT LOMA NAZARENE UNIVERSITY
Pastoral Ministry and Counseling M
Religion M

POINT PARK UNIVERSITY
Clinical Psychology M
Communication—General M
Criminal Justice and Criminology M
Journalism M
Mass Communication M
Music M
Theater M

POLYTECHNIC UNIVERSITY OF PUERTO RICO
Landscape Architecture M

PONCE HEALTH SCIENCES UNIVERSITY
Clinical Psychology D

PONTIFICAL CATHOLIC UNIVERSITY OF PUERTO RICO
Art/Fine Arts M
Clinical Psychology D
Criminal Justice and Criminology M
Hispanic Studies M,O
History M
Industrial and Organizational Psychology D
Psychology—General M,D
Public Administration M
Rehabilitation Counseling M
Spanish M,O
Theology M

PONTIFICAL COLLEGE JOSEPHINUM
Theology M

PONTIFICIA UNIVERSIDAD CATOLICA MADRE Y MAESTRA
Architecture M
Building Science M
Clinical Psychology M
Criminal Justice and Criminology M
Developmental Psychology M
Forensic Psychology M
Interior Design M
International Affairs M
Landscape Architecture M
Psychology—General M

POPE ST. JOHN XXIII NATIONAL SEMINARY
Theology M

PORTLAND STATE UNIVERSITY
Anthropology M,D,O
Applied Economics M,D
Applied Social Research M,D
Architecture M
Art/Fine Arts M
Conflict Resolution and Mediation/Peace Studies M
Criminal Justice and Criminology M,D
Economics M,D,O
English M
French M
Geography M,D
German M
Gerontology O
History M
Japanese M
Music M
Political Science M,D
Psychology—General M,D,O
Public Administration M,D
Public Affairs M,D
Public Policy M,D
Sociology M,D,O
Spanish M
Speech and Interpersonal Communication M,O
Theater M
Urban and Regional Planning M
Urban Studies M,D

POST UNIVERSITY
Addictions/Substance Abuse Counseling M
Public Administration M

PRAIRIE VIEW A&M UNIVERSITY
Architecture M
Clinical Psychology M,D
English M
Family and Consumer Sciences-General M
Forensic Psychology M,D
Sociology M
Urban Design M

PRATT INSTITUTE
Applied Arts and Design—General M,O*
Architecture M*
Art History M
Art Therapy M
Art/Fine Arts M*
Arts Administration M
Graphic Design M
Historic Preservation M
Industrial Design M
Interior Design M
Internet and Interactive Multimedia M
Media Studies M*
Music M
Photography M
Sustainable Development M
Therapies—Dance, Drama, and Music M
Urban and Regional Planning M
Urban Design M
Writing M

PRESCOTT COLLEGE
Art Therapy M
Counseling Psychology M
Health Psychology M
Humanities M
Psychoanalysis and Psychotherapy M

PRINCETON THEOLOGICAL SEMINARY
Religion M,D
Theology M,D

PRINCETON UNIVERSITY
Anthropology D
Archaeology D
Architecture M,D
Asian Studies D
Classics D
Comparative Literature D
Demography and Population Studies D,O
Economics D,O
English D
French D
German D
History of Science and Technology D
History D
International Affairs M,D
Music D
Near and Middle Eastern Studies M,D
Philosophy D
Political Science D
Portuguese D
Psychology—General D
Public Affairs M,D,O
Public Policy M,D
Religion D
Russian D
Slavic Languages D
Sociology D,O
Spanish D

PROVIDENCE COLLEGE
American Studies M
History M
Religion M
Theology M

PROVIDENCE UNIVERSITY COLLEGE & THEOLOGICAL SEMINARY
Counseling Psychology M,D,O
Missions and Missiology M,D,O
Pastoral Ministry and Counseling M,D,O
Theology M,D,O

PURCHASE COLLEGE, STATE UNIVERSITY OF NEW YORK
Art History M
Art/Fine Arts M
Music M
Theater M

PURDUE UNIVERSITY
Agricultural Economics and Agribusiness M,D
American Studies M,D
Anthropology M,D
Applied Arts and Design—General M
Art/Fine Arts M
Child and Family Studies M,D
Child Development M,D
Clinical Psychology D
Cognitive Sciences D
Communication—General M,D
Comparative Literature M,D
Computer Art and Design M,D
Consumer Economics M,D
Economics D
English M,D
Family and Consumer Sciences-General M,D
French M,D
German M,D
History M,D
Human Development M,D
Industrial and Organizational Psychology D
Japanese M,D
Linguistics M,D
Marriage and Family Therapy M,D
Philosophy M,D
Political Science M,D
Psychology—General D
Sociology M,D
Spanish M,D
Sport Psychology M,D
Theater M
Writing M,D

PURDUE UNIVERSITY CALUMET
Child and Family Studies M
Child Development M
Communication—General M
Counseling Psychology M
English M
History M
Marriage and Family Therapy M
School Psychology M

QUEENS COLLEGE OF THE CITY UNIVERSITY OF NEW YORK
Art History M
Art/Fine Arts M
Clinical Psychology M
English M
Family and Consumer Sciences-General M
French M
Hispanic and Latin American Languages M
History M
Italian M
Liberal Studies M
Linguistics M
Music M
Psychology—General M
Romance Languages M
School Psychology M,O
Social Sciences M
Sociology M
Spanish M
Urban Studies M
Writing M

QUEEN'S UNIVERSITY AT KINGSTON
Canadian Studies M,D
Classics M
Clinical Psychology M,D
Cognitive Sciences M,D
Communication—General M,D
Developmental Psychology M,D
English M,D
French M,D
Gender Studies M,D
Geography M,D
German M,D
Hispanic Studies M
Industrial and Labor Relations M
International Affairs M,D
Philosophy M,D
Political Science M,D
Psychology—General M,D
Public Policy M
Religion M
Social Psychology M,D
Sociology M,D
Spanish M
Sport Psychology M,D
Theology M,O
Urban and Regional Planning M
Women's Studies M,D

QUEENS UNIVERSITY OF CHARLOTTE
Corporate and Organizational Communication M
Writing M

QUINCY UNIVERSITY
Communication—General M
School Psychology M

QUINNIPIAC UNIVERSITY
Broadcast Journalism M
Communication—General M
Film, Television, and Video Production M
Internet and Interactive Multimedia M
Journalism M

RABBI ISAAC ELCHANAN THEOLOGICAL SEMINARY
Theology O

RABBINICAL ACADEMY MESIVTA RABBI CHAIM BERLIN
Theology O

RABBINICAL COLLEGE BETH SHRAGA
Theology

RABBINICAL COLLEGE BOBOVER YESHIVA B'NEI ZION
Theology

RABBINICAL COLLEGE CH'SAN SOFER
Theology

RABBINICAL COLLEGE OF LONG ISLAND
Theology

RABBINICAL SEMINARY OF AMERICA
Theology

RADFORD UNIVERSITY
Applied Arts and Design—General M
Art/Fine Arts M
Clinical Psychology M
Corporate and Organizational Communication M
Counseling Psychology M,D
Criminal Justice and Criminology M,O
English M
Experimental Psychology M
Industrial and Organizational Psychology M
Music M
Psychology—General M,D,O
School Psychology O
Therapies—Dance, Drama, and Music M

RAMAPO COLLEGE OF NEW JERSEY
Liberal Studies M
Sustainable Development M

RECONSTRUCTIONIST RABBINICAL COLLEGE
Jewish Studies M,D,O
Theology M,D,O
Women's Studies M,D,O

REED COLLEGE
Liberal Studies M

REFORMED EPISCOPAL SEMINARY
Theology M

REFORMED PRESBYTERIAN THEOLOGICAL SEMINARY
Theology M,D

REFORMED THEOLOGICAL SEMINARY–ATLANTA CAMPUS
Theology M,D,O

REFORMED THEOLOGICAL SEMINARY–CHARLOTTE CAMPUS
Pastoral Ministry and Counseling M,D
Religion M,D
Theology M,D

REFORMED THEOLOGICAL SEMINARY–HOUSTON CAMPUS
Religion M

REFORMED THEOLOGICAL SEMINARY–JACKSON CAMPUS
Marriage and Family Therapy M,D,O
Missions and Missiology M,D,O
Pastoral Ministry and Counseling M,D,O
Religion M,D,O
Theology M,D,O

REFORMED THEOLOGICAL SEMINARY–ORLANDO CAMPUS
Pastoral Ministry and Counseling M,D,O
Theology M,D,O

REFORMED THEOLOGICAL SEMINARY–WASHINGTON D.C.
Religion M
Theology M

REGENT COLLEGE
Theology M,O

REGENT'S UNIVERSITY LONDON
International Affairs M

REGENT UNIVERSITY
American Studies M
Clinical Psychology M,D,O
Communication—General M,D
Corporate and Organizational Communication M,D

Counseling Psychology M,D,O
Cultural Studies M,D
Emergency Management M
Film, Television, and Video Production M,D
History M,D
Homeland Security M
Interdisciplinary Studies M,D
International Affairs M
Journalism M,D
Marriage and Family Therapy M,D,O
Missions and Missiology M,D
Pastoral Ministry and Counseling M,D
Political Science M
Psychoanalysis and Psychotherapy M,D
Public Administration M
Religion M,D
Theater M,D
Theology M,D
Writing M,D

REGIS COLLEGE (CANADA)
Pastoral Ministry and Counseling M,D,O
Philosophy M,D,O
Theology M,D,O

REGIS COLLEGE (MA)
Applied Behavior Analysis M,D,O
Corporate and Organizational Communication M
Cultural Studies M
Writing M,O

REGIS UNIVERSITY
Counseling Psychology M,O
Criminal Justice and Criminology M
Liberal Studies M
Marriage and Family Therapy M,O

REINHARDT UNIVERSITY
Music M

RENSSELAER POLYTECHNIC INSTITUTE
Architecture M,D
Art/Fine Arts M,D
Building Science M,D
Cognitive Sciences D
Computer Art and Design M,D
History of Science and Technology M,D
Interdisciplinary Studies M,D
Lighting Design M,D
Rhetoric M,D
Speech and Interpersonal Communication M,D
Technical Communication M

RHODE ISLAND COLLEGE
Art/Fine Arts M
Arts Administration M
Counseling Psychology M,O
English M,O
Health Psychology M,O
History M
Psychology—General M,O
Public Administration M
School Psychology M,O
Writing M,O

RHODE ISLAND SCHOOL OF DESIGN
Applied Arts and Design—General M
Architecture M
Art/Fine Arts M
Computer Art and Design M
Graphic Design M
Industrial Design M
Interior Design M
Landscape Architecture M
Photography M
Textile Design M

RICE UNIVERSITY
African Studies D
American Studies D
Anthropology M,D
Archaeology M,D
Architecture M,D
Art History D
Cognitive Sciences M,D
Cultural Anthropology M,D
Economics M,D
English M,D
History M,D
Industrial and Organizational Psychology M,D
Jewish Studies D
Liberal Studies M
Linguistics M,D
Music M,D
Near and Middle Eastern Studies D
Philosophy M,D
Political Science D
Psychology—General M,D
Religion D
Sociology D
Urban Design M,D

RICHMOND, THE AMERICAN INTERNATIONAL UNIVERSITY IN LONDON
Art History M
International Affairs M

RICHMONT GRADUATE UNIVERSITY
Counseling Psychology M
Marriage and Family Therapy M
Pastoral Ministry and Counseling M
Psychology—General M

RIDER UNIVERSITY
Applied Psychology M
Corporate and Organizational Communication M
French O
German O
Music M
School Psychology O
Spanish O

RIVIER UNIVERSITY
Clinical Psychology M
Counseling Psychology M,D,O
English M
Experimental Psychology M
Psychology—General M
Writing M

THE ROBERT E. WEBBER INSTITUTE FOR WORSHIP STUDIES
Religion M,D

ROBERT MORRIS UNIVERSITY
Internet and Interactive Multimedia M,D

ROBERT MORRIS UNIVERSITY ILLINOIS
Arts Administration M
Criminal Justice and Criminology M
Media Studies M

ROBERTS WESLEYAN COLLEGE
Child and Family Studies M

ROCHESTER COLLEGE
Missions and Missiology M

ROCHESTER INSTITUTE OF TECHNOLOGY
Architecture M
Art/Fine Arts M,O
Communication—General M,O
Computer Art and Design M
Criminal Justice and Criminology M
Experimental Psychology M
Film, Television, and Video Production M
Graphic Design M
Industrial Design M
Interdisciplinary Studies M
Internet and Interactive Multimedia M,O
Media Studies M,O
Medical Illustration M
Photography M
Psychology—General M,O
Public Policy M
School Psychology M,O
Sustainable Development M,D

ROCKY MOUNTAIN COLLEGE OF ART + DESIGN
Arts Administration M
Internet and Interactive Multimedia M

ROGER WILLIAMS UNIVERSITY
Architectural History M
Architecture M
Art History M
Clinical Psychology M
Criminal Justice and Criminology M
Forensic Psychology M
Historic Preservation M
Public Administration M

ROLLINS COLLEGE
Liberal Studies M

ROOSEVELT UNIVERSITY
Anthropology M
Applied Economics M
Clinical Psychology M
Communication—General M
Corporate and Organizational Communication M
Economics M
English M
Gender Studies M,O
History M
Industrial and Organizational Psychology M,D
Journalism M
Music M,O
Political Science M
Psychology—General M,D
Public Administration M
Sociology M
Spanish M
Theater M
Women's Studies M,O
Writing M

ROSALIND FRANKLIN UNIVERSITY OF MEDICINE AND SCIENCE
Interdisciplinary Studies D
Psychology—General M,D

ROSEMONT COLLEGE
Counseling Psychology M
Publishing M
Writing M

ROWAN UNIVERSITY
Applied Behavior Analysis M,O
Arts Administration M
Clinical Psychology M,O
Corporate and Organizational Communication O
Criminal Justice and Criminology M
History M,O
Media Studies O
Music M
Psychology—General M,O
Publishing O
Rhetoric O
School Psychology M,O
Theater M
Writing M,O

ROYAL MILITARY COLLEGE OF CANADA
Military and Defense Studies M,D

ROYAL ROADS UNIVERSITY
Conflict Resolution and Mediation/Peace Studies M,O
Emergency Management M,O

RUTGERS, THE STATE UNIVERSITY OF NEW JERSEY, CAMDEN
Child Development M,D
Criminal Justice and Criminology M
English M
History M
International Affairs M
International Development M
Liberal Studies M
Psychology—General M
Public Administration M
Public History M
Public Policy M
Writing M

RUTGERS, THE STATE UNIVERSITY OF NEW JERSEY, NEWARK
American Studies M,D
Cognitive Sciences D
Criminal Justice and Criminology M,D
Economics M,D
English M
History M
International Affairs M,D
Music M
Political Science M
Psychology—General D
Public Administration M,D
Public Policy M,D,O
Rehabilitation Counseling M,D
Social Psychology D
Urban Studies M,D
Writing M

RUTGERS, THE STATE UNIVERSITY OF NEW JERSEY, NEW BRUNSWICK
African Studies D
African-American Studies D
Agricultural Economics and Agribusiness M
Anthropology M,D
Applied Arts and Design—General M
Applied Psychology M,D
Art History M,D,O
Art/Fine Arts M
Asian Studies M,D
Classics M,D
Clinical Psychology M,D
Cognitive Sciences D
Communication—General D
Comparative Literature M,D
Counseling Psychology M
Economics M,D
Emergency Management M,D,O
English D
French M,D
Gender Studies M,D
Geography M,D
German M,D
Health Psychology D
Historic Preservation M,D,O
History of Medicine D
History of Science and Technology D
History D
Industrial and Labor Relations M,D
Interdisciplinary Studies D
International Affairs M,D
Italian M,D
Jewish Studies M,O
Linguistics D
Media Studies D
Medieval and Renaissance Studies D
Music M,D,O
Philosophy D
Political Science M,D
Psychology—General D
Public Policy M,D
Religion M,O
School Psychology M,D
Social Psychology D
Sociology M,D
Spanish M,D
Theater M
Translation and Interpretation M,D
Urban and Regional Planning M,D
Women's Studies M,D
Writing M

RYERSON UNIVERSITY
Arts Administration M

SACRED HEART MAJOR SEMINARY
Pastoral Ministry and Counseling M
Theology M

SACRED HEART SCHOOL OF THEOLOGY
Theology M,O

SACRED HEART UNIVERSITY
Applied Psychology M
Communication—General M,O
Corporate and Organizational Communication M,O
Criminal Justice and Criminology M
Film, Television, and Video Production M,O
Internet and Interactive Multimedia M,O
Journalism M,O
Religion M

SAGE GRADUATE SCHOOL
Applied Behavior Analysis M,O
Child and Family Studies M
Counseling Psychology M
Forensic Psychology M,O
Gerontology M,O
Psychology—General M,O
Public Administration M
Social Psychology M

SAGINAW VALLEY STATE UNIVERSITY
Communication—General M
Media Studies M
Public Administration M

ST. AMBROSE UNIVERSITY
Criminal Justice and Criminology M
Pastoral Ministry and Counseling M

ST. ANDREW'S COLLEGE
Theology M,D,O

ST. ANDREW'S COLLEGE IN WINNIPEG
Theology M

ST. AUGUSTINE'S SEMINARY OF TORONTO
Pastoral Ministry and Counseling M,O
Theology M,O

ST. BERNARD'S SCHOOL OF THEOLOGY AND MINISTRY
Pastoral Ministry and Counseling M,O
Theology M,O

ST. BONAVENTURE UNIVERSITY
Corporate and Organizational Communication M
Counseling Psychology M,O
English M
Rehabilitation Counseling M,O
Religion M
Social Psychology M,O

ST. CATHARINE COLLEGE
Urban and Regional Planning M

ST. CATHERINE UNIVERSITY
Pastoral Ministry and Counseling M,O
Theology M,O

SAINT CHARLES BORROMEO SEMINARY, OVERBROOK
Religion M
Theology M

ST. CLOUD STATE UNIVERSITY
Applied Behavior Analysis M
Applied Economics M
Archaeology M
Child and Family Studies M
Criminal Justice and Criminology M
Economics M
English M
Geography M
Gerontology M
Historic Preservation M
History M
Industrial and Organizational Psychology M
Marriage and Family Therapy M
Mass Communication M
Music M
Psychology—General M,D
Rehabilitation Counseling M
Social Psychology M

ST. EDWARD'S UNIVERSITY
Computer Art and Design M
Counseling Psychology M
Ethics M
Humanities M,O
Liberal Studies M,O
Media Studies M
Social Sciences M,O
Sustainable Development M

ST. FRANCIS XAVIER UNIVERSITY
Cultural Studies M

ST. JOHN FISHER COLLEGE
Counseling Psychology M

ST. JOHN'S COLLEGE (MD)
Liberal Studies M

ST. JOHN'S COLLEGE (NM)
Asian Languages M
Asian Studies M
Liberal Studies M

ST. JOHN'S SEMINARY (CA)
Pastoral Ministry and Counseling M
Theology M

SAINT JOHN'S SEMINARY (MA)
Religion M
Theology M

SAINT JOHN'S UNIVERSITY (MN)
Music M
Pastoral Ministry and Counseling M
Theology M

ST. JOHN'S UNIVERSITY (NY)
Asian Studies M,O
Clinical Psychology M,D,O
Counseling Psychology M,O
Criminal Justice and Criminology M
English M,D
Experimental Psychology M
History M,D
International Affairs M,O
Liberal Studies M
Museum Studies M
Political Science M,O
Psychology—General M,D
Public Administration M,O

*M—masters degree; D—doctorate; O—other advanced degree; *—Close-Up and/or Display*

Public History — M,D
School Psychology — M,D
Sociology — M
Spanish — M
Theology — M

SAINT JOSEPH'S COLLEGE
Music — M,O

ST. JOSEPH'S COLLEGE, NEW YORK
Writing — M

SAINT JOSEPH'S COLLEGE OF MAINE
Pastoral Ministry and Counseling — M

ST. JOSEPH'S SEMINARY
Pastoral Ministry and Counseling — M
Religion — M
Theology — M

SAINT JOSEPH'S UNIVERSITY
Criminal Justice and Criminology — M,O
Gerontology — M
Homeland Security — M
Industrial and Organizational Psychology — M
Psychology—General — M,O
Writing — M

ST. LAWRENCE UNIVERSITY
Human Development — M,O

SAINT LEO UNIVERSITY
Criminal Justice and Criminology — M
Forensic Sciences — M
Pastoral Ministry and Counseling — M

SAINT LOUIS UNIVERSITY
American Studies — M,D
Clinical Psychology — M,D
Communication—General — M
English — M,D
Experimental Psychology — M,D
French — M
Geographic Information Systems — M,D,O
History — M,D
Human Development — M,D,O
Industrial and Organizational Psychology — M,D
Marriage and Family Therapy — M,D,O
Philosophy — M,D
Political Science — M
Psychology—General — M,D
Public Administration — M,D,O
Public Policy — M,D,O
Spanish — M
Theology — M,D
Urban Studies — M,D,O

SAINT LOUIS UNIVERSITY—MADRID CAMPUS
English — M
Spanish — M

SAINT MARTIN'S UNIVERSITY
Counseling Psychology — M
Social Psychology — M

SAINT MARY-OF-THE-WOODS COLLEGE
Art Therapy — M,O
Pastoral Ministry and Counseling — M,O
Theology — M,O
Therapies—Dance, Drama, and Music — M

SAINT MARY'S COLLEGE OF CALIFORNIA
Dance — M
Marriage and Family Therapy — M
Writing — M

SAINT MARY SEMINARY AND GRADUATE SCHOOL OF THEOLOGY
Theology — M,D

ST. MARY'S SEMINARY AND UNIVERSITY
Theology — M,D,O

SAINT MARY'S UNIVERSITY (CANADA)
Applied Psychology — M,D
Canadian Studies — M,O
Criminal Justice and Criminology — M
Gender Studies — M
History — M
Industrial and Organizational Psychology — M,D
International Development — M,O
Philosophy — M
Psychology—General — M,D
Religion — M
Theology — M
Women's Studies — M

ST. MARY'S UNIVERSITY (UNITED STATES)
Communication—General — M,O
Conflict Resolution and Mediation/Peace Studies — M,O
Counseling Psychology — M
English — M
Homeland Security — M,O
Industrial and Organizational Psychology — M
International Affairs — M,O
Marriage and Family Therapy — M,D
Political Science — M
Public Administration — M,O
Public Policy — M,O
Theology — M

SAINT MARY'S UNIVERSITY OF MINNESOTA
Addictions/Substance Abuse Counseling — M,O
Arts Administration — M
Counseling Psychology — M,D,O
Geographic Information Systems — M,O

Human Development — M
International Development — M
Marriage and Family Therapy — M,O
Philanthropic Studies — M

SAINT MEINRAD SCHOOL OF THEOLOGY
Pastoral Ministry and Counseling — M
Theology — M

SAINT MICHAEL'S COLLEGE
Clinical Psychology — M

ST. NORBERT COLLEGE
Liberal Studies — M
Theology — M

ST. PATRICK'S SEMINARY & UNIVERSITY
Theology — M,O

SAINT PAUL SCHOOL OF THEOLOGY
Theology — M,D

SAINT PAUL UNIVERSITY
Conflict Resolution and Mediation/Peace Studies — M
Counseling Psychology — M
Marriage and Family Therapy — M
Missions and Missiology — M
Pastoral Ministry and Counseling — M,D,O
Theology — M,D,O

ST. PETER'S SEMINARY
Theology — M

SAINT PETER'S UNIVERSITY
Applied Behavior Analysis — M,D,O
Criminal Justice and Criminology — M
Public Administration — M

SAINTS CYRIL AND METHODIUS SEMINARY
Pastoral Ministry and Counseling — M
Theology — M

ST. STEPHEN'S COLLEGE
Pastoral Ministry and Counseling — M,D
Theology — M,D

ST. THOMAS UNIVERSITY
Arts Administration — M
Communication—General — M,D,O
Counseling Psychology — M
Criminal Justice and Criminology — M,O
Film, Television, and Video Production — M
Hispanic Studies — M,O
Marriage and Family Therapy — M,O
Pastoral Ministry and Counseling — M,D,O
Public Administration — M,O
Theology — M,D,O

ST. TIKHON'S ORTHODOX THEOLOGICAL SEMINARY
Theology — M

ST. VINCENT DE PAUL REGIONAL SEMINARY
Theology — M

SAINT VINCENT SEMINARY
Pastoral Ministry and Counseling — M
Theology — M

ST. VLADIMIR'S ORTHODOX THEOLOGICAL SEMINARY
Music — M,D
Theology — M,D

SAINT XAVIER UNIVERSITY
Spanish — M

SALEM STATE UNIVERSITY
Counseling Psychology — M,O
Criminal Justice and Criminology — M
English — M
Geography — M
History — M
Psychology—General — M,O
Spanish — M

SALISBURY UNIVERSITY
Conflict Resolution and Mediation/Peace Studies — M
English — M
Geographic Information Systems — M
History — M
Music — M
Rhetoric — M

SALVE REGINA UNIVERSITY
Addictions/Substance Abuse Counseling — M,O
Conflict Resolution and Mediation/Peace Studies — M,D
Counseling Psychology — M,O
Criminal Justice and Criminology — M,O
Homeland Security — M,O
Humanities — M,D
International Affairs — M,O
Rehabilitation Counseling — M,O
Religion — M,D

SAMFORD UNIVERSITY
Music — M
Theology — M,D

SAM HOUSTON STATE UNIVERSITY
Clinical Psychology — M,D,O
Communication—General — M
Criminal Justice and Criminology — M,D
Dance — M
English — M
Family and Consumer Sciences-General — M
Forensic Sciences — M,D
Geographic Information Systems — M,O
History — M
Homeland Security — M
Humanities — M,D,O

Internet and Interactive Multimedia — M
Music — M
Political Science — M
Psychology—General — M,D,O
Public Administration — M
Publishing — M
School Psychology — M,D,O
Sociology — M
Spanish — M
Writing — M

SAN DIEGO STATE UNIVERSITY
Anthropology — M
Applied Arts and Design— General — M
Art History — M
Art/Fine Arts — M
Asian Studies — M
Child and Family Studies — M
Child Development — M
Clinical Psychology — M,D
Communication—General — M
Criminal Justice and Criminology — M
Economics — M
Emergency Management — M
English — M
Environmental Design — M
Film, Television, and Video Production — M
Gender Studies — O
Geography — M,D
Gerontology — M
Graphic Design — M
Health Psychology — M,D
History — M
Industrial and Organizational Psychology — M,D
Interdisciplinary Studies — M
Interior Design — M
Internet and Interactive Multimedia — M
Latin American Studies — M
Liberal Studies — M
Linguistics — M
Media Studies — M
Music — M
Philosophy — M
Political Science — M
Psychology—General — M,D
Public Administration — M
Rehabilitation Counseling — M
Rhetoric — M
Romance Languages — M
School Psychology — M
Sociology — M
Spanish — M
Theater — M
Urban and Regional Planning — M
Western European Studies — M
Women's Studies — M
Writing — M

SAN FRANCISCO ART INSTITUTE
Applied Arts and Design— General — M
Art History — M
Art/Fine Arts — M,O
Film, Television, and Video Production — M
Museum Studies — M
Photography — M

SAN FRANCISCO CONSERVATORY OF MUSIC
Music — M

SAN FRANCISCO STATE UNIVERSITY
Anthropology — M
Archaeology — M
Art History — M
Art/Fine Arts — M
Asian-American Studies — M
Chinese — M
Classics — M
Comparative Literature — M
Counseling Psychology — M,O
Criminal Justice and Criminology — M
Cultural Anthropology — M
Cultural Studies — M
Economics — M
English — M,O
Ethnic Studies — M
Family and Consumer Sciences-General — M
Film, Television, and Video Production — M
Film, Television, and Video Theory and Criticism — M
French — M
Geography — M
German — M
Gerontology — M
History — M
Humanities — M
Industrial and Organizational Psychology — M,O
Industrial Design — M
International Affairs — M
Italian — M
Japanese — M
Linguistics — M
Marriage and Family Therapy — M,O
Media Studies — M
Museum Studies — M
Music — M
Philosophy — M
Political Science — M
Psychology—General — M,O
Public Administration — M
Public Policy — M
Rehabilitation Counseling — M,O
School Psychology — M,O
Social Psychology — M,O
Spanish — M

Speech and Interpersonal Communication — M
Theater — M
Women's Studies — M
Writing — M

SAN FRANCISCO THEOLOGICAL SEMINARY
Theology — M,D

SAN JOSE STATE UNIVERSITY
Anthropology — M
Applied Arts and Design— General — M
Applied Economics — M
Art History — M
Art/Fine Arts — M
Child and Family Studies — M
Clinical Psychology — M
Communication—General — M
Comparative Literature — M
Computer Art and Design — M
Criminal Justice and Criminology — M
Economics — M
English — M
Experimental Psychology — M
Film, Television, and Video Production — M
French — M
Geographic Information Systems — M,O
Geography — M,O
Gerontology — M,O
Hispanic Studies — M
History — M
Illustration — M
Industrial and Organizational Psychology — M
Interdisciplinary Studies — M
Linguistics — M,O
Mass Communication — M
Music — M
Philosophy — M
Photography — M
Psychology—General — M
Public Administration — M
Sociology — M
Spanish — M
Speech and Interpersonal Communication — M
Theater — M
Urban and Regional Planning — M,O

SANTA CLARA UNIVERSITY
Counseling Psychology — M,O
Interdisciplinary Studies — M,O
Pastoral Ministry and Counseling — M
Theology — M,D,O

SARAH LAWRENCE COLLEGE
Child Development — M
Dance — M
Genetic Counseling — M
History — M
Theater — M
Women's Studies — M
Writing — M

SAVANNAH COLLEGE OF ART AND DESIGN
Applied Arts and Design— General — M,O
Architectural History — M
Architecture — M
Art History — M
Art/Fine Arts — M
Arts Administration — M
Clothing and Textiles — M
Computer Art and Design — M,O
Film, Television, and Video Production — M
Film, Television, and Video Theory and Criticism — M
Graphic Design — M
Historic Preservation — M,O
Illustration — M
Industrial Design — M
Interior Design — M
Internet and Interactive Multimedia — M,O
Media Studies — M
Music — M
Photography — M
Sustainable Development — M
Textile Design — M
Theater — M
Urban Design — M
Writing — M

SAVANNAH STATE UNIVERSITY
Public Administration — M
Urban and Regional Planning — M
Urban Studies — M

SAYBROOK UNIVERSITY
Clinical Psychology — M
Counseling Psychology — M
Health Psychology — M,D
Marriage and Family Therapy — M,D
Psychology—General — M,D
Sustainable Development — M,D
Transpersonal and Humanistic Psychology — M,D

SCHILLER INTERNATIONAL UNIVERSITY
International Affairs — M

SCHOOL OF ADVANCED AIR AND SPACE STUDIES
Military and Defense Studies — M

THE SCHOOL OF PROFESSIONAL PSYCHOLOGY AT FOREST INSTITUTE
Applied Behavior Analysis — M,D,O
Clinical Psychology — M,D,O
Counseling Psychology — M,D,O

Marriage and Family Therapy — M,D,O
Psychology—General — M,D,O

SCHOOL OF THE ART INSTITUTE OF CHICAGO
Applied Arts and Design—
  General — M
Architecture — M
Art History — M
Art Therapy — M
Art/Fine Arts — M
Arts Administration — M
Arts Journalism — M
Film, Television, and Video
  Production — M
Graphic Design — M
Historic Preservation — M
Interior Design — M
Journalism — M
Music — M
Photography — M
Textile Design — M,O
Writing — M,O

SCHOOL OF THE MUSEUM OF FINE ARTS, BOSTON
Art/Fine Arts — M,O

SCHOOL OF VISUAL ARTS (NY)
Applied Arts and Design—
  General — M
Art Therapy — M
Art/Fine Arts — M
Computer Art and Design — M
Cultural Studies — M
Film, Television, and Video
  Production — M
Graphic Design — M
Illustration — M
Internet and Interactive
  Multimedia — M
Photography — M
Writing — M

SCHREINER UNIVERSITY
Ethics — M

SEABURY-WESTERN THEOLOGICAL SEMINARY
Music — M,D,O
Theology — M,D,O

SEATTLE PACIFIC UNIVERSITY
Clinical Psychology — D
Industrial and Organizational
  Psychology — M,D
Marriage and Family Therapy — M,O
Theology — M,O
Writing — M

THE SEATTLE SCHOOL OF THEOLOGY AND PSYCHOLOGY
Counseling Psychology — M
Psychology—General — M
Religion — M
Theology — M

SEATTLE UNIVERSITY
Arts Administration — M
Criminal Justice and Criminology — M,O
Forensic Sciences — M,O
Pastoral Ministry and Counseling — M
Psychology—General — M
Public Administration — M
School Psychology — M,O
Theology — M,O
Transpersonal and Humanistic
  Psychology — M

SEMINARY OF THE IMMACULATE CONCEPTION
Pastoral Ministry and Counseling — M,D,O
Theology — M,D,O

SEMINARY OF THE SOUTHWEST
Theology — M,O

SETON HALL UNIVERSITY
Asian Studies — M
Communication—General — M
Corporate and Organizational
  Communication — M
Counseling Psychology — M,D
English — M
Experimental Psychology — M
History — M
International Affairs — M,O
Jewish Studies — M,O
Marriage and Family Therapy — M,O
Museum Studies — M
Pastoral Ministry and Counseling — M,O
Psychology—General — M,D,O
Public Administration — M,O
Public Policy — M,O
Religion — M,O
School Psychology — M
Speech and Interpersonal
  Communication — M
Sport Psychology — M
Theology — M,O

SETON HILL UNIVERSITY
Art Therapy — M
Holocaust and Genocide Studies — O
Marriage and Family Therapy — M
Writing — M,O

SEWANEE: THE UNIVERSITY OF THE SOUTH
English — M
Theology — M,D
Writing — M

SHASTA BIBLE COLLEGE
Pastoral Ministry and Counseling — M

SHAW UNIVERSITY
Theology — M

SHENANDOAH UNIVERSITY
Applied Behavior Analysis — M
Music — M,D,O

SHEPHERDS THEOLOGICAL SEMINARY
Pastoral Ministry and Counseling — M
Theology — M

SHEPHERD UNIVERSITY (CA)
Computer Art and Design — M
Music — M
Theology — M,D

SHILOH UNIVERSITY
Pastoral Ministry and Counseling — M
Theology — M

SHIPPENSBURG UNIVERSITY OF PENNSYLVANIA
Communication—General — M
Criminal Justice and Criminology — M
Geography — M
History — M
Marriage and Family Therapy — M,O
Psychology—General — M
Public Administration — M
Public History — M
Sociology — M

SH'OR YOSHUV RABBINICAL COLLEGE
Theology — M

SIENA HEIGHTS UNIVERSITY
Clinical Psychology — M,O
Counseling Psychology — M,O

SIMMONS COLLEGE
Applied Behavior Analysis — M,D,O
Communication—General — M
Public Policy — M,D,O

SIMON FRASER UNIVERSITY
Anthropology — M,D
Archaeology — M,D
Communication—General — M,D
Comparative and Interdisciplinary
  Arts — M
Criminal Justice and Criminology — M,D
Cultural Studies — D
Economics — M,D
English — M
French — M
Gender Studies — M
Geography — M,D
Gerontology — M
History — M,D
Humanities — M
International Affairs — M
Latin American Studies — M
Liberal Studies — M
Linguistics — M,D
Philosophy — M,D
Political Science — M,D
Psychology—General — M,D
Public Policy — M
Publishing — M
Sociology — M,D
Urban Studies — M,O
Women's Studies — M,D

SIMPSON COLLEGE
Criminal Justice and Criminology — M

SIMPSON UNIVERSITY
Counseling Psychology — M
Missions and Missiology — M

SIOUX FALLS SEMINARY
Marriage and Family Therapy — M
Pastoral Ministry and Counseling — M
Religion — M
Theology — M,D,O

SIT GRADUATE INSTITUTE
International Affairs — M
Sustainable Development — M

SKIDMORE COLLEGE
Liberal Studies — M

SLIPPERY ROCK UNIVERSITY OF PENNSYLVANIA
Addictions/Substance Abuse
  Counseling — M
Clinical Psychology — M
Counseling Psychology — M
Criminal Justice and Criminology — M
Gerontology — M
History — M
School Psychology — M

SMITH COLLEGE
Dance — M
French — M
History — M
Theater — M
Women's Studies — O

SOFIA UNIVERSITY
Clinical Psychology — M,D
Counseling Psychology — M,D,O
Pastoral Ministry and Counseling — M,D,O
Psychology—General — M,D
Transpersonal and Humanistic
  Psychology — M,D,O
Women's Studies — M,D,O

SONOMA STATE UNIVERSITY
Anthropology — M
Clinical Psychology — M
Counseling Psychology — M
English — M
Ethics — M
History — M

Interdisciplinary Studies — M
Marriage and Family Therapy — M
Political Science — M,O
Public Administration — M,O
Public History — M
Writing — M

SOTHEBY'S INSTITUTE OF ART–LONDON
Art/Fine Arts — M
Arts Administration — M
Decorative Arts — M
Photography — M

SOTHEBY'S INSTITUTE OF ART–NEW YORK
Art/Fine Arts — M
Arts Administration — M
Decorative Arts — M

SOUTH CAROLINA STATE UNIVERSITY
Agricultural Economics and
  Agribusiness — M
Child and Family Studies — M
Family and Consumer
  Sciences-General — M

SOUTH DAKOTA STATE UNIVERSITY
Clothing and Textiles — M
Communication—General — M
Consumer Economics — M
Economics — M
English — M
Family and Consumer
  Sciences-General — M
Geography — M
Interior Design — M
Journalism — M
Sociology — M,D

SOUTHEASTERN BAPTIST THEOLOGICAL SEMINARY
Ethics — M,D
Missions and Missiology — M,D
Music — M,D
Philosophy — M,D
Psychology—General — M,D
Theology — M,D
Women's Studies — M,D

SOUTHEASTERN LOUISIANA UNIVERSITY
Communication—General — M
English — M
History — M
Music — M
Psychology—General — M
Sociology — M
Writing — M

SOUTHEASTERN OKLAHOMA STATE UNIVERSITY
Clinical Psychology — M
Counseling Psychology — M

SOUTHEASTERN UNIVERSITY (FL)
Counseling Psychology — M
Pastoral Ministry and Counseling — M

SOUTHEAST MISSOURI STATE UNIVERSITY
Counseling Psychology — M,O
Criminal Justice and Criminology — M
English — M
Historic Preservation — M,O
History — M,O
Public Administration — M
Public History — M,O
Writing — M

SOUTHERN ADVENTIST UNIVERSITY
Counseling Psychology — M
Missions and Missiology — M
Psychology—General — M
Religion — M
Theology — M

SOUTHERN ARKANSAS UNIVERSITY–MAGNOLIA
Public Administration — M

SOUTHERN BAPTIST THEOLOGICAL SEMINARY
Missions and Missiology — M,D
Music — M,D
Pastoral Ministry and Counseling — M,D
Philosophy — M,D
Religion — M,D
Theology — M,D

SOUTHERN CALIFORNIA INSTITUTE OF ARCHITECTURE
Architecture — M

SOUTHERN CALIFORNIA SEMINARY
Counseling Psychology — M,D
Marriage and Family Therapy — M,D
Psychology—General — M,D
Religion — M
Theology — M,D

SOUTHERN CONNECTICUT STATE UNIVERSITY
English — M
History — M
Political Science — M
Psychology—General — M
School Psychology — M,O
Sociology — M
Sport Psychology — M
Women's Studies — M

SOUTHERN EVANGELICAL SEMINARY
Jewish Studies — M,D,O
Missions and Missiology — M,D,O
Near and Middle Eastern Studies — M,D,O

Pastoral Ministry and Counseling — M,D,O
Philosophy — M,D,O
Religion — M,D,O
Theology — M,D,O

SOUTHERN ILLINOIS UNIVERSITY CARBONDALE
Agricultural Economics and
  Agribusiness — M
Anthropology — M,D
Applied Arts and Design—
  General — M
Architecture — M
Art/Fine Arts — M
Clinical Psychology — M,D
Communication—General — M,D
Counseling Psychology — M,D
Criminal Justice and Criminology — M
Cultural Studies — M
Economics — M,D
English — M,D
Experimental Psychology — M,D
Geography — M,D
History — M,D
Homeland Security — M
Journalism — D
Linguistics — M
Mass Communication — M
Media Studies — M
Music — M
Philosophy — M,D
Political Science — M,D
Psychology—General — M,D
Public Administration — M
Rhetoric — M,D
Sociology — M,D
Speech and Interpersonal
  Communication — M,D
Theater — M,D
Writing — M

SOUTHERN ILLINOIS UNIVERSITY EDWARDSVILLE
Art Therapy — M
Art/Fine Arts — M
Clinical Psychology — M
Corporate and Organizational
  Communication — M
Economics — M
English — M,O
Geography — M
Health Communication — M
History — M
Industrial and Organizational
  Psychology — M
Mass Communication — M
Media Studies — O
Museum Studies — O
Music — M
Psychology—General — M,O
Public Administration — M
School Psychology — O
Sociology — M
Speech and Interpersonal
  Communication — M
Sport Psychology — M
Writing — M

SOUTHERN METHODIST UNIVERSITY
Anthropology — M,D
Applied Economics — M,D
Art History — M,D
Art/Fine Arts — M
Arts Administration — M
Clinical Psychology — D
Conflict Resolution and
  Mediation/Peace Studies — M
Economics — M,D
English — M,D
Ethics — M,D
Experimental Psychology — M,D
History — M,D
Liberal Studies — M
Medieval and Renaissance Studies — M
Music — M
Photography — M
Psychology—General — D
Religion — M,D
Sustainable Development — M,D
Theater — M
Theology — M,D

SOUTHERN NAZARENE UNIVERSITY
Counseling Psychology — M
Marriage and Family Therapy — M
Psychology—General — M

SOUTHERN NEW HAMPSHIRE UNIVERSITY
Child Development — M,D,O
Conflict Resolution and
  Mediation/Peace Studies — M,O
Ethics — M,O
Industrial and Labor Relations — M,O
Internet and Interactive
  Multimedia — M,O
Psychology—General — M,O
Writing — M,O

SOUTHERN OREGON UNIVERSITY
Counseling Psychology — M
French — M
Interdisciplinary Studies — M
Music — M
Psychology—General — M
Spanish — M
Theater — M

SOUTHERN POLYTECHNIC STATE UNIVERSITY
Communication—General — M,O
Graphic Design — M,O

---

*M—masters degree; D—doctorate; O—other advanced degree; *—Close-Up and/or Display*

Internet and Interactive Multimedia M,O
Technical Communication M,O

SOUTHERN UNIVERSITY AND AGRICULTURAL AND MECHANICAL COLLEGE
Criminal Justice and Criminology M
History M
Mass Communication M
Political Science M
Psychology—General M
Public Administration M
Public Policy D
Rehabilitation Counseling M
Social Sciences M

SOUTHERN UNIVERSITY AT NEW ORLEANS
Criminal Justice and Criminology M
Museum Studies M

SOUTHERN UTAH UNIVERSITY
Arts Administration M
Communication—General M
Public Administration M

SOUTHERN WESLEYAN UNIVERSITY
Pastoral Ministry and Counseling M

SOUTH UNIVERSITY (AL)
Counseling Psychology M
Criminal Justice and Criminology M
Public Administration M

SOUTH UNIVERSITY
Counseling Psychology M
Criminal Justice and Criminology M
Public Administration M

SOUTH UNIVERSITY
Criminal Justice and Criminology M

SOUTH UNIVERSITY (GA)
Counseling Psychology M
Criminal Justice and Criminology M
Pastoral Ministry and Counseling D
Public Administration M

SOUTH UNIVERSITY (MI)
Counseling Psychology M
Pastoral Ministry and Counseling D

SOUTH UNIVERSITY (NC)
Counseling Psychology M

SOUTH UNIVERSITY (OH)
Clinical Psychology M
Counseling Psychology M

SOUTH UNIVERSITY (SC)
Counseling Psychology M
Criminal Justice and Criminology M

SOUTH UNIVERSITY (TX)
Counseling Psychology M

SOUTH UNIVERSITY
Counseling Psychology M

SOUTH UNIVERSITY
Counseling Psychology M

SOUTHWESTERN ASSEMBLIES OF GOD UNIVERSITY
Counseling Psychology M
History M
Missions and Missiology M
Pastoral Ministry and Counseling M
Religion M
Theology M

SOUTHWESTERN BAPTIST THEOLOGICAL SEMINARY
Music M,D
Pastoral Ministry and Counseling M,D
Theology M,D

SOUTHWESTERN CHRISTIAN UNIVERSITY
Missions and Missiology M
Pastoral Ministry and Counseling M

SOUTHWESTERN COLLEGE (KS)
Criminal Justice and Criminology M
Theology M

SOUTHWESTERN COLLEGE (NM)
Art Therapy M
Counseling Psychology M,O
Health Psychology O
Psychology—General O
Social Psychology O
Thanatology M,O

SOUTHWESTERN OKLAHOMA STATE UNIVERSITY
Music M
School Psychology M

SOUTHWEST UNIVERSITY
Criminal Justice and Criminology M

SOUTHWEST UNIVERSITY OF VISUAL ARTS
Art/Fine Arts M
Photography M

SPALDING UNIVERSITY
Applied Behavior Analysis M
Clinical Psychology M,D
Corporate and Organizational Communication M
Psychology—General M,D
Writing M

SPERTUS INSTITUTE FOR JEWISH LEARNING AND LEADERSHIP
Jewish Studies M,D

SPRING ARBOR UNIVERSITY
Child and Family Studies M
Communication—General M
Counseling Psychology M
Pastoral Ministry and Counseling M
Theology M

SPRINGFIELD COLLEGE
Addictions/Substance Abuse Counseling M
Art Therapy M,O
Clinical Psychology M,D,O
Counseling Psychology M,D,O
Industrial and Organizational Psychology M,D,O
Rehabilitation Counseling M
Sport Psychology M,D,O

SPRING HILL COLLEGE
Art/Fine Arts M,O
English M,O
Ethics M,O
History M,O
Liberal Studies M,O
Pastoral Ministry and Counseling M,O
Theology M,O

STANFORD UNIVERSITY
Anthropology M,D
Applied Arts and Design—General M,D,O
Archaeology M,D
Art/Fine Arts M,D
Asian Languages M,D
Asian Studies M
Chinese M,D
Classics M,D
Communication—General M,D
Comparative Literature D
Cultural Studies M,D
East European and Russian Studies M
Economics D
English M,D
Film, Television, and Video Production M,D
French M,D
Genetic Counseling M,D
German M,D
History M,D
International Affairs M
International Development M
Italian M,D
Japanese M,D
Journalism M,D
Linguistics M,D
Media Studies M,D
Music M,D
National Security M
Philosophy M,D
Political Science D
Psychology—General D
Religion M,D
Slavic Languages M,D
Sociology D
Spanish M,D
Sustainable Development M,D,O
Theater D

STARR KING SCHOOL FOR THE MINISTRY
Theology M

STATE UNIVERSITY OF NEW YORK AT FREDONIA
Interdisciplinary Studies M

STATE UNIVERSITY OF NEW YORK AT NEW PALTZ
Art/Fine Arts M
Counseling Psychology M,O
English M
French M,O
Music M
Psychology—General M,O
Spanish M,O
Therapies—Dance, Drama, and Music M

STATE UNIVERSITY OF NEW YORK AT OSWEGO
Art/Fine Arts M
Child and Family Studies M
Consumer Economics M
Counseling Psychology M
English M
History M

STATE UNIVERSITY OF NEW YORK AT PLATTSBURGH
Clinical Psychology M,O
Counseling Psychology M,O
Psychology—General M,O
School Psychology M,O

STATE UNIVERSITY OF NEW YORK COLLEGE AT CORTLAND
English M
History M

STATE UNIVERSITY OF NEW YORK COLLEGE AT OLD WESTBURY
Counseling Psychology M

STATE UNIVERSITY OF NEW YORK COLLEGE AT ONEONTA
Museum Studies M

STATE UNIVERSITY OF NEW YORK COLLEGE AT POTSDAM
Communication—General M
English M
Music M

STATE UNIVERSITY OF NEW YORK COLLEGE OF ENVIRONMENTAL SCIENCE AND FORESTRY
Economics M,D
Geographic Information Systems M,D
Landscape Architecture M
Sustainable Development M,D,O
Urban and Regional Planning M,D
Urban Design M

STATE UNIVERSITY OF NEW YORK EMPIRE STATE COLLEGE
Economic Development M
Industrial and Labor Relations M
Liberal Studies M
Public Policy M

STEPHEN F. AUSTIN STATE UNIVERSITY
Applied Arts and Design—General M
Art/Fine Arts M
Communication—General M
English M
Family and Consumer Sciences-General M
History M
Interdisciplinary Studies M
Mass Communication M
Music M
Psychology—General M
Public Administration M
School Psychology M

STEPHENS COLLEGE
Counseling Psychology M,O
Marriage and Family Therapy M,O

STETSON UNIVERSITY
Marriage and Family Therapy M

STEVENS INSTITUTE OF TECHNOLOGY
Communication—General M,D,O
Computer Art and Design M,D,O
Corporate and Organizational Communication O
Ethics M,O
Internet and Interactive Multimedia M,D,O

STEVENSON UNIVERSITY
Communication—General M
Forensic Sciences M

STOCKTON UNIVERSITY
American Studies M,O
Criminal Justice and Criminology M
Holocaust and Genocide Studies M

STONY BROOK UNIVERSITY, STATE UNIVERSITY OF NEW YORK
Addictions/Substance Abuse Counseling M,O
African Studies M,O
Anthropology M,D
Art History M,D
Art/Fine Arts M
Clinical Psychology D
Cognitive Sciences D
Comparative Literature M,D,O
Cultural Studies M,D,O
Economics M,D
English M,D,O
Experimental Psychology D
French M
Geographic Information Systems O
Health Communication M,O
Health Psychology D
Hispanic and Latin American Languages M,D
History M,D
Italian M
Journalism M,O
Liberal Studies M,O
Linguistics M,D
Music M,D
Philosophy M,D,O
Political Science M,D
Psychology—General M,D
Public Policy M
Romance Languages M
Social Psychology D
Social Sciences M,O
Sociology M,D
Theater M
Women's Studies O
Writing M,O

STRAYER UNIVERSITY
Public Administration M

SUFFOLK UNIVERSITY
Applied Arts and Design—General M
Clinical Psychology M,D,O
Communication—General M
Corporate and Organizational Communication M
Counseling Psychology M,D,O
Criminal Justice and Criminology M
Economics M
Ethics M,O
Graphic Design M
Interior Design M
Political Science M,O
Psychology—General M,D,O
Public Administration M,O
Public Policy M,O
School Psychology M,D,O

SUL ROSS STATE UNIVERSITY
Art History M
Art/Fine Arts M
Clinical Psychology M
Criminal Justice and Criminology M
English M
History M
Political Science M
Psychology—General M

SUMMIT UNIVERSITY
Communication—General M,D
Cultural Studies M
English M
Missions and Missiology M,D
Pastoral Ministry and Counseling M,D
Philosophy M
Religion M,D
Theology M,D

SYRACUSE UNIVERSITY
Addictions/Substance Abuse Counseling O
African Studies M
African-American Studies M
Anthropology M,D
Applied Arts and Design—General M
Architecture M
Art History M
Art/Fine Arts M
Arts Administration M,O
Arts Journalism M
Broadcast Journalism M
Child and Family Studies M,D
Clinical Psychology M,D
Communication—General M,D
Computer Art and Design M
Conflict Resolution and Mediation/Peace Studies O
Disability Studies O
Economics M,D
English M,D
Experimental Psychology D
Film, Television, and Video Production M
Film, Television, and Video Theory and Criticism M
Forensic Sciences M
French M
Geography M,D
Historic Preservation O
History M,D
Illustration M
International Affairs M
Journalism M
Linguistics M
Marriage and Family Therapy M
Mass Communication M,D
Media Studies M
Museum Studies M
Music M
Philosophy M,D
Photography M
Political Science M,D,O
Public Administration M,D,O
Religion M,D
Rhetoric M,D
School Psychology M,D,O
Social Psychology D
Social Sciences M,D
Sociology D
Spanish M
Urban and Regional Planning O
Writing M,D

TALMUDIC COLLEGE OF FLORIDA
Theology M

TARLETON STATE UNIVERSITY
Counseling Psychology M,O
Criminal Justice and Criminology M
English M
History M
Political Science M
School Psychology M,O

TAYLOR COLLEGE AND SEMINARY
Cultural Studies M,O
Missions and Missiology M,O
Theology M,O

TEACHERS COLLEGE, COLUMBIA UNIVERSITY
Anthropology M,D
Applied Behavior Analysis M,D
Applied Psychology M,D
Arts Administration M
Clinical Psychology D
Communication—General M,D
Counseling Psychology M,D
Developmental Psychology M,D
Economics M,D
Industrial and Organizational Psychology M
Interdisciplinary Studies M,D
Linguistics M,D
Political Science M,D
School Psychology M,D
Social Psychology M
Sociology M,D

TELSHE YESHIVA–CHICAGO
Jewish Studies O

TEMPLE BAPTIST SEMINARY
Archaeology M,D
Religion M,D
Theology M,D

TEMPLE UNIVERSITY
African-American Studies M,D
Anthropology D
Architecture M
Art History M,D
Art/Fine Arts M
Arts Administration M,D
Communication—General M,D
Corporate and Organizational Communication M
Counseling Psychology M,D,O
Criminal Justice and Criminology M,D
Dance M,D
Economics M,D
English M,D
Film, Television, and Video Production M
Geography M,D
Gerontology M,D
Graphic Design M
History M,D
Industrial and Organizational Psychology M,D,O

Journalism M
Landscape Architecture M
Media Studies M
Music M,D
Philosophy M,D
Photography M
Political Science M,D
Psychology—General D
Religion M,D
School Psychology M,D,O
Social Psychology M,D,O
Sociology M,D
Spanish M,D
Sustainable Development M
Textile Design M
Theater M
Therapies—Dance, Drama, and
　Music M,D
Urban and Regional Planning M
Urban Design M,D
Urban Studies M,D
Writing M

TENNESSEE STATE UNIVERSITY
Counseling Psychology M,D
Criminal Justice and Criminology M
Family and Consumer
　Sciences-General M,D
Psychology—General M,D
Public Administration M,D
School Psychology M,D

TENNESSEE TECHNOLOGICAL UNIVERSITY
Applied Behavior Analysis D
Counseling Psychology M,O
English M
Internet and Interactive
　Multimedia M
School Psychology M,O

TEXAS A&M INTERNATIONAL UNIVERSITY
Counseling Psychology M
Criminal Justice and Criminology M
English M,D
Hispanic Studies M,D
History M,D
Political Science M,D
Psychology—General M
Public Administration M
Social Sciences M
Translation and Interpretation M,D

TEXAS A&M UNIVERSITY
Agricultural Economics and
　Agribusiness M,D
Anthropology M,D
Architecture M,D,O
Art/Fine Arts M
Clinical Psychology M,D
Cognitive Sciences M,D
Communication—General M,D
Counseling Psychology M,D
Cultural Studies M
Developmental Psychology M,D
Economics M,D
English M,D
Geography M,D
History M,D
Homeland Security M,O
Industrial and Organizational
　Psychology M,D
International Affairs M,O
Landscape Architecture M,D
Music M
National Security M,O
Philosophy M,D
Political Science M,D
Psychology—General M,D
Public Administration M,O
Public Affairs M,O
School Psychology M,D
Social Psychology M,D
Sociology M,D
Spanish M,D
Urban and Regional Planning M,D

TEXAS A&M UNIVERSITY–CENTRAL TEXAS
Clinical Psychology M,O
Criminal Justice and Criminology M,O
Experimental Psychology M,O
History M,O
Liberal Studies M,O
Marriage and Family Therapy M,O
Political Science M,O
School Psychology M,O

TEXAS A&M UNIVERSITY–CORPUS CHRISTI
Art/Fine Arts M
Communication—General M
English M
History M
Psychology—General M
Public Administration M

TEXAS A&M UNIVERSITY–KINGSVILLE
Criminal Justice and Criminology M
Cultural Studies M
English M
Family and Consumer
　Sciences-General M
Hispanic Studies D
History M
Political Science M
Psychology—General M
Sociology M
Spanish M
Sustainable Development D

TEXAS A&M UNIVERSITY–SAN ANTONIO
English M

TEXAS A&M UNIVERSITY–TEXARKANA
Counseling Psychology M
English M
Interdisciplinary Studies M
Psychology—General M

TEXAS CHRISTIAN UNIVERSITY
American Studies M,D
Art History M
Art/Fine Arts M
Cognitive Sciences M,D
Criminal Justice and Criminology M
Dance M
Developmental Psychology M,D
English M,D
Experimental Psychology M,D
History M,D
Journalism M
Liberal Studies M
Mass Communication M
Music M,D
Photography M
Psychology—General M,D
Rhetoric M,D
Social Psychology M,D
Speech and Interpersonal
　Communication M

TEXAS SOUTHERN UNIVERSITY
Art/Fine Arts M
Communication—General M
Criminal Justice and Criminology M,D
English M
Family and Consumer
　Sciences-General M
History M
Music M
Psychology—General M
Public Administration M
Sociology M
Urban and Regional Planning M,D

TEXAS STATE UNIVERSITY
Anthropology M
Child and Family Studies M
Communication—General M
Computer Art and Design M
Criminal Justice and Criminology M,D
English M
Ethics M
Family and Consumer
　Sciences-General M
Geographic Information Systems M,D
Geography M,D
Gerontology M
Graphic Design M
History M
Interdisciplinary Studies M
International Affairs M
Mass Communication M
Music M
Philosophy M
Political Science M
Psychology—General M
Public Administration M
Rhetoric M
School Psychology O
Social Psychology M
Sociology M
Spanish M
Sustainable Development M
Technical Communication M
Theater M
Urban and Regional Planning M
Writing M

TEXAS TECH UNIVERSITY
Agricultural Economics and
　Agribusiness M,D
Anthropology M
Applied Economics M,D
Architecture M,D
Art History M
Art/Fine Arts M,D
Child and Family Studies M,D
Classics M,D
Clinical Psychology M,D
Communication—General M
Consumer Economics M,D
Counseling Psychology M,D
Cultural Studies M,D
Economics M,D
English M,D
Environmental Design M,D
Experimental Psychology M,D
Family and Consumer
　Sciences-General M,D
Forensic Sciences M
Geography M,D
German M,D
Historic Preservation M,D
History M,D
Human Development M,D
Interdisciplinary Studies M,D
Interior Design M,D
Landscape Architecture M
Linguistics M,D
Marriage and Family Therapy M,D
Mass Communication M,D
Museum Studies M,D
Music M,D
Philosophy M
Political Science M,D
Psychology—General M,D
Public Administration M,D
Rhetoric M
Romance Languages M,D
Sociology M

Spanish M,D
Sustainable Development M,D
Technical Writing M,D
Theater M

TEXAS TECH UNIVERSITY HEALTH SCIENCES CENTER
Rehabilitation Counseling M

TEXAS WESLEYAN UNIVERSITY
Counseling Psychology M,D
Marriage and Family Therapy M,D

TEXAS WOMAN'S UNIVERSITY
Art/Fine Arts M
Child and Family Studies M,D
Child Development M
Counseling Psychology M,D,O
Dance M,D
English M,D
History M
Marriage and Family Therapy M,D
Music M
Political Science M
Psychology—General M,D,O
Rhetoric M
School Psychology M,D,O
Sociology M,D
Theater M
Women's Studies M,D

THOMAS EDISON STATE COLLEGE
Homeland Security O
Liberal Studies M
Public Administration M

THOMAS JEFFERSON UNIVERSITY
Applied Economics M,D,O
Marriage and Family Therapy M

THOMAS UNIVERSITY
Rehabilitation Counseling M
Social Psychology M

TIFFIN UNIVERSITY
Art/Fine Arts M
Communication—General M
Criminal Justice and Criminology M
English M
Film, Television, and Video
　Theory and Criticism M
Forensic Psychology M
Homeland Security M
Humanities M
Psychology—General M
Writing M

TORONTO SCHOOL OF THEOLOGY
Theology M,D

TOURO COLLEGE
Counseling Psychology M
Industrial and Organizational
　Psychology M
Internet and Interactive
　Multimedia M
Jewish Studies M
Psychology—General M
School Psychology M

TOWSON UNIVERSITY
Art History M
Art/Fine Arts M
Child and Family Studies M,O
Clinical Psychology M
Communication—General M
Corporate and Organizational
　Communication M
Counseling Psychology O
Forensic Sciences M
Geography M
Gerontology M,O
Homeland Security M,O
Humanities M
Internet and Interactive
　Multimedia M,D,O
Jewish Studies M,O
Liberal Studies M
Music M
School Psychology O
Social Sciences M
Theater M
Women's Studies M,O
Writing M

TRENT UNIVERSITY
American Indian/Native American
　Studies M,D
Anthropology M
Canadian Studies M
Cultural Studies D
Geography M,D

TREVECCA NAZARENE UNIVERSITY
Pastoral Ministry and Counseling M
Religion M
Theology M

TRIDENT UNIVERSITY INTERNATIONAL
Conflict Resolution and
　Mediation/Peace Studies M,D
Criminal Justice and Criminology M,D
Emergency Management M,D,O
Public Administration M,D

TRINE UNIVERSITY
Criminal Justice and Criminology M
Emergency Management M
Forensic Psychology M
Public Administration M

TRINITY CHRISTIAN COLLEGE
Counseling Psychology M

TRINITY COLLEGE (CANADA)
Music M,D,O

Spanish M,D
Sustainable Development M,D
Technical Writing M,D
Theater M

Pastoral Ministry and Counseling M,D,O
Theology M,D,O

TRINITY COLLEGE (UNITED STATES)
American Studies M
Cultural Studies M
English M
Media Studies M
Museum Studies M
Public Policy M
Writing M

TRINITY INTERNATIONAL UNIVERSITY
Archaeology M,D,O
Communication—General M
Counseling Psychology M,D,O
Missions and Missiology M,D,O
Pastoral Ministry and Counseling M,D,O
Theology M,D,O

TRINITY INTERNATIONAL UNIVERSITY, SOUTH FLORIDA CAMPUS
Counseling Psychology M
Religion M,O

TRINITY LUTHERAN SEMINARY
African-American Studies M
Missions and Missiology M
Music M
Pastoral Ministry and Counseling M
Theology M

TRINITY SCHOOL FOR MINISTRY
Missions and Missiology M,D,O
Pastoral Ministry and Counseling M,D,O
Religion M,D,O
Theology M,D,O

TRINITY UNIVERSITY
School Psychology M

TRINITY WASHINGTON UNIVERSITY
Clinical Psychology M
Communication—General M
Counseling Psychology M
National Security M

TRINITY WESTERN UNIVERSITY
Counseling Psychology M
English M
History M
Humanities M
Interdisciplinary Studies M
Linguistics M
Pastoral Ministry and Counseling M,D
Philosophy M
Theology M,D

TRI-STATE BIBLE COLLEGE
Theology M

TROPICAL AGRICULTURE RESEARCH AND HIGHER EDUCATION CENTER
Agricultural Economics and
　Agribusiness M,D

TROY UNIVERSITY
Addictions/Substance Abuse
　Counseling M,O
Clinical Psychology M,O
Communication—General M
Corporate and Organizational
　Communication M
Criminal Justice and Criminology M,O
Economic Development M
History M
International Affairs M
National Security M
Public Administration M
Rehabilitation Counseling M,O
School Psychology M,O
Social Psychology M,O
Social Sciences M

TRUMAN STATE UNIVERSITY
English M
Music M

TUFTS UNIVERSITY
Archaeology M
Art History M
Art/Fine Arts M
Child and Family Studies M,D
Child Development M,D
Classics M
Cognitive Sciences M,D
Conflict Resolution and
　Mediation/Peace Studies M,D
Economics M,D
English M,D
Family and Consumer
　Sciences-General M,D
French M
German M
Health Communication M,D,O
History M
Human Development M,D
Interdisciplinary Studies D
International Affairs M,D
International Development M,D
Museum Studies M,D,O
Music M
Philosophy M
Psychology—General M,D
Public Administration O
Public Policy M
School Psychology M,O
Theater M
Urban and Regional Planning M
Urban Studies M

TULANE UNIVERSITY
Anthropology M,D
Architecture M
Art History M,D
Art/Fine Arts M,D

Classics — M
Dance — M
Economics — M,D
Emergency Management — M,D
English — M,D
French — M,D
Health Communication — M,D
History — M,D
Interdisciplinary Studies — D
International Development — M,D
Latin American Studies — M,D
Liberal Studies — M
Music — M
Philosophy — M,D
Political Science — D
Portuguese — M,D
Psychology—General — M,D
Sociology — D
Spanish — M,D
Theater — M

TUSKEGEE UNIVERSITY
Agricultural Economics and
  Agribusiness — M

TYNDALE UNIVERSITY COLLEGE & SEMINARY
Missions and Missiology — M,O
Pastoral Ministry and Counseling — M,O
Theology — M,O

UNIFICATION THEOLOGICAL SEMINARY
Pastoral Ministry and Counseling — M,D
Religion — M,D
Theology — M,D

UNIFORMED SERVICES UNIVERSITY OF THE HEALTH SCIENCES
Clinical Psychology — D
Psychology—General — D

UNION COLLEGE (KY)
Clinical Psychology — M
Counseling Psychology — M
Psychology—General — M
School Psychology — M

UNION GRADUATE COLLEGE
Chinese — M,O
Ethics — M,O

UNION INSTITUTE & UNIVERSITY
Clinical Psychology — M,D
Cultural Studies — M
Ethics — D
History — M,D
Humanities — D
Interdisciplinary Studies — M,D
Psychology—General — M,D
Public Policy — M,D
Writing — M

UNION THEOLOGICAL SEMINARY IN THE CITY OF NEW YORK
Theology — M,D

UNION UNIVERSITY
Cultural Studies — M
Pastoral Ministry and Counseling — M,D
Religion — M

UNITED STATES ARMY COMMAND AND GENERAL STAFF COLLEGE
Military and Defense Studies — M

UNITED STATES INTERNATIONAL UNIVERSITY
Addictions/Substance Abuse
  Counseling — M
Conflict Resolution and
  Mediation/Peace Studies — M
Counseling Psychology — M
Health Psychology — M
International Affairs — M

UNITED TALMUDICAL SEMINARY
Theology

UNITED THEOLOGICAL SEMINARY
Theology — M,D

UNITED THEOLOGICAL SEMINARY OF THE TWIN CITIES
Art/Fine Arts — M,D,O
Asian Studies — M,D,O
Conflict Resolution and
  Mediation/Peace Studies — M,D,O
Ethnic Studies — M,D,O
Humanities — M,D,O
Pastoral Ministry and Counseling — M,D,O
Religion — M,D,O
Theology — M,D,O
Women's Studies — M,D,O

UNIVERSIDAD AUTONOMA DE GUADALAJARA
Architecture — M,D
Computer Art and Design — M,D
Corporate and Organizational
  Communication — M,D
Film, Television, and Video
  Production — M,D
Internet and Interactive
  Multimedia — M,D
Philosophy — M,D
Public Policy — M,D
Spanish — M,D
Translation and Interpretation — M,D

UNIVERSIDAD CENTRAL DEL CARIBE
Addictions/Substance Abuse
  Counseling — M

UNIVERSIDAD DE IBEROAMERICA
Clinical Psychology — M,D
Forensic Psychology — M,D

UNIVERSIDAD DE LAS AMERICAS, A.C.
International Affairs — M

Marriage and Family Therapy — M
Psychology—General — M

UNIVERSIDAD DE LAS AMÉRICAS PUEBLA
American Studies — M
Anthropology — M
Archaeology — M
Computer Art and Design — M
Economics — M
English — M
Linguistics — M
Psychology—General — M

UNIVERSIDAD DEL ESTE
Agricultural Economics and
  Agribusiness — M
Criminal Justice and Criminology — M
Public Policy — M

UNIVERSIDAD DEL TURABO
Art/Fine Arts — M
Arts Administration — M
Conflict Resolution and
  Mediation/Peace Studies — M
Counseling Psychology — M,D,O
Criminal Justice and Criminology — M
Forensic Sciences — M

UNIVERSIDAD IBEROAMERICANA
Corporate and Organizational
  Communication — M,D

UNIVERSIDAD METROPOLITANA
Counseling Psychology — M

UNIVERSIDAD NACIONAL PEDRO HENRIQUEZ URENA
Architecture — M
Historic Preservation — M
International Affairs — M
Political Science — M

UNIVERSITÉ DE MONCTON
Economics — M
French — M,D
History — M
Public Administration — M

UNIVERSITÉ DE MONTRÉAL
Anthropology — M,D
Art History — M,D
Classics — M
Communication—General — M,D
Comparative Literature — M,D
Criminal Justice and Criminology — M,D
Demography and Population Studies — M,D
Developmental Psychology — M,D
Economics — M,D,O
Emergency Management — O
English — M,D
Environmental Design — M,D,O
Film, Television, and Video
  Theory and Criticism — M,D
French — M,D
Genetic Counseling — O
Geography — M,D,O
German — M
Hispanic and Latin American
  Languages — M,D
History — M,D
Industrial and Labor Relations — M,D,O
International Affairs — M,O
Linguistics — M,D,O
Museum Studies — M
Music — M,D,O
Philosophy — M,D
Political Science — M,D
Psychology—General — M,D
Public Policy — O
Religion — M,D,O
Sociology — M,D
Spanish — M
Theology — M,D,O
Translation and Interpretation — M,D,O
Urban and Regional Planning — M,D,O

UNIVERSITÉ DE SAINT-BONIFACE
Canadian Studies — M

UNIVERSITÉ DE SHERBROOKE
Canadian Studies — M,D
Comparative Literature — M,D
Conflict Resolution and
  Mediation/Peace Studies — M,D,O
Corporate and Organizational
  Communication — M
Economic Development — D
Economics — M
Ethics — M,D,O
French — M,D
Geography — M
Gerontology — M
History — M
Linguistics — M,D
Philosophy — M,D,O
Psychology—General — M
Public Administration — M
Religion — M,D,O
Theater — M,D
Theology — M,D,O

UNIVERSITÉ DU QUÉBEC À CHICOUTIMI
Art/Fine Arts — M
Canadian Studies — M
Comparative Literature — M
Ethics — O
French — M
Linguistics — M
Theology — M,D

UNIVERSITÉ DU QUÉBEC À MONTRÉAL
Art History — M,D
Art/Fine Arts — M
Communication—General — M,D
Comparative Literature — M,D
Dance — M
Economics — M,D

Geographic Information Systems — O
Geography — M
History — M,D
Linguistics — M,D
Museum Studies — M
Philosophy — M,D
Political Science — M,D
Psychology—General — D
Public Administration — M
Religion — M,D
Sociology — M,D
Urban Studies — M,D

UNIVERSITÉ DU QUÉBEC À RIMOUSKI
Comparative Literature — M,D
Ethics — M,O
Social Psychology — M
Urban and Regional Planning — M,D,O

UNIVERSITÉ DU QUÉBEC À TROIS-RIVIÈRES
Communication—General — M,O
Comparative Literature — M
Industrial and Labor Relations — O
Philosophy — M,D
Psychology—General — D,O

UNIVERSITÉ DU QUÉBEC, ÉCOLE NATIONALE D'ADMINISTRATION PUBLIQUE
Public Administration — D,O
Urban Studies — M

UNIVERSITÉ DU QUÉBEC EN OUTAOUAIS
Industrial and Labor Relations — M,D,O
Urban and Regional Planning — M

UNIVERSITÉ DU QUÉBEC, INSTITUT NATIONAL DE LA RECHERCHE SCIENTIFIQUE
Demography and Population Studies — M,D,O
Urban Studies — M,D,O

UNIVERSITÉ LAVAL
Agricultural Economics and
  Agribusiness — M
Anthropology — M,D
Archaeology — M,D
Architecture — M
Art History — M,D
Art/Fine Arts — M
Clinical Psychology — D
Comparative Literature — M,D
Consumer Economics — O
Economics — M,D
English — M,D
Ethics — O
Ethnic Studies — M,D
Film, Television, and Video
  Theory and Criticism — M,D
Geographic Information Systems — M,O
Geography — M,D
Gerontology — O
Graphic Design — M
History — M,D
Industrial and Labor Relations — M,D
International Affairs — M,D
Journalism — O
Linguistics — M,D
Mass Communication — M,D
Museum Studies — O
Music — M,D
Philosophy — M,D
Political Science — M,D
Psychology—General — D
Religion — M,D
Rural Planning and Studies — O
Social Psychology — D
Sociology — M,D
Spanish — M,D
Theater — M,D
Theology — M,D
Translation and Interpretation — M,O
Urban and Regional Planning — M,D
Women's Studies — M

UNIVERSITY AT ALBANY, STATE UNIVERSITY OF NEW YORK
African Studies — M
African-American Studies — M
Anthropology — M,D
Art/Fine Arts — M
Clinical Psychology — M,D
Cognitive Sciences — M,D
Communication—General — M,D
Counseling Psychology — M,D
Criminal Justice and Criminology — M,D
Demography and Population Studies — M,D,O
Economics — M,D,O
English — M,D
Forensic Sciences — M,D
Geography — M
History — M,D,O
Homeland Security — M,D,O
Industrial and Organizational
  Psychology — M,D
Latin American Studies — M,D,O
Liberal Studies — M
Philosophy — M,D
Political Science — M,D
Psychology—General — M,D
Public Administration — M,D,O
Public History — M,D,O
Public Policy — M,D,O
School Psychology — M,D
Social Psychology — M,D
Sociology — M,D
Spanish — M,D
Urban and Regional Planning — M
Urban Studies — M,D,O
Women's Studies — M

UNIVERSITY AT BUFFALO, THE STATE UNIVERSITY OF NEW YORK
American Studies — M,D,O

Anthropology — M,D
Architecture — M
Art History — M,D
Art/Fine Arts — M,D
Arts Administration — M
Canadian Studies — M,D,O
Classics — M,D,O
Communication—General — M,D
Comparative Literature — M,D
Counseling Psychology — M,D,O
Cultural Studies — M,D,O
Economics — M,D
English — M,D
Film, Television, and Video
  Theory and Criticism — M,D,O
French — M,D,O
Gender Studies — M,D,O
Geographic Information Systems — M,D,O
Geography — M,D,O
German — M,D,O
Historic Preservation — M,D,O
History — M,D
Latin American Studies — M,D,O
Linguistics — M,D
Media Studies — M,D,O
Music — M,D,O
Philosophy — M,D
Political Science — M,D
Psychology—General — M,D
Rehabilitation Counseling — M,D,O
Romance Languages — M,D
Sociology — M,D
Spanish — M,D
Theater — M
Urban and Regional Planning — M,D
Urban Design — M,D,O

UNIVERSITY OF ADVANCING TECHNOLOGY
Internet and Interactive
  Multimedia — M

THE UNIVERSITY OF AKRON
Arts Administration — M
Child and Family Studies — M,D
Child Development — M
Clinical Psychology — M,D
Clothing and Textiles — M
Communication—General — M
Counseling Psychology — M,D
Economics — M
English — M
Gerontology — M
History — M,D
Industrial and Organizational
  Psychology — M,D
Marriage and Family Therapy — M
Music — M
Political Science — M
Psychology—General — M,D
Public Administration — M
School Psychology — M,D
Sociology — M,D
Spanish — M
Theater — M
Writing — M

THE UNIVERSITY OF ALABAMA
American Studies — M
Anthropology — M,D
Art History — M
Art/Fine Arts — M
Child and Family Studies — M
Clinical Psychology — D
Clothing and Textiles — M
Communication—General — M,D
Consumer Economics — M
Criminal Justice and Criminology — M
Economics — M,D
English — M,D
Experimental Psychology — D
Family and Consumer
  Sciences-General — M,D
Film, Television, and Video
  Production — M
French — M,D
Geographic Information Systems — M
Geography — M
German — M,D
History — M,D
Human Development — M
Interdisciplinary Studies — D
Journalism — M
Linguistics — M,D
Mass Communication — D
Media Studies — M
Music — M
Photography — M
Political Science — M
Psychology—General — D
Public Administration — M,D
Rhetoric — M
Romance Languages — M
Spanish — M,D
Speech and Interpersonal
  Communication — M
Theater — M
Urban and Regional Planning — M
Women's Studies — M
Writing — M,D

THE UNIVERSITY OF ALABAMA AT BIRMINGHAM
Anthropology — M
Art History — M
Clinical Psychology — M
Communication—General — M
Criminal Justice and Criminology — M
Developmental Psychology — M,D
English — M
Forensic Sciences — M
Genetic Counseling — M
Health Psychology — M,D
History — M
Interdisciplinary Studies — D

Music	M
Psychology—General	M,D
Public Administration	M
Rhetoric	M
Sociology	M
Writing	M

THE UNIVERSITY OF ALABAMA IN HUNTSVILLE

Criminal Justice and Criminology	M,O
English	M,O
History	M
Industrial and Organizational Psychology	M
Interdisciplinary Studies	M,D,O
Psychology—General	M
Public Affairs	M
Technical Writing	M,O

UNIVERSITY OF ALASKA ANCHORAGE

Anthropology	M
Clinical Psychology	M,D
English	M
Interdisciplinary Studies	M
Psychology—General	M,D
Public Administration	M
Social Psychology	M
Writing	M

UNIVERSITY OF ALASKA FAIRBANKS

Anthropology	M,D
Art/Fine Arts	M
Clinical Psychology	D
Communication—General	M
Computer Art and Design	M
Corporate and Organizational Communication	M
Criminal Justice and Criminology	M
Cultural Studies	M
Economics	M
English	M
Geographic Information Systems	M
History	M
Interdisciplinary Studies	M,D
Linguistics	M
Music	M
Northern Studies	M
Photography	M
Psychology—General	D
Rural Planning and Studies	M
Social Psychology	M,D,O
Sustainable Development	M,D
Writing	M

UNIVERSITY OF ALASKA SOUTHEAST

Public Administration	M

UNIVERSITY OF ALBERTA

Agricultural Economics and Agribusiness	M,D
Anthropology	M,D
Applied Arts and Design—General	M
Archaeology	M,D
Art History	M
Art/Fine Arts	M
Asian Studies	M
Chinese	M
Classics	M,D
Clothing and Textiles	M,D
Communication—General	M
Counseling Psychology	M,D
Criminal Justice and Criminology	M
Demography and Population Studies	M,D
East European and Russian Studies	M,D
Economics	M,D
English	M,D
Family and Consumer Sciences-General	M,D
Folklore	M,D
French	M,D
German	M,D
Hispanic Studies	M,D
History	M,D
Industrial and Labor Relations	D
Italian	M,D
Japanese	M
Linguistics	M,D
Music	M,D
Philosophy	M,D
Political Science	M,D
Psychology—General	M,D
Rural Sociology	M,D
School Psychology	M,D
Slavic Languages	M,D
Sociology	M,D
Theater	M

UNIVERSITY OF ANTELOPE VALLEY

Criminal Justice and Criminology	M

THE UNIVERSITY OF ARIZONA

Agricultural Economics and Agribusiness	M
American Indian/Native American Studies	M,D
Anthropology	M,D
Architecture	M
Art History	M,D
Art/Fine Arts	M
Asian Studies	M,D
Child and Family Studies	M,D,O
Classics	M
Communication—General	M
Counseling Psychology	M
Dance	M
Economics	M,D
English	M,D
Family and Consumer Sciences-General	M,D
French	M
Gender Studies	M,D,O
Geographic Information Systems	M,D,O

Geography	M,D,O
German	M,D
History	M,D
Human Development	M,D,O
Interdisciplinary Studies	M,D
Journalism	M
Landscape Architecture	M
Latin American Studies	M
Linguistics	M,D
Music	M,D
Near and Middle Eastern Studies	M,D
Philosophy	M,D
Political Science	M,D
Psychology—General	M,D
Public Administration	M,D
Public Policy	M,D
Rehabilitation Counseling	M,D
Rhetoric	M,D
Russian	M
School Psychology	D,O
Sociology	D
Spanish	M,D
Theater	M
Urban and Regional Planning	M
Women's Studies	M,D,O
Writing	M

UNIVERSITY OF ARKANSAS

Agricultural Economics and Agribusiness	M
Anthropology	M,D
Art/Fine Arts	M
Communication—General	M
Comparative Literature	M,D
Economics	M,D
English	M,D
Family and Consumer Sciences-General	M
French	M
Geography	M
German	M
History	M,D
Interdisciplinary Studies	M,D
Journalism	M
Music	M
Philosophy	M,D
Political Science	M
Psychology—General	M,D
Public Administration	M
Public Policy	D
Rehabilitation Counseling	M,D
Sociology	M
Spanish	M
Theater	M
Writing	M

UNIVERSITY OF ARKANSAS AT LITTLE ROCK

Applied Psychology	M
Art History	M
Art/Fine Arts	M
Conflict Resolution and Mediation/Peace Studies	O
Criminal Justice and Criminology	M,D
Gerontology	O
Interdisciplinary Studies	M
Mass Communication	M
Psychology—General	M
Public Administration	M
Public Affairs	M,O
Public History	M
Rehabilitation Counseling	M,O
Rhetoric	M
Speech and Interpersonal Communication	M
Technical Writing	M
Writing	M

UNIVERSITY OF ARKANSAS AT PINE BLUFF

Addictions/Substance Abuse Counseling	M

UNIVERSITY OF ARKANSAS FOR MEDICAL SCIENCES

Genetic Counseling	M,D

UNIVERSITY OF BALTIMORE

Applied Arts and Design—General	M
Applied Psychology	M
Conflict Resolution and Mediation/Peace Studies	M
Counseling Psychology	M
Criminal Justice and Criminology	M
Ethics	M
Graphic Design	M,D
Public Administration	M,D
Public Affairs	M,D
Publishing	M
Writing	M

UNIVERSITY OF BRIDGEPORT

Applied Arts and Design—General	M
Asian Studies	M
Clinical Psychology	M
Communication—General	M
Conflict Resolution and Mediation/Peace Studies	M
Counseling Psychology	M
International Affairs	M
Media Studies	M
Social Psychology	M

THE UNIVERSITY OF BRITISH COLUMBIA

Agricultural Economics and Agribusiness	M
Anthropology	M,D
Archaeology	M,D
Architecture	M
Art History	M,D,O

Art/Fine Arts	M,D,O
Asian Studies	M,D
Classics	M,D
Clinical Psychology	M,D
Cognitive Sciences	M,D
Counseling Psychology	M,D,O
Developmental Psychology	M,D
East European and Russian Studies	M,D
Economics	M,D
English	M,D
Film, Television, and Video Production	M,O
Film, Television, and Video Theory and Criticism	M,O
French	M,D
Gender Studies	M,D
Genetic Counseling	M
Geography	M,D
German	M,D
Health Psychology	M,D
Hispanic Studies	M,D
History	M,D
Human Development	M,D,O
International Affairs	M
Journalism	M
Landscape Architecture	M
Linguistics	M,D
Museum Studies	M,D,O
Music	M,D
Philosophy	M,D
Political Science	M,D
Psychology—General	M,D
Religion	M,D
School Psychology	M,D,O
Social Psychology	M,D
Sociology	M,D
Theater	M
Urban and Regional Planning	M,D
Writing	M,O

UNIVERSITY OF CALGARY

Anthropology	M,D
Applied Psychology	M,D
Archaeology	M
Architecture	M,D
Art/Fine Arts	M
Classics	M,D
Clinical Psychology	M,D
Communication—General	M,D
Counseling Psychology	M,D
Economics	M,D
English	M,D
Environmental Design	M,D
French	M,D
Geography	M,D
German	M,D
History	M,D
Linguistics	M,D
Military and Defense Studies	M,D
Music	M,D
Philosophy	M,D
Political Science	M,D
Psychology—General	M,D
Religion	M,D
School Psychology	M,D
Sociology	M,D
Spanish	M,D
Sustainable Development	M,D
Theater	M

UNIVERSITY OF CALIFORNIA, BERKELEY

Addictions/Substance Abuse Counseling	O
African-American Studies	D
Agricultural Economics and Agribusiness	D
Anthropology	D
Applied Arts and Design—General	M,O
Archaeology	M,D
Architectural History	M,D
Architecture	M,D
Art History	D
Art/Fine Arts	M,O
Asian Languages	M,D
Asian Studies	M,D
Building Science	M,D
Chinese	D
Classics	M,D
Comparative Literature	D
Counseling Psychology	O
Demography and Population Studies	M,D
Economics	D
English	D
Environmental Design	M,D
Ethnic Studies	D
Folklore	M
French	D
Geography	D
German	D
Hispanic and Latin American Languages	D
History of Science and Technology	D
History	M,D
Human Development	M,D
Industrial and Labor Relations	D
Interior Design	O
International Affairs	M,D
Italian	D
Japanese	D
Jewish Studies	D
Journalism	M
Landscape Architecture	M,D,O
Latin American Studies	M
Linguistics	D
Music	D
Near and Middle Eastern Studies	M,D
Philosophy	D
Political Science	D
Psychology—General	D

Public Policy	M,D
Religion	D
Rhetoric	D
Romance Languages	M,D
Russian	D
Scandinavian Languages	D
Slavic Languages	D
Sociology	D
Spanish	D
Sustainable Development	O
Theater	D
Urban and Regional Planning	M,D
Urban Design	M,D
Writing	O

UNIVERSITY OF CALIFORNIA, DAVIS

Agricultural Economics and Agribusiness	M,D
American Indian/Native American Studies	M,D
Anthropology	M,D
Art History	M
Art/Fine Arts	M
Child Development	M
Clothing and Textiles	M
Communication—General	M
Comparative Literature	D
Cultural Studies	M,D
Economics	M,D
English	M,D
Forensic Sciences	M
French	D
Geography	M,D
German	M,D
History	M,D
Human Development	D
Linguistics	M,D
Music	M,D
Philosophy	M,D
Political Science	M,D
Psychology—General	D
Sociology	M,D
Spanish	M,D
Textile Design	M
Theater	M,D
Urban and Regional Planning	M
Writing	M,D

UNIVERSITY OF CALIFORNIA, IRVINE

Anthropology	M,D
Art/Fine Arts	M,D
Asian Languages	M,D
Chinese	M,D
Classics	M,D
Comparative Literature	M,D
Criminal Justice and Criminology	M,D
Cultural Studies	D
Dance	M
Demography and Population Studies	M
Economics	M,D
English	M,D
Environmental Design	D
French	M,D
Genetic Counseling	M
German	M,D
History	M,D
Japanese	M,D
Music	M
Philosophy	M,D
Political Science	D
Psychology—General	D
Sociology	D
Spanish	M,D
Theater	M,D
Urban and Regional Planning	M,D
Urban Studies	M,D
Writing	M

UNIVERSITY OF CALIFORNIA, LOS ANGELES

African Studies	M
African-American Studies	M
American Indian/Native American Studies	M
Anthropology	M,D
Applied Arts and Design—General	M
Applied Social Research	M,D
Archaeology	M,D
Architecture	M,D
Art History	M,D
Art/Fine Arts	M
Asian Languages	M,D
Asian Studies	M,D
Asian-American Studies	M
Classics	M,D
Comparative Literature	M,D
Dance	M,D
Economics	M,D
English	M,D
Film, Television, and Video Production	M,D
French	M,D
Gender Studies	M,D
Geography	M,D
German	M,D
Hispanic and Latin American Languages	D
Historic Preservation	M
History	M,D
Italian	M,D
Latin American Studies	M
Linguistics	M,D
Media Studies	M,D
Music	M
Near and Middle Eastern Languages	M,D
Near and Middle Eastern Studies	M,D
Philosophy	M,D
Political Science	M,D
Portuguese	M
Psychology—General	M,D
Public Policy	M

Scandinavian Languages M
Slavic Languages M,D
Sociology M,D
Spanish M
Theater M,D
Urban and Regional Planning M,D
Urban Design M,D

UNIVERSITY OF CALIFORNIA, MERCED
Cognitive Sciences M,D
Cultural Studies M,D
Psychology—General M,D
Social Sciences M,D

UNIVERSITY OF CALIFORNIA, RIVERSIDE
Anthropology M,D
Art History M
Art/Fine Arts M
Asian Studies M
Classics D
Comparative Literature M,D
Cultural Studies D
Dance M,D
Economics M,D
English M,D
Ethnic Studies D
Hispanic Studies M,D
Historic Preservation M,D
History M,D
Museum Studies M,D
Music M,D
Philosophy M,D
Political Science M,D
Psychology—General M,D
Religion D
School Psychology M,D,O
Sociology M,D
Spanish M,D
Writing M

UNIVERSITY OF CALIFORNIA, SAN DIEGO
Anthropology D
Art History M,D
Art/Fine Arts M,D
Clinical Psychology D
Cognitive Sciences D
Communication—General D
Dance M,D
Economics D
English M,D
Ethnic Studies D
History of Science and Technology D
History M,D
International Affairs M,D
Jewish Studies M,D
Latin American Studies M
Linguistics D
Music M,D
Philosophy D
Political Science M,D
Psychology—General D
Public Policy M
Sociology D
Theater M,D
Writing M,D

UNIVERSITY OF CALIFORNIA, SAN FRANCISCO
Anthropology D
History of Science and Technology M,D
Sociology D

UNIVERSITY OF CALIFORNIA, SANTA BARBARA
African-American Studies D
Agricultural Economics and Agribusiness M,D
Anthropology M,D
Archaeology M,D
Art History D
Art/Fine Arts M
Asian Languages M,D
Asian Studies M,D
Classics M,D
Clinical Psychology M,D,O
Cognitive Sciences M,D
Communication—General D
Comparative Literature D
Counseling Psychology M,D,O
Cultural Anthropology M,D
Cultural Studies M,D
Economics M,D
English D
Film, Television, and Video Production D
French D
Geography M,D
Hispanic and Latin American Languages M,D
Hispanic Studies M,D
History D
Industrial and Labor Relations M,D
Interdisciplinary Studies D
International Affairs M,D
Latin American Studies M
Linguistics M,D
Media Studies M,D
Medieval and Renaissance Studies M,D
Music M,D
Philosophy D
Political Science M,D
Portuguese M,D
Psychology—General D
Public History D
Religion M,D
School Psychology M,D,O
Social Sciences D
Sociology D
Spanish M,D
Speech and Interpersonal Communication D
Sustainable Development M,D
Theater M,D
Translation and Interpretation M,D
Women's Studies M,D
Writing D

UNIVERSITY OF CALIFORNIA, SANTA CRUZ
Anthropology D
Applied Economics M
Art/Fine Arts M,D
Communication—General O
Comparative Literature M,D
Computer Art and Design M,D
Cultural Anthropology D
Economics D
English M,D
Film, Television, and Video Theory and Criticism D
History M,D
Humanities D
Interdisciplinary Studies M,D
International Affairs D
Linguistics M,D
Music M,D
Philosophy M,D
Political Science D
Psychology—General D
Social Sciences D
Sociology D
Theater O
Writing M

UNIVERSITY OF CENTRAL ARKANSAS
Computer Art and Design M
Counseling Psychology M
Economic Development M,O
Economics M,O
English M
Family and Consumer Sciences-General M
Film, Television, and Video Production M
Geographic Information Systems M,O
Geography M,O
History M
Music M,O
Psychology—General M,D,O
School Psychology M,D,O
Social Psychology M
Urban and Regional Planning M,O
Writing M

UNIVERSITY OF CENTRAL FLORIDA
Anthropology M,O
Applied Psychology M,D
Art/Fine Arts M
Clinical Psychology M,D
Communication—General M,O
Computer Art and Design M
Criminal Justice and Criminology M,D,O
Emergency Management M,O
English M,D,O
Experimental Psychology M,D
Film, Television, and Video Production M
Forensic Sciences M,D
Gender Studies M,O
History M
Homeland Security M,O
Industrial and Organizational Psychology M,D
Interdisciplinary Studies M,O
Marriage and Family Therapy M,O
Music M
National Security M,D
Political Science M,D
Psychology—General M,D
Public Administration M,O
Public Affairs M,D,O
School Psychology O
Sociology M,D
Spanish M
Theater M
Urban and Regional Planning M,O

UNIVERSITY OF CENTRAL MISSOURI
Communication—General M,D,O
Counseling Psychology M,D,O
Criminal Justice and Criminology M,D,O
English M,D,O
Gerontology M,D,O
History M,D,O
Music M,D,O
Psychology—General M,D,O
Sociology M,D,O
Theater M,D,O

UNIVERSITY OF CENTRAL OKLAHOMA
Addictions/Substance Abuse Counseling M
Applied Arts and Design—General M
Child and Family Studies M
Counseling Psychology M
Criminal Justice and Criminology M
English M
Experimental Psychology M
Family and Consumer Sciences-General M
Forensic Psychology M
Forensic Sciences M
Gerontology M
History M
Human Development M
Interdisciplinary Studies M
International Affairs M
Marriage and Family Therapy M
Museum Studies M
Music M
Political Science M
Psychology—General M
Public Administration M
School Psychology M
Sociology M
Writing M

UNIVERSITY OF CHARLESTON
Forensic Sciences M

UNIVERSITY OF CHICAGO
Anthropology D
Archaeology D
Art History M,D
Art/Fine Arts M
Asian Languages D
Asian Studies M,D
Classics M,D
Comparative Literature M,D
Economics M,D,O
Emergency Management M
English M,D
Ethics D
Film, Television, and Video Theory and Criticism D
French D
German M,D
History D
Human Development D
Humanities M
Interdisciplinary Studies D
International Affairs M
Italian D
Latin American Studies M
Liberal Studies M
Linguistics M,D
Media Studies D
Music M,D
Near and Middle Eastern Languages D
Near and Middle Eastern Studies M,D
Pastoral Ministry and Counseling M
Philosophy M,D
Political Science D
Psychology—General D
Public Policy M,D
Religion M,D
Romance Languages M,D
Social Sciences M,D
Sociology D
Spanish D
Theology D
Writing M

UNIVERSITY OF CINCINNATI
Anthropology M
Applied Arts and Design—General M
Applied Economics M
Architecture M
Art History M
Art/Fine Arts M
Arts Administration M,D
Classics M,D
Clinical Psychology D
Communication—General M
Criminal Justice and Criminology M,D
Economics M,D
English M,D
Experimental Psychology D
French M,D
Genetic Counseling M
Geography M,D
German M,D
Graphic Design M
History M,D
Industrial and Labor Relations M
Industrial Design M
Interdisciplinary Studies D
Interior Design M
Music M,D,O
Philosophy M,D
Political Science M,D
Psychology—General D
Romance Languages M,D
School Psychology D,O
Sociology M,D
Spanish M,D
Textile Design M
Theater M,D
Urban and Regional Planning M
Women's Studies M,O

UNIVERSITY OF COLORADO BOULDER
Anthropology M,D
Art History M
Art/Fine Arts M
Asian Studies M,D
Chinese M,D
Classics M,D
Communication—General M,D
Comparative Literature M,D
Dance M,D
Economics M,D
English M,D
French M,D
Geography M,D
German M
Hispanic and Latin American Languages M,D
History M,D
International Affairs M,D
Japanese M,D
Journalism M,D
Linguistics M,D
Mass Communication M,D
Media Studies M,D
Museum Studies M
Music M,D
Philosophy M,D
Photography M
Political Science M,D
Psychology—General M,D
Public Policy M,D
Religion M
Sociology D
Spanish M,D
Theater M,D
Writing M,D

UNIVERSITY OF COLORADO COLORADO SPRINGS
Communication—General M
Criminal Justice and Criminology M
Geography M
History M
Interdisciplinary Studies M
Psychology—General M,D
Public Administration M
Public Affairs M
Sociology M

UNIVERSITY OF COLORADO DENVER
American Studies M
Anthropology M
Archaeology M
Architectural History D
Architecture M
Art/Fine Arts M
Clinical Psychology M,D
Communication—General M
Corporate and Organizational Communication M
Counseling Psychology M
Criminal Justice and Criminology M,D
Economic Development M
Economics M
Emergency Management M,D
English M
Forensic Sciences M
Gender Studies M
Genetic Counseling M,D
Geographic Information Systems M,D
Health Psychology M,D
Historic Preservation M
History M
Homeland Security M,D
Human Development M,O
Humanities M
International Affairs M
Landscape Architecture M
Linguistics M
Marriage and Family Therapy M
Military and Defense Studies M,D
Music M
Political Science M,D
Public Administration M,D
Public Affairs M,D
Public History M
Rhetoric M
School Psychology M,O
Sociology M
Spanish M
Sustainable Development M,D
Urban and Regional Planning M,D
Urban Design M,D
Western European Studies M
Women's Studies M
Writing M

UNIVERSITY OF CONNECTICUT
African Studies M
Agricultural Economics and Agribusiness M,D
Anthropology M,D
Art History M
Art/Fine Arts M
Child and Family Studies M,D,O
Clinical Psychology M,D,O
Cognitive Sciences M,D,O
Communication—General M
Comparative Literature M,D
Corporate and Organizational Communication D
Counseling Psychology M,D,O
Developmental Psychology M,D,O
Economics M,D
English M,D
Experimental Psychology M,D,O
French M,D,O
Geographic Information Systems M,D,O
Geography M,D,O
German M,D
Health Psychology M,D,O
History M,D
Homeland Security M
Human Development M,D,O
Industrial and Organizational Psychology M,D,O
International Affairs M
Italian M,D
Jewish Studies M
Latin American Studies M
Linguistics M,D
Medieval and Renaissance Studies M,D
Music M,D,O
Philosophy M,D
Political Science M,D
Psychology—General M,D,O
Public Administration M,D
School Psychology M,D,O
Social Psychology M,D,O
Sociology M,D
Spanish M,D
Sustainable Development M
Theater M
Western European Studies M

UNIVERSITY OF DALLAS
American Studies M
Art/Fine Arts M
Comparative Literature D
English M
Humanities M
Pastoral Ministry and Counseling M
Philosophy M,D
Political Science M,D
Psychology—General M
Theology M

UNIVERSITY OF DAYTON
Clinical Psychology M,O
Communication—General M
Counseling Psychology M,O
English M
Human Development M,O
Pastoral Ministry and Counseling M,D
Public Administration M

School Psychology — M,O
Theology — M,D

UNIVERSITY OF DELAWARE
Agricultural Economics and
   Agribusiness — M
American Studies — M
Applied Arts and Design—
   General — M
Art History — M,D
Art/Fine Arts — M
Child and Family Studies — M,D
Chinese — M
Clinical Psychology — D
Clothing and Textiles — M
Cognitive Sciences — M,D
Communication—General — M
Criminal Justice and Criminology — M,D
Economics — M,D
Emergency Management — M,D
English — M,D
French — M
Geography — M,D
German — M
Historic Preservation — M,D
History of Science and Technology — M
History — M,D
Human Development — M,D
International Affairs — M,D
Liberal Studies — M
Linguistics — M,D
Music — M
Political Science — M,D
Psychology—General — D
Public Administration — M*
Public Policy — M
School Psychology — M,D,O
Social Psychology — D
Sociology — M,D
Spanish — M
Theater — M
Translation and Interpretation — M
Urban Studies — M,D

UNIVERSITY OF DENVER
Anthropology — M
Archaeology — M
Art History — M
Art/Fine Arts — M
Child and Family Studies — M,D,O
Clinical Psychology — M,D
Cognitive Sciences — D
Computer Art and Design — M
Conflict Resolution and
   Mediation/Peace Studies — M,O
Corporate and Organizational
   Communication — M,O
Counseling Psychology — M,D,O
Criminal Justice and Criminology — M,O
Cultural Anthropology — M
Cultural Studies — M,O
Developmental Psychology — D
Economics — M
Emergency Management — M,O
English — M,D
Film, Television, and Video
   Production — M
Forensic Psychology — M,D
Geographic Information Systems — M,O
Geography — M,D
History — M,O
International Affairs — M,D,O
Internet and Interactive
   Multimedia — M,O
Mass Communication — M
Museum Studies — M
Music — M,O
Psychology—General — M,D
Public Policy — M
Religion — M,D
School Psychology — M,D,O
Social Psychology — D
Speech and Interpersonal
   Communication — M,D
Sport Psychology — M,D
Theology — D
Translation and Interpretation — M,O
Writing — M,D

UNIVERSITY OF DETROIT MERCY
Addictions/Substance Abuse
   Counseling — M,O
Clinical Psychology — M,D
Criminal Justice and Criminology — M
Industrial and Organizational
   Psychology — M
Liberal Studies — M
Military and Defense Studies — M
Psychology—General — M,D,O
Religion — M
School Psychology — O

UNIVERSITY OF DUBUQUE
Communication—General — M
Theology — M,D

UNIVERSITY OF EVANSVILLE
Public Administration — M

THE UNIVERSITY OF FINDLAY
Public Administration — M,D
Rhetoric — M,D
Writing — M,D

UNIVERSITY OF FLORIDA
African Studies — O
Agricultural Economics and
   Agribusiness — M,D
Anthropology — M,D
Architecture — M,D
Art History — M,D
Art/Fine Arts — M,D
Child Development — M

Classics — M,D
Clinical Psychology — M,D
Communication—General — M,D
Computer Art and Design — M,D
Counseling Psychology — M,D
Criminal Justice and Criminology — M,D
Economics — M,D
Emergency Management — M
English — M,D
Family and Consumer
   Sciences-General — M
Forensic Sciences — M
French — M,D
Gender Studies — M,O
Geographic Information Systems — M,D
Geography — M,D
German — M,D
Health Communication — M,D,O
Health Psychology — M,D
Historic Preservation — M,D
History — M,D
Interdisciplinary Studies — M,D
Interior Design — M,D
International Affairs — M
International Development — M,D,O
Jewish Studies — M,D
Journalism — M,D
Landscape Architecture — M,D
Latin American Studies — M,O
Linguistics — M,D,O
Marriage and Family Therapy — M,D,O
Mass Communication — M,D
Media Studies — M,D
Museum Studies — M,D
Music — M,D
Philosophy — M,D
Political Science — M,D,O
Psychology—General — M,D
Public Affairs — M,D,O
Religion — M,D
School Psychology — M,D,O
Social Sciences — M,D,O
Sociology — M,D
Spanish — M,D
Sustainable Development — M,O
Theater — M
Urban and Regional Planning — M,D
Women's Studies — M,D
Writing — M

UNIVERSITY OF FORT LAUDERDALE
Pastoral Ministry and Counseling — M

UNIVERSITY OF GEORGIA
Agricultural Economics and
   Agribusiness — M,D
Anthropology — M,D
Applied Economics — M,D
Archaeology — M,D
Art History — M,D
Art/Fine Arts — M,D
Child and Family Studies — M,D,O
Classics — M
Clothing and Textiles — M,D
Communication—General — M,D
Comparative Literature — M,D
Consumer Economics — M,D
Economics — M,D
English — M,D
Environmental Design — M
Family and Consumer
   Sciences-General — M,D
French — M,D
Geography — M,D
German — M
Gerontology — O
Historic Preservation — M
History — M,D
Interior Design — M,D
International Affairs — M,D
Internet and Interactive
   Multimedia — M
Journalism — M,D
Landscape Architecture — M
Linguistics — M,D
Mass Communication — M,D
Music — M,D
Philosophy — M,D
Political Science — M,D
Psychology—General — M,D
Public Administration — M,D
Public Policy — M,D
Religion — M
Romance Languages — M,D
Sociology — M,D
Spanish — M,D
Speech and Interpersonal
   Communication — M,D
Sustainable Development — M,D
Theater — M,D
Women's Studies — O
Writing — M

UNIVERSITY OF GREAT FALLS
Counseling Psychology — M
Criminal Justice and Criminology — M

UNIVERSITY OF GUAM
Art/Fine Arts — M
English — M
Graphic Design — M
Pacific Area/Pacific Rim Studies — M
Public Administration — M

UNIVERSITY OF GUELPH
Agricultural Economics and
   Agribusiness — M,D
Anthropology — M,D
Applied Psychology — M,D
Art/Fine Arts — M
Child and Family Studies — M,D
Clinical Psychology — M,D

Cognitive Sciences — M,D
Comparative Literature — D
Consumer Economics — M
Criminal Justice and Criminology — M,D
Demography and Population Studies — M,D
Economics — M,D
English — M
French — M
Geography — M,D
History — M,D
Human Development — M,D
Industrial and Organizational
   Psychology — M,D
International Development — M,D
Landscape Architecture — M
Marriage and Family Therapy — M,D
Medieval and Renaissance Studies — D
Philosophy — M,D
Political Science — M
Psychology—General — M,D
Public Administration — M
Public Policy — M
Rural Planning and Studies — M
Social Psychology — M,D
Sociology — M,D
Theater — M
Western European Studies — M

UNIVERSITY OF HARTFORD
Architecture — M
Art/Fine Arts — M
Clinical Psychology — M,D
Communication—General — M
Experimental Psychology — M
Music — M,D,O
Psychology—General — M,D
School Psychology — M

UNIVERSITY OF HAWAII AT HILO
Counseling Psychology — M
Cultural Studies — M,D

UNIVERSITY OF HAWAII AT MANOA
American Studies — M,D,O
Anthropology — M,D
Architecture — D
Art History — M
Art/Fine Arts — M
Asian Languages — M,D
Asian Studies — O
Chinese — M,D,O
Clinical Psychology — M,D,O
Communication—General — M,O
Conflict Resolution and
   Mediation/Peace Studies — O
Cultural Studies — M,D
Dance — M
Demography and Population Studies — O
Disability Studies — O
Economics — M,D
Emergency Management — O
English — M,D
French — M
Geography — M,D,O
Gerontology — O
Historic Preservation — O
History — M,D
International Affairs — O
Japanese — M,D,O
Linguistics — M,D
Museum Studies — O
Music — M,D
Pacific Area/Pacific Rim Studies — M,O
Philosophy — M,D
Political Science — M,D
Psychology—General — M,D,O
Public Administration — M,O
Public Policy — O
Religion — M
Social Psychology — M,D,O
Sociology — M,D
Spanish — M
Speech and Interpersonal
   Communication — M
Theater — M,D
Urban and Regional Planning — M,D,O
Women's Studies — O

UNIVERSITY OF HOUSTON
Anthropology — M
Applied Economics — M,D
Architecture — M
Art History — M
Art/Fine Arts — M
Clinical Psychology — M,D
Communication—General — M
Comparative Literature — M
Counseling Psychology — M,D
Cultural Studies — M
Developmental Psychology — M,D
Economics — M,D
Family and Consumer
   Sciences-General — M
Health Communication — M
Hispanic Studies — M,D
History — M,D
Industrial and Organizational
   Psychology — M,D
Linguistics — M,D
Mass Communication — M
Music — M,D
Philosophy — M
Political Science — M,D
Psychology—General — M,D
Public Administration — M,D
Social Psychology — M,D
Sociology — M
Spanish — M,D
Speech and Interpersonal
   Communication — M
Theater — M
Writing — M,D

UNIVERSITY OF HOUSTON–CLEAR LAKE
Clinical Psychology — M
Criminal Justice and Criminology — M
Cultural Studies — M
English — M
History — M
Humanities — M
Marriage and Family Therapy — M
Psychology—General — M
School Psychology — M
Sociology — M

UNIVERSITY OF HOUSTON–DOWNTOWN
Criminal Justice and Criminology — M
English — M
Rhetoric — M
Technical Communication — M

UNIVERSITY OF HOUSTON–VICTORIA
Counseling Psychology — M
Economic Development — M
Forensic Psychology — M
Forensic Sciences — M
Interdisciplinary Studies — M
Psychology—General — M
Publishing — M
School Psychology — M
Writing — M

UNIVERSITY OF IDAHO
Agricultural Economics and
   Agribusiness — M
American Indian/Native American
   Studies — D
Anthropology — M
Applied Economics — M
Architecture — M
Art/Fine Arts — M
Conflict Resolution and
   Mediation/Peace Studies — D
Consumer Economics — M
English — M
Geography — M,D
History — M,D
Interdisciplinary Studies — M
Landscape Architecture — M
Music — M
Philosophy — M
Political Science — M,D
Psychology—General — M
Public Administration — M,D
Rehabilitation Counseling — M,O
Theater — M
Urban and Regional Planning — M
Writing — M

UNIVERSITY OF ILLINOIS AT CHICAGO
Anthropology — M,D
Applied Arts and Design—
   General — M
Architecture — M
Art History — M,D
Art/Fine Arts — M,D
Communication—General — M,D
Criminal Justice and Criminology — M,D
Developmental Psychology — M,D
Disability Studies — M,D
East European and Russian Studies — M,D
Economics — M,D
English — M,D
Forensic Sciences — M
French — M,D
Geography — M,D
German — M,D
Graphic Design — M
Hispanic and Latin American
   Languages — M,D
Hispanic Studies — M,D
History — M,D
Human Development — M,D
Interdisciplinary Studies — D
Latin American Studies — M
Linguistics — M
Medical Illustration — M
Museum Studies — M,D
Philosophy — M,D
Political Science — M,D
Psychology—General — M,D
Public Administration — M,D
Slavic Languages — M,D
Sociology — M,D
Spanish — M,D
Urban and Regional Planning — M,D

UNIVERSITY OF ILLINOIS AT SPRINGFIELD
Addictions/Substance Abuse
   Counseling — M,O
Child and Family Studies — M,O
Communication—General — M
Emergency Management — M,O
English — M,O
Gerontology — M,O
History — M
Homeland Security — M,O
Human Development — M
Interdisciplinary Studies — M
Journalism — M
Political Science — M
Public Administration — M,D,O
Public History — M
Social Sciences — M,O

UNIVERSITY OF ILLINOIS AT URBANA–CHAMPAIGN
African Studies — M
Agricultural Economics and
   Agribusiness — M,D
Anthropology — M,D

---

*M—masters degree; D—doctorate; O—other advanced degree; *—Close-Up and/or Display*

Applied Arts and Design—General	M,D
Applied Economics	M,D
Architecture	M,D
Art History	M,D
Art/Fine Arts	M
Asian Languages	M,D
Asian Studies	M,D
Classics	M,D
Communication—General	M,D
Comparative Literature	M,D
Consumer Economics	M,D
Dance	M
East European and Russian Studies	M
Economics	M,D
English	M,D
French	M,D
Geography	M,D
German	M,D
Graphic Design	M
History	M,D
Human Development	M,D
Industrial and Labor Relations	M,D
Industrial Design	M
Interdisciplinary Studies	D
Italian	M,D
Journalism	M
Landscape Architecture	M,D
Latin American Studies	M
Linguistics	M,D
Media Studies	M,D
Music	M,D
Near and Middle Eastern Studies	M
Philosophy	M,D
Photography	M
Political Science	M,D
Portuguese	M,D
Psychology—General	M,D
Religion	M
Romance Languages	D
Slavic Languages	M,D
Sociology	M,D
Spanish	M,D
Theater	M,D
Translation and Interpretation	M
Urban and Regional Planning	M,D
Western European Studies	M
Writing	M,D

UNIVERSITY OF INDIANAPOLIS

Anthropology	M
Art/Fine Arts	M
Clinical Psychology	M,D
Counseling Psychology	M,D
English	M
Gerontology	M,D,O
History	M
International Affairs	M
Psychology—General	M,D
Sociology	M

THE UNIVERSITY OF IOWA

American Studies	M,D
Anthropology	M,D
Art History	M,D
Art/Fine Arts	M
Asian Languages	M
Asian Studies	M
Chinese	M
Classics	M,D
Communication—General	M,D
Counseling Psychology	M,D,O
Dance	M
Economics	D
English	M,D
Film, Television, and Video Production	M
Film, Television, and Video Theory and Criticism	M,D
French	M,D
Geographic Information Systems	M,D,O
Geography	M,D,O
History	M,D
Journalism	M,D
Linguistics	M,D
Marriage and Family Therapy	M,D
Mass Communication	M,D
Media Studies	M,D
Music	M,D
Philosophy	D
Political Science	D
Psychology—General	M,D,O
Rehabilitation Counseling	M,D
Religion	M,D
Rhetoric	M,D
School Psychology	M,D,O
Sociology	M,D
Spanish	M,D
Speech and Interpersonal Communication	M,D
Theater	M
Urban and Regional Planning	M
Women's Studies	O
Writing	M,D

THE UNIVERSITY OF KANSAS

African Studies	M,O
African-American Studies	M,O
American Indian/Native American Studies	M,O
American Studies	M,D
Anthropology	M,D
Applied Arts and Design—General	M
Applied Behavior Analysis	M,D
Architecture	M,D,O
Art History	M,D
Art/Fine Arts	M
Asian Languages	M
Asian Studies	M
Classics	M
Clinical Psychology	M,D
Cognitive Sciences	M,D
Communication—General	M,D
Computer Art and Design	M
Counseling Psychology	M,D
Developmental Psychology	M,D
East European and Russian Studies	M,O
Economics	M,D
English	M,D
Film, Television, and Video Theory and Criticism	M,D
French	M,D
Geography	M,D
German	M,D
Gerontology	M,D,O
History	M,D
Interdisciplinary Studies	M,D
International Affairs	M
Journalism	M
Latin American Studies	M,O
Linguistics	M,D
Media Studies	M,O
Museum Studies	M,O
Music	M,D
Near and Middle Eastern Studies	M,O
Philosophy	M,D
Political Science	M,D
Psychology—General	M,D
Public Administration	M,D
Rehabilitation Counseling	M,D
Religion	M
School Psychology	D,O
Slavic Languages	M,D
Social Psychology	M,D
Sociology	M,D
Spanish	M,D
Textile Design	M
Theater	M,D
Therapies—Dance, Drama, and Music	M
Urban and Regional Planning	M
Writing	M,D

UNIVERSITY OF KENTUCKY

Agricultural Economics and Agribusiness	M,D
Anthropology	M,D
Applied Arts and Design—General	M
Architecture	M
Art History	M
Art/Fine Arts	M
Arts Administration	M
Child and Family Studies	M,D
Classics	M
Communication—General	M,D
Counseling Psychology	M,D,O
Economics	M,D
English	M,D
Geography	M,D
German	M
Gerontology	D,O
Hispanic Studies	M,D
Historic Preservation	M
History	M,D
Interior Design	M
International Affairs	M
Music	M,D
Philosophy	M,D
Political Science	M,D
Psychology—General	M,D
Public Administration	M,D
Public Policy	M,D
Rehabilitation Counseling	M,D
School Psychology	M,D,O
Sociology	M,D
Therapies—Dance, Drama, and Music	M,D

UNIVERSITY OF KING'S COLLEGE

Journalism	M
Writing	M

UNIVERSITY OF LA VERNE

Child and Family Studies	M
Child Development	M
Clinical Psychology	D
Gerontology	M,O
Marriage and Family Therapy	M
Psychology—General	M,D
Public Administration	M,D
School Psychology	M,O

UNIVERSITY OF LETHBRIDGE

Addictions/Substance Abuse Counseling	M,D
American Indian/Native American Studies	M,D
Anthropology	M,D
Archaeology	M,D
Art/Fine Arts	M,D
Canadian Studies	M,D
Counseling Psychology	M,D
Economics	M,D
English	M,D
French	M,D
Gender Studies	M,D
Geographic Information Systems	M,D
Geography	M,D
German	M,D
Media Studies	M,D
Music	M,D
Philosophy	M,D
Political Science	M,D
Psychology—General	M,D
Religion	M,D
Sociology	M,D
Spanish	M,D
Theater	M,D
Urban Studies	M,D
Women's Studies	M,D

UNIVERSITY OF LOUISIANA AT LAFAYETTE

American Studies	D
Cognitive Sciences	D
Communication—General	M
English	M,D
Folklore	M,D
French	M,D
History	M
Mass Communication	M
Music	M
Psychology—General	M
Rehabilitation Counseling	M
Rhetoric	M,D
Writing	M,D

UNIVERSITY OF LOUISIANA AT MONROE

Clinical Psychology	M
Communication—General	M
Counseling Psychology	M
Criminal Justice and Criminology	M
English	M
Family and Consumer Sciences-General	M,D
Forensic Psychology	M
Gerontology	M,O
History	M
Marriage and Family Therapy	M,D
Psychology—General	M
Speech and Interpersonal Communication	M,D

UNIVERSITY OF LOUISVILLE

Addictions/Substance Abuse Counseling	M,D,O
African Studies	M
African-American Studies	M
Anthropology	M
Art History	M,D
Art/Fine Arts	M,D
Asian Studies	O
Clinical Psychology	D
Communication—General	M
Criminal Justice and Criminology	M,D
English	M,D
Experimental Psychology	D
French	M
Geography	M
Gerontology	M,D,O
History	M,O
Humanities	M,D
Interdisciplinary Studies	M,D
Marriage and Family Therapy	M,D,O
Museum Studies	M,D
Music	M
Philosophy	M
Political Science	M
Psychology—General	D
Public Administration	M,D
Public Affairs	M,D
Public History	M,O
Public Policy	M,D
Rhetoric	M,D
Sociology	M,D
Spanish	M
Theater	M
Urban and Regional Planning	M,D
Urban Studies	M,D
Women's Studies	M,O
Writing	M,D

UNIVERSITY OF MAINE

Agricultural Economics and Agribusiness	M
Anthropology	D
Art/Fine Arts	M
Asian Studies	M,D
Canadian Studies	M,D
Communication—General	M,D
Economics	M
English	M
Gender Studies	M
Geographic Information Systems	M,D,O
History	M,D
Human Development	M,D,O
Interdisciplinary Studies	M,D
International Affairs	M
Mass Communication	M,D
Music	M
Psychology—General	M,D
Western European Studies	M,D

UNIVERSITY OF MANAGEMENT AND TECHNOLOGY

Criminal Justice and Criminology	M,O
Homeland Security	M
Public Administration	M,O

THE UNIVERSITY OF MANCHESTER

Anthropology	M,D
Archaeology	M,D
Architecture	M,D
Art History	D
Art/Fine Arts	M,D
Arts Administration	D
Asian Studies	M,D
Chinese	M,D
Classics	D
Clinical Psychology	M,D
Clothing and Textiles	M,D
Conflict Resolution and Mediation/Peace Studies	D
Counseling Psychology	M,D
Criminal Justice and Criminology	M,D
Cultural Studies	M,D
Developmental Psychology	M,D
Economics	D
English	D
Environmental Design	M,D
French	M,D
Geography	M,D
German	M,D
Hispanic Studies	M,D
History of Medicine	M,D
History of Science and Technology	M,D
History	D
International Affairs	D
International Development	M,D
Italian	M,D
Japanese	M,D
Landscape Architecture	M,D
Latin American Studies	M,D
Linguistics	M,D
Museum Studies	D
Music	D
Near and Middle Eastern Languages	M,D
Near and Middle Eastern Studies	M,D
Philosophy	M,D
Political Science	M,D
Psychology—General	M,D
Religion	D
Russian	M,D
Slavic Languages	M,D
Social Sciences	M,D
Sociology	M,D
Spanish	M,D
Textile Design	M,D
Theater	D
Theology	D
Translation and Interpretation	M,D
Writing	D

UNIVERSITY OF MANITOBA

Agricultural Economics and Agribusiness	M,D
American Indian/Native American Studies	M
Anthropology	M,D
Architecture	M
Canadian Studies	M
Child and Family Studies	M
Classics	M
Clinical Psychology	M,D
Clothing and Textiles	M
Disability Studies	M
Economics	M,D
English	M,D
Family and Consumer Sciences-General	M
French	M,D
Geography	M,D
German	M
History	M,D
Interdisciplinary Studies	M,D
Interior Design	M
Landscape Architecture	M
Linguistics	M,D
Music	M
Northern Studies	M
Philosophy	M
Political Science	M
Psychology—General	M,D
Public Administration	M
Religion	M,D
School Psychology	M,D
Slavic Languages	M
Sociology	M,D
Urban and Regional Planning	M

UNIVERSITY OF MARY

Addictions/Substance Abuse Counseling	M
Clinical Psychology	M
Counseling Psychology	M
School Psychology	M

UNIVERSITY OF MARY HARDIN-BAYLOR

Clinical Psychology	M
Counseling Psychology	M
Marriage and Family Therapy	M

UNIVERSITY OF MARYLAND, BALTIMORE

Ethics	O
Genetic Counseling	M
Gerontology	M,D

UNIVERSITY OF MARYLAND, BALTIMORE COUNTY

Applied Psychology	D
Cognitive Sciences	D
Communication—General	M
Computer Art and Design	M
Dance	M
Developmental Psychology	D
Economics	M,D
English	M
Geographic Information Systems	M,O
Geography	M,D
Gerontology	M,D
History	M
Industrial and Organizational Psychology	M
Linguistics	M
Music	O
Psychology—General	M,D
Public History	M,D
Public Policy	M,D
Social Sciences	D
Sociology	M
Theater	M
Urban Studies	M,D
Women's Studies	O

UNIVERSITY OF MARYLAND, COLLEGE PARK

Agricultural Economics and Agribusiness	M,D
American Studies	M,D
Anthropology	M
Architecture	M
Art History	M,D
Art Therapy	M,D,O
Art/Fine Arts	M
Broadcast Journalism	M,D
Child and Family Studies	M,D
Classics	M
Clinical Psychology	M,D
Cognitive Sciences	D
Communication—General	M,D
Comparative Literature	M,D
Counseling Psychology	M,D,O
Criminal Justice and Criminology	M,D
Dance	M
Developmental Psychology	M,D
Economics	M,D
English	M,D
Experimental Psychology	M,D

Family and Consumer
  Sciences-General — M,D
French — M,D
Geography — M,D
German — M,D
Historic Preservation — M,O
History — M,D
Human Development — M,D
Industrial and Organizational
  Psychology — M,D
Jewish Studies — M
Journalism — M,D
Landscape Architecture — M
Linguistics — M,D
Marriage and Family Therapy — M,D
Media Studies — M,D
Music — M,D
Philosophy — M,D
Political Science — D
Portuguese — M,D
Psychology—General — M,D
Public Administration — M
Public Policy — M,D
Rehabilitation Counseling — M,D,O
School Psychology — M,D,O
Social Psychology — M,D
Sociology — M,D
Spanish — M,D
Speech and Interpersonal
  Communication — M,D
Survey Methodology — M,D
Sustainable Development — M
Theater — M,D
Urban and Regional Planning — M,D
Women's Studies — M,D
Writing — M,D

UNIVERSITY OF MARYLAND EASTERN SHORE
Criminal Justice and Criminology — M
Rehabilitation Counseling — M

UNIVERSITY OF MASSACHUSETTS AMHERST
African-American Studies — M,D
Agricultural Economics and
  Agribusiness — M,D
American Studies — M,D
Anthropology — M,D
Architecture — M
Art History — M
Art/Fine Arts — M
Child and Family Studies — M,D,O
Chinese — M
Classics — M
Clinical Psychology — M,D
Cognitive Sciences — M,D
Communication—General — M,D
Comparative Literature — M,D
Conflict Resolution and
  Mediation/Peace Studies — M,D
Developmental Psychology — M,D
Economics — M,D
English — M,D
French — M
Geography — M
German — M,D
Hispanic and Latin American
  Languages — M,D
Historic Preservation — M
History — M,D
Industrial and Labor Relations — M
Interior Design — M
Italian — M
Japanese — M
Landscape Architecture — M
Linguistics — M,D
Music — M,D
Philosophy — M,D
Political Science — M,D
Portuguese — M,D
Psychology—General — M,D
Public Administration — M
Public Policy — M,D
Rhetoric — M,D
Scandinavian Languages — M,D
School Psychology — M,D,O
Social Psychology — M,D
Sociology — M,D
Spanish — M,D
Sustainable Development — M
Theater — M
Urban and Regional Planning — M
Writing — M,D

UNIVERSITY OF MASSACHUSETTS BOSTON
American Studies — M
Applied Economics — M
Archaeology — M
Classics — M
Clinical Psychology — D
Cognitive Sciences — M
Conflict Resolution and
  Mediation/Peace Studies — M,O
Counseling Psychology — M,D
English — M
Gerontology — M,D,O
History — M*
International Affairs — M
International Development — M,D
Linguistics — M
Marriage and Family Therapy — M
Public Affairs — M
Public Policy — M,D
Rehabilitation Counseling — M
School Psychology — M,D
Sociology — M,D
Writing — M

UNIVERSITY OF MASSACHUSETTS DARTMOUTH
Applied Arts and Design—
  General — M,O
Art/Fine Arts — M,O
Computer Art and Design — M,O
Latin American Studies — M,D
Portuguese — M,O
Psychology—General — M,O
Public Administration — M,O
Public Policy — M,O
Writing — M

UNIVERSITY OF MASSACHUSETTS LOWELL
Conflict Resolution and
  Mediation/Peace Studies — M,O
Criminal Justice and Criminology — M,D
Economic Development — M,O
Economics — M,O
Homeland Security — M,D
Music — M
Psychology—General — M
Social Psychology — M
Sociology — M,O
Sustainable Development — M,D,O
Urban and Regional Planning — M,O

UNIVERSITY OF MASSACHUSETTS WORCESTER
Interdisciplinary Studies — M,D

UNIVERSITY OF MEMPHIS
African-American Studies — M,D,O
Anthropology — M
Archaeology — M,D,O
Architecture — M
Art History — M,O
Art/Fine Arts — M,O
Communication—General — M,D
Comparative Literature — M,D,O
Counseling Psychology — M,D
Criminal Justice and Criminology — M
Economics — M,D
English — M,D,O
Family and Consumer
  Sciences-General — M
Film, Television, and Video
  Production — M,D
French — M
Geographic Information Systems — M,D,O
Geography — M,D,O
Graphic Design — M,O
History — M,D
Interdisciplinary Studies — M,D,O
Interior Design — M,O
Journalism — M
Liberal Studies — M
Linguistics — M,D,O
Music — M,D
Near and Middle Eastern Studies — M,D
Philosophy — M,D
Photography — M,O
Political Science — M
Psychology—General — M,D,O
Public Administration — M
Public Policy — M,D
Rehabilitation Counseling — M,D
School Psychology — M,D,O
Social Sciences — M
Sociology — M
Theater — M
Urban and Regional Planning — M
Writing — M,D,O

UNIVERSITY OF MIAMI
Architecture — M
Art History — M
Art/Fine Arts — M
Broadcast Journalism — M,D
Clinical Psychology — M,D
Communication—General — M,D
Counseling Psychology — D
Developmental Psychology — M,D
Economic Development — M,D
Economics — M,D
English — M,D
Film, Television, and Video
  Production — M,D
Film, Television, and Video
  Theory and Criticism — D
French — M,D
Geography — M
Graphic Design — M
History — M,D
Industrial and Labor Relations — M,D,O
International Affairs — M,D
International Economics — M,D
Internet and Interactive
  Multimedia — M
Journalism — M,D
Latin American Studies — M
Liberal Studies — M
Marriage and Family Therapy — M,O
Music — M,D,O
Philosophy — M,D
Photography — M
Political Science — M
Psychology—General — M,D
Romance Languages — D
Sociology — M,D
Spanish — M,D
Therapies—Dance, Drama, and
  Music — M,D,O
Urban Design — M
Writing — M,D

UNIVERSITY OF MICHIGAN
American Studies — M,D
Anthropology — D
Applied Arts and Design—
  General — M,D

Applied Economics — M
Archaeology — M,D
Architecture — M,D
Art History — M,D
Art/Fine Arts — M
Asian Languages — D
Asian Studies — M,D,O
Classics — M,D,O
Clinical Psychology — D
Cognitive Sciences — D
Communication—General — D
Comparative Literature — D
Cultural Anthropology — D
Dance — M
Developmental Psychology — D
East European and Russian Studies — M,D
Economics — M,D
English — M,D,O
Film, Television, and Video
  Theory and Criticism — D,O
French — D
Genetic Counseling — M,D
German — M,D
History — D,O
Interdisciplinary Studies — M,D
Italian — D
Jewish Studies — M,D,O
Landscape Architecture — M,D
Linguistics — D
Mass Communication — D
Media Studies — M
Music — M,D,O
Near and Middle Eastern Languages — M,D
Near and Middle Eastern Studies — M,D
Philosophy — M,D
Political Science — D
Psychology—General — D,O
Public Policy — M,D
Religion — M,D
Russian — M,D
Slavic Languages — M,D
Social Psychology — D
Social Sciences — D
Sociology — D
Spanish — D
Survey Methodology — M,D,O
Sustainable Development — M,D
Theater — M,D
Urban and Regional Planning — M,D
Urban Design — M
Women's Studies — D,O
Writing — M

UNIVERSITY OF MICHIGAN–DEARBORN
Clinical Psychology — M
Health Psychology — M
Public Administration — M
Public Policy — M

UNIVERSITY OF MICHIGAN–FLINT
American Studies — M
Art/Fine Arts — M
Arts Administration — M
Criminal Justice and Criminology — M
English — M
Gender Studies — M
International Affairs — M
Museum Studies — M
Music — M
Political Science — M
Public Administration — M
Rhetoric — M
Social Sciences — M
Writing — M

UNIVERSITY OF MINNESOTA, DULUTH
Anthropology — M
Art/Fine Arts — M
Criminal Justice and Criminology — M
English — M
Graphic Design — M
Liberal Studies — M
Music — M
Sociology — M

UNIVERSITY OF MINNESOTA, TWIN CITIES CAMPUS
American Studies — D
Anthropology — M,D
Applied Arts and Design—
  General — M,D,O
Applied Economics — M,D
Archaeology — M,D
Architecture — M
Art History — M,D
Art/Fine Arts — M
Asian Languages — D
Asian Studies — D
Child and Family Studies — M,D
Child Development — M,D
Classics — M,D
Clinical Psychology — D
Clothing and Textiles — M,D,O
Cognitive Sciences — D
Communication—General — M,D,O
Comparative Literature — D
Counseling Psychology — D
Cultural Studies — D
Economics — D
English — M,D
French — M,D
Genetic Counseling — M,D
Geographic Information Systems — M,D
Geography — M,D
German — M,D
Hispanic and Latin American
  Languages — M,D
History of Medicine — M,D
History of Science and Technology — M,D
History — M,D
Industrial and Labor Relations — M

Industrial and Organizational
  Psychology — D
Interdisciplinary Studies — D
Interior Design — M,D,O
International Development — M
Landscape Architecture — M
Linguistics — M,D
Marriage and Family Therapy — M,D
Mass Communication — M,D
Medieval and Renaissance Studies — M,D
Music — M,D
Philosophy — M,D
Political Science — D
Portuguese — M,D
Psychology—General — D
Public Affairs — M
Public Policy — M
Religion — M,D
Scandinavian Languages — M,D
School Psychology — M,D,O
Social Psychology — D
Sociology — M,D
Spanish — M,D
Textile Design — M,D,O
Theater — M,D
Urban and Regional Planning — M
Women's Studies — D

UNIVERSITY OF MISSISSIPPI
American Studies — M
Anthropology — M
Art History — M
Art/Fine Arts — M
Clinical Psychology — M,D
Economics — M,D
English — M,D
Experimental Psychology — M,D
French — M
German — M
History — M,D
Journalism — M
Music — M,D
Philosophy — M
Political Science — M,D
Psychology—General — M,D
Sociology — M
Spanish — M

UNIVERSITY OF MISSOURI
Agricultural Economics and
  Agribusiness — M,D,O
Anthropology — M,D
Archaeology — M,D
Architecture — M
Art History — M,D
Art/Fine Arts — M,D
Child and Family Studies — M,D
Classics — M,D
Clothing and Textiles — M,D
Communication—General — M,D,O
Comparative Literature — M,D
Computer Art and Design — M
Conflict Resolution and
  Mediation/Peace Studies — M,D,O
Consumer Economics — M,D,O
Corporate and Organizational
  Communication — M,D,O
Counseling Psychology — M,D,O
Economics — M,D
English — M,D
Environmental Design — M
Ethics — M,D,O
Family and Consumer
  Sciences-General — M,D,O
French — M,D
Geographic Information Systems — M,O
Geography — M,O
German — M
Gerontology — M,D,O
Health Communication — M,D,O
History — M,D
Human Development — M,D
Interdisciplinary Studies — O
Internet and Interactive
  Multimedia — M,D,O
Journalism — M,D,O
Media Studies — M,D,O
Music — M
Philosophy — M,D
Political Science — M,D
Psychology—General — M,D
Public Administration — M,D,O
Public Affairs — M,D,O
Public Policy — M,D,O
Religion — M
Romance Languages — M,D
Rural Sociology — M
Russian — M
School Psychology — M,D,O
Sociology — M,D
Spanish — M,D
Theater — M,D

UNIVERSITY OF MISSOURI–KANSAS CITY
Art History — M,D
Art/Fine Arts — M,D
Clinical Psychology — M,D
Counseling Psychology — M,D,O
Criminal Justice and Criminology — M
Economics — M,D
English — M,D
French — M
Health Psychology — M,D
History — M,D
Interdisciplinary Studies — D
Media Studies — M,D
Music — M,D
Political Science — M
Psychology—General — M,D
Public Administration — M,D
Public Affairs — M,D

Romance Languages	M
Social Psychology	M,D
Sociology	M
Spanish	M
Theater	M
Therapies—Dance, Drama, and Music	M,D
Writing	M,D

UNIVERSITY OF MISSOURI–ST. LOUIS

American Studies	M,D
Clinical Psychology	M,D,O
Communication—General	M
Counseling Psychology	M
Criminal Justice and Criminology	M,D
Cultural Studies	O
Economics	M
English	M
Gender Studies	O
Gerontology	M,O
Industrial and Organizational Psychology	M,D,O
Interdisciplinary Studies	O
Museum Studies	M,O
Philosophy	M
Political Science	M,D
Psychology—General	M,D,O
Public Administration	M,D,O
Public Policy	M,D,O
School Psychology	M,O

UNIVERSITY OF MOBILE

Marriage and Family Therapy	M

THE UNIVERSITY OF MONTANA

Anthropology	M,D
Art History	M
Art/Fine Arts	M
Child and Family Studies	M,D,O
Clinical Psychology	M,D,O
Communication—General	M
Computer Art and Design	M
Counseling Psychology	M,D,O
Criminal Justice and Criminology	M
Cultural Studies	M,D,O
Developmental Psychology	M,D,O
Economics	M
English	M
Experimental Psychology	M,D,O
Film, Television, and Video Production	M
French	M
Geography	M
German	M
History	M,D
Interdisciplinary Studies	M,D
Internet and Interactive Multimedia	M
Journalism	M
Linguistics	M,D
Music	M
Philosophy	M
Photography	M
Political Science	M
Psychology—General	M,D,O
Public Administration	M
Rural Planning and Studies	M
Rural Sociology	M
School Psychology	M,D,O
Sociology	M
Spanish	M
Theater	M
Writing	M

UNIVERSITY OF MONTEVALLO

English	M
Marriage and Family Therapy	M
Social Psychology	M

UNIVERSITY OF NEBRASKA AT KEARNEY

Counseling Psychology	M,O
English	M
History	M
School Psychology	M,O
Writing	M

UNIVERSITY OF NEBRASKA AT OMAHA

Communication—General	M,O
Criminal Justice and Criminology	M,D
Economics	M
English	M,O
Geographic Information Systems	M,O
Geography	M,O
Gerontology	M,O
History	M
Industrial and Organizational Psychology	M,D,O
Music	M
Political Science	M,O
Psychology—General	M,D,O
Public Administration	M,D,O
School Psychology	M,D,O
Sociology	M
Technical Communication	M,O
Theater	M
Writing	M,O

UNIVERSITY OF NEBRASKA–LINCOLN

Agricultural Economics and Agribusiness	M,D
Anthropology	M
Archaeology	M,D
Architecture	M,D
Art History	M
Art/Fine Arts	M
Child and Family Studies	M,D
Child Development	M,D
Classics	M
Clinical Psychology	M,D
Clothing and Textiles	M,D
Cognitive Sciences	M,D,O
Communication—General	M,D
Comparative Literature	M,D
Consumer Economics	M,D
Corporate and Organizational Communication	M,D
Counseling Psychology	M,D,O
Developmental Psychology	M,D,O
Economics	M,D
English	M,D
Family and Consumer Sciences-General	M,D
French	M,D
Geography	M,D
German	M,D
Gerontology	M,D
History	M,D
Human Development	M,D,O
Interior Design	M,D
Journalism	M
Marriage and Family Therapy	M,D
Mass Communication	M
Music	M,D
Philosophy	M,D
Political Science	M,D,O
Psychology—General	M,D
Public Policy	M,D,O
Rhetoric	M,D
School Psychology	M,D,O
Social Psychology	M,D
Sociology	M,D
Spanish	M,D
Speech and Interpersonal Communication	M,D
Survey Methodology	M,D
Theater	M
Urban and Regional Planning	M,D
Writing	M,D

UNIVERSITY OF NEBRASKA MEDICAL CENTER

Emergency Management	M

UNIVERSITY OF NEVADA, LAS VEGAS

Addictions/Substance Abuse Counseling	M,D,O
Anthropology	M,D
Architecture	M,O
Art/Fine Arts	M
Clinical Psychology	M,D,O
Communication—General	M
Counseling Psychology	M,D,O
Criminal Justice and Criminology	M,D
Economics	M
Emergency Management	M,D,O
English	M,D
Ethnic Studies	M,D
Film, Television, and Video Production	M,O
Hispanic Studies	M
History	M,D
Journalism	M
Marriage and Family Therapy	M
Media Studies	M
Music	M,D,O
Political Science	M,D
Psychology—General	M,D
Public Administration	M,D,O
Public Affairs	M,D,O
Sociology	M,D
Theater	M
Writing	M,D,O

UNIVERSITY OF NEVADA, RENO

Agricultural Economics and Agribusiness	M,D
Anthropology	M,D
Applied Economics	M,D
Art/Fine Arts	M
Child and Family Studies	M
Clinical Psychology	D
Cognitive Sciences	M,D
Criminal Justice and Criminology	M
Economics	M
English	M,D
French	M
Geography	M,D
German	M
History	M,D
Human Development	M
Journalism	M
Music	M
Philosophy	M
Political Science	M,D
Psychology—General	M,D
Public Administration	M
Social Psychology	D
Sociology	M
Spanish	M
Speech and Interpersonal Communication	M
Western European Studies	D

UNIVERSITY OF NEW BRUNSWICK FREDERICTON

Anthropology	M
Applied Economics	M
Classics	M
Conflict Resolution and Mediation/Peace Studies	M
Economics	M
English	M,D
History	M,D
Interdisciplinary Studies	M,D
International Development	M
Political Science	M
Psychology—General	M,D
Public Administration	M
Public Policy	M
Sociology	M,D
Sustainable Development	M
Urban and Regional Planning	M

UNIVERSITY OF NEW BRUNSWICK SAINT JOHN

Clinical Psychology	M,D
Experimental Psychology	M,D
Psychology—General	M,D

UNIVERSITY OF NEW ENGLAND

Ethics	M,O

UNIVERSITY OF NEW HAMPSHIRE

Art/Fine Arts	M
Child and Family Studies	M,O
Comparative Literature	M,D
Economics	M,D
English	M,D
Geographic Information Systems	O
History	M,D
International Development	M
Liberal Studies	M
Linguistics	M,D
Marriage and Family Therapy	M,O
Museum Studies	M,D
Music	M
Political Science	M,O
Psychology—General	D
Public Administration	M,O
Sociology	M,D
Spanish	M
Urban and Regional Planning	M

UNIVERSITY OF NEW HAVEN

Conflict Resolution and Mediation/Peace Studies	M,O
Criminal Justice and Criminology	M,D,O
Emergency Management	M,O
Forensic Psychology	M,D,O
Forensic Sciences	M,D,O
Geographic Information Systems	M,O
Homeland Security	M,O
Industrial and Labor Relations	M,O
Industrial and Organizational Psychology	M,O
National Security	M,O
Public Administration	M,O
Social Psychology	M,O
Urban and Regional Planning	M,O

UNIVERSITY OF NEW MEXICO

American Indian/Native American Studies	M,D
American Studies	M,D
Anthropology	M,D
Archaeology	M,D
Architecture	M,D
Art History	M,D
Art/Fine Arts	M
Child and Family Studies	M,D
Clinical Psychology	D
Cognitive Sciences	D
Communication—General	M,D
Comparative Literature	M,D
Cultural Studies	M,D
Dance	M
Developmental Psychology	D
Economics	M,D
English	M,D
Ethnic Studies	M,D
French	M,D
Geography	M
German	M,D
Health Psychology	D
Historic Preservation	O
History	M,D
Human Development	M,D
International Development	M,D
International Economics	M,D
Landscape Architecture	M
Latin American Studies	M,D
Linguistics	M,D
Music	M
Philosophy	M,D
Photography	M,D
Political Science	M,D
Portuguese	M,D
Psychology—General	D
Public Administration	M
Sociology	M,D
Spanish	M,D
Theater	M
Urban and Regional Planning	M
Urban Design	O
Women's Studies	O
Writing	M

UNIVERSITY OF NEW ORLEANS

Art/Fine Arts	M
Arts Administration	M
Economics	D
English	M
Film, Television, and Video Production	M
Geography	M
History	M
Music	M
Political Science	M,D
Psychology—General	M,D
Public Administration	M
Romance Languages	M
Sociology	M
Theater	M
Urban and Regional Planning	M
Urban Studies	M,D

UNIVERSITY OF NORTH ALABAMA

Child and Family Studies	M
Criminal Justice and Criminology	M
English	M
Geographic Information Systems	M
History	M
School Psychology	M
Urban and Regional Planning	M

UNIVERSITY OF NORTH CAROLINA AT ASHEVILLE

Liberal Studies	M

THE UNIVERSITY OF NORTH CAROLINA AT CHAPEL HILL

Anthropology	M,D
Archaeology	M,D
Art History	M,D
Art/Fine Arts	M
Classics	M,D
Clinical Psychology	D
Cognitive Sciences	D
Communication—General	D
Developmental Psychology	D
East European and Russian Studies	M
Economics	M,D
English	M,D
Folklore	M
French	M,D
Geography	M,D
German	M,D
Health Psychology	M,D
History	M,D
Italian	M,D
Latin American Studies	M,D,O
Linguistics	M,D
Mass Communication	M,D
Music	M,D
Philosophy	M,D
Political Science	M,D,O
Portuguese	M,D
Psychology—General	D
Public Administration	M
Public Policy	D
Rehabilitation Counseling	M,D
Religion	M,D
Romance Languages	M,D
Russian	M,D
School Psychology	M,D
Slavic Languages	M,D
Social Psychology	D
Sociology	M,D
Spanish	M,D
Theater	M
Urban and Regional Planning	M,D

THE UNIVERSITY OF NORTH CAROLINA AT CHARLOTTE

Addictions/Substance Abuse Counseling	M,D,O
African Studies	O
Anthropology	M
Architecture	M
Arts Administration	M,O
Child Development	M,D,O
Clinical Psychology	M,D,O
Cognitive Sciences	M,D,O
Communication—General	M,O
Corporate and Organizational Communication	M,O
Criminal Justice and Criminology	M
Dance	M,O
Economics	M
Emergency Management	M,O
English	M,D,O
Ethics	M,O
Ethnic Studies	M
Gender Studies	M
Geographic Information Systems	M,D
Geography	M,D
Gerontology	M,D,O
Health Communication	M,O
Health Psychology	M,D,O
History	M
Industrial and Organizational Psychology	M,D,O
Interdisciplinary Studies	M,D,O
Latin American Studies	M,D,O
Liberal Studies	M,D,O
Media Studies	M,O
Music	O
Philosophy	M,O
Political Science	M
Psychology—General	M,D,O
Public Administration	M,O
Public Policy	M,D,O
Religion	M
Rhetoric	M,O
Social Psychology	M,D,O
Social Sciences	M
Sociology	M
Spanish	M,O
Technical Communication	M,O
Theater	M,O
Translation and Interpretation	M,O
Urban and Regional Planning	M,O
Urban Design	M
Women's Studies	M,D,O

THE UNIVERSITY OF NORTH CAROLINA AT GREENSBORO

Applied Economics	M
Architecture	M,O
Art/Fine Arts	M
Child and Family Studies	M,D
Classics	M
Clinical Psychology	M,D
Cognitive Sciences	M,D
Communication—General	M
Conflict Resolution and Mediation/Peace Studies	M,O
Counseling Psychology	M,D,O
Criminal Justice and Criminology	M
Dance	M
Developmental Psychology	M,D
Economic Development	M,D,O
Economics	D
English	M,D
Film, Television, and Video Production	M
French	M
Gender Studies	M,O
Genetic Counseling	M
Geographic Information Systems	M,D,O
Geography	M,D,O
Gerontology	M,O
Hispanic and Latin American Languages	M,O
Hispanic Studies	M,O
Historic Preservation	M,O
History	M,D,O
Human Development	M,D
Interior Design	M,O

Liberal Studies — M
Marriage and Family Therapy — M,D,O
Media Studies — M
Museum Studies — M,D,O
Music — M,D
Political Science — M,O
Psychology—General — M,D
Public Affairs — M,O
Rhetoric — M,D
School Psychology — M,D,O
Social Psychology — M,D
Sociology — M
Spanish — M,O
Technical Writing — M,D,O
Textile Design — M,D
Theater — M
Women's Studies — M,D,O
Writing — M

THE UNIVERSITY OF NORTH CAROLINA AT PEMBROKE
Counseling Psychology — M
Music — M
Public Administration — M

UNIVERSITY OF NORTH CAROLINA SCHOOL OF THE ARTS
Arts Administration — M
Film, Television, and Video Production — M
Music — M
Theater — M

THE UNIVERSITY OF NORTH CAROLINA WILMINGTON
Conflict Resolution and Mediation/Peace Studies — M,O
Criminal Justice and Criminology — M
English — M
Gerontology — M,O
Hispanic Studies — M,O
History — M
Liberal Studies — M
Psychology—General — M
Public Administration — M,O
Sociology — M
Spanish — M,O
Writing — M

UNIVERSITY OF NORTH DAKOTA
Applied Economics — M
Art/Fine Arts — M
Clinical Psychology — M,D
Communication—General — M,D
Counseling Psychology — M
Criminal Justice and Criminology — D
English — M,D
Experimental Psychology — M,D
Forensic Psychology — M,D
Geography — M
History — M,D
Linguistics — M
Music — M,D
Psychology—General — M,D
Public Administration — M
Sociology — M
Theater — M

UNIVERSITY OF NORTHERN BRITISH COLUMBIA
Disability Studies — M,D,O
Gender Studies — M,D,O
History — M,D,O
Interdisciplinary Studies — M,D,O
International Affairs — M,D,O
Political Science — M,D,O
Psychology—General — M,D,O

UNIVERSITY OF NORTHERN COLORADO
Art/Fine Arts — M
Communication—General — M
Criminal Justice and Criminology — M
English — M
Gerontology — M
History — M
Music — M,D
Psychology—General — M,D
Rehabilitation Counseling — M,D
School Psychology — D,O
Sociology — M
Spanish — M

UNIVERSITY OF NORTHERN IOWA
Art/Fine Arts — M
Communication—General — M
Counseling Psychology — M
English — M
Gender Studies — M
Geography — M
History — M
Music — M
Psychology—General — M
Public History — M
Public Policy — M
School Psychology — M,O
Social Sciences — M
Spanish — M
Women's Studies — M
Writing — M

UNIVERSITY OF NORTH FLORIDA
Applied Behavior Analysis — M
Counseling Psychology — M
Criminal Justice and Criminology — M
Economics — M
English — M
Ethics — M,O
Gerontology — M,O
History — M
Philosophy — M,O
Psychology—General — M
Public Administration — M,O

Rehabilitation Counseling — M,O
Translation and Interpretation — M
Writing — M

UNIVERSITY OF NORTH GEORGIA — M
Clinical Psychology — M
Counseling Psychology — M
Criminal Justice and Criminology — M
History — M
International Affairs — M
Music — M
Public Administration — M

UNIVERSITY OF NORTH TEXAS
Anthropology — M,D,O
Applied Arts and Design—General — M,D,O
Applied Behavior Analysis — M,D,O
Art History — M,D,O
Art/Fine Arts — M,D,O
Child and Family Studies — M,D,O
Clinical Psychology — M,D,O
Communication—General — M,D,O
Counseling Psychology — M,D,O
Criminal Justice and Criminology — M,D,O
Economics — M,D,O
Emergency Management — M,D,O
English — M,D,O
Film, Television, and Video Production — M,D,O
French — M,D,O
Geography — M,D,O
Gerontology — M,D,O
History — M,D,O
Human Development — M,D,O
Interdisciplinary Studies — M,D,O
Interior Design — M,D,O
International Affairs — M,D,O
Internet and Interactive Multimedia — M,D,O
Journalism — M,D,O
Linguistics — M,D,O
Museum Studies — M,D,O
Music — M,D,O
Philosophy — M,D,O
Political Science — M,D,O
Psychology—General — M,D,O
Public Administration — M,D,O
Rehabilitation Counseling — M,D,O
Sociology — M,D,O
Spanish — M,D,O
Textile Design — M,D,O
Writing — M,D,O

UNIVERSITY OF NORTH TEXAS HEALTH SCIENCE CENTER AT FORT WORTH
Forensic Sciences — M,D

UNIVERSITY OF NORTHWESTERN–ST. PAUL
Family and Consumer Sciences-General — M
Pastoral Ministry and Counseling — M
Theology — M

UNIVERSITY OF NOTRE DAME
Applied Arts and Design—General — M
Architecture — M
Art History — M
Art/Fine Arts — M
Cognitive Sciences — D
Comparative Literature — D
Conflict Resolution and Mediation/Peace Studies — M,D
Counseling Psychology — D
Developmental Psychology — D
Economics — M,D
English — M,D
French — M
Graphic Design — M
History of Science and Technology — M,D
History — M,D
Industrial Design — M
Italian — M
Latin American Studies — M
Medieval and Renaissance Studies — M,D
Philosophy — D
Photography — M
Political Science — D
Psychology—General — D
Religion — M
Romance Languages — M
Sociology — D
Spanish — M
Theology — M,D
Writing — M

UNIVERSITY OF OKLAHOMA
Addictions/Substance Abuse Counseling — M,O
American Indian/Native American Studies — M,D
Anthropology — M,D
Applied Economics — M,D
Archaeology — M,D
Architecture — M
Art History — M,D
Art/Fine Arts — M
Communication—General — M,D
Corporate and Organizational Communication — M,D
Counseling Psychology — M,D
Dance — M
Economics — M,D
English — M,D
Film, Television, and Video Production — M,D
French — M,D
Gender Studies — O
Geography — M
German — M
History of Science and Technology — M,D

History — M,D
Industrial and Organizational Psychology — M,D
Interdisciplinary Studies — M,D
Interior Design — M
International Affairs — M,O
Journalism — M,D
Landscape Architecture — M
Liberal Studies — M,O
Lighting Design — M
Mass Communication — M,D
Museum Studies — M,O
Music — M,D
Philosophy — M,D
Photography — M,D
Political Science — M,D
Psychology—General — M,D
Public Administration — M
Public Policy — M
Sociology — M,D
Spanish — M,D
Sustainable Development — M,D
Theater — M
Urban and Regional Planning — M
Urban Studies — M
Women's Studies — O
Writing — M

UNIVERSITY OF OKLAHOMA HEALTH SCIENCES CENTER
Genetic Counseling — M
Homeland Security — M

UNIVERSITY OF OREGON
Anthropology — M,D
Architecture — M
Art History — M,D
Art/Fine Arts — M
Arts Administration — M
Asian Languages — M,D
Asian Studies — M
Chinese — M,D
Classics — M
Clinical Psychology — D
Cognitive Sciences — M,D
Communication—General — M,D
Comparative Literature — M,D
Dance — M
Developmental Psychology — M,D
Economics — M,D
English — M,D
Folklore — M
French — M
Geography — M,D
German — M,D
Historic Preservation — M
History — M,D
Interdisciplinary Studies — M
Interior Design — M
International Affairs — M
Italian — M
Japanese — M,D
Journalism — M,D
Landscape Architecture — M
Linguistics — M,D
Media Studies — M,D
Music — M,D
Philosophy — M,D
Political Science — M,D
Psychology—General — M,D
Public Policy — M
Romance Languages — M,D
Russian — M
Social Psychology — M,D
Sociology — M,D
Spanish — M,D
Theater — M,D
Urban and Regional Planning — M
Writing — M

UNIVERSITY OF OTTAWA
Anthropology — M
Canadian Studies — D
Classics — M,D
Communication—General — M
Criminal Justice and Criminology — M,D
Economics — M,D
English — M,D
French — M,D
Geography — M,D
History — M,D
Interdisciplinary Studies — D,O
International Development — M
Linguistics — M,D
Music — M,O
Philosophy — M,D
Political Science — M,D
Psychology—General — D
Public Administration — D,O
Religion — M,D
Sociology — M
Spanish — M,D
Theater — M
Translation and Interpretation — M,D
Women's Studies — M

UNIVERSITY OF PENNSYLVANIA
African Studies — M,D
Anthropology — M,D
Applied Economics — D
Applied Psychology — M,D
Archaeology — M,D
Architecture — M,D,O
Art History — M,D
Art/Fine Arts — M,O
Asian Studies — M,D
Classics — M,D
Communication—General — D
Comparative Literature — M,D
Computer Art and Design — M
Counseling Psychology — M
Criminal Justice and Criminology — M,D

Demography and Population Studies — M,D
Economic Development — M,O
Economics — M,D
English — M,D
Ethics — M,D
French — M,D
Geographic Information Systems — M,D,O
German — M,O
Graphic Design — M,O
Historic Preservation — M,O
History of Science and Technology — M,D
History — M,D
Human Development — M,D
International Affairs — M
Internet and Interactive Multimedia — M,O
Italian — M,D
Landscape Architecture — M,O
Liberal Studies — M
Linguistics — M,D
Music — M,D
Near and Middle Eastern Studies — M,D
Philosophy — M,D
Political Science — M,D,O
Psychology—General — D
Public Administration — M,O
Public Policy — M,D
Religion — D
Romance Languages — M,D
Sociology — M,D
Spanish — M,D
Urban and Regional Planning — M,D,O
Urban Design — M,D,O
Writing — M

UNIVERSITY OF PHILOSOPHICAL RESEARCH
Psychology—General — M
Theology — M

UNIVERSITY OF PHOENIX–ATLANTA CAMPUS
Public Administration — M

UNIVERSITY OF PHOENIX–AUGUSTA CAMPUS
Criminal Justice and Criminology — M
Public Administration — M

UNIVERSITY OF PHOENIX–AUSTIN CAMPUS
Criminal Justice and Criminology — M
Public Administration — M

UNIVERSITY OF PHOENIX–BAY AREA CAMPUS
Criminal Justice and Criminology — M
Marriage and Family Therapy — M
Public Administration — M,D

UNIVERSITY OF PHOENIX–BIRMINGHAM CAMPUS
Criminal Justice and Criminology — M
Gerontology — M
Psychology—General — M
Public Administration — M

UNIVERSITY OF PHOENIX–CENTRAL VALLEY CAMPUS
Gerontology — M
Marriage and Family Therapy — M
Public Administration — M

UNIVERSITY OF PHOENIX–CHARLOTTE CAMPUS
Gerontology — M

UNIVERSITY OF PHOENIX–CLEVELAND CAMPUS
Public Administration — M

UNIVERSITY OF PHOENIX–COLORADO CAMPUS
Public Administration — M
School Psychology — M

UNIVERSITY OF PHOENIX–COLORADO SPRINGS DOWNTOWN CAMPUS
Gerontology — M
Public Administration — M
School Psychology — M,O

UNIVERSITY OF PHOENIX–COLUMBUS GEORGIA CAMPUS
Public Administration — M

UNIVERSITY OF PHOENIX–DALLAS CAMPUS
Criminal Justice and Criminology — M
Public Administration — M

UNIVERSITY OF PHOENIX–DES MOINES CAMPUS
Criminal Justice and Criminology — M
Gerontology — M,D
Public Administration — M

UNIVERSITY OF PHOENIX–HAWAII CAMPUS
Gerontology — M
Public Administration — M

UNIVERSITY OF PHOENIX–HOUSTON CAMPUS
Public Administration — M

UNIVERSITY OF PHOENIX–IDAHO CAMPUS
Public Administration — M

UNIVERSITY OF PHOENIX–INDIANAPOLIS CAMPUS
Public Administration — M

---

*M—masters degree; D—doctorate; O—other advanced degree; *—Close-Up and/or Display*

UNIVERSITY OF PHOENIX–JERSEY CITY CAMPUS
Criminal Justice and Criminology M
Psychology—General M
Public Administration M

UNIVERSITY OF PHOENIX–KANSAS CITY CAMPUS
Criminal Justice and Criminology M
Public Administration M

UNIVERSITY OF PHOENIX–LAS VEGAS CAMPUS
Counseling Psychology M
Marriage and Family Therapy M
Public Administration M
School Psychology M

UNIVERSITY OF PHOENIX–MEMPHIS CAMPUS
Criminal Justice and Criminology M
Public Administration M

UNIVERSITY OF PHOENIX–MINNEAPOLIS/ST. PAUL CAMPUS
Public Administration M
Social Psychology M

UNIVERSITY OF PHOENIX–NORTH FLORIDA CAMPUS
Public Administration M

UNIVERSITY OF PHOENIX–ONLINE CAMPUS
Conflict Resolution and Mediation/Peace Studies M,O
Criminal Justice and Criminology M
Homeland Security M
Industrial and Organizational Psychology M,D,O
Psychology—General M,O
Public Administration M,O

UNIVERSITY OF PHOENIX–OREGON CAMPUS
Public Administration M

UNIVERSITY OF PHOENIX–PHILADELPHIA CAMPUS
Psychology—General M
Public Administration M

UNIVERSITY OF PHOENIX–PHOENIX CAMPUS
Clinical Psychology M
Counseling Psychology M
Criminal Justice and Criminology M
Homeland Security M
Marriage and Family Therapy M
Psychology—General M
Public Administration M
Social Psychology M

UNIVERSITY OF PHOENIX–PUERTO RICO CAMPUS
Counseling Psychology M
Marriage and Family Therapy M
School Psychology M

UNIVERSITY OF PHOENIX–RICHMOND-VIRGINIA BEACH CAMPUS
Public Administration M

UNIVERSITY OF PHOENIX–SACRAMENTO VALLEY CAMPUS
Public Administration M

UNIVERSITY OF PHOENIX–ST. LOUIS CAMPUS
Criminal Justice and Criminology M
Public Administration M

UNIVERSITY OF PHOENIX–SAN ANTONIO CAMPUS
Criminal Justice and Criminology M
Public Administration M

UNIVERSITY OF PHOENIX–SAN DIEGO CAMPUS
Public Administration M

UNIVERSITY OF PHOENIX–SAVANNAH CAMPUS
Criminal Justice and Criminology M
Public Administration M

UNIVERSITY OF PHOENIX–SOUTHERN ARIZONA CAMPUS
Psychology—General M

UNIVERSITY OF PHOENIX–SOUTHERN CALIFORNIA CAMPUS
Criminal Justice and Criminology M
Homeland Security M
Marriage and Family Therapy M
Psychology—General M
Public Administration M

UNIVERSITY OF PHOENIX–SOUTH FLORIDA CAMPUS
Public Administration M

UNIVERSITY OF PHOENIX–UTAH CAMPUS
School Psychology M

UNIVERSITY OF PHOENIX–WASHINGTON D.C. CAMPUS
Criminal Justice and Criminology M
Gerontology M,D
Industrial and Organizational Psychology M,D
Psychology—General M,D
Public Administration M,D

UNIVERSITY OF PHOENIX–WESTERN WASHINGTON CAMPUS
Criminal Justice and Criminology M

UNIVERSITY OF PITTSBURGH
African Studies O
Anthropology M,D
Applied Behavior Analysis M,D
Applied Psychology M,D
Architectural History M,D
Art History M,D
Asian Studies M,O
Communication—General M,D
Criminal Justice and Criminology M
Cultural Studies O
Developmental Psychology M,D
Disability Studies O
East European and Russian Studies O
Economics M,D
English M,D
Film, Television, and Video Theory and Criticism M,D,O
French M,D
Genetic Counseling M,D,O
Geographic Information Systems M,D
Hispanic and Latin American Languages M,D
History of Science and Technology M,D
History M,D
Interdisciplinary Studies D
International Affairs M,D,O
International Development M
Italian M
Latin American Studies O
Linguistics M,D
Medieval and Renaissance Studies O
Military and Defense Studies M
Music M,D
Philosophy M,D
Political Science M,D
Psychology—General M,D
Public Administration M,D
Public Policy M,D
Slavic Languages M,D
Sociology M,D
Spanish M,D
Theater M,D
Urban and Regional Planning M
Western European Studies O
Women's Studies O
Writing M,D

UNIVERSITY OF PORTLAND
Communication—General M
Corporate and Organizational Communication M
Pastoral Ministry and Counseling M
Theater M

UNIVERSITY OF PRINCE EDWARD ISLAND
Geography M

UNIVERSITY OF PUERTO RICO, MAYAGÜEZ CAMPUS
Agricultural Economics and Agribusiness M
English M
Hispanic Studies M

UNIVERSITY OF PUERTO RICO, MEDICAL SCIENCES CAMPUS
Demography and Population Studies M
Gerontology M,O

UNIVERSITY OF PUERTO RICO, RÍO PIEDRAS CAMPUS
Architecture M
Clinical Psychology M,D
Communication—General M
Comparative Literature M
Economic Development M
Economics M
English M,D
Family and Consumer Sciences-General M
Hispanic Studies M,D
History M,D
Industrial and Organizational Psychology M,D
Journalism M
Linguistics M,D
Mass Communication M
Philosophy M
Psychology—General M,D
Public Administration M
Public Policy M
Rehabilitation Counseling M
Social Psychology M,D
Sociology M
Translation and Interpretation M,O
Urban and Regional Planning M

UNIVERSITY OF PUGET SOUND
Counseling Psychology M

UNIVERSITY OF REDLANDS
Geographic Information Systems M
Music M

UNIVERSITY OF REGINA
Anthropology M
Applied Economics M
Applied Psychology M,D
Art/Fine Arts M
Canadian Studies M,D
Clinical Psychology M,D
Criminal Justice and Criminology M
Economics M,D,O
English M
Experimental Psychology M,D
Film, Television, and Video Production M
French M
Geography M,D
Gerontology M
History M
Interdisciplinary Studies M
Journalism M
Linguistics M

Music M
Philosophy M
Political Science M
Psychology—General M,D
Public Administration M,D,O
Public Policy M,D,O
Religion M
Social Sciences M
Sociology M
Women's Studies M
Writing M

UNIVERSITY OF RHODE ISLAND
Child and Family Studies M
Clinical Psychology M,D
Clothing and Textiles M
Communication—General M
Counseling Psychology M
Economics M,D
English M,D
Forensic Sciences M,D,O
Gerontology M,D
History M
Industrial and Labor Relations M
International Affairs M
Music M
Political Science M
Psychology—General M,D
Public Administration M
Public Policy M
School Psychology M,D
Spanish M
Sport Psychology M

UNIVERSITY OF ROCHESTER
American Studies M,D
Art History M,D
Art/Fine Arts M,D
Clinical Psychology D
Cognitive Sciences D
Developmental Psychology D
Economics M,D
English M,D
Historic Preservation M
History M,D
Human Development M,D
International Affairs M,D
Linguistics M
Marriage and Family Therapy M
Music M,D
Philosophy M,D
Photography M
Political Science D
Psychology—General D
Public Policy M
Social Psychology M,D
Translation and Interpretation M,O
Western European Studies M,D

UNIVERSITY OF ST. FRANCIS (IL)
Forensic Sciences M,O

UNIVERSITY OF SAINT FRANCIS (IN)
Art/Fine Arts M
Clinical Psychology M,O
Counseling Psychology M,O
Pastoral Ministry and Counseling M,O
Psychology—General M,O
Rehabilitation Counseling M,O
Theology M

UNIVERSITY OF SAINT JOSEPH
Applied Behavior Analysis M,O
Clinical Psychology M
Counseling Psychology M
Gerontology O
Marriage and Family Therapy M

UNIVERSITY OF SAINT MARY
Counseling Psychology M
Psychology—General M

UNIVERSITY OF SAINT MARY OF THE LAKE–MUNDELEIN SEMINARY
Pastoral Ministry and Counseling M,D
Theology M,D

UNIVERSITY OF ST. MICHAEL'S COLLEGE
Jewish Studies M,D,O
Pastoral Ministry and Counseling M,D,O
Theology M,D,O

UNIVERSITY OF ST. THOMAS (MN)
Art History M
Corporate and Organizational Communication M
Counseling Psychology M,D,O
English M
Ethics M,D
Human Development M,D
Marriage and Family Therapy M,D,O
Music M
Pastoral Ministry and Counseling M
Psychology—General M,D,O
Religion M
Theology M

UNIVERSITY OF ST. THOMAS (TX)
Liberal Studies M
Pastoral Ministry and Counseling M
Philosophy M,D
Religion M
Theology M

UNIVERSITY OF SAN DIEGO
Conflict Resolution and Mediation/Peace Studies M
Counseling Psychology M
History M
International Affairs M
Theater M

UNIVERSITY OF SAN FRANCISCO
Asian Studies M
Counseling Psychology M
Economics M
International Affairs M

International Development M
Internet and Interactive Multimedia M
Marriage and Family Therapy M
Museum Studies M
Pacific Area/Pacific Rim Studies M
Public Administration M
Public Affairs M
Urban Studies M
Writing M

UNIVERSITY OF SASKATCHEWAN
Agricultural Economics and Agribusiness M,D,O
Anthropology M
Archaeology M,D
Art/Fine Arts M
Canadian Studies M,D
East European and Russian Studies M
Economics M,O
English M,D
French M
Gender Studies M,D
Geography M,D
German M
History M,D
Music M
Philosophy M
Political Science M
Psychology—General M,D
Public Affairs M,D
Public Policy M,D
Religion M
Sociology M,D
Theater M
Women's Studies M,D

THE UNIVERSITY OF SCRANTON
Clinical Psychology M
Counseling Psychology M
Rehabilitation Counseling M
Theology M

UNIVERSITY OF SOUTH AFRICA
Anthropology M,D
Archaeology M,D
Art History M,D
Classics M,D
Clinical Psychology M,D
Communication—General M,D
Counseling Psychology M,D
Criminal Justice and Criminology M,D
Economics M,D
English M,D
Ethics M,D
Family and Consumer Sciences-General M,D
French M,D
Geography M,D
German M,D
History M,D
Human Development M,D
Industrial and Organizational Psychology M,D
Italian M,D
Linguistics M,D
Missions and Missiology M,D
Music M,D
Near and Middle Eastern Languages M,D
Near and Middle Eastern Studies M,D
Pastoral Ministry and Counseling M,D
Philosophy M,D
Political Science M,D
Portuguese M,D
Psychology—General M,D
Public Administration M,D
Religion M,D
Romance Languages M,D
Russian M,D
Sociology M,D
Spanish M,D
Theology M,D

UNIVERSITY OF SOUTH ALABAMA
Clinical Psychology D
Communication—General M
Counseling Psychology D
English M
History M
Interdisciplinary Studies M,D
Music M
Public Administration M

UNIVERSITY OF SOUTH CAROLINA
Anthropology M,D
Art History M
Art/Fine Arts M
Clinical Psychology M,D
Comparative Literature M,D
Consumer Economics M
Criminal Justice and Criminology M,D
Economics M,D
English M,D
Experimental Psychology M,D
French M,D
Genetic Counseling M
Geography M,D
German M,D
Gerontology O
Historic Preservation M,O
History M,D,O
International Affairs M,D
Journalism M,D
Linguistics M,D,O
Media Studies M
Museum Studies M,O
Music M,D,O
Philosophy M,D
Political Science M,D
Psychology—General M,D
Public Administration M
Public History M,O
Rehabilitation Counseling M,O
Religion M
School Psychology D
Social Psychology M,D

Sociology M,D
Spanish M,D
Speech and Interpersonal
Communication M,D
Theater M,D
Women's Studies O
Writing M,D

UNIVERSITY OF SOUTH CAROLINA AIKEN
Applied Psychology M
Clinical Psychology M

THE UNIVERSITY OF SOUTH DAKOTA
Addictions/Substance Abuse
Counseling M,D,O
Art/Fine Arts M
Clinical Psychology M,D
Communication—General M
Criminal Justice and Criminology M
English M,D
Graphic Design M
History M
Human Development M,D,O
Interdisciplinary Studies M
Music M
Political Science M,D
Psychology—General M,D
Public Administration M,D
Public Policy M,D
School Psychology M,D,O
Theater M

UNIVERSITY OF SOUTHERN CALIFORNIA
American Studies D
Architecture M,D
Art History M,D,O
Art/Fine Arts M,D,O
Arts Administration M
Asian Languages M,D
Asian Studies M,D
Child and Family Studies M,D
Classics M,D
Clinical Psychology M,D
Cognitive Sciences M,D
Communication—General M,D
Comparative Literature D
Computer Art and Design M
Corporate and Organizational
Communication M
Cultural Studies D
Developmental Psychology M,D
Economic Development M,D
Economics M,D
English M,D
Film, Television, and Video
Production M
Film, Television, and Video
Theory and Criticism M,D
Geographic Information Systems M,O
Geography M,O
Gerontology M,D,O
Health Communication M,D
History D
Homeland Security M,O
International Affairs M,D
Internet and Interactive
Multimedia M,D,O
Journalism M
Latin American Studies D
Linguistics M,D
Marriage and Family Therapy M
Media Studies M,D
Music M,D,O
Philosophy M,D
Photography M
Political Science M,D
Psychology—General M,D
Public Administration M,O
Public Policy M,D,O
Rhetoric D
Slavic Languages M,D
Social Psychology M,D
Sociology D
Spanish D
Sustainable Development M,D,O
Theater
Urban and Regional Planning M,D,O
Writing M,D

UNIVERSITY OF SOUTHERN INDIANA
Communication—General M
English M
Liberal Studies M
Public Administration M

UNIVERSITY OF SOUTHERN MAINE
Addictions/Substance Abuse
Counseling M,O
American Studies M,O
Applied Behavior Analysis M,O
Counseling Psychology M,O
Cultural Studies M
Music M
Public Policy M
Rehabilitation Counseling M,O
School Psychology M,D
Urban and Regional Planning M,O
Writing M

UNIVERSITY OF SOUTHERN MISSISSIPPI
Anthropology M
Child and Family Studies M
Clinical Psychology M,D
Counseling Psychology M,D
Criminal Justice and Criminology M,D
Economic Development M,D
Economics M,D
English M,D
Experimental Psychology M,D
Forensic Sciences M,D

Geography M,D
History M,D
International Affairs M,D
International Development M,D
Marriage and Family Therapy M
Mass Communication M,D
Music M,D
Political Science M,D
Psychology—General M,D
School Psychology M,D
Speech and Interpersonal
Communication M,D
Theater M
Writing M,D

UNIVERSITY OF SOUTH FLORIDA
Addictions/Substance Abuse
Counseling M
African Studies M,O
American Studies M
Anthropology M,D,O
Applied Behavior Analysis M,D
Archaeology M,D,O
Architecture M
Art History M
Art/Fine Arts M
Child and Family Studies M,D,O
Clinical Psychology D
Cognitive Sciences D
Communication—General M,D
Comparative Literature O
Corporate and Organizational
Communication M,O
Counseling Psychology O
Criminal Justice and Criminology M,D,O
Cultural Anthropology M,D,O
Economics M,D
Emergency Management O
English M,D,O
Film, Television, and Video
Theory and Criticism M
French M
Gender Studies M,O
Geographic Information Systems M,D,O
Geography M,D,O
Gerontology M,D,O
History M,D
Humanities M
Industrial and Organizational
Psychology D
Interdisciplinary Studies M,D
International Affairs M,D,O
Internet and Interactive
Multimedia M,O
Journalism M,O
Latin American Studies M,D,O
Liberal Studies M
Marriage and Family Therapy M,O
Mass Communication M,O
Media Studies M
Museum Studies O
Music M,D
Philosophy M,D
Political Science M,D,O
Psychology—General D
Public Administration O
Public Affairs O
Public Policy M,D
Rehabilitation Counseling M,O
Religion M,D
Rhetoric M,D
School Psychology M,D,O
Sociology M,D
Spanish M
Sustainable Development M,O
Technical Communication O
Urban and Regional Planning M,D,O
Women's Studies M
Writing M,D,O

UNIVERSITY OF SOUTH FLORIDA, ST. PETERSBURG
Computer Art and Design M
Journalism M
Liberal Studies M
Media Studies M
Psychology—General M

UNIVERSITY OF SOUTH FLORIDA SARASOTA-MANATEE
Criminal Justice and Criminology M

THE UNIVERSITY OF TAMPA
Writing M

THE UNIVERSITY OF TENNESSEE
Anthropology M,D
Applied Psychology M,D
Archaeology M,D
Architecture M
Art/Fine Arts M
Child and Family Studies M,D
Clinical Psychology M,D
Clothing and Textiles M,D
Communication—General M,D
Consumer Economics M,D
Counseling Psychology M,D
Criminal Justice and Criminology M,D
Cultural Anthropology M,D
Economics M,D
English M,D
Experimental Psychology M,D
Family and Consumer
Sciences-General D
French M,D
Geography M,D
German M,D
Gerontology M
Graphic Design M
History M,D
Industrial and Organizational
Psychology D

Italian D
Journalism M,D
Landscape Architecture M
Linguistics D
Media Studies M,D
Music M
Philosophy M,D
Photography M
Political Science M,D
Portuguese D
Psychology—General M,D
Public Administration M,D
Rehabilitation Counseling M,D
Religion M
Russian D
School Psychology M,D,O
Sociology M,D
Spanish M,D
Speech and Interpersonal
Communication M,D
Theater M

THE UNIVERSITY OF TENNESSEE AT CHATTANOOGA
Criminal Justice and Criminology M
English M,O
Ethics M,O
Experimental Psychology M
Industrial and Organizational
Psychology M
Music M
Psychology—General M
Public Administration M,O
Rhetoric M,O
School Psychology M,D,O
Social Psychology M,D,O
Writing M,O

THE UNIVERSITY OF TENNESSEE AT MARTIN
Child and Family Studies M
Child Development M
Family and Consumer
Sciences-General M
Interdisciplinary Studies M
Social Psychology M

THE UNIVERSITY OF TEXAS AT ARLINGTON
Anthropology M
Architecture M
Art/Fine Arts M
Communication—General M
Criminal Justice and Criminology M
Economics M
English M,D
Experimental Psychology M,D
Film, Television, and Video
Production M
French M
Health Psychology M,D
History M,D
Industrial and Organizational
Psychology M,D
Interdisciplinary Studies M
Landscape Architecture M
Linguistics M,D
Music M
Political Science M
Psychology—General M,D
Public Administration M
Public Affairs D
Sociology M
Spanish M
Sustainable Development M
Urban and Regional Planning M,D
Urban Studies M

THE UNIVERSITY OF TEXAS AT AUSTIN
African Studies M,D
American Studies M,D
Anthropology M,D
Applied Arts and Design—
General M
Archaeology M,D
Architectural History M,D
Architecture M
Art History M,D
Art/Fine Arts M
Asian Languages M,D
Asian Studies M,D
Child and Family Studies M,D
Child Development M,D
Classics M,D
Clinical Psychology D
Communication—General M,D
Comparative Literature M,D
Counseling Psychology M,D
Cultural Studies M,D
Dance M,D
Developmental Psychology D
East European and Russian Studies M
Economics M,D
English M,D
Family and Consumer
Sciences-General M,D
Film, Television, and Video
Production M,D
Folklore M,D
French M,D
Geography M,D
German M,D
Hispanic and Latin American
Languages M,D
Hispanic Studies M
Historic Preservation M
History M,D
Human Development M,D
Interior Design M
Italian M,D
Journalism M,D
Landscape Architecture M

Latin American Studies M
Linguistics M,D
Media Studies M,D
Mineral Economics M
Music M,D
Near and Middle Eastern Languages M,D
Near and Middle Eastern Studies M,D
Philosophy D
Political Science M,D
Portuguese M,D
Psychology—General D
Public Administration M,D
Public Affairs M,D
Public History M,D
Public Policy M,D
Rehabilitation Counseling M,D
Romance Languages M,D
School Psychology M,D
Slavic Languages M,D
Sociology M,D
Spanish M,D
Sport Psychology M,D
Sustainable Development M
Theater M,D
Urban and Regional Planning M,D
Urban Design M
Writing M,D

THE UNIVERSITY OF TEXAS AT BROWNSVILLE
English M
History M
Political Science M
Psychology—General M
Sociology M
Spanish M
Translation and Interpretation M

THE UNIVERSITY OF TEXAS AT DALLAS
Child and Family Studies M,D
Cognitive Sciences M,D
Communication—General M,D
Comparative Literature M,D
Criminal Justice and Criminology M,D
Economics M,D
English M,D
Geographic Information Systems M,D
Geography M,D
History M,D
Humanities M,D
Interdisciplinary Studies M
Internet and Interactive
Multimedia M,D
Latin American Studies M,D
Philosophy M,D
Political Science M,D
Psychology—General M,D
Public Affairs M,D
Public Policy M,D
Sociology M,D

THE UNIVERSITY OF TEXAS AT EL PASO
Anthropology M,O
Applied Psychology M,O
Art/Fine Arts M
Clinical Psychology M,D
Communication—General M
Economics M
English M,D,O
Experimental Psychology M,D
History M,D
Interdisciplinary Studies M
Liberal Studies M
Linguistics M,O
Music M
Philosophy M
Political Science M
Psychology—General M,D
Rehabilitation Counseling M
Rhetoric M,D,O
Sociology M,O
Spanish M,O
Writing M,D,O

THE UNIVERSITY OF TEXAS AT SAN ANTONIO
Anthropology M,D
Applied Behavior Analysis M,O
Architecture M
Art History M
Art/Fine Arts M
Communication—General M
Criminal Justice and Criminology M
Cultural Studies M,D
Demography and Population Studies D
Economics M
English M,D
History M
Interdisciplinary Studies M,D
Music M
Philosophy M
Political Science M
Psychology—General M,D
Public Administration M
School Psychology M,O
Sociology M
Spanish M
Urban and Regional Planning M

THE UNIVERSITY OF TEXAS AT TYLER
Art History M
Art/Fine Arts M
Clinical Psychology M
Communication—General M
Counseling Psychology M
Criminal Justice and Criminology M,D
English M
History M
Interdisciplinary Studies M
Marriage and Family Therapy M
Political Science M

*M—masters degree; D—doctorate; O—other advanced degree; *—Close-Up and/or Display*

Psychology—General M
Public Administration M
School Psychology M
Social Sciences M
Sociology M

THE UNIVERSITY OF TEXAS HEALTH SCIENCE CENTER AT HOUSTON
Genetic Counseling M

THE UNIVERSITY OF TEXAS HEALTH SCIENCE CENTER AT SAN ANTONIO
Interdisciplinary Studies D

THE UNIVERSITY OF TEXAS MEDICAL BRANCH
Humanities M,D

THE UNIVERSITY OF TEXAS OF THE PERMIAN BASIN
Applied Psychology M
Clinical Psychology M
Criminal Justice and Criminology M
English M
Experimental Psychology M
History M
Political Science M
Psychology—General M
Spanish M

THE UNIVERSITY OF TEXAS–PAN AMERICAN
Anthropology M
Art/Fine Arts M
Clinical Psychology M
Communication—General M,O
Criminal Justice and Criminology M
English M
Experimental Psychology M
History M
Interdisciplinary Studies M
Music M
Psychology—General M
Public Administration M
Rehabilitation Counseling M,D
School Psychology M
Sociology M
Spanish M,D
Theater M,O
Writing M

THE UNIVERSITY OF TEXAS SOUTHWESTERN MEDICAL CENTER
Clinical Psychology D
Rehabilitation Counseling M

THE UNIVERSITY OF THE ARTS
Art/Fine Arts M
Industrial Design M
Museum Studies M
Music M

UNIVERSITY OF THE CUMBERLANDS
Clinical Psychology D
Counseling Psychology M
Religion M
Theater M,D,O

UNIVERSITY OF THE DISTRICT OF COLUMBIA
Clinical Psychology M
Counseling Psychology M
English M
Public Administration M

UNIVERSITY OF THE FRASER VALLEY
Criminal Justice and Criminology M

UNIVERSITY OF THE INCARNATE WORD
Communication—General M
Industrial and Organizational Psychology M
Interdisciplinary Studies M
Psychology—General M
Religion M

UNIVERSITY OF THE PACIFIC
Communication—General M
International Affairs M,D
Music M
Psychology—General M
Public Policy M,D
School Psychology M,D,O
Therapies—Dance, Drama, and Music M

UNIVERSITY OF THE ROCKIES
Psychology—General M,D

UNIVERSITY OF THE SACRED HEART
Broadcast Journalism M,O
Communication—General M,O
Conflict Resolution and Mediation/Peace Studies M
Cultural Studies M
Film, Television, and Video Production M,O
Internet and Interactive Multimedia M,O
Writing M,O

UNIVERSITY OF THE SCIENCES
Health Psychology M
Technical Writing M,O

UNIVERSITY OF THE SOUTHWEST
Counseling Psychology M

UNIVERSITY OF THE VIRGIN ISLANDS
Public Administration M

UNIVERSITY OF THE WEST
Psychology—General M
Religion M,D
Theology M

THE UNIVERSITY OF TOLEDO
Clinical Psychology M,D
Communication—General O
Criminal Justice and Criminology M,O

Economics M,D,O
Emergency Management M,O
English M,O
Experimental Psychology M,D
French M
Gender Studies O
Geographic Information Systems M,D,O
Geography M,D,O
German M
Gerontology M,O
History M
Liberal Studies M
Music M,O
Philosophy M
Political Science M,O
Psychology—General M,D
Public Administration M,O
School Psychology M,D,O
Sociology M
Spanish M
Urban and Regional Planning M,D,O
Women's Studies O
Writing M,O

UNIVERSITY OF TORONTO
Anthropology M,D
Architecture M
Art History M,D
Asian Studies M,D
Classics M,D
Comparative Literature M,D
Criminal Justice and Criminology M,D
East European and Russian Studies M
Economics M,D
English M,D
Film, Television, and Video Theory and Criticism M,D
French M,D
Gender Studies M,D
Genetic Counseling M
Geography M,D
German M,D
History of Science and Technology M,D
History M,D
Industrial and Labor Relations M,D
International Affairs M
Italian M,D
Landscape Architecture M
Linguistics M,D
Medieval and Renaissance Studies M,D
Museum Studies M
Music M,D
Near and Middle Eastern Studies M,D
Philosophy M,D
Political Science M,D
Portuguese M,D
Psychology—General M,D
Religion M,D
Slavic Languages M,D
Social Sciences M,D
Sociology M,D
Spanish M,D
Theater M,D
Urban and Regional Planning M,D
Urban Design M,D
Women's Studies M,D
Writing M,D

THE UNIVERSITY OF TULSA
American Indian/Native American Studies M,D,O
Anthropology M,D
Art/Fine Arts M
Clinical Psychology M,D
English M,D
History M
Industrial and Organizational Psychology M,D
Museum Studies M
Psychology—General M,D

UNIVERSITY OF UTAH
American Studies M,D
Anthropology M,D
Architecture M
Art History M
Art/Fine Arts M
Asian Studies M
Child and Family Studies M
Clinical Psychology M,D
Communication—General M,D
Comparative Literature M,D
Consumer Economics M
Counseling Psychology M,D
Dance M
Economics M,D
English M,D
Film, Television, and Video Production M
French M,D
Geographic Information Systems M,D
Geography M,D
Gerontology M,O
Graphic Design M
History M,D
Human Development M
Humanities M
International Affairs M,D
Internet and Interactive Multimedia M
Latin American Studies M
Linguistics M,D
Music M,D
Near and Middle Eastern Languages M,D
Near and Middle Eastern Studies M,D
Philosophy M,D
Photography M
Political Science M
Psychology—General D
Public Administration M,D
Public Policy M
Rhetoric M,D
School Psychology M,D
Sociology M,D
Spanish M,D

Urban and Regional Planning M,D
Writing M,D

UNIVERSITY OF VALLEY FORGE
Music M
Religion M
Theology M

UNIVERSITY OF VERMONT
Agricultural Economics and Agribusiness M
Applied Economics M
Classics M
Clinical Psychology D
Communication—General M
Counseling Psychology M
English M
French M
German M
Historic Preservation M
History M
Interdisciplinary Studies M
Psychology—General D
Public Administration M

UNIVERSITY OF VICTORIA
Anthropology M
Art History M,D
Art/Fine Arts M
Asian Studies M
Child and Family Studies M,D
Classics M,D
Clinical Psychology M,D
Computer Art and Design M
Conflict Resolution and Mediation/Peace Studies M,D
Counseling Psychology M,D
Developmental Psychology M,D
Economics M,D
English M,D
Experimental Psychology M,D
Film, Television, and Video Production M
French M
Geography M,D
German M
Hispanic Studies M
History M,D
Human Development M,D
Italian M
Linguistics M,D
Music M
Pacific Area/Pacific Rim Studies M
Philosophy M
Photography M
Political Science M,D
Psychology—General M,D
Public Administration M,D
Social Psychology M,D
Sociology M,D
Theater M
Writing M

UNIVERSITY OF VIRGINIA
Anthropology M,D
Architectural History M,D
Art History M,D
Asian Studies M
Classics M,D
Clinical Psychology D
Economics M,D
English M,D,O
French M,D
German M,D
History M,D
Interdisciplinary Studies M,D
International Affairs M,D
Italian M
Landscape Architecture M
Linguistics M
Music M,D
Near and Middle Eastern Studies M
Philosophy M,D
Political Science M,D
Psychology—General M,D
Public Policy M
Religion M,D
Romance Languages M,D
School Psychology M,D
Slavic Languages M,D
Sociology M,D
Spanish M,D
Theater M
Urban and Regional Planning M
Writing M

UNIVERSITY OF WASHINGTON
Anthropology M,D
Applied Arts and Design—General M
Architecture M,D,O
Art History M,D
Art/Fine Arts M
Asian Languages M,D
Asian Studies M,D
Chinese M,D
Classics M,D
Clinical Psychology D
Cognitive Sciences D
Communication—General M,D
Comparative Literature M,D
Dance M
Developmental Psychology D
East European and Russian Studies M
Economics M,D
English M,D
French M,D
Geography M,D
German M,D
Hispanic and Latin American Languages M
Historic Preservation O
History M,D
Human Development M,D
Industrial Design M
International Affairs D

Urban and Regional Planning M,D
Writing M,D

Italian M,D
Japanese M,D
Landscape Architecture M
Lighting Design M,D,O
Linguistics M,D
Museum Studies M
Music M,D
Near and Middle Eastern Studies M,D
Philosophy M,D
Photography M
Political Science M,D
Portuguese M
Psychology—General D
Public Administration M,D
Public Affairs M,D
Public Policy M,D
Religion M,D
Russian M,D
Scandinavian Languages M,D
School Psychology M,D
Slavic Languages M,D
Social Psychology D
Social Sciences M,D
Sociology M,D
Spanish M
Sustainable Development M,D
Technical Communication M,D
Theater M,D
Urban and Regional Planning M,D
Urban Design M,D,O
Women's Studies D
Writing M

UNIVERSITY OF WASHINGTON, BOTHELL
Cultural Studies M
Public Policy M
Writing M

UNIVERSITY OF WASHINGTON, TACOMA
Interdisciplinary Studies M

UNIVERSITY OF WATERLOO
Anthropology M
Architecture M
Art/Fine Arts M
Economic Development M
Economics M,D
English M,D
French M,D
Geography M,D
German M,D
History M,D
International Affairs M,D
Near and Middle Eastern Studies M
Philosophy M,D
Political Science M,D
Psychology—General M,D
Public Affairs M
Religion D
Russian M,D
Sociology M,D
Technical Writing M,D
Urban and Regional Planning M,D

THE UNIVERSITY OF WEST ALABAMA
Child Development M
History M
Marriage and Family Therapy M
School Psychology M,O

THE UNIVERSITY OF WESTERN ONTARIO
Anthropology M,D
Classics M
Comparative Literature M,D
Counseling Psychology M
Economics M,D
English M,D
French M,D
Geography M,D
History M,D
Interdisciplinary Studies M,D
Journalism M
Media Studies M,D
Music M,D
Philosophy M,D
Political Science M,D
Psychology—General M,D
Sociology M,D
Spanish M,D
Sustainable Development M,D

UNIVERSITY OF WEST FLORIDA
Anthropology M
Archaeology M
Communication—General M
Counseling Psychology M
Criminal Justice and Criminology M,O
English M
Gerontology M
History M
Industrial and Organizational Psychology M
Military and Defense Studies M
Political Science M
Psychology—General M
Public Administration M,O
Public History M
Sociology M
Writing M

UNIVERSITY OF WEST GEORGIA
Criminal Justice and Criminology M
English M
Geographic Information Systems O
History M,O
Museum Studies M,O
Music M
Psychology—General M,D,O
Public Administration M,O
Public History M,O
Sociology M,O

UNIVERSITY OF WINDSOR
Applied Psychology M,D

Art/Fine Arts M
Clinical Psychology M,D
Communication—General M
Criminal Justice and Criminology M,D
Economics M
English M
History M
Philosophy M
Political Science M
Psychology—General M,D
Social Psychology M,D
Sociology M,D
Writing M

THE UNIVERSITY OF WINNIPEG
History M
Marriage and Family Therapy M
Public Administration M
Religion M
Theology M,O

UNIVERSITY OF WISCONSIN–EAU CLAIRE
English M
History M
Psychology—General M,O
School Psychology M,O
Writing M

UNIVERSITY OF WISCONSIN–LA CROSSE
Psychology—General M,O
School Psychology M,O

UNIVERSITY OF WISCONSIN–MADISON
African Studies M,D
African-American Studies M
Agricultural Economics and
  Agribusiness M,D
American Studies M,D
Anthropology D
Applied Arts and Design—
  General M,D
Applied Economics M,D
Archaeology D
Art History M,D
Art/Fine Arts M
Arts Administration M
Asian Languages M,D
Asian Studies M,D
Child and Family Studies M,D
Chinese M,D
Classics M,D
Clinical Psychology D
Cognitive Sciences D
Communication—General M,D
Comparative Literature M,D
Consumer Economics M,D
Counseling Psychology D
Cultural Anthropology D
Developmental Psychology D
Economics D
English M,D
Family and Consumer
  Sciences-General M,D
Film, Television, and Video
  Theory and Criticism M,D
Folklore M,D
French M,D,O
Genetic Counseling M
Geographic Information Systems M,D,O
Geography M,D,O
German M,D
History of Science and Technology M,D
History M,D
Human Development M,D
Italian M,D
Japanese M,D
Jewish Studies M,D
Journalism M,D
Landscape Architecture M
Latin American Studies M,D
Linguistics M,D
Mass Communication M,D
Media Studies M,D
Music M,D
Near and Middle Eastern Languages M,D
Near and Middle Eastern Studies M,D
Philosophy M,D
Political Science D
Portuguese M,D
Psychology—General D
Public Affairs M
Rehabilitation Counseling M,D
Rhetoric M,D
Rural Sociology M,D
Scandinavian Languages M,D
Slavic Languages M,D
Social Psychology M,D
Sociology M,D
Spanish M,D
Speech and Interpersonal
  Communication M,D
Sustainable Development M
Theater M,D
Urban and Regional Planning M,D
Women's Studies M,D
Writing M,D

UNIVERSITY OF WISCONSIN–MILWAUKEE
African Studies D
Anthropology M,D,O
Architecture M,D,O
Art History M,O
Art/Fine Arts M
Classics M,O
Clinical Psychology M,D
Communication—General M,D,O
Comparative Literature M,D,O
Conflict Resolution and
  Mediation/Peace Studies M,D,O

Counseling Psychology M,D
Criminal Justice and Criminology M
Dance M
Developmental Psychology M,D
Economics M,D
English M,D,O
Film, Television, and Video
  Production M,O
French M,O
Geographic Information Systems M,O
Geography M,D
German M,D
Gerontology M,D,O
Historic Preservation M,D,O
History M,D
Industrial and Labor Relations M
Interdisciplinary Studies D
Italian M,O
Jewish Studies M,O
Liberal Studies M
Linguistics M,D,O
Marriage and Family Therapy M,D,O
Media Studies M
Museum Studies M,D,O
Music M,O
Philosophy M
Political Science M,D
Psychology—General M,D
Public Administration M,D,O
Rhetoric M,D,O
School Psychology D,O
Slavic Languages M,O
Social Psychology M,D
Sociology M
Spanish M,O
Technical Communication M,D,O
Theater M
Translation and Interpretation M,O
Urban and Regional Planning M,O
Urban Studies M,D
Women's Studies M
Writing M,D,O

UNIVERSITY OF WISCONSIN–OSHKOSH
English M
Experimental Psychology M
Industrial and Organizational
  Psychology M
Psychology—General M
Public Administration M

UNIVERSITY OF WISCONSIN–PLATTEVILLE
Criminal Justice and Criminology M

UNIVERSITY OF WISCONSIN–RIVER FALLS
Art/Fine Arts M
School Psychology M,O

UNIVERSITY OF WISCONSIN–STEVENS POINT
Communication—General M
Corporate and Organizational
  Communication M
English M
Family and Consumer
  Sciences-General M
History M
Human Development M
Media Studies M
Speech and Interpersonal
  Communication M

UNIVERSITY OF WISCONSIN–STOUT
Applied Psychology M
Clinical Psychology M
Counseling Psychology M
Marriage and Family Therapy M
Rehabilitation Counseling M
School Psychology M,O

UNIVERSITY OF WISCONSIN–SUPERIOR
Art History M
Art Therapy M
Art/Fine Arts M
Communication—General M
Mass Communication M
School Psychology M
Social Psychology M
Speech and Interpersonal
  Communication M
Theater M

UNIVERSITY OF WISCONSIN–WHITEWATER
Communication—General M
Corporate and Organizational
  Communication M
Mass Communication M
Psychology—General M,O
School Psychology M,O
Social Psychology M

UNIVERSITY OF WYOMING
Agricultural Economics and
  Agribusiness M
American Studies M
Anthropology M,D
Applied Economics M
Child Development M
Communication—General M
Consumer Economics M
Economics M,D
English M
French M
Geography M
German M
History M
International Affairs M
Music M
Philosophy M
Political Science M

Psychology—General M,D
Public Administration M
Rural Planning and Studies M
Sociology M
Spanish M
Writing M

UPPER IOWA UNIVERSITY
Criminal Justice and Criminology M
Homeland Security M
Public Administration M

URBANA UNIVERSITY
Criminal Justice and Criminology M

URSHAN GRADUATE SCHOOL OF THEOLOGY
Theology M

URSULINE COLLEGE
Art Therapy M
Historic Preservation M
Liberal Studies M
Theology M

UTAH STATE UNIVERSITY
American Studies M
Applied Economics M
Art/Fine Arts M
Child and Family Studies M,D
Clinical Psychology M,D
Communication—General M
Consumer Economics M
Counseling Psychology M,D
Disability Studies M,D,O
Economics M,D
English M
Family and Consumer
  Sciences-General M,D
Folklore M
Geography M,D
History M
Human Development M,D
Interior Design M
Landscape Architecture M
Marriage and Family Therapy M,D
Political Science M
Psychology—General M,D
Rehabilitation Counseling M
School Psychology M,D
Sociology M,D
Theater M
Urban and Regional Planning M,D
Writing M

UTICA COLLEGE
Criminal Justice and Criminology M
Forensic Sciences M
Gerontology O
Liberal Studies M

VALDOSTA STATE UNIVERSITY
Criminal Justice and Criminology M
English M
History M
Music M
Psychology—General M,O
Rhetoric M
Sociology M

VALPARAISO UNIVERSITY
Arts Administration M
Asian Studies M
Clinical Psychology M
Communication—General M,O
English M,O
Ethics M,O
Gerontology M,O
History M,O
International Economics M
Liberal Studies M,O
Media Studies M,O
Pastoral Ministry and Counseling M
Psychology—General M
School Psychology M
Theology M,O

VANCOUVER SCHOOL OF THEOLOGY
Religion M,O
Theology M,O

VANDERBILT UNIVERSITY
Anthropology M,D
Child and Family Studies M
Classics M
Economic Development M,D
Economics M,D
English M,D
French M,D
German M,D
History M,D
Human Development M
Latin American Studies M
Liberal Studies M
Philosophy M,D
Political Science M,D
Portuguese M,D
Psychology—General M,D
Public Policy M,D
Religion M,D
Sociology M,D
Spanish M,D
Theology M
Urban and Regional Planning M
Writing M

VANGUARD UNIVERSITY OF SOUTHERN CALIFORNIA
Clinical Psychology M
Religion M
Theology M

VERMONT COLLEGE OF FINE ARTS
Art/Fine Arts M

Film, Television, and Video
  Production M
Graphic Design M
Music M
Writing M

VICTORIA UNIVERSITY
Theology M,D,O

VILLANOVA UNIVERSITY
American Studies M,O
Classics M
Communication—General M
English M
Hispanic Studies M
History M
Liberal Studies M,O
Missions and Missiology M
Philosophy D
Political Science M
Psychology—General M
Public Administration M
Theater M
Theology M

VIRGINIA BEACH THEOLOGICAL SEMINARY
Theology M

VIRGINIA COLLEGE IN BIRMINGHAM
Criminal Justice and Criminology M

VIRGINIA COMMONWEALTH UNIVERSITY
Applied Arts and Design—
  General M
Applied Social Research M,O
Architectural History M,D
Art History M,D
Art/Fine Arts M,D
Clinical Psychology D
Communication—General D
Counseling Psychology M,D,O
Criminal Justice and Criminology M,O
Developmental Psychology D
Economics M
Emergency Management M,O
English M
Forensic Sciences M
Geographic Information Systems O
Gerontology M,D,O
Health Psychology D
Historic Preservation O
History M,D
Homeland Security M,O
Humanities M,D,O
Interdisciplinary Studies M
Interior Design M
Internet and Interactive
  Multimedia M
Journalism M
Mass Communication M
Media Studies M,D
Museum Studies M,D
Music M
Photography M,D
Political Science M,D,O
Psychology—General D
Public Administration M,O
Public Affairs M,D,O
Public Policy D
Rehabilitation Counseling M,O
Rhetoric M
Social Psychology D
Sociology M,O
Theater M
Urban and Regional Planning M,D
Writing M

VIRGINIA INTERNATIONAL UNIVERSITY
Computer Art and Design M,O
Linguistics M

VIRGINIA POLYTECHNIC INSTITUTE AND STATE UNIVERSITY
Agricultural Economics and
  Agribusiness M,D
Applied Economics M,D
Architecture M,D,O
Building Science M,D,O
Communication—General M,D,O
Economics M,D
English M,D
Environmental Design M,D
Geographic Information Systems M,D
Geography M,D
History of Science and Technology M,D,O
History M,D,O
Human Development M,D,O
Humanities M,D,O
Interdisciplinary Studies M,D
International Affairs M,D,O
Internet and Interactive
  Multimedia M,D,O
Landscape Architecture M,D,O
Liberal Studies M,O
National Security M,O
Philosophy M,D,O
Political Science M,D,O
Psychology—General M,D
Public Administration M,D,O
Public Affairs M,D,O
Public Policy M,D,O
Rhetoric M,D,O
Sociology M,D,O
Theater M,D,O
Urban and Regional Planning M,D,O
Urban Studies M,D,O
Writing M,D,O

VIRGINIA STATE UNIVERSITY
Clinical Psychology M,D
Criminal Justice and Criminology M

---

*M—masters degree; D—doctorate; O—other advanced degree; *—Close-Up and/or Display*

- Economics M
- English M
- Health Psychology M,D
- Interdisciplinary Studies M
- Media Studies M
- Psychology—General M,D

VIRGINIA THEOLOGICAL SEMINARY
- Theology M,D

VIRGINIA UNION UNIVERSITY
- Theology M,D

VIRGINIA UNIVERSITY OF LYNCHBURG
- Religion M

VITERBO UNIVERSITY
- Addictions/Substance Abuse Counseling M
- Counseling Psychology M
- Developmental Psychology M
- Health Psychology M
- Pastoral Ministry and Counseling M

WAKE FOREST UNIVERSITY
- Communication—General M
- English M
- Liberal Studies M
- Psychology—General M
- Religion M
- Speech and Interpersonal Communication M

WALDEN UNIVERSITY
- Addictions/Substance Abuse Counseling M,D
- Applied Psychology M,D,O
- Child and Family Studies M,D
- Clinical Psychology M,D,O
- Communication—General M,D,O
- Conflict Resolution and Mediation/Peace Studies M,D,O
- Counseling Psychology M,D,O
- Criminal Justice and Criminology M,D,O
- Emergency Management M,D,O
- Forensic Psychology M,D,O
- Forensic Sciences M,D
- Health Psychology M,D,O
- Homeland Security M,D,O
- Industrial and Organizational Psychology M,D,O
- Interdisciplinary Studies M,D,O
- International Affairs M,D,O
- International Development M,D,O
- Marriage and Family Therapy M,D
- Psychology—General M,D,O
- Public Administration M,D,O
- Public Policy M,D,O
- Social Psychology M,D,O
- Sustainable Development M,D,O

WALLA WALLA UNIVERSITY
- Counseling Psychology M

WALSH UNIVERSITY
- Counseling Psychology M
- Pastoral Ministry and Counseling M
- Theology M

WARREN WILSON COLLEGE
- Writing M

WARTBURG THEOLOGICAL SEMINARY
- Theology M

WASHBURN UNIVERSITY
- Addictions/Substance Abuse Counseling M
- Clinical Psychology M
- Criminal Justice and Criminology M
- Liberal Studies M
- Psychology—General M

WASHINGTON ADVENTIST UNIVERSITY
- Counseling Psychology M
- Public Administration M
- Religion M

WASHINGTON COLLEGE
- English M
- History M
- Psychology—General M

WASHINGTON STATE UNIVERSITY
- Agricultural Economics and Agribusiness M,D,O
- American Studies M,D
- Anthropology M,D
- Archaeology M,D
- Architecture M
- Art/Fine Arts M
- Clinical Psychology M,D
- Clothing and Textiles M
- Communication—General M,D
- Corporate and Organizational Communication M,D
- Counseling Psychology M,D
- Criminal Justice and Criminology M,D
- Cultural Anthropology M,D
- Cultural Studies M,D
- Economics M,D,O
- English M,D
- Experimental Psychology M,D
- History M,D
- Human Development D
- Interdisciplinary Studies D
- Interior Design M
- Landscape Architecture M
- Music M
- Political Science M,D,O
- Psychology—General M,D
- Public Affairs M,D,O
- Sociology M,D

WASHINGTON UNIVERSITY IN ST. LOUIS
- American Indian/Native American Studies M,D,O
- Anthropology D
- Archaeology M,D
- Architecture M
- Art History M,D
- Art/Fine Arts M
- Asian Languages M,D
- Asian Studies M,D
- Child and Family Studies M,D,O
- Chinese M,D
- Classics M
- Clinical Psychology D
- Cognitive Sciences D
- Comparative Literature M,D
- Counseling Psychology M,D,O
- Developmental Psychology D
- Economic Development M,D,O
- Economics D
- English M,D
- French M,D
- German D
- Gerontology M,D,O
- History D
- Japanese M,D
- Jewish Studies M
- Music M,D
- Near and Middle Eastern Studies M
- Philosophy D
- Political Science M,D
- Psychology—General D
- Public Policy M
- Religion M
- Romance Languages M,D
- Social Psychology D
- Spanish M,D
- Speech and Interpersonal Communication M,D
- Theater M
- Urban Design M
- Writing M

WAYLAND BAPTIST UNIVERSITY
- Counseling Psychology M
- Criminal Justice and Criminology M
- History M
- Homeland Security M
- Interdisciplinary Studies M
- Pastoral Ministry and Counseling M
- Religion M
- Theology M

WAYNESBURG UNIVERSITY
- Addictions/Substance Abuse Counseling M,D
- Clinical Psychology M,D
- Counseling Psychology M,D

WAYNE STATE COLLEGE
- Communication—General M

WAYNE STATE UNIVERSITY
- African Studies M,D,O
- American Studies M,D,O
- Anthropology M,D
- Applied Arts and Design—General M
- Art History M
- Art Therapy M,D,O
- Art/Fine Arts M
- Classics M
- Clinical Psychology M,D
- Cognitive Sciences M,D
- Communication—General M,D
- Comparative Literature M
- Conflict Resolution and Mediation/Peace Studies M,O
- Criminal Justice and Criminology M
- Developmental Psychology M,D
- Economic Development M,D,O
- Economics M,D
- English M,D
- French M,D
- Gender Studies M,D,O
- Genetic Counseling M
- German M
- Gerontology M,D,O
- Graphic Design M
- Health Communication M,D,O
- History of Science and Technology M,D,O
- History M,D,O
- Industrial and Labor Relations M,D
- Industrial and Organizational Psychology M
- Industrial Design M
- Interior Design M
- International Economics M,D
- Italian M
- Journalism M,D,O
- Linguistics M
- Media Studies M,D,O
- Music M,O
- Near and Middle Eastern Languages M
- Near and Middle Eastern Studies M
- Philosophy M,D
- Photography M
- Political Science M,D
- Psychology—General M,D
- Public Administration M
- Public Policy M,D
- Rehabilitation Counseling M,D,O
- Romance Languages M
- School Psychology M,D,O
- Social Psychology M,D
- Sociology M,D
- Spanish M,D
- Sustainable Development O
- Textile Design M
- Theater M
- Urban and Regional Planning M,O
- Urban Studies M,D
- Western European Studies M,D,O
- Writing M,D

WEBBER INTERNATIONAL UNIVERSITY
- Criminal Justice and Criminology M

WEBER STATE UNIVERSITY
- Communication—General M
- English M

WEBSTER UNIVERSITY
- Art/Fine Arts M
- Arts Administration M
- Communication—General M
- Corporate and Organizational Communication M
- Counseling Psychology M
- Criminal Justice and Criminology M
- Forensic Sciences M
- Gerontology M
- International Affairs M
- Media Studies M
- Music M
- Public Administration M

WENTWORTH INSTITUTE OF TECHNOLOGY
- Architecture M

WESLEYAN UNIVERSITY
- Liberal Studies M
- Music M,D

WESLEY BIBLICAL SEMINARY
- Linguistics M
- Missions and Missiology M
- Pastoral Ministry and Counseling M
- Religion M
- Theology M
- Translation and Interpretation M

WESLEY THEOLOGICAL SEMINARY
- Theology M,D

WEST CHESTER UNIVERSITY OF PENNSYLVANIA
- Clinical Psychology M,O
- Communication—General M
- Criminal Justice and Criminology M
- Emergency Management M,O
- English M,O
- Ethics M,O
- French M,O
- Geographic Information Systems M,O
- Geography M,O
- History M,O
- Holocaust and Genocide Studies M,O
- Industrial and Organizational Psychology M,O
- Music M,O
- Philosophy M,O
- Psychology—General M,O
- Public Administration M,O
- Public Affairs M,O
- Spanish M,O
- Sustainable Development M,O
- Urban and Regional Planning M,O

WESTERN CAROLINA UNIVERSITY
- Applied Arts and Design—General M
- Art/Fine Arts M
- English M
- History M
- Music M
- Psychology—General M
- Public Affairs M
- School Psychology M
- Social Psychology M

WESTERN CONNECTICUT STATE UNIVERSITY
- Art/Fine Arts M
- Criminal Justice and Criminology M
- English M
- History M
- Illustration M
- Social Psychology M
- Writing M

WESTERN ILLINOIS UNIVERSITY
- Applied Arts and Design—General M
- Clinical Psychology M,O
- Communication—General M
- Criminal Justice and Criminology M,O
- Economic Development M,O
- Economics M,O
- English M,O
- Geographic Information Systems M,O
- Geography M,O
- Graphic Design M,O
- History M
- Internet and Interactive Multimedia M,O
- Liberal Studies M
- Museum Studies M,O
- Music M
- Political Science M
- Psychology—General M,O
- School Psychology M,O
- Social Psychology M,O
- Sociology M
- Sustainable Development M,O
- Theater M
- Writing M,O

WESTERN INTERNATIONAL UNIVERSITY
- Public Administration M

WESTERN KENTUCKY UNIVERSITY
- Anthropology M
- Applied Economics M
- Clinical Psychology M,O
- Communication—General M,O
- Comparative Literature M
- Corporate and Organizational Communication M,O
- Counseling Psychology M
- Criminal Justice and Criminology M
- English M
- Experimental Psychology M,O
- French M
- German M
- History M
- Homeland Security M
- Industrial and Organizational Psychology M,O
- Interdisciplinary Studies M,O
- Marriage and Family Therapy M,O
- Political Science M
- Psychology—General M,O
- Public Administration M
- School Psychology M,O
- Sociology M
- Spanish M
- Writing M

WESTERN MICHIGAN UNIVERSITY
- Anthropology M
- Applied Arts and Design—General M
- Applied Economics M,D
- Clinical Psychology M,D
- Communication—General M
- Counseling Psychology M,D
- Economics M,D*
- English M,D
- Family and Consumer Sciences-General M
- Geographic Information Systems M,O
- Geography M,D,O
- History M,D
- Industrial and Organizational Psychology M,D
- International Affairs M,D
- Music M,O
- Philosophy M
- Political Science M,D
- Psychology—General M,D
- Public Administration M,D,O
- Public Affairs M,D,O
- Rehabilitation Counseling M
- Religion M,O
- Sociology M,D
- Spanish M,D
- Therapies—Dance, Drama, and Music M,O
- Writing M,D

WESTERN MICHIGAN UNIVERSITY COOLEY LAW SCHOOL
- Homeland Security M,D
- National Security M,D

WESTERN NEW ENGLAND UNIVERSITY
- Applied Behavior Analysis M,D
- Communication—General M
- Writing M

WESTERN NEW MEXICO UNIVERSITY
- Interdisciplinary Studies M

WESTERN OREGON UNIVERSITY
- Criminal Justice and Criminology M
- Music M
- Rehabilitation Counseling M

WESTERN SEMINARY
- Pastoral Ministry and Counseling M,D,O
- Religion M,O
- Theology M,O
- Women's Studies M

WESTERN SEMINARY–SACRAMENTO CAMPUS
- Marriage and Family Therapy M
- Pastoral Ministry and Counseling M,O
- Theology M,O
- Women's Studies O

WESTERN SEMINARY–SAN JOSE CAMPUS
- Marriage and Family Therapy M,O
- Pastoral Ministry and Counseling M,O
- Theology M,O
- Women's Studies M,O

WESTERN STATE COLORADO UNIVERSITY
- Film, Television, and Video Production M
- Writing M

WESTERN THEOLOGICAL SEMINARY
- Pastoral Ministry and Counseling M,D,O
- Theology M,D,O

WESTERN WASHINGTON UNIVERSITY
- Anthropology M
- Counseling Psychology M
- English M
- Experimental Psychology M
- Geography M
- History M
- Music M
- Political Science M
- Psychology—General M
- Rehabilitation Counseling M

WESTFIELD STATE UNIVERSITY
- Applied Behavior Analysis M
- Counseling Psychology M
- Criminal Justice and Criminology M
- English M
- History M
- Psychology—General M

WEST LIBERTY UNIVERSITY
- Criminal Justice and Criminology M

WESTMINSTER COLLEGE (UT)
- Communication—General M
- Counseling Psychology M
- Writing M

WESTMINSTER SEMINARY CALIFORNIA
- Religion M
- Theology M

WESTMINSTER THEOLOGICAL SEMINARY

Missions and Missiology	M,D,O
Pastoral Ministry and Counseling	M,D,O
Religion	M,D,O
Theology	M,D,O

WEST TEXAS A&M UNIVERSITY

Agricultural Economics and Agribusiness	M
Art/Fine Arts	M
Communication—General	M
Criminal Justice and Criminology	M
Economics	M
English	M
History	M
Interdisciplinary Studies	M
Music	M
Psychology—General	M

WEST VIRGINIA STATE UNIVERSITY

Criminal Justice and Criminology	M
Media Studies	M

WEST VIRGINIA UNIVERSITY

African Studies	M,D
African-American Studies	M,D
Agricultural Economics and Agribusiness	M
American Studies	M,D
Applied Social Research	M
Art History	M
Art/Fine Arts	M
Asian Studies	M,D
Child and Family Studies	M
Clinical Psychology	M,D
Communication—General	M,D
Corporate and Organizational Communication	M,D,O
Counseling Psychology	D
Developmental Psychology	M,D
Economic Development	M,D
Economics	M,D
English	M,D
Forensic Sciences	M,D
French	M
Geographic Information Systems	M,D
Geography	M,D
Graphic Design	M
History of Science and Technology	M,D
History	M,D
Human Development	M,D
Industrial and Labor Relations	M
International Affairs	M,D
International Economics	M,D
Journalism	M,O
Latin American Studies	M,D
Liberal Studies	M
Linguistics	M
Music	M,D
Political Science	M,D
Psychology—General	M,D
Public Administration	M
Public Policy	M,D
Rehabilitation Counseling	M
Sociology	M
Spanish	M
Sport Psychology	M,D
Sustainable Development	D
Theater	M
Urban and Regional Planning	M,D
Writing	M

WEST VIRGINIA WESLEYAN COLLEGE

Writing	M

WHEATON COLLEGE

Archaeology	M,D
Clinical Psychology	M,D
Counseling Psychology	M,D
Cultural Studies	M,O
Marriage and Family Therapy	M,D
Missions and Missiology	M,O
Pastoral Ministry and Counseling	M,D
Psychology—General	M,D
Theology	M,D

WHEELOCK COLLEGE

Child and Family Studies	M
Human Development	M

WHITTIER COLLEGE

Child Development	M

WHITWORTH UNIVERSITY

Theology	M

WICHITA STATE UNIVERSITY

Anthropology	M
Art/Fine Arts	M
Clinical Psychology	D
Communication—General	M
Criminal Justice and Criminology	M
Economics	M
English	M
Gerontology	M

History	M
Liberal Studies	M
Music	M
Psychology—General	D
Public Administration	M
School Psychology	M,D,O
Social Psychology	D
Sociology	M
Spanish	M
Writing	M

WIDENER UNIVERSITY

Clinical Psychology	D
Criminal Justice and Criminology	M
Liberal Studies	M
Psychology—General	M
Public Administration	M

WILBERFORCE UNIVERSITY

Rehabilitation Counseling	M

WILFRID LAURIER UNIVERSITY

American Studies	M,D
Canadian Studies	M,D
Cognitive Sciences	M,D
Communication—General	M
Conflict Resolution and Mediation/Peace Studies	D
Criminal Justice and Criminology	M
Cultural Studies	M
Developmental Psychology	M,D
Economics	M,D
English	M,D
Film, Television, and Video Theory and Criticism	M,D
Gender Studies	M
Geography	M,D
History	M,D
International Affairs	M
International Economics	M
Media Studies	M
Pastoral Ministry and Counseling	M,D,O
Philosophy	M
Political Science	M,D
Psychology—General	M,D
Public Policy	M
Religion	M,D
Social Psychology	M,D
Social Sciences	M
Sociology	M
Theology	M,D,O
Therapies—Dance, Drama, and Music	M

WILKES UNIVERSITY

Writing	M

WILLAMETTE UNIVERSITY

Conflict Resolution and Mediation/Peace Studies	M,D

WILLIAM CAREY UNIVERSITY

Counseling Psychology	M
Psychology—General	M

WILLIAM PATERSON UNIVERSITY OF NEW JERSEY

Art/Fine Arts	M
Clinical Psychology	M,D
Communication—General	M
Counseling Psychology	M,D
English	M,D
History	M,D
Music	M
Public Policy	M,D
Sociology	M,D
Writing	M,D

WILLIAMS COLLEGE

Art History	M
Economic Development	M

WILMINGTON UNIVERSITY

Clinical Psychology	M
Counseling Psychology	M
Criminal Justice and Criminology	M
Geographic Information Systems	M
Homeland Security	M,D
Internet and Interactive Multimedia	M
Public Administration	M,D

WINEBRENNER THEOLOGICAL SEMINARY

Counseling Psychology	M,D
Theology	M,D

WINONA STATE UNIVERSITY

English	M

WINSTON-SALEM STATE UNIVERSITY

Rehabilitation Counseling	M

WINTHROP UNIVERSITY

Art/Fine Arts	M
Arts Administration	M
English	M

History	M
Liberal Studies	M
Music	M
Psychology—General	M,O
Spanish	M

WISCONSIN SCHOOL OF PROFESSIONAL PSYCHOLOGY

Clinical Psychology	M,D
Psychology—General	M,D

WON INSTITUTE OF GRADUATE STUDIES

Religion	M,O

WOODBURY UNIVERSITY

Architecture	M

WORCESTER POLYTECHNIC INSTITUTE

Interdisciplinary Studies	M,D,O
Internet and Interactive Multimedia	M
Social Sciences	M,D,O

WORCESTER STATE UNIVERSITY

History	M
School Psychology	O
Spanish	M

WRIGHT INSTITUTE

Clinical Psychology	D
Counseling Psychology	M
Psychology—General	D

WRIGHT STATE UNIVERSITY

Applied Behavior Analysis	M
Applied Economics	M
Clinical Psychology	D
Criminal Justice and Criminology	M
Economics	M
English	M
History	M
Humanities	M
Industrial and Organizational Psychology	M,D
Interdisciplinary Studies	M
Music	M
Psychology—General	M,D
Public Administration	M
Rehabilitation Counseling	M
Rhetoric	M
Urban Studies	M
Writing	M

WYCLIFFE COLLEGE

Religion	M,D,O
Theology	M,D,O

XAVIER UNIVERSITY

Clinical Psychology	M,D
Counseling Psychology	M
Criminal Justice and Criminology	M
English	M
Ethics	M
Industrial and Organizational Psychology	M,D
Pastoral Ministry and Counseling	M
Psychology—General	M,D
Sustainable Development	M
Theology	M

XAVIER UNIVERSITY OF LOUISIANA

Pastoral Ministry and Counseling	M
Theology	M

YALE UNIVERSITY

African Studies	M
African-American Studies	D
American Studies	D
Anthropology	M,D
Applied Arts and Design—General	M
Archaeology	M,D
Architecture	M,D
Art History	D
Art/Fine Arts	M
Asian Languages	D
Asian Studies	M
Classics	M,D
Clinical Psychology	D
Cognitive Sciences	D
Comparative Literature	D
Developmental Psychology	D
East European and Russian Studies	M,D
Economic Development	M
Economics	M,D
English	M,D
Environmental Design	M,D
Film, Television, and Video Theory and Criticism	D
French	M,D
German	D
Graphic Design	M
History of Medicine	M,D
History of Science and Technology	M,D
History	M,D
International Affairs	M

International Economics	M
Italian	D
Latin American Studies	D
Linguistics	D
Medieval and Renaissance Studies	M,D
Music	M,D,O
Near and Middle Eastern Languages	M,D
Near and Middle Eastern Studies	M,D
Philosophy	D
Photography	M
Political Science	D
Portuguese	D
Psychology—General	D
Religion	D
Russian	D
Slavic Languages	D
Social Psychology	D
Social Sciences	M,D
Sociology	D
Spanish	D
Theater	M,D,O
Theology	M
Writing	M,D,O

YESHIVA BETH MOSHE

Theology	O

YESHIVA DERECH CHAIM

Religion	D

YESHIVA KARLIN STOLIN RABBINICAL INSTITUTE

Theology	O

YESHIVA OF NITRA RABBINICAL COLLEGE

Theology	

YESHIVA SHAAR HATORAH TALMUDIC RESEARCH INSTITUTE

Theology	

YESHIVATH ZICHRON MOSHE

Theology	O

YESHIVA TORAS CHAIM TALMUDICAL SEMINARY

Theology	

YESHIVA UNIVERSITY

Clinical Psychology	D
Conflict Resolution and Mediation/Peace Studies	M,D
Counseling Psychology	M
Health Psychology	D
Jewish Studies	M,D
Psychology—General	M,D
School Psychology	D

YORK UNIVERSITY

Anthropology	M,D
Applied Arts and Design—General	M
Art History	M,D
Art/Fine Arts	M,D
Communication—General	M,D
Dance	M,D
Disability Studies	M,D
Economics	M,D
Emergency Management	M
English	M,D
Film, Television, and Video Production	M,D
French	M,D
Gender Studies	M,D
Geography	M,D
History	M,D
Humanities	M,D
Interdisciplinary Studies	M
International Affairs	M
Linguistics	M,D
Music	M,D
Philosophy	M,D
Political Science	M,D
Psychology—General	M,D
Public Administration	M
Public Affairs	M
Public Policy	M
Sociology	M,D
Theater	M,D
Translation and Interpretation	M
Women's Studies	M,D

YOUNGSTOWN STATE UNIVERSITY

Applied Behavior Analysis	M
Counseling Psychology	M
Criminal Justice and Criminology	M
Economics	M
English	M
Gerontology	M
History	M
Music	M
Psychology—General	M
School Psychology	M

---

*M—masters degree; D—doctorate; O—other advanced degree; *—Close-Up and/or Display*

ACADEMIC AND PROFESSIONAL PROGRAMS IN THE ARTS AND ARCHITECTURE

Section 1
Applied Arts and Design

This section contains a directory of institutions offering graduate work in applied arts and design, followed by in-depth entries submitted by institutions that chose to prepare detailed program descriptions. Additional information about programs listed in the directory but not augmented by an in-depth entry may be obtained by writing directly to the dean of a graduate school or chair of a department at the address given in the directory.

For programs offering related work, see also in this book *Architecture* and *Art and Art History*. In another guide in this series:

Graduate Programs in Business, Education, Information Studies, Law & Social Work
See *Advertising and Public Relations*

CONTENTS

Program Directories

Displays and Close-Ups

See also:

Applied Arts and Design—General

Academy of Art University, Graduate Program, School of Advertising, San Francisco, CA 94105-3410. Offers MFA. Part-time programs available. Postbaccalaureate distance learning degree programs offered (no on-campus study). *Faculty:* 9 full-time (2 women), 31 part-time/adjunct (7 women). *Students:* 166 full-time (95 women), 53 part-time (33 women); includes 29 minority (9 Black or African American, non-Hispanic/Latino; 10 Asian, non-Hispanic/Latino; 9 Hispanic/Latino; 1 Two or more races, non-Hispanic/Latino), 150 international. Average age 28. 59 applicants, 100% accepted, 27 enrolled. In 2014, 62 master's awarded. *Degree requirements:* For master's, final review. *Entrance requirements:* For master's, statement of intent; resume; portfolio/reel; official college transcripts. *Application deadline:* Applications are processed on a rolling basis. Application fee: $100. Electronic applications accepted. *Expenses: Tuition:* Part-time $910 per unit. *Financial support:* Career-related internships or fieldwork and Federal Work-Study available. Support available to part-time students. Financial award application deadline: 8/10; financial award applicants required to submit FAFSA. *Unit head:* 800-544-ARTS, E-mail: info@academyart.edu. *Application contact:* 800-544-ARTS, E-mail: info@academyart.edu.
Website: http://www.academyart.edu/advertising-school/index.html

Alfred University, Graduate School, New York State College of Ceramics, School of Art and Design, Alfred, NY 14802. Offers ceramic art (MFA); electronic integrated art (MFA); glass art (MFA); sculpture (MFA). *Accreditation:* NASAD. *Degree requirements:* For master's, thesis, exhibit. *Entrance requirements:* For master's, portfolio. Additional exam requirements/recommendations for international students: Required—TOEFL (minimum score 550 paper-based; 80 iBT), IELTS (minimum score 6). Electronic applications accepted. *Faculty research:* Ceramic art, sculpture, glass art, new media, time-based media.

Arizona State University at the Tempe campus, Herberger Institute for Design and the Arts, The Design School, Tempe, AZ 85287-1605. Offers architecture (M Arch); building design/built environment (MS); design (MSD), including arts, media, and engineering, healthcare and healing environments (MSD, PhD), industrial design, interaction design, interior design, new product innovation, visual communication design; design, environment and the arts (PhD), including design, digital culture, healthcare and healing environments (MSD, PhD), history, theory, and criticism; landscape architecture (MLA); urban design (MUD); MA/MBA. *Accreditation:* NASAD. Terminal master's awarded for partial completion of doctoral program. *Degree requirements:* For master's, thesis optional, interactive Program of Study (iPOS) submitted before completing 50 percent of required credit hours; for doctorate, comprehensive exam, thesis/dissertation, interactive Program of Study (iPOS) submitted before completing 50 percent of required credit hours. *Entrance requirements:* For master's, GRE General Test, minimum GPA of 3.0 or equivalent in last 2 years of work leading to bachelor's degree, design/creative works portfolio, 3 references, statement of intent; for doctorate, GRE, master's degree in architecture, graphic design, industrial design, interior design, landscape architecture, or art history or equivalent standing; statement of purpose; 3 letters of recommendation; indication of potential faculty mentor; sample of written work. Additional exam requirements/recommendations for international students: Required—TOEFL (minimum score 600 paper-based; 100 iBT). Electronic applications accepted.

The Art Institute of Dallas, a campus of South University, Program in Design and Media Management, Dallas, TX 75231-5993. Offers MA.

Bowling Green State University, Graduate College, College of Arts and Sciences, School of Art, Bowling Green, OH 43403. Offers 2-D studio art (MA, MFA); 3-D studio art (MA, MFA); art education (MA); art history (MA); computer art (MA); design (MFA); digital arts (MFA); graphics (MFA). *Accreditation:* NASAD. Part-time programs available. *Degree requirements:* For master's, thesis or alternative, final exhibit (MFA). *Entrance requirements:* For master's, GRE General Test (MA), slide portfolio (15-20 slides). Additional exam requirements/recommendations for international students: Required—TOEFL. Electronic applications accepted. *Faculty research:* Computer animation and virtual reality, Spanish still-life painting from 1600 to 1800, art and psychotherapy, Japanese wood-firing techniques in ceramics, non-toxic printmaking technologies.

California College of the Arts, Graduate Programs, Design Program, San Francisco, CA 94107. Offers graphic design (MFA); industrial design (MFA); interaction design (MFA). *Accreditation:* NASAD. *Degree requirements:* For master's, thesis, exhibit. *Entrance requirements:* For master's, appropriate bachelor's degree, portfolio, resume, letters of recommendation, transcripts. Additional exam requirements/recommendations for international students: Required—TOEFL (minimum score 600 paper-based; 100 iBT). Electronic applications accepted.

California College of the Arts, Graduate Programs, MBA in Design Strategy Program, San Francisco, CA 94107. Offers MBA. *Accreditation:* NASAD. *Degree requirements:* For master's, thesis. *Entrance requirements:* Additional exam requirements/recommendations for international students: Required—TOEFL (minimum score 600 paper-based; 100 iBT).

California Institute of the Arts, School of Art, Valencia, CA 91355-2340. Offers art (MFA, Adv C); graphic design (MFA, Adv C); photography (MFA, Adv C). *Accreditation:* NASAD (one or more programs are accredited). *Degree requirements:* For master's, final project. *Entrance requirements:* For master's, portfolio. Additional exam requirements/recommendations for international students: Required—TOEFL. Electronic applications accepted.

California State University, Fresno, Division of Graduate Studies, College of Arts and Humanities, Department of Art and Design, Fresno, CA 93740-8027. Offers art (MA). Part-time and evening/weekend programs available. *Degree requirements:* For master's, thesis or alternative. *Entrance requirements:* For master's, GRE General Test, minimum GPA of 3.0, portfolio. Additional exam requirements/recommendations for international students: Required—TOEFL. Electronic applications accepted. *Faculty research:* Art history, graphic design, studio art.

California State University, Fullerton, Graduate Studies, College of the Arts, Department of Visual Arts, Fullerton, CA 92834-9480. Offers art (MA, MFA), including art history (MA), ceramics (MFA), crafts, creative photography, exhibition design, glass, graphic design, illustration, sculpture. *Accreditation:* NASAD (one or more programs are accredited). Part-time programs available. *Students:* 28 full-time (16 women), 29 part-time (22 women); includes 20 minority (3 Black or African American, non-Hispanic/Latino; 8 Asian, non-Hispanic/Latino; 8 Hispanic/Latino; 1 Two or more races, non-Hispanic/Latino), 7 international. Average age 35. 58 applicants, 38% accepted, 14 enrolled. In 2014, 17 master's awarded. *Degree requirements:* For master's, project or thesis. *Entrance requirements:* For master's, minimum GPA of 2.5 in last 60 units of course work, portfolio. Application fee: $55. *Financial support:* Career-related internships or fieldwork, Federal Work-Study, institutionally sponsored loans, and scholarships/grants available. Support available to part-time students. Financial award application deadline: 3/1; financial award applicants required to submit FAFSA. *Unit head:* Dana Lamb, Chair, 657-278-2076. *Application contact:* Admissions/Applications, 657-278-2371.

California State University, Los Angeles, Graduate Studies, College of Arts and Letters, Department of Art, Los Angeles, CA 90032-8530. Offers art (MA), including art education, art history, art therapy, ceramics, metals, and textiles, design (MA, MFA), painting, sculpture, and graphic arts, photography; fine arts (MFA), including crafts, design (MA, MFA), studio arts. *Accreditation:* NASAD (one or more programs are accredited). Part-time and evening/weekend programs available. *Degree requirements:* For master's, comprehensive exam, project or thesis. *Entrance requirements:* For master's, portfolio. Additional exam requirements/recommendations for international students: Required—TOEFL (minimum score 500 paper-based). Electronic applications accepted. *Expenses:* Tuition, state resident: full-time $6738; part-time $3609 per year. Tuition, nonresident: full-time $15,666; part-time $8073 per year. Tuition and fees vary according to course load, degree level and program. *Faculty research:* The artist and the book, conceptual art, ceramic processes, computer graphics, architectural graphics.

Cardinal Stritch University, College of Arts and Sciences, Department of Art, Milwaukee, WI 53217-3985. Offers visual studies (MA). Part-time and evening/weekend programs available. *Degree requirements:* For master's, thesis, portfolio, exhibit. *Entrance requirements:* For master's, minimum GPA of 2.75; 3 letters of recommendation.

Carnegie Mellon University, College of Fine Arts, School of Design, Program in Design, Pittsburgh, PA 15213-3891. Offers MA, D Des, PhD. *Accreditation:* NASAD. *Degree requirements:* For doctorate, one foreign language, comprehensive exam, thesis/dissertation. *Entrance requirements:* For doctorate, GRE, portfolio of relevant work. Additional exam requirements/recommendations for international students: Required—TOEFL (minimum score 600 paper-based). *Faculty research:* Design theory, typography and information design, new product development, organizational behavior, interaction design.

College for Creative Studies, Graduate Programs, Detroit, MI 48202-4034. Offers interdisciplinary design (MFA); transportation design (MFA).

Concordia University, School of Graduate Studies, Faculty of Fine Arts, Department of Design and Computation Arts, Montréal, QC H3G 1M8, Canada. Offers digital technologies in design art practice (Certificate).

Cranbrook Academy of Art, Graduate School, Program in Fine Arts, Bloomfield Hills, MI 48303-0801. Offers 2D design (MFA); ceramics (MFA); fiber (MFA); metalsmithing (MFA); painting (MFA); photography (MFA); print media (MFA); sculpture (MFA). *Accreditation:* NASAD. *Faculty:* 9 full-time (3 women). *Students:* 138 full-time (93 women); includes 18 minority (7 Asian, non-Hispanic/Latino; 5 Hispanic/Latino; 6 Two or more races, non-Hispanic/Latino), 31 international. Average age 27. 390 applicants, 35% accepted, 72 enrolled. *Degree requirements:* For master's, thesis, exhibit. *Entrance requirements:* Additional exam requirements/recommendations for international students: Required—TOEFL. *Application deadline:* For fall admission, 2/1 priority date for domestic and international students; for spring admission, 11/1 for domestic students. Application fee: $85. Electronic applications accepted. *Expenses: Tuition:* Full-time $31,916. *Required fees:* $2387. *Financial support:* Federal Work-Study available. Financial award application deadline: 2/15; financial award applicants required to submit FAFSA. *Unit head:* Christopher Scoates, Director, 248-645-3301, Fax: 248-645-3591. *Application contact:* Leslie Tobakos, Registrar/Financial Aid and Admissions Manager, 248-645-3360, Fax: 248-645-3591, E-mail: ltobakos@cranbrook.edu.

Drexel University, Antoinette Westphal College of Media Arts and Design, Philadelphia, PA 19104-2875. Offers arts administration (MS); digital media (MS); fashion design (MS); interior architecture and design (MS); television management (MS); MS/MBA. *Accreditation:* NASAD. Part-time and evening/weekend programs available. *Entrance requirements:* For master's, interview. Additional exam requirements/recommendations for international students: Required—TOEFL. Electronic applications accepted. *Expenses:* Contact institution.

Emily Carr University of Art + Design, Program in Applied Arts, Vancouver, BC V6H 3R9, Canada. Offers design (M Des); media arts (MAA); visual arts (MAA). *Degree requirements:* For master's, internship, thesis project. *Entrance requirements:* For master's, minimum overall GPA of 3.0, visual portfolio, 3 letters of recommendation, resume/curriculum vitae. Additional exam requirements/recommendations for international students: Required—TOEFL (minimum score 570 paper-based; 84 iBT), IELTS (minimum score 6.5), Michigan English Language Assessment Battery (minimum score 81). *Application deadline:* For fall admission, 1/15 for domestic students. Application fee: $100 Canadian dollars. Electronic applications accepted. One-time fee: $600 Canadian dollars full-time. *Unit head:* Chris Jones, Coordinator, 604-844-3850, E-mail: masters@ecuad.ca.

★ **Fashion Institute of Technology,** School of Graduate Studies, New York, NY 10001-5992. Offers art market, principles and practices (MA); cosmetics and fragrance marketing and management (MPS); exhibition design (MA); fashion and textile studies (MA); global fashion management (MPS); illustration (MFA); sustainable interior environments (MA). *Accreditation:* NASAD. Part-time and evening/weekend programs available. *Degree requirements:* For master's, thesis. *Entrance requirements:* For master's, portfolio, letters of recommendation, resume, interview. Additional exam requirements/recommendations for international students: Required—TOEFL (minimum score 550 paper-based; 80 iBT). Electronic applications accepted. *Faculty research:* Fashion history, material conservation, international marketing and global sourcing, sustainable economic development, luxury braiding in China.

See Display on next page and Close-Up on page 97.

Ferris State University, Kendall College of Art and Design, Grand Rapids, MI 49503. Offers MAE, MFA. *Accreditation:* NASAD. Part-time programs available. *Faculty:* 21 full-time (14 women). *Students:* 34 full-time (19 women), 3 part-time (all women); includes 10 minority (2 Black or African American, non-Hispanic/Latino; 5 Asian, non-Hispanic/Latino; 2 Hispanic/Latino; 1 Two or more races, non-Hispanic/Latino), 3 international. Average age 32. 24 applicants, 67% accepted, 10 enrolled. In 2014, 12 master's awarded. *Degree requirements:* For master's, thesis, seminars. *Entrance requirements:* For master's, portfolio, 3 letters of recommendation, curriculum vitae. Additional exam requirements/recommendations for international students: Required—TOEFL (minimum score 70 iBT). *Application deadline:* For fall admission, 2/1 priority date for domestic and international students; for spring admission, 11/1 priority date for domestic and international students. Applications are processed on a rolling basis.

Application fee: $0. Tuition and fees vary according to degree level and program. *Financial support:* In 2014–15, 36 students received support, including 9 fellowships (averaging $16,638 per year); scholarships (averaging $7665 per year), graduate assistantships (averaging $3900 per year) also available. Support available to part-time students. Financial award application deadline: 2/1; financial award applicants required to submit FAFSA. *Unit head:* Dr. David M. Rosen, President and Vice Chancellor, 616-451-2787. *Application contact:* Krostopher Jones, Director of Talent Acquisition, 616-451-2787, Fax: 616-831-9689, E-mail: kcadadmissions@ferris.edu. Website: http://www.kcad.edu/

Florida Atlantic University, Dorothy F. Schmidt College of Arts and Letters, Department of Visual Arts and Art History, Boca Raton, FL 33431-0991. Offers visual art (MFA), including ceramics, graphic design, visual art. *Degree requirements:* For master's, one foreign language, project. *Entrance requirements:* For master's, GRE General Test, minimum GPA of 3.0 during last 60 hours of course work, slide portfolio. Electronic applications accepted. *Expenses:* Tuition, state resident: full-time $7396; part-time $369.82 per credit hour. Tuition, nonresident: full-time $19,392; part-time $1024.81 per credit hour. Tuition and fees vary according to course load. *Faculty research:* Painting, ceramics (traditional and non-traditional), installation, video and interactive sculpture.

Howard University, Graduate School, Division of Fine Arts, Department of Art, Program in Fine Arts, Washington, DC 20059-0002. Offers 3D reality (sculpture and ceramics) (MFA); design (MFA); electronic studio (MFA); painting (MFA); photography (MFA). *Accreditation:* NASAD. *Degree requirements:* For master's, comprehensive exam, thesis, exhibit. *Entrance requirements:* For master's, minimum GPA of 3.0, portfolio.

Illinois Institute of Technology, Graduate College, Institute of Design, Chicago, IL 60654. Offers M Des, MDM, PhD, M Des/MBA. Part-time programs available. *Faculty:* 13 full-time (2 women), 23 part-time/adjunct (8 women). *Students:* 88 full-time (51 women), 9 part-time (3 women); includes 10 minority (3 Black or African American, non-Hispanic/Latino; 5 Asian, non-Hispanic/Latino; 1 Hispanic/Latino; 1 Two or more races, non-Hispanic/Latino), 39 international. Average age 31. 158 applicants, 54% accepted, 31 enrolled. In 2014, 55 master's awarded. Terminal master's awarded for partial completion of doctoral program. *Degree requirements:* For master's, comprehensive exam (for some programs), thesis (for some programs); for doctorate, one foreign language, comprehensive exam, thesis/dissertation. *Entrance requirements:* For master's, GRE (minimum score 310); GMAT (minimum score 600), bachelor's degree, minimum GPA of 3.0, official transcripts, portfolio, minimum of two years of professional experience; Portfolios are required for applicants who possess design degrees; For those without design degrees, the quality of this professional work substitutes for GRE/GMAT test scores; for doctorate, GRE General Test (minimum score 1000 Quantitative and Verbal, 3.5 Analytical Writing), master's degree in design from accredited institution, official transcripts, portfolio, distinguished record of academic achievement, and be very highly recommended; Doctoral applicants with a master's degree in design must show evidence of distinguished academic and, if appropriate, professional work in their fields. Additional exam requirements/recommendations for international students: Required—TOEFL (minimum score 100 iBT); Recommended—IELTS (minimum score 7). *Application deadline:* For fall admission, 2/15 for domestic and international students; for spring admission, 10/15 for domestic students, 9/15 for international students. Application fee: $100. Electronic applications accepted. *Expenses:* Expenses: Contact institution. *Financial support:* Fellowships with full and partial tuition reimbursements, research assistantships, career-related internships or fieldwork, Federal Work-Study, institutionally sponsored loans, scholarships/grants, health care benefits, tuition waivers (partial), and unspecified assistantships available. Support available to part-time students. Financial award applicants required to submit FAFSA. *Faculty research:* Data

visualization, urbanism, big data, digital tools, future of work. *Unit head:* Patrick Whitney, Dean, 312-595-4900, Fax: 312-595-4901, E-mail: patrick.whitney@iit.edu. *Application contact:* Rachel Dean, Director of Admissions and Retention, 312-595-4906, Fax: 312-596-4901, E-mail: rdean@id.iit.edu. Website: http://www.id.iit.edu/

Indiana University–Purdue University Indianapolis, Herron School of Art and Design, Indianapolis, IN 46202. Offers art education (MAE); furniture design (MFA); printmaking (MFA); sculpture (MFA); visual communication (MFA). *Accreditation:* NASAD. *Faculty:* 40 full-time (22 women). *Students:* 60 full-time (41 women), 3 part-time (all women); includes 8 minority (3 Black or African American, non-Hispanic/Latino; 2 Asian, non-Hispanic/Latino; 1 Hispanic/Latino; 2 Two or more races, non-Hispanic/Latino), 7 international. Average age 30. 103 applicants, 67% accepted, 38 enrolled. In 2014, 26 master's awarded. *Degree requirements:* For master's, thesis. *Entrance requirements:* For master's, portfolio, 44 hours of course work in art history and studio art, Art Therapy requires 12 credits of psychology and 18 credits of studio art. Additional exam requirements/recommendations for international students: Recommended—TOEFL (minimum score 550 paper-based; 79 iBT), IELTS (minimum score 6.5). *Application deadline:* For fall admission, 1/15 priority date for domestic and international students; for spring admission, 11/1 for domestic students, 10/15 for international students. Application fee: $60 ($65 for international students). Electronic applications accepted. *Financial support:* In 2014–15, 55 students received support, including 30 fellowships (averaging $3,325 per year), 1 research assistantship (averaging $6,000 per year), 23 teaching assistantships (averaging $3,500 per year); career-related internships or fieldwork, Federal Work-Study, institutionally sponsored loans, scholarships/grants, health care benefits, and tuition waivers (partial) also available. *Unit head:* Prof. Valerie Eickmeier, Dean, 317-278-9470, Fax: 317-278-9471, E-mail: herron@iupui.edu. *Application contact:* Herron Office of Admissions and Student Services, 317-378-9400, E-mail: herron4u@iupui.edu. Website: http://www.herron.iupui.edu/

Kansas State University, Graduate School, College of Human Ecology, Department of Apparel, Textiles, and Interior Design, Manhattan, KS 66506. Offers apparel and textiles (MS), including design, general apparel and textiles, marketing, merchandising, product development. Postbaccalaureate distance learning degree programs offered (no on-campus study). *Faculty:* 12 full-time (9 women). *Students:* 4 full-time (all women), 13 part-time (12 women); includes 6 minority (4 Black or African American, non-Hispanic/Latino; 1 Asian, non-Hispanic/Latino; 1 Hispanic/Latino), 2 international. Average age 32. 7 applicants, 43% accepted, 1 enrolled. In 2014, 9 master's awarded. *Degree requirements:* For master's, comprehensive exam (for some programs), thesis (for some programs). *Entrance requirements:* For master's, GRE General Test (except for merchandising applicants), minimum undergraduate GPA of 3.0. Additional exam requirements/recommendations for international students: Required—TOEFL (minimum score 550 paper-based; 79 iBT), IELTS (minimum score 6.1). *Application deadline:* For fall admission, 1/1 priority date for domestic and international students; for spring admission, 8/1 priority date for domestic and international students; for summer admission, 12/1 priority date for domestic and international students. Applications are processed on a rolling basis. Application fee: $50 ($75 for international students). Electronic applications accepted. *Financial support:* In 2014–15, 7 students received support, including 1 fellowship (averaging $17,304 per year), 3 research assistantships (averaging $16,200 per year), 3 teaching assistantships with full tuition reimbursements available (averaging $14,053 per year); career-related internships or fieldwork, Federal Work-Study, institutionally sponsored loans, scholarships/grants, and unspecified assistantships also available. Support available to part-time students. Financial award application deadline: 2/1; financial award applicants required to submit FAFSA. *Faculty research:* Apparel marketing and consumer

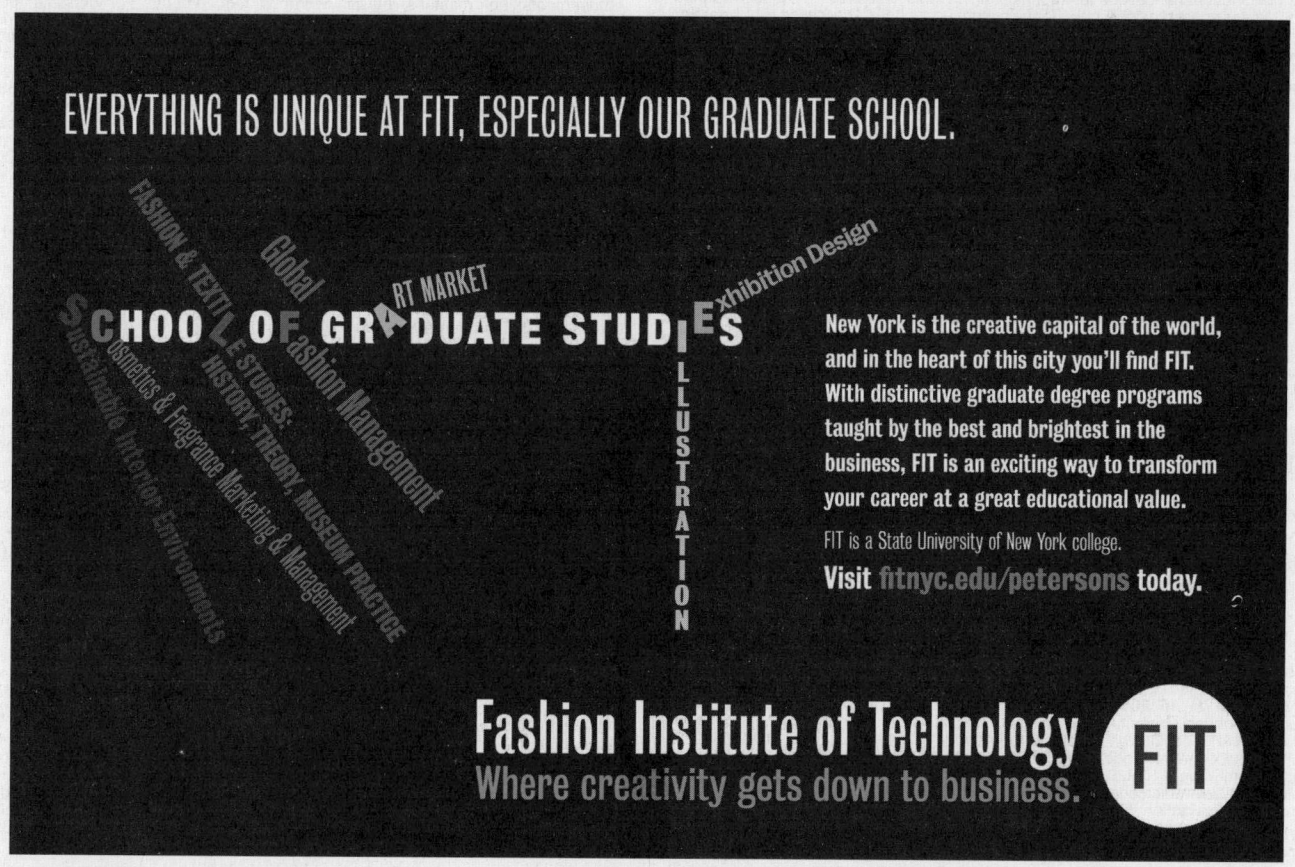

behavior, social and environmental responsibility, apparel design, new product development. *Total annual research expenditures:* $222,454. *Unit head:* Prof. Barbara G. Anderson, Head, 785-532-6993, Fax: 785-532-3796, E-mail: barbara@ksu.edu. *Application contact:* Gina Jackson, Application Contact, 785-532-6693, Fax: 785-532-3796, E-mail: gjackson@ksu.edu.
Website: http://www.he.k-state.edu/atid/

Louisiana State University and Agricultural & Mechanical College, Graduate School, College of Art and Design, Baton Rouge, LA 70803. Offers M Arch, MA, MFA, MLA. *Accreditation:* ASLA (one or more programs are accredited); NASAD (one or more programs are accredited). Part-time programs available. *Students:* 111 full-time (79 women), 2 part-time (1 woman); includes 8 minority (5 Black or African American, non-Hispanic/Latino; 1 Asian, non-Hispanic/Latino; 2 Hispanic/Latino), 46 international. Average age 27. 172 applicants, 54% accepted, 44 enrolled. In 2014, 54 master's awarded. *Degree requirements:* For master's, thesis. *Entrance requirements:* For master's, GRE General Test, minimum GPA of 3.0. Additional exam requirements/recommendations for international students: Required—TOEFL (minimum score 550 paper-based; 79 IBT), IELTS (minimum score 6.5), or PTE (minimum score 59). *Application deadline:* For fall admission, 1/1 priority date for domestic students, 5/15 for international students; for spring admission, 10/15 for domestic and international students; for summer admission, 5/15 for domestic and international students. Applications are processed on a rolling basis. Application fee: $50 ($70 for international students). Electronic applications accepted. *Financial support:* In 2014–15, 85 students received support, including 24 research assistantships with partial tuition reimbursements available (averaging $8,462 per year), 52 teaching assistantships with partial tuition reimbursements available (averaging $6,945 per year); fellowships, career-related internships or fieldwork, Federal Work-Study, institutionally sponsored loans, scholarships/grants, health care benefits, tuition waivers (full and partial), and unspecified assistantships also available. Support available to part-time students. Financial award applicants required to submit FAFSA. *Faculty research:* Creative studio work, site design, computer applications, historic preservation, energy conservation. *Total annual research expenditures:* $772,989. *Unit head:* Dr. Alkis Tsolakis, Interim Dean, 225-578-5400, Fax: 225-578-5040, E-mail: atsolakis@lsu.edu. *Application contact:* Theresa Mooney, Academic Counselor, 225-578-5400, Fax: 225-578-5040, E-mail: deacon1@lsu.edu.
Website: http://www.design.lsu.edu/

Louisiana Tech University, Graduate School, College of Liberal Arts, MFA Program, Ruston, LA 71272. Offers communication design (MFA); photography (MFA); studio (MFA). *Accreditation:* NASAD. Part-time programs available. *Degree requirements:* For master's, exhibit. *Entrance requirements:* For master's, GRE General Test, portfolio. *Application deadline:* For fall admission, 7/29 for domestic students; for spring admission, 2/3 for domestic students. Applications are processed on a rolling basis. Application fee: $40. *Financial support:* Fellowships, career-related internships or fieldwork, Federal Work-Study, institutionally sponsored loans, and unspecified assistantships available. Financial award application deadline: 2/1. *Unit head:* Joey Slaughter, Graduate Coordinator, 318-257-3909, Fax: 318-257-4890, E-mail: joey@latech.edu. *Application contact:* Marilyn J. Robinson, Assistant to the Dean of the Graduate School, 318-257-2924, Fax: 318-257-4487.

Maryland Institute College of Art, Graduate Studies, The Business of Art and Design Program, Baltimore, MD 21201. Offers MPS. Part-time programs available. *Faculty:* 15 part-time/adjunct (6 women). *Students:* 20 part-time (10 women); includes 5 minority (2 Black or African American, non-Hispanic/Latino; 1 Asian, non-Hispanic/Latino; 2 Hispanic/Latino). Average age 27. 53 applicants, 47% accepted, 20 enrolled. In 2014, 20 master's awarded. *Degree requirements:* For master's, business plan presentation. *Entrance requirements:* For master's, essay, resume. Additional exam requirements/recommendations for international students: Required—TOEFL (minimum score 550 paper-based; 80 iBT), IELTS (minimum score 6.5). *Application deadline:* For fall admission, 1/15 for domestic and international students; for spring admission, 4/1 for domestic and international students. Application fee: $70. *Expenses:* Expenses: Contact institution. *Financial support:* In 2014–15, 20 students received support, including 20 fellowships (averaging $3,400 per year); scholarships/grants also available. Financial award application deadline: 1/15; financial award applicants required to submit FAFSA. *Unit head:* Heather Bradbury, Manager, 410-225-2220, Fax: 410-225-2229, E-mail: hbradbury@mica.edu. *Application contact:* Chris D. Harring, Director of Graduate Admission, 410-225-2256, Fax: 410-225-5275, E-mail: graduate@mica.edu.
Website: http://www.mica.edu/Programs_of_Study/Graduate_Programs/The_Business_of_Art_and_Design_(Online_MPS).html

Maryland Institute College of Art, Graduate Studies, Design Leadership MBA/MA Program, Baltimore, MD 21201. Offers MBA/MA. Program offered in collaboration with The Johns Hopkins University. *Students:* 20 full-time (10 women); includes 7 minority (2 Black or African American, non-Hispanic/Latino; 2 Asian, non-Hispanic/Latino; 1 Hispanic/Latino; 2 Two or more races, non-Hispanic/Latino), 3 international. *Entrance requirements:* Additional exam requirements/recommendations for international students: Required—TOEFL (minimum score 100 iBT) or IELTS (minimum score 7). *Application deadline:* For fall admission, 1/15 priority date for domestic and international students; for spring admission, 4/1 for domestic and international students. Application fee: $100. Electronic applications accepted. *Expenses:* Expenses: Contact institution. *Financial support:* Scholarships/grants available. Financial award applicants required to submit FAFSA. *Unit head:* David Gracyalny, Vice Provost for Research/Dean, 410-225-5273, E-mail: dgracyalny@mica.edu. *Application contact:* Chris D. Harring, Director of Graduate Admission, 410-225-2256, Fax: 410-225-5275, E-mail: graduate@mica.edu.
Website: http://www.designleadershipmba.com/

Maryland Institute College of Art, Graduate Studies, Program in Information Visualization, Baltimore, MD 21201. Offers MPS. Part-time programs available. Postbaccalaureate distance learning degree programs offered (minimal on-campus study). *Faculty:* 13 part-time/adjunct (8 women). *Students:* 20 full-time (11 women); includes 2 minority (1 Black or African American, non-Hispanic/Latino; 1 Hispanic/Latino). Average age 31. 35 applicants, 71% accepted, 20 enrolled. In 2014, 20 degrees awarded. *Entrance requirements:* For master's, curriculum vitae/resume, visualization portfolio, bachelor's degree in any field. Additional exam requirements/recommendations for international students: Required—TOEFL (minimum score 550 paper-based; 80 iBT). *Application deadline:* For fall admission, 1/15 priority date for domestic students, 1/15 for international students. Application fee: $75. Electronic applications accepted. *Expenses:* Expenses: $17,000 tuition and fees for online study. *Financial support:* In 2014–15, 20 fellowships (averaging $3,500 per year) were awarded; scholarships/grants also available. *Unit head:* Heather Bradbury, Manager of Business of Art and Design Master's Program, 410-225-2220, Fax: 410-225-2229, E-mail: hbradbury@mica.edu. *Application contact:* Chris D. Harring, Director of Graduate Admission, 410-225-2256, Fax: 410-225-5275, E-mail: graduate@mica.edu.
Website: http://www.mica.edu/Programs_of_Study/Graduate_Programs/Information_Visualization_(Online_MPS).html

Maryland Institute College of Art, Graduate Studies, Program in Social Design, Baltimore, MD 21201. Offers MA. *Faculty:* 2 full-time (0 women), 1 (woman) part-time/adjunct. *Students:* 14 full-time (9 women); includes 5 minority (1 Black or African American, non-Hispanic/Latino; 1 Asian, non-Hispanic/Latino; 2 Hispanic/Latino; 1 Two or more races, non-Hispanic/Latino), 3 international. Average age 27. 60 applicants, 30% accepted, 14 enrolled. In 2014, 14 master's awarded. *Degree requirements:* For master's, thesis, thesis project, exhibition, project presentation. *Entrance requirements:* For master's, portfolio, bachelor's degree in any field. Additional exam requirements/recommendations for international students: Required—TOEFL (minimum score 550 paper-based; 80 iBT), IELTS (minimum score 6.5). *Application deadline:* For fall admission, 1/15 priority date for domestic students, 1/15 for international students. Application fee: $75. Electronic applications accepted. *Expenses:* Expenses: $42,390 combined tuition and fees. *Financial support:* In 2014–15, 8 students received support, including 14 fellowships (averaging $13,000 per year), 14 teaching assistantships (averaging $3,200 per year); scholarships/grants also available. Financial award application deadline: 1/15. *Unit head:* Michael S. Weikert, Director, 410-276-2015, E-mail: graduate@mica.edu. *Application contact:* Chris D. Harring, Director of Graduate Admission, 410-225-2256, Fax: 410-225-5275, E-mail: graduate@mica.edu.
Website: http://www.mica.edu/Programs_of_Study/Graduate_Programs/Social_Design_(MA).html

Massachusetts College of Art and Design, Graduate Programs, MFA Program, Boston, MA 02115-5882. Offers 2D fine arts (MFA), including painting; 3D fine arts (MFA), including ceramics, fibers, glass, jewelry and metalsmithing, sculpture; design (MFA, Postbaccalaureate Certificate), including dynamic media; fine arts (MFA), including interdisciplinary; media arts (MFA, Postbaccalaureate Certificate), including film/video (MFA), photography. *Accreditation:* NASAD. *Faculty:* 31 full-time (15 women), 42 part-time/adjunct (19 women). *Students:* 59 full-time (36 women), 32 part-time (23 women); includes 12 minority (2 Black or African American, non-Hispanic/Latino; 5 Asian, non-Hispanic/Latino; 5 Hispanic/Latino), 18 international. 278 applicants, 38% accepted, 40 enrolled. In 2014, 33 master's, 7 other advanced degrees awarded. *Degree requirements:* For master's, thesis, Exhibition for MFA non design. Thesis document MFA in design and low-residency. *Entrance requirements:* For master's, portfolio, college transcripts, resume, statement of purpose, letters of reference, interview; 6 credits of art history taken prior to or during MFA program; for Postbaccalaureate Certificate, portfolio, college transcripts, resume, statement of purpose, letters of reference, interview. Additional exam requirements/recommendations for international students: Required—TOEFL (minimum score 550 paper-based; 85 iBT); Recommended—IELTS (minimum score 6.5). *Application deadline:* For fall admission, 1/6 priority date for domestic and international students. Application fee: $75. Electronic applications accepted. *Expenses:* Tuition, state resident: full-time $23,400; part-time $780 per credit. Tuition, nonresident: full-time $23,400; part-time $780 per credit. Tuition and fees vary according to course load and program. *Financial support:* In 2014–15, 37 students received support, including 40 teaching assistantships (averaging $2,160 per year); career-related internships or fieldwork, scholarships/grants, tuition waivers (partial), and unspecified assistantships also available. Support available to part-time students. Financial award application deadline: 1/6. *Unit head:* Paul Paturzo, Interim Dean of Graduate Studies, 617-879-7166, E-mail: pjpaturzo@massart.edu. *Application contact:* Isaac Goldstein, Graduate Admissions Counselor, 617-879-7203, Fax: 617-879-7250, E-mail: igoldstein@massart.edu.
Website: http://www.massart.edu/Admissions/Graduate_Programs.html

Memphis College of Art, Graduate Programs, Memphis, TN 38104-2764. Offers MA, MAT, MFA. *Accreditation:* NASAD. Part-time and evening/weekend programs available. *Faculty:* 23 full-time (14 women), 13 part-time/adjunct (8 women). *Students:* 28 full-time (16 women), 41 part-time (29 women); includes 14 minority (9 Black or African American, non-Hispanic/Latino; 2 Asian, non-Hispanic/Latino; 1 Hispanic/Latino; 2 Two or more races, non-Hispanic/Latino), 2 international. Average age 36. 57 applicants, 67% accepted, 19 enrolled. In 2014, 14 master's awarded. *Degree requirements:* For master's, thesis. *Entrance requirements:* For master's, portfolio, interview, resume. Additional exam requirements/recommendations for international students: Required—TOEFL (minimum score 525 paper-based). *Application deadline:* For fall admission, 2/1 for domestic students, 3/1 for international students; for spring admission, 11/1 for domestic and international students. Application fee: $50. Electronic applications accepted. *Expenses: Tuition:* Full-time $29,470; part-time $3685 per course. *Required fees:* $700; $125 per course. Tuition and fees vary according to course load. *Financial support:* In 2014–15, 5 fellowships, 5 teaching assistantships were awarded; career-related internships or fieldwork, Federal Work-Study, scholarships/grants, and unspecified assistantships also available. Financial award application deadline: 7/27; financial award applicants required to submit FAFSA. *Application contact:* Gail Massey, Director of Enrollment, 901-272-5153, Fax: 901-272-5158, E-mail: gmassey@mca.edu.

Miami International University of Art & Design, Program in Design and Media Management, Miami, FL 33132-1418. Offers MA.

Minneapolis College of Art and Design, Program in Visual Studies, Minneapolis, MN 55404-4347. Offers animation (MFA); comic art (MFA); drawing (MFA); filmmaking (MFA); fine arts (MFA); furniture design (MFA); graphic design (MFA); illustration (MFA); interactive media (MFA); painting (MFA); photography (MFA); printmaking (MFA); sculpture (MFA). *Accreditation:* NASAD. Part-time programs available. *Degree requirements:* For master's, thesis, thesis exhibit. *Entrance requirements:* For master's, portfolio of visual artwork, resume, 3 letters of recommendation. Additional exam requirements/recommendations for international students: Required—TOEFL (minimum score 550 paper-based; 79 iBT). Electronic applications accepted. *Faculty research:* Visual arts: animation, comic art, drawing, filmmaking, furniture design, graphic design, illustration, interactive media, painting, photography, printmaking, sculpture.

The New School, Parsons The New School for Design, Program in Design Studies, New York, NY 10011. Offers MA.

The New School, Parsons The New School for Design, Program in Transdisciplinary Design (TransDesign), New York, NY 10011. Offers MFA. *Degree requirements:* For master's, thesis.

New York University, Tisch School of the Arts, Department of Design for Stage and Film, New York, NY 10012-1019. Offers MFA. *Faculty:* 10 full-time, 11 part-time/adjunct. *Students:* 50 full-time (29 women); includes 8 minority (1 Black or African American, non-Hispanic/Latino; 1 American Indian or Alaska Native, non-Hispanic/Latino; 1 Asian, non-Hispanic/Latino; 4 Hispanic/Latino; 1 Two or more races, non-Hispanic/Latino), 18 international. 94 applicants, 23% accepted, 18 enrolled. In 2014, 20 master's awarded. *Degree requirements:* For master's, thesis. *Entrance requirements:* For master's, interview, portfolio. Additional exam requirements/recommendations for international students: Required—TOEFL (minimum score 620 paper-based; 105 iBT), IELTS. *Application deadline:* For fall admission, 1/1 priority date for domestic and international students. Application fee: $60. Electronic applications accepted. *Financial support:* In 2014–15, 28 students received support, including 12 fellowships with full and partial tuition reimbursements available; Federal Work-Study, institutionally sponsored loans, tuition waivers (partial), and unspecified assistantships also available. Financial award application deadline: 2/15; financial award applicants required to submit FAFSA. *Unit head:* Susan Hilferty, Chair, 212-998-1950, Fax: 212-998-1953, E-mail:

tisch.design@nyu.edu. *Application contact:* Dan Sandford, Director of Graduate Admissions, 212-998-1918, Fax: 212-995-4060, E-mail: tisch.gradadmissions@nyu.edu. Website: http://www.design.tisch.nyu.edu/

North Carolina State University, Graduate School, College of Design, Program in Art and Design, Raleigh, NC 27695. Offers MAD. *Degree requirements:* For master's, thesis optional. Electronic applications accepted.

North Carolina State University, Graduate School, College of Design, Program in Design, Raleigh, NC 27695. Offers PhD. *Degree requirements:* For doctorate, thesis/dissertation. *Entrance requirements:* For doctorate, GRE. Electronic applications accepted. *Faculty research:* Design and cognition, children's environments, community design, ecological design, sustainable communities and urban spatial development.

Northeastern University, College of Arts, Media and Design, Boston, MA 02115-5096. Offers architecture (M Arch); information design and visualization (MFA); journalism (MA); studio art (MFA). *Entrance requirements:* Additional exam requirements/recommendations for international students: Required—TOEFL (minimum score 100 iBT), IELTS. Electronic applications accepted.

NSCAD University, Program in Fine Arts, Halifax, NS B3J 3J6, Canada. Offers craft (MFA); design (M Des); fine and media arts (MFA). *Degree requirements:* For master's, thesis, exhibit. *Entrance requirements:* For master's, portfolio, at least 5 art history classes. Additional exam requirements/recommendations for international students: Required—Michigan English Language Assessment Battery (minimum score: 80), CanTEST (minimum score: 4.5), CAEL (minimum score: 70); Recommended—TOEFL (minimum score 575 paper-based; 90 iBT), IELTS (minimum score 6.5).

Oklahoma State University, College of Human Sciences, Department of Design, Housing and Merchandising, Stillwater, OK 74078. Offers MS, PhD. *Faculty:* 16 full-time (11 women). *Students:* 4 full-time (3 women), 9 part-time (6 women); includes 1 minority (Asian, non-Hispanic/Latino), 7 international. Average age 29. 14 applicants, 57% accepted, 7 enrolled. In 2014, 1 master's, 3 doctorates awarded. *Degree requirements:* For master's, thesis (for some programs); for doctorate, comprehensive exam, thesis/dissertation. *Entrance requirements:* For master's and doctorate, GRE or GMAT. Additional exam requirements/recommendations for international students: Required—TOEFL (minimum score 550 paper-based; 79 iBT). *Application deadline:* For fall admission, 3/1 priority date for international students; for spring admission, 8/1 priority date for international students. Applications are processed on a rolling basis. Application fee: $40 ($75 for international students). Electronic applications accepted. *Expenses:* Tuition, state resident: full-time $4488; part-time $187 per credit hour. Tuition, nonresident: full-time $18,360; part-time $765 per credit hour. *Required fees:* $2413; $100.55 per credit hour. Tuition and fees vary according to campus/location. *Financial support:* In 2014–15, 9 research assistantships (averaging $12,150 per year), 6 teaching assistantships (averaging $10,058 per year) were awarded; career-related internships or fieldwork, Federal Work-Study, scholarships/grants, health care benefits, tuition waivers (partial), and unspecified assistantships also available. Support available to part-time students. Financial award application deadline: 3/1; financial award applicants required to submit FAFSA. *Faculty research:* Environmental sciences design, housing and merchandising; creativity and physical environment; product development, production and evaluation; experimental learning and critical thinking; technology strategies and assessment; customer expectation and satisfaction. *Unit head:* Dr. Kathleen Robinette, Department Head, 405-744-5049, Fax: 405-744-6910, E-mail: kath.robinette@okstate.edu. *Application contact:* Dr. Christine Johnson, Associate Dean for Research and Graduate Studies, 405-744-1744, E-mail: christine.johnson@okstate.edu. Website: http://humansciences.okstate.edu/dhm/

Pacific Northwest College of Art, Program in Applied Craft and Design, Portland, OR 97209. Offers MFA. Program offered in collaboration with Oregon College of Art & Craft. *Accreditation:* NASAD. *Entrance requirements:* For master's, resume, 2 letters of recommendation, portfolio.

Pacific Northwest College of Art, Program in Collaborative Design, Portland, OR 97209. Offers MFA.

Pratt Institute, School of Art and Design, Brooklyn, NY 11205-3899. Offers MFA, MID, MPS, MS, Adv C, MS/MFA, MS/MS. *Accreditation:* NASAD (one or more programs are accredited). Part-time programs available. *Students:* 366 full-time (281 women), 13 part-time (9 women); includes 89 minority (28 Black or African American, non-Hispanic/Latino; 1 American Indian or Alaska Native, non-Hispanic/Latino; 28 Asian, non-Hispanic/Latino; 29 Hispanic/Latino; 1 Native Hawaiian or other Pacific Islander, non-Hispanic/Latino; 2 Two or more races, non-Hispanic/Latino), 160 international. 890 applicants, 42% accepted, 146 enrolled. In 2014, 172 master's awarded. *Degree requirements:* For master's, thesis. *Entrance requirements:* Additional exam requirements/recommendations for international students: Required—TOEFL. *Application deadline:* For fall admission, 1/5 for domestic and international students; for spring admission, 10/1 for domestic and international students. Application fee: $50 ($90 for international students). Electronic applications accepted. *Financial support:* Career-related internships or fieldwork, Federal Work-Study, institutionally sponsored loans, scholarships/grants, health care benefits, and unspecified assistantships available. Support available to part-time students. Financial award application deadline: 2/1; financial award applicants required to submit FAFSA. *Faculty research:* Painting, sculpture, and printmaking; package, interior, and communications design; art therapy; graphic and industrial design; four-dimensional design. *Unit head:* Gerry Snyder, Dean, 718-636-3619, E-mail: gsnyder@pratt.edu. *Application contact:* Young Hah, Director of Graduate Admissions, 718-636-3683, Fax: 718-399-4242, E-mail: yhah@pratt.edu. Website: https://www.pratt.edu/academics/school-of-art/graduate-school-of-art/
See Display on this page and Close-Up on page 203.

Pratt Institute, School of Design, Brooklyn, NY 11205-3899. Offers MFA, MID, MS. Part-time programs available. *Faculty:* 12 full-time (5 women), 136 part-time/adjunct (56 women). *Students:* 382 full-time (285 women), 26 part-time (19 women); includes 74 minority (16 Black or African American, non-Hispanic/Latino; 34 Asian, non-Hispanic/Latino; 21 Hispanic/Latino; 1 Native Hawaiian or other Pacific Islander, non-Hispanic/Latino; 2 Two or more races, non-Hispanic/Latino), 188 international. Average age 27. 904 applicants, 45% accepted, 143 enrolled. In 2014, 153 master's awarded. *Degree requirements:* For master's, thesis. *Entrance requirements:* Additional exam requirements/recommendations for international students: Required—TOEFL (minimum score 575 paper-based; 90 iBT). *Application deadline:* For fall admission, 1/5 for domestic and international students; for spring admission, 10/1 for domestic and international students. Application fee: $50 ($90 for international students). Electronic applications accepted. *Financial support:* Application deadline: 2/1; applicants required to submit FAFSA. *Unit head:* Anita Cooney, Dean, School of Design, 718-687-5744, Fax: 718-636-3410, E-mail: acooney@pratt.edu. *Application contact:* Young Hah, Director of Graduate Admissions, 718-636-3683, Fax: 718-636-3670, E-mail: yhah@pratt.edu. Website: https://www.pratt.edu/academics/school-of-design/graduate-school-of-design/
See Display on this page and Close-Up on page 103.

Applied Arts and Design—General

Purdue University, Graduate School, College of Liberal Arts, Department of Visual and Performing Arts, West Lafayette, IN 47907. Offers art and design (MA); theatre (MA, MFA). *Accreditation:* NASAD; NAST. Part-time programs available. *Degree requirements:* For master's, terminal exhibit, project, or thesis. *Entrance requirements:* For master's, GRE General Test (for art education), minimum undergraduate GPA of 3.0 or equivalent; 9 undergraduate hours in an art or design history; BA in art (for MA in art education). Additional exam requirements/recommendations for international students: Required—TOEFL (minimum score 550 paper-based; 77 iBT). Electronic applications accepted. *Faculty research:* Design, fine arts, photography, acting, directing, theatre technology.

Radford University, College of Graduate and Professional Studies, College of Visual and Performing Arts, Program in Art, Radford, VA 24142. Offers design thinking (MFA); studio art (MFA). Part-time programs available. *Faculty:* 11 full-time (5 women), 1 (woman) part-time/adjunct. *Students:* 21 full-time (18 women), 12 part-time (7 women); includes 6 minority (2 Black or African American, non-Hispanic/Latino; 1 American Indian or Alaska Native, non-Hispanic/Latino; 1 Asian, non-Hispanic/Latino; 1 Hispanic/Latino; 1 Two or more races, non-Hispanic/Latino), 1 international. Average age 35. 21 applicants, 100% accepted, 15 enrolled. In 2014, 4 master's awarded. *Degree requirements:* For master's, comprehensive exam. *Entrance requirements:* For master's, statement of philosophy; minimum GPA of 2.75, 2 letters of reference, BFA or commensurate collegiate course work, 20 slides or CD of recent work, resume, and official transcripts (for studio art); minimum GPA of 3.0 (preferred) and three letters of reference (for design thinking). Additional exam requirements/recommendations for international students: Required—TOEFL (minimum score 550 paper-based; 79 iBT), IELTS (minimum score 6.5). *Application deadline:* For fall admission, 2/15 priority date for domestic students, 12/1 for international students; for spring admission, 7/1 for international students. Applications are processed on a rolling basis. Application fee: $50. Electronic applications accepted. *Expenses:* Tuition, state resident: full-time $7187; part-time $299 per credit hour. Tuition, nonresident: full-time $16,394; part-time $683 per credit hour. *Required fees:* $2974; $125 per credit hour. Tuition and fees vary according to course load and program. *Financial support:* In 2014–15, 14 students received support, including 7 research assistantships (averaging $8,214 per year), 6 teaching assistantships with partial tuition reimbursements available (averaging $8,750 per year); career-related internships or fieldwork, Federal Work-Study, institutionally sponsored loans, scholarships/grants, and unspecified assistantships also available. Financial award application deadline: 3/1; financial award applicants required to submit FAFSA. *Unit head:* Dr. Eloise Philpot, Graduate Coordinator, 540-831-5030, Fax: 540-831-6799, E-mail: ephilpot@radford.edu. *Application contact:* Rebecca Conner, Director, Graduate Enrollment, 540-831-6296, Fax: 540-831-6061, E-mail: gradcollege@radford.edu.
Website: http://www.radford.edu/content/cvpa/home/art.html

Rhode Island School of Design, Graduate Studies, Providence, RI 02903-2784. Offers M Arch, M Des, MA, MAT, MFA, MID, MLA. *Accreditation:* NASAD (one or more programs are accredited). *Faculty:* 15 full-time (8 women), 20 part-time/adjunct (15 women). *Students:* 39 full-time (30 women); includes 8 minority (1 Black or African American, non-Hispanic/Latino; 6 Asian, non-Hispanic/Latino; 1 Two or more races, non-Hispanic/Latino), 17 international. Average age 25. 140 applicants, 31% accepted, 25 enrolled. In 2014, 31 master's awarded. *Degree requirements:* For master's, thesis, exhibit. *Entrance requirements:* For master's, portfolio, statement of purpose, three letters of recommendation. Additional exam requirements/recommendations for international students: Required—TOEFL (minimum score 580 paper-based; 93 iBT). *Application deadline:* For fall admission, 2/1 for domestic and international students. Application fee: $60. Electronic applications accepted. *Expenses:* Expenses: $44,594. *Financial support:* Fellowships, teaching assistantships, career-related internships or fieldwork, Federal Work-Study, institutionally sponsored loans, scholarships/grants, and unspecified assistantships available. Financial award application deadline: 2/15; financial award applicants required to submit FAFSA. *Unit head:* Patricia Phillips, Dean of Graduate Studies, 401-454-6134, Fax: 401-454-6706, E-mail: pphillip02@risd.edu. *Application contact:* Molly Pettengil, Graduate Admissions Officer, 401-454-6312, Fax: 401-454-6309, E-mail: mpetteng@risd.edu.
Website: http://www.risd.edu/academics/graduate-studies/

Rutgers, The State University of New Jersey, New Brunswick, Mason Gross School of the Arts, Theater Arts Department, New Brunswick, NJ 08901. Offers acting (MFA); design (MFA); directing (MFA); playwriting (MFA); stage management (MFA). *Degree requirements:* For master's, thesis (for some programs), performance project. *Entrance requirements:* For master's, audition, interview, portfolio. Additional exam requirements/recommendations for international students: Required—TOEFL (minimum score 550 paper-based), IELTS (minimum score 7). Electronic applications accepted. *Faculty research:* Faculty of working professional.

San Diego State University, Graduate and Research Affairs, College of Professional Studies and Fine Arts, School of Art, Design and Art History, San Diego, CA 92182. Offers art history (MA); studio arts (MA, MFA), including applied design, environmental design, graphic design, interior design, painting and printmaking, sculpture. *Accreditation:* NASAD (one or more programs are accredited). *Degree requirements:* For master's, variable foreign language requirement, thesis. *Entrance requirements:* For master's, GRE General Test, bachelor's degree in related field, slide portfolio, typed slide information sheet, 2 letters of recommendation. Additional exam requirements/recommendations for international students: Required—TOEFL. Electronic applications accepted.

San Francisco Art Institute, Dual-Degree MFA/MA Program in Studio Art and History and Theory of Contemporary Art, San Francisco, CA 94133. Offers MFA/MA. Specializations available in art and technology, film, new genres, painting, photography, printmaking, and sculpture. *Faculty:* 15 full-time (7 women), 46 part-time/adjunct (23 women). *Students:* 6 full-time (4 women); includes 1 minority (Black or African American, non-Hispanic/Latino). Average age 27. 15 applicants, 40% accepted, 4 enrolled. *Entrance requirements:* Additional exam requirements/recommendations for international students: Required—TOEFL (minimum score 600 paper-based; 100 iBT), IELTS (minimum score 7.5). *Application deadline:* For fall admission, 1/15 priority date for domestic and international students. Applications are processed on a rolling basis. Application fee: $85. Electronic applications accepted. *Expenses: Tuition:* Full-time $41,100; part-time $1805 per credit. *Required fees:* $870. *Financial support:* In 2014–15, 8 students received support, including fellowships (averaging $30,000 per year), teaching assistantships (averaging $2,500 per year); career-related internships or fieldwork, Federal Work-Study, scholarships/grants, and unspecified assistantships also available. Support available to part-time students. Financial award application deadline: 3/1; financial award applicants required to submit FAFSA. *Unit head:* Tony Labat, Chair, Master of Fine Arts Department, 415-771-7020, Fax: 415-641-1205, E-mail: tlabat@sfai.edu. *Application contact:* Jana Rumberger, Associate Director of Recruitment, 415-351-3507, Fax: 415-749-4592, E-mail: jrumberger@sfai.edu.
Website: http://www.sfai.edu/degree-programs/graduate/dual-degree-ma-mfa

San Jose State University, Graduate Studies and Research, College of Humanities and the Arts, School of Art and Design, San Jose, CA 95192-0001. Offers animation/illustration (MA); art history (MA); digital media arts (MFA); photography

(MFA); pictorial arts (MFA); spatial arts (MFA). *Accreditation:* NASAD (one or more programs are accredited). *Entrance requirements:* For master's, GRE. Electronic applications accepted.

Savannah College of Art and Design, Graduate School, Savannah, GA 31402-3146. Offers M Arch, MA, MFA, MUD, Graduate Certificate. Part-time programs available. Postbaccalaureate distance learning degree programs offered (no on-campus study). *Faculty:* 508 full-time (208 women), 147 part-time/adjunct (74 women). *Students:* 1,571 full-time (977 women), 706 part-time (428 women); includes 462 minority (282 Black or African American, non-Hispanic/Latino; 9 American Indian or Alaska Native, non-Hispanic/Latino; 67 Asian, non-Hispanic/Latino; 100 Hispanic/Latino; 2 Native Hawaiian or other Pacific Islander, non-Hispanic/Latino; 2 Two or more races, non-Hispanic/Latino), 846 international. Average age 28. 2,504 applicants, 45% accepted, 611 enrolled. In 2014, 755 master's awarded. *Degree requirements:* For master's, thesis (for some programs), internships and/or final projects (for some programs). *Entrance requirements:* For master's, college transcript; resume; statement of purpose; 2 letters of recommendation; interview (recommended); audition or portfolio (for some programs of study); proof of English proficiency. Additional exam requirements/recommendations for international students: Required—TOEFL (minimum score 550 paper-based, 85 iBT), IELTS (minimum score 6.5), or ACTFL. *Application deadline:* For fall admission, 4/1 for domestic and international students. Applications are processed on a rolling basis. Application fee: $40. Electronic applications accepted. *Expenses: Tuition:* Full-time $34,605; part-time $3845 per course. One-time fee: $500. Tuition and fees vary according to course load. *Financial support:* Fellowships, career-related internships or fieldwork, Federal Work-Study, and scholarships/grants available. Financial award application deadline: 4/1; financial award applicants required to submit FAFSA. *Unit head:* Sarah McCarn, Director of Graduate Programs. *Application contact:* Jenny Jaquillard, Executive Director of Admissions, Recruitment and Events, 912-525-5100, Fax: 912-525-5985, E-mail: admission@scad.edu.

School of the Art Institute of Chicago, Graduate Division, Department of Architecture, Interior Architecture, and Designed Objects, Program in Designed Objects, Chicago, IL 60603-3103. Offers M Des. *Entrance requirements:* Additional exam requirements/recommendations for international students: Required—TOEFL, IELTS.

School of the Art Institute of Chicago, Graduate Division, Department of Architecture, Interior Architecture, and Designed Objects, Program in Design for Emerging Technologies, Chicago, IL 60603-3103. Offers MFA. *Entrance requirements:* Additional exam requirements/recommendations for international students: Required—TOEFL, IELTS.

School of the Art Institute of Chicago, Graduate Division, Department of Architecture, Interior Architecture, and Designed Objects, Program in Interior Architecture, Chicago, IL 60603-3103. Offers M Arc. *Entrance requirements:* Additional exam requirements/recommendations for international students: Required—TOEFL, IELTS.

School of Visual Arts, Graduate Programs, Branding Department, New York, NY 10010-3994. Offers MPS. *Degree requirements:* For master's, thesis, 36 credits, including all required courses; minimum cumulative GPA of 3.0; residency of one academic year. *Entrance requirements:* For master's, writing sample, statement of purpose. Additional exam requirements/recommendations for international students: Required—TOEFL (minimum score 550 paper-based; 79 iBT). *Expenses:* Contact institution.

School of Visual Arts, Graduate Programs, Design Criticism Department, New York, NY 10010-3994. Offers MFA. *Degree requirements:* For master's, thesis, 64 credits, including all required courses, with minimum cumulative GPA of 3.0; residency of two academic years. *Entrance requirements:* For master's, short essay critiquing design object, event or concept; writing sample of published or unpublished writing between 1,000 and 2,000 words; personal interview. Additional exam requirements/recommendations for international students: Required—TOEFL (minimum score 550 paper-based; 79 iBT). Electronic applications accepted.

School of Visual Arts, Graduate Programs, Design Department, New York, NY 10010-3994. Offers MFA. *Accreditation:* NASAD. *Degree requirements:* For master's, thesis, 60 credits, including all required courses; minimum cumulative GPA of 3.0; residency of two academic years. *Entrance requirements:* For master's, portfolio that reflects wide range of design work and fluency in type and typography. Additional exam requirements/recommendations for international students: Required—TOEFL (minimum score 550 paper-based; 79 iBT). *Expenses:* Contact institution. *Faculty research:* Design, graphic design, multimedia.

School of Visual Arts, Graduate Programs, Design for Social Innovation Department, New York, NY 10010-3994. Offers MFA. *Degree requirements:* For master's, thesis, 60 credits, including all required courses, with minimum cumulative GPA of 3.0; residency of two academic years. *Entrance requirements:* For master's, resume/curriculum vitae; statement of purpose; portfolio; personal interview. Additional exam requirements/recommendations for international students: Required—TOEFL (minimum score 550 paper-based; 79 iBT). Electronic applications accepted. *Expenses:* Contact institution.

School of Visual Arts, Graduate Programs, Products of Design Department, New York, NY 10010-3994. Offers MFA. *Degree requirements:* For master's, thesis, 60 credits, including all required courses; minimum cumulative GPA 3.0; residency of two academic years. *Entrance requirements:* For master's, portfolio. Additional exam requirements/recommendations for international students: Required—TOEFL (minimum score 550 paper-based; 79 iBT). Electronic applications accepted.

Southern Illinois University Carbondale, Graduate School, College of Liberal Arts, School of Art and Design, Carbondale, IL 62901-4701. Offers drawing (MFA); fiber/weaving (MFA); glass (MFA); metalsmithing/blacksmithing (MFA); painting (MFA). *Accreditation:* NASAD. *Faculty:* 23 full-time (7 women). *Students:* 41 full-time (21 women); includes 2 minority (1 American Indian or Alaska Native, non-Hispanic/Latino; 1 Asian, non-Hispanic/Latino), 5 international. Average age 29. 44 applicants, 32% accepted, 11 enrolled. In 2014, 13 master's awarded. *Degree requirements:* For master's, thesis or alternative. *Entrance requirements:* For master's, minimum GPA of 2.7, portfolio, slides. Additional exam requirements/recommendations for international students: Required—TOEFL. *Application deadline:* For fall admission, 3/1 priority date for domestic students. Applications are processed on a rolling basis. Application fee: $50. *Expenses:* Tuition, state resident: full-time $10,176; part-time $1153 per credit. Tuition, nonresident: full-time $20,814; part-time $1744 per credit. *Required fees:* $7092; $394 per credit. $2364 per semester. *Financial support:* In 2014–15, 3 fellowships with full tuition reimbursements, 5 research assistantships with full tuition reimbursements, 40 teaching assistantships with full tuition reimbursements were awarded; Federal Work-Study, institutionally sponsored loans, and tuition waivers (full) also available. Support available to part-time students. Financial award application deadline: 4/1. *Faculty research:* Prints/woodcuts, foundry, watercolor. *Unit head:* Jerry Monteith, Director, 618-453-7760, Fax: 618-453-7710, E-mail: monteith@siu.edu. *Application contact:* Diane McClain-Inman, Office Specialist, 618-453-4313, Fax: 618-453-7710, E-mail: dinman@siu.edu.

Stanford University, School of Engineering, Department of Civil and Environmental Engineering, Stanford, CA 94305-9991. Offers atmosphere and energy (MS, PhD); construction (MS), including construction engineering and management, design-construction integration, sustainable design and construction; environmental engineering and science (MS, PhD, Eng); environmental fluid mechanics and hydrology (PhD); geomechanics (MS); structural engineering (MS). Terminal master's awarded for partial completion of doctoral program. *Degree requirements:* For doctorate, thesis/dissertation, qualifying exam; for Eng, thesis. *Entrance requirements:* For master's, doctorate, and Eng, GRE General Test. Additional exam requirements/recommendations for international students: Required—TOEFL. Electronic applications accepted. *Expenses: Tuition:* Full-time $44,184; part-time $982 per credit hour. *Required fees:* $191.

Stanford University, School of Humanities and Sciences, Department of Art and Art History, Stanford, CA 94305-9991. Offers art history (PhD); art practice (MFA); design (MFA, MS); documentary film and video (MFA); MS/MFA. *Degree requirements:* For master's, thesis (for some programs), faculty reviews; for doctorate, 2 foreign languages, thesis/dissertation. *Entrance requirements:* For master's and doctorate, GRE General Test. Additional exam requirements/recommendations for international students: Required—TOEFL. Electronic applications accepted. *Expenses: Tuition:* Full-time $44,184; part-time $982 per credit hour. *Required fees:* $191.

Stephen F. Austin State University, Graduate School, College of Fine Arts, School of Art, Nacogdoches, TX 75962. Offers art (MA); design (MFA); drawing (MFA); painting (MFA); sculpture (MFA). *Accreditation:* NASAD. Part-time programs available. *Degree requirements:* For master's, comprehensive exam, thesis, exhibit. *Entrance requirements:* For master's, GRE General Test, portfolio. Additional exam requirements/recommendations for international students: Required—TOEFL. *Faculty research:* Printmaking, jewelry, photography, ceramics, art history.

Suffolk University, New England School of Art and Design, Boston, MA 02108-2770. Offers graphic design (MA); interior architecture (MA, MFA). *Accreditation:* NASAD. Part-time and evening/weekend programs available. *Faculty:* 13 full-time (9 women), 22 part-time/adjunct (10 women). *Students:* 60 full-time (50 women), 47 part-time (44 women); includes 10 minority (3 Black or African American, non-Hispanic/Latino; 6 Asian, non-Hispanic/Latino; 1 Hispanic/Latino), 42 international. Average age 28. 112 applicants, 60% accepted, 13 enrolled. In 2014, 31 master's awarded. *Entrance requirements:* For master's, GRE (for MFA), art portfolio, interview, 2 letters of recommendation, resume; letter of intent (for MFA). Additional exam requirements/recommendations for international students: Required—TOEFL (minimum score 550 paper-based; 80 iBT). *Application deadline:* For fall admission, 6/15 priority date for domestic students, 6/15 for international students; for spring admission, 11/1 priority date for domestic students, 11/1 for international students. Applications are processed on a rolling basis. Application fee: $50. Electronic applications accepted. *Expenses:* Expenses: Contact institution. *Financial support:* In 2014–15, 72 students received support, including 69 fellowships (averaging $6,358 per year). Financial award application deadline: 4/1; financial award applicants required to submit FAFSA. *Faculty research:* Sustainable design, lighting and technology, design education, environmental graphic design, designing for the non-profit sector. *Unit head:* Audrey Goldstein, Department Chair, 617-997-4290, E-mail: agoldstein@suffolk.edu. *Application contact:* Cory Meyers, Director of Graduate Admissions, 617-573-8302, Fax: 617-305-1733, E-mail: grad.admission@suffolk.edu.
Website: http://www.suffolk.edu/nesad/

Syracuse University, College of Visual and Performing Arts, Program in Art Video, Syracuse, NY 13244. Offers MFA. *Accreditation:* NASAD. Part-time programs available. Postbaccalaureate distance learning degree programs offered (no on-campus study). *Students:* 5 full-time (1 woman); includes 2 minority (1 Asian, non-Hispanic/Latino; 1 Hispanic/Latino), 3 international. Average age 26. 26 applicants, 42% accepted, 3 enrolled. In 2014, 2 master's awarded. *Degree requirements:* For master's, thesis or alternative. *Entrance requirements:* For master's, portfolio. Additional exam requirements/recommendations for international students: Required—TOEFL (minimum score 100 iBT), IELTS. *Application deadline:* For fall admission, 2/1 priority date for domestic and international students. Application fee: $75. Electronic applications accepted. *Expenses: Tuition:* Part-time $1341 per credit. *Financial support:* Fellowships with full tuition reimbursements, teaching assistantships with full and partial tuition reimbursements, and tuition waivers available. Financial award application deadline: 1/1; financial award applicants required to submit FAFSA. *Unit head:* Prof. Tom Sherman, Department of Transmedia 11202, twsherma@syr.edu, 315-443-1202, E-mail: admissg@syr.edu. *Application contact:* Therese West, Information Contact, 315-443-0137, E-mail: admissg@syr.edu.
Website: http://vpa.syr.edu/art-design/transmedia/graduate

University of Alberta, Faculty of Graduate Studies and Research, Department of Art and Design, Edmonton, AB T6G 2E1, Canada. Offers drawing (MFA); history of art, design, and visual culture (MA); industrial design (M Des); painting (MFA); printmaking (MFA); sculpture (MFA); visual communication design (M Des). *Degree requirements:* For master's, thesis. *Entrance requirements:* For master's, portfolio (MFA and MDES). Additional exam requirements/recommendations for international students: Required—TOEFL (minimum score 550 paper-based).

University of Baltimore, Graduate School, Yale Gordon College of Arts and Sciences, Program in Integrated Design, Baltimore, MD 21201-5779. Offers MFA. Part-time and evening/weekend programs available. *Entrance requirements:* Additional exam requirements/recommendations for international students: Required—TOEFL (minimum score 550 paper-based). Electronic applications accepted. *Expenses:* Contact institution. *Faculty research:* Information and graphics design, economics, hypermedia communications.

University of Bridgeport, Shintaro Akatsu School of Design, Bridgeport, CT 06604. Offers design management (MPS). Part-time and evening/weekend programs available. *Entrance requirements:* Additional exam requirements/recommendations for international students: Recommended—TOEFL (minimum score 550 paper-based; 80 iBT), IELTS (minimum score 6.5). Electronic applications accepted.

University of California, Berkeley, Graduate Division, College of Environmental Design, Master of Arts in Design Program, Berkeley, CA 94720-1500. Offers MA. *Degree requirements:* For master's, thesis. *Entrance requirements:* For master's, GRE General Test, minimum GPA of 3.0, portfolio, 3 letters of recommendation. Additional exam requirements/recommendations for international students: Required—TOEFL.

University of California, Berkeley, UC Berkeley Extension, Certificate Programs in Art and Design, Berkeley, CA 94720-1500. Offers interior design and interior architecture (Certificate); landscape architecture (Certificate); visual arts (Postbaccalaureate Certificate).

University of California, Los Angeles, Graduate Division, School of the Arts and Architecture, Department of Design Media Arts, Los Angeles, CA 90095. Offers MFA. *Degree requirements:* For master's, comprehensive exam. *Entrance requirements:* For master's, bachelor's degree; minimum undergraduate GPA of 3.0 (or its equivalent if letter grade system not used); portfolio. Additional exam requirements/recommendations for international students: Required—TOEFL. Electronic applications accepted. *Expenses:* Contact institution.

University of Central Oklahoma, The Jackson College of Graduate Studies, College of Fine Arts and Design, Department of Design and Interior Design, Edmond, OK 73034-5209. Offers design (MFA). Part-time programs available. Postbaccalaureate distance learning degree programs offered (minimal on-campus study). *Degree requirements:* For master's, thesis. *Entrance requirements:* For master's, essay, portfolio. Additional exam requirements/recommendations for international students: Required—TOEFL (minimum score 550 paper-based; 79 iBT), IELTS (minimum score 6.5). Electronic applications accepted. *Faculty research:* Design pedagogy in foundations curriculum, social media in design education, typography and its evolution in digital media, cross-cultural design, historical preservation for adaptive reuse.

University of Cincinnati, Graduate School, College of Design, Architecture, Art, and Planning, School of Design, Cincinnati, OH 45221. Offers fashion design (M Des); graphic design (M Des); industrial design (M Des); interaction design (M Des); product development (M Des). *Accreditation:* NASAD. *Students:* 34 full-time (16 women), 3 part-time (1 woman); includes 3 minority (1 Black or African American, non-Hispanic/Latino; 1 Asian, non-Hispanic/Latino; 1 Hispanic/Latino), 24 international. In 2014, 7 master's awarded. *Degree requirements:* For master's, thesis. *Entrance requirements:* For master's, undergraduate degree in design or related field, 2 years of work experience in design or related field. Additional exam requirements/recommendations for international students: Required—TOEFL. *Application deadline:* For fall admission, 2/1 for domestic students. Application fee: $30. Electronic applications accepted. *Financial support:* Fellowships, career-related internships or fieldwork, Federal Work-Study, tuition waivers (partial), and unspecified assistantships available. *Faculty research:* Design theory, interdisciplinary design topics. *Unit head:* Brigid O'Kane, Director, 513-556-0833, E-mail: brigid.okane@uc.edu. *Application contact:* Dr. J. Chewning, Information Contact, 513-556-2996, Fax: 513-556-0240, E-mail: j.chewning@uc.edu.
Website: http://www.daap.uc.edu/

University of Delaware, College of Arts and Sciences, Department of Art, Newark, DE 19716. Offers MA, MFA. *Degree requirements:* For master's, exposition paper final exhibition. *Entrance requirements:* For master's, portfolio of creative work. Electronic applications accepted. *Faculty research:* Painting, printmaking, ceramics, photography, sculpture.

University of Illinois at Chicago, Graduate College, College of Architecture, Design and the Arts, School of Design, Chicago, IL 60607-7128. Offers graphic design (M Des); industrial design (M Des). *Accreditation:* NASAD (one or more programs are accredited). *Faculty:* 20 full-time (7 women), 18 part-time/adjunct (6 women). *Students:* 23 full-time (17 women), 5 part-time (3 women); includes 8 minority (2 Black or African American, non-Hispanic/Latino; 3 Asian, non-Hispanic/Latino; 3 Hispanic/Latino), 13 international. Average age 28. 118 applicants, 19% accepted, 11 enrolled. In 2014, 11 master's awarded. *Degree requirements:* For master's, thesis, exhibit. *Entrance requirements:* For master's, MAT, portfolio. Additional exam requirements/recommendations for international students: Required—TOEFL. *Application deadline:* For fall admission, 12/15 priority date for domestic and international students. Applications are processed on a rolling basis. Application fee: $40 ($50 for international students). Electronic applications accepted. *Expenses:* Expenses: $19,134 in-state; $31,132 out-of-state. *Financial support:* Fellowships with full tuition reimbursements, research assistantships with full tuition reimbursements, teaching assistantships with full tuition reimbursements, career-related internships or fieldwork, Federal Work-Study, traineeships, tuition waivers (full), and unspecified assistantships available. Financial award application deadline: 2/1; financial award applicants required to submit FAFSA. *Unit head:* Marcia Lausen, Director, 312-996-5699, E-mail: mlausen@uic.edu. *Application contact:* Bonnie Osborne, Graduate Secretary, 312-996-3337.
Website: http://design.uic.edu/

University of Illinois at Urbana–Champaign, Graduate College, College of Fine and Applied Arts, School of Art and Design, Champaign, IL 61820. Offers Ed M, MA, MFA, PhD. *Accreditation:* NASAD. *Students:* 56 (45 women). *Entrance requirements:* For master's, minimum GPA of 3.0. Application fee: $70 ($90 for international students). *Unit head:* Nan Goggin, Director, 217-333-0855, Fax: 217-244-7688, E-mail: goggin@illinois.edu. *Application contact:* Ellen de Waard, Coordinator of Graduate Academic Affairs, 217-333-0642, Fax: 217-244-7688, E-mail: edewaard@illinois.edu.
Website: http://www.art.illinois.edu/

The University of Kansas, Graduate Studies, School of Architecture, Design, and Planning, Department of Design, Lawrence, KS 66045. Offers design (MA, MFA); design management (MA); interaction design (MA). *Accreditation:* NASAD (one or more programs are accredited). *Faculty:* 17 full-time, 16 part-time/adjunct. *Students:* 10 full-time (8 women), 17 part-time (8 women); includes 4 minority (2 Asian, non-Hispanic/Latino; 1 Hispanic/Latino; 1 Two or more races, non-Hispanic/Latino), 8 international. Average age 29. 19 applicants, 63% accepted, 8 enrolled. In 2014, 6 master's awarded. *Degree requirements:* For master's, thesis. *Entrance requirements:* For master's, portfolio, 3 letters of recommendation, minimum GPA of 3.0. Additional exam requirements/recommendations for international students: Required—TOEFL, IELTS. *Application deadline:* For fall admission, 4/1 for domestic and international students; for spring admission, 11/1 for domestic students. Applications are processed on a rolling basis. Application fee: $55 ($65 for international students). Electronic applications accepted. *Financial support:* Fellowships, teaching assistantships with full and partial tuition reimbursements, Federal Work-Study, scholarships/grants, and unspecified assistantships available. Financial award application deadline: 2/1; financial award applicants required to submit FAFSA. *Faculty research:* Interaction design, design management, photography, graphic design, industrial design. *Unit head:* Andrea Herstowski, Chair, 785-864-2956, E-mail: hestow@ku.edu. *Application contact:* Gera Elliott, Coordinator of Student Services, 785-864-3167, E-mail: archku@ku.edu.
Website: http://design.ku.edu/

University of Kentucky, Graduate School, College of Design, Lexington, KY 40506-0032. Offers M Arch, MAIDM, MHP, MSIDM. *Accreditation:* NASAD. *Entrance requirements:* For master's, GRE, minimum GPA of 2.75. Additional exam requirements/recommendations for international students: Required—TOEFL (minimum score 550 paper-based). Electronic applications accepted.

University of Massachusetts Dartmouth, Graduate School, College of Visual and Performing Arts, Department of Design, North Dartmouth, MA 02747-2300. Offers digital multi-media (MFA). *Accreditation:* NASAD. Part-time programs available. *Faculty:* 16 full-time (7 women), 3 part-time/adjunct (1 woman). *Students:* 10 full-time (4 women), 1 (woman) part-time; includes 1 minority (Black or African American, non-Hispanic/Latino), 7 international. Average age 27. 37 applicants, 24% accepted, 3 enrolled. In 2014, 2 master's awarded. *Degree requirements:* For master's, visual thesis, written thesis. *Entrance requirements:* For master's, statement of purpose (minimum of 300 words), resume, 2 letters of recommendation, official transcripts, portfolio (20 images representing applicant's art work); for Postbaccalaureate Certificate, statement of purpose (minimum of 300 words), resume, 3 letters of recommendation, official transcripts, portfolio (10 images representing applicant's art work). Additional exam

requirements/recommendations for international students: Required—TOEFL (minimum score 533 paper-based; 72 iBT), IELTS (minimum score 6). *Application deadline:* For fall admission, 1/9 priority date for domestic students, 12/9 priority date for international students; for spring admission, 10/15 priority date for domestic students, 9/15 priority date for international students. Applications are processed on a rolling basis. Application fee: $60. Electronic applications accepted. *Expenses:* Tuition, state resident: full-time $2071; part-time $86.29 per credit. Tuition, nonresident: full-time $8099; part-time $337.46 per credit. *Required fees:* $16,520; $712.33 per credit. Tuition and fees vary according to course load and reciprocity agreements. *Financial support:* In 2014–15, 1 teaching assistantship with partial tuition reimbursement (averaging $2,600 per year) was awarded; Federal Work-Study and unspecified assistantships also available. Support available to part-time students. Financial award application deadline: 3/1; financial award applicants required to submit FAFSA. *Faculty research:* Web design, animation (2D and 3D), multimedia design, broadcast design, product design, typography. *Total annual research expenditures:* $49,666. *Unit head:* Charlotte Hamlin, Coordinator for Graduate Studies, College of Visual and Preforming Arts, 508-999-8911, Fax: 508-999-8912, E-mail: chamlin@umassd.edu. *Application contact:* Steven Briggs, Director of Marketing and Recruitment for Graduate Studies, 508-999-8604, Fax: 508-999-8183, E-mail: graduate@umassd.edu.
Website: http://www.umassd.edu/cvpa/graduate/visualdesign/

University of Michigan, College of Engineering, Interpro Programs in Engineering, Ann Arbor, MI 48109. Offers automotive engineering (M Eng); design science (PhD); energy systems engineering (MS); financial engineering (MS); global automotive and manufacturing engineering (M Eng); manufacturing engineering (M Eng, D Eng); pharmaceutical engineering (M Eng); robotics and autonomous vehicles (M Eng); MBA/M Eng; MSE/MS. Part-time programs available. Postbaccalaureate distance learning degree programs offered (no on-campus study). *Students:* 187 full-time (46 women), 250 part-time (40 women). 364 applicants, 2% accepted, 3 enrolled. In 2014, 171 master's, 1 doctorate awarded. Terminal master's awarded for partial completion of doctoral program. *Degree requirements:* For master's, capstone project; for doctorate, thesis/dissertation. *Entrance requirements:* For master's, GRE; for doctorate, GRE, 2 years of work experience. Additional exam requirements/recommendations for international students: Required—TOEFL (minimum score 560 paper-based). *Application deadline:* Applications are processed on a rolling basis. Electronic applications accepted. *Financial support:* Fellowships, research assistantships with full tuition reimbursements, teaching assistantships with full tuition reimbursements, career-related internships or fieldwork, scholarships/grants, and unspecified assistantships available. Financial award application deadline: 2/15; financial award applicants required to submit FAFSA. *Faculty research:* Automotive engineering, design science, energy systems engineering, engineering sustainable systems, financial engineering, global automotive and manufacturing engineering, integrated microsystems, manufacturing engineering, pharmaceutical engineering, robotics and autonomous vehicles. *Total annual research expenditures:* $263,643. *Unit head:* Prof. Panos Papalambros, Director, 734-647-8401, Fax: 734-647-0079, E-mail: pyp@umich.edu. *Application contact:* Patti Mackmiller, Program Manager, 734-764-3071, Fax: 734-647-2243, E-mail: pmackmil@umich.edu.
Website: http://www.isd.engin.umich.edu

University of Michigan, Horace H. Rackham School of Graduate Studies, Penny W. Stamps School of Art and Design, Ann Arbor, MI 48109. Offers MFA. *Accreditation:* NASAD. *Degree requirements:* For master's, thesis, exhibit (MFA), slide lecture. *Entrance requirements:* For master's, portfolio. Additional exam requirements/recommendations for international students: Required—TOEFL, IELTS. Electronic applications accepted. *Faculty research:* Creative expression, commercial design, preparation for teaching.

University of Minnesota, Twin Cities Campus, Graduate School, College of Design, Department of Design, Housing, and Apparel, Minneapolis, MN 55455-0213. Offers apparel (MA, MS, PhD); design communication (MA, MS, PhD); housing studies (MA, MS, PhD, Postbaccalaureate Certificate); interactive design (MFA); interior design (MA, MS, PhD). Part-time programs available. *Degree requirements:* For master's and Postbaccalaureate Certificate, comprehensive exam, thesis (for some programs); for doctorate, comprehensive exam, thesis/dissertation. *Entrance requirements:* For master's, GRE General Test, minimum GPA of 3.0 (preferred), portfolio, 3 letters of recommendation; for doctorate, GRE General Test, minimum GPA of 3.0 (preferred), portfolio, 3 letters of recommendation, writing sample; for Postbaccalaureate Certificate, GRE General Test, minimum GPA of 3.0 (preferred). Additional exam requirements/recommendations for international students: Required—TOEFL (minimum score 550 paper-based; 79 iBT). Electronic applications accepted. *Faculty research:* Housing policy and community development; consumer behavior; interactive design; design history; social, cultural, and behavioral issues related to designed environments.

University of North Texas, Robert B. Toulouse School of Graduate Studies, Denton, TX 76203-5459. Offers accounting (MS); applied anthropology (MA, MS); applied behavior analysis (Certificate); applied geography (MA); applied technology and performance improvement (M Ed, MS); art education (MA); art history (MA); art museum education (Certificate); arts leadership (Certificate); audiology (Au D); behavior analysis (MS); behavioral science (PhD); biochemistry and molecular biology (MS); biology (MA, MS); biomedical engineering (MS); business analysis (MS); chemistry (MS); clinical health psychology (PhD); communication studies (MA, MS); computer engineering (MS); computer science (MS); counseling (M Ed, MS), including clinical mental health counseling (MS), college and university counseling, elementary school counseling, secondary school counseling; creative writing (MA); criminal justice (MS); curriculum and instruction (M Ed); decision sciences (MBA); design (MA, MFA), including fashion design (MFA), innovation studies, interior design (MFA); early childhood studies (MS); economics (MS); educational leadership (M Ed, Ed D); educational psychology (MS, PhD), including family studies (MS), gifted and talented (MS), human development (MS), learning and cognition (MS), research, measurement and evaluation (MS); electrical engineering (MS); emergency management (MPA); engineering technology (MS); English (MA); English as a second language (MA); environmental science (MS); finance (MBA, MS); financial management (MPA); French (MA); health services management (MBA); higher education (M Ed, Ed D); history (MA, MS); hospitality management (MS); human resources management (MPA); information science (MS); information systems (PhD); information technologies (MBA); interdisciplinary studies (MA, MS); international studies (MA); international sustainable tourism (MS); jazz studies (MM); journalism (MA, MJ, Graduate Certificate), including interactive and virtual digital communication (Graduate Certificate), narrative journalism (Graduate Certificate), public relations (Graduate Certificate); kinesiology (MS); linguistics (MA); local government management (MPA); logistics (PhD); logistics and supply chain management (MBA); long-term care, senior housing, and aging services (MA); management (PhD); marketing (MBA); mathematics (MA, MS); mechanical and energy engineering (MS, PhD); music (MA), including ethnomusicology, music theory, musicology, performance; music composition (PhD); music education (MM Ed, PhD); nonprofit management (MPA); operations and supply chain management (MBA); performance (MM, DMA); philosophy (MA); political science (MA); professional and technical communication (MA); radio, television and film (MA, MFA); rehabilitation counseling (Certificate); sociology (MA); Spanish (MA); special education (M Ed); speech-language pathology (MA); strategic management (MBA); studio art (MFA); teaching (M Ed); MBA/MS. Part-time and evening/weekend programs available. Postbaccalaureate distance learning degree programs offered. *Faculty:* 651 full-time (215 women), 233 part-time/adjunct (139 women). *Students:* 3,040 full-time (1,598 women), 3,401 part-time (2,097 women); includes 1,740 minority (533 Black or African American, non-Hispanic/Latino; 15 American Indian or Alaska Native, non-Hispanic/Latino; 286 Asian, non-Hispanic/Latino; 746 Hispanic/Latino; 3 Native Hawaiian or other Pacific Islander, non-Hispanic/Latino; 157 Two or more races, non-Hispanic/Latino), 1,145 international. Terminal master's awarded for partial completion of doctoral program. *Degree requirements:* For master's, variable foreign language requirement, comprehensive exam (for some programs), thesis (for some programs); for doctorate, variable foreign language requirement, comprehensive exam (for some programs), thesis/dissertation; for other advanced degree, variable foreign language requirement, comprehensive exam (for some programs). *Entrance requirements:* For master's and doctorate, GRE, GMAT. Additional exam requirements/recommendations for international students: Required—TOEFL (minimum score 550 paper-based; 79 iBT). *Application deadline:* For fall admission, 7/15 for domestic students, 3/15 for international students; for spring admission, 11/15 for domestic students, 9/15 for international students; for summer admission, 5/1 for domestic students. Applications are processed on a rolling basis. Application fee: $60. Electronic applications accepted. *Expenses:* Tuition, state resident: full-time $5450; part-time $3633 per year. Tuition, nonresident: full-time $11,966; part-time $7977 per year. *Required fees:* $1301; $398 per credit hour. $685 per semester. Tuition and fees vary according to program and reciprocity agreements. *Financial support:* Fellowships with partial tuition reimbursements, research assistantships with partial tuition reimbursements, teaching assistantships, career-related internships or fieldwork, Federal Work-Study, institutionally sponsored loans, scholarships/grants, health care benefits, and library assistantships available. Support available to part-time students. Financial award applicants required to submit FAFSA. *Unit head:* Mark Wardell, Dean, 940-565-2383, E-mail: mark.wardell@unt.edu. *Application contact:* Toulouse School of Graduate Studies, 940-565-2383, Fax: 940-565-2141, E-mail: gradsch@unt.edu.
Website: http://tsgs.unt.edu/

University of Notre Dame, Graduate School, College of Arts and Letters, Division of Humanities, Department of Art, Art History, and Design, Notre Dame, IN 46556. Offers art history (MA); design (MFA), including graphic design, industrial design; studio art (MFA), including ceramics, painting, photography, printmaking, sculpture. *Accreditation:* NASAD. *Degree requirements:* For master's, comprehensive exam (for some programs), thesis. *Entrance requirements:* For master's, GRE General Test, minimum GPA of 3.0. Additional exam requirements/recommendations for international students: Required—TOEFL (minimum score 600 paper-based; 80 iBT). Electronic applications accepted. *Faculty research:* Studio art practice in ceramics, printing, photography, printmaking and sculpture, graphic design and industrial design, digital imaging in design and photography, Renaissance and American art history, contemporary art theory and criticism.

The University of Texas at Austin, Graduate School, College of Fine Arts, Department of Art and Art History, Program in Design, Austin, TX 78712-1111. Offers MFA. *Accreditation:* NASAD. *Degree requirements:* For master's, thesis, oral exam, exhibition. *Entrance requirements:* For master's, minimum GPA of 3.0, portfolio. Electronic applications accepted.

University of Washington, Graduate School, College of Arts and Sciences, School of Art, Division of Design, Seattle, WA 98195. Offers industrial design (MFA); visual communication design (MFA).

University of Wisconsin–Madison, Graduate School, School of Human Ecology, Program in Design Studies, Madison, WI 53706. Offers MFA, MS, PhD. *Degree requirements:* For master's, thesis (for some programs); for doctorate, comprehensive exam, thesis/dissertation. *Entrance requirements:* For master's, portfolio, scholarly paper, 3 letters of recommendation from faculty; for doctorate, letters of recommendation, scholarly paper. Additional exam requirements/recommendations for international students: Required—TOEFL (minimum score 580 paper-based; 92 iBT). *Expenses:* Tuition, state resident: full-time $10,723; part-time $745 per credit. Tuition, nonresident: full-time $24,054; part-time $1578 per credit. *Required fees:* $374 per semester. Tuition and fees vary according to course load, program and reciprocity agreements. *Faculty research:* Feng shui, material culture, behavior and environment, use of pattern to enhance environment, design visualization.

Virginia Commonwealth University, Graduate School, School of the Arts, Department of Graphic Design, Richmond, VA 23284-9005. Offers design/visual communications (MFA); interior environment (MFA). *Accreditation:* NASAD. *Degree requirements:* For master's, thesis, exhibition. *Entrance requirements:* For master's, portfolio. Additional exam requirements/recommendations for international students: Required—TOEFL (minimum score 600 paper-based; 100 iBT). Electronic applications accepted. *Faculty research:* Conducting visual or theoretical research, and in investigating the intersection of function and expression in design problem solving.

Wayne State University, College of Fine, Performing and Communication Arts, James Pearson Duffy Department of Art and Art History, Program in Design and Merchandising, Detroit, MI 48202. Offers MA. *Students:* 2 full-time (both women), 1 part-time (0 women); includes 1 minority (Two or more races, non-Hispanic/Latino). Average age 30. 10 applicants, 20% accepted, 2 enrolled. *Degree requirements:* For master's, one foreign language, essay or thesis. *Entrance requirements:* For master's, GRE, minimum GPA of 2.8 with minimum 12 credits in clothing and textiles, merchandising, consumer affairs, with supporting courses in closely-related fields, portfolio, personal interview. Additional exam requirements/recommendations for international students: Required—TOEFL (minimum score 550 paper-based; 79 iBT), TWE (minimum score 5.5), Michigan English Language Assessment Battery (minimum score 85); Recommended—IELTS (minimum score 6.5). *Application deadline:* For fall admission, 2/1 for domestic and international students; for winter admission, 10/1 for domestic and international students. Application fee: $0. Electronic applications accepted. *Expenses:* Expenses: Contact institution. *Financial support:* In 2014–15, 3 students received support. Teaching assistantships with tuition reimbursements available, scholarships/grants, and unspecified assistantships available. Financial award application deadline: 3/31; financial award applicants required to submit FAFSA. *Unit head:* Dr. John Richardson, Chair, 313-577-2980, Fax: 313-577-3491, E-mail: af5343@wayne.edu. *Application contact:* Prof. Evan Larson-Voltz, Graduate Officer, 313-577-2983, E-mail: evanlarson@wayne.edu.
Website: http://art.wayne.edu/

Western Carolina University, Graduate School, College of Fine and Performing Arts, School of Art and Design, Cullowhee, NC 28723. Offers MFA. *Accreditation:* NASAD. Part-time programs available. *Degree requirements:* For master's, thesis. *Entrance requirements:* For master's, GRE, appropriate undergraduate degree, portfolio, letters of recommendation. Additional exam requirements/recommendations for international students: Required—TOEFL (minimum score 550 paper-based; 79 iBT). *Faculty research:* Art and society, visual literacy, vernacular cultural studies and oral history, environments for aging, health and leisure.

Western Illinois University, School of Graduate Studies, College of Fine Arts and Communication, Department of Theatre and Dance, Macomb, IL 61455-1390. Offers acting (MFA); design (MFA); directing (MFA). *Accreditation:* NAST. Part-time programs available. *Students:* 20 full-time (4 women), 1 part-time (0 women); includes 3 minority (2 Black or African American, non-Hispanic/Latino; 1 Two or more races, non-Hispanic/Latino). Average age 28. 42 applicants, 40% accepted, 15 enrolled. In 2014, 9 master's awarded. *Degree requirements:* For master's, comprehensive exam, thesis or alternative, creative project, written exam. *Entrance requirements:* For master's, audition or interview. Additional exam requirements/recommendations for international students: Required—TOEFL (minimum score 550 paper-based; 80 iBT). *Application deadline:* Applications are processed on a rolling basis. Application fee: $30. Electronic applications accepted. *Financial support:* In 2014–15, 14 students received support, including 6 research assistantships with full tuition reimbursements available (averaging $7,544 per year), 8 teaching assistantships with full tuition reimbursements available (averaging $8,688 per year). Financial award applicants required to submit FAFSA. *Unit head:* Dr. David Patrick, Chairperson, 309-298-1543. *Application contact:* Dr. Nancy Parsons, Associate Provost and Director of Graduate Studies, 309-298-1806, Fax: 309-298-2345, E-mail: grad-office@wiu.edu.
Website: http://wiu.edu/theatre/

Western Michigan University, Graduate College, College of Fine Arts, Gwen Frostic School of Art, Kalamazoo, MI 49008. Offers art education (MA). *Accreditation:* NASAD. *Degree requirements:* For master's, thesis or alternative. *Application deadline:* For fall admission, 2/15 for domestic students. *Financial support:* Application deadline: 2/15. *Application contact:* Admissions and Orientation, 269-387-2000, Fax: 269-387-2096.

Yale University, School of Art, New Haven, CT 06520-8339. Offers graphic design (MFA); painting/printmaking (MFA); photography (MFA); sculpture (MFA). *Degree requirements:* For master's, thesis (for some programs). *Entrance requirements:* Additional exam requirements/recommendations for international students: Required—TOEFL (minimum score 550 paper-based; 100 iBT). Electronic applications accepted. *Expenses:* Contact institution.

York University, Faculty of Graduate Studies, Faculty of Fine Arts, Program in Design, Toronto, ON M3J 1P3, Canada. Offers M Des. Electronic applications accepted.

Computer Art and Design

Academy of Art University, Graduate Program, School of Visual Development, San Francisco, CA 94105-3410. Offers MFA. Part-time and evening/weekend programs available. Postbaccalaureate distance learning degree programs offered (no on-campus study). *Faculty:* 4 full-time (0 women), 9 part-time/adjunct (1 woman). *Students:* 150 full-time (85 women), 47 part-time (21 women); includes 36 minority (7 Black or African American, non-Hispanic/Latino; 1 American Indian or Alaska Native, non-Hispanic/Latino; 17 Asian, non-Hispanic/Latino; 9 Hispanic/Latino; 2 Two or more races, non-Hispanic/Latino), 101 international. Average age 28. 56 applicants, 100% accepted, 39 enrolled. In 2014, 7 master's awarded. *Degree requirements:* For master's, final review. *Entrance requirements:* For master's, statement of intent; resume; portfolio/reel; official college transcripts. *Application deadline:* Applications are processed on a rolling basis. Application fee: $100. Electronic applications accepted. *Expenses: Tuition:* Part-time $910 per unit. *Financial support:* Career-related internships or fieldwork and Federal Work-Study available. Support available to part-time students. Financial award application deadline: 8/10; financial award applicants required to submit FAFSA. *Unit head:* 800-544-ARTS, E-mail: info@academyart.edu. *Application contact:* 800-544-ARTS, E-mail: info@academyart.edu.
Website: http://www.academyart.edu/visual-development-school/

Academy of Art University, Graduate Program, School of Web Design and New Media, San Francisco, CA 94105-3410. Offers MFA. Part-time and evening/weekend programs available. Postbaccalaureate distance learning degree programs offered (no on-campus study). *Faculty:* 11 full-time (2 women), 40 part-time/adjunct (8 women). *Students:* 262 full-time (167 women), 179 part-time (106 women); includes 86 minority (24 Black or African American, non-Hispanic/Latino; 39 Asian, non-Hispanic/Latino; 17 Hispanic/Latino; 6 Two or more races, non-Hispanic/Latino), 220 international. Average age 31. 98 applicants, 100% accepted, 50 enrolled. In 2014, 72 master's awarded. *Degree requirements:* For master's, final review. *Entrance requirements:* For master's, statement of intent; resume; portfolio/reel; official college transcripts. *Application deadline:* Applications are processed on a rolling basis. Application fee: $100. Electronic applications accepted. *Expenses: Tuition:* Part-time $910 per unit. *Financial support:* Career-related internships or fieldwork and Federal Work-Study available. Support available to part-time students. Financial award application deadline: 8/10; financial award applicants required to submit FAFSA. *Unit head:* 800-544-ARTS, E-mail: info@academyart.edu. *Application contact:* 800-544-ARTS, E-mail: info@academyart.edu.
Website: http://www.academyart.edu/computer-arts-school/index.html

Alfred University, Graduate School, New York State College of Ceramics, School of Art and Design, Alfred, NY 14802. Offers ceramic art (MFA); electronic integrated art (MFA); glass art (MFA); sculpture (MFA). *Accreditation:* NASAD. *Degree requirements:* For master's, thesis, exhibit. *Entrance requirements:* For master's, portfolio. Additional exam requirements/recommendations for international students: Required—TOEFL (minimum score 550 paper-based; 80 iBT), IELTS (minimum score 6). Electronic applications accepted. *Faculty research:* Ceramic art, sculpture, glass art, new media, time-based media.

Art Center College of Design, Graduate Media Design Practices Program, Pasadena, CA 91103. Offers MFA. *Accreditation:* NASAD. *Students:* 43 full-time (29 women), 2 part-time (1 woman); includes 12 minority (8 Asian, non-Hispanic/Latino; 3 Hispanic/Latino; 1 Native Hawaiian or other Pacific Islander, non-Hispanic/Latino), 18 international. Average age 26. 94 applicants, 53% accepted, 22 enrolled. In 2014, 11 master's awarded. *Degree requirements:* For master's, thesis, studio project. *Entrance requirements:* For master's, portfolio. Additional exam requirements/recommendations for international students: Required—TOEFL (minimum score 100 iBT), IELTS (minimum score 7). *Application deadline:* For fall admission, 2/1 priority date for domestic and international students. Application fee: $50 ($70 for international students). Electronic applications accepted. *Financial support:* Career-related internships or fieldwork, Federal Work-Study, and scholarships/grants available. Support available to part-time students. Financial award application deadline: 2/1; financial award applicants required to submit FAFSA. *Unit head:* Anne Burdick, Chair, 626-396-2359, E-mail: anne.burdick@artcenter.edu. *Application contact:* Kevin Wingate, Director, 626-396-2469, E-mail: kevin.wingate@artcenter.edu.

The Art Institute of California–San Francisco, a campus of Argosy University, Program in Computer Animation, San Francisco, CA 94102. Offers MFA.

Bowling Green State University, Graduate College, College of Arts and Sciences, School of Art, Bowling Green, OH 43403. Offers 2-D studio art (MA, MFA); 3-D studio art (MA, MFA); art education (MA); art history (MA); computer art (MA); design (MFA); digital arts (MFA); graphics (MFA). *Accreditation:* NASAD. Part-time programs available. *Degree requirements:* For master's, thesis or alternative, final exhibit (MFA). *Entrance requirements:* For master's, GRE General Test (MA), slide portfolio (15-20 slides). Additional exam requirements/recommendations for international students: Required—TOEFL. Electronic applications accepted. *Faculty research:* Computer animation and virtual reality, Spanish still-life painting from 1600 to 1800, art and psychotherapy, Japanese wood-firing techniques in ceramics, non-toxic printmaking technologies.

California College of the Arts, Graduate Programs, Design Program, San Francisco, CA 94107. Offers graphic design (MFA); industrial design (MFA); interaction design (MFA). *Accreditation:* NASAD. *Degree requirements:* For master's, thesis, exhibit. *Entrance requirements:* For master's, appropriate bachelor's degree, portfolio, resume, letters of recommendation, transcripts. Additional exam requirements/recommendations for international students: Required—TOEFL (minimum score 600 paper-based; 100 iBT). Electronic applications accepted.

Carnegie Mellon University, College of Fine Arts, School of Design, Program in Design for Interactions, Pittsburgh, PA 15213-3891. Offers M Des. Part-time programs available. *Degree requirements:* For master's, thesis. *Entrance requirements:* For master's, GRE, portfolio of relevant work. Additional exam requirements/recommendations for international students: Required—TOEFL (minimum score 600 paper-based). *Faculty research:* Interaction and emotion, visual interface design, robotics, visualization and diagramming, design theory.

Chatham University, Program in Film and Digital Technology, Pittsburgh, PA 15232-2826. Offers MFA. Part-time and evening/weekend programs available. *Faculty:* 1 (woman) part-time/adjunct. *Students:* 5 full-time (4 women), 2 part-time (both women); includes 4 minority (2 Black or African American, non-Hispanic/Latino; 1 Hispanic/Latino; 1 Two or more races, non-Hispanic/Latino), 1 international. Average age 28. 12 applicants, 83% accepted, 4 enrolled. In 2014, 6 master's awarded. *Degree requirements:* For master's, thesis, capstone project. *Entrance requirements:* Additional exam requirements/recommendations for international students: Required—TOEFL (minimum score 600 paper-based; 100 iBT), IELTS (minimum score 7), TWE. *Application deadline:* For fall admission, 4/1 priority date for domestic and international students; for spring admission, 11/1 priority date for domestic students, 10/1 priority date for international students. Applications are processed on a rolling basis. Application fee: $45. Electronic applications accepted. Application fee is waived when completed online. *Expenses: Tuition:* Full-time $15,318; part-time $851 per credit hour. *Required fees:* $440; $24 per credit hour. Tuition and fees vary according to course load, program and reciprocity agreements. *Financial support:* Applicants required to submit FAFSA. *Unit head:* Dr. Prajna Parasher, Director, 412-365-1182, E-mail: parasher@chatham.edu. *Application contact:* Katie Noel, Assistant Director of Graduate Admission, 412-365-2758, Fax: 412-365-1609, E-mail: gradadmissions@chatham.edu.
Website: http://www.chatham.edu/mfafilm

Claremont Graduate University, Graduate Programs, School of Arts and Humanities, Department of Art, Claremont, CA 91711. Offers digital media (MFA); drawing (MFA); installation (MFA); painting (MFA); performance (MFA); photography (MFA); sculpture (MFA); studio (MFA). Part-time programs available. *Faculty:* 4 full-time (1 woman). *Students:* 37 full-time (26 women), 3 part-time (1 woman); includes 11 minority (2 Black or African American, non-Hispanic/Latino; 1 Asian, non-Hispanic/Latino; 7 Hispanic/Latino; 1 Two or more races, non-Hispanic/Latino), 12 international. Average age 32. In 2014, 22 master's awarded. *Degree requirements:* For master's, final project show. *Entrance requirements:* For master's, BA in art or BFA, slide review. Additional exam requirements/recommendations for international students: Required—TOEFL (minimum score 550 paper-based; 80 iBT). *Application deadline:* For fall admission, 2/1 priority date for domestic and international students. Applications are processed on a rolling basis. Application fee: $80. Electronic applications accepted. *Expenses:* Expenses: Contact institution. *Financial support:* Fellowships, research assistantships, teaching assistantships, Federal Work-Study, institutionally sponsored loans, and scholarships/grants available. Support available to part-time students. Financial award application deadline: 2/15; financial award applicants required to submit FAFSA. *Faculty research:* Acoustic sculpture, feminization of abstraction, installation sculpture. *Unit head:* David Amico, Chair, 909-607-8216, Fax: 909-607-1276, E-mail: david.amico@cgu.edu. *Application contact:* Jennifer Gracia, Program Coordinator, 909-621-8071, E-mail: jennifer.gracia@cgu.edu.
Website: http://art.cgu.edu/

Clemson University, Graduate School, College of Engineering and Science, School of Computing, MFA Program in Digital Production Arts, Clemson, SC 29634. Offers MFA. *Accreditation:* NASAD. *Faculty:* 12 full-time (1 woman), 1 part-time/adjunct (0 women). *Students:* 25 full-time (10 women), 6 part-time (1 woman); includes 4 minority (2 Black or African American, non-Hispanic/Latino; 2 Two or more races, non-Hispanic/Latino), 8 international. Average age 26. 19 applicants, 74% accepted, 10 enrolled. In 2014, 12 master's awarded. *Degree requirements:* For master's, thesis. *Entrance requirements:* For master's, GRE General Test, portfolio. Additional exam requirements/recommendations for international students: Required—TOEFL. *Application deadline:* For fall admission, 1/15 for domestic and international students. Applications are processed on a rolling basis. Application fee: $80 ($90 for international students). Electronic applications accepted. *Financial support:* In 2014–15, 6 students received support, including 3 research assistantships with partial tuition reimbursements available (averaging $17,867 per year), 3 teaching assistantships with partial tuition reimbursements available (averaging $19,733 per year); fellowships with full and partial tuition reimbursements available, career-related internships or fieldwork, institutionally sponsored loans, scholarships/grants, health care benefits, and unspecified assistantships also available. Support available to part-time students. *Faculty research:* Distributed rendering, fluids and simulation, computer animation/graphics, game design, motion. *Unit head:* Dr. Robert M. Geist, III, Interim Director, 864-656-2258, Fax: 864-656-0145, E-mail: geist@clemson.edu. *Application contact:* Dida Weeks, Administrative Coordinator, 864-656-5577, Fax: 864-656-0145, E-mail: didaw@clemson.edu.
Website: http://www.clemson.edu/dpa

Computer Art and Design

Concordia University, School of Graduate Studies, Faculty of Fine Arts, Department of Design and Computation Arts, Montréal, QC H3G 1M8, Canada. Offers digital technologies in design art practice (Certificate).

Cornell University, Graduate School, Graduate Fields of Architecture, Art and Planning, Field of Architecture, Ithaca, NY 14853-0001. Offers architectural design (M Arch); architectural science (MS); computer graphics (MS); history of architecture (MA, PhD); history of urban development (MA, PhD); theory and criticism of architecture (M Arch); urban design (M Arch). *Degree requirements:* For master's, one foreign language, thesis (MA, MS); for doctorate, 2 foreign languages, comprehensive exam, thesis/dissertation. *Entrance requirements:* For master's, GRE General Test, 5-year bachelor's degree in architecture, portfolio (M Arch), 3 letters of recommendation; for doctorate, GRE General Test, 3 letters of recommendation. Additional exam requirements/recommendations for international students: Required—TOEFL (minimum score 600 paper-based; 77 iBT). Electronic applications accepted. *Faculty research:* Architectural design and urban design, theory and criticism of architecture, computer graphics, building technology and environmental science, history of architecture and history of urban-development.

DePaul University, College of Computing and Digital Media, Chicago, IL 60604. Offers animation (MA, MFA); business information technology (MS); cinema (MFA); cinema production (MS); computational finance (MS); computer and information sciences (PhD); computer game development (MS); computer information and network security (MS); computer science (MS); e-commerce technology (MS); health informatics (MS); human-computer interaction (MS); information systems (MS); information technology project management (MS); network engineering and management (MS); predictive analytics (MS); screenwriting (MFA); software engineering (MS); JD/MS. Part-time and evening/weekend programs available. Postbaccalaureate distance learning degree programs offered (no on-campus study). *Degree requirements:* For master's, thesis (for some programs); for doctorate, comprehensive exam, thesis/dissertation. *Entrance requirements:* For master's, GRE or GMAT (for MS in computational finance only), bachelor's degree, resume (MS in predictive analytics only), IT experience (MS in information technology project management only), portfolio review (all MFA programs and MA in animation); for doctorate, GRE, master's degree in computer science. Additional exam requirements/recommendations for international students: Required—TOEFL (minimum score 590 paper-based; 80 iBT), IELTS (minimum score 6.5), PTE (minimum score 53). Electronic applications accepted. *Expenses:* Contact institution. *Faculty research:* Data mining, computer science, human-computer interaction, security, animation and film.

DigiPen Institute of Technology, Graduate Programs, Redmond, WA 98052. Offers computer science (MS); digital arts (MFA). Part-time and evening/weekend programs available. *Faculty:* 25 full-time (5 women), 7 part-time/adjunct (0 women). *Students:* 63 full-time (13 women), 22 part-time (3 women); includes 35 minority (2 Black or African American, non-Hispanic/Latino; 1 American Indian or Alaska Native, non-Hispanic/Latino; 20 Asian, non-Hispanic/Latino; 12 Hispanic/Latino), 27 international. Average age 26. 204 applicants, 23% accepted, 30 enrolled. In 2014, 7 master's awarded. *Degree requirements:* For master's, comprehensive exam (for some programs), thesis (for some programs). *Entrance requirements:* For master's, GRE General Test or DigiPen computer science exam for applicants with non-computer science degrees (for MS), art portfolio (for MFA). Additional exam requirements/recommendations for international students: Required—TOEFL (minimum score 550 paper-based; 80 iBT). *Application deadline:* For fall admission, 2/1 priority date for domestic and international students; for spring admission, 7/1 for domestic and international students. Applications are processed on a rolling basis. Application fee: $35. Electronic applications accepted. *Expenses:* Expenses: $17,100, $18,920 international (for MS in computer science); $23,200, $25,200 international (for MFA in digital arts). *Financial support:* In 2014–15, 1 student received support, including 1 fellowship (averaging $15,450 per year); career-related internships or fieldwork and scholarships/grants also available. Financial award application deadline: 5/1; financial award applicants required to submit FAFSA. *Faculty research:* Procedural modeling, computer graphics and visualization, human-computer interaction, fuzzy numbers and fuzzy analysis, modeling under spistemic uncertainty, nonlinear image processing, mathematical representation of surfaces, advanced computer graphic rendering techniques, mathematical physics, computer music and sound synthesis. *Unit head:* Angela Kugler, Vice President of External Affairs, 425-895-4438, Fax: 425-558-0378, E-mail: akugler@digipen.edu. *Application contact:* Danial Powers, Director of Admissions, 425-629-5071, Fax: 425-558-0378, E-mail: dpowers@digipen.edu.

Digital Media Arts College, Graduate Programs, Boca Raton, FL 33487. Offers graphic design (MFA); special FX animation (MFA).

Drexel University, Antoinette Westphal College of Media Arts and Design, Program in Digital Media, Philadelphia, PA 19104-2875. Offers MS. *Degree requirements:* For master's, thesis (including oral presentation, written statement, and copy of completed media work). *Entrance requirements:* For master's, interview. Additional exam requirements/recommendations for international students: Required—TOEFL. Electronic applications accepted.

East Tennessee State University, School of Graduate Studies, College of Business and Technology, Department of Engineering Technology, Surveying and Digital Media, Johnson City, TN 37614. Offers MS, Postbaccalaureate Certificate. Part-time programs available. *Faculty:* 17 full-time (3 women). *Students:* 18 full-time (2 women), 10 part-time (2 women); includes 1 minority (Black or African American, non-Hispanic/Latino), 8 international. Average age 32. 51 applicants, 41% accepted, 12 enrolled. In 2014, 14 master's awarded. *Degree requirements:* For master's, comprehensive exam, thesis optional, capstone. *Entrance requirements:* For master's, bachelor's degree in technical or related area, minimum GPA of 3.0; for Postbaccalaureate Certificate, minimum GPA of 2.5, three letters of recommendation. Additional exam requirements/recommendations for international students: Required—TOEFL (minimum score 550 paper-based; 79 iBT). *Application deadline:* For fall admission, 6/1 for domestic students, 4/30 for international students; for spring admission, 11/1 for domestic students, 9/30 for international students. Application fee: $35 ($45 for international students). Electronic applications accepted. *Financial support:* In 2014–15, 16 students received support, including 14 research assistantships with full tuition reimbursements available (averaging $6,000 per year); career-related internships or fieldwork, institutionally sponsored loans, scholarships/grants, and unspecified assistantships also available. Financial award application deadline: 7/1; financial award applicants required to submit FAFSA. *Faculty research:* Computer-integrated manufacturing, alternative energy, sustainability, CAD/CAM, organizational change. *Unit head:* Dr. Keith V. Johnson, Chair, 423-439-7822, Fax: 423-439-7750, E-mail: johnsonk@etsu.edu. *Application contact:* Kimberly Brockman, Graduate Specialist, 423-439-6165, Fax: 423-439-5624, E-mail: brockmank@etsu.edu.
Website: http://applieddesign.etsu.edu/

Emily Carr University of Art + Design, Program in Digital Media, Vancouver, BC V5T 0C6, Canada. Offers MDM. *Degree requirements:* For master's, internship. *Entrance requirements:* For master's, portfolio, minimum undergraduate B+ average, 3 reference letters. Additional exam requirements/recommendations for international students: Required—TOEFL (minimum score 93 iBT), IELTS (minimum score 6.5), PTE (minimum score 62). *Application deadline:* For fall admission, 2/15 for domestic students. Application fee: $90 ($125 for international students). Electronic applications accepted. One-time fee: $600 Canadian dollars full-time. *Financial support:* Scholarships/grants available. *Application contact:* Yasmeen Awadh, Senior Student Recruitment Officer, 778-370-1010, E-mail: yasmeen_awadh@thecdm.ca.
Website: http://thecdm.ca/program/mdm

Full Sail University, Game Design Master of Science Program - Campus, Winter Park, FL 32792-7437. Offers MS.

Georgia Institute of Technology, Graduate Studies, Ivan Allen College of Liberal Arts, School of Literature, Media, and Communication, Atlanta, GA 30332-0001. Offers digital media (MS, PhD). Part-time programs available. *Students:* 33 full-time (11 women), 3 part-time (1 woman); includes 10 minority (4 Black or African American, non-Hispanic/Latino; 4 Asian, non-Hispanic/Latino; 2 Hispanic/Latino), 3 international. Average age 28. 68 applicants, 51% accepted, 8 enrolled. In 2014, 14 master's, 1 doctorate awarded. Terminal master's awarded for partial completion of doctoral program. *Degree requirements:* For master's, thesis optional, project studio, paid internship, responsible conduct of research training; for doctorate, comprehensive exam, thesis/dissertation, portfolio review, responsible conduct of research training. *Entrance requirements:* For master's, GRE, cumulative GPA of 3.0 or better (MS HCI), three letters of recommendation, transcripts from each college/university attended, design portfolio, statement of purpose; for doctorate, GRE, three letters of recommendation, transcripts from each college/university attended, design portfolio, statement of purpose. Additional exam requirements/recommendations for international students: Required—TOEFL (minimum score 650 paper-based; 114 iBT). *Application deadline:* For fall admission, 1/8 priority date for domestic and international students. Applications are processed on a rolling basis. Application fee: $75. Electronic applications accepted. *Expenses:* Tuition, state resident: full-time $12,344; part-time $515 per credit hour. Tuition, nonresident: full-time $27,600; part-time $1150 per credit hour. *Required fees:* $1196 per term. Part-time tuition and fees vary according to course load. *Financial support:* Fellowships, research assistantships, teaching assistantships, career-related internships or fieldwork, Federal Work-Study, institutionally sponsored loans, tuition waivers (partial), and unspecified assistantships available. Support available to part-time students. Financial award application deadline: 5/1. *Faculty research:* New media studies. *Total annual research expenditures:* $1.2 million. *Unit head:* Michael Nitsche, Director, 404-894-7000, E-mail: michael.nitsche@lmc.gatech.edu. *Application contact:* Michael Terrell, Graduate Coordinator, 404-385-7551, E-mail: michael.terrell@lmc.gatech.edu.
Website: http://lmc.gatech.edu

Goucher College, MA and MFA Programs, Baltimore, MD 21204-2794. Offers arts administration (MA); creative nonfiction (MFA); cultural sustainability (MA); digital arts (MFA); environmental studies (MA); historic preservation (MA); management (MA). Part-time and evening/weekend programs available. Postbaccalaureate distance learning degree programs offered (minimal on-campus study). *Faculty:* 83 part-time/adjunct (42 women). *Students:* 72 full-time (58 women), 65 part-time (54 women); includes 39 minority (15 Black or African American, non-Hispanic/Latino; 16 American Indian or Alaska Native, non-Hispanic/Latino; 2 Asian, non-Hispanic/Latino; 4 Hispanic/Latino; 2 Two or more races, non-Hispanic/Latino), 4 international. 120 applicants, 95% accepted, 50 enrolled. In 2014, 63 master's awarded. *Degree requirements:* For master's, thesis, e-portfolio completion. *Entrance requirements:* Additional exam requirements/recommendations for international students: Required—TOEFL (minimum score 550 paper-based; 80 iBT), IELTS (minimum score 7). *Application deadline:* Applications are processed on a rolling basis. Application fee: $75. *Expenses:* Expenses: $825 per credit; fees vary according to program. *Financial support:* Unspecified assistantships available. Financial award application deadline: 4/15; financial award applicants required to submit FAFSA. *Unit head:* Lynne Lochte, Vice President for New Ventures and Business Strategies, 410-337-6572, E-mail: lynne.lochte@goucher.edu. *Application contact:* Hanora Barron, Admissions Coordinator, 410-337-6200, Fax: 410-337-6085, E-mail: hanora.barron@goucher.edu.
Website: http://www.goucher.edu/grad

Indiana University Bloomington, School of Informatics and Computing, Bloomington, IN 47408. Offers computer science (MS, PhD); informatics (MS, PhD), including informatics; information and library science (MIS, MLS, PhD, Graduate Certificate, Sp LIS), including information architecture (Graduate Certificate), information science (MIS, PhD), library and information science (Sp LIS), library science (MLS); media arts and science (MS); JD/MLS; MIS/MA; MLS/MA; MPA/MIS; MPA/MLS; MS/PhD. PhD offered through University Graduate School. Part-time programs available. Postbaccalaureate distance learning degree programs offered (no on-campus study). *Faculty:* 63 full-time (12 women). *Students:* 652 full-time (228 women), 139 part-time (61 women); includes 67 minority (21 Black or African American, non-Hispanic/Latino; 26 Asian, non-Hispanic/Latino; 12 Hispanic/Latino; 8 Two or more races, non-Hispanic/Latino), 441 international. Average age 27. 1,495 applicants, 33% accepted, 251 enrolled. In 2014, 271 master's, 26 doctorates, 2 other advanced degrees awarded. Terminal master's awarded for partial completion of doctoral program. *Degree requirements:* For master's, thesis optional; for doctorate, comprehensive exam, thesis/dissertation, oral and written exams. *Entrance requirements:* For master's and doctorate, GRE, letters of reference. Additional exam requirements/recommendations for international students: Required—TOEFL. *Application deadline:* For fall admission, 1/15 for domestic students, 12/1 for international students. Application fee: $55 ($65 for international students). Electronic applications accepted. *Financial support:* Fellowships with full and partial tuition reimbursements, research assistantships, teaching assistantships, Federal Work-Study, institutionally sponsored loans, scholarships/grants, health care benefits, tuition waivers (full and partial), and unspecified assistantships available. Support available to part-time students. *Total annual research expenditures:* $2 million. *Unit head:* Dr. Howard Rosenbaum, Associate Dean for Graduate Studies, 812-855-3250, E-mail: hrosenba@indiana.edu. *Application contact:* Patty Reyes-Cooksey, Director of Graduate Administration, 812-856-3622, Fax: 812-856-3825, E-mail: patreyes@indiana.edu.
Website: http://www.soic.indiana.edu/

International Technological University, Program in Digital Arts, San Jose, CA 95113. Offers MA. Part-time programs available. *Faculty:* 1 full-time (0 women), 5 part-time/adjunct (1 woman). *Students:* 23 full-time (16 women), 5 part-time (3 women), all international. Average age 29. 12 applicants, 83% accepted, 7 enrolled. In 2014, 4 master's awarded. *Degree requirements:* For master's, capstone project. *Entrance requirements:* Additional exam requirements/recommendations for international students: Required—TOEFL, IELTS. *Application deadline:* For fall admission, 8/1 for domestic and international students; for spring admission, 12/1 for domestic and international students; for summer admission, 4/1 for domestic and international students. Applications are processed on a rolling basis. Application fee: $80. Electronic applications accepted. *Expenses: Tuition:* Full-time $13,500; part-time $500 per credit. *Required fees:* $265 per trimester. *Unit head:* Wes Takahashi, Interim Department Chair, 888-488-4968. *Application contact:* Mary Tran, Admissions Manager, 888-488-4968, E-mail: admissions@itu.edu.

Lindenwood University–Belleville, Graduate Programs, Belleville, IL 62226. Offers business administration (MBA); communications (MA), including digital and multimedia, media management, promotions, training and development; counseling (MA); criminal justice administration (MS); education (MA); healthcare administration (MS); human resource management (MS); school administration (MA); teaching (MAT).

Michigan State University, The Graduate School, College of Communication Arts and Sciences, Department of Telecommunication, Information Studies, and Media, East Lansing, MI 48824. Offers digital media arts and technology (MA); information and telecommunication management (MA); information, policy and society (MA); serious game design (MA). *Entrance requirements:* Additional exam requirements/recommendations for international students: Required—TOEFL. Electronic applications accepted.

Minneapolis College of Art and Design, Certificate Programs, Minneapolis, MN 55404-4347. Offers design (Certificate); fine arts (Certificate); graphic design (Certificate); media (Certificate); sustainable design (Certificate). Part-time programs available. Postbaccalaureate distance learning degree programs offered. *Degree requirements:* For Certificate, final project. *Entrance requirements:* For degree, resume, portfolio, letter of recommendation. Additional exam requirements/recommendations for international students: Required—TOEFL (minimum score 550 paper-based; 79 iBT). Electronic applications accepted. *Faculty research:* Visual arts.

New Mexico Highlands University, Graduate Studies, School of Business, Media and Technology, Department of Media Arts and Technology, Las Vegas, NM 87701. Offers media arts and computer science (MA), including media arts. *Faculty:* 5 full-time (1 woman), 4 part-time/adjunct (0 women). *Students:* 10 full-time (7 women), 3 part-time (1 woman); includes 5 minority (1 American Indian or Alaska Native, non-Hispanic/Latino; 4 Hispanic/Latino), 5 international. Average age 35. 3 applicants, 100% accepted, 3 enrolled. In 2014, 4 master's awarded. *Financial support:* In 2014–15, 8 teaching assistantships were awarded. *Unit head:* Dr. Kerry Loewen, Dean, 505-454-3184, Fax: 505-454-3354, E-mail: kclowen@nmhu.edu. *Application contact:* Diane Trujillo, Administrative Assistant, Graduate Studies, 505-454-3266, Fax: 505-426-2117, E-mail: dtrujillo@nmhu.edu.

The New School, Parsons The New School for Design, Program in Design and Technology, New York, NY 10011. Offers MFA. *Accreditation:* NASAD. *Degree requirements:* For master's, thesis, exam, written essay. *Entrance requirements:* For master's, portfolio. Additional exam requirements/recommendations for international students: Required—TOEFL (minimum score 580 paper-based; 92 iBT). Electronic applications accepted.

New York Institute of Technology, College of Arts and Sciences, Department of Fine Arts, Old Westbury, NY 11568-8000. Offers computer graphics (MFA), including animation, fine arts and technology, graphic design. Part-time and evening/weekend programs available. *Degree requirements:* For master's, thesis. *Entrance requirements:* For master's, minimum QPA of 2.85, portfolio. Additional exam requirements/recommendations for international students: Required—TOEFL (minimum score 550 paper-based; 79 iBT), IELTS (minimum score 6). Electronic applications accepted. *Faculty research:* Graphic design, animation, art and technology, digital art and science, sculpture.

New York University, School of Continuing and Professional Studies, Division of Programs in Business, Program in Graphic Communications Management and Technology, New York, NY 10012-1019. Offers MA. Part-time and evening/weekend programs available. *Faculty:* 16 part-time/adjunct (3 women). *Students:* 16 full-time (13 women), 45 part-time (32 women); includes 15 minority (5 Black or African American, non-Hispanic/Latino; 1 American Indian or Alaska Native, non-Hispanic/Latino; 4 Asian, non-Hispanic/Latino; 3 Hispanic/Latino; 1 Native Hawaiian or other Pacific Islander, non-Hispanic/Latino; 1 Two or more races, non-Hispanic/Latino), 17 international. Average age 29. 29 applicants, 66% accepted, 11 enrolled. In 2014, 49 master's awarded. *Degree requirements:* For master's, thesis, capstone, research course. *Entrance requirements:* For master's, GRE or GMAT (only upon request), relevant professional work, internship or volunteer experience. Additional exam requirements/recommendations for international students: Required—TOEFL (minimum score 600 paper-based; 100 iBT), IELTS (minimum score 7). *Application deadline:* For fall admission, 2/1 priority date for domestic and international students; for spring admission, 10/15 priority date for domestic students, 8/15 priority date for international students. Applications are processed on a rolling basis. Application fee: $150. Electronic applications accepted. *Financial support:* In 2014–15, 37 students received support, including 24 fellowships (averaging $2,032 per year); Federal Work-Study and scholarships/grants also available. Support available to part-time students. Financial award application deadline: 4/1; financial award applicants required to submit FAFSA. *Unit head:* Angela Ambrosini, Director, 212-992-3228, E-mail: pp64@nyu.edu. *Application contact:* Admissions Office, 212-998-7100, E-mail: scps.gradadmissions@nyu.edu.
Website: http://www.sps.nyu.edu/academics/departments/graphic-comm-management-tech.html

New York University, School of Continuing and Professional Studies, Division of Programs in Business, Program in Interactive Motion Graphics and Visual Effects, New York, NY 10012-1019. Offers MS. Part-time programs available. *Faculty:* 2 full-time (1 woman), 12 part-time/adjunct (4 women). *Students:* 14 full-time (7 women), 9 part-time (3 women); includes 3 minority (2 Black or African American, non-Hispanic/Latino; 1 Asian, non-Hispanic/Latino), 7 international. Average age 28. 22 applicants, 82% accepted, 9 enrolled. *Degree requirements:* For master's, thesis, project. *Entrance requirements:* For master's, bachelor's degree, resume with relevant professional work, internship or volunteer experience, two letters of recommendation, statement of purpose. Additional exam requirements/recommendations for international students: Required—TOEFL (minimum score 600 paper-based; 100 iBT), IELTS (minimum score 7). *Application deadline:* For fall admission, 2/1 priority date for domestic and international students; for spring admission, 8/15 priority date for domestic and international students. Applications are processed on a rolling basis. Application fee: $150. Electronic applications accepted. *Financial support:* In 2014–15, 5 students received support, including 5 fellowships with tuition reimbursements available (averaging $3,520 per year). *Unit head:* Vish Ganpati, Academic Director, 212-998-7112, E-mail: vg36@nyu.edu. *Application contact:* Admissions Office, 212-998-7100, E-mail: scps.gradadmissions@nyu.edu.
Website: http://www.scps.nyu.edu/areas-of-study/media-industry-design/

North Carolina Agricultural and Technical State University, School of Graduate Studies, School of Technology, Department of Graphic Communication Systems and Technological Studies, Greensboro, NC 27411. Offers graphic communication systems (MSTM); technology education (MAT). *Accreditation:* NCATE (one or more programs are accredited). Part-time and evening/weekend programs available. *Degree requirements:* For master's, comprehensive exam, thesis or alternative, qualifying exam. *Entrance requirements:* For master's, GRE General Test, minimum GPA of 3.0.

North Carolina State University, Graduate School, College of Humanities and Social Sciences, Program in Communication, Rhetoric, and Digital Media, Raleigh, NC 27695. Offers PhD.

The Ohio State University, Graduate School, College of Arts and Sciences, Division of Arts and Humanities, Department of Design, Columbus, OH 43210. Offers design (MA); design research and development (MFA); digital animation and interactive media (MFA). *Accreditation:* NASAD. Part-time programs available. *Faculty:* 16. *Students:* 20 full-time (11 women), 3 part-time (2 women); includes 6 minority (2 Black or African American, non-Hispanic/Latino; 3 Asian, non-Hispanic/Latino; 1 Hispanic/Latino), 8 international. Average age 29. In 2014, 6 master's awarded. *Degree requirements:* For master's, project or thesis. *Entrance requirements:* For master's, GRE General Test (for all applicants with cumulative GPA below 3.0), portfolio. Additional exam requirements/recommendations for international students: Recommended—TOEFL (minimum score 550 paper-based; 79 iBT). *Application deadline:* For fall admission, 12/13 priority date for domestic students, 11/30 priority date for international students; for winter admission, 12/1 for domestic students, 11/1 for international students; for spring admission, 3/1 for domestic students, 2/1 for international students. Applications are processed on a rolling basis. Application fee: $60 ($70 for international students). Electronic applications accepted. *Financial support:* Fellowships with tuition reimbursements, research assistantships with tuition reimbursements, teaching assistantships with tuition reimbursements, career-related internships or fieldwork, Federal Work-Study, institutionally sponsored loans, and unspecified assistantships available. Support available to part-time students. Financial award application deadline: 5/1. *Unit head:* Mary Anne Beecher, PhD, Chair, 614-688-6746, E-mail: beecher.17@osu.edu. *Application contact:* Graduate and Professional Admissions, 614-292-9444, Fax: 614-292-3895, E-mail: gpadmissions@osu.edu.
Website: http://design.osu.edu/

Old Dominion University, College of Arts and Letters, Program in Lifespan and Digital Communication, Norfolk, VA 23529. Offers MA. *Accreditation:* NASAD. Part-time and evening/weekend programs available. *Faculty:* 15 full-time (5 women). *Students:* 11 full-time (9 women), 14 part-time (10 women); includes 11 minority (8 Black or African American, non-Hispanic/Latino; 1 Hispanic/Latino; 2 Two or more races, non-Hispanic/Latino), 1 international. Average age 30. 14 applicants, 86% accepted, 12 enrolled. In 2014, 4 master's awarded. *Degree requirements:* For master's, thesis optional, comprehensive exam (for non-thesis students of a project). *Entrance requirements:* For master's, GRE. Additional exam requirements/recommendations for international students: Recommended—TOEFL (minimum score 550 paper-based; 79 iBT). *Application deadline:* For fall admission, 6/15 for domestic students, 4/15 for international students. Applications are processed on a rolling basis. Application fee: $50. Electronic applications accepted. *Expenses:* Tuition, state resident: full-time $10,488; part-time $437 per credit. Tuition, nonresident: full-time $26,136; part-time $1089 per credit. *Required fees:* $64 per semester. One-time fee: $50. *Financial support:* In 2014–15, 8 students received support, including 1 research assistantship (averaging $10,000 per year), 4 teaching assistantships (averaging $10,000 per year); 3 graduate assistantships ($5000 per term) also available. Financial award application deadline: 6/15. *Faculty research:* Family communication, digital media studies, lifespan communication, social media, screenwriting. *Unit head:* Dr. Thomas J. Socha, Graduate Program Director, 757-683-3833, E-mail: tsocha@odu.edu. *Application contact:* Dr. David C. Earnest, Associate Dean, 757-683-6077, Fax: 757-683-5746, E-mail: dearnest@odu.edu.
Website: http://www.odu.edu/~tsocha/Masters/ma-index.shtml

Purdue University, Graduate School, College of Technology, Department of Computer Graphics Technology, West Lafayette, IN 47907. Offers MS, PhD. *Degree requirements:* For master's, thesis; for doctorate, thesis/dissertation. *Entrance requirements:* For master's, GRE (minimum scores: 50th percentile, 150 on verbal, 150 on quantitative, 4.0 analytical). Additional exam requirements/recommendations for international students: Required—TOEFL (minimum score 550 paper-based; 77 iBT); Recommended—TWE. Electronic applications accepted.

Rensselaer Polytechnic Institute, Graduate School, School of Humanities, Arts, and Social Sciences, Program in Electronic Arts, Troy, NY 12180-3590. Offers MFA, PhD. *Faculty:* 32 full-time (10 women), 3 part-time/adjunct (0 women). *Students:* 15 full-time (6 women), 1 part-time (0 women); includes 2 minority (both Hispanic/Latino), 1 international. Average age 31. 49 applicants, 45% accepted, 9 enrolled. In 2014, 3 master's, 2 doctorates awarded. *Degree requirements:* For doctorate, comprehensive exam. *Entrance requirements:* Additional exam requirements/recommendations for international students: Required—TOEFL (minimum score 570 paper-based; 88 iBT), IELTS (minimum score 6.5), PTE (minimum score 60). *Application deadline:* For fall admission, 1/1 priority date for domestic and international students. Applications are processed on a rolling basis. Application fee: $75. Electronic applications accepted. *Expenses: Tuition:* Full-time $46,700; part-time $1945 per credit. Tuition and fees vary according to course load. *Financial support:* In 2014–15, 12 students received support, including research assistantships (averaging $18,500 per year), teaching assistantships with full tuition reimbursements available (averaging $18,500 per year); scholarships/grants also available. Financial award application deadline: 1/1. *Unit head:* Dr. Curtis Bahn, Graduate Program Director, 518-276-4032, E-mail: crb@rpi.edu. *Application contact:* Office of Graduate Admissions, 518-276-6216, E-mail: gradadmissions@rpi.edu.
Website: http://www.arts.rpi.edu/

Rhode Island School of Design, Graduate Studies, Department of Digital Media, Providence, RI 02903-2784. Offers MFA. *Faculty:* 7 full-time (5 women), 19 part-time/adjunct (11 women). *Students:* 29 full-time (20 women); includes 5 minority (4 Asian, non-Hispanic/Latino; 1 Two or more races, non-Hispanic/Latino), 17 international. Average age 26. 117 applicants, 24% accepted, 15 enrolled. In 2014, 14 master's awarded. *Degree requirements:* For master's, thesis, exhibit. *Entrance requirements:* For master's, portfolio, statement of purpose, 3 letters of recommendation. Additional exam requirements/recommendations for international students: Required—TOEFL (minimum score 580 paper-based; 93 iBT). *Application deadline:* For fall admission, 2/1 for domestic and international students. Application fee: $60. *Financial support:* Application deadline: 2/15; applicants required to submit FAFSA. *Unit head:* Shona Kitchen, Head, 401-454-6139, Fax: 401-277-4966, E-mail: skitchen@risd.edu. *Application contact:* Molly Pettengil, Graduate Admissions Officer, 401-454-6312, Fax: 401-454-6309, E-mail: mpetteng@risd.edu.

Rochester Institute of Technology, Graduate Enrollment Services, College of Imaging Arts and Sciences, School of Design, MFA Program in Visual Communication Design, Rochester, NY 14623-5603. Offers MFA. *Accreditation:* NASAD. Part-time programs available. *Students:* 44 full-time (26 women), 2 part-time; includes 4 minority (2 Hispanic/Latino; 2 Two or more races, non-Hispanic/Latino), 31 international. Average age 26. 221 applicants, 27% accepted, 23 enrolled. *Degree requirements:* For master's, thesis, thesis exhibition. *Entrance requirements:* For master's, GRE and TOEFL, IELTS, or PTE for non-native English speakers, portfolio, recommended minimum GPA of 3.0. Additional exam requirements/recommendations for international students: Required—PTE (minimum score 58), TOEFL (minimum score 550 paper-based; 79 iBT) or IELTS (minimum score 6.5). *Application deadline:* For fall admission,

2/15 priority date for domestic and international students. Applications are processed on a rolling basis. Application fee: $60. Electronic applications accepted. *Expenses:* Expenses: $1,673 per credit hour. *Financial support:* In 2014–15, 43 students received support. Research assistantships with partial tuition reimbursements available, teaching assistantships with partial tuition reimbursements available, career-related internships or fieldwork, Federal Work-Study, institutionally sponsored loans, scholarships/grants, and unspecified assistantships available. Support available to part-time students. Financial award application deadline: 2/15; financial award applicants required to submit FAFSA. *Unit head:* Chris Jackson, Graduate Program Director, 585-475-5823, Fax: 585-475-7533, E-mail: cbjpgd@rit.edu. *Application contact:* Diane Ellison, Associate Vice President, Graduate Enrollment Services, 585-475-2229, Fax: 585-475-7164, E-mail: gradinfo@rit.edu.
Website: http://cias.rit.edu/schools/design/graduate-visual-communication-design

Rochester Institute of Technology, Graduate Enrollment Services, College of Imaging Arts and Sciences, School of Film and Animation, MFA Program in Film and Animation, Rochester, NY 14623-5603. Offers MFA. Part-time programs available. *Students:* 31 full-time (12 women), 28 part-time (15 women); includes 9 minority (2 Black or African American, non-Hispanic/Latino; 4 Asian, non-Hispanic/Latino; 2 Hispanic/Latino; 1 Two or more races, non-Hispanic/Latino), 36 international. Average age 28. 146 applicants, 28% accepted, 12 enrolled. In 2014, 14 master's awarded. *Degree requirements:* For master's, thesis. *Entrance requirements:* For master's, GRE and TOEFL, IELTS, or PTE for non-native English speakers, portfolio, recommended minimum GPA of 3.0. Additional exam requirements/recommendations for international students: Required—PTE (minimum score 58), TOEFL (minimum score 550 paper-based; 79 iBT) or IELTS (minimum score 6.5). *Application deadline:* For fall admission, 2/15 priority date for domestic and international students. Applications are processed on a rolling basis. Application fee: $60. Electronic applications accepted. *Expenses:* Expenses: $1,673 per credit hour. *Financial support:* In 2014–15, 14 students received support. Research assistantships with partial tuition reimbursements available, teaching assistantships with partial tuition reimbursements available, career-related internships or fieldwork, Federal Work-Study, institutionally sponsored loans, scholarships/grants, and unspecified assistantships available. Support available to part-time students. Financial award applicants required to submit FAFSA. *Unit head:* Thomas Gasek, Graduate Program Director, 585-475-7403, E-mail: tdgpph@rit.edu. *Application contact:* Diane Ellison, Associate Vice President, Graduate Enrollment Services, 585-475-2229, Fax: 585-475-7164, E-mail: gradinfo@rit.edu.
Website: http://cias.rit.edu/schools/film-animation/graduate-film-and-animation

Rochester Institute of Technology, Graduate Enrollment Services, College of Imaging Arts and Sciences, School of Photographic Arts and Sciences, Rochester, NY 14623. Offers imaging arts, photography and related media (MFA). Part-time programs available. *Students:* 12 full-time (7 women), 3 part-time (all women); includes 1 minority (Two or more races, non-Hispanic/Latino), 7 international. Average age 28. 74 applicants, 22% accepted, 6 enrolled. In 2014, 4 master's awarded. *Degree requirements:* For master's, thesis, exhibit. *Entrance requirements:* For master's, GRE and TOEFL, IELTS, or PTE for non-native English speakers, recommended minimum GPA of 3.0, portfolio. Additional exam requirements/recommendations for international students: Required—PTE (minimum score 58), TOEFL (minimum score 550 paper-based; 79 iBT) or IELTS (minimum score 6.5). *Application deadline:* For fall admission, 2/15 priority date for domestic and international students. Applications are processed on a rolling basis. Application fee: $60. Electronic applications accepted. *Expenses:* Expenses: $1,673 per credit hour. *Financial support:* In 2014–15, 6 students received support. Research assistantships with partial tuition reimbursements available, teaching assistantships with partial tuition reimbursements available, career-related internships or fieldwork, Federal Work-Study, institutionally sponsored loans, scholarships/grants, and unspecified assistantships available. Support available to part-time students. Financial award application deadline: 8/30; financial award applicants required to submit FAFSA. *Faculty research:* Fine art photography, digital imaging, moving media. *Unit head:* Dr. Therese Mulligan, Administrative Chair, 585-475-2884, E-mail: mtmpph@rit.edu. *Application contact:* Diane Ellison, Associate Vice President, Graduate Enrollment Services, 585-475-2229, Fax: 585-475-7164, E-mail: gradinfo@rit.edu.
Website: http://cias.rit.edu/schools/photographic-arts-sciences

St. Edward's University, Bill Munday School of Business, Area of Digital Media Management, Austin, TX 78704. Offers MBA. *Students:* 37 full-time (16 women), 1 part-time (0 women); includes 17 minority (3 Black or African American, non-Hispanic/Latino; 1 American Indian or Alaska Native, non-Hispanic/Latino; 4 Asian, non-Hispanic/Latino; 8 Hispanic/Latino; 1 Two or more races, non-Hispanic/Latino), 3 international. Average age 27. 69 applicants, 46% accepted, 23 enrolled. In 2014, 18 master's awarded. *Entrance requirements:* For master's, GRE or GMAT, interview, 2 letters of recommendation, minimum GPA of 3.0 in last 60 hours of course work. Additional exam requirements/recommendations for international students: Required—TOEFL (minimum score 79 iBT) or IELTS (minimum score 6). *Application deadline:* For fall admission, 2/15 priority date for domestic and international students. Applications are processed on a rolling basis. Application fee: $50. Electronic applications accepted. *Expenses:* Expenses: Contact institution. *Unit head:* Russell Rains, Director, 512-428-1220, Fax: 512-448-8492, E-mail: russellr@stedwards.edu. *Application contact:* Office of Admission, 512-448-8500, Fax: 512-464-8877, E-mail: seu.admit@stedwards.edu.
Website: http://www.stedwards.edu

San Jose State University, Graduate Studies and Research, College of Humanities and the Arts, School of Art and Design, San Jose, CA 95192-0001. Offers animation/illustration (MA); art history (MA); digital media arts (MFA); photography (MFA); pictorial arts (MFA); spatial arts (MFA). *Accreditation:* NASAD (one or more programs are accredited). *Entrance requirements:* For master's, GRE. Electronic applications accepted.

Savannah College of Art and Design, Graduate School, Program in Animation, Savannah, GA 31402-3146. Offers MA, MFA. Part-time programs available. *Faculty:* 26 full-time (4 women), 4 part-time/adjunct (1 woman). *Students:* 153 full-time (79 women), 51 part-time (25 women); includes 30 minority (17 Black or African American, non-Hispanic/Latino; 1 American Indian or Alaska Native, non-Hispanic/Latino; 7 Asian, non-Hispanic/Latino; 5 Hispanic/Latino), 106 international. Average age 26. 160 applicants, 48% accepted, 49 enrolled. In 2014, 50 master's awarded. *Degree requirements:* For master's, thesis (for some programs), internship (for MFA). *Entrance requirements:* For master's, portfolio. Additional exam requirements/recommendations for international students: Required—TOEFL (minimum score 550 paper-based, 85 iBT), IELTS (minimum score 6.5), or ACTFL. *Application deadline:* For fall admission, 4/1 for domestic and international students. Applications are processed on a rolling basis. Application fee: $40. Electronic applications accepted. *Expenses: Tuition:* Full-time $34,605; part-time $3845 per course. One-time fee: $500. Tuition and fees vary according to course load. *Financial support:* Fellowships, career-related internships or fieldwork, Federal Work-Study, and scholarships/grants available. Financial award application deadline: 4/1; financial award applicants required to submit FAFSA. *Unit head:* Scott Bogoniewski, Chair. *Application contact:* Jenny Jaquillard, Executive Director of Admissions, Recruitment and Events, 912-525-5100, Fax: 912-525-5985, E-mail: admission@scad.edu.
Website: http://www.scad.edu/academics/programs/animation

Savannah College of Art and Design, Graduate School, Program in Interactive Design and Game Development, Savannah, GA 31402-3146. Offers MA, MFA, Graduate Certificate. Part-time programs available. Postbaccalaureate distance learning degree programs offered (no on-campus study). *Faculty:* 16 full-time (4 women), 5 part-time/adjunct (1 woman). *Students:* 53 full-time (17 women), 44 part-time (14 women); includes 14 minority (6 Black or African American, non-Hispanic/Latino; 6 Asian, non-Hispanic/Latino; 2 Hispanic/Latino), 37 international. Average age 28. 113 applicants, 42% accepted, 24 enrolled. In 2014, 22 master's awarded. *Degree requirements:* For master's, thesis (for some programs), final project (for MA); internship (for MFA). *Entrance requirements:* For master's, portfolio (in digital or multimedia format). Additional exam requirements/recommendations for international students: Required—TOEFL (minimum score 550 paper-based, 85 iBT), IELTS (minimum score 6.5), or ACTFL. *Application deadline:* For fall admission, 4/1 for domestic and international students. Applications are processed on a rolling basis. Application fee: $40. Electronic applications accepted. *Expenses: Tuition:* Full-time $34,605; part-time $3845 per course. One-time fee: $500. Tuition and fees vary according to course load. *Financial support:* Fellowships, career-related internships or fieldwork, Federal Work-Study, and scholarships/grants available. Financial award application deadline: 4/1; financial award applicants required to submit FAFSA. *Unit head:* SuAnne Fu, Interim Chair. *Application contact:* Jenny Jaquillard, Executive Director of Admissions, Recruitment and Events, 912-525-5100, Fax: 912-525-5985, E-mail: admission@scad.edu.
Website: http://www.scad.edu/academics/programs/interactive-design-and-game-development

Savannah College of Art and Design, Graduate School, Program in Motion Media Design, Savannah, GA 31402-3146. Offers MA, MFA. Part-time programs available. Postbaccalaureate distance learning degree programs offered (no on-campus study). *Faculty:* 10 full-time (2 women), 5 part-time/adjunct (2 women). *Students:* 38 full-time (21 women), 37 part-time (18 women); includes 21 minority (15 Black or African American, non-Hispanic/Latino; 3 Asian, non-Hispanic/Latino; 3 Hispanic/Latino), 28 international. Average age 30. 47 applicants, 47% accepted, 15 enrolled. In 2014, 23 master's awarded. *Degree requirements:* For master's, thesis (for some programs), final project (for MA); internship (for MFA). *Entrance requirements:* For master's, portfolio. Additional exam requirements/recommendations for international students: Required—TOEFL (minimum score 550 paper-based, 85 iBT), IELTS (minimum score 6.5), or ACTFL. *Application deadline:* For fall admission, 4/1 for domestic and international students. Applications are processed on a rolling basis. Application fee: $40. Electronic applications accepted. *Expenses: Tuition:* Full-time $34,605; part-time $3845 per course. One-time fee: $500. Tuition and fees vary according to course load. *Financial support:* Fellowships, career-related internships or fieldwork, Federal Work-Study, and scholarships/grants available. Financial award application deadline: 4/1; financial award applicants required to submit FAFSA. *Unit head:* John Colette, Chair. *Application contact:* Jenny Jaquillard, Executive Director of Admissions, Recruitment and Events, 912-525-5100, Fax: 912-525-5985, E-mail: admission@scad.edu.
Website: http://www.scad.edu/academics/programs/motion-media-design

School of Visual Arts, Graduate Programs, Computer Art Department, New York, NY 10010-3994. Offers MFA. *Accreditation:* NASAD. *Degree requirements:* For master's, thesis, 60 credits, including all required courses; minimum GPA of 3.0; matriculation of two academic years. *Entrance requirements:* For master's, portfolio; 3-5 minute sample reel showing best work; statement of purpose; official transcript; 3 letters of recommendation; resume/curriculum vitae. Additional exam requirements/recommendations for international students: Required—TOEFL (minimum score 550 paper-based; 79 iBT). Electronic applications accepted. *Expenses:* Contact institution.

Shepherd University, Hollywood CG School of Digital Arts, Los Angeles, CA 90065. Offers game art and design (MSIT); visual effects and animation (MSIT). *Degree requirements:* For master's, exam, thesis, or portfolio.

Stevens Institute of Technology, Graduate School, Charles V. Schaefer Jr. School of Engineering, Department of Computer Science, Hoboken, NJ 07030. Offers computer graphics (Certificate); computer science (MS, PhD); computer systems (Certificate); database management systems (Certificate); distributed systems (Certificate); elements of computer science (Certificate); enterprise computing (Certificate); enterprise security and information assurance (Certificate); health informatics (Certificate); multimedia experience and management (Certificate); networks and systems administration (Certificate); security and privacy (Certificate); service oriented computing (Certificate); software design (Certificate); theoretical computer science (Certificate). Part-time and evening/weekend programs available. Terminal master's awarded for partial completion of doctoral program. *Degree requirements:* For master's, thesis optional; for doctorate, variable foreign language requirement, comprehensive exam, thesis/dissertation. *Entrance requirements:* For master's and doctorate, GRE, minimum GPA of 3.0. Additional exam requirements/recommendations for international students: Required—TOEFL. Electronic applications accepted. *Faculty research:* Semantics, reliability theory, programming language, cyber security.

Syracuse University, College of Visual and Performing Arts, Program in Computer Art, Syracuse, NY 13244. Offers MFA. *Students:* 5 full-time (2 women), 1 (woman) part-time, 4 international. Average age 25. 40 applicants, 13% accepted, 2 enrolled. *Degree requirements:* For master's, thesis or alternative. *Entrance requirements:* For master's, portfolio. Additional exam requirements/recommendations for international students: Required—TOEFL (minimum score 100 iBT), IELTS. *Application deadline:* For fall admission, 2/1 priority date for domestic and international students. Application fee: $75. Electronic applications accepted. *Expenses: Tuition:* Part-time $1341 per credit. *Financial support:* Fellowships with full tuition reimbursements and teaching assistantships with full and partial tuition reimbursements available. Financial award application deadline: 1/1; financial award applicants required to submit FAFSA. *Unit head:* Prof. Annina Ruest,, Department of Transmedia, 315-443-1033, E-mail: rust@syr.edu. *Application contact:* Therese West, Information Contact, 315-443-0137, E-mail: admissg@syr.edu.
Website: http://vpa.syr.edu/art-design/transmedia/graduate/computer-art

Texas State University, The Graduate College, College of Fine Arts and Communication, School of Art and Design, Program in Communication Design, San Marcos, TX 78666. Offers MFA. *Faculty:* 8 full-time (4 women), 1 part-time/adjunct (0 women). *Students:* 13 full-time (4 women), 31 part-time (20 women); includes 12 minority (1 Black or African American, non-Hispanic/Latino; 2 Asian, non-Hispanic/Latino; 8 Hispanic/Latino; 1 Two or more races, non-Hispanic/Latino), 1 international. Average age 35. 26 applicants, 54% accepted, 9 enrolled. In 2014, 11 master's awarded. *Degree requirements:* For master's, comprehensive exam, thesis (for some programs). *Entrance requirements:* For master's, GRE (preferred), baccalaureate degree from regionally-accredited institution with minimum GPA of 2.75 in last 60 hours of undergraduate course work. Additional exam requirements/recommendations for international students: Required—TOEFL (minimum score 550 paper-based; 78 iBT). *Application deadline:* For fall admission, 3/31 for domestic and international students; for spring admission, 10/31 for domestic students, 10/1 for international students. Applications are processed on a rolling basis. Application fee: $40 ($90 for international

students). Electronic applications accepted. *Expenses:* Expenses: $8,834 (tuition and fees combined). *Financial support:* In 2014–15, 21 students received support, including 1 research assistantship (averaging $11,855 per year), 6 teaching assistantships (averaging $13,875 per year); Federal Work-Study, institutionally sponsored loans, scholarships/grants, and unspecified assistantships also available. Support available to part-time students. Financial award application deadline: 4/1; financial award applicants required to submit FAFSA. *Unit head:* Claudia Roschmann, Graduate Advisor, 512-245-7450, E-mail: cr29@txstate.edu. *Application contact:* Dr. Andrea Golato, Dean of Graduate School, 512-245-2581, Fax: 512-245-8365, E-mail: gradcollege@txstate.edu.
Website: http://www.finearts.txstate.edu/Art/mfacomdes/

Universidad Autonoma de Guadalajara, Graduate Programs, Guadalajara, Mexico. Offers administrative law and justice (LL M); advertising and corporate communications (MA); architecture (M Arch); business (MBA); computational science (MCC); education (Ed M, Ed D); English-Spanish translation (MA); entrepreneurship and management (MBA); integrated management of digital animation (MA); international business (MIB); international corporate law (LL M); internet technologies (MS); manufacturing systems (MMS); occupational health (MS); philosophy (MA, PhD); power electronics (MS); quality systems (MQS); renewable energy (MS); social evaluation of projects (MBA); strategic market research (MBA); tax law (MA); teaching mathematics (MA).

Universidad de las Américas Puebla, Division of Graduate Studies, School of Humanities, Program in Information Design, Puebla, Mexico. Offers MA. Part-time and evening/weekend programs available. *Degree requirements:* For master's, one foreign language, thesis. *Entrance requirements:* Additional exam requirements/recommendations for international students: Required—TOEFL. *Faculty research:* Typography, project development, organizational image.

University of Alaska Fairbanks, College of Liberal Arts, Department of Art, Fairbanks, AK 99775-5640. Offers art (MFA); ceramics (MFA); computer art (MFA); drawing (MFA); painting (MFA); photography (MFA); printmaking (MFA); sculpture (MFA). Part-time programs available. *Faculty:* 8 full-time (4 women). *Students:* 6 full-time (all women), 1 (woman) part-time; includes 2 minority (1 Asian, non-Hispanic/Latino; 1 Hispanic/Latino), 1 international. Average age 32. 6 applicants, 17% accepted, 1 enrolled. In 2014, 3 master's awarded. *Degree requirements:* For master's, comprehensive exam, oral defense of project or thesis. *Entrance requirements:* For master's, portfolio of work including about 20 slides or appropriate equivalent depending on field of study. Additional exam requirements/recommendations for international students: Required—TOEFL (minimum score 550 paper-based; 79 iBT), IELTS (minimum score 6.5). *Application deadline:* For fall admission, 6/1 for domestic students, 3/1 for international students; for spring admission, 10/15 for domestic students, 9/1 for international students. Applications are processed on a rolling basis. Application fee: $60. Electronic applications accepted. *Expenses:* Tuition, state resident: full-time $7614; part-time $423 per credit. Tuition, nonresident: full-time $15,552; part-time $864 per credit. Tuition and fees vary according to course level, course load and reciprocity agreements. *Financial support:* In 2014–15, 6 teaching assistantships with full tuition reimbursements (averaging $9,319 per year) were awarded; fellowships with full tuition reimbursements, research assistantships with full tuition reimbursements, Federal Work-Study, scholarships/grants, health care benefits, and unspecified assistantships also available. Support available to part-time students. Financial award application deadline: 7/1; financial award applicants required to submit FAFSA. *Faculty research:* Computer art, survey of arts in Alaska, found object art, visualization and animation, painting from the wilderness. *Unit head:* David Mollett, Chair, 907-474-7530, Fax: 907-474-5853, E-mail: uaf-art@alaska.edu. *Application contact:* Mary Kreta, Director of Admissions, 907-474-7500, Fax: 907-474-7097, E-mail: admissions@uaf.edu.
Website: http://www.uaf.edu/art/

University of California, Santa Cruz, Division of Graduate Studies, Division of the Arts, Department of Film and Digital Media, Santa Cruz, CA 95064. Offers PhD. *Degree requirements:* For doctorate, one foreign language, thesis/dissertation, qualifying exams. *Entrance requirements:* For doctorate, GRE. Additional exam requirements/recommendations for international students: Required—TOEFL (minimum score 550 paper-based; 83 iBT); Recommended—IELTS (minimum score 8). Electronic applications accepted. *Faculty research:* Integrating critical and creative practice, working across media, pursuing new modes of social and political engagement, fostering global cultural citizenship.

University of California, Santa Cruz, Division of Graduate Studies, Division of the Arts, Program in Digital Arts and New Media, Santa Cruz, CA 95064. Offers MFA. *Degree requirements:* For master's, thesis, written paper. *Entrance requirements:* Additional exam requirements/recommendations for international students: Required—TOEFL (minimum score 550 paper-based; 83 iBT); Recommended—IELTS (minimum score 8). Electronic applications accepted. *Faculty research:* Mechatronics, participatory culture, performative technologies, playable media.

University of Central Arkansas, Graduate School, College of Fine Arts and Communication, Program in Digital Filmmaking, Conway, AR 72035-0001. Offers MFA. *Degree requirements:* For master's, thesis. *Entrance requirements:* For master's, GRE General Test, minimum GPA of 2.7. Additional exam requirements/recommendations for international students: Required—TOEFL (minimum score 550 paper-based). Electronic applications accepted.

University of Central Florida, College of Arts and Humanities, School of Visual Arts and Design, Orlando, FL 32816. Offers digital media (MA); emerging media (MFA), including digital media, entrepreneurial digital cinema, studio art and the computer. *Faculty:* 51 full-time (20 women), 20 part-time/adjunct (4 women). *Students:* 40 full-time (18 women), 9 part-time (1 woman); includes 8 minority (1 Black or African American, non-Hispanic/Latino; 1 American Indian or Alaska Native, non-Hispanic/Latino; 1 Asian, non-Hispanic/Latino; 5 Hispanic/Latino), 7 international. Average age 32. 43 applicants, 56% accepted, 14 enrolled. In 2014, 12 master's awarded. Application fee: $30. Electronic applications accepted. *Expenses:* Tuition, state resident: part-time $288.16 per credit hour. Tuition, nonresident: part-time $1073.31 per credit hour. *Financial support:* In 2014–15, 25 students received support, including 11 fellowships (averaging $8,500 per year), 16 teaching assistantships (averaging $6,300 per year); scholarships/grants and unspecified assistantships also available. *Unit head:* Byron Clercx, Director, 407-823-3145, E-mail: byron.clercx@ucf.edu. *Application contact:* Barbara Rodriguez Lamas, Director, Admissions and Student Services, 407-823-2766, Fax: 407-823-6442, E-mail: gradadmissions@ucf.edu.
Website: http://svad.cah.ucf.edu/

University of Denver, Division of Arts, Humanities and Social Sciences, Department of Media, Film and Journalism Studies, Denver, CO 80208. Offers emergent digital practices (MA); international and intercultural communication (MA); strategic communication (MS); student designed emphasis (MA); video production (MA). Part-time programs available. *Faculty:* 14 full-time (8 women), 6 part-time/adjunct (2 women). *Students:* 24 full-time (17 women), 25 part-time (17 women); includes 10 minority (1 Asian, non-Hispanic/Latino; 4 Hispanic/Latino; 5 Two or more races, non-Hispanic/Latino), 4 international. Average age 27. 73 applicants, 89% accepted, 21 enrolled. In 2014, 17 master's awarded. *Degree requirements:* For master's, thesis (for some programs). *Entrance requirements:* For master's, GRE General Test, bachelor's degree, transcripts, personal statement, three letters of recommendation. Additional exam requirements/recommendations for international students: Required—TOEFL (minimum score 620 paper-based; 105 iBT). *Application deadline:* For fall admission, 2/15 priority date for domestic students, 1/1 priority date for international students. Applications are processed on a rolling basis. Application fee: $65. Electronic applications accepted. *Expenses:* Expenses: $1,199 per credit hour. *Financial support:* In 2014–15, 41 students received support, including 7 teaching assistantships with full and partial tuition reimbursements available (averaging $9,515 per year); career-related internships or fieldwork, Federal Work-Study, institutionally sponsored loans, scholarships/grants, and unspecified assistantships also available. Support available to part-time students. Financial award application deadline: 2/15; financial award applicants required to submit FAFSA. *Faculty research:* International and intercultural communication; media law; film history; youth, families, and social media; activist media. *Total annual research expenditures:* $50,000. *Unit head:* Dr. Lynn Schofield Clark, Chair, 303-871-3984, Fax: 303-871-4949, E-mail: lynn.clark@du.edu. *Application contact:* Information Contact, 303-871-2166, E-mail: mfjs@du.edu. Website: http://www.du.edu/ahss/mfjs/index.html

University of Denver, Division of Arts, Humanities and Social Sciences, Program in Emergent Digital Practices, Denver, CO 80208. Offers MA. Part-time programs available. *Faculty:* 10 full-time (2 women). *Students:* 4 full-time (2 women), 10 part-time (6 women); includes 1 minority (Hispanic/Latino), 2 international. Average age 28. 10 applicants, 50% accepted. *Degree requirements:* For master's, thesis (for some programs), project or thesis. *Entrance requirements:* For master's, GRE General Test, bachelor's degree, transcripts, personal statement, resume or curriculum vitae, three letters of recommendation. Additional exam requirements/recommendations for international students: Required—TOEFL (minimum score 620 paper-based; 105 iBT). *Application deadline:* For fall admission, 1/20 priority date for domestic and international students. Applications are processed on a rolling basis. Application fee: $65. Electronic applications accepted. *Expenses:* Expenses: $1,199 per credit hour. *Financial support:* In 2014–15, 14 students received support, including 9 teaching assistantships with full and partial tuition reimbursements available (averaging $5,185 per year); Federal Work-Study, scholarships/grants, and unspecified assistantships also available. Financial award application deadline: 2/15; financial award applicants required to submit FAFSA. *Faculty research:* Biomimetics, interactive installations, creative coding, humane games, locative networks, sonic arts. *Unit head:* Dr. Christopher Coleman, Director, 303-871-7716, E-mail: christopher.coleman@du.edu. *Application contact:* Dr. Laleh Mehran, Assistant Professor and Graduate Director, 303-871-3264, E-mail: laleh.mehran@du.edu.
Website: http://dms.du.edu

University of Denver, Division of Arts, Humanities and Social Sciences, School of Art and Art History, Denver, CO 80208. Offers art history (MA); art history/museum studies (MA); emergent digital practices (MFA). *Accreditation:* NASAD. Part-time programs available. *Faculty:* 16 full-time (11 women), 3 part-time/adjunct (1 woman). *Students:* 7 full-time (6 women), 17 part-time (16 women); includes 7 minority (1 Black or African American, non-Hispanic/Latino; 1 American Indian or Alaska Native, non-Hispanic/Latino; 5 Hispanic/Latino). Average age 25. 24 applicants, 83% accepted, 14 enrolled. In 2014, 7 master's awarded. *Degree requirements:* For master's, one foreign language, comprehensive exam, research paper or thesis project. *Entrance requirements:* For master's, GRE General Test, transcripts, personal statement, writing sample, three letters of recommendation. Additional exam requirements/recommendations for international students: Required—TOEFL (minimum score 550 paper-based; 80 iBT). *Application deadline:* For fall admission, 1/31 priority date for domestic and international students. Applications are processed on a rolling basis. Application fee: $65. Electronic applications accepted. *Expenses:* Expenses: $1,199 per credit hour. *Financial support:* In 2014–15, 18 students received support, including 8 teaching assistantships with full and partial tuition reimbursements available (averaging $7,817 per year); career-related internships or fieldwork, Federal Work-Study, institutionally sponsored loans, scholarships/grants, and unspecified assistantships also available. Support available to part-time students. Financial award application deadline: 2/15; financial award applicants required to submit FAFSA. *Faculty research:* Images of women in alchemical manuscripts and books, Giovanni Benedetto and Salvatore Castiglione. *Unit head:* Dr. Sarah Gjertson, Director, 303-871-3263, E-mail: sgjertso@du.edu. *Application contact:* Dr. Annabeth Headrick, Graduate Art History Advisor, 303-871-3574, E-mail: annabeth.headrick@du.edu.
Website: http://www.du.edu/art/

University of Florida, Graduate School, College of Engineering and College of Liberal Arts and Sciences, Department of Computer and Information Science and Engineering, Gainesville, FL 32611. Offers computer engineering (ME, MS, PhD); computer science (MS); digital arts and sciences (MS). Part-time programs available. Postbaccalaureate distance learning degree programs offered (minimal on-campus study). *Faculty:* 42 full-time (6 women), 32 part-time/adjunct (4 women). *Students:* 364 full-time (91 women), 90 part-time (9 women); includes 30 minority (8 Black or African American, non-Hispanic/Latino; 1 American Indian or Alaska Native, non-Hispanic/Latino; 12 Asian, non-Hispanic/Latino; 9 Hispanic/Latino), 370 international. 2,043 applicants, 22% accepted, 156 enrolled. In 2014, 218 master's, 18 doctorates awarded. Terminal master's awarded for partial completion of doctoral program. *Degree requirements:* For master's, comprehensive exam, thesis optional; for doctorate, comprehensive exam, thesis/dissertation. *Entrance requirements:* For master's and doctorate, minimum GPA of 3.0. Additional exam requirements/recommendations for international students: Required—TOEFL (minimum score 550 paper-based; 80 iBT), IELTS (minimum score 6). *Application deadline:* For fall admission, 12/15 priority date for domestic students, 2/1 for international students; for spring admission, 9/1 for domestic and international students. Applications are processed on a rolling basis. Application fee: $30. Electronic applications accepted. *Financial support:* In 2014–15, 4 fellowships, 92 research assistantships, 63 teaching assistantships were awarded; unspecified assistantships also available. Financial award application deadline: 2/1; financial award applicants required to submit FAFSA. *Faculty research:* Computer systems and computer networking; high-performance computing and algorithm; database and machine learning; computer graphics, vision, and intelligent systems; human center computing and digital art. *Unit head:* Paul Gader, PhD, Chair, 352-392-1527, Fax: 352-392-1220, E-mail: pgader@cise.ufl.edu. *Application contact:* Jih-Kwon Peir, PhD, Graduate Coordinator, 352-505-1573, Fax: 352-392-1220, E-mail: peir@cise.ufl.edu.
Website: http://www.cise.ufl.edu/

University of Florida, Graduate School, College of The Arts, School of Art and Art History, Gainesville, FL 32611-5800. Offers art (MA), including digital arts and sciences; art education (MA); art history (MA, PhD); museology (MA), including historic preservation. *Accreditation:* NASAD. Postbaccalaureate distance learning degree programs offered (minimal on-campus study). *Faculty:* 32 full-time (14 women), 5 part-time/adjunct (3 women). *Students:* 91 full-time (66 women), 117 part-time (100 women); includes 50 minority (14 Black or African American, non-Hispanic/Latino; 4 American Indian or Alaska Native, non-Hispanic/Latino; 6 Asian, non-Hispanic/Latino; 26 Hispanic/Latino), 14 international. 199 applicants, 41% accepted, 55 enrolled. In 2014, 69 master's awarded. *Degree requirements:* For master's, project or thesis (MFA); 1 foreign

language (MA in art history); for doctorate, 2 foreign languages, comprehensive exam, thesis/dissertation. *Entrance requirements:* For master's, GRE General Test, portfolio (MFA), writing sample (MA), minimum GPA 3.0; for doctorate, GRE General Test, minimum GPA of 3.0. Additional exam requirements/recommendations for international students: Required—TOEFL (minimum score 550 paper-based; 80 iBT), IELTS (minimum score 6). *Application deadline:* For fall admission, 1/1 priority date for domestic students, 1/1 for international students; for spring admission, 11/1 for domestic and international students. Applications are processed on a rolling basis. Application fee: $30. Electronic applications accepted. *Financial support:* In 2014–15, 4 fellowships, 8 research assistantships, 76 teaching assistantships were awarded; Federal Work-Study, institutionally sponsored loans, and unspecified assistantships also available. Financial award applicants required to submit FAFSA. *Faculty research:* Studio production, art historical studies of style context. *Unit head:* Richard Heipp, Professor and Interim Director, 352-273-3021, Fax: 352-392-8453, E-mail: heipp@ufl.edu. *Application contact:* Maya Stanfield-Mazzi, PhD, Assistant Professor/Director of Graduate Studies for Art History, 352-273-3070, Fax: 352-392-8453, E-mail: mstanfield@ufl.edu. Website: http://www.arts.ufl.edu/art

The University of Kansas, Graduate Studies, School of Architecture, Design, and Planning, Department of Design, Lawrence, KS 66045. Offers design (MA, MFA); design management (MA); interaction design (MA). *Accreditation:* NASAD (one or more programs are accredited). *Faculty:* 17 full-time, 16 part-time/adjunct. *Students:* 10 full-time (8 women), 17 part-time (8 women); includes 4 minority (2 Asian, non-Hispanic/Latino; 1 Hispanic/Latino; 1 Two or more races, non-Hispanic/Latino), 8 international. Average age 29. 19 applicants, 63% accepted, 8 enrolled. In 2014, 6 master's awarded. *Degree requirements:* For master's, thesis. *Entrance requirements:* For master's, portfolio, 3 letters of recommendation, minimum GPA of 3.0. Additional exam requirements/recommendations for international students: Required—TOEFL, IELTS. *Application deadline:* For fall admission, 4/1 for domestic and international students; for spring admission, 11/1 for domestic students. Applications are processed on a rolling basis. Application fee: $55 ($65 for international students). Electronic applications accepted. *Financial support:* Fellowships, teaching assistantships with full and partial tuition reimbursements, Federal Work-Study, scholarships/grants, and unspecified assistantships available. Financial award application deadline: 2/1; financial award applicants required to submit FAFSA. *Faculty research:* Interaction design, design management, photography, graphic design, industrial design. *Unit head:* Andrea Herstowski, Chair, 785-864-2956, E-mail: hestow@ku.edu. *Application contact:* Gera Elliott, Coordinator of Student Services, 785-864-3167, E-mail: archku@ku.edu. Website: http://design.ku.edu/

University of Maryland, Baltimore County, The Graduate School, College of Arts, Humanities and Social Sciences, Department of Visual Arts, Program in Intermedia and Digital Arts, Baltimore, MD 21250. Offers MFA. *Faculty:* 24 full-time (13 women), 15 part-time/adjunct (7 women). *Students:* 15 full-time (8 women); includes 1 minority (Hispanic/Latino), 2 international. Average age 30. 19 applicants, 32% accepted, 5 enrolled. In 2014, 6 master's awarded. *Degree requirements:* For master's, oral defense, exhibition, written thesis. *Entrance requirements:* For master's, minimum GPA of 3.0. Additional exam requirements/recommendations for international students: Required—TOEFL. *Application deadline:* For fall admission, 2/1 for domestic and international students. Applications are processed on a rolling basis. Application fee: $50. Electronic applications accepted. *Expenses:* Expenses: Contact institution. *Financial support:* In 2014–15, 14 students received support, including 14 research assistantships with full and partial tuition reimbursements available (averaging $22,325 per year); institutionally sponsored loans, scholarships/grants, health care benefits, and unspecified assistantships also available. Financial award application deadline: 3/15. *Faculty research:* Interactive art, video, electronic media, photography, animation, print media, sound, performance, installation, cinematic arts. *Unit head:* Prof. Lisa Moren, Graduate Program Director, 410-455-2490, Fax: 410-455-1053, E-mail: lmoren@umbc.edu. Website: http://imda.umbc.edu

University of Massachusetts Dartmouth, Graduate School, College of Visual and Performing Arts, Department of Design, North Dartmouth, MA 02747-2300. Offers digital multi-media (MFA). *Accreditation:* NASAD. Part-time programs available. *Faculty:* 16 full-time (7 women), 3 part-time/adjunct (1 woman). *Students:* 10 full-time (4 women), 1 (woman) part-time; includes 1 minority (Black or African American, non-Hispanic/Latino), 7 international. Average age 27. 37 applicants, 24% accepted, 3 enrolled. In 2014, 2 master's awarded. *Degree requirements:* For master's, visual thesis, written thesis. *Entrance requirements:* For master's, statement of purpose (minimum of 300 words), resume, 2 letters of recommendation, official transcripts, portfolio (20 images representing applicant's art work); for Postbaccalaureate Certificate, statement of purpose (minimum of 300 words), resume, 3 letters of recommendation, official transcripts, portfolio (10 images representing applicant's art work). Additional exam requirements/recommendations for international students: Required—TOEFL (minimum score 533 paper-based; 72 iBT), IELTS (minimum score 6). *Application deadline:* For fall admission, 1/9 priority date for domestic students, 12/9 priority date for international students; for spring admission, 10/15 priority date for domestic students, 9/15 priority date for international students. Applications are processed on a rolling basis. Application fee: $60. Electronic applications accepted. *Expenses:* Tuition, state resident: full-time $2071; part-time $86.29 per credit. Tuition, nonresident: full-time $8099; part-time $337.46 per credit. *Required fees:* $16,520; $712.33 per credit. Tuition and fees vary according to course load and reciprocity agreements. *Financial support:* In 2014–15, 1 teaching assistantship with partial tuition reimbursement (averaging $2,600 per year) was awarded; Federal Work-Study and unspecified assistantships also available. Support available to part-time students. Financial award application deadline: 3/1; financial award applicants required to submit FAFSA. *Faculty research:* Web design, animation (2D and 3D), multimedia design, broadcast design, product design, typography. *Total annual research expenditures:* $49,666. *Unit head:* Charlotte Hamlin, Coordinator for Graduate Studies, College of Visual and Preforming Arts, 508-999-8911, Fax: 508-999-8912, E-mail: chamlin@umassd.edu. *Application contact:* Steven Briggs, Director of Marketing and Recruitment for Graduate Studies, 508-999-8604, Fax: 508-999-8183, E-mail: graduate@umassd.edu. Website: http://www.umassd.edu/cvpa/graduate/visualdesign/

University of Missouri, Office of Research and Graduate Studies, College of Human Environmental Sciences, Department of Architectural Studies, Columbia, MO 65211. Offers design with digital media (MA, MS); environmental design (MS). *Faculty:* 7 full-time (2 women). *Students:* 14 full-time (11 women), 23 part-time (14 women); includes 5 minority (1 Black or African American, non-Hispanic/Latino; 2 Asian, non-Hispanic/Latino; 1 Hispanic/Latino; 1 Two or more races, non-Hispanic/Latino), 4 international. Average age 41. 33 applicants, 30% accepted, 7 enrolled. In 2014, 4 master's awarded. *Entrance requirements:* For master's, GRE General Test, minimum GPA of 3.0. Additional exam requirements/recommendations for international students: Required—TOEFL (minimum score 500 paper-based; 61 iBT). *Application deadline:* For fall admission, 4/1 for domestic students; for winter admission, 10/1 for domestic students; for spring admission, 4/1 for domestic students. Applications are processed on a rolling basis. Application fee: $55 ($75 for international students). Electronic applications accepted. *Financial support:* Fellowships, research assistantships, teaching assistantships, institutionally sponsored loans, scholarships/grants, health care benefits, and unspecified assistantships available. Support available to part-time students. *Faculty research:* Environment and aging, design education and research, place attachment, residential environments, computer-mediated simulation, architectural design process. *Unit head:* Dr. Ruth Brent Tofle, Department Chair, 573-882-6311, E-mail: tofler@missouri.edu. *Application contact:* Laura Franklin, Business Support Specialist II, 573-882-7224, E-mail: franklinl@missouri.edu. Website: http://arch.missouri.edu/

The University of Montana, Graduate School, College of Visual and Performing Arts, School of Media Arts, Missoula, MT 59812-0002. Offers digital filmmaking (MFA); integrated digital media (MFA).

University of Pennsylvania, School of Engineering and Applied Science, Computer Graphics and Game Technology Program, Philadelphia, PA 19104. Offers MSE. *Students:* 34 full-time (13 women), 1 part-time (0 women), 29 international. 123 applicants, 36% accepted, 15 enrolled. In 2014, 21 master's awarded. Application fee: $70. *Unit head:* Eduardo D. Glandt, Dean, 215-898-7244, E-mail: seasdean@seas.upenn.edu. *Application contact:* School of Engineering and Applied Science Graduate Admissions, 215-898-4542, E-mail: gradstudies@seas.upenn.edu. Website: http://www.seas.upenn.edu

University of Southern California, Graduate School, School of Cinematic Arts, Division of Animation and Digital Arts, Los Angeles, CA 90089. Offers MFA. *Degree requirements:* For master's, thesis, digital media and research documentation. *Entrance requirements:* Additional exam requirements/recommendations for international students: Recommended—TOEFL. Electronic applications accepted. *Expenses:* Contact institution. *Faculty research:* Character animation, visual effects, motion graphics, documentary animation, experimental animation.

University of South Florida, St. Petersburg, College of Arts and Sciences, St. Petersburg, FL 33701. Offers digital journalism and design (MA); environmental science and policy (MA, MS); Florida studies (MLA); journalism and media studies (MA); liberal studies (MLA); psychology (MA). Part-time programs available. Postbaccalaureate distance learning degree programs offered (no on-campus study). *Degree requirements:* For master's, comprehensive exam, thesis or project. *Entrance requirements:* For master's, GRE, LSAT, MCAT (varies by program), letter of intent, 3 letters of recommendation, writing samples, bachelor's degree from regionally-accredited institution with minimum GPA of 3.0 overall or in upper two years. Additional exam requirements/recommendations for international students: Required—TOEFL (minimum score 550 paper-based; 79 iBT); Recommended—IELTS. Electronic applications accepted.

University of Victoria, Faculty of Graduate Studies, Faculty of Fine Arts, Department of Visual Arts, Victoria, BC V8W 2Y2, Canada. Offers digital multimedia (MFA); drawing (MFA); painting (MFA); photography (MFA); sculpture (MFA); video (MFA). *Degree requirements:* For master's, exhibit, oral exam. *Entrance requirements:* For master's, portfolio, BFA. Additional exam requirements/recommendations for international students: Required—TOEFL (minimum score 575 paper-based), IELTS (minimum score 7). Electronic applications accepted.

Virginia International University, School of Computer Information Systems, Fairfax, VA 22030. Offers business intelligence (Graduate Certificate); business intelligence and data analytics (MIS); computer science (MS), including computer animation and gaming, cybersecurity, data management networking, intelligent systems, software applications development, software engineering; cybersecurity (MIS); data management (MIS); enterprise project management (MIS); health informatics (MIS); information assurance (MIS); information systems (Graduate Certificate); information systems management (MS, Graduate Certificate); information technology (MS); information technology audit and compliance (Graduate Certificate); knowledge management (MIS); software engineering (MS). Part-time programs available. Postbaccalaureate distance learning degree programs offered (no on-campus study). *Faculty:* 2 full-time (both women), 4 part-time/adjunct (0 women). *Students:* 62 full-time (30 women). Average age 26. 175 applicants, 26% accepted, 9 enrolled. In 2014, 26 master's awarded. *Entrance requirements:* For master's, bachelor's degree. Additional exam requirements/recommendations for international students: Required—TOEFL (minimum score 550 paper-based; 80 iBT), IELTS. *Application deadline:* For fall admission, 7/31 for domestic students, 7/3 for international students; for spring admission, 12/18 for domestic students, 11/20 for international students. Applications are processed on a rolling basis. Application fee: $100. Electronic applications accepted. *Expenses: Tuition:* Full-time $26,200. Full-time tuition and fees vary according to course load and program. *Financial support:* In 2014–15, 9 students received support. Scholarships/grants available. Financial award application deadline: 7/1. *Unit head:* Dean, 703-591-7042, E-mail: emilia@viu.edu. *Application contact:* Dean, 703-591-7042, E-mail: emilia@viu.edu. Website: http://viu.edu/scis

Graphic Design

Academy of Art University, Graduate Program, School of Graphic Design, San Francisco, CA 94105-3410. Offers MFA. *Accreditation:* NASAD. Part-time programs available. Postbaccalaureate distance learning degree programs offered (no on-campus study). *Faculty:* 11 full-time (2 women), 30 part-time/adjunct (14 women). *Students:* 219 full-time (160 women), 133 part-time (97 women); includes 53 minority (14 Black or African American, non-Hispanic/Latino; 1 American Indian or Alaska Native, non-Hispanic/Latino; 19 Asian, non-Hispanic/Latino; 17 Hispanic/Latino; 1 Native Hawaiian or other Pacific Islander, non-Hispanic/Latino; 1 Two or more races, non-Hispanic/Latino), 214 international. Average age 28. 198 applicants, 100% accepted, 103 enrolled. In 2014, 29 master's awarded. *Degree requirements:* For master's, final review. *Entrance requirements:* For master's, statement of intent; resume; portfolio/reel; official college transcripts. *Application deadline:* Applications are processed on a rolling

basis. Application fee: $100. Electronic applications accepted. *Expenses: Tuition:* Part-time $910 per unit. *Financial support:* Career-related internships or fieldwork and Federal Work-Study available. Support available to part-time students. Financial award application deadline: 8/10; financial award applicants required to submit FAFSA. *Unit head:* 800-544-ARTS, E-mail: info@academyart.edu. *Application contact:* 800-544-ARTS, E-mail: info@academyart.edu.
Website: http://www.academyart.edu/graphic-design-school/index.html

Atlantic University College, Program in Graphic Arts, Guaynabo, PR 00970. Offers digital graphic design (MGD). Part-time programs available. *Degree requirements:* For master's, thesis. *Entrance requirements:* For master's, minimum GPA of 3.0, 2 letters of recommendation, portfolio, interview. *Faculty research:* Digital design, technology.

Bob Jones University, Graduate Programs, Greenville, SC 29614. Offers accountancy (MS); Bible (MA); Bible translation (MA); Biblical studies (Certificate); broadcast management (MS); business administration (MBA); church history (MA, PhD); church ministries (MA); church music (MM); cinema and video production (MA); counseling (MS); curriculum and instruction (Ed D); divinity (M Div); dramatic production (MA); educational leadership (MS, Ed D, Ed S); elementary education (M Ed, MAT); English (M Ed, MA, MAT); fine arts (MA); graphic design (MA); history (M Ed, MA); illustration (MA); interpretative speech (MA); mathematics (M Ed, MAT); medical missions (Certificate); ministry (MM, D Min); multi-categorical special education (M Ed, MAT); music (M Ed); New Testament interpretation (PhD); Old Testament interpretation (PhD); orchestral instrument performance (MM); organ performance (MM); pastoral studies (MA); personnel services (MS, Ed S); piano pedagogy (MM); piano performance (MM); platform arts (MA); radio and television broadcasting (MS); rhetoric and public address (MA); secondary education (M Ed); studio art (MA); teaching Bible (MA); theology (MA, PhD); voice performance (MM); youth ministries (MA); M Div/MM.

Boston University, College of Fine Arts, School of Visual Arts, Boston, MA 02215. Offers art education (MA); graphic design (MFA); painting (MFA); sculpture (MFA); studio teaching (MA). *Faculty:* 17 full-time, 4 part-time/adjunct. *Students:* 188 full-time (159 women), 9 part-time (7 women); includes 22 minority (3 Black or African American, non-Hispanic/Latino; 5 Asian, non-Hispanic/Latino; 11 Hispanic/Latino; 3 Two or more races, non-Hispanic/Latino), 39 international. Average age 31. 257 applicants, 27% accepted, 21 enrolled. In 2014, 53 master's awarded. *Entrance requirements:* For master's, portfolio. Additional exam requirements/recommendations for international students: Required—TOEFL, IELTS. *Application deadline:* For fall admission, 2/2 for domestic and international students. Applications are processed on a rolling basis. Application fee: $80. *Expenses: Tuition:* Full-time $45,686; part-time $1428 per credit hour. *Required fees:* $660; $60 per semester. Tuition and fees vary according to program. *Financial support:* Fellowships and teaching assistantships available. Financial award application deadline: 2/15. *Unit head:* Jeannette Guillemin, Interim Director, 617-353-3371. *Application contact:* Mark Krone, Manager, Graduate Admissions and Online Marketing, 617-353-3350, E-mail: arts@bu.edu.

Bowling Green State University, Graduate College, College of Arts and Sciences, School of Art, Bowling Green, OH 43403. Offers 2-D studio art (MA, MFA); 3-D studio art (MA, MFA); art education (MA); art history (MA); computer art (MA); design (MFA); digital arts (MFA); graphics (MFA). *Accreditation:* NASAD. Part-time programs available. *Degree requirements:* For master's, thesis or alternative, final exhibit (MFA). *Entrance requirements:* For master's, GRE General Test (MA), slide portfolio (15-20 slides). Additional exam requirements/recommendations for international students: Required—TOEFL. Electronic applications accepted. *Faculty research:* Computer animation and virtual reality, Spanish still-life painting from 1600 to 1800, art and psychotherapy, Japanese wood-firing techniques in ceramics, non-toxic printmaking technologies.

California College of the Arts, Graduate Programs, Design Program, San Francisco, CA 94107. Offers graphic design (MFA); industrial design (MFA); interaction design (MFA). *Accreditation:* NASAD. *Degree requirements:* For master's, thesis, exhibit. *Entrance requirements:* For master's, appropriate bachelor's degree, portfolio, resume, letters of recommendation, transcripts. Additional exam requirements/recommendations for international students: Required—TOEFL (minimum score 600 paper-based; 100 iBT). Electronic applications accepted.

California Institute of the Arts, School of Art, Valencia, CA 91355-2340. Offers art (MFA, Adv C); graphic design (MFA, Adv C); photography (MFA, Adv C). *Accreditation:* NASAD (one or more programs are accredited). *Degree requirements:* For master's, final project. *Entrance requirements:* For master's, portfolio. Additional exam requirements/recommendations for international students: Required—TOEFL. Electronic applications accepted.

California State University, Fullerton, Graduate Studies, College of the Arts, Department of Visual Arts, Fullerton, CA 92834-9480. Offers art (MA, MFA), including art history (MA), ceramics (MFA), crafts, creative photography, exhibition design, glass, graphic design, illustration, sculpture. *Accreditation:* NASAD (one or more programs are accredited). Part-time programs available. *Students:* 28 full-time (16 women), 29 part-time (22 women); includes 20 minority (3 Black or African American, non-Hispanic/Latino; 8 Asian, non-Hispanic/Latino; 8 Hispanic/Latino; 1 Two or more races, non-Hispanic/Latino), 7 international. Average age 35. 58 applicants, 38% accepted, 14 enrolled. In 2014, 17 master's awarded. *Degree requirements:* For master's, project or thesis. *Entrance requirements:* For master's, minimum GPA of 2.5 in last 60 units of course work, portfolio. Application fee: $55. *Financial support:* Career-related internships or fieldwork, Federal Work-Study, institutionally sponsored loans, and scholarships/grants available. Support available to part-time students. Financial award application deadline: 3/1; financial award applicants required to submit FAFSA. *Unit head:* Dana Lamb, Chair, 657-278-2076. *Application contact:* Admissions/Applications, 657-278-2371.

California State University, Los Angeles, Graduate Studies, College of Arts and Letters, Department of Art, Los Angeles, CA 90032-8530. Offers art (MA), including art education, art history, art therapy, ceramics, metals, and textiles, design (MA, MFA), painting, sculpture, and graphic arts, photography; fine arts (MFA), including crafts, design (MA, MFA), studio arts. *Accreditation:* NASAD (one or more programs are accredited). Part-time and evening/weekend programs available. *Degree requirements:* For master's, comprehensive exam, project or thesis. *Entrance requirements:* For master's, portfolio. Additional exam requirements/recommendations for international students: Required—TOEFL (minimum score 500 paper-based). Electronic applications accepted. *Expenses:* Tuition, state resident: full-time $6738; part-time $3609 per year. Tuition, nonresident: full-time $15,666; part-time $8073 per year. Tuition and fees vary according to course load, degree level and program. *Faculty research:* The artist and the book, conceptual art, ceramic processes, computer graphics, architectural graphics.

Cardinal Stritch University, College of Arts and Sciences, Department of Art, Milwaukee, WI 53217-3985. Offers visual studies (MA). Part-time and evening/weekend programs available. *Degree requirements:* For master's, thesis, portfolio, exhibit. *Entrance requirements:* For master's, minimum GPA of 2.75; 3 letters of recommendation.

City College of the City University of New York, Graduate School, College of Liberal Arts and Science, Division of the Humanities and Arts, Department of Art, Program in Fine Arts, New York, NY 10031-9198. Offers advertising design (MFA); ceramic design (MFA); painting (MFA); printmaking (MFA); sculpture (MFA); wood and metal design (MFA). *Degree requirements:* For master's, thesis exhibit. *Entrance requirements:* For master's, 20 slide portfolio. Additional exam requirements/recommendations for international students: Required—TOEFL (minimum score 577 paper-based; 90 iBT). Electronic applications accepted.

Digital Media Arts College, Graduate Programs, Boca Raton, FL 33487. Offers graphic design (MFA); special FX animation (MFA).

East Carolina University, Graduate School, College of Fine Arts and Communication, School of Art and Design, Greenville, NC 27858-4353. Offers art education (MA Ed); ceramics (MFA); graphic design (MFA); illustration (MFA); metal design (MFA); painting and drawing (MFA); photography (MFA); printmaking (MFA); sculpture (MFA); textile design (MFA); wood design (MFA). *Accreditation:* NASAD (one or more programs are accredited). Part-time and evening/weekend programs available. *Degree requirements:* For master's, comprehensive exam, thesis (for some programs). *Entrance requirements:* For master's, GRE General Test or MAT, portfolio. Additional exam requirements/recommendations for international students: Required—TOEFL. *Expenses:* Tuition, state resident: full-time $4223. Tuition, nonresident: full-time $16,540. *Required fees:* $2184.

Florida Atlantic University, Dorothy F. Schmidt College of Arts and Letters, Department of Visual Arts and Art History, Boca Raton, FL 33431-0991. Offers visual art (MFA), including ceramics, graphic design, visual art. *Degree requirements:* For master's, one foreign language, project. *Entrance requirements:* For master's, GRE General Test, minimum GPA of 3.0 during last 60 hours of course work, slide portfolio. Electronic applications accepted. *Expenses:* Tuition, state resident: full-time $7396; part-time $369.82 per credit hour. Tuition, nonresident: full-time $19,392; part-time $1024.81 per credit hour. Tuition and fees vary according to course load. *Faculty research:* Painting, ceramics (traditional and non-traditional), installation, video and interactive sculpture.

Full Sail University, Game Design Master of Science Program - Campus, Winter Park, FL 32792-7437. Offers MS.

George Mason University, College of Visual and Performing Arts, Art and Visual Technology Program, Fairfax, VA 22030. Offers drawing (MFA); graphic design (MFA); new media art (MFA); painting (MFA); photography (MFA); printmaking (MFA); sculpture (MFA). *Accreditation:* NASAD. *Faculty:* 21 full-time (11 women), 36 part-time/adjunct (22 women). *Students:* 5 full-time (4 women), 12 part-time (2 women); includes 3 minority (1 Black or African American, non-Hispanic/Latino; 2 Two or more races, non-Hispanic/Latino). Average age 40. 25 applicants, 20% accepted, 3 enrolled. In 2014, 4 master's awarded. *Degree requirements:* For master's, comprehensive experience, studio project or thesis. *Entrance requirements:* For master's, official transcripts; 3 letters of recommendation; letter of intent; resume; professional goals statement. Additional exam requirements/recommendations for international students: Required—TOEFL (minimum score 570 paper-based; 80 iBT), IELTS (minimum score 6.5), PTE. *Application deadline:* For fall admission, 1/15 for domestic and international students. Application fee: $65 ($80 for international students). Electronic applications accepted. *Expenses:* Tuition, state resident: full-time $9794; part-time $408 per credit hour. Tuition, nonresident: full-time $26,978; part-time $1124 per credit hour. *Required fees:* $2820; $118 per credit hour. Tuition and fees vary according to course load and program. *Financial support:* In 2014–15, 2 students received support, including 2 teaching assistantships with full and partial tuition reimbursements available (averaging $6,696 per year); career-related internships or fieldwork, Federal Work-Study, scholarships/grants, unspecified assistantships, and health care benefits (for full-time research or teaching assistantship recipients) also available. Support available to part-time students. Financial award application deadline: 3/1; financial award applicants required to submit FAFSA. *Faculty research:* Digital arts, painting, photography, print-making, sculpture; combined art forms in in-disciplinary projects including installation, performance, publishing, time or writing-based; combined creative and critical approaches. *Unit head:* Peter Winant, Director, 703-993-8385, Fax: 703-993-8798, E-mail: pwinant@gmu.edu. *Application contact:* Asma Ormazad, Graduate Studies Administrative Assistant, 703-993-9773, Fax: 703-993-8255, E-mail: aomarzad@gmu.edu.
Website: http://soa.gmu.edu

George Mason University, College of Visual and Performing Arts, Program in Graphic Design, Fairfax, VA 22030. Offers MA. *Faculty:* 22 full-time (12 women), 11 part-time/adjunct (8 women). *Students:* 2 full-time (both women), 9 part-time (4 women); includes 3 minority (1 Black or African American, non-Hispanic/Latino; 1 Asian, non-Hispanic/Latino; 1 Hispanic/Latino), 1 international. Average age 35. 9 applicants. *Degree requirements:* For master's, final project. *Entrance requirements:* For master's, 2 official transcripts; goals statement; 3 letters of recommendation; writing sample; portfolio CD/DVD with 20 examples of design work. Additional exam requirements/recommendations for international students: Required—TOEFL (minimum score 570 paper-based; 80 iBT), IELTS (minimum score 6.5), PTE. *Application deadline:* For fall admission, 4/1 for domestic students; for spring admission, 10/1 for domestic students. Application fee: $65 ($80 for international students). Electronic applications accepted. *Expenses:* Tuition, state resident: full-time $9794; part-time $408 per credit hour. Tuition, nonresident: full-time $26,978; part-time $1124 per credit hour. *Required fees:* $2820; $118 per credit hour. Tuition and fees vary according to course load and program. *Financial support:* In 2014–15, 1 student received support, including 1 teaching assistantship (averaging $7,664 per year); career-related internships or fieldwork, Federal Work-Study, scholarships/grants, and unspecified assistantships also available. Support available to part-time students. Financial award application deadline: 3/1; financial award applicants required to submit FAFSA. *Unit head:* Jandos Rothstein, Associate Professor/Division Coordinator, 703-993-9437, Fax: 703-993-8798, E-mail: jrothste@gmu.edu. *Application contact:* Don Starr, Concentration Coordinator, 703-993-8642, Fax: 703-993-8798, E-mail: dstarr@gmu.edu.
Website: http://soa.gmu.edu/areasofconcentration/graphicdesign/

Georgia Southern University, Jack N. Averitt College of Graduate Studies, College of Liberal Arts and Social Sciences, Program in Art, Statesboro, GA 30460. Offers fine arts (MFA), including 2D graphic design, 2D studio art, 3D studio art. *Accreditation:* NASAD. Part-time programs available. *Students:* 10 full-time (6 women), 5 part-time (3 women); includes 3 minority (all Hispanic/Latino), 2 international. Average age 37. 13 applicants, 77% accepted, 5 enrolled. In 2014, 5 master's awarded. *Degree requirements:* For master's, thesis, exhibition. *Entrance requirements:* For master's, minimum GPA of 3.0; 18 semester hours of course work in studio art, 9 in art history; portfolio; letters of reference. Additional exam requirements/recommendations for international students: Required—TOEFL (minimum score 550 paper-based), IELTS (minimum score 6). *Application deadline:* For fall admission, 3/1 priority date for domestic and international students; for spring admission, 10/1 priority date for domestic students, 10/1 for international students. Applications are processed on a rolling basis. Application fee: $50. Electronic applications accepted. *Expenses:* Tuition, state resident: full-time $7236; part-time $277 per semester hour. Tuition, nonresident: full-time $27,118; part-time $1105 per semester hour. *Required fees:* $2092. *Financial*

support: In 2014–15, 8 students received support, including research assistantships with partial tuition reimbursements available (averaging $7,200 per year), teaching assistantships with partial tuition reimbursements available (averaging $7,200 per year); career-related internships or fieldwork, Federal Work-Study, scholarships/grants, tuition waivers (partial), and unspecified assistantships also available. Support available to part-time students. Financial award application deadline: 4/15; financial award applicants required to submit FAFSA. *Faculty research:* International design trends; graphic design social awareness campaigns; functional design; public sculpture; fine art painting, drawing, printmaking, paper and book arts; folk art; Georgia artists archive, technology, design, contemporary, traditional studio. *Unit head:* Dr. Marc Moulton, Graduate Director, 912-478-7665, Fax: 912-478-5104, E-mail: marcmoulton@georgiasouthern.edu.
Website: http://class.georgiasouthern.edu/art

Georgia State University, College of Arts and Sciences, Ernest G. Welch School of Art and Design, Program in Studio Art, Atlanta, GA 30302-3083. Offers ceramics (MFA); drawing and painting (MFA); graphic design (MFA); interior design (MFA); photography (MFA); printmaking (MFA); sculpture (MFA); textiles (MFA). *Accreditation:* NASAD. *Degree requirements:* For master's, thesis. *Application deadline:* For fall admission, 1/6 for domestic and international students; for spring admission, 1/15 priority date for domestic and international students. Application fee: $50. Electronic applications accepted. *Expenses:* Tuition, state resident: full-time $6516; part-time $362 per credit hour. Tuition, nonresident: full-time $22,014; part-time $1223 per credit hour. *Required fees:* $2128 per semester. Tuition and fees vary according to course load and program. *Financial support:* In 2014–15, fellowships with full tuition reimbursements (averaging $11,000 per year), teaching assistantships with full tuition reimbursements (averaging $7,000 per year) were awarded; research assistantships, scholarships/grants, and unspecified assistantships also available. Financial award application deadline: 4/15. *Faculty research:* Advertising and typography, new media, traditional media, three-dimensional art, architectural and environmental design. *Unit head:* Michael White, Director, Welch School of Art and Design, 404-413-5221, Fax: 404-413-5261, E-mail: mwhite@gsu.edu. *Application contact:* Hubert Stanley Anderson, Director of Graduate Studies, 404-413-5229, Fax: 404-413-5261, E-mail: artgrad@gsu.edu.
Website: http://artdesign.gsu.edu/graduate/admissions/masters-of-fine-arts-in-studio/

Illinois State University, Graduate School, College of Fine Arts, School of Art, Normal, IL 61790-2200. Offers art history (MA, MS); ceramics (MFA, MS); drawing (MFA, MS); fibers (MFA, MS); glass (MFA, MS); graphic design (MFA, MS); metals (MFA, MS); painting (MFA, MS); photography (MFA, MS); printmaking (MFA, MS); sculpture (MFA, MS). *Accreditation:* NASAD (one or more programs are accredited). *Degree requirements:* For master's, thesis or alternative, internship. *Entrance requirements:* For master's, portfolio, sample of scholarly writing.

Indiana State University, College of Graduate and Professional Studies, College of Arts and Sciences, Department of Art, Terre Haute, IN 47809. Offers ceramics (MA, MFA); drawing (MA, MFA); graphic design (MA, MFA); painting (MA, MFA); photography (MA, MFA); printmaking (MA, MFA); sculpture (MA, MFA). *Accreditation:* NASAD (one or more programs are accredited). Part-time programs available. *Degree requirements:* For master's, thesis or alternative, departmental qualifying exam. *Entrance requirements:* For master's, portfolio. Additional exam requirements/recommendations for international students: Required—TOEFL (minimum score 550 paper-based).

Inter American University of Puerto Rico, San Germán Campus, Graduate Studies Center, Program in Fine Arts, San Germán, PR 00683-5008. Offers drawing (MFA); graphic design (MFA); painting (MFA); photography (MFA); printmaking (MFA); sculpture (MFA). Part-time and evening/weekend programs available. *Degree requirements:* For master's, comprehensive exam, thesis. *Entrance requirements:* For master's, GRE General Test or EXADEP, minimum GPA of 3.0.

Iowa State University of Science and Technology, Program in Graphic Design, Ames, IA 50011. Offers MFA. *Accreditation:* NASAD. *Entrance requirements:* Additional exam requirements/recommendations for international students: Required—TOEFL (minimum score 550 paper-based; 79 iBT), IELTS (minimum score 6). Electronic applications accepted.

Kent State University, College of Communication and Information, School of Visual Communication Design, Kent, OH 44242-0001. Offers MA, MFA. *Accreditation:* NASAD. Part-time programs available. *Faculty:* 13 full-time (6 women). *Students:* 17 full-time (10 women), 11 part-time (6 women); includes 2 minority (1 Black or African American, non-Hispanic/Latino; 1 Hispanic/Latino), 2 international. Average age 32. 50 applicants, 60% accepted, 26 enrolled. In 2014, 5 master's awarded. *Degree requirements:* For master's, thesis (for some programs), thesis or project (for MA). *Entrance requirements:* For master's, minimum GPA of 3.0, transcripts, autobiographical statement, goal statement, portfolio, 3 letters of recommendation. Additional exam requirements/recommendations for international students: Required—TOEFL (minimum score: paper-based 525, iBT 71), Michigan English Language Assessment Battery (minimum score of 75), IELTS (minimum score of 6.0), PTE Academic (minimum score of 48), or completion of ELS level 112 Intensive Program. *Application deadline:* For fall admission, 3/1 for domestic and international students; for spring admission, 10/1 for domestic and international students. Application fee: $45 ($70 for international students). Electronic applications accepted. *Expenses:* Tuition, state resident: full-time $8730; part-time $485 per credit hour. Tuition, nonresident: full-time $14,886; part-time $827 per credit hour. Tuition and fees vary according to campus/location and program. *Financial support:* Research assistantships with full and partial tuition reimbursements, teaching assistantships with full and partial tuition reimbursements, career-related internships or fieldwork, Federal Work-Study, scholarships/grants, and unspecified assistantships available. Financial award application deadline: 2/1. *Unit head:* Sanda Katila, Professor and Acting Director, 330-672-7856, E-mail: skatila@kent.edu. *Application contact:* Ken Visocky O'Grady, Graduate Coordinator and Associate Professor, 330-672-7856, E-mail: kogrady@kent.edu.
Website: http://www.kent.edu/vcd/

Louisiana State University and Agricultural & Mechanical College, Graduate School, College of Art and Design, School of Art, Program in Studio Art, Baton Rouge, LA 70803. Offers ceramics (MFA); graphic design (MFA); painting and drawing (MFA); photography (MFA); printmaking (MFA); sculpture (MFA). *Accreditation:* NASAD. *Students:* 37 full-time (29 women), 1 (woman) part-time; includes 2 minority (both Hispanic/Latino), 10 international. Average age 29. 72 applicants, 31% accepted, 17 enrolled. In 2014, 20 master's awarded. *Degree requirements:* For master's, thesis. *Entrance requirements:* For master's, GRE General Test, minimum GPA of 3.0. Additional exam requirements/recommendations for international students: Required—TOEFL (minimum score 550 paper-based; 79 IBT), IELTS (minimum score 6.5), or PTE (minimum score 59). *Application deadline:* For fall admission, 1/1 priority date for domestic students, 5/15 for international students; for spring admission, 10/15 for domestic and international students; for summer admission, 5/15 for domestic and international students. Applications are processed on a rolling basis. Application fee: $50 ($70 for international students). Electronic applications accepted. *Financial support:* Research assistantships with partial tuition reimbursements, teaching assistantships, career-related internships or fieldwork, Federal Work-Study, institutionally sponsored loans, scholarships/grants, and unspecified assistantships available. Support available to part-time students. Financial award application deadline: 3/15. *Faculty research:* Ceramics, painting and drawing, photography, printmaking, and sculpture. *Unit head:* Kelli Scott Kelly, Graduate Coordinator, 225-578-8448, Fax: 225-578-5424, E-mail: kskelly@lsu.edu.
Website: http://design.lsu.edu/art/?page_id-582

Louisiana Tech University, Graduate School, College of Liberal Arts, MFA Program, Ruston, LA 71272. Offers communication design (MFA); photography (MFA); studio (MFA). *Accreditation:* NASAD. Part-time programs available. *Degree requirements:* For master's, exhibit. *Entrance requirements:* For master's, GRE General Test, portfolio. *Application deadline:* For fall admission, 7/29 for domestic students; for spring admission, 2/3 for domestic students. Applications are processed on a rolling basis. Application fee: $40. *Financial support:* Fellowships, career-related internships or fieldwork, Federal Work-Study, institutionally sponsored loans, and unspecified assistantships available. Financial award application deadline: 2/1. *Unit head:* Joey Slaughter, Graduate Coordinator, 318-257-3909, Fax: 318-257-4890, E-mail: joey@latech.edu. *Application contact:* Marilyn J. Robinson, Assistant to the Dean of the Graduate School, 318-257-2924, Fax: 318-257-4487.

Maryland Institute College of Art, Graduate Studies, Graphic Design Post-Baccalaureate Certificate Program, Baltimore, MD 21201. Offers Postbaccalaureate Certificate. *Faculty:* 1 (woman) full-time. *Students:* 17 full-time (11 women); includes 4 minority (2 Black or African American, non-Hispanic/Latino; 1 Asian, non-Hispanic/Latino; 1 Two or more races, non-Hispanic/Latino), 4 international. Average age 26. *Degree requirements:* For Postbaccalaureate Certificate, thesis, portfolio and documentation. *Entrance requirements:* For degree, portfolio, bachelor's degree in any field. Additional exam requirements/recommendations for international students: Required—TOEFL (minimum score 550 paper-based; 80 iBT), IELTS (minimum score 6.5). *Application deadline:* For fall admission, 1/15 priority date for domestic and international students; for spring admission, 4/1 for domestic and international students. Application fee: $75. Electronic applications accepted. *Financial support:* In 2014–15, 17 students received support, including 17 fellowships (averaging $5,500 per year); scholarships/grants also available. Financial award application deadline: 1/15; financial award applicants required to submit FAFSA. *Unit head:* Sandra Maxa, Director, 410-669-2382, Fax: 410-225-2408, E-mail: graduate@mica.edu. *Application contact:* Chris D. Harring, Director of Graduate Admission, 410-225-2256, Fax: 410-225-5275, E-mail: graduate@mica.edu.
Website: http://www.mica.edu/Programs_of_Study/Post-Baccalaureate_Certificate_in_Graphic_Design.html

Maryland Institute College of Art, Graduate Studies, MFA Program in Graphic Design, Baltimore, MD 21201. Offers MFA. *Faculty:* 2 full-time (both women), 7 part-time/adjunct (2 women). *Students:* 28 full-time (17 women); includes 4 minority (1 Asian, non-Hispanic/Latino; 1 Hispanic/Latino; 2 Two or more races, non-Hispanic/Latino), 8 international. Average age 27. 250 applicants, 10% accepted, 15 enrolled. In 2014, 15 master's awarded. *Degree requirements:* For master's, thesis, exhibit and thesis documentation. *Entrance requirements:* For master's, portfolio, bachelor's degree in any field. Additional exam requirements/recommendations for international students: Required—TOEFL (minimum score 550 paper-based; 80 iBT), IELTS (minimum score 6.5). *Application deadline:* For fall admission, 1/15 for domestic and international students. Application fee: $75. Electronic applications accepted. *Expenses:* Expenses: Contact institution. *Financial support:* In 2014–15, 28 students received support, including 28 fellowships (averaging $13,000 per year), 28 teaching assistantships (averaging $3,200 per year); career-related internships or fieldwork and scholarships/grants also available. Financial award application deadline: 1/15. *Unit head:* Ellen Lupton, Director, 410-225-5274, Fax: 410-225-5275. *Application contact:* Chris D. Harring, Director, Graduate Admission, 410-225-2256, Fax: 410-225-5275, E-mail: graduate@mica.edu.

Marywood University, Academic Affairs, Insalaco College of Creative and Performing Arts, Art Department, Program in Visual Arts, Scranton, PA 18509-1598. Offers clay (MFA); graphic design (MFA); illustration (MFA); painting (MFA); photography (MFA); printmaking (MFA); sculpture (MFA). *Accreditation:* NASAD. Part-time programs available. *Students:* 25 full-time (18 women), 3 part-time (all women); includes 1 minority (Hispanic/Latino), 2 international. Average age 36. In 2014, 5 master's awarded. *Application deadline:* For fall admission, 4/1 for domestic students, 3/31 for international students; for spring admission, 11/1 for domestic students, 8/31 for international students. Applications are processed on a rolling basis. Application fee: $35. Electronic applications accepted. *Expenses:* Expenses: Contact institution. *Financial support:* Application deadline: 6/30; applicants required to submit FAFSA. *Unit head:* Matthew Povse, Chair, 570-348-6211 Ext. 2476, E-mail: povse@marywood.edu. *Application contact:* Tammy Manka, Assistant Director of Graduate Admissions, 570-348-6211 Ext. 2322, E-mail: tmanka@marywood.edu.
Website: http://www.marywood.edu/art/graduate-programs/master-visual-arts.html

Minneapolis College of Art and Design, Certificate Programs, Minneapolis, MN 55404-4347. Offers design (Certificate); fine arts (Certificate); graphic design (Certificate); media (Certificate); sustainable design (Certificate). Part-time programs available. Postbaccalaureate distance learning degree programs offered. *Degree requirements:* For Certificate, final project. *Entrance requirements:* For degree, resume, portfolio, letter of recommendation. Additional exam requirements/recommendations for international students: Required—TOEFL (minimum score 550 paper-based; 79 iBT). Electronic applications accepted. *Faculty research:* Visual arts.

Minneapolis College of Art and Design, Program in Visual Studies, Minneapolis, MN 55404-4347. Offers animation (MFA); comic art (MFA); drawing (MFA); filmmaking (MFA); fine arts (MFA); furniture design (MFA); graphic design (MFA); illustration (MFA); interactive media (MFA); painting (MFA); photography (MFA); printmaking (MFA); sculpture (MFA). *Accreditation:* NASAD. Part-time programs available. *Degree requirements:* For master's, thesis, thesis exhibit. *Entrance requirements:* For master's, portfolio of visual artwork, resume, 3 letters of recommendation. Additional exam requirements/recommendations for international students: Required—TOEFL (minimum score 550 paper-based; 79 iBT). Electronic applications accepted. *Faculty research:* Visual arts: animation, comic art, drawing, filmmaking, furniture design, graphic design, illustration, interactive media, painting, photography, printmaking, sculpture.

Morehead State University, Graduate Programs, Caudill College of Arts, Humanities and Social Sciences, Department of Art and Design, Morehead, KY 40351. Offers art education (MA); graphic design (MA); studio art (MA). Part-time and evening/weekend programs available. *Degree requirements:* For master's, comprehensive exam, thesis (for some programs), oral exam during exhibition. *Entrance requirements:* For master's, GRE General Test, minimum undergraduate GPA of 3.0 in major, 2.5 overall; portfolio; bachelor's degree in art. Additional exam requirements/recommendations for international students: Required—TOEFL (minimum score 500 paper-based). Electronic applications accepted. *Faculty research:* Computer art, painting, drawing, ceramics, photography.

New York Institute of Technology, College of Arts and Sciences, Department of Fine Arts, Old Westbury, NY 11568-8000. Offers computer graphics (MFA), including

animation, fine arts and technology, graphic design. Part-time and evening/weekend programs available. *Degree requirements:* For master's, thesis. *Entrance requirements:* For master's, minimum QPA of 2.85, portfolio. Additional exam requirements/recommendations for international students: Required—TOEFL (minimum score 550 paper-based; 79 iBT), IELTS (minimum score 6). Electronic applications accepted. *Faculty research:* Graphic design, animation, art and technology, digital art and science, sculpture.

New York University, School of Continuing and Professional Studies, Division of Programs in Business, Program in Graphic Communications Management and Technology, New York, NY 10012-1019. Offers MA. Part-time and evening/weekend programs available. *Faculty:* 16 part-time/adjunct (3 women). *Students:* 16 full-time (13 women), 45 part-time (32 women); includes 15 minority (5 Black or African American, non-Hispanic/Latino; 1 American Indian or Alaska Native, non-Hispanic/Latino; 4 Asian, non-Hispanic/Latino; 3 Hispanic/Latino; 1 Native Hawaiian or other Pacific Islander, non-Hispanic/Latino; 1 Two or more races, non-Hispanic/Latino), 17 international. Average age 29. 29 applicants, 66% accepted, 11 enrolled. In 2014, 49 master's awarded. *Degree requirements:* For master's, thesis, capstone, research course. *Entrance requirements:* For master's, GRE or GMAT (only upon request), relevant professional work, internship or volunteer experience. Additional exam requirements/recommendations for international students: Required—TOEFL (minimum score 600 paper-based; 100 iBT), IELTS (minimum score 7). *Application deadline:* For fall admission, 2/1 priority date for domestic and international students; for spring admission, 10/15 priority date for domestic students, 8/15 priority date for international students. Applications are processed on a rolling basis. Application fee: $150. Electronic applications accepted. *Financial support:* In 2014–15, 37 students received support, including 24 fellowships (averaging $2,032 per year); Federal Work-Study and scholarships/grants also available. Support available to part-time students. Financial award application deadline: 4/1; financial award applicants required to submit FAFSA. *Unit head:* Angela Ambrosini, Director, 212-992-3228, E-mail: pp64@nyu.edu. *Application contact:* Admissions Office, 212-998-7100, E-mail: scps.gradadmissions@nyu.edu. Website: http://www.sps.nyu.edu/academics/departments/graphic-comm-management-tech.html

North Carolina Agricultural and Technical State University, School of Graduate Studies, School of Technology, Department of Graphic Communication Systems and Technological Studies, Greensboro, NC 27411. Offers graphic communication systems (MSTM); technology education (MAT). *Accreditation:* NCATE (one or more programs are accredited). Part-time and evening/weekend programs available. *Degree requirements:* For master's, comprehensive exam, thesis or alternative, qualifying exam. *Entrance requirements:* For master's, GRE General Test, minimum GPA of 3.0.

North Carolina State University, Graduate School, College of Design, Department of Graphic Design, Raleigh, NC 27695. Offers MGD. *Accreditation:* NASAD. *Degree requirements:* For master's, thesis optional, oral exam. *Entrance requirements:* For master's, GRE General Test, portfolio. Electronic applications accepted. *Faculty research:* Typography, graphic design, interaction design, design and cognition, design and culture.

Ohio University, Graduate College, College of Fine Arts, School of Art, Athens, OH 45701-2979. Offers art history (MA); ceramics (MFA); graphic design (MFA); painting (MFA); photography (MFA); printmaking (MFA); sculpture (MFA). Part-time programs available. *Degree requirements:* For master's, thesis. *Entrance requirements:* For master's, portfolio. Additional exam requirements/recommendations for international students: Required—TOEFL (minimum score 550 paper-based; 80 iBT) or IELTS (minimum score 6.5). Electronic applications accepted. *Faculty research:* Vapor-fired ceramics, video installation, art theory, digital photography, mixed and interdisciplinary media work.

Otis College of Art and Design, Program in Graphic Design, Los Angeles, CA 90045-9785. Offers MFA. *Entrance requirements:* Additional exam requirements/recommendations for international students: Required—TOEFL (minimum score 600 paper-based). Electronic applications accepted.

Pittsburg State University, Graduate School, College of Technology, Department of Graphics and Imaging Technologies, Pittsburg, KS 66762. Offers commercial graphics (MST); printing management (MST). *Degree requirements:* For master's, thesis or alternative.

Pratt Institute, School of Art and Design, Program in Digital Arts, Brooklyn, NY 11205-3899. Offers MFA, MS/MFA. *Accreditation:* NASAD. *Faculty:* 5 full-time (1 woman), 27 part-time/adjunct (8 women). *Students:* 65 full-time (40 women), 6 part-time (4 women); includes 5 minority (3 Asian, non-Hispanic/Latino; 2 Hispanic/Latino), 59 international. Average age 25. 218 applicants, 20% accepted, 20 enrolled. In 2014, 27 master's awarded. *Degree requirements:* For master's, thesis, exhibit. *Entrance requirements:* For master's, portfolio or video tape, letters of recommendation. Additional exam requirements/recommendations for international students: Required—TOEFL (minimum score 550 paper-based; 79 iBT). *Application deadline:* For fall admission, 1/5 for domestic and international students; for spring admission, 10/1 for domestic and international students. Applications are processed on a rolling basis. Application fee: $50 ($90 for international students). Electronic applications accepted. *Financial support:* Career-related internships or fieldwork, Federal Work-Study, institutionally sponsored loans, scholarships/grants, health care benefits, and unspecified assistantships available. Support available to part-time students. Financial award application deadline: 2/1; financial award applicants required to submit FAFSA. *Unit head:* Peter Patchen, Chair, 718-636-3693, E-mail: ppatchen@pratt.edu. *Application contact:* Young Hah, Director of Graduate Admissions, 718-636-3683, Fax: 718-399-4242, E-mail: yhah@pratt.edu. Website: https://www.pratt.edu/academics/school-of-art/graduate-school-of-art/digital-arts-grad/

See Display on page 153 and Close-Up on page 203.

Pratt Institute, School of Design, Program in Communications Design, New York, NY 10011. Offers MFA. *Accreditation:* NASAD. Part-time programs available. *Faculty:* 5 full-time (2 women), 35 part-time/adjunct (14 women). *Students:* 140 full-time (95 women), 15 part-time (12 women); includes 28 minority (5 Black or African American, non-Hispanic/Latino; 11 Asian, non-Hispanic/Latino; 12 Hispanic/Latino), 77 international. Average age 27. 351 applicants, 49% accepted, 50 enrolled. In 2014, 74 master's awarded. *Degree requirements:* For master's, thesis. *Entrance requirements:* For master's, portfolio, letters of recommendation. Additional exam requirements/recommendations for international students: Required—TOEFL (minimum score 575 paper-based; 90 iBT). *Application deadline:* For fall admission, 1/5 for domestic and international students; for spring admission, 10/1 for domestic and international students. Application fee: $50 ($90 for international students). Electronic applications accepted. *Financial support:* Career-related internships or fieldwork, Federal Work-Study, institutionally sponsored loans, scholarships/grants, and unspecified assistantships available. Support available to part-time students. Financial award application deadline: 2/1; financial award applicants required to submit FAFSA. *Faculty*

research: Graphics, film, photography, media presentations, computer graphics for community service organizations. *Unit head:* Santiago Piedrafita Iglesias, Chairperson, 212-647-7640, Fax: 212-367-2481, E-mail: spiedraf@pratt.edu. *Application contact:* Young Hah, Director of Graduate Admissions, 718-636-3683, Fax: 718-399-4242, E-mail: yhah@pratt.edu. Website: https://www.pratt.edu/academics/school-of-design/graduate-school-of-design/grad-communications-design/

See Display on page 65 and Close-Up on page 103.

Rhode Island School of Design, Graduate Studies, Division of Architecture and Design, Department of Graphic Design, Providence, RI 02903-2784. Offers MFA. *Accreditation:* NASAD. *Faculty:* 11 full-time (6 women), 11 part-time/adjunct (3 women). *Students:* 37 full-time (24 women); includes 8 minority (1 Black or African American, non-Hispanic/Latino; 3 Asian, non-Hispanic/Latino; 2 Hispanic/Latino; 2 Two or more races, non-Hispanic/Latino), 12 international. Average age 27. 265 applicants, 12% accepted, 17 enrolled. In 2014, 16 master's awarded. *Degree requirements:* For master's, thesis, exhibit. *Entrance requirements:* For master's, portfolio, statement of purpose, 3 letters of recommendation. Additional exam requirements/recommendations for international students: Required—TOEFL (minimum score 580 paper-based; 93 iBT). *Application deadline:* For fall admission, 2/1 for domestic and international students. Application fee: $60. *Expenses:* Expenses: $44,594. *Financial support:* Fellowships, teaching assistantships, career-related internships or fieldwork, Federal Work-Study, institutionally sponsored loans, scholarships/grants, and unspecified assistantships available. Financial award application deadline: 2/15; financial award applicants required to submit FAFSA. *Unit head:* John Caserta, Department Head, 401-454-6170, Fax: 401-454-6117, E-mail: jcaserta@risd.edu. *Application contact:* Molly Pettengil, Graduate Admissions Officer, 401-454-6312, Fax: 401-454-6309, E-mail: mpettengil@risd.edu. Website: http://www.risd.edu/academics/graphic-design/

Rochester Institute of Technology, Graduate Enrollment Services, College of Imaging Arts and Sciences, School of Design, MFA Program in Visual Communication Design, Rochester, NY 14623-5603. Offers MFA. *Accreditation:* NASAD. Part-time programs available. *Students:* 44 full-time (26 women), 2 part-time; includes 4 minority (2 Hispanic/Latino; 2 Two or more races, non-Hispanic/Latino), 31 international. Average age 26. 221 applicants, 27% accepted, 23 enrolled. *Degree requirements:* For master's, thesis, thesis exhibition. *Entrance requirements:* For master's, GRE and TOEFL, IELTS, or PTE for non-native English speakers, portfolio, recommended minimum GPA of 3.0. Additional exam requirements/recommendations for international students: Required—PTE (minimum score 58), TOEFL (minimum score 550 paper-based; 79 iBT) or IELTS (minimum score 6.5). *Application deadline:* For fall admission, 2/15 priority date for domestic and international students. Applications are processed on a rolling basis. Application fee: $60. Electronic applications accepted. *Expenses:* Expenses: $1,673 per credit hour. *Financial support:* In 2014–15, 43 students received support. Research assistantships with partial tuition reimbursements available, teaching assistantships with partial tuition reimbursements available, career-related internships or fieldwork, Federal Work-Study, institutionally sponsored loans, scholarships/grants, and unspecified assistantships available. Support available to part-time students. Financial award application deadline: 2/15; financial award applicants required to submit FAFSA. *Unit head:* Chris Jackson, Graduate Program Director, 585-475-5823, Fax: 585-475-7533, E-mail: cbjpgd@rit.edu. *Application contact:* Diane Ellison, Associate Vice President, Graduate Enrollment Services, 585-475-2229, Fax: 585-475-7164, E-mail: gradinfo@rit.edu. Website: http://cias.rit.edu/schools/design/graduate-visual-communication-design

Rochester Institute of Technology, Graduate Enrollment Services, College of Imaging Arts and Sciences, School of Media Sciences, Rochester, NY 14623-5603. Offers print media (MS). Part-time programs available. *Students:* 11 full-time (5 women), 1 part-time, 11 international. Average age 24. 16 applicants, 56% accepted, 4 enrolled. In 2014, 6 master's awarded. *Degree requirements:* For master's, thesis. *Entrance requirements:* For master's, GRE and TOEFL, IELTS, or PTE for non-native English speakers, recommended minimum GPA of 3.0. Additional exam requirements/recommendations for international students: Required—PTE (minimum score 58), TOEFL (minimum score 550 paper-based; 79 iBT) or IELTS (minimum score 6.5). *Application deadline:* For fall admission, 2/15 priority date for domestic and international students; for spring admission, 12/15 priority date for domestic and international students. Applications are processed on a rolling basis. Application fee: $60. Electronic applications accepted. *Expenses:* Expenses: $1,673 per credit hour. *Financial support:* In 2014–15, 8 students received support. Research assistantships with partial tuition reimbursements available, teaching assistantships with partial tuition reimbursements available, career-related internships or fieldwork, Federal Work-Study, institutionally sponsored loans, scholarships/grants, and unspecified assistantships available. Support available to part-time students. Financial award application deadline: 8/30; financial award applicants required to submit FAFSA. *Faculty research:* Content management, publishing workflows, typography and layout, business trends, color management, electronic publishing, multi-media, digital printing/publishing and applications of printing. *Unit head:* Dr. Gregory D'Amico, Graduate Program Director, 585-475-5992, E-mail: mxcppr@rit.edu. *Application contact:* Diane Ellison, Associate Vice President, Graduate Enrollment Services, 585-475-2229, Fax: 585-475-7164, E-mail: gradinfo@rit.edu. Website: http://cias.rit.edu/schools/media-sciences

San Diego State University, Graduate and Research Affairs, College of Professional Studies and Fine Arts, School of Art, Design and Art History, San Diego, CA 92182. Offers art history (MA); studio arts (MA, MFA), including applied design, environmental design, graphic design, interior design, painting and printmaking, sculpture. *Accreditation:* NASAD (one or more programs are accredited). *Degree requirements:* For master's, variable foreign language requirement, thesis. *Entrance requirements:* For master's, GRE General Test, bachelor's degree in related field, slide portfolio, typed slide information sheet, 2 letters of recommendation. Additional exam requirements/recommendations for international students: Required—TOEFL. Electronic applications accepted.

Savannah College of Art and Design, Graduate School, Program in Advertising, Savannah, GA 31402-3146. Offers MA, MFA. Part-time programs available. *Faculty:* 11 full-time (3 women), 4 part-time/adjunct (1 woman). *Students:* 37 full-time (22 women), 12 part-time (9 women); includes 13 minority (8 Black or African American, non-Hispanic/Latino; 4 Hispanic/Latino; 1 Native Hawaiian or other Pacific Islander, non-Hispanic/Latino), 21 international. Average age 26. 51 applicants, 24% accepted, 9 enrolled. In 2014, 13 master's awarded. *Degree requirements:* For master's, final project (for MA); thesis (for MFA). *Entrance requirements:* For master's, portfolio. Additional exam requirements/recommendations for international students: Required—TOEFL (minimum score 550 paper-based, 85 iBT), IELTS (minimum score 6.5), or ACTFL. *Application deadline:* For fall admission, 4/1 for domestic and international students. Applications are processed on a rolling basis. Application fee: $40. Electronic applications accepted. *Expenses:* Tuition: Full-time $34,605; part-time $3845 per course. One-time fee: $500. Tuition and fees vary according to course load. *Financial support:* Fellowships, career-related internships or fieldwork, Federal Work-Study, and scholarships/grants available. Financial award application deadline: 4/1; financial award applicants required to submit FAFSA. *Unit head:* Luke Longstreet Sullivan, Chair.

Graphic Design

Application contact: Jenny Jaquillard, Executive Director of Admissions, Recruitment and Events, 912-525-5100, Fax: 912-525-5985, E-mail: admission@scad.edu. Website: http://www.scad.edu/academics/programs/advertising

Savannah College of Art and Design, Graduate School, Program in Graphic Design, Savannah, GA 31402-3146. Offers MA, MFA. Part-time programs available. Postbaccalaureate distance learning degree programs offered (no on-campus study). *Faculty:* 25 full-time (11 women), 8 part-time/adjunct (4 women). *Students:* 110 full-time (77 women), 52 part-time (34 women); includes 21 minority (12 Black or African American, non-Hispanic/Latino; 3 Asian, non-Hispanic/Latino; 6 Hispanic/Latino), 69 international. Average age 29. 265 applicants, 26% accepted, 35 enrolled. In 2014, 64 master's awarded. *Degree requirements:* For master's, thesis (for some programs). *Entrance requirements:* For master's, portfolio. Additional exam requirements/recommendations for international students: Required—TOEFL (minimum score 550 paper-based, 85 iBT), IELTS (minimum score 6.5), or ACTFL. *Application deadline:* For fall admission, 4/1 for domestic and international students. Applications are processed on a rolling basis. Application fee: $40. Electronic applications accepted. *Expenses: Tuition:* Full-time $34,605; part-time $3845 per course. One-time fee: $500. Tuition and fees vary according to course load. *Financial support:* Fellowships, career-related internships or fieldwork, Federal Work-Study, and scholarships/grants available. Financial award application deadline: 4/1; financial award applicants required to submit FAFSA. *Unit head:* Jason Fox, Chair. *Application contact:* Jenny Jaquillard, Executive Director of Admissions, Recruitment and Events, 912-525-5100, Fax: 912-525-5985, E-mail: admission@scad.edu. Website: http://www.scad.edu/academics/programs/graphic-design

School of the Art Institute of Chicago, Graduate Division, Department of Visual Communication, Chicago, IL 60603-3103. Offers MFA. *Entrance requirements:* Additional exam requirements/recommendations for international students: Required—TOEFL, IELTS.

School of Visual Arts, Graduate Programs, Program in Visual Narrative, New York, NY 10010-3994. Offers MFA. Summer admission only. *Degree requirements:* For master's, thesis, 60 credits, including all required courses. *Entrance requirements:* For master's, portfolio, statement of purpose; unique and complete short story/visual narrative (minimum 2-5 pages/images, or 2-5 minutes for video or animation submissions). Additional exam requirements/recommendations for international students: Required—TOEFL (minimum score 550 paper-based; 79 iBT). Electronic applications accepted. *Faculty research:* Storytelling, animation, design, illustration, art history, painting, printmaking, writing, graphic novels.

Southern Polytechnic State University, School of Arts and Sciences, Department of English, Technical Communication, and Media Arts, Marietta, GA 30060-2896. Offers communications management (Postbaccalaureate Certificate); content development (Postbaccalaureate Certificate); information and instructional design (MSIID); information design and communication (MS); instructional design (Postbaccalaureate Certificate); technical communication (Graduate Certificate); visual communication and graphics (Postbaccalaureate Certificate). Part-time and evening/weekend programs available. Postbaccalaureate distance learning degree programs offered (no on-campus study). *Degree requirements:* For master's, thesis optional; for other advanced degree, thesis optional, 18 hours completed through thesis option (6 hours), internship option (6 hours) or advanced coursework option (6 hours). *Entrance requirements:* For master's, GRE, statement of purpose, writing sample, timed essay; for other advanced degree, writing sample, professional recommendations. Additional exam requirements/recommendations for international students: Required—TOEFL (minimum score 550 paper-based; 79 iBT), IELTS (minimum score 6.5). Electronic applications accepted. *Faculty research:* Usability, user-centered design, instructional design, information architecture, information design, content strategy.

Suffolk University, New England School of Art and Design, Boston, MA 02108-2770. Offers graphic design (MA); interior architecture (MA, MFA). *Accreditation:* NASAD. Part-time and evening/weekend programs available. *Faculty:* 13 full-time (9 women), 22 part-time/adjunct (10 women). *Students:* 60 full-time (50 women), 47 part-time (44 women); includes 10 minority (3 Black or African American, non-Hispanic/Latino; 6 Asian, non-Hispanic/Latino; 1 Hispanic/Latino), 42 international. Average age 28. 112 applicants, 60% accepted, 13 enrolled. In 2014, 31 master's awarded. *Entrance requirements:* For master's, GRE (for MFA), art portfolio, interview, 2 letters of recommendation, resume; letter of intent (for MFA). Additional exam requirements/recommendations for international students: Required—TOEFL (minimum score 550 paper-based; 80 iBT). *Application deadline:* For fall admission, 6/15 priority date for domestic students, 6/15 for international students; for spring admission, 11/1 priority date for domestic students, 11/1 for international students. Applications are processed on a rolling basis. Application fee: $50. Electronic applications accepted. *Expenses:* Expenses: Contact institution. *Financial support:* In 2014–15, 72 students received support, including 69 fellowships (averaging $6,358 per year). Financial award application deadline: 4/1; financial award applicants required to submit FAFSA. *Faculty research:* Sustainable design, lighting and technology, design education, environmental graphic design, designing for the non-profit sector. *Unit head:* Audrey Goldstein, Department Chair, 617-997-4290, E-mail: agoldstein@suffolk.edu. *Application contact:* Cory Meyers, Director of Graduate Admissions, 617-573-8302, Fax: 617-305-1733, E-mail: grad.admission@suffolk.edu. Website: http://www.suffolk.edu/nesad/

Temple University, Center for the Arts, Tyler School of Art, Department of Graphic Arts and Design, Philadelphia, PA 19122-6096. Offers graphic and interactive design (MFA); photography (MFA); printmaking (MFA). *Faculty:* 13 full-time (5 women), 22 part-time/adjunct (9 women). *Students:* 19 full-time (13 women); includes 2 minority (both Hispanic/Latino). 155 applicants, 12% accepted, 8 enrolled. In 2014, 8 master's awarded. *Degree requirements:* For master's, essay, exhibit. *Entrance requirements:* For master's, minimum GPA of 3.0, slide portfolio, 40 credits in studio art, 12 credits in art history, letters of recommendation, resume/curriculum vitae. Additional exam requirements/recommendations for international students: Required—TOEFL (minimum score 550 paper-based; 79 iBT), IELTS (minimum score 6.5). *Application deadline:* For fall admission, 1/15 for domestic students, 12/15 for international students. Application fee: $60. Electronic applications accepted. *Expenses:* Expenses: Contact institution. *Financial support:* Fellowships with full tuition reimbursements, research assistantships with full tuition reimbursements, teaching assistantships with full tuition reimbursements, and Federal Work-Study available. Support available to part-time students. Financial award application deadline: 1/15; financial award applicants required to submit FAFSA. *Unit head:* Stephanie Knopp, Chair, 215-782-2932, Fax: 215-782-2799, E-mail: stephanie.knopp@temple.edu. *Application contact:* Nicole Hall, Director of Admissions, 215-777-9090, E-mail: tylerart@temple.edu. Website: http://tyler.temple.edu/graduate

Texas State University, The Graduate College, College of Fine Arts and Communication, School of Art and Design, Program in Communication Design, San Marcos, TX 78666. Offers MFA. *Faculty:* 8 full-time (4 women), 1 part-time/adjunct (0 women). *Students:* 13 full-time (4 women), 31 part-time (20 women); includes 12 minority (1 Black or African American, non-Hispanic/Latino; 2 Asian, non-Hispanic/Latino; 8 Hispanic/Latino; 1 Two or more races, non-Hispanic/Latino), 1 international. Average age 35. 26 applicants, 54% accepted, 9 enrolled. In 2014, 11 master's awarded. *Degree requirements:* For master's, comprehensive exam, thesis (for some programs). *Entrance requirements:* For master's, GRE (preferred), baccalaureate degree from regionally-accredited institution with minimum GPA of 2.75 in last 60 hours of undergraduate course work. Additional exam requirements/recommendations for international students: Required—TOEFL (minimum score 550 paper-based; 78 iBT). *Application deadline:* For fall admission, 3/31 for domestic and international students; for spring admission, 10/31 for domestic students, 10/1 for international students. Applications are processed on a rolling basis. Application fee: $40 ($90 for international students). Electronic applications accepted. *Expenses:* Expenses: $8,834 (tuition and fees combined). *Financial support:* In 2014–15, 21 students received support, including 1 research assistantship (averaging $11,855 per year), 6 teaching assistantships (averaging $13,875 per year); Federal Work-Study, institutionally sponsored loans, scholarships/grants, and unspecified assistantships also available. Support available to part-time students. Financial award application deadline: 4/1; financial award applicants required to submit FAFSA. *Unit head:* Claudia Roschmann, Graduate Advisor, 512-245-7450, E-mail: cr29@txstate.edu. *Application contact:* Dr. Andrea Golato, Dean of Graduate School, 512-245-2581, Fax: 512-245-8365, E-mail: gradcollege@txstate.edu. Website: http://www.finearts.txstate.edu/Art/mfacomdes/

Université Laval, Faculty of Architecture, Planning and Visual Arts, School of Visual Arts, Programs in Visual Arts, Québec, QC G1K 7P4, Canada. Offers graphic design and multimedia (MA); visual arts (MA). *Degree requirements:* For master's, thesis (for some programs). *Entrance requirements:* For master's, technical exam, interview, mastery of pertinent software, knowledge of French. Electronic applications accepted.

University of Baltimore, Graduate School, Yale Gordon College of Arts and Sciences, Doctoral Program in Information and Interaction Design, Baltimore, MD 21201-5779. Offers DS. Part-time and evening/weekend programs available. *Entrance requirements:* For doctorate, minimum GPA of 3.2, previous graduate study in related discipline, portfolio, resume. Electronic applications accepted.

University of Baltimore, Graduate School, Yale Gordon College of Arts and Sciences, Program in Publications Design, Baltimore, MD 21201-5779. Offers MA. Part-time and evening/weekend programs available. *Degree requirements:* For master's, seminar project. *Entrance requirements:* For master's, minimum GPA of 3.0, portfolio, interview. Additional exam requirements/recommendations for international students: Required—TOEFL (minimum score 550 paper-based). Electronic applications accepted. *Faculty research:* Communication theory, graphic design, media technology.

University of Cincinnati, Graduate School, College of Design, Architecture, Art, and Planning, School of Design, Cincinnati, OH 45221. Offers fashion design (M Des); graphic design (M Des); industrial design (M Des); interaction design (M Des); product development (M Des). *Accreditation:* NASAD. *Students:* 34 full-time (16 women), 3 part-time (1 woman); includes 3 minority (1 Black or African American, non-Hispanic/Latino; 1 Asian, non-Hispanic/Latino; 1 Hispanic/Latino), 24 international. In 2014, 7 master's awarded. *Degree requirements:* For master's, thesis. *Entrance requirements:* For master's, undergraduate degree in design or related field, 2 years of work experience in design or related field. Additional exam requirements/recommendations for international students: Required—TOEFL. *Application deadline:* For fall admission, 2/1 for domestic students. Application fee: $30. Electronic applications accepted. *Financial support:* Fellowships, career-related internships or fieldwork, Federal Work-Study, tuition waivers (partial), and unspecified assistantships available. *Faculty research:* Design theory, interdisciplinary design topics. *Unit head:* Brigid O'Kane, Director, 513-556-0833, E-mail: brigid.okane@uc.edu. *Application contact:* Dr. J. Chewning, Information Contact, 513-556-2996, Fax: 513-556-0240, E-mail: j.chewning@uc.edu. Website: http://www.daap.uc.edu/

University of Guam, Office of Graduate Studies, College of Liberal Arts and Social Sciences, Division of Fine Arts, Mangilao, GU 96923. Offers ceramics (MA); graphics (MA); painting (MA). *Degree requirements:* For master's, thesis or alternative, exhibit, final oral exam. *Entrance requirements:* For master's, GRE General Test, portfolio. Additional exam requirements/recommendations for international students: Required—TOEFL.

University of Illinois at Chicago, Graduate College, College of Architecture, Design and the Arts, School of Design, Chicago, IL 60607-7128. Offers graphic design (M Des); industrial design (M Des). *Accreditation:* NASAD (one or more programs are accredited). *Faculty:* 20 full-time (7 women), 18 part-time/adjunct (6 women). *Students:* 23 full-time (17 women), 5 part-time (3 women); includes 8 minority (2 Black or African American, non-Hispanic/Latino; 3 Asian, non-Hispanic/Latino; 3 Hispanic/Latino), 13 international. Average age 28. 118 applicants, 19% accepted, 11 enrolled. In 2014, 11 master's awarded. *Degree requirements:* For master's, thesis, exhibit. *Entrance requirements:* For master's, MAT, portfolio. Additional exam requirements/recommendations for international students: Required—TOEFL. *Application deadline:* For fall admission, 12/15 priority date for domestic and international students. Applications are processed on a rolling basis. Application fee: $40 ($50 for international students). Electronic applications accepted. *Expenses:* Expenses: $19,134 in-state; $31,132 out-of-state. *Financial support:* Fellowships with full tuition reimbursements, research assistantships with full tuition reimbursements, teaching assistantships with full tuition reimbursements, career-related internships or fieldwork, Federal Work-Study, traineeships, tuition waivers (full), and unspecified assistantships available. Financial award application deadline: 2/1; financial award applicants required to submit FAFSA. *Unit head:* Marcia Lausen, Director, 312-996-5699, E-mail: mlausen@uic.edu. *Application contact:* Bonnie Osborne, Graduate Secretary, 312-996-3337. Website: http://design.uic.edu/

University of Illinois at Urbana–Champaign, Graduate College, College of Fine and Applied Arts, School of Art and Design, Program in Design and Media, Champaign, IL 61820. Offers art and design (MFA), including new media; graphic design (MFA); industrial design (MFA). *Accreditation:* NASAD. *Students:* 11 (8 women). Application fee: $70 ($90 for international students). *Unit head:* Ernest Scott, Chair, 217-333-1579, E-mail: ernscott@illinois.edu. *Application contact:* Ellen de Waard, Coordinator of Graduate Academic Affairs, 217-333-0642, Fax: 217-244-7688, E-mail: edewaard@illinois.edu. Website: http://www.art.illinois.edu

University of Memphis, Graduate School, College of Communication and Fine Arts, Department of Art, Memphis, TN 38152. Offers art (Graduate Certificate); art history (MA), including Egyptian art and archaeology, general art history; ceramics (MFA); graphic design (MFA); interior design (MFA); painting (MFA); printmaking/photography (MFA). *Accreditation:* NASAD (one or more programs are accredited). *Faculty:* 19 full-time (7 women), 4 part-time/adjunct (2 women). *Students:* 34 full-time (28 women), 3 part-time (2 women); includes 5 minority (2 Asian, non-Hispanic/Latino; 2 Hispanic/Latino; 1 Two or more races, non-Hispanic/Latino). Average age 30. 24 applicants, 63% accepted, 10 enrolled. In 2014, 14 master's, 14 other advanced degrees awarded. *Degree requirements:* For master's, 2 foreign languages, comprehensive exam, thesis. *Entrance requirements:* For master's, GRE General Test or MAT, portfolio (MFA). *Application deadline:* For fall admission, 8/1 for domestic students; for spring admission, 12/1 for domestic students. Applications are processed

on a rolling basis. Application fee: $35 ($60 for international students). *Financial support:* In 2014–15, 38 students received support. Research assistantships with full tuition reimbursements available, teaching assistantships with full tuition reimbursements available, Federal Work-Study, scholarships/grants, and unspecified assistantships available. Financial award application deadline: 2/15; financial award applicants required to submit FAFSA. *Faculty research:* Online collaborative learning, advanced art history studies, electronic publishing/design, studio arts, architectural studies. *Unit head:* Prof. Richard Lou, Chair, 901-678-2216, Fax: 901-678-2735, E-mail: gmyatt@memphis.edu. *Application contact:* Greely Myat, Graduate Studies Coordinator, 901-678-2650. Website: http://memphis.edu/art/

University of Miami, Graduate School, College of Arts and Sciences, Department of Art and Art History, Coral Gables, FL 33124. Offers art history (MA); ceramics/glass (MFA); graphic design/multimedia (MFA); painting (MFA); photography/digital imaging (MFA); printmaking (MFA); sculpture (MFA). Part-time programs available. *Degree requirements:* For master's, variable foreign language requirement, thesis, exhibit (MFA), comprehensive exam (MA). *Entrance requirements:* For master's, GRE General Test (MA), research paper (MA), slide portfolio (MFA). Additional exam requirements/recommendations for international students: Required—TOEFL. Electronic applications accepted. *Faculty research:* Installation art, public art.

University of Minnesota, Duluth, Graduate School, School of Fine Arts, Department of Art and Design, Duluth, MN 55812-2496. Offers graphic design (MFA). Part-time programs available. *Degree requirements:* For master's, final exhibit, project, supporting paper. *Entrance requirements:* For master's, minimum GPA of 3.0, writing sample, slide portfolio. Additional exam requirements/recommendations for international students: Required—TOEFL (minimum score 550 paper-based). *Faculty research:* Motion graphics, graphic design history, interactive design, typography, education.

University of Notre Dame, Graduate School, College of Arts and Letters, Division of Humanities, Department of Art, Art History, and Design, Notre Dame, IN 46556. Offers art history (MA); design (MFA), including graphic design, industrial design; studio art (MFA), including ceramics, painting, photography, printmaking, sculpture. *Accreditation:* NASAD. *Degree requirements:* For master's, comprehensive exam (for some programs), thesis. *Entrance requirements:* For master's, GRE General Test, minimum GPA of 3.0. Additional exam requirements/recommendations for international students: Required—TOEFL (minimum score 600 paper-based; 80 iBT). Electronic applications accepted. *Faculty research:* Studio art practice in ceramics, printing, photography, printmaking and sculpture, graphic design and industrial design, digital imaging in design and photography, Renaissance and American art history, contemporary art theory and criticism.

University of Pennsylvania, School of Design, Department of Fine Arts, Philadelphia, PA 19104. Offers emerging design and research (Certificate); fine arts (MFA); time-based and interactive media (Certificate). *Faculty:* 5 full-time (2 women). *Students:* 36 full-time (22 women), 1 part-time (0 women); includes 14 minority (4 Black or African American, non-Hispanic/Latino; 1 American Indian or Alaska Native, non-Hispanic/Latino; 1 Asian, non-Hispanic/Latino; 4 Hispanic/Latino; 4 Two or more races, non-Hispanic/Latino), 4 international. 119 applicants, 41% accepted, 18 enrolled. In 2014, 19 master's, 13 other advanced degrees awarded. *Entrance requirements:* For master's, portfolio. Additional exam requirements/recommendations for international students: Required—TOEFL, IELTS. *Application deadline:* For fall admission, 1/14 priority date for domestic and international students. Application fee: $80. Electronic applications accepted. *Financial support:* Teaching assistantships and scholarships/grants available. Financial award application deadline: 2/15; financial award applicants required to submit FAFSA. *Faculty research:* Painting, sculpture, printmaking, animation, video, installation, sound, emerging design practices, photography. *Unit head:* Marilyn Jordan Taylor, Dean, 215-898-6520, E-mail: mjtaylor@design.upenn.edu. *Application contact:* Office of Admissions and Financial Aid, 215-898-6520, E-mail: admissions@design.upenn.edu. Website: http://www.design.upenn.edu/fine-arts

The University of South Dakota, Graduate School, College of Fine Arts, Department of Art, Vermillion, SD 57069-2390. Offers graphic design (MFA); painting (MFA); printmaking (MFA); sculpture (MFA). *Accreditation:* NASAD. *Degree requirements:* For master's, thesis or alternative. *Entrance requirements:* For master's, portfolio, minimum GPA of 2.7. Additional exam requirements/recommendations for international students: Required—TOEFL (minimum score 550 paper-based; 79 iBT). Electronic applications accepted.

The University of Tennessee, Graduate School, College of Arts and Sciences, School of Art, Knoxville, TN 37996. Offers ceramics (MFA); drawing (MFA); graphic design (MFA); inter-area studies (MFA); media arts (MFA); painting (MFA); printmaking (MFA); sculpture (MFA); watercolor (MFA). *Accreditation:* NASAD. *Degree requirements:* For master's, thesis or alternative, exhibit. *Entrance requirements:* For master's, portfolio, minimum GPA of 2.7. Additional exam requirements/recommendations for international students: Required—TOEFL. Electronic applications accepted.

University of Utah, Graduate School, College of Fine Arts, Department of Art and Art History, Salt Lake City, UT 84112-0380. Offers art history (MA); ceramics (MFA); community-based art education (MFA); drawing (MFA); graphic design (MFA); painting (MFA); photography/digital imaging (MFA); printmaking (MFA); sculpture/intermedia (MFA). *Faculty:* 19 full-time (10 women), 22 part-time/adjunct (10 women). *Students:* 11 full-time (9 women), 5 part-time (2 women); includes 2 minority (both Hispanic/Latino), 1 international. Average age 30. 48 applicants, 31% accepted, 10 enrolled. In 2014, 5 master's awarded. *Degree requirements:* For master's, variable foreign language requirement, comprehensive exam (for some programs), thesis or alternative, exhibit and final project paper (for MFA). *Entrance requirements:* For master's, CD portfolio (MFA), writing sample (MA), curriculum vitae, letters of recommendation, letter of intent. Additional exam requirements/recommendations for international students: Required—TOEFL (minimum score 575 paper-based; 75 iBT). *Application deadline:* For fall admission, 1/15 priority date for domestic and international students. Application fee: $55 ($65 for international students). Electronic applications accepted. *Financial support:* In 2014–15, 2 fellowships, 6 research assistantships with partial tuition reimbursements, 34 teaching assistantships with partial tuition reimbursements were awarded; Federal Work-Study, institutionally sponsored loans, scholarships/grants, tuition waivers

(partial), unspecified assistantships, and stipends also available. Financial award application deadline: 1/2; financial award applicants required to submit FAFSA. *Faculty research:* Studio art, European art history, Asian art history, Latin American art history, twentieth century/contemporary art history. *Total annual research expenditures:* $54,906. *Unit head:* Prof. Brian Snapp, Chair, 801-581-8677, Fax: 801-585-6171, E-mail: b.snapp@utah.edu. *Application contact:* Prof. Kim Martinez, Director of Graduate Studies, 801-581-8677, Fax: 801-585-6171, E-mail: kim.martinez@art.utah.edu. Website: http://www.art.utah.edu/

Vermont College of Fine Arts, MFA in Graphic Design Program, Montpelier, VT 05602. Offers MFA. Postbaccalaureate distance learning degree programs offered (minimal on-campus study). *Faculty:* 11 part-time/adjunct (5 women). *Students:* 28 full-time (17 women); includes 4 minority (2 Black or African American, non-Hispanic/Latino; 1 Asian, non-Hispanic/Latino; 1 Hispanic/Latino). Average age 41. 31 applicants, 74% accepted, 14 enrolled. In 2014, 24 master's awarded. *Application deadline:* For fall admission, 7/13 priority date for domestic and international students; for spring admission, 1/15 priority date for domestic and international students. Applications are processed on a rolling basis. Application fee: $75. Electronic applications accepted. Full-time tuition and fees vary according to program. *Financial support:* Scholarships/grants available. Financial award applicants required to submit FAFSA. *Unit head:* Jennifer Renko, Program Director, 866-934-8232 Ext. 8896, E-mail: jennifer.renko@vcfa.edu. Website: http://www.vcfa.edu/graphic-design

Wayne State University, College of Fine, Performing and Communication Arts, James Pearson Duffy Department of Art and Art History, Detroit, MI 48202. Offers art (MA, MFA), including ceramics, drawing, fibers, graphic design, industrial design (MA), interior design (MA), metalsmithing, painting, photography, printmaking, sculpture; art history (MA); design and merchandising (MA). *Students:* 14 full-time (10 women), 13 part-time (8 women); includes 4 minority (1 Black or African American, non-Hispanic/Latino; 1 Hispanic/Latino; 2 Two or more races, non-Hispanic/Latino), 1 international. Average age 34. 49 applicants, 18% accepted, 6 enrolled. In 2014, 15 master's awarded. *Degree requirements:* For master's, thesis (for some programs), essay or thesis. *Entrance requirements:* For master's, GRE (for fashion and design merchandising applicants), BFA or another degree and equivalent course work, portfolio, personal interview, reference letters, statement of intent (except for art history program). Additional exam requirements/recommendations for international students: Required—TOEFL (minimum score 550 paper-based; 79 iBT), TWE (minimum score 5.5), Michigan English Language Assessment Battery (minimum score 85); Recommended—IELTS (minimum score 6.5). *Application deadline:* For fall admission, 2/1 for domestic and international students; for winter admission, 10/1 for domestic and international students. Application fee: $0. Electronic applications accepted. *Expenses:* Expenses: Contact institution. *Financial support:* In 2014–15, 11 students received support, including 1 fellowship with tuition reimbursement available (averaging $16,000 per year), 5 teaching assistantships with tuition reimbursements available (averaging $16,540 per year); scholarships/grants and unspecified assistantships also available. Support available to part-time students. Financial award application deadline: 3/31; financial award applicants required to submit FAFSA. *Faculty research:* Integration of the human figure into urban and rural landscape in painting; performance art utilizing digital media and video; exploration of race, gender, and culture through creative practice (including art, design, and art history); ongoing investigation and elaboration of visual art traditions in diverse media; continued scholarship in the history of art. *Unit head:* Dr. John Richardson, Chair, 313-577-2980, Fax: 313-577-3491, E-mail: af5343@wayne.edu. *Application contact:* Prof. Evan Larson-Voltz, Graduate Officer/Associate Professor, 313-577-2983, E-mail: evanlarson@wayne.edu. Website: http://art.wayne.edu/

Western Illinois University, School of Graduate Studies, College of Education and Human Services, Department of Instructional Design and Technology, Macomb, IL 61455-1390. Offers distance learning (Certificate); educational technology specialist (Certificate); graphic applications (Certificate); instructional design and technology (MS); multimedia (Certificate); technology integration in education (Certificate); training development (Certificate). Part-time programs available. Postbaccalaureate distance learning degree programs offered (no on-campus study). *Students:* 18 full-time (12 women), 59 part-time (32 women); includes 16 minority (11 Black or African American, non-Hispanic/Latino; 1 American Indian or Alaska Native, non-Hispanic/Latino; 3 Asian, non-Hispanic/Latino; 1 Hispanic/Latino), 5 international. Average age 35. 20 applicants, 85% accepted, 12 enrolled. In 2014, 25 master's, 11 other advanced degrees awarded. *Degree requirements:* For master's, thesis or alternative. *Entrance requirements:* Additional exam requirements/recommendations for international students: Required—TOEFL (minimum score 550 paper-based; 80 iBT). *Application deadline:* Applications are processed on a rolling basis. Application fee: $30. Electronic applications accepted. *Financial support:* In 2014–15, 11 students received support, including 5 research assistantships with full tuition reimbursements available (averaging $7,544 per year), 7 teaching assistantships with full tuition reimbursements available (averaging $8,688 per year). Financial award applicants required to submit FAFSA. *Unit head:* Dr. Hoyet Hemphill, Chairperson, 309-298-1952. *Application contact:* Dr. Nancy Parsons, Associate Provost and Director of Graduate Studies, 309-298-1806, Fax: 309-298-2345, E-mail: grad-office@wiu.edu. Website: http://wiu.edu/idt

West Virginia University, College of Creative Arts, Division of Art and Design, Morgantown, WV 26506. Offers art education (MA); art history (MA); ceramics (MFA); graphic design (MFA); painting (MFA); printmaking (MFA); sculpture (MFA); studio art (MA). *Accreditation:* NASAD. *Degree requirements:* For master's, thesis, exhibit. *Entrance requirements:* For master's, minimum GPA of 2.75, portfolio. Additional exam requirements/recommendations for international students: Required—TOEFL. *Expenses:* Contact institution. *Faculty research:* Medieval art history.

Yale University, School of Art, New Haven, CT 06520-8339. Offers graphic design (MFA); painting/printmaking (MFA); photography (MFA); sculpture (MFA). *Degree requirements:* For master's, thesis (for some programs). *Entrance requirements:* Additional exam requirements/recommendations for international students: Required—TOEFL (minimum score 550 paper-based; 100 iBT). Electronic applications accepted. *Expenses:* Contact institution.

Illustration

Academy of Art University, Graduate Program, School of Illustration, San Francisco, CA 94105-3410. Offers MFA. *Accreditation:* NASAD. Part-time programs available. Postbaccalaureate distance learning degree programs offered (no on-campus study). *Faculty:* 11 full-time (2 women), 40 part-time/adjunct (13 women). *Students:* 173

Illustration

full-time (114 women), 148 part-time (91 women); includes 45 minority (13 Black or African American, non-Hispanic/Latino; 13 Asian, non-Hispanic/Latino; 15 Hispanic/Latino; 4 Two or more races, non-Hispanic/Latino), 135 international. Average age 31. 86 applicants, 100% accepted, 47 enrolled. In 2014, 72 master's awarded. *Degree requirements:* For master's, final review. *Entrance requirements:* For master's, statement of intent; resume; portfolio/reel; official college transcripts. *Application deadline:* Applications are processed on a rolling basis. Application fee: $100. Electronic applications accepted. *Expenses: Tuition:* Part-time $910 per unit. *Financial support:* Career-related internships or fieldwork and Federal Work-Study available. Support available to part-time students. Financial award application deadline: 8/10; financial award applicants required to submit FAFSA. *Unit head:* 800-544-ARTS, E-mail: info@academyart.edu. *Application contact:* 800-544-ARTS, E-mail: info@academyart.edu.
Website: http://www.academyart.edu/illustration-school/index.html

Bob Jones University, Graduate Programs, Greenville, SC 29614. Offers accountancy (MS); Bible (MA); Bible translation (MA); Biblical studies (Certificate); broadcast management (MS); business administration (MBA); church history (MA, PhD); church ministries (MA); church music (MM); cinema and video production (MA); counseling (MS); curriculum and instruction (Ed D); divinity (M Div); dramatic production (MA); educational leadership (MS, Ed D, Ed S); elementary education (M Ed, MAT); English (M Ed, MA, MAT); fine arts (MA); graphic design (MA); history (M Ed, MA); illustration (MA); interpretative speech (MA); mathematics (M Ed, MAT); medical missions (Certificate); ministry (MM, D Min); multi-categorical special education (M Ed, MAT); music (M Ed); New Testament interpretation (PhD); Old Testament interpretation (PhD); orchestral instrument performance (MM); organ performance (MM); pastoral studies (MA); personnel services (MS, Ed S); piano pedagogy (MM); piano performance (MM); platform arts (MA); radio and television broadcasting (MS); rhetoric and public address (MA); secondary education (M Ed); studio art (MA); teaching Bible (MA); theology (MA, PhD); voice performance (MM); youth ministries (MA); M Div/MM.

California State University, Fullerton, Graduate Studies, College of the Arts, Department of Visual Arts, Fullerton, CA 92834-9480. Offers art (MA, MFA), including art history (MA), ceramics (MFA), crafts, creative photography, exhibition design, glass, graphic design, illustration, sculpture. *Accreditation:* NASAD (one or more programs are accredited). Part-time programs available. *Students:* 28 full-time (16 women), 29 part-time (22 women); includes 20 minority (3 Black or African American, non-Hispanic/Latino; 8 Asian, non-Hispanic/Latino; 8 Hispanic/Latino; 1 Two or more races, non-Hispanic/Latino), 7 international. Average age 35. 58 applicants, 38% accepted, 14 enrolled. In 2014, 17 master's awarded. *Degree requirements:* For master's, project or thesis. *Entrance requirements:* For master's, minimum GPA of 2.5 in last 60 units of course work, portfolio. Application fee: $55. *Financial support:* Career-related internships or fieldwork, Federal Work-Study, institutionally sponsored loans, and scholarships/grants available. Support available to part-time students. Financial award application deadline: 3/1; financial award applicants required to submit FAFSA. *Unit head:* Dana Lamb, Chair, 657-278-2076. *Application contact:* Admissions/Applications, 657-278-2371.

East Carolina University, Graduate School, College of Fine Arts and Communication, School of Art and Design, Greenville, NC 27858-4353. Offers art education (MA Ed); ceramics (MFA); graphic design (MFA); illustration (MFA); metal design (MFA); painting and drawing (MFA); photography (MFA); printmaking (MFA); sculpture (MFA); textile design (MFA); wood design (MFA). *Accreditation:* NASAD (one or more programs are accredited). Part-time and evening/weekend programs available. *Degree requirements:* For master's, comprehensive exam, thesis (for some programs). *Entrance requirements:* For master's, GRE General Test or MAT, portfolio. Additional exam requirements/recommendations for international students: Required—TOEFL.

Expenses: Tuition, state resident: full-time $4223. Tuition, nonresident: full-time $16,540. *Required fees:* $2184.

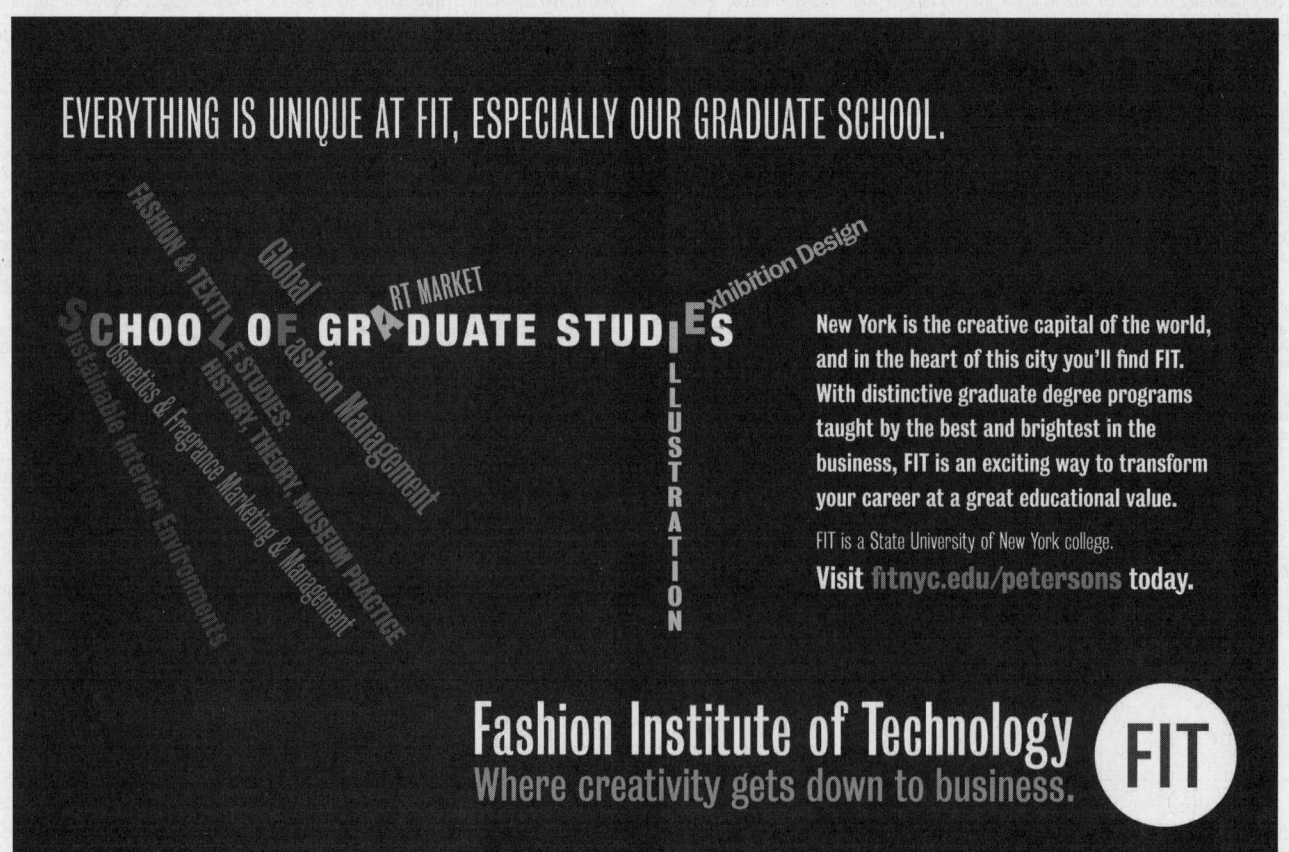 **Fashion Institute of Technology,** School of Graduate Studies, Program in Illustration, New York, NY 10001-5992. Offers MFA. *Entrance requirements:* Additional exam requirements/recommendations for international students: Required—TOEFL (minimum score 550 paper-based). Electronic applications accepted.

See Display below and Close-Up on page 99.

Hollins University, Graduate Programs, Program in Children's Literature, Roanoke, VA 24020. Offers children's book writing and illustrating (MFA); children's literature (MA, MFA). Program offered during summer only. Part-time programs available. *Faculty:* 1 (woman) full-time, 9 part-time/adjunct (8 women). *Students:* 41 full-time (38 women), 11 part-time (all women); includes 4 minority (1 Asian, non-Hispanic/Latino; 3 Hispanic/Latino). Average age 34. 35 applicants, 100% accepted, 24 enrolled. In 2014, 11 degrees awarded. *Degree requirements:* For master's, one foreign language, comprehensive exam, thesis. *Entrance requirements:* For master's, letters of recommendation, portfolio. Additional exam requirements/recommendations for international students: Required—TOEFL (minimum score 550 paper-based; 79 iBT). *Application deadline:* For fall admission, 2/15 for domestic and international students. Application fee: $40. Electronic applications accepted. *Expenses:* Expenses: $775 per credit hour, technology fee $85. *Financial support:* In 2014–15, 23 students received support, including 23 fellowships (averaging $1,000 per year); Federal Work-Study and scholarships/grants also available. Support available to part-time students. Financial award application deadline: 2/15; financial award applicants required to submit FAFSA. *Faculty research:* Fantasy, children's film, young adult fiction, gender studies, mythology and folk tales, children's poetry, picture books. *Unit head:* Amanda Cockrell, Director, 540-362-6024, Fax: 540-362-6642, E-mail: acockrell@hollins.edu. *Application contact:* Cathy S. Koon, Manager of Graduate Services, 540-362-6326, Fax: 540-362-6288, E-mail: ckoon@hollins.edu.
Website: http://www.hollins.edu/

Kent State University, College of Communication and Information, School of Visual Communication Design, Kent, OH 44242-0001. Offers MA, MFA. *Accreditation:* NASAD. Part-time programs available. *Faculty:* 13 full-time (6 women). *Students:* 17 full-time (10 women), 11 part-time (6 women); includes 2 minority (1 Black or African American, non-Hispanic/Latino; 1 Hispanic/Latino), 2 international. Average age 32. 50 applicants, 60% accepted, 26 enrolled. In 2014, 5 master's awarded. *Degree requirements:* For master's, thesis (for some programs), thesis or project (for MA). *Entrance requirements:* For master's, minimum GPA of 3.0, transcripts, autobiographical statement, goal statement, portfolio, 3 letters of recommendation. Additional exam requirements/recommendations for international students: Required—TOEFL (minimum score: paper-based 525, iBT 71), Michigan English Language Assessment Battery (minimum score of 75), IELTS (minimum score of 6.0), PTE Academic (minimum score of 48), or completion of ELS level 112 Intensive Program. *Application deadline:* For fall admission, 3/1 for domestic and international students; for spring admission, 10/1 for domestic and international students. Application fee: $45 ($70 for international students). Electronic applications accepted. *Expenses:* Tuition, state resident: full-time $8730; part-time $485 per credit hour. Tuition, nonresident: full-time $14,886; part-time $827 per credit hour. Tuition and fees vary according to campus/location and program. *Financial support:* Research assistantships with full and partial tuition reimbursements, teaching assistantships with full and partial tuition reimbursements, career-related internships or fieldwork, Federal Work-Study, scholarships/grants, and unspecified assistantships available. Financial award application deadline: 2/1. *Unit head:* Sanda Katila, Professor and Acting Director, 330-672-7856, E-mail: skatila@kent.edu. *Application contact:* Ken Visocky O'Grady,

Graduate Coordinator and Associate Professor, 330-672-7856, E-mail: kogrady@kent.edu.
Website: http://www.kent.edu/vcd/

Maryland Institute College of Art, Graduate Studies, Program in Illustration Practice, Baltimore, MD 21201. Offers MFA. *Faculty:* 4 full-time (all women). *Students:* 29 full-time (17 women); includes 13 minority (8 Asian, non-Hispanic/Latino; 3 Hispanic/Latino; 2 Two or more races, non-Hispanic/Latino), 8 international. Average age 24. 100 applicants, 20% accepted, 14 enrolled. In 2014, 14 master's awarded. *Degree requirements:* For master's, thesis, exhibition. *Entrance requirements:* For master's, portfolio, writing sample, bachelors degree in any field. Additional exam requirements/recommendations for international students: Required—TOEFL (minimum score 550 paper-based; 80 iBT), IELTS (minimum score 6.5). *Application deadline:* For fall admission, 1/15 for domestic and international students. Application fee: $75. Electronic applications accepted. *Financial support:* In 2014–15, 10 students received support, including 14 fellowships (averaging $13,000 per year), 14 teaching assistantships (averaging $3,200 per year); career-related internships or fieldwork and scholarships/grants also available. Financial award application deadline: 1/15. *Unit head:* Whitney Sherman, Director, 410-225-3177, Fax: 410-225-2408, E-mail: graduate@mica.edu. *Application contact:* Chris D. Harring, Director of Graduate Admission, 410-225-2256, Fax: 410-225-5275, E-mail: graduate@mica.edu.
Website: http://www.mica.edu/Programs_of_Study/Graduate_Programs/Illustration_Practice_(MFA).html

Marywood University, Academic Affairs, Insalaco College of Creative and Performing Arts, Art Department, Program in Visual Arts, Scranton, PA 18509-1598. Offers clay (MFA); graphic design (MFA); illustration (MFA); painting (MFA); photography (MFA); printmaking (MFA); sculpture (MFA). *Accreditation:* NASAD. Part-time programs available. *Students:* 25 full-time (18 women), 3 part-time (all women); includes 1 minority (Hispanic/Latino), 2 international. Average age 36. In 2014, 5 master's awarded. *Application deadline:* For fall admission, 4/1 for domestic students, 3/31 for international students; for spring admission, 11/1 for domestic students, 8/31 for international students. Applications are processed on a rolling basis. Application fee: $35. Electronic applications accepted. *Expenses:* Expenses: Contact institution. *Financial support:* Application deadline: 6/30; applicants required to submit FAFSA. *Unit head:* Matthew Povse, Chair, 570-348-6211 Ext. 2476, E-mail: povse@marywood.edu. *Application contact:* Tammy Manka, Assistant Director of Graduate Admissions, 570-348-6211 Ext. 2322, E-mail: tmanka@marywood.edu.
Website: http://www.marywood.edu/art/graduate-programs/master-visual-arts.html

Mills College, Graduate Studies, Department of English, Oakland, CA 94613-1000. Offers book art and creative writing (MFA); literature (MA); poetry (MFA); prose (MFA). Part-time programs available. *Faculty:* 12 full-time (10 women), 15 part-time/adjunct (13 women). *Students:* 60 full-time (50 women), 5 part-time (3 women); includes 24 minority (8 Black or African American, non-Hispanic/Latino; 1 American Indian or Alaska Native, non-Hispanic/Latino; 2 Asian, non-Hispanic/Latino; 8 Hispanic/Latino; 1 Native Hawaiian or other Pacific Islander, non-Hispanic/Latino; 4 Two or more races, non-Hispanic/Latino), 1 international. Average age 31. 128 applicants, 86% accepted, 32 enrolled. In 2014, 28 master's awarded. *Degree requirements:* For master's, comprehensive exam, thesis. *Entrance requirements:* For master's, 15-20 page writing sample. Additional exam requirements/recommendations for international students: Required—TOEFL (minimum score 600 paper-based; 100 iBT), IELTS (minimum score 7). *Application deadline:* For fall admission, 12/15 priority date for domestic students, 12/15 for international students. Applications are processed on a rolling basis. Application fee: $50. Electronic applications accepted. *Expenses: Tuition:* Full-time $31,620; part-time $7905 per course. *Required fees:* $1118. *Financial support:* In 2014–15, 70 students received support, including 60 fellowships (averaging $8,921 per year), 11 research assistantships (averaging $2,386 per year), 34 teaching assistantships with full and partial tuition reimbursements available (averaging $9,932 per year); scholarships/grants also available. Support available to part-time students. Financial award application deadline: 2/1; financial award applicants required to submit FAFSA. *Faculty research:* Creative writing, African-American literature, Victorian women writers, theories of sexuality, Shakespeare. *Unit head:* Dr. Ajuan Mance, Chair of the English Department, 510-430-2218, E-mail: dcady@mills.edu. *Application contact:* Shrim Bathey, Director of Graduate Admission, 510-430-3309, Fax: 510-430-2159, E-mail: grad-admission@mills.edu.
Website: http://www.mills.edu/english/

Mills College, Graduate Studies, Program in Book Art and Creative Writing, Oakland, CA 94613-1000. Offers MFA. *Faculty:* 1 (woman) full-time, 1 (woman) part-time/adjunct. *Students:* 9 full-time (8 women), 2 part-time (both women); includes 4 minority (1 Black or African American, non-Hispanic/Latino; 1 Hispanic/Latino; 2 Two or more races, non-Hispanic/Latino). Average age 28. 20 applicants, 60% accepted, 4 enrolled. In 2014, 2 master's awarded. *Degree requirements:* For master's, thesis project. *Entrance requirements:* For master's, visual portfolio of 15-25 images, written portfolio sample (for creative writing program). Additional exam requirements/recommendations for international students: Required—TOEFL (minimum score 600 paper-based; 100 iBT), IELTS (minimum score 7). *Application deadline:* For fall admission, 12/15 priority date for domestic students, 12/15 for international students. Application fee: $50. *Expenses: Tuition:* Full-time $31,620; part-time $7905 per course. *Required fees:* $1118. *Financial support:* In 2014–15, 10 students received support, including 11 fellowships with full and partial tuition reimbursements available (averaging $8,035 per year), 4 teaching assistantships with full and partial tuition reimbursements available (averaging $3,625 per year). Financial award application deadline: 2/1; financial award applicants required to submit FAFSA. *Unit head:* Kathleen Walkup, Professor of Book Arts, 510-430-2001, Fax: 510-430-2159, E-mail: kwalk@mills.edu. *Application contact:* Shrim Bathey, Director of Graduate Admission, 510-430-3309, Fax: 510-430-2159, E-mail: grad-admission@mills.edu.
Website: http://www.mills.edu/academics/graduate/eng/programs/MFA_in_bookart.php

Minneapolis College of Art and Design, Program in Visual Studies, Minneapolis, MN 55404-4347. Offers animation (MFA); comic art (MFA); drawing (MFA); filmmaking (MFA); fine arts (MFA); furniture design (MFA); graphic design (MFA); illustration (MFA); interactive media (MFA); painting (MFA); photography (MFA); printmaking (MFA); sculpture (MFA). *Accreditation:* NASAD. Part-time programs available. *Degree requirements:* For master's, thesis, thesis exhibit. *Entrance requirements:* For master's, portfolio of visual artwork, resume, 3 letters of recommendation. Additional exam requirements/recommendations for international students: Required—TOEFL (minimum score 550 paper-based; 79 iBT). Electronic applications accepted. *Faculty research:* Visual arts: animation, comic art, drawing, filmmaking, furniture design, graphic design, illustration, interactive media, painting, photography, printmaking, sculpture.

San Jose State University, Graduate Studies and Research, College of Humanities and the Arts, School of Art and Design, San Jose, CA 95192-0001. Offers animation/illustration (MA); art history (MA); digital media arts (MFA); photography (MFA); pictorial arts (MFA); spatial arts (MFA). *Accreditation:* NASAD (one or more programs are accredited). *Entrance requirements:* For master's, GRE. Electronic applications accepted.

Savannah College of Art and Design, Graduate School, Program in Illustration, Savannah, GA 31402-3146. Offers MA, MFA. Part-time programs available. Postbaccalaureate distance learning degree programs offered (no on-campus study). *Faculty:* 14 full-time (4 women), 5 part-time/adjunct (3 women). *Students:* 79 full-time (64 women), 36 part-time (21 women); includes 13 minority (6 Black or African American, non-Hispanic/Latino; 2 Asian, non-Hispanic/Latino; 4 Hispanic/Latino; 1 Native Hawaiian or other Pacific Islander, non-Hispanic/Latino), 44 international. Average age 30. 126 applicants, 44% accepted, 25 enrolled. In 2014, 28 master's awarded. *Degree requirements:* For master's, thesis (for some programs), final project (for MA); internship (for MFA). *Entrance requirements:* For master's, portfolio. Additional exam requirements/recommendations for international students: Required—TOEFL (minimum score 550 paper-based, 85 iBT), IELTS (minimum score 6.5), or ACTFL. *Application deadline:* For fall admission, 4/1 for domestic and international students. Applications are processed on a rolling basis. Application fee: $40. Electronic applications accepted. *Expenses: Tuition:* Full-time $34,605; part-time $3845 per course. One-time fee: $500. Tuition and fees vary according to course load. *Financial support:* In 2014–15, 4 fellowships were awarded; career-related internships or fieldwork, Federal Work-Study, and scholarships/grants also available. Financial award application deadline: 4/1; financial award applicants required to submit FAFSA. *Unit head:* Ron Spears, Chair. *Application contact:* Jenny Jaquillard, Executive Director of Admissions, Recruitment and Events, 912-525-5100, Fax: 912-525-5985, E-mail: admission@scad.edu.
Website: http://www.scad.edu/academics/programs/illustration

Savannah College of Art and Design, Graduate School, Program in Sequential Art, Savannah, GA 31402-3146. Offers MA, MFA. Part-time programs available. *Faculty:* 13 full-time (2 women), 5 part-time/adjunct (3 women). *Students:* 31 full-time (18 women), 12 part-time (5 women); includes 10 minority (5 Black or African American, non-Hispanic/Latino; 3 Asian, non-Hispanic/Latino; 2 Hispanic/Latino), 10 international. Average age 27. 32 applicants, 50% accepted, 13 enrolled. In 2014, 16 master's awarded. *Degree requirements:* For master's, thesis (for some programs), final project (for MA); internship (for MFA). *Entrance requirements:* For master's, portfolio. Additional exam requirements/recommendations for international students: Required—TOEFL (minimum score 550 paper-based, 85 iBT), IELTS (minimum score 6.5), or ACTFL. *Application deadline:* For fall admission, 4/1 for domestic and international students. Applications are processed on a rolling basis. Application fee: $40. Electronic applications accepted. *Expenses: Tuition:* Full-time $34,605; part-time $3845 per course. One-time fee: $500. Tuition and fees vary according to course load. *Financial support:* Fellowships, career-related internships or fieldwork, Federal Work-Study, and scholarships/grants available. Financial award application deadline: 4/1; financial award applicants required to submit FAFSA. *Unit head:* Ron Spears, Chair. *Application contact:* Jenny Jaquillard, Executive Director of Admissions, Recruitment and Events, 912-525-5100, Fax: 912-525-5985, E-mail: admission@scad.edu.
Website: http://www.scad.edu/academics/programs/sequential-art

School of Visual Arts, Graduate Programs, Illustration as Visual Essay Department, New York, NY 10010-3994. Offers MFA. *Accreditation:* NASAD. *Degree requirements:* For master's, thesis, 60 credits, including all required courses; residency of two academic years. *Entrance requirements:* For master's, portfolio of work (still images) submitted through SlideRoom. Additional exam requirements/recommendations for international students: Required—TOEFL (minimum score 100 iBT). Electronic applications accepted. *Faculty research:* Illustration, fine arts, computer art, writing, art history, art direction.

Syracuse University, College of Visual and Performing Arts, Program in Illustration, Syracuse, NY 13244. Offers MFA. *Students:* 6 full-time (5 women), 3 part-time (2 women), 6 international. Average age 26. 43 applicants, 16% accepted, 4 enrolled. In 2014, 1 master's awarded. *Degree requirements:* For master's, thesis or alternative. *Entrance requirements:* For master's, portfolio. Additional exam requirements/recommendations for international students: Required—TOEFL (minimum score 100 iBT), IELTS. *Application deadline:* For fall admission, 2/1 priority date for domestic and international students. Application fee: $75. Electronic applications accepted. *Expenses: Tuition:* Part-time $1341 per credit. *Financial support:* Fellowships with full tuition reimbursements and teaching assistantships with full and partial tuition reimbursements available. Financial award application deadline: 1/1. *Unit head:* Prof. Martha Blake,, Department of Art, 315-443-4613, E-mail: mablake@syr.edu. *Application contact:* Therese West, Information Contact, 315-443-0137, E-mail: admissg@syr.edu.
Website: http://vpa.syr.edu/art-design/art/graduate/illustration

Western Connecticut State University, Division of Graduate Studies, School of Visual and Performing Arts, Department of Art, Danbury, CT 06810-6885. Offers illustration (MFA); painting (MFA). Part-time programs available. *Degree requirements:* For master's, individual exhibition of artwork, review of student's progress prior to admission to final semester, completion of program in 6 years. *Entrance requirements:* For master's, portfolio review, minimum GPA of 2.5. Additional exam requirements/recommendations for international students: Recommended—TOEFL (minimum score 550 paper-based; 79 iBT), IELTS (minimum score 6). *Expenses:* Contact institution. *Faculty research:* Proficiency in both traditional and digital processes.

Industrial Design

Academy of Art University, Graduate Program, School of Industrial Design, San Francisco, CA 94105-3410. Offers MFA. Part-time programs available. Postbaccalaureate distance learning degree programs offered (no on-campus study). *Faculty:* 4 full-time (0 women), 31 part-time/adjunct (6 women). *Students:* 121 full-time (42 women), 44 part-time (24 women); includes 12 minority (2 Black or African American, non-Hispanic/Latino; 3 Asian, non-Hispanic/Latino; 6 Hispanic/Latino; 1 Native Hawaiian or other Pacific Islander, non-Hispanic/Latino), 122 international. Average age 28. 106 applicants, 100% accepted, 38 enrolled. In 2014, 25 master's

awarded. *Degree requirements:* For master's, final review. *Entrance requirements:* For master's, statement of intent; resume; portfolio/reel; official college transcripts. *Application deadline:* Applications are processed on a rolling basis. Application fee: $100. Electronic applications accepted. *Expenses: Tuition:* Part-time $910 per unit. *Financial support:* Career-related internships or fieldwork and Federal Work-Study available. Support available to part-time students. Financial award application deadline: 8/10; financial award applicants required to submit FAFSA. *Unit head:* 800-544-ARTS, E-mail: info@academyart.edu. *Application contact:* 800-544-ARTS, E-mail: info@academyart.edu.
Website: http://www.academyart.edu/industrial-design-school/index.html

Art Center College of Design, Graduate Industrial Design Program, Pasadena, CA 91103. Offers MS. *Accreditation:* NASAD. *Students:* 26 full-time (11 women), 18 part-time (7 women); includes 9 minority (5 Asian, non-Hispanic/Latino; 3 Hispanic/Latino; 1 Two or more races, non-Hispanic/Latino), 14 international. Average age 31. 102 applicants, 23% accepted, 13 enrolled. In 2014, 15 master's awarded. *Degree requirements:* For master's, thesis, studio project. *Entrance requirements:* For master's, portfolio. Additional exam requirements/recommendations for international students: Required—TOEFL (minimum score 100 iBT), IELTS (minimum score 7). *Application deadline:* For fall admission, 2/1 priority date for domestic and international students. Application fee: $50 ($70 for international students). Electronic applications accepted. *Financial support:* Career-related internships or fieldwork, Federal Work-Study, and scholarships/grants available. Financial award application deadline: 2/1; financial award applicants required to submit FAFSA. *Unit head:* Andy Ogden, Chair, 626-396-2465, E-mail: andy.ogden@artcenter.edu. *Application contact:* Maritza Herrera, Senior Coordinator, 626-396-2464, E-mail: maritza.herrera@artcenter.edu.

Auburn University, Graduate School, College of Architecture, Design, and Construction, Department of Industrial Design, Auburn University, AL 36849. Offers MID. *Accreditation:* NASAD. Part-time programs available. *Faculty:* 18 full-time (5 women), 1 part-time/adjunct (0 women). *Students:* 17 full-time (8 women), 7 part-time (1 woman); includes 2 minority (1 Asian, non-Hispanic/Latino; 1 Hispanic/Latino), 13 international. Average age 26. 38 applicants, 61% accepted, 10 enrolled. In 2014, 3 master's awarded. *Entrance requirements:* For master's, GRE General Test. *Application deadline:* For fall admission, 9/1 for domestic students; for spring admission, 3/1 for domestic students. Applications are processed on a rolling basis. Application fee: $50 ($60 for international students). Electronic applications accepted. *Expenses:* Tuition, state resident: full-time $8586; part-time $477 per credit hour. Tuition, nonresident: full-time $25,758; part-time $1431 per credit hour. *Required fees:* $804 per semester. Tuition and fees vary according to degree level and program. *Financial support:* Federal Work-Study available. Support available to part-time students. Financial award application deadline: 3/15; financial award applicants required to submit FAFSA. *Faculty research:* Design of space living facilities, color use in business communications. *Unit head:* Clark E. Lundell, Head, 334-844-2364. *Application contact:* Dr. George Flowers, Dean of the Graduate School, 334-844-2125.
Website: http://www.auburn.edu/academic/architecture/ind/menu.html

Brigham Young University, Graduate Studies, Ira A. Fulton College of Engineering and Technology, School of Technology, Provo, UT 84602-1001. Offers construction management (MS); information technology (MS); manufacturing systems (MS); technology and engineering education (MS). *Faculty:* 27 full-time (0 women). *Students:* 40 full-time (4 women); includes 6 minority (3 Asian, non-Hispanic/Latino; 2 Hispanic/Latino; 1 Native Hawaiian or other Pacific Islander, non-Hispanic/Latino), 1 international. Average age 30. 19 applicants, 63% accepted, 12 enrolled. In 2014, 12 master's awarded. *Degree requirements:* For master's, thesis. *Entrance requirements:* For master's, GRE General Test; GMAT or GRE (for construction management emphasis), minimum GPA of 3.0 in last 60 hours of course work. Additional exam requirements/recommendations for international students: Required—TOEFL (minimum score 580 paper-based; 85 iBT). *Application deadline:* For fall admission, 2/15 for domestic and international students; for winter admission, 9/10 for domestic students, 9/15 for international students; for spring admission, 2/15 for domestic and international students; for summer admission, 2/15 for domestic students. Application fee: $50. Electronic applications accepted. *Expenses: Tuition:* Full-time $6310; part-time $371 per credit hour. Tuition and fees vary according to program and student's religious affiliation. *Financial support:* In 2014–15, 40 students received support, including 17 research assistantships (averaging $4,305 per year), 18 teaching assistantships (averaging $4,257 per year); scholarships/grants also available. *Faculty research:* Information assurance and security, HEI and databases, manufacturing materials, processes and systems, innovation in construction management scheduling and delivery methods. *Total annual research expenditures:* $534,164. *Unit head:* Richard E. Fry, Director, 801-422-4445, Fax: 801-422-0490, E-mail: rfry@byu.edu. *Application contact:* Barry M. Lunt, Graduate Coordinator, 801-422-2264, Fax: 801-422-0490, E-mail: sotadminasst@byu.edu.
Website: http://www.et.byu.edu/sot/

California College of the Arts, Graduate Programs, Design Program, San Francisco, CA 94107. Offers graphic design (MFA); industrial design (MFA); interaction design (MFA). *Accreditation:* NASAD. *Degree requirements:* For master's, thesis, exhibit. *Entrance requirements:* For master's, appropriate bachelor's degree, portfolio, resume, letters of recommendation, transcripts. Additional exam requirements/recommendations for international students: Required—TOEFL (minimum score 600 paper-based; 100 iBT). Electronic applications accepted.

Carleton University, Faculty of Graduate Studies, Faculty of Engineering and Design, School of Industrial Design, Ottawa, ON K1S 5B6, Canada. Offers M Des. *Degree requirements:* For master's, thesis optional. *Entrance requirements:* For master's, honors degree. Additional exam requirements/recommendations for international students: Required—TOEFL.

Florida State University, The Graduate School, College of Human Sciences, Department of Retail, Merchandising and Product Development, Tallahassee, FL 32306. Offers MS. Part-time programs available. *Faculty:* 7 full-time (all women). *Students:* 14 full-time (12 women); includes 12 minority (3 Black or African American, non-Hispanic/Latino; 1 Asian, non-Hispanic/Latino; 6 Hispanic/Latino; 1 Native Hawaiian or other Pacific Islander, non-Hispanic/Latino; 1 Two or more races, non-Hispanic/Latino). 23 applicants, 52% accepted, 9 enrolled. In 2014, 15 master's awarded. *Degree requirements:* For master's, thesis optional. *Entrance requirements:* For master's, GRE General Test, minimum upper-division GPA of 3.0. Additional exam requirements/recommendations for international students: Required—TOEFL (minimum score 550 paper-based; 80 iBT). *Application deadline:* For fall admission, 7/1 for domestic and international students; for spring admission, 11/1 for domestic and international students. Applications are processed on a rolling basis. Application fee: $30. Electronic applications accepted. *Expenses:* Tuition, state resident: part-time $403.51 per credit hour. Tuition, nonresident: part-time $1004.85 per credit hour. *Required fees:* $75.81 per credit hour. One-time fee: $20 part-time. Tuition and fees vary according to campus/location. *Financial support:* In 2014–15, 19 teaching assistantships with full tuition reimbursements (averaging $5,642 per year) were awarded; career-related internships or fieldwork, institutionally sponsored loans, scholarships/grants, and unspecified assistantships also available. Financial award application deadline: 1/15; financial award applicants required to submit FAFSA. *Faculty research:* Global merchandising and product development. *Total annual research expenditures:* $34,011. *Unit head:* Dr. Sherry Schofield, Department Chair, 850-644-2498, Fax: 850-645-4673, E-mail: sschofield2@fsu.edu.
Website: http://www.chs.fsu.edu/Retail-Merchandising-Product-Development

Georgia Institute of Technology, Graduate Studies, College of Architecture, School of Industrial Design, Atlanta, GA 30332-0001. Offers MID. *Degree requirements:* For master's, thesis optional. *Expenses:* Tuition, state resident: full-time $12,344; part-time $515 per credit hour. Tuition, nonresident: full-time $27,600; part-time $1150 per credit hour. *Required fees:* $1196 per term. Part-time tuition and fees vary according to course load.

Iowa State University of Science and Technology, Program in Industrial Design, Ames, IA 50011. Offers MID. *Accreditation:* NASAD. *Entrance requirements:* For master's, GRE, curriculum vitae, portfolio, letters of recommendation, interview. Additional exam requirements/recommendations for international students: Required—TOEFL (minimum score 587 paper-based; 95 iBT), IELTS (minimum score 7). Electronic applications accepted.

North Carolina State University, Graduate School, College of Design, Department of Industrial Design, Raleigh, NC 27695. Offers MID. *Accreditation:* NASAD. Part-time programs available. *Degree requirements:* For master's, thesis optional, oral exam, project. *Entrance requirements:* For master's, GRE General Test (recommended), portfolio. Electronic applications accepted. *Faculty research:* Computer graphics, ergonomics, product design.

The Ohio State University, Graduate School, College of Arts and Sciences, Division of Arts and Humanities, Department of Design, Columbus, OH 43210. Offers design (MA); design research and development (MFA); digital animation and interactive media (MFA). *Accreditation:* NASAD. Part-time programs available. *Faculty:* 16. *Students:* 20 full-time (11 women), 3 part-time (2 women); includes 6 minority (2 Black or African American, non-Hispanic/Latino; 3 Asian, non-Hispanic/Latino; 1 Hispanic/Latino), 8 international. Average age 29. In 2014, 6 master's awarded. *Degree requirements:* For master's, project or thesis. *Entrance requirements:* For master's, GRE General Test (for all applicants with cumulative GPA below 3.0), portfolio. Additional exam requirements/recommendations for international students: Recommended—TOEFL (minimum score 550 paper-based; 79 iBT). *Application deadline:* For fall admission, 12/13 priority date for domestic students, 11/30 priority date for international students; for winter admission, 12/1 for domestic students, 11/1 for international students; for spring admission, 3/1 for domestic students, 2/1 for international students. Applications are processed on a rolling basis. Application fee: $60 ($70 for international students). Electronic applications accepted. *Financial support:* Fellowships with tuition reimbursements, research assistantships with tuition reimbursements, teaching assistantships with tuition reimbursements, career-related internships or fieldwork, Federal Work-Study, institutionally sponsored loans, and unspecified assistantships available. Support available to part-time students. Financial award application deadline: 5/1. *Unit head:* Mary Anne Beecher, PhD, Chair, 614-688-6746, E-mail: beecher.17@osu.edu. *Application contact:* Graduate and Professional Admissions, 614-292-9444, Fax: 614-292-3895, E-mail: gpadmissions@osu.edu.
Website: http://design.osu.edu/

Philadelphia University, School of Engineering and Textiles, Program in Industrial Design, Philadelphia, PA 19144. Offers MS. *Accreditation:* NASAD. Part-time and evening/weekend programs available. *Degree requirements:* For master's, project. *Entrance requirements:* For master's, essay; portfolio (recommended). Additional exam requirements/recommendations for international students: Required—TOEFL (minimum score 79 iBT), IELTS (minimum score 6.5).

Pratt Institute, School of Design, Program in Industrial Design, Brooklyn, NY 11205-3899. Offers MID. *Accreditation:* NASAD. Part-time programs available. *Faculty:* 4 full-time (1 woman), 39 part-time/adjunct (13 women). *Students:* 74 full-time (46 women); includes 14 minority (4 Black or African American, non-Hispanic/Latino; 7 Asian, non-Hispanic/Latino; 1 Hispanic/Latino; 2 Two or more races, non-Hispanic/Latino), 28 international. Average age 28. 269 applicants, 26% accepted, 27 enrolled. In 2014, 22 master's awarded. *Degree requirements:* For master's, thesis. *Entrance requirements:* For master's, portfolio, letters of recommendation. Additional exam requirements/recommendations for international students: Required—TOEFL (minimum score 575 paper-based; 90 iBT). *Application deadline:* For fall admission, 1/5 for domestic and international students; for spring admission, 10/1 for domestic and international students. Application fee: $50 ($90 for international students). Electronic applications accepted. *Financial support:* Career-related internships or fieldwork, Federal Work-Study, institutionally sponsored loans, scholarships/grants, health care benefits, and unspecified assistantships available. Support available to part-time students. Financial award application deadline: 2/1; financial award applicants required to submit FAFSA. *Faculty research:* Universal design, design ethics, sustainability in design. *Unit head:* Steve Diskin, Chairperson, 718-636-3631, E-mail: sdiskin@pratt.edu. *Application contact:* Young Hah, Director of Graduate Admissions, 718-636-3683, Fax: 718-399-4242, E-mail: yhah@pratt.edu.
Website: https://www.pratt.edu/academics/school-of-design/graduate-school-of-design/industrial-design-grad/

See Display on page 65 and Close-Up on page 103.

Pratt Institute, School of Design, Program in Package Design, New York, NY 10011. Offers MS. *Accreditation:* NASAD. Part-time programs available. *Faculty:* 5 full-time (2 women), 35 part-time/adjunct (14 women). *Students:* 30 full-time (23 women), 3 part-time (1 woman); includes 8 minority (5 Asian, non-Hispanic/Latino; 3 Hispanic/Latino), 19 international. Average age 25. 28 applicants, 75% accepted, 14 enrolled. In 2014, 14 master's awarded. *Degree requirements:* For master's, thesis. *Entrance requirements:* For master's, portfolio, letters of recommendation. Additional exam requirements/recommendations for international students: Required—TOEFL (minimum score 575 paper-based; 90 iBT). *Application deadline:* For fall admission, 1/5 for domestic and international students; for spring admission, 10/1 for domestic and international students. Application fee: $50 ($90 for international students). Electronic applications accepted. *Financial support:* Career-related internships or fieldwork, Federal Work-Study, institutionally sponsored loans, scholarships/grants, health care benefits, and unspecified assistantships available. Support available to part-time students. Financial award application deadline: 2/1; financial award applicants required to submit FAFSA. *Unit head:* Santiago Piedrafita Iglesias, Chairperson, 212-647-7640, Fax: 212-367-2481, E-mail: spiedraf@pratt.edu. *Application contact:* Young Hah, Director of Graduate Admissions, 718-636-3683, Fax: 718-399-4242, E-mail: yhah@pratt.edu.
Website: https://www.pratt.edu/academics/school-of-design/graduate-school-of-design/grad-communications-design/

See Display on page 65 and Close-Up on page 103.

Rhode Island School of Design, Graduate Studies, Division of Architecture and Design, Department of Industrial Design, Providence, RI 02903-2784. Offers MID. *Accreditation:* NASAD. *Faculty:* 7 full-time (1 woman), 19 part-time/adjunct (10 women). *Students:* 32 full-time (18 women); includes 4 minority (1 Black or African American,

non-Hispanic/Latino; 1 Hispanic/Latino; 2 Two or more races, non-Hispanic/Latino), 16 international. Average age 26. 204 applicants, 14% accepted, 12 enrolled. In 2014, 8 master's awarded. *Degree requirements:* For master's, thesis, exhibit. *Entrance requirements:* For master's, portfolio, statement of purpose, 3 letters of recommendation. Additional exam requirements/recommendations for international students: Required—TOEFL (minimum score 580 paper-based; 93 iBT). *Application deadline:* For fall admission, 2/1 for domestic and international students. Application fee: $60. *Expenses:* Expenses: $44,594. *Financial support:* Fellowships, teaching assistantships, career-related internships or fieldwork, Federal Work-Study, institutionally sponsored loans, scholarships/grants, and unspecified assistantships available. Financial award application deadline: 2/15; financial award applicants required to submit FAFSA. *Unit head:* Soojung Ham, Head, 401-454-6169, Fax: 401-454-6157, E-mail: sham01@risd.edu. *Application contact:* Molly Pettengil, Graduate Admissions Officer, 401-454-6312, E-mail: enewhall@risd.edu.
Website: http://www.risd.edu/academics/industrial-design/

Rochester Institute of Technology, Graduate Enrollment Services, College of Imaging Arts and Sciences, School of Design, MFA Program in Industrial Design, Rochester, NY 14623-5603. Offers MFA. *Accreditation:* NASAD. Part-time programs available. *Students:* 33 full-time (18 women), 7 part-time (4 women); includes 2 minority (both American Indian or Alaska Native, non-Hispanic/Latino), 30 international. Average age 26. 191 applicants, 21% accepted, 14 enrolled. In 2014, 14 master's awarded. *Degree requirements:* For master's, thesis, thesis exhibition. *Entrance requirements:* For master's, GRE and TOEFL, IELTS, or PTE for non-native English speakers, portfolio, recommended minimum GPA of 3.0. Additional exam requirements/recommendations for international students: Required—PTE (minimum score 58), TOEFL (minimum score 550 paper-based; 79 iBT) or IELTS (minimum score 6.5). *Application deadline:* For fall admission, 2/15 priority date for domestic and international students. Applications are processed on a rolling basis. Application fee: $60. Electronic applications accepted. *Expenses:* Expenses: $1,673 per credit hour. *Financial support:* In 2014–15, 24 students received support. Research assistantships with partial tuition reimbursements available, teaching assistantships with partial tuition reimbursements available, career-related internships or fieldwork, Federal Work-Study, institutionally sponsored loans, scholarships/grants, and unspecified assistantships available. Support available to part-time students. Financial award application deadline: 8/30; financial award applicants required to submit FAFSA. *Unit head:* Stan Rickel, Graduate Program Director, 585-475-4745, E-mail: srrfaa@rit.edu. *Application contact:* Diane Ellison, Associate Vice President, Graduate Enrollment Services, 585-475-2229, Fax: 585-475-7164, E-mail: gradinfo@rit.edu.
Website: http://cias.rit.edu/schools/design/graduate-industrial-design

San Francisco State University, Division of Graduate Studies, College of Liberal and Creative Arts, Department of Design and Industry, San Francisco, CA 94132-1722. Offers MA. *Expenses:* Tuition, state resident: full-time $6738. Tuition, nonresident: full-time $17,898; part-time $372 per credit hour. *Required fees:* $498 per semester. *Unit head:* Dr. Jane Veeder, Chair, 415-338-1547, Fax: 415-338-7770, E-mail: jveeder@sfsu.edu. *Application contact:* Prof. Hsiao-Yun Chu, Graduate Coordinator, 415-338-2430, Fax: 415-338-7770, E-mail: hychu@sfsu.edu.
Website: http://design.sfsu.edu

Savannah College of Art and Design, Graduate School, Program in Industrial Design, Savannah, GA 31402-3146. Offers MA, MFA. Part-time programs available. *Faculty:* 12 full-time (0 women), 2 part-time/adjunct (0 women). *Students:* 83 full-time (34 women), 18 part-time (7 women); includes 8 minority (4 Black or African American, non-Hispanic/Latino; 4 Asian, non-Hispanic/Latino), 78 international. Average age 26. 132 applicants, 69% accepted, 28 enrolled. In 2014, 26 master's awarded. *Degree requirements:* For master's, thesis (for some programs), final project (for MA); internship (for MFA). *Entrance requirements:* For master's, portfolio. Additional exam requirements/recommendations for international students: Required—TOEFL (minimum score 550 paper-based, 85 iBT), IELTS (minimum score 6.5), or ACTFL. *Application deadline:* For fall admission, 4/1 for domestic and international students. Applications are processed on a rolling basis. Application fee: $40. Electronic applications accepted. *Expenses:* Tuition: Full-time $34,605; part-time $3845 per course. One-time fee: $500. Tuition and fees vary according to course load. *Financial support:* Fellowships, career-related internships or fieldwork, Federal Work-Study, and scholarships/grants available. Financial award application deadline: 4/1; financial award applicants required to submit FAFSA. *Unit head:* Owen Foster, Chair. *Application contact:* Jenny Jaquillard, Executive Director of Admissions, Recruitment and Events, 912-525-5100, Fax: 912-525-5985, E-mail: admission@scad.edu.
Website: http://www.scad.edu/academics/programs/industrial-design

University of Cincinnati, Graduate School, College of Design, Architecture, Art, and Planning, School of Design, Cincinnati, OH 45221. Offers fashion design (M Des); graphic design (M Des); industrial design (M Des); interaction design (M Des); product development (M Des). *Accreditation:* NASAD. *Students:* 34 full-time (16 women), 3 part-time (1 woman); includes 3 minority (1 Black or African American, non-Hispanic/Latino; 1 Asian, non-Hispanic/Latino; 1 Hispanic/Latino), 24 international. In 2014, 7 master's awarded. *Degree requirements:* For master's, thesis. *Entrance requirements:* For master's, undergraduate degree in design or related field, 2 years of work experience in

design or related field. Additional exam requirements/recommendations for international students: Required—TOEFL. *Application deadline:* For fall admission, 2/1 for domestic students. Application fee: $30. Electronic applications accepted. *Financial support:* Fellowships, career-related internships or fieldwork, Federal Work-Study, tuition waivers (partial), and unspecified assistantships available. *Faculty research:* Design theory, interdisciplinary design topics. *Unit head:* Brigid O'Kane, Director, 513-556-0833, E-mail: brigid.okane@uc.edu. *Application contact:* Dr. J. Chewning, Information Contact, 513-556-2996, Fax: 513-556-0240, E-mail: j.chewning@uc.edu.
Website: http://www.daap.uc.edu/

University of Illinois at Urbana–Champaign, Graduate College, College of Fine and Applied Arts, School of Art and Design, Program in Design and Media, Champaign, IL 61820. Offers art and design (MFA), including new media; graphic design (MFA); industrial design (MFA). *Accreditation:* NASAD. *Students:* 11 (8 women). Application fee: $70 ($90 for international students). *Unit head:* Ernest Scott, Chair, 217-333-1579, E-mail: ernscott@illinois.edu. *Application contact:* Ellen de Waard, Coordinator of Graduate Academic Affairs, 217-333-0642, Fax: 217-244-7688, E-mail: edewaard@illinois.edu.
Website: http://www.art.illinois.edu

University of Notre Dame, Graduate School, College of Arts and Letters, Division of Humanities, Department of Art, Art History, and Design, Notre Dame, IN 46556. Offers art history (MA); design (MFA), including graphic design, industrial design; studio art (MFA), including ceramics, painting, photography, printmaking, sculpture. *Accreditation:* NASAD. *Degree requirements:* For master's, comprehensive exam (for some programs), thesis. *Entrance requirements:* For master's, GRE General Test, minimum GPA of 3.0. Additional exam requirements/recommendations for international students: Required—TOEFL (minimum score 600 paper-based; 80 iBT). Electronic applications accepted. *Faculty research:* Studio art practice in ceramics, printing, photography, printmaking and sculpture, graphic design and industrial design, digital imaging in design and photography, Renaissance and American art history, contemporary art theory and criticism.

The University of the Arts, College of Art, Media and Design, Department of Industrial Design, Philadelphia, PA 19102-4944. Offers MID. *Accreditation:* NASAD. *Degree requirements:* For master's, thesis. *Entrance requirements:* For master's, portfolio of 20 pieces that showcases self-generated projects, professional assignments or projects developed in a previous program; official transcripts; three letters of recommendation; one- to two-page statement of professional plans and goals; personal interview; resume or curriculum vitae; statement of intent. Additional exam requirements/recommendations for international students: Required—TOEFL (minimum score 580 paper-based, 92 iBT) or IELTS (minimum score 6.5).

University of Washington, Graduate School, College of Arts and Sciences, School of Art, Division of Design, Seattle, WA 98195. Offers industrial design (MFA); visual communication design (MFA).

Wayne State University, College of Fine, Performing and Communication Arts, James Pearson Duffy Department of Art and Art History, Detroit, MI 48202. Offers art (MA, MFA), including ceramics, drawing, fibers, graphic design, industrial design (MA), interior design (MA), metalsmithing, painting, photography, printmaking, sculpture; art history (MA); design and merchandising (MA). *Students:* 14 full-time (10 women), 13 part-time (8 women); includes 4 minority (1 Black or African American, non-Hispanic/Latino; 1 Hispanic/Latino; 2 Two or more races, non-Hispanic/Latino), 1 international. Average age 34. 49 applicants, 18% accepted, 6 enrolled. In 2014, 15 master's awarded. *Degree requirements:* For master's, thesis (for some programs), essay or thesis. *Entrance requirements:* For master's, GRE (for fashion and design merchandising applicants), BFA or another degree and equivalent course work, portfolio, personal interview, reference letters, statement of intent (except for art history program). Additional exam requirements/recommendations for international students: Required—TOEFL (minimum score 550 paper-based; 79 iBT), TWE (minimum score 5.5), Michigan English Language Assessment Battery (minimum score 85); Recommended—IELTS (minimum score 6.5). *Application deadline:* For fall admission, 2/1 for domestic and international students; for winter admission, 10/1 for domestic and international students. Application fee: $0. Electronic applications accepted. *Expenses:* Expenses: Contact institution. *Financial support:* In 2014–15, 11 students received support, including 1 fellowship with tuition reimbursement available (averaging $16,000 per year), 5 teaching assistantships with tuition reimbursements available (averaging $16,540 per year); scholarships/grants and unspecified assistantships also available. Support available to part-time students. Financial award application deadline: 3/31; financial award applicants required to submit FAFSA. *Faculty research:* Integration of the human figure into urban and rural landscape in painting; performance art utilizing digital media and video; exploration of race, gender, and culture through creative practice (including art, design, and art history); ongoing investigation and elaboration of visual art traditions in diverse media; continued scholarship in the history of art. *Unit head:* Dr. John Richardson, Chair, 313-577-2980, Fax: 313-577-3491, E-mail: af5343@wayne.edu. *Application contact:* Prof. Evan Larson-Voltz, Graduate Officer/Associate Professor, 313-577-2983, E-mail: evanlarson@wayne.edu.
Website: http://art.wayne.edu/

Interior Design

Academy of Art University, Graduate Program, School of Interior Architecture and Design, San Francisco, CA 94105-3410. Offers MFA. *Accreditation:* CIDA. Part-time programs available. Postbaccalaureate distance learning degree programs offered (no on-campus study). *Faculty:* 5 full-time (4 women), 29 part-time/adjunct (13 women). *Students:* 167 full-time (118 women), 127 part-time (108 women); includes 48 minority (8 Black or African American, non-Hispanic/Latino; 17 Asian, non-Hispanic/Latino; 15 Hispanic/Latino; 2 Native Hawaiian or other Pacific Islander, non-Hispanic/Latino; 6 Two or more races, non-Hispanic/Latino), 144 international. Average age 32. 96 applicants, 100% accepted, 28 enrolled. In 2014, 63 master's awarded. *Degree requirements:* For master's, final review. *Entrance requirements:* For master's, statement of intent; resume; portfolio/reel; official college transcripts. *Application deadline:* Applications are processed on a rolling basis. Application fee: $100. Electronic applications accepted. *Expenses:* Tuition: Part-time $910 per unit. *Financial support:* Career-related internships or fieldwork and Federal Work-Study available. Support available to part-time students. Financial award application deadline: 8/10; financial award applicants required to submit FAFSA. *Unit head:* 800-544-ARTS, E-mail: info@academyart.edu. *Application contact:* 800-544-ARTS, E-mail: info@academyart.edu.
Website: http://www.academyart.edu/interior-design-school/index.html

Boston Architectural College, Graduate Programs, Boston, MA 02115-2795. Offers architecture (M Arch); historic preservation (MDS); interior design (MID); landscape architecture (MLA); sustainable design (MDS). *Accreditation:* CIDA. *Degree requirements:* For master's, thesis. *Entrance requirements:* For master's, portfolio (recommended). Electronic applications accepted.

Brenau University, Sydney O. Smith Graduate School, School of Fine Arts and Humanities, Gainesville, GA 30501. Offers interior design (MID). *Accreditation:* CIDA. Part-time programs available. *Degree requirements:* For master's, internship; portfolio. *Entrance requirements:* For master's, portfolio review, minimum GPA of 3.0, resume. Additional exam requirements/recommendations for international students: Required—TOEFL (minimum score 500 paper-based; 61 iBT); Recommended—IELTS (minimum score 5). Electronic applications accepted.

California State Polytechnic University, Pomona, Program in Interior Architecture, Pomona, CA 91768-2557. Offers MIA. Program held jointly with UCLA Extension. *Accreditation:* CIDA. *Students:* 10 full-time (9 women), 64 part-time (52 women); includes 16 minority (1 Black or African American, non-Hispanic/Latino; 8 Asian, non-Hispanic/Latino; 4 Hispanic/Latino; 3 Two or more races, non-Hispanic/Latino), 30 international. Average age 30. 45 applicants, 76% accepted, 22 enrolled. In

2014, 39 master's awarded. *Degree requirements:* For master's, project. *Expenses:* Tuition, state resident: full-time $6738. Tuition, nonresident: full-time $12,300. *Required fees:* $1400. *Unit head:* Kip A. Dickson, Graduate Coordinator, 909-869-2682, Fax: 909-869-4331, E-mail: kadickson@cpp.edu.
Website: http://www.ceu.cpp.edu/specialsessions/degree_programs/mia.html

Chatham University, Program in Interior Architecture, Pittsburgh, PA 15232-2826. Offers MIA. *Accreditation:* CIDA. Part-time and evening/weekend programs available. Postbaccalaureate distance learning degree programs offered (no on-campus study). *Faculty:* 2 full-time (0 women), 6 part-time/adjunct (4 women). *Students:* 17 full-time (15 women), 10 part-time (9 women); includes 3 minority (1 Black or African American, non-Hispanic/Latino; 1 Asian, non-Hispanic/Latino; 1 Hispanic/Latino), 5 international. Average age 29. 23 applicants, 61% accepted, 6 enrolled. In 2014, 13 master's awarded. *Entrance requirements:* Additional exam requirements/recommendations for international students: Required—TOEFL (minimum score 600 paper-based; 100 iBT), IELTS (minimum score 7), TWE. *Application deadline:* For fall admission, 4/1 priority date for domestic and international students; for spring admission, 11/1 priority date for domestic students, 10/1 priority date for international students. Applications are processed on a rolling basis. Application fee: $45. Electronic applications accepted. Application fee is waived when completed online. *Expenses: Tuition:* Full-time $15,318; part-time $851 per credit hour. *Required fees:* $440; $24 per credit hour. Tuition and fees vary according to course load, program and reciprocity agreements. *Financial support:* Applicants required to submit FAFSA. *Faculty research:* Sustainability. *Unit head:* Dr. Thelma Lazo-Flores, Director, 412-365-2977, E-mail: tlazoflores@chatham.edu. *Application contact:* Ashlee Bartko, Senior Assistant Director of Graduate Admission, 412-365-1115, Fax: 412-365-1609, E-mail: gradadmissions@chatham.edu.
Website: http://www.chatham.edu/departments/artdesign/graduate/MIA/index.cfm

Cornell University, Graduate School, Graduate Fields of Human Ecology, Field of Design and Environmental Analysis, Ithaca, NY 14853. Offers applied research in human-environment relations (MS); facilities planning and management (MS); housing and design (MS); human factors and ergonomics (MS); human-environment relations (MS); interior design (MA, MPS). *Degree requirements:* For master's, thesis. *Entrance requirements:* For master's, GRE General Test, portfolio or slides of recent work; bachelor's degree in interior design, architecture or related design discipline; 2 letters of recommendation. Additional exam requirements/recommendations for international students: Required—TOEFL (minimum score 600 paper-based; 105 iBT). Electronic applications accepted. *Faculty research:* Facility planning and management, environmental psychology, housing, interior design, ergonomics and human factors.

Drexel University, Antoinette Westphal College of Media Arts and Design, Program in Interior Architecture and Design, Philadelphia, PA 19104-2875. Offers MS. *Accreditation:* CIDA; NASAD. *Degree requirements:* For master's, comprehensive exam, thesis, graduate review. *Entrance requirements:* For master's, interview. Additional exam requirements/recommendations for international students: Required—TOEFL. Electronic applications accepted. *Faculty research:* History of commercial interiors, hospice spaces, environmental sculpture, painting.

Eastern Michigan University, Graduate School, College of Technology, School of Visual and Built Environments, Program in Interior Design, Ypsilanti, MI 48197. Offers MS. Part-time and evening/weekend programs available. Postbaccalaureate distance learning degree programs offered (minimal on-campus study). *Students:* 8 full-time (all women), 9 part-time (6 women); includes 1 minority (Black or African American, non-Hispanic/Latino), 8 international. Average age 32. 14 applicants, 71% accepted, 4 enrolled. In 2014, 7 master's awarded. *Entrance requirements:* Additional exam requirements/recommendations for international students: Required—TOEFL.

Application deadline: Applications are processed on a rolling basis. Application fee: $45. *Financial support:* Fellowships, research assistantships with full tuition reimbursements, teaching assistantships with full tuition reimbursements, career-related internships or fieldwork, Federal Work-Study, institutionally sponsored loans, scholarships/grants, tuition waivers (partial), and unspecified assistantships available. Support available to part-time students. Financial award applicants required to submit FAFSA. *Application contact:* Dr. Shinming Shyu, Graduate Program Coordinator, 734-487-2040, Fax: 734-487-8755, E-mail: sshyu@emich.edu.

Endicott College, Van Loan School of Graduate and Professional Studies, Program in Interior Architecture, Beverly, MA 01915-2096. Offers MA, MFA. *Accreditation:* NASAD. Part-time programs available. *Faculty:* 3 full-time (1 woman), 6 part-time/adjunct (4 women). *Students:* 10 full-time (9 women), 2 part-time (both women), 1 international. Average age 29. 14 applicants, 86% accepted, 4 enrolled. In 2014, 8 master's awarded. *Degree requirements:* For master's, thesis. *Entrance requirements:* For master's, statement of professional goals, two letters of recommendation, interview, A design portfolio is required for Post-Professional degree applicants. A design portfolio is optional for First-Professional degree applications. Undergraduate Transcript. Additional exam requirements/recommendations for international students: Required—TOEFL (minimum score 550 paper-based; 79 iBT). *Application deadline:* Applications are processed on a rolling basis. Application fee: $50. Electronic applications accepted. *Financial support:* Applicants required to submit FAFSA. *Faculty research:* Community outreach design studio, interior design practice. *Unit head:* Myoung Joo Chun, Director of Graduate Interior Design Programs, 978-232-2545, Fax: 978-232-3000, E-mail: mchun@endicott.edu. *Application contact:* Ian Menchini, Director, Graduate Enrollment and Advising, 978-232-5292, Fax: 978-232-3000, E-mail: imenchin@endicott.edu.
Website: http://www.endicott.edu/VanLoan/Graduate-Studies/Interior-Architecture.aspx

 Fashion Institute of Technology, School of Graduate Studies, Program in Sustainable Interior Environments, New York, NY 10001-5992. Offers MA.

See Display below and Close-Up on page 101.

Florida International University, College of Architecture and the Arts, School of Architecture, Department of Interior Architecture, Miami, FL 33199. Offers MA, MIA, Certificate. *Accreditation:* CIDA. *Entrance requirements:* For master's, GRE or minimum GPA of 3.0 in upper-level undergraduate work, portfolio. Additional exam requirements/recommendations for international students: Required—TOEFL (minimum score 550 paper-based; 80 iBT). Electronic applications accepted.

Florida State University, The Graduate School, College of Fine Arts, Department of Interior Design, Tallahassee, FL 32306-1231. Offers MFA, MS. *Accreditation:* NASAD (one or more programs are accredited). Part-time programs available. *Faculty:* 8 full-time (6 women), 2 part-time/adjunct (both women). *Students:* 33 full-time (26 women), 2 part-time (both women); includes 7 minority (2 Asian, non-Hispanic/Latino; 5 Hispanic/Latino). Average age 27. 49 applicants, 43% accepted, 19 enrolled. In 2014, 12 master's awarded. *Degree requirements:* For master's, thesis or alternative. *Entrance requirements:* For master's, GRE General Test, minimum GPA of 3.0 during previous 2 years. Additional exam requirements/recommendations for international students: Required—TOEFL (minimum score 550 paper-based; 80 iBT). *Application deadline:* For fall admission, 5/1 for domestic and international students; for spring admission, 11/1 for domestic and international students; for summer admission, 3/1 for domestic and international students. Applications are processed on a rolling basis. Application fee: $30. Electronic applications accepted. *Expenses:* Tuition, state resident: part-time $403.51 per credit hour. Tuition, nonresident: part-time $1004.85 per credit hour. *Required fees:* $75.81 per credit hour. One-time fee: $20 part-time. Tuition and fees vary according to campus/location. *Financial support:* In 2014–15, 13 teaching

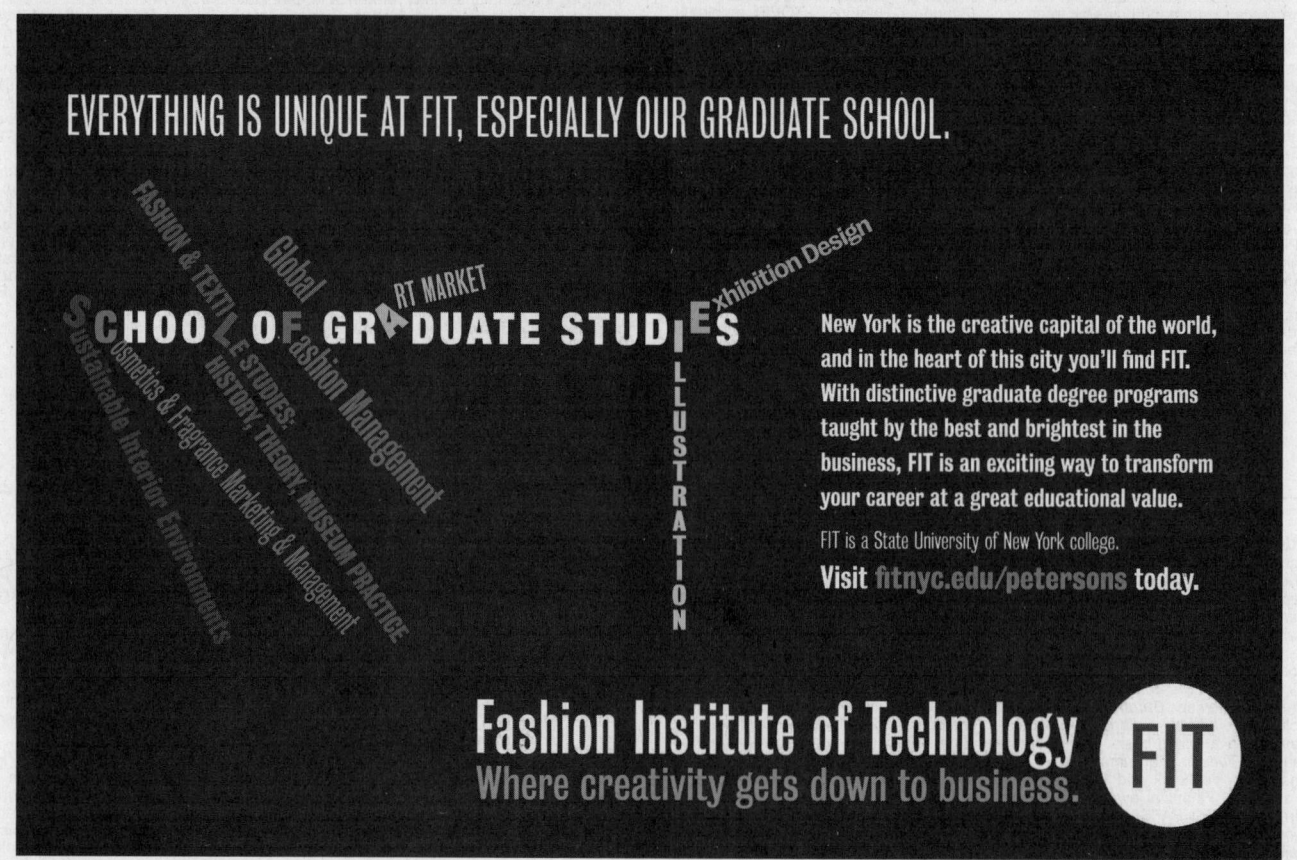

assistantships with tuition reimbursements (averaging $5,000 per year) were awarded; career-related internships or fieldwork and unspecified assistantships also available. Financial award applicants required to submit FAFSA. *Faculty research:* Social responsibility issues, graphics techniques, history of interiors, computer-aided design and drafting, pedagogy. *Unit head:* Dr. Lisa K. Waxman, Chairman, 850-644-8326, Fax: 850-644-3112, E-mail: lwaxman@fsu.edu. *Application contact:* Dr. Jill Pable, Director of Graduate Studies, 850-645-6831, Fax: 850-644-3112, E-mail: jpable@fsu.edu.
Website: http://interiordesign.fsu.edu/

The George Washington University, Columbian College of Arts and Sciences, Corcoran School of the Arts and Design, Washington, DC 20007. Offers art and the book (MA); art education (MA, MAT); exhibition design (MA); interior design (MA); new media photojournalism (MA). *Accreditation:* NASAD. Part-time programs available. *Entrance requirements:* Additional exam requirements/recommendations for international students: Required—TOEFL (minimum score 95 iBT).

The George Washington University, Columbian College of Arts and Sciences, Department of Fine Arts and Art History, Program in Interior Design, Washington, DC 20052. Offers MA, MFA. *Faculty:* 2 full-time (both women). *Students:* 78 full-time (71 women), 43 part-time (41 women); includes 26 minority (15 Black or African American, non-Hispanic/Latino; 4 Asian, non-Hispanic/Latino; 6 Hispanic/Latino; 1 Two or more races, non-Hispanic/Latino), 22 international. Average age 32. 31 applicants, 77% accepted, 10 enrolled. In 2014, 10 master's awarded. *Entrance requirements:* Additional exam requirements/recommendations for international students: Required—TOEFL (minimum score 550 paper-based; 80 iBT). *Application deadline:* For fall admission, 3/1 for domestic students, 1/15 for international students; for spring admission, 10/1 for domestic students, 9/1 for international students. *Financial support:* Application deadline: 1/15. *Unit head:* Stephanie Travis, Chair, E-mail: stravis@gwu.edu. *Application contact:* Information Contact, 202-994-6085, Fax: 202-994-8657, E-mail: art@gwu.edu.

Georgia State University, College of Arts and Sciences, Ernest G. Welch School of Art and Design, Program in Studio Art, Atlanta, GA 30302-3083. Offers ceramics (MFA); drawing and painting (MFA); graphic design (MFA); interior design (MFA); photography (MFA); printmaking (MFA); sculpture (MFA); textiles (MFA). *Accreditation:* NASAD. *Degree requirements:* For master's, thesis. *Application deadline:* For fall admission, 1/6 for domestic and international students; for spring admission, 1/15 priority date for domestic and international students. Application fee: $50. Electronic applications accepted. *Expenses:* Tuition, state resident: full-time $6516; part-time $362 per credit hour. Tuition, nonresident: full-time $22,014; part-time $1223 per credit hour. *Required fees:* $2128 per semester. Tuition and fees vary according to course load and program. *Financial support:* In 2014–15, fellowships with full tuition reimbursements (averaging $11,000 per year), teaching assistantships with full tuition reimbursements (averaging $7,000 per year) were awarded; research assistantships, scholarships/grants, and unspecified assistantships also available. Financial award application deadline: 4/15. *Faculty research:* Advertising and typography, new media, traditional media, three-dimensional art, architectural and environmental design. *Unit head:* Michael White, Director, Welch School of Art and Design, 404-413-5221, Fax: 404-413-5261, E-mail: mwhite@gsu.edu. *Application contact:* Hubert Stanley Anderson, Director of Graduate Studies, 404-413-5229, Fax: 404-413-5261, E-mail: artgrad@gsu.edu.
Website: http://artdesign.gsu.edu/graduate/admissions/masters-of-fine-arts-in-studio/

Interior Designers Institute, Graduate Program, Newport Beach, CA 92660. Offers MA.

Iowa State University of Science and Technology, Program in Interior Design, Ames, IA 50011. Offers MFA. *Accreditation:* NASAD. *Entrance requirements:* For master's, GRE. Additional exam requirements/recommendations for international students: Required—TOEFL (minimum score 550 paper-based; 79 iBT), IELTS (minimum score 6.5). Electronic applications accepted.

Lawrence Technological University, College of Architecture and Design, Southfield, MI 48075-1058. Offers architecture (M Arch); urban design (MUD). *Accreditation:* NASAD. Part-time and evening/weekend programs available. *Faculty:* 15 full-time (3 women), 30 part-time/adjunct (10 women). *Students:* 13 full-time (8 women), 208 part-time (84 women); includes 49 minority (6 Black or African American, non-Hispanic/Latino; 1 American Indian or Alaska Native, non-Hispanic/Latino; 26 Asian, non-Hispanic/Latino; 11 Hispanic/Latino; 5 Two or more races, non-Hispanic/Latino), 14 international. Average age 30. 139 applicants, 46% accepted, 43 enrolled. In 2014, 91 master's awarded. *Degree requirements:* For master's, thesis. *Entrance requirements:* Additional exam requirements/recommendations for international students: Required—TOEFL (minimum score 550 paper-based; 79 iBT). *Application deadline:* For fall admission, 5/15 priority date for domestic students, 5/29 for international students; for spring admission, 9/15 priority date for domestic students, 10/15 for international students; for summer admission, 2/15 for domestic students. Applications are processed on a rolling basis. Application fee: $50. Electronic applications accepted. *Expenses: Tuition:* Full-time $14,700; part-time $1050 per credit hour. *Required fees:* $150. One-time fee: $150 part-time. *Financial support:* In 2014–15, 66 students received support, including 5 research assistantships (averaging $6,090 per year); Federal Work-Study also available. Financial award application deadline: 4/1; financial award applicants required to submit FAFSA. *Unit head:* Glen LeRoy, Dean, 248-204-2800, Fax: 248-204-2900, E-mail: archdean@ltu.edu. *Application contact:* Jane Rohrback, Director of Admissions, 248-204-3160, Fax: 248-204-2228, E-mail: admissions@ltu.edu.
Website: http://www.ltu.edu/architecture_and_design/index.asp

Marymount University, School of Arts and Sciences, Program in Interior Design, Arlington, VA 22207-4299. Offers MA. *Accreditation:* CIDA. Part-time and evening/weekend programs available. *Faculty:* 4 full-time (all women), 3 part-time/adjunct (1 woman). *Students:* 20 full-time (18 women), 11 part-time (all women); includes 6 minority (2 Black or African American, non-Hispanic/Latino; 1 Asian, non-Hispanic/Latino; 3 Hispanic/Latino), 5 international. Average age 31. 20 applicants, 95% accepted, 16 enrolled. In 2014, 8 master's awarded. *Degree requirements:* For master's, thesis or alternative. *Entrance requirements:* For master's, 2 letters of recommendation, interview, resume, personal statement, portfolio. Additional exam requirements/recommendations for international students: Required—TOEFL (minimum score 600 paper-based; 96 iBT), IELTS (minimum score 6.5). *Application deadline:* For fall admission, 7/15 priority date for domestic students, 7/1 for international students; for spring admission, 11/15 priority date for domestic students, 10/15 for international students; for summer admission, 4/15 priority date for domestic students. Applications are processed on a rolling basis. Application fee: $40. Electronic applications accepted. *Expenses: Tuition:* Part-time $885 per credit. *Required fees:* $10 per credit. One-time fee: $220 part-time. Tuition and fees vary according to program. *Financial support:* In 2014–15, 11 students received support, including 3 research assistantships with full and partial tuition reimbursements available; career-related internships or fieldwork, Federal Work-Study, scholarships/grants, and unspecified assistantships also available. Support available to part-time students. Financial award applicants required to submit FAFSA. *Unit head:* Douglas R. Seidler, Chair, 703-284-1671, Fax: 703-284-3859, E-mail: bridget.may@marymount.edu. *Application contact:* Francesca Reed, Director, Graduate Admissions, 703-284-5901, Fax: 703-527-3815, E-mail: grad.admissions@marymount.edu.
Website: http://www.marymount.edu/Academics/School-of-Arts-Sciences/Graduate-Programs/Interior-Design-MA

Marywood University, Academic Affairs, School of Architecture, Program in Interior Architecture/Design, Scranton, PA 18509-1598. Offers MA. *Students:* 6 full-time (5 women), 2 international. Average age 23. In 2014, 9 master's awarded. *Degree requirements:* For master's, thesis. *Entrance requirements:* For master's, resume, personal essay, portfolio. Application fee: $35. *Expenses: Tuition:* Part-time $775 per credit. *Required fees:* $688 per semester. Tuition and fees vary according to degree level and campus/location. *Financial support:* Application deadline: 6/30; applicants required to submit FAFSA. *Unit head:* Gregory K. Hunt, Dean, 570-348-6211 Ext. 4536, E-mail: gkhunt@marywood.edu. *Application contact:* Tammy Manka, Assistant Director of Graduate Admissions, 866-279-9663, E-mail: tmanka@marywood.edu.
Website: http://www.marywood.edu/architecture/programs/m-iarc/

Michigan State University, The Graduate School, College of Agriculture and Natural Resources and College of Social Science, School of Planning, Design and Construction, East Lansing, MI 48824. Offers construction management (MS, PhD); environmental design (MA); interior design and facilities management (MA); international planning studies (MIPS); urban and regional planning (MURP). *Degree requirements:* For master's, thesis or alternative. *Entrance requirements:* Additional exam requirements/recommendations for international students: Required—TOEFL. Electronic applications accepted.

Moore College of Art & Design, Program in Interior Design, Philadelphia, PA 19103. Offers MFA. *Accreditation:* NASAD. Evening/weekend programs available. *Faculty:* 1 full-time (0 women). *Degree requirements:* For master's, thesis, internship, thesis exhibition. *Entrance requirements:* For master's, minimum GPA of 3.0, on-site interview, portfolio, 3 letters of recommendation, resume. *Expenses: Tuition:* Full-time $31,584; part-time $1504 per credit. *Unit head:* Dr. Mark Karlen, Graduate Program Manager, 215-965-4030, E-mail: mkarlen@moore.edu.

Mount Ida College, Program in Interior Design, Newton, MA 02459-3310. Offers MSM. Part-time and evening/weekend programs available. Postbaccalaureate distance learning degree programs offered (minimal on-campus study). *Entrance requirements:* For master's, portfolio. Additional exam requirements/recommendations for international students: Required—TOEFL (minimum score 550 paper-based; 79 iBT); Recommended—IELTS (minimum score 5.5). Electronic applications accepted.

The New School, Parsons The New School for Design, Program in Interior Design, New York, NY 10011. Offers MFA. *Degree requirements:* For master's, thesis. *Entrance requirements:* For master's, portfolio. Additional exam requirements/recommendations for international students: Required—TOEFL (minimum score 580 paper-based; 92 iBT). Electronic applications accepted.

The New School, Parsons The New School for Design, Program in Lighting Design, New York, NY 10011. Offers MFA. *Accreditation:* NASAD. *Degree requirements:* For master's, thesis. *Entrance requirements:* For master's, portfolio. Additional exam requirements/recommendations for international students: Required—TOEFL (minimum score 580 paper-based; 92 iBT). Electronic applications accepted.

New York School of Interior Design, Program in Healthcare Interior Design, New York, NY 10021-5110. Offers MPS. *Entrance requirements:* For master's, portfolio, resume, undergraduate degree in interior design or closely-related field. Additional exam requirements/recommendations for international students: Required—TOEFL (minimum score 550 paper-based; 79 iBT). Electronic applications accepted.

New York School of Interior Design, Program in Interior Design (Post-Professional Level), New York, NY 10021-5110. Offers MFA. *Degree requirements:* For master's, thesis. *Entrance requirements:* For master's, portfolio, resume, undergraduate degree in interior design or closely-related field. Additional exam requirements/recommendations for international students: Required—TOEFL (minimum score 550 paper-based; 79 iBT). Electronic applications accepted.

New York School of Interior Design, Program in Interior Design (Professional-Level), New York, NY 10021-5110. Offers MFA. *Accreditation:* CIDA; NASAD. *Degree requirements:* For master's, thesis. *Entrance requirements:* For master's, portfolio, resume, undergraduate degree in interior design or closely-related field. Additional exam requirements/recommendations for international students: Required—TOEFL (minimum score 550 paper-based; 79 iBT). Electronic applications accepted. *Faculty research:* History, theory, aesthetics, sociology, and green design; landscape, lighting, furniture, product, and set design.

The Ohio State University, Graduate School, College of Arts and Sciences, Division of Arts and Humanities, Department of Design, Columbus, OH 43210. Offers design (MA); design research and development (MFA); digital animation and interactive media (MFA). *Accreditation:* NASAD. Part-time programs available. *Faculty:* 16. *Students:* 20 full-time (11 women), 3 part-time (2 women); includes 6 minority (2 Black or African American, non-Hispanic/Latino; 3 Asian, non-Hispanic/Latino; 1 Hispanic/Latino), 8 international. Average age 29. In 2014, 6 master's awarded. *Degree requirements:* For master's, project or thesis. *Entrance requirements:* For master's, GRE General Test (for all applicants with cumulative GPA below 3.0), portfolio. Additional exam requirements/recommendations for international students: Recommended—TOEFL (minimum score 550 paper-based; 79 iBT). *Application deadline:* For fall admission, 12/13 priority date for domestic students, 11/30 priority date for international students; for winter admission, 12/1 for domestic students, 11/1 for international students; for spring admission, 3/1 for domestic students, 2/1 for international students. Applications are processed on a rolling basis. Application fee: $60 ($70 for international students). Electronic applications accepted. *Financial support:* Fellowships with tuition reimbursements, research assistantships with tuition reimbursements, teaching assistantships with tuition reimbursements, career-related internships or fieldwork, Federal Work-Study, institutionally sponsored loans, and unspecified assistantships available. Support available to part-time students. Financial award application deadline: 5/1. *Unit head:* Mary Anne Beecher, PhD, Chair, 614-688-6746, E-mail: beecher.17@osu.edu. *Application contact:* Graduate and Professional Admissions, 614-292-9444, Fax: 614-292-3895, E-mail: gpadmissions@osu.edu.
Website: http://design.osu.edu/

Philadelphia University, College of Architecture and the Built Environment, Program in Interior Architecture, Philadelphia, PA 19144. Offers MS.

Pontificia Universidad Catolica Madre y Maestra, Graduate School, Faculty of Sciences and Humanities, Santiago, Dominican Republic. Offers architecture (M Arch), including architecture of interiors, architecture of tourist lodgings, landscaping; early childhood education (M Ed).

Pratt Institute, School of Design, Program in Interior Design, Brooklyn, NY 11205-3899. Offers MS. *Accreditation:* NASAD. Part-time programs available. *Faculty:* 3 full-time (2 women), 62 part-time/adjunct (29 women). *Students:* 138 full-time (121 women), 8 part-time (6 women); includes 24 minority (7 Black or African American, non-Hispanic/Latino; 11 Asian, non-Hispanic/Latino; 5 Hispanic/Latino; 1 Native Hawaiian or other Pacific Islander, non-Hispanic/Latino), 64 international. Average age 27. 256 applicants, 56% accepted, 52 enrolled. In 2014, 43 master's awarded. *Degree requirements:* For master's, thesis. *Entrance requirements:* For master's, portfolio, letters of

recommendation. Additional exam requirements/recommendations for international students: Required—TOEFL (minimum score 575 paper-based; 90 iBT). *Application deadline:* For fall admission, 1/5 for domestic and international students; for spring admission, 10/1 for domestic and international students. Application fee: $50 ($90 for international students). Electronic applications accepted. *Financial support:* Career-related internships or fieldwork, Federal Work-Study, institutionally sponsored loans, scholarships/grants, health care benefits, and unspecified assistantships available. Support available to part-time students. Financial award application deadline: 2/1; financial award applicants required to submit FAFSA. *Unit head:* Karin Tehve, Chairperson of Interior Design, 718-636-3630, E-mail: ktehve@pratt.edu. *Application contact:* Young Hah, Director of Graduate Admissions, 718-636-3683, Fax: 718-636-3670, E-mail: yhah@pratt.edu.
Website: https://www.pratt.edu/academics/school-of-design/graduate-school-of-design/interior-design-grad/

See Display on page 65 and Close-Up on page 103.

Rhode Island School of Design, Graduate Studies, Division of Architecture and Design, Department of Interior Architecture, Providence, RI 02903-2784. Offers M Des, MA. *Faculty:* 9 full-time (4 women), 21 part-time/adjunct (9 women). *Students:* 61 full-time (49 women); includes 2 minority (1 Black or African American, non-Hispanic/Latino; 1 Hispanic/Latino), 44 international. Average age 24. 106 applicants, 64% accepted, 34 enrolled. In 2014, 38 master's awarded. *Degree requirements:* For master's, thesis, exhibit. *Entrance requirements:* For master's, portfolio, statement of purpose, 3 letters of recommendation. Additional exam requirements/recommendations for international students: Required—TOEFL (minimum score 580 paper-based; 93 iBT). *Application deadline:* For fall admission, 2/1 for domestic and international students. Application fee: $60. *Expenses:* Expenses: $44,594. *Financial support:* Fellowships, teaching assistantships, career-related internships or fieldwork, Federal Work-Study, institutionally sponsored loans, scholarships/grants, and unspecified assistantships available. Financial award application deadline: 2/15; financial award applicants required to submit FAFSA. *Unit head:* Liliane Wong, Head, 401-454-6274, Fax: 401-277-4962, E-mail: lwong@risd.edu. *Application contact:* Molly Pettengil, Graduate Admissions Officer, 401-454-6312, Fax: 401-454-6309, E-mail: mpetteng@risd.edu.
Website: http://www.risd.edu/academics/interior-architecture/

San Diego State University, Graduate and Research Affairs, College of Professional Studies and Fine Arts, School of Art, Design and Art History, San Diego, CA 92182. Offers art history (MA); studio arts (MA, MFA), including applied design, environmental design, graphic design, interior design, painting and printmaking, sculpture. *Accreditation:* NASAD (one or more programs are accredited). *Degree requirements:* For master's, variable foreign language requirement, thesis. *Entrance requirements:* For master's, GRE General Test, bachelor's degree in related field, slide portfolio, typed slide information sheet, 2 letters of recommendation. Additional exam requirements/recommendations for international students: Required—TOEFL. Electronic applications accepted.

Savannah College of Art and Design, Graduate School, Program in Interior Design, Savannah, GA 31402-3146. Offers MA, MFA. Part-time programs available. Postbaccalaureate distance learning degree programs offered (no on-campus study). *Faculty:* 17 full-time (12 women), 3 part-time/adjunct (2 women). *Students:* 61 full-time (47 women), 21 part-time (19 women); includes 12 minority (6 Black or African American, non-Hispanic/Latino; 1 American Indian or Alaska Native, non-Hispanic/Latino; 3 Asian, non-Hispanic/Latino; 2 Hispanic/Latino), 52 international. Average age 28. 139 applicants, 32% accepted, 22 enrolled. In 2014, 31 master's awarded. *Degree requirements:* For master's, thesis (for some programs), final project (for MA); internship (for MFA). *Entrance requirements:* For master's, portfolio (for MFA applicants); research paper (for MA applicants). Additional exam requirements/recommendations for international students: Required—TOEFL (minimum score 550 paper-based, 85 iBT), IELTS (minimum score 6.5), or ACTFL. *Application deadline:* For fall admission, 4/1 for domestic and international students. Applications are processed on a rolling basis. Application fee: $40. Electronic applications accepted. *Expenses: Tuition:* Full-time $34,605; part-time $3845 per course. One-time fee: $500. Tuition and fees vary according to course load. *Financial support:* Fellowships, career-related internships or fieldwork, Federal Work-Study, and scholarships/grants available. Financial award application deadline: 4/1; financial award applicants required to submit FAFSA. *Unit head:* Khoi Vo, Chair. *Application contact:* Jenny Jaquillard, Executive Director of Admissions, Recruitment and Events, 912-525-5100, Fax: 912-525-5985, E-mail: admission@scad.edu.
Website: http://www.scad.edu/academics/programs/interior-design

School of the Art Institute of Chicago, Graduate Division, Department of Architecture, Interior Architecture, and Designed Objects, Chicago, IL 60603-3103. Offers architecture (M Arc); design for emerging technologies (MFA); designed objects (M Des); interior architecture (M Arc). *Entrance requirements:* Additional exam requirements/recommendations for international students: Required—TOEFL, IELTS.

South Dakota State University, Graduate School, College of Education and Human Sciences, Department of Apparel Merchandising and Interior Design, Brookings, SD 57007. Offers MFCS. Part-time and evening/weekend programs available. Postbaccalaureate distance learning degree programs offered. *Entrance requirements:* Additional exam requirements/recommendations for international students: Required—TOEFL (minimum score 550 paper-based; 79 iBT). *Faculty research:* Rural internet shopping, professional development in apparel merchandising, gender, aesthetics.

Suffolk University, New England School of Art and Design, Boston, MA 02108-2770. Offers graphic design (MA); interior architecture (MA, MFA). *Accreditation:* NASAD. Part-time and evening/weekend programs available. *Faculty:* 13 full-time (9 women), 22 part-time/adjunct (10 women). *Students:* 60 full-time (50 women), 47 part-time (44 women); includes 10 minority (3 Black or African American, non-Hispanic/Latino; 6 Asian, non-Hispanic/Latino; 1 Hispanic/Latino), 42 international. Average age 28. 112 applicants, 60% accepted, 13 enrolled. In 2014, 31 master's awarded. *Entrance requirements:* For master's, GRE (for MFA), art portfolio, interview, 2 letters of recommendation, resume; letter of intent (for MFA). Additional exam requirements/recommendations for international students: Required—TOEFL (minimum score 550 paper-based; 80 iBT). *Application deadline:* For fall admission, 6/15 priority date for domestic students, 6/15 for international students; for spring admission, 11/1 priority date for domestic students, 11/1 for international students. Applications are processed on a rolling basis. Application fee: $50. Electronic applications accepted. *Expenses:* Expenses: Contact institution. *Financial support:* In 2014–15, 72 students received support, including 69 fellowships (averaging $6,358 per year). Financial award application deadline: 4/1; financial award applicants required to submit FAFSA. *Faculty research:* Sustainable design, lighting and technology, design education, environmental graphic design, designing for the non-profit sector. *Unit head:* Audrey Goldstein, Department Chair, 617-997-4290, E-mail: agoldstein@suffolk.edu. *Application contact:* Cory Meyers, Director of Graduate Admissions, 617-573-8302, Fax: 617-305-1733, E-mail: grad.admission@suffolk.edu.
Website: http://www.suffolk.edu/nesad/

Texas Tech University, Graduate School, College of Human Sciences, Department of Design, Lubbock, TX 79409-1220. Offers environmental design (MS); interior and environmental design (PhD). Part-time programs available. *Faculty:* 10 full-time (8 women), 2 part-time/adjunct (both women). *Students:* 27 full-time (21 women), 9 part-time (6 women); includes 6 minority (1 Asian, non-Hispanic/Latino; 5 Hispanic/Latino), 19 international. Average age 31. 24 applicants, 50% accepted, 5 enrolled. In 2014, 10 master's, 2 doctorates awarded. *Degree requirements:* For master's, comprehensive exam, thesis or alternative; for doctorate, thesis/dissertation. *Entrance requirements:* For master's and doctorate, GRE, 3 recommendation letters, design portfolio, 500-word written statement (reason for pursuing degree), resume. Additional exam requirements/recommendations for international students: Required—TOEFL (minimum score 550 paper-based; 79 iBT). *Application deadline:* For fall admission, 6/1 priority date for domestic students, 1/15 priority date for international students; for spring admission, 9/1 priority date for domestic students, 6/15 priority date for international students. Applications are processed on a rolling basis. Application fee: $60. Electronic applications accepted. *Expenses:* Tuition, state resident: full-time $6310; part-time $262.92 per credit hour. Tuition, nonresident: full-time $14,998; part-time $624.92 per credit hour. *Required fees:* $2701; $36.50 per credit. $912.50 per semester. Tuition and fees vary according to course load. *Financial support:* In 2014–15, 22 students received support, including 21 fellowships (averaging $4,293 per year), 3 research assistantships (averaging $14,124 per year), 3 teaching assistantships (averaging $14,833 per year); scholarships/grants and unspecified assistantships also available. Financial award application deadline: 4/15; financial award applicants required to submit FAFSA. *Faculty research:* Healthcare and the built environment, sustainability, vulnerable populations, historic preservation, evidence-based design. *Total annual research expenditures:* $139,399. *Unit head:* Dr. Sharran F. Parkinson, Chair, 806-742-3031, Fax: 806-742-1639, E-mail: sharran.parkinson@ttu.edu. *Application contact:* Dr. Kristi Gaines, Graduate Programs Director, 806-742-3050, Fax: 806-742-1639, E-mail: kristi.gaines@ttu.edu.
Website: http://www.depts.ttu.edu/hs/dod/

University of California, Berkeley, UC Berkeley Extension, Certificate Programs in Art and Design, Berkeley, CA 94720-1500. Offers interior design and interior architecture (Certificate); landscape architecture (Certificate); visual arts (Postbaccalaureate Certificate).

University of Cincinnati, Graduate School, College of Design, Architecture, Art, and Planning, School of Architecture and Interior Design, Cincinnati, OH 45221. Offers architecture (M Arch). *Accreditation:* NASAD. *Degree requirements:* For master's, one foreign language, thesis. *Entrance requirements:* Additional exam requirements/recommendations for international students: Required—TOEFL. *Faculty research:* Theory and history of architecture.

University of Florida, Graduate School, College of Design, Construction and Planning, Department of Interior Design, Gainesville, FL 32611-5704. Offers historic preservation (MID); interior design (MID); sustainable design (MID). *Faculty:* 6 full-time (4 women). *Students:* 8 full-time (all women), 1 (woman) part-time; includes 2 minority (both Hispanic/Latino), 2 international. 7 applicants, 14% accepted. In 2014, 4 master's awarded. *Degree requirements:* For master's, thesis. *Entrance requirements:* For master's, GRE General Test, minimum GPA of 3.0. Additional exam requirements/recommendations for international students: Required—TOEFL (minimum score 550 paper-based; 80 iBT), IELTS (minimum score 6). *Application deadline:* For fall admission, 4/1 for domestic students, 2/1 for international students. Application fee: $30. *Financial support:* In 2014–15, 2 research assistantships, 2 teaching assistantships were awarded; fellowships also available. Financial award applicants required to submit FAFSA. *Faculty research:* Sustainable design and environmentally significant behaviors; design innovation, creativity, methods and pedagogy; lighting and color design and perception; historic preservation; design for special populations. *Unit head:* Margaret Portillo, PhD, Professor and Chair, 352-392-0252 Ext. 333, Fax: 352-392-7266, E-mail: mportill@ufl.edu. *Application contact:* Nam-Kyu Park, PhD, Assistant Professor and Graduate Coordinator, 352-392-0252 Ext. 338, Fax: 352-392-7266, E-mail: npark@ufl.edu.
Website: http://www.dcp.ufl.edu/interior

University of Florida, Graduate School, College of Design, Construction and Planning, Doctoral Program in Design, Construction and Planning, Gainesville, FL 32611. Offers construction management (PhD); design, construction and planning (PhD); geographic information systems (PhD); historic preservation (PhD); interior design (PhD); landscape architecture (PhD); urban and regional planning (PhD). *Students:* 79 full-time (32 women), 21 part-time (7 women); includes 12 minority (4 Black or African American, non-Hispanic/Latino; 1 American Indian or Alaska Native, non-Hispanic/Latino; 4 Asian, non-Hispanic/Latino; 3 Hispanic/Latino), 51 international. 92 applicants, 25% accepted, 14 enrolled. In 2014, 18 doctorates awarded. *Degree requirements:* For doctorate, thesis/dissertation. *Entrance requirements:* For doctorate, GRE General Test, minimum GPA of 3.0. Additional exam requirements/recommendations for international students: Required—TOEFL (minimum score 550 paper-based; 80 iBT), IELTS (minimum score 6). *Application deadline:* For fall admission, 2/1 for domestic and international students. Applications are processed on a rolling basis. Application fee: $30. Electronic applications accepted. *Financial support:* In 2014–15, 3 fellowships, 26 research assistantships, 30 teaching assistantships were awarded; unspecified assistantships also available. Financial award applicants required to submit FAFSA. *Faculty research:* Architecture, building construction, urban and regional planning. *Unit head:* Zhong-Ren Peng, PhD, Professor/Director, 352-392-0997 Ext. 429, Fax: 352-392-3308, E-mail: zpeng@ufl.edu. *Application contact:* Zhong-Ren Peng, PhD, Professor/Director, 352-392-0997 Ext. 429, Fax: 352-392-3308, E-mail: zpeng@ufl.edu.
Website: http://www.dcp.ufl.edu/docprogram/

University of Georgia, College of Family and Consumer Sciences, Department of Textiles, Merchandising, and Interiors, Athens, GA 30602. Offers historical/cultural aspects of dress and textiles (MS); interior environments (MS); merchandising/international trade (MS); textile analysis (PhD); textile chemical processes (PhD); textile products and standards (PhD); textile science (MS). *Degree requirements:* For master's, thesis; for doctorate, thesis/dissertation. *Entrance requirements:* For master's and doctorate, GRE General Test. Electronic applications accepted.

University of Kentucky, Graduate School, College of Design, Program in Interior Design, Merchandising, and Textiles, Lexington, KY 40506-0032. Offers interior design (MA). *Degree requirements:* For master's, comprehensive exam, thesis optional. *Entrance requirements:* For master's, GRE General Test, minimum undergraduate GPA of 2.75. Additional exam requirements/recommendations for international students: Required—TOEFL (minimum score 550 paper-based). Electronic applications accepted. *Faculty research:* Interior design, apparel merchandising, textile evaluation, creativity in design, social-psychological aspects of dress and interiors.

University of Manitoba, Faculty of Graduate Studies, Faculty of Architecture, Department of Interior Design, Winnipeg, MB R3T 2N2, Canada. Offers MID. *Accreditation:* CIDA.

University of Massachusetts Amherst, Graduate School, College of Humanities and Fine Arts, Programs in Architecture and Design, Amherst, MA 01003. Offers architecture (M Arch); design (MS); design in historic preservation (MS). Part-time programs available. *Students:* 37 full-time (17 women); includes 2 minority (both Hispanic/Latino), 15 international. Average age 29. 105 applicants, 67% accepted, 11 enrolled. In 2014, 21 master's awarded. *Degree requirements:* For master's, thesis or alternative, project. *Entrance requirements:* For master's, GRE General Test (for M Arch only), 3 letters of recommendation (M Arch only); portfolio. Additional exam requirements/recommendations for international students: Required—TOEFL (minimum score 550 paper-based; 80 iBT), IELTS (minimum score 6.5). *Application deadline:* For fall admission, 2/1 for domestic and international students. Applications are processed on a rolling basis. Application fee: $75. Electronic applications accepted. *Expenses:* Tuition, state resident: full-time $1980; part-time $110 per credit. Tuition, nonresident: full-time $14,644; part-time $414 per credit. *Required fees:* $11,417. One-time fee: $357. *Financial support:* Fellowships with full and partial tuition reimbursements, research assistantships with full and partial tuition reimbursements, teaching assistantships with full and partial tuition reimbursements, career-related internships or fieldwork, Federal Work-Study, scholarships/grants, traineeships, health care benefits, tuition waivers (full and partial), and unspecified assistantships available. Support available to part-time students. Financial award application deadline: 2/1. *Unit head:* Dr. Kathleen Lugosch, Graduate Program Director, 413-577-0943, Fax: 413-545-3929. *Application contact:* Lindsay DeSantis, Supervisor of Admissions, 413-545-0722, Fax: 413-577-0100, E-mail: gradadm@grad.umass.edu.
Website: http://www.umass.edu/architecture/

University of Memphis, Graduate School, College of Communication and Fine Arts, Department of Art, Memphis, TN 38152. Offers art (Graduate Certificate); art history (MA), including Egyptian art and archaeology, general art history; ceramics (MFA); graphic design (MFA); interior design (MFA); painting (MFA); printmaking/photography (MFA). *Accreditation:* NASAD (one or more programs are accredited). *Faculty:* 19 full-time (7 women), 4 part-time/adjunct (2 women). *Students:* 34 full-time (28 women), 3 part-time (2 women); includes 5 minority (2 Asian, non-Hispanic/Latino; 2 Hispanic/Latino; 1 Two or more races, non-Hispanic/Latino). Average age 30. 24 applicants, 63% accepted, 10 enrolled. In 2014, 14 master's, 14 other advanced degrees awarded. *Degree requirements:* For master's, 2 foreign languages, comprehensive exam, thesis. *Entrance requirements:* For master's, GRE General Test or MAT, portfolio (MFA). *Application deadline:* For fall admission, 8/1 for domestic students; for spring admission, 12/1 for domestic students. Applications are processed on a rolling basis. Application fee: $35 ($60 for international students). *Financial support:* In 2014–15, 38 students received support. Research assistantships with full tuition reimbursements available, teaching assistantships with full tuition reimbursements available, Federal Work-Study, scholarships/grants, and unspecified assistantships available. Financial award application deadline: 2/15; financial award applicants required to submit FAFSA. *Faculty research:* Online collaborative learning, advanced art history studies, electronic publishing/design, studio arts, architectural studies. *Unit head:* Prof. Richard Lou, Chair, 901-678-2216, Fax: 901-678-2735, E-mail: gmyatt@memphis.edu. *Application contact:* Greely Myat, Graduate Studies Coordinator, 901-678-2650.
Website: http://memphis.edu/art/

University of Minnesota, Twin Cities Campus, Graduate School, College of Design, Department of Design, Housing, and Apparel, Minneapolis, MN 55455-0213. Offers apparel (MA, MS, PhD); design communication (MA, MS, PhD); housing studies (MA, MS, PhD, Postbaccalaureate Certificate); interactive design (MFA); interior design (MA, MS, PhD). Part-time programs available. *Degree requirements:* For master's and Postbaccalaureate Certificate, comprehensive exam, thesis (for some programs); for doctorate, comprehensive exam, thesis/dissertation. *Entrance requirements:* For master's, GRE General Test, minimum GPA of 3.0 (preferred), portfolio, 3 letters of recommendation; for doctorate, GRE General Test, minimum GPA of 3.0 (preferred), portfolio, 3 letters of recommendation, writing sample; for Postbaccalaureate Certificate, GRE General Test, minimum GPA of 3.0 (preferred). Additional exam requirements/recommendations for international students: Required—TOEFL (minimum score 550 paper-based; 79 iBT). Electronic applications accepted. *Faculty research:* Housing policy and community development; consumer behavior; interactive design; design history; social, cultural, and behavioral issues related to designed environments.

University of Nebraska–Lincoln, Graduate College, College of Architecture, Department of Architecture, Lincoln, NE 68588. Offers architecture (M Arch, MS, PhD); interior design (MS); M Arch/MBA; M Arch/MCRP. *Entrance requirements:* Additional exam requirements/recommendations for international students: Required—TOEFL. Electronic applications accepted.

The University of North Carolina at Greensboro, Graduate School, College of Arts and Sciences, Department of Interior Architecture, Greensboro, NC 27412-5001. Offers historic preservation (Certificate); interior architecture (MS); museum studies (Certificate). *Degree requirements:* For master's, thesis. *Entrance requirements:* For master's, GRE General Test or MAT, bachelor's degree in interior design, interview, portfolio. Additional exam requirements/recommendations for international students: Required—TOEFL. Electronic applications accepted.

University of North Texas, Robert B. Toulouse School of Graduate Studies, Denton, TX 76203-5459. Offers accounting (MS); applied anthropology (MA, MS); applied behavior analysis (Certificate); applied geography (MA); applied technology and performance improvement (M Ed, MS); art education (MA); art history (MA); art museum education (Certificate); arts leadership (Certificate); audiology (Au D); behavior analysis (MS); behavioral science (PhD); biochemistry and molecular biology (MS); biology (MA, MS); biomedical engineering (MS); business analysis (MS); chemistry (MS); clinical health psychology (PhD); communication studies (MA, MS); computer engineering (MS); computer science (MS); counseling (M Ed, MS), including clinical mental health counseling (MS), college and university counseling, elementary school counseling, secondary school counseling; creative writing (MA); criminal justice (MS); curriculum and instruction (M Ed); decision sciences (MBA); design (MA, MFA), including fashion design (MFA), innovation studies, interior design (MFA); early childhood studies (MS); economics (MS); educational leadership (M Ed, Ed D); educational psychology (MS, PhD), including family studies (MS), gifted and talented (MS), human development (MS), learning and cognition (MS), research, measurement and evaluation (MS); electrical engineering (MS); emergency management (MPA); engineering technology (MS); English (MA); English as a second language (MA); environmental science (MS); finance (MBA, MS); financial management (MPA); French (MA); health services management (MBA); higher education (M Ed, Ed D); history (MA, MS); hospitality management (MS); human resources management (MPA); information science (MS); information systems (PhD); information technologies (MBA); interdisciplinary studies (MA, MS); international studies (MA); international sustainable tourism (MS); jazz studies (MM); journalism (MA, MJ, Graduate Certificate), including interactive and virtual digital communication (Graduate Certificate), narrative journalism (Graduate Certificate), public relations (Graduate Certificate); kinesiology (MS); linguistics (MA); local government management (MPA); logistics (PhD); logistics and supply chain management (MBA); long-term care, senior housing, and aging services (MA); management (PhD); marketing (MBA); mathematics (MA, MS); mechanical and energy engineering (MS, PhD); music (MA), including ethnomusicology, music theory, musicology, performance; music composition (PhD); music education (MM Ed, PhD); nonprofit management (MPA); operations and supply chain management (MBA); performance (MM, DMA); philosophy (MA); political science (MA); professional and technical communication (MA); radio, television and film (MA, MFA); rehabilitation counseling (Certificate); sociology (MA); Spanish (MA); special education (M Ed); speech-language pathology (MA); strategic management (MBA); studio art (MFA); teaching (M Ed); MBA/MS. Part-time and evening/weekend programs available. Postbaccalaureate distance learning degree programs offered. *Faculty:* 651 full-time (215 women), 233 part-time/adjunct (139 women). *Students:* 3,040 full-time (1,598 women), 3,401 part-time (2,097 women); includes 1,740 minority (533 Black or African American, non-Hispanic/Latino; 15 American Indian or Alaska Native, non-Hispanic/Latino; 286 Asian, non-Hispanic/Latino; 746 Hispanic/Latino; 3 Native Hawaiian or other Pacific Islander, non-Hispanic/Latino; 157 Two or more races, non-Hispanic/Latino), 1,145 international. Terminal master's awarded for partial completion of doctoral program. *Degree requirements:* For master's, variable foreign language requirement, comprehensive exam (for some programs), thesis (for some programs); for doctorate, variable foreign language requirement, comprehensive exam (for some programs), thesis/dissertation; for other advanced degree, variable foreign language requirement, comprehensive exam (for some programs). *Entrance requirements:* For master's and doctorate, GRE, GMAT. Additional exam requirements/recommendations for international students: Required—TOEFL (minimum score 550 paper-based; 79 iBT). *Application deadline:* For fall admission, 7/15 for domestic students, 3/15 for international students; for spring admission, 11/15 for domestic students, 9/15 for international students; for summer admission, 5/1 for domestic students. Applications are processed on a rolling basis. Application fee: $60. Electronic applications accepted. *Expenses:* Tuition, state resident: full-time $5450; part-time $3633 per year. Tuition, nonresident: full-time $11,966; part-time $7977 per year. *Required fees:* $1301; $398 per credit hour. $685 per semester. Tuition and fees vary according to program and reciprocity agreements. *Financial support:* Fellowships with partial tuition reimbursements, research assistantships with partial tuition reimbursements, teaching assistantships, career-related internships or fieldwork, Federal Work-Study, institutionally sponsored loans, scholarships/grants, health care benefits, and library assistantships available. Support available to part-time students. Financial award applicants required to submit FAFSA. *Unit head:* Mark Wardell, Dean, 940-565-2383, E-mail: mark.wardell@unt.edu. *Application contact:* Toulouse School of Graduate Studies, 940-565-2383, Fax: 940-565-2141, E-mail: gradsch@unt.edu.
Website: http://tsgs.unt.edu/

University of Oklahoma, College of Architecture, Division of Interior Design, Norman, OK 73019. Offers architectural lighting (MID); design process management (MID); interior design (MID); sustainable living (MID). Part-time and evening/weekend programs available. *Students:* 2 full-time (both women), 1 international. Average age 26. 3 applicants, 67% accepted. In 2014, 3 master's awarded. *Degree requirements:* For master's, comprehensive exam, project or thesis. *Entrance requirements:* For master's, undergraduate degree in interior design or related field, portfolio of design work, letter of intent, three letters of recommendation. Additional exam requirements/recommendations for international students: Required—TOEFL (minimum score 79 iBT). *Application deadline:* For fall admission, 6/1 for domestic and international students; for spring admission, 10/15 for domestic and international students. Application fee: $50 ($100 for international students). Electronic applications accepted. *Expenses:* Tuition, state resident: full-time $4394; part-time $183.10 per credit hour. Tuition, nonresident: full-time $16,970; part-time $707.10 per credit hour. *Required fees:* $2892; $109.95 per credit hour. $126.50 per semester. *Financial support:* In 2014–15, 1 student received support, including 1 research assistantship (averaging $10,372 per year), 2 teaching assistantships with partial tuition reimbursements available (averaging $10,372 per year); career-related internships or fieldwork, scholarships/grants, and unspecified assistantships also available. Financial award application deadline: 6/1; financial award applicants required to submit FAFSA. *Faculty research:* Environmental and human behavior, indoor environmental quality, pedagogical exploration, building information modeling for cognitive spatial problem solving, community health and environmental design. *Unit head:* Mia Kile, Academic Director, 405-325-1051, Fax: 405-325-7558, E-mail: mkile@ou.edu. *Application contact:* Hans-Peter Wachter, Graduate Liaison and Associate Professor, 405-325-8780, Fax: 405-325-7558, E-mail: hepw@ou.edu.
Website: http://www.ou.edu/content/architecture/interior_design.html

University of Oregon, Graduate School, School of Architecture and Allied Arts, Department of Architecture, Eugene, OR 97403. Offers architecture (M Arch); interior architecture (MI Arch). *Accreditation:* CIDA. *Degree requirements:* For master's, thesis (for some programs). *Entrance requirements:* For master's, GRE General Test. Additional exam requirements/recommendations for international students: Required—TOEFL. *Faculty research:* Innovation in housing design and design production, climate responsive design, passive heating and cooling, computer software development for design applications, vernacular architecture.

The University of Texas at Austin, Graduate School, School of Architecture, Program in Interior Design, Austin, TX 78712-1111. Offers MID.

Utah State University, School of Graduate Studies, College of Humanities, Arts and Social Sciences, Program in Interior Design, Logan, UT 84322. Offers MS. Part-time programs available. Postbaccalaureate distance learning degree programs offered. *Entrance requirements:* For master's, GRE General Test, MAT, minimum GPA of 3.0. Additional exam requirements/recommendations for international students: Required—TOEFL.

Virginia Commonwealth University, Graduate School, School of the Arts, Department of Graphic Design, Richmond, VA 23284-9005. Offers design/visual communications (MFA); interior environment (MFA). *Accreditation:* NASAD. *Degree requirements:* For master's, thesis, exhibition. *Entrance requirements:* For master's, portfolio. Additional exam requirements/recommendations for international students: Required—TOEFL (minimum score 600 paper-based; 100 iBT). Electronic applications accepted. *Faculty research:* Conducting visual or theoretical research, and in investigating the intersection of function and expression in design problem solving.

Washington State University, College of Agricultural, Human, and Natural Resource Sciences, Program in Interior Design and Landscape Architecture, Pullman, WA 99164-2220. Offers MA, MS. Programs offered at the Pullman campus. Part-time programs available. *Faculty:* 13 full-time (0 women), 1 part-time/adjunct (0 women). *Students:* 9 full-time (8 women), 2 part-time (both women), 6 international. Average age 36. 32 applicants, 34% accepted, 3 enrolled. In 2014, 1 master's awarded. *Degree requirements:* For master's, comprehensive exam, thesis (for some programs), oral exam. *Entrance requirements:* For master's, portfolio. Additional exam requirements/recommendations for international students: Required—TOEFL or IELTS. *Application deadline:* For fall admission, 1/10 priority date for domestic and international students. Application fee: $75. Electronic applications accepted. *Expenses:* Tuition, state resident: full-time $11,768. Tuition, nonresident: full-time $25,200. *Required fees:* $960. Tuition and fees vary according to program. *Financial support:* In 2014–15, 1 student received support, including 5 teaching assistantships with partial tuition reimbursements available (averaging $7,308 per year); career-related internships or fieldwork, Federal

Work-Study, scholarships/grants, and unspecified assistantships also available. Financial award applicants required to submit FAFSA. *Faculty research:* Digital fabrication, design pedagogy, proportional systems, American architecture and urbanism, design leadership. *Unit head:* Prof. Matt Melcher, Program Coordinator, 509-335-1737, Fax: 509-335-6132, E-mail: melcher@wsu.edu. *Application contact:* Jaime L. Rice, Academic Coordinator, 509-335-5318, Fax: 509-335-6132, E-mail: jlrice@wsu.edu.
Website: http://sdc.wsu.edu

Wayne State University, College of Fine, Performing and Communication Arts, James Pearson Duffy Department of Art and Art History, Detroit, MI 48202. Offers art (MA, MFA), including ceramics, drawing, fibers, graphic design, industrial design (MA), interior design (MA), metalsmithing, painting, photography, printmaking, sculpture; art history (MA); design and merchandising (MA). *Students:* 14 full-time (10 women), 13 part-time (8 women); includes 4 minority (1 Black or African American, non-Hispanic/Latino; 1 Hispanic/Latino; 2 Two or more races, non-Hispanic/Latino), 1 international. Average age 34. 49 applicants, 18% accepted, 6 enrolled. In 2014, 15 master's awarded. *Degree requirements:* For master's, thesis (for some programs), essay or thesis. *Entrance requirements:* For master's, GRE (for fashion and design merchandising applicants), BFA or another degree and equivalent course work, portfolio, personal interview, reference letters, statement of intent (except for art history program). Additional exam requirements/recommendations for international students: Required—TOEFL (minimum score 550 paper-based; 79 iBT), TWE (minimum score 5.5), Michigan English Language Assessment Battery (minimum score 85); Recommended—IELTS (minimum score 6.5). *Application deadline:* For fall admission, 2/1 for domestic and international students; for winter admission, 10/1 for domestic and international students. Application fee: $0. Electronic applications accepted. *Expenses:* Expenses: Contact institution. *Financial support:* In 2014–15, 11 students received support, including 1 fellowship with tuition reimbursement available (averaging $16,000 per year), 5 teaching assistantships with tuition reimbursements available (averaging $16,540 per year); scholarships/grants and unspecified assistantships also available. Support available to part-time students. Financial award application deadline: 3/31; financial award applicants required to submit FAFSA. *Faculty research:* Integration of the human figure into urban and rural landscape in painting; performance art utilizing digital media and video; exploration of race, gender, and culture through creative practice (including art, design, and art history); ongoing investigation and elaboration of visual art traditions in diverse media; continued scholarship in the history of art. *Unit head:* Dr. John Richardson, Chair, 313-577-2980, Fax: 313-577-3491, E-mail: af5343@wayne.edu. *Application contact:* Prof. Evan Larson-Voltz, Graduate Officer/Associate Professor, 313-577-2983, E-mail: evanlarson@wayne.edu.
Website: http://art.wayne.edu/

Medical Illustration

Georgia Regents University, The Graduate School, Program in Medical Illustration, Augusta, GA 30912. Offers MS. *Accreditation:* ARCMI. *Degree requirements:* For master's, thesis or alternative, project. *Entrance requirements:* For master's, GRE General Test, portfolio. Additional exam requirements/recommendations for international students: Required—TOEFL (minimum score 550 paper-based; 79 iBT). Electronic applications accepted. *Faculty research:* Digital visual communication modalities, information science education, Southwestern Native American art pedagogy, medical illustration pedagogy, public health/visual education.

Johns Hopkins University, School of Medicine, Graduate Programs in Medicine, Department of Art as Applied to Medicine, Baltimore, MD 21205. Offers medical and biological illustration (MA). *Accreditation:* ARCMI. *Degree requirements:* For master's, thesis. *Entrance requirements:* Additional exam requirements/recommendations for international students: Recommended—TOEFL. Electronic applications accepted. *Faculty research:* Visualization, digital media, animation and 3D modeling, instructional design, facial prosthetics and anaplastology.

Rochester Institute of Technology, Graduate Enrollment Services, College of Health Sciences and Technology, Health Sciences Department, MFA Program in Medical Illustration, Rochester, NY 14623-5603. Offers MFA. Part-time programs available. *Students:* 13 full-time (11 women); includes 2 minority (both Black or African American, non-Hispanic/Latino), 2 international. Average age 24. 18 applicants, 67% accepted, 8 enrolled. In 2014, 1 master's awarded. *Degree requirements:* For master's, thesis. *Entrance requirements:* For master's, TOEFL, IELTS, or PTE for non-native English speakers, portfolio, recommended minimum GPA of 3.0. Additional exam requirements/recommendations for international students: Required—PTE (minimum score 58), TOEFL (minimum score 550 paper-based; 79 iBT) or IELTS (minimum score 6.5). *Application deadline:* For fall admission, 2/15 priority date for domestic and international students. Applications are processed on a rolling basis. Application fee: $60. Electronic applications accepted. *Expenses:* Expenses: $1,673 per credit hour. *Financial support:* In 2014–15, 14 students received support. Research assistantships with partial tuition reimbursements available, teaching assistantships with partial tuition reimbursements available, career-related internships or fieldwork, Federal Work-Study, institutionally sponsored loans, scholarships/grants, and unspecified assistantships available. Support available to part-time students. Financial award applicants required to submit FAFSA. *Faculty research:* Translating complex scientific information into visual images that support medical education, science research, patient care, advertising, litigation. *Unit head:* James Perkins, Graduate Program Director, Fax: 585-475-6447, E-mail: japfaa@rit.edu. *Application contact:* Diane Ellison, Associate Vice President, Graduate Enrollment Services, 585-475-2229, Fax: 585-475-7164, E-mail: gradinfo@rit.edu.
Website: http://www.rit.edu/healthsciences/graduate-programs/medical-illustration

University of Illinois at Chicago, Graduate College, College of Applied Health Sciences, Program in Biomedical Visualization, Chicago, IL 60607-7128. Offers MS. *Accreditation:* ARCMI. *Students:* 35 full-time (32 women), 5 part-time (4 women); includes 12 minority (3 Black or African American, non-Hispanic/Latino; 2 Asian, non-Hispanic/Latino; 4 Hispanic/Latino; 1 Native Hawaiian or other Pacific Islander, non-Hispanic/Latino; 2 Two or more races, non-Hispanic/Latino), 2 international. Average age 27. 48 applicants, 56% accepted, 16 enrolled. In 2014, 17 master's awarded. *Degree requirements:* For master's, thesis. *Entrance requirements:* For master's, GRE General Test, minimum GPA of 2.75. Additional exam requirements/recommendations for international students: Required—TOEFL. *Application deadline:* For fall admission, 2/1 for domestic students. Applications are processed on a rolling basis. Application fee: $60. Electronic applications accepted. *Expenses:* Expenses: Contact institution. *Financial support:* Fellowships with full tuition reimbursements, research assistantships with full tuition reimbursements, teaching assistantships with full tuition reimbursements, Federal Work-Study, institutionally sponsored loans, and tuition waivers (full) available. Financial award application deadline: 3/1; financial award applicants required to submit FAFSA. *Faculty research:* Medical illustration, graphics, reconstruction, anatomical modeling. *Unit head:* Dr. Larry Pawola, Department Head and Professor, 312-996-1446, Fax: 312-996-8342, E-mail: lpawola@uic.edu.
Website: http://www.ahs.uic.edu/bhis/academics/bvis/

Photography

Academy of Art University, Graduate Program, School of Photography, San Francisco, CA 94105-3410. Offers MFA. *Accreditation:* NASAD. Part-time programs available. Postbaccalaureate distance learning degree programs offered (no on-campus study). *Faculty:* 10 full-time (4 women), 27 part-time/adjunct (8 women). *Students:* 123 full-time (60 women), 187 part-time (117 women); includes 65 minority (20 Black or African American, non-Hispanic/Latino; 2 American Indian or Alaska Native, non-Hispanic/Latino; 18 Asian, non-Hispanic/Latino; 16 Hispanic/Latino; 2 Native Hawaiian or other Pacific Islander, non-Hispanic/Latino; 7 Two or more races, non-Hispanic/Latino), 76 international. Average age 36. 81 applicants, 100% accepted, 31 enrolled. In 2014, 72 master's awarded. *Degree requirements:* For master's, final review. *Entrance requirements:* For master's, statement of intent; resume; portfolio/reel; official college transcripts. *Application deadline:* Applications are processed on a rolling basis. Application fee: $100. Electronic applications accepted. *Expenses: Tuition:* Part-time $910 per unit. *Financial support:* Career-related internships or fieldwork and Federal Work-Study available. Support available to part-time students. Financial award application deadline: 8/10; financial award applicants required to submit FAFSA. *Unit head:* 800-544-ARTS, E-mail: info@academyart.edu. *Application contact:* 800-544-ARTS, E-mail: info@academyart.edu.
Website: http://www.academyart.edu/photography-school/index.html

Bard College, International Center of Photography, Annandale-on-Hudson, NY 12504. Offers advanced photographic studies (MFA).

Barry University, College of Arts and Sciences, Department of Fine Arts, Miami Shores, FL 33161-6695. Offers photography (MA, MFA). *Degree requirements:* For master's, thesis (for some programs). *Entrance requirements:* For master's, GRE General Test, minimum GPA of 3.0. Electronic applications accepted. *Faculty research:* Inclusion education, exceptional education, art-based assessments.

Bradley University, Graduate School, Slane College of Communications and Fine Arts, Department of Art, Peoria, IL 61625-0002. Offers ceramics (MA, MFA); drawing (MA, MFA); interdisciplinary art (MA, MFA); painting (MA, MFA); photography (MA, MFA); printmaking (MA, MFA); sculpture (MA, MFA); visual communications (MA, MFA). *Accreditation:* NASAD. Part-time programs available. *Faculty:* 11 full-time (2 women), 2 part-time/adjunct (both women). *Students:* 7 full-time (3 women), 3 part-time (2 women). 22 applicants, 41% accepted, 2 enrolled. In 2014, 4 master's awarded. *Degree requirements:* For master's, comprehensive exam, thesis, final exhibit. *Entrance requirements:* For master's, portfolio, 2 letters of recommendation. Additional exam requirements/recommendations for international students: Required—TOEFL (minimum score 550 paper-based; 79 iBT). *Application deadline:* For fall admission, 4/1 priority date for domestic and international students; for spring admission, 11/1 priority date for domestic and international students. Applications are processed on a rolling basis. Application fee: $40 ($50 for international students). Electronic applications accepted. *Expenses: Tuition:* Full-time $14,580; part-time $810 per credit. *Required fees:* $224. Full-time tuition and fees vary according to course load. *Financial support:* In 2014–15, 4 teaching assistantships with full and partial tuition reimbursements (averaging $19,640 per year) were awarded; scholarships/grants, tuition waivers (partial), and unspecified assistantships also available. Support available to part-time students. Financial award application deadline: 4/1. *Unit head:* Dr. Paul Krainak, Chairperson, 309-677-2967, E-mail: pkrainak@bradley.edu. *Application contact:* Kayla Carroll, Director of International Admission and Student Services, 309-677-2375, E-mail: klcarroll@fsmail.bradley.edu.

Brooklyn College of the City University of New York, School of Visual, Media and Performing Arts, Department of Art, Brooklyn, NY 11210-2889. Offers art history (MA); digital art (MFA); drawing and painting (MFA); photography (MFA); printmaking (MFA); sculpture (MFA). Part-time programs available. *Degree requirements:* For master's, thesis. *Entrance requirements:* For master's, bachelor's degree in art, portfolio, 2 letters of recommendation. Additional exam requirements/recommendations for international students: Required—TOEFL (minimum score 500 paper-based; 61 iBT). Electronic applications accepted.

Brooks Institute, Graduate Program in Professional Photography, Ventura, CA 93001. Offers MFA. Evening/weekend programs available. *Degree requirements:* For master's, thesis. *Entrance requirements:* For master's, portfolio review testing procedure (written exam), minimum GPA of 3.0, 3 letters of recommendation. Additional exam requirements/recommendations for international students: Required—TOEFL (minimum score 580 paper-based). Electronic applications accepted.

California College of the Arts, Graduate Programs, Fine Arts Programs, San Francisco, CA 94107. Offers ceramics (MFA); comics (MFA); film/video/performance (MFA); glass (MFA); interdisciplinary studies (MFA); jewelry/metal arts (MFA); media studies (MFA); painting/drawing (MFA); photography (MFA); printmaking (MFA); sculpture (MFA); social practice (MFA); textiles (MFA); wood/furniture (MFA). *Accreditation:* NASAD. *Degree requirements:* For master's, thesis, exhibit. *Entrance requirements:* For master's, appropriate bachelor's degree, portfolio, resume, 2 letters of recommendation, transcript. Additional exam requirements/recommendations for international students: Required—TOEFL (minimum score 600 paper-based; 100 iBT). Electronic applications accepted.

California Institute of the Arts, School of Art, Valencia, CA 91355-2340. Offers art (MFA, Adv C); graphic design (MFA, Adv C); photography (MFA, Adv C). *Accreditation:* NASAD (one or more programs are accredited). *Degree requirements:* For master's, final project. *Entrance requirements:* For master's, portfolio. Additional exam requirements/recommendations for international students: Required—TOEFL. Electronic applications accepted.

California State University, Fullerton, Graduate Studies, College of the Arts, Department of Visual Arts, Fullerton, CA 92834-9480. Offers art (MA, MFA), including art history (MA), ceramics (MFA), crafts, creative photography, exhibition design, glass, graphic design, illustration, sculpture. *Accreditation:* NASAD (one or more programs are accredited). Part-time programs available. *Students:* 28 full-time (16 women), 29 part-time (22 women); includes 20 minority (3 Black or African American, non-Hispanic/Latino; 8 Asian, non-Hispanic/Latino; 8 Hispanic/Latino; 1 Two or more races, non-Hispanic/Latino), 7 international. Average age 35. 58 applicants, 38% accepted, 14 enrolled. In 2014, 17 master's awarded. *Degree requirements:* For master's, project or thesis. *Entrance requirements:* For master's, minimum GPA of 2.5 in last 60 units of course work, portfolio. Application fee: $55. *Financial support:* Career-related internships or fieldwork, Federal Work-Study, institutionally sponsored loans, and scholarships/grants available. Support available to part-time students. Financial award application deadline: 3/1; financial award applicants required to submit FAFSA. *Unit head:* Dana Lamb, Chair, 657-278-2076. *Application contact:* Admissions/Applications, 657-278-2371.

California State University, Los Angeles, Graduate Studies, College of Arts and Letters, Department of Art, Los Angeles, CA 90032-8530. Offers art (MA), including art education, art history, art therapy, ceramics, metals, and textiles, design (MA, MFA), painting, sculpture, and graphic arts, photography; fine arts (MFA), including crafts, design (MA, MFA), studio arts. *Accreditation:* NASAD (one or more programs are accredited). Part-time and evening/weekend programs available. *Degree requirements:* For master's, comprehensive exam, project or thesis. *Entrance requirements:* For master's, portfolio. Additional exam requirements/recommendations for international students: Required—TOEFL (minimum score 500 paper-based). Electronic applications accepted. *Expenses:* Tuition, state resident: full-time $6738; part-time $3609 per year. Tuition, nonresident: full-time $15,666; part-time $8073 per year. Tuition and fees vary according to course load, degree level and program. *Faculty research:* The artist and the book, conceptual art, ceramic processes, computer graphics, architectural graphics.

Claremont Graduate University, Graduate Programs, School of Arts and Humanities, Department of Art, Claremont, CA 91711. Offers digital media (MFA); drawing (MFA); installation (MFA); painting (MFA); performance (MFA); photography (MFA); sculpture (MFA); studio (MFA). Part-time programs available. *Faculty:* 4 full-time (1 woman). *Students:* 37 full-time (26 women), 3 part-time (1 woman); includes 11 minority (2 Black or African American, non-Hispanic/Latino; 1 Asian, non-Hispanic/Latino; 7 Hispanic/Latino; 1 Two or more races, non-Hispanic/Latino), 12 international. Average age 32. In 2014, 22 master's awarded. *Degree requirements:* For master's, final project show. *Entrance requirements:* For master's, BA in art or BFA, slide review. Additional exam requirements/recommendations for international students: Required—TOEFL (minimum score 550 paper-based; 80 iBT). *Application deadline:* For fall admission, 2/1 priority date for domestic and international students. Applications are processed on a rolling basis. Application fee: $80. Electronic applications accepted. *Expenses:* Expenses: Contact institution. *Financial support:* Fellowships, research assistantships, teaching assistantships, Federal Work-Study, institutionally sponsored loans, and scholarships/grants available. Support available to part-time students. Financial award application deadline: 2/15; financial award applicants required to submit FAFSA. *Faculty research:* Acoustic sculpture, feminization of abstraction, installation sculpture. *Unit head:* David Amico, Chair, 909-607-8216, Fax: 909-607-1276, E-mail: david.amico@cgu.edu. *Application contact:* Jennifer Gracia, Program Coordinator, 909-621-8071, E-mail: jennifer.gracia@cgu.edu.
Website: http://art.cgu.edu/

Columbia College Chicago, Graduate School, Department of Photography, Chicago, IL 60605-1996. Offers MFA. *Faculty:* 4 full-time (1 woman). *Students:* 22 full-time (13 women); includes 6 minority (2 Black or African American, non-Hispanic/Latino; 1 Asian, non-Hispanic/Latino; 3 Hispanic/Latino), 1 international. Average age 28. *Degree requirements:* For master's, thesis. *Entrance requirements:* For master's, self-assessment essay, portfolio, resume, letters of recommendation. Additional exam requirements/recommendations for international students: Required—TOEFL (minimum score 600 paper-based; 100 iBT). *Application deadline:* For fall admission, 1/15 for domestic and international students. Application fee: $55 ($100 for international students). Electronic applications accepted. *Expenses:* Expenses: $1,033 per credit hour; fees: $352 per semester. *Financial support:* In 2014–15, 22 students received support, including 12 fellowships, 10 teaching assistantships; Federal Work-Study, scholarships/grants, and unspecified assistantships also available. Support available to part-time students. Financial award application deadline: 8/15; financial award applicants required to submit FAFSA. *Unit head:* Paul D'Amato, Co-Coordinator, 312-369-7036, E-mail: pdamato@colum.edu. *Application contact:* Kara Leffler, Associate Director of Graduate Admissions, 312-369-7262, Fax: 312-369-8024, E-mail: kleffler@colum.edu.
Website: http://www.colum.edu/Admissions/Graduate/programs/mfa-in-photography/index.php

Columbia University, School of the Arts, Visual Arts Program, New York, NY 10027. Offers new genres (MFA); painting (MFA); photography (MFA); printmaking (MFA); sculpture (MFA). *Degree requirements:* For master's, thesis. *Entrance requirements:* For master's, 3 letters of recommendation, portfolio, resume. Additional exam requirements/recommendations for international students: Required—TOEFL (minimum score 600 paper-based; 100 iBT). Electronic applications accepted.

See Display on page 257 and Close-Up on page 273.

Cornell University, Graduate School, Graduate Fields of Architecture, Art and Planning, Field of Art, Ithaca, NY 14853-0001. Offers creative visual arts (MFA), including painting, photography, printmaking, sculpture. *Degree requirements:* For master's, thesis, exhibit. *Entrance requirements:* For master's, slide portfolio of 10-20 slides, 3 letters of recommendation, resume. Additional exam requirements/recommendations for international students: Required—TOEFL (minimum score 550 paper-based; 77 iBT). Electronic applications accepted. *Faculty research:* Painting, sculpture, photography, printmaking.

Cornell University, Graduate School, Graduate Fields of Arts and Sciences, Field of History of Art, Archaeology and Visual Studies, Ithaca, NY 14853. Offers 19th century art (PhD); African, African American and African diaspora (PhD); American art (PhD); ancient art and archaeology (PhD); Asian American art (PhD); Baroque art (PhD); comparative modernities (PhD); digital art (PhD); East Asian art (PhD); history of photography (PhD); Islamic art (PhD); Latin American art (PhD); medieval art (PhD); modern art (PhD); Renaissance art (PhD); Southeast Asian art (PhD); theory and criticism (PhD); visual studies (PhD). *Degree requirements:* For doctorate, one foreign language, comprehensive exam, thesis/dissertation, general exams in 3 areas. *Entrance requirements:* For doctorate, GRE General Test, sample of written work, 3 letters of recommendation. Additional exam requirements/recommendations for international students: Required—TOEFL (minimum score 550 paper-based; 77 iBT). Electronic applications accepted.

Cranbrook Academy of Art, Graduate School, Program in Fine Arts, Bloomfield Hills, MI 48303-0801. Offers 2D design (MFA); ceramics (MFA); fiber (MFA); metalsmithing (MFA); painting (MFA); photography (MFA); print media (MFA); sculpture (MFA). *Accreditation:* NASAD. *Faculty:* 9 full-time (3 women). *Students:* 138 full-time (93 women); includes 18 minority (7 Asian, non-Hispanic/Latino; 5 Hispanic/Latino; 6 Two or more races, non-Hispanic/Latino), 31 international. Average age 27. 390 applicants, 35% accepted, 72 enrolled. *Degree requirements:* For master's, thesis, exhibit. *Entrance requirements:* Additional exam requirements/recommendations for international students: Required—TOEFL. *Application deadline:* For fall admission, 2/1 priority date for domestic and international students; for spring admission, 11/1 for domestic students. Application fee: $85. Electronic applications accepted. *Expenses: Tuition:* Full-time $31,916. *Required fees:* $2387. *Financial support:* Federal Work-Study available. Financial award application deadline: 2/15; financial award applicants required to submit FAFSA. *Unit head:* Christopher Scoates, Director, 248-645-3301, Fax: 248-645-3591. *Application contact:* Leslie Tobakos, Registrar/Financial Aid and Admissions Manager, 248-645-3360, Fax: 248-645-3591, E-mail: ltobakos@cranbrook.edu.

East Carolina University, Graduate School, College of Fine Arts and Communication, School of Art and Design, Greenville, NC 27858-4353. Offers art education (MA Ed); ceramics (MFA); graphic design (MFA); illustration (MFA); metal design (MFA); painting and drawing (MFA); photography (MFA); printmaking (MFA); sculpture (MFA); textile design (MFA); wood design (MFA). *Accreditation:* NASAD (one or more programs are accredited). Part-time and evening/weekend programs available. *Degree requirements:* For master's, comprehensive exam, thesis (for some programs). *Entrance requirements:* For master's, GRE General Test or MAT, portfolio. Additional exam requirements/recommendations for international students: Required—TOEFL. *Expenses:* Tuition, state resident: full-time $4223. Tuition, nonresident: full-time $16,540. *Required fees:* $2184.

George Mason University, College of Visual and Performing Arts, Art and Visual Technology Program, Fairfax, VA 22030. Offers drawing (MFA); graphic design (MFA); new media art (MFA); painting (MFA); photography (MFA); printmaking (MFA); sculpture (MFA). *Accreditation:* NASAD. *Faculty:* 21 full-time (11 women), 36 part-time/adjunct (22 women). *Students:* 5 full-time (4 women), 12 part-time (2 women); includes 3 minority (1 Black or African American, non-Hispanic/Latino; 2 Two or more races, non-Hispanic/Latino). Average age 40. 25 applicants, 20% accepted, 3 enrolled. In 2014, 4 master's awarded. *Degree requirements:* For master's, comprehensive experience, studio project or thesis. *Entrance requirements:* For master's, official transcripts; 3 letters of recommendation; letter of intent; resume; professional goals statement. Additional exam requirements/recommendations for international students: Required—TOEFL (minimum score 570 paper-based; 80 iBT), IELTS (minimum score 6.5), PTE. *Application deadline:* For fall admission, 1/15 for domestic and international students. Application fee: $65 ($80 for international students). Electronic applications accepted. *Expenses:* Tuition, state resident: full-time $9794; part-time $408 per credit hour. Tuition, nonresident: full-time $26,978; part-time $1124 per credit hour. *Required fees:* $2820; $118 per credit hour. Tuition and fees vary according to course load and program. *Financial support:* In 2014–15, 2 students received support, including 2 teaching assistantships with full and partial tuition reimbursements available (averaging $6,696 per year); career-related internships or fieldwork, Federal Work-Study, scholarships/grants, unspecified assistantships, and health care benefits (for full-time research or teaching assistantship recipients) also available. Support available to part-time students. Financial award application deadline: 3/1; financial award applicants required to submit FAFSA. *Faculty research:* Digital arts, painting, photography, print-making, sculpture; combined art forms in in-disciplinary projects including installation, performance, publishing, time or writing-based; combined creative and critical approaches. *Unit head:* Peter Winant, Director, 703-993-8385, Fax: 703-993-8798, E-mail: pwinant@gmu.edu. *Application contact:* Asma Ormazad, Graduate Studies Administrative Assistant, 703-993-9773, Fax: 703-993-8255, E-mail: aomarzad@gmu.edu.
Website: http://soa.gmu.edu

The George Washington University, Columbian College of Arts and Sciences, Corcoran School of the Arts and Design, Washington, DC 20007. Offers art and the book (MA); art education (MA, MAT); exhibition design (MA); interior design (MA); new media photojournalism (MA). *Accreditation:* NASAD. Part-time programs available. *Entrance requirements:* Additional exam requirements/recommendations for international students: Required—TOEFL (minimum score 95 iBT).

The George Washington University, Columbian College of Arts and Sciences, Department of Fine Arts and Art History, Washington, DC 20052. Offers art history (MA), including art history, museum training; ceramics (MFA); drawing/painting (MFA); interior design (MFA), including interior architecture and design; new media (MFA); photography (MFA); sculpture (MFA). *Accreditation:* CIDA. Part-time and evening/weekend programs available. *Faculty:* 17 full-time (10 women). *Students:* 81 full-time (66 women), 24 part-time (20 women); includes 15 minority (5 Black or African American, non-Hispanic/Latino; 1 American Indian or Alaska Native, non-Hispanic/Latino; 3 Asian, non-Hispanic/Latino; 3 Hispanic/Latino; 1 Native Hawaiian or other Pacific Islander, non-Hispanic/Latino; 2 Two or more races, non-Hispanic/Latino), 5 international. Average age 31. 79 applicants, 65% accepted, 12 enrolled. In 2014, 15 master's awarded. *Entrance requirements:* For master's, GRE General Test, bachelor's degree in field, minimum GPA of 3.0. Additional exam requirements/recommendations for international students: Required—TOEFL (minimum score 550 paper-based; 80 iBT). *Application deadline:* For fall admission, 3/1 priority date for domestic students, 1/15 priority date for international students; for spring admission, 10/1 priority date for domestic students, 9/1 priority date for international students. Applications are processed on a rolling basis. Application fee: $75. Electronic applications accepted. *Financial support:* In 2014–15, 12 students received support. Fellowships, teaching assistantships, career-related internships or fieldwork, Federal Work-Study, and tuition waivers available. Financial award application deadline: 1/15. *Unit head:* Phil Jacks, Chair, 202-994-6085, E-mail: pjacks@gwu.edu. *Application contact:* Information Contact, 202-994-6085, Fax: 202-994-8657, E-mail: art@gwu.edu.
Website: http://art.columbian.gwu.edu/

Georgia State University, College of Arts and Sciences, Department of Communication, Atlanta, GA 30302-3083. Offers film, video, and digital imaging (MA), including critical studies, production, screenwriting; human communication and social

influence (MA); mass communication (MA); media and society (PhD); moving image studies (PhD); public communication (PhD); rhetoric and politics (PhD). Part-time programs available. *Faculty:* 35 full-time (18 women). *Students:* 102 full-time (51 women), 40 part-time (15 women); includes 37 minority (20 Black or African American, non-Hispanic/Latino; 4 Asian, non-Hispanic/Latino; 6 Hispanic/Latino; 7 Two or more races, non-Hispanic/Latino), 14 international. Average age 33. 154 applicants, 39% accepted, 30 enrolled. In 2014, 25 master's, 5 doctorates awarded. *Degree requirements:* For master's, variable foreign language requirement, thesis (for some programs); for doctorate, comprehensive exam, thesis/dissertation. *Entrance requirements:* For master's, GRE; for doctorate, GRE. Additional exam requirements/recommendations for international students: Required—TOEFL (minimum score 550 paper-based; 80 iBT), IELTS (minimum score 6.5). *Application deadline:* For fall admission, 2/10 for domestic and international students; for spring admission, 10/15 for domestic and international students. Application fee: $50. Electronic applications accepted. *Expenses:* Tuition, state resident: full-time $6516; part-time $362 per credit hour. Tuition, nonresident: full-time $22,014; part-time $1223 per credit hour. *Required fees:* $2128 per semester. Tuition and fees vary according to course load and program. *Financial support:* In 2014–15, fellowships with tuition reimbursements (averaging $15,000 per year), teaching assistantships with tuition reimbursements (averaging $15,000 per year) were awarded; career-related internships or fieldwork and unspecified assistantships also available. Financial award applicants required to submit FAFSA. *Faculty research:* New media, mass media and journalism, rhetoric, film and media studies, film production. *Unit head:* Dr. David Cheshier, Chair, 404-413-5649, Fax: 404-413-5634, E-mail: dcheshier@gsu.edu. *Application contact:* Dr. Jennifer Barker, Associate Professor, 404-413-5793, Fax: 404-413-5634, E-mail: jmbarker@gsu.edu.
Website: http://communication.gsu.edu

Georgia State University, College of Arts and Sciences, Ernest G. Welch School of Art and Design, Program in Studio Art, Atlanta, GA 30302-3083. Offers ceramics (MFA); drawing and painting (MFA); graphic design (MFA); interior design (MFA); photography (MFA); printmaking (MFA); sculpture (MFA); textiles (MFA). *Accreditation:* NASAD. *Degree requirements:* For master's, thesis. *Application deadline:* For fall admission, 1/6 for domestic and international students; for spring admission, 1/15 priority date for domestic and international students. Application fee: $50. Electronic applications accepted. *Expenses:* Tuition, state resident: full-time $6516; part-time $362 per credit hour. Tuition, nonresident: full-time $22,014; part-time $1223 per credit hour. *Required fees:* $2128 per semester. Tuition and fees vary according to course load and program. *Financial support:* In 2014–15, fellowships with full tuition reimbursements (averaging $11,000 per year), teaching assistantships with full tuition reimbursements (averaging $7,000 per year) were awarded; research assistantships, scholarships/grants, and unspecified assistantships also available. Financial award application deadline: 4/15. *Faculty research:* Advertising and typography, new media, traditional media, three-dimensional art, architectural and environmental design. *Unit head:* Michael White, Director, Welch School of Art and Design, 404-413-5221, Fax: 404-413-5261, E-mail: mwhite@gsu.edu. *Application contact:* Hubert Stanley Anderson, Director of Graduate Studies, 404-413-5229, Fax: 404-413-5261, E-mail: artgrad@gsu.edu.
Website: http://artdesign.gsu.edu/graduate/admissions/masters-of-fine-arts-in-studio/

Howard University, Graduate School, Division of Fine Arts, Department of Art, Program in Fine Arts, Washington, DC 20059-0002. Offers 3D reality (sculpture and ceramics) (MFA); design (MFA); electronic studio (MFA); painting (MFA); photography (MFA). *Accreditation:* NASAD. *Degree requirements:* For master's, comprehensive exam, thesis, exhibit. *Entrance requirements:* For master's, minimum GPA of 3.0, portfolio.

Illinois State University, Graduate School, College of Fine Arts, School of Art, Normal, IL 61790-2200. Offers art history (MA, MS); ceramics (MFA, MS); drawing (MFA, MS); fibers (MFA, MS); glass (MFA, MS); graphic design (MFA, MS); metals (MFA, MS); painting (MFA, MS); photography (MFA, MS); printmaking (MFA, MS); sculpture (MFA, MS). *Accreditation:* NASAD (one or more programs are accredited). *Degree requirements:* For master's, thesis or alternative, internship. *Entrance requirements:* For master's, portfolio, sample of scholarly writing.

Indiana State University, College of Graduate and Professional Studies, College of Arts and Sciences, Department of Art, Terre Haute, IN 47809. Offers ceramics (MA, MFA); drawing (MA, MFA); graphic design (MA, MFA); painting (MA, MFA); photography (MA, MFA); printmaking (MA, MFA); sculpture (MA, MFA). *Accreditation:* NASAD (one or more programs are accredited). Part-time programs available. *Degree requirements:* For master's, thesis or alternative, departmental qualifying exam. *Entrance requirements:* For master's, portfolio. Additional exam requirements/recommendations for international students: Required—TOEFL (minimum score 550 paper-based).

Inter American University of Puerto Rico, San Germán Campus, Graduate Studies Center, Program in Fine Arts, San Germán, PR 00683-5008. Offers drawing (MFA); graphic design (MFA); painting (MFA); photography (MFA); printmaking (MFA); sculpture (MFA). Part-time and evening/weekend programs available. *Degree requirements:* For master's, comprehensive exam, thesis. *Entrance requirements:* For master's, GRE General Test or EXADEP, minimum GPA of 3.0.

James Madison University, The Graduate School, College of Visual and Performing Arts, School of Art, Design and Art History, Harrisonburg, VA 22807. Offers art education (MA); studio art (MFA), including drawing/painting, metal/jewelry, photography. *Accreditation:* NASAD. Part-time programs available. *Faculty:* 25 full-time (15 women). *Students:* 11 full-time (7 women), 1 (woman) part-time; includes 4 minority (1 Black or African American, non-Hispanic/Latino; 3 Two or more races, non-Hispanic/Latino), 1 international. Average age 28. 18 applicants, 39% accepted, 6 enrolled. In 2014, 7 master's awarded. *Degree requirements:* For master's, thesis (for some programs). *Application deadline:* For fall admission, 2/15 for domestic and international students; for spring admission, 10/15 for domestic and international students. Application fee: $55. Electronic applications accepted. *Expenses:* Tuition, state resident: full-time $7812; part-time $434 per credit hour. Tuition, nonresident: full-time $20,430; part-time $1135 per credit hour. *Financial support:* In 2014–15, 11 students received support, including 2 teaching assistantships with full tuition reimbursements available (averaging $8,837 per year); Federal Work-Study and 9 assistantships (averaging $2748) also available. Financial award application deadline: 3/1; financial award applicants required to submit FAFSA. *Unit head:* Dr. Kathy A. Schwartz, Director of School of Art, Design and Art History, 540-568-6216, E-mail: art-arthistory@jmu.edu. *Application contact:* Lynette D. Michael, Director of Graduate Admissions and Student Admissions, 540-568-6131 Ext. 6395, Fax: 540-568-7860, E-mail: michaeld@jmu.edu.
Website: http://www.jmu.edu/artandarthistory/

Lesley University, College of Art and Design, Cambridge, MA 02138-2790. Offers photography (MFA); visual arts (MFA). Part-time programs available. *Faculty:* 7 full-time (4 women), 17 part-time/adjunct (7 women). *Students:* 77 full-time (58 women), 1 (woman) part-time; includes 5 minority (3 Asian, non-Hispanic/Latino; 2 Two or more races, non-Hispanic/Latino), 5 international. Average age 39. In 2014, 34 master's awarded. *Degree requirements:* For master's, thesis, final exhibition of thesis work. *Entrance requirements:* For master's, portfolio, resume, personal statement. Additional exam requirements/recommendations for international students: Required—TOEFL (minimum score 550 paper-based; 80 iBT). *Application deadline:* For fall admission, 3/1 for domestic students; for spring admission, 9/1 for domestic students. Applications are processed on a rolling basis. Application fee: $50. Electronic applications accepted. *Financial support:* Fellowships, career-related internships or fieldwork, and scholarships/grants available. Financial award applicants required to submit FAFSA. *Faculty research:* Graphic design; Web and multimedia design; book, advertising and editorial illustration; animation; documentary photography; photojournalism; fine arts photography; fine arts; art education. *Unit head:* Dr. Stanley Trecker, Dean, 617-585-6651, E-mail: strecker@lesley.edu. *Application contact:* Martha Sheehan, Director, Graduate Admissions, 800-LESLEYU, E-mail: info@lesley.edu.
Website: http://www.lesley.edu/college-art-and-design/

Louisiana State University and Agricultural & Mechanical College, Graduate School, College of Art and Design, School of Art, Program in Studio Art, Baton Rouge, LA 70803. Offers ceramics (MFA); graphic design (MFA); painting and drawing (MFA); photography (MFA); printmaking (MFA); sculpture (MFA). *Accreditation:* NASAD. *Students:* 37 full-time (29 women), 1 (woman) part-time; includes 2 minority (both Hispanic/Latino), 10 international. Average age 29. 72 applicants, 31% accepted, 17 enrolled. In 2014, 20 master's awarded. *Degree requirements:* For master's, thesis. *Entrance requirements:* For master's, GRE General Test, minimum GPA of 3.0. Additional exam requirements/recommendations for international students: Required—TOEFL (minimum score 550 paper-based; 79 IBT), IELTS (minimum score 6.5), or PTE (minimum score 59). *Application deadline:* For fall admission, 1/1 priority date for domestic students, 5/15 for international students; for spring admission, 10/15 for domestic and international students; for summer admission, 5/15 for domestic and international students. Applications are processed on a rolling basis. Application fee: $50 ($70 for international students). Electronic applications accepted. *Financial support:* Research assistantships with partial tuition reimbursements, teaching assistantships, career-related internships or fieldwork, Federal Work-Study, institutionally sponsored loans, scholarships/grants, and unspecified assistantships available. Support available to part-time students. Financial award application deadline: 3/15. *Faculty research:* Ceramics, painting and drawing, photography, printmaking, and sculpture. *Unit head:* Kelli Scott Kelly, Graduate Coordinator, 225-578-8448, Fax: 225-578-5424, E-mail: kskelly@lsu.edu.
Website: http://design.lsu.edu/art/?page_id-582

Louisiana Tech University, Graduate School, College of Liberal Arts, MFA Program, Ruston, LA 71272. Offers communication design (MFA); photography (MFA); studio (MFA). *Accreditation:* NASAD. Part-time programs available. *Degree requirements:* For master's, exhibit. *Entrance requirements:* For master's, GRE General Test, portfolio. *Application deadline:* For fall admission, 7/29 for domestic students; for spring admission, 2/3 for domestic students. Applications are processed on a rolling basis. Application fee: $40. *Financial support:* Fellowships, career-related internships or fieldwork, Federal Work-Study, institutionally sponsored loans, and unspecified assistantships available. Financial award application deadline: 2/1. *Unit head:* Joey Slaughter, Graduate Coordinator, 318-257-3909, Fax: 318-257-4890, E-mail: joey@latech.edu. *Application contact:* Marilyn J. Robinson, Assistant to the Dean of the Graduate School, 318-257-2924, Fax: 318-257-4487.

Maryland Institute College of Art, Graduate Studies, Program in Photographic and Electronic Media, Baltimore, MD 21201. Offers MFA. *Accreditation:* NASAD. *Faculty:* 1 (woman) full-time, 5 part-time/adjunct (1 woman). *Students:* 28 full-time (18 women); includes 6 minority (1 Black or African American, non-Hispanic/Latino; 1 Asian, non-Hispanic/Latino; 1 Hispanic/Latino; 3 Two or more races, non-Hispanic/Latino), 5 international. Average age 27. 100 applicants, 30% accepted, 14 enrolled. In 2014, 14 master's awarded. *Degree requirements:* For master's, thesis, exhibit and thesis documentation. *Entrance requirements:* For master's, portfolio, bachelor's degree in any field. Additional exam requirements/recommendations for international students: Required—TOEFL (minimum score 550 paper-based; 80 iBT), IELTS (minimum score 6.5). *Application deadline:* For fall admission, 1/15 for domestic and international students. Application fee: $75. *Expenses:* Expenses: Contact institution. *Financial support:* In 2014–15, 28 students received support, including 28 fellowships (averaging $13,000 per year), 28 teaching assistantships (averaging $3,200 per year); career-related internships or fieldwork and scholarships/grants also available. Financial award application deadline: 1/15. *Unit head:* Timothy Druckrey, Director, 410-225-5274, Fax: 410-225-5275, E-mail: graduate@mica.edu. *Application contact:* Chris D. Harring, Director, Graduate Admission, 410-225-2256, Fax: 410-225-5275, E-mail: graduate@mica.edu.
Website: http://www.mica.edu/Programs_of_Study/Graduate_Programs/Photographic_and_Electronic_Media_(MFA).html

Marywood University, Academic Affairs, Insalaco College of Creative and Performing Arts, Art Department, Program in Studio Art, Scranton, PA 18509-1598. Offers clay (MA); painting (MA); photography (MA); printmaking (MA); sculpture (MA). *Accreditation:* NASAD. *Students:* 5 full-time (all women), 2 part-time (1 woman), 1 international. Average age 44. In 2014, 1 master's awarded. *Application deadline:* For fall admission, 4/1 priority date for domestic students, 3/31 priority date for international students; for spring admission, 11/1 priority date for domestic students, 8/31 priority date for international students. Applications are processed on a rolling basis. Application fee: $35. Electronic applications accepted. *Expenses: Tuition:* Part-time $775 per credit. *Required fees:* $688 per semester. Tuition and fees vary according to degree level and campus/location. *Financial support:* Application deadline: 6/30; applicants required to submit FAFSA. *Faculty research:* Texture and line in clay, cast bronze sculpture, color theories, book art and illustration, sculptural form. *Unit head:* Matthew Povse, Chair, 570-348-6211 Ext. 2476, E-mail: povse@marywood.edu. *Application contact:* Tammy Manka, Assistant Director of Graduate Admissions, 570-348-6211 Ext. 2322, E-mail: tmanka@marywood.edu.
Website: http://www.marywood.edu/art/graduate-programs/master-studio-art.html

Marywood University, Academic Affairs, Insalaco College of Creative and Performing Arts, Art Department, Program in Visual Arts, Scranton, PA 18509-1598. Offers clay (MFA); graphic design (MFA); illustration (MFA); painting (MFA); photography (MFA); printmaking (MFA); sculpture (MFA). *Accreditation:* NASAD. Part-time programs available. *Students:* 25 full-time (18 women), 3 part-time (all women); includes 1 minority (Hispanic/Latino), 2 international. Average age 36. In 2014, 5 master's awarded. *Application deadline:* For fall admission, 4/1 for domestic students, 3/31 for international students; for spring admission, 11/1 for domestic students, 8/31 for international students. Applications are processed on a rolling basis. Application fee: $35. Electronic applications accepted. *Expenses:* Expenses: Contact institution. *Financial support:* Application deadline: 6/30; applicants required to submit FAFSA. *Unit head:* Matthew Povse, Chair, 570-348-6211 Ext. 2476, E-mail: povse@marywood.edu. *Application contact:* Tammy Manka, Assistant Director of Graduate Admissions, 570-348-6211 Ext. 2322, E-mail: tmanka@marywood.edu.
Website: http://www.marywood.edu/art/graduate-programs/master-visual-arts.html

Massachusetts College of Art and Design, Graduate Programs, MFA Program, Boston, MA 02115-5882. Offers 2D fine arts (MFA), including painting; 3D fine arts (MFA), including ceramics, fibers, glass, jewelry and metalsmithing, sculpture; design (MFA, Postbaccalaureate Certificate), including dynamic media; fine arts (MFA), including interdisciplinary; media arts (MFA, Postbaccalaureate Certificate), including

film/video (MFA), photography. *Accreditation:* NASAD. *Faculty:* 31 full-time (15 women), 42 part-time/adjunct (19 women). *Students:* 59 full-time (36 women), 32 part-time (23 women); includes 12 minority (2 Black or African American, non-Hispanic/Latino; 5 Asian, non-Hispanic/Latino; 5 Hispanic/Latino), 18 international. 278 applicants, 38% accepted, 40 enrolled. In 2014, 33 master's, 7 other advanced degrees awarded. *Degree requirements:* For master's, thesis, Exhibition for MFA non design. Thesis document MFA in design and low-residency. *Entrance requirements:* For master's, portfolio, college transcripts, resume, statement of purpose, letters of reference, interview; 6 credits of art history taken prior to or during MFA program; for Postbaccalaureate Certificate, portfolio, college transcripts, resume, statement of purpose, letters of reference, interview. Additional exam requirements/recommendations for international students: Required—TOEFL (minimum score 550 paper-based; 85 iBT); Recommended—IELTS (minimum score 6.5). *Application deadline:* For fall admission, 1/6 priority date for domestic and international students. Application fee: $75. Electronic applications accepted. *Expenses:* Tuition, state resident: full-time $23,400; part-time $780 per credit. Tuition, nonresident: full-time $23,400; part-time $780 per credit. Tuition and fees vary according to course load and program. *Financial support:* In 2014–15, 37 students received support, including 40 teaching assistantships (averaging $2,160 per year); career-related internships or fieldwork, scholarships/grants, tuition waivers (partial), and unspecified assistantships also available. Support available to part-time students. Financial award application deadline: 1/6. *Unit head:* Paul Paturzo, Interim Dean of Graduate Studies, 617-879-7166, E-mail: pjpaturzo@massart.edu. *Application contact:* Isaac Goldstein, Graduate Admissions Counselor, 617-879-7203, Fax: 617-879-7250, E-mail: igoldstein@massart.edu.
Website: http://www.massart.edu/Admissions/Graduate_Programs.html

Mills College, Graduate Studies, Department of Art, Oakland, CA 94613-1000. Offers ceramics (MFA); intermedia (MFA); painting (MFA); photography (MFA); sculpture (MFA). *Faculty:* 5 full-time (all women), 8 part-time/adjunct (3 women). *Students:* 19 full-time (14 women); includes 3 minority (1 Black or African American, non-Hispanic/Latino; 1 Asian, non-Hispanic/Latino; 1 Hispanic/Latino), 1 international. Average age 32. 44 applicants, 48% accepted, 9 enrolled. In 2014, 12 master's awarded. *Degree requirements:* For master's, thesis or alternative, exhibit. *Entrance requirements:* For master's, portfolio, artist statement. Additional exam requirements/recommendations for international students: Required—TOEFL (minimum score 550 paper-based; 80 iBT) or IELTS (minimum score 6). *Application deadline:* For fall admission, 2/1 for domestic students, 12/15 for international students. Application fee: $50. Electronic applications accepted. *Expenses:* Expenses: Contact institution. *Financial support:* In 2014–15, 22 students received support, including 17 fellowships (averaging $12,285 per year), 10 teaching assistantships with full and partial tuition reimbursements available (averaging $14,760 per year); scholarships/grants and unspecified assistantships also available. Financial award application deadline: 2/1; financial award applicants required to submit FAFSA. *Faculty research:* Experimental film and video, public art projects, ecological design, contemporary art philosophy, sound installations. *Unit head:* Dr. Mary-Ann Milford, Professor of Art History, 510-430-2117. *Application contact:* Shrim Bathey, Director of Graduate Admission, 510-430-3309, Fax: 510-430-2159, E-mail: grad-admission@mills.edu.
Website: http://www.mills.edu/art

Minneapolis College of Art and Design, Program in Visual Studies, Minneapolis, MN 55404-4347. Offers animation (MFA); comic art (MFA); drawing (MFA); filmmaking (MFA); fine arts (MFA); furniture design (MFA); graphic design (MFA); illustration (MFA); interactive media (MFA); painting (MFA); photography (MFA); printmaking (MFA); sculpture (MFA). *Accreditation:* NASAD. Part-time programs available. *Degree requirements:* For master's, thesis, thesis exhibit. *Entrance requirements:* For master's, portfolio of visual artwork, resume, 3 letters of recommendation. Additional exam requirements/recommendations for international students: Required—TOEFL (minimum score 550 paper-based; 79 iBT). Electronic applications accepted. *Faculty research:* Visual arts: animation, comic art, drawing, filmmaking, furniture design, graphic design, illustration, interactive media, painting, photography, printmaking, sculpture.

New Hampshire Institute of Art, Graduate Programs, Manchester, NH 03104. Offers art education (MA); creative writing (MFA); photography (MFA); visual arts (MFA); writing for stage and screen (MFA). Part-time programs available. *Faculty:* 31 part-time/adjunct (14 women). *Students:* 43 full-time (25 women), 20 part-time (17 women). Average age 44. 36 applicants, 72% accepted, 24 enrolled. *Degree requirements:* For master's, thesis. *Entrance requirements:* For master's, writing sample or visual art portfolio; curriculum vitae; transcripts; letters of recommendation. Additional exam requirements/recommendations for international students: Required—TOEFL (minimum score 530 paper-based; 71 iBT). *Application deadline:* For fall admission, 5/15 for domestic students; for spring admission, 10/1 for domestic students. Applications are processed on a rolling basis. Application fee: $50. Electronic applications accepted. *Expenses:* Expenses: $9,500 per semester plus $495 residency fee (for MFA in visual arts or photography); $9,000 per semester plus $495 residency fee (for MFA in creative writing or writing for stage and screen); $7,155 per semester for full-time student (for MA in art education). *Financial support:* In 2014–15, 54 students received support, including 8 teaching assistantships with partial tuition reimbursements available; scholarships/grants and unspecified assistantships also available. Support available to part-time students. *Unit head:* Alison Williams, Dean of Graduate Studies, 603-836 2522, E-mail: alisonwilliams@nhia.edu. *Application contact:* Graduate Admissions, 603-836 2122, E-mail: gradadmissions@nhia.edu.

The New School, Parsons The New School for Design, Program in Photography, New York, NY 10011. Offers MFA. *Degree requirements:* For master's, thesis. *Entrance requirements:* For master's, portfolio. Additional exam requirements/recommendations for international students: Required—TOEFL (minimum score 580 paper-based; 93 iBT). Electronic applications accepted.

New York Film Academy, Program in Filmmaking–Hollywood, Los Angeles, CA 90068. Offers acting for film (MFA); cinematography (MFA); filmmaking (MFA); photography (MFA); producing (MFA); screenwriting (MFA). *Accreditation:* NASAD.

Ohio University, Graduate College, College of Fine Arts, School of Art, Athens, OH 45701-2979. Offers art history (MA); ceramics (MFA); graphic design (MFA); painting (MFA); photography (MFA); printmaking (MFA); sculpture (MFA). Part-time programs available. *Degree requirements:* For master's, thesis. *Entrance requirements:* For master's, portfolio. Additional exam requirements/recommendations for international students: Required—TOEFL (minimum score 550 paper-based; 80 iBT) or IELTS (minimum score 6.5). Electronic applications accepted. *Faculty research:* Vapor-fired ceramics, video installation, art theory, digital photography, mixed and interdisciplinary media work.

Ohio University, Graduate College, Scripps College of Communication, School of Visual Communication, Athens, OH 45701-2979. Offers MA. *Accreditation:* NASAD. *Entrance requirements:* For master's, minimum GPA of 2.5, portfolio. Additional exam requirements/recommendations for international students: Required—TOEFL (minimum score 600 paper-based; 100 iBT) or IELTS (minimum score 7). Electronic applications accepted. *Faculty research:* Photojournalism (including documentary photography), commercial photography (including illustrative photography), picture editing,

informational graphics/publication design, interactive multimedia, visual media management.

Otis College of Art and Design, Program in Fine Arts, Los Angeles, CA 90045-9785. Offers new genres (MFA); painting (MFA); photography (MFA); sculpture (MFA). *Accreditation:* NASAD. *Degree requirements:* For master's, thesis. *Entrance requirements:* For master's, portfolio. Additional exam requirements/recommendations for international students: Required—TOEFL (minimum score 600 paper-based). Electronic applications accepted.

Pratt Institute, School of Art and Design, Program in Fine Arts, Brooklyn, NY 11205-3899. Offers new forms (MFA); painting and drawing (MFA); photography (MFA); printmaking (MFA); sculpture (MFA). *Accreditation:* NASAD. Part-time programs available. *Faculty:* 10 full-time (5 women), 78 part-time/adjunct (33 women). *Students:* 94 full-time (59 women), 4 part-time (2 women); includes 19 minority (2 Black or African American, non-Hispanic/Latino; 11 Asian, non-Hispanic/Latino; 6 Hispanic/Latino), 42 international. Average age 28. 264 applicants, 47% accepted, 49 enrolled. In 2014, 45 master's awarded. *Degree requirements:* For master's, thesis, exhibit. *Entrance requirements:* For master's, portfolio, letters of recommendation. Additional exam requirements/recommendations for international students: Required—TOEFL (minimum score 550 paper-based; 79 iBT). *Application deadline:* For fall admission, 1/5 for domestic and international students; for spring admission, 10/1 for domestic and international students. Application fee: $50 ($90 for international students). Electronic applications accepted. *Financial support:* Career-related internships or fieldwork, Federal Work-Study, institutionally sponsored loans, scholarships/grants, health care benefits, and unspecified assistantships available. Support available to part-time students. Financial award application deadline: 2/1; financial award applicants required to submit FAFSA. *Unit head:* Deborah Bright, Chairperson, 718-636-3634, E-mail: dbright2@pratt.edu. *Application contact:* Young Hah, Director of Graduate Admissions, 718-636-3683, Fax: 718-399-4242, E-mail: yhah@pratt.edu.
Website: https://www.pratt.edu/academics/school-of-art/graduate-school-of-art/graduate-fine-arts/

See Display on page 153 and Close-Up on page 203.

Rhode Island School of Design, Graduate Studies, Division of Fine Arts, Department of Photography, Providence, RI 02903-2784. Offers MFA. *Accreditation:* NASAD. *Faculty:* 7 full-time (5 women), 8 part-time/adjunct (5 women). *Students:* 13 full-time (5 women); includes 4 minority (1 Black or African American, non-Hispanic/Latino; 2 Asian, non-Hispanic/Latino; 1 Hispanic/Latino), 2 international. Average age 31. 130 applicants, 10% accepted, 7 enrolled. In 2014, 6 master's awarded. *Degree requirements:* For master's, thesis, exhibit. *Entrance requirements:* For master's, portfolio, statement of purpose, 3 letters of recommendation. Additional exam requirements/recommendations for international students: Required—TOEFL (minimum score 580 paper-based; 93 iBT). *Application deadline:* For fall admission, 2/1 for domestic and international students. Application fee: $60. *Financial support:* Fellowships, teaching assistantships, career-related internships or fieldwork, Federal Work-Study, institutionally sponsored loans, scholarships/grants, and unspecified assistantships available. Financial award application deadline: 2/15; financial award applicants required to submit FAFSA. *Unit head:* Eva Sutton, Head, 401-454-6135, Fax: 401-454-6385, E-mail: esutton@risd.edu. *Application contact:* Molly Pettengil, Graduate Admissions Officer, 401-454-6312, Fax: 401-454-6309, E-mail: mpettengil@risd.edu.

Rochester Institute of Technology, Graduate Enrollment Services, College of Imaging Arts and Sciences, School of Photographic Arts and Sciences, MFA Program in Imaging Arts, Photography and Related Media, Rochester, NY 14623-5603. Offers MFA. *Accreditation:* NASAD. Part-time programs available. *Students:* 12 full-time (7 women), 3 part-time (all women); includes 1 minority (Two or more races, non-Hispanic/Latino), 7 international. Average age 28. 74 applicants, 22% accepted, 6 enrolled. In 2014, 4 master's awarded. *Degree requirements:* For master's, thesis, exhibit. *Entrance requirements:* For master's, GRE and TOEFL, IELTS, or PTE for non-native English speakers, portfolio, recommended minimum GPA of 3.0. Additional exam requirements/recommendations for international students: Required—PTE (minimum score 58), TOEFL (minimum score 550 paper-based; 79 iBT) or IELTS (minimum score 6.5). *Application deadline:* For fall admission, 2/15 priority date for domestic and international students. Applications are processed on a rolling basis. Application fee: $60. Electronic applications accepted. *Expenses:* Expenses: $1,673 per credit hour. *Financial support:* In 2014–15, 6 students received support. Research assistantships with partial tuition reimbursements available, teaching assistantships with partial tuition reimbursements available, career-related internships or fieldwork, Federal Work-Study, institutionally sponsored loans, scholarships/grants, tuition waivers (partial), and unspecified assistantships available. Support available to part-time students. Financial award application deadline: 8/30; financial award applicants required to submit FAFSA. *Faculty research:* Fine art photography, digital imaging, moving media. *Unit head:* Christine Shank, Graduate Program Director, 585-475-2616, Fax: 585-475-5804, E-mail: crspph@rit.edu. *Application contact:* Diane Ellison, Associate Vice President, Graduate Enrollment Services, 585-475-2229, Fax: 585-475-7164, E-mail: gradinfo@rit.edu.
Website: http://cias.rit.edu/schools/photographic-arts-sciences/graduate-imaging-arts

San Francisco Art Institute, Dual-Degree MFA/MA Program in Studio Art and History and Theory of Contemporary Art, San Francisco, CA 94133. Offers MFA/MA. Specializations available in art and technology, film, new genres, painting, photography, printmaking, and sculpture. *Faculty:* 15 full-time (7 women), 46 part-time/adjunct (23 women). *Students:* 6 full-time (4 women); includes 1 minority (Black or African American, non-Hispanic/Latino). Average age 27. 15 applicants, 40% accepted, 4 enrolled. *Entrance requirements:* Additional exam requirements/recommendations for international students: Required—TOEFL (minimum score 600 paper-based; 100 iBT), IELTS (minimum score 7.5). *Application deadline:* For fall admission, 1/15 priority date for domestic and international students. Applications are processed on a rolling basis. Application fee: $85. Electronic applications accepted. *Expenses:* Tuition: Full-time $41,100; part-time $1805 per credit. *Required fees:* $870. *Financial support:* In 2014–15, 8 students received support, including fellowships (averaging $30,000 per year), teaching assistantships (averaging $2,500 per year); career-related internships or fieldwork, Federal Work-Study, scholarships/grants, and unspecified assistantships also available. Support available to part-time students. Financial award application deadline: 3/1; financial award applicants required to submit FAFSA. *Unit head:* Tony Labat, Chair, Master of Fine Arts Department, 415-771-7020, Fax: 415-641-1205, E-mail: tlabat@sfai.edu. *Application contact:* Jana Rumberger, Associate Director of Recruitment, 415-351-3507, Fax: 415-749-4592, E-mail: jrumberger@sfai.edu.
Website: http://www.sfai.edu/degree-programs/graduate/dual-degree-ma-mfa

San Jose State University, Graduate Studies and Research, College of Humanities and the Arts, School of Art and Design, San Jose, CA 95192-0001. Offers animation/illustration (MA); art history (MA); digital media arts (MFA); photography (MFA); pictorial arts (MFA); spatial arts (MFA). *Accreditation:* NASAD (one or more programs are accredited). *Entrance requirements:* For master's, GRE. Electronic applications accepted.

Savannah College of Art and Design, Graduate School, Program in Photography, Savannah, GA 31402-3146. Offers MA, MFA. Part-time programs

available. Postbaccalaureate distance learning degree programs offered (no on-campus study). *Faculty:* 20 full-time (8 women), 9 part-time/adjunct (4 women). *Students:* 58 full-time (31 women), 46 part-time (21 women); includes 24 minority (14 Black or African American, non-Hispanic/Latino; 4 Asian, non-Hispanic/Latino; 5 Hispanic/Latino; 1 Native Hawaiian or other Pacific Islander, non-Hispanic/Latino), 16 international. Average age 33. 117 applicants, 28% accepted, 16 enrolled. In 2014, 32 master's awarded. *Degree requirements:* For master's, thesis (for some programs), final portfolio (for MA); internship (for MFA). *Entrance requirements:* For master's, portfolio. Additional exam requirements/recommendations for international students: Required—TOEFL (minimum score 550 paper-based, 85 iBT), IELTS (minimum score 6.5), or ACTFL. *Application deadline:* For fall admission, 4/1 for domestic and international students. Applications are processed on a rolling basis. Application fee: $40. Electronic applications accepted. *Expenses: Tuition:* Full-time $34,605; part-time $3845 per course. One-time fee: $500. Tuition and fees vary according to course load. *Financial support:* Fellowships, career-related internships or fieldwork, Federal Work-Study, and scholarships/grants available. Financial award application deadline: 4/1; financial award applicants required to submit FAFSA. *Unit head:* Rebecca Nolan, Chair. *Application contact:* Jenny Jaquillard, Executive Director of Admissions, Recruitment and Events, 912-525-5100, Fax: 912-525-5985, E-mail: admission@scad.edu.
Website: http://www.scad.edu/academics/programs/photography

School of the Art Institute of Chicago, Graduate Division, Department of Photography, Chicago, IL 60603-3103. Offers MFA. *Accreditation:* NASAD. *Entrance requirements:* Additional exam requirements/recommendations for international students: Required—TOEFL.

School of Visual Arts, Graduate Programs, Digital Photography Department, New York, NY 10010-3994. Offers MPS. Part-time programs available. Postbaccalaureate distance learning degree programs offered (minimal on-campus study). *Degree requirements:* For master's, thesis, 33 credits, including all required courses; minimum GPA of 3.0; thesis project culminating in online project, printed book and exhibition. *Entrance requirements:* For master's, image portfolio which represents 1-3 photographically cohesive bodies of work based on style, concept and execution. Additional exam requirements/recommendations for international students: Required—TOEFL (minimum score 550 paper-based; 79 iBT). Electronic applications accepted. *Faculty research:* Professional photography, digital-imaging technologies.

School of Visual Arts, Graduate Programs, Fashion Photography Department, New York, NY 10010-3994. Offers MPS. *Degree requirements:* For master's, 30 credits, including all required courses; minimum cumulative GPA of 3.0; original, challenging and provocative portfolio of images. *Entrance requirements:* For master's, portfolio, writing sample. Additional exam requirements/recommendations for international students: Required—TOEFL (minimum score 550 paper-based; 79 iBT). Electronic applications accepted. *Expenses:* Contact institution.

School of Visual Arts, Graduate Programs, Program in Photography, Video and Related Media, New York, NY 10010-3994. Offers MFA. *Accreditation:* NASAD. *Degree requirements:* For master's, thesis, 60 credits and all course requirements; minimum GPA of 3.3; thesis project. *Entrance requirements:* For master's, portfolio (still images and/or videos) through SlideRoom. Additional exam requirements/recommendations for international students: Required—TOEFL (minimum score 550 paper-based; 79 iBT). Electronic applications accepted. *Faculty research:* Contemporary and responsible creative initiatives, including experimental, narrative or documentary video, installation and conceptual art, tableau and real-world-witness photography.

Sotheby's Institute of Art–London, Graduate Programs, London, United Kingdom. Offers art business (MA); contemporary art (MA); contemporary design (MA); East Asian art (MA); fine and decorative art (MA); photography (MA). *Faculty:* 38 full-time (22 women). *Students:* 175 full-time (153 women). *Application contact:* Melba Remice, Director, Global Admissions, 212-517-2834, E-mail: admissions@sothebysinstitute.com.

Southern Methodist University, Meadows School of the Arts, Division of Art, Dallas, TX 75275. Offers studio art (MFA), including ceramics, drawing, painting, photography, printmaking, sculpture. *Accreditation:* NASAD. *Degree requirements:* For master's, thesis or alternative, exhibit. *Entrance requirements:* For master's, BFA or equivalent, letters of recommendation, portfolio. Additional exam requirements/recommendations for international students: Required—TOEFL (minimum score 550 paper-based; 80 iBT). *Faculty research:* American stoneware, Southwestern furniture traditions, photographic apparatus and techniques, American ceramists, architecture.

Southwest University of Visual Arts, MFA Programs, Tucson, AZ 85716-2505. Offers motion arts (MFA); painting and drawing (MFA); photography (MFA).

Syracuse University, College of Visual and Performing Arts, Program in Art Photography, Syracuse, NY 13244. Offers MFA. *Accreditation:* NASAD. *Students:* 13 full-time (5 women); includes 3 minority (2 Hispanic/Latino; 1 Two or more races, non-Hispanic/Latino), 2 international. Average age 27. 34 applicants, 32% accepted, 7 enrolled. In 2014, 4 master's awarded. *Degree requirements:* For master's, thesis or alternative. *Entrance requirements:* For master's, portfolio. Additional exam requirements/recommendations for international students: Required—TOEFL (minimum score 100 iBT). *Application deadline:* For fall admission, 2/1 priority date for domestic and international students. Application fee: $75. Electronic applications accepted. *Expenses: Tuition:* Part-time $1341 per credit. *Financial support:* Fellowships with full tuition reimbursements, teaching assistantships with full and partial tuition reimbursements, and tuition waivers available. Financial award application deadline: 1/1; financial award applicants required to submit FAFSA. *Unit head:* Prof. Laura Heyman, Department of Transmedia, 315-443-1103, E-mail: lheyman@syr.edu. *Application contact:* Therese West, 315-443-0137, E-mail: admissg@syr.edu.
Website: http://vpa.syr.edu/

Syracuse University, S. I. Newhouse School of Public Communications, Program in Photography, Syracuse, NY 13244. Offers MS. *Students:* 18 full-time (10 women), 8 part-time (4 women); includes 4 minority (1 Black or African American, non-Hispanic/Latino; 1 Asian, non-Hispanic/Latino; 2 Hispanic/Latino), 5 international. Average age 29. 25 applicants, 92% accepted, 13 enrolled. In 2014, 4 master's awarded. *Degree requirements:* For master's, thesis optional, special project. *Entrance requirements:* For master's, portfolio. Additional exam requirements/recommendations for international students: Required—TOEFL (minimum score 600 paper-based; 100 iBT). *Application deadline:* For fall admission, 2/1 for domestic and international students; for summer admission, 1/15 priority date for domestic and international students. Application fee: $45. Electronic applications accepted. *Expenses: Tuition:* Part-time $1341 per credit. *Financial support:* Fellowships with full tuition reimbursements, research assistantships with partial tuition reimbursements, teaching assistantships with partial tuition reimbursements, and Federal Work-Study available. Financial award application deadline: 2/1. *Unit head:* Prof. Bruce Strong, Chair, Multimedia Photography and Design, 315-443-2304, Fax: 315-443-3946, E-mail: pcgrad@syr.edu. *Application contact:* Graduate Records, 315-443-4039, Fax: 315-443-1834, E-mail: pcgrad@syr.edu.
Website: http://newhouse.syr.edu/

Temple University, Center for the Arts, Tyler School of Art, Department of Graphic Arts and Design, Philadelphia, PA 19122-6096. Offers graphic and interactive design (MFA); photography (MFA); printmaking (MFA). *Faculty:* 13 full-time (5 women), 22 part-time/adjunct (9 women). *Students:* 19 full-time (13 women); includes 2 minority (both Hispanic/Latino). 155 applicants, 12% accepted, 8 enrolled. In 2014, 8 master's awarded. *Degree requirements:* For master's, essay, exhibit. *Entrance requirements:* For master's, minimum GPA of 3.0, slide portfolio, 40 credits in studio art, 12 credits in art history, letters of recommendation, resume/curriculum vitae. Additional exam requirements/recommendations for international students: Required—TOEFL (minimum score 550 paper-based; 79 iBT), IELTS (minimum score 6.5). *Application deadline:* For fall admission, 1/15 for domestic students, 12/15 for international students. Application fee: $60. Electronic applications accepted. *Expenses:* Expenses: Contact institution. *Financial support:* Fellowships with full tuition reimbursements, research assistantships with full tuition reimbursements, teaching assistantships with full tuition reimbursements, and Federal Work-Study available. Support available to part-time students. Financial award application deadline: 1/15; financial award applicants required to submit FAFSA. *Unit head:* Stephanie Knopp, Chair, 215-782-2932, Fax: 215-782-2799, E-mail: stephanie.knopp@temple.edu. *Application contact:* Nicole Hall, Director of Admissions, 215-777-9090, E-mail: tylerart@temple.edu.
Website: http://tyler.temple.edu/graduate

Texas Christian University, College of Fine Arts, School of Art, Fort Worth, TX 76129. Offers art history (MA); studio art (MFA), including painting, photography, sculpture. *Accreditation:* NASAD. *Faculty:* 12 full-time (6 women), 3 part-time/adjunct (2 women). *Students:* 18 full-time (13 women); includes 5 minority (all Hispanic/Latino). Average age 28. 27 applicants, 41% accepted, 7 enrolled. In 2014, 7 master's awarded. *Degree requirements:* For master's, variable foreign language requirement, comprehensive exam, thesis. *Entrance requirements:* For master's, GRE General Test (for MA). Additional exam requirements/recommendations for international students: Required—TOEFL (minimum score 550 paper-based; 80 iBT). *Application deadline:* For fall admission, 2/1 for domestic and international students. Application fee: $60. Electronic applications accepted. *Expenses: Tuition:* Full-time $22,860; part-time $1270 per credit hour. *Financial support:* In 2014–15, 18 students received support, including 17 teaching assistantships (averaging $10,000 per year); institutionally sponsored loans, scholarships/grants, tuition waivers, and unspecified assistantships also available. Financial award application deadline: 4/15. *Unit head:* Dr. Sally Packard, Director, 817-257-7643, E-mail: s.packard@tcu.edu. *Application contact:* Donna Smolik, TCU College of Fine Arts Graduate Office, 817-257-7603, Fax: 817-257-5672, E-mail: cfagradinfo@tcu.edu.
Website: http://www.art.tcu.edu/

The University of Alabama, Graduate School, College of Arts and Sciences, Department of Art, Tuscaloosa, AL 35487. Offers art history (MA); studio art (MA, MFA), including ceramics, painting, photography, printmaking, sculpture. *Accreditation:* NASAD. Part-time programs available. *Faculty:* 16 full-time (9 women). *Students:* 22 full-time (16 women), 5 part-time (4 women); includes 3 minority (2 Black or African American, non-Hispanic/Latino; 1 Asian, non-Hispanic/Latino), 1 international. Average age 28. 22 applicants, 68% accepted, 10 enrolled. In 2014, 7 master's awarded. *Degree requirements:* For master's, one foreign language, comprehensive exam (for some programs), oral exam, thesis statement, exhibit (studio art), thesis (art history). *Entrance requirements:* For master's, GRE General Test or MAT (art history), minimum GPA of 3.0, BFA or equivalent (studio art). Additional exam requirements/recommendations for international students: Required—TOEFL (minimum score 550 paper-based). *Application deadline:* For fall admission, 3/15 for domestic and international students; for spring admission, 10/15 for domestic and international students. Applications are processed on a rolling basis. Application fee: $50 ($60 for international students). Electronic applications accepted. *Expenses:* Tuition, state resident: full-time $9826. Tuition, nonresident: full-time $24,950. *Financial support:* In 2014–15, 2 fellowships with full tuition reimbursements (averaging $14,000 per year), 13 teaching assistantships with full and partial tuition reimbursements (averaging $9,206 per year) were awarded; career-related internships or fieldwork, institutionally sponsored loans, scholarships/grants, and unspecified assistantships also available. Financial award application deadline: 7/14. *Faculty research:* Nineteenth-century American, Chinese, Baroque, twentieth-century, Asian art history. *Unit head:* William T. Dooley, Chairperson, 205-348-1890, Fax: 205-348-0287, E-mail: wtdooley@bama.ua.edu. *Application contact:* Craig R. Wedderspoon, Graduate Coordinator, 205-348-1898, Fax: 205-348-0287, E-mail: cwedders@bama.edu.
Website: http://www.art.ua.edu/

University of Alaska Fairbanks, College of Liberal Arts, Department of Art, Fairbanks, AK 99775-5640. Offers art (MFA); ceramics (MFA); computer art (MFA); drawing (MFA); painting (MFA); photography (MFA); printmaking (MFA); sculpture (MFA). Part-time programs available. *Faculty:* 8 full-time (4 women). *Students:* 6 full-time (all women), 1 (woman) part-time; includes 2 minority (1 Asian, non-Hispanic/Latino; 1 Hispanic/Latino), 1 international. Average age 32. 6 applicants, 17% accepted, 1 enrolled. In 2014, 3 master's awarded. *Degree requirements:* For master's, comprehensive exam, oral defense of project or thesis. *Entrance requirements:* For master's, portfolio of work including about 20 slides or appropriate equivalent depending on field of study. Additional exam requirements/recommendations for international students: Required—TOEFL (minimum score 550 paper-based; 79 iBT), IELTS (minimum score 6.5). *Application deadline:* For fall admission, 6/1 for domestic students, 3/1 for international students; for spring admission, 10/15 for domestic students, 9/1 for international students. Applications are processed on a rolling basis. Application fee: $60. Electronic applications accepted. *Expenses:* Tuition, state resident: full-time $7614; part-time $423 per credit. Tuition, nonresident: full-time $15,552; part-time $864 per credit. Tuition and fees vary according to course level, course load and reciprocity agreements. *Financial support:* In 2014–15, 6 teaching assistantships with full tuition reimbursements (averaging $9,319 per year) were awarded; fellowships with full tuition reimbursements, research assistantships with full tuition reimbursements, Federal Work-Study, scholarships/grants, health care benefits, and unspecified assistantships also available. Support available to part-time students. Financial award application deadline: 7/1; financial award applicants required to submit FAFSA. *Faculty research:* Computer art, survey of arts in Alaska, found object art, visualization and animation, painting from the wilderness. *Unit head:* David Mollett, Chair, 907-474-7530, Fax: 907-474-5853, E-mail: uaf-art@alaska.edu. *Application contact:* Mary Kreta, Director of Admissions, 907-474-7500, Fax: 907-474-7097, E-mail: admissions@uaf.edu.
Website: http://www.uaf.edu/art/

University of Colorado Boulder, Graduate School, College of Arts and Sciences, Department of Art and Art History, Boulder, CO 80309. Offers art history (MA), including contemporary art criticism, early twentieth-century art, nineteenth-century art, Russian and Soviet art; ceramics (MFA); drawing (MFA); painting (MFA); photography and media arts (MFA); printmaking (MFA); sculpture (MFA). *Faculty:* 23 full-time (11 women). *Students:* 50 full-time (32 women), 1 (woman) part-time; includes 6 minority (all Hispanic/Latino), 2 international. Average age 29. 213 applicants, 17% accepted, 21 enrolled. In 2014, 21 master's awarded. Terminal master's awarded for partial completion of doctoral program. *Degree requirements:* For master's, variable foreign language requirement, comprehensive exam, thesis (for some programs). *Entrance*

requirements: For master's, GRE General Test, minimum undergraduate GPA of 3.0, portfolio. *Application deadline:* For fall admission, 1/15 for domestic students, 12/1 for international students. Application fee: $50 ($70 for international students). Electronic applications accepted. *Financial support:* In 2014–15, 126 students received support, including 16 fellowships (averaging $1,206 per year), 43 teaching assistantships with full and partial tuition reimbursements available (averaging $26,856 per year); institutionally sponsored loans, scholarships/grants, health care benefits, and unspecified assistantships also available. Financial award application deadline: 1/15; financial award applicants required to submit FAFSA. *Faculty research:* Visual arts, fine arts, sculpture, installation art, inter-arts: interdisciplinary art forms.
Website: http://www.colorado.edu/arts/

University of Illinois at Urbana–Champaign, Graduate College, College of Fine and Applied Arts, School of Art and Design, Program in Studio Arts, Champaign, IL 61820. Offers art and design (MFA); crafts (MFA); metals (MFA); painting (MFA); photography (MFA); sculpture (MFA). *Accreditation:* NASAD. *Students:* 23 (16 women). *Entrance requirements:* For master's, minimum GPA of 3.0. Application fee: $70 ($90 for international students). *Unit head:* Timothy Van Laar, Chair, 217-333-6611, E-mail: tvanlaar@illinois.edu. *Application contact:* Ellen de Waard, Assistant to the Associate Director, 217-333-0642, Fax: 217-244-7688, E-mail: edewaard@illinois.edu.
Website: http://www.art.illinois.edu

University of Memphis, Graduate School, College of Communication and Fine Arts, Department of Art, Memphis, TN 38152. Offers art (Graduate Certificate); art history (MA), including Egyptian art and archaeology, general art history; ceramics (MFA); graphic design (MFA); interior design (MFA); painting (MFA); printmaking/photography (MFA). *Accreditation:* NASAD (one or more programs are accredited). *Faculty:* 19 full-time (7 women), 4 part-time/adjunct (2 women). *Students:* 34 full-time (28 women), 3 part-time (2 women); includes 5 minority (2 Asian, non-Hispanic/Latino; 2 Hispanic/Latino; 1 Two or more races, non-Hispanic/Latino). Average age 30. 24 applicants, 63% accepted, 10 enrolled. In 2014, 14 master's, 14 other advanced degrees awarded. *Degree requirements:* For master's, 2 foreign languages, comprehensive exam, thesis. *Entrance requirements:* For master's, GRE General Test or MAT, portfolio (MFA). *Application deadline:* For fall admission, 8/1 for domestic students; for spring admission, 12/1 for domestic students. Applications are processed on a rolling basis. Application fee: $35 ($60 for international students). *Financial support:* In 2014–15, 38 students received support. Research assistantships with full tuition reimbursements available, teaching assistantships with full tuition reimbursements available, Federal Work-Study, scholarships/grants, and unspecified assistantships available. Financial award application deadline: 2/15; financial award applicants required to submit FAFSA. *Faculty research:* Online collaborative learning, advanced art history studies, electronic publishing/design, studio arts, architectural studies. *Unit head:* Prof. Richard Lou, Chair, 901-678-2216, Fax: 901-678-2735, E-mail: gmyatt@memphis.edu. *Application contact:* Greely Myat, Graduate Studies Coordinator, 901-678-2650.
Website: http://memphis.edu/art/

University of Miami, Graduate School, College of Arts and Sciences, Department of Art and Art History, Coral Gables, FL 33124. Offers art history (MA); ceramics/glass (MFA); graphic design/multimedia (MFA); painting (MFA); photography/digital imaging (MFA); printmaking (MFA); sculpture (MFA). Part-time programs available. *Degree requirements:* For master's, variable foreign language requirement, thesis, exhibit (MFA), comprehensive exam (MA). *Entrance requirements:* For master's, GRE General Test (MA), research paper (MA), slide portfolio (MFA). Additional exam requirements/recommendations for international students: Required—TOEFL. Electronic applications accepted. *Faculty research:* Installation art, public art.

The University of Montana, Graduate School, College of Visual and Performing Arts, School of Art, Missoula, MT 59812-0002. Offers fine arts (MA), including art, art history; photography (MFA). *Accreditation:* NASAD (one or more programs are accredited). *Degree requirements:* For master's, thesis exhibit. *Entrance requirements:* For master's, GRE General Test, portfolio.

University of New Mexico, Graduate School, College of Fine Arts, Program in Art History, Albuquerque, NM 87131. Offers art history (MA); arts of the Americas (MA); history of architecture (PhD); history of graphic arts (PhD); history of photography (PhD); modern Latin American art history (PhD); Native American art history (PhD); Pre-Columbian art history (PhD); Spanish colonial art history (PhD). Part-time programs available. *Faculty:* 9 full-time (7 women). *Students:* 14 full-time (10 women), 22 part-time (16 women); includes 8 minority (2 American Indian or Alaska Native, non-Hispanic/Latino; 6 Hispanic/Latino), 5 international. Average age 32. 34 applicants, 26% accepted, 5 enrolled. In 2014, 5 master's, 1 doctorate awarded. *Degree requirements:* For master's, one foreign language, comprehensive exam (for some programs), thesis, symposium; for doctorate, 2 foreign languages, comprehensive exam, thesis/dissertation, symposium. *Entrance requirements:* Additional exam requirements/recommendations for international students: Required—TOEFL (minimum score 550 paper-based), IELTS (minimum score 6). *Application deadline:* For fall admission, 1/15 for domestic students; for spring admission, 1/15 for domestic students. Application fee: $50. Electronic applications accepted. *Financial support:* In 2014–15, fellowships (averaging $7,433 per year), research assistantships with tuition reimbursements (averaging $5,216 per year), teaching assistantships with partial tuition reimbursements (averaging $4,005 per year) were awarded; Federal Work-Study, institutionally sponsored loans, scholarships/grants, health care benefits, and unspecified assistantships also available. Support available to part-time students. Financial award application deadline: 3/1; financial award applicants required to submit FAFSA. *Faculty research:* Native American, modern Latin American, pre-Columbian, architectural, American, medieval, Spanish Colonial, and Latin American art; history of photography. *Unit head:* Prof. Mary Tsiongas, Chair, 505-277-5861, Fax: 505-277-5955, E-mail: tsiongas@unm.edu. *Application contact:* Kat Heatherington, Graduate Advisor, 505-277-6672, Fax: 505-277-5955, E-mail: art255@unm.edu.
Website: http://art.unm.edu/

University of Notre Dame, Graduate School, College of Arts and Letters, Division of Humanities, Department of Art, Art History, and Design, Notre Dame, IN 46556. Offers art history (MA); design (MFA), including graphic design, industrial design; studio art (MFA), including ceramics, painting, photography, printmaking, sculpture. *Accreditation:* NASAD. *Degree requirements:* For master's, comprehensive exam (for some programs), thesis. *Entrance requirements:* For master's, GRE General Test, minimum GPA of 3.0. Additional exam requirements/recommendations for international students: Required—TOEFL (minimum score 600 paper-based; 80 iBT). Electronic applications accepted. *Faculty research:* Studio art practice in ceramics, printing, photography, printmaking and sculpture, graphic design and industrial design, digital imaging in design and photography, Renaissance and American art history, contemporary art theory and criticism.

University of Oklahoma, Weitzenhoffer Family College of Fine Arts, School of Art and Art History, Norman, OK 73019. Offers art (MFA), including ceramics, film, painting, photography, printmaking, sculpture, video, visual communication; art history (MA, PhD), including art history (MA), art of the American West (PhD), Native American art (PhD). Part-time programs available. *Faculty:* 25 full-time (6 women). *Students:* 21 full-time (11 women), 11 part-time (7 women); includes 6 minority (4 American Indian or Alaska Native, non-Hispanic/Latino; 2 Two or more races, non-Hispanic/Latino), 1 international. Average age 32. 23 applicants, 48% accepted, 3 enrolled. In 2014, 7 master's awarded. Terminal master's awarded for partial completion of doctoral program. *Degree requirements:* For master's, comprehensive exam, thesis; for doctorate, comprehensive exam, thesis/dissertation. *Entrance requirements:* Additional exam requirements/recommendations for international students: Required—TOEFL (minimum score 79 iBT). *Application deadline:* For fall admission, 1/15 for domestic and international students; for spring admission, 10/1 for domestic and international students. Application fee: $50 ($100 for international students). Electronic applications accepted. *Expenses:* Tuition, state resident: full-time $4394; part-time $183.10 per credit hour. Tuition, nonresident: full-time $16,970; part-time $707.10 per credit hour. *Required fees:* $2892; $109.95 per credit hour. $126.50 per semester. *Financial support:* In 2014–15, 28 students received support, including 1 fellowship (averaging $5,000 per year), 16 teaching assistantships with partial tuition reimbursements available (averaging $10,377 per year); career-related internships or fieldwork, Federal Work-Study, institutionally sponsored loans, scholarships/grants, health care benefits, tuition waivers (full and partial), and unspecified assistantships also available. Support available to part-time students. Financial award application deadline: 6/1; financial award applicants required to submit FAFSA. *Faculty research:* Sculpture, painting, printmaking, technology, ceramics, Native American art, art of American West, Byzantine, Contemporary, Renaissance, Baroque, nineteenth-twentieth century. *Unit head:* 405-325-2691, Fax: 405-325-1668. *Application contact:* 405-325-2691, Fax: 405-325-1668.
Website: http://www.ou.edu/finearts/art_arthistory.html

University of Rochester, School of Arts and Sciences, Program in Photographic Preservation and Collections Management, Rochester, NY 14627. Offers MA. Program offered jointly with George Eastman House. Part-time programs available. *Students:* 9 full-time (7 women); includes 1 minority (Asian, non-Hispanic/Latino). 25 applicants, 48% accepted, 9 enrolled. *Degree requirements:* For master's, thesis (for some programs). *Entrance requirements:* Additional exam requirements/recommendations for international students: Required—TOEFL. *Application deadline:* For fall admission, 1/1 priority date for domestic students. Application fee: $60. Electronic applications accepted. *Expenses: Tuition:* Full-time $46,150; part-time $1442 per credit hour. *Required fees:* $504. *Financial support:* Fellowships, research assistantships, teaching assistantships, and tuition waivers (partial) available. *Faculty research:* Photographic preservation, collections management, photography. *Unit head:* Joan Saab, Director, E-mail: joan.saab@rochester.edu. *Application contact:* Gretchen Briscoe, Recruiting and Marketing Manager, 585-275-5029, E-mail: graduate.admissions@rochester.edu.
Website: http://www.rochester.edu/college/ppcm

University of Southern California, Graduate School, Roski School of Fine Arts, Graduate Programs in Fine Arts, Los Angeles, CA 90089. Offers new genres (MFA); painting/drawing (MFA); photography (MFA); sculpture (MFA). *Degree requirements:* For master's, thesis. *Entrance requirements:* For master's, portfolio, artist statement, 3 letters of recommendation. Additional exam requirements/recommendations for international students: Required—TOEFL (minimum score 600 paper-based; 100 iBT). Electronic applications accepted. *Faculty research:* Fine art production in the areas of photography, video, sculpture, drawing, and performance.

The University of Tennessee, Graduate School, College of Arts and Sciences, School of Art, Knoxville, TN 37996. Offers ceramics (MFA); drawing (MFA); graphic design (MFA); inter-area studies (MFA); media arts (MFA); painting (MFA); printmaking (MFA); sculpture (MFA); watercolor (MFA). *Accreditation:* NASAD. *Degree requirements:* For master's, thesis or alternative, exhibit. *Entrance requirements:* For master's, portfolio, minimum GPA of 2.7. Additional exam requirements/recommendations for international students: Required—TOEFL. Electronic applications accepted.

University of Utah, Graduate School, College of Fine Arts, Department of Art and Art History, Salt Lake City, UT 84112-0380. Offers art history (MA); ceramics (MFA); community-based art education (MFA); drawing (MFA); graphic design (MFA); painting (MFA); photography/digital imaging (MFA); printmaking (MFA); sculpture/intermedia (MFA). *Faculty:* 19 full-time (10 women), 22 part-time/adjunct (10 women). *Students:* 11 full-time (9 women), 5 part-time (2 women); includes 2 minority (both Hispanic/Latino), 1 international. Average age 30. 48 applicants, 31% accepted, 10 enrolled. In 2014, 5 master's awarded. *Degree requirements:* For master's, variable foreign language requirement, comprehensive exam (for some programs), thesis or alternative, exhibit and final project paper (for MFA). *Entrance requirements:* For master's, CD portfolio (MFA), writing sample (MA), curriculum vitae, letters of recommendation, letter of intent. Additional exam requirements/recommendations for international students: Required—TOEFL (minimum score 575 paper-based; 75 iBT). *Application deadline:* For fall admission, 1/15 priority date for domestic and international students. Application fee: $55 ($65 for international students). Electronic applications accepted. *Financial support:* In 2014–15, 2 fellowships, 6 research assistantships with partial tuition reimbursements, 34 teaching assistantships with partial tuition reimbursements were awarded; Federal Work-Study, institutionally sponsored loans, scholarships/grants, tuition waivers (partial), unspecified assistantships, and stipends also available. Financial award application deadline: 1/2; financial award applicants required to submit FAFSA. *Faculty research:* Studio art, European art history, Asian art history, Latin American art history, twentieth century/contemporary art history. *Total annual research expenditures:* $54,906. *Unit head:* Prof. Brian Snapp, Chair, 801-581-8677, Fax: 801-585-6171, E-mail: b.snapp@utah.edu. *Application contact:* Prof. Kim Martinez, Director of Graduate Studies, 801-581-8677, Fax: 801-585-6171, E-mail: kim.martinez@art.utah.edu.
Website: http://www.art.utah.edu/

University of Victoria, Faculty of Graduate Studies, Faculty of Fine Arts, Department of Visual Arts, Victoria, BC V8W 2Y2, Canada. Offers digital multimedia (MFA); drawing (MFA); painting (MFA); photography (MFA); sculpture (MFA); video (MFA). *Degree requirements:* For master's, exhibit, oral exam. *Entrance requirements:* For master's, portfolio, BFA. Additional exam requirements/recommendations for international students: Required—TOEFL (minimum score 575 paper-based), IELTS (minimum score 7). Electronic applications accepted.

University of Washington, Graduate School, College of Arts and Sciences, School of Art, Division of Art, Seattle, WA 98195. Offers painting and drawing (MFA); photography (MFA). *Degree requirements:* For master's, thesis, exhibit. *Entrance requirements:* For master's, BFA or equivalent academic work in art, 20 slide portfolio. Additional exam requirements/recommendations for international students: Required—TOEFL. Electronic applications accepted.

Virginia Commonwealth University, Graduate School, School of the Arts, Richmond, VA 23284-9005. Offers art education (MAE); art history (MA, PhD), including architectural history (MA), art history, historical studies (MA), museum studies (MA); ceramics (MFA); fibers (MFA); furniture design (MFA); glassworking (MFA); graphic design (MFA), including design/visual communications, interior environment, photography and film; jewelry/metalworking (MFA); kinetic imaging (MFA); music (MM), including education; painting (MFA); printmaking (MFA); sculpture (MFA); theatre (MFA), including acting, costume design, directing, pedagogy, scene design/technical

theater. Part-time programs available. *Entrance requirements:* For doctorate, GRE General Test, writing sample. Additional exam requirements/recommendations for international students: Required—TOEFL (minimum score 600 paper-based; 100 iBT). Electronic applications accepted.

Wayne State University, College of Fine, Performing and Communication Arts, James Pearson Duffy Department of Art and Art History, Program in Art, Detroit, MI 48202. Offers fibers (MFA); photography (MA); sculpture (MA). *Students:* 9 full-time (5 women), 8 part-time (5 women); includes 2 minority (1 Hispanic/Latino; 1 Two or more races, non-Hispanic/Latino), 1 international. Average age 35. 33 applicants, 15% accepted, 4 enrolled. In 2014, 9 master's awarded. *Degree requirements:* For master's, thesis exhibition (MFA), essay (MA). *Entrance requirements:* For master's, portfolio, personal interview, reference letters, statement of intent, BFA or equivalent coursework (for MA); superior portfolio, BFA or MA in art (for MFA). Additional exam requirements/recommendations for international students: Required—TOEFL (minimum score 550 paper-based), TWE (minimum score 5.5), Michigan English Language Assessment Battery (minimum score 85); Recommended—IELTS (minimum score 6.5). *Application deadline:* For fall admission, 2/1 for domestic and international students; for winter admission, 10/1 for domestic and international students. Application fee: $0. Electronic applications accepted. *Expenses:* Expenses: Contact institution. *Financial support:* In 2014–15, 9 students received support. Fellowships with tuition reimbursements available, teaching assistantships with tuition reimbursements available, scholarships/grants, and unspecified assistantships available. Financial award application deadline: 3/31; financial award applicants required to submit FAFSA. *Faculty research:* Painting, drawing, computer art. *Unit head:* Dr. John Richardson, Chair, 313-577-2980, Fax: 313-577-3491, E-mail: af5343@wayne.edu. *Application contact:* Jeffrey Abt, Professor, 313-993-6785, E-mail: jeffrey.abt@wayne.edu.
Website: http://art.wayne.edu/

Yale University, School of Art, New Haven, CT 06520-8339. Offers graphic design (MFA); painting/printmaking (MFA); photography (MFA); sculpture (MFA). *Degree requirements:* For master's, thesis (for some programs). *Entrance requirements:* Additional exam requirements/recommendations for international students: Required—TOEFL (minimum score 550 paper-based; 100 iBT). Electronic applications accepted. *Expenses:* Contact institution.

Textile Design

Academy of Art University, Graduate Program, School of Fashion, San Francisco, CA 94105-3410. Offers fashion design (MFA); fashion merchandising (MFA); fashion textiles (MFA); knitwear (MFA). Part-time programs available. Postbaccalaureate distance learning degree programs offered (no on-campus study). *Faculty:* 22 full-time (15 women), 65 part-time/adjunct (47 women). *Students:* 468 full-time (408 women), 232 part-time (215 women); includes 186 minority (88 Black or African American, non-Hispanic/Latino; 1 American Indian or Alaska Native, non-Hispanic/Latino; 53 Asian, non-Hispanic/Latino; 31 Hispanic/Latino; 1 Native Hawaiian or other Pacific Islander, non-Hispanic/Latino; 12 Two or more races, non-Hispanic/Latino), 389 international. Average age 28. 239 applicants, 100% accepted, 115 enrolled. In 2014, 197 master's awarded. *Degree requirements:* For master's, final review. *Entrance requirements:* For master's, statement of intent; resume; portfolio/reel; official college transcripts. *Application deadline:* Applications are processed on a rolling basis. Application fee: $100. Electronic applications accepted. *Expenses: Tuition:* Part-time $910 per unit. *Financial support:* Career-related internships or fieldwork and Federal Work-Study available. Support available to part-time students. Financial award application deadline: 8/10; financial award applicants required to submit FAFSA. *Unit head:* 800-544-ARTS, E-mail: info@academyart.edu. *Application contact:* 800-544-ARTS, E-mail: info@academyart.edu.
Website: http://www.academyart.edu/fashion-school/index.html

Arizona State University at the Tempe campus, Herberger Institute for Design and the Arts, School of Art, Tempe, AZ 85287-1505. Offers art education (MA); art history (MA); ceramics (MFA); design, environment and the arts (PhD), including history, theory and criticism; drawing (MFA); fibers (MFA); intermedia (MFA); metals (MFA); museum studies (MFA); painting (MFA); printmaking (MFA); sculpture (MFA); wood (MFA); MFA/MA. Terminal master's awarded for partial completion of doctoral program. *Degree requirements:* For master's, thesis/exhibition (MFA, MA in art education); interactive Program of Study (iPOS) submitted before completing 50 percent of required credit hours; for doctorate, comprehensive exam, thesis/dissertation, interactive Program of Study (iPOS) submitted before completing 50 percent of required credit hours. *Entrance requirements:* For master's, GRE or MAT, minimum GPA of 3.0 or equivalent in last 2 years of work leading to bachelor's degree; for doctorate, GRE, master's degree in architecture, graphic design, industrial design, interior design, landscape architecture, or art history or equivalent standing; statement of purpose; 3 letters of recommendation; indication of potential faculty mentor; sample of written work. Additional exam requirements/recommendations for international students: Required—TOEFL, IELTS, or PTE. Electronic applications accepted.

California College of the Arts, Graduate Programs, Fine Arts Programs, San Francisco, CA 94107. Offers ceramics (MFA); comics (MFA); film/video/performance (MFA); glass (MFA); interdisciplinary studies (MFA); jewelry/metal arts (MFA); media studies (MFA); painting/drawing (MFA); photography (MFA); printmaking (MFA); sculpture (MFA); social practice (MFA); textiles (MFA); wood/furniture (MFA). *Accreditation:* NASAD. *Degree requirements:* For master's, thesis, exhibit. *Entrance requirements:* For master's, appropriate bachelor's degree, portfolio, resume, 2 letters of recommendation, transcript. Additional exam requirements/recommendations for international students: Required—TOEFL (minimum score 600 paper-based; 100 iBT). Electronic applications accepted.

California State University, Los Angeles, Graduate Studies, College of Arts and Letters, Department of Art, Los Angeles, CA 90032-8530. Offers art (MA), including art education, art history, art therapy, ceramics, metals, and textiles, design (MA, MFA), painting, sculpture, and graphic arts, photography; fine arts (MFA), including crafts, design (MA, MFA), studio arts. *Accreditation:* NASAD (one or more programs are accredited). Part-time and evening/weekend programs available. *Degree requirements:* For master's, comprehensive exam, project or thesis. *Entrance requirements:* For master's, portfolio. Additional exam requirements/recommendations for international students: Required—TOEFL (minimum score 500 paper-based). Electronic applications accepted. *Expenses:* Tuition, state resident: full-time $6738; part-time $3609 per year. Tuition, nonresident: full-time $15,666; part-time $8073 per year. Tuition and fees vary according to course load, degree level and program. *Faculty research:* The artist and the book, conceptual art, ceramic processes, computer graphics, architectural graphics.

Cornell University, Graduate School, Graduate Fields of Human Ecology, Field of Fiber Science and Apparel Design, Ithaca, NY 14853. Offers apparel design (MA, MPS); fiber science (MS, PhD); polymer science (MS, PhD); textile science (MS, PhD). *Degree requirements:* For master's, thesis (MA, MS), project paper (MPS); for doctorate, comprehensive exam, thesis/dissertation. *Entrance requirements:* For master's, GRE General Test, 2 letters of recommendation, portfolio (for functional apparel design); for doctorate, GRE General Test, 2 letters of recommendation. Additional exam requirements/recommendations for international students: Required—TOEFL (minimum score 600 paper-based; 77 iBT). Electronic applications accepted. *Faculty research:* Apparel design, consumption, mass customization, 3-D body scanning.

Cranbrook Academy of Art, Graduate School, Program in Fine Arts, Bloomfield Hills, MI 48303-0801. Offers 2D design (MFA); ceramics (MFA); fiber (MFA); metalsmithing (MFA); painting (MFA); photography (MFA); print media (MFA); sculpture (MFA). *Accreditation:* NASAD. *Faculty:* 9 full-time (3 women). *Students:* 138 full-time (93 women); includes 18 minority (7 Asian, non-Hispanic/Latino; 5 Hispanic/Latino; 6 Two or more races, non-Hispanic/Latino), 31 international. Average age 27. 390 applicants, 35% accepted, 72 enrolled. *Degree requirements:* For master's, thesis, exhibit. *Entrance requirements:* Additional exam requirements/recommendations for international students: Required—TOEFL. *Application deadline:* For fall admission, 2/1 priority date for domestic and international students; for spring admission, 11/1 for domestic students. Application fee: $85. Electronic applications accepted. *Expenses: Tuition:* Full-time $31,916. *Required fees:* $2387. *Financial support:* Federal Work-Study available. Financial award application deadline: 2/15; financial award applicants required to submit FAFSA. *Unit head:* Christopher Scoates, Director, 248-645-3301, Fax: 248-645-3591. *Application contact:* Leslie Tobakos, Registrar/Financial Aid and Admissions Manager, 248-645-3360, Fax: 248-645-3591, E-mail: ltobakos@cranbrook.edu.

Drexel University, Antoinette Westphal College of Media Arts and Design, Program in Fashion Design, Philadelphia, PA 19104-2875. Offers MS. *Accreditation:* NASAD. *Degree requirements:* For master's, thesis, portfolio review. *Entrance requirements:* For master's, interview. Additional exam requirements/recommendations for international students: Required—TOEFL. Electronic applications accepted.

East Carolina University, Graduate School, College of Fine Arts and Communication, School of Art and Design, Greenville, NC 27858-4353. Offers art education (MA Ed); ceramics (MFA); graphic design (MFA); illustration (MFA); metal design (MFA); painting and drawing (MFA); photography (MFA); printmaking (MFA); sculpture (MFA); textile design (MFA); wood design (MFA). *Accreditation:* NASAD (one or more programs are accredited). Part-time and evening/weekend programs available. *Degree requirements:* For master's, comprehensive exam, thesis (for some programs). *Entrance requirements:* For master's, GRE General Test or MAT, portfolio. Additional exam requirements/recommendations for international students: Required—TOEFL. *Expenses:* Tuition, state resident: full-time $4223. Tuition, nonresident: full-time $16,540. *Required fees:* $2184.

Illinois State University, Graduate School, College of Fine Arts, School of Art, Normal, IL 61790-2200. Offers art history (MA, MS); ceramics (MFA, MS); drawing (MFA, MS); fibers (MFA, MS); glass (MFA, MS); graphic design (MFA, MS); metals (MFA, MS); painting (MFA, MS); photography (MFA, MS); printmaking (MFA, MS); sculpture (MFA, MS). *Accreditation:* NASAD (one or more programs are accredited). *Degree requirements:* For master's, thesis or alternative, internship. *Entrance requirements:* For master's, portfolio, sample of scholarly writing.

LIM College, MBA Program, New York, NY 10022-5268. Offers entrepreneurship (MBA); fashion management (MBA). *Accreditation:* ACBSP. *Entrance requirements:* For master's, interview. Additional exam requirements/recommendations for international students: Required—TOEFL (minimum score 550 paper-based; 80 iBT), IELTS (minimum score 6.5).

Lindenwood University, Graduate Programs, School of Fine and Performing Arts, St. Charles, MO 63301-1695. Offers fashion design (MA, MFA); studio art (MA, MFA); theatre (MFA). Part-time programs available. *Faculty:* 9 full-time (4 women), 4 part-time/adjunct (2 women). *Students:* 5 full-time (2 women), 6 part-time (4 women); includes 1 minority (Hispanic/Latino), 1 international. Average age 30. 16 applicants, 25% accepted, 4 enrolled. In 2014, 15 master's awarded. *Degree requirements:* For master's, thesis (for some programs), minimum cumulative GPA of 3.0. *Entrance requirements:* For master's, audition or interview, minimum GPA of 3.0, portfolio, letter of recommendation. Additional exam requirements/recommendations for international students: Required—TOEFL (minimum score 550 paper-based; 80 iBT). *Application deadline:* For fall admission, 8/24 priority date for domestic and international students; for spring admission, 1/24 priority date for domestic students, 1/25 priority date for international students. Applications are processed on a rolling basis. Application fee: $30 ($100 for international students). Electronic applications accepted. *Expenses: Tuition:* Full-time $15,230; part-time $440 per credit hour. *Required fees:* $205 per semester. Tuition and fees vary according to course level, course load and degree level. *Financial support:* In 2014–15, 1 student received support. Career-related internships or fieldwork, institutionally sponsored loans, scholarships/grants, tuition waivers (partial), and unspecified assistantships available. Financial award application deadline: 6/30; financial award applicants required to submit FAFSA. *Unit head:* Dr. Joseph Alsobrook, Dean of Fine and Performing Arts, 636-949-4164, Fax: 636-949-4910, E-mail: jalsobrook@lindenwood.edu. *Application contact:* Tyler Kostich, Dean of Evening Admissions and Extension Campuses, 636-949-4138, Fax: 636-949-4109, E-mail: adultadmissions@lindenwood.edu.

Massachusetts College of Art and Design, Graduate Programs, MFA Program, Boston, MA 02115-5882. Offers 2D fine arts (MFA), including painting; 3D fine arts (MFA), including ceramics, fibers, glass, jewelry and metalsmithing, sculpture; design (MFA, Postbaccalaureate Certificate), including dynamic media; fine arts (MFA), including interdisciplinary; media arts (MFA, Postbaccalaureate Certificate), including film/video (MFA), photography. *Accreditation:* NASAD. *Faculty:* 31 full-time (15 women), 42 part-time/adjunct (19 women). *Students:* 59 full-time (36 women), 32 part-time (23 women); includes 12 minority (2 Black or African American, non-Hispanic/Latino; 5 Asian, non-Hispanic/Latino; 5 Hispanic/Latino), 18 international. 278 applicants, 38% accepted, 40 enrolled. In 2014, 33 master's, 7 other advanced degrees awarded. *Degree requirements:* For master's, thesis, Exhibition for MFA non design. Thesis document MFA in design and low-residency. *Entrance requirements:* For master's, portfolio, college transcripts, resume, statement of purpose, letters of reference,

interview; 6 credits of art history taken prior to or during MFA program; for Postbaccalaureate Certificate, portfolio, college transcripts, resume, statement of purpose, letters of reference, interview. Additional exam requirements/recommendations for international students: Required—TOEFL (minimum score 550 paper-based; 85 iBT); Recommended—IELTS (minimum score 6.5). *Application deadline:* For fall admission, 1/6 priority date for domestic and international students. Application fee: $75. Electronic applications accepted. *Expenses:* Tuition, state resident: full-time $23,400; part-time $780 per credit. Tuition, nonresident: full-time $23,400; part-time $780 per credit. Tuition and fees vary according to course load and program. *Financial support:* In 2014–15, 37 students received support, including 40 teaching assistantships (averaging $2,160 per year); career-related internships or fieldwork, scholarships/grants, tuition waivers (partial), and unspecified assistantships also available. Support available to part-time students. Financial award application deadline: 1/6. *Unit head:* Paul Paturzo, Interim Dean of Graduate Studies, 617-879-7166, E-mail: pjpaturzo@massart.edu. *Application contact:* Isaac Goldstein, Graduate Admissions Counselor, 617-879-7203, Fax: 617-879-7250, E-mail: igoldstein@massart.edu. Website: http://www.massart.edu/Admissions/Graduate_Programs.html

The New School, Parsons The New School for Design, Program in Fashion Design and Society, New York, NY 10011. Offers MFA.

The New School, Parsons The New School for Design, Program in Fashion Studies, New York, NY 10011. Offers MA. *Degree requirements:* For master's, thesis.

Philadelphia University, School of Engineering and Textiles, Program in Textile Design, Philadelphia, PA 19144. Offers MS. Part-time programs available. *Entrance requirements:* For master's, GRE or MAT, minimum GPA of 2.8. Additional exam requirements/recommendations for international students: Required—TOEFL (minimum score 550 paper-based; 79 iBT). Electronic applications accepted.

Rhode Island School of Design, Graduate Studies, Division of Fine Arts, Department of Textiles, Providence, RI 02903-2784. Offers MFA. *Accreditation:* NASAD. *Faculty:* 8 full-time (4 women), 13 part-time/adjunct (9 women). *Students:* 12 full-time (10 women); includes 2 minority (1 Asian, non-Hispanic/Latino; 1 Hispanic/Latino), 5 international. Average age 27. 31 applicants, 29% accepted, 6 enrolled. In 2014, 6 master's awarded. *Degree requirements:* For master's, thesis, exhibit. *Entrance requirements:* For master's, portfolio, statement of purpose, 3 letters of recommendation. Additional exam requirements/recommendations for international students: Required—TOEFL (minimum score 580 paper-based; 93 iBT). *Application deadline:* For fall admission, 2/1 for domestic and international students. Application fee: $60. *Financial support:* Fellowships, teaching assistantships, career-related internships or fieldwork, Federal Work-Study, institutionally sponsored loans, scholarships/grants, and unspecified assistantships available. Financial award application deadline: 2/15; financial award applicants required to submit FAFSA. *Unit head:* Brooks Hagan, Head, 401-427-6916, Fax: 401-277-4883, E-mail: bhagan@risd.edu. *Application contact:* Molly Pettengil, Graduate Admissions Officer, 401-454-6312, Fax: 401-454-6309, E-mail: mpetteng@risd.edu.

Savannah College of Art and Design, Graduate School, Program in Fashion, Savannah, GA 31402-3146. Offers MA, MFA. Part-time programs available. *Faculty:* 22 full-time (15 women), 4 part-time/adjunct (all women). *Students:* 37 full-time (33 women), 23 part-time (18 women); includes 18 minority (15 Black or African American, non-Hispanic/Latino; 1 Asian, non-Hispanic/Latino; 2 Hispanic/Latino), 34 international. Average age 27. 79 applicants, 37% accepted, 19 enrolled. In 2014, 17 master's awarded. *Degree requirements:* For master's, thesis (for some programs), final project (for MA); internship (for MFA). *Entrance requirements:* For master's, portfolio. Additional exam requirements/recommendations for international students: Required—TOEFL (minimum score 550 paper-based, 85 iBT), IELTS (minimum score 6.5), or ACTFL. *Application deadline:* For fall admission, 4/1 for domestic and international students. Applications are processed on a rolling basis. Application fee: $40. Electronic applications accepted. *Expenses: Tuition:* Full-time $34,605; part-time $3845 per course. One-time fee: $500. Tuition and fees vary according to course load. *Financial support:* Fellowships, career-related internships or fieldwork, Federal Work-Study, and scholarships/grants available. Financial award application deadline: 4/1; financial award applicants required to submit FAFSA. *Unit head:* Jurgen Oeltjenbruns, Chair. *Application contact:* Jenny Jaquillard, Executive Director of Admissions, Recruitment and Events, 912-525-5100, Fax: 912-525-5985, E-mail: admission@scad.edu. Website: http://www.scad.edu/academics/programs/fashion

Savannah College of Art and Design, Graduate School, Program in Fibers, Savannah, GA 31402-3146. Offers MA, MFA. Part-time programs available. *Faculty:* 7 full-time (6 women), 3 part-time/adjunct (all women). *Students:* 13 full-time (10 women), 3 part-time (all women); includes 1 minority (Hispanic/Latino), 6 international. Average age 33. 16 applicants, 31% accepted, 5 enrolled. In 2014, 4 master's awarded. *Degree requirements:* For master's, thesis (for some programs), final project (for MA); internship (for MFA). *Entrance requirements:* For master's, portfolio. Additional exam requirements/recommendations for international students: Required—TOEFL (minimum score 550 paper-based, 85 iBT), IELTS (minimum score 6.5), or ACTFL. *Application deadline:* For fall admission, 4/1 for domestic and international students. Applications are processed on a rolling basis. Application fee: $40. Electronic applications accepted. *Expenses: Tuition:* Full-time $34,605; part-time $3845 per course. One-time fee: $500. Tuition and fees vary according to course load. *Financial support:* Fellowships, career-related internships or fieldwork, Federal Work-Study, and scholarships/grants available. Financial award application deadline: 4/1; financial award applicants required to submit FAFSA. *Unit head:* Cayewah Easley, Chair. *Application contact:* Jenny Jaquillard, Executive Director of Admissions, Recruitment and Events, 912-525-5100, Fax: 912-525-5985, E-mail: admission@scad.edu. Website: http://www.scad.edu/academics/programs/fibers

Savannah College of Art and Design, Graduate School, Program in Luxury and Fashion Management, Savannah, GA 31402-3146. Offers MA, MFA. Part-time programs available. *Students:* 84 full-time (76 women), 32 part-time (29 women); includes 42 minority (31 Black or African American, non-Hispanic/Latino; 6 Asian, non-Hispanic/Latino; 5 Hispanic/Latino), 40 international. Average age 27. 127 applicants, 46% accepted, 44 enrolled. In 2014, 36 master's awarded. *Degree requirements:* For master's, thesis (for some programs), final project (for MA); internship (for MFA). *Entrance requirements:* For master's, portfolio. Additional exam requirements/recommendations for international students: Required—TOEFL (minimum score 550 paper-based, 85 iBT), IELTS (minimum score 6.5), or ACTFL. *Application deadline:* For fall admission, 4/1 for domestic and international students. Applications are processed on a rolling basis. Application fee: $40. Electronic applications accepted. *Expenses: Tuition:* Full-time $34,605; part-time $3845 per course. One-time fee: $500. Tuition and fees vary according to course load. *Financial support:* Fellowships, career-related internships or fieldwork, Federal Work-Study, and scholarships/grants available. Financial award application deadline: 4/1; financial award applicants required to submit FAFSA. *Unit head:* Dan Green, Chair. *Application contact:* Jenny Jaquillard, Executive Director of Admissions, Recruitment and Events, 912-525-5100, Fax: 912-525-5985, E-mail: admission@scad.edu. Website: http://www.scad.edu/academics/programs/luxury-and-fashion-management

School of the Art Institute of Chicago, Graduate Division, Program in Fashion, Body, and Garment, Chicago, IL 60603-3103. Offers M Des, Certificate.

Temple University, Center for the Arts, Tyler School of Art, Department of Crafts, Philadelphia, PA 19122-6096. Offers ceramics/glass (MFA); fibers and material studies (MFA); metals/jewelry/CAD-CAM (MFA). *Faculty:* 7 full-time (3 women), 18 part-time/adjunct (14 women). *Students:* 17 full-time (11 women), 1 part-time (0 women); includes 2 minority (1 Asian, non-Hispanic/Latino; 1 Hispanic/Latino), 2 international. 65 applicants, 28% accepted, 9 enrolled. In 2014, 8 master's awarded. *Degree requirements:* For master's, essay, exhibit. *Entrance requirements:* For master's, minimum GPA of 3.0, slide portfolio, 40 credits in studio art, 12 credits in art history, letters of recommendation, resume/curriculum vitae. Additional exam requirements/recommendations for international students: Required—TOEFL (minimum score 550 paper-based; 79 iBT), IELTS (minimum score 6.5). *Application deadline:* For fall admission, 1/15 for domestic students, 12/15 for international students. Application fee: $60. Electronic applications accepted. *Expenses:* Expenses: Contact institution. *Financial support:* Fellowships with full tuition reimbursements, research assistantships with full tuition reimbursements, teaching assistantships with full tuition reimbursements, and Federal Work-Study available. Support available to part-time students. Financial award application deadline: 1/15; financial award applicants required to submit FAFSA. *Unit head:* Nicholas Kripal, Chair, 215-782-2790, Fax: 215-782-2799, E-mail: nkripal@temple.edu. *Application contact:* Nicole Hall, Director of Admissions, 215-777-9090, E-mail: tylerart@temple.edu.

University of California, Davis, Graduate Studies, Program in Textile Arts and Costume Design, Davis, CA 95616. Offers MFA. *Degree requirements:* For master's, presentation of an individual project/body of work. *Entrance requirements:* For master's, minimum GPA of 3.0, portfolio. Additional exam requirements/recommendations for international students: Required—TOEFL (minimum score 550 paper-based). Electronic applications accepted. *Faculty research:* Historic ethnographic and contemporary costume and textile design, computer-aided design.

University of Cincinnati, Graduate School, College of Design, Architecture, Art, and Planning, School of Design, Cincinnati, OH 45221. Offers fashion design (M Des); graphic design (M Des); industrial design (M Des); interaction design (M Des); product development (M Des). *Accreditation:* NASAD. *Students:* 34 full-time (16 women), 3 part-time (1 woman); includes 3 minority (1 Black or African American, non-Hispanic/Latino; 1 Asian, non-Hispanic/Latino; 1 Hispanic/Latino), 24 international. In 2014, 7 master's awarded. *Degree requirements:* For master's, thesis. *Entrance requirements:* For master's, undergraduate degree in design or related field, 2 years of work experience in design or related field. Additional exam requirements/recommendations for international students: Required—TOEFL. *Application deadline:* For fall admission, 2/1 for domestic students. Application fee: $30. Electronic applications accepted. *Financial support:* Fellowships, career-related internships or fieldwork, Federal Work-Study, tuition waivers (partial), and unspecified assistantships available. *Faculty research:* Design theory, interdisciplinary design topics. *Unit head:* Brigid O'Kane, Director, 513-556-0833, E-mail: brigid.okane@uc.edu. *Application contact:* Dr. J. Chewning, Information Contact, 513-556-2996, Fax: 513-556-0240, E-mail: j.chewning@uc.edu. Website: http://www.daap.uc.edu/

The University of Kansas, Graduate Studies, College of Liberal Arts and Sciences, Department of Visual Art, Lawrence, KS 66045. Offers ceramics (MFA); drawing and painting (MFA); metalsmithing/jewelry (MFA); printmaking (MFA); sculpture (MFA); textiles/fibers (MFA); visual art education (MA). *Accreditation:* NASAD. *Faculty:* 24 full-time, 7 part-time/adjunct. *Students:* 23 full-time (10 women), 1 (woman) part-time; includes 2 minority (1 American Indian or Alaska Native, non-Hispanic/Latino; 1 Two or more races, non-Hispanic/Latino), 4 international. Average age 29. 34 applicants, 38% accepted, 7 enrolled. In 2014, 13 master's awarded. *Degree requirements:* For master's, thesis (for some programs), oral examinations, thesis exhibition. *Entrance requirements:* For master's, portfolio, minimum GPA of 3.0, 3 letters of recommendation, image inventory. Additional exam requirements/recommendations for international students: Required—TOEFL. *Application deadline:* For fall admission, 1/15 priority date for domestic and international students. Application fee: $55 ($65 for international students). Electronic applications accepted. *Financial support:* Fellowships, teaching assistantships with full and partial tuition reimbursements, Federal Work-Study, scholarships/grants, and unspecified assistantships available. Financial award application deadline: 1/15; financial award applicants required to submit FAFSA. *Faculty research:* Metal and glass casting; mapping, indigenous lands and history; wood fire kilns; Japanese block printing techniques. *Unit head:* Mary Anne Jordan, Chair, 785-864-2952, E-mail: majordan@ku.edu. *Application contact:* Kay Isbell, Graduate Admissions Contact, 785-864-2957, E-mail: kisbell@ku.edu. Website: http://art.ku.edu/

The University of Manchester, School of Materials, Manchester, United Kingdom. Offers advanced aerospace materials engineering (M Sc); advanced metallic systems (PhD); biomedical materials (M Phil, M Sc, PhD); ceramics and glass (M Phil, M Sc, PhD); composite materials (M Sc, PhD); corrosion and protection (M Phil, M Sc, PhD); materials (M Phil, PhD); metallic materials (M Phil, M Sc, PhD); nanostructural materials (M Phil, M Sc, PhD); paper science (M Phil, M Sc, PhD); polymer science and engineering (M Phil, M Sc, PhD); technical textiles (M Sc); textile design, fashion and management (M Phil, M Sc, PhD); textile science and technology (M Phil, M Sc, PhD); textiles (M Phil, PhD); textiles and fashion (M Ent).

University of Minnesota, Twin Cities Campus, Graduate School, College of Design, Department of Design, Housing, and Apparel, Minneapolis, MN 55455-0213. Offers apparel (MA, MS, PhD); design communication (MA, MS, PhD); housing studies (MA, MS, PhD, Postbaccalaureate Certificate); interactive design (MFA); interior design (MA, MS, PhD). Part-time programs available. *Degree requirements:* For master's and Postbaccalaureate Certificate, comprehensive exam, thesis (for some programs); for doctorate, comprehensive exam, thesis/dissertation. *Entrance requirements:* For master's, GRE General Test, minimum GPA of 3.0 (preferred), portfolio, 3 letters of recommendation; for doctorate, GRE General Test, minimum GPA of 3.0 (preferred), portfolio, 3 letters of recommendation, writing sample; for Postbaccalaureate Certificate, GRE General Test, minimum GPA of 3.0 (preferred). Additional exam requirements/recommendations for international students: Required—TOEFL (minimum score 550 paper-based; 79 iBT). Electronic applications accepted. *Faculty research:* Housing policy and community development; consumer behavior; interactive design; design history; social, cultural, and behavioral issues related to designed environments.

The University of North Carolina at Greensboro, Graduate School, Bryan School of Business and Economics, Department of Consumer, Apparel, and Retail Studies, Greensboro, NC 27412-5001. Offers MS, PhD. *Degree requirements:* For master's, one foreign language; for doctorate, one foreign language, thesis/dissertation. *Entrance requirements:* For master's and doctorate, GRE General Test. Additional exam requirements/recommendations for international students: Required—TOEFL. Electronic applications accepted. *Faculty research:* Impact of phosphate removal, protective clothing for pesticide workers, fabric hand: subjective and objective measurements.

Textile Design

University of North Texas, Robert B. Toulouse School of Graduate Studies, Denton, TX 76203-5459. Offers accounting (MS); applied anthropology (MA, MS); applied behavior analysis (Certificate); applied geography (MA); applied technology and performance improvement (M Ed, MS); art education (MA); art history (MA); art museum education (Certificate); arts leadership (Certificate); audiology (Au D); behavior analysis (MS); behavioral science (PhD); biochemistry and molecular biology (MS); biology (MA, MS); biomedical engineering (MS); business analysis (MS); chemistry (MS); clinical health psychology (PhD); communication studies (MA, MS); computer engineering (MS); computer science (MS); counseling (M Ed, MS), including clinical mental health counseling (MS), college and university counseling, elementary school counseling, secondary school counseling; creative writing (MA); criminal justice (MS); curriculum and instruction (M Ed); decision sciences (MBA); design (MA, MFA), including fashion design (MFA), innovation studies, interior design (MFA); early childhood studies (MS); economics (MS); educational leadership (M Ed, Ed D); educational psychology (MS, PhD), including family studies (MS), gifted and talented (MS), human development (MS), learning and cognition (MS), research, measurement and evaluation (MS); electrical engineering (MS); emergency management (MPA); engineering technology (MS); English (MA); English as a second language (MA); environmental science (MS); finance (MBA, MS); financial management (MPA); French (MA); health services management (MBA); higher education (M Ed, Ed D); history (MA, MS); hospitality management (MS); human resources management (MPA); information science (MS); information systems (PhD); information technologies (MBA); interdisciplinary studies (MA, MS); international studies (MA); international sustainable tourism (MS); jazz studies (MM); journalism (MA, MJ, Graduate Certificate), including interactive and virtual digital communication (Graduate Certificate), narrative journalism (Graduate Certificate), public relations (Graduate Certificate); kinesiology (MS); linguistics (MA); local government management (MPA); logistics (PhD); logistics and supply chain management (MBA); long-term care, senior housing, and aging services (MA); management (PhD); marketing (MBA); mathematics (MA, MS); mechanical and energy engineering (MS, PhD); music (MA), including ethnomusicology, music theory, musicology, performance; music composition (PhD); music education (MM Ed, PhD); nonprofit management (MPA); operations and supply chain management (MBA); performance (MM, DMA); philosophy (MA); political science (MA); professional and technical communication (MA); radio, television and film (MA, MFA); rehabilitation counseling (Certificate); sociology (MA); Spanish (MA); special education (M Ed); speech-language pathology (MA); strategic management (MBA); studio art (MFA); teaching (M Ed); MBA/MS. Part-time and evening/weekend programs available. Postbaccalaureate distance learning degree programs offered. *Faculty:* 651 full-time (215 women), 233 part-time/adjunct (139 women). *Students:* 3,040 full-time (1,598 women), 3,401 part-time (2,097 women); includes 1,740 minority (533 Black or African American, non-Hispanic/Latino; 15 American Indian or Alaska Native, non-Hispanic/Latino; 286 Asian, non-Hispanic/Latino; 746 Hispanic/Latino; 3 Native Hawaiian or other Pacific Islander, non-Hispanic/Latino; 157 Two or more races, non-Hispanic/Latino), 1,145 international. Terminal master's awarded for partial completion of doctoral program. *Degree requirements:* For master's, variable foreign language requirement, comprehensive exam (for some programs), thesis (for some programs); for doctorate, variable foreign language requirement, comprehensive exam (for some programs), thesis/dissertation; for other advanced degree, variable foreign language requirement, comprehensive exam (for some programs). *Entrance requirements:* For master's and doctorate, GRE, GMAT. Additional exam requirements/recommendations for international students: Required—TOEFL (minimum score 550 paper-based; 79 iBT). *Application deadline:* For fall admission, 7/15 for domestic students, 3/15 for international students; for spring admission, 11/15 for domestic students, 9/15 for international students; for summer admission, 5/1 for domestic students. Applications are processed on a rolling basis. Application fee: $60. Electronic applications accepted. *Expenses:* Tuition, state resident: full-time $5450; part-time $3633 per year. Tuition, nonresident: full-time $11,966; part-time $7977 per year. *Required fees:* $1301; $398 per credit hour. $685 per semester. Tuition and fees vary according to program and reciprocity agreements. *Financial support:* Fellowships with partial tuition reimbursements, research assistantships with partial tuition reimbursements, teaching assistantships, career-related internships or fieldwork, Federal Work-Study, institutionally sponsored loans, scholarships/grants, health care benefits, and library assistantships available. Support available to part-time students. Financial award applicants required to submit FAFSA. *Unit head:* Mark Wardell, Dean, 940-565-2383, E-mail: mark.wardell@unt.edu. *Application contact:* Toulouse School of Graduate Studies, 940-565-2383, Fax: 940-565-2141, E-mail: gradsch@unt.edu. Website: http://tsgs.unt.edu/

Wayne State University, College of Fine, Performing and Communication Arts, James Pearson Duffy Department of Art and Art History, Program in Art, Detroit, MI 48202. Offers fibers (MFA); photography (MA); sculpture (MA). *Students:* 9 full-time (5 women), 8 part-time (5 women); includes 2 minority (1 Hispanic/Latino; 1 Two or more races, non-Hispanic/Latino), 1 international. Average age 35. 33 applicants, 15% accepted, 4 enrolled. In 2014, 9 master's awarded. *Degree requirements:* For master's, thesis exhibition (MFA), essay (MA). *Entrance requirements:* For master's, portfolio, personal interview, reference letters, statement of intent, BFA or equivalent coursework (for MA); superior portfolio, BFA or MA in art (for MFA). Additional exam requirements/recommendations for international students: Required—TOEFL (minimum score 550 paper-based), TWE (minimum score 5.5), Michigan English Language Assessment Battery (minimum score 85); Recommended—IELTS (minimum score 6.5). *Application deadline:* For fall admission, 2/1 for domestic and international students; for winter admission, 10/1 for domestic and international students. Application fee: $0. Electronic applications accepted. *Expenses:* Expenses: Contact institution. *Financial support:* In 2014–15, 9 students received support. Fellowships with tuition reimbursements available, teaching assistantships with tuition reimbursements available, scholarships/grants, and unspecified assistantships available. Financial award application deadline: 3/31; financial award applicants required to submit FAFSA. *Faculty research:* Painting, drawing, computer art. *Unit head:* Dr. John Richardson, Chair, 313-577-2980, Fax: 313-577-3491, E-mail: af5343@wayne.edu. *Application contact:* Jeffrey Abt, Professor, 313-993-6785, E-mail: jeffrey.abt@wayne.edu. Website: http://art.wayne.edu/

FASHION INSTITUTE OF TECHNOLOGY
State University of New York
M.A. in Exhibition Design

 For more information, visit http://petersons.to/fitexhibitiondesign

Programs of Study

The Fashion Institute of Technology (FIT), a State University of New York (SUNY) college of art and design, business, and technology, is home to a mix of innovative achievers, creative thinkers, and industry pioneers. FIT fosters interdisciplinary initiatives, advances research, and provides access to an international network of professionals. With a reputation for excellence, FIT offers its diverse student body access to world-class faculty, dynamic and relevant curricula, and a superior education at an affordable cost. It offers seven programs of graduate study. The programs in Art Market; Exhibition Design; Fashion and Textile Studies: History, Theory, Museum Practice; and Sustainable Interior Environments lead to the Master of Arts (M.A.) degree. The Illustration program leads to the Master of Fine Arts (M.F.A.) degree. The Master of Professional Studies (M.P.S.) degree programs are Cosmetics and Fragrance Marketing and Management, and Global Fashion Management.

The 39-credit, full-time Exhibition Design M.A. program prepares students for careers in the exhibition design profession, teaching them how to convey intellectual content, incite emotion, and engage audiences within the designed environment. The studio-driven, 16-month course of study centers on the designer's role within the exhibition team, with emphasis on the development of both design and conceptual development skills. Students explore exhibitions in museums, historic sites, expositions, retail venues, and public arenas, while working with narrative, audience research, architecture, environmental graphics, lighting, rendering, model-making, and production. An international travel seminar focusing on professional practices in the industry is available to interested students. All graduating students complete an independent qualifying paper and applied exhibition design project. An internship elective is available to interested students upon completion of their degree requirements.

Research Facilities

The School of Graduate Studies is primarily located in the campus's Shirley Goodman Resource Center, which also houses the Gladys Marcus Library and The Museum at FIT. School of Graduate Studies facilities include conference rooms; a fully equipped conservation laboratory; a multipurpose laboratory for conservation projects and the dressing of mannequins; storage facilities for costume and textile materials; a graduate student lounge with computer and printer access; a graduate student library reading room with computers, reference materials, and copies of past classes' qualifying and thesis papers; specialized wireless classrooms; traditional and digital illustration studios; and classrooms equipped with model stands, easels, and drafting tables.

The Gladys Marcus Library houses more than 300,000 volumes of print, nonprint, and digital resources. Specialized holdings include industry reference materials, manufacturers' catalogues, original fashion sketches and scrapbooks, photographs, portfolios of plates, and sample books. The FIT Digital Library provides access to over 90 searchable online databases.

The Museum at FIT houses one of the world's most important collections of clothing and textiles and is the only museum in New York City dedicated to the art of fashion. The permanent collection encompasses more than 50,000 garments and accessories dating from the eighteenth century, with particular strength in twentieth-century fashion, as well as 30,000 textiles and 100,000 textile swatches. Each year, nearly 100,000 visitors are drawn to the museum's award-winning exhibitions and public programs.

Financial Aid

FIT directly administers its institutional grants, scholarships, and loans. Federal funding administered by the college may include Federal Perkins Loans, federally subsidized and unsubsidized Direct Loans for students, Grad PLUS loans, and the Federal Work-Study Program. Priority for institutionally administered funds is given to students enrolled and designated as full-time.

Cost of Study

Tuition for New York State residents is $5,435 per semester, or $453 per credit. Out-of-state residents' tuition is $11,105 per semester, or $925 per credit. Tuition and fees are subject to change at the discretion of FIT's Board of Trustees. Additional expenses—for class materials, textbooks, and travel—may apply and vary per program.

Living and Housing Costs

On-campus housing is available to graduate students. Traditional residence hall accommodations (including meal plan) cost from $6,548 to $6,743 per semester. Apartment-style housing options (not including meal plan) cost from $6,060 to $10,095 per semester.

Student Group

Enrollment in the School of Graduate Studies is approximately 200 students per academic year, allowing considerable individual advisement. Students come to FIT from throughout the country and around the world.

Student Outcomes

Graduates of the Exhibition Design program find employment with architectural and exhibition design firms, museums, historic trusts, and special-events companies.

Location

FIT is located in Manhattan's Chelsea neighborhood, at the heart of the advertising, visual arts, marketing, fashion, business, design, and communications industries. Students are connected to New York City and gain unparalleled exposure to their field through guest lectures, field trips, internships, and sponsored competitions. The location provides access to major museums, galleries, and auction houses as well as dining, entertainment, and shopping options. The campus is near subway, bus, and commuter rail lines.

Fashion Institute of Technology

Applying

Applicants to all School of Graduate Studies programs must hold a baccalaureate degree in an appropriate major from a college or university, with a cumulative GPA of 3.0 or higher. International students from non-English-speaking countries are required to submit minimum TOEFL scores of 550 on the written test, 213 on the computer test, or 80 on the Internet test. Each major has additional, specialized prerequisites for admission; for detailed information, students should visit the School of Graduate Studies on FIT's website.

Domestic and international students use the same application when seeking admission. The deadline for completed applications with transcripts and supplemental materials is February 15 for the Exhibition Design program. After the deadline date, applicants are considered on a rolling admissions basis. Candidates may apply online at fitnyc.edu/gradstudies.

Correspondence and Information

School of Graduate Studies
Shirley Goodman Resource Center, Room E315
Fashion Institute of Technology
227 West 27 Street
New York, New York 10001-5992
Phone: 212-217-4300
Fax: 212-217-4301
E-mail: gradinfo@fitnyc.edu
Websites: http://www.fitnyc.edu/gradstudies
　　　　　http://www.fitnyc.edu/exhibitiondesign

THE FACULTY

A partial list of faculty members is below. Guest lecturers are not included.

Brenda Cowan, Associate Chairperson; M.S.Ed., Bank Street College of Education.

Robin Drake, B.S., Pratt.

Joseph Karadin.

Lynda Kennedy, Ph.D., CUNY Graduate Center.

Christina Lyons, M.S., Pratt.

Karl Matsuda, Exhibition Design Certificate, Cooper Union.

John Newman, M.A., Parsons.

Rick Orlosky, B.F.A., Hartford Art School.

Michael Stiller, B.A., Bard.

Kate Schein Waisman, M.S.Ed., Bank Street College of Education.

Michele Y. Washington, M.S., Pratt.

FASHION INSTITUTE OF TECHNOLOGY
State University of New York
M.F.A. in Illustration

 For more information, visit http://petersons.to/fitillustration

Programs of Study

The Fashion Institute of Technology (FIT), a State University of New York (SUNY) college of art and design, business, and technology, is home to a mix of innovative achievers, creative thinkers, and industry pioneers. FIT fosters interdisciplinary initiatives, advances research, and provides access to an international network of professionals. With a reputation for excellence, FIT offers its diverse student body access to world-class faculty, dynamic and relevant curricula, and a superior education at an affordable cost. It offers seven programs of graduate study. The programs in Art Market; Exhibition Design; Fashion and Textile Studies: History, Theory, Museum Practice; and Sustainable Interior Environments lead to the Master of Arts (M.A.) degree. The Illustration program leads to the Master of Fine Arts (M.F.A.). The Master of Professional Studies (M.P.S.) programs are Cosmetics and Fragrance Marketing and Management, and Global Fashion Management.

The 60-credit evening and weekend Illustration M.F.A. program is designed for working professionals seeking advanced study to further develop their skills as master illustrators. The program focuses on high-level techniques, new media applications, and illustration business practices. The curriculum encompasses digital and traditional studio methods, entrepreneurial research and writing, and opportunities in new and emerging markets. The program features assignments that mirror marketplace demands and specifications, regular guest lecturers, an intensive trip to the West Coast that provides opportunities for interactions with artists at film and entertainment studios, and regular off-campus engagement with New York City's art and design world. Students complete a visual thesis project and an independently researched and written master's thesis.

Research Facilities

The School of Graduate Studies is primarily located in the campus's Shirley Goodman Resource Center, which also houses the Gladys Marcus Library and The Museum at FIT. School of Graduate Studies facilities include conference rooms; a fully equipped conservation laboratory; a multipurpose laboratory for conservation projects and the dressing of mannequins; storage facilities for costume and textile materials; a graduate student lounge with computer and printer access; a graduate student library reading room with computers, reference materials, and copies of past classes' qualifying and thesis papers; specialized wireless classrooms; traditional and digital illustration studios; and classrooms equipped with model stands, easels, and drafting tables.

The Gladys Marcus Library houses more than 300,000 volumes of print, nonprint, and digital resources. Specialized holdings include industry reference materials, manufacturers' catalogues, original fashion sketches and scrapbooks, photographs, portfolios of plates, and sample books. The FIT Digital Library provides access to over 90 searchable online databases.

The Museum at FIT houses one of the world's most important collections of clothing and textiles and is the only museum in New York City dedicated to the art of fashion. The permanent collection encompasses more than 50,000 garments and accessories dating from the eighteenth century to the present, with particular strength in twentieth-century fashion, as well as 30,000 textiles and 100,000 textile swatches. Each year, nearly 100,000 visitors are drawn to the museum's award-winning exhibitions and public programs.

Financial Aid

FIT directly administers its institutional grants, scholarships, and loans. Federal funding administered by the college may include Federal Perkins Loans, federally subsidized and unsubsidized Direct Loans for students, Grad PLUS loans, and the Federal Work-Study Program. Priority for institutionally administered funds is given to students enrolled and designated as full-time.

Cost of Study

Tuition for New York State residents is $5,435 per semester, or $453 per credit. Out-of-state residents' tuition is $11,105 per semester, or $925 per credit. Tuition and fees are subject to change at the discretion of FIT's Board of Trustees. Additional expenses—for class materials, textbooks, and travel—may apply and vary per program.

Living and Housing Costs

On-campus housing is available to graduate students. Traditional residence hall accommodations (including meal plan) cost from $6,548 to $6,743 per semester. Apartment-style housing options (not including meal plan) cost from $6,060 to $10,095 per semester.

Student Group

Enrollment in the School of Graduate Studies is approximately 200 students per academic year, allowing considerable individualized advisement. Students come to FIT from throughout the country and around the world.

Student Outcomes

Students in the Illustration program graduate with a personal vision, an entrepreneurial spirit, and the skills needed to succeed as freelance illustrators.

Location

FIT is located in Manhattan's Chelsea neighborhood, at the heart of the advertising, visual arts, marketing, fashion, business, design, and communications industries. Students are connected to New York City and gain unparalleled exposure to their field through guest lectures, field trips, internships, and sponsored competitions. The location provides access to major museums, galleries, and auction houses as well as dining, entertainment, and shopping options. The campus is near subway, bus, and commuter rail lines.

Applying

Applicants to all School of Graduate Studies programs must hold a baccalaureate degree in an appropriate major from a college or university, with a cumulative GPA of 3.0 or higher. International students from non-English-speaking countries are required to submit minimum TOEFL scores of 550 on the written test, 213 on the computer test, or 80 on the Internet test. Each major has additional, specialized prerequisites for admission; for detailed information, students should visit the School of Graduate Studies on FIT's website.

Domestic and international students use the same application when seeking admission. The deadline for completed applications with transcripts and supplemental materials is February 15 for the Illustration program. After the deadline date, applicants are considered on a rolling admissions basis. Candidates may apply online at fitnyc.edu/gradstudies.

SECTION 1: APPLIED ARTS AND DESIGN

Fashion Institute of Technology

Correspondence and Information

School of Graduate Studies
Shirley Goodman Resource Center, Room E315
Fashion Institute of Technology
227 West 27 Street
New York, New York 10001-5992
Phone: 212-217-4300
Fax: 212-217-4301
E-mail: gradinfo@fitnyc.edu
Websites: http://www.fitnyc.edu/gradstudies
             http://www.fitnyc.edu/gradillustration

THE FACULTY

A partial list of faculty members is below. Guest lecturers are not included.

Melanie Reim, Associate Chairperson; M.F.A., Syracuse.
Daniel Abraham, J.D., Miami (Florida).
Steve Brodner, B.F.A., Cooper Union.
Celia Bullwinkel, M.F.A., School of Visual Arts.
Michael De Feo.
Dennis Dittrich, M.F.A., Syracuse.
Rudy Gutierrez, B.F.A., Pratt.
Michael Hyde, Ph.D., NYU.
Brendan Leach, M.F.A., School of Visual Arts.
Aya Kakeda, M.F.A., School of Visual Arts.
Monika Maniecki, M.F.A., Fashion Institute of Technology.
Anelle Miller, B.F.A., Parsons.
Bruno Nadalin, M.F.A., Fashion Institute of Technology, M.A., New Jersey City.
John Nickle, M.F.A., South Florida.
Cheryl Phelps, B.F.A., Memphis College of Art.
Martha Rich, M.F.A., Pennsylvania.
Jack Tom, M.F.A., Hartford.
Martin Wittfooth, M.F.A., School of Visual Arts.
Carmile S. Zaino.

FASHION INSTITUTE OF TECHNOLOGY

State University of New York

M.A. in Sustainable Interior Environments

 For more information, visit http://petersons.to/fitsustainableinterior

Programs of Study

The Fashion Institute of Technology (FIT), a State University of New York (SUNY) college of art and design, business, and technology, is home to a mix of innovative achievers, creative thinkers, and industry pioneers. FIT fosters interdisciplinary initiatives, advances research, and provides access to an international network of professionals. With a reputation for excellence, FIT offers its diverse student body access to world-class faculty, dynamic and relevant curricula, and a superior education at an affordable cost. It offers seven programs of graduate study. The programs in Art Market; Exhibition Design; Fashion and Textile Studies: History, Theory, Museum Practice; and Sustainable Interior Environments lead to the Master of Arts (M.A.) degree. The Illustration program leads to the Master of Fine Arts (M.F.A.) degree. The Master of Professional Studies (M.P.S.) degree programs are Cosmetics and Fragrance Marketing and Management, and Global Fashion Management.

Sustainable Interior Environments is a 36-credit, two-year, part-time evening M.A. program for established professionals, including practicing interior designers, architects, facilities planners, and managers. The program's intensive, hands-on curriculum focuses on the principles and theories of sustainable design as they apply to the built environment. Through experiential learning, specialized science courses, case studies, and research, students acquire a deep understanding of human psychological, physiological, and ergonomic needs, as well as information about toxic substances, pollution prevention, environmental systems, energy efficiency, and resource conservation. A graduate seminar guides students toward their research-oriented thesis project.

Research Facilities

The School of Graduate Studies is primarily located in the campus's Shirley Goodman Resource Center, which also houses the Gladys Marcus Library and The Museum at FIT. School of Graduate Studies facilities include conference rooms; a fully equipped conservation laboratory; a multipurpose laboratory for conservation projects and the dressing of mannequins; storage facilities for costume and textile materials; a graduate student lounge with computer and printer access; a graduate student library reading room with computers, reference materials, and copies of past classes' qualifying and thesis papers; specialized wireless classrooms; traditional and digital illustration studios; classrooms equipped with model stands, easels, and drafting tables; and specialized lighting and chemistry labs.

The Gladys Marcus Library houses more than 300,000 volumes of print, nonprint, and digital resources. Specialized holdings include industry reference materials, manufacturers' catalogues, original fashion sketches and scrapbooks, photographs, portfolios of plates, and sample books. The FIT Digital Library provides access to over 90 searchable online databases.

Financial Aid

FIT directly administers its institutional grants, scholarships, and loans. Federal funding administered by the college may include Federal Perkins Loans, federally subsidized and unsubsidized Direct Loans for students, Grad PLUS loans, and the Federal Work-Study Program. Priority for institutionally administered funds is given to students enrolled and designated as full-time.

Cost of Study

Sustainable Interior Environments is a part-time program and tuition is paid per credit. Tuition for New York State residents is $453 per credit. Out-of-state residents' tuition is $925 per credit. Tuition and fees are subject to change at the discretion of FIT's Board of Trustees. Additional expenses—for class materials, textbooks, and travel—may apply.

Living and Housing Costs

Residence facilities are available to graduate students. Traditional residence hall accommodations (including meal plan) cost from $6,548 to $6,743 per semester. Apartment-style housing options (not including meal plan) cost from $6,060 to $10,095 per semester.

Student Group

Enrollment in the School of Graduate Studies is approximately 200 students per academic year, allowing considerable individualized advisement. Students come to FIT from throughout the country and around the world.

Student Outcomes

Students in the Sustainable Interior Environments program gain highly marketable expertise that enables them to advance in their current employment, as well as assume leadership positions in the design industry, educational institutions, and research centers.

Location

FIT is located in Manhattan's Chelsea neighborhood, at the heart of the advertising, visual arts, marketing, fashion, business, design, and communications industries. Students are connected to New York City and gain unparalleled exposure to their field through guest lectures, field trips, internships, and sponsored competitions. The location provides access to major museums, galleries, and auction houses as well as dining, entertainment, and shopping options. The campus is near subway, bus, and commuter rail lines.

Applying

Applicants to all School of Graduate Studies programs must hold a baccalaureate degree in an appropriate major from a college or university, with a cumulative GPA of 3.0 or higher. International students from non-English-speaking countries are required to submit minimum TOEFL scores of 550 on the written test, 213 on the computer test, or 80 on the Internet test. Each major has additional, specialized prerequisites for admission; for detailed information, students should visit the School of Graduate Studies on FIT's website.

Domestic and international students use the same application when seeking admission. (Please note that as a part-time graduate program Sustainable Interior Environments is not able to provide support for international study visas.) The deadline for completed applications with transcripts and supplemental materials is February 15. After the deadline date, applicants are considered on a rolling admissions basis. Candidates may apply online at fitnyc.edu/gradstudies.

Correspondence and Information

School of Graduate Studies
Shirley Goodman Resource Center, Room E315
Fashion Institute of Technology
227 West 27 Street
New York, New York 10001-5992
Phone: 212-217-4300
Fax: 212-217-4301
E-mail: gradinfo@fitnyc.edu
Websites: http://www.fitnyc.edu/gradstudies
　　　　　 http://www.fitnyc.edu/SIE

Fashion Institute of Technology

THE FACULTY

A partial list of faculty members is below. Guest lecturers are not included.

Barbara Campagna, Acting Chairperson; M.S., Columbia.

Catherine Bobenhausen, M.S., NJIT.

Kacper Dolatowski, Ph.D. candidate, Academy of Fine Arts (Poland).

Ronald Eligator, M.S., Yale.

Brian Fallon, Ph.D., Indiana.

Mandi Gibbons.

Susan Kaplan, B.Arch., CUNY, City College.

Arthur H. Kopelman, Ph.D., CUNY Graduate Center.

Murray Levi, B.Arch., Cooper Union.

Eleanor Luken, Ph.D. candidate, CUNY Graduate Center.

Seema Pandya, B.F.A., Rocky Mountain College.

Karen R. Pearson, Ph.D., Washington State.

PRATT INSTITUTE
School of Design

Programs of Study

Pratt has been educating professionals for productive careers in the field of design since its founding in 1887. Pratt's School of Design, one of the largest of its kind, offers an outstanding professional art and design education taught by a faculty of working professionals who bring high standards and current practices to the classroom. Faculty members have received more than eighteen Tiffany, Fulbright, and Guggenheim awards as well as other prestigious professional awards. Pratt's graduate interior design program was ranked second nationally by *DesignIntelligence* in 2015; graduate industrial design was ranked fourth. *U.S. News & World Report* ranked Pratt's interior design program first in the country, communications design was ranked twelfth, and industrial design was ranked fifth.

Pratt offers master's degrees in a variety of programs, including Master of Fine Arts in Communications Design, Master of Science in Package Design or Interior Design, and Master of Industrial Design.

Graduates of Pratt's design programs have the competitive edge needed to obtain top administrative and creative positions in design studios, businesses, various industries, and arts organizations.

All graduate design curricula include supportive course work in the humanities. Students can choose from a wide array of course offerings, including art and design history, comparative literature, philosophy, foreign languages, and social sciences. The graduate programs require the completion of 30 to 68 credits and last from 1½ to 3 years, depending on the curriculum and the number of prerequisites that have not been met at the time of admission. For the granting of degrees, all of the graduate programs require the submission of a thesis or a comparable effort. For the M.F.A., an exhibition and supporting corollary statement are required. Candidates for the M.S. and the M.I.D. degrees must present a thesis project that demonstrates a meaningful contribution to design and documents the supportive research that informs all phases of design and construction.

Research Facilities

The Pratt Library contains 186,589 bound volumes, serial backfiles, and other material (including government documents); 251,603 audiovisual materials; and 3,996 microforms and subscribes to 925 periodicals.

Pratt maintains numerous studios, shops, and technical facilities for work in all media as well as state-of-the-art computer facilities. Digital arts labs include state-of-the-art Macintosh, PC/NT, and UNIX operating systems as well as digital video and audio systems. Pratt also has extensive gallery space for exhibitions.

Financial Aid

Financial aid awards are offered through a variety of institutional, state, and federally funded programs. These include Graduate Scholarships awarded by departments to incoming students on the basis of merit, endowed and restricted scholarships for continuing students, and student employment. Assistantships are awarded on a competitive basis to continuing students in all departments. Special alumni-sponsored fellowships are also available.

Cost of Study

Graduate tuition for 2015–16 is $28,638 per year (full-time 18 credits, $1,591 per credit) and student fees are $1,932 per year. The cost of books and supplies varies widely, depending on the program in which the student is enrolled.

Living and Housing Costs

Campus housing continues to be expanded to meet students' needs and is available for single students on a first-come, first-served basis. Housing costs average $17,646 per academic year. Pratt offers limited graduate student housing two blocks away from the campus. There is a plentiful supply of moderately priced rentals in the immediate area and in adjacent neighborhoods for married students seeking housing and for those students choosing to reside off campus.

Student Group

In educating more than four generations of students to be creative, technically skilled, and adaptable professionals, Pratt has gained an international reputation that attracts about 4,550 undergraduate and graduate students annually from forty-eight states and eighty-one countries.

Location

Pratt Institute's 25-acre, parklike main campus is situated among the turn-of-the-century mansions, Victorian brownstones, and wide, tree-lined boulevards of Clinton Hill, one of Brooklyn's historic neighborhoods. Midtown Manhattan, the heart of New York City, is only 25 minutes away by subway and offers students a vast array of professional, cultural, and recreational opportunities. Pratt also maintains a satellite facility in Manhattan's Chelsea district. Pratt Manhattan houses the Institute's communications/packaging design degree program.

The Institute

A private, nonsectarian institute of higher education, Pratt Institute was founded by the industrialist and philanthropist Charles Pratt. Changing with the needs and requirements of the professional world for which it prepares its graduates, Pratt today educates 3,145 undergraduate and 1,411 graduate students for careers in art and design, architecture, and library and information science.

Applying

The deadline for applications and all supporting materials, including portfolio, is January 5. Applicants should complete the application process online. Early submission of applications with all necessary credentials is highly desirable. For applicants who intend to file for financial aid, applications and all supporting documents should be received no later than January 5 for the fall semester and October 1 for the spring semester. Applications received after these dates are considered if openings exist in a particular program.

Correspondence and Information

Graduate Admissions Office
Pratt Institute
200 Willoughby Avenue
Brooklyn, New York 11205
United States
Phone: 718-636-3514
      800-331-0834 (toll-free)
Fax: 718-399-4242
E-mail: admissions@pratt.edu
Website: http://www.pratt.edu
      http://www.pratt.edu/admissions/request-information (to request information)

THE FACULTY

Anita Cooney, Dean

Communications/Package Design

Santiago Piedrafita, Chair, Associate Professor; M.S. Pratt.
Warren Bernard, Assistant Chair, Adjunct Assistant Professor; M.S., Pratt.
Michelle Hinebrook, Assistant Chair and Adjunct Assistant Instructor; M.F.A., Cranbrook Academy of Art.
Berry Berger, Visiting Associate Professor; B.I.D., Pratt.
Eric Bintner, Visiting Instructor; M.F.A., Cranbrook.
Jean Brennan, Adjunct Associate Professor; M.S., Pratt.
Tom Delaney, Visiting Instructor.
Antonio DiSpigna, Professor; M.S., Pratt.
Thomas Dolle, Adjunct Professor; B.F.A., Rhode Island School of Design; CCE.
Tyra Nicole Dumars, Visiting Instructor; M.P.S., Pratt.
David Frisco, Adjunct Associate Professor; M.F.A., Yale.
Kevin Gatta, Professor; M.S., Pratt.
J. Roger Guilfoyle, Adjunct Professor; B.A., Creighton; CCE.
J. Graham Hanson, Adjunct Associate Professor; B.F.A., Iowa State.
William Hilson, Adjunct Professor; CCE.
Allen Hori, Visiting Associate Professor; M.F.A., Cranbrook Academy of Art.
Thomas Klinkowstein, Adjunct Professor; M.S., Syracuse; CCE.
Gusty Lange, Adjunct Professor; M.P.S., Pratt, CCE.
Eunsun Lee, Adjunct Associate Professor; M.S., Pratt.
Alex Liebergesell, Associate Professor; M.F.A., Yale.
Brenda McManus, Adjunct Assistant Professor; M.S., Pratt.
Scott Menchin, Adjunct Associate Professor.
Kelli Miller, Visiting Assistant Professor; M.F.A., Cranbrook.
Katya Moorman, Adjunct Associate Professor; M.F.A., Cranbrook.
Ann Morris, Adjunct Assistant Professor; M.A., CUNY, Hunter.
Eric O'Toole, Adjunct Assistant Professor; B.I.D., Pratt.
Alan Rapp, Visiting Assistant Professor; M.F.A., School of Visual Arts.
Marc Rosen, Visiting Associate Professor; M.S., Pratt.
Andrew Shea, Visiting Assistant Professor; M.F.A., Maryland Institute College of Art.
Ryan Waller, Adjunct Assistant Professor; M.F.A., Yale.
Pirco Wolfframm, Adjunct Associate Professor; M.F.A., California Institute of the Arts; CCE.
Alisa Zamir, Professor; M.S., Pratt.

Industrial Design

Scott Lundberg, Chair, Adjunct Associate Professor; M.I.D., Pratt; CCE.
Harvey Bernstein, Adjunct Professor; M.S., Pratt; CCE.
Meri Bourgard-Rohrs, Visiting Professor; M.F.A., Pratt; CCE.
Gina Caspi, Visiting Professor; M.I.D., Pratt.
Gihyun Cho, Adjunct Professor; M.I.D., Syracuse.

SECTION 1: DESIGN

Pratt Institute

Kevin Crowley, Visiting Assistant Professor; B.I.D., Pratt.
Lucia DeRespinis, Adjunct Professor; B.I.D., Pratt; CCE.
Peter Erickson, Visiting Instructor.
Patrick Fenton, Visiting Instructor; M.F.A., Stanford.
Colin Gentle, Visiting Assistant Professor; B.Eng., Connecticut.
Mark Goetz, Adjunct Professor; B.I.D., Pratt.
Bruce Hannah, Professor; B.I.D., Pratt.
Kate Hixon, Adjunct Associate Professor; CCE.
Jay Levy, Visiting Assistant Professor; M.Arch., Columbia.
Jong. S. (Mark) Lim, Adjunct Professor; M.F.A., Pratt, CCE.
Frank Millero, Visiting Assistant Professor; M.I.D., Pratt.
Katrin Mueller-Russo, Associate Professor.
Rebeccah Pailes-Friedman, Adjunct Associate Professor; M.I.D., Pratt.
Jeanne Pfordresher, Adjunct Assistant Professor; B.F.A., Cleveland Institute of Art.
Arthur Sempliner, Adjunct Professor; M.B.A., Michigan.
Martin Skalski, Professor; M.I.D., Pratt.
Irvin Tepper, Adjunct Professor; M.F.A., Washington (Seattle), CCE.
William Jeffrey Tolbert, Adjunct Associate Professor; M.F.A., Yale.
Ignacio Urbina Polo, Associate Professor; M.S., Universidad Federal de Santa Catarina (Brazil).
Rebecca Welz, Adjunct Professor; B.A., SUNY Empire State College; CCE.
Henry Yoo, Adjunct Professor; M.I.D., Pratt, CCE.

Interior Design

Karin Tehve, Acting Chair; M.Arch., Harvard.
T. Camille Martin, Acting Assistant Chair; M.Arch., Washington (St. Louis).
Doreen Adengo, Visiting Assistant Professor; M.Arch., Yale.
Goil Amornvivat, Visiting Assistant Professor; M.Arch., Yale.
Brook Anderson, Visiting Assistant Professor; B.F.A., Kansas.
Eric Ansel, Visiting Assistant Professor; M.Arch., Pratt.
Tarek Ashkar, Visiting Assistant Professor; M.Arch., Harvard.
Francesca Bastianini, Visiting Assistant Professor; M.F.A., Parsons.
Tania Branquinho, Visiting Assistant Professor; M.Arch., Pratt.
Mary Burke, Adjunct Associate Professor; M.S., Columbia.
Tania Chau, Visiting Assistant Professor; M.S., Pratt.
Der Sean Chou, Visiting Assistant Professor; M.S., NYU.
Melissa Cicetti, Visiting Assistant Professor; M.Arch., Pennsylvania.
Annie Coggan, Visiting Assistant Professor; M.Arch., Southern California Institute of Architecture.
James Conti, Adjunct Associate Professor; M.F.A., Ohio State.
James Counts Jr., Visiting Assistant Professor; M.S., Columbia.
Wendy Cronk, Visiting Assistant Professor; M.Arch., Harvard.
Ron Eng, Visiting Assistant Professor; M.Arch., MIT.
Philip Farrell, Adjunct Professor; M.S., Pratt.
David C. Foley, Visiting Professor; M.Arch., Notre Dame.
Pavlina Gantcheva, Visiting Assistant Professor; M.S., Columbia.
Nicolas Guillin, Visiting Assistant Professor; M.F.A., École Nationale Supérieure de Création Industrielle (Paris).
Adam Hayes, Visiting Instructor; B.Arch., Rice.
John Heida, Visiting Assistant Professor; B.Arch., California College of the Arts.
Claudia Hernandez, Visiting Assistant Professor; M.S., Columbia.
Sarah Hill, Visiting Assistant Professor; M.S., Pratt.
Lindsay Homer, Visiting Associate Professor; M.S., Pratt.
Ben Howes, Visiting Assistant Professor; M.S., Stevens.
Latoya Nelson Kamdang, Visiting Assistant Professor; M.Arch., George Washington.
Sheryl Kasak, Adjunct Associate Professor; M.S., Columbia.
Ted Kilcommons, Visiting Instructor; B.A., Texas.
Margaret Kirk, Visiting Assistant Professor; M.Arch., Pratt.
Eugene Kwak, Visiting Assistant Professor; M.S., Columbia.
Annie K. Kwon, Visiting Assistant Professor; M.S., Columbia.
Chelsea Limbird, Visiting Assistant Professor; M.Arch., Rhode Island School of Design.
Jason Livingston, Visiting Assistant Professor; M.F.A., NYU.
Jennifer Logun, Visiting Assistant Professor; M.Arch., Florida.
Cam Lorendo, Adjunct Associate Professor; B.A., Parsons.
William Mangold, Adjunct Associate Professor; Ph.D., CUNY Graduate Center.
Anthony Mekel, Adjunct Assistant Professor; B.Arch., Pratt.
Francine Monaco, Adjunct Associate Professor; B.Arch., Cincinnati.
John Nafziger, Visiting Professor; M.Arch. II, Yale.
Robert Nassar, Visiting Assistant Professor; B.F.A., Syracuse.
Joseph E. Nocella, Visiting Assistant Professor; M.Arch., Kansas.
Tetsu Ohara, Visiting Assistant Professor; certificate of architecture, Harvard.
Jon Otis, Professor; M.S., Massachusetts.
Danny Ka Ho Pang, Visiting Assistant Professor; M.S., Pratt.
Andrew Pettit, Adjunct Associate Professor; B.Arch., Pratt.
J. Woodson Rainey, Visiting Assistant Professor; B.Arch., Utah.
Eduardo Rega, Visiting Assistant Professor; M.S., Columbia.
Christian Rietzke, Visiting Assistant Professor; M.Arch., Pratt.
Rachely Rotem, Visiting Assistant Professor; M.S., Columbia.
Mary-Jo Schlachter, Visiting Assistant Professor; M.Arch., Pennsylvania.
Irina Schneid; M.Arch., Cornell.
Deborah Schneiderman, Associate Professor; M.Arch., Southern California Institute of Architecture, RA, LEED AP.
Corie Sharples, Visiting Assistant Professor.
Hazel Siegel, Visiting Assistant Professor; M.F.A., CUNY, Hunter.

Andrew Simons, Visiting Assistant Professor; B.F.A., Carnegie Mellon.
Darius Somers, Visiting Assistant Professor; M.S., Columbia.
Sarah Strauss, Visiting Associate Professor; M.Arch., Yale.
Keena Suh, Adjunct Associate Professor; M.Arch., Columbia.
Myonggi Sul, Professor; M.S., Pratt.
Madeleine Taylor; Adjunct Assistant Professor; M.S., Columbia.
Jack Travis, Adjunct Assistant Professor; M.Arch., Illinois at Urbana–Champaign.
Loukia Tsafoulia, Visiting Assistant Professor; M.S.A.A.D., Columbia.
Kevin Walz, Visiting Associate Professor; Pratt.
William Watson, Visiting Assistant Professor; M.Arch., Texas at Austin.
Henry Weintraub, Visiting Assistant Professor; M.Arch., Harvard.
Alexandra Griffith Winton, Visiting Associate Professor; M.A., Bard.
Piotr Woronkowicz, Visiting Instructor; B.S., Art Center College of Design.
Corey Yurkovich, Visiting Assistant Professor; M.S., Harvard.
Edwin Zawadzki, Visiting Assistant Professor; M.Arch., Yale.
Michael Zuckerman, Adjunct Associate Professor; B.Arch., CUNY, City College; RA, LEED, AP.

© 2015 Bob Handelman

© 2015 Bob Handelman

Section 2
Architecture

This section contains a directory of institutions offering graduate work in architecture, followed by in-depth entries submitted by institutions that chose to prepare detailed program descriptions. Additional information about programs listed in the directory but not augmented by an in-depth entry may be obtained by writing directly to the dean of a graduate school or chair of a department at the address given in the directory.

For programs offering related work, see also in this book *Applied Arts and Design, Art and Art History,* and *Public, Regional, and Industrial Affairs.* In another guide in this series:

Graduate Programs in Engineering & Applied Sciences
See *Civil and Environmental Engineering*

CONTENTS

Architectural History

Arizona State University at the Tempe campus, Herberger Institute for Design and the Arts, The Design School, PhD Program in Design, Environment and the Arts, Tempe, AZ 85287-2105. Offers design (PhD); digital culture (PhD); healthcare and healing environments (PhD); history, theory, and criticism (PhD). *Degree requirements:* For doctorate, comprehensive exam, thesis/dissertation, interactive Program of Study (iPOS) submitted before completing 50 percent of required credit hours. *Entrance requirements:* For doctorate, GRE, master's degree in architecture, graphic design, industrial design, interior design, landscape architecture, or art history or equivalent standing; statement of purpose; 3 letters of recommendation; indication of potential faculty mentor; sample of written work. Additional exam requirements/recommendations for international students: Required—TOEFL, IELTS, or PTE. Electronic applications accepted. *Expenses:* Contact institution.

Cornell University, Graduate School, Graduate Fields of Architecture, Art and Planning, Field of Architecture, Ithaca, NY 14853-0001. Offers architectural design (M Arch); architectural science (MS); computer graphics (MS); history of architecture (MA, PhD); history of urban development (MA, PhD); theory and criticism of architecture (M Arch); urban design (M Arch). *Degree requirements:* For master's, one foreign language, thesis (MA, MS); for doctorate, 2 foreign languages, comprehensive exam, thesis/dissertation. *Entrance requirements:* For master's, GRE General Test, 5-year bachelor's degree in architecture, portfolio (M Arch), 3 letters of recommendation; for doctorate, GRE General Test, 3 letters of recommendation. Additional exam requirements/recommendations for international students: Required—TOEFL (minimum score 600 paper-based; 77 iBT). Electronic applications accepted. *Faculty research:* Architectural design and urban design, theory and criticism of architecture, computer graphics, building technology and environmental science, history of architecture and history of urban-development.

The Graduate Center, City University of New York, Graduate Studies, Program in Art History, New York, NY 10016-4039. Offers architecture (PhD); graphic arts (PhD); painting (PhD); photography (PhD); sculpture (PhD). *Degree requirements:* For doctorate, 2 foreign languages, thesis/dissertation. *Entrance requirements:* For doctorate, GRE General Test. Additional exam requirements/recommendations for international students: Required—TOEFL. Electronic applications accepted.

Harvard University, Graduate School of Arts and Sciences, Department of History of Art and Architecture, Cambridge, MA 02138. Offers ancient art (PhD); ancient Near Eastern art (PhD); Baroque art (PhD); Byzantine art (PhD); classical art (PhD); Indian art (PhD); Islamic art (PhD); Japanese and Chinese art (PhD); medieval art (PhD); modern art (PhD); Renaissance and modern architecture (PhD); Renaissance art (PhD). *Degree requirements:* For doctorate, variable foreign language requirement, thesis/dissertation, general exams; reading exams in French, German, and Italian. *Entrance requirements:* For doctorate, GRE General Test. Additional exam requirements/recommendations for international students: Required—TOEFL.

Massachusetts Institute of Technology, School of Architecture and Planning, Department of Architecture, Cambridge, MA 02139. Offers architecture (M Arch, PhD), including building technology (PhD), design and computation (PhD), history and theory of architecture (PhD), history and theory of art (PhD); architecture studies (SM Arch S); art, culture and technology (SMACT); building technology (SMBT). *Faculty:* 33 full-time (12 women), 1 part-time/adjunct (0 women). *Students:* 213 full-time (97 women); includes 42 minority (5 Black or African American, non-Hispanic/Latino; 20 Asian, non-Hispanic/Latino; 13 Hispanic/Latino; 4 Two or more races, non-Hispanic/Latino), 100 international. Average age 28. 1,179 applicants, 12% accepted, 79 enrolled. In 2014, 65 master's, 6 doctorates awarded. *Degree requirements:* For master's, thesis; for doctorate, comprehensive exam, thesis/dissertation. *Entrance requirements:* For master's and doctorate, GRE General Test. Additional exam requirements/recommendations for international students: Required—TOEFL, IELTS (minimum score 7). *Application deadline:* For fall admission, 12/31 for domestic and international students. Application fee: $75. Electronic applications accepted. *Expenses: Tuition:* Full-time $44,720; part-time $699 per unit. *Required fees:* $296. *Financial support:* In 2014–15, 171 students received support, including 139 fellowships (averaging $22,100 per year), 25 research assistantships (averaging $32,000 per year), 23 teaching assistantships (averaging $34,500 per year); Federal Work-Study, institutionally sponsored loans, scholarships/grants, health care benefits, and unspecified assistantships also available. Financial award application deadline: 4/15; financial award applicants required to submit FAFSA. *Faculty research:* Architecture; urbanism; building technology and sustainability; computation and design; history, theory, and criticism; art, culture, and technology. *Total annual research expenditures:* $1.2 million. *Unit head:* J. Meejin Yoon, Professor and Head of Department, 617-253-7791, E-mail: arch@mit.edu. *Application contact:* Admissions Coordinator, 617-715-4490, Fax: 617-253-8993, E-mail: arch@mit.edu.
Website: http://architecture.mit.edu/

New York University, Graduate School of Arts and Science, Program in Historical and Sustainable Architecture, New York, NY 10012-1019. Offers MA. *Students:* 12 full-time (8 women); includes 2 minority (both Hispanic/Latino). Average age 25. 17 applicants, 100% accepted, 12 enrolled. In 2014, 14 master's awarded. *Entrance requirements:* For master's, GRE, writing sample. *Application deadline:* For fall admission, 3/1 for domestic and international students. Application fee: $100. *Financial support:* Application deadline: 3/1. *Unit head:* Mosette Broderick, Director of Graduate Studies, 212-998-8180, Fax: 212-995-4152, E-mail: histsust@nyu.edu. *Application contact:* Jon Ritter, Assistant Director, 212-998-8180, Fax: 212-995-4152, E-mail: histsust@nyu.edu.
Website: http://arthistory.as.nyu.edu/

Roger Williams University, School of Architecture, Art and Historic Preservation, Bristol, RI 02809. Offers architecture (M Arch); art and architectural history (MA); historical preservation (MS). *Faculty:* 14 full-time (3 women), 16 part-time/adjunct (4 women). *Students:* 80 full-time (24 women), 18 part-time (8 women); includes 12 minority (1 Black or African American, non-Hispanic/Latino; 2 Asian, non-Hispanic/Latino; 8 Hispanic/Latino; 1 Two or more races, non-Hispanic/Latino), 7 international. Average age 25. 77 applicants, 87% accepted, 46 enrolled. In 2014, 49 master's awarded. *Degree requirements:* For master's, thesis. *Entrance requirements:* For master's, portfolio, 2 letters of recommendation. Additional exam requirements/recommendations for international students: Recommended—TOEFL (minimum score 85 iBT), IELTS. *Application deadline:* For fall admission, 3/1 priority date for domestic students. Application fee: $50. Electronic applications accepted. *Expenses:* Expenses: $33,792 (for M Arch); $20,644 (for MS in historical preservation). *Financial support:* In 2014–15, 84 students received support, including fellowships with partial tuition reimbursements available (averaging $6,000 per year), 80 research assistantships (averaging $3,000 per year). Financial award application deadline: 6/15; financial award applicants required to submit FAFSA. *Unit head:* Stephen White, Dean, 401-254-3607, E-mail: swhite@rwu.edu. *Application contact:* Lori Vales, Director of Graduate Admissions, 401-254-6200, Fax: 401-254-3557, E-mail: gradadmit@rwu.edu.
Website: http://www.rwu.edu/academics/departments/architecture.htm#dual

Savannah College of Art and Design, Graduate School, Program in Architectural History, Savannah, GA 31402-3146. Offers MA, MFA. Part-time programs available. *Faculty:* 8 full-time (1 woman). *Students:* 6 full-time (5 women), 6 part-time (5 women); includes 1 minority (Hispanic/Latino). Average age 30. 4 applicants, 50% accepted, 2 enrolled. In 2014, 3 master's awarded. *Degree requirements:* For master's, one foreign language, thesis (for some programs), internship (for MFA). *Entrance requirements:* For master's, research paper. Additional exam requirements/recommendations for international students: Required—TOEFL (minimum score 550 paper-based, 85 iBT), IELTS (minimum score 6.5), or ACTFL. *Application deadline:* For fall admission, 4/1 for domestic and international students. Applications are processed on a rolling basis. Application fee: $40. Electronic applications accepted. *Expenses: Tuition:* Full-time $34,605; part-time $3845 per course. One-time fee: $500. Tuition and fees vary according to course load. *Financial support:* Fellowships, career-related internships or fieldwork, Federal Work-Study, and scholarships/grants available. Financial award application deadline: 4/1; financial award applicants required to submit FAFSA. *Unit head:* Dr. Robin Williams, Chair. *Application contact:* Jenny Jaquillard, Executive Director of Admissions, Recruitment and Events, 912-525-5100, Fax: 912-525-5985, E-mail: admission@scad.edu.
Website: http://www.scad.edu/academics/programs/architectural-history

University of California, Berkeley, Graduate Division, College of Environmental Design, Department of Architecture, Berkeley, CA 94720-1500. Offers architecture (M Arch); building science (MS, PhD); building structures, construction and materials (MS, PhD); design theories, methods, and practices (MS, PhD); environmental design in developing countries (MS, PhD); history of architecture and urbanism (MS, PhD); social and cultural processes in architecture and urbanism (MS, PhD); M Arch/MCP; M Arch/MS; MLA/M Arch. *Degree requirements:* For master's, thesis; for doctorate, thesis/dissertation, qualifying exam. *Entrance requirements:* For master's and doctorate, GRE General Test, minimum GPA of 3.0, 3 letters of recommendation. Additional exam requirements/recommendations for international students: Required—TOEFL. Electronic applications accepted.

University of Colorado Denver, College of Architecture and Planning, Program in Design and Planning, Denver, CO 80217. Offers history of architecture, landscape and urbanism (PhD); sustainable and healthy environments (PhD). Part-time programs available. *Students:* 9 full-time (3 women), 11 part-time (9 women); includes 1 minority (Hispanic/Latino), 7 international. Average age 38. 32 applicants, 6% accepted, 1 enrolled. In 2014, 4 doctorates awarded. *Degree requirements:* For doctorate, comprehensive exam, thesis/dissertation. *Entrance requirements:* For doctorate, GRE (minimum score of 158 for both verbal and quantitative; writing 4.0), minimum undergraduate GPA of 3.0, graduate 3.5; writing sample; three letters of recommendation; statement of personal and professional goals. Additional exam requirements/recommendations for international students: Required—TOEFL (minimum score 80 iBT); Recommended—IELTS (minimum score 6.8). *Application deadline:* For fall admission, 2/2 for domestic students, 1/2 for international students; for spring admission, 10/1 for domestic students. Application fee: $50 ($75 for international students). Electronic applications accepted. *Expenses:* Expenses: Contact institution. *Financial support:* In 2014–15, 2 students received support. Fellowships, research assistantships, teaching assistantships, Federal Work-Study, institutionally sponsored loans, scholarships/grants, traineeships, and unspecified assistantships available. Financial award application deadline: 4/1; financial award applicants required to submit FAFSA. *Faculty research:* Land use and environmental planning and design; design and planning processes and practices; history, theory, and criticism of the built environment. *Unit head:* Dr. Osman Attmann, Director, 303-315-0032, Fax: 303-556-3687, E-mail: o.attmann@ucdenver.edu. *Application contact:* Rachael Kuroiwa, Manager of Admissions and Outreach, 303-315-2325, E-mail: rachael.kuroiwa@ucdenver.edu.
Website: http://www.ucdenver.edu/academics/colleges/ArchitecturePlanning/Academics/DegreePrograms/PhD/Pages/PhD.aspx

University of Pittsburgh, Dietrich School of Arts and Sciences, Department of History of Art and Architecture, Pittsburgh, PA 15260. Offers MA, PhD. *Faculty:* 14 full-time (7 women). *Students:* 34 full-time (28 women); includes 7 minority (2 American Indian or Alaska Native, non-Hispanic/Latino; 3 Asian, non-Hispanic/Latino; 2 Hispanic/Latino). Average age 33. 60 applicants, 12% accepted, 5 enrolled. In 2014, 2 master's, 3 doctorates awarded. *Degree requirements:* For master's, one foreign language, thesis; for doctorate, 2 foreign languages, comprehensive exam, thesis/dissertation. *Entrance requirements:* For doctorate, GRE General Test, 3 letters of recommendation, writing sample, statement of purpose. Additional exam requirements/recommendations for international students: Required—TOEFL (minimum score 550 paper-based; 90 iBT). *Application deadline:* For fall admission, 12/15 for domestic and international students. Application fee: $50. Electronic applications accepted. *Expenses:* Tuition, state resident: full-time $20,742; part-time $838 per credit. Tuition, nonresident: full-time $33,960; part-time $1389 per credit. *Required fees:* $800; $205 per term. Tuition and fees vary according to program. *Financial support:* In 2014–15, 28 students received support, including 9 fellowships with full tuition reimbursements available (averaging $21,262 per year), 12 teaching assistantships with full tuition reimbursements available (averaging $17,800 per year); research assistantships with full tuition reimbursements available, career-related internships or fieldwork, Federal Work-Study, scholarships/grants, health care benefits, and tuition waivers (partial) also available. Financial award application deadline: 12/15. *Faculty research:* Asian, medieval, modern art and architecture, contemporary, history of photography. *Unit head:* Dr. Barbara McCloskey, Associate Professor and Department Chair, 412-648-2417, Fax: 412-648-2792, E-mail: bmcc@pitt.edu. *Application contact:* Dr. Josh Ellenbogen, Director of Graduate Studies, 412-648-2400, Fax: 412-648-2792, E-mail: jme23@pitt.edu.
Website: http://www.haa.pitt.edu

The University of Texas at Austin, Graduate School, School of Architecture, Program in Architectural History, Austin, TX 78712-1111. Offers MA, PhD. *Degree requirements:* For doctorate, thesis/dissertation.

University of Virginia, School of Architecture, Department of Architectural History, Charlottesville, VA 22903. Offers M Arch H, PhD. *Faculty:* 6 full-time (3 women). *Students:* 15 full-time (10 women), 2 part-time (1 woman); includes 4 minority (2 Black or African American, non-Hispanic/Latino; 1 Hispanic/Latino; 1 Two or more races, non-Hispanic/Latino), 1 international. Average age 31. 21 applicants, 81% accepted, 10 enrolled. In 2014, 12 master's awarded. *Degree requirements:* For master's, one foreign language, thesis. *Entrance requirements:* For master's, GRE General Test, 3 letters of

recommendation. Additional exam requirements/recommendations for international students: Required—TOEFL (minimum score 600 paper-based; 90 iBT). *Application deadline:* For fall admission, 1/5 for domestic and international students. Applications are processed on a rolling basis. Application fee: $60. Electronic applications accepted. *Expenses:* Tuition, state resident: full-time $14,164; part-time $349 per credit hour. Tuition, nonresident: full-time $23,722; part-time $1300 per credit hour. *Required fees:* $2514. *Financial support:* Career-related internships or fieldwork, Federal Work-Study, and institutionally sponsored loans available. Financial award applicants required to submit FAFSA. *Faculty research:* Urban form, nineteenth and twentieth century American architecture. *Unit head:* Richard Guy Wilson, Chair, 434-924-6462, Fax: 434-982-2678, E-mail: rgw4h@virginia.edu. *Application contact:* Kristine Nelson, Director of Admissions and Financial Aid, 434-924-6442, Fax: 434-982-2678, E-mail: arch-admissions@virginia.edu. Website: http://www.arch.virginia.edu/academics/disciplines/history

Virginia Commonwealth University, Graduate School, School of the Arts, Department of Art History, Richmond, VA 23284-9005. Offers architectural history (MA); art history (MA, PhD); historical studies (MA); museum studies (MA). *Accreditation:* NASAD. *Degree requirements:* For master's, thesis; for doctorate, comprehensive exam, thesis/dissertation. *Entrance requirements:* For master's and doctorate, GRE General Test. Electronic applications accepted. *Faculty research:* Modern, nineteenth-century, Renaissance, American, and medieval art.

Architecture

Academy of Art University, Graduate Program, School of Architecture, San Francisco, CA 94105-3410. Offers M Arch. Part-time programs available. Postbaccalaureate distance learning degree programs offered (no on-campus study). *Faculty:* 8 full-time (2 women), 35 part-time/adjunct (14 women). *Students:* 146 full-time (49 women), 86 part-time (35 women); includes 44 minority (11 Black or African American, non-Hispanic/Latino; 12 Asian, non-Hispanic/Latino; 19 Hispanic/Latino; 1 Native Hawaiian or other Pacific Islander, non-Hispanic/Latino; 1 Two or more races, non-Hispanic/Latino), 91 international. Average age 33. 127 applicants, 100% accepted, 35 enrolled. In 2014, 41 master's awarded. *Degree requirements:* For master's, final review. *Entrance requirements:* For master's, statement of intent; resume; portfolio/reel; official college transcripts. *Application deadline:* Applications are processed on a rolling basis. Application fee: $100. Electronic applications accepted. *Expenses: Tuition:* Part-time $910 per unit. *Financial support:* Career-related internships or fieldwork and Federal Work-Study available. Support available to part-time students. Financial award application deadline: 8/10; financial award applicants required to submit FAFSA. *Unit head:* 800-544-ARTS, E-mail: info@academyart.edu. *Application contact:* 800-544-ARTS, E-mail: info@academyart.edu.
Website: http://www.academyart.edu/architecture-school/index.html

Andrews University, School of Graduate Studies, School of Architecture, Art and Design, Berrien Springs, MI 49104. Offers M Arch. *Faculty:* 8 full-time (3 women), 3 part-time/adjunct (1 woman). *Students:* 13 full-time (5 women); includes 6 minority (3 Black or African American, non-Hispanic/Latino; 3 Hispanic/Latino), 2 international. Average age 28. 21 applicants, 62% accepted, 3 enrolled. In 2014, 20 master's awarded. *Entrance requirements:* For master's, GRE. Additional exam requirements/recommendations for international students: Required—TOEFL (minimum score 550 paper-based). Application fee: $40. Tuition and fees vary according to course level. *Unit head:* Carey Carscallen, Dean, 269-471-6003. *Application contact:* Monica Wringer, Supervisor of Graduate Admission, 800-253-2874, Fax: 269-471-6321, E-mail: graduate@andrews.edu.

Arizona State University at the Tempe campus, Herberger Institute for Design and the Arts, The Design School, Tempe, AZ 85287-1605. Offers architecture (M Arch); building design/built environment (MS); design (MSD), including arts, media, and engineering, healthcare and healing environments (MSD, PhD), industrial design, interaction design, interior design, new product innovation, visual communication design; design, environment and the arts (PhD), including design, digital culture, healthcare and healing environments (MSD, PhD), history, theory, and criticism; landscape architecture (MLA); urban design (MUD); MA/MBA. *Accreditation:* NASAD. Terminal master's awarded for partial completion of doctoral program. *Degree requirements:* For master's, thesis optional, interactive Program of Study (iPOS) submitted before completing 50 percent of required credit hours; for doctorate, comprehensive exam, thesis/dissertation, interactive Program of Study (iPOS) submitted before completing 50 percent of required credit hours. *Entrance requirements:* For master's, GRE General Test, minimum GPA of 3.0 or equivalent in last 2 years of work leading to bachelor's degree, design/creative works portfolio, 3 references, statement of intent; for doctorate, GRE, master's degree in architecture, graphic design, industrial design, interior design, landscape architecture, or art history or equivalent standing; statement of purpose; 3 letters of recommendation; indication of potential faculty mentor; sample of written work. Additional exam requirements/recommendations for international students: Required—TOEFL (minimum score 600 paper-based; 100 iBT). Electronic applications accepted.

Auburn University, Graduate School, College of Architecture, Design, and Construction, Auburn University, AL 36849. Offers MBC, MCP, MID, MIDC, ML Arch, MPA/MCP. Part-time programs available. *Faculty:* 62 full-time (16 women), 12 part-time/adjunct (2 women). *Students:* 89 full-time (34 women), 56 part-time (16 women); includes 19 minority (9 Black or African American, non-Hispanic/Latino; 5 Asian, non-Hispanic/Latino; 5 Hispanic/Latino), 29 international. Average age 30. 207 applicants, 77% accepted, 85 enrolled. In 2014, 73 master's awarded. *Entrance requirements:* For master's, GRE General Test. *Application deadline:* For fall admission, 7/7 for domestic students; for spring admission, 11/24 for domestic students. Applications are processed on a rolling basis. Application fee: $50 ($60 for international students). Electronic applications accepted. *Expenses:* Expenses: Contact institution. *Financial support:* Fellowships and Federal Work-Study available. Support available to part-time students. Financial award application deadline: 3/15; financial award applicants required to submit FAFSA. *Unit head:* Dr. Vini Nathan, Dean, 334-844-4285. *Application contact:* Dr. George Flowers, Dean of the Graduate School, 334-844-2125.
Website: http://www.cadc.auburn.edu/

★ **Ball State University,** Graduate School, College of Architecture and Planning, Department of Architecture, Program in Architecture, Muncie, IN 47306-1099. Offers M Arch. *Students:* 61 full-time (19 women), 12 part-time (5 women); includes 7 minority (3 Black or African American, non-Hispanic/Latino; 4 Hispanic/Latino), 9 international. Average age 24. 76 applicants, 79% accepted, 20 enrolled. In 2014, 36 master's awarded. *Degree requirements:* For master's, thesis. *Entrance requirements:* For master's, minimum undergraduate B average, portfolio, writing sample. Application fee: $50. *Financial support:* In 2014–15, 26 students received support, including 11 research assistantships with partial tuition reimbursements available (averaging $5,169 per year), 20 teaching assistantships with partial tuition reimbursements available (averaging $4,741 per year); unspecified assistantships also available. Financial award application deadline: 3/1. *Unit head:* Dr. Mahesh Daas, Department Chairperson, 765-285-1904, Fax: 765-285-1765, E-mail: mahesh@bsu.edu. Website: http://www.bsu.edu/cap/arch/arch.html/

See Display on next page and Close-Up on page 135.

Boston Architectural College, Graduate Programs, Boston, MA 02115-2795. Offers architecture (M Arch); historic preservation (MDS); interior design (MID); landscape architecture (MLA); sustainable design (MDS). *Accreditation:* CIDA. *Degree requirements:* For master's, thesis. *Entrance requirements:* For master's, portfolio (recommended). Electronic applications accepted.

California Baptist University, Program in Architecture, Riverside, CA 92504-3206. Offers M Arch. *Faculty:* 6 full-time (3 women), 3 part-time/adjunct (0 women). *Students:* 47 full-time (24 women), 2 part-time (1 woman); includes 22 minority (3 Black or African American, non-Hispanic/Latino; 3 Asian, non-Hispanic/Latino; 13 Hispanic/Latino; 1 Native Hawaiian or other Pacific Islander, non-Hispanic/Latino; 2 Two or more races, non-Hispanic/Latino), 12 international. Average age 21. *Degree requirements:* For master's, thesis, internship, professional practice, minimum cumulative GPA of 2.75 by the end of the first semester of the third year, progress review after the fifth full-time semester in the program. *Entrance requirements:* Additional exam requirements/recommendations for international students: Required—TOEFL (minimum score 80 iBT). *Application deadline:* For fall admission, 8/1 priority date for domestic students, 7/1 for international students; for spring admission, 12/1 priority date for domestic students, 11/1 for international students. Applications are processed on a rolling basis. Application fee: $45. Electronic applications accepted. *Expenses:* Expenses: Contact institution. *Financial support:* Applicants required to submit CSS PROFILE or FAFSA. *Faculty research:* Architectural design, urbanism, interdisciplinary design thought. *Unit head:* Mark Roberson, Dean, College of Architecture, Visual Arts, and Design, 951-552-8652, E-mail: maroberson@calbaptist.edu. *Application contact:* Mark Roberson, Dean, College of Architecture, Visual Arts, and Design, 951-552-8652, E-mail: mroberson@calbaptist.edu.
Website: http://cbucavad.com/architecture/

California College of the Arts, Graduate Programs, Master of Architecture Program, San Francisco, CA 94107. Offers advanced architecture design (MAAD); architecture (M Arch). *Degree requirements:* For master's, thesis. *Entrance requirements:* For master's, appropriate bachelor's degree, portfolio, resume, minimum 2 letters of recommendation, essay, transcripts. Additional exam requirements/recommendations for international students: Required—TOEFL (minimum score 600 paper-based; 100 iBT).

California Polytechnic State University, San Luis Obispo, College of Architecture and Environmental Design, Department of Architecture, San Luis Obispo, CA 93407. Offers MS. Part-time programs available. *Faculty:* 5 full-time (1 woman). *Students:* 18 full-time (7 women), 8 part-time (2 women); includes 8 minority (2 Asian, non-Hispanic/Latino; 5 Hispanic/Latino; 1 Two or more races, non-Hispanic/Latino), 3 international. Average age 25. 35 applicants, 51% accepted, 12 enrolled. In 2014, 17 master's awarded. *Degree requirements:* For master's, thesis. *Application deadline:* For fall admission, 4/1 for domestic and international students; for winter admission, 11/1 for domestic students, 6/30 for international students. Applications are processed on a rolling basis. Application fee: $55. Electronic applications accepted. *Expenses:* Tuition, state resident: full-time $6738; part-time $3906 per year. Tuition, nonresident: full-time $15,666; part-time $8370 per year. *Required fees:* $3447; $1001 per quarter. One-time fee: $3447 full-time; $3003 part-time. *Financial support:* Fellowships, research assistantships, teaching assistantships, Federal Work-Study, and institutionally sponsored loans available. Support available to part-time students. Financial award application deadline: 3/2; financial award applicants required to submit FAFSA. *Faculty research:* Computer-assisted design, decision support systems, building science, facilities management. *Unit head:* Thomas Fowler, Graduate Coordinator, 805-756-2981, Fax: 805-756-1500, E-mail: tfowler@calpoly.edu. *Application contact:* Dr. James Maraviglia, Associate Vice Provost for Marketing and Enrollment Development, 805-756-2311, Fax: 805-756-5400, E-mail: admissions@calpoly.edu.
Website: http://www.architecture.calpoly.edu/

California State Polytechnic University, Pomona, Program in Architecture, Pomona, CA 91768-2557. Offers M Arch. Part-time programs available. *Students:* 47 full-time (24 women), 6 part-time (1 woman); includes 24 minority (9 Asian, non-Hispanic/Latino; 12 Hispanic/Latino; 3 Two or more races, non-Hispanic/Latino), 9 international. Average age 28. 84 applicants, 19% accepted, 16 enrolled. In 2014, 17 master's awarded. *Degree requirements:* For master's, thesis or alternative. *Application deadline:* For fall admission, 5/1 for domestic students; for winter admission, 10/15 priority date for domestic students; for spring admission, 1/20 priority date for domestic students. Applications are processed on a rolling basis. Application fee: $55. Electronic applications accepted. *Expenses:* Tuition, state resident: full-time $6738. Tuition, nonresident: full-time $12,300. *Required fees:* $1400. *Financial support:* Career-related internships or fieldwork, Federal Work-Study, and institutionally sponsored loans available. Support available to part-time students. Financial award application deadline: 3/2; financial award applicants required to submit FAFSA. *Unit head:* Kip A. Dickson, Graduate Coordinator, 909-869-2682, Fax: 909-869-4331, E-mail: kadickson@cpp.edu.
Website: http://www.cpp.edu/~arc/

Carleton University, Faculty of Graduate Studies, Faculty of Engineering and Design, School of Architecture, Ottawa, ON K1S 5B6, Canada. Offers design studies (M Arch). *Degree requirements:* For master's, thesis. *Entrance requirements:* For master's, honors degree. Additional exam requirements/recommendations for international students: Required—TOEFL. *Faculty research:* Theoretical issues in architecture and culture, cultural diversity, architecture and technoscientific culture.

Carnegie Mellon University, College of Fine Arts, School of Architecture, Pittsburgh, PA 15213-3891. Offers architecture (MSA); architecture, engineering, and construction management (PhD); building performance and diagnostics (MS, PhD); computational design (MS, PhD); engineering construction management (MSA); tangible interaction design (MTID); urban design (MUD). Terminal master's awarded for

partial completion of doctoral program. *Degree requirements:* For doctorate, thesis/dissertation. *Entrance requirements:* For master's and doctorate, GRE General Test. Additional exam requirements/recommendations for international students: Required—TOEFL.

The Catholic University of America, School of Architecture and Planning, Washington, DC 20064. Offers MS Arch St. Part-time programs available. *Faculty:* 22 full-time (9 women), 31 part-time/adjunct (9 women). *Students:* 90 full-time (38 women), 31 part-time (14 women); includes 33 minority (10 Black or African American, non-Hispanic/Latino; 5 Asian, non-Hispanic/Latino; 10 Hispanic/Latino; 8 Two or more races, non-Hispanic/Latino), 16 international. Average age 28. 93 applicants, 97% accepted, 45 enrolled. In 2014, 42 master's awarded. *Degree requirements:* For master's, thesis. *Entrance requirements:* For master's, GRE (minimum score: 1000), minimum GPA of 2.8, portfolio, statement of purpose, official copies of academic transcripts, three letters of recommendation. Additional exam requirements/recommendations for international students: Required—TOEFL (minimum score 580 paper-based). *Application deadline:* For fall admission, 1/15 priority date for domestic students, 1/15 for international students; for spring admission, 10/15 priority date for domestic students, 10/15 for international students. Applications are processed on a rolling basis. Application fee: $55. Electronic applications accepted. *Expenses:* Expenses: Contact institution. *Financial support:* Fellowships, research assistantships, teaching assistantships, Federal Work-Study, scholarships/grants, tuition waivers (full and partial), and unspecified assistantships available. Financial award application deadline: 2/1; financial award applicants required to submit FAFSA. *Faculty research:* Architectural history, cultural studies/sacred space, design technologies, digital media, real estate development, urban design. *Total annual research expenditures:* $98,238. *Unit head:* Randall Ott, Dean, 202-319-5784, Fax: 202-319-2023, E-mail: ott@cua.edu. *Application contact:* Director of Graduate Admissions, 202-319-5057, Fax: 202-319-6533, E-mail: cua-admissions@cua.edu.
Website: http://architecture.cua.edu/

City College of the City University of New York, Graduate School, School of Architecture and Environmental Studies, Program in Architecture, New York, NY 10031-9198. Offers M Arch. *Entrance requirements:* For master's, GRE. Additional exam requirements/recommendations for international students: Required—TOEFL (minimum score 550 paper-based).

Clemson University, Graduate School, College of Architecture, Arts, and Humanities, Department of Architecture, Clemson, SC 29634. Offers architecture (M Arch, MS). *Faculty:* 23 full-time (5 women), 12 part-time/adjunct (4 women). *Students:* 103 full-time (43 women), 1 part-time (0 women); includes 7 minority (3 Asian, non-Hispanic/Latino; 2 Hispanic/Latino; 2 Two or more races, non-Hispanic/Latino), 17 international. Average age 26. 277 applicants, 35% accepted, 39 enrolled. In 2014, 43 master's awarded. Terminal master's awarded for partial completion of doctoral program. *Degree requirements:* For master's, thesis. *Entrance requirements:* For master's, GRE General Test (including Analytical Writing), design portfolio. Additional exam requirements/recommendations for international students: Required—TOEFL. *Application deadline:* 1/15 for domestic and international students. Applications are processed on a rolling basis. Application fee: $70 ($80 for international students). Electronic applications accepted. *Financial support:* In 2014–15, 22 students received support, including 30 fellowships with partial tuition reimbursements available (averaging $1,242 per year), 5 research assistantships with partial tuition reimbursements available (averaging $9,280 per year); teaching assistantships with partial tuition reimbursements available, career-related internships or fieldwork, institutionally sponsored loans, scholarships/grants, health care benefits, and unspecified assistantships also available. Financial award application deadline: 1/15. *Faculty research:* Architecture and health, sustainable design, community design-build, architectural robotics, architectural and urban history and theory, digital fabrication. *Total annual research expenditures:* $190,289. *Unit head:* Dr. Kate Schwennsen, Chair, 864-656-3898, Fax: 864-656-0204, E-mail: kschwen@clemson.edu. *Application contact:* Michelle McLane, Student Services Coordinator, 864-656-3938, Fax: 864-656-1810, E-mail: wking@clemson.edu. Website: http://www.clemson.edu/caah/architecture/

Columbia University, Graduate School of Architecture, Planning, and Preservation, Program in Advanced Architectural Design, New York, NY 10027. Offers MS. *Entrance requirements:* For master's, GRE General Test.

Columbia University, Graduate School of Architecture, Planning, and Preservation, Program in Architecture, New York, NY 10027. Offers M Arch, PhD, M Arch/MS. PhD offered through the Graduate School of Arts and Science. *Degree requirements:* For master's, thesis optional. *Entrance requirements:* For master's, GRE General Test.

Cooper Union for the Advancement of Science and Art, Irwin S. Chanin School of Architecture, New York, NY 10003-7120. Offers M Arch II. *Faculty:* 14 full-time (3 women), 19 part-time/adjunct (6 women). *Students:* 8 full-time (5 women), all international. Average age 26. 75 applicants, 23% accepted, 8 enrolled. In 2014, 9 master's awarded. *Degree requirements:* For master's, thesis. *Entrance requirements:* For master's, GRE, 1 year of work experience, 3 letters of recommendation, resume or curriculum vitae, essay, portfolio, interview. Additional exam requirements/recommendations for international students: Required—TOEFL (minimum score 600 paper-based; 100 iBT). *Application deadline:* For fall admission, 3/2 for domestic and international students. Application fee: $70. Electronic applications accepted. *Expenses:* Expenses: $19,800 per semester, $925 student and studio/lab fee, $1,960 annual fee for international students. *Financial support:* In 2014–15, 8 fellowships with partial tuition reimbursements (averaging $13,300 per year) were awarded; tuition waivers (partial) and tuition scholarships offered to exceptional students also available. Financial award application deadline: 5/1; financial award applicants required to submit FAFSA. *Unit head:* Elizabeth O'Donnell, Acting Dean, 212-353-4223, E-mail: odonne@cooper.edu. *Application contact:* Student Contact, 212-353-4120, E-mail: admissions@cooper.edu.
Website: http://cooper.edu/architecture

Cornell University, Graduate School, Graduate Fields of Architecture, Art and Planning, Field of Architecture, Ithaca, NY 14853-0001. Offers architectural design (M Arch); architectural science (MS); computer graphics (MS); history of architecture (MA, PhD); history of urban development (MA, PhD); theory and criticism of architecture (M Arch); urban design (M Arch). *Degree requirements:* For master's, one foreign language, thesis (MA, MS); for doctorate, 2 foreign languages, comprehensive exam, thesis/dissertation. *Entrance requirements:* For master's, GRE General Test, 5-year bachelor's degree in architecture, portfolio (M Arch), 3 letters of recommendation; for doctorate, GRE General Test, 3 letters of recommendation. Additional exam requirements/recommendations for international students: Required—TOEFL (minimum score 600 paper-based; 77 iBT). Electronic applications accepted. *Faculty research:* Architectural design and urban design, theory and criticism of architecture, computer graphics, building technology and environmental science, history of architecture and history of urban-development.

Cranbrook Academy of Art, Graduate School, Program in Architecture, Bloomfield Hills, MI 48303-0801. Offers M Arch. *Faculty:* 1 full-time (0 women). *Students:* 17 full-time (10 women); includes 3 minority (2 Asian, non-Hispanic/Latino; 1

Hispanic/Latino), 5 international. Average age 31. *Degree requirements:* For master's, thesis, exhibit. *Entrance requirements:* Additional exam requirements/recommendations for international students: Required—TOEFL. *Application deadline:* For fall admission, 2/1 priority date for domestic and international students; for spring admission, 11/1 for domestic students. Application fee: $85. Electronic applications accepted. *Expenses: Tuition:* Full-time $31,916. *Required fees:* $2387. *Financial support:* Federal Work-Study and scholarships/grants available. Financial award application deadline: 2/15; financial award applicants required to submit FAFSA. *Unit head:* William Massie, Head, 248-645-3462, Fax: 248-645-3591, E-mail: wmassie@cranbrook.edu. *Application contact:* Leslie Tobakos, Registrar/Financial Aid and Admissions Manager, 248-645-3360, Fax: 248-645-3591, E-mail: ltobakos@cranbrook.edu.

Dalhousie University, Faculty of Architecture and Planning, Halifax, NS B3J 2X4, Canada. Offers M Arch, M Eng, M Plan, MEDS, MPS. *Degree requirements:* For master's, thesis. *Entrance requirements:* Additional exam requirements/recommendations for international students: Required—1 of 5 approved tests: TOEFL, IELTS, CANTEST, CAEL, Michigan English Language Assessment Battery. Electronic applications accepted.

Drury University, Hammons School of Architecture, Springfield, MO 65802. Offers M Arch. *Degree requirements:* For master's, thesis project.

Florida Agricultural and Mechanical University, Division of Graduate Studies, Research, and Continuing Education, School of Architecture, Tallahassee, FL 32307-3200. Offers architectural studies (MS Arch); architecture (professional) (M Arch); landscape architecture (MLA). Part-time programs available. *Degree requirements:* For master's, thesis. *Entrance requirements:* For master's, GRE General Test, minimum GPA of 3.0, portfolio. Additional exam requirements/recommendations for international students: Required—TOEFL (minimum score 550 paper-based). *Faculty research:* Environmental technology, post-occupancy evaluation, building economics, design methods, computer-aided design.

Florida International University, College of Architecture and the Arts, Miami, FL 33199. Offers M Arch, MA, MFA, MIA, MLA, MM, MS, Certificate, Graduate Certificate. *Accreditation:* ASLA. Part-time and evening/weekend programs available. *Degree requirements:* For master's, thesis (for some programs). *Entrance requirements:* For master's, GRE (depending on program), minimum GPA of 3.0 (upper-level coursework). Additional exam requirements/recommendations for international students: Required—TOEFL (minimum score 550 paper-based; 80 iBT). Electronic applications accepted.

Florida International University, College of Architecture and the Arts, School of Architecture, Department of Architecture, Miami, FL 33199. Offers M Arch, MA. Part-time and evening/weekend programs available. *Entrance requirements:* For master's, GRE or minimum GPA of 3.0 in upper-level undergraduate work, portfolio. Additional exam requirements/recommendations for international students: Required—TOEFL (minimum score 550 paper-based; 80 iBT). Electronic applications accepted.

★ **Frank Lloyd Wright School of Architecture,** Graduate Program, Scottsdale, AZ 85261-4430. Offers M Arch. Summer session held in Spring Green, WI. *Faculty:* 3 full-time (1 woman), 17 part-time/adjunct (4 women). *Students:* 19 full-time (4 women); includes 1 minority (Hispanic/Latino), 5 international. Average age 25. 15 applicants, 67% accepted. In 2014, 2 master's awarded. *Degree requirements:* For master's, thesis or alternative. *Entrance requirements:* For master's, interviews, portfolio. Additional exam requirements/recommendations for international students: Required—TOEFL. *Application deadline:* For fall admission, 3/20 for domestic and international students. Applications are processed on a rolling basis. Application fee: $50. *Expenses: Tuition:* Full-time $40,800. Full-time tuition and fees vary according to degree level. *Financial support:* In 2014–15, 15 students received support. Career-related internships or fieldwork, scholarships/grants, and traineeships available. Financial award application deadline: 6/1; financial award applicants required to submit FAFSA. *Faculty research:* Architecture, landscape architecture, materials design, design. *Unit head:* Aaron A. Betsky, Dean, 480-860-2700, Fax: 480-391-4009, E-mail: abetsky@taliesin.edu. *Application contact:* Jerry Kavalieratos, Director of Admissions and Student Services, 480-627-5345, E-mail: jkavalieratos@taliesin.edu.

See Display on this page and Close-Up on page 137.

Georgia Institute of Technology, Graduate Studies, College of Architecture, Doctoral Program in Architecture, Atlanta, GA 30332-0001. Offers PhD. Part-time programs available. Postbaccalaureate distance learning degree programs offered. *Degree requirements:* For doctorate, comprehensive exam, thesis/dissertation. *Entrance requirements:* For doctorate, GRE General Test. Additional exam requirements/recommendations for international students: Required—TOEFL (minimum score 600 paper-based). Electronic applications accepted. *Expenses:* Tuition, state resident: full-time $12,344; part-time $515 per credit hour. Tuition, nonresident: full-time $27,600; part-time $1150 per credit hour. *Required fees:* $1196 per term. Part-time tuition and fees vary according to course load.

Georgia Institute of Technology, Graduate Studies, College of Architecture, Master's Program in Architecture, Atlanta, GA 30332-0001. Offers M Arch, MS, M Arch/MCRP. Part-time programs available. *Degree requirements:* For master's, thesis or alternative. *Entrance requirements:* For master's, GRE General Test. Additional exam requirements/recommendations for international students: Required—TOEFL (minimum score 600 paper-based). Electronic applications accepted. *Expenses:* Tuition, state resident: full-time $12,344; part-time $515 per credit hour. Tuition, nonresident: full-time $27,600; part-time $1150 per credit hour. *Required fees:* $1196 per term. Part-time tuition and fees vary according to course load.

Georgia Institute of Technology, Graduate Studies, College of Architecture, School of City and Regional Planning, Atlanta, GA 30332-0001. Offers city and regional planning (PhD); economic development (MCRP); environmental planning and management (MCRP); geographic information systems (MCRP); land and community development (MCRP); land use planning (MCRP); transportation (MCRP); urban design (MCRP); MCP/MSCE. *Accreditation:* ACSP. *Degree requirements:* For master's, thesis, internship. *Entrance requirements:* For master's, GRE General Test, minimum GPA of 2.7. Additional exam requirements/recommendations for international students: Required—TOEFL. Electronic applications accepted. *Expenses:* Tuition, state resident: full-time $12,344; part-time $515 per credit hour. Tuition, nonresident: full-time $27,600; part-time $1150 per credit hour. *Required fees:* $1196 per term. Part-time tuition and fees vary according to course load.

Hampton University, School of Engineering and Technology, Hampton, VA 23668. Offers architecture (M Arch). Students enter program as freshmen. *Faculty:* 2 full-time (1 woman). *Students:* 23 full-time (10 women); includes 13 minority (all Black or African American, non-Hispanic/Latino). Average age 23. In 2014, 1 master's awarded. *Entrance requirements:* For master's, N/A. Electronic applications accepted. *Expenses: Tuition:* Full-time $20,526; part-time $522 per credit. *Required fees:* $100. *Financial support:* Applicants required to submit FAFSA. *Faculty research:* Design at the water's edge, impact of climate change on coastal regions, innovation in design, historic preservation and documentation, sustainability and energy efficiency. *Total annual research expenditures:* $10,000. *Unit head:* Dr. Eric J. Sheppard, Dean, 757-728-6970,

TALIESIN

FRANK LLOYD WRIGHT SCHOOL OF ARCHITECTURE

challenge
architectural
conventions

Master of Architecture
&
Immersion Experience

Architecture

Fax: 757-728-6972, E-mail: eric.sheppard@hamptonu.edu. *Application contact:* Robert Easter, Chair, Architecture Department, 757-727-5441, Fax: 757-728-6680.
Website: http://set.hamptonu.edu/

Harvard University, Graduate School of Arts and Sciences, Committee on Architecture, Landscape Architecture, and Urban Planning, Cambridge, MA 02138. Offers architecture (PhD); landscape architecture (PhD); urban planning (PhD). *Degree requirements:* For doctorate, one foreign language, thesis/dissertation, oral exam. *Entrance requirements:* For doctorate, GRE General Test. Additional exam requirements/recommendations for international students: Required—TOEFL.

Harvard University, Graduate School of Design, Department of Architecture, Cambridge, MA 02138. Offers M Arch. *Degree requirements:* For master's, thesis (for some programs). *Entrance requirements:* For master's, GRE General Test. Additional exam requirements/recommendations for international students: Required—TOEFL (minimum score 600 paper-based; 104 iBT). Electronic applications accepted.

Harvard University, Graduate School of Design, Program in Design, Cambridge, MA 02138. Offers Dr DES. *Entrance requirements:* For doctorate, GRE General Test. Additional exam requirements/recommendations for international students: Required—TOEFL (minimum score 600 paper-based; 104 iBT). Electronic applications accepted.

Harvard University, Graduate School of Design, Program in Design Studies, Cambridge, MA 02138. Offers M Des S. *Entrance requirements:* For master's, GRE General Test. Additional exam requirements/recommendations for international students: Required—TOEFL (minimum score 600 paper-based; 104 iBT). Electronic applications accepted.

Illinois Institute of Technology, Graduate College, College of Architecture, Chicago, IL 60616. Offers M Arch, MLA, MS Arch, PhD, MLA/M Arch. *Accreditation:* ASLA. Part-time programs available. *Faculty:* 36 full-time (9 women), 69 part-time/adjunct (19 women). *Students:* 160 full-time (67 women), 16 part-time (9 women); includes 7 minority (1 Black or African American, non-Hispanic/Latino; 2 Asian, non-Hispanic/Latino; 3 Hispanic/Latino; 1 Two or more races, non-Hispanic/Latino), 100 international. Average age 28. 481 applicants, 62% accepted, 55 enrolled. In 2014, 70 master's, 2 doctorates awarded. Terminal master's awarded for partial completion of doctoral program. *Degree requirements:* For master's, comprehensive exam (for some programs), thesis (for some programs); for doctorate, comprehensive exam, thesis/dissertation. *Entrance requirements:* For master's, GRE General Test (minimum score 292 Quantitative and Verbal, 2.5 Analytical Writing), minimum college GPA of 3.0, official transcripts, portfolio, 3 letters of recommendation, professional statement;; for doctorate, GRE General Test (minimum score 900 Quantitative and Verbal, 2.5 Analytical Writing), minimum GPA of 3.5, official transcripts, portfolio, 3 letters of recommendation, professional statement. Additional exam requirements/recommendations for international students: Required—TOEFL (minimum score 550 paper-based; 80 iBT). *Application deadline:* For fall admission, 4/15 for domestic and international students; for spring admission, 11/15 for domestic and international students. Applications are processed on a rolling basis. Application fee: $50. Electronic applications accepted. *Expenses: Tuition:* Full-time $22,500; part-time $1250 per credit hour. *Required fees:* $30 per course. $260 per semester. One-time fee: $235. Tuition and fees vary according to course load and program. *Financial support:* Fellowships with full and partial tuition reimbursements, research assistantships, teaching assistantships with full and partial tuition reimbursements, career-related internships or fieldwork, Federal Work-Study, institutionally sponsored loans, scholarships/grants, health care benefits, tuition waivers (partial), and unspecified assistantships available. Support available to part-time students. Financial award applicants required to submit FAFSA. *Faculty research:* Sustainable design and efficiency; the influence of climate and environment on building form; emerging urbanisms; computer applications (such as 3-D modeling); the design, planning and structure of high-rise buildings. *Unit head:* Wiel Arets, Dean, 312-567-3230, Fax: 312-567-5820, E-mail: wiel.arets@iit.edu. *Application contact:* Rishab Malhotra, Director of Graduate and Professional Admission, 866-472-3448, Fax: 312-567-3138, E-mail: inquiry.grad@iit.edu.
Website: http://www.iit.edu/arch/

Instituto Tecnológico y de Estudios Superiores de Monterrey, Campus Estado de México, Professional and Graduate Division, Estado de Mexico, Mexico. Offers administration of information technologies (MITA); architecture (M Arch); business administration (GMBA, MBA); computer sciences (MCS, PhD); education (M Ed); educational institution administration (MAD); educational technology and innovation (PhD); electronic commerce (MEC); environmental systems (MS); finance (MAF); humanistic studies (MHS); information sciences and knowledge management (MISKM); information systems (MS); manufacturing systems (MS); marketing (MEM); quality systems and productivity (MS); science and materials engineering (PhD); telecommunications management (MTM). Part-time programs available. Postbaccalaureate distance learning degree programs offered (minimal on-campus study). *Degree requirements:* For master's, one foreign language, thesis (for some programs); for doctorate, one foreign language, thesis/dissertation. *Entrance requirements:* For master's, E-PAEP 500, interview; for doctorate, E-PAEP 500, research proposal. Additional exam requirements/recommendations for international students: Required—TOEFL (minimum score 550 paper-based). *Faculty research:* Surface treatments by plasmas, mechanical properties, robotics, graphical computing, mechatronics security protocols.

Instituto Tecnológico y de Estudios Superiores de Monterrey, Campus Irapuato, Graduate Programs, Irapuato, Mexico. Offers administration (MBA); administration of information technology (MAIT); administration of telecommunications (MAT); architecture (M Arch); computer science (MCS); education (M Ed); educational administration (MEA); educational innovation and technology (DEIT); educational technology (MET); electronic commerce (MBA); environmental administration and planning (MEAP); environmental systems (MES); finances (MBA); humanistic studies (MHS); international management for Latin American executives (MIMLAE); library and information science (MLIS); manufacturing quality management (MMQM); marketing research (MBA).

Iowa State University of Science and Technology, Department of Architecture, Ames, IA 50011. Offers architectural studies (MSAS); architecture (M Arch); M Arch/MBA; M Arch/MCRP; M Arch/MS. *Degree requirements:* For master's, thesis (for some programs). *Entrance requirements:* For master's, GRE General Test, portfolio, letters of reference. Additional exam requirements/recommendations for international students: Required—TOEFL (minimum score 600 paper-based; 79 iBT), IELTS (minimum score 7). Electronic applications accepted. *Faculty research:* Computer-aided architectural design, social dimensions of urban architecture, designing for the elderly, energy utilization in buildings, architectural theory.

Judson University, Graduate Programs, Master of Architecture Program, Elgin, IL 60123-1498. Offers architecture (M Arch); sustainable design (M Arch); traditional architecture and urbanism (M Arch). Part-time programs available. *Degree requirements:* For master's, thesis optional, 1600-hour practicum/preceptorship completed prior to enrollment. *Entrance requirements:* For master's, GRE, Judson BA in architecture or equivalent; minimum cumulative undergraduate GPA of 2.75, 3.0 in architecture; comprehensive portfolio; letter of intent. Additional exam requirements/recommendations for international students: Required—TOEFL (minimum score 550 paper-based), IELTS (minimum score 6.5). *Application deadline:* For fall admission, 2/15 priority date for domestic and international students; for winter admission, 11/15 for domestic students; for spring admission, 11/15 for domestic and international students. Applications are processed on a rolling basis. Application fee: $100. Electronic applications accepted. *Expenses:* Expenses: Contact institution. *Financial support:* Teaching assistantships with partial tuition reimbursements, career-related internships or fieldwork, Federal Work-Study, and unspecified assistantships available. Financial award application deadline: 7/1; financial award applicants required to submit FAFSA. *Faculty research:* Sustainable design, urbanism, daylighting, acoustics, digital media and fabrication. *Unit head:* Keelan Kaiser, Chair, 847-628-1011, E-mail: kkaiser@judsonu.edu. *Application contact:* Nathan McNeely, Director of Admissions, 847-628-2510, E-mail: nmcneely@judsonu.edu.
Website: http://www.judsonu.edu/ArchMaster/

Kansas State University, Graduate School, College of Architecture, Planning and Design, Department of Architecture, Manhattan, KS 66506. Offers M Arch, MS Arch. Part-time programs available. *Faculty:* 18 full-time (3 women), 6 part-time/adjunct (2 women). *Students:* 160 full-time (65 women); includes 25 minority (2 Black or African American, non-Hispanic/Latino; 1 American Indian or Alaska Native, non-Hispanic/Latino; 10 Asian, non-Hispanic/Latino; 8 Hispanic/Latino; 4 Two or more races, non-Hispanic/Latino), 19 international. Average age 23. 86 applicants, 85% accepted, 73 enrolled. In 2014, 71 master's awarded. *Degree requirements:* For master's, thesis optional, residency. *Entrance requirements:* For master's, portfolio, minimum GPA of 3.0. Additional exam requirements/recommendations for international students: Required—TOEFL (minimum score 95 iBT), IELTS (minimum score 7). *Application deadline:* For fall admission, 2/1 priority date for domestic students, 1/1 priority date for international students; for spring admission, 8/1 priority date for domestic and international students. Applications are processed on a rolling basis. Application fee: $90 ($100 for international students). Electronic applications accepted. *Financial support:* In 2014–15, 18 teaching assistantships with full tuition reimbursements (averaging $7,500 per year) were awarded; research assistantships, institutionally sponsored loans, and scholarships/grants also available. Support available to part-time students. Financial award application deadline: 3/1; financial award applicants required to submit FAFSA. *Faculty research:* Design theory, environment behavior and place studies, ecological and sustainable design, computer-assisted design and fabrication. *Unit head:* Matthew Knox, Professor and Head, 785-532-5953, Fax: 785-532-6722, E-mail: mknox@ksu.edu. *Application contact:* R. Todd Gabbard, Associate Head and Director of Graduate Programs, 785-532-1129, Fax: 785-532-6722, E-mail: rtodd@ksu.edu.
Website: http://apdesign.k-state.edu/arch/

Kent State University, College of Architecture and Environmental Design, Kent, OH 44242-0001. Offers architecture (M Arch); architecture and environmental design (MS); health care design (MHCD); landscape architecture (ML Arch); urban design (MUD). Part-time programs available. *Faculty:* 24 full-time (5 women). *Students:* 66 full-time (25 women), 8 part-time (3 women); includes 5 minority (3 Black or African American, non-Hispanic/Latino; 1 American Indian or Alaska Native, non-Hispanic/Latino; 1 Asian, non-Hispanic/Latino), 4 international. Average age 25. 242 applicants, 67% accepted, 116 enrolled. In 2014, 45 degrees awarded. *Degree requirements:* For master's, thesis. *Entrance requirements:* For master's, GRE, minimum GPA of 3.0, writing sample, resume/curriculum vitae, letter of intent, portfolio, 3 letters of recommendation. Additional exam requirements/recommendations for international students: Required—TOEFL (minimum score: paper-based 525, iBT 71), Michigan English Language Assessment Battery (minimum score of 75), IELTS (minimum score of 6.0), PTE Academic (minimum score of 48), or completion of ELS level 112 Intensive Program. *Application deadline:* For fall admission, 1/15 for domestic and international students. Application fee: $45 ($70 for international students). Electronic applications accepted. *Expenses:* Tuition, state resident: full-time $8730; part-time $485 per credit hour. Tuition, nonresident: full-time $14,886; part-time $827 per credit hour. Tuition and fees vary according to campus/location and program. *Financial support:* Research assistantships with full tuition reimbursements, teaching assistantships with full tuition reimbursements, career-related internships or fieldwork, Federal Work-Study, scholarships/grants, and unspecified assistantships available. Financial award application deadline: 2/1. *Unit head:* Douglas Steidl, Dean, 330-672-2917, Fax: 330-672-3809, E-mail: dsteidl@kent.edu. *Application contact:* Lisa Pozo, Administrative Secretary, 330-672-2917, Fax: 330-672-3809, E-mail: caed_info@kent.edu.
Website: http://www.kent.edu/caed

Lawrence Technological University, College of Architecture and Design, Southfield, MI 48075-1058. Offers architecture (M Arch); urban design (MUD). *Accreditation:* NASAD. Part-time and evening/weekend programs available. *Faculty:* 15 full-time (3 women), 30 part-time/adjunct (10 women). *Students:* 13 full-time (8 women), 208 part-time (84 women); includes 49 minority (6 Black or African American, non-Hispanic/Latino; 1 American Indian or Alaska Native, non-Hispanic/Latino; 26 Asian, non-Hispanic/Latino; 11 Hispanic/Latino; 5 Two or more races, non-Hispanic/Latino), 14 international. Average age 30. 139 applicants, 46% accepted, 43 enrolled. In 2014, 91 master's awarded. *Degree requirements:* For master's, thesis. *Entrance requirements:* Additional exam requirements/recommendations for international students: Required—TOEFL (minimum score 550 paper-based; 79 iBT). *Application deadline:* For fall admission, 5/15 priority date for domestic students, 5/29 for international students; for spring admission, 9/15 priority date for domestic students, 10/15 for international students; for summer admission, 2/15 for domestic students. Applications are processed on a rolling basis. Application fee: $50. Electronic applications accepted. *Expenses: Tuition:* Full-time $14,700; part-time $1050 per credit hour. *Required fees:* $150. One-time fee: $150 part-time. *Financial support:* In 2014–15, 66 students received support, including 5 research assistantships (averaging $6,090 per year); Federal Work-Study also available. Financial award application deadline: 4/1; financial award applicants required to submit FAFSA. *Unit head:* Glen LeRoy, Dean, 248-204-2800, Fax: 248-204-2900, E-mail: archdean@ltu.edu. *Application contact:* Jane Rohrback, Director of Admissions, 248-204-3160, Fax: 248-204-2228, E-mail: admissions@ltu.edu.
Website: http://www.ltu.edu/architecture_and_design/index.asp

Louisiana State University and Agricultural & Mechanical College, Graduate School, College of Art and Design, School of Architecture, Baton Rouge, LA 70803. Offers M Arch. Part-time programs available. *Faculty:* 12 full-time (3 women). *Students:* 22 full-time (13 women), 1 part-time (0 women); includes 2 minority (both Black or African American, non-Hispanic/Latino), 1 international. Average age 27. 14 applicants, 43% accepted, 4 enrolled. In 2014, 10 master's awarded. *Degree requirements:* For master's, thesis. *Entrance requirements:* For master's, GRE General Test, minimum GPA of 3.0. Additional exam requirements/recommendations for international students: Required—TOEFL (minimum score 550 paper-based; 79 IBT), IELTS (minimum score 6.5), or PTE (minimum score 59). *Application deadline:* For fall admission, 1/1 priority date for domestic students, 5/15 for international students; for spring admission, 10/15 for domestic and international students; for summer admission, 5/15 for domestic and international students. Applications are processed on a rolling basis. Application fee: $50 ($70 for international students). Electronic applications accepted. *Financial support:* In 2014–15, 19 students received support, including 15

research assistantships with full and partial tuition reimbursements available (averaging $8,565 per year), 2 teaching assistantships with full and partial tuition reimbursements available (averaging $15,070 per year); fellowships, career-related internships or fieldwork, Federal Work-Study, institutionally sponsored loans, scholarships/grants, health care benefits, tuition waivers (full and partial), and unspecified assistantships also available. Support available to part-time students. Financial award application deadline: 3/1; financial award applicants required to submit FAFSA. *Faculty research:* Architectural design, history of architecture, sustainable design, digital fabrication, community design. *Total annual research expenditures:* $108,452. *Unit head:* Jori Erdman, Director, 225-578-6885, Fax: 225-578-2168, E-mail: jerdman@lsu.edu. *Application contact:* Ursula Emery-McClure, Graduate Coordinator, 225-578-4259, Fax: 225-578-2168, E-mail: uemery@lsu.edu.
Website: http://www.arch.lsu.edu/

Louisiana Tech University, Graduate School, College of Liberal Arts, Architecture Program, Ruston, LA 71272. Offers M Arch, D Arch. *Entrance requirements:* For master's, GRE General Test. *Application deadline:* For fall admission, 7/29 for domestic students; for spring admission, 2/3 for domestic students. Applications are processed on a rolling basis. Application fee: $40. *Financial support:* Application deadline: 2/1. *Unit head:* Damon Caldwell, Graduate Coordinator, 318-257-5259, Fax: 318-257-4687, E-mail: caldwell@latech.edu. *Application contact:* Marilyn J. Robinson, Assistant to the Dean of the Graduate School, 318-257-2924, Fax: 318-257-4487.
Website: http://www.latech.edu/tech/liberal-arts/architecture/

Marywood University, Academic Affairs, School of Architecture, Program in Architecture, Scranton, PA 18509-1598. Offers M Arch. Part-time programs available. *Students:* 2 full-time (1 woman). Average age 24. *Degree requirements:* For master's, thesis project. *Application fee:* $35. *Expenses: Tuition:* Part-time $775 per credit. *Required fees:* $688 per semester. Tuition and fees vary according to degree level and campus/location. *Financial support:* Application deadline: 6/30; applicants required to submit FAFSA. *Unit head:* Gregory K. Hunt, Dean, 570-348-6211 Ext. 4536, E-mail: gkhunt@marywood.edu. *Application contact:* Tammy Manka, Assistant Director of Graduate Admissions, 866-279-9663, E-mail: tmanka@marywood.edu.
Website: http://www.marywood.edu/architecture/programs/m-arch/

Massachusetts College of Art and Design, Graduate Programs, Program in Architecture, Boston, MA 02115-5882. Offers M Arch. *Faculty:* 6 full-time (4 women), 20 part-time/adjunct (7 women). *Students:* 19 full-time (11 women), 1 part-time (0 women); includes 3 minority (1 Black or African American, non-Hispanic/Latino; 1 Hispanic/Latino; 1 Two or more races, non-Hispanic/Latino), 5 international. 30 applicants, 93% accepted, 5 enrolled. In 2014, 10 master's awarded. *Degree requirements:* For master's, thesis. *Entrance requirements:* For master's, portfolio, college transcripts, resume, statement of purpose, letters of reference, interview. Additional exam requirements/recommendations for international students: Required—TOEFL (minimum score 550 paper-based; 85 iBT); Recommended—IELTS (minimum score 6). *Application deadline:* For fall admission, 1/6 for domestic and international students; for summer admission, 1/6 priority date for domestic and international students. Application fee: $75. Electronic applications accepted. *Expenses: Tuition:* state resident: full-time $23,400; part-time $780 per credit. Tuition, nonresident: full-time $23,400; part-time $780 per credit. Tuition and fees vary according to course load and program. *Financial support:* In 2014-15, 8 students received support, including 6 teaching assistantships (averaging $2,160 per year); career-related internships or fieldwork, scholarships/grants, tuition waivers (partial), and unspecified assistantships also available. Support available to part-time students. Financial award application deadline: 1/6. *Unit head:* Paul Paturzo, Interim Dean of Graduate Studies, 617-879-7166, E-mail: pjpaturzo@massart.edu. *Application contact:* Isaac Goldstein, Graduate Admissions Counselor, 617-879-7203, Fax: 617-879-7250, E-mail: igoldstein@massart.edu.
Website: http://www.massart.edu/Admissions/Graduate_Programs.html

Massachusetts Institute of Technology, School of Architecture and Planning, Department of Architecture, Cambridge, MA 02139. Offers architecture (M Arch, PhD), including building technology (PhD), design and computation (PhD), history and theory of architecture (PhD), history and theory of art (PhD); architecture studies (SM Arch S); art, culture and technology (SMACT); building technology (SMBT). *Faculty:* 33 full-time (12 women), 1 part-time/adjunct (0 women). *Students:* 213 full-time (97 women); includes 42 minority (5 Black or African American, non-Hispanic/Latino; 20 Asian, non-Hispanic/Latino; 13 Hispanic/Latino; 4 Two or more races, non-Hispanic/Latino), 100 international. Average age 28. 1,179 applicants, 12% accepted, 79 enrolled. In 2014, 65 master's, 6 doctorates awarded. *Degree requirements:* For master's, thesis; for doctorate, comprehensive exam, thesis/dissertation. *Entrance requirements:* For master's and doctorate, GRE General Test. Additional exam requirements/recommendations for international students: Required—TOEFL, IELTS (minimum score 7). *Application deadline:* For fall admission, 12/31 for domestic and international students. Application fee: $75. Electronic applications accepted. *Expenses: Tuition:* Full-time $44,720; part-time $699 per unit. *Required fees:* $296. *Financial support:* In 2014-15, 171 students received support, including 139 fellowships (averaging $22,100 per year), 25 research assistantships (averaging $32,000 per year), 23 teaching assistantships (averaging $34,500 per year); Federal Work-Study, institutionally sponsored loans, scholarships/grants, health care benefits, and unspecified assistantships also available. Financial award application deadline: 4/15; financial award applicants required to submit FAFSA. *Faculty research:* Architecture; urbanism; building technology and sustainability; computation and design; history, theory, and criticism; art, culture, and technology. *Total annual research expenditures:* $1.2 million. *Unit head:* J. Meejin Yoon, Professor and Head of Department, 617-253-7791, E-mail: arch@mit.edu. *Application contact:* Admissions Coordinator, 617-715-4490, Fax: 617-253-8993, E-mail: arch@mit.edu.
Website: http://architecture.mit.edu/

McGill University, Faculty of Graduate and Postdoctoral Studies, Faculty of Engineering, School of Architecture, Montréal, QC H3A 2T5, Canada. Offers affordable homes (M Arch II, Diploma); architectural history and theory (M Arch II); architecture (PhD); domestic environment (M Arch II); domestic environments (Diploma); minimum cost housing in developing countries (M Arch II, Diploma); professional architecture (M Arch I).

Miami University, College of Creative Arts, Department of Architecture, Oxford, OH 45056. Offers M Arch. *Students:* 32 full-time (18 women); includes 8 minority (2 Black or African American, non-Hispanic/Latino; 2 Asian, non-Hispanic/Latino; 3 Hispanic/Latino; 1 Two or more races, non-Hispanic/Latino), 9 international. Average age 28. In 2014, 15 master's awarded. *Entrance requirements:* For master's, GRE, portfolio; writing sample; three letters of recommendation; personal statement; curriculum vitae or resume. Additional exam requirements/recommendations for international students: Recommended—TOEFL (minimum score 80 iBT), IELTS (minimum score 6.5), TSE (minimum score 54). *Application deadline:* For fall admission, 1/15 for domestic and international students. Application fee: $50. Electronic applications accepted. *Expenses:* Tuition, state resident: full-time $12,887; part-time $537 per credit hour. Tuition, nonresident: full-time $28,449; part-time $1186 per credit hour. *Required fees:* $530; $24 per credit hour. $30 per quarter. Part-time tuition and fees vary according to course load and program. *Financial support:* Research assistantships with full and partial

tuition reimbursements and teaching assistantships with full and partial tuition reimbursements available. Financial award application deadline: 2/15; financial award applicants required to submit FAFSA. *Unit head:* Dr. John Weigand, Chair, 513-529-4903, E-mail: weiganjb@miamioh.edu. *Application contact:* Craig Hinrichs, Professor/Director of Graduate Studies, 513-529-7036, E-mail: hinriccl@miamioh.edu.
Website: http://www.MiamiOH.edu/architecture

Montana State University, The Graduate School, College of Arts and Architecture, School of Architecture, Bozeman, MT 59717. Offers M Arch. Part-time programs available. *Degree requirements:* For master's, comprehensive exam. *Entrance requirements:* For master's, GRE General Test, minimum cumulative GPA of 3.0, portfolio, 3 letters of recommendation. Additional exam requirements/recommendations for international students: Required—TOEFL (minimum score 550 paper-based). Electronic applications accepted. *Faculty research:* Sustainability, architecture as craft, visualization, stewardship, community design, design build.

Morgan State University, School of Graduate Studies, Institute of Architecture and Planning, Program in Architecture, Baltimore, MD 21251. Offers M Arch. *Degree requirements:* For master's, thesis. *Entrance requirements:* Additional exam requirements/recommendations for international students: Required—TOEFL (minimum score 550 paper-based).

New Jersey Institute of Technology, College of Architecture, Newark, NJ 07102. Offers architecture (M Arch, MS Arch); infrastructure planning (MIP); urban systems (PhD); M Arch/MIP; M Arch/MS. Part-time and evening/weekend programs available. Terminal master's awarded for partial completion of doctoral program. *Degree requirements:* For master's, thesis (for some programs). *Entrance requirements:* For master's, GRE General Test, minimum GPA of 3.0. Additional exam requirements/recommendations for international students: Required—TOEFL (minimum score 550 paper-based; 79 iBT). Electronic applications accepted. *Faculty research:* Building sciences, community and urban design history and theory, computer-aided architecture.

The New School, Parsons The New School for Design, Program in Architecture, New York, NY 10011. Offers M Arch. *Degree requirements:* For master's, thesis. *Entrance requirements:* For master's, GRE General Test, portfolio. Additional exam requirements/recommendations for international students: Required—TOEFL (minimum score 580 paper-based; 92 iBT). Electronic applications accepted.

NewSchool of Architecture and Design, Program in Architecture, San Diego, CA 92101-6634. Offers M Arch, MS. Part-time programs available. Postbaccalaureate distance learning degree programs offered (no on-campus study). *Degree requirements:* For master's, thesis. *Entrance requirements:* For master's, portfolio, interview. Additional exam requirements/recommendations for international students: Required—TOEFL, IELTS. *Faculty research:* Urban studies, regional studies, environmental design, structures, cross-cultural studies.

New York Institute of Technology, School of Architecture and Design, Old Westbury, NY 11568-8000. Offers urban and regional design (M Arch). Part-time programs available. *Degree requirements:* For master's, thesis. *Entrance requirements:* For master's, minimum QPA of 2.85, portfolio. Additional exam requirements/recommendations for international students: Required—TOEFL (minimum score 550 paper-based; 79 iBT), IELTS (minimum score 6). Electronic applications accepted. *Faculty research:* Resilient cities, compact morphology, new town development, pedestrian-friendly public realm.

North Carolina State University, Graduate School, College of Design, School of Architecture, Raleigh, NC 27695. Offers M Arch. *Degree requirements:* For master's, thesis optional, oral exam, project. *Entrance requirements:* For master's, GRE General Test, portfolio. Electronic applications accepted. *Faculty research:* Architectural design, architectural history and theory, construction materials, sustainable design.

North Dakota State University, College of Graduate and Interdisciplinary Studies, College of Engineering and Architecture, Department of Architecture and Landscape Architecture, Fargo, ND 58108. Offers architecture (M Arch). Electronic applications accepted.

Northeastern University, College of Arts, Media and Design, Boston, MA 02115-5096. Offers architecture (M Arch); information design and visualization (MFA); journalism (MA); studio art (MFA). *Entrance requirements:* Additional exam requirements/recommendations for international students: Required—TOEFL (minimum score 100 iBT), IELTS. Electronic applications accepted.

The Ohio State University, Graduate School, College of Engineering, Austin E. Knowlton School of Architecture, Columbus, OH 43210. Offers architecture (M Arch); city and regional planning (MCRP, PhD); landscape architecture (M Land Arch). *Accreditation:* ACSP; ASLA. *Faculty:* 33. *Students:* 187 full-time (83 women), 6 part-time (1 woman); includes 22 minority (5 Black or African American, non-Hispanic/Latino; 1 American Indian or Alaska Native, non-Hispanic/Latino; 5 Asian, non-Hispanic/Latino; 10 Hispanic/Latino; 1 Two or more races, non-Hispanic/Latino), 41 international. Average age 26. In 2014, 51 master's, 2 doctorates awarded. *Degree requirements:* For doctorate, thesis/dissertation. *Entrance requirements:* For master's, GRE or GMAT (city and regional planning), portfolio (for architecture and landscape architecture); for doctorate, GRE or GMAT (city and regional planning), example of research or written work. Additional exam requirements/recommendations for international students: Required—TOEFL (minimum score 600 paper-based; 100 iBT), Michigan English Language Assessment Battery (minimum score 86); Recommended—IELTS (minimum score 8). *Application deadline:* For fall admission, 1/1 priority date for domestic students, 12/1 priority date for international students; for winter admission, 12/1 for domestic students, 11/1 for international students; for spring admission, 12/1 for domestic students, 11/1 for international students; for summer admission, 4/1 for domestic students, 5/30 for international students. Applications are processed on a rolling basis. Application fee: $60 ($70 for international students). Electronic applications accepted. *Financial support:* Fellowships with tuition reimbursements, research assistantships with tuition reimbursements, Federal Work-Study, institutionally sponsored loans, and unspecified assistantships available. Support available to part-time students. *Unit head:* Michael B. Cadwell, Director and Walter H. Kidd Professor, 614-292-3174, E-mail: cadwell.1@osu.edu. *Application contact:* Graduate and Professional Admissions, 614-292-9444, Fax: 614-292-3895, E-mail: gpadmissions@osu.edu.
Website: http://knowlton.osu.edu/

Penn State University Park, Graduate School, College of Arts and Architecture, Stuckeman School of Architecture and Landscape Architecture, University Park, PA 16802. Offers architecture (M Arch, PhD); landscape architecture (MLA, MS). *Accreditation:* ASLA. *Unit head:* Dr. Barbara O. Korner, Dean, 814-865-2592, Fax: 814-865-2018, E-mail: bok2@psu.edu. *Application contact:* Lori A. Stania, Director, Graduate Student Services, 814-867-5278, Fax: 814-863-4627, E-mail: gswww@psu.edu.
Website: https://stuckeman.psu.edu/

Philadelphia University, College of Architecture and the Built Environment, Program in Architecture, Philadelphia, PA 19144. Offers high performance building (MS). *Entrance requirements:* For master's, bachelor?s degree, official undergraduate

Architecture

transcripts, current resume, two letters of recommendation, portfolio of relevant work, personal essay describing intended research.

Pontificia Universidad Catolica Madre y Maestra, Graduate School, Faculty of Sciences and Humanities, Santiago, Dominican Republic. Offers architecture (M Arch), including architecture of interiors, architecture of tourist lodgings, landscaping; early childhood education (M Ed).

Portland State University, Graduate Studies, School of Fine and Performing Arts, School of Architecture, Portland, OR 97207-0751. Offers M Arch. *Faculty:* 13 full-time (4 women), 14 part-time/adjunct (5 women). *Students:* 47 full-time (21 women), 5 part-time (4 women); includes 7 minority (2 Black or African American, non-Hispanic/Latino; 3 Asian, non-Hispanic/Latino; 1 Hispanic/Latino; 1 Two or more races, non-Hispanic/Latino), 2 international. Average age 29. 70 applicants, 43% accepted, 28 enrolled. In 2014, 13 master's awarded. *Degree requirements:* For master's, thesis optional. *Entrance requirements:* Additional exam requirements/recommendations for international students: Required—TOEFL (minimum score 550 paper-based; 80 iBT), IELTS (minimum score 6.5). *Application deadline:* For fall admission, 6/22 for domestic students; for summer admission, 5/23 for domestic students. Applications are processed on a rolling basis. Application fee: $50. Electronic applications accepted. *Expenses:* Tuition, state resident: part-time $222 per credit. Tuition, nonresident: part-time $527 per credit. *Required fees:* $22 per contact hour. $100 per quarter. Tuition and fees vary according to program. *Financial support:* In 2014–15, 3 research assistantships with full and partial tuition reimbursements (averaging $4,767 per year), 6 teaching assistantships with full and partial tuition reimbursements (averaging $4,766 per year) were awarded; Federal Work-Study, institutionally sponsored loans, scholarships/grants, and unspecified assistantships also available. Support available to part-time students. *Total annual research expenditures:* $72,282. *Unit head:* Prof. Clive Knights, Director, 503-725-8405, Fax: 503-725-8318, E-mail: knightsc@pdx.edu. *Application contact:* 503-725-3511, Fax: 503-725-5525.
Website: http://www.pdx.edu/the-arts/architecture

Prairie View A&M University, School of Architecture, Prairie View, TX 77446-0519. Offers architecture (M Arch); community development (MCD). Part-time and evening/weekend programs available. *Faculty:* 6 full-time (2 women), 5 part-time/adjunct (2 women). *Students:* 40 full-time (20 women), 15 part-time (9 women); includes 46 minority (41 Black or African American, non-Hispanic/Latino; 1 Asian, non-Hispanic/Latino; 2 Hispanic/Latino; 2 Two or more races, non-Hispanic/Latino), 5 international. Average age 30. 27 applicants, 100% accepted, 19 enrolled. In 2014, 36 master's awarded. *Degree requirements:* For master's, comprehensive exam, thesis. *Entrance requirements:* For master's, GRE General Test, portfolio (M Arch), minimum GPA of 2.75. Additional exam requirements/recommendations for international students: Required—TOEFL (minimum score 550 paper-based; 79 iBT). *Application deadline:* For fall admission, 7/1 priority date for domestic students, 6/1 priority date for international students; for spring admission, 11/1 priority date for domestic students, 10/1 priority date for international students; for summer admission, 3/1 priority date for domestic students, 2/1 priority date for international students. Applications are processed on a rolling basis. Application fee: $50. Electronic applications accepted. *Expenses:* Expenses: $6,686 tuition and fees. *Financial support:* Career-related internships or fieldwork, Federal Work-Study, institutionally sponsored loans, scholarships/grants, tuition waivers (full and partial), and unspecified assistantships available. Support available to part-time students. Financial award application deadline: 4/1; financial award applicants required to submit FAFSA. *Faculty research:* Community management, sustainable design. *Unit head:* Dr. Ikhlas Sabouni, Dean, 936-261-9800, Fax: 936-261-2350, E-mail: isabouni@pvamu.edu. *Application contact:* Pauline Walker, Administrative Assistant II, Research and Graduate Studies, 936-261-3521, Fax: 936-261-3529, E-mail: pmwalker@pvamu.edu.

★ **Pratt Institute,** School of Architecture, Program in Architecture, Brooklyn, NY 11205-3899. Offers architecture (first-professional) (M Arch); architecture (post-professional) (MS Arch). *Faculty:* 4 full-time (1 woman), 40 part-time/adjunct (11 women). *Students:* 190 full-time (94 women); includes 40 minority (2 Black or African American, non-Hispanic/Latino; 16 Asian, non-Hispanic/Latino; 21 Hispanic/Latino; 1 Two or more races, non-Hispanic/Latino), 64 international. Average age 26. 496 applicants, 74% accepted, 69 enrolled. In 2014, 66 master's awarded. *Degree requirements:* For master's, thesis. *Entrance requirements:* For master's, GRE (for M Arch only), B Arch (for MS Arch only), portfolio, letters of recommendation. Additional exam requirements/recommendations for international students: Required—TOEFL (minimum score 550 paper-based; 79 iBT). *Application deadline:* For fall admission, 1/5 for domestic and international students; for spring admission, 10/1 for domestic and international students. Application fee: $50 ($90 for international students). Electronic applications accepted. *Financial support:* Career-related internships or fieldwork, Federal Work-Study, institutionally sponsored loans, scholarships/grants, health care benefits, and unspecified assistantships available. Support available to part-time students. Financial award application deadline: 2/1; financial award applicants required to submit FAFSA. *Faculty research:* Design theory, advanced structural systems, urban investigations. *Unit head:* William J. Mac Donald, Chairperson, 718-636-4308, E-mail: wmacdona@pratt.edu. *Application contact:* Young Hah, Director of Graduate Admissions, 718-636-3683, Fax: 718-399-4242, E-mail: yhah@pratt.edu.
Website: https://www.pratt.edu/academics/architecture/grad-arch-urban-design/grad-dept-architecture/

See Display on this page and Close-Up on page 139.

Princeton University, Graduate School, School of Architecture, Princeton, NJ 08544-1019. Offers M Arch, PhD. Terminal master's awarded for partial completion of doctoral program. *Degree requirements:* For master's, thesis; for doctorate, 2 foreign languages, comprehensive exam, thesis/dissertation. *Entrance requirements:* For master's, GRE General Test, design portfolio, math, 2 semesters of physics, and art/architecture survey; for doctorate, GRE General Test, samples of written work. Additional exam requirements/recommendations for international students: Required—TOEFL (minimum score 600 paper-based). Electronic applications accepted. *Faculty research:* Design, urban studies, landscape architecture, media and information technologies in architecture.

Rensselaer Polytechnic Institute, Graduate School, School of Architecture, Program in Architectural Acoustics, Troy, NY 12180-3590. Offers architectural sciences (MS, PhD). Terminal master's awarded for partial completion of doctoral program. *Degree requirements:* For master's, thesis; for doctorate, comprehensive exam, thesis/dissertation. *Entrance requirements:* For master's and doctorate, GRE General Test. Additional exam requirements/recommendations for international students: Required—TOEFL (minimum score 570 paper-based; 88 iBT), IELTS (minimum score 6.5), PTE (minimum score 60). *Application deadline:* For fall admission, 1/1 priority date for domestic and international students. Applications are processed on a rolling basis. Application fee: $75. Electronic applications accepted. *Expenses: Tuition:* Full-time $46,700; part-time $1945 per credit. Tuition and fees vary according to course load. *Financial support:* In 2014–15, fellowships (averaging $18,500 per year), research assistantships (averaging $18,500 per year), teaching assistantships (averaging

$18,500 per year) were awarded. Financial award application deadline: 1/1. *Unit head:* Chris Perry, Graduate Program Director, 518-276-3034, E-mail: perryc3@rpi.edu. *Application contact:* Office of Graduate Admissions, 518-276-6216, E-mail: gradadmissions@rpi.edu.
Website: http://www.arch.rpi.edu/academic/graduate/architectural-acoustics/

Rensselaer Polytechnic Institute, Graduate School, School of Architecture, Program in Built Ecologies, Troy, NY 12180-3590. Offers MS, PhD. *Degree requirements:* For master's, thesis; for doctorate, comprehensive exam, thesis/dissertation. *Entrance requirements:* For master's and doctorate, GRE General Test. Additional exam requirements/recommendations for international students: Required—TOEFL (minimum score 570 paper-based; 88 iBT), IELTS (minimum score 6.5), PTE (minimum score 60). *Application deadline:* For fall admission, 1/1 priority date for domestic and international students. Applications are processed on a rolling basis. Application fee: $75. Electronic applications accepted. *Expenses: Tuition:* Full-time $46,700; part-time $1945 per credit. Tuition and fees vary according to course load. *Financial support:* In 2014–15, fellowships (averaging $18,500 per year), research assistantships (averaging $18,500 per year), teaching assistantships (averaging $18,500 per year) were awarded. Financial award application deadline: 1/1. *Unit head:* Chris Perry, Graduate Program Director, 518-276-3034, E-mail: perryc3@rpi.edu. *Application contact:* Office of Graduate Admissions, 518-276-6216, E-mail: gradadmissions@rpi.edu.
Website: http://www.arch.rpi.edu/academic/graduate/built-ecologies/

Rensselaer Polytechnic Institute, Graduate School, School of Architecture, Program in Lighting, Troy, NY 12180-3590. Offers architectural sciences (MS, PhD); lighting (MS). *Faculty:* 4 full-time (1 woman). *Students:* 2 full-time (0 women), 1 international. Average age 29. 7 applicants, 43% accepted, 2 enrolled. In 2014, 3 master's awarded. *Degree requirements:* For master's, comprehensive exam, thesis; for doctorate, comprehensive exam, thesis/dissertation. *Entrance requirements:* For master's and doctorate, GRE. Additional exam requirements/recommendations for international students: Required—TOEFL (minimum score 570 paper-based; 88 iBT), IELTS (minimum score 6.5), PTE (minimum score 60). *Application deadline:* For fall admission, 1/1 priority date for domestic and international students. Applications are processed on a rolling basis. Application fee: $75. Electronic applications accepted. *Expenses: Tuition:* Full-time $46,700; part-time $1945 per credit. Tuition and fees vary according to course load. *Financial support:* In 2014–15, 2 students received support, including research assistantships (averaging $18,500 per year), teaching assistantships with full tuition reimbursements available (averaging $18,500 per year); fellowships also available. Financial award application deadline: 1/1. *Faculty research:* Applications and design, automotive and street lighting, aviation lighting, controls, daylighting, energy and environment, health and vision, LEDs, outdoor lighting, residential lighting, security lighting. *Unit head:* Russ Leslie, Graduate Program Director, 518-687-7100, E-mail: leslir@rpi.edu. *Application contact:* Office of Graduate Admissions, 518-276-6216, E-mail: gradadmissions@rpi.edu.
Website: http://www.arch.rpi.edu/academic/graduate/lighting/

Rhode Island School of Design, Graduate Studies, Division of Architecture and Design, Department of Architecture, Providence, RI 02903-2784. Offers M Arch. *Faculty:* 26 full-time (12 women), 43 part-time/adjunct (15 women). *Students:* 96 full-time (56 women); includes 15 minority (2 Black or African American, non-Hispanic/Latino; 8 Asian, non-Hispanic/Latino; 4 Hispanic/Latino; 1 Two or more races, non-Hispanic/Latino), 41 international. Average age 26. 194 applicants, 62% accepted, 28 enrolled. In 2014, 26 master's awarded. *Degree requirements:* For master's, thesis, exhibit. *Entrance requirements:* For master's, portfolio, statement of purpose, 3 letters of recommendation. Additional exam requirements/recommendations for international students: Required—TOEFL (minimum score 580 paper-based; 93 iBT). *Application deadline:* For fall admission, 2/1 for domestic and international students. Application fee: $60. *Expenses:* Expenses: $44,594. *Financial support:* Fellowships, teaching assistantships, career-related internships or fieldwork, Federal Work-Study, and institutionally sponsored loans available. Financial award application deadline: 2/15; financial award applicants required to submit FAFSA. *Unit head:* Laura Briggs, Department Head, 401-454-6281, Fax: 401-454-6299, E-mail: lbriggs@risd.edu. *Application contact:* Molly Pettengil, Graduate Admissions Officer, 401-454-6312, Fax: 401-454-6309, E-mail: mpetteng@risd.edu.
Website: http://www.risd.edu/academics/architecture/

Rice University, Graduate Programs, School of Architecture, Houston, TX 77251-1892. Offers architecture (M Arch, D Arch); urban design (M Arch). *Degree requirements:* For master's, thesis optional; for doctorate, thesis/dissertation. *Entrance requirements:* For master's and doctorate, GRE. Additional exam requirements/recommendations for international students: Required—TOEFL (minimum score 600 paper-based; 100 iBT). Electronic applications accepted.

Rochester Institute of Technology, Graduate Enrollment Services, Golisano Institute for Sustainability, Architecture and Sustainability Department, M Arch Program in Architecture, Rochester, NY 14623-5608. Offers M Arch. *Students:* 44 full-time (22 women), 5 part-time (2 women); includes 3 minority (all Hispanic/Latino), 23 international. Average age 27. 57 applicants, 82% accepted, 22 enrolled. *Degree requirements:* For master's, thesis. *Entrance requirements:* For master's, GRE, and TOEFL, IELTS, or PTE for non-native English speakers, recommended minimum GPA of 3.0, portfolio. Additional exam requirements/recommendations for international students: Required—PTE (minimum score 58), TOEFL (minimum score 550 paper-based; 79 iBT) or IELTS (minimum score 6.5). *Application deadline:* For fall admission, 2/15 priority date for domestic and international students. Applications are processed on a rolling basis. Application fee: $60. Electronic applications accepted. *Expenses:* Expenses: $1,673 per credit hour. *Financial support:* In 2014–15, 14 students received support. Research assistantships with partial tuition reimbursements available, teaching assistantships with partial tuition reimbursements available, career-related internships or fieldwork, Federal Work-Study, institutionally sponsored loans, scholarships/grants, and unspecified assistantships available. Support available to part-time students. Financial award applicants required to submit FAFSA. *Faculty research:* Sustainable design and practice, practices and principles of preservation and adaptive reuse. *Unit head:* Dennis Andrejko, Program Chairman, 585-475-7363, E-mail: info@sustainability.rit.edu. *Application contact:* Diane Ellison, Associate Vice President, Graduate Enrollment Services, 585-475-2229, Fax: 585-475-7164, E-mail: gradinfo@rit.edu.
Website: http://www.rit.edu/gis/architecture/program

Roger Williams University, School of Architecture, Art and Historic Preservation, Bristol, RI 02809. Offers architecture (M Arch); art and architectural history (MA); historical preservation (MS). *Faculty:* 14 full-time (3 women), 16 part-time/adjunct (4 women). *Students:* 80 full-time (24 women), 18 part-time (8 women); includes 12 minority (1 Black or African American, non-Hispanic/Latino; 2 Asian, non-Hispanic/Latino; 8 Hispanic/Latino; 1 Two or more races, non-Hispanic/Latino), 7 international. Average age 25. 77 applicants, 87% accepted, 46 enrolled. In 2014, 49 master's awarded. *Degree requirements:* For master's, thesis. *Entrance requirements:* For master's, portfolio, 2 letters of recommendation. Additional exam requirements/recommendations for international students: Recommended—TOEFL (minimum score 85 iBT), IELTS. *Application deadline:* For fall admission, 3/1 priority date for domestic students. Application fee: $50. Electronic applications accepted. *Expenses:* Expenses: $33,792 (for M Arch); $20,644 (for MS in historical preservation). *Financial support:* In 2014–15, 84 students received support, including fellowships with partial tuition reimbursements available (averaging $6,000 per year), 80 research assistantships (averaging $3,000 per year). Financial award application deadline: 6/15; financial award applicants required to submit FAFSA. *Unit head:* Stephen White, Dean, 401-254-3607, E-mail: swhite@rwu.edu. *Application contact:* Lori Vales, Director of Graduate Admissions, 401-254-6200, Fax: 401-254-3557, E-mail: gradadmit@rwu.edu.
Website: http://www.rwu.edu/academics/departments/architecture.htm#dual

Savannah College of Art and Design, Graduate School, Program in Architecture, Savannah, GA 31402-3146. Offers M Arch. Part-time programs available. *Faculty:* 22 full-time (7 women), 7 part-time/adjunct (1 woman). *Students:* 94 full-time (43 women), 20 part-time (5 women); includes 17 minority (3 Black or African American, non-Hispanic/Latino; 1 Asian, non-Hispanic/Latino; 13 Hispanic/Latino), 47 international. Average age 25. 149 applicants, 66% accepted, 51 enrolled. In 2014, 79 master's awarded. *Degree requirements:* For master's, thesis, internship. *Entrance requirements:* For master's, portfolio. Additional exam requirements/recommendations for international students: Required—TOEFL (minimum score 550 paper-based, 85 iBT), IELTS (minimum score 6.5), or ACTFL. *Application deadline:* For fall admission, 4/1 for domestic and international students. Applications are processed on a rolling basis. Application fee: $40. Electronic applications accepted. *Expenses: Tuition:* Full-time $34,605; part-time $3845 per course. One-time fee: $500. Tuition and fees vary according to course load. *Financial support:* Fellowships, career-related internships or fieldwork, Federal Work-Study, and scholarships/grants available. Financial award application deadline: 4/1; financial award applicants required to submit FAFSA. *Faculty research:* Computer-aided design, photovoltaic-powered environmental control. *Unit head:* Ivan Chow. *Application contact:* Jenny Jaquillard, Executive Director of Admissions, Recruitment and Events, 912-525-5100, Fax: 912-525-5985, E-mail: admission@scad.edu.
Website: http://www.scad.edu/academics/programs/architecture

School of the Art Institute of Chicago, Graduate Division, Department of Architecture, Interior Architecture, and Designed Objects, Chicago, IL 60603-3103. Offers architecture (M Arc); design for emerging technologies (MFA); designed objects (M Des); interior architecture (M Arc). *Entrance requirements:* Additional exam requirements/recommendations for international students: Required—TOEFL, IELTS.

Southern California Institute of Architecture, Graduate Program in Architecture, Los Angeles, CA 90013. Offers M Arch. *Faculty:* 20 full-time (8 women), 16 part-time/adjunct (3 women). *Students:* 255 full-time (105 women), 5 part-time (0 women); includes 47 minority (2 Black or African American, non-Hispanic/Latino; 23 Asian, non-Hispanic/Latino; 16 Hispanic/Latino; 1 Native Hawaiian or other Pacific Islander, non-Hispanic/Latino; 5 Two or more races, non-Hispanic/Latino), 139 international. Average age 27. 502 applicants, 75% accepted, 124 enrolled. In 2014, 97 master's awarded. *Degree requirements:* For master's, thesis, final thesis project. *Entrance requirements:* For master's, GRE General Test, portfolio, 3 letters of recommendation, transcripts, statement of purpose, resume. Additional exam requirements/recommendations for international students: Required—TOEFL (minimum score 583 paper-based, 90 iBT) or IELTS (minimum score 6.5). *Application deadline:* For fall admission, 12/15 for domestic and international students. Application fee: $85. Electronic applications accepted. *Expenses: Tuition:* Full-time $39,162. *Required fees:* $2195. *Financial support:* In 2014–15, 8 teaching assistantships (averaging $750 per year) were awarded; Federal Work-Study and scholarships/grants also available. Financial award application deadline: 8/20; financial award applicants required to submit FAFSA. *Unit head:* Hernan Diaz Alonso, Graduate Program Chair, 213-613-2200, Fax: 213-613-2260, E-mail: hernan@sciarc.edu. *Application contact:* Sandy Frigo, Director of Admissions, 213-356-5321, Fax: 213-613-2260, E-mail: admissions@sciarc.edu.

Southern Illinois University Carbondale, Graduate School, College of Applied Science, School of Architecture, Carbondale, IL 62901-4701. Offers M Arch. *Students:* 82 full-time (22 women), 17 part-time (4 women); includes 8 minority (4 Black or African American, non-Hispanic/Latino; 2 Asian, non-Hispanic/Latino; 2 Hispanic/Latino), 9 international. 80 applicants, 38% accepted, 28 enrolled. In 2014, 26 master's awarded. *Entrance requirements:* Additional exam requirements/recommendations for international students: Required—TOEFL. Application fee: $50. *Expenses:* Tuition, state resident: full-time $10,176; part-time $1153 per credit. Tuition, nonresident: full-time $20,814; part-time $1744 per credit. *Required fees:* $7092; $394 per credit. $2364 per semester. *Unit head:* John Dobbins, Director of Graduate Studies, 618-453-3734, E-mail: jdobbins@siu.edu.

Syracuse University, School of Architecture, Syracuse, NY 13244. Offers M Arch, MS. *Faculty:* 38 full-time (13 women), 8 part-time/adjunct (1 woman). *Students:* 112 full-time (38 women), 1 (woman) part-time; includes 18 minority (5 Black or African American, non-Hispanic/Latino; 1 American Indian or Alaska Native, non-Hispanic/Latino; 6 Asian, non-Hispanic/Latino; 5 Hispanic/Latino; 1 Two or more races, non-Hispanic/Latino), 57 international. Average age 25. 248 applicants, 46% accepted, 37 enrolled. In 2014, 30 master's awarded. *Degree requirements:* For master's, thesis. *Entrance requirements:* For master's, GRE General Test, interview, portfolio. Additional exam requirements/recommendations for international students: Required—TOEFL (minimum score 100 iBT). *Application deadline:* For fall admission, 2/1 priority date for domestic and international students. Application fee: $75. Electronic applications accepted. *Expenses: Tuition:* Part-time $1341 per credit. *Financial support:* Fellowships with full tuition reimbursements, research assistantships with full and partial tuition reimbursements, and teaching assistantships with full and partial tuition reimbursements available. Financial award application deadline: 1/1. *Faculty research:* Urban design, urban mapping, building systems, landscape, theory. *Unit head:* Jean Francois Bedard, Graduate Director, 315-443-1041, Fax: 315-443-5082. *Application contact:* Speranza Migliore, Admissions Contact, 315-443-1041, Fax: 315-443-5082, E-mail: smiglior@syr.edu.
Website: http://soa.syr.edu/

Temple University, Center for the Arts, Tyler School of Art, Department of Architecture, Philadelphia, PA 19122-6096. Offers M Arch. Part-time programs available. *Faculty:* 11 full-time (5 women), 16 part-time/adjunct (7 women). *Students:* 23 full-time (9 women); includes 3 minority (1 Black or African American, non-Hispanic/Latino; 1 Asian, non-Hispanic/Latino; 1 Hispanic/Latino), 4 international. 52 applicants, 81% accepted, 13 enrolled. In 2014, 1 master's awarded. *Degree requirements:* For master's, thesis optional. *Entrance requirements:* For master's, GRE, portfolio, letters of recommendation, resume/curriculum vitae, minimum GPA of 3.0. Additional exam requirements/recommendations for international students: Required—TOEFL (minimum score 550 paper-based; 79 iBT), IELTS (minimum score 6.5). *Application deadline:* For fall admission, 1/15 for domestic students, 1/15 priority date for international students. Applications are processed on a rolling basis. Application fee: $60. Electronic applications accepted. *Expenses:* Expenses: Contact institution. *Financial support:* Career-related internships or fieldwork, Federal Work-Study, and institutionally sponsored loans available. Support available to part-time students. Financial award application deadline: 1/15; financial award applicants required to submit FAFSA. *Unit head:* Kate Wingert-Playdon, Chair, 215-204-8813, Fax: 215-204-5481, E-mail:

architecture@temple.edu. *Application contact:* Nicole Hall, Director of Admissions, 215-777-9090, E-mail: tylerart@temple.edu.
Website: http://www.temple.edu/architecture/

Texas A&M University, College of Architecture, Department of Architecture, College Station, TX 77843. Offers architecture (M Arch, MS, PhD); health systems and design (Certificate). *Faculty:* 30. *Students:* 139 full-time (63 women), 18 part-time (6 women); includes 16 minority (2 Black or African American, non-Hispanic/Latino; 4 Asian, non-Hispanic/Latino; 10 Hispanic/Latino), 84 international. Average age 30. 219 applicants, 56% accepted, 42 enrolled. In 2014, 45 master's, 10 doctorates awarded. *Degree requirements:* For master's, comprehensive exam, thesis; for doctorate, comprehensive exam, thesis/dissertation. *Entrance requirements:* For master's, GRE General Test, portfolio, letters of recommendation; for doctorate, GRE General Test. Additional exam requirements/recommendations for international students: Required—TOEFL. *Application deadline:* For fall admission, 12/15 priority date for domestic and international students. Applications are processed on a rolling basis. Application fee: $50 ($90 for international students). Electronic applications accepted. *Expenses:* Tuition, state resident: full-time $4078; part-time $226.55 per credit hour. Tuition, nonresident: full-time $10,594; part-time $577.55 per credit hour. *Required fees:* $2813; $237.70 per credit hour. $278.50 per semester. Tuition and fees vary according to degree level and student level. *Financial support:* In 2014–15, 107 students received support, including 4 fellowships with full and partial tuition reimbursements available (averaging $10,125 per year), 18 research assistantships with full and partial tuition reimbursements available (averaging $4,525 per year), 45 teaching assistantships with full and partial tuition reimbursements available (averaging $4,183 per year); career-related internships or fieldwork, institutionally sponsored loans, scholarships/grants, traineeships, health care benefits, tuition waivers (full and partial), and unspecified assistantships also available. Support available to part-time students. Financial award application deadline: 1/15; financial award applicants required to submit FAFSA. *Faculty research:* Energy optimization, architecture pedagogy, environment and behavior. *Unit head:* Dr. Ward Wells, Head, 979-845-1015, Fax: 979-862-1571, E-mail: ward-wells@tamu.edu. *Application contact:* Graduate Admissions, 979-845-1060, E-mail: graduate-admissions@tamu.edu.
Website: http://dept.arch.tamu.edu/

Texas Tech University, Graduate School, College of Architecture, Lubbock, TX 79409. Offers architecture (M Arch, MS); land use planning, management, and design (PhD); MBA/M Arch. Part-time programs available. *Faculty:* 41 full-time (12 women), 6 part-time/adjunct (1 woman). *Students:* 76 full-time (14 women), 34 part-time (7 women); includes 38 minority (1 Black or African American, non-Hispanic/Latino; 3 Asian, non-Hispanic/Latino; 32 Hispanic/Latino; 2 Two or more races, non-Hispanic/Latino), 12 international. Average age 25. 81 applicants, 46% accepted, 14 enrolled. In 2014, 64 master's awarded. *Degree requirements:* For master's, thesis; for doctorate, thesis/dissertation. *Entrance requirements:* For master's, GRE General Test, portfolio; for doctorate, GRE General Test. Additional exam requirements/recommendations for international students: Required—TOEFL (minimum score 550 paper-based; 79 iBT). *Application deadline:* For fall admission, 6/1 priority date for domestic students, 1/15 priority date for international students; for spring admission, 9/1 priority date for domestic students, 6/15 priority date for international students. Applications are processed on a rolling basis. Application fee: $60. Electronic applications accepted. *Expenses:* Expenses: Contact institution. *Financial support:* In 2014–15, 71 students received support, including 71 fellowships (averaging $4,212 per year), 1 research assistantship (averaging $17,400 per year); teaching assistantships, career-related internships or fieldwork, Federal Work-Study, institutionally sponsored loans, scholarships/grants, traineeships, health care benefits, and unspecified assistantships also available. Support available to part-time students. Financial award application deadline: 4/15; financial award applicants required to submit FAFSA. *Faculty research:* Historic preservation, vernacular architecture, community development and design, visualization, sustainable architecture, digital design construction and fabrication. *Total annual research expenditures:* $17,341. *Unit head:* Prof. Andrew Vernooy, Dean, 806-742-3136, Fax: 806-742-1400, E-mail: andrew.vernooy@ttu.edu. *Application contact:* Jess Schwintz, Coordinator of Academic Programs, 806-742-3169 Ext. 247, Fax: 806-742-1400, E-mail: jess.schwintz@ttu.edu.
Website: http://www.arch.ttu.edu/architecture/

Tulane University, School of Architecture, New Orleans, LA 70118-5669. Offers M Arch, MPS, MSRED. Part-time programs available. *Degree requirements:* For master's, thesis. *Entrance requirements:* For master's, GRE, portfolio. Additional exam requirements/recommendations for international students: Required—TOEFL. *Expenses:* Contact institution. *Faculty research:* Design topics, preservation and environmental conservation, architecture and human health, computing.

Universidad Autonoma de Guadalajara, Graduate Programs, Guadalajara, Mexico. Offers administrative law and justice (LL M); advertising and corporate communications (MA); architecture (M Arch); business (MBA); computational science (MCC); education (Ed M, Ed D); English-Spanish translation (MA); entrepreneurship and management (MBA); integrated management of digital animation (MA); international business (MIB); international corporate law (LL M); internet technologies (MS); manufacturing systems (MMS); occupational health (MS); philosophy (MA, PhD); power electronics (MS); quality systems (MQS); renewable energy (MS); social evaluation of projects (MBA); strategic market research (MBA); tax law (MA); teaching mathematics (MA).

Universidad Nacional Pedro Henriquez Urena, Graduate School, Santo Domingo, Dominican Republic. Offers agricultural diversity (MS), including horticultural/fruit production, tropical animal production; conservation of monuments and cultural assets (M Arch); ecology and environment (MS); environmental engineering (MEE); international relations (MA); natural resource management (MS); political science (MA); project optimization (MPM); project feasibility (MPM); project management (MPM); sanitation engineering (ME); science for teachers (MS); tropical Caribbean architecture (M Arch).

Université Laval, Faculty of Architecture, Planning and Visual Arts, School of Architecture, Program in Architecture, Québec, QC G1K 7P4, Canada. Offers M Arch, M Sc. Part-time programs available. *Degree requirements:* For master's, thesis (for some programs). *Entrance requirements:* For master's, mastery of software (CAO), knowledge of French and English. Electronic applications accepted.

University at Buffalo, the State University of New York, Graduate School, School of Architecture and Planning, Department of Architecture, Buffalo, NY 14214. Offers architecture (M Arch); flexible track (MS Arch); inclusive design (MS Arch); real estate development (MS Arch); situated technologies (MS Arch); urban design and historic preservation (MS Arch); M Arch/MBA; M Arch/MFA; M Arch/MUP. *Faculty:* 27 full-time (9 women), 13 part-time/adjunct (4 women). *Students:* 123 full-time (43 women), 4 part-time (1 woman); includes 19 minority (3 Black or African American, non-Hispanic/Latino; 7 Asian, non-Hispanic/Latino; 5 Hispanic/Latino; 4 Two or more races, non-Hispanic/Latino), 40 international. Average age 25. 181 applicants, 89% accepted, 65 enrolled. In 2014, 40 master's awarded. *Degree requirements:* For master's, thesis or alternative, project. *Entrance requirements:* For master's, GRE, portfolio, 3 letters of recommendation, transcripts, 500-word personal statement. Additional exam requirements/recommendations for international students: Required—TOEFL (minimum score 550 paper-based; 79 iBT), IELTS (minimum score 6.5). *Application deadline:* For fall admission, 1/15 priority date for domestic and international students. Application fee: $75. Electronic applications accepted. *Expenses:* Expenses: $7,017.50 per semester resident tuition and fees, $11,152.50 non-resident. *Financial support:* In 2014–15, 2 fellowships with full tuition reimbursements (averaging $20,618 per year), 10 research assistantships with full and partial tuition reimbursements (averaging $7,515 per year), 29 teaching assistantships with partial tuition reimbursements (averaging $4,865 per year) were awarded; career-related internships or fieldwork, Federal Work-Study, institutionally sponsored loans, scholarships/grants, health care benefits, tuition waivers (partial), and unspecified assistantships also available. Support available to part-time students. Financial award application deadline: 3/1; financial award applicants required to submit FAFSA. *Faculty research:* Inclusive design, material culture, situated technologies, ecological practices. *Total annual research expenditures:* $2.6 million. *Unit head:* Prof. Omar Khan, Chair, 716-829-3483 Ext. 105, Fax: 716-829-3256, E-mail: omar.khan@buffalo.edu. *Application contact:* Debra Eggebrecht, Assistant to the Chair, 716-829-3485 Ext. 105, Fax: 716-829-3256, E-mail: dle2@buffalo.edu.
Website: http://www.ap.buffalo.edu/architecture/

The University of Arizona, College of Architecture, Planning, and Landscape Architecture, School of Architecture, Tucson, AZ 85721. Offers M Arch. *Entrance requirements:* For master's, GRE, 3 letters of recommendation, statement of purpose, portfolio, resume. Additional exam requirements/recommendations for international students: Required—TOEFL (minimum score 550 paper-based; 79 iBT). Electronic applications accepted.

The University of British Columbia, Faculty of Applied Science, School of Architecture and Landscape Architecture, Vancouver, BC V6T 1Z2, Canada. Offers architecture (M Arch, MASA); landscape architecture (MASLA, MLA). *Degree requirements:* For master's, thesis. *Entrance requirements:* For master's, portfolio, resume, statement of interest, 3 reference letters. Additional exam requirements/recommendations for international students: Required—TOEFL (minimum score 600 paper-based; 100 iBT), IELTS (minimum score 7). Electronic applications accepted. *Expenses:* Contact institution. *Faculty research:* Energy and resource use of buildings, advanced design research, urban design and community activism, advanced research in computer applications, cultural studies.

University of Calgary, Faculty of Graduate Studies, Faculty of Environmental Design, Calgary, AB T2N 1N4, Canada. Offers architecture (M Arch); environmental design (M Env Des, PhD); planning (M Plan). *Degree requirements:* For master's, thesis; for doctorate, thesis/dissertation. *Entrance requirements:* For master's, minimum GPA of 3.0; for doctorate, minimum GPA of 3.5. Additional exam requirements/recommendations for international students: Required—TOEFL (minimum score 550 paper-based). *Faculty research:* Sustainable development in architecture, planning and product design, energy and environment, impact assessment, ecotourism.

University of California, Berkeley, Graduate Division, College of Environmental Design, Department of Architecture, Berkeley, CA 94720-1500. Offers architecture (M Arch); building science (MS, PhD); building structures, construction and materials (MS, PhD); design theories, methods, and practices (MS, PhD); environmental design in developing countries (MS, PhD); history of architecture and urbanism (MS, PhD); social and cultural processes in architecture and urbanism (MS, PhD); M Arch/MCP; M Arch/MS; MLA/M Arch. *Degree requirements:* For master's, thesis; for doctorate, thesis/dissertation, qualifying exam. *Entrance requirements:* For master's and doctorate, GRE General Test, minimum GPA of 3.0, 3 letters of recommendation. Additional exam requirements/recommendations for international students: Required—TOEFL. Electronic applications accepted.

University of California, Los Angeles, Graduate Division, School of the Arts and Architecture, Department of Architecture and Urban Design, Los Angeles, CA 90095. Offers M Arch, MA, PhD. *Degree requirements:* For master's, comprehensive exam (M Arch I, II); thesis (MA) ; for doctorate, 2 foreign languages, thesis/dissertation, oral and written qualifying exams. *Entrance requirements:* For master's, GRE General Test, bachelor's degree; minimum undergraduate GPA of 3.0 (or its equivalent if letter grade system not used); writing sample (MA only); portfolio (M Arch only); for doctorate, GRE General Test, bachelor's degree; minimum undergraduate GPA of 3.5 (or its equivalent if letter grade system not used); writing sample. Additional exam requirements/recommendations for international students: Required—TOEFL. Electronic applications accepted. *Expenses:* Contact institution.

University of Cincinnati, Graduate School, College of Design, Architecture, Art, and Planning, School of Architecture and Interior Design, Cincinnati, OH 45221. Offers architecture (M Arch). *Accreditation:* NASAD. *Degree requirements:* For master's, one foreign language, thesis. *Entrance requirements:* Additional exam requirements/recommendations for international students: Required—TOEFL. *Faculty research:* Theory and history of architecture.

University of Colorado Denver, College of Architecture and Planning, Program in Architecture, Denver, CO 80217. Offers M Arch. Part-time programs available. *Students:* 189 full-time (76 women), 7 part-time (5 women); includes 33 minority (2 American Indian or Alaska Native, non-Hispanic/Latino; 7 Asian, non-Hispanic/Latino; 18 Hispanic/Latino; 6 Two or more races, non-Hispanic/Latino), 10 international. Average age 27. 204 applicants, 84% accepted, 63 enrolled. In 2014, 96 master's awarded. *Degree requirements:* For master's, thesis optional. *Entrance requirements:* For master's, GRE, portfolio; sample of writing or work project; three letters of recommendation; statement of purpose. Additional exam requirements/recommendations for international students: Required—TOEFL (minimum score 75 iBT). *Application deadline:* For fall admission, 1/15 for domestic students, 12/15 for international students; for spring admission, 10/1 for domestic and international students. Application fee: $50 ($75 for international students). Electronic applications accepted. *Expenses:* Expenses: Contact institution. *Financial support:* In 2014–15, 42 students received support. Fellowships, research assistantships, teaching assistantships, Federal Work-Study, institutionally sponsored loans, scholarships/grants, and traineeships available. Financial award application deadline: 4/1; financial award applicants required to submit FAFSA. *Faculty research:* Architectural design; history, theory, and criticism of architecture; regional and environmental issues; sustainability; intervention and transformation in the urban and rural landscape. *Unit head:* Ekaterini Vlahos, Chair/Director of the Center of Preservation Research, 303-315-0573, E-mail: kat.vlahos@ucdenver.edu. *Application contact:* Rachael Kuroiwa, Manager of Admissions and Outreach, 303-315-2325, E-mail: rachael.kuroiwa@ucdenver.edu.
Website: http://www.ucdenver.edu/academics/colleges/ArchitecturePlanning/Academics/DegreePrograms/MArch/Pages/MArch.aspx

University of Florida, Graduate School, College of Design, Construction and Planning, Doctoral Program in Design, Construction and Planning, Gainesville, FL 32611. Offers construction management (PhD); design, construction and planning (PhD); geographic information systems (PhD); historic preservation (PhD); interior design (PhD); landscape architecture (PhD); urban and regional planning (PhD). *Students:* 79 full-time (32 women), 21 part-time (7 women); includes 12 minority (4 Black or African American, non-Hispanic/Latino; 1 American Indian or Alaska Native, non-

Hispanic/Latino; 4 Asian, non-Hispanic/Latino; 3 Hispanic/Latino), 51 international. 92 applicants, 25% accepted, 14 enrolled. In 2014, 18 doctorates awarded. *Degree requirements:* For doctorate, thesis/dissertation. *Entrance requirements:* For doctorate, GRE General Test, minimum GPA of 3.0. Additional exam requirements/recommendations for international students: Required—TOEFL (minimum score 550 paper-based; 80 iBT), IELTS (minimum score 6). *Application deadline:* For fall admission, 2/1 for domestic and international students. Applications are processed on a rolling basis. Application fee: $30. Electronic applications accepted. *Financial support:* In 2014–15, 3 fellowships, 26 research assistantships, 30 teaching assistantships were awarded; unspecified assistantships also available. Financial award applicants required to submit FAFSA. *Faculty research:* Architecture, building construction, urban and regional planning. *Unit head:* Zhong-Ren Peng, PhD, Professor/Director, 352-392-0997 Ext. 429, Fax: 352-392-3308, E-mail: zpeng@ufl.edu. *Application contact:* Zhong-Ren Peng, PhD, Professor/Director, 352-392-0997 Ext. 429, Fax: 352-392-3308, E-mail: zpeng@ufl.edu.
Website: http://www.dcp.ufl.edu/docprogram/

University of Florida, Graduate School, College of Design, Construction and Planning, School of Architecture, Gainesville, FL 32611-5702. Offers architecture (M Arch, MSAS); historic preservation (M Arch, MSAS); sustainable architecture (M Arch, MSAS); sustainable design (M Arch, MSAS). Postbaccalaureate distance learning degree programs offered. *Faculty:* 19 full-time (5 women), 1 part-time/adjunct (0 women). *Students:* 115 full-time (43 women), 6 part-time (3 women); includes 30 minority (3 Black or African American, non-Hispanic/Latino; 6 Asian, non-Hispanic/Latino; 21 Hispanic/Latino), 33 international. 209 applicants, 60% accepted, 44 enrolled. In 2014, 62 master's awarded. *Entrance requirements:* For master's, GRE General Test, minimum GPA of 3.0. Additional exam requirements/recommendations for international students: Required—TOEFL (minimum score 550 paper-based; 80 iBT), IELTS (minimum score 6). Application fee: $30. *Financial support:* In 2014–15, 1 research assistantship, 18 teaching assistantships were awarded; fellowships also available. Financial award applicants required to submit FAFSA. *Unit head:* Martin Gold, Director/Associate Professor, 352-392-0205, E-mail: mgold@ufl.edu. *Application contact:* Nancy M. Clark, Assistant Director for Graduate Program, 352-392-0205 Ext. 220, E-mail: nmclark@ufl.edu.
Website: http://soa.dcp.ufl.edu/

University of Hartford, College of Engineering, Technology and Architecture, Program in Architecture, West Hartford, CT 06117-1599. Offers M Arch. *Entrance requirements:* For master's, 3 letters of recommendation, portfolio. Additional exam requirements/recommendations for international students: Required—TOEFL (minimum score 550 paper-based).

University of Hawaii at Manoa, School of Architecture, Honolulu, HI 96822. Offers D Arch. Part-time programs available. *Entrance requirements:* Additional exam requirements/recommendations for international students: Required—TOEFL, IELTS. *Faculty research:* Housing, future cities, environmental studies, preservation, professional practice.

University of Houston, College of Architecture, Houston, TX 77204. Offers architecture (MS); architecture studies (MA); space architecture (MS). *Entrance requirements:* For master's, GRE General Test. Additional exam requirements/recommendations for international students: Required—TOEFL (minimum score 550 paper-based; 79 iBT), IELTS (minimum score 6.5). Electronic applications accepted. *Faculty research:* Community-based design; twentieth century architecture, urbanism, and design; extreme environments; design build; green building components and digital technology.

University of Idaho, College of Graduate Studies, College of Art and Architecture, Moscow, ID 83844-2461. Offers architecture (M Arch); art (MFA); bioregional planning and community design (MS); integrated architecture and design (MS); landscape architecture (MLA); teaching art (MAT). *Accreditation:* NASAD. *Faculty:* 17 full-time, 4 part-time/adjunct. *Students:* 88 full-time (34 women), 18 part-time (6 women). Average age 31. In 2014, 38 master's awarded. *Entrance requirements:* Additional exam requirements/recommendations for international students: Required—TOEFL (minimum score 550 paper-based). *Application deadline:* For fall admission, 8/1 for domestic students; for spring admission, 12/15 for domestic students. Applications are processed on a rolling basis. Application fee: $60. Electronic applications accepted. *Expenses:* Tuition, state resident: full-time $4784; part-time $280.50 per credit hour. Tuition, nonresident: full-time $18,314; part-time $957.50 per credit hour. *Required fees:* $2000; $58.50 per credit hour. Tuition and fees vary according to program. *Financial support:* Applicants required to submit FAFSA. *Faculty research:* Sustainability in communities, urban research, virtual technology, bioregional planning, environment and behavior interaction. *Unit head:* Dr. Mark Hoversten, Dean, 208-885-4409, E-mail: caa@uidaho.edu. *Application contact:* Sean Scoggin, Graduate Recruitment Coordinator, 208-885-4001, Fax: 208-885-4406, E-mail: graduateadmissions@uidaho.edu.
Website: http://www.uidaho.edu/caa

University of Illinois at Chicago, Graduate College, College of Architecture, Design and the Arts, School of Architecture, Chicago, IL 60607-7128. Offers M Arch, MA, MS, MS Arch. *Faculty:* 20 full-time (7 women), 18 part-time/adjunct (6 women). *Students:* 57 full-time (25 women), 1 (woman) part-time; includes 19 minority (1 Black or African American, non-Hispanic/Latino; 8 Asian, non-Hispanic/Latino; 8 Hispanic/Latino; 2 Two or more races, non-Hispanic/Latino), 9 international. Average age 26. 183 applicants, 57% accepted, 21 enrolled. In 2014, 31 master's awarded. *Entrance requirements:* For master's, GRE General Test, portfolio, minimum GPA of 3.0 in the last 60 hours of coursework, 3 letters of recommendation, statement of intent. Additional exam requirements/recommendations for international students: Required—TOEFL or IELTS. *Application deadline:* For fall admission, 1/15 priority date for domestic and international students. Applications are processed on a rolling basis. Application fee: $60. Electronic applications accepted. *Expenses:* Expenses: $19,134 in-state, $31,132 out-of-state (for MA Arch); $20,134 in-state, $32,132 out-of-state (for M Arch); $22,700 in-state, $34,698 out-of-state (for MS in architecture in health design); $18,718 in-state, $30,176 out-of-state (for MA in architecture design criticism). *Financial support:* Fellowships with full tuition reimbursements, research assistantships with full tuition reimbursements, teaching assistantships with full tuition reimbursements, institutionally sponsored loans, scholarships/grants, traineeships, and tuition waivers (full) available. Financial award application deadline: 1/15; financial award applicants required to submit FAFSA. *Faculty research:* Contemporary design, history and theory, technology, urbanism. *Total annual research expenditures:* $25,000. *Unit head:* Dr. Robert Somol, Director, 312-996-3335, E-mail: somol@uic.edu. *Application contact:* Stephanie Niebuhr, Graduate Academic Advisor, 312-996-3335.
Website: http://www.arch.uic.edu/

University of Illinois at Urbana–Champaign, Graduate College, College of Fine and Applied Arts, School of Architecture, Champaign, IL 61820. Offers architectural studies (MS); architecture (M Arch, PhD); M Arch/MBA; M Arch/MS; M Arch/MUP; MCS/M Arch. *Students:* 163 (63 women). Application fee: $70 ($90 for international students). *Unit head:* Peter Mortensen, Director, 217-333-1331, Fax: 217-244-8866, E-mail: pmortens@illinois.edu. *Application contact:* Christopher R. Wilcock, Admissions and

Records Officer, 217-244-4723, Fax: 217-244-8866, E-mail: cwilcock@illinois.edu.
Website: http://www.arch.illinois.edu/

The University of Kansas, Graduate Studies, School of Architecture, Design, and Planning, Department of Architecture, Lawrence, KS 66045. Offers architecture (M Arch, MA, PhD); facility management (Certificate); M Arch/MBA; M Arch/MUP. *Faculty:* 18 full-time, 21 part-time/adjunct. *Students:* 122 full-time (53 women), 19 part-time (9 women); includes 11 minority (3 Black or African American, non-Hispanic/Latino; 3 Asian, non-Hispanic/Latino; 2 Hispanic/Latino; 3 Two or more races, non-Hispanic/Latino), 32 international. Average age 26. 134 applicants, 56% accepted, 24 enrolled. In 2014, 76 master's, 1 doctorate awarded. Terminal master's awarded for partial completion of doctoral program. *Degree requirements:* For master's, thesis or alternative, 1 summer abroad; for doctorate, comprehensive exam, thesis/dissertation. *Entrance requirements:* For master's, portfolio, minimum GPA of 3.0, letters of recommendation; for doctorate, GRE, portfolio, master's degree, letters of recommendation. Additional exam requirements/recommendations for international students: Required—TOEFL, IELTS. *Application deadline:* For fall admission, 3/1 for domestic and international students; for spring admission, 11/1 for domestic and international students. Applications are processed on a rolling basis. Application fee: $55 ($75 for international students). Electronic applications accepted. *Financial support:* Fellowships, research assistantships with partial tuition reimbursements, teaching assistantships with full and partial tuition reimbursements, scholarships/grants, health care benefits, and unspecified assistantships available. Financial award application deadline: 2/1; financial award applicants required to submit FAFSA. *Faculty research:* Design build, sustainability, emergent technology, healthy places, urban design. *Unit head:* Prof. Paola Sanguinetti, Chair, 785-864-1577, E-mail: paolas@ku.edu. *Application contact:* Gera Elliott, Admissions Coordinator, 785-864-3167, Fax: 785-864-5185, E-mail: archku@ku.edu.
Website: http://architecture.ku.edu/

University of Kentucky, Graduate School, College of Design, School of Architecture, Lexington, KY 40506-0032. Offers M Arch. *Degree requirements:* For master's, comprehensive exam. *Entrance requirements:* For master's, GRE General Test, minimum undergraduate GPA of 2.75. Additional exam requirements/recommendations for international students: Required—TOEFL (minimum score 550 paper-based). Electronic applications accepted.

The University of Manchester, School of Environment and Development, Manchester, United Kingdom. Offers architecture (M Phil, PhD); development policy and management (M Phil, PhD); human geography (M Phil, PhD); physical geography (M Phil, PhD); planning and landscape (M Phil, PhD).

University of Manitoba, Faculty of Graduate Studies, Faculty of Architecture, Department of Architecture, Winnipeg, MB R3T 2N2, Canada. Offers M Arch. *Degree requirements:* For master's, thesis or alternative.

University of Maryland, College Park, Academic Affairs, School of Architecture, Planning and Preservation, Program in Architecture, College Park, MD 20742. Offers M Arch, M Arch/MCP. Part-time and evening/weekend programs available. *Entrance requirements:* For master's, GRE General Test, portfolio, minimum GPA of 3.0, letters of recommendation. Additional exam requirements/recommendations for international students: Required—TOEFL. Electronic applications accepted. *Faculty research:* Design, history, theory.

University of Massachusetts Amherst, Graduate School, College of Humanities and Fine Arts, Programs in Architecture and Design, Amherst, MA 01003. Offers architecture (M Arch); design (MS); design in historic preservation (MS). Part-time programs available. *Students:* 37 full-time (17 women); includes 2 minority (both Hispanic/Latino), 15 international. Average age 29. 105 applicants, 67% accepted, 11 enrolled. In 2014, 21 master's awarded. *Degree requirements:* For master's, thesis or alternative, project. *Entrance requirements:* For master's, GRE General Test (for M Arch only), 3 letters of recommendation (M Arch only); portfolio. Additional exam requirements/recommendations for international students: Required—TOEFL (minimum score 550 paper-based; 80 iBT), IELTS (minimum score 6.5). *Application deadline:* For fall admission, 2/1 for domestic and international students. Applications are processed on a rolling basis. Application fee: $75. Electronic applications accepted. *Expenses:* Tuition, state resident: full-time $1980; part-time $110 per credit. Tuition, nonresident: full-time 14,644; part-time $414 per credit. *Required fees:* $11,417. One-time fee: $357. *Financial support:* Fellowships with full and partial tuition reimbursements, research assistantships with full and partial tuition reimbursements, teaching assistantships with full and partial tuition reimbursements, career-related internships or fieldwork, Federal Work-Study, scholarships/grants, traineeships, health care benefits, tuition waivers (full and partial), and unspecified assistantships available. Support available to part-time students. Financial award application deadline: 2/1. *Unit head:* Dr. Kathleen Lugosch, Graduate Program Director, 413-577-0943, Fax: 413-545-3929. *Application contact:* Lindsay DeSantis, Supervisor of Admissions, 413-545-0722, Fax: 413-577-0100, E-mail: gradadm@grad.umass.edu.
Website: http://www.umass.edu/architecture/

University of Memphis, Graduate School, College of Communication and Fine Arts, Department of Architecture, Memphis, TN 38152. Offers M Arch. *Faculty:* 6 full-time (2 women), 1 part-time/adjunct (0 women). *Students:* 8 full-time (2 women), 3 part-time (2 women); includes 5 minority (4 Black or African American, non-Hispanic/Latino; 1 Hispanic/Latino). Average age 29. 7 applicants, 100% accepted, 2 enrolled. In 2014, 4 master's awarded. *Financial support:* In 2014–15, 7 students received support. Research assistantships with full tuition reimbursements available, teaching assistantships with full tuition reimbursements available, Federal Work-Study, scholarships/grants, and unspecified assistantships available. Financial award application deadline: 2/15; financial award applicants required to submit FAFSA. *Unit head:* Dr. Michael D. Hagge, Chair, 901-678-2724, Fax: 901-678-1755, E-mail: mdhagge@memphis.edu. *Application contact:* Sherry Brian, Coordinator of Graduate Studies, 901-678-3302, Fax: 901-678-1755.
Website: http://architecture.memphis.edu

University of Miami, Graduate School, School of Architecture, Coral Gables, FL 33124. Offers architecture (M Arch); suburb and town design (M Arch). *Entrance requirements:* For master's, GRE General Test, minimum GPA of 3.0, portfolio. Additional exam requirements/recommendations for international students: Required—TOEFL. Electronic applications accepted. *Faculty research:* Housing, town planning, retrofit.

University of Michigan, Taubman College of Architecture and Urban Planning, Doctoral Studies in Architecture, Ann Arbor, MI 48109. Offers PhD. Terminal master's awarded for partial completion of doctoral program. *Degree requirements:* For doctorate, comprehensive exam, thesis/dissertation. *Application deadline:* For fall admission, 12/15 for domestic and international students. Electronic applications accepted. *Financial support:* Application deadline: 12/15.

University of Michigan, Taubman College of Architecture and Urban Planning, Master of Architecture Program, Ann Arbor, MI 48109. Offers M Arch, M Arch/M Eng, M Arch/MSE, M Arch/MUP, MBA/M Arch. *Application deadline:* For fall admission, 1/6 for domestic and international students. Electronic applications accepted. *Financial*

support: Application deadline: 1/15. *Application contact:* Admissions Counselor. Website: http://taubmancollege.umich.edu/architecture/degrees/master-architecture

University of Minnesota, Twin Cities Campus, Graduate School, College of Design, School of Architecture, Minneapolis, MN 55455-0213. Offers architecture (M Arch); sustainable design (MS). First professional and post-professional tracks available in M Arch program. *Degree requirements:* For master's, thesis (for some programs). *Entrance requirements:* For master's, GRE General Test, suggested GPA of 3.0, portfolio. Additional exam requirements/recommendations for international students: Required—TOEFL (minimum score 550 paper-based; 79 iBT). *Expenses:* Contact institution. *Faculty research:* History, daylighting, computer-aided design, sustainable design, structures.

University of Missouri, Office of Research and Graduate Studies, College of Human Environmental Sciences, Department of Architectural Studies, Columbia, MO 65211. Offers design with digital media (MA, MS); environmental design (MS). *Faculty:* 7 full-time (2 women). *Students:* 14 full-time (11 women), 23 part-time (14 women); includes 5 minority (1 Black or African American, non-Hispanic/Latino; 2 Asian, non-Hispanic/Latino; 1 Hispanic/Latino; 1 Two or more races, non-Hispanic/Latino), 4 international. Average age 41. 33 applicants, 30% accepted, 7 enrolled. In 2014, 4 master's awarded. *Entrance requirements:* For master's, GRE General Test, minimum GPA of 3.0. Additional exam requirements/recommendations for international students: Required—TOEFL (minimum score 500 paper-based; 61 iBT). *Application deadline:* For fall admission, 4/1 for domestic students; for winter admission, 10/1 for domestic students; for spring admission, 4/1 for domestic students. Applications are processed on a rolling basis. Application fee: $55 ($75 for international students). Electronic applications accepted. *Financial support:* Fellowships, research assistantships, teaching assistantships, institutionally sponsored loans, scholarships/grants, health care benefits, and unspecified assistantships available. Support available to part-time students. *Faculty research:* Environment and aging, design education and research, place attachment, residential environments, computer-mediated simulation, architectural design process. *Unit head:* Dr. Ruth Brent Tofle, Department Chair, 573-882-6311, E-mail: tofler@missouri.edu. *Application contact:* Laura Franklin, Business Support Specialist II, 573-882-7224, E-mail: franklinl@missouri.edu. Website: http://arch.missouri.edu/

University of Nebraska–Lincoln, Graduate College, College of Architecture, Department of Architecture, Graduate Program in Architecture, Lincoln, NE 68588. Offers MS, PhD. *Degree requirements:* For master's, comprehensive exam, thesis. *Entrance requirements:* For master's, GRE General Test. Additional exam requirements/recommendations for international students: Required—TOEFL (minimum score 550 paper-based). Electronic applications accepted. *Faculty research:* Housing, environmental design, architectural history, sustainable design, rural architecture.

University of Nebraska–Lincoln, Graduate College, College of Architecture, Department of Architecture, Professional Program in Architecture, Lincoln, NE 68588. Offers M Arch, M Arch/MBA, M Arch/MCRP. *Entrance requirements:* For master's, GRE General Test. Additional exam requirements/recommendations for international students: Required—TOEFL. *Faculty research:* Housing, environmental design, architectural history, sustainable design, rural architecture.

University of Nevada, Las Vegas, Graduate College, College of Fine Arts, School of Architecture, Las Vegas, NV 89154. Offers architecture (M Arch); hospitality design (Certificate). Part-time programs available. *Faculty:* 11 full-time (3 women), 3 part-time/adjunct (0 women). *Students:* 44 full-time (17 women), 9 part-time (3 women); includes 19 minority (5 Asian, non-Hispanic/Latino; 11 Hispanic/Latino; 1 Native Hawaiian or other Pacific Islander, non-Hispanic/Latino; 2 Two or more races, non-Hispanic/Latino), 4 international. Average age 30. 31 applicants, 90% accepted, 24 enrolled. In 2014, 13 master's awarded. *Degree requirements:* For master's, thesis (for some programs), professional project. *Entrance requirements:* For master's, GRE General Test (minimum score 410 verbal, 430 quantitative). Additional exam requirements/recommendations for international students: Required—TOEFL (minimum score 550 paper-based; 80 iBT), IELTS (minimum score 7). *Application deadline:* For fall admission, 1/15 for domestic students, 5/1 for international students; for spring admission, 10/1 for international students. Application fee: $60 ($95 for international students). Electronic applications accepted. *Financial support:* In 2014–15, 12 students received support, including 12 teaching assistantships with partial tuition reimbursements available (averaging $10,417 per year); institutionally sponsored loans, scholarships/grants, health care benefits, and unspecified assistantships also available. Financial award application deadline: 3/1. *Faculty research:* Sustainability, hospitality/entertainment design, educational design, urban studies/design. *Total annual research expenditures:* $14,118. *Unit head:* Dr. David Baird, Director/Professor, 702-895-0939, Fax: 702-895-1119, E-mail: david.baird@unlv.edu. *Application contact:* Graduate College Admissions Evaluator, 702-895-3320, Fax: 702-895-4180, E-mail: gradcollege@unlv.edu. Website: http://architecture.unlv.edu/

University of New Mexico, Graduate School, College of Fine Arts, Program in Art History, Albuquerque, NM 87131. Offers art history (MA); arts of the Americas (MA); history of architecture (PhD); history of graphic arts (PhD); history of photography (PhD); modern Latin American art history (PhD); Native American art history (PhD); Pre-Columbian art history (PhD); Spanish colonial art history (PhD). Part-time programs available. *Faculty:* 9 full-time (7 women). *Students:* 14 full-time (10 women), 22 part-time (16 women); includes 8 minority (2 American Indian or Alaska Native, non-Hispanic/Latino; 6 Hispanic/Latino), 5 international. Average age 32. 34 applicants, 26% accepted, 5 enrolled. In 2014, 5 master's, 1 doctorate awarded. *Degree requirements:* For master's, one foreign language, comprehensive exam (for some programs), thesis, symposium; for doctorate, 2 foreign languages, comprehensive exam, thesis/dissertation, symposium. *Entrance requirements:* Additional exam requirements/recommendations for international students: Required—TOEFL (minimum score 550 paper-based), IELTS (minimum score 6). *Application deadline:* For fall admission, 1/15 for domestic students; for spring admission, 1/15 for domestic students. Application fee: $50. Electronic applications accepted. *Financial support:* In 2014–15, fellowships (averaging $7,433 per year), research assistantships with tuition reimbursements (averaging $5,216 per year), teaching assistantships with partial tuition reimbursements (averaging $4,005 per year) were awarded; Federal Work-Study, institutionally sponsored loans, scholarships/grants, health care benefits, and unspecified assistantships also available. Support available to part-time students. Financial award application deadline: 3/1; financial award applicants required to submit FAFSA. *Faculty research:* Native American, modern Latin American, pre-Columbian, architectural, American, medieval, Spanish Colonial, and Latin American art; history of photography. *Unit head:* Prof. Mary Tsiongas, Chair, 505-277-5861, Fax: 505-277-5955, E-mail: tsiongas@unm.edu. *Application contact:* Kat Heatherington, Graduate Advisor, 505-277-6672, Fax: 505-277-5955, E-mail: art255@unm.edu. Website: http://art.unm.edu/

University of New Mexico, Graduate School, School of Architecture and Planning, Program in Architecture, Albuquerque, NM 87131-2039. Offers M Arch. *Faculty:* 17 full-time (7 women), 7 part-time/adjunct (2 women). *Students:* 62 full-time (25 women), 7 part-time (5 women); includes 27 minority (1 Black or African American, non-Hispanic/

Latino; 3 American Indian or Alaska Native, non-Hispanic/Latino; 4 Asian, non-Hispanic/Latino; 19 Hispanic/Latino), 12 international. Average age 29. 57 applicants, 49% accepted, 18 enrolled. In 2014, 30 master's awarded. *Degree requirements:* For master's, thesis (for some programs), review. *Entrance requirements:* For master's, experience in field. Additional exam requirements/recommendations for international students: Required—TOEFL (minimum score 550 paper-based; 79 iBT). *Application deadline:* For fall admission, 2/1 priority date for domestic students. Application fee: $50. Electronic applications accepted. *Financial support:* In 2014–15, 77 students received support, including 1 research assistantship with partial tuition reimbursement available (averaging $7,500 per year); fellowships, scholarships/grants, health care benefits, and unspecified assistantships also available. Financial award application deadline: 3/1; financial award applicants required to submit FAFSA. *Faculty research:* Professional practice, design theory, sustainable environments, architecture and children, environment and behavior. *Unit head:* Geraldine Forbes Isais, Director, 505-277-3303, Fax: 505-277-0076, E-mail: gforbes@unm.edu. *Application contact:* Elizabeth M. Rowe, Senior Academic Advisor, 505-277-1303, Fax: 505-277-0076, E-mail: mitziv@unm.edu. Website: http://saap.unm.edu/

The University of North Carolina at Charlotte, College of Arts and Architecture, School of Architecture, Charlotte, NC 28223-0001. Offers M Arch I, M Arch II, MUD. *Faculty:* 26 full-time (7 women), 1 part-time/adjunct (0 women). *Students:* 79 full-time (44 women), 2 part-time (0 women); includes 18 minority (9 Black or African American, non-Hispanic/Latino; 1 Asian, non-Hispanic/Latino; 6 Hispanic/Latino; 2 Two or more races, non-Hispanic/Latino), 11 international. Average age 25. 125 applicants, 82% accepted, 43 enrolled. In 2014, 35 master's awarded. *Degree requirements:* For master's, thesis or alternative, project. *Entrance requirements:* For master's, GRE, statement of purpose, letters of recommendation, portfolio. Additional exam requirements/recommendations for international students: Required—TOEFL (minimum score 557 paper-based; 83 iBT). *Application deadline:* For fall admission, 1/15 for domestic and international students. Application fee: $75. Electronic applications accepted. *Expenses:* Tuition, state resident: full-time $4008. Tuition, nonresident: full-time $16,295. *Required fees:* $2755. Tuition and fees vary according to course load and program. *Financial support:* In 2014–15, 36 students received support, including 31 research assistantships (averaging $6,886 per year), 5 teaching assistantships (averaging $2,000 per year); unspecified assistantships also available. Financial award applicants required to submit FAFSA. *Faculty research:* Urban design studies for local and regional municipalities and community groups, high performance building and optimization protocols, daylighting and energy analysis, digital design and fabrication components, and interactive visualization; refinement of regionally specific computer-aided analysis tools used to evaluate total building energy performance, and the economic valuation of architectural systems and their design attributes. *Total annual research expenditures:* $201,227. *Unit head:* Kenneth A. Lambla, Dean, 704-687-0090, Fax: 704-687-0105, E-mail: kalambla@uncc.edu. *Application contact:* Kathy B. Giddings, Director of Graduate Admissions, 704-687-5503, Fax: 704-687-1668, E-mail: gradadm@uncc.edu. Website: http://coaa.uncc.edu/academics/school-of-architecture

The University of North Carolina at Greensboro, Graduate School, College of Arts and Sciences, Department of Interior Architecture, Greensboro, NC 27412-5001. Offers historic preservation (Certificate); interior architecture (MS); museum studies (Certificate). *Degree requirements:* For master's, thesis. *Entrance requirements:* For master's, GRE General Test or MAT, bachelor's degree in interior design, interview, portfolio. Additional exam requirements/recommendations for international students: Required—TOEFL. Electronic applications accepted.

University of Notre Dame, Graduate School, School of Architecture, Notre Dame, IN 46556. Offers architectural design and urbanism (M ADU); architecture (M Arch). *Degree requirements:* For master's, thesis or alternative. *Entrance requirements:* For master's, GRE General Test, portfolio. Additional exam requirements/recommendations for international students: Required—TOEFL (minimum score 600 paper-based; 80 iBT). Electronic applications accepted. *Faculty research:* Architectural theory, urban design, classical and traditional architecture and urbanism.

University of Oklahoma, College of Architecture, Division of Architecture, Norman, OK 73019. Offers architectural urban studies (MS), including architectural urban studies, environmental technology, human resources; architecture (M Arch). *Faculty:* 41 full-time (15 women), 2 part-time/adjunct (both women). *Students:* 16 full-time (5 women), 15 part-time (9 women); includes 11 minority (2 Asian, non-Hispanic/Latino; 4 Hispanic/Latino; 5 Two or more races, non-Hispanic/Latino), 5 international. Average age 31. 25 applicants, 84% accepted, 10 enrolled. In 2014, 6 master's awarded. *Degree requirements:* For master's, thesis or alternative, portfolio, project. *Entrance requirements:* For master's, GRE General Test, portfolio. Additional exam requirements/recommendations for international students: Required—TOEFL (minimum score 79 iBT). *Application deadline:* For fall admission, 4/1 for domestic and international students. Application fee: $50 ($100 for international students). Electronic applications accepted. *Expenses:* Tuition, state resident: full-time $4394; part-time $183.10 per credit hour. Tuition, nonresident: full-time $16,970; part-time $707.10 per credit hour. *Required fees:* $2892; $109.95 per credit hour. $126.50 per semester. *Financial support:* In 2014–15, 16 students received support, including 2 research assistantships with partial tuition reimbursements available (averaging $10,372 per year), 2 teaching assistantships with partial tuition reimbursements available (averaging $10,372 per year); scholarships/grants and unspecified assistantships also available. Financial award application deadline: 6/1; financial award applicants required to submit FAFSA. *Faculty research:* Rammed earth bricks, energy sustainability, acoustics, Italian architecture, architectural design. *Total annual research expenditures:* $132,781. *Unit head:* Dr. Hans Butzer, Director, 405-325-2444, Fax: 405-325-7558, E-mail: butzer@ou.edu. *Application contact:* Joel Dietrich, Professor Emeritus, 405-325-2444, Fax: 405-325-7558, E-mail: dietrich@ou.edu. Website: http://arch.ou.edu

University of Oregon, Graduate School, School of Architecture and Allied Arts, Department of Architecture, Eugene, OR 97403. Offers architecture (M Arch); interior architecture (MI Arch). *Accreditation:* CIDA. *Degree requirements:* For master's, thesis (for some programs). *Entrance requirements:* For master's, GRE General Test. Additional exam requirements/recommendations for international students: Required—TOEFL. *Faculty research:* Innovation in housing design and design production, climate responsive design, passive heating and cooling, computer software development for design applications, vernacular architecture.

University of Pennsylvania, School of Design, Graduate Group in Architecture, Philadelphia, PA 19104. Offers architecture (M Arch, PhD); ecological architecture (Certificate); environmental building design (MEBD). Part-time programs available. *Faculty:* 13 full-time (4 women), 12 part-time/adjunct (2 women). *Students:* 297 full-time (149 women), 4 part-time (2 women); includes 64 minority (3 Black or African American, non-Hispanic/Latino; 1 American Indian or Alaska Native, non-Hispanic/Latino; 32 Asian, non-Hispanic/Latino; 18 Hispanic/Latino; 10 Two or more races, non-Hispanic/Latino), 155 international. 884 applicants, 44% accepted, 147 enrolled. In 2014, 102 master's, 2 doctorates, 31 other advanced degrees awarded. *Degree requirements:* For doctorate, thesis/dissertation, qualifying examination, final defense, 2 language exams,

20 approved courses, preliminary examination, teaching experience. *Entrance requirements:* For master's and doctorate, GRE General Test, portfolio, writing sample. Additional exam requirements/recommendations for international students: Required—TOEFL or IELTS. *Application deadline:* For fall admission, 1/2 priority date for domestic students. Application fee: $80. Electronic applications accepted. *Financial support:* Fellowships, research assistantships, teaching assistantships, institutionally sponsored loans, scholarships/grants, and health care benefits available. Financial award application deadline: 2/15; financial award applicants required to submit FAFSA. *Faculty research:* Contemporary architectural theory, structure and technology, metropolitan and regional urbanism, computer modeling. *Unit head:* Marilyn Jordan Taylor, Dean, 215-898-6520, E-mail: mjtaylor@design.upenn.edu. *Application contact:* Office of Admissions and Financial Aid, 215-898-6520, E-mail: admissions@design.upenn.edu.
Website: http://www.design.upenn.edu/architecture

University of Puerto Rico, Río Piedras Campus, School of Architecture, San Juan, PR 00931-3300. Offers M Arch. Part-time programs available. *Degree requirements:* For master's, comprehensive exam, thesis, design project. *Entrance requirements:* For master's, PAEG or GRE, bachelor's degree in architecture, interview, minimum GPA of 3.0, portfolio, 2 letters of recommendation.

University of Southern California, Graduate School, School of Architecture, Los Angeles, CA 90089. Offers M Arch, MBS, MHP, MLA, PhD, M Arch/M Pl, MLA/M Pl. Terminal master's awarded for partial completion of doctoral program. *Degree requirements:* For master's, thesis (for some programs); for doctorate, thesis/dissertation. *Entrance requirements:* For master's and doctorate, GRE. Additional exam requirements/recommendations for international students: Required—TOEFL (minimum score 100 iBT). Electronic applications accepted. *Faculty research:* Urban housing; advanced digital simulation, computation, and representation; building skins; parametric design; advanced seismic research.

University of South Florida, College of The Arts, School of Architecture and Community Design, Tampa, FL 33620-9951. Offers M Arch, MUCD. *Faculty:* 9 full-time (0 women). *Students:* 86 full-time (35 women), 42 part-time (14 women); includes 55 minority (5 Black or African American, non-Hispanic/Latino; 1 American Indian or Alaska Native, non-Hispanic/Latino; 5 Asian, non-Hispanic/Latino; 39 Hispanic/Latino; 2 Native Hawaiian or other Pacific Islander, non-Hispanic/Latino; 3 Two or more races, non-Hispanic/Latino), 6 international. Average age 27. 74 applicants, 41% accepted, 22 enrolled. In 2014, 33 master's awarded. *Degree requirements:* For master's, comprehensive exam, thesis. *Entrance requirements:* For master's, GRE General Test, minimum undergraduate GPA of 3.0 in last 60 hours of coursework; three letters of recommendation; portfolio or creative work; written statement of intent; prerequisite courses in physics, calculus, and AutoCAD. Additional exam requirements/recommendations for international students: Required—TOEFL (minimum score 550 paper-based; 79 iBT) or IELTS (minimum score 6.5). *Application deadline:* For fall admission, 2/1 priority date for domestic students, 1/2 for international students. Applications are processed on a rolling basis. Application fee: $30. Electronic applications accepted. *Financial support:* In 2014–15, 3 students received support, including 3 teaching assistantships with tuition reimbursements available (averaging $9,360 per year); Federal Work-Study, scholarships/grants, and unspecified assistantships also available. *Faculty research:* Urban community design and planning; public space infrastructure; conditions of suburban sprawl; redevelopment strategies for abandoned commercial centers and edges; sustainability; influences of technology, cultural identity and interpretation and social values on architectural design; epistemology of design thinking; tropical architecture; high-density urbanism; design benevolence; economic development/community revitalization; housing/residential development; development regulations. *Total annual research expenditures:* $132,864. *Unit head:* Dr. Robert MacLeod, Director and Professor, School of Architecture and Community Design, 813-974-6015, Fax: 813-974-2557, E-mail: rmacleod@arch.usf.edu. *Application contact:* Mildred Abreu, Academic Advisor, 813-974-1216, Fax: 813-974-2557, E-mail: abreu@arch.usf.edu.
Website: http://www.arch.usf.edu/

The University of Tennessee, Graduate School, College of Architecture and Design, Program in Architecture, Knoxville, TN 37996. Offers architecture (professional) (M Arch); architecture (research) (M Arch). *Degree requirements:* For master's, thesis. *Entrance requirements:* For master's, GRE General Test, minimum GPA of 3.0, 3 letters of recommendation, samples of portfolio work (highly recommended for professional track). Additional exam requirements/recommendations for international students: Required—TOEFL (minimum score 550 paper-based).

The University of Texas at Arlington, Graduate School, School of Architecture, Program in Architecture, Arlington, TX 76019. Offers M Arch, M Arch/MCRP. *Degree requirements:* For master's, thesis. *Entrance requirements:* For master's, GRE General Test, minimum GPA of 3.0, portfolio (for those with previous design degrees). Additional exam requirements/recommendations for international students: Required—TOEFL (minimum score 575 paper-based; 91 iBT). *Faculty research:* Regional landscapes/native materials, urban densification, urban design, sustainable design principles.

The University of Texas at Austin, Graduate School, School of Architecture, Program in Architecture, Austin, TX 78712-1111. Offers M Arch, MSAS. *Entrance requirements:* For master's, GRE, transcripts, portfolio, statement of interest, references.

The University of Texas at San Antonio, College of Architecture, Department of Architecture, San Antonio, TX 78249-0617. Offers M Arch, MS Arch. Part-time programs available. *Faculty:* 19 full-time (6 women), 2 part-time/adjunct (0 women). *Students:* 71 full-time (35 women), 12 part-time (4 women); includes 40 minority (1 Black or African American, non-Hispanic/Latino; 39 Hispanic/Latino), 17 international. Average age 29. 68 applicants, 94% accepted, 26 enrolled. In 2014, 42 master's awarded. *Degree requirements:* For master's, comprehensive exam (for some programs), thesis optional. *Entrance requirements:* For master's, GRE General Test, bachelor's degree with 18 credit hours in field of study or in another appropriate field of study, 2 letters of recommendation, statement of purpose. Additional exam requirements/recommendations for international students: Required—TOEFL (minimum score 550 paper-based; 79 iBT), IELTS (minimum score 6.5). Application fee: $45 ($80 for international students). Electronic applications accepted. *Expenses:* Tuition, state resident: full-time $4671; part-time $260 per credit hour. Tuition, nonresident: full-time $18,022; part-time $1001 per credit hour. *Financial support:* In 2014–15, research assistantships (averaging $3,500 per year) were awarded; teaching assistantships and tuition waivers (partial) also available. Financial award applicants required to submit FAFSA. *Faculty research:* Building energy performance and sustainability, architectural and heritage tourism, regionalism and architectural theory, Mexican and Latin American architecture, medieval and Renaissance architecture, historic preservation and conservation, urban and regional planning, materials. *Unit head:* Dr. Vincent B. Canizaro, Chair, 210-458-2634, E-mail: vincent.canizaro@utsa.edu. *Application contact:* Dr. Sedef Doganer, Graduate Advisor of Record, 210-458-3037, Fax: 210-458-3016, E-mail: sedef.doganer@utsa.edu.
Website: http://architecture.utsa.edu/academic-programs/department-of-architecture/

University of Toronto, School of Graduate Studies, John H. Daniels Faculty of Architecture, Landscape, and Design, Toronto, ON M5S 2J7, Canada. Offers M Arch, MLA, MUD, MVS. *Accreditation:* ASLA. *Entrance requirements:* For master's, minimum B average; 3 letters of reference; resume; 3 writing samples; 5 samples of design work, drawing, or work in a related field, statement of interest. Additional exam requirements/recommendations for international students: Required—TOEFL (minimum score 580 paper-based; 93 iBT), IELTS (minimum score 7), TWE (minimum score 5), Michigan English Language Assessment Battery (minimum score 85), COPE (minimum score 76). Electronic applications accepted. *Expenses:* Contact institution.

University of Utah, Graduate School, College of Architecture and Planning, School of Architecture, Salt Lake City, UT 84112. Offers architectural studies (MS); architecture (M Arch). Part-time programs available. *Faculty:* 13 full-time (6 women), 18 part-time/adjunct (5 women). *Students:* 64 full-time (24 women), 2 part-time (0 women); includes 8 minority (3 Asian, non-Hispanic/Latino; 3 Hispanic/Latino; 2 Two or more races, non-Hispanic/Latino), 10 international. Average age 30. 72 applicants, 86% accepted, 37 enrolled. In 2014, 32 master's awarded. *Degree requirements:* For master's, thesis (for some programs), comprehensive project. *Entrance requirements:* For master's, minimum undergraduate GPA of 3.0; portfolio; statement of purpose; letters of recommendation. Additional exam requirements/recommendations for international students: Required—TOEFL (minimum score 550 paper-based). *Application deadline:* For fall admission, 1/1 for domestic students, 12/1 for international students. Application fee: $55 ($65 for international students). Electronic applications accepted. *Financial support:* In 2014–15, 36 students received support, including 15 fellowships with partial tuition reimbursements available (averaging $3,375 per year), 29 teaching assistantships with partial tuition reimbursements available (averaging $3,375 per year); career-related internships or fieldwork, Federal Work-Study, and scholarships/grants also available. Financial award application deadline: 3/1; financial award applicants required to submit FAFSA. *Faculty research:* History, design, acoustics, photography, structures, architecture of the American West, architectural communication and representation, impact of technology, design-build. *Total annual research expenditures:* $73,383. *Unit head:* Mira Locher, Chair, 801-5858946, E-mail: locher@arch.utah.edu. *Application contact:* Mayra Godin Focht, Administrative Assistant/Advisor, 801-585-5354, Fax: 801-581-8217, E-mail: mayra@arch.utah.edu.
Website: http://www.arch.utah.edu/?school_of_architecture

University of Washington, Graduate School, College of Built Environments, Department of Architecture, Seattle, WA 98195. Offers architecture (M Arch, MS); built environment (PhD); design computing (Certificate); design firm leadership and management (Certificate); historic preservation (Certificate); lighting (Certificate); urban design (Certificate). *Degree requirements:* For master's, thesis. *Entrance requirements:* For master's, GRE General Test, minimum GPA of 3.0, portfolio, 3 letters of recommendation. Additional exam requirements/recommendations for international students: Required—TOEFL. *Faculty research:* Lighting, materials, computing theory, media, culture, environment.

University of Waterloo, Graduate Studies, Faculty of Engineering, School of Architecture, Waterloo, ON N2L 3G1, Canada. Offers M Arch. Part-time programs available. *Degree requirements:* For master's, thesis. *Entrance requirements:* For master's, bachelor's degree in pre-professional architecture. Electronic applications accepted.

University of Wisconsin–Milwaukee, Graduate School, School of Architecture and Urban Planning, Department of Architecture, Milwaukee, WI 53201-0413. Offers architecture (PhD); preservation studies (Certificate); M Arch/MUP. *Degree requirements:* For master's, comprehensive exam, thesis; for doctorate, comprehensive exam, thesis/dissertation. *Entrance requirements:* For master's, GRE General Test, portfolio. Additional exam requirements/recommendations for international students: Required—TOEFL (minimum score 600 paper-based; 100 iBT), IELTS (minimum score 7). Electronic applications accepted.

Virginia Polytechnic Institute and State University, Graduate School, College of Architecture and Urban Studies, Blacksburg, VA 24061. Offers architecture (MS Arch); architecture and design research (PhD); building/construction science and management (MS); creative technologies (MFA); environmental design and planning (PhD); landscape architecture (MLA); planning, governance, and globalization (PhD); public administration (MPA); public administration/public affairs (PhD, Certificate); public and international affairs (MPIA); urban and regional planning (MURP); MS/MA. *Accreditation:* ASLA (one or more programs are accredited). *Faculty:* 133 full-time (54 women), 2 part-time/adjunct (1 woman). *Students:* 316 full-time (166 women), 237 part-time (108 women); includes 104 minority (46 Black or African American, non-Hispanic/Latino; 1 American Indian or Alaska Native, non-Hispanic/Latino; 20 Asian, non-Hispanic/Latino; 21 Hispanic/Latino; 16 Two or more races, non-Hispanic/Latino), 108 international. Average age 32. 609 applicants, 50% accepted, 108 enrolled. In 2014, 155 master's, 29 doctorates awarded. *Degree requirements:* For master's, comprehensive exam (for some programs), thesis (for some programs); for doctorate, comprehensive exam (for some programs), thesis/dissertation (for some programs). *Entrance requirements:* For master's and doctorate, GRE/GMAT (may vary by department). Additional exam requirements/recommendations for international students: Required—TOEFL (minimum score 550 paper-based). *Application deadline:* For fall admission, 8/1 for domestic students, 4/1 for international students; for spring admission, 1/1 for domestic students, 9/1 for international students. Applications are processed on a rolling basis. Application fee: $75. Electronic applications accepted. *Expenses:* Tuition, state resident: full-time $11,656; part-time $647.50 per credit hour. Tuition, nonresident: full-time $23,351; part-time $1297.25 per credit hour. *Required fees:* $2533; $465.75 per semester. Tuition and fees vary according to course load, campus/location and program. *Financial support:* In 2014–15, 13 research assistantships with full tuition reimbursements (averaging $20,302 per year), 44 teaching assistantships with full tuition reimbursements (averaging $19,484 per year) were awarded. Financial award application deadline: 3/1; financial award applicants required to submit FAFSA. *Total annual research expenditures:* $3.2 million. *Unit head:* Dr. A. J. Davis, Dean, 540-231-6416, Fax: 540-231-6332, E-mail: davisa@vt.edu. *Application contact:* Christine Mattsson-Coon, Executive Assistant, 540-231-6416, Fax: 540-231-6332, E-mail: cmattsso@vt.edu.
Website: http://www.caus.vt.edu/

Washington State University, Voiland College of Engineering and Architecture, Program in Architecture, Pullman, WA 99164-2220. Offers architecture (M Arch). *Faculty:* 20 full-time (5 women). *Students:* 31 full-time (14 women), 2 part-time (1 woman); includes 7 minority (5 Hispanic/Latino; 2 Two or more races, non-Hispanic/Latino), 3 international. Average age 27. 46 applicants, 46% accepted, 10 enrolled. In 2014, 10 master's awarded. *Degree requirements:* For master's, comprehensive exam, thesis, oral exam. *Entrance requirements:* For master's, minimum GPA of 3.0, 3 letters of recommendation, personal statement, portfolio. Additional exam requirements/recommendations for international students: Required—TOEFL (minimum score 80 iBT), IELTS. *Application deadline:* For fall admission, 1/10 priority date for domestic and international students. Applications are processed on a rolling basis. Application fee: $75. *Expenses:* Tuition, state resident: full-time $11,768. Tuition, nonresident: full-time $25,200. *Required fees:* $960. Tuition and fees vary according to program. *Financial*

support: In 2014–15, 25 students received support, including 23 teaching assistantships with full and partial tuition reimbursements available (averaging $6,582 per year); research assistantships with full and partial tuition reimbursements available, career-related internships or fieldwork, Federal Work-Study, institutionally sponsored loans, scholarships/grants, tuition waivers (partial), and unspecified assistantships also available. Financial award application deadline: 3/1; financial award applicants required to submit FAFSA. *Faculty research:* Cultural, technological, and environmental design; integrated project delivery; American architecture and urbanism; land use and planning; design for rural communities and aging populations. *Unit head:* Prof. Greg Kessler, Director, 509-335-5539, Fax: 509-335-6132, E-mail: gkessler@acm.wsu.edu. *Application contact:* Jaime L. Rice, Academic Coordinator, 509-335-5318, Fax: 509-335-6132, E-mail: jlrice@wsu.edu.
Website: http://sdc.wsu.edu/

Washington University in St. Louis, Sam Fox School of Design and Visual Arts, Program in Architecture, St. Louis, MO 63130-4899. Offers M Arch, MLA, M Arch/MBA, M Arch/MCM, M Arch/MSW, M Arch/MUD, MLA/M Arch. *Degree requirements:* For master's, final project. *Entrance requirements:* For master's, GRE General Test, portfolio. Additional exam requirements/recommendations for international students: Required—TOEFL (minimum score 550 paper-based; 80 iBT), TWE. Electronic applications accepted. *Faculty research:* Urban design development issues.

Wentworth Institute of Technology, Department of Architecture, Boston, MA 02115-5998. Offers M Arch. *Faculty:* 21 full-time (9 women), 26 part-time/adjunct (9 women). *Students:* 91 full-time (26 women), 2 part-time (0 women); includes 9 minority (1 Black or African American, non-Hispanic/Latino; 5 Hispanic/Latino; 3 Two or more races, non-Hispanic/Latino), 6 international. Average age 23. 112 applicants, 98% accepted, 93 enrolled. In 2014, 87 master's awarded. *Degree requirements:* For master's, thesis project. *Entrance requirements:* For master's, portfolio, references, minimum GPA of 3.0. Additional exam requirements/recommendations for international students: Required—TOEFL (minimum score 525 paper-based). *Application deadline:* For fall admission, 1/15 priority date for domestic and international students. Applications are processed on a rolling basis. Application fee: $50. Electronic applications accepted. *Financial support:* In 2014–15, 88 students received support, including 88 fellowships (averaging $5,886 per year), 35 teaching assistantships (averaging $3,000 per year). Financial award application deadline: 5/1; financial award applicants required to submit FAFSA. *Unit head:* Michael Macphail, Architecture Department Chair, 617-989-4455, E-mail: macphailm@wit.edu. *Application contact:* Michael Macphail, Architecture Department Chair, 617-989-4455, E-mail: macphailm@wit.edu.
Website: http://www.wit.edu/arch/

Woodbury University, School of Architecture, Burbank, CA 91504-1099. Offers M Arch, MIA, MS Arch. *Degree requirements:* For master's, thesis. *Entrance requirements:* For master's, GRE (if undergraduate GPA is below 3.0), 3 letters of recommendation, portfolio, essay, interview, resume, academic transcripts. Additional exam requirements/recommendations for international students: Required—TOEFL (minimum score 550 paper-based; 83 iBT), IELTS (minimum score 6.5). *Expenses:* Contact institution.

Yale University, School of Architecture, New Haven, CT 06520. Offers M Arch, M Env Des, MEM, PhD, M Arch/M Env Des, M Arch/MBA. *Faculty:* 20 full-time (6 women), 86 part-time/adjunct (20 women). *Students:* 200 full-time (81 women); includes 36 minority (2 Black or African American, non-Hispanic/Latino; 20 Asian, non-Hispanic/Latino; 9 Hispanic/Latino; 5 Two or more races, non-Hispanic/Latino), 60 international. 919 applicants, 18% accepted, 76 enrolled. In 2014, 81 master's awarded. *Entrance requirements:* For master's, GRE General Test, design portfolio. Additional exam requirements/recommendations for international students: Required—TOEFL. *Application deadline:* For fall admission, 1/10 for domestic and international students. Application fee: $85. Electronic applications accepted. *Expenses:* Expenses: Contact institution. *Financial support:* In 2014–15, 157 students received support. Fellowships, teaching assistantships, Federal Work-Study, and institutionally sponsored loans available. Financial award application deadline: 2/1; financial award applicants required to submit FAFSA. *Unit head:* Robert A. M. Stern, Dean, 203-432-2279, Fax: 203-432-7175. *Application contact:* Marilyn Weiss, Registrar, 203-432-2288, Fax: 203-432-7175, E-mail: gradarch.admissions@yale.edu.
Website: http://www.architecture.yale.edu/

Building Science

Arizona State University at the Tempe campus, Herberger Institute for Design and the Arts, The Design School, Tempe, AZ 85287-1605. Offers architecture (M Arch); building design/built environment (MS); design (MSD), including arts, media, and engineering, healthcare and healing environments (MSD, PhD), industrial design, interaction design, interior design, new product innovation, visual communication design; design, environment and the arts (PhD), including design, digital culture, healthcare and healing environments (MSD, PhD), history, theory, and criticism; landscape architecture (MLA); urban design (MUD); MA/MBA. *Accreditation:* NASAD. Terminal master's awarded for partial completion of doctoral program. *Degree requirements:* For master's, thesis optional, interactive Program of Study (iPOS) submitted before completing 50 percent of required credit hours; for doctorate, comprehensive exam, thesis/dissertation, interactive Program of Study (iPOS) submitted before completing 50 percent of required credit hours. *Entrance requirements:* For master's, GRE General Test, minimum GPA of 3.0 or equivalent in last 2 years of work leading to bachelor's degree, design/creative works portfolio, 3 references, statement of intent; for doctorate, GRE, master's degree in architecture, graphic design, industrial design, interior design, landscape architecture, or art history or equivalent standing; statement of purpose; 3 letters of recommendation; indication of potential faculty mentor; sample of written work. Additional exam requirements/recommendations for international students: Required—TOEFL (minimum score 600 paper-based; 100 iBT). Electronic applications accepted.

Auburn University, Graduate School, College of Architecture, Design, and Construction, Department of Building Science, Auburn University, AL 36849. Offers building construction (MBC); construction management (MBC); integrated design and construction (MIDC). *Faculty:* 17 full-time (1 woman), 2 part-time/adjunct (1 woman). *Students:* 25 full-time (4 women), 47 part-time (13 women); includes 9 minority (3 Black or African American, non-Hispanic/Latino; 2 Asian, non-Hispanic/Latino; 4 Hispanic/Latino), 4 international. Average age 33. 84 applicants, 85% accepted, 52 enrolled. In 2014, 36 master's awarded. *Entrance requirements:* For master's, GRE General Test. *Application deadline:* For fall admission, 7/7 for domestic students; for spring admission, 11/24 for domestic students. Applications are processed on a rolling basis. Application fee: $50 ($60 for international students). Electronic applications accepted. *Expenses:* Tuition, state resident: full-time $8586; part-time $477 per credit hour. Tuition, nonresident: full-time $25,758; part-time $1431 per credit hour. *Required fees:* $804 per semester. Tuition and fees vary according to degree level and program. *Financial support:* Application deadline: 3/15; applicants required to submit FAFSA. *Unit head:* Dr. Richard Burt, Head, 334-844-5260. *Application contact:* Dr. George Flowers, Dean of the Graduate School, 334-844-2125.
Website: http://cadc.auburn.edu/bsci/Pages/default.aspx

Auburn University, Graduate School, College of Architecture, Design, and Construction, Program in Design-Build, Auburn University, AL 36849. Offers MIDC. *Faculty:* 17 full-time (1 woman), 2 part-time/adjunct (1 woman). *Students:* 13 full-time (3 women); includes 1 minority (Black or African American, non-Hispanic/Latino), 3 international. Average age 26. 29 applicants, 83% accepted, 12 enrolled. In 2014, 15 master's awarded. Application fee: $50 ($60 for international students). *Expenses:* Tuition, state resident: full-time $8586; part-time $477 per credit hour. Tuition, nonresident: full-time $25,758; part-time $1431 per credit hour. *Required fees:* $804 per semester. Tuition and fees vary according to degree level and program. *Financial support:* Applicants required to submit FAFSA. *Unit head:* Dr. Vini Nathan, Dean, 334-844-4524. *Application contact:* Dr. George Flowers, Dean of the Graduate School, 334-844-2125.
Website: http://cadc.auburn.edu/construction/construction-masters-degrees-programs/integrated-design-and-const

Carnegie Mellon University, College of Fine Arts, School of Architecture, Pittsburgh, PA 15213-3891. Offers architecture (MSA); architecture, engineering, and construction management (PhD); building performance and diagnostics (MS, PhD); computational design (MS, PhD); engineering construction management (MSA); tangible interaction design (MTID); urban design (MUD). Terminal master's awarded for partial completion of doctoral program. *Degree requirements:* For doctorate, thesis/dissertation. *Entrance requirements:* For master's and doctorate, GRE General Test. Additional exam requirements/recommendations for international students: Required—TOEFL.

Georgia Institute of Technology, Graduate Studies, College of Architecture, School of Building Construction, Atlanta, GA 30332-0001. Offers building construction (PhD); integrated facility and property management (MS); integrated project delivery systems (MS); program management (MS); residential construction development (MS). Part-time and evening/weekend programs available. *Entrance requirements:* For master's and doctorate, GRE or GMAT. Additional exam requirements/recommendations for international students: Required—TOEFL (minimum score 550 paper-based). Electronic applications accepted. *Expenses:* Tuition, state resident: full-time $12,344; part-time $515 per credit hour. Tuition, nonresident: full-time $27,600; part-time $1150 per credit hour. *Required fees:* $1196 per term. Part-time tuition and fees vary according to course load. *Faculty research:* Design-build, mold, indoor air quality, real estate.

Pontificia Universidad Catolica Madre y Maestra, Graduate School, Faculty of Engineering Sciences, Santiago, Dominican Republic. Offers earthquake engineering (ME); logistics management (ME).

Rensselaer Polytechnic Institute, Graduate School, School of Architecture, Program in Built Ecologies, Troy, NY 12180-3590. Offers MS, PhD. *Degree requirements:* For master's, thesis; for doctorate, comprehensive exam, thesis/dissertation. *Entrance requirements:* For master's and doctorate, GRE General Test. Additional exam requirements/recommendations for international students: Required—TOEFL (minimum score 570 paper-based; 88 iBT), IELTS (minimum score 6.5), PTE (minimum score 60). *Application deadline:* For fall admission, 1/1 priority date for domestic and international students. Applications are processed on a rolling basis. Application fee: $75. Electronic applications accepted. *Expenses: Tuition:* Full-time $46,700; part-time $1945 per credit. Tuition and fees vary according to course load. *Financial support:* In 2014–15, fellowships (averaging $18,500 per year), research assistantships (averaging $18,500 per year), teaching assistantships (averaging $18,500 per year) were awarded. Financial award application deadline: 1/1. *Unit head:* Chris Perry, Graduate Program Director, 518-276-3034, E-mail: perryc3@rpi.edu. *Application contact:* Office of Graduate Admissions, 518-276-6216, E-mail: gradadmissions@rpi.edu.
Website: http://www.arch.rpi.edu/academic/graduate/built-ecologies/

University of California, Berkeley, Graduate Division, College of Environmental Design, Department of Architecture, Berkeley, CA 94720-1500. Offers architecture (M Arch); building science (MS, PhD); building structures, construction and materials (MS, PhD); design theories, methods, and practices (MS, PhD); environmental design in developing countries (MS, PhD); history of architecture and urbanism (MS, PhD); social and cultural processes in architecture and urbanism (MS, PhD); M Arch/MCP; M Arch/MS; MLA/M Arch. *Degree requirements:* For master's, thesis; for doctorate, thesis/dissertation, qualifying exam. *Entrance requirements:* For master's and doctorate, GRE General Test, minimum GPA of 3.0, 3 letters of recommendation. Additional exam requirements/recommendations for international students: Required—TOEFL. Electronic applications accepted.

Virginia Polytechnic Institute and State University, Graduate School, College of Architecture and Urban Studies, Blacksburg, VA 24061. Offers architecture (MS Arch); architecture and design research (PhD); building/construction science and management (MS); creative technologies (MFA); environmental design and planning (PhD); landscape architecture (MLA); planning, governance, and globalization (PhD); public administration (MPA); public administration/public affairs (PhD, Certificate); public and international affairs (MPIA); urban and regional planning (MURP); MS/MA. *Accreditation:* ASLA (one or more programs are accredited). *Faculty:* 133 full-time (54 women), 2 part-time/adjunct (1 woman). *Students:* 316 full-time (166 women), 237 part-time (108 women); includes 104 minority (46 Black or African American, non-Hispanic/Latino; 1 American Indian or Alaska Native, non-Hispanic/Latino; 20 Asian, non-Hispanic/Latino; 21 Hispanic/Latino; 16 Two or more races, non-Hispanic/Latino), 108 international. Average age 32. 609 applicants, 50% accepted, 108 enrolled. In 2014, 155

master's, 29 doctorates awarded. *Degree requirements:* For master's, comprehensive exam (for some programs), thesis (for some programs); for doctorate, comprehensive exam (for some programs), thesis/dissertation (for some programs). *Entrance requirements:* For master's and doctorate, GRE/GMAT (may vary by department). Additional exam requirements/recommendations for international students: Required—TOEFL (minimum score 550 paper-based). *Application deadline:* For fall admission, 8/1 for domestic students, 4/1 for international students; for spring admission, 1/1 for domestic students, 9/1 for international students. Applications are processed on a rolling basis. Application fee: $75. Electronic applications accepted. *Expenses:* Tuition, state resident: full-time $11,656; part-time $647.50 per credit hour. Tuition, nonresident: full-time $23,351; part-time $1297.25 per credit hour. *Required fees:* $2533; $465.75 per semester. Tuition and fees vary according to course load, campus/location and program. *Financial support:* In 2014–15, 13 research assistantships with full tuition reimbursements (averaging $20,302 per year), 44 teaching assistantships with full tuition reimbursements (averaging $19,484 per year) were awarded. Financial award application deadline: 3/1; financial award applicants required to submit FAFSA. *Total annual research expenditures:* $3.2 million. *Unit head:* Dr. A. J. Davis, Dean, 540-231-6416, Fax: 540-231-6332, E-mail: davisa@vt.edu. *Application contact:* Christine Mattsson-Coon, Executive Assistant, 540-231-6416, Fax: 540-231-6332, E-mail: cmattsso@vt.edu. Website: http://www.caus.vt.edu/

Environmental Design

Arizona State University at the Tempe campus, Herberger Institute for Design and the Arts, The Design School, PhD Program in Design, Environment and the Arts, Tempe, AZ 85287-2105. Offers design (PhD); digital culture (PhD); healthcare and healing environments (PhD); history, theory, and criticism (PhD). *Degree requirements:* For doctorate, comprehensive exam, thesis/dissertation, interactive Program of Study (iPOS) submitted before completing 50 percent of required credit hours. *Entrance requirements:* For doctorate, GRE, master's degree in architecture, graphic design, industrial design, interior design, landscape architecture, or art history or equivalent standing; statement of purpose; 3 letters of recommendation; indication of potential faculty mentor; sample of written work. Additional exam requirements/recommendations for international students: Required—TOEFL, IELTS, or PTE. Electronic applications accepted. *Expenses:* Contact institution.

Art Center College of Design, Graduate Environmental Design Program, Pasadena, CA 91103. Offers furniture and fixtures (MS); spatial experience (MS). *Students:* 19 full-time (13 women); includes 6 minority (5 Asian, non-Hispanic/Latino; 1 Hispanic/Latino), 9 international. Average age 29. 47 applicants, 74% accepted, 17 enrolled. *Degree requirements:* For master's, thesis. *Entrance requirements:* For master's, portfolio. Additional exam requirements/recommendations for international students: Required—TOEFL (minimum score 100 iBT), IELTS (minimum score 7). *Application deadline:* For fall admission, 2/1 priority date for domestic and international students. Application fee: $50 ($70 for international students). Electronic applications accepted. *Financial support:* Application deadline: 2/1; applicants required to submit FAFSA. *Unit head:* David Mocarski, Chair, 626-396-2220, E-mail: david.mocarski@artcenter.edu. *Application contact:* Helen Cahng, Director, 626-396-2495, E-mail: helen.cahng@artcenter.edu.

Bastyr University, School of Natural Health Arts and Sciences, Kenmore, WA 98028-4966. Offers counseling psychology (MA); holistic landscape design (Certificate); midwifery (MS); nutrition (MS); nutrition and clinical health psychology (MS). *Accreditation:* AND. Part-time programs available. *Students:* 373 full-time (334 women), 39 part-time (37 women); includes 71 minority (11 Black or African American, non-Hispanic/Latino; 1 American Indian or Alaska Native, non-Hispanic/Latino; 24 Asian, non-Hispanic/Latino; 14 Hispanic/Latino; 21 Two or more races, non-Hispanic/Latino), 20 international. Average age 30. *Degree requirements:* For master's, thesis optional. *Entrance requirements:* For master's, 1-2 years' basic sciences course work (depending on program). Additional exam requirements/recommendations for international students: Required—TOEFL (minimum score 550 paper-based; 79 iBT). *Application deadline:* For fall admission, 3/15 priority date for domestic and international students. Applications are processed on a rolling basis. Application fee: $75. *Financial support:* In 2014–15, 47 students received support. Career-related internships or fieldwork, Federal Work-Study, and scholarships/grants available. Support available to part-time students. Financial award application deadline: 4/15; financial award applicants required to submit FAFSA. *Faculty research:* Whole-food nutrition for type 2 diabetes; meditation in end-of-life care; stress management; Qi Gong, Tai Chi and yoga for older adults; Echinacea and immunology. *Unit head:* Dr. Timothy Callahan, Vice President and Provost, 425-602-3110, Fax: 425-823-6222. *Application contact:* Admissions Office, 425-602-3330, Fax: 425-602-3090, E-mail: admissions@bastyr.edu. Website: http://www.bastyr.edu/academics/schools-departments/school-natural-health-arts-sciences

Clemson University, Graduate School, College of Architecture, Arts, and Humanities, Program in Planning, Design and the Built Environment, Clemson, SC 29634. Offers PhD. *Students:* 17 full-time (8 women), 2 part-time (1 woman); includes 3 minority (1 Black or African American, non-Hispanic/Latino; 1 American Indian or Alaska Native, non-Hispanic/Latino; 1 Hispanic/Latino), 9 international. Average age 35. 36 applicants, 25% accepted, 6 enrolled. In 2014, 4 doctorates awarded. *Degree requirements:* For doctorate, comprehensive exam, thesis/dissertation. *Entrance requirements:* For doctorate, GRE General Test. Additional exam requirements/recommendations for international students: Required—TOEFL. *Application deadline:* For fall admission, 1/5 priority date for domestic and international students. Applications are processed on a rolling basis. Application fee: $70 ($80 for international students). Electronic applications accepted. *Financial support:* In 2014–15, 14 students received support, including 2 fellowships with partial tuition reimbursements available (averaging $5,000 per year), 1 research assistantship with partial tuition reimbursement available (averaging $9,280 per year), 13 teaching assistantships with partial tuition reimbursements available (averaging $18,800 per year); career-related internships or fieldwork, institutionally sponsored loans, scholarships/grants, health care benefits, and unspecified assistantships also available. Support available to part-time students. Financial award application deadline: 1/5. *Faculty research:* Built environment and health; restoration, sustainability and land ecology; regional/community design and development; technology, materials and construction processes; real estate development. *Unit head:* Dr. Mickey Lauria, Director, 864-656-0520, Fax: 864-656-0520, E-mail: mlauria@clemson.edu. Website: http://virtual.clemson.edu/caah/pdbe/

Columbia University, School of Continuing Education, Program in Landscape Design, New York, NY 10027. Offers MS. Part-time programs available. *Entrance requirements:* For master's, minimum undergraduate GPA of 3.0. Additional exam requirements/recommendations for international students: Required—American Language Program placement test.

Cornell University, Graduate School, Graduate Fields of Human Ecology, Field of Design and Environmental Analysis, Ithaca, NY 14853. Offers applied research in human-environment relations (MS); facilities planning and management (MS); housing and design (MS); human factors and ergonomics (MS); human-environment relations (MS); interior design (MA, MPS). *Degree requirements:* For master's, thesis. *Entrance requirements:* For master's, GRE General Test, portfolio or slides of recent work; bachelor's degree in interior design, architecture or related design discipline; 2 letters of recommendation. Additional exam requirements/recommendations for international students: Required—TOEFL (minimum score 600 paper-based; 105 iBT). Electronic applications accepted. *Faculty research:* Facility planning and management, environmental psychology, housing, interior design, ergonomics and human factors.

Florida Atlantic University, College of Design and Social Inquiry, School of Urban and Regional Planning, Boca Raton, FL 33431-0991. Offers economic development and tourism (Certificate); environmental planning (Certificate); sustainable community planning (Certificate); urban and regional planning (MURP); visual planning technology (Certificate). *Accreditation:* ACSP. Part-time and evening/weekend programs available. *Entrance requirements:* For master's, GRE General Test, minimum GPA of 3.0. Additional exam requirements/recommendations for international students: Required—TOEFL (minimum score 500 paper-based; 61 iBT), IELTS (minimum score 6). *Expenses:* Tuition, state resident: full-time $7396; part-time $369.82 per credit hour. Tuition, nonresident: full-time $19,392; part-time $1024.81 per credit hour. Tuition and fees vary according to course load. *Faculty research:* Growth management, urban design, computer applications/geographical information systems, environmental planning.

Kansas State University, Graduate School, College of Architecture, Planning and Design, Program in Environmental Design and Planning, Manhattan, KS 66506. Offers PhD. *Faculty:* 3 full-time (2 women). *Students:* 9 full-time (6 women), 2 part-time (1 woman); includes 2 minority (1 Black or African American, non-Hispanic/Latino; 1 Asian, non-Hispanic/Latino), 4 international. Average age 34. 15 applicants. In 2014, 2 doctorates awarded. *Degree requirements:* For doctorate, comprehensive exam, thesis/dissertation. *Entrance requirements:* For doctorate, GRE, transcript(s), statement of intent, three letters of recommendation, portfolio. Additional exam requirements/recommendations for international students: Required—TOEFL (minimum score 600 paper-based; 100 iBT). *Application deadline:* For fall admission, 1/1 for domestic and international students. Application fee: $90 ($100 for international students). Electronic applications accepted. *Expenses:* Expenses: Contact institution. *Financial support:* In 2014–15, 5 students received support. *Faculty research:* Design, planning, sustainability, place-making. *Unit head:* Dr. David H. Sachs, Director of Graduate Studies, 785-532-1183, E-mail: sachs@ksu.edu. *Application contact:* Ann Cook, Administrative Assistant, 785-532-5950, E-mail: amcook@ksu.edu. Website: http://apdesign.k-state.edu/academics/phd/

Kent State University, College of Architecture and Environmental Design, Kent, OH 44242-0001. Offers architecture (M Arch); architecture and environmental design (MS); health care design (MHCD); landscape architecture (ML Arch); urban design (MUD). Part-time programs available. *Faculty:* 24 full-time (5 women). *Students:* 66 full-time (25 women), 8 part-time (3 women); includes 5 minority (3 Black or African American, non-Hispanic/Latino; 1 American Indian or Alaska Native, non-Hispanic/Latino; 1 Asian, non-Hispanic/Latino), 4 international. Average age 25. 242 applicants, 67% accepted, 116 enrolled. In 2014, 45 degrees awarded. *Degree requirements:* For master's, thesis. *Entrance requirements:* For master's, GRE, minimum GPA of 3.0, writing sample, resume/curriculum vitae, letter of intent, portfolio, 3 letters of recommendation. Additional exam requirements/recommendations for international students: Required—TOEFL (minimum score: paper-based 525, iBT 71), Michigan English Language Assessment Battery (minimum score of 75), IELTS (minimum score of 6.0), PTE Academic (minimum score of 48), or completion of ELS level 112 Intensive Program. *Application deadline:* For fall admission, 1/15 for domestic and international students. Application fee: $45 ($70 for international students). Electronic applications accepted. *Expenses:* Tuition, state resident: full-time $8730; part-time $485 per credit hour. Tuition, nonresident: full-time $14,886; part-time $827 per credit hour. Tuition and fees vary according to campus/location and program. *Financial support:* Research assistantships with full tuition reimbursements, teaching assistantships with full tuition reimbursements, career-related internships or fieldwork, Federal Work-Study, scholarships/grants, and unspecified assistantships available. Financial award application deadline: 2/1. *Unit head:* Douglas Steidl, Dean, 330-672-2917, Fax: 330-672-3809, E-mail: dsteidl@kent.edu. *Application contact:* Lisa Pozo, Administrative Secretary, 330-672-2917, Fax: 330-672-3809, E-mail: caed_info@kent.edu. Website: http://www.kent.edu/caed

Michigan State University, The Graduate School, College of Agriculture and Natural Resources and College of Social Science, School of Planning, Design and Construction, East Lansing, MI 48824. Offers construction management (MS, PhD); environmental design (MA); interior design and facilities management (MA); international planning studies (MIPS); urban and regional planning (MURP). *Degree requirements:* For master's, thesis or alternative. *Entrance requirements:* Additional exam requirements/recommendations for international students: Required—TOEFL. Electronic applications accepted.

San Diego State University, Graduate and Research Affairs, College of Professional Studies and Fine Arts, School of Art, Design and Art History, San Diego, CA 92182. Offers art history (MA); studio arts (MA, MFA), including applied design, environmental design, graphic design, interior design, painting and printmaking, sculpture. *Accreditation:* NASAD (one or more programs are accredited). *Degree requirements:* For master's, variable foreign language requirement, thesis. *Entrance requirements:* For master's, GRE General Test, bachelor's degree in related field, slide portfolio, typed slide information sheet, 2 letters of recommendation. Additional exam requirements/recommendations for international students: Required—TOEFL. Electronic applications accepted.

Texas Tech University, Graduate School, College of Human Sciences, Department of Design, Lubbock, TX 79409-1220. Offers environmental design (MS); interior and environmental design (PhD). Part-time programs available. *Faculty:* 10 full-time (8 women), 2 part-time/adjunct (both women). *Students:* 27 full-time (21 women), 9 part-

time (6 women); includes 6 minority (1 Asian, non-Hispanic/Latino; 5 Hispanic/Latino), 19 international. Average age 31. 24 applicants, 50% accepted, 5 enrolled. In 2014, 10 master's, 2 doctorates awarded. *Degree requirements:* For master's, comprehensive exam, thesis or alternative; for doctorate, thesis/dissertation. *Entrance requirements:* For master's and doctorate, GRE, 3 recommendation letters, design portfolio, 500-word written statement (reason for pursuing degree), resume. Additional exam requirements/recommendations for international students: Required—TOEFL (minimum score 550 paper-based; 79 iBT). *Application deadline:* For fall admission, 6/1 priority date for domestic students, 1/15 priority date for international students; for spring admission, 9/1 priority date for domestic students, 6/15 priority date for international students. Applications are processed on a rolling basis. Application fee: $60. Electronic applications accepted. *Expenses:* Tuition, state resident: full-time $6310; part-time $262.92 per credit hour. Tuition, nonresident: full-time $14,998; part-time $624.92 per credit hour. *Required fees:* $2701; $36.50 per credit. $912.50 per semester. Tuition and fees vary according to course load. *Financial support:* In 2014–15, 22 students received support, including 21 fellowships (averaging $4,293 per year), 3 research assistantships (averaging $14,124 per year), 3 teaching assistantships (averaging $14,833 per year); scholarships/grants and unspecified assistantships also available. Financial award application deadline: 4/15; financial award applicants required to submit FAFSA. *Faculty research:* Healthcare and the built environment, sustainability, vulnerable populations, historic preservation, evidence-based design. *Total annual research expenditures:* $139,399. *Unit head:* Dr. Sharran F. Parkinson, Chair, 806-742-3031, Fax: 806-742-1639, E-mail: sharran.parkinson@ttu.edu. *Application contact:* Dr. Kristi Gaines, Graduate Programs Director, 806-742-3050, Fax: 806-742-1639, E-mail: kristi.gaines@ttu.edu.
Website: http://www.depts.ttu.edu/hs/dod/

Université de Montréal, Faculty of Environmental Design and Planning, Montréal, QC H3C 3J7, Canada. Offers environmental design and planning (M Sc A, PhD); environmental planning and design projects (DESS); game design (DESS); urban management for developing countries (DESS); urban planning (M Urb). DESS programs offered jointly with HEC Montreal and École Polytechnique de Montréal. *Accreditation:* ACSP. *Degree requirements:* For doctorate, thesis/dissertation, general exam. Electronic applications accepted. *Expenses:* Contact institution. *Faculty research:* Wayfinding, environmental evaluation, housing studies, urban design, urban and regional planning.

University of Calgary, Faculty of Graduate Studies, Faculty of Environmental Design, Calgary, AB T2N 1N4, Canada. Offers architecture (M Arch); environmental design (M Env Des, PhD); planning (M Plan). *Degree requirements:* For master's, thesis; for doctorate, thesis/dissertation. *Entrance requirements:* For master's, minimum GPA of 3.0; for doctorate, minimum GPA of 3.5. Additional exam requirements/recommendations for international students: Required—TOEFL (minimum score 550 paper-based). *Faculty research:* Sustainable development in architecture, planning and product design, energy and environment, impact assessment, ecotourism.

University of California, Berkeley, Graduate Division, College of Environmental Design, Department of Landscape Architecture and Environmental Planning, Berkeley, CA 94720-1500. Offers landscape architecture (MLA), including environmental planning, landscape design and site planning, urban and community design; landscape architecture and environmental planning (PhD); MLA/M Arch; MLA/MCP. *Accreditation:* ASLA (one or more programs are accredited). *Degree requirements:* For master's, professional project or thesis; for doctorate, one foreign language, thesis/dissertation, qualifying exam. *Entrance requirements:* For master's, GRE General Test, minimum GPA of 3.0, portfolio; for doctorate, GRE General Test, master's degree (strongly recommended), minimum GPA of 3.0, sample of written work, 3 letters of recommendation.

University of California, Berkeley, Graduate Division, College of Environmental Design, Master of Arts in Design Program, Berkeley, CA 94720-1500. Offers MA. *Degree requirements:* For master's, thesis. *Entrance requirements:* For master's, GRE General Test, minimum GPA of 3.0, portfolio, 3 letters of recommendation. Additional exam requirements/recommendations for international students: Required—TOEFL.

University of California, Irvine, School of Social Ecology, Programs in Social Ecology, Irvine, CA 92697. Offers environmental analysis and design (PhD); epidemiology and public health (PhD); social ecology (PhD). *Students:* 9 full-time (8 women), 1 part-time (0 women); includes 1 minority (Hispanic/Latino), 1 international. Average age 32. 11 applicants, 9% accepted, 1 enrolled. In 2014, 1 doctorate awarded. Application fee: $90 ($110 for international students). *Unit head:* Valerie Jenness, Dean, 949-824-6094, Fax: 949-824-1845, E-mail: jenness@uci.edu. *Application contact:* Jennnifer Craig, Director of Graduate Student Services, 949-824-5918, Fax: 949-824-1845, E-mail: craigj@uci.edu.
Website: http://socialecology.uci.edu/core/graduate-se-core-programs

University of Georgia, College of Environment and Design, Athens, GA 30602. Offers environmental planning and design (MEPD); historic preservation (MHP); landscape architecture (MLA).

The University of Manchester, School of Environment and Development, Manchester, United Kingdom. Offers architecture (M Phil, PhD); development policy and management (M Phil, PhD); human geography (M Phil, PhD); physical geography (M Phil, PhD); planning and landscape (M Phil, PhD).

University of Missouri, Office of Research and Graduate Studies, College of Human Environmental Sciences, Department of Architectural Studies, Columbia, MO 65211. Offers design with digital media (MA, MS); environmental design (MS). *Faculty:* 7 full-time (2 women). *Students:* 14 full-time (11 women), 23 part-time (14 women); includes 5 minority (1 Black or African American, non-Hispanic/Latino; 2 Asian, non-Hispanic/Latino; 1 Hispanic/Latino; 1 Two or more races, non-Hispanic/Latino), 4 international. Average age 41. 33 applicants, 30% accepted, 7 enrolled. In 2014, 4 master's awarded. *Entrance requirements:* For master's, GRE General Test, minimum GPA of 3.0. Additional exam requirements/recommendations for international students: Required—TOEFL (minimum score 500 paper-based; 61 iBT). *Application deadline:* For fall admission, 4/1 for domestic students; for winter admission, 10/1 for domestic students; for spring admission, 4/1 for domestic students. Applications are processed on a rolling basis. Application fee: $55 ($75 for international students). Electronic applications accepted. *Financial support:* Fellowships, research assistantships, teaching assistantships, institutionally sponsored loans, scholarships/grants, health care benefits, and unspecified assistantships available. Support available to part-time students. *Faculty research:* Environment and aging, design education and research, place attachment, residential environments, computer-mediated simulation, architectural design process. *Unit head:* Dr. Ruth Brent Tofle, Department Chair, 573-882-6311, E-mail: tofler@missouri.edu. *Application contact:* Laura Franklin, Business Support Specialist II, 573-882-7224, E-mail: franklinl@missouri.edu.
Website: http://arch.missouri.edu/

Virginia Polytechnic Institute and State University, Graduate School, College of Architecture and Urban Studies, Blacksburg, VA 24061. Offers architecture (MS Arch); architecture and design research (PhD); building/construction science and management (MS); creative technologies (MFA); environmental design and planning (PhD); landscape architecture (MLA); planning, governance, and globalization (PhD); public administration (MPA); public administration/public affairs (PhD, Certificate); public and international affairs (MPIA); urban and regional planning (MURP); MS/MA. *Accreditation:* ASLA (one or more programs are accredited). *Faculty:* 133 full-time (54 women), 2 part-time/adjunct (1 woman). *Students:* 316 full-time (166 women), 237 part-time (108 women); includes 104 minority (46 Black or African American, non-Hispanic/Latino; 1 American Indian or Alaska Native, non-Hispanic/Latino; 20 Asian, non-Hispanic/Latino; 21 Hispanic/Latino; 16 Two or more races, non-Hispanic/Latino), 108 international. Average age 32. 609 applicants, 50% accepted, 108 enrolled. In 2014, 155 master's, 29 doctorates awarded. *Degree requirements:* For master's, comprehensive exam (for some programs), thesis (for some programs); for doctorate, comprehensive exam (for some programs), thesis/dissertation (for some programs). *Entrance requirements:* For master's and doctorate, GRE/GMAT (may vary by department). Additional exam requirements/recommendations for international students: Required—TOEFL (minimum score 550 paper-based). *Application deadline:* For fall admission, 8/1 for domestic students, 4/1 for international students; for spring admission, 1/1 for domestic students, 9/1 for international students. Applications are processed on a rolling basis. Application fee: $75. Electronic applications accepted. *Expenses:* Tuition, state resident: full-time $11,656; part-time $647.50 per credit hour. Tuition, nonresident: full-time $23,351; part-time $1297.25 per credit hour. *Required fees:* $2533; $465.75 per semester. Tuition and fees vary according to course load, campus/location and program. *Financial support:* In 2014–15, 13 research assistantships with full tuition reimbursements (averaging $20,302 per year), 44 teaching assistantships with full tuition reimbursements (averaging $19,484 per year) were awarded. Financial award application deadline: 3/1; financial award applicants required to submit FAFSA. *Total annual research expenditures:* $3.2 million. *Unit head:* Dr. A. J. Davis, Dean, 540-231-6416, Fax: 540-231-6332, E-mail: davisa@vt.edu. *Application contact:* Christine Mattsson-Coon, Executive Assistant, 540-231-6416, Fax: 540-231-6332, E-mail: cmattsso@vt.edu.
Website: http://www.caus.vt.edu/

Yale University, School of Architecture, New Haven, CT 06520. Offers M Arch, M Env Des, MEM, PhD, M Arch/M Env Des, M Arch/MBA. *Faculty:* 20 full-time (6 women), 86 part-time/adjunct (20 women). *Students:* 200 full-time (81 women); includes 36 minority (2 Black or African American, non-Hispanic/Latino; 20 Asian, non-Hispanic/Latino; 9 Hispanic/Latino; 5 Two or more races, non-Hispanic/Latino), 60 international. 919 applicants, 18% accepted, 76 enrolled. In 2014, 81 master's awarded. *Entrance requirements:* For master's, GRE General Test, design portfolio. Additional exam requirements/recommendations for international students: Required—TOEFL. *Application deadline:* For fall admission, 1/10 for domestic and international students. Application fee: $85. Electronic applications accepted. *Expenses:* Expenses: Contact institution. *Financial support:* In 2014–15, 157 students received support. Fellowships, teaching assistantships, Federal Work-Study, and institutionally sponsored loans available. Financial award application deadline: 2/1; financial award applicants required to submit FAFSA. *Unit head:* Robert A. M. Stern, Dean, 203-432-2279, Fax: 203-432-7175. *Application contact:* Marilyn Weiss, Registrar, 203-432-2288, Fax: 203-432-7175, E-mail: gradarch.admissions@yale.edu.
Website: http://www.architecture.yale.edu/

Historic Preservation

The American University of Rome, Graduate School, Rome, Italy. Offers religious studies (MA); sustainable cultural heritage (MA). *Faculty:* 1 (woman) full-time, 13 part-time/adjunct (3 women). *Students:* 4 full-time (2 women). Average age 37. 8 applicants, 75% accepted, 4 enrolled. *Degree requirements:* For master's, thesis, internship. *Entrance requirements:* For master's, bachelor's degree in the liberal arts, humanities or social sciences; minimum GPA of 2.75. Additional exam requirements/recommendations for international students: Required—TOEFL (minimum score 550 paper-based; 80 iBT), IELTS (minimum score 6.5). *Application deadline:* For fall admission, 5/1 for domestic and international students. Applications are processed on a rolling basis. Application fee: $60. Electronic applications accepted. *Expenses: Tuition:* Full-time 13,000 euros. *Faculty research:* Sustainable cultural heritage, archaeology in Europe and Italy. *Unit head:* Dr. Maria Grazia Quieti, Dean of Graduate Studies, 39 06 5833 0919 Ext. 711, E-mail: m.quieti@aur.edu. *Application contact:* Arianna D'Amico, Director of Admissions and Financial Aid, 39 06-5833-0919, E-mail: admissions@aur.edu.
Website: http://www.aur.edu/gradschool

Arkansas State University, Graduate School, College of Humanities and Social Sciences, Heritage Studies Program, State University, AR 72467. Offers MA, PhD. Part-time programs available. *Faculty:* 2 full-time (1 woman). *Students:* 12 full-time (6 women), 22 part-time (13 women); includes 4 minority (all Black or African American, non-Hispanic/Latino), 3 international. Average age 47. 12 applicants, 33% accepted, 4 enrolled. In 2014, 4 master's, 4 doctorates awarded. *Degree requirements:* For master's, comprehensive exam, thesis or alternative, portfolio; for doctorate, comprehensive exam, thesis/dissertation, portfolio. *Entrance requirements:* For master's, GRE, MAT or GMAT, appropriate bachelor's degree, letters of reference, official transcript, interview, letter of interest, writing sample, immunization records; for doctorate, GRE, MAT, or GMAT, appropriate bachelor's or master's degree, interview, letters of reference, official transcript, letter of interest, writing sample, immunization records. Additional exam requirements/recommendations for international students: Required—TOEFL (minimum score 550 paper-based; 79 iBT), IELTS (minimum score 6), PTE (minimum score 56). *Application deadline:* For fall admission, 7/1 for domestic and international students. Applications are processed on a rolling basis. Application fee: $50. Electronic applications accepted. *Expenses:* Tuition, state resident: full-time $4392; part-time $244 per credit hour. Tuition, nonresident: full-time $8784; part-time $488 per credit hour. *International tuition:* $9484 full-time. *Required fees:* $1134; $63 per credit hour. $25 per term. Tuition and fees vary according to course load and program. *Financial support:* In

2014–15, 16 students received support. Fellowships, teaching assistantships, career-related internships or fieldwork, scholarships/grants, tuition waivers (partial), and unspecified assistantships available. Financial award application deadline: 7/1; financial award applicants required to submit FAFSA. *Unit head:* Dr. Brady Banta, Interim Director, 870-972-3509, Fax: 870-972-3207, E-mail: bbanta@astate.edu. *Application contact:* Vickey Ring, Graduate Admissions Coordinator, 870-972-3029, Fax: 870-972-3857, E-mail: vickeyring@astate.edu.
Website: http://www.astate.edu/college/humanities-and-social-sciences/departments/heritage-studies/

Ball State University, Graduate School, College of Architecture and Planning, Department of Architecture, Program in Historic Preservation, Muncie, IN 47306-1099. Offers MS. *Students:* 11 full-time (7 women), 2 part-time (1 woman). Average age 25. 11 applicants, 82% accepted, 6 enrolled. In 2014, 7 master's awarded. *Degree requirements:* For master's, thesis. *Entrance requirements:* For master's, minimum undergraduate B average, portfolio, writing sample. Application fee: $50. *Financial support:* In 2014–15, 11 students received support, including 2 research assistantships with partial tuition reimbursements available (averaging $1,996 per year), 7 teaching assistantships with partial tuition reimbursements available (averaging $4,680 per year). Financial award application deadline: 3/1. *Unit head:* Dr. Mahesh Daas, Chairperson, 765-285-1904, Fax: 765-285-1765, E-mail: mahesh@bsu.edu. *Application contact:* Mary Ann Heidemann, Director, 765-285-1911, Fax: 765-285-1765, E-mail: maheidemann@bsu.edu.
Website: http://cms.bsu.edu/Academics/CollegesandDepartments/CAP/Programs/Architecture/AboutUs/Centers/CenterHistoric.aspx

See Display on page 108 and Close-Up on page 135.

Boston Architectural College, Graduate Programs, Boston, MA 02115-2795. Offers architecture (M Arch); historic preservation (MDS); interior design (MID); landscape architecture (MLA); sustainable design (MDS). *Accreditation:* CIDA. *Degree requirements:* For master's, thesis. *Entrance requirements:* For master's, portfolio (recommended). Electronic applications accepted.

Boston University, Graduate School of Arts and Sciences, Program in Preservation Studies, Boston, MA 02215. Offers MA, JD/MA. *Students:* 3 part-time (2 women). Average age 30. 10 applicants, 90% accepted, 2 enrolled. *Degree requirements:* For master's, one foreign language, thesis or alternative, internship. *Entrance requirements:* For master's, GRE General Test, scholarly writing sample, 3 letters of recommendation. Additional exam requirements/recommendations for international students: Required—TOEFL (minimum score 550 paper-based; 84 iBT). *Application deadline:* For fall admission, 4/1 for domestic and international students; for spring admission, 11/15 for domestic and international students. Application fee: $80. Electronic applications accepted. *Expenses: Tuition:* Full-time $45,686; part-time $1428 per credit hour. *Required fees:* $660; $60 per semester. Tuition and fees vary according to program. *Financial support:* In 2014–15, 4 students received support. Career-related internships or fieldwork, Federal Work-Study, and unspecified assistantships available. Support available to part-time students. Financial award application deadline: 1/15. *Unit head:* Daniel Bluestone, Director, 617-358-7332, Fax: 617-353-2556, E-mail: dblues@bu.edu. *Application contact:* Benjamin Tocchi, Senior Program Coordinator, 617-353-2948, Fax: 617-353-2556, E-mail: btocchi@bu.edu.
Website: http://www.bu.edu/amnesp/ma/

Buffalo State College, State University of New York, The Graduate School, Faculty of Arts and Humanities, Department of Art Conservation, Buffalo, NY 14222-1095. Offers art conservation (CAS); conservation of historic works and art works (MA). *Degree requirements:* For master's, final oral exam; for CAS, internship. *Entrance requirements:* For master's, GRE General Test, minimum GPA of 2.8. Additional exam requirements/recommendations for international students: Required—TOEFL (minimum score 550 paper-based). *Faculty research:* Mechanics of deterioration of art, conservation of materials.

Clemson University, Graduate School, College of Architecture, Arts, and Humanities, Department of Planning, Development and Preservation, Program in Historic Preservation, Charleston, SC 29401. Offers MS. *Faculty:* 2 full-time (1 woman), 10 part-time/adjunct (4 women). *Students:* 27 full-time (24 women); includes 3 minority (all Hispanic/Latino). Average age 25. 39 applicants, 82% accepted, 15 enrolled. In 2014, 12 master's awarded. *Degree requirements:* For master's, thesis. *Entrance requirements:* For master's, GRE General Test. Additional exam requirements/recommendations for international students: Required—TOEFL. *Application deadline:* For fall admission, 2/15 for domestic and international students. Applications are processed on a rolling basis. Application fee: $70 ($80 for international students). Electronic applications accepted. *Financial support:* In 2014–15, 26 students received support, including 52 fellowships with partial tuition reimbursements available (averaging $3,077 per year); research assistantships with partial tuition reimbursements available, teaching assistantships with partial tuition reimbursements available, career-related internships or fieldwork, scholarships/grants, and unspecified assistantships also available. Financial award application deadline: 2/15. *Faculty research:* Early American architecture, microscopy of historic architectural finishes, cultural landscapes of Elizabethan Ireland, stone conservation, XRF and XRD application to architectural forensics. *Total annual research expenditures:* $46,000. *Unit head:* Dr. Carter L. Hudgins, Director, 864-937-9567, E-mail: chudgin@clemson.edu. *Application contact:* Mary Margaret Schley, Coordinator, 864-937-9596, E-mail: mschley@clemson.edu.
Website: http://www.clemson.edu/caah/pdp/historic-preservation/index.html

Cleveland State University, College of Graduate Studies, Maxine Goodman Levin College of Urban Affairs, Program in Urban Planning, Design, and Development, Cleveland, OH 44115. Offers economic development (MUPDD); environmental sustainability (MUPDD); geographic information systems (MUPDD, Certificate); historic preservation (MUPDD); housing and neighborhood development (MUPDD); urban economic development (Certificate); urban real estate development and finance (MUPDD, Certificate); JD/MUPDD. *Accreditation:* ACSP. Part-time and evening/weekend programs available. *Faculty:* 23 full-time (11 women), 23 part-time/adjunct (6 women). *Students:* 11 full-time (5 women), 25 part-time (10 women); includes 8 minority (2 Black or African American, non-Hispanic/Latino; 1 Asian, non-Hispanic/Latino; 2 Hispanic/Latino; 3 Two or more races, non-Hispanic/Latino), 3 international. Average age 38. 48 applicants, 56% accepted, 5 enrolled. In 2014, 16 master's awarded. *Degree requirements:* For master's, thesis or alternative, planning studio. *Entrance requirements:* For master's, GRE General Test (minimum score: 50th percentile combined verbal and quantitative, 4.0 analytical writing), minimum GPA of 3.0. Additional exam requirements/recommendations for international students: Required—TOEFL (minimum score 525 paper-based; 65 iBT), IELTS, or ITEP. *Application deadline:* For fall admission, 7/15 priority date for domestic students, 5/15 for international students; for spring admission, 11/1 for international students. Applications are processed on a rolling basis. Application fee: $30. Electronic applications accepted. *Expenses:* Expenses: $9,615 full-time, in-state tuition and fees. *Financial support:* In 2014–15, 10 students received support, including 7 research assistantships with full and partial tuition reimbursements available (averaging $5,600 per year), 2 teaching assistantships with full and partial tuition reimbursements available (averaging $2,000 per year); career-related internships or fieldwork, Federal Work-Study, scholarships/grants, tuition waivers, and unspecified assistantships also available. Support available to part-time students. Financial award application deadline: 3/1; financial award applicants required to submit FAFSA. *Faculty research:* Housing and neighborhood development, urban housing policy, environmental sustainability, economic development, GIS and planning decision support. *Unit head:* Dr. Dennis Keating, Director, 216-687-2298, Fax: 216-687-2013, E-mail: w.keating@csuohio.edu. *Application contact:* David Arrighi, Graduate Academic Advisor, 216-523-7522, Fax: 216-687-5398, E-mail: urbanprograms@csuohio.edu.
Website: http://urban.csuohio.edu/academics/graduate/mupdd/

College of Charleston, Graduate School, School of the Arts, Program in Historic Preservation, Charleston, SC 29424-0001. Offers MS. *Degree requirements:* For master's, thesis optional. *Entrance requirements:* For master's, GRE. Additional exam requirements/recommendations for international students: Required—TOEFL (minimum score 81 iBT). Electronic applications accepted.

Columbia University, Graduate School of Architecture, Planning, and Preservation, Program in Historic Preservation, New York, NY 10027. Offers MS, Certificate, M Arch/MS, MS/MS. *Degree requirements:* For master's, thesis. *Entrance requirements:* For master's, GRE General Test.

Cornell University, Graduate School, Graduate Fields of Architecture, Art and Planning, Field of City and Regional Planning, Ithaca, NY 14853-0001. Offers city and regional planning (MRP, PhD); environmental planning and design (MRP, PhD); historic preservation planning (MA); international development planning (MRP, PhD); planning theory and systems analysis (MRP, PhD); regional economics and development planning (MRP, PhD); regional science (MRP, PhD); social and health systems planning (MRP, PhD); urban and regional theory (MRP, PhD); urban planning history (MRP, PhD). *Accreditation:* ACSP (one or more programs are accredited). *Degree requirements:* For master's, thesis (MA); for doctorate, comprehensive exam, thesis/dissertation. *Entrance requirements:* For master's and doctorate, GRE General Test, 2 letters of recommendation. Additional exam requirements/recommendations for international students: Required—TOEFL (minimum score 600 paper-based; 77 iBT). Electronic applications accepted. *Faculty research:* Land use planning, economic development, international development, historic preservation, community development.

Delaware State University, Graduate Programs, Department of History, Philosophy and Political Sciences, Dover, DE 19901-2277. Offers historic preservation (MA). *Entrance requirements:* Additional exam requirements/recommendations for international students: Required—TOEFL (minimum score 550 paper-based). Electronic applications accepted.

Eastern Michigan University, Graduate School, College of Arts and Sciences, Department of Geography and Geology, Programs in Historic Preservation, Ypsilanti, MI 48197. Offers heritage interpretation and tourism (MS). Part-time and evening/weekend programs available. Postbaccalaureate distance learning degree programs offered (minimal on-campus study). *Students:* 26 full-time (20 women), 47 part-time (31 women); includes 4 minority (1 Black or African American, non-Hispanic/Latino; 1 Hispanic/Latino; 2 Two or more races, non-Hispanic/Latino), 1 international. Average age 34. 38 applicants, 87% accepted, 19 enrolled. In 2014, 15 master's awarded. *Entrance requirements:* Additional exam requirements/recommendations for international students: Required—TOEFL. *Application deadline:* Applications are processed on a rolling basis. Application fee: $45. *Financial support:* Fellowships, research assistantships with full tuition reimbursements, teaching assistantships with full tuition reimbursements, career-related internships or fieldwork, Federal Work-Study, institutionally sponsored loans, scholarships/grants, tuition waivers (partial), and unspecified assistantships available. Support available to part-time students. Financial award applicants required to submit FAFSA. *Application contact:* Dr. Ted Ligibel, Program Director, 734-487-0232, Fax: 734-487-6979, E-mail: ted.ligibel@emich.edu.

The George Washington University, Columbian College of Arts and Sciences, Department of American Studies, Washington, DC 20052. Offers American studies (PhD); folklife (MA); historic preservation (MA); material culture (MA). Part-time and evening/weekend programs available. *Faculty:* 14 full-time (7 women). *Students:* 18 full-time (12 women), 28 part-time (22 women); includes 7 minority (5 Black or African American, non-Hispanic/Latino; 1 Asian, non-Hispanic/Latino; 1 Two or more races, non-Hispanic/Latino), 3 international. Average age 30. 97 applicants, 30% accepted, 12 enrolled. In 2014, 13 master's, 4 doctorates awarded. Terminal master's awarded for partial completion of doctoral program. *Degree requirements:* For master's, comprehensive exam; for doctorate, one foreign language, thesis/dissertation, general exam. *Entrance requirements:* For master's and doctorate, GRE General Test, minimum GPA of 3.0. Additional exam requirements/recommendations for international students: Required—TOEFL (minimum score 550 paper-based; 80 iBT). *Application deadline:* For fall admission, 1/15 priority date for domestic and international students; for spring admission, 10/1 for domestic students. Application fee: $75. *Financial support:* In 2014–15, 22 students received support. Fellowships, research assistantships, teaching assistantships, career-related internships or fieldwork, Federal Work-Study, institutionally sponsored loans, and tuition waivers available. Financial award application deadline: 1/15. *Unit head:* Melanie McAlister, Chair, 202-994-7244, E-mail: jam@gwu.edu. *Application contact:* Information Contact, 202-994-6070, Fax: 202-994-8651, E-mail: amst@gwu.edu.
Website: http://departments.columbian.gwu.edu/americanstudies/

Georgia State University, College of Arts and Sciences, Department of History, Program in Heritage Preservation, Atlanta, GA 30302-3083. Offers MHP. Part-time programs available. *Degree requirements:* For master's, comprehensive exam, thesis optional, 42 hours of credit. *Entrance requirements:* For master's, GRE General Test, statement of purpose, three letters of recommendation, official transcripts. Additional exam requirements/recommendations for international students: Required—TOEFL (minimum score 550 paper-based; 80 iBT). *Application deadline:* For fall admission, 3/15 priority date for domestic and international students; for spring admission, 10/15 priority date for domestic and international students. Applications are processed on a rolling basis. Application fee: $50. Electronic applications accepted. *Expenses:* Tuition, state resident: full-time $6516; part-time $362 per credit hour. Tuition, nonresident: full-time $22,014; part-time $1223 per credit hour. *Required fees:* $2128 per semester. Tuition and fees vary according to course load and program. *Financial support:* In 2014–15, 1 fellowship with full tuition reimbursement (averaging $5,100 per year), 40 research assistantships with full tuition reimbursements (averaging $5,100 per year) were awarded; career-related internships or fieldwork, Federal Work-Study, scholarships/grants, and unspecified assistantships also available. Support available to part-time students. Financial award application deadline: 7/15. *Faculty research:* Materials conservation, preservation planning, cultural preservation, public history, oral history, twentieth-century American history. *Unit head:* Dr. Michelle Brattain, Chair, 404-413-6352, E-mail: mbrattain@gsu.edu. *Application contact:* Richard Laub, Director of Heritage Preservation Program, 404-413-6365, E-mail: rlaub@gsu.edu.
Website: http://www.gsu.edu/~wwwhis/

Georgia State University, College of Arts and Sciences, Department of History, Program in History, Atlanta, GA 30302-3083. Offers historic preservation (MA); history

(PhD); public history (MA); world history (MA). Part-time and evening/weekend programs available. Terminal master's awarded for partial completion of doctoral program. *Degree requirements:* For master's, one foreign language, comprehensive exam, thesis optional, continuous enrollment; 6 hours of thesis credits; for doctorate, 2 foreign languages, comprehensive exam, thesis/dissertation, dissertation prospectus and prospectus defense; dissertation defense; residency; continuous enrollment; 6 hours of thesis credits. *Entrance requirements:* For master's, GRE, BA in history; statement of purpose; writing sample; three letters of recommendation; official transcripts; for doctorate, GRE, MA in history; master's thesis; statement of purpose; writing sample; three letters of recommendation; official transcripts; appropriate language skills. Additional exam requirements/recommendations for international students: Required—TOEFL (minimum score 550 paper-based; 80 iBT). *Application deadline:* For fall admission, 3/15 for domestic and international students; for spring admission, 10/15 for domestic and international students. Applications are processed on a rolling basis. Application fee: $50. Electronic applications accepted. *Expenses:* Tuition, state resident: full-time $6516; part-time $362 per credit hour. Tuition, nonresident: full-time $22,014; part-time $1223 per credit hour. *Required fees:* $2128 per semester. Tuition and fees vary according to course load and program. *Financial support:* Research assistantships with tuition reimbursements, teaching assistantships with tuition reimbursements, and scholarships/grants available. Financial award application deadline: 2/15. *Faculty research:* Nineteenth- and twentieth-century U.S. history, early modern European history, modern European history, world history, public history. *Unit head:* Dr. Michelle Brattain, Chair, 404-413-6352, Fax: 404-413-6384, E-mail: mbrattain@gsu.edu. *Application contact:* Dr. Joe Perry, Director of Graduate Studies, 404-413-6374, Fax: 404-413-6384, E-mail: jbperry@gsu.edu.
Website: http://www.gsu.edu/~wwwhis/

Goucher College, MA and MFA Programs, Baltimore, MD 21204-2794. Offers arts administration (MA); creative nonfiction (MFA); cultural sustainability (MA); digital arts (MFA); environmental studies (MA); historic preservation (MA); management (MA). Part-time and evening/weekend programs available. Postbaccalaureate distance learning degree programs offered (minimal on-campus study). *Faculty:* 83 part-time/adjunct (42 women). *Students:* 72 full-time (58 women), 65 part-time (54 women); includes 39 minority (15 Black or African American, non-Hispanic/Latino; 16 American Indian or Alaska Native, non-Hispanic/Latino; 2 Asian, non-Hispanic/Latino; 4 Hispanic/Latino; 2 Two or more races, non-Hispanic/Latino), 4 international. 120 applicants, 95% accepted, 50 enrolled. In 2014, 63 master's awarded. *Degree requirements:* For master's, thesis, e-portfolio completion. *Entrance requirements:* Additional exam requirements/recommendations for international students: Required—TOEFL (minimum score 550 paper-based; 80 iBT), IELTS (minimum score 7). *Application deadline:* Applications are processed on a rolling basis. Application fee: $75. *Expenses:* Expenses: $825 per credit; fees vary according to program. *Financial support:* Unspecified assistantships available. Financial award application deadline: 4/15; financial award applicants required to submit FAFSA. *Unit head:* Lynne Lochte, Vice President for New Ventures and Business Strategies, 410-337-6572, E-mail: lynne.lochte@goucher.edu. *Application contact:* Hanora Barron, Admissions Coordinator, 410-337-6200, Fax: 410-337-6085, E-mail: hanora.barron@goucher.edu.
Website: http://www.goucher.edu/grad

Michigan Technological University, Graduate School, College of Sciences and Arts, Department of Social Sciences, Houghton, MI 49931. Offers environmental and energy policy (MS, PhD); industrial archaeology (MS); industrial heritage and archeology (PhD). Part-time programs available. *Faculty:* 29 full-time (12 women), 13 part-time/adjunct (4 women). *Students:* 29 full-time (14 women), 18 part-time (6 women); includes 8 minority (1 Black or African American, non-Hispanic/Latino; 1 American Indian or Alaska Native, non-Hispanic/Latino; 4 Asian, non-Hispanic/Latino; 1 Hispanic/Latino; 1 Two or more races, non-Hispanic/Latino), 10 international. Average age 33. 57 applicants, 32% accepted, 10 enrolled. In 2014, 9 master's awarded. Terminal master's awarded for partial completion of doctoral program. *Degree requirements:* For master's, comprehensive exam (for some programs), thesis (for some programs); for doctorate, comprehensive exam, thesis/dissertation. *Entrance requirements:* For master's and doctorate, GRE, statement of purpose, official transcripts, 3 letters of recommendation, writing sample, resume/curriculum vitae. Additional exam requirements/recommendations for international students: Required—TOEFL (recommended score 100 iBT) or IELTS. *Application deadline:* For fall admission, 2/1 priority date for domestic and international students. Applications are processed on a rolling basis. Electronic applications accepted. *Expenses:* Tuition, state resident: full-time $14,769; part-time $820.50 per credit. Tuition, nonresident: full-time $14,769; part-time $820.50 per credit. *Required fees:* $248; $248 per year. Tuition and fees vary according to course load and program. *Financial support:* In 2014–15, 35 students received support, including 3 fellowships with full and partial tuition reimbursements available (averaging $13,824 per year), 10 research assistantships with full and partial tuition reimbursements available (averaging $13,824 per year), 12 teaching assistantships with full and partial tuition reimbursements available (averaging $13,824 per year); career-related internships or fieldwork, Federal Work-Study, scholarships/grants, health care benefits, unspecified assistantships, and cooperative program also available. Financial award applicants required to submit FAFSA. *Faculty research:* Industrial archeology of early American industry, mining history, environmental and energy policy, land-use policy, environmental decision-making. *Total annual research expenditures:* $746,653. *Unit head:* Dr. Patrick E. Martin, Chair, 906-487-2070, Fax: 906-487-2284, E-mail: pemartin@mtu.edu. *Application contact:* Amy Spahn, Office Assistant, 906-487-2113, Fax: 906-487-2284, E-mail: gradadms@mtu.edu.
Website: http://www.social.mtu.edu/

Morgan State University, School of Graduate Studies, College of Liberal Arts, Department of History and Geography, Baltimore, MD 21251. Offers African-American studies (MA); history (MA, PhD); museum studies and historic preservation (MA). Part-time and evening/weekend programs available. *Degree requirements:* For master's, comprehensive exam, thesis; for doctorate, comprehensive exam, thesis/dissertation. *Entrance requirements:* For master's, minimum GPA of 2.5; for doctorate, GRE or MAT. Additional exam requirements/recommendations for international students: Required—TOEFL (minimum score 550 paper-based). *Faculty research:* Women's history, African diaspora history, urban history.

New York University, Graduate School of Arts and Science, Institute of Fine Arts, Program in Conservation Training, New York, NY 10012-1019. Offers MA/Diploma. *Students:* 5 full-time (all women); includes 1 minority (Two or more races, non-Hispanic/Latino), 1 international. 35 applicants, 31% accepted, 4 enrolled. *Application deadline:* For fall admission, 12/18 for domestic and international students. Application fee: $95. *Financial support:* Career-related internships or fieldwork, Federal Work-Study, and institutionally sponsored loans available. Financial award application deadline: 12/18; financial award applicants required to submit FAFSA. *Unit head:* Michele Marincola, Chair, Conservation Center, 212-992-5800, Fax: 212-992-5807, E-mail: ifa.program@nyu.edu. *Application contact:* Kevin Martin, Graduate Advisor, 212-992-5800, Fax: 212-992-5807, E-mail: ifa.program@nyu.edu.
Website: http://www.nyu.edu/gsas/dept/fineart/

Penn State Harrisburg, Graduate School, School of Humanities, Middletown, PA 17057-4898. Offers American studies (MA, PhD); communications (MA); folklore and ethnography (Certificate); heritage and museum practice (Certificate); humanities (MA); writing instruction specialist (Certificate). Evening/weekend programs available. *Unit head:* Dr. Mukund S. Kulkarni, Chancellor, 717-948-6105, Fax: 717-948-6452, E-mail: msk5@psu.edu. *Application contact:* Robert W. Coffman, Jr., Director of Enrollment Management, Admissions, 717-948-6250, Fax: 717-948-6325, E-mail: ric1@psu.edu.
Website: http://harrisburg.psu.edu/humanities

Plymouth State University, Program in Historic Preservation, Plymouth, NH 03264-1595. Offers MA. *Degree requirements:* For master's, thesis or practicum.

★ **Pratt Institute,** School of Architecture, Program in Historic Preservation, New York, NY 10011. Offers MS. Part-time programs available. *Faculty:* 5 full-time (2 women), 8 part-time/adjunct (4 women). *Students:* 18 full-time (14 women), 3 part-time (all women); includes 3 minority (all Hispanic/Latino), 3 international. Average age 32. 34 applicants, 88% accepted, 7 enrolled. In 2014, 7 master's awarded. *Entrance requirements:* For master's, writing sample, bachelor's degree, transcripts, letters of recommendation, portfolio. Additional exam requirements/recommendations for international students: Required—TOEFL (minimum score 550 paper-based; 79 iBT). *Application deadline:* For fall admission, 1/5 for domestic and international students; for spring admission, 10/1 for domestic and international students. Application fee: $50 ($90 for international students). Electronic applications accepted. *Financial support:* Career-related internships or fieldwork, Federal Work-Study, institutionally sponsored loans, scholarships/grants, health care benefits, and unspecified assistantships available. Support available to part-time students. Financial award application deadline: 2/1; financial award applicants required to submit FAFSA. *Unit head:* Thomas Hanrahan, Dean of Architecture, 718-399-4308, E-mail: hanrahan@pratt.edu. *Application contact:* Young Hah, Director of Graduate Admissions, 718-636-3683, Fax: 718-399-4242, E-mail: yhah@pratt.edu.
Website: https://www.pratt.edu/academics/architecture/historic-preservation/
See Display on page 112 and Close-Up on page 139.

Roger Williams University, School of Architecture, Art and Historic Preservation, Bristol, RI 02809. Offers architecture (M Arch); art and architectural history (MA); historical preservation (MS). *Faculty:* 14 full-time (3 women), 16 part-time/adjunct (4 women). *Students:* 80 full-time (24 women), 18 part-time (8 women); includes 12 minority (1 Black or African American, non-Hispanic/Latino; 2 Asian, non-Hispanic/Latino; 8 Hispanic/Latino; 1 Two or more races, non-Hispanic/Latino), 7 international. Average age 25. 77 applicants, 87% accepted, 46 enrolled. In 2014, 49 master's awarded. *Degree requirements:* For master's, thesis. *Entrance requirements:* For master's, portfolio, 2 letters of recommendation. Additional exam requirements/recommendations for international students: Recommended—TOEFL (minimum score 85 iBT), IELTS. *Application deadline:* For fall admission, 3/1 priority date for domestic students. Application fee: $50. Electronic applications accepted. *Expenses:* Expenses: $33,792 (for M Arch); $20,644 (for MS in historical preservation). *Financial support:* In 2014–15, 84 students received support, including fellowships with partial tuition reimbursements available (averaging $6,000 per year), 80 research assistantships (averaging $3,000 per year). Financial award application deadline: 6/15; financial award applicants required to submit FAFSA. *Unit head:* Stephen White, Dean, 401-254-3607, E-mail: swhite@rwu.edu. *Application contact:* Lori Vales, Director of Graduate Admissions, 401-254-6200, Fax: 401-254-3557, E-mail: gradadmit@rwu.edu.
Website: http://www.rwu.edu/academics/departments/architecture.htm#dual

Rutgers, The State University of New Jersey, New Brunswick, Graduate School-New Brunswick, Program in Art History, Piscataway, NJ 08854-8097. Offers art history (MA, PhD); curatorial studies (Certificate); historic preservation (Certificate). Part-time programs available. Terminal master's awarded for partial completion of doctoral program. *Degree requirements:* For master's, one foreign language, comprehensive exam; for doctorate, 2 foreign languages, comprehensive exam, thesis/dissertation. *Entrance requirements:* For master's and doctorate, GRE General Test, writing sample. Additional exam requirements/recommendations for international students: Required—TOEFL (minimum score 550 paper-based). Electronic applications accepted. *Faculty research:* Ancient and medieval art and architecture; Renaissance and Baroque art and architecture; modern and contemporary art and architecture; Italian studies; the arts of Asia, Africa, and the Americas.

Rutgers, The State University of New Jersey, New Brunswick, Graduate School-New Brunswick, Program in Cultural Heritage and Preservation Studies, Piscataway, NJ 08854-8097. Offers cultural heritage and preservation studies (MA); historic preservation (Certificate).

St. Cloud State University, School of Graduate Studies, College of Social Sciences, Program in Cultural Resource Management Archeology, St. Cloud, MN 56301-4498. Offers MS. *Entrance requirements:* For master's, GRE General Test, minimum GPA of 2.75. Additional exam requirements/recommendations for international students: Required—Michigan English Language Assessment Battery; Recommended—TOEFL (minimum score 550 paper-based).

Savannah College of Art and Design, Graduate School, Program in Historic Preservation, Savannah, GA 31402-3146. Offers MA, MFA, Graduate Certificate. Part-time programs available. Postbaccalaureate distance learning degree programs offered (no on-campus study). *Faculty:* 7 full-time (1 woman), 2 part-time/adjunct (1 woman). *Students:* 38 full-time (32 women), 26 part-time (21 women); includes 5 minority (4 Black or African American, non-Hispanic/Latino; 1 Asian, non-Hispanic/Latino). Average age 34. 49 applicants, 57% accepted, 14 enrolled. In 2014, 22 master's awarded. *Degree requirements:* For master's, thesis (for some programs), final project (for MA); internship (for MFA). *Entrance requirements:* For master's, portfolio, including research paper. Additional exam requirements/recommendations for international students: Required—TOEFL (minimum score 550 paper-based, 85 iBT), IELTS (minimum score 6.5), or ACTFL. *Application deadline:* For fall admission, 4/1 for domestic and international students. Applications are processed on a rolling basis. Application fee: $40. Electronic applications accepted. *Expenses: Tuition:* Full-time $34,605; part-time $3845 per course. One-time fee: $500. Tuition and fees vary according to course load. *Financial support:* Fellowships, career-related internships or fieldwork, Federal Work-Study, and scholarships/grants available. Financial award application deadline: 4/1; financial award applicants required to submit FAFSA. *Unit head:* Jeff Eley, Chair. *Application contact:* Jenny Jaquillard, Executive Director of Admissions, Recruitment and Events, 912-525-5100, Fax: 912-525-5985, E-mail: admission@scad.edu.
Website: http://www.scad.edu/academics/programs/historic-preservation

School of the Art Institute of Chicago, Graduate Division, Program in Historic Preservation, Chicago, IL 60603-3103. Offers MSHP. *Entrance requirements:* Additional exam requirements/recommendations for international students: Required—TOEFL, IELTS.

Southeast Missouri State University, School of Graduate Studies, Department of History, Cape Girardeau, MO 63701-4799. Offers heritage education (Certificate); historic preservation (Certificate); history (MA); public history (MA). Part-time and evening/weekend programs available. *Faculty:* 11 full-time (4 women). *Students:* 9 full-

time (8 women), 12 part-time (3 women); includes 1 minority (Hispanic/Latino). Average age 30. 16 applicants, 81% accepted, 12 enrolled. In 2014, 11 master's awarded. *Degree requirements:* For master's, comprehensive exam (for some programs), thesis optional, thesis or exam, plus capstone project/paper (for history); thesis or internship, plus project in applied history and comprehensive exams (for public history). *Entrance requirements:* For master's and Certificate, minimum undergraduate GPA of 2.75; 2 letters of recommendation; writing sample; letter of intent; 24 semester hours of undergraduate history credit. Additional exam requirements/recommendations for international students: Required—TOEFL (minimum score 550 paper-based; 79 iBT), IELTS (minimum score 6), PTE (minimum score 53). *Application deadline:* For fall admission, 8/1 for domestic students, 6/1 for international students; for spring admission, 11/21 for domestic students, 10/1 for international students; for summer admission, 5/15 for domestic students. Applications are processed on a rolling basis. Application fee: $30 ($40 for international students). Electronic applications accepted. *Expenses:* Tuition, state resident: full-time $5256; part-time $292 per credit hour. Tuition, nonresident: full-time $9288; part-time $516 per credit hour. *Financial support:* In 2014–15, 8 students received support, including 1 research assistantship with full tuition reimbursement available (averaging $7,907 per year), 4 teaching assistantships with full tuition reimbursements available (averaging $7,907 per year); career-related internships or fieldwork, Federal Work-Study, scholarships/grants, traineeships, tuition waivers (full), and unspecified assistantships also available. Financial award application deadline: 6/30; financial award applicants required to submit FAFSA. *Faculty research:* Medieval Europe; modern Europe including Britain, Germany, France, Russia, and Spain; Colonial and nineteenth-century America; twentieth-century America and American West; public history and historic preservation; Latin America. *Unit head:* Dr. Wayne Bowen, Chairperson/Professor of History, 573-651-2179, Fax: 573-651-5114, E-mail: wbowen@semo.edu. *Application contact:* Dr. Erika Hosselkus, Graduate Coordinator/Assistant Professor of History, 573-651-2763, Fax: 573-651-5114, E-mail: ehosselkus@semo.edu.
Website: http://www.semo.edu/history/

Syracuse University, School of Information Studies, Program in Cultural Heritage Preservation, Syracuse, NY 13244. Offers CAS. Part-time programs available. *Students:* Average age 50. 5 applicants, 100% accepted. In 2014, 4 CASs awarded. *Degree requirements:* For CAS, internships. *Entrance requirements:* Additional exam requirements/recommendations for international students: Required—TOEFL (minimum score 100 iBT). *Application deadline:* For fall admission, 1/1 priority date for domestic and international students; for spring admission, 10/15 for domestic students, 10/15 priority date for international students. Applications are processed on a rolling basis. Application fee: $75. Electronic applications accepted. *Expenses: Tuition:* Part-time $1341 per credit. *Unit head:* Prof. Jill Hurst-Wahl, Program Director, 315-443-1070, E-mail: igrad@syr.edu. *Application contact:* Susan Corieri, Director of Enrollment Management, 315-443-2575, E-mail: ischool@syr.edu.
Website: http://ischool.syr.edu/academics/graduate/ch/index.aspx

Texas Tech University, Graduate School, Interdisciplinary Programs, Lubbock, TX 79409-1030. Offers arid land studies (MS); biotechnology (MS); heritage management (MS); interdisciplinary studies (MA, MS); museum science (MA); wind science and engineering (PhD); JD/MS. Part-time programs available. *Faculty:* 4 full-time (3 women). *Students:* 112 full-time (70 women), 122 part-time (70 women); includes 71 minority (20 Black or African American, non-Hispanic/Latino; 1 American Indian or Alaska Native, non-Hispanic/Latino; 4 Asian, non-Hispanic/Latino; 40 Hispanic/Latino; 6 Two or more races, non-Hispanic/Latino), 43 international. Average age 30. 172 applicants, 65% accepted, 70 enrolled. In 2014, 56 master's, 4 doctorates awarded. Terminal master's awarded for partial completion of doctoral program. *Degree requirements:* For master's, comprehensive exam (for some programs), thesis (for some programs); for doctorate, comprehensive exam, thesis/dissertation (for some programs). *Entrance requirements:* Additional exam requirements/recommendations for international students: Required—TOEFL (minimum score 550 paper-based; 79 iBT). *Application deadline:* For fall admission, 6/1 priority date for domestic students, 1/15 priority date for international students; for spring admission, 9/1 priority date for domestic students, 6/15 priority date for international students. Applications are processed on a rolling basis. Application fee: $60. Electronic applications accepted. *Expenses:* Tuition, state resident: full-time $6310; part-time $262.92 per credit hour. Tuition, nonresident: full-time $14,998; part-time $624.92 per credit hour. *Required fees:* $2701; $36.50 per credit. $912.50 per semester. Tuition and fees vary according to course load. *Financial support:* In 2014–15, 201 students received support, including 196 fellowships (averaging $2,655 per year), 5 research assistantships (averaging $12,144 per year), 2 teaching assistantships (averaging $7,785 per year); scholarships/grants and unspecified assistantships also available. Financial award application deadline: 4/15; financial award applicants required to submit FAFSA. *Total annual research expenditures:* $241,842. *Unit head:* Dr. Mark Sheridan, Vice Provost for Graduate and Postdoctoral Affairs/Dean of the Graduate School, 806-742-2787, Fax: 806-742-1746, E-mail: mark.sheridan@ttu.edu. *Application contact:* Shannon Samson, Coordinator of Graduate School Recruitment, 806-834-5201, Fax: 806-742-1746, E-mail: gradschool@ttu.edu.
Website: http://www.depts.ttu.edu/gradschool/about/INDS/index.php

Universidad Nacional Pedro Henriquez Urena, Graduate School, Santo Domingo, Dominican Republic. Offers agricultural diversity (MS), including horticultural/fruit production, tropical animal production; conservation of monuments and cultural assets (M Arch); ecology and environment (MS); environmental engineering (MEE); international relations (MA); natural resource management (MS); political science (MA); project optimization (MPM); project feasibility (MPM); project management (MPM); sanitation engineering (ME); science for teachers (MS); tropical Caribbean architecture (M Arch).

University at Buffalo, the State University of New York, Graduate School, School of Architecture and Planning, Department of Architecture, Buffalo, NY 14214. Offers architecture (M Arch); flexible track (MS Arch); inclusive design (MS Arch); real estate development (MS Arch); situated technologies (MS Arch); urban design and historic preservation (MS Arch); M Arch/MBA; M Arch/MFA; M Arch/MUP. *Faculty:* 27 full-time (9 women), 13 part-time/adjunct (4 women). *Students:* 123 full-time (43 women), 4 part-time (1 woman); includes 19 minority (3 Black or African American, non-Hispanic/Latino; 7 Asian, non-Hispanic/Latino; 5 Hispanic/Latino; 4 Two or more races, non-Hispanic/Latino), 40 international. Average age 25. 181 applicants, 89% accepted, 65 enrolled. In 2014, 40 master's awarded. *Degree requirements:* For master's, thesis or alternative, project. *Entrance requirements:* For master's, GRE, portfolio, 3 letters of recommendation, transcripts, 500-word personal statement. Additional exam requirements/recommendations for international students: Required—TOEFL (minimum score 550 paper-based; 79 iBT), IELTS (minimum score 6.5). *Application deadline:* For fall admission, 1/15 priority date for domestic and international students. Application fee: $75. Electronic applications accepted. *Expenses:* Expenses: $7,017.50 per semester resident tuition and fees, $11,152.50 non-resident. *Financial support:* In 2014–15, 2 fellowships with full tuition reimbursements (averaging $20,618 per year), 10 research assistantships with full and partial tuition reimbursements (averaging $7,515 per year), 29 teaching assistantships with partial tuition reimbursements (averaging $4,865 per year) were awarded; career-related internships or fieldwork, Federal Work-Study, institutionally sponsored loans, scholarships/grants, health care benefits, tuition waivers (partial), and unspecified assistantships also available. Support available to part-time students. Financial award application deadline: 3/1; financial award applicants required to submit FAFSA. *Faculty research:* Inclusive design, material culture, situated technologies, ecological practices. *Total annual research expenditures:* $2.6 million. *Unit head:* Prof. Omar Khan, Chair, 716-829-3483 Ext. 105, Fax: 716-829-3256, E-mail: omar.khan@buffalo.edu. *Application contact:* Debra Eggebrecht, Assistant to the Chair, 716-829-3485 Ext. 105, Fax: 716-829-3256, E-mail: dle2@buffalo.edu.
Website: http://www.ap.buffalo.edu/architecture/

University at Buffalo, the State University of New York, Graduate School, School of Architecture and Planning, Department of Urban and Regional Planning, Buffalo, NY 14214. Offers historic preservation (Certificate); urban and regional planning (PhD); JD/MUP; M Arch/MUP. *Accreditation:* ACSP. Part-time programs available. *Faculty:* 14 full-time (4 women), 13 part-time/adjunct (2 women). *Students:* 97 full-time (45 women), 8 part-time (3 women); includes 12 minority (7 Black or African American, non-Hispanic/Latino; 2 Asian, non-Hispanic/Latino; 3 Two or more races, non-Hispanic/Latino), 39 international. Average age 25. 183 applicants, 62% accepted, 45 enrolled. In 2014, 34 master's awarded. *Degree requirements:* For master's, thesis or alternative, project; for doctorate, thesis/dissertation. *Entrance requirements:* For master's, minimum GPA of 3.0, resume, 3 letters of recommendation, 500-word personal statement, transcripts; for doctorate, GRE, transcripts, 3 letters of recommendation, minimum GPA of 3.0, resume, research statement, writing sample. Additional exam requirements/recommendations for international students: Required—TOEFL (minimum score 550 paper-based; 79 iBT), IELTS (minimum score 6.5). *Application deadline:* For fall admission, 3/1 priority date for domestic and international students; for spring admission, 10/31 priority date for domestic students, 10/1 priority date for international students. Applications are processed on a rolling basis. Application fee: $75. Electronic applications accepted. *Expenses:* Expenses: $6,242.50 per semester resident tuition and fees, $11,125.50 non-resident. *Financial support:* In 2014–15, 2 fellowships with full tuition reimbursements (averaging $21,878 per year), 20 research assistantships with full and partial tuition reimbursements (averaging $6,604 per year), 13 teaching assistantships with partial tuition reimbursements (averaging $4,834 per year) were awarded; career-related internships or fieldwork, Federal Work-Study, institutionally sponsored loans, scholarships/grants, health care benefits, tuition waivers (partial), and unspecified assistantships also available. Support available to part-time students. Financial award application deadline: 3/1; financial award applicants required to submit FAFSA. *Faculty research:* Economic and international development, environmental and land use planning, GIS and spatial modeling, urban design and physical planning, neighborhood planning and community development. *Total annual research expenditures:* $1.1 million. *Unit head:* Dr. Ernest Sternberg, Professor, 716-829-3671 Ext. 109, Fax: 716-829-3256, E-mail: ezs@buffalo.edu. *Application contact:* Norma Everett, Assistant to the Chair, 716-829-3283, Fax: 716-829-3256, E-mail: norma.everett@buffalo.edu.
Website: http://www.ap.buffalo.edu/planning/

University of California, Los Angeles, Graduate Division, College of Letters and Science, Interdepartmental Program in Conservation of Archaeological and Ethnographic Materials, Los Angeles, CA 90095. Offers MA. *Degree requirements:* For master's, one foreign language, thesis, eleven-month internship. *Entrance requirements:* For master's, GRE General Test, bachelor's degree; minimum undergraduate GPA of 3.0 (or its equivalent if letter grade system not used); proficiency in one foreign language; portfolio; writing sample; documented practical experience; interview. Additional exam requirements/recommendations for international students: Required—TOEFL.

University of California, Riverside, Graduate Division, Department of History, Riverside, CA 92521-0102. Offers archival management (MA); historic preservation (MA); history (MA, PhD); museum curatorship (MA). Part-time programs available. Terminal master's awarded for partial completion of doctoral program. *Degree requirements:* For master's, one foreign language, comprehensive exam, internship report and oral exams, or thesis; for doctorate, 2 foreign languages, thesis/dissertation, qualifying exams. *Entrance requirements:* For master's and doctorate, GRE General Test, minimum GPA of 3.2. Additional exam requirements/recommendations for international students: Required—TOEFL (minimum score 550 paper-based; 80 iBT). Electronic applications accepted. *Expenses:* Tuition, state resident: full-time $5399. Tuition, nonresident: full-time $10,433. *Faculty research:* Native American history, United States, public history, Europe, Latin America.

University of Colorado Denver, College of Architecture and Planning, Program in Historic Preservation, Denver, CO 80217. Offers MS. *Students:* 14 full-time (11 women), 5 part-time (2 women); includes 4 minority (1 Asian, non-Hispanic/Latino; 3 Hispanic/Latino). Average age 36. 16 applicants, 88% accepted, 4 enrolled. In 2014, 7 master's awarded. *Degree requirements:* For master's, thesis, 45 credit hours. *Entrance requirements:* For master's, GRE (recommended, especially for students with an undergraduate GPA of less than 3.0), portfolio of creative work; sample of writing or work project. Additional exam requirements/recommendations for international students: Required—TOEFL (minimum score 75 iBT). *Application deadline:* For fall admission, 3/15 priority date for domestic students, 2/15 priority date for international students. Applications are processed on a rolling basis. Application fee: $50 ($75 for international students). Electronic applications accepted. *Expenses:* Expenses: Contact institution. *Financial support:* In 2014–15, 3 students received support. Fellowships, research assistantships, teaching assistantships, Federal Work-Study, institutionally sponsored loans, scholarships/grants, and traineeships available. Financial award application deadline: 4/1; financial award applicants required to submit FAFSA. *Faculty research:* Rural cultural landscapes; vernacular architecture; cultural preservation; architectural conservation, heritage, and policy. *Unit head:* Dr. Christopher Koziol, Director, 303-556-6516, E-mail: christopher.koziol@ucdenver.edu. *Application contact:* Rachael Kuroiwa, Manager of Admissions and Outreach, 303-315-2325, E-mail: rachael.kuroiwa@ucdenver.edu.
Website: http://www.ucdenver.edu/academics/colleges/ArchitecturePlanning/Academics/DegreePrograms/MSHP/Pages/MSHP.aspx

University of Delaware, College of Arts and Sciences, Department of Art Conservation, Newark, DE 19716. Offers art conservation (MS); preservation studies (PhD). *Degree requirements:* For master's, internship, portfolio, oral exam, oral presentation. *Entrance requirements:* For master's, GRE General Test, course work in chemistry, art history/anthropology and studio art; minimum of 400 hours of conservation experience. Additional exam requirements/recommendations for international students: Recommended—TOEFL. Electronic applications accepted. *Faculty research:* Emergency response cleaning techniques, degradation process, art history, artists, materials, techniques of preservation and treatment.

University of Delaware, College of Arts and Sciences, School of Public Policy and Administration, Program in Urban Affairs and Public Policy, Newark, DE 19716. Offers governance planning and management (PhD); historic preservation (MA); social and urban policy (PhD); technology, environment and society (PhD); urban affairs and public policy (MA). Part-time programs available. Terminal master's awarded for partial completion of doctoral program. *Degree requirements:* For master's, analytical paper or thesis; for doctorate, thesis/dissertation. *Entrance requirements:* For master's, GRE

General Test, minimum GPA of 3.0; for doctorate, GRE General Test, minimum GPA of 3.5. Additional exam requirements/recommendations for international students: Required—TOEFL. Electronic applications accepted. *Faculty research:* Political economy; social policy analysis; technology and society; historic preservation; urban policy.

University of Florida, Graduate School, College of Liberal Arts and Sciences, Department of History, Gainesville, FL 32611. Offers historic preservation (MA, PhD); history (MA, PhD); Jewish studies (MA); women's and gender studies (PhD); JD/MA; JD/PhD. Part-time programs available. *Faculty:* 26 full-time (9 women), 9 part-time/adjunct (5 women). *Students:* 59 full-time (21 women), 14 part-time (6 women); includes 7 minority (4 Black or African American, non-Hispanic/Latino; 3 Hispanic/Latino), 6 international. 112 applicants, 21% accepted, 11 enrolled. In 2014, 6 master's, 14 doctorates awarded. Terminal master's awarded for partial completion of doctoral program. *Degree requirements:* For master's, variable foreign language requirement, thesis optional, 30 credit hours; for doctorate, variable foreign language requirement, comprehensive exam, thesis/dissertation, 90 credit hours. *Entrance requirements:* For master's and doctorate, GRE General Test, minimum GPA of 3.0. Additional exam requirements/recommendations for international students: Required—TOEFL (minimum score 550 paper-based; 80 iBT), IELTS (minimum score 6). *Application deadline:* For fall admission, 1/1 priority date for domestic students, 1/1 for international students. Applications are processed on a rolling basis. Application fee: $30. Electronic applications accepted. *Financial support:* In 2014–15, 15 fellowships, 9 research assistantships, 44 teaching assistantships were awarded; career-related internships or fieldwork and unspecified assistantships also available. Financial award application deadline: 1/15; financial award applicants required to submit FAFSA. *Faculty research:* Latin American and Caribbean history, nineteenth century U.S. history, medieval European history, African history and Atlantic world history. *Unit head:* Ida L. Altman, PhD, Professor and Chair, 352-392-6927, Fax: 352-392-6927, E-mail: ialtman@ufl.edu. *Application contact:* Elizabeth Dale, PhD, Graduate Coordinator, 352-273-3387, Fax: 352-392-6927, E-mail: edale@ufl.edu.
Website: http://www.history.ufl.edu/

University of Georgia, College of Environment and Design, Athens, GA 30602. Offers environmental planning and design (MEPD); historic preservation (MHP); landscape architecture (MLA).

University of Hawaii at Manoa, Graduate Division, College of Arts and Humanities, Department of American Studies, Program in Historic Preservation, Honolulu, HI 96822. Offers Graduate Certificate. Part-time programs available. *Entrance requirements:* Additional exam requirements/recommendations for international students: Required—TOEFL (minimum score 600 paper-based; 100 iBT), IELTS (minimum score 7).

University of Kentucky, Graduate School, College of Design, Department of Historic Preservation, Lexington, KY 40506-0032. Offers MHP. *Degree requirements:* For master's, comprehensive exam. *Entrance requirements:* For master's, GRE General Test, minimum undergraduate GPA of 2.75. Additional exam requirements/recommendations for international students: Required—TOEFL (minimum score 550 paper-based). Electronic applications accepted.

University of Maryland, College Park, Academic Affairs, School of Architecture, Planning and Preservation, Program in Historic Preservation, College Park, MD 20742. Offers MHP, Certificate. *Degree requirements:* For Certificate, thesis. *Entrance requirements:* For master's, GRE, minimum GPA of 3.0, 3 letters of recommendation, writing sample. Additional exam requirements/recommendations for international students: Required—TOEFL. Electronic applications accepted.

University of Massachusetts Amherst, Graduate School, College of Humanities and Fine Arts, Programs in Architecture and Design, Amherst, MA 01003. Offers architecture (M Arch); design (MS); design in historic preservation (MS). Part-time programs available. *Students:* 37 full-time (17 women); includes 2 minority (both Hispanic/Latino), 15 international. Average age 29. 105 applicants, 67% accepted, 11 enrolled. In 2014, 21 master's awarded. *Degree requirements:* For master's, thesis or alternative, project. *Entrance requirements:* For master's, GRE General Test (for M Arch only), 3 letters of recommendation (M Arch only); portfolio. Additional exam requirements/recommendations for international students: Required—TOEFL (minimum score 550 paper-based; 80 iBT), IELTS (minimum score 6.5). *Application deadline:* For fall admission, 2/1 for domestic and international students. Applications are processed on a rolling basis. Application fee: $75. Electronic applications accepted. *Expenses:* Tuition, state resident: full-time $1980; part-time $110 per credit. Tuition, nonresident: full-time $14,644; part-time $414 per credit. *Required fees:* $11,417. One-time fee: $357. *Financial support:* Fellowships with full and partial tuition reimbursements, research assistantships with full and partial tuition reimbursements, teaching assistantships with full and partial tuition reimbursements, career-related internships or fieldwork, Federal Work-Study, scholarships/grants, traineeships, health care benefits, tuition waivers (full and partial), and unspecified assistantships available. Support available to part-time students. Financial award application deadline: 2/1. *Unit head:* Dr. Kathleen Lugosch, Graduate Program Director, 413-577-0943, Fax: 413-545-3929. *Application contact:* Lindsay DeSantis, Supervisor of Admissions, 413-545-0722, Fax: 413-577-0100, E-mail: gradadm@grad.umass.edu.
Website: http://www.umass.edu/architecture/

University of New Mexico, Graduate School, School of Architecture and Planning, Program in Historic Preservation and Regionalism, Albuquerque, NM 87131-2039. Offers Graduate Certificate. Part-time and evening/weekend programs available. *Faculty:* 1 (woman) part-time/adjunct. *Students:* 3 full-time (1 woman), 8 part-time (4 women); includes 6 minority (1 American Indian or Alaska Native, non-Hispanic/Latino; 1 Asian, non-Hispanic/Latino; 4 Hispanic/Latino). Average age 40. 8 applicants, 100% accepted, 5 enrolled. In 2014, 9 Graduate Certificates awarded. *Application deadline:* For fall admission, 11/1 priority date for domestic students; for spring admission, 3/1 priority date for domestic students. Application fee: $50. Electronic applications accepted. *Financial support:* In 2014–15, 1 student received support, including 1 research assistantship (averaging $7,500 per year); career-related internships or fieldwork and scholarships/grants also available. Support available to part-time students. *Unit head:* Chris Wilson, Director, 505-277-3303, Fax: 505-277-0897, E-mail: chwilson@unm.edu. *Application contact:* Elizabeth M. Rowe, Senior Academic Adviser, 505-277-1303, Fax: 505-277-0076, E-mail: erowe@unm.edu.
Website: http://saap.unm.edu/

The University of North Carolina at Greensboro, Graduate School, College of Arts and Sciences, Department of Interior Architecture, Greensboro, NC 27412-5001. Offers historic preservation (Certificate); interior architecture (MS); museum studies (Certificate). *Degree requirements:* For master's, thesis. *Entrance requirements:* For master's, GRE General Test or MAT, bachelor's degree in interior design, interview,

portfolio. Additional exam requirements/recommendations for international students: Required—TOEFL. Electronic applications accepted.

University of Oregon, Graduate School, School of Architecture and Allied Arts, Program in Historic Preservation, Eugene, OR 97403. Offers MS. *Degree requirements:* For master's, thesis, internship. *Entrance requirements:* For master's, participation in Pacific Northwest Field School. Additional exam requirements/recommendations for international students: Required—TOEFL. *Faculty research:* Vernacular architecture, Native American architecture, masonry structure and details, wood construction systems, cultural landscapes.

University of Pennsylvania, School of Design, Graduate Group in Historic Preservation, Philadelphia, PA 19104. Offers MS, Certificate. Part-time programs available. *Faculty:* 3 full-time (0 women), 1 part-time/adjunct (0 women). *Students:* 44 full-time (35 women), 2 part-time (both women); includes 10 minority (2 Black or African American, non-Hispanic/Latino; 3 Asian, non-Hispanic/Latino; 4 Hispanic/Latino; 1 Two or more races, non-Hispanic/Latino), 12 international. 54 applicants, 94% accepted, 27 enrolled. In 2014, 29 master's, 1 other advanced degree awarded. *Degree requirements:* For master's, thesis. *Entrance requirements:* For master's, GRE General Test. Additional exam requirements/recommendations for international students: Required—TOEFL, IELTS. *Application deadline:* For fall admission, 1/14 priority date for domestic and international students. Application fee: $80. Electronic applications accepted. *Financial support:* Teaching assistantships and scholarships/grants available. Financial award application deadline: 2/15; financial award applicants required to submit FAFSA. *Faculty research:* Historic building technology, conservation of building materials and archaeological sites, theory and methods of preservation planning, cultural policy, economics of preservation, historic site management, history of historic preservation. *Unit head:* Marilyn Jordan Taylor, Dean, 215-898-6520, E-mail: mjtaylor@design.upenn.edu. *Application contact:* Office of Admissions and Financial Aid, 215-898-6520, E-mail: admissions@design.upenn.edu.
Website: http://www.design.upenn.edu/historic-preservation

University of Rochester, School of Arts and Sciences, Program in Photographic Preservation and Collections Management, Rochester, NY 14627. Offers MA. Program offered jointly with George Eastman House. Part-time programs available. *Students:* 9 full-time (7 women); includes 1 minority (Asian, non-Hispanic/Latino). 25 applicants, 48% accepted, 9 enrolled. *Degree requirements:* For master's, thesis (for some programs). *Entrance requirements:* Additional exam requirements/recommendations for international students: Required—TOEFL. *Application deadline:* For fall admission, 1/1 priority date for domestic students. Application fee: $60. Electronic applications accepted. *Expenses: Tuition:* Full-time $46,150; part-time $1442 per credit hour. *Required fees:* $504. *Financial support:* Fellowships, research assistantships, teaching assistantships, and tuition waivers (partial) available. *Faculty research:* Photographic preservation, collections management, photography. *Unit head:* Joan Saab, Director, E-mail: joan.saab@rochester.edu. *Application contact:* Gretchen Briscoe, Recruiting and Marketing Manager, 585-275-5029, E-mail: graduate.admissions@rochester.edu.
Website: http://www.rochester.edu/college/ppcm

University of South Carolina, The Graduate School, College of Arts and Sciences, Department of History, Program in Public History, Columbia, SC 29208. Offers archive management (MA); historic preservation (MA); museum administration (MA); museum management (Certificate); MLIS/MA. *Degree requirements:* For master's, one foreign language, thesis, internship. *Entrance requirements:* For master's, GRE General Test, writing sample. Additional exam requirements/recommendations for international students: Required—TOEFL. Electronic applications accepted. *Faculty research:* Museum studies, historic preservation, archives administration.

The University of Texas at Austin, Graduate School, School of Architecture, Program in Historic Preservation, Austin, TX 78712-1111. Offers M Arch, MS, MSCRP.

University of Vermont, Graduate College, College of Arts and Sciences, Program in Historic Preservation, Burlington, VT 05405. Offers MS. *Entrance requirements:* For master's, GRE General Test, sample project or equivalent. Additional exam requirements/recommendations for international students: Required—TOEFL (minimum score 550 paper-based; 80 iBT). Electronic applications accepted. *Faculty research:* Architectural environment.

University of Washington, Graduate School, College of Built Environments, Interdisciplinary Program in Historic Preservation, Seattle, WA 98195. Offers Certificate. Offered in cooperation with the Departments of Architecture, Landscape Architecture, and Urban Design and Planning. Part-time programs available. Electronic applications accepted. *Faculty research:* History of the built environment, historic preservation planning, vernacular architecture, ethnic and gender issues in preservation, restoration.

University of Wisconsin–Milwaukee, Graduate School, School of Architecture and Urban Planning, Department of Architecture, Milwaukee, WI 53201-0413. Offers architecture (PhD); preservation studies (Certificate); M Arch/MUP. *Degree requirements:* For master's, comprehensive exam, thesis; for doctorate, comprehensive exam, thesis/dissertation. *Entrance requirements:* For master's, GRE General Test, portfolio. Additional exam requirements/recommendations for international students: Required—TOEFL (minimum score 600 paper-based; 100 iBT), IELTS (minimum score 7). Electronic applications accepted.

Ursuline College, School of Graduate Studies, Program in Historic Preservation, Pepper Pike, OH 44124-4398. Offers MA. Part-time programs available. *Faculty:* 1 (woman) full-time. *Students:* 1 (woman) full-time, 3 part-time (2 women). Average age 32. 4 applicants, 50% accepted. In 2014, 1 master's awarded. *Degree requirements:* For master's, thesis. *Entrance requirements:* For master's, minimum undergraduate GPA of 3.0. Additional exam requirements/recommendations for international students: Required—TOEFL (minimum score 500 paper-based). *Application deadline:* For fall admission, 8/1 priority date for domestic students. Applications are processed on a rolling basis. Application fee: $25. *Financial support:* In 2014–15, 2 students received support. Federal Work-Study available. Financial award application deadline: 3/1. *Unit head:* Dr. Bari Stith, Director, 440-646-8135, Fax: 440-684-6088, E-mail: bstith@ursuline.edu. *Application contact:* Stephanie Pratt, Graduate Admission Coordinator, 440-646-8119, Fax: 440-684-6138, E-mail: graduateadmissions@ursuline.edu.

Virginia Commonwealth University, Graduate School, College of Humanities and Sciences, Wilder School of Government and Public Affairs, Department of Urban Studies and Planning, Program in Historic Preservation Planning, Richmond, VA 23284-9005. Offers Certificate. *Entrance requirements:* Additional exam requirements/recommendations for international students: Required—TOEFL (minimum score 600 paper-based; 100 iBT); Recommended—IELTS (minimum score 6.5). Electronic applications accepted.

Landscape Architecture

Academy of Art University, Graduate Program, School of Landscape Architecture, San Francisco, CA 94105-3410. Offers MFA. Part-time programs available. Postbaccalaureate distance learning degree programs offered (no on-campus study). *Faculty:* 1 (woman) full-time, 17 part-time/adjunct (7 women). *Students:* 37 full-time (21 women), 4 part-time (1 woman), 37 international. Average age 26. 33 applicants, 100% accepted, 9 enrolled. *Degree requirements:* For master's, final review. *Entrance requirements:* For master's, statement of intent; resume; portfolio/reel; official college transcripts. *Application deadline:* Applications are processed on a rolling basis. Application fee: $100. Electronic applications accepted. *Expenses: Tuition:* Part-time $910 per unit. *Financial support:* Career-related internships or fieldwork and Federal Work-Study available. Support available to part-time students. Financial award application deadline: 8/10; financial award applicants required to submit FAFSA. *Unit head:* 800-544-ARTS, E-mail: info@academyart.edu. *Application contact:* 800-544-ARTS, E-mail: info@academyart.edu.
Website: http://www.academyart.edu/landscape-architecture-school/index.html

Arizona State University at the Tempe campus, Herberger Institute for Design and the Arts, The Design School, Tempe, AZ 85287-1605. Offers architecture (M Arch); building design/built environment (MS); design (MSD), including arts, media, and engineering, healthcare and healing environments (MSD, PhD), industrial design, interaction design, interior design, new product innovation, visual communication design; design, environment and the arts (PhD), including design, digital culture, healthcare and healing environments (MSD, PhD), history, theory, and criticism; landscape architecture (MLA); urban design (MUD); MA/MBA. *Accreditation:* NASAD. Terminal master's awarded for partial completion of doctoral program. *Degree requirements:* For master's, thesis optional, interactive Program of Study (iPOS) submitted before completing 50 percent of required credit hours; for doctorate, comprehensive exam, thesis/dissertation, interactive Program of Study (iPOS) submitted before completing 50 percent of required credit hours. *Entrance requirements:* For master's, GRE General Test, minimum GPA of 3.0 or equivalent in last 2 years of work leading to bachelor's degree, design/creative works portfolio, 3 references, statement of intent; for doctorate, GRE, master's degree in architecture, graphic design, industrial design, interior design, landscape architecture, or art history or equivalent standing; statement of purpose; 3 letters of recommendation; indication of potential faculty mentor; sample of written work. Additional exam requirements/recommendations for international students: Required—TOEFL (minimum score 600 paper-based; 100 iBT). Electronic applications accepted.

Auburn University, Graduate School, College of Architecture, Design, and Construction, Program in Landscape Architecture, Auburn University, AL 36849. Offers ML Arch. *Accreditation:* ASLA. *Faculty:* 27 full-time (10 women), 9 part-time/adjunct (1 woman). *Students:* 24 full-time (11 women), 1 (woman) part-time; includes 2 minority (1 Black or African American, non-Hispanic/Latino; 1 Asian, non-Hispanic/Latino), 8 international. Average age 28. 46 applicants, 65% accepted, 15 enrolled. In 2014, 16 master's awarded. *Entrance requirements:* For master's, 3 letters of recommendation. Application fee: $50 ($60 for international students). *Expenses:* Tuition, state resident: full-time $8586; part-time $477 per credit hour. Tuition, nonresident: full-time $25,758; part-time $1431 per credit hour. *Required fees:* $804 per semester. Tuition and fees vary according to degree level and program. *Financial support:* Applicants required to submit FAFSA. *Unit head:* Rod Barnett, Chair, 334-844-5449. *Application contact:* Dr. George Flowers, Dean of the Graduate School, 334-844-2125.

★ **Ball State University,** Graduate School, College of Architecture and Planning, Department of Landscape Architecture, Muncie, IN 47306-1099. Offers MLA. *Accreditation:* ASLA. *Faculty:* 11 full-time (5 women). *Students:* 38 full-time (22 women), 9 part-time (3 women); includes 1 minority (Two or more races, non-Hispanic/Latino), 30 international. Average age 26. 40 applicants, 68% accepted, 13 enrolled. In 2014, 6 master's awarded. *Degree requirements:* For master's, thesis. *Entrance requirements:* For master's, writing sample. Application fee: $50. *Financial support:* In 2014–15, 16 students received support, including 9 research assistantships with partial tuition reimbursements available (averaging $3,105 per year), 10 teaching assistantships with partial tuition reimbursements available (averaging $3,461 per year); unspecified assistantships also available. Financial award application deadline: 3/1. *Unit head:* Jody Rosenblatt, Chairperson, 765-285-1971, Fax: 765-285-1983, E-mail: jrnaderi@bsu.edu. *Application contact:* Dr. Joseph Blalock, Associate Professor, 765-285-4258, E-mail: jblalock@bsu.edu.
Website: http://www.bsu.edu/cap/landscape/landscape.html/

See Display on page 108 and Close-Up on page 135.

Bastyr University, School of Natural Health Arts and Sciences, Kenmore, WA 98028-4966. Offers counseling psychology (MA); holistic landscape design (Certificate); midwifery (MS); nutrition (MS); nutrition and clinical health psychology (MS). *Accreditation:* AND. Part-time programs available. *Students:* 373 full-time (334 women), 39 part-time (37 women); includes 71 minority (11 Black or African American, non-Hispanic/Latino; 1 American Indian or Alaska Native, non-Hispanic/Latino; 24 Asian, non-Hispanic/Latino; 14 Hispanic/Latino; 21 Two or more races, non-Hispanic/Latino), 20 international. Average age 30. *Degree requirements:* For master's, thesis optional. *Entrance requirements:* For master's, 1-2 years' basic sciences course work (depending on program). Additional exam requirements/recommendations for international students: Required—TOEFL (minimum score 550 paper-based; 79 iBT). *Application deadline:* For fall admission, 3/15 priority date for domestic and international students. Applications are processed on a rolling basis. Application fee: $75. *Financial support:* In 2014–15, 47 students received support. Career-related internships or fieldwork, Federal Work-Study, and scholarships/grants available. Support available to part-time students. Financial award application deadline: 4/15; financial award applicants required to submit FAFSA. *Faculty research:* Whole-food nutrition for type 2 diabetes; meditation in end-of-life care; stress management; Qi Gong, Tai Chi and yoga for older adults; Echinacea and immunology. *Unit head:* Dr. Timothy Callahan, Vice President and Provost, 425-602-3110, Fax: 425-823-6222. *Application contact:* Admissions Office, 425-602-3330, Fax: 425-602-3090, E-mail: admissions@bastyr.edu.
Website: http://www.bastyr.edu/academics/schools-departments/school-natural-health-arts-sciences

Boston Architectural College, Graduate Programs, Boston, MA 02115-2795. Offers architecture (M Arch); historic preservation (MDS); interior design (MID); landscape architecture (MLA); sustainable design (MDS). *Accreditation:* CIDA. *Degree requirements:* For master's, thesis. *Entrance requirements:* For master's, portfolio (recommended). Electronic applications accepted.

California State Polytechnic University, Pomona, Program in Landscape Architecture, Pomona, CA 91768-2557. Offers M Land Arch. *Accreditation:* ASLA. Part-time programs available. *Students:* 36 full-time (18 women), 2 part-time (both women); includes 7 minority (2 Asian, non-Hispanic/Latino; 4 Hispanic/Latino; 1 Two or more races, non-Hispanic/Latino), 10 international. Average age 30. 46 applicants, 28% accepted, 11 enrolled. In 2014, 9 master's awarded. *Degree requirements:* For master's, thesis or alternative. *Application deadline:* For fall admission, 5/1 priority date for domestic students; for winter admission, 10/15 priority date for domestic students; for spring admission, 1/20 priority date for domestic students. Applications are processed on a rolling basis. Application fee: $55. Electronic applications accepted. *Expenses:* Tuition, state resident: full-time $6738. Tuition, nonresident: full-time $12,300. *Required fees:* $1400. *Financial support:* Career-related internships or fieldwork, Federal Work-Study, and institutionally sponsored loans available. Support available to part-time students. Financial award application deadline: 3/2; financial award applicants required to submit FAFSA. *Unit head:* Gerald O. Taylor, Graduate Coordinator, 909-869-6891, Fax: 909-869-4460, E-mail: jotaylor@cpp.edu.
Website: http://www.cpp.edu/~la/mla.html

Chatham University, Program in Landscape Architecture, Pittsburgh, PA 15232-2826. Offers landscape architecture (ML Arch); landscape design and development (MA). *Accreditation:* ASLA. Part-time and evening/weekend programs available. *Faculty:* 2 full-time (1 woman), 3 part-time/adjunct (1 woman). *Students:* 7 full-time (3 women), 2 part-time (both women); includes 1 minority (Black or African American, non-Hispanic/Latino), 4 international. Average age 30. 16 applicants, 50% accepted. In 2014, 1 master's awarded. *Degree requirements:* For master's, thesis, capstone project. *Entrance requirements:* For master's, portfolio. Additional exam requirements/recommendations for international students: Required—TOEFL (minimum score 600 paper-based; 100 iBT), IELTS (minimum score 7), TWE. *Application deadline:* For fall admission, 4/1 priority date for domestic and international students; for spring admission, 11/1 priority date for domestic students, 10/1 priority date for international students. Applications are processed on a rolling basis. Application fee: $45. Electronic applications accepted. Application fee is waived when completed online. *Expenses: Tuition:* Full-time $15,318; part-time $851 per credit hour. *Required fees:* $440; $24 per credit hour. Tuition and fees vary according to course load, program and reciprocity agreements. *Financial support:* Career-related internships or fieldwork available. Financial award applicants required to submit FAFSA. *Faculty research:* Sustainability. *Unit head:* Dr. Thelma Lazo-Flores, Director, 412-365-2977, E-mail: tlazoflores@chatham.edu. *Application contact:* Katie Noel, Assistant Director of Graduate Admission, 412-365-2758, Fax: 412-365-1609, E-mail: gradadmissions@chatham.edu.
Website: http://www.chatham.edu/departments/artdesign/graduate/landscapearch/index.cfm

City College of the City University of New York, Graduate School, School of Architecture and Environmental Studies, New York, NY 10031-9198. Offers architecture (M Arch); landscape architecture (MLA); urban design (MUP). Part-time programs available. *Degree requirements:* For master's, thesis. *Entrance requirements:* For master's, portfolio, professional degree in architecture or equivalent. Additional exam requirements/recommendations for international students: Required—TOEFL (minimum score 550 paper-based).

Clemson University, Graduate School, College of Architecture, Arts, and Humanities, Department of Planning, Development and Preservation, Clemson, SC 29634. Offers city and regional planning (MCRP), including developmental planning; historic preservation (MS); landscape architecture (MLA); real estate development (MRED). *Accreditation:* ACSP. *Faculty:* 20 full-time (5 women), 5 part-time/adjunct (2 women). *Students:* 103 full-time (56 women), 1 (woman) part-time; includes 9 minority (1 Black or African American, non-Hispanic/Latino; 2 Asian, non-Hispanic/Latino; 4 Hispanic/Latino; 2 Two or more races, non-Hispanic/Latino), 26 international. Average age 25. 214 applicants, 79% accepted, 60 enrolled. In 2014, 52 master's awarded. *Degree requirements:* For master's, departmental paper or thesis. *Entrance requirements:* For master's, GRE General Test. Additional exam requirements/recommendations for international students: Required—TOEFL. *Application deadline:* For fall admission, 2/1 priority date for domestic and international students. Applications are processed on a rolling basis. Application fee: $70 ($80 for international students). Electronic applications accepted. *Financial support:* In 2014–15, 46 students received support, including 70 fellowships with full and partial tuition reimbursements available (averaging $2,693 per year), 12 research assistantships with partial tuition reimbursements available (averaging $7,337 per year); teaching assistantships with partial tuition reimbursements available, career-related internships or fieldwork, institutionally sponsored loans, scholarships/grants, health care benefits, and unspecified assistantships also available. Support available to part-time students. Financial award application deadline: 4/15; financial award applicants required to submit FAFSA. *Faculty research:* Coastal planning, regional economic development, health care access. *Total annual research expenditures:* $118,757. *Unit head:* Dr. Elaine M. Worzala, Chair, 864-656-3657, Fax: 864-656-7519, E-mail: eworzal@clemson.edu. *Application contact:* Dr. Terry Farris, Coordinator, 864-656-3903, Fax: 864-656-7519, E-mail: jfarris@clemson.edu.
Website: http://www.clemson.edu/caah/pdp/

Clemson University, Graduate School, College of Architecture, Arts, and Humanities, Program in Landscape Architecture, Clemson, SC 29634. Offers MLA. *Accreditation:* ASLA. *Students:* 22 full-time (16 women); includes 1 minority (Asian, non-Hispanic/Latino), 15 international. Average age 24. 45 applicants, 60% accepted, 6 enrolled. In 2014, 11 master's awarded. *Entrance requirements:* For master's, GRE General Test. Additional exam requirements/recommendations for international students: Required—TOEFL. *Application deadline:* For fall admission, 2/15 for domestic students, 4/15 for international students. Applications are processed on a rolling basis. Application fee: $70 ($80 for international students). Electronic applications accepted. *Financial support:* In 2014–15, 4 students received support, including 2 fellowships with partial tuition reimbursements available (averaging $1,500 per year), 4 research assistantships with partial tuition reimbursements available (averaging $8,812 per year); teaching assistantships with partial tuition reimbursements available, career-related internships or fieldwork, institutionally sponsored loans, scholarships/grants, health care benefits, and unspecified assistantships also available. Support available to part-time students. *Unit head:* Dr. Elaine M. Worzala, Chair, 864-656-3657, Fax: 864-656-7519, E-mail: eworzal@clemson.edu. *Application contact:* Dr. Umit Yilmaz, Coordinator, 864-656-7349, Fax: 864-656-7519, E-mail: uyilmaz@clemson.edu.
Website: http://www.clemson.edu/caah/la/

Colorado State University, Graduate School, College of Agricultural Sciences, Department of Horticulture and Landscape Architecture, Fort Collins, CO 80523-1173. Offers horticulture (MS, PhD); landscape architecture (MLA). Part-time programs available. *Faculty:* 16 full-time (4 women), 1 part-time/adjunct (0 women). *Students:* 23 full-time (11 women), 22 part-time (9 women); includes 5 minority (1 American Indian or

Alaska Native, non-Hispanic/Latino; 3 Hispanic/Latino; 1 Two or more races, non-Hispanic/Latino), 12 international. Average age 34. 30 applicants, 50% accepted, 8 enrolled. In 2014, 11 master's, 3 doctorates awarded. *Degree requirements:* For master's, thesis (for some programs); for doctorate, comprehensive exam, thesis/dissertation. *Entrance requirements:* For master's, GRE General Test (minimum score in upper 50th percentile, 1100 verbal and quantitative), minimum GPA of 3.0, letters of reference, related bachelor's degree or experience, transcript, resume, statement of purpose; for doctorate, GRE General Test (minimum score in upper 50th percentile and combined minimum score of 1100 for the Verbal and Quantitative sections), minimum GPA of 3.0, letters of reference, statement of purpose, related bachelor's degree or experience, resume, transcripts. Additional exam requirements/recommendations for international students: Required—TOEFL (minimum score 550 paper-based; 80 iBT). *Application deadline:* For fall admission, 1/15 for domestic and international students; for spring admission, 9/1 for domestic and international students. Applications are processed on a rolling basis. Application fee: $50. Electronic applications accepted. *Expenses:* Tuition, state resident: full-time $9348; part-time $519 per credit. Tuition, nonresident: full-time $22,916; part-time $1273 per credit. *Required fees:* $1584. *Financial support:* In 2014–15, 17 students received support, including 9 research assistantships with partial tuition reimbursements available (averaging $13,719 per year), 8 teaching assistantships with partial tuition reimbursements available (averaging $10,412 per year); fellowships, scholarships/grants, and unspecified assistantships also available. Financial award applicants required to submit FAFSA. *Faculty research:* Antioxidants in food crops, environmental physiology, water conservation, tissue culture, rhizosphere biology, cancer prevention through dietary intervention. *Total annual research expenditures:* $4.6 million. *Unit head:* Dr. Stephen J. Wallner, Head, 970-491-7018, Fax: 970-491-7745, E-mail: stephen.wallner@colostate.edu. *Application contact:* Kathi Nietfeld, Coordinator, 970-491-7018, Fax: 970-491-7745, E-mail: kathi.nietfeld@colostate.edu.
Website: http://hortla.agsci.colostate.edu

Columbia University, School of Continuing Education, Program in Landscape Design, New York, NY 10027. Offers MS. Part-time programs available. *Entrance requirements:* For master's, minimum undergraduate GPA of 3.0. Additional exam requirements/recommendations for international students: Required—American Language Program placement test.

The Conway School, Graduate Program in Sustainable Landscape Planning and Design, Conway, MA 01341-0179. Offers landscape design (MA). *Degree requirements:* For master's, projects. *Faculty research:* Restoration of native plant communities; integration of humanities, environment, and design.

Cornell University, Graduate School, Graduate Fields of Agriculture and Life Sciences and Graduate Fields of Architecture, Art and Planning, Field of Landscape Architecture, Ithaca, NY 14853-0001. Offers MLA, MPS. *Accreditation:* ASLA. *Degree requirements:* For master's, project or thesis. *Entrance requirements:* For master's, GRE General Test (recommended), portfolio, 2 letters of recommendation. Additional exam requirements/recommendations for international students: Required—TOEFL (minimum score 550 paper-based; 77 iBT). Electronic applications accepted. *Faculty research:* Urban horticulture and landscape design, urban design research, cultural landscape history, women in landscape architecture, landscape design language, Japanese landscape architecture.

Florida Agricultural and Mechanical University, Division of Graduate Studies, Research, and Continuing Education, School of Architecture, Tallahassee, FL 32307-3200. Offers architectural studies (MS Arch); architecture (professional) (M Arch); landscape architecture (MLA). Part-time programs available. *Degree requirements:* For master's, thesis. *Entrance requirements:* For master's, GRE General Test, minimum GPA of 3.0, portfolio. Additional exam requirements/recommendations for international students: Required—TOEFL (minimum score 550 paper-based). *Faculty research:* Environmental technology, post-occupancy evaluation, building economics, design methods, computer-aided design.

Florida International University, College of Architecture and the Arts, School of Architecture, Department of Landscape Architecture, Miami, FL 33199. Offers MLA. Part-time programs available. *Entrance requirements:* For master's, GRE or minimum GPA of 3.0 in upper-level undergraduate work, portfolio. Additional exam requirements/recommendations for international students: Required—TOEFL (minimum score 550 paper-based; 80 iBT). Electronic applications accepted.

Harvard University, Graduate School of Arts and Sciences, Committee on Architecture, Landscape Architecture, and Urban Planning, Cambridge, MA 02138. Offers architecture (PhD); landscape architecture (PhD); urban planning (PhD). *Degree requirements:* For doctorate, one foreign language, thesis/dissertation, oral exam. *Entrance requirements:* For doctorate, GRE General Test. Additional exam requirements/recommendations for international students: Required—TOEFL.

Harvard University, Graduate School of Design, Department of Landscape Architecture, Cambridge, MA 02138. Offers MLA. *Accreditation:* ASLA. *Entrance requirements:* For master's, GRE General Test. Additional exam requirements/recommendations for international students: Required—TOEFL (minimum score 600 paper-based; 104 iBT). Electronic applications accepted.

Illinois Institute of Technology, Graduate College, College of Architecture, Chicago, IL 60616. Offers M Arch, MLA, MS Arch, PhD, MLA/M Arch. *Accreditation:* ASLA. Part-time programs available. *Faculty:* 36 full-time (9 women), 69 part-time/adjunct (19 women). *Students:* 160 full-time (67 women), 16 part-time (9 women); includes 7 minority (1 Black or African American, non-Hispanic/Latino; 2 Asian, non-Hispanic/Latino; 3 Hispanic/Latino; 1 Two or more races, non-Hispanic/Latino), 100 international. Average age 28. 481 applicants, 62% accepted, 55 enrolled. In 2014, 70 master's, 2 doctorates awarded. Terminal master's awarded for partial completion of doctoral program. *Degree requirements:* For master's, comprehensive exam (for some programs), thesis (for some programs); for doctorate, comprehensive exam, thesis/dissertation. *Entrance requirements:* For master's, GRE General Test (minimum score 292 Quantitative and Verbal, 2.5 Analytical Writing), minimum college GPA of 3.0, official transcripts, portfolio, 3 letters of recommendation, professional statement;; for doctorate, GRE General Test (minimum score 900 Quantitative and Verbal, 2.5 Analytical Writing), minimum GPA of 3.5, official transcripts, portfolio, 3 letters of recommendation, professional statement. Additional exam requirements/recommendations for international students: Required—TOEFL (minimum score 550 paper-based; 80 iBT). *Application deadline:* For fall admission, 4/15 for domestic and international students; for spring admission, 11/15 for domestic and international students. Applications are processed on a rolling basis. Application fee: $50. Electronic applications accepted. *Expenses: Tuition:* Full-time $22,500; part-time $1250 per credit hour. *Required fees:* $30 per course. $260 per semester. One-time fee: $235. Tuition and fees vary according to course load and program. *Financial support:* Fellowships with full and partial tuition reimbursements, research assistantships, teaching assistantships with full and partial tuition reimbursements, career-related internships or fieldwork, Federal Work-Study, institutionally sponsored loans, scholarships/grants, health care benefits, tuition waivers (partial), and unspecified assistantships available. Support available to part-time students. Financial award applicants required to submit FAFSA. *Faculty research:* Sustainable design and efficiency; the influence of climate and environment on building form; emerging urbanisms; computer applications (such as 3-D modeling); the design, planning and structure of high-rise buildings. *Unit head:* Wiel Arets, Dean, 312-567-3230, Fax: 312-567-5820, E-mail: wiel.arets@iit.edu. *Application contact:* Rishab Malhotra, Director of Graduate and Professional Admission, 866-472-3448, Fax: 312-567-3138, E-mail: inquiry.grad@iit.edu.
Website: http://www.iit.edu/arch/

Iowa State University of Science and Technology, Department of Landscape Architecture, Ames, IA 50011. Offers MLA, MCRP/MLA. *Accreditation:* ASLA. Part-time programs available. *Degree requirements:* For master's, thesis. *Entrance requirements:* For master's, GRE (highly recommended), portfolio. Additional exam requirements/recommendations for international students: Required—TOEFL (minimum score 600 paper-based; 79 iBT), IELTS (minimum score 7). Electronic applications accepted. *Faculty research:* Landscape ecology, geographic information systems, landscape perception, historic preservation, resource management, design.

Kansas State University, Graduate School, College of Architecture, Planning and Design, Department of Landscape Architecture and Regional and Community Planning, Manhattan, KS 66506. Offers community development (MS); landscape architecture (MLA); regional and community planning (MRCP). *Accreditation:* ASLA. Part-time programs available. *Faculty:* 17 full-time (6 women), 1 (woman) part-time/adjunct. *Students:* 50 full-time (25 women), 25 part-time (13 women); includes 11 minority (4 Black or African American, non-Hispanic/Latino; 7 Hispanic/Latino), 3 international. Average age 24. 53 applicants, 43% accepted, 21 enrolled. In 2014, 38 master's awarded. *Degree requirements:* For master's, thesis, residency, oral exam. *Entrance requirements:* For master's, portfolio. Additional exam requirements/recommendations for international students: Required—TOEFL (minimum score 600 paper-based). *Application deadline:* For fall admission, 2/1 priority date for domestic and international students; for spring admission, 8/1 priority date for domestic and international students. Applications are processed on a rolling basis. Application fee: $80. Electronic applications accepted. *Financial support:* In 2014–15, 2 research assistantships (averaging $9,500 per year), 10 teaching assistantships with full tuition reimbursements (averaging $7,366 per year) were awarded; fellowships, career-related internships or fieldwork, Federal Work-Study, institutionally sponsored loans, and scholarships/grants also available. Support available to part-time students. Financial award application deadline: 3/15; financial award applicants required to submit FAFSA. *Faculty research:* Community planning and design, design and planning theory, geospatial technology infrastructure, watershed restoration, landscape ecology. *Total annual research expenditures:* $110,033. *Unit head:* Prof. Stephanie Rolley, Head, 785-532-5961, Fax: 785-532-6722, E-mail: srolley@ksu.edu. *Application contact:* Rachel Robillard, Application Contact, 785-532-5961, Fax: 785-532-6722, E-mail: rjack@ksu.edu.
Website: http://apdesign.k-state.edu/larcp/

Louisiana State University and Agricultural & Mechanical College, Graduate School, College of Art and Design, School of Landscape Architecture, Baton Rouge, LA 70803. Offers MLA. *Accreditation:* ASLA. *Faculty:* 11 full-time (3 women). *Students:* 48 full-time (34 women); includes 3 minority (2 Black or African American, non-Hispanic/Latino; 1 Asian, non-Hispanic/Latino), 34 international. Average age 26. 82 applicants, 76% accepted, 22 enrolled. In 2014, 20 master's awarded. *Degree requirements:* For master's, thesis. *Entrance requirements:* For master's, GRE General Test, minimum GPA of 3.0. Additional exam requirements/recommendations for international students: Required—TOEFL (minimum score 550 paper-based; 79 IBT), IELTS (minimum score 6.5), or PTE (minimum score 59). *Application deadline:* For fall admission, 1/1 priority date for domestic students, 5/15 for international students; for spring admission, 10/15 for domestic and international students; for summer admission, 5/15 for domestic and international students. Applications are processed on a rolling basis. Application fee: $50 ($70 for international students). Electronic applications accepted. *Financial support:* In 2014–15, 25 students received support, including 6 research assistantships with full and partial tuition reimbursements available (averaging $8,918 per year), 13 teaching assistantships (averaging $6,300 per year); fellowships, career-related internships or fieldwork, Federal Work-Study, institutionally sponsored loans, health care benefits, and unspecified assistantships also available. Financial award application deadline: 7/1; financial award applicants required to submit FAFSA. *Faculty research:* Digital representation, cultural landscapes, urban infrastructure, community design. *Total annual research expenditures:* $32,550. *Unit head:* Prof. Bradley Cantrell, Director, 225-578-1434, Fax: 225-578-1445, E-mail: cantrell@lsu.edu.
Website: http://landscape.lsu.edu/

Mississippi State University, College of Agriculture and Life Sciences, Department of Landscape Architecture, Mississippi State, MS 39762. Offers MLA. *Accreditation:* ASLA. Part-time programs available. *Faculty:* 8 full-time (3 women). *Students:* 18 full-time (9 women), 6 part-time (1 woman); includes 1 minority (Hispanic/Latino), 12 international. Average age 30. 15 applicants, 53% accepted, 4 enrolled. In 2014, 5 master's awarded. *Degree requirements:* For master's, thesis. *Entrance requirements:* For master's, GRE or minimum GPA of 3.0 in upper-division major emphasis courses from accredited university, minimum GPA of 2.8 on bachelor's degree. Additional exam requirements/recommendations for international students: Required—TOEFL (minimum score 600 paper-based; 100 iBT); Recommended—IELTS (minimum score 7.5). *Application deadline:* For fall admission, 7/1 for domestic students, 5/1 for international students; for spring admission, 10/1 for domestic students, 9/1 for international students. Applications are processed on a rolling basis. Application fee: $60. Electronic applications accepted. *Expenses:* Tuition, state resident: full-time $7140; part-time $783 per credit hour. Tuition, nonresident: full-time $18,478; part-time $2043 per credit hour. *Financial support:* In 2014–15, 2 research assistantships (averaging $16,360 per year), 4 teaching assistantships with full and partial tuition reimbursements (averaging $7,120 per year) were awarded; Federal Work-Study, institutionally sponsored loans, tuition waivers (partial), and unspecified assistantships also available. Financial award application deadline: 4/1; financial award applicants required to submit FAFSA. *Faculty research:* Design pedagogy, low impact development, conservation planning, wildlife/urban interfacing planning, sustainable communities, watershed planning, historical landscapes, decision support system development, Center for Sustainable Design. *Unit head:* Sadik C. Artunc, Professor and Head, 662-325-4554, Fax: 662-325-7893, E-mail: sartunc@lalc.msstate.edu. *Application contact:* Dr. Michael Seymour, Associate Professor and Graduate Coordinator, 662-325-7897, Fax: 662-325-7893, E-mail: ms641@msstate.edu.
Website: http://www.lalc.msstate.edu

Morgan State University, School of Graduate Studies, Institute of Architecture and Planning, Program in Landscape Architecture, Baltimore, MD 21251. Offers MLA. *Accreditation:* ASLA. *Degree requirements:* For master's, thesis. *Entrance requirements:* Additional exam requirements/recommendations for international students: Required—TOEFL (minimum score 550 paper-based). *Faculty research:* Philosophy and design, urban design, design history and theory, computer-aided design and community design.

North Carolina State University, Graduate School, College of Design, Department of Landscape Architecture, Raleigh, NC 27695. Offers MLA. *Accreditation:* ASLA. *Degree requirements:* For master's, thesis optional, oral exam, project. *Entrance*

requirements: For master's, GRE General Test (recommended), portfolio. Electronic applications accepted. *Faculty research:* Community development and co-operative engagement, landscape planning and design.

The Ohio State University, Graduate School, College of Engineering, Austin E. Knowlton School of Architecture, Columbus, OH 43210. Offers architecture (M Arch); city and regional planning (MCRP, PhD); landscape architecture (M Land Arch). *Accreditation:* ACSP; ASLA. *Faculty:* 33. *Students:* 187 full-time (83 women), 6 part-time (1 woman); includes 22 minority (5 Black or African American, non-Hispanic/Latino; 1 American Indian or Alaska Native, non-Hispanic/Latino; 5 Asian, non-Hispanic/Latino; 10 Hispanic/Latino; 1 Two or more races, non-Hispanic/Latino), 41 international. Average age 26. In 2014, 51 master's, 2 doctorates awarded. *Degree requirements:* For doctorate, thesis/dissertation. *Entrance requirements:* For master's, GRE or GMAT (city and regional planning), portfolio (for architecture and landscape architecture); for doctorate, GRE or GMAT (city and regional planning), example of research or written work. Additional exam requirements/recommendations for international students: Required—TOEFL (minimum score 600 paper-based; 100 iBT), Michigan English Language Assessment Battery (minimum score 86); Recommended—IELTS (minimum score 8). *Application deadline:* For fall admission, 1/1 priority date for domestic students, 12/1 priority date for international students; for winter admission, 12/1 for domestic students, 11/1 for international students; for spring admission, 12/1 for domestic students, 11/1 for international students; for summer admission, 4/1 for domestic students, 5/30 for international students. Applications are processed on a rolling basis. Application fee: $60 ($70 for international students). Electronic applications accepted. *Financial support:* Fellowships with tuition reimbursements, research assistantships with tuition reimbursements, Federal Work-Study, institutionally sponsored loans, and unspecified assistantships available. Support available to part-time students. *Unit head:* Michael B. Cadwell, Director and Walter H. Kidd Professor, 614-292-3174, E-mail: cadwell.1@osu.edu. *Application contact:* Graduate and Professional Admissions, 614-292-9444, Fax: 614-292-3895, E-mail: gpadmissions@osu.edu.
Website: http://knowlton.osu.edu/

Oklahoma State University, College of Agricultural Science and Natural Resources, Department of Horticulture and Landscape Architecture, Stillwater, OK 74078. Offers crop science (PhD); environmental science (PhD); horticulture (M Ag, MS); plant science (PhD). *Faculty:* 17 full-time (4 women), 4 part-time/adjunct (0 women). *Students:* 3 full-time (2 women), 9 part-time (4 women); includes 1 minority (Asian, non-Hispanic/Latino), 6 international. Average age 29. 9 applicants, 22% accepted, 2 enrolled. In 2014, 3 master's awarded. *Degree requirements:* For master's, thesis (for some programs); for doctorate, comprehensive exam, thesis/dissertation. *Entrance requirements:* For master's and doctorate, GRE or GMAT. Additional exam requirements/recommendations for international students: Required—TOEFL (minimum score 550 paper-based; 79 iBT). *Application deadline:* For fall admission, 3/1 priority date for international students; for spring admission, 8/1 priority date for international students. Applications are processed on a rolling basis. Application fee: $40 ($75 for international students). Electronic applications accepted. *Expenses:* Tuition, state resident: full-time $4488; part-time $187 per credit hour. Tuition, nonresident: full-time $18,360; part-time $765 per credit hour. *Required fees:* $2413; $100.55 per credit hour. Tuition and fees vary according to campus/location. *Financial support:* In 2014–15, 8 research assistantships (averaging $14,400 per year), 2 teaching assistantships (averaging $18,702 per year) were awarded; career-related internships or fieldwork, Federal Work-Study, scholarships/grants, health care benefits, tuition waivers (partial), and unspecified assistantships also available. Support available to part-time students. Financial award application deadline: 3/1; financial award applicants required to submit FAFSA. *Faculty research:* Stress and postharvest physiology; water utilization and runoff; integrated pest management (IPM) systems and nursery, turf, floriculture, vegetable, net and fruit produces and natural resources, food extraction, and processing; public garden management. *Unit head:* Dr. Janet Cole, Interim Department Head, 405-744-5414, Fax: 405-744-9709. *Application contact:* Dr. Sheryl Tucker, Dean, 405-744-7099, Fax: 405-744-0355, E-mail: gradi@okstate.edu.
Website: http://www.hortla.okstate.edu/

Penn State University Park, Graduate School, College of Arts and Architecture, Stuckeman School of Architecture and Landscape Architecture, University Park, PA 16802. Offers architecture (M Arch, PhD); landscape architecture (MLA, MS). *Accreditation:* ASLA. *Unit head:* Dr. Barbara O. Korner, Dean, 814-865-2592, Fax: 814-865-2018, E-mail: bok2@psu.edu. *Application contact:* Lori A. Stania, Director, Graduate Student Services, 814-867-5278, Fax: 814-863-4627, E-mail: gswww@psu.edu.
Website: https://stuckeman.psu.edu/

Polytechnic University of Puerto Rico, Graduate School, Hato Rey, PR 00919. Offers business administration (MBA), including computer information systems, general management, management of information systems, management of international enterprises; civil engineering (ME, MS); computer engineering (ME, MS); computer science (MCS, MS); electrical engineering (ME, MS); engineering management (MEM); environmental management (MEM); landscape architecture (M Land Arch); manufacturing competitiveness (MMC, MS); manufacturing engineering (ME, MS); mechanical engineering (M Mech E). Part-time and evening/weekend programs available. *Entrance requirements:* For master's, 3 letters of recommendation.

Pontificia Universidad Catolica Madre y Maestra, Graduate School, Faculty of Sciences and Humanities, Santiago, Dominican Republic. Offers architecture (M Arch), including architecture of interiors, architecture of tourist lodgings, landscaping; early childhood education (M Ed).

Rhode Island School of Design, Graduate Studies, Division of Architecture and Design, Department of Landscape Architecture, Providence, RI 02903-2784. Offers MLA. *Accreditation:* ASLA. *Faculty:* 13 full-time (7 women), 26 part-time/adjunct (10 women). *Students:* 57 full-time (40 women); includes 4 minority (2 Asian, non-Hispanic/Latino; 1 Hispanic/Latino; 1 Two or more races, non-Hispanic/Latino), 42 international. Average age 24. 124 applicants, 65% accepted, 34 enrolled. In 2014, 15 master's awarded. *Degree requirements:* For master's, thesis, exhibit. *Entrance requirements:* For master's, portfolio, statement of purpose, 3 letters of recommendation. Additional exam requirements/recommendations for international students: Required—TOEFL (minimum score 580 paper-based; 93 iBT). *Application deadline:* For fall admission, 2/1 for domestic students, 1/1 for international students. Application fee: $60. *Expenses:* Expenses: $44,594. *Financial support:* Fellowships, teaching assistantships, career-related internships or fieldwork, Federal Work-Study, institutionally sponsored loans, scholarships/grants, and unspecified assistantships available. Financial award application deadline: 2/15; financial award applicants required to submit FAFSA. *Unit head:* Scheri Fultineer, Department Head and Graduate Program Director, 401-454-6286, Fax: 401-454-6299, E-mail: sfultine@risd.edu. *Application contact:* Molly Pettengil, Director of Admissions, 401-454-6312, Fax: 401-454-6309, E-mail: mpetteng@risd.edu.
Website: http://www.risd.edu/academics/landscape-architecture/

State University of New York College of Environmental Science and Forestry, Department of Landscape Architecture, Syracuse, NY 13210-2779. Offers community design and planning (MLA, MS); cultural landscape studies and conservation (MLA, MS); landscape and urban ecology (MLA, MS). *Accreditation:* ASLA (one or more programs are accredited). *Degree requirements:* For master's, comprehensive exam (for some programs), thesis (for some programs). *Entrance requirements:* For master's, GRE General Test, minimum GPA of 3.0. Additional exam requirements/recommendations for international students: Required—TOEFL (minimum score 550 paper-based; 80 iBT), IELTS (minimum score 6), or STEP Aiken (grade 1). *Faculty research:* Site analysis and design, city and regional planning, community environments.

Temple University, School of Environmental Design, Department of Landscape Architecture and Horticulture, Ambler, PA 19002. Offers landscape architecture (ML Arch), including ecological restoration. *Accreditation:* ASLA. Part-time programs available. *Faculty:* 7 full-time (4 women), 10 part-time/adjunct (4 women). *Students:* 27 full-time (16 women), 10 part-time (7 women); includes 2 minority (1 Hispanic/Latino; 1 Native Hawaiian or other Pacific Islander, non-Hispanic/Latino), 4 international. 22 applicants, 64% accepted, 9 enrolled. In 2014, 10 master's awarded. *Entrance requirements:* For master's, GRE or GMAT, 2 letters of recommendation, minimum undergraduate GPA of 3.0, statement of goals. Additional exam requirements/recommendations for international students: Required—TOEFL (minimum score 550 paper-based; 79 iBT). *Application deadline:* For fall admission, 7/1 for domestic students, 12/15 for international students; for spring admission, 11/1 for domestic students, 8/1 for international students. Applications are processed on a rolling basis. Application fee: $60. *Expenses:* Tuition, state resident: full-time $14,490; part-time $805 per credit hour. Tuition, nonresident: full-time $19,850; part-time $1103 per credit hour. *Required fees:* $690. Full-time tuition and fees vary according to class time, course load, degree level, campus/location and program. *Financial support:* In 2014–15, 8 students received support. Application deadline: 1/15; applicants required to submit FAFSA. *Faculty research:* Seasonal landscape performance, landscape performance, green urban schoolyards, intersection of landscape arch practice and research, community engagement and service. *Unit head:* Pauline Hurley-Kurtz, Chair, 267-468-8173, Fax: 267-468-8188, E-mail: phurleyk@temple.edu.
Website: http://www.ambler.temple.edu/la-hort/default.html

Texas A&M University, College of Architecture, Department of Landscape Architecture and Urban Planning, College Station, TX 77843. Offers land and property development (MLPD); landscape architecture (MLA); urban and regional planning (MUP); urban and regional science (PhD). *Accreditation:* ACSP (one or more programs are accredited); ASLA (one or more programs are accredited). *Faculty:* 28. *Students:* 157 full-time (80 women), 20 part-time (10 women); includes 26 minority (9 Black or African American, non-Hispanic/Latino; 4 Asian, non-Hispanic/Latino; 13 Hispanic/Latino), 105 international. Average age 29. 247 applicants, 63% accepted, 70 enrolled. In 2014, 54 master's, 7 doctorates awarded. Terminal master's awarded for partial completion of doctoral program. *Degree requirements:* For master's, thesis optional, professional internship; for doctorate, comprehensive exam, thesis/dissertation, seminar. *Entrance requirements:* For master's, GMAT or GRE General Test, portfolio (MLA), minimum GPA of 3.0; for doctorate, GMAT or GRE General Test. Additional exam requirements/recommendations for international students: Required—TOEFL. *Application deadline:* For fall admission, 12/1 priority date for domestic and international students; for spring admission, 8/1 for domestic students. Applications are processed on a rolling basis. Application fee: $50 ($90 for international students). Electronic applications accepted. *Expenses:* Tuition, state resident: full-time $4078; part-time $226.55 per credit hour. Tuition, nonresident: full-time $10,594; part-time $577.55 per credit hour. *Required fees:* $2813; $237.70 per credit hour. $278.50 per semester. Tuition and fees vary according to degree level and student level. *Financial support:* In 2014–15, 135 students received support, including 3 fellowships with full and partial tuition reimbursements available (averaging $20,750 per year), 41 research assistantships with full and partial tuition reimbursements available (averaging $5,280 per year), 11 teaching assistantships with full and partial tuition reimbursements available (averaging $6,281 per year); career-related internships or fieldwork, institutionally sponsored loans, scholarships/grants, traineeships, health care benefits, tuition waivers (full and partial), and unspecified assistantships also available. Support available to part-time students. Financial award application deadline: 4/1; financial award applicants required to submit FAFSA. *Faculty research:* Erosion control/water quality, geographic information systems/spatial information technology, transport hazards, international sustainable development. *Unit head:* Dr. Forster Ndubisi, Head, 979-845-1019, Fax: 979-862-1784. *Application contact:* Thena Morris, Administrative Assistant, 979-845-6582, Fax: 979-845-4491, E-mail: t-morris@tamu.edu.
Website: http://laup.arch.tamu.edu/

Texas Tech University, Graduate School, College of Agricultural Sciences and Natural Resources, Department of Landscape Architecture, Lubbock, TX 79409-2121. Offers MLA. *Accreditation:* ASLA. Part-time programs available. *Faculty:* 8 full-time (4 women). *Students:* 10 full-time (4 women), 2 part-time (1 woman); includes 2 minority (both Hispanic/Latino), 3 international. Average age 28. 17 applicants, 65% accepted, 5 enrolled. In 2014, 4 master's awarded. *Degree requirements:* For master's, thesis or alternative. *Entrance requirements:* For master's, formal approval from departmental committee. Additional exam requirements/recommendations for international students: Required—TOEFL (minimum score 550 paper-based; 79 iBT). *Application deadline:* For fall admission, 6/1 priority date for domestic students, 1/15 priority date for international students; for spring admission, 9/1 priority date for domestic students, 6/15 priority date for international students. Applications are processed on a rolling basis. Application fee: $60. Electronic applications accepted. *Expenses:* Tuition, state resident: full-time $6310; part-time $262.92 per credit hour. Tuition, nonresident: full-time $14,998; part-time $624.92 per credit hour. *Required fees:* $2701; $36.50 per credit. $912.50 per semester. Tuition and fees vary according to course load. *Financial support:* In 2014–15, 11 students received support, including 11 fellowships (averaging $3,899 per year). Financial award application deadline: 4/15; financial award applicants required to submit FAFSA. *Faculty research:* Environmental planning and design, therapeutic landscapes, geographic information systems in planning, service-learning, landscape performance. *Unit head:* Dr. Charles H. Klein, Interim Chair/Associate Professor, 806-834-8409, Fax: 806-742-0770, E-mail: charles.klein@ttu.edu. *Application contact:* Dr. Charles H. Klein, Interim Chair/Associate Professor, 806-834-8409, Fax: 806-742-0770, E-mail: charles.klein@ttu.edu.
Website: http://www.larc.ttu.edu/

The University of Arizona, College of Architecture, Planning, and Landscape Architecture, School of Landscape Architecture, Tucson, AZ 85721. Offers ML Arch. *Accreditation:* ASLA. *Degree requirements:* For master's, thesis. *Entrance requirements:* For master's, minimum GPA of 3.2, 3 letters of reference, statement of intent, portfolio, transcripts. Additional exam requirements/recommendations for international students: Required—TOEFL (minimum score 600 paper-based). Electronic applications accepted. *Faculty research:* Children's environments, cultural landscapes, arid lands plant communities, geographic information systems and science, computer-aided drafting and design (CAD).

The University of British Columbia, Faculty of Applied Science, School of Architecture and Landscape Architecture, Program in Landscape Architecture, Vancouver, BC V6T 1Z1, Canada. Offers MASLA, MLA. *Accreditation:* ASLA (one or more programs are accredited). *Degree requirements:* For master's, comprehensive

exam or thesis. *Entrance requirements:* For master's, portfolio. Additional exam requirements/recommendations for international students: Required—TOEFL (minimum score 560 paper-based). Electronic applications accepted. *Faculty research:* Landscape design, urban-rural interface, urban ecology, sustainable development, collaborative planning and community forestry.

University of California, Berkeley, Graduate Division, College of Environmental Design, Department of Landscape Architecture and Environmental Planning, Berkeley, CA 94720-1500. Offers landscape architecture (MLA), including environmental planning, landscape design and site planning, urban and community design; landscape architecture and environmental planning (PhD); MLA/M Arch; MLA/MCP. *Accreditation:* ASLA (one or more programs are accredited). *Degree requirements:* For master's, professional project or thesis; for doctorate, one foreign language, thesis/dissertation, qualifying exam. *Entrance requirements:* For master's, GRE General Test, minimum GPA of 3.0, portfolio; for doctorate, GRE General Test, master's degree (strongly recommended), minimum GPA of 3.0, sample of written work, 3 letters of recommendation.

University of California, Berkeley, UC Berkeley Extension, Certificate Programs in Art and Design, Berkeley, CA 94720-1500. Offers interior design and interior architecture (Certificate); landscape architecture (Certificate); visual arts (Postbaccalaureate Certificate).

University of Colorado Denver, College of Architecture and Planning, Program in Landscape Architecture, Denver, CO 80217. Offers MLA. *Accreditation:* ASLA. Part-time programs available. *Students:* 58 full-time (30 women), 3 part-time (2 women); includes 5 minority (1 American Indian or Alaska Native, non-Hispanic/Latino; 3 Hispanic/Latino; 1 Two or more races, non-Hispanic/Latino), 11 international. Average age 28. 61 applicants, 82% accepted, 22 enrolled. In 2014, 18 master's awarded. *Degree requirements:* For master's, thesis optional, six-semester sequence of course work totaling 90 semester hours. *Entrance requirements:* For master's, GRE (recommended for students with an undergraduate GPA of 3.0 or lower), portfolio of creative work; statement of purpose; three letters of recommendation. Additional exam requirements/recommendations for international students: Required—TOEFL (minimum score 75 iBT). *Application deadline:* For fall admission, 2/1 for domestic students, 1/1 priority date for international students. Application fee: $50 ($75 for international students). Electronic applications accepted. *Expenses:* Expenses: Contact institution. *Financial support:* In 2014–15, 24 students received support. Fellowships, research assistantships, teaching assistantships, Federal Work-Study, institutionally sponsored loans, scholarships/grants, traineeships, and unspecified assistantships available. Financial award application deadline: 4/1; financial award applicants required to submit FAFSA. *Faculty research:* Landscape architectural design theory and process, urban design, advanced landscape technologies, landscape planning. *Unit head:* Ann Komara, Associate Professor and Chair, 303-315-2428, E-mail: ann.komara@ucdenver.edu. *Application contact:* Rachael Kuroiwa, Manager of Admissions and Outreach, 303-315-2325, E-mail: rachael.kuroiwa@ucdenver.edu.
Website: http://www.ucdenver.edu/academics/colleges/ArchitecturePlanning/Academics/DegreePrograms/MLA/Pages/MLA.aspx

University of Florida, Graduate School, College of Design, Construction and Planning, Department of Landscape Architecture, Gainesville, FL 32611-5704. Offers geographic information systems (MLA); historic preservation (MLA); landscape architecture (MLA); sustainable design (MLA); wetland sciences (MLA). *Accreditation:* ASLA. Part-time programs available. *Faculty:* 5 full-time (2 women). *Students:* 22 full-time (17 women), 3 part-time (2 women); includes 7 minority (2 Black or African American, non-Hispanic/Latino; 1 Asian, non-Hispanic/Latino; 4 Hispanic/Latino), 7 international. 30 applicants, 83% accepted, 4 enrolled. In 2014, 5 master's awarded. *Degree requirements:* For master's, thesis, internship. *Entrance requirements:* For master's, GRE General Test, minimum GPA of 3.0. Additional exam requirements/recommendations for international students: Required—TOEFL (minimum score 550 paper-based; 80 iBT), IELTS (minimum score 6). *Application deadline:* For fall admission, 2/15 priority date for domestic students. Applications are processed on a rolling basis. Application fee: $30. Electronic applications accepted. *Financial support:* In 2014–15, 2 research assistantships, 2 teaching assistantships were awarded; fellowships and career-related internships or fieldwork also available. Financial award applicants required to submit FAFSA. *Faculty research:* Landscape reclamation, community development, landscape ethics, land-use planning, international conservation. *Unit head:* Maria C. Gurucharri, Chair/Associate Professor, 352-392-6098 Ext. 328, Fax: 352-392-7266, E-mail: guruch@ufl.edu. *Application contact:* Kevin R. Thompson, Assistant Professor/Graduate Coordinator/Co-Director, Center for International Design and Planning, 352-392-6098 Ext. 329, Fax: 352-392-7266, E-mail: gday@ufl.edu.
Website: http://www.dcp.ufl.edu/landscape

University of Florida, Graduate School, College of Design, Construction and Planning, Doctoral Program in Design, Construction and Planning, Gainesville, FL 32611. Offers construction management (PhD); design, construction and planning (PhD); geographic information systems (PhD); historic preservation (PhD); interior design (PhD); landscape architecture (PhD); urban and regional planning (PhD). *Students:* 79 full-time (32 women), 21 part-time (7 women); includes 12 minority (4 Black or African American, non-Hispanic/Latino; 1 American Indian or Alaska Native, non-Hispanic/Latino; 4 Asian, non-Hispanic/Latino; 3 Hispanic/Latino), 51 international. 92 applicants, 25% accepted, 14 enrolled. In 2014, 18 doctorates awarded. *Degree requirements:* For doctorate, thesis/dissertation. *Entrance requirements:* For doctorate, GRE General Test, minimum GPA of 3.0. Additional exam requirements/recommendations for international students: Required—TOEFL (minimum score 550 paper-based; 80 iBT), IELTS (minimum score 6). *Application deadline:* For fall admission, 2/1 for domestic and international students. Applications are processed on a rolling basis. Application fee: $30. Electronic applications accepted. *Financial support:* In 2014–15, 3 fellowships, 26 research assistantships, 30 teaching assistantships were awarded; unspecified assistantships also available. Financial award applicants required to submit FAFSA. *Faculty research:* Architecture, building construction, urban and regional planning. *Unit head:* Zhong-Ren Peng, PhD, Professor/Director, 352-392-0997 Ext. 429, Fax: 352-392-3308, E-mail: zpeng@ufl.edu. *Application contact:* Zhong-Ren Peng, PhD, Professor/Director, 352-392-0997 Ext. 429, Fax: 352-392-3308, E-mail: zpeng@ufl.edu.
Website: http://www.dcp.ufl.edu/docprogram/

University of Georgia, College of Environment and Design, Athens, GA 30602. Offers environmental planning and design (MEPD); historic preservation (MHP); landscape architecture (MLA).

University of Guelph, Graduate Studies, Ontario Agricultural College, School of Environmental Design and Rural Development, Landscape Architecture Program, Guelph, ON N1G 2W1, Canada. Offers MLA. *Accreditation:* ASLA. *Degree requirements:* For master's, thesis. *Entrance requirements:* For master's, minimum B-average during previous 2 years of honors degree, portfolio and questionnaire. Additional exam requirements/recommendations for international students: Required—TOEFL (minimum score 600 paper-based; 89 iBT), IELTS (minimum score 7), Canadian Academic Language Assessment, Michigan English Language Assessment Battery. Electronic applications accepted. *Faculty research:* Land planning, human factors in design, landscape assessment (biophysical and cultural), landscape ecology and restoration, community design.

University of Idaho, College of Graduate Studies, College of Art and Architecture, Moscow, ID 83844-2461. Offers architecture (M Arch); art (MFA); bioregional planning and community design (MS); integrated architecture and design (MS); landscape architecture (MLA); teaching art (MAT). *Accreditation:* NASAD. *Faculty:* 17 full-time, 4 part-time/adjunct. *Students:* 88 full-time (34 women), 18 part-time (6 women). Average age 31. In 2014, 38 master's awarded. *Entrance requirements:* Additional exam requirements/recommendations for international students: Required—TOEFL (minimum score 550 paper-based). *Application deadline:* For fall admission, 8/1 for domestic students; for spring admission, 12/15 for domestic students. Applications are processed on a rolling basis. Application fee: $60. Electronic applications accepted. *Expenses:* Tuition, state resident: full-time $4784; part-time $280.50 per credit hour. Tuition, nonresident: full-time $18,314; part-time $957.50 per credit hour. *Required fees:* $2000; $58.50 per credit hour. Tuition and fees vary according to program. *Financial support:* Applicants required to submit FAFSA. *Faculty research:* Sustainability in communities, urban research, virtual technology, bioregional planning, environment and behavior interaction. *Unit head:* Dr. Mark Hoversten, Dean, 208-885-4409, E-mail: caa@uidaho.edu. *Application contact:* Sean Scoggin, Graduate Recruitment Coordinator, 208-885-4001, Fax: 208-885-4406, E-mail: graduateadmissions@uidaho.edu.
Website: http://www.uidaho.edu/caa

University of Illinois at Urbana–Champaign, Graduate College, College of Fine and Applied Arts, Department of Landscape Architecture, Champaign, IL 61820. Offers MLA, PhD, MLA/MUP. *Accreditation:* ASLA. *Students:* 51 (37 women). Application fee: $70 ($90 for international students). *Unit head:* D. Ruggles, Interim Head, 217-333-0176, Fax: 217-244-4568, E-mail: dfr1@illinois.edu. *Application contact:* Carol Emmerling-Dinovo, Office Manager, 214-333-4511, Fax: 214-244-4568, E-mail: cemmer@illinois.edu.
Website: http://www.landarch.illinois.edu/

The University of Manchester, School of Environment and Development, Manchester, United Kingdom. Offers architecture (M Phil, PhD); development policy and management (M Phil, PhD); human geography (M Phil, PhD); physical geography (M Phil, PhD); planning and landscape (M Phil, PhD).

University of Manitoba, Faculty of Graduate Studies, Faculty of Architecture, Department of Landscape Architecture, Winnipeg, MB R3T 2N2, Canada. Offers M Land Arch. *Accreditation:* ASLA. *Degree requirements:* For master's, thesis or alternative.

University of Maryland, College Park, Academic Affairs, College of Agriculture and Natural Resources, Department of Plant Science and Landscape Architecture, Landscape Architecture Program, College Park, MD 20742. Offers MLA. *Accreditation:* ASLA. *Entrance requirements:* Additional exam requirements/recommendations for international students: Required—TOEFL. Electronic applications accepted. *Faculty research:* Cereal crop production, soil and water conservation, turf management, x-ray diffraction.

University of Massachusetts Amherst, Graduate School, College of Social and Behavioral Sciences, Department of Landscape Architecture and Regional Planning, Dual Program in Landscape Architecture and Regional Planning, Amherst, MA 01003. Offers MLA/MRP. *Accreditation:* ACSP; ASLA. Part-time programs available. *Students:* 3 full-time (2 women), 1 part-time (0 women). Average age 30. 4 applicants, 100% accepted, 2 enrolled. *Entrance requirements:* Additional exam requirements/recommendations for international students: Required—TOEFL (minimum score 550 paper-based; 80 iBT), IELTS (minimum score 6.5). *Application deadline:* For fall admission, 2/1 for domestic and international students. Applications are processed on a rolling basis. Application fee: $75. Electronic applications accepted. *Expenses:* Tuition, state resident: full-time $1980; part-time $110 per credit. Tuition, nonresident: full-time $14,644; part-time $414 per credit. *Required fees:* $11,417. One-time fee: $357. *Financial support:* Fellowships with full and partial tuition reimbursements, research assistantships with full and partial tuition reimbursements, teaching assistantships with full and partial tuition reimbursements, career-related internships or fieldwork, Federal Work-Study, scholarships/grants, traineeships, health care benefits, tuition waivers (full and partial), and unspecified assistantships available. Support available to part-time students. Financial award application deadline: 2/1; financial award applicants required to submit FAFSA. *Unit head:* Dr. Robert L. Ryan, Graduate Program Director, 413-545-2266, Fax: 413-545-1772. *Application contact:* Lindsay DeSantis, Supervisor of Admissions, 413-545-0721, Fax: 413-577-0010, E-mail: gradadm@grad.umass.edu.
Website: http://www.umass.edu/larp/academics/dual-degrees/mlamrp

University of Massachusetts Amherst, Graduate School, College of Social and Behavioral Sciences, Department of Landscape Architecture and Regional Planning, Program in Landscape Architecture, Amherst, MA 01003. Offers MLA, MLA/M Arch. *Accreditation:* ASLA. Part-time programs available. *Students:* 27 full-time (17 women), 4 part-time (2 women), 18 international. Average age 27. 83 applicants, 47% accepted, 8 enrolled. In 2014, 13 master's awarded. *Degree requirements:* For master's, thesis or alternative. *Entrance requirements:* For master's, GRE General Test, portfolio. Additional exam requirements/recommendations for international students: Required—TOEFL (minimum score 550 paper-based; 80 iBT), IELTS (minimum score 6.5). *Application deadline:* For fall admission, 2/1 for domestic and international students. Applications are processed on a rolling basis. Application fee: $75. Electronic applications accepted. *Expenses:* Tuition, state resident: full-time $1980; part-time $110 per credit. Tuition, nonresident: full-time $14,644; part-time $414 per credit. *Required fees:* $11,417. One-time fee: $357. *Financial support:* Fellowships with full and partial tuition reimbursements, research assistantships with full and partial tuition reimbursements, teaching assistantships with full and partial tuition reimbursements, career-related internships or fieldwork, Federal Work-Study, scholarships/grants, traineeships, health care benefits, tuition waivers (full and partial), and unspecified assistantships available. Support available to part-time students. Financial award application deadline: 2/1; financial award applicants required to submit FAFSA. *Unit head:* Dr. Ethan Carr, Graduate Program Director, 413-545-2266, Fax: 413-545-1772. *Application contact:* Lindsay DeSantis, Supervisor of Admissions, 413-545-0722, Fax: 413-577-0010, E-mail: gradadm@grad.umass.edu.
Website: http://www.umass.edu/larp/

University of Michigan, School of Natural Resources and Environment, Program in Landscape Architecture, Ann Arbor, MI 48109-1041. Offers MLA, PhD, MLA/M Arch, MLA/MBA, MLA/MUP. Offered through the Horace H. Rackham School of Graduate Studies. *Accreditation:* ASLA (one or more programs are accredited). *Degree requirements:* For master's, thesis, practicum or group project; for doctorate, comprehensive exam, thesis/dissertation, oral defense of dissertation, preliminary exam. *Entrance requirements:* For master's, GRE General Test; for doctorate, GRE General Test, master's degree, portfolio. Additional exam requirements/recommendations for international students: Required—TOEFL (minimum score 560 paper-based; 84 iBT) or IELTS (minimum score 6.5). *Faculty research:* Historic

landscape documentation, landscape architecture, landscape perception, sustainable design, ecological design.

University of Minnesota, Twin Cities Campus, Graduate School, College of Design, Department of Landscape Architecture, Minneapolis, MN 55455-0213. Offers MLA, MS. *Accreditation:* ASLA (one or more programs are accredited). *Degree requirements:* For master's, thesis (MS). *Entrance requirements:* For master's, GRE General Test (MS), suggested GPA of 3.0. Additional exam requirements/recommendations for international students: Required—TOEFL (minimum score 550 paper-based; 79 iBT). Electronic applications accepted. *Expenses:* Contact institution. *Faculty research:* Landscape history, landscape ecology, urban design, sustainable design, public art/space.

University of New Mexico, Graduate School, School of Architecture and Planning, Program in Landscape Architecture, Albuquerque, NM 87131-2039. Offers MLA. *Accreditation:* ASLA. Part-time programs available. *Faculty:* 1 full-time (0 women), 4 part-time/adjunct (1 woman). *Students:* 23 full-time (13 women), 5 part-time (3 women); includes 6 minority (1 Black or African American, non-Hispanic/Latino; 1 American Indian or Alaska Native, non-Hispanic/Latino; 1 Asian, non-Hispanic/Latino; 3 Hispanic/Latino), 5 international. Average age 32. 22 applicants, 82% accepted, 12 enrolled. In 2014, 22 master's awarded. *Degree requirements:* For master's, comprehensive exam, thesis optional, portfolio review, thesis studio. *Entrance requirements:* For master's, minimum GPA of 3.0. Additional exam requirements/recommendations for international students: Required—TOEFL. *Application deadline:* For fall admission, 2/15 priority date for domestic students, 2/15 for international students; for spring admission, 11/1 for domestic and international students. Applications are processed on a rolling basis. Application fee: $50. Electronic applications accepted. *Expenses:* Expenses: Contact institution. *Financial support:* In 2014–15, 43 students received support, including 4 research assistantships with partial tuition reimbursements available (averaging $7,306 per year), 1 teaching assistantship with partial tuition reimbursement available (averaging $3,698 per year); scholarships/grants, health care benefits, tuition waivers (partial), and unspecified assistantships also available. Financial award application deadline: 3/1; financial award applicants required to submit FAFSA. *Faculty research:* Cultural landscape studies, urban design and sustainability, landscape and infrastructure. *Unit head:* Dr. Alfred Simon, Director, 505-277-4120, Fax: 505-277-0897, E-mail: asimon@unm.edu. *Application contact:* Elizabeth M. Rowe, Senior Academic Advisor, 505-277-1303, Fax: 505-277-0076, E-mail: erowe@unm.edu.
Website: http://saap.unm.edu/

University of Oklahoma, College of Architecture, Division of Landscape Architecture, Norman, OK 73019. Offers MLA, MRCP/MLA. *Accreditation:* ASLA. *Students:* 6 full-time (2 women); includes 1 minority (Black or African American, non-Hispanic/Latino), 3 international. Average age 30. 10 applicants, 70% accepted, 2 enrolled. In 2014, 7 master's awarded. *Degree requirements:* For master's, comprehensive exam, thesis optional. *Entrance requirements:* For master's, minimum GPA of 3.0, statement of interest, 3 letters of recommendation. Additional exam requirements/recommendations for international students: Required—TOEFL (minimum score 79 iBT). *Application deadline:* For fall admission, 4/1 for domestic and international students; for spring admission, 9/1 for domestic and international students. Applications are processed on a rolling basis. Application fee: $50 ($100 for international students). Electronic applications accepted. *Expenses:* Tuition, state resident: full-time $4394; part-time $183.10 per credit hour. Tuition, nonresident: full-time $16,970; part-time $707.10 per credit hour. *Required fees:* $2892; $109.95 per credit hour. $126.50 per semester. *Financial support:* In 2014–15, 6 students received support, including 2 research assistantships with partial tuition reimbursements available (averaging $10,372 per year); scholarships/grants and unspecified assistantships also available. Financial award application deadline: 6/1; financial award applicants required to submit FAFSA. *Faculty research:* Green roof, exterior landscape lighting, social behavior in the environment, geodesign, urban design, landscape architecture. *Unit head:* Dr. Leehu Loon, Director and Associate Professor, 405-325-1519, E-mail: lloon@ou.edu. *Application contact:* Leehu Loon, Director and Associate Professor, 405-325-1519, E-mail: lloon@ou.edu.
Website: http://la.ou.edu

University of Oregon, Graduate School, School of Architecture and Allied Arts, Department of Landscape Architecture, Eugene, OR 97403. Offers MLA. *Accreditation:* ASLA. *Degree requirements:* For master's, thesis or alternative, project. *Entrance requirements:* For master's, portfolio. Additional exam requirements/recommendations for international students: Required—TOEFL. *Faculty research:* Design, landscape planning analysis, history and theory, computer applications.

University of Pennsylvania, School of Design, Department of Landscape Architecture, Philadelphia, PA 19104. Offers landscape architecture (MLA); landscape studies (Certificate). *Accreditation:* ASLA (one or more programs are accredited). Part-time programs available. *Faculty:* 7 full-time (3 women), 7 part-time/adjunct (2 women). *Students:* 108 full-time (61 women), 1 (woman) part-time; includes 10 minority (1 Black or African American, non-Hispanic/Latino; 3 Asian, non-Hispanic/Latino; 3 Hispanic/Latino; 3 Two or more races, non-Hispanic/Latino), 75 international. 340 applicants, 35% accepted, 53 enrolled. In 2014, 44 master's, 9 Certificates awarded. *Entrance requirements:* For master's, GRE General Test, portfolio. Additional exam requirements/recommendations for international students: Required—TOEFL or IELTS. *Application deadline:* For fall admission, 1/14 priority date for domestic and international students. Application fee: $80. Electronic applications accepted. *Financial support:* Teaching assistantships and scholarships/grants available. Financial award application deadline: 2/15; financial award applicants required to submit FAFSA. *Faculty research:* Contemporary landscape architecture design, urbanism and urban design, history and theory of landscape architecture, landscape visualization, geographic information systems, flood and disaster landscapes, the design of the public realm, social space, Renaissance gardens, garden art and theory, design theory, aesthetics and criticism. *Unit head:* Marilyn Jordan Taylor, Dean, 215-898-6520, E-mail: mjtaylor@design.upenn.edu. *Application contact:* Office of Admissions and Financial Aid, 215-898-6520, E-mail: admissions@design.upenn.edu.
Website: http://www.design.upenn.edu/landscape-architecture

The University of Tennessee, Graduate School, College of Architecture and Design, Program in Landscape Architecture, Knoxville, TN 37996. Offers landscape architecture (MLA); landscape architecture (research) (MA, MS). *Accreditation:* ASLA. *Degree requirements:* For master's, oral exam, project and thesis optional (MLA), oral exam and thesis (MA, MS). *Entrance requirements:* For master's, GRE General Test, minimum GPA of 3.0, 3 letters of recommendation, samples of portfolio work. Additional exam requirements/recommendations for international students: Required—TOEFL (minimum score 550 paper-based).

The University of Texas at Arlington, Graduate School, School of Architecture, Program in Landscape Architecture, Arlington, TX 76019. Offers MLA. *Accreditation:* ASLA. Part-time and evening/weekend programs available. *Degree requirements:* For master's, thesis. *Entrance requirements:* For master's, GRE General Test, minimum GPA of 3.0, portfolio. Additional exam requirements/recommendations for international students: Required—TOEFL (minimum score 575 paper-based; 80 iBT).

The University of Texas at Austin, Graduate School, School of Architecture, Program in Landscape Architecture, Austin, TX 78712-1111. Offers MLA. *Accreditation:* ASLA.

University of Toronto, School of Graduate Studies, John H. Daniels Faculty of Architecture, Landscape, and Design, Toronto, ON M5S 2J7, Canada. Offers M Arch, MLA, MUD, MVS. *Accreditation:* ASLA. *Entrance requirements:* For master's, minimum B average; 3 letters of reference; resume; 3 writing samples; 5 samples of design work, drawing, or work in a related field, statement of interest. Additional exam requirements/recommendations for international students: Required—TOEFL (minimum score 580 paper-based; 93 iBT), IELTS (minimum score 7), TWE (minimum score 5), Michigan English Language Assessment Battery (minimum score 85), COPE (minimum score 76). Electronic applications accepted. *Expenses:* Contact institution.

University of Virginia, School of Architecture, Department of Landscape Architecture, Charlottesville, VA 22903. Offers M Land Arch. *Accreditation:* ASLA. *Faculty:* 6 full-time (3 women), 1 (woman) part-time/adjunct. *Students:* 40 full-time (28 women); includes 3 minority (1 Black or African American, non-Hispanic/Latino; 2 Asian, non-Hispanic/Latino), 8 international. Average age 26. 198 applicants, 32% accepted, 22 enrolled. In 2014, 14 master's awarded. *Entrance requirements:* For master's, GRE General Test, 3 letters of recommendation; portfolio. Additional exam requirements/recommendations for international students: Required—TOEFL (minimum score 600 paper-based; 90 iBT). *Application deadline:* For fall admission, 1/15 for domestic students, 1/16 for international students. Applications are processed on a rolling basis. Application fee: $60. Electronic applications accepted. *Expenses:* Tuition, state resident: full-time $14,164; part-time $349 per credit hour. Tuition, nonresident: full-time $23,722; part-time $1300 per credit hour. *Required fees:* $2514. *Financial support:* Applicants required to submit FAFSA. *Faculty research:* History of landscape architecture. *Unit head:* Teresa Gali-Izard, Chair, 434-924-6465, Fax: 434-982-2678, E-mail: teg2q@virginia.edu. *Application contact:* Kristine Nelson, Director of Graduate Admissions and Financial Aid, 434-924-6442, Fax: 434-982-2678, E-mail: arch-admissions@virginia.edu.
Website: http://www.arch.virginia.edu/academics/disciplines/landscape

University of Washington, Graduate School, College of Built Environments, Department of Landscape Architecture, Seattle, WA 98195. Offers MLA. *Accreditation:* ASLA. *Degree requirements:* For master's, thesis. *Entrance requirements:* For master's, GRE, minimum GPA of 3.0. Additional exam requirements/recommendations for international students: Required—TOEFL. *Faculty research:* Cultural landscape, history of gardens, urban stream restoration, campus master planning, urban ecology.

University of Wisconsin–Madison, Graduate School, College of Agricultural and Life Sciences, Department of Landscape Architecture, Madison, WI 53076. Offers MA, MS. Part-time programs available. *Degree requirements:* For master's, thesis. *Entrance requirements:* For master's, GRE (recommended), samples of creative work. Additional exam requirements/recommendations for international students: Required—TOEFL (minimum score 580 paper-based). Electronic applications accepted. *Expenses:* Tuition, state resident: full-time $10,723; part-time $745 per credit. Tuition, nonresident: full-time $24,054; part-time $1578 per credit. *Required fees:* $374 per semester. Tuition and fees vary according to course load, program and reciprocity agreements. *Faculty research:* Urban/landscape ecology, land restoration, cultural resource preservation, community design, conservation design.

Utah State University, School of Graduate Studies, College of Humanities, Arts and Social Sciences, Department of Landscape Architecture and Environmental Planning, Logan, UT 84322. Offers bioregional planning (MS); landscape architecture (MLA). *Accreditation:* ASLA (one or more programs are accredited). *Degree requirements:* For master's, thesis. *Entrance requirements:* For master's, GRE General Test, minimum GPA of 3.0. Additional exam requirements/recommendations for international students: Required—TOEFL. *Faculty research:* Visual resource management, planning for wildlife, agricultural land preservation, watershed planning, community planning and design.

Virginia Polytechnic Institute and State University, Graduate School, College of Architecture and Urban Studies, Blacksburg, VA 24061. Offers architecture (MS Arch); architecture and design research (PhD); building/construction science and management (MS); creative technologies (MFA); environmental design and planning (PhD); landscape architecture (MLA); planning, governance, and globalization (PhD); public administration (MPA); public administration/public affairs (PhD, Certificate); public and international affairs (MPIA); urban and regional planning (MURP); MS/MA. *Accreditation:* ASLA (one or more programs are accredited). *Faculty:* 133 full-time (54 women), 2 part-time/adjunct (1 woman). *Students:* 316 full-time (166 women), 237 part-time (108 women); includes 104 minority (46 Black or African American, non-Hispanic/Latino; 1 American Indian or Alaska Native, non-Hispanic/Latino; 20 Asian, non-Hispanic/Latino; 21 Hispanic/Latino; 16 Two or more races, non-Hispanic/Latino), 108 international. Average age 32. 609 applicants, 50% accepted, 108 enrolled. In 2014, 155 master's, 29 doctorates awarded. *Degree requirements:* For master's, comprehensive exam (for some programs), thesis (for some programs); for doctorate, comprehensive exam (for some programs), thesis/dissertation (for some programs). *Entrance requirements:* For master's and doctorate, GRE/GMAT (may vary by department). Additional exam requirements/recommendations for international students: Required—TOEFL (minimum score 550 paper-based). *Application deadline:* For fall admission, 8/1 for domestic students, 4/1 for international students; for spring admission, 1/1 for domestic students, 9/1 for international students. Applications are processed on a rolling basis. Application fee: $75. Electronic applications accepted. *Expenses:* Tuition, state resident: full-time $11,656; part-time $647.50 per credit hour. Tuition, nonresident: full-time $23,351; part-time $1297.25 per credit hour. *Required fees:* $2533; $465.75 per semester. Tuition and fees vary according to course load, campus/location and program. *Financial support:* In 2014–15, 13 research assistantships with full tuition reimbursements (averaging $20,302 per year), 44 teaching assistantships with full tuition reimbursements (averaging $19,484 per year) were awarded. Financial award application deadline: 3/1; financial award applicants required to submit FAFSA. *Total annual research expenditures:* $3.2 million. *Unit head:* Dr. A. J. Davis, Dean, 540-231-6416, Fax: 540-231-6332, E-mail: davisa@vt.edu. *Application contact:* Christine Mattsson-Coon, Executive Assistant, 540-231-6416, Fax: 540-231-6332, E-mail: cmattsso@vt.edu.
Website: http://www.caus.vt.edu/

Washington State University, College of Agricultural, Human, and Natural Resource Sciences, Program in Interior Design and Landscape Architecture, Pullman, WA 99164-2220. Offers MA, MS. Programs offered at the Pullman campus. Part-time programs available. *Faculty:* 13 full-time (0 women), 1 part-time/adjunct (0 women). *Students:* 9 full-time (8 women), 2 part-time (both women), 6 international. Average age 36. 32 applicants, 34% accepted, 3 enrolled. In 2014, 1 master's awarded. *Degree requirements:* For master's, comprehensive exam, thesis (for some programs), oral exam. *Entrance requirements:* For master's, portfolio. Additional exam requirements/recommendations for international students: Required—TOEFL or IELTS. *Application deadline:* For fall admission, 1/10 priority date for domestic and international students. Application fee: $75. Electronic applications accepted. *Expenses:* Tuition, state

resident: full-time $11,768. Tuition, nonresident: full-time $25,200. *Required fees:* $960. Tuition and fees vary according to program. *Financial support:* In 2014–15, 1 student received support, including 5 teaching assistantships with partial tuition reimbursements available (averaging $7,308 per year); career-related internships or fieldwork, Federal Work-Study, scholarships/grants, and unspecified assistantships also available. Financial award applicants required to submit FAFSA. *Faculty research:* Digital fabrication, design pedagogy, proportional systems, American architecture and urbanism, design leadership. *Unit head:* Prof. Matt Melcher, Program Coordinator, 509-335-1737, Fax: 509-335-6132, E-mail: melcher@wsu.edu. *Application contact:* Jaime L. Rice, Academic Coordinator, 509-335-5318, Fax: 509-335-6132, E-mail: jlrice@wsu.edu. Website: http://sdc.wsu.edu

Lighting Design

The New School, Parsons The New School for Design, Program in Lighting Design, New York, NY 10011. Offers MFA. *Accreditation:* NASAD. *Degree requirements:* For master's, thesis. *Entrance requirements:* For master's, portfolio. Additional exam requirements/recommendations for international students: Required—TOEFL (minimum score 580 paper-based; 92 iBT). Electronic applications accepted.

New York School of Interior Design, Program in Interior Lighting Design, New York, NY 10021-5110. Offers MPS. *Entrance requirements:* For master's, portfolio, resume, undergraduate degree in interior design or closely-related field. Additional exam requirements/recommendations for international students: Required—TOEFL (minimum score 79 iBT). Electronic applications accepted.

Rensselaer Polytechnic Institute, Graduate School, School of Architecture, PhD Program in Architectural Sciences, Troy, NY 12180-3590. Offers architectural acoustics (PhD); built ecologies (PhD); lighting (PhD). *Faculty:* 41 full-time (10 women), 5 part-time/adjunct (1 woman). *Students:* 29 full-time (10 women), 10 part-time (3 women); includes 6 minority (1 Asian, non-Hispanic/Latino; 2 Hispanic/Latino; 3 Two or more races, non-Hispanic/Latino), 9 international. Average age 31. 68 applicants, 35% accepted, 17 enrolled. In 2014, 4 doctorates awarded. *Degree requirements:* For doctorate, comprehensive exam (for some programs), thesis/dissertation. *Entrance requirements:* For doctorate, GRE. Additional exam requirements/recommendations for international students: Required—TOEFL (minimum score 570 paper-based; 88 iBT), IELTS (minimum score 6.5), PTE (minimum score 60). *Application deadline:* For fall admission, 1/1 priority date for domestic and international students; for spring admission, 8/15 priority date for domestic and international students. Applications are processed on a rolling basis. Application fee: $75. Electronic applications accepted. *Expenses:* Tuition: Full-time $46,700; part-time $1945 per credit. Tuition and fees vary according to course load. *Financial support:* In 2014–15, 29 students received support, including research assistantships (averaging $18,500 per year), teaching assistantships with full tuition reimbursements available (averaging $18,500 per year); fellowships also available. Financial award application deadline: 1/1. *Faculty research:* Architectural acoustics, built ecologies, lighting. *Unit head:* Chris Perry, Graduate Program Director, 518-276-3034, E-mail: perryc3@rpi.edu. *Application contact:* Office of Graduate Admissions, 518-276-6216, E-mail: gradadmissions@rpi.edu. Website: http://www.arch.rpi.edu/academic/graduate/phd-program/

Rensselaer Polytechnic Institute, Graduate School, School of Architecture, Program in Lighting, Troy, NY 12180-3590. Offers architectural sciences (MS, PhD); lighting (MS). *Faculty:* 4 full-time (1 woman). *Students:* 2 full-time (0 women), 1 international. Average age 29. 7 applicants, 43% accepted, 2 enrolled. In 2014, 3 master's awarded. *Degree requirements:* For master's, comprehensive exam, thesis; for doctorate, comprehensive exam, thesis/dissertation. *Entrance requirements:* For master's and doctorate, GRE. Additional exam requirements/recommendations for international students: Required—TOEFL (minimum score 570 paper-based; 88 iBT), IELTS (minimum score 6.5), PTE (minimum score 60). *Application deadline:* For fall admission, 1/1 priority date for domestic and international students. Applications are processed on a rolling basis. Application fee: $75. Electronic applications accepted. *Expenses:* Tuition: Full-time $46,700; part-time $1945 per credit. Tuition and fees vary according to course load. *Financial support:* In 2014–15, 2 students received support, including research assistantships (averaging $18,500 per year), teaching assistantships with full tuition reimbursements available (averaging $18,500 per year); fellowships also available. Financial award application deadline: 1/1. *Faculty research:* Applications and design, automotive and street lighting, aviation lighting, controls, daylighting, energy and environment, health and vision, LEDs, outdoor lighting, residential lighting, security lighting. *Unit head:* Russ Leslie, Graduate Program Director, 518-687-7100, E-mail: leslir@rpi.edu. *Application contact:* Office of Graduate Admissions, 518-276-6216, E-mail: gradadmissions@rpi.edu. Website: http://www.arch.rpi.edu/academic/graduate/lighting/

University of Oklahoma, College of Architecture, Division of Interior Design, Norman, OK 73019. Offers architectural lighting (MID); design process management (MID); interior design (MID); sustainable living (MID). Part-time and evening/weekend programs available. *Students:* 2 full-time (both women), 1 international. Average age 26. 3 applicants, 67% accepted. In 2014, 3 master's awarded. *Degree requirements:* For master's, comprehensive exam, project or thesis. *Entrance requirements:* For master's, undergraduate degree in interior design or related field, portfolio of design work, letter of intent, three letters of recommendation. Additional exam requirements/recommendations for international students: Required—TOEFL (minimum score 79 iBT). *Application deadline:* For fall admission, 6/1 for domestic and international students; for spring admission, 10/15 for domestic and international students. Application fee: $50 ($100 for international students). Electronic applications accepted. *Expenses:* Tuition, state resident: full-time $4394; part-time $183.10 per credit hour. Tuition, nonresident: full-time $16,970; part-time $707.10 per credit hour. *Required fees:* $2892; $109.95 per credit hour. $126.50 per semester. *Financial support:* In 2014–15, 1 student received support, including 1 research assistantship (averaging $10,372 per year), 2 teaching assistantships with partial tuition reimbursements available (averaging $10,372 per year); career-related internships or fieldwork, scholarships/grants, and unspecified assistantships also available. Financial award application deadline: 6/1; financial award applicants required to submit FAFSA. *Faculty research:* Environmental and human behavior, indoor environmental quality, pedagogical exploration, building information modeling for cognitive spatial problem solving, community health and environmental design. *Unit head:* Mia Kile, Academic Director, 405-325-1051, Fax: 405-325-7558, E-mail: mkile@ou.edu. *Application contact:* Hans-Peter Wachter, Graduate Liaison and Associate Professor, 405-325-8780, Fax: 405-325-7558, E-mail: hepw@ou.edu. Website: http://www.ou.edu/content/architecture/interior_design.html

University of Washington, Graduate School, College of Built Environments, Department of Architecture, Seattle, WA 98195. Offers architecture (M Arch, MS); built environment (PhD); design computing (Certificate); design firm leadership and management (Certificate); historic preservation (Certificate); lighting (Certificate); urban design (Certificate). *Degree requirements:* For master's, thesis. *Entrance requirements:* For master's, GRE General Test, minimum GPA of 3.0, portfolio, 3 letters of recommendation. Additional exam requirements/recommendations for international students: Required—TOEFL. *Faculty research:* Lighting, materials, computing theory, media, culture, environment.

Urban Design

American University of Beirut, Graduate Programs, Faculty of Engineering and Architecture, Beirut, Lebanon. Offers applied energy (ME); civil engineering (PhD); electrical and computer engineering (PhD); engineering management (MEM); environmental and water resources (ME); environmental technology (MSES); mechanical engineering (ME, PhD); urban design (MUD); urban planning and policy (MUPP). Part-time programs available. *Faculty:* 93 full-time (18 women), 3 part-time/adjunct (1 woman). *Students:* 268 full-time (111 women), 58 part-time (27 women). Average age 26. 225 applicants, 68% accepted, 79 enrolled. In 2014, 114 master's, 9 doctorates awarded. Terminal master's awarded for partial completion of doctoral program. *Degree requirements:* For master's, one foreign language, comprehensive exam, thesis (for some programs); for doctorate, one foreign language, comprehensive exam, thesis/dissertation, publications. *Entrance requirements:* For master's, letters of recommendation; for doctorate, GRE, letters of recommendation, master's degree, transcripts, curriculum vitae, interview. Additional exam requirements/recommendations for international students: Required—TOEFL (minimum score 600 paper-based; 100 iBT), IELTS (minimum score 7.5). *Application deadline:* For fall admission, 2/5 priority date for domestic and international students; for spring admission, 11/1 priority date for domestic students, 11/1 for international students. Application fee: $50. Electronic applications accepted. *Expenses: Tuition:* Full-time $15,462; part-time $859 per credit. *Required fees:* $692. Tuition and fees vary according to course load and program. *Financial support:* In 2014–15, 190 students received support, including 2 fellowships with full tuition reimbursements available (averaging $24,800 per year), 64 research assistantships with full tuition reimbursements available (averaging $24,800 per year), 124 teaching assistantships with full tuition reimbursements available (averaging $9,800 per year); career-related internships or fieldwork, institutionally sponsored loans, scholarships/grants, health care benefits, and unspecified assistantships also available. *Total annual research expenditures:* $1.5 million. *Unit head:* Prof. Makram T. Suidan, Dean, 961-1350000 Ext. 3400, Fax: 961-1744462, E-mail: msuidan@aub.edu.lb. *Application contact:* Dr. Salim Kanaan, Director, Admissions Office, 961-1350000 Ext. 2594, Fax: 961-1750775, E-mail: sk00@aub.edu.lb. Website: http://staff.aub.edu.lb/~webfea

Arizona State University at the Tempe campus, Herberger Institute for Design and the Arts, The Design School, Tempe, AZ 85287-1605. Offers architecture (M Arch); building design/built environment (MS); design (MSD), including arts, media, and engineering, healthcare and healing environments (MSD, PhD), industrial design, interaction design, interior design, new product innovation, visual communication design; design, environment and the arts (PhD), including design, digital culture, healthcare and healing environments (MSD, PhD), history, theory, and criticism; landscape architecture (MLA); urban design (MUD); MA/MBA. *Accreditation:* NASAD. Terminal master's awarded for partial completion of doctoral program. *Degree requirements:* For master's, thesis optional, interactive Program of Study (iPOS) submitted before completing 50 percent of required credit hours; for doctorate, comprehensive exam, thesis/dissertation, interactive Program of Study (iPOS) submitted before completing 50 percent of required credit hours. *Entrance requirements:* For master's, GRE General Test, minimum GPA of 3.0 or equivalent in last 2 years of work leading to bachelor's degree, design/creative works portfolio, 3 references, statement of intent; for doctorate, GRE, master's degree in architecture, graphic design, industrial design, interior design, landscape architecture, or art history or equivalent standing; statement of purpose; 3 letters of recommendation; indication of potential faculty mentor; sample of written work. Additional exam requirements/recommendations for international students: Required—TOEFL (minimum score 600 paper-based; 100 iBT). Electronic applications accepted.

★ **Ball State University,** Graduate School, College of Architecture and Planning, Department of Architecture, Program in Urban Design, Muncie, IN 47306-1099. Offers MUD. *Students:* 13 full-time (2 women); includes 1 minority (Hispanic/Latino), 4 international. Average age 23. 22 applicants, 73% accepted, 11 enrolled. In 2014, 12 master's awarded. Application fee: $50. *Financial support:* In 2014–15, 2 research assistantships with partial tuition reimbursements (averaging $11,226 per year) were awarded. *Unit head:* Dr. Michel Mounayar, Associate Dean, 765-285-5859, E-mail: mmounaya@bsu.edu.
See Display on page 108 and Close-Up on page 135.

Carnegie Mellon University, College of Fine Arts, School of Architecture, Pittsburgh, PA 15213-3891. Offers architecture (MSA); architecture, engineering, and construction management (PhD); building performance and diagnostics (MS, PhD); computational design (MS, PhD); engineering construction management (MSA); tangible interaction design (MTID); urban design (MUD). Terminal master's awarded for partial completion of doctoral program. *Degree requirements:* For doctorate, thesis/dissertation. *Entrance requirements:* For master's and doctorate, GRE General Test. Additional exam requirements/recommendations for international students: Required—TOEFL.

City College of the City University of New York, Graduate School, School of Architecture and Environmental Studies, Program in Urban Design, New York, NY 10031-9198. Offers MUP. Part-time programs available. *Degree requirements:* For master's, thesis. *Entrance requirements:* For master's, portfolio, professional degree in architecture or equivalent. Additional exam requirements/recommendations for international students: Required—TOEFL (minimum score 550 paper-based). *Faculty research:* Real estate, planning, law.

Cornell University, Graduate School, Graduate Fields of Architecture, Art and Planning, Field of Architecture, Ithaca, NY 14853-0001. Offers architectural design (M Arch); architectural science (MS); computer graphics (MS); history of architecture (MA, PhD); history of urban development (MA, PhD); theory and criticism of architecture (M Arch); urban design (M Arch). *Degree requirements:* For master's, one foreign language, thesis (MA, MS); for doctorate, 2 foreign languages, comprehensive exam, thesis/dissertation. *Entrance requirements:* For master's, GRE General Test, 5-year bachelor's degree in architecture, portfolio (M Arch), 3 letters of recommendation; for doctorate, GRE General Test, 3 letters of recommendation. Additional exam requirements/recommendations for international students: Required—TOEFL (minimum score 600 paper-based; 77 iBT). Electronic applications accepted. *Faculty research:* Architectural design and urban design, theory and criticism of architecture, computer graphics, building technology and environmental science, history of architecture and history of urban-development.

DePaul University, College of Liberal Arts and Social Sciences, Chicago, IL 60614. Offers Arabic (MA); Chinese (MA); English (MA); French (MA); German (MA); history (MA); interdisciplinary studies (MA, MS); international public service (MS); international studies (MA); Italian (MA); Japanese (MA); leadership and policy studies (MS); liberal studies (MA); new media studies (MA); nonprofit management (MNM); public administration (MPA); public health (MPH); public service management (MS); social work (MSW); sociology (MA); Spanish (MA); sustainable urban development (MA); women and gender studies (MA); writing and publishing (MA); writing, rhetoric, and discourse (MA); MA/PhD. Part-time and evening/weekend programs available. Postbaccalaureate distance learning degree programs offered (no on-campus study). Terminal master's awarded for partial completion of doctoral program. *Degree requirements:* For master's, variable foreign language requirement, comprehensive exam (for some programs), thesis (for some programs). Electronic applications accepted.

Georgia Institute of Technology, Graduate Studies, College of Architecture, School of City and Regional Planning, Atlanta, GA 30332-0001. Offers city and regional planning (PhD); economic development (MCRP); environmental planning and management (MCRP); geographic information systems (MCRP); land and community development (MCRP); land use planning (MCRP); transportation (MCRP); urban design (MCRP); MCP/MSCE. *Accreditation:* ACSP. *Degree requirements:* For master's, thesis, internship. *Entrance requirements:* For master's, GRE General Test, minimum GPA of 2.7. Additional exam requirements/recommendations for international students: Required—TOEFL. Electronic applications accepted. *Expenses:* Tuition, state resident: full-time $12,344; part-time $515 per credit hour. Tuition, nonresident: full-time $27,600; part-time $1150 per credit hour. *Required fees:* $1196 per term. Part-time tuition and fees vary according to course load.

Harvard University, Graduate School of Design, Department of Urban Planning and Design, Cambridge, MA 02138. Offers urban planning (MUP); urban planning and design (MAUD, MLAUD). *Accreditation:* ACSP (one or more programs are accredited). *Entrance requirements:* For master's, GRE General Test. Additional exam requirements/recommendations for international students: Required—TOEFL (minimum score 600 paper-based; 104 iBT). Electronic applications accepted.

Hofstra University, College of Liberal Arts and Sciences, Programs in Biology, Hempstead, NY 11549. Offers biology (MA, MS); urban ecology (MA, MS). Part-time and evening/weekend programs available. *Students:* 15 full-time (9 women), 8 part-time (5 women); includes 4 minority (1 Black or African American, non-Hispanic/Latino; 2 Hispanic/Latino; 1 Two or more races, non-Hispanic/Latino). Average age 26. 24 applicants, 75% accepted, 7 enrolled. In 2014, 6 master's awarded. *Degree requirements:* For master's, thesis, minimum GPA of 3.0. *Entrance requirements:* For master's, GRE, bachelor's degree in biology or equivalent, 2 letters of recommendation, essay. Additional exam requirements/recommendations for international students: Required—TOEFL (minimum score 550 paper-based; 80 iBT). *Application deadline:* Applications are processed on a rolling basis. Application fee: $70 ($75 for international students). Electronic applications accepted. *Expenses: Tuition:* Full-time $20,610; part-time $1145 per credit hour. *Required fees:* $970; $165 per term. Tuition and fees vary according to program. *Financial support:* In 2014–15, 16 students received support, including 11 fellowships with full and partial tuition reimbursements available (averaging $5,859 per year); research assistantships with full and partial tuition reimbursements available, Federal Work-Study, institutionally sponsored loans, scholarships/grants, and tuition waivers (full and partial) also available. Support available to part-time students. Financial award applicants required to submit FAFSA. *Faculty research:* Genomic, hormonal and neurobiological bases for behavior; applied and environmental microbiology; developmental genetics, tissue-specific gene regulation; plant and soil ecology, urbanization, global environmental change; systematics and biology of marine polychaete worms and crustaceans. *Unit head:* Dr. Maureen K. Krause, Program Director, 516-463-6178, Fax: 516-463-5112, E-mail: biomkk@hofstra.edu. *Application contact:* Sunil Samuel, Assistant Vice President of Admissions, 516-463-4723516, Fax: 516-463-4664, E-mail: graduateadmission@hofstra.edu. Website: http://www.hofstra.edu/hclas

Judson University, Graduate Programs, Master of Architecture Program, Elgin, IL 60123-1498. Offers architecture (M Arch); sustainable design (M Arch); traditional architecture and urbanism (M Arch). Part-time programs available. *Degree requirements:* For master's, thesis optional, 1600-hour practicum/preceptorship completed prior to enrollment. *Entrance requirements:* For master's, GRE, Judson BA in architecture or equivalent; minimum cumulative undergraduate GPA of 2.75, 3.0 in architecture; comprehensive portfolio; letter of intent. Additional exam requirements/recommendations for international students: Required—TOEFL (minimum score 550 paper-based), IELTS (minimum score 6.5). *Application deadline:* For fall admission, 2/15 priority date for domestic and international students; for winter admission, 11/15 for domestic students; for spring admission, 11/15 for domestic and international students. Applications are processed on a rolling basis. Application fee: $100. Electronic applications accepted. *Expenses:* Expenses: Contact institution. *Financial support:* Teaching assistantships with partial tuition reimbursements, career-related internships or fieldwork, Federal Work-Study, and unspecified assistantships available. Financial award application deadline: 7/1; financial award applicants required to submit FAFSA. *Faculty research:* Sustainable design, urbanism, daylighting, acoustics, digital media and fabrication. *Unit head:* Keelan Kaiser, Chair, 847-628-1011, E-mail: kkaiser@judsonu.edu. *Application contact:* Nathan McNeely, Director of Admissions, 847-628-2510, E-mail: nmcneely@judsonu.edu. Website: http://www.judsonu.edu/ArchMaster/

Kent State University, College of Architecture and Environmental Design, Kent, OH 44242-0001. Offers architecture (M Arch); architecture and environmental design (MS); health care design (MHCD); landscape architecture (ML Arch); urban design (MUD). Part-time programs available. *Faculty:* 24 full-time (5 women). *Students:* 66 full-time (25 women), 8 part-time (3 women); includes 5 minority (3 Black or African American, non-Hispanic/Latino; 1 American Indian or Alaska Native, non-Hispanic/Latino; 1 Asian, non-Hispanic/Latino), 4 international. Average age 25. 242 applicants, 67% accepted, 116 enrolled. In 2014, 45 degrees awarded. *Degree requirements:* For master's, thesis. *Entrance requirements:* For master's, GRE, minimum GPA of 3.0, writing sample, resume/curriculum vitae, letter of intent, portfolio, 3 letters of recommendation. Additional exam requirements/recommendations for international students: Required—TOEFL (minimum score: paper-based 525, iBT 71), Michigan English Language Assessment Battery (minimum score of 75), IELTS (minimum score of 6.0), PTE Academic (minimum score of 48), or completion of ELS level 112 Intensive Program. *Application deadline:* For fall admission, 1/15 for domestic and international students. Application fee: $45 ($70 for international students). Electronic applications accepted. *Expenses:* Tuition, state resident: full-time $8730; part-time $485 per credit hour. Tuition, nonresident: full-time $14,886; part-time $827 per credit hour. Tuition and fees vary according to campus/location and program. *Financial support:* Research assistantships with full tuition reimbursements, teaching assistantships with full tuition reimbursements, career-related internships or fieldwork, Federal Work-Study, scholarships/grants, and unspecified assistantships available. Financial award application deadline: 2/1. *Unit head:* Douglas Steidl, Dean, 330-672-2917, Fax: 330-672-3809, E-mail: dsteidl@kent.edu. *Application contact:* Lisa Pozo, Administrative Secretary, 330-672-2917, Fax: 330-672-3809, E-mail: caed_info@kent.edu. Website: http://www.kent.edu/caed

Lawrence Technological University, College of Architecture and Design, Southfield, MI 48075-1058. Offers architecture (M Arch); urban design (MUD). *Accreditation:* NASAD. Part-time and evening/weekend programs available. *Faculty:* 15 full-time (3 women), 30 part-time/adjunct (10 women). *Students:* 13 full-time (8 women), 208 part-time (84 women); includes 49 minority (6 Black or African American, non-Hispanic/Latino; 1 American Indian or Alaska Native, non-Hispanic/Latino; 26 Asian, non-Hispanic/Latino; 11 Hispanic/Latino; 5 Two or more races, non-Hispanic/Latino), 14 international. Average age 30. 139 applicants, 46% accepted, 43 enrolled. In 2014, 91 master's awarded. *Degree requirements:* For master's, thesis. *Entrance requirements:* Additional exam requirements/recommendations for international students: Required—TOEFL (minimum score 550 paper-based; 79 iBT). *Application deadline:* For fall admission, 5/15 priority date for domestic students, 5/29 for international students; for spring admission, 9/15 priority date for domestic students, 10/15 for international students; for summer admission, 2/15 for domestic students. Applications are processed on a rolling basis. Application fee: $50. Electronic applications accepted. *Expenses: Tuition:* Full-time $14,700; part-time $1050 per credit hour. *Required fees:* $150. One-time fee: $150 part-time. *Financial support:* In 2014–15, 66 students received support, including 5 research assistantships (averaging $6,090 per year); Federal Work-Study also available. Financial award application deadline: 4/1; financial award applicants required to submit FAFSA. *Unit head:* Glen LeRoy, Dean, 248-204-2800, Fax: 248-204-2900, E-mail: archdean@ltu.edu. *Application contact:* Jane Rohrback, Director of Admissions, 248-204-3160, Fax: 248-204-2228, E-mail: admissions@ltu.edu. Website: http://www.ltu.edu/architecture_and_design/index.asp

The New School, Parsons The New School for Design, Program in Design and Urban Ecologies, New York, NY 10011. Offers MS.

The New School, Parsons The New School for Design, Program in Theories of Urban Practice, New York, NY 10011. Offers MA.

New York Institute of Technology, School of Architecture and Design, Old Westbury, NY 11568-8000. Offers urban and regional design (M Arch). Part-time programs available. *Degree requirements:* For master's, thesis. *Entrance requirements:* For master's, minimum QPA of 2.85, portfolio. Additional exam requirements/recommendations for international students: Required—TOEFL (minimum score 550 paper-based; 79 iBT), IELTS (minimum score 6). Electronic applications accepted. *Faculty research:* Resilient cities, compact morphology, new town development, pedestrian-friendly public realm.

Prairie View A&M University, School of Architecture, Prairie View, TX 77446-0519. Offers architecture (M Arch); community development (MCD). Part-time and evening/weekend programs available. *Faculty:* 6 full-time (2 women), 5 part-time/adjunct (2 women). *Students:* 40 full-time (20 women), 15 part-time (9 women); includes 46 minority (41 Black or African American, non-Hispanic/Latino; 1 Asian, non-Hispanic/Latino; 2 Hispanic/Latino; 2 Two or more races, non-Hispanic/Latino), 5 international. Average age 30. 27 applicants, 100% accepted, 19 enrolled. In 2014, 36 master's awarded. *Degree requirements:* For master's, comprehensive exam, thesis. *Entrance requirements:* For master's, GRE General Test, portfolio (M Arch), minimum GPA of 2.75. Additional exam requirements/recommendations for international students: Required—TOEFL (minimum score 550 paper-based; 79 iBT). *Application deadline:* For fall admission, 7/1 priority date for domestic students, 6/1 priority date for international students; for spring admission, 11/1 priority date for domestic students, 10/1 priority date for international students; for summer admission, 3/1 priority date for domestic students, 2/1 priority date for international students. Applications are processed on a rolling basis. Application fee: $50. Electronic applications accepted. *Expenses:* Expenses: $6,686 tuition and fees. *Financial support:* Career-related internships or fieldwork, Federal Work-Study, institutionally sponsored loans, scholarships/grants, tuition waivers (full and partial), and unspecified assistantships available. Support available to part-time students. Financial award application deadline: 4/1; financial award applicants required to submit FAFSA. *Faculty research:* Community management, sustainable design. *Unit head:* Dr. Ikhlas Sabouni, Dean, 936-261-9800, Fax: 936-261-2350, E-mail: isabouni@pvamu.edu. *Application contact:* Pauline Walker, Administrative Assistant II, Research and Graduate Studies, 936-261-3521, Fax: 936-261-3529, E-mail: pmwalker@pvamu.edu.

★ **Pratt Institute,** School of Architecture, Program in Architecture and Urban Design, Brooklyn, NY 11205-3899. Offers MS. *Faculty:* 4 part-time/adjunct (2 women). *Students:* 6 full-time (2 women); includes 1 minority (Asian, non-Hispanic/Latino), 5 international. Average age 28. 62 applicants, 77% accepted, 5 enrolled. In 2014, 8 master's awarded. *Degree requirements:* For master's, thesis. *Entrance requirements:* For master's, portfolio, letters of recommendation. Additional exam requirements/recommendations for international students: Required—TOEFL (minimum score 550 paper-based; 79 iBT). *Application deadline:* For fall admission, 1/5 for domestic and international students. Application fee: $50 ($90 for international students). Electronic applications accepted. *Financial support:* Career-

related internships or fieldwork, Federal Work-Study, institutionally sponsored loans, scholarships/grants, health care benefits, and unspecified assistantships available. Support available to part-time students. Financial award application deadline: 2/1; financial award applicants required to submit FAFSA. *Faculty research:* Urban development process; historical, social, and economic implications of planning. *Unit head:* William J. Mac Donald, Chairperson, 718-399-4357, E-mail: wmacdona@pratt.edu. *Application contact:* Young Hah, Director of Graduate Admissions, 718-636-3683, Fax: 718-399-4242, E-mail: yhah@pratt.edu. Website: https://www.pratt.edu/academics/architecture/grad-arch-urban-design/

See Display on page 112 and Close-Up on page 139.

Rice University, Graduate Programs, School of Architecture, Houston, TX 77251-1892. Offers architecture (M Arch, D Arch); urban design (M Arch). *Degree requirements:* For master's, thesis optional; for doctorate, thesis/dissertation. *Entrance requirements:* For master's and doctorate, GRE. Additional exam requirements/recommendations for international students: Required—TOEFL (minimum score 600 paper-based; 100 iBT). Electronic applications accepted.

Savannah College of Art and Design, Graduate School, Program in Urban Design and Development, Savannah, GA 31402-3146. Offers MUD. Part-time programs available. *Faculty:* 1 full-time (0 women), 1 part-time/adjunct (0 women). *Students:* 21 full-time (7 women), 3 part-time (1 woman); includes 2 minority (1 Asian, non-Hispanic/Latino; 1 Hispanic/Latino), 17 international. Average age 27. 43 applicants, 58% accepted, 5 enrolled. In 2014, 6 master's awarded. *Degree requirements:* For master's, thesis, internship. *Entrance requirements:* For master's, portfolio. Additional exam requirements/recommendations for international students: Required—TOEFL (minimum score 550 paper-based, 85 iBT), IELTS (minimum score 6.5), or ACTFL. *Application deadline:* For fall admission, 4/1 for domestic and international students. Applications are processed on a rolling basis. Application fee: $40. Electronic applications accepted. *Expenses: Tuition:* Full-time $34,605; part-time $3845 per course. One-time fee: $500. Tuition and fees vary according to course load. *Financial support:* Fellowships, career-related internships or fieldwork, Federal Work-Study, and scholarships/grants available. Financial award application deadline: 4/1; financial award applicants required to submit FAFSA. *Unit head:* Ivan Chow, Interim Chair. *Application contact:* Jenny Jaquillard, Executive Director of Admissions, Recruitment and Events, 912-525-5100, Fax: 912-525-5985, E-mail: admission@scad.edu. Website: http://www.scad.edu/academics/programs/urban-design

State University of New York College of Environmental Science and Forestry, Department of Landscape Architecture, Syracuse, NY 13210-2779. Offers community design and planning (MLA, MS); cultural landscape studies and conservation (MLA, MS); landscape and urban ecology (MLA, MS). *Accreditation:* ASLA (one or more programs are accredited). *Degree requirements:* For master's, comprehensive exam (for some programs), thesis (for some programs). *Entrance requirements:* For master's, GRE General Test, minimum GPA of 3.0. Additional exam requirements/recommendations for international students: Required—TOEFL (minimum score 550 paper-based; 80 iBT), IELTS (minimum score 6), or STEP Aiken (grade 1). *Faculty research:* Site analysis and design, city and regional planning, community environments.

Temple University, College of Liberal Arts, Department of Geography and Urban Studies, Philadelphia, PA 19122-6096. Offers geography and urban studies (MA); urban studies (PhD). *Faculty:* 9 full-time (3 women), 1 (woman) part-time/adjunct. *Students:* 23 full-time (12 women), 4 part-time (2 women); includes 7 minority (5 Black or African American, non-Hispanic/Latino; 1 Hispanic/Latino; 1 Two or more races, non-Hispanic/Latino), 3 international. 48 applicants, 38% accepted, 10 enrolled. In 2014, 6 master's, 2 doctorates awarded. *Degree requirements:* For master's, comprehensive exam, thesis or alternative. *Entrance requirements:* For master's, GRE General Test, minimum GPA of 3.0, 3 letters of recommendation; for doctorate, GRE, minimum GPA of 3.0, 3 letters of recommendation. Additional exam requirements/recommendations for international students: Required—TOEFL (minimum score 575 paper-based; 88 iBT). *Application deadline:* For fall admission, 1/15 for domestic students, 12/15 for international students; for spring admission, 10/15 for domestic students, 8/1 for international students. Applications are processed on a rolling basis. Application fee: $60. Electronic applications accepted. *Expenses:* Tuition, state resident: full-time $14,490; part-time $805 per credit hour. Tuition, nonresident: full-time $19,850; part-time $1103 per credit hour. *Required fees:* $690. Full-time tuition and fees vary according to class time, course load, degree level, campus/location and program. *Financial support:* Fellowships, teaching assistantships, career-related internships or fieldwork, Federal Work-Study, and tuition waivers (partial) available. Financial award application deadline: 1/15; financial award applicants required to submit FAFSA. *Faculty research:* Social justice, sustainability, globalization, geographic methods, urban processes. *Unit head:* Dr. C. Hamil Pearsall, Graduate Director, 215-204-3074, Fax: 215-204-7833, E-mail: hamil.pearsall@temple.edu. *Application contact:* Tycina Cousin, Coordinator, 215-204-7692, Fax: 215-204-7833, E-mail: tcousin@temple.edu. Website: http://www.cla.temple.edu/gus/

University at Buffalo, the State University of New York, Graduate School, School of Architecture and Planning, Department of Architecture, Buffalo, NY 14214. Offers architecture (M Arch); flexible track (MS Arch); inclusive design (MS Arch); real estate development (MS Arch); situated technologies (MS Arch); urban design and historic preservation (MS Arch); M Arch/MBA; M Arch/MFA; M Arch/MUP. *Faculty:* 27 full-time (9 women), 13 part-time/adjunct (4 women). *Students:* 123 full-time (43 women), 4 part-time (1 woman); includes 19 minority (3 Black or African American, non-Hispanic/Latino; 7 Asian, non-Hispanic/Latino; 5 Hispanic/Latino; 4 Two or more races, non-Hispanic/Latino), 40 international. Average age 25. 181 applicants, 89% accepted, 65 enrolled. In 2014, 40 master's awarded. *Degree requirements:* For master's, thesis or alternative, project. *Entrance requirements:* For master's, GRE, portfolio, 3 letters of recommendation, transcripts, 500-word personal statement. Additional exam requirements/recommendations for international students: Required—TOEFL (minimum score 550 paper-based; 79 iBT), IELTS (minimum score 6.5). *Application deadline:* For fall admission, 1/15 priority date for domestic and international students. Application fee: $75. Electronic applications accepted. *Expenses:* Expenses: $7,017.50 per semester resident tuition and fees, $11,152.50 non-resident. *Financial support:* In 2014–15, 2 fellowships with full tuition reimbursements (averaging $20,618 per year), 10 research assistantships with full and partial tuition reimbursements (averaging $7,515 per year), 29 teaching assistantships with partial tuition reimbursements (averaging $4,865 per year) were awarded; career-related internships or fieldwork, Federal Work-Study, institutionally sponsored loans, scholarships/grants, health care benefits, tuition waivers (partial), and unspecified assistantships also available. Support available to part-time students. Financial award application deadline: 3/1; financial award applicants required to submit FAFSA. *Faculty research:* Inclusive design, material culture, situated technologies, ecological practices. *Total annual research expenditures:* $2.6 million. *Unit head:* Prof. Omar Khan, Chair, 716-829-3483 Ext. 105, Fax: 716-829-3256, E-mail: omar.khan@buffalo.edu. *Application contact:* Debra Eggebrecht, Assistant to the Chair, 716-829-3485 Ext. 105, Fax: 716-829-3256, E-mail: dle2@buffalo.edu. Website: http://www.ap.buffalo.edu/architecture/

University at Buffalo, the State University of New York, Graduate School, School of Architecture and Planning, Department of Urban and Regional Planning, Buffalo, NY 14214. Offers historic preservation (Certificate); urban and regional planning (PhD); JD/MUP; M Arch/MUP. *Accreditation:* ACSP. Part-time programs available. *Faculty:* 14 full-time (4 women), 13 part-time/adjunct (2 women). *Students:* 97 full-time (45 women), 8 part-time (3 women); includes 12 minority (7 Black or African American, non-Hispanic/Latino; 2 Asian, non-Hispanic/Latino; 3 Two or more races, non-Hispanic/Latino), 39 international. Average age 25. 183 applicants, 62% accepted, 45 enrolled. In 2014, 34 master's awarded. *Degree requirements:* For master's, thesis or alternative, project; for doctorate, thesis/dissertation. *Entrance requirements:* For master's, minimum GPA of 3.0, resume, 3 letters of recommendation, 500-word personal statement, transcripts; for doctorate, GRE, transcripts, 3 letters of recommendation, minimum GPA of 3.0, resume, research statement, writing sample. Additional exam requirements/recommendations for international students: Required—TOEFL (minimum score 550 paper-based; 79 iBT), IELTS (minimum score 6.5). *Application deadline:* For fall admission, 3/1 priority date for domestic and international students; for spring admission, 10/31 priority date for domestic students, 10/1 priority date for international students. Applications are processed on a rolling basis. Application fee: $75. Electronic applications accepted. *Expenses:* Expenses: $6,242.50 per semester resident tuition and fees, $11,125.50 non-resident. *Financial support:* In 2014–15, 2 fellowships with full tuition reimbursements (averaging $21,878 per year), 20 research assistantships with full and partial tuition reimbursements (averaging $6,604 per year), 13 teaching assistantships with partial tuition reimbursements (averaging $4,834 per year) were awarded; career-related internships or fieldwork, Federal Work-Study, institutionally sponsored loans, scholarships/grants, health care benefits, tuition waivers (partial), and unspecified assistantships also available. Support available to part-time students. Financial award application deadline: 3/1; financial award applicants required to submit FAFSA. *Faculty research:* Economic and international development, environmental and land use planning, GIS and spatial modeling, urban design and physical planning, neighborhood planning and community development. *Total annual research expenditures:* $1.1 million. *Unit head:* Dr. Ernest Sternberg, Professor, 716-829-3671 Ext. 109, Fax: 716-829-3256, E-mail: ezs@buffalo.edu. *Application contact:* Norma Everett, Assistant to the Chair, 716-829-3283, Fax: 716-829-3256, E-mail: norma.everett@buffalo.edu. Website: http://www.ap.buffalo.edu/planning/

University of California, Berkeley, Graduate Division, College of Environmental Design, Department of Architecture, Berkeley, CA 94720-1500. Offers architecture (M Arch); building science (MS, PhD); building structures, construction and materials (MS, PhD); design theories, methods, and practices (MS, PhD); environmental design in developing countries (MS, PhD); history of architecture and urbanism (MS, PhD); social and cultural processes in architecture and urbanism (MS, PhD); M Arch/MCP; M Arch/MS; MLA/M Arch. *Degree requirements:* For master's, thesis; for doctorate, thesis/dissertation, qualifying exam. *Entrance requirements:* For master's and doctorate, GRE General Test, minimum GPA of 3.0, 3 letters of recommendation. Additional exam requirements/recommendations for international students: Required—TOEFL. Electronic applications accepted.

University of California, Berkeley, Graduate Division, College of Environmental Design, Department of Landscape Architecture and Environmental Planning, Berkeley, CA 94720-1500. Offers landscape architecture (MLA), including environmental planning, landscape design and site planning, urban and community design; landscape architecture and environmental planning (PhD); MLA/M Arch; MLA/MCP. *Accreditation:* ASLA (one or more programs are accredited). *Degree requirements:* For master's, professional project or thesis; for doctorate, one foreign language, thesis/dissertation, qualifying exam. *Entrance requirements:* For master's, GRE General Test, minimum GPA of 3.0, portfolio; for doctorate, GRE General Test, master's degree (strongly recommended), minimum GPA of 3.0, sample of written work, 3 letters of recommendation.

University of California, Berkeley, Graduate Division, College of Environmental Design, Group in Urban Design, Berkeley, CA 94720-1500. Offers MUD. *Degree requirements:* For master's, professional project or thesis. *Entrance requirements:* For master's, GRE General Test, minimum GPA of 3.0, portfolio, 3 letters of recommendation.

University of California, Los Angeles, Graduate Division, School of the Arts and Architecture, Department of Architecture and Urban Design, Los Angeles, CA 90095. Offers M Arch, MA, PhD. *Degree requirements:* For master's, comprehensive exam (M Arch I, II); thesis (MA) ; for doctorate, 2 foreign languages, thesis/dissertation, oral and written qualifying exams. *Entrance requirements:* For master's, GRE General Test, bachelor's degree; minimum undergraduate GPA of 3.0 (or its equivalent if letter grade system not used); writing sample (MA only); portfolio (M Arch only); for doctorate, GRE General Test, bachelor's degree; minimum undergraduate GPA of 3.5 (or its equivalent if letter grade system not used); writing sample. Additional exam requirements/recommendations for international students: Required—TOEFL. Electronic applications accepted. *Expenses:* Contact institution.

University of Colorado Denver, College of Architecture and Planning, Program in Design and Planning, Denver, CO 80217. Offers history of architecture, landscape and urbanism (PhD); sustainable and healthy environments (PhD). Part-time programs available. *Students:* 9 full-time (3 women), 11 part-time (9 women); includes 1 minority (Hispanic/Latino), 7 international. Average age 38. 32 applicants, 6% accepted, 1 enrolled. In 2014, 4 doctorates awarded. *Degree requirements:* For doctorate, comprehensive exam, thesis/dissertation. *Entrance requirements:* For doctorate, GRE (minimum score of 158 for both verbal and quantitative; writing 4.0), minimum undergraduate GPA of 3.0, graduate 3.5; writing sample; three letters of recommendation; statement of personal and professional goals. Additional exam requirements/recommendations for international students: Required—TOEFL (minimum score 80 iBT); Recommended—IELTS (minimum score 6.8). *Application deadline:* For fall admission, 2/2 for domestic students, 1/2 for international students; for spring admission, 10/1 for domestic students. Application fee: $50 ($75 for international students). Electronic applications accepted. *Expenses:* Expenses: Contact institution. *Financial support:* In 2014–15, 2 students received support. Fellowships, research assistantships, teaching assistantships, Federal Work-Study, institutionally sponsored loans, scholarships/grants, traineeships, and unspecified assistantships available. Financial award application deadline: 4/1; financial award applicants required to submit FAFSA. *Faculty research:* Land use and environmental planning and design; design and planning processes and practices; history, theory, and criticism of the built environment. *Unit head:* Dr. Osman Attmann, Director, 303-315-0032, Fax: 303-556-3687, E-mail: o.attmann@ucdenver.edu. *Application contact:* Rachael Kuroiwa, Manager of Admissions and Outreach, 303-315-2325, E-mail: rachael.kuroiwa@ucdenver.edu. Website: http://www.ucdenver.edu/academics/colleges/ArchitecturePlanning/Academics/DegreePrograms/PhD/Pages/PhD.aspx

University of Colorado Denver, College of Architecture and Planning, Program in Urban Design, Denver, CO 80217. Offers MUD. Part-time programs available. *Students:* 14 full-time (1 woman), 2 part-time (1 woman); includes 2 minority (both Hispanic/Latino), 6 international. Average age 30. 24 applicants, 58% accepted, 6 enrolled. In

2014, 15 master's awarded. *Degree requirements:* For master's, thesis optional, 36 credits, including an independent study, internship, or additional elective. *Entrance requirements:* For master's, GRE (for students with an undergraduate GPA below 3.0), BA in related field and a prior professional degree, portfolio of creative work; statement of purpose; resume. Additional exam requirements/recommendations for international students: Required—TOEFL (minimum score 75 iBT). *Application deadline:* For fall admission, 2/15 priority date for domestic students, 1/15 priority date for international students; for spring admission, 10/1 for domestic students. Applications are processed on a rolling basis. Application fee: $50 ($75 for international students). Electronic applications accepted. *Expenses:* Expenses: Contact institution. *Financial support:* In 2014–15, 3 students received support. Fellowships, research assistantships, teaching assistantships, Federal Work-Study, institutionally sponsored loans, scholarships/grants, and traineeships available. Financial award application deadline: 4/1; financial award applicants required to submit FAFSA. *Faculty research:* Architecture of the city, architectural experimentation and exploration, composition and decomposition, intervention and transformation in the urban and rural landscape. *Unit head:* Jeremy Nemeth, Co-Director of Urban Design Program, 303-315-0069, E-mail: jeremy.nemeth@ucdenver.edu. *Application contact:* Rachael Kuroiwa, Manager of Admissions and Outreach, 303-315-2325, E-mail: rachael.kuroiwa@ucdenver.edu.
Website: http://www.ucdenver.edu/academics/colleges/ArchitecturePlanning/Academics/DegreePrograms/MUD/Pages/MUD.aspx

University of Colorado Denver, School of Education and Human Development, Program in Educational Leadership and Innovation, Denver, CO 80217. Offers educational studies and research (PhD), including administrative leadership and policy, early childhood special education, math education, research, assessment and evaluation, science education, urban ecologies. Part-time and evening/weekend programs available. *Students:* 22 full-time (19 women), 11 part-time (9 women); includes 10 minority (3 Black or African American, non-Hispanic/Latino; 2 American Indian or Alaska Native, non-Hispanic/Latino; 3 Asian, non-Hispanic/Latino; 2 Hispanic/Latino), 3 international. Average age 39. 24 applicants, 46% accepted, 7 enrolled. In 2014, 2 doctorates awarded. *Degree requirements:* For doctorate, comprehensive exam, thesis/dissertation, 75 credit hours (for PhD). *Entrance requirements:* For doctorate, GRE or equivalent, resume or curriculum vitae, letters of recommendation, master's degree or equivalent, completion of basic or advanced statistics course with minimum B grade. Additional exam requirements/recommendations for international students: Required—TOEFL (minimum score 537 paper-based; 75 iBT); Recommended—IELTS (minimum score 6.5). *Application deadline:* For fall admission, 12/1 priority date for domestic students, 11/1 priority date for international students. Applications are processed on a rolling basis. Application fee: $50 ($75 for international students). Electronic applications accepted. *Expenses:* Expenses: Contact institution. *Financial support:* In 2014–15, 14 students received support. Fellowships, research assistantships, teaching assistantships, Federal Work-Study, institutionally sponsored loans, scholarships/grants, and traineeships available. Financial award application deadline: 4/1; financial award applicants required to submit FAFSA. *Faculty research:* Administrative leadership and policy studies, early childhood education, research in diversity, paraprofessionals in education, urban schools lab. *Unit head:* Shelley Zion, Executive Director, Continuing and Professional Education, 303-315-4985, E-mail: shelley.zion@ucdenver.edu. *Application contact:* Jason Clark, Director of Recruitment and Retention, 303-315-0183, E-mail: jason.clark@ucdenver.edu.
Website: http://www.ucdenver.edu/academics/colleges/SchoolOfEducation/Academics/Doctorate/Pages/PhD%20in%20Education%20and%20Human%20Development.aspx

University of Miami, Graduate School, School of Architecture, Program in Suburb and Town Design, Coral Gables, FL 33124. Offers M Arch. *Entrance requirements:* For master's, GRE General Test, minimum GPA of 3.0, portfolio. Additional exam requirements/recommendations for international students: Required—TOEFL. Electronic applications accepted.

University of Michigan, Taubman College of Architecture and Urban Planning, Master of Urban Design Program, Ann Arbor, MI 48109. Offers MUD. *Application deadline:* For fall admission, 1/15 for domestic and international students.
Website: http://taubmancollege.umich.edu/architecture/degrees/master-urban-design

University of New Mexico, Graduate School, School of Architecture and Planning, Program in Town Design, Albuquerque, NM 87131-2039. Offers Graduate Certificate. Part-time programs available. *Students:* 1 applicant. *Application deadline:* For fall admission, 3/1 for domestic students; for spring admission, 11/1 for domestic students. Application fee: $50. Electronic applications accepted. *Unit head:* Mark C. Childs, Director, 505-277-5059, Fax: 505-277-0076, E-mail: mchilds@unm.edu. *Application contact:* Elizabeth M. Rowe, Senior Academic Adviser, 505-277-1303, Fax: 505-277-0076, E-mail: erowe@unm.edu.
Website: http://saap.unm.edu

The University of North Carolina at Charlotte, College of Arts and Architecture, School of Architecture, Charlotte, NC 28223-0001. Offers M Arch I, M Arch II, MUD. *Faculty:* 26 full-time (7 women), 1 part-time/adjunct (0 women). *Students:* 79 full-time (44 women), 2 part-time (0 women); includes 18 minority (9 Black or African American, non-Hispanic/Latino; 1 Asian, non-Hispanic/Latino; 6 Hispanic/Latino; 2 Two or more races, non-Hispanic/Latino), 11 international. Average age 25. 125 applicants, 82% accepted, 43 enrolled. In 2014, 35 master's awarded. *Degree requirements:* For master's, thesis or alternative, project. *Entrance requirements:* For master's, GRE, statement of purpose, letters of recommendation, portfolio. Additional exam requirements/recommendations for international students: Required—TOEFL (minimum score 557 paper-based; 83 iBT). *Application deadline:* For fall admission, 1/15 for domestic and international students. Application fee: $75. Electronic applications accepted. *Expenses:* Tuition, state resident: full-time $4008. Tuition, nonresident: full-time $16,295. *Required fees:* $2755. Tuition and fees vary according to course load and program. *Financial support:* In 2014–15, 36 students received support, including 31 research assistantships (averaging $6,886 per year), 5 teaching assistantships (averaging $2,000 per year); unspecified assistantships also available. Financial award applicants required to submit FAFSA. *Faculty research:* Urban design studies for local and regional municipalities and community groups, high performance building and optimization protocols, daylighting and energy analysis, digital design and fabrication components, and interactive visualization; refinement of regionally specific computer-aided analysis tools used to evaluate total building energy performance, and the economic valuation of architectural systems and their design attributes. *Total annual research expenditures:* $201,227. *Unit head:* Kenneth A. Lambla, Dean, 704-687-0090, Fax: 704-687-0105, E-mail: kalambla@uncc.edu. *Application contact:* Kathy B. Giddings, Director of Graduate Admissions, 704-687-5503, Fax: 704-687-1668, E-mail: gradadm@uncc.edu.
Website: http://coaa.uncc.edu/academics/school-of-architecture

University of Pennsylvania, School of Design, Department of City and Regional Planning, Philadelphia, PA 19104. Offers city and regional planning (PhD); city planning (MCP); GIS and spatial analysis (Certificate); land preservation (Certificate); urban design (Certificate); urban redevelopment (Certificate); urban spatial analytics (MUSA). *Accreditation:* ACSP (one or more programs are accredited). *Faculty:* 15 full-time (6 women), 6 part-time/adjunct (0 women). *Students:* 158 full-time (87 women), 9 part-time (8 women); includes 32 minority (3 Black or African American, non-Hispanic/Latino; 15 Asian, non-Hispanic/Latino; 6 Hispanic/Latino; 1 Native Hawaiian or other Pacific Islander, non-Hispanic/Latino; 7 Two or more races, non-Hispanic/Latino), 62 international. 475 applicants, 46% accepted, 75 enrolled. In 2014, 89 master's, 3 other advanced degrees awarded. *Degree requirements:* For doctorate, thesis/dissertation, 20 approved courses, 4 seminars, 2 methods courses, writing and presentation/scholarly preparation, qualifying examination, final defense. *Entrance requirements:* For master's, GRE General Test; for doctorate, GRE General Test, writing sample. Additional exam requirements/recommendations for international students: Required—TOEFL, IELTS. *Application deadline:* For fall admission, 1/14 priority date for domestic and international students. Application fee: $80. Electronic applications accepted. *Financial support:* Fellowships, research assistantships, teaching assistantships, institutionally sponsored loans, scholarships/grants, and health care benefits available. Financial award application deadline: 2/15; financial award applicants required to submit FAFSA. *Faculty research:* Growth management, transportation planning, urban simulation modeling, housing, development planning. *Unit head:* Marilyn Jordan Taylor, Dean, 215-898-6520, E-mail: mjtaylor@design.upenn.edu. *Application contact:* Office of Admissions and Financial Aid, 215-898-6520, E-mail: admissions@design.upenn.edu.
Website: http://www.design.upenn.edu/city-regional-planning/graduate/work

The University of Texas at Austin, Graduate School, School of Architecture, Program in Urban Design, Austin, TX 78712-1111. Offers M Arch, MSUD.

University of Toronto, School of Graduate Studies, Faculty of Arts and Science, Department of Geography, Program in Planning, Toronto, ON M5S 2J7, Canada. Offers M Sc Pl, MUDS, PhD. Part-time programs available. *Degree requirements:* For master's, summer internship. *Entrance requirements:* For master's, bachelor's degree in planning, geography, social science or a closely related professional field, minimum B+ average in final year, 3 letters of reference; for doctorate, minimum A- or equivalent standing in previous master's program. Additional exam requirements/recommendations for international students: Required—TOEFL (minimum score 580 paper-based; 93 iBT), TWE (minimum score 5). Electronic applications accepted. *Expenses:* Contact institution.

University of Toronto, School of Graduate Studies, John H. Daniels Faculty of Architecture, Landscape, and Design, Toronto, ON M5S 2J7, Canada. Offers M Arch, MLA, MUD, MVS. *Accreditation:* ASLA. *Entrance requirements:* For master's, minimum B average; 3 letters of reference; resume; 3 writing samples; 5 samples of design work, drawing, or work in a related field, statement of interest. Additional exam requirements/recommendations for international students: Required—TOEFL (minimum score 580 paper-based; 93 iBT), IELTS (minimum score 7), TWE (minimum score 5), Michigan English Language Assessment Battery (minimum score 85), COPE (minimum score 76). Electronic applications accepted. *Expenses:* Contact institution.

University of Washington, Graduate School, College of Built Environments, Department of Urban Design and Planning, Seattle, WA 98195. Offers urban design and planning (PhD); urban planning (MUP). *Accreditation:* ACSP (one or more programs are accredited). *Degree requirements:* For master's, thesis or alternative; for doctorate, thesis/dissertation. *Entrance requirements:* For master's and doctorate, GRE General Test, minimum GPA of 3.0. Additional exam requirements/recommendations for international students: Required—TOEFL. *Faculty research:* Land-use and growth management, urban form and travel behavior, geographic information systems/remote sensing, historic preservation, urban ecology and environmental planning.

University of Washington, Graduate School, College of Built Environments, Interdisciplinary Program in Urban Design, Seattle, WA 98195. Offers Certificate. Electronic applications accepted. *Faculty research:* Urban design process; urban form; place theory; place analysis; race, class, and gender in community design.

Washington University in St. Louis, Sam Fox School of Design and Visual Arts, Program in Urban Design, St. Louis, MO 63130-4899. Offers MUD, M Arch/MUD, MUD/MSW. *Entrance requirements:* For master's, GRE General Test, portfolio. Additional exam requirements/recommendations for international students: Required—TOEFL (minimum score 600 paper-based; 100 iBT), TWE. *Faculty research:* Urban design development issues: city revitalization, sustainability and suburbanization; urban history and visualization of urban form.

BALL STATE UNIVERSITY
College of Architecture and Planning

 For more information, visit http://petersons.to/ballstatearchitecture

Programs of Study

The College of Architecture and Planning (CAP) at Ball State University is consistently recognized for the high quality of its graduate and undergraduate programs. *Design Intelligence* named the college among "America's World-Class Schools of Architecture" and among the Top 10 in the nation for landscape architecture. In addition to academic rigor, CAP stresses community-based learning, sustainability, digital fabrication, and social justice.

Ball State's College of Architecture and Planning divides the study of the art and science of environmental design and planning into three distinct departments: the Department of Architecture, the Department of Landscape Architecture, and the Department of Urban Planning. The following graduate professional degrees are offered: Master of Architecture (M.Arch. professional and M.Arch. II professional), Master of Science in Historic Preservation, Master of Landscape Architecture, Master of Urban and Regional Planning, and Master of Urban Design.

Since its founding in 1965, CAP has established and promoted specific programs that combine teaching, research, and service activities that focus on the environmental design and planning professions. Students studying in the College of Architecture and Planning have been all over the world. They take part in focused field study programs arranged by their departments or programs. They also may choose from a range of university-wide programs, such as CAP Italia, CAP Asia, World Tour, and the Ball State Study Abroad Program.

The studio method of education is central to the College of Architecture and Planning's success and provides students with hands-on design experience almost every semester. That makes the design studios the hub of activity in the college.

Throughout their college career, students are assigned their own personal studio space, accessible 24/7 while the University is in session. Each design studio offers state-of-the-art tools and materials for creating drawings, models, and other hands-on assignments. All departmental and faculty offices are located near the studios to enhance mentoring and student/faculty rapport.

Students have access to a variety of digital design and presentation tools, including 3-D modeling and animation software, video filming and editing equipment, and live interactive media. In addition, students have access to the equipment needed for working with wood, metal, plastics, glass, and other materials. Equipment includes woodworking machines, welding equipment, vacuum forming machines, laser cutters, 3-D printers, a CNC router, Kuka robotic arm, and virtual reality helmet.

Research Facilities

CAP's outreach, applied research, and research initiatives provide low- or no-cost expertise to communities while offering students excellent opportunities for real-world experience. Resources include the following:

- CAP Indianapolis Center (CAP:IC) offers research and academic opportunities, forums, and lab experiences for students and professionals in the state's largest urban area. Additional information is available at bsu.edu/capic.

- Center for Energy Research/Education/Service (CERES) is an interdisciplinary resource focusing on issues related to energy and resource use, alternatives, and conservation. More information is online at bsu.edu/ceres.
- Center for Historic Preservation (CHP) provides experiences for students and services to communities seeking economic development through preservation. Additional details can be found online at bsu.edu/chp.
- Design–Build Lab, offering on-site building and learning space.
- Drawings and Documents Archive collects and preserves records about Indiana's historic sites and structures.
- Digital Fabrication Lab (DFL) contains equipment for designing and making 1:1 prototypes of building and furniture components, as well as smaller-scale models.
- Hybrid Design Technologies (HDT) supports the design and production of virtual, immersive and interactive environments, developing innovative immersive solutions for cultural heritage, museums, arts, teaching and learning. (http://cms.bsu.edu/about/administrativeoffices/hybriddesigntech)

Financial Aid

More than 75 percent of Ball State students receive financial aid in the form of loans, scholarships, grants, and other options. Graduate students are eligible to apply for Federal Direct Stafford loans, Federal Direct Graduate PLUS loans, and student employment. Priority for Federal Perkins and Federal Work-Study is given to undergraduate students, with graduate students considered on a funds-available basis.

A number of graduate assistantships and doctoral fellowships are available to qualified graduate students and may provide a stipend and partial fee remission for the academic year.

Cost of Study

The most current information regarding tuition and fees can be accessed by contacting the Ball State University Bursar's office at bursar@bsu.edu or 765-285-1643.

Living and Housing

Ball State has on-campus housing available for graduate students. Shively Hall in the LaFollette complex offers accommodations for students age 21 or older. Graduate students may also apply to live in one of the 580 units for married students and families in the Anthony or Schiedler apartment complexes. Students also take advantage of local apartment complexes and rental homes, many within walking or bicycle distance to the campus.

Student Organizations

The College of Architecture and Planning has many established student professional organizations that include the American Institute of Architecture Students (AIAS), Student Planning Association, a student chapter of the American Society of Landscape Architecture, National Organization of Minority Architects, Emerging Green Builders, Freedom by Design, Associated Students for Historic Preservation, and Sigma Lambda Alpha. There are also another 350 student organizations active at Ball State University.

SECTION 2: ARCHITECTURE

Ball State University

The Faculty

There are more than 50 full-time professors, instructors, and visiting scholars in the College of Architecture and Planning. All are committed to teaching, research, practice, and public service. These teacher–scholars have studied and taught in leading academic institutions throughout the world. Most have professional experience in the subject areas they teach. They apply their knowledge and skills through projects in communities throughout the state and region.

The University

Founded in 1918, Ball State University is a state-assisted residential university in Muncie, Indiana, a midsize Midwestern city 1 hour northeast of Indianapolis. About 21,000 undergraduate and graduate students enroll each year in diverse academic programs on and off campus.

Ball State is ranked a research university, high research activity by the Carnegie Foundation for the Advancement of Teaching and is accredited by the Higher Learning Commission of the North Central Association of Colleges and Schools. Individual programs are accredited by various regional and national organizations. All College of Architecture and Planning professional programs are accredited.

Applying

To apply to the graduate programs in the College of Architecture and Planning, students must have a bachelor's degree or equivalent from an accredited college or university and meet admission requirements developed by their degree-department. In addition, prospective students must also meet the requirements of the Ball State Graduate School or the Rinker Center for International Programs. More application information is available at bsu.edu/cap.

Correspondence and Information
College of Architecture and Planning
Ball State University
2000 West University Avenue, AB104
Muncie, Indiana 47306
United States
Phone: 765-285-5861 (College of Architecture and Planning)
            866-285-4723 (toll-free) (Graduate School)
E-mail: cap@bsu.edu
Website: bsu.edu/cap (College of Architecture and Planning)
            bsu.edu/gradschool (Ball State University Graduate School)
Facebook: facebook.com/BallStateCAP
Instagram: Instagram.com/BallStateCAP
Twitter: @BallStateCAP

FRANK LLOYD WRIGHT SCHOOL OF ARCHITECTURE
Master of Architecture Program

 For more information, visit http://petersons.to/franklloydwrightarchitecture

Programs of Study

Founded by Frank Lloyd Wright in 1932 as an alternative to traditional architectural education, Taliesin, the Frank Lloyd Wright School of Architecture today provides a professional Master of Architecture (M.Arch.) degree in an intensive, in-residence academic environment. The program is designed for self-motivated students who thrive in a multifaceted environment focusing on rigorous design, critical thinking, exploration, and hands-on learning.

The Master of Architecture (M.Arch.) program prepares students in advanced design, professional practice, and hands-on application while emerging them in the communities Wright designed at Taliesin in Spring Green, Wisconsin, and Taliesin West in Scottsdale, Arizona.

The School's small scale facilitates an individualized educational experience and fosters a close and dynamic relationship between students, faculty, and staff. Students explore the discipline through work in the design studio, through architectural practice, in seminars with noted scholars, and on design-build projects.

The Taliesin community empowers students to be leaders within the framework of residence life and provides a rich set of experiences outside the architectural discipline. Students host key events, create design identities for campus initiatives, help prepare meals, garden in on-campus gardens, perform music, and exhibit design projects to an invited audiences. More information is available at http://www.taliesin.edu/program.html.

Philosophy

Before new apprentices would arrive, Frank Lloyd Wright would famously tell them to bring four things: a drafting pencil, a hammer, a sleeping bag, and a tuxedo. The logic behind these requirements remains the same today: to learn by drawing, by making, by being there, and by being part of a civilized conversation about the past, present, and future of our culture. Students learn how to embrace and celebrate diverse cultures and customs while also developing the art and methods they need to explain their designs and converse with others. Once a month, students participate in Taliesin Evenings, which fill the campus with music, dance, and dialogue with members of the community. Students thus have the opportunity to meet with faculty and visitors both for formal education and for cultural and social events, participating in everything from making music to doing the dishes.

The education at Taliesin is immersive and offers the opportunity to work side by side with professors, participating in hands-on projects all day and into the evening. The Frank Lloyd Wright School of Architecture also embodies Wright's concepts of organic architecture; to build with the land rather than just upon it. The design process unfolds out of existing cultural and physical condition, materials, and landscapes into well-crafted frameworks for human activities.

Curriculum

The mission of the Frank Lloyd Wright School of Architecture is to be a place where students learn how to make a human-made environment that is more sustainable, open, and aesthetically beautiful. The School's curriculum is based on the notion of learning by doing and experience through experimentation. The School trains the next generation of architects to be designers, thinkers, and visionaries, but also fully formed citizens and human beings. All of the core faculty members are practicing architects, and thus bring to the studio not only the principles and methodology of architecture, but also real-world experience.

The Core Curriculum comprises three phases: foundation, exploration, and synthesis. Studios, workshops, and classes designated as Core are required activities, and occur at intervals throughout the student's course of study. The Core Curriculum includes design studios, classes, architectural practice activities, research, and shelter construction and preservation projects. Students are required to attend all Core offerings, which may be complimented with independent study as approved by faculty. Core requirements may be adjusted based on evaluation of prior work. Twice a year, students demonstrate their comprehensive ability in design by choosing and developing a project.

Originally a present to Frank Lloyd Wright for Christmas and his birthday, the "box" project is now a celebration of innovation, imagination, and synthesis of knowledge. Students research and develop their projects under the support of a chosen mentor, and document all stages of the process for their ongoing learning portfolio. These projects are presented to faculty and peers, and are critiqued after the presentation. Students are required to

represent and critically examine all Core Curriculum work in their portfolios due at the end of each semester.

Living and Self-Discovery

Continuing a tradition begun in 1937, the School operates seasonally at two locations. From mid-October through mid-May, the School is in session at Taliesin West in Scottsdale, Arizona. Mid-May through mid-October is spent at Taliesin in Spring Green, Wisconsin. The Taliesin educational experience is closely linked to its two architecturally stunning campuses and is fueled by the year-round educational community. This intense and rewarding residential experience is shaped by two forces that bear essential relevance on the experience of architecture: the force of the landscape as captured in the genius loci (spirit of place) of the two campuses, and the force of self-discovery in the context of a living culture of architecture. The migration travels provide opportunities to visit places of interest, architectural sites, and experience the vast landscapes between Arizona and Wisconsin.

Taliesin students live on-campus and participate in the life of the academic community. Housing is available in rooms within the historic campus and in the experimental dwellings designed by previous students built in the landscape surrounding the campus core. In keeping with Taliesin tradition, students are provided the opportunity to design, build, and live in their own experimental structures as a component of their learning program and personal portfolio.

The community component of the program is based on Wright's strongly-held belief that, "a great architect is not made by way of a brain nearly so much as he is made by way of a cultivated, enriched heart." Community involvement at Taliesin provides opportunities for students to explore the social and cultural contexts of architecture and to integrate and apply the content, philosophies, and disciplines of all learning through the experience and social interaction of daily living and community maintenance.

Through participation in community, students learn to apply critical thinking and creative problem solving in challenging situations that arise as part of projects of any size; and they learn to resolve the human problems that occur whenever people attempt to work together cooperatively. Students come from a wide variety of cultural and socioeconomic backgrounds, yet are expected to leave Taliesin prepared to function as professionals. Community participation, by providing students with opportunities to develop social skills, conversational skills, leadership and collaborative skills, and cultural awareness, prepares them to enter the architectural profession with the poise and confidence needed to interact with clients of all kinds.

With nearly 90 percent of all graduates actively working in the architectural field, the Frank Lloyd Wright School of Architecture's practice of discovery and invention builds architects who can thrive within the context of the rapidly changing world.

Cost of Study

The cost of attendance is $40,500 annually and covers tuition, room /board, food, accident insurance, and facility fee. There are scholarships and financial aid available for those who qualify.

Correspondence and Information
Director of Admissions
Frank Lloyd Wright School of Architecture
Taliesin West
P.O. Box 4430
Scottsdale, Arizona 85261-4430
United States
Phone: 480-627-5345
E-mail: admissions@taliesin.edu
Website: http://www.taliesin.edu

The historic studio at Taliesin West.

PRATT INSTITUTE
School of Architecture

 For more information, visit http://petersons.to/prattarchitecture

Programs of Study

The School of Architecture is dedicated to maintaining the connection between design theory and practice and to extending the range of knowledge necessary to an understanding of the built environment. The diversity of programs within the School and the accessibility of other programs within the Institute enable students to pursue a wide range of interests. Students can take electives in fine arts, film, digital arts, industrial design, furniture design, interior design, and photography as well as electives in advanced architectural theory, design, technology, and management. The School has many internationally recognized faculty members who bring to the graduate programs a strong theoretical base and the high standards of their professional work. The programs are distinguished by strong studio cultures and creative approaches to architectural design. Many special courses are offered in contemporary theoretical and critical issues, advanced computing and media, building technology, architectural history, and experimental structures. Students are exposed to the professional world through optional internship programs that place them in outstanding New York architectural offices, public agencies, and nonprofit design institutions, giving them firsthand work experience and credit towards their degree.

The School of Architecture offers a total of eight graduate programs. There are two graduate architecture programs: the first-professional accredited Master of Architecture (M.Arch.) and the post-professional Master of Architecture (M.S.Arch.). There are also six Master of Science programs: Architecture and Urban Design, City and Regional Planning, Environmental Systems Management, Facilities Management, Historic Preservation, and Urban Placemaking and Management.

The three-year M.Arch. first-professional program is designed for students holding a four-year undergraduate program in any field, including architecture. Graduate courses and seminars are designed to familiarize students with all aspects of the discipline and practice of architecture. Design studios at Pratt find many of their coordinates within the rich territory of New York City. However, the program also reaches into areas worldwide and into other frames, such as global marketplaces, digital worlds, and historical, theoretical, and political networks. This program is fully accredited by NAAB. Students with a B.S. in Architecture or other non-professional degree should apply for this M.Arch. program. The post-professional M.S.Arch., a summer/fall/spring program, is for those who hold an accredited architecture degree or the equivalent. The program takes three semesters to complete. Students with significant professional experience can also apply for work credit, which reduces total credit-hour requirements. The post-professional M.S.Arch. allows intensive theoretical and technical engagement of architecture and the city and stresses research and experimentation concentrating on the relations between architecture and other urban forms, scales, and forces. Research is conducted primarily within the analytic and synthetic content of the design studio and culminates in a required thesis.

The Master of Science in Architecture and Urban Design program is intended for students who are interested in careers that enhance the growth and development of the built urban environments, the context for an urban laboratory. The 33-credit program requires 17 hours of design studio and research, with the balance of the credits in required courses in urban history, theory, infrastructure, and implementation and electives in law, transportation, housing, and preservation. The program is open to those with professional undergraduate degrees in architecture and is a summer/fall/spring program.

The five programs offered by Pratt's Programs for Sustainable Planning and Development (PSPD)—the M.S. in City and Regional Planning (CRP), the M.S. in Environmental Systems Management (ESM), the M.S. in Historic Preservation, the M.S. in Urban Placemaking and Management and the M.S. in Facilities Management (FM)—emphasize planning and preservation practice rooted in the principles of sustainability, equity, and public participation.

The curricula are designed to build the professional skills and knowledge of students who desire to affect the built, natural, and social environments of the nation's cities and communities in positive ways. CRP and ESM courses are offered in the evenings, enabling students to work full-time. The City and Regional planning program offers specializations in community development, environmental planning, physical planning, and preservation planning. The CRP program requires the completion of 60 credits, including the thesis or the Demonstration of Professional Competence course. The Urban Placemaking and Management program requires the completion of 40 credits. The curriculum of study includes Design and Infrastructure, Economics, Planning and Policy and Management. The ESM program requires 40 credits of course work and includes a focus on sustainability.

Students with undergraduate degrees in architecture and engineering may have up to 9 credits waived in either the CRP or ESM program.

PSPD's Historic Preservation program is a two-year graduate program leading to the M.S. in Historic Preservation. The program, designed primarily for full-time students and based at the Brooklyn campus, is a 44-credit sequence of courses that provides studies in community planning, history, interpretation, design, policy, and regulatory practice.

Recognizing that today's field of preservation requires more than curatorial management, the program fosters the knowledge preservationists must have in order to participate in policy-making to revitalize urban areas, suburban communities, and rural landscapes. With its urban focus, the program emphasizes hands-on work and makes extensive use of New York City's rich resources.

All five graduate programs in the PSPD maintain strong ties with Pratt's architecture and design programs and with the Pratt Center for Community Development, an innovative center for the practice of planning, design, and policy work that focuses on increasing quality of life and affecting social change in New York City's diverse communities.

The M.S. in Facilities Management program prepares individuals to assume leadership roles in corporations, institutions, and government. The degree requires the completion of 45 credits of course work and the 5-credit Demonstration of Professional Competence course, for a total of 50 credits. Students entering the program with prior professional experience or graduate work in related fields may be eligible for advanced standing; up to 12 credits may be waived. The facilities management program, accredited by IFMA, is offered at the Pratt Manhattan Center on an evening schedule, allowing maximum flexibility to combine full-time work with study and research. Students may take courses in any of the programs in PSPD.

Research Facilities

The Pratt Library has grown with the Institute to house one of the finest collections of reference material on art, design, and architecture.

Pratt maintains numerous studios, shops, and technical facilities for work in all media, as well as state-of-the-art computer facilities. Pratt also has extensive gallery space for the exhibition of works by the student body, alumni, faculty members, and well-known architects and designers.

Financial Aid

Financial aid awards are offered through a variety of institutional, state, and federally funded programs. These include Graduate Scholarships awarded by departments to incoming students on the basis of merit, endowed and restricted scholarships for continuing students, and student employment. Assistantships are awarded on a competitive basis to continuing students in all departments. Special alumni-sponsored fellowships are also available.

Cost of Study

Graduate tuition for 2015–16 is $ $28,638 per year (full-time 18 credits, $1,591 per credit). Student fees are $1,932 per semester. The cost of books and supplies varies widely, depending on the program in which the student is enrolled.

Living and Housing Costs

Campus housing continues to be expanded to meet student needs and is available for single students on a first-come, first-served basis. Housing costs average $21,712 per academic year. There is a plentiful supply of moderately priced rentals in the immediate area and in adjacent neighborhoods for married students seeking housing as well as for those students choosing to reside off campus.

Student Group

There are 338 students enrolled in Pratt's School of Architecture graduate programs; 53 percent are women. They come from all parts of the United States and the world. The graduate programs are noted for an exceptional placement ratio, with more than 85 percent of the graduating students finding employment before graduation.

Location

Pratt Institute is located in the Clinton Hill section of Brooklyn, on a 25-acre park-like campus. Pratt's Manhattan campus houses the Institute's graduate arts and cultural management, communications design, design management, facilities management, historic preservation, and library and information science programs as well as offering courses in architecture, city and regional planning, creative arts therapy, and urban design.

The Institute

A private, nonsectarian institute of higher education, Pratt Institute was founded in 1887 by the industrialist and philanthropist Charles Pratt. Today, Pratt educates 3,145 undergraduates and 1,411 graduate students for careers in art and design, architecture, and library and information science.

Applying

The deadline for applications and all supporting materials, including portfolio, is January 5. Applicants should complete the application process online. Early submission of applications with all necessary credentials is highly desirable. For applicants who intend to file for financial aid, applications and all supporting documents should be received no later than January 5 for the fall semester and October 1 for the spring semester. Applications received after these dates are considered if openings exist in a particular program.

Correspondence and Information

Graduate Admissions Office
Pratt Institute
200 Willoughby Avenue
Brooklyn, New York 11205
Phone: 718-636-3514
       800-331-0834 (toll-free outside New York State)
Fax: 718-399-4242
E-mail: admissions@pratt.edu
Website: http://www.pratt.edu

THE FACULTY

Thomas Hanrahan, Dean; M.Arch., Harvard; AIA, NCARB.

Architecture

William MacDonald, Professor and Chair; M.S., Columbia.
Philip Parker, Assistant Chair, Adjunct Associate Professor; M.Arch., Yale.
Vito Acconci, Adjunct Associate Professor; M.F.A., Iowa.
Nick Agneta, Adjunct Associate Professor; B.Arch., Cooper Union; AIA.
Carlos Arnaiz, Adjunct Assistant Professor; M.Arch., Harvard.
Kutan Ayata, Adjunct Assistant Professor; M.Arch., Princeton.
Alexandra Barker, Adjunct Assistant Professor; M.Arch., Harvard.
Stephanie Bayard, Adjunct Assistant Professor; M.S., Columbia.
Meta Brunzema, Adjunct Associate Professor; M.Arch., Columbia.
Robert Cervellione, Visiting Instructor; M.Arch., Pratt.
Steven J. Chang, Adjunct Assistant Professor; B.Arch., Berkeley; AIA.
Cristobal Correa, Assistant Professor; M.S.C.E., MIT.
Theo David, Professor; M.Arch., Yale.
Manuel DeLanda, Adjunct Professor; B.F.A., School of Visual Arts.
Deborah Gans, Professor; M.Arch., Princeton.
James Garrison, Adjunct Associate Professor; B.Arch., Syracuse.
Erik Ghenoiu, Adjunct Associate Professor; Ph.D., Harvard.
Jose Gonzalez, Visiting Assistant Professor; M.S., Columbia.
Catherine Ingraham, Professor; Ph.D., Johns Hopkins.
Hina Jamelle, Visiting Assistant Professor; M.Arch., Michigan.
Robert Kearns, Visiting Assistant Professor; M.A.E., Penn State.
Karel Klein, Adjunct Associate Professor; M.Arch., Columbia.
Carisima Koenig, Visiting Instructor; M.Arch., Iowa State.

Pratt Institute

Mehmet Ferda Kolatan, Visiting Assistant Professor; M.S.A.A.D., Columbia.
Sulan Kolatan, Adjunct Professor; M.S.Arch., Columbia.
Craig Konyk, Adjunct Associate Professor; M.Arch., Virginia.
Christopher Kroner, Adjunct Assistant Professor; M.Arch., Columbia.
Sameer Kumar, Adjunct Assistant Professor; M.Arch., Pennsylvania.
Sanford Kwinter, Professor, Ph.D., Columbia.
Thomas Leeser, Associate Professor.
Carla Leitao, Adjunct Assistant Professor; M.S.AAD., Columbia.
John Lobell, Professor; M.Arch., Pennsylvania.
Ariane Lourie-Harrison, Adjunct Associate Professor, Ph.D., NYU.
Peter Macapia, Adjunct Assistant Professor; Ph.D., Columbia.
Radhi Majmuder, Adjunct Assistant Professor; M.S., Columbia.
Rosalinda Malibiran, Visiting Assistant Professor; M.Arch., Columbia.
Elliott Maltby, Adjunct Associate Professor; M.L.A., Berkeley.
Deborah McGuinness, Visiting Associate Professor, B.S., Villanova.
Benjamin Martinson, Visiting Instructor; M.Arch., Pratt.
Bruce Nichol, Visiting Professor, Graduate Diploma, Architecture, Oxford Brookes University; ARB, RIBA.
Signe Nielsen, Adjunct Professor; B.S., Pratt.
Brian Ringley, Visiting Assistant Professor; M.Arch., Cincinnati.
David Ruy, Associate Professor; M.Arch., Columbia.
Richard Scherr, Director, Facilities Planning; M.S.Arch., Columbia.
Erich Schoenenberger, Adjunct Associate Professor; M.S.AAD., Columbia.
Paul Segal, Adjunct Professor; M.F.A., Princeton; FAIA.
Benjamin Shepherd, Adjunct Associate Professor; M.A., Yale.
Maria Sieira, Adjunct Assistant Instructor; M.Arch., Pennsylvania.
Henry Smith-Miller, Adjunct Professor; M.Arch., Pennsylvania.
Roland Snooks, Adjunct Assistant Professor; M.S.AAD., Columbia.
Michael Szivos, Visiting Assistant Professor; M.S.AAD., Columbia.
Jeffrey Taras, Visiting Instructor; M.Arch., Columbia.
Maria Ludovica Tramontin, Adjunct Assistant Professor; Ph.D., Cagliari (Italy).
Nanako Umemoto-Reiser, Adjunct Professor; B.Arch., Cooper Union.
Jason Vigneri-Beane, Adjunct Associate Professor; M.Arch., Iowa State.
John Christopher Whitelaw, Visiting Instructor; M.Arch., Columbia.

Urban Design

William MacDonald, Professor and Chair; M.S., Columbia.
Philip Parker, Assistant Chair; M.Arch., Yale.
Vito Acconci, Adjunct Associate Professor; M.F.A., Iowa.
Carlos Arnaiz, Adjunct Assistant Professor; M.Arch., Harvard.
Stephanie Bayard, Adjunct Assistant Professor; M.S.AAD, Columbia.
Meta Brunzema, Adjunct Associate Professor; M.Arch., Columbia.
Jose Gonzales, Visiting Assistant Professor; M.S.AAD., Columbia.
Mehmet Ferda Kolatan, Visiting Assistant Professor; M.S.AAD., Columbia.
Sulan Kolatan, Adjunct Professor; M.S.Arch., Columbia.
Carla Leitao, Adjunct Associate Professor; M.S.AAD., Columbia.
Elliot Maltby, Adjunct Associate Professor; M.L.A., Berkeley.
Benjamin Martinson, Visiting Instructor; M.Arch., Pratt.
Signe Nielsen, Adjunct Professor; B.S., Pratt.
David Ruy, Associate Professor; M.Arch., Columbia.
Erich Schoenenberger, Visiting Instructor; M.S.AAD., Columbia.
Nanako Umemoto-Reiser, Adjunct Professor; B.Arch., Cooper Union.

Planning and the Environment (City and Regional Planning and Sustainable Environmental Systems and Urban Placemaking and Management)

John Shapiro, Chair, Associate Professor; M.S.C.R.P., Pratt; AICP.
Jaime Stein, Coordinator, Urban Environmental Systems Management; M.S., Pratt.
Moshe Adler, Visiting Associate Professor; Ph.D., UCLA.
Bridget Anderson, Visiting Assistant Professor; M.P.A., Columbia.
Alec Appelbaum, Visiting Assistant Professor; M.B.A., Yale.
Caron Atlas, Visiting Assistant Professor; M.A., Chicago.
Eddie Bautista, Visiting Assistant Professor; M.S.C.R.P., Pratt.
Jennifer Becker, Visiting Assistant Professor; M.S., Pratt.
Bethany Bingham, Visiting Assistant Professor, M.S., Pratt.
Michael Bobker, Visiting Assistant Professor; M.S., NYIT.
Jessica Braden, Visiting Assistant Professor; M.A., Toledo.
Carlton Brown, Visiting Assistant Professor; B.Arch., Princeton.
David Burney, Associate Professor; M.S., London.
Joan Byron, Visiting Assistant Professor; B.Arch., Pratt.
Damon Chaky, Assistant Professor; Ph.D., Rensselaer Polytechnic Institute.
Carter Craft, Visiting Assistant Professor; M.U.P., NYU.
Mike Flynn, Visiting Assistant Professor; M.S.C.R.P., Pratt.
Michael Freedman-Schnapp, Visiting Assistant Professor; M.S.U.P., NYU.
Adam Friedman, Visiting Assistant Professor; J.D., Yeshiva.
Mindy Fullilove, Visiting Assistant Professor; M.D., Columbia.
Moses Gates, Visiting Assistant Professor; M.U.P., Hunter College.
Ben Gibberd, Visiting Assistant Professor; M.A., Edinburgh.
Eva Hanhardt, Visiting Assistant Professor; M.U.P., NYU.
Daniel Hernandez, Visiting Assistant Professor; M.Arch., UCLA.
George Jacquemart, Visiting Assistant Professor; M.S.U.P., Stanford; PE.
Tom Jost, Visiting Assistant Professor; M.U.D., Pratt.
David Kallick, Visiting Assistant Professor; B.A., Yale.
Gavin Kearney, Visiting Assistant Professor; J.D., Minnesota.
Katie Kendall, Visiting Assisting Professor; J.D., Brooklyn Law School.
Nicholas Klein, Visiting Assistant Professor; Ph.D. Candidate, Rutgers.
Sarah Kogel-Smucker, Visiting Assistant Professor; J.D., Boston College.
Raj Kottamasu, Visiting Assistant Professor; M.C.P. with Urban Design Certificate, MIT.
Tanu Kumar, Visiting Assistant Professor; M.S., Cornell.
Frank Lang, Visiting Assistant Professor; M.Arch., Pennsylvania; RA.
Matthew Lister, Visiting Assistant Professor.
Alan Mallach, Visiting Assistant Professor; B.A., Yale.
Elliott Maltby, Adjunct Associate Professor; M.L.A., Berkeley.
Paul Mankiewicz, Visiting Associate Professor; Ph.D., CUNY.
Michael Marella, Visiting Assistant Professor; M.C.P. with Urban Design Certificate, MIT.
Jonathan Martin, Associate Professor; Ph.D., Cornell.
William Menking, Professor; M.S.C.R.P., Pratt.
Gita Nandan, Visiting Assistant Professor; M.Arch., Berkeley.
Mercedes Narciso, Adjunct Associate Professor; M.S.C.R.P., Pratt.
Signe Nielsen, Adjunct Professor; B.L.Arch., CUNY, City College.
Larisa Ortiz Pu-Folkes, Visiting Assistant Professor; M.S., Massachusetts.
Juan Camilo Osorio, Visiting Assistant Professor; M.S., Massachusetts.
Stuart Pertz, Visiting Assistant Professor; M.Arch., Princeton.
Steven Romalewski, Visiting Assistant Professor; M.S., Columbia.
Carolyn Schaeberle, Visiting Assistant Professor; M.S.I.D., Pratt.

David Seiter, Visiting Assistant Professor; M.L.A., Pennsylvania.
Ronald Shiffman, Professor; M.S.C.R.P., Pratt; FAICP, FAIA.
Toby Snyder, Visiting Assistant Professor; M.Arch., Rhode Island School of Design.
Daniel Steinberg, Visiting Assistant Professor; Ph.D. candidate, Columbia.
Ira Stern, Visiting Assistant Professor; M.S.C.R.P., Pratt.
Gelvin Stevenson, Visiting Associate Professor; Ph.D., Washington (St. Louis).
Samara Swanston, Visiting Assistant Professor; J.D., St. John's (New York).
Lacey Tauber, Visiting Assistant Professor; M.S., Pratt.
Petra Todorovich, Visiting Assistant Professor; M.S.C.R.P., Rutgers.
Evren Uzer, Visiting Assistant Professor; Ph.D., Istanbul Technical University.
Meg Walker, Visiting Assistant Professor; M.Arch., Columbia.
Ben Wellington, Visiting Assistant Professor; Ph.D., NYU.
Andrew Wiley-Schwartz, Visiting Assistant Professor; B.A., Hampshire College.
Barika Williams, Visiting Assistant Professor; M.C.P., MIT.
Edward Perry Winston, Visiting Assistant Professor; M.Arch., Rice; RA.
Ayse Yonder, Professor; Ph.D., Berkeley.

Historic Preservation

Nadya Nenadick, Academic Coordinator, Graduate Center for Planning; Ph.D., Polytechnic University of Cataluna.
Lisa Ackerman, Visiting Assistant Professor; M.B.A., NYU.
Beth Bingham, Visiting Assistant Professor; M.S., Pratt.
Patrick Ciccone, Visiting Asssistant Professor; M.S., Columbia.
Carol Clark, Visiting Associate Professor; M.S., Columbia.
Peter Destabler, Visiting Assistant Professor; Ph.D., NYU.
Pat Fisher-Olsen, Visiting Assistant Professor; M.S., Pratt.
Eric Ghenoui, Adjunct Associate Professor; Ph.D., Harvard.
Bill Higgins, Visiting Assistant Professor; M.S., Columbia.
Anne Hrychuk, Visiting Assistant Professor; Ph.D., NYU.
Ben Margolis, Visiting Assistant Professor; M.P.A., Columbia.
Norman Mintz, Visiting Associate Professor; M.S., Columbia.
Christopher Neville, Visiting Assistant Professor; M.S., Columbia
Theodore Prudon, Adjunct Professor; Ph.D., Columbia; FAIA.
Lacey Tauber Visiting Assistant Professor; M.S., Pratt.
Vicki Weiner, Adjunct Associate Professor; M.S., Columbia.
Kevin Wolfe, Visiting Assistant Professor; M.Arch., Columbia.
Arthur Zabarkas, Visiting Assistant Professor; M.S., Columbia.

Facilities Management and Construction Management

Regina Ford Cahill, Chair; M.S., Pratt.
Lennart Andersson, Visiting Assistant Professor; M.Arch., Savannah College of Art and Design.
Matthias Ebinger, Visiting Assistant Professor; M.S., NYU.
William Henry, Visiting Assistant Professor; B.Arch., NYU.
Stephen LoGrasso, Visiting Assistant Professor; B.S., NYIT.
Harriet Markis, Adjunct Associate Professor; M.Eng., Cornell.
Mary J. Matthews, Professor Emerita; M.S., Boston College.
Gerald F. McGowan, Visiting Associate Professor; M.B.A., NYU.
Martin McManus, Visiting Assistant Professor; B.B.A., Pace.
Russell Olson, Visiting Assistant Professor; M.S., Pratt.
John Osborn, Visiting Associate Professor; J.D., South Carolina.
Edward Re, Adjunct Associate Professor; M.S., Pratt.
Norman Rosenfeld, Adjunct Assistant Professor; B.Arch., Pratt.
Audrey L. Schultz, Associate Professor; Ph.D., Salford; FMP, ASC, CIB.
Marjorie St. Ellin, Visiting Assistant Professor; B.S., Pratt.
Mira Tsymuk, Visiting Assistant Professor; M.A., CUNY, Hunter.

© 2015 Bob Handelman

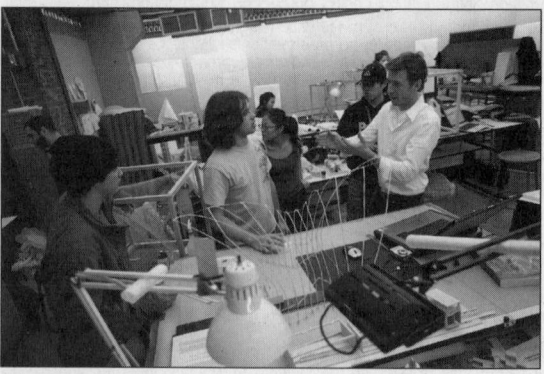

© 2015 Bob Handelman

Section 3
Art and Art History

This section contains a directory of institutions offering graduate work in art and art history, followed by in-depth entries submitted by institutions that chose to prepare detailed program descriptions. Additional information about programs listed in the directory but not augmented by an in-depth entry may be obtained by writing directly to the dean of a graduate school or chair of a department at the address given in the directory.

For programs offering related work, see also in this book *Applied Arts and Design; Architecture; Area and Cultural Studies; Film, Television, and Video; Performing Arts;* and *Sociology, Anthropology, and Archaeology.* In another guide in this series:

Graduate Programs in Business, Education, Information Studies, Law & Social Work
See *Subject Areas (Art Education)*

CONTENTS

Program Directories

Displays and Close-Ups

See also:

Art/Fine Arts

Academy of Art University, Graduate Program, School of Fine Art, San Francisco, CA 94105-3410. Offers figurative painting (MFA); non-figurative painting (MFA); printmaking (MFA); sculpture (MFA). *Accreditation:* NASAD. Part-time programs available. Postbaccalaureate distance learning degree programs offered (no on-campus study). *Faculty:* 20 full-time (7 women), 45 part-time/adjunct (19 women). *Students:* 121 full-time (73 women), 175 part-time (126 women); includes 53 minority (12 Black or African American, non-Hispanic/Latino; 3 American Indian or Alaska Native, non-Hispanic/Latino; 17 Asian, non-Hispanic/Latino; 16 Hispanic/Latino; 1 Native Hawaiian or other Pacific Islander, non-Hispanic/Latino; 4 Two or more races, non-Hispanic/Latino), 88 international. Average age 40. 97 applicants, 100% accepted, 41 enrolled. In 2014, 77 master's awarded. *Degree requirements:* For master's, final review. *Entrance requirements:* For master's, statement of intent; resume; portfolio/reel; official college transcripts. *Application deadline:* Applications are processed on a rolling basis. Application fee: $100. Electronic applications accepted. *Expenses: Tuition:* Part-time $910 per unit. *Financial support:* Career-related internships or fieldwork and Federal Work-Study available. Support available to part-time students. Financial award application deadline: 8/10; financial award applicants required to submit FAFSA. *Unit head:* 800-544-ARTS, E-mail: info@academyart.edu. *Application contact:* 800-544-ARTS, E-mail: info@academyart.edu.
Website: http://www.academyart.edu/fine-art-school/index.html

Academy of Art University, Graduate Program, School of Jewelry and Metal Arts, San Francisco, CA 94105-3410. Offers MFA. Part-time and evening/weekend programs available. Postbaccalaureate distance learning degree programs offered (no on-campus study). *Faculty:* 1 (woman) full-time, 5 part-time/adjunct (3 women). *Students:* 28 full-time (23 women), 10 part-time (8 women); includes 5 minority (1 Black or African American, non-Hispanic/Latino; 2 Asian, non-Hispanic/Latino; 2 Hispanic/Latino), 23 international. Average age 30. 21 applicants, 100% accepted, 10 enrolled. In 2014, 2 master's awarded. *Degree requirements:* For master's, final review. *Entrance requirements:* For master's, statement of intent; resume; portfolio/reel; official college transcripts. *Application deadline:* Applications are processed on a rolling basis. Application fee: $100. Electronic applications accepted. *Expenses: Tuition:* Part-time $910 per unit. *Financial support:* Career-related internships or fieldwork and Federal Work-Study available. Support available to part-time students. Financial award application deadline: 8/10; financial award applicants required to submit FAFSA. *Unit head:* 800-544-ARTS, E-mail: info@academyart.edu. *Application contact:* 800-544-ARTS, E-mail: info@academyart.edu.
Website: http://www.academyart.edu/jewelry-and-metal-arts-school/

Adams State University, The Graduate School, Department of Art, Alamosa, CO 81101. Offers MA. Part-time programs available. *Degree requirements:* For master's, thesis, departmental qualifying exam. *Entrance requirements:* For master's, GRE General Test or MAT, minimum undergraduate GPA of 2.75.

Adelphi University, College of Arts and Sciences, Department of Art and Art History, Garden City, NY 11530-0701. Offers studio art (MA). Part-time programs available. *Students:* 2 full-time (both women), 4 part-time (3 women). Average age 32. In 2014, 4 master's awarded. *Degree requirements:* For master's, art exhibit. *Entrance requirements:* For master's, essay, portfolio, 2 letters of recommendation. Additional exam requirements/recommendations for international students: Required—TOEFL (minimum score 550 paper-based; 80 iBT). *Application deadline:* For fall admission, 5/1 for international students; for spring admission, 12/1 for international students. Applications are processed on a rolling basis. Application fee: $50. Electronic applications accepted. *Financial support:* Research assistantships with full and partial tuition reimbursements, career-related internships or fieldwork, Federal Work-Study, institutionally sponsored loans, and unspecified assistantships available. Financial award application deadline: 2/15; financial award applicants required to submit FAFSA. *Unit head:* David Hornung, Chairperson, 516-877-4458, E-mail: hornung@adelphi.edu. *Application contact:* Christine Murphy, Director of Admissions, 516-877-3050, Fax: 516-877-3039, E-mail: graduateadmissions@adelphi.edu.
Website: http://academics.adelphi.edu/artsci/art/

Alfred University, Graduate School, New York State College of Ceramics, Kazuo Inamori School of Engineering, Alfred, NY 14802. Offers biomaterials engineering (MS); ceramic engineering (MS); ceramics (PhD); electrical engineering (MS); glass science (MS, PhD); materials science and engineering (MS, PhD); mechanical engineering (MS). Part-time programs available. *Degree requirements:* For master's, thesis; for doctorate, thesis/dissertation. *Entrance requirements:* Additional exam requirements/recommendations for international students: Required—TOEFL (minimum score 590 paper-based; 90 iBT), IELTS (minimum score 6.5). Electronic applications accepted. *Expenses:* Contact institution. *Faculty research:* X-ray diffraction, biomaterials and polymers, thin-film processing, electronic and optical ceramics, solid-state chemistry.

Alfred University, Graduate School, New York State College of Ceramics, School of Art and Design, Alfred, NY 14802. Offers ceramic art (MFA); electronic integrated art (MFA); glass art (MFA); sculpture (MFA). *Accreditation:* NASAD. *Degree requirements:* For master's, thesis, exhibit. *Entrance requirements:* For master's, portfolio. Additional exam requirements/recommendations for international students: Required—TOEFL (minimum score 550 paper-based; 80 iBT), IELTS (minimum score 6). Electronic applications accepted. *Faculty research:* Ceramic art, sculpture, glass art, new media, time-based media.

Anna Maria College, Graduate Division, Program in Education, Paxton, MA 01612. Offers early childhood education (M Ed); education (CAGS); elementary education (M Ed); English language arts (M Ed); visual arts (M Ed). Part-time and evening/weekend programs available. *Entrance requirements:* For master's, bachelor's degree in liberal arts or sciences, minimum GPA of 3.0. Additional exam requirements/recommendations for international students: Required—TOEFL (minimum score 500 paper-based). Electronic applications accepted.

Anna Maria College, Graduate Division, Program in Visual Arts, Paxton, MA 01612. Offers art and visual art (MA); teacher of visual art (M Ed). Part-time and evening/weekend programs available. *Degree requirements:* For master's, thesis. *Entrance requirements:* For master's, minimum GPA of 2.7, undergraduate major in art, portfolio. Additional exam requirements/recommendations for international students: Required—TOEFL (minimum score 500 paper-based). Electronic applications accepted.

Antioch University Midwest, Graduate Programs, Individualized Liberal and Professional Studies Program, Yellow Springs, OH 45387-1609. Offers liberal and professional studies (MA), including counseling, creative writing, education, liberal studies, management, modern literature, psychology, visual arts. Part-time and evening/weekend programs available. Postbaccalaureate distance learning degree programs offered (minimal on-campus study). *Degree requirements:* For master's, thesis or

alternative. *Entrance requirements:* For master's, resume, goal statement, interview. Electronic applications accepted. *Expenses:* Contact institution.

Arizona State University at the Tempe campus, Herberger Institute for Design and the Arts, School of Art, Tempe, AZ 85287-1505. Offers art education (MA); art history (MA); ceramics (MFA); design, environment and the arts (PhD), including history, theory and criticism; drawing (MFA); fibers (MFA); intermedia (MFA); metals (MFA); museum studies (MFA); painting (MFA); printmaking (MFA); sculpture (MFA); wood (MFA); MFA/MA. Terminal master's awarded for partial completion of doctoral program. *Degree requirements:* For master's, thesis/exhibition (MFA, MA in art education); interactive Program of Study (iPOS) submitted before completing 50 percent of required credit hours; for doctorate, comprehensive exam, thesis/dissertation, interactive Program of Study (iPOS) submitted before completing 50 percent of required credit hours. *Entrance requirements:* For master's, GRE or MAT, minimum GPA of 3.0 or equivalent in last 2 years of work leading to bachelor's degree; for doctorate, GRE, master's degree in architecture, graphic design, industrial design, interior design, landscape architecture, or art history or equivalent standing; statement of purpose; 3 letters of recommendation; indication of potential faculty mentor; sample of written work. Additional exam requirements/recommendations for international students: Required—TOEFL, IELTS, or PTE. Electronic applications accepted.

Art Center College of Design, Graduate Art Program, Pasadena, CA 91103. Offers MFA. *Accreditation:* NASAD. *Students:* 22 full-time (12 women), 6 part-time (2 women); includes 9 minority (4 Asian, non-Hispanic/Latino; 4 Hispanic/Latino; 1 Native Hawaiian or other Pacific Islander, non-Hispanic/Latino), 6 international. Average age 30. 80 applicants, 35% accepted, 8 enrolled. In 2014, 5 master's awarded. *Degree requirements:* For master's, thesis. *Entrance requirements:* For master's, portfolio. Additional exam requirements/recommendations for international students: Required—TOEFL (minimum score 100 iBT), IELTS (minimum score 7). *Application deadline:* For fall admission, 2/1 priority date for domestic and international students; for winter admission, 9/15 for domestic students; for spring admission, 10/1 priority date for domestic and international students. Application fee: $50 ($70 for international students). Electronic applications accepted. *Financial support:* Application deadline: 2/1; applicants required to submit FAFSA. *Unit head:* Diana Thater, Chair, E-mail: dthater@artcenter.edu. *Application contact:* Jimmy Stambrandt, Administrative Assistant, 626-396-2373, E-mail: jimmy.stambrandt@artcenter.edu.

Azusa Pacific University, College of Liberal Arts and Sciences, Program in Fine Arts in Visual Art, Azusa, CA 91702-7000. Offers MFA. *Accreditation:* NASAD.

Ball State University, Graduate School, College of Fine Arts, Department of Art, Muncie, IN 47306-1099. Offers MA, MFA. *Accreditation:* NASAD. *Faculty:* 17 full-time (7 women). *Students:* 15 full-time (1 woman), 2 part-time (1 woman); includes 3 minority (1 Black or African American, non-Hispanic/Latino; 1 Asian, non-Hispanic/Latino; 1 Hispanic/Latino). Average age 24. 16 applicants, 56% accepted. In 2014, 2 master's awarded. Application fee: $50. *Financial support:* In 2014–15, 7 students received support, including 1 research assistantship with partial tuition reimbursement available (averaging $9,396 per year), 11 teaching assistantships with partial tuition reimbursements available (averaging $7,818 per year); unspecified assistantships also available. Financial award application deadline: 3/1. *Unit head:* Thomas Riesing, Head, 765-285-5838, Fax: 765-285-5275, E-mail: tjriesing@bsu.edu. *Application contact:* Kenton Hall, Director, 765-285-5838, Fax: 765-285-5275, E-mail: khall@bsu.edu.

Bard College, Milton Avery Graduate School of the Arts, Annandale-on-Hudson, NY 12504. Offers MFA. *Degree requirements:* For master's, thesis, project, 8-week summer residency, independent study. *Entrance requirements:* For master's, interview, portfolio, 2 letters of recommendation, history of work in the arts. Additional exam requirements/recommendations for international students: Required—TOEFL (minimum score 550 paper-based). Electronic applications accepted. *Faculty research:* Original work in painting, writing, sculpture, photography, video/film, sound/music.

Barry University, College of Arts and Sciences, Department of Fine Arts, Miami Shores, FL 33161-6695. Offers photography (MA, MFA). *Degree requirements:* For master's, thesis (for some programs). *Entrance requirements:* For master's, GRE General Test, minimum GPA of 3.0. Electronic applications accepted. *Faculty research:* Inclusion education, exceptional education, art-based assessments.

Bob Jones University, Graduate Programs, Greenville, SC 29614. Offers accountancy (MS); Bible (MA); Bible translation (MA); Biblical studies (Certificate); broadcast management (MS); business administration (MBA); church history (MA, PhD); church ministries (MA); church music (MM); cinema and video production (MA); counseling (MS); curriculum and instruction (Ed D); divinity (M Div); dramatic production (MA); educational leadership (MS, Ed D, Ed S); elementary education (M Ed, MAT); English (M Ed, MA, MAT); fine arts (MA); graphic design (MA); history (M Ed, MA); illustration (MA); interpretative speech (MA); mathematics (M Ed, MAT); medical missions (Certificate); ministry (MM, D Min); multi-categorical special education (M Ed, MAT); music (M Ed); New Testament interpretation (PhD); Old Testament interpretation (PhD); orchestral instrument performance (MM); organ performance (MM); pastoral studies (MA); personnel services (MS, Ed S); piano pedagogy (MM); piano performance (MM); platform arts (MA); radio and television broadcasting (MS); rhetoric and public address (MA); secondary education (M Ed); studio art (MA); teaching Bible (MA); theology (MA, PhD); voice performance (MM); youth ministries (MA); M Div/MM.

Boise State University, College of Arts and Sciences, Department of Art, Boise, ID 83725-0399. Offers art education (MA); visual arts (MFA). *Faculty:* 21 full-time, 7 part-time/adjunct. *Students:* 9 full-time (5 women), 5 part-time (all women), 1 international. Average age 38. 34 applicants, 94% accepted, 3 enrolled. In 2014, 4 master's awarded. *Degree requirements:* For master's, thesis optional. *Entrance requirements:* For master's, minimum GPA of 3.0, portfolio. *Application deadline:* For fall admission, 3/1 priority date for domestic students; for spring admission, 10/1 priority date for domestic students. Applications are processed on a rolling basis. Application fee: $55. Electronic applications accepted. *Expenses: Tuition,* state resident: part-time $331 per credit hour. Tuition, nonresident: part-time $531 per credit hour. *Financial support:* In 2014–15, 6 students received support. Career-related internships or fieldwork, institutionally sponsored loans, and unspecified assistantships available. Support available to part-time students. *Unit head:* Richard Young, Department Chair, 208-426-3561. *Application contact:* Chad Erpelding, Graduate Program Director, 208-426-4081, E-mail: chaderpelding@boisestate.edu.
Website: http://art.boisestate.edu/gradprogram/

Boston University, College of Fine Arts, School of Visual Arts, Boston, MA 02215. Offers art education (MA); graphic design (MFA); painting (MFA); sculpture (MFA); studio teaching (MA). *Faculty:* 17 full-time, 4 part-time/adjunct. *Students:* 188 full-time (159 women), 9 part-time (7 women); includes 22 minority (3 Black or African American,

non-Hispanic/Latino; 5 Asian, non-Hispanic/Latino; 11 Hispanic/Latino; 3 Two or more races, non-Hispanic/Latino), 39 international. Average age 31. 257 applicants, 27% accepted, 21 enrolled. In 2014, 53 master's awarded. *Entrance requirements:* For master's, portfolio. Additional exam requirements/recommendations for international students: Required—TOEFL, IELTS. *Application deadline:* For fall admission, 2/2 for domestic and international students. Applications are processed on a rolling basis. Application fee: $80. *Expenses: Tuition:* Full-time $45,686; part-time $1428 per credit hour. *Required fees:* $660; $60 per semester. Tuition and fees vary according to program. *Financial support:* Fellowships and teaching assistantships available. Financial award application deadline: 2/15. *Unit head:* Jeannette Guillemin, Interim Director, 617-353-3371. *Application contact:* Mark Krone, Manager, Graduate Admissions and Online Marketing, 617-353-3350, E-mail: arts@bu.edu.

Bowling Green State University, Graduate College, College of Arts and Sciences, School of Art, Bowling Green, OH 43403. Offers 2-D studio art (MA, MFA); 3-D studio art (MA, MFA); art education (MA); art history (MA); computer art (MA); design (MFA); digital arts (MFA); graphics (MFA). *Accreditation:* NASAD. Part-time programs available. *Degree requirements:* For master's, thesis or alternative, final exhibit (MFA). *Entrance requirements:* For master's, GRE General Test (MA), slide portfolio (15-20 slides). Additional exam requirements/recommendations for international students: Required—TOEFL. Electronic applications accepted. *Faculty research:* Computer animation and virtual reality, Spanish still-life painting from 1600 to 1800, art and psychotherapy, Japanese wood-firing techniques in ceramics, non-toxic printmaking technologies.

Bradley University, Graduate School, Slane College of Communications and Fine Arts, Department of Art, Peoria, IL 61625-0002. Offers ceramics (MA, MFA); drawing (MA, MFA); interdisciplinary art (MA, MFA); painting (MA, MFA); photography (MA, MFA); printmaking (MA, MFA); sculpture (MA, MFA); visual communications (MA, MFA). *Accreditation:* NASAD. Part-time programs available. *Faculty:* 11 full-time (2 women), 2 part-time/adjunct (both women). *Students:* 7 full-time (3 women), 3 part-time (2 women). 22 applicants, 41% accepted, 2 enrolled. In 2014, 4 master's awarded. *Degree requirements:* For master's, comprehensive exam, thesis, final exhibit. *Entrance requirements:* For master's, portfolio, 2 letters of recommendation. Additional exam requirements/recommendations for international students: Required—TOEFL (minimum score 550 paper-based; 79 iBT). *Application deadline:* For fall admission, 4/1 priority date for domestic and international students; for spring admission, 11/1 priority date for domestic and international students. Applications are processed on a rolling basis. Application fee: $40 ($50 for international students). Electronic applications accepted. *Expenses: Tuition:* Full-time $14,580; part-time $810 per credit. *Required fees:* $224. Full-time tuition and fees vary according to course load. *Financial support:* In 2014–15, 4 teaching assistantships with full and partial tuition reimbursements (averaging $19,640 per year) were awarded; scholarships/grants, tuition waivers (partial), and unspecified assistantships also available. Support available to part-time students. Financial award application deadline: 4/1. *Unit head:* Dr. Paul Krainak, Chairperson, 309-677-2967, E-mail: pkrainak@bradley.edu. *Application contact:* Kayla Carroll, Director of International Admission and Student Services, 309-677-2375, E-mail: klcarroll@fsmail.bradley.edu.

Brigham Young University, Graduate Studies, College of Fine Arts and Communications, Department of Art, Provo, UT 84602-6414. Offers art education (MA); studio arts (MFA). Art education applications accepted biennially. *Accreditation:* NASAD. *Faculty:* 9 full-time (0 women). *Students:* 22 full-time (13 women); includes 3 minority (1 Asian, non-Hispanic/Latino; 1 Hispanic/Latino; 1 Native Hawaiian or other Pacific Islander, non-Hispanic/Latino). Average age 26. 15 applicants, 33% accepted, 5 enrolled. In 2014, 9 master's awarded. *Degree requirements:* For master's, one foreign language, comprehensive exam, selected project (for MFA); curriculum project (for art education). *Entrance requirements:* For master's, GRE (for MA), minimum GPA of 3.0 (for MFA, MA in art education), 3.5 (for MA in art history and curatorial studies); portfolio in CD format (for MFA); writing samples (for MA). Additional exam requirements/recommendations for international students: Required—TOEFL (minimum score 580 paper-based; 85 iBT). *Application deadline:* For fall admission, 2/1 for domestic and international students. Application fee: $50. Electronic applications accepted. *Expenses: Tuition:* Full-time $6310; part-time $371 per credit hour. Tuition and fees vary according to program and student's religious affiliation. *Financial support:* In 2014–15, 20 students received support. Teaching assistantships with partial tuition reimbursements available, scholarships/grants, and tuition waivers (partial) available. Financial award application deadline: 2/1. *Faculty research:* Methodology-standards-assessment, medieval architecture, classical/Islamic eighteenth and nineteenth century art, Netherlandish art, contemporary art, modern art, history of photography, exploration of art making processes, new genre. *Unit head:* Prof. Garold (Gary) C. Barton, Chair, 801-422-4429, Fax: 801-422-0695, E-mail: garold_barton@byu.edu. *Application contact:* Sharon Lyn Heelis, Secretary, 801-422-4429, Fax: 801-422-0695, E-mail: sharon_heelis@byu.edu. Website: http://visualarts.byu.edu

Brooklyn College of the City University of New York, School of Visual, Media and Performing Arts, Department of Art, Brooklyn, NY 11210-2889. Offers art history (MA); digital art (MFA); drawing and painting (MFA); photography (MFA); printmaking (MFA); sculpture (MFA). Part-time programs available. *Degree requirements:* For master's, thesis. *Entrance requirements:* For master's, bachelor's degree in art, portfolio, 2 letters of recommendation. Additional exam requirements/recommendations for international students: Required—TOEFL (minimum score 500 paper-based; 61 iBT). Electronic applications accepted.

California College of the Arts, Graduate Programs, Fine Arts Programs, San Francisco, CA 94107. Offers ceramics (MFA); comics (MFA); film/video/performance (MFA); glass (MFA); interdisciplinary studies (MFA); jewelry/metal arts (MFA); media studies (MFA); painting/drawing (MFA); photography (MFA); printmaking (MFA); sculpture (MFA); social practice (MFA); textiles (MFA); wood/furniture (MFA). *Accreditation:* NASAD. *Degree requirements:* For master's, thesis, exhibit. *Entrance requirements:* For master's, appropriate bachelor's degree, portfolio, resume, 2 letters of recommendation, transcript. Additional exam requirements/recommendations for international students: Required—TOEFL (minimum score 600 paper-based; 100 iBT). Electronic applications accepted.

California College of the Arts, Graduate Programs, Visual and Critical Studies Program, San Francisco, CA 94107. Offers MA. *Degree requirements:* For master's, thesis. *Entrance requirements:* For master's, portfolio, resume, 2 letters of recommendation, transcripts, essay, interview. Additional exam requirements/recommendations for international students: Required—TOEFL (minimum score 600 paper-based; 100 iBT). Electronic applications accepted.

California Institute of the Arts, School of Art, Valencia, CA 91355-2340. Offers art (MFA, Adv C); graphic design (MFA, Adv C); photography (MFA, Adv C). *Accreditation:* NASAD (one or more programs are accredited). *Degree requirements:* For master's, final project. *Entrance requirements:* For master's, portfolio. Additional exam requirements/recommendations for international students: Required—TOEFL. Electronic applications accepted.

California State University, Chico, Office of Graduate Studies, College of Humanities and Fine Arts, Department of Art and Art History, Program in Fine Arts, Chico, CA 95929-0722. Offers MFA. *Accreditation:* NASAD. *Faculty:* 11 full-time (6 women). *Students:* 2 full-time (1 woman), 2 part-time (both women); includes 1 minority (Hispanic/Latino). Average age 33. 12 applicants, 50% accepted, 5 enrolled. In 2014, 3 master's awarded. *Degree requirements:* For master's, thesis or alternative, exhibition with written evaluation of work. *Entrance requirements:* For master's, three letters of recommendation, statement of purpose, media portfolio due March 1st. Additional exam requirements/recommendations for international students: Required—TOEFL (minimum score 550 paper-based; 80 iBT), IELTS (minimum score 6.5), PTE (minimum score 59). *Application deadline:* For fall admission, 3/1 priority date for domestic students, 3/1 for international students; for spring admission, 9/15 priority date for domestic students, 9/15 for international students. Application fee: $55. Electronic applications accepted. *Expenses:* Tuition, state resident: full-time $7002. Tuition, nonresident: full-time $18,162. *Required fees:* $1530. Tuition and fees vary according to program. *Financial support:* Scholarships/grants available. Financial award application deadline: 3/1; financial award applicants required to submit FAFSA. *Unit head:* Dr. Robert Herhusky, Chair, 530-898-5331, Fax: 530-898-4171, E-mail: art@csuchico.edu. *Application contact:* Judy L. Rice, Graduate Admissions Coordinator, 530-898-5416, Fax: 530-898-3342, E-mail: jlrice@csuchico.edu.
Website: http://catalog.csuchico.edu/viewer/15/ARTS/ARTSARTSMF.html

California State University, Fresno, Division of Graduate Studies, College of Arts and Humanities, Department of Art and Design, Fresno, CA 93740-8027. Offers art (MA). Part-time and evening/weekend programs available. *Degree requirements:* For master's, thesis or alternative. *Entrance requirements:* For master's, GRE General Test, minimum GPA of 3.0, portfolio. Additional exam requirements/recommendations for international students: Required—TOEFL. Electronic applications accepted. *Faculty research:* Art history, graphic design, studio art.

California State University, Fullerton, Graduate Studies, College of the Arts, Department of Visual Arts, Fullerton, CA 92834-9480. Offers art (MA, MFA), including art history (MA), ceramics (MFA), crafts, creative photography, exhibition design, glass, graphic design, illustration, sculpture. *Accreditation:* NASAD (one or more programs are accredited). Part-time programs available. *Students:* 28 full-time (16 women), 29 part-time (22 women); includes 20 minority (3 Black or African American, non-Hispanic/Latino; 8 Asian, non-Hispanic/Latino; 8 Hispanic/Latino; 1 Two or more races, non-Hispanic/Latino), 7 international. Average age 35. 58 applicants, 38% accepted, 14 enrolled. In 2014, 17 master's awarded. *Degree requirements:* For master's, project or thesis. *Entrance requirements:* For master's, minimum GPA of 2.5 in last 60 units of course work, portfolio. Application fee: $55. *Financial support:* Career-related internships or fieldwork, Federal Work-Study, institutionally sponsored loans, and scholarships/grants available. Support available to part-time students. Financial award application deadline: 3/1; financial award applicants required to submit FAFSA. *Unit head:* Dana Lamb, Chair, 657-278-2076. *Application contact:* Admissions/Applications, 657-278-2371.

California State University, Long Beach, Graduate Studies, College of the Arts, Department of Art, Long Beach, CA 90840. Offers art education (MA); art history (MA); studio art (MA, MFA). *Accreditation:* NASAD. Part-time programs available. *Degree requirements:* For master's, thesis (for some programs). *Entrance requirements:* For master's, minimum GPA of 3.0 in last 60 hours. Electronic applications accepted.

California State University, Los Angeles, Graduate Studies, College of Arts and Letters, Department of Art, Los Angeles, CA 90032-8530. Offers art (MA), including art education, art history, art therapy, ceramics, metals, and textiles, design (MA, MFA), painting, sculpture, and graphic arts, photography; fine arts (MFA), including crafts, design (MA, MFA), studio arts. *Accreditation:* NASAD (one or more programs are accredited). Part-time and evening/weekend programs available. *Degree requirements:* For master's, comprehensive exam, project or thesis. *Entrance requirements:* For master's, portfolio. Additional exam requirements/recommendations for international students: Required—TOEFL (minimum score 500 paper-based). Electronic applications accepted. *Expenses:* Tuition, state resident: full-time $6738; part-time $3609 per year. Tuition, nonresident: full-time $15,666; part-time $8073 per year. Tuition and fees vary according to course load, degree level and program. *Faculty research:* The artist and the book, conceptual art, ceramic processes, computer graphics, architectural graphics.

California State University, Northridge, Graduate Studies, College of Arts, Media, and Communication, Department of Art, Northridge, CA 91330. Offers art education (MA); art history (MA); studio art (MA, MFA); visual communications (MA, MFA). *Accreditation:* NASAD. *Students:* 34 full-time (26 women), 11 part-time (8 women); includes 14 minority (3 Asian, non-Hispanic/Latino; 9 Hispanic/Latino; 2 Two or more races, non-Hispanic/Latino), 4 international. Average age 30. *Application deadline:* For fall admission, 11/30 for domestic students. Application fee: $55. *Expenses: Required fees:* $12,402. *Financial support:* Application deadline: 3/1. *Unit head:* Prof. Edward Alfano, Chair, 818-677-2242, E-mail: art.dept@csun.edu.
Website: http://www.csun.edu/art/

California State University, Sacramento, Office of Graduate Studies, College of Arts and Letters, Department of Art, Sacramento, CA 95819. Offers studio art (MA). *Accreditation:* NASAD. Part-time programs available. *Entrance requirements:* For master's, minimum GPA of 3.0 during previous 2 years. Additional exam requirements/recommendations for international students: Required—TOEFL. Electronic applications accepted.

California State University, San Bernardino, Graduate Studies, College of Arts and Letters, Department of Art, San Bernardino, CA 92407-2397. Offers art education (MA); studio art (MA). *Accreditation:* NASAD. *Students:* 12 full-time (5 women), 2 part-time (0 women); includes 5 minority (all Hispanic/Latino). Average age 31. 14 applicants, 29% accepted, 4 enrolled. In 2014, 3 master's awarded. *Entrance requirements:* Additional exam requirements/recommendations for international students: Required—TOEFL. *Application deadline:* For fall admission, 7/17 priority date for domestic students. Application fee: $55. *Expenses:* Tuition, state resident: full-time $6738; part-time $1302 per term. Tuition, nonresident: full-time $17,898; part-time $248 per unit. *Required fees:* $365 per quarter. Tuition and fees vary according to degree level and program. *Unit head:* Dr. Margaret Perry, Chair/Professor, 909-537-5808, Fax: 909-537-7068, E-mail: mperry@csusb.edu. *Application contact:* Dr. Jeffrey Thompson, Director of Admissions, 909-537-5058, Fax: 909-537-5078, E-mail: jthompso@csusb.edu.

Carnegie Mellon University, College of Fine Arts, School of Art, Pittsburgh, PA 15213-3891. Offers MFA. *Accreditation:* NASAD. *Degree requirements:* For master's, thesis, exhibit. *Entrance requirements:* For master's, portfolio. Additional exam requirements/recommendations for international students: Required—TOEFL.

Central Washington University, Graduate Studies and Research, College of Arts and Humanities, Department of Art, Ellensburg, WA 98926. Offers MA, MFA. *Degree requirements:* For master's, thesis or alternative. *Entrance requirements:* For master's, minimum GPA of 3.0, portfolio. Additional exam requirements/recommendations for international students: Required—TOEFL (minimum score 550 paper-based; 79 iBT) or IELTS (minimum score 6.5). Electronic applications accepted.

Christie's Education, Certificate Program in Collecting Contemporary Art, New York, NY 10036. Offers Certificate. *Application contact:* Catherine Warden, Short Course Coordinator, 212-355-1501 Ext. 3300, Fax: 212-355-7370, E-mail:

cwarden@christies.edu. Website: http://www.christies.edu/new-york/courses/certificate-collecting.aspx

Christie's Education, Certificate Program in Modern and Contemporary Art in New York, New York, NY 10036. Offers Certificate. Part-time programs available. *Faculty:* 5 full-time (4 women), 1 (woman) part-time/adjunct. *Students:* 8 (all women). *Application deadline:* Applications are processed on a rolling basis. Application fee: $35. *Application contact:* Margaret Conklin, Business Manager, 212-355-1501 Ext. 302, Fax: 212-355-7370, E-mail: mconklin@christies.edu.
Website: http://www.christies.edu/new-york/courses/certificate-modern-contemporary-art.aspx

City College of the City University of New York, Graduate School, College of Liberal Arts and Science, Division of the Humanities and Arts, Department of Art, Program in Fine Arts, New York, NY 10031-9198. Offers advertising design (MFA); ceramic design (MFA); painting (MFA); printmaking (MFA); sculpture (MFA); wood and metal design (MFA). *Degree requirements:* For master's, thesis exhibit. *Entrance requirements:* For master's, 20 slide portfolio. Additional exam requirements/recommendations for international students: Required—TOEFL (minimum score 577 paper-based; 90 iBT). Electronic applications accepted.

Claremont Graduate University, Graduate Programs, School of Arts and Humanities, Department of Art, Claremont, CA 91711. Offers digital media (MFA); drawing (MFA); installation (MFA); painting (MFA); performance (MFA); photography (MFA); sculpture (MFA); studio (MFA). Part-time programs available. *Faculty:* 4 full-time (1 woman). *Students:* 37 full-time (26 women), 3 part-time (1 woman); includes 11 minority (2 Black or African American, non-Hispanic/Latino; 1 Asian, non-Hispanic/Latino; 7 Hispanic/Latino; 1 Two or more races, non-Hispanic/Latino), 12 international. Average age 32. In 2014, 22 master's awarded. *Degree requirements:* For master's, final project show. *Entrance requirements:* For master's, BA in art or BFA, slide review. Additional exam requirements/recommendations for international students: Required—TOEFL (minimum score 550 paper-based; 80 iBT). *Application deadline:* For fall admission, 2/1 priority date for domestic and international students. Applications are processed on a rolling basis. Application fee: $80. Electronic applications accepted. *Expenses:* Expenses: Contact institution. *Financial support:* Fellowships, research assistantships, teaching assistantships, Federal Work-Study, institutionally sponsored loans, and scholarships/grants available. Support available to part-time students. Financial award application deadline: 2/15; financial award applicants required to submit FAFSA. *Faculty research:* Acoustic sculpture, feminization of abstraction, installation sculpture. *Unit head:* David Amico, Chair, 909-607-8216, Fax: 909-607-1276, E-mail: david.amico@cgu.edu. *Application contact:* Jennifer Gracia, Program Coordinator, 909-621-8071, E-mail: jennifer.gracia@cgu.edu.
Website: http://art.cgu.edu/

Clemson University, Graduate School, College of Architecture, Arts, and Humanities, Department of Art, Clemson, SC 29634. Offers visual arts (MFA). *Accreditation:* NASAD. *Faculty:* 13 full-time (7 women), 1 (woman) part-time/adjunct. *Students:* 14 full-time (10 women), 1 international. Average age 29. 16 applicants, 38% accepted, 4 enrolled. In 2014, 6 master's awarded. *Entrance requirements:* For master's, portfolio. Additional exam requirements/recommendations for international students: Required—TOEFL, IELTS. *Application deadline:* For fall admission, 3/15 for domestic and international students; for spring admission, 9/15 for international students. Application fee: $80 ($90 for international students). Electronic applications accepted. *Financial support:* In 2014–15, 7 students received support, including 10 fellowships with partial tuition reimbursements available (averaging $1,540 per year), 2 teaching assistantships with partial tuition reimbursements available (averaging $9,293 per year); career-related internships or fieldwork, institutionally sponsored loans, scholarships/grants, health care benefits, and unspecified assistantships also available. Support available to part-time students. Financial award applicants required to submit FAFSA. *Total annual research expenditures:* $5,000. *Unit head:* Prof. Greg Shelnutt, Chair, 864-656-3881, E-mail: gshelnu@clemson.edu. *Application contact:* Prof. Dave Detrich, Program Coordinator, 864-656-3890, Fax: 864-656-0204, E-mail: ddavid@clemson.edu.
Website: http://www.clemson.edu/caah/art/

The College at Brockport, State University of New York, School of the Arts, Humanities and Social Sciences, Visual Studies Workshop, Brockport, NY 14420-2997. Offers MFA. *Faculty:* 2 full-time (1 woman). *Students:* 7 full-time (3 women), 6 part-time (4 women); includes 3 minority (1 Hispanic/Latino; 2 Two or more races, non-Hispanic/Latino). 10 applicants, 90% accepted, 3 enrolled. In 2014, 4 master's awarded. *Degree requirements:* For master's, thesis or alternative, internship, final project. *Entrance requirements:* For master's, slides, portfolio, video or CD/DVD, including work description; letters of recommendation; minimum GPA of 3.0; statement of objectives. Additional exam requirements/recommendations for international students: Required—TOEFL (minimum score 550 paper-based; 79 iBT), IELTS (minimum score 6.5). *Application deadline:* For fall admission, 2/15 priority date for domestic and international students. Application fee: $50. Electronic applications accepted. *Financial support:* Federal Work-Study and scholarships/grants available. Support available to part-time students. Financial award application deadline: 3/15; financial award applicants required to submit FAFSA. *Faculty research:* Photography, film, video, digital media, artists' books. *Unit head:* Tate Shaw, Executive Director, 585-442-8676, Fax: 585-442-1992, E-mail: tshaw@brockport.edu. *Application contact:* Danielle A. Welch, Graduate Admissions Counselor, 585-395-5465, Fax: 585-395-2515.
Website: http://www.vsw.org

College for Creative Studies, Graduate Programs, Detroit, MI 48202-4034. Offers interdisciplinary design (MFA); transportation design (MFA).

Colorado State University, Graduate School, College of Liberal Arts, Department of Art, Fort Collins, CO 80523-1779. Offers MFA. *Faculty:* 24 full-time (11 women), 1 part-time/adjunct (0 women). *Students:* 11 full-time (6 women), 5 part-time (2 women); includes 1 minority (Two or more races, non-Hispanic/Latino), 1 international. Average age 33. 55 applicants, 16% accepted, 3 enrolled. In 2014, 8 master's awarded. *Degree requirements:* For master's, comprehensive exam (for some programs), thesis (for some programs), exhibition. *Entrance requirements:* For master's, portfolio, letters of recommendation, transcripts, statement of purpose, resume, artist statement. Additional exam requirements/recommendations for international students: Required—TOEFL (minimum score 550 paper-based; 80 iBT). *Application deadline:* For fall admission, 2/1 priority date for domestic students; for spring admission, 10/15 priority date for domestic students. Applications are processed on a rolling basis. Application fee: $50. Electronic applications accepted. *Expenses:* Expenses: Contact institution. *Financial support:* In 2014–15, 9 students received support, including 9 teaching assistantships with tuition reimbursements available (averaging $9,313 per year); Federal Work-Study, institutionally sponsored loans, scholarships/grants, health care benefits, and unspecified assistantships also available. Support available to part-time students. Financial award application deadline: 3/1; financial award applicants required to submit FAFSA. *Faculty research:* African art history, bronze castings, etching/lithography, pre-Columbian art history, contemporary crafts. *Total annual research expenditures:* $12,103. *Unit head:* Gary W. Voss, Chair, 970-491-5895, E-mail: gary.voss@colostate.edu. *Application contact:* Kathleen Chynoweth, Graduate Contact, 970-491-6775, E-mail: kathleen.chynoweth@colostate.edu.
Website: http://art.colostate.edu/

Columbia University, Graduate School of Arts and Sciences, New York, NY 10027. Offers African-American studies (MA); American studies (MA); anthropology (MA, PhD); art history and archaeology (MA, PhD); astronomy (PhD); biological sciences (PhD); biotechnology (MA); chemical physics (PhD); chemistry (PhD); classical studies (MA, PhD); classics (MA, PhD); climate and society (MA); earth and environmental sciences (PhD); East Asia: regional studies (MA); East Asian languages and cultures (MA, PhD); ecology, evolution and environmental biology (MA), including conservation biology; ecology, evolution, and environmental biology (PhD), including ecology and evolutionary biology, evolutionary primatology; economics (PhD); English and comparative literature (MA, PhD); French and Romance philology (MA, PhD); Germanic languages (MA, PhD); global French studies (MA); Hispanic cultural studies (MA); history (PhD); history and literature (MA); human rights studies (MA); Islamic studies (MA); Italian (MA, PhD); Japanese pedagogy (MA); Jewish studies (MA); Latin America and the Caribbean: regional studies (MA); Latin American and Iberian cultures (PhD); mathematics (MA, PhD), including finance (MA); medieval and Renaissance studies (MA); Middle Eastern, South Asian, and African studies (MA, PhD); modern art: critical and curatorial studies (MA); modern European studies (MA); museum anthropology (MA); music (DMA, PhD); oral history (MA); philosophical foundations of physics (MA); philosophy (MA, PhD); physics (PhD); political science (MA, PhD); psychology (PhD); quantitative methods in the social sciences (MA); religion (MA, PhD); Russia, Eurasia and East Europe: regional studies (MA); Russian translation (MA); Slavic cultures (MA); Slavic languages (MA, PhD); sociology (MA, PhD); South Asian studies (MA); statistics (MA, PhD); theatre (PhD); JD/PhD; MA/MS; MD/PhD; MPA/MA. Dual-degree programs require admission to both Graduate School of Arts and Sciences and another Columbia school. Part-time and evening/weekend programs available. Terminal master's awarded for partial completion of doctoral program. *Degree requirements:* For master's, thesis (for some programs); for doctorate, comprehensive exam, thesis/dissertation. *Entrance requirements:* For master's and doctorate, GRE General Test, GRE Subject Test (for some programs). Electronic applications accepted. *Faculty research:* Humanities, natural sciences, social sciences.

Columbia University, School of the Arts, Visual Arts Program, New York, NY 10027. Offers new genres (MFA); painting (MFA); photography (MFA); printmaking (MFA); sculpture (MFA). *Degree requirements:* For master's, thesis. *Entrance requirements:* For master's, 3 letters of recommendation, portfolio, resume. Additional exam requirements/recommendations for international students: Required—TOEFL (minimum score 600 paper-based; 100 iBT). Electronic applications accepted.

See Display on page 257 and Close-Up on page 273.

Columbus College of Art & Design, Program in Visual Arts: New Projects, Columbus, OH 43215-1758. Offers MFA. *Accreditation:* NASAD. *Entrance requirements:* For master's, portfolio, resume/curriculum vitae, three letters of recommendation. Electronic applications accepted.

Concordia University, School of Graduate Studies, Faculty of Fine Arts, Department of Studio Arts, Montréal, QC H3G 1M8, Canada. Offers studio arts (MFA), including film production, open media, painting, photography, print media, sculpture, ceramics and fibers. *Degree requirements:* For master's, thesis or alternative. *Entrance requirements:* For master's, portfolio.

Cornell University, Graduate School, Graduate Fields of Architecture, Art and Planning, Field of Art, Ithaca, NY 14853-0001. Offers creative visual arts (MFA), including painting, photography, printmaking, sculpture. *Degree requirements:* For master's, thesis, exhibit. *Entrance requirements:* For master's, slide portfolio of 10-20 slides, 3 letters of recommendation, resume. Additional exam requirements/recommendations for international students: Required—TOEFL (minimum score 550 paper-based; 77 iBT). Electronic applications accepted. *Faculty research:* Painting, sculpture, photography, printmaking.

Cranbrook Academy of Art, Graduate School, Program in Fine Arts, Bloomfield Hills, MI 48303-0801. Offers 2D design (MFA); ceramics (MFA); fiber (MFA); metalsmithing (MFA); painting (MFA); photography (MFA); print media (MFA); sculpture (MFA). *Accreditation:* NASAD. *Faculty:* 9 full-time (3 women). *Students:* 138 full-time (93 women); includes 18 minority (7 Asian, non-Hispanic/Latino; 5 Hispanic/Latino; 6 Two or more races, non-Hispanic/Latino), 31 international. Average age 27. 390 applicants, 35% accepted, 72 enrolled. *Degree requirements:* For master's, thesis, exhibit. *Entrance requirements:* Additional exam requirements/recommendations for international students: Required—TOEFL. *Application deadline:* For fall admission, 2/1 priority date for domestic and international students; for spring admission, 11/1 for domestic students. Application fee: $85. Electronic applications accepted. *Expenses: Tuition:* Full-time $31,916. *Required fees:* $2387. *Financial support:* Federal Work-Study available. Financial award application deadline: 2/15; financial award applicants required to submit FAFSA. *Unit head:* Christopher Scoates, Director, 248-645-3301, Fax: 248-645-3591. *Application contact:* Leslie Tobakos, Registrar/Financial Aid and Admissions Manager, 248-645-3360, Fax: 248-645-3591, E-mail: ltobakos@cranbrook.edu.

Drury University, Program in Studio Art and Theory, Springfield, MO 65802. Offers MA. *Entrance requirements:* For master's, GRE or MAT. Additional exam requirements/recommendations for international students: Required—TOEFL. Electronic applications accepted.

Duke University, Graduate School, Department of Art, Art History and Visual Studies, Durham, NC 27708-0764. Offers historical and cultural visualization (MA); history of art (PhD). *Degree requirements:* For doctorate, thesis/dissertation. *Entrance requirements:* For doctorate, GRE General Test. Additional exam requirements/recommendations for international students: Required—TOEFL (minimum score 577 paper-based; 90 iBT) or IELTS (minimum score 7). Electronic applications accepted. *Expenses: Tuition:* Full-time $45,760; part-time $2765 per credit. *Required fees:* $978. Full-time tuition and fees vary according to program.

East Carolina University, Graduate School, College of Fine Arts and Communication, School of Art and Design, Greenville, NC 27858-4353. Offers art education (MA Ed); ceramics (MFA); graphic design (MFA); illustration (MFA); metal design (MFA); painting and drawing (MFA); photography (MFA); printmaking (MFA); sculpture (MFA); textile design (MFA); wood design (MFA). *Accreditation:* NASAD (one or more programs are accredited). Part-time and evening/weekend programs available. *Degree requirements:* For master's, comprehensive exam, thesis (for some programs). *Entrance requirements:* For master's, GRE General Test or MAT, portfolio. Additional exam requirements/recommendations for international students: Required—TOEFL. *Expenses:* Tuition, state resident: full-time $4223. Tuition, nonresident: full-time $16,540. *Required fees:* $2184.

Eastern Illinois University, Graduate School, College of Arts and Humanities, Department of Art, Charleston, IL 61920. Offers art (MA); art education (MA); community arts (MA). *Accreditation:* NASAD. Part-time and evening/weekend programs available. Postbaccalaureate distance learning degree programs offered (minimal on-campus study). *Faculty:* 15. *Students:* 9 full-time (5 women), 15 part-time (14 women); includes 1 minority (Hispanic/Latino). Average age 32. 26 applicants, 58% accepted, 11 enrolled. In

2014, 10 master's awarded. *Degree requirements:* For master's, comprehensive exam (for some programs), thesis (for some programs). *Entrance requirements:* For master's, GMAT or GRE. Additional exam requirements/recommendations for international students: Required—TOEFL (minimum score 500 paper-based; 61 iBT), IELTS (minimum score 6). *Application deadline:* For fall admission, 5/15 for domestic and international students; for spring admission, 10/15 for domestic and international students. Applications are processed on a rolling basis. Application fee: $30. Electronic applications accepted. *Expenses:* Tuition, state resident: full-time $3113; part-time $283 per credit hour. Tuition, nonresident: full-time $7469; part-time $679 per credit hour. *Required fees:* $2287; $96 per credit hour. Tuition and fees vary according to course load. *Financial support:* In 2014–15, 17 students received support, including 5 teaching assistantships with tuition reimbursements available (averaging $7,650 per year); career-related internships or fieldwork, Federal Work-Study, and unspecified assistantships also available. Support available to part-time students. Financial award application deadline: 3/1; financial award applicants required to submit FAFSA. *Unit head:* David Griffin, Department Chair, 217-581-3410, Fax: 217-581-6199, E-mail: dfgriffin@eiu.edu. *Application contact:* Chris Kahler, Graduate Coordinator, 217-581-6259, Fax: 217-581-6199, E-mail: cbkahler@eiu.edu.
Website: http://www.eiu.edu/artgrad/index.php

Eastern Michigan University, Graduate School, College of Arts and Sciences, Department of Art, Program in Studio Art, Ypsilanti, MI 48197. Offers MA, MFA. Part-time and evening/weekend programs available. Postbaccalaureate distance learning degree programs offered (minimal on-campus study). *Students:* 8 full-time (5 women), 12 part-time (8 women); includes 4 minority (1 Black or African American, non-Hispanic/Latino; 1 American Indian or Alaska Native, non-Hispanic/Latino; 2 Asian, non-Hispanic/Latino), 1 international. Average age 33. 17 applicants, 35% accepted, 5 enrolled. In 2014, 10 master's awarded. *Application deadline:* Applications are processed on a rolling basis. Application fee: $45. *Financial support:* Fellowships, research assistantships with full tuition reimbursements, teaching assistantships with full tuition reimbursements, career-related internships or fieldwork, Federal Work-Study, institutionally sponsored loans, scholarships/grants, and unspecified assistantships available. Support available to part-time students. *Unit head:* Dr. Colin Blakely, Department Head, 734-487-1268, Fax: 734-487-2324, E-mail: cblakely@emich.edu. *Application contact:* Michael Reedy, Graduate Coordinator, 734-487-1268, Fax: 734-487-2324, E-mail: mreedy@emich.edu.

East Tennessee State University, School of Graduate Studies, College of Arts and Sciences, Department of Art and Design, Johnson City, TN 37614. Offers studio art (MFA). *Accreditation:* NASAD. *Faculty:* 8 full-time (3 women). *Students:* 15 full-time (11 women), 4 part-time (2 women); includes 3 minority (1 Black or African American, non-Hispanic/Latino; 1 American Indian or Alaska Native, non-Hispanic/Latino; 1 Hispanic/Latino). Average age 36. 21 applicants, 38% accepted, 5 enrolled. In 2014, 1 master's awarded. *Degree requirements:* For master's, thesis, exhibit, oral exam. *Entrance requirements:* For master's, GRE General Test, portfolio, bachelor's degree in art, minimum GPA of 3.0, three letters of recommendation. Additional exam requirements/recommendations for international students: Required—TOEFL (minimum score 550 paper-based; 79 iBT). *Application deadline:* For fall admission, 2/1 for domestic and international students. Application fee: $35 ($45 for international students). Electronic applications accepted. *Financial support:* In 2014–15, 10 students received support, including 1 research assistantship with full tuition reimbursement available (averaging $9,000 per year), 14 teaching assistantships with full tuition reimbursements available (averaging $6,000 per year); career-related internships or fieldwork, institutionally sponsored loans, scholarships/grants, and unspecified assistantships also available. Financial award application deadline: 7/1; financial award applicants required to submit FAFSA. *Faculty research:* Art history, ceramics, drawing, fibers, graphic design, installation, jewelry/metalsmithing, mixed media, new media, painting, photography, printmaking, sculpture, video. *Unit head:* Prof. Mira Geard, Chair, 423-439-4247, Fax: 423-439-4393, E-mail: gerard@etsu.edu. *Application contact:* Angela Edwards, Graduate Specialist, 423-439-4703, Fax: 423-439-5624, E-mail: edwardag@etsu.edu.
Website: http://www.etsu.edu/cas/art/

Edinboro University of Pennsylvania, Department of Art, Edinboro, PA 16444. Offers art education (MA); fine arts (MFA), including ceramics, jewelry/metalsmithing, painting, printmaking, sculpture. *Accreditation:* NASAD. Evening/weekend programs available. *Degree requirements:* For master's, comprehensive exam, thesis or alternative, competency exam, exhibit, portfolio. *Entrance requirements:* For master's, GRE or MAT, interview, minimum QPA of 2.5, portfolio. Electronic applications accepted.

Emily Carr University of Art + Design, Program in Applied Arts, Vancouver, BC V6H 3R9, Canada. Offers design (M Des); media arts (MAA); visual arts (MAA). *Degree requirements:* For master's, internship, thesis project. *Entrance requirements:* For master's, minimum overall GPA of 3.0, visual portfolio, 3 letters of recommendation, resume/curriculum vitae. Additional exam requirements/recommendations for international students: Required—TOEFL (minimum score 570 paper-based; 84 iBT), IELTS (minimum score 6.5), Michigan English Language Assessment Battery (minimum score 81). *Application deadline:* For fall admission, 1/15 for domestic students. Application fee: $100 Canadian dollars. Electronic applications accepted. One-time fee: $600 Canadian dollars full-time. *Unit head:* Chris Jones, Coordinator, 604-844-3850, E-mail: masters@ecuad.ca.

Fairleigh Dickinson University, Metropolitan Campus, University College: Arts, Sciences, and Professional Studies, School of Art and Media Studies, Teaneck, NJ 07666-1914. Offers MA.

Ferris State University, Kendall College of Art and Design, Grand Rapids, MI 49503. Offers MAE, MFA. *Accreditation:* NASAD. Part-time programs available. *Faculty:* 21 full-time (14 women). *Students:* 34 full-time (19 women), 3 part-time (all women); includes 10 minority (2 Black or African American, non-Hispanic/Latino; 5 Asian, non-Hispanic/Latino; 2 Hispanic/Latino; 1 Two or more races, non-Hispanic/Latino), 3 international. Average age 32. 24 applicants, 67% accepted, 10 enrolled. In 2014, 12 master's awarded. *Degree requirements:* For master's, thesis, seminars. *Entrance requirements:* For master's, portfolio, 3 letters of recommendation, curriculum vitae. Additional exam requirements/recommendations for international students: Required—TOEFL (minimum score 70 iBT). *Application deadline:* For fall admission, 2/1 priority date for domestic and international students; for spring admission, 11/1 priority date for domestic and international students. Applications are processed on a rolling basis. Application fee: $0. Tuition and fees vary according to degree level and program. *Financial support:* In 2014–15, 36 students received support, including 9 fellowships (averaging $16,638 per year); scholarships (averaging $7665 per year), graduate assistantships (averaging $3900 per year) also available. Support available to part-time students. Financial award application deadline: 2/1; financial award applicants required to submit FAFSA. *Unit head:* Dr. David M. Rosen, President and Vice Chancellor, 616-451-2787. *Application contact:* Krostopher Jones, Director of Talent Acquisition, 616-451-2787, Fax: 616-831-9689, E-mail: kcadadmissions@ferris.edu.
Website: http://www.kcad.edu/

Florida Atlantic University, Dorothy F. Schmidt College of Arts and Letters, Department of Visual Arts and Art History, Boca Raton, FL 33431-0991. Offers visual art (MFA), including ceramics, graphic design, visual art. *Degree requirements:* For master's, one foreign language, project. *Entrance requirements:* For master's, GRE General Test, minimum GPA of 3.0 during last 60 hours of course work, slide portfolio. Electronic applications accepted. *Expenses:* Tuition, state resident: full-time $7396; part-time $369.82 per credit hour. Tuition, nonresident: full-time $19,392; part-time $1024.81 per credit hour. Tuition and fees vary according to course load. *Faculty research:* Painting, ceramics (traditional and non-traditional), installation, video and interactive sculpture.

Florida International University, College of Architecture and the Arts, School of Art and Art History, Miami, FL 33199. Offers museum studies (Graduate Certificate); studio art (MFA). *Accreditation:* NASAD. Part-time and evening/weekend programs available. *Entrance requirements:* For master's, minimum GPA of 3.0 (upper level coursework), 3 letters of recommendation, 20 slides of creative work. Additional exam requirements/recommendations for international students: Required—TOEFL (minimum score 550 paper-based; 80 iBT). Electronic applications accepted.

Florida State University, The Graduate School, College of Fine Arts, Department of Art, Tallahassee, FL 32306. Offers MFA. *Accreditation:* NASAD. *Faculty:* 18 full-time (10 women), 33 part-time/adjunct (22 women). *Students:* 31 full-time (24 women); includes 7 minority (1 Black or African American, non-Hispanic/Latino; 1 American Indian or Alaska Native, non-Hispanic/Latino; 2 Asian, non-Hispanic/Latino; 3 Hispanic/Latino). Average age 26. 85 applicants, 18% accepted, 11 enrolled. In 2014, 14 master's awarded. *Degree requirements:* For master's, thesis, creative thesis project, short thesis paper. *Entrance requirements:* Additional exam requirements/recommendations for international students: Required—TOEFL (minimum score 550 paper-based). *Application deadline:* For fall admission, 2/1 priority date for domestic and international students. Application fee: $40. Electronic applications accepted. *Expenses:* Tuition, state resident: part-time $403.51 per credit hour. Tuition, nonresident: part-time $1004.85 per credit hour. *Required fees:* $75.81 per credit hour. One-time fee: $20 part-time. Tuition and fees vary according to campus/location. *Financial support:* In 2014–15, 31 students received support, including 31 teaching assistantships (averaging $5,000 per year); fellowships, tuition waivers (full), and unspecified assistantships also available. *Faculty research:* Photography, painting, sculpture, printmaking, ceramics. *Unit head:* Carolyn Henne, Department Chair, 850-644-7254, E-mail: chenne@fsu.edu. *Application contact:* Elizabeth DiDonna, Graduate Admissions Officer, 850-644-8252, E-mail: edidonna@fsu.edu.
Website: http://art.fsu.edu/

Fontbonne University, Graduate Programs, Department of Fine Arts, St. Louis, MO 63105-3098. Offers art (MA); fine arts (MFA); theater education (MA). Part-time and evening/weekend programs available. *Degree requirements:* For master's, thesis exhibit (MFA). *Entrance requirements:* For master's, minimum GPA of 3.0, portfolio.

Fort Hays State University, Graduate School, College of Arts and Sciences, Department of Art, Hays, KS 67601-4099. Offers studio art (MFA). Part-time programs available. *Degree requirements:* For master's, comprehensive exam, thesis. *Entrance requirements:* For master's, slides. Additional exam requirements/recommendations for international students: Required—TOEFL (minimum score 550 paper-based; 79 iBT). Electronic applications accepted. *Faculty research:* Migration art of Germanic tribes, iconographic and stylistic development, graphic design, photography, lithography.

Framingham State University, Continuing Education, Program in Art, Framingham, MA 01701-9101. Offers M Ed.

Full Sail University, Education Media Design and Technology Master of Science Program - Online, Winter Park, FL 32792-7437. Offers MS. Postbaccalaureate distance learning degree programs offered (no on-campus study). *Entrance requirements:* Additional exam requirements/recommendations for international students: Required—TOEFL (minimum score 550 paper-based; 79 iBT).

Full Sail University, Media Design Master of Fine Arts Program - Online, Winter Park, FL 32792-7437. Offers MFA. Postbaccalaureate distance learning degree programs offered.

George Mason University, College of Visual and Performing Arts, Art and Visual Technology Program, Fairfax, VA 22030. Offers drawing (MFA); graphic design (MFA); new media art (MFA); painting (MFA); photography (MFA); printmaking (MFA); sculpture (MFA). *Accreditation:* NASAD. *Faculty:* 21 full-time (11 women), 36 part-time/adjunct (22 women). *Students:* 5 full-time (4 women), 12 part-time (2 women); includes 3 minority (1 Black or African American, non-Hispanic/Latino; 2 Two or more races, non-Hispanic/Latino). Average age 40. 25 applicants, 20% accepted, 3 enrolled. In 2014, 4 master's awarded. *Degree requirements:* For master's, comprehensive experience, studio project or thesis. *Entrance requirements:* For master's, official transcripts; 3 letters of recommendation; letter of intent; resume; professional goals statement. Additional exam requirements/recommendations for international students: Required—TOEFL (minimum score 570 paper-based; 80 iBT), IELTS (minimum score 6.5), PTE. *Application deadline:* For fall admission, 1/15 for domestic and international students. Application fee: $65 ($80 for international students). Electronic applications accepted. *Expenses:* Tuition, state resident: full-time $9794; part-time $408 per credit hour. Tuition, nonresident: full-time $26,978; part-time $1124 per credit hour. *Required fees:* $2820; $118 per credit hour. Tuition and fees vary according to course load and program. *Financial support:* In 2014–15, 2 students received support, including 2 teaching assistantships with full and partial tuition reimbursements available (averaging $6,696 per year); career-related internships or fieldwork, Federal Work-Study, scholarships/grants, unspecified assistantships, and health care benefits (for full-time research or teaching assistantship recipients) also available. Support available to part-time students. Financial award application deadline: 3/1; financial award applicants required to submit FAFSA. *Faculty research:* Digital arts, painting, photography, print-making, sculpture; combined art forms in in-disciplinary projects including installation, performance, publishing, time or writing-based; combined creative and critical approaches. *Unit head:* Peter Winant, Director, 703-993-8385, Fax: 703-993-8798, E-mail: pwinant@gmu.edu. *Application contact:* Asma Ormazad, Graduate Studies Administrative Assistant, 703-993-9773, Fax: 703-993-8255, E-mail: aomarzad@gmu.edu.
Website: http://soa.gmu.edu

The George Washington University, Columbian College of Arts and Sciences, Department of Fine Arts and Art History, Washington, DC 20052. Offers art history (MA), including art history, museum training; ceramics (MFA); drawing/painting (MFA); interior design (MFA), including interior architecture and design; new media (MFA); photography (MFA); sculpture (MFA). *Accreditation:* CIDA. Part-time and evening/weekend programs available. *Faculty:* 17 full-time (10 women). *Students:* 81 full-time (66 women), 24 part-time (20 women); includes 15 minority (5 Black or African American, non-Hispanic/Latino; 1 American Indian or Alaska Native, non-Hispanic/Latino; 3 Asian, non-Hispanic/Latino; 3 Hispanic/Latino; 1 Native Hawaiian or other Pacific Islander, non-Hispanic/Latino; 2 Two or more races, non-Hispanic/Latino), 5 international. Average age 31. 79 applicants, 65% accepted, 12 enrolled. In 2014, 15 master's awarded. *Entrance requirements:* For master's, GRE General Test, bachelor's degree in field, minimum GPA of 3.0. Additional exam requirements/recommendations for international students: Required—TOEFL (minimum score 550 paper-based; 80 iBT). *Application deadline:* For fall admission, 3/1 priority date for domestic students, 1/15 priority date for international students; for spring admission, 10/1 priority date for domestic students, 9/1 priority date

for international students. Applications are processed on a rolling basis. Application fee: $75. Electronic applications accepted. *Financial support:* In 2014–15, 12 students received support. Fellowships, teaching assistantships, career-related internships or fieldwork, Federal Work-Study, and tuition waivers available. Financial award application deadline: 1/15. *Unit head:* Phil Jacks, Chair, 202-994-6085, E-mail: pjacks@gwu.edu. *Application contact:* Information Contact, 202-994-6085, Fax: 202-994-8657, E-mail: art@gwu.edu.
Website: http://art.columbian.gwu.edu/

Georgia Southern University, Jack N. Averitt College of Graduate Studies, College of Liberal Arts and Social Sciences, Program in Art, Statesboro, GA 30460. Offers fine arts (MFA), including 2D graphic design, 2D studio art, 3D studio art. *Accreditation:* NASAD. Part-time programs available. *Students:* 10 full-time (6 women), 5 part-time (3 women); includes 3 minority (all Hispanic/Latino), 2 international. Average age 37. 13 applicants, 77% accepted, 5 enrolled. In 2014, 5 master's awarded. *Degree requirements:* For master's, thesis, exhibition. *Entrance requirements:* For master's, minimum GPA of 3.0; 18 semester hours of course work in studio art, 9 in art history; portfolio; letters of reference. Additional exam requirements/recommendations for international students: Required—TOEFL (minimum score 550 paper-based), IELTS (minimum score 6). *Application deadline:* For fall admission, 3/1 priority date for domestic and international students; for spring admission, 10/1 priority date for domestic students, 10/1 for international students. Applications are processed on a rolling basis. Application fee: $50. Electronic applications accepted. *Expenses:* Tuition, state resident: full-time $7236; part-time $277 per semester hour. Tuition, nonresident: full-time $27,118; part-time $1105 per semester hour. *Required fees:* $2092. *Financial support:* In 2014–15, 8 students received support, including research assistantships with partial tuition reimbursements available (averaging $7,200 per year), teaching assistantships with partial tuition reimbursements available (averaging $7,200 per year); career-related internships or fieldwork, Federal Work-Study, scholarships/grants, tuition waivers (partial), and unspecified assistantships also available. Support available to part-time students. Financial award application deadline: 4/15; financial award applicants required to submit FAFSA. *Faculty research:* International design trends; graphic design social awareness campaigns; functional design; public sculpture; fine art painting, drawing, printmaking, paper and book arts; folk art; Georgia artists archive, technology, design, contemporary, traditional studio. *Unit head:* Dr. Marc Moulton, Graduate Director, 912-478-7665, Fax: 912-478-5104, E-mail: marcmoulton@georgiasouthern.edu.
Website: http://class.georgiasouthern.edu/art

Georgia State University, College of Arts and Sciences, Ernest G. Welch School of Art and Design, Program in Studio Art, Atlanta, GA 30302-3083. Offers ceramics (MFA); drawing and painting (MFA); graphic design (MFA); interior design (MFA); photography (MFA); printmaking (MFA); sculpture (MFA); textiles (MFA). *Accreditation:* NASAD. *Degree requirements:* For master's, thesis. *Application deadline:* For fall admission, 1/6 for domestic and international students; for spring admission, 1/15 priority date for domestic and international students. Application fee: $50. Electronic applications accepted. *Expenses:* Tuition, state resident: full-time $6516; part-time $362 per credit hour. Tuition, nonresident: full-time $22,014; part-time $1223 per credit hour. *Required fees:* $2128 per semester. Tuition and fees vary according to course load and program. *Financial support:* In 2014–15, fellowships with full tuition reimbursements (averaging $11,000 per year), teaching assistantships with full tuition reimbursements (averaging $7,000 per year) were awarded; research assistantships, scholarships/grants, and unspecified assistantships also available. Financial award application deadline: 4/15. *Faculty research:* Advertising and typography, new media, traditional media, three-dimensional art, architectural and environmental design. *Unit head:* Michael White, Director, Welch School of Art and Design, 404-413-5221, Fax: 404-413-5261, E-mail: mwhite@gsu.edu. *Application contact:* Hubert Stanley Anderson, Director of Graduate Studies, 404-413-5229, Fax: 404-413-5261, E-mail: artgrad@gsu.edu.
Website: http://artdesign.gsu.edu/graduate/admissions/masters-of-fine-arts-in-studio/

Governors State University, College of Arts and Sciences, Program in Art, University Park, IL 60484. Offers MA. Part-time and evening/weekend programs available. *Degree requirements:* For master's, thesis or alternative. *Entrance requirements:* For master's, portfolio, bachelor's degree in humanities. *Faculty research:* Historical study of art of selected ethnic groups of southwestern Zaire.

Hofstra University, School of Education, Programs in Teacher Education, Hempstead, NY 11549. Offers bilingual education (MA), including biology (MA, MS Ed), geology; business education (MS Ed); early childhood and childhood education (MS Ed), including French; early childhood education (MA); education technology (Advanced Certificate); elementary education (MA), including math. science, technology (STEM); English education (MS Ed); fine arts education (MS Ed), including biology (MA, MS Ed); foreign language and TESOL (MS Ed); learning and teaching (Ed D), including applied linguistics, art education, arts and humanities, early childhood education, English education, human development, math education, math, science, and technology, multicultural education, physical education, science education, social studies education, special education; mathematics education (MA, MS Ed); secondary education (Advanced Certificate); social studies education (MA, MS Ed). Part-time and evening/weekend programs available. Postbaccalaureate distance learning degree programs offered (minimal on-campus study). *Students:* 141 full-time (111 women), 119 part-time (84 women); includes 58 minority (13 Black or African American, non-Hispanic/Latino; 14 Asian, non-Hispanic/Latino; 28 Hispanic/Latino; 1 Native Hawaiian or other Pacific Islander, non-Hispanic/Latino; 2 Two or more races, non-Hispanic/Latino), 18 international. Average age 30. 301 applicants, 87% accepted, 112 enrolled. In 2014, 133 master's, 5 doctorates, 28 other advanced degrees awarded. *Degree requirements:* For master's, comprehensive exam, thesis (for some programs), exit project, student teaching, fieldwork, electronic portfolio, curriculum project, minimum GPA of 3.0; for doctorate, thesis/dissertation; for Advanced Certificate, 3 foreign languages, comprehensive exam (for some programs), thesis project. *Entrance requirements:* For master's, 2 letters of recommendation, portfolio, teacher certification (MA), interview, essay; for doctorate, GMAT, GRE, LSAT, or MAT; for Advanced Certificate, 2 letters of recommendation, essay, interview and/or portfolio, teaching certificate. Additional exam requirements/recommendations for international students: Required—TOEFL (minimum score 550 paper-based; 80 iBT). *Application deadline:* Applications are processed on a rolling basis. Application fee: $70 ($75 for international students). Electronic applications accepted. *Expenses: Tuition:* Full-time $20,610; part-time $1145 per credit hour. *Required fees:* $970; $165 per term. Tuition and fees vary according to program. *Financial support:* In 2014–15, 153 students received support, including 60 fellowships with full and partial tuition reimbursements available (averaging $5,084 per year), 4 research assistantships with full and partial tuition reimbursements available (averaging $7,095 per year); Federal Work-Study, institutionally sponsored loans, scholarships/grants, health care benefits, and tuition waivers (full and partial) also available. Support available to part-time students. Financial award applicants required to submit FAFSA. *Faculty research:* Appropriate content in secondary school disciplines, lesson development across content, interdisciplinary curriculum, multicultural education. *Unit head:* Dr. Eustace Thompson, Chairperson, 516-463-5749, Fax: 516-463-6275, E-mail: edaegt@hofstra.edu. *Application contact:* Sunil Samuel, Assistant Vice President of Admissions, 516-463-4723, Fax: 516-463-4664, E-mail: graduateadmission@hofstra.edu.
Website: http://www.hofstra.edu/education/

Hollins University, Graduate Programs, Program in Liberal Studies, Roanoke, VA 24020. Offers humanities (MALS); interdisciplinary studies (MALS); leadership (MALS); liberal studies (CAS); social science (MALS); visual and performing arts (MALS). Part-time and evening/weekend programs available. *Students:* 3 full-time (all women), 37 part-time (32 women); includes 6 minority (4 Black or African American, non-Hispanic/Latino; 1 Hispanic/Latino; 1 Two or more races, non-Hispanic/Latino). Average age 44. 13 applicants, 100% accepted, 9 enrolled. In 2014, 15 master's awarded. *Degree requirements:* For master's, thesis. *Entrance requirements:* For master's, letters of recommendation, interview. Additional exam requirements/recommendations for international students: Required—TOEFL (minimum score 550 paper-based; 79 iBT). *Application deadline:* For fall admission, 7/1 priority date for domestic and international students; for spring admission, 12/10 priority date for domestic and international students. Applications are processed on a rolling basis. Application fee: $40. Electronic applications accepted. *Financial support:* In 2014–15, 7 students received support, including 7 fellowships (averaging $1,000 per year); scholarships/grants also available. Support available to part-time students. Financial award application deadline: 7/15; financial award applicants required to submit FAFSA. *Faculty research:* Diversity, gender and women's studies, political science, leadership. *Unit head:* Dr. Joe Leedom, Director, 540-362-6326, Fax: 540-362-6288, E-mail: jleedom@hollins.edu. *Application contact:* Cathy S. Koon, Manager of Graduate Services, 540-362-6326, Fax: 540-362-6288, E-mail: ckoon@hollins.edu.
Website: http://www.hollins.edu/

Hood College, Graduate School, Program in Ceramic Arts, Frederick, MD 21701-8575. Offers ceramic arts (Certificate); ceramics (MA, MFA). Part-time and evening/weekend programs available. *Degree requirements:* For master's, comprehensive exam. *Entrance requirements:* For master's, minimum GPA of 2.75; for Certificate, portfolio. Additional exam requirements/recommendations for international students: Required—TOEFL (minimum score 575 paper-based; 89 iBT), IELTS (minimum score 6.5). Electronic applications accepted. Application fee is waived when completed online.

Houston Baptist University, School of Fine Arts, Houston, TX 77074-3298. Offers MFA. Part-time and evening/weekend programs available. *Students:* 21 full-time (11 women); includes 11 minority (3 Black or African American, non-Hispanic/Latino; 1 Asian, non-Hispanic/Latino; 6 Hispanic/Latino; 1 Two or more races, non-Hispanic/Latino), 2 international. Average age 37. 32 applicants, 44% accepted, 13 enrolled. In 2014, 9 master's awarded. *Degree requirements:* For master's, comprehensive exam. *Entrance requirements:* For master's, minimum GPA of 2.5, two recommendations, resume, bachelor's degree, transcript, digital portfolio. Additional exam requirements/recommendations for international students: Required—TOEFL. *Application deadline:* For fall admission, 4/1 for domestic students, 2/1 for international students; for winter admission, 10/1 for domestic and international students; for spring admission, 1/1 for domestic and international students. Applications are processed on a rolling basis. Application fee: $0. Electronic applications accepted. *Expenses:* Expenses: Contact institution. *Financial support:* Federal Work-Study and scholarships/grants available. Support available to part-time students. Financial award application deadline: 4/1; financial award applicants required to submit FAFSA. *Unit head:* Dr. Matthew Boyleston, Dean, 281-649-3607, E-mail: mboyleston@hbu.edu. *Application contact:* Michael Collins, Program Director, E-mail: mcollins@hbu.edu.
Website: http://www.hbu.edu/mfa

Howard University, Graduate School, Division of Fine Arts, Department of Art, Program in Fine Arts, Washington, DC 20059-0002. Offers 3D reality (sculpture and ceramics) (MFA); design (MFA); electronic studio (MFA); painting (MFA); photography (MFA). *Accreditation:* NASAD. *Degree requirements:* For master's, comprehensive exam, thesis, exhibit. *Entrance requirements:* For master's, minimum GPA of 3.0, portfolio.

Hunter College of the City University of New York, Graduate School, School of Arts and Sciences, Department of Art, Program in Studio Art, New York, NY 10065-5085. Offers MFA. Part-time and evening/weekend programs available. *Faculty:* 5 full-time (1 woman), 1 (woman) part-time/adjunct. *Students:* 12 full-time (7 women), 93 part-time (44 women); includes 19 minority (7 Black or African American, non-Hispanic/Latino; 4 Asian, non-Hispanic/Latino; 8 Hispanic/Latino), 25 international. Average age 31. 590 applicants, 7% accepted, 20 enrolled. In 2014, 45 master's awarded. *Degree requirements:* For master's, exhibit, project. *Entrance requirements:* For master's, minimum of 24 credits of course work in studio art, 9 in art history; portfolio. Additional exam requirements/recommendations for international students: Required—TOEFL. *Application deadline:* For fall admission, 2/1 for domestic students; for spring admission, 10/1 for domestic students. *Financial support:* Career-related internships or fieldwork, Federal Work-Study, scholarships/grants, and tuition waivers (partial) available. Support available to part-time students. Financial award application deadline: 4/15. *Faculty research:* Color theory, public printmaking and environmental commissions in painting and sculpture, graphics, ceramics, contemporary film and video. *Unit head:* Joel Carreiro, Graduate Adviser, 212-650-3398, E-mail: grad.arthistoryadvisor@hunter.cuny.edu. *Application contact:* William Zlata, Director for Graduate Admissions, 212-772-4482, Fax: 212-650-3336, E-mail: admissions@hunter.cuny.edu.

Idaho State University, Office of Graduate Studies, College of Arts and Letters, Department of Art and Pre-Architecture, Pocatello, ID 83209-8004. Offers art (MFA). Part-time programs available. *Degree requirements:* For master's, comprehensive exam, thesis, exhibit, 2 year minimum participation in program, oral exam. *Entrance requirements:* For master's, GRE General Test, GMAT or MAT, minimum GPA of 3.0 in all upper-division classes, portfolio of work, 3 letters of recommendation. Additional exam requirements/recommendations for international students: Required—TOEFL (minimum score 550 paper-based; 80 iBT). Electronic applications accepted. *Faculty research:* Computerized weaving, anodizing refractory metals, viscosity printing, neon, ceramic shell casting.

Illinois State University, Graduate School, College of Fine Arts, Program in Arts Technology, Normal, IL 61790-2200. Offers MS. *Accreditation:* NASAD. *Degree requirements:* For master's, thesis or alternative.

Illinois State University, Graduate School, College of Fine Arts, School of Art, Normal, IL 61790-2200. Offers art history (MA, MS); ceramics (MFA, MS); drawing (MFA, MS); fibers (MFA, MS); glass (MFA, MS); graphic design (MFA, MS); metals (MFA, MS); painting (MFA, MS); photography (MFA, MS); printmaking (MFA, MS); sculpture (MFA, MS). *Accreditation:* NASAD (one or more programs are accredited). *Degree requirements:* For master's, thesis or alternative, internship. *Entrance requirements:* For master's, portfolio, sample of scholarly writing.

Indiana State University, College of Graduate and Professional Studies, College of Arts and Sciences, Department of Art, Terre Haute, IN 47809. Offers ceramics (MA, MFA); drawing (MA, MFA); graphic design (MA, MFA); painting (MA, MFA); photography (MA, MFA); printmaking (MA, MFA); sculpture (MA, MFA). *Accreditation:* NASAD (one or more programs are accredited). Part-time programs available. *Degree requirements:* For master's, thesis or alternative, departmental qualifying exam. *Entrance*

requirements: For master's, portfolio. Additional exam requirements/recommendations for international students: Required—TOEFL (minimum score 550 paper-based).

Indiana University Bloomington, University Graduate School, College of Arts and Sciences, Henry Radford Hope School of Fine Arts, Bloomington, IN 47405-7000. Offers MA, MFA, PhD. *Accreditation:* NASAD (one or more programs are accredited). *Faculty:* 17 full-time (10 women). *Students:* 97 full-time (63 women), 4 part-time (1 woman); includes 16 minority (1 Black or African American, non-Hispanic/Latino; 5 Asian, non-Hispanic/Latino; 8 Hispanic/Latino; 2 Two or more races, non-Hispanic/Latino), 4 international. Average age 29. 211 applicants, 23% accepted, 33 enrolled. In 2014, 30 master's, 6 doctorates awarded. *Degree requirements:* For doctorate, 2 foreign languages, thesis/dissertation. *Entrance requirements:* For master's, portfolio (MFA); for doctorate, minimum GPA of 3.0. Additional exam requirements/recommendations for international students: Required—TOEFL. *Application deadline:* For fall admission, 1/15 priority date for domestic students, 12/15 for international students; for spring admission, 9/1 for domestic and international students. Applications are processed on a rolling basis. Application fee: $55 ($65 for international students). Electronic applications accepted. *Financial support:* Fellowships with tuition reimbursements, research assistantships with tuition reimbursements, teaching assistantships with tuition reimbursements, career-related internships or fieldwork, Federal Work-Study, scholarships/grants, tuition waivers (full and partial), and stipends available. Financial award application deadline: 2/15. *Faculty research:* Infrared reflectography, Italian Renaissance painters, hand papermaking, British Romantic landscape painting, late nineteenth century American art. *Unit head:* Patrick McNaughton, Chair, 812-855-5277, E-mail: mcnaught@indiana.edu. *Application contact:* Erin Kirchhofer, Graduate Services Coordinator, 812-855-0188, E-mail: sofagrad@indiana.edu.
Website: http://www.indiana.edu/~finaweb/

Indiana University of Pennsylvania, School of Graduate Studies and Research, College of Fine Arts, Department of Art, MA Program in Art, Indiana, PA 15705-1087. Offers MA. *Accreditation:* NASAD. Part-time programs available. *Faculty:* 10 full-time (4 women). *Students:* 1 (woman) full-time, all international. Average age 25. 5 applicants, 40% accepted, 1 enrolled. In 2014, 5 master's awarded. *Degree requirements:* For master's, thesis optional. *Entrance requirements:* For master's, 3 letters of recommendation, portfolio. Additional exam requirements/recommendations for international students: Required—TOEFL (minimum score 540 paper-based). *Application deadline:* For fall admission, 4/15 priority date for domestic students. Applications are processed on a rolling basis. Application fee: $50. Electronic applications accepted. *Financial support:* In 2014–15, 1 research assistantship with full and partial tuition reimbursement (averaging $2,000 per year) was awarded; fellowships, career-related internships or fieldwork, Federal Work-Study, scholarships/grants, and unspecified assistantships also available. Support available to part-time students. Financial award application deadline: 4/15; financial award applicants required to submit FAFSA. *Unit head:* Dr. Susan Palmisano, Graduate Coordinator, 724-357-2530, E-mail: palmisan@iup.edu.
Website: http://www.iup.edu/upper.aspx?id-88993

Indiana University of Pennsylvania, School of Graduate Studies and Research, College of Fine Arts, Department of Art, Master of Fine Arts Program, Indiana, PA 15705-1087. Offers MFA. Part-time programs available. *Faculty:* 10 full-time (4 women). *Students:* 13 full-time (8 women), 9 part-time (3 women); includes 4 minority (2 Hispanic/Latino; 2 Two or more races, non-Hispanic/Latino), 1 international. Average age 28. 18 applicants, 44% accepted, 5 enrolled. In 2014, 4 master's awarded. *Degree requirements:* For master's, thesis/exhibition. *Entrance requirements:* For master's, 2 letters of recommendation, art slides. Additional exam requirements/recommendations for international students: Required—TOEFL (minimum score 540 paper-based). *Application deadline:* For fall admission, 2/15 priority date for domestic students. Application fee: $50. Electronic applications accepted. *Financial support:* In 2014–15, 1 fellowship with full tuition reimbursement (averaging $1,000 per year), 9 research assistantships with full and partial tuition reimbursements (averaging $4,040 per year) were awarded; career-related internships or fieldwork, Federal Work-Study, scholarships/grants, and unspecified assistantships also available. Support available to part-time students. Financial award application deadline: 4/15; financial award applicants required to submit FAFSA. *Unit head:* Dr. Susan Palmisano, Graduate Coordinator, 724-357-2536, E-mail: palmisan@iup.edu.
Website: http://www.iup.edu/upper.aspx?id-88993

Indiana University–Purdue University Indianapolis, Herron School of Art and Design, Indianapolis, IN 46202. Offers art education (MAE); furniture design (MFA); printmaking (MFA); sculpture (MFA); visual communication (MFA). *Accreditation:* NASAD. *Faculty:* 40 full-time (22 women). *Students:* 60 full-time (41 women), 3 part-time (all women); includes 8 minority (3 Black or African American, non-Hispanic/Latino; 2 Asian, non-Hispanic/Latino; 1 Hispanic/Latino; 2 Two or more races, non-Hispanic/Latino), 7 international. Average age 30. 103 applicants, 67% accepted, 38 enrolled. In 2014, 26 master's awarded. *Degree requirements:* For master's, thesis. *Entrance requirements:* For master's, portfolio, 44 hours of course work in art history and studio art, Art Therapy requires 12 credits of psychology and 18 credits of studio art. Additional exam requirements/recommendations for international students: Recommended—TOEFL (minimum score 550 paper-based; 79 iBT), IELTS (minimum score 6.5). *Application deadline:* For fall admission, 1/15 priority date for domestic and international students; for spring admission, 11/1 for domestic students, 10/15 for international students. Application fee: $60 ($65 for international students). Electronic applications accepted. *Financial support:* In 2014–15, 55 students received support, including 30 fellowships (averaging $3,325 per year), 1 research assistantship (averaging $6,000 per year), 23 teaching assistantships (averaging $3,500 per year); career-related internships or fieldwork, Federal Work-Study, institutionally sponsored loans, scholarships/grants, health care benefits, and tuition waivers (partial) also available. *Unit head:* Prof. Valerie Eickmeier, Dean, 317-278-9470, Fax: 317-278-9471, E-mail: herron@iupui.edu. *Application contact:* Herron Office of Admissions and Student Services, 317-378-9400, E-mail: herron4u@iupui.edu.
Website: http://www.herron.iupui.edu/

Institute for Doctoral Studies in the Visual Arts, PhD Program in Visual Art: Philosophy, Aesthetics, and Art Theory, Portland, ME 04102. Offers aesthetics (PhD); art theory (PhD); philosophy (PhD). Postbaccalaureate distance learning degree programs offered (minimal on-campus study). *Faculty:* 3 full-time, 7 part-time/adjunct. *Students:* 56 full-time. *Degree requirements:* For doctorate, comprehensive exam, thesis/dissertation, dissertation defense. *Entrance requirements:* For doctorate, curriculum vitae, writing sample, portfolio, interview. *Application deadline:* Applications are processed on a rolling basis. Application fee: $56. Electronic applications accepted. Application fee is waived when completed online. *Financial support:* Fellowships and scholarships/grants available. Financial award applicants required to submit FAFSA. *Faculty research:* Visual culture, cultural studies, feminism, contemporary art. *Application contact:* Molly Davis, Co-Director of Admissions, 800-240-7357, E-mail: info@idsva.org.
Website: http://idsva.org

Inter American University of Puerto Rico, San Germán Campus, Graduate Studies Center, Program in Fine Arts, San Germán, PR 00683-5008. Offers drawing (MFA); graphic design (MFA); painting (MFA); photography (MFA); printmaking (MFA); sculpture (MFA). Part-time and evening/weekend programs available. *Degree requirements:* For master's, comprehensive exam, thesis. *Entrance requirements:* For master's, GRE General Test or EXADEP, minimum GPA of 3.0.

Iowa State University of Science and Technology, Program in Integrated Visual Arts, Ames, IA 50011. Offers MFA. *Accreditation:* NASAD. *Entrance requirements:* Additional exam requirements/recommendations for international students: Required—TOEFL (minimum score 550 paper-based; 79 iBT), IELTS (minimum score 6.5).

James Madison University, The Graduate School, College of Visual and Performing Arts, School of Art, Design and Art History, Harrisonburg, VA 22807. Offers art education (MA); studio art (MFA), including drawing/painting, metal/jewelry, photography. *Accreditation:* NASAD. Part-time programs available. *Faculty:* 25 full-time (15 women). *Students:* 11 full-time (7 women), 1 (woman) part-time; includes 4 minority (1 Black or African American, non-Hispanic/Latino; 3 Two or more races, non-Hispanic/Latino), 1 international. Average age 28. 18 applicants, 39% accepted, 6 enrolled. In 2014, 7 master's awarded. *Degree requirements:* For master's, thesis (for some programs). *Application deadline:* For fall admission, 2/15 for domestic and international students; for spring admission, 10/15 for domestic and international students. Application fee: $55. Electronic applications accepted. *Expenses:* Tuition, state resident: full-time $7812; part-time $434 per credit hour. Tuition, nonresident: full-time $20,430; part-time $1135 per credit hour. *Financial support:* In 2014–15, 11 students received support, including 2 teaching assistantships with full tuition reimbursements available (averaging $8,837 per year); Federal Work-Study and 9 assistantships (averaging $2748) also available. Financial award application deadline: 3/1; financial award applicants required to submit FAFSA. *Unit head:* Dr. Kathy A. Schwartz, Director of School of Art, Design and Art History, 540-568-6216, E-mail: art-arthistory@jmu.edu. *Application contact:* Lynette D. Michael, Director of Graduate Admissions and Student Admissions, 540-568-6131 Ext. 6395, Fax: 540-568-7860, E-mail: michaeld@jmu.edu.
Website: http://www.jmu.edu/artandarthistory/

John F. Kennedy University, Graduate School of Holistic Studies, Department of Arts and Consciousness, Program in Studio Arts, Pleasant Hill, CA 94523-4817. Offers MFA. Part-time and evening/weekend programs available. *Degree requirements:* For master's, thesis or alternative. *Entrance requirements:* For master's, interview, portfolio. Additional exam requirements/recommendations for international students: Required—TOEFL. *Expenses:* Contact institution.

Johnson State College, Program in Studio Arts, Johnson, VT 05656. Offers drawing (MFA); mixed media (MFA); painting (MFA); printmaking (MFA); sculpture (MFA). Part-time programs available. Postbaccalaureate distance learning degree programs offered (minimal on-campus study). *Degree requirements:* For master's, thesis. *Entrance requirements:* For master's, portfolio. Additional exam requirements/recommendations for international students: Required—TOEFL. *Expenses:* Contact institution.

Kansas State University, Graduate School, College of Arts and Sciences, Department of Art, Manhattan, KS 66506. Offers MFA. *Accreditation:* NASAD. *Faculty:* 18 full-time (7 women), 2 part-time/adjunct (0 women). *Students:* 16 full-time (12 women), 1 part-time (0 women); includes 1 minority (Hispanic/Latino). Average age 28. 24 applicants, 21% accepted, 3 enrolled. In 2014, 3 master's awarded. *Degree requirements:* For master's, thesis, gallery exhibit. *Entrance requirements:* For master's, images of artistic work, portfolio, official transcripts, recommendation form/letters, statement of purpose. Additional exam requirements/recommendations for international students: Required—TOEFL (minimum score 550 paper-based; 79 iBT). *Application deadline:* For fall admission, 1/15 for domestic students, 1/1 for international students; for spring admission, 10/1 for domestic students, 8/1 for international students. Application fee: $50 ($75 for international students). Electronic applications accepted. *Financial support:* In 2014–15, 16 students received support, including 16 teaching assistantships with full tuition reimbursements available (averaging $8,323 per year); career-related internships or fieldwork, institutionally sponsored loans, scholarships/grants, and unspecified assistantships also available. Support available to part-time students. Financial award application deadline: 3/1; financial award applicants required to submit FAFSA. *Faculty research:* Drawing, painting, sculpture, metalsmithing, visual communication. *Unit head:* Stephen Kiefer, Interim Head, 785-532-6605, Fax: 785-532-0334, E-mail: swkiefer@ksu.edu. *Application contact:* Prof. Glen Brown, Director of Graduate Studies, 785-532-6605, Fax: 785-532-1751, E-mail: gbrown@ksu.edu.
Website: http://art.ksu.edu

Kean University, College of Visual and Performing Arts, Union, NJ 07083. Offers MA. Part-time programs available. *Faculty:* 8 full-time (3 women). *Students:* 11 full-time (10 women), 21 part-time (14 women); includes 8 minority (2 Black or African American, non-Hispanic/Latino; 6 Hispanic/Latino), 1 international. Average age 35. 8 applicants, 100% accepted, 8 enrolled. In 2014, 12 master's awarded. *Degree requirements:* For master's, thesis (for some programs). *Entrance requirements:* Additional exam requirements/recommendations for international students: Required—TOEFL (minimum score 550 paper-based; 79 iBT). *Application deadline:* For fall admission, 6/1 for domestic and international students; for spring admission, 12/1 for domestic and international students. Applications are processed on a rolling basis. Application fee: $75 ($150 for international students). Electronic applications accepted. *Expenses:* Tuition, state resident: full-time $12,461; part-time $607 per credit. Tuition, nonresident: full-time $16,889; part-time $744 per credit. *Required fees:* $3141; $143 per credit. Tuition and fees vary according to course load, degree level and program. *Financial support:* In 2014–15, 4 research assistantships with full tuition reimbursements (averaging $3,742 per year) were awarded; scholarships/grants and unspecified assistantships also available. Financial award applicants required to submit FAFSA. *Unit head:* Dr. George Arasimowicz, Dean, 908-737-4376, Fax: 908-737-4377, E-mail: garasimo@kean.edu. *Application contact:* Steven Koch, Assistant Director for Graduate Admissions, 908-737-7136, Fax: 908-737-7135, E-mail: skoch@kean.edu.
Website: http://www.kean.edu/KU/College-of-Visual-Performing-Arts

Kent State University, College of the Arts, School of Art, Kent, OH 44242-0001. Offers art education (MA); art history (MA); crafts (MA, MFA), including glass. *Accreditation:* NASAD (one or more programs are accredited). Part-time programs available. *Faculty:* 22 full-time (14 women). *Students:* 38 full-time (25 women), 31 part-time (23 women); includes 5 minority (1 Black or African American, non-Hispanic/Latino; 2 Hispanic/Latino; 2 Two or more races, non-Hispanic/Latino), 6 international. Average age 33. 106 applicants, 49% accepted, 24 enrolled. In 2014, 21 master's awarded. *Degree requirements:* For master's, one foreign language, comprehensive exam, thesis. *Entrance requirements:* For master's, minimum GPA of 3.0, transcript, goal statement, philosophy of art education (for MA in art education), curriculum vitae, portfolio, 3 letters of recommendation. Additional exam requirements/recommendations for international students: Required—TOEFL (minimum score: paper-based 525, iBT 71), Michigan English Language Assessment Battery (minimum score of 75), IELTS (minimum score of 6.0), PTE Academic (minimum score of 48), or completion of ELS level 112 Intensive Program. *Application deadline:* For fall admission, 2/2 priority date for domestic students; for spring admission, 9/15 priority date for domestic students. Applications are processed on a rolling basis. Application fee: $45 ($70 for international students). Electronic applications accepted. *Expenses:* Tuition, state resident: full-time $8730; part-time $485 per credit hour. Tuition, nonresident: full-time $14,886; part-time $827

per credit hour. Tuition and fees vary according to campus/location and program. *Financial support:* Research assistantships with full tuition reimbursements, teaching assistantships with full tuition reimbursements, career-related internships or fieldwork, Federal Work-Study, scholarships/grants, and unspecified assistantships available. Financial award application deadline: 2/15. *Unit head:* Dr. Christine Havice, Director, 330-672-2192, Fax: 330-672-4729, E-mail: chavice@kent.edu. *Application contact:* Lisa Everson, Clerical Specialist, 330-672-2192, E-mail: lheld2@kent.edu.
Website: http://www.kent.edu/art

Laguna College of Art & Design, Graduate Program, Laguna Beach, CA 92651-1136. Offers painting (MFA). *Accreditation:* NASAD. *Entrance requirements:* For master's, BA with a studio concentration or BFA, minimum GPA of 3.0 in studio subjects, portfolio, resume. Additional exam requirements/recommendations for international students: Required—TOEFL (minimum score 550 paper-based). Electronic applications accepted.

Lake Forest College, Master of Arts in Teaching Program, Lake Forest, IL 60045. Offers elementary education (MAT); K-12 French (MAT); K-12 music (MAT); K-12 Spanish (MAT); K-12 visual art (MAT); secondary biology (MAT); secondary chemistry (MAT); secondary English (MAT); secondary history (MAT); secondary mathematics (MAT). *Degree requirements:* For master's, comprehensive exam, portfolio. *Entrance requirements:* For master's, GRE.

La Salle University, School of Arts and Sciences, Program in English, Philadelphia, PA 19141-1199. Offers American studies (Certificate); English for educators (MA); English in literary and cultural studies (MA); global literature (Certificate); media studies and the performing and visual arts (Certificate); Philadelphia and regional studies (Certificate). Part-time and evening/weekend programs available. *Degree requirements:* For master's, critical-pedagogical project (for English for educators), thesis or comprehensive examination (for English in literary and cultural studies). *Entrance requirements:* For master's, GRE General Test or MAT, 18 hours of undergraduate course work in English or a related discipline with minimum GPA of 3.0; three letters of recommendation; brief personal statement; writing sample; for Certificate, undergraduate degree in English or a related discipline with minimum GPA of 3.0; 3 letters of recommendation. Additional exam requirements/recommendations for international students: Required—TOEFL. Electronic applications accepted. Application fee is waived when completed online.

Lehman College of the City University of New York, Division of Arts and Humanities, Department of Art, Bronx, NY 10468-1589. Offers MA, MFA. Part-time and evening/weekend programs available. *Entrance requirements:* For master's, 33 undergraduate credits in art, interview, portfolio. *Faculty research:* Graphic art, modern and contemporary art, sculpture, primitive and pre-Columbian art, medieval art.

Lesley University, College of Art and Design, Cambridge, MA 02138-2790. Offers photography (MFA); visual arts (MFA). Part-time programs available. *Faculty:* 7 full-time (4 women), 17 part-time/adjunct (7 women). *Students:* 77 full-time (58 women), 1 (woman) part-time; includes 5 minority (3 Asian, non-Hispanic/Latino; 2 Two or more races, non-Hispanic/Latino), 5 international. Average age 39. In 2014, 34 master's awarded. *Degree requirements:* For master's, thesis, final exhibition of thesis work. *Entrance requirements:* For master's, portfolio, resume, personal statement. Additional exam requirements/recommendations for international students: Required—TOEFL (minimum score 550 paper-based; 80 iBT). *Application deadline:* For fall admission, 3/1 for domestic students; for spring admission, 9/1 for domestic students. Applications are processed on a rolling basis. Application fee: $50. Electronic applications accepted. *Financial support:* Fellowships, career-related internships or fieldwork, and scholarships/grants available. Financial award applicants required to submit FAFSA. *Faculty research:* Graphic design; Web and multimedia design; book, advertising and editorial illustration; animation; documentary photography; photojournalism; fine arts photography; fine arts; art education. *Unit head:* Dr. Stanley Trecker, Dean, 617-585-6651, E-mail: strecker@lesley.edu. *Application contact:* Martha Sheehan, Director, Graduate Admissions, 800-LESLEYU, E-mail: info@lesley.edu.
Website: http://www.lesley.edu/college-art-and-design/

Lesley University, Graduate School of Education, Cambridge, MA 02138-2790. Offers arts, community, and education (M Ed); autism studies (Certificate); curriculum and instruction (M Ed, CAGS); early childhood education (M Ed); ecological teaching and learning (MS); educational studies (PhD), including adult learning, educational leadership, individually designed; elementary education (M Ed); emergent technologies for educators (Certificate); ESLArts: language learning through the arts (M Ed); high school education (M Ed); individually designed (M Ed); integrated teaching through the arts (M Ed); literacy for K-8 classroom teachers (M Ed); mathematics education (M Ed); middle school education (M Ed); moderate disabilities (M Ed); online learning (Certificate); reading (CAGS); science in education (M Ed); severe disabilities (M Ed); special needs (CAGS); specialist teacher of reading (M Ed); teacher of visual art (M Ed); technology in education (M Ed, CAGS). *Accreditation:* Teacher Education Accreditation Council. Part-time and evening/weekend programs available. Postbaccalaureate distance learning degree programs offered (no on-campus study). *Faculty:* 49 full-time (38 women), 66 part-time/adjunct (52 women). *Students:* 364 full-time (304 women), 1,333 part-time (1,121 women); includes 258 minority (127 Black or African American, non-Hispanic/Latino; 8 American Indian or Alaska Native, non-Hispanic/Latino; 30 Asian, non-Hispanic/Latino; 56 Hispanic/Latino; 2 Native Hawaiian or other Pacific Islander, non-Hispanic/Latino; 35 Two or more races, non-Hispanic/Latino), 23 international. Average age 34. In 2014, 925 master's, 15 doctorates, 36 other advanced degrees awarded. *Degree requirements:* For master's, practicum; for doctorate, thesis/dissertation. *Entrance requirements:* For master's, Massachusetts Tests for Educator Licensure (MTEL), transcripts, statement of purpose, recommendations; interview (for special education); for doctorate, GRE General Test, transcripts, statement of purpose, recommendations, interview, master's degree, resume; for other advanced degree, interview, master's degree. Additional exam requirements/recommendations for international students: Required—TOEFL (minimum score 550 paper-based; 80 iBT). *Application deadline:* Applications are processed on a rolling basis. Application fee: $50. Electronic applications accepted. *Financial support:* Fellowships, career-related internships or fieldwork, Federal Work-Study, scholarships/grants, tuition waivers, and unspecified assistantships available. Financial award application deadline: 4/15; financial award applicants required to submit FAFSA. *Faculty research:* Assessment in literacy, mathematics and science; autism spectrum disorders; instructional technology and online learning; multicultural education and English language learners. *Unit head:* Dr. Jack Gillette, Dean, 617-349-8401, Fax: 617-349-8607, E-mail: jgillett@lesley.edu. *Application contact:* Martha Sheehan, Director of Admissions, 888-LESLEYU, Fax: 617-349-8313, E-mail: info@lesley.edu.
Website: http://www.lesley.edu/soe.html

Liberty University, School of Communication and Creative Arts, Lynchburg, VA 24515. Offers strategic communication (MA); studio and digital arts (MFA). Part-time programs available. *Students:* 68 full-time (49 women), 97 part-time (62 women); includes 36 minority (28 Black or African American, non-Hispanic/Latino; 2 Asian, non-Hispanic/Latino; 2 Hispanic/Latino; 4 Two or more races, non-Hispanic/Latino), 16 international. Average age 32. 278 applicants, 40% accepted, 67 enrolled. In 2014, 15 degrees awarded. *Degree requirements:* For master's, thesis (for some programs). *Entrance requirements:* For master's, minimum undergraduate GPA of 3.0, faculty recommendation, written statement of purpose, writing sample. Additional exam requirements/recommendations for international students: Required—TOEFL (minimum score 600 paper-based; 100 iBT). *Application deadline:* For fall admission, 6/1 for domestic students; for spring admission, 11/1 for domestic students. Applications are processed on a rolling basis. Application fee: $50. Electronic applications accepted. *Financial support:* Federal Work-Study and unspecified assistantships available. Financial award applicants required to submit FAFSA. *Unit head:* Dr. Norman Mintle, Dean, 434-582-2077, E-mail: cvkramer@liberty.edu. *Application contact:* Dr. Terry Elam, Director of Graduate Admissions, 434-582-2111, Fax: 434-582-7836, E-mail: gradadmissions@liberty.edu.

Lindenwood University, Graduate Programs, School of Fine and Performing Arts, St. Charles, MO 63301-1695. Offers fashion design (MA, MFA); studio art (MA, MFA); theatre (MFA). Part-time programs available. *Faculty:* 9 full-time (4 women), 4 part-time/adjunct (2 women). *Students:* 5 full-time (2 women), 6 part-time (4 women); includes 1 minority (Hispanic/Latino), 1 international. Average age 30. 16 applicants, 25% accepted, 4 enrolled. In 2014, 15 master's awarded. *Degree requirements:* For master's, thesis (for some programs), minimum cumulative GPA of 3.0. *Entrance requirements:* For master's, audition or interview, minimum GPA of 3.0, portfolio, letter of recommendation. Additional exam requirements/recommendations for international students: Required—TOEFL (minimum score 550 paper-based; 80 iBT). *Application deadline:* For fall admission, 8/24 priority date for domestic and international students; for spring admission, 1/24 priority date for domestic students, 1/25 priority date for international students. Applications are processed on a rolling basis. Application fee: $30 ($100 for international students). Electronic applications accepted. *Expenses: Tuition:* Full-time $15,230; part-time $440 per credit hour. *Required fees:* $205 per semester. Tuition and fees vary according to course level, course load and degree level. *Financial support:* In 2014–15, 1 student received support. Career-related internships or fieldwork, institutionally sponsored loans, scholarships/grants, tuition waivers (partial), and unspecified assistantships available. Financial award application deadline: 6/30; financial award applicants required to submit FAFSA. *Unit head:* Dr. Joseph Alsobrook, Dean of Fine and Performing Arts, 636-949-4164, Fax: 636-949-4910, E-mail: jalsobrook@lindenwood.edu. *Application contact:* Tyler Kostich, Dean of Evening Admissions and Extension Campuses, 636-949-4138, Fax: 636-949-4109, E-mail: adultadmissions@lindenwood.edu.

Louisiana State University and Agricultural & Mechanical College, Graduate School, College of Art and Design, School of Art, Program in Studio Art, Baton Rouge, LA 70803. Offers ceramics (MFA); graphic design (MFA); painting and drawing (MFA); photography (MFA); printmaking (MFA); sculpture (MFA). *Accreditation:* NASAD. *Students:* 37 full-time (29 women), 1 (woman) part-time; includes 2 minority (both Hispanic/Latino), 10 international. Average age 29. 72 applicants, 31% accepted, 17 enrolled. In 2014, 20 master's awarded. *Degree requirements:* For master's, thesis. *Entrance requirements:* For master's, GRE General Test, minimum GPA of 3.0. Additional exam requirements/recommendations for international students: Required—TOEFL (minimum score 550 paper-based; 79 IBT), IELTS (minimum score 6.5), or PTE (minimum score 59). *Application deadline:* For fall admission, 1/1 priority date for domestic students, 5/15 for international students; for spring admission, 10/15 for domestic and international students; for summer admission, 5/15 for domestic and international students. Applications are processed on a rolling basis. Application fee: $50 ($70 for international students). Electronic applications accepted. *Financial support:* Research assistantships with partial tuition reimbursements, teaching assistantships, career-related internships or fieldwork, Federal Work-Study, institutionally sponsored loans, scholarships/grants, and unspecified assistantships available. Support available to part-time students. Financial award application deadline: 3/15. *Faculty research:* Ceramics, painting and drawing, photography, printmaking, and sculpture. *Unit head:* Kelli Scott Kelly, Graduate Coordinator, 225-578-8448, Fax: 225-578-5424, E-mail: kskelly@lsu.edu.
Website: http://design.lsu.edu/art/?page_id-582

Louisiana Tech University, Graduate School, College of Liberal Arts, MFA Program, Ruston, LA 71272. Offers communication design (MFA); photography (MFA); studio (MFA). *Accreditation:* NASAD. Part-time programs available. *Degree requirements:* For master's, exhibit. *Entrance requirements:* For master's, GRE General Test, portfolio. *Application deadline:* For fall admission, 7/29 for domestic students; for spring admission, 2/3 for domestic students. Applications are processed on a rolling basis. Application fee: $40. *Financial support:* Fellowships, career-related internships or fieldwork, Federal Work-Study, institutionally sponsored loans, and unspecified assistantships available. Financial award application deadline: 2/1. *Unit head:* Joey Slaughter, Graduate Coordinator, 318-257-3909, Fax: 318-257-4890, E-mail: joey@latech.edu. *Application contact:* Marilyn J. Robinson, Assistant to the Dean of the Graduate School, 318-257-2924, Fax: 318-257-4487.

Maine College of Art, Program in Studio Art, Portland, ME 04101. Offers MA, MFA. *Accreditation:* NASAD. *Faculty:* 1 (woman) full-time, 25 part-time/adjunct (15 women). *Students:* 75 applicants, 49% accepted, 16 enrolled. In 2014, 8 master's awarded. *Degree requirements:* For master's, thesis, studio thesis exhibition. *Entrance requirements:* Additional exam requirements/recommendations for international students: Required—TOEFL (minimum score 550 paper-based). *Application deadline:* For fall admission, 2/15 for domestic students; for summer admission, 2/6 priority date for domestic students, 2/6 for international students. Applications are processed on a rolling basis. Application fee: $50 ($70 for international students). Electronic applications accepted. *Expenses: Tuition:* Full-time $30,940. *Required fees:* $350. *Financial support:* Teaching assistantships, Federal Work-Study, scholarships/grants, and resident advisor positions available. Financial award application deadline: 3/1; financial award applicants required to submit FAFSA. *Unit head:* Rachel Katz, Administrative Director, 207-699-5030, Fax: 207-775-5069, E-mail: rkatz@meca.edu. *Application contact:* Megan Lloyd, Admissions, 207-699-5024, Fax: 207-775-5069, E-mail: admissions@meca.edu.
Website: http://www.meca.edu/mfa/

Marshall University, Academic Affairs Division, College of Arts and Media, Department of Art, Huntington, WV 25755. Offers MA. Evening/weekend programs available. *Faculty:* 6 full-time (3 women). *Students:* 3 full-time (1 woman). Average age 40. *Degree requirements:* For master's, thesis optional. *Entrance requirements:* For master's, GRE General Test, portfolio. Application fee: $40. *Unit head:* Dr. Maribea Barnes, Interim Director, 304-696-2895, Fax: 304-696-6505, E-mail: barnesm@marshall.edu. *Application contact:* Information Contact, 304-746-1900, Fax: 304-746-1902, E-mail: services@marshall.edu.
Website: http://www.marshall.edu/art/

Maryland Institute College of Art, Graduate Studies, The Business of Art and Design Program, Baltimore, MD 21201. Offers MPS. Part-time programs available. *Faculty:* 15 part-time/adjunct (6 women). *Students:* 20 part-time (10 women); includes 5 minority (2 Black or African American, non-Hispanic/Latino; 1 Asian, non-Hispanic/Latino; 2 Hispanic/Latino). Average age 27. 53 applicants, 47% accepted, 20 enrolled. In 2014, 20 master's awarded. *Degree requirements:* For master's, business plan presentation. *Entrance requirements:* For master's, essay, resume. Additional exam requirements/recommendations for international students: Required—TOEFL (minimum score 550 paper-based; 80 iBT), IELTS (minimum score 6.5). *Application deadline:* For fall

admission, 1/15 for domestic and international students; for spring admission, 4/1 for domestic and international students. Application fee: $70. *Expenses:* Expenses: Contact institution. *Financial support:* In 2014–15, 20 students received support, including 20 fellowships (averaging $3,400 per year); scholarships/grants also available. Financial award application deadline: 1/15; financial award applicants required to submit FAFSA. *Unit head:* Heather Bradbury, Manager, 410-225-2220, Fax: 410-225-2229, E-mail: hbradbury@mica.edu. *Application contact:* Chris D. Harring, Director of Graduate Admission, 410-225-2256, Fax: 410-225-5275, E-mail: graduate@mica.edu.
Website: http://www.mica.edu/Programs_of_Study/Graduate_Programs/The_Business_of_Art_and_Design_(Online_MPS).html

Maryland Institute College of Art, Graduate Studies, Fine Arts Post Baccalaureate Certificate Program, Baltimore, MD 21201. Offers Postbaccalaureate Certificate. *Faculty:* 1 full-time (0 women), 1 (woman) part-time/adjunct. *Students:* 23 full-time (13 women); includes 4 minority (3 Asian, non-Hispanic/Latino; 1 Hispanic/Latino), 3 international. Average age 27. In 2014, 23 Postbaccalaureate Certificates awarded. *Degree requirements:* For Postbaccalaureate Certificate, thesis, exhibition and documentation. *Entrance requirements:* For degree, portfolio, 40 studio credits, 6 credits in art history. Additional exam requirements/recommendations for international students: Required—TOEFL (minimum score 550 paper-based; 80 iBT), IELTS (minimum score 6.5). *Application deadline:* For fall admission, 1/15 priority date for domestic and international students; for spring admission, 11/15 for domestic and international students. Application fee: $75. Electronic applications accepted. *Financial support:* In 2014–15, 22 students received support, including 22 fellowships with partial tuition reimbursements available (averaging $7,000 per year); scholarships/grants also available. Financial award application deadline: 1/15; financial award applicants required to submit FAFSA. *Unit head:* William Schmidt, Director, 410-230-0568. *Application contact:* Chris D. Harring, Director of Graduate Admission, 410-225-2256, Fax: 410-225-5275, E-mail: graduate@mica.edu.
Website: http://www.mica.edu/Programs_of_Study/Post-Baccalaureate_Certificate_in_Fine_Art.html

Maryland Institute College of Art, Graduate Studies, Hoffberger School of Painting, Baltimore, MD 21201. Offers MFA. *Accreditation:* NASAD. *Faculty:* 1 (woman) full-time, 2 part-time/adjunct (0 women). *Students:* 20 full-time (12 women); includes 4 minority (1 Black or African American, non-Hispanic/Latino; 1 Asian, non-Hispanic/Latino; 1 Hispanic/Latino; 1 Two or more races, non-Hispanic/Latino), 4 international. Average age 27. 200 applicants, 10% accepted, 10 enrolled. In 2014, 10 master's awarded. *Degree requirements:* For master's, thesis, exhibit and thesis documentation. *Entrance requirements:* For master's, portfolio, bachelor's degree in any field. Additional exam requirements/recommendations for international students: Required—TOEFL (minimum score 550 paper-based; 80 iBT), IELTS (minimum score 6.5). *Application deadline:* For fall admission, 1/15 for domestic and international students. Application fee: $75. *Expenses:* Expenses: Contact institution. *Financial support:* In 2014–15, 20 students received support, including 20 fellowships (averaging $13,000 per year), 20 teaching assistantships (averaging $3,200 per year); career-related internships or fieldwork and scholarships/grants also available. Financial award application deadline: 1/15. *Unit head:* Joan Waltemath, Director, 410-225-5274, Fax: 410-225-5275, E-mail: graduate@mica.edu. *Application contact:* Chris D. Harring, Director of Graduate Admission, 410-225-2256, Fax: 410-225-5275, E-mail: graduate@mica.edu.
Website: http://www.mica.edu/Programs_of_Study/Graduate_Programs/Hoffberger_School_of_Painting.html

Maryland Institute College of Art, Graduate Studies, Mount Royal School of Art, Baltimore, MD 21217. Offers painting (MFA). *Faculty:* 1 full-time (0 women), 6 part-time/adjunct (3 women). *Students:* 28 full-time (17 women); includes 3 minority (1 Asian, non-Hispanic/Latino; 2 Two or more races, non-Hispanic/Latino), 5 international. Average age 27. 175 applicants, 11% accepted, 15 enrolled. In 2014, 15 master's awarded. *Degree requirements:* For master's, thesis, exhibit and thesis documentation. *Entrance requirements:* For master's, 40 credits in studio art, bachelor's degree in any field. Additional exam requirements/recommendations for international students: Required—TOEFL (minimum score 550 paper-based; 80 iBT), IELTS (minimum score 6.5). *Application deadline:* For fall admission, 1/15 for domestic and international students. Application fee: $75. Electronic applications accepted. *Expenses:* Expenses: Contact institution. *Financial support:* In 2014–15, 28 students received support, including 28 fellowships (averaging $13,000 per year), 28 teaching assistantships (averaging $3,200 per year); career-related internships or fieldwork and scholarships/grants also available. Financial award application deadline: 1/15. *Unit head:* Luca Buvoli, Director, 410-225-5274, Fax: 410-225-5275, E-mail: graduate@mica.edu. *Application contact:* Chris D. Harring, Director, Graduate Admission, 410-225-2256, Fax: 410-225-5275, E-mail: graduate@mica.edu.
Website: http://www.mica.edu/Programs_of_Study/Graduate_Programs/Mount_Royal_School_of_Art_(Multidisciplinary_MFA).html

Maryland Institute College of Art, Graduate Studies, Program in Community Arts, Baltimore, MD 21201. Offers MFA. Part-time programs available. *Faculty:* 3 full-time (2 women), 2 part-time/adjunct (both women). *Students:* 20 full-time (18 women); includes 4 minority (2 Black or African American, non-Hispanic/Latino; 1 Hispanic/Latino; 1 Two or more races, non-Hispanic/Latino), 1 international. Average age 27. 35 applicants, 43% accepted, 10 enrolled. In 2014, 10 master's awarded. *Degree requirements:* For master's, thesis, exhibition and thesis documentation. *Entrance requirements:* For master's, portfolio, bachelor's degree in any field. Additional exam requirements/recommendations for international students: Required—TOEFL (minimum score 550 paper-based; 80 iBT), IELTS (minimum score 6.5). *Application deadline:* For fall admission, 1/15 for domestic and international students. Application fee: $75. Electronic applications accepted. *Expenses:* Expenses: Contact institution. *Financial support:* In 2014–15, 20 students received support, including 20 fellowships (averaging $13,000 per year), 20 teaching assistantships (averaging $3,200 per year); career-related internships or fieldwork and scholarships/grants also available. Financial award application deadline: 1/15. *Unit head:* Ken Krafchek, Director, 410-225-5274, Fax: 410-225-5275, E-mail: graduate@mica.edu. *Application contact:* Chris D. Harring, Director, Graduate Admission, 410-225-2256, Fax: 410-225-5275, E-mail: graduate@mica.edu.

Maryland Institute College of Art, Graduate Studies, Program in Studio Art, Baltimore, MD 21201. Offers MFA. Offered during summer only. *Faculty:* 3 full-time (1 woman), 1 (woman) part-time/adjunct. *Students:* 37 full-time (26 women); includes 8 minority (2 Black or African American, non-Hispanic/Latino; 2 Asian, non-Hispanic/Latino; 2 Hispanic/Latino; 2 Two or more races, non-Hispanic/Latino), 1 international. Average age 38. 85 applicants, 18% accepted, 10 enrolled. In 2014, 10 master's awarded. *Degree requirements:* For master's, thesis, exhibition, final paper. *Entrance requirements:* For master's, portfolio, 40 studio credits, 6 credits in art history, bachelor's degree in any field. Additional exam requirements/recommendations for international students: Required—TOEFL (minimum score 550 paper-based; 80 iBT), IELTS (minimum score 6.5). *Application deadline:* For fall admission, 1/15 priority date for domestic students, 1/15 for international students. Application fee: $75. *Financial support:* In 2014–15, 37 fellowships (averaging $6,500 per year) were awarded; career-related internships or fieldwork and scholarships/grants also available. Financial award application deadline: 1/15. *Unit head:* Zlata Baum, Director, 410-225-2297, Fax: 410-225-2257. *Application contact:* Chris D. Harring, Director of Graduate Admission, 410-225-2256, Fax: 410-225-5275, E-mail: graduate@mica.edu.
Website: http://www.mica.edu/Programs_of_Study/Graduate_Programs/Studio_Art_(Online_and_Low-Residency_MFA).html

Maryland Institute College of Art, Graduate Studies, Rinehart School of Sculpture, Baltimore, MD 21202. Offers MFA. *Accreditation:* NASAD. *Faculty:* 3 full-time (2 women), 2 part-time/adjunct (both women). *Students:* 15 full-time (9 women); includes 4 minority (3 Asian, non-Hispanic/Latino; 1 Native Hawaiian or other Pacific Islander, non-Hispanic/Latino), 4 international. Average age 27. 80 applicants, 25% accepted, 8 enrolled. In 2014, 5 master's awarded. *Degree requirements:* For master's, thesis, exhibition. *Entrance requirements:* For master's, portfolio, bachelor's degree in any field. Additional exam requirements/recommendations for international students: Required—TOEFL (minimum score 550 paper-based; 80 iBT), IELTS (minimum score 6.5). *Application deadline:* For fall admission, 1/15 for domestic and international students. Application fee: $75. *Expenses:* Expenses: $42,390 combined tuition and fees. *Financial support:* In 2014–15, 11 students received support, including 15 fellowships with partial tuition reimbursements available (averaging $13,000 per year), 11 teaching assistantships (averaging $3,200 per year); career-related internships or fieldwork and scholarships/grants also available. Financial award application deadline: 1/15; financial award applicants required to submit FAFSA. *Unit head:* Maren Hassinger, Director, 410-225-2271, Fax: 410-225-2408. *Application contact:* Chris D. Harring, Director of Graduate Admission, 410-225-2256, Fax: 410-225-2408, E-mail: graduate@mica.edu.
Website: http://www.mica.edu/Programs_of_Study/Graduate_Programs/Rinehart_School_of_Sculpture_(MFA).html

Marywood University, Academic Affairs, Insalaco College of Creative and Performing Arts, Art Department, Program in Studio Art, Scranton, PA 18509-1598. Offers clay (MA); painting (MA); photography (MA); printmaking (MA); sculpture (MA). *Accreditation:* NASAD. *Students:* 5 full-time (all women), 2 part-time (1 woman), 1 international. Average age 44. In 2014, 1 master's awarded. *Application deadline:* For fall admission, 4/1 priority date for domestic students, 3/31 priority date for international students; for spring admission, 11/1 priority date for domestic students, 8/31 priority date for international students. Applications are processed on a rolling basis. Application fee: $35. Electronic applications accepted. *Expenses: Tuition:* Part-time $775 per credit. *Required fees:* $688 per semester. Tuition and fees vary according to degree level and campus/location. *Financial support:* Application deadline: 6/30; applicants required to submit FAFSA. *Faculty research:* Texture and line in clay, cast bronze sculpture, color theories, book art and illustration, sculptural form. *Unit head:* Matthew Povse, Chair, 570-348-6211 Ext. 2476, E-mail: povse@marywood.edu. *Application contact:* Tammy Manka, Assistant Director of Graduate Admissions, 570-348-6211 Ext. 2322, E-mail: tmanka@marywood.edu.
Website: http://www.marywood.edu/art/graduate-programs/master-studio-art.html

Marywood University, Academic Affairs, Insalaco College of Creative and Performing Arts, Art Department, Program in Visual Arts, Scranton, PA 18509-1598. Offers clay (MFA); graphic design (MFA); illustration (MFA); painting (MFA); photography (MFA); printmaking (MFA); sculpture (MFA). *Accreditation:* NASAD. Part-time programs available. *Students:* 25 full-time (18 women), 3 part-time (all women); includes 1 minority (Hispanic/Latino), 2 international. Average age 36. In 2014, 5 master's awarded. *Application deadline:* For fall admission, 4/1 for domestic students, 3/31 for international students; for spring admission, 11/1 for domestic students, 8/31 for international students. Applications are processed on a rolling basis. Application fee: $35. Electronic applications accepted. *Expenses:* Expenses: Contact institution. *Financial support:* Application deadline: 6/30; applicants required to submit FAFSA. *Unit head:* Matthew Povse, Chair, 570-348-6211 Ext. 2476, E-mail: povse@marywood.edu. *Application contact:* Tammy Manka, Assistant Director of Graduate Admissions, 570-348-6211 Ext. 2322, E-mail: tmanka@marywood.edu.
Website: http://www.marywood.edu/art/graduate-programs/master-visual-arts.html

Massachusetts College of Art and Design, Graduate Programs, MFA Program, Boston, MA 02115-5882. Offers 2D fine arts (MFA), including painting; 3D fine arts (MFA), including ceramics, fibers, glass, jewelry and metalsmithing, sculpture; design (MFA, Postbaccalaureate Certificate), including dynamic media; fine arts (MFA), including interdisciplinary; media arts (MFA, Postbaccalaureate Certificate), including film/video (MFA), photography. *Accreditation:* NASAD. *Faculty:* 31 full-time (15 women), 42 part-time/adjunct (19 women). *Students:* 59 full-time (36 women), 32 part-time (23 women); includes 12 minority (2 Black or African American, non-Hispanic/Latino; 5 Asian, non-Hispanic/Latino; 5 Hispanic/Latino), 18 international. 278 applicants, 38% accepted, 40 enrolled. In 2014, 33 master's, 7 other advanced degrees awarded. *Degree requirements:* For master's, thesis, Exhibition for MFA non design. Thesis document MFA in design and low-residency. *Entrance requirements:* For master's, portfolio, college transcripts, resume, statement of purpose, letters of reference, interview; 6 credits of art history taken prior to or during MFA program; for Postbaccalaureate Certificate, portfolio, college transcripts, resume, statement of purpose, letters of reference, interview. Additional exam requirements/recommendations for international students: Required—TOEFL (minimum score 550 paper-based; 85 iBT); Recommended—IELTS (minimum score 6.5). *Application deadline:* For fall admission, 1/6 priority date for domestic and international students. Application fee: $75. Electronic applications accepted. *Expenses:* Tuition, state resident: full-time $23,400; part-time $780 per credit. Tuition, nonresident: full-time $23,400; part-time $780 per credit. Tuition and fees vary according to course load and program. *Financial support:* In 2014–15, 37 students received support, including 40 teaching assistantships (averaging $2,160 per year); career-related internships or fieldwork, scholarships/grants, tuition waivers (partial), and unspecified assistantships also available. Support available to part-time students. Financial award application deadline: 1/6. *Unit head:* Paul Paturzo, Interim Dean of Graduate Studies, 617-879-7166, E-mail: pjpaturzo@massart.edu. *Application contact:* Isaac Goldstein, Graduate Admissions Counselor, 617-879-7203, Fax: 617-879-7250, E-mail: igoldstein@massart.edu.
Website: http://www.massart.edu/Admissions/Graduate_Programs.html

Memphis College of Art, Graduate Programs, MFA Program, Memphis, TN 38104-2764. Offers studio art (MFA). *Accreditation:* NASAD. Part-time programs available. *Faculty:* 23 full-time (14 women), 13 part-time/adjunct (8 women). *Students:* 28 full-time (15 women), 6 part-time (5 women); includes 4 minority (2 Asian, non-Hispanic/Latino; 1 Hispanic/Latino; 1 Two or more races, non-Hispanic/Latino), 2 international. Average age 26. 38 applicants, 68% accepted, 11 enrolled. In 2014, 6 master's awarded. *Degree requirements:* For master's, thesis, thesis exhibit. *Entrance requirements:* For master's, portfolio, interview, resume. Additional exam requirements/recommendations for international students: Required—TOEFL (minimum score 525 paper-based). *Application deadline:* For fall admission, 2/1 priority date for domestic and international students; for spring admission, 11/1 priority date for domestic and international students. Application fee: $50. *Expenses: Tuition:* Full-time $29,470; part-time $3685 per course. *Required fees:* $700; $125 per course. Tuition and fees vary according to course load. *Financial support:* In 2014–15, 5 fellowships (averaging $5,000 per year), 5 teaching assistantships (averaging $2,000 per year) were awarded; career-related internships or fieldwork, Federal Work-Study, scholarships/grants, and unspecified assistantships also available. Financial award application deadline: 8/1; financial award applicants required

to submit FAFSA. *Unit head:* Eszter Sziksz, Director, 901-272-5100, E-mail: esziksz@mca.edu. *Application contact:* Gail Massey, Director of Enrollment, 901-272-5153, Fax: 901-272-5158, E-mail: gmassey@mca.edu.

Miami University, College of Creative Arts, Department of Art, Oxford, OH 45056. Offers art education (MA); studio art (MFA). *Accreditation:* NASAD (one or more programs are accredited). *Students:* 18 full-time (9 women), 1 part-time (0 women); includes 1 minority (Asian, non-Hispanic/Latino), 2 international. Average age 29. In 2014, 5 master's awarded. *Entrance requirements:* Additional exam requirements/recommendations for international students: Recommended—TOEFL (minimum score 80 iBT), IELTS (minimum score 6.5), TSE (minimum score 54). *Application deadline:* For fall admission, 2/1 for domestic and international students. Application fee: $50. Electronic applications accepted. *Expenses:* Tuition, state resident: full-time $12,887; part-time $537 per credit hour. Tuition, nonresident: full-time $28,449; part-time $1186 per credit hour. *Required fees:* $530; $24 per credit hour. $30 per quarter. Part-time tuition and fees vary according to course load and program. *Financial support:* Research assistantships with full and partial tuition reimbursements and teaching assistantships with full and partial tuition reimbursements available. Financial award application deadline: 2/15; financial award applicants required to submit FAFSA. *Unit head:* Dr. Peg Faimon, Chair/Professor, 513-529-2900, E-mail: faimonma@miamioh.edu.
Website: http://www.MiamiOH.edu/art

Michigan State University, The Graduate School, College of Arts and Letters, Department of Art and Art History, East Lansing, MI 48824. Offers studio art (MFA). *Entrance requirements:* For master's, minimum GPA of 3.0, portfolio, resume. Additional exam requirements/recommendations for international students: Required—TOEFL, Michigan State University ELT (minimum score 85), Michigan English Language Assessment Battery (minimum score 83). Electronic applications accepted.

Millersville University of Pennsylvania, College of Graduate and Professional Studies, School of Humanities and Social Sciences, Department of Art, Millersville, PA 17551-0302. Offers M Ed. *Accreditation:* NASAD; NCATE. Part-time programs available. *Faculty:* 13 full-time (9 women), 3 part-time/adjunct (2 women). *Students:* 2 full-time (both women), 8 part-time (4 women); includes 2 minority (1 Asian, non-Hispanic/Latino; 1 Hispanic/Latino). Average age 32. 2 applicants, 100% accepted, 1 enrolled. *Degree requirements:* For master's, comprehensive exam, thesis optional. *Entrance requirements:* For master's, GRE or MAT, 3 letters of recommendation, portfolio, goal statement, official transcripts. Additional exam requirements/recommendations for international students: Required—TOEFL (minimum score 500 paper-based, 65 iBT) or IELTS (minimum score 6). *Application deadline:* For fall admission, 1/15 priority date for domestic and international students; for winter admission, 6/1 priority date for domestic and international students; for spring admission, 10/1 priority date for domestic and international students. Applications are processed on a rolling basis. Application fee: $40. Electronic applications accepted. *Expenses:* Tuition, state resident: full-time $8172. Tuition, nonresident: full-time $12,258. *Required fees:* $2300. Tuition and fees vary according to course load and program. *Financial support:* Research assistantships with full tuition reimbursements, institutionally sponsored loans, and unspecified assistantships available. Support available to part-time students. Financial award application deadline: 3/15; financial award applicants required to submit FAFSA. *Faculty research:* Art education curriculum, democratic education, assessment in arts education, collaborative action research. *Total annual research expenditures:* $10,000. *Unit head:* Deborah S. Sigel, Chair, 717-871-7249, Fax: 717-871-7929, E-mail: deborah.sigel@millersville.edu. *Application contact:* Dr. Victor S. DeSantis, Dean of College of Graduate and Professional Studies/Associate Provost for Civic and Community Engagement, 717-871-7619, Fax: 717-871-7954, E-mail: victor.desantis@millersville.edu.
Website: http://www.millersville.edu/art/

Mills College, Graduate Studies, Department of Art, Oakland, CA 94613-1000. Offers ceramics (MFA); intermedia (MFA); painting (MFA); photography (MFA); sculpture (MFA). *Faculty:* 5 full-time (all women), 8 part-time/adjunct (3 women). *Students:* 19 full-time (14 women); includes 3 minority (1 Black or African American, non-Hispanic/Latino; 1 Asian, non-Hispanic/Latino; 1 Hispanic/Latino), 1 international. Average age 32. 44 applicants, 48% accepted, 9 enrolled. In 2014, 12 master's awarded. *Degree requirements:* For master's, thesis or alternative, exhibit. *Entrance requirements:* For master's, portfolio, artist statement. Additional exam requirements/recommendations for international students: Required—TOEFL (minimum score 550 paper-based; 80 iBT) or IELTS (minimum score 6). *Application deadline:* For fall admission, 2/1 for domestic students, 12/15 for international students. Application fee: $50. Electronic applications accepted. *Expenses:* Expenses: Contact institution. *Financial support:* In 2014–15, 22 students received support, including 17 fellowships (averaging $12,285 per year), 10 teaching assistantships with full and partial tuition reimbursements available (averaging $14,760 per year); scholarships/grants and unspecified assistantships also available. Financial award application deadline: 2/1; financial award applicants required to submit FAFSA. *Faculty research:* Experimental film and video, public art projects, ecological design, contemporary art philosophy, sound installations. *Unit head:* Dr. Mary-Ann Milford, Professor of Art History, 510-430-2117. *Application contact:* Shrim Bathey, Director of Graduate Admission, 510-430-3309, Fax: 510-430-2159, E-mail: grad-admission@mills.edu.
Website: http://www.mills.edu/art

Minneapolis College of Art and Design, Certificate Programs, Minneapolis, MN 55404-4347. Offers design (Certificate); fine arts (Certificate); graphic design (Certificate); media (Certificate); sustainable design (Certificate). Part-time programs available. Postbaccalaureate distance learning degree programs offered. *Degree requirements:* For Certificate, final project. *Entrance requirements:* For degree, resume, portfolio, letter of recommendation. Additional exam requirements/recommendations for international students: Required—TOEFL (minimum score 550 paper-based; 79 iBT). Electronic applications accepted. *Faculty research:* Visual arts.

Minneapolis College of Art and Design, Program in Visual Studies, Minneapolis, MN 55404-4347. Offers animation (MFA); comic art (MFA); drawing (MFA); filmmaking (MFA); fine arts (MFA); furniture design (MFA); graphic design (MFA); illustration (MFA); interactive media (MFA); painting (MFA); photography (MFA); printmaking (MFA); sculpture (MFA). *Accreditation:* NASAD. Part-time programs available. *Degree requirements:* For master's, thesis, thesis exhibit. *Entrance requirements:* For master's, portfolio of visual artwork, resume, 3 letters of recommendation. Additional exam requirements/recommendations for international students: Required—TOEFL (minimum score 550 paper-based; 79 iBT). Electronic applications accepted. *Faculty research:* Visual arts: animation, comic art, drawing, filmmaking, furniture design, graphic design, illustration, interactive media, painting, photography, printmaking, sculpture.

Minnesota State University Mankato, College of Graduate Studies, College of Arts and Humanities, Department of Art, Mankato, MN 56001. Offers studio art (MA); teaching art (MAT). *Accreditation:* NASAD (one or more programs are accredited). Part-time programs available. *Students:* 6 full-time (3 women), 10 part-time (5 women). *Degree requirements:* For master's, one foreign language, comprehensive exam, thesis or alternative. *Entrance requirements:* For master's, minimum GPA of 3.0 during previous 2 years, portfolio (MA). Additional exam requirements/recommendations for international students: Required—TOEFL. *Application deadline:* For fall admission, 7/1 priority date for domestic students, 5/1 for international students; for spring admission, 11/1 for domestic students, 10/1 for international students. Applications are processed on a rolling basis. Application fee: $40. Electronic applications accepted. *Financial support:* Research assistantships, teaching assistantships with full tuition reimbursements, and unspecified assistantships available. Financial award application deadline: 3/15; financial award applicants required to submit FAFSA. *Faculty research:* Photographic documentation. *Unit head:* David Rogers, Graduate Coordinator, 507-389-2728. *Application contact:* 507-389-2321, E-mail: grad@mnsu.edu.
Website: http://www.mnsu.edu/artdept/

Mississippi College, Graduate School, College of Arts and Sciences, School of Christian Studies and the Arts, Department of Art, Clinton, MS 39058. Offers M Ed, MA, MFA. Part-time and evening/weekend programs available. *Degree requirements:* For master's, one foreign language, comprehensive exam, thesis (for some programs). *Entrance requirements:* For master's, GRE or NTE, minimum GPA of 2.5. Additional exam requirements/recommendations for international students: Recommended—TOEFL, IELTS. Electronic applications accepted.

Montana State University, The Graduate School, College of Arts and Architecture, School of Art, Bozeman, MT 59717. Offers art (MFA); art history (MA). *Accreditation:* NASAD (one or more programs are accredited). Part-time programs available. *Degree requirements:* For master's, comprehensive exam, thesis. *Entrance requirements:* For master's, GRE General Test, undergraduate degree in art. Additional exam requirements/recommendations for international students: Required—TOEFL (minimum score 550 paper-based). Electronic applications accepted. *Faculty research:* Encaustic painting, wild clay research, environmentally friendly kiln fuel, Roman wall paintings, French revolutionary portraiture.

Montclair State University, The Graduate School, College of the Arts, Program in Fine Art, Montclair, NJ 07043-1624. Offers museum management (MA); studio (MA). Part-time and evening/weekend programs available. *Students:* 10 full-time (7 women), 23 part-time (16 women); includes 6 minority (1 Black or African American, non-Hispanic/Latino; 1 Asian, non-Hispanic/Latino; 2 Hispanic/Latino; 2 Two or more races, non-Hispanic/Latino). Average age 35. 18 applicants, 39% accepted, 6 enrolled. In 2014, 14 master's awarded. *Degree requirements:* For master's, project. *Entrance requirements:* For master's, GRE or MAT, 2 letters of recommendation, essay. *Application deadline:* Applications are processed on a rolling basis. Application fee: $60. Electronic applications accepted. *Expenses:* Tuition, state resident: full-time $9960; part-time $553.35 per credit. Tuition, nonresident: full-time $15,074; part-time $837.43 per credit. *Required fees:* $1595; $88.63 per credit. Tuition and fees vary according to degree level and program. *Financial support:* Federal Work-Study, scholarships/grants, and unspecified assistantships available. Support available to part-time students. Financial award application deadline: 3/1; financial award applicants required to submit FAFSA. *Unit head:* Dr. Scott Gordley, Chairperson, 973-655-7295. *Application contact:* Amy Aiello, Director of Graduate Admissions and Operations, 973-655-5147, E-mail: graduate.school@montclair.edu.
Website: http://www.montclair.edu/Arts/

Montclair State University, The Graduate School, College of the Arts, Program in Studio Art, Montclair, NJ 07043-1624. Offers MFA. Part-time and evening/weekend programs available. *Students:* 24 full-time (17 women), 2 part-time (1 woman); includes 4 minority (2 Asian, non-Hispanic/Latino; 2 Hispanic/Latino), 5 international. Average age 34. 54 applicants, 33% accepted, 13 enrolled. In 2014, 9 master's awarded. *Degree requirements:* For master's, project. *Entrance requirements:* For master's, 2 letters of recommendation, essay. Additional exam requirements/recommendations for international students: Required—TOEFL (minimum score 83 iBT), IELTS (minimum score 6.5). *Application deadline:* Applications are processed on a rolling basis. Application fee: $60. Electronic applications accepted. *Expenses:* Tuition, state resident: full-time $9960; part-time $553.35 per credit. Tuition, nonresident: full-time $15,074; part-time $837.43 per credit. *Required fees:* $1595; $88.63 per credit. Tuition and fees vary according to degree level and program. *Financial support:* In 2014–15, 6 research assistantships with full tuition reimbursements (averaging $7,000 per year) were awarded; Federal Work-Study, scholarships/grants, and unspecified assistantships also available. Support available to part-time students. Financial award application deadline: 3/1; financial award applicants required to submit FAFSA. *Unit head:* Dr. Scott Gordley, Chairperson, 973-655-7295. *Application contact:* Amy Aiello, Executive Director of The Graduate School, 973-655-5147, E-mail: graduate.school@montclair.edu.
Website: http://www.montclair.edu/arts/art-and-design/academic-programs/graduate-programs/art-studio-mfa/

Moore College of Art & Design, Program in Studio Art, Philadelphia, PA 19103. Offers MFA. *Accreditation:* NASAD. *Faculty:* 1 full-time (0 women), 7 part-time/adjunct (4 women). *Degree requirements:* For master's, thesis. *Entrance requirements:* For master's, bachelor's degree in visual arts or another field with completion of 15 art history credits; minimum GPA of 3.0; on-site interview; portfolio; 3 letters of recommendation; resume. *Expenses: Tuition:* Full-time $31,584; part-time $1504 per credit. *Unit head:* Paul Hubbard, Graduate Program Manager, 215-965-4016, E-mail: phubbard@moore.edu.

Morehead State University, Graduate Programs, Caudill College of Arts, Humanities and Social Sciences, Department of Art and Design, Morehead, KY 40351. Offers art education (MA); graphic design (MA); studio art (MA). Part-time and evening/weekend programs available. *Degree requirements:* For master's, comprehensive exam, thesis (for some programs), oral exam during exhibition. *Entrance requirements:* For master's, GRE General Test, minimum undergraduate GPA of 3.0 in major, 2.5 overall; portfolio; bachelor's degree in art. Additional exam requirements/recommendations for international students: Required—TOEFL (minimum score 500 paper-based). Electronic applications accepted. *Faculty research:* Computer art, painting, drawing, ceramics, photography.

New Hampshire Institute of Art, Graduate Programs, Manchester, NH 03104. Offers art education (MA); creative writing (MFA); photography (MFA); visual arts (MFA); writing for stage and screen (MFA). Part-time programs available. *Faculty:* 31 part-time/adjunct (14 women). *Students:* 43 full-time (25 women), 20 part-time (17 women). Average age 44. 36 applicants, 72% accepted, 24 enrolled. *Degree requirements:* For master's, thesis. *Entrance requirements:* For master's, writing sample or visual art portfolio; curriculum vitae; transcripts; letters of recommendation. Additional exam requirements/recommendations for international students: Required—TOEFL (minimum score 530 paper-based; 71 iBT). *Application deadline:* For fall admission, 5/15 for domestic students; for spring admission, 10/1 for domestic students. Applications are processed on a rolling basis. Application fee: $50. Electronic applications accepted. *Expenses:* Expenses: $9,500 per semester plus $495 residency fee (for MFA in visual arts or photography); $9,000 per semester plus $495 residency fee (for MFA in creative writing or writing for stage and screen); $7,155 per semester for full-time student (for MA in art education). *Financial support:* In 2014–15, 54 students received support, including 8 teaching assistantships with partial tuition reimbursements available; scholarships/grants and unspecified assistantships also available. Support available to part-time students. *Unit head:* Alison Williams, Dean of Graduate Studies, 603-836 2522, E-mail:

alisonwilliams@nhia.edu. *Application contact:* Graduate Admissions, 603-836 2122, E-mail: gradadmissions@nhia.edu.

New Jersey City University, Graduate Studies and Continuing Education, William J. Maxwell College of Arts and Sciences, Department of Art, Jersey City, NJ 07305-1597. Offers art (MFA); art education (MA); studio art (MFA). *Accreditation:* NASAD. Part-time and evening/weekend programs available. *Faculty:* 6 full-time (3 women), 8 part-time/adjunct (4 women). *Students:* 5 full-time (3 women), 8 part-time (6 women); includes 8 minority (3 Black or African American, non-Hispanic/Latino; 2 Asian, non-Hispanic/Latino; 3 Hispanic/Latino), 2 international. Average age 40. 4 applicants, 100% accepted, 4 enrolled. In 2014, 4 master's awarded. *Degree requirements:* For master's, thesis or alternative, exhibit. *Entrance requirements:* For master's, portfolio. Additional exam requirements/recommendations for international students: Required—TOEFL (minimum score 79 iBT). *Application deadline:* For fall admission, 8/1 priority date for domestic students; for spring admission, 12/1 for domestic students. Applications are processed on a rolling basis. Application fee: $0. *Expenses: Tuition, area resident:* Part-time $538 per credit. Tuition, state resident: part-time $538 per credit. Tuition, nonresident: part-time $948 per credit. *Financial support:* Unspecified assistantships available. *Unit head:* Martin Kruck, 201-200-2367, E-mail: mkruck@njcu.edu. *Application contact:* Jose Balda, E-mail: jbalda@njcu.edu.

New Mexico State University, College of Arts and Sciences, Department of Art, Las Cruces, NM 88003-8001. Offers art history (MA); studio art (MFA). Part-time programs available. *Faculty:* 10 full-time (8 women). *Students:* 10 full-time (9 women), 3 part-time (2 women); includes 2 minority (1 Black or African American, non-Hispanic/Latino; 1 Hispanic/Latino), 2 international. Average age 39. 11 applicants, 36% accepted, 3 enrolled. In 2014, 4 master's awarded. *Degree requirements:* For master's, one foreign language, comprehensive exam (for some programs), thesis, thesis exhibit. *Entrance requirements:* For master's, portfolio (MFA); 10-20 page paper (MA). Additional exam requirements/recommendations for international students: Required—TOEFL (minimum score 550 paper-based; 79 iBT), IELTS (minimum score 6.5). *Application deadline:* For fall admission, 1/20 for domestic students; for spring admission, 11/15 for domestic students. Application fee: $40 ($50 for international students). Electronic applications accepted. *Expenses:* Tuition, state resident: full-time $3969; part-time $220.50 per credit hour. Tuition, nonresident: full-time $13,838; part-time $768.80 per credit hour. *Required fees:* $853; $47.40 per credit hour. *Financial support:* In 2014–15, 13 students received support, including 10 teaching assistantships (averaging $15,225 per year); career-related internships or fieldwork, Federal Work-Study, scholarships/grants, traineeships, health care benefits, and unspecified assistantships also available. Support available to part-time students. Financial award application deadline: 3/1. *Faculty research:* Art history, painting, graphic design, sculpture, ceramics, photography. *Total annual research expenditures:* $11,222. *Unit head:* Dr. Julia Barello, Academic Department Head, 575-646-1705, Fax: 575-646-8036, E-mail: jbarello@nmsu.edu. *Application contact:* 575-646-1705, Fax: 575-646-8036, E-mail: artdept@nmsu.edu.
Website: http://artdepartment.nmsu.edu/

The New School, Parsons The New School for Design, Program in Fine Arts, New York, NY 10011. Offers MFA. *Degree requirements:* For master's, thesis. *Entrance requirements:* For master's, portfolio. Additional exam requirements/recommendations for international students: Required—TOEFL (minimum score 580 paper-based; 92 iBT). Electronic applications accepted.

New York Academy of Art, Master of Fine Arts Program, New York, NY 10013-2911. Offers drawing (MFA), including anatomy, printmaking; painting (MFA), including anatomy, printmaking; sculpture (MFA), including anatomy, printmaking. *Accreditation:* NASAD. *Degree requirements:* For master's, thesis. *Entrance requirements:* For master's, slide portfolio, two letters of recommendation, essay, official undergraduate transcripts. Additional exam requirements/recommendations for international students: Required—TOEFL, IELTS. Application fee is waived when completed online.

New York Institute of Technology, College of Arts and Sciences, Department of Fine Arts, Old Westbury, NY 11568-8000. Offers computer graphics (MFA), including animation, fine arts and technology, graphic design. Part-time and evening/weekend programs available. *Degree requirements:* For master's, thesis. *Entrance requirements:* For master's, minimum QPA of 2.85, portfolio. Additional exam requirements/recommendations for international students: Required—TOEFL (minimum score 550 paper-based; 79 iBT), IELTS (minimum score 6). Electronic applications accepted. *Faculty research:* Graphic design, animation, art and technology, digital art and science, sculpture.

New York Studio School of Drawing, Painting and Sculpture, Certificate Program, New York, NY 10011. Offers studio art (Certificate).

★ **New York Studio School of Drawing, Painting and Sculpture,** MFA Program, New York, NY 10011. Offers painting (MFA); sculpture (MFA). **See Display below and Close-Up on page 201.**

New York University, Graduate School of Arts and Science, Institute of Fine Arts, New York, NY 10012-1019. Offers art history and archaeology (MA, PhD), including architectural studies (PhD), art history and archaeology, classical art and archaeology (PhD), curatorial studies (PhD), East and South Asian art (PhD), Near Eastern art and archaeology (PhD); MA/Diploma; PhD/Certificate. Part-time programs available. *Faculty:* 19 full-time (5 women). *Students:* 181 full-time (145 women), 56 part-time (46 women); includes 28 minority (2 Black or African American, non-Hispanic/Latino; 12 Asian, non-Hispanic/Latino; 9 Hispanic/Latino; 5 Two or more races, non-Hispanic/Latino), 37 international. Average age 31. 346 applicants, 43% accepted, 52 enrolled. In 2014, 47 master's, 24 doctorates awarded. Terminal master's awarded for partial completion of doctoral program. *Degree requirements:* For master's, 2 foreign languages, thesis or alternative, 2 qualifying papers; for doctorate, 2 foreign languages, thesis/dissertation. *Entrance requirements:* For master's, GRE General Test; for doctorate, GRE General Test, MA. Additional exam requirements/recommendations for international students: Required—TOEFL. *Application deadline:* For fall admission, 12/18 for domestic and international students. Application fee: $100. *Financial support:* Fellowships with tuition reimbursements, research assistantships with tuition reimbursements, teaching assistantships with tuition reimbursements, career-related internships or fieldwork, Federal Work-Study, institutionally sponsored loans, and tuition waivers (partial) available. Financial award application deadline: 12/18; financial award applicants required to submit FAFSA. *Unit head:* Patricia Rubin, Chair, 212-992-5800, Fax: 212-992-5807, E-mail: ifa.program@nyu.edu. *Application contact:* Alexander Nagel, Director of Graduate Studies, 212-992-5800, Fax: 212-992-5807, E-mail: ifa.program@nyu.edu. Website: http://www.nyu.edu/gsas/dept/fineart/

New York University, Steinhardt School of Culture, Education, and Human Development, Department of Art and Art Professions, Program in Studio Art, New York, NY 10003. Offers MA, MFA, Advanced Certificate. Part-time programs available. *Faculty:* 14 full-time (8 women). *Students:* 20 full-time (11 women), 3 part-time (all women); includes 4 minority (1 Asian, non-Hispanic/Latino; 2 Hispanic/Latino; 1 Two or more races, non-Hispanic/Latino), 3 international. Average age 48. 159 applicants, 10% accepted, 12 enrolled. In 2014, 24 master's, 3 other advanced degrees awarded. *Degree requirements:* For master's, thesis (for some programs). *Entrance requirements:* For master's, portfolio, interview, presentation. Additional exam requirements/recommendations for international students: Required—TOEFL (minimum score 100 iBT). *Application deadline:* For fall admission, 12/1 priority date for domestic and international students. Applications are processed on a rolling basis. Application fee:

$75. Electronic applications accepted. *Financial support:* Teaching assistantships, career-related internships or fieldwork, Federal Work-Study, institutionally sponsored loans, scholarships/grants, tuition waivers (partial), and unspecified assistantships available. Support available to part-time students. Financial award application deadline: 2/1; financial award applicants required to submit FAFSA. *Faculty research:* Media and culture, video art and digital media, multimedia works, critical theory, memory and history, performance and text. *Unit head:* Prof. Maureen Gallace, Program Director, 212-998-5700, Fax: 212-995-4320, E-mail: mag6@nyu.edu. *Application contact:* 212-998-5030, Fax: 212-995-4328, E-mail: steinhardt.gradadmissions@nyu.edu.
Website: http://steinhardt.nyu.edu/art

New York University, Steinhardt School of Culture, Education, and Human Development, Department of Art and Art Professions, Program in Visual Culture, New York, NY 10003. Offers costume studies (MA); MA/MS. Part-time programs available. *Faculty:* 1 (woman) full-time, 1 (woman) part-time/adjunct. *Students:* 19 full-time (17 women), 12 part-time (8 women); includes 7 minority (2 Black or African American, non-Hispanic/Latino; 1 Asian, non-Hispanic/Latino; 4 Hispanic/Latino), 8 international. Average age 26. 36 applicants, 53% accepted, 12 enrolled. In 2014, 15 master's awarded. *Degree requirements:* For master's, thesis (for some programs). *Entrance requirements:* Additional exam requirements/recommendations for international students: Required—TOEFL (minimum score 100 iBT). *Application deadline:* For fall admission, 12/1 priority date for domestic and international students. Applications are processed on a rolling basis. Application fee: $75. Electronic applications accepted. *Financial support:* Career-related internships or fieldwork, Federal Work-Study, institutionally sponsored loans, scholarships/grants, and tuition waivers available. Support available to part-time students. Financial award application deadline: 2/1; financial award applicants required to submit FAFSA. *Faculty research:* Textiles as material culture, contemporary visual culture and globalization, cultural theory. *Unit head:* Prof. Nancy Diehl, Director, 212-998-5700, E-mail: nbd2012@nyu.edu. *Application contact:* 212-998-5030, Fax: 212-995-4328, E-mail: steinhardt.gradadmissions@nyu.edu.
Website: http://steinhardt.nyu.edu/art/costume

New York University, Tisch School of the Arts, Program in Arts Politics, New York, NY 10012-1019. Offers MA. *Faculty:* 3 full-time (2 women), 4 part-time/adjunct (3 women). *Students:* 14 full-time (9 women), 1 (woman) part-time; includes 4 minority (1 Asian, non-Hispanic/Latino; 2 Hispanic/Latino; 1 Two or more races, non-Hispanic/Latino), 8 international. Average age 25. 33 applicants, 97% accepted, 15 enrolled. *Degree requirements:* For master's, thesis. *Entrance requirements:* For master's, professional resume, writing sample, statement of purpose. Additional exam requirements/recommendations for international students: Required—TOEFL or IELTS. *Application deadline:* For fall admission, 1/1 for domestic and international students. Application fee: $60. *Financial support:* In 2014–15, 2 students received support. Federal Work-Study and scholarships/grants available. Financial award application deadline: 2/15; financial award applicants required to submit FAFSA. *Unit head:* Randy Martin, Director, 212-992-8248. *Application contact:* Dan Sandford, Director of Graduate Admissions, 212-998-1918, Fax: 212-995-4060, E-mail: tisch.gradadmissions@nyu.edu.

Norfolk State University, School of Graduate Studies, School of Liberal Arts, Department of Fine Arts, Norfolk, VA 23504. Offers visual studies (MA, MFA). Part-time programs available. *Degree requirements:* For master's, thesis or alternative. *Entrance requirements:* For master's, portfolio, interview, letters of recommendation. Additional exam requirements/recommendations for international students: Required—TOEFL (minimum score 500 paper-based).

Northeastern University, College of Arts, Media and Design, Boston, MA 02115-5096. Offers architecture (M Arch); information design and visualization (MFA); journalism (MA); studio art (MFA). *Entrance requirements:* Additional exam requirements/recommendations for international students: Required—TOEFL (minimum score 100 iBT), IELTS. Electronic applications accepted.

Northern Illinois University, Graduate School, College of Visual and Performing Arts, School of Art, De Kalb, IL 60115-2854. Offers MA, MFA, MS. *Accreditation:* NASAD (one or more programs are accredited). Part-time and evening/weekend programs available. *Faculty:* 36 full-time (15 women), 1 (woman) part-time/adjunct. *Students:* 43 full-time (28 women), 21 part-time (13 women); includes 9 minority (1 Black or African American, non-Hispanic/Latino; 1 Asian, non-Hispanic/Latino; 4 Hispanic/Latino; 3 Two or more races, non-Hispanic/Latino), 2 international. Average age 31. 81 applicants, 30% accepted, 9 enrolled. In 2014, 22 master's awarded. *Degree requirements:* For master's, variable foreign language requirement, comprehensive exam, thesis (for some programs), show or project. *Entrance requirements:* For master's, GRE General Test, minimum GPA of 2.75, portfolio. Additional exam requirements/recommendations for international students: Required—TOEFL (minimum score 550 paper-based). *Application deadline:* For fall and spring admission, 3/1 for domestic and international students. Applications are processed on a rolling basis. Application fee: $40. Electronic applications accepted. *Financial support:* In 2014–15, 28 research assistantships with full tuition reimbursements, 33 teaching assistantships with full tuition reimbursements were awarded; fellowships with full tuition reimbursements, career-related internships or fieldwork, Federal Work-Study, scholarships/grants, tuition waivers (full), and staff assistantships also available. Support available to part-time students. Financial award applicants required to submit FAFSA. *Faculty research:* Art education, portfolio assessment, central European design history, relationship between modern art and industrialism. *Unit head:* Dr. Douglas Boughton, Director, 815-753-7850, Fax: 815-753-7701, E-mail: dboughton@niu.edu. *Application contact:* Kurt Schultz, Graduate Coordinator, 815-753-1473, E-mail: artgradcoordinator@niu.edu.
Website: http://www.niu.edu/art/

Northwestern State University of Louisiana, Graduate Studies and Research, School of Creative and Performing Arts, Program in Art, Natchitoches, LA 71497. Offers fine and graphic arts (MA). *Accreditation:* NASAD. *Degree requirements:* For master's, comprehensive exam, thesis or alternative. *Entrance requirements:* For master's, GRE General Test, minimum undergraduate GPA of 2.5. Additional exam requirements/recommendations for international students: Required—TOEFL. Electronic applications accepted.

Northwestern University, The Graduate School, Judd A. and Marjorie Weinberg College of Arts and Sciences, Department of Art Theory and Practice, Evanston, IL 60208. Offers visual arts (MFA). Admissions and degrees offered through The Graduate School. *Degree requirements:* For master's, essay, exhibit. *Entrance requirements:* For master's, 20 slides of recent work. Additional exam requirements/recommendations for international students: Required—TOEFL. Electronic applications accepted.

NSCAD University, Program in Fine Arts, Halifax, NS B3J 3J6, Canada. Offers craft (MFA); design (M Des); fine and media arts (MFA). *Degree requirements:* For master's, thesis, exhibit. *Entrance requirements:* For master's, portfolio, at least 5 art history classes. Additional exam requirements/recommendations for international students: Required—Michigan English Language Assessment Battery (minimum score: 80), CanTEST (minimum score: 4.5), CAEL (minimum score: 70); Recommended—TOEFL (minimum score 575 paper-based; 90 iBT), IELTS (minimum score 6.5).

The Ohio State University, Graduate School, College of Arts and Sciences, Division of Arts and Humanities, Department of Art, Columbus, OH 43210. Offers MFA. *Accreditation:* NASAD. *Faculty:* 24. *Students:* 42 full-time (25 women); includes 6 minority (1 Black or African American, non-Hispanic/Latino; 2 Asian, non-Hispanic/Latino; 2 Hispanic/Latino; 1 Two or more races, non-Hispanic/Latino), 4 international. Average age 30. In 2014, 5 master's awarded. *Degree requirements:* For master's, thesis, exhibit, oral exams. *Entrance requirements:* For master's, GRE General Test (if GPA cumulative average is less than 3.0), electronic portfolio. Additional exam requirements/recommendations for international students: Required—Michigan English Language Assessment Battery (minimum score 82); Recommended—TOEFL (minimum score 550 paper-based; 79 iBT), IELTS (minimum score 7). *Application deadline:* For fall admission, 12/31 priority date for domestic students, 11/30 priority date for international students; for winter admission, 12/1 for domestic students, 11/1 for international students; for spring admission, 3/1 for domestic students, 2/1 for international students. Applications are processed on a rolling basis. Application fee: $60 ($70 for international students). Electronic applications accepted. *Financial support:* Fellowships with tuition reimbursements, teaching assistantships with tuition reimbursements, Federal Work-Study, institutionally sponsored loans, and unspecified assistantships available. Support available to part-time students. *Unit head:* Rebecca Harvey, Interim Chair, 614-292-5072, E-mail: harvey.113@osu.edu. *Application contact:* Graduate and Professional Admissions, 614-292-9444, Fax: 614-292-3895, E-mail: gpadmissions@osu.edu.
Website: http://art.osu.edu/

Ohio University, Graduate College, College of Fine Arts, School of Art, Athens, OH 45701-2979. Offers art history (MA); ceramics (MFA); graphic design (MFA); painting (MFA); photography (MFA); printmaking (MFA); sculpture (MFA). Part-time programs available. *Degree requirements:* For master's, thesis. *Entrance requirements:* For master's, portfolio. Additional exam requirements/recommendations for international students: Required—TOEFL (minimum score 550 paper-based; 80 iBT) or IELTS (minimum score 6.5). Electronic applications accepted. *Faculty research:* Vapor-fired ceramics, video installation, art theory, digital photography, mixed and interdisciplinary media work.

Oregon College of Art & Craft, MFA Program, Portland, OR 97225. Offers craft (MFA). *Accreditation:* NASAD.

Otis College of Art and Design, Program in Fine Arts, Los Angeles, CA 90045-9785. Offers new genres (MFA); painting (MFA); photography (MFA); sculpture (MFA). *Accreditation:* NASAD. *Degree requirements:* For master's, thesis. *Entrance requirements:* For master's, portfolio. Additional exam requirements/recommendations for international students: Required—TOEFL (minimum score 600 paper-based). Electronic applications accepted.

Otis College of Art and Design, Program in Public Practice, Los Angeles, CA 90045-9785. Offers MFA. *Entrance requirements:* Additional exam requirements/recommendations for international students: Required—TOEFL (minimum score 600 paper-based). Electronic applications accepted.

Pacific Northwest College of Art, Program in Visual Studies, Portland, OR 97209. Offers MFA. *Accreditation:* NASAD.

Penn State University Park, Graduate School, College of Arts and Architecture, School of Visual Arts, University Park, PA 16802. Offers art (MFA); art education (MPS, MS, PhD, Certificate). *Accreditation:* NASAD. *Unit head:* Dr. Barbara O. Korner, Dean, 814-865-2592, Fax: 814-865-2018, E-mail: bok2@psu.edu. *Application contact:* Lori A. Stania, Director, Graduate Student Services, 814-867-5278, Fax: 814-863-4627, E-mail: gswww@psu.edu.
Website: http://sova.psu.edu/

Pennsylvania Academy of the Fine Arts, Division of Graduate Studies, Philadelphia, PA 19102. Offers drawing (MFA, Postbaccalaureate Certificate); painting (MFA, Postbaccalaureate Certificate); printmaking (MFA, Postbaccalaureate Certificate); sculpture (MFA, Postbaccalaureate Certificate). MFA program also available in a low-residency format. *Accreditation:* NASAD (one or more programs are accredited). *Faculty:* 8 full-time (2 women), 20 part-time/adjunct (11 women). *Students:* 86 full-time (50 women); includes 10 minority (4 Black or African American, non-Hispanic/Latino; 4 Asian, non-Hispanic/Latino; 2 Hispanic/Latino), 4 international. *Degree requirements:* For master's, thesis, thesis exhibit. *Entrance requirements:* For master's, 10-20 slides of work and slide list or SlideRoom submission, 3 letters of recommendation, bachelor's degree, statement of purpose. Additional exam requirements/recommendations for international students: Required—TOEFL (minimum score 600 paper-based; 100 iBT), IELTS (minimum score 6). *Application deadline:* For fall admission, 1/15 for domestic and international students. Application fee: $60. Electronic applications accepted. *Expenses: Tuition:* Full-time $36,215. *Financial support:* Teaching assistantships, Federal Work-Study, institutionally sponsored loans, scholarships/grants, and unspecified assistantships available. Financial award application deadline: 3/1; financial award applicants required to submit FAFSA. *Unit head:* Clint Jukkala, Chair of Graduate Programs, 215-972-2027, Fax: 215-569-0153, E-mail: cjukkala@pafa.edu. *Application contact:* Andre S. F. van de Putte, Dean of Enrollment, 215-972-2047, Fax: 215-569-0153, E-mail: avandeputte@pafa.edu.

Philadelphia University, School of Engineering and Textiles, Program in Surface Imaging, Philadelphia, PA 19144. Offers MS.

Pittsburg State University, Graduate School, College of Arts and Sciences, Department of Art, Pittsburg, KS 66762. Offers art education (MA); studio art (MA). *Degree requirements:* For master's, thesis or alternative.

Pontifical Catholic University of Puerto Rico, College of Arts and Humanities, Department of Fine Arts, Ponce, PR 00717-0777. Offers painting and drawing (MA).

Portland State University, Graduate Studies, School of Fine and Performing Arts, Department of Art, Portland, OR 97207-0751. Offers drawing (MFA); mixed media (MFA); painting (MFA); printmaking (MFA); sculpture (MFA). *Faculty:* 33 full-time (23 women), 44 part-time/adjunct (23 women). *Students:* 21 full-time (15 women), 3 part-time (all women); includes 5 minority (1 Asian, non-Hispanic/Latino; 4 Hispanic/Latino), 1 international. Average age 31. 64 applicants, 22% accepted, 12 enrolled. In 2014, 33 master's awarded. *Degree requirements:* For master's, variable foreign language requirement, thesis, exhibit. *Entrance requirements:* For master's, minimum GPA of 3.0 in upper-division course work or 2.75 overall, portfolio, 3 letters of recommendation. Additional exam requirements/recommendations for international students: Required—TOEFL (minimum score 550 paper-based; 80 iBT), IELTS (minimum score 6.5). *Application deadline:* For fall admission, 3/1 for domestic and international students. Application fee: $50. *Expenses:* Tuition, state resident: part-time $222 per credit. Tuition, nonresident: part-time $527 per credit. *Required fees:* $22 per contact hour. $100 per quarter. Tuition and fees vary according to program. *Financial support:* In 2014–15, 8 research assistantships (averaging $1,490 per year), 4 teaching assistantships with partial tuition reimbursements (averaging $1,986 per year) were awarded; Federal Work-Study, scholarships/grants, and unspecified assistantships also available. Support available to part-time students. Financial award application deadline: 3/1; financial award applicants required to submit FAFSA. *Total annual research expenditures:* $4,000. *Unit head:* Ethan Seltzer, Interim School Director, 503-725-5169,

Fax: 503-725-4541, E-mail: seltzere@pdx.edu. *Application contact:* 503-725-3515, Fax: 503-725-4541, E-mail: askmfa@pdx.edu.
Website: http://www.pdx.edu/the-arts/art-design

Pratt Institute, School of Art and Design, Program in Fine Arts, Brooklyn, NY 11205-3899. Offers new forms (MFA); painting and drawing (MFA); photography (MFA); printmaking (MFA); sculpture (MFA). *Accreditation:* NASAD. Part-time programs available. *Faculty:* 10 full-time (5 women), 78 part-time/adjunct (33 women). *Students:* 94 full-time (59 women), 4 part-time (2 women); includes 19 minority (2 Black or African American, non-Hispanic/Latino; 11 Asian, non-Hispanic/Latino; 6 Hispanic/Latino), 42 international. Average age 28. 264 applicants, 47% accepted, 49 enrolled. In 2014, 45 master's awarded. *Degree requirements:* For master's, thesis, exhibit. *Entrance requirements:* For master's, portfolio, letters of recommendation. Additional exam requirements/recommendations for international students: Required—TOEFL (minimum score 550 paper-based; 79 iBT). *Application deadline:* For fall admission, 1/5 for domestic and international students; for spring admission, 10/1 for domestic and international students. Application fee: $50 ($90 for international students). Electronic applications accepted. *Financial support:* Career-related internships or fieldwork, Federal Work-Study, institutionally sponsored loans, scholarships/grants, health care benefits, and unspecified assistantships available. Support available to part-time students. Financial award application deadline: 2/1; financial award applicants required to submit FAFSA. *Unit head:* Deborah Bright, Chairperson, 718-636-3634, E-mail: dbright2@pratt.edu. *Application contact:* Young Hah, Director of Graduate Admissions, 718-636-3683, Fax: 718-399-4242, E-mail: yhah@pratt.edu.
Website: https://www.pratt.edu/academics/school-of-art/graduate-school-of-art/graduate-fine-arts/

See Display on this page and Close-Up on page 203.

Purchase College, State University of New York, School of Art and Design, Purchase, NY 10577-1400. Offers MFA. *Accreditation:* NASAD. *Students:* 12 full-time (8 women); includes 3 minority (1 Asian, non-Hispanic/Latino; 2 Hispanic/Latino), 3 international. 81 applicants, 22% accepted, 14 enrolled. *Degree requirements:* For master's, thesis, exhibit. *Entrance requirements:* For master's, portfolio. *Application deadline:* For fall admission, 3/1 for domestic students. Applications are processed on a rolling basis. Application fee: $50. Electronic applications accepted. *Expenses:* Tuition, state resident: full-time $10,370; part-time $432 per credit. Tuition, nonresident: full-time $20,190; part-time $831 per credit. *Required fees:* $1763. *Financial support:* Fellowships, teaching assistantships, Federal Work-Study, scholarships/grants, and tuition waivers (partial) available. Support available to part-time students. Financial award application deadline: 3/15; financial award applicants required to submit FAFSA. *Unit head:* Steven Lam, Director, 914-251-6750, Fax: 914-251-6793. *Application contact:* Sabrina Johnston, Admission Counselor, 914-251-6479, Fax: 914-251-6314, E-mail: admissn@purchase.edu.
Website: http://www.purchase.edu/Departments/AcademicPrograms/Arts/ArtDesign/

Purdue University, Graduate School, College of Liberal Arts, Department of Visual and Performing Arts, West Lafayette, IN 47907. Offers art and design (MA); theatre (MA, MFA). *Accreditation:* NASAD; NAST. Part-time programs available. *Degree requirements:* For master's, terminal exhibit, project, or thesis. *Entrance requirements:* For master's, GRE General Test (for art education), minimum undergraduate GPA of 3.0 or equivalent; 9 undergraduate hours in an art or design history; BA in art (for MA in art education). Additional exam requirements/recommendations for international students: Required—TOEFL (minimum score 550 paper-based; 77 iBT). Electronic applications accepted. *Faculty research:* Design, fine arts, photography, acting, directing, theatre technology.

Queens College of the City University of New York, Division of Graduate Studies, Arts and Humanities Division, Department of Art, Program in Fine Arts, Flushing, NY 11367-1597. Offers MFA. *Degree requirements:* For master's, art show. *Entrance requirements:* For master's, minimum GPA of 3.0, portfolio. Additional exam requirements/recommendations for international students: Required—TOEFL.

Radford University, College of Graduate and Professional Studies, College of Visual and Performing Arts, Program in Art, Radford, VA 24142. Offers design thinking (MFA); studio art (MFA). Part-time programs available. *Faculty:* 11 full-time (5 women), 1 (woman) part-time/adjunct. *Students:* 21 full-time (18 women), 12 part-time (7 women); includes 6 minority (2 Black or African American, non-Hispanic/Latino; 1 American Indian or Alaska Native, non-Hispanic/Latino; 1 Asian, non-Hispanic/Latino; 1 Hispanic/Latino; 1 Two or more races, non-Hispanic/Latino), 1 international. Average age 35. 21 applicants, 100% accepted, 15 enrolled. In 2014, 4 master's awarded. *Degree requirements:* For master's, comprehensive exam. *Entrance requirements:* For master's, statement of philosophy; minimum GPA of 2.75, 2 letters of reference, BFA or commensurate collegiate course work, 20 slides or CD of recent work, resume, and official transcripts (for studio art); minimum GPA of 3.0 (preferred) and three letters of reference (for design thinking). Additional exam requirements/recommendations for international students: Required—TOEFL (minimum score 550 paper-based; 79 iBT), IELTS (minimum score 6.5). *Application deadline:* For fall admission, 2/15 priority date for domestic students, 12/1 for international students; for spring admission, 7/1 for international students. Applications are processed on a rolling basis. Application fee: $50. Electronic applications accepted. *Expenses:* Tuition, state resident: full-time $7187; part-time $299 per credit hour. Tuition, nonresident: full-time $16,394; part-time $683 per credit hour. *Required fees:* $2974; $125 per credit hour. Tuition and fees vary according to course load and program. *Financial support:* In 2014–15, 14 students received support, including 7 research assistantships (averaging $8,214 per year), 6 teaching assistantships with partial tuition reimbursements available (averaging $8,750 per year); career-related internships or fieldwork, Federal Work-Study, institutionally sponsored loans, scholarships/grants, and unspecified assistantships also available. Financial award application deadline: 3/1; financial award applicants required to submit FAFSA. *Unit head:* Dr. Eloise Philpot, Graduate Coordinator, 540-831-5030, Fax: 540-831-6799, E-mail: ephilpot@radford.edu. *Application contact:* Rebecca Conner, Director, Graduate Enrollment, 540-831-6296, Fax: 540-831-6061, E-mail: gradcollege@radford.edu.
Website: http://www.radford.edu/content/cvpa/home/art.html

Rensselaer Polytechnic Institute, Graduate School, School of Humanities, Arts, and Social Sciences, Program in Electronic Arts, Troy, NY 12180-3590. Offers MFA, PhD. *Faculty:* 32 full-time (10 women), 3 part-time/adjunct (0 women). *Students:* 15 full-time (6 women), 1 part-time (0 women); includes 2 minority (both Hispanic/Latino), 1 international. Average age 31. 49 applicants, 45% accepted, 9 enrolled. In 2014, 3 master's, 2 doctorates awarded. *Degree requirements:* For doctorate, comprehensive exam. *Entrance requirements:* Additional exam requirements/recommendations for international students: Required—TOEFL (minimum score 570 paper-based; 88 iBT), IELTS (minimum score 6.5), PTE (minimum score 60). *Application deadline:* For fall admission, 1/1 priority date for domestic and international students. Applications are processed on a rolling basis. Application fee: $75. Electronic applications accepted. *Expenses: Tuition:* Full-time $46,700; part-time $1945 per credit. Tuition and fees vary according to course load. *Financial support:* In 2014–15, 12 students received support, including research assistantships (averaging $18,500 per year), teaching assistantships

with full tuition reimbursements available (averaging $18,500 per year); scholarships/grants also available. Financial award application deadline: 1/1. *Unit head:* Dr. Curtis Bahn, Graduate Program Director, 518-276-4032, E-mail: crb@rpi.edu. *Application contact:* Office of Graduate Admissions, 518-276-6216, E-mail: gradadmissions@rpi.edu.
Website: http://www.arts.rpi.edu/

Rhode Island College, School of Graduate Studies, Faculty of Arts and Sciences, Department of Art, Providence, RI 02908-1991. Offers art education (MA, MAT); media studies (MA). *Accreditation:* NASAD (one or more programs are accredited). Part-time and evening/weekend programs available. *Faculty:* 6 full-time (3 women), 5 part-time/adjunct (2 women). *Students:* 9 full-time (6 women), 10 part-time (7 women), 1 international. Average age 35. In 2014, 8 master's awarded. *Degree requirements:* For master's, thesis. *Entrance requirements:* For master's, GRE General Test, portfolio (MA), 3 letters of recommendation, interview. Additional exam requirements/recommendations for international students: Recommended—TOEFL (minimum score 550 paper-based; 79 iBT). *Application deadline:* For fall admission, 3/1 for domestic students. Applications are processed on a rolling basis. Application fee: $50. *Expenses:* Tuition, state resident: full-time $8928; part-time $372 per credit hour. Tuition, nonresident: full-time $17,376; part-time $724 per credit hour. *Required fees:* $602; $22 per credit. $72 per term. *Financial support:* In 2014–15, 2 teaching assistantships with full tuition reimbursements (averaging $1,500 per year) were awarded; career-related internships or fieldwork, Federal Work-Study, scholarships/grants, health care benefits, and unspecified assistantships also available. Support available to part-time students. Financial award application deadline: 5/15; financial award applicants required to submit FAFSA. *Unit head:* Prof. Nancy Bockbrader, Chair, 401-456-8054. *Application contact:* Graduate Studies, 401-456-8700.
Website: http://www.ric.edu/art/index.php

Rhode Island School of Design, Graduate Studies, Division of Fine Arts, Department of Ceramics, Providence, RI 02903-2784. Offers MFA. *Accreditation:* NASAD. *Faculty:* 2 full-time (1 woman), 6 part-time/adjunct (4 women). *Students:* 9 full-time (5 women); includes 1 minority (Hispanic/Latino), 4 international. Average age 28. 21 applicants, 43% accepted, 6 enrolled. In 2014, 3 master's awarded. *Degree requirements:* For master's, thesis, exhibit. *Entrance requirements:* For master's, portfolio, 3 letters of recommendation. Additional exam requirements/recommendations for international students: Required—TOEFL (minimum score 580 paper-based; 93 iBT). *Application deadline:* For fall admission, 2/1 for domestic and international students. Application fee: $60. *Financial support:* Fellowships, teaching assistantships, career-related internships or fieldwork, Federal Work-Study, institutionally sponsored loans, scholarships/grants, and unspecified assistantships available. Financial award application deadline: 2/15; financial award applicants required to submit FAFSA. *Unit head:* Katy Schimert, Department Head and Graduate Program Director, 401-454-6190, Fax: 401-454-6191, E-mail: kchimer@risd.edu. *Application contact:* Molly Pettengil, Graduate Admissions Officer, 401-454-6312, Fax: 401-454-6309, E-mail: mpetteng@risd.edu.

Rhode Island School of Design, Graduate Studies, Division of Fine Arts, Department of Glass, Providence, RI 02903-2784. Offers MFA. *Accreditation:* NASAD. *Faculty:* 1 (woman) full-time, 3 part-time/adjunct (2 women). *Students:* 3 full-time (all women), 2 international. Average age 25. 8 applicants, 50% accepted, 2 enrolled. In 2014, 2 master's awarded. *Degree requirements:* For master's, thesis, exhibit. *Entrance requirements:* For master's, portfolio, statement of purpose, 3 letters of recommendation. Additional exam requirements/recommendations for international students: Required—TOEFL (minimum score 580 paper-based; 93 iBT). *Application deadline:* For fall admission, 2/1 for domestic and international students. Application fee: $60. *Financial support:* Fellowships, teaching assistantships, career-related internships or fieldwork, Federal Work-Study, institutionally sponsored loans, scholarships/grants, and unspecified assistantships available. Financial award application deadline: 2/15; financial award applicants required to submit FAFSA. *Unit head:* Rachel Berwick, Department Head and Graduate Program Director, 401-454-6190, Fax: 401-454-6680, E-mail: rberwick@risd.edu. *Application contact:* Molly Pettengil, Graduate Admissions Officer, 401-454-6312, Fax: 401-454-6309, E-mail: mpetteng@risd.edu.

Rhode Island School of Design, Graduate Studies, Division of Fine Arts, Department of Jewelry and Metalsmithing, Providence, RI 02903-2784. Offers MFA. *Accreditation:* NASAD. *Faculty:* 3 full-time (2 women), 8 part-time/adjunct (7 women). *Students:* 10 full-time (8 women); includes 3 minority (2 Asian, non-Hispanic/Latino; 1 Hispanic/Latino), 3 international. Average age 27. 43 applicants, 19% accepted, 6 enrolled. In 2014, 3 master's awarded. *Degree requirements:* For master's, thesis, exhibit. *Entrance requirements:* For master's, portfolio, statement of purpose, 3 letters of recommendation. Additional exam requirements/recommendations for international students: Required—TOEFL (minimum score 580 paper-based; 93 iBT). *Application deadline:* For fall admission, 2/1 for domestic and international students. Application fee: $60. *Financial support:* Fellowships, teaching assistantships, career-related internships or fieldwork, Federal Work-Study, institutionally sponsored loans, scholarships/grants, and unspecified assistantships available. Financial award application deadline: 2/15; financial award applicants required to submit FAFSA. *Unit head:* Robin Quigley, Head, 401-454-6190, Fax: 401-454-6191, E-mail: rquigley@risd.edu. *Application contact:* Molly Pettengil, Graduate Admissions Officer, 401-454-6312, Fax: 401-454-6309, E-mail: empetteng@risd.edu.

Rhode Island School of Design, Graduate Studies, Division of Fine Arts, Department of Painting, Providence, RI 02903-2784. Offers MFA. *Accreditation:* NASAD. *Faculty:* 7 full-time (3 women), 8 part-time/adjunct (6 women). *Students:* 20 full-time (8 women); includes 4 minority (all Hispanic/Latino), 6 international. Average age 27. 241 applicants, 7% accepted, 10 enrolled. In 2014, 10 master's awarded. *Degree requirements:* For master's, thesis, exhibit. *Entrance requirements:* For master's, portfolio, statement of purpose, letters of recommendation. Additional exam requirements/recommendations for international students: Required—TOEFL (minimum score 580 paper-based; 93 iBT). *Application deadline:* For fall admission, 2/1 for domestic and international students. Application fee: $60. *Financial support:* Fellowships, teaching assistantships, career-related internships or fieldwork, Federal Work-Study, institutionally sponsored loans, scholarships/grants, and unspecified assistantships available. Financial award application deadline: 2/15; financial award applicants required to submit FAFSA. *Unit head:* Duane Slick, Head, 401-454-6158, Fax: 401-454-6681, E-mail: dslick@risd.edu. *Application contact:* Molly Pettengil, Graduate Admissions Officer, 401-454-6312, Fax: 401-454-6309, E-mail: mpetteng@risd.edu.

Rhode Island School of Design, Graduate Studies, Division of Fine Arts, Department of Printmaking, Providence, RI 02903-2784. Offers MFA. *Faculty:* 8 full-time (3 women), 12 part-time/adjunct (6 women). *Students:* 16 full-time (10 women); includes 6 minority (1 Black or African American, non-Hispanic/Latino; 1 Asian, non-Hispanic/Latino; 3 Hispanic/Latino; 1 Two or more races, non-Hispanic/Latino). Average age 28. 45 applicants, 31% accepted, 8 enrolled. In 2014, 6 master's awarded. *Degree requirements:* For master's, thesis, exhibit. *Entrance requirements:* For master's, portfolio, statement of purpose, 3 letters of recommendation. Additional exam requirements/recommendations for international students: Required—TOEFL (minimum score 580 paper-based; 93 iBT). *Application deadline:* For fall admission, 2/1 for domestic and international students. Application fee: $60. *Financial support:* Fellowships, teaching assistantships, Federal Work-Study, institutionally sponsored loans, scholarships/grants, and unspecified assistantships available. Financial award application deadline: 2/15; financial award applicants required to submit FAFSA. *Unit head:* Henry Ferreira, Head, 401-454-6224, Fax: 401-454-6707, E-mail: hferreir@risd.edu. *Application contact:* Molly Pettengil, Graduate Admissions Officer, 401-454-6312, Fax: 401-454-6309, E-mail: mpetteng@risd.edu.

Rhode Island School of Design, Graduate Studies, Division of Fine Arts, Department of Sculpture, Providence, RI 02903-2784. Offers MFA. *Accreditation:* NASAD. *Faculty:* 6 full-time (3 women), 10 part-time/adjunct (6 women). *Students:* 14 full-time (8 women), 1 international. Average age 27. 76 applicants, 16% accepted, 6 enrolled. In 2014, 7 master's awarded. *Degree requirements:* For master's, thesis, exhibit. *Entrance requirements:* For master's, portfolio, statement of purpose, 3 letters of recommendation. Additional exam requirements/recommendations for international students: Required—TOEFL (minimum score 580 paper-based; 93 iBT). *Application deadline:* For fall admission, 2/1 for domestic and international students. Application fee: $60. *Financial support:* Fellowships, teaching assistantships, career-related internships or fieldwork, Federal Work-Study, institutionally sponsored loans, scholarships/grants, and unspecified assistantships available. Financial award application deadline: 2/15; financial award applicants required to submit FAFSA. *Unit head:* Dean Snyder, Head, 401-454-6190, Fax: 401-454-6191, E-mail: dsnyder@risd.edu. *Application contact:* Molly Pettengil, Graduate Admissions Officer, 401-454-6312, Fax: 401-454-6309, E-mail: mpettengil@risd.edu.

Rochester Institute of Technology, Graduate Enrollment Services, College of Imaging Arts and Sciences, School for American Crafts, MFA Program in Ceramics, Rochester, NY 14623. Offers MFA. *Accreditation:* NASAD. Part-time programs available. *Students:* 7 full-time (4 women); includes 2 minority (both Black or African American, non-Hispanic/Latino), 5 international. Average age 31. 4 applicants, 75% accepted, 1 enrolled. In 2014, 1 master's awarded. *Degree requirements:* For master's, thesis. *Entrance requirements:* For master's, GRE and TOEFL, IELTS, or PTE for non-native English speakers, portfolio, recommended minimum GPA of 3.0. Additional exam requirements/recommendations for international students: Required—PTE (minimum score 58), TOEFL (minimum score 550 paper-based; 79 iBT) or IELTS (minimum score 6.5). *Application deadline:* For fall admission, 2/15 priority date for domestic and international students. Applications are processed on a rolling basis. Application fee: $60. Electronic applications accepted. *Expenses:* Expenses: $1,673 per credit hour. *Financial support:* In 2014–15, 5 students received support. Research assistantships with partial tuition reimbursements available, teaching assistantships with partial tuition reimbursements available, career-related internships or fieldwork, Federal Work-Study, institutionally sponsored loans, scholarships/grants, and unspecified assistantships available. Support available to part-time students. Financial award applicants required to submit FAFSA. *Unit head:* Len Urso, Graduate Program Director, 585-475-6114, Fax: 585-475-6447, E-mail: sac@rit.edu. *Application contact:* Diane Ellison, Associate Vice President, Graduate Enrollment Services, 585-475-2229, Fax: 585-475-7164, E-mail: gradinfo@rit.edu.
Website: http://cias.rit.edu/schools/american-crafts/graduate-ceramics-graduate

Rochester Institute of Technology, Graduate Enrollment Services, College of Imaging Arts and Sciences, School for American Crafts, MFA Program in Furniture Design, Rochester, NY 14623-5603. Offers MFA. Part-time programs available. *Students:* 12 full-time (6 women), 1 part-time, 8 international. Average age 28. 14 applicants, 71% accepted, 4 enrolled. In 2014, 5 master's awarded. *Degree requirements:* For master's, thesis project/exhibition. *Entrance requirements:* For master's, GRE and TOEFL, IELTS, or PTE for non-native English speakers, portfolio, recommended minimum GPA of 3.0. Additional exam requirements/recommendations for international students: Required—PTE (minimum score 58), TOEFL (minimum score 550 paper-based; 79 iBT) or IELTS (minimum score 6.5). *Application deadline:* For fall admission, 2/15 priority date for domestic and international students. Applications are processed on a rolling basis. Application fee: $60. Electronic applications accepted. *Expenses:* Expenses: $1,673 per credit hour. *Financial support:* In 2014–15, 8 students received support. Research assistantships with partial tuition reimbursements available, teaching assistantships with partial tuition reimbursements available, career-related internships or fieldwork, Federal Work-Study, institutionally sponsored loans, scholarships/grants, and unspecified assistantships available. Support available to part-time students. Financial award application deadline: 8/30; financial award applicants required to submit FAFSA. *Unit head:* Len Urso, Graduate Program Director, 585-475-6114, Fax: 585-475-6447, E-mail: sac@rit.edu. *Application contact:* Diane Ellison, Associate Vice President, Graduate Enrollment Services, 585-475-2229, Fax: 585-475-7164, E-mail: gradinfo@rit.edu.
Website: http://cias.rit.edu/schools/american-crafts/graduate-woodworking-graduate

Rochester Institute of Technology, Graduate Enrollment Services, College of Imaging Arts and Sciences, School for American Crafts, MFA Program in Glass, Rochester, NY 14623-5603. Offers MFA. *Accreditation:* NASAD. Part-time programs available. *Students:* 4 full-time (1 woman), 1 part-time, 2 international. Average age 31. 7 applicants, 57% accepted, 2 enrolled. In 2014, 5 master's awarded. *Degree requirements:* For master's, thesis. *Entrance requirements:* For master's, GRE and TOEFL, IELTS, or PTE for non-native English speakers, portfolio, recommended minimum GPA of 3.0. Additional exam requirements/recommendations for international students: Required—PTE (minimum score 58), TOEFL (minimum score 550 paper-based; 79 iBT) or IELTS (minimum score 6.5). *Application deadline:* For fall admission, 2/15 priority date for domestic and international students. Applications are processed on a rolling basis. Application fee: $60. Electronic applications accepted. *Expenses:* Expenses: $1,673 per credit hour. *Financial support:* In 2014–15, 4 students received support. Research assistantships with partial tuition reimbursements available, teaching assistantships with partial tuition reimbursements available, career-related internships or fieldwork, Federal Work-Study, institutionally sponsored loans, scholarships/grants, and unspecified assistantships available. Support available to part-time students. Financial award application deadline: 8/30; financial award applicants required to submit FAFSA. *Unit head:* Len Urso, Graduate Program Director, 585-475-6114, Fax: 585-475-6447, E-mail: sac@rit.edu. *Application contact:* Diane Ellison, Associate Vice President, Graduate Enrollment Services, 585-475-2229, Fax: 585-475-7164, E-mail: gradinfo@rit.edu.
Website: http://cias.rit.edu/schools/american-crafts/graduate-glass

Rochester Institute of Technology, Graduate Enrollment Services, College of Imaging Arts and Sciences, School for American Crafts, MFA Program in Metals and Jewelry Design, Rochester, NY 14623-5603. Offers MFA. *Accreditation:* NASAD. Part-time programs available. *Students:* 12 full-time (11 women), 6 part-time (all women); includes 3 minority (all Asian, non-Hispanic/Latino), 14 international. Average age 26. 27 applicants, 52% accepted, 8 enrolled. In 2014, 4 master's awarded. *Degree requirements:* For master's, thesis. *Entrance requirements:* For master's, GRE and TOEFL, IELTS, or PTE for non-native English speakers, portfolio, recommended minimum GPA of 3.0. Additional exam requirements/recommendations for international students: Required—PTE (minimum score 58), TOEFL (minimum score 550 paper-based; 79 iBT) or IELTS (minimum score 6.5). *Application deadline:* For fall admission, 2/15 priority date for domestic and international students. Applications are processed on

a rolling basis. Application fee: $60. Electronic applications accepted. *Expenses:* Expenses: $1,673 per credit hour. *Financial support:* In 2014–15, 9 students received support. Research assistantships with partial tuition reimbursements available, teaching assistantships with partial tuition reimbursements available, career-related internships or fieldwork, Federal Work-Study, institutionally sponsored loans, scholarships/grants, and unspecified assistantships available. Support available to part-time students. Financial award application deadline: 8/30; financial award applicants required to submit FAFSA. *Unit head:* Len Urso, Graduate Program Director, 585-475-6114, Fax: 585-475-6447, E-mail: sac@rit.edu. *Application contact:* Diane Ellison, Associate Vice President, Graduate Enrollment Services, 585-475-2229, Fax: 585-475-7164, E-mail: gradinfo@rit.edu.
Website: http://cias.rit.edu/schools/american-crafts/graduate-metalcrafts-graduate

Rochester Institute of Technology, Graduate Enrollment Services, College of Imaging Arts and Sciences, School of Art, MFA Program in Fine Arts Studio, Rochester, NY 14623-5603. Offers fine arts studio (MFA); non-toxic printmaking (Advanced Certificate). *Accreditation:* NASAD. Part-time programs available. *Students:* 14 full-time (7 women), 2 part-time (1 woman); includes 1 minority (Black or African American, non-Hispanic/Latino), 2 international. Average age 29. 34 applicants, 56% accepted, 9 enrolled. In 2014, 7 master's awarded. *Degree requirements:* For master's, thesis (for some programs). *Entrance requirements:* For master's, GRE and TOEFL, IELTS, or PTE for non-native English speakers, portfolio, recommended minimum GPA of 3.0. Additional exam requirements/recommendations for international students: Required—TOEFL (minimum score 550 paper-based; 79 iBT) or IELTS (minimum score 6.5). *Application deadline:* For fall admission, 2/15 priority date for domestic and international students. Applications are processed on a rolling basis. Application fee: $60. Electronic applications accepted. *Expenses:* Expenses: $1,673 per credit hour. *Financial support:* In 2014–15, 11 students received support. Research assistantships with partial tuition reimbursements available, teaching assistantships with partial tuition reimbursements available, career-related internships or fieldwork, Federal Work-Study, institutionally sponsored loans, scholarships/grants, and unspecified assistantships available. Support available to part-time students. Financial award application deadline: 8/30; financial award applicants required to submit FAFSA. *Unit head:* Elizabeth Kronfield, Graduate Program Director, 585-475-7562, E-mail: edkfaa@rit.edu. *Application contact:* Diane Ellison, Associate Vice President, Graduate Enrollment Services, 585-475-2229, Fax: 585-475-7164, E-mail: gradinfo@rit.edu.
Website: http://cias.rit.edu/schools/art/graduate-fine-arts-studio

Rutgers, The State University of New Jersey, New Brunswick, Mason Gross School of the Arts, Visual Arts Department, New Brunswick, NJ 08901. Offers drawing (MFA); painting (MFA); sculpture (MFA); visual arts (MFA). *Degree requirements:* For master's, thesis, exhibit. *Entrance requirements:* For master's, portfolio. Additional exam requirements/recommendations for international students: Required—TOEFL (minimum score 550 paper-based), IELTS (minimum score 7). Electronic applications accepted. *Faculty research:* Media, painting, sculpture, photography, film.

San Diego State University, Graduate and Research Affairs, College of Professional Studies and Fine Arts, School of Art, Design and Art History, San Diego, CA 92182. Offers art history (MA); studio arts (MA, MFA), including applied design, environmental design, graphic design, interior design, painting and printmaking, sculpture. *Accreditation:* NASAD (one or more programs are accredited). *Degree requirements:* For master's, variable foreign language requirement, thesis. *Entrance requirements:* For master's, GRE General Test, bachelor's degree in related field, slide portfolio, typed slide information sheet, 2 letters of recommendation. Additional exam requirements/recommendations for international students: Required—TOEFL. Electronic applications accepted.

San Francisco Art Institute, Dual-Degree MFA/MA Program in Studio Art and History and Theory of Contemporary Art, San Francisco, CA 94133. Offers MFA/MA. Specializations available in art and technology, film, new genres, painting, photography, printmaking, and sculpture. *Faculty:* 15 full-time (7 women), 46 part-time/adjunct (23 women). *Students:* 6 full-time (4 women); includes 1 minority (Black or African American, non-Hispanic/Latino). Average age 27. 15 applicants, 40% accepted, 4 enrolled. *Entrance requirements:* Additional exam requirements/recommendations for international students: Required—TOEFL (minimum score 600 paper-based; 100 iBT), IELTS (minimum score 7.5). *Application deadline:* For fall admission, 1/15 priority date for domestic and international students. Applications are processed on a rolling basis. Application fee: $85. Electronic applications accepted. *Expenses: Tuition:* Full-time $41,100; part-time $1805 per credit. *Required fees:* $870. *Financial support:* In 2014–15, 8 students received support, including fellowships (averaging $30,000 per year), teaching assistantships (averaging $2,500 per year); career-related internships or fieldwork, Federal Work-Study, scholarships/grants, and unspecified assistantships also available. Support available to part-time students. Financial award application deadline: 3/1; financial award applicants required to submit FAFSA. *Unit head:* Tony Labat, Chair, Master of Fine Arts Department, 415-771-7020, Fax: 415-641-1205, E-mail: tlabat@sfai.edu. *Application contact:* Jana Rumberger, Associate Director of Recruitment, 415-351-3507, Fax: 415-749-4592, E-mail: jrumberger@sfai.edu.
Website: http://www.sfai.edu/degree-programs/graduate/dual-degree-ma-mfa

San Francisco Art Institute, Master of Fine Arts Programs, San Francisco, CA 94133. Offers studio art (MFA, Certificate), including film (MFA), new genres (MFA), painting (MFA), photography (MFA), printmaking (MFA), sculpture (MFA). *Accreditation:* NASAD. Part-time programs available. *Faculty:* 15 full-time (7 women), 46 part-time/adjunct (23 women). *Students:* 201 full-time (114 women), 13 part-time (9 women); includes 46 minority (1 Black or African American, non-Hispanic/Latino; 1 American Indian or Alaska Native, non-Hispanic/Latino; 10 Asian, non-Hispanic/Latino; 22 Hispanic/Latino; 12 Two or more races, non-Hispanic/Latino), 72 international. Average age 29. 380 applicants, 61% accepted, 90 enrolled. In 2014, 72 master's, 4 other advanced degrees awarded. *Degree requirements:* For master's, thesis. *Entrance requirements:* For master's and Certificate, portfolio. Additional exam requirements/recommendations for international students: Required—TOEFL (minimum score 580 paper-based; 92 iBT), IELTS (minimum score 7). *Application deadline:* For fall admission, 1/15 priority date for domestic and international students; for spring admission, 11/15 priority date for domestic and international students. Applications are processed on a rolling basis. Application fee: $85. Electronic applications accepted. *Expenses: Tuition:* Full-time $41,100; part-time $1805 per credit. *Required fees:* $870. *Financial support:* In 2014–15, 142 students received support, including 20 fellowships (averaging $30,000 per year), teaching assistantships (averaging $2,500 per year); career-related internships or fieldwork, Federal Work-Study, scholarships/grants, and unspecified assistantships also available. Support available to part-time students. Financial award application deadline: 3/1; financial award applicants required to submit FAFSA. *Unit head:* Tony Labat, Chair, Master of Fine Arts Department, 415-771-7020, Fax: 415-641-1205, E-mail: tlabat@sfai.edu. *Application contact:* Nicole Crescenzi, Senior Associate Director of Graduate Admissions, 415-351-3517, Fax: 415-749-4592, E-mail: ncrescenzi@sfai.edu.
Website: http://www.sfai.edu/degree-programs/graduate

San Francisco State University, Division of Graduate Studies, College of Liberal and Creative Arts, Department of Art, San Francisco, CA 94132-1722. Offers art (MFA); art history (MA). *Accreditation:* NASAD (one or more programs are accredited). *Expenses:* Tuition, state resident: full-time $6738. Tuition, nonresident: full-time $17,898; part-time $372 per credit hour. *Required fees:* $498 per semester. *Unit head:* Gail Dawson, Chair, 415-338-2176, Fax: 415-338-6537, E-mail: artdept@sfsu.edu. *Application contact:* Prof. Susan Belau, Associate Professor and Graduate Coordinator, 415-338-1591, Fax: 415-338-6537, E-mail: artgrad@sfsu.edu.
Website: http://www.art.sfsu.edu

San Jose State University, Graduate Studies and Research, College of Humanities and the Arts, School of Art and Design, San Jose, CA 95192-0001. Offers animation/illustration (MA); art history (MA); digital media arts (MFA); photography (MFA); pictorial arts (MFA); spatial arts (MFA). *Accreditation:* NASAD (one or more programs are accredited). *Entrance requirements:* For master's, GRE. Electronic applications accepted.

Savannah College of Art and Design, Graduate School, Program in Accessory Design, Savannah, GA 31402-3146. Offers MA, MFA. Part-time programs available. *Faculty:* 4 full-time (2 women). *Students:* 8 full-time (7 women), 2 part-time (1 woman); includes 4 minority (2 Black or African American, non-Hispanic/Latino; 1 Asian, non-Hispanic/Latino; 1 Hispanic/Latino), 2 international. Average age 25. 9 applicants, 67% accepted, 4 enrolled. In 2014, 1 master's awarded. *Degree requirements:* For master's, thesis (for some programs), final project (for MA); internship (for MFA). *Entrance requirements:* For master's, portfolio (submitted in digital format). Additional exam requirements/recommendations for international students: Required—TOEFL (minimum score 550 paper-based, 85 iBT), IELTS (minimum score 6.5), or ACTFL. *Application deadline:* For fall admission, 4/1 for domestic and international students. Applications are processed on a rolling basis. Application fee: $40. Electronic applications accepted. *Expenses: Tuition:* Full-time $34,605; part-time $3845 per course. One-time fee: $500. Tuition and fees vary according to course load. *Financial support:* Fellowships, career-related internships or fieldwork, Federal Work-Study, and scholarships/grants available. Financial award application deadline: 4/1; financial award applicants required to submit FAFSA. *Unit head:* Michael Fink, Dean, School of Fashion. *Application contact:* Jenny Jaquillard, Executive Director of Admissions, Recruitment and Events, 912-525-5100, Fax: 912-525-5985, E-mail: admission@scad.edu.
Website: http://www.scad.edu/academics/programs/accessory-design

Savannah College of Art and Design, Graduate School, Program in Furniture Design, Savannah, GA 31402-3146. Offers MA, MFA. Part-time programs available. *Faculty:* 4 full-time (1 woman), 1 part-time/adjunct (0 women). *Students:* 14 full-time (7 women), 4 part-time (3 women); includes 2 minority (both Hispanic/Latino), 11 international. Average age 29. 14 applicants, 50% accepted, 4 enrolled. In 2014, 8 master's awarded. *Degree requirements:* For master's, thesis (for some programs), final project (for MA); internship (for MFA). *Entrance requirements:* For master's, portfolio. Additional exam requirements/recommendations for international students: Required—TOEFL (minimum score 550 paper-based, 85 iBT), IELTS (minimum score 6.5), or ACTFL. *Application deadline:* For fall admission, 4/1 for domestic and international students. Applications are processed on a rolling basis. Application fee: $40. Electronic applications accepted. *Expenses: Tuition:* Full-time $34,605; part-time $3845 per course. One-time fee: $500. Tuition and fees vary according to course load. *Financial support:* Fellowships, career-related internships or fieldwork, Federal Work-Study, and scholarships/grants available. Financial award application deadline: 4/1; financial award applicants required to submit FAFSA. *Unit head:* Fred Spector, Program Coordinator. *Application contact:* Jenny Jaquillard, Executive Director of Admissions, Recruitment and Events, 912-525-5100, Fax: 912-525-5985, E-mail: admission@scad.edu.
Website: http://www.scad.edu/academics/programs/furniture-design

Savannah College of Art and Design, Graduate School, Program in Jewelry, Savannah, GA 31402-3146. Offers MA, MFA. Part-time programs available. *Faculty:* 5 full-time (4 women). *Students:* 12 full-time (11 women), 3 part-time (all women), 9 international. Average age 29. 21 applicants, 52% accepted, 3 enrolled. In 2014, 4 master's awarded. *Degree requirements:* For master's, thesis (for some programs), final project (for MA); internship (for MFA). *Entrance requirements:* For master's, portfolio. Additional exam requirements/recommendations for international students: Required—TOEFL (minimum score 550 paper-based, 85 iBT), IELTS (minimum score 6.5), or ACTFL. *Application deadline:* For fall admission, 4/1 for domestic and international students. Applications are processed on a rolling basis. Application fee: $40. Electronic applications accepted. *Expenses: Tuition:* Full-time $34,605; part-time $3845 per course. One-time fee: $500. Tuition and fees vary according to course load. *Financial support:* Fellowships, career-related internships or fieldwork, Federal Work-Study, and scholarships/grants available. Financial award application deadline: 4/1; financial award applicants required to submit FAFSA. *Unit head:* Jay Song, Chair. *Application contact:* Jenny Jaquillard, Executive Director of Admissions, Recruitment and Events, 912-525-5100, Fax: 912-525-5985, E-mail: admission@scad.edu.
Website: http://www.scad.edu/academics/programs/jewelry

Savannah College of Art and Design, Graduate School, Program in Painting, Savannah, GA 31402-3146. Offers MA, MFA. Part-time programs available. Postbaccalaureate distance learning degree programs offered (minimal on-campus study). *Faculty:* 10 full-time (3 women), 1 (woman) part-time/adjunct. *Students:* 52 full-time (33 women), 25 part-time (14 women); includes 13 minority (5 Black or African American, non-Hispanic/Latino; 1 American Indian or Alaska Native, non-Hispanic/Latino; 2 Asian, non-Hispanic/Latino; 5 Hispanic/Latino), 21 international. Average age 33. 59 applicants, 53% accepted, 9 enrolled. In 2014, 25 master's awarded. *Degree requirements:* For master's, thesis (for some programs), final project (for MA); internship (for MFA). *Entrance requirements:* For master's, portfolio. Additional exam requirements/recommendations for international students: Required—TOEFL (minimum score 550 paper-based, 85 iBT), IELTS (minimum score 6.5), or ACTFL. *Application deadline:* For fall admission, 4/1 for domestic and international students. Applications are processed on a rolling basis. Application fee: $40. Electronic applications accepted. *Expenses: Tuition:* Full-time $34,605; part-time $3845 per course. One-time fee: $500. Tuition and fees vary according to course load. *Financial support:* Fellowships, career-related internships or fieldwork, Federal Work-Study, and scholarships/grants available. Financial award application deadline: 4/1; financial award applicants required to submit FAFSA. *Unit head:* Denise Carson, Chair. *Application contact:* Jenny Jaquillard, Executive Director of Admissions, Recruitment and Events, 912-525-5100, Fax: 912-525-5985, E-mail: admission@scad.edu.
Website: http://www.scad.edu/academics/programs/painting

Savannah College of Art and Design, Graduate School, Program in Printmaking, Savannah, GA 31402-3146. Offers MFA. Part-time programs available. *Faculty:* 4 full-time (3 women), 1 part-time/adjunct (0 women). *Students:* 8 full-time (7 women), 1 (woman) part-time, 5 international. Average age 28. 3 applicants, 33% accepted. In 2014, 4 master's awarded. *Degree requirements:* For master's, thesis, internship. *Entrance requirements:* For master's, portfolio. Additional exam requirements/recommendations for international students: Required—TOEFL (minimum score 550 paper-based, 85 iBT), IELTS (minimum score 6.5), or ACTFL. *Application deadline:* For fall admission, 4/1 for domestic and international students. Applications are processed on a rolling basis. Application fee: $40. Electronic applications accepted. *Expenses: Tuition:* Full-time $34,605; part-time $3845 per course. One-time fee: $500. Tuition and fees vary according to course load. *Financial support:* Fellowships, career-related

internships or fieldwork, Federal Work-Study, and scholarships/grants available. Financial award application deadline: 4/1; financial award applicants required to submit FAFSA. *Unit head:* Robert Brown, Chair. *Application contact:* Jenny Jaquillard, Executive Director of Admissions, Recruitment and Events, 912-525-5100, Fax: 912-525-5985, E-mail: admission@scad.edu.
Website: http://www.scad.edu/academics/programs/printmaking

Savannah College of Art and Design, Graduate School, Program in Sculpture, Savannah, GA 31402-3146. Offers MA, MFA. Part-time programs available. *Faculty:* 2 full-time (1 woman), 2 part-time/adjunct (0 women). *Students:* 12 full-time (7 women), 5 part-time (3 women); includes 1 minority (American Indian or Alaska Native, non-Hispanic/Latino), 5 international. Average age 31. 9 applicants, 22% accepted, 2 enrolled. In 2014, 4 master's awarded. *Degree requirements:* For master's, thesis (for some programs), final project (for MA); internship (for MFA). *Entrance requirements:* For master's, portfolio. Additional exam requirements/recommendations for international students: Required—TOEFL (minimum score 550 paper-based, 85 iBT), IELTS (minimum score 6.5), or ACTFL. *Application deadline:* For fall admission, 4/1 for domestic and international students. Applications are processed on a rolling basis. Application fee: $40. Electronic applications accepted. *Expenses: Tuition:* Full-time $34,605; part-time $3845 per course. One-time fee: $500. Tuition and fees vary according to course load. *Financial support:* Fellowships, career-related internships or fieldwork, Federal Work-Study, and scholarships/grants available. Financial award application deadline: 4/1; financial award applicants required to submit FAFSA. *Unit head:* Susan Krause, Chair. *Application contact:* Jenny Jaquillard, Executive Director of Admissions, Recruitment and Events, 912-525-5100, Fax: 912-525-5985, E-mail: admission@scad.edu.
Website: http://www.scad.edu/academics/programs/sculpture

Savannah College of Art and Design, Graduate School, Program in Visual Effects, Savannah, GA 31402-3146. Offers MA, MFA. Part-time programs available. *Faculty:* 15 full-time (5 women). *Students:* 57 full-time (20 women), 12 part-time (4 women); includes 8 minority (3 Black or African American, non-Hispanic/Latino; 1 Asian, non-Hispanic/Latino; 4 Hispanic/Latino), 41 international. Average age 26. 51 applicants, 53% accepted, 21 enrolled. In 2014, 22 master's awarded. *Degree requirements:* For master's, thesis (for some programs), internship (for MFA). *Entrance requirements:* For master's, portfolio (in digital or multimedia format). Additional exam requirements/recommendations for international students: Required—TOEFL (minimum score 550 paper-based, 85 iBT), IELTS (minimum score 6.5), or ACTFL. *Application deadline:* For fall admission, 4/1 for domestic and international students. Applications are processed on a rolling basis. Application fee: $40. Electronic applications accepted. *Expenses: Tuition:* Full-time $34,605; part-time $3845 per course. One-time fee: $500. Tuition and fees vary according to course load. *Financial support:* Fellowships available. Financial award application deadline: 4/1; financial award applicants required to submit FAFSA. *Unit head:* Barbara McCullough, Chair. *Application contact:* Jenny Jaquillard, Executive Director of Admissions, Recruitment and Events, 912-525-5100, Fax: 912-525-5985, E-mail: admission@scad.edu.
Website: http://www.scad.edu/academics/programs/visual-effects

School of the Art Institute of Chicago, Graduate Division, Department of Art and Technology Studies, Chicago, IL 60603-3103. Offers MFA. *Entrance requirements:* Additional exam requirements/recommendations for international students: Required—TOEFL, IELTS. Electronic applications accepted.

School of the Art Institute of Chicago, Graduate Division, Department of Ceramics, Chicago, IL 60603-3103. Offers MFA. *Accreditation:* NASAD. *Entrance requirements:* Additional exam requirements/recommendations for international students: Required—TOEFL, IELTS. Electronic applications accepted.

School of the Art Institute of Chicago, Graduate Division, Department of Fiber and Material Studies, Chicago, IL 60603-3103. Offers MFA. *Accreditation:* NASAD. *Entrance requirements:* Additional exam requirements/recommendations for international students: Required—TOEFL, IELTS.

School of the Art Institute of Chicago, Graduate Division, Department of Painting and Drawing, Chicago, IL 60603-3103. Offers MFA. *Accreditation:* NASAD. *Entrance requirements:* Additional exam requirements/recommendations for international students: Required—TOEFL, IELTS.

School of the Art Institute of Chicago, Graduate Division, Department of Printmaking, Chicago, IL 60603-3103. Offers MFA. *Accreditation:* NASAD. *Entrance requirements:* Additional exam requirements/recommendations for international students: Required—TOEFL (minimum score 550 paper-based; 80 iBT), IELTS (minimum score 6.5).

School of the Art Institute of Chicago, Graduate Division, Department of Sculpture, Chicago, IL 60603-3103. Offers MFA. *Accreditation:* NASAD. *Entrance requirements:* Additional exam requirements/recommendations for international students: Required—TOEFL, IELTS.

School of the Art Institute of Chicago, Graduate Division, Program in Visual and Critical Studies, Chicago, IL 60603-3103. Offers MA.

School of the Museum of Fine Arts, Boston, Graduate Programs, Boston, MA 02115. Offers art education (MAT); studio art (MFA, Postbaccalaureate Certificate). *Accreditation:* NASAD (one or more programs are accredited). Postbaccalaureate distance learning degree programs offered. *Faculty:* 37 full-time (21 women), 30 part-time/adjunct (17 women). *Students:* 156 full-time (115 women), 7 part-time (4 women); includes 28 minority (6 Black or African American, non-Hispanic/Latino; 1 American Indian or Alaska Native, non-Hispanic/Latino; 6 Asian, non-Hispanic/Latino; 11 Hispanic/Latino; 4 Two or more races, non-Hispanic/Latino), 35 international. Average age 30. 275 applicants, 82% accepted, 102 enrolled. In 2014, 85 master's, 29 other advanced degrees awarded. Terminal master's awarded for partial completion of doctoral program. *Degree requirements:* For master's, thesis (for some programs), exhibition thesis. *Entrance requirements:* For master's, BFA, bachelor's degree or equivalent in related area, portfolio; for Postbaccalaureate Certificate, portfolio, BFA or equivalent. Additional exam requirements/recommendations for international students: Required—TOEFL (minimum score 550 paper-based). *Application deadline:* For fall admission, 2/1 priority date for domestic and international students. Applications are processed on a rolling basis. Application fee: $65. Electronic applications accepted. *Expenses: Tuition:* Full-time $40,676; part-time $1500 per credit. *Required fees:* $782; $391 per semester. Tuition and fees vary according to degree level and student level. *Financial support:* In 2014–15, 14 fellowships (averaging $3,000 per year), 30 teaching assistantships (averaging $1,500 per year) were awarded; career-related internships or fieldwork, Federal Work-Study, scholarships/grants, tuition waivers (partial), and unspecified assistantships also available. Support available to part-time students. Financial award application deadline: 2/15; financial award applicants required to submit FAFSA. *Faculty research:* Public art commissions, National Endowment for the Arts grant recipients, international exhibitions. *Unit head:* Lisa Bynoe, Associate Dean of Graduate Programs, 617-369-3870, E-mail: lbynoe@smfa.edu. *Application contact:* Admissions Representative, 617-369-3626, Fax: 617-369-4264, E-mail: admissions@smfa.edu.
Website: http://www.smfa.edu/

School of Visual Arts, Graduate Programs, Art Practice Department, New York, NY 10010-3994. Offers MFA. *Degree requirements:* For master's, thesis. *Entrance requirements:* For master's, portfolio submitted through SlideRoom; 500- to 750-word writing sample. Additional exam requirements/recommendations for international students: Required—TOEFL (minimum score 550 paper-based; 100 iBT), IELTS (minimum score 8). Electronic applications accepted.

School of Visual Arts, Graduate Programs, Computer Art Department, New York, NY 10010-3994. Offers MFA. *Accreditation:* NASAD. *Degree requirements:* For master's, thesis, 60 credits, including all required courses; minimum GPA of 3.0; matriculation of two academic years. *Entrance requirements:* For master's, portfolio; 3-5 minute sample reel showing best work; statement of purpose; official transcript; 3 letters of recommendation; resume/curriculum vitae. Additional exam requirements/recommendations for international students: Required—TOEFL (minimum score 550 paper-based; 79 iBT). Electronic applications accepted. *Expenses:* Contact institution.

School of Visual Arts, Graduate Programs, Design Department, New York, NY 10010-3994. Offers MFA. *Accreditation:* NASAD. *Degree requirements:* For master's, thesis, 60 credits, including all required courses; minimum cumulative GPA of 3.0; residency of two academic years. *Entrance requirements:* For master's, portfolio that reflects wide range of design work and fluency in type and typography. Additional exam requirements/recommendations for international students: Required—TOEFL (minimum score 550 paper-based; 79 iBT). *Expenses:* Contact institution. *Faculty research:* Design, graphic design, multimedia.

School of Visual Arts, Graduate Programs, Fine Arts Department, New York, NY 10010-3994. Offers painting (MFA). *Accreditation:* NASAD. *Degree requirements:* For master's, thesis, 60 credits, including all required courses; residency of two academic years. *Entrance requirements:* For master's, CD portfolio of work with exactly 12 images. Additional exam requirements/recommendations for international students: Required—TOEFL (minimum score 550 paper-based; 79 iBT). Electronic applications accepted.

School of Visual Arts, Graduate Programs, Illustration as Visual Essay Department, New York, NY 10010-3994. Offers MFA. *Accreditation:* NASAD. *Degree requirements:* For master's, thesis, 60 credits, including all required courses; residency of two academic years. *Entrance requirements:* For master's, portfolio of work (still images) submitted through SlideRoom. Additional exam requirements/recommendations for international students: Required—TOEFL (minimum score 100 iBT). Electronic applications accepted. *Faculty research:* Illustration, fine arts, computer art, writing, art history, art direction.

School of Visual Arts, Graduate Programs, Program in Photography, Video and Related Media, New York, NY 10010-3994. Offers MFA. *Accreditation:* NASAD. *Degree requirements:* For master's, thesis, 60 credits and all course requirements; minimum GPA of 3.3; thesis project. *Entrance requirements:* For master's, portfolio (still images and/or videos) through SlideRoom. Additional exam requirements/recommendations for international students: Required—TOEFL (minimum score 550 paper-based; 79 iBT). Electronic applications accepted. *Faculty research:* Contemporary and responsible creative initiatives, including experimental, narrative or documentary video, installation and conceptual art, tableau and real-world-witness photography.

Sotheby's Institute of Art–London, Graduate Programs, London, United Kingdom. Offers art business (MA); contemporary art (MA); contemporary design (MA); East Asian art (MA); fine and decorative art (MA); photography (MA). *Faculty:* 38 full-time (22 women). *Students:* 175 full-time (153 women). *Application contact:* Melba Remice, Director, Global Admissions, 212-517-2834, E-mail: admissions@sothebysinstitute.com.

Sotheby's Institute of Art–New York, Graduate Programs, New York, NY 10021. Offers American fine and decorative art (MA); art business (MA); contemporary art (MA). *Accreditation:* NASAD. *Faculty:* 25 full-time (12 women). *Students:* 153 full-time (141 women). *Entrance requirements:* For master's, academic transcripts, two letters of academic reference, personal statement, writing sample, curriculum vitae/resume, interview. Application fee: $100. Electronic applications accepted. *Application contact:* Melba Remice, Director of Global Admissions, 212-517-2834, E-mail: admissions@sothebysinstitute.com.
Website: http://www.sothebysinstitute.com/Programmes/PNewyork.aspx

Southern Illinois University Carbondale, Graduate School, College of Liberal Arts, School of Art and Design, Carbondale, IL 62901-4701. Offers drawing (MFA); fiber/weaving (MFA); glass (MFA); metalsmithing/blacksmithing (MFA); painting (MFA). *Accreditation:* NASAD. *Faculty:* 23 full-time (7 women). *Students:* 41 full-time (21 women); includes 2 minority (1 American Indian or Alaska Native, non-Hispanic/Latino; 1 Asian, non-Hispanic/Latino), 5 international. Average age 29. 44 applicants, 32% accepted, 11 enrolled. In 2014, 13 master's awarded. *Degree requirements:* For master's, thesis or alternative. *Entrance requirements:* For master's, minimum GPA of 2.7, portfolio, slides. Additional exam requirements/recommendations for international students: Required—TOEFL. *Application deadline:* For fall admission, 3/1 priority date for domestic students. Applications are processed on a rolling basis. Application fee: $50. *Expenses:* Tuition, state resident: full-time $10,176; part-time $1153 per credit. Tuition, nonresident: full-time $20,814; part-time $1744 per credit. *Required fees:* $7092; $394 per credit. $2364 per semester. *Financial support:* In 2014–15, 3 fellowships with full tuition reimbursements, 5 research assistantships with full tuition reimbursements, 40 teaching assistantships with full tuition reimbursements were awarded; Federal Work-Study, institutionally sponsored loans, and tuition waivers (full) also available. Support available to part-time students. Financial award application deadline: 4/1. *Faculty research:* Prints/woodcuts, foundry, watercolor. *Unit head:* Jerry Monteith, Director, 618-453-7760, Fax: 618-453-7710, E-mail: monteith@siu.edu. *Application contact:* Diane McClain-Inman, Office Specialist, 618-453-4313, Fax: 618-453-7710, E-mail: dinman@siu.edu.

Southern Illinois University Edwardsville, Graduate School, College of Arts and Sciences, Department of Art and Design, Program in Art Studio, Edwardsville, IL 62026-0001. Offers MFA. Part-time programs available. *Students:* 17 full-time (11 women), 3 part-time (2 women); includes 1 minority (Two or more races, non-Hispanic/Latino), 1 international. 20 applicants, 35% accepted. In 2014, 3 master's awarded. *Degree requirements:* For master's, thesis, exhibition. *Entrance requirements:* For master's, portfolio. Additional exam requirements/recommendations for international students: Required—TOEFL (minimum score 550 paper-based; 79 iBT), IELTS (minimum score 6.5). *Application deadline:* For fall admission, 2/1 for domestic and international students. Application fee: $30. Electronic applications accepted. *Expenses:* Tuition, state resident: full-time $5026. Tuition, nonresident: full-time $12,566. *International tuition:* $25,136 full-time. *Required fees:* $1682. Tuition and fees vary according to course load, campus/location and program. *Financial support:* In 2014–15, 16 students received support, including 1 fellowship with full tuition reimbursement available (averaging $8,370 per year), 6 research assistantships with full tuition reimbursements available, 9 teaching assistantships with full tuition reimbursements available; Federal Work-Study, institutionally sponsored loans, and unspecified assistantships also available. Support available to part-time students. Financial award application deadline: 3/1; financial award applicants required to submit FAFSA. *Unit head:* Dr. Barbara Nwacha, Chair, 618-650-3074, E-mail: bnwacha@siue.edu. *Application contact:* Melissa

K. Mace, Assistant Director of Admissions for Graduate and International Recruitment, 618-650-2756, Fax: 618-650-3618, E-mail: mmace@siue.edu.
Website: http://www.siue.edu/artsandsciences/art/master_fine_studio.shtml

Southern Methodist University, Meadows School of the Arts, Division of Art, Dallas, TX 75275. Offers studio art (MFA), including ceramics, drawing, painting, photography, printmaking, sculpture. *Accreditation:* NASAD. *Degree requirements:* For master's, thesis or alternative, exhibit. *Entrance requirements:* For master's, BFA or equivalent, letters of recommendation, portfolio. Additional exam requirements/recommendations for international students: Required—TOEFL (minimum score 550 paper-based; 80 iBT). *Faculty research:* American stoneware, Southwestern furniture traditions, photographic apparatus and techniques, American ceramists, architecture.

Southwest University of Visual Arts, MFA Programs, Tucson, AZ 85716-2505. Offers motion arts (MFA); painting and drawing (MFA); photography (MFA).

Spring Hill College, Graduate Programs, Program in Liberal Arts, Mobile, AL 36608-1791. Offers fine arts (MLA); history and social science (MLA); leadership and ethics (MLA, Postbaccalaureate Certificate); literature (MLA); studio art (Postbaccalaureate Certificate). Part-time and evening/weekend programs available. *Faculty:* 6 full-time (1 woman), 3 part-time/adjunct (all women). *Students:* 3 full-time (1 woman), 33 part-time (18 women); includes 9 minority (8 Black or African American, non-Hispanic/Latino; 1 American Indian or Alaska Native, non-Hispanic/Latino), 1 international. Average age 36. In 2014, 8 master's awarded. *Degree requirements:* For master's, capstone course, completion of program within 6 years of initial admittance. *Entrance requirements:* For master's, bachelor's degree with minimum undergraduate GPA of 3.0 or graduate/professional degree. Additional exam requirements/recommendations for international students: Required—TOEFL (minimum score 550 paper-based; 80 iBT), IELTS (minimum score 6.5), CPE or CAE (minimum score C), Michigan English Language Assessment Battery (minimum score 90). *Application deadline:* For fall admission, 8/1 priority date for domestic and international students; for spring admission, 12/1 priority date for domestic and international students. Applications are processed on a rolling basis. Application fee: $25 ($35 for international students). Electronic applications accepted. *Expenses:* Expenses: Contact institution. *Financial support:* Applicants required to submit FAFSA. *Unit head:* Dr. Thomas J. Hoffman, Director, 251-380-4184, Fax: 251-460-2115, E-mail: thoffman@shc.edu. *Application contact:* Robert Stewart, Vice President of Enrollment, 251-380-3030, Fax: 251-460-2186, E-mail: rstewart@shc.edu.
Website: http://ug.shc.edu/graduate-degrees/master-liberal-arts/

Stanford University, School of Humanities and Sciences, Department of Art and Art History, Stanford, CA 94305-9991. Offers art history (PhD); art practice (MFA); design (MFA, MS); documentary film and video (MFA); MS/MFA. *Degree requirements:* For master's, thesis (for some programs), faculty reviews; for doctorate, 2 foreign languages, thesis/dissertation. *Entrance requirements:* For master's and doctorate, GRE General Test. Additional exam requirements/recommendations for international students: Required—TOEFL. Electronic applications accepted. *Expenses: Tuition:* Full-time $44,184; part-time $982 per credit hour. *Required fees:* $191.

State University of New York at New Paltz, Graduate School, School of Fine and Performing Arts, Department of Fine Arts, New Paltz, NY 12561. Offers art studio (MA); ceramics (MFA); metal (MFA); painting/drawing (MFA); printmaking (MFA); sculpture (MFA). *Accreditation:* NASAD (one or more programs are accredited). Part-time and evening/weekend programs available. *Faculty:* 17 full-time (8 women), 1 part-time/adjunct (0 women). *Students:* 36 full-time (29 women), 1 (woman) part-time; includes 5 minority (1 Black or African American, non-Hispanic/Latino; 1 American Indian or Alaska Native, non-Hispanic/Latino; 1 Asian, non-Hispanic/Latino; 2 Hispanic/Latino), 8 international. Average age 30. 87 applicants, 56% accepted, 23 enrolled. In 2014, 18 master's awarded. *Degree requirements:* For master's, thesis, portfolio, exhibit (MFA). *Entrance requirements:* For master's, minimum GPA of 3.0, portfolio. Additional exam requirements/recommendations for international students: Required—TOEFL (minimum score 550 paper-based; 80 iBT), IELTS (minimum score 6.5). *Application deadline:* For fall admission, 2/15 priority date for domestic and international students. Applications are processed on a rolling basis. Application fee: $50. Electronic applications accepted. *Financial support:* . In 2014–15, 7 teaching assistantships with partial tuition reimbursements (averaging $5,000 per year) were awarded. Financial award application deadline: 8/1. *Unit head:* Prof. Anne Galperin, Chair, 845-257-3833, E-mail: galperia@newpaltz.edu. *Application contact:* Prof. Matthew Friday, Graduate Coordinator, 845-257-2609, E-mail: fridaym@newpaltz.edu.
Website: http://www.newpaltz.edu/art/

State University of New York at Oswego, Graduate Studies, Department of Art, Oswego, NY 13126. Offers MA. *Accreditation:* NASAD. Part-time programs available. *Degree requirements:* For master's, exhibit, final presentation. *Entrance requirements:* For master's, slides of previous work. Additional exam requirements/recommendations for international students: Required—TOEFL (minimum score 560 paper-based). *Faculty research:* Ancient and primitive art, nineteenth century art, medieval art, Renaissance art.

Stephen F. Austin State University, Graduate School, College of Fine Arts, School of Art, Nacogdoches, TX 75962. Offers art (MA); design (MFA); drawing (MFA); painting (MFA); sculpture (MFA). *Accreditation:* NASAD. Part-time programs available. *Degree requirements:* For master's, comprehensive exam, thesis, exhibit. *Entrance requirements:* For master's, GRE General Test, portfolio. Additional exam requirements/recommendations for international students: Required—TOEFL. *Faculty research:* Printmaking, jewelry, photography, ceramics, art history.

Stony Brook University, State University of New York, Graduate School, College of Arts and Sciences, Department of Art, Program in Studio Art, Stony Brook, NY 11794. Offers MFA. *Students:* 12 full-time (10 women); includes 4 minority (1 Black or African American, non-Hispanic/Latino; 3 Hispanic/Latino), 2 international. Average age 32. In 2014, 1 master's awarded. *Degree requirements:* For master's, comprehensive exam, thesis, reading knowledge of German, French, or Italian; exhibition. *Entrance requirements:* For master's, GRE General Test, minimum undergraduate GPA of 3.0. Additional exam requirements/recommendations for international students: Required—TOEFL. *Application deadline:* For fall admission, 1/15 priority date for domestic students. Application fee: $100. *Expenses:* Tuition, state resident: full-time $10,370; part-time $432 per credit. Tuition, nonresident: full-time $20,190; part-time $841 per credit. *Required fees:* $1431. *Unit head:* Dr. John Lutterbie, Director, 631-632-7250, E-mail: john.lutterbie@stonybrook.edu. *Application contact:* Lisa Perez, Coordinator, 631-632-7270, Fax: 631-632-7261, E-mail: lisa.perez@stonybrook.edu.
Website: http://art.stonybrook.edu/graduate-programs/mfa-program/

Sul Ross State University, School of Arts and Sciences, Department of Fine Arts and Communication, Alpine, TX 79832. Offers art history (MA); studio art (MA), including art education, ceramics, painting, sculpture. Part-time programs available. *Degree requirements:* For master's, oral or written exam. *Entrance requirements:* For master's, GRE General Test, minimum GPA of 2.5 in last 60 hours of undergraduate work. *Faculty research:* Ceramic sculpture, watercolor, wood sculpture, rock art.

Syracuse University, College of Visual and Performing Arts, Program in Ceramics, Syracuse, NY 13244. Offers MFA. *Accreditation:* NASAD. Part-time programs available. *Students:* 7 full-time (3 women), 1 part-time (0 women); includes 3 minority (1 Hispanic/Latino; 2 Two or more races, non-Hispanic/Latino). Average age 28. 24 applicants, 33% accepted, 3 enrolled. In 2014, 2 master's awarded. *Degree requirements:* For master's, thesis or alternative. *Entrance requirements:* For master's, portfolio. Additional exam requirements/recommendations for international students: Required—TOEFL (minimum score 100 iBT). *Application deadline:* For fall admission, 2/1 priority date for domestic and international students. Application fee: $75. Electronic applications accepted. *Expenses: Tuition:* Part-time $1341 per credit. *Financial support:* Fellowships with full tuition reimbursements, teaching assistantships with full and partial tuition reimbursements, and tuition waivers available. Financial award application deadline: 1/1; financial award applicants required to submit FAFSA. *Unit head:* Prof. Errol Willet,, Department of Art C, 315-443-3700, E-mail: eswillet@syr.edu. *Application contact:* Therese West, Information Contact, 315-443-0137, E-mail: admissg@syr.edu.
Website: http://vpa.syr.edu/

Syracuse University, College of Visual and Performing Arts, Program in Jewelry and Metalsmithing, Syracuse, NY 13244. Offers MFA. *Students:* 4 full-time (all women), 2 international. Average age 30. 11 applicants, 9% accepted, 1 enrolled. In 2014, 1 master's awarded. *Degree requirements:* For master's, thesis or alternative. *Entrance requirements:* For master's, portfolio. Additional exam requirements/recommendations for international students: Required—TOEFL (minimum score 100 iBT). *Application deadline:* For fall admission, 2/1 priority date for domestic and international students. Application fee: $75. Electronic applications accepted. *Expenses: Tuition:* Part-time $1341 per credit. *Financial support:* Fellowships with full tuition reimbursements and teaching assistantships with full and partial tuition reimbursements available. Financial award application deadline: 1/1; financial award applicants required to submit FAFSA. *Unit head:* Barbara Walter,, Department of Art, 315-443-3700, E-mail: bewalter@syr.edu. *Application contact:* Therese West, Information Contact, 315-443-0137, E-mail: admissg@syr.edu.
Website: http://vpa.syr.edu/art-design/art/graduate/jewelry-and-metalsmithing

Syracuse University, College of Visual and Performing Arts, Program in Painting, Syracuse, NY 13244. Offers MFA. *Students:* 8 full-time (4 women); includes 1 minority (Two or more races, non-Hispanic/Latino), 1 international. Average age 28. 29 applicants, 28% accepted, 2 enrolled. In 2014, 4 master's awarded. *Degree requirements:* For master's, thesis or alternative. *Entrance requirements:* For master's, portfolio. Additional exam requirements/recommendations for international students: Required—TOEFL (minimum score 100 iBT). *Application deadline:* For fall admission, 2/1 priority date for domestic and international students. Application fee: $75. Electronic applications accepted. *Expenses: Tuition:* Part-time $1341 per credit. *Financial support:* Fellowships with full tuition reimbursements and teaching assistantships with full and partial tuition reimbursements available. Financial award application deadline: 1/1; financial award applicants required to submit FAFSA. *Unit head:* Kevin Larmon, Kevin Larmon, Department of Art, 315-443-4613, E-mail: klarmon@syr.edu. *Application contact:* Therese West, Information Contact, 315-443-0137, E-mail: admissg@syr.edu.
Website: http://vpa.syr.edu/art-design/art/graduate/painting

Syracuse University, College of Visual and Performing Arts, Program in Printmaking, Syracuse, NY 13244. Offers MFA. *Students:* 6 full-time (1 woman), 1 part-time (0 women); includes 2 minority (1 Asian, non-Hispanic/Latino; 1 Hispanic/Latino). Average age 31. 16 applicants, 19% accepted, 2 enrolled. In 2014, 2 master's awarded. *Degree requirements:* For master's, thesis or alternative. *Entrance requirements:* For master's, portfolio. Additional exam requirements/recommendations for international students: Required—TOEFL (minimum score 100 iBT). *Application deadline:* For fall admission, 2/1 priority date for domestic and international students. Application fee: $75. Electronic applications accepted. *Expenses: Tuition:* Part-time $1341 per credit. *Financial support:* Fellowships with full tuition reimbursements and teaching assistantships with full and partial tuition reimbursements available. Financial award application deadline: 1/1; financial award applicants required to submit FAFSA. *Unit head:* Dusty Herbig,, Department of Art, 315-443-3700, E-mail: dtherbig@syr.edu. *Application contact:* Therese West, Information Contact, 315-443-0137, E-mail: admissg@syr.edu.
Website: http://vpa.syr.edu/art-design/art/graduate/printmaking

Syracuse University, College of Visual and Performing Arts, Program in Sculpture, Syracuse, NY 13244. Offers MFA. *Students:* 5 full-time (1 woman); includes 2 minority (1 Asian, non-Hispanic/Latino; 1 Two or more races, non-Hispanic/Latino), 2 international. Average age 26. 23 applicants, 17% accepted, 2 enrolled. In 2014, 1 master's awarded. *Degree requirements:* For master's, thesis or alternative. *Entrance requirements:* For master's, portfolio. Additional exam requirements/recommendations for international students: Required—TOEFL (minimum score 100 iBT). *Application deadline:* For fall admission, 2/1 priority date for domestic and international students. Application fee: $75. Electronic applications accepted. *Expenses: Tuition:* Part-time $1341 per credit. *Financial support:* Fellowships with full tuition reimbursements and teaching assistantships with full and partial tuition reimbursements available. Financial award application deadline: 1/1; financial award applicants required to submit FAFSA. *Unit head:* Jude Lewis,, Department of Art, 315-443-3700, E-mail: jllewis@syr.edu. *Application contact:* Therese West, Information Contact, 315-443-0137, E-mail: admissg@syr.edu.
Website: http://vpa.syr.edu/art-design/art/graduate/sculpture

Temple University, Center for the Arts, Tyler School of Art, Department of Crafts, Philadelphia, PA 19122-6096. Offers ceramics/glass (MFA); fibers and material studies (MFA); metals/jewelry/CAD-CAM (MFA). *Faculty:* 7 full-time (3 women), 18 part-time/adjunct (14 women). *Students:* 17 full-time (11 women), 1 part-time (0 women); includes 2 minority (1 Asian, non-Hispanic/Latino; 1 Hispanic/Latino), 2 international. 65 applicants, 28% accepted, 9 enrolled. In 2014, 8 master's awarded. *Degree requirements:* For master's, essay, exhibit. *Entrance requirements:* For master's, minimum GPA of 3.0, slide portfolio, 40 credits in studio art, 12 credits in art history, letters of recommendation, resume/curriculum vitae. Additional exam requirements/recommendations for international students: Required—TOEFL (minimum score 550 paper-based; 79 iBT), IELTS (minimum score 6.5). *Application deadline:* For fall admission, 1/15 for domestic students, 12/15 for international students. Application fee: $60. Electronic applications accepted. *Expenses:* Expenses: Contact institution. *Financial support:* Fellowships with full tuition reimbursements, research assistantships with full tuition reimbursements, teaching assistantships with full tuition reimbursements, and Federal Work-Study available. Support available to part-time students. Financial award application deadline: 1/15; financial award applicants required to submit FAFSA. *Unit head:* Nicholas Kripal, Chair, 215-782-2790, Fax: 215-782-2799, E-mail: nkripal@temple.edu. *Application contact:* Nicole Hall, Director of Admissions, 215-777-9090, E-mail: tylerart@temple.edu.

Temple University, Center for the Arts, Tyler School of Art, Department of Graphic Arts and Design, Philadelphia, PA 19122-6096. Offers graphic and interactive design (MFA); photography (MFA); printmaking (MFA). *Faculty:* 13 full-time (5 women), 22 part-time/adjunct (9 women). *Students:* 19 full-time (13 women); includes 2 minority (both Hispanic/Latino). 155 applicants, 12% accepted, 8 enrolled. In 2014, 8 master's awarded. *Degree requirements:* For master's, essay, exhibit. *Entrance requirements:* For master's, minimum GPA of 3.0, slide portfolio, 40 credits in studio art, 12 credits in art history, letters of recommendation, resume/curriculum vitae. Additional exam

requirements/recommendations for international students: Required—TOEFL (minimum score 550 paper-based; 79 iBT), IELTS (minimum score 6.5). *Application deadline:* For fall admission, 1/15 for domestic students, 12/15 for international students. Application fee: $60. Electronic applications accepted. *Expenses:* Expenses: Contact institution. *Financial support:* Fellowships with full tuition reimbursements, research assistantships with full tuition reimbursements, teaching assistantships with full tuition reimbursements, and Federal Work-Study available. Support available to part-time students. Financial award application deadline: 1/15; financial award applicants required to submit FAFSA. *Unit head:* Stephanie Knopp, Chair, 215-782-2932, Fax: 215-782-2799, E-mail: stephanie.knopp@temple.edu. *Application contact:* Nicole Hall, Director of Admissions, 215-777-9090, E-mail: tylerart@temple.edu.
Website: http://tyler.temple.edu/graduate

Temple University, Center for the Arts, Tyler School of Art, Department of Painting, Drawing, and Sculpture, Philadelphia, PA 19122-6096. Offers painting (MFA); sculpture (MFA). *Faculty:* 13 full-time (8 women), 3 part-time/adjunct (1 woman). *Students:* 22 full-time (7 women); includes 7 minority (2 Black or African American, non-Hispanic/Latino; 4 Hispanic/Latino; 1 Native Hawaiian or other Pacific Islander, non-Hispanic/Latino), 1 international. 207 applicants, 8% accepted, 13 enrolled. In 2014, 11 master's awarded. *Degree requirements:* For master's, essay, exhibit. *Entrance requirements:* For master's, minimum GPA of 3.0, slide portfolio, 40 credits in studio art, 12 credits in art history, letters of recommendation, resume/curriculum vitae. Additional exam requirements/recommendations for international students: Required—TOEFL (minimum score 550 paper-based; 79 iBT), IELTS (minimum score 6.5). *Application deadline:* For fall admission, 1/15 for domestic students, 12/15 for international students. Application fee: $60. Electronic applications accepted. *Expenses:* Expenses: Contact institution. *Financial support:* Fellowships with full tuition reimbursements, research assistantships with full tuition reimbursements, teaching assistantships with full tuition reimbursements, and Federal Work-Study available. Support available to part-time students. Financial award application deadline: 1/15; financial award applicants required to submit FAFSA. *Unit head:* Margo Margolis, Chair, 215-782-2870, Fax: 215-782-2799, E-mail: margom@temple.edu. *Application contact:* Nicole Hall, Director of Admissions, 215-777-9090, E-mail: tylerart@temple.edu.

Texas A&M University, College of Architecture, Department of Visualization, College Station, TX 77843. Offers MFA, MS. *Faculty:* 12. *Students:* 73 full-time (29 women), 23 part-time (7 women); includes 19 minority (6 Asian, non-Hispanic/Latino; 10 Hispanic/Latino; 3 Two or more races, non-Hispanic/Latino), 23 international. Average age 26. 42 applicants, 93% accepted, 30 enrolled. In 2014, 14 master's awarded. *Application deadline:* For fall admission, 1/5 for domestic students. Application fee: $50 ($90 for international students). *Expenses:* Tuition, state resident: full-time $4078; part-time $226.55 per credit hour. Tuition, nonresident: full-time $10,594; part-time $577.55 per credit hour. *Required fees:* $2813; $237.70 per credit hour. $278.50 per semester. Tuition and fees vary according to degree level and student level. *Financial support:* In 2014–15, 73 students received support, including 1 fellowship with full and partial tuition reimbursement available (averaging $30,563 per year), 23 research assistantships with full and partial tuition reimbursements available (averaging $3,742 per year), 42 teaching assistantships with full and partial tuition reimbursements available (averaging $3,374 per year); career-related internships or fieldwork, institutionally sponsored loans, scholarships/grants, traineeships, health care benefits, tuition waivers (full and partial), and unspecified assistantships also available. Support available to part-time students. Financial award applicants required to submit FAFSA. *Unit head:* Dr. Tim McLaughlin, Department Head, 979-845-3465, E-mail: timm@viz.tamu.edu. *Application contact:* Dr. Frederic Parke, Associate Head of Department/Graduate Program Coordinator, 979-845-6596, E-mail: parke@viz.tamu.edu.
Website: http://viz.arch.tamu.edu/

Texas A&M University–Corpus Christi, College of Graduate Studies, College of Liberal Arts, Program in Studio Art, Corpus Christi, TX 78412-5503. Offers MA, MFA. Part-time and evening/weekend programs available. *Students:* 19 full-time (6 women), 6 part-time (4 women); includes 9 minority (1 Asian, non-Hispanic/Latino; 8 Hispanic/Latino). Average age 29. 34 applicants, 56% accepted, 12 enrolled. In 2014, 10 master's awarded. *Degree requirements:* For master's, comprehensive exam, thesis (for some programs). *Entrance requirements:* For master's, GRE General Test. Additional exam requirements/recommendations for international students: Required—TOEFL. *Application deadline:* For fall admission, 7/15 priority date for domestic students, 5/1 priority date for international students; for spring admission, 11/15 priority date for domestic students, 9/1 priority date for international students. Applications are processed on a rolling basis. Application fee: $50 ($70 for international students). Electronic applications accepted. *Financial support:* Research assistantships, teaching assistantships, career-related internships or fieldwork, Federal Work-Study, institutionally sponsored loans, scholarships/grants, health care benefits, and unspecified assistantships available. Support available to part-time students. Financial award application deadline: 3/15; financial award applicants required to submit FAFSA. *Unit head:* Jack Gron, Head, 361-825-3473, E-mail: jack.gron@tamucc.edu. *Application contact:* Graduate Admissions Coordinator, 361-825-2177, Fax: 361-825-2755, E-mail: gradweb@tamucc.edu.
Website: http://cla.tamucc.edu/art/graduate/art_grad.html

Texas Christian University, College of Fine Arts, School of Art, Fort Worth, TX 76129. Offers art history (MA); studio art (MFA), including painting, photography, sculpture. *Accreditation:* NASAD. *Faculty:* 12 full-time (6 women), 3 part-time/adjunct (2 women). *Students:* 18 full-time (13 women); includes 5 minority (all Hispanic/Latino). Average age 28. 27 applicants, 41% accepted, 7 enrolled. In 2014, 7 master's awarded. *Degree requirements:* For master's, variable foreign language requirement, comprehensive exam, thesis. *Entrance requirements:* For master's, GRE General Test (for MA). Additional exam requirements/recommendations for international students: Required—TOEFL (minimum score 550 paper-based; 80 iBT). *Application deadline:* For fall admission, 2/1 for domestic and international students. Application fee: $60. Electronic applications accepted. *Expenses: Tuition:* Full-time $22,860; part-time $1270 per credit hour. *Financial support:* In 2014–15, 18 students received support, including 17 teaching assistantships (averaging $10,000 per year); institutionally sponsored loans, scholarships/grants, tuition waivers, and unspecified assistantships also available. Financial award application deadline: 4/15. *Unit head:* Dr. Sally Packard, Director, 817-257-7643, E-mail: s.packard@tcu.edu. *Application contact:* Donna Smolik, TCU College of Fine Arts Graduate Office, 817-257-7603, Fax: 817-257-5672, E-mail: cfagradinfo@tcu.edu.
Website: http://www.art.tcu.edu/

Texas Southern University, College of Liberal Arts and Behavioral Sciences, Department of Fine Arts, Houston, TX 77004-4584. Offers fine arts (MA); music (MA). Part-time programs available. *Degree requirements:* For master's, one foreign language, comprehensive exam, recital. *Entrance requirements:* For master's, GRE General Test, minimum GPA of 2.5. Additional exam requirements/recommendations for international students: Required—TOEFL. Electronic applications accepted. *Faculty research:* Music theory, choral music, composition, percussion composition, ethnic musicology.

Texas Tech University, Graduate School, College of Visual and Performing Arts, Fine Arts Doctoral Program, Lubbock, TX 79409-5060. Offers art (PhD). *Accreditation:* NAST. Part-time programs available. *Students:* 51 full-time (30 women), 41 part-time (24 women); includes 11 minority (6 Black or African American, non-Hispanic/Latino; 1 Asian, non-Hispanic/Latino; 2 Hispanic/Latino; 2 Two or more races, non-Hispanic/Latino), 16 international. Average age 37. 36 applicants, 47% accepted, 14 enrolled. In 2014, 11 doctorates awarded. *Degree requirements:* For doctorate, variable foreign language requirement, comprehensive exam, thesis/dissertation. *Entrance requirements:* For doctorate, GRE General Test. Additional exam requirements/recommendations for international students: Required—TOEFL (minimum score 550 paper-based; 79 iBT). *Application deadline:* For fall admission, 6/1 for domestic students, 1/15 for international students; for spring admission, 9/1 for domestic students, 6/15 for international students. Applications are processed on a rolling basis. Application fee: $60. Electronic applications accepted. *Expenses:* Tuition, state resident: full-time $6310; part-time $262.92 per credit hour. Tuition, nonresident: full-time $14,998; part-time $624.92 per credit hour. *Required fees:* $2701; $36.50 per credit. $912.50 per semester. Tuition and fees vary according to course load. *Financial support:* In 2014–15, 130 students received support, including 81 fellowships (averaging $3,650 per year), 4 research assistantships (averaging $14,970 per year), 45 teaching assistantships (averaging $8,784 per year); Federal Work-Study, institutionally sponsored loans, scholarships/grants, health care benefits, tuition waivers (partial), and unspecified assistantships also available. Financial award application deadline: 4/15; financial award applicants required to submit FAFSA. *Faculty research:* Art criticism and theory, music, theatre arts, arts education, history of arts, interdisciplinary arts. *Unit head:* Dr. Brian D. Steele, Director/Associate Dean, College of Visual and Performing Arts, 806-742-0700, Fax: 806-742-0695, E-mail: brian.steele@ttu.edu.
Website: http://www.fadp.vpa.ttu.edu

Texas Tech University, Graduate School, College of Visual and Performing Arts, School of Art, Lubbock, TX 79409. Offers art (MFA); art education (MAE); art history (MA). *Accreditation:* NASAD (one or more programs are accredited). Part-time programs available. Postbaccalaureate distance learning degree programs offered (minimal on-campus study). *Faculty:* 33 full-time (18 women), 10 part-time/adjunct (7 women). *Students:* 32 full-time (20 women), 25 part-time (21 women); includes 19 minority (2 Black or African American, non-Hispanic/Latino; 15 Hispanic/Latino; 2 Two or more races, non-Hispanic/Latino), 5 international. Average age 32. 53 applicants, 55% accepted, 17 enrolled. In 2014, 12 master's awarded. *Degree requirements:* For master's, variable foreign language requirement, comprehensive exam, thesis (for some programs), exhibition (for MFA). *Entrance requirements:* For master's, GRE (for MA). Additional exam requirements/recommendations for international students: Required—TOEFL (minimum score 550 paper-based; 79 iBT), IELTS (minimum score 6.5). *Application deadline:* For fall admission, 6/1 priority date for domestic students, 1/15 priority date for international students; for spring admission, 9/1 priority date for domestic students, 6/15 priority date for international students. Applications are processed on a rolling basis. Application fee: $60. Electronic applications accepted. *Expenses:* Tuition, state resident: full-time $6310; part-time $262.92 per credit hour. Tuition, nonresident: full-time $14,998; part-time $624.92 per credit hour. *Required fees:* $2701; $36.50 per credit. $912.50 per semester. Tuition and fees vary according to course load. *Financial support:* In 2014–15, 58 students received support, including 58 fellowships (averaging $3,219 per year), 3 research assistantships (averaging $14,600 per year), 42 teaching assistantships (averaging $8,087 per year); Federal Work-Study, institutionally sponsored loans, scholarships/grants, health care benefits, tuition waivers (partial), and unspecified assistantships also available. Financial award application deadline: 2/15; financial award applicants required to submit FAFSA. *Faculty research:* Modern and contemporary art; contemporary Chicano/a art; transformation of multidisciplinary approach to printmaking; figurative painting and an intense interest in space as metaphor for community; working-class, sexuality and race issues; letter press posters; creating and crafting of metalsmithing. *Unit head:* Prof. Lydia Thompson, Director and Professor, 806-742-3825 Ext. 255, E-mail: lydia.thompson@ttu.edu. *Application contact:* Ryan Scheckel, Academic Advisor, 806-742-3825 Ext. 222, E-mail: ryan.scheckel@ttu.edu.
Website: http://www.art.ttu.edu

Texas Woman's University, Graduate School, College of Arts and Sciences, School of the Arts, Department of Visual Arts, Denton, TX 76201. Offers art (MA, MFA). *Degree requirements:* For master's, comprehensive exam, thesis (for some programs), exhibit (MFA), oral exam, thesis or professional paper (MA). *Entrance requirements:* For master's, portfolio, interview, current curriculum vitae, letter of intent, 3 letters of recommendation (for MFA only). Additional exam requirements/recommendations for international students: Required—TOEFL (minimum score 550 paper-based; 79 iBT). Electronic applications accepted. *Faculty research:* Art education and electronic technology, film noir, handmade paper, one-of-a kind art books, new media.

Tiffin University, Program in Humanities, Tiffin, OH 44883-2161. Offers art and visual media (MH); communication (MH); creative writing (MH); English (MH); film studies (MH); humanities (MH); individualized studies (MH). Part-time and evening/weekend programs available. Postbaccalaureate distance learning degree programs offered (no on-campus study). *Entrance requirements:* For master's, work experience. Additional exam requirements/recommendations for international students: Required—TOEFL (minimum score 550 paper-based; 79 iBT).

Towson University, Program in Studio Arts, Towson, MD 21252-0001. Offers MFA. *Students:* 12 full-time (7 women), 9 part-time (3 women); includes 3 minority (2 Asian, non-Hispanic/Latino; 1 Hispanic/Latino), 1 international. *Entrance requirements:* For master's, bachelor's degree preferably in art, portfolio, minimum GPA of 3.0, letter of intent, current resume, 2 letters of recommendation. *Application deadline:* For fall admission, 2/1 for domestic students; for spring admission, 11/1 for domestic students. Application fee: $45. Electronic applications accepted. *Financial support:* Application deadline: 4/1. *Unit head:* Prof. Tonia Matthews, Graduate Program Director, 410-704-2803, E-mail: tmatthews@towson.edu. *Application contact:* Alicia Arkell-Kleis, Information Contact, 410-704-6004, E-mail: grads@towson.edu.
Website: http://grad.towson.edu/program/master/arts-mfa/index.asp

Tufts University, Graduate School of Arts and Sciences, Department of Art and Art History, Medford, MA 02155. Offers art history (MA); art history and museum studies (MA); studio art (MFA). *Faculty:* 11 full-time (6 women), 4 part-time/adjunct (3 women). *Students:* 100 full-time (74 women), 32 part-time (21 women); includes 18 minority (5 Black or African American, non-Hispanic/Latino; 4 Asian, non-Hispanic/Latino; 6 Hispanic/Latino; 3 Two or more races, non-Hispanic/Latino), 20 international. Average age 29. 89 applicants, 40% accepted, 13 enrolled. In 2014, 82 master's awarded. *Degree requirements:* For master's, one foreign language, thesis (for some programs). *Entrance requirements:* For master's, GRE General Test. Additional exam requirements/recommendations for international students: Required—TOEFL (minimum score 550 paper-based; 80 iBT), IELTS (minimum score 6.5). *Application deadline:* For fall admission, 1/15 for domestic and international students. Application fee: $75. Electronic applications accepted. *Expenses: Tuition:* Full-time $45,590; part-time $1161 per credit hour. *Required fees:* $782. Full-time tuition and fees vary according to degree level, program and student level. Part-time tuition and fees vary according to course load. *Financial support:* Teaching assistantships with partial tuition reimbursements, Federal Work-Study, scholarships/grants, tuition waivers (partial), and unspecified

assistantships available. Financial award application deadline: 5/15; financial award applicants required to submit FAFSA. *Unit head:* Karen Overbey, Graduate Program Director, 617-627-3395. *Application contact:* Office of Graduate Admissions, 617-627-3395, E-mail: gradadmissions@tufts.edu.
Website: http://ase.tufts.edu/art/

Tulane University, School of Liberal Arts, Department of Art, New Orleans, LA 70118-5669. Offers history and Latin American studies (PhD); history of art (MA); studio art (MFA). PhD held jointly with Roger Thayer Stone Center for Latin American Studies. *Degree requirements:* For master's, one foreign language, thesis. *Entrance requirements:* For master's, GRE General Test, minimum B average in undergraduate course work. Additional exam requirements/recommendations for international students: Required—TOEFL. Electronic applications accepted. *Expenses: Tuition:* Full-time $46,326; part-time $2574 per credit hour. *Required fees:* $1980; $44.50 per credit hour. $550 per term. Tuition and fees vary according to course load and program.

United Theological Seminary of the Twin Cities, Graduate Programs, New Brighton, MN 55112-2598. Offers advanced theological studies (Diploma); justice and peace studies (M Div, MA); leadership toward racial justice (M Div, MA, Certificate); Methodist studies (M Div, MA, Certificate); ministry (D Min); ministry renewal and professional development (Certificate); pastoral care and counseling (M Div, MA, MARL); religion and theology (MA); theological and religious studies (Certificate); theology and the arts (M Div, MA); urban ministry (M Div, MA, MARL); women's studies: religion, theology and ministry (M Div, MA). *Accreditation:* ACIPE; ATS. Part-time and evening/weekend programs available. *Degree requirements:* For master's, thesis; for doctorate, comprehensive exam, thesis/dissertation. *Entrance requirements:* For master's, minimum GPA of 2.75; strong analytical, reflective thinking and writing skills; vocational and academic goals compatible with those of Seminary; for doctorate, M Div or equivalent, minimum GPA of 3.0, 3 years experience in professional ministry; for other advanced degree, BA or equivalent life experience; strong analytical, reflective thinking and writing skills (Certificate); proficiency in English language, previous study of theology at a theological school, recommendation of student's denomination (Diploma). Additional exam requirements/recommendations for international students: Required—TOEFL (minimum score 550 paper-based).

Universidad del Turabo, Graduate Programs, Programs in Education, Program in Teaching of Fine Arts, Gurabo, PR 00778-3030. Offers M Ed.

Université du Québec à Chicoutimi, Graduate Programs, Program in Fine Arts, Chicoutimi, QC G7H 2B1, Canada. Offers MA. Program offered jointly with Université du Québec à Montréal. Part-time programs available. *Degree requirements:* For master's, thesis optional. *Entrance requirements:* For master's, appropriate bachelor's degree, proficiency in French.

Université du Québec à Montréal, Graduate Programs, Program in Fine Arts, Montréal, QC H3C 3P8, Canada. Offers MA. Program offered jointly with Université du Québec à Chicoutimi. Part-time programs available. *Degree requirements:* For master's, thesis optional. *Entrance requirements:* For master's, appropriate bachelor's degree or equivalent, proficiency in French.

Université Laval, Faculty of Architecture, Planning and Visual Arts, School of Visual Arts, Programs in Visual Arts, Québec, QC G1K 7P4, Canada. Offers graphic design and multimedia (MA); visual arts (MA). *Degree requirements:* For master's, thesis (for some programs). *Entrance requirements:* For master's, technical exam, interview, mastery of pertinent software, knowledge of French. Electronic applications accepted.

University at Albany, State University of New York, College of Arts and Sciences, Department of Art and Art History, Albany, NY 12222-0001. Offers art (MA, MFA). *Degree requirements:* For master's, exhibit. *Entrance requirements:* For master's, portfolio. Additional exam requirements/recommendations for international students: Required—TOEFL (minimum score 550 paper-based). *Faculty research:* Art history, sculpture, painting and drawing, photography, digital media.

University at Buffalo, the State University of New York, Graduate School, College of Arts and Sciences, Department of Visual Studies, Buffalo, NY 14260-6010. Offers art (MFA); art history (MA); visual studies (MA). *Degree requirements:* For master's, thesis, exhibition, written research paper; for doctorate, thesis/dissertation. *Entrance requirements:* For master's, bachelor's degree with minimum GPA of 3.0, work samples, three letters of reference, statement of purpose; for doctorate, GRE. Additional exam requirements/recommendations for international students: Required—TOEFL (minimum score 550 paper-based; 79 iBT). Electronic applications accepted. *Faculty research:* Studio practice, visual studies, design, new media.

The University of Alabama, Graduate School, College of Arts and Sciences, Department of Art, Tuscaloosa, AL 35487. Offers art history (MA); studio art (MA, MFA), including ceramics, painting, photography, printmaking, sculpture. *Accreditation:* NASAD. Part-time programs available. *Faculty:* 16 full-time (9 women). *Students:* 22 full-time (16 women), 5 part-time (4 women); includes 3 minority (2 Black or African American, non-Hispanic/Latino; 1 Asian, non-Hispanic/Latino), 1 international. Average age 28. 22 applicants, 68% accepted, 10 enrolled. In 2014, 7 master's awarded. *Degree requirements:* For master's, one foreign language, comprehensive exam (for some programs), oral exam, thesis statement, exhibit (studio art), thesis (art history). *Entrance requirements:* For master's, GRE General Test or MAT (art history), minimum GPA of 3.0, BFA or equivalent (studio art). Additional exam requirements/recommendations for international students: Required—TOEFL (minimum score 550 paper-based). *Application deadline:* For fall admission, 3/15 for domestic and international students; for spring admission, 10/15 for domestic and international students. Applications are processed on a rolling basis. Application fee: $50 ($60 for international students). Electronic applications accepted. *Expenses:* Tuition, state resident: full-time $9826. Tuition, nonresident: full-time $24,950. *Financial support:* In 2014–15, 2 fellowships with full tuition reimbursements (averaging $14,000 per year), 13 teaching assistantships with full and partial tuition reimbursements (averaging $9,206 per year) were awarded; career-related internships or fieldwork, institutionally sponsored loans, scholarships/grants, and unspecified assistantships also available. Financial award application deadline: 7/14. *Faculty research:* Nineteenth-century American, Chinese, Baroque, twentieth-century, Asian art history. *Unit head:* William T. Dooley, Chairperson, 205-348-1890, Fax: 205-348-0287, E-mail: wtdooley@bama.ua.edu. *Application contact:* Craig R. Wedderspoon, Graduate Coordinator, 205-348-1898, Fax: 205-348-0287, E-mail: cwedders@bama.edu.
Website: http://www.art.ua.edu/

University of Alaska Fairbanks, College of Liberal Arts, Department of Art, Fairbanks, AK 99775-5640. Offers art (MFA); ceramics (MFA); computer art (MFA); drawing (MFA); painting (MFA); photography (MFA); printmaking (MFA); sculpture (MFA). Part-time programs available. *Faculty:* 8 full-time (4 women). *Students:* 6 full-time (all women), 1 (woman) part-time; includes 2 minority (1 Asian, non-Hispanic/Latino; 1 Hispanic/Latino), 1 international. Average age 32. 6 applicants, 17% accepted, 1 enrolled. In 2014, 3 master's awarded. *Degree requirements:* For master's, comprehensive exam, oral defense of project or thesis. *Entrance requirements:* For master's, portfolio of work including about 20 slides or appropriate equivalent depending on field of study. Additional exam requirements/recommendations for international students: Required—TOEFL (minimum score 550 paper-based; 79 iBT), IELTS (minimum score 6.5). *Application deadline:* For fall admission, 6/1 for domestic students, 3/1 for international students; for spring admission, 10/15 for domestic students, 9/1 for international students. Applications are processed on a rolling basis. Application fee: $60. Electronic applications accepted. *Expenses:* Tuition, state resident: full-time $7614; part-time $423 per credit. Tuition, nonresident: full-time $15,552; part-time $864 per credit. Tuition and fees vary according to course level, course load and reciprocity agreements. *Financial support:* In 2014–15, 6 teaching assistantships with full tuition reimbursements (averaging $9,319 per year) were awarded; fellowships with full tuition reimbursements, research assistantships with full tuition reimbursements, Federal Work-Study, scholarships/grants, health care benefits, and unspecified assistantships also available. Support available to part-time students. Financial award application deadline: 7/1; financial award applicants required to submit FAFSA. *Faculty research:* Computer art, survey of arts in Alaska, found object art, visualization and animation, painting from the wilderness. *Unit head:* David Mollett, Chair, 907-474-7530, Fax: 907-474-5853, E-mail: uaf-art@alaska.edu. *Application contact:* Mary Kreta, Director of Admissions, 907-474-7500, Fax: 907-474-7097, E-mail: admissions@uaf.edu.
Website: http://www.uaf.edu/art/

University of Alberta, Faculty of Graduate Studies and Research, Department of Art and Design, Edmonton, AB T6G 2E1, Canada. Offers drawing (MFA); history of art, design, and visual culture (MA); industrial design (M Des); painting (MFA); printmaking (MFA); sculpture (MFA); visual communication design (M Des). *Degree requirements:* For master's, thesis. *Entrance requirements:* For master's, portfolio (MFA and MDES). Additional exam requirements/recommendations for international students: Required—TOEFL (minimum score 550 paper-based).

The University of Arizona, College of Fine Arts, School of Art, Program in Art, Tucson, AZ 85721. Offers MFA. *Entrance requirements:* Additional exam requirements/recommendations for international students: Required—TOEFL (minimum score 550 paper-based; 79 iBT). Electronic applications accepted.

University of Arkansas, Graduate School, J. William Fulbright College of Arts and Sciences, Department of Art, Fayetteville, AR 72701-1201. Offers MFA. *Degree requirements:* For master's, exhibit or thesis. Electronic applications accepted.

University of Arkansas at Little Rock, Graduate School, College of Arts, Humanities, and Social Science, Department of Art, Little Rock, AR 72204-1099. Offers art education (MA); art history (MA); studio art (MA). *Accreditation:* NASAD. Part-time programs available. *Degree requirements:* For master's, 4 foreign languages, oral exam, oral defense of thesis or exhibit. *Entrance requirements:* For master's, portfolio review or term paper evaluation, minimum GPA of 2.7. *Application deadline:* For fall admission, 4/1 for domestic students; for spring admission, 11/1 for domestic students. Applications are processed on a rolling basis. Application fee: $40. *Expenses:* Tuition, state resident: full-time $6000; part-time $300 per credit hour. Tuition, nonresident: full-time $13,800; part-time $690 per credit hour. *Required fees:* $1126; $603 per term. One-time fee: $40 full-time. *Financial support:* Research assistantships with tuition reimbursements, teaching assistantships with tuition reimbursements, Federal Work-Study, institutionally sponsored loans, and unspecified assistantships available. Support available to part-time students. *Unit head:* Tom Clifton, Chair, 501-569-3182, E-mail: tgclifton@ualr.edu. *Application contact:* Dr. Marjorie Williams-Smith, Program Coordinator, 501-569-3591, E-mail: mwsmith@ualr.edu.
Website: http://ualr.edu/art/

The University of British Columbia, Faculty of Arts and Faculty of Graduate Studies, Department of Art History, Visual Art, and Theory, Vancouver, BC V6T1Z2, Canada. Offers art history (MA, PhD, Diploma); critical and curatorial studies (MA); visual art (MFA). *Degree requirements:* For master's, one foreign language, thesis, final exhibition (MFA, MA in critical and curatorial studies); for doctorate, 2 foreign languages, comprehensive exam, thesis/dissertation. *Entrance requirements:* For master's, bachelor's degree with minimum B+ average (MFA, MA in critical and curatorial studies), A- (MA in art history); for doctorate, master's degree with minimum A- average. Additional exam requirements/recommendations for international students: Required—TOEFL (minimum score 600 paper-based). Electronic applications accepted. *Faculty research:* Conceptual art, Asian art, indigenous North American art, post-second war art, eighteenth and nineteenth century art, curatorial, digital art.

University of Calgary, Faculty of Graduate Studies, Faculty of Arts, Department of Art, Calgary, AB T2N 1N4, Canada. Offers MA, MFA. *Degree requirements:* For master's, thesis. *Entrance requirements:* Additional exam requirements/recommendations for international students: Required—TOEFL. *Faculty research:* Painting, sculpture, drawing, photography, printmaking, new media.

University of California, Berkeley, Graduate Division, College of Letters and Science, Department of Art Practice, Berkeley, CA 94720-1500. Offers MFA. *Entrance requirements:* For master's, GRE General Test, minimum GPA of 3.0, sample of work, 3 letters of recommendation. Additional exam requirements/recommendations for international students: Required—TOEFL (minimum score 570 paper-based). Electronic applications accepted.

University of California, Berkeley, UC Berkeley Extension, Certificate Programs in Art and Design, Berkeley, CA 94720-1500. Offers interior design and interior architecture (Certificate); landscape architecture (Certificate); visual arts (Postbaccalaureate Certificate).

University of California, Davis, Graduate Studies, Program in Art, Davis, CA 95616. Offers MFA. *Degree requirements:* For master's, final exhibit. *Entrance requirements:* For master's, minimum GPA of 3.0, portfolio. Additional exam requirements/recommendations for international students: Required—TOEFL (minimum score 550 paper-based). Electronic applications accepted. *Faculty research:* Drawing, painting, photography, video, interactive art.

University of California, Irvine, Claire Trevor School of the Arts, Department of Art, Irvine, CA 92697. Offers MFA. *Students:* 29 full-time (17 women); includes 10 minority (1 Asian, non-Hispanic/Latino; 6 Hispanic/Latino; 3 Two or more races, non-Hispanic/Latino), 3 international. Average age 31. 145 applicants, 6% accepted, 8 enrolled. In 2014, 13 master's awarded. *Degree requirements:* For master's, thesis. *Entrance requirements:* For master's, minimum GPA of 3.0. *Application deadline:* For fall admission, 1/15 for domestic and international students. Applications are processed on a rolling basis. Application fee: $90 ($110 for international students). Electronic applications accepted. *Financial support:* Fellowships with tuition reimbursements, research assistantships with tuition reimbursements, teaching assistantships with tuition reimbursements, institutionally sponsored loans, traineeships, health care benefits, and unspecified assistantships available. Financial award application deadline: 3/1; financial award applicants required to submit FAFSA. *Faculty research:* Experimental concepts, processes relevant to contemporary issues. *Unit head:* John Medina, Department Manager, 949-824-4917, Fax: 949-824-4106, E-mail: jcmedina@uci.edu. *Application contact:* Kevin Appel, Graduate Advisor, Fax: 949-824-5297, E-mail: kappel@uci.edu.
Website: http://www.arts.uci.edu/ctsa-academic-departments-art-department

University of California, Irvine, School of Humanities, Department of Art History, Irvine, CA 92697. Offers visual studies (MA, PhD). Program offoered jointly with Department of Film and Media Studies. *Students:* 27 full-time (17 women); includes 6

minority (1 Black or African American, non-Hispanic/Latino; 2 Asian, non-Hispanic/Latino; 2 Hispanic/Latino; 1 Two or more races, non-Hispanic/Latino), 2 international. Average age 32. 89 applicants, 10% accepted, 3 enrolled. In 2014, 4 master's, 5 doctorates awarded. *Degree requirements:* For doctorate, thesis/dissertation. *Entrance requirements:* For master's, GRE, minimum GPA of 3.0; for doctorate, GRE General Test, writing sample. Additional exam requirements/recommendations for international students: Required—TOEFL (minimum score 550 paper-based). *Application deadline:* For fall admission, 12/15 for domestic and international students. Application fee: $80 ($100 for international students). Electronic applications accepted. *Financial support:* Fellowships, teaching assistantships, institutionally sponsored loans, traineeships, health care benefits, and unspecified assistantships available. Financial award application deadline: 3/1; financial award applicants required to submit FAFSA. *Faculty research:* Interdisciplinary study and research in art history, critical theory, women's studies, cultural studies, film studies. *Unit head:* Prof. Douglas E. Winther, Department Chair, 949-824-2464, E-mail: dewinthe@uci.edu. *Application contact:* Heidi E. Tinsman, Graduate Faculty Advisors, 949-824-6521, Fax: 949-824-2865, E-mail: hetinsma@uci.edu.
Website: http://www.hnet.uci.edu/arthistory/

University of California, Los Angeles, Graduate Division, School of the Arts and Architecture, Department of Art, Los Angeles, CA 90095. Offers MFA. *Degree requirements:* For master's, comprehensive exam. *Entrance requirements:* For master's, bachelor's degree; minimum undergraduate GPA of 3.0 (or its equivalent if letter grade system not used); portfolio. Additional exam requirements/recommendations for international students: Required—TOEFL. Electronic applications accepted. *Expenses:* Contact institution.

University of California, Riverside, Graduate Division, Program in Visual Arts, Riverside, CA 92521-0102. Offers MFA. *Degree requirements:* For master's, thesis. *Entrance requirements:* For master's, portfolio, minimum GPA of 3.2. Additional exam requirements/recommendations for international students: Required—TOEFL (minimum score 550 paper-based; 80 iBT). Electronic applications accepted. *Expenses:* Tuition, state resident: full-time $5399. Tuition, nonresident: full-time $10,433. *Faculty research:* Painting, photography, sculpture, digital art, video.

University of California, San Diego, Graduate Division, Department of Visual Arts, La Jolla, CA 92093. Offers art history, theory and criticism (PhD), including anthropogeny, art practice; visual arts (MFA). *Students:* 72 full-time (48 women); includes 14 minority (3 Black or African American, non-Hispanic/Latino; 2 American Indian or Alaska Native, non-Hispanic/Latino; 3 Asian, non-Hispanic/Latino; 6 Hispanic/Latino), 12 international. 205 applicants, 14% accepted, 15 enrolled. In 2014, 15 master's, 2 doctorates awarded. *Degree requirements:* For master's, thesis; for doctorate, 2 foreign languages, comprehensive exam, thesis/dissertation, reading knowledge of at least two of the foreign languages commonly used by scholars engaged in the advanced study in art history, theory, and criticism. *Entrance requirements:* For master's, electronic portfolio; for doctorate, GRE General Test, electronic portfolio. Additional exam requirements/recommendations for international students: Required—TOEFL (minimum score 550 paper-based; 80 iBT), IELTS (minimum score 7). *Application deadline:* For fall admission, 11/26 priority date for domestic students. Application fee: $90 ($110 for international students). Electronic applications accepted. *Expenses:* Tuition, state resident: full-time $11,220; part-time $5610 per quarter. Tuition, nonresident: full-time $26,322; part-time $13,161 per quarter. *Required fees:* $570 per quarter. Tuition and fees vary according to program. *Financial support:* Fellowships, research assistantships, teaching assistantships, career-related internships or fieldwork, scholarships/grants, and readerships available. Financial award applicants required to submit FAFSA. *Faculty research:* Contemporary art, ancient art, critical design, digital/new media/software/hardware, nano/bio/neuro. *Unit head:* Jordan Crandall, Chair, 858-534-0418, E-mail: jcrandall@ucsd.edu. *Application contact:* Asia Marks, Graduate Program Coordinator, 858-822-3884, E-mail: vis-grad@ucsd.edu.
Website: http://visarts.ucsd.edu/

University of California, Santa Barbara, Graduate Division, College of Letters and Sciences, Division of Humanities and Fine Arts, Department of Art, Santa Barbara, CA 93106-7120. Offers MFA. *Degree requirements:* For master's, thesis, exhibition. *Entrance requirements:* Additional exam requirements/recommendations for international students: Required—TOEFL (minimum score 550 paper-based; 80 iBT), IELTS (minimum score 7). Electronic applications accepted. *Faculty research:* Digital media, interactive media, spatial studies, public space art, book arts.

University of California, Santa Cruz, Division of Graduate Studies, Division of the Arts, Program in Digital Arts and New Media, Santa Cruz, CA 95064. Offers MFA. *Degree requirements:* For master's, thesis, written paper. *Entrance requirements:* Additional exam requirements/recommendations for international students: Required—TOEFL (minimum score 550 paper-based; 83 iBT); Recommended—IELTS (minimum score 8). Electronic applications accepted. *Faculty research:* Mechatronics, participatory culture, performative technologies, playable media.

University of California, Santa Cruz, Division of Graduate Studies, Division of the Arts, Program in Visual Studies, Santa Cruz, CA 95064. Offers PhD. *Degree requirements:* For doctorate, one foreign language, thesis/dissertation, qualifying exams. *Entrance requirements:* For doctorate, GRE, writing sample under 20 pages, 3 letters of recommendation. Additional exam requirements/recommendations for international students: Required—TOEFL (minimum score 550 paper-based; 83 iBT); Recommended—IELTS (minimum score 8). Electronic applications accepted. *Faculty research:* Opportunity to consider the role of social and cultural forces in guiding how and what their members see, concentration on cultures in Africa, the Americas, Asia, Europe, and the Pacific Islands.

University of Central Florida, College of Arts and Humanities, School of Visual Arts and Design, Orlando, FL 32816. Offers digital media (MA); emerging media (MFA), including digital media, entrepreneurial digital cinema, studio art and the computer. *Faculty:* 51 full-time (20 women), 20 part-time/adjunct (4 women). *Students:* 40 full-time (18 women), 9 part-time (1 woman); includes 8 minority (1 Black or African American, non-Hispanic/Latino; 1 American Indian or Alaska Native, non-Hispanic/Latino; 1 Asian, non-Hispanic/Latino; 5 Hispanic/Latino), 7 international. Average age 32. 43 applicants, 56% accepted, 14 enrolled. In 2014, 12 master's awarded. Application fee: $30. Electronic applications accepted. *Expenses:* Tuition, state resident: part-time $288.16 per credit hour. Tuition, nonresident: part-time $1073.31 per credit hour. *Financial support:* In 2014–15, 25 students received support, including 11 fellowships (averaging $8,500 per year), 16 teaching assistantships (averaging $6,300 per year); scholarships/grants and unspecified assistantships also available. *Unit head:* Byron Clercx, Director, 407-823-3145, E-mail: byron.clercx@ucf.edu. *Application contact:* Barbara Rodriguez Lamas, Director, Admissions and Student Services, 407-823-2766, Fax: 407-823-6442, E-mail: gradadmissions@ucf.edu.
Website: http://svad.cah.ucf.edu/

University of Chicago, Division of the Humanities, Department of Visual Arts, Chicago, IL 60637. Offers MFA. *Students:* 16 full-time (9 women); includes 4 minority (2 Black or African American, non-Hispanic/Latino; 2 Hispanic/Latino). 82 applicants, 18% accepted, 8 enrolled. *Entrance requirements:* Additional exam requirements/recommendations for international students: Required—TOEFL (minimum score 104 iBT), IELTS (minimum score 7). *Application deadline:* For fall admission, 12/15 for domestic and international students. Application fee: $90. Electronic applications accepted. *Expenses: Tuition:* Full-time $46,899. *Required fees:* $347. *Financial support:* Fellowships and tuition waivers (full and partial) available. Financial award application deadline: 12/15; financial award applicants required to submit FAFSA. *Unit head:* Dr. Jessica Stockholder, Chair, 773-753-4821. *Application contact:* Braden Grams, Assistant Dean of Students, Admissions and Fellowships, 773-702-1552, Fax: 773-834-9148, E-mail: humanitiesadmissions@uchicago.edu.
Website: http://dova.uchicago.edu/

University of Cincinnati, Graduate School, College of Design, Architecture, Art, and Planning, School of Art, Program in Fine Arts, Cincinnati, OH 45221. Offers MFA. *Accreditation:* NASAD. Part-time programs available. *Degree requirements:* For master's, thesis, oral exam. *Entrance requirements:* Additional exam requirements/recommendations for international students: Required—TOEFL. Electronic applications accepted. *Faculty research:* Painting, drawing, ceramics, printmaking, sculpture.

University of Colorado Boulder, Graduate School, College of Arts and Sciences, Department of Art and Art History, Boulder, CO 80309. Offers art history (MA), including contemporary art criticism, early twentieth-century art, nineteenth-century art, Russian and Soviet art; ceramics (MFA); drawing (MFA); painting (MFA); photography and media arts (MFA); printmaking (MFA); sculpture (MFA). *Faculty:* 23 full-time (11 women). *Students:* 50 full-time (32 women), 1 (woman) part-time; includes 6 minority (all Hispanic/Latino), 2 international. Average age 29. 213 applicants, 17% accepted, 21 enrolled. In 2014, 21 master's awarded. Terminal master's awarded for partial completion of doctoral program. *Degree requirements:* For master's, variable foreign language requirement, comprehensive exam, thesis (for some programs). *Entrance requirements:* For master's, GRE General Test, minimum undergraduate GPA of 3.0, portfolio. *Application deadline:* For fall admission, 1/15 for domestic students, 12/1 for international students. Application fee: $50 ($70 for international students). Electronic applications accepted. *Financial support:* In 2014–15, 126 students received support, including 16 fellowships (averaging $1,206 per year), 43 teaching assistantships with full and partial tuition reimbursements available (averaging $26,856 per year); institutionally sponsored loans, scholarships/grants, health care benefits, and unspecified assistantships also available. Financial award application deadline: 1/15; financial award applicants required to submit FAFSA. *Faculty research:* Visual arts, fine arts, sculpture, installation art, inter-arts: interdisciplinary art forms.
Website: http://www.colorado.edu/arts/

University of Colorado Denver, College of Liberal Arts and Sciences, Program in Humanities, Denver, CO 80217. Offers community health science (MSS); humanities (MH); international studies (MSS); philosophy and theory (MH); social justice (MSS); society and the environment (MSS); visual studies (MH); women's and gender studies (MSS). Part-time and evening/weekend programs available. *Faculty:* 1 full-time (0 women), 1 (woman) part-time/adjunct. *Students:* 49 full-time (37 women), 26 part-time (19 women); includes 14 minority (3 Black or African American, non-Hispanic/Latino; 1 American Indian or Alaska Native, non-Hispanic/Latino; 1 Asian, non-Hispanic/Latino; 6 Hispanic/Latino; 3 Two or more races, non-Hispanic/Latino), 1 international. Average age 35. 27 applicants, 63% accepted, 11 enrolled. In 2014, 16 master's awarded. *Degree requirements:* For master's, 36 credit hours, project or thesis. *Entrance requirements:* For master's, writing sample, statement of purpose/letter of intent, three letters of recommendation. Additional exam requirements/recommendations for international students: Required—TOEFL (minimum score 537 paper-based; 75 iBT); Recommended—IELTS (minimum score 6.5). *Application deadline:* For fall admission, 5/15 for domestic students, 5/15 priority date for international students; for spring admission, 10/15 for domestic students, 10/15 priority date for international students; for summer admission, 3/15 for domestic and international students. Application fee: $50 ($75 for international students). Electronic applications accepted. *Financial support:* In 2014–15, 4 students received support. Fellowships, research assistantships, teaching assistantships, Federal Work-Study, institutionally sponsored loans, scholarships/grants, and traineeships available. Financial award application deadline: 4/1; financial award applicants required to submit FAFSA. *Faculty research:* Women and gender in the classical Mediterranean, communication theory and democracy, relationship between psychology and philosophy. *Unit head:* Margaret Woodhull, Director of Humanities, 303-315-3568, E-mail: margaret.woodhull@ucdenver.edu. *Application contact:* Angela Beale, Program Assistant, 303-315-3565, E-mail: angela.beale@ucdenver.edu.
Website: http://www.ucdenver.edu/academics/colleges/CLAS/Programs/HumanitiesSocialSciences/Programs/Pages/MasterofHumanities.aspx

University of Connecticut, Graduate School, School of Fine Arts, Department of Art and Art History, Field of Studio Art, Storrs, CT 06269. Offers MFA. *Accreditation:* NASAD. *Entrance requirements:* Additional exam requirements/recommendations for international students: Required—TOEFL (minimum score 550 paper-based). Electronic applications accepted.

University of Dallas, Braniff Graduate School of Liberal Arts, Program in Art, Irving, TX 75062-4736. Offers MA, MFA. Part-time programs available. *Degree requirements:* For master's, exhibit, oral exam. *Entrance requirements:* For master's, GRE General Test, portfolio. Additional exam requirements/recommendations for international students: Required—TOEFL (minimum score 550 paper-based). *Faculty research:* Ceramics, printmaking, sculpture, art history, religious imagery and architecture.

University of Delaware, College of Arts and Sciences, Department of Art, Newark, DE 19716. Offers MA, MFA. *Degree requirements:* For master's, exposition paper final exhibition. *Entrance requirements:* For master's, portfolio of creative work. Electronic applications accepted. *Faculty research:* Painting, printmaking, ceramics, photography, sculpture.

University of Denver, Division of Arts, Humanities and Social Sciences, School of Art and Art History, Denver, CO 80208. Offers art history (MA); art history/museum studies (MA); emergent digital practices (MFA). *Accreditation:* NASAD. Part-time programs available. *Faculty:* 16 full-time (11 women), 3 part-time/adjunct (1 woman). *Students:* 7 full-time (6 women), 17 part-time (16 women); includes 7 minority (1 Black or African American, non-Hispanic/Latino; 1 American Indian or Alaska Native, non-Hispanic/Latino; 5 Hispanic/Latino). Average age 25. 24 applicants, 83% accepted, 14 enrolled. In 2014, 7 master's awarded. *Degree requirements:* For master's, one foreign language, comprehensive exam, research paper or thesis project. *Entrance requirements:* For master's, GRE General Test, transcripts, personal statement, writing sample, three letters of recommendation. Additional exam requirements/recommendations for international students: Required—TOEFL (minimum score 550 paper-based; 80 iBT). *Application deadline:* For fall admission, 1/31 priority date for domestic and international students. Applications are processed on a rolling basis. Application fee: $65. Electronic applications accepted. *Expenses:* Expenses: $1,199 per credit hour. *Financial support:* In 2014–15, 18 students received support, including 8 teaching assistantships with full and partial tuition reimbursements available (averaging $7,817 per year); career-related internships or fieldwork, Federal Work-Study, institutionally sponsored loans, scholarships/grants, and unspecified assistantships also available. Support available to part-time students. Financial award application deadline: 2/15; financial award

applicants required to submit FAFSA. *Faculty research:* Images of women in alchemical manuscripts and books, Giovanni Benedetto and Salvatore Castiglione. *Unit head:* Dr. Sarah Gjertson, Director, 303-871-3263, E-mail: sgjertso@du.edu. *Application contact:* Dr. Annabeth Headrick, Graduate Art History Advisor, 303-871-3574, E-mail: annabeth.headrick@du.edu.
Website: http://www.du.edu/art/

University of Florida, Graduate School, College of The Arts, School of Art and Art History, Gainesville, FL 32611-5800. Offers art (MA), including digital arts and sciences; art education (MA); art history (MA, PhD); museology (MA), including historic preservation. *Accreditation:* NASAD. Postbaccalaureate distance learning degree programs offered (minimal on-campus study). *Faculty:* 32 full-time (14 women), 5 part-time/adjunct (3 women). *Students:* 91 full-time (66 women), 117 part-time (100 women); includes 50 minority (14 Black or African American, non-Hispanic/Latino; 4 American Indian or Alaska Native, non-Hispanic/Latino; 6 Asian, non-Hispanic/Latino; 26 Hispanic/Latino), 14 international. 199 applicants, 41% accepted, 55 enrolled. In 2014, 69 master's awarded. *Degree requirements:* For master's, project or thesis (MFA); 1 foreign language (MA in art history); for doctorate, 2 foreign languages, comprehensive exam, thesis/dissertation. *Entrance requirements:* For master's, GRE General Test, portfolio (MFA), writing sample (MA), minimum GPA 3.0; for doctorate, GRE General Test, minimum GPA of 3.0. Additional exam requirements/recommendations for international students: Required—TOEFL (minimum score 550 paper-based; 80 iBT), IELTS (minimum score 6). *Application deadline:* For fall admission, 1/1 priority date for domestic students, 1/1 for international students; for spring admission, 11/1 for domestic and international students. Applications are processed on a rolling basis. Application fee: $30. Electronic applications accepted. *Financial support:* In 2014–15, 4 fellowships, 8 research assistantships, 76 teaching assistantships were awarded; Federal Work-Study, institutionally sponsored loans, and unspecified assistantships also available. Financial award applicants required to submit FAFSA. *Faculty research:* Studio production, art historical studies of style context. *Unit head:* Richard Heipp, Professor and Interim Director, 352-273-3021, Fax: 352-392-8453, E-mail: heipp@ufl.edu. *Application contact:* Maya Stanfield-Mazzi, PhD, Assistant Professor/Director of Graduate Studies for Art History, 352-273-3070, Fax: 352-392-8453, E-mail: mstanfield@ufl.edu.
Website: http://www.arts.ufl.edu/art

University of Georgia, Franklin College of Arts and Sciences, Lamar Dodd School of Art, Athens, GA 30602. Offers art (MFA, PhD); art history (MA). *Accreditation:* NASAD (one or more programs are accredited). *Degree requirements:* For doctorate, one foreign language, thesis/dissertation. *Entrance requirements:* For master's and doctorate, GRE General Test. Electronic applications accepted.

University of Guam, Office of Graduate Studies, College of Liberal Arts and Social Sciences, Division of Fine Arts, Mangilao, GU 96923. Offers ceramics (MA); graphics (MA); painting (MA). *Degree requirements:* For master's, thesis or alternative, exhibit, final oral exam. *Entrance requirements:* For master's, GRE General Test, portfolio. Additional exam requirements/recommendations for international students: Required—TOEFL.

University of Guelph, Graduate Studies, College of Arts, School of Fine Art and Music, Guelph, ON N1G 2W1, Canada. Offers studio art (MFA). *Degree requirements:* For master's, exhibition, support paper, oral defense. *Entrance requirements:* For master's, minimum B- average during previous 2 years of course work. Additional exam requirements/recommendations for international students: Required—TOEFL. Electronic applications accepted. *Faculty research:* Studio practice in painting, sculpture, print, photo, drawing, video.

University of Hartford, Hartford Art School, West Hartford, CT 06117-1599. Offers MFA. *Accreditation:* NASAD. Part-time programs available. *Degree requirements:* For master's, thesis. *Entrance requirements:* For master's, portfolio, 3 letters of recommendation. Additional exam requirements/recommendations for international students: Required—TOEFL (minimum score 550 paper-based). Electronic applications accepted. *Expenses:* Contact institution.

University of Hawaii at Manoa, Graduate Division, College of Arts and Humanities, Department of Art and Art History, Honolulu, HI 96822. Offers art history (MA); visual arts (MFA). Part-time programs available. *Degree requirements:* For master's, thesis optional. *Entrance requirements:* For master's, GRE General Test, BFA, 18 hours of course work in art history. Additional exam requirements/recommendations for international students: Required—TOEFL (minimum score 550 paper-based; 79 iBT), IELTS (minimum score 7). *Faculty research:* Painting, sculpture, glass, design, printmaking.

University of Houston, College of Liberal Arts and Social Sciences, Department of Art, Houston, TX 77204. Offers art history (MA); interdisciplinary practice and emerging forms (MFA); painting (MFA); studio art (MFA). *Entrance requirements:* For master's, baccalaureate degree, portfolio. Electronic applications accepted. *Faculty research:* Painting, sculpture, photography/installation/video, graphic design and typography, art history (Pre-Columbian to Surrealism).

University of Idaho, College of Graduate Studies, College of Art and Architecture, Moscow, ID 83844-2461. Offers architecture (M Arch); art (MFA); bioregional planning and community design (MS); integrated architecture and design (MS); landscape architecture (MLA); teaching art (MAT). *Accreditation:* NASAD. *Faculty:* 17 full-time, 4 part-time/adjunct. *Students:* 88 full-time (34 women), 18 part-time (6 women). Average age 31. In 2014, 38 master's awarded. *Entrance requirements:* Additional exam requirements/recommendations for international students: Required—TOEFL (minimum score 550 paper-based). *Application deadline:* For fall admission, 8/1 for domestic students; for spring admission, 12/15 for domestic students. Applications are processed on a rolling basis. Application fee: $60. Electronic applications accepted. *Expenses:* Tuition, state resident: full-time $4784; part-time $280.50 per credit hour. Tuition, nonresident: full-time $18,314; part-time $957.50 per credit hour. *Required fees:* $2000; $58.50 per credit hour. Tuition and fees vary according to program. *Financial support:* Applicants required to submit FAFSA. *Faculty research:* Sustainability in communities, urban research, virtual technology, bioregional planning, environment and behavior interaction. *Unit head:* Dr. Mark Hoversten, Dean, 208-885-4409, E-mail: caa@uidaho.edu. *Application contact:* Sean Scoggin, Graduate Recruitment Coordinator, 208-885-4001, Fax: 208-885-4406, E-mail: graduateadmissions@uidaho.edu.
Website: http://www.uidaho.edu/caa

University of Illinois at Chicago, Graduate College, College of Architecture, Design and the Arts, School of Art and Art History, Chicago, IL 60607-7128. Offers art history (MA); electronic visualization (MFA); museum and exhibition studies (MA); new media arts (MFA). Part-time and evening/weekend programs available. *Faculty:* 84 full-time (40 women), 70 part-time/adjunct (20 women). *Students:* 160 full-time (105 women), 23 part-time (17 women); includes 18 minority (3 Black or African American, non-Hispanic/Latino; 4 Asian, non-Hispanic/Latino; 10 Hispanic/Latino; 1 Two or more races, non-Hispanic/Latino), 13 international. Average age 29. 211 applicants, 32% accepted, 34 enrolled. In 2014, 21 master's, 3 doctorates awarded. Terminal master's awarded for partial completion of doctoral program. *Degree requirements:* For master's, one foreign language, thesis or alternative; for doctorate, thesis/dissertation. *Entrance requirements:* For master's, GRE General Test, minimum GPA of 2.75, 3 letters of recommendation; for doctorate, GRE General Test, MA in art history or equivalent, minimum GPA of 3.0. Additional exam requirements/recommendations for international students: Required—TOEFL. *Application deadline:* For fall admission, 1/1 priority date for domestic and international students; for spring admission, 10/1 for domestic students, 7/15 for international students. Application fee: $60. Electronic applications accepted. *Expenses:* Expenses: $19,134 in-state, $31,132 out-of-state (for art); $17,932 in-state, $29,930 out-of-state (for art history). *Financial support:* Fellowships with full tuition reimbursements, research assistantships with full tuition reimbursements, teaching assistantships with full tuition reimbursements, career-related internships or fieldwork, Federal Work-Study, scholarships/grants, traineeships, tuition waivers (full), and unspecified assistantships available. Support available to part-time students. Financial award application deadline: 3/1; financial award applicants required to submit FAFSA. *Faculty research:* Modern painting and sculpture, history of architecture, city planning and design, history of photography. *Unit head:* Prof. Lisa Yun Lee, Director, 312-413-5358, E-mail: lisalee@uic.edu. *Application contact:* Receptionist, 312-413-2550, E-mail: gradcoll@uic.edu.
Website: http://artandarthistory.uic.edu/art-history

University of Illinois at Urbana–Champaign, Graduate College, College of Fine and Applied Arts, School of Art and Design, Program in Design and Media, Champaign, IL 61820. Offers art and design (MFA), including new media; graphic design (MFA); industrial design (MFA). *Accreditation:* NASAD. *Students:* 11 (8 women). Application fee: $70 ($90 for international students). *Unit head:* Ernest Scott, Chair, 217-333-1579, E-mail: ernscott@illinois.edu. *Application contact:* Ellen de Waard, Coordinator of Graduate Academic Affairs, 217-333-0642, Fax: 217-244-7688, E-mail: edewaard@illinois.edu.
Website: http://www.art.illinois.edu

University of Illinois at Urbana–Champaign, Graduate College, College of Fine and Applied Arts, School of Art and Design, Program in Studio Arts, Champaign, IL 61820. Offers art and design (MFA); crafts (MFA); metals (MFA); painting (MFA); photography (MFA); sculpture (MFA). *Accreditation:* NASAD. *Students:* 23 (16 women). *Entrance requirements:* For master's, minimum GPA of 3.0. Application fee: $70 ($90 for international students). *Unit head:* Timothy Van Laar, Chair, 217-333-6611, E-mail: tvanlaar@illinois.edu. *Application contact:* Ellen de Waard, Assistant to the Associate Director, 217-333-0642, Fax: 217-244-7688, E-mail: edewaard@illinois.edu.
Website: http://www.art.illinois.edu

University of Indianapolis, Graduate Programs, College of Arts and Sciences, Department of Art, Indianapolis, IN 46227-3697. Offers MA. *Accreditation:* NASAD. Part-time and evening/weekend programs available. *Faculty:* 4 full-time (1 woman). *Students:* 2 full-time (1 woman), 4 part-time (3 women); includes 1 minority (Hispanic/Latino), 2 international. Average age 37. In 2014, 3 master's awarded. *Entrance requirements:* For master's, GRE Subject Test, 3 letters of recommendation, portfolio. Additional exam requirements/recommendations for international students: Required—TOEFL. *Application deadline:* Applications are processed on a rolling basis. Application fee: $30. *Financial support:* Federal Work-Study, scholarships/grants, and tuition waivers (full and partial) available. Support available to part-time students. Financial award application deadline: 5/1; financial award applicants required to submit FAFSA. *Unit head:* James Vieweigh, Chair, 317-788-3509, E-mail: jvieweigh@uindy.edu. *Application contact:* Hazel Augustin, Administrative Assistant, Art and Design, 317-788-3253, E-mail: augustinh@uindy.edu.
Website: http://art.uindy.edu/

The University of Iowa, Graduate College, College of Liberal Arts and Sciences, School of Art and Art History, Programs in Studio Art, Iowa City, IA 52242-1316. Offers MA, MFA. *Degree requirements:* For master's, thesis, final exam. *Entrance requirements:* For master's, portfolio. Additional exam requirements/recommendations for international students: Required—TOEFL (minimum score 550 paper-based; 81 iBT). Electronic applications accepted. *Faculty research:* Ceramics, painting and drawing, design, printmaking, photography.

The University of Kansas, Graduate Studies, College of Liberal Arts and Sciences, Department of Visual Art, Program in Visual Art Education, Lawrence, KS 66045. Offers MA. Part-time programs available. *Faculty:* 24 full-time (0 women), 7 part-time/adjunct (0 women). *Students:* 4 full-time (all women), 9 part-time (8 women); includes 1 minority (Two or more races, non-Hispanic/Latino). Average age 29. 7 applicants, 71% accepted, 3 enrolled. In 2014, 1 master's awarded. *Degree requirements:* For master's, thesis or alternative. *Entrance requirements:* For master's, portfolio, 3 letters of recommendation, minimum GPA of 3.0. Additional exam requirements/recommendations for international students: Required—TOEFL (minimum score 570 paper-based) or IELTS (minimum score 6.5). *Application deadline:* For fall admission, 5/1 for domestic and international students; for spring admission, 10/15 for domestic and international students. Application fee: $55 ($65 for international students). Electronic applications accepted. *Financial support:* Teaching assistantships with full tuition reimbursements, Federal Work-Study, scholarships/grants, and unspecified assistantships available. Financial award application deadline: 5/1. *Faculty research:* Museum education, art educator education. *Unit head:* Mary Anne Jordan, Chairperson, 785-864-2952, E-mail: majordan@ku.edu. *Application contact:* Kay Isbell, Graduate Admissions Contact, 785-864-2957, E-mail: kisbell@ku.edu.
Website: http://art.ku.edu/programs/visual_art_education/

University of Kentucky, Graduate School, College of Fine Arts, Program in Art Studio, Lexington, KY 40506-0032. Offers MFA. *Accreditation:* NASAD. *Degree requirements:* For master's, comprehensive exam. *Entrance requirements:* For master's, GRE General Test, minimum undergraduate GPA of 2.75. Additional exam requirements/recommendations for international students: Required—TOEFL (minimum score 550 paper-based). Electronic applications accepted.

University of Lethbridge, School of Graduate Studies, Lethbridge, AB T1K 3M4, Canada. Offers addictions counseling (M Sc); agricultural biotechnology (M Sc); agricultural studies (M Sc, MA); anthropology (MA); archaeology (M Sc, MA); art (MA, MFA); biochemistry (M Sc); biological sciences (M Sc); biomolecular science (PhD); biosystems and biodiversity (PhD); Canadian studies (MA); chemistry (M Sc); computer science (M Sc); computer science and geographical information science (M Sc); counseling (MC); counseling psychology (M Ed); dramatic arts (MA); earth, space, and physical science (PhD); economics (MA); education (MA); educational leadership (M Ed); English (MA); environmental science (M Sc); evolution and behavior (PhD); exercise science (M Sc); French (MA); French/German (MA); French/Spanish (MA); general education (M Ed); geography (M Sc, MA); German (MA); health sciences (M Sc); individualized multidisciplinary (M Sc, MA); kinesiology (M Sc, MA); management (M Sc), including accounting, finance, general management, human resource management and labor relations, information systems, international management, marketing, policy and strategy; mathematics (M Sc); modern languages (MA); music (M Mus, MA); Native American studies (MA); neuroscience (M Sc, PhD); new media (MA, MFA); nursing (M Sc, MN); philosophy (MA); physics (M Sc); political science (MA); psychology (M Sc, MA); religious studies (MA); sociology (MA); theatre and dramatic arts (MFA); theoretical and computational science (PhD); urban and

regional studies (MA); women and gender studies (MA). Part-time and evening/weekend programs available. *Faculty:* 358. *Students:* 445 full-time (243 women), 116 part-time (72 women). Average age 31. 351 applicants, 26% accepted, 87 enrolled. In 2014, 129 master's, 13 doctorates awarded. *Degree requirements:* For master's, thesis (for some programs); for doctorate, comprehensive exam, thesis/dissertation. *Entrance requirements:* For master's, GMAT (for M Sc in management), bachelor's degree in related field, minimum GPA of 3.0 during previous 20 graded semester courses, 2 years' teaching or related experience (M Ed); for doctorate, master's degree, minimum graduate GPA of 3.5. Additional exam requirements/recommendations for international students: Required—TOEFL. Application fee: $100 Canadian dollars. *Financial support:* Fellowships, research assistantships, teaching assistantships, scholarships/grants, health care benefits, and unspecified assistantships available. *Faculty research:* Movement and brain plasticity, gibberellin physiology, photosynthesis, carbon cycling, molecular properties of main-group ring components. *Application contact:* School of Graduate Studies, 403-329-5194, E-mail: sgsinquiries@uleth.ca. Website: http://www.uleth.ca/graduatestudies/

University of Louisville, Graduate School, College of Arts and Sciences, Department of Fine Arts, Louisville, KY 40292. Offers art history (MA, PhD); creative art (MA); curatorial studies (MA). *Students:* 15 full-time (10 women), 9 part-time (5 women); includes 5 minority (2 Black or African American, non-Hispanic/Latino; 2 Asian, non-Hispanic/Latino; 1 Hispanic/Latino), 2 international. Average age 36. 27 applicants, 63% accepted, 8 enrolled. In 2014, 3 master's, 1 doctorate awarded. *Degree requirements:* For master's, thesis; for doctorate, 2 foreign languages, comprehensive exam, thesis/dissertation. *Entrance requirements:* For master's and doctorate, GRE General Test. Additional exam requirements/recommendations for international students: Required—TOEFL (minimum score 550 paper-based; 79 iBT). *Application deadline:* For fall admission, 1/15 for domestic students, 5/1 priority date for international students; for spring admission, 11/1 priority date for international students; for summer admission, 4/1 priority date for international students. Applications are processed on a rolling basis. Application fee: $60. *Expenses:* Tuition, state resident: full-time $11,326; part-time $630 per credit hour. Tuition, nonresident: full-time $23,568; part-time $1311 per credit hour. *Required fees:* $196. Tuition and fees vary according to program and reciprocity agreements. *Financial support:* Teaching assistantships with full tuition reimbursements available. Financial award application deadline: 1/15. *Faculty research:* Art history in the periods from ancient to contemporary and various regions, 2D and 3D studio areas, intermedia, curatorial studies. *Unit head:* Prof. Ying Kit Chan, Chair, 502-852-6794, Fax: 502-852-6791, E-mail: chan@louisville.edu. *Application contact:* Libby Leggett, Director, Graduate Admissions, 502-852-3101, Fax: 502-852-6536, E-mail: gradadm@louisville.edu.
Website: http://art.louisville.edu

University of Maine, Graduate School, College of Liberal Arts and Sciences, Intermedia Program, Orono, ME 04469. Offers MFA. *Faculty:* 7 full-time (3 women), 10 part-time/adjunct (4 women). *Students:* 25 full-time (8 women), 21 part-time (15 women); includes 5 minority (4 American Indian or Alaska Native, non-Hispanic/Latino; 1 Hispanic/Latino), 2 international. Average age 42. 11 applicants, 91% accepted, 5 enrolled. In 2014, 7 master's awarded. *Degree requirements:* For master's, comprehensive exam, thesis. *Entrance requirements:* For master's, portfolio. Additional exam requirements/recommendations for international students: Required—TOEFL. *Application deadline:* For fall admission, 1/15 for domestic students. Application fee: $65. *Expenses:* Tuition, state resident: part-time $658 per credit hour. Tuition, nonresident: part-time $1550 per credit hour. *Financial support:* In 2014–15, 14 students received support, including 8 research assistantships (averaging $7,300 per year), 4 teaching assistantships (averaging $14,600 per year); Federal Work-Study, scholarships/grants, health care benefits, and unspecified assistantships also available. Financial award application deadline: 3/1; financial award applicants required to submit FAFSA. *Faculty research:* Variable media, arts research and innovation, permaculture, wearable computing, interactive environments. *Total annual research expenditures:* $750,000. *Unit head:* Dr. Owen Smith, Director, 207-581-4389, E-mail: owen.smith@umit.maine.edu. *Application contact:* Scott G. Delcourt, Assistant Vice President for Graduate Studies and Senior Associate Dean, 207-581-3291, Fax: 207-581-3232, E-mail: graduate@maine.edu.
Website: http://intermediamfa.org

The University of Manchester, School of Arts, Histories and Cultures, Manchester, United Kingdom. Offers anthropology, media and performance (PhD); applied theatre professional (PhD); archaeology (PhD); art history and visual studies (PhD); arts management and cultural policy (PhD); classics and ancient history (PhD); composition (PhD); creative writing (PhD); drama (PhD); economic and social history (PhD); electroacoustic composition (PhD); English and American studies (PhD); history (PhD); humanitarianism and conflict response (PhD); museology (PhD); music (PhD); musicology (PhD); religions and theology (PhD).

The University of Manchester, School of Materials, Manchester, United Kingdom. Offers advanced aerospace materials engineering (M Sc); advanced metallic systems (PhD); biomedical materials (M Phil, M Sc, PhD); ceramics and glass (M Phil, M Sc, PhD); composite materials (M Sc, PhD); corrosion and protection (M Phil, M Sc, PhD); materials (M Phil, PhD); metallic materials (M Phil, M Sc, PhD); nanostructural materials (M Phil, M Sc, PhD); paper science (M Phil, M Sc, PhD); polymer science and engineering (M Phil, M Sc, PhD); technical textiles (M Sc); textile design, fashion and management (M Phil, M Sc, PhD); textile science and technology (M Phil, M Sc, PhD); textiles (M Phil, PhD); textiles and fashion (M Ent).

University of Maryland, College Park, Academic Affairs, College of Arts and Humanities, Department of Art, College Park, MD 20742. Offers MFA. *Degree requirements:* For master's, thesis, oral defense. *Entrance requirements:* For master's, minimum GPA of 3.0, portfolio, 20 digital images, 3 letters of recommendation. Electronic applications accepted. *Faculty research:* Studio art.

University of Massachusetts Amherst, Graduate School, College of Humanities and Fine Arts, Department of Art, Amherst, MA 01003. Offers art (MA, MFA), including art education (MA), studio art (MFA); history of art and architecture (MA). Part-time programs available. *Faculty:* 45 full-time (28 women). *Students:* 18 full-time (6 women), 7 part-time (6 women); includes 1 minority (Hispanic/Latino), 1 international. Average age 34. 43 applicants, 33% accepted, 10 enrolled. In 2014, 7 master's awarded. *Degree requirements:* For master's, comprehensive exam (for some programs), thesis (for some programs). *Entrance requirements:* For master's, portfolio. Additional exam requirements/recommendations for international students: Required—TOEFL (minimum score 550 paper-based; 80 iBT), IELTS (minimum score 6.5). *Application deadline:* For fall admission, 2/1 for domestic and international students. Applications are processed on a rolling basis. Application fee: $75. Electronic applications accepted. *Expenses:* Tuition, state resident: full-time $1980; part-time $110 per credit. Tuition, nonresident: full-time $14,644; part-time $414 per credit. *Required fees:* $11,417. One-time fee: $357. *Financial support:* Fellowships with full and partial tuition reimbursements, research assistantships with full and partial tuition reimbursements, teaching assistantships with full and partial tuition reimbursements, career-related internships or fieldwork, Federal Work-Study, scholarships/grants, traineeships, health care benefits, tuition waivers (full and partial), and unspecified assistantships available. Support

available to part-time students. Financial award application deadline: 2/1. *Unit head:* Dr. Shona Macdonald, Graduate Program Director, 413-545-1903, Fax: 413-545-3929. *Application contact:* Lindsay DeSantis, Supervisor of Admissions, 413-545-0722, Fax: 413-577-0100, E-mail: gradadm@grad.umass.edu.
Website: http://www.umass.edu/art/

University of Massachusetts Dartmouth, Graduate School, College of Visual and Performing Arts, Department of Artisanry, North Dartmouth, MA 02747-2300. Offers MFA, Postbaccalaureate Certificate. *Accreditation:* NASAD. Part-time programs available. *Faculty:* 6 full-time (4 women), 2 part-time/adjunct (0 women). *Students:* 14 full-time (10 women), 13 part-time (8 women); includes 4 minority (2 Asian, non-Hispanic/Latino; 1 Hispanic/Latino; 1 Two or more races, non-Hispanic/Latino), 2 international. Average age 33. 45 applicants, 71% accepted, 9 enrolled. In 2014, 7 master's, 3 other advanced degrees awarded. *Degree requirements:* For master's, visual thesis, written thesis. *Entrance requirements:* For master's, statement of purpose (minimum of 300 words), resume, 2 letters of recommendation, official transcripts, portfolio (20 images representing applicant's art work); for Postbaccalaureate Certificate, statement of purpose (minimum of 300 words), resume, 3 letters of recommendation, official transcripts, portfolio (10 images representing applicant's art work). Additional exam requirements/recommendations for international students: Required—TOEFL (minimum score 533 paper-based; 72 iBT), IELTS (minimum score 6). *Application deadline:* For fall admission, 1/9 priority date for domestic students, 12/9 priority date for international students; for spring admission, 10/15 priority date for domestic students, 9/15 priority date for international students. Applications are processed on a rolling basis. Application fee: $60. Electronic applications accepted. *Expenses:* Tuition, state resident: full-time $2071; part-time $86.29 per credit. Tuition, nonresident: full-time $8099; part-time $337.46 per credit. *Required fees:* $16,520; $712.33 per credit. Tuition and fees vary according to course load and reciprocity agreements. *Financial support:* In 2014–15, 1 fellowship with full tuition reimbursement (averaging $12,000 per year), 6 teaching assistantships with partial tuition reimbursements (averaging $2,400 per year) were awarded; Federal Work-Study and unspecified assistantships also available. Support available to part-time students. Financial award application deadline: 3/1; financial award applicants required to submit FAFSA. *Faculty research:* Hand-building, wheeling-throwing, fabrication of jewelry, sculptural objects, slip casting. *Total annual research expenditures:* $49,667. *Unit head:* Charlotte Hamlin, Coordinator for Graduate Studies, College of Visual and Preforming Arts, 508-999-8911, Fax: 508-999-8912, E-mail: chamlin@umassd.edu. *Application contact:* Steven Briggs, Director of Marketing and Recruitment for Graduate Studies, 508-999-8604, Fax: 508-999-8183, E-mail: graduate@umassd.edu.
Website: http://www.umassd.edu/cvpa/graduate/artisanry

University of Massachusetts Dartmouth, Graduate School, College of Visual and Performing Arts, Department of Fine Arts, North Dartmouth, MA 02747-2300. Offers painting (Postbaccalaureate Certificate); printmaking (Postbaccalaureate Certificate); sculpture (Postbaccalaureate Certificate). Part-time programs available. *Faculty:* 11 full-time (4 women), 4 part-time/adjunct (2 women). *Students:* 15 full-time (10 women), 3 part-time (2 women); includes 4 minority (2 Hispanic/Latino; 2 Two or more races, non-Hispanic/Latino), 1 international. Average age 42. 21 applicants, 86% accepted, 10 enrolled. In 2014, 7 master's, 2 other advanced degrees awarded. *Degree requirements:* For master's, visual thesis, written thesis. *Entrance requirements:* For master's, statement of purpose (minimum of 300 words), resume, 2 letters of recommendation, official transcripts, portfolio (20 images representing applicant's art work); for Postbaccalaureate Certificate, statement of purpose (minimum of 300 words), resume, 3 letters of recommendation, official transcripts, portfolio (10 images representing applicant's art work). Additional exam requirements/recommendations for international students: Required—TOEFL (minimum score 533 paper-based; 72 iBT), IELTS (minimum score 6). *Application deadline:* For fall admission, 1/9 priority date for domestic students, 12/9 priority date for international students; for spring admission, 10/15 priority date for domestic students, 9/15 priority date for international students. Applications are processed on a rolling basis. Application fee: $60. Electronic applications accepted. *Expenses:* Tuition, state resident: full-time $2071; part-time $86.29 per credit. Tuition, nonresident: full-time $8099; part-time $337.46 per credit. *Required fees:* $16,520; $712.33 per credit. Tuition and fees vary according to course load and reciprocity agreements. *Financial support:* In 2014–15, 1 fellowship with full tuition reimbursement (averaging $12,000 per year), 5 teaching assistantships with partial tuition reimbursements (averaging $2,360 per year) were awarded; Federal Work-Study and unspecified assistantships also available. Support available to part-time students. Financial award application deadline: 3/1; financial award applicants required to submit FAFSA. *Faculty research:* Painting, printmaking, drawing, figurative sculpture/plaster media. *Total annual research expenditures:* $49,667. *Unit head:* Charlotte Hamlin, Coordinator for Graduate Studies, College of Visual and Preforming Arts, 508-999-8911, Fax: 508-999-8912, E-mail: chamlin@umassd.edu. *Application contact:* Steven Briggs, Director of Marketing and Recruitment for Graduate Studies, 508-999-8604, Fax: 508-999-8183, E-mail: graduate@umassd.edu.
Website: http://www.umassd.edu/cvpa/graduate/finearts

University of Memphis, Graduate School, College of Communication and Fine Arts, Department of Art, Memphis, TN 38152. Offers art (Graduate Certificate); art history (MA), including Egyptian art and archaeology, general art history; ceramics (MFA); graphic design (MFA); interior design (MFA); painting (MFA); printmaking/photography (MFA). *Accreditation:* NASAD (one or more programs are accredited). *Faculty:* 19 full-time (7 women), 4 part-time/adjunct (2 women). *Students:* 34 full-time (28 women), 3 part-time (2 women); includes 5 minority (2 Asian, non-Hispanic/Latino; 2 Hispanic/Latino; 1 Two or more races, non-Hispanic/Latino). Average age 30. 24 applicants, 63% accepted, 10 enrolled. In 2014, 14 master's, 14 other advanced degrees awarded. *Degree requirements:* For master's, 2 foreign languages, comprehensive exam, thesis. *Entrance requirements:* For master's, GRE General Test or MAT, portfolio (MFA). *Application deadline:* For fall admission, 8/1 for domestic students; for spring admission, 12/1 for domestic students. Applications are processed on a rolling basis. Application fee: $35 ($60 for international students). *Financial support:* In 2014–15, 38 students received support. Research assistantships with full tuition reimbursements available, teaching assistantships with full tuition reimbursements available, Federal Work-Study, scholarships/grants, and unspecified assistantships available. Financial award application deadline: 2/15; financial award applicants required to submit FAFSA. *Faculty research:* Online collaborative learning, advanced art history studies, electronic publishing/design, studio arts, architectural studies. *Unit head:* Prof. Richard Lou, Chair, 901-678-2216, Fax: 901-678-2735, E-mail: gmyatt@memphis.edu. *Application contact:* Greely Myat, Graduate Studies Coordinator, 901-678-2650.
Website: http://memphis.edu/art/

University of Miami, Graduate School, College of Arts and Sciences, Department of Art and Art History, Coral Gables, FL 33124. Offers art history (MA); ceramics/glass (MFA); graphic design/multimedia (MFA); painting (MFA); photography/digital imaging (MFA); printmaking (MFA); sculpture (MFA). Part-time programs available. *Degree requirements:* For master's, variable foreign language requirement, thesis, exhibit (MFA), comprehensive exam (MA). *Entrance requirements:* For master's, GRE General Test (MA), research paper (MA), slide portfolio (MFA). Additional exam requirements/

recommendations for international students: Required—TOEFL. Electronic applications accepted. *Faculty research:* Installation art, public art.

University of Michigan, Horace H. Rackham School of Graduate Studies, Penny W. Stamps School of Art and Design, Ann Arbor, MI 48109. Offers MFA. *Accreditation:* NASAD. *Degree requirements:* For master's, thesis, exhibit (MFA), slide lecture. *Entrance requirements:* For master's, portfolio. Additional exam requirements/recommendations for international students: Required—TOEFL, IELTS. Electronic applications accepted. *Faculty research:* Creative expression, commercial design, preparation for teaching.

University of Michigan–Flint, Graduate Programs, Program in Arts Administration, Flint, MI 48502-1950. Offers museum and visual arts (MA); performance (MA). Part-time programs available. *Faculty:* 2 part-time/adjunct (1 woman). *Students:* 7 full-time (5 women), 11 part-time (8 women); includes 3 minority (all Black or African American, non-Hispanic/Latino), 1 international. Average age 36. 10 applicants, 100% accepted, 9 enrolled. In 2014, 10 master's awarded. *Degree requirements:* For master's, thesis, internship. *Entrance requirements:* For master's, bachelor's degree in the arts (visual art, theatre, dance, music, etc.) from accredited institution with minimum undergraduate GPA of 3.0. Additional exam requirements/recommendations for international students: Required—TOEFL (minimum score 84 iBT), IELTS (minimum score 6.5). *Application deadline:* For fall admission, 8/1 for domestic students, 5/1 for international students; for winter admission, 11/15 for domestic students, 9/15 for international students. Applications are processed on a rolling basis. Application fee: $55. Electronic applications accepted. Application fee is waived when completed online. *Financial support:* Federal Work-Study and scholarships/grants available. Support available to part-time students. Financial award application deadline: 3/1; financial award applicants required to submit FAFSA. *Unit head:* Dr. Sarah Lippert, Interim Director, 810-766-6679, E-mail: sarlipp@umflint.edu. *Application contact:* Bradley T. Maki, Director of Graduate Admissions, 810-762-3171, Fax: 810-766-6789, E-mail: bmaki@umflint.edu. Website: http://www.umflint.edu/graduateprograms/arts-administration-ma

University of Minnesota, Duluth, Graduate School, School of Fine Arts, Department of Art and Design, Duluth, MN 55812-2496. Offers graphic design (MFA). Part-time programs available. *Degree requirements:* For master's, final exhibit, project, supporting paper. *Entrance requirements:* For master's, minimum GPA of 3.0, writing sample, slide portfolio. Additional exam requirements/recommendations for international students: Required—TOEFL (minimum score 550 paper-based). *Faculty research:* Motion graphics, graphic design history, interactive design, typography, education.

University of Minnesota, Twin Cities Campus, Graduate School, College of Liberal Arts, Department of Art, Minneapolis, MN 55455. Offers MFA. *Degree requirements:* For master's, oral exam, supporting paper, thesis exhibit. *Entrance requirements:* For master's, portfolio, letters of recommendation, minimum GPA of 3.0. Additional exam requirements/recommendations for international students: Required—TOEFL (minimum score 550 paper-based; 79 iBT). Recommended—IELTS (minimum score 6.5). Electronic applications accepted. *Faculty research:* Performed photography, image as code and symbol, cast metal sculpture, performance and installations, high-fired salt glazed and utilitarian ceramic earthenware, contemporary theory, multimedia, video and electronic technology.

University of Mississippi, Graduate School, College of Liberal Arts, Department of Art, University, MS 38677. Offers art education (MA); art history (MA); fine arts (MFA). *Accreditation:* NASAD (one or more programs are accredited). Part-time programs available. *Degree requirements:* For master's, thesis (for some programs). *Entrance requirements:* For master's, GRE General Test, minimum GPA of 3.0. Additional exam requirements/recommendations for international students: Required—TOEFL. Electronic applications accepted.

University of Missouri, Office of Research and Graduate Studies, College of Arts and Science, Department of Art, Columbia, MO 65211. Offers MFA. *Faculty:* 20 full-time (8 women), 5 part-time/adjunct (all women). *Students:* 20 full-time (12 women), 2 part-time (1 woman); includes 3 minority (1 Black or African American, non-Hispanic/Latino; 1 American Indian or Alaska Native, non-Hispanic/Latino; 1 Hispanic/Latino). Average age 32. 23 applicants, 30% accepted, 7 enrolled. In 2014, 2 master's awarded. *Degree requirements:* For master's, thesis. *Entrance requirements:* For master's, GRE General Test, minimum GPA of 3.0. Additional exam requirements/recommendations for international students: Required—TOEFL (minimum score 550 paper-based; 80 iBT), IELTS (minimum score 5.5). *Application deadline:* For fall admission, 1/1 priority date for domestic students, 1/1 for international students; for winter admission, 9/1 for domestic and international students; for spring admission, 2/1 for domestic students. Applications are processed on a rolling basis. Application fee: $55 ($75 for international students). Electronic applications accepted. *Financial support:* In 2014–15, 2 research assistantships with full tuition reimbursements, 14 teaching assistantships with full tuition reimbursements were awarded; institutionally sponsored loans, health care benefits, and unspecified assistantships also available. Support available to part-time students. *Faculty research:* Painting, digital art, new media, photography, ceramics. *Unit head:* Dr. Melvin C. Platt, Department Chair, 573-882-3638, E-mail: plattm@missouri.edu. *Application contact:* Brenda J. Warren, Administrative Assistant, 573-882-4037, E-mail: warrenb@missouri.edu. Website: http://art.missouri.edu/mfa-program.html

University of Missouri–Kansas City, College of Arts and Sciences, Department of Art and Art History, Kansas City, MO 64110-2499. Offers art history (MA, PhD); studio art (MA). PhD (interdisciplinary) offered through the School of Graduate Studies. Part-time programs available. *Faculty:* 11 full-time (5 women), 11 part-time/adjunct (4 women). *Students:* 12 full-time (7 women), 27 part-time (23 women); includes 4 minority (2 Black or African American, non-Hispanic/Latino; 2 Hispanic/Latino), 2 international. Average age 34. 19 applicants, 79% accepted, 13 enrolled. In 2014, 11 master's awarded. Terminal master's awarded for partial completion of doctoral program. *Degree requirements:* For master's, thesis, qualifying exam; for doctorate, thesis/dissertation, exams. *Entrance requirements:* For master's, good general education in the humanities. Additional exam requirements/recommendations for international students: Required—TOEFL (minimum score 550 paper-based; 80 iBT). *Application deadline:* For fall admission, 3/1 priority date for domestic and international students; for spring admission, 10/15 for domestic and international students. Applications are processed on a rolling basis. Application fee: $45 ($50 for international students). Electronic applications accepted. *Financial support:* In 2014–15, 9 teaching assistantships with partial tuition reimbursements (averaging $9,933 per year) were awarded; career-related internships or fieldwork, Federal Work-Study, institutionally sponsored loans, and tuition waivers (full and partial) also available. Support available to part-time students. Financial award application deadline: 3/1; financial award applicants required to submit FAFSA. *Faculty research:* Painting, electronic media, Western and non-Western art history, photography. *Unit head:* Elijah Gowin, Department Chair, 816-235-5301, Fax: 816-235-5507, E-mail: gowinp@umkc.edu. *Application contact:* Tamera Byland, Director of Admissions, 816-235-1111, Fax: 816-235-5544, E-mail: admit@umkc.edu. Website: http://cas.umkc.edu/art

The University of Montana, Graduate School, College of Visual and Performing Arts, School of Art, Missoula, MT 59812-0002. Offers fine arts (MA), including art, art history;

photography (MFA). *Accreditation:* NASAD (one or more programs are accredited). *Degree requirements:* For master's, thesis exhibit. *Entrance requirements:* For master's, GRE General Test, portfolio.

University of Nebraska–Lincoln, Graduate College, College of Fine and Performing Arts, Department of Art and Art History, Lincoln, NE 68588. Offers art history (MA); studio art (MFA). *Accreditation:* NASAD. *Degree requirements:* For master's, thesis. *Entrance requirements:* For master's, slide portfolio. Additional exam requirements/recommendations for international students: Required—TOEFL (minimum score 550 paper-based). Electronic applications accepted. *Faculty research:* Classical archaeology, contemporary art, printmaking, photography.

University of Nevada, Las Vegas, Graduate College, College of Fine Arts, Department of Art, Las Vegas, NV 89154-5013. Offers MFA. *Accreditation:* NASAD. Part-time programs available. *Faculty:* 8 full-time (3 women), 2 part-time/adjunct (both women). *Students:* 12 full-time (9 women); includes 1 minority (Two or more races, non-Hispanic/Latino), 3 international. Average age 27. 20 applicants, 20% accepted, 4 enrolled. In 2014, 4 master's awarded. *Degree requirements:* For master's, comprehensive exam, thesis. *Entrance requirements:* Additional exam requirements/recommendations for international students: Required—TOEFL (minimum score 550 paper-based; 80 iBT), IELTS (minimum score 7). *Application deadline:* For fall admission, 2/1 for domestic students, 5/1 for international students; for spring admission, 10/1 for international students. Application fee: $60 ($95 for international students). Electronic applications accepted. *Financial support:* In 2014–15, 12 students received support, including 12 teaching assistantships with partial tuition reimbursements available (averaging $13,000 per year); institutionally sponsored loans, scholarships/grants, health care benefits, and unspecified assistantships also available. Financial award application deadline: 3/1. *Faculty research:* Studio arts: printmaking, sculpture, mixed media, photography, film and digital; graphic design; art history, theory and criticism. *Total annual research expenditures:* $1,325. *Unit head:* Dr. Louisa McDonald, Chair/Professor, 702-895-2717, Fax: 702-895-4346, E-mail: louisa.mcdonald@unlv.edu. *Application contact:* Graduate College Admissions Evaluator, 702-895-3320, Fax: 702-895-4180, E-mail: gradcollege@unlv.edu. Website: http://art.unlv.edu/

University of Nevada, Reno, Graduate School, College of Liberal Arts, Department of Fine Arts, Reno, NV 89557. Offers MFA. *Degree requirements:* For master's, thesis optional. *Entrance requirements:* For master's, minimum GPA of 2.75. Additional exam requirements/recommendations for international students: Required—TOEFL (minimum score 500 paper-based; 61 iBT), IELTS (minimum score 6). Electronic applications accepted. *Faculty research:* Ceramics; digital-media; drawing; painting; performance; photography; printmaking; sculpture; video; studio program supported by a strong emphasis in the areas of contemporary art, theory and criticism.

University of New Hampshire, Graduate School, College of Liberal Arts, Program in Painting, Durham, NH 03824. Offers MFA. Program offered in fall only. Part-time programs available. *Faculty:* 9 full-time (3 women). *Students:* 7 full-time (5 women), 1 international. Average age 33. 12 applicants, 58% accepted, 3 enrolled. In 2014, 4 master's awarded. *Degree requirements:* For master's, thesis or alternative. *Entrance requirements:* For master's, slide portfolio. Additional exam requirements/recommendations for international students: Required—TOEFL (minimum score 550 paper-based; 80 iBT). *Application deadline:* For fall admission, 2/15 priority date for domestic students, 2/15 for international students. Applications are processed on a rolling basis. Application fee: $65. Electronic applications accepted. *Expenses:* Tuition, state resident: full-time $13,500; part-time $750 per credit hour. Tuition, nonresident: full-time $26,460; part-time $1110 per credit hour. *Required fees:* $1788; $447 per semester. *Financial support:* In 2014–15, 7 students received support, including 2 teaching assistantships; fellowships, research assistantships, career-related internships or fieldwork, Federal Work-Study, and scholarships/grants also available. Support available to part-time students. Financial award application deadline: 2/15. *Unit head:* Jennifer Moses, Chair, 603-862-2497. *Application contact:* Eileen Wong, Administrative Assistant, 603-862-3820, E-mail: mfa.painting@unh.edu. Website: http://cola.unh.edu/art-and-art-history/program/painting-mfa

University of New Mexico, Graduate School, College of Fine Arts, Program in Studio Art, Albuquerque, NM 87131. Offers MFA. *Faculty:* 22 full-time (13 women), 1 (woman) part-time/adjunct. *Students:* 41 full-time (28 women), 4 part-time (2 women); includes 9 minority (1 American Indian or Alaska Native, non-Hispanic/Latino; 4 Hispanic/Latino; 4 Two or more races, non-Hispanic/Latino), 2 international. Average age 32. 115 applicants, 23% accepted, 16 enrolled. In 2014, 14 master's awarded. *Degree requirements:* For master's, comprehensive exam, thesis or alternative, studio reviews, qualifying exams. *Entrance requirements:* Additional exam requirements/recommendations for international students: Required—TOEFL (minimum score 550 paper-based), IELTS (minimum score 6). *Application deadline:* For fall admission, 1/15 for domestic and international students. Application fee: $50. Electronic applications accepted. *Financial support:* In 2014–15, 46 students received support, including 1 fellowship (averaging $3,600 per year), 6 research assistantships with tuition reimbursements available (averaging $2,714 per year), 33 teaching assistantships with partial tuition reimbursements available (averaging $6,233 per year); Federal Work-Study, institutionally sponsored loans, scholarships/grants, health care benefits, and unspecified assistantships also available. Support available to part-time students. Financial award application deadline: 3/1; financial award applicants required to submit FAFSA. *Faculty research:* Photography, painting, drawing, print making, sculpture, ceramics, electronic arts, art and ecology. *Unit head:* Prof. Mary Tsiongas, Chair, 505-277-5861, Fax: 505-277-5955, E-mail: tsiongas@unm.edu. *Application contact:* Kat Heatherington, Graduate Advisor, 505-277-6672, Fax: 505-277-5955, E-mail: art255@unm.edu. Website: http://art.unm.edu/graduate-programs/

University of New Orleans, Graduate School, College of Liberal Arts, Department of Fine Arts, New Orleans, LA 70148. Offers MFA. *Accreditation:* NASAD. *Degree requirements:* For master's, thesis. *Entrance requirements:* For master's, GRE General Test, slide review. Additional exam requirements/recommendations for international students: Required—TOEFL (minimum score 550 paper-based; 79 iBT), IELTS (minimum score 6.5). Electronic applications accepted. *Faculty research:* Large-scale painting and sculpture, black-and-white and color photography, computer graphics.

The University of North Carolina at Chapel Hill, Graduate School, College of Arts and Sciences, Department of Art, Studio Art Program, Chapel Hill, NC 27599. Offers MFA. *Degree requirements:* For master's, variable foreign language requirement. *Entrance requirements:* For master's, minimum GPA of 3.0, portfolio. Electronic applications accepted. *Faculty research:* Environmental installation, painting, photography, mixed media, printmaking.

The University of North Carolina at Greensboro, Graduate School, College of Arts and Sciences, Department of Art, Greensboro, NC 27412-5001. Offers studio arts (MFA). *Degree requirements:* For master's, thesis (for some programs). *Entrance requirements:* For master's, GRE General Test, 39 hours of course work in studio art, 15 hours of course work in art history, portfolio. Additional exam requirements/

recommendations for international students: Required—TOEFL. Electronic applications accepted.

University of North Dakota, Graduate School, College of Arts and Sciences, Department of Visual Arts, Grand Forks, ND 58202. Offers MFA. *Accreditation:* NASAD. *Degree requirements:* For master's, thesis or alternative, comprehensive evaluation, professional exhibition. *Entrance requirements:* For master's, minimum GPA of 3.0. Additional exam requirements/recommendations for international students: Required—TOEFL (minimum score 550 paper-based; 79 iBT), IELTS (minimum score 6.5). Electronic applications accepted. *Faculty research:* Ceramics, drawing, metalsmithing, printmaking, painting.

University of Northern Colorado, Graduate School, College of Performing and Visual Arts, School of Visual Arts, Greeley, CO 80639. Offers MA. Part-time programs available. *Degree requirements:* For master's, comprehensive exam, thesis. *Entrance requirements:* For master's, GRE General Test, portfolio, 3 letters of recommendation, minimum undergraduate GPA of 3.0. Electronic applications accepted.

University of Northern Iowa, Graduate College, College of Humanities, Arts and Sciences, Department of Art, Cedar Falls, IA 50614. Offers art education (MA). *Accreditation:* NASAD. Part-time and evening/weekend programs available. *Degree requirements:* For master's, comprehensive exam (for some programs), thesis or alternative. *Entrance requirements:* For master's, minimum GPA of 3.0, portfolio. Additional exam requirements/recommendations for international students: Required—TOEFL (minimum score 500 paper-based; 61 iBT). *Application deadline:* For fall admission, 8/1 priority date for domestic students. Applications are processed on a rolling basis. Application fee: $50 ($70 for international students). Electronic applications accepted. *Expenses:* Tuition, state resident: full-time $7912; part-time $880 per credit. Tuition, nonresident: full-time $17,906; part-time $880 per credit. *Required fees:* $1101; $325.50 per credit. $465.63 per semester. Tuition and fees vary according to course load and program. *Financial support:* Career-related internships or fieldwork, Federal Work-Study, scholarships/grants, and tuition waivers (full and partial) available. Support available to part-time students. Financial award application deadline: 2/1. *Unit head:* Dr. Jeffery Byrd, Department Head/Professor, 319-273-2077, Fax: 319-273-7333, E-mail: jeffery.byrd@uni.edu. *Application contact:* Laurie S. Russell, Record Analyst, 319-273-2623, Fax: 319-273-2885, E-mail: laurie.russell@uni.edu.
Website: http://www.uni.edu/artdept/

University of North Texas, Robert B. Toulouse School of Graduate Studies, Denton, TX 76203-5459. Offers accounting (MS); applied anthropology (MA, MS); applied behavior analysis (Certificate); applied geography (MA); applied technology and performance improvement (M Ed, MS); art education (MA); art history (MA); art museum education (Certificate); arts leadership (Certificate); audiology (Au D); behavior analysis (MS); behavioral science (PhD); biochemistry and molecular biology (MS); biology (MA, MS); biomedical engineering (MS); business analysis (MS); chemistry (MS); clinical health psychology (PhD); communication studies (MA, MS); computer engineering (MS); computer science (MS); counseling (M Ed, MS), including clinical mental health counseling (MS), college and university counseling, elementary school counseling, secondary school counseling; creative writing (MA); criminal justice (MS); curriculum and instruction (M Ed); decision sciences (MBA); design (MA, MFA), including fashion design (MFA), innovation studies, interior design (MFA); early childhood studies (MS); economics (MS); educational leadership (M Ed, Ed D); educational psychology (MS, PhD), including family studies (MS), gifted and talented (MS), human development (MS), learning and cognition (MS), research, measurement and evaluation (MS); electrical engineering (MS); emergency management (MPA); engineering technology (MS); English (MA); English as a second language (MA); environmental science (MS); finance (MBA, MS); financial management (MPA); French (MA); health services management (MBA); higher education (M Ed, Ed D); history (MA, MS); hospitality management (MS); human resources management (MPA); information science (MS); information systems (PhD); information technologies (MBA); interdisciplinary studies (MA, MS); international studies (MA); international sustainable tourism (MS); jazz studies (MM); journalism (MA, MJ, Graduate Certificate), including interactive and virtual digital communication (Graduate Certificate), narrative journalism (Graduate Certificate), public relations (Graduate Certificate); kinesiology (MS); linguistics (MA); local government management (MPA); logistics (PhD); logistics and supply chain management (MBA); long-term care, senior housing, and aging services (MA); management (PhD); marketing (MBA); mathematics (MA, MS); mechanical and energy engineering (MS, PhD); music (MA), including ethnomusicology, music theory, musicology, performance; music composition (PhD); music education (MM Ed, PhD); nonprofit management (MPA); operations and supply chain management (MBA); performance (MM, DMA); philosophy (MA); political science (MA); professional and technical communication (MA); radio, television and film (MA, MFA); rehabilitation counseling (Certificate); sociology (MA); Spanish (MA); special education (M Ed); speech-language pathology (MA); strategic management (MBA); studio art (MFA); teaching (M Ed); MBA/MS. Part-time and evening/weekend programs available. Postbaccalaureate distance learning degree programs offered. *Faculty:* 651 full-time (215 women), 233 part-time/adjunct (139 women). *Students:* 3,040 full-time (1,598 women), 3,401 part-time (2,097 women); includes 1,740 minority (533 Black or African American, non-Hispanic/Latino; 15 American Indian or Alaska Native, non-Hispanic/Latino; 286 Asian, non-Hispanic/Latino; 746 Hispanic/Latino; 3 Native Hawaiian or other Pacific Islander, non-Hispanic/Latino; 157 Two or more races, non-Hispanic/Latino), 1,145 international. Terminal master's awarded for partial completion of doctoral program. *Degree requirements:* For master's, variable foreign language requirement, comprehensive exam (for some programs), thesis (for some programs); for doctorate, variable foreign language requirement, comprehensive exam (for some programs), thesis/dissertation; for other advanced degree, variable foreign language requirement, comprehensive exam (for some programs). *Entrance requirements:* For master's and doctorate, GRE, GMAT. Additional exam requirements/recommendations for international students: Required—TOEFL (minimum score 550 paper-based; 79 iBT). *Application deadline:* For fall admission, 7/15 for domestic students, 3/15 for international students; for spring admission, 11/15 for domestic students, 9/15 for international students; for summer admission, 5/1 for domestic students. Applications are processed on a rolling basis. Application fee: $60. Electronic applications accepted. *Expenses:* Tuition, state resident: full-time $5450; part-time $3633 per year. Tuition, nonresident: full-time $11,966; part-time $7977 per year. *Required fees:* $1301; $398 per credit hour. $685 per semester. Tuition and fees vary according to program and reciprocity agreements. *Financial support:* Fellowships with partial tuition reimbursements, research assistantships with partial tuition reimbursements, teaching assistantships, career-related internships or fieldwork, Federal Work-Study, institutionally sponsored loans, scholarships/grants, health care benefits, and library assistantships available. Support available to part-time students. Financial award applicants required to submit FAFSA. *Unit head:* Mark Wardell, Dean, 940-565-2383, E-mail: mark.wardell@unt.edu. *Application contact:* Toulouse School of Graduate Studies, 940-565-2383, Fax: 940-565-2141, E-mail: gradsch@unt.edu.
Website: http://tsgs.unt.edu/

University of Notre Dame, Graduate School, College of Arts and Letters, Division of Humanities, Department of Art, Art History, and Design, Notre Dame, IN 46556. Offers art history (MA); design (MFA), including graphic design, industrial design; studio art (MFA), including ceramics, painting, photography, printmaking, sculpture. *Accreditation:* NASAD. *Degree requirements:* For master's, comprehensive exam (for some programs), thesis. *Entrance requirements:* For master's, GRE General Test, minimum GPA of 3.0. Additional exam requirements/recommendations for international students: Required—TOEFL (minimum score 600 paper-based; 80 iBT). Electronic applications accepted. *Faculty research:* Studio art practice in ceramics, printing, photography, printmaking and sculpture, graphic design and industrial design, digital imaging in design and photography, Renaissance and American art history, contemporary art theory and criticism.

University of Oklahoma, Weitzenhoffer Family College of Fine Arts, School of Art and Art History, Program in Art, Norman, OK 73019. Offers visual communication (MFA). Applicants admitted in Fall only. *Students:* 13 full-time (3 women), 1 part-time (0 women); includes 4 minority (2 American Indian or Alaska Native, non-Hispanic/Latino; 2 Two or more races, non-Hispanic/Latino), 1 international. Average age 31. 20 applicants, 40% accepted, 2 enrolled. In 2014, 5 master's awarded. *Degree requirements:* For master's, comprehensive exam, thesis. *Entrance requirements:* For master's, bachelor's degree in art-related field, portfolio, writing sample, curriculum vitae, letters of recommendation. Additional exam requirements/recommendations for international students: Required—TOEFL (minimum score 79 iBT). *Application deadline:* For fall admission, 1/15 for domestic and international students. Application fee: $50 ($100 for international students). Electronic applications accepted. *Expenses:* Tuition, state resident: full-time $4394; part-time $183.10 per credit hour. Tuition, nonresident: full-time $16,970; part-time $707.10 per credit hour. *Required fees:* $2892; $109.95 per credit hour. $126.50 per semester. *Financial support:* In 2014–15, 14 students received support. Federal Work-Study, scholarships/grants, health care benefits, tuition waivers (partial), and unspecified assistantships available. Financial award application deadline: 6/1; financial award applicants required to submit FAFSA. *Faculty research:* Sculpture, painting, printmaking, technology, ceramics. *Unit head:* Todd Stewart, Interim Co-Director, 405-325-2691, Fax: 405-325-1668, E-mail: stewart@ou.edu. *Application contact:* Curtis Jones, Associate Professor, 405-325-2691, Fax: 405-325-1668, E-mail: chivo@ou.edu.
Website: http://art.ou.edu

University of Oregon, Graduate School, School of Architecture and Allied Arts, Department of Art, Eugene, OR 97403. Offers MFA. *Accreditation:* NASAD. *Degree requirements:* For master's, thesis or alternative. *Entrance requirements:* For master's, BFA or equivalent. Additional exam requirements/recommendations for international students: Required—TOEFL.

University of Pennsylvania, School of Design, Department of Fine Arts, Philadelphia, PA 19104. Offers emerging design and research (Certificate); fine arts (MFA); time-based and interactive media (Certificate). *Faculty:* 5 full-time (2 women). *Students:* 36 full-time (22 women), 1 part-time (0 women); includes 14 minority (4 Black or African American, non-Hispanic/Latino; 1 American Indian or Alaska Native, non-Hispanic/Latino; 1 Asian, non-Hispanic/Latino; 4 Hispanic/Latino; 4 Two or more races, non-Hispanic/Latino), 4 international. 119 applicants, 41% accepted, 18 enrolled. In 2014, 19 master's, 13 other advanced degrees awarded. *Entrance requirements:* For master's, portfolio. Additional exam requirements/recommendations for international students: Required—TOEFL, IELTS. *Application deadline:* For fall admission, 1/14 priority date for domestic and international students. Application fee: $80. Electronic applications accepted. *Financial support:* Teaching assistantships and scholarships/grants available. Financial award application deadline: 2/15; financial award applicants required to submit FAFSA. *Faculty research:* Painting, sculpture, printmaking, animation, video, installation, sound, emerging design practices, photography. *Unit head:* Marilyn Jordan Taylor, Dean, 215-898-6520, E-mail: mjtaylor@design.upenn.edu. *Application contact:* Office of Admissions and Financial Aid, 215-898-6520, E-mail: admissions@design.upenn.edu.
Website: http://www.design.upenn.edu/fine-arts

University of Regina, Faculty of Graduate Studies and Research, Faculty of Fine Arts, Department of Visual Arts, Regina, SK S4S 0A2, Canada. Offers ceramics (MFA); drawing (MFA); interdisciplinary studies (MA, MFA); intermedia (MFA); painting (MFA); sculpture (MFA). *Faculty:* 11 full-time (6 women), 3 part-time/adjunct (1 woman). *Students:* 7 full-time (all women), 2 part-time (both women). 11 applicants, 55% accepted. In 2014, 5 master's awarded. *Degree requirements:* For master's, exhibition, support paper, oral defense. *Entrance requirements:* For master's, documentation of recent work. Additional exam requirements/recommendations for international students: Required—TOEFL (minimum score 580 paper-based; 80 iBT), IELTS (minimum score 6.5), PTE (minimum score 59). *Application deadline:* For fall admission, 1/15 for domestic and international students. Application fee: $100. Electronic applications accepted. *Expenses: Tuition, area resident:* Full-time $4900 Canadian dollars; part-time $837.65 Canadian dollars per semester. *International tuition:* $7900 Canadian dollars full-time. *Required fees:* $396 Canadian dollars; $86.90 Canadian dollars per semester. *Financial support:* In 2014–15, 1 fellowship (averaging $6,000 per year), 6 teaching assistantships (averaging $2,427 per year) were awarded; research assistantships and scholarships/grants also available. Financial award application deadline: 6/15. *Faculty research:* Contemporary visual art theory and practice; art history; curatorial practice; print media; drawing/painting, sculpture, and ceramics. *Unit head:* Dr. David Garneau, Department Head, 306-585-5615, Fax: 306-585-5526, E-mail: david.garneau@uregina.ca. *Application contact:* Dr. Robert Truszkowski, Graduate Coordinator, Visual Arts, 306-585-5574, Fax: 306-585-5526, E-mail: robert.truszkowski@uregina.ca.

University of Rochester, School of Arts and Sciences, Department of Art and Art History, Rochester, NY 14627. Offers visual and cultural studies (MA, PhD). *Faculty:* 13 full-time (7 women). *Students:* 30 full-time (19 women); includes 6 minority (1 Black or African American, non-Hispanic/Latino; 2 Asian, non-Hispanic/Latino; 2 Hispanic/Latino; 1 Two or more races, non-Hispanic/Latino), 8 international. 73 applicants, 11% accepted, 3 enrolled. In 2014, 3 master's, 6 doctorates awarded. Terminal master's awarded for partial completion of doctoral program. *Degree requirements:* For master's, thesis optional; for doctorate, one foreign language, thesis/dissertation, qualifying exam. *Entrance requirements:* For master's and doctorate, GRE General Test, personal statement, three letters of recommendation, official undergraduate and graduate transcripts, writing sample. Additional exam requirements/recommendations for international students: Required—TOEFL. *Application deadline:* For fall admission, 1/15 for domestic students. Application fee: $60. *Expenses: Tuition:* Full-time $46,150; part-time $1442 per credit hour. *Required fees:* $504. *Financial support:* Fellowships, research assistantships, teaching assistantships, and tuition waivers (full and partial) available. Financial award application deadline: 2/1. *Faculty research:* Visual culture from a social-historical perspective. *Unit head:* Allen C. Topolski, Chair, 585-275-4287. *Application contact:* Martin Collier, Administrator, 585-275-7451.
Website: http://www.rochester.edu/College/aah/

University of Saint Francis, Graduate School, Department of Visual Art and Communication, Fort Wayne, IN 46808-3994. Offers studio art (MA). *Accreditation:* NASAD. Part-time and evening/weekend programs available. Postbaccalaureate distance learning degree programs offered (minimal on-campus study). *Faculty:* 6 full-time (4 women), 3 part-time/adjunct (1 woman). *Students:* 1 (woman) full-time, 3 part-

time (all women); includes 1 minority (Asian, non-Hispanic/Latino). Average age 41. 3 applicants, 100% accepted, 3 enrolled. In 2014, 4 master's awarded. *Degree requirements:* For master's, thesis, exhibit. *Entrance requirements:* For master's, undergraduate degree in art; minimum undergraduate GPA of 3.0; portfolio. Additional exam requirements/recommendations for international students: Required—TOEFL or IELTS. *Application deadline:* For fall admission, 7/1 for domestic students; for spring admission, 11/1 for domestic students. Applications are processed on a rolling basis. Application fee: $0. Electronic applications accepted. *Expenses:* Expenses: $830 per credit hour. *Financial support:* In 2014–15, 1 student received support. Federal Work-Study, scholarships/grants, and unspecified assistantships available. Support available to part-time students. Financial award application deadline: 3/10; financial award applicants required to submit FAFSA. *Unit head:* Rick Cartwright, Dean, 260-399-7700 Ext. 8015, Fax: 260-399-8171, E-mail: rcartwright@sf.edu. *Application contact:* Kyle Richardson, Enrollment Specialist, 260-399-7700 Ext. 6310, Fax: 260-399-8152, E-mail: krichardson@sf.edu.
Website: http://art.sf.edu/graduate/

University of Saskatchewan, College of Graduate Studies and Research, College of Arts and Science, Department of Art and Art History, Saskatoon, SK S7N 5A2, Canada. Offers MFA. Part-time programs available. *Degree requirements:* For master's, thesis. *Entrance requirements:* Additional exam requirements/recommendations for international students: Required—TOEFL (minimum score 80 iBT); Recommended—IELTS (minimum score 6.5).

University of South Carolina, The Graduate School, College of Arts and Sciences, Department of Art, Columbia, SC 29208. Offers art education (IMA, MA, MAT); art history (MA); art studio (MA); media arts (MMA); studio art (MFA). *Accreditation:* NASAD. *Degree requirements:* For master's, comprehensive exam (for some programs), thesis (for some programs). *Entrance requirements:* For master's, GRE General Test or MAT, portfolio. Additional exam requirements/recommendations for international students: Required—TOEFL. Electronic applications accepted. *Faculty research:* Script writing, teaching art at the elementary and secondary levels of education, history of art and architecture.

The University of South Dakota, Graduate School, College of Fine Arts, Department of Art, Vermillion, SD 57069-2390. Offers graphic design (MFA); painting (MFA); printmaking (MFA); sculpture (MFA). *Accreditation:* NASAD. *Degree requirements:* For master's, thesis or alternative. *Entrance requirements:* For master's, portfolio, minimum GPA of 2.7. Additional exam requirements/recommendations for international students: Required—TOEFL (minimum score 550 paper-based; 79 iBT). Electronic applications accepted.

University of Southern California, Graduate School, Dana and David Dornsife College of Letters, Arts and Sciences, Department of Art History, Los Angeles, CA 90089. Offers art history (MA, PhD); visual studies (Graduate Certificate). *Degree requirements:* For doctorate, 2 foreign languages, comprehensive exam, thesis/dissertation, 60 units. *Entrance requirements:* For doctorate, GRE. Additional exam requirements/recommendations for international students: Required—TOEFL. *Faculty research:* Ancient, medieval, Renaissance, eighteenth-nineteenth century, contemporary.

University of Southern California, Graduate School, Roski School of Fine Arts, Graduate Programs in Fine Arts, Los Angeles, CA 90089. Offers new genres (MFA); painting/drawing (MFA); photography (MFA); sculpture (MFA). *Degree requirements:* For master's, thesis. *Entrance requirements:* For master's, portfolio, artist statement, 3 letters of recommendation. Additional exam requirements/recommendations for international students: Required—TOEFL (minimum score 600 paper-based; 100 iBT). Electronic applications accepted. *Faculty research:* Fine art production in the areas of photography, video, sculpture, drawing, and performance.

University of South Florida, College of The Arts, School of Art and Art History, Tampa, FL 33620-9951. Offers art (MFA); art history (MA). *Accreditation:* NASAD. Part-time programs available. *Faculty:* 17 full-time (8 women). *Students:* 42 full-time (25 women), 2 part-time (1 woman); includes 9 minority (1 Black or African American, non-Hispanic/Latino; 7 Hispanic/Latino; 1 Two or more races, non-Hispanic/Latino), 4 international. Average age 29. 62 applicants, 39% accepted, 17 enrolled. In 2014, 10 master's awarded. *Degree requirements:* For master's, thesis, exhibition (for MFA). *Entrance requirements:* For master's, GRE General Test, bachelor's degree from regionally-accredited institution with minimum GPA of 3.0 in upper-division coursework or graduate degree from regionally-accredited institution; portfolio; goals statement (for MA in art history). Additional exam requirements/recommendations for international students: Required—TOEFL (minimum score 550 paper-based; 79 iBT) or IELTS (minimum score 6.5). *Application deadline:* For fall admission, 1/15 for domestic students, 1/2 for international students. Application fee: $30. *Financial support:* In 2014–15, 37 students received support, including 37 teaching assistantships with partial tuition reimbursements available (averaging $9,440 per year); scholarships/grants, health care benefits, and unspecified assistantships also available. Support available to part-time students. Financial award application deadline: 2/15; financial award applicants required to submit FAFSA. *Faculty research:* Contemporary art and role of the artist, identity strategies, political iconography, art practice and technology, the construction of race in art. *Total annual research expenditures:* $126,118. *Unit head:* Prof. Wallace Wilson, Director, 813-974-2360, Fax: 813-974-9226, E-mail: wwilson2@usf.edu. *Application contact:* Prof. Neil Bender, Associate Professor and Graduate Program Director, 813-974-2360, Fax: 813-974-9226, E-mail: nb2@usf.edu.
Website: http://www.art.usf.edu

The University of Tennessee, Graduate School, College of Arts and Sciences, School of Art, Knoxville, TN 37996. Offers ceramics (MFA); drawing (MFA); graphic design (MFA); inter-area studies (MFA); media arts (MFA); painting (MFA); printmaking (MFA); sculpture (MFA); watercolor (MFA). *Accreditation:* NASAD. *Degree requirements:* For master's, thesis or alternative, exhibit. *Entrance requirements:* For master's, portfolio, minimum GPA of 2.7. Additional exam requirements/recommendations for international students: Required—TOEFL. Electronic applications accepted.

The University of Texas at Arlington, Graduate School, College of Liberal Arts, Department of Art and Art History, Arlington, TX 76019. Offers film and video (MFA); glass (MFA); intermedia (MFA); visual communication (MFA). *Accreditation:* NASAD. *Degree requirements:* For master's, thesis or alternative, mid- and final program reviews; exhibition. *Entrance requirements:* For master's, GRE, minimum GPA of 3.0, 3 letters of recommendation, portfolio, resume. Additional exam requirements/recommendations for international students: Required—TOEFL (minimum score 550 paper-based). Electronic applications accepted.

The University of Texas at Austin, Graduate School, College of Fine Arts, Department of Art and Art History, Program in Studio Art, Austin, TX 78712-1111. Offers MFA. *Accreditation:* NASAD. *Degree requirements:* For master's, thesis, oral exam. *Entrance requirements:* For master's, minimum GPA of 3.0, portfolio of 15 slides. Electronic applications accepted. *Faculty research:* Painting, sculpture, transmedia, photography, printmaking.

The University of Texas at El Paso, Graduate School, College of Liberal Arts, Department of Art, El Paso, TX 79968-0001. Offers art education (MA); studio art (MA). Part-time and evening/weekend programs available. *Degree requirements:* For master's, thesis optional. *Entrance requirements:* For master's, minimum GPA of 3.0, digital portfolio, letters of recommendation. Additional exam requirements/recommendations for international students: Required—TOEFL; Recommended—IELTS. Electronic applications accepted.

The University of Texas at San Antonio, College of Liberal and Fine Arts, Department of Art and Art History, San Antonio, TX 78249-0617. Offers art (MFA); art history (MA). *Accreditation:* NASAD (one or more programs are accredited). *Faculty:* 15 full-time (8 women), 1 part-time/adjunct (0 women). *Students:* 22 full-time (13 women), 3 part-time (all women); includes 11 minority (all Hispanic/Latino). Average age 28. 24 applicants, 46% accepted, 5 enrolled. In 2014, 10 master's awarded. *Entrance requirements:* For master's, GRE General Test, portfolio, minimum GPA of 3.0 in last 60 hours, 3 letters of recommendation, statement of purpose. Additional exam requirements/recommendations for international students: Required—TOEFL (minimum score 550 paper-based; 79 iBT), IELTS (minimum score 6.5). *Application deadline:* For fall admission, 7/1 for domestic students, 4/1 for international students; for spring admission, 11/1 for domestic students, 9/1 for international students. Application fee: $45 ($80 for international students). *Expenses:* Tuition, state resident: full-time $4671; part-time $260 per credit hour. Tuition, nonresident: full-time $18,022; part-time $1001 per credit hour. *Unit head:* Dr. Gregory Elliott, Department Chair, 210-458-4362, Fax: 210-458-4356, E-mail: greg.elliott@utsa.edu. *Application contact:* Monica Rodriguez, Director of Graduate Admissions, 210-458-4331, Fax: 210-458-4332, E-mail: graduatestudies@utsa.edu.
Website: http://art.utsa.edu/

The University of Texas at Tyler, College of Arts and Sciences, Department of Art and Art History, Tyler, TX 75799-0001. Offers art history (MA); interdisciplinary (MAIS); studio art (MFA). *Degree requirements:* For master's, thesis, graduate committee review. *Entrance requirements:* For master's, minimum GPA of 3.0. Additional exam requirements/recommendations for international students: Required—TOEFL. *Faculty research:* Classical myths in contemporary art, social issues in contemporary art, casting methods, Renaissance art.

The University of Texas–Pan American, College of Arts and Humanities, Department of Art, Edinburg, TX 78539. Offers MFA. Part-time programs available. *Degree requirements:* For master's, thesis, thesis show of artwork. *Entrance requirements:* For master's, bachelor's degree in fine arts, portfolio, 3 letters of reference. *Expenses:* Tuition, state resident: full-time $4187; part-time $232.60 per credit hour. Tuition, nonresident: full-time $10,857; part-time $603.16 per credit hour. *Required fees:* $782; $27.50 per credit hour. $143.35 per semester. *Faculty research:* Creative art, ceramics, painting, sculpture, computer art.

The University of the Arts, College of Art, Media and Design, Department of Book Arts/Printmaking, Philadelphia, PA 19102-4944. Offers MFA. *Accreditation:* NASAD. *Degree requirements:* For master's, thesis. *Entrance requirements:* For master's, portfolio of 20-30 digital images showing work that represents applicant's full range of studio experience, preferrably including printmaking and book arts; official transcripts from each undergraduate or graduate school attended; three letters of recommendation; one-to two-page statement of professional plans and goals; personal interview. Additional exam requirements/recommendations for international students: Required—TOEFL (minimum score 580 paper-based, 92 iBT) or IELTS (minimum score 6.5).

The University of the Arts, College of Art, Media and Design, Program in Studio Art, Philadelphia, PA 19102-4944. Offers MFA. *Degree requirements:* For master's, thesis, summer residency. *Entrance requirements:* For master's, official transcripts from each undergraduate or graduate school attended, three letters of recommendation, one- to two-page statement of professional plans and goals, personal interview, portfolio. Additional exam requirements/recommendations for international students: Required—TOEFL (minimum score 580 paper-based, 92 iBT) or IELTS (minimum score 6.5).

The University of Tulsa, Graduate School, Kendall College of Arts and Sciences, School of Art, Tulsa, OK 74104-3189. Offers MA, MFA, MTA. Part-time programs available. *Faculty:* 9 full-time (5 women), 2 part-time/adjunct (0 women). *Students:* 10 full-time (6 women), 1 part-time (0 women); includes 3 minority (all American Indian or Alaska Native, non-Hispanic/Latino). Average age 35. 9 applicants, 67% accepted, 4 enrolled. In 2014, 4 master's awarded. *Degree requirements:* For master's, comprehensive exam (for some programs), thesis (for some programs). *Entrance requirements:* For master's, portfolio. Additional exam requirements/recommendations for international students: Required—TOEFL (minimum score 577 paper-based; 91 iBT), IELTS (minimum score 6.5). *Application deadline:* For fall admission, 2/1 for domestic and international students. Application fee: $55. Electronic applications accepted. *Expenses: Tuition:* Full-time $20,160; part-time $1120 per credit hour. *Required fees:* $6 per credit hour. Tuition and fees vary according to course level and course load. *Financial support:* In 2014–15, 9 students received support, including 9 teaching assistantships with full and partial tuition reimbursements available (averaging $12,417 per year); fellowships, career-related internships or fieldwork, Federal Work-Study, scholarships/grants, traineeships, health care benefits, tuition waivers (full and partial), and unspecified assistantships also available. Support available to part-time students. Financial award application deadline: 2/1; financial award applicants required to submit FAFSA. *Faculty research:* Drawing, painting, printmaking, ceramics, graphic design, photography. *Unit head:* Prof. Teresa Valero, Chairperson, 918-631-3513, Fax: 918-631-3423, E-mail: maria-valero@utulsa.edu. *Application contact:* Prof. Teresa Valero, Adviser, 918-631-3513, Fax: 918-631-3423, E-mail: maria-valero@utulsa.edu.
Website: http://artsandsciences.utulsa.edu/academics/departments-schools/art/

The University of Tulsa, Graduate School, Kendall College of Arts and Sciences, School of Education, Program in Teaching Arts, Tulsa, OK 74104-3189. Offers art (MTA); biology (MTA); English (MTA); history (MTA); mathematics (MTA). Part-time programs available. *Students:* 2 full-time (1 woman), 1 part-time (0 women); includes 1 minority (Black or African American, non-Hispanic/Latino). Average age 30. 2 applicants, 100% accepted, 1 enrolled. *Entrance requirements:* For master's, GRE General Test. Additional exam requirements/recommendations for international students: Required—TOEFL (minimum score 577 paper-based), IELTS (minimum score 6.5). *Application deadline:* Applications are processed on a rolling basis. Application fee: $55. Electronic applications accepted. *Expenses: Tuition:* Full-time $20,160; part-time $1120 per credit hour. *Required fees:* $6 per credit hour. Tuition and fees vary according to course level and course load. *Financial support:* In 2014–15, 2 students received support, including 1 research assistantship with full and partial tuition reimbursement available (averaging $13,148 per year), 1 teaching assistantship with full and partial tuition reimbursement available (averaging $13,148 per year); fellowships with full and partial tuition reimbursements available, career-related internships or fieldwork, Federal Work-Study, scholarships/grants, health care benefits, tuition waivers (full and partial), and unspecified assistantships also available. Support available to part-time students. Financial award application deadline: 2/1; financial award applicants required to submit FAFSA. *Unit head:* Dr. Kara Gae Neal, Chair, 918-631-2238, Fax: 918-631-3721, E-mail: karagae-neal@utulsa.edu. *Application contact:* Dr. David Brown, Advisor, 918-631-2719, Fax: 918-631-2133, E-mail: david-brown@utulsa.edu.

University of Utah, Graduate School, College of Fine Arts, Department of Art and Art History, Salt Lake City, UT 84112-0380. Offers art history (MA); ceramics (MFA);

community-based art education (MFA); drawing (MFA); graphic design (MFA); painting (MFA); photography/digital imaging (MFA); printmaking (MFA); sculpture/intermedia (MFA). *Faculty:* 19 full-time (10 women), 22 part-time/adjunct (10 women). *Students:* 11 full-time (9 women), 5 part-time (2 women); includes 2 minority (both Hispanic/Latino), 1 international. Average age 30. 48 applicants, 31% accepted, 10 enrolled. In 2014, 5 master's awarded. *Degree requirements:* For master's, variable foreign language requirement, comprehensive exam (for some programs), thesis or alternative, exhibit and final project paper (for MFA). *Entrance requirements:* For master's, CD portfolio (MFA), writing sample (MA), curriculum vitae, letters of recommendation, letter of intent. Additional exam requirements/recommendations for international students: Required—TOEFL (minimum score 575 paper-based; 75 iBT). *Application deadline:* For fall admission, 1/15 priority date for domestic and international students. Application fee: $55 ($65 for international students). Electronic applications accepted. *Financial support:* In 2014–15, 2 fellowships, 6 research assistantships with partial tuition reimbursements, 34 teaching assistantships with partial tuition reimbursements were awarded; Federal Work-Study, institutionally sponsored loans, scholarships/grants, tuition waivers (partial), unspecified assistantships, and stipends also available. Financial award application deadline: 1/2; financial award applicants required to submit FAFSA. *Faculty research:* Studio art, European art history, Asian art history, Latin American art history, twentieth century/contemporary art history. *Total annual research expenditures:* $54,906. *Unit head:* Prof. Brian Snapp, Chair, 801-581-8677, Fax: 801-585-6171, E-mail: b.snapp@utah.edu. *Application contact:* Prof. Kim Martinez, Director of Graduate Studies, 801-581-8677, Fax: 801-585-6171, E-mail: kim.martinez@art.utah.edu.
Website: http://www.art.utah.edu/

University of Victoria, Faculty of Graduate Studies, Faculty of Fine Arts, Department of Visual Arts, Victoria, BC V8W 2Y2, Canada. Offers digital multimedia (MFA); drawing (MFA); painting (MFA); photography (MFA); sculpture (MFA); video (MFA). *Degree requirements:* For master's, exhibit, oral exam. *Entrance requirements:* For master's, portfolio, BFA. Additional exam requirements/recommendations for international students: Required—TOEFL (minimum score 575 paper-based), IELTS (minimum score 7). Electronic applications accepted.

University of Washington, Graduate School, College of Arts and Sciences, School of Art, Division of Art, Seattle, WA 98195. Offers painting and drawing (MFA); photography (MFA). *Degree requirements:* For master's, thesis, exhibit. *Entrance requirements:* For master's, BFA or equivalent academic work in art, 20 slide portfolio. Additional exam requirements/recommendations for international students: Required—TOEFL. Electronic applications accepted.

University of Waterloo, Graduate Studies, Faculty of Arts, Department of Fine Arts, Waterloo, ON N2L 3G1, Canada. Offers studio art (MFA). *Degree requirements:* For master's, thesis exhibit. *Entrance requirements:* For master's, honors degree, minimum A- average, sample of work. Additional exam requirements/recommendations for international students: Required—TOEFL, TWE. Electronic applications accepted. *Faculty research:* Ceramic sculpture, computer imaging, painting, drawing, contemporary art theory.

University of Windsor, Faculty of Graduate Studies, Faculty of Arts and Social Sciences, School of Visual Arts, Windsor, ON N9B 3P4, Canada. Offers MFA. *Degree requirements:* For master's, thesis. *Entrance requirements:* For master's, minimum B average, portfolio. Additional exam requirements/recommendations for international students: Required—TOEFL (minimum score 560 paper-based). Electronic applications accepted.

University of Wisconsin–Madison, Graduate School, School of Education, Department of Art, Madison, WI 53706-1380. Offers art (MA, MFA); art education (MA). *Accreditation:* NASAD. Electronic applications accepted. *Expenses:* Tuition, state resident: full-time $10,723; part-time $745 per credit. Tuition, nonresident: full-time $24,054; part-time $1578 per credit. *Required fees:* $374 per semester. Tuition and fees vary according to course load, program and reciprocity agreements.

University of Wisconsin–Milwaukee, Graduate School, Peck School of the Arts, Department of Art, Milwaukee, WI 53201-0413. Offers art education (MS); studio art (MA, MFA). Part-time programs available. *Degree requirements:* For master's, comprehensive exam, thesis or alternative. *Entrance requirements:* For master's, portfolio. Additional exam requirements/recommendations for international students: Required—TOEFL (minimum score 550 paper-based; 79 iBT), IELTS (minimum score 6.5). Electronic applications accepted.

University of Wisconsin–River Falls, Outreach and Graduate Studies, College of Arts and Science, Program in Fine Arts, River Falls, WI 54022. Offers MSE.

University of Wisconsin–Superior, Graduate Division, Department of Visual Arts, Superior, WI 54880-4500. Offers art education (MA); art history (MA); art therapy (MA); studio arts (MA). Part-time programs available. *Degree requirements:* For master's, comprehensive exam, exhibit. *Entrance requirements:* For master's, minimum GPA of 2.75, portfolio. Electronic applications accepted.

Utah State University, School of Graduate Studies, College of Humanities, Arts and Social Sciences, Department of Art, Logan, UT 84322. Offers MA, MFA. *Degree requirements:* For master's, thesis, exhibit. *Entrance requirements:* For master's, GRE General Test or MAT, minimum GPA of 3.0, slide portfolio of art. Additional exam requirements/recommendations for international students: Required—TOEFL. *Faculty research:* Painting, drawing, sculpture, ceramics, photography.

Vermont College of Fine Arts, MFA in Visual Art Program, Montpelier, VT 05602. Offers MFA. Postbaccalaureate distance learning degree programs offered (minimal on-campus study). *Faculty:* 13 part-time/adjunct (7 women). *Students:* 49 full-time (34 women); includes 3 minority (1 American Indian or Alaska Native, non-Hispanic/Latino; 2 Hispanic/Latino), 3 international. Average age 43. 45 applicants, 58% accepted, 16 enrolled. In 2014, 29 master's awarded. *Entrance requirements:* For master's, BFA, BA, or BS from accredited college or university, or Diploma from recognized professional art school, substantial experience in making art; thirty semester hours in undergraduate study (preferred). *Application deadline:* For fall admission, 2/15 priority date for domestic students, 2/15 for international students; for spring admission, 9/15 priority date for domestic students, 9/15 for international students. Applications are processed on a rolling basis. Application fee: $75. Electronic applications accepted. Full-time tuition and fees vary according to program. *Financial support:* Scholarships/grants available. Financial award applicants required to submit FAFSA. *Unit head:* Danielle Dahline, Program Director, 802-828-8703, E-mail: danielle.dahline@vcfa.edu. *Application contact:* Renee Lauzon, Assistant Director of Admissions, 802-828-8636, E-mail: renee.lauzon@vcfa.edu.
Website: http://www.vcfa.edu/visual-art

Virginia Commonwealth University, Graduate School, College of Humanities and Sciences, School of Mass Communications, Program in Media, Art, and Text, Richmond, VA 23284-9005. Offers PhD. *Entrance requirements:* For doctorate, GRE. Additional exam requirements/recommendations for international students: Required—TOEFL (minimum score 600 paper-based; 100 iBT); Recommended—IELTS (minimum score 6.5). Electronic applications accepted.

Virginia Commonwealth University, Graduate School, School of the Arts, Richmond, VA 23284-9005. Offers art education (MAE); art history (MA, PhD), including architectural history (MA), art history, historical studies (MA), museum studies (MA); ceramics (MFA); fibers (MFA); furniture design (MFA); glassworking (MFA); graphic design (MFA), including design/visual communications, interior environment, photography and film; jewelry/metalworking (MFA); kinetic imaging (MFA); music (MM), including education; painting (MFA); printmaking (MFA); sculpture (MFA); theatre (MFA), including acting, costume design, directing, pedagogy, scene design/technical theater. Part-time programs available. *Entrance requirements:* For doctorate, GRE General Test, writing sample. Additional exam requirements/recommendations for international students: Required—TOEFL (minimum score 600 paper-based; 100 iBT). Electronic applications accepted.

Washington State University, College of Liberal Arts, Department of Fine Arts, Pullman, WA 99164. Offers MFA. Programs offered at the Pullman campus. *Students:* 14 full-time (9 women). Average age 27. 25 applicants, 24% accepted, 6 enrolled. In 2014, 7 master's awarded. *Degree requirements:* For master's, comprehensive exam (for some programs), thesis, exhibit, oral exam. *Entrance requirements:* For master's, statement of intent, portfolio of no more than 15 images on CD/DVD. Additional exam requirements/recommendations for international students: Required—TOEFL (minimum score 550 paper-based), IELTS. *Application deadline:* For fall admission, 1/10 for domestic and international students. Application fee: $75. Electronic applications accepted. *Expenses:* Tuition, state resident: full-time $11,768. Tuition, nonresident: full-time $25,200. *Required fees:* $960. Tuition and fees vary according to program. *Financial support:* In 2014–15, 14 teaching assistantships with full and partial tuition reimbursements (averaging $12,423 per year) were awarded; research assistantships, career-related internships or fieldwork, Federal Work-Study, institutionally sponsored loans, tuition waivers (partial), and unspecified assistantships also available. Financial award application deadline: 2/15; financial award applicants required to submit FAFSA. *Faculty research:* Polynesian art, museum representation, number theory. *Unit head:* Dr. Thom Brown, Chair, 509-335-8686, Fax: 509-335-7742, E-mail: thom.brown@wsu.edu. *Application contact:* Graduate School Admissions, 800-GRADWSU, Fax: 509-335-1949, E-mail: gradsch@wsu.edu.
Website: http://finearts.wsu.edu/

Washington University in St. Louis, Sam Fox School of Design and Visual Arts, Graduate School of Art, St. Louis, MO 63130-4899. Offers visual art (MFA). *Accreditation:* NASAD. *Degree requirements:* For master's, thesis, exhibition. *Entrance requirements:* For master's, portfolio, resume. Additional exam requirements/recommendations for international students: Required—TOEFL (minimum score 577 paper-based; 90 iBT), IELTS (minimum score 7.5). Electronic applications accepted. *Expenses:* Contact institution. *Faculty research:* New media, design, fine arts.

Wayne State University, College of Fine, Performing and Communication Arts, James Pearson Duffy Department of Art and Art History, Program in Art, Detroit, MI 48202. Offers fibers (MFA); photography (MA); sculpture (MA). *Students:* 9 full-time (5 women), 8 part-time (5 women); includes 2 minority (1 Hispanic/Latino; 1 Two or more races, non-Hispanic/Latino), 1 international. Average age 35. 33 applicants, 15% accepted, 4 enrolled. In 2014, 9 master's awarded. *Degree requirements:* For master's, thesis exhibition (MFA), essay (MA). *Entrance requirements:* For master's, portfolio, personal interview, reference letters, statement of intent, BFA or equivalent coursework (for MA); superior portfolio, BFA or MA in art (for MFA). Additional exam requirements/recommendations for international students: Required—TOEFL (minimum score 550 paper-based), TWE (minimum score 5.5), Michigan English Language Assessment Battery (minimum score 85); Recommended—IELTS (minimum score 6.5). *Application deadline:* For fall admission, 2/1 for domestic and international students; for winter admission, 10/1 for domestic and international students. Application fee: $0. Electronic applications accepted. *Expenses:* Expenses: Contact institution. *Financial support:* In 2014–15, 9 students received support. Fellowships with tuition reimbursements available, teaching assistantships with tuition reimbursements available, scholarships/grants, and unspecified assistantships available. Financial award application deadline: 3/31; financial award applicants required to submit FAFSA. *Faculty research:* Painting, drawing, computer art. *Unit head:* Dr. John Richardson, Chair, 313-577-2980, Fax: 313-577-3491, E-mail: af5343@wayne.edu. *Application contact:* Jeffrey Abt, Professor, 313-993-6785, E-mail: jeffrey.abt@wayne.edu.
Website: http://art.wayne.edu/

Webster University, Leigh Gerdine College of Fine Arts, Department of Art, St. Louis, MO 63119-3194. Offers art (MA); arts management and leadership (MFA). Part-time programs available. *Degree requirements:* For master's, thesis. *Entrance requirements:* For master's, BA or BFA in related field, interview, portfolio. Additional exam requirements/recommendations for international students: Required—TOEFL.

Western Carolina University, Graduate School, College of Fine and Performing Arts, Cullowhee, NC 28723. Offers MFA, MM. *Accreditation:* NASAD. Part-time programs available. *Degree requirements:* For master's, comprehensive exam, thesis optional. *Entrance requirements:* For master's, GRE, appropriate undergraduate degree, portfolio, letters of recommendation, letter of intent, live audition and/or interview. Additional exam requirements/recommendations for international students: Required—TOEFL (minimum score 550 paper-based; 79 iBT). *Faculty research:* Vernacular cultural studies and oral history, sound mixing for television, music technology.

Western Connecticut State University, Division of Graduate Studies, School of Visual and Performing Arts, Department of Art, Danbury, CT 06810-6885. Offers illustration (MFA); painting (MFA). Part-time programs available. *Degree requirements:* For master's, individual exhibition of artwork, review of student's progress prior to admission to final semester, completion of program in 6 years. *Entrance requirements:* For master's, portfolio review, minimum GPA of 2.5. Additional exam requirements/recommendations for international students: Recommended—TOEFL (minimum score 550 paper-based; 79 iBT), IELTS (minimum score 6). *Expenses:* Contact institution. *Faculty research:* Proficiency in both traditional and digital processes.

West Texas A&M University, College of Fine Arts and Humanities, Department of Art, Theatre and Dance, Program in Art, Canyon, TX 79016-0001. Offers MA. Part-time programs available. *Degree requirements:* For master's, comprehensive exam, thesis optional, exhibit, portfolio review. *Entrance requirements:* For master's, GRE General Test, interview, portfolio. Additional exam requirements/recommendations for international students: Required—TOEFL (minimum score 550 paper-based). Electronic applications accepted. *Faculty research:* Ceramics, graphic design, woodblock prints, art history, aesthetics, glassblowing.

West Texas A&M University, College of Fine Arts and Humanities, Department of Art, Theatre and Dance, Program in Studio Art, Canyon, TX 79016-0001. Offers MFA. Part-time programs available. *Degree requirements:* For master's, comprehensive exam, thesis optional, exhibit, portfolio review, professional paper. *Entrance requirements:* For master's, GRE General Test, interview, portfolio. Additional exam requirements/recommendations for international students: Required—TOEFL (minimum score 550 paper-based). *Faculty research:* Ceramics, printmaking, graphic design, art history, aesthetics, glass blowing.

West Virginia University, College of Creative Arts, Division of Art and Design, Morgantown, WV 26506. Offers art education (MA); art history (MA); ceramics (MFA); graphic design (MFA); painting (MFA); printmaking (MFA); sculpture (MFA); studio art (MA). *Accreditation:* NASAD. *Degree requirements:* For master's, thesis, exhibit. *Entrance requirements:* For master's, minimum GPA of 2.75, portfolio. Additional exam requirements/recommendations for international students: Required—TOEFL. *Expenses:* Contact institution. *Faculty research:* Medieval art history.

Wichita State University, Graduate School, College of Fine Arts, School of Art and Design, Wichita, KS 67260. Offers studio arts (MFA), including ceramics, painting, printmaking, sculpture. *Accreditation:* NASAD. *Unit head:* Prof. Royce Smith, Director, 316-978-3555, Fax: 316-978-5418, E-mail: royce.smith@wichita.edu. *Application contact:* Jordan Oleson, Admissions Coordinator, 316-978-3095, Fax: 316-978-3253, E-mail: jordan.oleson@wichita.edu.
Website: http://www.wichita.edu/artdesign

William Paterson University of New Jersey, College of the Arts and Communication, Wayne, NJ 07470-8420. Offers art (MFA); music (MM); professional communication (MA). *Accreditation:* NASAD. Part-time and evening/weekend programs available. *Faculty:* 23 full-time (15 women), 11 part-time/adjunct (6 women). *Students:* 32 full-time (13 women), 18 part-time (11 women); includes 9 minority (2 Black or African American, non-Hispanic/Latino; 3 Asian, non-Hispanic/Latino; 4 Hispanic/Latino), 5 international. Average age 32. 79 applicants, 59% accepted, 24 enrolled. In 2014, 26 master's awarded. *Degree requirements:* For master's, comprehensive exam (for some programs), thesis (for some programs). *Entrance requirements:* For master's, GRE, minimum GPA of 2.75; audition; 2 letters of recommendation; portfolio with letter of intent. Additional exam requirements/recommendations for international students: Required—TOEFL (minimum score 550 paper-based; 79 iBT), IELTS (minimum score 6). *Application deadline:* For fall admission, 6/1 for domestic students, 3/1 for international students; for spring admission, 11/5 for domestic students, 10/15 for international students. Applications are processed on a rolling basis. Application fee: $50. Electronic applications accepted. *Expenses:* Tuition, state resident: full-time $12,413; part-time $564.21 per credit. Tuition, nonresident: full-time $20,487; part-time $931.21 per credit. *Required fees:* $2107; $95.79 per credit. $478.95 per semester. Tuition and fees vary according to course load and degree level. *Financial support:* Research assistantships with full tuition reimbursements, career-related internships or fieldwork, Federal Work-Study, scholarships/grants, and unspecified assistantships available. Support available to part-time students. Financial award application deadline: 4/1; financial award applicants required to submit FAFSA. *Unit head:* Daryl Moore, Dean, 973-720-2232, E-mail: moored@wpunj.edu. *Application contact:* Christina Aiello, Assistant Director, Graduate Admissions, 973-720-2506, Fax: 973-720-2035, E-mail: aielloc@wpunj.edu.
Website: http://www.wpunj.edu/coac

Winthrop University, College of Visual and Performing Arts, Department of Art, Rock Hill, SC 29733. Offers art (MFA); art administration (MA); art education (MA). *Accreditation:* NASAD. Part-time programs available. *Degree requirements:* For master's, thesis, documented exhibit, oral exam. *Entrance requirements:* For master's, GRE General Test or MAT, PRAXIS (MA), minimum GPA of 3.0, resume, slide portfolio, teaching certificate (MA). Electronic applications accepted.

Yale University, School of Art, New Haven, CT 06520-8339. Offers graphic design (MFA); painting/printmaking (MFA); photography (MFA); sculpture (MFA). *Degree requirements:* For master's, thesis (for some programs). *Entrance requirements:* Additional exam requirements/recommendations for international students: Required—TOEFL (minimum score 550 paper-based; 100 iBT). Electronic applications accepted. *Expenses:* Contact institution.

York University, Faculty of Graduate Studies, Faculty of Fine Arts, Program in Visual Arts, Toronto, ON M3J 1P3, Canada. Offers MFA, PhD. *Degree requirements:* For master's, thesis. *Entrance requirements:* For master's, portfolio. Electronic applications accepted.

Art History

Academy of Art University, Graduate Program, School of Art History, San Francisco, CA 94105-3410. Offers MA. Part-time and evening/weekend programs available. Postbaccalaureate distance learning degree programs offered (no on-campus study). *Students:* 4 full-time (3 women), 17 part-time (16 women); includes 5 minority (1 Black or African American, non-Hispanic/Latino; 1 Asian, non-Hispanic/Latino; 2 Hispanic/Latino; 1 Two or more races, non-Hispanic/Latino). Average age 35. 25 applicants, 100% accepted, 10 enrolled. *Degree requirements:* For master's, final review. *Entrance requirements:* For master's, statement of intent; resume; portfolio/reel; official college transcripts. *Application deadline:* Applications are processed on a rolling basis. Application fee: $100. Electronic applications accepted. *Expenses: Tuition:* Part-time $910 per unit. *Financial support:* Career-related internships or fieldwork and Federal Work-Study available. Support available to part-time students. Financial award application deadline: 8/10; financial award applicants required to submit FAFSA. *Unit head:* 800-544-ARTS, E-mail: info@academyart.edu. *Application contact:* 800-544-ARTS, E-mail: info@academyart.edu.
Website: http://www.academyart.edu/art-history/

Arizona State University at the Tempe campus, Herberger Institute for Design and the Arts, School of Art, Tempe, AZ 85287-1505. Offers art education (MA); art history (MA); ceramics (MFA); design, environment and the arts (PhD), including history, theory and criticism; drawing (MFA); fibers (MFA); intermedia (MFA); metals (MFA); museum studies (MFA); painting (MFA); printmaking (MFA); sculpture (MFA); wood (MFA); MFA/MA. Terminal master's awarded for partial completion of doctoral program. *Degree requirements:* For master's, thesis/exhibition (MFA, MA in art education); interactive Program of Study (iPOS) submitted before completing 50 percent of required credit hours; for doctorate, comprehensive exam, thesis/dissertation, interactive Program of Study (iPOS) submitted before completing 50 percent of required credit hours. *Entrance requirements:* For master's, GRE or MAT, minimum GPA of 3.0 or equivalent in last 2 years of work leading to bachelor's degree; for doctorate, GRE, master's degree in architecture, graphic design, industrial design, interior design, landscape architecture, or art history or equivalent standing; statement of purpose; 3 letters of recommendation; indication of potential faculty mentor; sample of written work. Additional exam requirements/recommendations for international students: Required—TOEFL, IELTS, or PTE. Electronic applications accepted.

Bard Graduate Center: Decorative Arts, Design History, Material Culture, Graduate Studies, New York, NY 10024-3602. Offers M Phil, MA, PhD. Part-time programs available. *Faculty:* 17 full-time (7 women), 5 part-time/adjunct (4 women). *Students:* 70 full-time (56 women), 13 part-time (all women). 100 applicants, 35% accepted, 21 enrolled. In 2014, 22 master's, 4 doctorates awarded. Terminal master's awarded for partial completion of doctoral program. *Degree requirements:* For master's, one foreign language, internship, qualifying paper; for doctorate, 2 foreign languages, thesis/dissertation, exams. *Entrance requirements:* For master's, GRE General Test, writing sample, 3 letters of recommendation; for doctorate, GRE General Test, master's thesis or equivalent, 3 letters of recommendation. Additional exam requirements/recommendations for international students: Required—TOEFL. *Application deadline:* For fall admission, 1/8 for domestic and international students. Application fee: $70. *Financial support:* Fellowships with tuition reimbursements, research assistantships, teaching assistantships, career-related internships or fieldwork, institutionally sponsored loans, scholarships/grants, traineeships, health care benefits, and unspecified assistantships available. Financial award application deadline: 1/8; financial award applicants required to submit FAFSA. *Faculty research:* English craftsmen; ancient furniture; aesthetics and politics; Art Nouveau jewelry; European sculpture; New York and American material culture; modern design history; early modern Europe; history and theory of museums; comparative medieval material culture (China, Islam, Europe); archaeology, anthropology, and material culture. *Unit head:* Susan Weber, Director, 212-501-3000, Fax: 212-501-3079. *Application contact:* Elena Pinto Simon, Dean, Academic Administration and Student Affairs, 212-501-3057, Fax: 212-501-3065, E-mail: simon@bgc.bard.edu.

See Display on next page and Close-Up on page 195.

Binghamton University, State University of New York, Graduate School, School of Arts and Sciences, Department of Art History, Vestal, NY 13850. Offers MA, PhD. *Faculty:* 8 full-time (4 women), 1 part-time/adjunct (0 women). *Students:* 16 full-time (13 women), 14 part-time (11 women); includes 3 minority (1 Asian, non-Hispanic/Latino; 1 Hispanic/Latino; 1 Native Hawaiian or other Pacific Islander, non-Hispanic/Latino), 14 international. Average age 34. 22 applicants, 68% accepted, 5 enrolled. In 2014, 4 master's, 5 doctorates awarded. *Degree requirements:* For master's, one foreign language, comprehensive exam, thesis; for doctorate, 2 foreign languages, comprehensive exam, thesis/dissertation. *Entrance requirements:* For master's and doctorate, GRE General Test, writing sample. Additional exam requirements/recommendations for international students: Required—TOEFL (minimum score 80 iBT). *Application deadline:* For fall admission, 1/15 priority date for domestic and international students; for spring admission, 10/1 priority date for domestic and international students. Applications are processed on a rolling basis. Application fee: $75. Electronic applications accepted. *Expenses:* Tuition, state resident: full-time $7776; part-time $432 per credit. Tuition, nonresident: full-time $15,138; part-time $841 per credit. *Required fees:* $1754; $213 per credit. Tuition and fees vary according to degree level and program. *Financial support:* In 2014–15, 15 students received support, including 9 teaching assistantships with full tuition reimbursements available (averaging $15,000 per year); career-related internships or fieldwork, Federal Work-Study, institutionally sponsored loans, scholarships/grants, health care benefits, and unspecified assistantships also available. Financial award application deadline: 2/15; financial award applicants required to submit FAFSA. *Faculty research:* History of art and architecture. *Unit head:* Dr. Nancy Um, Interim Chair, 607-777-5864, E-mail: nancyum@binghamton.edu. *Application contact:* Kishan Zuber, Recruiting and Admissions Coordinator, 607-777-2151, Fax: 607-777-2501, E-mail: kzuber@binghamton.edu.
Website: http://www.binghamton.edu/art-history/

Boston University, Graduate School of Arts and Sciences, Department of History of Art and Architecture, Boston, MA 02215. Offers art history (MA, PhD); museum studies (Certificate). *Students:* 58 full-time (54 women), 6 part-time (4 women); includes 10 minority (3 Black or African American, non-Hispanic/Latino; 3 Asian, non-Hispanic/Latino; 2 Hispanic/Latino; 2 Two or more races, non-Hispanic/Latino), 4 international. Average age 32. 188 applicants, 32% accepted, 12 enrolled. In 2014, 13 master's, 4 doctorates awarded. Terminal master's awarded for partial completion of doctoral program. *Degree requirements:* For master's, one foreign language, comprehensive exam, thesis; for doctorate, 2 foreign languages, comprehensive exam, thesis/dissertation. *Entrance requirements:* For master's and doctorate, GRE General Test, 3 letters of recommendation, writing sample, foreign language proficiency; for Certificate, GRE General Test. Additional exam requirements/recommendations for international students: Required—TOEFL (minimum score 550 paper-based; 84 iBT). *Application deadline:* For fall admission, 1/5 for domestic and international students; for spring admission, 10/15 for domestic and international students. Application fee: $80. *Expenses: Tuition:* Full-time $45,686; part-time $1428 per credit hour. *Required fees:* $660; $60 per semester. Tuition and fees vary according to program. *Financial support:* In 2014–15, 49 students received support, including 13 fellowships with full tuition reimbursements available (averaging $20,500 per year), 7 teaching assistantships with full tuition reimbursements available (averaging $20,500 per year); career-related internships or fieldwork, Federal Work-Study, health care benefits, and unspecified assistantships also available. Support available to part-time students. Financial award application deadline: 1/5. *Unit head:* Bruce Redford, Chairman, 617-353-1455, Fax: 617-353-3243, E-mail: bredford@bu.edu. *Application contact:* Cheryl Crombie, Administrative Assistant, 617-353-2522, Fax: 617-353-3243, E-mail: ccrombie@bu.edu.
Website: http://www.bu.edu/AH/

Bowling Green State University, Graduate College, College of Arts and Sciences, School of Art, Bowling Green, OH 43403. Offers 2-D studio art (MA, MFA); 3-D studio art (MA, MFA); art education (MA); art history (MA); computer art (MA); design (MFA); digital arts (MFA); graphics (MFA). *Accreditation:* NASAD. Part-time programs available. *Degree requirements:* For master's, thesis or alternative, final exhibit (MFA). *Entrance requirements:* For master's, GRE General Test (MA), slide portfolio (15-20 slides). Additional exam requirements/recommendations for international students: Required—TOEFL. Electronic applications accepted. *Faculty research:* Computer animation and virtual reality, Spanish still-life painting from 1600 to 1800, art and psychotherapy, Japanese wood-firing techniques in ceramics, non-toxic printmaking technologies.

Brooklyn College of the City University of New York, School of Visual, Media and Performing Arts, Department of Art, Brooklyn, NY 11210-2889. Offers art history (MA); digital art (MFA); drawing and painting (MFA); photography (MFA); printmaking (MFA); sculpture (MFA). Part-time programs available. *Degree requirements:* For master's, thesis. *Entrance requirements:* For master's, bachelor's degree in art, portfolio, 2 letters

Art History

of recommendation. Additional exam requirements/recommendations for international students: Required—TOEFL (minimum score 500 paper-based; 61 iBT). Electronic applications accepted.

Brown University, Graduate School, Department of History of Art and Architecture, Providence, RI 02912. Offers PhD. *Degree requirements:* For doctorate, 2 foreign languages, thesis/dissertation, oral exam. *Entrance requirements:* For doctorate, GRE General Test, MA with distinction.

Brown University, Graduate School, Joukowsky Institute for Archaeology and the Ancient World, Providence, RI 02912. Offers PhD. *Degree requirements:* For doctorate, thesis/dissertation.

Bryn Mawr College, Graduate School of Arts and Sciences, Department of History of Art, Bryn Mawr, PA 19010-2899. Offers MA, PhD. Part-time programs available. *Faculty:* 7 full-time (5 women), 1 (woman) part-time/adjunct. *Students:* 23 full-time (20 women), 1 (woman) part-time; includes 5 minority (1 Asian, non-Hispanic/Latino; 3 Hispanic/Latino; 1 Native Hawaiian or other Pacific Islander, non-Hispanic/Latino), 1 international. Average age 30. 38 applicants, 21% accepted, 3 enrolled. In 2014, 2 master's, 4 doctorates awarded. *Degree requirements:* For master's, 2 foreign languages, thesis; for doctorate, 2 foreign languages, comprehensive exam, thesis/dissertation. *Entrance requirements:* For master's and doctorate, GRE General Test. Additional exam requirements/recommendations for international students: Required—TOEFL (minimum score 600 paper-based). *Application deadline:* For fall admission, 1/3 for domestic and international students. Application fee: $50. *Expenses: Tuition:* Full-time $37,920. *Financial support:* In 2014–15, 15 fellowships with partial tuition reimbursements (averaging $15,335 per year), 6 teaching assistantships with full tuition reimbursements (averaging $13,875 per year) were awarded; Federal Work-Study, scholarships/grants, tuition waivers (full and partial), and unspecified assistantships also available. Support available to part-time students. Financial award application deadline: 1/3. *Unit head:* Maria Dantis, Graduate Program Administrator, 610-526-5074, E-mail: gsas@brynmawr.edu.

California State University, Chico, Office of Graduate Studies, College of Humanities and Fine Arts, Department of Art and Art History, Program in Art History, Chico, CA 95929-0722. Offers MA. *Accreditation:* NASAD. *Students:* 4 applicants, 100% accepted, 2 enrolled. In 2014, 2 master's awarded. *Degree requirements:* For master's, thesis, examination. *Entrance requirements:* For master's, 2 letters of recommendation; statement of purpose; two upper-division art history papers; department letter of recommendation access waiver form. Additional exam requirements/recommendations for international students: Required—TOEFL (minimum score 550 paper-based; 80 iBT), IELTS (minimum score 6.5), PTE (minimum score 59). *Application deadline:* For fall admission, 3/1 priority date for domestic students, 3/1 for international students; for spring admission, 9/15 priority date for domestic students, 9/15 for international students. Application fee: $55. Electronic applications accepted. *Expenses:* Tuition, state resident: full-time $7002. Tuition, nonresident: full-time $18,162. *Required fees:* $1530. Tuition and fees vary according to program. *Financial support:* Scholarships/grants available. Financial award application deadline: 3/1; financial award applicants required to submit FAFSA. *Unit head:* Dr. Robert Herhusky, Chair, 530-898-4560, Fax: 530-898-4171, E-mail: art@csuchico.edu. *Application contact:* Judy L. Rice, Graduate Admissions Coordinator, 530-898-5416, Fax: 530-898-3342, E-mail: jlrice@csuchico.edu.
Website: http://catalog.csuchico.edu/viewer/15/ARTS/ARTSNONEMA.html

California State University, Fullerton, Graduate Studies, College of the Arts, Department of Visual Arts, Fullerton, CA 92834-9480. Offers art (MA, MFA), including art history (MA), ceramics (MFA), crafts, creative photography, exhibition design, glass, graphic design, illustration, sculpture. *Accreditation:* NASAD (one or more programs are accredited). Part-time programs available. *Students:* 28 full-time (16 women), 29 part-time (22 women); includes 20 minority (3 Black or African American, non-Hispanic/Latino; 8 Asian, non-Hispanic/Latino; 8 Hispanic/Latino; 1 Two or more races, non-Hispanic/Latino), 7 international. Average age 35. 58 applicants, 38% accepted, 14 enrolled. In 2014, 17 master's awarded. *Degree requirements:* For master's, project or thesis. *Entrance requirements:* For master's, minimum GPA of 2.5 in last 60 units of course work, portfolio. Application fee: $55. *Financial support:* Career-related internships or fieldwork, Federal Work-Study, institutionally sponsored loans, and scholarships/grants available. Support available to part-time students. Financial award application deadline: 3/1; financial award applicants required to submit FAFSA. *Unit head:* Dana Lamb, Chair, 657-278-2076. *Application contact:* Admissions/Applications, 657-278-2371.

California State University, Long Beach, Graduate Studies, College of the Arts, Department of Art, Long Beach, CA 90840. Offers art education (MA); art history (MA); studio art (MA, MFA). *Accreditation:* NASAD. Part-time programs available. *Degree requirements:* For master's, minimum GPA of 3.0 in last 60 hours. Electronic applications accepted.

California State University, Los Angeles, Graduate Studies, College of Arts and Letters, Department of Art, Los Angeles, CA 90032-8530. Offers art (MA), including art education, art history, art therapy, ceramics, metals, and textiles, design (MA, MFA), painting, sculpture, and graphic arts, photography; fine arts (MFA), including crafts, design (MA, MFA), studio arts. *Accreditation:* NASAD (one or more programs are accredited). Part-time and evening/weekend programs available. *Degree requirements:* For master's, comprehensive exam, project or thesis. *Entrance requirements:* For master's, portfolio. Additional exam requirements/recommendations for international students: Required—TOEFL (minimum score 500 paper-based). Electronic applications accepted. *Expenses:* Tuition, state resident: full-time $6738; part-time $3609 per year. Tuition, nonresident: full-time $15,666; part-time $8073 per year. Tuition and fees vary according to course load, degree level and program. *Faculty research:* The artist and the book, conceptual art, ceramic processes, computer graphics, architectural graphics.

California State University, Northridge, Graduate Studies, College of Arts, Media, and Communication, Department of Art, Northridge, CA 91330. Offers art education (MA); art history (MA); studio art (MA, MFA); visual communications (MA, MFA). *Accreditation:* NASAD. *Students:* 34 full-time (26 women), 11 part-time (8 women); includes 14 minority (3 Asian, non-Hispanic/Latino; 9 Hispanic/Latino; 2 Two or more races, non-Hispanic/Latino), 4 international. Average age 30. *Application deadline:* For fall admission, 11/30 for domestic students. Application fee: $55. *Expenses: Required fees:* $12,402. *Financial support:* Application deadline: 3/1. *Unit head:* Prof. Edward Alfano, Chair, 818-677-2242, E-mail: art.dept@csun.edu.
Website: http://www.csun.edu/art/

Caribbean University, Graduate School, Bayamón, PR 00960-0493. Offers administration and supervision (MA Ed); criminal justice (MA); curriculum and instruction (MA Ed, PhD), including elementary education (MA Ed), English education (MA Ed), history education (MA Ed), mathematics education (MA Ed), primary education (MA Ed), science education (MA Ed), Spanish education (MA Ed); educational technology in instructional systems (MA Ed); gerontology (MSN); human resources (MBA); museology, archiving and art history (MA Ed); neonatal pediatrics (MSN); physical education (MA Ed); special education (MA Ed). *Entrance requirements:* For master's, interview, minimum GPA of 2.5.

Carleton University, Faculty of Graduate Studies, Faculty of Arts and Social Sciences, School for Studies in Art and Culture, Program in Art History: Art and its Institutions, Ottawa, ON K1S 5B6, Canada. Offers MA. *Degree requirements:* For master's, thesis. *Entrance requirements:* For master's, honors degree.

Case Western Reserve University, School of Graduate Studies, Department of Art History and Art, Program in Art History, Cleveland, OH 44106. Offers MA, PhD. Programs offered jointly with The Cleveland Museum of Art. Part-time programs available. *Faculty:* 7 full-time (6 women), 13 part-time/adjunct (7 women). *Students:* 10 full-time (8 women), 1 (woman) part-time; includes 1 minority (Asian, non-Hispanic/Latino). Average age 33. 36 applicants, 39% accepted, 8 enrolled. In 2014, 1 master's, 3 doctorates awarded. *Degree requirements:* For master's, one foreign language, thesis or alternative; for doctorate, 2 foreign languages, comprehensive exam, thesis/dissertation. *Entrance requirements:* For master's, GRE General Test, 2 samples of written work; for doctorate, GRE General Test, 2 samples of written work, MA thesis. Additional exam requirements/recommendations for international students: Required—TOEFL (minimum score 600 paper-based; 100 iBT). *Application deadline:* For fall admission, 1/1 priority date for domestic students. Applications are processed on a rolling basis. Application fee: $50. Electronic applications accepted. *Financial support:* Fellowships, research assistantships, teaching assistantships, career-related internships or fieldwork, and tuition waivers available. Financial award application deadline: 1/1; financial award applicants required to submit FAFSA. *Faculty research:* Greek art and architecture, Northern Baroque art, Italian Baroque sculpture, abstract expressionism, Indian art, nineteenth century French art, American and contemporary art. *Unit head:* Catherine Scallen, Chair, 216-368-2383, Fax: 216-368-4681, E-mail: catherine.scallen@case.edu. *Application contact:* Debby Tenenbaum, Assistant, 216-368-4118, Fax: 216-368-4681, E-mail: deborah.tenenbaum@case.edu.
Website: http://arthistory.case.edu/graduate/art-history/

Christie's Education, MA Program in Modern Art and its Markets, New York, NY 10036. Offers MA. Part-time programs available. *Faculty:* 6 full-time (5 women). *Students:* 33 full-time (31 women), 3 part-time (all women). In 2014, 27 master's awarded. *Degree requirements:* For master's, one foreign language, thesis, internship. *Entrance requirements:* For master's, GRE, writing sample, 3 letters of recommendation. Additional exam requirements/recommendations for international students: Required—TOEFL. *Application deadline:* For fall admission, 1/15 priority date for domestic and international students. Applications are processed on a rolling basis. Application fee: $90. *Financial support:* Scholarships/grants and unspecified assistantships available. Financial award applicants required to submit FAFSA. *Unit head:* Dr. Julie Reiss, Director of Studies, 212-355-1501 Ext. 3307, Fax: 212-355-7370, E-mail: jreiss@christies.edu. *Application contact:* Margaret Conklin, Business Manager, 212-355-1501 Ext. 302, Fax: 212-355-7370, E-mail: mconklin@christies.edu.
Website: http://www.christies.edu/new-york/courses/masters-modern-art-markets.aspx

City College of the City University of New York, Graduate School, College of Liberal Arts and Science, Division of the Humanities and Arts, Department of Art, Concentrations in Art History and Museum Studies, New York, NY 10031-9198. Offers art history (MA); museum studies (MA). Part-time programs available. *Degree requirements:* For master's, one foreign language, thesis. *Entrance requirements:* For master's, minimum GPA of 3.0, portfolio, art history paper. Additional exam requirements/recommendations for international students: Required—TOEFL (minimum score 577 paper-based; 90 iBT). Electronic applications accepted. *Faculty research:* Egyptian, Greek, medieval, Romanesque, and Ottoman art.

Cleveland State University, College of Graduate Studies, College of Liberal Arts and Social Sciences, Department of History, Cleveland, OH 44115. Offers art history (MA); history (MA); museum studies (MA). Part-time and evening/weekend programs available. *Faculty:* 13 full-time (4 women). *Students:* 9 full-time (4 women), 15 part-time (9 women); includes 4 minority (3 Black or African American, non-Hispanic/Latino; 1 Two or more races, non-Hispanic/Latino). Average age 32. 13 applicants, 85% accepted, 6 enrolled. In 2014, 10 master's awarded. *Degree requirements:* For master's, thesis optional. *Entrance requirements:* For master's, minimum GPA of 3.0, bachelor's degree in history (or related field for art history). Additional exam requirements/recommendations for international students: Required—TOEFL (minimum score 525 paper-based). *Application deadline:* For fall admission, 7/15 priority date for domestic students. Applications are processed on a rolling basis. Application fee: $30. Electronic applications accepted. *Expenses:* Tuition, state resident: full-time $9566; part-time $531 per credit hour. Tuition, nonresident: full-time $17,980; part-time $999 per credit hour. *Required fees:* $25 per semester. Tuition and fees vary according to degree level and program. *Financial support:* In 2014–15, 7 students received support, including research assistantships with full tuition reimbursements available (averaging $8,600 per year); career-related internships or fieldwork, tuition waivers (full and partial), and unspecified assistantships also available. Financial award application deadline: 4/15. *Faculty research:* Africa and African diaspora, European history, Middle Eastern history, Latin American/Caribbean history, American history, gender and sexuality. *Unit head:* Dr. Elizabeth A. Lehfeldt, Chairperson, 216-687-3920, Fax: 216-687-5592, E-mail: e.lehfeldt@csuohio.edu. *Application contact:* Dr. Karen Sotiropoulos, Graduate Director, 216-687-3940, E-mail: r.s.shelton@csuohio.edu.
Website: http://www.csuohio.edu/history/

Columbia University, Graduate School of Arts and Sciences, New York, NY 10027. Offers African-American studies (MA); American studies (MA); anthropology (MA, PhD); art history and archaeology (MA, PhD); astronomy (PhD); biological sciences (PhD); biotechnology (MA); chemical physics (PhD); chemistry (PhD); classical studies (MA, PhD); classics (MA, PhD); climate and society (MA); earth and environmental sciences (PhD); East Asia: regional studies (MA); East Asian languages and cultures (MA, PhD); ecology, evolution and environmental biology (MA), including conservation biology; ecology, evolution, and environmental biology (PhD), including ecology and evolutionary biology, evolutionary primatology; economics (PhD); English and comparative literature (MA, PhD); French and Romance philology (MA, PhD); Germanic languages (MA, PhD); global French studies (MA); Hispanic cultural studies (MA); history (PhD); history and literature (MA); human rights studies (MA); Islamic studies (MA); Italian (MA, PhD); Japanese pedagogy (MA); Jewish studies (MA); Latin America and the Caribbean: regional studies (MA); Latin American and Iberian cultures (PhD); mathematics (MA, PhD), including finance (MA); medieval and Renaissance studies (MA); Middle Eastern, South Asian, and African studies (MA, PhD); modern art: critical and curatorial studies (MA); modern European studies (MA); museum anthropology (MA); music (DMA, PhD); oral history (MA); philosophical foundations of physics (MA); philosophy (MA, PhD); physics (PhD); political science (MA, PhD); psychology (PhD); quantitative methods in the social sciences (MA); religion (MA, PhD); Russia, Eurasia and East Europe: regional studies (MA); Russian translation (MA); Slavic cultures (MA); Slavic languages (MA, PhD); sociology (MA, PhD); South Asian studies (MA); statistics (MA, PhD); theatre (PhD); JD/PhD; MA/MS; MD/PhD; MPA/MA. Dual-degree programs require admission to both Graduate School of Arts and Sciences and another Columbia school. Part-time and evening/weekend programs available. Terminal master's awarded for partial completion of doctoral program. *Degree requirements:* For master's, thesis (for some programs); for doctorate, comprehensive exam, thesis/dissertation. *Entrance requirements:* For master's and doctorate, GRE General Test, GRE Subject Test (for some programs). Electronic applications accepted. *Faculty research:* Humanities, natural sciences, social sciences.

Concordia University, School of Graduate Studies, Faculty of Fine Arts, Department of Art History, Montréal, QC H3G 1M8, Canada. Offers MA, PhD. PhD program offered jointly with Université Laval, Université de Montréal, and Université du Québec à Montréal. *Degree requirements:* For master's, one foreign language, thesis. *Entrance requirements:* For master's, BFA or equivalent, minimum B average in major. *Faculty research:* Ancient and modern Canadian art and architecture, Canadian decorative arts, museum studies.

Cornell University, Graduate School, Graduate Fields of Arts and Sciences, Field of History of Art, Archaeology and Visual Studies, Ithaca, NY 14853. Offers 19th century art (PhD); African, African American and African diaspora (PhD); American art (PhD); ancient art and archaeology (PhD); Asian American art (PhD); Baroque art (PhD); comparative modernities (PhD); digital art (PhD); East Asian art (PhD); history of photography (PhD); Islamic art (PhD); Latin American art (PhD); medieval art (PhD); modern art (PhD); Renaissance art (PhD); Southeast Asian art (PhD); theory and criticism (PhD); visual studies (PhD). *Degree requirements:* For doctorate, one foreign language, comprehensive exam, thesis/dissertation, general exams in 3 areas. *Entrance requirements:* For doctorate, GRE General Test, sample of written work, 3 letters of recommendation. Additional exam requirements/recommendations for international students: Required—TOEFL (minimum score 550 paper-based; 77 iBT). Electronic applications accepted.

Dominican University of California, School of Arts, Humanities and Social Sciences, Humanities Program, San Rafael, CA 94901-2298. Offers applied music (MA); art history (MA); creative writing (MA); history (MA); literature (MA); philosophy (MA); political theory (MA); religion (MA); women and gender studies (MA). Part-time programs available. *Faculty:* 11 full-time (5 women), 5 part-time/adjunct (2 women). *Students:* 2 full-time (1 woman), 25 part-time (16 women); includes 7 minority (1 Black or African American, non-Hispanic/Latino; 1 American Indian or Alaska Native, non-Hispanic/Latino; 3 Hispanic/Latino; 2 Two or more races, non-Hispanic/Latino). Average age 46. 12 applicants, 83% accepted, 7 enrolled. *Degree requirements:* For master's, thesis or alternative. *Entrance requirements:* For master's, minimum GPA of 3.0, interview. Additional exam requirements/recommendations for international students: Required—TOEFL (minimum score 550 paper-based; 80 iBT), IELTS (minimum score 6.5). *Application deadline:* For fall admission, 5/15 priority date for domestic and international students; for spring admission, 11/15 priority date for domestic and international students. Applications are processed on a rolling basis. Electronic applications accepted. Application fee is waived when completed online. *Expenses:* Expenses: $935 per unit. *Financial support:* Scholarships/grants available. Support available to part-time students. Financial award application deadline: 3/2; financial award applicants required to submit FAFSA. *Unit head:* Dr. Laura Stivers, Acting Dean, 415-458-3734, E-mail: laura.stivers@dominican.edu. *Application contact:* Ryan Purtill, Director, 415-458-3748, Fax: 415-485-3214, E-mail: ryan.purtill@dominican.edu.
Website: http://www.dominican.edu/academics/ahss/graduate-program/index_html

Duke University, Graduate School, Department of Art, Art History and Visual Studies, Durham, NC 27708-0764. Offers historical and cultural visualization (MA); history of art (PhD). *Degree requirements:* For doctorate, thesis/dissertation. *Entrance requirements:* For doctorate, GRE General Test. Additional exam requirements/recommendations for international students: Required—TOEFL (minimum score 577 paper-based; 90 iBT) or IELTS (minimum score 7). Electronic applications accepted. *Expenses: Tuition:* Full-time $45,760; part-time $2765 per credit. *Required fees:* $978. Full-time tuition and fees vary according to program.

Emory University, Laney Graduate School, Department of Art History, Atlanta, GA 30322-1100. Offers PhD. *Degree requirements:* For doctorate, 2 foreign languages, comprehensive exam, thesis/dissertation, oral exam. *Entrance requirements:* For doctorate, GRE General Test. Additional exam requirements/recommendations for international students: Required—TOEFL. Electronic applications accepted.

★ **Fashion Institute of Technology,** School of Graduate Studies, Program in Art Market, New York, NY 10001-5992. Offers MA. *Accreditation:* NASAD. *Degree requirements:* For master's, one foreign language, thesis, internship. *Entrance requirements:* For master's, GRE General Test, previous course work in art history, 4 semesters of a foreign language. Additional exam requirements/recommendations for international students: Required—TOEFL (minimum score 550 paper-based). Electronic applications accepted.

See Display on page 189 and Close-Up on page 197.

Florida State University, The Graduate School, College of Fine Arts, Department of Art History, Tallahassee, FL 32306. Offers art history (MA, PhD); museum and cultural heritage studies (MA); museum studies (Certificate). *Accreditation:* NASAD. Part-time programs available. *Faculty:* 10 full-time (4 women), 10 part-time/adjunct (5 women). *Students:* 52 full-time (46 women), 4 part-time (3 women); includes 8 minority (1 Asian, non-Hispanic/Latino; 4 Hispanic/Latino; 3 Two or more races, non-Hispanic/Latino). Average age 25. 43 applicants, 77% accepted, 17 enrolled. In 2014, 8 master's, 2 doctorates awarded. Terminal master's awarded for partial completion of doctoral program. *Degree requirements:* For master's, one foreign language, thesis (for some programs), capstone project (for some programs); for doctorate, 2 foreign languages, comprehensive exam, thesis/dissertation. *Entrance requirements:* For master's, GRE General Test, minimum GPA of 3.0; for doctorate, GRE General Test, minimum GPA of 3.5. Additional exam requirements/recommendations for international students: Required—TOEFL (minimum score 80 iBT). *Application deadline:* For fall admission, 12/10 for domestic and international students. Applications are processed on a rolling basis. Application fee: $35. Electronic applications accepted. *Expenses:* Expenses: $17,745 in-state, $40,932 out-of-state (for MA and PhD in art history and Certificate in museum studies); $23,660 in-state, $54,576 out-of-state (for MA in museum and cultural heritage studies). *Financial support:* In 2014–15, 33 students received support, including 8 fellowships with full tuition reimbursements available (averaging $10,827 per year), 15 research assistantships with full tuition reimbursements available (averaging $5,175 per year), 8 teaching assistantships with full tuition reimbursements available (averaging $6,109 per year); career-related internships or fieldwork, Federal Work-Study, institutionally sponsored loans, scholarships/grants, and unspecified assistantships also available. Financial award application deadline: 12/10; financial award applicants required to submit FAFSA. *Faculty research:* Modern art and critical theory, medieval, Renaissance and Baroque, Pre-Columbian and Spanish Colonial, visual arts of the Americas. *Unit head:* Dr. Adam Jolles, Associate Professor of Art History/Department Chair, 850-644-7066, E-mail: ajolles@fsu.edu. *Application contact:* Leah Sherman, Academic Program Specialist/Graduate Student Advisor, 850-644-8207, E-mail: lrsherman@fsu.edu.
Website: http://arthistory.fsu.edu/

George Mason University, College of Humanities and Social Sciences, Department of History and Art History, Program in Art History, Fairfax, VA 22030. Offers MA. *Accreditation:* NASAD. *Faculty:* 10 full-time (7 women), 6 part-time/adjunct (5 women). *Students:* 7 full-time (6 women), 15 part-time (11 women); includes 3 minority (1 Black or African American, non-Hispanic/Latino; 2 Hispanic/Latino). Average age 28. 21 applicants, 67% accepted, 8 enrolled. In 2014, 12 master's awarded. *Degree requirements:* For master's, variable foreign language requirement, comprehensive exam, thesis optional. *Entrance requirements:* For master's, GRE (waived for those who hold another graduate degree or received their undergraduate degree 10 or more years

ago), expanded goals statement; 2 letters of recommendation; resume; official transcript. Additional exam requirements/recommendations for international students: Required—TOEFL (minimum score 570 paper-based; 80 iBT), IELTS (minimum score 6.5), PTE. *Application deadline:* For fall admission, 3/15 priority date for domestic students; for spring admission, 11/1 for domestic students. Application fee: $65 ($80 for international students). Electronic applications accepted. *Expenses:* Tuition, state resident: full-time $9794; part-time $408 per credit hour. Tuition, nonresident: full-time $26,978; part-time $1124 per credit hour. *Required fees:* $2820; $118 per credit hour. Tuition and fees vary according to course load and program. *Financial support:* Career-related internships or fieldwork, Federal Work-Study, scholarships/grants, unspecified assistantships, and health care benefits (for full-time research or teaching assistantship recipients) available. Support available to part-time students. Financial award application deadline: 3/1; financial award applicants required to submit FAFSA. *Faculty research:* Exhibit on Pompeii: ancient art, southeast Asia; history on Buddhist art, twentieth century Latin America interchange, Silk Road Project, American art on visual imagery. *Unit head:* Robert DeCaroli, Director, 703-993-3479, Fax: 703-993-1251, E-mail: rdecarol@gmu.edu. *Application contact:* Nicole Anne Roth, Graduate Coordinator, 703-993-1248, Fax: 703-993-1251, E-mail: nroth@gmu.edu.
Website: http://historyarthistory.gmu.edu/programs/la-ma-ah

The George Washington University, Columbian College of Arts and Sciences, Department of Fine Arts and Art History, Program in Art History, Washington, DC 20052. Offers art history (MA); museum training (MA). Part-time and evening/weekend programs available. *Faculty:* 5 full-time (all women), 15 part-time/adjunct (all women). *Students:* 14 full-time (11 women), 3 part-time (all women). Average age 27. 51 applicants, 75% accepted, 8 enrolled. In 2014, 12 master's awarded. *Degree requirements:* For master's, one foreign language, comprehensive exam, thesis or alternative. *Entrance requirements:* For master's, GRE General Test, bachelor's degree in field, minimum GPA of 3.0. Additional exam requirements/recommendations for international students: Required—TOEFL (minimum score 550 paper-based; 80 iBT). *Application deadline:* For fall admission, 3/1 priority date for domestic students, 1/15 priority date for international students; for spring admission, 10/1 priority date for domestic students, 9/1 priority date for international students. Applications are processed on a rolling basis. Application fee: $75. Electronic applications accepted. *Financial support:* In 2014–15, 3 students received support. Fellowships, teaching assistantships, career-related internships or fieldwork, and Federal Work-Study available. Financial award application deadline: 1/15. *Unit head:* Thomas K. Brown, Chair, 202-994-9067, E-mail: thbrown@gwu.edu. *Application contact:* Information Contact, 202-994-6085, Fax: 202-994-8657, E-mail: art@gwu.edu.

Georgia State University, College of Arts and Sciences, Ernest G. Welch School of Art and Design, Program in Art History, Atlanta, GA 30302-3083. Offers MA. *Accreditation:* NASAD. *Degree requirements:* For master's, one foreign language, comprehensive exam, thesis. *Application deadline:* For fall admission, 1/6 for domestic and international students; for spring admission, 1/15 priority date for domestic and international students. Application fee: $50. Electronic applications accepted. *Expenses:* Tuition, state resident: full-time $6516; part-time $362 per credit hour. Tuition, nonresident: full-time $22,014; part-time $1223 per credit hour. *Required fees:* $2128 per semester. Tuition and fees vary according to course load and program. *Financial support:* In 2014–15, research assistantships with full tuition reimbursements (averaging $6,000 per year) were awarded; fellowships, scholarships/grants, and unspecified assistantships also available. Financial award application deadline: 4/15. *Faculty research:* Ancient Egyptian tomb painting, nineteenth- and early twentieth-century French representations of primitive mankind, contemporary women artists, early modern images of devotion and death, images of the wet nurse in Afro-Brazilian art. *Unit head:* Michael White, Director, Welch School of Art and Design, 404-413-5221, Fax: 404-413-5261, E-mail: mwhite@gsu.edu. *Application contact:* Hubert Stanley Anderson, Director of Graduate Studies, 404-413-5229, Fax: 404-413-5261, E-mail: artgrad@gsu.edu.
Website: http://artdesign.gsu.edu/graduate/admissions/master-of-arts-in-art-history/

The Graduate Center, City University of New York, Graduate Studies, Program in Art History, New York, NY 10016-4039. Offers architecture (PhD); graphic arts (PhD); painting (PhD); photography (PhD); sculpture (PhD). *Degree requirements:* For doctorate, 2 foreign languages, thesis/dissertation. *Entrance requirements:* For doctorate, GRE General Test. Additional exam requirements/recommendations for international students: Required—TOEFL. Electronic applications accepted.

Graduate Theological Union, Graduate Programs, Berkeley, CA 94709-1212. Offers art and religion (MA, PhD, Th D); biblical languages (MA); biblical studies (MA); Biblical studies (PhD, Th D); Buddhist studies (MA); Christian spirituality (MA, PhD, Th D); cultural and historical studies of religions (MA, PhD, Th D); ethics and social theory (PhD, Th D); history (MA, PhD, Th D); homiletics (MA, PhD, Th D); interdisciplinary studies (PhD, Th D); Jewish studies (MA, PhD, Th D, Certificate); liturgical studies (MA, PhD, Th D); Near Eastern religions (PhD, Th D); Orthodox Christian studies (MA); religion and psychology (MA, PhD, Th D); religion and society/ethics and social theory (MA); systematic and philosophical theology (MA, PhD, Th D). PhD programs in Jewish studies and Near Eastern religions offered jointly with University of California, Berkeley. *Accreditation:* ATS. Terminal master's awarded for partial completion of doctoral program. *Degree requirements:* For master's, one foreign language, thesis; for doctorate, one foreign language, comprehensive exam, thesis/dissertation. *Entrance requirements:* For master's, GRE General Test; for doctorate, GRE General Test, MA or M Div. Additional exam requirements/recommendations for international students: Required—TOEFL. Electronic applications accepted.

Harvard University, Graduate School of Arts and Sciences, Department of History of Art and Architecture, Cambridge, MA 02138. Offers ancient art (PhD); ancient Near Eastern art (PhD); Baroque art (PhD); Byzantine art (PhD); classical art (PhD); Indian art (PhD); Islamic art (PhD); Japanese and Chinese art (PhD); medieval art (PhD); modern art (PhD); Renaissance and modern architecture (PhD); Renaissance art (PhD). *Degree requirements:* For doctorate, variable foreign language requirement, thesis/dissertation, general exams; reading exams in French, German, and Italian. *Entrance requirements:* For doctorate, GRE General Test. Additional exam requirements/recommendations for international students: Required—TOEFL.

Howard University, Graduate School, Division of Fine Arts, Department of Art, Program in Art History, Washington, DC 20059-0002. Offers art history (MA); history of art and visual culture (MA). *Accreditation:* NASAD. Part-time programs available. *Degree requirements:* For master's, comprehensive exam, thesis. *Entrance requirements:* For master's, GRE General Test, minimum GPA of 3.0, BA in art history or related field, portfolio.

Hunter College of the City University of New York, Graduate School, School of Arts and Sciences, Department of Art, Program in Art History, New York, NY 10065-5085. Offers MA. Part-time and evening/weekend programs available. *Faculty:* 5 full-time (1 woman), 1 (woman) part-time/adjunct. *Students:* 1 (woman) full-time, 93 part-time (79 women); includes 12 minority (4 Black or African American, non-Hispanic/Latino; 6 Asian, non-Hispanic/Latino; 2 Hispanic/Latino), 15 international. Average age 32. 72 applicants, 74% accepted, 17 enrolled. In 2014, 31 master's awarded. *Degree requirements:* For master's, one foreign language, comprehensive exam, thesis. *Entrance requirements:* For master's, GRE General Test, minimum 12 credits of course work in art history, reading knowledge of a foreign language (Italian, French or German), 2 letters of recommendation. Additional exam requirements/recommendations for international students: Required—TOEFL. *Application deadline:* For fall admission, 3/1 for domestic students; for spring admission, 10/1 for domestic students. *Financial support:* Teaching assistantships, career-related internships or fieldwork, Federal Work-Study, scholarships/grants, and tuition waivers (partial) available. Support available to part-time students. Financial award application deadline: 4/15. *Faculty research:* Islamic art, Renaissance and Baroque, Impressionism, critical theory, Modernism. *Unit head:* Dr. Richard Stapleford, Graduate Adviser, 212-650-5052, E-mail: grad.arthisotryadvisor@hunter.cuny.edu. *Application contact:* William Zlata, Director for Graduate Admissions, 212-772-4482, Fax: 212-650-3336, E-mail: admissions@hunter.cuny.edu.

Illinois State University, Graduate School, College of Fine Arts, School of Art, Normal, IL 61790-2200. Offers art history (MA, MS); ceramics (MFA, MS); drawing (MFA, MS); fibers (MFA, MS); glass (MFA, MS); graphic design (MFA, MS); metals (MFA, MS); painting (MFA, MS); photography (MFA, MS); printmaking (MFA, MS); sculpture (MFA, MS). *Accreditation:* NASAD (one or more programs are accredited). *Degree requirements:* For master's, thesis or alternative, internship. *Entrance requirements:* For master's, portfolio, sample of scholarly writing.

Indiana University Bloomington, University Graduate School, College of Arts and Sciences, Henry Radford Hope School of Fine Arts, Department of the History of Art, Bloomington, IN 47405-7000. Offers MA, PhD. *Accreditation:* NASAD. *Faculty:* 11 full-time (7 women), 1 (woman) part-time/adjunct. *Students:* 27 full-time (23 women); includes 1 minority (Asian, non-Hispanic/Latino). Average age 30. 41 applicants, 27% accepted, 3 enrolled. In 2014, 6 master's, 6 doctorates awarded. *Degree requirements:* For master's, one foreign language, thesis; for doctorate, 2 foreign languages, comprehensive exam, thesis/dissertation. *Entrance requirements:* For master's, GRE, writing sample, 3 letters of recommendation; for doctorate, GRE, transcript, writing samples, 3 letters of recommendation. Additional exam requirements/recommendations for international students: Required—TOEFL (minimum score 550 paper-based). *Application deadline:* For fall admission, 1/1 for domestic students, 12/1 for international students; for spring admission, 8/15 for domestic and international students. Application fee: $55 ($65 for international students). Electronic applications accepted. *Financial support:* Fellowships with full tuition reimbursements, research assistantships with full tuition reimbursements, teaching assistantships with full tuition reimbursements, career-related internships or fieldwork, and Federal Work-Study available. Financial award application deadline: 2/15. *Faculty research:* Art and social history, consumer culture, feminist art and theory, classical revivals. *Unit head:* Patrick McNaughton, Chair, 812-855-4924, Fax: 812-855-7498, E-mail: mcnaught@indiana.edu. *Application contact:* Fenella Jean Alice Flinn, Administrative Assistant, 812-855-9556, Fax: 812-855-7498, E-mail: fflinn@indiana.edu.
Website: http://www.indiana.edu/~arthist/

James Madison University, The Graduate School, College of Visual and Performing Arts, School of Art, Design and Art History, Harrisonburg, VA 22807. Offers art education (MA); studio art (MFA), including drawing/painting, metal/jewelry, photography. *Accreditation:* NASAD. Part-time programs available. *Faculty:* 25 full-time (15 women). *Students:* 11 full-time (7 women), 1 (woman) part-time; includes 4 minority (1 Black or African American, non-Hispanic/Latino; 3 Two or more races, non-Hispanic/Latino), 1 international. Average age 28. 18 applicants, 39% accepted, 6 enrolled. In 2014, 7 master's awarded. *Degree requirements:* For master's, thesis (for some programs). *Application deadline:* For fall admission, 2/15 for domestic and international students; for spring admission, 10/15 for domestic and international students. Application fee: $55. Electronic applications accepted. *Expenses:* Tuition, state resident: full-time $7812; part-time $434 per credit hour. Tuition, nonresident: full-time $20,430; part-time $1135 per credit hour. *Financial support:* In 2014–15, 11 students received support, including 2 teaching assistantships with full tuition reimbursements available (averaging $8,837 per year); Federal Work-Study and 9 assistantships (averaging $2748) also available. Financial award application deadline: 3/1; financial award applicants required to submit FAFSA. *Unit head:* Dr. Kathy A. Schwartz, Director of School of Art, Design and Art History, 540-568-6216, E-mail: art-arthistory@jmu.edu. *Application contact:* Lynette D. Michael, Director of Graduate Admissions and Student Admissions, 540-568-6131 Ext. 6395, Fax: 540-568-7860, E-mail: michaeld@jmu.edu.
Website: http://www.jmu.edu/artandarthistory/

Johns Hopkins University, Zanvyl Krieger School of Arts and Sciences, Department of History of Art, Baltimore, MD 21218. Offers MA, PhD. Terminal master's awarded for partial completion of doctoral program. *Degree requirements:* For master's, 2 foreign languages; for doctorate, 2 foreign languages, thesis/dissertation. *Entrance requirements:* For master's and doctorate, GRE General Test. Additional exam requirements/recommendations for international students: Required—TOEFL (minimum score 600 paper-based; 100 iBT), IELTS. Electronic applications accepted. *Faculty research:* Modern art, Renaissance art, medieval art, Roman art.

Kent State University, College of the Arts, School of Art, Kent, OH 44242-0001. Offers art education (MA); art history (MA); crafts (MA, MFA), including glass. *Accreditation:* NASAD (one or more programs are accredited). Part-time programs available. *Faculty:* 22 full-time (14 women). *Students:* 38 full-time (25 women), 31 part-time (23 women); includes 5 minority (1 Black or African American, non-Hispanic/Latino; 2 Hispanic/Latino; 2 Two or more races, non-Hispanic/Latino), 6 international. Average age 33. 106 applicants, 49% accepted, 24 enrolled. In 2014, 21 master's awarded. *Degree requirements:* For master's, one foreign language, comprehensive exam, thesis. *Entrance requirements:* For master's, minimum GPA of 3.0, transcript, goal statement, philosophy of art education (for MA in art education), curriculum vitae, portfolio, 3 letters of recommendation. Additional exam requirements/recommendations for international students: Required—TOEFL (minimum score: paper-based 525, iBT 71), Michigan English Language Assessment Battery (minimum score of 75), IELTS (minimum score of 6.0), PTE Academic (minimum score of 48), or completion of ELS level 112 Intensive Program. *Application deadline:* For fall admission, 2/2 priority date for domestic students; for spring admission, 9/15 priority date for domestic students. Applications are processed on a rolling basis. Application fee: $45 ($70 for international students). Electronic applications accepted. *Expenses:* Tuition, state resident: full-time $8730; part-time $485 per credit hour. Tuition, nonresident: full-time $14,886; part-time $827 per credit hour. Tuition and fees vary according to campus/location and program. *Financial support:* Research assistantships with full tuition reimbursements, teaching assistantships with full tuition reimbursements, career-related internships or fieldwork, Federal Work-Study, scholarships/grants, and unspecified assistantships available. Financial award application deadline: 2/15. *Unit head:* Dr. Christine Havice, Director, 330-672-2192, Fax: 330-672-4729, E-mail: chavice@kent.edu. *Application contact:* Lisa Everson, Clerical Specialist, 330-672-2192, E-mail: lheld2@kent.edu.
Website: http://www.kent.edu/art

Lancaster Theological Seminary, Graduate and Professional Programs, Lancaster, PA 17603-2812. Offers biblical studies (MAR); Christian education (MAR); Christianity and the arts (MAR); church history (MAR); congregational life (MAR); lay leadership (Certificate); theological studies (M Div); theology (D Min); theology and ethics (MAR). *Accreditation:* ACIPE; ATS. *Degree requirements:* For doctorate, thesis/dissertation.

Louisiana State University and Agricultural & Mechanical College, Graduate School, College of Art and Design, School of Art, Program in Art History, Baton Rouge, LA 70803. Offers MA. *Accreditation:* NASAD. *Students:* 4 full-time (3 women); includes 1 minority (Black or African American, non-Hispanic/Latino), 1 international. Average age 29. 4 applicants, 100% accepted, 2 enrolled. In 2014, 8 master's awarded. *Degree requirements:* For master's, one foreign language, thesis. *Entrance requirements:* For master's, GRE General Test, minimum GPA of 3.0. Additional exam requirements/recommendations for international students: Required—TOEFL (minimum score 550 paper-based; 79 IBT), IELTS (minimum score 6.5), or PTE (minimum score 59). *Application deadline:* For fall admission, 1/1 priority date for domestic students, 5/15 for international students; for spring admission, 10/15 for domestic and international students; for summer admission, 5/15 for domestic and international students. Applications are processed on a rolling basis. Application fee: $50 ($70 for international students). Electronic applications accepted. *Financial support:* Research assistantships with partial tuition reimbursements, teaching assistantships with partial tuition reimbursements, career-related internships or fieldwork, Federal Work-Study, institutionally sponsored loans, scholarships/grants, traineeships, health care benefits, and unspecified assistantships available. Support available to part-time students. Financial award application deadline: 3/15. *Faculty research:* Liturgical art, Greco-Roman art, Renaissance prints, American twentieth century art, performance art. *Unit head:* Kelli Scott Kelly, Graduate Advisor, 225-578-8813, Fax: 225-578-5424, E-mail: kskelly@lsu.edu.
Website: http://design.lsu.edu/art/?page_id-582

Massachusetts Institute of Technology, School of Architecture and Planning, Department of Architecture, Cambridge, MA 02139. Offers architecture (M Arch, PhD), including building technology (PhD), design and computation (PhD), history and theory of architecture (PhD), history and theory of art (PhD); architecture studies (SM Arch S); art, culture and technology (SMACT); building technology (SMBT). *Faculty:* 33 full-time (12 women), 1 part-time/adjunct (0 women). *Students:* 213 full-time (97 women); includes 42 minority (5 Black or African American, non-Hispanic/Latino; 20 Asian, non-Hispanic/Latino; 13 Hispanic/Latino; 4 Two or more races, non-Hispanic/Latino), 100 international. Average age 28. 1,179 applicants, 12% accepted, 79 enrolled. In 2014, 65 master's, 6 doctorates awarded. *Degree requirements:* For master's, thesis; for doctorate, comprehensive exam, thesis/dissertation. *Entrance requirements:* For master's and doctorate, GRE General Test. Additional exam requirements/recommendations for international students: Required—TOEFL, IELTS (minimum score 7). *Application deadline:* For fall admission, 12/31 for domestic and international students. Application fee: $75. Electronic applications accepted. *Expenses: Tuition:* Full-time $44,720; part-time $699 per unit. *Required fees:* $296. *Financial support:* In 2014–15, 171 students received support, including 139 fellowships (averaging $22,100 per year), 25 research assistantships (averaging $32,000 per year), 23 teaching assistantships (averaging $34,500 per year); Federal Work-Study, institutionally sponsored loans, scholarships/grants, health care benefits, and unspecified assistantships also available. Financial award application deadline: 4/15; financial award applicants required to submit FAFSA. *Faculty research:* Architecture; urbanism; building technology and sustainability; computation and design; history, theory, and criticism; art, culture, and technology. *Total annual research expenditures:* $1.2 million. *Unit head:* J. Meejin Yoon, Professor and Head of Department, 617-253-7791, E-mail: arch@mit.edu. *Application contact:* Admissions Coordinator, 617-715-4490, Fax: 617-253-8993, E-mail: arch@mit.edu.
Website: http://architecture.mit.edu/

McGill University, Faculty of Graduate and Postdoctoral Studies, Faculty of Arts, Department of Art History and Communication Studies, Montréal, QC H3A 2T5, Canada. Offers MA, PhD.

Montana State University, The Graduate School, College of Arts and Architecture, School of Art, Bozeman, MT 59717. Offers art (MFA); art history (MA). *Accreditation:* NASAD (one or more programs are accredited). Part-time programs available. *Degree requirements:* For master's, comprehensive exam, thesis. *Entrance requirements:* For master's, GRE General Test, undergraduate degree in art. Additional exam requirements/recommendations for international students: Required—TOEFL (minimum score 550 paper-based). Electronic applications accepted. *Faculty research:* Encaustic painting, wild clay research, environmentally friendly kiln fuel, Roman wall paintings, French revolutionary portraiture.

New Mexico State University, College of Arts and Sciences, Department of Art, Las Cruces, NM 88003-8001. Offers art history (MA); studio art (MFA). Part-time programs available. *Faculty:* 10 full-time (8 women). *Students:* 10 full-time (9 women), 3 part-time (2 women); includes 2 minority (1 Black or African American, non-Hispanic/Latino; 1 Hispanic/Latino), 2 international. Average age 39. 11 applicants, 36% accepted, 3 enrolled. In 2014, 4 master's awarded. *Degree requirements:* For master's, one foreign language, comprehensive exam (for some programs), thesis, thesis exhibit. *Entrance requirements:* For master's, portfolio (MFA); 10-20 page paper (MA). Additional exam requirements/recommendations for international students: Required—TOEFL (minimum score 550 paper-based; 79 iBT), IELTS (minimum score 6.5). *Application deadline:* For fall admission, 1/20 for domestic students; for spring admission, 11/15 for domestic students. Application fee: $40 ($50 for international students). Electronic applications accepted. *Expenses:* Tuition, state resident: full-time $3969; part-time $220.50 per credit hour. Tuition, nonresident: full-time $13,838; part-time $768.80 per credit hour. *Required fees:* $853; $47.40 per credit hour. *Financial support:* In 2014–15, 13 students received support, including 10 teaching assistantships (averaging $15,225 per year); career-related internships or fieldwork, Federal Work-Study, scholarships/grants, traineeships, health care benefits, and unspecified assistantships also available. Support available to part-time students. Financial award application deadline: 3/1. *Faculty research:* Art history, painting, graphic design, sculpture, ceramics, photography. *Total annual research expenditures:* $11,222. *Unit head:* Dr. Julia Barello, Academic Department Head, 575-646-1705, Fax: 575-646-8036, E-mail: jbarello@nmsu.edu. *Application contact:* 575-646-1705, Fax: 575-646-8036, E-mail: artdept@nmsu.edu.
Website: http://artdepartment.nmsu.edu/

New York University, Graduate School of Arts and Science, Institute of Fine Arts, Program in Art History and Archaeology, New York, NY 10012-1019. Offers architectural studies (PhD); art history and archaeology (MA, PhD); classical art and archaeology (PhD); curatorial studies (PhD); East and South Asian art (PhD); Near Eastern art and archaeology (PhD); MA/Diploma; PhD/Certificate. Part-time programs available. *Students:* 181 full-time (145 women), 56 part-time (46 women); includes 28 minority (2 Black or African American, non-Hispanic/Latino; 12 Asian, non-Hispanic/Latino; 9 Hispanic/Latino; 5 Two or more races, non-Hispanic/Latino), 37 international. Average age 31. 346 applicants, 43% accepted, 52 enrolled. In 2014, 47 master's, 24 doctorates awarded. Terminal master's awarded for partial completion of doctoral program. *Degree requirements:* For master's, 2 foreign languages, thesis or alternative, 2 qualifying papers; for doctorate, 2 foreign languages, thesis/dissertation. *Entrance requirements:* For master's, GRE General Test; for doctorate, GRE General Test, MA. Additional exam requirements/recommendations for international students: Required—TOEFL. *Application deadline:* For fall admission, 12/18 for domestic and international students. Application fee: $100. *Financial support:* Fellowships with tuition reimbursements, research assistantships with tuition reimbursements, teaching assistantships with tuition reimbursements, career-related internships or fieldwork, Federal Work-Study, and institutionally sponsored loans available. Financial award application deadline: 12/18; financial award applicants required to submit FAFSA. *Unit head:* Patricia Rubin, Chair, 212-992-5800, Fax: 212-992-5807, E-mail: ifa.program@nyu.edu. *Application contact:* Alexander Nagel, Director of Graduate Studies, 212-992-5800, Fax: 212-992-5807, E-mail: ifa.program@nyu.edu.
Website: http://www.nyu.edu/gsas/dept/fineart/

Northwestern University, The Graduate School, Judd A. and Marjorie Weinberg College of Arts and Sciences, Department of Art History, Evanston, IL 60208. Offers PhD. Admissions and degrees offered through The Graduate School. *Degree requirements:* For doctorate, 2 foreign languages, comprehensive exam, thesis/dissertation, major and minor field exercises. *Entrance requirements:* For doctorate, GRE General Test. Additional exam requirements/recommendations for international students: Required—TOEFL. Electronic applications accepted. *Faculty research:* Modern American and European art and architecture, prehistoric and ancient art, central Asian art, medieval manuscripts and early printed books, history of museums, art of Western Africa, theory of culture.

The Ohio State University, Graduate School, College of Arts and Sciences, Division of Arts and Humanities, Department of History of Art, Columbus, OH 43210. Offers MA, PhD. *Accreditation:* NASAD. *Faculty:* 12. *Students:* 31 full-time (26 women), 2 part-time (both women); includes 7 minority (4 Asian, non-Hispanic/Latino; 3 Hispanic/Latino), 8 international. Average age 32. In 2014, 5 doctorates awarded. Terminal master's awarded for partial completion of doctoral program. *Degree requirements:* For master's, one foreign language, thesis optional; for doctorate, 2 foreign languages, thesis/dissertation. *Entrance requirements:* For master's and doctorate, GRE General Test. Additional exam requirements/recommendations for international students: Required—TOEFL (minimum score 550 paper-based; 79 iBT), Michigan English Language Assessment Battery (minimum score 82); Recommended—IELTS (minimum score 7). *Application deadline:* For fall admission, 12/1 priority date for domestic and international students; for winter admission, 12/1 for domestic students, 11/1 for international students; for spring admission, 3/1 for domestic students, 2/1 for international students. Applications are processed on a rolling basis. Application fee: $60 ($70 for international students). Electronic applications accepted. *Financial support:* Fellowships with tuition reimbursements, teaching assistantships with tuition reimbursements, Federal Work-Study, and institutionally sponsored loans available. Support available to part-time students. *Faculty research:* Western and Oriental art, African art and archaeology. *Unit head:* Dr. Lisa Florman, Chair and Professor, 614-292-7481, E-mail: florman.4@osu.edu. *Application contact:* Graduate and Professional Admissions, 614-292-9444, Fax: 614-292-3895, E-mail: gpadmissions@osu.edu.
Website: http://history-of-art.osu.edu/

Ohio University, Graduate College, College of Fine Arts, School of Art, Athens, OH 45701-2979. Offers art history (MA); ceramics (MFA); graphic design (MFA); painting (MFA); photography (MFA); printmaking (MFA); sculpture (MFA). Part-time programs available. *Degree requirements:* For master's, thesis. *Entrance requirements:* For master's, portfolio. Additional exam requirements/recommendations for international students: Required—TOEFL (minimum score 550 paper-based; 80 iBT) or IELTS (minimum score 6.5). Electronic applications accepted. *Faculty research:* Vapor-fired ceramics, video installation, art theory, digital photography, mixed and interdisciplinary media work.

Penn State University Park, Graduate School, College of Arts and Architecture, Department of Art History, University Park, PA 16802. Offers MA, PhD. *Unit head:* Dr. Barbara O. Korner, Dean, 814-865-2592, Fax: 814-865-2018, E-mail: bok2@psu.edu. *Application contact:* Lori A. Stania, Director, Graduate Student Services, 814-867-5278, Fax: 814-863-4627, E-mail: gswww@psu.edu.
Website: http://arthistory.psu.edu/

Pratt Institute, School of Liberal Arts and Sciences, Program in Art History, Brooklyn, NY 11205-3899. Offers art history (MS); art history theory and criticism (MS); MS/MFA; MS/MS. *Accreditation:* NASAD. Part-time programs available. *Faculty:* 7 full-time (6 women), 35 part-time/adjunct (22 women). *Students:* 44 full-time (40 women), 7 part-time (all women); includes 9 minority (3 Black or African American, non-Hispanic/Latino; 3 Asian, non-Hispanic/Latino; 3 Hispanic/Latino), 8 international. Average age 28. 59 applicants, 90% accepted, 14 enrolled. In 2014, 22 master's awarded. *Degree requirements:* For master's, one foreign language, thesis. *Entrance requirements:* For master's, GRE General Test, letters of recommendation, portfolio. Additional exam requirements/recommendations for international students: Required—TOEFL (minimum score 600 paper-based; 100 iBT). *Application deadline:* For fall admission, 1/5 for domestic and international students; for spring admission, 10/1 for domestic and international students. Application fee: $50 ($90 for international students). Electronic applications accepted. *Financial support:* Career-related internships or fieldwork, Federal Work-Study, institutionally sponsored loans, scholarships/grants, health care benefits, and unspecified assistantships available. Support available to part-time students. Financial award application deadline: 2/1; financial award applicants required to submit CSS PROFILE or FAFSA. *Faculty research:* Conservation techniques, women artists from previous centuries, art of sixteenth-century Veneto, design history, nineteenth century Germany. *Unit head:* Dorothea Dietrich, Chairperson, 718-636-3532, Fax: 718-687-5925, E-mail: ddietric@pratt.edu. *Application contact:* Young Hah, Director of Graduate Admissions, 718-636-3683, Fax: 718-399-4242, E-mail: yhah@pratt.edu.
Website: https://www.pratt.edu/academics/liberal-arts-and-sciences/history-of-art-design-grad/

Purchase College, State University of New York, School of Humanities, Purchase, NY 10577-1400. Offers art history (MA). *Accreditation:* NASAD. *Students:* 6 full-time (5 women), 11 part-time (10 women); includes 3 minority (1 Asian, non-Hispanic/Latino; 2 Hispanic/Latino), 2 international. Average age 31. 17 applicants, 41% accepted, 3 enrolled. *Degree requirements:* For master's, one foreign language, thesis. *Entrance requirements:* For master's, BA or BFA, previous course work in art history, three letters of recommendation, personal statement, 1-2 writing samples, official transcripts. Additional exam requirements/recommendations for international students: Required—TOEFL or IELTS. *Application deadline:* For fall admission, 2/1 for domestic students. Application fee: $80. Electronic applications accepted. *Expenses:* Tuition, state resident: full-time $10,370; part-time $432 per credit. Tuition, nonresident: full-time $20,190; part-time $831 per credit. *Required fees:* $1763. *Financial support:* Fellowships, Federal Work-Study, scholarships/grants, and tuition waivers (partial) available. Support available to part-time students. Financial award application deadline: 3/15; financial award applicants required to submit FAFSA. *Unit head:* Ross Daly, Chair, 914-251-6550. *Application contact:* Sabrina Johnston, Admissions Counselor, 914-251-6479, Fax: 914-251-6314, E-mail: admissn@purchase.edu.
Website: http://www.purchase.edu/Departments/AcademicPrograms/LAS/Humanities/

Queens College of the City University of New York, Division of Graduate Studies, Arts and Humanities Division, Department of Art, Program in Art History, Flushing, NY 11367-1597. Offers MA. Part-time and evening/weekend programs available. *Degree*

requirements: For master's, 2 foreign languages, thesis, qualifying exam. *Entrance requirements:* For master's, minimum GPA of 3.0. Additional exam requirements/recommendations for international students: Required—TOEFL.

Rice University, Graduate Programs, School of Humanities, Department of Art History, Houston, TX 77251-1892. Offers PhD.

Richmond, The American International University in London, MA in Art History Program, Richmond, United Kingdom. Offers MA. Part-time programs available. *Degree requirements:* For master's, thesis. *Entrance requirements:* For master's, minimum GPA of 3.0. Additional exam requirements/recommendations for international students: Required—TOEFL, IELTS. Electronic applications accepted. *Expenses:* Contact institution. *Faculty research:* Archaeology of art and representation, contemporary paganisms, nineteenth century modernisms, American twentieth century art, sound media.

Roger Williams University, School of Architecture, Art and Historic Preservation, Bristol, RI 02809. Offers architecture (M Arch); art and architectural history (MA); historical preservation (MS). *Faculty:* 14 full-time (3 women), 16 part-time/adjunct (4 women). *Students:* 80 full-time (24 women), 18 part-time (8 women); includes 12 minority (1 Black or African American, non-Hispanic/Latino; 2 Asian, non-Hispanic/Latino; 8 Hispanic/Latino; 1 Two or more races, non-Hispanic/Latino), 7 international. Average age 25. 77 applicants, 87% accepted, 46 enrolled. In 2014, 49 master's awarded. *Degree requirements:* For master's, thesis. *Entrance requirements:* For master's, portfolio, 2 letters of recommendation. Additional exam requirements/recommendations for international students: Recommended—TOEFL (minimum score 85 iBT), IELTS. *Application deadline:* For fall admission, 3/1 priority date for domestic students. Application fee: $50. Electronic applications accepted. *Expenses:* Expenses: $33,792 (for M Arch); $20,644 (for MS in historical preservation). *Financial support:* In 2014–15, 84 students received support, including fellowships with partial tuition reimbursements available (averaging $6,000 per year), 80 research assistantships (averaging $3,000 per year). Financial award application deadline: 6/15; financial award applicants required to submit FAFSA. *Unit head:* Stephen White, Dean, 401-254-3607, E-mail: swhite@rwu.edu. *Application contact:* Lori Vales, Director of Graduate Admissions, 401-254-6200, Fax: 401-254-3557, E-mail: gradadmit@rwu.edu. Website: http://www.rwu.edu/academics/departments/architecture.htm#dual

Rutgers, The State University of New Jersey, New Brunswick, Graduate School-New Brunswick, Program in Art History, Piscataway, NJ 08854-8097. Offers art history (MA, PhD); curatorial studies (Certificate); historic preservation (Certificate). Part-time programs available. Terminal master's awarded for partial completion of doctoral program. *Degree requirements:* For master's, one foreign language, comprehensive exam; for doctorate, 2 foreign languages, comprehensive exam, thesis/dissertation. *Entrance requirements:* For master's and doctorate, GRE General Test, writing sample. Additional exam requirements/recommendations for international students: Required—TOEFL (minimum score 550 paper-based). Electronic applications accepted. *Faculty research:* Ancient and medieval art and architecture; Renaissance and Baroque art and architecture; modern and contemporary art and architecture; Italian studies; the arts of Asia, Africa, and the Americas.

San Diego State University, Graduate and Research Affairs, College of Professional Studies and Fine Arts, School of Art, Design and Art History, San Diego, CA 92182. Offers art history (MA); studio arts (MA, MFA), including applied design, environmental design, graphic design, interior design, painting and printmaking, sculpture. *Accreditation:* NASAD (one or more programs are accredited). *Degree requirements:* For master's, variable foreign language requirement, thesis. *Entrance requirements:* For master's, GRE General Test, bachelor's degree in related field, slide portfolio, typed slide information sheet, 2 letters of recommendation. Additional exam requirements/recommendations for international students: Required—TOEFL. Electronic applications accepted.

San Francisco Art Institute, Dual-Degree MFA/MA Program in Studio Art and History and Theory of Contemporary Art, San Francisco, CA 94133. Offers MFA/MA. Specializations available in art and technology, film, new genres, painting, photography, printmaking, and sculpture. *Faculty:* 15 full-time (7 women), 46 part-time/adjunct (23 women). *Students:* 6 full-time (4 women); includes 1 minority (Black or African American, non-Hispanic/Latino). Average age 27. 15 applicants, 40% accepted, 4 enrolled. *Entrance requirements:* Additional exam requirements/recommendations for international students: Required—TOEFL (minimum score 600 paper-based; 100 iBT), IELTS (minimum score 7.5). *Application deadline:* For fall admission, 1/15 priority date for domestic and international students. Applications are processed on a rolling basis. Application fee: $85. Electronic applications accepted. *Expenses:* Tuition: Full-time $41,100; part-time $1805 per credit. *Required fees:* $870. *Financial support:* In 2014–15, 8 students received support, including fellowships (averaging $30,000 per year), teaching assistantships (averaging $2,500 per year); career-related internships or fieldwork, Federal Work-Study, scholarships/grants, and unspecified assistantships also available. Support available to part-time students. Financial award application deadline: 3/1; financial award applicants required to submit FAFSA. *Unit head:* Tony Labat, Chair, Master of Fine Arts Department, 415-771-7020, Fax: 415-641-1205, E-mail: tlabat@sfai.edu. *Application contact:* Jana Rumberger, Associate Director of Recruitment, 415-351-3507, Fax: 415-749-4592, E-mail: jrumberger@sfai.edu. Website: http://www.sfai.edu/degree-programs/graduate/dual-degree-ma-mfa

San Francisco Art Institute, Master of Arts Programs, San Francisco, CA 94133. Offers exhibition and museum studies (MA); history and theory of contemporary art (MA). *Faculty:* 4 full-time (all women), 17 part-time/adjunct (10 women). *Students:* 12 full-time (all women); includes 2 minority (1 Hispanic/Latino; 1 Two or more races, non-Hispanic/Latino), 2 international. Average age 26. 32 applicants, 72% accepted, 6 enrolled. In 2014, 18 master's awarded. *Degree requirements:* For master's, thesis. *Entrance requirements:* For master's, critical writing sample. Additional exam requirements/recommendations for international students: Required—TOEFL (minimum score 600 paper-based; 100 iBT), IELTS (minimum score 7.5). *Application deadline:* For fall admission, 1/15 priority date for domestic and international students. Applications are processed on a rolling basis. Application fee: $85. Electronic applications accepted. *Expenses:* Tuition: Full-time $41,100; part-time $1805 per credit. *Required fees:* $870. *Financial support:* In 2014–15, 9 students received support, including 3 fellowships (averaging $25,000 per year), teaching assistantships (averaging $2,500 per year); career-related internships or fieldwork, Federal Work-Study, scholarships/grants, and unspecified assistantships also available. Support available to part-time students. Financial award application deadline: 3/1; financial award applicants required to submit FAFSA. *Unit head:* Claire Daigle, Chair, Master of Arts Department, 415-641-1241 Ext. 1004, Fax: 415-641-1205, E-mail: cdaigle@sfai.edu. *Application contact:* Jana Rumberger, Associate Director of Recruitment, 415-351-3507, Fax: 415-749-4592, E-mail: jrumberger@sfai.edu. Website: http://www.sfai.edu/degree-programs/graduate/ma

San Francisco State University, Division of Graduate Studies, College of Liberal and Creative Arts, Department of Art, San Francisco, CA 94132-1722. Offers art (MFA); art history (MA). *Accreditation:* NASAD (one or more programs are accredited). *Expenses:* Tuition, state resident: full-time $6738. Tuition, nonresident: full-time $17,898; part-time

$372 per credit hour. *Required fees:* $498 per semester. *Unit head:* Gail Dawson, Chair, 415-338-2176, Fax: 415-338-6537, E-mail: artdept@sfsu.edu. *Application contact:* Prof. Susan Belau, Associate Professor and Graduate Coordinator, 415-338-1591, Fax: 415-338-6537, E-mail: artgrad@sfsu.edu. Website: http://www.art.sfsu.edu

San Jose State University, Graduate Studies and Research, College of Humanities and the Arts, School of Art and Design, San Jose, CA 95192-0001. Offers animation/illustration (MA); art history (MA); digital media arts (MFA); photography (MFA); pictorial arts (MFA); spatial arts (MFA). *Accreditation:* NASAD (one or more programs are accredited). *Entrance requirements:* For master's, GRE. Electronic applications accepted.

Savannah College of Art and Design, Graduate School, Program in Art History, Savannah, GA 31402-3146. Offers MA. Part-time programs available. *Faculty:* 37 full-time (22 women), 7 part-time/adjunct (5 women). *Students:* 8 full-time (7 women), 5 part-time (all women); includes 1 minority (Asian, non-Hispanic/Latino), 2 international. Average age 26. 21 applicants, 38% accepted, 5 enrolled. In 2014, 3 master's awarded. *Degree requirements:* For master's, one foreign language, comprehensive exam, thesis. *Entrance requirements:* For master's, research paper. Additional exam requirements/recommendations for international students: Required—TOEFL (minimum score 550 paper-based, 85 iBT), IELTS (minimum score 6.5), or ACTFL. *Application deadline:* For fall admission, 4/1 for domestic and international students. Applications are processed on a rolling basis. Application fee: $40. Electronic applications accepted. *Expenses:* Tuition: Full-time $34,605; part-time $3845 per course. One-time fee: $500. Tuition and fees vary according to course load. *Financial support:* Fellowships, career-related internships or fieldwork, Federal Work-Study, and scholarships/grants available. Financial award application deadline: 4/1; financial award applicants required to submit FAFSA. *Faculty research:* Contemporary art. *Unit head:* Dr. Geoffrey Taylor, Chair. *Application contact:* Jenny Jaquillard, Executive Director of Admissions, Recruitment and Events, 912-525-5100, Fax: 912-525-5985, E-mail: admission@scad.edu. Website: http://www.scad.edu/academics/programs/art-history

School of the Art Institute of Chicago, Graduate Division, Program in Modern Art History, Theory, and Criticism, Chicago, IL 60603-3103. Offers MA. *Accreditation:* NASAD. *Entrance requirements:* For master's, GRE. Additional exam requirements/recommendations for international students: Required—TOEFL, IELTS.

Southern Methodist University, Meadows School of the Arts, Division of Art History, Dallas, TX 75275. Offers art history (MA); rhetorics of art, space and culture (PhD). Part-time and evening/weekend programs available. *Degree requirements:* For master's, one foreign language, thesis, translation exam. *Entrance requirements:* For master's, GRE, 12 upper-level hours in art history, sample research paper. Additional exam requirements/recommendations for international students: Required—TOEFL (minimum score 550 paper-based; 80 iBT). *Faculty research:* American art, nineteenth- and twentieth-century art, classical and Byzantine art, Hispanic art, Mesoamerican art, Renaissance-Baroque.

Stony Brook University, State University of New York, Graduate School, College of Arts and Sciences, Department of Art, Program in Art History and Criticism, Stony Brook, NY 11794. Offers MA, PhD. Part-time programs available. *Students:* 37 full-time (30 women), 2 part-time (0 women); includes 5 minority (1 American Indian or Alaska Native, non-Hispanic/Latino; 3 Hispanic/Latino; 1 Two or more races, non-Hispanic/Latino), 8 international. Average age 30. 32 applicants, 84% accepted, 9 enrolled. In 2014, 1 master's, 3 doctorates awarded. *Degree requirements:* For master's, comprehensive exam, thesis, reading knowledge of German or French; for doctorate, comprehensive exam, thesis/dissertation, qualifying paper, reading knowledge of German and French, qualifying examination. *Entrance requirements:* For master's, GRE General Test, minimum undergraduate GPA of 3.0; for doctorate, GRE General Test, minimum graduate GPA of 3.0. Additional exam requirements/recommendations for international students: Required—TOEFL (minimum score 550 paper-based), IELTS (minimum score 6.5). *Application deadline:* For fall admission, 1/15 for domestic students; for spring admission, 10/1 for domestic students. Application fee: $100. *Expenses:* Tuition, state resident: full-time $10,370; part-time $432 per credit. Tuition, nonresident: full-time $20,190; part-time $841 per credit. *Required fees:* $1431. *Financial support:* In 2014–15, 2 fellowships, 16 teaching assistantships were awarded; research assistantships also available. *Unit head:* Dr. John Lutterbie, Director, 631-632-7250, E-mail: john.lutterbie@stonybrook.edu. *Application contact:* Lisa Perez, Coordinator, 631-632-7270, E-mail: lisa.a.perez@stonybrook.edu. Website: http://art.stonybrook.edu/graduate-programs/maph-d-programs/

Sul Ross State University, School of Arts and Sciences, Department of Fine Arts and Communication, Alpine, TX 79832. Offers art history (MA); studio art (MA), including art education, ceramics, painting, sculpture. Part-time programs available. *Degree requirements:* For master's, oral or written exam. *Entrance requirements:* For master's, GRE General Test, minimum GPA of 2.5 in last 60 hours of undergraduate work. *Faculty research:* Ceramic sculpture, watercolor, wood sculpture, rock art.

Syracuse University, College of Arts and Sciences, Program in Art History, Syracuse, NY 13244. Offers MA. *Students:* 19 full-time (16 women), 2 part-time (both women); includes 3 minority (1 Asian, non-Hispanic/Latino; 2 Hispanic/Latino), 1 international. Average age 27. 26 applicants, 77% accepted, 8 enrolled. In 2014, 7 master's awarded. *Degree requirements:* For master's, one foreign language, symposium presentation. *Entrance requirements:* For master's, GRE, research writing sample; second language. Additional exam requirements/recommendations for international students: Required—TOEFL (minimum score 100 iBT). *Application deadline:* For fall admission, 1/1 priority date for domestic and international students. Application fee: $75. Electronic applications accepted. *Expenses:* Tuition: Part-time $1341 per credit. *Financial support:* Fellowships with full tuition reimbursements and teaching assistantships with full and partial tuition reimbursements available. Financial award application deadline: 1/1; financial award applicants required to submit FAFSA. *Unit head:* Prof. Laurinda Dixon, Graduate Director, 315-443-5031, E-mail: amhweb@syr.edu. *Application contact:* Maureen Verone, Information Contact, 315-443-4185, E-mail: mverone@syr.edu. Website: http://amh.syr.edu/

Temple University, Center for the Arts, Tyler School of Art, Department of Art History, Philadelphia, PA 19122-6096. Offers MA, PhD. Part-time programs available. *Faculty:* 13 full-time (8 women), 5 part-time/adjunct (4 women). *Students:* 52 full-time (44 women), 5 part-time (4 women); includes 9 minority (3 Asian, non-Hispanic/Latino; 5 Hispanic/Latino; 1 Two or more races, non-Hispanic/Latino), 3 international. 44 applicants, 73% accepted, 13 enrolled. In 2014, 6 master's, 5 doctorates awarded. Terminal master's awarded for partial completion of doctoral program. *Degree requirements:* For master's, 2 foreign languages, thesis, comprehensive slide exam; for doctorate, 2 foreign languages, thesis/dissertation, qualifying exam. *Entrance requirements:* For master's, GRE General Test, minimum GPA of 3.0, letters of recommendation, resume/curriculum vitae, writing sample; for doctorate, GRE, MA in art history, minimum GPA of 3.0, letters of recommendation, resume/curriculum vitae, writing sample. Additional exam requirements/recommendations for international students: Required—TOEFL (minimum score 550 paper-based; 79 iBT), IELTS (minimum score 6.5). *Application deadline:* For fall admission, 12/15 for domestic and

international students; for spring admission, 11/1 for domestic students, 10/1 for international students. Applications are processed on a rolling basis. Application fee: $60. Electronic applications accepted. *Expenses:* Expenses: Contact institution. *Financial support:* Fellowships, research assistantships with full tuition reimbursements, teaching assistantships with full tuition reimbursements, career-related internships or fieldwork, institutionally sponsored loans, and technical assistantships available. Financial award application deadline: 1/15. *Faculty research:* Aegean, Greek, and Roman art; early Christian art; medieval art and architecture; Renaissance and Baroque painting, sculpture, and architecture; nineteenth and twentieth century painting and sculpture. *Unit head:* Dr. Gerald Silk, Chair, 215-204-7837, Fax: 215-204-6951, E-mail: gsilk@temple.edu. *Application contact:* Nicole Hall, Director of Admissions, 215-777-9090, E-mail: nicoleh@temple.edu.
Website: http://www.temple.edu/tyler/arthistory/

Texas Christian University, College of Fine Arts, School of Art, Fort Worth, TX 76129. Offers art history (MA); studio art (MFA), including painting, photography, sculpture. *Accreditation:* NASAD. *Faculty:* 12 full-time (6 women), 3 part-time/adjunct (2 women). *Students:* 18 full-time (13 women); includes 5 minority (all Hispanic/Latino). Average age 28. 27 applicants, 41% accepted, 7 enrolled. In 2014, 7 master's awarded. *Degree requirements:* For master's, variable foreign language requirement, comprehensive exam, thesis. *Entrance requirements:* For master's, GRE General Test (for MA). Additional exam requirements/recommendations for international students: Required—TOEFL (minimum score 550 paper-based; 80 iBT). *Application deadline:* For fall admission, 2/1 for domestic and international students. Application fee: $60. Electronic applications accepted. *Expenses: Tuition:* Full-time $22,860; part-time $1270 per credit hour. *Financial support:* In 2014–15, 18 students received support, including 17 teaching assistantships (averaging $10,000 per year); institutionally sponsored loans, scholarships/grants, tuition waivers, and unspecified assistantships also available. Financial award application deadline: 4/15. *Unit head:* Dr. Sally Packard, Director, 817-257-7643, E-mail: s.packard@tcu.edu. *Application contact:* Donna Smolik, TCU College of Fine Arts Graduate Office, 817-257-7603, Fax: 817-257-5672, E-mail: cfagradinfo@tcu.edu.
Website: http://www.art.tcu.edu/

Texas Tech University, Graduate School, College of Visual and Performing Arts, School of Art, Lubbock, TX 79409. Offers art (MFA); art education (MAE); art history (MA). *Accreditation:* NASAD (one or more programs are accredited). Part-time programs available. Postbaccalaureate distance learning degree programs offered (minimal on-campus study). *Faculty:* 33 full-time (18 women), 10 part-time/adjunct (7 women). *Students:* 32 full-time (20 women), 25 part-time (21 women); includes 19 minority (2 Black or African American, non-Hispanic/Latino; 15 Hispanic/Latino; 2 Two or more races, non-Hispanic/Latino), 5 international. Average age 32. 53 applicants, 55% accepted, 17 enrolled. In 2014, 12 master's awarded. *Degree requirements:* For master's, variable foreign language requirement, comprehensive exam, thesis (for some programs), exhibition (for MFA). *Entrance requirements:* For master's, GRE (for MA). Additional exam requirements/recommendations for international students: Required—TOEFL (minimum score 550 paper-based; 79 iBT), IELTS (minimum score 6.5). *Application deadline:* For fall admission, 6/1 priority date for domestic students, 1/15 priority date for international students; for spring admission, 9/1 priority date for domestic students, 6/15 priority date for international students. Applications are processed on a rolling basis. Application fee: $60. Electronic applications accepted. *Expenses:* Tuition, state resident: full-time $6310; part-time $262.92 per credit hour. Tuition, nonresident: full-time $14,998; part-time $624.92 per credit hour. *Required fees:* $2701; $36.50 per credit. $912.50 per semester. Tuition and fees vary according to course load. *Financial support:* In 2014–15, 58 students received support, including 58 fellowships (averaging $3,219 per year), 3 research assistantships (averaging $14,600 per year), 42 teaching assistantships (averaging $8,087 per year); Federal Work-Study, institutionally sponsored loans, scholarships/grants, health care benefits, tuition waivers (partial), and unspecified assistantships also available. Financial award application deadline: 2/15; financial award applicants required to submit FAFSA. *Faculty research:* Modern and contemporary art; contemporary Chicano/a art; transformation of multidisciplinary approach to printmaking; figurative painting and an intense interest in space as metaphor for community; working-class, sexuality and race issues; letter press posters; creating and crafting of metalsmithing. *Unit head:* Prof. Lydia Thompson, Director and Professor, 806-742-3825 Ext. 255, E-mail: lydia.thompson@ttu.edu. *Application contact:* Ryan Scheckel, Academic Advisor, 806-742-3825 Ext. 222, E-mail: ryan.scheckel@ttu.edu.
Website: http://www.art.ttu.edu

Towson University, Program in Professional Studies, Towson, MD 21252-0001. Offers art history (MA); individualized plan (MA). Part-time and evening/weekend programs available. *Students:* 9 full-time (6 women), 27 part-time (21 women); includes 10 minority (7 Black or African American, non-Hispanic/Latino; 2 Asian, non-Hispanic/Latino; 1 Two or more races, non-Hispanic/Latino), 2 international. *Degree requirements:* For master's, thesis optional. *Entrance requirements:* For master's, minimum GPA of 3.0, essay. *Application deadline:* Applications are processed on a rolling basis. Application fee: $45. Electronic applications accepted. *Financial support:* Application deadline: 4/1. *Unit head:* Dr. James Smith, Graduate Program Director, 410-704-4620, E-mail: jmsmith@towson.edu. *Application contact:* Alicia Arkell-Kleis, Information Contact, 410-704-6004, E-mail: grads@towson.edu.
Website: http://grad.towson.edu/program/master/lbps-ma/index.asp

Tufts University, Graduate School of Arts and Sciences, Department of Art and Art History, Medford, MA 02155. Offers art history (MA); art history and museum studies (MA); studio art (MFA). *Faculty:* 11 full-time (6 women), 4 part-time/adjunct (3 women). *Students:* 100 full-time (74 women), 32 part-time (21 women); includes 18 minority (5 Black or African American, non-Hispanic/Latino; 4 Asian, non-Hispanic/Latino; 6 Hispanic/Latino; 3 Two or more races, non-Hispanic/Latino), 20 international. Average age 29. 89 applicants, 40% accepted, 13 enrolled. In 2014, 82 master's awarded. *Degree requirements:* For master's, one foreign language, thesis (for some programs). *Entrance requirements:* For master's, GRE General Test. Additional exam requirements/recommendations for international students: Required—TOEFL (minimum score 550 paper-based; 80 iBT), IELTS (minimum score 6.5). *Application deadline:* For fall admission, 1/15 for domestic and international students. Application fee: $75. Electronic applications accepted. *Expenses: Tuition:* Full-time $45,590; part-time $1161 per credit hour. *Required fees:* $782. Full-time tuition and fees vary according to degree level, program and student level. Part-time tuition and fees vary according to course load. *Financial support:* Teaching assistantships with partial tuition reimbursements, Federal Work-Study, scholarships/grants, tuition waivers (partial), and unspecified assistantships available. Financial award application deadline: 5/15; financial award applicants required to submit FAFSA. *Unit head:* Karen Overbey, Graduate Program Director, 617-627-3395. *Application contact:* Office of Graduate Admissions, 617-627-3395, E-mail: gradadmissions@tufts.edu.
Website: http://ase.tufts.edu/art/

Tulane University, School of Liberal Arts, Department of Art, New Orleans, LA 70118-5669. Offers history and Latin American studies (PhD); history of art (MA); studio art (MFA). PhD held jointly with Roger Thayer Stone Center for Latin American Studies. *Degree requirements:* For master's, one foreign language, thesis. *Entrance requirements:* For master's, GRE General Test, minimum B average in undergraduate course work. Additional exam requirements/recommendations for international students: Required—TOEFL. Electronic applications accepted. *Expenses: Tuition:* Full-time $46,326; part-time $2574 per credit hour. *Required fees:* $1980; $44.50 per credit hour. $550 per term. Tuition and fees vary according to course load and program.

Université de Montréal, Faculty of Arts and Sciences, Department of Art History and Film Studies, Montréal, QC H3C 3J7, Canada. Offers art history (MA, PhD); film studies (MA, PhD). Programs offered jointly with Concordia University, Université Laval, and Université du Québec à Montréal. *Degree requirements:* For master's, thesis. Electronic applications accepted. *Faculty research:* Western art from the Middle Ages, classic and modern theory, modern and contemporary art, Canadian art.

Université du Québec à Montréal, Graduate Programs, Program in Art Studies, Montréal, QC H3C 3P8, Canada. Offers art history (PhD); art studies (MA); study and practices of the arts (PhD). Part-time programs available. *Degree requirements:* For master's, thesis; for doctorate, thesis/dissertation. *Entrance requirements:* For master's, appropriate bachelor's degree or equivalent, proficiency in French; for doctorate, appropriate master's degree or equivalent, proficiency in French.

Université Laval, Faculty of Letters, Department of History, Programs in Art History, Québec, QC G1K 7P4, Canada. Offers MA, PhD. PhD offered jointly with Concordia University, Université de Montréal, and Université du Québec à Montréal. Terminal master's awarded for partial completion of doctoral program. *Degree requirements:* For master's, thesis; for doctorate, comprehensive exam, thesis/dissertation. *Entrance requirements:* For master's, English test (comprehension of written English), knowledge of French; for doctorate, English test (comprehension of written English), knowledge of French and English, knowledge of a third language. Electronic applications accepted.

University at Buffalo, the State University of New York, Graduate School, College of Arts and Sciences, Department of Visual Studies, Program in Art History, Buffalo, NY 14260. Offers MA. Part-time programs available. *Degree requirements:* For master's, one foreign language, thesis, field exam. *Entrance requirements:* Additional exam requirements/recommendations for international students: Required—TOEFL (minimum score 79 iBT). Electronic applications accepted. *Faculty research:* Frank Lloyd Wright, non-Western art, Renaissance, Bronze Age Crete, American art.

The University of Alabama, Graduate School, College of Arts and Sciences, Department of Art, Tuscaloosa, AL 35487. Offers art history (MA); studio art (MA, MFA), including ceramics, painting, photography, printmaking, sculpture. *Accreditation:* NASAD. Part-time programs available. *Faculty:* 16 full-time (9 women). *Students:* 22 full-time (16 women), 5 part-time (4 women); includes 3 minority (2 Black or African American, non-Hispanic/Latino; 1 Asian, non-Hispanic/Latino), 1 international. Average age 28. 22 applicants, 68% accepted, 10 enrolled. In 2014, 7 master's awarded. *Degree requirements:* For master's, one foreign language, comprehensive exam (for some programs), oral exam, thesis statement, exhibit (studio art), thesis (art history). *Entrance requirements:* For master's, GRE General Test or MAT (art history), minimum GPA of 3.0, BFA or equivalent (studio art). Additional exam requirements/recommendations for international students: Required—TOEFL (minimum score 550 paper-based). *Application deadline:* For fall admission, 3/15 for domestic and international students; for spring admission, 10/15 for domestic and international students. Applications are processed on a rolling basis. Application fee: $50 ($60 for international students). Electronic applications accepted. *Expenses:* Tuition, state resident: full-time $9826. Tuition, nonresident: full-time $24,950. *Financial support:* In 2014–15, 2 fellowships with full tuition reimbursements (averaging $14,000 per year), 13 teaching assistantships with full and partial tuition reimbursements (averaging $9,206 per year) were awarded; career-related internships or fieldwork, institutionally sponsored loans, scholarships/grants, and unspecified assistantships also available. Financial award application deadline: 7/14. *Faculty research:* Nineteenth-century American, Chinese, Baroque, twentieth-century, Asian art history. *Unit head:* William T. Dooley, Chairperson, 205-348-1890, Fax: 205-348-0287, E-mail: wtdooley@bama.ua.edu. *Application contact:* Craig R. Wedderspoon, Graduate Coordinator, 205-348-1898, Fax: 205-348-0287, E-mail: cwedders@bama.edu.
Website: http://www.art.ua.edu/

The University of Alabama at Birmingham, College of Arts and Sciences, Program in Art History, Birmingham, AL 35294. Offers MA. Program offered jointly with The University of Alabama (Tuscaloosa). *Accreditation:* NASAD. *Students:* 4 full-time (3 women), 4 part-time (3 women); includes 1 minority (Two or more races, non-Hispanic/Latino), 2 international. Average age 29. In 2014, 4 master's awarded. *Degree requirements:* For master's, one foreign language, comprehensive exam, thesis optional. *Entrance requirements:* For master's, GRE General Test or MAT, minimum GPA of 3.0. *Application deadline:* For fall admission, 4/1 for domestic students; for spring admission, 10/1 for domestic students. Applications are processed on a rolling basis. Electronic applications accepted. *Expenses:* Tuition, state resident: full-time $7090; part-time $370 per credit hour. Tuition, nonresident: full-time $16,072; part-time $869 per credit hour. Full-time tuition and fees vary according to course load and program. *Financial support:* Research assistantships, Federal Work-Study, and tuition waivers (partial) available. Financial award application deadline: 5/1. *Unit head:* Dr. Cathleen Cummings, Graduate Advisor, 205-934-7909, E-mail: cathleen@uab.edu. *Application contact:* Susan Noblitt Banks, Director of Graduate School Operations, 205-934-8227, Fax: 205-934-8413, E-mail: gradschool@uab.edu.
Website: http://www.uab.edu/cas/art/areas-of-study/ma-art-history

University of Alberta, Faculty of Graduate Studies and Research, Department of Art and Design, Edmonton, AB T6G 2E1, Canada. Offers drawing (MFA); history of art, design, and visual culture (MA); industrial design (M Des); painting (MFA); printmaking (MFA); sculpture (MFA); visual communication design (M Des). *Degree requirements:* For master's, thesis. *Entrance requirements:* For master's, portfolio (MFA and MDES). Additional exam requirements/recommendations for international students: Required—TOEFL (minimum score 550 paper-based).

The University of Arizona, College of Fine Arts, School of Art, Program in Art History, Tucson, AZ 85721. Offers MA. *Accreditation:* NASAD. Part-time programs available. Terminal master's awarded for partial completion of doctoral program. *Degree requirements:* For master's, one foreign language, thesis. *Entrance requirements:* For master's, GRE, 3 letters of recommendation, resume or curriculum vitae, writing sample. Additional exam requirements/recommendations for international students: Required—TOEFL (minimum score 550 paper-based; 79 iBT). Electronic applications accepted. *Faculty research:* American art, history of photography, Mexican art, contemporary African art.

The University of Arizona, College of Fine Arts, School of Art, Program in Art History and Education, Tucson, AZ 85721. Offers PhD. *Degree requirements:* For doctorate, thesis/dissertation. *Entrance requirements:* Additional exam requirements/recommendations for international students: Required—TOEFL (minimum score 550 paper-based; 79 iBT). Electronic applications accepted.

The University of Arizona, College of Fine Arts, School of Art, Program in History and Theory of Art, Tucson, AZ 85721. Offers PhD. *Entrance requirements:* Additional exam

requirements/recommendations for international students: Required—TOEFL (minimum score 550 paper-based; 79 iBT).

University of Arkansas at Little Rock, Graduate School, College of Arts, Humanities, and Social Science, Department of Art, Little Rock, AR 72204-1099. Offers art education (MA); art history (MA); studio art (MA). *Accreditation:* NASAD. Part-time programs available. *Degree requirements:* For master's, 4 foreign languages, oral exam, oral defense of thesis or exhibit. *Entrance requirements:* For master's, portfolio review or term paper evaluation, minimum GPA of 2.7. *Application deadline:* For fall admission, 4/1 for domestic students; for spring admission, 11/1 for domestic students. Applications are processed on a rolling basis. Application fee: $40. *Expenses:* Tuition, state resident: full-time $6000; part-time $300 per credit hour. Tuition, nonresident: full-time $13,800; part-time $690 per credit hour. *Required fees:* $1126; $603 per term. One-time fee: $40 full-time. *Financial support:* Research assistantships with tuition reimbursements, teaching assistantships with tuition reimbursements, Federal Work-Study, institutionally sponsored loans, and unspecified assistantships available. Support available to part-time students. *Unit head:* Tom Clifton, Chair, 501-569-3182, E-mail: tgclifton@ualr.edu. *Application contact:* Dr. Marjorie Williams-Smith, Program Coordinator, 501-569-3591, E-mail: mwsmith@ualr.edu.
Website: http://ualr.edu/art/

The University of British Columbia, Faculty of Arts and Faculty of Graduate Studies, Department of Art History, Visual Art, and Theory, Vancouver, BC V6T1Z2, Canada. Offers art history (MA, PhD, Diploma); critical and curatorial studies (MA); visual art (MFA). *Degree requirements:* For master's, one foreign language, thesis, final exhibition (MFA, MA in critical and curatorial studies); for doctorate, 2 foreign languages, comprehensive exam, thesis/dissertation. *Entrance requirements:* For master's, bachelor's degree with minimum B+ average (MFA, MA in critical and curatorial studies), A- (MA in art history); for doctorate, master's degree with minimum A- average. Additional exam requirements/recommendations for international students: Required—TOEFL (minimum score 600 paper-based). Electronic applications accepted. *Faculty research:* Conceptual art, Asian art, indigenous North American art, post-second war art, eighteenth and nineteenth century art, curatorial, digital art.

University of California, Berkeley, Graduate Division, College of Letters and Science, Department of History of Art, Berkeley, CA 94720-1500. Offers PhD. *Degree requirements:* For doctorate, 2 foreign languages, thesis/dissertation, qualifying exam. *Entrance requirements:* For doctorate, GRE General Test, minimum GPA of 3.0, 3 letters of recommendation. Additional exam requirements/recommendations for international students: Required—TOEFL. *Faculty research:* Modernism, Italian Renaissance art and architecture, Gothic art and architecture, women artists' representations of the body, the body in ancient Greece.

University of California, Davis, Graduate Studies, Program in Art History, Davis, CA 95616. Offers MA. *Degree requirements:* For master's, thesis. *Entrance requirements:* For master's, GRE, minimum GPA of 3.0, writing sample. Additional exam requirements/recommendations for international students: Required—TOEFL (minimum score 550 paper-based). Electronic applications accepted.

University of California, Los Angeles, Graduate Division, College of Letters and Science, Department of Art History, Los Angeles, CA 90095. Offers MA, PhD. Terminal master's awarded for partial completion of doctoral program. *Degree requirements:* For master's, one foreign language, thesis; for doctorate, one foreign language, thesis/dissertation, oral and written qualifying exams. *Entrance requirements:* For doctorate, GRE General Test, master's degree; minimum undergraduate GPA of 3.0 (or its equivalent if letter grade system not used); thesis or research paper, language survey. Additional exam requirements/recommendations for international students: Required—TOEFL. Electronic applications accepted.

University of California, Riverside, Graduate Division, Department of Art History, Riverside, CA 92521-0102. Offers MA. Part-time programs available. *Degree requirements:* For master's, one foreign language, thesis. *Entrance requirements:* For master's, GRE General Test, sample of written work, minimum GPA of 3.2. Additional exam requirements/recommendations for international students: Required—TOEFL (minimum score 550 paper-based; 80 iBT). Electronic applications accepted. *Expenses:* Tuition, state resident: full-time $5399. Tuition, nonresident: full-time $10,433. *Faculty research:* Ancient, medieval, Renaissance, seventeenth and eighteenth century art; modern European art; contemporary art and theory; modern architecture and urbanism; history of photography.

University of California, San Diego, Graduate Division, Department of Visual Arts, La Jolla, CA 92093. Offers art history, theory and criticism (PhD), including anthropogeny, art practice; visual arts (MFA). *Students:* 72 full-time (48 women); includes 14 minority (3 Black or African American, non-Hispanic/Latino; 2 American Indian or Alaska Native, non-Hispanic/Latino; 3 Asian, non-Hispanic/Latino; 6 Hispanic/Latino), 12 international. 205 applicants, 14% accepted, 15 enrolled. In 2014, 15 master's, 2 doctorates awarded. *Degree requirements:* For master's, thesis; for doctorate, 2 foreign languages, comprehensive exam, thesis/dissertation, reading knowledge of at least two of the foreign languages commonly used by scholars engaged in the advanced study in art history, theory, and criticism. *Entrance requirements:* For master's, electronic portfolio; for doctorate, GRE General Test, electronic portfolio. Additional exam requirements/recommendations for international students: Required—TOEFL (minimum score 550 paper-based; 80 iBT), IELTS (minimum score 7). *Application deadline:* For fall admission, 11/26 priority date for domestic students. Application fee: $90 ($110 for international students). Electronic applications accepted. *Expenses:* Tuition, state resident: full-time $11,220; part-time $5610 per quarter. Tuition, nonresident: full-time $26,322; part-time $13,161 per quarter. *Required fees:* $570 per quarter. Tuition and fees vary according to program. *Financial support:* Fellowships, research assistantships, teaching assistantships, career-related internships or fieldwork, scholarships/grants, and readerships available. Financial award applicants required to submit FAFSA. *Faculty research:* Contemporary art, ancient art, critical design, digital/new media/software/hardware, nano/bio/neuro. *Unit head:* Jordan Crandall, Chair, 858-534-0418, E-mail: jcrandall@ucsd.edu. *Application contact:* Asia Marks, Graduate Program Coordinator, 858-822-3884, E-mail: vis-grad@ucsd.edu.
Website: http://visarts.ucsd.edu/

University of California, Santa Barbara, Graduate Division, College of Letters and Sciences, Division of Humanities and Fine Arts, Department of History of Art and Architecture, Santa Barbara, CA 93106-2014. Offers art history (PhD), including art history, European medieval studies, feminist studies; MA/PhD. Terminal master's awarded for partial completion of doctoral program. *Degree requirements:* For doctorate, 2 foreign languages, comprehensive exam, thesis/dissertation. *Entrance requirements:* For doctorate, GRE. Additional exam requirements/recommendations for international students: Required—TOEFL (minimum score 550 paper-based; 80 iBT), IELTS (minimum score 7). Electronic applications accepted. *Faculty research:* History of architecture, Renaissance-Italian, Baroque, American, Chinese, Japanese, contemporary, Northern Renaissance.

University of Chicago, Division of the Humanities, Department of Art History, Chicago, IL 60637. Offers PhD. *Students:* 54 full-time (42 women); includes 10 minority (2 Black or African American, non-Hispanic/Latino; 6 Asian, non-Hispanic/Latino; 2 Hispanic/Latino), 12 international. 168 applicants, 31% accepted, 6 enrolled. Terminal master's awarded for partial completion of doctoral program. *Degree requirements:* For doctorate, variable foreign language requirement, thesis/dissertation. *Entrance requirements:* For doctorate, GRE General Test. Additional exam requirements/recommendations for international students: Required—TOEFL (minimum score 104 iBT), IELTS (minimum score 7). *Application deadline:* For fall admission, 12/15 for domestic and international students. Application fee: $90. Electronic applications accepted. *Expenses: Tuition:* Full-time $46,899. *Required fees:* $347. *Financial support:* Fellowships with full tuition reimbursements, teaching assistantships with full tuition reimbursements, Federal Work-Study, institutionally sponsored loans, and scholarships/grants available. Financial award application deadline: 12/15; financial award applicants required to submit FAFSA. *Unit head:* Christine Mehring, Chair. *Application contact:* Braden Grams, Assistant Dean of Students, Admissions and Fellowships, 773-702-1552, Fax: 773-834-9148, E-mail: humanitiesadmissions@uchicago.edu.
Website: http://arthistory.uchicago.edu

University of Chicago, Division of the Humanities, Master of Arts Program in the Humanities, Chicago, IL 60637. Offers art history (MA); classics (MA); comparative literature (MA); creative writing (MA); digital humanities (MA); English language and literature (MA); Germanic studies (MA); linguistics (MA); music (MA); philosophy (MA); Romance languages and literatures (MA); South Asian languages and civilizations (MA). *Students:* 83 full-time (41 women), 8 part-time (6 women); includes 14 minority (1 Black or African American, non-Hispanic/Latino; 6 Asian, non-Hispanic/Latino; 6 Hispanic/Latino; 1 Two or more races, non-Hispanic/Latino), 17 international. Average age 26. 153 applicants, 67% accepted, 80 enrolled. *Degree requirements:* For master's, thesis. *Entrance requirements:* For master's, GRE General Test. Additional exam requirements/recommendations for international students: Required—TOEFL (minimum score 600 paper-based; 104 iBT), IELTS (minimum score 7). *Application deadline:* For fall admission, 3/15 for domestic and international students. Application fee: $90. Electronic applications accepted. *Expenses: Tuition:* Full-time $46,899. *Required fees:* $347. *Financial support:* In 2014–15, 100 students received support, including 8 fellowships with partial tuition reimbursements available (averaging $12,000 per year); Federal Work-Study, institutionally sponsored loans, and tuition waivers (partial) also available. Financial award application deadline: 3/15; financial award applicants required to submit FAFSA. *Unit head:* Prof. David Wray, Director, 773-834-1201, E-mail: ma-humanities@uchicago.edu. *Application contact:* Program Coordinator, 773-834-1201, Fax: 773-834-7526, E-mail: ma-humanities@uchicago.edu.
Website: http://maph.uchicago.edu/

University of Cincinnati, Graduate School, College of Design, Architecture, Art, and Planning, School of Art, Program in Art History, Cincinnati, OH 45221. Offers MA. *Accreditation:* NASAD. Part-time programs available. *Degree requirements:* For master's, one foreign language, comprehensive exam, thesis. Electronic applications accepted.

University of Colorado Boulder, Graduate School, College of Arts and Sciences, Department of Art and Art History, Boulder, CO 80309. Offers art history (MA), including contemporary art criticism, early twentieth-century art, nineteenth-century art, Russian and Soviet art; ceramics (MFA); drawing (MFA); painting (MFA); photography and media arts (MFA); printmaking (MFA); sculpture (MFA). *Faculty:* 23 full-time (11 women). *Students:* 50 full-time (32 women), 1 (woman) part-time; includes 6 minority (all Hispanic/Latino), 2 international. Average age 29. 213 applicants, 17% accepted, 21 enrolled. In 2014, 21 master's awarded. Terminal master's awarded for partial completion of doctoral program. *Degree requirements:* For master's, variable foreign language requirement, comprehensive exam, thesis (for some programs). *Entrance requirements:* For master's, GRE General Test, minimum undergraduate GPA of 3.0, portfolio. *Application deadline:* For fall admission, 1/15 for domestic students, 12/1 for international students. Application fee: $50 ($70 for international students). Electronic applications accepted. *Financial support:* In 2014–15, 126 students received support, including 16 fellowships (averaging $1,206 per year), 43 teaching assistantships with full and partial tuition reimbursements available (averaging $26,856 per year); institutionally sponsored loans, scholarships/grants, health care benefits, and unspecified assistantships also available. Financial award application deadline: 1/15; financial award applicants required to submit FAFSA. *Faculty research:* Visual arts, fine arts, sculpture, installation art, inter-arts: interdisciplinary art forms.
Website: http://www.colorado.edu/arts/

University of Connecticut, Graduate School, School of Fine Arts, Department of Art and Art History, Field of Art History, Storrs, CT 06269. Offers MA. *Accreditation:* NASAD. *Degree requirements:* For master's, comprehensive exam. *Entrance requirements:* Additional exam requirements/recommendations for international students: Required—TOEFL (minimum score 550 paper-based). Electronic applications accepted.

University of Delaware, College of Arts and Sciences, Department of Art History, Newark, DE 19716. Offers MA, PhD. Part-time programs available. *Degree requirements:* For master's, one foreign language, thesis; for doctorate, 2 foreign languages, comprehensive exam, thesis/dissertation. *Entrance requirements:* For master's and doctorate, GRE General Test, writing sample. Additional exam requirements/recommendations for international students: Required—TOEFL. Electronic applications accepted. *Faculty research:* Art of Europe and the United States, art theory, vernacular architecture, medieval manuscripts, African art and architecture.

University of Denver, Division of Arts, Humanities and Social Sciences, School of Art and Art History, Denver, CO 80208. Offers art history (MA); art history/museum studies (MA); emergent digital practices (MFA). *Accreditation:* NASAD. Part-time programs available. *Faculty:* 16 full-time (11 women), 3 part-time/adjunct (1 woman). *Students:* 7 full-time (6 women), 17 part-time (16 women); includes 7 minority (1 Black or African American, non-Hispanic/Latino; 1 American Indian or Alaska Native, non-Hispanic/Latino; 5 Hispanic/Latino). Average age 25. 24 applicants, 83% accepted, 14 enrolled. In 2014, 7 master's awarded. *Degree requirements:* For master's, one foreign language, comprehensive exam, research paper or thesis project. *Entrance requirements:* For master's, GRE General Test, transcripts, personal statement, writing sample, three letters of recommendation. Additional exam requirements/recommendations for international students: Required—TOEFL (minimum score 550 paper-based; 80 iBT). *Application deadline:* For fall admission, 1/31 priority date for domestic and international students. Applications are processed on a rolling basis. Application fee: $65. Electronic applications accepted. *Expenses:* Expenses: $1,199 per credit hour. *Financial support:* In 2014–15, 18 students received support, including 8 teaching assistantships with full and partial tuition reimbursements available (averaging $7,817 per year); career-related internships or fieldwork, Federal Work-Study, institutionally sponsored loans, scholarships/grants, and unspecified assistantships also available. Support available to part-time students. Financial award application deadline: 2/15; financial award applicants required to submit FAFSA. *Faculty research:* Images of women in alchemical manuscripts and books, Giovanni Benedetto and Salvatore Castiglione. *Unit head:* Dr. Sarah Gjertson, Director, 303-871-3263, E-mail: sgjertso@du.edu. *Application contact:* Dr. Annabeth Headrick, Graduate Art History Advisor, 303-871-3574, E-mail: annabeth.headrick@du.edu.
Website: http://www.du.edu/art/

University of Florida, Graduate School, College of The Arts, School of Art and Art History, Gainesville, FL 32611-5800. Offers art (MA), including digital arts and sciences; art education (MA); art history (MA, PhD); museology (MA), including historic preservation. *Accreditation:* NASAD. Postbaccalaureate distance learning degree programs offered (minimal on-campus study). *Faculty:* 32 full-time (14 women), 5 part-time/adjunct (3 women). *Students:* 91 full-time (66 women), 117 part-time (100 women); includes 50 minority (14 Black or African American, non-Hispanic/Latino; 4 American Indian or Alaska Native, non-Hispanic/Latino; 6 Asian, non-Hispanic/Latino; 26 Hispanic/Latino), 14 international. 199 applicants, 41% accepted, 55 enrolled. In 2014, 69 master's awarded. *Degree requirements:* For master's, project or thesis (MFA); 1 foreign language (MA in art history); for doctorate, 2 foreign languages, comprehensive exam, thesis/dissertation. *Entrance requirements:* For master's, GRE General Test, portfolio (MFA), writing sample (MA), minimum GPA 3.0; for doctorate, GRE General Test, minimum GPA of 3.0. Additional exam requirements/recommendations for international students: Required—TOEFL (minimum score 550 paper-based; 80 iBT), IELTS (minimum score 6). *Application deadline:* For fall admission, 1/1 priority date for domestic students, 1/1 for international students; for spring admission, 11/1 for domestic and international students. Applications are processed on a rolling basis. Application fee: $30. Electronic applications accepted. *Financial support:* In 2014–15, 4 fellowships, 8 research assistantships, 76 teaching assistantships were awarded; Federal Work-Study, institutionally sponsored loans, and unspecified assistantships also available. Financial award applicants required to submit FAFSA. *Faculty research:* Studio production, art historical studies of style context. *Unit head:* Richard Heipp, Professor and Interim Director, 352-273-3021, Fax: 352-392-8453, E-mail: heipp@ufl.edu. *Application contact:* Maya Stanfield-Mazzi, PhD, Assistant Professor/Director of Graduate Studies for Art History, 352-273-3070, Fax: 352-392-8453, E-mail: mstanfield@ufl.edu.
Website: http://www.arts.ufl.edu/art

University of Georgia, Franklin College of Arts and Sciences, Lamar Dodd School of Art, Athens, GA 30602. Offers art (MFA, PhD); art history (MA). *Accreditation:* NASAD (one or more programs are accredited). *Degree requirements:* For doctorate, one foreign language, thesis/dissertation. *Entrance requirements:* For master's and doctorate, GRE General Test. Electronic applications accepted.

University of Hawaii at Manoa, Graduate Division, College of Arts and Humanities, Department of Art and Art History, Program in Art History, Honolulu, HI 96822. Offers MA. Part-time programs available. *Entrance requirements:* Additional exam requirements/recommendations for international students: Required—TOEFL (minimum score 600 paper-based; 100 iBT); Recommended—IELTS.

University of Houston, College of Liberal Arts and Social Sciences, Department of Art, Houston, TX 77204. Offers art history (MA); interdisciplinary practice and emerging forms (MFA); painting (MFA); studio art (MFA). *Entrance requirements:* For master's, baccalaureate degree, portfolio. Electronic applications accepted. *Faculty research:* Painting, sculpture, photography/installation/video, graphic design and typography, art history (Pre-Columbian to Surrealism).

University of Illinois at Chicago, Graduate College, College of Architecture, Design and the Arts, School of Art and Art History, Chicago, IL 60607-7128. Offers art history (MA); electronic visualization (MFA); museum and exhibition studies (MA); new media arts (MFA). Part-time and evening/weekend programs available. *Faculty:* 84 full-time (40 women), 70 part-time/adjunct (20 women). *Students:* 160 full-time (105 women), 23 part-time (17 women); includes 18 minority (3 Black or African American, non-Hispanic/Latino; 4 Asian, non-Hispanic/Latino; 10 Hispanic/Latino; 1 Two or more races, non-Hispanic/Latino), 13 international. Average age 29. 211 applicants, 32% accepted, 34 enrolled. In 2014, 21 master's, 3 doctorates awarded. Terminal master's awarded for partial completion of doctoral program. *Degree requirements:* For master's, one foreign language, thesis or alternative; for doctorate, thesis/dissertation. *Entrance requirements:* For master's, GRE General Test, minimum GPA of 2.75, 3 letters of recommendation; for doctorate, GRE General Test, MA in art history or equivalent, minimum GPA of 3.0. Additional exam requirements/recommendations for international students: Required—TOEFL. *Application deadline:* For fall admission, 1/1 priority date for domestic and international students; for spring admission, 10/1 for domestic students, 7/15 for international students. Application fee: $60. Electronic applications accepted. *Expenses:* Expenses: $19,134 in-state, $31,132 out-of-state (for art); $17,932 in-state, $29,930 out-of-state (for art history). *Financial support:* Fellowships with full tuition reimbursements, research assistantships with full tuition reimbursements, teaching assistantships with full tuition reimbursements, career-related internships or fieldwork, Federal Work-Study, scholarships/grants, traineeships, tuition waivers (full), and unspecified assistantships available. Support available to part-time students. Financial award application deadline: 3/1; financial award applicants required to submit FAFSA. *Faculty research:* Modern painting and sculpture, history of architecture, city planning and design, history of photography. *Unit head:* Prof. Lisa Yun Lee, Director, 312-413-5358, E-mail: lisalee@uic.edu. *Application contact:* Receptionist, 312-413-2550, E-mail: gradcoll@uic.edu.
Website: http://artandarthistory.uic.edu/art-history

University of Illinois at Urbana–Champaign, Graduate College, College of Fine and Applied Arts, School of Art and Design, Program in Art History, Champaign, IL 61820. Offers MA, PhD. *Accreditation:* NASAD. *Students:* 19 (all women). Application fee: $70 ($90 for international students). *Unit head:* Lisa Rosenthal, Chair, 217-265-5236, Fax: 217-244-7688, E-mail: lrosenth@illinois.edu. *Application contact:* Ellen de Waard, Coordinator of Graduate Academic Affairs, 217-333-0642, Fax: 217-244-7688, E-mail: edewaard@illinois.edu.
Website: http://www.art.illinois.edu

The University of Iowa, Graduate College, College of Liberal Arts and Sciences, School of Art and Art History, Program in Art History, Iowa City, IA 52242-1316. Offers MA, PhD. *Degree requirements:* For master's, one foreign language, thesis, exam; for doctorate, 2 foreign languages, comprehensive exam, thesis/dissertation, final exams. *Entrance requirements:* For master's, GRE General Test; for doctorate, GRE General Test, MA in art history. Additional exam requirements/recommendations for international students: Required—TOEFL (minimum score 550 paper-based; 81 iBT). Electronic applications accepted. *Faculty research:* African (Oceanic), Asian, Ancient (3000 B.C.-300 A.D.), medieval, Renaissance, Baroque, eighteenth and nineteenth century European, American (includes Pre-Columbian, Native American, and African American), and Modern/Contemporary.

The University of Kansas, Graduate Studies, College of Liberal Arts and Sciences, The Kress Foundation Department of Art History, Lawrence, KS 66045. Offers MA, PhD. Part-time programs available. *Faculty:* 14 full-time. *Students:* 35 full-time (29 women), 5 part-time (4 women); includes 1 minority (Asian, non-Hispanic/Latino), 9 international. Average age 31. 31 applicants, 77% accepted, 7 enrolled. In 2014, 9 master's, 2 doctorates awarded. Terminal master's awarded for partial completion of doctoral program. *Degree requirements:* For master's, one foreign language, comprehensive exam, thesis optional; for doctorate, 2 foreign languages, comprehensive exam, thesis/dissertation, 1-year full-time enrollment. *Entrance requirements:* For master's, GRE, minimum undergraduate GPA of 3.3, 18 credit hours of art history; for doctorate, GRE, MA in art history or related field. Additional exam requirements/recommendations for international students: Required—TOEFL. *Application deadline:* For fall admission, 1/1 for domestic and international students. Application fee: $55 ($65 for international students). Electronic applications accepted. *Financial support:* Fellowships with full tuition reimbursements, research assistantships with partial tuition reimbursements, teaching assistantships with full tuition reimbursements, career-related internships or fieldwork, scholarships/grants, health care benefits, and unspecified assistantships available. Financial award application deadline: 1/1. *Faculty research:* American, Asian, European, and modern art; medieval/Renaissance. *Unit head:* Linda Stone-Ferrier, Chair, 785-864-4713, Fax: 785-864-5091, E-mail: lsf@ku.edu. *Application contact:* Lisa Cloar, Graduate Admissions Contact, 785-864-4713, Fax: 785-864-5091, E-mail: arthist@ku.edu.
Website: http://arthistory.ku.edu/

University of Kentucky, Graduate School, College of Fine Arts, Program in Art History, Lexington, KY 40506-0032. Offers MA. *Accreditation:* NASAD. *Degree requirements:* For master's, 2 foreign languages, comprehensive exam, thesis. *Entrance requirements:* For master's, GRE General Test, minimum undergraduate GPA of 2.75. Additional exam requirements/recommendations for international students: Required—TOEFL (minimum score 550 paper-based). Electronic applications accepted. *Faculty research:* Northern European prints and drawings, nineteenth century French painting and drawing, Roman sarcophagus sculpture, manuscript illumination, history and theory of photography.

University of Louisville, Graduate School, College of Arts and Sciences, Department of Fine Arts, Louisville, KY 40292. Offers art history (MA, PhD); creative art (MA); curatorial studies (MA). *Students:* 15 full-time (10 women), 9 part-time (5 women); includes 5 minority (2 Black or African American, non-Hispanic/Latino; 2 Asian, non-Hispanic/Latino; 1 Hispanic/Latino), 2 international. Average age 36. 27 applicants, 63% accepted, 8 enrolled. In 2014, 3 master's, 1 doctorate awarded. *Degree requirements:* For master's, thesis; for doctorate, 2 foreign languages, comprehensive exam, thesis/dissertation. *Entrance requirements:* For master's and doctorate, GRE General Test. Additional exam requirements/recommendations for international students: Required—TOEFL (minimum score 550 paper-based; 79 iBT). *Application deadline:* For fall admission, 1/15 for domestic students, 5/1 priority date for international students; for spring admission, 11/1 priority date for international students; for summer admission, 4/1 priority date for international students. Applications are processed on a rolling basis. Application fee: $60. *Expenses:* Tuition, state resident: full-time $11,326; part-time $630 per credit hour. Tuition, nonresident: full-time $23,568; part-time $1311 per credit hour. *Required fees:* $196. Tuition and fees vary according to program and reciprocity agreements. *Financial support:* Teaching assistantships with full tuition reimbursements available. Financial award application deadline: 1/15. *Faculty research:* Art history in the periods from ancient to contemporary and various regions, 2D and 3D studio areas, intermedia, curatorial studies. *Unit head:* Prof. Ying Kit Chan, Chair, 502-852-6794, Fax: 502-852-6791, E-mail: chan@louisville.edu. *Application contact:* Libby Leggett, Director, Graduate Admissions, 502-852-3101, Fax: 502-852-6536, E-mail: gradadm@louisville.edu.
Website: http://art.louisville.edu

The University of Manchester, School of Arts, Histories and Cultures, Manchester, United Kingdom. Offers anthropology, media and performance (PhD); applied theatre professional (PhD); archaeology (PhD); art history and visual studies (PhD); arts management and cultural policy (PhD); classics and ancient history (PhD); composition (PhD); creative writing (PhD); drama (PhD); economic and social history (PhD); electroacoustic composition (PhD); English and American studies (PhD); history (PhD); humanitarianism and conflict response (PhD); museology (PhD); music (PhD); musicology (PhD); religions and theology (PhD).

University of Maryland, College Park, Academic Affairs, College of Arts and Humanities, Department of Art History and Archaeology, College Park, MD 20742. Offers art history (MA, PhD). *Degree requirements:* For master's, one foreign language, thesis, oral exam; for doctorate, 2 foreign languages, thesis/dissertation, oral exam. *Entrance requirements:* For master's, GRE General Test, minimum GPA of 3.0, writing sample, 3 letters of recommendation. Additional exam requirements/recommendations for international students: Required—TOEFL. Electronic applications accepted. *Faculty research:* Western, African, pre-Columbian, American, and East Asian art.

University of Massachusetts Amherst, Graduate School, College of Humanities and Fine Arts, Department of Art, Department of the History of Art and Architecture, Amherst, MA 01003. Offers MA. Part-time programs available. *Students:* 7 full-time (6 women), 10 part-time (7 women); includes 2 minority (both Hispanic/Latino). Average age 27. 33 applicants, 36% accepted, 7 enrolled. In 2014, 6 master's awarded. *Degree requirements:* For master's, comprehensive exam, journal-level knowledge of French, German, or Italian. *Entrance requirements:* For master's, GRE General Test, 7-20 page writing sample. Additional exam requirements/recommendations for international students: Required—TOEFL (minimum score 550 paper-based; 80 iBT), IELTS (minimum score 6.5). *Application deadline:* For fall admission, 1/15 for domestic and international students; for spring admission, 10/1 for domestic and international students. Applications are processed on a rolling basis. Application fee: $75. Electronic applications accepted. *Expenses:* Tuition, state resident: full-time $1980; part-time $110 per credit. Tuition, nonresident: full-time $14,644; part-time $414 per credit. *Required fees:* $11,417. One-time fee: $357. *Financial support:* Fellowships with full and partial tuition reimbursements, research assistantships with full and partial tuition reimbursements, teaching assistantships with full and partial tuition reimbursements, career-related internships or fieldwork, Federal Work-Study, scholarships/grants, traineeships, health care benefits, tuition waivers (full and partial), and unspecified assistantships available. Support available to part-time students. Financial award application deadline: 1/15. *Unit head:* Dr. Monika Schmitter, Graduate Program Director, 413-545-2751, Fax: 413-545-3135. *Application contact:* Lindsay DeSantis, Supervisor of Admissions, 413-545-0722, Fax: 413-577-0100, E-mail: gradadm@grad.umass.edu.
Website: http://www.umass.edu/arthist/

University of Memphis, Graduate School, College of Communication and Fine Arts, Department of Art, Memphis, TN 38152. Offers art (Graduate Certificate); art history (MA), including Egyptian art and archaeology, general art history; ceramics (MFA); graphic design (MFA); interior design (MFA); painting (MFA); printmaking/photography (MFA). *Accreditation:* NASAD (one or more programs are accredited). *Faculty:* 19 full-time (7 women), 4 part-time/adjunct (2 women). *Students:* 34 full-time (28 women), 3 part-time (2 women); includes 5 minority (2 Asian, non-Hispanic/Latino; 2 Hispanic/Latino; 1 Two or more races, non-Hispanic/Latino). Average age 30. 24 applicants, 63% accepted, 10 enrolled. In 2014, 14 master's, 14 other advanced degrees awarded. *Degree requirements:* For master's, 2 foreign languages, comprehensive exam, thesis. *Entrance requirements:* For master's, GRE General Test or MAT, portfolio (MFA). *Application deadline:* For fall admission, 8/1 for domestic students; for spring admission, 12/1 for domestic students. Applications are processed on a rolling basis. Application fee: $35 ($60 for international students). *Financial support:* In 2014–15, 38 students received support. Research assistantships with full tuition reimbursements available, teaching assistantships with full tuition reimbursements available, Federal Work-Study, scholarships/grants, and unspecified assistantships available. Financial award application deadline: 2/15; financial award applicants required to submit FAFSA. *Faculty research:* Online collaborative learning, advanced art history studies, electronic

publishing/design, studio arts, architectural studies. *Unit head:* Prof. Richard Lou, Chair, 901-678-2216, Fax: 901-678-2735, E-mail: gmyatt@memphis.edu. *Application contact:* Greely Myat, Graduate Studies Coordinator, 901-678-2650.
Website: http://memphis.edu/art/

University of Miami, Graduate School, College of Arts and Sciences, Department of Art and Art History, Coral Gables, FL 33124. Offers art history (MA); ceramics/glass (MFA); graphic design/multimedia (MFA); painting (MFA); photography/digital imaging (MFA); printmaking (MFA); sculpture (MFA). Part-time programs available. *Degree requirements:* For master's, variable foreign language requirement, thesis, exhibit (MFA), comprehensive exam (MA). *Entrance requirements:* For master's, GRE General Test (MA), research paper (MA), slide portfolio (MFA). Additional exam requirements/recommendations for international students: Required—TOEFL. Electronic applications accepted. *Faculty research:* Installation art, public art.

University of Michigan, Horace H. Rackham School of Graduate Studies, College of Literature, Science, and the Arts, Department of History of Art, Ann Arbor, MI 48109-1357. Offers PhD. *Degree requirements:* For doctorate, 2 foreign languages, thesis/dissertation, preliminary examinations, oral defense of dissertation. *Entrance requirements:* For doctorate, GRE General Test. Additional exam requirements/recommendations for international students: Recommended—TOEFL. Electronic applications accepted. *Faculty research:* Asian, African and African-American, ancient, medieval and Byzantine, early modern, and modern art.

University of Michigan, Horace H. Rackham School of Graduate Studies, College of Literature, Science, and the Arts, Interdepartmental Program in Classical Art and Archaeology, Ann Arbor, MI 48109. Offers MA, PhD. *Faculty:* 20 full-time (8 women), 1 (woman) part-time/adjunct. *Students:* 23 full-time (15 women), 6 international. 42 applicants, 12% accepted, 3 enrolled. In 2014, 4 doctorates awarded. *Degree requirements:* For doctorate, 4 foreign languages, comprehensive exam, thesis/dissertation, ancient history exam, preliminary exam. *Entrance requirements:* For doctorate, GRE General Test. Additional exam requirements/recommendations for international students: Required—TOEFL (minimum score 560 paper-based; 84 iBT). *Application deadline:* For fall admission, 12/15 for domestic and international students. Application fee: $75 ($90 for international students). Electronic applications accepted. *Financial support:* In 2014–15, 21 students received support, including 9 fellowships with full tuition reimbursements available (averaging $18,234 per year), 1 research assistantship with full tuition reimbursement available (averaging $18,925 per year), 7 teaching assistantships with full tuition reimbursements available (averaging $18,234 per year); career-related internships or fieldwork, health care benefits, and summer research funding (average of $3,500 per student), ad hoc conference travel funding also available. Financial award application deadline: 4/15. *Faculty research:* Greek art and archaeology, Roman art and archaeology, Near Eastern art and archaeology, archaeological theory and methodology. *Unit head:* Prof. Lisa Nevett, Program Director, 734-764-8581, Fax: 734-763-8976, E-mail: lcnevett@umich.edu. *Application contact:* Alexander Zwinak, Graduate Program Coordinator, 734-764-6323, Fax: 734-763-8976, E-mail: ipcaa.office@umich.edu.
Website: http://www.lsa.umich.edu/ipcaa/

University of Minnesota, Twin Cities Campus, Graduate School, College of Liberal Arts, Department of Art History, Minneapolis, MN 55455. Offers MA, PhD. Part-time programs available. *Faculty:* 10 full-time (3 women), 1 (woman) part-time/adjunct. *Students:* 22 full-time (20 women); includes 4 minority (2 Asian, non-Hispanic/Latino; 2 Hispanic/Latino). Average age 35. 37 applicants, 16% accepted, 3 enrolled. In 2014, 2 master's, 3 doctorates awarded. Terminal master's awarded for partial completion of doctoral program. *Degree requirements:* For master's, one foreign language, comprehensive exam, thesis or alternative; for doctorate, 2 foreign languages, comprehensive exam, thesis/dissertation. *Entrance requirements:* For master's, GRE, 3 letters of recommendation, writing sample; for doctorate, GRE, transcripts, 3 letters of recommendation, writing sample. Additional exam requirements/recommendations for international students: Required—TOEFL. *Application deadline:* For fall admission, 12/1 for domestic and international students. Application fee: $75 ($95 for international students). Electronic applications accepted. *Financial support:* In 2014–15, 15 students received support, including 2 fellowships with full tuition reimbursements available (averaging $22,500 per year), 4 research assistantships with full tuition reimbursements available (averaging $15,140 per year), 12 teaching assistantships with full tuition reimbursements available (averaging $15,140 per year); career-related internships or fieldwork, Federal Work-Study, institutionally sponsored loans, scholarships/grants, health care benefits, and unspecified assistantships also available. Financial award application deadline: 6/30; financial award applicants required to submit FAFSA. *Faculty research:* North American, Latin American, modern/contemporary, early modern, East Asian, South Asian, and ancient art. *Total annual research expenditures:* $13,000. *Unit head:* Steven F. Ostrow, Chair, 612-624-4500, Fax: 612-626-8679, E-mail: ostro133@umn.edu. *Application contact:* Erik Farseth, Information Contact, 612-624-4500, Fax: 612-626-8679, E-mail: arthist@umn.edu.
Website: http://www.arthist.umn.edu/

University of Minnesota, Twin Cities Campus, Graduate School, College of Liberal Arts, Department of Classical and Near Eastern Studies, Minneapolis, MN 55455-0213. Offers ancient and medieval art and archaeology (MA, PhD); classics (MA, PhD); Greek (MA, PhD); Latin (MA, PhD); religions in antiquity (MA). Part-time programs available. Terminal master's awarded for partial completion of doctoral program. *Degree requirements:* For master's, 2 foreign languages, comprehensive exam, thesis or alternative; for doctorate, variable foreign language requirement, comprehensive exam, thesis/dissertation. *Entrance requirements:* For master's and doctorate, GRE, 3 letters of recommendation, writing sample, copies of transcripts, personal statement. Additional exam requirements/recommendations for international students: Required—TOEFL. Electronic applications accepted. *Faculty research:* Greek and Latin literature, religions in antiquity, ancient Near East.

University of Mississippi, Graduate School, College of Liberal Arts, Department of Art, University, MS 38677. Offers art education (MA); art history (MA); fine arts (MFA). *Accreditation:* NASAD (one or more programs are accredited). Part-time programs available. *Degree requirements:* For master's, thesis (for some programs). *Entrance requirements:* For master's, GRE General Test, minimum GPA of 3.0. Additional exam requirements/recommendations for international students: Required—TOEFL. Electronic applications accepted.

University of Missouri, Office of Research and Graduate Studies, College of Arts and Science, Department of Art History and Archaeology, Columbia, MO 65211. Offers MA, PhD. *Faculty:* 9 full-time (3 women), 1 (woman) part-time/adjunct. *Students:* 25 full-time (21 women), 4 part-time (all women); includes 1 minority (Hispanic/Latino), 1 international. Average age 30. 34 applicants, 12% accepted, 4 enrolled. In 2014, 1 master's, 2 doctorates awarded. Terminal master's awarded for partial completion of doctoral program. *Degree requirements:* For master's, 2 foreign languages, thesis; for doctorate, 2 foreign languages, thesis/dissertation. *Entrance requirements:* For master's, GRE General Test (minimum score 1000 verbal and quantitative, 4.5 analytical), minimum GPA of 3.0, 3.3 in major field; at least 3 semesters in appropriate foreign language; for doctorate, GRE General Test, minimum GPA of 3.0; MA or equivalent in art history or classical archaeology; master's thesis. Additional exam

requirements/recommendations for international students: Required—TOEFL (minimum score 500 paper-based; 61 iBT), IELTS (minimum score 5.5). *Application deadline:* For fall admission, 1/18 priority date for domestic students. Applications are processed on a rolling basis. Application fee: $55 ($75 for international students). Electronic applications accepted. *Financial support:* In 2014–15, 4 fellowships with full tuition reimbursements, 13 research assistantships with full tuition reimbursements, 5 teaching assistantships with full tuition reimbursements were awarded; institutionally sponsored loans, health care benefits, and unspecified assistantships also available. *Faculty research:* Classical Mediterranean archaeology, medieval and Renaissance art, art and architecture of modern Europe and the Americas. *Unit head:* Dr. Susan Langdon, Department Chair, 573-882-6711, E-mail: langdons@missouri.edu. *Application contact:* Linda Garrison, Administrative Associate I, 573-882-2757, E-mail: garrisonl@missouri.edu.
Website: http://aha.missouri.edu/

University of Missouri–Kansas City, College of Arts and Sciences, Department of Art and Art History, Kansas City, MO 64110-2499. Offers art history (MA, PhD); studio art (MA). PhD (interdisciplinary) offered through the School of Graduate Studies. Part-time programs available. *Faculty:* 11 full-time (5 women), 11 part-time/adjunct (4 women). *Students:* 12 full-time (7 women), 27 part-time (23 women); includes 4 minority (2 Black or African American, non-Hispanic/Latino; 2 Hispanic/Latino), 2 international. Average age 34. 19 applicants, 79% accepted, 13 enrolled. In 2014, 11 master's awarded. Terminal master's awarded for partial completion of doctoral program. *Degree requirements:* For master's, thesis, qualifying exam; for doctorate, thesis/dissertation, exams. *Entrance requirements:* For master's, good general education in the humanities. Additional exam requirements/recommendations for international students: Required—TOEFL (minimum score 550 paper-based; 80 iBT). *Application deadline:* For fall admission, 3/1 priority date for domestic and international students; for spring admission, 10/15 for domestic and international students. Applications are processed on a rolling basis. Application fee: $45 ($50 for international students). Electronic applications accepted. *Financial support:* In 2014–15, 9 teaching assistantships with partial tuition reimbursements (averaging $9,933 per year) were awarded; career-related internships or fieldwork, Federal Work-Study, institutionally sponsored loans, and tuition waivers (full and partial) also available. Support available to part-time students. Financial award application deadline: 3/1; financial award applicants required to submit FAFSA. *Faculty research:* Painting, electronic media, Western and non-Western art history, photography. *Unit head:* Elijah Gowin, Department Chair, 816-235-5301, Fax: 816-235-5507, E-mail: gowinp@umkc.edu. *Application contact:* Tamera Byland, Director of Admissions, 816-235-1111, Fax: 816-235-5544, E-mail: admit@umkc.edu.
Website: http://cas.umkc.edu/art

The University of Montana, Graduate School, College of Visual and Performing Arts, School of Art, Missoula, MT 59812-0002. Offers fine arts (MA), including art, art history; photography (MFA). *Accreditation:* NASAD (one or more programs are accredited). *Degree requirements:* For master's, thesis exhibit. *Entrance requirements:* For master's, GRE General Test, portfolio.

University of Nebraska–Lincoln, Graduate College, College of Fine and Performing Arts, Department of Art and Art History, Lincoln, NE 68588. Offers art history (MA); studio art (MFA). *Accreditation:* NASAD. *Degree requirements:* For master's, thesis. *Entrance requirements:* For master's, slide portfolio. Additional exam requirements/recommendations for international students: Required—TOEFL (minimum score 550 paper-based). Electronic applications accepted. *Faculty research:* Classical archaeology, contemporary art, printmaking, photography.

University of New Mexico, Graduate School, College of Fine Arts, Program in Art History, Albuquerque, NM 87131. Offers art history (MA); arts of the Americas (MA); history of architecture (PhD); history of graphic arts (PhD); history of photography (PhD); modern Latin American art history (PhD); Native American art history (PhD); Pre-Columbian art history (PhD); Spanish colonial art history (PhD). Part-time programs available. *Faculty:* 9 full-time (7 women). *Students:* 14 full-time (10 women), 22 part-time (16 women); includes 8 minority (2 American Indian or Alaska Native, non-Hispanic/Latino; 6 Hispanic/Latino), 5 international. Average age 32. 34 applicants, 26% accepted, 5 enrolled. In 2014, 5 master's, 1 doctorate awarded. *Degree requirements:* For master's, one foreign language, comprehensive exam (for some programs), thesis, symposium; for doctorate, 2 foreign languages, comprehensive exam, thesis/dissertation, symposium. *Entrance requirements:* Additional exam requirements/recommendations for international students: Required—TOEFL (minimum score 550 paper-based), IELTS (minimum score 6). *Application deadline:* For fall admission, 1/15 for domestic students; for spring admission, 1/15 for domestic students. Application fee: $50. Electronic applications accepted. *Financial support:* In 2014–15, fellowships (averaging $7,433 per year), research assistantships with tuition reimbursements (averaging $5,216 per year), teaching assistantships with partial tuition reimbursements (averaging $4,005 per year) were awarded; Federal Work-Study, institutionally sponsored loans, scholarships/grants, health care benefits, and unspecified assistantships also available. Support available to part-time students. Financial award application deadline: 3/1; financial award applicants required to submit FAFSA. *Faculty research:* Native American, modern Latin American, pre-Columbian, architectural, American, medieval, Spanish Colonial, and Latin American art; history of photography. *Unit head:* Prof. Mary Tsiongas, Chair, 505-277-5861, Fax: 505-277-5955, E-mail: tsiongas@unm.edu. *Application contact:* Kat Heatherington, Graduate Advisor, 505-277-6672, Fax: 505-277-5955, E-mail: art255@unm.edu.
Website: http://art.unm.edu/

The University of North Carolina at Chapel Hill, Graduate School, College of Arts and Sciences, Department of Art, Program in Art History, Chapel Hill, NC 27599. Offers MA, PhD. *Degree requirements:* For master's, one foreign language, comprehensive exam, thesis; for doctorate, one foreign language, comprehensive exam, thesis/dissertation. *Entrance requirements:* For master's and doctorate, GRE General Test, minimum GPA of 3.0.

University of North Texas, Robert B. Toulouse School of Graduate Studies, Denton, TX 76203-5459. Offers accounting (MS); applied anthropology (MA, MS); applied behavior analysis (Certificate); applied geography (MA); applied technology and performance improvement (M Ed, MS); art education (MA); art history (MA); art museum education (Certificate); arts leadership (Certificate); audiology (Au D); behavior analysis (MS); behavioral science (PhD); biochemistry and molecular biology (MS); biology (MA, MS); biomedical engineering (MS); business analysis (MS); chemistry (MS); clinical health psychology (PhD); communication studies (MA, MS); computer engineering (MS); computer science (MS); counseling (M Ed, MS), including clinical mental health counseling (MS), college and university counseling, elementary school counseling, secondary school counseling; creative writing (MA); criminal justice (MS); curriculum and instruction (M Ed); decision sciences (MBA); design (MA, MFA), including fashion design (MFA), innovation studies, interior design (MFA); early childhood studies (MS); economics (MS); educational leadership (M Ed, Ed D); educational psychology (MS, PhD), including family studies (MS), gifted and talented (MS), human development (MS), learning and cognition (MS), research, measurement and evaluation (MS); electrical engineering (MS); emergency management (MPA); engineering technology (MS); English (MA); English as a second language (MA); environmental science (MS); finance (MBA, MS); financial management (MPA); French (MA); health services management

(MBA); higher education (M Ed, Ed D); history (MA, MS); hospitality management (MS); human resources management (MPA); information science (MS); information systems (PhD); information technologies (MBA); interdisciplinary studies (MA, MS); international studies (MA); international sustainable tourism (MS); jazz studies (MM); journalism (MA, MJ, Graduate Certificate), including interactive and virtual digital communication (Graduate Certificate), narrative journalism (Graduate Certificate), public relations (Graduate Certificate); kinesiology (MS); linguistics (MA); local government management (MPA); logistics (PhD); logistics and supply chain management (MBA); long-term care, senior housing, and aging services (MA); management (PhD); marketing (MBA); mathematics (MA, MS); mechanical and energy engineering (MS, PhD); music (MA), including ethnomusicology, music theory, musicology, performance; music composition (PhD); music education (MM Ed, PhD); nonprofit management (MPA); operations and supply chain management (MBA); performance (MM, DMA); philosophy (MA); political science (MA); professional and technical communication (MA); radio, television and film (MA, MFA); rehabilitation counseling (Certificate); sociology (MA); Spanish (MA); special education (M Ed); speech-language pathology (MA); strategic management (MBA); studio art (MFA); teaching (M Ed); MBA/MS. Part-time and evening/weekend programs available. Postbaccalaureate distance learning degree programs offered. *Faculty:* 651 full-time (215 women), 233 part-time/adjunct (139 women). *Students:* 3,040 full-time (1,598 women), 3,401 part-time (2,097 women); includes 1,740 minority (533 Black or African American, non-Hispanic/Latino; 15 American Indian or Alaska Native, non-Hispanic/Latino; 286 Asian, non-Hispanic/Latino; 746 Hispanic/Latino; 3 Native Hawaiian or other Pacific Islander, non-Hispanic/Latino; 157 Two or more races, non-Hispanic/Latino), 1,145 international. Terminal master's awarded for partial completion of doctoral program. *Degree requirements:* For master's, variable foreign language requirement, comprehensive exam (for some programs), thesis (for some programs); for doctorate, variable foreign language requirement, comprehensive exam (for some programs), thesis/dissertation; for other advanced degree, variable foreign language requirement, comprehensive exam (for some programs). *Entrance requirements:* For master's and doctorate, GRE, GMAT. Additional exam requirements/recommendations for international students: Required—TOEFL (minimum score 550 paper-based; 79 iBT). *Application deadline:* For fall admission, 7/15 for domestic students, 3/15 for international students; for spring admission, 11/15 for domestic students, 9/15 for international students; for summer admission, 5/1 for domestic students. Applications are processed on a rolling basis. Application fee: $60. Electronic applications accepted. *Expenses:* Tuition, state resident: full-time $5450; part-time $3633 per year. Tuition, nonresident: full-time $11,966; part-time $7977 per year. *Required fees:* $1301; $398 per credit hour. $685 per semester. Tuition and fees vary according to program and reciprocity agreements. *Financial support:* Fellowships with partial tuition reimbursements, research assistantships with partial tuition reimbursements, teaching assistantships, career-related internships or fieldwork, Federal Work-Study, institutionally sponsored loans, scholarships/grants, health care benefits, and library assistantships available. Support available to part-time students. Financial award applicants required to submit FAFSA. *Unit head:* Mark Wardell, Dean, 940-565-2383, E-mail: mark.wardell@unt.edu. *Application contact:* Toulouse School of Graduate Studies, 940-565-2383, Fax: 940-565-2141, E-mail: gradsch@unt.edu.
Website: http://tsgs.unt.edu/

University of Notre Dame, Graduate School, College of Arts and Letters, Division of Humanities, Department of Art, Art History, and Design, Notre Dame, IN 46556. Offers art history (MA); design (MFA), including graphic design, industrial design; studio art (MFA), including ceramics, painting, photography, printmaking, sculpture. *Accreditation:* NASAD. *Degree requirements:* For master's, comprehensive exam (for some programs), thesis. *Entrance requirements:* For master's, GRE General Test, minimum GPA of 3.0. Additional exam requirements/recommendations for international students: Required—TOEFL (minimum score 600 paper-based; 80 iBT). Electronic applications accepted. *Faculty research:* Studio art practice in ceramics, printing, photography, printmaking and sculpture, graphic design and industrial design, digital imaging in design and photography, Renaissance and American art history, contemporary art theory and criticism.

University of Oklahoma, Weitzenhoffer Family College of Fine Arts, School of Art and Art History, Program in Art History, Norman, OK 73019. Offers art history (MA); art of the American West (PhD). Part-time programs available. *Students:* 8 full-time (all women), 10 part-time (7 women); includes 2 minority (both American Indian or Alaska Native, non-Hispanic/Latino). Average age 33. 3 applicants, 100% accepted, 1 enrolled. In 2014, 2 master's awarded. Terminal master's awarded for partial completion of doctoral program. *Degree requirements:* For master's, one foreign language, comprehensive exam, thesis, 36 hours; for doctorate, one foreign language, comprehensive exam, thesis/dissertation, 90 total hours. *Entrance requirements:* For master's, GRE, minimum GPA of 3.0 in art history courses or related field, evidence of strong writing skills, 3 letters of recommendation; for doctorate, GRE, minimum GPA of 3.0 on art history courses, evidence of research and writing skills in art history, 3 letters of recommendation. Additional exam requirements/recommendations for international students: Required—TOEFL (minimum score 79 iBT). *Application deadline:* For fall admission, 1/15 for domestic and international students; for spring admission, 10/1 for domestic and international students. Application fee: $50 ($100 for international students). Electronic applications accepted. *Expenses:* Tuition, state resident: full-time $4394; part-time $183.10 per credit hour. Tuition, nonresident: full-time $16,970; part-time $707.10 per credit hour. *Required fees:* $2892; $109.95 per credit hour. $126.50 per semester. *Financial support:* In 2014–15, 13 students received support. Career-related internships or fieldwork, Federal Work-Study, institutionally sponsored loans, scholarships/grants, health care benefits, tuition waivers (full and partial), and unspecified assistantships available. Support available to part-time students. Financial award application deadline: 6/1; financial award applicants required to submit FAFSA. *Faculty research:* Byzantine, Renaissance, Baroque, nineteenth-twentieth century, contemporary, Native American art, art of the American West. *Unit head:* Dr. Rozmeri Basic, Interim Co-Director, 405-325-2691, Fax: 405-325-1668, E-mail: rozmeri@ou.edu. *Application contact:* Dr. Jackson Rushing, Graduate Coordinator, 405-325-2691, Fax: 405-325-1668, E-mail: jackson_rushing@ou.edu.
Website: http://www.ou.edu/finearts/art_arthistory/programs/master_of_art_in_art_history.html

University of Oregon, Graduate School, School of Architecture and Allied Arts, Department of Art History, Eugene, OR 97403. Offers MA, PhD. *Degree requirements:* For master's, one foreign language, thesis or alternative; for doctorate, 2 foreign languages, thesis/dissertation. *Entrance requirements:* For master's, GRE General Test, minimum GPA of 3.0; for doctorate, minimum GPA of 3.0. Additional exam requirements/recommendations for international students: Required—TOEFL. *Faculty research:* Scytho-Siberian art, modern Chinese painting, European landscape painting, American architecture, German expressionist graphics.

University of Pennsylvania, School of Arts and Sciences, Graduate Group in the History of Art, Philadelphia, PA 19104. Offers AM, PhD. *Faculty:* 27 full-time (12 women), 6 part-time/adjunct (3 women). *Students:* 43 full-time (35 women), 2 part-time (1 woman); includes 8 minority (1 Black or African American, non-Hispanic/Latino; 3 Asian, non-Hispanic/Latino; 2 Hispanic/Latino; 2 Two or more races, non-Hispanic/Latino), 3 international. 164 applicants, 12% accepted, 9 enrolled. In 2014, 6 master's, 6 doctorates awarded. Terminal master's awarded for partial completion of doctoral program. *Degree requirements:* For master's, 2 foreign languages, thesis; for doctorate, 2 foreign languages, thesis/dissertation. *Entrance requirements:* For master's and doctorate, GRE, language background according to subfield of interest. Additional exam requirements/recommendations for international students: Required—TOEFL. *Application deadline:* For fall admission, 12/1 priority date for domestic students. Application fee: $70. Electronic applications accepted. *Financial support:* Fellowships, research assistantships, teaching assistantships, institutionally sponsored loans, scholarships/grants, traineeships, health care benefits, and unspecified assistantships available. Financial award application deadline: 12/15. *Unit head:* Dr. Ralph M. Rosen, Associate Dean for Graduate Studies, 215-898-7156, Fax: 215-573-8068, E-mail: grad-dean@sas.upenn.edu. *Application contact:* Arts and Sciences Graduate Admissions, 215-573-5816, Fax: 215-573-8068, E-mail: gdasadmis@sas.upenn.edu.
Website: http://www.sas.upenn.edu/arthistory/graduate/about-the-program

University of Pittsburgh, Dietrich School of Arts and Sciences, Department of History of Art and Architecture, Pittsburgh, PA 15260. Offers MA, PhD. *Faculty:* 14 full-time (7 women). *Students:* 34 full-time (28 women); includes 7 minority (2 American Indian or Alaska Native, non-Hispanic/Latino; 3 Asian, non-Hispanic/Latino; 2 Hispanic/Latino). Average age 33. 60 applicants, 12% accepted, 5 enrolled. In 2014, 2 master's, 3 doctorates awarded. *Degree requirements:* For master's, one foreign language, thesis; for doctorate, 2 foreign languages, comprehensive exam, thesis/dissertation. *Entrance requirements:* For doctorate, GRE General Test, 3 letters of recommendation, writing sample, statement of purpose. Additional exam requirements/recommendations for international students: Required—TOEFL (minimum score 550 paper-based; 90 iBT). *Application deadline:* For fall admission, 12/15 for domestic and international students. Application fee: $50. Electronic applications accepted. *Expenses:* Tuition, state resident: full-time $20,742; part-time $838 per credit. Tuition, nonresident: full-time $33,960; part-time $1389 per credit. *Required fees:* $800; $205 per term. Tuition and fees vary according to program. *Financial support:* In 2014–15, 28 students received support, including 9 fellowships with full tuition reimbursements available (averaging $21,262 per year), 12 teaching assistantships with full tuition reimbursements available (averaging $17,800 per year); research assistantships with full tuition reimbursements available, career-related internships or fieldwork, Federal Work-Study, scholarships/grants, health care benefits, and tuition waivers (partial) also available. Financial award application deadline: 12/15. *Faculty research:* Asian, medieval, modern art and architecture, contemporary, history of photography. *Unit head:* Dr. Barbara McCloskey, Associate Professor and Department Chair, 412-648-2417, Fax: 412-648-2792, E-mail: bmcc@pitt.edu. *Application contact:* Dr. Josh Ellenbogen, Director of Graduate Studies, 412-648-2400, Fax: 412-648-2792, E-mail: jme23@pitt.edu.
Website: http://www.haa.pitt.edu

University of Rochester, School of Arts and Sciences, Department of Art and Art History, Rochester, NY 14627. Offers visual and cultural studies (MA, PhD). *Faculty:* 13 full-time (7 women). *Students:* 30 full-time (19 women); includes 6 minority (1 Black or African American, non-Hispanic/Latino; 2 Asian, non-Hispanic/Latino; 2 Hispanic/Latino; 1 Two or more races, non-Hispanic/Latino), 8 international. 73 applicants, 11% accepted, 3 enrolled. In 2014, 3 master's, 6 doctorates awarded. Terminal master's awarded for partial completion of doctoral program. *Degree requirements:* For master's, thesis optional; for doctorate, one foreign language, thesis/dissertation, qualifying exam. *Entrance requirements:* For master's and doctorate, GRE General Test, personal statement, three letters of recommendation, official undergraduate and graduate transcripts, writing sample. Additional exam requirements/recommendations for international students: Required—TOEFL. *Application deadline:* For fall admission, 1/15 for domestic students. Application fee: $60. *Expenses: Tuition:* Full-time $46,150; part-time $1442 per credit hour. *Required fees:* $504. *Financial support:* Fellowships, research assistantships, teaching assistantships, and tuition waivers (full and partial) available. Financial award application deadline: 2/1. *Faculty research:* Visual culture from a social-historical perspective. *Unit head:* Allen C. Topolski, Chair, 585-275-4287. *Application contact:* Martin Collier, Administrator, 585-275-7451.
Website: http://www.rochester.edu/College/aah/

University of St. Thomas, Graduate Studies, College of Arts and Sciences, Department of Art History, St. Paul, MN 55105-1096. Offers MA. Part-time and evening/weekend programs available. *Degree requirements:* For master's, thesis, oral exam, reading proficiency in 1 foreign language. *Entrance requirements:* For master's, bachelor's degree in art history or related field; 3 letters of recommendation; writing sample; personal statement. Additional exam requirements/recommendations for international students: Required—TOEFL. Electronic applications accepted. Application fee is waived when completed online. *Faculty research:* Pictorial narrative and theory, Mesoamerican art, Chinese manuscript painting, Africa and African diaspora, architectural history, modernism.

University of South Africa, College of Human Sciences, Pretoria, South Africa. Offers adult education (M Ed); African languages (MA, PhD); African politics (MA, PhD); Afrikaans (MA, PhD); ancient history (MA, PhD); ancient Near Eastern studies (MA, PhD); anthropology (MA, PhD); applied linguistics (MA); Arabic (MA, PhD); archaeology (MA); art history (MA); Biblical archaeology (MA); Biblical studies (M Th, D Th, PhD); Christian spirituality (M Th, D Th); church history (M Th, D Th); classical studies (MA, PhD); clinical psychology (MA); communication (MA, PhD); comparative education (M Ed, Ed D); consulting psychology (D Admin, D Com, PhD); curriculum studies (M Ed, Ed D); development studies (M Admin, MA, D Admin, PhD); didactics (M Ed, Ed D); education (M Tech); education management (M Ed, Ed D); educational psychology (M Ed); English (MA); environmental education (M Ed); French (MA, PhD); German (MA, PhD); Greek (MA); guidance and counseling (M Ed); health studies (MA, PhD), including health sciences education (MA), health services management (MA), medical and surgical nursing science (critical care general) (MA), midwifery and neonatal nursing science (MA), trauma and emergency care (MA); history (MA, PhD); history of education (Ed D); inclusive education (M Ed, Ed D); information and communications technology policy and regulation (MA); information science (MA, MIS, PhD); international politics (MA, PhD); Islamic studies (MA, PhD); Italian (MA, PhD); Judaica (MA, PhD); linguistics (MA, PhD); mathematical education (M Ed); mathematics education (MA); missiology (M Th, D Th); modern Hebrew (MA, PhD); musicology (MA, MMus, D Mus, PhD); natural science education (M Ed); New Testament (M Th, D Th); Old Testament (D Th); pastoral therapy (M Th, D Th); philosophy (MA); philosophy of education (M Ed, Ed D); politics (MA, PhD); Portuguese (MA, PhD); practical theology (M Th, D Th); psychology (MA, MS, PhD); psychology of education (M Ed, Ed D); public health (MA); religious studies (MA, D Th, PhD); Romance languages (MA); Russian (MA, PhD); Semitic languages (MA, PhD); social behavior studies in HIV/AIDS (MA); social science (mental health) (MA); social science in development studies (MA); social science in psychology (MA); social science in social work (MA); social science in sociology (MA); social work (MSW, DSW, PhD); socio-education (M Ed, Ed D); sociolinguistics (MA); sociology (MA, PhD); Spanish (MA, PhD); systematic theology (M Th, D Th); TESOL (teaching English to speakers of other languages) (MA); theological ethics (M Th, D Th); theory of literature (MA, PhD); urban ministries (D Th); urban ministry (M Th).

University of South Carolina, The Graduate School, College of Arts and Sciences, Department of Art, Program in Art History, Columbia, SC 29208. Offers MA.

Art History

Accreditation: NASAD. Part-time programs available. *Degree requirements:* For master's, one foreign language, comprehensive exam, thesis. *Entrance requirements:* For master's, GRE General Test or MAT, writing sample. Additional exam requirements/recommendations for international students: Required—TOEFL. Electronic applications accepted. *Faculty research:* History of art and architecture.

University of Southern California, Graduate School, Dana and David Dornsife College of Letters, Arts and Sciences, Department of Art History, Los Angeles, CA 90089. Offers art history (MA, PhD); visual studies (Graduate Certificate). *Degree requirements:* For doctorate, 2 foreign languages, comprehensive exam, thesis/dissertation, 60 units. *Entrance requirements:* For doctorate, GRE. Additional exam requirements/recommendations for international students: Required—TOEFL. *Faculty research:* Ancient, medieval, Renaissance, eighteenth-nineteenth century, contemporary.

University of South Florida, College of The Arts, School of Art and Art History, Tampa, FL 33620-9951. Offers art (MFA); art history (MA). *Accreditation:* NASAD. Part-time programs available. *Faculty:* 17 full-time (8 women). *Students:* 42 full-time (25 women), 2 part-time (1 woman); includes 9 minority (1 Black or African American, non-Hispanic/Latino; 7 Hispanic/Latino; 1 Two or more races, non-Hispanic/Latino), 4 international. Average age 29. 62 applicants, 39% accepted, 17 enrolled. In 2014, 10 master's awarded. *Degree requirements:* For master's, thesis, exhibition (for MFA). *Entrance requirements:* For master's, GRE General Test, bachelor's degree from regionally-accredited institution with minimum GPA of 3.0 in upper-division coursework or graduate degree from regionally-accredited institution; portfolio; goals statement (for MA in art history). Additional exam requirements/recommendations for international students: Required—TOEFL (minimum score 550 paper-based; 79 iBT) or IELTS (minimum score 6.5). *Application deadline:* For fall admission, 1/15 for domestic students, 1/2 for international students. Application fee: $30. *Financial support:* In 2014–15, 37 students received support, including 37 teaching assistantships with partial tuition reimbursements available (averaging $9,440 per year); scholarships/grants, health care benefits, and unspecified assistantships also available. Support available to part-time students. Financial award application deadline: 2/15; financial award applicants required to submit FAFSA. *Faculty research:* Contemporary art and role of the artist, identity strategies, political iconography, art practice and technology, the construction of race in art. *Total annual research expenditures:* $126,118. *Unit head:* Prof. Wallace Wilson, Director, 813-974-2360, Fax: 813-974-9226, E-mail: wwilson2@usf.edu. *Application contact:* Prof. Neil Bender, Associate Professor and Graduate Program Director, 813-974-2360, Fax: 813-974-9226, E-mail: nb2@usf.edu.
Website: http://www.art.usf.edu

The University of Texas at Austin, Graduate School, College of Fine Arts, Department of Art and Art History, Program in Art History, Austin, TX 78712-1111. Offers MA, PhD. *Accreditation:* NASAD. Part-time programs available. *Degree requirements:* For master's, one foreign language, thesis; for doctorate, 2 foreign languages, thesis/dissertation, oral and written qualifying exam. *Entrance requirements:* For master's, GRE General Test, 2 samples of written work; for doctorate, GRE General Test, minimum GPA of 3.0, 2 samples of written work. Electronic applications accepted.

The University of Texas at San Antonio, College of Liberal and Fine Arts, Department of Art and Art History, San Antonio, TX 78249-0617. Offers art (MFA); art history (MA). *Accreditation:* NASAD (one or more programs are accredited). *Faculty:* 15 full-time (8 women), 1 part-time/adjunct (0 women). *Students:* 22 full-time (13 women), 3 part-time (all women); includes 11 minority (all Hispanic/Latino). Average age 28. 24 applicants, 46% accepted, 5 enrolled. In 2014, 10 master's awarded. *Entrance requirements:* For master's, GRE General Test, portfolio, minimum GPA of 3.0 in last 60 hours, 3 letters of recommendation, statement of purpose. Additional exam requirements/recommendations for international students: Required—TOEFL (minimum score 550 paper-based; 79 iBT), IELTS (minimum score 6.5). *Application deadline:* For fall admission, 7/1 for domestic students, 4/1 for international students; for spring admission, 11/1 for domestic students, 9/1 for international students. Application fee: $45 ($80 for international students). *Expenses:* Tuition, state resident: full-time $4671; part-time $260 per credit hour. Tuition, nonresident: full-time $18,022; part-time $1001 per credit hour. *Unit head:* Dr. Gregory Elliott, Department Chair, 210-458-4362, Fax: 210-458-4356, E-mail: greg.elliott@utsa.edu. *Application contact:* Monica Rodriguez, Director of Graduate Admissions, 210-458-4331, Fax: 210-458-4332, E-mail: graduatestudies@utsa.edu.
Website: http://art.utsa.edu/

The University of Texas at Tyler, College of Arts and Sciences, Department of Art and Art History, Tyler, TX 75799-0001. Offers art history (MA); interdisciplinary (MAIS); studio art (MFA). *Degree requirements:* For master's, thesis, graduate committee review. *Entrance requirements:* For master's, minimum GPA of 3.0. Additional exam requirements/recommendations for international students: Required—TOEFL. *Faculty research:* Classical myths in contemporary art, social issues in contemporary art, casting methods, Renaissance art.

University of Toronto, School of Graduate Studies, Faculty of Arts and Science, Department of Art, Toronto, ON M5S 2J7, Canada. Offers art history (MA, PhD). Part-time programs available. *Degree requirements:* For master's, 2 foreign languages, language proficiency exams; for doctorate, 2 foreign languages, comprehensive exam, thesis/dissertation. *Entrance requirements:* For master's, coursework in a foreign language, 3 letters of reference, sample research paper, minimum B+ average in senior art history and/or humanities courses; for doctorate, minimum A– average in senior art history and/or humanities courses, 2 letters of reference, sample research paper. Electronic applications accepted.

University of Utah, Graduate School, College of Fine Arts, Department of Art and Art History, Program in Art History, Salt Lake City, UT 84112-0380. Offers MA. *Faculty:* 7 full-time (5 women), 2 part-time/adjunct (1 woman). *Students:* 8 full-time (6 women), 1 part-time (0 women); includes 2 minority (both Hispanic/Latino), 1 international. Average age 27. 19 applicants, 26% accepted, 2 enrolled. In 2014, 3 master's awarded. Terminal master's awarded for partial completion of doctoral program. *Degree requirements:* For master's, one foreign language, comprehensive exam, thesis, thesis defense. *Entrance requirements:* For master's, curriculum vitae, academic writing sample, letters of recommendation. Additional exam requirements/recommendations for international students: Required—TOEFL (minimum score 80 iBT). *Application deadline:* For fall admission, 1/15 for domestic and international students. Application fee: $55 ($65 for international students). *Financial support:* In 2014–15, 10 students received support, including 4 fellowships (averaging $3,000 per year), 6 teaching assistantships with partial tuition reimbursements available (averaging $6,250 per year); research assistantships with partial tuition reimbursements available and stipends and tuition reduction also available. Financial award application deadline: 2/1; financial award applicants required to submit FAFSA. *Faculty research:* Asian, Latin American, Baroque, European/American, twentieth century/contemporary, and medieval art. *Unit head:* Prof. Elizabeth A. Peterson, Director, 801-581-8677, Fax: 801-585-6171. *Application contact:* Dr. Elena Shtromberg, Director of Graduate Studies, 801-581-8677, Fax: 801-585-6171, E-mail: e.shtromberg@utah.edu.
Website: http://www.arthistory.utah.edu/

University of Victoria, Faculty of Graduate Studies, Faculty of Fine Arts, Department of History in Art, Victoria, BC V8W 2Y2, Canada. Offers MA, PhD. *Degree requirements:* For master's, one foreign language, thesis (for some programs), oral defense; for doctorate, 2 foreign languages, comprehensive exam, thesis/dissertation, oral defense. *Entrance requirements:* For master's, minimum B+ average in undergraduate course work; for doctorate, minimum B+ average in graduate course work. Additional exam requirements/recommendations for international students: Required—TOEFL (minimum score 575 paper-based), IELTS (minimum score 7). Electronic applications accepted. *Faculty research:* Europe, Southeast Asia, China and Islamic world, architecture of North America and the Islamic World, film.

University of Virginia, College and Graduate School of Arts and Sciences, Program in Art and Architectural History, Charlottesville, VA 22903. Offers MA, PhD. *Faculty:* 21 full-time (10 women), 2 part-time/adjunct (both women). *Students:* 32 full-time (22 women); includes 4 minority (2 Asian, non-Hispanic/Latino; 1 Hispanic/Latino; 1 Two or more races, non-Hispanic/Latino), 1 international. Average age 32. 52 applicants, 15% accepted, 4 enrolled. In 2014, 4 master's, 10 doctorates awarded. *Degree requirements:* For master's, one foreign language, comprehensive exam, thesis; for doctorate, 2 foreign languages, thesis/dissertation, oral exam. *Entrance requirements:* For master's and doctorate, GRE, 2 letters of recommendation. *Application deadline:* For fall admission, 12/7 for domestic and international students. Applications are processed on a rolling basis. Application fee: $60. Electronic applications accepted. *Expenses:* Tuition, state resident: full-time $14,164; part-time $349 per credit hour. Tuition, nonresident: full-time $23,722; part-time $1300 per credit hour. *Required fees:* $2514. *Financial support:* Application deadline: 12/7. *Unit head:* Larry Goedde, Chair, 434-924-3541, Fax: 434-924-3647, E-mail: artdept@virginia.edu.
Website: http://www.virginia.edu/art/phd-program/

University of Washington, Graduate School, College of Arts and Sciences, School of Art, Division of Art History, Seattle, WA 98195. Offers MA, PhD. Terminal master's awarded for partial completion of doctoral program. *Degree requirements:* For master's, 2 foreign languages, practicum or thesis; for doctorate, 2 foreign languages, thesis/dissertation. *Entrance requirements:* For master's, GRE General Test, minimum undergraduate GPA of 3.0, undergraduate major in art history or equivalent; for doctorate, GRE General Test, MA in art history, minimum graduate GPA of 3.0. Additional exam requirements/recommendations for international students: Required—TOEFL (minimum score 580 paper-based). Electronic applications accepted. *Faculty research:* European-American (all periods), Japanese, Chinese, African, and Native American art.

University of Wisconsin–Madison, Graduate School, College of Letters and Science, Department of Art History, Madison, WI 53706-1380. Offers MA, PhD. Part-time programs available. Terminal master's awarded for partial completion of doctoral program. *Degree requirements:* For master's, one foreign language; for doctorate, 2 foreign languages, thesis/dissertation. *Entrance requirements:* For master's and doctorate, GRE. Additional exam requirements/recommendations for international students: Required—TOEFL. Electronic applications accepted. *Expenses:* Tuition, state resident: full-time $10,723; part-time $745 per credit. Tuition, nonresident: full-time $24,054; part-time $1578 per credit. *Required fees:* $374 per semester. Tuition and fees vary according to course load, program and reciprocity agreements. *Faculty research:* Twentieth-century, African art, Italian Renaissance, Dutch, material culture.

University of Wisconsin–Milwaukee, Graduate School, College of Letters and Sciences, Department of Art History, Milwaukee, WI 53201-0413. Offers art history (MA); art museum studies (Certificate). Part-time programs available. *Degree requirements:* For master's, one foreign language, comprehensive exam, thesis or alternative. *Entrance requirements:* For master's, GRE. Additional exam requirements/recommendations for international students: Required—TOEFL (minimum score 550 paper-based; 79 iBT), IELTS (minimum score 6.5). *Faculty research:* Ancient Mediterranean art through contemporary Western art, Chinese art, Pre-Columbian art, film, theory.

University of Wisconsin–Superior, Graduate Division, Department of Visual Arts, Superior, WI 54880-4500. Offers art education (MA); art history (MA); art therapy (MA); studio arts (MA). Part-time programs available. *Degree requirements:* For master's, comprehensive exam, exhibit. *Entrance requirements:* For master's, minimum GPA of 2.75, portfolio. Electronic applications accepted.

Virginia Commonwealth University, Graduate School, School of the Arts, Department of Art History, Richmond, VA 23284-9005. Offers architectural history (MA); art history (MA, PhD); historical studies (MA); museum studies (MA). *Accreditation:* NASAD. *Degree requirements:* For master's, thesis; for doctorate, comprehensive exam, thesis/dissertation. *Entrance requirements:* For master's and doctorate, GRE General Test. Electronic applications accepted. *Faculty research:* Modern, nineteenth-century, Renaissance, American, and medieval art.

Washington University in St. Louis, Graduate School of Arts and Sciences, Department of Art History and Archaeology, St. Louis, MO 63130-4899. Offers AM, PhD. *Degree requirements:* For doctorate, 2 foreign languages, comprehensive exam, thesis/dissertation. *Entrance requirements:* For master's and doctorate, GRE General Test, sample of written work. Electronic applications accepted. *Faculty research:* Ancient, medieval, Renaissance, early modern European, modern and contemporary European and American, and Asian art history; classical archaeology.

Wayne State University, College of Fine, Performing and Communication Arts, James Pearson Duffy Department of Art and Art History, Program in Art History, Detroit, MI 48202. Offers MA. *Students:* 3 full-time (all women), 4 part-time (3 women); includes 1 minority (Black or African American, non-Hispanic/Latino). Average age 34. 9 applicants, 22% accepted. In 2014, 2 master's awarded. *Degree requirements:* For master's, one foreign language, essay or thesis. *Entrance requirements:* For master's, minimum GPA of 3.0; undergraduate degree in art history; three semesters of college-level work in one foreign language (appropriate to scholarly study within this field). Additional exam requirements/recommendations for international students: Required—TOEFL (minimum score 550 paper-based; 79 iBT), TWE (minimum score 5.5), Michigan English Language Assessment Battery (minimum score 85); Recommended—IELTS (minimum score 6.5). *Application deadline:* For fall admission, 2/1 for domestic and international students; for winter admission, 10/1 for domestic and international students. Application fee: $0. Electronic applications accepted. *Expenses:* Expenses: Contact institution. *Financial support:* In 2014–15, 4 students received support. Fellowships with tuition reimbursements available, teaching assistantships with tuition reimbursements available, scholarships/grants, and unspecified assistantships available. Financial award application deadline: 3/31; financial award applicants required to submit FAFSA. *Faculty research:* Ancient, medieval, and nineteenth- and twentieth-century art history; theory and criticism. *Unit head:* Dr. John Richardson, Chair, 313-577-2980, Fax: 313-577-3491, E-mail: af5343@wayne.edu. *Application contact:* Prof. Evan Larson-Voltz, Professor of Art/Graduate Officer, 313-577-2983, E-mail: evanlarson@wayne.edu.
Website: http://art.wayne.edu/

West Virginia University, College of Creative Arts, Division of Art and Design, Morgantown, WV 26506. Offers art education (MA); art history (MA); ceramics (MFA);

graphic design (MFA); painting (MFA); printmaking (MFA); sculpture (MFA); studio art (MA). *Accreditation:* NASAD. *Degree requirements:* For master's, thesis, exhibit. *Entrance requirements:* For master's, minimum GPA of 2.75, portfolio. Additional exam requirements/recommendations for international students: Required—TOEFL. *Expenses:* Contact institution. *Faculty research:* Medieval art history.

Williams College, Graduate Programs, Williamstown, MA 01267. Offers development economics (MA); history of art (MA). MA in history of art offered jointly with Sterling and Francine Clark Art Institute. *Degree requirements:* For master's, 2 foreign languages, symposium paper and lecture. *Entrance requirements:* For master's, GRE General Test. Additional exam requirements/recommendations for international students: Recommended—TOEFL. Electronic applications accepted.

Yale University, Graduate School of Arts and Sciences, Department of History of Art, New Haven, CT 06520. Offers PhD. *Degree requirements:* For doctorate, 2 foreign languages, thesis/dissertation. *Entrance requirements:* For doctorate, GRE General Test.

York University, Faculty of Graduate Studies, Faculty of Fine Arts, Program in Art History, Toronto, ON M3J 1P3, Canada. Offers MA, PhD. Part-time programs available. *Degree requirements:* For master's, one foreign language, thesis or alternative. Electronic applications accepted.

Arts Administration

Arizona State University at the Tempe campus, Herberger Institute for Design and the Arts, School of Film, Dance and Theatre, Tempe, AZ 85287-2002. Offers dance (MFA), including dance, interdisciplinary digital media and performance; theatre (MA, MFA, PhD), including arts entrepreneurship and management (MFA), directing (MFA), dramatic writing (MFA), interdisciplinary digital media and performance (MFA), performance (MFA), performance design (MFA), theatre (MFA), theatre and performance of the Americas (PhD), theatre for youth (MFA, PhD). Terminal master's awarded for partial completion of doctoral program. *Degree requirements:* For master's, comprehensive exam (for some programs), thesis (for some programs), applied project (for some programs); interactive Program of Study (iPOS) submitted before completing 50 percent of required credit hours; for doctorate, comprehensive exam, thesis/dissertation, interactive Program of Study (iPOS) submitted before completing 50 percent of required credit hours. *Entrance requirements:* For master's, GRE or MAT, minimum GPA of 3.0 in last 2 years of work leading to bachelor's degree (depending on program); for doctorate, GRE, minimum GPA of 3.0 or equivalent in last 2 years of work leading to bachelor's degree, 3 letters of recommendation, resume, scholarly writing sample, statement of purpose. Additional exam requirements/recommendations for international students: Required—TOEFL, IELTS, or PTE. Electronic applications accepted.

Baruch College of the City University of New York, Weissman School of Arts and Sciences, Program in Arts Administration, New York, NY 10010-5585. Offers MA. Part-time and evening/weekend programs available. *Degree requirements:* For master's, thesis or alternative, Students complete an arts consultancy project. *Entrance requirements:* For master's, GRE/GMAT (may be waived). Additional exam requirements/recommendations for international students: Required—TOEFL. *Application deadline:* For fall admission, 5/1 for domestic and international students; for spring admission, 11/1 for domestic and international students. Electronic applications accepted. *Unit head:* Michael J. Lovaglio, Director of Graduate Programs, 646-312-3897, E-mail: michael.lovaglio@baruch.cuny.edu. *Application contact:* Michael J. Lovaglio, Director of Graduate Programs, 646-312-3897, Fax: 646-312-3871, E-mail: wsas.graduate.studies@baruch.cuny.edu.
Website: http://www.baruch.cuny.edu/wsas/academics/ma-arts-administration/index.html

Boston University, Metropolitan College, Program in Arts Administration, Boston, MA 02215. Offers arts administration (MS, Graduate Certificate); fundraising management (Graduate Certificate). Part-time and evening/weekend programs available. *Faculty:* 2 full-time (0 women), 16 part-time/adjunct (5 women). *Students:* 15 full-time (13 women), 74 part-time (64 women); includes 6 minority (2 Asian, non-Hispanic/Latino; 3 Hispanic/Latino; 1 Two or more races, non-Hispanic/Latino), 24 international. Average age 28. 136 applicants, 55% accepted, 30 enrolled. In 2014, 25 master's awarded. *Degree requirements:* For master's, internship. *Entrance requirements:* Additional exam requirements/recommendations for international students: Required—TOEFL (minimum score 95 iBT). *Application deadline:* For fall admission, 4/1 priority date for domestic students, 2/1 priority date for international students; for spring admission, 11/15 priority date for domestic and international students. Applications are processed on a rolling basis. Application fee: $80. Electronic applications accepted. *Expenses: Tuition:* Full-time $45,686; part-time $1428 per credit hour. *Required fees:* $660; $60 per semester. Tuition and fees vary according to program. *Financial support:* In 2014–15, 4 research assistantships (averaging $8,400 per year) were awarded; career-related internships or fieldwork, unspecified assistantships, and 6 office assistantships (averaging $4200) also available. Support available to part-time students. Financial award applicants required to submit FAFSA. *Faculty research:* Cultural policy, artists' rights, museum practices, audience development. *Unit head:* Dr. Rich Maloney, Assistant Professor/Interim Director, 617-353-4064, Fax: 617-353-1230, E-mail: artsad@bu.edu. *Application contact:* Jeannie Motherwell, Program Administrator, 617-353-4064, Fax: 617-358-1230, E-mail: jmoth@bu.edu.
Website: http://www.bu.edu/artsadmin/programs/

Brooklyn College of the City University of New York, School of Visual, Media and Performing Arts, Department of Theater, Brooklyn, NY 11210-2889. Offers acting (MFA); design and technical theater (MFA); directing (MFA); performing arts management (MFA); theater history and criticism (MA). Part-time programs available. *Degree requirements:* For master's, thesis, professional residency. *Entrance requirements:* For master's, audition or interview, 18 credits in theater, 2 letters of recommendation, essay. Additional exam requirements/recommendations for international students: Required—TOEFL. Electronic applications accepted. *Faculty research:* Multiculturalism and the arts, art education, arts collaboration.

Carnegie Mellon University, H. John Heinz III College, School of Public Policy and Management, Master of Arts Management Program, Pittsburgh, PA 15213-3891. Offers MAM. *Degree requirements:* For master's, internship. *Entrance requirements:* For master's, GRE or GMAT, college-level course in advanced algebra/pre-calculus; college-level courses in economics and statistics (recommended). Additional exam requirements/recommendations for international students: Required—TOEFL or IELTS. Electronic applications accepted.

Christie's Education, Certificate Program in Art Business, New York, NY 10036. Offers Certificate. *Application deadline:* Applications are processed on a rolling basis. Application fee: $35. Electronic applications accepted. *Unit head:* Marisa Kayyem, Associate Professor/Director of Short Courses, 212-355-1501, Fax: 212-355-7370, E-mail: mkayyem@christies.edu. *Application contact:* Catherine Warden, Short Course Coordinator, 212-355-1501, Fax: 212-355-7370, E-mail: shortcoursesus@christies.edu.
Website: http://www.christies.edu/new-york/courses/certificate-art-business.aspx

Claremont Graduate University, Graduate Programs, Peter F. Drucker and Masatoshi Ito Graduate School of Management, Program in Art Business, Claremont, CA 91711-6160. Offers MA. Program offered in conjunction with Sotheby's Institute of Art–Los Angeles. *Faculty:* 2 full-time (1 woman). *Students:* 46 full-time (45 women), 2 part-time (both women); includes 9 minority (1 Asian, non-Hispanic/Latino; 6 Hispanic/Latino; 2 Two or more races, non-Hispanic/Latino), 12 international. Average age 28. *Degree requirements:* For master's, project seminar. *Entrance requirements:* Additional exam requirements/recommendations for international students: Required—TOEFL. *Application deadline:* For fall admission, 2/1 for domestic and international students. Application fee: $80. Electronic applications accepted. *Expenses: Tuition:* Full-time $41,784; part-time $1741 per credit. *Required fees:* $600; $300 per semester. *Financial support:* Federal Work-Study, institutionally sponsored loans, and scholarships/grants available. Support available to part-time students. *Unit head:* Jonathan Neil, Director, 909-607-0619, E-mail: jonathan.neil@cgu.edu. *Application contact:* Tory Benoit, External Relations Specialist, 909-607-9049, E-mail: t.benoit@sothebysinstitute.com.
Website: http://www.cgu.edu/pages/10149.asp

Claremont Graduate University, Graduate Programs, Program in Arts Management, Claremont, CA 91711-6160. Offers MA. *Students:* 16 full-time (15 women), 16 part-time (15 women); includes 10 minority (1 Black or African American, non-Hispanic/Latino; 4 Asian, non-Hispanic/Latino; 4 Hispanic/Latino; 1 Two or more races, non-Hispanic/Latino), 11 international. Average age 30. In 2014, 17 master's awarded. *Entrance requirements:* For master's, GRE General Test. Additional exam requirements/recommendations for international students: Required—TOEFL (minimum score 550 paper-based; 80 iBT). *Application deadline:* For fall admission, 2/1 priority date for domestic and international students. Applications are processed on a rolling basis. Application fee: $80. Electronic applications accepted. *Expenses: Tuition:* Full-time $41,784; part-time $1741 per credit. *Required fees:* $600; $300 per semester. *Financial support:* Fellowships, research assistantships, teaching assistantships, Federal Work-Study, institutionally sponsored loans, and scholarships/grants available. Support available to part-time students. Financial award application deadline: 2/15; financial award applicants required to submit FAFSA. *Unit head:* Laura Zucker, Director, 909-607-9109, Fax: 909-621-8330, E-mail: laura.zucker@cgu.edu. *Application contact:* Amy Sandefur, Assistant Director of Admissions, 909-607-9101, E-mail: amy.sandefur@cgu.edu.
Website: http://www.cgu.edu/am

The College at Brockport, State University of New York, School of Education and Human Services, Department of Public Administration, Brockport, NY 14420-2997. Offers arts administration (AGC); nonprofit management (AGC); public administration (MPA), including health care management, nonprofit management, public management. *Accreditation:* NASPAA. Part-time and evening/weekend programs available. *Faculty:* 4 full-time (3 women), 4 part-time/adjunct (2 women). *Students:* 42 full-time (24 women), 56 part-time (39 women); includes 22 minority (12 Black or African American, non-Hispanic/Latino; 2 Asian, non-Hispanic/Latino; 3 Hispanic/Latino; 5 Two or more races, non-Hispanic/Latino). 89 applicants, 79% accepted, 50 enrolled. In 2014, 34 master's, 7 other advanced degrees awarded. *Degree requirements:* For master's, thesis or alternative. *Entrance requirements:* For master's, GRE or minimum GPA of 3.0, letters of recommendation, statement of objectives, current resume. Additional exam requirements/recommendations for international students: Required—TOEFL (minimum score 550 paper-based; 79 iBT), IELTS (minimum score 6.5). *Application deadline:* For fall admission, 8/15 priority date for domestic and international students; for spring admission, 1/15 priority date for domestic and international students; for summer admission, 4/15 priority date for domestic and international students. Application fee: $50. Electronic applications accepted. *Financial support:* In 2014–15, 1 fellowship with full tuition reimbursement (averaging $7,500 per year), 1 teaching assistantship with full tuition reimbursement (averaging $6,000 per year) were awarded; Federal Work-Study, scholarships/grants, and unspecified assistantships also available. Support available to part-time students. Financial award application deadline: 3/15; financial award applicants required to submit FAFSA. *Faculty research:* E-government, performance management, nonprofits and policy implementation, Medicaid and disabilities. *Unit head:* Dr. Celia Watt, Graduate Director, 585-395-5538, Fax: 585-395-2172, E-mail: cwatt@brockport.edu. *Application contact:* Danielle A. Welch, Graduate Admissions Counselor, 585-395-2525, Fax: 585-395-2515.
Website: http://www.brockport.edu/pubadmin

College of Charleston, Graduate School, School of the Arts, Program in Arts Management, Charleston, SC 29424-0001. Offers MPA, Certificate. Part-time and evening/weekend programs available. *Entrance requirements:* For degree, minimum GPA of 3.0, writing sample. Additional exam requirements/recommendations for international students: Required—TOEFL (minimum score 81 iBT).

Columbia College Chicago, Graduate School, Department of Business and Entrepreneurship, Chicago, IL 60605-1996. Offers arts, entertainment and media management (MA), including visual arts management. Part-time programs available. *Faculty:* 13 full-time (6 women). *Students:* 39 full-time (27 women); includes 13 minority (8 Black or African American, non-Hispanic/Latino; 3 Asian, non-Hispanic/Latino; 1 Hispanic/Latino; 1 Two or more races, non-Hispanic/Latino), 5 international. Average age 28. *Degree requirements:* For master's, thesis, internship. *Entrance requirements:* For master's, GRE (recommended), self-assessment essay, resume, letters of recommendation. Additional exam requirements/recommendations for international students: Required—TOEFL (minimum score 600 paper-based; 100 iBT). *Application deadline:* For fall admission, 1/15 for domestic and international students. Application fee: $55. Electronic applications accepted. *Expenses:* Expenses: $1,113 per credit hour; fees: $352 per semester. *Financial support:* In 2014–15, 11 students received support, including 8 fellowships, 3 research assistantships; career-related internships or fieldwork, Federal Work-Study, scholarships/grants, and unspecified assistantships also available. Support available to part-time students. Financial award application deadline: 8/13; financial award applicants required to submit FAFSA. *Unit head:* Prof. Dawn

Arts Administration

Larsen, Director of Graduate Studies, 312-369-7639, E-mail: dlarsen@colum.edu. *Application contact:* Kara Leffler, Associate Director of Graduate Admissions, 312-369-7262, Fax: 312-369-8024, E-mail: kleffler@colum.edu.
Website: http://www.colum.edu/Admissions/Graduate/programs/business-and-entrepreneurship/index.php

Daemen College, Department of Visual and Performing Arts, Amherst, NY 14226-3592. Offers arts administration (MS). *Entrance requirements:* For master's, bachelor?s degree from an accredited institution; at least two letters of recommendation; minimum undergraduate GPA of 2.75 or GRE/GMAT.

Drexel University, Antoinette Westphal College of Media Arts and Design, Program in Arts Administration, Philadelphia, PA 19104-2875. Offers MS. *Accreditation:* NASAD. Part-time and evening/weekend programs available. *Degree requirements:* For master's, thesis, internship. *Entrance requirements:* For master's, GRE, interview, minimum GPA of 3.0, previous course work in arts and business. Additional exam requirements/recommendations for international students: Required—TOEFL. Electronic applications accepted. *Faculty research:* Evaluation of art administration structures, funding for the arts, impact of politics in the arts, computer applications.

Eastern Michigan University, Graduate School, College of Arts and Sciences, Department of Communication, Media and Theatre Arts, Program in Arts Administration, Ypsilanti, MI 48197. Offers MA. Part-time and evening/weekend programs available. Postbaccalaureate distance learning degree programs offered (minimal on-campus study). *Students:* 6 full-time (4 women), 4 part-time (all women); includes 1 minority (Asian, non-Hispanic/Latino), 1 international. Average age 26. 15 applicants, 60% accepted, 5 enrolled. In 2014, 6 master's awarded. *Entrance requirements:* Additional exam requirements/recommendations for international students: Required—TOEFL. *Application deadline:* Applications are processed on a rolling basis. Application fee: $45. *Financial support:* Fellowships, research assistantships with full tuition reimbursements, teaching assistantships with full tuition reimbursements, career-related internships or fieldwork, Federal Work-Study, institutionally sponsored loans, scholarships/grants, tuition waivers (partial), and unspecified assistantships available. Support available to part-time students. Financial award applicants required to submit FAFSA. *Unit head:* Dr. Susan Booth, Coordinator, 734-487-1883, Fax: 734-487-3443, E-mail: sbooth1@emich.edu.

★ **Fashion Institute of Technology,** School of Graduate Studies, Program in Art Market, Principles and Practices, New York, NY 10001-5992. Offers MA. *Accreditation:* NASAD. *Degree requirements:* For master's, one foreign language, thesis, internship. *Entrance requirements:* For master's, GRE General Test, previous course work in art history, 4 semesters of a foreign language. Additional exam requirements/recommendations for international students: Required—TOEFL (minimum score 550 paper-based).
See Display below and Close-Up on page 197.

Florida State University, The Graduate School, College of Music, Tallahassee, FL 32306. Offers accompanying (MM); arts administration (MA); choral conducting (MM); composition (MM, DM); ethnomusicology (MM); general music (MA); instrumental accompanying (MM); instrumental conducting (MM); jazz studies (MM); music education (MM Ed, PhD); music theory (MM, PhD); music therapy (MM); musicology (MM, PhD), including ethnomusicology (PhD), historical musicology; opera (MM); performance (MM, DM); piano pedagogy (MM); piano technology (MA); vocal accompanying (MM). *Accreditation:* NASM. *Faculty:* 87 full-time, 13 part-time/adjunct. *Students:* 368 full-time (191 women); includes 86 minority (31 Black or African American, non-Hispanic/Latino; 2 American Indian or Alaska Native, non-Hispanic/Latino; 18 Asian, non-Hispanic/Latino; 25 Hispanic/Latino; 1 Native Hawaiian or other Pacific Islander, non-Hispanic/Latino; 9 Two or more races, non-Hispanic/Latino). Average age 26. 737 applicants,

42% accepted, 138 enrolled. In 2014, 108 master's, 42 doctorates awarded. *Degree requirements:* For master's, comprehensive exam (for some programs), thesis (for some programs), departmental qualifying exam; for doctorate, comprehensive exam (for some programs), thesis/dissertation, departmental qualifying exam. *Entrance requirements:* For master's, GRE General Test (for some programs), audition, minimum GPA of 3.0; for doctorate, GRE General Test (for some programs), audition, master's degree, minimum GPA of 3.0. Additional exam requirements/recommendations for international students: Required—TOEFL (minimum score 590 paper-based; 97 iBT), IELTS (minimum score 7.5). *Application deadline:* For fall admission, 7/1 for domestic and international students; for spring admission, 11/1 for domestic and international students; for summer admission, 3/1 for domestic students. Applications are processed on a rolling basis. Application fee: $30. Electronic applications accepted. *Expenses:* Expenses: $479.32 per credit hour for in-state students; $1,110.72 for out-of-state students. *Financial support:* In 2014–15, 223 students received support, including fellowships (averaging $15,000 per year), 9 research assistantships (averaging $4,750 per year), 173 teaching assistantships (averaging $4,750 per year); career-related internships or fieldwork, Federal Work-Study, tuition waivers, and unspecified assistantships also available. Support available to part-time students. Financial award application deadline: 2/28; financial award applicants required to submit FAFSA. *Faculty research:* Musicology. *Unit head:* Dr. Patricia Flowers, Dean, 850-644-4361, Fax: 850-644-2033, E-mail: pjflowers@fsu.edu. *Application contact:* Dr. James Mathes, Interim Associate Dean for Academic Affairs/Director of Graduate Studies in Music, 850-644-5888, Fax: 850-644-2033, E-mail: jmathes@fsu.edu.
Website: http://www.music.fsu.edu/

George Mason University, College of Visual and Performing Arts, Program in Arts Management, Fairfax, VA 22030. Offers MA, Certificate. *Accreditation:* NASAD. *Faculty:* 2 full-time (both women), 7 part-time/adjunct (5 women). *Students:* 39 full-time (36 women), 45 part-time (40 women); includes 17 minority (7 Black or African American, non-Hispanic/Latino; 1 Asian, non-Hispanic/Latino; 5 Hispanic/Latino; 4 Two or more races, non-Hispanic/Latino), 12 international. Average age 29. 96 applicants, 50% accepted, 27 enrolled. In 2014, 28 master's, 1 other advanced degree awarded. *Degree requirements:* For master's, internship. *Entrance requirements:* For master's and Certificate, GRE (recommended), undergraduate degree with minimum GPA of 3.0, official transcripts, 2 letters of recommendation, statement of purpose, resume. Additional exam requirements/recommendations for international students: Required—TOEFL (minimum score 570 paper-based; 80 iBT), IELTS (minimum score 6.5), PTE. *Application deadline:* For fall admission, 3/1 for domestic students, 2/15 for international students; for spring admission, 10/1 for domestic students, 9/15 for international students. Application fee: $65 ($80 for international students). Electronic applications accepted. *Expenses:* Tuition, state resident: full-time $9794; part-time $408 per credit hour. Tuition, nonresident: full-time $26,978; part-time $1124 per credit hour. *Required fees:* $2820; $118 per credit hour. Tuition and fees vary according to course load and program. *Financial support:* Career-related internships or fieldwork, Federal Work-Study, scholarships/grants, unspecified assistantships, and health care benefits (for full-time research or teaching assistantship recipients) available. Support available to part-time students. Financial award application deadline: 3/1; financial award applicants required to submit FAFSA. *Faculty research:* Information technology for arts managers, special topics in arts management, directions in gallery management, arts in society, public relations/marketing strategies for art organizations. *Unit head:* Claire Huschle, Interim Program Director, 703-993-8719, Fax: 703-993-9829, E-mail: chuschle@gmu.edu. *Application contact:* Allison Byers, Administrative Assistant, 703-993-8926, Fax: 703-993-9829, E-mail: abyers3@gmu.edu.
Website: http://artsmanagement.gmu.edu/arts-management-ma/

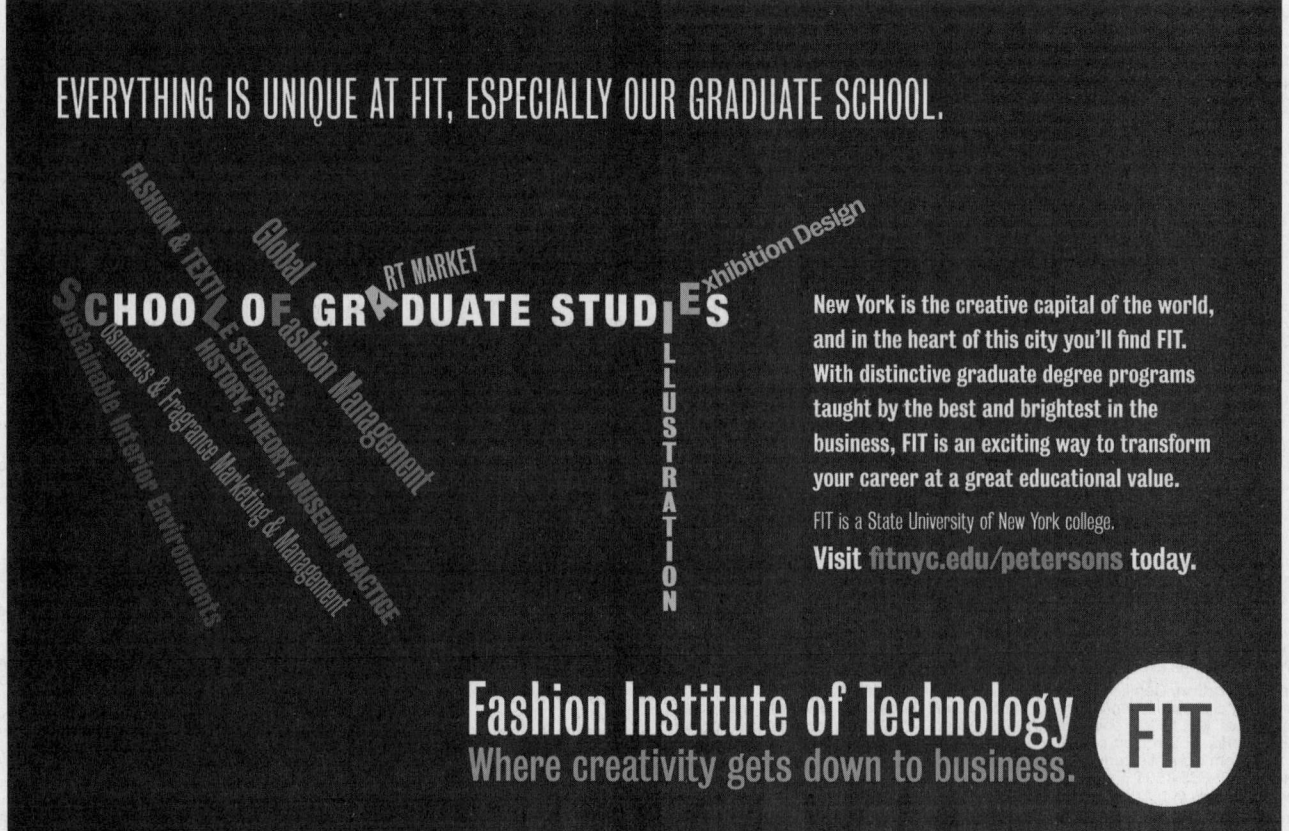

Goucher College, MA and MFA Programs, Baltimore, MD 21204-2794. Offers arts administration (MA); creative nonfiction (MFA); cultural sustainability (MA); digital arts (MFA); environmental studies (MA); historic preservation (MA); management (MA). Part-time and evening/weekend programs available. Postbaccalaureate distance learning degree programs offered (minimal on-campus study). *Faculty:* 83 part-time/adjunct (42 women). *Students:* 72 full-time (58 women), 65 part-time (54 women); includes 39 minority (15 Black or African American, non-Hispanic/Latino; 16 American Indian or Alaska Native, non-Hispanic/Latino; 2 Asian, non-Hispanic/Latino; 4 Hispanic/Latino; 2 Two or more races, non-Hispanic/Latino), 4 international. 120 applicants, 95% accepted, 50 enrolled. In 2014, 63 master's awarded. *Degree requirements:* For master's, thesis, e-portfolio completion. *Entrance requirements:* Additional exam requirements/recommendations for international students: Required—TOEFL (minimum score 550 paper-based; 80 iBT), IELTS (minimum score 7). *Application deadline:* Applications are processed on a rolling basis. Application fee: $75. *Expenses:* Expenses: $825 per credit; fees vary according to program. *Financial support:* Unspecified assistantships available. Financial award application deadline: 4/15; financial award applicants required to submit FAFSA. *Unit head:* Lynne Lochte, Vice President for New Ventures and Business Strategies, 410-337-6572, E-mail: lynne.lochte@goucher.edu. *Application contact:* Hanora Barron, Admissions Coordinator, 410-337-6200, Fax: 410-337-6085, E-mail: hanora.barron@goucher.edu.
Website: http://www.goucher.edu/grad

HEC Montreal, School of Business Administration, Graduate Diploma Programs in Administration, Program in Management of Cultural Organizations, Montréal, QC H3T 2A7, Canada. Offers Graduate Diploma. All courses are given in French. *Students:* 50 full-time (41 women), 138 part-time (116 women). 96 applicants, 88% accepted, 71 enrolled. In 2014, 68 Graduate Diplomas awarded. *Degree requirements:* For Graduate Diploma, one foreign language. *Entrance requirements:* For degree, bachelor's degree (not in administration, preferably cultural field), one year of work experience. *Application deadline:* For fall admission, 4/15 for domestic and international students; for winter admission, 9/15 for domestic and international students. Application fee: $83 Canadian dollars. Electronic applications accepted. *Financial support:* Research assistantships, teaching assistantships, and scholarships/grants available. Financial award application deadline: 9/2. *Unit head:* Silvia Ponce, Director, 514-340-6393, Fax: 514-340-6915, E-mail: silvia.ponce@hec.ca. *Application contact:* Jo Anne Audet, Administrative Director, 514-340-1315, Fax: 514-340-6411, E-mail: joanne.audet@hec.ca.
Website: http://www.hec.ca/programmes_formations/des/dess/dess_gestion_organismes_culturels/index.html

Indiana University Bloomington, School of Public and Environmental Affairs, Program in Arts Administration, Bloomington, IN 47405-7000. Offers MAAA. Part-time programs available. *Degree requirements:* For master's, final internship. *Entrance requirements:* For master's, GRE or GMAT. Additional exam requirements/recommendations for international students: Required—TOEFL or IELTS. Electronic applications accepted. *Faculty research:* Cultural policy, nonprofit management, and pricing for the arts.

Montclair State University, The Graduate School, College of the Arts, MA Program in Theatre, Montclair, NJ 07043-1624. Offers arts management (MA); production/stage management (MA); theatre studies (MA). *Accreditation:* NAST. Part-time and evening/weekend programs available. *Students:* 9 full-time (5 women), 17 part-time (10 women); includes 6 minority (2 Black or African American, non-Hispanic/Latino; 4 Hispanic/Latino), 1 international. Average age 33. 14 applicants, 71% accepted, 6 enrolled. In 2014, 6 master's awarded. *Degree requirements:* For master's, comprehensive exam, thesis or alternative. *Entrance requirements:* For master's, GRE General Test, 2 letters of recommendation. Additional exam requirements/recommendations for international students: Required—TOEFL (minimum score 83 iBT) or IELTS (minimum score 6.5). *Application deadline:* For fall admission, 6/1 for international students; for spring admission, 10/1 for international students. Applications are processed on a rolling basis. Application fee: $60. Electronic applications accepted. *Expenses:* Tuition, state resident: full-time $9960; part-time $553.35 per credit. Tuition, nonresident: full-time $15,074; part-time $837.43 per credit. *Required fees:* $1595; $88.63 per credit. Tuition and fees vary according to degree level and program. *Financial support:* In 2014–15, 2 research assistantships with full tuition reimbursements (averaging $7,000 per year) were awarded; Federal Work-Study, scholarships/grants, and unspecified assistantships also available. Support available to part-time students. Financial award application deadline: 3/1; financial award applicants required to submit FAFSA. *Faculty research:* Danceturgy, Arab and Muslim images in American drama, Neil LaBute and playwriting, directing, Robert Edmond Jones. *Unit head:* Dr. Eric Diamond, Chairperson, 973-655-4217, E-mail: peterson@mail.montclair.edu. *Application contact:* Amy Aiello, Executive Director of The Graduate School, 973-655-5147, E-mail: petersonj@mail.montclair.edu.

Moore College of Art & Design, Program in Community Practice, Philadelphia, PA 19103. Offers MFA. *Degree requirements:* For master's, thesis. *Expenses: Tuition:* Full-time $31,584; part-time $1504 per credit. *Unit head:* Daniel Tucker, Program Manager, E-mail: dtucker@moore.edu. *Application contact:* Stefan Schechs, Associate Director of Admissions, 215-965-4016, Fax: 215-568-3547, E-mail: sschechs@moore.edu.
Website: http://moore.edu/academics/graduate-studies/mfa-in-community-practice

New York University, Steinhardt School of Culture, Education, and Human Development, Department of Art and Art Professions, Program in Visual Arts Administration, New York, NY 10003. Offers MA. Part-time programs available. *Faculty:* 5 full-time (3 women). *Students:* 69 full-time (65 women), 25 part-time (18 women); includes 20 minority (3 Black or African American, non-Hispanic/Latino; 10 Asian, non-Hispanic/Latino; 4 Hispanic/Latino; 3 Two or more races, non-Hispanic/Latino), 37 international. Average age 27. 161 applicants, 47% accepted, 52 enrolled. In 2014, 38 master's awarded. *Degree requirements:* For master's, thesis (for some programs). *Entrance requirements:* For master's, interview. Additional exam requirements/recommendations for international students: Required—TOEFL (minimum score 100 iBT). *Application deadline:* For fall admission, 12/1 priority date for domestic and international students. Applications are processed on a rolling basis. Application fee: $75. Electronic applications accepted. *Financial support:* Career-related internships or fieldwork, Federal Work-Study, institutionally sponsored loans, scholarships/grants, and tuition waivers (partial) available. Support available to part-time students. Financial award application deadline: 2/1; financial award applicants required to submit FAFSA. *Faculty research:* Corporate philanthropy, contemporary art and culture, public art and urban development, cultural policy, arts advocacy. *Unit head:* Prof. Sandra Lang, Director, 212-998-5723, Fax: 212-995-4320, E-mail: sandra.lang@nyu.edu. *Application contact:* 212-998-5030, Fax: 212-995-4328, E-mail: steinhardt.gradadmissions@nyu.edu.
Website: http://steinhardt.nyu.edu/art/admin

New York University, Steinhardt School of Culture, Education, and Human Development, Department of Music and Performing Arts Professions, Program in Performing Arts Administration, New York, NY 10012. Offers MA. Part-time programs available. *Faculty:* 1 full-time (0 women). *Students:* 40 full-time (30 women), 10 part-time (8 women); includes 5 minority (1 Black or African American, non-Hispanic/Latino; 2 Asian, non-Hispanic/Latino; 2 Hispanic/Latino), 19 international. Average age 27. 132 applicants, 42% accepted, 27 enrolled. In 2014, 26 master's awarded. *Degree requirements:* For master's, thesis (for some programs). *Entrance requirements:* For master's, interview. Additional exam requirements/recommendations for international students: Required—TOEFL (minimum score 100 iBT). *Application deadline:* For fall admission, 12/1 priority date for domestic students, 12/1 for international students. Applications are processed on a rolling basis. Application fee: $75. Electronic applications accepted. *Financial support:* Career-related internships or fieldwork, Federal Work-Study, institutionally sponsored loans, scholarships/grants, and tuition waivers (partial) available. Support available to part-time students. Financial award application deadline: 2/1; financial award applicants required to submit FAFSA. *Faculty research:* Legal dimensions of arts management, global arts management, cultural policy. *Unit head:* Prof. Brann J. Wry, Director, 212-998-5424, E-mail: brann.wry@nyu.edu. *Application contact:* 212-998-5030, Fax: 212-995-4328, E-mail: steinhardt.gradadmissions@nyu.edu.
Website: http://steinhardt.nyu.edu/music/artsadmin

New York University, Tisch School of the Arts, Program in Arts Politics, New York, NY 10012-1019. Offers MA. *Faculty:* 3 full-time (2 women), 4 part-time/adjunct (3 women). *Students:* 14 full-time (9 women), 1 (woman) part-time; includes 4 minority (1 Asian, non-Hispanic/Latino; 2 Hispanic/Latino; 1 Two or more races, non-Hispanic/Latino), 8 international. Average age 25. 33 applicants, 97% accepted, 15 enrolled. *Degree requirements:* For master's, thesis. *Entrance requirements:* For master's, professional resume, writing sample, statement of purpose. Additional exam requirements/recommendations for international students: Required—TOEFL or IELTS. *Application deadline:* For fall admission, 1/1 for domestic and international students. Application fee: $60. *Financial support:* In 2014–15, 2 students received support. Federal Work-Study and scholarships/grants available. Financial award application deadline: 2/15; financial award applicants required to submit FAFSA. *Unit head:* Randy Martin, Director, 212-992-8248. *Application contact:* Dan Sandford, Director of Graduate Admissions, 212-998-1918, Fax: 212-995-4060, E-mail: tisch.gradadmissions@nyu.edu.

Northwestern University, The Graduate School, School of Communication, Program in Leadership for Creative Enterprises, Evanston, IL 60208. Offers MS.

The Ohio State University, Graduate School, College of Arts and Sciences, Division of Arts and Humanities, Department of Arts Administration, Education and Policy, Program in Arts Policy and Administration, Columbus, OH 43210. Offers MA. *Faculty:* 14. *Students:* 16 full-time (11 women); includes 2 minority (both Black or African American, non-Hispanic/Latino), 4 international. Average age 26. In 2014, 5 master's awarded. *Degree requirements:* For master's, thesis. *Entrance requirements:* For master's, GRE General Test. Additional exam requirements/recommendations for international students: Required—TOEFL (minimum score 600 paper-based; 100 iBT); Recommended—IELTS (minimum score 8). *Application deadline:* For fall admission, 11/30 priority date for domestic and international students; for winter admission, 12/1 for domestic students, 11/1 for international students; for spring admission, 11/30 priority date for domestic and international students. Applications are processed on a rolling basis. Application fee: $60 ($70 for international students). Electronic applications accepted. *Financial support:* Fellowships with tuition reimbursements, teaching assistantships with tuition reimbursements, career-related internships or fieldwork, and unspecified assistantships available. Support available to part-time students. Financial award application deadline: 4/5. *Faculty research:* Public policy and advocacy. *Unit head:* Dr. Karen Hutzel, Graduate Studies Chair, 614-292-0285, E-mail: hutzel.4@osu.edu. *Application contact:* Graduate and Professional Admissions, 614-292-6031, Fax: 614-292-3656, E-mail: gpadmissions@osu.edu.
Website: http://aaep.osu.edu/arts-policy-administration-ma-program

Pratt Institute, School of Art and Design, Program in Arts and Cultural Management, New York, NY 10011. Offers MPS. Part-time and evening/weekend programs available. *Faculty:* 4 part-time/adjunct (2 women). *Students:* 47 full-time (37 women); includes 13 minority (4 Black or African American, non-Hispanic/Latino; 2 Asian, non-Hispanic/Latino; 6 Hispanic/Latino; 1 Native Hawaiian or other Pacific Islander, non-Hispanic/Latino), 21 international. Average age 28. 145 applicants, 30% accepted, 21 enrolled. In 2014, 24 master's awarded. *Degree requirements:* For master's, thesis. *Entrance requirements:* For master's, letters of recommendation, portfolio. Additional exam requirements/recommendations for international students: Required—TOEFL (minimum score 600 paper-based; 100 iBT). *Application deadline:* For fall admission, 1/5 for domestic and international students; for spring admission, 10/1 for domestic and international students. Application fee: $50 ($90 for international students). Electronic applications accepted. *Financial support:* Career-related internships or fieldwork, Federal Work-Study, institutionally sponsored loans, scholarships/grants, health care benefits, and unspecified assistantships available. Support available to part-time students. Financial award application deadline: 2/1; financial award applicants required to submit FAFSA. *Unit head:* Dr. Mary McBride, Director, 212-647-7538, E-mail: mmcb1033@pratt.edu. *Application contact:* Young Hah, Director of Graduate Admissions, 718-636-3683, Fax: 718-399-4242, E-mail: yhah@pratt.edu.
Website: https://www.pratt.edu/academics/school-of-art/graduate-school-of-art/arts-cultural-management/

Pratt Institute, School of Art and Design, Program in Design Management, New York, NY 10011. Offers MPS. Part-time programs available. *Faculty:* 7 part-time/adjunct (3 women). *Students:* 45 full-time (36 women), 1 (woman) part-time; includes 13 minority (5 Black or African American, non-Hispanic/Latino; 3 Asian, non-Hispanic/Latino; 5 Hispanic/Latino), 27 international. Average age 30. 83 applicants, 53% accepted, 22 enrolled. In 2014, 24 master's awarded. *Degree requirements:* For master's, thesis. *Entrance requirements:* For master's, letters of recommendation, portfolio. Additional exam requirements/recommendations for international students: Required—TOEFL (minimum score 600 paper-based; 100 iBT). *Application deadline:* For fall admission, 1/5 for domestic and international students; for spring admission, 10/1 for domestic and international students. Application fee: $50 ($90 for international students). Electronic applications accepted. *Financial support:* Career-related internships or fieldwork, Federal Work-Study, institutionally sponsored loans, scholarships/grants, health care benefits, and unspecified assistantships available. Support available to part-time students. Financial award application deadline: 2/1; financial award applicants required to submit FAFSA. *Unit head:* Dr. Mary McBride, Chairperson, 212-647-7538, E-mail: mmcb1033@pratt.edu. *Application contact:* Young Hah, Director of Graduate Admissions, 718-636-3683, Fax: 718-399-4242, E-mail: yhah@pratt.edu.
Website: https://www.pratt.edu/academics/school-of-art/graduate-school-of-art/design-management/

See Display on page 153 and Close-Up on page 203.

Rhode Island College, School of Graduate Studies, Faculty of Arts and Sciences, Department of Art, Providence, RI 02908-1991. Offers art education (MA, MAT); media studies (MA). *Accreditation:* NASAD (one or more programs are accredited). Part-time and evening/weekend programs available. *Faculty:* 6 full-time (3 women), 5 part-time/adjunct (2 women). *Students:* 9 full-time (6 women), 10 part-time (7 women), 1 international. Average age 35. In 2014, 8 master's awarded. *Degree requirements:* For master's, thesis. *Entrance requirements:* For master's, GRE General Test, portfolio (MA), 3 letters of recommendation, interview. Additional exam requirements/recommendations for international students: Recommended—TOEFL (minimum score 550 paper-based; 79 iBT). *Application deadline:* For fall admission, 3/1 for domestic

students. Applications are processed on a rolling basis. Application fee: $50. *Expenses:* Tuition, state resident: full-time $8928; part-time $372 per credit hour. Tuition, nonresident: full-time $17,376; part-time $724 per credit hour. *Required fees:* $602; $22 per credit. $72 per term. *Financial support:* In 2014–15, 2 teaching assistantships with full tuition reimbursements (averaging $1,500 per year) were awarded; career-related internships or fieldwork, Federal Work-Study, scholarships/grants, health care benefits, and unspecified assistantships also available. Support available to part-time students. Financial award application deadline: 5/15; financial award applicants required to submit FAFSA. *Unit head:* Prof. Nancy Bockbrader, Chair, 401-456-8054. *Application contact:* Graduate Studies, 401-456-8700.
Website: http://www.ric.edu/art/index.php

Robert Morris University Illinois, Morris Graduate School of Management, Chicago, IL 60605. Offers accounting (MBA); accounting/finance (MBA); business analytics (MIS); design and media (MM); educational technology (MM); health care administration (MM); higher education administration (MM); human resource management (MBA); information security (MIS); information systems (MIS); law enforcement administration (MM); management (MBA); management/finance (MBA); management/human resource management (MBA); mobile computing (MIS); sports administration (MM). Part-time and evening/weekend programs available. *Faculty:* 5 full-time (2 women), 27 part-time/adjunct (8 women). *Students:* 237 full-time (122 women), 180 part-time (109 women); includes 222 minority (128 Black or African American, non-Hispanic/Latino; 2 American Indian or Alaska Native, non-Hispanic/Latino; 18 Asian, non-Hispanic/Latino; 68 Hispanic/Latino; 1 Native Hawaiian or other Pacific Islander, non-Hispanic/Latino; 5 Two or more races, non-Hispanic/Latino), 26 international. Average age 33. 191 applicants, 63% accepted, 104 enrolled. In 2014, 234 master's awarded. *Entrance requirements:* For master's, official transcripts, two letters of recommendation. Additional exam requirements/recommendations for international students: Required—TOEFL (minimum score 550 paper-based). *Application deadline:* Applications are processed on a rolling basis. Application fee: $20 ($100 for international students). Electronic applications accepted. *Expenses: Tuition:* Full-time $14,400; part-time $2400 per course. *Financial support:* In 2014–15, 339 students received support. Federal Work-Study and scholarships/grants available. Support available to part-time students. Financial award applicants required to submit FAFSA. *Unit head:* Kayed Akkawi, Dean, 312-935-6050, Fax: 312-935-6020, E-mail: kakkawi@robertmorris.edu. *Application contact:* Catherine Lockwood, Vice President of Adult Undergraduate and Graduate Education, 312-935-6050, Fax: 312-935-6020, E-mail: clockwood@robertmorris.edu.

Rocky Mountain College of Art + Design, Program in Education, Leadership + Emerging Technologies, Lakewood, CO 80214. Offers MA. Postbaccalaureate distance learning degree programs offered (no on-campus study).

Rowan University, Graduate School, College of Performing Arts, Department of Theatre and Dance, Glassboro, NJ 08028-1701. Offers theatre arts administration (MA). *Faculty:* 1 (woman) full-time, 3 part-time/adjunct (all women). *Students:* 1 (woman) full-time, 20 part-time (14 women); includes 3 minority (all Black or African American, non-Hispanic/Latino). Average age 32. In 2014, 2 master's awarded. *Application deadline:* For summer admission, 2/15 for domestic students. Applications are processed on a rolling basis. Application fee: $65. Electronic applications accepted. *Expenses: Tuition, area resident:* Part-time $648 per credit. Tuition, state resident: part-time $648 per credit. Tuition, nonresident: part-time $648 per credit. *Required fees:* $145 per credit. Tuition and fees vary according to degree level, campus/location, program and student level. *Unit head:* Dr. Horacio Sosa, Vice President, Global Learning and Partnerships, 856-256-4747, Fax: 856-256-5638, E-mail: sosa@rowan.edu. *Application contact:* Admissions and Enrollment Services, 856-256-4747, Fax: 856-256-5637, E-mail: globaladmissions@rowan.edu.
Website: http://www.rowan.edu/colleges/cpa/theatre_dance/

Ryerson University, School of Graduate Studies, Program in Photographic Preservation and Collections Management, Toronto, ON M5B 2K3, Canada. Offers MA.

Saint Mary's University of Minnesota, Schools of Graduate and Professional Programs, Graduate School of Business and Technology, Arts and Cultural Management Program, Winona, MN 55987-1399. Offers MA.

St. Thomas University, School of Leadership Studies, Program in Art Management, Miami Gardens, FL 33054-6459. Offers MA.

Savannah College of Art and Design, Graduate School, Program in Arts Administration, Savannah, GA 31402-3146. Offers MA. Part-time programs available. Postbaccalaureate distance learning degree programs offered (no on-campus study). *Faculty:* 4 full-time (2 women), 4 part-time/adjunct (2 women). *Students:* 59 full-time (55 women), 71 part-time (59 women); includes 34 minority (26 Black or African American, non-Hispanic/Latino; 2 Asian, non-Hispanic/Latino; 5 Hispanic/Latino; 1 Two or more races, non-Hispanic/Latino), 34 international. Average age 29. 155 applicants, 51% accepted, 54 enrolled. In 2014, 76 master's awarded. *Degree requirements:* For master's, thesis, internship, final project. *Entrance requirements:* For master's, portfolio of writing samples. Additional exam requirements/recommendations for international students: Required—TOEFL (minimum score 550 paper-based, 85 iBT), IELTS (minimum score 6.5), or ACTFL. *Application deadline:* For fall admission, 4/1 for domestic and international students. Applications are processed on a rolling basis. Application fee: $40. Electronic applications accepted. *Expenses: Tuition:* Full-time $34,605; part-time $3845 per course. One-time fee: $500. Tuition and fees vary according to course load. *Financial support:* Fellowships, career-related internships or fieldwork, Federal Work-Study, and scholarships/grants available. Financial award application deadline: 4/1; financial award applicants required to submit FAFSA. *Unit head:* Anita Akella, Program Coordinator. *Application contact:* Jenny Jaquillard, Executive Director of Admissions, Recruitment and Events, 912-525-5100, Fax: 912-525-5985, E-mail: admission@scad.edu.
Website: http://www.scad.edu/academics/programs/arts-administration

Savannah College of Art and Design, Graduate School, Program in Design Management, Savannah, GA 31402-3146. Offers MA, MFA. Part-time programs available. Postbaccalaureate distance learning degree programs offered (no on-campus study). *Faculty:* 2 full-time (1 woman), 5 part-time/adjunct (4 women). *Students:* 47 full-time (31 women), 63 part-time (43 women); includes 23 minority (6 Black or African American, non-Hispanic/Latino; 1 American Indian or Alaska Native, non-Hispanic/Latino; 5 Asian, non-Hispanic/Latino; 11 Hispanic/Latino), 37 international. Average age 30. 80 applicants, 39% accepted, 19 enrolled. In 2014, 37 master's awarded. *Degree requirements:* For master's, thesis (for some programs), final project (for MA). *Entrance requirements:* For master's, portfolio. Additional exam requirements/recommendations for international students: Required—TOEFL (minimum score 550 paper-based, 85 iBT), IELTS (minimum score 6.5), or ACTFL. *Application deadline:* For fall admission, 4/1 for domestic and international students. Applications are processed on a rolling basis. Application fee: $40. Electronic applications accepted. *Expenses: Tuition:* Full-time $34,605; part-time $3845 per course. One-time fee: $500. Tuition and fees vary according to course load. *Financial support:* Fellowships, career-related internships or fieldwork, Federal Work-Study, and scholarships/grants available. *Unit head:* Owen Foster, Chair. *Application contact:* Jenny Jaquillard, Executive Director of Admissions, Recruitment and Events, 912-525-5100, Fax: 912-525-5985, E-mail: admission@scad.edu.
Website: http://www.scad.edu/academics/programs/design-management

School of the Art Institute of Chicago, Graduate Division, Program in Arts Administration and Policy, Chicago, IL 60603-3103. Offers MAAAP. *Accreditation:* NASAD. *Degree requirements:* For master's, thesis, telephone interview. *Entrance requirements:* Additional exam requirements/recommendations for international students: Required—TOEFL, IELTS. *Faculty research:* Latin American artists, activist art, community-based art.

Seattle University, College of Arts and Sciences, Program in Arts Leadership, Seattle, WA 98122-1090. Offers MFA. Part-time and evening/weekend programs available. *Students:* 5 full-time (all women), 68 part-time (54 women); includes 19 minority (4 Black or African American, non-Hispanic/Latino; 1 American Indian or Alaska Native, non-Hispanic/Latino; 3 Asian, non-Hispanic/Latino; 6 Hispanic/Latino; 5 Two or more races, non-Hispanic/Latino), 6 international. Average age 30. 96 applicants, 76% accepted, 49 enrolled. In 2014, 19 master's awarded. *Degree requirements:* For master's, summary capstone project presentation and paper. *Entrance requirements:* For master's, minimum GPA of 3.0, 2 years of management in nonprofit or comparable work or volunteer experience. Additional exam requirements/recommendations for international students: Required—TOEFL, IELTS. *Application deadline:* For fall admission, 3/15 for domestic students, 4/1 for international students. Applications are processed on a rolling basis. Application fee: $55. Electronic applications accepted. *Financial support:* Application deadline: 3/15; applicants required to submit FAFSA. *Faculty research:* Leadership succession planning, social media in arts marketing, audience development. *Unit head:* Kevin Maifeld, Director, 206-296-5370, E-mail: maifeldk@seattleu.edu. *Application contact:* Janet Shandley, Associate Dean of Graduate Admissions, 206-296-5900, Fax: 206-298-5656, E-mail: grad_admissions@seattleu.edu.
Website: https://www.seattleu.edu/artsci/mfa/

Sotheby's Institute of Art–London, Graduate Programs, London, United Kingdom. Offers art business (MA); contemporary art (MA); contemporary design (MA); East Asian art (MA); fine and decorative art (MA); photography (MA). *Faculty:* 38 full-time (22 women). *Students:* 175 full-time (153 women). *Application contact:* Melba Remice, Director, Global Admissions, 212-517-2834, E-mail: admissions@sothebysinstitute.com.

Sotheby's Institute of Art–New York, Graduate Programs, New York, NY 10021. Offers American fine and decorative art (MA); art business (MA); contemporary art (MA). *Accreditation:* NASAD. *Faculty:* 25 full-time (12 women). *Students:* 153 full-time (141 women). *Entrance requirements:* For master's, academic transcripts, two letters of academic reference, personal statement, writing sample, curriculum vitae/resume, interview. Application fee: $100. Electronic applications accepted. *Application contact:* Melba Remice, Director of Global Admissions, 212-517-2834, E-mail: admissions@sothebysinstitute.com.
Website: http://www.sothebysinstitute.com/Programmes/PNewyork.aspx

Southern Methodist University, Meadows School of the Arts, Division of Arts Management and Arts Entrepreneurship, Dallas, TX 75275. Offers international arts management (MM); MA/MBA. MM offered jointly with Bocconi University Graduate School of Management in Milan and HEC Montreal. *Entrance requirements:* For master's, GMAT. Additional exam requirements/recommendations for international students: Required—TOEFL (minimum score 600 paper-based; 100 iBT). Electronic applications accepted.

Southern Utah University, Program in Arts Administration, Cedar City, UT 84720-2498. Offers MA, MFA. Part-time programs available. *Students:* 6 full-time (all women), 19 part-time (14 women); includes 1 minority (Native Hawaiian or other Pacific Islander, non-Hispanic/Latino). Average age 36. 34 applicants, 50% accepted, 13 enrolled. In 2014, 3 master's awarded. *Entrance requirements:* For master's, bachelor's degree, interview, 3 letters of recommendation, resume, minimum undergraduate GPA of 3.0, written statement of purpose, transcripts. Additional exam requirements/recommendations for international students: Required—TOEFL (minimum score 550 paper-based, 79 iBT) or IELTS (minimum score 6). *Application deadline:* For fall admission, 2/15 for domestic and international students. Applications are processed on a rolling basis. Application fee: $60 ($75 for international students). Electronic applications accepted. *Expenses:* Expenses: Contact institution. *Financial support:* Tuition waivers and unspecified assistantships available. *Unit head:* Rachel Bishop, Interim Program Director/Assistant Professor, 435-586-7873, Fax: 435-865-8657, E-mail: bishopr@suu.edu.
Website: http://www.suu.edu/pva/aa/index.html

Syracuse University, College of Arts and Sciences, Program in Arts Leadership, Syracuse, NY 13244. Offers MA, CAS. *Students:* 13 full-time (12 women), 1 (woman) part-time; includes 3 minority (1 Asian, non-Hispanic/Latino; 1 Hispanic/Latino; 1 Two or more races, non-Hispanic/Latino), 5 international. Average age 25. 43 applicants, 63% accepted, 10 enrolled. In 2014, 2 master's awarded. *Degree requirements:* For master's, final project. *Entrance requirements:* For master's, GRE, essay. Additional exam requirements/recommendations for international students: Required—TOEFL (minimum score 100 iBT). *Application deadline:* For fall admission, 1/1 for international students; for summer admission, 1/1 priority date for domestic and international students. Application fee: $75. Electronic applications accepted. *Expenses: Tuition:* Part-time $1341 per credit. *Financial support:* Fellowships with full tuition reimbursements available. Financial award application deadline: 1/1; financial award applicants required to submit FAFSA. *Unit head:* Prof. Mark Nerenhausen, Program Director, 315-443-1796, E-mail: manerenh@syr.edu. *Application contact:* Christine Conroy, Coordinator, 315-443-4184, E-mail: cconroy@syr.edu.
Website: http://janklow.syr.edu/

Teachers College, Columbia University, Graduate Faculty of Education, Department of Arts and Humanities, Program in Arts Administration, New York, NY 10027-6696. Offers MA. *Faculty:* 2 full-time, 5 part-time/adjunct. *Students:* 52 full-time (47 women), 5 part-time (4 women); includes 13 minority (4 Black or African American, non-Hispanic/Latino; 3 Asian, non-Hispanic/Latino; 5 Hispanic/Latino; 1 Two or more races, non-Hispanic/Latino), 22 international. Average age 26. 155 applicants, 34% accepted, 27 enrolled. In 2014, 23 master's awarded. *Degree requirements:* For master's, thesis, internship. *Entrance requirements:* For master's, GRE, approximately 3 years of related experience. Additional exam requirements/recommendations for international students: Required—TOEFL (minimum score 600 paper-based). *Application deadline:* For fall admission, 1/15 priority date for domestic students. Application fee: $65. Electronic applications accepted. *Expenses: Tuition:* Full-time $33,552; part-time $1398 per credit. *Required fees:* $418 per semester. *Financial support:* Career-related internships or fieldwork, Federal Work-Study, institutionally sponsored loans, tuition waivers (partial), and unspecified assistantships available. Financial award application deadline: 2/1. *Faculty research:* Artists' career development, arts law, American culture, strategic management, international training. *Unit head:* Prof. Steve Dubin, Program Coordinator, 212-678-3134, E-mail: sed2188@columbia.edu. *Application contact:* Thomas P. Rock, Director of Admissions, 212-678-3083, Fax: 212-678-4171, E-mail: rock@tc.edu.
Website: http://www.tc.columbia.edu/academic/arad/

Temple University, Center for the Arts, Tyler School of Art, Department of Art History, Philadelphia, PA 19122-6096. Offers MA, PhD. Part-time programs available. *Faculty:*

13 full-time (8 women), 5 part-time/adjunct (4 women). *Students:* 52 full-time (44 women), 5 part-time (4 women); includes 9 minority (3 Asian, non-Hispanic/Latino; 5 Hispanic/Latino; 1 Two or more races, non-Hispanic/Latino), 3 international. 44 applicants, 73% accepted, 13 enrolled. In 2014, 6 master's, 5 doctorates awarded. Terminal master's awarded for partial completion of doctoral program. *Degree requirements:* For master's, 2 foreign languages, thesis, comprehensive slide exam; for doctorate, 2 foreign languages, thesis/dissertation, qualifying exam. *Entrance requirements:* For master's, GRE General Test, minimum GPA of 3.0, letters of recommendation, resume/curriculum vitae, writing sample; for doctorate, GRE, MA in art history, minimum GPA of 3.0, letters of recommendation, resume/curriculum vitae, writing sample. Additional exam requirements/recommendations for international students: Required—TOEFL (minimum score 550 paper-based; 79 iBT), IELTS (minimum score 6.5). *Application deadline:* For fall admission, 12/15 for domestic and international students; for spring admission, 11/1 for domestic students, 10/1 for international students. Applications are processed on a rolling basis. Application fee: $60. Electronic applications accepted. *Expenses:* Expenses: Contact institution. *Financial support:* Fellowships, research assistantships with full tuition reimbursements, teaching assistantships with full tuition reimbursements, career-related internships or fieldwork, institutionally sponsored loans, and technical assistantships available. Financial award application deadline: 1/15. *Faculty research:* Aegean, Greek, and Roman art; early Christian art; medieval art and architecture; Renaissance and Baroque painting, sculpture, and architecture; nineteenth and twentieth century painting and sculpture. *Unit head:* Dr. Gerald Silk, Chair, 215-204-7837, Fax: 215-204-6951, E-mail: gsilk@temple.edu. *Application contact:* Nicole Hall, Director of Admissions, 215-777-9090, E-mail: nicoleh@temple.edu.
Website: http://www.temple.edu/tyler/arthistory/

Universidad del Turabo, Graduate Programs, School of Social Sciences and Humanities, Programs in Public Affairs, Program in Arts Administration, Gurabo, PR 00778-3030. Offers MPA.

University at Buffalo, the State University of New York, Graduate School, College of Arts and Sciences, Arts Management Program, Buffalo, NY 14260. Offers MA. Part-time programs available. *Faculty:* 2 full-time (both women), 6 part-time/adjunct (3 women). *Students:* 24 full-time (22 women); includes 13 minority (2 Black or African American, non-Hispanic/Latino; 8 Asian, non-Hispanic/Latino; 1 Native Hawaiian or other Pacific Islander, non-Hispanic/Latino; 2 Two or more races, non-Hispanic/Latino). Average age 24. 70 applicants, 41% accepted, 12 enrolled. In 2014, 1 master's awarded. *Degree requirements:* For master's, thesis. *Entrance requirements:* Additional exam requirements/recommendations for international students: Required—TOEFL or IELTS; Recommended—TOEFL (minimum score 79 iBT). *Application deadline:* For fall admission, 1/10 priority date for domestic and international students. Applications are processed on a rolling basis. Application fee: $75. Electronic applications accepted. *Expenses:* Expenses: Contact institution. *Financial support:* In 2014–15, 3 students received support, including 2 fellowships with full tuition reimbursements available; career-related internships or fieldwork and scholarships/grants also available. Financial award application deadline: 8/15; financial award applicants required to submit FAFSA. *Faculty research:* Cultural policy, arts management, museums and the public space, cultural diplomacy. *Unit head:* Prof. Royal Roussel, Acting Director, 716-645-2437, Fax: 716-645-6737, E-mail: artsmgmt@buffalo.edu. *Application contact:* Joseph C. Syracuse, Graduate Enrollment Manager, 716-645-2711, Fax: 716-645-3888, E-mail: jcs32@buffalo.edu.
Website: http://www.artsmanagement.buffalo.edu/

The University of Akron, Graduate School, Buchtel College of Arts and Sciences, School of Dance, Theatre, and Arts Administration, Program in Arts Administration, Akron, OH 44325. Offers MA. *Accreditation:* NASAD. *Students:* 16 full-time (10 women), 8 part-time (7 women); includes 4 minority (2 Black or African American, non-Hispanic/Latino; 2 Two or more races, non-Hispanic/Latino), 2 international. Average age 31. 15 applicants, 80% accepted, 7 enrolled. In 2014, 9 master's awarded. *Degree requirements:* For master's, thesis optional. *Entrance requirements:* For master's, minimum GPA of 2.75, 300-word statement of intent summarizing student background and outlining career goals. Additional exam requirements/recommendations for international students: Required—TOEFL (minimum score 550 paper-based; 79 iBT), IELTS (minimum score 6.5). *Application deadline:* For fall admission, 3/15 for domestic and international students. Application fee: $45 ($70 for international students). Electronic applications accepted. *Expenses:* Tuition, state resident: full-time $7578; part-time $421 per credit hour. Tuition, nonresident: full-time $12,977; part-time $721 per credit hour. *Required fees:* $1388; $35 per credit hour. Tuition and fees vary according to course load. *Total annual research expenditures:* $1,928. *Unit head:* Dr. Neil Sapienza, Interim Director, 330-972-7408, E-mail: nbs@uakron.edu. *Application contact:* Kara Stewart, Coordinator, Arts Administration, 330-972-7948, E-mail: kms140@uakron.edu.
Website: http://www.uakron.edu/dtaa/artsadmin/

University of Cincinnati, Graduate School, College-Conservatory of Music, Divisions of Opera, Musical Theater, Drama, and Arts Administration, Cincinnati, OH 45221. Offers arts administration (MA); directing (MFA); theater design and production (MFA); voice and opera (MM, DMA); MBA/MA. *Accreditation:* NAST (one or more programs are accredited). *Degree requirements:* For master's, final project. *Entrance requirements:* For master's, GMAT (MA), audition/interview. Additional exam requirements/recommendations for international students: Required—TOEFL (minimum score 520 paper-based). Electronic applications accepted.

University of Kentucky, Graduate School, College of Fine Arts, Program in Arts Administration, Lexington, KY 40506-0032. Offers MA.

The University of Manchester, School of Arts, Histories and Cultures, Manchester, United Kingdom. Offers anthropology, media and performance (PhD); applied theatre professional (PhD); archaeology (PhD); art history and visual studies (PhD); arts management and cultural policy (PhD); classics and ancient history (PhD); composition (PhD); creative writing (PhD); drama (PhD); economic and social history (PhD); electroacoustic composition (PhD); English and American studies (PhD); history (PhD); humanitarianism and conflict response (PhD); museology (PhD); music (PhD); musicology (PhD); religions and theology (PhD).

University of Michigan–Flint, Graduate Programs, Program in Arts Administration, Flint, MI 48502-1950. Offers museum and visual arts (MA); performance (MA). Part-time programs available. *Faculty:* 2 part-time/adjunct (1 woman). *Students:* 7 full-time (5 women), 11 part-time (8 women); includes 3 minority (all Black or African American, non-Hispanic/Latino), 1 international. Average age 36. 10 applicants, 100% accepted, 9 enrolled. In 2014, 10 master's awarded. *Degree requirements:* For master's, thesis, internship. *Entrance requirements:* For master's, bachelor's degree in the arts (visual art, theatre, dance, music, etc.) from accredited institution with minimum undergraduate GPA of 3.0. Additional exam requirements/recommendations for international students: Required—TOEFL (minimum score 84 iBT), IELTS (minimum score 6.5). *Application deadline:* For fall admission, 8/1 for domestic students, 5/1 for international students; for winter admission, 11/15 for domestic students, 9/15 for international students. Applications are processed on a rolling basis. Application fee: $55. Electronic applications accepted. Application fee is waived when completed online. *Financial*

support: Federal Work-Study and scholarships/grants available. Support available to part-time students. Financial award application deadline: 3/1; financial award applicants required to submit FAFSA. *Unit head:* Dr. Sarah Lippert, Interim Director, 810-766-6679, E-mail: sarlipp@umflint.edu. *Application contact:* Bradley T. Maki, Director of Graduate Admissions, 810-762-3171, Fax: 810-766-6789, E-mail: bmaki@umflint.edu.
Website: http://www.umflint.edu/graduateprograms/arts-administration-ma

University of New Orleans, Graduate School, College of Liberal Arts, Program in Arts Administration, New Orleans, LA 70148. Offers MA. Part-time programs available. *Degree requirements:* For master's, internship. *Entrance requirements:* For master's, GRE General Test. Additional exam requirements/recommendations for international students: Required—TOEFL (minimum score 550 paper-based; 79 iBT), IELTS (minimum score 6.5). Electronic applications accepted.

The University of North Carolina at Charlotte, College of Liberal Arts and Sciences, Department of Political Science and Public Administration, Charlotte, NC 28223-0001. Offers emergency management (Graduate Certificate); non-profit management (Graduate Certificate); public administration (MPA), including arts administration, emergency management, non-profit management, public finance; public finance (Graduate Certificate); urban management and policy (Graduate Certificate). *Accreditation:* NASPAA. Part-time and evening/weekend programs available. *Faculty:* 15 full-time (8 women), 4 part-time/adjunct (1 woman). *Students:* 16 full-time (10 women), 83 part-time (51 women); includes 32 minority (21 Black or African American, non-Hispanic/Latino; 1 Asian, non-Hispanic/Latino; 7 Hispanic/Latino; 3 Two or more races, non-Hispanic/Latino). Average age 30. 60 applicants, 65% accepted, 25 enrolled. In 2014, 23 master's, 11 other advanced degrees awarded. Terminal master's awarded for partial completion of doctoral program. *Degree requirements:* For master's, thesis or alternative. *Entrance requirements:* For master's, GRE General Test or MAT, minimum GPA of 3.0 in undergraduate major, 2.75 overall. Additional exam requirements/recommendations for international students: Required—TOEFL (minimum score 557 paper-based; 83 iBT). *Application deadline:* For fall admission, 5/1 priority date for domestic students, 5/1 for international students; for spring admission, 10/1 priority date for domestic students, 10/1 for international students. Applications are processed on a rolling basis. Application fee: $75. Electronic applications accepted. *Expenses:* Tuition, state resident: full-time $4008. Tuition, nonresident: full-time $16,295. *Required fees:* $2755. Tuition and fees vary according to course load and program. *Financial support:* In 2014–15, 7 students received support, including 7 research assistantships (averaging $6,857 per year); career-related internships or fieldwork, Federal Work-Study, institutionally sponsored loans, scholarships/grants, and unspecified assistantships also available. Support available to part-time students. Financial award application deadline: 4/1; financial award applicants required to submit FAFSA. *Faculty research:* Health policy and politics, managed care, issues of ethnic and racial disparities in health, aging policies, Central Asia. *Total annual research expenditures:* $348,793. *Unit head:* Dr. Greg Weeks, Chair, 704-687-7574, Fax: 704-687-1400, E-mail: gbweeks@uncc.edu. *Application contact:* Kathy B. Giddings, Director of Graduate Admissions, 704-687-5503, Fax: 704-687-1668, E-mail: gradadm@uncc.edu.
Website: https://politicalscience.uncc.edu/graduate

University of North Carolina School of the Arts, School of Design and Production, Winston-Salem, NC 27127-2738. Offers costume design (MFA); costume technology (MFA); performance arts management (MFA); scene design (MFA); scene painting/properties (MFA); sound design (MFA); stage automation (MFA); technical direction (MFA); wig and make-up design (MFA). *Degree requirements:* For master's, thesis (for some programs), project. *Entrance requirements:* For master's, interview, portfolio. Additional exam requirements/recommendations for international students: Required—TOEFL. Electronic applications accepted.

University of Oregon, Graduate School, School of Architecture and Allied Arts, Program in Arts and Administration, Eugene, OR 97403. Offers arts management (MA, MS); media management (MA, MS). *Degree requirements:* For master's, summer internship, thesis/project. *Entrance requirements:* For master's, minimum GPA of 3.0; bachelor's degree in history, practice of visual, performing arts or other related degree. Additional exam requirements/recommendations for international students: Required—TOEFL. *Faculty research:* Museum education, arts program evaluation, community arts, information management, arts marketing.

University of Southern California, Graduate School, Roski School of Fine Arts, Art and Curatorial Practices in the Public Sphere Program, Los Angeles, CA 90089. Offers MA. *Degree requirements:* For master's, thesis, practicum exhibition. *Entrance requirements:* For master's, GRE, personal statement, writing sample, three letters of recommendation. Additional exam requirements/recommendations for international students: Required—TOEFL (minimum score 600 paper-based; 100 iBT). Electronic applications accepted. *Faculty research:* Curatorial studies, exhibition histories, modern and contemporary art, public art.

University of Wisconsin–Madison, Graduate School, Wisconsin School of Business, Wisconsin Full-Time MBA Program, Madison, WI 53706. Offers applied security analysis (MBA); arts administration (MBA); brand and product management (MBA); corporate finance and investment banking (MBA); marketing research (MBA); operations and technology management (MBA); real estate (MBA); risk management and insurance (MBA); strategic human resource management (MBA); supply chain management (MBA). *Faculty:* 55 full-time (9 women), 13 part-time/adjunct (4 women). *Students:* 199 full-time (72 women); includes 30 minority (11 Black or African American, non-Hispanic/Latino; 1 American Indian or Alaska Native, non-Hispanic/Latino; 3 Asian, non-Hispanic/Latino; 12 Hispanic/Latino; 3 Two or more races, non-Hispanic/Latino), 39 international. Average age 28. 473 applicants, 29% accepted, 100 enrolled. In 2014, 92 master's awarded. *Entrance requirements:* For master's, GMAT or GRE, bachelor's or equivalent degree, 2 years of work experience, essay, one letter of recommendation, resume. Additional exam requirements/recommendations for international students: Required—TOEFL (minimum score 100 iBT), IELTS (minimum score 7.5). *Application deadline:* For fall admission, 11/4 for domestic and international students; for winter admission, 2/3 for domestic and international students; for spring admission, 4/28 for domestic students, 4/2 for international students. Applications are processed on a rolling basis. Application fee: $56. Electronic applications accepted. *Expenses:* Expenses: Contact institution. *Financial support:* In 2014–15, 157 students received support, including 10 fellowships with full tuition reimbursements available (averaging $37,956 per year), 82 research assistantships with full tuition reimbursements available (averaging $28,175 per year), 50 teaching assistantships with full tuition reimbursements available (averaging $28,175 per year); scholarships/grants, health care benefits, and unspecified assistantships also available. Financial award application deadline: 4/28; financial award applicants required to submit FAFSA. *Faculty research:* Market consequences of International Financial Reporting Standards (IFRS), inter-firm relationships and strategic partnerships, application of Bayesian statistical methods and applied probability models to understanding individuals' behaviors in the context of customer relationship management (CRM) applications, liquidity provision and the structure of financial markets, strategic management of global startups. *Unit head:* Prof. Ella Mae Matsumura, Associate Dean Full-time MBA Program, 608-262-9731, E-mail: ematsumura@bus.wisc.edu. *Application contact:* Betsy Kacizak, Director of Admissions and Recruiting, Full-time MBA Program, 608-262-4000, E-mail:

mlewitzke@bus.wisc.edu.
Website: http://www.bus.wisc.edu/mba

Valparaiso University, Graduate School, Program in Arts and Entertainment Administration, Valparaiso, IN 46383. Offers MA. Part-time and evening/weekend programs available. *Students:* 9 full-time (all women), 6 part-time (3 women); includes 1 minority (Hispanic/Latino), 12 international. Average age 26. In 2014, 11 master's awarded. *Degree requirements:* For master's, internship or research project. *Entrance requirements:* Additional exam requirements/recommendations for international students: Required—TOEFL (minimum score 550 paper-based; 80 iBT), IELTS (minimum score 6). *Application deadline:* Applications are processed on a rolling basis. Application fee: $30 ($50 for international students). Electronic applications accepted. *Expenses: Tuition:* Full-time $10,710; part-time $595 per credit hour. *Required fees:* $378; $101 per term. Tuition and fees vary according to course load and program. *Financial support:* Available to part-time students. Applicants required to submit FAFSA. *Unit head:* Dr. Jennifer A. Ziegler, Dean, Graduate School and Continuing Education, 219-464-5313, Fax: 219-464-5381, E-mail: jennifer.ziegler@valpo.edu. *Application contact:* Jessica Choquette, Graduate Admissions Specialist, 219-464-5313, Fax: 219-464-5381, E-mail: jessica.choquette@valpo.edu.
Website: http://www.valpo.edu/grad/aea/

Webster University, Leigh Gerdine College of Fine Arts, Department of Art, Program in Arts Management and Leadership, St. Louis, MO 63119-3194. Offers MFA. Part-time and evening/weekend programs available. *Degree requirements:* For master's, thesis. *Entrance requirements:* For master's, GRE, BA or BFA in related field, interview.

Winthrop University, College of Visual and Performing Arts, Department of Art, Rock Hill, SC 29733. Offers art (MFA); art administration (MA); art education (MA). *Accreditation:* NASAD. Part-time programs available. *Degree requirements:* For master's, thesis, documented exhibit, oral exam. *Entrance requirements:* For master's, GRE General Test or MAT, PRAXIS (MA), minimum GPA of 3.0, resume, slide portfolio, teaching certificate (MA). Electronic applications accepted.

Art Therapy

Adler Graduate School, Program in Adlerian Counseling and Psychotherapy, Richfield, MN 55423. Offers Adlerian studies (MA); art therapy (MA); clinical counseling (MA); co-occurring substance abuse and mental health disorders (MA); marriage and family therapy (MA); school counseling (MA). Part-time and evening/weekend programs available. *Faculty:* 7 full-time (6 women), 68 part-time/adjunct (49 women). *Students:* 368 part-time (283 women); includes 61 minority (41 Black or African American, non-Hispanic/Latino; 4 American Indian or Alaska Native, non-Hispanic/Latino; 8 Asian, non-Hispanic/Latino; 8 Hispanic/Latino). Average age 40. In 2014, 90 master's awarded. *Degree requirements:* For master's, thesis or alternative, 500-700 hour internship (depending on license choice). *Entrance requirements:* For master's, personal goal statement, three letters of reference, resume or work history, official transcripts. *Application deadline:* Applications are processed on a rolling basis. Application fee: $50. Electronic applications accepted. *Expenses: Tuition:* Full-time $6060; part-time $505 per credit. *Financial support:* Career-related internships or fieldwork and tuition waivers available. Support available to part-time students. Financial award applicants required to submit FAFSA. *Unit head:* Dr. Dan Haugen, President, 612-767-7048, Fax: 612-861-7559, E-mail: haugen@alfredadler.edu. *Application contact:* Evelyn B. Haas, Director of Admissions, 612-767-7044, Fax: 612-861-7559, E-mail: ev@alfredadler.edu.

Adler University, Programs in Psychology, Chicago, IL 60602. Offers advanced Adlerian psychotherapy (Certificate); art therapy (MA); clinical neuropsychology (Certificate); clinical psychology (Psy D); community psychology (MA); counseling and organizational psychology (MA); counseling psychology (MA); criminology (MA); emergency management leadership (MA); forensic psychology (MA); marriage and family counseling (MA); marriage and family therapy (Certificate); military psychology (MA); nonprofit management (MA); organizational psychology (MA); police psychology (MA); public policy and administration (MA); rehabilitation counseling (MA); sport and health psychology (MA); substance abuse counseling (Certificate); Psy D/Certificate; Psy D/MACAT; Psy D/MACP; Psy D/MAMFC; Psy D/MASAC. *Accreditation:* APA. Part-time and evening/weekend programs available. Postbaccalaureate distance learning degree programs offered (minimal on-campus study). Terminal master's awarded for partial completion of doctoral program. *Degree requirements:* For master's, thesis or alternative, oral exam, practicum; for doctorate, thesis/dissertation, clinical exam, internship, oral exam, practicum, written qualifying exam. *Entrance requirements:* For master's, 12 semester hours in psychology, minimum GPA of 3.0; for doctorate, 18 semester hours in psychology, minimum GPA of 3.25; for Certificate, appropriate master's or doctoral degree. Additional exam requirements/recommendations for international students: Required—TOEFL (minimum score 550 paper-based; 79 iBT). Electronic applications accepted.

See Display on page 968 and Close-Up on page 1207.

Albertus Magnus College, Master of Arts in Art Therapy Program, New Haven, CT 06511-1189. Offers MAAT. Part-time programs available. *Faculty:* 3 full-time (all women), 13 part-time/adjunct (10 women). *Students:* 44 full-time (41 women); includes 3 minority (1 American Indian or Alaska Native, non-Hispanic/Latino; 2 Hispanic/Latino). Average age 34. 20 applicants, 65% accepted, 10 enrolled. *Degree requirements:* For master's, thesis, 725-hour internship; 60 credits. *Entrance requirements:* For master's, 15 credits in psychology; 18 credits in studio art, interview, writing sample, portfolio (original art). Additional exam requirements/recommendations for international students: Required—TOEFL (minimum score 120 iBT). *Application deadline:* For fall admission, 5/1 for domestic students; for spring admission, 11/1 for domestic students. Applications are processed on a rolling basis. Application fee: $50. Electronic applications accepted. *Expenses:* Expenses: $1,878 per three-credit course; information technology fee $35 per session; registration fee $25 per semester; materials fee $50 per semester (for studio courses). *Financial support:* Unspecified assistantships available. Support available to part-time students. Financial award application deadline: 8/15; financial award applicants required to submit FAFSA. *Unit head:* Abbe Miller, Director, 203-773-8543, Fax: 203-773-3117, E-mail: amiller@albertus.edu. *Application contact:* Dr. Sean O'Connell, Interim Vice President for Academic Affairs, 203-777-8539, Fax: 203-777-3701, E-mail: soconnell@albertus.edu.

Athabasca University, Graduate Centre for Applied Psychology, Athabasca, AB T9S 3A3, Canada. Offers art therapy (MC); career counseling (MC); counseling (Advanced Certificate); counseling psychology (MC); school counseling (MC).

Caldwell University, Graduate Studies, Department of Psychology, Caldwell, NJ 07006-6195. Offers art therapy (MA); counseling (MA), including art therapy, mental health, school counseling; director of school counseling (Post-Master's Certificate); professional counselor (Post-Master's Certificate); school counselor (Post-Master's Certificate). *Accreditation:* ACA. Part-time and evening/weekend programs available. *Faculty:* 6 full-time (4 women), 13 part-time/adjunct (8 women). *Students:* 64 full-time (62 women), 70 part-time (62 women); includes 31 minority (14 Black or African American, non-Hispanic/Latino; 2 Asian, non-Hispanic/Latino; 12 Hispanic/Latino; 3 Two or more races, non-Hispanic/Latino). Average age 34. 83 applicants, 35% accepted, 29 enrolled. In 2014, 64 master's awarded. *Degree requirements:* For master's, comprehensive exam. *Entrance requirements:* For master's, GRE or MAT, interview. *Application deadline:* For fall admission, 7/1 for domestic and international students; for spring admission, 12/1 for domestic and international students. Applications are processed on a rolling basis. Application fee: $40. Electronic applications accepted. *Expenses: Tuition:* Part-time $930 per credit. *Financial support:* Career-related internships or fieldwork available. Financial award applicants required to submit FAFSA. *Faculty research:* Counseling, school counseling, art therapy. *Unit head:* Dr. Stacey Solomon, Program Coordinator, 973-618-3387, E-mail: ssolomon@caldwell.edu. *Application contact:* Vilma Mueller, Director of Graduate Studies, 973-618-3544, E-mail: graduate@caldwell.edu.

California Institute of Integral Studies, School of Professional Psychology and Health, San Francisco, CA 94103. Offers clinical psychology (Psy D); community mental health (MA); drama therapy (MA); expressive arts therapy (MA); integral counseling psychology (MA); integrative health studies (MA); psychological studies (MA); somatic psychology (MA). *Accreditation:* APA. Part-time and evening/weekend programs available. *Students:* 522 full-time (397 women), 105 part-time (83 women); includes 155 minority (27 Black or African American, non-Hispanic/Latino; 3 American Indian or Alaska Native, non-Hispanic/Latino; 31 Asian, non-Hispanic/Latino; 62 Hispanic/Latino; 3 Native Hawaiian or other Pacific Islander, non-Hispanic/Latino; 29 Two or more races, non-Hispanic/Latino), 49 international. Average age 34. 351 applicants, 86% accepted, 175 enrolled. In 2014, 168 master's, 24 doctorates awarded. *Degree requirements:* For doctorate, comprehensive exam, thesis/dissertation. *Entrance requirements:* For master's, minimum GPA of 3.0, letters of recommendation, writing sample; for doctorate, GRE, MA in psychology or social work with appropriate practical experience for advanced standing, or BA with a minimum GPA of 3.1; letters of recommendation; writing sample. Additional exam requirements/recommendations for international students: Required—TOEFL. *Application deadline:* For fall admission, 2/1 priority date for domestic and international students; for spring admission, 10/15 priority date for domestic and international students. Applications are processed on a rolling basis. Application fee: $65. Electronic applications accepted. *Expenses: Tuition:* Full-time $18,270; part-time $1015 per credit. *Required fees:* $85 per semester hour. *Financial support:* In 2014–15, 464 students received support, including 5 research assistantships with tuition reimbursements available (averaging $800 per year), 36 teaching assistantships with tuition reimbursements available (averaging $825 per year); career-related internships or fieldwork, Federal Work-Study, and scholarships/grants also available. Support available to part-time students. Financial award application deadline: 4/15; financial award applicants required to submit FAFSA. *Faculty research:* Transpersonal psychology, somatic psychology, expressive arts therapy, drama therapy, community mental health, ecopsychology, integrative health. *Application contact:* David Townes, Senior Admissions Counselor, 415-575-6152, Fax: 415-575-1268, E-mail: admissions@ciis.edu.

California State University, Los Angeles, Graduate Studies, College of Arts and Letters, Department of Art, Los Angeles, CA 90032-8530. Offers art (MA), including art education, art history, art therapy, ceramics, metals, and textiles, design (MA, MFA), painting, sculpture, and graphic arts, photography; fine arts (MFA), including crafts, design (MA, MFA), studio arts. *Accreditation:* NASAD (one or more programs are accredited). Part-time and evening/weekend programs available. *Degree requirements:* For master's, comprehensive exam, project or thesis. *Entrance requirements:* For master's, portfolio. Additional exam requirements/recommendations for international students: Required—TOEFL (minimum score 500 paper-based). Electronic applications accepted. *Expenses:* Tuition, state resident: full-time $6738; part-time $3609 per year. Tuition, nonresident: full-time $15,666; part-time $8073 per year. Tuition and fees vary according to course load, degree level and program. *Faculty research:* The artist and the book, conceptual art, ceramic processes, computer graphics, architectural graphics.

Cedar Crest College, Program in Art Therapy, Allentown, PA 18104-6196. Offers MA. Evening/weekend programs available. Postbaccalaureate distance learning degree programs offered (no on-campus study). *Faculty:* 2 full-time (both women), 3 part-time/adjunct (all women). *Students:* 17 full-time (all women), 3 part-time (all women). *Unit head:* Rebecca Arnold, Director, 610-437-4471 Ext. 3594, E-mail: rarnold@cedarcrest.edu. *Application contact:* Mary Ellen Hickes, Director of School of Adult and Graduate Education, 610-437-4471, E-mail: sage@cedarcrest.edu.
Website: http://sage.cedarcrest.edu/graduate/master-of-arts-in-art-therapy/

The College of New Rochelle, Graduate School, Division of Art and Communication Studies, Program in Art Therapy, New Rochelle, NY 10805-2308. Offers art therapy (MS); art therapy/counseling (MS). Part-time and evening/weekend programs available. *Degree requirements:* For master's, thesis, practicum, fieldwork, internship. *Entrance requirements:* For master's, 12 credits in psychology, portfolio. *Expenses: Tuition:* Part-time $894 per credit. *Required fees:* $325 per semester. *Faculty research:* Phototherapy, assessment and evaluation, developmental stages in art, creativity and mental illness.

Concordia University, School of Graduate Studies, Faculty of Fine Arts, Department of Creative Arts Therapies, Montréal, QC H3G 1M8, Canada. Offers MA.

Drexel University, College of Nursing and Health Professions, Department of Creative Arts Therapies, Specialization in Art Therapy, Philadelphia, PA 19104-2875. Offers MA, PMC. *Accreditation:* NASAD. *Degree requirements:* For master's, comprehensive exam, thesis. *Entrance requirements:* For master's, GRE General Test or MAT, interview, minimum GPA of 2.75, portfolio. Electronic applications accepted.

Eastern Virginia Medical School, Graduate Art Therapy and Counseling Program, Norfolk, VA 23501-1980. Offers MS. *Degree requirements:* For master's, thesis, internship. *Entrance requirements:* For master's, 12 credit hours in psychology, including abnormal and developmental; 18 credit hours in studio art; face-to-face interview; portfolio (diverse media preferred). Electronic applications accepted. *Expenses:* Contact institution.

Edinboro University of Pennsylvania, Department of Counseling, School Psychology and Special Education, Edinboro, PA 16444. Offers counseling (MA), including art therapy, clinical mental health counseling, college counseling, rehabilitation counseling, school counseling; educational psychology (M Ed); school psychology (Ed S); special education (M Ed), including autism, behavior management. Part-time and evening/weekend programs available. *Degree requirements:* For master's, thesis or alternative, competency exam; for Ed S, thesis or alternative. *Entrance requirements:* For master's and Ed S, GRE or MAT, minimum QPA of 2.5. Electronic applications accepted.

Emporia State University, Program in Art Therapy, Emporia, KS 66801-5415. Offers MS. *Accreditation:* NASAD. Part-time programs available. *Students:* 24 full-time (22 women), 9 part-time (6 women); includes 3 minority (1 American Indian or Alaska Native, non-Hispanic/Latino; 2 Hispanic/Latino), 3 international. 12 applicants, 92% accepted, 11 enrolled. In 2014, 7 master's awarded. *Degree requirements:* For master's, comprehensive exam or thesis, internship. *Entrance requirements:* For master's, GRE General Test or MAT, essay exam, appropriate bachelor's degree. Additional exam requirements/recommendations for international students: Required—TOEFL (minimum score 520 paper-based; 68 iBT). *Application deadline:* For fall admission, 6/1 for domestic students; for spring admission, 10/1 for domestic students. Applications are processed on a rolling basis. Application fee: $30 ($75 for international students). Electronic applications accepted. *Expenses:* Tuition, state resident: part-time $227 per credit hour. Tuition, nonresident: part-time $706 per credit hour. *Required fees:* $75 per credit hour. Tuition and fees vary according to campus/location. *Financial support:* Career-related internships or fieldwork, Federal Work-Study, institutionally sponsored loans, health care benefits, and unspecified assistantships available. Financial award application deadline: 3/15; financial award applicants required to submit FAFSA. *Unit head:* Dr. James Costello, Chair, 620-341-5791, E-mail: jcostell@emporia.edu. *Application contact:* Mary Sewell, Admissions Coordinator, 800-950-GRAD, Fax: 620-341-5909, E-mail: msewell@emporia.edu.

The George Washington University, Columbian College of Arts and Sciences, Program in Art Therapy, Washington, DC 20052. Offers MA, Graduate Certificate. *Faculty:* 5 full-time (all women). *Students:* 48 full-time (47 women), 21 part-time (19 women); includes 17 minority (6 Black or African American, non-Hispanic/Latino; 7 Asian, non-Hispanic/Latino; 3 Hispanic/Latino; 1 Two or more races, non-Hispanic/Latino), 5 international. Average age 28. 70 applicants, 66% accepted, 27 enrolled. In 2014, 29 master's awarded. *Degree requirements:* For master's, internship, practicum paper. *Entrance requirements:* For master's, GRE General Test, interview, minimum GPA of 3.0; for Graduate Certificate, interview, minimum GPA of 3.0. Additional exam requirements/recommendations for international students: Required—TOEFL (minimum score 550 paper-based; 80 iBT). *Application deadline:* For fall admission, 1/1 priority date for domestic students. Application fee: $75. *Financial support:* In 2014–15, 11 students received support. Fellowships with partial tuition reimbursements available, career-related internships or fieldwork, Federal Work-Study, institutionally sponsored loans, and tuition waivers available. *Unit head:* Heidi Bardot, Director, 202-994-4148, E-mail: hbardot@gwu.edu. *Application contact:* Information Contact, 202-994-6285, Fax: 202-994-1404, E-mail: artx@gwu.edu.
Website: http://arttherapy.columbian.gwu.edu/program-options

Georgia College & State University, Graduate School, College of Health Sciences, Program in Art Therapy, Milledgeville, GA 31061. Offers MA. *Students:* 11 full-time (all women), 1 (woman) part-time; includes 2 minority (1 Black or African American, non-Hispanic/Latino; 1 Hispanic/Latino). Average age 32. 5 applicants, 100% accepted, 4 enrolled. *Degree requirements:* For master's, comprehensive exam, thesis or alternative, minimum GPA of 3.0. *Entrance requirements:* For master's, GRE or MAT, art portfolio, 3 letters of recommendation, minimum GPA of 2.75. *Application deadline:* For fall admission, 1/1 for domestic students; for spring admission, 11/15 for domestic students; for summer admission, 3/1 for domestic students. Application fee: $40. Electronic applications accepted. *Expenses: Tuition, area resident:* Part-time $283 per credit hour. Tuition, nonresident: part-time $1027 per credit hour. *Required fees:* $995 per semester. Full-time tuition and fees vary according to course load, degree level, campus/location and program. *Financial support:* In 2014–15, 1 research assistantship was awarded. Financial award applicants required to submit FAFSA. *Unit head:* Dr. Patrick Varallo, Director of Art Therapy Graduatete Program, 478-445-2646, Fax: 478-445-4532, E-mail: patrick.varallo@gcsu.edu. *Application contact:* Kate Marshall, Graduate Admissions Coordinator, 478-445-1184, Fax: 478-445-1336, E-mail: grad-admit@gcsu.edu.

Hofstra University, School of Health Sciences and Human Services, Programs in Counseling, Hempstead, NY 11549. Offers counseling (MS Ed, PD); creative arts therapy (MA); interdisciplinary transition specialist (Advanced Certificate); marriage and family therapy (MA); mental health counseling (MA); rehabilitation administration (PD); rehabilitation counseling (MS Ed, Advanced Certificate); rehabilitation counseling in mental health (MS Ed, Advanced Certificate); school counselor bilingual extension (Advanced Certificate). Part-time and evening/weekend programs available. *Students:* 138 full-time (128 women), 54 part-time (51 women); includes 53 minority (24 Black or African American, non-Hispanic/Latino; 1 American Indian or Alaska Native, non-Hispanic/Latino; 9 Asian, non-Hispanic/Latino; 18 Hispanic/Latino; 1 Two or more races, non-Hispanic/Latino), 6 international. Average age 30. 117 applicants, 83% accepted, 57 enrolled. In 2014, 72 master's, 4 other advanced degrees awarded. *Degree requirements:* For master's, comprehensive exam (for some programs), thesis (for some programs), internship, practicum, student teaching, seminars, minimum GPA of 3.0. *Entrance requirements:* For master's, GRE, interview, letters of recommendation, portfolio, essay, professional experience, certification; for other advanced degree, GRE, interview, letters of recommendation, essay, professional experience, resume, master's degree. Additional exam requirements/recommendations for international students: Required—TOEFL (minimum score 550 paper-based; 80 iBT). *Application deadline:* Applications are processed on a rolling basis. Application fee: $70 ($75 for international students). Electronic applications accepted. *Expenses: Tuition:* Full-time $20,610; part-time $1145 per credit hour. *Required fees:* $970; $165 per term. Tuition and fees vary according to program. *Financial support:* In 2014–15, 109 students received support, including 29 fellowships with full and partial tuition reimbursements available (averaging $3,381 per year), 4 research assistantships with full and partial tuition reimbursements available (averaging $7,324 per year); career-related internships or fieldwork, Federal Work-Study, institutionally sponsored loans, scholarships/grants, health care benefits, and tuition waivers (full and partial) also available. Support available to part-time students. Financial award applicants required to submit FAFSA. *Faculty research:* Bereavement, loss, and trauma counseling; conflict transformation, the impact of hope on academic success; student persistence; GLBTQ issues. *Unit head:* Dr. Holly Seirup, Chairperson, 516-463-5752, Fax: 516-463-6184, E-mail: vpshjs@hofstra.edu. *Application contact:* Sunil Samuel, Assistant Vice President of Admissions, 516-463-4723, Fax: 516-463-4664, E-mail: graduateadmission@hofstra.edu.
Website: http://www.hofstra.edu/academics/colleges/healthscienceshumanservices/

Lesley University, Graduate School of Arts and Social Sciences, Cambridge, MA 02138-2790. Offers clinical mental health counseling (MA), including holistic counseling, school and community counseling, trauma studies; counseling psychology (MA, CAGS), including professional counseling (MA), school counseling (MA); creative writing (MFA); expressive therapies (MA, PhD, CAGS), including art (MA), clinical mental health counseling (MA), dance (MA), expressive therapies (MA), music (MA); independent studies (CAGS); independent study (MA); intercultural relations (MA, CAGS); interdisciplinary studies (MA), including individualized studies, integrative holistic health, mindfulness studies, peace and conflict transformation, trauma sensitive assessment, intervention, and consultation, women's studies; urban environmental leadership (MA). Part-time programs available. Postbaccalaureate distance learning degree programs offered (no on-campus study). *Faculty:* 35 full-time (25 women), 115 part-time/adjunct (90 women). *Students:* 420 full-time (379 women), 514 part-time (414 women); includes 142 minority (50 Black or African American, non-Hispanic/Latino; 5 American Indian or Alaska Native, non-Hispanic/Latino; 16 Asian, non-Hispanic/Latino; 48 Hispanic/Latino; 23 Two or more races, non-Hispanic/Latino), 46 international. Average age 33. In 2014, 475 master's, 11 doctorates, 4 other advanced degrees awarded. *Degree requirements:* For master's, internship, practicum, thesis (for expressive therapies); for doctorate, thesis/dissertation, arts apprenticeship, field placement; for CAGS, thesis, internship (for counseling psychology, expressive therapies). *Entrance requirements:* For master's, MAT (counseling psychology), interview, writing samples, art portfolio; for doctorate, GRE or MAT, interview, master's degree; for CAGS, interview, master's degree. Additional exam requirements/recommendations for international students: Required—TOEFL (minimum score 550 paper-based; 80 iBT). *Application deadline:* Applications are processed on a rolling basis. Application fee: $50. Electronic applications accepted. *Financial support:* Fellowships, career-related internships or fieldwork, Federal Work-Study, scholarships/grants, tuition waivers, and unspecified assistantships available. Financial award applicants required to submit FAFSA. *Faculty research:* Psychotherapy and culture; psychotherapy and psychological trauma; women's issues in art, teaching and psychotherapy; community-based art, psycho-spiritual inquiry. *Unit head:* Dr. Catherine Koverola, Dean, 617-349-8317, Fax: 617-349-8366, E-mail: koverola@lesley.edu. *Application contact:* Martha Sheehan, Director, Graduate Admissions, 888-LESLEYU, Fax: 617-349-8313, E-mail: info@lesley.edu.
Website: http://www.lesley.edu/graduate-school-of-arts-and-social-sciences/

Marylhurst University, Department of Art Therapy Counseling, Marylhurst, OR 97036-0261. Offers art therapy (PGC); art therapy counseling (MA); counseling (PGC). Part-time programs available. *Students:* 38 full-time (35 women), 2 part-time (both women); includes 4 minority (3 Hispanic/Latino; 1 Two or more races, non-Hispanic/Latino). In 2014, 9 master's awarded. *Degree requirements:* For master's, comprehensive exam, practica. *Entrance requirements:* For master's, MAT, transcripts from all previous institutions attended, minimum undergraduate GPA of 3.0, letters of recommendation, course work in psychology and art, art portfolio, resume, autobiography. Additional exam requirements/recommendations for international students: Required—TOEFL (minimum score 550 paper-based; 79 iBT), IELTS (minimum score 6.5), PTE (minimum score 53). *Application deadline:* For fall admission, 1/31 priority date for domestic and international students. Applications are processed on a rolling basis. Application fee: $50. Electronic applications accepted. *Expenses:* Expenses: Contact institution. *Financial support:* Scholarships/grants available. Support available to part-time students. Financial award applicants required to submit FAFSA. *Faculty research:* Scientific approaches to art therapy research, child and adolescent psychotherapy, multicultural counseling. *Unit head:* Christine Turner, Chair, 503-636-8141, Fax: 503-636-9526, E-mail: cturner@marylhurst.edu. *Application contact:* Maruska Lynch, Graduate Admissions Counselor, 800-634-9982 Ext. 6322, Fax: 503-699-6320, E-mail: admissions@marylhurst.edu.
Website: http://marylhurst.edu/academics/schools-colleges-departments/art-music-creative-art-therapies/art-therapy-counseling/ma-art-therapy.html

Marywood University, Academic Affairs, Insalaco College of Creative and Performing Arts, Art Department, Program in Art Therapy, Scranton, PA 18509-1598. Offers MA, Graduate Certificate. *Accreditation:* NASAD. Part-time programs available. *Students:* 22 full-time (19 women), 2 part-time (both women); includes 4 minority (1 Black or African American, non-Hispanic/Latino; 2 Hispanic/Latino; 1 Two or more races, non-Hispanic/Latino), 1 international. Average age 28. In 2014, 4 master's awarded. *Application deadline:* For fall admission, 4/1 for domestic students, 3/31 for international students; for spring admission, 11/1 for domestic students, 8/31 for international students. Applications are processed on a rolling basis. Application fee: $35. Electronic applications accepted. *Expenses: Tuition:* Part-time $775 per credit. *Required fees:* $688 per semester. Tuition and fees vary according to degree level and campus/location. *Financial support:* Application deadline: 6/30; applicants required to submit FAFSA. *Unit head:* Matthew Povse, Chair, 570-348-6211 Ext. 2476, E-mail: povse@marywood.edu. *Application contact:* Tammy Manka, Assistant Director of Graduate Admissions, 570-348-6211 Ext. 2322, E-mail: tmanka@marywood.edu.
Website: http://www.marywood.edu/art/graduate-programs/master-art-therapy.html

Mount Mary University, Graduate Division, Program in Art Therapy, Milwaukee, WI 53222-4597. Offers MS, DAT. Part-time and evening/weekend programs available. *Faculty:* 4 full-time (2 women), 12 part-time/adjunct (11 women). *Students:* 64 full-time (62 women), 17 part-time (13 women); includes 6 minority (2 Black or African American, non-Hispanic/Latino; 1 Asian, non-Hispanic/Latino; 1 Hispanic/Latino; 2 Two or more races, non-Hispanic/Latino). Average age 32. 76 applicants, 63% accepted, 20 enrolled. In 2014, 33 master's, 4 doctorates awarded. *Degree requirements:* For master's, thesis or alternative, internship; for doctorate, culminating project and pre-graduation defense. *Entrance requirements:* For master's, minimum GPA of 3.0; for doctorate, minimum GPA of 3.5. Additional exam requirements/recommendations for international students: Required—TOEFL (minimum score 550 paper-based, 80 iBT) or IELTS (minimum score 6.5). *Application deadline:* For fall admission, 10/31 priority date for domestic and international students; for summer admission, 3/15 for domestic and international students. Application fee: $50 ($0 for international students). Electronic applications accepted. *Expenses:* Expenses: Contact institution. *Financial support:* Career-related internships or fieldwork, Federal Work-Study, and unspecified assistantships available. Support available to part-time students. Financial award application deadline: 5/1; financial award applicants required to submit FAFSA. *Faculty research:* Art-based research in art therapy, consensus-group supervision, art therapy in public school programs. *Unit head:* Dr. Chris Belkofer, Graduate Program Director, 414-258-4810 Ext. 489, E-mail: belkofec@mtmary.edu. *Application contact:* Dr. Douglas J. Mickelson, Dean for Graduate Education, 414-256-1252, Fax: 414-256-0167, E-mail: mickelsd@mtmary.edu.
Website: http://www.mtmary.edu/majors-programs/graduate/art-therapy/

Naropa University, Graduate Programs, Program in Transpersonal Counseling Psychology, Concentration in Art Therapy, Boulder, CO 80302-6697. Offers MA. *Faculty:* 10 full-time (6 women), 26 part-time/adjunct (19 women). *Students:* 50 full-time (49 women), 2 part-time (both women); includes 8 minority (4 Hispanic/Latino; 4 Two or more races, non-Hispanic/Latino), 1 international. Average age 30. 52 applicants, 50% accepted, 20 enrolled. In 2014, 16 master's awarded. *Degree requirements:* For master's, internships, 180 direct art contact hours of studio-based work, counseling practicum. *Entrance requirements:* For master's, visual art portfolio, in-person interview, course work in psychology and art, transcripts, resume, letter of interest, 2 letters of recommendation. Additional exam requirements/recommendations for international students: Required—TOEFL (minimum score 600 paper-based; 80 iBT). *Application deadline:* For fall admission, 1/15 priority date for domestic and international students.

Art Therapy

Applications are processed on a rolling basis. Application fee: $60. Electronic applications accepted. *Expenses: Tuition:* Full-time $23,400; part-time $975 per credit. *Required fees:* $335 per semester. Tuition and fees vary according to course load. *Financial support:* In 2014–15, 22 students received support, including 2 research assistantships with partial tuition reimbursements available (averaging $6,125 per year); career-related internships or fieldwork, scholarships/grants, tuition waivers (partial), and unspecified assistantships also available. Support available to part-time students. Financial award application deadline: 3/1; financial award applicants required to submit FAFSA. *Unit head:* Dr. Deborah Bowman, Dean, Graduate School of Psychology, 303-546-3559, E-mail: bowman@naropa.edu. *Application contact:* Office of Admissions, 303-546-3572, Fax: 303-546-3583, E-mail: admissions@naropa.edu.
Website: http://www.naropa.edu/academics/gsp/grad/transpersonal-counseling-psychology-ma/art-therapy/index.php

Nazareth College of Rochester, Graduate Studies, Department of Creative Arts Therapy, Program in Art Therapy, Rochester, NY 14618-3790. Offers MS. Part-time programs available. *Entrance requirements:* For master's, minimum GPA of 3.0, portfolio review.

New York University, Steinhardt School of Culture, Education, and Human Development, Department of Art and Art Professions, Program in Art Therapy, New York, NY 10003. Offers MA. Part-time programs available. *Faculty:* 1 (woman) full-time. *Students:* 41 full-time (40 women), 9 part-time (8 women); includes 9 minority (2 Black or African American, non-Hispanic/Latino; 2 Asian, non-Hispanic/Latino; 4 Hispanic/Latino; 1 Two or more races, non-Hispanic/Latino), 9 international. Average age 29. 130 applicants, 23% accepted, 18 enrolled. In 2014, 21 master's awarded. *Degree requirements:* For master's, thesis (for some programs). *Entrance requirements:* For master's, interview, portfolio. Additional exam requirements/recommendations for international students: Required—TOEFL (minimum score 100 iBT). *Application deadline:* For fall admission, 12/1 priority date for domestic and international students. Applications are processed on a rolling basis. Application fee: $75. Electronic applications accepted. *Financial support:* Career-related internships or fieldwork, Federal Work-Study, institutionally sponsored loans, scholarships/grants, and tuition waivers (partial) available. Support available to part-time students. Financial award application deadline: 2/1; financial award applicants required to submit FAFSA. *Faculty research:* Art therapy in non-clinical settings, international art therapy. *Unit head:* Prof. Ikuko Acosta, Director, 212-998-5700, Fax: 212-995-4320, E-mail: ia4@nyu.edu. *Application contact:* 212-998-5030, Fax: 212-995-4328, E-mail: steinhardt.gradadmissions@nyu.edu.
Website: http://steinhardt.nyu.edu/art/therapy

Notre Dame de Namur University, Division of Academic Affairs, College of Arts and Sciences, Program in Art Therapy Psychology, Belmont, CA 94002-1908. Offers art therapy (MA, PhD); marriage and family therapy (MA). Part-time programs available. *Degree requirements:* For master's, thesis, oral presentation, portfolio; for doctorate, thesis/dissertation. *Entrance requirements:* For master's, interview, minimum GPA of 2.5; for doctorate, master's degree from accredited university in art therapy or in a related field; minimum of two years of clinical work in the field; portfolio; three professional recommendations; one published article or scholarly academic writing on an art therapy subject in publication acceptable form; interview. Additional exam requirements/recommendations for international students: Required—TOEFL (minimum score 550 paper-based; 79 iBT). Electronic applications accepted.

Ottawa University, Graduate Studies-Arizona, Program in Professional Counseling, Ottawa, KS 66067-3399. Offers Christian counseling (MA); expressive arts therapy (MA); marriage and family therapy (MA); treatment of trauma, abuse and deprivation (MA). Programs offered in Mesa, Phoenix, Tempe and West Valley, AZ. Part-time and evening/weekend programs available. Postbaccalaureate distance learning degree programs offered. *Degree requirements:* For master's, comprehensive exam, thesis or alternative, field experience, practicum. *Entrance requirements:* For master's, minimum undergraduate GPA of 3.0; course work in theories of personality, abnormal psychology, and human growth and development. Additional exam requirements/recommendations for international students: Required—TOEFL (minimum score 550 paper-based).

Phillips Graduate Institute, Programs in Marriage and Family Therapy and School Counseling, Encino, CA 91316-1509. Offers art therapy (MA); marriage and family therapy (MA); school counseling (MA). Evening/weekend programs available. *Degree requirements:* For master's, comprehensive exam, thesis. *Entrance requirements:* For master's, minimum GPA of 2.5. Electronic applications accepted. *Faculty research:* Integration of interpersonal psychological theory, systems approach, firsthand experiential learning.

Pratt Institute, School of Art and Design, Programs in Creative Arts Therapy, Brooklyn, NY 11205-3899. Offers art therapy and creativity development (MPS); art therapy-special education (MPS); dance/movement therapy (MS). *Accreditation:* NASAD (one or more programs are accredited). Part-time programs available. *Faculty:* 3 full-time (all women), 22 part-time/adjunct (19 women). *Students:* 106 full-time (101 women), 1 (woman) part-time; includes 37 minority (16 Black or African American, non-Hispanic/Latino; 9 Asian, non-Hispanic/Latino; 10 Hispanic/Latino; 2 Two or more races, non-Hispanic/Latino), 8 international. Average age 29. 160 applicants, 46% accepted, 30 enrolled. In 2014, 45 master's awarded. *Degree requirements:* For master's, thesis. *Entrance requirements:* For master's, letters of recommendation, portfolio. Additional exam requirements/recommendations for international students: Required—TOEFL (minimum score 600 paper-based; 100 iBT). *Application deadline:* For fall admission, 1/5 for domestic and international students; for spring admission, 10/1 for domestic and international students. Applications are processed on a rolling basis. Application fee: $50 ($90 for international students). Electronic applications accepted. *Financial support:* Career-related internships or fieldwork, Federal Work-Study, institutionally sponsored loans, scholarships/grants, health care benefits, tuition waivers (full), and unspecified assistantships available. Support available to part-time students. Financial award application deadline: 2/1; financial award applicants required to submit FAFSA. *Faculty research:* Psychology and aesthetic interaction, art therapy and AIDS, art therapy and autism, art diagnosis. *Unit head:* Julie Miller, Chairperson, 718-636-3428, E-mail: jmiller2@pratt.edu. *Application contact:* Young Hah, Director of Graduate Admissions, 718-636-3683, Fax: 718-399-4242, E-mail: yhah@pratt.edu.
Website: https://www.pratt.edu/academics/school-of-art/graduate-school-of-art/creative-arts-therapy/

See Display on page 153 and Close-Up on page 203.

Prescott College, Graduate Programs, Program in Counseling and Psychology, Prescott, AZ 86301. Offers adventure-based psychotherapy (MA); counseling psychology (MA); ecopsychology (MA); ecotherapy (MA); equine-assisted mental health (MA); expressive arts therapy (MA); somatic psychology (MA); student-directed independent study (MA). Part-time programs available. Postbaccalaureate distance learning degree programs offered (minimal on-campus study). *Degree requirements:* For master's, thesis, fieldwork or internship, practicum. *Entrance requirements:* For master's, 2 letters of recommendation, resume. Additional exam requirements/recommendations for international students: Required—TOEFL (minimum score 500 paper-based). Electronic applications accepted.

Saint Mary-of-the-Woods College, Program in Art Therapy, Saint Mary of the Woods, IN 47876. Offers MA, Post-Master's Certificate. Part-time and evening/weekend programs available. Postbaccalaureate distance learning degree programs offered (minimal on-campus study). *Degree requirements:* For master's, thesis or project. *Entrance requirements:* For master's, minimum GPA of 2.5; for Post-Master's Certificate, 12 credit hours in abnormal and developmental psychology, 15 credit hours in studio art skills, art portfolio, interview, minimum GPA of 2.5. Electronic applications accepted.

School of the Art Institute of Chicago, Graduate Division, Program in Art Therapy, Chicago, IL 60603-3103. Offers MAAT. Program offered jointly with Rush University. *Accreditation:* NASAD. *Degree requirements:* For master's, thesis, personal interview. *Entrance requirements:* Additional exam requirements/recommendations for international students: Required—TOEFL, IELTS. *Faculty research:* Migrane, ousider art, community-based practice.

School of Visual Arts, Graduate Programs, Art Therapy Department, New York, NY 10010-3994. Offers MPS. *Degree requirements:* For master's, thesis, 60 credits, including all required courses; minimum cumulative GPA of 3.0; residency of two academic years; internship. *Entrance requirements:* For master's, interview; 18 credits (or equivalent) in studio art and 12 credits in psychology (developmental and abnormal required; courses in introduction to psychology and theories of personality recommended); 15 to 20 digital images on CD. Additional exam requirements/recommendations for international students: Required—TOEFL (minimum score 550 paper-based; 79 iBT). Electronic applications accepted.

Seton Hill University, Program in Art Therapy, Greensburg, PA 15601. Offers MA. Part-time programs available. *Faculty:* 2 full-time (both women), 3 part-time/adjunct (all women). *Students:* 40 full-time (39 women), 15 part-time (all women); includes 5 minority (3 Black or African American, non-Hispanic/Latino; 2 Asian, non-Hispanic/Latino), 2 international. Average age 28. 56 applicants, 61% accepted, 15 enrolled. In 2014, 16 master's awarded. *Entrance requirements:* For master's, portfolio; 3 letters of recommendation; letter of intent; transcripts; writing sample (APA style); resume. Additional exam requirements/recommendations for international students: Required—TOEFL (minimum score 650 paper-based; 114 iBT), IELTS (minimum score 7). *Application deadline:* For fall admission, 7/1 for domestic and international students; for spring admission, 11/30 for domestic and international students. Applications are processed on a rolling basis. Application fee: $0. Electronic applications accepted. *Expenses: Tuition:* Full-time $7362; part-time $818 per credit. *Required fees:* $34 per credit. *Financial support:* In 2014–15, 49 students received support. Federal Work-Study, scholarships/grants, and tuition discounts available. Financial award application deadline: 8/15; financial award applicants required to submit FAFSA. *Faculty research:* Medical art therapy, art-based supervision, self-care for practitioners, participatory action research with undergrads using the PhotoVoice project to research student perceptions of root causes of gender based violence. *Unit head:* Lori Mackey, Director, 724-830-1047, E-mail: lmackey@setonhill.edu. *Application contact:* Lisa Glessner, Program Counselor, 724-830-4209, E-mail: lglessner@setonhill.edu.
Website: http://www.setonhill.edu/academics/graduate_programs/art_therapy

Southern Illinois University Edwardsville, Graduate School, College of Arts and Sciences, Department of Art and Design, Program in Art Therapy Counseling, Edwardsville, IL 62026-0001. Offers MA. Part-time programs available. *Students:* 16 full-time (all women), 13 part-time (12 women); includes 2 minority (both Asian, non-Hispanic/Latino). 20 applicants, 55% accepted. In 2014, 8 master's awarded. *Degree requirements:* For master's, thesis or alternative, project. *Entrance requirements:* For master's, MAT, portfolio. Additional exam requirements/recommendations for international students: Required—TOEFL (minimum score 550 paper-based; 79 iBT), IELTS (minimum score 6.5). *Application deadline:* For fall admission, 2/1 for domestic and international students. Application fee: $30. Electronic applications accepted. *Expenses:* Tuition, state resident: full-time $5026. Tuition, nonresident: full-time $12,566. International tuition: $25,136 full-time. *Required fees:* $1682. Tuition and fees vary according to course load, campus/location and program. *Financial support:* In 2014–15, 10 students received support, including 1 fellowship with full tuition reimbursement available (averaging $8,370 per year), 3 research assistantships with full tuition reimbursements available, 6 teaching assistantships with full tuition reimbursements available; career-related internships or fieldwork, scholarships/grants, and unspecified assistantships also available. Financial award application deadline: 3/1; financial award applicants required to submit FAFSA. *Unit head:* Dr. Shelly Goebl-Parker, Program Director, 618-650-3183, E-mail: egoeblp@siue.edu. *Application contact:* Melissa K. Mace, Assistant Director of Admissions for Graduate and International Recruitment, 618-650-2756, Fax: 618-650-3618, E-mail: mmace@siue.edu.
Website: http://www.siue.edu/artsandsciences/art/arttherapy/

Southwestern College, Program in Art Therapy/Counseling, Santa Fe, NM 87502-4788. Offers MA. Part-time and evening/weekend programs available. *Degree requirements:* For master's, internship. *Entrance requirements:* For master's, resume, slide portfolio, interview, 3 letters of reference. Additional exam requirements/recommendations for international students: Required—TOEFL.

Springfield College, Graduate Programs, Program in Art Therapy, Springfield, MA 01109-3797. Offers M Ed, MS, CAGS. Part-time programs available. *Faculty:* 2 full-time (1 woman), 9 part-time/adjunct (8 women). *Students:* 28. Average age 30. 36 applicants, 72% accepted, 9 enrolled. In 2014, 6 master's, 1 other advanced degree awarded. *Degree requirements:* For master's, research project, final art exhibition. *Entrance requirements:* For master's, portfolio. Additional exam requirements/recommendations for international students: Required—TOEFL (minimum score 550 paper-based). *Application deadline:* For fall admission, 7/15 for domestic and international students; for winter admission, 11/1 for domestic and international students; for spring admission, 11/1 for domestic and international students. Applications are processed on a rolling basis. Application fee: $50. Electronic applications accepted. *Financial support:* Fellowships with partial tuition reimbursements, teaching assistantships with partial tuition reimbursements, career-related internships or fieldwork, Federal Work-Study, institutionally sponsored loans, and unspecified assistantships available. Financial award application deadline: 3/1; financial award applicants required to submit FAFSA. *Faculty research:* Stage development in art, psychopathology of expression, art history and art therapy. *Unit head:* Dr. Simone Alter-Muri, Director, 413-748-3752, E-mail: saltermuri@spfldcol.edu. *Application contact:* Evelyn Cohen, Director of Graduate Admissions, 413-748-3225, Fax: 413-748-3694, E-mail: ecohen@springfieldcollege.edu.

University of Maryland, College Park, Academic Affairs, College of Education, Department of Counseling, Higher Education and Special Education, College Park, MD 20742. Offers college student personnel (M Ed, MA); college student personnel administration (PhD); community counseling (CAGS); community/career counseling (M Ed, MA); counseling and personnel services (M Ed, MA, PhD), including art therapy (M Ed), college student personnel (M Ed), counseling and personnel services (PhD), counseling psychology (M Ed), mental health counseling (M Ed), school counseling (M Ed); counseling psychology (PhD); counselor education (PhD); rehabilitation counseling (M Ed, MA, AGSC); school counseling (M Ed, MA); school psychology

(M Ed, MA, PhD). *Accreditation:* ACA (one or more programs are accredited); APA (one or more programs are accredited); NCATE. Part-time and evening/weekend programs available. Postbaccalaureate distance learning degree programs offered (no on-campus study). *Degree requirements:* For master's, thesis (for some programs); for doctorate, thesis/dissertation. *Entrance requirements:* For master's, GRE General Test or MAT, minimum GPA of 3.0, 3 letters of recommendation; for doctorate, GRE General Test or MAT, minimum GPA of 3.5, 3 letters of recommendation. Additional exam requirements/recommendations for international students: Required—TOEFL. Electronic applications accepted. *Faculty research:* Educational psychology, counseling, health.

University of Wisconsin–Superior, Graduate Division, Department of Visual Arts, Superior, WI 54880-4500. Offers art education (MA); art history (MA); art therapy (MA); studio arts (MA). Part-time programs available. *Degree requirements:* For master's, comprehensive exam, exhibit. *Entrance requirements:* For master's, minimum GPA of 2.75, portfolio. Electronic applications accepted.

Ursuline College, School of Graduate Studies, Program in Art Therapy Counseling, Pepper Pike, OH 44124-4398. Offers MA. Part-time programs available. *Faculty:* 5 full-time (all women), 7 part-time/adjunct (6 women). *Students:* 40 full-time (39 women), 49 part-time (48 women); includes 12 minority (2 Black or African American, non-Hispanic/Latino; 2 American Indian or Alaska Native, non-Hispanic/Latino; 4 Hispanic/Latino; 4 Two or more races, non-Hispanic/Latino), 1 international. Average age 29. 42 applicants, 79% accepted, 20 enrolled. In 2014, 25 master's awarded. *Degree requirements:* For master's, thesis, 700-hour internship. *Entrance requirements:* For master's, BA in psychology, social sciences, or related field; minimum undergraduate GPA of 3.0; portfolio; work experience with human service agency. Additional exam requirements/recommendations for international students: Required—TOEFL (minimum score 500 paper-based). *Application deadline:* For fall admission, 8/1 priority date for domestic students. Applications are processed on a rolling basis. Application fee: $25. *Financial support:* In 2014–15, 12 students received support. Federal Work-Study available. Financial award application deadline: 3/1; financial award applicants required to submit FAFSA. *Faculty research:* Art therapy used with psychiatric and geriatric populations, art therapy used in treatment of chemical dependency, family therapy, child art therapy. *Unit head:* Gale Rule-Hoffman, Director, 440-646-8138, Fax: 440-684-6135. *Application contact:* Stephanie Pratt, Graduate Admission Coordinator, 440-646-8119, Fax: 440-684-6138, E-mail: graduateadmissions@ursuline.edu.

Wayne State University, College of Education, Division of Teacher Education, Detroit, MI 48202. Offers art education (M Ed); art therapy (M Ed); autism spectrum disorders (Certificate); bilingual/bicultural education (M Ed, Certificate); career and technical education (M Ed, Certificate); cognitive impairment (Certificate); curriculum and instruction (Ed D, PhD, Ed S), including art education (PhD), bilingual education (Ed D, Ed S), bilingual-bicultural education (PhD), career and technical education (MAT, Ed D, PhD, Ed S), early childhood education (MAT, Ed D, PhD, Ed S), elementary education, English as a second language (Ed D, Ed S), English education (MAT, Ed D, PhD, Ed S), foreign language education (MAT, PhD), K-12 curriculum, mathematics education, science education, secondary education, social studies education; early childhood education (M Ed, Certificate); elementary education (M Ed, MAT), including children's literature (MAT), early childhood education (MAT, Ed D, PhD, Ed S), general elementary education (MAT); emotionally impaired (Certificate); English as a second language (Certificate); English education (M Ed); foreign language education (M Ed); K-12 reading specialist (Certificate); learning disabilities (Certificate); mathematics education (M Ed); reading (M Ed, Ed S); reading, language and literature (Ed D); science education (M Ed); secondary education (MAT), including art education (K-12), career and technical education (MAT, Ed D, PhD, Ed S), English education (MAT, Ed D, PhD, Ed S), foreign language education (MAT, PhD), kinesiology; social studies education (M Ed); special education (M Ed, MAT, Ed D, PhD, Ed S); visual arts education (Certificate). Part-time programs available. Postbaccalaureate distance learning degree programs offered. *Faculty:* 36 full-time (25 women), 55 part-time/adjunct (43 women). *Students:* 200 full-time (159 women), 400 part-time (320 women); includes 222 minority (167 Black or African American, non-Hispanic/Latino; 3 American Indian or Alaska Native, non-Hispanic/Latino; 12 Asian, non-Hispanic/Latino; 26 Hispanic/Latino; 1 Native Hawaiian or other Pacific Islander, non-Hispanic/Latino; 13 Two or more races, non-Hispanic/Latino), 11 international. Average age 37. 239 applicants, 41% accepted, 70 enrolled. In 2014, 203 master's, 8 doctorates, 29 other advanced degrees awarded. *Degree requirements:* For master's, thesis, essay or project (for some M Ed programs), professional field experience (for MAT programs); for doctorate, thesis/dissertation. *Entrance requirements:* For master's, Michigan Test for Teacher Certification (MA in teaching), verification of participation in group work with children and Michigan State Police Criminal Background check; for doctorate, minimum undergraduate GPA of 3.0, graduate 3.5; interview; curriculum vitae; references. Additional exam requirements/recommendations for international students: Required—TOEFL (minimum score 550 paper-based; 79 iBT), TWE (minimum score 5.5), Michigan English Language Assessment Battery (minimum score 85); Recommended—IELTS (minimum score 6.5). *Application deadline:* For fall admission, 6/1 priority date for domestic students, 5/1 priority date for international students; for winter admission, 10/1 priority date for domestic students, 9/1 priority date for international students; for spring admission, 2/1 priority date for domestic students, 1/1 priority date for international students. Applications are processed on a rolling basis. Application fee: $0. Electronic applications accepted. *Expenses:* Tuition, state resident: full-time $10,294; part-time $571.90 per credit hour. Tuition, nonresident: full-time $29,730; part-time $1238.75 per credit hour. *Required fees:* $1365; $43.50 per credit hour. $291.10 per semester. Tuition and fees vary according to course load and program. *Financial support:* In 2014–15, 120 students received support, including 2 fellowships (averaging $14,146 per year); research assistantships with tuition reimbursements available, Federal Work-Study, scholarships/grants, health care benefits, and unspecified assistantships also available. Support available to part-time students. Financial award application deadline: 3/31; financial award applicants required to submit FAFSA. *Faculty research:* Improving students' skill achievement in mathematics, improving elementary children's understanding of informational text, teachers' use of their pedagogical and mathematical knowledge in the interactive work of teaching, the intersection of identity construction in teaching and learning, identifying effective methods of literacy instruction and assessments for bilingual students in elementary language arts classrooms. *Unit head:* Dr. Kathleen Crawford-McKinney, Assistant Dean, 313-577-0122. *Application contact:* Janice Green, Assistant Dean, 313-577-1605, E-mail: jwgreen@wayne.edu. Website: http://coe.wayne.edu/ted/index.php

Decorative Arts

Bard Graduate Center: Decorative Arts, Design History, Material Culture, Graduate Studies, New York, NY 10024-3602. Offers M Phil, MA, PhD. Part-time programs available. *Faculty:* 17 full-time (7 women), 5 part-time/adjunct (4 women). *Students:* 70 full-time (56 women), 13 part-time (all women). 100 applicants, 35% accepted, 21 enrolled. In 2014, 22 master's, 4 doctorates awarded. Terminal master's awarded for partial completion of doctoral program. *Degree requirements:* For master's, one foreign language, internship, qualifying paper; for doctorate, 2 foreign languages, thesis/dissertation, exams. *Entrance requirements:* For master's, GRE General Test, writing sample, 3 letters of recommendation; for doctorate, GRE General Test, master's thesis or equivalent, 3 letters of recommendation. Additional exam requirements/recommendations for international students: Required—TOEFL. *Application deadline:* For fall admission, 1/8 for domestic and international students. Application fee: $70. *Financial support:* Fellowships with tuition reimbursements, research assistantships, teaching assistantships, career-related internships or fieldwork, institutionally sponsored loans, scholarships/grants, traineeships, health care benefits, and unspecified assistantships available. Financial award application deadline: 1/8; financial award applicants required to submit FAFSA. *Faculty research:* English craftsmen; ancient furniture; aesthetics and politics; Art Nouveau jewelry; European sculpture; New York and American material culture; modern design history; early modern Europe; history and theory of museums; comparative medieval material culture (China, Islam, Europe); archaeology, anthropology, and material culture. *Unit head:* Susan Weber, Director, 212-501-3000, Fax: 212-501-3079. *Application contact:* Elena Pinto Simon, Dean, Academic Administration and Student Affairs, 212-501-3057, Fax: 212-501-3065, E-mail: simon@bgc.bard.edu.

See Display on page 167 and Close-Up on page 195.

The New School, Parsons The New School for Design, Program in the History of Decorative Arts and Design, New York, NY 10011. Offers MA. Offered jointly with the Cooper-Hewitt Museum and the Smithsonian Institution. *Accreditation:* NASAD. Part-time programs available. *Degree requirements:* For master's, one foreign language, comprehensive exam or thesis project. *Entrance requirements:* For master's, sample of written work. Additional exam requirements/recommendations for international students: Required—TOEFL (minimum score 580 paper-based; 92 iBT). Electronic applications accepted.

Sotheby's Institute of Art–London, Graduate Programs, London, United Kingdom. Offers art business (MA); contemporary art (MA); contemporary design (MA); East Asian art (MA); fine and decorative art (MA); photography (MA). *Faculty:* 38 full-time (22 women). *Students:* 175 full-time (153 women). *Application contact:* Melba Remice, Director, Global Admissions, 212-517-2834, E-mail: admissions@sothebysinstitute.com.

Sotheby's Institute of Art–New York, Graduate Programs, New York, NY 10021. Offers American fine and decorative art (MA); art business (MA); contemporary art (MA). *Accreditation:* NASAD. *Faculty:* 25 full-time (12 women). *Students:* 153 full-time (141 women). *Entrance requirements:* For master's, academic transcripts, two letters of academic reference, personal statement, writing sample, curriculum vitae/resume, interview. Application fee: $100. Electronic applications accepted. *Application contact:* Melba Remice, Director of Global Admissions, 212-517-2834, E-mail: admissions@sothebysinstitute.com. Website: http://www.sothebysinstitute.com/Programmes/PNewyork.aspx

Museum Studies

American Museum of Natural History–Richard Gilder Graduate School, Program in Comparative Biology, New York, NY 10024. Offers PhD. *Degree requirements:* For doctorate, thesis/dissertation, qualifying examination. *Entrance requirements:* For doctorate, GRE General Test (taken within the past five years); GRE Subject Test (recommended), BA, BS, or equivalent degree from accredited institution; official transcripts; essay;. Additional exam requirements/recommendations for international students: Required—TOEFL (minimum score 600 paper-based; 100 iBT), IELTS (minimum score 7).

Arizona State University at the Tempe campus, College of Liberal Arts and Sciences, School of Human Evolution and Social Change, Tempe, AZ 85287-2402. Offers anthropology (MA, PhD), including anthropology (PhD), archaeology (PhD), bioarchaeology (PhD), evolutionary (PhD), museum studies (MA), sociocultural (PhD); applied mathematics for the life and social sciences (PhD); environmental social science (PhD), including environmental social science, urbanism; global health (MA, PhD), including complex adaptive systems science (PhD), evolutionary global health sciences (PhD), health and culture (PhD), urbanism (PhD); immigration studies (Graduate Certificate). Terminal master's awarded for partial completion of doctoral program. *Degree requirements:* For master's, thesis or alternative, interactive Program of Study (iPOS) submitted before completing 50 percent of required credit hours; for doctorate, comprehensive exam, thesis/dissertation, interactive Program of Study (iPOS) submitted before completing 50 percent of required credit hours. *Entrance requirements:* For master's and doctorate, GRE, minimum GPA of 3.0 or equivalent in last 2 years of

work leading to bachelor's degree. Additional exam requirements/recommendations for international students: Required—TOEFL, IELTS, or PTE. Electronic applications accepted.

Arizona State University at the Tempe campus, Herberger Institute for Design and the Arts, School of Art, Tempe, AZ 85287-1505. Offers art education (MA); art history (MA); ceramics (MFA); design, environment and the arts (PhD), including history, theory and criticism; drawing (MFA); fibers (MFA); intermedia (MFA); metals (MFA); museum studies (MFA); painting (MFA); printmaking (MFA); sculpture (MFA); wood (MFA); MFA/MA. Terminal master's awarded for partial completion of doctoral program. *Degree requirements:* For master's, thesis/exhibition (MFA, MA in art education); interactive Program of Study (iPOS) submitted before completing 50 percent of required credit hours; for doctorate, comprehensive exam, thesis/dissertation, interactive Program of Study (iPOS) submitted before completing 50 percent of required credit hours. *Entrance requirements:* For master's, GRE or MAT, minimum GPA of 3.0 or equivalent in last 2 years of work leading to bachelor's degree; for doctorate, GRE, master's degree in architecture, graphic design, industrial design, interior design, landscape architecture, or art history or equivalent standing; statement of purpose; 3 letters of recommendation; indication of potential faculty mentor; sample of written work. Additional exam requirements/recommendations for international students: Required—TOEFL, IELTS, or PTE. Electronic applications accepted.

Bard College, Center for Curatorial Studies, Annandale-on-Hudson, NY 12504. Offers MA. *Degree requirements:* For master's, thesis, exhibition. *Entrance requirements:* For master's, exhibition review, 3 letters of recommendation. Additional exam requirements/recommendations for international students: Required—TOEFL (minimum score 550 paper-based). Electronic applications accepted. *Expenses:* Contact institution. *Faculty research:* Contemporary art, history of exhibition, curatorial practice.

Baylor University, Graduate School, College of Arts and Sciences, Department of Museum Studies, Waco, TX 76798. Offers MA. *Degree requirements:* For master's, comprehensive exam, thesis or alternative. *Entrance requirements:* For master's, GRE General Test. Electronic applications accepted. *Faculty research:* Paleontology/archaeology, preservation.

Boston University, Graduate School of Arts and Sciences, Department of History of Art and Architecture, Boston, MA 02215. Offers art history (MA, PhD); museum studies (Certificate). *Students:* 58 full-time (54 women), 6 part-time (4 women); includes 10 minority (3 Black or African American, non-Hispanic/Latino; 3 Asian, non-Hispanic/Latino; 2 Hispanic/Latino; 2 Two or more races, non-Hispanic/Latino), 4 international. Average age 32. 188 applicants, 32% accepted, 12 enrolled. In 2014, 13 master's, 4 doctorates awarded. Terminal master's awarded for partial completion of doctoral program. *Degree requirements:* For master's, one foreign language, comprehensive exam, thesis; for doctorate, 2 foreign languages, comprehensive exam, thesis/dissertation. *Entrance requirements:* For master's and doctorate, GRE General Test, 3 letters of recommendation, writing sample, foreign language proficiency; for Certificate, GRE General Test. Additional exam requirements/recommendations for international students: Required—TOEFL (minimum score 550 paper-based; 84 iBT). *Application deadline:* For fall admission, 1/5 for domestic and international students; for spring admission, 10/15 for domestic and international students. Application fee: $80. *Expenses:* Tuition: Full-time $45,686; part-time $1428 per credit hour. *Required fees:* $660; $60 per semester. Tuition and fees vary according to program. *Financial support:* In 2014–15, 49 students received support, including 13 fellowships with full tuition reimbursements available (averaging $20,500 per year), 7 teaching assistantships with full tuition reimbursements available (averaging $20,500 per year), career-related internships or fieldwork, Federal Work-Study, health care benefits, and unspecified assistantships also available. Support available to part-time students. Financial award application deadline: 1/5. *Unit head:* Bruce Redford, Chairman, 617-353-1455, Fax: 617-353-3243, E-mail: bredford@bu.edu. *Application contact:* Cheryl Crombie, Administrative Assistant, 617-353-2522, Fax: 617-353-3243, E-mail: ccrombie@bu.edu. Website: http://www.bu.edu/AH/

California College of the Arts, Graduate Programs, Curatorial Practice Program, San Francisco, CA 94107. Offers MA. *Degree requirements:* For master's, thesis, exhibit. *Entrance requirements:* For master's, appropriate bachelor's degree, portfolio, resume, letters of recommendation, transcript. Additional exam requirements/recommendations for international students: Required—TOEFL (minimum score 600 paper-based; 100 iBT). Electronic applications accepted.

California State University, Chico, Office of Graduate Studies, College of Behavioral and Social Sciences, Department of Anthropology, Chico, CA 95929-0722. Offers anthropology (MA); museum studies (MA). *Faculty:* 3 full-time (2 women), 2 part-time/adjunct (1 woman). *Students:* 11 full-time (9 women), 17 part-time (12 women); includes 4 minority (all Hispanic/Latino). Average age 26. 65 applicants, 29% accepted, 9 enrolled. In 2014, 7 master's awarded. *Degree requirements:* For master's, comprehensive exam, thesis, oral examination. *Entrance requirements:* For master's, GRE General Test, two letters of recommendation, statement of purpose, curriculum vitae, writing sample. Additional exam requirements/recommendations for international students: Required—TOEFL (minimum score 550 paper-based; 80 iBT), IELTS (minimum score 6.5), PTE (minimum score 59). *Application deadline:* For fall admission, 1/15 for domestic and international students. Application fee: $55. Electronic applications accepted. *Expenses:* Tuition, state resident: full-time $7002. Tuition, nonresident: full-time $18,162. *Required fees:* $1530. Tuition and fees vary according to program. *Financial support:* Fellowships, career-related internships or fieldwork, institutionally sponsored loans, scholarships/grants, and unspecified assistantships available. Financial award application deadline: 3/1; financial award applicants required to submit FAFSA. *Unit head:* Antoinette Martinez, Chair, 530-898-6192, Fax: 530-898-6143, E-mail: anth@csuchico.edu. *Application contact:* Judy L. Rice, Graduate Admissions Coordinator, 530-898-6880, Fax: 530-898-6889, E-mail: jlrice@csuchico.edu.
Website: http://www.csuchico.edu/anth/

California State University, Fullerton, Graduate Studies, College of the Arts, Department of Visual Arts, Fullerton, CA 92834-9480. Offers art (MA, MFA), including art history (MA), ceramics (MFA), crafts, creative photography, exhibition design, glass, graphic design, illustration, sculpture. *Accreditation:* NASAD (one or more programs are accredited). Part-time programs available. *Students:* 28 full-time (16 women), 29 part-time (22 women); includes 20 minority (3 Black or African American, non-Hispanic/Latino; 8 Asian, non-Hispanic/Latino; 8 Hispanic/Latino; 1 Two or more races, non-Hispanic/Latino), 7 international. Average age 35. 58 applicants, 38% accepted, 14 enrolled. In 2014, 17 master's awarded. *Degree requirements:* For master's, project or thesis. *Entrance requirements:* For master's, minimum GPA of 2.5 in last 60 units of course work, portfolio. Application fee: $55. *Financial support:* Career-related internships or fieldwork, Federal Work-Study, institutionally sponsored loans, and scholarships/grants available. Support available to part-time students. Financial award application deadline: 3/1; financial award applicants required to submit FAFSA. *Unit head:* Dana Lamb, Chair, 657-278-2076. *Application contact:* Admissions/Applications, 657-278-2371.

Caribbean University, Graduate School, Bayamón, PR 00960-0493. Offers administration and supervision (MA Ed); criminal justice (MA); curriculum and instruction (MA Ed, PhD), including elementary education (MA Ed), English education (MA Ed), history education (MA Ed), mathematics education (MA Ed), primary education (MA Ed), science education (MA Ed), Spanish education (MA Ed); educational technology in instructional systems (MA Ed); gerontology (MSN); human resources (MBA); museology, archiving and art history (MA Ed); neonatal pediatrics (MSN); physical education (MA Ed); special education (MA Ed). *Entrance requirements:* For master's, interview, minimum GPA of 2.5.

Case Western Reserve University, School of Graduate Studies, Department of Art History and Art, Program in Art History and Museum Studies, Cleveland, OH 44106. Offers MA. Part-time programs available. *Faculty:* 7 full-time (6 women), 10 part-time/adjunct (6 women). *Students:* 1 (woman) full-time, 5 part-time (all women). Average age 24. 25 applicants, 32% accepted, 1 enrolled. In 2014, 5 master's awarded. *Degree requirements:* For master's, one foreign language, thesis or alternative. *Entrance requirements:* For master's, GRE General Test, 2 samples of written work. Additional exam requirements/recommendations for international students: Required—TOEFL (minimum score 600 paper-based; 100 iBT). *Application deadline:* For fall admission, 1/1 priority date for domestic students. Applications are processed on a rolling basis. Application fee: $50. Electronic applications accepted. *Financial support:* Fellowships, research assistantships, teaching assistantships, career-related internships or fieldwork, and tuition waivers available. Financial award application deadline: 1/1. *Faculty research:* Greek art and architecture, Northern Baroque art, Italian Renaissance and Baroque, abstract expressionism, East Asian art, nineteenth century French art, American and contemporary art. *Unit head:* Catherine Scallen, Chair, 216-368-2383, Fax: 216-368-4681, E-mail: catherine.scallen@case.edu. *Application contact:* Debby Tenenbaum, Assistant, 216-368-4118, Fax: 216-368-4681, E-mail: deborah.tenenbaum@case.edu.
Website: http://arthistory.case.edu/graduate/art-history/

Christie's Education, MA Program in Modern Art and its Markets, New York, NY 10036. Offers MA. Part-time programs available. *Faculty:* 6 full-time (5 women). *Students:* 33 full-time (31 women), 3 part-time (all women). In 2014, 27 master's awarded. *Degree requirements:* For master's, one foreign language, thesis, internship. *Entrance requirements:* For master's, GRE, writing sample, 3 letters of recommendation. Additional exam requirements/recommendations for international students: Required—TOEFL. *Application deadline:* For fall admission, 1/15 priority date for domestic and international students. Applications are processed on a rolling basis. Application fee: $90. *Financial support:* Scholarships/grants and unspecified assistantships available. Financial award applicants required to submit FAFSA. *Unit head:* Dr. Julie Reiss, Director of Studies, 212-355-1501 Ext. 3307, Fax: 212-355-7370, E-mail: jreiss@christies.edu. *Application contact:* Margaret Conklin, Business Manager, 212-355-1501 Ext. 302, Fax: 212-355-7370, E-mail: mconklin@christies.edu.
Website: http://www.christies.edu/new-york/courses/masters-modern-art-markets.aspx

City College of the City University of New York, Graduate School, College of Liberal Arts and Science, Division of the Humanities and Arts, Department of Art, Concentrations in Art History and Museum Studies, New York, NY 10031-9198. Offers art history (MA); museum studies (MA). Part-time programs available. *Degree requirements:* For master's, one foreign language, thesis. *Entrance requirements:* For master's, minimum GPA of 3.0, portfolio, art history paper. Additional exam requirements/recommendations for international students: Required—TOEFL (minimum score 577 paper-based; 90 iBT). Electronic applications accepted. *Faculty research:* Egyptian, Greek, medieval, Romanesque, and Ottoman art.

Claremont Graduate University, Graduate Programs, School of Arts and Humanities, Department of Cultural Studies, Claremont, CA 91711-6160. Offers Africana studies (Certificate); cultural studies (MA, PhD); media studies (MA, PhD); museum studies (MA). Part-time programs available. *Faculty:* 6 full-time (2 women). *Students:* 35 full-time (22 women), 15 part-time (11 women); includes 20 minority (6 Black or African American, non-Hispanic/Latino; 1 American Indian or Alaska Native, non-Hispanic/Latino; 5 Asian, non-Hispanic/Latino; 8 Hispanic/Latino), 7 international. Average age 35. In 2014, 6 master's, 3 doctorates, 1 other advanced degree awarded. *Entrance requirements:* For master's and doctorate, GRE General Test. Additional exam requirements/recommendations for international students: Required—TOEFL (minimum score 550 paper-based; 80 iBT). *Application deadline:* For fall admission, 2/1 priority date for domestic and international students. Applications are processed on a rolling basis. Application fee: $80. Electronic applications accepted. *Expenses: Tuition:* Full-time $41,784; part-time $1741 per credit. *Required fees:* $600; $300 per semester. *Financial support:* Fellowships, research assistantships, Federal Work-Study, institutionally sponsored loans, and scholarships/grants available. Support available to part-time students. Financial award application deadline: 2/15; financial award applicants required to submit FAFSA. *Unit head:* Eve Oishi, Chair, 909-607-7587, E-mail: eve.oishi@cgu.edu. *Application contact:* Amy Sandefur, Assistant Director of Admissions, 909-607-9101, E-mail: amy.sandefur@cgu.edu.
Website: http://www.cgu.edu/pages/441.asp

Cleveland State University, College of Graduate Studies, College of Liberal Arts and Social Sciences, Department of History, Cleveland, OH 44115. Offers art history (MA); history (MA); museum studies (MA). Part-time and evening/weekend programs available. *Faculty:* 13 full-time (4 women). *Students:* 9 full-time (4 women), 15 part-time (9 women); includes 4 minority (3 Black or African American, non-Hispanic/Latino; 1 Two or more races, non-Hispanic/Latino). Average age 32. 13 applicants, 85% accepted, 6 enrolled. In 2014, 10 master's awarded. *Degree requirements:* For master's, thesis optional. *Entrance requirements:* For master's, minimum GPA of 3.0, bachelor's degree in history (or related field for art history). Additional exam requirements/recommendations for international students: Required—TOEFL (minimum score 525 paper-based). *Application deadline:* For fall admission, 7/15 priority date for domestic students. Applications are processed on a rolling basis. Application fee: $30. Electronic applications accepted. *Expenses:* Tuition, state resident: full-time $9566; part-time $531 per credit hour. Tuition, nonresident: full-time $17,980; part-time $999 per credit hour. *Required fees:* $25 per semester. Tuition and fees vary according to degree level and program. *Financial support:* In 2014–15, 7 students received support, including research assistantships with full tuition reimbursements available (averaging $8,600 per year); career-related internships or fieldwork, tuition waivers (full and partial), and unspecified assistantships also available. Financial award application deadline: 4/15. *Faculty research:* Africa and African diaspora, European history, Middle Eastern history, Latin American/Caribbean history, American history, gender and sexuality. *Unit head:* Dr. Elizabeth A. Lehfeldt, Chairperson, 216-687-3920, Fax: 216-687-5592, E-mail: e.lehfeldt@csuohio.edu. *Application contact:* Dr. Karen Sotiropoulos, Graduate Director, 216-687-3940, E-mail: r.s.shelton@csuohio.edu.
Website: http://www.csuohio.edu/history/

Columbia University, Graduate School of Arts and Sciences, New York, NY 10027. Offers African-American studies (MA); American studies (MA); anthropology (MA, PhD); art history and archaeology (MA, PhD); astronomy (PhD); biological sciences (PhD); biotechnology (MA); chemical physics (PhD); chemistry (PhD); classical studies (MA, PhD); classics (MA, PhD); climate and society (MA); earth and environmental sciences

(PhD); East Asia: regional studies (MA); East Asian languages and cultures (MA, PhD); ecology, evolution and environmental biology (MA), including conservation biology; ecology, evolution, and environmental biology (PhD), including ecology and evolutionary biology, evolutionary primatology; economics (PhD); English and comparative literature (MA, PhD); French and Romance philology (MA, PhD); Germanic languages (MA, PhD); global French studies (MA); Hispanic cultural studies (MA); history (PhD); history and literature (MA); human rights studies (MA); Islamic studies (MA); Italian (MA, PhD); Japanese pedagogy (MA); Jewish studies (MA); Latin America and the Caribbean: regional studies (MA); Latin American and Iberian cultures (PhD); mathematics (MA, PhD), including finance (MA); medieval and Renaissance studies (MA); Middle Eastern, South Asian, and African studies (MA, PhD); modern art: critical and curatorial studies (MA); modern European studies (MA); museum anthropology (MA); music (DMA, PhD); oral history (MA); philosophical foundations of physics (MA); philosophy (MA, PhD); physics (PhD); political science (MA, PhD); psychology (PhD); quantitative methods in the social sciences (MA); religion (MA, PhD); Russia, Eurasia and East Europe: regional studies (MA); Russian translation (MA); Slavic cultures (MA); Slavic languages (MA, PhD); sociology (MA, PhD); South Asian studies (MA); statistics (MA, PhD); theatre (PhD); JD/PhD; MA/MS; MD/PhD; MPA/MA. Dual-degree programs require admission to both Graduate School of Arts and Sciences and another Columbia school. Part-time and evening/weekend programs available. Terminal master's awarded for partial completion of doctoral program. *Degree requirements:* For master's, thesis (for some programs); for doctorate, comprehensive exam, thesis/dissertation. *Entrance requirements:* For master's and doctorate, GRE General Test, GRE Subject Test (for some programs). Electronic applications accepted. *Faculty research:* Humanities, natural sciences, social sciences.

Fashion Institute of Technology, School of Graduate Studies, Program in Exhibition Design, New York, NY 10001-5992. Offers MA. *Entrance requirements:* Additional exam requirements/recommendations for international students: Required—TOEFL (minimum score 550 paper-based). Electronic applications accepted.

See Display on this page and Close-Up on page 97.

⭐ **Fashion Institute of Technology,** School of Graduate Studies, Program in Fashion and Textile Studies, New York, NY 10001-5992. Offers MA. *Accreditation:* NASAD. *Degree requirements:* For master's, one foreign language, thesis, internship. *Entrance requirements:* For master's, GRE General Test or GRE Subject Test, previous course work in art history and chemistry, 4 semesters of a foreign language. Additional exam requirements/recommendations for international students: Required—TOEFL (minimum score 550 paper-based). Electronic applications accepted.

See Display below and Close-Up on page 199.

Florida International University, College of Architecture and the Arts, School of Art and Art History, Miami, FL 33199. Offers museum studies (Graduate Certificate); studio art (MFA). *Accreditation:* NASAD. Part-time and evening/weekend programs available. *Entrance requirements:* For master's, minimum GPA of 3.0 (upper level coursework), 3 letters of recommendation, 20 slides of creative work. Additional exam requirements/recommendations for international students: Required—TOEFL (minimum score 550 paper-based; 80 iBT). Electronic applications accepted.

Florida State University, The Graduate School, College of Fine Arts, Department of Art History, Tallahassee, FL 32306. Offers art history (MA, PhD); museum and cultural heritage studies (MA); museum studies (Certificate). *Accreditation:* NASAD. Part-time programs available. *Faculty:* 10 full-time (4 women), 10 part-time/adjunct (5 women). *Students:* 52 full-time (46 women), 4 part-time (3 women); includes 8 minority (1 Asian, non-Hispanic/Latino; 4 Hispanic/Latino; 3 Two or more races, non-Hispanic/Latino).

Average age 25. 43 applicants, 77% accepted, 17 enrolled. In 2014, 8 master's, 2 doctorates awarded. Terminal master's awarded for partial completion of doctoral program. *Degree requirements:* For master's, one foreign language, thesis (for some programs), capstone project (for some programs); for doctorate, 2 foreign languages, comprehensive exam, thesis/dissertation. *Entrance requirements:* For master's, GRE General Test, minimum GPA of 3.0; for doctorate, GRE General Test, minimum GPA of 3.5. Additional exam requirements/recommendations for international students: Required—TOEFL (minimum score 80 iBT). *Application deadline:* For fall admission, 12/10 for domestic and international students. Applications are processed on a rolling basis. Application fee: $35. Electronic applications accepted. *Expenses:* Expenses: $17,745 in-state, $40,932 out-of-state (for MA and PhD in art history and Certificate in museum studies); $23,660 in-state, $54,576 out-of-state (for MA in museum and cultural heritage studies). *Financial support:* In 2014–15, 33 students received support, including 8 fellowships with full tuition reimbursements available (averaging $10,827 per year), 15 research assistantships with full tuition reimbursements available (averaging $5,175 per year), 8 teaching assistantships with full tuition reimbursements available (averaging $6,109 per year); career-related internships or fieldwork, Federal Work-Study, institutionally sponsored loans, scholarships/grants, and unspecified assistantships also available. Financial award application deadline: 12/10; financial award applicants required to submit FAFSA. *Faculty research:* Modern art and critical theory, medieval, Renaissance and Baroque, Pre-Columbian and Spanish Colonial, visual arts of the Americas. *Unit head:* Dr. Adam Jolles, Associate Professor of Art History/Department Chair, 850-644-7066, E-mail: ajolles@fsu.edu. *Application contact:* Leah Sherman, Academic Program Specialist/Graduate Student Advisor, 850-644-8207, E-mail: lrsherman@fsu.edu.
Website: http://arthistory.fsu.edu/

Florida State University, The Graduate School, College of Fine Arts, Specialized Study in Museum Theory and Practice, Tallahassee, FL 32306. Offers Graduate Certificate. Part-time programs available. *Students:* 46 part-time (37 women); includes 5 minority (3 Asian, non-Hispanic/Latino; 2 Hispanic/Latino). Average age 24. 10 applicants, 100% accepted, 10 enrolled. In 2014, 7 Graduate Certificates awarded. *Degree requirements:* For Graduate Certificate, internship. *Entrance requirements:* For degree, GRE, graduate degree or current study towards a graduate degree. Additional exam requirements/recommendations for international students: Recommended—TOEFL. *Application deadline:* For fall admission, 8/15 priority date for domestic and international students; for spring admission, 12/15 for domestic and international students. Applications are processed on a rolling basis. Application fee: $30. *Expenses:* Tuition, state resident: part-time $403.51 per credit hour. Tuition, nonresident: part-time $1004.85 per credit hour. *Required fees:* $75.81 per credit hour. One-time fee: $20 part-time. Tuition and fees vary according to campus/location. *Financial support:* Career-related internships or fieldwork available. *Unit head:* Dr. Teri R. Abstein, Academic Coordinator, 850-645-4681, Fax: 850-644-7229, E-mail: tabstein@fsu.edu.
Website: http://museumstudies.cfa.fsu.edu/specialized-study-in-museum-theory-practice/

The George Washington University, Columbian College of Arts and Sciences, Department of Anthropology, Washington, DC 20052. Offers anthropology (MA, PhD); international development (MA); medical antropology (MA); museum training (MA). Part-time and evening/weekend programs available. *Faculty:* 15 full-time (5 women). *Students:* 38 full-time (29 women), 7 part-time (5 women); includes 6 minority (1 Black or African American, non-Hispanic/Latino; 2 Hispanic/Latino; 3 Two or more races, non-Hispanic/Latino), 6 international. Average age 27. 98 applicants, 39% accepted, 15 enrolled. In 2014, 13 master's, 4 doctorates awarded. *Degree requirements:* For master's, one foreign language, comprehensive exam, thesis or alternative. *Entrance requirements:* For master's, GRE General Test, minimum GPA of 3.0. Additional exam

requirements/recommendations for international students: Required—TOEFL (minimum score 550 paper-based; 80 iBT). *Application deadline:* For fall admission, 1/15 priority date for international students; for spring admission, 9/15 priority date for domestic students, 9/1 priority date for international students. Applications are processed on a rolling basis. Application fee: $75. Electronic applications accepted. *Financial support:* In 2014–15, 8 students received support. Fellowships, teaching assistantships, career-related internships or fieldwork, and Federal Work-Study available. Financial award application deadline: 1/15. *Unit head:* Richard Grinker, Chair, 202-994-6984, E-mail: rgrink@email.gwu.edu. *Application contact:* Information Contact, 202-994-6075, E-mail: anth@gwu.edu.
Website: http://anthropology.columbian.gwu.edu/

The George Washington University, Columbian College of Arts and Sciences, Department of Fine Arts and Art History, Program in Art History, Washington, DC 20052. Offers art history (MA); museum training (MA). Part-time and evening/weekend programs available. *Faculty:* 5 full-time (all women), 15 part-time/adjunct (all women). *Students:* 14 full-time (11 women), 3 part-time (all women). Average age 27. 51 applicants, 75% accepted, 8 enrolled. In 2014, 12 master's awarded. *Degree requirements:* For master's, one foreign language, comprehensive exam, thesis or alternative. *Entrance requirements:* For master's, GRE General Test, bachelor's degree in field, minimum GPA of 3.0. Additional exam requirements/recommendations for international students: Required—TOEFL (minimum score 550 paper-based; 80 iBT). *Application deadline:* For fall admission, 3/1 priority date for domestic students, 1/15 priority date for international students; for spring admission, 10/1 priority date for domestic students, 9/1 priority date for international students. Applications are processed on a rolling basis. Application fee: $75. Electronic applications accepted. *Financial support:* In 2014–15, 3 students received support. Fellowships, teaching assistantships, career-related internships or fieldwork, and Federal Work-Study available. Financial award application deadline: 1/15. *Unit head:* Thomas K. Brown, Chair, 202-994-9067, E-mail: thbrown@gwu.edu. *Application contact:* Information Contact, 202-994-6085, Fax: 202-994-8657, E-mail: art@gwu.edu.

The George Washington University, Columbian College of Arts and Sciences, Program in Museum Studies, Washington, DC 20052. Offers museum collections management and care (Graduate Certificate); museum studies (MA). Part-time and evening/weekend programs available. *Faculty:* 5 full-time (all women). *Students:* 88 full-time (79 women), 51 part-time (42 women); includes 13 minority (3 Black or African American, non-Hispanic/Latino; 1 American Indian or Alaska Native, non-Hispanic/Latino; 1 Asian, non-Hispanic/Latino; 6 Hispanic/Latino; 2 Two or more races, non-Hispanic/Latino), 7 international. Average age 27. 222 applicants, 74% accepted, 62 enrolled. In 2014, 58 master's, 21 other advanced degrees awarded. *Degree requirements:* For master's, comprehensive exam, internship. *Entrance requirements:* For master's, GRE General Test, minimum GPA of 3.0. Additional exam requirements/recommendations for international students: Required—TOEFL (minimum score 550 paper-based; 80 iBT). *Application deadline:* For fall admission, 2/1 priority date for domestic students, 1/15 priority date for international students; for spring admission, 10/15 priority date for domestic students, 9/1 priority date for international students. Applications are processed on a rolling basis. Application fee: $75. Electronic applications accepted. *Financial support:* In 2014–15, 15 students received support. Fellowships with tuition reimbursements available, career-related internships or fieldwork, Federal Work-Study, institutionally sponsored loans, and tuition waivers available. Financial award application deadline: 1/15. *Unit head:* Kym S. Rice, Director, 202-994-0165, Fax: 202-994-7034, E-mail: kym@gwu.edu. *Application contact:* Information Contact, 202-994-7030, Fax: 202-994-7034, E-mail: mstd@gwu.edu.
Website: http://www.gwu.edu/~mstd/

Harvard University, Extension School, Cambridge, MA 02138-3722. Offers applied sciences (CAS); biotechnology (ALM); educational technologies (ALM); educational technology (CET); English for graduate and professional studies (DGP); environmental management (ALM, CEM); information technology (ALM); journalism (ALM); liberal arts (ALM); management (ALM, CM); mathematics for teaching (ALM); museum studies (ALM); premedical studies (Diploma); publication and communication (CPC). Part-time and evening/weekend programs available. *Degree requirements:* For master's, thesis. *Entrance requirements:* For master's, 3 completed graduate courses with grade of B or higher. Additional exam requirements/recommendations for international students: Required—TOEFL (minimum score 600 paper-based), TWE (minimum score 5). *Expenses:* Contact institution.

Indiana University–Purdue University Indianapolis, School of Liberal Arts, Department of Museum Studies, Indianapolis, IN 46202. Offers MS, Certificate. *Students:* 30 full-time (29 women), 5 part-time (all women); includes 4 minority (2 Black or African American, non-Hispanic/Latino; 2 Two or more races, non-Hispanic/Latino). Average age 27. 48 applicants, 81% accepted, 19 enrolled. In 2014, 9 master's, 1 other advanced degree awarded. *Entrance requirements:* For master's, GRE. *Application deadline:* For fall admission, 2/1 for domestic students; for spring admission, 10/1 for domestic students. Application fee: $55 ($65 for international students). *Financial support:* Fellowships with partial tuition reimbursements and teaching assistantships available. Financial award application deadline: 2/1; financial award applicants required to submit FAFSA. *Unit head:* Dr. Elee Wood, Director, 317-274-7332. *Application contact:* Becky Ellis, Information Contact, 317-274-1490, E-mail: museum@iupui.edu.
Website: http://www.liberalarts.iupui.edu/mstd/

John F. Kennedy University, School of Education and Liberal Arts, Department of Museum Studies, Berkeley, CA 94702. Offers museum studies (MA, Certificate), including administration, collections management, public programming. Part-time programs available. *Degree requirements:* For master's, project. *Entrance requirements:* For master's, interview. Additional exam requirements/recommendations for international students: Required—TOEFL, TWE. *Faculty research:* Emerging museum philosophies, multicultural diversity issues in museums, trends in collections management and preventive conservation, effective programming techniques and application for diverse audiences.

Johns Hopkins University, Zanvyl Krieger School of Arts and Sciences, Advanced Academic Programs, Program in Museum Studies, Washington, DC 20036. Offers digital curation (Certificate); museum studies (MA). Part-time and evening/weekend programs available. Postbaccalaureate distance learning degree programs offered (minimal on-campus study). *Entrance requirements:* For master's, minimum GPA of 3.0. Additional exam requirements/recommendations for international students: Required—TOEFL (minimum score 100 iBT). Electronic applications accepted.

Marist College, Graduate Programs, School of Communication and the Arts, Poughkeepsie, NY 12601-1387. Offers communication (MA); integrated marketing communication (MA); museum studies (MA). Part-time programs available. Postbaccalaureate distance learning degree programs offered (no on-campus study). *Degree requirements:* For master's, thesis or comprehensive exam. *Entrance requirements:* For master's, GRE, minimum undergraduate GPA of 3.0, resume, 3 letters of recommendation. Additional exam requirements/recommendations for international students: Required—TOEFL (minimum score 550 paper-based; 80 iBT); Recommended—IELTS (minimum score 6.5). Electronic applications accepted.

Maryland Institute College of Art, Graduate Studies, Program in Curatorial Practice, Baltimore, MD 21201. Offers MFA. *Faculty:* 2 full-time (0 women), 4 part-time/adjunct (1 woman). *Students:* 20 full-time (18 women); includes 9 minority (3 Black or African American, non-Hispanic/Latino; 1 Asian, non-Hispanic/Latino; 2 Hispanic/Latino; 3 Two or more races, non-Hispanic/Latino), 3 international. Average age 27. 40 applicants, 38% accepted, 10 enrolled. In 2014, 10 master's awarded. *Degree requirements:* For master's, thesis, exhibit and thesis documentation. *Entrance requirements:* For master's, portfolio, bachelor's degree in any field. Additional exam requirements/recommendations for international students: Required—TOEFL (minimum score 550 paper-based; 80 iBT), IELTS (minimum score 6.5). *Application deadline:* For fall admission, 1/15 for domestic and international students. Application fee: $75. Electronic applications accepted. *Expenses:* Expenses: Contact institution. *Financial support:* In 2014–15, 10 students received support, including 20 fellowships (averaging $13,000 per year), 10 teaching assistantships (averaging $3,200 per year); career-related internships or fieldwork and scholarships/grants also available. Financial award application deadline: 1/15. *Unit head:* George Ciscle, Director, 410-225-5274, Fax: 410-225-5275, E-mail: graduate@mica.edu. *Application contact:* Chris D. Harring, Director, Graduate Admission, 410-225-2256, Fax: 410-225-5275, E-mail: graduate@mica.edu.
Website: http://www.mica.edu/Programs_of_Study/Graduate_Programs/Curatorial_Practice_(MFA).html

Morgan State University, School of Graduate Studies, College of Liberal Arts, Department of History and Geography, Baltimore, MD 21251. Offers African-American studies (MA); history (MA, PhD); museum studies and historic preservation (MA). Part-time and evening/weekend programs available. *Degree requirements:* For master's, comprehensive exam, thesis; for doctorate, comprehensive exam, thesis/dissertation. *Entrance requirements:* For master's, minimum GPA of 2.5; for doctorate, GRE or MAT. Additional exam requirements/recommendations for international students: Required—TOEFL (minimum score 550 paper-based). *Faculty research:* Women's history, African diaspora history, urban history.

New Mexico State University, College of Arts and Sciences, Department of Anthropology, Las Cruces, NM 88003-8001. Offers anthropology (MA); cultural resource management (Graduate Certificate); museum studies (Graduate Certificate). Part-time programs available. *Faculty:* 8 full-time (4 women), 4 part-time/adjunct (2 women). *Students:* 47 full-time (33 women), 31 part-time (22 women); includes 17 minority (1 Black or African American, non-Hispanic/Latino; 1 American Indian or Alaska Native, non-Hispanic/Latino; 13 Hispanic/Latino; 2 Two or more races, non-Hispanic/Latino), 2 international. Average age 32. 44 applicants, 64% accepted, 16 enrolled. In 2014, 17 master's, 6 other advanced degrees awarded. *Degree requirements:* For master's, comprehensive exam (for some programs), thesis optional. *Entrance requirements:* For master's, minimum undergraduate GPA of 3.0. Additional exam requirements/recommendations for international students: Required—TOEFL (minimum score 550 paper-based; 79 iBT), IELTS (minimum score 6.5). *Application deadline:* For fall admission, 2/1 priority date for domestic and international students; for spring admission, 10/1 priority date for domestic and international students. Applications are processed on a rolling basis. Application fee: $40 ($50 for international students). Electronic applications accepted. *Expenses:* Tuition, state resident: full-time $3969; part-time $220.50 per credit hour. Tuition, nonresident: full-time $13,838; part-time $768.80 per credit hour. *Required fees:* $853; $47.40 per credit hour. *Financial support:* In 2014–15, 28 students received support, including 3 fellowships (averaging $3,970 per year), 1 research assistantship (averaging $23,100 per year), 13 teaching assistantships (averaging $8,902 per year); career-related internships or fieldwork, Federal Work-Study, scholarships/grants, traineeships, health care benefits, and unspecified assistantships also available. Support available to part-time students. Financial award application deadline: 3/1. *Faculty research:* Native American culture and society, Latin America and border studies, prehistoric and historic archaeology, medical anthropology, applied anthropology, museum studies. *Total annual research expenditures:* $63,773. *Unit head:* Dr. Rani Alexander, Head, 575-646-2826, Fax: -, E-mail: raalexan@nmsu.edu. *Application contact:* Dr. Lois Stanford, Graduate Advisor, 575-646-6092, E-mail: lstanfor@nmsu.edu.
Website: http://anthropology.nmsu.edu

New York University, Graduate School of Arts and Science, Program in Museum Studies, New York, NY 10012-1019. Offers museum studies (MA, Advanced Certificate), including Africana studies (MA), Hebrew and Judaic studies (MA), Latin American and Caribbean studies (MA), Near Eastern studies (MA). Part-time and evening/weekend programs available. *Students:* 45 full-time (39 women), 23 part-time (19 women); includes 15 minority (2 American Indian or Alaska Native, non-Hispanic/Latino; 3 Asian, non-Hispanic/Latino; 6 Hispanic/Latino; 4 Two or more races, non-Hispanic/Latino), 19 international. Average age 26. 123 applicants, 81% accepted, 29 enrolled. In 2014, 35 master's, 1 other advanced degree awarded. *Entrance requirements:* For master's, GRE General Test; for Advanced Certificate, master's degree or PhD. Additional exam requirements/recommendations for international students: Required—TOEFL. *Application deadline:* For fall admission, 2/15 for domestic and international students; for spring admission, 11/1 for domestic and international students. Application fee: $100. *Financial support:* Application deadline: 2/15. *Faculty research:* Modern and contemporary art, history of museums and exhibitions, conservation of cultural materials, museum anthropology, ethnography. *Unit head:* Bruce Altshuler, Director, 212-998-8080, Fax: 212-995-4185, E-mail: museum.studies@nyu.edu. *Application contact:* Tatiana Kamorina, Department Administrator, 212-998-8080, Fax: 212-995-4185, E-mail: museum.studies@nyu.edu.
Website: http://www.nyu.edu/fas/program/museumstudies/

Penn State Harrisburg, Graduate School, School of Humanities, Middletown, PA 17057-4898. Offers American studies (MA, PhD); communications (MA); folklore and ethnography (Certificate); heritage and museum practice (Certificate); humanities (MA); writing instruction specialist (Certificate). Evening/weekend programs available. *Unit head:* Dr. Mukund S. Kulkarni, Chancellor, 717-948-6105, Fax: 717-948-6452, E-mail: msk5@psu.edu. *Application contact:* Robert W. Coffman, Jr., Director of Enrollment Management, Admissions, 717-948-6250, Fax: 717-948-6325, E-mail: ric1@psu.edu.
Website: http://harrisburg.psu.edu/humanities

St. John's University, St. John's College of Liberal Arts and Sciences, Department of Art and Design, Queens, NY 11439. Offers MA. *Students:* 4 applicants, 50% accepted. *Degree requirements:* For master's, internship. *Entrance requirements:* For master's, BA with at least 24 credits in art history or a major in a related area in the humanities and coursework in art history; minimum cumulative undergraduate GPA of 3.0 overall and in major. *Expenses: Tuition:* Full-time $20,610; part-time $1145 per credit. *Required fees:* $170 per semester. *Financial support:* Unspecified assistantships available. *Unit head:* Dr. Susan Rosenberg, Director, 718-990-5239, E-mail: rosenbs3@stjohns.edu. *Application contact:* Robert Medrano, Director of Graduate Admission, 718-990-1601, Fax: 718-990-5686, E-mail: gradhelp@stjohns.edu.

San Francisco Art Institute, Master of Arts Programs, San Francisco, CA 94133. Offers exhibition and museum studies (MA); history and theory of contemporary art (MA). *Faculty:* 4 full-time (all women), 17 part-time/adjunct (10 women). *Students:* 12 full-time (all women); includes 2 minority (1 Hispanic/Latino; 1 Two or more races, non-Hispanic/Latino), 2 international. Average age 26. 32 applicants, 72% accepted, 6

enrolled. In 2014, 18 master's awarded. *Degree requirements:* For master's, thesis. *Entrance requirements:* For master's, critical writing sample. Additional exam requirements/recommendations for international students: Required—TOEFL (minimum score 600 paper-based; 100 iBT), IELTS (minimum score 7.5). *Application deadline:* For fall admission, 1/15 priority date for domestic and international students. Applications are processed on a rolling basis. Application fee: $85. Electronic applications accepted. *Expenses: Tuition:* Full-time $41,100; part-time $1805 per credit. *Required fees:* $870. *Financial support:* In 2014–15, 9 students received support, including 3 fellowships (averaging $25,000 per year), teaching assistantships (averaging $2,500 per year); career-related internships or fieldwork, Federal Work-Study, scholarships/grants, and unspecified assistantships also available. Support available to part-time students. Financial award application deadline: 3/1; financial award applicants required to submit FAFSA. *Unit head:* Claire Daigle, Chair, Master of Arts Department, 415-641-1241 Ext. 1004, Fax: 415-641-1205, E-mail: cdaigle@sfai.edu. *Application contact:* Jana Rumberger, Associate Director of Recruitment, 415-351-3507, Fax: 415-749-4592, E-mail: jrumberger@sfai.edu.
Website: http://www.sfai.edu/degree-programs/graduate/ma

San Francisco State University, Division of Graduate Studies, College of Liberal and Creative Arts, Museum Studies Program, San Francisco, CA 94132-1722. Offers MA. Part-time programs available. *Expenses:* Tuition, state resident: full-time $6738. Tuition, nonresident: full-time $17,898; part-time $372 per credit hour. *Required fees:* $498 per semester. *Financial support:* Career-related internships or fieldwork and Federal Work-Study available. *Unit head:* Dr. Edward Luby, Professor/Program Director, 415-338-3163, Fax: 415-338-6537, E-mail: emluby@sfsu.edu. *Application contact:* Christine Fogarty, Program Coordinator, 415-405-0599, Fax: 415-338-6537, E-mail: cfog@sfsu.edu.
Website: http://museumstudies.sfsu.edu/

Seton Hall University, College of Arts and Sciences, Department of Communication, South Orange, NJ 07079-2697. Offers corporate and professional communication (MA); museum professions (MA), including exhibition development, museum education, museum management, museum registration; strategic communication (MA); strategic communication and leadership (MA). Part-time and evening/weekend programs available. Postbaccalaureate distance learning degree programs offered (minimal on-campus study). *Faculty:* 3 full-time (1 woman), 15 part-time/adjunct (6 women). *Students:* 31 full-time (21 women), 105 part-time (69 women); includes 47 minority (34 Black or African American, non-Hispanic/Latino; 3 Asian, non-Hispanic/Latino; 10 Hispanic/Latino), 6 international. Average age 32. 114 applicants, 74% accepted, 40 enrolled. In 2014, 65 master's awarded. *Degree requirements:* For master's, thesis. *Entrance requirements:* Additional exam requirements/recommendations for international students: Required—TOEFL. *Application deadline:* For fall admission, 7/1 priority date for domestic and international students; for spring admission, 11/1 priority date for domestic and international students. Applications are processed on a rolling basis. Application fee: $75. Electronic applications accepted. *Financial support:* Research assistantships, career-related internships or fieldwork, Federal Work-Study, and unspecified assistantships available. Financial award applicants required to submit FAFSA. *Faculty research:* Managerial communication, communication consulting, communication and development. *Unit head:* Prof. Deirdre Yates, Chair, 973-761-9474, Fax: 973-761-9234, E-mail: deirdre.yates@shu.edu. *Application contact:* Dr. Richard Dool, Director of Graduate Studies, 973-761-9490, Fax: 973-761-9234, E-mail: rrichard.dool@shu.edu.
Website: http://www.shu.edu/academics/artsci/communication-arts/

Southern Illinois University Edwardsville, Graduate School, College of Arts and Sciences, Department of Historical Studies, Program in Museum Studies, Edwardsville, IL 62026-0001. Offers Postbaccalaureate Certificate. Part-time and evening/weekend programs available. *Students:* 4 part-time (3 women); includes 1 minority (Black or African American, non-Hispanic/Latino). 3 applicants, 100% accepted. In 2014, 5 Postbaccalaureate Certificates awarded. *Entrance requirements:* Additional exam requirements/recommendations for international students: Required—TOEFL (minimum score 550 paper-based; 79 iBT), IELTS (minimum score 6.5). *Application deadline:* For fall admission, 7/24 for domestic students, 7/15 for international students; for spring admission, 12/11 for domestic students, 11/15 for international students; for summer admission, 4/29 for domestic students, 4/15 for international students. Applications are processed on a rolling basis. Application fee: $30. Electronic applications accepted. *Expenses:* Tuition, state resident: full-time $5026. Tuition, nonresident: full-time $12,566. *International tuition:* $25,136 full-time. *Required fees:* $1682. Tuition and fees vary according to course load, campus/location and program. *Financial support:* Fellowships with full tuition reimbursements, research assistantships with full tuition reimbursements, teaching assistantships with full tuition reimbursements, institutionally sponsored loans, scholarships/grants, and unspecified assistantships available. Financial award application deadline: 3/1; financial award applicants required to submit FAFSA. *Unit head:* Dr. Laura Fowler, Program Director, 618-650-2145, E-mail: lmilsk@siue.edu. *Application contact:* Melissa K. Mace, Assistant Director of Admissions for Graduate and International Recruitment, 618-650-2756, Fax: 618-650-3618, E-mail: mmace@siue.edu.
Website: http://www.siue.edu/artsandsciences/historicalstudies/museumstudies/

Southern University at New Orleans, School of Graduate Studies, New Orleans, LA 70126-1009. Offers criminal justice (MA); management information systems (MS); museum studies (MA); social work (MSW). *Accreditation:* CSWE. Part-time and evening/weekend programs available. *Degree requirements:* For master's, thesis. *Entrance requirements:* For master's, GRE/GMAT. Additional exam requirements/recommendations for international students: Required—TOEFL.

State University of New York College at Oneonta, Graduate Education, Cooperstown Graduate Program in History Museum Studies, Cooperstown, NY 13326. Offers MA. *Degree requirements:* For master's, research paper or thesis. *Entrance requirements:* For master's, GRE General Test. *Expenses:* Contact institution.

Syracuse University, College of Visual and Performing Arts, Program in Museum Studies, Syracuse, NY 13244. Offers MA. *Accreditation:* NASAD. *Students:* 29 full-time (25 women), 4 part-time (all women); includes 3 minority (2 Black or African American, non-Hispanic/Latino; 1 Two or more races, non-Hispanic/Latino). Average age 25. 62 applicants, 74% accepted, 18 enrolled. In 2014, 15 master's awarded. *Degree requirements:* For master's, thesis or alternative. *Entrance requirements:* For master's, writing sample, curriculum vitae. Additional exam requirements/recommendations for international students: Required—TOEFL (minimum score 100 iBT), IELTS. *Application deadline:* For fall admission, 2/1 priority date for domestic and international students. Application fee: $75. Electronic applications accepted. *Expenses: Tuition:* Part-time $1341 per credit. *Financial support:* Fellowships with full tuition reimbursements and teaching assistantships with full and partial tuition reimbursements available. Financial award application deadline: 1/1; financial award applicants required to submit FAFSA. *Unit head:* Edward Aiken, Professor/Program Coordinator, Museum Studies, 315-443-4098, Fax: 315-443-1303, E-mail: eaaiken@syr.edu. *Application contact:* Therese West, Information Contact, 315-443-0137, E-mail: admissg@syr.edu.
Website: http://vpa.syr.edu/

Texas Tech University, Graduate School, Interdisciplinary Programs, Lubbock, TX 79409-1030. Offers arid land studies (MS); biotechnology (MS); heritage management (MS); interdisciplinary studies (MA, MS); museum science (MA); wind science and engineering (PhD); JD/MS. Part-time programs available. *Faculty:* 4 full-time (3 women). *Students:* 112 full-time (70 women), 122 part-time (70 women); includes 71 minority (20 Black or African American, non-Hispanic/Latino; 1 American Indian or Alaska Native, non-Hispanic/Latino; 4 Asian, non-Hispanic/Latino; 40 Hispanic/Latino; 6 Two or more races, non-Hispanic/Latino), 43 international. Average age 30. 172 applicants, 65% accepted, 70 enrolled. In 2014, 56 master's, 4 doctorates awarded. Terminal master's awarded for partial completion of doctoral program. *Degree requirements:* For master's, comprehensive exam (for some programs), thesis (for some programs); for doctorate, comprehensive exam, thesis/dissertation (for some programs). *Entrance requirements:* Additional exam requirements/recommendations for international students: Required—TOEFL (minimum score 550 paper-based; 79 iBT). *Application deadline:* For fall admission, 6/1 priority date for domestic students, 1/15 priority date for international students; for spring admission, 9/1 priority date for domestic students, 6/15 priority date for international students. Applications are processed on a rolling basis. Application fee: $60. Electronic applications accepted. *Expenses:* Tuition, state resident: full-time $6310; part-time $262.92 per credit hour. Tuition, nonresident: full-time $14,998; part-time $624.92 per credit hour. *Required fees:* $2701; $36.50 per credit. $912.50 per semester. Tuition and fees vary according to course load. *Financial support:* In 2014–15, 201 students received support, including 196 fellowships (averaging $2,655 per year), 5 research assistantships (averaging $12,144 per year), 2 teaching assistantships (averaging $7,785 per year); scholarships/grants and unspecified assistantships also available. Financial award application deadline: 4/15; financial award applicants required to submit FAFSA. *Total annual research expenditures:* $241,842. *Unit head:* Dr. Mark Sheridan, Vice Provost for Graduate and Postdoctoral Affairs/Dean of the Graduate School, 806-742-2787, Fax: 806-742-1746, E-mail: mark.sheridan@ttu.edu. *Application contact:* Shannon Samson, Coordinator of Graduate School Recruitment, 806-834-5201, Fax: 806-742-1746, E-mail: gradschool@ttu.edu.
Website: http://www.depts.ttu.edu/gradschool/about/INDS/index.php

Trinity College, Graduate Programs, Program in American Studies, Hartford, CT 06106-3100. Offers American culture studies (MA); museums and communities (MA). Part-time and evening/weekend programs available. *Degree requirements:* For master's, thesis or alternative. *Entrance requirements:* For master's, minimum GPA of 3.0.

Tufts University, Graduate School of Arts and Sciences, Department of Art and Art History, Medford, MA 02155. Offers art history (MA); art history and museum studies (MA); studio art (MFA). *Faculty:* 11 full-time (6 women), 4 part-time/adjunct (3 women). *Students:* 100 full-time (74 women), 32 part-time (21 women); includes 18 minority (5 Black or African American, non-Hispanic/Latino; 4 Asian, non-Hispanic/Latino; 6 Hispanic/Latino; 3 Two or more races, non-Hispanic/Latino), 20 international. Average age 29. 89 applicants, 40% accepted, 13 enrolled. In 2014, 82 master's awarded. *Degree requirements:* For master's, one foreign language, thesis (for some programs). *Entrance requirements:* For master's, GRE General Test. Additional exam requirements/recommendations for international students: Required—TOEFL (minimum score 550 paper-based; 80 iBT), IELTS (minimum score 6.5). *Application deadline:* For fall admission, 1/15 for domestic and international students. Application fee: $75. Electronic applications accepted. *Expenses: Tuition:* Full-time $45,590; part-time $1161 per credit hour. *Required fees:* $782. Full-time tuition and fees vary according to degree level, program and student level. Part-time tuition and fees vary according to course load. *Financial support:* Teaching assistantships with partial tuition reimbursements, Federal Work-Study, scholarships/grants, tuition waivers (partial), and unspecified assistantships available. Financial award application deadline: 5/15; financial award applicants required to submit FAFSA. *Unit head:* Karen Overbey, Graduate Program Director, 617-627-3395. *Application contact:* Office of Graduate Admissions, 617-627-3395, E-mail: gradadmissions@tufts.edu.
Website: http://ase.tufts.edu/art/

Tufts University, Graduate School of Arts and Sciences, Department of History, Medford, MA 02155. Offers history (MA, PhD); history and museum studies (MA). *Faculty:* 21 full-time (10 women). *Students:* 14 full-time (6 women), 4 part-time (3 women); includes 1 minority (Asian, non-Hispanic/Latino), 2 international. Average age 26. 54 applicants, 39% accepted, 5 enrolled. In 2014, 8 master's awarded. Terminal master's awarded for partial completion of doctoral program. *Degree requirements:* For master's, one foreign language; for doctorate, 2 foreign languages, thesis/dissertation. *Entrance requirements:* For master's and doctorate, GRE General Test, writing sample. Additional exam requirements/recommendations for international students: Required—TOEFL (minimum score 550 paper-based; 80 iBT), IELTS (minimum score 6.5). *Application deadline:* For fall admission, 1/15 for domestic and international students. Applications are processed on a rolling basis. Application fee: $75. Electronic applications accepted. *Expenses: Tuition:* Full-time $45,590; part-time $1161 per credit hour. *Required fees:* $782. Full-time tuition and fees vary according to degree level, program and student level. Part-time tuition and fees vary according to course load. *Financial support:* Teaching assistantships with full and partial tuition reimbursements, Federal Work-Study, scholarships/grants, tuition waivers (partial), and unspecified assistantships available. Financial award application deadline: 1/15. *Unit head:* Dr. Steven Marrone, Graduate Program Director. *Application contact:* Office of Graduate Admissions, 617-627-3395, E-mail: gradadmissions@tufts.edu.
Website: http://www.ase.tufts.edu/history/

Tufts University, Graduate School of Arts and Sciences, Graduate Certificate Programs, Museum Studies Program, Medford, MA 02155. Offers Certificate. Part-time and evening/weekend programs available. *Expenses:* Contact institution.

Université de Montréal, Faculty of Arts and Sciences, Program in Museology, Montréal, QC H3C 3J7, Canada. Offers MA. Program offered jointly with Université du Québec à Montréal. Electronic applications accepted. *Faculty research:* Museum exhibits, museum education, natural science and museums, new technologies and museums.

Université du Québec à Montréal, Graduate Programs, Program in Museology, Montréal, QC H3C 3P8, Canada. Offers MA. Part-time programs available. *Entrance requirements:* For master's, appropriate bachelor's degree or equivalent and proficiency in French.

Université Laval, Faculty of Letters, Department of History, Program in Museology, Québec, QC G1K 7P4, Canada. Offers Diploma. Part-time programs available. *Entrance requirements:* For degree, English exam (comprehension of English), knowledge of French. Electronic applications accepted.

The University of British Columbia, Faculty of Arts and Faculty of Graduate Studies, Department of Art History, Visual Art, and Theory, Vancouver, BC V6T1Z2, Canada. Offers art history (MA, PhD, Diploma); critical and curatorial studies (MA); visual art (MFA). *Degree requirements:* For master's, one foreign language, thesis, final exhibition (MFA, MA in critical and curatorial studies); for doctorate, 2 foreign languages, comprehensive exam, thesis/dissertation. *Entrance requirements:* For master's, bachelor's degree with minimum B+ average (MFA, MA in critical and curatorial studies),

A- (MA in art history); for doctorate, master's degree with minimum A- average. Additional exam requirements/recommendations for international students: Required—TOEFL (minimum score 600 paper-based). Electronic applications accepted. *Faculty research:* Conceptual art, Asian art, indigenous North American art, post-second war art, eighteenth and nineteenth century art, curatorial, digital art.

University of California, Riverside, Graduate Division, Department of History, Riverside, CA 92521-0102. Offers archival management (MA); historic preservation (MA); history (MA, PhD); museum curatorship (MA). Part-time programs available. Terminal master's awarded for partial completion of doctoral program. *Degree requirements:* For master's, one foreign language, comprehensive exam, internship report and oral exams, or thesis; for doctorate, 2 foreign languages, thesis/dissertation, qualifying exams. *Entrance requirements:* For master's and doctorate, GRE General Test, minimum GPA of 3.2. Additional exam requirements/recommendations for international students: Required—TOEFL (minimum score 550 paper-based; 80 iBT). Electronic applications accepted. *Expenses:* Tuition, state resident: full-time $5399. Tuition, nonresident: full-time $10,433. *Faculty research:* Native American history, United States, public history, Europe, Latin America.

University of Central Oklahoma, The Jackson College of Graduate Studies, College of Liberal Arts, Department of History, Edmond, OK 73034-5209. Offers history (MA); museum studies (MA). Part-time programs available. *Degree requirements:* For master's, one foreign language, comprehensive exam (for some programs), thesis (for some programs). *Entrance requirements:* For master's, GRE, writing sample, essay. Additional exam requirements/recommendations for international students: Required—TOEFL (minimum score 550 paper-based; 79 iBT), IELTS (minimum score 6.5). Electronic applications accepted. *Faculty research:* China, Russia, civil war, American naval logistics.

University of Colorado Boulder, Graduate School, Museum and Field Studies Program, Boulder, CO 80309. Offers MS. *Students:* 14 full-time (all women), 5 part-time (4 women); includes 5 minority (1 Black or African American, non-Hispanic/Latino; 3 Hispanic/Latino; 1 Two or more races, non-Hispanic/Latino). Average age 27. 45 applicants, 11% accepted, 3 enrolled. In 2014, 6 master's awarded. Terminal master's awarded for partial completion of doctoral program. *Degree requirements:* For master's, comprehensive exam, thesis or alternative. *Entrance requirements:* For master's, GRE General Test, GRE Subject Test, minimum undergraduate GPA of 3.0. *Application deadline:* For fall admission, 1/15 for domestic students, 12/1 for international students. Application fee: $50 ($70 for international students). Electronic applications accepted. *Financial support:* In 2014–15, 35 students received support, including 4 fellowships (averaging $6,006 per year), 3 research assistantships with full and partial tuition reimbursements available (averaging $15,286 per year), 13 teaching assistantships with full and partial tuition reimbursements available (averaging $24,452 per year); institutionally sponsored loans, scholarships/grants, health care benefits, and unspecified assistantships also available. Financial award application deadline: 2/1; financial award applicants required to submit FAFSA. *Total annual research expenditures:* $456,916. Website: http://cumuseum.colorado.edu/

University of Denver, Division of Arts, Humanities and Social Sciences, Department of Anthropology, Denver, CO 80208. Offers archaeology (MA); cultural anthropology (MA); museum studies (MA). Part-time programs available. *Faculty:* 7 full-time (3 women). *Students:* 1 full-time (0 women), 20 part-time (14 women); includes 5 minority (2 Hispanic/Latino; 3 Two or more races, non-Hispanic/Latino), 1 international. Average age 25. 47 applicants, 49% accepted, 11 enrolled. In 2014, 4 master's awarded. *Degree requirements:* For master's, one foreign language, comprehensive exam, thesis (for some programs), tool, foreign language literacy, or course work. *Entrance requirements:* For master's, GRE General Test, bachelor's degree, transcripts, personal statement, two letters of recommendation. Additional exam requirements/recommendations for international students: Required—TOEFL (minimum score 550 paper-based; 80 iBT). *Application deadline:* For fall admission, 2/4 priority date for domestic and international students. Applications are processed on a rolling basis. Application fee: $65. Electronic applications accepted. *Expenses:* Expenses: $1,199 per credit hour. *Financial support:* In 2014–15, 18 students received support, including 12 teaching assistantships with partial tuition reimbursements available (averaging $5,000 per year); career-related internships or fieldwork, Federal Work-Study, institutionally sponsored loans, scholarships/grants, and unspecified assistantships also available. Support available to part-time students. Financial award application deadline: 2/15; financial award applicants required to submit FAFSA. *Faculty research:* Human diversity, human rights, historic archaeology, museums and heritage, high-tech field methods. *Unit head:* Dr. Dean J. Saitta, Chair, 303-871-2680, E-mail: dsaitta@du.edu. *Application contact:* Dr. Larry Conyers, Professor/Director of Graduate and Undergraduate Programs, 303-871-2684, E-mail: lconyers@du.edu. Website: http://www.du.edu/ahss/schools/anthropology/

University of Denver, Division of Arts, Humanities and Social Sciences, School of Art and Art History, Denver, CO 80208. Offers art history (MA); art history/museum studies (MA); emergent digital practices (MFA). *Accreditation:* NASAD. Part-time programs available. *Faculty:* 16 full-time (11 women), 3 part-time/adjunct (1 woman). *Students:* 7 full-time (6 women), 17 part-time (16 women); includes 7 minority (1 Black or African American, non-Hispanic/Latino; 1 American Indian or Alaska Native, non-Hispanic/Latino; 5 Hispanic/Latino). Average age 25. 24 applicants, 83% accepted, 14 enrolled. In 2014, 7 master's awarded. *Degree requirements:* For master's, one foreign language, comprehensive exam, research paper or thesis project. *Entrance requirements:* For master's, GRE General Test, transcripts, personal statement, writing sample, three letters of recommendation. Additional exam requirements/recommendations for international students: Required—TOEFL (minimum score 550 paper-based; 80 iBT). *Application deadline:* For fall admission, 1/31 priority date for domestic and international students. Applications are processed on a rolling basis. Application fee: $65. Electronic applications accepted. *Expenses:* Expenses: $1,199 per credit hour. *Financial support:* In 2014–15, 18 students received support, including 8 teaching assistantships with full and partial tuition reimbursements available (averaging $7,817 per year); career-related internships or fieldwork, Federal Work-Study, institutionally sponsored loans, scholarships/grants, and unspecified assistantships also available. Support available to part-time students. Financial award application deadline: 2/15; financial award applicants required to submit FAFSA. *Faculty research:* Images of women in alchemical manuscripts and books, Giovanni Benedetto and Salvatore Castiglione. *Unit head:* Dr. Sarah Gjertson, Director, 303-871-3263, E-mail: sgjertso@du.edu. *Application contact:* Dr. Annabeth Headrick, Graduate Art History Advisor, 303-871-3574, E-mail: annabeth.headrick@du.edu. Website: http://www.du.edu/art/

University of Florida, Graduate School, College of The Arts, School of Art and Art History, Gainesville, FL 32611-5800. Offers art (MA), including digital arts and sciences; art education (MA); art history (MA, PhD); museology (MA), including historic preservation. *Accreditation:* NASAD. Postbaccalaureate distance learning degree programs offered (minimal on-campus study). *Faculty:* 32 full-time (14 women), 5 part-time/adjunct (3 women). *Students:* 91 full-time (66 women), 117 part-time (100 women); includes 50 minority (14 Black or African American, non-Hispanic/Latino; 4 American

Indian or Alaska Native, non-Hispanic/Latino; 6 Asian, non-Hispanic/Latino; 26 Hispanic/Latino), 14 international. 199 applicants, 41% accepted, 55 enrolled. In 2014, 69 master's awarded. *Degree requirements:* For master's, project or thesis (MFA); 1 foreign language (MA in art history); for doctorate, 2 foreign languages, comprehensive exam, thesis/dissertation. *Entrance requirements:* For master's, GRE General Test, portfolio (MFA), writing sample (MA), minimum GPA 3.0; for doctorate, GRE General Test, minimum GPA of 3.0. Additional exam requirements/recommendations for international students: Required—TOEFL (minimum score 550 paper-based; 80 iBT), IELTS (minimum score 6). *Application deadline:* For fall admission, 1/1 priority date for domestic students, 1/1 for international students; for spring admission, 11/1 for domestic and international students. Applications are processed on a rolling basis. Application fee: $30. Electronic applications accepted. *Financial support:* In 2014–15, 4 fellowships, 8 research assistantships, 76 teaching assistantships were awarded; Federal Work-Study, institutionally sponsored loans, and unspecified assistantships also available. Financial award applicants required to submit FAFSA. *Faculty research:* Studio production, art historical studies of style context. *Unit head:* Richard Heipp, Professor and Interim Director, 352-273-3021, Fax: 352-392-8453, E-mail: heipp@ufl.edu. *Application contact:* Maya Stanfield-Mazzi, PhD, Assistant Professor/Director of Graduate Studies for Art History, 352-273-3070, Fax: 352-392-8453, E-mail: mstanfield@ufl.edu. Website: http://www.arts.ufl.edu/art

University of Hawaii at Manoa, Graduate Division, College of Arts and Humanities, Department of American Studies, Program in Museum Studies, Honolulu, HI 96822. Offers Graduate Certificate. Part-time programs available. *Entrance requirements:* Additional exam requirements/recommendations for international students: Required—TOEFL (minimum score 600 paper-based; 100 iBT), IELTS (minimum score 7).

University of Illinois at Chicago, Graduate College, College of Architecture, Design and the Arts, School of Art and Art History, Chicago, IL 60607-7128. Offers art history (MA); electronic visualization (MFA); museum and exhibition studies (MA); new media arts (MFA). Part-time and evening/weekend programs available. *Faculty:* 84 full-time (40 women), 70 part-time/adjunct (20 women). *Students:* 160 full-time (105 women), 23 part-time (17 women); includes 18 minority (3 Black or African American, non-Hispanic/Latino; 4 Asian, non-Hispanic/Latino; 10 Hispanic/Latino; 1 Two or more races, non-Hispanic/Latino), 13 international. Average age 29. 211 applicants, 32% accepted, 34 enrolled. In 2014, 21 master's, 3 doctorates awarded. Terminal master's awarded for partial completion of doctoral program. *Degree requirements:* For master's, one foreign language, thesis or alternative; for doctorate, thesis/dissertation. *Entrance requirements:* For master's, GRE General Test, minimum GPA of 2.75, 3 letters of recommendation; for doctorate, GRE General Test, MA in art history or equivalent, minimum GPA of 3.0. Additional exam requirements/recommendations for international students: Required—TOEFL. *Application deadline:* For fall admission, 1/1 priority date for domestic and international students; for spring admission, 10/1 for domestic students, 7/15 for international students. Application fee: $60. Electronic applications accepted. *Expenses:* Expenses: $19,134 in-state, $31,132 out-of-state (for art); $17,932 in-state, $29,930 out-of-state (for art history). *Financial support:* Fellowships with full tuition reimbursements, research assistantships with full tuition reimbursements, teaching assistantships with full tuition reimbursements, career-related internships or fieldwork, Federal Work-Study, scholarships/grants, traineeships, tuition waivers (full), and unspecified assistantships available. Support available to part-time students. Financial award application deadline: 3/1; financial award applicants required to submit FAFSA. *Faculty research:* Modern painting and sculpture, history of architecture, city planning and design, history of photography. *Unit head:* Prof. Lisa Yun Lee, Director, 312-413-5358, E-mail: lisalee@uic.edu. *Application contact:* Receptionist, 312-413-2550, E-mail: gradcoll@uic.edu. Website: http://artandarthistory.uic.edu/art-history

The University of Kansas, Graduate Studies, College of Liberal Arts and Sciences, Museum Studies Program, Lawrence, KS 66045-7545. Offers MA, Graduate Certificate. Part-time programs available. *Faculty:* 2 full-time, 1 part-time/adjunct. *Students:* 15 full-time (12 women), 3 part-time (all women). Average age 25. 47 applicants, 28% accepted, 10 enrolled. In 2014, 16 master's awarded. *Degree requirements:* For master's, comprehensive exam, 18 credit hours of required courses; 18 credit hours in academic track courses; 6 credit hours of supervised internship. *Entrance requirements:* For master's, GRE, 3 letters of recommendation, resume, writing sample, statement of purpose, official transcripts. Additional exam requirements/recommendations for international students: Required—TOEFL. *Application deadline:* For fall admission, 1/15 priority date for domestic and international students; for spring admission, 10/1 for domestic and international students. Applications are processed on a rolling basis. Application fee: $55 ($65 for international students). Electronic applications accepted. *Financial support:* Research assistantships with partial tuition reimbursements, career-related internships or fieldwork, and unspecified assistantships available. *Faculty research:* Museum studies, audience evaluation, community engagement, material culture, anthropology, historical and legal backgrounds by which museums have come to control culturally-sensitive objects. *Unit head:* Dr. Peter H. Welsh, Director, 785-864-5702, E-mail: phwelsh@ku.edu. *Application contact:* Kay Isbell, Graduate Academic Advisor, 785-864-2306, E-mail: kisbell@ku.edu. Website: http://museumstudies.ku.edu/

University of Louisville, Graduate School, College of Arts and Sciences, Department of Fine Arts, Louisville, KY 40292. Offers art history (MA, PhD); creative art (MA); curatorial studies (MA). *Students:* 15 full-time (10 women), 9 part-time (5 women); includes 5 minority (2 Black or African American, non-Hispanic/Latino; 2 Asian, non-Hispanic/Latino; 1 Hispanic/Latino), 2 international. Average age 36. 27 applicants, 63% accepted, 8 enrolled. In 2014, 3 master's, 1 doctorate awarded. *Degree requirements:* For master's, thesis; for doctorate, 2 foreign languages, comprehensive exam, thesis/dissertation. *Entrance requirements:* For master's and doctorate, GRE General Test. Additional exam requirements/recommendations for international students: Required—TOEFL (minimum score 550 paper-based; 79 iBT). *Application deadline:* For fall admission, 1/15 for domestic students, 5/1 priority date for international students; for spring admission, 11/1 priority date for international students; for summer admission, 4/1 priority date for international students. Applications are processed on a rolling basis. Application fee: $60. *Expenses:* Tuition, state resident: full-time $11,326; part-time $630 per credit hour. Tuition, nonresident: full-time $23,568; part-time $1311 per credit hour. *Required fees:* $196. Tuition and fees vary according to program and reciprocity agreements. *Financial support:* Teaching assistantships with full tuition reimbursements available. Financial award application deadline: 1/15. *Faculty research:* Art history in the periods from ancient to contemporary and various regions, 2D and 3D studio areas, intermedia, curatorial studies. *Unit head:* Prof. Ying Kit Chan, Chair, 502-852-6794, Fax: 502-852-6791, E-mail: chan@louisville.edu. *Application contact:* Libby Leggett, Director, Graduate Admissions, 502-852-3101, Fax: 502-852-6536, E-mail: gradadm@louisville.edu. Website: http://art.louisville.edu

The University of Manchester, School of Arts, Histories and Cultures, Manchester, United Kingdom. Offers anthropology, media and performance (PhD); applied theatre professional (PhD); archaeology (PhD); art history and visual studies (PhD); arts

management and cultural policy (PhD); classics and ancient history (PhD); composition (PhD); creative writing (PhD); drama (PhD); economic and social history (PhD); electroacoustic composition (PhD); English and American studies (PhD); history (PhD); humanitarianism and conflict response (PhD); museology (PhD); music (PhD); musicology (PhD); religions and theology (PhD).

University of Michigan–Flint, Graduate Programs, Program in Arts Administration, Flint, MI 48502-1950. Offers museum and visual arts (MA); performance (MA). Part-time programs available. *Faculty:* 2 part-time/adjunct (1 woman). *Students:* 7 full-time (5 women), 11 part-time (8 women); includes 3 minority (all Black or African American, non-Hispanic/Latino), 1 international. Average age 36. 10 applicants, 100% accepted, 9 enrolled. In 2014, 10 master's awarded. *Degree requirements:* For master's, thesis, internship. *Entrance requirements:* For master's, bachelor's degree in the arts (visual art, theatre, dance, music, etc.) from accredited institution with minimum undergraduate GPA of 3.0. Additional exam requirements/recommendations for international students: Required—TOEFL (minimum score 84 iBT), IELTS (minimum score 6.5). *Application deadline:* For fall admission, 8/1 for domestic students, 5/1 for international students; for winter admission, 11/15 for domestic students, 9/15 for international students. Applications are processed on a rolling basis. Application fee: $55. Electronic applications accepted. Application fee is waived when completed online. *Financial support:* Federal Work-Study and scholarships/grants available. Support available to part-time students. Financial award application deadline: 3/1; financial award applicants required to submit FAFSA. *Unit head:* Dr. Sarah Lippert, Interim Director, 810-766-6679, E-mail: sarlipp@umflint.edu. *Application contact:* Bradley T. Maki, Director of Graduate Admissions, 810-762-3171, Fax: 810-766-6789, E-mail: bmaki@umflint.edu. Website: http://www.umflint.edu/graduateprograms/arts-administration-ma

University of Missouri–St. Louis, College of Arts and Sciences, Department of History, St. Louis, MO 63121. Offers history (MA); museum studies (MA, Certificate). Part-time and evening/weekend programs available. *Faculty:* 16 full-time (5 women), 2 part-time/adjunct (0 women). *Students:* 19 full-time (14 women), 25 part-time (8 women); includes 2 minority (both Black or African American, non-Hispanic/Latino). Average age 35. 54 applicants, 52% accepted, 11 enrolled. In 2014, 7 master's awarded. *Degree requirements:* For master's, thesis (for some programs). *Entrance requirements:* For master's, writing sample; minimum GPA of 2.75 (for history), 3.2 (for museum studies). Additional exam requirements/recommendations for international students: Required—TOEFL (minimum score 550 paper-based; 79 iBT), IELTS (minimum score 6.5). *Application deadline:* For fall admission, 3/15 for domestic and international students; for spring admission, 10/15 for domestic and international students. Applications are processed on a rolling basis. Application fee: $50 ($40 for international students). Electronic applications accepted. *Expenses:* Tuition, state resident: full-time $7364; part-time $409.10 per hour. Tuition, nonresident: full-time $18,153; part-time $1008.50 per hour. *Financial support:* In 2014–15, 4 teaching assistantships with full and partial tuition reimbursements (averaging $9,000 per year) were awarded; research assistantships with full and partial tuition reimbursements and career-related internships or fieldwork also available. Financial award applicants required to submit FAFSA. *Faculty research:* United States, European, East Asian, Latin American, and African history. *Unit head:* Dr. Andrew Hurley, Director of Graduate Studies, 314-516-5680, Fax: 314-516-5781, E-mail: ahurley@umsl.edu. *Application contact:* 314-516-5458, Fax: 314-516-6996, E-mail: gradadm@umsl.edu. Website: http://www.umsl.edu/~history/

University of New Hampshire, Graduate School, College of Liberal Arts, Department of History, Durham, NH 03824. Offers history (MA); museum studies (MA). Part-time programs available. *Faculty:* 21 full-time (11 women). *Students:* 27 full-time (12 women), 12 part-time (5 women); includes 1 minority (Two or more races, non-Hispanic/Latino), 2 international. Average age 34. 71 applicants, 51% accepted, 13 enrolled. In 2014, 10 master's, 3 doctorates awarded. *Degree requirements:* For master's, thesis or alternative; for doctorate, 2 foreign languages, thesis/dissertation. *Entrance requirements:* For master's and doctorate, GRE General Test. Additional exam requirements/recommendations for international students: Required—TOEFL (minimum score 550 paper-based; 80 iBT). *Application deadline:* For fall admission, 6/1 priority date for domestic students, 4/15 for international students; for spring admission, 12/1 for domestic students. Applications are processed on a rolling basis. Application fee: $65. Electronic applications accepted. *Expenses:* Tuition, state resident: full-time $13,500; part-time $750 per credit hour. Tuition, nonresident: full-time $26,460; part-time $1110 per credit hour. *Required fees:* $1788; $447 per semester. *Financial support:* In 2014–15, 18 students received support, including 1 fellowship, 14 teaching assistantships; research assistantships, career-related internships or fieldwork, Federal Work-Study, scholarships/grants, and tuition waivers (full and partial) also available. Support available to part-time students. Financial award application deadline: 2/15. *Unit head:* Dr. Eliga Gould, Chairperson, 603-862-3012. *Application contact:* Lara Demarest, Administrative Assistant, 603-862-1765, E-mail: history.grad@unh.edu. Website: http://cola.unh.edu/history

The University of North Carolina at Greensboro, Graduate School, College of Arts and Sciences, Department of History, Greensboro, NC 27412-5001. Offers historic preservation (Certificate); history (MA); museum studies (Certificate); U.S. history (PhD). Part-time programs available. *Entrance requirements:* For master's, GRE General Test. Additional exam requirements/recommendations for international students: Required—TOEFL. Electronic applications accepted. *Faculty research:* Simultaneous discovery in science, progressive social reform, Robert Mayer.

The University of North Carolina at Greensboro, Graduate School, College of Arts and Sciences, Department of Interior Architecture, Greensboro, NC 27412-5001. Offers historic preservation (Certificate); interior architecture (MS); museum studies (Certificate). *Degree requirements:* For master's, thesis. *Entrance requirements:* For master's, GRE General Test or MAT, bachelor's degree in interior design, interview, portfolio. Additional exam requirements/recommendations for international students: Required—TOEFL. Electronic applications accepted.

University of North Texas, Robert B. Toulouse School of Graduate Studies, Denton, TX 76203-5459. Offers accounting (MS); applied anthropology (MA, MS); applied behavior analysis (Certificate); applied geography (MA); applied technology and performance improvement (M Ed, MS); art education (MA); art history (MA); art museum education (Certificate); arts leadership (Certificate); audiology (Au D); behavior analysis (MS); behavioral science (PhD); biochemistry and molecular biology (MS); biology (MA, MS); biomedical engineering (MS); business analysis (MS); chemistry (MS); clinical health psychology (PhD); communication studies (MA, MS); computer engineering (MS); computer science (MS); counseling (M Ed, MS), including clinical mental health counseling (MS), college and university counseling, elementary school counseling, secondary school counseling; creative writing (MA); criminal justice (MS); curriculum and instruction (M Ed); decision sciences (MBA); design (MA, MFA), including fashion design (MFA), innovation studies, interior design (MFA); early childhood studies (MS); economics (MS); educational leadership (M Ed, Ed D); educational psychology (MS, PhD), including family studies (MS), gifted and talented (MS), human development (MS), learning and cognition (MS), research, measurement and evaluation (MS); electrical engineering (MS); emergency management (MPA); engineering technology (MS); English (MA); English as a second language (MA); environmental science (MS); finance

(MBA, MS); financial management (MPA); French (MA); health services management (MBA); higher education (M Ed, Ed D); history (MA, MS); hospitality management (MS); human resources management (MPA); information science (MS); information systems (PhD); information technologies (MBA); interdisciplinary studies (MA, MS); international studies (MA); international sustainable tourism (MS); jazz studies (MM); journalism (MA, MJ, Graduate Certificate), including interactive and virtual digital communication (Graduate Certificate), narrative journalism (Graduate Certificate), public relations (Graduate Certificate); kinesiology (MS); linguistics (MA); local government management (MPA); logistics (PhD); logistics and supply chain management (MBA); long-term care, senior housing, and aging services (MA); management (PhD); marketing (MBA); mathematics (MA, MS); mechanical and energy engineering (MS, PhD); music (MA), including ethnomusicology, music theory, musicology, performance; music composition (PhD); music education (MM Ed, PhD); nonprofit management (MPA); operations and supply chain management (MBA); performance (MM, DMA); philosophy (MA); political science (MA); professional and technical communication (MA); radio, television and film (MA, MFA); rehabilitation counseling (Certificate); sociology (MA); Spanish (MA); special education (M Ed); speech-language pathology (MA); strategic management (MBA); studio art (MFA); teaching (M Ed); MBA/MS. Part-time and evening/weekend programs available. Postbaccalaureate distance learning degree programs offered. *Faculty:* 651 full-time (215 women), 233 part-time/adjunct (139 women). *Students:* 3,040 full-time (1,598 women), 3,401 part-time (2,097 women); includes 1,740 minority (533 Black or African American, non-Hispanic/Latino; 15 American Indian or Alaska Native, non-Hispanic/Latino; 286 Asian, non-Hispanic/Latino; 746 Hispanic/Latino; 3 Native Hawaiian or other Pacific Islander, non-Hispanic/Latino; 157 Two or more races, non-Hispanic/Latino), 1,145 international. Terminal master's awarded for partial completion of doctoral program. *Degree requirements:* For master's, variable foreign language requirement, comprehensive exam (for some programs), thesis (for some programs); for doctorate, variable foreign language requirement, comprehensive exam (for some programs), thesis/dissertation; for other advanced degree, variable foreign language requirement, comprehensive exam (for some programs). *Entrance requirements:* For master's and doctorate, GRE, GMAT. Additional exam requirements/recommendations for international students: Required—TOEFL (minimum score 550 paper-based; 79 iBT). *Application deadline:* For fall admission, 7/15 for domestic students, 3/15 for international students; for spring admission, 11/15 for domestic students, 9/15 for international students; for summer admission, 5/1 for domestic students. Applications are processed on a rolling basis. Application fee: $60. Electronic applications accepted. *Expenses:* Tuition, state resident: full-time $5450; part-time $3633 per year. Tuition, nonresident: full-time $11,966; part-time $7977 per year. *Required fees:* $1301; $398 per credit hour. $685 per semester. Tuition and fees vary according to program and reciprocity agreements. *Financial support:* Fellowships with partial tuition reimbursements, research assistantships with partial tuition reimbursements, teaching assistantships, career-related internships or fieldwork, Federal Work-Study, institutionally sponsored loans, scholarships/grants, health care benefits, and library assistantships available. Support available to part-time students. Financial award applicants required to submit FAFSA. *Unit head:* Mark Wardell, Dean, 940-565-2383, E-mail: mark.wardell@unt.edu. *Application contact:* Toulouse School of Graduate Studies, 940-565-2383, Fax: 940-565-2141, E-mail: gradsch@unt.edu. Website: http://tsgs.unt.edu/

University of Oklahoma, College of Liberal Studies, Norman, OK 73019. Offers administrative leadership (MA Ed); liberal studies (MA), including human and health services administration, museum studies; prevention science (MPS). Part-time programs available. Postbaccalaureate distance learning degree programs offered (no on-campus study). *Faculty:* 14 full-time (8 women), 3 part-time/adjunct (1 woman). *Students:* 65 full-time (33 women), 600 part-time (301 women); includes 184 minority (57 Black or African American, non-Hispanic/Latino; 37 American Indian or Alaska Native, non-Hispanic/Latino; 8 Asian, non-Hispanic/Latino; 44 Hispanic/Latino; 3 Native Hawaiian or other Pacific Islander, non-Hispanic/Latino; 35 Two or more races, non-Hispanic/Latino), 1 international. Average age 35. 217 applicants, 97% accepted, 141 enrolled. In 2014, 155 master's, 5 other advanced degrees awarded. Terminal master's awarded for partial completion of doctoral program. *Degree requirements:* For master's, comprehensive exam (for some programs), thesis optional, practicum (for museum studies only); for Graduate Certificate, comprehensive exam (for some programs), thesis optional. *Entrance requirements:* For master's and Graduate Certificate, minimum cumulative GPA of 3.0 in previous undergraduate/graduate coursework. Additional exam requirements/recommendations for international students: Required—TOEFL (minimum score 79 iBT). *Application deadline:* For fall admission, 7/1 for domestic and international students; for winter admission, 12/1 for domestic and international students; for spring admission, 5/1 for domestic and international students. Application fee: $50 ($100 for international students). Electronic applications accepted. *Expenses:* Tuition, state resident: full-time $4394; part-time $183.10 per credit hour. Tuition, nonresident: full-time $16,970; part-time $707.10 per credit hour. *Required fees:* $2892; $109.95 per credit hour. $126.50 per semester. *Financial support:* In 2014–15, 107 students received support. Career-related internships or fieldwork, Federal Work-Study, institutionally sponsored loans, scholarships/grants, health care benefits, and tuition waivers (partial) available. Support available to part-time students. Financial award application deadline: 6/1; financial award applicants required to submit FAFSA. *Faculty research:* Race, crime, and class inequality; human trafficking; textual analysis and early Christianity; drug policy implementation; professionalism in police practice; service-learning; Chinese cultural studies. *Unit head:* Dr. James Pappas, Dean/Vice President of OU Outreach, 405-325-6361, Fax: 405-325-7132, E-mail: jpappas@ou.edu. *Application contact:* Missy Heinze, Recruitment Coordinator, 405-325-0559, Fax: 405-325-7132, E-mail: mheinze@ou.edu. Website: http://www.ou.edu/cls/

University of San Francisco, College of Arts and Sciences, Museum Studies Program, San Francisco, CA 94117-1080. Offers MA. *Faculty:* 2 full-time (both women), 5 part-time/adjunct (all women). *Students:* 25 full-time (22 women), 18 part-time (14 women); includes 11 minority (1 Black or African American, non-Hispanic/Latino; 3 Asian, non-Hispanic/Latino; 6 Hispanic/Latino; 1 Two or more races, non-Hispanic/Latino), 1 international. Average age 29. 105 applicants, 44% accepted, 22 enrolled. *Application deadline:* For fall admission, 2/1 for domestic students. *Expenses:* Tuition: Full-time $21,762; part-time $1209 per credit hour. Tuition and fees vary according to degree level, campus/location and program. *Financial support:* In 2014–15, 13 students received support. *Unit head:* Dr. Marjorie Schwarzer, Dean, 415-422-5685. *Application contact:* Mark Landerghini, Information Contact, 415-422-5101, Fax: 415-422-2217, E-mail: asgraduate@usfca.edu. Website: http://www.usfca.edu/artsci/muse/

University of South Carolina, The Graduate School, College of Arts and Sciences, Department of History, Program in Public History, Columbia, SC 29208. Offers archive management (MA); historic preservation (MA); museum administration (MA); museum management (Certificate); MLIS/MA. *Degree requirements:* For master's, one foreign language, thesis, internship. *Entrance requirements:* For master's, GRE General Test, writing sample. Additional exam requirements/recommendations for international students: Required—TOEFL. Electronic applications accepted. *Faculty research:* Museum studies, historic preservation, archives administration.

Museum Studies

University of South Florida, Innovative Education, Tampa, FL 33620-9951. *Unit head:* Kathy Barnes, Interdisciplinary Programs Coordinator, 813-974-8031, Fax: 813-974-7061, E-mail: barnesk@usf.edu. *Application contact:* Karen Tylinski, Metro Initiatives, 813-974-9943, Fax: 813-974-7061, E-mail: ktylinsk@usf.edu.
Website: http://www.usf.edu/innovative-education/

The University of the Arts, College of Art, Media and Design, Department of Museum Studies, Philadelphia, PA 19102-4944. Offers museum communication (MA); museum education (MA); museum exhibition planning and design (MFA). *Accreditation:* NASAD. *Degree requirements:* For master's, thesis, internship. *Entrance requirements:* For master's, official transcripts, three letters of recommendation, one- to two-page statement, personal interview; academic writing sample and examples of work (for museum communication); two examples of academic and professional writing (for museum education); portfolio and/or writing samples (for museum exhibition planning and design). Additional exam requirements/recommendations for international students: Required—TOEFL (minimum score 580 paper-based, 92 iBT) or IELTS (minimum score 6.5).

University of Toronto, School of Graduate Studies, Faculty of Information Studies, Program in Museum Studies, Toronto, ON M5S 2J7, Canada. Offers MM St. *Entrance requirements:* Additional exam requirements/recommendations for international students: Required—TOEFL (minimum score 580 paper-based; 93 iBT), TWE (minimum score 5). Electronic applications accepted. *Expenses:* Contact institution.

The University of Tulsa, Graduate School, Program in Museum Science and Management, Tulsa, OK 74104-3189. Offers MA. Part-time programs available. *Faculty:* 9 full-time (1 woman). *Students:* 6 full-time (all women), 4 part-time (3 women); includes 3 minority (1 Black or African American, non-Hispanic/Latino; 2 American Indian or Alaska Native, non-Hispanic/Latino). Average age 33. 6 applicants, 50% accepted, 1 enrolled. In 2014, 4 master's awarded. *Degree requirements:* For master's, final semester internship or independent research project. *Entrance requirements:* For master's, GRE General Test. Additional exam requirements/recommendations for international students: Required—TOEFL (minimum score 575 paper-based; 91 iBT), IELTS (minimum score 6.5). *Application deadline:* Applications are processed on a rolling basis. Application fee: $55. Electronic applications accepted. *Expenses: Tuition:* Full-time $20,160; part-time $1120 per credit hour. *Required fees:* $6 per credit hour. Tuition and fees vary according to course level and course load. *Financial support:* In 2014–15, 8 students received support, including 3 fellowships with full and partial tuition reimbursements available (averaging $4,882 per year), 5 research assistantships with full and partial tuition reimbursements available (averaging $10,056 per year), 2 teaching assistantships with full and partial tuition reimbursements available (averaging $6,570 per year); career-related internships or fieldwork, Federal Work-Study, scholarships/grants, health care benefits, tuition waivers (full and partial), and unspecified assistantships also available. Support available to part-time students. *Total annual research expenditures:* $40,000. *Unit head:* Dr. Bob Pickering, Director, 918-596-2706, Fax: 918-596-2770, E-mail: bob-pickering@utulsa.edu. *Application contact:* Graduate School, 918-631-2336, Fax: 918-631-2156, E-mail: grad@utulsa.edu.
Website: http://graduate.utulsa.edu/academics/museum-science-management-program/

University of Washington, Graduate School, Museology Graduate Program, Seattle, WA 98195. Offers MA. *Degree requirements:* For master's, thesis or alternative. *Entrance requirements:* For master's, GRE General Test, minimum GPA of 3.0. Additional exam requirements/recommendations for international students: Required—TOEFL (minimum score 580 paper-based; 92 iBT). Electronic applications accepted. *Expenses:* Contact institution. *Faculty research:* Collection management, conservation, art history, anthropology, administration.

University of West Georgia, College of Arts and Humanities, Department of History, Carrollton, GA 30118. Offers history (MA); museum studies (Certificate); public history (Certificate). Part-time and evening/weekend programs available. *Faculty:* 15 full-time (6 women). *Students:* 24 full-time (12 women), 15 part-time (9 women); includes 6 minority (5 Black or African American, non-Hispanic/Latino; 1 Hispanic/Latino). Average age 35. 15 applicants, 87% accepted, 7 enrolled. In 2014, 12 master's, 5 other advanced degrees awarded. *Degree requirements:* For master's, one foreign language, comprehensive exam, thesis or alternative. *Entrance requirements:* For master's, GRE General Test (minimum score of 151 on verbal, 4.0 on analytical writing), undergraduate degree in history or related social studies, minimum GPA of 3.0; for Certificate, GRE General Test (minimum score 151 verbal, 4.0 writing), MA from another institution or enrolled in MA at UWG. Additional exam requirements/recommendations for international students: Required—TOEFL (minimum score 523 paper-based; 69 iBT); Recommended—IELTS (minimum score 6). *Application deadline:* For fall admission, 8/1 for domestic students, 6/1 for international students; for spring admission, 11/15 for domestic students, 10/15 for international students. Applications are processed on a rolling basis. Application fee: $40. Electronic applications accepted. *Financial support:* In 2014–15, 1 student received support, including 21 research assistantships with full tuition reimbursements available (averaging $6,000 per year), 2 teaching assistantships (averaging $5,000 per year); career-related internships or fieldwork, scholarships/grants, and unspecified assistantships also available. Support available to part-time students. Financial award application deadline: 4/1; financial award applicants required to submit FAFSA. *Faculty research:* Public history, United States, Europe, Atlantic, world war and society. *Unit head:* Dr. Howard Steven Goodson, Chair, 678-839-6042, E-mail: hgoodson@westga.edu. *Application contact:* Dr. Nadya Williams, Graduate Coordinator, 678-839-5453, E-mail: nwilliam@westga.edu.
Website: http://westga.edu/~history/

University of Wisconsin–Milwaukee, Graduate School, College of Letters and Sciences, Department of Anthropology, Milwaukee, WI 53201-0413. Offers anthropology (PhD); museum studies (Certificate). *Degree requirements:* For master's, thesis or alternative; for doctorate, one foreign language, thesis/dissertation, departmental qualifying exam. *Entrance requirements:* For master's, GRE; for doctorate, GRE, minimum GPA of 3.0, master's degree. Additional exam requirements/recommendations for international students: Required—TOEFL (minimum score 550 paper-based; 79 iBT), IELTS (minimum score 6.5).

University of Wisconsin–Milwaukee, Graduate School, College of Letters and Sciences, Department of Art History, Milwaukee, WI 53201-0413. Offers art history (MA); art museum studies (Certificate). Part-time programs available. *Degree requirements:* For master's, one foreign language, comprehensive exam, thesis or alternative. *Entrance requirements:* For master's, GRE. Additional exam requirements/recommendations for international students: Required—TOEFL (minimum score 550 paper-based; 79 iBT), IELTS (minimum score 6.5). *Faculty research:* Ancient Mediterranean art through contemporary Western art, Chinese art, Pre-Columbian art, film, theory.

Virginia Commonwealth University, Graduate School, School of the Arts, Department of Art History, Richmond, VA 23284-9005. Offers architectural history (MA); art history (MA, PhD); historical studies (MA); museum studies (MA). *Accreditation:* NASAD. *Degree requirements:* For master's, thesis; for doctorate, comprehensive exam, thesis/dissertation. *Entrance requirements:* For master's and doctorate, GRE General Test. Electronic applications accepted. *Faculty research:* Modern, nineteenth-century, Renaissance, American, and medieval art.

Western Illinois University, School of Graduate Studies, College of Fine Arts and Communication, Program in Museum Studies, Macomb, IL 61455-1390. Offers MA, Certificate. *Accreditation:* NASAD. Part-time programs available. *Students:* 15 full-time (13 women), 8 part-time (6 women); includes 4 minority (2 Black or African American, non-Hispanic/Latino; 1 Asian, non-Hispanic/Latino; 1 Hispanic/Latino). Average age 30. 15 applicants, 100% accepted, 6 enrolled. In 2014, 8 master's awarded. *Entrance requirements:* For master's, minimum GPA of 3.0. Additional exam requirements/recommendations for international students: Required—TOEFL (minimum score 600 paper-based; 100 iBT). *Application deadline:* Applications are processed on a rolling basis. Application fee: $30. Electronic applications accepted. *Financial support:* In 2014–15, 5 students received support, including 5 research assistantships with full tuition reimbursements available (averaging $7,544 per year). Financial award applicants required to submit FAFSA. *Unit head:* Dr. Ann Rowson Love, Director, 309-762-9481 Ext. 266, E-mail: a-rowsonlove@wiu.edu. *Application contact:* Dr. Nancy Parsons, Associate Provost and Director of Graduate Studies, 309-298-1806, Fax: 309-298-2345, E-mail: grad-office@wiu.edu.
Website: http://wiu.edu/museumstudies/

BARD GRADUATE CENTER: DECORATIVE ARTS, DESIGN HISTORY, MATERIAL CULTURE

Programs of Study

Bard Graduate Center is a graduate institute affiliated with Bard College that studies the cultural history of the material world. Founded in 1993, it offers M.A. and Ph.D. degrees. Its teaching, research, and exhibitions draw on methodologies and approaches from art and design history, decorative arts, economic history, history of technology, philosophy, anthropology, and archaeology. Areas of particular strength include New York and American material culture, modern design history, history and theory of museums, early modern Europe, global Middle Ages, archaeology, anthropology, and material culture, and cultures of conservation. Hands-on examination of materials and objects is a key part of the curriculum and there is an extensive connection to special programs and exhibition projects with the Metropolitan Museum of Art, the New-York Historical Society, the Brooklyn Museum of Art, the American Museum of Natural History, the Frick Collection, and the Museum of Arts and Design, among other major cultural institutions. As part of their studies, all M.A. students undertake an internship at one of more than 250 institutions around the world and participate in an international study trip. Bard Graduate Center's programs prepare students for careers or career advancement in museums and galleries; auction houses; government agencies; art-related education, research, publishing, and communications; and landscape and historic preservation.

A semiannual interdisciplinary journal, *West 86th: A Journal of Decorative Arts, Design History, and Material Culture,* is published in collaboration with the University of Chicago Press and features scholarly articles that focus on the wider crossroads where the decorative arts meet design history and material culture. Advanced graduate students are invited to submit articles for possible publication.

Research Facilities

Bard Graduate Center occupies two six-story town houses at 18 and 38 West 86th Street in Manhattan. The buildings' elegantly appointed rooms provide an aesthetically appropriate setting for the study of the decorative arts. Its facilities include a 50,000-volume research library, a digital media research lab, exhibition galleries, classrooms, faculty offices, student lounges, outdoor terraces, symposium spaces, and administrative offices.

Financial Aid

Bard Graduate Center offers fellowships, scholarships, and a student campus employment program. Aid is awarded on the basis of need and merit. Financial aid applications are due by January 8. About 85 percent of students receive some financial aid.

Cost of Study

The average annual tuition for incoming full-time students in the 2015–16 academic year was $35,235 for M.A. students, based on a cost of $1,305 per credit. Tuition and fees for Ph.D. students averaged $31,320 for incoming full-time students in the 2015–16 academic year; they vary for subsequent years of doctoral work. Students may contact the Office of Admissions for more detailed and updated fee schedules.

Living and Housing Costs

Bard Hall, located at 410 West 58th Street, provides housing for students, faculty members, and visiting scholars. Nine residential floors offer a variety of furnished studios and one- and two-bedroom suites with kitchens and baths. Apartments are offered year-round. For the 2015–16 academic year, the cost of a studio unit was approximately $17,040, a one-bedroom unit was $20,400, and a two-bedroom unit was $16,860 per student.

Student Group

Bard Graduate Center enrolls approximately 20–25 full-time and a limited number of part-time M.A. students into the program annually and approximately 3 Ph.D. students. Applications are received from many countries and from across the United States. Bard Graduate Center welcomes students of all ages and backgrounds as well as working professionals.

Location

Bard Graduate Center is located on the Upper West Side of Manhattan, near Central Park. It is situated in a landmark neighborhood conveniently served by public transportation, with easy access to the innumerable museums, libraries, auction houses, and galleries of metropolitan New York.

Applying

Students are admitted to the graduate programs annually for fall admission. The application deadline for admission and financial aid is January 8. Applicants to the M.A. program must have a bachelor's degree or the equivalent; applicants to the Ph.D. program are expected to have completed a master's degree in either the decorative arts or a related field. Because of the interdisciplinary nature of the program, there are no limitations on the M.A. applicant's prior field of study. Successful applicants, however, will have had some previous study, training, or work experience in the history of art, architecture, archeology, history, the decorative arts, cultural history, or material culture studies.

Applications should include scores on the General Test of the Graduate Record Examinations (GRE), three letters of recommendation, a short resume, a sample of scholarly writing, and a statement of intent describing academic and professional objectives. International candidates must submit TOEFL scores and a Certification of Finances. An interview is required. The application fee for 2015–16 is $70.

Correspondence and Information
Office of Admissions
Bard Graduate Center
38 West 86th Street
New York, New York 10024
Phone: 212-501-3057
Fax: 212-501-3065
E-mail: admissions@bgc.bard.edu
Website: http://www.bgc.bard.edu/admissions

Bard Graduate Center: Decorative Arts, Design History, Material Culture

THE FACULTY AND THEIR RESEARCH

Bard Graduate Center maintains a distinguished core of full-time faculty members, supplemented by eminent decorative arts scholars visiting from a broad range of national and international museums and institutions of higher learning.

Bard Graduate Center Faculty

Susan Weber, Iris Horowitz Professor in the History of the Decorative Arts and Director; Ph.D., Royal College of Art. Eighteenth- and nineteenth-century decorative arts topics.

Peter N. Miller, Professor and Dean; Ph.D., University of Cambridge. History of historical research.

Kenneth Ames, Professor; Ph.D., University of Pennsylvania. American and European decorative arts and material culture.

Abigail Krasner Balbale, Assistant Professor; Ph.D., Harvard University. Islamic art and material culture studies.

Jeffrey Collins, Professor and Chair of Academic Programs; Ph.D., Yale University. Seventeenth- and eighteenth-century art and culture.

Ivan Gaskell, Professor; Ph.D., University of Cambridge. Material culture of North America and Europe, sixteenth through twentieth centuries.

Aaron Glass, Associate Professor; Ph.D., New York University. Native peoples of the Northwest Coast, museums and anthropology.

Freyja Hartzell, Assistant Professor; Ph.D., Yale University. Nineteenth- and twentieth-century European decorative arts and material culture.

David Jaffee, Professor; Ph.D., Harvard University. Early American material culture, cultural geography and landscape.

Deborah L. Krohn, Associate Professor; Ph.D., Harvard University. Italian renaissance decorative arts and material culture.

François Louis, Associate Professor; Ph.D., University of Zurich. History of Chinese design and visual culture, material culture of Medieval China.

Michele Majer, Assistant Professor; M.A., New York University. European and American clothing and textiles, costume historian.

Andrew Morrall, Professor; Ph.D., Courtauld Institute of Art, London University. Early modern Northern European fine and applied arts.

Elizabeth Simpson, Professor; Ph.D., University of Pennsylvania. Greek, Roman, Ancient Near Eastern, and Egyptian art and archaeology.

Paul Stirton, Associate Professor; Ph.D. University of Glasgow. Nineteenth- and twentieth-century European design and architecture.

Ittai Weinryb, Assistant Professor; Ph.D., Johns Hopkins University. Medieval European artistic and material culture.

Catherine Whalen, Associate Professor; Ph.D., Yale University. American material culture studies, craft and design history.

Elissa Auther, Windgate Research Curator, Museum of Arts and Design and Visiting Associate Professor; Ph.D., University of Maryland, College Park.

Shawn C. Rowlands, BGC-AMNH Postdoctoral Fellow in Museum Anthropology; Ph.D., University of New England.

Vera Solovyeva, Andrew W. Mellon Fellow, Cultures of Conservation; Ph.D. candidate, George Mason University.

Charlotte Vignon, Curator of Decorative Arts, The Frick Collection and Visiting Assistant Professor; Ph.D., Paris-Sorbonne University.

Pat Kirkham, Professor Emeritus; Ph.D., University of London. Histories of design, architecture, and objects; material culture; film; gender.

Professor Michele Majer and her students admire Bard Graduate Center's Focus Gallery's Staging Fashion exhibition, the culmination of a multipart seminar course.

An M.A. student studies the progress of a 3-D printer, one of the pieces of equipment available in Bard Graduate Center's digital media lab.

FASHION INSTITUTE OF TECHNOLOGY
State University of New York
M.A. in Art Market

 For more information, visit http://petersons.to/fitartmarket

Programs of Study

The Fashion Institute of Technology (FIT), a State University of New York (SUNY) college of art and design, business, and technology, is home to a mix of innovative achievers, creative thinkers, and industry pioneers. FIT fosters interdisciplinary initiatives, advances research, and provides access to an international network of professionals. With a reputation for excellence, FIT offers its diverse student body access to world-class faculty, dynamic and relevant curricula, and a superior education at an affordable cost. It offers seven programs of graduate study. The programs in Art Market; Exhibition Design; Fashion and Textile Studies: History, Theory, Museum Practice; and Sustainable Interior Environments lead to the Master of Arts (M.A.) degree. The Illustration program leads to the Master of Fine Arts (M.F.A.) degree. The Master of Professional Studies (M.P.S.) degree programs are Cosmetics and Fragrance Marketing and Management and Global Fashion Management.

Art Market is a 48-credit M.A. program preparing students for careers in the business, collection, and exhibition of art. The curriculum includes art history, writing for the art market, gallery design and operation, business practices, computer technology for the art world, marketing, valuation and appraisal, and art law and professional ethics. Students are required to complete a relevant internship and research and write a qualifying paper. Graduating students also complete a practicum in which they work as a team to assemble a group show from concept to execution at an off-campus commercial space.

Research Facilities

The School of Graduate Studies is primarily located in the campus's Shirley Goodman Resource Center, which also houses the Gladys Marcus Library and The Museum at FIT. School of Graduate Studies facilities include conference rooms; a fully equipped conservation laboratory; a multipurpose laboratory for conservation projects and the dressing of mannequins; storage facilities for costume and textile materials; a graduate student lounge with computer and printer access; a graduate student library reading room with computers, reference materials, and copies of past classes' qualifying and thesis papers; specialized wireless classrooms; traditional and digital illustration studios; and classrooms equipped with model stands, easels, and drafting tables.

The Gladys Marcus Library houses more than 300,000 volumes of print, nonprint, and digital resources. Specialized holdings include industry reference materials, manufacturers' catalogues, original fashion sketches and scrapbooks, photographs, portfolios of plates, and sample books. The FIT Digital Library provides access to over 90 searchable online databases.

The Museum at FIT houses one of the world's most important collections of clothing and textiles and is the only museum in New York City dedicated to the art of fashion. The permanent collection encompasses more than 50,000 garments and accessories dating from the eighteenth century to the present, with particular strength in twentieth-century fashion, as well as 30,000 textiles and 100,000 textile swatches. Each year, nearly 100,000 visitors are drawn to the museum's award-winning exhibitions and public programs.

Financial Aid

FIT directly administers its institutional grants, scholarships, and loans. Federal funding administered by the college may include Federal Perkins Loans, federally subsidized and unsubsidized Direct Loans for students, Grad PLUS loans, and the Federal Work-Study Program. Priority for institutionally administered funds is given to students enrolled and designated as full-time.

Cost of Study

Tuition for New York State residents is $5,435 per semester, or $453 per credit. Out-of-state residents' tuition is $11,105 per semester, or $925 per credit. Tuition and fees are subject to change at the discretion of FIT's Board of Trustees. Additional expenses—for class materials, textbooks, and travel—may apply and vary per program.

Living and Housing Costs

On-campus housing is available to graduate students. Traditional residence hall accommodations (including meal plan) cost from $6,548 to $6,743 per semester. Apartment-style housing options (not including meal plan) cost from $6,060 to $10,095 per semester.

Student Group

Enrollment in the School of Graduate Studies is approximately 200 students per academic year, allowing considerable individual advisement. Students come to FIT from throughout the country and around the world.

Student Outcomes

Art Market graduates find employment as art gallery directors, public art program directors, art consultants for private and corporate collections, art foundation administrators, museum marketing and development directors, independent curators, auction house department heads, and artists' representatives.

Location

FIT is located in Manhattan's Chelsea neighborhood, at the heart of the advertising, visual arts, marketing, fashion, business, design, and communications industries. Students are connected to New York City and gain unparalleled exposure to their field through guest lectures, field trips, internships, and sponsored competitions. The location provides access to major museums, galleries, and auction houses as well as dining, entertainment, and shopping options. The campus is near subway, bus, and commuter rail lines.

Applying

Applicants to all School of Graduate Studies programs must hold a baccalaureate degree in an appropriate major from a college or university, with a cumulative GPA of 3.0 or higher. International students from non-English-speaking countries are required to submit minimum TOEFL scores of 550 on the written test, 213 on the computer test, or 80 on the Internet test. Each major has additional, specialized prerequisites for admission; for detailed information, students should visit the School of Graduate Studies on FIT's website. Students applying to the Art Market program must submit GRE scores.

Domestic and international students use the same application when seeking admission. The deadline for completed applications with transcripts and supplemental materials is February 15 for the Art Market program. After the deadline date, applicants are considered on a rolling admissions basis. Candidates may apply online at fitnyc.edu/gradstudies.

Fashion Institute of Technology

Correspondence and Information

School of Graduate Studies
Shirley Goodman Resource Center, Room E315
Fashion Institute of Technology
227 West 27 Street
New York, New York 10001-5992
Phone: 212-217-4300
Fax: 212-217-4301
E-mail: gradinfo@fitnyc.edu
Websites: http://www.fitnyc.edu/gradstudies
           http://www.fitnyc.edu/artmarket

THE FACULTY
A partial list of faculty members is below. Guest lecturers are not included.

Katherine Jánszky Michaelsen, Associate Chairperson; Ph.D., Columbia.

Catherine Hannah Behrend, M.B.A., NYU; Certificate in Executive Education, INSEAD (France).

David Cohen, M.A., Courtauld Institute of Art, London.

Mari Dumett, Ph.D., Boston University.

John Lee, B.A., Vassar.

Florence Lynch, M.A., Fashion Institute of Technology.

Donald McMichael, M.B.A., Duke.

Enrique Paz, B.F.A., Fashion Institute of Technology.

Alexander Rich, Ph.D., Institute of Fine Arts, NYU.

Lucille A. Roussin, Ph.D., Columbia; J.D., Yeshiva.

Beth Miller Servetar, M.F.A., Bennington.

Gayle M. Skluzacek, B.A., Barat.

Helen Toomer, B.F.A., Arts Institute at Bournemouth (England).

Andrew Weinstein, Ph.D., NYU.

FASHION INSTITUTE OF TECHNOLOGY
State University of New York

M.A. in Fashion and Textile Studies: History, Theory, Museum Practice

 For more information, visit http://petersons.to/fitfashiontextile

Programs of Study

The Fashion Institute of Technology (FIT), a State University of New York (SUNY) college of art and design, business, and technology, is home to a mix of innovative achievers, creative thinkers, and industry pioneers. FIT fosters interdisciplinary initiatives, advances research, and provides access to an international network of professionals. With a reputation for excellence, FIT offers its diverse student body access to world-class faculty, dynamic and relevant curricula, and a superior education at an affordable cost. It offers seven programs of graduate study. The programs in Art Markets; Exhibition Design; Fashion and Textile Studies: History, Theory, Museum Practice; and Sustainable Interior Environments lead to the Master of Arts (M.A.) degree. The Illustration program leads to the Master of Fine Arts (M.F.A.) degree. The Master of Professional Studies (M.P.S.) degree programs are Cosmetics and Fragrance Marketing and Management, and Global Fashion Management.

The 48-credit, full- or part-time Fashion and Textile Studies: History, Theory, Museum Practice M.A. program prepares students for professional curatorial, conservation, education, and other scholarly careers that focus on historical clothing, accessories, textiles, and related materials. The curriculum incorporates conservation skills, current collections management methods, exhibition techniques, art historical methodologies, material culture studies, and gender studies. The program draws on the resources of The Museum at FIT, one of the world's largest collections of clothing, textiles, and accessories. Students may elect either a conservation or curatorial emphasis; they may also select up to two independent study courses with an appropriate focus on their chosen specialization. All students are required to complete an internship in the field, write a qualifying paper based on original research, and take an active role in a yearlong course culminating in a professional exhibition.

Research Facilities

The School of Graduate Studies is primarily located in the campus's Shirley Goodman Resource Center, which also houses the Gladys Marcus Library and The Museum at FIT. School of Graduate Studies facilities include conference rooms; a fully equipped conservation laboratory; a multipurpose laboratory for conservation projects and the dressing of mannequins; storage facilities for costume and textile materials; a graduate student lounge with computer and printer access; a graduate student library reading room with computers, reference materials, and copies of past classes' qualifying and thesis papers; specialized wireless classrooms; traditional and digital illustration studios; and classrooms equipped with model stands, easels, and drafting tables.

The Gladys Marcus Library houses more than 300,000 volumes of print, nonprint, and digital resources. Specialized holdings include industry reference materials, manufacturers' catalogues, original fashion sketches and scrapbooks, photographs, portfolios of plates, and sample books. The FIT Digital Library provides access to over 90 searchable online databases.

The Museum at FIT houses one of the world's most important collections of clothing and textiles and is the only museum in New York City dedicated to the art of fashion. The permanent collection encompasses more than 50,000 garments and accessories dating from the eighteenth century, with particular strength in twentieth-century fashion, as well as 30,000 textiles and 100,000 textile swatches. Each year, nearly 100,000 visitors are drawn to the museum's award-winning exhibitions and public programs.

Financial Aid

FIT directly administers its institutional grants, scholarships, and loans. Federal funding administered by the college may include Federal Perkins Loans, federally subsidized and unsubsidized Direct Loans for students, Grad PLUS loans, and the Federal Work-Study Program. Priority for institutionally administered funds is given to students enrolled and designated as full-time.

Cost of Study

Tuition for New York State residents is $5,435 per semester, or $453 per credit. Out-of-state residents' tuition is $11,105 per semester, or $925 per credit. Tuition and fees are subject to change at the discretion of FIT's Board of Trustees. Additional expenses—for class materials, textbooks, and travel—may apply and vary per program.

Living and Housing Costs

On-campus housing is available to graduate students. Traditional residence hall accommodations (including meal plan) cost from $6,548 to $6,743 per semester. Apartment-style housing options (not including meal plan) cost from $6,060 to $10,095 per semester.

Student Group

Enrollment in the School of Graduate Studies is approximately 200 students per academic year, allowing considerable individualized advisement. Students come to FIT from throughout the country and around the world.

Student Outcomes

Graduates of the Fashion and Textile Studies: History, Theory, Museum Practice program find positions as museum curators, research specialists, collections managers and registrars, historic house directors, museum educators, independent exhibition curators, corporate curators, fashion and textile historians, costume and textile conservators, auction house department specialists and researchers, vintage clothing and textile dealers, and consultants.

Location

FIT is located in Manhattan's Chelsea neighborhood, at the heart of the advertising, visual arts, marketing, fashion, business, design, and communications industries. Students are connected to New York City and gain unparalleled exposure to their field through guest lectures, field trips, internships, and sponsored competitions. The location provides access to major museums, galleries, and auction houses as well as dining, entertainment, and shopping options. The campus is near subway, bus, and commuter rail lines.

Applying

Applicants to all School of Graduate Studies programs must hold a baccalaureate degree in an appropriate major from a college or university, with a cumulative GPA of 3.0 or higher. International students from non-English-speaking countries are required to submit minimum TOEFL scores of 550 on the written test, 213 on the computer test, or 80 on the Internet test. Students applying to the Fashion and Textile Studies: History, Theory, Museum Practice program must submit GRE scores. Each major has additional, specialized prerequisites for admission; for detailed information, students should visit the School of Graduate Studies on FIT's website.

Fashion Institute of Technology

Domestic and international students use the same application when seeking admission. The deadline for completed applications with transcripts and supplemental materials is February 15 for the Fashion and Textile Studies: History, Theory, Museum Practice program. After the deadline date, applicants are considered on a rolling admissions basis. Candidates may apply online at fitnyc.edu/gradstudies.

Correspondence and Information

School of Graduate Studies
Shirley Goodman Resource Center, Room E315
Fashion Institute of Technology
227 West 27 Street
New York, New York 10001-5992
Phone: 212-217-4300
Fax: 212-217-4301
E-mail: gradinfo@fitnyc.edu
Websites: http://www.fitnyc.edu/gradstudies
        http://www.fitnyc.edu/fashiontextilehistory

THE FACULTY

A partial list of faculty members is below. Guest lecturers are not included.

Denyse Montegut, Associate Chairperson; Ph.D. candidate, Delaware.
June Burns Bové, M.A., NYU.
Sarah Byrd, M.A., Fashion Institute of Technology.
Joyce Denney, Ph.D. candidate, Bard Graduate Studies.
Lourdes M. Font, Ph.D., NYU.
Rebecca Kelly, M.S., University of Rhode Island.
Sarah Scaturro, B.A., Colorado.
Valerie Soll, B.A., Oregon.
Deborah Trupin, M.A., NYU.

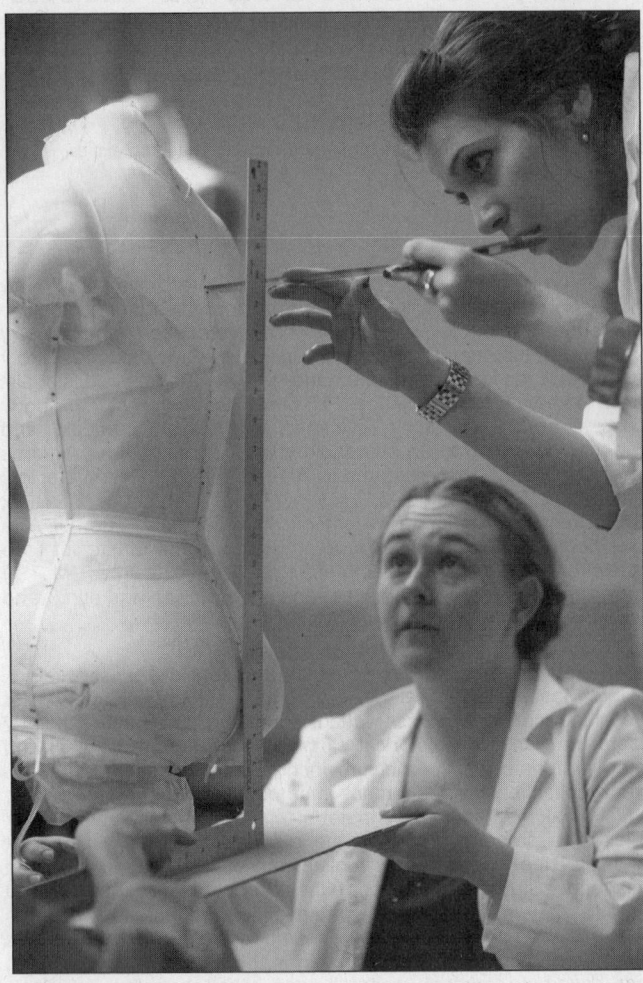

NEW YORK STUDIO SCHOOL OF DRAWING, PAINTING & SCULPTURE

Master of Fine Arts Program

 http://petersons.to/nystudioschoolmfa

Programs of Study

The New York Studio School is committed to providing aspiring artists with a significant education that will last a lifetime. Students are encouraged to question and think about the practice of drawing, painting, and sculpture at all times. Master of Fine Arts (MFA) students graduate from the program with an ambitious studio practice, a developed understanding of the language of art, and an enlarged imagination stirred by an established work ethic.

During the first year of study, students choose a core faculty member with whom they work alongside in an atelier model. Faculty members are present in the classrooms two days each week, and students are expected to work on the objectives set by the instructors throughout the week. Faculty contact hours are reduced as students develop in their second year. MFA candidates work in semi-private studios toward the completion of their individual thesis projects.

The MFA programs are offered with concentrations in painting or in sculpture and are based on maintaining a full-time, rigorous studio practice. Students are engaged in their work a minimum of 40 hours per week for the duration of their two years at the School. Studio practice is balanced with Critical Studies courses, in addition to peer and instructed critiques. Lectures and seminars are held throughout the semester, as well as small group discussion with current and visiting faculty. Students must complete 60 credits to successfully achieve the Master of Fine Arts degree, and credits must include all required courses. A residency of at least two academic years is necessary to complete the degree. Students have access to their studios on a full-time basis. While enrolled, students are immersed in New York City's museums, arts organizations, and culture as a resource for their research.

The School's internationally recognized Marathon Programs were developed in 1988 by Dean Graham Nickson, initially as a measure for the rest of the semester at the start of the program year. The program has since expanded to become a core component of the School's curriculum. The interest in the Marathon Programs has led to a wider audience of participants outside the full-time student body. Renowned artists, art historians, dealers, collectors, art educators, writers, journalists, and students of all levels and affiliations have since experienced the intensity of the program. The Marathon Sessions are offered three times during the academic year: fall, spring, and summer.

Research Facilities

The John McEnroe Library's mission is to support the New York Studio School's programs and courses by providing materials and information for students, faculty, staff, and visiting lecturers. Holdings include monographs on artists, art historical texts, art periodicals, and exhibition catalogs, as well as an extensive lecture archive, comprising audio and video recordings of lectures from the past thirty years, featuring artists, historians, critics, and philosophers.

The library provides an online catalog to check the holdings of the collection, as well as access to research databases and indexes that aid in scholarly research.

Financial Aid

The financial aid programs are part of the School's desire to attract qualified students from diverse backgrounds. Any student who would like to be considered for financial assistance from the School must complete a financial aid application and submit it to Student Services by the deadline date each year. Financial aid scholarships are contingent on the continuation of satisfactory progress in all enrolled courses and are available to all full-time enrolled students. Scholarships are available for part-time students during the summer session.

Cost of Study

For the 2015–16 academic year, the cost for the MFA program is $11,437.50 per semester. The cost for the Certificate program is $7,425 per semester. For additional, up-to-date cost information, prospective students should visit www.nyss.org/admissions-services/tuition-fees-financial-aid/.

Living and Housing Costs

The School does not have facilities to house students. Upon acceptance, students receive information on housing opportunities in New York, including listings of temporary accommodations and help on searching for suitable living situations. The School is easily accessible by public transport from the outer boroughs and New Jersey. Rents in the outer boroughs tend to be lower than in Manhattan. Less expensive situations can be found through sublets or by living with roommates. Students should plan to find proper accommodations prior to enrolling.

Student Group

The Studio School welcomes a diverse demographic of students varying in ages and geographical origins; one third of the full-time student body is composed of international students. At the Studio School, the incentive to work comes from the students themselves without the distraction of too many diversionary projects or assignments. The students here are excited to remain in the studio and to concentrate on their independent work.

The measure of each student's development is particular to that individual, and progresses without the pressure of producing accomplished works. The amount learned in the process is the criterion of success. At the School, the pursuit of authenticity tends to reject the distractions of style or the rush for novelty. Response to the contemporary does not lessen the excitement of discovery within the art of the past. No dichotomy between realism and abstraction is assumed at the School. On the contrary, perceptual experience is encouraged to lead the student to the discovery of abstract equivalents, to a deepening grasp of the plastic means.

Location

The School is located on West 8th Street, between Sixth Avenue/Avenue of the Americas and Fifth Avenue. It accessible by subway or the PATH train. The School occupies eight historic buildings with an extraordinary cultural and artistic history. Occupied by various artists, and the original home of the Whitney Museum of American Art from 1931 to 1954, the School's physical home has been a place where art has been created, discussed, and displayed for over a century. In the 45 years that the School has been on West 8th Street, artists and students alike have found both inspiration and comfort in continuing the tradition of drawing, painting, and sculpting in the historic spaces that have played such an important role in the history of art in America.

New York Studio School of Drawing, Painting & Sculpture

Applying

The application deadline for MFA applicants is February 15. Late applications are reviewed on a case-by-case basis; however late applicants may not be eligible for financial aid. MFA candidates are accepted exclusively for enrollment in the fall semester. Applicants must have a bachelor's degree or equivalent to be considered for admission. Forms must be completed online at https://nyss.slideroom.com/#/Login.

Completed applications include the application form, two required essays, a $90 nonrefundable application fee, two letters of recommendation, 20 jpeg images of student work with an image list accompanying the images, and official transcripts from all previous institutions that resulted in the applicant's undergraduate degree. Detailed instructions are available as part of the application form. Partial applications will not be considered. Prospective candidates will be invited for an interview with the Admissions Committee.

For additional information, prospective students should visit http://www.nyss.org/admissions-services/application-requirements/.

Correspondence and Information

New York Studio School
8 West 8th Street
New York, New York 10011
United States
Phone: 212-673-6466
Fax: 212-777-0996
E-mail: info@nyss.org
Website: http://www.nyss.org/programs-courses/mfa-painting-sculpture/

The School's internationally recognized Marathon programs were developed by Dean Graham Nickson, initially as a measure for the rest of the semester at the start of the program year. All MFA and Certificate candidates begin in the Fall and Spring semesters with either a Drawing or Sculpture Marathon.

THE FACULTY

David Cohen, art critic and curator; Gallery Director at the New York Studio School and publisher of *artcritical.com.*

Garth Evans, sculptor; studied at Manchester Junior and Regional Colleges of Art and the Slade School of Fine Art (London).

Bruce Gagnier, sculptor; M.F.A., Columbia. National Academician represented by Lori Bookstein Fine Art.

Judy Glantzman, painter; B.F.A., Rhode Island School of Design. Represented by the Betty Cuningham Gallery, New York City.

Bill Jensen, painter; B.F.A. and M.F.A., University of Minnesota. Represented by Cheim & Read Gallery, New York.

Elisa Jensen, painter; M.A., Smith College and the New York Studio School.

John Lees, painter; B.F.A. and M.F.A., Otis Art Institute. Represented by Betty Cuningham Gallery.

Margrit Lewczuk, painter; studied at Queens College and the Brooklyn Museum Art School.

John Newman, sculptor; B.A., Oberlin College; M.F.A., Yale School of Art.

Graham Nickson, painting and drawing; B.A., Camberwell School of Arts & Crafts; M.A., Royal College of Art (London).

Lee Tribe, sculptor; educated at Saint Martin's School of Art and Birmingham School of Art (England) and the New York Studio School.

Karen Wilkin, art historian and critic; educated at Barnard College and Columbia University. Fulbright and Woodrow Wilson Fellow.

Second-year MFA candidates are provided with semi-private to private studios, allowing for growth and development of their creative practice.

PRATT INSTITUTE
School of Art

Programs of Study

Pratt has been educating professionals for productive careers in the fields of art and design since its founding in 1887. Pratt's School of Art offers an outstanding professional art education taught by a faculty of working professionals that brings high standards and current practices to the classroom. Faculty members have received more than eighteen Tiffany, Fulbright, and Guggenheim awards as well as other prestigious professional awards.

Pratt offers master's degrees in a variety of programs, including Master of Fine Arts in Digital Arts (including animation) or Studio Arts (new forms–nontraditional investigations, painting and drawing, photography, printmaking, sculpture); Master of Science in Art and Design Education (teacher certification) and Dance/Movement Therapy; and Master of Professional Studies in Art Therapy, Art Therapy–Special Needs, Arts and Cultural Management, or Design Management. A postbaccalaureate New York State certification program for the teaching of art in grades pre-K–12 is available for fine arts graduate students. Art Therapy majors electing a special needs concentration are eligible for provisional New York State teaching certification. Pratt also offers a dual degree in Fine Arts and Library and Information Science and a dual degree in Digital Arts and Library Science as well as various certificates for holders of the M.S. in Library Science including Museum Studies, Archives, and Library and Information Studies.

Art and Design Education graduates are prepared to pursue teaching careers in pre-K–12 schools, museums and cultural institutions, or colleges. Graduates of the Creative Arts Therapy program work in psychiatric, medical rehabilitation, geriatric and family therapy, school, substance abuse, and child-life settings. They also learn to work with a variety of patient populations, including patients with eating disorders and the homeless.

All graduate art curricula include supportive course work in the humanities. Students can choose from a wide array of course offerings, including art and design history, comparative literature, philosophy, foreign languages, and social sciences. The graduate programs require the completion of 30 to 68 credits (75 credits for the M.S./M.F.A. dual-degree program) and last from 1½ to 3 years, depending on the curriculum and the number of prerequisites that have not been met at the time of admission. For the granting of degrees, all of the graduate programs require the submission of a thesis or a comparable effort. For the M.F.A., an exhibition and supporting corollary statement are required. For the M.P.S. in Art Therapy and the M.S. in Dance/Movement Therapy, the thesis project may involve research, an extended case study, the development of a project implementing innovative techniques in therapy, or the opportunity to publish an article. For the M.P.S. in Design Management, the thesis project is the preparation of a business case study.

Research Facilities

The Pratt Library contains 186,589 bound volumes, serial backfiles, and other material (including government documents); 251,603 audiovisual materials; and 3,996 microforms and subscribes to 925 periodicals.

Pratt maintains numerous studios, shops, and technical facilities for work in all media as well as state-of-the-art computer facilities. Digital arts labs include state-of-the-art Macintosh, PC/NT, and UNIX operating systems as well as digital video and audio systems. Pratt also has extensive gallery space for exhibitions.

Financial Aid

Financial aid awards are offered through a variety of institutional, state, and federally funded programs. These include Graduate Scholarships awarded by departments to incoming students on the basis of merit, endowed and restricted scholarships for continuing students, and student employment. Assistantships are awarded on a competitive basis to continuing students in all departments. Special alumni-sponsored fellowships are also available.

Cost of Study

Graduate tuition for 2015–16 is $28,638 per year (full-time 18 credits, $1,591 per credit) and student fees are $1,932 per year. The cost of books and supplies varies widely, depending on the program in which the student is enrolled.

Living and Housing Costs

Campus housing continues to be expanded to meet students' needs and is available for single students on a first-come, first-served basis. Housing costs average $17,646 per academic year. Pratt offers limited graduate student housing two blocks away from the campus. There is a plentiful supply of moderately priced rentals in the immediate area and in adjacent neighborhoods for married students seeking housing and for those students choosing to reside off campus.

Student Group

In educating more than five generations of students to be creative, technically skilled, and adaptable professionals, Pratt has gained an international reputation that attracts about 4,600 undergraduate and graduate students annually from forty-eight states and seventy-nine countries.

Location

Pratt Institute's 25-acre, parklike main campus is situated among the turn-of-the-century mansions, Victorian brownstones, and wide, tree-lined boulevards of Clinton Hill, one of Brooklyn's historic neighborhoods. Midtown Manhattan, the heart of New York City, is only 25 minutes away by subway and offers students a vast array of professional, cultural, and recreational opportunities. Pratt also maintains a campus in Manhattan's Chelsea district. Pratt Manhattan houses the Institute's graduate arts and cultural management and design management programs.

The Institute

A private, nonsectarian institute of higher education, Pratt Institute was founded by the industrialist and philanthropist Charles Pratt. Changing with the needs and requirements of the professional world for which it prepares its graduates, Pratt today educates 3,145 undergraduate and 1,411 graduate students for careers in art and design, architecture, and library and information science.

Applying

The deadline for applications and all supporting materials, including portfolio, is January 5. Applicants should complete the application process online. Early submission of applications with all necessary credentials is highly desirable. For applicants who intend to file for financial aid, applications and all supporting documents should be received no later than January 5 for the fall semester and October 1 for the spring semester. Applications received after these dates are considered if openings exist in a particular program.

Correspondence and Information

Graduate Admissions Office
Pratt Institute
200 Willoughby Avenue
Brooklyn, New York 11205
United States
Phone: 718-636-3514
　　　800-331-0834 (toll-free)
Fax: 718-399-4242
E-mail: admissions@pratt.edu
Website: http://www.pratt.edu
　　　http://www.pratt.edu/admissions/request-information (to request information)

THE FACULTY

Gerry Snyder, Dean

Art and Design Education
Heather Lewis, Chair, Associate Professor; Ph.D., NYU.
Lisa Baumwell, Visiting Associate Instructor; Ph.D., NYU.
Lisa Capone, Adjunct Instructor; M.F.A., Pratt.
Mary Elmer-Dewitt, Adjunct Assistant Professor; M.S., Pratt.
Shari Fischberg, Adjunct Instructor; M.F.A., CUNY, Queens.
Borinquen Gallo, Assistant Professor; M.F.A., CUNY, Hunter.
Christopher Kennedy, Assistant Professor; Ph.D., North Carolina at Greensboro.
Tonya Leslie, Visiting Instructor; M.A., NYU.
Joshua Millis, Visiting Instructor, M.F.A., Art Institute of Chicago.
Theodora Skipitares, Associate Professor; M.F.A., NYU.
Aileen Wilson, Professor, Ed.D., Columbia.

Arts and Cultural Management
Mary McBride, Chair; Professor, Ph.D., NYU.
Christopher Shrum, Visiting Assistant Professor; Ph.D., Fielding Graduate University.
Catherine Ashcraft, Visiting Assistant Professor; Ph.D., MIT.
Catherine Cacho-Leary, Visiting Assistant Professor; M.B.A., Keller Graduate School of Management.
Tyra Nicole Dumars, Visiting Assistant Professor; M.P.S., Pratt.
Kristen Earls; M.A., NYU.
Richard Green, Professor.
Daniel Hayek.
Jeffrey Klein, Visiting Assistant Professor; J.D., Fordham.
Christina Rosan, Visiting Assistant Professor; Ph.D., MIT.
Susan Schear, Visiting Assistant Professor.
JoJo Spiker; M.P.S., Pratt.
Denise Tahara, Visiting Associate Professor; Ph.D., NYU.
Kelly Kocinski Trager, Visiting Associate Professor; J.D., Brooklyn Law.
Alicia Whiteman, M.P.S., Pratt.

Creative Arts Therapy
Julie Miller, Chair; M.A./M.S., Hunter.
Linda Siegel, Director of Graduate Art Therapy Program, Assistant Professor.
Joan Wittig, Director of Graduate Dance/Movement Therapy Program, Associate Professor; M.S., CUNY, Hunter.
Claudia Bader, Visiting Instructor; M.P.S., Pratt.
Joachim Boenig, Adjunct Assistant Professor.
Shannon Bradley, Visiting Instructor; M.S., Pratt.
Corinna Brown, Visiting Instructor; M.S., CUNY, Hunter.
Kimberly Bush, Adjunct Assistant Professor; M.F.A., Parsons.
Jean Davis, Adjunct Associate Professor; M.P.S., Pratt.
Christina Devereaux, Visiting Assistant Professor; Ph.D., Santa Barbara Graduate Institute.
Ted Ehrhardt, Adjunct Assistant Professor; M.S., CUNY, Hunter.
Alison Gigl-George, Adjunct Assistant Professor.
Valerie Hubbs, Visiting Instructor; M.S., CUNY, Hunter.
Melissa Klay, Adjunct Instructor; Ph.D., Pacifica Graduate.
Fred Landers, Visiting Instructor; Ph.D., Union (Ohio).
Judith R. Levy, Visiting Instructor.
Judith Luongo, Adjunct Associate Professor; M.P.S., Pratt.
Deborah Rice, Visiting Professor; M.P.S., Pratt.
Maria Romani De Goes, Visiting Instructor; M.P.S., Pratt.
Sara Rothstein, Visiting Instructor; M.P.S., Pratt.
Madeline Rugh, Visiting Associate Professor; Ph.D., Oklahoma.
Dina Schapiro, Adjunct Assistant Professor; M.P.S., Pratt.
Jean Seibel, Visiting Instructor.
Jennifer Frank Tantia, Visiting Instructor; Ph.D., Chicago School of Professional Psychology.
Laurel Thompson, Associate Professor; Ph.D., Union (Ohio).
Susan Tortora, Visiting Assistant Professor; Ph.D.
Elissa White, Visiting Assistant Professor.
Eva Teirstein Young, Visiting Instructor; M.P.S., Pratt.

Design Management
Mary McBride, Chair, Professor; Ph.D., NYU.
Catherine Ashcraft, Visiting Assistant Professor; Ph.D., MIT.
Laurence DeGaetano, Adjunct Assistant Professor; M.B.A., NYU.
Dyanis DeJesus, Visiting Assistant Professor; M.P.S., Pratt.
Tyra Nicole Dumars, Visiting Assistant Professor, M.P.S., Pratt.
Roger Dunbar, Visiting Professor; Ph.D., Cornell.
Scott Fiaschetti, Visiting Associate Professor.
Larry Gibbs, Visiting Assistant Professor.
Richard Green, Professor.

Pratt Institute

Jacqueline McCormack, Adjunct Associate Professor; M.P.S., Pratt.
James Murray, Visiting Assistant Professor; M.P.S., Pratt.
Christina Rosan, Visiting Assistant Professor; Ph.D., MIT.
Jo Ann Stonier, Visiting Assistant Professor; J.D., St. John's (New York).
Marvin Waldman, Visiting Assistant Professor; M.B.A., CUNY, Baruch.
Denise Tahara, Visiting Associate Professor; Ph.D., NYU.
Kelly Kocinski Trager, Visiting Associate Professor; J.D., Brooklyn Law.

Digital Arts
Peter Patchen, Chair; M.F.A., Oregon.
Carla Gannis, Assistant Chair; M.F.A., Boston University.
Justin Berry, Visiting Assistant Professor; M.F.A., Art Institute of Chicago.
Thomas Bonè, Visiting Assistant Professor.
Liubomir Borissov, Associate Professor; Ph.D., Columbia.
Svjetlana Bukvich-Nichols, Visiting Associate Professor; M.F.A., Rensselaer.
Jonathan Cohrs, Visiting Instructor; M.F.A., Parsons.
Elliot Cowan, Visiting Instructor; B.A., Independent College of Art and Design.
Edward Darino, Adjunct Assistant Professor; Ph.D.
Marianna Ellenberg, Visiting Instructor; M.A., Slade School of Art.
Mike Enright, Adjunct Assistant Professor; M.F.A., California Institute of the Arts.
Kay Hines, Adjunct Assistant Professor; B.A., Barnard.
Kenneth Hughes, Visiting Instructor.
Stephen Jackett, Visiting Instructor; M.F.A., School of Visual Arts.
Everett Kane, Assistant Professor; M.F.A., Art Center College of Design.
Hyunsuk Kim, Visiting Instructor.
Linda Lauro-Lazin, Adjunct Associate Professor, M.A., NYIT.
Peter Mackey, Professor; M.F.A., USC.
David Mattingly, Visiting Instructor; M.F.A., Art Center.
Nicholas O'Brien, Visiting Instructor; M.F.A., Colorado at Boulder.
Genevieve Okupniak, Visiting Instructor, M.F.A., California Institute of the Arts.
Michael J. O'Rourke, Professor; Ed.M., Harvard.
Mira Scharf, Visiting Instructor; M.F.A., UCLA.
Claudia Tait, Associate Professor; M.F.A., Maryland.
Katherine Torn, Visiting Instructor; M.F.A., Art Institute of Chicago.
Lukas Wadya, Visiting Instructor; M.F.A., School of Visual Arts.
Gregory Webb, Adjunct Instructor.
Daniel Weisbard, Visiting Instructor; M.F.A., RIT.
Elizabeth White, Visiting Instructor; M.F.A., School of Visual Arts.
Bryan Zanisnik, Visiting Instructor; M.F.A., Hunter.

Fine Arts
Deborah Bright, Chair; M.F.A., Chicago.
Nat Meade, Assistant Chair of Fine Arts, Visiting Instructor; M.F.A., Pratt.
Dina Weiss, Assistant Chair, Visiting Instructor; M.F.A., Parsons.
David Alban, Visiting Assistant Professor; M.F.A., Cranbrook Academy of Art.
Adam Apostolos, Visiting Instructor.
Karen Bachmann, Visiting Assistant Professor; B.F.A., Pratt.
Lisha Bai, Adjunct Assistant Professor; M.F.A., Yale.
Hannah Barrett, Visiting Assistant Professor; M.F.A., Boston University.
Lisa Bateman, Adjunct Associate Professor; M.F.A., Virginia Commonwealth.
Michael Brennan, Adjunct Assistant Professor; M.F.A., Pratt.
Mona Brody, Visiting Assistant Professor; M.F.A., Vermont College.
Howard Buchwald, Professor; M.A., CUNY, Hunter.
David Butler, Adjunct Associate Professor; M.F.A., Washington (Seattle).
Blake Carrington, Visiting Instructor; M.F.A., Syracuse.
William Carroll, Visiting Associate Professor; M.F.A., CUNY, Queens.
Nanette Carter, Adjunct Associate Professor; M.F.A., Pratt.
Cammi Climaco, Visiting Associate Professor; M.F.A., Cranbrook Academy of Art.
Ian Cofre, Visiting Instructor; Columbia.
David Cohen, Visiting Associate Professor; M.A., Courtauld Institute of Art (London).
Alexia Cohen-Tortoledo, Visiting Instructor; B.F.A., Massachusetts College of Art and Design.
James Costanzo, Adjunct Associate Professor; M.F.A., Iowa.
Grayson Cox, Visiting Assistant Professor; M.F.A., Columbia.
Peggy Cyphers, Adjunct Professor; M.F.A., Pratt.
Pradeep Dalal, Visiting Assistant Director; M.F.A., Bard.
Gregory Drasler, Adjunct Associate Professor; M.F.A., University of Illinois.
Kelly Driscoll, Assistant Professor; M.F.A., CUNY, City College.
Samuel Evensen, Visiting Assistant Professor; M.F.A., New York Academy of Art.
Brad Ewing, Visiting Instructor; M.F.A., Rhode Island School of Design.
Patrick Fenton, Visiting Assistant Professor; M.F.A., Stanford.
Allen Frame, Adjunct Associate Professor; B.A., Harvard.
Linda Francis, Adjunct Professor; M.A., CUNY, Hunter.
Michael Fujita, Visiting Assistant Professor; M.F.A., Alfred.
Joseph Fyfe, Adjunct Associate Professor; B.F.A., University of the Arts.
Mariam Ghani, Visiting Associate Professor; M.F.A., School of Visual Arts.
Anne Gilman, Adjunct Associate Professor; M.F.A., CUNY, Brooklyn.
Jonathan Goodman, Visiting Assistant Professor; M.A., Pennsylvania.
David Gothard, Visiting Assistant Professor; B.F.A., Pratt.
Toni Greenbaum, Visiting Associate Professor; M.A., Hunter.
Nancy Grimes, Adjunct Associate Professor; M.F.A., Art Institute of Chicago.
Dave Hardy, Visiting Professor; M.F.A., Yale.
Eric Heist, Visiting Assistant Professor; M.F.A., CUNY, Hunter.
Vera Iliatova, Visiting Assistant Professor; M.F.A., Yale.
Martine Kacynski, Adjunct Associate Professor; M.F.A., Parsons.
Yael Kanarek, Visiting Assistant Professor; M.F.A., Rensselaer.
Shirley Kaneda, Professor; B.F.A., Parsons.
Michael Kirk, Adjunct Professor; M.F.A., Pratt.
Ross Knight, Visiting Assistant Professor; B.F.A., Minnesota, Twin Cities.
Vivien Knussi, Adjunct Instructor; Ph.D., Columbia.
Peter Kruty, Visiting Assistant Professor; M.A., Alabama.
Alexander Kvares, Visiting Assistant Professor, M.F.A., University of Texas
Benjamin LaRocco, Visiting Assistant Professor; M.F.A., Pratt.
David Lantow, Visiting Associate Professor; M.F.A., CUNY, Brooklyn.
Catherine Lecleire, Adjunct Assistant Professor; M.F.A., USC.
Jenny Lee, Adjunct Professor; B.F.A., Cooper Union.
Marc Lepson, Visiting Associate Professor; M.F.A., Art Institute of Chicago.
Frank Lind, Professor; M.F.A., Pratt.
Omar Lopez-Chahoud, Visiting Assistant Professor; M.F.A., Yale.
Patricia Madeja, Associate Professor; B.F.A., Pratt.
Ann Mandelbaum, Adjunct Professor; M.F.A., Pratt.
Dennis Masback, Adjunct Professor; M.F.A., Washington (St. Louis).
J. Martin Mazorra, Visiting Assistant Professor; M.F.A., American.
Dennis McNett, Adjunct Assistant Professor; M.F.A., Pratt.

Jennifer Melby, Adjunct Associate Professor; M.F.A., Pratt.
Anne Messner, Adjunct Professor; B.F.A., Pratt.
Curtis Mitchell, Adjunct Associate Professor; M.F.A., Yale.
John Monti, Professor; M.F.A., Pratt.
Donna Moran, Professor; M.F.A., Pratt.
Robert Morgan, Adjunct Professor; Ph.D., NYU.
Carlos Motta, Visiting Associate Professor; M.F.A., Bard.
Cyrilla Mozenter, Adjunct Professor; M.F.A., Pratt.
Dominique Nahas, Adjunct Associate Professor; M.A., NYU.
Mario Naves, Adjunct Assistant Professor; M.F.A., Pratt.
Ross Neher, Adjunct Professor; M.F.A., Pratt.
Sarah Nicholls, Visiting Assistant Professor; B.A., Sarah Lawrence.
Thirwell Nolen, Adjunct Associate Professor; M.Arch., Georgia Tech.
John O'Connor, Visiting Assistant Professor; M.F.A., Pratt.
Bethany Pelle, Visiting Assistant Professor; M.F.A., Temple.
Sheila Pepe, Adjunct Associate Professor; M.F.A., Tufts.
Catherine Redmond, Adjunct Associate Professor; B.A., SUNY at Binghamton.
Max Reinhardt; Visiting Assistant Professor; M.F.A., Art Institute of Chicago.
William Richards, Adjunct Associate Professor; M.F.A., New Mexico.
Howard Rosenthal, Adjunct Associate Professor; M.F.A., Pratt.
Mary Beth Rozkewicz, Adjunct Associate Professor; B.F.A., SUNY.
Stuart Sachs, Visiting Assistant Professor.
Analia Segal, Visiting Assistant Professor; M.A., NYU.
Beverly Semmes, Visiting Professor; M.F.A., Yale.
Carla Shapiro, Adjunct Assistant Professor; B.F.A., Syracuse.
Jean Shin, Adjunct Associate Professor; M.S., Pratt.
Gerald Siciliano, Adjunct Associate Professor; M.S., Pratt.
Robbin Silverberg, Adjunct Associate Professor; B.A., Princeton.
Keith Simpson, Visiting Instructor; M.F.A., Ohio State.
Joseph Smith, Professor; M.F.A., NYU.
Judith Solodkin, Visiting Associate Professor; M.F.A., Columbia.
Jane South, Visiting Assistant Professor; M.F.A., North Carolina at Greensboro.
Tim Spelios, Visiting Associate Professor; B.F.A., Illinois at Urbana-Champaign.
Joseph Stauber, Adjunct Assistant Professor; M.F.A., SUNY Purchase.
Jason Stopa, Visiting Assistant Professor; M.F.A., Pratt.
Anthony Tammaro, Visiting Assistant Professor; M.F.A., Temple.
Irvin Tepper, Adjunct Professor; M.F.A., Washington (Seattle).
Christopher Verstegen, Visiting Instructor; M.F.A., Pratt.
Emily Weiner, Visiting Assistant Professor; M.F.A., School of Visual Arts.
Christopher White, Adjunct Associate Professor; B.A., Harvard.
Rachel Wiecking, Visiting Assistant Professor; M.F.A., Purchase, SUNY.
Martha Wilson, Visiting Associate Professor.
Chris Wright, Adjunct Associate Professor; M.F.A., Pratt.
Robert Zakarian, Professor; M.F.A., Pratt.
Katrin Zimmerman, Visiting Assistant Professor; M.A., School of Oriental and African Studies (London).

©2015 Bob Handelman

©2015 Bob Handelman

Section 4
Comparative and Interdisciplinary Arts

This section contains a directory of institutions offering graduate work in comparative and interdisciplinary arts. Additional information about programs listed in the directory may be obtained by writing directly to the dean of a graduate school or chair of a department at the address given in the directory.

For programs offering related work, see also in this book *Applied Arts and Design, Architecture, Art and Art History,* and *Performing Arts.* In another guide in this series:

Graduate Programs in Business, Education, Information Studies, Law & Social Work
See *Subject Areas (Art Education)*

CONTENTS

Program Directory

Comparative and Interdisciplinary Arts

Bradley University, Graduate School, Slane College of Communications and Fine Arts, Department of Art,, Peoria, IL 61625-0002. Offers ceramics (MA, MFA); drawing (MA, MFA); interdisciplinary art (MA, MFA); painting (MA, MFA); photography (MA, MFA); printmaking (MA, MFA); sculpture (MA, MFA); visual communications (MA, MFA). *Accreditation:* NASAD. Part-time programs available. *Faculty:* 11 full-time (2 women), 2 part-time/adjunct (both women). *Students:* 7 full-time (3 women), 3 part-time (2 women). 22 applicants, 41% accepted, 2 enrolled. In 2014, 4 master's awarded. *Degree requirements:* For master's, comprehensive exam, thesis, final exhibit. *Entrance requirements:* For master's, portfolio, 2 letters of recommendation. Additional exam requirements/recommendations for international students: Required—TOEFL (minimum score 550 paper-based; 79 iBT). *Application deadline:* For fall admission, 4/1 priority date for domestic and international students; for spring admission, 11/1 priority date for domestic and international students. Applications are processed on a rolling basis. Application fee: $40 ($50 for international students). Electronic applications accepted. *Expenses: Tuition:* Full-time $14,580; part-time $810 per credit. *Required fees:* $224. Full-time tuition and fees vary according to course load. *Financial support:* In 2014–15, 4 teaching assistantships with full and partial tuition reimbursements (averaging $19,640 per year) were awarded; scholarships/grants, tuition waivers (partial), and unspecified assistantships also available. Support available to part-time students. Financial award application deadline: 4/1. *Unit head:* Dr. Paul Krainak, Chairperson, 309-677-2967, E-mail: pkrainak@bradley.edu. *Application contact:* Kayla Carroll, Director of International Admission and Student Services, 309-677-2375, E-mail: klcarroll@fsmail.bradley.edu.

Brigham Young University, Graduate Studies, College of Humanities, Department of Humanities, Classics, and Comparative Literature, Provo, UT 84602. Offers comparative studies (MA). *Faculty:* 24 full-time (5 women). *Students:* 14 full-time (10 women), 8 part-time (5 women). Average age 26. 14 applicants, 50% accepted, 7 enrolled. In 2014, 6 master's awarded. *Degree requirements:* For master's, 2 foreign languages, thesis. *Entrance requirements:* For master's, GRE, minimum GPA of 3.0 in last 60 hours. Additional exam requirements/recommendations for international students: Required—TOEFL (minimum score 580 paper-based; 85 iBT), IELTS (minimum score 7). *Application deadline:* For fall admission, 3/1 for domestic and international students. Application fee: $50. Electronic applications accepted. *Expenses: Tuition:* Full-time $6310; part-time $371 per credit hour. Tuition and fees vary according to program and student's religious affiliation. *Financial support:* In 2014–15, 17 students received support, including 31 fellowships with partial tuition reimbursements available (averaging $1,604 per year), 4 research assistantships (averaging $1,500 per year), 29 teaching assistantships (averaging $2,503 per year); career-related internships or fieldwork, institutionally sponsored loans, scholarships/grants, tuition waivers (full and partial), and student instructorships also available. Support available to part-time students. *Unit head:* Dr. Carl Sederholm, Coordinator, 801-422-9078, Fax: 801-422-0305, E-mail: carl_sederholm@byu.edu. *Application contact:* Carolyn Hone, Graduate Secretary for Humanities and Comparative Literature, 801-422-4430, Fax: 801-422-0305, E-mail: carolyn_hone@byu.edu.

Columbia College Chicago, Graduate School, Department of Interdisciplinary Arts, Chicago, IL 60605-1996. Offers interdisciplinary arts (MA); interdisciplinary arts and media (MFA); interdisciplinary book and paper arts (MFA). Part-time and evening/weekend programs available. Postbaccalaureate distance learning degree programs offered (minimal on-campus study). *Faculty:* 10 full-time (7 women), 4 part-time/adjunct (3 women). *Students:* 45 full-time (28 women); includes 14 minority (6 Black or African American, non-Hispanic/Latino; 1 Asian, non-Hispanic/Latino; 4 Hispanic/Latino; 3 Two or more races, non-Hispanic/Latino), 2 international. Average age 31. In 2014, 25 master's awarded. *Degree requirements:* For master's, thesis. *Entrance requirements:* For master's, self-assessment essay, work sample, interview, letters of recommendation. Additional exam requirements/recommendations for international students: Required—TOEFL (minimum score 600 paper-based; 100 iBT). *Application deadline:* For fall admission, 1/15 priority date for domestic and international students. Application fee: $55 ($100 for international students). Electronic applications accepted.

Expenses: Expenses: $1,033 per credit hour; fees: $352 per semester. *Financial support:* In 2014–15, 26 students received support, including 15 fellowships, 8 research assistantships, 3 teaching assistantships; career-related internships or fieldwork, Federal Work-Study, scholarships/grants, and unspecified assistantships also available. Support available to part-time students. Financial award application deadline: 8/15; financial award applicants required to submit FAFSA. *Unit head:* Niki Nolin, Interim Chair, 312-369-7345, E-mail: nnolin@colum.edu. *Application contact:* Kara Leffler, Associate Director of Graduate Admissions, 312-369-7262, Fax: 312-369-8024, E-mail: kleffler@colum.edu.

Florida Atlantic University, Dorothy F. Schmidt College of Arts and Letters, Department of Comparative Studies, Boca Raton, FL 33431-0991. Offers PhD. Part-time programs available. *Degree requirements:* For doctorate, one foreign language, comprehensive exam, thesis/dissertation. *Entrance requirements:* For doctorate, GRE, minimum GPA of 3.5, 3 references. Additional exam requirements/recommendations for international students: Required—TOEFL (minimum score 500 paper-based; 61 iBT), IELTS (minimum score 6). *Expenses:* Tuition, state resident: full-time $7396; part-time $369.82 per credit hour. Tuition, nonresident: full-time $19,392; part-time $1024.81 per credit hour. Tuition and fees vary according to course load. *Faculty research:* Arts, humanities, social sciences.

Goddard College, Graduate Division, Master of Fine Arts in Interdisciplinary Arts Program, Plainfield, VT 05667-9432. Offers MFA. Postbaccalaureate distance learning degree programs offered (minimal on-campus study). *Faculty:* 4 full-time (3 women), 14 part-time/adjunct (12 women). *Students:* 93 full-time. Average age 39. 55 applicants, 47% accepted, 17 enrolled. In 2014, 36 master's awarded. *Degree requirements:* For master's, thesis. *Entrance requirements:* For master's, relevant undergraduate degree, 3 letters of recommendation, interview, portfolio, artistic resume. *Application deadline:* Applications are processed on a rolling basis. Application fee: $40. Electronic applications accepted. *Expenses: Tuition:* Full-time $16,578. Tuition and fees vary according to course load and program. *Financial support:* Scholarships/grants and tuition waivers (full and partial) available. Financial award applicants required to submit FAFSA. *Unit head:* Prof. Ju-Pong Lin, Director, 802-454-8311, Fax: 802-454-7835, E-mail: jupong.lin@goddard.edu. *Application contact:* Chip Cummings, Admissions Counselor, 800-906-8312 Ext. 221, Fax: 802-454-1029, E-mail: chip.cummings@goddard.edu.
Website: http://www.goddard.edu/academics/mfa/mfa-interdisciplinary-arts/

John F. Kennedy University, Graduate School of Holistic Studies, Department of Arts and Consciousness, Program in Transformative Arts, Pleasant Hill, CA 94523-4817. Offers MA. Part-time and evening/weekend programs available. *Degree requirements:* For master's, thesis or alternative. *Entrance requirements:* For master's, interview. Additional exam requirements/recommendations for international students: Required—TOEFL. *Expenses:* Contact institution.

Ohio University, Graduate College, College of Fine Arts, School of Interdisciplinary Arts, Athens, OH 45701-2979. Offers PhD. *Degree requirements:* For doctorate, 2 foreign languages, comprehensive exam, thesis/dissertation. *Entrance requirements:* For doctorate, GRE or MAT, master's degree. Additional exam requirements/recommendations for international students: Required—TOEFL (minimum score 575 paper-based; 91 iBT) or IELTS (minimum score 7). Electronic applications accepted. *Faculty research:* Comparative studies of theater, music, and the visual arts.

Simon Fraser University, Office of Graduate Studies, School for the Contemporary Arts, Vancouver, BC V6B 1H4, Canada. Offers MA, MFA. *Degree requirements:* For master's, thesis or alternative. *Entrance requirements:* For master's, portfolio; minimum GPA of 3.0 (on scale of 4.33), or 3.33 based on last 60 credits of undergraduate courses. Additional exam requirements/recommendations for international students: Recommended—TOEFL (minimum score 580 paper-based; 93 iBT), IELTS (minimum score 7), TWE (minimum score 5). Electronic applications accepted. *Faculty research:* Dance theory, screenplays, drawing and painting, acting, electroacoustic music.

Section 5
Film, Television, and Video

This section contains a directory of institutions offering graduate work in film, television, and video. Additional information about programs listed in the directory but not augmented by an in-depth entry may be obtained by writing directly to the dean of a graduate school or chair of a department at the address given in the directory.

For programs offering related work, see also in this book *Art and Art History* and *Communication and Media.* In the other guides in this series:

Graduate Programs in Engineering & Applied Sciences
See *Telecommunications*

Graduate Programs in Business, Education, Information Studies, Law & Social Work
See *Advertising and Public Relations*

CONTENTS

Program Directories

Displays and Close-Ups

See:

Film, Television, and Video Production

Academy of Art University, Graduate Program, School of Animation and Visual Effects, San Francisco, CA 94105-3410. Offers 3D animation (MFA); 3D modeling (MFA); storyboarding (MFA); traditional animation (MFA); visual effects (MFA). Part-time programs available. Postbaccalaureate distance learning degree programs offered (no on-campus study). *Faculty:* 22 full-time (5 women), 71 part-time/adjunct (16 women). *Students:* 383 full-time (168 women), 206 part-time (77 women); includes 94 minority (24 Black or African American, non-Hispanic/Latino; 3 American Indian or Alaska Native, non-Hispanic/Latino; 30 Asian, non-Hispanic/Latino; 30 Hispanic/Latino; 2 Native Hawaiian or other Pacific Islander, non-Hispanic/Latino; 5 Two or more races, non-Hispanic/Latino), 353 international. Average age 29. 165 applicants, 100% accepted, 87 enrolled. In 2014, 202 master's awarded. *Degree requirements:* For master's, final review. *Entrance requirements:* For master's, statement of intent; resume; portfolio/reel; official college transcripts. *Application deadline:* Applications are processed on a rolling basis. Application fee: $100. Electronic applications accepted. *Expenses: Tuition:* Part-time $910 per unit. *Financial support:* Career-related internships or fieldwork and Federal Work-Study available. Support available to part-time students. Financial award application deadline: 8/10; financial award applicants required to submit FAFSA. *Unit head:* 800-544-ARTS, E-mail: info@academyart.edu. *Application contact:* 800-544-ARTS, E-mail: info@academyart.edu.
Website: http://www.academyart.edu/animation-school/index.html

Academy of Art University, Graduate Program, School of Motion Pictures and Television, San Francisco, CA 94105-3410. Offers MFA. Part-time programs available. Postbaccalaureate distance learning degree programs offered (no on-campus study). *Faculty:* 9 full-time (1 woman), 54 part-time/adjunct (13 women). *Students:* 252 full-time (108 women), 120 part-time (46 women); includes 68 minority (35 Black or African American, non-Hispanic/Latino; 5 American Indian or Alaska Native, non-Hispanic/Latino; 11 Asian, non-Hispanic/Latino; 12 Hispanic/Latino; 2 Native Hawaiian or other Pacific Islander, non-Hispanic/Latino; 3 Two or more races, non-Hispanic/Latino), 206 international. Average age 30. 151 applicants, 100% accepted, 65 enrolled. In 2014, 82 master's awarded. *Degree requirements:* For master's, final review. *Entrance requirements:* For master's, statement of intent; resume; portfolio/reel; official college transcripts. *Application deadline:* Applications are processed on a rolling basis. Application fee: $100. Electronic applications accepted. *Expenses: Tuition:* Part-time $910 per unit. *Financial support:* Career-related internships or fieldwork and Federal Work-Study available. Support available to part-time students. Financial award application deadline: 8/10; financial award applicants required to submit FAFSA. *Unit head:* 800-544-ARTS, E-mail: info@academyart.edu. *Application contact:* 800-544-ARTS, E-mail: info@academyart.edu.
Website: http://www.academyart.edu/film-school/index.html

Academy of Art University, Graduate Program, School of Music Production and Sound Design for Visual Media, San Francisco, CA 94105-3410. Offers MFA. Part-time programs available. Postbaccalaureate distance learning degree programs offered (no on-campus study). *Faculty:* 4 full-time (0 women), 24 part-time/adjunct (3 women). *Students:* 115 full-time (49 women), 32 part-time (12 women); includes 27 minority (15 Black or African American, non-Hispanic/Latino; 1 American Indian or Alaska Native, non-Hispanic/Latino; 3 Asian, non-Hispanic/Latino; 5 Hispanic/Latino; 3 Two or more races, non-Hispanic/Latino), 83 international. Average age 29. 50 applicants, 100% accepted, 27 enrolled. In 2014, 29 master's awarded. *Degree requirements:* For master's, final review. *Entrance requirements:* For master's, statement of intent; resume; portfolio/reel; official college transcripts. *Application deadline:* Applications are processed on a rolling basis. Application fee: $100. Electronic applications accepted. *Expenses: Tuition:* Part-time $910 per unit. *Financial support:* Career-related internships or fieldwork and Federal Work-Study available. Support available to part-time students. Financial award application deadline: 8/10; financial award applicants required to submit FAFSA. *Unit head:* 800-544-ARTS, E-mail: info@academyart.edu. *Application contact:* 800-544-ARTS, E-mail: info@academyart.edu.
Website: http://www.academyart.edu/music-for-visual-media/index.html

Academy of Art University, Graduate Program, School of Writing for Film, Television and Digital Media, San Francisco, CA 94105-3410. Offers MFA. Part-time programs available. Postbaccalaureate distance learning degree programs offered (no on-campus study). *Faculty:* 1 full-time (0 women). *Students:* 1 (woman) full-time; minority (Black or African American, non-Hispanic/Latino). Average age 24. *Degree requirements:* For master's, final review. *Entrance requirements:* For master's, statement of intent; resume; portfolio/reel; official college transcripts. *Application deadline:* Applications are processed on a rolling basis. Application fee: $100. Electronic applications accepted. *Expenses: Tuition:* Part-time $910 per unit. *Financial support:* Career-related internships or fieldwork and Federal Work-Study available. Support available to part-time students. Financial award application deadline: 8/10; financial award applicants required to submit FAFSA. *Unit head:* 800-544-ARTS, E-mail: info@academyart.edu. *Application contact:* 800-544-ARTS, E-mail: info@academyart.edu.
Website: http://www.academyart.edu/academics/writing-film-television-digital-media

American Film Institute Conservatory, Graduate Program, Los Angeles, CA 90027-1657. Offers cinematography (MFA); directing (MFA); editing (MFA); producing (MFA); production design (MFA); screenwriting (MFA). *Degree requirements:* For master's, one foreign language, thesis. *Entrance requirements:* Additional exam requirements/recommendations for international students: Required—TOEFL (minimum score 600 paper-based; 100 iBT). *Faculty research:* Film production, TV production.

American University, School of Communication, Film and Electronic Media Program, Washington, DC 20016-8001. Offers MFA. Part-time and evening/weekend programs available. *Degree requirements:* For master's, comprehensive exam, thesis or alternative. *Entrance requirements:* For master's, GRE General Test. Additional exam requirements/recommendations for international students: Required—TOEFL (minimum score 600 paper-based; 100 iBT), IELTS. *Application deadline:* For fall admission, 2/1 priority date for domestic and international students; for spring admission, 11/15 for domestic and international students. Applications are processed on a rolling basis. Application fee: $50. Electronic applications accepted. *Financial support:* Fellowships with partial tuition reimbursements, research assistantships with partial tuition reimbursements, teaching assistantships with partial tuition reimbursements, career-related internships or fieldwork, Federal Work-Study, institutionally sponsored loans, scholarships/grants, tuition waivers (partial), and unspecified assistantships available. Financial award application deadline: 2/1; financial award applicants required to submit FAFSA. *Faculty research:* Documentary film production, social media, media and public policy, visual literacy, new technology. *Unit head:* Prof. John Douglass, Director, Film and Media Arts Division, 202-885-2045, Fax: 202-885-2019, E-mail: jdougla@american.edu. *Application contact:* Sharmeen Ahsan-Bracciale, Director of Graduate Student Services, 202-885-3940, Fax: 202-885-2019, E-mail: sharmeen@american.edu.
Website: http://www.american.edu/soc/film/degrees/MFA-FLEM.cfm

American University, School of Communication, Film and Video Program, Washington, DC 20016-8001. Offers MA. Part-time and evening/weekend programs available. *Degree requirements:* For master's, comprehensive exam, thesis or alternative. *Entrance requirements:* For master's, GRE General Test. Additional exam requirements/recommendations for international students: Required—TOEFL (minimum score 660 paper-based; 100 iBT), IELTS (minimum score 7). *Application deadline:* For fall admission, 2/1 priority date for domestic and international students; for spring admission, 11/15 for domestic and international students. Applications are processed on a rolling basis. Application fee: $50. Electronic applications accepted. *Financial support:* Research assistantships with partial tuition reimbursements, teaching assistantships with partial tuition reimbursements, career-related internships or fieldwork, Federal Work-Study, institutionally sponsored loans, scholarships/grants, tuition waivers (partial), and unspecified assistantships available. Financial award application deadline: 2/1; financial award applicants required to submit FAFSA. *Faculty research:* Documentary film and video production, visual literacy, Eastern European cinema, media and public policy, social media. *Unit head:* Prof. John Douglass, Director, Film and Media Arts Division, 202-885-2045, Fax: 202-885-2019, E-mail: jdougla@american.edu. *Application contact:* Sharmeen Ahsan-Bracciale, Director of Graduate Services, 202-885-3940, Fax: 202-885-2019, E-mail: sharmeen@american.edu.
Website: http://www.american.edu/soc/film/degrees/MA-FLVD.cfm

American University, School of Communication, Weekend Programs in Communication, Washington, DC 20016-8001. Offers interactive journalism (MA); media entrepreneurship (MA); producing for film and video (MA); strategic communication (MA). *Accreditation:* ACEJMC. Part-time and evening/weekend programs available. *Degree requirements:* For master's, comprehensive exam, thesis or alternative. *Entrance requirements:* Additional exam requirements/recommendations for international students: Required—TOEFL (minimum score 600 paper-based; 100 iBT). *Application deadline:* For fall admission, 8/1 for domestic students. Applications are processed on a rolling basis. Application fee: $50. Electronic applications accepted. *Financial support:* Fellowships and institutionally sponsored loans available. Financial award applicants required to submit FAFSA. *Unit head:* Prof. Rose Ann Robertson, Associate Dean for Academic Administration, 202-885-2002, E-mail: rrobert@american.edu. *Application contact:* Sharmeen Ahsan-Bracciale, Director of Graduate Services, 202-885-3940, Fax: 202-885-2019, E-mail: sharmeen@american.edu.
Website: http://american.edu/soc/admissions/weekend.cfm

Arizona State University at the Tempe campus, College of Liberal Arts and Sciences, Department of English, Program in Film and Media Studies, Tempe, AZ 85287-0402. Offers American media and popular culture (MAS). Part-time and evening/weekend programs available. Postbaccalaureate distance learning degree programs offered (no on-campus study). *Degree requirements:* For master's, integrated project. *Entrance requirements:* For master's, minimum GPA of 3.0 or equivalent in last 2 years of work leading to bachelor's degree. Additional exam requirements/recommendations for international students: Required—TOEFL, IELTS, or PTE. Electronic applications accepted. *Expenses:* Contact institution.

Art Center College of Design, Graduate Film Program, Pasadena, CA 91103. Offers MFA. *Accreditation:* NASAD. *Students:* 35 full-time (9 women), 27 part-time (6 women); includes 18 minority (4 Black or African American, non-Hispanic/Latino; 7 Asian, non-Hispanic/Latino; 4 Hispanic/Latino; 1 Native Hawaiian or other Pacific Islander, non-Hispanic/Latino; 2 Two or more races, non-Hispanic/Latino), 26 international. Average age 28. 108 applicants, 43% accepted, 19 enrolled. In 2014, 20 master's awarded. *Degree requirements:* For master's, thesis. *Entrance requirements:* For master's, portfolio. Additional exam requirements/recommendations for international students: Required—TOEFL (minimum score 100 iBT), IELTS (minimum score 7). *Application deadline:* For fall admission, 2/1 priority date for domestic and international students; for spring admission, 10/1 priority date for domestic and international students. Applications are processed on a rolling basis. Application fee: $50 ($70 for international students). Electronic applications accepted. *Financial support:* Application deadline: 2/1; applicants required to submit FAFSA. *Unit head:* Ross La Manna, Chair, 626-396-2354, E-mail: ross.lamanna@artcenter.edu. *Application contact:* Tom Stern, Managing Director, Admissions, 626-396-2369, E-mail: tom.stern@artcenter.edu.

The Art Institute of California–San Francisco, a campus of Argosy University, Program in Computer Animation, San Francisco, CA 94102. Offers MFA.

Bob Jones University, Graduate Programs, Greenville, SC 29614. Offers accountancy (MS); Bible (MA); Bible translation (MA); Biblical studies (Certificate); broadcast management (MS); business administration (MBA); church history (MA, PhD); church ministries (MA); church music (MM); cinema and video production (MA); counseling (MS); curriculum and instruction (Ed D); divinity (M Div); dramatic production (MA); educational leadership (MS, Ed D, Ed S); elementary education (M Ed, MAT); English (M Ed, MA, MAT); fine arts (MA); graphic design (MA); history (M Ed, MA); illustration (MA); interpretative speech (MA); mathematics (M Ed, MAT); medical missions (Certificate); ministry (MM, D Min); multi-categorical special education (M Ed, MAT); music (M Ed); New Testament interpretation (PhD); Old Testament interpretation (PhD); orchestral instrument performance (MM); organ performance (MM); pastoral studies (MA); personnel services (MS, Ed S); piano pedagogy (MM); piano performance (MM); platform arts (MA); radio and television broadcasting (MS); rhetoric and public address (MA); secondary education (M Ed); studio art (MA); teaching Bible (MA); theology (MA, PhD); voice performance (MM); youth ministries (MA); M Div/MM.

Boston University, College of Communication, Department of Film and Television, Boston, MA 02215. Offers MFA, MS, MBA/MS. Part-time programs available. *Faculty:* 17 full-time, 25 part-time/adjunct. *Students:* 68 full-time (52 women), 7 part-time (5 women); includes 11 minority (7 Black or African American, non-Hispanic/Latino; 3 Hispanic/Latino; 1 Two or more races, non-Hispanic/Latino), 16 international. Average age 25. 223 applicants, 51% accepted, 53 enrolled. In 2014, 14 master's awarded. *Degree requirements:* For master's, thesis. *Entrance requirements:* For master's, GRE General Test, resume, writing and creative samples, letters of recommendation. Additional exam requirements/recommendations for international students: Required—TOEFL (minimum score 600 paper-based; 100 iBT), IELTS. *Application deadline:* For fall admission, 5/1 for domestic and international students. Applications are processed on a rolling basis. Application fee: $80. Electronic applications accepted. *Expenses: Tuition:* Full-time $45,686; part-time $1428 per credit hour. *Required fees:* $660; $60 per semester. Tuition and fees vary according to program. *Financial support:* Teaching assistantships with partial tuition reimbursements, career-related internships or

fieldwork, Federal Work-Study, institutionally sponsored loans, scholarships/grants, and unspecified assistantships available. Support available to part-time students. Financial award application deadline: 5/1; financial award applicants required to submit FAFSA. *Unit head:* Paul Schneider, Chairman, 617-353-3483, Fax: 617-353-1084, E-mail: ftvchair@bu.edu. *Application contact:* Manny Dotel, Assistant Director, Graduate Affairs, 617-353-3481, E-mail: comgrad@bu.edu.
Website: http://www.bu.edu/com/academics/film-tv/

Bowling Green State University, Graduate College, College of Arts and Sciences, Department of Theatre and Film, Bowling Green, OH 43403. Offers MA, PhD. *Accreditation:* NAST. Part-time programs available. Terminal master's awarded for partial completion of doctoral program. *Degree requirements:* For master's, thesis or alternative; for doctorate, comprehensive exam, thesis/dissertation, 9 hour research tool. *Entrance requirements:* For master's and doctorate, GRE General Test. Additional exam requirements/recommendations for international students: Required—TOEFL. Electronic applications accepted. *Faculty research:* Theatre history, dramatic theory, cultural studies, performance studies, American theatre history.

Brigham Young University, Graduate Studies, College of Fine Arts and Communications, Department of Theatre and Media Arts, Provo, UT 84602-6404. Offers MA. Program accepts applications in odd-numbered years only. *Accreditation:* NAST. Evening/weekend programs available. *Faculty:* 18 full-time (6 women). *Students:* 8 full-time (5 women). Average age 29. In 2014, 2 master's awarded. *Degree requirements:* For master's, comprehensive exam, thesis, 32 hours, oral defense. *Entrance requirements:* For master's, GRE, two samples of scholarly writing, letter of intent, three letters of recommendation. Additional exam requirements/recommendations for international students: Required—TOEFL (minimum score 580 paper-based; 85 iBT). *Application deadline:* For fall admission, 4/1 priority date for domestic and international students. Application fee: $50. Electronic applications accepted. *Expenses: Tuition:* Full-time $6310; part-time $371 per credit hour. Tuition and fees vary according to program and student's religious affiliation. *Financial support:* In 2014–15, 8 students received support. Career-related internships or fieldwork, institutionally sponsored loans, scholarships/grants, tuition waivers (partial), and unspecified assistantships available. Support available to part-time students. *Unit head:* Dr. Megan Sanborn, Graduate Coordinator, 801-422-1321, E-mail: msjones@byu.edu. *Application contact:* Lindsi Michelle Neilson, Graduate Secretary, 801-422-3750, E-mail: lindsi_neilson@byu.edu.
Website: http://cfac.byu.edu/departments/tma

Brooklyn College of the City University of New York, School of Visual, Media and Performing Arts, Department of Television and Radio, Brooklyn, NY 11210-2889. Offers media studies (MS); television production (MFA). Part-time and evening/weekend programs available. *Degree requirements:* For master's, comprehensive exam. *Entrance requirements:* For master's, GRE General Test or MAT, 12 credits in television/radio with a minimum B average, 2 letters of recommendation. Additional exam requirements/recommendations for international students: Required—TOEFL (minimum score 580 paper-based; 92 iBT). Electronic applications accepted. *Faculty research:* Criticism, research methods, audience behavior, policy and regulation, program history, international television and radio.

California College of the Arts, Graduate Programs, Fine Arts Programs, San Francisco, CA 94107. Offers ceramics (MFA); comics (MFA); film/video/performance (MFA); glass (MFA); interdisciplinary studies (MFA); jewelry/metal arts (MFA); media studies (MFA); painting/drawing (MFA); photography (MFA); printmaking (MFA); sculpture (MFA); social practice (MFA); textiles (MFA); wood/furniture (MFA). *Accreditation:* NASAD. *Degree requirements:* For master's, thesis, exhibit. *Entrance requirements:* For master's, appropriate bachelor's degree, portfolio, resume, 2 letters of recommendation, transcript. Additional exam requirements/recommendations for international students: Required—TOEFL (minimum score 600 paper-based; 100 iBT). Electronic applications accepted.

California Institute of the Arts, School of Film/Video, Valencia, CA 91355-2340. Offers experimental animation (MFA); film directing (MFA, Adv C); film/video (Adv C). *Entrance requirements:* For master's, portfolio. Additional exam requirements/recommendations for international students: Required—TOEFL. Electronic applications accepted. *Faculty research:* Experimental and character animation, experimental film/video, video graphics.

California State University, Fullerton, Graduate Studies, College of Communications, Department of Radio-TV-Film, Fullerton, CA 92834-9480. Offers screenwriting (MFA). *Students:* 20 full-time (8 women), 1 (woman) part-time; includes 10 minority (2 Black or African American, non-Hispanic/Latino; 7 Hispanic/Latino; 1 Two or more races, non-Hispanic/Latino), 2 international. Average age 30. 26 applicants, 65% accepted, 12 enrolled. In 2014, 14 master's awarded. *Degree requirements:* For master's, final project. *Entrance requirements:* For master's, bachelor's degree from accredited university; samples of competent and creative writing, such as original screenplays, teleplays, theatrical plays, or other narrative work; essay; three letters of recommendation. Application fee: $55. Electronic applications accepted. *Unit head:* Dr. Ed Fink, Head, 714-278-7883. *Application contact:* Admissions/Applications, 657-278-2371.
Website: http://communications.fullerton.edu/departments/rtvf/

California State University, Northridge, Graduate Studies, College of Arts, Media, and Communication, Department of Cinema and Television Arts, Northridge, CA 91330. Offers screenwriting (MA). *Students:* 23 full-time (7 women), 31 part-time (12 women); includes 11 minority (5 Black or African American, non-Hispanic/Latino; 4 Hispanic/Latino; 2 Two or more races, non-Hispanic/Latino), 4 international. Average age 42. *Entrance requirements:* For master's, GRE (if cumulative undergraduate GPA less than 3.0). Application fee: $55. *Expenses: Required fees:* $12,402. *Unit head:* Jon Stahl, Chair, 818-677-3192.
Website: http://www.ctva.csun.edu/

Carleton University, Faculty of Graduate Studies, Faculty of Arts and Social Sciences, School for Studies in Art and Culture, Program in Film Studies, Ottawa, ON K1S 5B6, Canada. Offers MA. *Degree requirements:* For master's, thesis. *Entrance requirements:* For master's, honors degree. Additional exam requirements/recommendations for international students: Required—TOEFL.

Carnegie Mellon University, College of Fine Arts, School of Drama, Pittsburgh, PA 15213-3891. Offers design (MFA); directing (MFA); dramatic writing (MFA); production technology and management (MFA); video and media design (MFA). *Degree requirements:* For master's, thesis (for some programs). *Entrance requirements:* For master's, audition, portfolio review, interview. Additional exam requirements/recommendations for international students: Required—TOEFL. *Faculty research:* Developing voice and speech compact disc.

Carnegie Mellon University, School of Computer Science and College of Fine Arts, Program in Entertainment Technology, Pittsburgh, PA 15213-3891. Offers MET.

Central Michigan University, College of Graduate Studies, College of Communication and Fine Arts, School of Broadcasting and Cinematic Arts, Mount Pleasant, MI 48859. Offers electronic media management (MA); electronic media production (MA); electronic media studies (MA); film theory and criticism (MA). Part-time programs available.

Degree requirements: For master's, thesis or alternative. *Entrance requirements:* For master's, undergraduate degree in broadcasting, film studies, or an associated discipline with minimum GPA of 2.7. Electronic applications accepted. *Faculty research:* Multimedia production, film history and criticism, writing and promotions, international broadcasting and media systems, history of American broadcasting.

Chapman University, Dodge College of Film and Media Arts, Orange, CA 92866. Offers film and television producing (MFA); film production (MFA); film studies (MA); production design (MFA); screenwriting (MFA); JD/MFA; MBA/MFA. Part-time and evening/weekend programs available. *Faculty:* 44 full-time (8 women), 72 part-time/adjunct (26 women). *Students:* 219 full-time (91 women), 3 part-time (1 woman); includes 53 minority (17 Black or African American, non-Hispanic/Latino; 10 Asian, non-Hispanic/Latino; 20 Hispanic/Latino; 6 Two or more races, non-Hispanic/Latino), 64 international. Average age 26. 475 applicants, 45% accepted, 96 enrolled. In 2014, 77 master's awarded. *Degree requirements:* For master's, thesis. *Entrance requirements:* For master's, GRE, minimum undergraduate GPA of 2.5, creative portfolio. Additional exam requirements/recommendations for international students: Required—TOEFL (minimum score 550 paper-based; 80 iBT). *Application deadline:* For fall admission, 2/1 priority date for domestic students. Application fee: $60. Electronic applications accepted. *Expenses:* Expenses: Contact institution. *Financial support:* Fellowships, Federal Work-Study, and scholarships/grants available. Financial award applicants required to submit FAFSA. *Unit head:* Eric Young, Chair, Film Division, 714-516-4544, E-mail: bdoyle@chapman.edu. *Application contact:* Lauren Kacura, Assistant Director of Admissions, 714-744-7856, E-mail: kacura@chapmna.edu.

Chatham University, Program in Film and Digital Technology, Pittsburgh, PA 15232-2826. Offers MFA. Part-time and evening/weekend programs available. *Faculty:* 1 (woman) part-time/adjunct. *Students:* 5 full-time (4 women), 2 part-time (both women); includes 4 minority (2 Black or African American, non-Hispanic/Latino; 1 Hispanic/Latino; 1 Two or more races, non-Hispanic/Latino), 1 international. Average age 28. 12 applicants, 83% accepted, 4 enrolled. In 2014, 6 master's awarded. *Degree requirements:* For master's, thesis, capstone project. *Entrance requirements:* Additional exam requirements/recommendations for international students: Required—TOEFL (minimum score 600 paper-based; 100 iBT), IELTS (minimum score 7), TWE. *Application deadline:* For fall admission, 4/1 priority date for domestic and international students; for spring admission, 11/1 priority date for domestic students, 10/1 priority date for international students. Applications are processed on a rolling basis. Application fee: $45. Electronic applications accepted. Application fee is waived when completed online. *Expenses: Tuition:* Full-time $15,318; part-time $851 per credit hour. *Required fees:* $440; $24 per credit hour. Tuition and fees vary according to course load, program and reciprocity agreements. *Financial support:* Applicants required to submit FAFSA. *Unit head:* Dr. Prajna Parasher, Director, 412-365-1182, E-mail: parasher@chatham.edu. *Application contact:* Katie Noel, Assistant Director of Graduate Admission, 412-365-2758, Fax: 412-365-1609, E-mail: gradadmissions@chatham.edu.
Website: http://www.chatham.edu/mfafilm

Columbia College Chicago, Graduate School, Department of Cinema Art and Science, Chicago, IL 60605-1996. Offers cinema directing (MFA); creative producing (MFA). Part-time programs available. In 2014, 31 master's awarded. *Degree requirements:* For master's, thesis, film project. *Entrance requirements:* For master's, self-assessment essay, work samples, interview, case study. Additional exam requirements/recommendations for international students: Required—TOEFL (minimum score 550 paper-based). *Application deadline:* For fall admission, 1/15 for domestic and international students. Application fee: $55 ($100 for international students). Electronic applications accepted. *Financial support:* In 2014–15, 26 students received support, including 19 fellowships with full and partial tuition reimbursements available, 12 research assistantships; career-related internships or fieldwork, Federal Work-Study, scholarships/grants, health care benefits, and unspecified assistantships also available. Support available to part-time students. Financial award application deadline: 8/15; financial award applicants required to submit FAFSA. *Unit head:* Josef Steiff, Associate Chair, 312-369-6719, E-mail: jsteiff@colum.edu. *Application contact:* Kara Leffler, Associate Director of Graduate Admissions, 312-369-7262, Fax: 312-369-8024, E-mail: kleffler@colum.edu.
Website: http://www.colum.edu/academics/media-arts/cinema-art-and-science/

Columbia University, School of the Arts, Film Program, New York, NY 10027. Offers creative producing (MFA); directing (MFA); film studies (MA); screenwriting (MFA). *Degree requirements:* For master's, thesis. *Entrance requirements:* For master's, 3 letters of recommendation, writing sample, complete a scene, feature film treatment (optional visual submission). Additional exam requirements/recommendations for international students: Required—TOEFL (minimum score 600 paper-based; 100 iBT). Electronic applications accepted.

See Display on page 257 and Close-Up on page 273.

Concordia University, School of Graduate Studies, Faculty of Fine Arts, Department of Studio Arts, Montréal, QC H3G 1M8, Canada. Offers studio arts (MFA), including film production, open media, painting, photography, print media, sculpture, ceramics and fibers. *Degree requirements:* For master's, thesis or alternative. *Entrance requirements:* For master's, portfolio.

Concordia University, School of Graduate Studies, Faculty of Fine Arts, Mel Hoppenheim School of Cinema, Montréal, QC H3G 1M8, Canada. Offers film studies (MA).

DePaul University, College of Computing and Digital Media, Chicago, IL 60604. Offers animation (MA, MFA); business information technology (MS); cinema (MFA); cinema production (MS); computational finance (MS); computer and information sciences (PhD); computer game development (MS); computer information and network security (MS); computer science (MS); e-commerce technology (MS); health informatics (MS); human-computer interaction (MS); information systems (MS); information technology project management (MS); network engineering and management (MS); predictive analytics (MS); screenwriting (MFA); software engineering (MS); JD/MS. Part-time and evening/weekend programs available. Postbaccalaureate distance learning degree programs offered (no on-campus study). *Degree requirements:* For master's, thesis (for some programs); for doctorate, comprehensive exam, thesis/dissertation. *Entrance requirements:* For master's, GRE or GMAT (for MS in computational finance only), bachelor's degree, resume (MS in predictive analytics only), IT experience (MS in information technology project management only), portfolio review (all MFA programs and MA in animation); for doctorate, GRE, master's degree in computer science. Additional exam requirements/recommendations for international students: Required—TOEFL (minimum score 590 paper-based; 80 iBT), IELTS (minimum score 6.5), PTE (minimum score 53). Electronic applications accepted. *Expenses:* Contact institution. *Faculty research:* Data mining, computer science, human-computer interaction, security, animation and film.

Drexel University, Antoinette Westphal College of Media Arts and Design, Program in Television Management, Philadelphia, PA 19104-2875. Offers MS, MS/MBA.

Florida Atlantic University, Dorothy F. Schmidt College of Arts and Letters, School of Communication and Multimedia Studies, Boca Raton, FL 33431-0991. Offers

communication studies (MA); film and video (Certificate); media, technology and entertainment (MFA). Part-time programs available. *Degree requirements:* For master's, one foreign language, comprehensive exam (for some programs), thesis (for some programs). *Entrance requirements:* For master's, GRE General Test, minimum GPA of 3.0, essay, letters of recommendation. Electronic applications accepted. *Expenses:* Tuition, state resident: full-time $7396; part-time $369.82 per credit hour. Tuition, nonresident: full-time $19,392; part-time $1024.81 per credit hour. Tuition and fees vary according to course load. *Faculty research:* Cultural studies, gender studies, film, communication theory, journalism, new media.

Florida State University, The Graduate School, College of Motion Picture Arts, Tallahassee, FL 32306-2350. Offers film production (MFA); screenwriting (MFA). *Faculty:* 24 full-time (9 women), 3 part-time/adjunct (1 woman). *Students:* 53 full-time (24 women); includes 22 minority (10 Black or African American, non-Hispanic/Latino; 7 Asian, non-Hispanic/Latino; 4 Hispanic/Latino; 1 Two or more races, non-Hispanic/Latino). Average age 25. 189 applicants, 16% accepted, 30 enrolled. In 2014, 30 master's awarded. *Degree requirements:* For master's, thesis, thesis film project. *Entrance requirements:* For master's, GRE (for MFA in writing), minimum GPA of 3.0, application documents (resume, statement of purpose, writing sample, 3 letters of recommendation, creative portfolio). Additional exam requirements/recommendations for international students: Required—TOEFL (minimum score 550 paper-based; 80 iBT). *Application deadline:* For fall admission, 12/1 for domestic and international students. Application fee: $30. Electronic applications accepted. *Expenses:* Tuition, state resident: part-time $403.51 per credit hour. Tuition, nonresident: part-time $1004.85 per credit hour. *Required fees:* $75.81 per credit hour. One-time fee: $20 part-time. Tuition and fees vary according to campus/location. *Financial support:* In 2014–15, 20 students received support, including 20 teaching assistantships with partial tuition reimbursements available (averaging $5,500 per year); institutionally sponsored loans and unspecified assistantships also available. Financial award application deadline: 12/1; financial award applicants required to submit FAFSA. *Faculty research:* Producing, screenwriting, directing, cinematography, editing. *Unit head:* Frank Patterson, Dean, 850-644-0453, Fax: 850-644-2626. *Application contact:* Emily Burgess, Director of Student Services, 850-644-4927, Fax: 850-644-2626, E-mail: eburgess@film.fsu.edu.
Website: http://film.fsu.edu/

Georgia State University, College of Arts and Sciences, Department of Communication, Atlanta, GA 30302-3083. Offers film, video, and digital imaging (MA), including critical studies, production, screenwriting; human communication and social influence (MA); mass communication (MA); media and society (PhD); moving image studies (PhD); public communication (PhD); rhetoric and politics (PhD). Part-time programs available. *Faculty:* 35 full-time (18 women). *Students:* 102 full-time (51 women), 40 part-time (15 women); includes 37 minority (20 Black or African American, non-Hispanic/Latino; 4 Asian, non-Hispanic/Latino; 6 Hispanic/Latino; 7 Two or more races, non-Hispanic/Latino), 14 international. Average age 33. 154 applicants, 39% accepted, 30 enrolled. In 2014, 25 master's, 5 doctorates awarded. *Degree requirements:* For master's, variable foreign language requirement, thesis (for some programs); for doctorate, comprehensive exam, thesis/dissertation. *Entrance requirements:* For master's, GRE; for doctorate, GRE. Additional exam requirements/recommendations for international students: Required—TOEFL (minimum score 550 paper-based; 80 iBT), IELTS (minimum score 6.5). *Application deadline:* For fall admission, 2/10 for domestic and international students; for spring admission, 10/15 for domestic and international students. Application fee: $50. Electronic applications accepted. *Expenses:* Tuition, state resident: full-time $6516; part-time $362 per credit hour. Tuition, nonresident: full-time $22,014; part-time $1223 per credit hour. *Required fees:* $2128 per semester. Tuition and fees vary according to course load and program. *Financial support:* In 2014–15, fellowships with tuition reimbursements (averaging $15,000 per year), teaching assistantships with tuition reimbursements (averaging $15,000 per year) were awarded; career-related internships or fieldwork and unspecified assistantships also available. Financial award applicants required to submit FAFSA. *Faculty research:* New media, mass media and journalism, rhetoric, film and media studies, film production. *Unit head:* Dr. David Cheshier, Chair, 404-413-5649, Fax: 404-413-5634, E-mail: dcheshier@gsu.edu. *Application contact:* Dr. Jennifer Barker, Associate Professor, 404-413-5793, Fax: 404-413-5634, E-mail: jmbarker@gsu.edu.
Website: http://communication.gsu.edu

Hofstra University, Lawrence Herbert School of Communication, Program in Documentary Studies and Production, Hempstead, NY 11549. Offers MFA. Part-time and evening/weekend programs available. *Students:* 10 full-time (9 women), 5 part-time (1 woman); includes 2 minority (both Hispanic/Latino), 7 international. Average age 31. 7 applicants, 57% accepted. In 2014, 4 master's awarded. *Degree requirements:* For master's, thesis, thesis project, minimum GPA of 3.0. *Entrance requirements:* For master's, 2 letters of recommendation, essay, portfolio, interview. Additional exam requirements/recommendations for international students: Required—TOEFL (minimum score 550 paper-based; 80 iBT). *Application deadline:* Applications are processed on a rolling basis. Application fee: $70 ($75 for international students). Electronic applications accepted. *Expenses: Tuition:* Full-time $20,610; part-time $1145 per credit hour. *Required fees:* $970; $165 per term. Tuition and fees vary according to program. *Financial support:* In 2014–15, 6 students received support, including 3 fellowships with full and partial tuition reimbursements available (averaging $7,500 per year), 2 research assistantships with full and partial tuition reimbursements available (averaging $7,578 per year); Federal Work-Study, institutionally sponsored loans, scholarships/grants, and tuition waivers (full and partial) also available. Support available to part-time students. Financial award applicants required to submit FAFSA. *Faculty research:* Cultural studies, women, urban studies, class, grassroots movements and personal documentary, documentary film aesthetics, history and theory, animation and feminism, community and citizens media, indigenous movements in Latin America, development and globalization, sports, music, culture, experimental documentary. *Unit head:* Dr. Rodney F. Hill, Program Director, 516-463-7038, Fax: 516-463-7043, E-mail: avfrfh@hofstra.edu. *Application contact:* Sunil Samuel, Assistant Vice President of Admissions, 516-463-4723, Fax: 516-463-4664, E-mail: graduateadmission@hofstra.edu.
Website: http://www.hofstra.edu/hclas

Hollins University, Graduate Programs, Program in Screenwriting and Film Studies, Roanoke, VA 24020. Offers screenwriting (MFA); screenwriting and film studies (MA). Program offered during summer only. Part-time programs available. *Faculty:* 1 (woman) full-time, 5 part-time/adjunct (0 women). *Students:* 30 full-time (7 women), 5 part-time (all women); includes 8 minority (5 Black or African American, non-Hispanic/Latino; 2 Asian, non-Hispanic/Latino; 1 Two or more races, non-Hispanic/Latino). Average age 39. 18 applicants, 100% accepted, 12 enrolled. In 2014, 5 master's awarded. *Degree requirements:* For master's, one foreign language, comprehensive exam, thesis. *Entrance requirements:* For master's, letters of recommendation, portfolio. Additional exam requirements/recommendations for international students: Required—TOEFL (minimum score 550 paper-based; 79 iBT). *Application deadline:* For fall admission, 2/15 for domestic and international students. Application fee: $40. Electronic applications accepted. *Expenses:* Expenses: $775 per credit hour, $85 technology fee. *Financial support:* In 2014–15, 18 students received support, including 18 fellowships (averaging $1,000 per year); Federal Work-Study and scholarships/grants also available. Support available to part-time students. Financial award application deadline: 2/15; financial award applicants required to submit FAFSA. *Faculty research:* Censorship, minorities in film, writing for television, new media. *Unit head:* Dr. Tim Albaugh, Director, 540-362-6326, E-mail: albaughtt@hollins.edu. *Application contact:* Cathy S. Koon, Manager of Graduate Services, 540-362-6326, Fax: 540-362-6288, E-mail: ckoon@hollins.edu.
Website: http://www.hollins.edu/

Howard University, School of Communications, Department of Radio, Television and Film, Washington, DC 20059-0002. Offers film (MFA). Part-time programs available. *Degree requirements:* For master's, thesis optional. *Entrance requirements:* For master's, GRE General Test, minimum GPA of 3.0.

Lipscomb University, Program in Film and Creative Media, Nashville, TN 37204-3951. Offers MA, MFA, MFA/MBA. Part-time and evening/weekend programs available. *Faculty:* 2 full-time (0 women), 4 part-time/adjunct (0 women). *Students:* 18 full-time (7 women), 3 part-time (0 women); includes 6 minority (3 Black or African American, non-Hispanic/Latino; 1 Asian, non-Hispanic/Latino; 1 Hispanic/Latino; 1 Two or more races, non-Hispanic/Latino). Average age 36. 24 applicants, 71% accepted, 12 enrolled. *Degree requirements:* For master's, professional practicum, portfolio. *Entrance requirements:* For master's, GRE or MAT, 2 references, resume, video portfolio. Additional exam requirements/recommendations for international students: Required—TOEFL (minimum score 570 paper-based; 80 iBT). *Application deadline:* Applications are processed on a rolling basis. Application fee: $50 ($75 for international students). *Expenses:* Expenses: $919 per credit hour. *Financial support:* Applicants required to submit FAFSA. *Unit head:* David DeBorde, Director, 615-966-7111, E-mail: david.deborde@lipscomb.edu. *Application contact:* Tessa Bryant, Administrative Assistant, 615-966-7111, E-mail: tessa.bryant@lipscomb.edu.
Website: http://www.lipscomb.edu/cinematicarts/graduate-programs

Loyola Marymount University, School of Film and Television, Department of Production, Program in Film and Television Production, Los Angeles, CA 90045-8347. Offers MFA. *Degree requirements:* For master's, thesis, film. *Entrance requirements:* For master's, GRE, creative work, 2 letters of recommendation, personal statement. Additional exam requirements/recommendations for international students: Required—TOEFL (minimum score 600 paper-based; 100 iBT). Electronic applications accepted.

Loyola Marymount University, School of Film and Television, Department of Screenwriting, Program in Writing and Producing for Television, Los Angeles, CA 90045. Offers MFA. *Entrance requirements:* For master's, GRE, personal statement, letters of recommendation, creative work or writing sample. Additional exam requirements/recommendations for international students: Required—TOEFL (minimum score 600 paper-based; 100 iBT).

Maryland Institute College of Art, Graduate Studies, Program in Filmmaking, Baltimore, MD 21201. Offers MFA. *Faculty:* 5 full-time (2 women). *Degree requirements:* For master's, thesis film and screening, written thesis. *Entrance requirements:* For master's, Portfolio, writing samples, bachelors degree in any field. Additional exam requirements/recommendations for international students: Required—TOEFL (minimum score 550 paper-based; 80 iBT), IELTS (minimum score 6.5). *Application deadline:* For fall admission, 1/15 priority date for domestic students. Application fee: $75. Electronic applications accepted. *Expenses:* Expenses: Contact institution. *Financial support:* In 2014–15, 12 students received support, including 12 fellowships (averaging $13,000 per year); career-related internships or fieldwork and scholarships/grants also available. Financial award application deadline: 1/15. *Unit head:* Patrick Wright, Director. *Application contact:* Chris D. Harring, Director of Graduate Admission, 410-225-2256, Fax: 410-225-5275, E-mail: graduate@mica.edu.
Website: http://www.mica.edu/Programs_of_Study/Graduate_Programs/Filmmaking_(MFA).html

Massachusetts College of Art and Design, Graduate Programs, MFA Program, Boston, MA 02115-5882. Offers 2D fine arts (MFA), including painting; 3D fine arts (MFA), including ceramics, fibers, glass, jewelry and metalsmithing, sculpture; design (MFA, Postbaccalaureate Certificate), including dynamic media; fine arts (MFA), including interdisciplinary; media arts (MFA, Postbaccalaureate Certificate), including film/video (MFA), photography. *Accreditation:* NASAD. *Faculty:* 31 full-time (15 women), 42 part-time/adjunct (19 women). *Students:* 59 full-time (36 women), 32 part-time (23 women); includes 12 minority (2 Black or African American, non-Hispanic/Latino; 5 Asian, non-Hispanic/Latino; 5 Hispanic/Latino), 18 international. 278 applicants, 38% accepted, 40 enrolled. In 2014, 33 master's, 7 other advanced degrees awarded. *Degree requirements:* For master's, thesis, Exhibition for MFA non design. Thesis document MFA in design and low-residency. *Entrance requirements:* For master's, portfolio, college transcripts, resume, statement of purpose, letters of reference, interview; 6 credits of art history taken prior to or during MFA program; for Postbaccalaureate Certificate, portfolio, college transcripts, resume, statement of purpose, letters of reference, interview. Additional exam requirements/recommendations for international students: Required—TOEFL (minimum score 550 paper-based; 85 iBT); Recommended—IELTS (minimum score 6.5). *Application deadline:* For fall admission, 1/6 priority date for domestic and international students. Application fee: $75. Electronic applications accepted. *Expenses:* Tuition, state resident: full-time $23,400; part-time $780 per credit. Tuition, nonresident: full-time $23,400; part-time $780 per credit. Tuition and fees vary according to course load and program. *Financial support:* In 2014–15, 37 students received support, including 40 teaching assistantships (averaging $2,160 per year); career-related internships or fieldwork, scholarships/grants, tuition waivers (partial), and unspecified assistantships also available. Support available to part-time students. Financial award application deadline: 1/6. *Unit head:* Paul Paturzo, Interim Dean of Graduate Studies, 617-879-7166, E-mail: pjpaturzo@massart.edu. *Application contact:* Isaac Goldstein, Graduate Admissions Counselor, 617-879-7203, Fax: 617-879-7250, E-mail: igoldstein@massart.edu.
Website: http://www.massart.edu/Admissions/Graduate_Programs.html

Miami International University of Art & Design, Program in Film, Miami, FL 33132-1418. Offers MFA. Postbaccalaureate distance learning degree programs offered.

Minneapolis College of Art and Design, Program in Visual Studies, Minneapolis, MN 55404-4347. Offers animation (MFA); comic art (MFA); drawing (MFA); filmmaking (MFA); fine arts (MFA); furniture design (MFA); graphic design (MFA); illustration (MFA); interactive media (MFA); painting (MFA); photography (MFA); printmaking (MFA); sculpture (MFA). *Accreditation:* NASAD. Part-time programs available. *Degree requirements:* For master's, thesis, thesis exhibit. *Entrance requirements:* For master's, portfolio of visual artwork, resume, 3 letters of recommendation. Additional exam requirements/recommendations for international students: Required—TOEFL (minimum score 550 paper-based; 79 iBT). Electronic applications accepted. *Faculty research:* Visual arts: animation, comic art, drawing, filmmaking, furniture design, graphic design, illustration, interactive media, painting, photography, printmaking, sculpture.

Montana State University, The Graduate School, College of Arts and Architecture, School of Film and Photography, Bozeman, MT 59717. Offers science and natural history filmmaking (MFA). Part-time programs available. *Degree requirements:* For master's, comprehensive exam. *Entrance requirements:* For master's, GRE General Test, minimum GPA of 3.0, resume, 3 letters of recommendation. Additional exam requirements/recommendations for international students: Required—TOEFL (minimum

score 550 paper-based). Electronic applications accepted. *Faculty research:* Science and natural history filmmaking, science communication, public outreach, new media production, environmental communication.

Mount Saint Mary's University, Graduate Division, Los Angeles, CA 90049-1599. Offers business administration (MBA); counseling psychology (MS); creative writing (MFA); education (MS, Certificate); film and television (MFA); health policy and management (MS); humanities (MA); nursing (MSN, Certificate); physical therapy (DPT); religious studies (MA). Part-time and evening/weekend programs available. *Faculty:* 15 full-time (11 women), 61 part-time/adjunct (33 women). *Students:* 462 full-time (345 women), 218 part-time (175 women); includes 417 minority (66 Black or African American, non-Hispanic/Latino; 3 American Indian or Alaska Native, non-Hispanic/Latino; 69 Asian, non-Hispanic/Latino; 254 Hispanic/Latino; 11 Native Hawaiian or other Pacific Islander, non-Hispanic/Latino; 14 Two or more races, non-Hispanic/Latino), 1 international. Average age 33. 1,086 applicants, 25% accepted, 241 enrolled. In 2014, 181 master's, 28 doctorates, 22 other advanced degrees awarded. *Entrance requirements:* Additional exam requirements/recommendations for international students: Required—TOEFL. *Application deadline:* For fall admission, 6/30 priority date for domestic and international students; for spring admission, 10/30 priority date for domestic and international students; for summer admission, 3/30 priority date for domestic and international students. Applications are processed on a rolling basis. Application fee: $50. Electronic applications accepted. *Expenses: Tuition:* Full-time $9756; part-time $813 per unit. One-time fee: $128. Tuition and fees vary according to degree level and program. *Financial support:* In 2014–15, 213 students received support. Career-related internships or fieldwork, Federal Work-Study, institutionally sponsored loans, and tuition waivers (full and partial) available. Support available to part-time students. Financial award application deadline: 3/15; financial award applicants required to submit FAFSA. *Unit head:* Dr. Linda Moody, Graduate Dean, 213-477-2800, E-mail: gradprograms@msmu.edu. *Application contact:* Tara Wessel, Senior Graduate Admission Counselor, 213-477-2800, E-mail: gradprograms@msmu.edu.
Website: http://www.msmu.edu/graduate-programs/admission/

National University, Academic Affairs, School of Professional Studies, La Jolla, CA 92037-1011. Offers criminal justice (MCJ); digital cinema (MFA); digital journalism (MA); juvenile justice (MS); professional screen writing (MFA); public administration (MPA), including human resource management, organizational leadership, public finance. Part-time and evening/weekend programs available. Postbaccalaureate distance learning degree programs offered (no on-campus study). *Faculty:* 19 full-time (8 women), 28 part-time/adjunct (7 women). *Students:* 277 full-time (141 women), 140 part-time (80 women); includes 248 minority (102 Black or African American, non-Hispanic/Latino; 23 Asian, non-Hispanic/Latino; 102 Hispanic/Latino; 5 Native Hawaiian or other Pacific Islander, non-Hispanic/Latino; 16 Two or more races, non-Hispanic/Latino), 8 international. Average age 37. *Degree requirements:* For master's, thesis (for some programs). *Entrance requirements:* For master's, interview, minimum GPA of 2.5. Additional exam requirements/recommendations for international students: Required—TOEFL (minimum score 550 paper-based; 79 iBT), IELTS (minimum score 6). *Application deadline:* Applications are processed on a rolling basis. Application fee: $60 ($65 for international students). Electronic applications accepted. *Expenses: Tuition:* Full-time $14,184; part-time $1773 per course. *Financial support:* Career-related internships or fieldwork, institutionally sponsored loans, scholarships/grants, and tuition waivers (partial) available. Support available to part-time students. Financial award application deadline: 6/30; financial award applicants required to submit FAFSA. *Unit head:* School of Professional Studies, 800-628-8648, E-mail: sops@nu.edu. *Application contact:* Frank Rojas, Vice President for Enrollment Services, 800-628-8648, E-mail: advisor@nu.edu.
Website: http://www.nu.edu/OurPrograms/School-of-Professional-Studies.html

New York Film Academy, Program in Filmmaking–Hollywood, Los Angeles, CA 90068. Offers acting for film (MFA); cinematography (MFA); filmmaking (MFA); photography (MFA); producing (MFA); screenwriting (MFA). *Accreditation:* NASAD.

New York Film Academy, Program in Filmmaking–New York, New York, NY 10003. Offers acting for film (MFA); filmmaking (MFA); producing (MFA); screenwriting (MFA).

New York Film Academy, Program in Filmmaking–United Arab Emirates, Abu Dhabi, CA 90068, United Arab Emirates. Offers acting for film (MFA); filmmaking (MFA); producing (MFA); screenwriting (MFA).

New York University, Tisch School of the Arts, Kanbar Institute of Film and Television, New York, NY 10012-1019. Offers MFA. *Faculty:* 19 full-time, 20 part-time/adjunct. *Students:* 143 full-time (62 women); includes 33 minority (15 Black or African American, non-Hispanic/Latino; 9 Asian, non-Hispanic/Latino; 4 Hispanic/Latino; 5 Two or more races, non-Hispanic/Latino), 57 international. 747 applicants, 7% accepted, 38 enrolled. In 2014, 30 master's awarded. *Degree requirements:* For master's, 4 films. *Entrance requirements:* For master's, portfolio. Additional exam requirements/recommendations for international students: Required—TOEFL or IELTS. *Application deadline:* For fall admission, 12/1 for domestic and international students. Application fee: $60. Electronic applications accepted. *Financial support:* In 2014–15, 60 students received support, including 16 fellowships with full and partial tuition reimbursements available, 6 teaching assistantships with tuition reimbursements available; Federal Work-Study, institutionally sponsored loans, scholarships/grants, tuition waivers (full and partial), and unspecified assistantships also available. Financial award application deadline: 2/15; financial award applicants required to submit FAFSA. *Unit head:* John Tintori, Chair, 212-998-1780, E-mail: jt42@nyu.edu. *Application contact:* Dan Sandford, Director of Graduate Admissions, 212-998-1918, Fax: 212-995-4060, E-mail: tisch.gradadmissions@nyu.edu.
Website: http://www.filmtv.tisch.nyu.edu/

New York University, Tisch School of the Arts, Program in Moving Image Archiving and Preservation, New York, NY 10012-1019. Offers MA. *Faculty:* 2 full-time, 4 part-time/adjunct. *Students:* 20 full-time (10 women), 3 part-time (1 woman); includes 7 minority (1 Asian, non-Hispanic/Latino; 5 Hispanic/Latino; 1 Two or more races, non-Hispanic/Latino), 2 international. Average age 28. 36 applicants, 50% accepted, 10 enrolled. In 2014, 6 master's awarded. *Degree requirements:* For master's, internship. *Entrance requirements:* For master's, GRE. Additional exam requirements/recommendations for international students: Required—TOEFL or IELTS. *Application deadline:* For fall admission, 12/1 for domestic and international students. Application fee: $60. Electronic applications accepted. *Financial support:* In 2014–15, 11 students received support, including 5 fellowships with full and partial tuition reimbursements available; tuition waivers (partial) also available. Financial award application deadline: 2/15. *Unit head:* Richard Allen, Head, 212-998-1618. *Application contact:* Dan Sandford, Director of Graduate Admissions, 212-998-1918, Fax: 212-995-4060, E-mail: tisch.gradadmissions@nyu.edu.
Website: http://www.cinema.tisch.nyu.edu/

Northwestern University, The Graduate School, School of Communication, Department of Radio, Television and Film, Evanston, IL 60208. Offers documentary media (MFA); screen cultures (MA, PhD); writing for the screen and stage (MFA). Admissions and degrees offered through The Graduate School. Part-time programs available. Terminal master's awarded for partial completion of doctoral program. *Degree requirements:* For master's, comprehensive exam or thesis; for doctorate, thesis/dissertation, qualifying exam. *Entrance requirements:* For master's and doctorate, GRE General Test. Additional exam requirements/recommendations for international students: Required—TOEFL. Electronic applications accepted. *Faculty research:* Art and new media, media theory and criticism, gender, media history, documentary.

Ohio University, Graduate College, College of Fine Arts, School of Film, Athens, OH 45701-2979. Offers film (MFA); film studies (MA). *Degree requirements:* For master's, one foreign language, thesis. *Entrance requirements:* Additional exam requirements/recommendations for international students: Required—TOEFL (minimum score 550 paper-based; 80 iBT) or IELTS (minimum score 6.5). Electronic applications accepted. *Faculty research:* Scriptwriting, sound, editing, cinematography, film theory, digital post production.

Pepperdine University, Seaver College, Master of Fine Arts Program in Writing for Screen and Television, Malibu, CA 90263. Offers MFA. *Students:* 7 full-time (5 women), 22 part-time (12 women); includes 4 minority (2 Black or African American, non-Hispanic/Latino; 1 Asian, non-Hispanic/Latino; 1 Hispanic/Latino). In 2014, 7 master's awarded. *Entrance requirements:* For master's, GRE General Test, statement of purpose and intent for writing as a vocation, script writing sample, letters of recommendation. Additional exam requirements/recommendations for international students: Required—TOEFL. *Application deadline:* For fall admission, 2/1 priority date for domestic students. Application fee: $55. Electronic applications accepted. *Unit head:* Dr. Maire Mullins, Chair/Professor of English, Humanities and Teacher Education Division, 310-506-4894, E-mail: maire.mullins@pepperdine.edu. *Application contact:* Michael Truschke, Dean of Admission and Enrollment Management, 310-506-6165, Fax: 310-506-4861, E-mail: admission-seaver@pepperdine.edu.
Website: http://seaver.pepperdine.edu/humanities/academics/ma-screenwriting.htm

Quinnipiac University, School of Communications, Program in Interactive Media, Hamden, CT 06518-1940. Offers interactive media (MS); production (MS); social media (MS). Part-time and evening/weekend programs available. Postbaccalaureate distance learning degree programs offered (no on-campus study). *Faculty:* 5 full-time (2 women), 12 part-time/adjunct (2 women). *Students:* 9 full-time (7 women), 96 part-time (67 women); includes 26 minority (14 Black or African American, non-Hispanic/Latino; 4 Asian, non-Hispanic/Latino; 7 Hispanic/Latino; 1 Two or more races, non-Hispanic/Latino). 24 applicants, 92% accepted, 18 enrolled. In 2014, 69 master's awarded. *Entrance requirements:* For master's, minimum GPA of 2.8, portfolio or writing sample. Additional exam requirements/recommendations for international students: Required—TOEFL (minimum score 575 paper-based; 90 iBT), IELTS (minimum score 6.5). *Application deadline:* For fall admission, 7/30 priority date for domestic students, 4/30 priority date for international students; for spring admission, 12/30 priority date for domestic students, 9/15 priority date for international students. Applications are processed on a rolling basis. Application fee: $45. Electronic applications accepted. *Expenses: Tuition:* Part-time $920 per credit. *Required fees:* $222 per semester. Tuition and fees vary according to course load and program. *Financial support:* Career-related internships or fieldwork and unspecified assistantships available. Support available to part-time students. Financial award application deadline: 6/1; financial award applicants required to submit FAFSA. *Faculty research:* User experience, social media, semiotics and communication, online distribution of news, Web-based interventions for research. *Unit head:* Phillip Simon, Director, 203-582-8274, E-mail: phillip.simon@quinnipiac.edu. *Application contact:* Quinnipiac University Online Admissions Office, 800-462-1944, E-mail: quonlineadmissions@quinnipiac.edu.
Website: https://quonline.quinnipiac.edu/online-programs/online-graduate-programs/ms-in-interactive-media/

Regent University, Graduate School, School of Communication and the Arts, Virginia Beach, VA 23464-9800. Offers acting (MFA); communication (MA, PhD), including political communication (MA), strategic communication (MA); directing for cinema/television (MFA); film and TV (MA), including producing, production, script writing; journalism (MA); producing for cinema/television (MFA); script and screenwriting (MFA); theatre (MA). Part-time programs available. Postbaccalaureate distance learning degree programs offered (minimal on-campus study). *Faculty:* 20 full-time (3 women), 26 part-time/adjunct (7 women). *Students:* 89 full-time (49 women), 211 part-time (125 women); includes 92 minority (69 Black or African American, non-Hispanic/Latino; 2 American Indian or Alaska Native, non-Hispanic/Latino; 2 Asian, non-Hispanic/Latino; 19 Hispanic/Latino), 10 international. Average age 35. 199 applicants, 53% accepted, 77 enrolled. In 2014, 48 master's, 8 doctorates awarded. *Degree requirements:* For master's, thesis or alternative; for doctorate, thesis/dissertation. *Entrance requirements:* For master's, GRE General Test or MAT, minimum undergraduate GPA of 3.0, writing sample, computer literacy survey, recommendation, resume, interview, audition (for MFA programs); for doctorate, GRE General Test, minimum graduate GPA of 3.0, writing sample, computer literacy survey, recommendation, interview, transcripts. Additional exam requirements/recommendations for international students: Required—TOEFL (minimum score 577 paper-based). *Application deadline:* For fall admission, 3/1 priority date for domestic students; for spring admission, 10/1 priority date for domestic students. Applications are processed on a rolling basis. Application fee: $50. Electronic applications accepted. *Expenses:* Expenses: Contact institution. *Financial support:* Fellowships with full and partial tuition reimbursements, career-related internships or fieldwork, scholarships/grants, tuition waivers (full and partial), and unspecified assistantships available. Support available to part-time students. Financial award application deadline: 9/1; financial award applicants required to submit FAFSA. *Faculty research:* Southern gospel music, education and entertainment, celebrities and the media, journalism and ethics, C.S. Lewis. *Unit head:* Dr. Mitch Land, Dean, 757-352-4916, Fax: 757-352-4291, E-mail: mland@regent.edu. *Application contact:* Matthew Chadwick, Director of Enrollment Support Services, 800-373-5504, Fax: 757-352-4381, E-mail: admissions@regent.edu.
Website: http://www.regent.edu/acad/schcom/

Rochester Institute of Technology, Graduate Enrollment Services, College of Imaging Arts and Sciences, School of Film and Animation, MFA Program in Film and Animation, Rochester, NY 14623-5603. Offers MFA. Part-time programs available. *Students:* 31 full-time (12 women), 28 part-time (15 women); includes 9 minority (2 Black or African American, non-Hispanic/Latino; 4 Asian, non-Hispanic/Latino; 2 Hispanic/Latino; 1 Two or more races, non-Hispanic/Latino), 36 international. Average age 28. 146 applicants, 28% accepted, 12 enrolled. In 2014, 14 master's awarded. *Degree requirements:* For master's, thesis. *Entrance requirements:* For master's, GRE and TOEFL, IELTS, or PTE for non-native English speakers, portfolio, recommended minimum GPA of 3.0. Additional exam requirements/recommendations for international students: Required—PTE (minimum score 58), TOEFL (minimum score 550 paper-based; 79 iBT) or IELTS (minimum score 6.5). *Application deadline:* For fall admission, 2/15 priority date for domestic and international students. Applications are processed on a rolling basis. Application fee: $60. Electronic applications accepted. *Expenses:* Expenses: $1,673 per credit hour. *Financial support:* In 2014–15, 14 students received support. Research assistantships with partial tuition reimbursements available, teaching assistantships with partial tuition reimbursements available, career-related internships or fieldwork, Federal Work-Study, institutionally sponsored loans, scholarships/grants, and unspecified assistantships available. Support available to part-time students. Financial award applicants required to submit FAFSA. *Unit head:* Thomas Gasek, Graduate Program

Director, 585-475-7403, E-mail: tdgpph@rit.edu. *Application contact:* Diane Ellison, Associate Vice President, Graduate Enrollment Services, 585-475-2229, Fax: 585-475-7164, E-mail: gradinfo@rit.edu.
Website: http://cias.rit.edu/schools/film-animation/graduate-film-and-animation

Rochester Institute of Technology, Graduate Enrollment Services, College of Imaging Arts and Sciences, School of Photographic Arts and Sciences, MFA Program in Imaging Arts, Photography and Related Media, Rochester, NY 14623-5603. Offers MFA. *Accreditation:* NASAD. Part-time programs available. *Students:* 12 full-time (7 women), 3 part-time (all women); includes 1 minority (Two or more races, non-Hispanic/Latino), 7 international. Average age 28. 74 applicants, 22% accepted, 6 enrolled. In 2014, 4 master's awarded. *Degree requirements:* For master's, thesis, exhibit. *Entrance requirements:* For master's, GRE and TOEFL, IELTS, or PTE for non-native English speakers, portfolio, recommended minimum GPA of 3.0. Additional exam requirements/recommendations for international students: Required—PTE (minimum score 58), TOEFL (minimum score 550 paper-based; 79 iBT) or IELTS (minimum score 6.5). *Application deadline:* For fall admission, 2/15 priority date for domestic and international students. Applications are processed on a rolling basis. Application fee: $60. Electronic applications accepted. *Expenses:* Expenses: $1,673 per credit hour. *Financial support:* In 2014–15, 6 students received support. Research assistantships with partial tuition reimbursements available, teaching assistantships with partial tuition reimbursements available, career-related internships or fieldwork, Federal Work-Study, institutionally sponsored loans, scholarships/grants, tuition waivers (partial), and unspecified assistantships available. Support available to part-time students. Financial award application deadline: 8/30; financial award applicants required to submit FAFSA. *Faculty research:* Fine art photography, digital imaging, moving media. *Unit head:* Christine Shank, Graduate Program Director, 585-475-2616, Fax: 585-475-5804, E-mail: crspph@rit.edu. *Application contact:* Diane Ellison, Associate Vice President, Graduate Enrollment Services, 585-475-2229, Fax: 585-475-7164, E-mail: gradinfo@rit.edu.
Website: http://cias.rit.edu/schools/photographic-arts-sciences/graduate-imaging-arts

Sacred Heart University, Graduate Programs, College of Arts and Sciences, Department of Communications, Fairfield, CT 06825-1000. Offers corporate communication and public relations (MA Comm); digital/multimedia journalism (MA Comm); digital/multimedia production (MA Comm). Part-time and evening/weekend programs available. *Faculty:* 10 full-time (2 women). *Students:* 62 full-time (31 women), 27 part-time (14 women); includes 25 minority (16 Black or African American, non-Hispanic/Latino; 8 Hispanic/Latino; 1 Native Hawaiian or other Pacific Islander, non-Hispanic/Latino), 4 international. Average age 26. 117 applicants, 90% accepted, 69 enrolled. In 2014, 40 master's awarded. *Degree requirements:* For master's, thesis or alternative. *Entrance requirements:* For master's, bachelor's degree. Additional exam requirements/recommendations for international students: Required—PTE; Recommended—TOEFL (minimum score 570 paper-based; 80 iBT), IELTS (minimum score 6.5). *Application deadline:* Applications are processed on a rolling basis. Application fee: $60. Electronic applications accepted. *Expenses: Tuition:* Full-time $24,559; part-time $649 per credit. *Financial support:* Unspecified assistantships available. Financial award applicants required to submit FAFSA. *Unit head:* Dr. Andrew Miller, Chair, 203-396-8087, E-mail: millera@sacredheart.edu. *Application contact:* Kathy Dilks, Executive Director of Graduate Admissions, 203-365-7619, Fax: 203-365-4732, E-mail: gradstudies@sacredheart.edu.
Website: http://www.sacredheart.edu/academics/collegeofartssciences/academicdepartments/communicationmediastudies/

St. Thomas University, School of Leadership Studies, Program in Electronic Media, Miami Gardens, FL 33054-6459. Offers MA.

San Diego State University, Graduate and Research Affairs, College of Professional Studies and Fine Arts, School of Theater, Television and Film, Program in Television, Film, and New Media Production, San Diego, CA 92182. Offers MA. *Entrance requirements:* For master's, GRE General Test, 3 letters of recommendation, resume, sample reel, influential book list, influential films list, hobby list. Additional exam requirements/recommendations for international students: Required—TOEFL. Electronic applications accepted. *Faculty research:* Experimental film and television programs, documentary film, television research and production.

San Francisco Art Institute, Dual-Degree MFA/MA Program in Studio Art and History and Theory of Contemporary Art, San Francisco, CA 94133. Offers MFA/MA. Specializations available in art and technology, film, new genres, painting, photography, printmaking, and sculpture. *Faculty:* 15 full-time (7 women), 46 part-time/adjunct (23 women). *Students:* 6 full-time (4 women); includes 1 minority (Black or African American, non-Hispanic/Latino). Average age 27. 15 applicants, 40% accepted, 4 enrolled. *Entrance requirements:* Additional exam requirements/recommendations for international students: Required—TOEFL (minimum score 600 paper-based; 100 iBT), IELTS (minimum score 7.5). *Application deadline:* For fall admission, 1/15 priority date for domestic and international students. Applications are processed on a rolling basis. Application fee: $85. Electronic applications accepted. *Expenses: Tuition:* Full-time $41,100; part-time $1805 per credit. *Required fees:* $870. *Financial support:* In 2014–15, 8 students received support, including fellowships (averaging $30,000 per year), teaching assistantships (averaging $2,500 per year); career-related internships or fieldwork, Federal Work-Study, scholarships/grants, and unspecified assistantships also available. Support available to part-time students. Financial award application deadline: 3/1; financial award applicants required to submit FAFSA. *Unit head:* Tony Labat, Chair, Master of Fine Arts Department, 415-771-7020, Fax: 415-641-1205, E-mail: tlabat@sfai.edu. *Application contact:* Jana Rumberger, Associate Director of Recruitment, 415-351-3507, Fax: 415-749-4592, E-mail: jrumberger@sfai.edu.
Website: http://www.sfai.edu/degree-programs/graduate/dual-degree-ma-mfa

San Francisco State University, Division of Graduate Studies, College of Liberal and Creative Arts, Department of Cinema, San Francisco, CA 94132-1722. Offers MA, MFA. *Expenses:* Tuition, state resident: full-time $6738. Tuition, nonresident: full-time $17,898; part-time $372 per credit hour. *Required fees:* $498 per semester. *Unit head:* Dr. Steven Kovacs, Interim Chair, 415-338-1629, Fax: 415-338-0906, E-mail: cinedept@sfsu.edu. *Application contact:* Dr. R.L. Rutsky, MA Coordinator, 415-405-3400, Fax: 415-338-0906, E-mail: cinegrad@sfsu.edu.
Website: http://www.cinema.sfsu.edu/

San Jose State University, Graduate Studies and Research, College of Humanities and the Arts, Department of Television, Radio, Film and Theatre, San Jose, CA 95192-0001. Offers theatre arts (MA). *Accreditation:* NAST. *Degree requirements:* For master's, written exam. *Entrance requirements:* Additional exam requirements/recommendations for international students: Required—TOEFL (minimum score 570 paper-based). Electronic applications accepted.

San Jose State University, Graduate Studies and Research, College of Humanities and the Arts, School of Art and Design, San Jose, CA 95192-0001. Offers animation/illustration (MA); art history (MA); digital media arts (MFA); photography (MFA); pictorial arts (MFA); spatial arts (MFA). *Accreditation:* NASAD (one or more programs are accredited). *Entrance requirements:* For master's, GRE. Electronic applications accepted.

Savannah College of Art and Design, Graduate School, Program in Animation, Savannah, GA 31402-3146. Offers MA, MFA. Part-time programs available. *Faculty:* 26 full-time (4 women), 4 part-time/adjunct (1 woman). *Students:* 153 full-time (79 women), 51 part-time (25 women); includes 30 minority (17 Black or African American, non-Hispanic/Latino; 1 American Indian or Alaska Native, non-Hispanic/Latino; 7 Asian, non-Hispanic/Latino; 5 Hispanic/Latino), 106 international. Average age 26. 160 applicants, 48% accepted, 49 enrolled. In 2014, 50 master's awarded. *Degree requirements:* For master's, thesis (for some programs), internship (for MFA). *Entrance requirements:* For master's, portfolio. Additional exam requirements/recommendations for international students: Required—TOEFL (minimum score 550 paper-based, 85 iBT), IELTS (minimum score 6.5), or ACTFL. *Application deadline:* For fall admission, 4/1 for domestic and international students. Applications are processed on a rolling basis. Application fee: $40. Electronic applications accepted. *Expenses: Tuition:* Full-time $34,605; part-time $3845 per course. One-time fee: $500. Tuition and fees vary according to course load. *Financial support:* Fellowships, career-related internships or fieldwork, Federal Work-Study, and scholarships/grants available. Financial award application deadline: 4/1; financial award applicants required to submit FAFSA. *Unit head:* Scott Bogoniewski, Chair. *Application contact:* Jenny Jaquillard, Executive Director of Admissions, Recruitment and Events, 912-525-5100, Fax: 912-525-5985, E-mail: admission@scad.edu.
Website: http://www.scad.edu/academics/programs/animation

Savannah College of Art and Design, Graduate School, Program in Film and Television, Savannah, GA 31402-3146. Offers MA, MFA. Part-time programs available. *Faculty:* 14 full-time (2 women), 3 part-time/adjunct (2 women). *Students:* 108 full-time (55 women), 27 part-time (6 women); includes 52 minority (42 Black or African American, non-Hispanic/Latino; 2 American Indian or Alaska Native, non-Hispanic/Latino; 2 Asian, non-Hispanic/Latino; 6 Hispanic/Latino), 43 international. Average age 27. 204 applicants, 48% accepted, 54 enrolled. In 2014, 25 master's awarded. *Degree requirements:* For master's, thesis (for some programs), final project (for MA); internship (for MFA). *Entrance requirements:* For master's, video recording. Additional exam requirements/recommendations for international students: Required—TOEFL (minimum score 550 paper-based, 85 iBT), IELTS (minimum score 6.5), or ACTFL. *Application deadline:* For fall admission, 4/1 for domestic and international students. Applications are processed on a rolling basis. Application fee: $40. Electronic applications accepted. *Expenses: Tuition:* Full-time $34,605; part-time $3845 per course. One-time fee: $500. Tuition and fees vary according to course load. *Financial support:* Fellowships, career-related internships or fieldwork, Federal Work-Study, and scholarships/grants available. Financial award application deadline: 4/1; financial award applicants required to submit FAFSA. *Application contact:* Jenny Jaquillard, Executive Director of Admissions, Recruitment and Events, 912-525-5100, Fax: 912-525-5985, E-mail: admission@scad.edu.
Website: http://www.scad.edu/academics/programs/film-and-television

Savannah College of Art and Design, Graduate School, Program in Sound Design, Savannah, GA 31402-3146. Offers MA, MFA. Part-time programs available. *Faculty:* 8 full-time (0 women). *Students:* 40 full-time (15 women), 8 part-time (2 women); includes 17 minority (12 Black or African American, non-Hispanic/Latino; 2 Asian, non-Hispanic/Latino; 3 Hispanic/Latino), 10 international. Average age 26. 31 applicants, 65% accepted, 11 enrolled. In 2014, 11 master's awarded. *Degree requirements:* For master's, thesis (for some programs), final project (for MA); internship (for MFA). *Entrance requirements:* For master's, portfolio (in digital or multimedia format). Additional exam requirements/recommendations for international students: Required—TOEFL (minimum score 550 paper-based, 85 iBT), IELTS (minimum score 6.5), or ACTFL. *Application deadline:* For fall admission, 4/1 for domestic and international students. Application fee: $40. *Expenses: Tuition:* Full-time $34,605; part-time $3845 per course. One-time fee: $500. Tuition and fees vary according to course load. *Financial support:* Fellowships, career-related internships or fieldwork, Federal Work-Study, and scholarships/grants available. Financial award application deadline: 4/1; financial award applicants required to submit FAFSA. *Unit head:* Robin Beauchamp, Chair. *Application contact:* Jenny Jaquillard, Executive Director of Admissions, Recruitment and Events, 912-525-5100, Fax: 912-525-5985, E-mail: admission@scad.edu.
Website: http://www.scad.edu/academics/programs/sound-design

School of the Art Institute of Chicago, Graduate Division, Department of Film, Video, and New Media, Chicago, IL 60603-3103. Offers MFA. *Accreditation:* NASAD. *Degree requirements:* For master's, thesis exhibit. *Entrance requirements:* Additional exam requirements/recommendations for international students: Required—TOEFL (minimum score 550 paper-based; 80 iBT), IELTS (minimum score 6.5). Electronic applications accepted.

School of the Art Institute of Chicago, Graduate Division, Department of Sound, Chicago, IL 60603-3103. Offers MFA. *Entrance requirements:* Additional exam requirements/recommendations for international students: Required—TOEFL, IELTS.

School of Visual Arts, Graduate Programs, Directing Department, New York, NY 10010-3994. Offers MPS. *Degree requirements:* For master's, thesis, 36 credits, including all required courses; minimum GPA of 3.0; completion and marketing of his or her thesis film. *Entrance requirements:* For master's, portfolio. Additional exam requirements/recommendations for international students: Required—TOEFL (minimum score 550 paper-based; 79 iBT).

School of Visual Arts, Graduate Programs, Program in Photography, Video and Related Media, New York, NY 10010-3994. Offers MFA. *Accreditation:* NASAD. *Degree requirements:* For master's, thesis, 60 credits and all course requirements; minimum GPA of 3.3; thesis project. *Entrance requirements:* For master's, portfolio (still images and/or videos) through SlideRoom. Additional exam requirements/recommendations for international students: Required—TOEFL (minimum score 550 paper-based; 79 iBT). Electronic applications accepted. *Faculty research:* Contemporary and responsible creative initiatives, including experimental, narrative or documentary video, installation and conceptual art, tableau and real-world-witness photography.

School of Visual Arts, Graduate Programs, Social Documentary Film Department, New York, NY 10010-3994. Offers MFA. *Degree requirements:* For master's, thesis, 60 credits, including all required courses; minimum cumulative GPA of 3.0; residency of two academic years. *Entrance requirements:* For master's, concise treatment for documentary film production; video work or still imagery; visual documentation of a subject (for applicants without prior filmmaking experience). Additional exam requirements/recommendations for international students: Required—TOEFL (minimum score 550 paper-based; 79 iBT). Electronic applications accepted. *Expenses:* Contact institution.

Stanford University, School of Humanities and Sciences, Department of Art and Art History, Stanford, CA 94305-9991. Offers art history (PhD); art practice (MFA); design (MFA, MS); documentary film and video (MFA); MS/MFA. *Degree requirements:* For master's, thesis (for some programs), faculty reviews; for doctorate, 2 foreign languages, thesis/dissertation. *Entrance requirements:* For master's and doctorate, GRE General Test. Additional exam requirements/recommendations for international

students: Required—TOEFL. Electronic applications accepted. *Expenses: Tuition:* Full-time $44,184; part-time $982 per credit hour. *Required fees:* $191.

Syracuse University, College of Visual and Performing Arts, Program in Film, Syracuse, NY 13244. Offers MFA. *Students:* 16 full-time (4 women), 1 part-time (0 women); includes 1 minority (Black or African American, non-Hispanic/Latino), 13 international. Average age 30. 149 applicants, 7% accepted, 6 enrolled. In 2014, 5 master's awarded. *Degree requirements:* For master's, thesis or alternative. *Entrance requirements:* For master's, portfolio. Additional exam requirements/recommendations for international students: Required—TOEFL (minimum score 100 iBT). *Application deadline:* For fall admission, 2/1 priority date for domestic and international students. Application fee: $75. Electronic applications accepted. *Expenses: Tuition:* Part-time $1341 per credit. *Financial support:* Fellowships with full tuition reimbursements and teaching assistantships with full and partial tuition reimbursements available. Financial award application deadline: 1/1; financial award applicants required to submit FAFSA. *Unit head:* Owen Shapiro,, 315-443-1033, E-mail: ojshapir@syr.edu. *Application contact:* Therese West, Information Contact, 315-443-0137, E-mail: admissg@syr.edu. Website: http://vpa.syr.edu/art-design/transmedia/graduate/film

Syracuse University, S. I. Newhouse School of Public Communications, Program in Documentary Film and History, Syracuse, NY 13244. Offers MA. *Students:* 6 full-time (3 women); includes 3 minority (1 Asian, non-Hispanic/Latino; 2 Hispanic/Latino). Average age 31. 15 applicants, 87% accepted, 5 enrolled. In 2014, 10 master's awarded. *Degree requirements:* For master's, thesis or alternative. *Entrance requirements:* For master's, GRE General Test. Additional exam requirements/recommendations for international students: Required—TOEFL (minimum score 100 iBT). *Application deadline:* For fall admission, 2/1 for domestic and international students; for summer admission, 1/15 priority date for domestic and international students. Application fee: $45. Electronic applications accepted. *Expenses: Tuition:* Part-time $1341 per credit. *Financial support:* Fellowships with full tuition reimbursements, research assistantships with partial tuition reimbursements, and teaching assistantships with partial tuition reimbursements available. Financial award application deadline: 2/1. *Unit head:* Richard Breyer, Director, 315-443-9249, E-mail: pcgrad@syr.edu. *Application contact:* Graduate Records Office, 315-443-4039, Fax: 315-443-1834, E-mail: pcgrad@syr.edu. Website: http://newhouse.syr.edu/

Temple University, Center for the Arts, Division of Theater, Film and Media Arts, Department of Film and Media Arts, Philadelphia, PA 19122. Offers MFA. Part-time programs available. *Faculty:* 17 full-time (4 women), 16 part-time/adjunct (3 women). *Students:* 36 full-time (24 women), 4 part-time (2 women); includes 7 minority (2 Black or African American, non-Hispanic/Latino; 4 Hispanic/Latino; 1 Two or more races, non-Hispanic/Latino), 12 international. 38 applicants, 34% accepted, 10 enrolled. In 2014, 10 master's awarded. *Degree requirements:* For master's, comprehensive exam, project. *Entrance requirements:* For master's, minimum GPA of 3.0; exhibit. Additional exam requirements/recommendations for international students: Required—TOEFL (minimum score 600 paper-based; 100 iBT). *Application deadline:* For fall admission, 2/2 for domestic and international students. Application fee: $60. Electronic applications accepted. *Expenses:* Expenses: Contact institution. *Financial support:* Fellowships, research assistantships, teaching assistantships, Federal Work-Study, institutionally sponsored loans, and unspecified assistantships available. Financial award application deadline: 3/1; financial award applicants required to submit FAFSA. *Faculty research:* Documentary/experimental film, narrative film, digital media arts, film and media studies, screenwriting. *Unit head:* Dr. Jeff Rush, Chair, 215-204-3859, Fax: 215-204-5280, E-mail: film@temple.edu. *Application contact:* Leah Dempsey, Assistant Director for Administration, 215-204-8791, E-mail: leahdempsey@temple.edu. Website: http://smc.temple.edu/fma/graduate/

Universidad Autonoma de Guadalajara, Graduate Programs, Guadalajara, Mexico. Offers administrative law and justice (LL M); advertising and corporate communications (MA); architecture (M Arch); business (MBA); computational science (MCC); education (Ed M, Ed D); English-Spanish translation (MA); entrepreneurship and management (MBA); integrated management of digital animation (MA); international business (MIB); international corporate law (LL M); internet technologies (MS); manufacturing systems (MMS); occupational health (MS); philosophy (MA, PhD); power electronics (MS); quality systems (MQS); renewable energy (MS); social evaluation of projects (MBA); strategic market research (MBA); tax law (MA); teaching mathematics (MA).

The University of Alabama, Graduate School, College of Communication and Information Sciences, Department of Telecommunication and Film, Tuscaloosa, AL 35487-0152. Offers MA. *Faculty:* 14 full-time (4 women). *Students:* 8 full-time (4 women), 1 part-time (0 women); includes 2 minority (1 Black or African American, non-Hispanic/Latino; 1 Two or more races, non-Hispanic/Latino), 3 international. Average age 25. 17 applicants, 53% accepted, 7 enrolled. In 2014, 4 master's awarded. Terminal master's awarded for partial completion of doctoral program. *Degree requirements:* For master's, comprehensive exam, thesis or alternative. *Entrance requirements:* For master's, GRE, minimum GPA of 3.0. Additional exam requirements/recommendations for international students: Required—TOEFL (minimum score 600 paper-based; 79 iBT). *Application deadline:* For fall admission, 4/15 priority date for domestic students, 1/15 priority date for international students; for spring admission, 11/1 for domestic students, 10/1 priority date for international students. Applications are processed on a rolling basis. Application fee: $50 ($60 for international students). Electronic applications accepted. *Expenses:* Tuition, state resident: full-time $9826. Tuition, nonresident: full-time $24,950. *Financial support:* In 2014–15, 6 students received support, including 2 research assistantships with tuition reimbursements available (averaging $9,825 per year), 2 teaching assistantships with tuition reimbursements available (averaging $9,825 per year); institutionally sponsored loans also available. Financial award application deadline: 2/15. *Faculty research:* Entertainment theory, news and public affairs, effects of telecommunications, management, media law and policy. *Unit head:* Dr. Gary A. Copeland, Chair, 205-348-6350, Fax: 205-348-5162, E-mail: copeland@ua.edu. *Application contact:* Dr. Shuhua Zhou, Graduate Coordinator, 205-348-8653, Fax: 205-348-5162, E-mail: szhou@bama.ua.edu. Website: http://www.tcf.ua.edu

The University of British Columbia, Faculty of Arts, Creative Writing Program, Vancouver, BC V6T 1Z1, Canada. Offers creative writing (MFA); creative writing and film production (MFA); creative writing and theatre (MFA). Part-time programs available. Postbaccalaureate distance learning degree programs offered (minimal on-campus study). *Degree requirements:* For master's, thesis. *Entrance requirements:* For master's, sample of written work. Additional exam requirements/recommendations for international students: Required—TOEFL (minimum score 550 paper-based). Electronic applications accepted. *Expenses:* Contact institution. *Faculty research:* Writing of fiction; poetry, creative nonfiction, plays for stage, screen, television, radio, writing for children and translation, song lyrics and libretto, new media and graphic novel.

The University of British Columbia, Faculty of Arts and Faculty of Graduate Studies, Department of Theatre and Film, Film Program, Vancouver, BC V6T 1Z2, Canada. Offers creative writing and film production (MFA); film production (MFA, Diploma); film studies (MA). *Degree requirements:* For master's, variable foreign language requirement, comprehensive exam, thesis (MA); thesis or project (MFA). *Entrance requirements:* For master's, portfolio (MFA). Additional exam requirements/

recommendations for international students: Required—TOEFL (minimum score 600 paper-based). *Faculty research:* Film theory and violence; American and European cinema; cult cinema; Irish cinema.

University of California, Los Angeles, Graduate Division, School of Theater, Film and Television, Department of Film, Television, and Digital Media, Los Angeles, CA 90034. Offers animation (MFA); cinema and media studies (MA, PhD); cinematography (MFA); production (MFA); screenwriting (MFA). *Degree requirements:* For master's, comprehensive exam; for doctorate, one foreign language, thesis/dissertation, oral and written qualifying exams. *Entrance requirements:* For master's, GRE General Test (for MA applicants), bachelor's degree; minimum undergraduate GPA of 3.0 (or its equivalent if letter grade system not used); writing sample (for MA); for doctorate, GRE General Test, master's degree; minimum undergraduate GPA of 3.0 (or its equivalent if letter grade system not used); writing sample. Additional exam requirements/recommendations for international students: Required—TOEFL. Electronic applications accepted. *Expenses:* Contact institution.

University of California, Los Angeles, Graduate Division, School of Theater, Film and Television, Interdepartmental Program in Moving Image Archive Studies, Los Angeles, CA 90095. Offers MA. *Degree requirements:* For master's, comprehensive exam, thesis. *Entrance requirements:* For master's, bachelor's degree; minimum undergraduate GPA of 3.0 (or its equivalent if letter grade system not used); writing sample. Additional exam requirements/recommendations for international students: Required—TOEFL. Electronic applications accepted.

University of California, Santa Barbara, Graduate Division, College of Letters and Sciences, Division of Humanities and Fine Arts, Department of Film and Media Studies, Santa Barbara, CA 93106-4010. Offers PhD, MA/PhD. Terminal master's awarded for partial completion of doctoral program. *Degree requirements:* For doctorate, one foreign language, comprehensive exam, thesis/dissertation. *Entrance requirements:* For doctorate, GRE, MA in film/media studies or equivalent. Additional exam requirements/recommendations for international students: Required—TOEFL (minimum score 600 paper-based; 100 iBT), IELTS (minimum score 7). Electronic applications accepted. *Faculty research:* Classical film theory, film and television history, historiography, cultural studies, global media, media industries, regulation and policy.

University of Central Arkansas, Graduate School, College of Fine Arts and Communication, Program in Digital Filmmaking, Conway, AR 72035-0001. Offers MFA. *Degree requirements:* For master's, thesis. *Entrance requirements:* For master's, GRE General Test, minimum GPA of 2.7. Additional exam requirements/recommendations for international students: Required—TOEFL (minimum score 550 paper-based). Electronic applications accepted.

University of Central Florida, College of Arts and Humanities, School of Visual Arts and Design, Orlando, FL 32816. Offers digital media (MA); emerging media (MFA), including digital media, entrepreneurial digital cinema, studio art and the computer. *Faculty:* 51 full-time (20 women), 20 part-time/adjunct (4 women). *Students:* 40 full-time (18 women), 9 part-time (1 woman); includes 8 minority (1 Black or African American, non-Hispanic/Latino; 1 American Indian or Alaska Native, non-Hispanic/Latino; 1 Asian, non-Hispanic/Latino; 5 Hispanic/Latino), 7 international. Average age 32. 43 applicants, 56% accepted, 14 enrolled. In 2014, 12 master's awarded. Application fee: $30. Electronic applications accepted. *Expenses:* Tuition, state resident: part-time $288.16 per credit hour. Tuition, nonresident: part-time $1073.31 per credit hour. *Financial support:* In 2014–15, 25 students received support, including 11 fellowships (averaging $8,500 per year), 16 teaching assistantships (averaging $6,300 per year); scholarships/grants and unspecified assistantships also available. *Unit head:* Byron Clercx, Director, 407-823-3145, E-mail: byron.clercx@ucf.edu. *Application contact:* Barbara Rodriguez Lamas, Director, Admissions and Student Services, 407-823-2766, Fax: 407-823-6442, E-mail: gradadmissions@ucf.edu. Website: http://svad.cah.ucf.edu/

University of Denver, Division of Arts, Humanities and Social Sciences, Department of Media, Film and Journalism Studies, Denver, CO 80208. Offers emergent digital practices (MA); international and intercultural communication (MA); strategic communication (MS); student designed emphasis (MA); video production (MA). Part-time programs available. *Faculty:* 14 full-time (8 women), 6 part-time/adjunct (2 women). *Students:* 24 full-time (17 women), 25 part-time (17 women); includes 10 minority (1 Asian, non-Hispanic/Latino; 4 Hispanic/Latino; 5 Two or more races, non-Hispanic/Latino), 4 international. Average age 27. 73 applicants, 89% accepted, 21 enrolled. In 2014, 17 master's awarded. *Degree requirements:* For master's, thesis (for some programs). *Entrance requirements:* For master's, GRE General Test, bachelor's degree, transcripts, personal statement, three letters of recommendation. Additional exam requirements/recommendations for international students: Required—TOEFL (minimum score 620 paper-based; 105 iBT). *Application deadline:* For fall admission, 2/15 priority date for domestic students, 1/1 priority date for international students. Applications are processed on a rolling basis. Application fee: $65. Electronic applications accepted. *Expenses:* Expenses: $1,199 per credit hour. *Financial support:* In 2014–15, 41 students received support, including 7 teaching assistantships with full and partial tuition reimbursements available (averaging $9,515 per year); career-related internships or fieldwork, Federal Work-Study, institutionally sponsored loans, scholarships/grants, and unspecified assistantships also available. Support available to part-time students. Financial award application deadline: 2/15; financial award applicants required to submit FAFSA. *Faculty research:* International and intercultural communication; media law; film history; youth, families, and social media; activist media. *Total annual research expenditures:* $50,000. *Unit head:* Dr. Lynn Schofield Clark, Chair, 303-871-3984, Fax: 303-871-4949, E-mail: lynn.clark@du.edu. *Application contact:* Information Contact, 303-871-2166, E-mail: mfjs@du.edu. Website: http://www.du.edu/ahss/mfjs/index.html

The University of Iowa, Graduate College, College of Liberal Arts and Sciences, Department of Cinema and Comparative Literature, Program in Film and Video Production, Iowa City, IA 52242-1316. Offers MFA. *Degree requirements:* For master's, thesis (for some programs), exam. *Entrance requirements:* For master's, GRE General Test, minimum GPA of 3.0. Additional exam requirements/recommendations for international students: Required—TOEFL (minimum score 550 paper-based; 81 iBT). Electronic applications accepted.

University of Memphis, Graduate School, College of Communication and Fine Arts, Department of Communication, Memphis, TN 38152. Offers communication (MA); communication arts (PhD); film and video production (MA). Part-time programs available. *Faculty:* 12 full-time (5 women). *Students:* 20 full-time (10 women), 18 part-time (6 women); includes 8 minority (4 Black or African American, non-Hispanic/Latino; 1 Asian, non-Hispanic/Latino; 2 Hispanic/Latino; 1 Two or more races, non-Hispanic/Latino). Average age 35. 47 applicants, 55% accepted, 6 enrolled. In 2014, 3 master's, 6 doctorates awarded. *Degree requirements:* For master's, comprehensive exam, thesis or alternative; for doctorate, comprehensive exam, thesis/dissertation. *Entrance requirements:* For master's and doctorate, GRE General Test. Additional exam requirements/recommendations for international students: Required—TOEFL (minimum score 600 paper-based). *Application deadline:* For fall admission, 2/1 for domestic and international students. Application fee: $35 ($60 for international students). *Financial*

support: In 2014–15, 27 students received support. Research assistantships with full tuition reimbursements available, teaching assistantships with full tuition reimbursements available, Federal Work-Study, scholarships/grants, and unspecified assistantships available. Financial award application deadline: 2/15; financial award applicants required to submit FAFSA. *Faculty research:* Rhetoric, media studies, applied communication (health communication). *Unit head:* Dr. Sandra Sarkela, Chair, 901-678-3173, Fax: 901-678-4331, E-mail: ssarkela@memphis.edu. *Application contact:* Dr. Amanda Young, Coordinator of Graduate Studies, 901-678-3612, Fax: 901-678-4331, E-mail: ajyoung@memphis.edu.
Website: http://www.memphis.edu/ccfa/index.php

University of Miami, Graduate School, School of Communication, Coral Gables, FL 33124. Offers communication (PhD); communication studies (MA); film studies (MA, PhD); motion pictures (MFA), including production, producing, and screenwriting; print journalism (MA); public relations (MA); Spanish language journalism (MA); television broadcast journalism (MA). Part-time programs available. *Degree requirements:* For master's, comprehensive exam (for some programs), thesis (for some programs); for doctorate, comprehensive exam, thesis/dissertation. *Entrance requirements:* For master's, GRE General Test; for doctorate, GRE General Test, master's thesis or scholarly research. Additional exam requirements/recommendations for international students: Required—TOEFL (minimum score 600 paper-based; 100 iBT). Electronic applications accepted. *Faculty research:* Communication studies, mass communication, international/interpersonal communication, film studies, journalism.

The University of Montana, Graduate School, College of Visual and Performing Arts, School of Media Arts, Missoula, MT 59812-0002. Offers digital filmmaking (MFA); integrated digital media (MFA).

University of Nevada, Las Vegas, Graduate College, College of Fine Arts, Department of Film, Las Vegas, NV 89154-5015. Offers writing for dramatic media (MFA). Part-time programs available. *Faculty:* 1 full-time (0 women). *Students:* 9 full-time (5 women), 1 (woman) part-time; includes 3 minority (1 Black or African American, non-Hispanic/Latino; 1 Asian, non-Hispanic/Latino; 1 Two or more races, non-Hispanic/Latino), 1 international. Average age 34. 19 applicants, 26% accepted, 4 enrolled. In 2014, 3 master's awarded. *Degree requirements:* For master's, comprehensive exam, creative project. *Entrance requirements:* Additional exam requirements/recommendations for international students: Required—TOEFL (minimum score 550 paper-based), IELTS (minimum score 7). *Application deadline:* For fall admission, 1/15 for domestic students, 5/1 for international students; for spring admission, 10/1 for international students. Application fee: $60 ($95 for international students). Electronic applications accepted. *Financial support:* In 2014–15, 7 students received support, including 7 teaching assistantships with partial tuition reimbursements available (averaging $13,000 per year); institutionally sponsored loans, scholarships/grants, health care benefits, and unspecified assistantships also available. Financial award application deadline: 3/1. *Faculty research:* Screenplay, stage play, television series, Web entertainment content, production. *Unit head:* Francisco Menendez, Chair/Professor, 702-895-4223, Fax: 702-895-4395, E-mail: francisco.menendez@unlv.edu. *Application contact:* Graduate College Admissions Evaluator, 702-895-3320, Fax: 702-895-4180, E-mail: gradcollege@unlv.edu.
Website: http://film.unlv.edu/

University of New Orleans, Graduate School, College of Liberal Arts, Department of Film and Theatre, New Orleans, LA 70148. Offers design (MFA); film production (MFA); theatre performance (MFA), including acting, directing. *Accreditation:* NAST. *Degree requirements:* For master's, comprehensive exam, thesis. *Entrance requirements:* Additional exam requirements/recommendations for international students: Required—TOEFL (minimum score 550 paper-based; 79 iBT), IELTS (minimum score 6.5). Electronic applications accepted. *Faculty research:* Mass communication theory, nineteenth and twentieth century theater history, film criticism and history.

The University of North Carolina at Greensboro, Graduate School, College of Arts and Sciences, Department of Media Studies, Greensboro, NC 27412-5001. Offers film and video production (MFA).

University of North Carolina School of the Arts, School of Filmmaking, Winston-Salem, NC 27127-2738. Offers film music composition (MFA). *Entrance requirements:* For master's, audition, performance, portfolio, interview. Additional exam requirements/recommendations for international students: Required—TOEFL.

University of North Texas, Robert B. Toulouse School of Graduate Studies, Denton, TX 76203-5459. Offers accounting (MS); applied anthropology (MA, MS); applied behavior analysis (Certificate); applied geography (MA); applied technology and performance improvement (M Ed, MS); art education (MA); art history (MA); art museum education (Certificate); arts leadership (Certificate); audiology (Au D); behavior analysis (MS); behavioral science (PhD); biochemistry and molecular biology (MS); biology (MA, MS); biomedical engineering (MS); business analysis (MS); chemistry (MS); clinical health psychology (PhD); communication studies (MA, MS); computer engineering (MS); computer science (MS); counseling (M Ed, MS), including clinical mental health counseling (MS), college and university counseling, elementary school counseling, secondary school counseling; creative writing (MA); criminal justice (MS); curriculum and instruction (M Ed); decision sciences (MBA); design (MA, MFA), including fashion design (MFA), innovation studies, interior design (MFA); early childhood studies (MS); economics (MS); educational leadership (M Ed, Ed D); educational psychology (MS, PhD), including family studies (MS), gifted and talented (MS), human development (MS), learning and cognition (MS), research, measurement and evaluation (MS); electrical engineering (MS); emergency management (MPA); engineering technology (MS); English (MA); English as a second language (MA); environmental science (MS); finance (MBA, MS); financial management (MPA); French (MA); health services management (MBA); higher education (M Ed, Ed D); history (MA, MS); hospitality management (MS); human resources management (MPA); information science (MS); information systems (PhD); information technologies (MBA); interdisciplinary studies (MA, MS); international studies (MA); international sustainable tourism (MS); jazz studies (MM); journalism (MA, MJ, Graduate Certificate), including interactive and virtual digital communication (Graduate Certificate), narrative journalism (Graduate Certificate), public relations (Graduate Certificate); kinesiology (MS); linguistics (MA); local government management (MPA); logistics (PhD); logistics and supply chain management (MBA); long-term care, senior housing, and aging services (MA); management (PhD); marketing (MBA); mathematics (MA, MS); mechanical and energy engineering (MS, PhD); music (MA), including ethnomusicology, music theory, musicology, performance; music composition (PhD); music education (MM Ed, PhD); nonprofit management (MPA); operations and supply chain management (MBA); performance (MM, DMA); philosophy (MA); political science (MA); professional and technical communication (MA); radio, television and film (MA, MFA); rehabilitation counseling (Certificate); sociology (MA); Spanish (MA); special education (M Ed); speech-language pathology (MA); strategic management (MBA); studio art (MFA); teaching (M Ed); MBA/MS. Part-time and evening/weekend programs available. Postbaccalaureate distance learning degree programs offered. *Faculty:* 651 full-time (215 women), 233 part-time/adjunct (139 women). *Students:* 3,040 full-time (1,598 women), 3,401 part-time (2,097 women); includes 1,740 minority (533 Black or African American, non-Hispanic/Latino; 15 American Indian or Alaska Native, non-Hispanic/Latino; 286 Asian, non-Hispanic/Latino; 746 Hispanic/Latino; 3 Native Hawaiian or other Pacific Islander, non-Hispanic/Latino; 157 Two or more races, non-Hispanic/Latino), 1,145 international. Terminal master's awarded for partial completion of doctoral program. *Degree requirements:* For master's, variable foreign language requirement, comprehensive exam (for some programs), thesis (for some programs); for doctorate, variable foreign language requirement, comprehensive exam (for some programs), thesis/dissertation; for other advanced degree, variable foreign language requirement, comprehensive exam (for some programs). *Entrance requirements:* For master's and doctorate, GRE, GMAT. Additional exam requirements/recommendations for international students: Required—TOEFL (minimum score 550 paper-based; 79 iBT). *Application deadline:* For fall admission, 7/15 for domestic students, 3/15 for international students; for spring admission, 11/15 for domestic students, 9/15 for international students; for summer admission, 5/1 for domestic students. Applications are processed on a rolling basis. Application fee: $60. Electronic applications accepted. *Expenses:* Tuition, state resident: full-time $5450; part-time $3633 per year. Tuition, nonresident: full-time $11,966; part-time $7977 per year. *Required fees:* $1301; $398 per credit hour. $685 per semester. Tuition and fees vary according to program and reciprocity agreements. *Financial support:* Fellowships with partial tuition reimbursements, research assistantships with partial tuition reimbursements, teaching assistantships, career-related internships or fieldwork, Federal Work-Study, institutionally sponsored loans, scholarships/grants, health care benefits, and library assistantships available. Support available to part-time students. Financial award applicants required to submit FAFSA. *Unit head:* Mark Wardell, Dean, 940-565-2383, E-mail: mark.wardell@unt.edu. *Application contact:* Toulouse School of Graduate Studies, 940-565-2383, Fax: 940-565-2141, E-mail: gradsch@unt.edu.
Website: http://tsgs.unt.edu/

University of Oklahoma, Weitzenhoffer Family College of Fine Arts, School of Art and Art History, Norman, OK 73019. Offers art (MFA), including ceramics, film, painting, photography, printmaking, sculpture, video, visual communication; art history (MA, PhD), including art history (MA), art of the American West (PhD), Native American art (PhD). Part-time programs available. *Faculty:* 25 full-time (6 women). *Students:* 21 full-time (11 women), 11 part-time (7 women); includes 6 minority (4 American Indian or Alaska Native, non-Hispanic/Latino; 2 Two or more races, non-Hispanic/Latino), 1 international. Average age 32. 23 applicants, 48% accepted, 3 enrolled. In 2014, 7 master's awarded. Terminal master's awarded for partial completion of doctoral program. *Degree requirements:* For master's, comprehensive exam, thesis; for doctorate, comprehensive exam, thesis/dissertation. *Entrance requirements:* Additional exam requirements/recommendations for international students: Required—TOEFL (minimum score 79 iBT). *Application deadline:* For fall admission, 1/15 for domestic and international students; for spring admission, 10/1 for domestic and international students. Application fee: $50 ($100 for international students). Electronic applications accepted. *Expenses:* Tuition, state resident: full-time $4394; part-time $183.10 per credit hour. Tuition, nonresident: full-time $16,970; part-time $707.10 per credit hour. *Required fees:* $2892; $109.95 per credit hour. $126.50 per semester. *Financial support:* In 2014–15, 28 students received support, including 1 fellowship (averaging $5,000 per year), 16 teaching assistantships with partial tuition reimbursements available (averaging $10,377 per year); career-related internships or fieldwork, Federal Work-Study, institutionally sponsored loans, scholarships/grants, health care benefits, tuition waivers (full and partial), and unspecified assistantships also available. Support available to part-time students. Financial award application deadline: 6/1; financial award applicants required to submit FAFSA. *Faculty research:* Sculpture, painting, printmaking, technology, ceramics, Native American art, art of American West, Byzantine, Contemporary, Renaissance, Baroque, nineteenth-twentieth century. *Unit head:* 405-325-2691, Fax: 405-325-1668. *Application contact:* 405-325-2691, Fax: 405-325-1668.
Website: http://www.ou.edu/finearts/art_arthistory.html

University of Regina, Faculty of Graduate Studies and Research, Faculty of Fine Arts, Department of Film, Regina, SK S4S 0A2, Canada. Offers media production (MFA); media studies (MA). Part-time programs available. *Faculty:* 11 full-time (6 women). *Students:* 8 full-time (6 women), 1 part-time (0 women). 15 applicants, 20% accepted. In 2014, 1 master's awarded. *Degree requirements:* For master's, thesis (for some programs). *Entrance requirements:* For master's, two writing samples (for MA); media-based support material (for MFA). Additional exam requirements/recommendations for international students: Required—TOEFL (minimum score 600 paper-based; 93 iBT), IELTS (minimum score 7), PTE (minimum score 59). *Application deadline:* For fall admission, 1/15 for domestic and international students. Application fee: $100. Electronic applications accepted. *Expenses: Tuition, area resident:* Full-time $4900 Canadian dollars; part-time $837.65 Canadian dollars per semester. *International tuition:* $7900 Canadian dollars full-time. *Required fees:* $396 Canadian dollars; $86.90 Canadian dollars per semester. *Financial support:* In 2014–15, 3 fellowships (averaging $6,000 per year), 3 teaching assistantships (averaging $2,427 per year) were awarded; research assistantships and scholarships/grants also available. Financial award application deadline: 6/15. *Faculty research:* Dramatic, documentary, and experimental film and video; new and interactive media; animation through a range of artistic, aesthetic, technical, and theoretical skills and knowledge; general and specialized study in media arts production; media arts theory. *Unit head:* Dr. Mark Wihak, Department Head and Graduate Program Coordinator, 306-337-2233, Fax: 306-585-4439, E-mail: mark.wihak@uregina.ca. *Application contact:* Andrea Stachowich, Administrative Assistant, 306-585-4796, Fax: 306-585-4439, E-mail: andrea.stachowich@uregina.ca.

University of Southern California, Graduate School, School of Cinematic Arts, Division of Animation and Digital Arts, Los Angeles, CA 90089. Offers MFA. *Degree requirements:* For master's, thesis, digital media and research documentation. *Entrance requirements:* Additional exam requirements/recommendations for international students: Recommended—TOEFL. Electronic applications accepted. *Expenses:* Contact institution. *Faculty research:* Character animation, visual effects, motion graphics, documentary animation, experimental animation.

University of Southern California, Graduate School, School of Cinematic Arts, Division of Film and Television Production, Los Angeles, CA 90089. Offers MFA. Terminal master's awarded for partial completion of doctoral program. *Degree requirements:* For master's, advanced project. *Entrance requirements:* Additional exam requirements/recommendations for international students: Required—TOEFL (minimum score 600 paper-based). Electronic applications accepted. *Faculty research:* Documentary filmmaking, narrative filmmaking, initiatives related to health issues, science foundation project, global workshops in China.

University of Southern California, Graduate School, School of Cinematic Arts, The Peter Stark Producing Program, Los Angeles, CA 90089. Offers motion picture producing (MFA). *Degree requirements:* For master's, thesis, set curriculum, oral examination. *Entrance requirements:* For master's, GRE. Additional exam requirements/recommendations for international students: Required—TOEFL (minimum score 600 paper-based; 100 iBT), IELTS (minimum score 7). Electronic applications accepted.

University of Southern California, Graduate School, School of Cinematic Arts, Writing for Screen and Television Division, Los Angeles, CA 90089. Offers MFA. *Degree requirements:* For master's, thesis or alternative. *Entrance requirements:* For master's, GRE. Additional exam requirements/recommendations for international students:

Required—TOEFL. Electronic applications accepted. *Faculty research:* Dramatic storytelling, new media content and distribution, television and film character development, theory of storytelling, interactive writing.

The University of Texas at Arlington, Graduate School, College of Liberal Arts, Department of Art and Art History, Arlington, TX 76019. Offers film and video (MFA); glass (MFA); intermedia (MFA); visual communication (MFA). *Accreditation:* NASAD. *Degree requirements:* For master's, thesis or alternative, mid- and final program reviews; exhibition. *Entrance requirements:* For master's, GRE, minimum GPA of 3.0, 3 letters of recommendation, portfolio, resume. Additional exam requirements/ recommendations for international students: Required—TOEFL (minimum score 550 paper-based). Electronic applications accepted.

The University of Texas at Austin, Graduate School, College of Communication, Department of Radio-Television-Film, Austin, TX 78712-1111. Offers film and media production (MFA); media studies (MA, PhD); screenwriting (MFA). *Degree requirements:* For master's, thesis (for some programs); for doctorate, thesis/ dissertation. *Entrance requirements:* For master's and doctorate, GRE General Test. Electronic applications accepted. *Faculty research:* International communication, film studies, media and culture, telecommunication and new media, gender and sexuality.

The University of Texas at Austin, Graduate School, Michener Center for Writers, Austin, TX 78712-1111. Offers fiction (MFA); playwriting (MFA); poetry (MFA); screenwriting (MFA). Electronic applications accepted.

University of the Sacred Heart, Graduate Programs, Department of Communication, San Juan, PR 00914-0383. Offers contemporary culture and media (MA); digital journalism (MA, Certificate); editing for media (MA, Certificate); public relations (MA, Certificate); publicity (MA, Certificate); scriptwriting (MA, Certificate). Part-time and evening/weekend programs available. *Degree requirements:* For master's, thesis.

University of Utah, Graduate School, College of Fine Arts, Film and Media Arts Department, Salt Lake City, UT 84112-0380. Offers MFA. Part-time programs available. *Faculty:* 7 full-time (3 women), 14 part-time/adjunct (2 women). *Students:* 14 full-time (9 women), 3 part-time (2 women); includes 2 minority (1 Asian, non-Hispanic/Latino; 1 Hispanic/Latino), 4 international. Average age 31. 27 applicants, 15% accepted, 4 enrolled. In 2014, 10 master's awarded. *Degree requirements:* For master's, comprehensive exam, film or video portfolio. *Entrance requirements:* For master's, minimum GPA of 3.0. Additional exam requirements/recommendations for international students: Required—TOEFL (minimum score 500 paper-based). *Application deadline:* For fall admission, 11/30 for domestic and international students. Application fee: $55 ($65 for international students). *Financial support:* In 2014–15, 14 students received support, including 14 teaching assistantships with full and partial tuition reimbursements available (averaging $8,800 per year); career-related internships or fieldwork, Federal Work-Study, institutionally sponsored loans, scholarships/grants, health care benefits, and unspecified assistantships also available. Financial award application deadline: 3/1;

financial award applicants required to submit FAFSA. *Faculty research:* Film history, criticism, cultural studies, production of narrative and documentary films. *Unit head:* Prof. Kevin D. Hanson, Chair, 801-581-7428, Fax: 801-585-3192, E-mail: kevin.hanson@utah.edu. *Application contact:* Prof. Chris Lippard, Director of Graduate Studies, 801-585-9358, Fax: 801-585-3192, E-mail: chris.lippard@utah.edu. Website: http://www.film.utah.edu

University of Victoria, Faculty of Graduate Studies, Faculty of Fine Arts, Department of Visual Arts, Victoria, BC V8W 2Y2, Canada. Offers digital multimedia (MFA); drawing (MFA); painting (MFA); photography (MFA); sculpture (MFA); video (MFA). *Degree requirements:* For master's, exhibit, oral exam. *Entrance requirements:* For master's, portfolio, BFA. Additional exam requirements/recommendations for international students: Required—TOEFL (minimum score 575 paper-based), IELTS (minimum score 7). Electronic applications accepted.

University of Wisconsin–Milwaukee, Graduate School, Peck School of the Arts, Program in Performing Arts, Milwaukee, WI 53201-0413. Offers dance (MFA); film (MFA); theatre (MFA). Part-time programs available. *Degree requirements:* For master's, variable foreign language requirement, comprehensive exam, thesis or alternative. *Entrance requirements:* For master's, audition, interview. Additional exam requirements/recommendations for international students: Required—TOEFL (minimum score 550 paper-based; 79 iBT), IELTS (minimum score 6.5). Electronic applications accepted.

Vermont College of Fine Arts, MFA in Film Program, Montpelier, VT 05602. Offers MFA. *Faculty:* 8 part-time/adjunct (3 women). *Students:* 33 full-time (13 women); includes 9 minority (3 Black or African American, non-Hispanic/Latino; 4 Hispanic/ Latino; 1 Native Hawaiian or other Pacific Islander, non-Hispanic/Latino; 1 Two or more races, non-Hispanic/Latino). *Application deadline:* For fall admission, 8/15 for domestic students; for spring admission, 2/15 for domestic students. Application fee: $75. Full-time tuition and fees vary according to program. *Financial support:* Application deadline: 6/15. *Unit head:* Stephen Pite, Director, 802-828-8529, E-mail: stephen.pite@vcfa.edu. *Application contact:* David Markow, Director of Enrollment Management, 802-828-8535, E-mail: admissions@vcfa.edu. Website: http://www.vcfa.edu/film

Western State Colorado University, Program in Creative Writing, Gunnison, CO 81231. Offers mainstream genre fiction (MFA); poetry (MFA); screenwriting (MFA). Postbaccalaureate distance learning degree programs offered (minimal on-campus study). *Degree requirements:* For master's, thesis.

York University, Faculty of Graduate Studies, Faculty of Fine Arts, Program in Film, Toronto, ON M3J 1P3, Canada. Offers MA, MFA, PhD. *Degree requirements:* For master's, thesis. *Entrance requirements:* For master's, portfolio. Electronic applications accepted.

Film, Television, and Video Theory and Criticism

California College of the Arts, Graduate Programs, Visual and Critical Studies Program, San Francisco, CA 94107. Offers MA. *Degree requirements:* For master's, thesis. *Entrance requirements:* For master's, portfolio, resume, 2 letters of recommendation, transcripts, essay, interview. Additional exam requirements/ recommendations for international students: Required—TOEFL (minimum score 600 paper-based; 100 iBT). Electronic applications accepted.

Central Michigan University, College of Graduate Studies, College of Communication and Fine Arts, School of Broadcasting and Cinematic Arts, Mount Pleasant, MI 48859. Offers electronic media management (MA); electronic media production (MA); electronic media studies (MA); film theory and criticism (MA). Part-time programs available. *Degree requirements:* For master's, thesis or alternative. *Entrance requirements:* For master's, undergraduate degree in broadcasting, film studies, or an associated discipline with minimum GPA of 2.7. Electronic applications accepted. *Faculty research:* Multimedia production, film history and criticism, writing and promotions, international broadcasting and media systems, history of American broadcasting.

Claremont Graduate University, Graduate Programs, School of Arts and Humanities, Department of English, Claremont, CA 91711-6160. Offers American studies (MA, PhD); critical theory (MA, PhD); early modern studies (MA, PhD); English (M Phil, MA, PhD); literary theory (PhD); literature (MA, PhD); literature and creative writing (MA); literature and film (MA); MBA/MA; MBA/PhD. Part-time programs available. *Faculty:* 4 full-time (2 women), 2 part-time/adjunct (0 women). *Students:* 70 full-time (51 women), 27 part-time (17 women); includes 31 minority (4 Black or African American, non-Hispanic/Latino; 1 American Indian or Alaska Native, non-Hispanic/Latino; 12 Asian, non-Hispanic/Latino; 6 Hispanic/Latino; 8 Two or more races, non-Hispanic/Latino), 8 international. Average age 36. In 2014, 9 master's, 7 doctorates awarded. *Entrance requirements:* For master's and doctorate, GRE General Test. Additional exam requirements/recommendations for international students: Required—TOEFL (minimum score 550 paper-based; 80 iBT). *Application deadline:* For fall admission, 2/1 priority date for domestic and international students. Applications are processed on a rolling basis. Application fee: $80. Electronic applications accepted. *Expenses:* Tuition: Full-time $41,784; part-time $1741 per credit. Required fees: $600; $300 per semester. *Financial support:* Fellowships, Federal Work-Study, institutionally sponsored loans, and scholarships/grants available. Support available to part-time students. Financial award application deadline: 2/15; financial award applicants required to submit FAFSA. *Faculty research:* American, comparative, and English Renaissance literature; modernism; feminist literature and theory. *Unit head:* David Luis-Brown, Chair, E-mail: david.luis-brown@cgu.edu. *Application contact:* Erma Cross, Admissions and Alumni Coordinator, 909-607-9843, E-mail: erminia.cross@cgu.edu. Website: http://www.cgu.edu/pages/568.asp

College of Staten Island of the City University of New York, Graduate Programs, Division of Humanities and Social Sciences, Program in Cinema and Media Studies, Staten Island, NY 10314-6600. Offers MA. Part-time and evening/weekend programs available. *Faculty:* 5 full-time (3 women). *Students:* 15 part-time (9 women). Average age 28. 16 applicants, 44% accepted, 5 enrolled. In 2014, 3 master's awarded. *Degree requirements:* For master's, comprehensive exam (for some programs), thesis optional, 36 credits in cinema and media studies courses. *Entrance requirements:* For master's, bachelor's degree with minimum B average in undergraduate cinema studies or communications courses; 10-12 page writing sample; three letters of recommendation; one- to two-page statement of intent detailing interest in field, background in film and media studies, and/or research interests. Additional exam requirements/ recommendations for international students: Required—TOEFL (minimum score 550

paper-based; 79 iBT), IELTS (minimum score 6.5). *Application deadline:* For fall admission, 4/15 priority date for domestic and international students; for spring admission, 11/25 priority date for domestic and international students. Applications are processed on a rolling basis. Application fee: $125. Electronic applications accepted. *Expenses:* Tuition, state resident: full-time $9650; part-time $405 per credit. Tuition, nonresident: full-time $17,880; part-time $745 per credit. *Required fees:* $141.10 per semester. Tuition and fees vary according to program. *Financial support:* In 2014–15, 2 students received support, including 2 fellowships (averaging $1,000 per year), 1 research assistantship (averaging $11,654 per year), 3 teaching assistantships (averaging $3,000 per year); career-related internships or fieldwork, Federal Work-Study, and scholarships/grants also available. Support available to part-time students. Financial award applicants required to submit FAFSA. *Unit head:* Dr. Cindy Wong, Graduate Program Coordinator, 718-982-2541, Fax: 718-982-2710, E-mail: cinemamasters@csi.cuny.edu. *Application contact:* Sasha Spence, Assistant Director for Graduate Admissions, 718-982-2019, Fax: 718-982-2500, E-mail: sasha.spence@csi.cuny.edu. Website: http://csivc.csi.cuny.edu/mediaculture/files

Concordia University, School of Graduate Studies, Faculty of Fine Arts, Mel Hoppenheim School of Cinema, Montréal, QC H3G 1M8, Canada. Offers film studies (MA).

DePaul University, College of Communication, Chicago, IL 60614. Offers digital communication and media arts (MA); health communication (MA); journalism (MA); media and cinema studies (MA); organizational and multicultural communication (MA); public relations and advertising (MA); relational communication (MA). Part-time and evening/weekend programs available. *Entrance requirements:* Additional exam requirements/recommendations for international students: Required—TOEFL (minimum score 590 paper-based; 96 iBT), IELTS (minimum score 7.5) or PTE. Electronic applications accepted.

Emory University, Laney Graduate School, Department of Film Studies, Atlanta, GA 30322-1100. Offers MA, PhD/Certificate. *Degree requirements:* For master's, comprehensive exam, thesis or alternative. *Entrance requirements:* For master's, GRE General Test, 3 letters of reference, 2 writing samples. Additional exam requirements/ recommendations for international students: Required—TOEFL. Electronic applications accepted. *Faculty research:* International film history, film theory, film style, feminism and film, reception.

Emory University, Laney Graduate School, Department of Spanish and Portuguese, Atlanta, GA 30322-1100. Offers comparative literature (Certificate); film studies (Certificate); Spanish (PhD); women's studies (Certificate). *Degree requirements:* For doctorate, 2 foreign languages, comprehensive exam, thesis/dissertation. *Entrance requirements:* For doctorate, GRE General Test. Additional exam requirements/ recommendations for international students: Required—TOEFL. Electronic applications accepted. *Faculty research:* Spanish literature, Spanish American literature, literary theory, criticism, cultural studies.

George Mason University, College of Humanities and Social Sciences, Interdisciplinary Studies Program, Fairfax, VA 22030. Offers community college teaching (MAIS); computational social science (MAIS); energy and sustainability (MAIS); film and video studies (MAIS); folklore studies (MAIS); higher education administration (MAIS); neuroethics (MAIS); religion, culture and values (MAIS); social entrepreneurship (MAIS); war and military in society (MAIS); women and gender studies (MAIS). *Faculty:* 11 full-time (3 women), 4 part-time/adjunct (all women). *Students:* 22 full-time (13

women), 87 part-time (51 women); includes 31 minority (21 Black or African American, non-Hispanic/Latino; 2 Asian, non-Hispanic/Latino; 6 Hispanic/Latino; 2 Two or more races, non-Hispanic/Latino), 6 international. Average age 32. 75 applicants, 75% accepted, 28 enrolled. In 2014, 31 master's awarded. *Degree requirements:* For master's, project or thesis. *Entrance requirements:* For master's, 3 letters of recommendation; writing sample; official transcript; resume. Additional exam requirements/recommendations for international students: Required—TOEFL (minimum score 570 paper-based; 80 iBT), IELTS (minimum score 6.5), PTE. *Application deadline:* For fall admission, 3/1 priority date for domestic students; for spring admission, 10/15 for domestic students. Application fee: $65 ($80 for international students). Electronic applications accepted. *Expenses:* Tuition, state resident: full-time $9794; part-time $408 per credit hour. Tuition, nonresident: full-time $26,978; part-time $1124 per credit hour. *Required fees:* $2820; $118 per credit hour. Tuition and fees vary according to course load and program. *Financial support:* In 2014–15, 10 students received support, including 1 fellowship (averaging $6,935 per year), 2 research assistantships with full and partial tuition reimbursements available (averaging $6,499 per year), 8 teaching assistantships with full and partial tuition reimbursements available (averaging $8,271 per year); career-related internships or fieldwork, Federal Work-Study, scholarships/grants, unspecified assistantships, and health care benefits (for full-time research or teaching assistantship recipients) also available. Support available to part-time students. Financial award application deadline: 3/1; financial award applicants required to submit FAFSA. *Faculty research:* Combined English and folklore, religious and cultural studies (Christianity and Muslim society). *Unit head:* Meredith H. Lair, Director, 703-993-2159, Fax: 703-993-1251, E-mail: mlair@gmu.edu. *Application contact:* Lisa Struckmeyer, Administrative Coordinator, 703-993-8762, Fax: 703-993-5585, E-mail: lstruckm@gmu.edu.
Website: http://mais.gmu.edu

Hollins University, Graduate Programs, Program in Screenwriting and Film Studies, Roanoke, VA 24020. Offers screenwriting (MFA); screenwriting and film studies (MA). Program offered during summer only. Part-time programs available. *Faculty:* 1 (woman) full-time, 5 part-time/adjunct (0 women). *Students:* 30 full-time (7 women), 5 part-time (all women); includes 8 minority (5 Black or African American, non-Hispanic/Latino; 2 Asian, non-Hispanic/Latino; 1 Two or more races, non-Hispanic/Latino). Average age 39. 18 applicants, 100% accepted, 12 enrolled. In 2014, 5 master's awarded. *Degree requirements:* For master's, one foreign language, comprehensive exam, thesis. *Entrance requirements:* For master's, letters of recommendation, portfolio. Additional exam requirements/recommendations for international students: Required—TOEFL (minimum score 550 paper-based; 79 iBT). *Application deadline:* For fall admission, 2/15 for domestic and international students. Application fee: $40. Electronic applications accepted. *Expenses:* Expenses: $775 per credit hour, $85 technology fee. *Financial support:* In 2014–15, 18 students received support, including 18 fellowships (averaging $1,000 per year); Federal Work-Study and scholarships/grants also available. Support available to part-time students. Financial award application deadline: 2/15; financial award applicants required to submit FAFSA. *Faculty research:* Censorship, minorities in film, writing for television, new media. *Unit head:* Dr. Tim Albaugh, Director, 540-362-6326, E-mail: albaughtt@hollins.edu. *Application contact:* Cathy S. Koon, Manager of Graduate Services, 540-362-6326, Fax: 540-362-6288, E-mail: ckoon@hollins.edu.
Website: http://www.hollins.edu/

Indiana University Bloomington, University Graduate School, College of Arts and Sciences, The Media School, Department of Communication and Culture, Bloomington, IN 47405-7000. Offers communication and culture (MA); film and media studies (PhD); performance and ethnography (PhD); rhetoric and public culture (PhD). *Faculty:* 22 full-time (13 women), 1 (woman) part-time/adjunct. *Students:* 75 full-time (41 women); includes 7 minority (1 Black or African American, non-Hispanic/Latino; 5 Hispanic/Latino; 1 Two or more races, non-Hispanic/Latino), 7 international. 116 applicants, 15% accepted, 8 enrolled. In 2014, 7 master's, 7 doctorates awarded. *Degree requirements:* For master's, comprehensive exam; for doctorate, one foreign language, comprehensive exam, thesis/dissertation, student teaching. *Entrance requirements:* For master's and doctorate, GRE General Test, minimum GPA of 3.0, 3 letters of recommendation, writing sample, personal statement. Additional exam requirements/recommendations for international students: Required—TOEFL (minimum score 550 paper-based) or IELTS. *Application deadline:* For fall admission, 1/2 for domestic students, 12/1 for international students; for winter admission, 1/2 for domestic students, 12/1 for international students. Application fee: $55 ($65 for international students). Electronic applications accepted. *Financial support:* Fellowships with full tuition reimbursements, research assistantships with full tuition reimbursements, and teaching assistantships with full tuition reimbursements available. Financial award application deadline: 1/2. *Faculty research:* Rhetoric and public culture, film and media studies, performance ethnography. *Unit head:* Prof. Jane Goodman, Chair, 812-855-3232, Fax: 812-855-6014, E-mail: cmcl@indiana.edu. *Application contact:* Kathy P. Teige, Graduate Secretary, 812-855-6389, Fax: 812-855-6014, E-mail: kteige@indiana.edu.
Website: http://www.indiana.edu/~cmcl/

National University, Academic Affairs, College of Letters and Sciences, La Jolla, CA 92037-1011. Offers applied linguistics (MA); biology (MS); counseling psychology (MA), including licensed professional clinical counseling, marriage and family therapy; creative writing (MFA); English (MA), including Gothic studies, rhetoric; film studies (MA); forensic and crime science (Certificate); forensic studies (MFS), including criminalistics, investigation; history (MA); human behavior (MA); mathematics for educators (MS); performance psychology (MA); strategic communications (MA). Part-time and evening/weekend programs available. Postbaccalaureate distance learning degree programs offered (no on-campus study). *Faculty:* 69 full-time (34 women), 100 part-time/adjunct (55 women). *Students:* 727 full-time (532 women), 349 part-time (240 women); includes 505 minority (128 Black or African American, non-Hispanic/Latino; 5 American Indian or Alaska Native, non-Hispanic/Latino; 52 Asian, non-Hispanic/Latino; 260 Hispanic/Latino; 9 Native Hawaiian or other Pacific Islander, non-Hispanic/Latino; 51 Two or more races, non-Hispanic/Latino), 4 international. Average age 34. In 2014, 569 master's awarded. *Degree requirements:* For master's, thesis (for some programs). *Entrance requirements:* For master's, interview, minimum GPA of 2.5. Additional exam requirements/recommendations for international students: Required—TOEFL (minimum score 550 paper-based; 79 iBT), IELTS (minimum score 6). *Application deadline:* Applications are processed on a rolling basis. Application fee: $60 ($65 for international students). Electronic applications accepted. *Expenses: Tuition:* Full-time $14,184; part-time $1773 per course. *Financial support:* Career-related internships or fieldwork, institutionally sponsored loans, scholarships/grants, and tuition waivers (partial) available. Support available to part-time students. Financial award application deadline: 6/30; financial award applicants required to submit FAFSA. *Unit head:* College of Letters and Sciences, 800-628-8648, E-mail: cols@nu.edu. *Application contact:* Frank Rojas, Interim Vice President for Enrollment Services, 800-628-8648, E-mail: advisor@nu.edu.
Website: http://www.nu.edu/OurPrograms/CollegeOfLettersAndSciences.html

Ohio University, Graduate College, College of Fine Arts, School of Film, Athens, OH 45701-2979. Offers film (MFA); film studies (MA). *Degree requirements:* For master's, one foreign language, thesis. *Entrance requirements:* Additional exam requirements/recommendations for international students: Required—TOEFL (minimum score 550 paper-based; 80 iBT) or IELTS (minimum score 6.5). Electronic applications accepted. *Faculty research:* Scriptwriting, sound, editing, cinematography, film theory, digital post production.

San Francisco State University, Division of Graduate Studies, College of Liberal and Creative Arts, Department of Cinema, San Francisco, CA 94132-1722. Offers MA, MFA. *Expenses:* Tuition, state resident: full-time $6738. Tuition, nonresident: full-time $17,898; part-time $372 per credit hour. *Required fees:* $498 per semester. *Unit head:* Dr. Steven Kovacs, Interim Chair, 415-338-1629, Fax: 415-338-0906, E-mail: cinedept@sfsu.edu. *Application contact:* Dr. R.L. Rutsky, MA Coordinator, 415-405-3400, Fax: 415-338-0906, E-mail: cinegrad@sfsu.edu.
Website: http://www.cinema.sfsu.edu/

Savannah College of Art and Design, Graduate School, Program in Cinema Studies, Savannah, GA 31402-3146. Offers MA. Part-time programs available. *Faculty:* 2 full-time (1 woman), 1 part-time/adjunct (0 women). *Students:* 2 full-time (both women), 7 part-time (5 women), 2 international. Average age 26. 4 applicants, 25% accepted, 1 enrolled. In 2014, 4 master's awarded. *Degree requirements:* For master's, thesis. *Entrance requirements:* For master's, portfolio of writing samples. Additional exam requirements/recommendations for international students: Required—TOEFL (minimum score 550 paper-based, 85 iBT), IELTS (minimum score 6.5), or ACTFL. *Application deadline:* For fall admission, 4/1 for domestic and international students. Applications are processed on a rolling basis. Application fee: $40. Electronic applications accepted. *Expenses: Tuition:* Full-time $34,605; part-time $3845 per course. One-time fee: $500. Tuition and fees vary according to course load. *Financial support:* Fellowships, career-related internships or fieldwork, Federal Work-Study, and scholarships/grants available. Financial award application deadline: 4/1; financial award applicants required to submit FAFSA. *Unit head:* Dr. Beth Concepcion, Dean, School of Liberal Arts. *Application contact:* Jenny Jaquillard, Executive Director of Admissions, Recruitment and Events, 912-525-5100, Fax: 912-525-5985, E-mail: admission@scad.edu.
Website: http://www.scad.edu/academics/programs/cinema-studies

Syracuse University, S. I. Newhouse School of Public Communications, Program in Documentary Film and History, Syracuse, NY 13244. Offers MA. *Students:* 6 full-time (3 women); includes 3 minority (1 Asian, non-Hispanic/Latino; 2 Hispanic/Latino). Average age 31. 15 applicants, 87% accepted, 5 enrolled. In 2014, 10 master's awarded. *Degree requirements:* For master's, thesis or alternative. *Entrance requirements:* For master's, GRE General Test. Additional exam requirements/recommendations for international students: Required—TOEFL (minimum score 100 iBT). *Application deadline:* For fall admission, 2/1 for domestic and international students; for summer admission, 1/15 priority date for domestic and international students. Application fee: $45. Electronic applications accepted. *Expenses: Tuition:* Part-time $1341 per credit. *Financial support:* Fellowships with full tuition reimbursements, research assistantships with partial tuition reimbursements, and teaching assistantships with partial tuition reimbursements available. Financial award application deadline: 2/1. *Unit head:* Richard Breyer, Director, 315-443-9249, E-mail: pcgrad@syr.edu. *Application contact:* Graduate Records Office, 315-443-4039, Fax: 315-443-1834, E-mail: pcgrad@syr.edu.
Website: http://newhouse.syr.edu/

Tiffin University, Program in Humanities, Tiffin, OH 44883-2161. Offers art and visual media (MH); communication (MH); creative writing (MH); English (MH); film studies (MH); humanities (MH); individualized studies (MH). Part-time and evening/weekend programs available. Postbaccalaureate distance learning degree programs offered (no on-campus study). *Entrance requirements:* For master's, work experience. Additional exam requirements/recommendations for international students: Required—TOEFL (minimum score 550 paper-based; 79 iBT).

Université de Montréal, Faculty of Arts and Sciences, Department of Art History and Film Studies, Montréal, QC H3C 3J7, Canada. Offers art history (MA, PhD); film studies (MA, PhD). Programs offered jointly with Concordia University, Université Laval, and Université du Québec à Montréal. *Degree requirements:* For master's, thesis. Electronic applications accepted. *Faculty research:* Western art from the Middle Ages, classic and modern theory, modern and contemporary art, Canadian art.

Université Laval, Faculty of Letters, Department of Literature, Programs in Literature and Arts of the Screen and Stage, Québec, QC G1K 7P4, Canada. Offers MA, PhD. Part-time programs available. Terminal master's awarded for partial completion of doctoral program. *Degree requirements:* For master's, thesis; for doctorate, comprehensive exam, thesis/dissertation. *Entrance requirements:* For master's and doctorate, linguistics exams, knowledge of French, knowledge of a second language. Electronic applications accepted.

University at Buffalo, the State University of New York, Graduate School, College of Arts and Sciences, Department of Media Study, Buffalo, NY 14260. Offers film studies (MAH); media arts production (MFA); media study (PhD); new media design (Certificate); M Arch/MFA. *Faculty:* 11 full-time (4 women), 3 part-time/adjunct (1 woman). *Students:* 59 (33 women); includes 20 minority (1 Black or African American, non-Hispanic/Latino; 17 Asian, non-Hispanic/Latino; 1 Hispanic/Latino; 1 Two or more races, non-Hispanic/Latino). Average age 26. 66 applicants, 20% accepted, 10 enrolled. In 2014, 15 master's awarded. Terminal master's awarded for partial completion of doctoral program. *Degree requirements:* For master's, thesis, Thesis and media project; for doctorate, thesis/dissertation, qualifying exam, dissertation includes media project. *Entrance requirements:* For master's, portfolio; for doctorate, GRE, portfolio. Additional exam requirements/recommendations for international students: Required—TOEFL (minimum score 550 paper-based; 79 iBT). *Application deadline:* For fall admission, 1/7 priority date for domestic and international students. Applications are processed on a rolling basis. Application fee: $75. Electronic applications accepted. *Financial support:* In 2014–15, 11 students received support, including 2 fellowships (averaging $4,000 per year), 11 teaching assistantships with full tuition reimbursements available (averaging $13,480 per year); career-related internships or fieldwork, Federal Work-Study, scholarships/grants, health care benefits, and unspecified assistantships also available. Support available to part-time students. Financial award application deadline: 1/5; financial award applicants required to submit FAFSA. *Faculty research:* Digital arts, video, documentary, film, game design, digital poetics, locative media. *Total annual research expenditures:* $44,875. *Unit head:* Prof. Josephine Anstey, Chair, 716-645-6902, Fax: 716-645-6979, E-mail: jranstey@buffalo.edu. *Application contact:* Ann Mangan, Academic Advisor & Graduate Coordinator, 716-645-0945, Fax: 716-645-6979, E-mail: annmanga@buffalo.edu.
Website: http://mediastudy.buffalo.edu/

The University of British Columbia, Faculty of Arts and Faculty of Graduate Studies, Department of Theatre and Film, Film Program, Vancouver, BC V6T 1Z2, Canada. Offers creative writing and film production (MFA); film production (MFA, Diploma); film studies (MA). *Degree requirements:* For master's, variable foreign language requirement, comprehensive exam, thesis (MA); thesis or project (MFA). *Entrance requirements:* For master's, portfolio (MFA). Additional exam requirements/recommendations for international students: Required—TOEFL (minimum score 600 paper-based). *Faculty research:* Film theory and violence; American and European cinema; cult cinema; Irish cinema.

University of California, Santa Cruz, Division of Graduate Studies, Division of the Arts, Department of Film and Digital Media, Santa Cruz, CA 95064. Offers PhD. *Degree*

requirements: For doctorate, one foreign language, thesis/dissertation, qualifying exams. *Entrance requirements:* For doctorate, GRE. Additional exam requirements/recommendations for international students: Required—TOEFL (minimum score 550 paper-based; 83 iBT); Recommended—IELTS (minimum score 8). Electronic applications accepted. *Faculty research:* Integrating critical and creative practice, working across media, pursuing new modes of social and political engagement, fostering global cultural citizenship.

University of Chicago, Division of the Humanities, Department of Cinema and Media Studies, Chicago, IL 60637. Offers PhD. *Students:* 37 full-time (21 women); includes 5 minority (3 Black or African American, non-Hispanic/Latino; 2 Two or more races, non-Hispanic/Latino), 13 international. 124 applicants, 31% accepted, 6 enrolled. Terminal master's awarded for partial completion of doctoral program. *Degree requirements:* For doctorate, 2 foreign languages, thesis/dissertation. *Entrance requirements:* For doctorate, GRE General Test. Additional exam requirements/recommendations for international students: Required—TOEFL (minimum score 104 iBT), IELTS (minimum score 7). *Application deadline:* For fall admission, 12/15 for domestic and international students. Application fee: $90. Electronic applications accepted. *Expenses: Tuition:* Full-time $46,899. *Required fees:* $347. *Financial support:* Fellowships with full tuition reimbursements, teaching assistantships with tuition reimbursements, institutionally sponsored loans, scholarships/grants, and health care benefits available. Financial award application deadline: 12/15; financial award applicants required to submit FAFSA. *Unit head:* Dr. James Chandler, Chair, 773-702-8274. *Application contact:* Braden Grams, Assistant Dean of Students, Admissions and Fellowships, 773-702-1552, Fax: 773-834-9148, E-mail: humanitiesadmissions@uchicago.edu.
Website: http://humanities.uchicago.edu/cmtes/cms/

The University of Iowa, Graduate College, College of Liberal Arts and Sciences, Department of Cinema and Comparative Literature, Program in Film Studies, Iowa City, IA 52242-1316. Offers MA, PhD. *Degree requirements:* For master's, thesis optional, exam; for doctorate, comprehensive exam, thesis/dissertation. *Entrance requirements:* For master's and doctorate, GRE General Test, minimum GPA of 3.0. Additional exam requirements/recommendations for international students: Required—TOEFL (minimum score 550 paper-based; 81 iBT). Electronic applications accepted.

The University of Kansas, Graduate Studies, College of Liberal Arts and Sciences, Department of Film and Media Studies, Lawrence, KS 66045. Offers MA, PhD. *Faculty:* 11 full-time, 4 part-time/adjunct. *Students:* 18 full-time (6 women), 1 (woman) part-time; includes 3 minority (1 American Indian or Alaska Native, non-Hispanic/Latino; 1 Asian, non-Hispanic/Latino; 1 Two or more races, non-Hispanic/Latino), 2 international. Average age 33. 13 applicants, 54% accepted, 1 enrolled. In 2014, 3 doctorates awarded. *Degree requirements:* For master's, thesis; for doctorate, one foreign language, comprehensive exam, thesis/dissertation. *Entrance requirements:* For master's, GRE General Test, minimum GPA of 3.0; for doctorate, GRE General Test, minimum GPA of 3.5; MA in film or related field. Additional exam requirements/recommendations for international students: Required—TOEFL or IELTS. *Application deadline:* For fall admission, 1/1 for domestic and international students. Application fee: $55 ($65 for international students). Electronic applications accepted. *Financial support:* Teaching assistantships with full and partial tuition reimbursements available. Financial award application deadline: 1/1; financial award applicants required to submit FAFSA. *Faculty research:* Latin American cinema, Japanese and East Asian cinema, new media/cultural geography of media, film history, film theory and visual culture. *Unit head:* Dr. Tamara L. Falicov, Chair, 785-864-1353, E-mail: tfalicov@ku.edu. *Application contact:* Karla Conrad, Graduate Secretary, 785-864-1340, E-mail: kmconrad@ku.edu.
Website: http://film.ku.edu/

University of Miami, Graduate School, School of Communication, Coral Gables, FL 33124. Offers communication (PhD); communication studies (MA); film studies (MA, PhD); motion pictures (MFA), including production, producing, and screenwriting; print journalism (MA); public relations (MA); Spanish language journalism (MA); television broadcast journalism (MA). Part-time programs available. *Degree requirements:* For master's, comprehensive exam (for some programs), thesis (for some programs); for doctorate, comprehensive exam, thesis/dissertation. *Entrance requirements:* For master's, GRE General Test; for doctorate, GRE General Test, master's thesis or scholarly research. Additional exam requirements/recommendations for international students: Required—TOEFL (minimum score 600 paper-based; 100 iBT). Electronic applications accepted. *Faculty research:* Communication studies, mass communication, international/interpersonal communication, film studies, journalism.

University of Michigan, Horace H. Rackham School of Graduate Studies, College of Literature, Science, and the Arts, Department of Screen Arts and Cultures, Ann Arbor, MI 48109. Offers PhD, Certificate. *Faculty:* 10 full-time (4 women). *Students:* 13 full-time (4 women); includes 3 minority (1 Asian, non-Hispanic/Latino; 2 Hispanic/Latino), 4 international. Average age 28. 49 applicants, 6% accepted, 2 enrolled. In 2014, 2 doctorates awarded. *Degree requirements:* For doctorate, one foreign language, comprehensive exam, thesis/dissertation; for Certificate, 15 credit hours (3 directed study). *Entrance requirements:* For doctorate, GRE. Additional exam requirements/recommendations for international students: Required—TOEFL. *Application deadline:* For fall admission, 12/15 for domestic and international students. Application fee: $75 ($90 for international students). Electronic applications accepted. *Financial support:* In 2014–15, 13 students received support, including 2 fellowships with full tuition reimbursements available (averaging $18,600 per year), 20 teaching assistantships with full tuition reimbursements available (averaging $18,600 per year); scholarships/grants, health care benefits, tuition waivers (full), unspecified assistantships, and summer research funds also available. Financial award application deadline: 12/15; financial award applicants required to submit FAFSA. *Faculty research:* Transnational cinema, new media, classical Hollywood cinema, silent cinema, film theory, television. *Unit head:* Prof. Caryl Flinn, Chair, 734-763-1314, Fax: 734-936-1846, E-mail: flinnc@umich.edu. *Application contact:* Carrie Moore, Student Services Coordinator, 734-647-6909, Fax: 734-936-1846, E-mail: ctave@umich.edu.
Website: http://www.lsa.umich.edu/sac/

University of Pittsburgh, Dietrich School of Arts and Sciences, Department of French and Italian, Program in French, Pittsburgh, PA 15260. Offers film studies (PhD); French (MA, PhD). Part-time programs available. *Faculty:* 7 full-time (3 women). *Students:* 20 full-time (11 women), 8 international. Average age 32. 12 applicants, 42% accepted, 3 enrolled. In 2014, 1 master's, 2 doctorates awarded. Terminal master's awarded for partial completion of doctoral program. *Degree requirements:* For master's, one foreign language, comprehensive exam, seminar paper; for doctorate, one foreign language, comprehensive exam, thesis/dissertation, dissertation defense. *Entrance requirements:* For master's, GRE General Test, phone interview, 2 writing samples (French and English); for doctorate, GRE General Test, phone interview, 2 writing samples (French and English), personal essay. Additional exam requirements/recommendations for international students: Required—TOEFL (minimum score 600 paper-based; 90 iBT). *Application deadline:* For fall admission, 1/10 priority date for domestic and international students. Application fee: $50. Electronic applications accepted. *Expenses:* Tuition, state resident: full-time $20,742; part-time $838 per credit. Tuition, nonresident: full-time $33,960; part-time $1389 per credit. *Required fees:* $800; $205 per term. Tuition and fees vary according to program. *Financial support:* In 2014–15, 16 students received support, including 3 fellowships with full tuition reimbursements available (averaging $19,615 per year), 12 teaching assistantships with full tuition reimbursements available (averaging $17,010 per year); career-related internships or fieldwork, Federal Work-Study, institutionally sponsored loans, scholarships/grants, traineeships, health care benefits, tuition waivers (partial), unspecified assistantships, and summer research stipends, summer teaching, teaching on study abroad program also available. Support available to part-time students. Financial award application deadline: 1/10. *Faculty research:* Literature and politics, constructs of the French nation, literary and cultural theory, French linguistics, gender and sexuality, French film, French and Francophone literature and culture of all periods. *Total annual research expenditures:* $3,200. *Unit head:* Dr. Lina Insana, Chair, 412-624-6269, Fax: 412-624-6263, E-mail: insana@pitt.edu. *Application contact:* Patrick Fogarty, Graduate Administrator, 412-624-5227, Fax: 412-624-6263, E-mail: pmf23@pitt.edu.
Website: http://www.frenchanditalian.pitt.edu/graduate/french/

University of Pittsburgh, Dietrich School of Arts and Sciences, Program in Film Studies, Pittsburgh, PA 15260. Offers MA, PhD, Certificate. *Faculty:* 19 full-time (6 women). *Students:* 18 full-time (10 women); includes 5 minority (2 Asian, non-Hispanic/Latino; 3 Hispanic/Latino). Average age 30. 60 applicants, 8% accepted, 5 enrolled. Terminal master's awarded for partial completion of doctoral program. *Degree requirements:* For master's, variable foreign language requirement, comprehensive exam (for some programs), thesis, proseminar; for doctorate, variable foreign language requirement, comprehensive exam, thesis/dissertation, proseminar. *Entrance requirements:* For master's and doctorate, BA. Additional exam requirements/recommendations for international students: Required—TOEFL (minimum score 90 iBT), IELTS. *Application deadline:* For fall admission, 1/15 for domestic and international students. Applications are processed on a rolling basis. Application fee: $50. Electronic applications accepted. *Expenses:* Tuition, state resident: full-time $20,742; part-time $838 per credit. Tuition, nonresident: full-time $33,960; part-time $1389 per credit. *Required fees:* $800; $205 per term. Tuition and fees vary according to program. *Faculty research:* International cinema, film history and historiography, cinema and national/international politics, theoretical studies of film, film and other media. *Unit head:* Dr. Adam Lowenstein, Director of the Film Studies Program, 412-624-6551, Fax: 412-383-6999, E-mail: alowen@pitt.edu. *Application contact:* Jennifer R. Florian, Administrative Secretary, 412-624-6564, Fax: 412-383-6999, E-mail: jrf16@pitt.edu.
Website: http://www.filmstudies.pitt.edu/

University of Southern California, Graduate School, School of Cinematic Arts, Division of Critical Studies, Los Angeles, CA 90089. Offers cinema-television (MA); cinema-television (critical studies) (PhD). *Degree requirements:* For master's, comprehensive exam; for doctorate, comprehensive exam, thesis/dissertation. *Entrance requirements:* For master's and doctorate, GRE. Additional exam requirements/recommendations for international students: Required—TOEFL (minimum score 100 iBT). Electronic applications accepted. *Faculty research:* Transnational cinema, race and cultural studies, global media, television studies, digital media, feminist studies.

University of South Florida, College of Arts and Sciences, Department of Humanities and Cultural Studies, Tampa, FL 33620-9951. Offers American studies (MA); liberal arts (MA), including Africana studies, film studies, humanities, social and political thought. Part-time and evening/weekend programs available. *Faculty:* 7 full-time (3 women). *Students:* 11 full-time (2 women), 8 part-time (2 women); includes 8 minority (4 Black or African American, non-Hispanic/Latino; 3 Hispanic/Latino; 1 Two or more races, non-Hispanic/Latino), 1 international. Average age 34. 9 applicants, 78% accepted, 5 enrolled. In 2014, 5 master's awarded. *Degree requirements:* For master's, comprehensive exam, thesis, language requirement (for humanities subconcentration). *Entrance requirements:* For master's, GRE General Test (minimum preferred score 59th percentile (153) verbal and 4.5 in analytical writing), minimum GPA of 3.0 in upper-division courses, personal statement, writing sample. Additional exam requirements/recommendations for international students: Required—TOEFL (minimum score 550 paper-based; 79 iBT) or IELTS (minimum score 6.5). *Application deadline:* For fall admission, 2/15 priority date for domestic students, 1/2 for international students; for spring admission, 10/15 priority date for domestic students, 6/1 for international students. Application fee: $30. *Financial support:* In 2014–15, 15 students received support, including 15 teaching assistantships with tuition reimbursements available (averaging $12,437 per year); scholarships/grants also available. Financial award application deadline: 4/1. *Faculty research:* American South, American autobiography, material culture, critical theory, cultural studies, film studies. *Unit head:* Dr. William Cummings, Professor and Chair, 813-974-9380, Fax: 813-974-9409, E-mail: wcummings@usf.edu. *Application contact:* Dr. Brook Sadler, Associate Professor and Graduate Program Director, 813-974-8841, Fax: 813-974-9409, E-mail: brooksadler@usf.edu.
Website: http://humanities.usf.edu/

University of Toronto, School of Graduate Studies, Faculty of Arts and Science, Cinema Studies Institute, Toronto, ON M5S 2J7, Canada. Offers MA, PhD. *Entrance requirements:* For master's, minimum B+ in final year or over a year's worth of senior courses, successful completion of minimum of six full-course equivalents in cinema studies or comparable program preparation. Additional exam requirements/recommendations for international students: Required—TOEFL (minimum score 580 paper-based; 93 iBT), TWE (minimum score 5). Electronic applications accepted.

University of Wisconsin–Madison, Graduate School, College of Letters and Science, Department of Communication Arts, Madison, WI 53706-1380. Offers communication science (MA, PhD); film (MA, PhD); media and cultural studies (MA, PhD); rhetoric (MA, PhD). Terminal master's awarded for partial completion of doctoral program. *Degree requirements:* For master's, one foreign language, thesis (for some programs); for doctorate, one foreign language, thesis/dissertation. *Entrance requirements:* For master's and doctorate, GRE General Test, minimum GPA of 3.5. Electronic applications accepted. *Expenses:* Tuition, state resident: full-time $10,723; part-time $745 per credit. Tuition, nonresident: full-time $24,054; part-time $1578 per credit. *Required fees:* $374 per semester. Tuition and fees vary according to course load, program and reciprocity agreements.

Wilfrid Laurier University, Faculty of Graduate and Postdoctoral Studies, Faculty of Arts, Department of English and Film Studies, Waterloo, ON N2L 3C5, Canada. Offers English (MA); English and film (PhD). *Degree requirements:* For master's, thesis optional; for doctorate, thesis/dissertation. *Entrance requirements:* For master's, honours BA or the equivalent in English, minimum B+ in English courses above first year level; for doctorate, MA in English, minimum A- average in graduate work. Additional exam requirements/recommendations for international students: Recommended—TOEFL (minimum score 89 iBT). Electronic applications accepted. *Faculty research:* Gender and genre, Canadian studies, early modern studies, postcolonial studies, nineteenth century studies.

SECTION 5: FILM, TELEVISION, AND VIDEO

Film, Television, and Video Theory and Criticism

Yale University, Graduate School of Arts and Sciences, Department of East Asian Languages and Literatures, New Haven, CT 06520. Offers East Asian languages and literatures (PhD); East Asian languages and literatures and film studies (PhD). *Degree requirements:* For doctorate, 2 foreign languages, thesis/dissertation. *Entrance requirements:* For doctorate, GRE General Test.

Yale University, Graduate School of Arts and Sciences, Department of Slavic Languages and Literatures, New Haven, CT 06520. Offers medieval Slavic literature and philology (PhD); Polish literature (PhD); Russian literature (PhD); Slavic languages and literatures and film studies (PhD). *Degree requirements:* For doctorate, 3 foreign languages, thesis/dissertation. *Entrance requirements:* For doctorate, GRE General Test.

Yale University, Graduate School of Arts and Sciences, Interdisciplinary Program in Film Studies, New Haven, CT 06520. Offers PhD.

Section 6
Performing Arts

This section contains a directory of institutions offering graduate work in performing arts, followed by an in-depth entry submitted by an institution that chose to prepare a detailed program description. Additional information about programs listed in the directory but not augmented by an in-depth entry may be obtained by writing directly to the dean of a graduate school or chair of a department at the address given in the directory.

For programs offering related work, see also in this book *Area and Cultural Studies, Art and Art History, Communication and Media,* and *Film, Television, and Video.* In another guide in this series:

Graduate Programs in Business, Education, Information Studies, Law & Social Work

See *Leisure Studies and Recreation, Subject Areas (Music Education),* and *Physical Education and Kinesiology*

CONTENTS

Program Directories

Displays and Close-Ups

See also:

Dance

Arizona State University at the Tempe campus, Herberger Institute for Design and the Arts, School of Film, Dance and Theatre, Department of Dance, Tempe, AZ 85287-0304. Offers dance (MFA); interdisciplinary digital media and performance (MFA). *Degree requirements:* For master's, thesis optional, project, written document and oral defense, interactive Program of Study (iPOS) submitted before completing 50 percent of required credit hours. *Entrance requirements:* For master's, personal statement relating to school's core values, resume, 3 letters of recommendation from professionals in the dance field. Electronic applications accepted.

Bennington College, Graduate Programs, MFA in Dance Program, Bennington, VT 05201. Offers MFA. Part-time programs available. *Degree requirements:* For master's, performances. *Faculty research:* Exploration of relationship between emergent improvisation and complex systems.

California Institute of the Arts, School of Dance, Valencia, CA 91355-2340. Offers MFA, Adv C. *Accreditation:* NASD. *Degree requirements:* For master's, thesis presentation. *Entrance requirements:* For master's, audition, video of choreography. Additional exam requirements/recommendations for international students: Required—TOEFL.

California State University, Fullerton, Graduate Studies, College of the Arts, Department of Theatre and Dance, Fullerton, CA 92834-9480. Offers theatre arts (MFA), including acting, design and technical production, directing. *Accreditation:* NAST. Part-time programs available. *Students:* 12 full-time (7 women), 7 part-time (3 women); includes 5 minority (1 Black or African American, non-Hispanic/Latino; 1 American Indian or Alaska Native, non-Hispanic/Latino; 2 Hispanic/Latino; 1 Two or more races, non-Hispanic/Latino), 1 international. Average age 30. 36 applicants, 31% accepted, 10 enrolled. In 2014, 7 master's awarded. *Degree requirements:* For master's, oral and written exam, project or thesis. *Entrance requirements:* For master's, major in theatre or related field, audition or interview, minimum GPA of 2.5 in last 60 units of course work. Application fee: $55. *Financial support:* Career-related internships or fieldwork, Federal Work-Study, institutionally sponsored loans, and scholarships/grants available. Support available to part-time students. Financial award application deadline: 3/1; financial award applicants required to submit FAFSA. *Unit head:* Dr. Bruce Goodrich, Chair, 657-278-3649. *Application contact:* Admissions/Applications, 657-278-2371.

California State University, Long Beach, Graduate Studies, College of the Arts, Department of Dance, Long Beach, CA 90840. Offers MA, MFA. *Accreditation:* NASD. Part-time programs available. *Degree requirements:* For master's, thesis. Electronic applications accepted.

Case Western Reserve University, School of Graduate Studies, Department of Dance, Cleveland, OH 44106. Offers MA, MFA. *Faculty:* 3 full-time (2 women). *Students:* 8 full-time (7 women), 1 part-time (0 women); includes 1 minority (Hispanic/Latino), 4 international. Average age 28. 5 applicants, 40% accepted, 2 enrolled. In 2014, 2 master's awarded. *Degree requirements:* For master's, thesis, performance thesis. *Entrance requirements:* For master's, professional video, statement of goals and objectives, audition, interview. Additional exam requirements/recommendations for international students: Required—TOEFL (minimum score 577 paper-based; 90 iBT); Recommended—IELTS (minimum score 7). *Application deadline:* For fall admission, 3/1 priority date for domestic students; for spring admission, 11/1 priority date for domestic students. Application fee: $50. Electronic applications accepted. *Financial support:* Fellowships, teaching assistantships, scholarships/grants, and stipends available. Financial award application deadline: 3/1. *Faculty research:* Dance medicine and science, dance/technology. *Unit head:* Karen Potter, Chair, 216-368-1491, E-mail: karen.potter@case.edu. *Application contact:* Lori Waugh, Admissions Coordinator, 216-368-2854, Fax: 216-368-4250, E-mail: lori.waugh@case.edu.
Website: http://dance.case.edu/

The College at Brockport, State University of New York, School of the Arts, Humanities and Social Sciences, Department of Dance, Brockport, NY 14420-2997. Offers dance (MA, MFA), including choreography/performance (MA), dance education (preK-12) (MA), dance studies (MA). *Accreditation:* NASD. Part-time programs available. *Faculty:* 13 full-time (7 women), 2 part-time/adjunct (both women). *Students:* 15 full-time (13 women), 2 part-time (1 woman); includes 2 minority (1 American Indian or Alaska Native, non-Hispanic/Latino; 1 Two or more races, non-Hispanic/Latino), 3 international. 30 applicants, 53% accepted, 10 enrolled. In 2014, 6 master's awarded. *Degree requirements:* For master's, thesis or alternative. *Entrance requirements:* For master's, local writing assessment assignment, audition/interview, minimum GPA of 3.0, letters of recommendation. Additional exam requirements/recommendations for international students: Required—TOEFL (minimum score 550 paper-based; 79 iBT), IELTS (minimum score 6.5). *Application deadline:* For fall admission, 4/15 priority date for domestic and international students. Application fee: $50. Electronic applications accepted. *Financial support:* In 2014–15, 1 fellowship with full tuition reimbursement (averaging $7,500 per year), 4 teaching assistantships with full tuition reimbursements (averaging $6,000 per year) were awarded; Federal Work-Study, scholarships/grants, and unspecified assistantships also available. Support available to part-time students. Financial award application deadline: 3/15; financial award applicants required to submit FAFSA. *Faculty research:* Choreography and performance, world dance and culture, dance process and theory, dance education, dance science and somatics. *Unit head:* Kevin Warner, Chairperson, 585-395-5304, Fax: 585-395-5134, E-mail: kwarner@brockport.edu. *Application contact:* Karl Rogers, Graduate Program Director, 585-395-5305, Fax: 585-395-5134, E-mail: krogers@brockport.edu.
Website: http://www.brockport.edu/dance/

Florida State University, The Graduate School, College of Fine Arts, School of Dance, Tallahassee, FL 32306-2120. Offers American dance studies (MFA); studio and related studies (MA). *Accreditation:* NASD. *Faculty:* 17 full-time (11 women), 3 part-time/adjunct (2 women). *Students:* 30 full-time (23 women); includes 14 minority (5 Black or African American, non-Hispanic/Latino; 2 Asian, non-Hispanic/Latino; 7 Hispanic/Latino). Average age 28. 25 applicants, 80% accepted, 18 enrolled. In 2014, 8 master's awarded. *Degree requirements:* For master's, comprehensive exam (for some programs), thesis optional, technical proficiency; 1 foreign language (for MA in American dance studies). *Entrance requirements:* For master's, GRE General Test (MA in American dance studies), audition, writing sample, interview (for MFA, MA in dance). Additional exam requirements/recommendations for international students: Required—TOEFL (minimum score 550 paper-based, 80 iBT), IELTS (minimum score 6.5) or Michigan English Language Assessment Battery (minimum score 77). *Application deadline:* For fall admission, 7/1 priority date for domestic and international students; for spring admission, 11/1 priority date for domestic and international students. Applications are processed on a rolling basis. Application fee: $30. Electronic applications accepted. *Expenses:* Tuition, state resident: part-time $403.51 per credit hour. Tuition, nonresident: part-time $1004.85 per credit hour. *Required fees:* $75.81 per credit hour. One-time fee: $20 part-time. Tuition and fees vary according to campus/location. *Financial support:* In 2014–15, 30 students received support, including 1 fellowship with full tuition reimbursement available (averaging $20,000 per year), 10 research assistantships with full tuition reimbursements available (averaging $5,000 per year), 11 teaching assistantships with full tuition reimbursements available (averaging $5,000 per year); scholarships/grants, health care benefits, and unspecified assistantships also available. Financial award application deadline: 6/30; financial award applicants required to submit FAFSA. *Faculty research:* Choreography, performance, dance and cultural significance, American dance history, dance technology. *Unit head:* Prof. Russell Sandifer, Professor and Co-Chair, 850-644-1024, Fax: 850-644-1277, E-mail: rsandifer@fsu.edu. *Application contact:* Stephanie Mills, Academic Coordinator, 850-644-1023, Fax: 850-644-1277, E-mail: smmills@fsu.edu.
Website: http://dance.fsu.edu/

The George Washington University, Columbian College of Arts and Sciences, Department of Theatre and Dance, Washington, DC 20052. Offers classical acting (MFA); dance (MFA); exhibit design (Graduate Certificate); production design (MFA). Part-time and evening/weekend programs available. *Faculty:* 12 full-time (7 women). *Students:* 26 full-time (16 women), 22 part-time (8 women); includes 9 minority (3 Black or African American, non-Hispanic/Latino; 1 Asian, non-Hispanic/Latino; 5 Hispanic/Latino), 4 international. Average age 35. 78 applicants, 46% accepted, 24 enrolled. In 2014, 20 master's, 4 other advanced degrees awarded. *Degree requirements:* For master's, thesis. *Entrance requirements:* For master's, minimum GPA of 3.0, portfolio. Additional exam requirements/recommendations for international students: Required—TOEFL (minimum score 550 paper-based; 80 iBT). *Application deadline:* For fall admission, 8/1 priority date for domestic students; for spring admission, 10/1 priority date for domestic students. Applications are processed on a rolling basis. Application fee: $75. Electronic applications accepted. *Financial support:* In 2014–15, 2 students received support. Fellowships with tuition reimbursements available, teaching assistantships with tuition reimbursements available, career-related internships or fieldwork, Federal Work-Study, and tuition waivers available. *Unit head:* Dana Tai Soon Burgess, Chair, 202-994-1660, E-mail: dtsb@gwu.edu. *Application contact:* Information Contact, 202-994-8072, E-mail: trdanews@gwu.edu.
Website: http://www.gwu.edu/~theatre/

Hollins University, Graduate Programs, Program in Dance, Roanoke, VA 24020. Offers MFA. Part-time programs available. *Faculty:* 2 full-time (1 woman), 10 part-time/adjunct (5 women). *Students:* 21 full-time (17 women), 1 part-time (0 women); includes 4 minority (3 Black or African American, non-Hispanic/Latino; 1 Asian, non-Hispanic/Latino), 6 international. Average age 34. 73 applicants, 70% accepted, 19 enrolled. In 2014, 15 master's awarded. *Degree requirements:* For master's, thesis. *Entrance requirements:* For master's, videotape of selected works, 3 letters of recommendation, resume. Additional exam requirements/recommendations for international students: Required—TOEFL (minimum score 550 paper-based; 79 iBT). *Application deadline:* For fall admission, 12/1 for domestic and international students. Application fee: $40. Electronic applications accepted. *Expenses:* Expenses: $867 per credit hour, technology fee: $325 for the year; advising fee: $300; portfolio fee: $250; thesis fee: $350. *Financial support:* In 2014–15, 14 students received support, including 14 fellowships; scholarships/grants also available. Support available to part-time students. Financial award application deadline: 2/2. *Unit head:* Jeffery Bullock, MFA Program Director & Chair of Dance, 540-362-6596, E-mail: jbullock@hollins.edu. *Application contact:* Cathy S. Koon, Manager of Graduate Services, 540-362-6326, Fax: 540-362-6288, E-mail: ckoon@hollins.edu.
Website: http://www.hollinsdance.org

Jacksonville University, College of Fine Arts, Jacksonville, FL 32211. Offers dance (MFA).

Mills College, Graduate Studies, Department of Dance, Oakland, CA 94613-1000. Offers choreography (MFA); dance (MA); performance and choreography (MFA). Part-time programs available. *Faculty:* 5 full-time (3 women), 5 part-time/adjunct (all women). *Students:* 19 full-time (17 women); includes 5 minority (1 Black or African American, non-Hispanic/Latino; 1 Hispanic/Latino; 3 Two or more races, non-Hispanic/Latino), 3 international. Average age 28. 28 applicants, 68% accepted, 9 enrolled. In 2014, 11 master's awarded. *Degree requirements:* For master's, comprehensive exam, thesis, performance. *Entrance requirements:* For master's, audition, DVD recording of original choreography of up to two choreographic works (for MFA); writing sample with topic related to field of dance studies (for MA). Additional exam requirements/recommendations for international students: Required—TOEFL (minimum score 550 paper-based; 80 iBT) or IELTS (minimum score 6). *Application deadline:* For fall admission, 2/1 priority date for domestic students, 12/15 for international students. Applications are processed on a rolling basis. Application fee: $50. *Expenses: Tuition:* Full-time $31,620; part-time $7905 per course. *Required fees:* $1118. *Financial support:* In 2014–15, 10 students received support, including 17 fellowships (averaging $8,131 per year), 13 teaching assistantships with full and partial tuition reimbursements available (averaging $4,160 per year); scholarships/grants and unspecified assistantships also available. Financial award application deadline: 2/1; financial award applicants required to submit FAFSA. *Faculty research:* Modern techniques, movement for actors, choreography, dance criticism and analysis, dance and literature. *Unit head:* Sonya Delwaide, Department Head, 510-430-3301, E-mail: sdelwaid@mills.edu. *Application contact:* Shrim Bathey, Director of Graduate Admission, 510-430-3309, Fax: 510-430-2159, E-mail: grad-admission@mills.edu.
Website: http://www.mills.edu/dance

New Mexico State University, College of Education, Department of Curriculum and Instruction, Las Cruces, NM 88003-8001. Offers curriculum and instruction (Ed D); dance (MAT). *Accreditation:* NCATE. Part-time and evening/weekend programs available. Postbaccalaureate distance learning degree programs offered (no on-campus study). *Faculty:* 29 full-time (22 women), 6 part-time/adjunct (4 women). *Students:* 134 full-time (90 women), 281 part-time (220 women); includes 227 minority (13 Black or African American, non-Hispanic/Latino; 6 American Indian or Alaska Native, non-Hispanic/Latino; 9 Asian, non-Hispanic/Latino; 191 Hispanic/Latino; 8 Two or more races, non-Hispanic/Latino), 32 international. Average age 36. 209 applicants, 68% accepted, 113 enrolled. In 2014, 107 master's, 17 doctorates awarded. *Degree requirements:* For master's, comprehensive exam, thesis optional; for doctorate, comprehensive exam, thesis/dissertation. *Entrance requirements:* For master's and Ed S, minimum cumulative GPA of 3.0; for doctorate, portfolio. Additional exam requirements/recommendations for international students: Required—TOEFL (minimum score 550 paper-based; 79 iBT), IELTS (minimum score 6.5). *Application deadline:* For fall admission, 12/15 priority date for domestic and international students; for spring admission, 11/1 for domestic students. Applications are processed on a rolling basis. Application fee: $40 ($50 for international students). Electronic applications accepted.

Expenses: Tuition, state resident: full-time $3969; part-time $220.50 per credit hour. Tuition, nonresident: full-time $13,838; part-time $768.80 per credit hour. *Required fees:* $853; $47.40 per credit hour. *Financial support:* In 2014–15, 114 students received support, including 5 research assistantships (averaging $10,203 per year), 10 teaching assistantships (averaging $14,142 per year); career-related internships or fieldwork, Federal Work-Study, scholarships/grants, traineeships, health care benefits, and unspecified assistantships also available. Support available to part-time students. Financial award application deadline: 3/1. *Faculty research:* STEM education, bilingual and English as a second language education, critical pedagogy/multicultural education, learning design and technology, early childhood education. *Total annual research expenditures:* $16,321. *Unit head:* Dr. Jeanette Haynes, Academic Department Head, 575-646-1834, Fax: 575-646-5436, E-mail: jeanette@nmsu.edu. *Application contact:* Dr. David Rutledge, Associate Department Head for Graduate Programs, 575-646-5411, Fax: 575-646-5436, E-mail: rutledge@nmsu.edu.
Website: http://ci.education.nmsu.edu

New York University, Steinhardt School of Culture, Education, and Human Development, Department of Music and Performing Arts Professions, Program in Dance Education, New York, NY 10010. Offers teachers of dance, all grades (MA); teaching dance in the professions (MA), including American Ballet Theatre pedagogy, teaching dance in the professions; MA/MA. Part-time programs available. *Faculty:* 2 full-time (both women). *Students:* 49 full-time (47 women), 7 part-time (6 women); includes 16 minority (10 Black or African American, non-Hispanic/Latino; 3 Asian, non-Hispanic/Latino; 1 Hispanic/Latino; 2 Two or more races, non-Hispanic/Latino), 15 international. Average age 28. 34 applicants, 82% accepted, 21 enrolled. In 2014, 25 master's awarded. *Degree requirements:* For master's, thesis (for some programs). *Entrance requirements:* For master's, audition, interview. Additional exam requirements/recommendations for international students: Required—TOEFL (minimum score 100 iBT). *Application deadline:* For fall admission, 12/1 priority date for domestic and international students; for spring admission, 10/1 for domestic and international students. Applications are processed on a rolling basis. Application fee: $75. Electronic applications accepted. *Financial support:* Career-related internships or fieldwork, Federal Work-Study, institutionally sponsored loans, and scholarships/grants available. Support available to part-time students. Financial award application deadline: 2/1; financial award applicants required to submit FAFSA. *Faculty research:* Dance cognition and creativity, technology in dance, development of teacher expertise, ballet pedagogy. *Unit head:* Prof. Susan R. Koff, Director, 212-992-9384, Fax: 212-995-4043, E-mail: susan.koff@nyu.edu. *Application contact:* 212-998-5030, Fax: 212-995-4328, E-mail: steinhardt.gradadmissions@nyu.edu.
Website: http://steinhardt.nyu.edu/music/dance

New York University, Tisch School of the Arts, Department of Dance, New York, NY 10012-1019. Offers MFA. *Faculty:* 11 full-time, 16 part-time/adjunct. *Students:* 28 full-time (19 women); includes 9 minority (2 Black or African American, non-Hispanic/Latino; 1 American Indian or Alaska Native, non-Hispanic/Latino; 2 Asian, non-Hispanic/Latino; 3 Hispanic/Latino; 1 Native Hawaiian or other Pacific Islander, non-Hispanic/Latino), 9 international. 61 applicants, 33% accepted, 14 enrolled. In 2014, 13 master's awarded. *Entrance requirements:* For master's, audition. Additional exam requirements/recommendations for international students: Required—TOEFL or IELTS. *Application deadline:* For fall admission, 1/1 priority date for domestic students, 1/1 for international students. Application fee: $60. Electronic applications accepted. *Financial support:* In 2014–15, 19 fellowships with full and partial tuition reimbursements were awarded; Federal Work-Study, institutionally sponsored loans, tuition waivers (partial), and unspecified assistantships also available. Financial award application deadline: 2/15; financial award applicants required to submit FAFSA. *Unit head:* Sean Curran, Chair, 212-998-1980, Fax: 212-995-4644. *Application contact:* Dan Sandford, Director of Graduate Admissions, 212-998-1918, Fax: 212-995-4060, E-mail: tisch.gradadmissions@nyu.edu.
Website: http://dance.tisch.nyu.edu/

New York University, Tisch School of the Arts and Graduate School of Arts and Science, Department of Performance Studies, New York, NY 10012-1019. Offers MA, PhD. *Faculty:* 12 full-time (7 women), 4 part-time/adjunct (3 women). *Students:* 37 full-time (23 women), 2 part-time (both women); includes 10 minority (4 Black or African American, non-Hispanic/Latino; 1 Asian, non-Hispanic/Latino; 3 Hispanic/Latino; 2 Two or more races, non-Hispanic/Latino), 16 international. 99 applicants, 90% accepted, 37 enrolled. In 2014, 36 master's, 7 doctorates awarded. *Degree requirements:* For doctorate, one foreign language, comprehensive exam, thesis/dissertation, dissertation defense, qualifying exam. *Entrance requirements:* For master's, sample of written work; for doctorate, master's degree, writing sample. Additional exam requirements/recommendations for international students: Required—TOEFL or IELTS. *Application deadline:* For fall admission, 12/1 for domestic and international students. Application fee: $60. Electronic applications accepted. *Expenses:* Expenses: Contact institution. *Financial support:* In 2014–15, 32 students received support, including 24 fellowships with full and partial tuition reimbursements available, 4 research assistantships, 4 teaching assistantships; Federal Work-Study, institutionally sponsored loans, tuition waivers (partial), and unspecified assistantships also available. Financial award application deadline: 2/15; financial award applicants required to submit CSS PROFILE or FAFSA. *Faculty research:* Performance theory, dance, folklore and festivals, postcolonial theory, anthropology and gender studies. *Unit head:* Karen Shimakawa, Chair, 212-998-1620, Fax: 212-995-4571, E-mail: performance.studies@nyu.edu. *Application contact:* Dan Sandford, Director of Graduate Admissions, 212-998-1918, Fax: 212-995-4060, E-mail: tisch.gradadmissions@nyu.edu.
Website: http://www.performance.tisch.nyu.edu/

Northern Illinois University, Graduate School, College of Visual and Performing Arts, School of Theatre and Dance, De Kalb, IL 60115-2854. Offers MFA. *Accreditation:* NAST. Part-time programs available. *Faculty:* 16 full-time (9 women). *Students:* 25 full-time (10 women); includes 4 minority (2 Hispanic/Latino; 2 Two or more races, non-Hispanic/Latino). Average age 27. 34 applicants, 56% accepted, 16 enrolled. In 2014, 23 master's awarded. *Degree requirements:* For master's, comprehensive exam, final project and defense. *Entrance requirements:* For master's, minimum GPA of 2.75, audition or portfolio. Additional exam requirements/recommendations for international students: Required—TOEFL (minimum score 550 paper-based). *Application deadline:* For fall admission, 4/1 priority date for domestic students, 5/1 for international students; for spring admission, 10/15 priority date for domestic students, 10/1 for international students. Applications are processed on a rolling basis. Application fee: $40. Electronic applications accepted. *Financial support:* In 2014–15, 27 teaching assistantships with full tuition reimbursements were awarded; fellowships with full tuition reimbursements, research assistantships with full tuition reimbursements, career-related internships or fieldwork, Federal Work-Study, scholarships/grants, tuition waivers (full), and staff assistantships also available. Support available to part-time students. Financial award applicants required to submit FAFSA. *Faculty research:* Theatre history, choreography, performance art spectacles, storytelling, computer visualization of the ethical space. *Unit head:* Alexander Gelman, Director, 815-753-8253, Fax: 815-753-8415, E-mail: agelman@niu.edu. *Application contact:* Graduate School Office, 815-753-0395, E-mail: gradsch@niu.edu.
Website: http://www.niu.edu/theatre/

The Ohio State University, Graduate School, College of Arts and Sciences, Division of Arts and Humanities, Department of Dance, Columbus, OH 43210. Offers choreography (MFA); dance (MFA, PhD); dance and technology (MFA); dance studies (PhD); history, theory and literature (MFA); lighting and production (MFA); movement analysis, Laban studies, notation and dance documentation (MFA); performance (MFA). *Accreditation:* NASD. *Faculty:* 15. *Students:* 33 full-time (24 women), 1 (woman) part-time; includes 5 minority (1 Asian, non-Hispanic/Latino; 3 Hispanic/Latino; 1 Two or more races, non-Hispanic/Latino), 6 international. Average age 31. In 2014, 2 master's awarded. *Degree requirements:* For master's, thesis optional. *Entrance requirements:* For master's, GRE General Test (for all applicants with cumulative GPA below 3.0), audition; for doctorate, GRE General Test, invitation-only interview. Additional exam requirements/recommendations for international students: Required—Michigan English Language Assessment Battery (minimum score 82); Recommended—TOEFL (minimum score 550 paper-based; 79 iBT), IELTS (minimum score 7). *Application deadline:* For fall admission, 11/15 priority date for domestic and international students; for winter admission, 12/1 for domestic students, 11/1 for international students; for spring admission, 3/1 for domestic students, 2/1 for international students. Applications are processed on a rolling basis. Application fee: $60 ($70 for international students). Electronic applications accepted. *Financial support:* Fellowships with tuition reimbursements, teaching assistantships with tuition reimbursements, Federal Work-Study, and institutionally sponsored loans available. Support available to part-time students. *Unit head:* Susan Van Pelt Petry, Chair, 614-292-0984, E-mail: petry.37@osu.edu. *Application contact:* Amy Schmidt, Academic Program Coordinator, 614-292-8933, E-mail: schmidt.442@osu.edu.
Website: http://dance.osu.edu/

Oklahoma City University, Margaret E. Petree College of Performing Arts, Ann Lacy School of American Dance and Arts Management, Oklahoma City, OK 73106-1402. Offers dance (MFA). *Degree requirements:* For master's, thesis. *Entrance requirements:* For master's, minimum GPA of 3.0, audition, interview, essay. Additional exam requirements/recommendations for international students: Required—TOEFL (minimum score 550 paper-based; 80 iBT). *Application deadline:* For fall admission, 2/23 for domestic students. Application fee: $50. *Expenses: Tuition:* Part-time $936 per credit hour. *Required fees:* $115 per credit hour. One-time fee: $250. Tuition and fees vary according to course load, degree level, program and student's religious affiliation. *Financial support:* Applicants required to submit FAFSA. *Unit head:* Melanie Shelley, Associate Dean, 405-208-5982, Fax: 405-208-5313, E-mail: mshelley@okcu.edu. *Application contact:* Michelle Cook, Director, Admissions, 405-208-5340, Fax: 405-208-5916, E-mail: gadmissions@okcu.edu.
Website: http://www.okcu.edu/dance/index

Saint Mary's College of California, School of Liberal Arts, MFA Program in Dance, Moraga, CA 94575. Offers dance: creative practice (MFA); dance: design and production (MFA).

Sam Houston State University, College of Fine Arts and Mass Communication, Department of Dance, Huntsville, TX 77341. Offers MFA. Part-time programs available. *Faculty:* 7 full-time (3 women). *Students:* 14 full-time (11 women); includes 4 minority (1 Black or African American, non-Hispanic/Latino; 3 Hispanic/Latino). Average age 26. 6 applicants, 100% accepted, 5 enrolled. In 2014, 5 master's awarded. *Degree requirements:* For master's, comprehensive exam, thesis, project. *Entrance requirements:* For master's, GRE General Test, writing sample, interview, audition, resume, video portfolio, letters of recommendation. Additional exam requirements/recommendations for international students: Required—TOEFL (minimum score 550 paper-based; 79 iBT), IELTS (minimum score 6.5). *Application deadline:* For fall admission, 8/1 for domestic students, 6/25 for international students; for spring admission, 12/1 for domestic students, 11/12 for international students; for summer admission, 5/15 for domestic students, 4/9 for international students. Applications are processed on a rolling basis. Application fee: $45 ($75 for international students). Electronic applications accepted. *Expenses:* Tuition, state resident: full-time $2286; part-time $254 per credit hour. Tuition, nonresident: full-time $5544; part-time $616 per credit hour. *Required fees:* $440 per semester. Tuition and fees vary according to course load and campus/location. *Financial support:* In 2014–15, 8 research assistantships (averaging $6,710 per year), 7 teaching assistantships (averaging $8,766 per year) were awarded; career-related internships or fieldwork, Federal Work-Study, scholarships/grants, tuition waivers (partial), and unspecified assistantships also available. Support available to part-time students. Financial award application deadline: 3/15; financial award applicants required to submit FAFSA. *Unit head:* Jennifer Pontius, Chair, 936-294-1300, Fax: 936-294-3954, E-mail: dnc_jkp@shsu.edu. *Application contact:* Dr. Dionne Noble, Academic Advisor, 936-294-1588, Fax: 936-294-3954, E-mail: dln008@shsu.edu.
Website: http://www.shsu.edu/~dnc_www/

Sarah Lawrence College, Graduate Studies, Program in Dance, Bronxville, NY 10708-5999. Offers MFA. *Degree requirements:* For master's, performance. *Entrance requirements:* For master's, audition, minimum B average in undergraduate course work. Additional exam requirements/recommendations for international students: Required—TOEFL. Electronic applications accepted.

Sarah Lawrence College, Graduate Studies, Program in Dance/Movement Therapy, Bronxville, NY 10708-5999. Offers MS. *Degree requirements:* For master's, thesis, practicum.

Smith College, Graduate and Special Programs, Department of Dance, Northampton, MA 01063. Offers MFA. *Faculty:* 2 full-time (1 woman), 1 (woman) part-time/adjunct. *Students:* 8 full-time (all women). Average age 33. 23 applicants, 17% accepted, 4 enrolled. In 2014, 4 master's awarded. *Degree requirements:* For master's, thesis performance. *Entrance requirements:* For master's, audition. Additional exam requirements/recommendations for international students: Required—TOEFL (minimum score 595 paper-based; 97 iBT). *Application deadline:* For fall admission, 12/1 for domestic and international students. Application fee: $60. *Expenses: Tuition:* Full-time $33,360; part-time $1390 per credit. *Financial support:* In 2014–15, 8 students received support, including 8 teaching assistantships with full tuition reimbursements available (averaging $6,785 per year); institutionally sponsored loans and scholarships/grants also available. Financial award application deadline: 12/1; financial award applicants required to submit CSS PROFILE or FAFSA. *Unit head:* Rodger Blum, Chair, 413-585-3234, E-mail: rblum@smith.edu. *Application contact:* Chris Aiken, Graduate Student Adviser, 413-585-3241, E-mail: caiken@smith.edu.
Website: http://www.smith.edu/dance/

Temple University, Center for the Arts, Esther Boyer College of Music and Dance, Department of Dance, Philadelphia, PA 19122-6096. Offers MA, MFA, PhD. *Accreditation:* NASD. Part-time programs available. Postbaccalaureate distance learning degree programs offered (minimal on-campus study). *Faculty:* 7 full-time (5 women), 11 part-time/adjunct (9 women). *Students:* 35 full-time (30 women), 5 part-time (3 women); includes 8 minority (4 Black or African American, non-Hispanic/Latino; 1 Asian, non-Hispanic/Latino; 3 Hispanic/Latino), 9 international. 51 applicants, 76% accepted, 14 enrolled. In 2014, 6 master's, 2 doctorates awarded. *Degree requirements:* For master's, thesis optional, professional project; for doctorate, thesis/dissertation. *Entrance requirements:* For master's and doctorate, minimum GPA of 3.0, audition/

interview, academic writing sample, dance questionnaire. Additional exam requirements/recommendations for international students: Required—TOEFL. *Application deadline:* For fall admission, 1/11 for domestic students, 12/1 for international students. Application fee: $60. Electronic applications accepted. *Expenses:* Tuition, state resident: full-time $14,490; part-time $805 per credit hour. Tuition, nonresident: full-time $19,850; part-time $1103 per credit hour. *Required fees:* $690. Full-time tuition and fees vary according to class time, course load, degree level, campus/location and program. *Financial support:* Fellowships with tuition reimbursements, research assistantships with tuition reimbursements, teaching assistantships with tuition reimbursements, Federal Work-Study, scholarships/grants, health care benefits, tuition waivers, and unspecified assistantships available. Financial award application deadline: 1/15; financial award applicants required to submit FAFSA. *Faculty research:* Cultural studies, dance technology, aesthetics, choreography, dance research. *Unit head:* Dr. Sherril Dodds, Department Chair, 215-204-6280, Fax: 215-204-4957, E-mail: sherril.dodds@temple.edu. *Application contact:* Norma Porter, Admissions Representative, 215-204-0533, Fax: 215-204-0533, E-mail: norma.porter@temple.edu.
Website: http://www.temple.edu/boyer/dance/

Texas Christian University, College of Fine Arts, School for Classical and Contemporary Dance, Fort Worth, TX 76129-0002. Offers MFA. *Degree requirements:* For master's, one foreign language, comprehensive exam, thesis. *Application deadline:* For fall admission, 12/1 for domestic students; for spring admission, 12/1 for domestic students. *Expenses: Tuition:* Full-time $22,860; part-time $1270 per credit hour. *Financial support:* Tuition waivers available. Financial award application deadline: 12/1. *Unit head:* Elizabeth Gillaspy, Director, 817-257-7615, E-mail: e.a.gillaspy@tcu.edu. *Application contact:* Dr. Joseph Butler, Associate Dean, College of Fine Arts, 817-257-7603, E-mail: j.butler@tcu.edu.
Website: http://www.dance.tcu.edu/graduate.asp

Texas Woman's University, Graduate School, College of Arts and Sciences, School of the Arts, Department of Dance, Denton, TX 76201. Offers MA, MFA, PhD. *Accreditation:* NASD. *Degree requirements:* For master's, comprehensive exam, thesis, choreography portfolio, professional paper; for doctorate, comprehensive exam, thesis/dissertation. *Entrance requirements:* For master's, audition, 3 letters of recommendation, interview, writing sample, resume, personal essay; for doctorate, interview, 3 letters of reference, personal essay, curriculum vitae, DVD portfolio of artistic work. Additional exam requirements/recommendations for international students: Required—TOEFL (minimum score 550 paper-based; 79 iBT). Electronic applications accepted. *Faculty research:* Performance, choreography, pedagogy, somatic practices, theorizing artistic practice.

Tulane University, School of Liberal Arts, Department of Theatre and Dance, New Orleans, LA 70118-5669. Offers design and technical production (MFA). *Entrance requirements:* For master's, GRE General Test, minimum B average in undergraduate course work. Additional exam requirements/recommendations for international students: Required—TOEFL. Electronic applications accepted. *Expenses: Tuition:* Full-time $46,326; part-time $2574 per credit hour. *Required fees:* $1980; $44.50 per credit hour. $550 per term. Tuition and fees vary according to course load and program. *Faculty research:* Scene design, stage management, costume design, technical direction, lighting design.

Université du Québec à Montréal, Graduate Programs, Program in Dance, Montréal, QC H3C 3P8, Canada. Offers MA. Part-time programs available. *Degree requirements:* For master's, thesis optional. *Entrance requirements:* For master's, appropriate bachelor's degree or equivalent and proficiency in French.

The University of Arizona, College of Fine Arts, School of Dance, Tucson, AZ 85721. Offers MFA. *Entrance requirements:* Additional exam requirements/recommendations for international students: Required—TOEFL (minimum score 550 paper-based; 79 iBT). Electronic applications accepted.

University of California, Irvine, Claire Trevor School of the Arts, Department of Dance, Irvine, CA 92697. Offers MFA. *Students:* 24 full-time (21 women); includes 7 minority (1 Asian, non-Hispanic/Latino; 3 Hispanic/Latino; 3 Two or more races, non-Hispanic/Latino), 4 international. Average age 30. 30 applicants, 43% accepted, 10 enrolled. In 2014, 7 master's awarded. *Degree requirements:* For master's, thesis. *Entrance requirements:* For master's, minimum GPA of 3.0. *Application deadline:* For fall admission, 1/15 priority date for domestic students, 1/15 for international students. Applications are processed on a rolling basis. Application fee: $90 ($110 for international students). Electronic applications accepted. *Financial support:* Fellowships, teaching assistantships, institutionally sponsored loans, traineeships, health care benefits, and unspecified assistantships available. Financial award application deadline: 3/1; financial award applicants required to submit FAFSA. *Faculty research:* Dance science, digital technology, history and theory, choreography. *Unit head:* Lisa Marie Naugle, Chair, 949-824-3209, E-mail: lnaugle@uci.edu. *Application contact:* Alan Terricciano, Graduate Advisor, 949-824-5744, Fax: 949-824-4563, E-mail: aterricc@uci.edu.
Website: http://dance.arts.uci.edu/

University of California, Los Angeles, Graduate Division, School of the Arts and Architecture, Department of World Arts and Cultures, Los Angeles, CA 90095. Offers culture and performance (MA, PhD); dance (MFA). *Degree requirements:* For master's, 1 foreign language, and comprehensive exam or thesis (MA); comprehensive exam (MFA); for doctorate, one foreign language, thesis/dissertation, oral and written qualifying exams. *Entrance requirements:* For master's, bachelor's degree; minimum undergraduate GPA of 3.0 (or its equivalent if letter grade system not used); audition and interview (MFA); writing sample (MA); for doctorate, master's degree; minimum undergraduate GPA of 3.0 (or its equivalent if letter grade system not used); writing sample. Additional exam requirements/recommendations for international students: Required—TOEFL. Electronic applications accepted.

University of California, Riverside, Graduate Division, Department of Dance, Riverside, CA 92521. Offers critical dance studies (PhD); experimental choreography (MFA). *Faculty:* 8 full-time (6 women). *Students:* 27 full-time (26 women); includes 4 minority (1 Black or African American, non-Hispanic/Latino; 3 Hispanic/Latino), 4 international. Average age 33. 27 applicants, 15% accepted, 3 enrolled. In 2014, 4 master's, 3 doctorates awarded. *Degree requirements:* For doctorate, one foreign language, thesis/dissertation, qualifying exams. *Entrance requirements:* For master's, Stable electronic link (such as Vimeo/YouTube) of a choreographed piece (for MFA program only); for doctorate, GRE General Test (Ph.D. program only), minimum GPA of 3.2, writing sample (Ph.D program only). Additional exam requirements/recommendations for international students: Required—TOEFL (minimum score 550 paper-based; 80 iBT). *Application deadline:* For fall admission, 12/5 priority date for domestic and international students. Application fee: $80 ($100 for international students). Electronic applications accepted. *Expenses:* Tuition, state resident: full-time $5399. Tuition, nonresident: full-time $10,433. *Financial support:* In 2014–15, 13 students received support, including fellowships with full tuition reimbursements available (averaging $12,000 per year), teaching assistantships with full tuition reimbursements available (averaging $15,600 per year); research assistantships with tuition reimbursements available, career-related internships or fieldwork, Federal Work-Study, institutionally sponsored loans, scholarships/grants, tuition waivers (full and partial), and unspecified assistantships also available. Financial award application deadline: 1/5; financial award applicants required to submit FAFSA. *Faculty research:* Movement analysis, cultural postcolonial gender studies of performance, theories of dance, anthropology of dance, history and reconstruction of dance. *Unit head:* Anthea Kraut, PhD, Chair, 951-827-3944, Fax: 951-827-4651, E-mail: danceadvising@ucr.edu. *Application contact:* Linda J. Tomko, PhD, Graduate Advisor, 951-827-3944, Fax: 951-827-4651, E-mail: danceadvising@ucr.edu.
Website: http://www.dance.ucr.edu

University of California, San Diego, Graduate Division, Department of Theatre and Dance, La Jolla, CA 92093. Offers acting (MFA); dance theatre (MFA); design (MFA); directing (MFA); drama and theatre (PhD); playwriting (MFA); stage management (MFA). PhD offered jointly with University of California, Irvine. *Students:* 81 full-time (47 women), 5 part-time (1 woman); includes 26 minority (15 Black or African American, non-Hispanic/Latino; 1 American Indian or Alaska Native, non-Hispanic/Latino; 7 Asian, non-Hispanic/Latino; 3 Hispanic/Latino), 7 international. 439 applicants, 7% accepted, 25 enrolled. In 2014, 19 master's, 4 doctorates awarded. *Degree requirements:* For master's, thesis; for doctorate, comprehensive exam, thesis/dissertation. *Entrance requirements:* For master's, GRE General Test (for playwriting only), minimum GPA of 3.5; audition or interview; for doctorate, GRE General Test, minimum GPA of 3.5; audition and/or interview. Additional exam requirements/recommendations for international students: Required—TOEFL (minimum score 550 paper-based; 80 iBT), IELTS (minimum score 7). *Application deadline:* For fall admission, 1/6 for domestic students. Application fee: $90 ($110 for international students). Electronic applications accepted. *Expenses:* Tuition, state resident: full-time $11,220; part-time $5610 per quarter. Tuition, nonresident: full-time $26,322; part-time $13,161 per quarter. *Required fees:* $570 per quarter. Tuition and fees vary according to program. *Financial support:* Scholarships/grants available. Financial award applicants required to submit FAFSA. *Faculty research:* Theatre of the Americas, European theatre, Asian theatre, gender studies, critical theory. *Unit head:* Jim Carmody, Chair, 858-534-6889, E-mail: jcarmody@ucsd.edu. *Application contact:* Marybeth Ward, Graduate Coordinator, 858-534-1046, E-mail: meward@ucsd.edu.
Website: http://theatre.ucsd.edu/

University of Colorado Boulder, Graduate School, College of Arts and Sciences, Department of Theatre and Dance, Boulder, CO 80309. Offers dance (MFA); theatre (MA, PhD). *Faculty:* 14 full-time (9 women). *Students:* 39 full-time (33 women); includes 6 minority (4 Black or African American, non-Hispanic/Latino; 2 Hispanic/Latino), 1 international. Average age 33. 40 applicants, 45% accepted, 8 enrolled. In 2014, 8 master's, 3 doctorates awarded. Terminal master's awarded for partial completion of doctoral program. *Degree requirements:* For master's, comprehensive exam, thesis; for doctorate, one foreign language, thesis/dissertation. *Entrance requirements:* For master's, GRE General Test (MA), audition (MFA), minimum undergraduate GPA of 2.75. *Application deadline:* For fall admission, 12/15 for domestic students, 12/1 for international students. Application fee: $50 ($70 for international students). Electronic applications accepted. *Financial support:* In 2014–15, 102 students received support, including 20 fellowships (averaging $1,284 per year), 31 teaching assistantships with full and partial tuition reimbursements available (averaging $19,505 per year); institutionally sponsored loans, scholarships/grants, health care benefits, and unspecified assistantships also available. Financial award application deadline: 1/15; financial award applicants required to submit FAFSA. *Faculty research:* Performing arts, drama, dramatic/theatre arts, dance, opera/musical theatre.
Website: http://www.colorado.edu/theatredance/

University of Hawaii at Manoa, Graduate Division, College of Arts and Humanities, Department of Theatre and Dance, Honolulu, HI 96822. Offers dance (MA, MFA); theatre (MA, MFA, PhD). Part-time programs available. *Degree requirements:* For master's, one foreign language, thesis optional; for doctorate, one foreign language, comprehensive exam, thesis/dissertation. *Entrance requirements:* For master's and doctorate, GRE General Test. Additional exam requirements/recommendations for international students: Required—TOEFL (minimum score 600 paper-based; 100 iBT), IELTS (minimum score 7). *Faculty research:* Asian theatre, feminist theatre and dance, Russian theatre, Australian theatre.

University of Illinois at Urbana–Champaign, Graduate College, College of Fine and Applied Arts, Department of Dance, Champaign, IL 61820. Offers MFA. *Accreditation:* NASD. *Students:* 13 (11 women). Application fee: $70 ($90 for international students). *Unit head:* Jan K. Erkert, Head, 217-333-1010, Fax: 217-333-3000, E-mail: erkert@illinois.edu. *Application contact:* Rebecca Ferrell, Assistant to the Head, 217-333-1011, Fax: 217-333-3000, E-mail: rferrel@illinois.edu.
Website: http://dance.illinois.edu/

The University of Iowa, Graduate College, College of Liberal Arts and Sciences, Department of Dance, Iowa City, IA 52242-1316. Offers MFA. *Accreditation:* NASD. *Degree requirements:* For master's, thesis, exam. *Entrance requirements:* For master's, minimum GPA of 3.0. Additional exam requirements/recommendations for international students: Required—TOEFL (minimum score 550 paper-based; 81 iBT). Electronic applications accepted.

University of Maryland, Baltimore County, The Graduate School, College of Arts, Humanities and Social Sciences, Department of Education, Program in Teaching, Baltimore, MD 21250. Offers early childhood education (MAT); elementary education (MAT); secondary education (MAT), including art, biology, chemistry, choral music, classical foreign language, dance, earth/space science, English, instrumental music, mathematics, modern foreign language, physical science, physics, social studies, theatre. Part-time and evening/weekend programs available. *Faculty:* 24 full-time (18 women), 25 part-time/adjunct (19 women). *Students:* 64 full-time (52 women), 34 part-time (22 women); includes 31 minority (12 Black or African American, non-Hispanic/Latino; 1 American Indian or Alaska Native, non-Hispanic/Latino; 7 Asian, non-Hispanic/Latino; 8 Hispanic/Latino; 3 Two or more races, non-Hispanic/Latino), 1 international. Average age 29. 40 applicants, 95% accepted, 35 enrolled. In 2014, 106 master's awarded. *Degree requirements:* For master's, comprehensive exam (for some programs), thesis (for some programs). *Entrance requirements:* For master's, PRAXIS I or SAT (minimum score of 1000), minimum GPA of 3.0. Additional exam requirements/recommendations for international students: Required—TOEFL. *Application deadline:* For fall admission, 6/1 for domestic students; for spring admission, 11/1 for domestic students. Applications are processed on a rolling basis. Application fee: $50. Electronic applications accepted. *Expenses:* Tuition, state resident: part-time $557. Tuition, nonresident: part-time $922. *Required fees:* $122 per semester. One-time fee: $200 part-time. *Financial support:* In 2014–15, 6 students received support, including teaching assistantships with full and partial tuition reimbursements available (averaging $12,000 per year); career-related internships or fieldwork, Federal Work-Study, scholarships/grants, tuition waivers, and unspecified assistantships also available. Financial award application deadline: 3/1. *Faculty research:* STEM teacher education, culturally sensitive pedagogy, ESOL/bilingual education, early childhood education, language, literacy and culture. *Unit head:* Dr. Susan M. Blunck, Graduate Program Director, 410-455-2869, Fax: 410-455-3986, E-mail: blunck@umbc.edu.
Website: http://www.umbc.edu/education/

University of Maryland, College Park, Academic Affairs, College of Arts and Humanities, School of Theatre, Dance and Performance Studies, Program in Dance,

College Park, MD 20742. Offers MFA. *Degree requirements:* For master's, final project. *Entrance requirements:* For master's, audition/interview, video tapes/writing sample, 3 letters of recommendation. Additional exam requirements/recommendations for international students: Required—TOEFL. Electronic applications accepted. *Faculty research:* Performance and choreography.

University of Michigan, Horace H. Rackham School of Graduate Studies, School of Music, Theatre, and Dance, Department of Dance, Ann Arbor, MI 48109-2217. Offers modern dance performance and choreography (MFA). Offered through the Horace H. Rackham School of Graduate Studies. *Accreditation:* NASD. *Degree requirements:* For master's, thesis. *Entrance requirements:* For master's, audition. Additional exam requirements/recommendations for international students: Required—TOEFL. Electronic applications accepted.

University of New Mexico, Graduate School, College of Fine Arts, Department of Theatre and Dance, Albuquerque, NM 87131-2039. Offers dance (MFA); dance history (MA); dramatic writing (MFA); theatre education and outreach (MA). *Accreditation:* NASD; NAST. *Faculty:* 8 full-time (4 women), 1 (woman) part-time/adjunct. *Students:* 9 full-time (6 women); includes 3 minority (all Hispanic/Latino). Average age 31. 9 applicants, 44% accepted, 1 enrolled. In 2014, 4 master's awarded. *Degree requirements:* For master's, comprehensive exam (for some programs), thesis (for some programs). *Entrance requirements:* For master's, minimum GPA of 3.0; undergraduate major in theatre, dance or closely-related field; 3 letters of recommendation; letter of intent; BA, BFA, BS, or MA in dance movement science or related field, or equivalent experience (for MFA in dance). *Application deadline:* For fall admission, 4/15 for domestic students; for spring admission, 11/10 for domestic students. Application fee: $50. Electronic applications accepted. *Financial support:* In 2014–15, 1 fellowship (averaging $7,200 per year), 1 research assistantship with partial tuition reimbursement (averaging $3,750 per year), 3 teaching assistantships with partial tuition reimbursements (averaging $4,482 per year) were awarded; Federal Work-Study, health care benefits, tuition waivers (partial), and unspecified assistantships also available. Financial award application deadline: 3/1; financial award applicants required to submit FAFSA. *Faculty research:* Theater education and outreach, choreography, dramatic writing, dance history/criticism. *Unit head:* Bill Liotta, Chair, 505-277-4332, Fax: 505-277-8921, E-mail: wliotta@unm.edu. *Application contact:* Christina Squire, Administrator II, 505-277-7362, Fax: 505-277-8921, E-mail: csquire@unm.edu.
Website: http://theatredance.unm.edu

The University of North Carolina at Charlotte, College of Education, Interdisciplinary Education Programs, Charlotte, NC 28223-0001. Offers art education (MAT); dance education (MAT); elementary education (MAT); English as a second language (MAT); foreign language education (MAT); middle grades education (MAT); music education (MAT); secondary education (MAT); special education (MAT); teacher certification (Graduate Certificate); teaching (Graduate Certificate); theater education (MAT). Part-time programs available. *Students:* 96 full-time (67 women), 703 part-time (569 women); includes 300 minority (211 Black or African American, non-Hispanic/Latino; 20 Asian, non-Hispanic/Latino; 56 Hispanic/Latino; 13 Two or more races, non-Hispanic/Latino), 15 international. Average age 33. 425 applicants, 94% accepted, 317 enrolled. In 2014, 199 master's, 257 other advanced degrees awarded. Terminal master's awarded for partial completion of doctoral program. *Degree requirements:* For master's, thesis. *Entrance requirements:* For master's, GRE or MAT. Additional exam requirements/recommendations for international students: Required—TOEFL (minimum score 550 paper-based; 83 iBT). *Application deadline:* For fall admission, 5/1 priority date for domestic and international students; for spring admission, 10/1 priority date for domestic and international students. Applications are processed on a rolling basis. Application fee: $75. Electronic applications accepted. *Expenses:* Tuition, state resident: full-time $4008. Tuition, nonresident: full-time $16,295. *Required fees:* $2755. Tuition and fees vary according to course load and program. *Total annual research expenditures:* $94,425. *Unit head:* Dr. Warren DiBiase, Chair, 704-687-8881, Fax: 704-687-4705, E-mail: wjdibias@uncc.edu. *Application contact:* Kathy B. Giddings, Director of Graduate Admissions, 704-687-5503, Fax: 704-687-1668, E-mail: gradadm@uncc.edu.
Website: http://education.uncc.edu/academic-programs

The University of North Carolina at Greensboro, Graduate School, School of Music, Theatre and Dance, Department of Dance, Greensboro, NC 27412-5001. Offers MA, MFA. *Accreditation:* NASD. *Degree requirements:* For master's, thesis. *Entrance requirements:* For master's, GRE General Test or MAT, audition or video (MFA). Additional exam requirements/recommendations for international students: Required—TOEFL. Electronic applications accepted. *Faculty research:* Consciousness-raising images, perspectives on ballet.

University of Oklahoma, Weitzenhoffer Family College of Fine Arts, School of Dance, Norman, OK 73019. Offers MFA. *Faculty:* 7 full-time (3 women). *Students:* 4 full-time (2 women). Average age 28. In 2014, 1 master's awarded. *Degree requirements:* For master's, comprehensive exam, thesis. *Entrance requirements:* For master's, BFA. Additional exam requirements/recommendations for international students: Required—TOEFL (minimum score 79 iBT). *Application deadline:* For fall admission, 4/15 for domestic students, 3/1 for international students; for spring admission, 11/1 for domestic students, 9/1 for international students. Application fee: $50 ($100 for international students). Electronic applications accepted. *Expenses:* Tuition, state resident: full-time $4394; part-time $183.10 per credit hour. Tuition, nonresident: full-time $16,970; part-time $707.10 per credit hour. *Required fees:* $2892; $109.95 per credit hour. $126.50 per semester. *Financial support:* In 2014–15, 4 students received support, including 1 fellowship with full tuition reimbursement available (averaging $5,000 per year), 2 research assistantships with partial tuition reimbursements available (averaging $12,686 per year), 3 teaching assistantships with partial tuition reimbursements available (averaging $10,994 per year); health care benefits and unspecified assistantships also available. Support available to part-time students. Financial award application deadline: 6/1; financial award applicants required to submit FAFSA. *Faculty research:* Dance history, body science, teaching methods, choreography, performance. *Unit head:* Dr. Mary Margaret Holt, Acting Dean, Weitzenhoffer Family College of Fine Arts/Chair/Professor/Director, School of Dance, 405-325-4051, Fax: 405-325-7024, E-mail: marymholt@ou.edu. *Application contact:* Jeremy Lindberg, Professor/Director, 405-325-4051, Fax: 405-325-7024, E-mail: jlindberg@ou.edu.
Website: http://www.ou.edu/finearts/dance

University of Oregon, Graduate School, School of Music, Department of Dance, Eugene, OR 97403. Offers MA, MS. *Degree requirements:* For master's, thesis or alternative. *Entrance requirements:* For master's, minimum GPA of 3.0. Additional exam requirements/recommendations for international students: Required—TOEFL. *Faculty research:* Choreography, dance history, dance pedagogy, scientific aspects of dance.

The University of Texas at Austin, Graduate School, College of Fine Arts, Department of Theatre and Dance, Austin, TX 78712-1111. Offers acting (MFA); dance (MFA); directing (MFA); drama and theatre for youth (MFA); performance as public practice (MA, MFA, PhD); playwriting (MFA); theatre technology (MFA); theatrical design (MFA). *Accreditation:* NASD. *Degree requirements:* For master's, thesis; for doctorate, variable foreign language requirement, thesis/dissertation. *Entrance requirements:* For master's and doctorate, GRE General Test.

University of Utah, Graduate School, College of Fine Arts, Department of Modern Dance, Salt Lake City, UT 84112-0280. Offers MFA. *Accreditation:* NASD. *Faculty:* 8 full-time (4 women), 8 part-time/adjunct (5 women). *Students:* 20 full-time (13 women), 1 (woman) part-time; includes 3 minority (1 Black or African American, non-Hispanic/Latino; 2 Hispanic/Latino), 5 international. Average age 28. 11 applicants, 73% accepted, 8 enrolled. In 2014, 6 master's awarded. *Degree requirements:* For master's, thesis, project, oral examination. *Entrance requirements:* For master's, audition, interview, minimum GPA of 3.0. Additional exam requirements/recommendations for international students: Required—TOEFL (minimum score 500 paper-based; 61 iBT). *Application deadline:* For fall admission, 3/1 priority date for domestic and international students. Applications are processed on a rolling basis. Application fee: $55 ($65 for international students). Electronic applications accepted. *Financial support:* In 2014–15, 17 students received support, including teaching assistantships with full and partial tuition reimbursements available (averaging $12,000 per year); fellowships with full and partial tuition reimbursements available, Federal Work-Study, institutionally sponsored loans, scholarships/grants, health care benefits, and unspecified assistantships also available. Financial award application deadline: 3/1; financial award applicants required to submit FAFSA. *Faculty research:* Choreography, teaching methods, performance, dance for camera, dance technology. *Total annual research expenditures:* $29,720. *Unit head:* Stephen Koester, Chair, 801-581-7327, Fax: 801-581-5442, E-mail: stephen.koester@utah.edu. *Application contact:* Eric Handman, Director of Graduate Studies, 801-587-9804, Fax: 801-581-5442, E-mail: eric.handman@utah.edu.
Website: http://www.dance.utah.edu

University of Washington, Graduate School, College of Arts and Sciences, Program in Dance, Seattle, WA 98195-1150. Offers MFA. *Degree requirements:* For master's, performance, project, course development. *Entrance requirements:* For master's, 8 years of professional dance experience, resume, performance DVD or VHS tape, 3 letters of reference. Additional exam requirements/recommendations for international students: Required—TOEFL. Electronic applications accepted. *Faculty research:* Choreography, history, anatomy, ethnography, integrated dance, social dance.

University of Wisconsin–Milwaukee, Graduate School, Peck School of the Arts, Program in Performing Arts, Milwaukee, WI 53201-0413. Offers dance (MFA); film (MFA); theatre (MFA). Part-time programs available. *Degree requirements:* For master's, variable foreign language requirement, comprehensive exam, thesis or alternative. *Entrance requirements:* For master's, audition, interview. Additional exam requirements/recommendations for international students: Required—TOEFL (minimum score 550 paper-based; 79 iBT), IELTS (minimum score 6.5). Electronic applications accepted.

York University, Faculty of Graduate Studies, Faculty of Fine Arts, Program in Dance, Toronto, ON M3J 1P3, Canada. Offers MA, MFA, PhD. *Degree requirements:* For master's, thesis or alternative. Electronic applications accepted.

Music

Academy of Art University, Graduate Program, School of Music Production and Sound Design for Visual Media, San Francisco, CA 94105-3410. Offers MFA. Part-time programs available. Postbaccalaureate distance learning degree programs offered (no on-campus study). *Faculty:* 4 full-time (0 women), 24 part-time/adjunct (3 women). *Students:* 115 full-time (49 women), 32 part-time (12 women); includes 27 minority (15 Black or African American, non-Hispanic/Latino; 1 American Indian or Alaska Native, non-Hispanic/Latino; 3 Asian, non-Hispanic/Latino; 5 Hispanic/Latino; 3 Two or more races, non-Hispanic/Latino), 83 international. Average age 29. 50 applicants, 100% accepted, 27 enrolled. In 2014, 29 master's awarded. *Degree requirements:* For master's, final review. *Entrance requirements:* For master's, statement of intent; resume; portfolio/reel; official college transcripts. *Application deadline:* Applications are processed on a rolling basis. Application fee: $100. Electronic applications accepted. *Expenses: Tuition:* Part-time $910 per unit. *Financial support:* Career-related internships or fieldwork and Federal Work-Study available. Support available to part-time students. Financial award application deadline: 8/10; financial award applicants required to submit FAFSA. *Unit head:* 800-544-ARTS, E-mail: info@academyart.edu. *Application contact:* 800-544-ARTS, E-mail: info@academyart.edu.
Website: http://www.academyart.edu/music-for-visual-media/index.html

Alabama Agricultural and Mechanical University, School of Graduate Studies, School of Education, Area in Music Education, Huntsville, AL 35811. Offers music (MS); music education (M Ed). *Accreditation:* NCATE. Part-time and evening/weekend programs available. *Degree requirements:* For master's, comprehensive exam. *Entrance requirements:* For master's, GRE General Test. Additional exam requirements/recommendations for international students: Required—TOEFL (minimum score 500 paper-based; 61 iBT). Electronic applications accepted. *Faculty research:* Jazz and black music, Alabama folk music.

Andrews University, School of Graduate Studies, College of Arts and Sciences, Department of Music, Berrien Springs, MI 49104. Offers M Mus, MA. *Accreditation:* NASM. *Faculty:* 10 full-time (4 women). *Students:* 16 full-time (8 women), 9 part-time (5 women); includes 4 minority (2 Black or African American, non-Hispanic/Latino; 1 Asian, non-Hispanic/Latino; 1 Hispanic/Latino), 11 international. Average age 29. 10 applicants, 60% accepted, 5 enrolled. In 2014, 7 master's awarded. *Degree requirements:* For master's, variable foreign language requirement. *Entrance requirements:* For master's, GRE Subject Test, minimum undergraduate GPA of 2.6. Additional exam requirements/recommendations for international students: Required—TOEFL (minimum score 550 paper-based). *Application deadline:* Applications are processed on a rolling basis. Application fee: $40. Tuition and fees vary according to course level. *Unit head:* Dr. Carlos Flores, Chairman, 269-471-3555. *Application contact:* Monica Wringer, Supervisor of Graduate Admission, 800-253-2874, Fax: 269-471-6321, E-mail: graduate@andrews.edu.

Music

Appalachian State University, Cratis D. Williams Graduate School, Center for Appalachian Studies, Boone, NC 28608. Offers culture (MA); roots and music (MA); sustainable development (MA). Part-time programs available. *Degree requirements:* For master's, one foreign language, comprehensive exam, thesis optional. *Entrance requirements:* For master's, GRE General Test, 3 letters of recommendation. Additional exam requirements/recommendations for international students: Required—TOEFL (minimum score 570 paper-based; 79 iBT), IELTS (minimum score 6.5). Electronic applications accepted. *Faculty research:* Appalachian culture, sustainable development, Appalachian music.

Appalachian State University, Cratis D. Williams Graduate School, School of Music, Boone, NC 28608. Offers music education (MM); music performance (MM); music therapy (MMT). *Accreditation:* NASM. Part-time programs available. *Degree requirements:* For master's, comprehensive exam, thesis or alternative. *Entrance requirements:* For master's, GRE General Test, 3 letters of reference, audition. Additional exam requirements/recommendations for international students: Required—TOEFL (minimum score 550 paper-based; 79 iBT), IELTS (minimum score 6.5). Electronic applications accepted. *Faculty research:* Music of the Holocaust, Celtic folk music, early nineteenth-century performance practice, hypermeter and phase rhythm, world music, music and psychoneuroimmunology.

Aquinas Institute of Theology, Graduate and Professional Programs, St. Louis, MO 63108. Offers biblical studies (Certificate); church music (MM); health care mission (MAHCM); ministry (M Div); pastoral care (Certificate); pastoral ministry (MAPM); pastoral studies (MAPS); preaching (D Min); spiritual direction (Certificate); theology (M Div, MA); Thomistic studies (Certificate); M Div/MA; MA/PhD; MAPS/MSW. *Accreditation:* ATS (one or more programs are accredited). Part-time and evening/weekend programs available. Postbaccalaureate distance learning degree programs offered (minimal on-campus study). *Faculty:* 14 full-time (7 women), 24 part-time/adjunct (8 women). *Students:* 87 full-time (24 women), 59 part-time (37 women); includes 21 minority (9 Black or African American, non-Hispanic/Latino; 1 American Indian or Alaska Native, non-Hispanic/Latino; 4 Asian, non-Hispanic/Latino; 6 Hispanic/Latino; 1 Native Hawaiian or other Pacific Islander, non-Hispanic/Latino), 8 international. Average age 46. In 2014, 25 master's, 5 doctorates awarded. *Degree requirements:* For master's, variable foreign language requirement, comprehensive exam (for some programs), thesis (for some programs); for doctorate, thesis/dissertation. *Entrance requirements:* For master's and Certificate, MAT; for doctorate, 3 years of ministerial experience, 6 hours of graduate course work in homiletics, M Div or the equivalent, minimum GPA of 3.0. Additional exam requirements/recommendations for international students: Required—TOEFL. *Application deadline:* For fall admission, 3/15 priority date for domestic and international students; for spring admission, 11/15 priority date for domestic and international students. Applications are processed on a rolling basis. Application fee: $50. *Expenses:* Expenses $680 per credit hour; $265 per semester in fees. *Financial support:* Scholarships/grants, health care benefits, and tuition waivers (partial) available. Support available to part-time students. Financial award application deadline: 3/15; financial award applicants required to submit CSS PROFILE or FAFSA. *Faculty research:* Theology of preaching, hermeneutics, lay ecclesial ministry, pastoral and practical theology. *Unit head:* Fr. Gregory Heille, Vice-President/Academic Dean, 314-256-8800, Fax: 314-256-8888, E-mail: heille@ai.edu. *Application contact:* David Werthmann, Director of Admissions, 314-256-8806, Fax: 314-256-8888, E-mail: admissions@ai.edu.
Website: http://www.ai.edu/

Arizona State University at the Tempe campus, Herberger Institute for Design and the Arts, School of Film, Dance and Theatre, Tempe, AZ 85287-2002. Offers dance (MFA), including dance, interdisciplinary digital media and performance; theatre (MA, MFA, PhD), including arts entrepreneurship and management (MFA), directing (MFA), dramatic writing (MFA), interdisciplinary digital media and performance (MFA), performance (MFA), performance design (MFA), theatre (MFA), theatre and performance of the Americas (PhD), theatre for youth (MFA, PhD). Terminal master's awarded for partial completion of doctoral program. *Degree requirements:* For master's, comprehensive exam (for some programs), thesis (for some programs), applied project (for some programs); interactive Program of Study (iPOS) submitted before completing 50 percent of required credit hours; for doctorate, comprehensive exam, thesis/dissertation, interactive Program of Study (iPOS) submitted before completing 50 percent of required credit hours. *Entrance requirements:* For master's, GRE or MAT, minimum GPA of 3.0 in last 2 years of work leading to bachelor's degree (depending on program); for doctorate, GRE, minimum GPA of 3.0 or equivalent in last 2 years of work leading to bachelor's degree, 3 letters of recommendation, resume, scholarly writing sample, statement of purpose. Additional exam requirements/recommendations for international students: Required—TOEFL, IELTS, or PTE. Electronic applications accepted.

Arizona State University at the Tempe campus, Herberger Institute for Design and the Arts, School of Music, Tempe, AZ 85287-0405. Offers composition (MM, DMA); conducting (DMA); ethnomusicology (MA); interdisciplinary digital media/performance (DMA); music education (MM, PhD); music history and literature (MA); music therapy (MM); performance (MM, DMA). *Accreditation:* NASM. Terminal master's awarded for partial completion of doctoral program. *Degree requirements:* For master's, thesis (for some programs), interactive Program of Study (iPOS) submitted before completing 50 percent of required credit hours; for doctorate, comprehensive exam, thesis/dissertation, interactive Program of Study (iPOS) submitted before completing 50 percent of required credit hours. *Entrance requirements:* For master's, minimum GPA of 3.0 or equivalent in last 2 years of work leading to bachelor's degree, 3 letters of recommendation, resume; for doctorate, GRE or MAT, minimum GPA of 3.0 or equivalent in last 2 years of work leading to bachelor's degree, 3 letters of recommendation, curriculum vitae, statement of intent. Additional exam requirements/recommendations for international students: Required—TOEFL, IELTS, or PTE. Electronic applications accepted.

Arkansas State University, Graduate School, College of Fine Arts, Department of Music, State University, AR 72467. Offers music education (MME, SCCT); performance (MM). *Accreditation:* NASM (one or more programs are accredited). Part-time programs available. *Faculty:* 21 full-time (6 women). *Students:* 5 full-time (2 women), 9 part-time (1 woman); includes 3 minority (all Black or African American, non-Hispanic/Latino), 1 international. Average age 27. 12 applicants, 58% accepted, 6 enrolled. In 2014, 8 master's, 1 other advanced degree awarded. *Degree requirements:* For master's, 2 foreign languages, comprehensive exam, thesis or alternative; for SCCT, comprehensive exam. *Entrance requirements:* For master's, GRE General Test or MAT, university entrance exam, appropriate bachelor's degree, audition, letters of recommendation, teaching experience, official transcripts, immunization records, valid teaching certificate; for SCCT, GRE General Test or MAT, interview, master's degree, official transcript, immunization records, letters of recommendation. Additional exam requirements/recommendations for international students: Required—TOEFL (minimum score 550 paper-based; 79 iBT), IELTS (minimum score 6), PTE (minimum score 56). *Application deadline:* For fall admission, 7/1 for domestic and international students; for spring admission, 11/15 for domestic students, 11/14 for international students. Applications are processed on a rolling basis. Application fee: $30 ($40 for international students). Electronic applications accepted. *Expenses:* Tuition, state resident: full-time

$4392; part-time $244 per credit hour. Tuition, nonresident: full-time $8784; part-time $488 per credit hour. *International tuition:* $9484 full-time. *Required fees:* $1134; $63 per credit hour. $25 per term. Tuition and fees vary according to course load and program. *Financial support:* In 2014–15, 1 student received support. Teaching assistantships, career-related internships or fieldwork, scholarships/grants, and unspecified assistantships available. Financial award application deadline: 7/1; financial award applicants required to submit FAFSA. *Unit head:* Dr. Marika Kyriakos, Chair, 870-972-2094, Fax: 870-972-3932, E-mail: mkyriakos@astate.edu. *Application contact:* Vickey Ring, Graduate Admissions Coordinator, 870-972-3029, Fax: 870-972-3857, E-mail: vickeyring@astate.edu.
Website: http://www.astate.edu/college/fine-arts/music/

Austin Peay State University, College of Graduate Studies, College of Arts and Letters, Department of Music, Clarksville, TN 37044. Offers music education (M Mu); music performance (M Mu). *Accreditation:* NASM. Part-time programs available. *Degree requirements:* For master's, comprehensive exam, thesis optional. *Entrance requirements:* For master's, GRE General Test, diagnostic exams, audition, bachelor's degree, 3 letters of recommendation. Additional exam requirements/recommendations for international students: Required—TOEFL (minimum score 500 paper-based). Electronic applications accepted.

Azusa Pacific University, School of Music, Azusa, CA 91702-7000. Offers education (M Mus); performance (M Mus). *Accreditation:* NASM. Part-time and evening/weekend programs available. *Degree requirements:* For master's, recital. *Entrance requirements:* For master's, interview, audition. Additional exam requirements/recommendations for international students: Required—TOEFL (minimum score 550 paper-based).

The Baptist College of Florida, Graduate Programs, Graceville, FL 32440-1898. Offers Christian studies (MA); music and worship leadership (MA). Part-time programs available. Postbaccalaureate distance learning degree programs offered (no on-campus study). *Faculty:* 12 full-time (0 women). *Students:* 33 full-time (6 women); includes 2 minority (1 Black or African American, non-Hispanic/Latino; 1 Hispanic/Latino). Average age 28. 10 applicants, 100% accepted, 10 enrolled. *Degree requirements:* For master's, variable foreign language requirement, comprehensive exam (for some programs), thesis (for some programs). *Entrance requirements:* For master's, regionally-accredited undergraduate degree, undergraduate courses in field, minimum GPA of 2.5. Additional exam requirements/recommendations for international students: Required—TOEFL. *Application deadline:* For fall admission, 8/15 for domestic students; for spring admission, 1/15 for domestic students. Applications are processed on a rolling basis. Application fee: $25. Electronic applications accepted. *Expenses:* Expenses: $310 per hour. *Financial support:* In 2014–15, 2 students received support. *Faculty research:* Biblical studies, ministry studies. *Unit head:* Dr. Ed Scott, Chair of the Graduate Division, 850-263-3261 Ext. 488, E-mail: eescott@baptistcollege.edu. *Application contact:* Sandra Richards, Director of Admissions, 850-263-3261 Ext. 415.

Bard College, Conservatory of Music, The Conductors Institute, Annandale-on-Hudson, NY 12504. Offers MFA. *Entrance requirements:* For master's, resume, 3 letters of recommendation.

Bard College, Conservatory of Music, Graduate Program in Vocal Arts, Annandale-on-Hudson, NY 12504. Offers MM. *Entrance requirements:* For master's, portfolio, 3 letters of recommendation, headshot, repertoire list.

Bard College, Longy School of Music, Cambridge, MA 02138. Offers chamber ensemble (Artist Diploma); collaborative piano (MM, Artist Diploma, GPD); composition (MM); Dalcroze eurhythmics (MM); early music (MM, Artist Diploma, GPD); instrumental performance (MM, Artist Diploma, GPD); modern American music (MM, GPD); opera performance (MM, GPD); organ performance (MM, Artist Diploma, GPD); piano performance (MM, Artist Diploma, GPD); vocal performance (MM, Artist Diploma, GPD). Part-time programs available. *Degree requirements:* For master's, thesis (for some programs), recital; for other advanced degree, recital. *Entrance requirements:* For master's and other advanced degree, audition. Additional exam requirements/recommendations for international students: Required—TOEFL (minimum score 550 paper-based; 79 iBT). Electronic applications accepted.

Baylor University, Graduate School, School of Music, Waco, TX 76798. Offers church music (MM, DMA); collaborative piano (MM); composition (MM); conducting (MM); music history and literature (MM); music theory (MM); performance (MM); piano pedagogy and performance (MM); M Div/MM. *Accreditation:* NASM. *Degree requirements:* For master's, variable foreign language requirement, thesis (for some programs). *Entrance requirements:* For master's, GRE General Test.

Belmont University, School of Music, Nashville, TN 37212-3757. Offers church music (MM); commercial music (MM); composition (MM); music education (MM); pedagogy (MM); performance (MM). *Accreditation:* NASM. Part-time programs available. *Students:* 51 full-time (27 women), 9 part-time (5 women); includes 11 minority (7 Black or African American, non-Hispanic/Latino; 2 Hispanic/Latino; 2 Two or more races, non-Hispanic/Latino), 1 international. Average age 27. 90 applicants, 42% accepted, 25 enrolled. *Degree requirements:* For master's, comprehensive exam, thesis (for some programs). *Entrance requirements:* For master's, placement exam, GRE or MAT, audition, interview, minimum GPA of 2.75. Additional exam requirements/recommendations for international students: Required—TOEFL (minimum score 500 paper-based). *Application deadline:* For fall admission, 5/1 priority date for domestic students, 5/1 for international students; for spring admission, 11/1 priority date for domestic students, 11/1 for international students. Applications are processed on a rolling basis. Application fee: $50. Electronic applications accepted. *Financial support:* Fellowships, teaching assistantships, career-related internships or fieldwork, scholarships/grants, and unspecified assistantships available. Financial award application deadline: 3/1; financial award applicants required to submit FAFSA. *Unit head:* Dr. Cynthia R. Curtis, Dean, 615-460-8118, Fax: 615-386-0239, E-mail: cynthia.curtis@belmont.edu. *Application contact:* Ben Craine, Graduate Secretary, 615-460-8117, Fax: 615-386-0239, E-mail: ben.craine@belmont.edu.

Bennington College, Graduate Programs, MFA in Music Program, Bennington, VT 05201. Offers MFA. Part-time programs available. *Degree requirements:* For master's, thesis, concert performances.

Berklee College of Music, Master's Programs, 46013 Valencia, Spain. Offers contemporary performance careers (MM); global entertainment and music business (MA); music technology innovation (MM); scoring for film, television, and video games (MM). Programs offered at Valencia, Spain campus.

Bethesda University, Graduate and Professional Programs, Anaheim, CA 92801. Offers biblical studies (MA); music (MA); theology (M Div). *Entrance requirements:* For master's, interview. Additional exam requirements/recommendations for international students: Recommended—TOEFL.

Binghamton University, State University of New York, Graduate School, School of Arts and Sciences, Department of Music, Vestal, NY 13850. Offers MM. *Accreditation:* NASM. *Faculty:* 12 full-time (1 woman), 27 part-time/adjunct (11 women). *Students:* 14 full-time (5 women), 3 part-time (1 woman); includes 1 minority (Black or African American, non-Hispanic/Latino). Average age 34. 38 applicants, 47% accepted, 10 enrolled. In 2014, 7 master's awarded. *Degree requirements:* For master's, variable

foreign language requirement, comprehensive exam, thesis (for some programs). *Entrance requirements:* Additional exam requirements/recommendations for international students: Required—TOEFL (minimum score 550 paper-based; 80 iBT). *Application deadline:* For fall admission, 6/15 priority date for domestic and international students; for spring admission, 10/15 priority date for domestic and international students. Applications are processed on a rolling basis. Application fee: $75. Electronic applications accepted. *Expenses:* Tuition, state resident: full-time $7776; part-time $432 per credit. Tuition, nonresident: full-time $15,138; part-time $841 per credit. *Required fees:* $1754; $213 per credit. Tuition and fees vary according to degree level and program. *Financial support:* In 2014–15, 12 students received support, including 10 teaching assistantships with full tuition reimbursements available (averaging $9,500 per year); career-related internships or fieldwork, Federal Work-Study, institutionally sponsored loans, scholarships/grants, health care benefits, tuition waivers (full and partial), and unspecified assistantships also available. Financial award application deadline: 2/15; financial award applicants required to submit FAFSA. *Unit head:* Dr. James Burns, Chairperson, 607-777-2592, E-mail: jburns@binghamton.edu. *Application contact:* Kishan Zuber, Recruiting and Admissions Coordinator, 607-777-2151, Fax: 607-777-2501, E-mail: kzuber@binghamton.edu.

Bob Jones University, Graduate Programs, Greenville, SC 29614. Offers accountancy (MS); Bible (MA); Bible translation (MA); Biblical studies (Certificate); broadcast management (MS); business administration (MBA); church history (MA, PhD); church ministries (MA); church music (MM); cinema and video production (MA); counseling (MS); curriculum and instruction (Ed D); divinity (M Div); dramatic production (MA); educational leadership (MS, Ed D, Ed S); elementary education (M Ed, MAT); English (M Ed, MA, MAT); fine arts (MA); graphic design (MA); history (M Ed, MA); illustration (MA); interpretative speech (MA); mathematics (M Ed, MAT); medical missions (Certificate); ministry (MM, D Min); multi-categorical special education (M Ed, MAT); music (M Ed); New Testament interpretation (PhD); Old Testament interpretation (PhD); orchestral instrument performance (MM); organ performance (MM); pastoral studies (MA); personnel services (MS, Ed S); piano pedagogy (MM); piano performance (MM); platform arts (MA); radio and television broadcasting (MS); rhetoric and public address (MA); secondary education (M Ed); studio art (MA); teaching Bible (MA); theology (MA, PhD); voice performance (MM); youth ministries (MA); M Div/MM.

Boise State University, College of Arts and Sciences, Department of Music, Boise, ID 83725-0399. Offers music (MM); music education (MM); pedagogy (MM); performance (MM). *Accreditation:* NASM. Part-time programs available. *Faculty:* 21 full-time, 3 part-time/adjunct. *Students:* 18 full-time (9 women), 3 part-time (2 women); includes 1 minority (Hispanic/Latino), 1 international. 26 applicants, 92% accepted, 14 enrolled. In 2014, 4 master's awarded. *Degree requirements:* For master's, thesis optional. *Entrance requirements:* For master's, minimum GPA of 3.0, performance demonstration. *Application deadline:* For fall admission, 7/17 priority date for domestic students; for spring admission, 12/5 priority date for domestic students. Applications are processed on a rolling basis. Application fee: $0. Electronic applications accepted. *Expenses:* Tuition, state resident: part-time $331 per credit hour. Tuition, nonresident: part-time $531 per credit hour. *Financial support:* In 2014–15, 11 students received support, including 4 fellowships; career-related internships or fieldwork, Federal Work-Study, institutionally sponsored loans, and unspecified assistantships also available. Support available to part-time students. Financial award application deadline: 3/1. *Unit head:* Dr. Mark Hansen, Chair, 208-426-1773, Fax: 208-426-1771. *Application contact:* Linda Platt, Office Services Supervisor, Graduate Admission and Degree Services, 208-426-1074, Fax: 208-426-2789, E-mail: lplatt@boisestate.edu.
Website: http://music.boisestate.edu/graduate-studies-in-music/

The Boston Conservatory, Graduate Division, Music Division, Boston, MA 02215. Offers contemporary music performance (MM); music (MM, ADP, Certificate); music education (MM). Part-time programs available. *Degree requirements:* For master's, thesis (for some programs), recital; for other advanced degree, recital. *Entrance requirements:* For master's and other advanced degree, audition. Electronic applications accepted.

Boston University, College of Fine Arts, School of Music, Boston, MA 02215. Offers choral conducting (MM); collaborative piano (DMA); composition and theory (DMA); conducting (Performance Diploma); historical performance (MM, Artist Diploma); music education (MM, DMA); music theory (MM); opera performance (Certificate); performance (MM). *Accreditation:* NASM. Part-time programs available. *Faculty:* 36 full-time, 21 part-time/adjunct. *Students:* 376 full-time (241 women), 1 (woman) part-time; includes 42 minority (9 Black or African American, non-Hispanic/Latino; 17 Asian, non-Hispanic/Latino; 10 Hispanic/Latino; 6 Two or more races, non-Hispanic/Latino), 184 international. Average age 27. 1,027 applicants, 35% accepted, 111 enrolled. In 2014, 165 master's, 33 doctorates awarded. *Degree requirements:* For master's, thesis; for doctorate, 2 foreign languages, thesis/dissertation. *Entrance requirements:* Additional exam requirements/recommendations for international students: Required—TOEFL, IELTS. *Application deadline:* For fall admission, 12/3 priority date for domestic and international students. Application fee: $80. Electronic applications accepted. *Expenses: Tuition:* Full-time $45,686; part-time $1428 per credit hour. *Required fees:* $660; $60 per semester. Tuition and fees vary according to program. *Financial support:* Fellowships and teaching assistantships available. Financial award application deadline: 12/15. *Unit head:* Richard Cornell, Interim Director, 617-353-3341, Fax: 617-353-7455, E-mail: cfamusic@bu.edu. *Application contact:* Shaun Ramsay, Assistant Director, Admissions and Student Affairs, 617-353-3341, E-mail: arts@bu.edu.

Boston University, Graduate School of Arts and Sciences, Department of Music, Boston, MA 02215. Offers composition (MA); music education (MA); music history/theory (PhD); musicology (MA, PhD). *Accreditation:* NASM. *Students:* 15 full-time (10 women), 3 part-time (0 women), 2 international. Average age 35. 52 applicants, 13% accepted, 4 enrolled. *Degree requirements:* For master's, 2 foreign languages, comprehensive exam, thesis; for doctorate, 2 foreign languages, comprehensive exam, thesis/dissertation. *Entrance requirements:* For master's and doctorate, GRE General Test, musical composition or research paper, 3 letters of recommendation. Additional exam requirements/recommendations for international students: Required—TOEFL (minimum score 550 paper-based; 84 iBT). *Application deadline:* For fall admission, 1/5 for domestic and international students. Application fee: $80. Electronic applications accepted. *Expenses: Tuition:* Full-time $45,686; part-time $1428 per credit hour. *Required fees:* $660; $60 per semester. Tuition and fees vary according to program. *Financial support:* In 2014–15, 10 students received support, including 4 fellowships (averaging $20,500 per year); Federal Work-Study, scholarships/grants, health care benefits, and unspecified assistantships also available. Support available to part-time students. Financial award application deadline: 1/5. *Unit head:* Victor Coelho, Director, 617-358-0628, Fax: 617-353-7455, E-mail: blues@bu.edu. *Application contact:* Melissa Riesgo, Administrative Coordinator, 617-353-6888, Fax: 617-353-7455, E-mail: riesgo@bu.edu.
Website: http://www.bu.edu/musicology/

Bowling Green State University, Graduate College, College of Musical Arts, Bowling Green, OH 43403. Offers composition (MM); contemporary music (DMA), including composition, performance; ethnomusicology (MM); music education (MM), including choral, comprehensive, instrumental; music history (MM); music theory (MM); performance (MM). *Accreditation:* NASM. Part-time programs available. *Degree requirements:* For master's, thesis or alternative, recitals; for doctorate, comprehensive exam, thesis/dissertation. *Entrance requirements:* For master's, GRE General Test, diagnostic placement exams in music history and theory, audition, interview. Additional exam requirements/recommendations for international students: Required—TOEFL. Electronic applications accepted. *Faculty research:* Ethnomusicology.

Brandeis University, Graduate School of Arts and Sciences, Department of Music, Waltham, MA 02454-9110. Offers composition and theory (MA, MFA, PhD); musicology (MA, MFA, PhD). Part-time programs available. Terminal master's awarded for partial completion of doctoral program. *Degree requirements:* For master's, variable foreign language requirement, comprehensive exam (for some programs), thesis (for some programs); for doctorate, one foreign language, comprehensive exam, thesis/dissertation, colloquia. *Entrance requirements:* For master's and doctorate, resume, 2 letters of recommendation, transcript(s), statement of purpose, writing sample, exam and examples of original work (for composition and theory applicants). Additional exam requirements/recommendations for international students: Required—TOEFL (minimum score 600 paper-based; 100 iBT), PTE (minimum score 68); Recommended—IELTS (minimum score 7). Electronic applications accepted.

Brandon University, School of Music, Brandon, MB R7A 6A9, Canada. Offers composition (M Mus); music education (M Mus); performance and literature (M Mus), including clarinet, conducting, jazz, piano, strings, trumpet. Part-time programs available. *Degree requirements:* For master's, comprehensive exam (for some programs), thesis (for some programs), 2 recitals. *Entrance requirements:* For master's, B Mus. Additional exam requirements/recommendations for international students: Required—TOEFL (minimum score 580 paper-based), IELTS (minimum score 7). Electronic applications accepted. *Faculty research:* Composition, evaluation and assessment, performance anxiety, philosophy of music, teacher education.

Brigham Young University, Graduate Studies, College of Fine Arts and Communications, School of Music, Provo, UT 84602-1001. Offers composition (MM); conducting (MM); music education (MA, MM); musicology (MA); performance (MM). *Accreditation:* NASM. *Faculty:* 49 full-time (8 women). *Students:* 21 full-time (14 women), 31 part-time (20 women); includes 4 minority (1 American Indian or Alaska Native, non-Hispanic/Latino; 1 Asian, non-Hispanic/Latino; 1 Hispanic/Latino; 1 Native Hawaiian or other Pacific Islander, non-Hispanic/Latino). Average age 29. 49 applicants, 47% accepted, 19 enrolled. In 2014, 16 master's awarded. *Degree requirements:* For master's, comprehensive exam (for some programs), thesis (for some programs), recital, project, or composition (for some programs). *Entrance requirements:* For master's, School of Music Entrance Exam, minimum GPA of 3.0, BM. Additional exam requirements/recommendations for international students: Required—TOEFL (minimum score 580 paper-based; 85 iBT). *Application deadline:* For fall admission, 12/15 priority date for domestic and international students. Application fee: $50. Electronic applications accepted. *Expenses: Tuition:* Full-time $6310; part-time $371 per credit hour. Tuition and fees vary according to program and student's religious affiliation. *Financial support:* In 2014–15, 60 students received support, including 50 research assistantships (averaging $3,000 per year), 46 teaching assistantships (averaging $3,500 per year); career-related internships or fieldwork, institutionally sponsored loans, scholarships/grants, tuition waivers (partial), and unspecified assistantships also available. Support available to part-time students. Financial award application deadline: 12/15; financial award applicants required to submit FAFSA. *Faculty research:* Adult musical/lifelong learning, Mormonism, race, media and cosplay. *Unit head:* Prof. Kory L. Katseanes, Director, 801-422-6304, Fax: 801-422-0533, E-mail: kory_katseanes@byu.edu. *Application contact:* Dr. A. Claudine Bigelow, Graduate Coordinator, 801-422-1315, Fax: 801-422-0533, E-mail: claudine_bigelow@byu.edu.
Website: https://cfac.byu.edu/music/

Brooklyn College of the City University of New York, School of Visual, Media and Performing Arts, Conservatory of Music, Brooklyn, NY 11210-2889. Offers composition (MM); music teacher (MA); musicology (MA); performance (MM). Part-time programs available. *Degree requirements:* For master's, one foreign language, comprehensive exam, thesis. *Entrance requirements:* For master's, placement exam, 36 credits in music, audition, completed composition, writing sample. Additional exam requirements/recommendations for international students: Required—TOEFL (minimum score 550 paper-based; 79 iBT). Electronic applications accepted. *Faculty research:* American music, computer music.

Brooklyn College of the City University of New York, School of Visual, Media and Performing Arts, Program in Performance and Interactive Media Arts, Brooklyn, NY 11210-2889. Offers MFA. *Entrance requirements:* For master's, 2 letters of recommendation, resume, portfolio, interview. Additional exam requirements/recommendations for international students: Required—TOEFL (minimum score 550 paper-based; 61 iBT). Electronic applications accepted.

Brown University, Graduate School, Department of Music, Providence, RI 02912. Offers computer music and multimedia (PhD); ethnomusicology (PhD). *Degree requirements:* For doctorate, 2 foreign languages, comprehensive exam, thesis/dissertation, departmental qualifying exam. *Entrance requirements:* For doctorate, GRE General Test. *Faculty research:* Ethnomusicology.

Butler University, Jordan College of Fine Arts, Indianapolis, IN 46208-3485. Offers MM. Part-time and evening/weekend programs available. *Faculty:* 25 full-time (6 women), 30 part-time/adjunct (14 women). *Students:* 17 full-time (10 women), 10 part-time (4 women), 1 international. Average age 28. 35 applicants, 66% accepted, 7 enrolled. In 2014, 12 master's awarded. *Entrance requirements:* For master's, GRE General Test, GRE Subject Test, audition, interview. Additional exam requirements/recommendations for international students: Required—TOEFL (minimum score 550 paper-based; 79 iBT), IELTS (minimum score 6). *Application deadline:* For fall admission, 8/15 priority date for domestic students. Applications are processed on a rolling basis. Application fee: $35. Electronic applications accepted. *Financial support:* Fellowships, teaching assistantships with tuition reimbursements, career-related internships or fieldwork, institutionally sponsored loans, and scholarships/grants available. Support available to part-time students. Financial award application deadline: 7/15; financial award applicants required to submit FAFSA. *Unit head:* Ronald Caltabiano, Dean, 317-940-9231, E-mail: rcalt@butler.edu. *Application contact:* Diane Dubord, Graduate Student Services Specialist, 317-940-8107, E-mail: ddubord@butler.edu.
Website: http://www.butler.edu/jca/

California Baptist University, Program in Music, Riverside, CA 92504-3206. Offers conducting (MM); music education (MM); performance (MM). *Accreditation:* NASM. Part-time and evening/weekend programs available. *Faculty:* 14 full-time (5 women), 17 part-time/adjunct (9 women). *Students:* 13 full-time (9 women), 4 part-time (1 woman); includes 5 minority (1 Black or African American, non-Hispanic/Latino; 1 Asian, non-Hispanic/Latino; 3 Hispanic/Latino), 5 international. Average age 25. 2 applicants, 100% accepted, 2 enrolled. In 2014, 5 master's awarded. *Degree requirements:* For master's, comprehensive exam (for some programs), comprehensive exam or thesis. *Entrance requirements:* For master's, minimum undergraduate GPA of 2.75; bachelor's degree in music; three recommendations; comprehensive essay; interview/audition. Additional

exam requirements/recommendations for international students: Required—TOEFL (minimum score 80 iBT). *Application deadline:* For fall admission, 8/1 priority date for domestic students, 7/1 for international students; for spring admission, 12/1 priority date for domestic students, 11/1 for international students. Applications are processed on a rolling basis. Application fee: $45. Electronic applications accepted. *Expenses:* Expenses: Contact institution. *Financial support:* Institutionally sponsored loans and scholarships/grants available. Financial award applicants required to submit CSS PROFILE or FAFSA. *Faculty research:* Choral conducting, church music, choir building, hymnology, music technology. *Unit head:* Dr. Judd Bonner, Dean, School of Music, 951-343-4256, Fax: 951-343-4570, E-mail: jbonner@calbaptist.edu. *Application contact:* Dr. Judd Bonner, Dean, School of Music, 951-343-4256, Fax: 951-343-4570, E-mail: jbonner@calbaptist.edu.
Website: http://www.calbaptist.edu/masterofmusic/

California Institute of the Arts, School of Music, Valencia, CA 91355-2340. Offers African music (MFA, Adv C); composition (MFA, Adv C); composition/new media (MFA, Adv C); Indonesian music (MFA, Adv C); jazz (MFA, Adv C); North Indian music (MFA, Adv C); performance (MFA, Adv C); performer/composer (MFA, Adv C); voice (MFA, Adv C); world music performance (MFA). *Accreditation:* NASM. Part-time programs available. *Degree requirements:* For master's, composition or recital. *Entrance requirements:* For master's, audition or portfolio. Additional exam requirements/recommendations for international students: Required—TOEFL. Electronic applications accepted. *Faculty research:* Music composition and twentieth century performance practice, interactive multimedia and computer music, music cognition.

California State University, East Bay, Office of Academic Programs and Graduate Studies, College of Letters, Arts, and Social Sciences, Department of Music, Hayward, CA 94542-3000. Offers MA. *Accreditation:* NASM. Part-time programs available. *Degree requirements:* For master's, variable foreign language requirement, comprehensive exam, project, recital, or thesis. *Entrance requirements:* For master's, minimum GPA of 3.0 in field; audition or work sample; 2 letters of recommendation. Additional exam requirements/recommendations for international students: Required—TOEFL (minimum score 550 paper-based). *Application deadline:* For fall admission, 3/1 for domestic and international students. Application fee: $55. Electronic applications accepted. *Expenses:* Tuition, state resident: full-time $7830; part-time $1302 per credit hour. Tuition, nonresident: full-time $16,368. *Required fees:* $327 per quarter. Tuition and fees vary according to course load and program. *Financial support:* Fellowships, Federal Work-Study, institutionally sponsored loans, and scholarships/grants available. Support available to part-time students. Financial award application deadline: 3/2. *Unit head:* John D. Eros, Chair, 510-885-3149, E-mail: john.eros@csueastbay.edu. *Application contact:* Prof. Peter Marsh, Graduate Advisor, 510-885-3132, Fax: 510-885-3461, E-mail: peter.marsh@csueastbay.edu.
Website: http://www20.csueastbay.edu/class/departments/music/

California State University, Fresno, Division of Graduate Studies, College of Arts and Humanities, Department of Music, Fresno, CA 93740-8027. Offers music (MA); music education (MA); performance (MA). *Accreditation:* NASM. Part-time programs available. *Degree requirements:* For master's, thesis or alternative. *Entrance requirements:* For master's, GRE General Test, BA in music, minimum GPA of 3.0. Additional exam requirements/recommendations for international students: Required—TOEFL. Electronic applications accepted. *Faculty research:* Technology transfer, folk art.

California State University, Fullerton, Graduate Studies, College of the Arts, Department of Music, Fullerton, CA 92834-9480. Offers music education (MA); music history and literature (MA); performance (MM); piano pedagogy (MA); theory-composition (MM). *Accreditation:* NASM. Part-time programs available. *Students:* 27 full-time (9 women), 26 part-time (14 women); includes 17 minority (7 Asian, non-Hispanic/Latino; 8 Hispanic/Latino; 2 Two or more races, non-Hispanic/Latino), 13 international. Average age 28. 74 applicants, 49% accepted, 26 enrolled. In 2014, 18 master's awarded. *Degree requirements:* For master's, comprehensive exam, project or thesis. *Entrance requirements:* For master's, audition, major in music or related field, minimum GPA of 2.5 in last 60 units of course work. Application fee: $55. *Financial support:* Career-related internships or fieldwork, Federal Work-Study, institutionally sponsored loans, and scholarships/grants available. Support available to part-time students. Financial award application deadline: 3/1; financial award applicants required to submit FAFSA. *Unit head:* Dr. Marc Dickey, Chair, 657-278-3511. *Application contact:* Admissions/Applications, 657-278-2371.

California State University, Long Beach, Graduate Studies, College of the Arts, Department of Music, Long Beach, CA 90840. Offers composition (MM); conducting-choral (MM); conducting-instrumental (MM); instrument/vocal performance (MM); jazz studies (MM); music (MA); opera performance (MM). *Accreditation:* NASM. Part-time programs available. *Degree requirements:* For master's, thesis or alternative, departmental qualifying exam. Electronic applications accepted.

California State University, Los Angeles, Graduate Studies, College of Arts and Letters, Department of Music, Los Angeles, CA 90032-8530. Offers music composition (MM); music education (MA); musicology (MA); performance (MM). *Accreditation:* NASM. Part-time and evening/weekend programs available. *Degree requirements:* For master's, comprehensive exam, project or thesis. *Entrance requirements:* For master's, audition. Additional exam requirements/recommendations for international students: Required—TOEFL (minimum score 500 paper-based). Electronic applications accepted. *Expenses:* Tuition, state resident: full-time $6738; part-time $3609 per year. Tuition, nonresident: full-time $15,666; part-time $8073 per year. Tuition and fees vary according to course load, degree level and program. *Faculty research:* Gregorian semiology, Baroque opera.

California State University, Northridge, Graduate Studies, College of Arts, Media, and Communication, Department of Music, Northridge, CA 91330. Offers composition (MM); conducting (MM); music education (MA); performance (MM). *Accreditation:* NASM. *Students:* 25 full-time (18 women), 26 part-time (13 women); includes 15 minority (5 Asian, non-Hispanic/Latino; 8 Hispanic/Latino; 2 Two or more races, non-Hispanic/Latino), 17 international. Average age 28. *Degree requirements:* For master's, thesis. *Entrance requirements:* For master's, audition, GRE General Test or minimum GPA of 3.0. Additional exam requirements/recommendations for international students: Required—TOEFL. *Application deadline:* For fall admission, 11/30 for domestic students. Application fee: $55. *Expenses: Required fees:* $12,402. *Financial support:* Application deadline: 3/1. *Faculty research:* Touring program. *Unit head:* Rick Alviso, Chair, 816-677-4752. *Application contact:* Julia Heinen, Graduate Advisor, 818-677-3168, E-mail: julia.heinen@csun.edu.
Website: http://www.csun.edu/music/

California State University, Sacramento, Office of Graduate Studies, College of Arts and Letters, Department of English, Sacramento, CA 95819. Offers composition (MA); creative writing (MA); literature (MA); teaching English to speakers of other languages (MA). Part-time programs available. *Degree requirements:* For master's, thesis, project, or comprehensive exam; TESOL exam; writing proficiency exam. *Entrance requirements:* For master's, portfolio (creative writing); minimum GPA of 3.0 in English, 2.75 overall during previous 2 years. Additional exam requirements/recommendations for international students: Required—TOEFL. Electronic applications accepted. *Faculty research:* Teaching composition, remedial writing.

California State University, Sacramento, Office of Graduate Studies, College of Arts and Letters, Department of Music, Sacramento, CA 95819. Offers MM. *Accreditation:* NASM. Part-time programs available. *Degree requirements:* For master's, thesis or project, writing proficiency exam. *Entrance requirements:* For master's, GRE, music exam, BA in music or equivalent, minimum GPA of 2.5 during previous 2 years of course work. Additional exam requirements/recommendations for international students: Required—TOEFL. Electronic applications accepted.

California State University, San Bernardino, Graduate Studies, College of Arts and Letters, Department of English, San Bernardino, CA 92407-2397. Offers creative writing (MFA), including fiction; English composition (MA), including composition. Part-time and evening/weekend programs available. *Students:* 31 full-time (17 women), 61 part-time (41 women); includes 46 minority (7 Black or African American, non-Hispanic/Latino; 1 Asian, non-Hispanic/Latino; 35 Hispanic/Latino; 3 Two or more races, non-Hispanic/Latino), 2 international. Average age 27. 74 applicants, 53% accepted, 37 enrolled. In 2014, 45 master's awarded. *Degree requirements:* For master's, one foreign language, thesis. *Entrance requirements:* Additional exam requirements/recommendations for international students: Required—TOEFL. *Application deadline:* For fall admission, 7/17 for domestic students. Application fee: $55. *Expenses:* Tuition, state resident: full-time $6738; part-time $1302 per term. Tuition, nonresident: full-time $17,898; part-time $248 per unit. *Required fees:* $365 per quarter. Tuition and fees vary according to degree level and program. *Financial support:* Application deadline: 3/1. *Unit head:* Dr. Sunny Hyon, Chair, 909-537-5834, Fax: 909-537-7086, E-mail: shyon@csusb.edu. *Application contact:* Dr. Jeffrey Thompson, Dean of Graduate Studies, 909-537-5058, Fax: 909-537-5078, E-mail: jthompso@csusb.edu.

Campbellsville University, School of Music, Campbellsville, KY 42718-2799. Offers church music (MM); music (MA); music education (MM); music performance (MMP). *Accreditation:* NASM. Part-time programs available. *Students:* 10 full-time (6 women), 14 part-time (6 women); includes 1 minority (Hispanic/Latino), 13 international. Average age 28. In 2014, 13 master's awarded. *Degree requirements:* For master's, thesis (for some programs), paper or recital. *Entrance requirements:* For master's, GRE General Test or PRAXIS, minimum GPA of 2.75. Additional exam requirements/recommendations for international students: Required—TOEFL (minimum score 550 paper-based). *Application deadline:* For fall admission, 6/1 priority date for domestic students, 5/1 priority date for international students; for spring admission, 11/1 priority date for domestic students, 10/1 priority date for international students. Applications are processed on a rolling basis. Application fee: $25. Electronic applications accepted. *Financial support:* In 2014–15, 24 students received support, including 1 fellowship (averaging $4,300 per year); institutionally sponsored loans and scholarships/grants also available. Support available to part-time students. Financial award application deadline: 6/1; financial award applicants required to submit FAFSA. *Unit head:* Dr. Tony Cunha, Dean, 270-789-5240, Fax: 270-789-5524, E-mail: accunha@campbellsville.edu. *Application contact:* Monica Bamwine, Assistant Director of Admissions, 270-789-5221, Fax: 270-789-5071, E-mail: mkbamwine@campbellsville.edu.
Website: http://www.campbellsville.edu/music

Capital University, Conservatory of Music, Columbus, OH 43209-2394. Offers music education (MM), including instrumental emphasis, Kodály emphasis. Program offered only in summer. *Accreditation:* NASM. Part-time programs available. *Degree requirements:* For master's, comprehensive exam, thesis or alternative, chamber performance exam. *Entrance requirements:* For master's, music theory exam, minimum undergraduate GPA of 3.0. Additional exam requirements/recommendations for international students: Required—TOEFL (minimum score 550 paper-based; 80 iBT). Electronic applications accepted. *Expenses:* Contact institution. *Faculty research:* Folk song research, Kodály method, performance, composition.

Cardinal Stritch University, College of Arts and Sciences, Music Department, Milwaukee, WI 53217-3985. Offers piano (MM). Part-time programs available. *Degree requirements:* For master's, comprehensive exam, recital permission audition. *Entrance requirements:* For master's, placement test in music theory and music history, 3 letters of recommendation, audition. Electronic applications accepted.

Carleton University, Faculty of Graduate Studies, Faculty of Arts and Social Sciences, School for Studies in Art and Culture, Program in Music and Culture, Ottawa, ON K1S 5B6, Canada. Offers MA.

Carnegie Mellon University, College of Fine Arts, School of Music, Pittsburgh, PA 15213-3891. Offers collaborative piano (MM); composition (MM); instrumental performance (MM); music and technology (MS); music education (MM); vocal performance (MM). *Accreditation:* NASM. Part-time programs available. *Degree requirements:* For master's, comprehensive exam, recital. *Entrance requirements:* For master's, audition. *Faculty research:* Computer music, music history.

Case Western Reserve University, School of Graduate Studies, Department of Music, Program in Historical Performance Practice, Cleveland, OH 44106. Offers MA, DMA, PhD. *Faculty:* 12 full-time (4 women). *Students:* 30 full-time (14 women), 1 (woman) part-time, 3 international. Average age 31. 33 applicants, 15% accepted, 5 enrolled. In 2014, 1 master's, 1 doctorate awarded. Terminal master's awarded for partial completion of doctoral program. *Degree requirements:* For master's, one foreign language, comprehensive exam (for some programs), juried lecture-recital, ensemble particpation; for doctorate, 2 foreign languages, comprehensive exam (for some programs), thesis/dissertation, ensemble partipation; juried lecture-recital. *Entrance requirements:* For master's and doctorate, GRE, Statement of purpose; two writing samples; CV; three letters of recommendation. Additional exam requirements/recommendations for international students: Required—TOEFL (minimum score 577 paper-based; 90 iBT); Recommended—IELTS (minimum score 7). *Application deadline:* For fall admission, 1/1 priority date for domestic students. Application fee: $50. Electronic applications accepted. *Financial support:* Fellowships, tuition waivers (full and partial), and stipends available. Financial award application deadline: 1/1; financial award applicants required to submit FAFSA. *Faculty research:* Early music, music history and historical performance practice. *Unit head:* David Ake, Chair, 216-368-2400, Fax: 216-368-6557, E-mail: info@music.case.edu. *Application contact:* Laura Stauffer, Admissions, 216-368-2400, Fax: 216-368-6557, E-mail: info@music.case.edu.
Website: http://music.case.edu/

Case Western Reserve University, School of Graduate Studies, Department of Music, Program in Music History, Cleveland, OH 44106. Offers historical musicology (PhD); music history (MA). *Unit head:* David Ake, Chair, 216-368-2400, Fax: 216-368-6557, E-mail: info@music.case.edu. *Application contact:* Laura Stauffer, Admissions, 216-368-2400, Fax: 216-368-6557, E-mail: info@music.case.edu.

The Catholic University of America, The Benjamin T. Rome School of Music, Washington, DC 20064. Offers MA, MM, MMSM, DMA, PhD, Certificate. *Accreditation:* NASM. Part-time programs available. *Faculty:* 19 full-time (4 women), 49 part-time/adjunct (21 women). *Students:* 32 full-time (18 women), 86 part-time (42 women); includes 26 minority (9 Black or African American, non-Hispanic/Latino; 13 Asian, non-Hispanic/Latino; 3 Hispanic/Latino; 1 Two or more races, non-Hispanic/Latino), 26 international. Average age 34. 83 applicants, 72% accepted, 28 enrolled. In 2014, 5

master's, 12 doctorates awarded. *Degree requirements:* For master's, comprehensive exam (for some programs), thesis (for some programs); for doctorate, comprehensive exam (for some programs), thesis/dissertation (for some programs), minimum GPA of 3.0, qualifying exam. *Entrance requirements:* For master's, theory placement test, 2 letters of recommendation, minimum undergraduate B average, BA in music, demonstration of performance proficiency; for doctorate, statement of purpose, official copies of academic transcripts, 4 letters of recommendation, audition/interview. Additional exam requirements/recommendations for international students: Required—TOEFL (minimum score 580 paper-based). *Application deadline:* For fall admission, 7/15 priority date for domestic students, 7/1 for international students; for spring admission, 11/15 priority date for domestic students, 11/1 for international students. Applications are processed on a rolling basis. Application fee: $55. Electronic applications accepted. *Expenses: Tuition:* Full-time $40,200; part-time $1600 per credit hour. *Required fees:* $400; $195 per semester. One-time fee: $425. *Financial support:* Fellowships, research assistantships, teaching assistantships, Federal Work-Study, scholarships/grants, tuition waivers (full and partial), and unspecified assistantships available. Financial award application deadline: 2/1; financial award applicants required to submit FAFSA. *Faculty research:* Composition, sacred music, orchestral instruments, piano, voice, music history and theory. *Unit head:* Dr. Grayson Wagstaff, Dean, 202-319-5417, Fax: 202-319-6280, E-mail: cua-music@cua.edu. *Application contact:* Director of Graduate Admissions, 202-319-5057, Fax: 202-319-6533, E-mail: cua-admissions@cua.edu.
Website: http://music.cua.edu/

Central Michigan University, College of Graduate Studies, College of Communication and Fine Arts, School of Music, Mount Pleasant, MI 48859. Offers composition (MM); conducting (MM); music education (MM); performance (MM). *Accreditation:* NASM. Part-time programs available. *Degree requirements:* For master's, thesis or alternative. Electronic applications accepted. *Faculty research:* Music education, music composition, conducting, music performance.

Central Washington University, Graduate Studies and Research, College of Arts and Humanities, Department of Music, Ellensburg, WA 98926. Offers MM. *Accreditation:* NASM. *Degree requirements:* For master's, thesis or alternative. *Entrance requirements:* For master's, minimum GPA of 3.0. Additional exam requirements/recommendations for international students: Required—TOEFL (minimum score 550 paper-based; 79 iBT) or IELTS (minimum score 6.5). Electronic applications accepted.

Charlotte Christian College and Theological Seminary, Graduate Program, Charlotte, NC 28205. Offers urban Christian ministry (MA), including church planting, multi-cultural studies, sacred music, youth ministry. Part-time and evening/weekend programs available. *Faculty:* 5 full-time (1 woman), 9 part-time/adjunct (2 women). *Students:* 2 full-time (1 woman), 25 part-time (15 women); includes 18 minority (17 Black or African American, non-Hispanic/Latino; 1 Hispanic/Latino), 2 international. Average age 47. 2 applicants, 100% accepted, 2 enrolled. In 2014, 2 master's awarded. *Degree requirements:* For master's, thesis. *Entrance requirements:* For master's, MAT, writing sample/essay. Additional exam requirements/recommendations for international students: Required—TOEFL, IELTS. *Application deadline:* For fall admission, 7/24 for domestic students, 7/18 for international students; for spring admission, 12/11 for domestic students, 12/5 for international students; for summer admission, 4/18 for domestic and international students. Application fee: $50 ($140 for international students). Electronic applications accepted. *Expenses:* Expenses: 1 course: $1,200; 2 courses: $2,300; 3 courses: $3,300; 4 courses $3,900. *Financial support:* In 2014–15, 5 students received support. Federal Work-Study and scholarships/grants available. Financial award application deadline: 4/1; financial award applicants required to submit FAFSA. *Unit head:* Anne Witt, Registrar/Director of International Students, 704-344-6882 Ext. 103, Fax: 704-334-6885, E-mail: abwitt@charlottechristian.edu. *Application contact:* Constance Hemphill, Director of Admissions, 704-334-6882 Ext. 115, Fax: 704-334-6885, E-mail: chemphill@charlottechristian.edu.
Website: http://www.charlottechristian.edu

City College of the City University of New York, Graduate School, College of Liberal Arts and Science, Division of the Humanities and Arts, Department of Music, New York, NY 10031-9198. Offers MA. Part-time programs available. *Degree requirements:* For master's, one foreign language, thesis. *Entrance requirements:* For master's, minimum GPA of 3.0, portfolio (composition), writing samples (history and theory), audition (performance). Additional exam requirements/recommendations for international students: Required—TOEFL (minimum score 575 paper-based; 90 iBT). Electronic applications accepted. *Faculty research:* Tonal theory, American music, musicology, atonal theory, performance.

Claremont Graduate University, Graduate Programs, School of Arts and Humanities, Department of Music, Claremont, CA 91711-6160. Offers church music (MA, DCM); composition (MA, DMA); historical performance practices (MA, DMA); musicology (MA, PhD); performance (MA, DMA); MBA/PhD. Part-time programs available. *Faculty:* 3 full-time (1 woman). *Students:* 37 full-time (18 women), 19 part-time (7 women); includes 16 minority (1 Black or African American, non-Hispanic/Latino; 8 Asian, non-Hispanic/Latino; 7 Hispanic/Latino), 12 international. Average age 36. In 2014, 4 master's, 4 doctorates awarded. Terminal master's awarded for partial completion of doctoral program. *Degree requirements:* For master's, one foreign language, comprehensive exam, thesis (for some programs), oral and written qualifying exams, recitals; for doctorate, 2 foreign languages, comprehensive exam, thesis/dissertation (for some programs), oral and written qualifying exams, oral defense of dissertation, recitals. *Entrance requirements:* For master's and doctorate, GRE General Test, auditions, compositions, or papers. Additional exam requirements/recommendations for international students: Required—TOEFL (minimum score 550 paper-based; 80 iBT). *Application deadline:* For fall admission, 2/1 priority date for domestic and international students. Applications are processed on a rolling basis. Application fee: $80. Electronic applications accepted. *Expenses: Tuition:* Full-time $41,784; part-time $1741 per credit. *Required fees:* $600; $300 per semester. *Financial support:* Fellowships, research assistantships, teaching assistantships, Federal Work-Study, institutionally sponsored loans, and scholarships/grants available. Support available to part-time students. Financial award application deadline: 2/15; financial award applicants required to submit FAFSA. *Unit head:* Robert Zappulla, Chair, 909-607-9664, Fax: 909-607-3694, E-mail: robert.zappulla@cgu.edu. *Application contact:* Erma Cross, Admissions and Alumni Coordinator, 909-607-9843, E-mail: erminia.cross@cgu.edu.
Website: http://www.cgu.edu/pages/368.asp

Cleveland Institute of Music, Graduate Programs, Cleveland, OH 44106-1776. Offers MM, DMA, AD, CPS. DMA and MM programs offered jointly with Case Western Reserve University. *Accreditation:* NASM (one or more programs are accredited). *Degree requirements:* For master's, comprehensive exam, recital; for doctorate, comprehensive exam, thesis/dissertation (for some programs), final projects; for other advanced degree, recital. *Entrance requirements:* For master's, theory placement tests, audition; for doctorate, diagnostic exams, theory placement test, audition; for other advanced degree, audition. Additional exam requirements/recommendations for international students: Required—TOEFL (minimum score 550 paper-based). Electronic applications accepted.

Cleveland State University, College of Graduate Studies, College of Liberal Arts and Social Sciences, Department of Music, Cleveland, OH 44115. Offers composition (MM); music education (MM); performance (MM). *Accreditation:* NASM. Part-time and evening/weekend programs available. *Faculty:* 9 full-time (2 women), 19 part-time/adjunct (6 women). *Students:* 25 full-time (11 women), 5 part-time (4 women); includes 7 minority (2 Black or African American, non-Hispanic/Latino; 3 Asian, non-Hispanic/Latino; 1 Hispanic/Latino; 1 Two or more races, non-Hispanic/Latino), 3 international. Average age 25. 25 applicants, 88% accepted, 15 enrolled. In 2014, 9 master's awarded. *Degree requirements:* For master's, comprehensive exam, thesis or recital. *Entrance requirements:* For master's, departmental assessment in music history, minimum undergraduate GPA of 2.75, audition on primary instrument, or submission of composition portfolio or written samples for Master in Music Education. Additional exam requirements/recommendations for international students: Required—TOEFL (minimum score 525 paper-based). *Application deadline:* For fall admission, 3/15 priority date for domestic students, 5/15 for international students. Applications are processed on a rolling basis. Application fee: $30. *Expenses:* Tuition, state resident: full-time $9566; part-time $531 per credit hour. Tuition, nonresident: full-time $17,980; part-time $999 per credit hour. *Required fees:* $25 per semester. Tuition and fees vary according to degree level and program. *Financial support:* In 2014–15, 14 students received support, including 14 research assistantships with full tuition reimbursements available (averaging $3,612 per year); tuition waivers (partial) and unspecified assistantships also available. Financial award application deadline: 3/15. *Faculty research:* Ethnomusicology, electronic music, interdisciplinary studies, music education, music therapy. *Total annual research expenditures:* $162,000. *Unit head:* Dr. Leo Jeffres, Chairperson, 216-687-2302, Fax: 216-687-9279, E-mail: l.jeffres@csuohio.edu. *Application contact:* Dr. Victor Liva, Coordinator of Graduate Studies and Admission, 216-687-6931, Fax: 216-687-9279, E-mail: v.liva@csuohio.edu.
Website: http://www.csuohio.edu/music/

The College of Saint Rose, Graduate Studies, School of Arts and Humanities, Music Department, Program in Music, Albany, NY 12203-1419. Offers MA. *Accreditation:* NASM. *Degree requirements:* For master's, final project. *Entrance requirements:* For master's, audition, minimum undergraduate GPA of 3.0. Additional exam requirements/recommendations for international students: Required—TOEFL (minimum score 550 paper-based). Electronic applications accepted.

Colorado State University, Graduate School, College of Liberal Arts, Department of Music, Theater, and Dance, Fort Collins, CO 80523-1779. Offers music (MM). *Accreditation:* NASM. Part-time programs available. *Faculty:* 36 full-time (11 women). *Students:* 63 full-time (44 women), 93 part-time (73 women); includes 16 minority (1 American Indian or Alaska Native, non-Hispanic/Latino; 5 Asian, non-Hispanic/Latino; 9 Hispanic/Latino; 1 Two or more races, non-Hispanic/Latino), 13 international. Average age 31. 93 applicants, 66% accepted, 41 enrolled. In 2014, 60 master's awarded. *Degree requirements:* For master's, variable foreign language requirement, comprehensive exam (for some programs), thesis (for some programs), 2 recitals, project. *Entrance requirements:* For master's, minimum GPA of 3.0, audition, bachelor's degree, 3 letters of recommendation, transcripts, statement of purpose. Additional exam requirements/recommendations for international students: Required—TOEFL (minimum score 550 paper-based; 80 iBT). *Application deadline:* For fall admission, 2/15 priority date for domestic students; for spring admission, 11/15 priority date for domestic students. Applications are processed on a rolling basis. Application fee: $50. Electronic applications accepted. *Expenses:* Tuition, state resident: full-time $9348; part-time $519 per credit. Tuition, nonresident: full-time $22,916; part-time $1273 per credit. *Required fees:* $1584. *Financial support:* In 2014–15, 31 students received support, including 31 teaching assistantships with full and partial tuition reimbursements available (averaging $7,931 per year); career-related internships or fieldwork, Federal Work-Study, scholarships/grants, traineeships, and unspecified assistantships also available. Financial award application deadline: 3/1; financial award applicants required to submit FAFSA. *Faculty research:* Neurobiology, musicology, music literacy, music learning, music therapy. *Total annual research expenditures:* $52,447. *Unit head:* Price Johnston, Interim Director, 970-491-7792, E-mail: price.johnston@colostate.edu. *Application contact:* Dr. Graeme Murray Oliver, Graduate Coordinator, 970-491-5193, Fax: 970-491-7541, E-mail: murray.oliver@colostate.edu.
Website: http://sota.colostate.edu/

Columbia College Chicago, Graduate School, MFA Program in Music Composition for the Screen, Chicago, IL 60605-1996. Offers MFA. *Faculty:* 3 full-time (0 women). *Students:* 23 full-time (9 women); includes 6 minority (1 Black or African American, non-Hispanic/Latino; 1 Asian, non-Hispanic/Latino; 2 Hispanic/Latino; 2 Two or more races, non-Hispanic/Latino), 4 international. Average age 26. *Entrance requirements:* For master's, self-assessment essay, work samples, resume, letters of recommendation. Additional exam requirements/recommendations for international students: Required—TOEFL (minimum score 600 paper-based; 100 iBT). *Application deadline:* For fall admission, 1/15 for domestic and international students. Application fee: $55 ($100 for international students). Electronic applications accepted. *Expenses:* Expenses: $1,033 per credit hour; fees: $352 per semester. *Financial support:* In 2014–15, 14 students received support, including 8 fellowships, 6 research assistantships; career-related internships or fieldwork, Federal Work-Study, scholarships/grants, and unspecified assistantships also available. Support available to part-time students. *Unit head:* Kubilay Uner, Program Director, 312-369-6300, E-mail: kuner@colum.edu. *Application contact:* Kara Leffler, Associate Director of Graduate Admissions, 312-369-7262, Fax: 312-369-8024, E-mail: kleffler@colum.edu.
Website: http://www.colum.edu/Admissions/Graduate/programs/writing-music-for-film/index.php

Columbia University, Graduate School of Arts and Sciences, New York, NY 10027. Offers African-American studies (MA); American studies (MA); anthropology (MA, PhD); art history and archaeology (MA, PhD); astronomy (PhD); biological sciences (PhD); biotechnology (MA); chemical physics (PhD); chemistry (PhD); classical studies (MA, PhD); classics (MA, PhD); climate and society (MA); earth and environmental sciences (PhD); East Asia: regional studies (MA); East Asian languages and cultures (MA, PhD); ecology, evolution and environmental biology (MA), including conservation biology; ecology, evolution, and environmental biology (PhD), including ecology and evolutionary biology, evolutionary primatology; economics (PhD); English and comparative literature (MA, PhD); French and Romance philology (MA, PhD); Germanic languages (MA, PhD); global French studies (MA); Hispanic cultural studies (MA); history (PhD); history and literature (MA); human rights studies (MA); Islamic studies (MA); Italian (MA, PhD); Japanese pedagogy (MA); Jewish studies (MA); Latin America and the Caribbean: regional studies (MA); Latin American and Iberian cultures (PhD); mathematics (MA, PhD), including finance (MA); medieval and Renaissance studies (MA); Middle Eastern, South Asian, and African studies (MA, PhD); modern art: critical and curatorial studies (MA); modern European studies (MA); museum anthropology (MA); music (DMA, PhD); oral history (MA); philosophical foundations of physics (MA); philosophy (MA, PhD); physics (PhD); political science (MA, PhD); psychology (PhD); quantitative methods in the social sciences (MA); religion (MA, PhD); Russia, Eurasia and East Europe: regional studies (MA); Russian translation (MA); Slavic cultures (MA); Slavic languages (MA, PhD); sociology (MA, PhD); South Asian studies (MA); statistics (MA, PhD); theatre (PhD); JD/PhD; MA/MS; MD/PhD; MPA/MA. Dual-degree programs require admission

to both Graduate School of Arts and Sciences and another Columbia school. Part-time and evening/weekend programs available. Terminal master's awarded for partial completion of doctoral program. *Degree requirements:* For master's, thesis (for some programs); for doctorate, comprehensive exam, thesis/dissertation. *Entrance requirements:* For master's and doctorate, GRE General Test, GRE Subject Test (for some programs). Electronic applications accepted. *Faculty research:* Humanities, natural sciences, social sciences.

Columbus State University, Graduate Studies, College of the Arts, Schwob School of Music, Columbus, GA 31907-5645. Offers music (Artist Diploma); music education (MM); music performance (MM). *Accreditation:* NASM; NCATE (one or more programs are accredited). Part-time and evening/weekend programs available. *Faculty:* 25 full-time (11 women), 3 part-time/adjunct (0 women). *Students:* 37 full-time (21 women), 6 part-time (2 women); includes 10 minority (1 Black or African American, non-Hispanic/Latino; 2 Asian, non-Hispanic/Latino; 5 Hispanic/Latino; 2 Two or more races, non-Hispanic/Latino), 15 international. Average age 25. 59 applicants, 49% accepted, 20 enrolled. In 2014, 11 master's, 7 Artist Diplomas awarded. *Degree requirements:* For master's, exit exam. *Entrance requirements:* For master's, GRE General Test, audition, letters of recommendation, minimum undergraduate GPA of 2.5. Additional exam requirements/recommendations for international students: Required—TOEFL (minimum score 550 paper-based; 79 iBT). *Application deadline:* For fall admission, 6/30 for domestic students, 5/1 for international students; for spring admission, 11/1 for domestic and international students; for summer admission, 3/1 for domestic and international students. Applications are processed on a rolling basis. Application fee: $40. Electronic applications accepted. *Financial support:* In 2014–15, 41 students received support, including 27 research assistantships with partial tuition reimbursements available (averaging $3,000 per year); career-related internships or fieldwork, Federal Work-Study, institutionally sponsored loans, scholarships/grants, tuition waivers (full), and unspecified assistantships also available. Support available to part-time students. Financial award application deadline: 5/1; financial award applicants required to submit FAFSA. *Unit head:* Dr. Edwin Scott Harris, Director, 706-507-8419, E-mail: harris_scott@columbusstate.edu. *Application contact:* Kristin Williams, Director of International and Graduate Recruitment, 706-507-8848, Fax: 706-568-5091, E-mail: williams_kristin@columbusstate.edu.
Website: http://music.columbusstate.edu/

Concordia University, School of Graduate Studies, Faculty of Fine Arts, Department of Music, Montréal, QC H3G 1M8, Canada. Offers advanced music performance studies (Diploma). *Degree requirements:* For Diploma, performance, 2 recitals.

Concordia University Chicago, College of Graduate and Innovative Programs, Program in Church Music, River Forest, IL 60305-1499. Offers MCM. *Accreditation:* NASM. Part-time programs available. *Degree requirements:* For master's, composition, recital, or thesis. *Entrance requirements:* For master's, minimum GPA of 2.9, audition. Additional exam requirements/recommendations for international students: Required—TOEFL (minimum score 550 paper-based). Electronic applications accepted. *Faculty research:* Twentieth-century sacred choral music, liturgical context of sacred music after the Council of Trent, dance and music of J.S. Bach.

Concordia University Chicago, College of Graduate and Innovative Programs, Program in Music, River Forest, IL 60305-1499. Offers MA. Part-time programs available. *Degree requirements:* For master's, composition, recital, or thesis. *Entrance requirements:* For master's, minimum GPA of 2.9, audition. Additional exam requirements/recommendations for international students: Required—TOEFL (minimum score 550 paper-based). Electronic applications accepted.

Concordia University Wisconsin, Graduate Programs, School of Arts and Sciences, Program in Church Music, Mequon, WI 53097-2402. Offers MCM. *Degree requirements:* For master's, comprehensive exam, thesis or alternative. *Entrance requirements:* For master's, minimum GPA of 3.0. Additional exam requirements/recommendations for international students: Required—TOEFL.

Conservatorio de Musica de Puerto Rico, Program in Musical Performance, San Juan, PR 00907. Offers guitar (Diploma); orchestral instruments (Diploma); piano (Diploma); vocal performance (Diploma). *Accreditation:* NASM. *Entrance requirements:* For degree, 3 letters of recommendation, audition, degree in music, minimum GPA of 2.5.

Converse College, School of Education and Graduate Studies, Petrie School of Music, Spartanburg, SC 29302-0006. Offers music education (M Mus); performance (M Mus). *Accreditation:* NASM. Part-time and evening/weekend programs available. *Degree requirements:* For master's, variable foreign language requirement, comprehensive exam, thesis (for some programs), recitals. *Entrance requirements:* For master's, NTE (music education), audition, 3 letters of recommendation. Additional exam requirements/recommendations for international students: Required—TOEFL. Electronic applications accepted. *Faculty research:* Chamber music, opera, performance, composition, recording.

Cornell University, Graduate School, Graduate Fields of Arts and Sciences, Field of Music, Ithaca, NY 14853-0001. Offers composition (DMA); musicology (PhD); performance practice (DMA); theory of music (MA). *Degree requirements:* For doctorate, comprehensive exam, thesis/dissertation, 1 foreign language (DMA), 2 foreign languages (PhD). *Entrance requirements:* For doctorate, GRE General Test, 2 music papers (PhD); 2 recent scores with recording and 1 music paper (DMA in composition); 1 music paper, recording and audition (DMA in performance practice). Additional exam requirements/recommendations for international students: Required—TOEFL (minimum score 600 paper-based; 77 iBT). Electronic applications accepted. *Faculty research:* Music history, music theory, performance practice, ethnomusicology, composition.

Curtis Institute of Music, Graduate Studies, Philadelphia, PA 19103-6107. Offers opera (MM). *Accreditation:* NASM. *Entrance requirements:* For master's, audition or performance in 2 or more principal roles or 6 major scenes.

Dalhousie University, Faculty of Arts and Social Science, Department of Musicology, Halifax, NS B3H 4R2, Canada. Offers MA. *Entrance requirements:* Additional exam requirements/recommendations for international students: Required—TOEFL, IELTS, CANTEST, CAEL, or Michigan English Language Assessment Battery. Electronic applications accepted.

Dallas Baptist University, Gary Cook School of Leadership, Program in Worship Leadership, Dallas, TX 75211-9299. Offers communication ministry (MA); worship leadership (MA); worship ministry (MA); worship music (MA); MA/MA. Part-time and evening/weekend programs available. *Entrance requirements:* For master's, minimum GPA of 3.0. Additional exam requirements/recommendations for international students: Required—TOEFL, IELTS. *Expenses: Tuition:* Full-time $14,130; part-time $785 per credit hour. *Required fees:* $200 per semester. Tuition and fees vary according to course level and course load.

Dartmouth College, Arts and Sciences Graduate Programs, Department of Music, Hanover, NH 03755. Offers electro-acoustic music (AM). *Faculty:* 9 full-time (1 woman), 27 part-time/adjunct (8 women). *Students:* 6 full-time (3 women); includes 1 minority (Asian, non-Hispanic/Latino), 1 international. Average age 24. 26 applicants, 12% accepted, 3 enrolled. In 2014, 3 master's awarded. *Degree requirements:* For master's, thesis or alternative. *Entrance requirements:* Additional exam requirements/recommendations for international students: Required—TOEFL. *Application deadline:* For fall admission, 2/1 priority date for domestic students. Application fee: $35. *Financial support:* Fellowships with full tuition reimbursements, career-related internships or fieldwork, institutionally sponsored loans, and tuition waivers (full) available. *Faculty research:* Composition and design of computer music software and related topics. *Unit head:* Michael Casey, Director, Graduate Program in Electro-Acoustic Music, 603-646-3531, Fax: 603-646-2551. *Application contact:* Catherine La Touche, Administrative Assistant, 603-646-2520, Fax: 603-646-2551.
Website: http://eamusic.dartmouth.edu/

DePaul University, School of Music, Chicago, IL 60614. Offers composition (MM); jazz studies (MM); music education (MM); music performance (MM); performance (Certificate). *Accreditation:* NASM (one or more programs are accredited). Part-time and evening/weekend programs available. *Degree requirements:* For master's, comprehensive exam. *Entrance requirements:* For master's, bachelor's degree in music or related field, minimum GPA of 3.0, auditions (performance), scores (composition); for Certificate, master's degree in performance or related field, auditions (for performance majors). Additional exam requirements/recommendations for international students: Required—TOEFL (minimum score 550 paper-based; 80 iBT). Electronic applications accepted. *Expenses:* Contact institution.

Dominican University of California, School of Arts, Humanities and Social Sciences, Humanities Program, San Rafael, CA 94901-2298. Offers applied music (MA); art history (MA); creative writing (MA); history (MA); literature (MA); philosophy (MA); political theory (MA); religion (MA); women and gender studies (MA). Part-time programs available. *Faculty:* 11 full-time (5 women), 5 part-time/adjunct (2 women). *Students:* 2 full-time (1 woman), 25 part-time (16 women); includes 7 minority (1 Black or African American, non-Hispanic/Latino; 1 American Indian or Alaska Native, non-Hispanic/Latino; 3 Hispanic/Latino; 2 Two or more races, non-Hispanic/Latino). Average age 46. 12 applicants, 83% accepted, 7 enrolled. *Degree requirements:* For master's, thesis or alternative. *Entrance requirements:* For master's, minimum GPA of 3.0, interview. Additional exam requirements/recommendations for international students: Required—TOEFL (minimum score 550 paper-based; 80 iBT), IELTS (minimum score 6.5). *Application deadline:* For fall admission, 5/15 priority date for domestic and international students; for spring admission, 11/15 priority date for domestic and international students. Applications are processed on a rolling basis. Electronic applications accepted. Application fee is waived when completed online. *Expenses:* Expenses: $935 per unit. *Financial support:* Scholarships/grants available. Support available to part-time students. Financial award application deadline: 3/2; financial award applicants required to submit FAFSA. *Unit head:* Dr. Laura Stivers, Acting Dean, 415-458-3734, E-mail: laura.stivers@dominican.edu. *Application contact:* Ryan Purtill, Director, 415-458-3748, Fax: 415-485-3214, E-mail: ryan.purtill@dominican.edu.
Website: http://www.dominican.edu/academics/ahss/graduate-program/index_html

Duke University, Graduate School, Department of Music, Durham, NC 27708. Offers music composition (PhD); musicology (PhD); performance practice (PhD). Part-time programs available. Terminal master's awarded for partial completion of doctoral program. *Degree requirements:* For doctorate, 3 foreign languages, thesis/dissertation. *Entrance requirements:* For doctorate, GRE General Test, paper on musical topic (for musicology); samples of compositions (for music composition). Additional exam requirements/recommendations for international students: Required—TOEFL (minimum score 577 paper-based; 90 iBT) or IELTS (minimum score 7). Electronic applications accepted. *Expenses: Tuition:* Full-time $45,760; part-time $2765 per credit. *Required fees:* $978. Full-time tuition and fees vary according to program.

Duquesne University, Mary Pappert School of Music, Pittsburgh, PA 15282-0001. Offers music education (MM). *Accreditation:* NASM. Part-time programs available. *Faculty:* 27 full-time (8 women), 82 part-time/adjunct (26 women). *Students:* 56 full-time (27 women), 16 part-time (9 women); includes 4 minority (1 Asian, non-Hispanic/Latino; 3 Hispanic/Latino), 21 international. Average age 27. 136 applicants, 52% accepted, 33 enrolled. In 2014, 39 master's awarded. *Degree requirements:* For master's, comprehensive exam, thesis (for some programs), recital (music performance); for AD, recital. *Entrance requirements:* For master's, audition, minimum undergraduate QPA of 3.0 in music, portfolio of original compositions, or music education experience; for AD, audition. Additional exam requirements/recommendations for international students: Required—TOEFL (minimum score 550 paper-based; 80 iBT). *Application deadline:* For fall admission, 7/1 priority date for domestic and international students; for spring admission, 12/1 priority date for domestic and international students; for summer admission, 6/1 priority date for domestic students, 5/1 priority date for international students. Applications are processed on a rolling basis. Application fee: $50. Electronic applications accepted. *Expenses:* Expenses: $1,267 per credit; fees: $100 per credit. *Financial support:* In 2014–15, 54 students received support, including 54 fellowships with full and partial tuition reimbursements available (averaging $15,818 per year); scholarships/grants, tuition waivers (full and partial), and unspecified assistantships also available. Financial award application deadline: 4/1. *Faculty research:* Performance; computer-assisted instruction in music at elementary and secondary levels; electronic music; contemporary music, theory, and analysis; development of online graduate music courses; interdisciplinary endeavors in music and philosophy. *Unit head:* Dr. Seth Beckman, Dean, 412-396-6082, Fax: 412-396-1524, E-mail: beckmans@duq.edu. *Application contact:* Peggy Eiseman, Administrative Assistant of Admissions, 412-396-5064, Fax: 412-396-5719, E-mail: eiseman@duq.edu.
Website: http://www.duq.edu/academics/schools/music

East Carolina University, Graduate School, College of Fine Arts and Communication, School of Music, Greenville, NC 27858-4353. Offers advanced performance studies (Certificate); music education (MM); music therapy (MM); performance (MM), including accompanying, choral conducting, instrumental conducting, jazz studies, organ, percussion, piano, piano pedagogy, sacred music, string (Suzuki) pedagogy, strings, vocal pedagogy, voice, woodwind specialist; Suzuki pedagogy (Certificate); theory and composition (MM). *Accreditation:* NASM. Part-time programs available. *Degree requirements:* For master's, comprehensive exam, thesis optional. *Entrance requirements:* For master's, GRE General Test or MAT. Additional exam requirements/recommendations for international students: Required—TOEFL. *Expenses:* Tuition, state resident: full-time $4223. Tuition, nonresident: full-time $16,540. *Required fees:* $2184.

East Carolina University, Graduate School, Thomas Harriot College of Arts and Sciences, Department of English, Greenville, NC 27858-4353. Offers creative writing (MA); English studies (MA); linguistics (MA); literature (MA); multicultural and transnational literatures (MA, Certificate); rhetoric and composition (MA); rhetoric, writing, and professional communication (PhD); teaching English in the two-year college (Certificate); teaching English to speakers of other languages (MA, Certificate); technical and professional communication (MA). Part-time and evening/weekend programs available. *Degree requirements:* For master's, one foreign language, comprehensive exam, thesis optional. *Entrance requirements:* For master's, GRE General Test, MAT (for MA Ed). Additional exam requirements/recommendations for international students: Required—TOEFL. *Expenses:* Tuition, state resident: full-time $4223. Tuition, nonresident: full-time $16,540. *Required fees:* $2184.

Eastern Illinois University, Graduate School, College of Arts and Humanities, Department of Music, Charleston, IL 61920. Offers MA. *Accreditation:* NASM. Part-time and evening/weekend programs available. Postbaccalaureate distance learning degree programs offered (minimal on-campus study). *Faculty:* 17. *Students:* 12 full-time (6 women), 8 part-time (6 women); includes 3 minority (1 Black or African American, non-Hispanic/Latino; 1 Asian, non-Hispanic/Latino; 1 Hispanic/Latino), 3 international. Average age 26. 16 applicants, 88% accepted, 5 enrolled. In 2014, 6 master's awarded. *Degree requirements:* For master's, comprehensive exam (for some programs), thesis (for some programs). *Entrance requirements:* For master's, Submit a personal statement, resume, and three letters of recommendation. Additional exam requirements/recommendations for international students: Required—TOEFL (minimum score 500 paper-based; 61 iBT), IELTS (minimum score 6). *Application deadline:* For fall admission, 5/15 for domestic and international students; for spring admission, 10/15 for domestic and international students. Applications are processed on a rolling basis. Application fee: $30. Electronic applications accepted. *Expenses:* Tuition, state resident: full-time $3113; part-time $283 per credit hour. Tuition, nonresident: full-time $7469; part-time $679 per credit hour. *Required fees:* $2287; $96 per credit hour. Tuition and fees vary according to course load. *Financial support:* In 2014–15, 13 students received support, including 1 teaching assistantship with full tuition reimbursement available (averaging $7,830 per year); career-related internships or fieldwork, Federal Work-Study, and unspecified assistantships also available. Support available to part-time students. Financial award application deadline: 3/1; financial award applicants required to submit FAFSA. *Unit head:* Jerry Daniels, Department Chair, 217-581-3010, Fax: 217-581-7137, E-mail: jldaniels@eiu.edu. *Application contact:* Marilyn Coles, Graduate Coordinator, 217-581-2723, Fax: 217-581-7137, E-mail: mjcoles@eiu.edu. Website: http://www.eiu.edu/musicgrad/

Eastern Kentucky University, The Graduate School, College of Arts and Sciences, Department of Music, Richmond, KY 40475-3102. Offers choral conducting (MM); performance (MM); theory/composition (MM). *Accreditation:* NASM. Part-time programs available. *Degree requirements:* For master's, thesis optional. *Entrance requirements:* For master's, GRE General Test, minimum GPA of 2.5. *Faculty research:* Technology.

Eastern Michigan University, Graduate School, College of Arts and Sciences, Department of Music and Dance, Ypsilanti, MI 48197. Offers MM. *Accreditation:* NASM. Part-time and evening/weekend programs available. Postbaccalaureate distance learning degree programs offered (minimal on-campus study). *Faculty:* 25 full-time (12 women). *Students:* 5 full-time (2 women), 11 part-time (7 women), 3 international. Average age 29. 17 applicants, 71% accepted, 7 enrolled. In 2014, 12 master's awarded. *Entrance requirements:* Additional exam requirements/recommendations for international students: Required—TOEFL. *Application deadline:* Applications are processed on a rolling basis. Application fee: $45. *Financial support:* Fellowships, research assistantships with full tuition reimbursements, teaching assistantships with full tuition reimbursements, career-related internships or fieldwork, Federal Work-Study, institutionally sponsored loans, scholarships/grants, tuition waivers (partial), and unspecified assistantships available. Support available to part-time students. Financial award applicants required to submit FAFSA. *Unit head:* Dr. Diane Winder, Department Head, 734-487-4380, Fax: 734-487-6939, E-mail: dwinder@emich.edu. *Application contact:* Dr. David Pierce, Coordinator of Music Advising, 734-487-4380, Fax: 734-487-6939, E-mail: david.pierce@emich.edu. Website: http://www.emich.edu/musicdance

Eastern Washington University, Graduate Studies, College of Arts, Letters and Education, Department of Music, Cheney, WA 99004-2431. Offers composition (MA); general (MA); instrumental/vocal performance (MA); jazz pedagogy (MA); music education (MA). *Accreditation:* NASM. Part-time programs available. *Degree requirements:* For master's, comprehensive exam, thesis or alternative. *Entrance requirements:* For master's, GRE General Test, minimum GPA of 3.0.

Emory University, Laney Graduate School, Department of Music, Atlanta, GA 30322-1100. Offers choral conducting (MM, MSM); organ performance (MM, MSM). Terminal master's awarded for partial completion of doctoral program. *Degree requirements:* For master's, comprehensive exam, recital or worship service. *Entrance requirements:* For master's, GRE General Test, audition, interview. Additional exam requirements/recommendations for international students: Required—TOEFL. Electronic applications accepted. *Faculty research:* Nineteenth century criticism, Heinrich Schenker, Bach aria styles, contemporary passion music, Louis Andriessen, cross-cultural research, organ performance.

Emporia State University, Department of Music, Emporia, KS 66801-5415. Offers MM. *Accreditation:* NASM. Part-time programs available. *Faculty:* 15 full-time (5 women), 3 part-time/adjunct (all women). *Students:* 7 full-time (3 women), 13 part-time (10 women); includes 1 minority (Hispanic/Latino), 9 international. 2 applicants, 100% accepted, 2 enrolled. In 2014, 10 master's awarded. *Degree requirements:* For master's, comprehensive exam or thesis. *Entrance requirements:* For master's, music qualifying exam, appropriate undergraduate degree. Additional exam requirements/recommendations for international students: Required—TOEFL (minimum score 520 paper-based; 68 iBT). *Application deadline:* For fall admission, 8/15 priority date for domestic students. Applications are processed on a rolling basis. Application fee: $30 ($75 for international students). Electronic applications accepted. *Expenses:* Tuition, state resident: part-time $227 per credit hour. Tuition, nonresident: part-time $706 per credit hour. *Required fees:* $75 per credit hour. Tuition and fees vary according to campus/location. *Financial support:* In 2014–15, 4 teaching assistantships with full tuition reimbursements (averaging $7,344 per year) were awarded; Federal Work-Study, institutionally sponsored loans, health care benefits, and unspecified assistantships also available. Financial award application deadline: 3/15; financial award applicants required to submit FAFSA. *Unit head:* Dr. Allan D. Comstock, Chair, 620-341-5431, E-mail: acomstoc@emporia.edu. *Application contact:* Dr. Andrew Houchins, Graduate Coordinator, 620-341-6089, E-mail: ahouchin@emporia.edu. Website: http://www.emporia.edu/music/

Evangel University, Department of Music, Springfield, MO 65802. Offers music education (MME); music performance (MM). *Accreditation:* NASM. Part-time programs available. *Faculty:* 4 full-time (1 woman), 2 part-time/adjunct (1 woman). *Students:* 1 full-time (0 women), 4 part-time (3 women). Average age 33. 1 applicant, 100% accepted, 1 enrolled. In 2014, 8 master's awarded. *Entrance requirements:* For master's, diagnostic exam, performance audition (MM), teaching certificate (MME). Additional exam requirements/recommendations for international students: Required—TOEFL (minimum score 550 paper-based). *Application deadline:* For fall admission, 7/15 priority date for domestic students, 8/1 for international students; for spring admission, 11/15 priority date for domestic students, 12/1 for international students. Applications are processed on a rolling basis. Application fee: $25. Electronic applications accepted. *Financial support:* In 2014–15, 1 student received support. Scholarships/grants and unspecified assistantships available. Support available to part-time students. Financial award application deadline: 4/1; financial award applicants required to submit FAFSA. *Unit head:* Dr. Greg Morris, Program Coordinator, 417-865-2811 Ext. 7326, Fax: 417-575-5484, E-mail: morrisg@evangel.edu. *Application contact:* Matt Petry, Admissions Representative, Graduate Studies, 417-865-2811 Ext. 7229, Fax: 417-575-5484, E-mail: petrym@evangel.edu. Website: http://www.evangel.edu/academics/graduate-studies/graduate-programs

Five Towns College, Graduate Programs, Dix Hills, NY 11746-6055. Offers childhood education (MS Ed); composition and arranging (DMA); jazz/commercial music (MM); music education (MM, DMA); music history and literature (DMA); music performance (DMA). Part-time programs available. *Faculty:* 12 full-time (3 women), 6 part-time/adjunct (0 women). *Students:* 22 full-time (7 women), 16 part-time (4 women); includes 6 minority (3 Black or African American, non-Hispanic/Latino; 1 Asian, non-Hispanic/Latino; 2 Hispanic/Latino), 7 international. *Degree requirements:* For master's, thesis, exams, major composition or capstone project, recital; for doctorate, comprehensive exam, thesis/dissertation, final oral exam. *Entrance requirements:* For master's, audition (for MM); New York state teaching certification (for MS Ed); personal statement, two letters of recommendation; for doctorate, 3 letters of recommendation, audition, essay. Additional exam requirements/recommendations for international students: Required—TOEFL (minimum score 520 paper-based; 85 iBT); Recommended—IELTS (minimum score 7). *Application deadline:* For fall admission, 9/1 for domestic and international students; for spring admission, 1/25 for domestic and international students. Applications are processed on a rolling basis. Application fee: $50. Electronic applications accepted. *Expenses:* Tuition: Full-time $11,250; part-time $625 per credit. *Required fees:* $900; $325 per term. *Financial support:* Fellowships with tuition reimbursements, teaching assistantships with tuition reimbursements, and tuition waivers (partial) available. Financial award applicants required to submit FAFSA. *Faculty research:* Teaching methods, teaching strategies and techniques, analysis of modern music, jazz. *Application contact:* Ronnie MacDonald, Director of Admissions, 631-656-2110, Fax: 631-656-2172, E-mail: admissions@ftc.edu.

Florida Atlantic University, College of Business, Program in Music Business Administration, Boca Raton, FL 33431-0991. Offers MS. *Expenses:* Tuition, state resident: full-time $7396; part-time $369.82 per credit hour. Tuition, nonresident: full-time $19,392; part-time $1024.81 per credit hour. Tuition and fees vary according to course load.

Florida Atlantic University, Dorothy F. Schmidt College of Arts and Letters, Department of English, Boca Raton, FL 33431-0991. Offers American literature (MA); British literature (MA); creative nonfiction (MFA); creative writing (MA); English (MAT); fiction (MFA); multicultural and world literacies (MA); poetry (MFA); rhetoric and composition (MA); science fiction and fantasy (MA). Part-time programs available. *Degree requirements:* For master's, one foreign language, thesis. *Entrance requirements:* For master's, GRE General Test, minimum GPA of 3.0, writing samples, 2 letters of recommendation. Additional exam requirements/recommendations for international students: Required—TOEFL (minimum score 500 paper-based; 61 iBT), IELTS (minimum score 6). Electronic applications accepted. *Expenses:* Tuition, state resident: full-time $7396; part-time $369.82 per credit hour. Tuition, nonresident: full-time $19,392; part-time $1024.81 per credit hour. Tuition and fees vary according to course load. *Faculty research:* African-American writers, critical theory, British-American, Asian-American.

Florida Atlantic University, Dorothy F. Schmidt College of Arts and Letters, Department of Music, Boca Raton, FL 33431-0991. Offers commercial music (MA); music history/literature (MA); performance (MA). *Accreditation:* NASM. Part-time programs available. *Degree requirements:* For master's, one foreign language, comprehensive exam, thesis (for some programs), lecture/recital or thesis. *Entrance requirements:* For master's, placement evaluations in music history and theory, audition, minimum GPA of 3.0 in last 60 hours of course work. Additional exam requirements/recommendations for international students: Required—TOEFL (minimum score 500 paper-based; 61 iBT), IELTS (minimum score 6). *Expenses:* Tuition, state resident: full-time $7396; part-time $369.82 per credit hour. Tuition, nonresident: full-time $19,392; part-time $1024.81 per credit hour. Tuition and fees vary according to course load. *Faculty research:* Classical guitar history and literature, women composers, Mozart opera, composition, performance.

Florida International University, College of Architecture and the Arts, School of Music, Miami, FL 33199. Offers music (MM); music education (MS). Part-time and evening/weekend programs available. *Degree requirements:* For master's, thesis (for some programs). *Entrance requirements:* For master's, GRE (depending on program), statement of intent; 2 letters of recommendation; audition, interview and/or writing sample (depending on the area). Additional exam requirements/recommendations for international students: Required—TOEFL (minimum score 550 paper-based; 80 iBT). Electronic applications accepted.

Florida State University, The Graduate School, College of Arts and Sciences, Department of English, Tallahassee, FL 32312. Offers creative writing (MFA); English (PhD), including creative writing, literature, rhetoric and composition; literature (MA); rhetoric and composition (MA). Part-time programs available. *Faculty:* 47 full-time (24 women), 2 part-time/adjunct (1 woman). *Students:* 142 full-time (80 women), 31 part-time (23 women); includes 44 minority (17 Black or African American, non-Hispanic/Latino; 1 American Indian or Alaska Native, non-Hispanic/Latino; 12 Asian, non-Hispanic/Latino; 5 Hispanic/Latino; 9 Two or more races, non-Hispanic/Latino), 9 international. Average age 30. 307 applicants, 20% accepted, 38 enrolled. In 2014, 21 master's, 24 doctorates awarded. *Degree requirements:* For master's, one foreign language, thesis (for some programs), 33 hours of coursework including capstone essay, thesis or portfolio (MA); 45 hours of coursework including 9-12 thesis hours (MFA); for doctorate, comprehensive exam, thesis/dissertation, 27 hours of coursework, 24 hours of dissertation work. *Entrance requirements:* For master's and doctorate, GRE General Test, sample of written work, 3 letters of recommendation, resume. Additional exam requirements/recommendations for international students: Required—TOEFL. *Application deadline:* For fall admission, 1/1 priority date for domestic and international students. Application fee: $30. Electronic applications accepted. *Expenses:* Tuition, state resident: part-time $403.51 per credit hour. Tuition, nonresident: part-time $1004.85 per credit hour. *Required fees:* $75.81 per credit hour. One-time fee: $20 part-time. Tuition and fees vary according to campus/location. *Financial support:* In 2014–15, 132 students received support, including 5 fellowships with full and partial tuition reimbursements available, teaching assistantships with full and partial tuition reimbursements available (averaging $13,250 per year); career-related internships or fieldwork, Federal Work-Study, and institutionally sponsored loans also available. Financial award application deadline: 8/1; financial award applicants required to submit FAFSA. *Faculty research:* British and Irish literature, American literature, creative writing, rhetoric and composition, multiethnic transnational literature, history of text technology. *Unit head:* Dr. Eric Walker, Chairman, 850-644-4230, Fax: 850-644-0811, E-mail: ewalker@fsu.edu. *Application contact:* Ginger Martin, Senior Graduate Academic Coordinator, 850-644-1081, Fax: 850-644-9656, E-mail: vmartin@fsu.edu. Website: http://english.fsu.edu/

Florida State University, The Graduate School, College of Music, Tallahassee, FL 32306. Offers accompanying (MM); arts administration (MA); choral conducting (MM); composition (MM, DM); ethnomusicology (MM); general music (MA); instrumental accompanying (MM); instrumental conducting (MM); jazz studies (MM); music education (MM Ed, PhD); music theory (MM, PhD); music therapy (MM); musicology (MM, PhD), including ethnomusicology (PhD), historical musicology; opera (MM); performance (MM,

DM); piano pedagogy (MM); piano technology (MA); vocal accompanying (MM). *Accreditation:* NASM. *Faculty:* 87 full-time, 13 part-time/adjunct. *Students:* 368 full-time (191 women); includes 86 minority (31 Black or African American, non-Hispanic/Latino; 2 American Indian or Alaska Native, non-Hispanic/Latino; 18 Asian, non-Hispanic/Latino; 25 Hispanic/Latino; 1 Native Hawaiian or other Pacific Islander, non-Hispanic/Latino; 9 Two or more races, non-Hispanic/Latino). Average age 26. 737 applicants, 42% accepted, 138 enrolled. In 2014, 108 master's, 42 doctorates awarded. *Degree requirements:* For master's, comprehensive exam (for some programs), thesis (for some programs), departmental qualifying exam; for doctorate, comprehensive exam (for some programs), thesis/dissertation, departmental qualifying exam. *Entrance requirements:* For master's, GRE General Test (for some programs), audition, minimum GPA of 3.0; for doctorate, GRE General Test (for some programs), audition, master's degree, minimum GPA of 3.0. Additional exam requirements/recommendations for international students: Required—TOEFL (minimum score 590 paper-based; 97 iBT), IELTS (minimum score 7.5). *Application deadline:* For fall admission, 7/1 for domestic and international students; for spring admission, 11/1 for domestic and international students; for summer admission, 3/1 for domestic students. Applications are processed on a rolling basis. Application fee: $30. Electronic applications accepted. *Expenses:* Expenses: $479.32 per credit hour for in-state students; $1,110.72 for out-of-state students. *Financial support:* In 2014–15, 223 students received support, including fellowships (averaging $15,000 per year), 9 research assistantships (averaging $4,750 per year), 173 teaching assistantships (averaging $4,750 per year); career-related internships or fieldwork, Federal Work-Study, tuition waivers, and unspecified assistantships also available. Support available to part-time students. Financial award application deadline: 2/28; financial award applicants required to submit FAFSA. *Faculty research:* Musicology. *Unit head:* Dr. Patricia Flowers, Dean, 850-644-4361, Fax: 850-644-2033, E-mail: pjflowers@fsu.edu. *Application contact:* Dr. James Mathes, Interim Associate Dean for Academic Affairs/Director of Graduate Studies in Music, 850-644-5848, Fax: 850-644-2033, E-mail: jmathes@fsu.edu.
Website: http://www.music.fsu.edu/

Fuller Theological Seminary, Graduate Programs, Pasadena, CA 91182. Offers Christian leadership (MACL); clinical psychology (PhD, Psy D); family studies (MA); global leadership (MA); global ministries (D Min); global ministries (Korean language) (D Min); intercultural studies (MA, Th M, PhD); intercultural studies (Korean language) (MA); marital and family therapy (MS); marriage and family enrichment (Certificate); ministry (M Div, D Min); missiology (D Miss); missiology (Korean language) (Th M); theology (MA, Th M, PhD), including evangelism (MA), family life education (MA), pastoral ministry (MA), recovery ministry (MA), worship music ministry (MA), worship, theology, and the arts (MA), youth, family, and culture (MA); theology and ministry (MA).

Garrett-Evangelical Theological Seminary, Graduate and Professional Programs, Evanston, IL 60201-3298. Offers Bible and culture (PhD); Christian education (MA); Christian education and congregational studies (PhD); contemporary theology and culture (PhD); divinity (M Div); ethics, church, and society (MA); liturgical studies (PhD); ministry (D Min); music ministry (MA); pastoral care and counseling (MA); pastoral theology, personality, and culture (PhD); spiritual formation and evangelism (MA); theological studies (MTS); M Div/MSW. M Div/MSW offered jointly with Loyola University Chicago. *Accreditation:* ACIPE; ATS (one or more programs are accredited). Part-time programs available. *Degree requirements:* For master's, thesis (for some programs); for doctorate, thesis/dissertation. *Entrance requirements:* For doctorate, GRE (PhD). Additional exam requirements/recommendations for international students: Required—TOEFL (minimum score 560 paper-based). Electronic applications accepted.

George Mason University, College of Visual and Performing Arts, School of Music, Program in Music, Fairfax, VA 22030. Offers composition (MM); conducting (MM); jazz studies (MM); music education (MM); pedagogy (MM); performance (MM). *Faculty:* 20 full-time (9 women), 45 part-time/adjunct (17 women). *Students:* 24 full-time (9 women), 29 part-time (18 women); includes 13 minority (6 Black or African American, non-Hispanic/Latino; 2 Asian, non-Hispanic/Latino; 3 Hispanic/Latino; 1 Native Hawaiian or other Pacific Islander, non-Hispanic/Latino; 1 Two or more races, non-Hispanic/Latino), 5 international. Average age 30. 42 applicants, 76% accepted, 21 enrolled. In 2014, 22 master's awarded. *Degree requirements:* For master's, comprehensive exam, foreign language in vocal emphasis. *Entrance requirements:* For master's, expanded goals statement; 2 letters of recommendation; official transcript. Additional exam requirements/recommendations for international students: Required—TOEFL (minimum score 570 paper-based; 80 iBT), IELTS (minimum score 6.5), PTE. *Application deadline:* For fall admission, 3/1 for domestic students; for spring admission, 11/1 for domestic students. Application fee: $65 ($80 for international students). Electronic applications accepted. *Expenses:* Tuition, state resident: full-time $9794; part-time $408 per credit hour. Tuition, nonresident: full-time $26,978; part-time $1124 per credit hour. *Required fees:* $2820; $118 per credit hour. Tuition and fees vary according to course load and program. *Financial support:* Career-related internships or fieldwork, Federal Work-Study, scholarships/grants, and unspecified assistantships available. Financial award application deadline: 3/1; financial award applicants required to submit FAFSA. *Unit head:* Dr. Dennis Layendecker, Chair/Director, 703-993-5082, Fax: 703-993-1394, E-mail: dlayende@gmu.edu. *Application contact:* Dr. Rachel Bergman, Graduate Director, 703-993-1395, Fax: 703-993-1394, E-mail: rbergman@gmu.edu.
Website: http://music.gmu.edu

George Mason University, College of Visual and Performing Arts, School of Music, Program in Musical Arts, Fairfax, VA 22030. Offers composition (DMA); conducting (DMA); performance (DMA). *Faculty:* 20 full-time (9 women), 45 part-time/adjunct (17 women). *Students:* 11 full-time (1 woman), 12 part-time (4 women); includes 4 minority (1 Asian, non-Hispanic/Latino; 3 Hispanic/Latino), 1 international. Average age 34. 17 applicants, 59% accepted, 7 enrolled. In 2014, 3 doctorates awarded. *Degree requirements:* For doctorate, one foreign language, comprehensive exam, thesis/dissertation. *Entrance requirements:* For doctorate, GRE, master's degree in music; minimum GPA of 3.0 in master's coursework, 3.25 in courses related to field of study; 3 letters of recommendation; writing sample; audition or portfolio (depending on area of study). Additional exam requirements/recommendations for international students: Required—TOEFL (minimum score 570 paper-based; 80 iBT), IELTS (minimum score 6.5), PTE. *Application deadline:* For fall admission, 2/15 for domestic students. Application fee: $65 ($80 for international students). *Expenses:* Tuition, state resident: full-time $9794; part-time $408 per credit hour. Tuition, nonresident: full-time $26,978; part-time $1124 per credit hour. *Required fees:* $2820; $118 per credit hour. Tuition and fees vary according to course load and program. *Financial support:* In 2014–15, 2 students received support, including 2 teaching assistantships with full and partial tuition reimbursements available (averaging $11,279 per year); career-related internships or fieldwork, Federal Work-Study, scholarships/grants, unspecified assistantships, and health care benefits (for full-time research or teaching assistantship recipients) also available. Support available to part-time students. Financial award application deadline: 3/1; financial award applicants required to submit FAFSA. *Unit head:* Dr. Dennis Layendecker, Chair/Director, 703-993-5082, Fax: 703-993-1394, E-mail: dlayende@gmu.edu. *Application contact:* Dr. Rachel Bergman, Graduate Director, 703-993-1395, Fax: 703-993-1394, E-mail: rbergman@gmu.edu.
Website: http://music.gmu.edu

Georgia Christian University, School of Music, Atlanta, GA 30360. Offers MA.

Georgia Institute of Technology, Graduate Studies, College of Architecture, School of Music, Atlanta, GA 30332-0001. Offers music technology (MS, PhD). *Expenses:* Tuition, state resident: full-time $12,344; part-time $515 per credit hour. Tuition, nonresident: full-time $27,600; part-time $1150 per credit hour. *Required fees:* $1196 per term. Part-time tuition and fees vary according to course load.

Georgia Southern University, Jack N. Averitt College of Graduate Studies, College of Liberal Arts and Social Sciences, Program in Music, Statesboro, GA 30460. Offers MM. *Accreditation:* NASM. Part-time and evening/weekend programs available. *Students:* 16 full-time (5 women), 17 part-time (10 women); includes 13 minority (5 Black or African American, non-Hispanic/Latino; 1 Asian, non-Hispanic/Latino; 6 Hispanic/Latino; 1 Two or more races, non-Hispanic/Latino), 5 international. Average age 25. 29 applicants, 72% accepted, 13 enrolled. In 2014, 12 master's awarded. *Degree requirements:* For master's, comprehensive exam, recital or final project. *Entrance requirements:* For master's, minimum GPA of 2.5, audition, letters of recommendation. Additional exam requirements/recommendations for international students: Required—TOEFL (minimum score 550 paper-based; 80 iBT), IELTS (minimum score 6). *Application deadline:* For fall admission, 3/1 priority date for domestic and international students; for spring admission, 10/1 priority date for domestic students, 10/1 for international students. Applications are processed on a rolling basis. Application fee: $50. Electronic applications accepted. *Expenses:* Tuition, state resident: full-time $7236; part-time $277 per semester hour. Tuition, nonresident: full-time $27,118; part-time $1105 per semester hour. *Required fees:* $2092. *Financial support:* In 2014–15, 15 students received support, including research assistantships with partial tuition reimbursements available (averaging $7,200 per year), teaching assistantships with partial tuition reimbursements available (averaging $7,200 per year); Federal Work-Study, scholarships/grants, tuition waivers (partial), and unspecified assistantships also available. Support available to part-time students. Financial award application deadline: 4/15; financial award applicants required to submit FAFSA. *Faculty research:* Performance, conducting, composition, technology, education. *Unit head:* Dr. Greg Harwood, Graduate Director, 912-478-5813, Fax: 912-478-1295, E-mail: gharwood@georgiasouthern.edu.
Website: http://class.georgiasouthern.edu/music/

Georgia State University, College of Arts and Sciences, School of Music, Atlanta, GA 30303. Offers choral conducting (MM); jazz studies (MM); music (Certificate); music composition (MM); music education (PhD); orchestral conducting (MM); performance (MM), including keyboard instruments: piano, harpsichord, organ, orchestral instruments, voice; piano pedagogy (MM); wind band conducting (MM). *Accreditation:* NASM. Part-time and evening/weekend programs available. *Faculty:* 28 full-time (7 women). *Students:* 59 full-time (26 women), 6 part-time (3 women); includes 19 minority (14 Black or African American, non-Hispanic/Latino; 2 Asian, non-Hispanic/Latino; 2 Hispanic/Latino; 1 Two or more races, non-Hispanic/Latino), 11 international. Average age 29. 73 applicants, 74% accepted, 27 enrolled. In 2014, 33 master's, 5 other advanced degrees awarded. *Degree requirements:* For master's, comprehensive exam, thesis (for some programs), recital; for doctorate, comprehensive exam, thesis/dissertation; for Certificate, recital. *Entrance requirements:* For master's, GRE (music education, composition only), BM; for doctorate, GRE, MM; for Certificate, MM. Additional exam requirements/recommendations for international students: Required—TOEFL (minimum score 550 paper-based; 80 iBT). *Application deadline:* For fall admission, 3/1 priority date for domestic and international students; for spring admission, 10/1 priority date for domestic and international students. Applications are processed on a rolling basis. Application fee: $50. Electronic applications accepted. *Expenses:* Tuition, state resident: full-time $6516; part-time $362 per credit hour. Tuition, nonresident: full-time $22,014; part-time $1223 per credit hour. *Required fees:* $2128 per semester. Tuition and fees vary according to course load and program. *Financial support:* In 2014–15, research assistantships with full tuition reimbursements (averaging $4,000 per year) were awarded; Federal Work-Study, scholarships/grants, health care benefits, tuition waivers (partial), and unspecified assistantships also available. Financial award application deadline: 3/1. *Faculty research:* Male changing voice, nineteenth-century chamber music, improvisation and learning, Garibunda, African-American classical musicians. *Unit head:* William Dwight Coleman, Director, School of Music, 404-413-5953, Fax: 404-413-5910, E-mail: wcoleman@gsu.edu. *Application contact:* Dr. Steven Andrew Harper, Graduate Director, 404-413-5943, Fax: 404-413-5910, E-mail: sharper@gsu.edu.
Website: http://www.music.gsu.edu/

The Graduate Center, City University of New York, Graduate Studies, Program in Music, New York, NY 10016-4039. Offers DMA, PhD. *Degree requirements:* For doctorate, 2 foreign languages, thesis/dissertation. *Entrance requirements:* For doctorate, GRE General Test. Additional exam requirements/recommendations for international students: Required—TOEFL. Electronic applications accepted.

Hardin-Simmons University, Graduate School, College of Fine Arts, Abilene, TX 79698-0001. Offers church music (MM); music education (MM); music performance (MM); theory-composition (MM). *Accreditation:* NASM. Part-time programs available. *Faculty:* 10 full-time (3 women), 1 part-time/adjunct (0 women). *Students:* 3 full-time (2 women), 1 part-time (0 women). Average age 27. In 2014, 3 master's awarded. *Degree requirements:* For master's, one foreign language, comprehensive exam, thesis (for some programs). *Entrance requirements:* For master's, minimum undergraduate GPA of 3.0 in major, 2.7 overall; performance; writing sample; demonstrated knowledge in chosen area. Additional exam requirements/recommendations for international students: Required—TOEFL (minimum score 550 paper-based; 75 iBT). *Application deadline:* For fall admission, 8/15 priority date for domestic students, 4/1 for international students; for spring admission, 1/5 priority date for domestic students, 9/1 for international students. Applications are processed on a rolling basis. Application fee: $50. *Expenses:* Tuition: Full-time $12,060; part-time $670 per credit hour. *Required fees:* $325; $110 per semester. Tuition and fees vary according to program. *Financial support:* In 2014–15, 5 students received support, including 4 fellowships (averaging $2,700 per year); career-related internships or fieldwork and scholarships/grants also available. Support available to part-time students. Financial award application deadline: 6/30; financial award applicants required to submit FAFSA. *Unit head:* Dr. Lynette Chambers, Program Director, 325-670-1430, Fax: 325-670-5873, E-mail: lchambers@hsutx.edu. *Application contact:* Dr. Nancy Kucinski, Dean of Graduate Studies, 325-670-1298, Fax: 325-670-1564, E-mail: gradoff@hsutx.edu.
Website: http://www.hsutx.edu/academics/cofa

Harvard University, Graduate School of Arts and Sciences, Department of Music, Cambridge, MA 02138. Offers composition (AM, PhD); musicology (AM); musicology and ethnomusicology (PhD); theory (AM, PhD). *Degree requirements:* For doctorate, 3 foreign languages, thesis/dissertation, composition, analytical paper. *Entrance requirements:* For master's and doctorate, GRE General Test. Additional exam requirements/recommendations for international students: Required—TOEFL.

Hebrew College, Program in Jewish Studies, Newton Centre, MA 02459. Offers Jewish liturgical music (Certificate); Jewish music education (Certificate); Jewish studies (MA). Part-time and evening/weekend programs available. Postbaccalaureate distance learning degree programs offered (minimal on-campus study). *Degree requirements:*

For master's, one foreign language. *Entrance requirements:* For master's, GRE, interview. Additional exam requirements/recommendations for international students: Required—TOEFL.

Hebrew Union College–Jewish Institute of Religion, School of Sacred Music, New York, NY 10012-1186. Offers MSM. *Degree requirements:* For master's, one foreign language, thesis, recital. *Entrance requirements:* For master's, GRE, minimum 2 years of college-level Hebrew, bachelor's degree in music or related area, trained singing voice. Additional exam requirements/recommendations for international students: Required—TOEFL. *Expenses:* Contact institution.

Hollins University, Graduate Programs, Program in Liberal Studies, Roanoke, VA 24020. Offers humanities (MALS); interdisciplinary studies (MALS); leadership (MALS); liberal studies (CAS); social science (MALS); visual and performing arts (MALS). Part-time and evening/weekend programs available. *Students:* 3 full-time (all women), 37 part-time (32 women); includes 6 minority (4 Black or African American, non-Hispanic/Latino; 1 Hispanic/Latino; 1 Two or more races, non-Hispanic/Latino). Average age 44. 13 applicants, 100% accepted, 9 enrolled. In 2014, 15 master's awarded. *Degree requirements:* For master's, thesis. *Entrance requirements:* For master's, letters of recommendation, interview. Additional exam requirements/recommendations for international students: Required—TOEFL (minimum score 550 paper-based; 79 iBT). *Application deadline:* For fall admission, 7/1 priority date for domestic and international students; for spring admission, 12/10 priority date for domestic and international students. Applications are processed on a rolling basis. Application fee: $40. Electronic applications accepted. *Financial support:* In 2014–15, 7 students received support, including 7 fellowships (averaging $1,000 per year); scholarships/grants also available. Support available to part-time students. Financial award application deadline: 7/15; financial award applicants required to submit FAFSA. *Faculty research:* Diversity, gender and women's studies, political science, leadership. *Unit head:* Dr. Joe Leedom, Director, 540-362-6326, Fax: 540-362-6288, E-mail: jleedom@hollins.edu. *Application contact:* Cathy S. Koon, Manager of Graduate Services, 540-362-6326, Fax: 540-362-6288, E-mail: ckoon@hollins.edu.
Website: http://www.hollins.edu/

Holy Names University, Graduate Division, Department of Music, Oakland, CA 94619-1699. Offers Kodaly (Certificate); music education with Kodaly emphasis (MM); piano pedagogy (MM); piano pedagogy with Suzuki emphasis (MM); vocal pedagogy (MM). *Faculty:* 9. *Students:* 4 full-time (all women), 11 part-time (7 women); includes 4 minority (3 Asian, non-Hispanic/Latino; 1 Native Hawaiian or other Pacific Islander, non-Hispanic/Latino), 2 international. Average age 33. 8 applicants, 63% accepted, 5 enrolled. In 2014, 11 master's, 1 Certificate awarded. *Degree requirements:* For master's, comprehensive exam, recital. *Entrance requirements:* For master's, audition; minimum undergraduate GPA of 2.6 overall, 3.0 in major. Additional exam requirements/recommendations for international students: Required—TOEFL (minimum score 550 paper-based; 79 iBT). *Application deadline:* For fall admission, 8/1 priority date for domestic students, 7/15 for international students; for spring admission, 12/1 priority date for domestic students, 12/1 for international students; for summer admission, 5/1 priority date for domestic students, 5/1 for international students. Applications are processed on a rolling basis. Application fee: $65. Electronic applications accepted. *Financial support:* Career-related internships or fieldwork, Federal Work-Study, scholarships/grants, and unspecified assistantships available. Support available to part-time students. Financial award application deadline: 3/2; financial award applicants required to submit FAFSA. *Faculty research:* Performance practice with special interest in Baroque, Romantic, and twentieth-century instrumental and vocal music; choral pedagogy; Hungarian music education. *Unit head:* Dr. Steven Hofer, Chair of Music Department, 510-436-1244, E-mail: hofer@hnu.edu. *Application contact:* 800-430-1321, Fax: 510-436-1325, E-mail: graduateadmissions@hnu.edu.

Hope International University, School of Graduate and Professional Studies, Programs in Ministry, Fullerton, CA 92831-3138. Offers Christian leadership (MCM); church music (MA); church music (Korean track) (MCM); church planting (MCM); intercultural studies (MCM); worship (MCM). Part-time and evening/weekend programs available. Postbaccalaureate distance learning degree programs offered (minimal on-campus study). *Degree requirements:* For master's, thesis (for some programs), project. *Entrance requirements:* For master's, minimum GPA of 3.0, MCM program requires an undergraduate degree in music, 2 references. Additional exam requirements/recommendations for international students: Required—TOEFL (minimum score 550 paper-based; 86 iBT); Recommended—IELTS (minimum score 6.5). Electronic applications accepted. *Expenses:* Contact institution. *Faculty research:* Church dynamics, growth methodologies.

Houghton College, Greatbatch School of Music, Houghton, NY 14744. Offers collaborative performance (MMus); composition (MMus); conducting (MMus); music (MA); performance (MMus); world music with theology and intercultural studies (MA). *Accreditation:* NASM. *Degree requirements:* For master's, comprehensive exam (for some programs), thesis (for some programs), recitals (for some programs). *Entrance requirements:* For master's, B Mus or equivalent. Additional exam requirements/recommendations for international students: Required—TOEFL (minimum score 600 paper-based). Electronic applications accepted. *Faculty research:* Bach Studies; original compositions; professional performance; contemporary women composers; music in Christian worship.

Howard University, Graduate School, Division of Fine Arts, Department of Music, Washington, DC 20059-0002. Offers applied music (MM); instrument (MM Ed); jazz studies (MM); organ (MM Ed); piano (MM Ed); voice (MM Ed). *Accreditation:* NASM. Part-time programs available. *Degree requirements:* For master's, comprehensive exam, thesis or alternative, departmental qualifying exam, recital. *Entrance requirements:* For master's, minimum GPA of 3.0, bachelor's degree in music or music education. Additional exam requirements/recommendations for international students: Required—TOEFL.

Hunter College of the City University of New York, Graduate School, School of Arts and Sciences, Department of Music, New York, NY 10065-5085. Offers MA. Part-time and evening/weekend programs available. *Faculty:* 6 full-time (2 women), 1 (woman) part-time/adjunct. *Students:* 1 full-time (0 women), 37 part-time (15 women); includes 4 minority (2 Black or African American, non-Hispanic/Latino; 2 Hispanic/Latino), 5 international. Average age 34. 21 applicants, 71% accepted, 11 enrolled. In 2014, 17 master's awarded. *Degree requirements:* For master's, one foreign language, thesis, composition, essay, or recital; proficiency exam. *Entrance requirements:* For master's, undergraduate major in music (minimum 24 credits) or equivalent, sample of work, research paper. Additional exam requirements/recommendations for international students: Required—TOEFL. *Application deadline:* For fall admission, 4/1 for domestic students, 2/1 for international students; for spring admission, 11/1 for domestic students, 9/1 for international students. Applications are processed on a rolling basis. *Financial support:* In 2014–15, 4 fellowships (averaging $1,000 per year) were awarded; Federal Work-Study, tuition waivers (partial), and lesson stipends also available. Support available to part-time students. Financial award application deadline: 4/15. *Faculty research:* African and African-American music, Bach, Renaissance music, early romantic music, theory of tonal music. *Unit head:* Dr. Paul Mueller, Department Chair, 212-772-5020, Fax: 212-772-5022, E-mail: music@hunter.cuny.edu. *Application*

contact: Pondie Burstein, Graduate Adviser, 212-772-5152, E-mail: huntermust@aol.com.
Website: http://www.hunter.cuny.edu/music/

Illinois State University, Graduate School, College of Fine Arts, School of Music, Normal, IL 61790-2200. Offers MM, MM Ed. *Accreditation:* NASM. *Degree requirements:* For master's, thesis or alternative, performance. *Entrance requirements:* For master's, minimum GPA of 3.0 in music, 2.6 overall; auditions. *Faculty research:* Concerts on the Quad summer concert series.

Indiana State University, College of Graduate and Professional Studies, College of Arts and Sciences, Department of Music, Terre Haute, IN 47809. Offers music performance (MM). *Accreditation:* NASM. *Degree requirements:* For master's, comprehensive exam, thesis, qualifying exam. Electronic applications accepted.

Indiana University Bloomington, Jacobs School of Music, Bloomington, IN 47405-7000. Offers MA, MM, MME, MS, DM, DME, PhD, AD, Performance Diploma, Spec, MA/MLS, MM/MLS. *Accreditation:* NASM (one or more programs are accredited). *Faculty:* 139 full-time (35 women), 11 part-time/adjunct (3 women). *Students:* 736 full-time (355 women), 130 part-time (77 women); includes 129 minority (23 Black or African American, non-Hispanic/Latino; 1 American Indian or Alaska Native, non-Hispanic/Latino; 46 Asian, non-Hispanic/Latino; 37 Hispanic/Latino; 22 Two or more races, non-Hispanic/Latino), 250 international. Average age 28. 1,351 applicants, 42% accepted, 303 enrolled. In 2014, 174 master's, 67 doctorates, 57 other advanced degrees awarded. Terminal master's awarded for partial completion of doctoral program. *Degree requirements:* For master's, comprehensive exam (for some programs); for doctorate, comprehensive exam, thesis/dissertation. *Entrance requirements:* For master's and doctorate, GRE, audition, 3 letters of recommendation. Additional exam requirements/recommendations for international students: Required—TOEFL (minimum score 560 paper-based; 84 iBT). *Application deadline:* For fall admission, 12/1 for domestic and international students; for spring admission, 9/1 for domestic and international students. Applications are processed on a rolling basis. Application fee: $135 ($145 for international students). Electronic applications accepted. *Expenses:* Expenses: Contact institution. *Financial support:* Fellowships with full and partial tuition reimbursements, research assistantships with tuition reimbursements, teaching assistantships with full tuition reimbursements, Federal Work-Study, institutionally sponsored loans, scholarships/grants, health care benefits, tuition waivers (full and partial), and unspecified assistantships available. Support available to part-time students. Financial award application deadline: 3/1; financial award applicants required to submit FAFSA. *Total annual research expenditures:* $8,300. *Unit head:* Gwyn Richards, Dean, 812-855-2435, E-mail: musdean@indiana.edu. *Application contact:* Rebecca Patrick Shipman, Music Admissions, 812-855-7998.
Website: http://www.music.indiana.edu/

Indiana University Bloomington, University Graduate School, College of Arts and Sciences, Department of Folklore and Ethnomusicology, Bloomington, IN 47408-3890. Offers folklore (MA, PhD), including ethnomusicology. Part-time programs available. *Faculty:* 15 full-time (6 women), 4 part-time/adjunct (0 women). *Students:* 81 full-time (48 women), 2 part-time (1 woman); includes 20 minority (9 Black or African American, non-Hispanic/Latino; 4 Asian, non-Hispanic/Latino; 5 Hispanic/Latino; 2 Two or more races, non-Hispanic/Latino), 19 international. Average age 33. 73 applicants, 16% accepted, 10 enrolled. In 2014, 12 master's, 13 doctorates awarded. *Degree requirements:* For master's, one foreign language, comprehensive exam, project, thesis, or exam; for doctorate, 2 foreign languages, comprehensive exam, thesis/dissertation. *Entrance requirements:* For master's, GRE General Test (minimum scores: 151 for Verbal, 150 for Quantitative, 4.5 for Analytical), minimum GPA of 3.0, writing sample; for doctorate, GRE General Test (minimum scores: 151 for Verbal, 150 for Quantitative, 4.5 for Analytical), minimum GPA of 3.0, writing sample. Additional exam requirements/recommendations for international students: Required—TOEFL (minimum score 550 paper-based; 79 iBT). *Application deadline:* For fall admission, 1/2 for domestic students, 12/1 for international students. Application fee: $55 ($65 for international students). Electronic applications accepted. *Financial support:* In 2014–15, 40 students received support, including 4 fellowships with full tuition reimbursements available (averaging $18,000 per year), 15 research assistantships with full tuition reimbursements available (averaging $15,750 per year), 21 teaching assistantships with full tuition reimbursements available (averaging $15,750 per year); Federal Work-Study, scholarships/grants, health care benefits, and unspecified assistantships also available. Financial award application deadline: 3/1; financial award applicants required to submit FAFSA. *Faculty research:* Narrative, performance studies, material culture, popular culture, music. *Unit head:* Dr. John McDowell, Chair, 812-855-0390, Fax: 812-855-4008, E-mail: mcdowell@indiana.edu. *Application contact:* Michelle Melhouse, Graduate Recorder, 812-855-0389, Fax: 812-855-4008, E-mail: mmelhous@indiana.edu.
Website: http://www.indiana.edu/~folklore/

Indiana University Bloomington, University Graduate School, College of Arts and Sciences, The Media School, Department of Communication and Culture, Bloomington, IN 47405-7000. Offers communication and culture (MA); film and media studies (PhD); performance and ethnography (PhD); rhetoric and public culture (PhD). *Faculty:* 22 full-time (13 women), 1 (woman) part-time/adjunct. *Students:* 75 full-time (41 women); includes 7 minority (1 Black or African American, non-Hispanic/Latino; 5 Hispanic/Latino; 1 Two or more races, non-Hispanic/Latino), 7 international. 116 applicants, 15% accepted, 8 enrolled. In 2014, 7 master's, 7 doctorates awarded. *Degree requirements:* For master's, comprehensive exam; for doctorate, one foreign language, comprehensive exam, thesis/dissertation, student teaching. *Entrance requirements:* For master's and doctorate, GRE General Test, minimum GPA of 3.0, 3 letters of recommendation, writing sample, personal statement. Additional exam requirements/recommendations for international students: Required—TOEFL (minimum score 550 paper-based) or IELTS. *Application deadline:* For fall admission, 1/2 for domestic students, 12/1 for international students; for winter admission, 1/2 for domestic students, 12/1 for international students. Application fee: $55 ($65 for international students). Electronic applications accepted. *Financial support:* Fellowships with full tuition reimbursements, research assistantships with full tuition reimbursements, and teaching assistantships with full tuition reimbursements available. Financial award application deadline: 1/2. *Faculty research:* Rhetoric and public culture, film and media studies, performance ethnography. *Unit head:* Prof. Jane Goodman, Chair, 812-855-3232, Fax: 812-855-6014, E-mail: cmcl@indiana.edu. *Application contact:* Kathy P. Teige, Graduate Secretary, 812-855-6389, Fax: 812-855-6014, E-mail: kteige@indiana.edu.
Website: http://www.indiana.edu/~cmcl/

Indiana University of Pennsylvania, School of Graduate Studies and Research, College of Fine Arts, Department of Music, Program in Music, Indiana, PA 15705-1087. Offers music education (MA); performance (MA). *Accreditation:* NASM. Part-time programs available. *Faculty:* 13 full-time (4 women), 1 part-time/adjunct (0 women). *Students:* 5 full-time (2 women), 15 part-time (7 women), 1 international. Average age 25. 24 applicants, 75% accepted, 12 enrolled. In 2014, 6 master's awarded. *Degree requirements:* For master's, thesis optional. *Entrance requirements:* For master's, 2 letters of recommendation, audition. Additional exam requirements/recommendations for international students: Required—TOEFL (minimum score 550 paper-based). *Application deadline:* Applications are processed on a rolling basis. Application fee: $50.

Electronic applications accepted. *Financial support:* In 2014–15, 2 fellowships with full tuition reimbursements (averaging $1,000 per year), 7 research assistantships with full and partial tuition reimbursements (averaging $3,138 per year) were awarded; career-related internships or fieldwork, Federal Work-Study, scholarships/grants, and unspecified assistantships also available. Support available to part-time students. Financial award application deadline: 4/15; financial award applicants required to submit FAFSA. *Unit head:* Dr. Matthew Baumer, Coordinator, 724-357-5646, E-mail: matthew.baumer@iup.edu.
Website: http://www.iup.edu/upper.aspx?id-89383

Indiana University–Purdue University Indianapolis, School of Engineering and Technology, School of Music, Indianapolis, IN 46202. Offers music technology (MS); music therapy (MS). *Accreditation:* NASM. Part-time and evening/weekend programs available. Postbaccalaureate distance learning degree programs offered. *Students:* 6 full-time (0 women), 16 part-time (3 women); includes 4 minority (2 Black or African American, non-Hispanic/Latino; 1 Hispanic/Latino; 1 Two or more races, non-Hispanic/Latino), 3 international. Average age 32. 21 applicants, 57% accepted, 9 enrolled. In 2014, 14 master's awarded. *Degree requirements:* For master's, internship or final project. *Entrance requirements:* For master's, audition, minimum GPA of 3.0. Additional exam requirements/recommendations for international students: Required—TOEFL. *Application deadline:* For fall admission, 4/15 priority date for domestic students, 3/15 for international students; for spring admission, 11/15 priority date for domestic students, 11/15 for international students. Applications are processed on a rolling basis. Application fee: $55 ($65 for international students). *Financial support:* Teaching assistantships with full tuition reimbursements, Federal Work-Study, institutionally sponsored loans, and scholarships/grants available. Support available to part-time students. Financial award application deadline: 11/15. *Unit head:* G. David Peters, Director, 317-278-2591, E-mail: gpeters@iupui.edu. *Application contact:* Kathleen Dusing, Administrative Support, Graduate Programs, 317-278-4960, E-mail: kdusing@iupui.edu.
Website: http://www.engr.iupui.edu/departments/mat/

Indiana University South Bend, Raclin School of the Arts, South Bend, IN 46634-7111. Offers music (MM); studio teaching (MM). Part-time programs available. *Faculty:* 1 full-time (0 women). *Students:* 10 full-time (4 women), 4 part-time (2 women); includes 3 minority (all Black or African American, non-Hispanic/Latino), 7 international. Average age 29. 17 applicants, 59% accepted, 6 enrolled. In 2014, 3 master's awarded. *Entrance requirements:* For master's, performance audition. *Application deadline:* For fall admission, 7/1 priority date for domestic students; for spring admission, 11/1 for domestic students. Applications are processed on a rolling basis. *Financial support:* Fellowships, teaching assistantships, and Federal Work-Study available. Support available to part-time students. Financial award application deadline: 3/1; financial award applicants required to submit FAFSA. *Faculty research:* Orchestral conducting. *Unit head:* Dr. Marvin V. Curtis, Dean, 574-520-4170, E-mail: mvcurtis@iusb.edu. *Application contact:* Admissions Counselor, 574-520-4839, Fax: 574-520-4834, E-mail: graduate@iusb.edu.
Website: https://www.iusb.edu/arts/

Inter American University of Puerto Rico, San Germán Campus, Graduate Studies Center, Program in Music Education, San Germán, PR 00683-5008. Offers music (MA); music teacher education (MA). Part-time and evening/weekend programs available.

Ithaca College, School of Music, Programs in Music and Music Education, Ithaca, NY 14850. Offers composition (MM); conducting (MM); music education (MM, MS); performance (MM); Suzuki pedagogy (MM). *Accreditation:* NASM. Part-time programs available. *Faculty:* 59 full-time (21 women), 4 part-time/adjunct (3 women). *Students:* 51 full-time (26 women), 4 part-time (all women); includes 7 minority (2 Black or African American, non-Hispanic/Latino; 2 Asian, non-Hispanic/Latino; 3 Hispanic/Latino), 10 international. Average age 25. 210 applicants, 28% accepted, 20 enrolled. In 2014, 34 master's awarded. *Degree requirements:* For master's, comprehensive exam (for some programs), thesis (for some programs). *Entrance requirements:* For master's, audition, minimum GPA of 3.0. Additional exam requirements/recommendations for international students: Required—TOEFL (minimum score 550 paper-based; 80 iBT). *Application deadline:* For fall admission, 3/1 for domestic and international students; for spring admission, 12/1 for domestic and international students. Applications are processed on a rolling basis. Application fee: $40. Electronic applications accepted. *Expenses:* Expenses: Contact institution. *Financial support:* In 2014–15, 42 students received support, including 42 teaching assistantships (averaging $9,497 per year); career-related internships or fieldwork, Federal Work-Study, scholarships/grants, and unspecified assistantships also available. Support available to part-time students. Financial award application deadline: 3/1; financial award applicants required to submit CSS PROFILE or FAFSA. *Faculty research:* Musical performance and performance studies, musical composition, music theory and analysis, music education, teaching and learning, musical direction and conducting. *Unit head:* Dr. Les Black, Chair, Graduate Studies in Music, 607-274-3143, Fax: 607-274-1263, E-mail: gps@ithaca.edu. *Application contact:* Gerard Turbide, Director, Office of Admission, 607-274-3143, Fax: 607-274-1263, E-mail: gps@ithaca.edu.
Website: http://www.ithaca.edu/gradprograms/music

Jacksonville State University, College of Graduate Studies and Continuing Education, College of Arts and Sciences, Department of Music, Jacksonville, AL 36265-1602. Offers MA. *Accreditation:* NASM. Part-time and evening/weekend programs available. *Faculty:* 22 full-time (7 women), 6 part-time/adjunct (2 women). *Students:* 5 full-time (1 woman), 9 part-time (3 women); includes 3 minority (all Black or African American, non-Hispanic/Latino), 1 international. Average age 30. 4 applicants, 75% accepted, 3 enrolled. In 2014, 3 master's awarded. *Degree requirements:* For master's, comprehensive exam, thesis (for some programs). *Entrance requirements:* For master's, GRE General Test or MAT. Additional exam requirements/recommendations for international students: Required—TOEFL (minimum score 500 paper-based; 61 iBT). *Application deadline:* Applications are processed on a rolling basis. Application fee: $35. Electronic applications accepted. *Financial support:* In 2014–15, 6 students received support. Available to part-time students. Application deadline: 4/1; applicants required to submit FAFSA. *Unit head:* Dr. Legare McIntosh, Head, 256-782-5560, E-mail: mcintosh@jsu.edu. *Application contact:* Dr. Jean Pugliese, Associate Dean, 256-782-8278, Fax: 256-782-5321, E-mail: pugliese@jsu.edu.

James Madison University, The Graduate School, College of Visual and Performing Arts, School of Music, Doctor of Musical Arts Program, Harrisonburg, VA 22807. Offers DMA. Part-time programs available. *Students:* 28 full-time (11 women), 9 part-time (6 women); includes 2 minority (1 Hispanic/Latino; 1 Two or more races, non-Hispanic/Latino), 12 international. Average age 28. 27 applicants, 78% accepted, 9 enrolled. In 2014, 4 doctorates awarded. *Degree requirements:* For doctorate, comprehensive exam. *Application deadline:* For fall and spring admission, 4/1 for domestic and international students. Application fee: $55. Electronic applications accepted. *Expenses:* Tuition, state resident: full-time $7812; part-time $434 per credit hour. Tuition, nonresident: full-time $20,430; part-time $1135 per credit hour. *Financial support:* In 2014–15, 24 students received support, including 1 fellowship; unspecified assistantships and 23 doctoral assistantships (averaging $12,935) also available. Financial award application deadline: 3/1; financial award applicants required to submit FAFSA. *Unit head:* Dr. Jeffrey E Bush, Director of the School of Music, 540-568-3614, E-mail: bushje@jmu.edu. *Application contact:* Lynette D. Michael, Director of Graduate Admissions and Student Records, 540-568-6131 Ext. 6395, Fax: 540-568-7860, E-mail: michaeld@jmu.edu.
Website: http://www.jmu.edu/music/degree-programs/dma.shtml

The Jewish Theological Seminary, H. L. Miller Cantorial School and College of Jewish Music, New York, NY 10027-4649. Offers MSM. *Degree requirements:* For master's, one foreign language, comprehensive exam, departmental qualifying exam, recitals. *Entrance requirements:* For master's, music aptitude test, audition, interview, 3 letters of recommendation. Additional exam requirements/recommendations for international students: Required—TOEFL. *Expenses:* Contact institution.

Johns Hopkins University, Peabody Conservatory, Baltimore, MD 21218-2699. Offers MA, MM, DMA, AD, GPD. *Accreditation:* NASM. *Degree requirements:* For master's, thesis (for some programs), departmental qualifying exam, recital; for doctorate, 2 foreign languages, thesis/dissertation (for some programs), departmental qualifying exam, recitals; for other advanced degree, recitals. *Entrance requirements:* For master's and other advanced degree, audition; for doctorate, audition, interview. Additional exam requirements/recommendations for international students: Required—TOEFL (minimum score 550 paper-based; 79 iBT). Electronic applications accepted. *Expenses:* Contact institution.

The Juilliard School, Program in Music, New York, NY 10023-6588. Offers MM, DMA, Artist Diploma, Diploma. *Degree requirements:* For master's and other advanced degree, performance jury, recital; for doctorate, one foreign language, thesis/dissertation, performance jury, 3 recitals. *Entrance requirements:* For master's and other advanced degree, audition; for doctorate, audition, interview, dossier. Additional exam requirements/recommendations for international students: Required—TOEFL (minimum score 570 paper-based; 89 iBT). Electronic applications accepted.

Kansas State University, Graduate School, College of Arts and Sciences, School of Music, Theatre and Dance, Manhattan, KS 66506. Offers MA, MM. *Accreditation:* NASM. Part-time programs available. Postbaccalaureate distance learning degree programs offered (minimal on-campus study). *Faculty:* 54 full-time (21 women), 6 part-time/adjunct (2 women). *Students:* 27 full-time (18 women), 42 part-time (26 women); includes 2 minority (1 Asian, non-Hispanic/Latino; 1 Hispanic/Latino), 4 international. Average age 30. 37 applicants, 57% accepted, 12 enrolled. In 2014, 31 master's awarded. *Degree requirements:* For master's, thesis optional. *Entrance requirements:* For master's, GRE, audition (in person or recording), interview (for music education). Additional exam requirements/recommendations for international students: Required—TOEFL (minimum score 600 paper-based). *Application deadline:* For fall admission, 2/1 priority date for domestic and international students; for spring admission, 8/1 priority date for domestic and international students. Applications are processed on a rolling basis. Application fee: $50 ($75 for international students). Electronic applications accepted. *Financial support:* In 2014–15, 16 teaching assistantships with full tuition reimbursements (averaging $8,419 per year) were awarded; fellowships, institutionally sponsored loans, scholarships/grants, and tuition waivers (full and partial) also available. Support available to part-time students. Financial award application deadline: 3/1; financial award applicants required to submit FAFSA. *Faculty research:* American music, opera, drama therapy, directing, costume and scenic design, music by women composers. *Total annual research expenditures:* $16,349. *Unit head:* Dr. Gary Mortenson, Head, 785-532-3802, Fax: 785-532-5740, E-mail: garym@ksu.edu. *Application contact:* Dr. Fred Burrack, Director of Graduate Music Programs, 785-532-3429, Fax: 785-532-5740, E-mail: fburrack@ksu.edu.
Website: http://www.k-state.edu/mtd/

Kent State University, College of the Arts, Hugh A. Glauser School of Music, Kent, OH 44242-0001. Offers conducting (MM), including choral conducting; ethnomusicology (MA); music composition (MA, Certificate); music conducting (Certificate); music education (MM, PhD); music performance (Certificate); music theory (MA, PhD); performance (MM), including chamber music. *Accreditation:* NASM. Part-time programs available. Postbaccalaureate distance learning degree programs offered. *Faculty:* 32 full-time (9 women). *Students:* 54 full-time (28 women), 193 part-time (107 women); includes 11 minority (5 Black or African American, non-Hispanic/Latino; 1 Asian, non-Hispanic/Latino; 3 Hispanic/Latino; 2 Two or more races, non-Hispanic/Latino), 20 international. Average age 31. 195 applicants, 76% accepted, 115 enrolled. In 2014, 98 master's, 5 doctorates, 1 other advanced degree awarded. *Degree requirements:* For master's, variable foreign language requirement, comprehensive exam, thesis (for all except MM in music education); for doctorate, variable foreign language requirement, comprehensive exam, thesis/dissertation, preliminary examinations, residency. *Entrance requirements:* For master's, minimum GPA of 3.0, transcript, goal statement, resume, audition or portfolio, teaching certificate and experience (for MM in music education), 3 letters of recommendation; for doctorate, minimum GPA of 3.0, transcript, resume, goal statement, scholarly writing sample, 3 letters of recommendation; three scores of original compositions (for music theory); teaching experience, certificate, statement of philosophy, and interview (for music education); for Certificate, minimum GPA of 3.0, transcript, audition or original score, 2 letters of recommendation. Additional exam requirements/recommendations for international students: Required—TOEFL (minimum score: paper-based 525, iBT 71), Michigan English Language Assessment Battery (minimum score of 75), IELTS (minimum score of 6.0), PTE Academic (minimum score of 48), or completion of ELS level 112 Intensive Program. *Application deadline:* For fall admission, 8/1 for domestic students; for spring admission, 12/1 for domestic students. Application fee: $45 ($70 for international students). Electronic applications accepted. *Expenses:* Tuition, state resident: full-time $8730; part-time $485 per credit hour. Tuition, nonresident: full-time $14,886; part-time $827 per credit hour. Tuition and fees vary according to campus/location and program. *Financial support:* Research assistantships with full tuition reimbursements, teaching assistantships with full tuition reimbursements, Federal Work-Study, scholarships/grants, and unspecified assistantships available. Financial award application deadline: 2/1. *Unit head:* Ralph Lorenz, Acting Director, 330-672-2172, E-mail: rlorenz@kent.edu. *Application contact:* Michael W. Chunn, Coordinator of Graduate Studies, 330-672-2172, Fax: 330-672-7837, E-mail: mchunn@kent.edu.
Website: http://www.kent.edu/music/

Lamar University, College of Graduate Studies, College of Fine Arts and Communication, Mary Morgan Moore Department of Music, Beaumont, TX 77710. Offers MM. *Accreditation:* NASM. *Faculty:* 7 full-time (2 women). *Students:* 7 full-time (1 woman), 3 part-time (1 woman); includes 2 minority (both Hispanic/Latino). Average age 27. 4 applicants, 75% accepted, 1 enrolled. In 2014, 3 master's awarded. *Degree requirements:* For master's, comprehensive exam, thesis optional. *Entrance requirements:* For master's, GRE General Test, theory placement exams, audition. Additional exam requirements/recommendations for international students: Required—TOEFL (minimum score 550 paper-based; 79 iBT), IELTS (minimum score 6.5). *Application deadline:* For fall admission, 8/10 for domestic students, 7/1 for international students; for spring admission, 1/5 for domestic students, 12/1 for international students. Applications are processed on a rolling basis. Application fee: $25 ($50 for international students). *Expenses:* Tuition, state resident: full-time $5724; part-time $1908 per semester. Tuition, nonresident: full-time $12,240; part-time $4080 per semester.

Required fees: $1940; $318 per credit hour. *Financial support:* In 2014–15, 4 fellowships with tuition reimbursements (averaging $2,000 per year), 2 teaching assistantships were awarded; institutionally sponsored loans and tuition waivers (partial) also available. Support available to part-time students. Financial award application deadline: 4/1. *Faculty research:* Performance: ensembles and personal. *Unit head:* Dr. Kurt Gilman, Chair, 409-880-8144, Fax: 409-880-8143. *Application contact:* Melissa Gallien, Director, Admissions and Academic Services, 409-880-8888, Fax: 409-880-7419, E-mail: gradmissions@lamar.edu.
Website: http://fineartscomm.lamar.edu/music

Lee University, Program in Music, Cleveland, TN 37320-3450. Offers conducting (MM); music education (MM); music performance (MM); religious/sacred music (MCM). *Accreditation:* NASM. Part-time programs available. *Faculty:* 19 full-time (5 women), 4 part-time/adjunct (1 woman). *Students:* 27 full-time (19 women), 20 part-time (8 women); includes 5 minority (2 Black or African American, non-Hispanic/Latino; 2 Asian, non-Hispanic/Latino; 1 Hispanic/Latino), 7 international. Average age 26. 21 applicants, 100% accepted, 19 enrolled. In 2014, 14 master's awarded. *Degree requirements:* For master's, variable foreign language requirement, comprehensive exam, thesis, internship. *Entrance requirements:* For master's, placement exercises in music theory, music history, diction, and piano proficiency, audition, resume, interview, minimum GPA of 2.75, official transcripts, essay, 3 recommendations. Additional exam requirements/recommendations for international students: Required—TOEFL (minimum score 450 paper-based). *Application deadline:* For fall admission, 4/1 priority date for domestic and international students; for spring admission, 10/1 priority date for domestic and international students. Applications are processed on a rolling basis. Application fee: $25. *Expenses: Tuition:* Full-time $10,260; part-time $570 per credit hour. *Required fees:* $35 per semester. One-time fee: $25. Tuition and fees vary according to program. *Financial support:* In 2014–15, 43 students received support. Career-related internships or fieldwork, Federal Work-Study, institutionally sponsored loans, and scholarships/grants available. Financial award application deadline: 3/1; financial award applicants required to submit FAFSA. *Unit head:* Dr. Brad J. Moffett, Director, 423-614-8240, Fax: 423-614-8242, E-mail: gradmusic@leeuniversity.edu. *Application contact:* Vicki Glasscock, Graduate Admissions Director, 423-614-8059, E-mail: vglasscock@leeuniversity.edu.
Website: http://www.leeuniversity.edu/academics/graduate/music

Liberty University, School of Music, Lynchburg, VA 24515. Offers ethnomusicology (MA); music and worship (MA); music education (MA); worship studies (MA, DWS), including church planting (MA), ethnomusicology (MA), leadership (MA). Part-time programs available. Postbaccalaureate distance learning degree programs offered (minimal on-campus study). *Students:* 57 full-time (19 women), 180 part-time (75 women); includes 48 minority (34 Black or African American, non-Hispanic/Latino; 1 American Indian or Alaska Native, non-Hispanic/Latino; 2 Asian, non-Hispanic/Latino; 2 Hispanic/Latino; 1 Native Hawaiian or other Pacific Islander, non-Hispanic/Latino; 8 Two or more races, non-Hispanic/Latino), 12 international. Average age 35. 330 applicants, 32% accepted, 57 enrolled. In 2014, 41 master's awarded. *Entrance requirements:* For master's, minimum GPA of 3.0; interview; letter of recommendation; statement of purpose; bachelor's/master's degree in music, worship, or related field, or 5 years of experience. Additional exam requirements/recommendations for international students: Required—TOEFL (minimum score 600 paper-based; 100 iBT). *Application deadline:* Applications are processed on a rolling basis. Application fee: $50. Electronic applications accepted. *Unit head:* Dr. Vernon Whaley, Dean, 434-592-3463, E-mail: vwhaley@liberty.edu. *Application contact:* Jay Bridge, Director of Admissions, 800-424-9595, Fax: 800-628-7977, E-mail: gradadmissions@liberty.edu.
Website: http://www.liberty.edu/academics/music/

Louisiana State University and Agricultural & Mechanical College, Graduate School, College of Music and Dramatic Arts, School of Music, Baton Rouge, LA 70803. Offers music (MM, DMA, PhD); music education (PhD). *Accreditation:* NASM. Part-time programs available. *Faculty:* 53 full-time (16 women), 1 (woman) part-time/adjunct. *Students:* 149 full-time (58 women), 31 part-time (10 women); includes 35 minority (21 Black or African American, non-Hispanic/Latino; 2 American Indian or Alaska Native, non-Hispanic/Latino; 5 Asian, non-Hispanic/Latino; 6 Hispanic/Latino; 1 Two or more races, non-Hispanic/Latino), 44 international. Average age 29. 201 applicants, 44% accepted, 45 enrolled. In 2014, 38 master's, 24 doctorates awarded. Terminal master's awarded for partial completion of doctoral program. *Degree requirements:* For doctorate, thesis/dissertation (for some programs). *Entrance requirements:* For master's, minimum GPA of 3.0, audition/interview; for doctorate, GRE General Test, minimum GPA of 3.0, audition/interview. Additional exam requirements/recommendations for international students: Required—TOEFL (minimum score 550 paper-based; 79 IBT), IELTS (minimum score 6.5), or PTE (minimum score 59). *Application deadline:* For fall admission, 1/1 priority date for domestic students, 5/15 for international students; for spring admission, 10/15 for domestic and international students; for summer admission, 5/15 for domestic and international students. Applications are processed on a rolling basis. Application fee: $50 ($70 for international students). Electronic applications accepted. *Financial support:* In 2014–15, 159 students received support, including 4 fellowships (averaging $29,117 per year), 3 research assistantships with full and partial tuition reimbursements available (averaging $14,367 per year), 90 teaching assistantships with full and partial tuition reimbursements available (averaging $9,995 per year); Federal Work-Study, institutionally sponsored loans, scholarships/grants, health care benefits, tuition waivers (full and partial), and unspecified assistantships also available. Support available to part-time students. Financial award applicants required to submit FAFSA. *Faculty research:* Music education, music literature, formal and harmonic analysis, pedagogy, performance. *Unit head:* Dr. Stephen David Beck, Dean, 225-578-3261, Fax: 225-578-2562, E-mail: sdbeck@lsu.edu. *Application contact:* -, Fax: -.
Website: http://www.music.lsu.edu/

Loyola University New Orleans, College of Music and Fine Arts, New Orleans, LA 70118-6195. Offers music therapy (MMT); performance (MM). *Accreditation:* NASM. Part-time programs available. *Faculty:* 15 full-time (8 women), 6 part-time/adjunct (3 women). *Students:* 16 full-time (8 women), 10 part-time (5 women); includes 6 minority (5 Black or African American, non-Hispanic/Latino; 1 Hispanic/Latino), 3 international. Average age 26. 33 applicants, 42% accepted, 14 enrolled. In 2014, 9 master's awarded. *Degree requirements:* For master's, comprehensive written and oral exams; thesis (for MMT). *Entrance requirements:* For master's, performance audition, appropriate bachelor's degree, transcripts, minimum GPA of 3.0, 2 letters of recommendation, resume. Additional exam requirements/recommendations for international students: Required—TOEFL (minimum score 580 paper-based; 92 iBT). *Application deadline:* For fall admission, 8/15 priority date for domestic and international students; for spring admission, 1/1 priority date for domestic and international students. Applications are processed on a rolling basis. Application fee: $20. Electronic applications accepted. *Expenses:* Expenses: Contact institution. *Financial support:* Career-related internships or fieldwork, Federal Work-Study, institutionally sponsored loans, scholarships/grants, unspecified assistantships, and talent-based music scholarships available. Support available to part-time students. Financial award application deadline: 5/1; financial award applicants required to submit FAFSA. *Faculty research:* Music business, music therapy, musicology, music theory, music education. *Unit head:* Dr. Victoria P. Vega, Associate Dean, 504-865-3037, Fax: 504-865-2852, E-mail: vpvega@loyno.edu. *Application contact:* Melissa L. Lightell, Director, Office of Professional and Continuing Studies, 504-865-3530, Fax: 504-865-2787, E-mail: evening@loyno.edu.
Website: http://cmfa.loyno.edu/

Lynchburg College, Graduate Studies, MA Program in Music, Lynchburg, VA 24501-3199. Offers MA. *Accreditation:* NASM. Part-time programs available. *Faculty:* 2 full-time (1 woman), 1 (woman) part-time/adjunct. *Students:* 1 part-time (0 women); minority (Black or African American, non-Hispanic/Latino). Average age 23. In 2014, 2 master's awarded. *Degree requirements:* For master's, comprehensive exam, recital. *Entrance requirements:* For master's, minimum undergraduate GPA of 3.0 (preferred); official transcripts (bachelor's, others as relevant), three letters of recommendation, career goals statement, minimum of 1 year of public or private school teaching experience or 2 years of experience as a conductor or associate conductor, performance portfolio. Additional exam requirements/recommendations for international students: Required—TOEFL (minimum score 550 paper-based; 79 iBT), IELTS (minimum score 6.5). *Application deadline:* For fall admission, 7/31 for domestic students, 6/1 for international students; for spring admission, 11/30 for domestic students, 10/15 for international students. Applications are processed on a rolling basis. Application fee: $30. Electronic applications accepted. Application fee is waived when completed online. *Financial support:* Fellowships, Federal Work-Study, scholarships/grants, health care benefits, and unspecified assistantships available. Support available to part-time students. Financial award application deadline: 7/31; financial award applicants required to submit FAFSA. *Unit head:* Dr. Jong Kim, Professor/Director of MA in Music, 434-544-8443, E-mail: kim@lynchburg.edu. *Application contact:* Christine Priller, Executive Assistant, Graduate Studies, 434-544-8383, Fax: 434-544-8483, E-mail: gradstudies@lynchburg.edu.
Website: http://www.lynchburg.edu/graduate/master-of-arts-in-music/

Lynn University, Conservatory of Music, Boca Raton, FL 33431-5598. Offers collaborative piano (MM); composition (MM); performance (MM); professional performance (Certificate). *Accreditation:* NASM. Part-time and evening/weekend programs available. *Faculty:* 17 full-time (3 women), 2 part-time/adjunct (1 woman). *Students:* 38 full-time (17 women), 23 part-time (10 women); includes 5 minority (3 Asian, non-Hispanic/Latino; 2 Hispanic/Latino), 33 international. Average age 26. 60 applicants, 100% accepted, 25 enrolled. In 2014, 9 master's, 6 Certificates awarded. *Degree requirements:* For master's, comprehensive exam, completion of program in 4 calendar years, minimum GPA of 3.0. *Entrance requirements:* For master's, bachelor's degree from accredited institution, essay/personal statement, resume, letter of recommendation, official transcripts, audition. Additional exam requirements/recommendations for international students: Required—TOEFL (minimum score 550 paper-based; 80 iBT), IELTS (minimum score 6.5). *Application deadline:* For fall admission, 3/31 priority date for domestic and international students; for spring admission, 12/1 priority date for domestic and international students. Applications are processed on a rolling basis. Application fee: $50. *Expenses:* Expenses: Contact institution. *Financial support:* In 2014–15, 61 students received support. Federal Work-Study, scholarships/grants, and unspecified assistantships available. Support available to part-time students. Financial award application deadline: 3/1; financial award applicants required to submit FAFSA. *Unit head:* Dr. Jon Robertson, Dean, 561-237-7702, Fax: 561-237-9002, E-mail: jrobertson@lynn.edu. *Application contact:* Steven Pruitt, Director of Graduate Admissions, 561-237-7834, Fax: 561-237-7100, E-mail: admission@lynn.edu.
Website: http://www.lynn.edu/academics/colleges/conservatory

Manhattan School of Music, Graduate Programs, New York, NY 10027-4698. Offers composition (MM, DMA); jazz (MM, DMA); music performance (MM, DMA); orchestral performance (MM). *Degree requirements:* For master's, recital; for doctorate, variable foreign language requirement, thesis/dissertation, departmental qualifying exam, recitals. *Entrance requirements:* For master's, audition, pre-screen CD, bachelor's degree; for doctorate, departmental exam, audition, interview, pre-screen CD, master's degree. Additional exam requirements/recommendations for international students: Required—TOEFL (minimum score 550 paper-based; 79 iBT). Electronic applications accepted.

Manhattan School of Music, Professional Studies Certificate Program, New York, NY 10027-4698. Offers instrumental music (CPS), including accompanying, brass, composition, guitar, orchestral performance, organ, piano, strings, voice, woodwinds; vocal music (CPS), including accompanying, brass, composition, guitar, orchestral performance, organ, piano, strings, voice, woodwinds. *Degree requirements:* For CPS, recital. *Entrance requirements:* For degree, audition, pre-screen CD. Additional exam requirements/recommendations for international students: Required—TOEFL (minimum score 550 paper-based). Electronic applications accepted.

Mansfield University of Pennsylvania, Graduate Studies, Department of Music, Mansfield, PA 16933. Offers band conducting (MA); choral conducting (MA); performance (MA). *Accreditation:* NASM. Part-time and evening/weekend programs available. *Degree requirements:* For master's, comprehensive exam, thesis optional. *Entrance requirements:* For master's, minimum GPA of 3.0, audition. Additional exam requirements/recommendations for international students: Required—TOEFL (minimum score 550 paper-based). Electronic applications accepted.

Marshall University, Academic Affairs Division, College of Arts and Media, Department of Music, Huntington, WV 25755. Offers MA. *Accreditation:* NASM. Evening/weekend programs available. *Faculty:* 9 full-time (1 woman), 1 (woman) part-time/adjunct. *Students:* 13 full-time (2 women), 5 part-time (2 women); includes 4 minority (1 Black or African American, non-Hispanic/Latino; 1 Asian, non-Hispanic/Latino; 1 Hispanic/Latino; 1 Two or more races, non-Hispanic/Latino), 1 international. Average age 27. In 2014, 6 master's awarded. *Degree requirements:* For master's, thesis optional. Application fee: $40. *Unit head:* Dr. Michael Stroeher, Chairperson, 304-696-3109, E-mail: stroeher@marshall.edu. *Application contact:* Information Contact, 304-746-1900, Fax: 304-746-1902, E-mail: services@marshall.edu.
Website: http://www.marshall.edu/somt/

McGill University, Faculty of Graduate and Postdoctoral Studies, Schulich School of Music, Montréal, QC H3A 2T5, Canada. Offers composition (M Mus, D Mus, PhD); music education (MA, PhD); music technology (MA, PhD); musicology (MA, PhD); performance (M Mus); performance studies (D Mus); sound recording (M Mus, PhD); theory (MA, PhD).

McNally Smith College of Music, Master of Music in Performance Program, Saint Paul, MN 55101. Offers bass performance (MM); brass and woodwind performance (MM); guitar performance (MM); keyboard performance (MM); percussion performance (MM); string performance (MM); vocal performance (MM). Part-time and evening/weekend programs available. *Degree requirements:* For master's, comprehensive exam, thesis, final project, final recital. *Entrance requirements:* For master's, audition, performance sample (2 recordings), artist statement, resume/curriculum vitae, 3 reference letters/letters of recommendation, undergraduate transcripts. Additional exam requirements/recommendations for international students: Required—TOEFL (minimum score 70 iBT), IELTS (minimum score 6.5). Electronic applications accepted.

Music

Memorial University of Newfoundland, School of Graduate Studies, Interdisciplinary Program in Ethnomusicology, St. John's, NL A1C 5S7, Canada. Offers MA, PhD. *Degree requirements:* For master's, thesis optional, research paper (non-thesis option); for doctorate, one foreign language, comprehensive exam, thesis/dissertation, oral defense of thesis. *Entrance requirements:* For master's, minimum B+ average with a B Mus or humanities/social sciences degree; for doctorate, MA in ethnomusicology or a related field.

Memorial University of Newfoundland, School of Graduate Studies, School of Music, St. John's, NL A1C 5S7, Canada. Offers conducting (MMus); performance pedagogy (MMus); performing (MMus). *Entrance requirements:* For master's, diagnostic exams measuring skills and knowledge in musical literacy, B Mus with first-class standing, audition (ca. 60 min. performance). Electronic applications accepted.

Mercer University, Graduate Studies, Macon Campus, School of Music, Macon, GA 31207. Offers choral conducting (MM); church music (MM); collaborative piano (MM); instrumental conducting (MM); performance (MM). Part-time programs available. *Faculty:* 14 full-time (6 women), 7 part-time/adjunct (5 women). *Students:* 17 full-time (7 women), 2 part-time (0 women); includes 6 minority (3 Black or African American, non-Hispanic/Latino; 3 Hispanic/Latino), 3 international. Average age 31. In 2014, 7 master's awarded. *Degree requirements:* For master's, comprehensive exam, recitals. *Entrance requirements:* For master's, GRE, audition. Additional exam requirements/recommendations for international students: Required—TOEFL (minimum score 550 paper-based; 80 iBT). *Application deadline:* Applications are processed on a rolling basis. Application fee: $100. Electronic applications accepted. *Expenses:* Expenses: Contact institution. *Financial support:* In 2014–15, 14 students received support. Tuition waivers and unspecified assistantships available. Financial award applicants required to submit FAFSA. *Faculty research:* Philosophy of church music, performance practices of the Baroque and Classical periods, organ repertoire of the High Baroque. *Total annual research expenditures:* $5,000. *Unit head:* Dr. Richard G. Kosowski, Director of Graduate Studies, 478-301-4167, Fax: 478-301-5633, E-mail: keith_cd@mercer.edu. *Application contact:* Director, 912-301-2700.
Website: http://music.mercer.edu

Messiah College, Program in Conducting, Mechanicsburg, PA 17055. Offers choral conducting (MM); orchestral conducting (MM); wind conducting (MM). *Accreditation:* NASM. Part-time programs available. Postbaccalaureate distance learning degree programs offered (minimal on-campus study). *Degree requirements:* For master's, advanced conducting project. Electronic applications accepted.

Miami University, College of Creative Arts, Department of Music, Oxford, OH 45056. Offers music education (MM); music performance (MM). *Accreditation:* NASM. *Students:* 19 full-time (7 women), 1 part-time (0 women); includes 7 minority (5 Black or African American, non-Hispanic/Latino; 1 Hispanic/Latino; 1 Two or more races, non-Hispanic/Latino), 2 international. Average age 24. In 2014, 18 master's awarded. *Entrance requirements:* Additional exam requirements/recommendations for international students: Recommended—TOEFL (minimum score 80 iBT), IELTS (minimum score 6.5), TSE (minimum score 54). Application fee: $50. Electronic applications accepted. *Expenses:* Tuition, state resident: full-time $12,887; part-time $537 per credit hour. Tuition, nonresident: full-time $28,449; part-time $1186 per credit hour. *Required fees:* $530; $24 per credit hour. $30 per quarter. Part-time tuition and fees vary according to course load and program. *Financial support:* Research assistantships with full and partial tuition reimbursements and teaching assistantships with full and partial tuition reimbursements available. Financial award application deadline: 2/15. *Unit head:* Dr. Bruce Murray, Chair and Professor, 513-529-3014, E-mail: bruce.murray@miamioh.edu. *Application contact:* Dr. Brenda Mitchell, Associate Professor of Music/Director of Graduate Studies, 513-529-1228, E-mail: mitchebs@miamioh.edu.
Website: http://www.MiamiOH.edu/music

Michigan State University, The Graduate School, College of Music, East Lansing, MI 48824. Offers collaborative piano (M Mus); jazz studies (M Mus); music (PhD); music composition (M Mus, DMA); music conducting (M Mus, DMA); music education (M Mus); music performance (M Mus, DMA); music theory (M Mus); music therapy (M Mus); musicology (MA); piano pedagogy (M Mus). *Accreditation:* NASM. *Entrance requirements:* Additional exam requirements/recommendations for international students: Required—TOEFL. Electronic applications accepted.

Middle Tennessee State University, College of Graduate Studies, College of Liberal Arts, School of Music, Murfreesboro, TN 37132. Offers MA. *Accreditation:* NASM. Part-time and evening/weekend programs available. Postbaccalaureate distance learning degree programs offered. *Faculty:* 27 full-time (8 women), 10 part-time/adjunct (3 women). *Students:* 17 full-time (6 women), 8 part-time (5 women); includes 5 minority (3 Black or African American, non-Hispanic/Latino; 1 Asian, non-Hispanic/Latino; 1 Two or more races, non-Hispanic/Latino), 4 international. 44 applicants, 73% accepted. In 2014, 7 master's awarded. *Degree requirements:* For master's, one foreign language, comprehensive exam, thesis optional. *Entrance requirements:* For master's, GRE or MAT. Additional exam requirements/recommendations for international students: Required—TOEFL (minimum score 525 paper-based; 71 iBT) or IELTS (minimum score 6). *Application deadline:* For fall admission, 6/1 for domestic and international students. Applications are processed on a rolling basis. Application fee: $30. Electronic applications accepted. *Financial support:* In 2014–15, 18 students received support. Tuition waivers available. Support available to part-time students. Financial award application deadline: 4/1; financial award applicants required to submit FAFSA. *Unit head:* Dr. Michael Parkinson, School Director, 615-898-5903, Fax: 615-898-5037, E-mail: michael.parkinson@mtsu.edu. *Application contact:* Dr. Michael D. Allen, Vice Provost for Research/Dean, 615-898-2840, Fax: 615-904-8020, E-mail: michael.allen@mtsu.edu.

Middle Tennessee State University, College of Graduate Studies, College of Mass Communication, Department of Recording Industry, Murfreesboro, TN 37132. Offers recording arts and technologies (MFA). Part-time and evening/weekend programs available. Postbaccalaureate distance learning degree programs offered. *Faculty:* 14 full-time (1 woman), 1 part-time/adjunct (0 women). *Students:* 24 full-time (6 women), 10 part-time (2 women); includes 8 minority (4 Black or African American, non-Hispanic/Latino; 2 Hispanic/Latino; 2 Two or more races, non-Hispanic/Latino), 5 international. 28 applicants, 86% accepted. In 2014, 11 master's awarded. *Degree requirements:* For master's, comprehensive exam, thesis or alternative. *Entrance requirements:* For master's, GRE. Additional exam requirements/recommendations for international students: Required—TOEFL (minimum score 525 paper-based; 71 iBT) or IELTS (minimum score 6). *Application deadline:* For fall admission, 6/1 for domestic and international students. Applications are processed on a rolling basis. Application fee: $30. *Financial support:* In 2014–15, 12 students received support. Tuition waivers available. Support available to part-time students. Financial award application deadline: 4/1. *Faculty research:* Digital audio, music production. *Unit head:* Beverly Keel, Chair, 615-904-8364, Fax: 615-494-7740, E-mail: beverly.keel@mtsu.edu. *Application contact:* Dr. Michael D. Allen, Vice Provost for Research/Dean, 615-898-2840, Fax: 615-904-8020, E-mail: michael.allen@mtsu.edu.
Website: http://www.mtsu.edu/mass-communication/recording-industry/

Midwestern Baptist Theological Seminary, Graduate and Professional Programs, Kansas City, MO 64118-4697. Offers Christian education (MACE); Christian foundations (Graduate Certificate); church music (MCM); counseling (MA); ministry (D Ed Min, D Min); Old or New Testament studies (PhD); theology (M Div). *Accreditation:* ATS. Part-time programs available. Postbaccalaureate distance learning degree programs offered (minimal on-campus study). *Degree requirements:* For doctorate, thesis/dissertation. *Entrance requirements:* For doctorate, MAT. Electronic applications accepted. *Faculty research:* Ministerial studies, Biblical and theological studies, missions, counseling.

Mills College, Graduate Studies, Department of Dance, Oakland, CA 94613-1000. Offers choreography (MFA); dance (MA); performance and choreography (MFA). Part-time programs available. *Faculty:* 5 full-time (3 women), 5 part-time/adjunct (all women). *Students:* 19 full-time (17 women); includes 5 minority (1 Black or African American, non-Hispanic/Latino; 1 Hispanic/Latino; 3 Two or more races, non-Hispanic/Latino), 3 international. Average age 28. 28 applicants, 68% accepted, 9 enrolled. In 2014, 11 master's awarded. *Degree requirements:* For master's, comprehensive exam, thesis, performance. *Entrance requirements:* For master's, audition, DVD recording of original choreography of up to two choreographic works (for MFA); writing sample with topic related to field of dance studies (for MA). Additional exam requirements/recommendations for international students: Required—TOEFL (minimum score 550 paper-based; 80 iBT) or IELTS (minimum score 6). *Application deadline:* For fall admission, 2/1 priority date for domestic students, 12/15 for international students. Applications are processed on a rolling basis. Application fee: $50. *Expenses: Tuition:* Full-time $31,620; part-time $7905 per course. *Required fees:* $1118. *Financial support:* In 2014–15, 10 students received support, including 17 fellowships (averaging $8,131 per year), 13 teaching assistantships with full and partial tuition reimbursements available (averaging $4,160 per year); scholarships/grants and unspecified assistantships also available. Financial award application deadline: 2/1; financial award applicants required to submit FAFSA. *Faculty research:* Modern techniques, movement for actors, choreography, dance criticism and analysis, dance and literature. *Unit head:* Sonya Delwaide, Department Head, 510-430-3301, E-mail: sdelwaid@mills.edu. *Application contact:* Shrim Bathey, Director of Graduate Admission, 510-430-3309, Fax: 510-430-2159, E-mail: grad-admission@mills.edu.
Website: http://www.mills.edu/dance

Mills College, Graduate Studies, Department of Music, Oakland, CA 94613-1000. Offers composition (MA); electronic music and recording media (MFA); performance and literature (MFA). Part-time programs available. *Faculty:* 6 full-time (2 women), 7 part-time/adjunct (2 women). *Students:* 42 full-time (11 women); includes 6 minority (4 Asian, non-Hispanic/Latino; 2 Hispanic/Latino), 3 international. Average age 31. 60 applicants, 72% accepted, 18 enrolled. In 2014, 20 master's awarded. *Degree requirements:* For master's, variable foreign language requirement, thesis, performance or recital. *Entrance requirements:* For master's, portfolio or audition. Additional exam requirements/recommendations for international students: Required—TOEFL (minimum score 550 paper-based; 80 iBT) or IELTS (minimum score 6). *Application deadline:* For fall admission, 1/15 priority date for domestic students, 12/15 for international students; for spring admission, 11/1 priority date for domestic students, 10/1 for international students. Applications are processed on a rolling basis. Application fee: $50. Electronic applications accepted. *Expenses: Tuition:* Full-time $31,620; part-time $7905 per course. *Required fees:* $1118. *Financial support:* In 2014–15, 48 students received support, including 35 fellowships with full and partial tuition reimbursements available (averaging $9,722 per year), 20 teaching assistantships with full and partial tuition reimbursements available (averaging $9,744 per year); scholarships/grants also available. Support available to part-time students. Financial award application deadline: 2/1; financial award applicants required to submit FAFSA. *Faculty research:* Composition and songwriting, nineteenth and twentieth century Western classical music and opera, interdisciplinary electroacoustic composition and performance, musical instrument building and new instrumental resources, sound installation. *Unit head:* David Bernstein, Head, Center for Contemporary Music, 510-430-2187, Fax: 510-430-3314, E-mail: maggi@mills.edu. *Application contact:* Shrim Bathey, Director of Graduate Admission, 510-430-3309, Fax: 510-430-2159, E-mail: grad-admission@mills.edu.
Website: http://www.mills.edu/music

Minnesota State University Mankato, College of Graduate Studies, College of Arts and Humanities, Department of Music, Mankato, MN 56001. Offers MAT, MM. *Accreditation:* NASM. *Students:* 3 full-time (0 women), 5 part-time (3 women). *Degree requirements:* For master's, comprehensive exam, thesis or alternative. *Entrance requirements:* For master's, minimum GPA of 3.0 during previous 2 years, audition or test. Additional exam requirements/recommendations for international students: Required—TOEFL. *Application deadline:* For fall admission, 7/1 priority date for domestic students; for spring admission, 11/1 for domestic students. Applications are processed on a rolling basis. Application fee: $40. Electronic applications accepted. *Financial support:* Research assistantships with full tuition reimbursements, teaching assistantships with full tuition reimbursements, career-related internships or fieldwork, Federal Work-Study, and institutionally sponsored loans available. Support available to part-time students. Financial award application deadline: 3/15. *Unit head:* Dr. David Dickau, Graduate Coordinator, 507-389-2118. *Application contact:* 507-389-2321, E-mail: grad@mnsu.edu.

Mississippi College, Graduate School, College of Arts and Sciences, School of Christian Studies and the Arts, Department of Music, Clinton, MS 39058. Offers applied music performance (MM); conducting (MM); music education (MM); music performance: organ (MM); vocal pedagogy (MM). *Accreditation:* NASM. Part-time and evening/weekend programs available. *Degree requirements:* For master's, comprehensive exam, recital. *Entrance requirements:* For master's, GRE, minimum GPA of 2.5. Additional exam requirements/recommendations for international students: Recommended—TOEFL, IELTS. Electronic applications accepted.

Missouri State University, Graduate College, College of Arts and Letters, Department of Music, Springfield, MO 65897. Offers MM, MS Ed. *Accreditation:* NASM. Part-time programs available. *Faculty:* 27 full-time (11 women), 1 (woman) part-time/adjunct. *Students:* 13 full-time (7 women), 27 part-time (13 women); includes 4 minority (2 Black or African American, non-Hispanic/Latino; 2 Hispanic/Latino), 6 international. Average age 28. 28 applicants, 86% accepted, 16 enrolled. In 2014, 17 master's awarded. *Degree requirements:* For master's, comprehensive exam, thesis or alternative. *Entrance requirements:* For master's, GRE, interview/audition (MM), 9-12 teaching certification (MS Ed). Additional exam requirements/recommendations for international students: Required—TOEFL (minimum score 550 paper-based; 79 iBT). *Application deadline:* For fall admission, 7/20 for domestic students, 5/1 for international students; for spring admission, 12/20 for domestic students, 9/1 for international students. Applications are processed on a rolling basis. Application fee: $35 ($50 for international students). Electronic applications accepted. *Expenses:* Tuition, state resident: full-time $2250; part-time $250 per credit hour. Tuition, nonresident: full-time $4509; part-time $501 per credit hour. Tuition and fees vary according to course level, course load and program. *Financial support:* In 2014–15, 5 teaching assistantships with full tuition reimbursements (averaging $8,450 per year) were awarded; Federal Work-Study, institutionally sponsored loans, scholarships/grants, tuition waivers (partial), and

unspecified assistantships also available. Financial award application deadline: 3/31; financial award applicants required to submit FAFSA. *Faculty research:* Musical theatre, Ozarks music, carillon, jazz studies. *Unit head:* Dr. Julie Combs, Head, 417-836-5648, Fax: 417-836-7665, E-mail: music@missouristate.edu. *Application contact:* Misty Stewart, Coordinator of Graduate Recruitment, 417-836-6079, Fax: 417-836-6200, E-mail: mistystewart@missouristate.edu.
Website: http://www.missouristate.edu/music/

Montclair State University, The Graduate School, College of the Arts, John J. Cali School of Music, Artist's Diploma Program, Montclair, NJ 07043-1624. Offers AD. Part-time and evening/weekend programs available. *Students:* 5 part-time (3 women), 3 international. Average age 29. 6 applicants, 83% accepted, 3 enrolled. In 2014, 10 ADs awarded. *Entrance requirements:* For degree, essay. Additional exam requirements/recommendations for international students: Required—TOEFL (minimum score 83 iBT), IELTS (minimum score 6.5). *Application deadline:* Applications are processed on a rolling basis. Application fee: $60. Electronic applications accepted. *Expenses:* Tuition, state resident: full-time $9960; part-time $553.35 per credit. Tuition, nonresident: full-time $15,074; part-time $837.43 per credit. *Required fees:* $1595; $88.63 per credit. Tuition and fees vary according to degree level and program. *Financial support:* Federal Work-Study, scholarships/grants, and unspecified assistantships available. Support available to part-time students. Financial award application deadline: 3/1; financial award applicants required to submit FAFSA. *Unit head:* Prof. Robert Aldridge, Chairperson, 973-655-7212. *Application contact:* Amy Aiello, Executive Director of The Graduate School, 973-655-5147, Fax: 973-655-7869, E-mail: graduate.school@montclair.edu.

Montclair State University, The Graduate School, College of the Arts, John J. Cali School of Music, Performer's Certificate Program, Montclair, NJ 07043-1624. Offers Performer's Certificate. *Students:* 8 part-time (5 women); includes 1 minority (Asian, non-Hispanic/Latino), 6 international. Average age 27. 8 applicants, 88% accepted, 6 enrolled. In 2014, 5 Performer's Certificates awarded. *Expenses:* Tuition, state resident: full-time $9960; part-time $553.35 per credit. Tuition, nonresident: full-time $15,074; part-time $837.43 per credit. *Required fees:* $1595; $88.63 per credit. Tuition and fees vary according to degree level and program. *Unit head:* Dr. Robert Cart, Coordinator. *Application contact:* Amy Aiello, Executive Director of The Graduate School, 973-655-5147, Fax: 973-655-7869, E-mail: graduate.school@montclair.edu.

Montclair State University, The Graduate School, College of the Arts, John J. Cali School of Music, Program in Music, Montclair, NJ 07043-1624. Offers music education (MA); music therapy (MA); performance (MA); theory/composition (MA). Part-time and evening/weekend programs available. *Students:* 24 full-time (12 women), 36 part-time (18 women); includes 9 minority (3 Black or African American, non-Hispanic/Latino; 3 Asian, non-Hispanic/Latino; 3 Hispanic/Latino), 5 international. Average age 31. 60 applicants, 45% accepted, 20 enrolled. In 2014, 13 master's awarded. *Degree requirements:* For master's, thesis. *Entrance requirements:* For master's, GRE General Test, 2 letters of recommendation, essay. Additional exam requirements/recommendations for international students: Required—TOEFL (minimum score 83 iBT), IELTS (minimum score 6.5). *Application deadline:* Applications are processed on a rolling basis. Application fee: $60. Electronic applications accepted. *Expenses:* Tuition, state resident: full-time $9960; part-time $553.35 per credit. Tuition, nonresident: full-time $15,074; part-time $837.43 per credit. *Required fees:* $1595; $88.63 per credit. Tuition and fees vary according to degree level and program. *Financial support:* In 2014–15, 3 research assistantships with full tuition reimbursements (averaging $7,000 per year) were awarded; Federal Work-Study, scholarships/grants, and unspecified assistantships also available. Support available to part-time students. Financial award application deadline: 3/1; financial award applicants required to submit FAFSA. *Unit head:* Prof. Robert Aldridge, Chairperson, 973-655-7212. *Application contact:* Amy Aiello, Executive Director of The Graduate School, 973-655-5147, Fax: 973-655-7869, E-mail: graduate.school@montclair.edu.
Website: http://www.montclair.edu/Arts/music/

Morehead State University, Graduate Programs, Caudill College of Arts, Humanities and Social Sciences, Department of Music, Theatre and Dance, Morehead, KY 40351. Offers music education (MM); music performance (MM). *Accreditation:* NASM. Part-time and evening/weekend programs available. *Degree requirements:* For master's, comprehensive exam, oral and written exams. *Entrance requirements:* For master's, music entrance exam, BA in music with minimum GPA of 3.0, 2.5 overall; audition. Additional exam requirements/recommendations for international students: Required—TOEFL (minimum score 550 paper-based). Electronic applications accepted. *Faculty research:* Musical instrument digital interface (MIDI) applications, tonal concepts of euphonium and baritone horn, digital synthesis, computer-assisted instruction in music, musical composition.

Morgan State University, School of Graduate Studies, College of Liberal Arts, Department of Fine and Performing Arts, Baltimore, MD 21251. Offers MA. *Accreditation:* NASM. Part-time and evening/weekend programs available. *Degree requirements:* For master's, comprehensive exam, thesis. *Entrance requirements:* Additional exam requirements/recommendations for international students: Required—TOEFL (minimum score 550 paper-based).

Murray State University, College of Humanities and Fine Arts, Program in Music, Murray, KY 42071. Offers music education (MME). *Accreditation:* NASM. Part-time programs available. *Entrance requirements:* For master's, GRE General Test or MAT. Additional exam requirements/recommendations for international students: Required—TOEFL.

New England Conservatory of Music, Graduate Program in Music, Boston, MA 02115-5000. Offers MM, DMA, Diploma. *Accreditation:* NASM (one or more programs are accredited). *Degree requirements:* For master's, thesis (for some programs), recital; for doctorate, one foreign language, comprehensive exam, thesis/dissertation, qualifying exams, recital. *Entrance requirements:* For master's and Diploma, audition; for doctorate, music theory and musicology exam, audition. Additional exam requirements/recommendations for international students: Required—TOEFL (minimum score 550 paper-based; 79 iBT).

New Jersey City University, Graduate Studies and Continuing Education, William J. Maxwell College of Arts and Sciences, Department of Music, Dance and Theatre, Jersey City, NJ 07305-1597. Offers music education (MA); performance (MM). *Accreditation:* NASM. Part-time and evening/weekend programs available. *Faculty:* 5 full-time (3 women), 4 part-time/adjunct (0 women). *Students:* 18 full-time (8 women), 12 part-time (4 women); includes 10 minority (3 Black or African American, non-Hispanic/Latino; 1 Asian, non-Hispanic/Latino; 5 Hispanic/Latino; 1 Two or more races, non-Hispanic/Latino), 4 international. Average age 31. 11 applicants, 100% accepted, 9 enrolled. In 2014, 6 master's awarded. *Degree requirements:* For master's, thesis optional, recital. *Entrance requirements:* Additional exam requirements/recommendations for international students: Required—TOEFL (minimum score 79 iBT). *Application deadline:* For fall admission, 8/1 priority date for domestic students; for spring admission, 12/1 for domestic students. Applications are processed on a rolling basis. Application fee: $0. *Expenses: Tuition, area resident:* Part-time $538 per credit. Tuition, state resident: part-time $538 per credit. Tuition, nonresident: part-time $948 per credit. *Financial support:* Unspecified assistantships available. *Unit head:* Dr. Min Kim, Chairperson, 201-200-3157, E-mail: mkim@njcu.edu. *Application contact:* Jose Balda, E-mail: jbalda@njcu.edu.

New Mexico State University, College of Arts and Sciences, Department of Music, Las Cruces, NM 88003-8001. Offers conducting (MM); music education (MM); performance (MM). *Accreditation:* NASM. Part-time programs available. *Faculty:* 16 full-time (5 women), 3 part-time/adjunct (1 woman). *Students:* 10 full-time (3 women), 8 part-time (3 women); includes 9 minority (1 American Indian or Alaska Native, non-Hispanic/Latino; 1 Asian, non-Hispanic/Latino; 7 Hispanic/Latino), 4 international. Average age 30. 9 applicants, 67% accepted, 6 enrolled. In 2014, 7 master's awarded. *Degree requirements:* For master's, comprehensive exam (for some programs), thesis (for some programs), recital. *Entrance requirements:* For master's, diagnostic exam, audition, bachelor's degree or equivalent from an accredited institution. Additional exam requirements/recommendations for international students: Required—TOEFL (minimum score 550 paper-based; 79 iBT), IELTS (minimum score 6.5). *Application deadline:* For fall admission, 7/1 priority date for domestic students; for spring admission, 11/1 for domestic students. Applications are processed on a rolling basis. Application fee: $40 ($50 for international students). Electronic applications accepted. *Expenses:* Expenses: Contact institution. *Financial support:* In 2014–15, 16 students received support, including 8 teaching assistantships (averaging $13,462 per year); career-related internships or fieldwork, Federal Work-Study, scholarships/grants, traineeships, health care benefits, and unspecified assistantships also available. Support available to part-time students. Financial award application deadline: 3/1. *Faculty research:* Music education, contemporary wind band literature, performance, music history, composition. *Total annual research expenditures:* $6,439. *Unit head:* Dr. Lon W. Chaffin, Academic Department Head, 575-646-2421, Fax: 575-646-8199, E-mail: lchaffin@nmsu.edu. *Application contact:* Dr. James Shearer, Coordinator of Graduate Studies, 575-646-2601, Fax: 575-646-8199, E-mail: jshearer@nmsu.edu.
Website: http://music.nmsu.edu

New Orleans Baptist Theological Seminary, Graduate and Professional Programs, Division of Church Music Ministries, New Orleans, LA 70126-4858. Offers M Div, MMCM, DMA. *Accreditation:* NASM. Postbaccalaureate distance learning degree programs offered. *Degree requirements:* For doctorate, one foreign language, thesis/dissertation. *Entrance requirements:* For doctorate, GRE General Test. Additional exam requirements/recommendations for international students: Required—TOEFL.

The New School, Mannes College The New School for Music, New York, NY 10024. Offers music performance and composition (MM). *Degree requirements:* For master's, recital, professional performance with graduation juries. *Entrance requirements:* For master's, audition. Additional exam requirements/recommendations for international students: Required—TOEFL. Electronic applications accepted.

New York University, Graduate School of Arts and Science, Department of Music, New York, NY 10012-1019. Offers composition and theory (MA, PhD); early music performance (Advanced Certificate); ethnomusicology (MA, PhD). *Students:* 41 full-time (20 women), 5 part-time (3 women); includes 5 minority (1 Black or African American, non-Hispanic/Latino; 1 Asian, non-Hispanic/Latino; 2 Hispanic/Latino; 1 Two or more races, non-Hispanic/Latino), 18 international. Average age 33. 126 applicants, 5% accepted, 5 enrolled. In 2014, 2 master's, 7 doctorates awarded. Terminal master's awarded for partial completion of doctoral program. *Degree requirements:* For master's, one foreign language, thesis (for some programs), general exam; for doctorate, 2 foreign languages, thesis/dissertation, general and special exams. *Entrance requirements:* For master's, GRE General Test, bachelor's degree in liberal arts or music; for doctorate, GRE General Test, master's degree in music. Additional exam requirements/recommendations for international students: Required—TOEFL. *Application deadline:* For fall admission, 1/4 for domestic and international students. Application fee: $100. *Financial support:* Fellowships with tuition reimbursements, teaching assistantships with tuition reimbursements, Federal Work-Study, institutionally sponsored loans, scholarships/grants, health care benefits, and unspecified assistantships available. Financial award application deadline: 1/4; financial award applicants required to submit FAFSA. *Faculty research:* Early music (nineteenth century), Wagner, Verdi, performance practice. *Unit head:* David Samuels, Chair, 212-998-8300, Fax: 212-995-4147, E-mail: fas.music.gradadmissions@nyu.edu. *Application contact:* Maureen Mahon, Director of Graduate Studies, 212-998-8300, Fax: 212-995-4147, E-mail: fas.music.gradadmissions@nuy.edu.
Website: http://www.nyu.edu/gsas/dept/music/

New York University, Steinhardt School of Culture, Education, and Human Development, Department of Music and Performing Arts Professions, Program in Music Business, New York, NY 10012. Offers music business (MA); music technology (MA). Part-time programs available. *Faculty:* 4 full-time (2 women). *Students:* 64 full-time (36 women), 17 part-time (6 women); includes 23 minority (9 Black or African American, non-Hispanic/Latino; 5 Asian, non-Hispanic/Latino; 9 Hispanic/Latino), 23 international. Average age 26. 99 applicants, 64% accepted, 41 enrolled. In 2014, 36 master's awarded. *Degree requirements:* For master's, thesis (for some programs). *Entrance requirements:* For master's, interview. Additional exam requirements/recommendations for international students: Required—TOEFL (minimum score 100 iBT). *Application deadline:* For fall admission, 12/1 priority date for domestic and international students. Applications are processed on a rolling basis. Application fee: $75. Electronic applications accepted. *Financial support:* Career-related internships or fieldwork, Federal Work-Study, scholarships/grants, and tuition waivers (partial) available. Support available to part-time students. Financial award application deadline: 2/1; financial award applicants required to submit FAFSA. *Faculty research:* Strategic marketing, new technologies, intellectual property, entrepreneurship, globalization, music in video games. *Unit head:* Dr. Catherine Moore-Broatman, Director, 212-998-5427, Fax: 212-998-4560, E-mail: catherine.moore@nyu.edu. *Application contact:* 212-998-5030, Fax: 212-995-4328, E-mail: steinhardt.gradadmissions@nyu.edu.
Website: http://steinhardt.nyu.edu/music/business

New York University, Steinhardt School of Culture, Education, and Human Development, Department of Music and Performing Arts Professions, Program in Music Performance and Composition, New York, NY 10012. Offers instrumental performance (MM), including instrumental performance, jazz instrumental performance; music performance and composition (PhD), including music performance and composition; music theory and composition (MM), including composition for music theater, computer music composition, music theory and composition, scoring for film and multimedia, songwriting; piano performance (MM), including collaborative piano, solo piano; vocal pedagogy (Advanced Certificate); vocal performance (MM), including classical voice, musical theatre performance; vocal performance/vocal pedagogy (MM), including classical voice, musical theatre performance. Part-time programs available. *Faculty:* 25 full-time (7 women). *Students:* 228 full-time (107 women), 79 part-time (37 women); includes 51 minority (9 Black or African American, non-Hispanic/Latino; 18 Asian, non-Hispanic/Latino; 14 Hispanic/Latino; 10 Two or more races, non-Hispanic/Latino), 130 international. Average age 27. 534 applicants, 50% accepted, 141 enrolled. In 2014, 130 master's, 2 doctorates, 12 other advanced degrees awarded. *Degree requirements:* For master's, thesis (for some programs); for doctorate, thesis/dissertation. *Entrance requirements:* For master's, audition; for doctorate, GRE General Test, audition,

interview. Additional exam requirements/recommendations for international students: Required—TOEFL (minimum score 100 iBT). *Application deadline:* For fall admission, 12/1 priority date for domestic and international students; for spring admission, 10/1 for domestic and international students. Applications are processed on a rolling basis. Application fee: $75. Electronic applications accepted. *Financial support:* Fellowships with full and partial tuition reimbursements, Federal Work-Study, scholarships/grants, and tuition waivers (partial) available. Support available to part-time students. Financial award application deadline: 2/1; financial award applicants required to submit FAFSA. *Faculty research:* Aesthetics, performance analysis, twentieth century music, music methodologies for arts criticism and analysis. *Unit head:* Dr. Tae Hong Park, Director, 212-998-5424, Fax: 212-995-4043, E-mail: tae.hong.park@nyu.edu. *Application contact:* 212-998-5030, Fax: 212-995-4328, E-mail: steinhardt.gradadmissions@nyu.edu.
Website: http://steinhardt.nyu.edu/music/composition/programs/graduate

New York University, Steinhardt School of Culture, Education, and Human Development, Department of Music and Performing Arts Professions, Program in Music Technology, New York, NY 10012. Offers MM, PhD. Part-time programs available. *Faculty:* 5 full-time (2 women). *Students:* 83 full-time (18 women), 33 part-time (5 women); includes 17 minority (6 Black or African American, non-Hispanic/Latino; 5 Asian, non-Hispanic/Latino; 4 Hispanic/Latino; 2 Two or more races, non-Hispanic/Latino), 48 international. Average age 30. 126 applicants, 70% accepted, 40 enrolled. In 2014, 24 master's, 2 doctorates awarded. *Degree requirements:* For master's, thesis (for some programs); for doctorate, thesis/dissertation. *Entrance requirements:* For master's, portfolio; for doctorate, essay, 3 letters of recommendation, master's degree. Additional exam requirements/recommendations for international students: Required—TOEFL (minimum score 100 iBT). *Application deadline:* For fall admission, 12/1 priority date for domestic and international students; for spring admission, 10/1 for domestic and international students. Applications are processed on a rolling basis. Application fee: $75. Electronic applications accepted. *Financial support:* Fellowships with full and partial tuition reimbursements, research assistantships with full and partial tuition reimbursements, career-related internships or fieldwork, Federal Work-Study, institutionally sponsored loans, scholarships/grants, and tuition waivers (partial) available. Support available to part-time students. Financial award application deadline: 2/1; financial award applicants required to submit FAFSA. *Faculty research:* Pattern processing in music, computer music, acoustics, music perception, interactive music systems. *Unit head:* Prof. Kenneth J. Peacock, Director, 212-998-5424, Fax: 212-995-4043, E-mail: kp3@nyu.edu. *Application contact:* 212-998-5030, Fax: 212-995-4328, E-mail: steinhardt.gradadmissions@nyu.edu.
Website: http://steinhardt.nyu.edu/music/technology

New York University, Tisch School of the Arts, Graduate Musical Theatre Writing Program, New York, NY 10012-1019. Offers MFA. *Faculty:* 6 full-time, 14 part-time/adjunct. *Students:* 56 full-time (30 women), 1 part-time (0 women); includes 11 minority (3 Black or African American, non-Hispanic/Latino; 2 Asian, non-Hispanic/Latino; 3 Hispanic/Latino; 3 Two or more races, non-Hispanic/Latino), 13 international. Average age 28. 60 applicants, 82% accepted, 31 enrolled. In 2014, 21 master's awarded. *Degree requirements:* For master's, full-length musical theatre work. *Entrance requirements:* For master's, interview, portfolio. Additional exam requirements/recommendations for international students: Required—TOEFL or IELTS. *Application deadline:* For fall admission, 2/1 priority date for domestic and international students. Application fee: $60. Electronic applications accepted. *Financial support:* In 2014–15, 18 students received support. Fellowships with tuition reimbursements available, career-related internships or fieldwork, Federal Work-Study, tuition waivers (partial), and unspecified assistantships available. Financial award application deadline: 2/15; financial award applicants required to submit FAFSA. *Unit head:* Sarah Schlesinger, Chair, 212-998-1830, Fax: 212-995-4873, E-mail: musical.theatre@nyu.edu. *Application contact:* Dan Sandford, Director of Graduate Admissions, 212-998-1918, Fax: 212-995-4060, E-mail: tisch.gradadmissions@nyu.edu.
Website: http://www.gmtw.tisch.nyu.edu/

Norfolk State University, School of Graduate Studies, School of Liberal Arts, Department of Music, Norfolk, VA 23504. Offers music (MM); music education (MM); performance (MM); theory and composition (MM). *Accreditation:* NASM. Part-time programs available. *Degree requirements:* For master's, thesis or alternative. *Entrance requirements:* For master's, minimum GPA of 2.7, letters of recommendation. Additional exam requirements/recommendations for international students: Required—TOEFL.

North Carolina Central University, College of Liberal Arts, Department of Music, Durham, NC 27707-3129. Offers jazz studies (MM).

North Dakota State University, College of Graduate and Interdisciplinary Studies, College of Arts, Humanities and Social Sciences, Department of Music, Fargo, ND 58108. Offers M Ed, MM, DMA. *Accreditation:* NASM. *Degree requirements:* For master's, 2 foreign languages, comprehensive exam, thesis or alternative, recitals; for doctorate, 2 foreign languages, comprehensive exam, thesis/dissertation or alternative, recitals. *Entrance requirements:* For master's and doctorate, music history, music theory, performance audition. Additional exam requirements/recommendations for international students: Required—TOEFL (minimum score 525 paper-based; 71 iBT). Electronic applications accepted. *Faculty research:* Performance, conducting.

Northeastern Illinois University, College of Graduate Studies and Research, College of Arts and Sciences, Program in Music, Chicago, IL 60625-4699. Offers MA. *Accreditation:* NASM. Part-time and evening/weekend programs available. *Degree requirements:* For master's, comprehensive exam, thesis optional. *Entrance requirements:* For master's, departmental exam, audition, minimum GPA of 2.75. Additional exam requirements/recommendations for international students: Required—TOEFL (minimum score 550 paper-based; 79 iBT). Electronic applications accepted. *Faculty research:* World music, computers as applied instruments, vocal pedagogy, vocal interpretation, jazz repertory.

Northern Arizona University, Graduate College, College of Arts and Letters, School of Music, Flagstaff, AZ 86011. Offers choral conducting (MM); composition (MM); instrumental conducting (MM); instrumental performance (MM); musicology (MM); performance (Certificate); piano and chamber music (MM); Suzuki violin/viola (MM); theory (MM); voice performance (MM). *Accreditation:* NASM. *Degree requirements:* For master's, comprehensive exam, thesis (for some programs), departmental exams. *Entrance requirements:* For master's, bachelor's degree in music, minimum GPA of 3.0, audition. Additional exam requirements/recommendations for international students: Required—TOEFL (minimum score 550 paper-based; 80 iBT), IELTS (minimum score 7). Electronic applications accepted.

Northern Illinois University, Graduate School, College of Visual and Performing Arts, School of Music, De Kalb, IL 60115-2854. Offers MM, Performer's Certificate. *Accreditation:* NASM. Part-time programs available. *Faculty:* 33 full-time (3 women), 14 part-time/adjunct (3 women). *Students:* 36 full-time (23 women), 50 part-time (26 women); includes 17 minority (6 Black or African American, non-Hispanic/Latino; 6 Asian, non-Hispanic/Latino; 4 Hispanic/Latino; 1 Two or more races, non-Hispanic/Latino), 27 international. Average age 29. 107 applicants, 58% accepted, 27 enrolled. In 2014, 47 master's, 8 other advanced degrees awarded. *Degree requirements:* For master's, comprehensive exam, thesis optional, recital or project; for Performer's Certificate, recitals. *Entrance requirements:* For master's, minimum GPA of 2.75, appropriate bachelor's degree, audition, interview; for Performer's Certificate, minimum GPA of 2.75 (undergraduate), 3.2 (graduate); audition. Additional exam requirements/recommendations for international students: Required—TOEFL (minimum score 550 paper-based). *Application deadline:* For fall admission, 4/1 for domestic students, 5/1 for international students; for spring admission, 11/1 for domestic students, 10/1 for international students. Applications are processed on a rolling basis. Application fee: $40. Electronic applications accepted. *Financial support:* In 2014–15, 33 teaching assistantships with full tuition reimbursements were awarded; fellowships with full tuition reimbursements, research assistantships with full tuition reimbursements, Federal Work-Study, scholarships/grants, tuition waivers (full), and staff assistantships also available. Support available to part-time students. Financial award applicants required to submit FAFSA. *Faculty research:* Impact of music on urban children and acquisition of language skills, music in seventeenth-century Madrid, Finnish music and culture, jazz studies. *Unit head:* Dr. Paul Bauer, Director, 815-753-1551, Fax: 815-753-1759, E-mail: paulbauer@niu.edu. *Application contact:* Lynn Slater, Coordinator of Admissions and Public Relations, 815-753-1546, E-mail: lslater@niu.edu.
Website: http://www.niu.edu/music/

Northern Kentucky University, Office of Graduate Programs, College of Arts and Sciences, Program in English, Highland Heights, KY 41099. Offers composition and rhetoric (Certificate); creative writing (Certificate); cultural studies and discourses (Certificate); English (MA); professional writing (Certificate). Part-time and evening/weekend programs available. *Faculty:* 13 full-time (6 women), 6 part-time/adjunct (0 women). *Students:* 2 full-time (1 woman), 51 part-time (39 women); includes 3 minority (2 Black or African American, non-Hispanic/Latino; 1 Two or more races, non-Hispanic/Latino). Average age 36. In 2014, 10 master's, 9 other advanced degrees awarded. *Degree requirements:* For master's, comprehensive exam (for some programs), capstone (thesis, portfolio, project, or exams); 30 hours of credit; for Certificate, 18 hours of credit. *Entrance requirements:* For master's, bachelor's degree in English or related field from regionally-accredited institution with minimum GPA of 3.0 in major or cognate area coursework; official transcripts for all undergraduate and graduate work; two letters of reference; for Certificate, official transcripts for all undergraduate and graduate work; bachelor's degree from regionally-accredited institution; minimum undergraduate GPA of 2.5. Additional exam requirements/recommendations for international students: Required—TOEFL (minimum score 79 iBT); Recommended—IELTS (minimum score 6.5). *Application deadline:* For fall admission, 7/1 priority date for domestic students, 6/1 priority date for international students; for spring admission, 11/1 priority date for domestic students, 10/1 for international students. Application fee: $40. Electronic applications accepted. *Expenses: Tuition, area resident:* Part-time $518 per credit hour. Tuition, state resident: part-time $630 per credit hour. Tuition, nonresident: part-time $797 per credit hour. *Required fees:* $192 per semester. Tuition and fees vary according to course load, degree level, campus/location, program and reciprocity agreements. *Financial support:* In 2014–15, 8 students received support. Unspecified assistantships available. Financial award applicants required to submit FAFSA. *Unit head:* Dr. John Alberti, Director of English Graduate Studies, 859-572-5619, Fax: 859-572-6093, E-mail: alberti@nku.edu. *Application contact:* Alison Swanson, Graduate Admissions Coordinator, 859-572-6971, E-mail: swansona1@nku.edu.
Website: http://english.nku.edu/gradprogram/

North Park University, School of Music, Chicago, IL 60625-4895. Offers vocal performance (MM). *Accreditation:* NASM.

Northwestern State University of Louisiana, Graduate Studies and Research, School of Creative and Performing Arts, Program in Music, Natchitoches, LA 71497. Offers MM. *Accreditation:* NASM. *Degree requirements:* For master's, comprehensive exam, thesis or alternative. *Entrance requirements:* For master's, GRE General Test, minimum undergraduate GPA of 2.5. Additional exam requirements/recommendations for international students: Required—TOEFL. Electronic applications accepted.

Northwestern University, The Graduate School, School of Communication, Department of Performance Studies, Evanston, IL 60208. Offers MA, PhD. Admissions and degrees offered through The Graduate School. Part-time programs available. Terminal master's awarded for partial completion of doctoral program. *Degree requirements:* For master's, recital; for doctorate, one foreign language, thesis/dissertation, recital. *Entrance requirements:* For master's and doctorate, GRE General Test. Additional exam requirements/recommendations for international students: Required—TOEFL. *Faculty research:* Adaptation/performance of literature, ethnography of performance, critical cultural studies, performance theory, intercultural performance, gender studies.

Northwestern University, Henry and Leigh Bienen School of Music, Department of Music Performance, Evanston, IL 60208. Offers brass performance (MM, DMA); conducting (MM, DMA); jazz studies (MM); percussion performance (MM, DMA); performance (MM); piano pedagogy (MME); piano performance (MM, DMA); piano performance and collaborative arts (MM, DMA); piano performance and pedagogy (MM, DMA); string performance (MM, DMA); voice and opera performance (MM, DMA); woodwind performance (MM, DMA). *Accreditation:* NASM. *Degree requirements:* For master's, recital; for doctorate, comprehensive exam, thesis/dissertation, 3 recitals. *Entrance requirements:* For master's, audition, preliminary tapes in voice, flute, percussion; for doctorate, written essay exam (theory and music history), audition, preliminary tapes. Additional exam requirements/recommendations for international students: Required—TOEFL (minimum score 600 paper-based; 100 iBT).

Northwestern University, Henry and Leigh Bienen School of Music, Department of Music Studies, Evanston, IL 60208. Offers composition (DMA); music education (MME, PhD); music theory and cognition (PhD); musicology (MM, PhD); theory (MM). PhD admissions and degree offered through The Graduate School. *Accreditation:* NASM. *Degree requirements:* For doctorate, comprehensive exam, thesis/dissertation. *Entrance requirements:* For master's, portfolio or research papers; for doctorate, GRE General Test (for PhD), portfolio, research papers. Additional exam requirements/recommendations for international students: Required—TOEFL (minimum score 600 paper-based; 100 iBT). *Faculty research:* Music cognition, cognitive learning, aesthetic education, computer music, technology in education.

Notre Dame de Namur University, Division of Academic Affairs, College of Arts and Sciences, Program in Musical Performance, Belmont, CA 94002-1908. Offers MFA, Certificate. Part-time programs available. *Degree requirements:* For master's, recital, final project. *Entrance requirements:* For master's, audition, appropriate bachelor's degree, minimum GPA of 2.5. Additional exam requirements/recommendations for international students: Required—TOEFL (minimum score 550 paper-based; 79 iBT). Electronic applications accepted.

Oakland University, Graduate Study and Lifelong Learning, College of Arts and Sciences, Department of Music, Rochester, MI 48309-4401. Offers music (MM); music education (PhD). *Accreditation:* NASM. *Entrance requirements:* For master's, minimum GPA of 3.0. Additional exam requirements/recommendations for international students: Required—TOEFL (minimum score 550 paper-based). Electronic applications accepted. *Expenses:* Contact institution.

Oberlin College, Conservatory of Music, Oberlin, OH 44074-1588. Offers contemporary chamber music (MM); historical performance (MM); music education (MMT); performance (AD). *Accreditation:* NASM. *Students:* 15 full-time (6 women). 81 applicants, 15% accepted, 9 enrolled. In 2014, 11 master's, 1 AD awarded. *Degree requirements:* For master's, 2 recitals. *Entrance requirements:* For master's and AD, audition. Additional exam requirements/recommendations for international students: Required—TOEFL (minimum score 100 iBT). *Application deadline:* For fall admission, 12/1 for domestic and international students. Application fee: $100. Electronic applications accepted. *Financial support:* Career-related internships or fieldwork, Federal Work-Study, and scholarships/grants available. Financial award application deadline: 2/15; financial award applicants required to submit CSS PROFILE or FAFSA. *Unit head:* Andrea Kalyn, Dean, 440-775-8200. *Application contact:* Michael Manderen, Director of Conservatory Admissions, 440-775-8413, Fax: 440-775-6972, E-mail: conservatory.admissions@oberlin.edu.
Website: http://new.oberlin.edu/conservatory/

The Ohio State University, Graduate School, College of Arts and Sciences, Division of Arts and Humanities, Department of Dance, Columbus, OH 43210. Offers choreography (MFA); dance (MFA, PhD); dance and technology (MFA); dance studies (PhD); history, theory and literature (MFA); lighting and production (MFA); movement analysis, Laban studies, notation and dance documentation (MFA); performance (MFA). *Accreditation:* NASD. *Faculty:* 15. *Students:* 33 full-time (24 women), 1 (woman) part-time; includes 5 minority (1 Asian, non-Hispanic/Latino; 3 Hispanic/Latino; 1 Two or more races, non-Hispanic/Latino), 6 international. Average age 31. In 2014, 2 master's awarded. *Degree requirements:* For master's, thesis optional. *Entrance requirements:* For master's, GRE General Test (for all applicants with cumulative GPA below 3.0), audition; for doctorate, GRE General Test, invitation-only interview. Additional exam requirements/recommendations for international students: Required—Michigan English Language Assessment Battery (minimum score 82); Recommended—TOEFL (minimum score 550 paper-based; 79 iBT), IELTS (minimum score 7). *Application deadline:* For fall admission, 11/15 priority date for domestic and international students; for winter admission, 12/1 for domestic students, 11/1 for international students; for spring admission, 3/1 for domestic students, 2/1 for international students. Applications are processed on a rolling basis. Application fee: $60 ($70 for international students). Electronic applications accepted. *Financial support:* Fellowships with tuition reimbursements, teaching assistantships with tuition reimbursements, Federal Work-Study, and institutionally sponsored loans available. Support available to part-time students. *Unit head:* Susan Van Pelt Petry, Chair, 614-292-0984, E-mail: petry.37@osu.edu. *Application contact:* Amy Schmidt, Academic Program Coordinator, 614-292-8933, E-mail: schmidt.442@osu.edu.
Website: http://dance.osu.edu/

The Ohio State University, Graduate School, College of Arts and Sciences, Division of Arts and Humanities, School of Music, Columbus, OH 43210. Offers MA, MM, DMA, PhD. *Accreditation:* NASM. Part-time programs available. *Faculty:* 50. *Students:* 97 full-time (54 women), 12 part-time (4 women); includes 12 minority (5 Black or African American, non-Hispanic/Latino; 3 Asian, non-Hispanic/Latino; 4 Hispanic/Latino), 19 international. Average age 29. In 2014, 29 master's, 16 doctorates awarded. *Degree requirements:* For master's, thesis optional; for doctorate, 2 foreign languages, thesis/dissertation. *Entrance requirements:* For master's, GRE General Test (for MA); GRE General Test (for MM if GPA is below 3.0), pre-screen video audition (for piano and voice); for doctorate, GRE General Test (for PhD); ; GRE General Test (for DMA if GPA is below 3.0), pre-screen video audition (for piano and voice). Additional exam requirements/recommendations for international students: Required—TOEFL (minimum score 550 paper-based; 79 iBT), Michigan English Language Assessment Battery (minimum score 82); Recommended—IELTS (minimum score 7). *Application deadline:* For fall admission, 12/13 priority date for domestic students, 11/30 priority date for international students; for winter admission, 12/1 for domestic students, 11/1 for international students; for spring admission, 12/14 for domestic students, 11/12 for international students; for summer admission, 5/15 for domestic students, 4/14 for international students. Applications are processed on a rolling basis. Application fee: $60 ($70 for international students). Electronic applications accepted. *Financial support:* Fellowships with tuition reimbursements, research assistantships with tuition reimbursements, teaching assistantships with tuition reimbursements, Federal Work-Study, institutionally sponsored loans, and unspecified assistantships available. Support available to part-time students. *Unit head:* Richard Blatti, Director, 614-292-7664, E-mail: blatti.1@osu.edu. *Application contact:* Becky Chappell, Graduate Studies Coordinator, 614-292-6389, Fax: 614-292-1102, E-mail: mus-grad@osu.edu.
Website: http://music.osu.edu/

Ohio University, Graduate College, College of Fine Arts, School of Music, Athens, OH 45701-2979. Offers accompanying (MM); composition (MM); conducting (MM); history/literature (MM); music education (MM); music therapy (MM); performance (MM, Certificate); performance/pedagogy (MM); theory (MM). *Accreditation:* NASM. Part-time and evening/weekend programs available. Postbaccalaureate distance learning degree programs offered (minimal on-campus study). *Degree requirements:* For master's, comprehensive exam, thesis (for some programs), oral exam. *Entrance requirements:* For master's, audition, interview, portfolio, recordings (varies by program). Additional exam requirements/recommendations for international students: Required—TOEFL (minimum score 550 paper-based; 80 iBT) or IELTS (minimum score 6.5). Electronic applications accepted.

Oklahoma City University, Margaret E. Petree College of Performing Arts, Wanda L. Bass School of Music, Oklahoma City, OK 73106-1402. Offers composition (MM); conducting (MM); musical theatre (MM); opera performance (MM). *Accreditation:* NASM. Part-time programs available. *Faculty:* 22 full-time (7 women), 13 part-time/adjunct (7 women). *Students:* 63 full-time (33 women), 3 part-time (1 woman); includes 12 minority (4 Black or African American, non-Hispanic/Latino; 1 Asian, non-Hispanic/Latino; 4 Hispanic/Latino; 3 Two or more races, non-Hispanic/Latino), 20 international. Average age 24. 91 applicants, 49% accepted, 27 enrolled. In 2014, 19 master's awarded. *Degree requirements:* For master's, thesis, departmental qualifying exam, recital. *Entrance requirements:* For master's, audition, bachelor's degree in music from NASM-accredited institution, minimum GPA of 3.0. Additional exam requirements/recommendations for international students: Required—TOEFL (minimum score 550 paper-based; 80 iBT). *Application deadline:* Applications are processed on a rolling basis. Application fee: $50. Electronic applications accepted. *Expenses: Tuition:* Part-time $936 per credit hour. *Required fees:* $115 per credit hour. One-time fee: $250. Tuition and fees vary according to course load, degree level, program and student's religious affiliation. *Financial support:* In 2014–15, 61 students received support. Career-related internships or fieldwork, Federal Work-Study, institutionally sponsored loans, scholarships/grants, and tuition waivers available. Support available to part-time students. Financial award application deadline: 6/1; financial award applicants required to submit FAFSA. *Unit head:* Mark Parker, Dean, 405-208-5474, Fax: 405-208-5971, E-mail: mparker@okcu.edu. *Application contact:* Michael Harrington, Director of Graduate Admission, 800-633-7242, Fax: 405-208-5916, E-mail: gadmissions@okcu.edu.
Website: http://www.okcu.edu/music/

Oklahoma State University, College of Arts and Sciences, Department of Music, Stillwater, OK 74078. Offers pedagogy and performance (MM). *Accreditation:* NASM. *Faculty:* 31 full-time (12 women), 3 part-time/adjunct (all women). *Students:* 11 full-time (4 women), 6 part-time (2 women); includes 3 minority (1 Black or African American, non-Hispanic/Latino; 1 Hispanic/Latino; 1 Two or more races, non-Hispanic/Latino), 1 international. Average age 24. 29 applicants, 45% accepted, 10 enrolled. In 2014, 9 master's awarded. *Degree requirements:* For master's, final project, oral exam. *Entrance requirements:* For master's, GRE, audition. Additional exam requirements/recommendations for international students: Required—TOEFL (minimum score 550 paper-based; 79 iBT). *Application deadline:* For fall admission, 3/1 priority date for international students; for spring admission, 8/1 priority date for international students. Applications are processed on a rolling basis. Application fee: $40 ($75 for international students). Electronic applications accepted. *Expenses:* Tuition, state resident: full-time $4488; part-time $187 per credit hour. Tuition, nonresident: full-time $18,360; part-time $765 per credit hour. *Required fees:* $2413; $100.55 per credit hour. Tuition and fees vary according to campus/location. *Financial support:* In 2014–15, 15 teaching assistantships (averaging $12,423 per year) were awarded; career-related internships or fieldwork, Federal Work-Study, scholarships/grants, health care benefits, tuition waivers (partial), and unspecified assistantships also available. Support available to part-time students. Financial award application deadline: 3/1; financial award applicants required to submit FAFSA. *Faculty research:* Discovery and presentation of music literature of other countries, transportation of ancient music literature to modern notation. *Unit head:* Dr. Brant Adams, Department Head, 405-744-6133, Fax: 405-744-9324, E-mail: osumusic@okstate.edu.
Website: http://music.okstate.edu/

Park University, School of Graduate and Professional Studies, Kansas City, MO 54105. Offers adult education (M Ed); business and government leadership (Graduate Certificate); business, government, and global society (MPA); communication and leadership (MA); creative and life writing (Graduate Certificate); disaster and emergency management (MPA, Graduate Certificate); educational leadership (M Ed); finance (MBA, Graduate Certificate); general business (MBA); global business (Graduate Certificate); healthcare administration (MHA); healthcare services management and leadership (Graduate Certificate); international business (MBA); language and literacy (M Ed), including English for speakers of other languages, special reading teacher/literacy coach; leadership of international healthcare organizations (Graduate Certificate); management information systems (MBA, Graduate Certificate); music performance (ADP, Graduate Certificate), including cello (MM, ADP), piano (MM, ADP), viola (MM, ADP), violin (MM, ADP); nonprofit and community services management (MPA); nonprofit leadership (Graduate Certificate); performance (MM), including cello (MM, ADP), piano (MM, ADP), viola (MM, ADP), violin (MM, ADP); public management (MPA); social work (MSW); teacher leadership (M Ed), including curriculum and assessment, instructional leader. Part-time and evening/weekend programs available. Postbaccalaureate distance learning degree programs offered (no on-campus study). *Degree requirements:* For master's, comprehensive exam (for some programs), thesis (for some programs), internship (for some programs); exam (for some programs). *Entrance requirements:* For master's, GRE or GMAT (for some programs), teacher certification (for some M Ed programs), letters of recommendation, essay, resume (for some programs). Additional exam requirements/recommendations for international students: Required—TOEFL (minimum score 550 paper-based; 79 iBT), IELTS (minimum score 6). Electronic applications accepted.

Penn State University Park, Graduate School, College of Arts and Architecture, School of Music, University Park, PA 16802. Offers composition theory (M Mus); conducting (M Mus); music education (Certificate); pedagogy and performance (M Mus); piano performance (DMA). *Accreditation:* NASM. *Unit head:* Dr. Barbara O. Korner, Dean, 814-865-2592, Fax: 814-865-2018, E-mail: bok2@psu.edu. *Application contact:* Lori A. Stania, Director, Graduate Student Services, 814-867-5278, Fax: 814-863-4627, E-mail: gswww@psu.edu.
Website: http://music.psu.edu/

Phillips Theological Seminary, Programs in Theology, Tulsa, OK 74116. Offers administration of church agencies (M Div); campus ministry (M Div); church-related social work (M Div); college and seminary teaching (M Div); global mission work (M Div); institutional chaplaincy (M Div); ministerial vocations in Christian education (M Div); ministry (D Min), including parish ministry, pastoral counseling, practices of ministry; ministry and culture (MAMC), including Christian education, congregational leadership, history and practice of Christian spirituality, theology, ethics, and culture; ministry of music (M Div); pastoral care and counseling (M Div); pastoral ministry (M Div); theological studies (MTS). *Accreditation:* ATS. Part-time programs available. Postbaccalaureate distance learning degree programs offered (minimal on-campus study). *Degree requirements:* For master's, thesis (for some programs); for doctorate, thesis/dissertation. *Entrance requirements:* For master's, minimum GPA of 2.5; for doctorate, M Div, minimum GPA of 3.0. *Faculty research:* Biblical studies, historical studies, theology and culture, practical theology, theology and film.

Pittsburg State University, Graduate School, College of Arts and Sciences, Department of Music, Pittsburg, KS 66762. Offers instrumental music education (MM); music history/music literature (MM); performance (MM), including orchestral performance, organ, piano, voice; theory and composition (MM); vocal music education (MM). *Accreditation:* NASM. *Degree requirements:* For master's, thesis or alternative.

Point Park University, Conservatory of Performing Arts, Pittsburgh, PA 15222-1984. Offers theatre arts-acting (MFA). *Degree requirements:* For master's, comprehensive exam (for some programs), thesis or alternative. *Entrance requirements:* For master's, interview, undergraduate degree in related field, theatre experience. Additional exam requirements/recommendations for international students: Required—TOEFL (minimum score 550 paper-based; 79 iBT). Electronic applications accepted.

Portland State University, Graduate Studies, School of Fine and Performing Arts, Department of Music, Portland, OR 97207-0751. Offers conducting (MMC); music education (MAT, MST); performance (MMP). *Accreditation:* NASM. Part-time programs available. *Faculty:* 23 full-time (9 women), 50 part-time/adjunct (19 women). *Students:* 24 full-time (8 women), 11 part-time (7 women); includes 10 minority (2 Black or African American, non-Hispanic/Latino; 2 Asian, non-Hispanic/Latino; 5 Hispanic/Latino; 1 Two or more races, non-Hispanic/Latino), 2 international. Average age 31. 45 applicants, 49% accepted, 12 enrolled. In 2014, 22 master's awarded. *Degree requirements:* For master's, variable foreign language requirement, exit exam. *Entrance requirements:* For master's, GRE General Test, departmental exam, minimum GPA of 3.0 in upper-division course work or 2.75 overall. Additional exam requirements/recommendations for international students: Required—TOEFL (minimum score 550 paper-based). *Application deadline:* For fall admission, 4/15 priority date for domestic students, 4/15 for international students; for winter admission, 10/1 for domestic and international students; for spring admission, 12/1 for domestic and international students; for summer admission, 1/15 for domestic and international students. Application fee: $50. *Expenses:* Tuition, state resident: part-time $222 per credit. Tuition, nonresident: part-time $527 per credit. *Required fees:* $22 per contact hour. $100 per quarter. Tuition and fees vary according to program. *Financial support:* In 2014–15, 9 teaching assistantships with partial tuition reimbursements (averaging $5,135 per year) were awarded; Federal

Work-Study, scholarships/grants, and unspecified assistantships also available. Support available to part-time students. Financial award application deadline: 3/1; financial award applicants required to submit FAFSA. *Faculty research:* Composition, music analysis, music history, jazz. *Unit head:* Bryan Johanson, Director, 503-725-3003, Fax: 503-725-8215, E-mail: johansonb@pdx.edu. *Application contact:* Evan Brown, Office Coordinator, 503-725-3011, Fax: 503-725-5525, E-mail: music@pdx.edu.
Website: http://www.pdx.edu/the-arts/music

Pratt Institute, School of Liberal Arts and Sciences, Program in Performance and Performance Studies, Brooklyn, NY 11205-3899. Offers MFA.

Princeton University, Graduate School, Department of Music, Princeton, NJ 08544-1019. Offers composition (PhD); musicology (PhD). *Degree requirements:* For doctorate, variable foreign language requirement, thesis/dissertation. *Entrance requirements:* For doctorate, GRE General Test, sample of written work. Additional exam requirements/recommendations for international students: Required—TOEFL (minimum score 600 paper-based). Electronic applications accepted. *Faculty research:* Computer synthesis, history of Western music, comparative musicology, theory.

Purchase College, State University of New York, Conservatory of Music, Purchase, NY 10577-1400. Offers composition (MM); instrumental performance (MM); jazz studies (MM); studio composition (MM); voice and opera studies (MM). *Students:* 60 full-time (17 women), 9 part-time (5 women); includes 6 minority (2 Black or African American, non-Hispanic/Latino; 1 Asian, non-Hispanic/Latino; 1 Hispanic/Latino; 2 Two or more races, non-Hispanic/Latino), 29 international. 172 applicants, 47% accepted, 75 enrolled. *Degree requirements:* For master's, thesis or alternative, composition, performance. *Entrance requirements:* For master's, audition. *Application deadline:* For fall admission, 3/1 for domestic students. Application fee: $50. Electronic applications accepted. *Expenses:* Tuition, state resident: full-time $10,370; part-time $432 per credit. Tuition, nonresident: full-time $20,190; part-time $831 per credit. *Required fees:* $1763. *Financial support:* Fellowships, teaching assistantships, career-related internships or fieldwork, Federal Work-Study, scholarships/grants, and tuition waivers (partial) available. Support available to part-time students. Financial award application deadline: 3/15; financial award applicants required to submit FAFSA. *Unit head:* James Undercofler, Interim Director, 914-251-6700, Fax: 914-251-6739, E-mail: james.undercofler@purchase.edu. *Application contact:* Sabrina Johnston, Admission Counselor, 914-251-6479, Fax: 914-251-6314, E-mail: admissn@purchase.edu.
Website: http://www.purchase.edu/Departments/AcademicPrograms/Arts/Music/

Queens College of the City University of New York, Division of Graduate Studies, Arts and Humanities Division, Aaron Copland School of Music, Flushing, NY 11367-1597. Offers MA. Part-time programs available. *Degree requirements:* For master's, one foreign language, qualifying exams, recital. *Entrance requirements:* For master's, audition, bachelor's degree in music, minimum GPA of 3.0. Additional exam requirements/recommendations for international students: Required—TOEFL.

Radford University, College of Graduate and Professional Studies, College of Visual and Performing Arts, Program in Music, Radford, VA 24142. Offers music (MA); music education (MS); music therapy (MS). *Accreditation:* NASM. Part-time programs available. *Faculty:* 8 full-time (0 women), 4 part-time/adjunct (0 women). *Students:* 14 full-time (10 women), 4 part-time (2 women). Average age 26. 10 applicants, 80% accepted, 7 enrolled. In 2014, 8 master's awarded. *Degree requirements:* For master's, comprehensive exam, thesis or alternative. *Entrance requirements:* For master's, GRE or PRAXIS II (music content knowledge), minimum GPA of 2.75, 3 letters of reference, resume, official transcripts. Additional exam requirements/recommendations for international students: Required—TOEFL (minimum score 550 paper-based; 79 iBT), IELTS (minimum score 6.5). *Application deadline:* For fall admission, 2/15 priority date for domestic students, 12/1 for international students; for spring admission, 7/1 for international students. Applications are processed on a rolling basis. Application fee: $50. Electronic applications accepted. *Expenses:* Tuition, state resident: full-time $7187; part-time $299 per credit hour. Tuition, nonresident: full-time $16,394; part-time $683 per credit hour. *Required fees:* $2974; $125 per credit hour. Tuition and fees vary according to course load and program. *Financial support:* In 2014–15, 12 students received support, including 5 research assistantships (averaging $7,300 per year), 6 teaching assistantships with partial tuition reimbursements available (averaging $8,250 per year); career-related internships or fieldwork, Federal Work-Study, institutionally sponsored loans, scholarships/grants, and unspecified assistantships also available. Financial award application deadline: 3/1; financial award applicants required to submit FAFSA. *Unit head:* Dr. Trish Winter, Graduate Music Program Coordinator, 540-831-6174, Fax: 540-831-6133, E-mail: pwinter3@radford.edu. *Application contact:* Rebecca Conner, Director, Graduate Enrollment, 540-831-6296, Fax: 540-831-6061, E-mail: gradcollege@radford.edu.
Website: http://www.radford.edu/content/cvpa/home/music.html

Reinhardt University, Program in Music, Waleska, GA 30183-2981. Offers conducting (MM); music education (MM); piano pedagogy (MM). *Accreditation:* NASM. Part-time and evening/weekend programs available. Postbaccalaureate distance learning degree programs offered. *Entrance requirements:* For master's, GRE, audition (for piano pedagogy and conducting), 2 letters of reference. Additional exam requirements/recommendations for international students: Required—TOEFL.

Rice University, Graduate Programs, Shepherd School of Music, Houston, TX 77251-1892. Offers composition (MM, DMA); conducting (MM); musicology (MM); performance (MM, DMA); theory (MM). *Degree requirements:* For master's, thesis (for some programs), 2 recitals; for doctorate, one foreign language, comprehensive exam, thesis/dissertation, 4 recitals. *Entrance requirements:* For master's, GRE General Test (musicology); for doctorate, GRE General Test. Additional exam requirements/recommendations for international students: Required—TOEFL (minimum score 600 paper-based; 100 iBT), IELTS (minimum score 7). *Faculty research:* Musicology, performance, theory, composition.

Rider University, Westminster Choir College, Programs in Music, Lawrenceville, NJ 08648-3001. Offers choral conducting (MM); composition (MM); organ performance (MM); piano accompanying and coaching (MM); piano pedagogy and performance (MM); piano performance (MM); sacred music (MM); vocal pedagogy and performance (MM); vocal training (MVP). Part-time programs available. *Degree requirements:* For master's, variable foreign language requirement, departmental qualifying exam. *Entrance requirements:* For master's, audition, interview, repertoire list, 2 letters of reference, resume. Additional exam requirements/recommendations for international students: Required—TOEFL (minimum score 525 paper-based). Electronic applications accepted.

Roosevelt University, Graduate Division, Chicago College of Performing Arts, The Music Conservatory, Chicago, IL 60605. Offers music (MM); piano pedagogy (Diploma). *Accreditation:* NASM. Part-time and evening/weekend programs available.

Rowan University, Graduate School, College of Performing Arts, Program in Performance, Glassboro, NJ 08028-1701. Offers MM. *Accreditation:* NASM. Part-time and evening/weekend programs available. *Faculty:* 3 full-time (1 woman), 3 part-time/adjunct (0 women). *Students:* 6 full-time (2 women), 5 part-time (1 woman); includes 2 minority (1 Black or African American, non-Hispanic/Latino; 1 Hispanic/Latino), 1 international. Average age 29. 12 applicants, 100% accepted, 5 enrolled. In 2014, 17 master's awarded. *Degree requirements:* For master's, thesis (for some programs). *Entrance requirements:* For master's, GRE General Test. Additional exam requirements/recommendations for international students: Required—TOEFL. *Application deadline:* For fall admission, 8/1 for domestic and international students; for spring admission, 11/1 for domestic and international students. Applications are processed on a rolling basis. Application fee: $65. Electronic applications accepted. *Expenses: Tuition, area resident:* Part-time $648 per credit. Tuition, state resident: part-time $648 per credit. Tuition, nonresident: part-time $648 per credit. *Required fees:* $145 per credit. Tuition and fees vary according to degree level, campus/location, program and student level. *Financial support:* Career-related internships or fieldwork, scholarships/grants, health care benefits, and unspecified assistantships available. Support available to part-time students. *Unit head:* Dr. Horacio Sosa, Vice President, Global Learning and Partnerships, 856-256-4747, Fax: 856-256-5638, E-mail: sosa@rowan.edu. *Application contact:* Admissions and Enrollment Services, 856-256-4747, Fax: 856-256-5637, E-mail: globaladmissions@rowan.edu.

Rutgers, The State University of New Jersey, Newark, Graduate School, Program in Jazz History and Research, Newark, NJ 07102. Offers MA. *Entrance requirements:* For master's, GRE, minimum B average. Electronic applications accepted.

Rutgers, The State University of New Jersey, New Brunswick, Mason Gross School of the Arts, Music Department, New Brunswick, NJ 08901. Offers collaborative piano (MM, DMA); conducting: choral (MM, DMA); conducting: instrumental (MM, DMA); conducting: orchestral (MM, DMA); jazz studies (MM); music (DMA, AD); music education (MM, DMA); music performance (MM). *Accreditation:* NASM. *Degree requirements:* For doctorate, one foreign language. *Entrance requirements:* For master's and doctorate, audition. Additional exam requirements/recommendations for international students: Required—TOEFL (minimum score 550 paper-based), IELTS (minimum score 7). Electronic applications accepted. *Faculty research:* Performance, twentieth century music, jazz, music education.

St. Cloud State University, School of Graduate Studies, College of Liberal Arts, Department of Music, St. Cloud, MN 56301-4498. Offers conducting and literature (MM); music education (MM); piano pedagogy (MM). *Degree requirements:* For master's, comprehensive exam (for some programs), thesis or alternative. *Entrance requirements:* For master's, GRE General Test, minimum GPA of 2.75. Additional exam requirements/recommendations for international students: Required—TOEFL (minimum score 550 paper-based; 79 iBT), IELTS (minimum score 6.5), Michigan English Language Assessment Battery. Electronic applications accepted.

Saint John's University, Saint John's School of Theology and Seminary, Collegeville, MN 56321. Offers divinity (M Div); liturgical music (MA); liturgical studies (MA); pastoral ministry (MA); theology (MA), including church history, liturgy, monastic studies, scripture, spirituality, systematics; M Div/MA. *Accreditation:* ATS. Part-time programs available. Postbaccalaureate distance learning degree programs offered (no on-campus study). *Degree requirements:* For master's, one foreign language, comprehensive exam (for some programs), thesis (for some programs). *Entrance requirements:* For master's, GRE General Test or MAT. Electronic applications accepted. *Faculty research:* Religious education, biblical literature.

Saint Joseph's College, Rensselaer Program of Church Music and Liturgy, Rensselaer, IN 47978. Offers church music and liturgy (MA); pastoral liturgy and music (Diploma). Offered during summer only. Part-time programs available. *Degree requirements:* For master's, thesis, research paper, service recital. *Entrance requirements:* For master's, entrance exams in music theory, conducting, keyboard, voice, and history.

St. Vladimir's Orthodox Theological Seminary, Graduate School of Theology, Crestwood, NY 10707-1699. Offers general theological studies (MA); liturgical music (MA); religious education (MA); theology (M Div, M Th, D Min); M Div/MA. MA in general theological studies, M Div offered jointly with St. Nersess Seminary. *Accreditation:* ATS. Part-time programs available. *Degree requirements:* For master's, one foreign language, thesis, fieldwork; for doctorate, thesis/dissertation, fieldwork. *Entrance requirements:* For doctorate, M Div, minimum GPA of 3.0. Additional exam requirements/recommendations for international students: Required—TOEFL.

Salisbury University, Program in English, Salisbury, MD 21801-6837. Offers composition and rhetoric (MA); English (MA); literature (MA); TESOL (MA). Part-time and evening/weekend programs available. *Faculty:* 11 full-time (5 women). *Students:* 9 full-time (6 women), 24 part-time (19 women); includes 6 minority (3 Black or African American, non-Hispanic/Latino; 2 Hispanic/Latino; 1 Two or more races, non-Hispanic/Latino), 3 international. Average age 32. 11 applicants, 100% accepted, 11 enrolled. In 2014, 20 master's awarded. *Degree requirements:* For master's, comprehensive exam (for some programs), thesis optional. *Entrance requirements:* For master's, GRE, MAT, PRAXIS I, 2 letters of recommendation; personal statement. Additional exam requirements/recommendations for international students: Required—TOEFL (minimum score 550 paper-based; 79 iBT), IELTS (minimum score 6.5). *Application deadline:* For fall admission, 3/15 for domestic and international students; for spring admission, 10/1 for domestic and international students. Applications are processed on a rolling basis. Application fee: $65. Electronic applications accepted. *Expenses:* Expenses: $358 per credit hour for residents; $647 for non-residents; $78 fees. *Financial support:* In 2014–15, 12 teaching assistantships with full tuition reimbursements (averaging $9,498 per year) were awarded; career-related internships or fieldwork, institutionally sponsored loans, and unspecified assistantships also available. Support available to part-time students. Financial award application deadline: 3/1; financial award applicants required to submit FAFSA. *Faculty research:* American literature; British literature; linguistics, film, rhetoric and composition. *Unit head:* Dr. Christopher Vilmar, Graduate Program Director, English, 410-677-6511, Fax: -, E-mail: csvilmar@salisbury.edu.
Website: http://www.salisbury.edu/gsr/gradstudies/ENGpage.html

Samford University, School of the Arts, Birmingham, AL 35229. Offers church music (MM); music education (MME); piano performance and pedagogy (MM). MME program offered in Traditional, Fifth Year Non-Traditional, and National Board Cohort formats. *Accreditation:* NASM. Part-time programs available. *Faculty:* 9 full-time (5 women), 5 part-time/adjunct (1 woman). *Students:* 12 full-time (6 women), 1 part-time (0 women); includes 3 minority (2 Black or African American, non-Hispanic/Latino; 1 Asian, non-Hispanic/Latino), 1 international. Average age 26. 17 applicants, 100% accepted, 5 enrolled. In 2014, 8 master's awarded. *Degree requirements:* For master's, comprehensive exam, comprehensive oral exam; juried public recital (for MM). *Entrance requirements:* For master's, PRAXIS II (for MME), minimum GPA of 3.0, undergraduate degree in music. Additional exam requirements/recommendations for international students: Required—TOEFL (minimum score 90 iBT). *Application deadline:* For fall admission, 11/15 priority date for domestic and international students; for spring admission, 4/15 priority date for domestic and international students. Applications are processed on a rolling basis. Application fee: $35. *Expenses: Tuition:* Full-time $11,904; part-time $744 per credit hour. *Required fees:* $500. Tuition and fees vary according to course load, degree level and student level. *Financial support:* In 2014–15, 9 students received support, including research assistantships with partial tuition reimbursements available (averaging $6,000 per year); Federal Work-Study, scholarships/grants, tuition waivers (partial), and unspecified assistantships also available. Financial award

application deadline: 9/1; financial award applicants required to submit FAFSA. *Faculty research:* Hymnology, choral techniques, assessment of music learning at elementary and secondary levels, piano pedagogy, special education and inclusion, learning theories, church music administration, worship and the arts. *Unit head:* Dr. Kathryn Fouse, Associate Dean, 205-726-2489, E-mail: klfouse@samford.edu. *Application contact:* Dr. Demondrae Thurman, Director, Graduate Studies, 205-726-2389, Fax: 205-726-2165, E-mail: dthurman@samford.edu.
Website: http://www.samford.edu/arts

Sam Houston State University, College of Fine Arts and Mass Communication, School of Music, Huntsville, TX 77341. Offers MM. *Accreditation:* NASM. Part-time programs available. *Faculty:* 27 full-time (8 women), 2 part-time/adjunct (1 woman). *Students:* 21 full-time (11 women), 23 part-time (11 women); includes 13 minority (3 Asian, non-Hispanic/Latino; 9 Hispanic/Latino; 1 Two or more races, non-Hispanic/Latino), 7 international. Average age 28. 18 applicants, 100% accepted, 15 enrolled. In 2014, 48 master's awarded. *Degree requirements:* For master's, comprehensive exam, thesis, departmental qualifying exam. *Entrance requirements:* For master's, GRE General Test, letters of recommendation, audition/interview. Additional exam requirements/recommendations for international students: Required—TOEFL (minimum score 550 paper-based; 79 iBT), IELTS (minimum score 6.5). *Application deadline:* For fall admission, 8/1 for domestic students, 6/25 for international students; for spring admission, 12/1 for domestic students, 11/12 for international students; for summer admission, 5/15 for domestic students, 4/9 for international students. Applications are processed on a rolling basis. Application fee: $45 ($75 for international students). Electronic applications accepted. *Expenses:* Tuition, state resident: full-time $2286; part-time $254 per credit hour. Tuition, nonresident: full-time $5544; part-time $616 per credit hour. *Required fees:* $440 per semester. Tuition and fees vary according to course load and campus/location. *Financial support:* In 2014–15, 13 research assistantships (averaging $7,649 per year), 1 teaching assistantship (averaging $7,658 per year) were awarded; career-related internships or fieldwork, Federal Work-Study, scholarships/grants, tuition waivers (partial), and unspecified assistantships also available. Support available to part-time students. Financial award application deadline: 3/15; financial award applicants required to submit FAFSA. *Unit head:* Dr. Scott Plugge, Director, 936-294-3808, Fax: 936-294-3765, E-mail: plugge@shsu.edu. *Application contact:* Kevin Clifton, Associate Director, 936-294-1393, Fax: 936-294-3765, E-mail: kmc053@shsu.edu.
Website: http://www.shsu.edu/academics/music/

San Diego State University, Graduate and Research Affairs, College of Professional Studies and Fine Arts, School of Music and Dance, San Diego, CA 92182. Offers composition (acoustic and electronic) (MM); conducting (MM); ethnomusicology (MA); jazz studies (MM); musicology (MA); performance (MM); piano pedagogy (MA); theory (MA). *Degree requirements:* For master's, comprehensive exam (for some programs), thesis (for some programs). *Entrance requirements:* For master's, GRE General Test, bachelor's degree in related field, 2 letters of reference. Additional exam requirements/recommendations for international students: Required—TOEFL. Electronic applications accepted.

San Francisco Conservatory of Music, Graduate Division, San Francisco, CA 94102. Offers brass (MM); chamber music (MM); collaborative piano (MM); composition (MM); conducting (MM); guitar (MM); harpsichord (MM); orchestral instruments (MM); percussion (MM); piano and organ (MM); strings (MM); timpani (MM); voice (MM); woodwinds (MM). *Accreditation:* NASM. *Degree requirements:* For master's, variable foreign language requirement, 1-2 recitals, 1-3 juried performances. *Entrance requirements:* For master's, audition, recommendations. Additional exam requirements/recommendations for international students: Required—TOEFL (minimum score 500 paper-based; 71 iBT). Electronic applications accepted. *Expenses: Tuition:* Full-time $40,000; part-time $1764 per semester. *Required fees:* $992; $496 per semester. Tuition and fees vary according to course load.

San Francisco State University, Division of Graduate Studies, College of Liberal and Creative Arts, School of Music and Dance, San Francisco, CA 94132-1722. Offers chamber music (MM); classical performance (MM); composition (MA); conducting (MM); music education (MA); music history (MA). *Accreditation:* NASM. *Expenses:* Tuition, state resident: full-time $6738. Tuition, nonresident: full-time $17,898; part-time $372 per credit hour. *Required fees:* $498 per semester. *Unit head:* Dr. Dianthe Spencer, Director, 415-338-1431, Fax: 415-338-3294, E-mail: smd@sfsu.edu. *Application contact:* Dr. Cyrus Ginwala, Graduate Coordinator, 415-338-1431, Fax: 415-338-3294, E-mail: cginwala@sfsu.edu.
Website: http://musicdance.sfsu.edu/

San Jose State University, Graduate Studies and Research, College of Humanities and the Arts, School of Music and Dance, San Jose, CA 95192-0001. Offers music (MA). *Accreditation:* NASM. *Degree requirements:* For master's, thesis or alternative. *Entrance requirements:* For master's, minimum GPA of 3.0 in last 60 units of undergraduate coursework; 3 letters of recommendation; audition or portfolio. Additional exam requirements/recommendations for international students: Required—TOEFL (minimum score 590 paper-based; 96 iBT). Electronic applications accepted.

Savannah College of Art and Design, Graduate School, Program in Performing Arts, Savannah, GA 31402-3146. Offers MFA. *Faculty:* 11 full-time (5 women), 5 part-time/adjunct (4 women). *Students:* 50 full-time (32 women), 2 part-time (1 woman); includes 22 minority (14 Black or African American, non-Hispanic/Latino; 1 American Indian or Alaska Native, non-Hispanic/Latino; 4 Asian, non-Hispanic/Latino; 2 Hispanic/Latino; 1 Two or more races, non-Hispanic/Latino), 3 international. Average age 27. 88 applicants, 49% accepted, 24 enrolled. In 2014, 12 master's awarded. *Degree requirements:* For master's, thesis. *Entrance requirements:* For master's, audition, interview. Additional exam requirements/recommendations for international students: Required—TOEFL (minimum score 550 paper-based, 85 iBT), IELTS (minimum score 6.5), or ACTFL. *Application deadline:* For fall admission, 4/1 for domestic and international students. Applications are processed on a rolling basis. Application fee: $40. Electronic applications accepted. *Expenses: Tuition:* Full-time $34,605; part-time $3845 per course. One-time fee: $500. Tuition and fees vary according to course load. *Financial support:* Fellowships, career-related internships or fieldwork, Federal Work-Study, and scholarships/grants available. Financial award application deadline: 4/1; financial award applicants required to submit FAFSA. *Unit head:* Michael Wainstein, Chair. *Application contact:* Jenny Jaquillard, Executive Director of Admissions, Recruitment and Events, 912-525-5100, Fax: 912-525-5985, E-mail: admission@scad.edu.
Website: http://www.scad.edu/academics/programs/performing-arts

School of the Art Institute of Chicago, Graduate Division, Department of Performance, Chicago, IL 60603-3103. Offers MFA. *Entrance requirements:* Additional exam requirements/recommendations for international students: Required—TOEFL, IELTS.

Seabury-Western Theological Seminary, School of Theology, Evanston, IL 60201-2976. Offers advanced theological studies (Certificate); church music and liturgy (MTS); congregational development (D Min); preaching (D Min); theological studies (MA); theology (M Div, L Th). D Min in congregational development offered in summer only; D Min in preaching offered jointly with Chicago Theological Seminary, Lutheran School of Theology at Chicago, McCormick Theological Seminary, and Northern Baptist Theological Seminary. *Accreditation:* ACIPE; ATS (one or more programs are accredited). Part-time programs available. *Degree requirements:* For master's, thesis; for doctorate, thesis/dissertation; for other advanced degree, thesis (for some programs). *Entrance requirements:* For master's, interview, sample of written work. *Faculty research:* Liturgical interpretations of baptism, trinitarian theology, congregational development, post modern biblical criticism-Matthew.

Shenandoah University, Shenandoah Conservatory, Winchester, VA 22601-5195. Offers church music (MM, Certificate); collaborative piano (MM); music (Artist Diploma); pedagogy (DMA); performance (MM, DMA). *Accreditation:* NASM. *Faculty:* 42 full-time (13 women), 18 part-time/adjunct (9 women). *Students:* 57 full-time (31 women), 75 part-time (42 women); includes 20 minority (7 Black or African American, non-Hispanic/Latino; 4 Asian, non-Hispanic/Latino; 9 Hispanic/Latino), 16 international. Average age 32. 107 applicants, 70% accepted, 38 enrolled. In 2014, 35 master's, 7 doctorates, 11 other advanced degrees awarded. *Degree requirements:* For master's, variable foreign language requirement, comprehensive exam, thesis (for some programs), minimum GPA of 3.0, internship (MS), recital (MM), research teaching project or thesis (MME), project (MA); for doctorate, variable foreign language requirement, comprehensive exam, minimum GPA of 3.0, dissertation or teaching project, recital; for other advanced degree, variable foreign language requirement, comprehensive exam, thesis, minimum GPA of 3.0, research project, recital. *Entrance requirements:* For master's, diagnostic examination in music theory, vocal diction assessment (for MM in voice and choral conducting), bachelor's degree with minimum of GPA of 2.5, performance audition, writing sample, resume, all academic transcripts; for doctorate, diagnostic examination in music theory and music literature, vocal diction assessment (for voice), master's degree with minimum GPA of 3.25, performance audition, 2 letters of recommendation, writing sample, resume, all academic transcripts; for other advanced degree, bachelor's or master's degree; minimum GPA of 2.5; performance audition (for Artist Diploma). Additional exam requirements/recommendations for international students: Required—TOEFL (minimum score 550 paper-based; 79 iBT), IELTS (minimum score 6.5), Sakae Institute of Study Abroad (SISA) test (minimum score 15). *Application deadline:* For fall admission, 1/15 for domestic and international students; for summer admission, 5/1 for domestic and international students. Applications are processed on a rolling basis. Application fee: $30. Electronic applications accepted. *Expenses: Tuition:* Full-time $19,512; part-time $813 per credit hour. *Required fees:* $365 per term. Tuition and fees vary according to course level, course load and program. *Financial support:* In 2014–15, 34 students received support, including 33 teaching assistantships with partial tuition reimbursements available (averaging $7,779 per year); career-related internships or fieldwork, scholarships/grants, and unspecified assistantships also available. Support available to part-time students. Financial award application deadline: 3/15; financial award applicants required to submit FAFSA. *Faculty research:* CD recording and release project, creative clinical therapy. *Unit head:* Michael J. Stepniak, EdD, Dean of Conservatory, 540-665-4600, Fax: 540-665-5402, E-mail: mstepnia@su.edu. *Application contact:* Andrew Woodall, Executive Director of Recruitment and Advancement, 540-665-4581, Fax: 540-665-4627, E-mail: admit@su.edu.
Website: http://www.conservatory.su.edu

Shepherd University, Cornel School of Contemporary Music, Los Angeles, CA 90065. Offers MM. *Entrance requirements:* For master's, official college/university transcripts, bachelor's degree, audition. Electronic applications accepted.

Southeastern Baptist Theological Seminary, Graduate and Professional Programs, Wake Forest, NC 27588-1889. Offers advanced biblical studies (M Div); Christian education (M Div, MACE); Christian ethics (PhD); Christian ministry (M Div); Christian planting (M Div); church music (MACM); counseling (MACO); evangelism (PhD); language (M Div); ministry (D Min); New Testament (PhD); Old Testament (PhD); philosophy (PhD); theology (Th M, PhD); women's studies (M Div). *Accreditation:* ACIPE; ATS (one or more programs are accredited). *Degree requirements:* For master's, thesis (for some programs), oral exam; for doctorate, thesis/dissertation, fieldwork. *Entrance requirements:* For master's, Cooperative English Test, minimum GPA of 2.0, M Div or equivalent (Th M); for doctorate, GRE General Test or MAT, Cooperative English Test, M Div or equivalent, 3 years of professional experience.

Southeastern Louisiana University, College of Arts, Humanities and Social Sciences, Department of Fine and Performing Arts, Hammond, LA 70402. Offers music (M Mus), including performance. *Accreditation:* NASM. *Faculty:* 12 full-time (2 women). *Students:* 19 full-time (7 women); includes 4 minority (2 Black or African American, non-Hispanic/Latino; 1 Asian, non-Hispanic/Latino; 1 Hispanic/Latino), 6 international. Average age 28. *Degree requirements:* For master's, comprehensive exam, thesis (for some programs). *Entrance requirements:* For master's, BM; senior recital (for performance program). Additional exam requirements/recommendations for international students: Required—TOEFL (minimum score 500 paper-based; 61 iBT), IELTS (minimum score 5.5). *Application deadline:* For fall admission, 7/15 priority date for domestic students, 6/1 priority date for international students; for spring admission, 12/1 priority date for domestic students, 10/1 priority date for international students. Applications are processed on a rolling basis. Application fee: $20 ($30 for international students). Electronic applications accepted. *Financial support:* In 2014–15, 3 research assistantships (averaging $7,800 per year), 11 teaching assistantships (averaging $9,600 per year) were awarded; career-related internships or fieldwork, Federal Work-Study, institutionally sponsored loans, scholarships/grants, traineeships, and unspecified assistantships also available. Support available to part-time students. Financial award application deadline: 5/1; financial award applicants required to submit FAFSA. *Faculty research:* Wind band performance and repertoire for young audiences, pedagogical piano music of contemporary American composers, spectral music composition, intonation and extended woodwind techniques. *Unit head:* Dr. Ken Boulton, Interim Department Head, 985-549-2184, Fax: 985-549-2892, E-mail: kenneth.boulton@selu.edu. *Application contact:* Sandra Meyers, Graduate Admissions Analyst, 985-549-5620, Fax: 985-549-5632, E-mail: admissions@selu.edu.
Website: http://www.selu.edu/acad_research/depts/arts/

Southern Baptist Theological Seminary, School of Church Ministries, Louisville, KY 40280-0004. Offers Biblical counseling (M Div, MA); children's and family ministry (M Div, MA); Christian education (MA); Christian worship (PhD); church ministries (M Div); church music (MCM); college ministry (M Div, MA); discipleship and family ministry (M Div, MA); education (Ed D); family ministry (D Min, PhD); higher education (PhD); leadership (M Div, MA, D Min, PhD); ministry (D Ed Min); missions and ethnodoxology (M Div); women's leadership (M Div, MA); worship leadership (M Div, MA); worship leadership and church ministry (MA); youth and family ministry (M Div, MA). Part-time programs available. Postbaccalaureate distance learning degree programs offered (minimal on-campus study). *Degree requirements:* For doctorate, thesis/dissertation. *Entrance requirements:* For doctorate, GRE General Test, interview, M Div or MACE. Additional exam requirements/recommendations for international students: Required—TWE. *Faculty research:* Gerontology, creative teaching methods, faith development in children, faith development in youth, transformational learning.

Southern Illinois University Carbondale, Graduate School, College of Liberal Arts, School of Music, Carbondale, IL 62901-4701. Offers MM. *Accreditation:* NASM. Part-

time programs available. *Faculty:* 22 full-time (6 women). *Students:* 33 full-time (20 women), 4 part-time (2 women); includes 2 minority (1 Black or African American, non-Hispanic/Latino; 1 Hispanic/Latino), 5 international. Average age 24. 30 applicants, 70% accepted, 15 enrolled. In 2014, 18 master's awarded. *Degree requirements:* For master's, one foreign language, thesis or alternative. *Entrance requirements:* For master's, audition, minimum GPA of 2.7. Additional exam requirements/recommendations for international students: Required—TOEFL. *Application deadline:* Applications are processed on a rolling basis. Application fee: $50. *Expenses:* Tuition, state resident: full-time $10,176; part-time $1153 per credit. Tuition, nonresident: full-time $20,814; part-time $1744 per credit. *Required fees:* $7092; $394 per credit. $2364 per semester. *Financial support:* In 2014–15, 16 students received support, including 2 fellowships with full tuition reimbursements available, 12 teaching assistantships with full tuition reimbursements available; research assistantships with full tuition reimbursements available, Federal Work-Study, institutionally sponsored loans, and tuition waivers (full) also available. Support available to part-time students. Financial award application deadline: 4/1. *Faculty research:* Performance practices, historical research, operatic development. *Unit head:* Dr. Frank Stemper, Director of Graduate Studies, 618-453-2541, E-mail: fstemp@siu.edu.

Southern Illinois University Edwardsville, Graduate School, College of Arts and Sciences, Department of Music, Program in Music, Edwardsville, IL 62026-0001. Offers music education (MM); music performance (MM). Part-time programs available. *Faculty:* 18 full-time (5 women). *Students:* 12 full-time (7 women), 8 part-time (5 women); includes 3 minority (1 Hispanic/Latino; 2 Two or more races, non-Hispanic/Latino), 2 international. 10 applicants, 90% accepted. In 2014, 9 master's awarded. *Degree requirements:* For master's, one foreign language, thesis (for some programs), recital. *Entrance requirements:* Additional exam requirements/recommendations for international students: Required—TOEFL (minimum score 550 paper-based; 79 iBT), IELTS (minimum score 6.5). *Application deadline:* For fall admission, 7/24 for domestic students, 7/15 for international students; for spring admission, 12/11 for domestic students, 11/15 for international students; for summer admission, 4/29 for domestic and international students. Applications are processed on a rolling basis. Application fee: $30. Electronic applications accepted. *Expenses:* Tuition, state resident: full-time $5026. Tuition, nonresident: full-time $12,566. *International tuition:* $25,136 full-time. *Required fees:* $1682. Tuition and fees vary according to course load, campus/location and program. *Financial support:* Institutionally sponsored loans, scholarships/grants, and unspecified assistantships available. Financial award application deadline: 3/1; financial award applicants required to submit FAFSA. *Unit head:* Dr. Marc Schapman, Program Director, 618-650-2034, E-mail: maschap@siue.edu. *Application contact:* Melissa K. Mace, Assistant Director of Admissions for Graduate and International Recruitment, 618-650-2756, Fax: 618-650-3618, E-mail: mmace@siue.edu.
Website: http://www.siue.edu/artsandsciences/music/

Southern Methodist University, Meadows School of the Arts, Division of Music, Dallas, TX 75275. Offers composition (MM); conducting (MM), including choral, instrumental; music education (MM); music history and literature (MM); performance (MM), including harpsichord, orchestral instrument, organ, piano, voice; piano performance and pedagogy (MM); theory pedagogy (MM). *Accreditation:* NASM. Part-time programs available. *Degree requirements:* For master's, variable foreign language requirement, comprehensive exam, project, recital, or thesis. *Entrance requirements:* For master's, placement exams in music history and theory, audition; bachelor's degree in music or equivalent; minimum GPA of 3.0; research paper in history, theory, education. Additional exam requirements/recommendations for international students: Required—TOEFL (minimum score 550 paper-based; 80 iBT). Electronic applications accepted. *Faculty research:* Music perception and cognition, computer-based instruction, music medicine and therapy, theoretical and historical analysis-medieval to contemporary.

Southern Oregon University, Graduate Studies, Department of Music, Ashland, OR 97520. Offers performance (MM). *Faculty:* 8 full-time (3 women), 1 part-time/adjunct (0 women). *Students:* 7 full-time (1 woman), 4 part-time (3 women), 2 international. Average age 35. 11 applicants, 82% accepted, 6 enrolled. *Entrance requirements:* For master's, undergraduate degree with music major, audition, three letters of recommendation. *Application deadline:* For fall admission, 7/31 priority date for domestic and international students; for winter admission, 11/15 priority date for domestic and international students; for spring admission, 1/7 priority date for domestic and international students. Application fee: $50. *Expenses:* Tuition, state resident: full-time $10,225; part-time $1515 per quarter. Tuition, nonresident: full-time $12,782; part-time $1894 per quarter. *Required fees:* $1395; $261 per quarter. *Financial support:* In 2014–15, 2 students received support, including 2 research assistantships with partial tuition reimbursements available. *Unit head:* Dr. Vicki Purslow, Graduate Program Coordinator, 541-552-6538, E-mail: purslowv@sou.edu. *Application contact:* Kelly Moutsatson, Director of Admissions, 541-552-6411, Fax: 541-552-8403, E-mail: admissions@sou.edu.

Southwestern Baptist Theological Seminary, School of Church Music, Fort Worth, TX 76122-0000. Offers MACM, MAWSHP, MM, DMA, PhD. *Accreditation:* NASM. Part-time programs available. Terminal master's awarded for partial completion of doctoral program. *Degree requirements:* For master's, comprehensive exam, thesis; for doctorate, comprehensive exam, thesis/dissertation. *Entrance requirements:* For master's, audition; for doctorate, MM or equivalent. Additional exam requirements/recommendations for international students: Required—TOEFL. *Application deadline:* For fall admission, 7/15 priority date for domestic students, 4/1 for international students; for spring admission, 12/15 priority date for domestic students, 10/1 for international students. Applications are processed on a rolling basis. Electronic applications accepted. *Financial support:* Teaching assistantships, career-related internships or fieldwork, institutionally sponsored loans, and scholarships/grants available. Support available to part-time students. Financial award application deadline: 11/1. *Unit head:* Dr. Stephen Johnson, Dean, 817-923-1921 Ext. 3111, Fax: 817-921-8762, E-mail: sjohnson@swbts.edu. *Application contact:* Director of Admissions, 817-923-1921 Ext. 2700, Fax: 817-921-8757, E-mail: admissions@swbts.edu.
Website: http://swbts.edu/academics/schools-programs/churchmusic/

Southwestern Oklahoma State University, College of Arts and Sciences, Department of Music, Weatherford, OK 73096-3098. Offers music education (MM); performance (MM). *Accreditation:* NASM. Part-time programs available. *Degree requirements:* For master's, comprehensive exam, recital (music performance). *Entrance requirements:* For master's, minimum GPA of 2.5. Additional exam requirements/recommendations for international students: Required—TOEFL.

Stanford University, School of Humanities and Sciences, Department of Music, Stanford, CA 94305-9991. Offers composition (DMA); computer-based music theory and acoustics (MA, PhD); music composition (MA); music history (MA); music, science, and technology (MA); musicology (PhD). Terminal master's awarded for partial completion of doctoral program. *Degree requirements:* For master's, variable foreign language requirement, thesis or alternative, project; for doctorate, variable foreign language requirement, thesis/dissertation (for some programs), qualifying, special area, and oral exams (PhD); composition project, lecture-demonstration exams (DMA). *Entrance requirements:* For master's and doctorate, GRE General Test, departmental theory/analysis test, samples of work. Additional exam requirements/recommendations for international students: Required—TOEFL. Electronic applications accepted. *Expenses:* *Tuition:* Full-time $44,184; part-time $982 per credit hour. *Required fees:* $191.

State University of New York at New Paltz, Graduate School, School of Fine and Performing Arts, Department of Music, New Paltz, NY 12561. Offers music therapy (MS). *Accreditation:* NASM. Part-time programs available. *Faculty:* 5 full-time (1 woman), 2 part-time/adjunct (both women). *Students:* 16 full-time (13 women), 22 part-time (17 women); includes 3 minority (1 Asian, non-Hispanic/Latino; 1 Hispanic/Latino; 1 Two or more races, non-Hispanic/Latino), 8 international. Average age 32. 22 applicants, 41% accepted, 6 enrolled. In 2014, 4 master's awarded. *Degree requirements:* For master's, thesis. *Entrance requirements:* For master's, audition, minimum GPA of 3.0. Additional exam requirements/recommendations for international students: Required—TOEFL (minimum score 550 paper-based; 80 iBT), IELTS (minimum score 6.5). *Application deadline:* For fall admission, 5/15 for domestic and international students; for spring admission, 11/15 for domestic and international students. Applications are processed on a rolling basis. Application fee: $50. Electronic applications accepted. *Financial support:* In 2014–15, 4 teaching assistantships with partial tuition reimbursements (averaging $5,000 per year) were awarded. Financial award application deadline: 8/1. *Unit head:* Dr. Daniel Kempton, Chair, 845-257-2701, E-mail: kemptond@newpaltz.edu. *Application contact:* Prof. John Mahoney, Graduate Coordinator, 845-257-2709, E-mail: mahoneyj@newpaltz.edu.

State University of New York College at Potsdam, Crane School of Music, Potsdam, NY 13676. Offers music education (MM); music performance (MM). *Accreditation:* NASM. Part-time programs available. *Degree requirements:* For master's, variable foreign language requirement, thesis (for some programs). *Entrance requirements:* For master's, audition, minimum GPA of 3.0. Additional exam requirements/recommendations for international students: Required—TOEFL (minimum score 550 paper-based; 80 iBT), IELTS (minimum score 6). Electronic applications accepted.

Stephen F. Austin State University, Graduate School, College of Fine Arts, School of Music, Nacogdoches, TX 75962. Offers MA, MM. *Accreditation:* NASM (one or more programs are accredited). Part-time programs available. *Degree requirements:* For master's, comprehensive exam, thesis optional. *Entrance requirements:* For master's, GRE General Test, audition. Additional exam requirements/recommendations for international students: Required—TOEFL. *Faculty research:* Music classroom methodology, serial music, seventeenth century sacred music, vocal pedagogy, organ duet literature.

Stony Brook University, State University of New York, Graduate School, College of Arts and Sciences, Department of Music, Program in Music History/Theory, Stony Brook, NY 11794. Offers MA, PhD. *Students:* 36 full-time (13 women), 1 part-time (0 women); includes 2 minority (1 Black or African American, non-Hispanic/Latino; 1 Hispanic/Latino), 8 international. 52 applicants, 31% accepted, 5 enrolled. In 2014, 2 master's, 1 doctorate awarded. *Degree requirements:* For doctorate, thesis/dissertation. *Entrance requirements:* For master's and doctorate, GRE General Test. Additional exam requirements/recommendations for international students: Required—TOEFL. *Application deadline:* For fall admission, 1/15 for domestic students; for spring admission, 10/1 for domestic students. Application fee: $100. Electronic applications accepted. *Expenses:* Tuition, state resident: full-time $10,370; part-time $432 per credit. Tuition, nonresident: full-time $20,190; part-time $841 per credit. *Required fees:* $1431. *Unit head:* Dr. Perry Goldstein, Chair, 631-632-7340, E-mail: perry.goldstein@stonybrook.edu. *Application contact:* Monica Gentile, Coordinator, 631-632-7340, Fax: 631-632-7404, E-mail: monica.gentile@stonybrook.edu.

Stony Brook University, State University of New York, Graduate School, College of Arts and Sciences, Department of Music, Program in Music Performance, Stony Brook, NY 11794. Offers MM, DMA. *Students:* 200 full-time (108 women), 7 part-time (4 women); includes 44 minority (2 Black or African American, non-Hispanic/Latino; 1 American Indian or Alaska Native, non-Hispanic/Latino; 26 Asian, non-Hispanic/Latino; 10 Hispanic/Latino; 5 Two or more races, non-Hispanic/Latino), 71 international. 287 applicants, 29% accepted, 40 enrolled. In 2014, 15 master's, 37 doctorates awarded. *Degree requirements:* For doctorate, thesis/dissertation. *Entrance requirements:* For master's and doctorate, GRE General Test. Additional exam requirements/recommendations for international students: Required—TOEFL. *Application deadline:* For fall admission, 1/15 for domestic students; for spring admission, 10/1 for domestic students. Application fee: $100. *Expenses:* Tuition, state resident: full-time $10,370; part-time $432 per credit. Tuition, nonresident: full-time $20,190; part-time $841 per credit. *Required fees:* $1431. *Unit head:* Dr. Perry Goldstein, Chair, 631-632-7340, Fax: 631-632-7404, E-mail: perry.goldstein@stonybrook.edu. *Application contact:* Monica Gentile, Coordinator, 631-632-7330, Fax: 631-632-7404, E-mail: monica.gentile@stonybrook.edu.

Syracuse University, College of Visual and Performing Arts, Program in Conducting, Syracuse, NY 13244. Offers M Mu. *Accreditation:* NASM. *Students:* 4 full-time (2 women); includes 2 minority (1 Asian, non-Hispanic/Latino; 1 Hispanic/Latino), 1 international. Average age 32. 7 applicants, 43% accepted, 3 enrolled. In 2014, 4 master's awarded. *Degree requirements:* For master's, thesis or alternative. *Entrance requirements:* For master's, audition, interview. Additional exam requirements/recommendations for international students: Required—TOEFL (minimum score 100 iBT). *Application deadline:* For fall admission, 2/1 priority date for domestic and international students. Application fee: $75. Electronic applications accepted. *Expenses:* *Tuition:* Part-time $1341 per credit. *Financial support:* Fellowships with full tuition reimbursements, teaching assistantships with full and partial tuition reimbursements, Federal Work-Study, and tuition waivers available. Financial award application deadline: 1/1; financial award applicants required to submit FAFSA. *Unit head:* Dr. Steven Heyman,, Chair, Department of Applied Music and Performance Setnor School of Music, 315-443-1638, E-mail: sheyman@syr.edu. *Application contact:* Therese West, Information Contact, 315-443-0137, E-mail: admissg@syr.edu.
Website: http://vpa.syr.edu/

Syracuse University, College of Visual and Performing Arts, Program in Music Composition, Syracuse, NY 13244. Offers M Mus. *Students:* 3 full-time (0 women), 2 international. Average age 25. 10 applicants, 20% accepted, 2 enrolled. In 2014, 1 master's awarded. *Degree requirements:* For master's, thesis or alternative. *Entrance requirements:* For master's, performance recording. Additional exam requirements/recommendations for international students: Required—TOEFL (minimum score 100 iBT). *Application deadline:* For fall admission, 2/1 priority date for domestic and international students. Application fee: $75. Electronic applications accepted. *Expenses:* *Tuition:* Part-time $1341 per credit. *Financial support:* Fellowships with full tuition reimbursements and teaching assistantships with full and partial tuition reimbursements available. Financial award application deadline: 1/1; financial award applicants required to submit FAFSA. *Unit head:* Nicolas Scherzinger, 315-443-3907, E-mail: nscherzi@syr.edu. *Application contact:* Therese West, Information Contact, 315-443-0137, E-mail: admissg@syr.edu.
Website: http://vpa.syr.edu/music/programs/graduate/composition

Syracuse University, College of Visual and Performing Arts, Program in Organ, Syracuse, NY 13244. Offers M Mus. *Degree requirements:* For master's, thesis or

alternative. *Entrance requirements:* For master's, in-person audition. Additional exam requirements/recommendations for international students: Required—TOEFL (minimum score 100 iBT). *Application deadline:* For fall admission, 2/1 priority date for domestic and international students. Application fee: $75. Electronic applications accepted. *Expenses: Tuition:* Part-time $1341 per credit. *Financial support:* Fellowships with full tuition reimbursements and teaching assistantships with full and partial tuition reimbursements available. Financial award application deadline: 1/1; financial award applicants required to submit FAFSA. *Unit head:* Steven Heyman Jones, hair, Department of Applied Music and Performance, 315-443-1638, E-mail: sheyman@syr.edu. *Application contact:* Therese West, Information Contact, 315-443-0137, E-mail: admissg@syr.edu.
Website: http://vpa.syr.edu/

Syracuse University, College of Visual and Performing Arts, Program in Percussion, Syracuse, NY 13244. Offers M Mus. *Degree requirements:* For master's, thesis or alternative. *Entrance requirements:* For master's, audition. Additional exam requirements/recommendations for international students: Required—TOEFL (minimum score 100 iBT). *Application deadline:* For fall admission, 2/1 priority date for domestic and international students. Application fee: $75. Electronic applications accepted. *Expenses: Tuition:* Part-time $1341 per credit. *Financial support:* Fellowships with full tuition reimbursements and teaching assistantships with full and partial tuition reimbursements available. Financial award application deadline: 1/1; financial award applicants required to submit FAFSA. *Unit head:* Steven Heyman, Heyman, Chair, Department of Applied Music and Performance, 315-443-1638, E-mail: sheyman@syr.edu. *Application contact:* Therese West, Information Contact, 315-443-0137, E-mail: admissg@syr.edu.
Website: http://vpa.syr.edu/

Syracuse University, College of Visual and Performing Arts, Program in Piano, Syracuse, NY 13244. Offers M Mus. *Students:* 14 full-time (12 women); includes 3 minority (1 Black or African American, non-Hispanic/Latino; 1 Asian, non-Hispanic/Latino; 1 Hispanic/Latino), 8 international. Average age 23. 14 applicants, 64% accepted, 8 enrolled. In 2014, 3 master's awarded. *Degree requirements:* For master's, thesis or alternative. *Entrance requirements:* For master's, audition. Additional exam requirements/recommendations for international students: Required—TOEFL (minimum score 100 iBT). *Application deadline:* For fall admission, 2/1 priority date for domestic and international students. Application fee: $75. Electronic applications accepted. *Expenses: Tuition:* Part-time $1341 per credit. *Financial support:* Fellowships with full tuition reimbursements and teaching assistantships with full and partial tuition reimbursements available. Financial award application deadline: 1/1; financial award applicants required to submit FAFSA. *Unit head:* Dr. Steven Heyman, Chair, 315-443-1638, E-mail: sheyman@syr.edu. *Application contact:* Therese West, Information Contact, 315-443-0137, E-mail: admissg@syr.edu.
Website: http://vpa.syr.edu/

Syracuse University, College of Visual and Performing Arts, Program in Strings, Syracuse, NY 13244. Offers M Mus. *Students:* 2 full-time (both women), 2 part-time (1 woman). Average age 24. 8 applicants, 75% accepted, 2 enrolled. In 2014, 1 master's awarded. *Degree requirements:* For master's, thesis or alternative. *Entrance requirements:* For master's, audition. Additional exam requirements/recommendations for international students: Required—TOEFL (minimum score 100 iBT). *Application deadline:* For fall admission, 2/1 priority date for domestic and international students. Application fee: $75. Electronic applications accepted. *Expenses: Tuition:* Part-time $1341 per credit. *Financial support:* Fellowships with full tuition reimbursements and teaching assistantships with full and partial tuition reimbursements available. Financial award application deadline: 1/1. *Unit head:* Steven Heyman,, Chair, 315-443-1638, E-mail: sheyman@syr.edu. *Application contact:* Therese West, Information Contact, 315-443-5755, E-mail: admissg@syr.edu.
Website: http://vpa.syr.edu/

Syracuse University, College of Visual and Performing Arts, Program in Voice, Syracuse, NY 13244. Offers M Mus. *Students:* 4 full-time (3 women); includes 1 minority (Asian, non-Hispanic/Latino), 1 international. Average age 24. 8 applicants, 38% accepted, 1 enrolled. In 2014, 2 master's awarded. *Degree requirements:* For master's, thesis or alternative. *Entrance requirements:* For master's, audition. Additional exam requirements/recommendations for international students: Required—TOEFL (minimum score 100 iBT). *Application deadline:* For fall admission, 2/1 priority date for domestic and international students. Application fee: $75. Electronic applications accepted. *Expenses: Tuition:* Part-time $1341 per credit. *Financial support:* Fellowships with full tuition reimbursements and teaching assistantships with full and partial tuition reimbursements available. Financial award application deadline: 1/1; financial award applicants required to submit FAFSA. *Unit head:* Dr. Steven Heyman, Steven Heyman, Chair, Department of Applied Music and Performance, 315-443-1638, E-mail: sheyman@syr.edu. *Application contact:* Therese West, Information Contact, 315-443-0137, E-mail: admissg@syr.edu.
Website: http://vpa.syr.edu/

Syracuse University, College of Visual and Performing Arts, Program in Wind Instruments, Syracuse, NY 13244. Offers M Mus. *Students:* 1 full-time (0 women); minority (Black or African American, non-Hispanic/Latino). Average age 24. 1 applicant, 100% accepted. *Degree requirements:* For master's, thesis or alternative. *Entrance requirements:* For master's, audition. Additional exam requirements/recommendations for international students: Required—TOEFL (minimum score 100 iBT). *Application deadline:* For fall admission, 2/1 priority date for domestic and international students. Application fee: $75. Electronic applications accepted. *Expenses: Tuition:* Part-time $1341 per credit. *Financial support:* Fellowships with full tuition reimbursements and teaching assistantships with full and partial tuition reimbursements available. Financial award application deadline: 1/1; financial award applicants required to submit FAFSA. *Unit head:* Steven Heyman,, Steven Heyman, Chair, Department of Applied Music and Performance 310 Crouse College, 315-443-1638, sheyman@syr.edu, 315-443-1638, E-mail: sheyman@syr.edu. *Application contact:* Therese West, Information Contact, 315-443-0137, E-mail: admissg@syr.edu.
Website: http://vpa.syr.edu/

Temple University, Center for the Arts, Esther Boyer College of Music and Dance, Department of Music, Philadelphia, PA 19122-6096. Offers choral conducting (MM); collaborative piano/chamber music (MM); collaborative piano/opera coaching (MM); composition (MM, PhD); instrumental conducting (MM); music education (MM, PhD); music history (MM); music performance (MM, DMA), including instrumental (MM), keyboard, voice (DMA), voice/opera (MM); music studies (PhD); music theory (MM, PhD); music therapy (MMT, PhD); musicology (MM, PhD); opera (MM); piano pedagogy (MM); string pedagogy (MM). Part-time programs available. Postbaccalaureate distance learning degree programs offered. *Faculty:* 46 full-time (21 women), 43 part-time/adjunct (21 women). *Students:* 182 full-time (110 women), 36 part-time (20 women); includes 30 minority (4 Black or African American, non-Hispanic/Latino; 17 Asian, non-Hispanic/Latino; 4 Hispanic/Latino; 5 Two or more races, non-Hispanic/Latino), 57 international. 344 applicants, 53% accepted, 77 enrolled. In 2014, 58 master's, 9 doctorates awarded. Terminal master's awarded for partial completion of doctoral program. *Degree requirements:* For doctorate, thesis/dissertation. *Entrance requirements:* Additional exam requirements/recommendations for international students: Required—TOEFL. *Application deadline:* For fall admission, 11/15 for international students; for spring admission, 8/1 for international students. Applications are processed on a rolling basis. Application fee: $60. Electronic applications accepted. *Expenses:* Tuition, state resident: full-time $14,490; part-time $805 per credit hour. Tuition, nonresident: full-time $19,850; part-time $1103 per credit hour. *Required fees:* $690. Full-time tuition and fees vary according to class time, course load, degree level, campus/location and program. *Financial support:* Fellowships with full and partial tuition reimbursements, research assistantships with full and partial tuition reimbursements, teaching assistantships with full and partial tuition reimbursements, career-related internships or fieldwork, Federal Work-Study, scholarships/grants, health care benefits, and unspecified assistantships available. Financial award application deadline: 3/1; financial award applicants required to submit FAFSA. *Unit head:* Dr. Robert Stroker, Dean, 215-204-5527, Fax: 215-204-4957, E-mail: rstroker@temple.edu. *Application contact:* James Short, Director, Graduate Admissions, 215-204-8301, Fax: 215-204-4957, E-mail: james.short@temple.edu.
Website: http://www.temple.edu/boyer/academicprograms/

Texas A&M University, College of Liberal Arts, Department of Performance Studies, College Station, TX 77843. Offers MA. *Faculty:* 4. *Students:* 14 full-time (12 women); includes 4 minority (2 Black or African American, non-Hispanic/Latino; 1 Hispanic/Latino; 1 Two or more races, non-Hispanic/Latino), 2 international. Average age 25. 12 applicants, 58% accepted, 6 enrolled. In 2014, 2 master's awarded. *Degree requirements:* For master's, comprehensive exam (for some programs), thesis or alternative. *Entrance requirements:* For master's, GRE General Test. Additional exam requirements/recommendations for international students: Required—TOEFL. *Application deadline:* For fall admission, 2/15 for domestic students; for spring admission, 10/15 for domestic students. Applications are processed on a rolling basis. Application fee: $50 ($90 for international students). Electronic applications accepted. *Expenses:* Tuition, state resident: full-time $4078; part-time $226.55 per credit hour. Tuition, nonresident: full-time $10,594; part-time $577.55 per credit hour. *Required fees:* $2813; $237.70 per credit hour. $278.50 per semester. Tuition and fees vary according to degree level and student level. *Financial support:* In 2014–15, 14 students received support. Unspecified assistantships available. Financial award applicants required to submit FAFSA. *Unit head:* Dr. Donnlee Dox, Interim Head, 979-458-1870, E-mail: dox@tamu.edu. *Application contact:* Dr. Kirsten Pullen, Director of Graduate Studies, 979-845-2899, Fax: 979-845-5164, E-mail: kpullen@tamu.edu.
Website: http://perf.tamu.edu/

Texas Christian University, College of Fine Arts, School of Music, Doctoral Programs in Music, Fort Worth, TX 76129. Offers composition (DMA), including music history; conducting (DMA), including music history; piano pedagogy (DMA). *Faculty:* 39 full-time (7 women), 16 part-time/adjunct (6 women). *Students:* 9 full-time (3 women), 2 part-time (1 woman); includes 3 minority (2 Hispanic/Latino; 1 Two or more races, non-Hispanic/Latino), 2 international. Average age 34. 23 applicants, 17% accepted, 3 enrolled. *Degree requirements:* For doctorate, comprehensive exam, thesis/dissertation. *Entrance requirements:* For doctorate, GRE General Test. Additional exam requirements/recommendations for international students: Required—TOEFL (minimum score 100 iBT). *Application deadline:* For spring admission, 12/15 for domestic and international students. Application fee: $80. Electronic applications accepted. *Expenses: Tuition:* Full-time $22,860; part-time $1270 per credit hour. *Financial support:* In 2014–15, 11 students received support, including 11 research assistantships with full tuition reimbursements available (averaging $9,000 per year); career-related internships or fieldwork, institutionally sponsored loans, scholarships/grants, tuition waivers, and unspecified assistantships also available. Financial award application deadline: 12/15; financial award applicants required to submit CSS PROFILE or FAFSA. *Unit head:* Dr. Richard C. Gipson, Director, 817-257-6606, Fax: 817-257-5818, E-mail: music@tcu.edu. *Application contact:* Donna Smolik, TCU College of Fine Arts Graduate Office, 817-257-7603, Fax: 817-257-5672, E-mail: cfagradinfo@tcu.edu.
Website: http://www.music.tcu.edu

Texas Christian University, College of Fine Arts, School of Music, Master's Programs in Music, Fort Worth, TX 76129. Offers music education (MM Ed); performance (M Mus), including piano, strings, voice, winds/percussion. *Faculty:* 39 full-time (7 women), 16 part-time/adjunct (6 women). *Students:* 40 full-time (20 women), 1 (woman) part-time; includes 6 minority (1 Asian, non-Hispanic/Latino; 5 Hispanic/Latino), 12 international. Average age 26. 82 applicants, 63% accepted, 21 enrolled. In 2014, 24 master's awarded. *Degree requirements:* For master's, comprehensive exam. *Entrance requirements:* For master's, GRE General Test. Additional exam requirements/recommendations for international students: Required—TOEFL (minimum score 80 iBT). *Application deadline:* For fall admission, 3/1 for domestic and international students. Application fee: $80. Electronic applications accepted. *Expenses: Tuition:* Full-time $22,860; part-time $1270 per credit hour. *Financial support:* In 2014–15, 41 students received support, including 41 research assistantships with full tuition reimbursements available (averaging $6,000 per year); career-related internships or fieldwork, institutionally sponsored loans, scholarships/grants, tuition waivers, and unspecified assistantships also available. Financial award application deadline: 3/1; financial award applicants required to submit CSS PROFILE or FAFSA. *Unit head:* Dr. Richard C. Gipson, Director, 817-257-6606, Fax: 817-257-5818, E-mail: music@tcu.edu. *Application contact:* Donna Smolik, TCU College of Fine Arts Graduate Office, 817-257-7603, Fax: 817-257-5672, E-mail: cfagradinfo@tcu.edu.
Website: http://www.music.tcu.edu

Texas Southern University, College of Liberal Arts and Behavioral Sciences, Department of Fine Arts, Houston, TX 77004-4584. Offers fine arts (MA); music (MA). Part-time programs available. *Degree requirements:* For master's, one foreign language, comprehensive exam, recital. *Entrance requirements:* For master's, GRE General Test, minimum GPA of 2.5. Additional exam requirements/recommendations for international students: Required—TOEFL. Electronic applications accepted. *Faculty research:* Music theory, choral music, composition, percussion composition, ethnic musicology.

Texas State University, The Graduate College, College of Fine Arts and Communication, School of Music, Program in Music, San Marcos, TX 78666. Offers MM. *Accreditation:* NASM. Part-time programs available. *Faculty:* 11 full-time (6 women), 1 part-time/adjunct (0 women). *Students:* 49 full-time (20 women), 9 part-time (5 women); includes 19 minority (1 Asian, non-Hispanic/Latino; 17 Hispanic/Latino; 1 Two or more races, non-Hispanic/Latino), 12 international. Average age 28. 61 applicants, 57% accepted, 18 enrolled. In 2014, 20 master's awarded. *Degree requirements:* For master's, comprehensive exam. *Entrance requirements:* For master's, GRE (preferred), baccalaureate degree from regionally-accredited institution with minimum GPA of 2.75 in last 60 hours of undergraduate course work. Additional exam requirements/recommendations for international students: Required—TOEFL (minimum score 550 paper-based; 78 iBT). *Application deadline:* For fall admission, 6/15 priority date for domestic students, 6/1 for international students; for spring admission, 10/15 priority date for domestic students, 10/1 for international students; for summer admission, 4/15 for domestic students, 3/15 for international students. Applications are processed on a rolling basis. Application fee: $40 ($90 for international students). Electronic applications accepted. *Expenses:* Expenses: $8,834 (tuition and fees

combined). *Financial support:* In 2014–15, 48 students received support, including 25 teaching assistantships (averaging $5,961 per year); research assistantships, career-related internships or fieldwork, Federal Work-Study, institutionally sponsored loans, scholarships/grants, and unspecified assistantships also available. Support available to part-time students. Financial award application deadline: 4/1; financial award applicants required to submit FAFSA. *Unit head:* Dr. Amy Simmons, Graduate Advisor, 512-245-2651, Fax: 512-245-8181, E-mail: as61@txstate.edu. *Application contact:* Dr. Andrea Golato, Dean of Graduate School, 512-245-2581, Fax: 512-245-8365, E-mail: gradcollege@txstate.edu.
Website: http://www.finearts.txstate.edu/music/

Texas State University, The Graduate College, College of Liberal Arts, Department of English, Program in Rhetoric and Composition, San Marcos, TX 78666. Offers MA. Part-time programs available. *Faculty:* 6 full-time (4 women). *Students:* 8 full-time (4 women), 6 part-time (3 women); includes 6 minority (1 Black or African American, non-Hispanic/Latino; 3 Hispanic/Latino; 2 Two or more races, non-Hispanic/Latino). Average age 33. 9 applicants, 67% accepted, 4 enrolled. In 2014, 10 master's awarded. *Degree requirements:* For master's, comprehensive exam, thesis optional. *Entrance requirements:* For master's, GRE (preferred), baccalaureate degree from regionally-accredited university with minimum GPA of 2.75 on last 60 undergraduate semester hours, 3.0 in minimum of 12 hours of undergraduate English courses. Additional exam requirements/recommendations for international students: Required—TOEFL (minimum score 550 paper-based; 78 iBT). *Application deadline:* For fall admission, 6/15 for domestic students, 6/1 for international students; for spring admission, 11/1 for domestic students, 10/1 for international students; for summer admission, 4/15 for domestic students, 3/15 for international students. Applications are processed on a rolling basis. Application fee: $40 ($90 for international students). Electronic applications accepted. *Expenses:* Expenses: $8,834 (tuition and fees combined). *Financial support:* In 2014–15, 8 students received support, including 1 research assistantship (averaging $14,579 per year), 6 teaching assistantships (averaging $13,485 per year); Federal Work-Study, institutionally sponsored loans, scholarships/grants, and unspecified assistantships also available. Support available to part-time students. Financial award application deadline: 4/1; financial award applicants required to submit FAFSA. *Unit head:* Dr. Rebecca Jackson, Graduate Advisor, 512-245-2163, E-mail: rj10@txstate.edu. *Application contact:* Dr. Andrea Golato, Dean of Graduate School, 512-245-2581, Fax: 512-245-8365, E-mail: gradcollege@txstate.edu.
Website: http://www.english.txstate.edu

Texas Tech University, Graduate School, College of Visual and Performing Arts, School of Music, Lubbock, TX 79409-2033. Offers music (MM, DMA); music education (MM Ed). *Accreditation:* NASM. Part-time programs available. *Faculty:* 57 full-time (21 women), 2 part-time/adjunct (1 woman). *Students:* 117 full-time (65 women), 20 part-time (8 women); includes 19 minority (3 Black or African American, non-Hispanic/Latino; 1 Asian, non-Hispanic/Latino; 10 Hispanic/Latino; 5 Two or more races, non-Hispanic/Latino), 39 international. Average age 30. 139 applicants, 61% accepted, 47 enrolled. In 2014, 26 master's, 10 doctorates awarded. *Degree requirements:* For master's, thesis or alternative; for doctorate, comprehensive exam (for some programs), thesis/dissertation. *Entrance requirements:* For master's, GRE General Test. Additional exam requirements/recommendations for international students: Required—TOEFL (minimum score 550 paper-based; 79 iBT). *Application deadline:* For fall admission, 6/1 priority date for domestic students, 1/15 priority date for international students; for spring admission, 9/1 priority date for domestic students, 6/15 priority date for international students. Applications are processed on a rolling basis. Application fee: $60. Electronic applications accepted. *Expenses:* Tuition, state resident: full-time $6310; part-time $262.92 per credit hour. Tuition, nonresident: full-time $14,998; part-time $624.92 per credit hour. *Required fees:* $2701; $36.50 per credit. $912.50 per semester. Tuition and fees vary according to course load. *Financial support:* In 2014–15, 149 students received support, including 134 fellowships (averaging $2,210 per year), 3 research assistantships (averaging $15,000 per year), 94 teaching assistantships (averaging $7,784 per year); Federal Work-Study, institutionally sponsored loans, scholarships/grants, health care benefits, tuition waivers (partial), and unspecified assistantships also available. Financial award application deadline: 4/15; financial award applicants required to submit FAFSA. *Faculty research:* Strategies for music pedagogy in grades K-12, performance practice of traditional music, role of the woman piano virtuoso, vernacular music center, voice health and culture. *Total annual research expenditures:* $3,400. *Unit head:* Prof. William Ballenger, Director, 806-834-1724, Fax: 806-742-2294, E-mail: william.ballenger@ttu.edu. *Application contact:* Emily Gifford, Admissions and Scholarship Coordinator, 806-834-5076, Fax: 806-742-2294, E-mail: emily.gifford@ttu.edu.
Website: http://www.depts.ttu.edu/music

Texas Woman's University, Graduate School, College of Arts and Sciences, School of the Arts, Department of Music and Drama, Denton, TX 76201. Offers drama (MA); music (MA). *Accreditation:* NASM. Part-time programs available. *Degree requirements:* For master's, comprehensive exam, thesis (for some programs), project recital, professional paper. *Entrance requirements:* For master's, music history/theory placement exam (for music only), audition and/or design portfolio, interview, resume, writing sample (for drama only). Additional exam requirements/recommendations for international students: Required—TOEFL (minimum score 550 paper-based; 79 iBT). Electronic applications accepted. *Faculty research:* Musical development in early childhood, little known or neglected compositions for flute (especially by women composers), relationship of visual art to piano music, pedagogical development of the singing voice, guided imagery and music.

Towson University, Program in Music Performance and Composition, Towson, MD 21252-0001. Offers MM. *Accreditation:* NASM. Part-time and evening/weekend programs available. *Students:* 5 full-time (1 woman), 5 part-time (3 women); includes 1 minority (Asian, non-Hispanic/Latino). *Entrance requirements:* For master's, audition, bachelor's degree in music, minimum GPA of 3.0. Additional exam requirements/recommendations for international students: Required—TOEFL (minimum score 550 paper-based). *Application deadline:* Applications are processed on a rolling basis. Application fee: $45. Electronic applications accepted. *Financial support:* Application deadline: 4/1. *Unit head:* Prof. Terry Ewell, Graduate Program Director, 410-704-2824, E-mail: tewell@towson.edu. *Application contact:* Alicia Arkell-Kleis, Information Contact, 410-704-6004, E-mail: grads@towson.edu.
Website: http://grad.towson.edu/program/master/musc-mm/

Trinity College, Faculty of Divinity, Toronto, ON M5S 1H8, Canada. Offers ministry (Diploma); ministry for church musicians (Diploma); theology (M Div, MA, MTS, Th M, D Min, PhD, Th D, Diploma, L Th); M Div/MA. *Accreditation:* ATS. Part-time programs available. *Degree requirements:* For master's, 2 foreign languages, thesis (for some programs); for doctorate, 3 foreign languages, comprehensive exam, thesis/dissertation; for other advanced degree, thesis (for some programs). *Entrance requirements:* For master's, 1 language (modern or ancient), interview; for doctorate, 2 languages (modern and ancient). Additional exam requirements/recommendations for international students: Required—TOEFL, TWE. *Faculty research:* Interreligious dialogue, feminist theology, systematic theology, philosophy of religion, pastoral theology.

Trinity Lutheran Seminary, Graduate and Professional Programs, Columbus, OH 43209-2334. Offers African American studies (MTS); Biblical studies (MTS, STM); Christian education (MA); Christian spirituality (STM); church in the world (MTS); church music (MA); divinity (M Div); general theological studies (MTS); mission and evangelism (STM); pastoral leadership and practice (STM); youth and family ministry (MA); MSN/MTS; MTS/JD. *Accreditation:* ACIPE; ATS. Part-time programs available. *Faculty:* 11 full-time (5 women), 2 part-time/adjunct (both women). *Students:* 68 full-time (24 women), 43 part-time (18 women); includes 12 minority (10 Black or African American, non-Hispanic/Latino; 1 Asian, non-Hispanic/Latino; 1 Two or more races, non-Hispanic/Latino), 1 international. Average age 35. 45 applicants, 96% accepted, 34 enrolled. In 2014, 34 master's awarded. *Degree requirements:* For master's, variable foreign language requirement, comprehensive exam (for some programs), thesis (for some programs), field experience (for some programs). *Entrance requirements:* For master's, BA or equivalent (for MA, M Div, MTS); M Div, MTS, or equivalent (for STM); audition (for MACM). Additional exam requirements/recommendations for international students: Required—TOEFL. *Application deadline:* For fall admission, 7/15 priority date for domestic and international students. Applications are processed on a rolling basis. Application fee: $25. Electronic applications accepted. *Expenses:* Expenses: $13,760 tuition and fees for degree completion (for D Min). *Financial support:* In 2014–15, 72 students received support. Career-related internships or fieldwork, Federal Work-Study, and scholarships/grants available. Support available to part-time students. Financial award application deadline: 5/1; financial award applicants required to submit FAFSA. *Unit head:* Dr. Brad A. Binau, Academic Dean, 614-235-4136 Ext. 4674, Fax: 614-384-4635, E-mail: bbinau@tlsohio.edu. *Application contact:* Rev. Seth Bridger, Director of Admissions, 614-235-4136 Ext. 4650, Fax: 866-610-8572, E-mail: sbridger@tlsohio.edu.
Website: http://www.tlsohio.edu

Truman State University, Graduate School, School of Arts and Letters, Program in Music, Kirksville, MO 63501-4221. Offers MA. *Accreditation:* NASM. *Degree requirements:* For master's, comprehensive exam, thesis or alternative. *Entrance requirements:* For master's, GRE General Test, minimum GPA of 3.0. Additional exam requirements/recommendations for international students: Required—TOEFL (minimum score 550 paper-based). Electronic applications accepted.

Tufts University, Graduate School of Arts and Sciences, Department of Music, Medford, MA 02155. Offers ethnomusicology (MA); music history and literature (MA); music theory and composition (MA). Part-time programs available. *Students:* 10 full-time (1 woman), 6 part-time (2 women); includes 3 minority (1 Asian, non-Hispanic/Latino; 2 Hispanic/Latino), 2 international. Average age 25. 27 applicants, 59% accepted, 8 enrolled. In 2014, 12 master's awarded. *Degree requirements:* For master's, one foreign language, thesis. *Entrance requirements:* For master's, GRE General Test, writing sample or musical score. Additional exam requirements/recommendations for international students: Required—TOEFL (minimum score 550 paper-based; 80 iBT), IELTS (minimum score 6.5). *Application deadline:* For fall admission, 2/1 for domestic and international students. Applications are processed on a rolling basis. Application fee: $75. Electronic applications accepted. *Expenses: Tuition:* Full-time $45,590; part-time $1161 per credit hour. *Required fees:* $782. Full-time tuition and fees vary according to degree level, program and student level. Part-time tuition and fees vary according to course load. *Financial support:* Teaching assistantships with full and partial tuition reimbursements, Federal Work-Study, scholarships/grants, tuition waivers (partial), and unspecified assistantships available. Financial award application deadline: 2/1. *Unit head:* Dr. Richard Jankowsky, Graduate Program Director, 617-627-3564. *Application contact:* Office of Graduate Admissions, 617-627-3395, E-mail: gradadmissions@tufts.edu.
Website: http://www.tufts.edu/as/music/

Tulane University, School of Liberal Arts, Department of Music, New Orleans, LA 70118-5669. Offers MA, MFA. *Degree requirements:* For master's, one foreign language, thesis (for some programs), recital or composition (MA). *Entrance requirements:* For master's, GRE General Test, minimum B average in undergraduate course work. Additional exam requirements/recommendations for international students: Required—TOEFL. Electronic applications accepted. *Expenses: Tuition:* Full-time $46,326; part-time $2574 per credit hour. *Required fees:* $1980; $44.50 per credit hour. $550 per term. Tuition and fees vary according to course load and program. *Faculty research:* New Orleans music, composition, piano, voice, music theatre, classical guitar.

Université de Montréal, Faculty of Music, Montréal, QC H3C 3J7, Canada. Offers composition (M Mus, D Mus); interpretation (M Mus, D Mus, DESS); music (MA, PhD); orchestral repertoire (DESS). *Degree requirements:* For doctorate, thesis/dissertation, general exam. Electronic applications accepted. *Faculty research:* Semiology, music in Creole areas, computer-assisted composition, Argentinean tango.

Université Laval, Faculty of Music, Programs in Music, Québec, QC G1K 7P4, Canada. Offers composition (M Mus); instrumental didactics (M Mus); interpretation (M Mus); music education (M Mus, PhD); musicology (M Mus, PhD). Terminal master's awarded for partial completion of doctoral program. *Degree requirements:* For master's, thesis (for some programs); for doctorate, comprehensive exam, thesis/dissertation. *Entrance requirements:* For master's, English exam, audition, knowledge of French; for doctorate, English exam, knowledge of French, third language. Electronic applications accepted.

University at Buffalo, the State University of New York, Graduate School, College of Arts and Sciences, Department of Music, Buffalo, NY 14260. Offers contemporary music (Advanced Certificate); historical musicology and music theory (PhD); music composition (MA, PhD); music history (MA); music performance (MM); music theory (MA). Part-time programs available. *Faculty:* 20 full-time (4 women), 17 part-time/adjunct (3 women). *Students:* 66 full-time (25 women), 7 part-time (3 women); includes 16 minority (3 Black or African American, non-Hispanic/Latino; 11 Asian, non-Hispanic/Latino; 2 Hispanic/Latino), 4 international. Average age 25. 56 applicants, 64% accepted, 16 enrolled. In 2014, 8 master's, 4 doctorates, 1 other advanced degree awarded. Terminal master's awarded for partial completion of doctoral program. *Degree requirements:* For master's, variable foreign language requirement, comprehensive exam (for some programs), thesis (for some programs), recitals (for MM); master's projects and/or thesis for MA in Music Theory, History, Composition; for doctorate, variable foreign language requirement, comprehensive exam, thesis/dissertation; for Advanced Certificate, recitals. *Entrance requirements:* For master's, audition (for MM), compositions, writing sample(s), essay, letters of recommendation; for doctorate, GRE General Test, compositions, writing sample(s), essay, letters of recommendation; for Advanced Certificate, audition for contemporary music performance certificate. Additional exam requirements/recommendations for international students: Required—TOEFL (minimum score 550 paper-based; 79 iBT). *Application deadline:* For fall admission, 1/1 priority date for domestic and international students; for spring admission, 10/1 for domestic students, 9/1 priority date for international students. Applications are processed on a rolling basis. Application fee: $75. Electronic applications accepted. *Financial support:* In 2014–15, 16 students received support, including 11 fellowships with full tuition reimbursements available (averaging $19,580 per year), 5 teaching assistantships with full tuition reimbursements available (averaging $13,580 per year); career-related internships or fieldwork, Federal Work-Study, institutionally sponsored loans, scholarships/grants, and unspecified assistantships also

available. Financial award application deadline: 1/1; financial award applicants required to submit FAFSA. *Faculty research:* Music composition, music theory, historical musicology, concert performance, contemporary music. *Unit head:* Prof. Jeffrey Stadelman, Chairperson, 716-645-0639, Fax: 716-645-3824, E-mail: stadelm@buffalo.edu. *Application contact:* Karen A. Sausner, Director of Student Programs, 716-645-2758, Fax: 716-645-6196, E-mail: ksausner@buffalo.edu. Website: http://www.music.buffalo.edu/

The University of Akron, Graduate School, Buchtel College of Arts and Sciences, School of Music, Program in Performance, Akron, OH 44325. Offers MM. *Students:* 40 full-time (15 women), 3 part-time (1 woman); includes 8 minority (2 Black or African American, non-Hispanic/Latino; 1 Asian, non-Hispanic/Latino; 2 Hispanic/Latino; 3 Two or more races, non-Hispanic/Latino), 8 international. Average age 25. 35 applicants, 97% accepted, 26 enrolled. In 2014, 24 master's awarded. *Degree requirements:* For master's, comprehensive exam. *Entrance requirements:* For master's, minimum GPA of 2.75, three letters of recommendation, audition. Additional exam requirements/recommendations for international students: Required—TOEFL (minimum score 550 paper-based; 79 iBT), IELTS (minimum score 6.5). *Application deadline:* Applications are processed on a rolling basis. Application fee: $45 ($70 for international students). Electronic applications accepted. *Expenses:* Tuition, state resident: full-time $7578; part-time $421 per credit hour. Tuition, nonresident: full-time $12,977; part-time $721 per credit hour. *Required fees:* $1388; $35 per credit hour. Tuition and fees vary according to course load. *Unit head:* Dr. Ann Usher, Director, 330-972-6923, E-mail: ausher@uakron.edu. *Application contact:* Dr. Brooks Toliver, Graduate Director, 330-972-5207, E-mail: brooks2@uakron.edu.

The University of Alabama, Graduate School, College of Arts and Sciences, Department of English, Tuscaloosa, AL 35487. Offers applied linguistics (PhD); composition and rhetoric (PhD); creative writing (MFA), including fiction, poetry; literature (MA, PhD); rhetoric and composition (MA); teaching English as a second language (MATESOL). *Faculty:* 34 full-time (19 women). *Students:* 129 full-time (70 women), 9 part-time (8 women); includes 18 minority (9 Black or African American, non-Hispanic/Latino; 1 Asian, non-Hispanic/Latino; 5 Hispanic/Latino; 3 Two or more races, non-Hispanic/Latino), 7 international. Average age 28. 318 applicants, 18% accepted, 42 enrolled. In 2014, 39 master's, 2 doctorates awarded. *Degree requirements:* For master's, one foreign language, comprehensive exam, thesis optional; for doctorate, 2 foreign languages, comprehensive exam, thesis/dissertation. *Entrance requirements:* For master's, GRE (minimum score of 300, except for MFA), minimum GPA of 3.0, critical writing sample; for doctorate, GRE (minimum score of 300), minimum GPA of 3.5 on master's or equivalent graduate work, critical writing sample. Additional exam requirements/recommendations for international students: Required—TOEFL (minimum score 100 iBT). *Application deadline:* For fall admission, 12/31 priority date for domestic and international students. Application fee: $50 ($60 for international students). Electronic applications accepted. *Expenses:* Tuition, state resident: full-time $9826. Tuition, nonresident: full-time $24,950. *Financial support:* In 2014–15, 11 fellowships with full tuition reimbursements (averaging $15,000 per year), 1 research assistantship with full tuition reimbursement (averaging $12,366 per year), 112 teaching assistantships with full tuition reimbursements (averaging $12,366 per year) were awarded; career-related internships or fieldwork, scholarships/grants, health care benefits, and unspecified assistantships also available. Financial award application deadline: 12/31. *Faculty research:* American literature, British literature, composition/rhetoric, applied linguistics, creative writing. *Unit head:* Prof. Joel Brouwer, Department Chair, 205-348-9524, Fax: 205-348-1388, E-mail: joel.brouwer@ua.edu. *Application contact:* Jennifer Fuqua, Graduate Coordinator, 205-348-0766, Fax: 205-348-1388, E-mail: jfuqua@ua.edu.

The University of Alabama, Graduate School, College of Arts and Sciences, School of Music, Tuscaloosa, AL 35487. Offers arranging (MM); choral conducting (MM, DMA); church music (MM); composition (MM, DMA); music education (MA, PhD); musicology (MM); performance (MM, DMA); theory (MM); wind conducting (MM, DMA). *Accreditation:* NASM. *Faculty:* 40 full-time (14 women), 1 (woman) part-time/adjunct. *Students:* 56 full-time (19 women), 11 part-time (2 women); includes 11 minority (5 Black or African American, non-Hispanic/Latino; 4 Hispanic/Latino; 2 Two or more races, non-Hispanic/Latino), 12 international. Average age 29. 83 applicants, 63% accepted, 24 enrolled. In 2014, 15 master's, 12 doctorates awarded. *Degree requirements:* For master's, variable foreign language requirement, comprehensive exam (for some programs), thesis (for some programs), recital; for doctorate, variable foreign language requirement, comprehensive exam, thesis/dissertation, oral exam; recital (for some majors). *Entrance requirements:* For master's and doctorate, School of Music Audition Exam, audition in the major instrument or area. Additional exam requirements/recommendations for international students: Required—PTE (minimum score 59), TOEFL (minimum score 550 paper-based, 79 iBT) or IELTS (minimum score 6.5). *Application deadline:* For fall admission, 3/15 priority date for domestic and international students; for winter admission, 9/1 priority date for domestic and international students; for spring admission, 9/1 priority date for domestic and international students. Applications are processed on a rolling basis. Application fee: $50 ($60 for international students). Electronic applications accepted. *Expenses:* Tuition, state resident: full-time $9826. Tuition, nonresident: full-time $24,950. *Financial support:* In 2014–15, 50 students received support, including 1 fellowship with full tuition reimbursement available (averaging $10,000 per year), 44 teaching assistantships with full and partial tuition reimbursements available (averaging $10,161 per year); institutionally sponsored loans, scholarships/grants, health care benefits, and unspecified assistantships also available. Financial award application deadline: 3/15. *Faculty research:* Performance practice, musicology, theory, composition. *Unit head:* Charles G. Snead, Director, 205-348-7110, Fax: 205-348-1473, E-mail: ssnead@music.ua.edu. *Application contact:* Dr. Linda Cummins, Director of Graduate Studies, 205-348-1465, Fax: 205-348-1473, E-mail: lcummins@ua.edu.
Website: http://www.music.ua.edu/

The University of Alabama at Birmingham, College of Arts and Sciences, Program in English, Birmingham, AL 35294. Offers creative writing (MA); literature (MA); rhetoric and composition (MA). Part-time programs available. *Students:* 13 full-time (12 women), 12 part-time (4 women); includes 1 minority (Black or African American, non-Hispanic/Latino). Average age 29. In 2014, 11 master's awarded. *Degree requirements:* For master's, one foreign language, comprehensive exam, thesis or alternative. *Entrance requirements:* For master's, GRE General Test or MAT, minimum GPA of 2.75. *Application deadline:* For fall admission, 7/1 for domestic students; for spring admission, 11/1 for domestic students. Applications are processed on a rolling basis. Application fee: $45 ($60 for international students). Electronic applications accepted. *Expenses:* Tuition, state resident: full-time $7090; part-time $370 per credit hour. Tuition, nonresident: full-time $16,072; part-time $869 per credit hour. Full-time tuition and fees vary according to course load and program. *Financial support:* Teaching assistantships and career-related internships or fieldwork available. *Unit head:* Dr. Gale Temple, Program Director, 205-934-8593, Fax: 205-975-6610, E-mail: gtemple@uab.edu. *Application contact:* Susan Noblitt Banks, Director of Graduate School Operations, 205-934-8227, Fax: 205-934-8413, E-mail: gradschool@uab.edu.
Website: http://www.uab.edu/cas/english/academic-programs

University of Alaska Fairbanks, College of Liberal Arts, Department of Music, Fairbanks, AK 99775-5660. Offers MM. *Accreditation:* NASM. Part-time programs available. *Faculty:* 11 full-time (3 women). *Students:* 7 full-time (2 women), 1 (woman) part-time, 3 international. Average age 25. 7 applicants, 71% accepted, 4 enrolled. In 2014, 1 master's awarded. *Degree requirements:* For master's, comprehensive exam, thesis or alternative, project, oral defense of project. *Entrance requirements:* For master's, diagnostic examinations in music theory, music history, and music literature, bachelor's degree from accredited institution with minimum cumulative undergraduate and major GPA of 3.0, performance audition. Additional exam requirements/recommendations for international students: Required—TOEFL (minimum score 550 paper-based; 79 iBT), IELTS (minimum score 6.5). *Application deadline:* For fall admission, 6/1 for domestic students, 3/1 for international students; for spring admission, 10/15 for domestic students, 9/1 for international students. Applications are processed on a rolling basis. Application fee: $60. Electronic applications accepted. *Expenses:* Tuition, state resident: full-time $7614; part-time $423 per credit. Tuition, nonresident: full-time $15,552; part-time $864 per credit. Tuition and fees vary according to course level, course load and reciprocity agreements. *Financial support:* In 2014–15, 7 teaching assistantships with full tuition reimbursements (averaging $12,176 per year) were awarded; fellowships with full tuition reimbursements, Federal Work-Study, scholarships/grants, health care benefits, and unspecified assistantships also available. Support available to part-time students. Financial award application deadline: 7/1; financial award applicants required to submit FAFSA. *Unit head:* Dr. Eduard Zilberkant, Department Chair, 907-474-7555, Fax: 907-474-6420, E-mail: uaf.music@alaska.edu. *Application contact:* Mary Kreta, Director of Admissions, 907-474-7500, Fax: 907-474-7097, E-mail: admissions@uaf.edu.
Website: http://www.uaf.edu/music/

University of Alberta, Faculty of Graduate Studies and Research, Department of Music, Edmonton, AB T6G 2E1, Canada. Offers applied music (M Mus); choral conducting (M Mus); composition (M Mus); music (PhD); organ and choral conductors (D Mus); piano (D Mus). *Degree requirements:* For master's, one foreign language, thesis; for doctorate, one foreign language, thesis/dissertation. *Entrance requirements:* Additional exam requirements/recommendations for international students: Required—TOEFL (minimum score 550 paper-based). Electronic applications accepted. *Faculty research:* Classical/Indian and West African music, popular music, choral conducting, theory and composition, musicology, applied music.

The University of Arizona, College of Fine Arts, School of Music, Program in Music, Tucson, AZ 85721. Offers composition (MM); ethnomusicology (MM); music education (MM, PhD); music theory (MM, PhD); musicology (MM); performance (MM), including conducting - choral, conducting - instrumental, instrumental, keyboard, piano accompanying, piano and dance accompanying, vocal. *Entrance requirements:* Additional exam requirements/recommendations for international students: Required—TOEFL (minimum score 550 paper-based; 79 iBT). Electronic applications accepted. *Faculty research:* Music in general education, psychology of music learning, innovation in string music education, Zarzuela, Franz Liszt's work.

The University of Arizona, College of Fine Arts, School of Music, Program in Musical Arts, Tucson, AZ 85721. Offers composition (DMA); conducting (DMA); performance (DMA), including instrumental, keyboard, vocal. *Entrance requirements:* Additional exam requirements/recommendations for international students: Required—TOEFL (minimum score 550 paper-based; 79 iBT). Electronic applications accepted. *Faculty research:* Music in general education, psychology of music learning, innovation in string music education, Zarzuela, Franz Liszt's work.

The University of Arizona, College of Humanities, Department of English, Rhetoric, Composition and the Teaching of English Program, Tucson, AZ 85721. Offers MA, PhD. *Degree requirements:* For master's, one foreign language, comprehensive exam; for doctorate, one foreign language, comprehensive exam, thesis/dissertation. *Entrance requirements:* For doctorate, GRE General Test, 3 letters of recommendation, writing sample. Additional exam requirements/recommendations for international students: Required—TOEFL (minimum score 550 paper-based; 79 iBT). Electronic applications accepted.

University of Arkansas, Graduate School, J. William Fulbright College of Arts and Sciences, Department of Music, Fayetteville, AR 72701-1201. Offers MM. *Accreditation:* NASM. *Entrance requirements:* For master's, GRE General Test. Electronic applications accepted.

The University of British Columbia, Faculty of Arts and Faculty of Graduate Studies, School of Music, Vancouver, BC V6T 1Z2, Canada. Offers M Mus, MA, DMA, PhD. Part-time programs available. *Degree requirements:* For master's, recital (M Mus), thesis (MA); for doctorate, one foreign language, comprehensive exam, public performance or composition (DMA), dissertation (PhD). *Entrance requirements:* For master's, audition/performance (M Mus); for doctorate, audition/performance (DMA). Additional exam requirements/recommendations for international students: Required—TOEFL (minimum score 580 paper-based; 93 iBT). Electronic applications accepted. *Faculty research:* Performance, composition, opera, musicology, ethnomusicology, theory.

University of Calgary, Faculty of Graduate Studies, Faculty of Arts, Department of Music, Calgary, AB T2N 1N4, Canada. Offers M Mus, MA, PhD. *Degree requirements:* For master's, one foreign language, thesis; for doctorate, 2 foreign languages, thesis/dissertation. *Entrance requirements:* For master's, audition (performance), 3 compositions. Additional exam requirements/recommendations for international students: Required—TOEFL. Electronic applications accepted. *Faculty research:* Musicology, theory and composition, performance and performance practice, teaching methodology, folk music collection and analyses.

University of California, Berkeley, Graduate Division, College of Letters and Science, Department of Music, Berkeley, CA 94720-1500. Offers composition (PhD); ethnomusicology (PhD); musicology (PhD). *Degree requirements:* For doctorate, 2 foreign languages, thesis/dissertation, qualifying exam. *Entrance requirements:* For doctorate, GRE General Test, minimum GPA of 3.0, examples of work, 3 letters of recommendation. Additional exam requirements/recommendations for international students: Required—TOEFL (minimum score 570 paper-based). *Faculty research:* Historical musicology, music criticism, computer music.

University of California, Davis, Graduate Studies, Program in Music, Davis, CA 95616. Offers composition (MA, PhD); conducting (MA, PhD); musicology (MA, PhD). Terminal master's awarded for partial completion of doctoral program. *Degree requirements:* For master's, one foreign language, thesis; for doctorate, 2 foreign languages, thesis/dissertation. *Entrance requirements:* For master's, minimum GPA of 3.0; for doctorate, GRE, minimum GPA of 3.0. Additional exam requirements/recommendations for international students: Required—TOEFL (minimum score 550 paper-based). Electronic applications accepted.

University of California, Davis, Graduate Studies, Program in Performance Studies, Davis, CA 95616. Offers dramatic art (PhD). *Degree requirements:* For doctorate, 2 foreign languages, thesis/dissertation. *Entrance requirements:* For doctorate, GRE, minimum GPA of 3.25. Additional exam requirements/recommendations for international students: Required—TOEFL (minimum score 550 paper-based). Electronic applications accepted.

Music

University of California, Irvine, Claire Trevor School of the Arts, Department of Music, Irvine, CA 92697. Offers accompanying (MFA); choral conducting (MFA); composition and technology (MFA); guitar/lute performance (MFA); instrumental performance (MFA); jazz instrumental/composition (MFA); piano performance (MFA); vocal performance (MFA). *Students:* 20 full-time (10 women); includes 6 minority (1 Black or African American, non-Hispanic/Latino; 4 Asian, non-Hispanic/Latino; 1 Two or more races, non-Hispanic/Latino), 3 international. Average age 27. 42 applicants, 36% accepted, 11 enrolled. In 2014, 8 master's awarded. *Degree requirements:* For master's, one foreign language, thesis. *Entrance requirements:* For master's, minimum GPA of 3.0. *Application deadline:* For fall admission, 1/15 priority date for domestic students, 1/15 for international students. Applications are processed on a rolling basis. Application fee: $90 ($110 for international students). Electronic applications accepted. *Financial support:* Fellowships, teaching assistantships, institutionally sponsored loans, traineeships, health care benefits, and unspecified assistantships available. Financial award application deadline: 3/1; financial award applicants required to submit FAFSA. *Faculty research:* Composition, instrumental and choral performance, African-American music, Italian Baroque music and performance practice. *Unit head:* David L. Brodbeck, Chair, 949-824-4281, Fax: 949-824-4914, E-mail: david.brodbeck@uci.edu. *Application contact:* Amy M. Bauer, Graduate Advisor, 949-824-6615, Fax: 949-824-4914, E-mail: abauer@uci.edu.
Website: http://www.arts.uci.edu/ctsa-academic-departments-music

University of California, Los Angeles, Graduate Division, College of Letters and Science, Department of Musicology, Los Angeles, CA 90095. Offers MA, PhD. Terminal master's awarded for partial completion of doctoral program. *Degree requirements:* For master's, one foreign language, comprehensive exam, thesis; for doctorate, one foreign language, thesis/dissertation, oral and written qualifying exams. *Entrance requirements:* For master's and doctorate, GRE General Test (recommended), bachelor's degree; minimum undergraduate GPA of 3.0 (or its equivalent if letter grade system not used); writing sample. Additional exam requirements/recommendations for international students: Required—TOEFL. Electronic applications accepted.

University of California, Los Angeles, Graduate Division, School of the Arts and Architecture, Department of Ethnomusicology, Los Angeles, CA 90095. Offers MA, PhD. *Degree requirements:* For master's, one foreign language, comprehensive exam; for doctorate, 2 foreign languages, thesis/dissertation, oral and written qualifying exams. *Entrance requirements:* For master's, bachelor's degree; minimum undergraduate GPA of 3.0 (or its equivalent if letter grade system not used); writing sample; for doctorate, master's degree; minimum undergraduate GPA of 3.0 (or its equivalent if letter grade system not used); writing sample. Additional exam requirements/recommendations for international students: Required—TOEFL. Electronic applications accepted.

University of California, Los Angeles, Graduate Division, School of the Arts and Architecture, Department of Music, Los Angeles, CA 90095. Offers composition (MA, PhD); performance (MM, DMA). *Degree requirements:* For master's, one foreign language, thesis, final recital (for MM); for doctorate, one foreign language, thesis/dissertation, oral and written qualifying exams; recital (DMA). *Entrance requirements:* For master's, departmental assessment exams, bachelor's degree; minimum undergraduate GPA of 3.0 (or its equivalent if letter grade system not used); portfolio; interview; audition; for doctorate, departmental assessment exams, master's degree; minimum undergraduate GPA of 3.0 (or its equivalent if letter grade system not used); portfolio; interview. Additional exam requirements/recommendations for international students: Required—TOEFL. Electronic applications accepted.

University of California, Riverside, Graduate Division, Department of Music, Riverside, CA 92521-0102. Offers composition (PhD); ethnomusicology (MA, PhD); musicology (PhD). Terminal master's awarded for partial completion of doctoral program. *Degree requirements:* For master's, one foreign language, comprehensive exam, thesis (for some programs), oral exams; for doctorate, 2 foreign languages, comprehensive exam, thesis/dissertation, written and oral qualifying examination. *Entrance requirements:* For master's and doctorate, GRE General Test, minimum GPA of 3.0. Additional exam requirements/recommendations for international students: Required—TOEFL (minimum score 550 paper-based; 80 iBT). Electronic applications accepted. *Expenses:* Tuition, state resident: full-time $5399. Tuition, nonresident: full-time $10,433. *Faculty research:* Composition, ethnomusicology (especially Southeast Asian and Asian-American music), cultural musicology, gender studies, performance practice.

University of California, San Diego, Graduate Division, Department of Music, La Jolla, CA 92093. Offers contemporary music performance (DMA); music (MA, PhD). *Students:* 90 full-time (29 women), 1 part-time (0 women); includes 15 minority (3 Black or African American, non-Hispanic/Latino; 1 American Indian or Alaska Native, non-Hispanic/Latino; 6 Asian, non-Hispanic/Latino; 5 Hispanic/Latino), 20 international. 128 applicants, 16% accepted, 14 enrolled. In 2014, 5 master's, 10 doctorates awarded. *Degree requirements:* For master's, thesis; for doctorate, thesis/dissertation (for some programs), 6 credit units of apprentice teaching; major composition (for some programs); major recital (for some programs). *Entrance requirements:* For master's, GRE General Test, supporting musical portfolio; for doctorate, GRE General Test, master's degree; supporting musical portfolio. Additional exam requirements/recommendations for international students: Required—TOEFL (minimum score 550 paper-based; 80 iBT), IELTS (minimum score 7). *Application deadline:* For fall admission, 12/1 for domestic students. Application fee: $90 ($110 for international students). Electronic applications accepted. *Expenses:* Tuition, state resident: full-time $11,220; part-time $5610 per quarter. Tuition, nonresident: full-time $26,322; part-time $13,161 per quarter. *Required fees:* $570 per quarter. Tuition and fees vary according to program. *Financial support:* Fellowships, research assistantships, teaching assistantships, scholarships/grants, unspecified assistantships, and readerships available. Financial award applicants required to submit FAFSA. *Faculty research:* Composition, computer music, integrative studies, performance. *Unit head:* Rand Steiger, Chair, 858-534-3230, E-mail: rpsteiger@ucsd.edu. *Application contact:* Diana Platero-Lopez, Graduate Coordinator, 858-534-3279, E-mail: dplatero@ucsd.edu.
Website: http://musicweb.ucsd.edu/

University of California, Santa Barbara, Graduate Division, College of Letters and Sciences, Division of Humanities and Fine Arts, Department of Music, Santa Barbara, CA 93106-2014. Offers brass (MM); composition (MA, PhD); conducting (MM, DMA); ethnomusicology (MA, PhD); keyboard (MM, DMA); musicology (MA, PhD); piano accompanying (MM); strings (MM, DMA); theory (MA, PhD); voice (MM, DMA); woodwinds (MM); MA/PhD; MM/DMA. *Degree requirements:* For master's, variable foreign language requirement, comprehensive exam (for some programs), thesis (for some programs); for doctorate, variable foreign language requirement, comprehensive exam, thesis/dissertation. *Entrance requirements:* For master's and doctorate, GRE. Additional exam requirements/recommendations for international students: Required—TOEFL (minimum score 550 paper-based; 80 iBT), IELTS (minimum score 7). Electronic applications accepted. *Faculty research:* Music theory, ethnomusicology, musicology, music performance, music composition.

University of California, Santa Cruz, Division of Graduate Studies, Division of the Arts, Department of Music, Santa Cruz, CA 95064. Offers ethnomusicology (MA); music (PhD), including cross-cultural and interdisciplinary studies; music composition (MA, DMA), including world music composition (DMA); music composition (DMA), including computer-assisted (algorithmic) composition ; performance practice (MA). *Degree requirements:* For master's, one foreign language, thesis, recital; for doctorate, one foreign language, thesis/dissertation, qualifying and final examinations. *Entrance requirements:* For master's, GRE General Test, 3 letters of recommendation, writing or composition sample, 10-20 minute unedited recording; for doctorate, GRE General Test, 3 letters of recommendation, writing sample. Additional exam requirements/recommendations for international students: Required—TOEFL (minimum score 550 paper-based; 83 iBT); Recommended—IELTS (minimum score 8). Electronic applications accepted. *Faculty research:* Western music history, new music, composition, ethnomusicology, musicology.

University of Central Arkansas, Graduate School, College of Fine Arts and Communication, Department of Music, Conway, AR 72035-0001. Offers choral conducting (MM); instrumental conducting (MM); music (PC); music education (MM); music theory (MM); performance (MM). *Accreditation:* NASM. Part-time programs available. *Degree requirements:* For master's, comprehensive exam, thesis optional. *Entrance requirements:* For master's, GRE General Test, minimum GPA of 2.7. Additional exam requirements/recommendations for international students: Required—TOEFL (minimum score 550 paper-based). Electronic applications accepted.

University of Central Florida, College of Arts and Humanities, Department of Music, Orlando, FL 32816. Offers music (MA); theatre (MA, MFA), including acting (MFA), design (MFA), theatre for young audiences (MFA). *Accreditation:* NASM; NCATE. Part-time and evening/weekend programs available. *Faculty:* 51 full-time (19 women), 14 part-time/adjunct (8 women). *Students:* 28 full-time (15 women), 24 part-time (15 women); includes 9 minority (2 Black or African American, non-Hispanic/Latino; 1 Asian, non-Hispanic/Latino; 3 Hispanic/Latino; 3 Two or more races, non-Hispanic/Latino), 1 international. Average age 32. 49 applicants, 49% accepted, 18 enrolled. In 2014, 22 master's awarded. *Entrance requirements:* For master's, GRE General Test. Additional exam requirements/recommendations for international students: Required—TOEFL. *Application deadline:* For fall admission, 7/15 for domestic students; for spring admission, 12/1 for domestic students. Application fee: $30. Electronic applications accepted. *Expenses:* Tuition, state resident: part-time $288.16 per credit hour. Tuition, nonresident: part-time $1073.31 per credit hour. *Financial support:* In 2014–15, 25 students received support, including 6 fellowships with partial tuition reimbursements available (averaging $5,500 per year), 4 research assistantships with tuition reimbursements available (averaging $7,500 per year), 19 teaching assistantships with partial tuition reimbursements available (averaging $7,800 per year); career-related internships or fieldwork, Federal Work-Study, institutionally sponsored loans, tuition waivers (partial), and unspecified assistantships also available. Financial award application deadline: 3/1; financial award applicants required to submit FAFSA. *Unit head:* Jeffrey Moore, Chair, 407-823-2879, Fax: 407-823-3378, E-mail: jeffrey.moore@ucf.edu. *Application contact:* Barbara Rodriguez Lamas, Director, Admissions and Student Services, 407-823-2766, Fax: 407-823-6442, E-mail: gradadmissions@ucf.edu.
Website: http://performingarts.cah.ucf.edu/

University of Central Missouri, The Graduate School, Warrensburg, MO 64093. Offers accountancy (MA); accounting (MBA); applied mathematics (MS); aviation safety (MA); biology (MS); business administration (MBA); career and technical education leadership (MS); college student personnel administration (MS); communication (MA); computer science (MS); counseling (MS); criminal justice (MS); educational leadership (Ed D); educational technology (MS); elementary and early childhood education (MSE); English (MA); environmental studies (MA); finance (MBA); history (MA); human services/educational technology (Ed S); human services/learning resources (Ed S); human services/professional counseling (Ed S); industrial hygiene (MS); industrial management (MS); information systems (MBA); information technology (MS); kinesiology (MS); library science and information services (MS); literacy education (MSE); marketing (MBA); mathematics (MS); music (MA); occupational safety management (MS); psychology (MS); rural family nursing (MS); school administration (MSE); social gerontology (MS); sociology (MA); special education (MSE); speech language pathology (MS); superintendency (Ed S); teaching (MAT); teaching English as a second language (MA); technology (MS); technology management (PhD); theatre (MA). Part-time programs available. *Faculty:* 314 full-time (137 women), 24 part-time/adjunct (14 women). *Students:* 1,624 full-time (542 women), 1,773 part-time (1,055 women); includes 194 minority (104 Black or African American, non-Hispanic/Latino; 6 American Indian or Alaska Native, non-Hispanic/Latino; 23 Asian, non-Hispanic/Latino; 41 Hispanic/Latino; 3 Native Hawaiian or other Pacific Islander, non-Hispanic/Latino; 17 Two or more races, non-Hispanic/Latino), 1,592 international. Average age 31. 2,800 applicants, 63% accepted, 1223 enrolled. In 2014, 796 master's, 81 other advanced degrees awarded. *Degree requirements:* For master's and Ed S, comprehensive exam (for some programs), thesis (for some programs). *Entrance requirements:* Additional exam requirements/recommendations for international students: Required—TOEFL (minimum score 550 paper-based; 79 iBT). *Application deadline:* For fall admission, 6/1 for domestic students; for spring admission, 10/1 for domestic and international students. Applications are processed on a rolling basis. Application fee: $30 ($75 for international students). Electronic applications accepted. *Expenses:* Tuition, state resident: full-time $6630; part-time $276.25 per credit hour. Tuition, nonresident: full-time $13,260; part-time $552.50 per credit hour. *Required fees:* $29 per credit hour. Tuition and fees vary according to campus/location. *Financial support:* In 2014–15, 118 students received support, including 271 research assistantships with full and partial tuition reimbursements available (averaging $7,500 per year), 109 teaching assistantships with full and partial tuition reimbursements available (averaging $7,500 per year); career-related internships or fieldwork, Federal Work-Study, scholarships/grants, and administrative and laboratory assistantships also available. Support available to part-time students. Financial award application deadline: 3/1; financial award applicants required to submit FAFSA. *Unit head:* Tina Church-Hockett, Director of Graduate School and International Admissions, 660-543-4621, Fax: 660-543-4778, E-mail: church@ucmo.edu. *Application contact:* Brittany Lawrence, Graduate Student Services Coordinator, 660-543-4621, Fax: 660-543-4778, E-mail: gradinfo@ucmo.edu.
Website: http://www.ucmo.edu/graduate/

University of Central Oklahoma, The Jackson College of Graduate Studies, College of Fine Arts and Design, Department of Music, Edmond, OK 73034-5209. Offers jazz (MM), including commercial music production, performance; music (MM). *Accreditation:* NASM. Part-time programs available. *Degree requirements:* For master's, comprehensive exam, recital or project. *Entrance requirements:* For master's, interview, audition. Additional exam requirements/recommendations for international students: Required—TOEFL (minimum score 550 paper-based; 79 iBT), IELTS (minimum score 6.5). Electronic applications accepted. *Faculty research:* Historical performance, history of music education.

University of Chicago, Division of the Humanities, Department of Music, Chicago, IL 60637. Offers PhD. *Students:* 71 full-time (31 women); includes 9 minority (5 Black or African American, non-Hispanic/Latino; 2 Hispanic/Latino; 2 Two or more races, non-Hispanic/Latino), 20 international. 157 applicants, 24% accepted, 6 enrolled. Terminal master's awarded for partial completion of doctoral program. *Degree requirements:* For

doctorate, 3 foreign languages, thesis/dissertation. *Entrance requirements:* For doctorate, GRE General Test. Additional exam requirements/recommendations for international students: Required—TOEFL (minimum score 104 iBT), IELTS (minimum score 7). *Application deadline:* For fall admission, 12/15 for domestic and international students. Application fee: $90. Electronic applications accepted. *Expenses: Tuition:* Full-time $46,899. *Required fees:* $347. *Financial support:* Fellowships with full tuition reimbursements, teaching assistantships with full tuition reimbursements, Federal Work-Study, institutionally sponsored loans, scholarships/grants, and health care benefits available. Financial award application deadline: 12/15; financial award applicants required to submit FAFSA. *Unit head:* Dr. Anne Walters Robertson, Chair. *Application contact:* Braden Grams, Assistant Dean of Students, Admissions and Fellowships, 773-702-1552, Fax: 773-834-9148, E-mail: humanitiesadmissions@uchicago.edu. Website: http://music.uchicago.edu/

University of Chicago, Division of the Humanities, Master of Arts Program in the Humanities, Chicago, IL 60637. Offers art history (MA); classics (MA); comparative literature (MA); creative writing (MA); digital humanities (MA); English language and literature (MA); Germanic studies (MA); linguistics (MA); music (MA); philosophy (MA); Romance languages and literatures (MA); South Asian languages and civilizations (MA). *Students:* 83 full-time (41 women), 8 part-time (6 women); includes 14 minority (1 Black or African American, non-Hispanic/Latino; 6 Asian, non-Hispanic/Latino; 6 Hispanic/Latino; 1 Two or more races, non-Hispanic/Latino), 17 international. Average age 26. 153 applicants, 67% accepted, 80 enrolled. *Degree requirements:* For master's, thesis. *Entrance requirements:* For master's, GRE General Test. Additional exam requirements/recommendations for international students: Required—TOEFL (minimum score 600 paper-based; 104 iBT), IELTS (minimum score 7). *Application deadline:* For fall admission, 3/15 for domestic and international students. Application fee: $90. Electronic applications accepted. *Expenses: Tuition:* Full-time $46,899. *Required fees:* $347. *Financial support:* In 2014–15, 100 students received support, including 8 fellowships with partial tuition reimbursements available (averaging $12,000 per year); Federal Work-Study, institutionally sponsored loans, and tuition waivers (partial) also available. Financial award application deadline: 3/15; financial award applicants required to submit FAFSA. *Unit head:* Prof. David Wray, Director, 773-834-1201, E-mail: ma-humanities@uchicago.edu. *Application contact:* Program Coordinator, 773-834-1201, Fax: 773-834-7526, E-mail: ma-humanities@uchicago.edu. Website: http://maph.uchicago.edu/

University of Cincinnati, Graduate School, College-Conservatory of Music, Division of Composition, Musicology and Theory, Cincinnati, OH 45221. Offers composition (MM, DMA); music history (MM); music theory (MM, PhD); musicology (PhD). *Accreditation:* NASM. *Faculty:* 13 full-time (5 women), 2 part-time/adjunct (0 women). *Students:* 52 full-time (18 women), 22 part-time (10 women); includes 5 minority (3 Black or African American, non-Hispanic/Latino; 2 Hispanic/Latino), 19 international. 63 applicants, 40% accepted. In 2014, 5 master's, 1 doctorate awarded. *Degree requirements:* For master's, variable foreign language requirement, comprehensive exam, thesis; for doctorate, variable foreign language requirement, comprehensive exam, thesis/dissertation. *Entrance requirements:* For master's and doctorate, GRE General Test, interview. Additional exam requirements/recommendations for international students: Required—TOEFL (minimum score 520 paper-based). *Application deadline:* For fall admission, 2/1 for domestic students. Applications are processed on a rolling basis. Application fee: $85. Electronic applications accepted. *Financial support:* In 2014–15, 21 teaching assistantships with full tuition reimbursements (averaging $7,020 per year) were awarded; fellowships, research assistantships, Federal Work-Study, scholarships/grants, tuition waivers (full and partial), and unspecified assistantships also available. Financial award application deadline: 3/1. *Unit head:* Dr. Joel Hoffman, Chair, 513-556-6046, E-mail: joel.hoffman@uc.edu. *Application contact:* Paul R. Hillner, Assistant Dean for Admissions and Student Services, 513-556-5462, Fax: 513-556-1028, E-mail: paul.hillner@uc.edu. Website: http://ccm.uc.edu/music/cmt.html

University of Cincinnati, Graduate School, College-Conservatory of Music, Division of Ensembles and Conducting, Cincinnati, OH 45221. Offers choral conducting (MM, DMA); orchestral conducting (MM, DMA); wind conducting (MM, DMA). *Accreditation:* NASM. *Degree requirements:* For master's, comprehensive exam, conducting performances; for doctorate, one foreign language, comprehensive exam, thesis/dissertation, conducting performances, lecture recital. *Entrance requirements:* For master's and doctorate, GRE General Test, audition, interview. Additional exam requirements/recommendations for international students: Required—TOEFL (minimum score 520 paper-based). Electronic applications accepted.

University of Cincinnati, Graduate School, College-Conservatory of Music, Division of Keyboard Studies, Cincinnati, OH 45221. Offers MM, DMA, AD. *Degree requirements:* For master's, comprehensive exam; for doctorate, one foreign language, comprehensive exam, thesis/dissertation. *Entrance requirements:* For master's and doctorate, GRE General Test, audition; for AD, audition. Additional exam requirements/recommendations for international students: Required—TOEFL (minimum score 520 paper-based). Electronic applications accepted.

University of Cincinnati, Graduate School, College-Conservatory of Music, Division of Performance Studies, Cincinnati, OH 45221. Offers performance (MM, DMA, AD). MM, DMA, and AD are available for every instrument. *Accreditation:* NASM. *Degree requirements:* For master's, comprehensive exam, recitals; for doctorate, one foreign language, comprehensive exam, thesis/dissertation, recitals; for AD, recitals. *Entrance requirements:* For master's and doctorate, GRE General Test, audition. Additional exam requirements/recommendations for international students: Required—TOEFL (minimum score 520 paper-based). Electronic applications accepted. *Faculty research:* Performance, guest teaching.

University of Cincinnati, Graduate School, College-Conservatory of Music, Divisions of Opera, Musical Theater, Drama, and Arts Administration, Cincinnati, OH 45221. Offers arts administration (MA); directing (MFA); theater design and production (MFA); voice and opera (MM, DMA); MBA/MA. *Accreditation:* NAST (one or more programs are accredited). *Degree requirements:* For master's, final project. *Entrance requirements:* For master's, GMAT (MA), audition/interview. Additional exam requirements/recommendations for international students: Required—TOEFL (minimum score 520 paper-based). Electronic applications accepted.

University of Colorado Boulder, Graduate School, College of Music, Boulder, CO 80309. Offers composition (M Mus, D Mus A); conducting (M Mus); instrumental conducting and literature (D Mus A); literature and performance of choral music (D Mus A); music education (M Mus Ed, PhD), including choral or wind instrument conducting (M Mus Ed), general (M Mus Ed), Kodaly concepts (M Mus Ed), piano pedagogy (M Mus Ed), primary instruments (M Mus Ed), secondary instruments (M Mus Ed), voice pedagogy (M Mus Ed); music theory (M Mus); musicology (PhD); performance (M Mus, D Mus A); performance and pedagogy (M Mus, D Mus A). *Accreditation:* NASM. *Faculty:* 58 full-time (20 women). *Students:* 175 full-time (82 women), 51 part-time (28 women); includes 33 minority (3 Black or African American, non-Hispanic/Latino; 12 Asian, non-Hispanic/Latino; 10 Hispanic/Latino; 1 Native Hawaiian or other Pacific Islander, non-Hispanic/Latino; 7 Two or more races, non-Hispanic/Latino), 18 international. Average age 29. 453 applicants, 32% accepted, 57

enrolled. In 2014, 37 master's, 17 doctorates awarded. Terminal master's awarded for partial completion of doctoral program. *Degree requirements:* For master's, variable foreign language requirement, comprehensive exam, thesis or alternative, recital; for doctorate, variable foreign language requirement, thesis/dissertation. *Entrance requirements:* For master's, GRE General Test, GRE Subject Test (music literature), minimum undergraduate GPA of 2.75; for doctorate, GRE General Test, GRE Subject Test, audition, sample of research. *Application deadline:* For fall admission, 12/1 for domestic and international students; for spring admission, 10/1 for domestic and international students. Applications are processed on a rolling basis. Application fee: $50 ($70 for international students). Electronic applications accepted. *Financial support:* In 2014–15, 360 students received support, including 118 fellowships (averaging $3,025 per year), 1 research assistantship with full and partial tuition reimbursement available (averaging $8,730 per year), 101 teaching assistantships with full and partial tuition reimbursements available (averaging $19,294 per year); institutionally sponsored loans, scholarships/grants, health care benefits, and unspecified assistantships also available. Financial award application deadline: 3/1; financial award applicants required to submit FAFSA. *Faculty research:* Music, instrumental music, performing arts, chamber music, musicology/music theory. Website: http://music.colorado.edu/

University of Colorado Denver, College of Arts and Media, Denver, CO 80217. Offers recording arts (MS), including media forensics, recording arts. Part-time and evening/weekend programs available. *Faculty:* 32 full-time (11 women), 2 part-time/adjunct (1 woman). *Students:* 23 full-time (5 women), 4 part-time (2 women); includes 6 minority (2 Asian, non-Hispanic/Latino; 3 Hispanic/Latino; 1 Two or more races, non-Hispanic/Latino), 1 international. Average age 34. 19 applicants, 74% accepted, 8 enrolled. In 2014, 8 master's awarded. *Degree requirements:* For master's, thesis, 34 credits, thesis/portfolio. *Entrance requirements:* For master's, GRE General Test (minimum scores higher than 50th percentile for all sections), minimum undergraduate GPA of 3.0, portfolio, resume, interview, 3 letters of recommendation. Additional exam requirements/recommendations for international students: Required—TOEFL (minimum score 70 iBT). *Application deadline:* For fall admission, 4/1 for domestic students, 3/1 for international students. Application fee: $50 ($75 for international students). Electronic applications accepted. *Expenses:* Expenses: Contact institution. *Financial support:* In 2014–15, 2 students received support. Federal Work-Study, institutionally sponsored loans, scholarships/grants, traineeships, and unspecified assistantships available. Financial award application deadline: 4/1; financial award applicants required to submit FAFSA. *Faculty research:* Audio forensics, audio pedagogy, concert recordings, digital audio workstations, music law. Total annual research expenditures: $29,822. *Unit head:* Laurence Kaptain, Dean, 303-352-3559, E-mail: laurence.kaptain@ucdenver.edu. *Application contact:* Megan Sforzini, Program Assistant, 303-352-3833, E-mail: megan.sforzini@ucdenver.edu. Website: http://www.ucdenver.edu/academics/colleges/CAM/programs/meis/masterdegree/Pages/index.aspx

University of Connecticut, Graduate School, School of Fine Arts, Department of Music, Storrs, CT 06269. Offers conducting (M Mus, DMA); historical musicology (MA); music (Performer's Certificate); music education (M Mus, PhD); music theory (MA); music theory and history (PhD); performance (M Mus, DMA). *Accreditation:* NASM. Terminal master's awarded for partial completion of doctoral program. *Degree requirements:* For master's, comprehensive exam; for doctorate, thesis/dissertation. *Entrance requirements:* For master's, GRE General Test, GRE Subject Test, audition; for doctorate, GRE Subject Test, MAT, audition. Additional exam requirements/recommendations for international students: Required—TOEFL (minimum score 550 paper-based).

University of Delaware, College of Arts and Sciences, Department of Music, Newark, DE 19716. Offers composition (MM); music education (MM); performance (MM). *Accreditation:* NASM. Part-time programs available. *Entrance requirements:* For master's, audition. Additional exam requirements/recommendations for international students: Required—TOEFL. Electronic applications accepted. *Faculty research:* Teaching of music.

University of Denver, Division of Arts, Humanities and Social Sciences, Lamont School of Music, Denver, CO 80208. Offers MA, MM, Certificate. *Accreditation:* NASM. Part-time programs available. *Faculty:* 28 full-time (8 women), 33 part-time/adjunct (16 women). *Students:* 28 full-time (14 women), 46 part-time (23 women); includes 12 minority (1 Black or African American, non-Hispanic/Latino; 1 Asian, non-Hispanic/Latino; 9 Hispanic/Latino; 1 Two or more races, non-Hispanic/Latino), 13 international. Average age 26. 108 applicants, 74% accepted, 38 enrolled. In 2014, 26 master's, 4 other advanced degrees awarded. *Degree requirements:* For master's, one foreign language, comprehensive exam, recital or project (for performance), thesis (for musicology, music theory, piano pedagogy). *Entrance requirements:* For master's, GRE General Test (for MA only), bachelor's degree, transcripts, personal statement, resume, three letters of recommendation, pre-screen audition (for performance), portfolio (for composition), essay or research paper (for MA only); for Certificate, bachelor's degree, transcripts, personal statement, resume, letters of recommendation, pre-screen video recording or music audition. Additional exam requirements/recommendations for international students: Required—TOEFL (minimum score 550 paper-based; 80 iBT). *Application deadline:* For fall admission, 12/15 priority date for domestic and international students. Applications are processed on a rolling basis. Application fee: $65. Electronic applications accepted. *Expenses:* Expenses: $1,199 per credit hour. *Financial support:* In 2014–15, 61 students received support, including 32 teaching assistantships with full and partial tuition reimbursements available (averaging $7,070 per year); career-related internships or fieldwork, Federal Work-Study, institutionally sponsored loans, scholarships/grants, tuition waivers, and unspecified assistantships also available. Support available to part-time students. Financial award application deadline: 2/15; financial award applicants required to submit FAFSA. *Faculty research:* Performance, jazz studies and commercial music, musicology, music theory, composition, music pedagogy, music recording and production. *Unit head:* Nancy Cochran, School Director, 303-871-6986, Fax: 303-871-3118, E-mail: nancy.cochran@du.edu. *Application contact:* Stephen Campbell, Director of Admission, 303-871-6973, Fax: 303-871-3118, E-mail: stephen.l.campbell@du.edu. Website: http://www.du.edu/ahss/schools/lamont/index.html

University of Florida, Graduate School, College of The Arts, School of Music, Gainesville, FL 32611-5800. Offers choral conducting (MM); composition (MM, PhD); electronic music (MM); ethnomusicology (MM); instrumental conducting (MM); music (MM, PhD); music education (MM, PhD), including choral conducting (MM), composition (MM), electronic music (MM), ethnomusicology (MM), instrumental conducting (MM), music education (MM), music history and literature (MM), music theory (MM), performance (MM), piano pedagogy (MM); music history and literature (MM, PhD); music theory (MM); performance (MM); sacred music (MM). *Accreditation:* NASM. *Faculty:* 28 full-time (8 women), 3 part-time/adjunct (0 women). *Students:* 80 full-time (31 women), 94 part-time (41 women); includes 36 minority (18 Black or African American, non-Hispanic/Latino; 2 American Indian or Alaska Native, non-Hispanic/Latino; 5 Asian, non-Hispanic/Latino; 11 Hispanic/Latino), 15 international. 115 applicants, 62% accepted, 52 enrolled. In 2014, 26 master's, 7 doctorates awarded.

Degree requirements: For master's, variable foreign language requirement, comprehensive exam, thesis, recital; for doctorate, thesis/dissertation. *Entrance requirements:* For master's and doctorate, GRE General Test, audition, minimum GPA of 3.0. Additional exam requirements/recommendations for international students: Required—TOEFL (minimum score 550 paper-based; 80 iBT), IELTS (minimum score 6). *Application deadline:* For fall admission, 1/1 priority date for domestic students, 1/1 for international students; for spring admission, 11/1 for domestic and international students. Applications are processed on a rolling basis. Application fee: $30. Electronic applications accepted. *Financial support:* In 2014–15, 1 fellowship, 76 teaching assistantships were awarded; research assistantships and unspecified assistantships also available. Financial award applicants required to submit FAFSA. *Unit head:* John A. Duff, PhD, Program Director and Professor, 352-392-8506, Fax: 352-392-0461, E-mail: jduff@arts.ufl.edu. *Application contact:* Dr. Leslie S. Odom, Associate Professor and Graduate Advisor, 352-273-3172, Fax: 352-352-0461, E-mail: lodom@arts.ufl.edu. Website: http://www.arts.ufl.edu/welcome/music/

University of Georgia, Franklin College of Arts and Sciences, Hugh Hodgson School of Music, Athens, GA 30602. Offers MA, MM, DMA, PhD. *Accreditation:* NASM. *Degree requirements:* For master's, variable foreign language requirement, thesis (MA); for doctorate, variable foreign language requirement, thesis/dissertation. *Entrance requirements:* For master's and doctorate, GRE General Test. Electronic applications accepted.

University of Hartford, The Hartt School, West Hartford, CT 06117-1599. Offers choral conducting (MM Ed); composition (MM, DMA, Artist Diploma, Diploma); conducting (MM, DMA, Artist Diploma, Diploma), including choral (MM, Diploma), instrumental (MM, Diploma); early childhood education (MM Ed); instrumental conducting (MM Ed); Kodály (MM Ed); music (CAGS); music education (DMA, PhD); music history (MM); music theory (MM); pedagogy (MM Ed); performance (MM, MM Ed, DMA, Artist Diploma, Diploma); research (MM Ed); technology (MM Ed). *Accreditation:* NASD. Part-time programs available. *Degree requirements:* For master's, variable foreign language requirement, thesis (for some programs), recital; for doctorate, variable foreign language requirement, thesis/dissertation (for some programs), recital; for other advanced degree, recital. *Entrance requirements:* For master's, audition, letters of recommendation; for doctorate, proficiency exam, audition, interview, research paper; for other advanced degree, audition. Additional exam requirements/recommendations for international students: Required—TOEFL. Electronic applications accepted. *Expenses:* Contact institution.

University of Hawaii at Manoa, Graduate Division, College of Arts and Humanities, Department of Music, Honolulu, HI 96822. Offers M Mus, MA, PhD. *Accreditation:* NASM. Part-time programs available. *Degree requirements:* For master's, variable foreign language requirement, thesis optional; for doctorate, variable foreign language requirement, comprehensive exam, thesis/dissertation. *Entrance requirements:* For master's, GRE General Test, diagnostic exams in acoustics theory; for doctorate, diagnostic exams in music history and theory, GRE General Test. Additional exam requirements/recommendations for international students: Required—TOEFL (minimum score 540 paper-based; 76 iBT), IELTS (minimum score 5). *Faculty research:* Original compositions, nineteenth century German music, Korean and Indonesian music, piano/voice performance, Pacific music.

University of Houston, College of Liberal Arts and Social Sciences, Moores School of Music, Houston, TX 77204. Offers accompanying and chamber music (MM); applied music (MM); composition (MM); music education (DMA); music theory (MM); performance (DMA). *Accreditation:* NASM. Part-time programs available. *Degree requirements:* For master's, one foreign language, comprehensive exam, recital; for doctorate, one foreign language, comprehensive exam, thesis/dissertation. *Entrance requirements:* For master's, audition, resume, 3 letters of recommendation; for doctorate, writing sample, audition, statement of purpose, resume. Additional exam requirements/recommendations for international students: Required—TOEFL (minimum score 550 paper-based; 79 iBT), IELTS (minimum score 6.5). Electronic applications accepted. *Faculty research:* Twentieth century music, Baroque music, history of music theory, music analysis.

University of Idaho, College of Graduate Studies, College of Letters, Arts and Social Sciences, Lionel Hampton School of Music, Moscow, ID 83844-4015. Offers M Mus, MA. *Accreditation:* NASM. *Faculty:* 18 full-time, 1 part-time/adjunct. *Students:* 10 full-time, 10 part-time. Average age 33. In 2014, 8 master's awarded. *Degree requirements:* For master's, one foreign language, thesis or alternative. *Entrance requirements:* For master's, minimum GPA of 2.8. Additional exam requirements/recommendations for international students: Required—TOEFL. *Application deadline:* For fall admission, 8/1 for domestic students; for spring admission, 12/15 for domestic students. Applications are processed on a rolling basis. Application fee: $60. Electronic applications accepted. *Expenses:* Tuition, state resident: full-time $4784; part-time $280.50 per credit hour. Tuition, nonresident: full-time $18,314; part-time $957.50 per credit hour. *Required fees:* $2000; $58.50 per credit hour. Tuition and fees vary according to program. *Financial support:* Research assistantships and teaching assistantships available. Financial award applicants required to submit FAFSA. *Unit head:* Dr. Torrey Lawrence, Director, 208-885-6231, E-mail: music@uidaho.edu. *Application contact:* Sean Scoggin, Director of Graduate Admissions, 208-885-4001, Fax: 208-885-4406, E-mail: graduateadmissions@uidaho.edu. Website: http://www.uidaho.edu/class/music

University of Illinois at Urbana–Champaign, Graduate College, College of Fine and Applied Arts, School of Music, Champaign, IL 61820. Offers music (M Mus, AD, DMA); music education (MME, PhD); musicology (PhD). *Accreditation:* NASM. *Students:* 347 (177 women). Application fee: $70 ($90 for international students). *Unit head:* Jeffrey S. Magee, Interim Director, 217-244-2676, Fax: 217-244-4585, E-mail: jmag@illinois.edu. *Application contact:* J. Michael Holmes, Enrollment Management Director, 217-244-9879, Fax: 217-244-4585, E-mail: holmes2@illinois.edu. Website: http://www.music.illinois.edu/

The University of Iowa, Graduate College, College of Liberal Arts and Sciences, School of Music, Iowa City, IA 52242-1316. Offers MA, MFA, DMA, PhD. *Accreditation:* NASM. *Degree requirements:* For master's, thesis (for some programs), exam; for doctorate, comprehensive exam, thesis/dissertation. *Entrance requirements:* For master's and doctorate, minimum GPA of 3.0. Additional exam requirements/recommendations for international students: Required—TOEFL (minimum score 550 paper-based; 81 iBT). Electronic applications accepted.

The University of Kansas, Graduate Studies, School of Music, Program in Music, Lawrence, KS 66045. Offers MM, DMA, PhD. *Accreditation:* NASM. *Faculty:* 53 full-time, 18 part-time/adjunct. *Students:* 148 full-time (71 women), 13 part-time (8 women); includes 17 minority (1 Black or African American, non-Hispanic/Latino; 1 American Indian or Alaska Native, non-Hispanic/Latino; 2 Asian, non-Hispanic/Latino; 8 Hispanic/Latino; 5 Two or more races, non-Hispanic/Latino), 43 international. Average age 30. 206 applicants, 50% accepted, 39 enrolled. In 2014, 29 master's, 29 doctorates awarded. *Degree requirements:* For master's, comprehensive exam, thesis, recitals; for doctorate, comprehensive exam, thesis/dissertation, recitals (for DMA). *Entrance requirements:* For master's, KU Musicology and Music Theory diagnostic exam,

minimum GPA of 3.0, audition (for performance); for doctorate, GRE (for PhD); KU Musicology and Music Theory diagnostic exam, minimum GPA of 3.0, audition (for DMA). Additional exam requirements/recommendations for international students: Required—TOEFL or IELTS (minimum score 6). *Application deadline:* For fall admission, 12/15 priority date for domestic and international students; for spring admission, 5/1 for domestic and international students. Applications are processed on a rolling basis. Application fee: $55 ($65 for international students). Electronic applications accepted. *Financial support:* Fellowships with full tuition reimbursements, teaching assistantships with full and partial tuition reimbursements, institutionally sponsored loans, scholarships/grants, and unspecified assistantships available. Financial award application deadline: 12/15; financial award applicants required to submit FAFSA. *Faculty research:* Musicology, music theory, composition, performance, conducting. *Unit head:* Dr. Robert Walzel, Dean, 785-864-3421, Fax: 785-864-5866, E-mail: music@ku.edu. *Application contact:* Jane Gnojek, Administrative Professional, 785-864-2862, E-mail: jgnojek@ku.edu. Website: http://www.music.ku.edu

University of Kentucky, Graduate School, College of Fine Arts, Program in Music, Lexington, KY 40506-0032. Offers composition (MM, DMA); conducting (MM, DMA); music education (MM, PhD); music theory (MA, PhD); music therapy (MM); musicology (MA, PhD); performance (MM, DMA); sacred music (MM). *Accreditation:* NASM. Part-time and evening/weekend programs available. *Degree requirements:* For master's, variable foreign language requirement, comprehensive exam, thesis (for some programs); for doctorate, variable foreign language requirement, comprehensive exam, thesis/dissertation. *Entrance requirements:* For master's, GRE General Test, minimum undergraduate GPA of 2.75; for doctorate, GRE General Test, minimum undergraduate GPA of 2.75, graduate 3.0. Additional exam requirements/recommendations for international students: Required—TOEFL (minimum score 550 paper-based). Electronic applications accepted. *Faculty research:* Musicology, music theory, jazz, music education, performance and conducting.

University of Lethbridge, School of Graduate Studies, Lethbridge, AB T1K 3M4, Canada. Offers addictions counseling (M Sc); agricultural biotechnology (M Sc); agricultural studies (M Sc, MA); anthropology (MA); archaeology (M Sc, MA); art (MA, MFA); biochemistry (M Sc); biological sciences (M Sc); biomolecular science (PhD); biosystems and biodiversity (PhD); Canadian studies (MA); chemistry (M Sc); computer science (M Sc); computer science and geographical information science (M Sc); counseling (MC); counseling psychology (M Ed); dramatic arts (MA); earth, space, and physical science (PhD); economics (MA); education (MA); educational leadership (M Ed); English (MA); environmental science (M Sc); evolution and behavior (PhD); exercise science (M Sc); French (MA); French/German (MA); French/Spanish (MA); general education (M Ed); geography (M Sc, MA); German (MA); health sciences (M Sc); individualized multidisciplinary (M Sc, MA); kinesiology (M Sc, MA); management (M Sc), including accounting, finance, general management, human resource management and labor relations, information systems, international management, marketing, policy and strategy; mathematics (M Sc); modern languages (MA); music (M Mus, MA); Native American studies (MA); neuroscience (M Sc, PhD); new media (MA, MFA); nursing (M Sc, MN); philosophy (MA); physics (M Sc); political science (MA); psychology (M Sc, MA); religious studies (MA); sociology (MA); theatre and dramatic arts (MFA); theoretical and computational science (PhD); urban and regional studies (MA); women and gender studies (MA). Part-time and evening/weekend programs available. *Faculty:* 358. *Students:* 445 full-time (243 women), 116 part-time (72 women). Average age 31. 351 applicants, 26% accepted, 87 enrolled. In 2014, 129 master's, 13 doctorates awarded. *Degree requirements:* For master's, thesis (for some programs); for doctorate, comprehensive exam, thesis/dissertation. *Entrance requirements:* For master's, GMAT (for M Sc in management), bachelor's degree in related field, minimum GPA of 3.0 during previous 20 graded semester courses, 2 years' teaching or related experience (M Ed); for doctorate, master's degree, minimum graduate GPA of 3.5. Additional exam requirements/recommendations for international students: Required—TOEFL. Application fee: $100 Canadian dollars. *Financial support:* Fellowships, research assistantships, teaching assistantships, scholarships/grants, health care benefits, and unspecified assistantships available. *Faculty research:* Movement and brain plasticity, gibberellin physiology, photosynthesis, carbon cycling, molecular properties of main-group ring components. *Application contact:* School of Graduate Studies, 403-329-5194, E-mail: sgsinquiries@uleth.ca. Website: http://www.uleth.ca/graduatestudies/

University of Louisiana at Lafayette, College of the Arts, School of Music, Lafayette, LA 70504. Offers conducting (MM); pedagogy (MM); vocal and instrumental performance (MM). *Accreditation:* NASM. *Degree requirements:* For master's, thesis or alternative. *Entrance requirements:* For master's, GRE General Test, minimum GPA of 2.75. Additional exam requirements/recommendations for international students: Required—TOEFL (minimum score 550 paper-based). Electronic applications accepted. *Faculty research:* Nineteenth century American music, trumpet pedagogy, fifteenth century Renaissance polyphony, Charles Ives.

University of Louisville, Graduate School, School of Music, Louisville, KY 40292-0001. Offers music composition (MM); music education (MME); music history and literature (MM); music theory (MM); performance (MM). *Accreditation:* NASM. Part-time and evening/weekend programs available. *Students:* 54 full-time (21 women), 4 part-time (1 woman); includes 10 minority (3 Black or African American, non-Hispanic/Latino; 4 Hispanic/Latino; 3 Two or more races, non-Hispanic/Latino), 10 international. Average age 26. 82 applicants, 66% accepted, 30 enrolled. In 2014, 29 master's awarded. *Degree requirements:* For master's, one foreign language, recital (for performance), paper or thesis (for music education), major composition (for composition). *Entrance requirements:* For master's, GRE General Test, music history and theory entrance exams, jazz entrance exam, audition, portfolio. Additional exam requirements/recommendations for international students: Required—TOEFL (minimum score 550 paper-based; 79 iBT). *Application deadline:* For fall admission, 3/15 priority date for domestic and international students; for spring admission, 11/15 priority date for domestic and international students. Applications are processed on a rolling basis. Application fee: $60. Electronic applications accepted. *Expenses:* Tuition, state resident: full-time $11,326; part-time $630 per credit hour. Tuition, nonresident: full-time $23,568; part-time $1311 per credit hour. *Required fees:* $196. Tuition and fees vary according to program and reciprocity agreements. *Financial support:* Fellowships with full tuition reimbursements, teaching assistantships with full tuition reimbursements, scholarships/grants, health care benefits, tuition waivers (full and partial), and unspecified assistantships available. Financial award application deadline: 3/1; financial award applicants required to submit FAFSA. *Faculty research:* Music therapy and autism, music composition, musicological research, music performance, contemporary music. *Total annual research expenditures:* $155,218. *Unit head:* Dr. Christopher Doane, Dean, 502-852-6907, Fax: 502-852-1874, E-mail: doane@louisville.edu. *Application contact:* Toni Robinson, Admissions Counselor, 502-852-1623, Fax: 502-852-0520, E-mail: toni.robinson@louisville.edu. Website: http://www.louisville.edu/music/

University of Maine, Graduate School, College of Liberal Arts and Sciences, Department of English, Orono, ME 04469. Offers composition and pedagogy (MA);

gender and literature (MA). Part-time and evening/weekend programs available. *Faculty:* 19 full-time (10 women). *Students:* 25 full-time (18 women), 3 part-time (2 women), 2 international. Average age 29. 41 applicants, 73% accepted, 14 enrolled. In 2014, 3 master's awarded. *Degree requirements:* For master's, one foreign language, thesis optional. *Entrance requirements:* For master's, GRE General Test, minimum GPA of 3.0. Additional exam requirements/recommendations for international students: Required—TOEFL. *Application deadline:* For fall admission, 1/15 priority date for domestic students. Applications are processed on a rolling basis. Application fee: $65. Electronic applications accepted. *Expenses:* Tuition, state resident: part-time $658 per credit hour. Tuition, nonresident: part-time $1550 per credit hour. *Financial support:* In 2014–15, 24 students received support, including 21 teaching assistantships with full tuition reimbursements available (averaging $14,600 per year); Federal Work-Study and tuition waivers (full and partial) also available. Financial award application deadline: 3/1. *Faculty research:* Poetry and poetics, critical studies, medieval studies, gender theory, nineteenth- and twentieth-century literature, Native American literature. *Unit head:* Dr. Richard Brucher, Chair, 207-581-3823, Fax: 207-581-1604. *Application contact:* Scott G. Delcourt, Assistant Vice President for Graduate Studies and Senior Associate Dean, 207-581-3291, Fax: 207-581-3232, E-mail: graduate@maine.edu. Website: http://english.umaine.edu/

University of Maine, Graduate School, College of Liberal Arts and Sciences, School of Performing Arts, Orono, ME 04469. Offers music performance (MM). Part-time programs available. *Faculty:* 8 full-time (3 women), 10 part-time/adjunct (5 women). *Students:* 8 full-time (4 women), 1 international. Average age 24. 9 applicants, 67% accepted, 5 enrolled. In 2014, 5 master's awarded. *Entrance requirements:* For master's, audition. Additional exam requirements/recommendations for international students: Required—TOEFL. *Application deadline:* For fall admission, 2/1 priority date for domestic students. Applications are processed on a rolling basis. Application fee: $65. Electronic applications accepted. *Expenses:* Tuition, state resident: part-time $658 per credit hour. Tuition, nonresident: part-time $1550 per credit hour. *Financial support:* In 2014–15, 4 students received support, including 4 teaching assistantships with full tuition reimbursements available (averaging $7,300 per year); career-related internships or fieldwork, Federal Work-Study, institutionally sponsored loans, scholarships/grants, and tuition waivers (full and partial) also available. Support available to part-time students. Financial award application deadline: 3/1. *Faculty research:* Percussion music of Carter and Varese, song-settings of the poetry of W.B. Yeats, philosophy of voice, Entartete Musik: music and composers banned by the Nazis. *Unit head:* Dr. Beth Wiemann, Chair, 207-581-1244, Fax: 207-581-4701. *Application contact:* Scott G. Delcourt, Assistant Vice President for Graduate Studies and Senior Associate Dean, 207-581-3291, Fax: 207-581-3232, E-mail: graduate@maine.edu. Website: http://umaine.edu/spa/academics/music/

The University of Manchester, School of Arts, Histories and Cultures, Manchester, United Kingdom. Offers anthropology, media and performance (PhD); applied theatre professional (PhD); archaeology (PhD); art history and visual studies (PhD); arts management and cultural policy (PhD); classics and ancient history (PhD); composition (PhD); creative writing (PhD); drama (PhD); economic and social history (PhD); electroacoustic composition (PhD); English and American studies (PhD); history (PhD); humanitarianism and conflict response (PhD); museology (PhD); music (PhD); musicology (PhD); religions and theology (PhD).

University of Manitoba, Faculty of Graduate Studies, Marcel A. Desautels Faculty of Music, Winnipeg, MB R3T 2N2, Canada. Offers M Mus.

University of Maryland, Baltimore County, The Graduate School, College of Arts, Humanities and Social Sciences, Department of Music, Baltimore, MD 21250. Offers American contemporary music (Postbaccalaureate Certificate). *Faculty:* 10 full-time (5 women), 22 part-time/adjunct (11 women). *Students:* 1 (woman) full-time. Average age 32. 2 applicants, 1 enrolled. *Entrance requirements:* For degree, minimum GPA of 3.0, resume, reference letters, DVD of performance. Additional exam requirements/recommendations for international students: Recommended—TOEFL. *Application deadline:* For fall admission, 12/1 for domestic and international students; for winter admission, 1/30 for domestic and international students; for spring admission, 5/15 priority date for domestic students, 4/15 for international students. Applications are processed on a rolling basis. Application fee: $50. *Expenses:* Expenses: Contact institution. *Financial support:* Applicants required to submit FAFSA. *Faculty research:* Music, composition, performance, music technology, contemporary music. *Unit head:* Dr. E. Michael Richards, Chair, 410-455-3064, E-mail: emrichards@umbc.edu. *Application contact:* Dr. Anna Rubin, Director, 410-455-3190, Fax: 410-455-1181, E-mail: airubin@umbc.edu. Website: http://www.umbc.edu/music/

University of Maryland, College Park, Academic Affairs, College of Arts and Humanities, School of Music, Program in Ethnomusicology, College Park, MD 20742. Offers MA. *Degree requirements:* For master's, comprehensive exam, thesis optional, oral defense. *Entrance requirements:* Additional exam requirements/recommendations for international students: Required—TOEFL.

University of Maryland, College Park, Academic Affairs, College of Arts and Humanities, School of Music, Program in Music, College Park, MD 20742. Offers M Ed, MA, MM, DMA, Ed D, PhD. *Entrance requirements:* For master's, GRE General Test (for ethnomusicology, historical musicology and music theory), 3 letters of recommendation, audition/interview. Additional exam requirements/recommendations for international students: Required—TOEFL.

University of Massachusetts Amherst, Graduate School, College of Humanities and Fine Arts, Department of English, Amherst, MA 01003. Offers American studies (PhD); composition and rhetoric (PhD); creative writing (MFA); English and American literature (MA, PhD). Part-time programs available. *Faculty:* 49 full-time (24 women). *Students:* 100 full-time (60 women), 76 part-time (50 women); includes 29 minority (2 Black or African American, non-Hispanic/Latino; 6 Asian, non-Hispanic/Latino; 10 Hispanic/Latino; 1 Native Hawaiian or other Pacific Islander, non-Hispanic/Latino; 10 Two or more races, non-Hispanic/Latino), 17 international. Average age 30. 600 applicants, 12% accepted, 29 enrolled. In 2014, 26 master's, 10 doctorates awarded. Terminal master's awarded for partial completion of doctoral program. *Degree requirements:* For master's, one foreign language, thesis optional; for doctorate, one foreign language, comprehensive exam, thesis/dissertation. *Entrance requirements:* For master's, manuscript; for doctorate, GRE General Test, manuscript. Additional exam requirements/recommendations for international students: Required—TOEFL (minimum score 550 paper-based; 80 iBT), IELTS (minimum score 6.5). *Application deadline:* For fall admission, 12/15 for domestic and international students. Applications are processed on a rolling basis. Application fee: $75. Electronic applications accepted. *Expenses:* Tuition, state resident: full-time $1980; part-time $110 per credit. Tuition, nonresident: full-time $14,644; part-time $414 per credit. Required fees: $11,417. One-time fee: $357. *Financial support:* Fellowships with full and partial tuition reimbursements, research assistantships with full and partial tuition reimbursements, teaching assistantships with full and partial tuition reimbursements, career-related internships or fieldwork, Federal Work-Study, scholarships/grants, traineeships, health care benefits, tuition waivers (full and partial), and unspecified assistantships available. Support available to part-time students. Financial award application deadline: 12/15.

Unit head: Dr. Jenny Spencer, Department Head, 413-545-2332, Fax: 413-545-3880. *Application contact:* Lindsay DeSantis, Supervisor of Admissions, 413-545-0722, Fax: 413-577-0010, E-mail: gradadm@grad.umass.edu. Website: http://www.umass.edu/english/

University of Massachusetts Amherst, Graduate School, College of Humanities and Fine Arts, Department of Music and Dance, Amherst, MA 01003. Offers collaborative piano (MM); composition (MM); conducting (MM); jazz composition/arranging (MM); music education (MM, PhD); music history (MM); music theory (PhD); performance (MM). *Accreditation:* NASM. Part-time programs available. *Faculty:* 22 full-time (6 women). *Students:* 60 full-time (28 women), 19 part-time (3 women); includes 9 minority (2 Asian, non-Hispanic/Latino; 5 Hispanic/Latino; 2 Two or more races, non-Hispanic/Latino), 10 international. Average age 28. 87 applicants, 67% accepted, 39 enrolled. In 2014, 39 master's, 1 doctorate awarded. Terminal master's awarded for partial completion of doctoral program. *Degree requirements:* For master's, thesis or alternative; for doctorate, comprehensive exam, thesis/dissertation. *Entrance requirements:* For master's and doctorate, placement tests, original scores, research, audition or tape. Additional exam requirements/recommendations for international students: Required—TOEFL (minimum score 550 paper-based; 80 iBT), IELTS (minimum score 6.5). *Application deadline:* For fall admission, 1/15 for domestic and international students; for spring admission, 10/1 for domestic and international students. Applications are processed on a rolling basis. Application fee: $75. Electronic applications accepted. *Expenses:* Tuition, state resident: full-time $1980; part-time $110 per credit. Tuition, nonresident: full-time $14,644; part-time $414 per credit. Required fees: $11,417. One-time fee: $357. *Financial support:* Fellowships with full and partial tuition reimbursements, research assistantships with full and partial tuition reimbursements, teaching assistantships with full and partial tuition reimbursements, career-related internships or fieldwork, Federal Work-Study, scholarships/grants, traineeships, health care benefits, tuition waivers (full and partial), and unspecified assistantships available. Support available to part-time students. Financial award application deadline: 1/15. *Unit head:* Dr. Brent Auerbach, Graduate Program Director, 413-545-0311, Fax: 413-545-2092. *Application contact:* Lindsay DeSantis, Supervisor of Admissions, 413-545-0722, Fax: 413-577-0010, E-mail: gradadm@grad.umass.edu. Website: http://www.umass.edu/music/

University of Massachusetts Lowell, College of Fine Arts, Humanities and Social Sciences, Department of Music, Lowell, MA 01854. Offers music education (MM); sound recording technology (MM). *Accreditation:* NASM. Part-time programs available. *Degree requirements:* For master's, one foreign language, thesis. *Entrance requirements:* For master's, MAT, audition. Electronic applications accepted.

University of Memphis, Graduate School, College of Communication and Fine Arts, Rudi E. Scheidt School of Music, Memphis, TN 38152. Offers conducting (M Mu, DMA); historical musicology (PhD); music education (M Mu, DMA); musicology (M Mu). *Accreditation:* NASM. Part-time programs available. *Faculty:* 34 full-time (8 women), 6 part-time/adjunct (3 women). *Students:* 75 full-time (25 women), 52 part-time (25 women); includes 24 minority (12 Black or African American, non-Hispanic/Latino; 3 Asian, non-Hispanic/Latino; 5 Hispanic/Latino; 4 Two or more races, non-Hispanic/Latino), 20 international. Average age 32. 101 applicants, 67% accepted, 23 enrolled. In 2014, 17 master's, 7 doctorates awarded. Terminal master's awarded for partial completion of doctoral program. *Degree requirements:* For master's, comprehensive exam, thesis or alternative; for doctorate, one foreign language, comprehensive exam, thesis/dissertation, exam. *Entrance requirements:* For master's, GRE General Test or MAT, proficiency exam, audition; for doctorate, GRE General Test or MAT, proficiency exam, audition, master's degree. Additional exam requirements/recommendations for international students: Required—TOEFL. *Application deadline:* For fall admission, 8/1 for domestic students; for spring admission, 12/1 for domestic students. Applications are processed on a rolling basis. Application fee: $35 ($60 for international students). *Financial support:* In 2014–15, 73 students received support. Research assistantships with full and partial tuition reimbursements available, teaching assistantships with full and partial tuition reimbursements available, Federal Work-Study, scholarships/grants, and unspecified assistantships available. Financial award application deadline: 2/15; financial award applicants required to submit FAFSA. *Faculty research:* Spanish Renaissance, twentieth century music, Project OPTIMUS, composition, musical performance, regional music, performance, performance practice, composition. *Unit head:* Dr. Patricia J. Hoy, Director, 901-678-2541, Fax: 901-678-3096, E-mail: phoy@memphis.edu. *Application contact:* Dr. John Baur, Assistant Director for Graduate Admissions, 901-678-3362, Fax: 901-678-3096, E-mail: jbaur@memphis.edu. Website: http://www.memphis.edu/music/

University of Miami, Graduate School, Frost School of Music, Department of Instrumental Performance, Coral Gables, FL 33124. Offers instrumental conducting (MM, DMA); instrumental performance (MM, DMA, AD); multiple woodwinds (MM, DMA). *Accreditation:* NASM. *Degree requirements:* For master's, thesis, recital paper, recital; for doctorate, thesis/dissertation, essay, 2 research tools, 3 recitals. *Entrance requirements:* For master's and doctorate, GRE General Test, audition. Additional exam requirements/recommendations for international students: Required—TOEFL (minimum score 550 paper-based; 59 iBT). Electronic applications accepted. *Faculty research:* Performance, conducting, composition.

University of Miami, Graduate School, Frost School of Music, Department of Keyboard Performance, Coral Gables, FL 33124. Offers accompanying and chamber music (MM, DMA); keyboard performance and pedagogy (MM, DMA); piano performance (MM, DMA, AD). *Accreditation:* NASM. *Degree requirements:* For master's, thesis, recital paper, recital; for doctorate, thesis/dissertation, essay, 2 research tools, 3 recitals. *Entrance requirements:* For master's and doctorate, GRE General Test, audition. Additional exam requirements/recommendations for international students: Required—TOEFL (minimum score 555 paper-based; 59 iBT). Electronic applications accepted.

University of Miami, Graduate School, Frost School of Music, Department of Music Media and Industry, Coral Gables, FL 33124. Offers music business and entertainment industries (MM); music engineering (MS). *Accreditation:* NASM. *Degree requirements:* For master's, thesis, internship (MM), research project (MS). *Entrance requirements:* For master's, GRE General Test. Additional exam requirements/recommendations for international students: Required—TOEFL (minimum score 550 paper-based; 59 iBT). Electronic applications accepted. *Faculty research:* Recording rights and property, digital sound design, recording industry, Internet-based music industries.

University of Miami, Graduate School, Frost School of Music, Department of Musicology, Coral Gables, FL 33124. Offers MM. *Accreditation:* NASM. *Degree requirements:* For master's, thesis. *Entrance requirements:* For master's, GRE General Test. Additional exam requirements/recommendations for international students: Required—TOEFL (minimum score 550 paper-based; 59 iBT). Electronic applications accepted.

University of Miami, Graduate School, Frost School of Music, Department of Music Theory-Composition, Coral Gables, FL 33124. Offers composition (MM, DMA); electronic music (MM); media writing and production (MM); music theory (MM). *Accreditation:* NASM. *Degree requirements:* For master's, thesis; for doctorate, thesis/dissertation, essay. *Entrance requirements:* For master's and doctorate, GRE General

Test, portfolio. Additional exam requirements/recommendations for international students: Required—TOEFL (minimum score 550 paper-based; 59 iBT). Electronic applications accepted. *Faculty research:* Composition, commercial music and media music.

University of Miami, Graduate School, Frost School of Music, Department of Studio Music and Jazz, Coral Gables, FL 33124. Offers jazz composition (DMA); jazz pedagogy (MM); jazz performance (MM, DMA); studio jazz writing (MM). *Accreditation:* NASM. *Degree requirements:* For master's, thesis. *Entrance requirements:* For master's and doctorate, GRE General Test, portfolio. Additional exam requirements/recommendations for international students: Required—TOEFL (minimum score 550 paper-based; 59 iBT). Electronic applications accepted. *Faculty research:* Jazz performance, jazz conducting, jjazz composition.

University of Miami, Graduate School, Frost School of Music, Department of Vocal Performance, Coral Gables, FL 33124. Offers choral conducting (MM, DMA); vocal pedagogy (DMA); vocal performance (MM, DMA, AD). *Accreditation:* NASM. *Degree requirements:* For master's, 2 foreign languages, thesis, recital paper; for doctorate, thesis/dissertation, essay. *Entrance requirements:* For master's and doctorate, GRE General Test, audition. Additional exam requirements/recommendations for international students: Required—TOEFL (minimum score 550 paper-based; 59 iBT). Electronic applications accepted. *Faculty research:* Opera, musical theatre, performance, directing, pedagogy.

University of Michigan, Horace H. Rackham School of Graduate Studies, School of Music, Theatre, and Dance, Program in Composition, Ann Arbor, MI 48109-2217. Offers MA, MM, A Mus D. *Degree requirements:* For doctorate, one foreign language, thesis/dissertation, oral exam, composition. *Entrance requirements:* For master's and doctorate, portfolio. Additional exam requirements/recommendations for international students: Required—TOEFL.

University of Michigan, Horace H. Rackham School of Graduate Studies, School of Music, Theatre, and Dance, Program in Composition and Theory, Ann Arbor, MI 48109-2085. Offers PhD. *Degree requirements:* For doctorate, one foreign language, thesis/dissertation, oral exam, composition. *Entrance requirements:* For doctorate, GRE, portfolio. Additional exam requirements/recommendations for international students: Required—TOEFL. Electronic applications accepted.

University of Michigan, Horace H. Rackham School of Graduate Studies, School of Music, Theatre, and Dance, Program in Conducting, Ann Arbor, MI 48109-2085. Offers MM, A Mus D. *Degree requirements:* For doctorate, one foreign language, thesis/dissertation, 3 concerts, oral exam. *Entrance requirements:* For doctorate, audition, portfolio. Additional exam requirements/recommendations for international students: Required—TOEFL. Electronic applications accepted.

University of Michigan, Horace H. Rackham School of Graduate Studies, School of Music, Theatre, and Dance, Program in Musicology, Ann Arbor, MI 48109-2085. Offers MA, PhD. *Degree requirements:* For doctorate, 2 foreign languages, thesis/dissertation, oral exam. *Entrance requirements:* For master's and doctorate, GRE General Test, writing sample. Additional exam requirements/recommendations for international students: Required—TOEFL. Electronic applications accepted.

University of Michigan, Horace H. Rackham School of Graduate Studies, School of Music, Theatre, and Dance, Program in Music Theory, Ann Arbor, MI 48109-2085. Offers PhD. *Degree requirements:* For doctorate, one foreign language, thesis/dissertation, oral exam. *Entrance requirements:* For doctorate, GRE, writing sample. Additional exam requirements/recommendations for international students: Required—TOEFL. Electronic applications accepted.

University of Michigan, Horace H. Rackham School of Graduate Studies, School of Music, Theatre, and Dance, Program in Performance, Ann Arbor, MI 48109-2085. Offers MM, A Mus D, Spec M. *Degree requirements:* For doctorate, one foreign language, thesis/dissertation, 3 concerts, oral exam. *Entrance requirements:* For doctorate, audition. Additional exam requirements/recommendations for international students: Required—TOEFL. Electronic applications accepted.

University of Michigan–Flint, Graduate Programs, Program in Arts Administration, Flint, MI 48502-1950. Offers museum and visual arts (MA); performance (MA). Part-time programs available. *Faculty:* 2 part-time/adjunct (1 woman). *Students:* 7 full-time (5 women), 11 part-time (8 women); includes 3 minority (all Black or African American, non-Hispanic/Latino), 1 international. Average age 36. 10 applicants, 100% accepted, 9 enrolled. In 2014, 10 master's awarded. *Degree requirements:* For master's, thesis, internship. *Entrance requirements:* For master's, bachelor's degree in the arts (visual art, theatre, dance, music, etc.) from accredited institution with minimum undergraduate GPA of 3.0. Additional exam requirements/recommendations for international students: Required—TOEFL (minimum score 84 iBT), IELTS (minimum score 6.5). *Application deadline:* For fall admission, 8/1 for domestic students, 5/1 for international students; for winter admission, 11/15 for domestic students, 9/15 for international students. Applications are processed on a rolling basis. Application fee: $55. Electronic applications accepted. Application fee is waived when completed online. *Financial support:* Federal Work-Study and scholarships/grants available. Support available to part-time students. Financial award application deadline: 3/1; financial award applicants required to submit FAFSA. *Unit head:* Dr. Sarah Lippert, Interim Director, 810-766-6679, E-mail: sarlipp@umflint.edu. *Application contact:* Bradley T. Maki, Director of Graduate Admissions, 810-762-3171, Fax: 810-766-6789, E-mail: bmaki@umflint.edu.
Website: http://www.umflint.edu/graduateprograms/arts-administration-ma

University of Minnesota, Duluth, Graduate School, School of Fine Arts, Department of Music, Duluth, MN 55812-2496. Offers music education (MM); performance (MM). *Accreditation:* NASM. Part-time programs available. *Degree requirements:* For master's, comprehensive exam, thesis (for some programs), recital (MM in performance). *Entrance requirements:* For master's, audition, minimum GPA of 3.0, sample of written work, interview, bachelor's degree in music, video of teaching. Additional exam requirements/recommendations for international students: Required—TOEFL (minimum score 550 paper-based). *Faculty research:* Band composition, music aesthetics, learning theory, value theory, music advocacy.

University of Minnesota, Twin Cities Campus, Graduate School, College of Liberal Arts, School of Music, Minneapolis, MN 55455-0213. Offers MA, MM, DMA, PhD. *Accreditation:* NASM. *Degree requirements:* For master's, comprehensive exam, thesis (for some programs), foreign language (MA), recital (MM); for doctorate, comprehensive exam, 5 recitals (DMA); 2 foreign languages or computer languages, dissertation (PhD). *Entrance requirements:* For master's, GRE (MA); for doctorate, GRE (PhD). Additional exam requirements/recommendations for international students: Required—TOEFL (minimum score 550 paper-based; 79 iBT: 21 writing, 19 reading), IELTS (minimum score 6.5). Electronic applications accepted.

University of Mississippi, Graduate School, College of Liberal Arts, Department of Music, University, MS 38677. Offers MM, DA. *Accreditation:* NASM. *Degree requirements:* For master's, thesis (for some programs); for doctorate, thesis/dissertation. *Entrance requirements:* For master's, GRE General Test, minimum GPA of 3.0; for doctorate, GRE General Test. Additional exam requirements/recommendations for international students: Required—TOEFL. Electronic applications accepted.

University of Missouri, Office of Research and Graduate Studies, College of Arts and Science, School of Music, Columbia, MO 65211. Offers MA, MM. *Accreditation:* NASM. *Faculty:* 38 full-time (14 women), 10 part-time/adjunct (6 women). *Students:* 42 full-time (15 women), 12 part-time (9 women); includes 6 minority (1 Black or African American, non-Hispanic/Latino; 1 Asian, non-Hispanic/Latino; 3 Hispanic/Latino; 1 Two or more races, non-Hispanic/Latino), 10 international. Average age 26. 75 applicants, 53% accepted, 23 enrolled. In 2014, 23 master's awarded. *Degree requirements:* For master's, 3 foreign languages, thesis. *Entrance requirements:* For master's, minimum GPA of 3.0. Additional exam requirements/recommendations for international students: Required—TOEFL (minimum score 500 paper-based; 61 iBT). *Application deadline:* For fall admission, 12/15 priority date for domestic and international students. Applications are processed on a rolling basis. Application fee: $55 ($75 for international students). Electronic applications accepted. *Financial support:* Fellowships with full tuition reimbursements, research assistantships, teaching assistantships with full tuition reimbursements, institutionally sponsored loans, health care benefits, and unspecified assistantships available. *Faculty research:* Preparing students to become professional musicians and music educators. *Unit head:* Dr. Robert Shay, Director, 573-882-2606, E-mail: shayr@missouri.edu. *Application contact:* Dr. Dan Willett, Associate Director, 573-882-0933, E-mail: willettd@missouri.edu.
Website: http://music.missouri.edu/

University of Missouri–Kansas City, Conservatory of Music and Dance, Kansas City, MO 64110-2499. Offers composition (MM, DMA); conducting (MM, DMA); music (MA); music education (MME, PhD); music history and literature (MM); music theory (MM); music therapy (MA); musicology (MM); performance (MM, DMA). PhD (interdisciplinary) offered through the School of Graduate Studies. *Accreditation:* NASM. Part-time programs available. *Faculty:* 51 full-time (17 women), 36 part-time/adjunct (14 women). *Students:* 162 full-time (71 women), 65 part-time (28 women); includes 25 minority (6 Black or African American, non-Hispanic/Latino; 10 Asian, non-Hispanic/Latino; 8 Hispanic/Latino; 1 Two or more races, non-Hispanic/Latino), 38 international. Average age 28. 418 applicants, 47% accepted, 97 enrolled. In 2014, 25 master's, 18 doctorates awarded. *Degree requirements:* For master's, variable foreign language requirement, comprehensive exam, thesis (for some programs); for doctorate, variable foreign language requirement, comprehensive exam, thesis/dissertation or alternative. *Entrance requirements:* For master's, minimum GPA of 3.0 in major, auditions (for MM in performance); for doctorate, minimum graduate GPA of 3.5, auditions (for DMA in performance), portfolio of compositions. Additional exam requirements/recommendations for international students: Required—TOEFL (minimum score 550 paper-based; 80 iBT). *Application deadline:* For fall admission, 1/15 priority date for domestic students, 1/15 for international students. Application fee: $45 ($50 for international students). *Financial support:* In 2014–15, 61 teaching assistantships with partial tuition reimbursements (averaging $8,991 per year) were awarded; career-related internships or fieldwork, Federal Work-Study, institutionally sponsored loans, scholarships/grants, tuition waivers (partial), and unspecified assistantships also available. Support available to part-time students. Financial award application deadline: 3/1; financial award applicants required to submit FAFSA. *Faculty research:* Electro-acoustic composition, affective music responses, American music theatre, Russian choral music, music therapy and Alzheimer's. *Unit head:* Peter Witte, Dean, 816-235-2731, Fax: 816-235-5265, E-mail: wittep@umkc.edu. *Application contact:* William Everett, Associate Dean for Graduate Studies, 816-235-2857, Fax: 816-235-5264, E-mail: everettw@umkc.edu.
Website: http://conservatory.umkc.edu/

The University of Montana, Graduate School, College of Visual and Performing Arts, School of Music, Missoula, MT 59812-0002. Offers performance (MM). *Accreditation:* NASM. *Entrance requirements:* For master's, GRE General Test, GRE Subject Test, portfolio.

University of Nebraska at Omaha, Graduate Studies, College of Communication, Fine Arts and Media, School of Music, Omaha, NE 68182. Offers MM. *Accreditation:* NASM. Part-time and evening/weekend programs available. *Faculty:* 16 full-time (6 women). *Students:* 6 full-time (3 women), 12 part-time (11 women); includes 1 minority (Asian, non-Hispanic/Latino), 1 international. Average age 29. 10 applicants, 60% accepted, 4 enrolled. In 2014, 15 master's awarded. *Degree requirements:* For master's, comprehensive exam (for some programs), thesis (for some programs). *Entrance requirements:* For master's, departmental diagnostic exam, minimum GPA of 3.0, resume, transcripts. Additional exam requirements/recommendations for international students: Required—TOEFL, IELTS, PTE. *Application deadline:* For fall admission, 6/15 priority date for domestic and international students; for spring admission, 11/15 priority date for domestic and international students; for summer admission, 4/15 for domestic and international students. Applications are processed on a rolling basis. Application fee: $45. Electronic applications accepted. *Financial support:* In 2014–15, 5 students received support, including 2 research assistantships with tuition reimbursements available, 3 teaching assistantships with tuition reimbursements available; career-related internships or fieldwork, Federal Work-Study, scholarships/grants, tuition waivers (partial), and unspecified assistantships also available. Support available to part-time students. Financial award application deadline: 3/1; financial award applicants required to submit FAFSA. *Unit head:* Dr. Ronald Tomm, Chairperson, 402-554-2341, E-mail: graduate@unomaha.edu. *Application contact:* Dr. Christine Beard, Graduate Program Chair, 402-554-2341, E-mail: graduate@unomaha.edu.

University of Nebraska–Lincoln, Graduate College, College of Arts and Sciences, Department of English, Lincoln, NE 68588-0333. Offers composition and rhetoric (MA, PhD); creative writing (MA, PhD); literature studies (MA, PhD). *Degree requirements:* For master's, thesis optional; for doctorate, one foreign language, comprehensive exam, thesis/dissertation. *Entrance requirements:* For master's, writing sample; for doctorate, GRE General Test, writing sample. Additional exam requirements/recommendations for international students: Required—TOEFL (minimum score 600 paper-based). Electronic applications accepted. *Faculty research:* Creative writing, composition and rhetoric, women's studies, North American literature, medieval/Renaissance studies.

University of Nebraska–Lincoln, Graduate College, College of Fine and Performing Arts, School of Music, Lincoln, NE 68588. Offers composition (MM, DMA); conducting (MM, DMA); music education (MM, PhD); music history (MM); music theory (MM); performance (MM, DMA); piano pedagogy (MM); woodwind specialties (MM). *Accreditation:* NASM. *Degree requirements:* For master's, thesis optional; for doctorate, comprehensive exam, thesis/dissertation. *Entrance requirements:* For master's and doctorate, audition. Additional exam requirements/recommendations for international students: Required—TOEFL. Electronic applications accepted. *Faculty research:* Mozart, Tchaikovsky, Josquin des Prez, practice of J.S. Bach's organ works, instructional strategies in music education.

University of Nevada, Las Vegas, Graduate College, College of Fine Arts, Department of Music, Las Vegas, NV 89154-5025. Offers music (MM); musical arts (DMA); teacher licensure (Certificate). *Accreditation:* NASM. Part-time programs available. *Faculty:* 23 full-time (7 women), 19 part-time/adjunct (3 women). *Students:* 67 full-time (26 women), 36 part-time (20 women); includes 26 minority (7 Black or African American, non-Hispanic/Latino; 1 American Indian or Alaska Native, non-Hispanic/Latino; 5 Asian, non-Hispanic/Latino; 7 Hispanic/Latino; 1 Native Hawaiian or other Pacific Islander, non-

Hispanic/Latino; 5 Two or more races, non-Hispanic/Latino), 10 international. Average age 33. 38 applicants, 79% accepted, 22 enrolled. In 2014, 24 master's, 3 doctorates awarded. *Degree requirements:* For master's, thesis optional, oral and/or written comprehensive exam; for doctorate, one foreign language, comprehensive exam, lecture-recital and document. *Entrance requirements:* Additional exam requirements/recommendations for international students: Required—TOEFL (minimum score 550 paper-based; 80 iBT), IELTS (minimum score 7). *Application deadline:* For fall admission, 5/1 for domestic and international students; for spring admission, 11/1 for domestic students, 10/1 for international students; for summer admission, 5/10 for domestic students. Application fee: $60 ($95 for international students). Electronic applications accepted. *Financial support:* In 2014–15, 37 students received support, including 1 research assistantship (averaging $13,000 per year), 36 teaching assistantships with partial tuition reimbursements available (averaging $12,083 per year); institutionally sponsored loans, scholarships/grants, health care benefits, and unspecified assistantships also available. Financial award application deadline: 3/1. *Faculty research:* Technology in preparing future teachers, professional development for music educators, public policy in arts education, Roman music history, Wagner. *Total annual research expenditures:* $2,890. *Unit head:* Sue Mueller, Chair/Professor, 702-895-5776, Fax: 702-895-4239, E-mail: susan.mueller@unlv.edu. *Application contact:* Graduate College Admissions Evaluator, 702-895-3320, Fax: 702-895-4180, E-mail: gradcollege@unlv.edu.
Website: http://music.unlv.edu/

University of Nevada, Reno, Graduate School, College of Liberal Arts, Department of Music, Reno, NV 89557. Offers MA, MM. *Accreditation:* NASM. *Degree requirements:* For master's, thesis optional. *Entrance requirements:* For master's, minimum GPA of 2.75. Additional exam requirements/recommendations for international students: Required—TOEFL (minimum score 500 paper-based; 61 iBT), IELTS (minimum score 6). Electronic applications accepted. *Faculty research:* Performance, conducting, music composition and arranging.

University of New Hampshire, Graduate School, College of Liberal Arts, Department of Music, Durham, NH 03824. Offers composition (MA); musicology (MA). *Accreditation:* NASM. *Faculty:* 17 full-time (4 women). *Students:* 8 full-time (4 women), 3 part-time (1 woman); includes 1 minority (Hispanic/Latino). Average age 25. 14 applicants, 86% accepted, 8 enrolled. In 2014, 3 master's awarded. *Degree requirements:* For master's, one foreign language. *Entrance requirements:* For master's, audition. Additional exam requirements/recommendations for international students: Required—TOEFL (minimum score 550 paper-based; 80 iBT). *Application deadline:* For fall admission, 4/1 priority date for domestic students, 4/1 for international students; for spring admission, 12/1 for domestic students. Applications are processed on a rolling basis. Application fee: $65. Electronic applications accepted. *Expenses:* Tuition, state resident: full-time $13,500; part-time $750 per credit hour. Tuition, nonresident: full-time $26,460; part-time $1110 per credit hour. *Required fees:* $1788; $447 per semester. *Financial support:* In 2014–15, 9 students received support, including 4 teaching assistantships; fellowships, research assistantships, career-related internships or fieldwork, Federal Work-Study, scholarships/grants, and tuition waivers (full and partial) also available. Support available to part-time students. Financial award application deadline: 2/15. *Unit head:* Dr. Nicholas Orovich, Chairperson, 603-862-3247. *Application contact:* Susan Adams, Administrative Assistant, 603-862-2404, E-mail: grad.music@unh.edu.
Website: http://cola.unh.edu/music

University of New Mexico, Graduate School, College of Fine Arts, Program in Music, Albuquerque, NM 87131-0001. Offers collaborative piano (M Mu); conducting (M Mu); music education (M Mu); music history and literature (M Mu); performance (M Mu); theory and composition (M Mu). *Accreditation:* NASM. Part-time programs available. *Faculty:* 34 full-time (9 women), 6 part-time/adjunct (4 women). *Students:* 52 full-time (25 women), 35 part-time (24 women); includes 17 minority (2 American Indian or Alaska Native, non-Hispanic/Latino; 14 Hispanic/Latino; 1 Two or more races, non-Hispanic/Latino), 11 international. Average age 28. 78 applicants, 50% accepted, 25 enrolled. In 2014, 30 master's awarded. *Degree requirements:* For master's, variable foreign language requirement, comprehensive exam, thesis (for some programs), recital (for some programs). *Entrance requirements:* For master's, placement exams in music history and theory. Additional exam requirements/recommendations for international students: Required—TOEFL (minimum score 550 paper-based). *Application deadline:* For fall admission, 7/1 for domestic students, 5/1 for international students; for spring admission, 11/1 for domestic students, 10/1 for international students. Applications are processed on a rolling basis. Application fee: $50. Electronic applications accepted. *Financial support:* In 2014–15, 74 students received support, including 2 research assistantships (averaging $4,062 per year), 10 teaching assistantships with full and partial tuition reimbursements available (averaging $4,761 per year); Federal Work-Study, scholarships/grants, and unspecified assistantships also available. Support available to part-time students. Financial award application deadline: 2/1; financial award applicants required to submit FAFSA. *Faculty research:* Opera, twentieth century and contemporary music, performance, conducting. *Total annual research expenditures:* $16,650. *Unit head:* Dr. Steven Block, Chair, 505-277-2127, Fax: 505-277-4202, E-mail: sblock@unm.edu. *Application contact:* Colleen M. Sheinberg, Graduate Coordinator, 505-277-8401, Fax: 505-277-4202, E-mail: colleens@unm.edu.
Website: http://music.unm.edu/

University of New Orleans, Graduate School, College of Liberal Arts, Department of Music, New Orleans, LA 70148. Offers MM. *Accreditation:* NASM. Evening/weekend programs available. *Degree requirements:* For master's, recital. *Entrance requirements:* For master's, GRE General Test, audition. Additional exam requirements/recommendations for international students: Required—TOEFL (minimum score 550 paper-based; 79 iBT), IELTS (minimum score 6.5). Electronic applications accepted. *Faculty research:* American jazz, Czech music, Hispanic music.

The University of North Carolina at Chapel Hill, Graduate School, College of Arts and Sciences, Department of Music, Chapel Hill, NC 27599. Offers MA, PhD. Terminal master's awarded for partial completion of doctoral program. *Degree requirements:* For master's, one foreign language, thesis, theory and keyboard exams; for doctorate, 2 foreign languages, comprehensive exam, thesis/dissertation, theory and keyboard exams. *Entrance requirements:* For master's and doctorate, GRE General Test, department diagnostic exam, minimum GPA of 3.0. Additional exam requirements/recommendations for international students: Required—TOEFL. Electronic applications accepted. *Expenses:* Contact institution. *Faculty research:* Music theory, ethnomusicology, music history.

The University of North Carolina at Charlotte, College of Arts and Architecture, Department of Music, Charlotte, NC 28223-0001. Offers violin (Graduate Certificate); vocal pedagogy (Graduate Certificate). *Faculty:* 9 full-time (3 women). In 2014, 1 Graduate Certificate awarded. *Entrance requirements:* Additional exam requirements/recommendations for international students: Required—TOEFL (minimum score 557 paper-based; 83 iBT). *Application deadline:* For fall admission, 5/1 priority date for domestic and international students; for spring admission, 10/1 priority date for domestic and international students. Application fee: $75. Electronic applications accepted. *Expenses:* Tuition, state resident: full-time $4008. Tuition, nonresident: full-time $16,295. *Required fees:* $2755. Tuition and fees vary according to course load and

program. *Unit head:* James A. Grymes, Interim Chair, 704-687-0251, E-mail: jagrymes@uncc.edu. *Application contact:* Kathy B. Giddings, Director of Graduate Admissions, 704-687-5503, Fax: 704-687-1668, E-mail: gradadm@uncc.edu.
Website: http://coaa.uncc.edu/academics/department-of-music

The University of North Carolina at Greensboro, Graduate School, School of Music, Theatre and Dance, Greensboro, NC 27412-5001. Offers composition (MM); dance (MA, MFA); education (MM); music education (PhD); performance (MM, DMA); theatre (M Ed, MFA), including acting (MFA), design (MFA), directing (MFA), theatre education (M Ed), theatre for youth (MFA); theory (MM). *Accreditation:* NASM. *Degree requirements:* For master's, variable foreign language requirement, thesis (for some programs), recital; for doctorate, comprehensive exam, thesis/dissertation, diagnostic exam, recital. *Entrance requirements:* For master's, GRE General Test, NTE, audition; for doctorate, GRE General Test, GRE Subject Test (music), audition. Additional exam requirements/recommendations for international students: Required—TOEFL. Electronic applications accepted.

The University of North Carolina at Pembroke, Graduate Studies, Department of Music, Pembroke, NC 28372-1510. Offers music (MAT); music education (MA). *Accreditation:* NASM. *Entrance requirements:* For master's, GRE or MAT, minimum GPA of 3.0 in major, 2.5 overall; audition. Additional exam requirements/recommendations for international students: Required—TOEFL.

University of North Carolina School of the Arts, School of Filmmaking, Winston-Salem, NC 27127-2738. Offers film music composition (MFA). *Entrance requirements:* For master's, audition, performance, portfolio, interview. Additional exam requirements/recommendations for international students: Required—TOEFL.

University of North Carolina School of the Arts, School of Music, Winston-Salem, NC 27127-2738. Offers music performance (MM), including chamber music performance. *Entrance requirements:* For master's, audition (music performance), interview, original score. Additional exam requirements/recommendations for international students: Required—TOEFL.

University of North Dakota, Graduate School, College of Arts and Sciences, Department of Music, Grand Forks, ND 58202. Offers music (M Mus); music education (M Mus, DMEd). *Accreditation:* NASM. Part-time programs available. *Degree requirements:* For master's, comprehensive exam, thesis or alternative. *Entrance requirements:* For master's, minimum GPA of 3.0. Additional exam requirements/recommendations for international students: Required—TOEFL (minimum score 550 paper-based; 79 iBT), IELTS (minimum score 6.5). Electronic applications accepted.

University of Northern Colorado, Graduate School, College of Performing and Visual Arts, School of Music, Greeley, CO 80639. Offers collaborative keyboard (MM); conducting (MM); instrumental performance (MM); jazz studies (MM); music conducting (DA); music education (MM, DA); music history and literature (MM, DA); music performance (DA); music theory and composition (MM, DA); vocal performance (MM). *Accreditation:* NASM; NCATE (one or more programs are accredited). Part-time programs available. *Degree requirements:* For master's, comprehensive exam, thesis or alternative; for doctorate, comprehensive exam, thesis/dissertation. *Entrance requirements:* For master's, audition; for doctorate, GRE General Test, audition, 3 letters of recommendation. Electronic applications accepted.

University of Northern Iowa, Graduate College, College of Humanities, Arts and Sciences, School of Music, MA Program in Music, Cedar Falls, IA 50614. Offers MA. *Accreditation:* NASM. *Students:* 8 full-time (3 women), 1 (woman) part-time, 2 international. 8 applicants, 63% accepted, 4 enrolled. In 2014, 1 master's awarded. *Degree requirements:* For master's, comprehensive exam, thesis or alternative. *Entrance requirements:* For master's, written diagnostic exam in theory, music history, expository writing skills, and in the area of claimed competency, portfolio, tape recordings of compositions, in-person auditions, minimum GPA of 3.0. Additional exam requirements/recommendations for international students: Required—TOEFL (minimum score 500 paper-based; 61 iBT). *Application deadline:* For fall admission, 8/1 priority date for domestic students. Applications are processed on a rolling basis. Application fee: $50 ($70 for international students). Electronic applications accepted. *Expenses:* Tuition, state resident: full-time $7912; part-time $880 per credit. Tuition, nonresident: full-time $17,906; part-time $880 per credit. *Required fees:* $1101; $325.50 per credit. $465.63 per semester. Tuition and fees vary according to course load and program. *Financial support:* Career-related internships or fieldwork, Federal Work-Study, and tuition waivers (full and partial) available. Support available to part-time students. Financial award application deadline: 2/1. *Unit head:* Dr. Julia Bullard, Coordinator, 319-273-3074, Fax: 319-273-7320, E-mail: julia.bullard@uni.edu. *Application contact:* Laurie S. Russell, Record Analyst, 319-273-2623, Fax: 319-273-2885, E-mail: laurie.russell@uni.edu.
Website: http://www.uni.edu/music/

University of Northern Iowa, Graduate College, College of Humanities, Arts and Sciences, School of Music, MM Program in Composition, Cedar Falls, IA 50614. Offers MM. *Students:* 1 part-time (0 women). In 2014, 1 master's awarded. *Degree requirements:* For master's, comprehensive exam. *Entrance requirements:* For master's, portfolio, recordings of compositions. Application fee: $50 ($70 for international students). *Expenses:* Tuition, state resident: full-time $7912; part-time $880 per credit. Tuition, nonresident: full-time $17,906; part-time $880 per credit. *Required fees:* $1101; $325.50 per credit. $465.63 per semester. Tuition and fees vary according to course load and program. *Unit head:* Dr. Jonathan Schwabe, Coordinator, E-mail: jonathan.schwabe@uni.edu. *Application contact:* Laurie S. Russell, Record Analyst, 319-273-2623, Fax: 319-273-2885, E-mail: laurie.russell@uni.edu.

University of Northern Iowa, Graduate College, College of Humanities, Arts and Sciences, School of Music, MM Program in Conducting, Cedar Falls, IA 50614. Offers MM. *Students:* 1 (woman) part-time. In 2014, 1 master's awarded. *Degree requirements:* For master's, comprehensive exam. *Entrance requirements:* For master's, audition, interview. Application fee: $50 ($70 for international students). *Expenses:* Tuition, state resident: full-time $7912; part-time $880 per credit. Tuition, nonresident: full-time $17,906; part-time $880 per credit. *Required fees:* $1101; $325.50 per credit. $465.63 per semester. Tuition and fees vary according to course load and program. *Unit head:* Dr. Ronald Johnson, Coordinator, 319-273-6058, E-mail: ronald.johnson@uni.edu. *Application contact:* Laurie S. Russell, Record Analyst, 319-273-2623, Fax: 319-273-2885, E-mail: laurie.russell@uni.edu.

University of Northern Iowa, Graduate College, College of Humanities, Arts and Sciences, School of Music, MM Program in Music History, Cedar Falls, IA 50614. Offers MM. *Students:* 2 part-time (1 woman). *Entrance requirements:* For master's, scholarly paper. Application fee: $50 ($70 for international students). *Expenses:* Tuition, state resident: full-time $7912; part-time $880 per credit. Tuition, nonresident: full-time $17,906; part-time $880 per credit. *Required fees:* $1101; $325.50 per credit. $465.63 per semester. Tuition and fees vary according to course load and program. *Unit head:* Dr. John F. Vallentine, Director, 319-273-2024, Fax: 319-273-7320, E-mail: john.vallentine@uni.edu. *Application contact:* Laurie S. Russell, Record Analyst, 319-273-2623, Fax: 319-273-2885, E-mail: laurie.russell@uni.edu.

Music

University of Northern Iowa, Graduate College, College of Humanities, Arts and Sciences, School of Music, MM Program in Performance, Cedar Falls, IA 50614. Offers percussion (MM); piano/organ (MM); string (MM); vocal (MM); woodwind (MM). *Students:* 15 full-time (12 women), 3 part-time (all women); includes 3 minority (2 Black or African American, non-Hispanic/Latino; 1 Two or more races, non-Hispanic/Latino), 1 international. 16 applicants, 38% accepted, 5 enrolled. In 2014, 7 master's awarded. *Degree requirements:* For master's, comprehensive exam. *Entrance requirements:* For master's, audition. Application fee: $50 ($70 for international students). *Expenses:* Tuition, state resident: full-time $7912; part-time $880 per credit. Tuition, nonresident: full-time $17,906; part-time $880 per credit. *Required fees:* $1101; $325.50 per credit. $465.63 per semester. Tuition and fees vary according to course load and program. *Unit head:* Dr. John F. Vallentine, Director, 319-273-2024, Fax: 319-273-7320, E-mail: john.vallentine@uni.edu. *Application contact:* Laurie S. Russell, Record Analyst, 319-273-2623, Fax: 319-273-2885, E-mail: laurie.russell@uni.edu.

University of Northern Iowa, Graduate College, College of Humanities, Arts and Sciences, School of Music, MM Program in Piano Performance and Pedagogy, Cedar Falls, IA 50614. Offers MM. *Students:* 2 full-time (both women), 2 part-time (0 women). 3 applicants, 67% accepted, 2 enrolled. In 2014, 3 master's awarded. Application fee: $50 ($70 for international students). *Expenses:* Tuition, state resident: full-time $7912; part-time $880 per credit. Tuition, nonresident: full-time $17,906; part-time $880 per credit. *Required fees:* $1101; $325.50 per credit. $465.63 per semester. Tuition and fees vary according to course load and program. *Unit head:* Dr. John F. Vallentine, Director, 319-273-2024, Fax: 319-273-7320, E-mail: john.vallentine@uni.edu. *Application contact:* Laurie S. Russell, Record Analyst, 319-273-2623, Fax: 319-273-2885, E-mail: laurie.russell@uni.edu.

University of North Georgia, Department of Performing Arts, Dahlonega, GA 30597. Offers music (MM). Part-time programs available. *Entrance requirements:* For master's, 3 recommendations, audition. Additional exam requirements/recommendations for international students: Required—TOEFL (minimum score 550 paper-based; 79 iBT), IELTS (minimum score 6.5). Electronic applications accepted.

University of North Texas, Robert B. Toulouse School of Graduate Studies, Denton, TX 76203-5459. Offers accounting (MS); applied anthropology (MA, MS); applied behavior analysis (Certificate); applied geography (MA); applied technology and performance improvement (M Ed, MS); art education (MA); art history (MA); art museum education (Certificate); arts leadership (Certificate); audiology (Au D); behavior analysis (MS); behavioral science (PhD); biochemistry and molecular biology (MS); biology (MA, MS); biomedical engineering (MS); business analysis (MS); chemistry (MS); clinical health psychology (PhD); communication studies (MA, MS); computer engineering (MS); computer science (MS); counseling (M Ed, MS), including clinical mental health counseling (MS), college and university counseling, elementary school counseling, secondary school counseling; creative writing (MA); criminal justice (MS); curriculum and instruction (M Ed); decision sciences (MBA); design (MA, MFA), including fashion design (MFA), innovation studies, interior design (MFA); early childhood studies (MS); economics (MS); educational leadership (M Ed, Ed D); educational psychology (MS, PhD), including family studies (MS), gifted and talented (MS), human development (MS), learning and cognition (MS), research, measurement and evaluation (MS); electrical engineering (MS); emergency management (MPA); engineering technology (MS); English (MA); English as a second language (MA); environmental science (MS); finance (MBA, MS); financial management (MPA); French (MA); health services management (MBA); higher education (M Ed, Ed D); history (MA, MS); hospitality management (MS); human resources management (MPA); information science (MS); information systems (PhD); information technologies (MBA); interdisciplinary studies (MA, MS); international studies (MA); international sustainable tourism (MS); jazz studies (MM); journalism (MA, MJ, Graduate Certificate), including interactive and virtual digital communication (Graduate Certificate), narrative journalism (Graduate Certificate), public relations (Graduate Certificate); kinesiology (MS); linguistics (MA); local government management (MPA); logistics (PhD); logistics and supply chain management (MBA); long-term care, senior housing, and aging services (MA); management (PhD); marketing (MBA); mathematics (MA, MS); mechanical and energy engineering (MS, PhD); music (MA), including ethnomusicology, music theory, musicology, performance; music composition (PhD); music education (MM Ed, PhD); nonprofit management (MPA); operations and supply chain management (MBA); performance (MM, DMA); philosophy (MA); political science (MA); professional and technical communication (MA); radio, television and film (MA, MFA); rehabilitation counseling (Certificate); sociology (MA); Spanish (MA); special education (M Ed); speech-language pathology (MA); strategic management (MBA); studio art (MFA); teaching (M Ed); MBA/MS. Part-time and evening/weekend programs available. Postbaccalaureate distance learning degree programs offered. *Faculty:* 651 full-time (215 women), 233 part-time/adjunct (139 women). *Students:* 3,040 full-time (1,598 women), 3,401 part-time (2,097 women); includes 1,740 minority (533 Black or African American, non-Hispanic/Latino; 15 American Indian or Alaska Native, non-Hispanic/Latino; 286 Asian, non-Hispanic/Latino; 746 Hispanic/Latino; 3 Native Hawaiian or other Pacific Islander, non-Hispanic/Latino; 157 Two or more races, non-Hispanic/Latino), 1,145 international. Terminal master's awarded for partial completion of doctoral program. *Degree requirements:* For master's, variable foreign language requirement, comprehensive exam (for some programs), thesis (for some programs); for doctorate, variable foreign language requirement, comprehensive exam (for some programs), thesis/dissertation; for other advanced degree, variable foreign language requirement, comprehensive exam (for some programs). *Entrance requirements:* For master's and doctorate, GRE, GMAT. Additional exam requirements/recommendations for international students: Required—TOEFL (minimum score 550 paper-based; 79 iBT). *Application deadline:* For fall admission, 7/15 for domestic students, 3/15 for international students; for spring admission, 11/15 for domestic students, 9/15 for international students; for summer admission, 5/1 for domestic students. Applications are processed on a rolling basis. Application fee: $60. Electronic applications accepted. *Expenses:* Tuition, state resident: full-time $5450; part-time $3633 per year. Tuition, nonresident: full-time $11,966; part-time $7977 per year. *Required fees:* $1301; $398 per credit hour. $685 per semester. Tuition and fees vary according to program and reciprocity agreements. *Financial support:* Fellowships with partial tuition reimbursements, research assistantships with partial tuition reimbursements, teaching assistantships, career-related internships or fieldwork, Federal Work-Study, institutionally sponsored loans, scholarships/grants, health care benefits, and library assistantships available. Support available to part-time students. Financial award applicants required to submit FAFSA. *Unit head:* Mark Wardell, Dean, 940-565-2383, E-mail: mark.wardell@unt.edu. *Application contact:* Toulouse School of Graduate Studies, 940-565-2383, Fax: 940-565-2141, E-mail: gradsch@unt.edu.
Website: http://tsgs.unt.edu/

University of Oklahoma, Weitzenhoffer Family College of Fine Arts, School of Music, Norman, OK 73019. Offers conducting (DMA); instrumental conducting (M Mus Ed); music composition (DMA); musicology (M Mus); vocal/general (M Mus Ed); voice (DMA), including performance. *Accreditation:* NASM. *Faculty:* 66 full-time (19 women), 5 part-time/adjunct (1 woman). *Students:* 104 full-time (52 women), 73 part-time (37 women); includes 31 minority (4 Black or African American, non-Hispanic/Latino; 5 American Indian or Alaska Native, non-Hispanic/Latino; 9 Asian, non-Hispanic/Latino; 7 Hispanic/Latino; 6 Two or more races, non-Hispanic/Latino), 26 international. Average age 30. 154 applicants, 63% accepted, 55 enrolled. In 2014, 28 master's, 15 doctorates awarded. *Degree requirements:* For master's, variable foreign language requirement, comprehensive exam (for some programs), thesis (for some programs), major recital (for performance, conducting and composition); for doctorate, variable foreign language requirement, comprehensive exam, thesis/dissertation, 3 public performances (for performance and conducting); 2 public performances (for composition). *Entrance requirements:* For master's, satisfactory auditions/teaching demonstrations/composition portfolios, recommendations, minimum GPA of 3.0; scholarly writing sample (for music theory and musicology programs); for doctorate, satisfactory auditions/teaching demonstrations/composition portfolios, scholarly writing sample, recommendations, minimum GPA of 3.0; 2 years of full-time, professional teaching experience (for PhD in music education). Additional exam requirements/recommendations for international students: Required—TOEFL (minimum score 79 iBT). *Application deadline:* For fall admission, 12/1 for domestic and international students; for spring admission, 9/1 for domestic and international students. Application fee: $50 ($100 for international students). Electronic applications accepted. *Expenses:* Tuition, state resident: full-time $4394; part-time $183.10 per credit hour. Tuition, nonresident: full-time $16,970; part-time $707.10 per credit hour. *Required fees:* $2892; $109.95 per credit hour. $126.50 per semester. *Financial support:* In 2014–15, 122 students received support, including 4 fellowships with full tuition reimbursements available (averaging $5,000 per year), 29 research assistantships with partial tuition reimbursements available (averaging $10,369 per year), 65 teaching assistantships with partial tuition reimbursements available (averaging $10,669 per year); Federal Work-Study and unspecified assistantships also available. Financial award application deadline: 6/1; financial award applicants required to submit FAFSA. *Faculty research:* Piano pedagogy, performance practice, music education, early music, non-Western music. *Unit head:* Dr. Lawrence Mallett, Director, 405-325-2081, Fax: 405-325-7574, E-mail: lmallett@ou.edu. *Application contact:* Jan Russell, Graduate Admissions and Recruiting Advisor, 405-325-5393, Fax: 405-325-7574, E-mail: jrussell@ou.edu.
Website: http://music.ou.edu

University of Oregon, Graduate School, School of Music, Program in Music, Eugene, OR 97403. Offers composition (M Mus, DMA, PhD); conducting (M Mus); jazz studies (M Mus); music (MA), including music history, music theory; music history (PhD); music theory (PhD); performance (M Mus, DMA); piano pedagogy (M Mus). *Entrance requirements:* For master's, minimum GPA of 3.0, audition (performance applicants), videotape or interview (conducting applicants); for doctorate, GRE General Test, minimum GPA of 3.0, audition (performance applicants), videotape or interview (conducting applicants). Additional exam requirements/recommendations for international students: Required—TOEFL.

University of Ottawa, Faculty of Graduate and Postdoctoral Studies, Faculty of Arts, Department of Music, Ottawa, ON K1N 6N5, Canada. Offers music (M Mus, MA); orchestral studies (Certificate); piano pedagogy research (Certificate). *Degree requirements:* For master's, thesis optional. *Entrance requirements:* For master's, honors degree or equivalent, minimum B+ average. Electronic applications accepted. *Faculty research:* Performance, theory, musicology.

University of Pennsylvania, School of Arts and Sciences, Graduate Group in Music, Philadelphia, PA 19104. Offers AM, PhD. *Faculty:* 11 full-time (3 women), 3 part-time/adjunct (0 women). *Students:* 36 full-time (18 women); includes 6 minority (2 Black or African American, non-Hispanic/Latino; 1 Asian, non-Hispanic/Latino; 1 Hispanic/Latino; 2 Two or more races, non-Hispanic/Latino), 13 international. 98 applicants, 12% accepted, 4 enrolled. In 2014, 1 master's, 7 doctorates awarded. Terminal master's awarded for partial completion of doctoral program. *Degree requirements:* For master's, variable foreign language requirement; for doctorate, variable foreign language requirement, thesis/dissertation. *Entrance requirements:* For master's and doctorate, GRE General Test, GRE Subject Test, samples of previous work. Additional exam requirements/recommendations for international students: Required—TOEFL. *Application deadline:* For fall admission, 12/1 priority date for domestic students. Application fee: $70. Electronic applications accepted. *Financial support:* Institutionally sponsored loans, scholarships/grants, traineeships, health care benefits, and unspecified assistantships available. Financial award application deadline: 12/15. *Unit head:* Dr. Ralph M. Rosen, Associate Dean for Graduate Studies, 215-898-7156, Fax: 215-573-8068, E-mail: grad-dean@sas.upenn.edu. *Application contact:* Arts and Sciences Graduate Admissions, 215-573-5816, Fax: 215-573-8068, E-mail: gdasadmis@sas.upenn.edu.
Website: http://www.sas.upenn.edu/graduate-division

University of Pittsburgh, Dietrich School of Arts and Sciences, Department of Music, Pittsburgh, PA 15260. Offers composition and theory (MA, PhD); ethnomusicology (PhD); jazz studies (MA, PhD); musicology (MA, PhD). Part-time programs available. *Faculty:* 11 full-time (6 women), 1 part-time/adjunct (0 women). *Students:* 35 full-time (11 women); includes 11 minority (2 Black or African American, non-Hispanic/Latino; 8 Asian, non-Hispanic/Latino; 1 Hispanic/Latino). Average age 33. 56 applicants, 14% accepted, 4 enrolled. In 2014, 5 doctorates awarded. Terminal master's awarded for partial completion of doctoral program. *Degree requirements:* For master's, comprehensive exam, thesis, 1 foreign language (for composition/theory, ethnomusicology, musicology); for doctorate, one foreign language, comprehensive exam, thesis/dissertation, 2 foreign languages (for musicology). *Entrance requirements:* For master's and doctorate, GRE General Test, samples of work, 3 letters of reference, minimum GPA of 3.0, bachelor's degree. Additional exam requirements/recommendations for international students: Required—TOEFL (minimum score 600 paper-based; 80 iBT). *Application deadline:* For fall admission, 1/5 for domestic and international students. Application fee: $50. Electronic applications accepted. *Expenses:* Tuition, state resident: full-time $20,742; part-time $838 per credit. Tuition, nonresident: full-time $33,960; part-time $1389 per credit. *Required fees:* $800; $205 per term. Tuition and fees vary according to program. *Financial support:* In 2014–15, 30 students received support, including 4 fellowships with full tuition reimbursements available (averaging $21,206 per year), 18 teaching assistantships with full and partial tuition reimbursements available (averaging $17,465 per year); scholarships/grants, health care benefits, tuition waivers (full and partial), and unspecified assistantships also available. Financial award application deadline: 1/5; financial award applicants required to submit FAFSA. *Faculty research:* Composition and theory, ethnomusicology, musicology, jazz studies. *Unit head:* Dr. Andrew Weintraub, Chair, 412-624-4126, Fax: 412-624-4186, E-mail: anwein@pitt.edu. *Application contact:* Dr. Amy Williams, Director of Graduate Admissions, 412-624-4126, Fax: 412-624-4186, E-mail: amywill@pitt.edu.
Website: http://www.music.pitt.edu/

University of Redlands, College of Arts and Sciences, School of Music, Redlands, CA 92373-0999. Offers MM. *Accreditation:* NASM. Part-time programs available. *Degree requirements:* For master's, comprehensive exam, thesis, 3 recitals, major conducted ensemble. *Entrance requirements:* For master's, GRE, bachelor's degree in music, minimum GPA of 2.75, audition, original scores. Additional exam requirements/recommendations for international students: Required—TOEFL (minimum score 550 paper-based). *Expenses:* Contact institution. *Faculty research:* Performance, composition.

University of Regina, Faculty of Graduate Studies and Research, Faculty of Fine Arts, Department of Music, Regina, SK S4S 0A2, Canada. Offers composition (MMus); conducting (MMus); music theory (MA); musicology (MA); performance (MMus), including piano, organ, voice, and orchestral instruments. *Faculty:* 9 full-time (6 women), 1 part-time/adjunct (0 women). *Students:* 4 applicants. *Degree requirements:* For master's, thesis (for some programs), recital, oral exam, jury examinations. *Entrance requirements:* For master's, B Mus or equivalent; recent compositions (composers only); audition; singing ability in French, Italian, German (vocalists only). Additional exam requirements/recommendations for international students: Required—TOEFL (minimum score 580 paper-based; 80 iBT), IELTS (minimum score 6.5), PTE (minimum score 59). *Application deadline:* For fall admission, 1/15 for domestic and international students. Application fee: $100. Electronic applications accepted. *Expenses: Tuition, area resident:* Full-time $4900 Canadian dollars; part-time $837.65 Canadian dollars per semester. *International tuition:* $7900 Canadian dollars full-time. *Required fees:* $396 Canadian dollars; $86.90 Canadian dollars per semester. *Financial support:* Fellowships, research assistantships, teaching assistantships, and scholarships/grants available. Financial award application deadline: 6/15. *Faculty research:* Renaissance, Baroque, and medieval music; music of the Classical and Romantic eras; analysis of music written since 1900; music theory; history of music theory. *Unit head:* Dr. Karen Finnsson, Head/Coordinator, 306-585-5507, Fax: 306-585-5549, E-mail: karen.finnsson@uregina.ca.

University of Rhode Island, Graduate School, College of Arts and Sciences, Department of Music, Kingston, RI 02881. Offers music education (MM); music performance (MM). *Accreditation:* NASM. Part-time programs available. *Faculty:* 11 full-time (5 women). *Students:* 6 full-time (3 women), 6 part-time (3 women); includes 2 minority (1 Black or African American, non-Hispanic/Latino; 1 American Indian or Alaska Native, non-Hispanic/Latino). *Entrance requirements:* For master's, 2 letters of recommendation, audition. Additional exam requirements/recommendations for international students: Required—TOEFL (minimum score 550 paper-based). *Application deadline:* For fall admission, 7/15 for domestic students, 2/1 for international students; for spring admission, 11/15 for domestic students, 7/15 for international students. Application fee: $65. Electronic applications accepted. *Expenses:* Tuition, state resident: full-time $11,532; part-time $641 per credit. Tuition, nonresident: full-time $23,606; part-time $1311 per credit. *Required fees:* $1442; $39 per credit. $35 per semester. One-time fee: $155. *Financial support:* In 2014–15, 3 teaching assistantships with full and partial tuition reimbursements (averaging $11,883 per year) were awarded. Financial award application deadline: 3/15; financial award applicants required to submit FAFSA. *Unit head:* Dr. Joe Parillo, Chair, 401-874-2431, Fax: 401-874-2772, E-mail: jparillo@uri.edu. *Application contact:* Dr. Manabu Takasawa, Co-Director of Graduate Studies, 401-874-2790, Fax: 401-874-2772, E-mail: takasawa@uri.edu.
Website: http://www.uri.edu/artsci/mus/

University of Rochester, Eastman School of Music, Program in Ethnomusicology, Rochester, NY 14627. Offers MA. *Expenses: Tuition:* Full-time $46,150; part-time $1442 per credit hour. *Required fees:* $504.

University of Rochester, Eastman School of Music, Program in Music Theory Pedagogy, Rochester, NY 14627. Offers MA. *Expenses: Tuition:* Full-time $46,150; part-time $1442 per credit hour. *Required fees:* $504.

University of Rochester, Eastman School of Music, Programs in Music Composition, Rochester, NY 14627. Offers MA, MM, DMA, PhD. *Expenses: Tuition:* Full-time $46,150; part-time $1442 per credit hour. *Required fees:* $504.

University of Rochester, Eastman School of Music, Programs in Musicology, Rochester, NY 14627. Offers PhD. *Expenses: Tuition:* Full-time $46,150; part-time $1442 per credit hour. *Required fees:* $504.

University of Rochester, Eastman School of Music, Programs in Music Theory, Rochester, NY 14627. Offers PhD. *Expenses: Tuition:* Full-time $46,150; part-time $1442 per credit hour. *Required fees:* $504.

University of St. Thomas, Graduate Studies, College of Arts and Sciences, Graduate Programs in Music Education, St. Paul, MN 55105-1096. Offers choral (MA); instrumental (MA); Kodaly (MA); Orff (MA); piano pedagogy (MA). *Accreditation:* NASM; NCATE. Part-time programs available. *Degree requirements:* For master's, comprehensive exam, thesis, music history theory and diagnostic exam, piano recital (for piano pedagogy students). *Entrance requirements:* For master's, performance assessment hearing, interview. Additional exam requirements/recommendations for international students: Required—TOEFL (minimum score 550 paper-based; 80 iBT). Electronic applications accepted. Application fee is waived when completed online. *Faculty research:* Kodaly, choral, piano pedagogy, Orff, instrumental.

University of Saskatchewan, College of Graduate Studies and Research, College of Arts and Science, Department of Music, Saskatoon, SK S7N 5A2, Canada. Offers M Mus, MA. *Degree requirements:* For master's, thesis. *Entrance requirements:* Additional exam requirements/recommendations for international students: Required—TOEFL (minimum score 80 iBT); Recommended—IELTS (minimum score 6.5). Electronic applications accepted.

University of South Africa, College of Human Sciences, Pretoria, South Africa. Offers adult education (M Ed); African languages (MA, PhD); African politics (MA, PhD); Afrikaans (MA, PhD); ancient history (MA, PhD); ancient Near Eastern studies (MA, PhD); anthropology (MA, PhD); applied linguistics (MA); Arabic (MA, PhD); archaeology (MA); art history (MA); Biblical archaeology (MA); Biblical studies (M Th, D Th, PhD); Christian spirituality (M Th, D Th); church history (M Th, D Th); classical studies (MA, PhD); clinical psychology (MA); communication (MA, PhD); comparative education (M Ed, Ed D); consulting psychology (D Admin, D Com, PhD); curriculum studies (M Ed, Ed D); development studies (M Admin, MA, D Admin, PhD); didactics (M Ed, Ed D); education (M Tech); education management (M Ed, Ed D); educational psychology (M Ed); English (MA); environmental education (M Ed); French (MA, PhD); German (MA, PhD); Greek (MA); guidance and counseling (M Ed); health studies (MA, PhD), including health sciences education (MA), health services management (MA), medical and surgical nursing science (critical care general) (MA), midwifery and neonatal nursing science (MA), trauma and emergency care (MA); history (MA, PhD); history of education (Ed D); inclusive education (M Ed, Ed D); information and communications technology policy and regulation (MA); information science (MA, MIS, PhD); international politics (MA, PhD); Islamic studies (MA, PhD); Italian (MA, PhD); Judaica (MA, PhD); linguistics (MA, PhD); mathematical education (M Ed); mathematics education (MA); missiology (M Th, D Th); modern Hebrew (MA, PhD); musicology (MA, MMus, D Mus, PhD); natural science education (M Ed); New Testament (M Th, D Th); Old Testament (D Th); pastoral therapy (M Th, D Th); philosophy (MA); philosophy of education (M Ed, Ed D); politics (MA, PhD); Portuguese (MA, PhD); practical theology (M Th, D Th); psychology (MA, MS, PhD); psychology of education (M Ed, Ed D); public health (MA); religious studies (MA, D Th, PhD); Romance languages (MA); Russian (MA, PhD); Semitic languages (MA, PhD); social behavior studies in HIV/AIDS (MA); social science (mental health) (MA); social science in development studies (MA); social science in psychology (MA); social science in social work (MA); social science in sociology (MA); social work (MSW, DSW, PhD); socio-education (M Ed, Ed D); sociolinguistics (MA); sociology (MA, PhD); Spanish (MA, PhD); systematic theology (M Th, D Th); TESOL (teaching English to speakers of other languages) (MA); theological ethics (M Th, D Th); theory of literature (MA, PhD); urban ministries (D Th); urban ministry (M Th).

University of South Alabama, College of Arts and Sciences, Department of Music, Mobile, AL 36688. Offers collaborative keyboard (MM); music education (MM); performance (MM). *Faculty:* 4 full-time (1 woman). *Students:* 4 full-time (1 woman), 3 part-time (1 woman). Average age 29. 6 applicants, 67% accepted, 4 enrolled. *Degree requirements:* For master's, comprehensive exam, final project. *Entrance requirements:* For master's, GRE/ GMAT, undergraduate degree in music with minimum GPA of 3.0, official transcript, resume, 3 recommendation letters; teaching certificate (for music education). Additional exam requirements/recommendations for international students: Required—TOEFL (minimum score 525 paper-based; 71 iBT). *Application deadline:* For fall admission, 7/15 priority date for domestic students, 6/15 priority date for international students; for spring admission, 12/1 priority date for domestic students, 11/1 priority date for international students; for summer admission, 5/1 priority date for domestic students, 4/1 priority date for international students. Applications are processed on a rolling basis. Application fee: $35. Electronic applications accepted. *Expenses:* Tuition, state resident: full-time $9288; part-time $387 per credit hour. Tuition, nonresident: full-time $18,576; part-time $774 per credit hour. Part-time tuition and fees vary according to course load and program. *Financial support:* Fellowships, research assistantships, teaching assistantships, career-related internships or fieldwork, Federal Work-Study, institutionally sponsored loans, scholarships/grants, and unspecified assistantships available. Support available to part-time students. Financial award application deadline: 5/31; financial award applicants required to submit FAFSA. *Unit head:* Dr. Greg Gruner, Chair, Music, 251-460-6804, Fax: 251-460-7328, E-mail: ggruner@southalabama.edu. *Application contact:* Dr. Jeannette Fresne, Graduate Coordinator, Music, 251-460-6697, Fax: 251-460-7328, E-mail: jfresne@southalabama.edu.
Website: http://www.southalabama.edu/colleges/music/

University of South Carolina, The Graduate School, School of Music, Columbia, SC 29208. Offers composition (MM, DMA); conducting (MM, DMA); jazz studies (MM); music education (MM Ed, PhD); music history (MM); music performance (Certificate); music theory (MM); opera theater (MM); performance (MM, DMA); piano pedagogy (MM, DMA). *Accreditation:* NASM (one or more programs are accredited). Part-time programs available. *Degree requirements:* For master's, 5 foreign languages, comprehensive exam, thesis (for some programs); for doctorate, one foreign language, comprehensive exam, thesis/dissertation; for Certificate, recitals. *Entrance requirements:* For master's and doctorate, GRE General Test or MAT, music diagnostic exam. Additional exam requirements/recommendations for international students: Required—TOEFL (minimum score 570 paper-based). Electronic applications accepted. *Expenses:* Contact institution. *Faculty research:* Music skills in pre-school children, evaluation of school performing ensembles.

The University of South Dakota, Graduate School, College of Fine Arts, Department of Music, Vermillion, SD 57069-2390. Offers history of musical instruments (MM); music education (MM); music history (MM); music performance (MM). *Accreditation:* NASM. *Degree requirements:* For master's, thesis or alternative. *Entrance requirements:* For master's, minimum GPA of 2.7, audition or performance tape. Additional exam requirements/recommendations for international students: Required—TOEFL (minimum score 550 paper-based; 79 iBT). Electronic applications accepted.

University of Southern California, Graduate School, Thornton School of Music, Los Angeles, CA 90089. Offers brass performance (MM, DMA, Graduate Certificate); choral and sacred music (MM, DMA); classical guitar (MM, DMA, Graduate Certificate); composition (MM, DMA); early music (MA, DMA); harp performance (MM, DMA, Graduate Certificate); historical musicology (PhD); jazz studies (MM, DMA, Graduate Certificate); keyboard collaborative arts (MM, DMA, Graduate Certificate); music education (MM, DMA); organ performance (MM, DMA, Graduate Certificate); percussion performance (MM, DMA, Graduate Certificate); piano performance (MM, DMA, Graduate Certificate); scoring for motion pictures and television (Graduate Certificate); strings performance (MM, DMA, Graduate Certificate); studio jazz guitar (MM, DMA, Graduate Certificate); teaching music (MA); vocal arts (classical voice/opera) (MM, DMA, Graduate Certificate); woodwind performance (MM, DMA, Graduate Certificate). *Accreditation:* NASM. Part-time and evening/weekend programs available. Terminal master's awarded for partial completion of doctoral program. *Degree requirements:* For master's, variable foreign language requirement, comprehensive exam (for some programs), thesis (for some programs); for doctorate, variable foreign language requirement, comprehensive exam, thesis/dissertation (for some programs). *Entrance requirements:* For master's, GRE (for MA in early music and MM in music education); for doctorate, GRE (for DMA). Additional exam requirements/recommendations for international students: Required—TOEFL (minimum score 560 paper-based; 83 iBT). Electronic applications accepted. *Expenses:* Contact institution. *Faculty research:* Early Modern musical improvisation and composition, maternal sound stimulation of the premature infant, physiological characteristics of jazz guitarists, the musical experience of the very young child, electronic music.

University of Southern Maine, College of Arts and Sciences, School of Music, Portland, ME 04104-9300. Offers composition (MM); conducting (MM); jazz studies (MM); music education (MM); performance (MM). *Accreditation:* NASM. *Faculty:* 7 full-time (1 woman), 5 part-time/adjunct (3 women). *Students:* 5 full-time (3 women), 7 part-time (3 women). Average age 32. 8 applicants, 100% accepted, 7 enrolled. In 2014, 8 master's awarded. Application fee: $65. *Expenses: Tuition, area resident:* Full-time $6840; part-time $380 per credit hour. Tuition, state resident: full-time $10,260; part-time $570 per credit hour. Tuition, nonresident: full-time $18,468; part-time $1026 per credit hour. *Required fees:* $830; $83 per credit hour. Tuition and fees vary according to course load and program. *Unit head:* Alan Kaschub, Director, 207-780-5387, E-mail: kaschulb@maine.edu. *Application contact:* Mary Sloan, Assistant Dean of Graduate Studies and Director of Graduate Admissions, 207-780-4812, Fax: 207-780-4969, E-mail: gradstudies@usm.maine.edu.
Website: http://usm.maine.edu/music

University of Southern Mississippi, Graduate School, College of Arts and Letters, Department of Theatre, Hattiesburg, MS 39406-0001. Offers design and technology (MFA); directing (MFA); performance (MFA). *Accreditation:* NAST. Part-time programs available. *Degree requirements:* For master's, comprehensive exam, thesis or alternative, creative project. *Entrance requirements:* For master's, GRE General Test, minimum GPA of 3.0. Additional exam requirements/recommendations for international students: Required—TOEFL, IELTS. *Faculty research:* Technical design, acting.

University of Southern Mississippi, Graduate School, College of Arts and Letters, School of Music, Hattiesburg, MS 39406-0001. Offers conducting (MM); history and literature (MM); music education (MME, PhD); performance (MM); performance and pedagogy (DMA); theory and composition (MM); woodwind performance (MM). *Accreditation:* NASM. Terminal master's awarded for partial completion of doctoral program. *Degree requirements:* For master's, comprehensive exam, thesis (for some programs); for doctorate, comprehensive exam, thesis/dissertation. *Entrance requirements:* For master's, GRE General Test, minimum GPA of 2.75 in last 60 hours; for doctorate, GRE General Test, minimum GPA of 3.5. Additional exam requirements/recommendations for international students: Required—TOEFL, IELTS. *Faculty research:* Music theory, composition, music performance.

Music

University of South Florida, College of Arts and Sciences, Department of English, Tampa, FL 33620-9951. Offers creative writing (MFA), including fiction, poetry; literature (MA, PhD); rhetoric and composition (MA, PhD). Part-time and evening/weekend programs available. *Faculty:* 24 full-time (12 women). *Students:* 73 full-time (52 women), 27 part-time (19 women); includes 16 minority (3 Black or African American, non-Hispanic/Latino; 4 Asian, non-Hispanic/Latino; 7 Hispanic/Latino; 2 Two or more races, non-Hispanic/Latino). Average age 32. 122 applicants, 44% accepted, 25 enrolled. In 2014, 26 master's, 5 doctorates awarded. *Degree requirements:* For master's, thesis (for MFA); thesis or comprehensive examination (for MA); for doctorate, one foreign language, comprehensive exam, thesis/dissertation. *Entrance requirements:* For master's, GRE General Test, minimum undergraduate GPA of 3.5 (for MA), 3.2 (for MFA); three letters of recommendation; personal statement; writing sample from 10 to 20 pages, depending on genre; for doctorate, GRE General Test, minimum graduate GPA of 3.7; three letters of recommendation; 2-3 page personal statement; 2500-word writing sample from English coursework. Additional exam requirements/recommendations for international students: Required—TOEFL (minimum score 550 paper-based; 79 iBT) or IELTS (minimum score 6.5) for MA and PhD; TOEFL (minimum score 600 paper-based) for MFA. *Application deadline:* For fall admission, 2/1 for domestic students, 1/2 for international students. Applications are processed on a rolling basis. Application fee: $30. Electronic applications accepted. *Financial support:* In 2014–15, 81 students received support, including 2 research assistantships (averaging $17,221 per year), 79 teaching assistantships with tuition reimbursements available (averaging $11,576 per year); unspecified assistantships also available. Financial award application deadline: 6/30; financial award applicants required to submit FAFSA. *Faculty research:* British and American literature, rhetoric and composition, world and comparative literatures, creative writing, gender and sexuality studies, women's literature, film and genre studies, literary theory, popular and visual culture, textual and translation studies. *Total annual research expenditures:* $63,565. *Unit head:* Dr. Hunt Hawkins, Professor and Chairperson, 813-974-9492, Fax: 813-974-2270, E-mail: hhawkins@usf.edu. *Application contact:* Dr. Marty Gould, Associate Professor and Graduate Director, 813-974-9474, Fax: 813-974-2270, E-mail: mgould@usf.edu.
Website: http://english.usf.edu/

University of South Florida, College of The Arts, School of Music, Tampa, FL 33620-9951. Offers chamber music (MM); choral conducting (MM); electro-acoustic music (MM); instrumental conducting (MM); jazz composition (MM); jazz performance (MM); music composition (MM); music education (MA, PhD); music performance (MM); music theory (MM); piano pedagogy (MM). *Accreditation:* NASM. Part-time and evening/weekend programs available. *Faculty:* 26 full-time (8 women), 1 part-time/adjunct (0 women). *Students:* 76 full-time (37 women), 22 part-time (10 women); includes 18 minority (2 Black or African American, non-Hispanic/Latino; 3 Asian, non-Hispanic/Latino; 10 Hispanic/Latino; 1 Native Hawaiian or other Pacific Islander, non-Hispanic/Latino; 2 Two or more races, non-Hispanic/Latino), 20 international. Average age 31. 99 applicants, 64% accepted, 32 enrolled. In 2014, 37 master's, 2 doctorates awarded. *Degree requirements:* For master's, comprehensive exam, thesis optional; for doctorate, comprehensive exam, thesis/dissertation. *Entrance requirements:* For master's, minimum GPA of 3.0 in upper-division courses and music courses for bachelor's degree; resume; three letters of recommendation; at least 2 years of K-12 music teaching experience (for MA in music education); audition or interview (for MM); for doctorate, GRE General Test, master's degree from accredited institution with minimum GPA of 3.5, 3.0 in upper-division undergraduate courses; at least 2 years of K-12 music teaching experience; interview with faculty; 3 letters of recommendation; academic writing sample; curriculum vitae; personal goals statement; 15-20 minute video of applicant teaching music. Additional exam requirements/recommendations for international students: Required—TOEFL (minimum score 550 paper-based; 79 iBT) or IELTS (minimum score 6.5). *Application deadline:* For fall admission, 2/15 priority date for domestic students, 3/15 for international students; for spring admission, 10/15 for domestic students, 6/1 for international students. Application fee: $30. *Financial support:* In 2014–15, 47 students received support, including 1 research assistantship with tuition reimbursement available (averaging $15,724 per year), 46 teaching assistantships with tuition reimbursements available (averaging $10,099 per year); unspecified assistantships also available. Financial award application deadline: 2/15. *Faculty research:* Music education: alternate methods, community collaboration, contemporary changes, early childhood, general music, international perspectives, multicultural issues, technology, teacher behaviors, philosophy, psychology, sociology; music: chamber music, composition, conducting, jazz studies, music performance, music theory, pedagogy, electronic music. *Total annual research expenditures:* $126,118. *Unit head:* Dr. Karen Bryan, Director, 813-974-2311, Fax: 813-974-8721, E-mail: kmbryan@usf.edu. *Application contact:* Dr. William Hayden, Associate Professor and Graduate Program Director, 813-974-1753, Fax: 813-974-8721, E-mail: wphayden@usf.edu.
Website: http://music.arts.usf.edu/

The University of Tennessee, Graduate School, College of Arts and Sciences, Department of Theatre, Knoxville, TN 37996. Offers costume design (MFA); lighting design (MFA); performance (MFA); scene design (MFA); theatre technology (MFA). *Degree requirements:* For master's, thesis or alternative. *Entrance requirements:* For master's, audition, minimum GPA of 2.7. Additional exam requirements/recommendations for international students: Required—TOEFL. Electronic applications accepted.

The University of Tennessee, Graduate School, College of Arts and Sciences, School of Music, Knoxville, TN 37996. Offers accompanying (MM); choral conducting (MM); composition (MM); instrumental conducting (MM); jazz (MM); music education (MM); music theory (MM); musicology (MM); performance (MM); piano pedagogy and literature (MM). *Accreditation:* NASM. Part-time programs available. *Degree requirements:* For master's, thesis (for some programs). *Entrance requirements:* For master's, audition, minimum GPA of 2.7. Additional exam requirements/recommendations for international students: Required—TOEFL. Electronic applications accepted.

The University of Tennessee at Chattanooga, Program in Music, Chattanooga, TN 37403. Offers music education (MM); performance (MM). *Accreditation:* NASM. Part-time programs available. *Faculty:* 9 full-time (2 women), 1 part-time/adjunct (0 women). *Students:* 7 full-time (4 women), 6 part-time (4 women); includes 2 minority (1 Black or African American, non-Hispanic/Latino; 1 Hispanic/Latino), 1 international. Average age 32. 4 applicants, 100% accepted, 3 enrolled. In 2014, 2 master's awarded. *Degree requirements:* For master's, comprehensive exam, thesis or alternative, recital. *Entrance requirements:* For master's, GRE General Test or MAT, bachelor's degree in music, audition for placement. Additional exam requirements/recommendations for international students: Required—TOEFL (minimum score 550 paper-based; 79 iBT), IELTS (minimum score 6). *Application deadline:* For fall admission, 6/13 priority date for domestic students, 6/1 for international students; for spring admission, 10/15 priority date for domestic students, 10/1 for international students. Applications are processed on a rolling basis. Application fee: $30 ($35 for international students). Electronic applications accepted. *Expenses:* Tuition, state resident: full-time $7708; part-time $428 per credit hour. Tuition, nonresident: full-time $23,826; part-time $1323 per credit hour. *Required fees:* $1708; $252 per credit hour. *Financial support:* In 2014–15, 4 research assistantships with tuition reimbursements (averaging $5,503 per year) were awarded;

Federal Work-Study, scholarships/grants, and unspecified assistantships also available. Financial award applicants required to submit FAFSA. *Faculty research:* Music education, conducting, opera, vocal instruction, orchestras. *Unit head:* Dr. Lee Harris, Department Head, 423-425-4601, Fax: 423-425-4603, E-mail: lee-harris@utc.edu. *Application contact:* Dr. J. Randy Walker, Interim Dean of Graduate Studies, 423-425-4478, Fax: 423-425-5223, E-mail: randy-walker@utc.edu.
Website: http://www.utc.edu/Academic/Music/

The University of Texas at Arlington, Graduate School, College of Liberal Arts, Department of Music, Arlington, TX 76019. Offers education (MM); performance (MM). *Accreditation:* NASM. Part-time and evening/weekend programs available. *Degree requirements:* For master's, comprehensive exam, thesis optional. *Entrance requirements:* For master's, GRE, 3 letters of recommendation, minimum GPA of 3.0 in last 60 hours of course work. Additional exam requirements/recommendations for international students: Required—TOEFL (minimum score 550 paper-based). Electronic applications accepted.

The University of Texas at Austin, Graduate School, College of Fine Arts, Sarah and Ernest Butler School of Music, Austin, TX 78712-1111. Offers band and wind conducting (M Music, DMA); brass/woodwind/percussion (MM, DMA); chamber music (MM); choral conducting (MM, DMA); collaborative piano (MM, DMA); composition (MM, DMA), including composition, jazz, jazz (DMA); ethnomusicology (MM, PhD); literature and pedagogy (MM); music and human learning (MM, PhD); music and human learning (DMA), including jazz (MM, DMA), piano pedagogy; musicology (MM, PhD); opera performance (MM, DMA); orchestral conducting (MM, DMA); organ (MM), including sacred music; organ performance (MM, DMA); performance (MM), including jazz (MM, DMA); performance (DMA), including jazz (MM, DMA); piano (DMA), including jazz (MM, DMA); piano literature and pedagogy (MM); piano performance (MM, DMA); string performance (MM, DMA); theory (MM, PhD); vocal performance (MM, DMA); voice (DMA), including opera; voice performance pedagogy (DMA); woodwind, brass, percussion performance (MM). *Accreditation:* NASM. Part-time programs available. *Degree requirements:* For master's, one foreign language, comprehensive exam, thesis (for some programs), recital (performance or composition majors); for doctorate, one foreign language, comprehensive exam, thesis/dissertation (for some programs), recital (for performance or composition majors). *Entrance requirements:* For master's and doctorate, GRE General Test (except for performance or composition majors), audition (performance majors). Electronic applications accepted.

The University of Texas at El Paso, Graduate School, College of Liberal Arts, Department of Music, El Paso, TX 79968-0001. Offers music education (MM); music performance (MM). *Accreditation:* NASM. Part-time and evening/weekend programs available. *Degree requirements:* For master's, thesis optional. *Entrance requirements:* For master's, audition, interview, letters of recommendation. Additional exam requirements/recommendations for international students: Required—TOEFL; Recommended—IELTS. Electronic applications accepted.

The University of Texas at San Antonio, College of Liberal and Fine Arts, Department of Music, San Antonio, TX 78249-0617. Offers MM. *Accreditation:* NASM. Part-time programs available. *Faculty:* 27 full-time (10 women), 3 part-time/adjunct (1 woman). *Students:* 12 full-time (9 women), 17 part-time (7 women); includes 11 minority (10 Hispanic/Latino; 1 Two or more races, non-Hispanic/Latino). Average age 27. 22 applicants, 100% accepted, 11 enrolled. In 2014, 13 master's awarded. *Degree requirements:* For master's, comprehensive exam, thesis (for some programs). *Entrance requirements:* For master's, GRE, audition, 3 letters of recommendation. Additional exam requirements/recommendations for international students: Required—TOEFL (minimum score 550 paper-based; 79 iBT), IELTS (minimum score 6.5). *Application deadline:* For fall admission, 7/1 for domestic students, 4/1 for international students; for spring admission, 11/1 for domestic students, 9/1 for international students. Application fee: $45 ($80 for international students). *Expenses:* Tuition, state resident: full-time $4671; part-time $260 per credit hour. Tuition, nonresident: full-time $18,022; part-time $1001 per credit hour. *Financial support:* Scholarships/grants and unspecified assistantships available. *Faculty research:* Music cognition and perception, dalcroze eurhythmics in therapy, vocology, music of the Americas, music and film. *Unit head:* Dr. R. J. David Frego, Department Chair, 210-458-4354, Fax: 210-458-4381, E-mail: david.frego@utsa.edu.
Website: http://music.utsa.edu

The University of Texas–Pan American, College of Arts and Humanities, Department of Music, Edinburg, TX 78539. Offers ethnomusicology (M Mus); interdisciplinary studies (MAIS); music education (M Mus); performance (M Mus). *Accreditation:* NASM. Part-time programs available. *Degree requirements:* For master's, comprehensive exam, thesis optional, recital (performance). *Entrance requirements:* For master's, audition for performance area, bachelor's degree in music. *Expenses:* Tuition, state resident: full-time $4187; part-time $232.60 per credit hour. Tuition, nonresident: full-time $10,857; part-time $603.16 per credit hour. *Required fees:* $782; $27.50 per credit hour. $143.35 per semester. *Faculty research:* Music history, instrumental pedagogy, vocal pedagogy, music education, ethnomusicology.

The University of the Arts, College of Performing Arts, School of Music, Program in Jazz Studies, Philadelphia, PA 19102-4944. Offers MM. *Degree requirements:* For master's, recital, thesis/project. *Entrance requirements:* For master's, audition consisting of a performance, interview and written examination to measure aural, theoretical, arranging and historical skills and knowledge; official transcripts from each undergraduate or graduate school attended; three letters of recommendation; one- to two-page statement of professional plans and goals. Additional exam requirements/recommendations for international students: Required—TOEFL (minimum score 580 paper-based, 92 iBT) or IELTS (minimum score 6.5).

University of the Pacific, Conservatory of Music, Stockton, CA 95211-0197. Offers music education (MM); music therapy (MA). *Accreditation:* NASM. *Students:* 8 full-time (6 women), 14 part-time (11 women); includes 4 minority (2 Asian, non-Hispanic/Latino; 1 Hispanic/Latino; 1 Two or more races, non-Hispanic/Latino), 2 international. Average age 31. 24 applicants, 50% accepted, 8 enrolled. In 2014, 3 master's awarded. *Entrance requirements:* For master's, GRE General Test. Additional exam requirements/recommendations for international students: Required—TOEFL (minimum score 475 paper-based). *Application deadline:* For fall admission, 3/1 priority date for domestic students; for spring admission, 10/1 priority date for domestic students. Applications are processed on a rolling basis. Application fee: $75. *Financial support:* Teaching assistantships and institutionally sponsored loans available. Support available to part-time students. Financial award application deadline: 3/1; financial award applicants required to submit FAFSA. *Unit head:* Dr. Giulio Ongaro, Dean, 209-946-2417, E-mail: musicdean@pacific.edu. *Application contact:* Dr. Ruth Brittin, Chairperson, 209-946-2408, E-mail: rbittin@pacific.edu.

The University of Toledo, College of Graduate Studies, College of Communication and the Arts, Department of Music, Toledo, OH 43606-3390. Offers music (Certificate); music performance (MMP). *Accreditation:* NASM. *Degree requirements:* For master's, comprehensive exam, diagnostic theory exam. *Entrance requirements:* For master's, GRE if GPA less than 2.7, minimum cumulative point-hour ratio of 2.7 for all previous academic work, audition. Additional exam requirements/recommendations for

international students: Required—TOEFL (minimum score 550 paper-based; 80 iBT). Electronic applications accepted.

University of Toronto, School of Graduate Studies, Faculty of Music, Toronto, ON M5S 2J7, Canada. Offers composition (M Mus, DMA); ethnomusicology (MA, PhD); jazz (M Mus); music education (MA, PhD); musicology/theory (MA, PhD); opera (M Mus); performance (M Mus, DMA). Part-time programs available. *Degree requirements:* For master's, comprehensive exam (for some programs), oral examination (M Mus in composition), 1 foreign language (MA); for doctorate, recital of original works (DMA), thesis (PhD). *Entrance requirements:* For master's, BM in area of specialization with minimum B average in final 2 years, original compositions (M Mus in composition); for doctorate, master's degree in area of specialization, minimum B+ average, at least 2 extended compositions (DMA). Additional exam requirements/recommendations for international students: Required—TOEFL (minimum score 580 paper-based; 93 iBT), TWE (minimum score 5). Electronic applications accepted.

University of Utah, Graduate School, College of Fine Arts, School of Music, Salt Lake City, UT 84112. Offers choral conducting (M Mus, DMA); collaborative piano (M Mus); composition (M Mus, PhD); instrumental conducting (M Mus); instrumental performance (M Mus, DMA); jazz studies (M Mus); music education (M Mus, PhD); music history and literature (M Mus); musicology (MA); organ performance (M Mus); piano performance (M Mus, DMA); string performance and pedagogy (M Mus); theory (M Mus); vocal performance (DMA). *Accreditation:* NASM. *Faculty:* 25 full-time (11 women), 50 part-time/adjunct (19 women). *Students:* 71 full-time (36 women), 27 part-time (14 women); includes 8 minority (1 Black or African American, non-Hispanic/Latino; 2 Asian, non-Hispanic/Latino; 2 Hispanic/Latino; 3 Two or more races, non-Hispanic/Latino), 19 international. Average age 32. 82 applicants, 74% accepted, 27 enrolled. In 2014, 25 master's, 17 doctorates awarded. *Degree requirements:* For master's, variable foreign language requirement, comprehensive exam (for some programs), thesis (for some programs), 1-2 recitals (MM), final oral exam; for doctorate, variable foreign language requirement, comprehensive exam (for some programs), thesis/dissertation, 4 recitals (DMA), thesis/dissertation defense. *Entrance requirements:* For master's, placement exams, minimum GPA of 3.0, audition, bachelor's degree in music; for doctorate, placement exams, minimum GPA of 3.0, audition, master's degree in music. Additional exam requirements/recommendations for international students: Required—TOEFL (minimum score 85 iBT). *Application deadline:* For fall admission, 2/15 for domestic students, 1/15 for international students; for spring admission, 10/1 for domestic students, 9/1 for international students; for summer admission, 3/15 for domestic students, 2/15 for international students. Applications are processed on a rolling basis. Application fee: $55 ($65 for international students). Electronic applications accepted. *Financial support:* In 2014–15, 61 students received support, including 51 teaching assistantships with full and partial tuition reimbursements available (averaging $10,814 per year); fellowships with full and partial tuition reimbursements available, research assistantships with full and partial tuition reimbursements available, scholarships/grants, health care benefits, and unspecified assistantships also available. Financial award application deadline: 2/1. *Faculty research:* Music education, conducting, musicology, composition, performance. *Total annual research expenditures:* $25,000. *Unit head:* Miguel Chuaqui, Director, 801-585-3720, E-mail: m.chauqui@utah.edu. *Application contact:* Heather Severson, Academic Coordinator, 801-585-6972, Fax: 801-581-5683, E-mail: heather.severson@utah.edu.
Website: http://www.music.utah.edu/

University of Valley Forge, Program in Music Technology, Phoenixville, PA 19460. Offers MM. Postbaccalaureate distance learning degree programs offered (minimal on-campus study).

University of Victoria, Faculty of Graduate Studies, Faculty of Fine Arts, School of Music, Victoria, BC V8W 2Y2, Canada. Offers composition (M Mus); musicology (MA, PhD); musicology with performance (MA); performance (M Mus). *Degree requirements:* For master's, 2 foreign languages, thesis; for doctorate, 2 foreign languages, thesis/dissertation, candidacy exam. *Entrance requirements:* For master's, theory placement test, audition or sample papers and compositions; for doctorate, audition or sample papers and compositions. Additional exam requirements/recommendations for international students: Required—TOEFL (minimum score 575 paper-based), IELTS (minimum score 7). Electronic applications accepted. *Faculty research:* Beethoven, Wagner, metrical structure in tonal music, French baroque, eighteenth-century opera.

University of Virginia, College and Graduate School of Arts and Sciences, Department of Music, Charlottesville, VA 22903. Offers MA, PhD. *Faculty:* 16 full-time (5 women), 14 part-time/adjunct (5 women). *Students:* 30 full-time (12 women); includes 4 minority (1 Black or African American, non-Hispanic/Latino; 3 Two or more races, non-Hispanic/Latino), 2 international. Average age 30. 42 applicants, 19% accepted, 5 enrolled. In 2014, 1 master's, 5 doctorates awarded. *Degree requirements:* For master's, one foreign language, article-length paper; for doctorate, one foreign language, comprehensive exam, thesis/dissertation. *Entrance requirements:* For master's and doctorate, GRE General Test, 2 writing samples or portfolio. Additional exam requirements/recommendations for international students: Required—TOEFL (minimum score 600 paper-based; 90 iBT), IELTS (minimum score 7). *Application deadline:* For fall admission, 1/1 for domestic students, 1/2 for international students. Applications are processed on a rolling basis. Application fee: $60. Electronic applications accepted. *Expenses:* Tuition, state resident: full-time $14,164; part-time $349 per credit hour. Tuition, nonresident: full-time $23,722; part-time $1300 per credit hour. *Required fees:* $2514. *Financial support:* Teaching assistantships available. Financial award applicants required to submit FAFSA. *Unit head:* Richard Will, Chair, 434-924-3052, Fax: 434-924-6033, E-mail: rw6w@virginia.edu. *Application contact:* Bonnie Gordon, Director of Graduate Studies, 434-924-3052, Fax: 434-924-6033, E-mail: bsg7v@virginia.edu.
Website: http://music.virginia.edu/

University of Washington, Graduate School, College of Arts and Sciences, School of Music, Concentration in Choral Conducting, Seattle, WA 98195. Offers MM, DMA.

University of Washington, Graduate School, College of Arts and Sciences, School of Music, Concentration in Ethnomusicology, Seattle, WA 98195. Offers MA.

University of Washington, Graduate School, College of Arts and Sciences, School of Music, Concentration in Music History, Seattle, WA 98195. Offers MA, PhD.

University of Washington, Graduate School, College of Arts and Sciences, School of Music, Department of Choral Music, Seattle, WA 98195. Offers choral conducting (MM, DMA).

The University of Western Ontario, Faculty of Graduate Studies, Don Wright Faculty of Music, London, ON N6A 5B8, Canada. Offers music (M Mus, PhD); popular music and culture (MA). Part-time programs available. Terminal master's awarded for partial completion of doctoral program. *Degree requirements:* For master's, 2 foreign languages, thesis (for some programs), recital; for doctorate, 2 foreign languages, thesis/dissertation. *Entrance requirements:* For master's, honors degree in music; minimum A average in proposed area of concentration, B average overall; for doctorate, MA or equivalent. *Faculty research:* Systematic musicology, musicology, theory, music education.

University of West Georgia, College of Arts and Humanities, Department of Music, Carrollton, GA 30118. Offers music education (M Mus); performance (M Mus). *Accreditation:* NASM. Part-time programs available. Postbaccalaureate distance learning degree programs offered (no on-campus study). *Faculty:* 8 full-time (3 women), 2 part-time/adjunct (both women). *Students:* 2 full-time (1 woman), 23 part-time (13 women); includes 8 minority (6 Black or African American, non-Hispanic/Latino; 1 American Indian or Alaska Native, non-Hispanic/Latino; 1 Hispanic/Latino). Average age 33. 12 applicants, 75% accepted, 7 enrolled. In 2014, 2 master's awarded. *Degree requirements:* For master's, comprehensive exam, thesis optional, recital (for MM in performance), qualifying exam. *Entrance requirements:* For master's, minimum GPA of 2.5, bachelor's degree in music education or teacher certification and essay (for music education); performance evaluation (for performance). Additional exam requirements/recommendations for international students: Required—TOEFL (minimum score 523 paper-based; 69 iBT); Recommended—IELTS (minimum score 6). *Application deadline:* For fall admission, 8/1 for domestic students, 6/1 for international students; for spring admission, 11/15 for domestic students, 10/15 for international students. Applications are processed on a rolling basis. Application fee: $40. Electronic applications accepted. *Financial support:* Unspecified assistantships available. Financial award application deadline: 4/1; financial award applicants required to submit FAFSA. *Faculty research:* Musicology, instrumental music/music education, jazz performance, French music. *Unit head:* Dr. Kevin Hibbard, Chair, 678-839-6516, Fax: 678-839-6259, E-mail: khibbard@westga.edu. *Application contact:* Alicia Freed, Graduate and International Admission, 678-839-1393, E-mail: afreed@westga.edu.
Website: http://www.westga.edu/music

University of Wisconsin–Madison, Graduate School, College of Letters and Science, School of Music, Program in Composition, Madison, WI 53706-1380. Offers MM, DMA. *Accreditation:* NASM. *Degree requirements:* For doctorate, thesis/dissertation. *Expenses:* Tuition, state resident: full-time $10,723; part-time $745 per credit. Tuition, nonresident: full-time $24,054; part-time $1578 per credit. *Required fees:* $374 per semester. Tuition and fees vary according to course load, program and reciprocity agreements.

University of Wisconsin–Madison, Graduate School, College of Letters and Science, School of Music, Program in Conducting, Madison, WI 53706-1380. Offers choral (MM, DMA); instrumental (MM, DMA); orchestral (MM, DMA). *Accreditation:* NASM. *Degree requirements:* For doctorate, thesis/dissertation. *Expenses:* Tuition, state resident: full-time $10,723; part-time $745 per credit. Tuition, nonresident: full-time $24,054; part-time $1578 per credit. *Required fees:* $374 per semester. Tuition and fees vary according to course load, program and reciprocity agreements.

University of Wisconsin–Madison, Graduate School, College of Letters and Science, School of Music, Program in Musicology and Ethnomusicology, Madison, WI 53706-1380. Offers ethnomusicology (MA, PhD); historical musicology (PhD); music history (MA). *Accreditation:* NASM. *Degree requirements:* For doctorate, 2 foreign languages, thesis/dissertation. *Entrance requirements:* For doctorate, GRE General Test. *Expenses:* Tuition, state resident: full-time $10,723; part-time $745 per credit. Tuition, nonresident: full-time $24,054; part-time $1578 per credit. *Required fees:* $374 per semester. Tuition and fees vary according to course load, program and reciprocity agreements.

University of Wisconsin–Madison, Graduate School, College of Letters and Science, School of Music, Program in Music Performance, Madison, WI 53706-1380. Offers MM, DMA. *Accreditation:* NASM. *Degree requirements:* For doctorate, one foreign language, thesis/dissertation. *Expenses:* Tuition, state resident: full-time $10,723; part-time $745 per credit. Tuition, nonresident: full-time $24,054; part-time $1578 per credit. *Required fees:* $374 per semester. Tuition and fees vary according to course load, program and reciprocity agreements.

University of Wisconsin–Madison, Graduate School, College of Letters and Science, School of Music, Program in Music Theory, Madison, WI 53706-1380. Offers MA, PhD. *Accreditation:* NASM. *Degree requirements:* For master's, thesis, 1 foreign language (MA); for doctorate, 2 foreign languages, thesis/dissertation. *Entrance requirements:* For master's, GRE General Test (MA); for doctorate, GRE General Test. *Expenses:* Tuition, state resident: full-time $10,723; part-time $745 per credit. Tuition, nonresident: full-time $24,054; part-time $1578 per credit. *Required fees:* $374 per semester. Tuition and fees vary according to course load, program and reciprocity agreements.

University of Wisconsin–Milwaukee, Graduate School, Peck School of the Arts, Department of Music, Milwaukee, WI 53201-0413. Offers chamber music performance (Certificate); music composition (MM); music education (MM); music history and literature (MM); opera and vocal arts (Certificate); string pedagogy (MM); MLIS/MM. *Accreditation:* NASM. Part-time programs available. *Degree requirements:* For master's, variable foreign language requirement, comprehensive exam, thesis or alternative. *Entrance requirements:* For master's, GRE General Test, GRE Subject Test, audition, interview. Additional exam requirements/recommendations for international students: Required—TOEFL (minimum score 550 paper-based; 79 iBT), IELTS (minimum score 6.5). Electronic applications accepted. *Expenses:* Contact institution.

University of Wyoming, College of Arts and Sciences, Department of Music, Laramie, WY 82071. Offers music education (MME); performance (MM). *Accreditation:* NASM. *Degree requirements:* For master's, comprehensive exam, thesis or alternative. *Entrance requirements:* For master's, minimum GPA of 3.0. Additional exam requirements/recommendations for international students: Required—TOEFL (minimum score 540 paper-based). Electronic applications accepted.

Valdosta State University, Department of English, Valdosta, GA 31698. Offers literature (MA); rhetoric and composition (MA); studies for language arts teachers (MA). Part-time programs available. *Faculty:* 12 full-time (9 women). *Students:* 6 full-time (5 women), 24 part-time (14 women); includes 2 minority (1 Black or African American, non-Hispanic/Latino; 1 Two or more races, non-Hispanic/Latino). Average age 24. 7 applicants, 71% accepted, 4 enrolled. *Degree requirements:* For master's, one foreign language, thesis, comprehensive written and/or oral exams. *Entrance requirements:* For master's, GRE General Test, minimum GPA of 3.0. Additional exam requirements/recommendations for international students: Required—TOEFL (minimum score 523 paper-based). *Application deadline:* For fall admission, 7/1 for domestic and international students; for spring admission, 11/1 for domestic and international students. Applications are processed on a rolling basis. Application fee: $35. Electronic applications accepted. *Expenses:* Tuition, state resident: part-time $236 per credit hour. Tuition, nonresident: part-time $850 per credit hour. *Required fees:* $1032 per semester. *Financial support:* In 2014–15, 11 students received support, including 6 research assistantships with full tuition reimbursements available (averaging $4,000 per year), 7 teaching assistantships with full tuition reimbursements available (averaging $8,000 per year); institutionally sponsored loans, scholarships/grants, and unspecified assistantships also available. Support available to part-time students. Financial award application deadline: 7/1; financial award applicants required to submit FAFSA. *Faculty research:* American literature, creative writing. *Unit head:* Dr. Mark Smith, Head, 229-333-5946, E-mail: marksmit@valdosta.edu. *Application contact:* Jessica Powers, Admissions Specialist, 229-333-5694, Fax: 229-245-3853, E-mail: jldevane@valdosta.edu.

Music

Vermont College of Fine Arts, MFA in Music Composition Program, Montpelier, VT 05602. Offers MFA. Postbaccalaureate distance learning degree programs offered (minimal on-campus study). *Faculty:* 11 part-time/adjunct (1 woman). *Students:* 34 full-time (10 women); includes 6 minority (2 Black or African American, non-Hispanic/Latino; 1 Hispanic/Latino; 3 Two or more races, non-Hispanic/Latino). Average age 42. 13 applicants, 77% accepted, 6 enrolled. In 2014, 16 master's awarded. *Entrance requirements:* For master's, resume of education and relevant professional experience, three samples of original compositions, official transcripts of all previous undergraduate and graduate coursework, two letters of recommendation, statement of purpose. *Application deadline:* For fall admission, 6/15 for domestic and international students; for spring admission, 12/15 for domestic and international students. Applications are processed on a rolling basis. Application fee: $75. Full-time tuition and fees vary according to program. *Financial support:* Scholarships/grants available. Financial award applicants required to submit FAFSA. *Unit head:* Carol Beatty, Program Director, 866-934-8232 Ext. 8610, E-mail: carol.beatty@vcfa.edu. *Application contact:* Sarah Madru, Assistant Program Director, 802-828-8534, E-mail: sarah.madru@vcfa.edu. Website: http://www.vcfa.edu/music-comp

Virginia Commonwealth University, Graduate School, School of the Arts, Department of Music, Richmond, VA 23284-9005. Offers education (MM). *Accreditation:* NASM. *Degree requirements:* For master's, departmental qualifying exam, recital. *Entrance requirements:* For master's, department examination, audition or tapes, portfolio. Additional exam requirements/recommendations for international students: Required—TOEFL (minimum score 600 paper-based; 100 iBT). Electronic applications accepted. *Faculty research:* Composition, conducting, education, performance.

Washington State University, College of Liberal Arts, School of Music, Pullman, WA 99164-5300. Offers MA. *Accreditation:* NASM. Part-time programs available. *Faculty:* 27 full-time (8 women), 5 part-time/adjunct (all women). *Students:* 16 full-time (4 women), 4 part-time (0 women); includes 3 minority (2 Asian, non-Hispanic/Latino; 1 Hispanic/Latino), 3 international. Average age 30. 29 applicants, 59% accepted, 10 enrolled. In 2014, 7 master's awarded. *Degree requirements:* For master's, one foreign language, comprehensive exam, thesis (for some programs), oral exam. *Entrance requirements:* For master's, audition, minimum GPA of 3.0, 3 letters of recommendation, composition portfolio and recording (for composition); writing sample and written philosophy (for music education); writing sample (for music history); in-depth audition (for performance). Additional exam requirements/recommendations for international students: Required—TOEFL, IELTS. *Application deadline:* For fall admission, 1/10 priority date for domestic students, 1/10 for international students; for spring admission, 7/1 for domestic and international students. Applications are processed on a rolling basis. Application fee: $75. Electronic applications accepted. *Expenses:* Tuition, state resident: full-time $11,768. Tuition, nonresident: full-time $25,200. *Required fees:* $960. Tuition and fees vary according to program. *Financial support:* In 2014–15, 12 students received support, including 13 teaching assistantships with full tuition reimbursements available (averaging $13,379 per year); health care benefits also available. Financial award application deadline: 2/15; financial award applicants required to submit FAFSA. *Faculty research:* Composition, education. *Unit head:* Dr. Gregory W. Yasinitsky, Director, 509-335-3898, Fax: 509-335-4245, E-mail: yasinits@wsu.edu. *Application contact:* Dr. Shannon Scott, Graduate Coordinator for School of Music, 509-335-5342, Fax: 509-335-4245, E-mail: shannonscott@wsu.edu. Website: http://libarts.wsu.edu/music/

Washington University in St. Louis, Graduate School of Arts and Sciences, Department of Music, St. Louis, MO 63130-4899. Offers MA, MM, PhD. Terminal master's awarded for partial completion of doctoral program. *Degree requirements:* For master's, thesis or alternative; for doctorate, thesis/dissertation. *Entrance requirements:* For master's, GRE General Test, departmental exam; for doctorate, departmental exam, GRE General Test. Additional exam requirements/recommendations for international students: Required—TOEFL. Electronic applications accepted. *Faculty research:* Performance, composition, musicology, ethnomusicology, theory.

Wayne State University, College of Fine, Performing and Communication Arts, Department of Music, Detroit, MI 48202. Offers composition/theory (MM); jazz performance (MM); music (MA); orchestral studies (Certificate); performance (MM). *Accreditation:* NASM. *Students:* 17 full-time (7 women), 7 part-time (1 woman); includes 7 minority (6 Black or African American, non-Hispanic/Latino; 1 American Indian or Alaska Native, non-Hispanic/Latino), 1 international. Average age 31. 29 applicants, 45% accepted, 11 enrolled. In 2014, 10 master's awarded. *Degree requirements:* For master's, thesis (for some programs), oral examination (for some programs), recital with program notes (for some programs). *Entrance requirements:* For master's, diagnostic exam in theory and history, undergraduate degree in same field as desired field of graduate study or equivalent in course work, private study, or experience; audition/interview; for Certificate, undergraduate degree in same field as desired field of graduate study or equivalent in course work, private study, or experience; audition/interview. Additional exam requirements/recommendations for international students: Required—TOEFL (minimum score 550 paper-based; 79 iBT), Michigan English Language Assessment Battery (minimum score 85); Recommended—IELTS (minimum score 6.5), TWE (minimum score 5.5). *Application deadline:* For fall admission, 1/1 for domestic and international students. Applications are processed on a rolling basis. Application fee: $0. Electronic applications accepted. *Expenses:* Expenses: Contact institution. *Financial support:* In 2014–15, 18 students received support. Career-related internships or fieldwork, institutionally sponsored loans, and scholarships/grants available. Support available to part-time students. Financial award application deadline: 3/31; financial award applicants required to submit FAFSA. *Faculty research:* Teacher training, pedagogy, musicology, composition/theory, conducting/performance practice. *Unit head:* Dr. Norah Duncan, Interim Chair, Department of Music, 313-577-1775, E-mail: norah.duncan@wayne.edu. *Application contact:* Danny DeRose, Academic Services Officer II, 313-577-1783, E-mail: danny.derose@wayne.edu. Website: http://music.wayne.edu/

Webster University, Leigh Gerdine College of Fine Arts, Department of Music, St. Louis, MO 63119-3194. Offers church music (MM); composition (MM); jazz studies (MM); music (MA); music education (MM); organ (MM); performance (MM); piano (MM); voice (MM). *Accreditation:* NASM. *Entrance requirements:* Additional exam requirements/recommendations for international students: Required—TOEFL.

Wesleyan University, Graduate Studies, Department of Music, Middletown, CT 06459. Offers composition (MA); ethnomusicology (MA, PhD). *Degree requirements:* For master's, one foreign language, thesis; for doctorate, 2 foreign languages, comprehensive exam, thesis/dissertation. *Entrance requirements:* For doctorate, MA. Additional exam requirements/recommendations for international students: Required—TOEFL. Electronic applications accepted. *Faculty research:* Ethnomusicology, musicology, music theory, composition, performance.

West Chester University of Pennsylvania, College of Visual and Performing Arts, Department of Applied Music, West Chester, PA 19383. Offers performance (MM); piano pedagogy (MM, Certificate). Part-time and evening/weekend programs available. *Faculty:* 16 full-time (4 women), 4 part-time/adjunct (2 women). *Students:* 17 full-time (10 women), 14 part-time (4 women); includes 4 minority (1 Black or African American, non-Hispanic/Latino; 1 Asian, non-Hispanic/Latino; 1 Native Hawaiian or other Pacific Islander, non-Hispanic/Latino; 1 Two or more races, non-Hispanic/Latino), 10 international. Average age 32. 20 applicants, 85% accepted, 3 enrolled. In 2014, 16 master's awarded. *Degree requirements:* For master's, comprehensive exam, thesis optional, recital. *Entrance requirements:* For master's and Certificate, School of Music Graduate Placement Test (GPT), audition, interview. Additional exam requirements/recommendations for international students: Required—TOEFL (minimum score 550 paper-based; 80 iBT). *Application deadline:* For fall admission, 4/15 priority date for domestic students, 3/15 for international students; for spring admission, 10/15 priority date for domestic students, 9/1 for international students. Applications are processed on a rolling basis. Application fee: $45. Electronic applications accepted. *Expenses:* Tuition, state resident: full-time $8172; part-time $454 per credit. Tuition, nonresident: full-time $12,258; part-time $681 per credit. *Required fees:* $2231; $110.78 per credit. Tuition and fees vary according to campus/location and program. *Financial support:* Unspecified assistantships available. Support available to part-time students. Financial award application deadline: 2/15; financial award applicants required to submit FAFSA. *Unit head:* Dr. Chris Hanning, Chair, 610-436-4178, Fax: 610-436-2873, E-mail: channing@wcupa.edu. *Application contact:* Dr. M. Gregory Martin, Graduate Coordinator, 610-436-2070, Fax: 610-436-2873, E-mail: mmartin@wcupa.edu. Website: http://catalog.wcupa.edu/graduate/visual-performing-arts/applied-music/

West Chester University of Pennsylvania, College of Visual and Performing Arts, Department of Music Education, West Chester, PA 19383. Offers Kodaly (MM); Kodaly methodology (Certificate); music education (MM, Teaching Certificate); music technology (MM, Certificate); Orff-Schulwerk (MM, Certificate); performance (MM). *Accreditation:* NASM; NCATE. Part-time programs available. *Faculty:* 4 full-time (2 women). *Students:* 5 full-time (2 women), 27 part-time (17 women); includes 2 minority (1 Asian, non-Hispanic/Latino; 1 Hispanic/Latino). Average age 28. 16 applicants, 88% accepted, 6 enrolled. In 2014, 9 master's, 5 Certificates awarded. *Degree requirements:* For master's, comprehensive exam, thesis optional, recital. *Entrance requirements:* For master's and other advanced degree, School of Music Graduate Placement Test (GPT), audition, interview. Additional exam requirements/recommendations for international students: Required—TOEFL (minimum score 550 paper-based; 80 iBT). *Application deadline:* For fall admission, 4/15 priority date for domestic students, 3/15 for international students; for spring admission, 10/15 priority date for domestic students, 9/1 for international students. Applications are processed on a rolling basis. Application fee: $45. Electronic applications accepted. *Expenses:* Tuition, state resident: full-time $8172; part-time $454 per credit. Tuition, nonresident: full-time $12,258; part-time $681 per credit. *Required fees:* $2231; $110.78 per credit. Tuition and fees vary according to campus/location and program. *Financial support:* Unspecified assistantships available. Support available to part-time students. Financial award application deadline: 2/15; financial award applicants required to submit FAFSA. *Faculty research:* Developing music listening skills. *Unit head:* Dr. J. Bryan Burton, Chair and Graduate Coordinator, 610-436-2222, Fax: 610-436-2873, E-mail: jburton@wcupa.edu. *Application contact:* Dr. M. Gregory Martin, Graduate Coordinator, 610-436-2070, E-mail: mmartin@wcupa.edu. Website: http://catalog.wcupa.edu/graduate/visual-performing-arts/music-education/

West Chester University of Pennsylvania, College of Visual and Performing Arts, Department of Music Theory, History and Composition, West Chester, PA 19383. Offers music (MM), including composition, history and literature; music history (MM); music theory/composition (MM). Part-time programs available. *Faculty:* 7 full-time (1 woman). *Students:* 5 full-time (0 women), 1 part-time (0 women); includes 1 minority (Asian, non-Hispanic/Latino). Average age 28. 3 applicants, 100% accepted, 1 enrolled. In 2014, 2 master's awarded. *Degree requirements:* For master's, variable foreign language requirement, comprehensive exam, thesis (for music theory/composition). *Entrance requirements:* For master's, interview. *Application deadline:* For fall admission, 4/15 for domestic students, 3/15 for international students; for spring admission, 10/15 for domestic students, 9/1 for international students. Applications are processed on a rolling basis. Application fee: $45. Electronic applications accepted. *Expenses:* Tuition, state resident: full-time $8172; part-time $454 per credit. Tuition, nonresident: full-time $12,258; part-time $681 per credit. *Required fees:* $2231; $110.78 per credit. Tuition and fees vary according to campus/location and program. *Financial support:* Unspecified assistantships available. Financial award application deadline: 2/15; financial award applicants required to submit FAFSA. *Faculty research:* Musicology, eighteenth century European music. *Unit head:* Dr. Robert Maggio, Chair, 610-436-2646, E-mail: musicinfo@wcupa.edu. *Application contact:* Dr. M. Gregory Martin, Graduate Coordinator, 610-436-2070, E-mail: gmartin@wcupa.edu. Website: http://catalog.wcupa.edu/graduate/visual-performing-arts/music-theory-history-composition/

Western Carolina University, Graduate School, College of Fine and Performing Arts, School of Music, Cullowhee, NC 28723. Offers MM. *Accreditation:* NASM. Part-time programs available. *Degree requirements:* For master's, comprehensive exam, thesis. *Entrance requirements:* For master's, GRE, music entrance exam, appropriate undergraduate degree, live audition and/or interview. Additional exam requirements/recommendations for international students: Required—TOEFL (minimum score 550 paper-based; 79 iBT). *Faculty research:* Music experiences for K-12 students, marching band, sound mixing for television, music technology, choral methods, music history.

Western Illinois University, School of Graduate Studies, College of Fine Arts and Communication, School of Music, Macomb, IL 61455-1390. Offers MM. *Accreditation:* NASM. Part-time programs available. *Students:* 24 full-time (9 women), 1 (woman) part-time; includes 4 minority (1 Black or African American, non-Hispanic/Latino; 2 Hispanic/Latino; 1 Native Hawaiian or other Pacific Islander, non-Hispanic/Latino), 7 international. Average age 27. 23 applicants, 70% accepted, 8 enrolled. In 2014, 19 master's awarded. *Degree requirements:* For master's, comprehensive exam, thesis or alternative. *Entrance requirements:* For master's, audition. Additional exam requirements/recommendations for international students: Required—TOEFL (minimum score 550 paper-based; 80 iBT). *Application deadline:* Applications are processed on a rolling basis. Application fee: $30. Electronic applications accepted. *Financial support:* In 2014–15, 22 students received support, including 1 research assistantship with full tuition reimbursement available (averaging $7,544 per year), 21 teaching assistantships with full tuition reimbursements available (averaging $8,688 per year). Financial award applicants required to submit FAFSA. *Unit head:* Dr. Bart Shanklin, Director, 309-298-1544. *Application contact:* Dr. Nancy Parsons, Associate Provost and Director of Graduate Studies, 309-298-1806, Fax: 309-298-2345, E-mail: grad-office@wiu.edu. Website: http://wiu.edu/music

Western Michigan University, Graduate College, College of Fine Arts, School of Music, Kalamazoo, MI 49008. Offers music (MA); music composition (MM); music conducting (MM); music education (MM); music performance (MM); music therapy (MM). *Accreditation:* NASM. *Application deadline:* For fall admission, 2/15 for domestic students. *Financial support:* Application deadline: 2/15. *Application contact:* Admissions and Orientation, 269-387-2000, Fax: 269-387-2096.

Western Oregon University, Graduate Programs, College of Liberal Arts and Sciences, Division of Creative Arts, Monmouth, OR 97361-1394. Offers contemporary music (MM). *Accreditation:* NASM. *Entrance requirements:* Additional exam requirements/recommendations for international students: Required—TOEFL (minimum score 550 paper-based; 79 iBT), IELTS (minimum score 6.5).

Western Washington University, Graduate School, College of Fine and Performing Arts, Department of Music, Bellingham, WA 98225-5996. Offers M Mus. *Accreditation:* NASM. Part-time programs available. *Degree requirements:* For master's, thesis. *Entrance requirements:* For master's, GRE General Test, department placement exams, audition, portfolio, minimum GPA of 3.0 in last 60 semester hours or last 90 quarter hours of course work. Additional exam requirements/recommendations for international students: Required—TOEFL (minimum score 567 paper-based). Electronic applications accepted. *Faculty research:* Baroque opera, historical music of the Silk Road, original composition, 20th century orchestral music, 13th century polyphony.

West Texas A&M University, College of Fine Arts and Humanities, School of Music, Program in Music, Canyon, TX 79016-0001. Offers MA. *Accreditation:* NASM. Part-time programs available. *Degree requirements:* For master's, comprehensive exam, thesis optional. *Entrance requirements:* For master's, GRE General Test. Additional exam requirements/recommendations for international students: Required—TOEFL (minimum score 550 paper-based). Electronic applications accepted.

West Texas A&M University, College of Fine Arts and Humanities, School of Music, Program in Performance, Canyon, TX 79016-0001. Offers MM. *Accreditation:* NASM. Part-time programs available. *Degree requirements:* For master's, comprehensive exam, thesis optional. *Entrance requirements:* For master's, GRE General Test. Additional exam requirements/recommendations for international students: Required—TOEFL (minimum score 550 paper-based). Electronic applications accepted.

West Virginia University, College of Creative Arts, Division of Music, Morgantown, WV 26506. Offers music composition (MM, DMA); music education (MM, PhD); music history (MM); music performance (MM, DMA); music theory (MM). *Accreditation:* NASM. *Degree requirements:* For master's, comprehensive exam, thesis (for some programs), recitals; for doctorate, variable foreign language requirement, comprehensive exam, thesis/dissertation, recitals (DMA). *Entrance requirements:* For master's, GRE General Test (music history), minimum GPA of 3.0, audition; for doctorate, GRE General Test (music education), minimum GPA of 3.0, audition. Additional exam requirements/recommendations for international students: Required—TOEFL. *Faculty research:* Jazz history, seventeenth century French court music, nineteenth century composition theory.

Wichita State University, Graduate School, College of Fine Arts, School of Music, Wichita, KS 67260. Offers music (MM); music education (MME). *Accreditation:* NASM. Part-time programs available. *Unit head:* Prof. Russ Widener, Director, 316-978-6435, Fax: 316-978-3625, E-mail: russ.widener@wichita.edu. *Application contact:* Jordan Oleson, Admissions Coordinator, 316-978-3095, Fax: 316-978-3253, E-mail: jordan.oleson@wichita.edu.
Website: http://www.wichita.edu/music

William Paterson University of New Jersey, College of the Arts and Communication, Wayne, NJ 07470-8420. Offers art (MFA); music (MM); professional communication (MA). *Accreditation:* NASAD. Part-time and evening/weekend programs available. *Faculty:* 23 full-time (15 women), 11 part-time/adjunct (6 women). *Students:* 32 full-time (13 women), 18 part-time (11 women); includes 9 minority (2 Black or African American, non-Hispanic/Latino; 3 Asian, non-Hispanic/Latino; 4 Hispanic/Latino), 5 international. Average age 32. 79 applicants, 59% accepted, 24 enrolled. In 2014, 26 master's awarded. *Degree requirements:* For master's, comprehensive exam (for some programs), thesis (for some programs). *Entrance requirements:* For master's, GRE, minimum GPA of 2.75; audition; 2 letters of recommendation; portfolio with letter of intent. Additional exam requirements/recommendations for international students: Required—TOEFL (minimum score 550 paper-based; 79 iBT), IELTS (minimum score 6). *Application deadline:* For fall admission, 6/1 for domestic students, 3/1 for international students; for spring admission, 11/5 for domestic students, 10/15 for international students. Applications are processed on a rolling basis. Application fee: $50. Electronic applications accepted. *Expenses:* Tuition, state resident: full-time $12,413; part-time $564.21 per credit. Tuition, nonresident: full-time $20,487; part-time $931.21 per credit. *Required fees:* $2107; $95.79 per credit. $478.95 per semester. Tuition and fees vary according to course load and degree level. *Financial support:* Research assistantships with full tuition reimbursements, career-related internships or fieldwork, Federal Work-Study, scholarships/grants, and unspecified assistantships available. Support available to part-time students. Financial award application deadline: 4/1; financial award applicants required to submit FAFSA. *Unit head:* Daryl Moore, Dean, 973-720-2232, E-mail: moored@wpunj.edu. *Application contact:* Christina Aiello, Assistant Director, Graduate Admissions, 973-720-2506, Fax: 973-720-2035, E-mail: aielloc@wpunj.edu.
Website: http://www.wpunj.edu/coac

Winthrop University, College of Visual and Performing Arts, Department of Music, Rock Hill, SC 29733. Offers conducting (MM); music education (MME); performance (MM). *Accreditation:* NASM. Part-time programs available. *Degree requirements:* For master's, oral and written exams, recital (MM). *Entrance requirements:* For master's, GRE General Test, audition, minimum GPA of 3.0, 2 recitals. Electronic applications accepted.

Wright State University, School of Graduate Studies, College of Liberal Arts, Department of Music, Dayton, OH 45435. Offers music education (M Mus); performance (M Mus). *Accreditation:* NASM. Part-time programs available. *Degree requirements:* For master's, thesis or alternative, oral exam. *Entrance requirements:* For master's, theory placement test, BA in music. Additional exam requirements/recommendations for international students: Required—TOEFL. *Faculty research:* General music, current needs, role of teacher, expectations in music education.

Yale University, Graduate School of Arts and Sciences, Department of Music, New Haven, CT 06520. Offers music history (MA); music theory (MA). *Accreditation:* NASM. Terminal master's awarded for partial completion of doctoral program. *Degree requirements:* For master's, one foreign language; for doctorate, 3 foreign languages, thesis/dissertation. *Entrance requirements:* For doctorate, GRE General Test, GRE Subject Test.

Yale University, School of Music, New Haven, CT 06520. Offers MM, MMA, DMA, AD, Certificate. *Accreditation:* NASM. *Faculty:* 28 full-time (9 women), 30 part-time/adjunct (6 women). *Students:* 211 full-time (79 women); includes 30 minority (3 Black or African American, non-Hispanic/Latino; 16 Asian, non-Hispanic/Latino; 2 Hispanic/Latino; 9 Two or more races, non-Hispanic/Latino), 83 international. Average age 25. 1,479 applicants, 10% accepted, 109 enrolled. In 2014, 68 master's, 8 doctorates, 37 ADs awarded. *Degree requirements:* For master's, one foreign language, thesis (for some programs), recitals; for doctorate, one foreign language, thesis/dissertation, oral and written exam, recitals; for other advanced degree, one foreign language, recitals. *Entrance requirements:* For master's and other advanced degree, departmental exams, audition; for doctorate, entrance exam in music history, analysis, and musicianship, audition. Additional exam requirements/recommendations for international students: Required—TOEFL (minimum score 567 paper-based; 86 iBT). *Application deadline:* For fall admission, 12/1 for domestic and international students. Application fee: $125. Electronic applications accepted. *Expenses:* Expenses: Contact institution. *Financial support:* In 2014–15, 211 students received support, including 211 fellowships (averaging $33,300 per year); Federal Work-Study and scholarships/grants also available. Financial award application deadline: 5/30; financial award applicants required to submit FAFSA. *Faculty research:* Performance, composition, conducting, music history and theory. *Unit head:* Robert Blocker, Dean, 203-432-4160, Fax: 203-432-7542. *Application contact:* Suzanne M. Stringer, Director of Students Services, 203-432-1962, Fax: 203-432-7448, E-mail: suzanne.stringer@yale.edu.
Website: http://music.yale.edu/

York University, Faculty of Graduate Studies, Faculty of Fine Arts, Program in Music, Toronto, ON M3J 1P3, Canada. Offers composition (MA); music (PhD); musicology and ethnomusicology (MA). Part-time programs available. *Degree requirements:* For master's, one foreign language, thesis optional; for doctorate, 2 foreign languages, comprehensive exam, thesis/dissertation. *Entrance requirements:* For master's, portfolio. Electronic applications accepted.

Youngstown State University, Graduate School, College of Fine and Performing Arts, Dana School of Music, Youngstown, OH 44555-0001. Offers jazz studies (MM); music education (MM); music history and literature (MM); music theory and composition (MM); performance (MM). *Accreditation:* NASM. Part-time and evening/weekend programs available. *Degree requirements:* For master's, one foreign language, thesis optional, final qualifying exam. *Entrance requirements:* For master's, audition; GRE General Test or minimum GPA of 2.7. Additional exam requirements/recommendations for international students: Required—TOEFL. *Faculty research:* Teaching education, use of computers, conducting.

Theater

Academy of Art University, Graduate Program, School of Acting, San Francisco, CA 94105-3410. Offers MFA. Part-time programs available. *Faculty:* 1 (woman) full-time, 11 part-time/adjunct (7 women). *Students:* 26 full-time (15 women), 1 part-time (0 women); includes 12 minority (2 Black or African American, non-Hispanic/Latino; 2 Asian, non-Hispanic/Latino; 6 Hispanic/Latino; 2 Two or more races, non-Hispanic/Latino), 6 international. Average age 28. 30 applicants, 100% accepted, 6 enrolled. *Degree requirements:* For master's, final review. *Entrance requirements:* For master's, statement of intent; resume; portfolio/reel; official college transcripts. *Application deadline:* Applications are processed on a rolling basis. Application fee: $100. Electronic applications accepted. *Expenses: Tuition:* Part-time $910 per unit. *Financial support:* Career-related internships or fieldwork and Federal Work-Study available. Support available to part-time students. Financial award application deadline: 8/10; financial award applicants required to submit FAFSA. *Unit head:* 800-544-ARTS, E-mail: info@academyart.edu. *Application contact:* 800-544-ARTS, E-mail: info@academyart.edu.
Website: http://www.academyart.edu/acting-school/index.html

American Conservatory Theater, Program in Acting, San Francisco, CA 94108-5800. Offers MFA, Certificate. *Degree requirements:* For master's, thesis (for some programs), stage performance. *Entrance requirements:* For master's, audition, interview, bachelor's degree from an accredited institution, 2 confidential letters of recommendation.

Arcadia University, Graduate Studies, School of Education, Glenside, PA 19038-3295. Offers art education (M Ed); computer education (CAS); curriculum (CAS); curriculum studies (M Ed); early childhood education (M Ed, CAS), including individualized (M Ed), master teacher (M Ed), research in child development (M Ed); educational leadership (M Ed, Ed D, CAS); elementary education (M Ed, CAS); English education (MA Ed); environmental education (MA Ed, CAS); history education (MA Ed); instructional technology (M Ed); language arts (M Ed, CAS); library science (M Ed); mathematics education (M Ed, MA Ed, CAS); music education (MA Ed); psychology (MA Ed); reading (M Ed, CAS); science education (M Ed, CAS); secondary education (M Ed, CAS); special education (M Ed, Ed D, CAS); theater arts (MA Ed); written communication (MA Ed). *Accreditation:* NASAD. Part-time and evening/weekend programs available. Postbaccalaureate distance learning degree programs offered (minimal on-campus study). Electronic applications accepted. *Expenses:* Contact institution.

Arizona State University at the Tempe campus, Herberger Institute for Design and the Arts, School of Film, Dance and Theatre, Tempe, AZ 85287-2002. Offers dance (MFA), including dance, interdisciplinary digital media and performance; theatre (MA, MFA, PhD), including arts entrepreneurship and management (MFA), directing (MFA), dramatic writing (MFA), interdisciplinary digital media and performance (MFA), performance (MFA), performance design (MFA), theatre (MFA), theatre and performance of the Americas (PhD), theatre for youth (MFA, PhD). Terminal master's awarded for partial completion of doctoral program. *Degree requirements:* For master's, comprehensive exam (for some programs), thesis (for some programs), applied project (for some programs); interactive Program of Study (iPOS) submitted before completing 50 percent of required credit hours; for doctorate, comprehensive exam, thesis/dissertation, interactive Program of Study (iPOS) submitted before completing 50 percent of required credit hours. *Entrance requirements:* For master's, GRE or MAT, minimum GPA of 3.0 in last 2 years of work leading to bachelor's degree (depending on program); for doctorate, GRE, minimum GPA of 3.0 or equivalent in last 2 years of work leading to bachelor's degree, 3 letters of recommendation, resume, scholarly writing sample, statement of purpose. Additional exam requirements/recommendations for international students: Required—TOEFL, IELTS, or PTE. Electronic applications accepted.

Averett University, Master in Education Program, Danville, VA 24541-3692. Offers administration and supervision (M Ed); art (M Ed); biology (M Ed); chemistry (M Ed); curriculum and instruction (M Ed); early childhood (M Ed); English (M Ed); English/theatre (M Ed); health/physical education (M Ed); history (M Ed); history/social science (M Ed); liberal studies (M Ed); mathematics (M Ed); middle grades (M Ed); physical science (M Ed); reading specialist (M Ed); special education (M Ed); special education learning disability (M Ed); theatre (M Ed). Program offered on Danville Campus only. Part-time and evening/weekend programs available. Postbaccalaureate distance

learning degree programs offered (no on-campus study). *Faculty:* 7 full-time (4 women), 4 part-time/adjunct (2 women). *Students:* 25 full-time (20 women), 21 part-time (20 women); includes 10 minority (3 Black or African American, non-Hispanic/Latino; 6 American Indian or Alaska Native, non-Hispanic/Latino; 1 Hispanic/Latino). Average age 37. In 2014, 50 master's awarded. *Degree requirements:* For master's, 30-credit core curriculum, minimum GPA of 3.0 throughout program, completion of degree requirements within six years from start of program. *Entrance requirements:* For master's, PRAXIS I, GRE, or MAT; writing proficiency test, minimum cumulative GPA of 3.0 over the last 60 hours of undergraduate study toward a baccalaureate degree, three letters of recommendation, Virginia teaching license (or eligibility). Additional exam requirements/recommendations for international students: Required—TOEFL (minimum score 600 paper-based; 100 iBT). *Application deadline:* Applications are processed on a rolling basis. Application fee: $100. Electronic applications accepted. *Expenses:* Expenses: Contact institution. *Financial support:* Career-related internships or fieldwork and scholarships/grants available. Financial award application deadline: 4/1; financial award applicants required to submit FAFSA. *Unit head:* Dr. Sue Davis, Acting Education Chair, 434-791-5741, E-mail: suedavis@averett.edu. *Application contact:* Christy Pack, Associate Vice President for Client Relations, 804-887-8612, E-mail: dpack@averett.edu.
Website: http://gps.averett.edu/programs/master-degrees/

Baylor University, Graduate School, College of Arts and Sciences, Department of Theatre Arts, Waco, TX 76798. Offers directing (MFA); theatre (MA). *Accreditation:* NAST. Part-time programs available. *Degree requirements:* For master's, thesis. *Entrance requirements:* For master's, GRE General Test. Electronic applications accepted. *Faculty research:* Military and theatre, Avant-garde Japanese theatre, Horton Foote, Post-War Japan, Modernism in theatre.

Binghamton University, State University of New York, Graduate School, School of Arts and Sciences, Department of Theater, Vestal, NY 13850. Offers MA. *Faculty:* 7 full-time (4 women), 15 part-time/adjunct (8 women). *Students:* 4 full-time (all women); includes 1 minority (Asian, non-Hispanic/Latino), 2 international. Average age 32. 7 applicants, 71% accepted, 2 enrolled. In 2014, 5 master's awarded. *Degree requirements:* For master's, thesis. *Entrance requirements:* For master's, GRE General Test. Additional exam requirements/recommendations for international students: Required—TOEFL (minimum score 550 paper-based; 80 iBT). *Application deadline:* For fall admission, 8/1 priority date for domestic and international students; for spring admission, 12/15 priority date for domestic and international students. Applications are processed on a rolling basis. Application fee: $75. Electronic applications accepted. *Expenses:* Tuition, state resident: full-time $7776; part-time $432 per credit. Tuition, nonresident: full-time $15,138; part-time $841 per credit. *Required fees:* $1754; $213 per credit. Tuition and fees vary according to degree level and program. *Financial support:* In 2014–15, 2 students received support. Career-related internships or fieldwork, Federal Work-Study, institutionally sponsored loans, scholarships/grants, health care benefits, and unspecified assistantships available. Financial award application deadline: 2/15; financial award applicants required to submit FAFSA. *Unit head:* Dr. Barbara Wolfe, Chairperson, 607-777-2360, E-mail: bwolfe@binghamton.edu. *Application contact:* Kishan Zuber, Recruiting and Admissions Coordinator, 607-777-2151, Fax: 607-777-2501, E-mail: kzuber@binghamton.edu.
Website: http://www2.binghamton.edu/theatre/

Bob Jones University, Graduate Programs, Greenville, SC 29614. Offers accountancy (MS); Bible (MA); Bible translation (MA); Biblical studies (Certificate); broadcast management (MS); business administration (MBA); church history (MA, PhD); church ministries (MA); church music (MM); cinema and video production (MA); counseling (MS); curriculum and instruction (Ed D); divinity (M Div); dramatic production (MA); educational leadership (MS, Ed D, Ed S); elementary education (M Ed, MAT); English (M Ed, MA, MAT); fine arts (MA); graphic design (MA); history (M Ed, MA); illustration (MA); interpretative speech (MA); mathematics (M Ed, MAT); medical missions (Certificate); ministry (MM, D Min); multi-categorical special education (M Ed, MAT); music (M Ed); New Testament interpretation (PhD); Old Testament interpretation (PhD); orchestral instrument performance (MM); organ performance (MM); pastoral studies (MA); personnel services (MS, Ed S); piano pedagogy (MM); piano performance (MM); platform arts (MA); radio and television broadcasting (MS); rhetoric and public address (MA); secondary education (M Ed); studio art (MA); teaching Bible (MA); theology (MA, PhD); voice performance (MM); youth ministries (MA); M Div/MM.

The Boston Conservatory, Graduate Division, Theater Division, Boston, MA 02215. Offers MM. Part-time programs available. *Degree requirements:* For master's, performances. *Entrance requirements:* For master's, audition. Additional exam requirements/recommendations for international students: Required—TOEFL (minimum score 580 paper-based). Electronic applications accepted.

Boston University, College of Fine Arts, School of Theatre, Boston, MA 02215. Offers design (MFA); lighting crafts (Certificate); management (MFA); production (MFA); scenic painting (Certificate). *Faculty:* 16 full-time, 9 part-time/adjunct. *Students:* 47 full-time (32 women), 1 (woman) part-time; includes 5 minority (1 Black or African American, non-Hispanic/Latino; 1 Asian, non-Hispanic/Latino; 2 Hispanic/Latino; 1 Two or more races, non-Hispanic/Latino), 3 international. Average age 28. 142 applicants, 15% accepted, 16 enrolled. In 2014, 27 master's awarded. *Entrance requirements:* For master's, interview, portfolio. Additional exam requirements/recommendations for international students: Required—TOEFL. *Application deadline:* For fall admission, 2/3 priority date for domestic and international students. Application fee: $80. *Expenses: Tuition:* Full-time $45,686; part-time $1428 per credit hour. *Required fees:* $660; $60 per semester. Tuition and fees vary according to program. *Financial support:* Fellowships and teaching assistantships available. Financial award application deadline: 2/3. *Unit head:* Jim Petosa, Director, 617-353-3390. *Application contact:* Mark Krone, Manager, Graduate Admissions and Online Marketing, 617-353-3350, E-mail: arts@bu.edu.

Bowling Green State University, Graduate College, College of Arts and Sciences, Department of Theatre and Film, Bowling Green, OH 43403. Offers MA, PhD. *Accreditation:* NAST. Part-time programs available. Terminal master's awarded for partial completion of doctoral program. *Degree requirements:* For master's, thesis or alternative; for doctorate, comprehensive exam, thesis/dissertation, 9 hour research tool. *Entrance requirements:* For master's and doctorate, GRE General Test. Additional exam requirements/recommendations for international students: Required—TOEFL. Electronic applications accepted. *Faculty research:* Theatre history, dramatic theory, cultural studies, performance studies, American theatre history.

Brandeis University, Graduate School of Arts and Sciences, Department of Theater Arts, Waltham, MA 02454-9110. Offers acting (MFA). *Entrance requirements:* For master's, curriculum vitae or resume, 2 letters of recommendation, interview, audition, head shot, artistic resume, transcript(s), statement of purpose. Additional exam requirements/recommendations for international students: Required—TOEFL (minimum score 600 paper-based; 100 iBT), PTE (minimum score 68); Recommended—IELTS (minimum score 7). Electronic applications accepted.

Brigham Young University, Graduate Studies, College of Fine Arts and Communications, Department of Theatre and Media Arts, Provo, UT 84602-6404. Offers MA. Program accepts applications in odd-numbered years only. *Accreditation:* NAST. Evening/weekend programs available. *Faculty:* 18 full-time (6 women). *Students:* 8 full-time (5 women). Average age 29. In 2014, 2 master's awarded. *Degree requirements:* For master's, comprehensive exam, thesis, 32 hours, oral defense. *Entrance requirements:* For master's, GRE, two samples of scholarly writing, letter of intent, three letters of recommendation. Additional exam requirements/recommendations for international students: Required—TOEFL (minimum score 580 paper-based; 85 iBT). *Application deadline:* For fall admission, 4/1 priority date for domestic and international students. Application fee: $50. Electronic applications accepted. *Expenses: Tuition:* Full-time $6310; part-time $371 per credit hour. Tuition and fees vary according to program and student's religious affiliation. *Financial support:* In 2014–15, 8 students received support. Career-related internships or fieldwork, institutionally sponsored loans, scholarships/grants, tuition waivers (partial), and unspecified assistantships available. Support available to part-time students. *Unit head:* Dr. Megan Sanborn, Graduate Coordinator, 801-422-1321, E-mail: msjones@byu.edu. *Application contact:* Lindsi Michelle Neilson, Graduate Secretary, 801-422-3750, E-mail: lindsi_neilson@byu.edu.
Website: http://cfac.byu.edu/departments/tma

Brooklyn College of the City University of New York, School of Visual, Media and Performing Arts, Department of Theater, Brooklyn, NY 11210-2889. Offers acting (MFA); design and technical theater (MFA); directing (MFA); performing arts management (MFA); theater history and criticism (MA). Part-time programs available. *Degree requirements:* For master's, thesis, professional residency. *Entrance requirements:* For master's, audition or interview, 18 credits in theater, 2 letters of recommendation, essay. Additional exam requirements/recommendations for international students: Required—TOEFL. Electronic applications accepted. *Faculty research:* Multiculturalism and the arts, art education, arts collaboration.

Brown University, Graduate School, Department of Theatre Arts and Performance Studies, Providence, RI 02912. Offers acting and directing (MFA); playwriting (MFA); theatre and performance studies (PhD). *Degree requirements:* For master's, thesis or alternative. *Entrance requirements:* For master's, GRE General Test.

California Institute of the Arts, School of Theatre, Valencia, CA 91355-2340. Offers acting (MFA, Adv C); design and technology (Adv C); directing (MFA); performing arts design and technology (MFA); theater management (MFA, Adv C); writing for performance (MFA). *Degree requirements:* For master's, thesis (for some programs), faculty review, performance or portfolio. *Entrance requirements:* For master's, audition or portfolio, interview. Additional exam requirements/recommendations for international students: Required—TOEFL. Electronic applications accepted.

California State University, Fullerton, Graduate Studies, College of the Arts, Department of Theatre and Dance, Fullerton, CA 92834-9480. Offers theatre arts (MFA), including acting, design and technical production, directing. *Accreditation:* NAST. Part-time programs available. *Students:* 12 full-time (7 women), 7 part-time (3 women); includes 5 minority (1 Black or African American, non-Hispanic/Latino; 1 American Indian or Alaska Native, non-Hispanic/Latino; 2 Hispanic/Latino; 1 Two or more races, non-Hispanic/Latino), 1 international. Average age 30. 36 applicants, 31% accepted, 10 enrolled. In 2014, 7 master's awarded. *Degree requirements:* For master's, oral and written exam, project or thesis. *Entrance requirements:* For master's, major in theatre or related field, audition or interview, minimum GPA of 2.5 in last 60 units of course work. Application fee: $55. *Financial support:* Career-related internships or fieldwork, Federal Work-Study, institutionally sponsored loans, and scholarships/grants available. Support available to part-time students. Financial award application deadline: 3/1; financial award applicants required to submit FAFSA. *Unit head:* Dr. Bruce Goodrich, Chair, 657-278-3649. *Application contact:* Admissions/Applications, 657-278-2371.

California State University, Long Beach, Graduate Studies, College of the Arts, Department of Theatre Arts, Long Beach, CA 90840. Offers acting (MFA); design (MFA); theatre management (MFA); MBA/MFA. *Accreditation:* NAST. Part-time programs available. *Degree requirements:* For master's, thesis or alternative. Electronic applications accepted.

California State University, Los Angeles, Graduate Studies, College of Arts and Letters, Department of Theatre Arts and Dance, Los Angeles, CA 90032-8530. Offers theater arts (MA). Part-time and evening/weekend programs available. *Degree requirements:* For master's, comprehensive exam, project or thesis. *Entrance requirements:* For master's, minimum GPA of 2.5, 30 units of course work in theater. Additional exam requirements/recommendations for international students: Required—TOEFL (minimum score 500 paper-based). Electronic applications accepted. *Expenses:* Tuition, state resident: full-time $6738; part-time $3609 per year. Tuition, nonresident: full-time $15,666; part-time $8073 per year. Tuition and fees vary according to course load, degree level and program. *Faculty research:* Sondheim, Taiwanese theater, Australian theater, absurdism, dramaturgy.

California State University, Northridge, Graduate Studies, College of Arts, Media, and Communication, Department of Theatre, Northridge, CA 91330. Offers MA. *Accreditation:* NAST. *Students:* 3 full-time (all women), 8 part-time (all women); includes 1 minority (Hispanic/Latino), 1 international. Average age 36. *Degree requirements:* For master's, thesis. *Entrance requirements:* For master's, GRE General Test or minimum GPA of 3.0. Additional exam requirements/recommendations for international students: Required—TOEFL. *Application deadline:* For fall admission, 11/30 for domestic students. Application fee: $55. *Expenses: Required fees:* $12,402. *Financial support:* Application deadline: 3/1. *Unit head:* Garry Lennon, Chair, 818-677-3086.
Website: http://www.csun.edu/theatre/

California State University, San Bernardino, Graduate Studies, College of Arts and Letters, Department of Theatre Arts, San Bernardino, CA 92407-2397. Offers MA. *Degree requirements:* For master's, thesis. *Entrance requirements:* Additional exam requirements/recommendations for international students: Required—TOEFL. *Application deadline:* For fall admission, 7/17 for domestic students. Application fee: $55. *Expenses:* Tuition, state resident: full-time $6738; part-time $1302 per term. Tuition, nonresident: full-time $17,898; part-time $248 per unit. *Required fees:* $365 per quarter. Tuition and fees vary according to degree level and program. *Unit head:* Terry D. Smith, Chair, 909-537-5797, E-mail: tdsmith@csusb.edu. *Application contact:* Dr. Jeffrey Thompson, Dean of Graduate Studies, 909-537-5058, E-mail: jthompso@csusb.edu.

Carnegie Mellon University, College of Fine Arts, School of Drama, Pittsburgh, PA 15213-3891. Offers design (MFA); directing (MFA); dramatic writing (MFA); production technology and management (MFA); video and media design (MFA). *Degree requirements:* For master's, thesis (for some programs). *Entrance requirements:* For master's, audition, portfolio review, interview. Additional exam requirements/recommendations for international students: Required—TOEFL. *Faculty research:* Developing voice and speech compact disc.

Case Western Reserve University, School of Graduate Studies, Department of Theater, Cleveland, OH 44106. Offers acting (MFA); theater (MFA). *Faculty:* 7 full-time (3 women), 2 part-time/adjunct (0 women). *Students:* 8 full-time (3 women). Average age 25. In 2014, 7 master's awarded. *Degree requirements:* For master's, comprehensive exam, thesis, oral presentation and defense, portfolio, thesis concert production and presentation (for MFA). *Entrance requirements:* For master's, audition, interview, letter of intent, three recommendations, headshots, resume. Additional exam

requirements/recommendations for international students: Required—TOEFL (minimum score 577 paper-based; 90 iBT); Recommended—IELTS (minimum score 7). *Application deadline:* For fall admission, 10/15 priority date for domestic students. Applications are processed on a rolling basis. Electronic applications accepted. *Financial support:* Fellowships, scholarships/grants, tuition waivers (full and partial), and stipends available. Financial award application deadline: 1/15. *Faculty research:* Playwriting; history of theater; participation in professional area theaters in performing, design, acting, coaching; choreography, performance and pedagogy, dance wellness medicine and science. *Unit head:* Ron Wilson, Chairman, 216-368-6142, Fax: 216-368-5184, E-mail: ron.wilson@case.edu. *Application contact:* Scarlett Grala, Administrative Assistant, 216-368-4868, Fax: 216-368-5184, E-mail: ksg@po.cwru.edu. Website: http://theater.case.edu

The Catholic University of America, School of Arts and Sciences, Department of Drama, Washington, DC 20064. Offers acting, directing, and playwriting (MFA); theatre education (MA); theatre history and criticism (MA). Part-time programs available. *Faculty:* 8 full-time (4 women), 5 part-time/adjunct (1 woman). *Students:* 4 full-time (2 women), 25 part-time (19 women); includes 8 minority (6 Black or African American, non-Hispanic/Latino; 1 Hispanic/Latino; 1 Two or more races, non-Hispanic/Latino). Average age 31. 15 applicants, 60% accepted, 5 enrolled. In 2014, 4 master's awarded. *Degree requirements:* For master's, variable foreign language requirement, comprehensive exam, thesis or alternative. *Entrance requirements:* For master's, GRE General Test, statement of purpose, official copies of academic transcripts, three letters of recommendation. Additional exam requirements/recommendations for international students: Required—TOEFL (minimum score 580 paper-based). *Application deadline:* For fall admission, 7/15 priority date for domestic students, 7/1 for international students; for spring admission, 11/15 priority date for domestic students, 11/1 for international students. Applications are processed on a rolling basis. Application fee: $55. Electronic applications accepted. *Expenses: Tuition:* Full-time $40,200; part-time $1600 per credit hour. *Required fees:* $400; $195 per semester. One-time fee: $425. *Financial support:* Fellowships, research assistantships, teaching assistantships, Federal Work-Study, scholarships/grants, tuition waivers (full and partial), and unspecified assistantships available. Financial award application deadline: 2/1; financial award applicants required to submit FAFSA. *Faculty research:* Acting, directing, playwriting, costume design, Shakespearean stage history. *Unit head:* Dr. Patrick Tuite, Chair, 202-319-5351, Fax: 202-319-5359, E-mail: tuite@cua.edu. *Application contact:* Director of Graduate Admissions, 202-319-5057, Fax: 202-319-6533, E-mail: cua-admissions@cua.edu. Website: http://drama.cua.edu/

Central Washington University, Graduate Studies and Research, College of Arts and Humanities, Department of Theatre Arts, Ellensburg, WA 98926. Offers theatre production (MA); theatre studies (MA). Part-time programs available. *Degree requirements:* For master's, thesis or alternative. *Entrance requirements:* For master's, minimum GPA of 3.0. Additional exam requirements/recommendations for international students: Required—TOEFL (minimum score 550 paper-based; 79 iBT). Electronic applications accepted.

Columbia University, Graduate School of Arts and Sciences, New York, NY 10027. Offers African-American studies (MA); American studies (MA); anthropology (MA, PhD); art history and archaeology (MA, PhD); astronomy (PhD); biological sciences (PhD); biotechnology (MA); chemical physics (PhD); chemistry (PhD); classical studies (MA, PhD); classics (MA, PhD); climate and society (MA); earth and environmental sciences (PhD); East Asia: regional studies (MA); East Asian languages and cultures (MA, PhD); ecology, evolution and environmental biology (MA), including conservation biology; ecology, evolution, and environmental biology (PhD), including ecology and evolutionary biology, evolutionary primatology; economics (PhD); English and comparative literature (MA, PhD); French and Romance philology (MA, PhD); Germanic languages (MA, PhD);

global French studies (MA); Hispanic cultural studies (MA); history (PhD); history and literature (MA); human rights studies (MA); Islamic studies (MA); Italian (MA, PhD); Japanese pedagogy (MA); Jewish studies (MA); Latin America and the Caribbean: regional studies (MA); Latin American and Iberian cultures (PhD); mathematics (MA, PhD), including finance (MA); medieval and Renaissance studies (MA); Middle Eastern, South Asian, and African studies (MA, PhD); modern art: critical and curatorial studies (MA); modern European studies (MA); museum anthropology (MA); music (DMA, PhD); oral history (MA); philosophical foundations of physics (MA); philosophy (MA, PhD); physics (PhD); political science (MA, PhD); psychology (PhD); quantitative methods in the social sciences (MA); religion (MA, PhD); Russia, Eurasia and East Europe: regional studies (MA); Russian translation (MA); Slavic cultures (MA); Slavic languages (MA, PhD); sociology (MA, PhD); South Asian studies (MA); statistics (MA, PhD); theatre (PhD); JD/PhD; MA/MS; MD/PhD; MPA/MA. Dual-degree programs require admission to both Graduate School of Arts and Sciences and another Columbia school. Part-time and evening/weekend programs available. Terminal master's awarded for partial completion of doctoral program. *Degree requirements:* For master's, thesis (for some programs); for doctorate, comprehensive exam, thesis/dissertation. *Entrance requirements:* For master's and doctorate, GRE General Test, GRE Subject Test (for some programs). Electronic applications accepted. *Faculty research:* Humanities, natural sciences, social sciences.

Columbia University, School of the Arts, Theatre Arts Program, New York, NY 10027. Offers acting (MFA); directing (MFA); dramaturgy (MFA); playwriting (MFA); stage management (MFA); theater management (MFA); JD/MFA. *Degree requirements:* For master's, thesis, 2 internships. *Entrance requirements:* For master's, 3 letters of recommendation, resume. Additional exam requirements/recommendations for international students: Required—TOEFL (minimum score 600 paper-based; 100 iBT). Electronic applications accepted.

See Display below and Close-Up on page 273.

Columbus State University, Graduate Studies, College of the Arts, Department of Theatre, Columbus, GA 31907-5645. Offers theatre education (M Ed, MAT). *Faculty:* 1 full-time (0 women). *Students:* 4 part-time (2 women). Average age 40. In 2014, 2 master's awarded. *Entrance requirements:* For master's, audition, letters of recommendation. Additional exam requirements/recommendations for international students: Required—TOEFL (minimum score 550 paper-based; 79 iBT). *Application deadline:* For fall admission, 6/1 for domestic and international students; for spring admission, 11/1 for domestic and international students; for summer admission, 3/1 for domestic and international students. Application fee: $50. *Financial support:* Research assistantships and scholarships/grants available. *Unit head:* Dr. Larry Dooley, Department Chair, 706-507-8402, E-mail: dooley_larry@columbusstate.edu. *Application contact:* Kristin Williams, Director of International and Graduate Recruitment, 706-507-8848, Fax: 706-568-5091, E-mail: thornton_katie@colstate.edu. Website: http://theatre.columbusstate.edu/

Cornell University, Graduate School, Graduate Fields of Arts and Sciences, Field of Theatre Arts, Ithaca, NY 14853-0001. Offers drama and the theatre (PhD); theatre history (PhD); theatre theory and aesthetics (PhD). *Degree requirements:* For doctorate, 2 foreign languages, comprehensive exam, thesis/dissertation. *Entrance requirements:* For doctorate, GRE General Test, sample of written work, 3 letters of recommendation. Additional exam requirements/recommendations for international students: Required—TOEFL (minimum score 600 paper-based; 77 iBT). Electronic applications accepted. *Faculty research:* Cultural studies and critical theory, seventeenth to twenty-first century European and American theater, theory of the performing arts, film history and theory, feminism and theater.

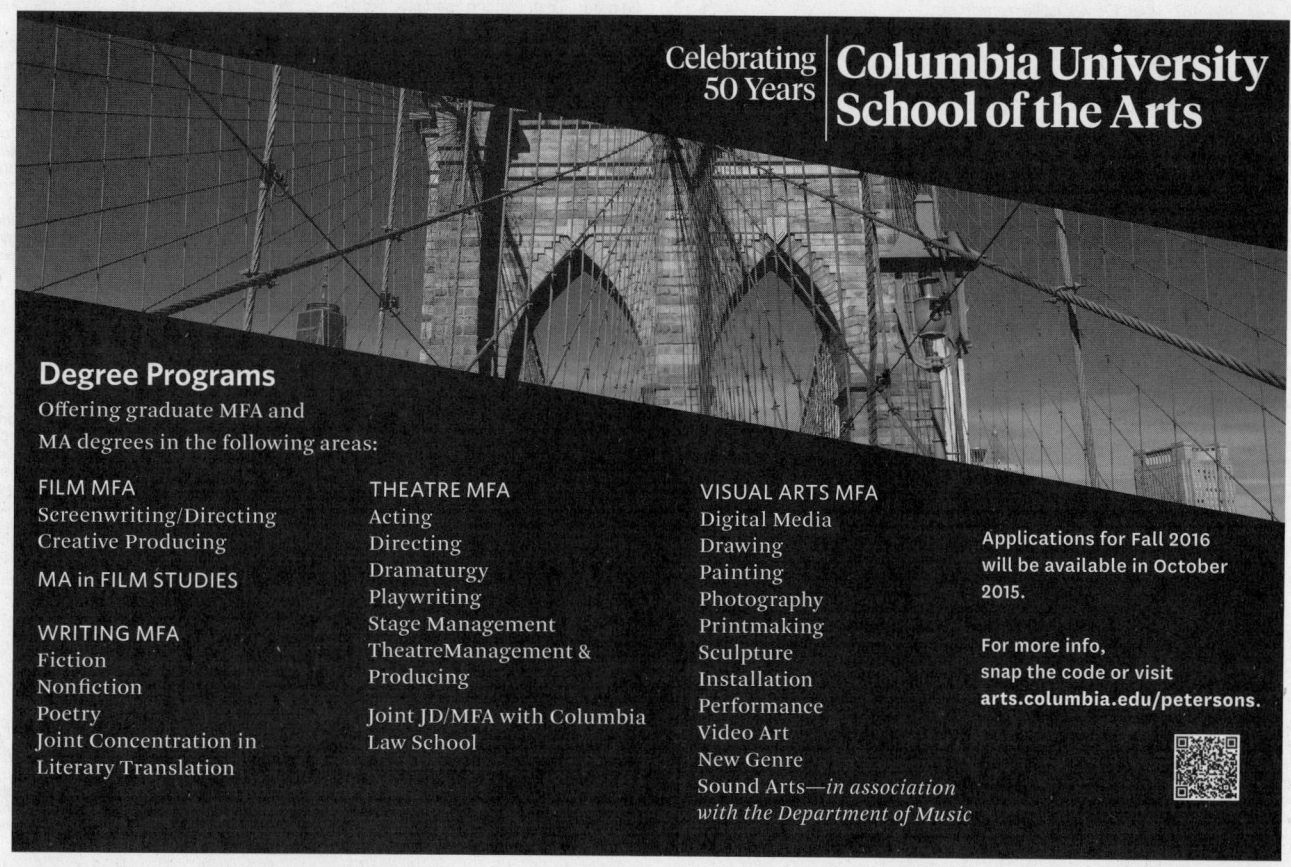

Theater

Dell'Arte International School of Physical Theatre, MFA Program, Blue Lake, CA 95525. Offers ensemble based physical theatre (MFA). *Accreditation:* NAST. *Degree requirements:* For master's, thesis. *Entrance requirements:* For master's, undergraduate degree, audition. Electronic applications accepted. *Faculty research:* Physical theatre, international theatre, ensemble, devised.

DePaul University, The Theatre School, Chicago, IL 60614. Offers acting (MFA); arts leadership (MFA); directing (MFA). *Degree requirements:* For master's, comprehensive exam, thesis. *Entrance requirements:* For master's, audition or interview, official transcripts, three letters of recommendation, resume, written statements (for directing program). Additional exam requirements/recommendations for international students: Required—TOEFL (minimum score 550 paper-based; 80 iBT), IELTS (minimum score 6.5). Electronic applications accepted. *Expenses:* Contact institution.

Drew University, Caspersen School of Graduate Studies, Program in Education, Madison, NJ 07940-1493. Offers biology (MAT); chemistry (MAT); English (MAT); French (MAT); Italian (MAT); math (MAT); physics (MAT); social studies (MAT); Spanish (MAT); theatre arts (MAT). *Accreditation:* Teacher Education Accreditation Council. Part-time programs available. *Degree requirements:* For master's, student teaching internship and seminar. *Entrance requirements:* For master's, transcripts, statement of purpose, three letters of recommendation. Additional exam requirements/ recommendations for international students: Required—TOEFL. *Expenses:* Contact institution.

Eastern Michigan University, Graduate School, College of Arts and Sciences, Department of Communication, Media and Theatre Arts, Programs in Applied Drama/ Theatre for the Young, Ypsilanti, MI 48197. Offers MA, MFA. Part-time programs available. Postbaccalaureate distance learning degree programs offered (minimal on-campus study). *Students:* 2 full-time (both women), 4 part-time (all women); includes 1 minority (Black or African American, non-Hispanic/Latino), 2 international. Average age 37. 8 applicants, 38% accepted, 3 enrolled. In 2014, 6 master's awarded. *Degree requirements:* For master's, thesis optional. *Entrance requirements:* Additional exam requirements/recommendations for international students: Required—TOEFL. *Application deadline:* Applications are processed on a rolling basis. Application fee: $45. *Financial support:* Fellowships, research assistantships with full tuition reimbursements, teaching assistantships with full tuition reimbursements, career-related internships or fieldwork, Federal Work-Study, institutionally sponsored loans, scholarships/grants, tuition waivers (partial), and unspecified assistantships available. Support available to part-time students. Financial award applicants required to submit FAFSA. *Unit head:* Prof. Patricia Zimmer, Coordinator, 734-487-0031, Fax: 734-487-3443, E-mail: patricia.zimmer@emich.edu.

Eastern Michigan University, Graduate School, College of Arts and Sciences, Department of Communication, Media and Theatre Arts, Programs in Theatre Arts, Ypsilanti, MI 48197. Offers interpretation/performance studies (MA); theatre arts (MA). Part-time and evening/weekend programs available. Postbaccalaureate distance learning degree programs offered (minimal on-campus study). *Students:* 5 full-time (3 women), 15 part-time (8 women); includes 6 minority (5 Black or African American, non-Hispanic/Latino; 1 Hispanic/Latino), 1 international. Average age 35. 7 applicants, 86% accepted, 3 enrolled. In 2014, 6 master's awarded. *Degree requirements:* For master's, thesis or alternative. *Entrance requirements:* Additional exam requirements/ recommendations for international students: Required—TOEFL. *Application deadline:* Applications are processed on a rolling basis. Application fee: $45. *Financial support:* Fellowships, research assistantships with full tuition reimbursements, teaching assistantships with full tuition reimbursements, career-related internships or fieldwork, Federal Work-Study, institutionally sponsored loans, scholarships/grants, and unspecified assistantships available. Support available to part-time students. Financial award applicants required to submit FAFSA. *Unit head:* Dr. Lee Stille, Coordinator, 734-487-6846, Fax: 734-487-3443, E-mail: lstille@emich.edu.

Emerson College, Graduate Studies, School of the Arts, Department of Performing Arts, Program in Theatre Education, Boston, MA 02116-4624. Offers MA. Part-time programs available. *Faculty:* 27 full-time (14 women), 16 part-time/adjunct (7 women). *Students:* 67 full-time (56 women), 14 part-time (11 women); includes 6 minority (4 Black or African American, non-Hispanic/Latino; 2 Two or more races, non-Hispanic/Latino), 4 international. Average age 29. 104 applicants, 70% accepted, 37 enrolled. In 2014, 35 master's awarded. *Entrance requirements:* For master's, GRE General Test. Additional exam requirements/recommendations for international students: Required—TOEFL (minimum score 550 paper-based; 80 iBT), IELTS (minimum score 6.5). *Application deadline:* For fall admission, 2/15 priority date for domestic and international students. Applications are processed on a rolling basis. Application fee: $60 ($75 for international students). Electronic applications accepted. *Expenses: Tuition:* Part-time $1145 per credit. *Financial support:* In 2014–15, 12 students received support, including 12 fellowships with partial tuition reimbursements available (averaging $9,583 per year); research assistantships with partial tuition reimbursements available, Federal Work-Study, scholarships/grants, and unspecified assistantships also available. Financial award application deadline: 3/1; financial award applicants required to submit FAFSA. *Faculty research:* Theater. *Unit head:* Robert Colby, Graduate Program Director, 617-824-8780, E-mail: robert_colby@emerson.edu. *Application contact:* Leanda Ferland, Office of Graduate Admission, 617-824-8610, Fax: 617-824-8614, E-mail: gradapp@emerson.edu.
Website: http://www.emerson.edu/graduate_admission

Florida Atlantic University, Dorothy F. Schmidt College of Arts and Letters, Department of Theatre and Dance, Boca Raton, FL 33431-0991. Offers acting (MFA); design and technology (MFA). *Degree requirements:* For master's, thesis, production. *Entrance requirements:* For master's, GRE General Test, minimum GPA of 3.0 during last 60 hours of undergraduate course work. *Expenses:* Tuition, state resident: full-time $7396; part-time $369.82 per credit hour. Tuition, nonresident: full-time $19,392; part-time $1024.81 per credit hour. Tuition and fees vary according to course load. *Faculty research:* Contemporary British theatre, Eastern European playwrights, Latin American drama.

Florida State University, The Graduate School, College of Fine Arts, School of Theatre, Tallahassee, FL 32306. Offers acting (MFA); costume design (MFA); directing (MFA); technical production (MFA); theatre (MA, MS, PhD); theatre management (MFA). *Accreditation:* NAST. *Faculty:* 17 full-time (8 women). *Students:* 71 full-time (34 women), 2 part-time (0 women); includes 6 minority (1 Black or African American, non-Hispanic/ Latino; 5 Hispanic/Latino). Average age 25. 125 applicants, 24% accepted, 26 enrolled. In 2014, 23 master's, 2 doctorates awarded. *Degree requirements:* For master's, one foreign language, comprehensive exam (for some programs), thesis (for some programs); for doctorate, one foreign language, comprehensive exam, thesis/ dissertation. *Entrance requirements:* For master's, GRE General Test, writing sample (MA), interview and portfolio (MFA), minimum undergraduate GPA of 3.0, audition (MFA in acting). Additional exam requirements/recommendations for international students: Required—TOEFL. *Application deadline:* For fall admission, 2/15 priority date for domestic and international students. Applications are processed on a rolling basis. Application fee: $30. Electronic applications accepted. *Expenses:* Tuition, state resident: part-time $403.51 per credit hour. Tuition, nonresident: part-time $1004.85 per credit hour. *Required fees:* $75.81 per credit hour. One-time fee: $20 part-time. Tuition and fees vary according to campus/location. *Financial support:* In 2014–15, 1 fellowship with full tuition reimbursement (averaging $18,000 per year), 30 research assistantships with full tuition reimbursements (averaging $8,300 per year), 24 teaching assistantships with full tuition reimbursements (averaging $8,900 per year) were awarded; career-related internships or fieldwork, Federal Work-Study, institutionally sponsored loans, scholarships/grants, health care benefits, and unspecified assistantships also available. Financial award application deadline: 1/1; financial award applicants required to submit FAFSA. *Faculty research:* Gender theatre, performance theory, computers in theatre, dramaturgy, music theatre performance. *Unit head:* Cameron Jackson, Director, 850-644-7257, Fax: 850-644-7408, E-mail: ccjackson@admin.fsu.edu. *Application contact:* Barbara Thomas, Program Assistant, 850-644-7234, Fax: 850-644-7246, E-mail: bgthomas@admin.fsu.edu.
Website: http://theatre.fsu.edu/

Fontbonne University, Graduate Programs, Department of Fine Arts, St. Louis, MO 63105-3098. Offers art (MA); fine arts (MFA); theater education (MA). Part-time and evening/weekend programs available. *Degree requirements:* For master's, thesis exhibit (MFA). *Entrance requirements:* For master's, minimum GPA of 3.0, portfolio.

Fordham University, Graduate School of Arts and Sciences, Program in Playwriting, New York, NY 10023. Offers MFA. Program offered jointly with Primary Stages theater company. *Students:* 4 full-time (1 woman). 16 applicants, 19% accepted, 2 enrolled. *Entrance requirements:* For master's, 3 letters of recommendation, resume/curriculum vitae, statement of intent, official transcripts, playwriting portfolio, bachelor's degree. Additional exam requirements/recommendations for international students: Required—TOEFL. *Application deadline:* Applications are processed on a rolling basis. Application fee: $70. Electronic applications accepted. *Unit head:* Matthew Maguire, Director, E-mail: mmaguire@fordham.edu. *Application contact:* Bernadette Valentino-Morrison, Director of Graduate Admissions, 718-817-4419, Fax: 718-817-3566, E-mail: valentinomor@fordham.edu.
Website: http://www.fordham.edu/info/21309/playwriting_mfa/2561/ playwriting_mfa_application_information

The George Washington University, Columbian College of Arts and Sciences, Department of Theatre and Dance, Washington, DC 20052. Offers classical acting (MFA); dance (MFA); exhibit design (Graduate Certificate); production design (MFA). Part-time and evening/weekend programs available. *Faculty:* 12 full-time (7 women). *Students:* 26 full-time (16 women), 22 part-time (8 women); includes 9 minority (3 Black or African American, non-Hispanic/Latino; 1 Asian, non-Hispanic/Latino; 5 Hispanic/ Latino), 4 international. Average age 35. 78 applicants, 46% accepted, 24 enrolled. In 2014, 20 master's, 4 other advanced degrees awarded. *Degree requirements:* For master's, thesis. *Entrance requirements:* For master's, minimum GPA of 3.0, portfolio. Additional exam requirements/recommendations for international students: Required—TOEFL (minimum score 550 paper-based; 80 iBT). *Application deadline:* For fall admission, 8/1 priority date for domestic students; for spring admission, 10/1 priority date for domestic students. Applications are processed on a rolling basis. Application fee: $75. Electronic applications accepted. *Financial support:* In 2014–15, 2 students received support. Fellowships with tuition reimbursements available, teaching assistantships with tuition reimbursements available, career-related internships or fieldwork, Federal Work-Study, and tuition waivers available. *Unit head:* Dana Tai Soon Burgess, Chair, 202-994-1660, E-mail: dtsb@gwu.edu. *Application contact:* Information Contact, 202-994-8072, E-mail: trdanews@gwu.edu.
Website: http://www.gwu.edu/~theatre/

The Graduate Center, City University of New York, Graduate Studies, Program in Theatre, New York, NY 10016-4039. Offers PhD. *Degree requirements:* For doctorate, 2 foreign languages, thesis/dissertation. *Entrance requirements:* For doctorate, GRE General Test, writing sample. Additional exam requirements/recommendations for international students: Required—TOEFL. Electronic applications accepted.

Hollins University, Graduate Programs, Program in Playwriting, Roanoke, VA 24020. Offers new play direction (Certificate); new play performance (Certificate); playwriting (MFA). Part-time programs available. *Faculty:* 1 full-time (0 women), 5 part-time/adjunct (3 women). *Students:* 29 full-time (21 women), 1 part-time (0 women); includes 4 minority (3 Black or African American, non-Hispanic/Latino; 1 American Indian or Alaska Native, non-Hispanic/Latino). Average age 40. 19 applicants, 89% accepted, 12 enrolled. In 2014, 6 master's awarded. *Degree requirements:* For master's, comprehensive exam, thesis. *Entrance requirements:* For master's, letters of recommendation, writing samples. Additional exam requirements/recommendations for international students: Required—TOEFL (minimum score 550 paper-based; 79 iBT). *Application deadline:* For summer admission, 2/15 priority date for domestic students. Application fee: $40. *Expenses:* Expenses: $775 per credit hour, $85 technology fee. *Financial support:* In 2014–15, 20 students received support, including 20 fellowships (averaging $1,000 per year). Financial award application deadline: 2/15. *Unit head:* Todd Ristau, Director, 540-362-6386, E-mail: tristau@hollins.edu. *Application contact:* Cathy S. Koon, Manager of Graduate Services, 540-362-6326, Fax: 540-362-6288, E-mail: ckoon@hollins.edu.
Website: http://www.hollins.edu/grad/playwriting/index.html

Hunter College of the City University of New York, Graduate School, School of Arts and Sciences, Department of Theatre, New York, NY 10065-5085. Offers playwriting (MFA); theatre (MA). Part-time and evening/weekend programs available. *Faculty:* 3 full-time (all women), 1 part-time/adjunct (0 women). *Students:* 20 part-time (10 women); includes 3 minority (1 Black or African American, non-Hispanic/Latino; 2 Hispanic/ Latino), 3 international. Average age 36. 29 applicants, 31% accepted, 6 enrolled. In 2014, 19 master's awarded. *Degree requirements:* For master's, comprehensive exam, thesis. *Entrance requirements:* For master's, GRE General Test. Additional exam requirements/recommendations for international students: Required—TOEFL. *Application deadline:* For fall admission, 4/1 for domestic students, 2/1 for international students; for spring admission, 11/1 for domestic students, 9/1 for international students. *Financial support:* In 2014–15, 1 fellowship (averaging $3,000 per year), 4 teaching assistantships were awarded; research assistantships, career-related internships or fieldwork, Federal Work-Study, and tuition waivers (partial) also available. Support available to part-time students. Financial award application deadline: 4/15. *Faculty research:* Modern French mimes, acting techniques, directing, New York avant-garde theater and popular entertainment, playwriting. *Unit head:* Dr. Joel Bassin, Chairperson, 212-650-3338, E-mail: jbassin@hunter.cuny.edu. *Application contact:* Milena Solo, Graduate Admissions Director, 212-772-4780, E-mail: admissions@hunter.cuny.edu.
Website: http://www.hunter.cuny.edu/theatre/

Idaho State University, Office of Graduate Studies, College of Arts and Letters, Program in Theatre and Dance, Pocatello, ID 83209-8006. Offers theatre (MA). *Accreditation:* NAST. Part-time programs available. *Degree requirements:* For master's, comprehensive exam, thesis optional, oral and written exam. *Entrance requirements:* For master's, GRE General Test (35th percentile or above on one of the 3 sections). Additional exam requirements/recommendations for international students: Required—TOEFL (minimum score 550 paper-based; 80 iBT). Electronic applications accepted. *Faculty research:* Theatre history, technical theatre.

Illinois State University, Graduate School, College of Fine Arts, School of Theatre, Normal, IL 61790-2200. Offers MA, MFA, MS. *Accreditation:* NAST. Part-time programs available. *Degree requirements:* For master's, variable foreign language requirement, thesis or alternative. *Entrance requirements:* For master's, sample of written work, minimum GPA of 3.0 in last 60 hours of course work. *Faculty research:* Illinois Shakespeare festival.

Indiana University Bloomington, University Graduate School, College of Arts and Sciences, Department of Theatre, Drama, and Contemporary Dance, Bloomington, IN 47405-1101. Offers acting (MFA); design and technology (MFA); directing (MFA); playwriting (MFA); theatre history, theory and literature (MA); theatre history, theory, and literature (PhD). *Accreditation:* NAST. *Faculty:* 12 full-time (5 women), 2 part-time/ adjunct (1 woman). *Students:* 57 full-time (29 women); includes 3 minority (1 Black or African American, non-Hispanic/Latino; 2 Hispanic/Latino), 4 international. Average age 31. 58 applicants, 41% accepted, 22 enrolled. In 2014, 16 master's, 1 doctorate awarded. Terminal master's awarded for partial completion of doctoral program. *Degree requirements:* For master's, one foreign language, comprehensive exam, thesis, 30 credit hours; for doctorate, 2 foreign languages, comprehensive exam, thesis/ dissertation, 90 credit hours. *Entrance requirements:* For master's, audition, interview, portfolio or script analysis; for doctorate, GRE General Test. Additional exam requirements/recommendations for international students: Required—TOEFL (minimum score 550 paper-based; 80 iBT). *Application deadline:* For fall admission, 1/15 priority date for domestic students, 12/1 for international students. Application fee: $55 ($65 for international students). Electronic applications accepted. *Financial support:* In 2014–15, 57 students received support. Fellowships with tuition reimbursements available, research assistantships with tuition reimbursements available, teaching assistantships with tuition reimbursements available, career-related internships or fieldwork, institutionally sponsored loans, scholarships/grants, health care benefits, and unspecified assistantships available. Financial award application deadline: 3/1. *Faculty research:* American, western European, world literature; history and theory; theatrical production, design and technology; acting; directing; playwriting. *Unit head:* Jonathan R. Michaelsen, Chairperson and Professor, 812-855-4535, Fax: 812-856-0698, E-mail: theatre@indiana.edu. *Application contact:* Catherine Richards, Academic Secretary, 812-855-4503, Fax: 812-855-0698, E-mail: car@indiana.edu.
Website: http://www.indiana.edu/~thtr/

Kansas State University, Graduate School, College of Arts and Sciences, School of Music, Theatre and Dance, Manhattan, KS 66506. Offers MA, MM. *Accreditation:* NASM. Part-time programs available. Postbaccalaureate distance learning degree programs offered (minimal on-campus study). *Faculty:* 54 full-time (21 women), 6 part-time/adjunct (2 women). *Students:* 27 full-time (18 women), 42 part-time (26 women); includes 2 minority (1 Asian, non-Hispanic/Latino; 1 Hispanic/Latino), 4 international. Average age 30. 37 applicants, 57% accepted, 12 enrolled. In 2014, 31 master's awarded. *Degree requirements:* For master's, thesis optional. *Entrance requirements:* For master's, GRE, audition (in person or recording), interview (for music education). Additional exam requirements/recommendations for international students: Required— TOEFL (minimum score 600 paper-based). *Application deadline:* For fall admission, 2/1 priority date for domestic and international students; for spring admission, 8/1 priority date for domestic and international students. Applications are processed on a rolling basis. Application fee: $50 ($75 for international students). Electronic applications accepted. *Financial support:* In 2014–15, 16 teaching assistantships with full tuition reimbursements (averaging $8,419 per year) were awarded; fellowships, institutionally sponsored loans, scholarships/grants, and tuition waivers (full and partial) also available. Support available to part-time students. Financial award application deadline: 3/1; financial award applicants required to submit FAFSA. *Faculty research:* American music, opera, drama therapy, directing, costume and scenic design, music by women composers. *Total annual research expenditures:* $16,349. *Unit head:* Dr. Gary Mortenson, Head, 785-532-3802, Fax: 785-532-5740, E-mail: garym@ksu.edu. *Application contact:* Dr. Fred Burrack, Director of Graduate Music Programs, 785-532-3429, Fax: 785-532-5740, E-mail: fburrack@ksu.edu.
Website: http://www.k-state.edu/mtd/

Kent State University, College of the Arts, School of Theatre and Dance, Kent, OH 44242-0001. Offers acting (MFA); design and technology (MFA), including costume design, lighting design, scenic design, theatre technology. *Accreditation:* NAST. Part-time programs available. *Faculty:* 19 full-time (13 women). *Students:* 13 full-time (5 women); includes 2 minority (both Black or African American, non-Hispanic/Latino), 1 international. Average age 33. 10 applicants, 60% accepted, 6 enrolled. In 2014, 2 master's awarded. *Degree requirements:* For master's, thesis, practicum, culminating project. *Entrance requirements:* For master's, minimum GPA of 3.0, transcript, audition or portfolio, letters of recommendation. Additional exam requirements/recommendations for international students: Required—TOEFL (minimum score: paper-based 525, iBT 71), Michigan English Language Assessment Battery (minimum score of 75), IELTS (minimum score of 6.0), PTE Academic (minimum score of 48), or completion of ELS level 112 Intensive Program. *Application deadline:* For fall admission, 7/12 for domestic students; for spring admission, 11/29 for domestic students. Applications are processed on a rolling basis. Application fee: $45 ($70 for international students). Electronic applications accepted. *Expenses:* Tuition, state resident: full-time $8730; part-time $485 per credit hour. Tuition, nonresident: full-time $14,886; part-time $827 per credit hour. Tuition and fees vary according to campus/location and program. *Financial support:* In 2014–15, 15 students received support. Career-related internships or fieldwork, Federal Work-Study, and scholarships/grants available. Financial award application deadline: 2/1. *Unit head:* Eric Can Baars, Associate Professor and Acting Director, 330-672-0102, E-mail: fvanbaar@kent.edu. *Application contact:* Yuko Kurahashi, Associate Professor and Graduate Coordinator, 330-672-2082, E-mail: theatre@kent.edu.
Website: http://www.kent.edu/theatredance

Lindenwood University, Graduate Programs, School of Fine and Performing Arts, St. Charles, MO 63301-1695. Offers fashion design (MA, MFA); studio art (MA, MFA); theatre (MFA). Part-time programs available. *Faculty:* 9 full-time (4 women), 4 part-time/ adjunct (2 women). *Students:* 5 full-time (2 women), 6 part-time (4 women); includes 1 minority (Hispanic/Latino), 1 international. Average age 30. 16 applicants, 25% accepted, 4 enrolled. In 2014, 15 master's awarded. *Degree requirements:* For master's, thesis (for some programs), minimum cumulative GPA of 3.0. *Entrance requirements:* For master's, audition or interview, minimum GPA of 3.0, portfolio, letter of recommendation. Additional exam requirements/recommendations for international students: Required—TOEFL (minimum score 550 paper-based; 80 iBT). *Application deadline:* For fall admission, 8/24 priority date for domestic and international students; for spring admission, 1/24 priority date for domestic students, 1/25 priority date for international students. Applications are processed on a rolling basis. Application fee: $30 ($100 for international students). Electronic applications accepted. *Expenses:* Tuition: Full-time $15,230; part-time $440 per credit hour. *Required fees:* $205 per semester. Tuition and fees vary according to course level, course load and degree level. *Financial support:* In 2014–15, 1 student received support. Career-related internships or fieldwork, institutionally sponsored loans, scholarships/grants, tuition waivers (partial), and unspecified assistantships available. Financial award application deadline: 6/30; financial award applicants required to submit FAFSA. *Unit head:* Dr. Joseph Alsobrook, Dean of Fine and Performing Arts, 636-949-4164, Fax: 636-949-4910, E-mail: jalsobrook@lindenwood.edu. *Application contact:* Tyler Kostich, Dean of Evening Admissions and Extension Campuses, 636-949-4138, Fax: 636-949-4109, E-mail: adultadmissions@lindenwood.edu.

Louisiana State University and Agricultural & Mechanical College, Graduate School, College of Music and Dramatic Arts, Department of Theatre, Baton Rouge, LA 70803. Offers acting (MFA); directing (MFA); theatre (PhD); theatre design/technology (MFA). *Accreditation:* NAST. *Faculty:* 18 full-time (6 women). *Students:* 23 full-time (13 women), 2 part-time (0 women); includes 4 minority (3 Black or African American, non-Hispanic/Latino; 1 Hispanic/Latino). Average age 30. 7 applicants, 43% accepted, 3 enrolled. *Degree requirements:* For master's, thesis; for doctorate, one foreign language, thesis/dissertation. *Entrance requirements:* For master's, GRE General Test, audition, minimum GPA of 3.0; for doctorate, GRE General Test, minimum GPA of 3.0. Additional exam requirements/recommendations for international students: Required— TOEFL (minimum score 550 paper-based; 79 iBT), IELTS (minimum score 6.5), or PTE (minimum score 59). *Application deadline:* For fall admission, 1/1 priority date for domestic students, 5/15 for international students; for spring admission, 10/15 for domestic and international students; for summer admission, 5/15 for domestic and international students. Applications are processed on a rolling basis. Application fee: $50 ($70 for international students). Electronic applications accepted. *Financial support:* In 2014–15, 24 students received support, including 1 fellowship with full and partial tuition reimbursement available (averaging $33,995 per year), 18 teaching assistantships with full and partial tuition reimbursements available (averaging $12,778 per year); research assistantships with full and partial tuition reimbursements available, Federal Work-Study, scholarships/grants, health care benefits, tuition waivers (full and partial), and unspecified assistantships also available. Support available to part-time students. Financial award application deadline: 6/15; financial award applicants required to submit FAFSA. *Faculty research:* Acting, American drama, arts administration, theatre history, dramatic theory/literature, black drama. *Unit head:* Dr. John Fletcher, Interim Chair, 225-578-9274, Fax: 225-578-4135, E-mail: jfletch@lsu.edu. *Application contact:* Dr. Femi Euba, Professor, 225-578-3537, E-mail: theuba@lsu.edu.
Website: http://www.theatre.lsu.edu/

Mary Baldwin College, Graduate Studies, Program in Shakespeare and Renaissance Literature in Performance, Staunton, VA 24401-3610. Offers acting (M Litt); directing (M Litt); Shakespeare and Renaissance literature in performance (MFA); teaching (M Litt). *Entrance requirements:* For master's, GRE (M Litt).

Miami University, College of Creative Arts, Department of Theatre, Oxford, OH 45056. Offers MA. *Accreditation:* NAST. *Students:* 8. In 2014, 2 master's awarded. *Entrance requirements:* For master's, writing sample; examples of artistic work (recommended); statement of purpose; letters of recommendation. Additional exam requirements/ recommendations for international students: Recommended—TOEFL (minimum score 80 iBT), IELTS (minimum score 6.5), TSE (minimum score 54). *Application deadline:* For fall admission, 2/1 priority date for domestic and international students. Application fee: $50. Electronic applications accepted. *Expenses:* Tuition, state resident: full-time $12,887; part-time $537 per credit hour. Tuition, nonresident: full-time $28,449; part-time $1186 per credit hour. *Required fees:* $530; $24 per credit hour. $30 per quarter. Part-time tuition and fees vary according to course load and program. *Financial support:* Research assistantships with full and partial tuition reimbursements and teaching assistantships with full and partial tuition reimbursements available. Financial award application deadline: 2/1; financial award applicants required to submit FAFSA. *Unit head:* Dr. Julia Guichard, Interim Chair and Associate Professor of Theatre, 513-529-1517, E-mail: theatre@miamioh.edu. *Application contact:* Dr. Paul Bryant-Jackson, Professor and Director of Graduate Studies, 513-529-1406, E-mail: jacksopk@miamioh.edu.
Website: http://www.MiamiOH.edu/theatre

Michigan State University, The Graduate School, College of Arts and Letters, Department of Theatre, East Lansing, MI 48824. Offers MA, MFA. *Entrance requirements:* Additional exam requirements/recommendations for international students: Required—TOEFL. Electronic applications accepted.

Minnesota State University Mankato, College of Graduate Studies, College of Arts and Humanities, Department of Theatre and Dance, Mankato, MN 56001. Offers theatre arts (MA, MFA). *Students:* 12 full-time (5 women), 6 part-time (3 women). *Degree requirements:* For master's, one foreign language, comprehensive exam, thesis. *Entrance requirements:* For master's, minimum GPA of 3.0 during previous 2 years, 3 letters of recommendation, resume of theatre work, audition. Additional exam requirements/recommendations for international students: Required—TOEFL. *Application deadline:* For fall admission, 7/1 priority date for domestic students, 5/1 for international students; for spring admission, 11/1 for domestic students, 10/1 for international students. Applications are processed on a rolling basis. Application fee: $40. Electronic applications accepted. *Financial support:* Research assistantships with full tuition reimbursements, teaching assistantships with full tuition reimbursements, career-related internships or fieldwork, Federal Work-Study, institutionally sponsored loans, and unspecified assistantships available. Support available to part-time students. Financial award application deadline: 3/15; financial award applicants required to submit FAFSA. *Unit head:* Dr. Paul Hustoles, Chairperson, 507-389-2118. *Application contact:* 507-389-2321, E-mail: grad@mnsu.edu.
Website: http://www.mnsu.edu/theatre/

Missouri State University, Graduate College, College of Arts and Letters, Department of Theatre and Dance, Springfield, MO 65897. Offers secondary education (MS Ed), including speech and theatre; theatre (MA). *Accreditation:* NAST. Part-time programs available. *Faculty:* 9 full-time (5 women). *Students:* 1 (woman) full-time, 6 part-time (5 women). Average age 33. In 2014, 5 master's awarded. *Degree requirements:* For master's, comprehensive exam, thesis or alternative. *Entrance requirements:* For master's, minimum GPA of 3.0 (MA), 9-12 teaching certification (MS Ed). Additional exam requirements/recommendations for international students: Required—TOEFL (minimum score 550 paper-based; 79 iBT). *Application deadline:* For fall admission, 7/20 for domestic students, 5/1 for international students; for spring admission, 12/20 for domestic students, 9/1 for international students. Applications are processed on a rolling basis. Application fee: $35 ($50 for international students). Electronic applications accepted. *Expenses:* Tuition, state resident: full-time $2250; part-time $250 per credit hour. Tuition, nonresident: full-time $4509; part-time $501 per credit hour. Tuition and fees vary according to course level, course load and program. *Financial support:* Federal Work-Study, institutionally sponsored loans, scholarships/grants, and unspecified assistantships available. Financial award application deadline: 3/31; financial award applicants required to submit FAFSA. *Unit head:* Dr. Christopher Herr, Interim Department Head, 417-836-4400, Fax: 417-836-4234, E-mail: theatreanddance@missouristate.edu. *Application contact:* Misty Stewart, Coordinator of Admissions and Recruitment, 417-836-6079, Fax: 417-836-6200, E-mail: mistystewart@missouristate.edu.
Website: http://theatreanddance.missouristate.edu/

Montclair State University, The Graduate School, College of the Arts, MA Program in Theatre, Montclair, NJ 07043-1624. Offers arts management (MA); production/stage management (MA); theatre studies (MA). *Accreditation:* NAST. Part-time and evening/ weekend programs available. *Students:* 9 full-time (5 women), 17 part-time (10 women);

includes 6 minority (2 Black or African American, non-Hispanic/Latino; 4 Hispanic/Latino), 1 international. Average age 33. 14 applicants, 71% accepted, 6 enrolled. In 2014, 6 master's awarded. *Degree requirements:* For master's, comprehensive exam, thesis or alternative. *Entrance requirements:* For master's, GRE General Test, 2 letters of recommendation. Additional exam requirements/recommendations for international students: Required—TOEFL (minimum score 83 iBT) or IELTS (minimum score 6.5). *Application deadline:* For fall admission, 6/1 for international students; for spring admission, 10/1 for international students. Applications are processed on a rolling basis. Application fee: $60. Electronic applications accepted. *Expenses:* Tuition, state resident: full-time $9960; part-time $553.35 per credit. Tuition, nonresident: full-time $15,074; part-time $837.43 per credit. *Required fees:* $1595; $88.63 per credit. Tuition and fees vary according to degree level and program. *Financial support:* In 2014–15, 2 research assistantships with full tuition reimbursements (averaging $7,000 per year) were awarded; Federal Work-Study, scholarships/grants, and unspecified assistantships also available. Support available to part-time students. Financial award application deadline: 3/1; financial award applicants required to submit FAFSA. *Faculty research:* Danceturgy, Arab and Muslim images in American drama, Neil LaBute and playwriting, directing, Robert Edmond Jones. *Unit head:* Dr. Eric Diamond, Chairperson, 973-655-4217, E-mail: peterson@mail.montclair.edu. *Application contact:* Amy Aiello, Executive Director of The Graduate School, 973-655-5147, E-mail: petersonj@mail.montclair.edu.

Naropa University, Graduate Programs, Program in Theater: Contemporary Performance, Boulder, CO 80302-6697. Offers MFA. *Faculty:* 1 (woman) full-time, 3 part-time/adjunct (2 women). *Students:* 16 full-time (12 women); includes 2 minority (both Hispanic/Latino). Average age 30. 12 applicants, 92% accepted, 7 enrolled. In 2014, 11 master's awarded. *Degree requirements:* For master's, thesis, culminating projects and performances. *Entrance requirements:* For master's, interview, head shot, resume, transcripts, 2 letters of recommendation, letter of interest, professional accomplishment in one of the following areas and a minimum degree of competence in all three: acting, dance/movement, voice. Additional exam requirements/recommendations for international students: Required—TOEFL (minimum score 600 paper-based; 80 iBT). *Application deadline:* For fall admission, 1/15 priority date for domestic and international students. Applications are processed on a rolling basis. Application fee: $60. Electronic applications accepted. *Expenses: Tuition:* Full-time $23,400; part-time $975 per credit. *Required fees:* $335 per semester. Tuition and fees vary according to course load. *Financial support:* In 2014–15, 13 students received support, including 3 research assistantships with partial tuition reimbursements available (averaging $4,667 per year); career-related internships or fieldwork, scholarships/grants, tuition waivers (partial), and unspecified assistantships also available. Support available to part-time students. Financial award application deadline: 3/1; financial award applicants required to submit FAFSA. *Unit head:* Sue Hammond West, Dean, School of the Arts, 303-546-3585, E-mail: suewest@naropa.edu. *Application contact:* Office of Admissions, 303-536-3572, Fax: 303-546-3583, E-mail: admissions@naropa.edu.
Website: http://www.naropa.edu/academics/arts/grad/contemporary-performance-mfa/index.php

The New School, The New School for Drama, New York, NY 10014. Offers acting (MFA); directing (MFA); playwriting (MFA). *Degree requirements:* For master's, thesis, student involvement in theatrical production and presentation. *Entrance requirements:* For master's, audition (acting), interview (directing and playwriting). Additional exam requirements/recommendations for international students: Required—TOEFL (minimum score 600 paper-based; 100 iBT). Electronic applications accepted. *Expenses:* Contact institution.

New York University, Steinhardt School of Culture, Education, and Human Development, Department of Music and Performing Arts Professions, Program in Educational Theatre, New York, NY 10012. Offers educational theatre and English 7-12 (MA); educational theatre and social studies 7-12 (MA); educational theatre for colleges and communities (MA, Ed D, PhD); educational theatre, all grades (MA). Part-time programs available. *Faculty:* 6 full-time (2 women). *Students:* 65 full-time (48 women), 22 part-time (14 women); includes 22 minority (7 Black or African American, non-Hispanic/Latino; 1 American Indian or Alaska Native, non-Hispanic/Latino; 3 Asian, non-Hispanic/Latino; 8 Hispanic/Latino; 3 Two or more races, non-Hispanic/Latino), 9 international. Average age 28. 90 applicants, 76% accepted, 37 enrolled. In 2014, 47 master's, 5 doctorates awarded. *Degree requirements:* For master's, thesis (for some programs); for doctorate, thesis/dissertation. *Entrance requirements:* For master's, audition; for doctorate, GRE General Test, interview. Additional exam requirements/recommendations for international students: Required—TOEFL (minimum score 100 iBT). *Application deadline:* For fall admission, 12/1 priority date for domestic and international students; for spring admission, 10/1 for domestic and international students. Applications are processed on a rolling basis. Application fee: $75. Electronic applications accepted. *Financial support:* Teaching assistantships with partial tuition reimbursements, career-related internships or fieldwork, Federal Work-Study, institutionally sponsored loans, and scholarships/grants available. Support available to part-time students. Financial award application deadline: 2/1; financial award applicants required to submit FAFSA. *Faculty research:* Theatre for young audiences, drama in education, applied theatre, arts education assessment, reflective praxis. *Unit head:* Prof. David Montgomery, Director, 212-998-5869, Fax: 212-995-4043, E-mail: dm635@nyu.edu. *Application contact:* 212-998-5030, Fax: 212-995-4328, E-mail: steinhardt.gradadmissions@nyu.edu.
Website: http://steinhardt.nyu.edu/music/edtheatre

New York University, Steinhardt School of Culture, Education, and Human Development, Department of Music and Performing Arts Professions, Program in Music Performance and Composition, New York, NY 10012. Offers instrumental performance (MM), including instrumental performance, jazz instrumental performance; music performance and composition (PhD), including music performance and composition; music theory and composition (MM), including composition for music theater, computer music composition, music theory and composition, scoring for film and multimedia, songwriting; piano performance (MM), including collaborative piano, solo piano; vocal pedagogy (Advanced Certificate); vocal performance (MM), including classical voice, musical theatre performance; vocal performance/vocal pedagogy (MM), including classical voice, musical theatre performance. Part-time programs available. *Faculty:* 25 full-time (7 women). *Students:* 228 full-time (107 women), 79 part-time (37 women); includes 51 minority (9 Black or African American, non-Hispanic/Latino; 18 Asian, non-Hispanic/Latino; 14 Hispanic/Latino; 10 Two or more races, non-Hispanic/Latino), 130 international. Average age 27. 534 applicants, 50% accepted, 141 enrolled. In 2014, 130 master's, 2 doctorates, 12 other advanced degrees awarded. *Degree requirements:* For master's, thesis (for some programs); for doctorate, thesis/dissertation. *Entrance requirements:* For master's, audition; for doctorate, GRE General Test, audition, interview. Additional exam requirements/recommendations for international students: Required—TOEFL (minimum score 100 iBT). *Application deadline:* For fall admission, 12/1 priority date for domestic and international students; for spring admission, 10/1 for domestic and international students. Applications are processed on a rolling basis. Application fee: $75. Electronic applications accepted. *Financial support:* Fellowships with full and partial tuition reimbursements, Federal Work-Study, scholarships/grants, and tuition waivers (partial) available. Support available to part-time students. Financial award application deadline: 2/1; financial award applicants required to submit FAFSA. *Faculty research:* Aesthetics, performance analysis, twentieth century music, music methodologies for arts criticism and analysis. *Unit head:* Dr. Tae Hong Park, Director, 212-998-5424, Fax: 212-995-4043, E-mail: tae.hong.park@nyu.edu. *Application contact:* 212-998-5030, Fax: 212-995-4328, E-mail: steinhardt.gradadmissions@nyu.edu.
Website: http://steinhardt.nyu.edu/music/composition/programs/graduate

New York University, Tisch School of the Arts and Graduate School of Arts and Science, Department of Performance Studies, New York, NY 10012-1019. Offers MA, PhD. *Faculty:* 12 full-time (7 women), 4 part-time/adjunct (3 women). *Students:* 37 full-time (23 women), 2 part-time (both women); includes 10 minority (4 Black or African American, non-Hispanic/Latino; 1 Asian, non-Hispanic/Latino; 3 Hispanic/Latino; 2 Two or more races, non-Hispanic/Latino), 16 international. 99 applicants, 90% accepted, 37 enrolled. In 2014, 36 master's, 7 doctorates awarded. *Degree requirements:* For doctorate, one foreign language, comprehensive exam, thesis/dissertation, dissertation defense, qualifying exam. *Entrance requirements:* For master's, sample of written work; for doctorate, master's degree, writing sample. Additional exam requirements/recommendations for international students: Required—TOEFL or IELTS. *Application deadline:* For fall admission, 12/1 for domestic and international students. Application fee: $60. Electronic applications accepted. *Expenses:* Expenses: Contact institution. *Financial support:* In 2014–15, 32 students received support, including 24 fellowships with full and partial tuition reimbursements available, 4 research assistantships, 4 teaching assistantships; Federal Work-Study, institutionally sponsored loans, tuition waivers (partial), and unspecified assistantships also available. Financial award application deadline: 2/15; financial award applicants required to submit CSS PROFILE or FAFSA. *Faculty research:* Performance theory, dance, folklore and festivals, postcolonial theory, anthropology and gender studies. *Unit head:* Karen Shimakawa, Chair, 212-998-1620, Fax: 212-995-4571, E-mail: performance.studies@nyu.edu. *Application contact:* Dan Sandford, Director of Graduate Admissions, 212-998-1918, Fax: 212-995-4060, E-mail: tisch.gradadmissions@nyu.edu.
Website: http://www.performance.tisch.nyu.edu/

New York University, Tisch School of the Arts, Graduate Acting Program, New York, NY 10012-1019. Offers MFA. *Faculty:* 9 full-time (6 women), 11 part-time/adjunct (5 women). *Students:* 44 full-time (19 women), 1 (woman) part-time; includes 17 minority (10 Black or African American, non-Hispanic/Latino; 1 Asian, non-Hispanic/Latino; 1 Hispanic/Latino; 1 Native Hawaiian or other Pacific Islander, non-Hispanic/Latino; 4 Two or more races, non-Hispanic/Latino). Average age 26. 731 applicants, 3% accepted, 16 enrolled. In 2014, 18 master's awarded. *Entrance requirements:* For master's, audition. *Application deadline:* For fall admission, 1/1 for domestic and international students. Application fee: $60. Electronic applications accepted. *Financial support:* In 2014–15, 30 students received support, including 4 fellowships with full and partial tuition reimbursements available; Federal Work-Study, institutionally sponsored loans, scholarships/grants, tuition waivers (full and partial), and unspecified assistantships also available. Financial award application deadline: 2/15; financial award applicants required to submit FAFSA. *Unit head:* Mark Wing-Davey, Chair, 212-998-1964, Fax: 212-995-4067. *Application contact:* Dan Sandford, Director of Graduate Admissions, 212-998-1918, Fax: 212-995-4060, E-mail: tisch.gradadmissions@nyu.edu.
Website: http://www.gradacting.tisch.nyu.edu/

Northern Illinois University, Graduate School, College of Visual and Performing Arts, School of Theatre and Dance, De Kalb, IL 60115-2854. Offers MFA. *Accreditation:* NAST. Part-time programs available. *Faculty:* 16 full-time (9 women). *Students:* 25 full-time (10 women); includes 4 minority (2 Hispanic/Latino; 2 Two or more races, non-Hispanic/Latino). Average age 27. 34 applicants, 56% accepted, 16 enrolled. In 2014, 23 master's awarded. *Degree requirements:* For master's, comprehensive exam, final project and defense. *Entrance requirements:* For master's, minimum GPA of 2.75, audition or portfolio. Additional exam requirements/recommendations for international students: Required—TOEFL (minimum score 550 paper-based). *Application deadline:* For fall admission, 4/1 priority date for domestic students, 5/1 for international students; for spring admission, 10/15 priority date for domestic students, 10/1 for international students. Applications are processed on a rolling basis. Application fee: $40. Electronic applications accepted. *Financial support:* In 2014–15, 27 teaching assistantships with full tuition reimbursements were awarded; fellowships with full tuition reimbursements, research assistantships with full tuition reimbursements, career-related internships or fieldwork, Federal Work-Study, scholarships/grants, tuition waivers (full), and staff assistantships also available. Support available to part-time students. Financial award applicants required to submit FAFSA. *Faculty research:* Theatre history, choreography, performance art spectacles, storytelling, computer visualization of the ethical space. *Unit head:* Alexander Gelman, Director, 815-753-8253, Fax: 815-753-8415, E-mail: agelman@niu.edu. *Application contact:* Graduate School Office, 815-753-0395, E-mail: gradsch@niu.edu.
Website: http://www.niu.edu/theatre/

Northern Michigan University, Office of Graduate Education and Research, College of Arts and Sciences, Department of English, Marquette, MI 49855-5301. Offers creative writing (MFA); literature (MA); pedagogy (MA); teaching English to speakers of other languages (Graduate Certificate); theater (MA); writing (MA). Part-time and evening/weekend programs available. *Faculty:* 14 full-time (9 women). *Students:* 55 full-time (32 women), 11 part-time (7 women); includes 8 minority (1 Black or African American, non-Hispanic/Latino; 1 American Indian or Alaska Native, non-Hispanic/Latino; 2 Hispanic/Latino; 4 Two or more races, non-Hispanic/Latino). Average age 27. 135 applicants, 43% accepted, 28 enrolled. In 2014, 21 master's awarded. Terminal master's awarded for partial completion of doctoral program. *Degree requirements:* For master's, capstone project: thesis, practicum or portfolio (for MA); thesis (for MFA); for Graduate Certificate, one foreign language. *Entrance requirements:* For master's, minimum GPA of 3.0; bachelor's degree in English or minimum of 30 credit hours in undergraduate English; statement of purpose; resume; critical essay; 3 letters of recommendation; for Graduate Certificate, bachelor's degree. Additional exam requirements/recommendations for international students: Required—TOEFL (minimum score 550 paper-based; 79 iBT), IELTS (minimum score 6.5). *Application deadline:* For fall admission, 2/1 for domestic students; for winter admission, 2/1 for domestic students; for spring admission, 3/17 for domestic students. Applications are processed on a rolling basis. Application fee: $50. Electronic applications accepted. *Expenses:* Tuition, state resident: full-time $7716; part-time $441 per credit hour. Tuition, nonresident: full-time $10,812; part-time $634.50 per credit hour. *Required fees:* $31.88 per semester. Tuition and fees vary according to course load, degree level and program. *Financial support:* In 2014–15, research assistantships with full tuition reimbursements (averaging $8,898 per year), teaching assistantships with full tuition reimbursements (averaging $8,898 per year) were awarded; Federal Work-Study, institutionally sponsored loans, and unspecified assistantships also available. Support available to part-time students. Financial award application deadline: 3/1; financial award applicants required to submit FAFSA. *Faculty research:* Modern Arabic literature, British literature (medieval to contemporary), postcolonial literature, Native and African-American literature, creative writing, critical theory, pedagogy. *Unit head:* Prof. Russell Prather, PhD, Director of MA Program/Professor, 906-227-2857, E-mail: rprather@nmu.edu. *Application contact:* Prof. Russell

Prather, PhD, Director of MA Program/Professor, 906-227-2857, E-mail: rprather@nmu.edu. Website: http://www.nmu.edu/english/

Northwestern University, The Graduate School, School of Communication, Department of Theatre, Evanston, IL 60208. Offers directing (MFA); stage design (MFA); theatre and drama (PhD). Admissions and degrees offered through The Graduate School. *Degree requirements:* For master's, thesis (MFA). *Entrance requirements:* For master's, GRE General Test. Additional exam requirements/recommendations for international students: Required—TOEFL. *Faculty research:* Critical analysis, theory and history of theatre and drama, philosophy of dance and movement, performance in multicultural contexts, storytelling, computer design process.

Northwestern University, The Graduate School, School of Communication, Interdisciplinary PhD Program in Theatre and Drama, Evanston, IL 60208. Offers PhD. Admissions and degree offered through The Graduate School. *Degree requirements:* For doctorate, thesis/dissertation, qualifying and final oral exams. *Entrance requirements:* For doctorate, GRE General Test, sample of written work. Additional exam requirements/recommendations for international students: Required—TOEFL. Electronic applications accepted. *Faculty research:* Theory and history of theatre and drama, performance theory, performance in multicultural contexts, critical analysis drama, theatre historiography.

The Ohio State University, Graduate School, College of Arts and Sciences, Division of Arts and Humanities, Department of Theatre, Columbus, OH 43210. Offers acting (MFA); design (MFA); theatre (PhD); theatre studies (MA). *Accreditation:* NAST. *Faculty:* 16. *Students:* 35 full-time (20 women), 2 part-time (0 women); includes 4 minority (3 Hispanic/Latino; 1 Two or more races, non-Hispanic/Latino), 7 international. Average age 32. In 2014, 4 master's, 6 doctorates awarded. Terminal master's awarded for partial completion of doctoral program. *Degree requirements:* For master's, thesis (for some programs); for doctorate, one foreign language, thesis/dissertation. *Entrance requirements:* For master's, GRE General Test (for MA); GRE (for MFA applicant with GPA below 3.0), audition (for MFA in acting); electronic design portfolio (for MFA in design); sample of published or unpublished research work (for MA); for doctorate, GRE General Test. Additional exam requirements/recommendations for international students: Required—Michigan English Language Assessment Battery (minimum score 82); Recommended—TOEFL (minimum score 550 paper-based; 79 iBT), IELTS (minimum score 7). *Application deadline:* For fall admission, 11/30 priority date for domestic and international students; for winter admission, 12/1 for domestic students, 11/1 for international students; for spring admission, 3/1 for domestic students, 2/1 for international students. Applications are processed on a rolling basis. Application fee: $60 ($70 for international students). Electronic applications accepted. *Financial support:* Fellowships, teaching assistantships, Federal Work-Study, and institutionally sponsored loans available. Support available to part-time students. Financial award application deadline: 3/1; financial award applicants required to submit FAFSA. *Unit head:* Dr. Lesley Ferris, Interim Chair, 614-292-0829, E-mail: ferris.36@osu.edu. *Application contact:* Graduate and Professional Admissions, 614-292-9444, Fax: 614-292-3895, E-mail: gpadmissions@osu.edu.
Website: http://theatre.osu.edu/

Ohio University, Graduate College, College of Fine Arts, School of Theater, Athens, OH 45701-2979. Offers MA, MFA. *Accreditation:* NAST. *Degree requirements:* For master's, thesis or alternative. *Entrance requirements:* For master's, minimum GPA of 3.0. Additional exam requirements/recommendations for international students: Required—TOEFL (minimum score 550 paper-based; 80 iBT) or IELTS (minimum score 6.5). Electronic applications accepted.

Oklahoma City University, Margaret E. Petree College of Performing Arts, School of Theatre, Oklahoma City, OK 73106-1402. Offers costume design (MA); technical theater (MA); theater (MA); theater for young audiences (MA). Part-time programs available. *Degree requirements:* For master's, thesis or alternative. *Entrance requirements:* For master's, interview, audition, writing sample. Additional exam requirements/recommendations for international students: Required—TOEFL (minimum score 550 paper-based; 80 iBT). *Application deadline:* Applications are processed on a rolling basis. Application fee: $50 ($70 for international students). *Expenses: Tuition:* Part-time $936 per credit hour. *Required fees:* $115 per credit hour. One-time fee: $250. Tuition and fees vary according to course load, degree level, program and student's religious affiliation. *Financial support:* Career-related internships or fieldwork and Federal Work-Study available. Financial award application deadline: 6/1; financial award applicants required to submit FAFSA. *Faculty research:* Translation of plays, writing plays, dramaturgical research for plays and educational outreach materials. *Unit head:* Dr. Mark Belcik, Associate Dean, 405-208-5474, Fax: 405-208-5971, E-mail: mbelcik@okcu.edu. *Application contact:* Michelle Cook, Director, Admissions, 800-633-7242, Fax: 405-208-5916, E-mail: gadmissions@okcu.edu.

Oklahoma State University, College of Arts and Sciences, Department of Theatre, Stillwater, OK 74078. Offers MA. *Accreditation:* NAST. *Faculty:* 10 full-time (5 women). *Students:* 2 full-time (1 woman), 5 part-time (all women); includes 1 minority (Two or more races, non-Hispanic/Latino). Average age 37. 7 applicants, 71% accepted, 3 enrolled. In 2014, 4 master's awarded. *Degree requirements:* For master's, creative component or thesis. *Entrance requirements:* For master's, GRE. Additional exam requirements/recommendations for international students: Required—TOEFL (minimum score 550 paper-based; 79 iBT). *Application deadline:* For fall admission, 3/1 priority date for international students; for spring admission, 8/1 priority date for international students. Applications are processed on a rolling basis. Application fee: $40 ($75 for international students). Electronic applications accepted. *Expenses:* Tuition, state resident: full-time $4488; part-time $187 per credit hour. Tuition, nonresident: full-time $18,360; part-time $765 per credit hour. *Required fees:* $2413; $100.55 per credit hour. Tuition and fees vary according to campus/location. *Financial support:* In 2014–15, 5 teaching assistantships (averaging $13,608 per year) were awarded; career-related internships or fieldwork, Federal Work-Study, scholarships/grants, health care benefits, tuition waivers (partial), and unspecified assistantships also available. Support available to part-time students. Financial award application deadline: 3/1; financial award applicants required to submit FAFSA. *Faculty research:* Historical scene painting and scenic art, Eastern European stage design, stage direction, voice and diction for the actor, stage choreography and dance. *Unit head:* Andrew Kimbrough, Department Head, 405-744-6094, Fax: 405-744-6509, E-mail: andrew.kimbrough@okstate.edu. *Application contact:* Dr. Maria Beach, Graduate Coordinator, 405-744-2966, Fax: 405-744-6509, E-mail: maria.beach@okstate.edu.
Website: http://theatre.okstate.edu/

Pace University, Dyson College of Arts and Sciences, The Actors Studio MFA, New York, NY 10038. Offers acting (MFA); directing (MFA); playwriting (MFA). *Faculty:* 7 full-time (3 women), 10 part-time/adjunct (3 women). *Students:* 115 full-time (72 women); includes 34 minority (16 Black or African American, non-Hispanic/Latino; 1 American Indian or Alaska Native, non-Hispanic/Latino; 2 Asian, non-Hispanic/Latino; 13 Hispanic/Latino; 2 Two or more races, non-Hispanic/Latino), 20 international. Average age 27. 149 applicants, 56% accepted, 44 enrolled. In 2014, 36 master's awarded. *Entrance requirements:* For master's, one academic and one professional recommendation. Additional exam requirements/recommendations for international students: Required—TOEFL. *Application deadline:* For fall admission, 1/1 for domestic students. Application fee: $70. *Expenses: Tuition:* Part-time $1120 per credit. *Required fees:* $266 per semester. Tuition and fees vary according to course load, degree level and program. *Unit head:* Andreas Manolikakis, Chair, 212-346-1131, E-mail: actorsstudiomfa@pace.edu. *Application contact:* Susan Ford-Goldschein, Director of Graduate Admissions, 212-346-1531, Fax: 212-346-1585, E-mail: gradnyc@pace.edu.
Website: http://www.pace.edu/dyson/academic-departments-and-programs/asds

Penn State University Park, Graduate School, College of Arts and Architecture, School of Theatre, University Park, PA 16802. Offers MFA. *Accreditation:* NAST. *Unit head:* Dr. Barbara O. Korner, Dean, 814-865-2592, Fax: 814-865-2018, E-mail: bok2@psu.edu. *Application contact:* Lori A. Stania, Director, Graduate Student Services, 814-867-5278, Fax: 814-863-4627, E-mail: gswww@psu.edu.
Website: http://theatre.psu.edu/

Pittsburg State University, Graduate School, College of Arts and Sciences, Department of Communication, Pittsburg, KS 66762. Offers applied communication (MA); communication education (MA); theatre (MA). *Degree requirements:* For master's, thesis or alternative.

Point Park University, Conservatory of Performing Arts, Pittsburgh, PA 15222-1984. Offers theatre arts-acting (MFA). *Degree requirements:* For master's, comprehensive exam (for some programs), thesis or alternative. *Entrance requirements:* For master's, interview, undergraduate degree in related field, theatre experience. Additional exam requirements/recommendations for international students: Required—TOEFL (minimum score 550 paper-based; 79 iBT). Electronic applications accepted.

Portland State University, Graduate Studies, School of Fine and Performing Arts, Department of Theater Arts, Portland, OR 97207-0751. Offers MA, MS, MA/MS. *Accreditation:* NAST. *Faculty:* 14 full-time (6 women), 17 part-time/adjunct (9 women). *Students:* 5 full-time (3 women), 3 part-time (2 women); includes 3 minority (1 Black or African American, non-Hispanic/Latino; 1 Hispanic/Latino; 1 Two or more races, non-Hispanic/Latino). Average age 34. 8 applicants, 63% accepted, 3 enrolled. In 2014, 3 master's awarded. *Degree requirements:* For master's, variable foreign language requirement, thesis or alternative. *Entrance requirements:* For master's, minimum GPA of 3.0 in upper-division course work or 2.75 overall, 24 credits in theater arts. Additional exam requirements/recommendations for international students: Required—TOEFL (minimum score 550 paper-based; 80 iBT). *Application deadline:* For fall admission, 4/1 priority date for domestic students, 3/1 priority date for international students; for winter admission, 9/1 for domestic students; for spring admission, 11/1 for domestic students; for summer admission, 2/1 for domestic students. Applications are processed on a rolling basis. Application fee: $50. *Expenses:* Tuition, state resident: part-time $222 per credit. Tuition, nonresident: part-time $527 per credit. *Required fees:* $22 per contact hour. $100 per quarter. Tuition and fees vary according to program. *Financial support:* In 2014–15, 1 teaching assistantship with partial tuition reimbursement (averaging $2,979 per year) was awarded; career-related internships or fieldwork, Federal Work-Study, and unspecified assistantships also available. Support available to part-time students. Financial award application deadline: 3/1; financial award applicants required to submit FAFSA. *Faculty research:* Design, acting/directing, scene/costume technology, dramatic literature, theater history. *Total annual research expenditures:* $1,621. *Unit head:* Mark Berrettini, Director, 503-725-4623, Fax: 503-725-4624, E-mail: mberre@pdx.edu. *Application contact:* Katie Sinback, Office Coordinator, 503-725-4604, Fax: 503-725-4624, E-mail: sinback@pdx.edu.
Website: http://www.pdx.edu/the-arts/theatre-film

Purchase College, State University of New York, Conservatory of Theatre Arts, Purchase, NY 10577-1400. Offers theatre design/technology (MFA). *Students:* 5 full-time (4 women), 1 international. 13 applicants, 46% accepted, 6 enrolled. *Degree requirements:* For master's, thesis or alternative, performance. *Entrance requirements:* For master's, BFA, interview, portfolio. *Application deadline:* For fall admission, 3/1 for domestic students. Application fee: $50. Electronic applications accepted. *Expenses:* Tuition, state resident: full-time $10,370; part-time $432 per credit. Tuition, nonresident: full-time $20,190; part-time $831 per credit. *Required fees:* $1763. *Financial support:* Fellowships, teaching assistantships, career-related internships or fieldwork, Federal Work-Study, scholarships/grants, and tuition waivers (partial) available. Support available to part-time students. Financial award application deadline: 3/15; financial award applicants required to submit FAFSA. *Unit head:* Dr. Gregory Taylor, Director, 914-251-6831, E-mail: gregory.taylor@purchase.edu. *Application contact:* Sabrina Johnston, Admission Counselor, 914-251-6479, Fax: 914-251-6314, E-mail: admissn@purchase.edu.
Website: http://www.purchase.edu/Departments/AcademicPrograms/Arts/TAF/

Purdue University, Graduate School, College of Liberal Arts, Department of Visual and Performing Arts, West Lafayette, IN 47907. Offers art and design (MA); theatre (MA, MFA). *Accreditation:* NASAD; NAST. Part-time programs available. *Degree requirements:* For master's, terminal exhibit, project, or thesis. *Entrance requirements:* For master's, GRE General Test (for art education), minimum undergraduate GPA of 3.0 or equivalent; 9 undergraduate hours in an art or design history; BA in art (for MA in art education). Additional exam requirements/recommendations for international students: Required—TOEFL (minimum score 550 paper-based; 77 iBT). Electronic applications accepted. *Faculty research:* Design, fine arts, photography, acting, directing, theatre technology.

Regent University, Graduate School, School of Communication and the Arts, Virginia Beach, VA 23464-9800. Offers acting (MFA); communication (MA, PhD), including political communication (MA), strategic communication (MA); directing for cinema/television (MFA); film and TV (MA), including producing, production, script writing; journalism (MA); producing for cinema/television (MFA); script and screenwriting (MFA); theatre (MA). Part-time programs available. Postbaccalaureate distance learning degree programs offered (minimal on-campus study). *Faculty:* 20 full-time (3 women), 26 part-time/adjunct (7 women). *Students:* 89 full-time (49 women), 211 part-time (125 women); includes 92 minority (69 Black or African American, non-Hispanic/Latino; 2 American Indian or Alaska Native, non-Hispanic/Latino; 2 Asian, non-Hispanic/Latino; 19 Hispanic/Latino), 10 international. Average age 35. 199 applicants, 53% accepted, 77 enrolled. In 2014, 48 master's, 8 doctorates awarded. *Degree requirements:* For master's, thesis or alternative; for doctorate, thesis/dissertation. *Entrance requirements:* For master's, GRE General Test or MAT, minimum undergraduate GPA of 3.0, writing sample, computer literacy survey, recommendation, resume, interview, audition (for MFA programs); for doctorate, GRE General Test, minimum graduate GPA of 3.0, writing sample, computer literacy survey, recommendation, interview, transcripts. Additional exam requirements/recommendations for international students: Required—TOEFL (minimum score 577 paper-based). *Application deadline:* For fall admission, 3/1 priority date for domestic students; for spring admission, 10/1 priority date for domestic students. Applications are processed on a rolling basis. Application fee: $50. Electronic applications accepted. *Expenses:* Expenses: Contact institution. *Financial support:* Fellowships with full and partial tuition reimbursements, career-related internships or fieldwork, scholarships/grants, tuition waivers (full and partial), and unspecified assistantships available. Support available to part-time students. Financial award application deadline: 9/1; financial award applicants required to submit FAFSA. *Faculty research:* Southern gospel music, education and entertainment, celebrities and the media, journalism and ethics, C.S. Lewis. *Unit head:* Dr. Mitch Land, Dean, 757-352-4916, Fax: 757-352-4291, E-mail:

mland@regent.edu. *Application contact:* Matthew Chadwick, Director of Enrollment Support Services, 800-373-5504, Fax: 757-352-4381, E-mail: admissions@regent.edu. Website: http://www.regent.edu/acad/schcom

Roosevelt University, Graduate Division, Chicago College of Performing Arts, Theatre Conservatory, Chicago, IL 60605. Offers directing and dramaturgy (MFA); musical theatre (MFA); theatre (MA, MFA); theatre-directing (MA); theatre-performance (MFA). MA is a special 3-summer program for high school teachers only. *Degree requirements:* For master's, thesis production/performance. *Entrance requirements:* For master's, audition, interview, minimum GPA of 2.5. *Faculty research:* Brecht, Shakespeare, contemporary and new work, fully mounted theatre.

Rowan University, Graduate School, College of Education, Department of Teacher Education, Program in Theatre Education, Glassboro, NJ 08028-1701. Offers MST. *Accreditation:* NAST. *Faculty:* 1 (woman) full-time, 4 part-time/adjunct (all women). *Students:* 3 full-time (2 women). Average age 25. In 2014, 3 master's awarded. *Application deadline:* For summer admission, 2/15 for domestic students. Applications are processed on a rolling basis. Application fee: $65. Electronic applications accepted. *Expenses: Tuition,* area resident: Part-time $648 per credit. Tuition, state resident: part-time $648 per credit. Tuition, nonresident: part-time $648 per credit. *Required fees:* $145 per credit. Tuition and fees vary according to degree level, campus/location, program and student level. *Unit head:* Dr. Horacio Sosa, Dean, College of Graduate and Continuing Education, 856-256-4747, Fax: 856-256-5638, E-mail: sosa@rowan.edu. *Application contact:* Admissions and Enrollment Services, 856-256-5435, Fax: 856-256-5637, E-mail: cgceadmissions@rowan.edu.
Website: http://rowanu.com/mst-theatre

Rowan University, Graduate School, College of Performing Arts, Department of Theatre and Dance, Glassboro, NJ 08028-1701. Offers theatre arts administration (MA). *Faculty:* 1 (woman) full-time, 3 part-time/adjunct (all women). *Students:* 1 (woman) full-time, 20 part-time (14 women); includes 3 minority (all Black or African American, non-Hispanic/Latino). Average age 32. In 2014, 2 master's awarded. *Application deadline:* For summer admission, 2/15 for domestic students. Applications are processed on a rolling basis. Application fee: $65. Electronic applications accepted. *Expenses: Tuition, area resident:* Part-time $648 per credit. Tuition, state resident: part-time $648 per credit. Tuition, nonresident: part-time $648 per credit. *Required fees:* $145 per credit. Tuition and fees vary according to degree level, campus/location, program and student level. *Unit head:* Dr. Horacio Sosa, Vice President, Global Learning and Partnerships, 856-256-4747, Fax: 856-256-5638, E-mail: sosa@rowan.edu. *Application contact:* Admissions and Enrollment Services, 856-256-4747, Fax: 856-256-5637, E-mail: globaladmissions@rowan.edu.
Website: http://www.rowan.edu/colleges/cpa/theatre_dance/

Rutgers, The State University of New Jersey, New Brunswick, Mason Gross School of the Arts, Theater Arts Department, New Brunswick, NJ 08901. Offers acting (MFA); design (MFA); directing (MFA); playwriting (MFA); stage management (MFA). *Degree requirements:* For master's, thesis (for some programs), performance project. *Entrance requirements:* For master's, audition, interview, portfolio. Additional exam requirements/recommendations for international students: Required—TOEFL (minimum score 550 paper-based), IELTS (minimum score 7). Electronic applications accepted. *Faculty research:* Faculty of working professional.

San Diego State University, Graduate and Research Affairs, College of Professional Studies and Fine Arts, School of Theater, Television and Film, San Diego, CA 92182. Offers television, film, and new media production (MA); theatre arts (MA, MFA). *Accreditation:* NAST. Part-time programs available. *Degree requirements:* For master's, thesis. *Entrance requirements:* For master's, GRE General Test, 3 letters of recommendation, interview. Additional exam requirements/recommendations for international students: Required—TOEFL. Electronic applications accepted.

San Francisco State University, Division of Graduate Studies, College of Liberal and Creative Arts, Department of Theatre Arts, San Francisco, CA 94132-1722. Offers theatre arts (MFA), including design/technical production. *Accreditation:* NAST. *Expenses:* Tuition, state resident: full-time $6738. Tuition, nonresident: full-time $17,898; part-time $372 per credit hour. *Required fees:* $498 per semester. *Unit head:* Dr. Rhonnie Washington, Interim Chair, 415-338-2519, Fax: 415-338-0575, E-mail: rhonnie@sfsu.edu. *Application contact:* Prof. Joel Schechter, MA Coordinator, 415-338-1331, Fax: 415-338-0575, E-mail: jschech@sfsu.edu.
Website: http://www.theatre.sfsu.edu

San Jose State University, Graduate Studies and Research, College of Humanities and the Arts, Department of Television, Radio, Film and Theatre, San Jose, CA 95192-0001. Offers theatre arts (MA). *Accreditation:* NAST. *Degree requirements:* For master's, written exam. *Entrance requirements:* Additional exam requirements/recommendations for international students: Required—TOEFL (minimum score 570 paper-based). Electronic applications accepted.

Sarah Lawrence College, Graduate Studies, Program in Theater, Bronxville, NY 10708-5999. Offers MFA. *Degree requirements:* For master's, portfolio. *Entrance requirements:* For master's, interview, minimum B average in undergraduate course work. Additional exam requirements/recommendations for international students: Required—TOEFL (minimum score 600 paper-based). Electronic applications accepted.

Savannah College of Art and Design, Graduate School, Program in Dramatic Writing, Savannah, GA 31402-3146. Offers MFA. Part-time programs available. *Faculty:* 1 full-time (0 women). *Students:* 14 full-time (6 women), 2 part-time (both women), 5 international. Average age 25. 14 applicants, 43% accepted, 4 enrolled. In 2014, 10 master's awarded. *Degree requirements:* For master's, thesis, internship. *Entrance requirements:* For master's, portfolio. Additional exam requirements/recommendations for international students: Required—TOEFL (minimum score 550 paper-based, 85 iBT), IELTS (minimum score 6.5), or ACTFL. *Application deadline:* For fall admission, 4/1 for domestic and international students. Applications are processed on a rolling basis. Application fee: $40. Electronic applications accepted. *Expenses: Tuition:* Full-time $34,605; part-time $3845 per course. One-time fee: $500. Tuition and fees vary according to course load. *Financial support:* Fellowships, career-related internships or fieldwork, Federal Work-Study, and scholarships/grants available. Financial award application deadline: 4/1; financial award applicants required to submit FAFSA. *Unit head:* Averie Storck, Program Coordinator. *Application contact:* Jenny Jaquillard, Executive Director of Admissions, Recruitment and Events, 912-525-5100, Fax: 912-525-5985, E-mail: admission@scad.edu.
Website: http://www.scad.edu/academics/programs/dramatic-writing

Savannah College of Art and Design, Graduate School, Program in Production Design, Savannah, GA 31402-3146. Offers MA, MFA. Part-time programs available. *Faculty:* 5 full-time (1 woman). *Students:* 9 full-time (8 women); includes 1 minority (Hispanic/Latino), 1 international. Average age 25. 12 applicants, 50% accepted, 2 enrolled. In 2014, 7 master's awarded. *Degree requirements:* For master's, thesis (for some programs), final project (for MA). *Entrance requirements:* For master's, portfolio. Additional exam requirements/recommendations for international students: Required—TOEFL (minimum score 550 paper-based, 85 iBT), IELTS (minimum score 6.5), or ACTFL. *Application deadline:* For fall admission, 4/1 for domestic and international students. Applications are processed on a rolling basis. Application fee: $40. Electronic

applications accepted. *Expenses: Tuition:* Full-time $34,605; part-time $3845 per course. One-time fee: $500. Tuition and fees vary according to course load. *Financial support:* Fellowships, career-related internships or fieldwork, Federal Work-Study, and scholarships/grants available. Financial award application deadline: 4/1; financial award applicants required to submit FAFSA. *Unit head:* Richard Tyler Tunney, Chair. *Application contact:* Jenny Jaquillard, Executive Director of Admissions, Recruitment and Events, 912-525-5100, Fax: 912-525-5985, E-mail: admission@scad.edu.
Website: http://www.scad.edu/academics/programs/production-design

Smith College, Graduate and Special Programs, Department of Theatre, Northampton, MA 01063. Offers playwriting (MFA). Part-time programs available. *Faculty:* 8 full-time (6 women). *Students:* 1 (woman) full-time. Average age 28. 3 applicants, 100% accepted, 1 enrolled. *Degree requirements:* For master's, one foreign language, thesis. *Entrance requirements:* Additional exam requirements/recommendations for international students: Required—TOEFL (minimum score 595 paper-based; 97 iBT). *Application deadline:* For fall admission, 4/1 for domestic students, 1/15 for international students; for spring admission, 12/1 for domestic students. Application fee: $60. *Expenses: Tuition:* Full-time $33,360; part-time $1390 per credit. *Financial support:* In 2014–15, 1 student received support. Institutionally sponsored loans and scholarships/grants available. Support available to part-time students. Financial award application deadline: 1/15; financial award applicants required to submit CSS PROFILE or FAFSA. *Unit head:* Leonard Berkman, Graduate Student Adviser, 413-585-3206, E-mail: lberkman@smith.edu. *Application contact:* Ruth Morgan, Program Assistant, 413-585-3050, Fax: 413-585-3054, E-mail: rmorgan@smith.edu.
Website: http://www.smith.edu/theatre/

Southern Illinois University Carbondale, Graduate School, College of Liberal Arts, Theater Department, Carbondale, IL 62901-4701. Offers speech/theater (PhD); theater (MFA). *Accreditation:* NAST (one or more programs are accredited). Part-time programs available. *Faculty:* 8 full-time (4 women). *Students:* 15 full-time (8 women), 1 (woman) part-time. Average age 26. 13 applicants, 31% accepted, 4 enrolled. In 2014, 4 master's awarded. *Degree requirements:* For master's, thesis; for doctorate, thesis/dissertation. *Entrance requirements:* For master's, minimum GPA of 2.7; for doctorate, minimum GPA of 3.25. Additional exam requirements/recommendations for international students: Required—TOEFL. *Application deadline:* For fall admission, 3/1 for domestic students. Applications are processed on a rolling basis. Application fee: $50. *Expenses:* Tuition, state resident: full-time $10,176; part-time $1153 per credit. Tuition, nonresident: full-time $20,814; part-time $1744 per credit. *Required fees:* $7092; $394 per credit. $2364 per semester. *Financial support:* In 2014–15, 13 research assistantships with full tuition reimbursements, 10 teaching assistantships with full tuition reimbursements were awarded; fellowships with full tuition reimbursements, career-related internships or fieldwork, Federal Work-Study, institutionally sponsored loans, and tuition waivers (full) also available. Support available to part-time students. Financial award application deadline: 3/15. *Faculty research:* Scenography, theater performance, theater history, dramatic criticism, theater technology, playwriting. *Unit head:* Dr. Tom Kidd, Chair, 618-453-7583, E-mail: tkidd@siu.edu. *Application contact:* Samantha Myers, Director, 618-453-7579, E-mail: samanthamyers@siu.edu.

Southern Methodist University, Meadows School of the Arts, Division of Theatre, Dallas, TX 75275. Offers acting (MFA); design (MFA). *Accreditation:* NAST. *Entrance requirements:* For master's, audition or interview. Additional exam requirements/recommendations for international students: Required—TOEFL (minimum score 550 paper-based; 80 iBT). Electronic applications accepted. *Faculty research:* European lighting techniques.

Southern Oregon University, Graduate Studies, Ashland Center for Theatre Studies, Ashland, OR 97520. Offers MTS. Part-time programs available. *Faculty:* 11 full-time (4 women), 8 part-time/adjunct (6 women). *Students:* 45 full-time (30 women), 3 part-time (2 women); includes 2 minority (both Two or more races, non-Hispanic/Latino), 1 international. Average age 39. 21 applicants, 90% accepted, 15 enrolled. In 2014, 28 master's awarded. *Degree requirements:* For master's, thesis (for some programs). *Entrance requirements:* For master's, GRE General Test, minimum cumulative GPA of 3.0 in the last 90 quarter credits (60 semester credits) of undergraduate coursework. Additional exam requirements/recommendations for international students: Required—TOEFL (minimum score 540 paper-based; 76 iBT), IELTS (minimum score 6), ELPT (minimum score 964) or ELS (minimum score 112). *Application deadline:* For fall admission, 7/31 priority date for domestic and international students; for winter admission, 11/15 priority date for domestic and international students; for spring admission, 1/7 priority date for domestic and international students. Applications are processed on a rolling basis. Application fee: $50. Electronic applications accepted. *Expenses:* Tuition, state resident: full-time $10,225; part-time $1515 per quarter. Tuition, nonresident: full-time $12,782; part-time $1894 per quarter. *Required fees:* $1395; $261 per quarter. *Financial support:* Career-related internships or fieldwork, institutionally sponsored loans, scholarships/grants, and unspecified assistantships available. *Unit head:* Dr. Eric Levin, Graduate Program Coordinator, 541-552-6364, E-mail: levine@sou.edu. *Application contact:* Kelly Moutsatson, Director of Admissions, 541-552-6411, Fax: 541-552-8403, E-mail: admissions@sou.edu.
Website: http://www.sou.edu/acts/

Stanford University, School of Humanities and Sciences, Department of Theater and Performance Studies, Stanford, CA 94305-9991. Offers PhD. *Degree requirements:* For doctorate, one foreign language, thesis/dissertation, qualifying exams. *Entrance requirements:* For doctorate, GRE General Test, summary of production experience. Additional exam requirements/recommendations for international students: Required—TOEFL. Electronic applications accepted. *Expenses: Tuition:* Full-time $44,184; part-time $982 per credit hour. *Required fees:* $191.

Stony Brook University, State University of New York, Graduate School, College of Arts and Sciences, Department of Theatre Arts, Program in Dramaturgy, Stony Brook, NY 11794. Offers MFA. *Students:* Average age 29. *Degree requirements:* For master's, one foreign language, thesis. *Entrance requirements:* For master's, GRE General Test. Additional exam requirements/recommendations for international students: Required—TOEFL. *Application deadline:* For fall admission, 1/15 for domestic students. Application fee: $100. *Expenses:* Tuition, state resident: full-time $10,370; part-time $432 per credit. Tuition, nonresident: full-time $20,190; part-time $841 per credit. *Required fees:* $1431. *Unit head:* Dr. John Lutterbie, Chair, 631-632-7245, Fax: 631-632-7261, E-mail: john.lutterbie@stonybrook.edu. *Application contact:* Lisa Perez, Coordinator, 631-632-7270, Fax: 631-632-7261, E-mail: lisa.perez@stonybrook.edu.

Stony Brook University, State University of New York, Graduate School, College of Arts and Sciences, Department of Theatre Arts, Program in Theatre Arts, Stony Brook, NY 11794. Offers MA. Evening/weekend programs available. *Students:* 5 full-time (4 women), 3 part-time (all women), 4 international. Average age 35. 7 applicants, 86% accepted, 3 enrolled. *Degree requirements:* For master's, one foreign language, thesis. *Entrance requirements:* For master's, GRE General Test. Additional exam requirements/recommendations for international students: Required—TOEFL. *Application deadline:* For fall admission, 1/15 for domestic students; for spring admission, 10/1 for domestic students. Application fee: $100. *Expenses:* Tuition, state resident: full-time $10,370; part-time $432 per credit. Tuition, nonresident: full-time $20,190; part-time $841 per credit. *Required fees:* $1431. *Unit head:* Dr. John Lutterbie, Chair, 631-632-7245, Fax:

631-632-7258, E-mail: john.lutterbie@stonybrook.edu. *Application contact:* Lisa Perez, Coordinator, 631-632-7270, Fax: 632-7258, E-mail: lisa.perez@stonybrook.edu.

Temple University, Center for the Arts, Division of Theater, Film and Media Arts, Department of Theater, Philadelphia, PA 19122. Offers acting (MFA); design (MFA); directing (MFA); playwriting (MFA). *Accreditation:* NAST. Part-time programs available. *Faculty:* 13 full-time (4 women), 18 part-time/adjunct (15 women). *Students:* 19 full-time (9 women), 4 part-time (1 woman); includes 4 minority (1 Black or African American, non-Hispanic/Latino; 3 Two or more races, non-Hispanic/Latino), 1 international. 10 applicants, 50% accepted, 4 enrolled. In 2014, 4 master's awarded. *Degree requirements:* For master's, thesis (for some programs). *Entrance requirements:* For master's, minimum GPA of 3.0; audition/interview, portfolio, or samples of written work. Additional exam requirements/recommendations for international students: Required—TOEFL (minimum score 550 paper-based; 79 iBT). *Application deadline:* For fall admission, 12/15 for international students. Application fee: $60. Electronic applications accepted. *Expenses:* Expenses: Contact institution. *Financial support:* Teaching assistantships with full tuition reimbursements, Federal Work-Study, institutionally sponsored loans, and unspecified assistantships available. Financial award application deadline: 3/1; financial award applicants required to submit FAFSA. *Faculty research:* Acting/voice/speech/movement, theatrical design and production, musical theater, directing, playwriting. *Unit head:* Dr. Douglas Wager, Associate Dean, 215-204-6127, E-mail: theater@temple.edu. *Application contact:* Leah Dempsey, Assistant Director for Administration, 215-204-8791, E-mail: leahdempsey@temple.edu.
Website: http://www.temple.edu/theater/

Texas State University, The Graduate College, College of Fine Arts and Communication, Department of Theatre Arts and Dance, Program in Theatre Arts, San Marcos, TX 78666. Offers directing (MFA); playwriting (MA); theatre history, dramatic criticism and dramaturgy (MA). Part-time and evening/weekend programs available. *Faculty:* 6 full-time (2 women), 2 part-time/adjunct (0 women). *Students:* 14 full-time (4 women); includes 5 minority (1 Black or African American, non-Hispanic/Latino; 4 Hispanic/Latino). Average age 34. 19 applicants, 63% accepted, 6 enrolled. In 2014, 6 master's awarded. *Degree requirements:* For master's, comprehensive exam, thesis (for some programs). *Entrance requirements:* For master's, GRE General Test (minimum preferred score of 300), baccalaureate degree from regionally-accredited institution with minimum GPA of 2.75 in last 60 hours of undergraduate course work. Additional exam requirements/recommendations for international students: Required—TOEFL (minimum score 550 paper-based; 78 iBT). *Application deadline:* For fall admission, 3/15 priority date for domestic students, 3/15 for international students. Applications are processed on a rolling basis. Application fee: $40 ($90 for international students). Electronic applications accepted. *Expenses:* Expenses: $8,834 (tuition and fees combined). *Financial support:* In 2014–15, 13 students received support, including 2 research assistantships (averaging $12,152 per year), 12 teaching assistantships (averaging $11,953 per year); Federal Work-Study, institutionally sponsored loans, scholarships/grants, and unspecified assistantships also available. Support available to part-time students. Financial award application deadline: 4/1; financial award applicants required to submit FAFSA. *Faculty research:* Theatre history (especially nineteenth century American theatre), stage productions, playwriting. *Unit head:* Dr. Sandra Mayo, Graduate Advisor, 512-245-2061, Fax: 512-245-8440, E-mail: sm37@txstate.edu. *Application contact:* Dr. Andrea Golato, Dean of Graduate School, 512-245-2581, Fax: 512-245-8365, E-mail: gradcollege@txstate.edu.
Website: http://www.theatreanddance.txstate.edu/

Texas Tech University, Graduate School, College of Visual and Performing Arts, Department of Theatre and Dance, Lubbock, TX 79409. Offers theatre arts (MA, MFA). *Accreditation:* NAST. Part-time programs available. *Faculty:* 19 full-time (9 women), 2 part-time/adjunct (both women). *Students:* 28 full-time (15 women); includes 5 minority (1 Black or African American, non-Hispanic/Latino; 3 Hispanic/Latino; 1 Two or more races, non-Hispanic/Latino). Average age 31. 28 applicants, 46% accepted, 10 enrolled. In 2014, 9 master's awarded. *Degree requirements:* For master's, variable foreign language requirement, comprehensive exam (for some programs), thesis (for some programs), direct a production (for some programs). *Entrance requirements:* For master's, GRE, samples of artistic work in area of interest and/or interview/audition with faculty (for MFA). Additional exam requirements/recommendations for international students: Required—TOEFL (minimum score 550 paper-based; 79 iBT), IELTS (minimum score 6.5), PTE (minimum score 60). *Application deadline:* For fall admission, 6/1 priority date for domestic students, 1/15 priority date for international students; for spring admission, 9/1 priority date for domestic students, 6/15 priority date for international students. Applications are processed on a rolling basis. Application fee: $60. Electronic applications accepted. *Expenses:* Tuition, state resident: full-time $6310; part-time $262.92 per credit hour. Tuition, nonresident: full-time $14,998; part-time $624.92 per credit hour. *Required fees:* $2701; $36.50 per credit. $912.50 per semester. Tuition and fees vary according to course load. *Financial support:* In 2014–15, 25 students received support, including 25 fellowships (averaging $2,642 per year), 2 research assistantships (averaging $15,000 per year), 44 teaching assistantships (averaging $10,350 per year); Federal Work-Study, institutionally sponsored loans, scholarships/grants, health care benefits, tuition waivers (partial), and unspecified assistantships also available. Financial award application deadline: 4/15; financial award applicants required to submit FAFSA. *Faculty research:* Translation/adaptation, early modern theatre studies, Lessac voice work, Bertolt Brecht studies, devised theatre. *Total annual research expenditures:* $16,636. *Unit head:* Dr. Mark Charney, Department Chairperson, 806-742-3601, Fax: 806-742-1338, E-mail: mark.charney@ttu.edu. *Application contact:* Beth Scheckel, Graduate Admissions Coordinator, 806-742-3601, E-mail: beth.scheckel@ttu.edu.
Website: http://www.depts.ttu.edu/theatreanddance/

Texas Woman's University, Graduate School, College of Arts and Sciences, School of the Arts, Department of Music and Drama, Denton, TX 76201. Offers drama (MA); music (MA). *Accreditation:* NASM. Part-time programs available. *Degree requirements:* For master's, comprehensive exam, thesis (for some programs), project recital, professional paper. *Entrance requirements:* For master's, music history/theory placement exam (for music only), audition and/or design portfolio, interview, resume, writing sample (for drama only). Additional exam requirements/recommendations for international students: Required—TOEFL (minimum score 550 paper-based; 79 iBT). Electronic applications accepted. *Faculty research:* Musical development in early childhood, little known or neglected compositions for flute (especially by women composers), relationship of visual art to piano music, pedagogical development of the singing voice, guided imagery and music.

Towson University, Program in Theatre, Towson, MD 21252-0001. Offers MFA. *Accreditation:* NAST. *Students:* 10 full-time (6 women); includes 1 minority (Two or more races, non-Hispanic/Latino), 1 international. *Degree requirements:* For master's, thesis. *Entrance requirements:* For master's, minimum GPA of 3.0, bachelor's degree, 3 letters of recommendation, artistic statement, current professional resume, 3 references, portfolio, interview. *Application deadline:* For fall admission, 3/1 for domestic students. Application fee: $45. Electronic applications accepted. *Financial support:* Application deadline: 4/1. *Unit head:* Prof. Naoko Maeshiba, Graduate Program Director, 410-704-2791, E-mail: nmaeshiba@towson.edu. *Application contact:* Alicia Arkell-Kleis, Information Contact, 410-704-6004, E-mail: grads@towson.edu.
Website: http://grad.towson.edu/program/master/thea-mfa/

Tufts University, Graduate School of Arts and Sciences, Department of Drama and Dance, Medford, MA 02155. Offers drama (MA); dramatic literature and criticism (PhD); theater history (PhD). *Faculty:* 6 full-time (4 women). *Students:* 21 full-time (11 women), 6 part-time (3 women); includes 2 minority (1 Black or African American, non-Hispanic/Latino; 1 Two or more races, non-Hispanic/Latino), 4 international. Average age 30. 25 applicants, 36% accepted, 4 enrolled. In 2014, 1 master's, 2 doctorates awarded. Terminal master's awarded for partial completion of doctoral program. *Degree requirements:* For master's, one foreign language, thesis; for doctorate, 2 foreign languages, thesis/dissertation, oral exam, written general exam. *Entrance requirements:* For master's and doctorate, GRE General Test, writing sample. Additional exam requirements/recommendations for international students: Required—TOEFL (minimum score 600 paper-based; 80 iBT), IELTS (minimum score 6.5). *Application deadline:* For fall admission, 1/15 for domestic and international students. Applications are processed on a rolling basis. Application fee: $75. Electronic applications accepted. *Expenses:* *Tuition:* Full-time $45,590; part-time $1161 per credit hour. *Required fees:* $782. Full-time tuition and fees vary according to degree level, program and student level. Part-time tuition and fees vary according to course load. *Financial support:* Fellowships with full and partial tuition reimbursements, teaching assistantships with full and partial tuition reimbursements, Federal Work-Study, scholarships/grants, tuition waivers (partial), and unspecified assistantships available. Financial award application deadline: 5/15; financial award applicants required to submit FAFSA. *Unit head:* Dr. Laurence Senelick, Graduate Program Director. *Application contact:* Office of Graduate Admissions, 617-627-3395, E-mail: gradadmissions@tufts.edu.
Website: http://www.tufts.edu/as/drama/

Tulane University, School of Liberal Arts, Department of Theatre and Dance, New Orleans, LA 70118-5669. Offers design and technical production (MFA). *Entrance requirements:* For master's, GRE General Test, minimum B average in undergraduate course work. Additional exam requirements/recommendations for international students: Required—TOEFL. Electronic applications accepted. *Expenses:* *Tuition:* Full-time $46,326; part-time $2574 per credit hour. *Required fees:* $1980; $44.50 per credit hour. $550 per term. Tuition and fees vary according to course load and program. *Faculty research:* Scene design, stage management, costume design, technical direction, lighting design.

Université de Sherbrooke, Faculty of Letters and Human Sciences, Department of Letters and Communications, Sherbrooke, QC J1K 2R1, Canada. Offers comparative Canadian literature (MA, PhD); French literature (MA, PhD); linguistics (MA); theatre (MA). *Degree requirements:* For master's, thesis or alternative; for doctorate, thesis/dissertation. *Entrance requirements:* For master's, minimum GPA of 2.8; for doctorate, minimum GPA of 3.0.

Université Laval, Faculty of Letters, Department of Literature, Programs in Literature and Arts of the Screen and Stage, Québec, QC G1K 7P4, Canada. Offers MA, PhD. Part-time programs available. Terminal master's awarded for partial completion of doctoral program. *Degree requirements:* For master's, thesis; for doctorate, comprehensive exam, thesis/dissertation. *Entrance requirements:* For master's and doctorate, linguistics exams, knowledge of French, knowledge of a second language. Electronic applications accepted.

University at Buffalo, the State University of New York, Graduate School, College of Arts and Sciences, Department of Theatre and Dance, Buffalo, NY 14260. Offers theatre and performance (MA, PhD). Part-time programs available. *Faculty:* 4 full-time (2 women). *Students:* 8 full-time (4 women), 1 part-time (0 women). Average age 32. 17 applicants, 59% accepted, 6 enrolled. *Degree requirements:* For master's, thesis, thesis project or written thesis; for doctorate, one foreign language, comprehensive exam, thesis/dissertation. *Entrance requirements:* For master's, statement of purpose; academic writing sample (e.g., scholarly essay, performance or book review); 3 letters of recommendation (sent electronically); portfolio of creative work; resume; completed BA, BFA, or BS; for doctorate, GRE, statement of purpose; academic writing sample (e.g., scholarly essay, performance or book review); 3 letters of recommendation (sent electronically); portfolio of creative work; a resume; completed MA degree. Additional exam requirements/recommendations for international students: Required—TOEFL (minimum score 550 paper-based). *Application deadline:* For fall admission, 2/1 for domestic and international students. Applications are processed on a rolling basis. Application fee: $75. Electronic applications accepted. *Financial support:* In 2014–15, 6 students received support, including 5 fellowships with full and partial tuition reimbursements available (averaging $3,200 per year), 1 teaching assistantship with full tuition reimbursement available (averaging $12,400 per year); scholarships/grants also available. Financial award application deadline: 12/1. *Faculty research:* Intermediality in theatre and performance; contemporary performance and theory; intersections of technology and performance; performances of authenticity and realness in intermedial theater, reality television, and immersive and pervasive gaming; digital dramaturgy; American theaters of the everyday. *Unit head:* Prof. Lynne Koscielniak, Chair, 716-645-0574, Fax: 716-645-6992, E-mail: lk2@buffalo.edu. *Application contact:* Dr. Sarah Bay-Cheng, Director of Graduate Studies, 716-645-0587, E-mail: baycheng@buffalo.edu.
Website: http://www.theatredance.buffalo.edu/

The University of Akron, Graduate School, Buchtel College of Arts and Sciences, School of Dance, Theatre, and Arts Administration, Akron, OH 44325. Offers arts administration (MA); theatre arts (MA). Part-time and evening/weekend programs available. *Faculty:* 6 full-time (2 women), 18 part-time/adjunct (10 women). *Students:* 16 full-time (10 women), 8 part-time (7 women); includes 4 minority (2 Black or African American, non-Hispanic/Latino; 2 Two or more races, non-Hispanic/Latino), 2 international. Average age 31. 15 applicants, 80% accepted, 7 enrolled. In 2014, 9 master's awarded. *Degree requirements:* For master's, thesis optional. *Entrance requirements:* For master's, minimum GPA of 2.75, 300-word statement of intent summarizing student background and outlining career goals. Additional exam requirements/recommendations for international students: Required—TOEFL (minimum score 550 paper-based; 79 iBT), IELTS (minimum score 6.5). *Application deadline:* For fall admission, 3/15 for domestic and international students. Application fee: $45 ($70 for international students). Electronic applications accepted. *Expenses:* Tuition, state resident: full-time $7578; part-time $421 per credit hour. Tuition, nonresident: full-time $12,977; part-time $721 per credit hour. *Required fees:* $1388; $35 per credit hour. Tuition and fees vary according to course load. *Financial support:* In 2014–15, 13 teaching assistantships with full tuition reimbursements were awarded. *Faculty research:* Theatre history; technical theatre; set, costume, and design; lighting; playwriting. *Total annual research expenditures:* $1,928. *Unit head:* Dr. Neil Sapienza, Interim Director, 330-972-7408, E-mail: nbs@uakron.edu. *Application contact:* Kara Stewart, Coordinator, Arts Administration, 330-972-7948, E-mail: kms140@uakron.edu.
Website: http://www.uakron.edu/dtaa/

The University of Alabama, Graduate School, College of Arts and Sciences, Department of Theatre and Dance, Tuscaloosa, AL 35487. Offers acting (MFA); costume design (MFA); directing (MFA); scene design/technical production (MFA); stage management (MFA); theatre (MFA); theatre management/administration (MFA). *Accreditation:* NAST. *Faculty:* 15 full-time (6 women). *Students:* 39 full-time (21 women),

1 part-time (0 women); includes 2 minority (1 Black or African American, non-Hispanic/Latino; 1 Two or more races, non-Hispanic/Latino), 1 international. Average age 29. 26 applicants, 58% accepted, 13 enrolled. In 2014, 6 master's awarded. *Degree requirements:* For master's, thesis project. *Entrance requirements:* For master's, auditions and/or portfolio review. *Application deadline:* For fall admission, 4/1 for domestic students, 3/1 for international students. Applications are processed on a rolling basis. Application fee: $50 ($60 for international students). Electronic applications accepted. *Expenses:* Tuition, state resident: full-time $9826. Tuition, nonresident: full-time $24,950. *Financial support:* In 2014–15, 21 research assistantships with full tuition reimbursements (averaging $13,140 per year), 19 teaching assistantships with full tuition reimbursements (averaging $13,140 per year) were awarded; career-related internships or fieldwork, health care benefits, and unspecified assistantships also available. Financial award application deadline: 4/16. *Faculty research:* Acting, theatre history, directing, design practice and production (scenery, costumes, and lighting), technical direction and production, theatre management. *Unit head:* Prof. William Teague, Chair and Professor, 205-348-5283, Fax: 205-348-9048, E-mail: wteague@ua.edu. *Application contact:* Nancy Calvert, Recruiting Contact, 205-348-5283, Fax: 205-348-9048, E-mail: ncalvert@ua.edu.
Website: http://www.as.ua.edu/theatre/

University of Alberta, Faculty of Graduate Studies and Research, Department of Drama, Edmonton, AB T6G 2E1, Canada. Offers design (MFA); directing (MFA); drama (MA). *Degree requirements:* For master's, one foreign language, production thesis. *Faculty research:* Dramaturgy, history, theory and criticism, design.

The University of Arizona, College of Fine Arts, School of Theatre Arts, Tucson, AZ 85721. Offers MA, MFA. *Accreditation:* NAST. *Degree requirements:* For master's, comprehensive exam (for some programs), thesis (for some programs), production monograph. *Entrance requirements:* For master's, 3 letters of recommendation, portfolio. Additional exam requirements/recommendations for international students: Required—TOEFL (minimum score 550 paper-based; 79 iBT). Electronic applications accepted. *Faculty research:* Modern and contemporary theater, cultural studies, musical theater, women and theater.

University of Arkansas, Graduate School, J. William Fulbright College of Arts and Sciences, Department of Drama, Fayetteville, AR 72701-1201. Offers MA, MFA. *Degree requirements:* For master's, thesis optional. Electronic applications accepted.

The University of British Columbia, Faculty of Arts, Creative Writing Program, Vancouver, BC V6T 1Z1, Canada. Offers creative writing (MFA); creative writing and film production (MFA); creative writing and theatre (MFA). Part-time programs available. Postbaccalaureate distance learning degree programs offered (minimal on-campus study). *Degree requirements:* For master's, thesis. *Entrance requirements:* For master's, sample of written work. Additional exam requirements/recommendations for international students: Required—TOEFL (minimum score 550 paper-based). Electronic applications accepted. *Expenses:* Contact institution. *Faculty research:* Writing of fiction; poetry, creative nonfiction, plays for stage, screen, television, radio, writing for children and translation, song lyrics and libretto, new media and graphic novel.

The University of British Columbia, Faculty of Arts and Faculty of Graduate Studies, Department of Theatre and Film, Theatre Program, Vancouver, BC V6T 1Z2, Canada. Offers theatre (MA, PhD); theatre design (MFA); theatre directing (MFA). Terminal master's awarded for partial completion of doctoral program. *Degree requirements:* For master's, variable foreign language requirement, comprehensive exam, thesis; for doctorate, one foreign language, comprehensive exam, thesis/dissertation. *Entrance requirements:* For master's, portfolio (MFA); for doctorate, MA or equivalent. Additional exam requirements/recommendations for international students: Required—TOEFL (minimum score 550 paper-based for MFA; 600 for MA and PhD). *Faculty research:* Devising theatre; Canadian theatre; multicultural and theatre arts; stage lighting and costume design.

University of Calgary, Faculty of Graduate Studies, Faculty of Arts, Department of Drama, Calgary, AB T2N 1N4, Canada. Offers design and technical theatre (MFA); directing (MFA); playwriting (MFA); theatre studies (MFA). *Degree requirements:* For master's, thesis. *Entrance requirements:* For master's, bachelor's degree in drama, minimum GPA of 3.0, portfolio (design and playwriting). Additional exam requirements/recommendations for international students: Required—TOEFL. *Faculty research:* Popular theatre, collective creation, technical design, dramaturgy, directing styles.

University of California, Berkeley, Graduate Division, College of Letters and Science, Group in Performance Studies, Berkeley, CA 94720-1500. Offers PhD. *Degree requirements:* For doctorate, one foreign language, thesis/dissertation, qualifying exam. *Entrance requirements:* For doctorate, GRE General Test, sample of critical writing, 3 letters of recommendation. Additional exam requirements/recommendations for international students: Required—TOEFL. Electronic applications accepted. *Faculty research:* Postcolonial performance; gender, sexuality, and performance; political performance; dramatic literature and theory; race, ethnicity, performance.

University of California, Davis, Graduate Studies, Program in Dramatic Art, Davis, CA 95616. Offers acting (MFA); dramatic art (PhD). *Entrance requirements:* For master's, minimum GPA of 3.0, portfolio. Additional exam requirements/recommendations for international students: Required—TOEFL (minimum score 550 paper-based). Electronic applications accepted. *Faculty research:* Twentieth century performance and culture.

University of California, Davis, Graduate Studies, Program in Performance Studies, Davis, CA 95616. Offers dramatic art (PhD). *Degree requirements:* For doctorate, 2 foreign languages, thesis/dissertation. *Entrance requirements:* For doctorate, GRE, minimum GPA of 3.25. Additional exam requirements/recommendations for international students: Required—TOEFL (minimum score 550 paper-based). Electronic applications accepted.

University of California, Irvine, Claire Trevor School of the Arts, Department of Drama, Irvine, CA 92697. Offers acting (MFA); design and stage management (MFA); directing (MFA); drama (MFA); drama and theatre (PhD). *Students:* 73 full-time (42 women), 1 part-time (0 women); includes 24 minority (7 Black or African American, non-Hispanic/Latino; 4 Asian, non-Hispanic/Latino; 8 Hispanic/Latino; 5 Two or more races, non-Hispanic/Latino). Average age 27. 181 applicants, 15% accepted, 23 enrolled. In 2014, 18 master's, 5 doctorates awarded. *Degree requirements:* For master's, comprehensive exam, thesis; for doctorate, one foreign language, thesis/dissertation. *Entrance requirements:* For master's, audition, interview, or portfolio; minimum GPA of 3.0; for doctorate, GRE, minimum GPA of 3.5, critical writing samples. *Application deadline:* For fall admission, 1/15 priority date for domestic students, 1/15 for international students. Applications are processed on a rolling basis. Application fee: $90 ($110 for international students). Electronic applications accepted. *Financial support:* Fellowships, teaching assistantships, institutionally sponsored loans, traineeships, health care benefits, and unspecified assistantships available. Financial award application deadline: 3/1; financial award applicants required to submit FAFSA. *Faculty research:* Costume, scenery, and lighting design; production; theatre history, literature, and criticism. *Unit head:* Daniel Gary Busby, Department Chair, 949-824-8243, Fax: 949-824-3475, E-mail: dgbusby@uci.edu. *Application contact:* Prof. Stephen F. Barker, Associate Dean, 949-824-5684, Fax: 949-824-2450, E-mail: barker@uci.edu.
Website: http://www.arts.uci.edu/ctsa-academic-departments-drama

University of California, Los Angeles, Graduate Division, School of Theater, Film and Television, Department of Theater, Los Angeles, CA 90095. Offers theater (MA, MFA); theater and performance studies (PhD). *Accreditation:* NAST. *Degree requirements:* For master's, comprehensive exam or thesis; for doctorate, one foreign language, thesis/dissertation, oral and written qualifying exams. *Entrance requirements:* For master's, bachelor's degree; minimum undergraduate GPA of 3.0 (or its equivalent if letter grade system not used); portfolio (MFA); writing sample (MA); for doctorate, GRE General Test, bachelor's degree; minimum undergraduate GPA of 3.0 (or its equivalent if letter grade system not used); writing sample. Additional exam requirements/recommendations for international students: Required—TOEFL. Electronic applications accepted. *Expenses:* Contact institution.

University of California, San Diego, Graduate Division, Department of Theatre and Dance, La Jolla, CA 92093. Offers acting (MFA); dance theatre (MFA); design (MFA); directing (MFA); drama and theatre (PhD); playwriting (MFA); stage management (MFA). PhD offered jointly with University of California, Irvine. *Students:* 81 full-time (47 women), 5 part-time (1 woman); includes 26 minority (15 Black or African American, non-Hispanic/Latino; 1 American Indian or Alaska Native, non-Hispanic/Latino; 7 Asian, non-Hispanic/Latino; 3 Hispanic/Latino), 7 international. 439 applicants, 7% accepted, 25 enrolled. In 2014, 19 master's, 4 doctorates awarded. *Degree requirements:* For master's, thesis; for doctorate, comprehensive exam, thesis/dissertation. *Entrance requirements:* For master's, GRE General Test (for playwriting only), minimum GPA of 3.5; audition or interview; for doctorate, GRE General Test, minimum GPA of 3.5; audition and/or interview. Additional exam requirements/recommendations for international students: Required—TOEFL (minimum score 550 paper-based; 80 iBT), IELTS (minimum score 7). *Application deadline:* For fall admission, 1/6 for domestic students. Application fee: $90 ($110 for international students). Electronic applications accepted. *Expenses:* Tuition, state resident: full-time $11,220; part-time $5610 per quarter. Tuition, nonresident: full-time $26,322; part-time $13,161 per quarter. *Required fees:* $570 per quarter. Tuition and fees vary according to program. *Financial support:* Scholarships/grants available. Financial award applicants required to submit FAFSA. *Faculty research:* Theatre of the Americas, European theatre, Asian theatre, gender studies, critical theory. *Unit head:* Jim Carmody, Chair, 858-534-6889, E-mail: jcarmody@ucsd.edu. *Application contact:* Marybeth Ward, Graduate Coordinator, 858-534-1046, E-mail: meward@ucsd.edu.
Website: http://theatre.ucsd.edu/

University of California, Santa Barbara, Graduate Division, College of Letters and Sciences, Division of Humanities and Fine Arts, Department of Theater and Dance, Santa Barbara, CA 93106-7060. Offers theater studies (MA, PhD), including European medieval studies (PhD), feminist studies (PhD), theatre studies (PhD); MA/PhD. Terminal master's awarded for partial completion of doctoral program. *Degree requirements:* For master's, comprehensive exam, thesis; for doctorate, one foreign language, comprehensive exam, thesis/dissertation. *Entrance requirements:* For master's and doctorate, GRE. Additional exam requirements/recommendations for international students: Required—TOEFL (minimum score 550 paper-based; 80 iBT), IELTS (minimum score 7). Electronic applications accepted. *Faculty research:* English and American theater and Ancient Greek; Spanish, Latin American and Caribbean performance; Renaissance and Baroque drama and intercultural theory; East Asian performance, gender and nationalism; Korean cultural studies, Russian literature, and Slavic folklore; history of German theater, Shakespeare, and European opera; postcolonialism, performance-based ethnography, globalism and national identity formation in Africa.

University of California, Santa Cruz, Division of Graduate Studies, Division of the Arts, Department of Theater Arts, Santa Cruz, CA 95064. Offers Certificate. *Entrance requirements:* Additional exam requirements/recommendations for international students: Required—TOEFL (minimum score 550 paper-based; 83 iBT); Recommended—IELTS (minimum score 8). Electronic applications accepted.

University of Central Florida, College of Arts and Humanities, Department of Music, Orlando, FL 32816. Offers music (MA); theatre (MA, MFA), including acting (MFA), design (MFA), theatre for young audiences (MFA). *Accreditation:* NASM; NCATE. Part-time and evening/weekend programs available. *Faculty:* 51 full-time (19 women), 14 part-time/adjunct (8 women). *Students:* 28 full-time (15 women), 24 part-time (15 women); includes 9 minority (2 Black or African American, non-Hispanic/Latino; 1 Asian, non-Hispanic/Latino; 3 Hispanic/Latino; 3 Two or more races, non-Hispanic/Latino), 1 international. Average age 32. 49 applicants, 49% accepted, 18 enrolled. In 2014, 22 master's awarded. *Entrance requirements:* For master's, GRE General Test. Additional exam requirements/recommendations for international students: Required—TOEFL. *Application deadline:* For fall admission, 7/15 for domestic students; for spring admission, 12/1 for domestic students. Application fee: $30. Electronic applications accepted. *Expenses:* Tuition, state resident: part-time $288.16 per credit hour. Tuition, nonresident: part-time $1073.31 per credit hour. *Financial support:* In 2014–15, 25 students received support, including 6 fellowships with partial tuition reimbursements available (averaging $5,500 per year), 4 research assistantships with tuition reimbursements available (averaging $7,500 per year), 19 teaching assistantships with partial tuition reimbursements available (averaging $7,800 per year); career-related internships or fieldwork, Federal Work-Study, institutionally sponsored loans, tuition waivers (partial), and unspecified assistantships also available. Financial award application deadline: 3/1; financial award applicants required to submit FAFSA. *Unit head:* Jeffrey Moore, Chair, 407-823-2879, Fax: 407-823-3378, E-mail: jeffrey.moore@ucf.edu. *Application contact:* Barbara Rodriguez Lamas, Director, Admissions and Student Services, 407-823-2766, Fax: 407-823-6442, E-mail: gradadmissions@ucf.edu.
Website: http://performingarts.cah.ucf.edu/

University of Central Missouri, The Graduate School, Warrensburg, MO 64093. Offers accountancy (MA); accounting (MBA); applied mathematics (MS); aviation safety (MA); biology (MS); business administration (MBA); career and technical education leadership (MS); college student personnel administration (MS); communication (MA); computer science (MS); counseling (MS); criminal justice (MS); educational leadership (Ed D); educational technology (MS); elementary and early childhood education (MSE); English (MA); environmental studies (MA); finance (MBA); history (MA); human services/educational technology (Ed S); human services/learning resources (Ed S); human services/professional counseling (Ed S); industrial hygiene (MS); industrial management (MS); information systems (MBA); information technology (MS); kinesiology (MS); library science and information services (MS); literacy education (MSE); marketing (MBA); mathematics (MS); music (MA); occupational safety management (MS); psychology (MS); rural family nursing (MS); school administration (MSE); social gerontology (MS); sociology (MA); special education (MSE); speech language pathology (MS); superintendency (Ed S); teaching (MAT); teaching English as a second language (MA); technology (MS); technology management (PhD); theatre (MA). Part-time programs available. *Faculty:* 314 full-time (137 women), 24 part-time/adjunct (14 women). *Students:* 1,624 full-time (542 women), 1,773 part-time (1,055 women); includes 194 minority (104 Black or African American, non-Hispanic/Latino; 6 American Indian or Alaska Native, non-Hispanic/Latino; 23 Asian, non-Hispanic/Latino; 41 Hispanic/Latino; 3 Native Hawaiian or other Pacific Islander, non-Hispanic/Latino; 17 Two or more races,

non-Hispanic/Latino), 1,592 international. Average age 31. 2,800 applicants, 63% accepted, 1223 enrolled. In 2014, 796 master's, 81 other advanced degrees awarded. *Degree requirements:* For master's and Ed S, comprehensive exam (for some programs), thesis (for some programs). *Entrance requirements:* Additional exam requirements/recommendations for international students: Required—TOEFL (minimum score 550 paper-based; 79 iBT). *Application deadline:* For fall admission, 6/1 for domestic students; for spring admission, 10/1 for domestic and international students. Applications are processed on a rolling basis. Application fee: $30 ($75 for international students). Electronic applications accepted. *Expenses:* Tuition, state resident: full-time $6630; part-time $276.25 per credit hour. Tuition, nonresident: full-time $13,260; part-time $552.50 per credit hour. *Required fees:* $29 per credit hour. Tuition and fees vary according to campus/location. *Financial support:* In 2014–15, 118 students received support, including 271 research assistantships with full and partial tuition reimbursements available (averaging $7,500 per year), 109 teaching assistantships with full and partial tuition reimbursements available (averaging $7,500 per year); career-related internships or fieldwork, Federal Work-Study, scholarships/grants, and administrative and laboratory assistantships also available. Support available to part-time students. Financial award application deadline: 3/1; financial award applicants required to submit FAFSA. *Unit head:* Tina Church-Hockett, Director of Graduate School and International Admissions, 660-543-4621, Fax: 660-543-4778, E-mail: church@ucmo.edu. *Application contact:* Brittany Lawrence, Graduate Student Services Coordinator, 660-543-4621, Fax: 660-543-4778, E-mail: gradinfo@ucmo.edu. Website: http://www.ucmo.edu/graduate/

University of Cincinnati, Graduate School, College-Conservatory of Music, Divisions of Opera, Musical Theater, Drama, and Arts Administration, Cincinnati, OH 45221. Offers arts administration (MA); directing (MFA); theater design and production (MFA); voice and opera (MM, DMA); MBA/MA. *Accreditation:* NAST (one or more programs are accredited). *Degree requirements:* For master's, final project. *Entrance requirements:* For master's, GMAT (MA), audition/interview. Additional exam requirements/recommendations for international students: Required—TOEFL (minimum score 520 paper-based). Electronic applications accepted.

University of Colorado Boulder, Graduate School, College of Arts and Sciences, Department of Theatre and Dance, Boulder, CO 80309. Offers dance (MFA); theatre (MA, PhD). *Faculty:* 14 full-time (9 women). *Students:* 39 full-time (33 women); includes 6 minority (4 Black or African American, non-Hispanic/Latino; 2 Hispanic/Latino), 1 international. Average age 33. 40 applicants, 45% accepted, 8 enrolled. In 2014, 8 master's, 3 doctorates awarded. Terminal master's awarded for partial completion of doctoral program. *Degree requirements:* For master's, comprehensive exam, thesis; for doctorate, one foreign language, thesis/dissertation. *Entrance requirements:* For master's, GRE General Test (MA), audition (MFA), minimum undergraduate GPA of 2.75. *Application deadline:* For fall admission, 12/15 for domestic students, 12/1 for international students. Application fee: $50 ($70 for international students). Electronic applications accepted. *Financial support:* In 2014–15, 102 students received support, including 20 fellowships (averaging $1,284 per year), 31 teaching assistantships with full and partial tuition reimbursements available (averaging $19,505 per year); institutionally sponsored loans, scholarships/grants, health care benefits, and unspecified assistantships also available. Financial award application deadline: 1/15; financial award applicants required to submit FAFSA. *Faculty research:* Performing arts, drama, dramatic/theatre arts, dance, opera/musical theatre. Website: http://www.colorado.edu/theatredance/

University of Connecticut, Graduate School, School of Fine Arts, Department of Dramatic Arts, Storrs, CT 06269. Offers acting (MFA); costume design (MFA); lighting design (MFA); puppetry (MA, MFA); scenic design (MFA). *Degree requirements:* For master's, comprehensive exam. *Entrance requirements:* Additional exam requirements/ recommendations for international students: Required—TOEFL (minimum score 550 paper-based). Electronic applications accepted.

University of Delaware, College of Arts and Sciences, Professional Theatre Training Program, Newark, DE 19716. Offers acting (MFA); stage management (MFA); technical production (MFA). Students are matriculated into program once every three years. *Entrance requirements:* For master's, audition, interview. Electronic applications accepted. *Faculty research:* Theatre training, acting, technical production, stage management.

University of Florida, Graduate School, College of The Arts, School of Theatre and Dance, Gainesville, FL 32611-5800. Offers theatre (MFA), including acting, costume design, lighting design, scene design. *Accreditation:* NAST. Postbaccalaureate distance learning degree programs offered. *Faculty:* 14 full-time (4 women), 2 part-time/adjunct (1 woman). *Students:* 31 full-time (20 women), 11 part-time (0 women); includes 11 minority (7 Black or African American, non-Hispanic/Latino; 2 American Indian or Alaska Native, non-Hispanic/Latino; 2 Hispanic/Latino). 21 applicants, 71% accepted, 15 enrolled. In 2014, 12 master's awarded. *Degree requirements:* For master's, thesis, creative project. *Entrance requirements:* For master's, GRE General Test, audition/ portfolio, bachelor's degree in theatre, interview, minimum GPA 3.0. Additional exam requirements/recommendations for international students: Required—TOEFL (minimum score 550 paper-based; 80 iBT), IELTS (minimum score 6). *Application deadline:* For fall admission, 1/1 priority date for domestic students, 1/1 for international students; for spring admission, 11/1 for domestic and international students. Applications are processed on a rolling basis. Application fee: $30. Electronic applications accepted. *Financial support:* In 2014–15, 31 teaching assistantships were awarded; career-related internships or fieldwork, Federal Work-Study, institutionally sponsored loans, and unspecified assistantships also available. Financial award applicants required to submit FAFSA. *Faculty research:* Aesthetics of lighting design for the theater, production, history of theatre, criticism. *Unit head:* Jerry Dickey, PhD, Professor and Director, 352-273-0501, Fax: 352-395-5114, E-mail: jdickey@arts.ufl.edu. *Application contact:* Dylan Klempner, Graduate Program Advisor, 352-273-1488, Fax: 352-392-5114, E-mail: dylanklempner@ufl.edu. Website: http://www.arts.ufl.edu/theatreanddance/

University of Georgia, Franklin College of Arts and Sciences, Department of Theatre and Film Studies, Athens, GA 30602. Offers theatre (MFA, PhD). *Accreditation:* NAST. *Degree requirements:* For master's, comprehensive exam, written report; for doctorate, one foreign language, comprehensive exam, thesis/dissertation. *Entrance requirements:* For master's and doctorate, GRE General Test. Additional exam requirements/ recommendations for international students: Required—TOEFL (minimum score 550 paper-based). Electronic applications accepted. *Faculty research:* Digital media, African-American theatre, Indian theatre, history of animation, Vaudeville and popular culture history.

University of Guelph, Graduate Studies, College of Arts, School of English and Theatre Studies, Program in Drama, Guelph, ON N1G 2W1, Canada. Offers MA. Part-time programs available. *Degree requirements:* For master's, thesis (for some programs). *Entrance requirements:* For master's, 2 letters of reference, 4 year honours undergraduate degree in English or drama. Additional exam requirements/ recommendations for international students: Required—TOEFL. Electronic applications accepted. *Faculty research:* Canadian theatre, Renaissance, nineteenth- and twentieth-

century drama and theatre, Shaw, theatre history, dramatic literature, performance theory.

University of Hawaii at Manoa, Graduate Division, College of Arts and Humanities, Department of Theatre and Dance, Honolulu, HI 96822. Offers dance (MA, MFA); theatre (MA, MFA, PhD). Part-time programs available. *Degree requirements:* For master's, one foreign language, thesis optional; for doctorate, one foreign language, comprehensive exam, thesis/dissertation. *Entrance requirements:* For master's and doctorate, GRE General Test. Additional exam requirements/recommendations for international students: Required—TOEFL (minimum score 600 paper-based; 100 iBT), IELTS (minimum score 7). *Faculty research:* Asian theatre, feminist theatre and dance, Russian theatre, Australian theatre.

University of Houston, College of Liberal Arts and Social Sciences, School of Theatre and Dance, Houston, TX 77204. Offers theatre (MA, MFA). Part-time programs available. *Degree requirements:* For master's, thesis optional. *Entrance requirements:* For master's, GRE General Test, audition/interview (for MFA). Electronic applications accepted.

University of Idaho, College of Graduate Studies, College of Letters, Arts and Social Sciences, Department of Theatre Arts, Moscow, ID 83844-2008. Offers theatre arts (MFA). *Faculty:* 5 full-time, 1 part-time/adjunct. *Students:* 14 full-time, 1 part-time. Average age 35. In 2014, 8 master's awarded. *Entrance requirements:* For master's, minimum GPA of 2.8. Additional exam requirements/recommendations for international students: Required—TOEFL (minimum score 550 paper-based). *Application deadline:* For fall admission, 8/1 for domestic students; for spring admission, 12/15 for domestic students. Applications are processed on a rolling basis. Application fee: $60. Electronic applications accepted. *Expenses:* Tuition, state resident: full-time $4784; part-time $280.50 per credit hour. Tuition, nonresident: full-time $18,314; part-time $957.50 per credit hour. *Required fees:* $2000; $58.50 per credit hour. Tuition and fees vary according to program. *Financial support:* Research assistantships and teaching assistantships available. Financial award applicants required to submit FAFSA. *Unit head:* Dr. Dean Fields Panttaja, Chair, 208-885-5182, E-mail: theatre@uidaho.edu. *Application contact:* Sean Scoggin, Graduate Recruitment Coordinator, 208-885-4001, E-mail: graduateadmissions@uidaho.edu. Website: http://www.uidaho.edu/class/theatre

University of Illinois at Urbana–Champaign, Graduate College, College of Fine and Applied Arts, Department of Theatre, Champaign, IL 61820. Offers MA, MFA, PhD. *Accreditation:* NAST. *Students:* 71 (36 women). Application fee: $70 ($90 for international students). *Unit head:* Jeffrey Eric Jenkins, Head, 217-333-2371, Fax: 217-244-1861, E-mail: jej@illinois.edu. *Application contact:* David Swinford, Admissions and Records Officer, 217-244-6189, Fax: 217-244-1861, E-mail: dswinfor@illinois.edu. Website: https://theatre.illinois.edu/

The University of Iowa, Graduate College, College of Liberal Arts and Sciences, Department of Theatre Arts, Iowa City, IA 52242-1316. Offers MFA. *Accreditation:* NAST. *Degree requirements:* For master's, thesis, exam. *Entrance requirements:* For master's, minimum GPA of 3.0. Additional exam requirements/recommendations for international students: Required—TOEFL (minimum score 550 paper-based; 81 iBT). Electronic applications accepted.

The University of Kansas, Graduate Studies, College of Liberal Arts and Sciences, Department of Theatre, Lawrence, KS 66045. Offers theatre (MA, PhD); theatre design (MFA), including scenography. *Faculty:* 15 full-time. *Students:* 20 full-time (13 women), 4 international. Average age 31. 13 applicants, 69% accepted, 3 enrolled. In 2014, 4 master's awarded. *Degree requirements:* For master's, thesis; for doctorate, one foreign language, comprehensive exam, thesis/dissertation. *Entrance requirements:* For master's, GRE General Test, minimum GPA of 3.2; for doctorate, GRE General Test, minimum GPA of 3.5; MA or MFA in theatre or related field. Additional exam requirements/recommendations for international students: Required—TOEFL. *Application deadline:* For fall admission, 1/1 priority date for domestic and international students. Application fee: $55 ($65 for international students). Electronic applications accepted. *Financial support:* In 2014–15, 2 research assistantships with full tuition reimbursements, 9 teaching assistantships with full and partial tuition reimbursements (averaging $12,650 per year) were awarded; fellowships with tuition reimbursements, Federal Work-Study, scholarships/grants, and unspecified assistantships also available. Financial award application deadline: 1/1. *Faculty research:* Theatre history, performance studies, scenography, theatre historiography, cultural studies. *Unit head:* Mechele Leon, Chair, 785-864-2062, E-mail: mleon@ku.edu. *Application contact:* Karen Hummel, Senior Administrative Associate, 785-864-3511, E-mail: khummel@ku.edu. Website: http://www.theatre.ku.edu/

University of Lethbridge, School of Graduate Studies, Lethbridge, AB T1K 3M4, Canada. Offers addictions counseling (M Sc); agricultural biotechnology (M Sc); agricultural studies (M Sc, MA); anthropology (MA); archaeology (M Sc, MA); art (MA, MFA); biochemistry (M Sc); biological sciences (M Sc); biomolecular science (PhD); biosystems and biodiversity (PhD); Canadian studies (MA); chemistry (M Sc; computer science (M Sc); computer science and geographical information science (M Sc); counseling (MC); counseling psychology (M Ed); dramatic arts (MA); earth, space, and physical science (PhD); economics (MA); education (MA); educational leadership (M Ed); English (MA); environmental science (M Sc); evolution and behavior (PhD); exercise science (M Sc); French (MA); French/German (MA); French/Spanish (MA); general education (M Ed); geography (M Sc, MA); German (MA); health sciences (M Sc); individualized multidisciplinary (M Sc, MA); kinesiology (M Sc, MA); management (M Sc), including accounting, finance, general management, human resource management and labor relations, information systems, international management, marketing, policy and strategy; mathematics (M Sc); modern languages (MA); music (M Mus, MA); Native American studies (MA); neuroscience (M Sc, PhD); new media (MA, MFA); nursing (M Sc, MN); philosophy (MA); physics (M Sc); political science (MA); psychology (M Sc, MA); religious studies (MA); sociology (MA); theatre and dramatic arts (MFA); theoretical and computational science (PhD); urban and regional studies (MA); women and gender studies (MA). Part-time and evening/weekend programs available. *Faculty:* 358. *Students:* 445 full-time (243 women), 116 part-time (72 women). Average age 31. 351 applicants, 26% accepted, 87 enrolled. In 2014, 129 master's, 13 doctorates awarded. *Degree requirements:* For master's, thesis (for some programs); for doctorate, comprehensive exam, thesis/dissertation. *Entrance requirements:* For master's, GMAT (for M Sc in management), bachelor's degree in related field, minimum GPA of 3.0 during previous 20 graded semester courses, 2 years' teaching or related experience (M Ed); for doctorate, master's degree, minimum graduate GPA of 3.5. Additional exam requirements/recommendations for international students: Required—TOEFL. Application fee: $100 Canadian dollars. *Financial support:* Fellowships, research assistantships, teaching assistantships, scholarships/grants, health care benefits, and unspecified assistantships available. *Faculty research:* Movement and brain plasticity, gibberellin physiology, photosynthesis, carbon cycling, molecular properties of main-group ring components. *Application contact:* School of Graduate Studies, 403-329-5194, E-mail: sgsinquiries@uleth.ca. Website: http://www.uleth.ca/graduatestudies/

Theater

University of Louisville, Graduate School, College of Arts and Sciences, Department of Theatre Arts, Louisville, KY 40292-0001. Offers performance (MFA). *Accreditation:* NAST. Part-time programs available. *Students:* 12 full-time (6 women); includes 8 minority (all Black or African American, non-Hispanic/Latino). Average age 25. 9 applicants, 67% accepted, 5 enrolled. In 2014, 3 master's awarded. *Degree requirements:* For master's, thesis, performance project, monograph. *Entrance requirements:* For master's, GRE General Test, auditions, portfolio review. Additional exam requirements/recommendations for international students: Required—TOEFL. *Application deadline:* For fall admission, 5/1 priority date for international students; for spring admission, 4/15 for domestic students, 11/1 priority date for international students; for summer admission, 4/1 priority date for international students. Applications are processed on a rolling basis. Application fee: $60. Electronic applications accepted. *Expenses:* Tuition, state resident: full-time $11,326; part-time $630 per credit hour. Tuition, nonresident: full-time $23,568; part-time $1311 per credit hour. *Required fees:* $196. Tuition and fees vary according to program and reciprocity agreements. *Financial support:* Teaching assistantships, scholarships/grants, and health care benefits available. Financial award application deadline: 3/15; financial award applicants required to submit FAFSA. *Faculty research:* Speech/dialects, especially for actors of color; African diaspora theatre; community acting and creation of new works; peace studies; African-American theatre. *Unit head:* Dr. Rinda Frye, Chair, 502-852-8444, Fax: 502-852-7235, E-mail: rlfrye01@louisville.edu. *Application contact:* Libby Leggett, Director, Graduate Admissions, 502-852-3101, Fax: 502-852-6536, E-mail: gradadm@louisville.edu.
Website: http://louisville.edu/theatrearts/

The University of Manchester, School of Arts, Histories and Cultures, Manchester, United Kingdom. Offers anthropology, media and performance (PhD); applied theatre professional (PhD); archaeology (PhD); art history and visual studies (PhD); arts management and cultural policy (PhD); classics and ancient history (PhD); composition (PhD); creative writing (PhD); drama (PhD); economic and social history (PhD); electroacoustic composition (PhD); English and American studies (PhD); history (PhD); humanitarianism and conflict response (PhD); museology (PhD); music (PhD); musicology (PhD); religions and theology (PhD).

University of Maryland, Baltimore County, The Graduate School, College of Arts, Humanities and Social Sciences, Department of Education, Program in Teaching, Baltimore, MD 21250. Offers early childhood education (MAT); elementary education (MAT); secondary education (MAT), including art, biology, chemistry, choral music, classical foreign language, dance, earth/space science, English, instrumental music, mathematics, modern foreign language, physical science, physics, social studies, theatre. Part-time and evening/weekend programs available. *Faculty:* 24 full-time (18 women), 25 part-time/adjunct (19 women). *Students:* 64 full-time (52 women), 34 part-time (22 women); includes 31 minority (12 Black or African American, non-Hispanic/Latino; 1 American Indian or Alaska Native, non-Hispanic/Latino; 7 Asian, non-Hispanic/Latino; 8 Hispanic/Latino; 3 Two or more races, non-Hispanic/Latino), 1 international. Average age 29. 40 applicants, 95% accepted, 35 enrolled. In 2014, 106 master's awarded. *Degree requirements:* For master's, comprehensive exam (for some programs), thesis (for some programs). *Entrance requirements:* For master's, PRAXIS I or SAT (minimum score of 1000), minimum GPA of 3.0. Additional exam requirements/recommendations for international students: Required—TOEFL. *Application deadline:* For fall admission, 6/1 for domestic students; for spring admission, 11/1 for domestic students. Applications are processed on a rolling basis. Application fee: $50. Electronic applications accepted. *Expenses:* Tuition, state resident: part-time $557. Tuition, nonresident: part-time $922. *Required fees:* $122 per semester. One-time fee: $200 part-time. *Financial support:* In 2014–15, 6 students received support, including teaching assistantships with full and partial tuition reimbursements available (averaging $12,000 per year); career-related internships or fieldwork, Federal Work-Study, scholarships/grants, tuition waivers, and unspecified assistantships also available. Financial award application deadline: 3/1. *Faculty research:* STEM teacher education, culturally sensitive pedagogy, ESOL/bilingual education, early childhood education, language, literacy and culture. *Unit head:* Dr. Susan M. Blunck, Graduate Program Director, 410-455-2869, Fax: 410-455-3986, E-mail: blunck@umbc.edu.
Website: http://www.umbc.edu/education/

University of Maryland, College Park, Academic Affairs, College of Arts and Humanities, School of Theatre, Dance and Performance Studies, Theatre Program, College Park, MD 20742. Offers performance (MFA); theatre and performance studies (MA, PhD); theatre design (MFA). *Degree requirements:* For master's, comprehensive exam, thesis optional. *Entrance requirements:* For master's, GRE General Test, portfolio, writing sample, 3 letters of recommendation. Additional exam requirements/recommendations for international students: Required—TOEFL. Electronic applications accepted.

University of Massachusetts Amherst, Graduate School, College of Humanities and Fine Arts, Department of Theater, Amherst, MA 01003. Offers costume design (MFA); directing (MFA); dramaturgy (MFA); lighting design (MFA); scenic design (MFA). Part-time programs available. *Faculty:* 17 full-time (9 women). *Students:* 13 full-time (6 women), 1 (woman) part-time; includes 1 minority (Black or African American, non-Hispanic/Latino), 1 international. Average age 29. 60 applicants, 12% accepted, 6 enrolled. In 2014, 2 master's awarded. *Degree requirements:* For master's, thesis. *Entrance requirements:* For master's, GRE (for dramaturgy and costume design only), two critical essays or design portfolios, resume of production experience. Additional exam requirements/recommendations for international students: Required—TOEFL (minimum score 550 paper-based; 80 iBT), IELTS (minimum score 6.5). *Application deadline:* For fall admission, 1/15 for domestic and international students. Applications are processed on a rolling basis. Application fee: $75. Electronic applications accepted. *Expenses:* Tuition, state resident: full-time $1980; part-time $110 per credit. Tuition, nonresident: full-time $14,644; part-time $414 per credit. *Required fees:* $11,417. One-time fee: $357. *Financial support:* Fellowships with full and partial tuition reimbursements, research assistantships with full and partial tuition reimbursements, teaching assistantships with full and partial tuition reimbursements, career-related internships or fieldwork, Federal Work-Study, scholarships/grants, traineeships, health care benefits, tuition waivers (full and partial), and unspecified assistantships available. Support available to part-time students. Financial award application deadline: 1/15. *Unit head:* Dr. Harley Erdman, Graduate Program Director, 413-545-3490, Fax: 413-577-0025. *Application contact:* Lindsay DeSantis, Supervisor of Admissions, 413-545-0722, Fax: 413-577-0010, E-mail: gradadm@grad.umass.edu.
Website: http://www.umass.edu/theater/

University of Memphis, Graduate School, College of Communication and Fine Arts, Department of Theatre and Dance, Memphis, TN 38152. Offers theatre (MFA). *Accreditation:* NAST. *Faculty:* 8 full-time (3 women), 1 (woman) part-time/adjunct. *Students:* 15 full-time (7 women), 7 part-time (0 women); includes 1 minority (Two or more races, non-Hispanic/Latino), 1 international. Average age 31. 10 applicants, 100% accepted, 5 enrolled. In 2014, 6 master's awarded. *Degree requirements:* For master's, comprehensive exam, practicum. *Entrance requirements:* For master's, minimum GPA of 3.0 in major, 2.5 overall. *Application deadline:* For fall admission, 8/1 for domestic students; for spring admission, 12/1 for domestic students. Applications are processed on a rolling basis. Application fee: $35 ($60 for international students). *Financial support:* In 2014–15, 12 students received support. Research assistantships with full tuition reimbursements available, teaching assistantships with full tuition reimbursements available, career-related internships or fieldwork, Federal Work-Study, institutionally sponsored loans, scholarships/grants, and unspecified assistantships available. Financial award application deadline: 2/15; financial award applicants required to submit FAFSA. *Faculty research:* Theatre design, production management, Lessac vocal training, movement styles, directing. *Unit head:* Prof. Robert A. Hetherington, Chair, 901-678-2523, Fax: 901-678-4331, E-mail: rhether@memphis.edu. *Application contact:* Moira J. Logan, Associate Dean/Director of Research and Graduate Studies, 901-678-2350, Fax: 901-678-5118, E-mail: mlogan1@memphis.edu.
Website: http://www.memphis.edu/theatre/

University of Michigan, Horace H. Rackham School of Graduate Studies, School of Music, Theatre, and Dance, Department of Theatre and Drama, Ann Arbor, MI 48109. Offers design (MFA); theatre (PhD). *Degree requirements:* For master's, thesis; for doctorate, one foreign language, thesis/dissertation, preliminary exam, qualifying exam. *Entrance requirements:* For master's, portfolio, interview, writing sample; for doctorate, GRE General Test, writing sample, interview. Additional exam requirements/recommendations for international students: Required—TOEFL. Electronic applications accepted. *Faculty research:* Silent film, avant-garde drama, popular entertainment.

University of Minnesota, Twin Cities Campus, Graduate School, College of Liberal Arts, Department of Theatre Arts and Dance, Minneapolis, MN 55455. Offers design technology (MFA); theatre arts (MA, PhD). *Accreditation:* NAST (one or more programs are accredited). Terminal master's awarded for partial completion of doctoral program. *Degree requirements:* For master's, thesis (for some programs), final creative project (MFA), foreign language (MA); for doctorate, one foreign language, thesis/dissertation, oral defense, written exams. *Entrance requirements:* For master's, GRE General Test (for MA), minimum GPA of 3.0 or portfolio; for doctorate, GRE General Test, minimum GPA of 3.0, writing sample, 1 foreign language. Additional exam requirements/recommendations for international students: Required—TOEFL (minimum score 550 paper-based; 79 iBT). Electronic applications accepted. *Faculty research:* Theatre historiography, theatre for social change, dance and performance studies, performance politics of ethnicity, migration, globalization, European avant-garde; theatre design and technology: costume, scenography, lighting, sound, multimedia.

University of Missouri, Office of Research and Graduate Studies, College of Arts and Science, Department of Theatre, Columbia, MO 65211. Offers MA, PhD. Part-time programs available. *Faculty:* 11 full-time (3 women), 1 (woman) part-time/adjunct. *Students:* 22 full-time (14 women), 2 part-time (1 woman); includes 2 minority (1 Hispanic/Latino; 1 Two or more races, non-Hispanic/Latino), 2 international. Average age 34. 10 applicants, 50% accepted, 5 enrolled. In 2014, 2 master's, 3 doctorates awarded. *Degree requirements:* For doctorate, thesis/dissertation. *Entrance requirements:* For master's, GRE General Test, minimum GPA of 3.0 overall and in last 60 hours; for doctorate, GRE General Test, minimum GPA of 3.0 overall and in last 60 hours, 3.5 in master's program. Additional exam requirements/recommendations for international students: Required—TOEFL (minimum score 650 paper-based; 114 iBT). *Application deadline:* For fall admission, 1/15 priority date for domestic and international students. Application fee: $55 ($75 for international students). Electronic applications accepted. *Financial support:* Fellowships with full tuition reimbursements, research assistantships with full tuition reimbursements, teaching assistantships with full tuition reimbursements, institutionally sponsored loans, health care benefits, and unspecified assistantships available. *Faculty research:* Theatrical history, production and design, interactive theatre, performance studies. *Unit head:* Dr. Heather M. Carver, Department Chair, 573-882-9263, E-mail: carverh@missouri.edu. *Application contact:* Phebe Nichols, Administrative Associate I, 573-882-2022, E-mail: nicholsa@missouri.edu.
Website: http://theatre.missouri.edu/gradprogram/index.html

University of Missouri–Kansas City, College of Arts and Sciences, Theatre Department, Kansas City, MO 64110-2499. Offers acting (MFA); design technology (MFA); theatre (MA). *Accreditation:* NAST. *Faculty:* 16 full-time (5 women), 7 part-time/adjunct (2 women). *Students:* 54 full-time (26 women), 19 part-time (10 women); includes 11 minority (4 Black or African American, non-Hispanic/Latino; 5 Hispanic/Latino; 2 Two or more races, non-Hispanic/Latino), 2 international. Average age 29. 25 applicants, 56% accepted, 14 enrolled. In 2014, 31 master's awarded. *Degree requirements:* For master's, thesis. *Entrance requirements:* For master's, audition or portfolio, interview. Additional exam requirements/recommendations for international students: Required—TOEFL (minimum score 550 paper-based; 80 iBT). *Application deadline:* For fall admission, 3/1 priority date for domestic and international students; for spring admission, 11/1 priority date for domestic and international students. Applications are processed on a rolling basis. Application fee: $45 ($50 for international students). Electronic applications accepted. *Financial support:* In 2014–15, 66 teaching assistantships with partial tuition reimbursements (averaging $6,810 per year) were awarded; career-related internships or fieldwork, Federal Work-Study, institutionally sponsored loans, and scholarships/grants also available. Financial award application deadline: 3/1; financial award applicants required to submit FAFSA. *Faculty research:* Contemporary Russian theatre, Shakespeare in performance, subtle energies in actor training, multi-channel sound, renovation of Zuni Pueblo historic Spanish mission. *Unit head:* Tom Mardikes, Chair, 816-235-2784, Fax: 816-235-6562, E-mail: mardikest@umkc.edu. *Application contact:* Cindy Stofiel, Student Affairs Representative, 816-235-6683, Fax: 816-235-6562, E-mail: stofielc@umkc.edu.
Website: http://cas.umkc.edu/theatre/

The University of Montana, Graduate School, College of Visual and Performing Arts, School of Theatre and Dance, Missoula, MT 59812-0002. Offers design/technology (MFA); theatre (MA). *Accreditation:* NAST (one or more programs are accredited). *Degree requirements:* For master's, thesis or alternative. *Entrance requirements:* For master's, GRE General Test, audition, portfolio, production notebook.

University of Nebraska at Omaha, Graduate Studies, College of Communication, Fine Arts and Media, Department of Theatre, Omaha, NE 68182. Offers MA. Part-time programs available. *Faculty:* 6 full-time (2 women). *Students:* 5 full-time (4 women), 1 part-time (0 women); includes 1 minority (Two or more races, non-Hispanic/Latino). Average age 27. 5 applicants, 60% accepted, 1 enrolled. In 2014, 1 master's awarded. *Degree requirements:* For master's, comprehensive exam, thesis (for some programs). *Entrance requirements:* For master's, minimum GPA of 3.0, statement of purpose, writing sample, 2 letters of recommendation, transcripts. Additional exam requirements/recommendations for international students: Required—TOEFL, IELTS, PTE. *Application deadline:* For fall admission, 2/22 for domestic students; for spring admission, 10/1 for domestic students. Applications are processed on a rolling basis. Application fee: $45. Electronic applications accepted. *Financial support:* In 2014–15, 3 students received support, including 3 research assistantships with tuition reimbursements available; fellowships, teaching assistantships with tuition reimbursements available, Federal Work-Study, scholarships/grants, tuition waivers (full), and unspecified assistantships also available. Support available to part-time students. Financial award application deadline: 3/1; financial award applicants required to submit FAFSA. *Unit head:* Dr. Scott Glasser, Chairperson, 402-554-2341, E-mail:

graduate@unomaha.edu. *Application contact:* Dr. Cynthia Phaneuf, Graduate Program Chair, 402-554-2341, E-mail: graduate@unomaha.edu.

University of Nebraska–Lincoln, Graduate College, College of Fine and Performing Arts, Johnny Carson School of Theatre and Film, Lincoln, NE 68588. Offers acting (MFA); costume (MFA); directing (MFA); stage design (MFA). *Accreditation:* NAST. *Degree requirements:* For master's, thesis. *Entrance requirements:* For master's, audition, portfolio. Additional exam requirements/recommendations for international students: Required—TOEFL (minimum score 500 paper-based). Electronic applications accepted. *Faculty research:* American theatre history, British theatre history, modern American drama, contemporary performance, Elizabethan theatre history.

University of Nevada, Las Vegas, Graduate College, College of Fine Arts, Department of Theatre, Las Vegas, NV 89154-5036. Offers MA, MFA. *Accreditation:* NAST. Part-time programs available. *Faculty:* 8 full-time (3 women), 2 part-time/adjunct (both women). *Students:* 30 full-time (18 women), 4 part-time (2 women); includes 8 minority (5 Black or African American, non-Hispanic/Latino; 1 Asian, non-Hispanic/Latino; 2 Hispanic/Latino), 3 international. Average age 32. 20 applicants, 65% accepted, 10 enrolled. In 2014, 6 master's awarded. *Degree requirements:* For master's, thesis (for some programs), creative project, oral exam. *Entrance requirements:* Additional exam requirements/recommendations for international students: Required—TOEFL (minimum score 550 paper-based; 80 iBT), IELTS (minimum score 7). *Application deadline:* For fall admission, 8/1 for domestic students, 5/1 for international students; for spring admission, 10/1 for international students. Application fee: $60 ($95 for international students). Electronic applications accepted. *Financial support:* In 2014–15, 29 students received support, including 14 research assistantships with partial tuition reimbursements available (averaging $12,786 per year), 15 teaching assistantships with partial tuition reimbursements available (averaging $12,752 per year); institutionally sponsored loans, scholarships/grants, health care benefits, and unspecified assistantships also available. Financial award application deadline: 3/1. *Faculty research:* Designing scenery, costumes or lighting, directing or stage managing, serving as technical director/consultant, or acting for a production for a regional theatre. *Unit head:* Brackley Frayer, Chair/Associate Professor, 702-895-3353, Fax: 702-895-0833, E-mail: brackley.frayer@unlv.edu. *Application contact:* Graduate College Admissions Evaluator, 702-895-3320, Fax: 702-895-4180, E-mail: gradcollege@unlv.edu.
Website: http://theatre.unlv.edu/

University of New Mexico, Graduate School, College of Fine Arts, Department of Theatre and Dance, Albuquerque, NM 87131-2039. Offers dance (MFA); dance history (MA); dramatic writing (MFA); theatre education and outreach (MA). *Accreditation:* NASD; NAST. *Faculty:* 8 full-time (4 women), 1 (woman) part-time/adjunct. *Students:* 9 full-time (6 women); includes 3 minority (all Hispanic/Latino). Average age 31. 9 applicants, 44% accepted, 1 enrolled. In 2014, 4 master's awarded. *Degree requirements:* For master's, comprehensive exam (for some programs), thesis (for some programs). *Entrance requirements:* For master's, minimum GPA of 3.0; undergraduate major in theatre, dance or closely-related field; 3 letters of recommendation; letter of intent; BA, BFA, BS, or MA in dance movement science or related field, or equivalent experience (for MFA in dance). *Application deadline:* For fall admission, 4/15 for domestic students; for spring admission, 11/10 for domestic students. Application fee: $50. Electronic applications accepted. *Financial support:* In 2014–15, 1 fellowship (averaging $7,200 per year), 1 research assistantship with partial tuition reimbursement (averaging $3,750 per year), 3 teaching assistantships with partial tuition reimbursements (averaging $4,482 per year) were awarded; Federal Work-Study, health care benefits, tuition waivers (partial), and unspecified assistantships also available. Financial award application deadline: 3/1; financial award applicants required to submit FAFSA. *Faculty research:* Theater education and outreach, choreography, dramatic writing, dance history/criticism. *Unit head:* Bill Liotta, Chair, 505-277-4332, Fax: 505-277-8921, E-mail: wliotta@unm.edu. *Application contact:* Christina Squire, Administrator II, 505-277-7362, Fax: 505-277-8921, E-mail: csquire@unm.edu.
Website: http://theatredance.unm.edu

University of New Orleans, Graduate School, College of Liberal Arts, Department of Film and Theatre, New Orleans, LA 70148. Offers design (MFA); film production (MFA); theatre performance (MFA), including acting, directing. *Accreditation:* NAST. *Degree requirements:* For master's, comprehensive exam, thesis. *Entrance requirements:* Additional exam requirements/recommendations for international students: Required—TOEFL (minimum score 550 paper-based; 79 iBT), IELTS (minimum score 6.5). Electronic applications accepted. *Faculty research:* Mass communication theory, nineteenth and twentieth century theater history, film criticism and history.

The University of North Carolina at Chapel Hill, Graduate School, College of Arts and Sciences, Department of Dramatic Art, Chapel Hill, NC 27599. Offers acting (MFA); costume production (MFA); technical production (MFA). *Entrance requirements:* For master's, audition or portfolio.

The University of North Carolina at Charlotte, College of Education, Interdisciplinary Education Programs, Charlotte, NC 28223-0001. Offers art education (MAT); dance education (MAT); elementary education (MAT); English as a second language (MAT); foreign language education (MAT); middle grades education (MAT); music education (MAT); secondary education (MAT); special education (MAT); teacher certification (Graduate Certificate); teaching (Graduate Certificate); theater education (MAT). Part-time programs available. *Students:* 96 full-time (67 women), 703 part-time (569 women); includes 300 minority (211 Black or African American, non-Hispanic/Latino; 20 Asian, non-Hispanic/Latino; 56 Hispanic/Latino; 13 Two or more races, non-Hispanic/Latino), 15 international. Average age 33. 425 applicants, 94% accepted, 317 enrolled. In 2014, 199 master's, 257 other advanced degrees awarded. Terminal master's awarded for partial completion of doctoral program. *Degree requirements:* For master's, thesis. *Entrance requirements:* For master's, GRE or MAT. Additional exam requirements/recommendations for international students: Required—TOEFL (minimum score 550 paper-based; 83 iBT). *Application deadline:* For fall admission, 5/1 priority date for domestic and international students; for spring admission, 10/1 priority date for domestic and international students. Applications are processed on a rolling basis. Application fee: $75. Electronic applications accepted. *Expenses:* Tuition, state resident: full-time $4008. Tuition, nonresident: full-time $16,295. *Required fees:* $2755. Tuition and fees vary according to course load and program. *Total annual research expenditures:* $94,425. *Unit head:* Dr. Warren DiBiase, Chair, 704-687-8881, Fax: 704-687-4705, E-mail: wjdibias@uncc.edu. *Application contact:* Kathy B. Giddings, Director of Graduate Admissions, 704-687-5503, Fax: 704-687-1668, E-mail: gradadm@uncc.edu.
Website: http://education.uncc.edu/academic-programs

The University of North Carolina at Greensboro, Graduate School, School of Music, Theatre and Dance, Department of Theatre, Greensboro, NC 27412-5001. Offers acting (MFA); design (MFA); directing (MFA); theater education (M Ed); theater for youth (MFA). *Accreditation:* NAST. *Entrance requirements:* For master's, portfolio, interviews. Electronic applications accepted.

University of North Carolina School of the Arts, School of Design and Production, Winston-Salem, NC 27127-2738. Offers costume design (MFA); costume technology (MFA); performance arts management (MFA); scene design (MFA); scene painting/properties (MFA); sound design (MFA); stage automation (MFA); technical direction (MFA); wig and make-up design (MFA). *Degree requirements:* For master's, thesis (for some programs), project. *Entrance requirements:* For master's, interview, portfolio. Additional exam requirements/recommendations for international students: Required—TOEFL. Electronic applications accepted.

University of North Dakota, Graduate School, College of Arts and Sciences, Department of Theatre Arts, Grand Forks, ND 58202. Offers MA. *Accreditation:* NAST. *Degree requirements:* For master's, comprehensive exam, thesis or alternative. *Entrance requirements:* For master's, minimum GPA of 3.0. Additional exam requirements/recommendations for international students: Required—TOEFL (minimum score 550 paper-based; 79 iBT), IELTS (minimum score 6.5). Electronic applications accepted.

University of Oklahoma, Weitzenhoffer Family College of Fine Arts, School of Drama, Norman, OK 73019. Offers MFA. *Accreditation:* NAST. *Faculty:* 10 full-time (5 women). *Students:* 3 full-time (1 woman), 2 part-time (both women); includes 1 minority (American Indian or Alaska Native, non-Hispanic/Latino). Average age 31. 2 applicants, 50% accepted. *Degree requirements:* For master's, comprehensive exam. *Entrance requirements:* For master's, writing sample, statement of professional goals, resume, recommendations. Additional exam requirements/recommendations for international students: Required—TOEFL (minimum score 79 iBT). *Application deadline:* For fall admission, 3/15 for domestic and international students; for spring admission, 11/1 for domestic and international students. Application fee: $50 ($100 for international students). Electronic applications accepted. *Expenses:* Tuition, state resident: full-time $4394; part-time $183.10 per credit hour. Tuition, nonresident: full-time $16,970; part-time $707.10 per credit hour. *Required fees:* $2892; $109.95 per credit hour. $126.50 per semester. *Financial support:* In 2014–15, 3 students received support, including 4 teaching assistantships with partial tuition reimbursements available (averaging $12,966 per year); unspecified assistantships also available. Financial award application deadline: 6/1; financial award applicants required to submit FAFSA. *Faculty research:* Dramaturgy, theatre history, criticism, stage management, directing, design. *Unit head:* Dr. Tom Orr, Director, 405-325-4021, Fax: 405-325-0400, E-mail: thorr@ou.edu. *Application contact:* Dr. Kae Koger, Graduate Liaison, 405-325-4021, Fax: 405-325-0400, E-mail: akoger@ou.edu.
Website: http://www.ou.edu/finearts/drama

University of Oregon, Graduate School, College of Arts and Sciences, Department of Theater Arts, Eugene, OR 97403. Offers MA, MFA, MS, PhD. *Degree requirements:* For master's, variable foreign language requirement, thesis or alternative; for doctorate, variable foreign language requirement, thesis/dissertation. *Entrance requirements:* For master's and doctorate, minimum GPA of 3.0. Additional exam requirements/recommendations for international students: Required—TOEFL.

University of Ottawa, Faculty of Graduate and Postdoctoral Studies, Faculty of Arts, Department of Theatre, Ottawa, ON K1N 6N5, Canada. Offers directing for theatre (MA). Electronic applications accepted. *Faculty research:* Lamise en scéne.

University of Pittsburgh, Dietrich School of Arts and Sciences, Department of Theatre Arts, Pittsburgh, PA 15260. Offers MA, MFA, PhD. *Accreditation:* NAST. *Faculty:* 4 full-time (3 women). *Students:* 20 full-time (13 women); includes 6 minority (1 Black or African American, non-Hispanic/Latino; 1 Asian, non-Hispanic/Latino; 4 Hispanic/Latino). Average age 33. 26 applicants, 27% accepted, 6 enrolled. In 2014, 6 doctorates awarded. Terminal master's awarded for partial completion of doctoral program. *Degree requirements:* For master's, comprehensive exam; for doctorate, one foreign language, comprehensive exam, thesis/dissertation, diagnostic exams. *Entrance requirements:* For master's and doctorate, GRE General Test, samples of written work. Additional exam requirements/recommendations for international students: Required—TOEFL (minimum score 550 paper-based; 90 iBT). *Application deadline:* For fall admission, 1/15 priority date for domestic and international students. Application fee: $50. Electronic applications accepted. *Expenses:* Tuition, state resident: full-time $20,742; part-time $838 per credit. Tuition, nonresident: full-time $33,960; part-time $1389 per credit. *Required fees:* $800; $205 per term. Tuition and fees vary according to program. *Financial support:* In 2014–15, 15 students received support, including 1 fellowship with partial tuition reimbursement available (averaging $24,296 per year), 14 teaching assistantships with full tuition reimbursements available (averaging $14,400 per year); research assistantships with full tuition reimbursements available, career-related internships or fieldwork, Federal Work-Study, institutionally sponsored loans, scholarships/grants, health care benefits, and unspecified assistantships also available. Support available to part-time students. Financial award application deadline: 1/15; financial award applicants required to submit FAFSA. *Faculty research:* American theatre, Renaissance theatre, Asian theatre, dramatic structure, performance theory. *Unit head:* Prof. Annmarie Duggan, Chairman, 412-624-7284, Fax: 412-624-6338, E-mail: duggan@pitt.edu. *Application contact:* Connie Anne Markiw, Department Secretary, 412-624-6568, Fax: 412-624-6338, E-mail: cam177@pitt.edu.
Website: http://www.play.pitt.edu/

University of Portland, Department of Performing and Fine Arts, Portland, OR 97203-5798. Offers directing (MFA). Part-time and evening/weekend programs available. *Faculty:* 3 full-time (1 woman). *Students:* 4 full-time (2 women). Average age 29. In 2014, 3 master's awarded. *Degree requirements:* For master's, thesis optional. *Entrance requirements:* For master's, GRE General Test, minimum GPA of 3.0, resume, 3 letters of recommendation, statement of goals, official transcripts. Additional exam requirements/recommendations for international students: Required—TOEFL (minimum score 600 paper-based; 100 iBT), IELTS (minimum score 7.5). *Application deadline:* For fall admission, 7/15 priority date for domestic and international students; for spring admission, 12/15 priority date for domestic and international students. Applications are processed on a rolling basis. Application fee: $50. *Expenses:* Tuition: Full-time $19,260; part-time $1070 per credit hour. Tuition and fees vary according to program. *Financial support:* Federal Work-Study, scholarships/grants, and tuition waivers (partial) available. Financial award application deadline: 3/1; financial award applicants required to submit FAFSA. *Unit head:* Dr. Andrew Golla, Director, 503-943-7228, E-mail: golla@up.edu. *Application contact:* Allison Able, Administrative Assistant, 503-943-7107, Fax: 503-943-7315, E-mail: able@up.edu.
Website: http://college.up.edu/pfa/drama/default.aspx?cid-9895&pid-4935

University of San Diego, College of Arts and Sciences, Graduate Acting Program, San Diego, CA 92110-2492. Offers MFA. *Faculty:* 6 full-time (2 women). *Students:* 14 full-time (6 women); includes 4 minority (3 Black or African American, non-Hispanic/Latino; 1 Two or more races, non-Hispanic/Latino), 1 international. Average age 28. 364 applicants, 2% accepted, 7 enrolled. In 2014, 7 master's awarded. *Entrance requirements:* For master's, audition. Additional exam requirements/recommendations for international students: Required—TOEFL (minimum score 580 paper-based; 83 iBT), TWE. *Application deadline:* For fall admission, 1/4 for domestic and international students. Application fee: $55. *Financial support:* In 2014–15, 14 students received support, including 14 fellowships with full tuition reimbursements available; career-related internships or fieldwork, Federal Work-Study, and institutionally sponsored loans also available. Financial award application deadline: 4/1; financial award applicants required to submit FAFSA. *Faculty research:* Voice and dialect coaching, directing, stage combat, movement choreography, acting. *Unit head:* Richard Seer, Graduate Program Director, 619-260-8813, Fax: 619-231-5879. *Application contact:* Monica

Mahon, Associate Director of Graduate Admissions, 619-260-4524, Fax: 619-260-4158, E-mail: grads@sandiego.edu. Website: http://www.globemfa.org/

University of Saskatchewan, College of Graduate Studies and Research, College of Arts and Science, Department of Drama, Saskatoon, SK S7N 5A2, Canada. Offers MA. *Degree requirements:* For master's, thesis. *Entrance requirements:* Additional exam requirements/recommendations for international students: Required—TOEFL (minimum score 80 iBT); Recommended—IELTS (minimum score 6.5). Electronic applications accepted.

University of South Carolina, The Graduate School, College of Arts and Sciences, Department of Theatre and Dance, Columbia, SC 29208. Offers theatre (MA, MAT, MFA). MA and MAT offered in cooperation with the College of Education. *Accreditation:* NAST (one or more programs are accredited). *Degree requirements:* For master's, comprehensive exam, thesis. *Entrance requirements:* For master's, GRE General Test, GRE or MAT (MAT), audition, interview (for MFA). Additional exam requirements/recommendations for international students: Required—TOEFL. Electronic applications accepted. *Faculty research:* Computer assisted design, rhetoric of science and technology, Alexander Technique, script analysis, Lessac Method.

University of South Carolina, The Graduate School, College of Education, Department of Instruction and Teacher Education, Program in Secondary Education, Columbia, SC 29208. Offers art education (IMA, MAT); business education (IMA, MAT); English (MAT); foreign language (MAT); health education (MAT); mathematics (MAT); science (IMA, MAT); secondary (Ed D); secondary education (MT, PhD); social studies (MAT); theatre and speech (MAT). IMA and MT offered jointly with the subject areas. *Accreditation:* NCATE. *Degree requirements:* For master's, comprehensive exam, thesis (for some programs), foreign language (MA); for doctorate, one foreign language, comprehensive exam, thesis/dissertation. *Entrance requirements:* For master's, GRE General Test or MAT, teaching certificate (IMA, M Ed), interview; for doctorate, GRE General Test or MAT, interview. *Faculty research:* Middle school programs, professional development, school collaboration.

The University of South Dakota, Graduate School, College of Fine Arts, Department of Theatre, Vermillion, SD 57069-2390. Offers design/technology (MFA); directing (MFA); theatre (MA). *Accreditation:* NAST. *Degree requirements:* For master's, thesis or alternative. *Entrance requirements:* For master's, GRE (MA), minimum GPA of 2.7, portfolio. Additional exam requirements/recommendations for international students: Required—TOEFL (minimum score 550 paper-based; 79 iBT). Electronic applications accepted.

University of Southern California, Graduate School, School of Theatre, Los Angeles, CA 90089. Offers acting (MFA); applied theatre arts (MA); dramatic writing (MFA). *Degree requirements:* For master's, comprehensive exam. *Entrance requirements:* For master's, GRE. Additional exam requirements/recommendations for international students: Required—TOEFL. Electronic applications accepted.

University of Southern Mississippi, Graduate School, College of Arts and Letters, Department of Theatre, Hattiesburg, MS 39406-0001. Offers design and technology (MFA); directing (MFA); performance (MFA). *Accreditation:* NAST. Part-time programs available. *Degree requirements:* For master's, comprehensive exam, thesis or alternative, creative project. *Entrance requirements:* For master's, GRE General Test, minimum GPA of 3.0. Additional exam requirements/recommendations for international students: Required—TOEFL, IELTS. *Faculty research:* Technical design, acting.

The University of Tennessee, Graduate School, College of Arts and Sciences, Department of Theatre, Knoxville, TN 37996. Offers costume design (MFA); lighting design (MFA); performance (MFA); scene design (MFA); theatre technology (MFA). *Degree requirements:* For master's, thesis or alternative. *Entrance requirements:* For master's, audition, minimum GPA of 2.7. Additional exam requirements/recommendations for international students: Required—TOEFL. Electronic applications accepted.

The University of Texas at Austin, Graduate School, College of Fine Arts, Department of Theatre and Dance, Austin, TX 78712-1111. Offers acting (MFA); dance (MFA); directing (MFA); drama and theatre for youth (MFA); performance as public practice (MA, MFA, PhD); playwriting (MFA); theatre technology (MFA); theatrical design (MFA). *Accreditation:* NASD. *Degree requirements:* For master's, thesis; for doctorate, variable foreign language requirement, thesis/dissertation. *Entrance requirements:* For master's and doctorate, GRE General Test.

The University of Texas at Austin, Graduate School, Michener Center for Writers, Austin, TX 78712-1111. Offers fiction (MFA); playwriting (MFA); poetry (MFA); screenwriting (MFA). Electronic applications accepted.

The University of Texas–Pan American, College of Arts and Humanities, Department of Communication, Edinburg, TX 78539. Offers communication (MA); communication training and consulting (Graduate Certificate); strategic communication and media relations (Graduate Certificate); theatre (MA). *Accreditation:* NAST. Part-time and evening/weekend programs available. *Degree requirements:* For master's, comprehensive exam, thesis or alternative. *Entrance requirements:* For master's, minimum GPA of 3.0. Additional exam requirements/recommendations for international students: Required—TOEFL. *Expenses:* Tuition, state resident: full-time $4187; part-time $232.60 per credit hour. Tuition, nonresident: full-time $10,857; part-time $603.16 per credit hour. *Required fees:* $782; $27.50 per credit hour. $143.35 per semester. *Faculty research:* Rhetorical theory, intercultural and mass communication, American theatre, multicultural theatre and drama, television and film.

University of the Cumberlands, Graduate Programs in Education, Williamsburg, KY 40769-1372. Offers all grades (P-12) (M Ed); business and marketing (MA Ed, MAT); counselor education and supervision (Ed D); director of pupil personnel (Certificate); director of special education (Certificate); educational administration and supervision (Ed S); educational leadership (Ed D); elementary education (MA Ed, MAT); instructional leadership - principalship (MA Ed); instructional leadership - school principal (Certificate); middle school education (MA Ed, MAT); reading and writing (MA Ed); school counseling (MA Ed); school superintendent (Certificate); secondary education (MA Ed, MAT); special education (MAT); supervisor of instruction (Certificate); teacher leader (MA Ed). Part-time and evening/weekend programs available. Postbaccalaureate distance learning degree programs offered. *Degree requirements:* For master's, comprehensive exam. Electronic applications accepted.

University of Toronto, School of Graduate Studies, Faculty of Arts and Science, Centre for Drama, Theatre and Performance Studies, Toronto, ON M5S 2J7, Canada. Offers MA, PhD. Part-time programs available. *Entrance requirements:* For master's, minimum B+ average, significant coursework in drama and related disciplines, resume, 2 letters of recommendation. Additional exam requirements/recommendations for international students: Required—TOEFL (minimum score 580 paper-based; 93 iBT), TWE (minimum score 5). Electronic applications accepted.

University of Victoria, Faculty of Graduate Studies, Faculty of Fine Arts, Department of Theatre, Victoria, BC V8W 2Y2, Canada. Offers design (MFA); directing (MFA); theatre history (MA). *Degree requirements:* For master's, thesis. *Entrance requirements:* Additional exam requirements/recommendations for international students: Required—

TOEFL (minimum score 575 paper-based), IELTS (minimum score 7). Electronic applications accepted.

University of Virginia, College and Graduate School of Arts and Sciences, Department of Drama, Charlottesville, VA 22903. Offers MFA. *Faculty:* 17 full-time (8 women), 2 part-time/adjunct (both women). *Students:* 18 full-time (9 women); includes 3 minority (1 Black or African American, non-Hispanic/Latino; 1 Hispanic/Latino; 1 Two or more races, non-Hispanic/Latino). Average age 27. 20 applicants, 70% accepted, 14 enrolled. In 2014, 14 master's awarded. *Degree requirements:* For master's, thesis project. *Entrance requirements:* For master's, GRE General Test, resume; 3 letters of recommendation. Additional exam requirements/recommendations for international students: Required—TOEFL (minimum score 600 paper-based; 90 iBT), IELTS (minimum score 7). *Application deadline:* For fall admission, 2/20 for domestic and international students. Applications are processed on a rolling basis. Application fee: $60. Electronic applications accepted. *Expenses:* Tuition, state resident: full-time $14,164; part-time $349 per credit hour. Tuition, nonresident: full-time $23,722; part-time $1300 per credit hour. *Required fees:* $2514. *Financial support:* Fellowships and teaching assistantships available. Financial award applicants required to submit FAFSA. *Faculty research:* Acting, scenic design, lighting design, technical direction, costume design/technology. *Unit head:* Tom Bloom, Chair, 434-924-3326, Fax: 434-924-1447, E-mail: drama@virginia.edu. *Application contact:* Barbara Koonin, Graduate Administrator, 434-924-3326, Fax: 434-924-1447, E-mail: blk2n@virginia.edu. Website: http://www.virginia.edu/drama/

University of Washington, Graduate School, College of Arts and Sciences, School of Drama, Seattle, WA 98195. Offers acting (MFA); costume design (MFA); directing (MFA); dramatic theory (PhD); lighting design (MFA); scenic design (MFA); theatre and performance history (PhD). *Degree requirements:* For master's, thesis; for doctorate, one foreign language, comprehensive exam, thesis/dissertation. *Entrance requirements:* For master's, interview, minimum GPA of 3.0, portfolio; for doctorate, GRE General Test, minimum GPA of 3.0, writing sample. Additional exam requirements/recommendations for international students: Required—TOEFL. *Faculty research:* Semiotics, Suzuki actor training, modern American theatre, ethnic American theatre.

University of Wisconsin–Madison, Graduate School, College of Letters and Science, Department of Theatre and Drama, Madison, WI 53706-1380. Offers MA, MFA, PhD. *Accreditation:* NAST. Part-time programs available. *Degree requirements:* For master's, thesis; for doctorate, thesis/dissertation. *Entrance requirements:* For master's and doctorate, GRE. Electronic applications accepted. *Expenses:* Tuition, state resident: full-time $10,723; part-time $745 per credit. Tuition, nonresident: full-time $24,054; part-time $1578 per credit. *Required fees:* $374 per semester. Tuition and fees vary according to course load, program and reciprocity agreements. *Faculty research:* Theories and histories of dance, theatre and performance studies; Russian theatre and dance; postmodern performance; Holocaust drama; race and representation.

University of Wisconsin–Milwaukee, Graduate School, Peck School of the Arts, Program in Performing Arts, Milwaukee, WI 53201-0413. Offers dance (MFA); film (MFA); theatre (MFA). Part-time programs available. *Degree requirements:* For master's, variable foreign language requirement, comprehensive exam, thesis or alternative. *Entrance requirements:* For master's, audition, interview. Additional exam requirements/recommendations for international students: Required—TOEFL (minimum score 550 paper-based; 79 iBT), IELTS (minimum score 6.5). Electronic applications accepted.

University of Wisconsin–Superior, Graduate Division, Department of Communicating Arts, Superior, WI 54880-4500. Offers mass communication (MA); speech communication (MA); theater (MA). Part-time programs available. *Degree requirements:* For master's, comprehensive exam, thesis or alternative, position paper or project. *Entrance requirements:* For master's, minimum GPA of 2.75. Electronic applications accepted. *Faculty research:* Multimedia technology, ethics in journalism, diversity, electronic portfolio assessment.

Utah State University, School of Graduate Studies, College of Humanities, Arts and Social Sciences, Department of Theatre Arts, Logan, UT 84322. Offers advanced technical practice (MFA); design (MFA); theatre arts (MA, MFA). *Degree requirements:* For master's, variable foreign language requirement, thesis (for some programs), summer internship (MFA). *Entrance requirements:* For master's, GRE General Test or MAT, portfolio (MFA), minimum GPA of 3.0, interview, BS or 20 semester credit. Additional exam requirements/recommendations for international students: Required—TOEFL. *Faculty research:* Seventeenth and eighteenth century Spanish theatre, Greek and Roman theatre, interpretation of literature for performance.

Villanova University, Graduate School of Liberal Arts and Sciences, Department of Theatre, Villanova, PA 19085-1699. Offers MA. Part-time and evening/weekend programs available. *Faculty:* 7. *Students:* 32 full-time (23 women), 6 part-time (2 women); includes 2 minority (1 Black or African American, non-Hispanic/Latino; 1 Two or more races, non-Hispanic/Latino). Average age 29. 26 applicants, 100% accepted, 20 enrolled. In 2014, 18 master's awarded. *Degree requirements:* For master's, comprehensive exam. *Entrance requirements:* For master's, GRE, minimum GPA of 3.0, resume, statement of goals, headshot. Additional exam requirements/recommendations for international students: Required—TOEFL. *Application deadline:* For fall admission, 3/1 for domestic students, 5/1 priority date for international students; for spring admission, 11/15 for domestic students, 10/15 priority date for international students; for summer admission, 5/1 for domestic students. Applications are processed on a rolling basis. Application fee: $50. Electronic applications accepted. *Financial support:* Research assistantships, teaching assistantships, scholarships/grants, and unspecified assistantships available. Financial award applicants required to submit FAFSA. *Unit head:* Fr. David Cregan, Chairperson, 610-519-4760. *Application contact:* Dean, Graduate School of Liberal Arts and Sciences. Website: http://www1.villanova.edu/villanova/artsci/theatre/graduate.html

Virginia Commonwealth University, Graduate School, School of the Arts, Department of Theatre, Richmond, VA 23284-9005. Offers costume design (MFA); pedagogy (MFA); scene design/technical theater (MFA). *Accreditation:* NAST. *Degree requirements:* For master's, thesis (for some programs). *Entrance requirements:* For master's, audition, portfolio. Additional exam requirements/recommendations for international students: Required—TOEFL (minimum score 600 paper-based; 100 iBT). Electronic applications accepted. *Faculty research:* Dramatic literature, speech.

Virginia Polytechnic Institute and State University, Graduate School, College of Liberal Arts and Human Sciences, Blacksburg, VA 24061. Offers career and technical education (MS Ed, Ed D, PhD, Ed S); communication (MA); counselor education (MA Ed, Ed D, PhD, Ed S); creative writing (MFA); curriculum and instruction (MA Ed, Ed D, PhD, Ed S); educational leadership and policy studies (MA Ed, Ed D, PhD, Ed S); educational research and evaluation (PhD); English (MA); foreign languages, cultures, and literatures (MA); higher education and student affairs (MA Ed); history (MA); human development (MS, PhD); material culture and public humanities (MA); philosophy (MA); political science (MA); rhetoric and writing (PhD); science and technology studies (MS, PhD); social, political, ethical, and cultural thought (PhD); sociology (MS, PhD); theater arts (MFA). *Faculty:* 421 full-time (216 women), 2 part-time/adjunct (both women). *Students:* 642 full-time (437 women), 537 part-time (344 women); includes 235 minority

(132 Black or African American, non-Hispanic/Latino; 2 American Indian or Alaska Native, non-Hispanic/Latino; 27 Asian, non-Hispanic/Latino; 52 Hispanic/Latino; 1 Native Hawaiian or other Pacific Islander, non-Hispanic/Latino; 21 Two or more races, non-Hispanic/Latino), 81 international. Average age 34. 890 applicants, 46% accepted, 303 enrolled. In 2014, 342 master's, 96 doctorates, 33 other advanced degrees awarded. *Degree requirements:* For master's, comprehensive exam (for some programs), thesis (for some programs); for doctorate, comprehensive exam (for some programs), thesis/dissertation (for some programs). *Entrance requirements:* For master's and doctorate, GRE/GMAT (may vary by department). Additional exam requirements/recommendations for international students: Required—TOEFL (minimum score 550 paper-based). *Application deadline:* For fall admission, 8/1 for domestic students, 4/1 for international students; for spring admission, 1/1 for domestic students, 9/1 for international students. Applications are processed on a rolling basis. Application fee: $75. Electronic applications accepted. *Expenses:* Tuition, state resident: full-time $11,656; part-time $647.50 per credit hour. Tuition, nonresident: full-time $23,351; part-time $1297.25 per credit hour. *Required fees:* $2533; $465.75 per semester. Tuition and fees vary according to course load, campus/location and program. *Financial support:* In 2014–15, 19 research assistantships with full tuition reimbursements (averaging $22,141 per year), 231 teaching assistantships with full tuition reimbursements (averaging $19,470 per year) were awarded. Financial award application deadline: 3/1; financial award applicants required to submit FAFSA. *Total annual research expenditures:* $6.5 million. *Unit head:* Elizabeth Spiller, Dean, 540-231-6779, Fax: 540-231-7157, E-mail: espiller@vt.edu. *Application contact:* Melissa Elliott, Executive Assistant, 540-231-6779, Fax: 540-231-7157, E-mail: elliott1@vt.edu.
Website: http://www.clahs.vt.edu/

Washington University in St. Louis, Graduate School of Arts and Sciences, Department of Performing Arts, St. Louis, MO 63130-4899. Offers theater and performance studies (MA). *Degree requirements:* For master's, thesis optional. *Entrance requirements:* For master's, GRE General Test, sample of written work. Additional exam requirements/recommendations for international students: Required—TOEFL. Electronic applications accepted. *Faculty research:* Theater and performance studies.

Wayne State University, College of Fine, Performing and Communication Arts, Department of Theatre and Dance, Detroit, MI 48202. Offers theatre (MA, MFA), including acting (MFA), costume design (MFA), lighting design (MFA), stage management (MFA), theatre (MA), theatre management (MFA), theatre stage design (MFA). *Accreditation:* NAST. *Students:* 42 full-time (24 women); includes 6 minority (2 Black or African American, non-Hispanic/Latino; 2 Hispanic/Latino; 2 Two or more races, non-Hispanic/Latino), 2 international. Average age 29. 158 applicants, 11% accepted, 17 enrolled. In 2014, 17 master's awarded. *Degree requirements:* For master's, thesis (for some programs). *Entrance requirements:* For master's, minimum GPA of 3.0 (MA, MFA); auditions, interviews, resume, 3 or 4 letters of recommendation, samples of work (except for acting), head shots (acting only) (for MFA). Additional exam requirements/recommendations for international students: Required—TOEFL (minimum score 550 paper-based; 79 iBT), TWE (minimum score 5.5), Michigan English Language Assessment Battery (minimum score 85); Recommended—IELTS (minimum score 6.5). *Application deadline:* For fall admission, 1/15 for domestic and international students. Application fee: $0. Electronic applications accepted. *Expenses:* Expenses: Contact institution. *Financial support:* In 2014–15, 40 students received support, including 2 fellowships with tuition reimbursements available (averaging $16,000 per year), 37 research assistantships with tuition reimbursements available (averaging $16,540 per year); teaching assistantships with tuition reimbursements available, scholarships/grants, and unspecified assistantships also available. Financial award application deadline: 3/31; financial award applicants required to submit FAFSA. *Faculty research:* Dramatic criticism, lighting design, acting, directing, scenography. *Unit head:* Dr. John Wolf, Chair, 313-577-4273, E-mail: fe3828@wayne.edu. *Application contact:* Prof. James Thomas, Professor and Graduate Officer, 313-577-3508, E-mail: theatreanddance@wayne.edu.
Website: http://theatreanddance.wayne.edu/

Western Illinois University, School of Graduate Studies, College of Fine Arts and Communication, Department of Theatre and Dance, Macomb, IL 61455-1390. Offers acting (MFA); design (MFA); directing (MFA). *Accreditation:* NAST. Part-time programs available. *Students:* 20 full-time (4 women), 1 part-time (0 women); includes 3 minority (2 Black or African American, non-Hispanic/Latino; 1 Two or more races, non-Hispanic/Latino). Average age 28. 42 applicants, 40% accepted, 15 enrolled. In 2014, 9 master's awarded. *Degree requirements:* For master's, comprehensive exam, thesis or alternative, creative project, written exam. *Entrance requirements:* For master's, audition or interview. Additional exam requirements/recommendations for international students: Required—TOEFL (minimum score 550 paper-based; 80 iBT). *Application deadline:* Applications are processed on a rolling basis. Application fee: $30. Electronic applications accepted. *Financial support:* In 2014–15, 14 students received support, including 6 research assistantships with full tuition reimbursements available (averaging $7,544 per year), 8 teaching assistantships with full tuition reimbursements available (averaging $8,688 per year). Financial award applicants required to submit FAFSA. *Unit head:* Dr. David Patrick, Chairperson, 309-298-1543. *Application contact:* Dr. Nancy Parsons, Associate Provost and Director of Graduate Studies, 309-298-1806, Fax: 309-298-2345, E-mail: grad-office@wiu.edu.
Website: http://wiu.edu/theatre/

West Virginia University, College of Creative Arts, Division of Theatre and Dance, Morgantown, WV 26506. Offers acting (MFA); theatre design/technology (MFA). *Accreditation:* NAST. Part-time programs available. *Degree requirements:* For master's, thesis, oral defense. *Entrance requirements:* For master's, minimum GPA of 3.0, audition or portfolio. Additional exam requirements/recommendations for international students: Required—TOEFL. *Faculty research:* Professional directing, consulting, design.

Yale University, School of Drama, New Haven, CT 06520. Offers acting (MFA, Certificate); design (MFA, Certificate), including costume design, lighting design, projection design, set design; directing (MFA, Certificate); dramaturgy and dramatic criticism (MFA, DFA); playwriting (MFA, Certificate); sound design (MFA, Certificate); stage management (MFA, Certificate); technical design and production (MFA, Certificate); theater management (MFA); MFA/MBA. *Faculty:* 41 full-time (16 women), 80 part-time/adjunct (30 women). *Students:* 211 full-time (113 women); includes 51 minority (19 Black or African American, non-Hispanic/Latino; 8 Asian, non-Hispanic/Latino; 14 Hispanic/Latino; 10 Two or more races, non-Hispanic/Latino), 32 international. Average age 28. 1,391 applicants, 5% accepted, 66 enrolled. In 2014, 62 master's, 3 doctorates awarded. *Degree requirements:* For master's, comprehensive exam (for some programs), thesis (for some programs); for doctorate, thesis/dissertation, oral and written comprehensive exams. *Entrance requirements:* For master's, GRE (verbal, quantitative, and analytical), in-person audition (for acting); portfolio review (for design). Additional exam requirements/recommendations for international students: Required—TOEFL. *Application deadline:* For fall admission, 1/2 for domestic and international students. Application fee: $110. Electronic applications accepted. *Financial support:* In 2014–15, 203 students received support. Career-related internships or fieldwork, Federal Work-Study, institutionally sponsored loans, scholarships/grants, and health care benefits available. Financial award application deadline: 2/15; financial award applicants required to submit FAFSA. *Unit head:* James Bundy, Dean/Artistic Director of Yale Repertory Theatre, 203-432-1505. *Application contact:* Maria R. Leveton, Registrar/Admissions Administrator, 203-432-1507, Fax: 203-432-9668, E-mail: maria.leveton@yale.edu.
Website: http://www.yale.edu/drama/

York University, Faculty of Graduate Studies, Faculty of Fine Arts, Program in Theatre, Toronto, ON M3J 1P3, Canada. Offers MFA. *Degree requirements:* For master's, thesis. Electronic applications accepted.

York University, Faculty of Graduate Studies, Faculty of Fine Arts, Program in Theatre and Performance Studies, Toronto, ON M3J 1P3, Canada. Offers MA, PhD.

Therapies—Dance, Drama, and Music

Antioch University New England, Graduate School, Department of Applied Psychology, Program in Dance/Movement Therapy and Counseling, Keene, NH 03431-3552. Offers M Ed, MA, PMC. *Degree requirements:* For master's, thesis, internship, practicum. *Entrance requirements:* For master's, previous course work and work experience in psychology, experience in dance or movement. Additional exam requirements/recommendations for international students: Required—TOEFL (minimum score 550 paper-based). Electronic applications accepted. *Expenses:* Contact institution. *Faculty research:* Research attitudes and needs of dance/movement therapists.

Appalachian State University, Cratis D. Williams Graduate School, School of Music, Boone, NC 28608. Offers music education (MM); music performance (MM); music therapy (MMT). *Accreditation:* NASM. Part-time programs available. *Degree requirements:* For master's, comprehensive exam, thesis or alternative. *Entrance requirements:* For master's, GRE General Test, 3 letters of reference, audition. Additional exam requirements/recommendations for international students: Required—TOEFL (minimum score 550 paper-based; 79 iBT), IELTS (minimum score 6.5). Electronic applications accepted. *Faculty research:* Music of the Holocaust, Celtic folk music, early nineteenth-century performance practice, hypermeter and phase rhythm, world music, music and psychoneuroimmunology.

Arizona State University at the Tempe campus, Herberger Institute for Design and the Arts, School of Music, Tempe, AZ 85287-0405. Offers composition (MM, DMA); conducting (DMA); ethnomusicology (MA); interdisciplinary digital media/performance (DMA); music education (MM, PhD); music history and literature (MA); music therapy (MM); performance (MM, DMA). *Accreditation:* NASM. Terminal master's awarded for partial completion of doctoral program. *Degree requirements:* For master's, thesis (for some programs), interactive Program of Study (iPOS) submitted before completing 50 percent of required credit hours; for doctorate, comprehensive exam, thesis/dissertation, interactive Program of Study (iPOS) submitted before completing 50 percent of required credit hours. *Entrance requirements:* For master's, minimum GPA of 3.0 or equivalent in last 2 years of work leading to bachelor's degree, 3 letters of recommendation, resume; for doctorate, GRE or MAT, minimum GPA of 3.0 or equivalent in last 2 years of work leading to bachelor's degree, 3 letters of recommendation, curriculum vitae, statement of intent. Additional exam requirements/recommendations for international students: Required—TOEFL, IELTS, or PTE. Electronic applications accepted.

California Institute of Integral Studies, School of Professional Psychology and Health, San Francisco, CA 94103. Offers clinical psychology (Psy D); community mental health (MA); drama therapy (MA); expressive arts therapy (MA); integral counseling psychology (MA); integrative health studies (MA); psychological studies (MA); somatic psychology (MA). *Accreditation:* APA. Part-time and evening/weekend programs available. *Students:* 522 full-time (397 women), 105 part-time (83 women); includes 155 minority (27 Black or African American, non-Hispanic/Latino; 3 American Indian or Alaska Native, non-Hispanic/Latino; 31 Asian, non-Hispanic/Latino; 62 Hispanic/Latino; 3 Native Hawaiian or other Pacific Islander, non-Hispanic/Latino; 29 Two or more races, non-Hispanic/Latino), 49 international. Average age 34. 351 applicants, 86% accepted, 175 enrolled. In 2014, 168 master's, 24 doctorates awarded. *Degree requirements:* For doctorate, comprehensive exam, thesis/dissertation. *Entrance requirements:* For master's, minimum GPA of 3.0, letters of recommendation, writing sample; for doctorate, GRE, MA in psychology or social work with appropriate practical experience for advanced standing, or BA with a minimum GPA of 3.1; letters of recommendation; writing sample. Additional exam requirements/recommendations for international students: Required—TOEFL. *Application deadline:* For fall admission, 2/1 priority date for domestic and international students; for spring admission, 10/15 priority date for domestic and international students. Applications are processed on a rolling basis. Application fee: $65. Electronic applications accepted. *Expenses:* Tuition: Full-time $18,270; part-time $1015 per credit. *Required fees:* $85 per semester hour. *Financial support:* In 2014–15, 464 students received support, including 5 research assistantships with tuition reimbursements available (averaging $800 per year), 36 teaching assistantships with tuition reimbursements available (averaging $825 per year); career-related internships or fieldwork, Federal Work-Study, and scholarships/grants also available. Support available to part-time students. Financial award application deadline: 4/15; financial award applicants required to submit FAFSA. *Faculty research:* Transpersonal psychology, somatic psychology, expressive arts therapy, drama therapy, community mental health, ecopsychology, integrative health. *Application contact:* David Townes, Senior Admissions Counselor, 415-575-6152, Fax: 415-575-1268, E-mail: admissions@ciis.edu.

Columbia College Chicago, Graduate School, Department of Creative Arts Therapies, Chicago, IL 60605-1996. Offers alternate route in dance/movement therapy and counseling (Certificate); dance/movement therapy and counseling (MA); Laban movement analysis (Certificate); movement pattern analysis consultant (Certificate). *Faculty:* 3 full-time (all women), 16 part-time/adjunct (14 women). *Students:* 59 full-time

(56 women), 14 part-time (12 women); includes 17 minority (7 Black or African American, non-Hispanic/Latino; 7 Hispanic/Latino; 3 Two or more races, non-Hispanic/Latino), 5 international. Average age 29. *Degree requirements:* For master's, thesis, internship. *Entrance requirements:* For master's, self-assessment essay, work sample, interview, letters of recommendation. Additional exam requirements/recommendations for international students: Required—TOEFL (minimum score 600 paper-based; 100 iBT). *Application deadline:* For fall admission, 12/15 for domestic and international students. Application fee: $55 ($100 for international students). Electronic applications accepted. *Financial support:* In 2014–15, 10 students received support, including 4 fellowships with full and partial tuition reimbursements available, 6 research assistantships; career-related internships or fieldwork, Federal Work-Study, scholarships/grants, and unspecified assistantships also available. Support available to part-time students. Financial award application deadline: 8/15; financial award applicants required to submit FAFSA. *Unit head:* Susan Imus, Chairperson, 312-369-7697, Fax: 312-369-8054, E-mail: simus@colum.edu. *Application contact:* Kara Leffler, Associate Director of Graduate Admissions, 312-369-7262, Fax: 312-369-8024, E-mail: kleffler@colum.edu.
Website: http://www.colum.edu/Admissions/Graduate/programs/dance-movement-therapy-and-counseling/index.php

Drexel University, College of Nursing and Health Professions, Department of Creative Arts Therapies, Specialization in Dance/Movement Therapy, Philadelphia, PA 19104-2875. Offers MA, PMC. Part-time programs available. *Degree requirements:* For master's, comprehensive exam, thesis. *Entrance requirements:* For master's, GRE General Test or MAT, audition, interview, minimum GPA of 2.75. Electronic applications accepted. *Faculty research:* Family nonverbal communication, early intervention, sexual abuse.

Drexel University, College of Nursing and Health Professions, Department of Creative Arts Therapies, Specialization in Music Therapy, Philadelphia, PA 19104-2875. Offers MA, PMC. Part-time programs available. *Degree requirements:* For master's, comprehensive exam, thesis. *Entrance requirements:* For master's, GRE General Test or MAT, audition, interview, minimum GPA of 2.75. Electronic applications accepted. *Faculty research:* Early childhood intervention through creative art therapies, rhythm and dementia, music therapy and bulimia, assessment of adolescent suicide.

East Carolina University, Graduate School, College of Fine Arts and Communication, School of Music, Greenville, NC 27858-4353. Offers advanced performance studies (Certificate); music education (MM); music therapy (MM); performance (MM), including accompanying, choral conducting, instrumental conducting, jazz studies, organ, percussion, piano, piano pedagogy, sacred music, string (Suzuki) pedagogy, strings, vocal pedagogy, voice, woodwind specialist; Suzuki pedagogy (Certificate); theory and composition (MM). *Accreditation:* NASM. Part-time programs available. *Degree requirements:* For master's, comprehensive exam, thesis optional. *Entrance requirements:* For master's, GRE General Test or MAT. Additional exam requirements/recommendations for international students: Required—TOEFL. *Expenses:* Tuition, state resident: full-time $4223. Tuition, nonresident: full-time $16,540. *Required fees:* $2184.

Florida State University, The Graduate School, College of Music, Tallahassee, FL 32306. Offers accompanying (MM); arts administration (MA); choral conducting (MM); composition (MM, DM); ethnomusicology (MM); general music (MA); instrumental accompanying (MM); instrumental conducting (MM); jazz studies (MM); music education (MM Ed, PhD); music theory (MM, PhD); music therapy (MM); musicology (MM, PhD), including ethnomusicology (PhD), historical musicology; opera (MM); performance (MM, DM); piano pedagogy (MM); piano technology (MA); vocal accompanying (MM). *Accreditation:* NASM. *Faculty:* 87 full-time, 13 part-time/adjunct. *Students:* 368 full-time (191 women); includes 86 minority (31 Black or African American, non-Hispanic/Latino; 2 American Indian or Alaska Native, non-Hispanic/Latino; 18 Asian, non-Hispanic/Latino; 25 Hispanic/Latino; 1 Native Hawaiian or other Pacific Islander, non-Hispanic/Latino; 9 Two or more races, non-Hispanic/Latino). Average age 26. 737 applicants, 42% accepted, 138 enrolled. In 2014, 108 master's, 42 doctorates awarded. *Degree requirements:* For master's, comprehensive exam (for some programs), thesis (for some programs), departmental qualifying exam; for doctorate, comprehensive exam (for some programs), thesis/dissertation, departmental qualifying exam. *Entrance requirements:* For master's, GRE General Test (for some programs), audition, minimum GPA of 3.0; for doctorate, GRE General Test (for some programs), audition, master's degree, minimum GPA of 3.0. Additional exam requirements/recommendations for international students: Required—TOEFL (minimum score 590 paper-based; 97 iBT), IELTS (minimum score 7.5). *Application deadline:* For fall admission, 7/1 for domestic and international students; for spring admission, 11/1 for domestic and international students; for summer admission, 3/1 for domestic students. Applications are processed on a rolling basis. Application fee: $30. Electronic applications accepted. *Expenses:* Expenses: $479.32 per credit hour for in-state students; $1,110.72 for out-of-state students. *Financial support:* In 2014–15, 223 students received support, including fellowships (averaging $15,000 per year), 9 research assistantships (averaging $4,750 per year), 173 teaching assistantships (averaging $4,750 per year); career-related internships or fieldwork, Federal Work-Study, tuition waivers, and unspecified assistantships also available. Support available to part-time students. Financial award application deadline: 2/28; financial award applicants required to submit FAFSA. *Faculty research:* Musicology. *Unit head:* Dr. Patricia Flowers, Dean, 850-644-4361, Fax: 850-644-2033, E-mail: pjflowers@fsu.edu. *Application contact:* Dr. James Mathes, Interim Associate Dean for Academic Affairs/Director of Graduate Studies in Music, 850-644-5848, Fax: 850-644-2033, E-mail: jmathes@fsu.edu.
Website: http://www.music.fsu.edu/

Georgia College & State University, Graduate School, College of Health Sciences, Program in Music Therapy, Milledgeville, GA 31061. Offers MMT. Part-time and evening/weekend programs available. Postbaccalaureate distance learning degree programs offered (minimal on-campus study). *Students:* 6 full-time (5 women), 5 part-time (3 women); includes 4 minority (3 Black or African American, non-Hispanic/Latino; 1 Hispanic/Latino), 1 international. Average age 32. 6 applicants, 100% accepted, 5 enrolled. In 2014, 8 master's awarded. *Degree requirements:* For master's, comprehensive exam, thesis or alternative, minimum GPA of 3.0. *Entrance requirements:* For master's, MAT or GRE, bachelor's degree in music therapy or equivalent, minimum undergraduate GPA of 2.75, 2 letters of recommendation, essay, interview. Additional exam requirements/recommendations for international students: Recommended—TOEFL (minimum score 550 paper-based; 79 iBT). *Application deadline:* For fall admission, 7/1 priority date for domestic students; for spring admission, 11/15 priority date for domestic students; for summer admission, 4/1 for domestic students. Application fee: $40. Electronic applications accepted. *Expenses: Tuition, area resident:* Part-time $283 per credit hour. Tuition, nonresident: part-time $1027 per credit hour. *Required fees:* $995 per semester. Full-time tuition and fees vary according to course load, degree level, campus/location and program. *Financial support:* In 2014–15, 4 research assistantships were awarded; career-related internships or fieldwork and unspecified assistantships also available. Support available to part-time students. Financial award application deadline: 3/1; financial award applicants required to submit FAFSA. *Unit head:* Dr. Chesley Mercado, Director, 478-445-2645, Fax: 478-445-2645, E-mail: chesley.mercado@gcsu.edu. *Application contact:* Kate Marshall, Graduate Admissions Coordinator, 478-445-1184, Fax: 478-445-1336, E-mail: grad-admit@gcsu.edu.
Website: http://www.gcsu.edu/mtherapy/graduate/index.htm

Immaculata University, College of Graduate Studies, Program in Music Therapy, Immaculata, PA 19345. Offers MA. *Accreditation:* NASM. Part-time and evening/weekend programs available. *Degree requirements:* For master's, comprehensive exam, thesis optional. *Entrance requirements:* For master's, GRE General Test or MAT, minimum GPA of 3.0. Additional exam requirements/recommendations for international students: Required—TOEFL. Electronic applications accepted. *Faculty research:* Biofeedback music laboratory, experimental music therapy, virtual arts therapies, sound beam.

Indiana University–Purdue University Indianapolis, School of Engineering and Technology, School of Music, Indianapolis, IN 46202. Offers music technology (MS); music therapy (MS). *Accreditation:* NASM. Part-time and evening/weekend programs available. Postbaccalaureate distance learning degree programs offered. *Students:* 6 full-time (0 women), 16 part-time (3 women); includes 4 minority (2 Black or African American, non-Hispanic/Latino; 1 Hispanic/Latino; 1 Two or more races, non-Hispanic/Latino), 3 international. Average age 32. 21 applicants, 57% accepted, 9 enrolled. In 2014, 14 master's awarded. *Degree requirements:* For master's, internship or final project. *Entrance requirements:* For master's, audition, minimum GPA of 3.0. Additional exam requirements/recommendations for international students: Required—TOEFL. *Application deadline:* For fall admission, 4/15 priority date for domestic students, 3/15 for international students; for spring admission, 11/15 priority date for domestic students, 11/15 for international students. Applications are processed on a rolling basis. Application fee: $55 ($65 for international students). *Financial support:* Teaching assistantships with full tuition reimbursements, Federal Work-Study, institutionally sponsored loans, and scholarships/grants available. Support available to part-time students. Financial award application deadline: 11/15. *Unit head:* G. David Peters, Director, 317-278-2591, E-mail: gpeters@iupui.edu. *Application contact:* Kathleen Dusing, Administrative Support, Graduate Programs, 317-278-4960, E-mail: kdusing@iupui.edu.
Website: http://www.engr.iupui.edu/departments/mat/

Lesley University, Graduate School of Arts and Social Sciences, Cambridge, MA 02138-2790. Offers clinical mental health counseling (MA), including holistic counseling, school and community counseling, trauma studies; counseling psychology (MA, CAGS), including professional counseling (MA), school counseling (MA); creative writing (MFA); expressive therapies (MA, PhD, CAGS), including art (MA), clinical mental health counseling (MA), dance (MA), expressive therapies (MA), music (MA); independent studies (CAGS); independent study (MA); intercultural relations (MA, CAGS); interdisciplinary studies (MA), including individualized studies, integrative holistic health, mindfulness studies, peace and conflict transformation, trauma sensitive assessment, intervention, and consultation, women's studies; urban environmental leadership (MA). Part-time programs available. Postbaccalaureate distance learning degree programs offered (no on-campus study). *Faculty:* 35 full-time (25 women), 115 part-time/adjunct (90 women). *Students:* 420 full-time (379 women), 514 part-time (414 women); includes 142 minority (50 Black or African American, non-Hispanic/Latino; 5 American Indian or Alaska Native, non-Hispanic/Latino; 16 Asian, non-Hispanic/Latino; 48 Hispanic/Latino; 23 Two or more races, non-Hispanic/Latino), 46 international. Average age 33. In 2014, 475 master's, 11 doctorates, 4 other advanced degrees awarded. *Degree requirements:* For master's, internship, practicum, thesis (for expressive therapies); for doctorate, thesis/dissertation, arts apprenticeship, field placement; for CAGS, thesis, internship (for counseling psychology, expressive therapies). *Entrance requirements:* For master's, MAT (counseling psychology), interview, writing samples, art portfolio; for doctorate, GRE or MAT, interview, master's degree; for CAGS, interview, master's degree. Additional exam requirements/recommendations for international students: Required—TOEFL (minimum score 550 paper-based; 80 iBT). *Application deadline:* Applications are processed on a rolling basis. Application fee: $50. Electronic applications accepted. *Financial support:* Fellowships, career-related internships or fieldwork, Federal Work-Study, scholarships/grants, tuition waivers, and unspecified assistantships available. Financial award applicants required to submit FAFSA. *Faculty research:* Psychotherapy and culture; psychotherapy and psychological trauma; women's issues in art, teaching and psychotherapy; community-based art, psycho-spiritual inquiry. *Unit head:* Dr. Catherine Koverola, Dean, 617-349-8317, Fax: 617-349-8366, E-mail: koverola@lesley.edu. *Application contact:* Martha Sheehan, Director, Graduate Admissions, 888-LESLEYU, Fax: 617-349-8313, E-mail: info@lesley.edu.
Website: http://www.lesley.edu/graduate-school-of-arts-and-social-sciences/

Loyola University New Orleans, College of Music and Fine Arts, New Orleans, LA 70118-6195. Offers music therapy (MMT); performance (MM). *Accreditation:* NASM. Part-time programs available. *Faculty:* 15 full-time (8 women), 6 part-time/adjunct (3 women). *Students:* 16 full-time (8 women), 10 part-time (5 women); includes 6 minority (5 Black or African American, non-Hispanic/Latino; 1 Hispanic/Latino), 3 international. Average age 26. 33 applicants, 42% accepted, 14 enrolled. In 2014, 9 master's awarded. *Degree requirements:* For master's, comprehensive written and oral exams; thesis (for MMT). *Entrance requirements:* For master's, performance audition, appropriate bachelor's degree, transcripts, minimum GPA of 3.0, 2 letters of recommendation, resume. Additional exam requirements/recommendations for international students: Required—TOEFL (minimum score 580 paper-based; 92 iBT). *Application deadline:* For fall admission, 8/15 priority date for domestic and international students; for spring admission, 1/1 priority date for domestic and international students. Applications are processed on a rolling basis. Application fee: $20. Electronic applications accepted. *Expenses:* Expenses: Contact institution. *Financial support:* Career-related internships or fieldwork, Federal Work-Study, institutionally sponsored loans, scholarships/grants, unspecified assistantships, and talent-based music scholarships available. Support available to part-time students. Financial award application deadline: 5/1; financial award applicants required to submit FAFSA. *Faculty research:* Music business, music therapy, musicology, music theory, music education. *Unit head:* Dr. Victoria P. Vega, Associate Dean, 504-865-3037, Fax: 504-865-2852, E-mail: vpvega@loyno.edu. *Application contact:* Melissa L. Lightell, Director, Office of Professional and Continuing Studies, 504-865-3530, Fax: 504-865-2787, E-mail: evening@loyno.edu.
Website: http://cmfa.loyno.edu/

Maryville University of Saint Louis, College of Health Professions, Program in Music Therapy, St. Louis, MO 63141-7299. Offers MMT. *Accreditation:* NASM. Part-time programs available. *Faculty:* 1 (woman) full-time, 1 (woman) part-time/adjunct. *Students:* 15 full-time (12 women), 3 part-time (0 women); includes 4 minority (2 Black or African American, non-Hispanic/Latino; 1 American Indian or Alaska Native, non-Hispanic/Latino; 1 Hispanic/Latino). Average age 26. In 2014, 2 master's awarded. *Entrance requirements:* For master's, music audition, interview, minimum undergraduate GPA of 3.0, 3 letters of recommendation. Additional exam requirements/recommendations for international students: Required—TOEFL (minimum score 550 paper-based). *Application deadline:* Applications are processed on a rolling basis. Application fee: $40 ($60 for international students). Electronic applications accepted. Application fee is

waived when completed online. *Expenses: Tuition:* Full-time $24,694; part-time $755 per credit hour. Part-time tuition and fees vary according to course load and degree level. *Financial support:* Application deadline: 3/1; applicants required to submit FAFSA. *Unit head:* Dr. Cynthia Briggs, Director, 314-529-9441, Fax: 314-529-9495, E-mail: cbriggs@maryville.edu. *Application contact:* Crystal Jacobsmeyer, Assistant Director, Graduate Enrollment Advising, 314-529-9654, Fax: 314-529-9927, E-mail: cjacobsmeyer@maryville.edu.
Website: http://www.maryville.edu/hp/music-therapy/

Michigan State University, The Graduate School, College of Music, East Lansing, MI 48824. Offers collaborative piano (M Mus); jazz studies (M Mus); music (PhD); music composition (M Mus, DMA); music conducting (M Mus, DMA); music education (M Mus); music performance (M Mus, DMA); music theory (M Mus); music therapy (M Mus); musicology (MA); piano pedagogy (M Mus). *Accreditation:* NASM. *Entrance requirements:* Additional exam requirements/recommendations for international students: Required—TOEFL. Electronic applications accepted.

Molloy College, Graduate Music Therapy Program, Rockville Centre, NY 11571-5002. Offers MS. *Faculty:* 4 full-time (3 women), 8 part-time/adjunct (7 women). *Students:* 13 full-time (10 women), 19 part-time (11 women); includes 8 minority (2 Black or African American, non-Hispanic/Latino; 2 Asian, non-Hispanic/Latino; 4 Hispanic/Latino), 5 international. Average age 31. 48 applicants, 46% accepted, 12 enrolled. In 2014, 9 master's awarded. *Application deadline:* Applications are processed on a rolling basis. Application fee: $60. *Expenses: Tuition:* Full-time $17,640; part-time $980 per credit. *Required fees:* $900. *Unit head:* Suzanne Sorel, Associate Dean/Director of Graduate Music Therapy, 516-323-3322, E-mail: ssorel@molloy.edu. *Application contact:* Alina Haitz, Assistant Director of Graduate Admissions, 516-323-4008, E-mail: ahaitz@molloy.edu.

Montclair State University, The Graduate School, College of the Arts, John J. Cali School of Music, Post Baccalaureate Certificate Program in Music Therapy, Montclair, NJ 07043-1624. Offers Postbaccalaureate Certificate. Part-time and evening/weekend programs available. *Students:* 1 (woman) full-time, 1 (woman) part-time. Average age 32. 5 applicants, 40% accepted, 2 enrolled. *Entrance requirements:* For degree, 2 letters of recommendation, essay. Additional exam requirements/recommendations for international students: Required—TOEFL (minimum score 83 iBT), IELTS (minimum score 6.5). *Application deadline:* Applications are processed on a rolling basis. Application fee: $60. Electronic applications accepted. *Expenses:* Tuition, state resident: full-time $9960; part-time $553.35 per credit. Tuition, nonresident: full-time $15,074; part-time $837.43 per credit. *Required fees:* $1595; $88.63 per credit. Tuition and fees vary according to degree level and program. *Financial support:* Federal Work-Study, scholarships/grants, and unspecified assistantships available. Support available to part-time students. Financial award application deadline: 3/1; financial award applicants required to submit FAFSA. *Unit head:* Prof. Robert Aldridge, Chairperson, 973-655-7212. *Application contact:* Amy Aiello, Executive Director of The Graduate School, 973-655-5147, Fax: 973-655-7869, E-mail: graduate.school@montclair.edu.
Website: http://www.montclair.edu/graduate/programs-of-study/therapy-post-baccalaureate/

Montclair State University, The Graduate School, College of the Arts, John J. Cali School of Music, Program in Music, Montclair, NJ 07043-1624. Offers music education (MA); music therapy (MA); performance (MA); theory/composition (MA). Part-time and evening/weekend programs available. *Students:* 24 full-time (12 women), 36 part-time (18 women); includes 9 minority (3 Black or African American, non-Hispanic/Latino; 3 Asian, non-Hispanic/Latino; 3 Hispanic/Latino), 5 international. Average age 31. 60 applicants, 45% accepted, 20 enrolled. In 2014, 13 master's awarded. *Degree requirements:* For master's, thesis. *Entrance requirements:* For master's, GRE General Test, 2 letters of recommendation, essay. Additional exam requirements/recommendations for international students: Required—TOEFL (minimum score 83 iBT), IELTS (minimum score 6.5). *Application deadline:* Applications are processed on a rolling basis. Application fee: $60. Electronic applications accepted. *Expenses:* Tuition, state resident: full-time $9960; part-time $553.35 per credit. Tuition, nonresident: full-time $15,074; part-time $837.43 per credit. *Required fees:* $1595; $88.63 per credit. Tuition and fees vary according to degree level and program. *Financial support:* In 2014–15, 3 research assistantships with full tuition reimbursements (averaging $7,000 per year) were awarded; Federal Work-Study, scholarships/grants, and unspecified assistantships also available. Support available to part-time students. Financial award application deadline: 3/1; financial award applicants required to submit FAFSA. *Unit head:* Prof. Robert Aldridge, Chairperson, 973-655-7212. *Application contact:* Amy Aiello, Executive Director of The Graduate School, 973-655-5147, Fax: 973-655-7869, E-mail: graduate.school@montclair.edu.
Website: http://www.montclair.edu/Arts/music/

Naropa University, Graduate Programs, Program in Somatic Counseling Psychology, Concentration in Dance/Movement Therapy, Boulder, CO 80302-6697. Offers MA. Part-time programs available. *Faculty:* 4 full-time (3 women), 7 part-time/adjunct (all women). *Students:* 17 full-time (all women), 14 part-time (all women); includes 4 minority (1 Black or African American, non-Hispanic/Latino; 2 Hispanic/Latino; 1 Two or more races, non-Hispanic/Latino). Average age 29. 35 applicants, 51% accepted, 7 enrolled. In 2014, 11 master's awarded. *Degree requirements:* For master's, comprehensive exam, thesis, internship, experiential counseling, clinical practicum. *Entrance requirements:* For master's, in-person interview, course work in psychology and anatomy, experience in 3 forms of dance, resume, letter of interest, 2 letters of recommendation, transcript, minimum of 100 hours' volunteer fieldwork experience in a supervised setting in the mental health field or through work in a community facility or service organization; supplemental essay. Additional exam requirements/recommendations for international students: Required—TOEFL (minimum score 600 paper-based; 80 iBT). *Application deadline:* For fall admission, 1/15 priority date for domestic and international students. Applications are processed on a rolling basis. Application fee: $60. Electronic applications accepted. *Expenses: Tuition:* Full-time $23,400; part-time $975 per credit. *Required fees:* $335 per semester. Tuition and fees vary according to course load. *Financial support:* In 2014–15, 6 students received support. Career-related internships or fieldwork, scholarships/grants, tuition waivers (partial), and unspecified assistantships available. Support available to part-time students. Financial award application deadline: 3/1; financial award applicants required to submit FAFSA. *Unit head:* Dr. Deborah Bowman, Dean, Graduate School of Psychology, 303-546-3559, E-mail: bowman@naropa.edu. *Application contact:* Office of Admissions, 303-546-3572, Fax: 303-546-3583, E-mail: admissions@naropa.edu.
Website: http://www.naropa.edu/academics/gsp/grad/somatic-counseling-psychology-ma/dance-movement-therapy/index.php

Nazareth College of Rochester, Graduate Studies, Department of Creative Arts Therapy, Program in Music Therapy, Rochester, NY 14618-3790. Offers MS. *Entrance requirements:* For master's, audition, minimum GPA of 3.0.

New York University, Steinhardt School of Culture, Education, and Human Development, Department of Music and Performing Arts Professions, Program in Drama Therapy, New York, NY 10012. Offers MA. Part-time programs available. *Faculty:* 1 (woman) full-time. *Students:* 28 full-time (23 women), 6 part-time (5 women); includes 8 minority (1 American Indian or Alaska Native, non-Hispanic/Latino; 1 Asian, non-Hispanic/Latino; 5 Hispanic/Latino; 1 Two or more races, non-Hispanic/Latino), 6 international. Average age 29. 41 applicants, 73% accepted, 18 enrolled. In 2014, 17 master's awarded. *Degree requirements:* For master's, thesis (for some programs). *Entrance requirements:* For master's, audition, interview. Additional exam requirements/recommendations for international students: Required—TOEFL (minimum score 100 iBT). *Application deadline:* For fall admission, 12/1 priority date for domestic and international students; for spring admission, 10/1 for domestic and international students. Applications are processed on a rolling basis. Application fee: $75. Electronic applications accepted. *Financial support:* Career-related internships or fieldwork, Federal Work-Study, institutionally sponsored loans, scholarships/grants, and tuition waivers (partial) available. Support available to part-time students. Financial award application deadline: 2/1; financial award applicants required to submit FAFSA. *Faculty research:* Meaning of role in drama, therapy, and everyday life; clinical approaches to drama therapy; trauma effects on children. *Unit head:* Prof. Robert Landy, Director, 212-998-5258, E-mail: rjl1@nyu.edu. *Application contact:* 212-998-5030, Fax: 212-995-4328, E-mail: steinhardt.gradadmissions@nyu.edu.
Website: http://steinhardt.nyu.edu/music/dramatherapy

New York University, Steinhardt School of Culture, Education, and Human Development, Department of Music and Performing Arts Professions, Program in Music Therapy, New York, NY 10010. Offers MA. Part-time programs available. *Faculty:* 2 full-time (1 woman). *Students:* 30 full-time (17 women), 12 part-time (8 women); includes 11 minority (2 Black or African American, non-Hispanic/Latino; 1 Asian, non-Hispanic/Latino; 6 Hispanic/Latino; 2 Two or more races, non-Hispanic/Latino), 10 international. Average age 30. 70 applicants, 31% accepted, 18 enrolled. In 2014, 17 master's awarded. *Degree requirements:* For master's, thesis (for some programs). *Entrance requirements:* For master's, audition, interview. Additional exam requirements/recommendations for international students: Required—TOEFL (minimum score 100 iBT). *Application deadline:* For fall admission, 12/1 priority date for domestic and international students. Applications are processed on a rolling basis. Application fee: $75. Electronic applications accepted. *Financial support:* Career-related internships or fieldwork, Federal Work-Study, institutionally sponsored loans, scholarships/grants, and tuition waivers (partial) available. Support available to part-time students. Financial award application deadline: 2/1; financial award applicants required to submit FAFSA. *Faculty research:* Music therapy in special education, including autism and emotional disabilities; guided imagery. *Unit head:* Prof. Barbara Hesser, Director, 212-998-5452, Fax: 212-995-4043, E-mail: barbara.hesser@nyu.edu. *Application contact:* 212-998-5030, Fax: 212-995-4328, E-mail: steinhardt.gradadmissions@nyu.edu.
Website: http://steinhardt.nyu.edu/music/therapy

Ohio University, Graduate College, College of Fine Arts, School of Music, Athens, OH 45701-2979. Offers accompanying (MM); composition (MM); conducting (MM); history/literature (MM); music education (MM); music therapy (MM); performance (MM, Certificate); performance/pedagogy (MM); theory (MM). *Accreditation:* NASM. Part-time and evening/weekend programs available. Postbaccalaureate distance learning degree programs offered (minimal on-campus study). *Degree requirements:* For master's, comprehensive exam, thesis (for some programs), oral exam. *Entrance requirements:* For master's, audition, interview, portfolio, recordings (varies by program). Additional exam requirements/recommendations for international students: Required—TOEFL (minimum score 550 paper-based; 80 iBT) or IELTS (minimum score 6.5). Electronic applications accepted.

Pratt Institute, School of Art and Design, Programs in Creative Arts Therapy, Brooklyn, NY 11205-3899. Offers art therapy and creativity development (MPS); art therapy-special education (MPS); dance/movement therapy (MS). *Accreditation:* NASAD (one or more programs are accredited). Part-time programs available. *Faculty:* 3 full-time (all women), 22 part-time/adjunct (19 women). *Students:* 106 full-time (101 women), 1 (woman) part-time; includes 37 minority (16 Black or African American, non-Hispanic/Latino; 9 Asian, non-Hispanic/Latino; 10 Hispanic/Latino; 2 Two or more races, non-Hispanic/Latino), 8 international. Average age 29. 160 applicants, 46% accepted, 30 enrolled. In 2014, 45 master's awarded. *Degree requirements:* For master's, thesis. *Entrance requirements:* For master's, letters of recommendation, portfolio. Additional exam requirements/recommendations for international students: Required—TOEFL (minimum score 600 paper-based; 100 iBT). *Application deadline:* For fall admission, 1/5 for domestic and international students; for spring admission, 10/1 for domestic and international students. Applications are processed on a rolling basis. Application fee: $50 ($90 for international students). Electronic applications accepted. *Financial support:* Career-related internships or fieldwork, Federal Work-Study, institutionally sponsored loans, scholarships/grants, health care benefits, tuition waivers (full), and unspecified assistantships available. Support available to part-time students. Financial award application deadline: 2/1; financial award applicants required to submit FAFSA. *Faculty research:* Psychology and aesthetic interaction, art therapy and AIDS, art therapy and autism, art diagnosis. *Unit head:* Julie Miller, Chairperson, 718-636-3428, E-mail: jmiller2@pratt.edu. *Application contact:* Young Hah, Director of Graduate Admissions, 718-636-3683, Fax: 718-399-4242, E-mail: yhah@pratt.edu.
Website: https://www.pratt.edu/academics/school-of-art/graduate-school-of-art/creative-arts-therapy/

See Display on page 153 and Close-Up on page 203.

Radford University, College of Graduate and Professional Studies, College of Visual and Performing Arts, Program in Music, Radford, VA 24142. Offers music (MA); music education (MS); music therapy (MS). *Accreditation:* NASM. Part-time programs available. *Faculty:* 8 full-time (0 women), 4 part-time/adjunct (0 women). *Students:* 14 full-time (10 women), 4 part-time (2 women). Average age 26. 10 applicants, 80% accepted, 7 enrolled. In 2014, 8 master's awarded. *Degree requirements:* For master's, comprehensive exam, thesis or alternative. *Entrance requirements:* For master's, GRE or PRAXIS II (music content knowledge), minimum GPA of 2.75, 3 letters of reference, resume, official transcripts. Additional exam requirements/recommendations for international students: Required—TOEFL (minimum score 550 paper-based; 79 iBT), IELTS (minimum score 6.5). *Application deadline:* For fall admission, 2/15 priority date for domestic students, 12/1 for international students; for spring admission, 7/1 for international students. Applications are processed on a rolling basis. Application fee: $50. Electronic applications accepted. *Expenses:* Tuition, state resident: full-time $7187; part-time $299 per credit hour. Tuition, nonresident: full-time $16,394; part-time $683 per credit hour. *Required fees:* $2974; $125 per credit hour. Tuition and fees vary according to course load and program. *Financial support:* In 2014–15, 12 students received support, including 5 research assistantships (averaging $7,300 per year), 6 teaching assistantships with partial tuition reimbursements available (averaging $8,250 per year); career-related internships or fieldwork, Federal Work-Study, institutionally sponsored loans, scholarships/grants, and unspecified assistantships also available. Financial award application deadline: 3/1; financial award applicants required to submit FAFSA. *Unit head:* Dr. Trish Winter, Graduate Music Program Coordinator, 540-831-6174, Fax: 540-831-6133, E-mail: pwinter3@radford.edu. *Application contact:* Rebecca Conner, Director, Graduate Enrollment, 540-831-6296, Fax: 540-831-6061, E-mail: gradcollege@radford.edu.
Website: http://www.radford.edu/content/cvpa/home/music.html

Therapies—Dance, Drama, and Music

Saint Mary-of-the-Woods College, Program in Music Therapy, Saint Mary of the Woods, IN 47876. Offers MA. *Accreditation:* NASM. Part-time programs available. Postbaccalaureate distance learning degree programs offered (minimal on-campus study). *Degree requirements:* For master's, thesis or alternative, qualifying exam, portfolio completion. *Entrance requirements:* For master's, diagnostic music exam, audition. Electronic applications accepted.

State University of New York at New Paltz, Graduate School, School of Fine and Performing Arts, Department of Music, New Paltz, NY 12561. Offers music therapy (MS). *Accreditation:* NASM. Part-time programs available. *Faculty:* 5 full-time (1 woman), 2 part-time/adjunct (both women). *Students:* 16 full-time (13 women), 22 part-time (17 women); includes 3 minority (1 Asian, non-Hispanic/Latino; 1 Hispanic/Latino; 1 Two or more races, non-Hispanic/Latino), 8 international. Average age 32. 22 applicants, 41% accepted, 6 enrolled. In 2014, 4 master's awarded. *Degree requirements:* For master's, thesis. *Entrance requirements:* For master's, audition, minimum GPA of 3.0. Additional exam requirements/recommendations for international students: Required—TOEFL (minimum score 550 paper-based; 80 iBT), IELTS (minimum score 6.5). *Application deadline:* For fall admission, 5/15 for domestic and international students; for spring admission, 11/15 for domestic and international students. Applications are processed on a rolling basis. Application fee: $50. Electronic applications accepted. *Financial support:* In 2014–15, 4 teaching assistantships with partial tuition reimbursements (averaging $5,000 per year) were awarded. Financial award application deadline: 8/1. *Unit head:* Dr. Daniel Kempton, Chair, 845-257-2701, E-mail: kemptond@newpaltz.edu. *Application contact:* Prof. John Mahoney, Graduate Coordinator, 845-257-2709, E-mail: mahoneyj@newpaltz.edu.

Temple University, Center for the Arts, Esther Boyer College of Music and Dance, Department of Music, Philadelphia, PA 19122-6096. Offers choral conducting (MM); collaborative piano/chamber music (MM); collaborative piano/opera coaching (MM); composition (MM, PhD); instrumental conducting (MM); music education (MM, PhD); music history (MM); music performance (MM, DMA), including instrumental (MM), keyboard, voice (DMA), voice/opera (MM); music studies (PhD); music theory (MM, PhD); music therapy (MMT, PhD); musicology (MM, PhD); opera (MM); piano pedagogy (MM); string pedagogy (MM). Part-time programs available. Postbaccalaureate distance learning degree programs offered. *Faculty:* 46 full-time (21 women), 43 part-time/adjunct (21 women). *Students:* 182 full-time (110 women), 36 part-time (20 women); includes 30 minority (4 Black or African American, non-Hispanic/Latino; 17 Asian, non-Hispanic/Latino; 4 Hispanic/Latino; 5 Two or more races, non-Hispanic/Latino), 57 international. 344 applicants, 53% accepted, 77 enrolled. In 2014, 58 master's, 9 doctorates awarded. Terminal master's awarded for partial completion of doctoral program. *Degree requirements:* For doctorate, thesis/dissertation. *Entrance requirements:* Additional exam requirements/recommendations for international students: Required—TOEFL. *Application deadline:* For fall admission, 11/15 for international students; for spring admission, 8/1 for international students. Applications are processed on a rolling basis. Application fee: $60. Electronic applications accepted. *Expenses:* Tuition, state resident: full-time $14,490; part-time $805 per credit hour. Tuition, nonresident: full-time $19,850; part-time $1103 per credit hour. *Required fees:* $690. Full-time tuition and fees vary according to class time, course load, degree level, campus/location and program. *Financial support:* Fellowships with full and partial tuition reimbursements, research assistantships with full and partial tuition reimbursements, teaching assistantships with full and partial tuition reimbursements, career-related internships or fieldwork, Federal Work-Study, scholarships/grants, health care benefits, and unspecified assistantships available. Financial award application deadline: 3/1; financial award applicants required to submit FAFSA. *Unit head:* Dr. Robert Stroker, Dean, 215-204-5527, Fax: 215-204-4957, E-mail: rstroker@temple.edu. *Application contact:* James Short, Director, Graduate Admissions, 215-204-8301, Fax: 215-204-4957, E-mail: james.short@temple.edu.
Website: http://www.temple.edu/boyer/academicprograms/

The University of Kansas, Graduate Studies, School of Music, Program in Music Therapy, Lawrence, KS 66045. Offers MME. *Faculty:* 53 full-time, 18 part-time/adjunct. *Students:* 22 full-time (18 women), 17 part-time (14 women); includes 1 minority (Black or African American, non-Hispanic/Latino), 6 international. Average age 27. 22 applicants, 59% accepted, 9 enrolled. In 2014, 4 master's awarded. *Degree requirements:* For master's, comprehensive exam, thesis or alternative. *Entrance requirements:* For master's, GRE General Test, minimum undergraduate GPA of 3.0, video, reference letters, transcripts. Additional exam requirements/recommendations for international students: Required—TOEFL (minimum score 570 paper-based; 92 iBT) or IELTS (minimum score 6). *Application deadline:* For fall admission, 2/15 priority date for domestic and international students. Applications are processed on a rolling basis. Application fee: $55 ($65 for international students). Electronic applications accepted. *Financial support:* Fellowships with tuition reimbursements, research assistantships, teaching assistantships with full and partial tuition reimbursements, institutionally sponsored loans, scholarships/grants, and unspecified assistantships available. Financial award application deadline: 12/15; financial award applicants required to submit FAFSA. *Faculty research:* Orff-based music therapy; music therapy in health, wellness, autism and hospice; changing attitudes toward individuals with disabilities; music therapy in medical settings; music therapy in pediatrics, early intervention. *Unit head:* Dr. Robert Walzel, Dean, 785-864-3421, Fax: 785-864-5366, E-mail: music@ku.edu. *Application contact:* Lois Elmer, Administrative Professional for Music, 785-864-4784, Fax: 785-864-9640, E-mail: elmer@ku.edu.
Website: http://www.memt.ku.edu

University of Kentucky, Graduate School, College of Fine Arts, Program in Music, Lexington, KY 40506-0032. Offers composition (MM, DMA); conducting (MM, DMA); music education (MM, PhD); music theory (MA, PhD); music therapy (MM); musicology (MA, PhD); performance (MM, DMA); sacred music (MM). *Accreditation:* NASM. Part-time and evening/weekend programs available. *Degree requirements:* For master's, variable foreign language requirement, comprehensive exam, thesis (for some programs); for doctorate, variable foreign language requirement, comprehensive exam, thesis/dissertation. *Entrance requirements:* For master's, GRE General Test, minimum undergraduate GPA of 2.75; for doctorate, GRE General Test, minimum undergraduate GPA of 2.75, graduate 3.0. Additional exam requirements/recommendations for international students: Required—TOEFL (minimum score 550 paper-based). Electronic applications accepted. *Faculty research:* Musicology, music theory, jazz, music education, performance and conducting.

University of Miami, Graduate School, Frost School of Music, Department of Music Education and Music Therapy, Coral Gables, FL 33124. Offers music education (MM, PhD, Spec M); music therapy (MM). *Accreditation:* NASM. *Degree requirements:* For master's, thesis; for doctorate, thesis/dissertation, 2 research tools; for Spec M, thesis, research project. *Entrance requirements:* For master's and doctorate, GRE General Test. Additional exam requirements/recommendations for international students: Required—TOEFL (minimum score 550 paper-based; 59 iBT). Electronic applications accepted. *Faculty research:* Motivation, quantitative research, early childhood, instrumental music, elementary music.

University of Missouri–Kansas City, Conservatory of Music and Dance, Kansas City, MO 64110-2499. Offers composition (MM, DMA); conducting (MM, DMA); music (MA); music education (MME, PhD); music history and literature (MM); music theory (MM); music therapy (MA); musicology (MM); performance (MM, DMA). PhD (interdisciplinary) offered through the School of Graduate Studies. *Accreditation:* NASM. Part-time programs available. *Faculty:* 51 full-time (17 women), 36 part-time/adjunct (14 women). *Students:* 162 full-time (71 women), 65 part-time (28 women); includes 25 minority (6 Black or African American, non-Hispanic/Latino; 10 Asian, non-Hispanic/Latino; 8 Hispanic/Latino; 1 Two or more races, non-Hispanic/Latino), 38 international. Average age 28. 418 applicants, 47% accepted, 97 enrolled. In 2014, 25 master's, 18 doctorates awarded. *Degree requirements:* For master's, variable foreign language requirement, comprehensive exam, thesis (for some programs); for doctorate, variable foreign language requirement, comprehensive exam, thesis/dissertation or alternative. *Entrance requirements:* For master's, minimum GPA of 3.0 in major, auditions (for MM in performance); for doctorate, minimum graduate GPA of 3.5, auditions (for DMA in performance), portfolio of compositions. Additional exam requirements/recommendations for international students: Required—TOEFL (minimum score 550 paper-based; 80 iBT). *Application deadline:* For fall admission, 1/15 priority date for domestic students, 1/15 for international students. Application fee: $45 ($50 for international students). *Financial support:* In 2014–15, 61 teaching assistantships with partial tuition reimbursements (averaging $8,991 per year) were awarded; career-related internships or fieldwork, Federal Work-Study, institutionally sponsored loans, scholarships/grants, tuition waivers (partial), and unspecified assistantships also available. Support available to part-time students. Financial award application deadline: 3/1; financial award applicants required to submit FAFSA. *Faculty research:* Electro-acoustic composition, affective music responses, American music theatre, Russian choral music, music therapy and Alzheimer's. *Unit head:* Peter Witte, Dean, 816-235-2731, Fax: 816-235-5265, E-mail: wittep@umkc.edu. *Application contact:* William Everett, Associate Dean for Graduate Studies, 816-235-2857, Fax: 816-235-5264, E-mail: everettw@umkc.edu.
Website: http://conservatory.umkc.edu/

University of the Pacific, Conservatory of Music, Stockton, CA 95211-0197. Offers music education (MM); music therapy (MA). *Accreditation:* NASM. *Students:* 8 full-time (6 women), 14 part-time (11 women); includes 4 minority (2 Asian, non-Hispanic/Latino; 1 Hispanic/Latino; 1 Two or more races, non-Hispanic/Latino), 2 international. Average age 31. 24 applicants, 50% accepted, 8 enrolled. In 2014, 3 master's awarded. *Entrance requirements:* For master's, GRE General Test. Additional exam requirements/recommendations for international students: Required—TOEFL (minimum score 475 paper-based). *Application deadline:* For fall admission, 3/1 priority date for domestic students; for spring admission, 10/1 priority date for domestic students. Applications are processed on a rolling basis. Application fee: $75. *Financial support:* Teaching assistantships and institutionally sponsored loans available. Support available to part-time students. Financial award application deadline: 3/1; financial award applicants required to submit FAFSA. *Unit head:* Dr. Giulio Ongaro, Dean, 209-946-2417, E-mail: musicdean@pacific.edu. *Application contact:* Dr. Ruth Brittin, Chairperson, 209-946-2408, E-mail: rbittin@pacific.edu.

Western Michigan University, Graduate College, College of Fine Arts, School of Music, Kalamazoo, MI 49008. Offers music (MA); music composition (MM); music conducting (MM); music education (MM); music performance (MM); music therapy (MM). *Accreditation:* NASM. *Application deadline:* For fall admission, 2/15 for domestic students. *Financial support:* Application deadline: 2/15. *Application contact:* Admissions and Orientation, 269-387-2000, Fax: 269-387-2096.

Wilfrid Laurier University, Faculty of Graduate and Postdoctoral Studies, Faculty of Music, Waterloo, ON N2L 3C5, Canada. Offers MMT. *Entrance requirements:* For master's, 4-year honours BA in music therapy with minimum B average in final year, grade 6 RCM and grade 10 performance ability (for 1-year program); 4-year honours BA in allied area (music or psychology) with minimum B average in final year, grade 6 RCM, grade 10 performance ability (for 2-year program). Additional exam requirements/recommendations for international students: Required—TOEFL (minimum score 89 iBT). Electronic applications accepted. *Faculty research:* Group analytic music therapy, music psychotherapy, low frequency sound wave, aesthetic music therapy.

COLUMBIA UNIVERSITY
School of the Arts
Programs in Film, Theatre, Visual Arts, and Writing

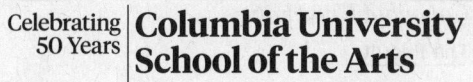

Programs of Study

The School of the Arts offers M.F.A. degree programs in Film (concentrations in screenwriting/directing and creative producing); Theatre (concentrations in acting, directing, dramaturgy, playwriting, stage management, and theatre management & producing); Visual Arts (areas of study include painting, photography, printmaking, sculpture, new genres, and a program in sound arts in association with the Department of Music); Writing (concentrations in fiction, nonfiction, and poetry, with the option of pursuing a joint course of study in writing and literary translation); and an M.A. degree program in Film Studies. In addition, a Ph.D. in Drama and Theatre Arts is available through the Graduate School of Arts and Sciences, and a joint J.D./M.F.A. in Theatre Management and Producing is available in conjunction with Columbia Law School. The School also offers summer programs, including master classes, workshops, and credit and noncredit courses in film, theatre, visual arts, and writing through the School of Continuing Education, and an array of international programs in partnership with Columbia University's Global Centers and Office of Global Programs.

The School of the Arts typically enrolls full-time students only, except in the M.A. in Film Studies program, where students can attend part-time. The M.F.A. degree programs require 60 points of completed course work. Once the 60 points of course work are completed, each student completes a thesis and/or internships, often under "research arts" student status.

For all specific program requirements and information, prospective students should visit http://arts.columbia.edu/petersonsguide.

Research Facilities

The School of the Arts is located on Columbia's Morningside Campus in the vibrant Upper West Side of Manhattan, with New York City's world-renowned museums, Broadway and Off-Broadway theaters, film centers, galleries, cultural foundations, poetry houses, and literary hubs all nearby. The School is also home to Miller Theatre, the LeRoy Neiman Center for Print Studies, the Columbia University Arts Initiative, and the Office of Community Outreach and Education. The University's 22 libraries and countless research centers and institutes are all also available for students.

Financial Aid

The School of the Arts and Columbia University Office of Student Financial Planning work carefully with students to arrange the financing of their degrees. Scholarships, fellowships, federal work-study, on-campus employment, loan packages, and other options are available for eligible students. Students are encouraged to actively explore all options, even before acceptance into the School, to develop a plan to support the costs of graduate study.

More information is available at http://arts.columbia.edu/financing-your-degree/petersonsguide.

Cost of Study

M.F.A. tuition and fees for 2015–16 are approximately $60,000 for each of the first two years, based on full-time matriculation of 12 to 18 credits per semester. M.F.A. students who have completed the two-year course work requirement pay a reduced tuition while progressing toward completion of the required thesis. M.A. students pay approximately $53,500 in 2015–16 tuition and fees for the first year, then pay a reduced tuition during their third and final semester.

Living and Housing Costs

The University estimates that students need about $28,000 per year to cover living expenses and housing in New York City. Students can find housing around campus in the Morningside Heights neighborhood, in surrounding Manhattan neighborhoods and boroughs, and in the greater New York area. Columbia University apartment housing consists of a limited number of apartment shares; dormitory-style rooms; and one-bedroom, studio, and family units for which priority is given to couples and families. This housing is primarily located within walking distance of campus.

For additional details, visit http://facilities.columbia.edu/housing.

Student Group

In fall 2014, the School enrolled nearly 800 students from 57 countries: 311 in film programs, 156 in theatre programs, 307 in writing programs, and 54 in visual arts programs.

Location

Columbia University (including Barnard College and Teachers College) occupies approximately eighteen square blocks in the Morningside Heights area of Manhattan. The School of the Arts is on the Morningside Campus, at 116th Street and Broadway on the Upper West Side of Manhattan.

The University and the School

Columbia, founded in 1754, is comprised of three undergraduate schools, fourteen graduate and professional schools, and affiliate Barnard College.

Additional information is available at http://arts.columbia.edu/columbia-university.

Columbia University

The Faculty

The faculty comprises acclaimed and internationally renowned artists, film and theatre directors, playwrights, producers, poets, writers of fiction and nonfiction, critics, and scholars.

Additional information about full-time and adjunct faculty members is available at http://arts.columbia.edu/petersonsguide.

Applying

Applications are accepted for the fall semester only. The application cost for fall 2015 is $110 for the online application. The GRE is not required for application. TOEFL scores are good for two years from the test date. Applicants whose scores were received over two years ago must retake the test and resubmit their current scores with the admissions application. Applicants should request that TOEFL direct results to school code 2171, department code 15.

Students whose transcripts reflect advanced study at an institution where English is the primary language of instruction may request to have the TOEFL requirement waived by e-mailing admissions-arts@columbia.edu. An original certified transcript from the institution, in English, will be required to verify the waiver request. If no transcript has been received, the offer of admission will be provisional until the School receives and approves the official transcript.

Deadlines and more information are available at http://arts.columbia.edu/apply/petersonsguide.

Correspondence and Information

Office of Admissions
School of the Arts
Columbia University
305 Dodge Hall, MC 1808
2960 Broadway
New York, New York 10027
Phone: 212-854-2134
E-mail: admissions-arts@columbia.edu
Website: http://arts.columbia.edu/petersonsguide

ACADEMIC AND PROFESSIONAL
PROGRAMS IN THE HUMANITIES

ACADEMIC AND PROFESSIONAL
PROGRAMS IN THE HUMANITIES

Section 7
History

This section contains a directory of institutions offering graduate work in history, followed by an in-depth entry submitted by an institution that chose to prepare a detailed program description. Additional information about programs listed in the directory but not augmented by an in-depth entry may be obtained by writing directly to the dean of a graduate school or chair of a department at the address given in the directory.

For programs offering related work, see also in this book *Area and Cultural Studies, Architecture, Humanities, Political Science and International Affairs,* and *Sociology, Anthropology, and Archaeology.*

CONTENTS

Program Directories

Displays and Close-Ups

History

Adams State University, The Graduate School, Department of History, Government and Philosophy, Alamosa, CO 81101. Offers history (MA).

American Public University System, AMU/APU Graduate Programs, Charles Town, WV 25414. Offers accounting (MBA, MS); criminal justice (MA), including business administration, emergency and disaster management, general (MA, MS); educational leadership (M Ed); emergency and disaster management (MA); entrepreneurship (MBA); environmental policy and management (MS), including environmental planning, environmental sustainability, fish and wildlife management, general (MA, MS), global environmental management; finance (MBA); general (MBA); global business management (MBA); history (MA), including American history, ancient and classical history, European history, global history, public history; homeland security (MA), including business administration, counter-terrorism studies, criminal justice, cyber, emergency management and public health, intelligence studies, transportation security; homeland security resource allocation (MBA); humanities (MA); information technology (MS), including digital forensics, enterprise software development, information assurance and security, IT project management; information technology management (MBA); intelligence studies (MA), including criminal intelligence, cyber, general (MA, MS), homeland security, intelligence analysis, intelligence collection, intelligence management, intelligence operations, terrorism studies; international relations and conflict resolution (MA), including comparative and security issues, conflict resolution, international and transnational security issues, peacekeeping; legal studies (MA); management (MA), including defense management, general (MA, MS), human resource management, organizational leadership, public administration; marketing (MBA); military history (MA), including American military history, American Revolution, civil war, war since 1945, World War II; military studies (MA), including joint warfare, strategic leadership; national security studies (MA), including general (MA, MS), homeland security, regional security studies, security and intelligence analysis, terrorism studies; nonprofit management (MBA); political science (MA), including American politics and government, comparative government and development, general (MA, MS), international relations, public policy; psychology (MA); public administration (MPA), including disaster management, environmental policy, health policy, human resources, national security, organizational management, security management; public health (MPH); reverse logistics management (MA); school counseling (M Ed); security management (MA); space studies (MS), including aerospace science, general (MA, MS), planetary science; sports and health sciences (MS); teaching (M Ed), including curriculum and instruction for elementary teachers, elementary reading, English language learners, instructional leadership, online learning, special education; transportation and logistics management (MA), including general (MA, MS), maritime engineering management, reverse logistics management. Programs offered via distance learning only. Part-time and evening/weekend programs available. Postbaccalaureate distance learning degree programs offered (no on-campus study). *Faculty:* 426 full-time (236 women), 1,864 part-time/adjunct (880 women). *Students:* 475 full-time (215 women), 10,067 part-time (4,085 women); includes 3,462 minority (1,863 Black or African American, non-Hispanic/Latino; 74 American Indian or Alaska Native, non-Hispanic/Latino; 273 Asian, non-Hispanic/Latino; 831 Hispanic/Latino; 78 Native Hawaiian or other Pacific Islander, non-Hispanic/Latino; 343 Two or more races, non-Hispanic/Latino), 131 international. Average age 36. In 2014, 3,740 master's awarded. *Degree requirements:* For master's, comprehensive exam or practicum. *Entrance requirements:* For master's, official transcript showing earned bachelor's degree from institution accredited by recognized accrediting body. Additional exam requirements/recommendations for international students: Required—TOEFL (minimum score 550 paper-based), IELTS (minimum score 6.5). *Application deadline:* Applications are processed on a rolling basis. Application fee: $0. Electronic applications accepted. *Financial support:* Applicants required to submit FAFSA. *Faculty research:* Military history, criminal justice, management performance, national security. *Unit head:* Dr. Karan Powell, Executive Vice President and Provost, 877-468-6268, Fax: 304-724-3780. *Application contact:* Terry Grant, Vice President of Enrollment Management, 877-468-6268, Fax: 304-724-3780, E-mail: info@apus.edu.
Website: http://www.apus.edu

American University of Beirut, Graduate Programs, Faculty of Arts and Sciences, Beirut, Lebanon. Offers anthropology (MA); Arab and Middle Eastern history (PhD); Arabic language and literature (MA, PhD); archaeology (MA); biology (MS); cell and molecular biology (PhD); chemistry (MS); clinical psychology (MA); computational sciences (MS); computer science (MS); economics (MA); English language (MA); English literature (MA); environmental policy planning (MS); financial economics (MAFE); geology (MS); history (MA); mathematics (MA, MS); media studies (MA); Middle Eastern studies (MA); physics (MS); political studies (MA); psychology (MA); public administration (MA); sociology (MA); statistics (MA, MS); theoretical physics (PhD); transnational American studies (MA). Part-time programs available. *Faculty:* 107 full-time (32 women), 6 part-time/adjunct (2 women). *Students:* 230 full-time (161 women), 209 part-time (146 women). Average age 26. 261 applicants, 70% accepted, 83 enrolled. In 2014, 68 master's, 2 doctorates awarded. *Degree requirements:* For master's, one foreign language, comprehensive exam, thesis (for some programs); for doctorate, one foreign language, comprehensive exam, thesis/dissertation. *Entrance requirements:* For master's, GRE (for some MA/MS programs), letter of recommendation; for doctorate, GRE, letters of recommendation. Additional exam requirements/recommendations for international students: Required—TOEFL (minimum score 600 paper-based; 97 iBT), IELTS (minimum score 7). *Application deadline:* For fall admission, 4/1 for domestic and international students; for spring admission, 11/1 for domestic and international students. Application fee: $50. Electronic applications accepted. *Expenses: Tuition:* Full-time $15,462; part-time $859 per credit. *Required fees:* $692. Tuition and fees vary according to course load and program. *Financial support:* Research assistantships, career-related internships or fieldwork, institutionally sponsored loans, scholarships/grants, health care benefits, and unspecified assistantships available. Financial award application deadline: 2/4; financial award applicants required to submit FAFSA. *Faculty research:* Determinants of language proficiency among Arab learners of English as a foreign language; opinion mining, information retrieval, runtime verification, high performance computing; solar and fuel cells, self-organizing systems, heterocyclic chemistry, air and water chemistry; complex analysis, harmonic analysis, number theory; social and political psychology, clinical psychology; thin films physics and technology; theory of soft matter; religious and ethnic conflict; sports and politics. *Total annual research expenditures:* $966,000. *Unit head:* Dr. Patrick McGreevy, Dean, 961-1374374 Ext. 3800, Fax: 961-1744461, E-mail: pm07@aub.edu.lb. *Application contact:* Dr. Salim Kanaan, Director, Admissions Office, 961-1350000 Ext. 2590, Fax: 961-1750775, E-mail: sk00@aub.edu.lb.
Website: http://www.aub.edu.lb/fas/

Appalachian State University, Cratis D. Williams Graduate School, Department of History, Boone, NC 28608. Offers general history (MA). Part-time programs available. Postbaccalaureate distance learning degree programs offered (no on-campus study). *Degree requirements:* For master's, one foreign language, comprehensive exam, thesis (for some programs). *Entrance requirements:* For master's, GRE General Test, 3 letters of recommendation. Additional exam requirements/recommendations for international students: Required—TOEFL (minimum score 570 paper-based; 79 iBT), IELTS (minimum score 6.5). Electronic applications accepted. *Faculty research:* Women's history, social/cultural history, U.S. history, Latin America, medieval studies.

Arizona State University at the Tempe campus, College of Liberal Arts and Sciences, School of Historical, Philosophical and Religious Studies, Tempe, AZ 85287-4301. Offers European history (MA, PhD); medieval studies (Graduate Certificate); North American history (MA, PhD); philosophy (MA, PhD); public history (MA); religious studies (MA, PhD); Renaissance studies (Graduate Certificate); scholarly publishing (Graduate Certificate). Part-time programs available. Terminal master's awarded for partial completion of doctoral program. *Degree requirements:* For master's, thesis or alternative, interactive Program of Study (iPOS) submitted before completing 50 percent of required credit hours; for doctorate, variable foreign language requirement, comprehensive exam, thesis/dissertation, interactive Program of Study (iPOS) submitted before completing 50 percent of required credit hours. *Entrance requirements:* For master's and doctorate, GRE, minimum GPA of 3.0 or equivalent in last 2 years of work leading to bachelor's degree. Additional exam requirements/recommendations for international students: Required—TOEFL, IELTS, or PTE. Electronic applications accepted.

Arkansas State University, Graduate School, College of Humanities and Social Sciences, Department of History, State University, AR 72467. Offers history (MA); history education (SCCT); social science education (MSE). Part-time programs available. *Faculty:* 13 full-time (7 women). *Students:* 2 full-time (1 woman), 29 part-time (11 women); includes 4 minority (3 Black or African American, non-Hispanic/Latino; 1 Hispanic/Latino). Average age 35. 15 applicants, 87% accepted, 10 enrolled. In 2014, 6 master's awarded. *Degree requirements:* For master's, comprehensive exam, thesis or alternative; for SCCT, comprehensive exam. *Entrance requirements:* For master's, GRE General Test or MAT, GMAT, appropriate bachelor's degree, letters of reference, official transcript, valid teaching certificate (for MSE), immunization records; for SCCT, GRE General Test or MAT, interview, master's degree, letters of reference, official transcript, immunization records. Additional exam requirements/recommendations for international students: Required—TOEFL (minimum score 550 paper-based; 79 iBT), IELTS (minimum score 6), PTE (minimum score 56). *Application deadline:* For fall admission, 7/1 for domestic and international students; for spring admission, 11/15 for domestic students, 11/14 for international students. Applications are processed on a rolling basis. Application fee: $30 ($40 for international students). Electronic applications accepted. *Expenses:* Tuition, state resident: full-time $4392; part-time $244 per credit hour. Tuition, nonresident: full-time $8784; part-time $488 per credit hour. *International tuition:* $9484 full-time. *Required fees:* $1134; $63 per credit hour. $25 per term. Tuition and fees vary according to course load and program. *Financial support:* In 2014–15, 1 student received support. Career-related internships or fieldwork, scholarships/grants, and unspecified assistantships available. Financial award application deadline: 7/1; financial award applicants required to submit FAFSA. *Unit head:* Dr. Joseph Key, Chair, 870-972-3046, Fax: 870-972-2880, E-mail: jkey@astate.edu. *Application contact:* Vickey Ring, Graduate Admissions Coordinator, 870-972-3029, Fax: 870-972-3857, E-mail: vickeyring@astate.edu.
Website: http://www.astate.edu/college/humanities-and-social-sciences/departments/history/

Arkansas Tech University, College of Arts and Humanities, Russellville, AR 72801. Offers English (M Ed, MA); history (MA); liberal arts (MLA); multi-media journalism (MA); psychology (MS); teaching English as a second language (MA). Part-time programs available. *Students:* 70 full-time (39 women), 105 part-time (72 women); includes 20 minority (3 Black or African American, non-Hispanic/Latino; 2 American Indian or Alaska Native, non-Hispanic/Latino; 1 Asian, non-Hispanic/Latino; 10 Hispanic/Latino; 4 Two or more races, non-Hispanic/Latino), 51 international. Average age 30. In 2014, 63 master's awarded. *Degree requirements:* For master's, comprehensive exam (for some programs), thesis (for some programs), project. *Entrance requirements:* For master's, GRE General Test or GMAT. Additional exam requirements/recommendations for international students: Required—TOEFL (minimum score 550 paper-based; 79 iBT), IELTS (minimum score 6). *Application deadline:* For fall admission, 3/1 priority date for domestic students, 5/1 priority date for international students; for spring admission, 10/1 priority date for domestic and international students. Applications are processed on a rolling basis. Application fee: $25 ($75 for international students). Electronic applications accepted. *Expenses:* Tuition, state resident: full-time $6264; part-time $261 per credit hour. Tuition, nonresident: full-time $12,528; part-time $522 per credit hour. *Required fees:* $423 per semester. Tuition and fees vary according to course load. *Financial support:* In 2014–15, research assistantships with full tuition reimbursements (averaging $4,800 per year), teaching assistantships with full tuition reimbursements (averaging $4,800 per year) were awarded; career-related internships or fieldwork, Federal Work-Study, scholarships/grants, health care benefits, and unspecified assistantships also available. Support available to part-time students. Financial award application deadline: 4/15; financial award applicants required to submit FAFSA. *Unit head:* Dr. Jeffrey Woods, Dean, 479-968-0274, Fax: 479-964-0812, E-mail: jwoods@atu.edu. *Application contact:* Dr. Mary B. Gunter, Dean of Graduate College, 479-968-0398, Fax: 479-964-0542, E-mail: gradcollege@atu.edu.
Website: http://www.atu.edu/humanities/

Armstrong State University, School of Graduate Studies, Program in History, Savannah, GA 31419-1997. Offers American and European history (MA); public history (MA). Part-time and evening/weekend programs available. *Faculty:* 5 full-time (2 women), 1 (woman) part-time/adjunct. *Students:* 6 full-time (5 women), 7 part-time (4 women); includes 3 minority (1 Black or African American, non-Hispanic/Latino; 1 Asian, non-Hispanic/Latino; 1 Hispanic/Latino). Average age 32. 9 applicants, 67% accepted, 5 enrolled. In 2014, 9 master's awarded. *Degree requirements:* For master's, one foreign language, comprehensive exam (for some programs), thesis (for some programs), thesis, internship, or advanced fieldwork. *Entrance requirements:* For master's, GRE General Test, minimum GPA of 3.0, letters of recommendation, BA in history or equivalent. Additional exam requirements/recommendations for international students: Required—TOEFL (minimum score 523 paper-based). *Application deadline:* For fall admission, 6/30 priority date for domestic students, 5/1 priority date for international students; for spring admission, 11/15 priority date for domestic students, 9/15 priority date for international students; for summer admission, 4/15 priority date for domestic students, 9/15 for international students. Applications are processed on a rolling basis.

Application fee: $30. Electronic applications accepted. *Expenses:* Tuition, state resident: part-time $206 per credit hour. Tuition, nonresident: part-time $763 per credit hour. *Required fees:* $612 per semester. Tuition and fees vary according to course load, campus/location and program. *Financial support:* In 2014–15, research assistantships with full tuition reimbursements (averaging $5,000 per year) were awarded; career-related internships or fieldwork, Federal Work-Study, and unspecified assistantships also available. Support available to part-time students. Financial award application deadline: 3/15; financial award applicants required to submit FAFSA. *Faculty research:* Public history; European, Latin American, African, and United States history. *Unit head:* Dr. Christopher Curtis, Department Head, 912-344-3051, Fax: 912-344-3451, E-mail: chris.curtis@armstrong.edu. *Application contact:* Kathy Ingram, Associate Director of Graduate/Adult and Nontraditional Students, 912-344-2503, Fax: 912-344-3417, E-mail: graduate@armstrong.edu.
Website: http://www.armstrong.edu/Liberal_Arts/history/history_graduate_program

Ashland University, College of Arts and Sciences, Program in American History and Government, Ashland, OH 44805-3702. Offers MAHG. Part-time programs available. *Degree requirements:* For master's, capstone project or thesis. *Entrance requirements:* For master's, minimum undergraduate GPA of 2.75, 3.0 graduate. Electronic applications accepted. *Expenses:* Contact institution. *Faculty research:* American founding, United States Civil War, Progressive Era.

Auburn University, Graduate School, College of Liberal Arts, Department of History, Auburn University, AL 36849. Offers MA, PhD, Graduate Certificate. Part-time programs available. *Faculty:* 29 full-time (11 women). *Students:* 30 full-time (7 women), 23 part-time (6 women); includes 2 minority (both Black or African American, non-Hispanic/Latino), 1 international. Average age 33. 48 applicants, 35% accepted, 5 enrolled. In 2014, 8 master's, 4 doctorates, 5 other advanced degrees awarded. *Degree requirements:* For master's, thesis, oral exam; for doctorate, 2 foreign languages, thesis/dissertation. *Entrance requirements:* For master's, GRE General Test; for doctorate, GRE General Test, master's degree with thesis. *Application deadline:* For fall admission, 7/7 for domestic students; for spring admission, 11/24 for domestic students. Applications are processed on a rolling basis. Application fee: $50 ($60 for international students). Electronic applications accepted. *Expenses:* Tuition, state resident: full-time $8586; part-time $477 per credit hour. Tuition, nonresident: full-time $25,758; part-time $1431 per credit hour. *Required fees:* $804 per semester. Tuition and fees vary according to degree level and program. *Financial support:* Teaching assistantships and Federal Work-Study available. Support available to part-time students. Financial award application deadline: 3/15; financial award applicants required to submit FAFSA. *Unit head:* Morris Bian, 334-844-4360. *Application contact:* Dr. George Flowers, Dean of the Graduate School, 334-844-2125.

Averett University, Master in Education Program, Danville, VA 24541-3692. Offers administration and supervision (M Ed); art (M Ed); biology (M Ed); chemistry (M Ed); curriculum and instruction (M Ed); early childhood (M Ed); English (M Ed); English/theatre (M Ed); health/physical education (M Ed); history (M Ed); history/social science (M Ed); liberal studies (M Ed); mathematics (M Ed); middle grades (M Ed); physical science (M Ed); reading specialist (M Ed); special education (M Ed); special education learning disability (M Ed); theatre (M Ed). Program offered on Danville Campus only. Part-time and evening/weekend programs available. Postbaccalaureate distance learning degree programs offered (no on-campus study). *Faculty:* 7 full-time (4 women), 4 part-time/adjunct (2 women). *Students:* 25 full-time (20 women), 21 part-time (20 women); includes 10 minority (3 Black or African American, non-Hispanic/Latino; 6 American Indian or Alaska Native, non-Hispanic/Latino; 1 Hispanic/Latino). Average age 37. In 2014, 50 master's awarded. *Degree requirements:* For master's, 30-credit core curriculum, minimum GPA of 3.0 throughout program, completion of degree requirements within six years from start of program. *Entrance requirements:* For master's, PRAXIS I, GRE, or MAT; writing proficiency test, minimum cumulative GPA of 3.0 over the last 60 hours of undergraduate study toward a baccalaureate degree, three letters of recommendation, Virginia teaching license (or eligibility). Additional exam requirements/recommendations for international students: Required—TOEFL (minimum score 600 paper-based; 100 iBT). *Application deadline:* Applications are processed on a rolling basis. Application fee: $100. Electronic applications accepted. *Expenses:* Expenses: Contact institution. *Financial support:* Career-related internships or fieldwork and scholarships/grants available. Financial award application deadline: 4/1; financial award applicants required to submit FAFSA. *Unit head:* Dr. Sue Davis, Acting Education Chair, 434-791-5741, E-mail: suedavis@averett.edu. *Application contact:* Christy Pack, Associate Vice President for Client Relations, 804-887-8612, E-mail: dpack@averett.edu.
Website: http://gps.averett.edu/programs/master-degrees/

Ball State University, Graduate School, College of Sciences and Humanities, Department of History, Muncie, IN 47306-1099. Offers MA. *Faculty:* 10 full-time (2 women). *Students:* 8 full-time (5 women), 18 part-time (9 women); includes 1 minority (Hispanic/Latino). Average age 28. 10 applicants, 90% accepted, 4 enrolled. In 2014, 6 master's awarded. Application fee: $50. *Financial support:* In 2014–15, 15 students received support, including 3 research assistantships with partial tuition reimbursements available (averaging $10,655 per year), 4 teaching assistantships with partial tuition reimbursements available (averaging $10,910 per year); unspecified assistantships also available. Financial award application deadline: 3/1. *Faculty research:* European, British, and American history. *Unit head:* Dr. Kevin Smith, Chairperson, 765-285-8700, E-mail: ksmith@bsu.edu. *Application contact:* Dr. Kenneth Swope, Graduate Program Director, 765-285-8778, Fax: 765-285-5612, E-mail: kswope@bsu.edu.
Website: http://www.bsu.edu/csh/history/

Baylor University, Graduate School, College of Arts and Sciences, Department of History, Waco, TX 76798. Offers history (MA); religion and culture (PhD); U.S. and Britain (PhD). Part-time programs available. Terminal master's awarded for partial completion of doctoral program. *Degree requirements:* For master's, one foreign language, comprehensive exam, thesis; for doctorate, one foreign language, comprehensive exam, thesis/dissertation. *Entrance requirements:* For master's and doctorate, GRE General Test, 18 semester hours in history. Additional exam requirements/recommendations for international students: Required—TOEFL. *Faculty research:* American religion and culture, medieval women and religion, U.S. women's history, Chinese missions, late nineteenth-century Germany, twentieth-century urban United States.

Binghamton University, State University of New York, Graduate School, School of Arts and Sciences, Department of History, Vestal, NY 13850. Offers MA, PhD. Part-time programs available. *Faculty:* 25 full-time (11 women), 11 part-time/adjunct (2 women). *Students:* 32 full-time (18 women), 46 part-time (26 women); includes 3 minority (1 Black or African American, non-Hispanic/Latino; 1 Hispanic/Latino; 1 Native Hawaiian or other Pacific Islander, non-Hispanic/Latino), 16 international. Average age 30. 83 applicants, 54% accepted, 16 enrolled. In 2014, 7 master's, 13 doctorates awarded. Terminal master's awarded for partial completion of doctoral program. *Degree requirements:* For master's, variable foreign language requirement, comprehensive exam, thesis; for doctorate, variable foreign language requirement, comprehensive exam, thesis/dissertation. *Entrance requirements:* For master's and doctorate, GRE General Test, writing sample. Additional exam requirements/recommendations for international students: Required—TOEFL (minimum score 550 paper-based; 80 iBT). *Application deadline:* For fall admission, 4/15 priority date for domestic and international students; for spring admission, 11/1 priority date for domestic and international students. Applications are processed on a rolling basis. Application fee: $75. Electronic applications accepted. *Expenses:* Tuition, state resident: full-time $7776; part-time $432 per credit. Tuition, nonresident: full-time $15,138; part-time $841 per credit. *Required fees:* $1754; $213 per credit. Tuition and fees vary according to degree level and program. *Financial support:* In 2014–15, 46 students received support, including 40 teaching assistantships with full tuition reimbursements available (averaging $15,000 per year); career-related internships or fieldwork, Federal Work-Study, institutionally sponsored loans, scholarships/grants, health care benefits, tuition waivers (full), and unspecified assistantships also available. Financial award application deadline: 2/15; financial award applicants required to submit FAFSA. *Unit head:* Dr. Howard G. Brown, Chairperson, 607-777-4562, E-mail: hgbrown@binghamton.edu. *Application contact:* Kishan Zuber, Recruiting and Admissions Coordinator, 607-777-2151, Fax: 607-777-2501, E-mail: kzuber@binghamton.edu.

Bob Jones University, Graduate Programs, Greenville, SC 29614. Offers accountancy (MS); Bible (MA); Bible translation (MA); Biblical studies (Certificate); broadcast management (MS); business administration (MBA); church history (MA, PhD); church ministries (MA); church music (MM); cinema and video production (MA); counseling (MS); curriculum and instruction (Ed D); divinity (M Div); dramatic production (MA); educational leadership (MS, Ed D, Ed S); elementary education (M Ed, MAT); English (M Ed, MA, MAT); fine arts (MA); graphic design (MA); history (M Ed, MA); illustration (MA); interpretative speech (MA); mathematics (M Ed, MAT); medical missions (Certificate); ministry (MM, D Min); multi-categorical special education (M Ed, MAT); music (M Ed); New Testament interpretation (PhD); Old Testament interpretation (PhD); orchestral instrument performance (MM); organ performance (MM); pastoral studies (MA); personnel services (MS, Ed S); piano pedagogy (MM); piano performance (MM); platform arts (MA); radio and television broadcasting (MS); rhetoric and public address (MA); secondary education (M Ed); studio art (MA); teaching Bible (MA); theology (MA, PhD); voice performance (MM); youth ministries (MA); M Div/MM.

Boise State University, College of Social Sciences and Public Affairs, Department of History, Boise, ID 83725-0399. Offers MA, MAHR. Part-time programs available. *Faculty:* 20 full-time, 15 part-time/adjunct. *Students:* 13 full-time (3 women), 15 part-time (9 women); includes 4 minority (1 Black or African American, non-Hispanic/Latino; 1 American Indian or Alaska Native, non-Hispanic/Latino; 2 Hispanic/Latino). 24 applicants, 92% accepted, 7 enrolled. In 2014, 4 master's awarded. *Degree requirements:* For master's, thesis. *Entrance requirements:* For master's, GRE General Test, minimum GPA of 3.0. *Application deadline:* For fall admission, 3/1 priority date for domestic students; for spring admission, 10/1 priority date for domestic students. Applications are processed on a rolling basis. Application fee: $55. Electronic applications accepted. *Expenses:* Tuition, state resident: part-time $331 per credit hour. Tuition, nonresident: part-time $531 per credit hour. *Financial support:* In 2014–15, 7 students received support, including 2 research assistantships, 4 teaching assistantships; career-related internships or fieldwork, Federal Work-Study, institutionally sponsored loans, and unspecified assistantships also available. Support available to part-time students. Financial award application deadline: 3/1. *Faculty research:* Public history, American social and cultural history, European history, Third World history. *Unit head:* Dr. Joanne Klein, Department Chair, 208-426-3248, Fax: 208-426-4058, E-mail: jklein@boisestate.edu. *Application contact:* Dr. Jill Gill, Graduate Coordinator, 208-426-1316, E-mail: jgill@boisestate.edu.
Website: http://sspa.boisestate.edu/history/graduate/

Boston College, Graduate School of Arts and Sciences, Department of History, Chestnut Hill, MA 02467-3800. Offers European national studies (MA); history (MA, PhD); medieval studies (MA). *Faculty:* 43 full-time. *Students:* 61 full-time (30 women); includes 4 minority (1 Black or African American, non-Hispanic/Latino; 1 Asian, non-Hispanic/Latino; 1 Hispanic/Latino; 1 Two or more races, non-Hispanic/Latino), 5 international. 194 applicants, 29% accepted, 20 enrolled. In 2014, 13 master's, 7 doctorates awarded. Terminal master's awarded for partial completion of doctoral program. *Degree requirements:* For master's, one foreign language, comprehensive exam, thesis optional; for doctorate, 2 foreign languages, comprehensive exam, thesis/dissertation. *Entrance requirements:* For master's and doctorate, GRE General Test, writing sample. Additional exam requirements/recommendations for international students: Required—TOEFL (minimum score 600 paper-based; 100 iBT), IELTS (minimum score 7). *Application deadline:* For fall admission, 1/2 for domestic and international students. Application fee: $75. Electronic applications accepted. *Financial support:* In 2014–15, fellowships with full tuition reimbursements (averaging $21,000 per year), teaching assistantships with full tuition reimbursements (averaging $21,000 per year) were awarded; Federal Work-Study, scholarships/grants, health care benefits, and unspecified assistantships also available. Support available to part-time students. Financial award application deadline: 3/1; financial award applicants required to submit FAFSA. *Faculty research:* U.S. history, medieval history, early modern European history, Latin American history, Asian history, transnational history. *Unit head:* Dr. Kevin Kenny, Chairperson, 617-552-1196, E-mail: kevin.kenny@bc.edu. *Application contact:* Dr. Prasannan Pathasarathi, Director of Graduate Studies, 617-552-3781, E-mail: pathasa@bc.edu.
Website: http://www.bc.edu/history

Boston University, Graduate School of Arts and Sciences, Department of History, Boston, MA 02215. Offers MA, PhD, JD/MA. *Students:* 35 full-time (18 women), 4 part-time (2 women); includes 3 minority (1 Black or African American, non-Hispanic/Latino; 1 Hispanic/Latino; 1 Two or more races, non-Hispanic/Latino), 1 international. Average age 31. 152 applicants, 13% accepted, 6 enrolled. In 2014, 7 master's, 3 doctorates awarded. Terminal master's awarded for partial completion of doctoral program. *Degree requirements:* For master's, one foreign language; for doctorate, 2 foreign languages, comprehensive exam, thesis/dissertation. *Entrance requirements:* For master's and doctorate, GRE General Test, 3 letters of recommendation, writing sample, foreign language proficiency. Additional exam requirements/recommendations for international students: Required—TOEFL (minimum score 550 paper-based; 84 iBT). *Application deadline:* For fall admission, 1/15 for domestic and international students. Application fee: $80. Electronic applications accepted. *Expenses: Tuition:* Full-time $45,686; part-time $1428 per credit hour. *Required fees:* $660; $60 per semester. Tuition and fees vary according to program. *Financial support:* In 2014–15, 34 students received support, including 4 fellowships with full tuition reimbursements available (averaging $20,500 per year), 1 research assistantship with full tuition reimbursement available (averaging $20,500 per year), 11 teaching assistantships with full tuition reimbursements available (averaging $20,500 per year); Federal Work-Study, scholarships/grants, health care benefits, and unspecified assistantships also available. Financial award application deadline: 1/15. *Unit head:* Louis Ferleger, Chairman, 617-353-2550, Fax: 617-353-2556, E-mail: ferleger@bu.edu. *Application contact:* Carrie Mountain, Department Administrator, 617-353-2555, Fax: 617-353-2556, E-mail: cmount@bu.edu.
Website: http://www.bu.edu/history/

History

Bowling Green State University, Graduate College, College of Arts and Sciences, Department of History, Bowling Green, OH 43403. Offers history (MA, MAT, PhD); public history (MA); MA/MA. Part-time programs available. *Degree requirements:* For master's, thesis or alternative; for doctorate, one foreign language, comprehensive exam, thesis/dissertation. *Entrance requirements:* For master's and doctorate, GRE General Test. Additional exam requirements/recommendations for international students: Required—TOEFL. Electronic applications accepted. *Faculty research:* Policy history, modern Europe, recent United States history, East Asia, Latin America.

Brandeis University, Graduate School of Arts and Sciences, Department of History, Waltham, MA 02454-9110. Offers MA, PhD. Terminal master's awarded for partial completion of doctoral program. *Degree requirements:* For master's, thesis or capstone; seminars; for doctorate, one foreign language, comprehensive exam, thesis/dissertation, regional colloquia; seminars; directed research analyzing primary sources. *Entrance requirements:* For master's, resume, writing sample, 2 letters of recommendation, statement of purpose, transcript(s); for doctorate, GRE General Test, resume, writing sample, 2 letters of recommendation, statement of purpose, transcript(s). Additional exam requirements/recommendations for international students: Required—TOEFL (minimum score 600 paper-based; 100 iBT); Recommended—IELTS (minimum score 7). Electronic applications accepted. *Faculty research:* American and European history, world history, regional and national history, medieval history, modern history, international and cultural history.

Brandeis University, Graduate School of Arts and Sciences, Joint Master's Programs in Women's and Gender Studies, Waltham, MA 02454-9110. Offers anthropology and women's and gender studies (MA); English and women's and gender studies (MA); history and women's and gender studies (MA); Near Eastern and Judaic studies and women's and gender studies (MA); psychology and women's and gender studies (MA); public policy and women's and gender studies (MA); social policy and women's and gender studies (MA); sociology and women's and gender studies (MA); sustainable international development and women's/gender studies (MA). *Degree requirements:* For master's, thesis. *Entrance requirements:* For master's, GRE, sample of written work, resume, statement of purpose, transcript(s), letters of recommendation. Additional exam requirements/recommendations for international students: Required—TOEFL (minimum score 600 paper-based; 100 iBT), PTE (minimum score 68); Recommended—IELTS (minimum score 7). Electronic applications accepted. *Faculty research:* Anthropology, English, history, music, Near Eastern and Judaic studies, public policy, psychology, sociology, and sustainable international development.

Brock University, Faculty of Graduate Studies, Faculty of Humanities, Program in History, St. Catharines, ON L2S 3A1, Canada. Offers MA. Part-time programs available. *Degree requirements:* For master's, thesis optional. *Entrance requirements:* For master's, honors degree in history. Additional exam requirements/recommendations for international students: Required—TOEFL (minimum score 550 paper-based; 80 iBT), IELTS (minimum score 6.5), TWE (minimum score 4). Electronic applications accepted.

Brooklyn College of the City University of New York, School of Humanities and Social Sciences, Department of History, Brooklyn, NY 11210-2889. Offers MA. Part-time and evening/weekend programs available. *Degree requirements:* For master's, 30 credits. *Entrance requirements:* For master's, 12 credits in history, minimum GPA of 3.0 in major, 2 letters of recommendation. Additional exam requirements/recommendations for international students: Required—TOEFL (minimum score 650 paper-based; 114 iBT). Electronic applications accepted. *Faculty research:* Modern European, U.S., medieval, women's, Asian, and Caribbean history.

Brown University, Graduate School, Department of History, Providence, RI 02912. Offers MA, PhD. *Degree requirements:* For master's, thesis or alternative; for doctorate, variable foreign language requirement, thesis/dissertation, preliminary exam.

Buffalo State College, State University of New York, The Graduate School, Faculty of Natural and Social Sciences, Department of History and Social Studies, Buffalo, NY 14222-1095. Offers history (MA); secondary education (MS Ed), including social studies. Part-time and evening/weekend programs available. *Degree requirements:* For master's, one foreign language, thesis (for some programs), project (MS Ed.). *Entrance requirements:* For master's, minimum GPA of 2.75, 30 hours in history (MA), 36 hours in history or social sciences (MS Ed). Additional exam requirements/recommendations for international students: Required—TOEFL (minimum score 550 paper-based).

Butler University, College of Liberal Arts and Sciences, Department of History, Indianapolis, IN 46208-3485. Offers MA. Part-time programs available. *Faculty:* 1 full-time (0 women). *Students:* 5 part-time (2 women). Average age 31. 3 applicants, 33% accepted, 1 enrolled. In 2014, 1 master's awarded. *Degree requirements:* For master's, thesis or alternative. *Entrance requirements:* For master's, GRE General Test, minimum GPA of 3.25 in undergraduate major. Additional exam requirements/recommendations for international students: Required—TOEFL (minimum score 550 paper-based; 79 iBT), IELTS (minimum score 6). *Application deadline:* For fall admission, 8/15 priority date for domestic students. Applications are processed on a rolling basis. Application fee: $35. Electronic applications accepted. *Financial support:* Institutionally sponsored loans available. Support available to part-time students. Financial award applicants required to submit FAFSA. *Unit head:* Dr. Elise Edwards, Chair, 317-940-9743, E-mail: emedwar1@butler.edu. *Application contact:* Diane Dubord, Student Services Specialist, 317-940-8100, Fax: 317-940-8250, E-mail: ddubord@butler.edu. Website: http://legacy.butler.edu/history-anthropology/history/graduate-degree

California Polytechnic State University, San Luis Obispo, College of Liberal Arts, Department of History, San Luis Obispo, CA 93407. Offers MA. Part-time programs available. *Faculty:* 5 full-time (2 women). *Students:* 6 full-time (3 women), 14 part-time (7 women); includes 4 minority (3 Hispanic/Latino; 1 Two or more races, non-Hispanic/Latino). Average age 27. 17 applicants, 71% accepted, 9 enrolled. In 2014, 6 master's awarded. *Degree requirements:* For master's, comprehensive exam (for some programs), thesis (for some programs). *Application deadline:* For fall admission, 6/1 for domestic students, 4/1 for international students; for winter admission, 10/1 for domestic students, 6/30 for international students; for spring admission, 2/1 for domestic students. Applications are processed on a rolling basis. Application fee: $55. Electronic applications accepted. *Expenses:* Tuition, state resident: full-time $6738; part-time $3906 per year. Tuition, nonresident: full-time $15,666; part-time $8370 per year. *Required fees:* $3447; $1001 per quarter. One-time fee: $3447 full-time; $3003 part-time. *Financial support:* Federal Work-Study and scholarships/grants available. Support available to part-time students. Financial award application deadline: 3/2; financial award applicants required to submit FAFSA. *Faculty research:* American history, European history, Asian history, African history, comparative world history. *Unit head:* Dr. Matthew Hopper, Graduate Coordinator, 805-756-2641, Fax: 805-756-5055, E-mail: mshopper@calpoly.edu. *Application contact:* Dr. James Maraviglia, Associate Vice Provost for Marketing and Enrollment Development, 805-756-2311, Fax: 805-756-5400, E-mail: admissions@calpoly.edu. Website: http://cla.calpoly.edu/hist.html

California State Polytechnic University, Pomona, Program in History, Pomona, CA 91768-2557. Offers MA. Part-time programs available. *Students:* 15 part-time (7 women); includes 4 minority (1 Black or African American, non-Hispanic/Latino; 2 Hispanic/Latino; 1 Two or more races, non-Hispanic/Latino). Average age 30. 17

applicants, 71% accepted, 5 enrolled. In 2014, 1 master's awarded. *Degree requirements:* For master's, comprehensive exam (for some programs), thesis (for some programs). *Application deadline:* For fall admission, 5/1 priority date for domestic students; for winter admission, 10/15 priority date for domestic students; for spring admission, 1/20 priority date for domestic students. Applications are processed on a rolling basis. Application fee: $55. Electronic applications accepted. *Expenses:* Tuition, state resident: full-time $6738. Tuition, nonresident: full-time $12,300. *Required fees:* $1400. *Unit head:* Dr. Mahmood Ibrahim, Graduate Coordinator, 909-869-3867, Fax: 909-869-4724, E-mail: mibrahim@cpp.edu. Website: http://www.cpp.edu/~class/history/graduate-students/

California State University, Bakersfield, Division of Graduate Studies, School of Arts and Humanities, Program in History, Bakersfield, CA 93311. Offers MA. *Degree requirements:* For master's, comprehensive exam or thesis. *Entrance requirements:* For master's, 2 letters of recommendation, letter of intent, writing sample, undergraduate transcripts. *Faculty research:* American, European, Latin American, and modern Chinese history.

California State University, Chico, Office of Graduate Studies, College of Humanities and Fine Arts, Department of History, Chico, CA 95929-0722. Offers MA. Part-time programs available. *Faculty:* 3 full-time (0 women). *Students:* 4 full-time (0 women), 4 part-time (1 woman). Average age 30. 6 applicants, 67% accepted, 2 enrolled. In 2014, 8 master's awarded. *Degree requirements:* For master's, thesis, oral exam. *Entrance requirements:* For master's, GRE General Test, 2 letters of recommendation, statement of purpose, writing sample. Additional exam requirements/recommendations for international students: Required—TOEFL (minimum score 550 paper-based; 80 iBT), IELTS (minimum score 6.5), PTE (minimum score 59). *Application deadline:* For fall admission, 3/1 priority date for domestic students, 3/1 for international students; for spring admission, 9/15 priority date for domestic students, 9/15 for international students. Application fee: $55. Electronic applications accepted. *Expenses:* Tuition, state resident: full-time $7002. Tuition, nonresident: full-time $18,162. *Required fees:* $1530. Tuition and fees vary according to program. *Financial support:* Teaching assistantships, career-related internships or fieldwork, scholarships/grants, and unspecified assistantships available. Financial award application deadline: 3/1; financial award applicants required to submit FAFSA. *Unit head:* Dr. Laird M. Easton, Chair, 530-898-5366, Fax: 530-898-6925, E-mail: hist@csuchico.edu. *Application contact:* Judy L. Rice, Graduate Admissions Coordinator, 530-898-5416, Fax: 530-898-3342, E-mail: ktranschel@csuchico.edu. Website: http://www.csuchico.edu/hist

California State University, East Bay, Office of Academic Programs and Graduate Studies, College of Letters, Arts, and Social Sciences, Department of History, Hayward, CA 94542-3000. Offers history (MA); public history (MA); teaching (MA). Part-time and evening/weekend programs available. *Degree requirements:* For master's, one foreign language, comprehensive exam, project, thesis, or exam. *Entrance requirements:* For master's, GRE (strongly recommended), minimum GPA of 3.0 in field, 3.3 in history; 2 letters of recommendation; writing sample. Additional exam requirements/recommendations for international students: Required—TOEFL (minimum score 550 paper-based). *Application deadline:* For fall admission, 5/16 for domestic and international students. Applications are processed on a rolling basis. Application fee: $55. Electronic applications accepted. *Expenses:* Tuition, state resident: full-time $7830; part-time $1302 per credit hour. Tuition, nonresident: full-time $16,368. *Required fees:* $327 per quarter. Tuition and fees vary according to course load and program. *Financial support:* Fellowships, teaching assistantships, career-related internships or fieldwork, Federal Work-Study, institutionally sponsored loans, and scholarships/grants available. Support available to part-time students. Financial award application deadline: 3/2; financial award applicants required to submit FAFSA. *Faculty research:* Digital history, American women, early America, Native Americans, medieval colonial India. *Unit head:* Dr. Linda L. Ivey, Chair, 510-885-4015, E-mail: linda.ivey@csueastbay.edu. *Application contact:* Dr. Khal Schneider, Graduate Coordinator, 510-885-3237, Fax: 510-885-4791, E-mail: khal.schneider@csueastbay.edu. Website: http://www20.csueastbay.edu/class/departments/history/

California State University, Fresno, Division of Graduate Studies, College of Social Sciences, Department of History, Fresno, CA 93740-8027. Offers history-teaching option (MA); history-traditional track (MA). Part-time and evening/weekend programs available. *Degree requirements:* For master's, thesis or alternative. *Entrance requirements:* For master's, GRE General Test, minimum GPA of 3.0. Additional exam requirements/recommendations for international students: Required—TOEFL. Electronic applications accepted. *Faculty research:* International education, classical art history, improving teacher quality.

California State University, Fullerton, Graduate Studies, College of Humanities and Social Sciences, Department of History, Fullerton, CA 92834-9480. Offers MA. Part-time programs available. *Students:* 36 full-time (20 women), 83 part-time (40 women); includes 48 minority (6 Black or African American, non-Hispanic/Latino; 5 Asian, non-Hispanic/Latino; 34 Hispanic/Latino; 3 Two or more races, non-Hispanic/Latino), 3 international. Average age 30. 62 applicants, 87% accepted, 35 enrolled. In 2014, 31 master's awarded. *Degree requirements:* For master's, comprehensive exam, project or thesis. *Entrance requirements:* For master's, undergraduate major in history or related field, minimum GPA of 3.0. Application fee: $55. *Financial support:* Career-related internships or fieldwork, Federal Work-Study, institutionally sponsored loans, and scholarships/grants available. Support available to part-time students. Financial award application deadline: 3/1; financial award applicants required to submit FAFSA. *Unit head:* Dr. Jochen Burgtorf, Chair, 657-278-3474. *Application contact:* Admissions/ Applications, 657-278-2371.

California State University, Long Beach, Graduate Studies, College of Liberal Arts, Department of History, Long Beach, CA 90840. Offers Africa and the Middle East (MA); ancient/medieval Europe (MA); Asia (MA); Latin America (MA); modern Europe (MA); United States (MA); world history (MA). Part-time and evening/weekend programs available. *Degree requirements:* For master's, one foreign language, comprehensive exam or thesis. Electronic applications accepted. *Faculty research:* All periods of European and American history, recent Asian and African history.

California State University, Los Angeles, Graduate Studies, College of Natural and Social Sciences, Department of History, Los Angeles, CA 90032-8530. Offers MA. Part-time and evening/weekend programs available. *Degree requirements:* For master's, one foreign language, comprehensive exam or thesis. *Entrance requirements:* For master's, minimum GPA of 3.0, undergraduate major in history. Additional exam requirements/recommendations for international students: Required—TOEFL (minimum score 500 paper-based). Electronic applications accepted. *Expenses:* Tuition, state resident: full-time $6738; part-time $3609 per year. Tuition, nonresident: full-time $15,666; part-time $8073 per year. Tuition and fees vary according to course load, degree level and program. *Faculty research:* Ancient and modern Europe, the Middle East, Latin America, U.S. history: Bill of Rights.

California State University, Northridge, Graduate Studies, College of Social and Behavioral Sciences, Department of History, Northridge, CA 91330. Offers MA.

Students: 20 full-time (11 women), 30 part-time (8 women); includes 12 minority (1 Black or African American, non-Hispanic/Latino; 1 Asian, non-Hispanic/Latino; 8 Hispanic/Latino; 2 Two or more races, non-Hispanic/Latino), 3 international. Average age 34. *Degree requirements:* For master's, one foreign language. *Entrance requirements:* For master's, GRE General Test or minimum GPA of 3.0, 2 letters of recommendation. Additional exam requirements/recommendations for international students: Required—TOEFL. *Application deadline:* For fall admission, 5/15 for domestic students; for spring admission, 11/1 for domestic students. Application fee: $55. *Expenses: Required fees:* $12,402. *Financial support:* Fellowships and scholarships/grants available. Financial award application deadline: 3/1. *Unit head:* Dr. Thomas R. Maddux, Chair, 818-677-3566, E-mail: thomas.maddux@csun.edu. *Application contact:* Prof. Jeffrey Auerbach, Graduate Coordinator, 818-677-3566.
Website: http://www.csun.edu/csbs/departments/history/index.html

California State University, San Marcos, College of Humanities, Arts, Behavioral and Social Sciences, Program in History, San Marcos, CA 92096-0001. Offers MA. *Students:* 9 full-time (3 women), 14 part-time (10 women); includes 4 minority (1 Black or African American, non-Hispanic/Latino; 3 Hispanic/Latino). Average age 33. *Degree requirements:* For master's, thesis. *Entrance requirements:* For master's, GRE General Test, three letters of recommendation, minimum GPA of 3.0 overall and in major, academic writing sample. Additional exam requirements/recommendations for international students: Required—TOEFL (minimum score 500 paper-based). *Application deadline:* For fall admission, 2/1 priority date for domestic students; for spring admission, 8/30 priority date for domestic students. *Expenses:* Tuition, state resident: full-time $6738. *Required fees:* $1692. Tuition and fees vary according to program. *Unit head:* Prof. Alyssa Sepinwall, Coordinator, 760-750-8053, E-mail: sepinwal@csusm.edu. *Application contact:* Admissions, 760-750-4848, Fax: 760-750-3248, E-mail: apply@csusm.edu.
Website: http://www.csusm.edu/history/masters/

California State University, Stanislaus, College of Humanities and Social Sciences, Program in History (MA), Turlock, CA 95382. Offers history (MA); international relations (MA); secondary school teachers (MA). Part-time programs available. *Degree requirements:* For master's, comprehensive exam, thesis or alternative. *Entrance requirements:* For master's, GRE, minimum GPA of 3.0, personal statement. Additional exam requirements/recommendations for international students: Required—TOEFL (minimum score 575 paper-based). Electronic applications accepted. *Faculty research:* History of Ancient Greece, history and ecology of the Central Valley, acculturation and gender.

Cardinal Stritch University, College of Arts and Sciences, Department of History, Milwaukee, WI 53217-3985. Offers MA. Part-time programs available. *Degree requirements:* For master's, comprehensive exam, research project. *Entrance requirements:* For master's, minimum GPA of 3.0, 2 letters of recommendation. Electronic applications accepted.

Carleton University, Faculty of Graduate Studies, Faculty of Arts and Social Sciences, Department of History, Ottawa, ON K1S 5B6, Canada. Offers MA, PhD. *Degree requirements:* For master's, one foreign language, thesis; for doctorate, one foreign language, thesis/dissertation. *Entrance requirements:* For master's, honors degree; for doctorate, master's degree. Additional exam requirements/recommendations for international students: Required—TOEFL. *Faculty research:* Canadian, American, British, modern French, and modern Russian history; international, medieval, and European intellectual history; women's history.

Carnegie Mellon University, Dietrich College of Humanities and Social Sciences, Department of History, Pittsburgh, PA 15213-3891. Offers African and African-American diaspora (PhD); culture and power (PhD); labor, politics and social movements (PhD); technology, environment, science and health (PhD); women, gender and the family (PhD). Part-time programs available. *Degree requirements:* For doctorate, oral and written comprehensive exams, dissertation defense. *Entrance requirements:* For doctorate, GRE General Test. Additional exam requirements/recommendations for international students: Required—TOEFL. Electronic applications accepted. *Faculty research:* Anthropology and history, African-American history, technology/environment, cultural history analysis.

Case Western Reserve University, School of Graduate Studies, Department of History, Cleveland, OH 44106. Offers MA, PhD. Part-time programs available. *Faculty:* 17 full-time (7 women), 4 part-time/adjunct (2 women). *Students:* 23 full-time (8 women), 5 part-time (all women), 2 international. Average age 33. 25 applicants, 44% accepted, 4 enrolled. In 2014, 4 master's, 2 doctorates awarded. Terminal master's awarded for partial completion of doctoral program. *Degree requirements:* For master's, thesis; for doctorate, thesis/dissertation. *Entrance requirements:* For master's and doctorate, GRE General Test, Statement of objective; three letters of recommendation; CV; writing sample; short essay. Additional exam requirements/recommendations for international students: Required—TOEFL (minimum score 577 paper-based; 90 iBT); Recommended—IELTS (minimum score 7). *Application deadline:* For fall admission, 1/31 priority date for domestic students. Application fee: $50. Electronic applications accepted. *Financial support:* Fellowships, research assistantships, teaching assistantships, career-related internships or fieldwork, tuition waivers (full and partial), and unspecified assistantships available. Financial award application deadline: 1/31; financial award applicants required to submit FAFSA. *Faculty research:* American social history, social policy history, history of technology, environment, science, medicine. *Unit head:* Prof. Jonathan Sadowsky, Chair, 216-368-2622, Fax: 216-368-4681, E-mail: jonathan.sadowsky@case.edu. *Application contact:* Daniel Cohen, Graduate Studies Director, 216-368-4165, Fax: 216-368-4681, E-mail: daniel.a.cohen@case.edu.
Website: http://history.case.edu/

The Catholic University of America, School of Arts and Sciences, Department of History, Washington, DC 20064. Offers history (MA, PhD); religion and society in the late medieval and early modern world (MA); MA/JD; MSLS/MA. Part-time programs available. *Faculty:* 15 full-time (6 women). *Students:* 11 full-time (4 women), 23 part-time (11 women); includes 2 minority (both Two or more races, non-Hispanic/Latino), 2 international. Average age 31. 24 applicants, 58% accepted, 1 enrolled. In 2014, 3 master's, 4 doctorates awarded. *Degree requirements:* For master's, one foreign language, comprehensive exam, thesis optional; for doctorate, 2 foreign languages, comprehensive exam, thesis/dissertation. *Entrance requirements:* For master's and doctorate, GRE General Test, statement of purpose, official copies of academic transcripts, three letters of recommendation, writing sample. Additional exam requirements/recommendations for international students: Required—TOEFL (minimum score 580 paper-based). *Application deadline:* For fall admission, 7/15 priority date for domestic students, 7/1 for international students; for spring admission, 11/15 priority date for domestic students, 11/1 for international students. Applications are processed on a rolling basis. Application fee: $55. Electronic applications accepted. *Expenses:* Tuition: Full-time $40,200; part-time $1600 per credit hour. *Required fees:* $400; $195 per semester. One-time fee: $425. *Financial support:* Fellowships, research assistantships, teaching assistantships, Federal Work-Study, scholarships/grants, tuition waivers (full and partial), and unspecified assistantships available. Financial award application deadline: 2/1; financial award applicants required to submit FAFSA. *Faculty research:* Modern European intellectual history, history of mathematics and

sciences, Renaissance, Catholic reformation, medieval women and gender. *Unit head:* Dr. Jerry Muller, Chair, 202-319-5484, Fax: 202-319-5569, E-mail: mullerj@cua.edu. *Application contact:* Director of Graduate Admissions, 202-319-5057, Fax: 202-319-6533, E-mail: cua-admissions@cua.edu.
Website: http://history.cua.edu/

Central Connecticut State University, School of Graduate Studies, College of Liberal Arts and Social Sciences, Department of History, New Britain, CT 06050-4010. Offers history (MA, Certificate); public history (MA); social studies (Certificate). Part-time and evening/weekend programs available. *Faculty:* 9 full-time (4 women). *Students:* 19 full-time (10 women), 33 part-time (16 women); includes 1 minority (Hispanic/Latino). Average age 35. 28 applicants, 75% accepted, 13 enrolled. In 2014, 14 master's, 2 other advanced degrees awarded. *Degree requirements:* For master's, comprehensive exam, thesis or alternative; for Certificate, qualifying exam. *Entrance requirements:* For master's, minimum undergraduate GPA of 3.0, essay, letters of recommendation. Additional exam requirements/recommendations for international students: Required—TOEFL (minimum score 550 paper-based; 79 iBT). *Application deadline:* For fall admission, 5/1 for domestic and international students; for spring admission, 11/1 for domestic and international students. Applications are processed on a rolling basis. Application fee: $50. Electronic applications accepted. *Expenses: Tuition, area resident:* Full-time $5730; part-time $534 per credit. Tuition, state resident: full-time $8596; part-time $534 per credit. Tuition, nonresident: full-time $15,964; part-time $548 per credit. *Required fees:* $4211; $215 per credit. *Financial support:* In 2014–15, 4 students received support, including 2 research assistantships; career-related internships or fieldwork, Federal Work-Study, scholarships/grants, and unspecified assistantships also available. Support available to part-time students. Financial award application deadline: 3/1; financial award applicants required to submit FAFSA. *Faculty research:* American West, African history, Eastern Europe, modern Middle East, East Asia. *Unit head:* Dr. Katherine Hermes, Chair, 860-832-2800, E-mail: hermesk@ccsu.edu. *Application contact:* Patricia Gardner, Associate Director of Graduate Studies, 860-832-2350, Fax: 860-832-2362, E-mail: graduateadmissions@ccsu.edu.
Website: http://www.ccsu.edu/history/

Central European University, Graduate Studies, Department of History, Budapest, Hungary. Offers MA, PhD. *Faculty:* 11 full-time (3 women), 13 part-time/adjunct (4 women). *Students:* 92 full-time (40 women). Average age 28. 145 applicants, 37% accepted, 45 enrolled. In 2014, 38 master's, 5 doctorates awarded. Terminal master's awarded for partial completion of doctoral program. *Degree requirements:* For master's, one foreign language, thesis; for doctorate, one foreign language, comprehensive exam, thesis/dissertation. *Entrance requirements:* For master's and doctorate, interview. Additional exam requirements/recommendations for international students: Required—TOEFL (minimum score 570 paper-based); Recommended—IELTS (minimum score 6.5). *Application deadline:* For fall admission, 1/24 priority date for domestic and international students. Application fee: $40. Electronic applications accepted. *Expenses: Tuition:* Full-time 12,000 euros. *Required fees:* 200 euros. One-time fee: 500 euros full-time. *Financial support:* In 2014–15, 81 students received support, including 81 fellowships with full and partial tuition reimbursements available (averaging $6,100 per year); career-related internships or fieldwork, institutionally sponsored loans, scholarships/grants, and tuition waivers (full and partial) also available. *Faculty research:* Early modern intellectual history, history of ideas, contemporary historiography, comparative history of empires, symbolic geography, history of cultural and religious coexistence. *Unit head:* Dr. Matthias Riedl, Head, 36 1 327-3022, Fax: 361-327-3191, E-mail: history@ceu.hu. *Application contact:* Agnes Bendik, Coordinator, 361-327-3000 Ext. 2591, Fax: 361-235-6145, E-mail: history@ceu.hu.
Website: http://history.ceu.hu/

Central Michigan University, College of Graduate Studies, College of Humanities and Social and Behavioral Sciences, Department of History, Mount Pleasant, MI 48859. Offers European history (Graduate Certificate); history (MA); modern history (Graduate Certificate); United States history (Graduate Certificate); MA/PhD. Part-time programs available. *Degree requirements:* For master's, thesis or alternative. Electronic applications accepted. *Faculty research:* Colonial and revolutionary United States history, modern European history, Latin American and transatlantic history, transnational and comparative history, United States social history.

Central Washington University, Graduate Studies and Research, College of Arts and Humanities, Department of History, Ellensburg, WA 98926. Offers MA. *Degree requirements:* For master's, thesis or alternative. *Entrance requirements:* For master's, GRE General Test, minimum GPA of 3.0, writing sample. Additional exam requirements/recommendations for international students: Required—TOEFL (minimum score 550 paper-based; 79 iBT). Electronic applications accepted.

Centro de Estudios Avanzados de Puerto Rico y el Caribe, Graduate Program in Puerto Rican and Caribbean Studies, Old San Juan, PR 00902-3970. Offers Puerto Rican and Caribbean history (MA, PhD); Puerto Rican and Caribbean literature (MA, PhD); Puerto Rican studies (MA). Part-time and evening/weekend programs available. *Degree requirements:* For master's, comprehensive exam, thesis; for doctorate, 2 foreign languages, comprehensive exam, thesis/dissertation. *Entrance requirements:* For master's and doctorate, interview. *Faculty research:* Literature, history, art, folklore, and culture of Puerto Rico and Caribbean countries.

Chicago State University, School of Graduate and Professional Studies, College of Arts and Sciences, Department of Geography, Sociology, History, African-American Studies and Anthropology, Chicago, IL 60628. Offers geographic information systems (MA); geography (MA); history (MA). *Entrance requirements:* For master's, minimum GPA of 3.0.

The Citadel, The Military College of South Carolina, Citadel Graduate College, Department of History, Charleston, SC 29409. Offers MA. Program offered jointly with The Graduate School of the College of Charleston. Part-time and evening/weekend programs available. *Degree requirements:* For master's, comprehensive exam, thesis optional. *Entrance requirements:* For master's, GRE (minimum combined verbal and quantitative score of 300) or MAT (minimum score 410), minimum undergraduate GPA of 2.5 (3.0 in major); 3 letters of recommendation; evidence of ability to conduct research and present findings. Additional exam requirements/recommendations for international students: Required—TOEFL (minimum score 550 paper-based). Electronic applications accepted.

City College of the City University of New York, Graduate School, College of Liberal Arts and Science, Division of the Humanities and Arts, Department of History, New York, NY 10031-9198. Offers MA. Part-time programs available. *Degree requirements:* For master's, one foreign language, comprehensive exam, thesis. *Entrance requirements:* Additional exam requirements/recommendations for international students: Required—TOEFL (minimum score 600 paper-based; 100 iBT). Electronic applications accepted. *Faculty research:* Latin American, European, Asian, urban, and architectural history.

Claremont Graduate University, Graduate Programs, School of Arts and Humanities, Department of History, Claremont, CA 91711-6160. Offers Africana history (Certificate); American studies and U.S. history (MA, PhD); archival studies (MA); early modern studies (MA, PhD); European studies (MA, PhD); oral history (MA, PhD); MBA/MA; MBA/PhD. *Faculty:* 4 full-time (2 women), 1 part-time/adjunct (0 women). *Students:* 41

full-time (19 women), 25 part-time (10 women); includes 18 minority (2 Black or African American, non-Hispanic/Latino; 1 American Indian or Alaska Native, non-Hispanic/Latino; 6 Asian, non-Hispanic/Latino; 6 Hispanic/Latino; 1 Native Hawaiian or other Pacific Islander, non-Hispanic/Latino; 2 Two or more races, non-Hispanic/Latino). Average age 37. In 2014, 7 master's, 6 doctorates, 1 other advanced degree awarded. Terminal master's awarded for partial completion of doctoral program. *Entrance requirements:* For master's and doctorate, GRE General Test. Additional exam requirements/recommendations for international students: Required—TOEFL (minimum score 550 paper-based; 80 iBT). *Application deadline:* For fall admission, 2/1 priority date for domestic and international students. Applications are processed on a rolling basis. Application fee: $80. Electronic applications accepted. *Expenses: Tuition:* Full-time $41,784; part-time $1741 per credit. *Required fees:* $600; $300 per semester. *Financial support:* Fellowships, research assistantships, Federal Work-Study, institutionally sponsored loans, and scholarships/grants available. Support available to part-time students. Financial award application deadline: 2/15; financial award applicants required to submit FAFSA. *Faculty research:* Intellectual and social history, cultural studies, gender studies, Western history, Chicano history. *Unit head:* Joshua Goode, Chair, 909-607-7430, E-mail: joshua.goode@cgu.edu. *Application contact:* Erma Cross, Admissions and Alumni Coordinator, 909-607-9843, E-mail: erminia.cross@cgu.edu.
Website: http://www.cgu.edu/pages/369.asp

Clark Atlanta University, School of Arts and Sciences, Department of History, Atlanta, GA 30314. Offers MA, DAH. Part-time programs available. *Faculty:* 2 full-time (both women). *Students:* 3 full-time (all women), 4 part-time (3 women); all minorities (all Black or African American, non-Hispanic/Latino). Average age 41. In 2014, 1 master's, 1 doctorate awarded. *Degree requirements:* For master's, one foreign language, comprehensive exam, thesis; for doctorate, one foreign language, comprehensive exam, thesis/dissertation. *Entrance requirements:* For master's, GRE General Test, minimum GPA of 2.5. Additional exam requirements/recommendations for international students: Required—TOEFL (minimum score 500 paper-based; 61 iBT). *Application deadline:* For fall admission, 4/1 for domestic and international students; for spring admission, 11/1 for domestic and international students. Applications are processed on a rolling basis. Application fee: $40 ($55 for international students). Electronic applications accepted. *Expenses: Tuition:* Full-time $14,904; part-time $828 per credit hour. *Required fees:* $746; $373 per semester. *Financial support:* Scholarships/grants and unspecified assistantships available. Financial award application deadline: 4/30; financial award applicants required to submit FAFSA. *Faculty research:* Education for public service. *Unit head:* Dr. Stephanie Evans, Dean, 404-880-6774, E-mail: sevans@cau.edu. *Application contact:* Michelle Clark-Davis, Graduate Program Admissions, 404-880-6605, E-mail: cauadmissions@cau.edu.

Clark University, Graduate School, Department of History, Worcester, MA 01610-1477. Offers American history (MA, PhD); history (MA, CAGS); Holocaust history (PhD). *Faculty:* 12 full-time (6 women), 1 part-time/adjunct (0 women). *Students:* 33 full-time (18 women), 6 part-time (2 women), 10 international. Average age 33. 54 applicants, 22% accepted, 9 enrolled. In 2014, 5 master's, 5 doctorates awarded. *Degree requirements:* For master's, thesis, oral exam; for doctorate, thesis/dissertation. *Entrance requirements:* Additional exam requirements/recommendations for international students: Required—TOEFL. *Application deadline:* For fall admission, 1/15 priority date for domestic students. Applications are processed on a rolling basis. Application fee: $75. *Expenses: Tuition:* Full-time $40,380; part-time $1262 per credit hour. *Required fees:* $30. *Financial support:* In 2014–15, fellowships with full and partial tuition reimbursements (averaging $12,090 per year), research assistantships with full and partial tuition reimbursements (averaging $12,090 per year), 4 teaching assistantships with full and partial tuition reimbursements (averaging $12,090 per year) were awarded; tuition waivers (full and partial) also available. *Faculty research:* American political history, comparative history, modern German and European history, Holocaust history, American family history. *Total annual research expenditures:* $84,000. *Unit head:* Dr. Willem Klooster, Chair, 508-421-3768. *Application contact:* Diane Fenner, Department Assistant, 508-793-7288, Fax: 508-793-8816, E-mail: dfenner@clarku.edu.
Website: http://www.clarku.edu/departments/history/

Clemson University, Graduate School, College of Architecture, Arts, and Humanities, Department of History, Clemson, SC 29634. Offers MA. Part-time programs available. *Faculty:* 26 full-time (9 women), 1 (woman) part-time/adjunct. *Students:* 17 full-time (9 women), 5 part-time (4 women); includes 1 minority (American Indian or Alaska Native, non-Hispanic/Latino), 1 international. Average age 29. 22 applicants, 77% accepted, 10 enrolled. In 2014, 7 master's awarded. *Degree requirements:* For master's, one foreign language, thesis. *Entrance requirements:* For master's, GRE General Test. Additional exam requirements/recommendations for international students: Required—TOEFL. *Application deadline:* For fall admission, 1/20 for domestic and international students; for spring admission, 11/1 for domestic students, 9/15 for international students. Application fee: $70 ($80 for international students). Electronic applications accepted. *Financial support:* Research assistantships with partial tuition reimbursements, teaching assistantships with partial tuition reimbursements, career-related internships or fieldwork, institutionally sponsored loans, scholarships/grants, health care benefits, and unspecified assistantships available. Support available to part-time students. Financial award application deadline: 1/20; financial award applicants required to submit FAFSA. *Faculty research:* U.S., U.S. South, British, European and non-Western history. *Unit head:* Dr. Thomas Kuehn, Chair, 864-656-5361, Fax: 864-656-1015, E-mail: tjkuehn@clemson.edu. *Application contact:* Dr. Paul Christopher Anderson, Graduate Coordinator, 864-656-3153, Fax: 864-656-1015, E-mail: pcander@clemson.edu.
Website: http://www.clemson.edu/caah/history/

Cleveland State University, College of Graduate Studies, College of Liberal Arts and Social Sciences, Department of History, Cleveland, OH 44115. Offers art history (MA); history (MA); museum studies (MA). Part-time and evening/weekend programs available. *Faculty:* 13 full-time (4 women). *Students:* 9 full-time (4 women), 15 part-time (9 women); includes 4 minority (3 Black or African American, non-Hispanic/Latino; 1 Two or more races, non-Hispanic/Latino). Average age 32. 13 applicants, 85% accepted, 6 enrolled. In 2014, 10 master's awarded. *Degree requirements:* For master's, thesis optional. *Entrance requirements:* For master's, minimum GPA of 3.0, bachelor's degree in history (or related field for art history). Additional exam requirements/recommendations for international students: Required—TOEFL (minimum score 525 paper-based). *Application deadline:* For fall admission, 7/15 priority date for domestic students. Applications are processed on a rolling basis. Application fee: $30. Electronic applications accepted. *Expenses:* Tuition, state resident: full-time $9566; part-time $531 per credit hour. Tuition, nonresident: full-time $17,980; part-time $999 per credit hour. *Required fees:* $25 per semester. Tuition and fees vary according to degree level and program. *Financial support:* In 2014–15, 7 students received support, including research assistantships with full tuition reimbursements available (averaging $8,600 per year); career-related internships or fieldwork, tuition waivers (full and partial), and unspecified assistantships also available. Financial award application deadline: 4/15. *Faculty research:* Africa and African diaspora, European history, Middle Eastern history, Latin American/Caribbean history, American history, gender and sexuality. *Unit head:* Dr. Elizabeth A. Lehfeldt, Chairperson, 216-687-3920, Fax: 216-687-5592, E-mail: e.lehfeldt@csuohio.edu. *Application contact:* Dr. Karen Sotiropoulos, Graduate Director, 216-687-3940, E-mail: r.s.shelton@csuohio.edu.
Website: http://www.csuohio.edu/history/

The College at Brockport, State University of New York, School of the Arts, Humanities and Social Sciences, Department of History, Brockport, NY 14420-2997. Offers history (MA), including American history, American/world history, world history. Part-time and evening/weekend programs available. *Faculty:* 11 full-time (5 women). *Students:* 15 full-time (4 women), 19 part-time (6 women); includes 3 minority (2 Hispanic/Latino; 1 Two or more races, non-Hispanic/Latino). 22 applicants, 91% accepted, 17 enrolled. In 2014, 17 master's awarded. *Degree requirements:* For master's, thesis or alternative. *Entrance requirements:* For master's, minimum GPA of 3.0, writing sample, letters of recommendation, statement of objectives. Additional exam requirements/recommendations for international students: Required—TOEFL (minimum score 550 paper-based; 79 iBT), IELTS (minimum score 6.5). *Application deadline:* For fall admission, 7/1 priority date for domestic and international students; for spring admission, 11/15 priority date for domestic and international students; for summer admission, 4/15 for domestic and international students. Application fee: $50. Electronic applications accepted. *Financial support:* In 2014–15, 1 fellowship with tuition reimbursement (averaging $3,750 per year), 2 teaching assistantships with full tuition reimbursements (averaging $6,000 per year) were awarded; Federal Work-Study, scholarships/grants, and unspecified assistantships also available. Support available to part-time students. Financial award application deadline: 3/15; financial award applicants required to submit FAFSA. *Faculty research:* American history, women's history, European history, world history, cultural history. *Unit head:* Dr. Owen Steve Ireland, Chairperson, 585-395-5627, Fax: 585-395-2620, E-mail: oireland@brockport.edu. *Application contact:* Dr. Morag Martin, Graduate Director, 585-395-5690, Fax: 585-395-2620, E-mail: mmartin@brockport.edu.
Website: http://www.brockport.edu/history/grad/

College of Charleston, Graduate School, School of Humanities and Social Sciences, Program in History, Charleston, SC 29424-0001. Offers MA. Program offered jointly with The Citadel, The Military College of South Carolina. Part-time and evening/weekend programs available. *Degree requirements:* For master's, comprehensive exam, thesis optional. *Entrance requirements:* For master's, GRE General Test or MAT, writing sample. Additional exam requirements/recommendations for international students: Required—TOEFL (minimum score 81 iBT). Electronic applications accepted. *Faculty research:* Modern West Africa, labor history, Southern women's' education, Native Americans, the Atlantic world.

The College of Saint Rose, Graduate Studies, School of Arts and Humanities, Program in History/Political Science, Albany, NY 12203-1419. Offers MA. Part-time and evening/weekend programs available. *Degree requirements:* For master's, final paper/project, thesis or comprehensive exam. *Entrance requirements:* For master's, minimum undergraduate GPA of 3.0, 12 undergraduate credits in US history and/or political science. Additional exam requirements/recommendations for international students: Required—TOEFL (minimum score 550 paper-based). Electronic applications accepted.

College of Staten Island of the City University of New York, Graduate Programs, Division of Humanities and Social Sciences, Program in History, Staten Island, NY 10314-6600. Offers MA. Part-time and evening/weekend programs available. *Faculty:* 3 full-time (1 woman). *Students:* 16 part-time (6 women). Average age 34. 9 applicants. In 2014, 8 master's awarded. *Degree requirements:* For master's, comprehensive exam (for some programs), thesis (for some programs), 32 credits; thesis or portfolio. *Entrance requirements:* For master's, bachelor's degree with minimum GPA of 3.0 overall and in undergraduate history courses; two letters of recommendation; letter of interest; research-based writing sample; one-page statement explaining why student is interested in pursuing graduate studies in history. Additional exam requirements/recommendations for international students: Required—TOEFL (minimum score 550 paper-based; 79 iBT), IELTS (minimum score 6.5). *Application deadline:* For fall admission, 5/20 priority date for domestic and international students; for spring admission, 12/2 priority date for domestic and international students. Applications are processed on a rolling basis. Application fee: $125. Electronic applications accepted. *Expenses:* Tuition, state resident: full-time $9650; part-time $405 per credit. Tuition, nonresident: full-time $17,880; part-time $745 per credit. *Required fees:* $141.10 per semester. Tuition and fees vary according to program. *Financial support:* In 2014–15, 2 students received support. Career-related internships or fieldwork, Federal Work-Study, and scholarships/grants available. Support available to part-time students. Financial award applicants required to submit FAFSA. *Unit head:* Dr. Samira Haj, Graduate Program Coordinator, 718-982-2866, E-mail: samira.haj@csi.cuny.edu. *Application contact:* Sasha Spence, Assistant Director for Graduate Admissions, 718-982-2019, Fax: 718-982-2500, E-mail: sasha.spence@csi.cuny.edu.
Website: http://www.csi.cuny.edu/catalog/graduate/master-of-arts-in-history-ma.htm

The College of William and Mary, Faculty of Arts and Sciences, Lyon Gardiner Tyler Department of History, Williamsburg, VA 23187-8795. Offers MA, PhD. *Faculty:* 35 full-time (12 women), 1 part-time/adjunct (0 women). *Students:* 43 full-time (27 women), 1 part-time (0 women); includes 3 minority (1 Black or African American, non-Hispanic/Latino; 1 Hispanic/Latino; 1 Two or more races, non-Hispanic/Latino), 1 international. Average age 29. 121 applicants, 16% accepted, 13 enrolled. In 2014, 12 master's, 2 doctorates awarded. Terminal master's awarded for partial completion of doctoral program. *Degree requirements:* For master's, one foreign language, comprehensive exam, thesis; for doctorate, one foreign language, comprehensive exam, thesis/dissertation. *Entrance requirements:* For master's and doctorate, GRE General Test, minimum GPA of 3.0. Additional exam requirements/recommendations for international students: Required—TOEFL. *Application deadline:* For fall admission, 12/5 for domestic and international students. Application fee: $45. Electronic applications accepted. *Financial support:* In 2014–15, 40 students received support, including 5 fellowships with full tuition reimbursements available (averaging $25,000 per year), 19 research assistantships with full tuition reimbursements available (averaging $20,400 per year), 6 teaching assistantships with full tuition reimbursements available (averaging $20,400 per year); career-related internships or fieldwork also available. Financial award application deadline: 12/5; financial award applicants required to submit FAFSA. *Faculty research:* Early American, U.S., and comparative and transitional history; early America and the Atlantic world; race and slavery; gender and sexuality. *Total annual research expenditures:* $331,689. *Unit head:* Dr. Cindy Hahamovitch, Chair, 757-221-6285, Fax: 757-221-2111, E-mail: cxhaha@wm.edu. *Application contact:* Dr. Hiroshi Kitamura, Director of Graduate Studies, 757-221-7654, Fax: 757-221-2111, E-mail: hxkita@wm.edu.
Website: http://www.wm.edu/as/history/gradprogram/index.php

Colorado State University, Graduate School, College of Liberal Arts, Department of History, Fort Collins, CO 80523-1776. Offers MA. Part-time programs available. *Faculty:* 17 full-time (9 women). *Students:* 23 full-time (14 women), 7 part-time (5 women); includes 1 minority (Hispanic/Latino). Average age 30. 41 applicants, 49% accepted, 14 enrolled. In 2014, 14 master's awarded. *Degree requirements:* For master's, variable foreign language requirement, comprehensive exam (for some programs), thesis (for some programs), written and oral exams. *Entrance requirements:* For master's, GRE General Test, minimum GPA of 3.0, minimum 21 credits in history, 3 letters of

recommendation, personal statement, transcripts, writing sample. Additional exam requirements/recommendations for international students: Required—TOEFL (minimum score 550 paper-based; 80 iBT). *Application deadline:* For fall admission, 2/1 priority date for domestic and international students; for spring admission, 11/1 for domestic and international students. Application fee: $50. Electronic applications accepted. *Expenses:* Tuition, state resident: full-time $9348; part-time $519 per credit. Tuition, nonresident: full-time $22,916; part-time $1273 per credit. *Required fees:* $1584. *Financial support:* In 2014–15, 22 students received support, including 22 teaching assistantships with tuition reimbursements available (averaging $12,733 per year); career-related internships or fieldwork, Federal Work-Study, institutionally sponsored loans, scholarships/grants, traineeships, and unspecified assistantships also available. Financial award application deadline: 3/1; financial award applicants required to submit FAFSA. *Faculty research:* U.S. history, world history, gender history, European history, environmental history. *Total annual research expenditures:* $666,724. *Unit head:* Dr. Douglas Yarrington, Professor and Chair, 970-491-6801, Fax: 970-491-2941, E-mail: doug.yarrington@colostate.edu. *Application contact:* Nancy Rehe, Graduate Contact, 970-491-6334, Fax: 970-491-2941, E-mail: nancy.rehe@colostate.edu.
Website: http://history.colostate.edu/

Columbia University, Graduate School of Arts and Sciences, New York, NY 10027. Offers African-American studies (MA); American studies (MA); anthropology (MA, PhD); art history and archaeology (MA, PhD); astronomy (PhD); biological sciences (PhD); biotechnology (MA); chemical physics (PhD); chemistry (PhD); classical studies (MA, PhD); classics (MA, PhD); climate and society (MA); earth and environmental sciences (PhD); East Asia: regional studies (MA); East Asian languages and cultures (MA, PhD); ecology, evolution and environmental biology (MA), including conservation biology; ecology, evolution, and environmental biology (PhD), including ecology and evolutionary biology, evolutionary primatology; economics (PhD); English and comparative literature (MA, PhD); French and Romance philology (MA, PhD); Germanic languages (MA, PhD); global French studies (MA); Hispanic cultural studies (MA); history (PhD); history and literature (MA); human rights studies (MA); Islamic studies (MA); Italian (MA, PhD); Japanese pedagogy (MA); Jewish studies (MA); Latin America and the Caribbean: regional studies (MA); Latin American and Iberian cultures (PhD); mathematics (MA, PhD), including finance (MA); medieval and Renaissance studies (MA); Middle Eastern, South Asian, and African studies (MA, PhD); modern art: critical and curatorial studies (MA); modern European studies (MA); museum anthropology (MA); music (DMA, PhD); oral history (MA); philosophical foundations of physics (MA); philosophy (MA, PhD); physics (PhD); political science (MA, PhD); psychology (PhD); quantitative methods in the social sciences (MA); religion (MA, PhD); Russia, Eurasia and East Europe: regional studies (MA); Russian translation (MA); Slavic cultures (MA); Slavic languages (MA, PhD); sociology (MA, PhD); South Asian studies (MA); statistics (MA, PhD); theatre (PhD); JD/PhD; MA/MS; MD/PhD; MPA/MA. Dual-degree programs require admission to both Graduate School of Arts and Sciences and another Columbia school. Part-time and evening/weekend programs available. Terminal master's awarded for partial completion of doctoral program. *Degree requirements:* For master's, thesis (for some programs); for doctorate, comprehensive exam, thesis/dissertation. *Entrance requirements:* For master's and doctorate, GRE General Test, GRE Subject Test (for some programs). Electronic applications accepted. *Faculty research:* Humanities, natural sciences, social sciences.

Columbus State University, Graduate Studies, College of Letters and Sciences, Department of History and Geography, Columbus, GA 31907-5645. Offers history (MA). *Faculty:* 3 full-time (1 woman). *Students:* 3 full-time (1 woman), 5 part-time (2 women); includes 4 minority (3 Black or African American, non-Hispanic/Latino; 1 American Indian or Alaska Native, non-Hispanic/Latino). Average age 31. 4 applicants, 75% accepted, 3 enrolled. In 2014, 1 master's awarded. *Degree requirements:* For master's, thesis. *Entrance requirements:* For master's, GRE. Additional exam requirements/recommendations for international students: Required—TOEFL (minimum score 550 paper-based; 79 iBT). *Application deadline:* For fall admission, 6/30 for domestic students, 5/1 for international students; for spring admission, 11/1 for domestic and international students; for summer admission, 3/1 for domestic and international students. Applications are processed on a rolling basis. Application fee: $50. Electronic applications accepted. *Financial support:* In 2014–15, 8 students received support, including 1 research assistantship; teaching assistantships, tuition waivers, and unspecified assistantships also available. Financial award application deadline: 5/1; financial award applicants required to submit FAFSA. *Unit head:* Dr. Gary Sprayberry, Chair, 706-507-8356, E-mail: sprayberry_gary@columbusstate.edu. *Application contact:* Kristin Williams, Director of International and Graduate Recruitment, 706-507-8848, Fax: 706-568-5091, E-mail: williams_kristin@columbusstate.edu.
Website: http://history.columbusstate.edu/

Concordia University, School of Graduate Studies, Faculty of Arts and Science, Department of History, Montréal, QC H3G 1M8, Canada. Offers MA, PhD. *Degree requirements:* For master's, one foreign language, thesis optional; for doctorate, one foreign language, comprehensive exam, thesis/dissertation. *Entrance requirements:* For master's, honors degree in history or equivalent. *Faculty research:* Canadian history, European social history, Canadian-American relations.

Converse College, School of Education and Graduate Studies, Program in Liberal Arts, Spartanburg, SC 29302-0006. Offers English (MLA); history (MLA); political science (MLA). *Degree requirements:* For master's, capstone paper. *Entrance requirements:* For master's, minimum GPA of 3.0, 2 recommendations.

Cornell University, Graduate School, Graduate Fields of Arts and Sciences, Field of History, Ithaca, NY 14853-0001. Offers African history (MA, PhD); American history (MA, PhD); ancient Greek history (PhD); ancient history (MA, PhD); ancient Roman history (PhD); early modern European history (MA, PhD); English history (MA, PhD); French history (MA, PhD); German history (MA, PhD); history of science (MA, PhD); Korean history (PhD); Latin American history (MA, PhD); medieval Chinese history (MA, PhD); medieval history (MA, PhD); modern Chinese history (MA, PhD); modern European history (MA, PhD); modern Japanese history (MA, PhD); modern Middle Eastern history (PhD); premodern Islamic history (MA, PhD); premodern Japanese history (MA, PhD); Renaissance history (MA, PhD); Russian history (MA, PhD); South Asian history (PhD); Southeast Asian history (MA, PhD). Terminal master's awarded for partial completion of doctoral program. *Degree requirements:* For master's, thesis; for doctorate, 2 foreign languages, comprehensive exam, thesis/dissertation, 1 year of teaching experience. *Entrance requirements:* For master's and doctorate, GRE General Test, writing sample, 3 letters of recommendation. Additional exam requirements/recommendations for international students: Required—TOEFL (minimum score 550 paper-based; 77 iBT). Electronic applications accepted.

Dalhousie University, Faculty of Arts and Social Science, Department of History, Halifax, NS B3H 4R2, Canada. Offers MA, PhD. *Entrance requirements:* Additional exam requirements/recommendations for international students: Required—TOEFL, IELTS, CANTEST, CAEL, or Michigan English Language Assessment Battery. Electronic applications accepted. *Faculty research:* African, British, Russian, Canadian and medieval history.

DePaul University, College of Liberal Arts and Social Sciences, Chicago, IL 60614. Offers Arabic (MA); Chinese (MA); English (MA); French (MA); German (MA); history (MA); interdisciplinary studies (MA, MS); international public service (MS); international studies (MA); Italian (MA); Japanese (MA); leadership and policy studies (MS); liberal studies (MA); new media studies (MA); nonprofit management (MNM); public administration (MPA); public health (MPH); public service management (MS); social work (MSW); sociology (MA); Spanish (MA); sustainable urban development (MA); women and gender studies (MA); writing and publishing (MA); writing, rhetoric, and discourse (MA); MA/PhD. Part-time and evening/weekend programs available. Postbaccalaureate distance learning degree programs offered (no on-campus study). Terminal master's awarded for partial completion of doctoral program. *Degree requirements:* For master's, variable foreign language requirement, comprehensive exam (for some programs), thesis (for some programs). Electronic applications accepted.

Dominican University of California, School of Arts, Humanities and Social Sciences, Humanities Program, San Rafael, CA 94901-2298. Offers applied music (MA); art history (MA); creative writing (MA); history (MA); literature (MA); philosophy (MA); political theory (MA); religion (MA); women and gender studies (MA). Part-time programs available. *Faculty:* 11 full-time (5 women), 5 part-time/adjunct (2 women). *Students:* 2 full-time (1 woman), 25 part-time (16 women); includes 7 minority (1 Black or African American, non-Hispanic/Latino; 1 American Indian or Alaska Native, non-Hispanic/Latino; 3 Hispanic/Latino; 2 Two or more races, non-Hispanic/Latino). Average age 46. 12 applicants, 83% accepted, 7 enrolled. *Degree requirements:* For master's, thesis or alternative. *Entrance requirements:* For master's, minimum GPA of 3.0, interview. Additional exam requirements/recommendations for international students: Required—TOEFL (minimum score 550 paper-based; 80 iBT), IELTS (minimum score 6.5). *Application deadline:* For fall admission, 5/15 priority date for domestic and international students; for spring admission, 11/15 priority date for domestic and international students. Applications are processed on a rolling basis. Electronic applications accepted. Application fee is waived when completed online. *Expenses:* Expenses: $935 per unit. *Financial support:* Scholarships/grants available. Support available to part-time students. Financial award application deadline: 3/2; financial award applicants required to submit FAFSA. *Unit head:* Dr. Laura Stivers, Acting Dean, 415-458-3734, E-mail: laura.stivers@dominican.edu. *Application contact:* Ryan Purtill, Director, 415-458-3748, Fax: 415-485-3214, E-mail: ryan.purtill@dominican.edu.
Website: http://www.dominican.edu/academics/ahss/graduate-program/index_html

Drew University, Caspersen School of Graduate Studies, Program in History and Culture, Madison, NJ 07940-1493. Offers modern intellectual and cultural history (MA, PhD). Part-time programs available. Terminal master's awarded for partial completion of doctoral program. *Degree requirements:* For master's, thesis; for doctorate, one foreign language, comprehensive exam (for some programs), thesis/dissertation. *Entrance requirements:* For master's and doctorate, GRE, transcripts, personal statement, writing sample, recommendations. Additional exam requirements/recommendations for international students: Required—TOEFL (minimum score 585 paper-based; 95 iBT), TWE.

Duke University, Graduate School, Department of History, Durham, NC 27708. Offers history (AM, PhD); Latin American studies (PhD); JD/AM. *Degree requirements:* For doctorate, 2 foreign languages, thesis/dissertation. *Entrance requirements:* For doctorate, GRE General Test. Additional exam requirements/recommendations for international students: Required—TOEFL (minimum score 577 paper-based; 90 iBT) or IELTS (minimum score 7). Electronic applications accepted. *Expenses: Tuition:* Full-time $45,760; part-time $2765 per credit. *Required fees:* $978. Full-time tuition and fees vary according to program.

Duquesne University, Graduate School of Liberal Arts, Department of History, Pittsburgh, PA 15282-0001. Offers historical studies (MA); public history (MA). Part-time and evening/weekend programs available. *Faculty:* 15 full-time (5 women), 5 part-time/adjunct (3 women). *Students:* 30 full-time (21 women), 7 part-time (2 women); includes 1 minority (Hispanic/Latino). Average age 28. 39 applicants, 69% accepted, 14 enrolled. In 2014, 19 master's awarded. *Degree requirements:* For master's, comprehensive exam (for some programs), thesis optional. *Entrance requirements:* For master's, GRE General Test, writing sample. Additional exam requirements/recommendations for international students: Required—TOEFL. *Application deadline:* For fall admission, 8/15 for domestic students, 5/1 for international students; for spring admission, 11/1 priority date for domestic students. Applications are processed on a rolling basis. Electronic applications accepted. *Expenses: Tuition:* Full-time $18,882; part-time $1049 per credit. *Required fees:* $1800; $100 per credit. Tuition and fees vary according to program. *Financial support:* In 2014–15, 4 teaching assistantships with full tuition reimbursements (averaging $6,000 per year) were awarded; career-related internships or fieldwork, Federal Work-Study, scholarships/grants, tuition waivers (full and partial), and unspecified assistantships also available. Support available to part-time students. Financial award application deadline: 5/1. *Faculty research:* American studies, immigration history, local social history, applied history, Eastern European history. *Unit head:* Dr. John Dwyer, Chair, 412-396-6470, E-mail: dwyer@duq.edu. *Application contact:* Linda Rendulic, Assistant to the Dean, 412-396-6400, E-mail: rendulic@duq.edu.
Website: http://www.duq.edu/academics/schools/liberal-arts/graduate-school/programs/history

East Carolina University, Graduate School, Thomas Harriot College of Arts and Sciences, Department of History, Greenville, NC 27858-4353. Offers American history (MA); Atlantic world (MA); European history (MA); history education (MA Ed); maritime studies (MA); military history (MA); public history (MA). Part-time and evening/weekend programs available. *Degree requirements:* For master's, one foreign language, comprehensive exam, thesis. *Entrance requirements:* For master's, GRE General Test, GRE Subject Test. Additional exam requirements/recommendations for international students: Required—TOEFL. *Expenses:* Tuition, state resident: full-time $4223. Tuition, nonresident: full-time $16,540. *Required fees:* $2184.

Eastern Illinois University, Graduate School, College of Arts and Humanities, Department of History, Charleston, IL 61920. Offers historical administration (MA); history (MA). Part-time and evening/weekend programs available. *Faculty:* 16. *Students:* 24 full-time (10 women), 27 part-time (15 women); includes 4 minority (2 Hispanic/Latino; 2 Two or more races, non-Hispanic/Latino). Average age 28. 42 applicants, 50% accepted, 17 enrolled. In 2014, 18 master's awarded. *Degree requirements:* For master's, comprehensive exam (for some programs), thesis (for some programs). *Entrance requirements:* For master's, GMAT or GRE. Additional exam requirements/recommendations for international students: Required—TOEFL (minimum score 500 paper-based; 61 iBT), IELTS (minimum score 6). *Application deadline:* For fall admission, 5/15 for domestic and international students; for spring admission, 10/15 for domestic and international students. Applications are processed on a rolling basis. Application fee: $30. Electronic applications accepted. *Expenses:* Tuition, state resident: full-time $3113; part-time $283 per credit hour. Tuition, nonresident: full-time $7469; part-time $679 per credit hour. *Required fees:* $2287; $96 per credit hour. Tuition and fees vary according to course load. *Financial support:* In 2014–15, 28 students received support, including 8 research assistantships with full tuition reimbursements available (averaging $8,820 per year); career-related internships or fieldwork, Federal Work-Study, and unspecified assistantships also available. Support available to part-

time students. Financial award application deadline: 3/1; financial award applicants required to submit FAFSA. *Unit head:* Anita Shelton, Department Chair, 217-581-6989, Fax: 217-581-7233, E-mail: ashelton@eiu.edu. *Application contact:* Ed Wehrle, Graduate Coordinator, 217-581-3310, Fax: 217-581-7233, E-mail: efwehrle@eiu.edu. Website: http://www.eiu.edu/history/

Eastern Kentucky University, The Graduate School, College of Arts and Sciences, Department of History, Richmond, KY 40475-3102. Offers MA. Part-time programs available. *Degree requirements:* For master's, comprehensive exam, thesis optional. *Entrance requirements:* For master's, GRE General Test, GRE Subject Test, minimum GPA of 2.5. *Faculty research:* Twentieth-century U.S. history, Kentucky history, British history, world history, Eastern Europe.

Eastern Michigan University, Graduate School, College of Arts and Sciences, Department of History and Philosophy, Programs in History, Ypsilanti, MI 48197. Offers history (MA); state and local history (Graduate Certificate). Part-time and evening/weekend programs available. Postbaccalaureate distance learning degree programs offered (minimal on-campus study). *Students:* 3 full-time (1 woman), 54 part-time (21 women); includes 2 minority (both Black or African American, non-Hispanic/Latino). Average age 34. 25 applicants, 84% accepted, 13 enrolled. In 2014, 9 master's awarded. *Degree requirements:* For master's, thesis optional. *Entrance requirements:* Additional exam requirements/recommendations for international students: Required—TOEFL. *Application deadline:* Applications are processed on a rolling basis. Application fee: $45. *Financial support:* Fellowships, research assistantships with full tuition reimbursements, teaching assistantships with full tuition reimbursements, career-related internships or fieldwork, Federal Work-Study, institutionally sponsored loans, scholarships/grants, tuition waivers (partial), and unspecified assistantships available. Support available to part-time students. Financial award applicants required to submit FAFSA. *Application contact:* Dr. Ronald Delph, Director, 734-487-1018, Fax: 734-487-6835, E-mail: rdelph@emich.edu.

Eastern Washington University, Graduate Studies, College of Arts, Letters and Education, Department of History, Cheney, WA 99004-2431. Offers MA. *Degree requirements:* For master's, comprehensive exam, thesis optional. *Entrance requirements:* For master's, minimum GPA of 3.0.

East Stroudsburg University of Pennsylvania, Graduate College, College of Arts and Sciences, Department of History, East Stroudsburg, PA 18301-2999. Offers M Ed, MA. Part-time and evening/weekend programs available. *Degree requirements:* For master's, comprehensive exam, thesis, thesis defense. *Entrance requirements:* For master's, Commonwealth of Pennsylvania Department of Education Certification Requirements (M Ed). Additional exam requirements/recommendations for international students: Required—TOEFL (minimum score 560 paper-based; 83 iBT) or IELTS. Electronic applications accepted.

East Tennessee State University, School of Graduate Studies, College of Arts and Sciences, Department of Appalachian Studies, Johnson City, TN 37614. Offers MA, Postbaccalaureate Certificate. Part-time programs available. *Faculty:* 7 full-time (2 women), 3 part-time/adjunct (1 woman). *Students:* 6 full-time (3 women), 7 part-time (5 women). Average age 40. 12 applicants, 58% accepted, 7 enrolled. In 2014, 4 master's awarded. *Entrance requirements:* For master's, GRE General Test, minimum undergraduate GPA of 3.0, writing sample; 3 letters of recommendation; for Postbaccalaureate Certificate, minimum undergraduate GPA of 3.0, writing sample. Additional exam requirements/recommendations for international students: Required—TOEFL (minimum score 550 paper-based; 79 iBT). *Application deadline:* For fall admission, 6/1 for domestic students, 4/29 for international students; for spring admission, 11/1 for domestic students, 9/30 for international students. Applications are processed on a rolling basis. Application fee: $35 ($45 for international students). Electronic applications accepted. *Financial support:* In 2014–15, 5 research assistantships with full tuition reimbursements (averaging $6,000 per year) were awarded; career-related internships or fieldwork, institutionally sponsored loans, scholarships/grants, and unspecified assistantships also available. Financial award applicants required to submit FAFSA. *Faculty research:* Appalachian culture, history, literature, art, environmental studies; bluegrass, old time, Celtic, and country music; community development and sustainability. *Unit head:* Dr. Roberta T. Herrin, Chair, 423-439-7865, Fax: 423-439-7870. *Application contact:* Kimberly Brockman, School of Graduate Studies, 423-439-6165, Fax: 423-439-5624, E-mail: brockmank@etsu.edu. Website: http://www.etsu.edu/cas/das/

East Tennessee State University, School of Graduate Studies, College of Arts and Sciences, Department of History, Johnson City, TN 37614. Offers MA. Part-time and evening/weekend programs available. *Faculty:* 20 full-time (4 women), 1 part-time/adjunct (0 women). *Students:* 32 full-time (10 women), 8 part-time (4 women); includes 5 minority (1 Black or African American, non-Hispanic/Latino; 1 American Indian or Alaska Native, non-Hispanic/Latino; 1 Asian, non-Hispanic/Latino; 2 Two or more races, non-Hispanic/Latino), 2 international. Average age 30. 43 applicants, 72% accepted, 22 enrolled. In 2014, 15 master's awarded. *Degree requirements:* For master's, comprehensive exam, thesis optional. *Entrance requirements:* For master's, bachelor's degree in history, minimum GPA of 3.0, three letters of recommendation. Additional exam requirements/recommendations for international students: Required—TOEFL (minimum score 550 paper-based; 79 iBT). *Application deadline:* For fall admission, 3/1 for domestic students, 1/30 for international students; for spring admission, 11/1 for domestic students, 9/30 for international students. Application fee: $35 ($45 for international students). Electronic applications accepted. *Financial support:* In 2014–15, 31 students received support, including 4 research assistantships with full tuition reimbursements available (averaging $6,000 per year), 21 teaching assistantships with full tuition reimbursements available (averaging $6,000 per year); career-related internships or fieldwork, institutionally sponsored loans, scholarships/grants, and unspecified assistantships also available. Financial award application deadline: 7/1; financial award applicants required to submit FAFSA. *Faculty research:* Post-World War II German occupation, biographies of Eleanor Copenhaver Anderson and Harry M. Candill, the Miss America Pageant, encyclopedia of colonialism, the new Georgia campaign in the Pacific war. *Unit head:* Dr. Philip Wilson, Chair, 423-439-4222, Fax: 423-439-5373, E-mail: wilsonpk@etsu.edu. *Application contact:* Angela Edwards, Graduate Specialist, 423-439-4703, Fax: 423-439-5624, E-mail: edwardag@etsu.edu. Website: http://www.etsu.edu/cas/history/

Edinboro University of Pennsylvania, Department of History, Anthropology and World Languages, Edinboro, PA 16444. Offers social sciences (MA), including anthropology, history. Part-time and evening/weekend programs available. *Degree requirements:* For master's, thesis or alternative, competency exam. *Entrance requirements:* For master's, GRE or MAT, minimum QPA of 2.5. Electronic applications accepted.

Emory & Henry College, Graduate Programs, Emory, VA 24327-0947. Offers American history (MA Ed); organizational leadership (MCOL); professional studies (M Ed); reading specialist (MA Ed). Part-time and evening/weekend programs available. *Entrance requirements:* For master's, GRE or PRAXIS I, recommendations, writing sample. Additional exam requirements/recommendations for international students: Recommended—TOEFL.

Emory University, Laney Graduate School, Department of History, Atlanta, GA 30322-1100. Offers PhD. *Degree requirements:* For doctorate, 2 foreign languages, comprehensive exam, thesis/dissertation. *Entrance requirements:* For doctorate, GRE General Test, minimum GPA of 3.0. Additional exam requirements/recommendations for international students: Recommended—TOEFL. Electronic applications accepted. *Faculty research:* United States, modern Europe, early modern Europe, medieval Europe, Latin America, Africa.

Emporia State University, Program in History, Emporia, KS 66801-5415. Offers American history (MA); world history (MA). Part-time programs available. *Faculty:* 14 full-time (6 women), 1 (woman) part-time/adjunct. *Students:* 2 full-time (0 women), 19 part-time (4 women); includes 3 minority (1 Black or African American, non-Hispanic/Latino; 1 Hispanic/Latino; 1 Two or more races, non-Hispanic/Latino). 10 applicants, 90% accepted, 7 enrolled. In 2014, 3 master's awarded. *Degree requirements:* For master's, comprehensive exam or thesis. *Entrance requirements:* For master's, 12 credit hours in history, minimum undergraduate GPA of 2.5, writing sample. Additional exam requirements/recommendations for international students: Required—TOEFL (minimum score 520 paper-based; 68 iBT). *Application deadline:* For fall admission, 8/15 priority date for domestic students. Applications are processed on a rolling basis. Application fee: $30 ($75 for international students). Electronic applications accepted. *Expenses:* Tuition, state resident: part-time $227 per credit hour. Tuition, nonresident: part-time $706 per credit hour. *Required fees:* $75 per credit hour. Tuition and fees vary according to campus/location. *Financial support:* In 2014–15, 1 research assistantship with full tuition reimbursement (averaging $7,344 per year), 6 teaching assistantships with full tuition reimbursements (averaging $7,344 per year) were awarded; Federal Work-Study, institutionally sponsored loans, health care benefits, and unspecified assistantships also available. Financial award application deadline: 3/15; financial award applicants required to submit FAFSA. *Faculty research:* Great Plains history. *Unit head:* Dr. Michael Smith, Chair, 620-341-5566, E-mail: msmith3@emporia.edu.

Fairleigh Dickinson University, Metropolitan Campus, University College: Arts, Sciences, and Professional Studies, School of History, Political and International Studies, Program in History, Teaneck, NJ 07666-1914. Offers MA.

Faulkner University, Great Books Honors College, Montgomery, AL 36109-3398. Offers M Litt.

Fayetteville State University, Graduate School, Department of Geography, History and Political Science, Fayetteville, NC 28301-4298. Offers history (MA). Part-time and evening/weekend programs available. *Faculty:* 13 full-time (4 women). *Students:* Average age 40. *Degree requirements:* For master's, comprehensive exam, internship. *Entrance requirements:* For master's, GRE General Test. *Application deadline:* For fall admission, 4/15 for domestic students; for spring admission, 10/15 for domestic students. Applications are processed on a rolling basis. Application fee: $40. Electronic applications accepted. *Unit head:* Dr. Adeguke Ademiluyi, Chairperson, 910-672-1137, E-mail: aademiluyi@uncfsu.edu. *Application contact:* Adeguke Ademiluyi, 910-672-1137, Fax: 910-672-1470, E-mail: aademiluyi@uncfsu.edu.

Fitchburg State University, Division of Graduate and Continuing Education, Programs in History and Teaching History (Secondary Level), Fitchburg, MA 01420-2697. Offers MA, MAT, Certificate. *Accreditation:* NCATE. Part-time and evening/weekend programs available. *Entrance requirements:* Additional exam requirements/recommendations for international students: Required—TOEFL (minimum score 550 paper-based; 79 iBT). Electronic applications accepted.

Florida Agricultural and Mechanical University, Division of Graduate Studies, Research, and Continuing Education, College of Social Sciences, Arts and Humanities, Department of History and Political Science, Program in Applied Social Science, Tallahassee, FL 32307-3200. Offers criminal justice (MASS); history (MASS); political science (MASS); public administration (MASS). Part-time programs available. *Degree requirements:* For master's, thesis optional. *Entrance requirements:* For master's, GRE General Test, minimum GPA of 3.0. *Faculty research:* Southern history, black history, election trends, Presidential history.

Florida Atlantic University, Dorothy F. Schmidt College of Arts and Letters, Department of History, Boca Raton, FL 33431-0991. Offers environmental studies (Certificate); history (MA). Part-time programs available. *Degree requirements:* For master's, one foreign language, thesis optional. *Entrance requirements:* For master's, GRE General Test, minimum GPA of 3.0. Additional exam requirements/recommendations for international students: Required—TOEFL (minimum score 500 paper-based; 61 iBT), IELTS (minimum score 6). Electronic applications accepted. *Expenses:* Tuition, state resident: full-time $7396; part-time $369.82 per credit hour. Tuition, nonresident: full-time $19,392; part-time $1024.81 per credit hour. Tuition and fees vary according to course load. *Faculty research:* Twentieth-century America, U.S. urban history, Florida history, history of socialism, Latin America.

Florida Gulf Coast University, College of Arts and Sciences, Program in History, Fort Myers, FL 33965-6565. Offers MA. Part-time and evening/weekend programs available. *Faculty:* 230 full-time (93 women), 158 part-time/adjunct (72 women). *Students:* 7 full-time (2 women), 9 part-time (4 women); includes 1 minority (Hispanic/Latino). Average age 29. 5 applicants, 100% accepted, 4 enrolled. In 2014, 2 master's awarded. *Entrance requirements:* Additional exam requirements/recommendations for international students: Required—TOEFL (minimum score 550 paper-based). *Application deadline:* For fall admission, 2/15 priority date for domestic students; for spring admission, 10/1 for domestic students. Applications are processed on a rolling basis. Electronic applications accepted. *Expenses:* Tuition, state resident: full-time $6974. Tuition, nonresident: full-time $28,170. *Required fees:* $1987. Tuition and fees vary according to course load. *Financial support:* In 2014–15, 3 students received support. Application deadline: 6/30; applicants required to submit FAFSA. *Unit head:* Scott Rohrer, Head, 239-590-7258, E-mail: srohrer@fgcu.edu. *Application contact:* Patricia Rice, Executive Secretary, 239-590-7196, Fax: 239-590-7200, E-mail: price@fgcu.edu.

Florida International University, College of Arts and Sciences, Department of History, Miami, FL 33199. Offers Atlantic civilization (PhD); history (MA). Part-time and evening/weekend programs available. *Degree requirements:* For master's, one foreign language, thesis optional; for doctorate, 2 foreign languages, comprehensive exam, thesis/dissertation. *Entrance requirements:* For master's, 12 credits of history courses (non-history majors), 2 letters of recommendation; writing sample, minimum GPA of 3.25; for doctorate, GRE General Test (minimum score of 1120), two letters of recommendation, statement of purpose, curriculum vitae, writing sample, minimum GPA of 3.25. Additional exam requirements/recommendations for international students: Required—TOEFL (minimum score 575 paper-based; 90 iBT). Electronic applications accepted. *Faculty research:* European social history, American culture, social and labor history, Latin American culture and social history, military history, Diaspora studies.

Florida State University, The Graduate School, College of Arts and Sciences, Department of Classics, Tallahassee, FL 32306-1510. Offers ancient history (MA); classical archaeology (MA); classical civilization (MA); classics (MA, PhD), including classical archaeology (PhD), classics (PhD); Greek (MA); Greek and Latin (MA); Latin (MA). Part-time programs available. *Faculty:* 15 full-time (5 women). *Students:* 42 full-time (23 women); includes 2 minority (1 Black or African American, non-Hispanic/Latino; 1 Asian, non-Hispanic/Latino), 2 international. Average age 24. 61 applicants, 51%

accepted, 10 enrolled. In 2014, 10 master's, 2 doctorates awarded. Terminal master's awarded for partial completion of doctoral program. *Degree requirements:* For master's, 2 foreign languages, comprehensive exam (for some programs), thesis or alternative; for doctorate, 4 foreign languages, comprehensive exam, thesis/dissertation. *Entrance requirements:* For master's, GRE General Test, minimum GPA of 3.0; for doctorate, GRE General Test, minimum GPA of 3.5. Additional exam requirements/recommendations for international students: Required—TOEFL. *Application deadline:* For fall admission, 1/15 priority date for domestic students, 2/15 for international students. Applications are processed on a rolling basis. Application fee: $30. Electronic applications accepted. *Expenses:* Tuition, state resident: part-time $403.51 per credit hour. Tuition, nonresident: part-time $1004.85 per credit hour. *Required fees:* $75.81 per credit hour. One-time fee: $20 part-time. Tuition and fees vary according to campus/location. *Financial support:* In 2014–15, 42 students received support, including 2 fellowships with full tuition reimbursements available (averaging $18,000 per year), research assistantships with full tuition reimbursements available (averaging $10,000 per year), 33 teaching assistantships with full tuition reimbursements available (averaging $10,000 per year); Federal Work-Study, institutionally sponsored loans, and tuition waivers (full and partial) also available. Support available to part-time students. Financial award application deadline: 1/15; financial award applicants required to submit FAFSA. *Faculty research:* Greek and Latin literature, classical archaeology, mythology, ancient history, religion. *Total annual research expenditures:* $100,000. *Unit head:* Dr. Daniel J. Pullen, Chairman, 850-644-0304, Fax: 850-644-4073, E-mail: dpullen@fsu.edu. *Application contact:* Dr. Allen Romano, Admissions Director, 850-644-0305, Fax: 850-644-4073, E-mail: aromano@fsu.edu.
Website: http://classics.fsu.edu/

Florida State University, The Graduate School, College of Arts and Sciences, Department of History, Tallahassee, FL 32306. Offers historical administration and public history (MA); history (MA, MS, PhD). Part-time programs available. *Faculty:* 26 full-time (8 women). *Students:* 50 full-time (18 women), 47 part-time (18 women); includes 14 minority (3 Black or African American, non-Hispanic/Latino; 1 American Indian or Alaska Native, non-Hispanic/Latino; 2 Asian, non-Hispanic/Latino; 1 Hispanic/Latino; 7 Two or more races, non-Hispanic/Latino), 5 international. Average age 34. 53 applicants, 60% accepted, 15 enrolled. In 2014, 21 master's, 14 doctorates awarded. *Degree requirements:* For master's, one foreign language, comprehensive exam (for some programs), thesis (for some programs), internships; for doctorate, one foreign language, comprehensive exam, thesis/dissertation. *Entrance requirements:* For master's, GRE General Test, minimum GPA of 3.3, minimum 18 hours of course work in history; for doctorate, GRE General Test, master's degree, minimum graduate GPA of 3.65. Additional exam requirements/recommendations for international students: Required—TOEFL (minimum score 550 paper-based; 80 iBT). *Application deadline:* For fall admission, 12/1 for domestic and international students. Applications are processed on a rolling basis. Application fee: $30. Electronic applications accepted. *Expenses:* Tuition, state resident: part-time $403.51 per credit hour. Tuition, nonresident: part-time $1004.85 per credit hour. *Required fees:* $75.81 per credit hour. One-time fee: $20 part-time. Tuition and fees vary according to campus/location. *Financial support:* In 2014–15, 50 students received support, including 10 fellowships with full tuition reimbursements available (averaging $15,458 per year), 32 research assistantships with full tuition reimbursements available (averaging $13,127 per year), 8 teaching assistantships with full tuition reimbursements available (averaging $14,785 per year); Federal Work-Study, institutionally sponsored loans, scholarships/grants, tuition waivers (full and partial), and unspecified assistantships also available. Financial award application deadline: 12/1; financial award applicants required to submit FAFSA. *Faculty research:* Napoleon and the French Revolution, modern Europe, Latin America, U.S. intellectual and cultural history, modern Asia. *Unit head:* Dr. Edward Gray, Chair, 850-644-5888, Fax: 850-644-6402, E-mail: egray@fsu.edu. *Application contact:* Lisa VanMiddlesworth, Academic Program Assistant, 850-644-2610, E-mail: lvanmiddlesworth@fsu.edu.
Website: http://history.fsu.edu/

Fordham University, Graduate School of Arts and Sciences, Department of History, New York, NY 10458. Offers MA, PhD. Part-time and evening/weekend programs available. *Faculty:* 32 full-time (14 women). *Students:* 40 full-time (21 women), 22 part-time (9 women); includes 6 minority (1 Black or African American, non-Hispanic/Latino; 2 Asian, non-Hispanic/Latino; 3 Hispanic/Latino), 3 international. Average age 33. 106 applicants, 55% accepted, 12 enrolled. In 2014, 9 master's, 3 doctorates awarded. Terminal master's awarded for partial completion of doctoral program. *Degree requirements:* For master's, one foreign language, thesis optional; for doctorate, 2 foreign languages, comprehensive exam, thesis/dissertation. *Entrance requirements:* For master's and doctorate, GRE General Test. Additional exam requirements/recommendations for international students: Required—TOEFL (minimum score 650 paper-based). *Application deadline:* For fall admission, 1/4 priority date for domestic students; for spring admission, 11/1 for domestic students. Application fee: $70. Electronic applications accepted. *Financial support:* In 2014–15, 23 students received support, including 4 fellowships with full and partial tuition reimbursements available (averaging $28,390 per year), 1 research assistantship with full and partial tuition reimbursement available (averaging $14,768 per year), 23 teaching assistantships with full and partial tuition reimbursements available (averaging $24,778 per year); institutionally sponsored loans, tuition waivers (full and partial), and unspecified assistantships also available. Financial award application deadline: 1/4; financial award applicants required to submit FAFSA. *Unit head:* Dr. Asif Siddiqi, Director of Graduate Studies, 718-817-3939, Fax: 718-817-4680, E-mail: siddiqi@fordham.edu. *Application contact:* Bernadette Valentino-Morrison, Director of Graduate Admissions, 718-817-4419, Fax: 718-817-3566, E-mail: valentinomor@fordham.edu.

Fort Hays State University, Graduate School, College of Arts and Sciences, Department of History, Hays, KS 67601-4099. Offers MA. *Degree requirements:* For master's, comprehensive exam, thesis or alternative. *Entrance requirements:* For master's, minimum undergraduate GPA of 3.0. Additional exam requirements/recommendations for international students: Required—TOEFL (minimum score 550 paper-based). Electronic applications accepted. *Faculty research:* Seventeenth century English legal history, Native American history, immigration history, Volga German settlement.

George Mason University, College of Education and Human Development, Programs in Curriculum and Instruction, Fairfax, VA 22030. Offers advanced studies in teaching and learning (M Ed), including advanced international baccalaureate; assistive/special education technology (M Ed); designing digital learning in schools (M Ed); early childhood education (M Ed); early childhood education for diverse learners (M Ed); elementary education (M Ed); English as a second langugae (M Ed); gifted child education (M Ed); history (M Ed); international education (M Ed), including ESOL PK-12; literacy (M Ed), including PK-12 classroom teachers, reading specialist; literacy leadership for diverse schools (M Ed), including K-12 reading specialis; physical education (M Ed); science K-12 (M Ed); secondary education (M Ed), including biology, chemistry, earth science, English, history/social science, math, physics; special education (M Ed); teacher leadership (M Ed); teaching culturally, linguistically diverse and exceptional learners (M Ed); transformative teaching (M Ed). *Faculty:* 38 full-time (31 women), 88 part-time/adjunct (78 women). *Students:* 206 full-time (171 women), 763 part-time (634 women); includes 214 minority (62 Black or African American, non-Hispanic/Latino; 2 American Indian or Alaska Native, non-Hispanic/Latino; 67 Asian, non-Hispanic/Latino; 61 Hispanic/Latino; 5 Native Hawaiian or other Pacific Islander, non-Hispanic/Latino; 17 Two or more races, non-Hispanic/Latino), 22 international. Average age 31. 527 applicants, 80% accepted, 318 enrolled. In 2014, 393 master's awarded. *Degree requirements:* For master's, comprehensive exam, thesis (for some programs). *Entrance requirements:* For master's, PRAXIS Core (for some programs), minimum GPA of 3.0 in last 60 hours, licensed as teacher or educational administrator, official transcripts, goals statement, 3 recommendation letters, interview or writing sample (depending on program), up to 3 years' teaching experience (depending on program). Additional exam requirements/recommendations for international students: Required—TOEFL (minimum score 575 paper-based; 80 iBT), IELTS (minimum score 6.5), PTE. *Application deadline:* Applications are processed on a rolling basis. Application fee: $65 ($80 for international students). Electronic applications accepted. *Expenses:* Tuition, state resident: full-time $9794; part-time $408 per credit hour. Tuition, nonresident: full-time $26,978; part-time $1124 per credit hour. *Required fees:* $2820; $118 per credit hour. Tuition and fees vary according to course load and program. *Financial support:* In 2014–15, 4 students received support, including 2 fellowships (averaging $1,000 per year), 2 teaching assistantships with full and partial tuition reimbursements available (averaging $22,750 per year); research assistantships, career-related internships or fieldwork, Federal Work-Study, scholarships/grants, unspecified assistantships, and health care benefits (for full-time research or teaching assistantship recipients) also available. Support available to part-time students. Financial award application deadline: 3/1; financial award applicants required to submit FAFSA. *Faculty research:* Achievement gaps and superintendent decisions, constructivist view of classroom teaching, cost of cheating, creating a critical literacy milieu in kindergarten. *Unit head:* Elizabeth Sturtevant, Professor and Division Director of Literacy, 703-993-2052, Fax: 703-993-2013, E-mail: esturtev@gmu.edu. *Application contact:* Rabia Ghani, Program Manager for Literacy, 703-993-7611, Fax: 703-993-5300, E-mail: rghani@gmu.edu.
Website: http://gse.gmu.edu/programs/gsemasters

George Mason University, College of Humanities and Social Sciences, Department of History and Art History, Program in History, Fairfax, VA 22030. Offers history (MA); new media and information technology (PhD); public and applied history (PhD). *Faculty:* 45 full-time (18 women), 8 part-time/adjunct (4 women). *Students:* 66 full-time (32 women), 136 part-time (58 women); includes 19 minority (4 Black or African American, non-Hispanic/Latino; 3 Asian, non-Hispanic/Latino; 9 Hispanic/Latino; 3 Two or more races, non-Hispanic/Latino), 4 international. Average age 36. 145 applicants, 54% accepted, 42 enrolled. In 2014, 42 master's, 4 doctorates awarded. *Degree requirements:* For master's, comprehensive exam, translation language exam; for doctorate, comprehensive exam, thesis/dissertation. *Entrance requirements:* For master's, GRE (waived for students who received their undergraduate degree 10 or more years ago or hold another graduate degree), expanded goals statement; 2 letters of recommendation; resume; official transcript; for doctorate, GRE, expanded goals statement; 3 letters of recommendation; writing sample; official transcripts. Additional exam requirements/recommendations for international students: Required—TOEFL (minimum score 570 paper-based; 80 iBT), IELTS (minimum score 6.5), PTE. *Application deadline:* For fall admission, 3/15 priority date for domestic students; for spring admission, 11/1 priority date for domestic students. Application fee: $65 ($80 for international students). Electronic applications accepted. *Expenses:* Tuition, state resident: full-time $9794; part-time $408 per credit hour. Tuition, nonresident: full-time $26,978; part-time $1124 per credit hour. *Required fees:* $2820; $118 per credit hour. Tuition and fees vary according to course load and program. *Financial support:* In 2014–15, 31 students received support, including 2 fellowships with full tuition reimbursements available (averaging $7,151 per year), 16 research assistantships with full and partial tuition reimbursements available (averaging $17,210 per year), 14 teaching assistantships with full and partial tuition reimbursements available (averaging $14,330 per year); career-related internships or fieldwork, Federal Work-Study, scholarships/grants, unspecified assistantships, and health care benefits (for full-time research or teaching assistantship recipients) also available. Support available to part-time students. Financial award application deadline: 3/1; financial award applicants required to submit FAFSA. *Faculty research:* History and new media, American history (digital), building digital archives in the 1930's. *Unit head:* Randolph Scully, History Program Director, 703-993-1259, Fax: 703-993-1251, E-mail: rscully@gmu.edu. *Application contact:* Nicole Anne Roth, Graduate Program Coordinator, 703-993-1248, Fax: 703-993-1251, E-mail: nroth@gmu.edu.
Website: http://historyarthistory.gmu.edu/programs/la-ma-hist

Georgetown University, Graduate School of Arts and Sciences, Department of History, Washington, DC 20057-1305. Offers global history (MA); global, international and comparative history (MA); history (MA, PhD); MA/PhD; MS/MA. MA in global history offered jointly with the history department at King's College London. *Degree requirements:* For master's, thesis (for some programs); for doctorate, 2 foreign languages, comprehensive exam, thesis/dissertation. *Entrance requirements:* For master's and doctorate, GRE General Test. Additional exam requirements/recommendations for international students: Required—TOEFL.

Georgetown University, Graduate School of Arts and Sciences, School of Continuing Studies, Washington, DC 20057. Offers American studies (MALS); Catholic studies (MALS); classical civilizations (MALS); emergency and disaster management (MPS); ethics and the professions (MALS); hospitality management (MPS); human resources management (MPS); humanities (MALS); individualized study (MALS); international affairs (MALS); Islam and Muslim-Christian relations (MALS); journalism (MPS); liberal studies (DLS); literature and society (MALS); medieval and early modern European studies (MALS); public relations and corporate communications (MPS); real estate (MPS); religious studies (MALS); social and public policy (MALS); sports industry management (MPS); systems engineering management (MPS); technology management (MPS); the theory and practice of American democracy (MALS); urban and regional planning (MPS); visual culture (MALS). MPS in systems engineering management offered jointly with Stevens Institute of Technology. *Entrance requirements:* Additional exam requirements/recommendations for international students: Required—TOEFL.

The George Washington University, Columbian College of Arts and Sciences, Department of History, Washington, DC 20052. Offers MA, PhD. Part-time and evening/weekend programs available. *Faculty:* 28 full-time (12 women). *Students:* 33 full-time (10 women), 29 part-time (14 women); includes 7 minority (3 Black or African American, non-Hispanic/Latino; 2 Asian, non-Hispanic/Latino; 2 Hispanic/Latino), 4 international. Average age 30. 166 applicants, 28% accepted, 19 enrolled. In 2014, 10 master's, 3 doctorates awarded. Terminal master's awarded for partial completion of doctoral program. *Degree requirements:* For master's, one foreign language, comprehensive exam, thesis or alternative; for doctorate, 2 foreign languages, thesis/dissertation, general exam. *Entrance requirements:* For master's and doctorate, GRE General Test, minimum GPA of 3.0. Additional exam requirements/recommendations for international students: Required—TOEFL (minimum score 550 paper-based; 80 iBT). *Application deadline:* For fall admission, 1/15 priority date for domestic and international students; for spring admission, 10/1 priority date for domestic students, 9/1 priority date for

international students. Applications are processed on a rolling basis. Application fee: $75. Electronic applications accepted. *Financial support:* In 2014–15, 28 students received support. Fellowships with full tuition reimbursements available, teaching assistantships with tuition reimbursements available, career-related internships or fieldwork, Federal Work-Study, and tuition waivers available. Financial award application deadline: 1/15. *Unit head:* William Becker, Chair, 202-994-6052, E-mail: whbecker@gwu.edu. *Application contact:* Information Contact, 202-994-6230, Fax: 202-994-6231, E-mail: history@gwu.edu.
Website: http://www.gwu.edu/~history/

Georgia College & State University, Graduate School, College of Arts and Sciences, Department of History, Geography and Philosophy, Milledgeville, GA 31061. Offers public history (MA); U. S., Europe and world (MA). Part-time and evening/weekend programs available. *Students:* 4 full-time (1 woman), 6 part-time (3 women); includes 2 minority (1 American Indian or Alaska Native, non-Hispanic/Latino; 1 Hispanic/Latino). Average age 32. 4 applicants, 100% accepted, 4 enrolled. In 2014, 3 master's awarded. *Degree requirements:* For master's, one foreign language, comprehensive exam (for some programs), thesis or alternative. *Entrance requirements:* For master's, GRE, 2 letters of reference, transcript, minimum GPA of 3.0, undergraduate degree in history or other major with substantial work in history, foreign language. Additional exam requirements/recommendations for international students: Recommended—TOEFL (minimum score 550 paper-based; 79 iBT). *Application deadline:* For fall admission, 4/15 for domestic and international students; for spring admission, 11/15 for domestic students, 9/1 for international students; for summer admission, 4/1 for domestic students. Application fee: $40. Electronic applications accepted. *Expenses: Tuition, area resident:* Part-time $283 per credit hour. Tuition, nonresident: part-time $1027 per credit hour. *Required fees:* $995 per semester. Full-time tuition and fees vary according to course load, degree level, campus/location and program. *Financial support:* In 2014–15, 6 research assistantships were awarded; unspecified assistantships also available. Support available to part-time students. Financial award applicants required to submit FAFSA. *Unit head:* Dr. Stephen Auerbach, Graduate Coordinator for MA in History, 478-445-8276, E-mail: stephen.auerbach@gcsu.edu. *Application contact:* Kate Marshall, Graduate Admissions Coordinator, 478-445-1184, Fax: 478-445-1336, E-mail: grad-admit@gcsu.edu.
Website: http://www.gcsu.edu/history/masters.htm

Georgia Southern University, Jack N. Averitt College of Graduate Studies, College of Liberal Arts and Social Sciences, Program in History, Statesboro, GA 30460. Offers MA, Graduate Certificate. Part-time programs available. *Students:* 16 full-time (10 women), 6 part-time (4 women); includes 9 minority (2 Black or African American, non-Hispanic/Latino; 7 Hispanic/Latino), 1 international. Average age 27. 11 applicants, 100% accepted, 7 enrolled. In 2014, 7 master's awarded. *Degree requirements:* For master's, one foreign language, thesis optional, terminal exams. *Entrance requirements:* For master's, GRE General Test, minimum GPA of 3.0, undergraduate major in history or equivalent, letters of reference. Additional exam requirements/recommendations for international students: Required—TOEFL (minimum score 550 paper-based; 80 iBT), IELTS (minimum score 6). *Application deadline:* For fall admission, 3/1 priority date for domestic and international students; for spring admission, 10/1 priority date for domestic students, 10/1 for international students. Applications are processed on a rolling basis. Application fee: $50. Electronic applications accepted. *Expenses:* Tuition, state resident: full-time $7236; part-time $277 per semester hour. Tuition, nonresident: full-time $27,118; part-time $1105 per semester hour. *Required fees:* $2092. *Financial support:* In 2014–15, 16 students received support, including research assistantships with partial tuition reimbursements available (averaging $7,200 per year), teaching assistantships with partial tuition reimbursements available (averaging $7,200 per year); career-related internships or fieldwork, Federal Work-Study, scholarships/grants, tuition waivers (partial), and unspecified assistantships also available. Support available to part-time students. Financial award application deadline: 4/15; financial award applicants required to submit FAFSA. *Faculty research:* Women's/gender history, the American South, military history, public history, modern Europe. *Unit head:* Dr. Timothy Teeter, Graduate Program Director, 912-478-0239, Fax: 912-478-0377, E-mail: tmteeter@georgiasouthern.edu. *Application contact:* -, Fax: -.
Website: http://class.georgiasouthern.edu/history/

Georgia State University, College of Arts and Sciences, Department of History, Program in History, Atlanta, GA 30302-3083. Offers historic preservation (MA); history (PhD); public history (MA); world history (MA). Part-time and evening/weekend programs available. Terminal master's awarded for partial completion of doctoral program. *Degree requirements:* For master's, one foreign language, comprehensive exam, thesis optional, continuous enrollment; 6 hours of thesis credits; for doctorate, 2 foreign languages, comprehensive exam, thesis/dissertation, dissertation prospectus and prospectus defense; dissertation defense; residency; continuous enrollment; 6 hours of thesis credits. *Entrance requirements:* For master's, GRE, BA in history; statement of purpose; writing sample; three letters of recommendation; official transcripts; for doctorate, GRE, MA in history; master's thesis; statement of purpose; writing sample; three letters of recommendation; official transcripts; appropriate language skills. Additional exam requirements/recommendations for international students: Required—TOEFL (minimum score 550 paper-based; 80 iBT). *Application deadline:* For fall admission, 3/15 for domestic and international students; for spring admission, 10/15 for domestic and international students. Applications are processed on a rolling basis. Application fee: $50. Electronic applications accepted. *Expenses:* Tuition, state resident: full-time $6516; part-time $362 per credit hour. Tuition, nonresident: full-time $22,014; part-time $1223 per credit hour. *Required fees:* $2128 per semester. Tuition and fees vary according to course load and program. *Financial support:* Research assistantships with tuition reimbursements, teaching assistantships with tuition reimbursements, and scholarships/grants available. Financial award application deadline: 2/15. *Faculty research:* Nineteenth- and twentieth-century U.S. history, early modern European history, modern European history, world history, public history. *Unit head:* Dr. Michelle Brattain, Chair, 404-413-6352, Fax: 404-413-6384, E-mail: mbrattain@gsu.edu. *Application contact:* Dr. Joe Perry, Director of Graduate Studies, 404-413-6374, Fax: 404-413-6384, E-mail: jbperry@gsu.edu.
Website: http://www.gsu.edu/~wwwhis/

Georgia State University, College of Education, Department of Middle-Secondary Education and Instructional Technology, Atlanta, GA 30302-3083. Offers curriculum and instruction (Ed D); English education (MAT); mathematics education (M Ed, MAT); middle level education (MAT); reading, language and literacy education (M Ed, MAT), including reading instruction (M Ed); science education (M Ed, MAT), including biology (MAT), broad field science (MAT), chemistry (MAT), earth science (MAT), physics (MAT); social studies education (M Ed, MAT), including economics (MAT), geography (MAT), history (MAT), political science (MAT); teaching and learning (PhD), including language and literacy, mathematics education, music education, science education, social studies education, teaching and teacher education. *Accreditation:* NCATE. Part-time and evening/weekend programs available. Postbaccalaureate distance learning degree programs offered (minimal on-campus study). *Faculty:* 20 full-time (16 women). *Students:* 155 full-time (112 women), 101 part-time (70 women); includes 112 minority (82 Black or African American, non-Hispanic/Latino; 10 Asian, non-Hispanic/Latino; 12 Hispanic/Latino; 8 Two or more races, non-Hispanic/Latino), 3 international. Average age 32. 155 applicants, 61% accepted, 65 enrolled. *Degree requirements:* For master's, comprehensive exam (for some programs), thesis or alternative, exit portfolio; for doctorate, comprehensive exam, thesis/dissertation. *Entrance requirements:* For master's, GRE; GACE I (for initial teacher preparation programs), baccalaureate degree or equivalent, resume, goals statement, two letters of recommendation, minimum undergraduate GPA of 2.5; proof of initial teacher certification in the content area (for M Ed); for doctorate, GRE, resume, goals statement, writing sample, two letters of recommendation, minimum graduate GPA of 3.3, interview. Additional exam requirements/recommendations for international students: Required—TOEFL (minimum score 550 paper-based; 79 iBT) or IELTS (minimum score 6.5). *Application deadline:* For fall admission, 1/15 priority date for domestic and international students; for spring admission, 10/1 for domestic and international students. Application fee: $50. Electronic applications accepted. *Expenses:* Tuition, state resident: full-time $6516; part-time $362 per credit hour. Tuition, nonresident: full-time $22,014; part-time $1223 per credit hour. *Required fees:* $2128 per semester. Tuition and fees vary according to course load and program. *Financial support:* In 2014–15, fellowships with full tuition reimbursements (averaging $19,667 per year), research assistantships with full tuition reimbursements (averaging $5,436 per year), teaching assistantships with full tuition reimbursements (averaging $2,779 per year) were awarded; career-related internships or fieldwork, Federal Work-Study, scholarships/grants, health care benefits, tuition waivers (full and partial), and unspecified assistantships also available. Financial award application deadline: 3/15. *Faculty research:* Teacher education in language and literacy, mathematics, science, and social studies in urban middle and secondary school settings; learning technologies in school, community, and corporate settings; multicultural education and education for social justice; urban education; international education. *Unit head:* Dr. Dana L. Fox, Chair, 404-413-8060, Fax: 404-413-8063, E-mail: dfox@gsu.edu. *Application contact:* Bobbie Turner, Administrative Coordinator I, 404-413-8405, Fax: 404-413-8063, E-mail: bnturner@gsu.edu.
Website: http://mse.education.gsu.edu/

The Graduate Center, City University of New York, Graduate Studies, Program in History, New York, NY 10016-4039. Offers PhD. *Degree requirements:* For doctorate, one foreign language, thesis/dissertation. *Entrance requirements:* For doctorate, GRE General Test, writing sample (15 pages). Additional exam requirements/recommendations for international students: Required—TOEFL. Electronic applications accepted.

Hardin-Simmons University, Graduate School, Cynthia Ann Parker College of Liberal Arts, Department of History, Abilene, TX 79698-0001. Offers MA. Part-time programs available. *Faculty:* 4 full-time (1 woman). *Students:* 1 (woman) full-time, 2 part-time (0 women). Average age 34. *Degree requirements:* For master's, one foreign language, comprehensive exam, thesis or alternative. *Entrance requirements:* For master's, GRE, minimum undergraduate GPA of 3.0 in history, 2.7 overall; 18 upper-level hours of course work in history; letters of recommendation; resume; writing sample. Additional exam requirements/recommendations for international students: Required—TOEFL (minimum score 550 paper-based; 75 iBT). *Application deadline:* For fall admission, 8/15 priority date for domestic students, 4/1 for international students; for spring admission, 1/5 priority date for domestic students, 9/1 for international students. Applications are processed on a rolling basis. Application fee: $50. *Expenses: Tuition:* Full-time $12,060; part-time $670 per credit hour. *Required fees:* $325; $110 per semester. Tuition and fees vary according to program. *Financial support:* Fellowships and scholarships/grants available. Support available to part-time students. Financial award application deadline: 6/30; financial award applicants required to submit FAFSA. *Faculty research:* Vietnam, diplomatic history, Texas politics, Mexico and NAFTA, classical warfare. *Unit head:* Dr. Mark Beasley, Program Director, 325-670-1279, Fax: 325-670-1526, E-mail: mbeasley@hsutx.edu. *Application contact:* Dr. Nancy Kucinski, Dean of Graduate Studies, 325-670-1298, Fax: 325-670-1564, E-mail: gradoff@hsutx.edu.
Website: http://www.hsutx.edu/academics/cap/graduate/history

Harvard University, Graduate School of Arts and Sciences, Department of History, Cambridge, MA 02138. Offers African history (PhD); American history (PhD); ancient, medieval, early modern, and modern Europe (PhD), including Central Europe, Russia, Southeastern Europe, Western Europe; diplomatic history (PhD); East Asian history (PhD); economic and social history (PhD); intellectual history (PhD); Latin American history (PhD); Near Eastern history (PhD); oceanic history (PhD). *Degree requirements:* For doctorate, variable foreign language requirement, thesis/dissertation, oral general exam. *Entrance requirements:* For doctorate, GRE General Test, proficiency in 2 languages. Additional exam requirements/recommendations for international students: Required—TOEFL.

High Point University, Norcross Graduate School, High Point, NC 27268. Offers business administration (MBA); educational leadership (M Ed); elementary education (M Ed); history (MA); nonprofit management (MA); secondary math (M Ed); special education (M Ed); strategic communication (MA); teaching elementary education k-6 (MAT); teaching secondary mathematics 9-12 (MAT). *Accreditation:* NCATE. Part-time and evening/weekend programs available. *Degree requirements:* For master's, comprehensive exam (for some programs), thesis (for some programs). *Entrance requirements:* For master's, GMAT (MBA), GRE, MAT, minimum GPA of 3.0. Additional exam requirements/recommendations for international students: Required—TOEFL (minimum score 550 paper-based). Electronic applications accepted.

Howard University, Graduate School, Department of History, Washington, DC 20059-0002. Offers African diaspora (MA, PhD); African history (MA, PhD); Latin America and the Caribbean (MA, PhD); public history (MA); United States history (MA, PhD). Part-time programs available. Terminal master's awarded for partial completion of doctoral program. *Degree requirements:* For master's, one foreign language, thesis optional; for doctorate, 2 foreign languages, comprehensive exam, thesis/dissertation. *Entrance requirements:* For master's, GRE General Test, minimum GPA of 3.0, 3 letters of recommendation; for doctorate, GRE General Test, minimum GPA of 3.5, 3 letters of recommendation. Additional exam requirements/recommendations for international students: Required—TOEFL. Electronic applications accepted. *Faculty research:* Africa diaspora, U.S. diplomatic relations, Caribbean economic history.

Hunter College of the City University of New York, Graduate School, School of Arts and Sciences, Department of History, New York, NY 10065-5085. Offers MA. *Faculty:* 4 full-time (3 women), 1 part-time/adjunct (0 women). *Students:* 2 full-time (1 woman), 27 part-time (8 women); includes 7 minority (2 Black or African American, non-Hispanic/Latino; 1 Asian, non-Hispanic/Latino; 4 Hispanic/Latino). Average age 38. 18 applicants, 72% accepted, 5 enrolled. In 2014, 5 master's awarded. *Degree requirements:* For master's, one foreign language, comprehensive exam, thesis, essay, language exam. *Entrance requirements:* For master's, GRE General Test, minimum of 18 credits in undergraduate history or related field. Additional exam requirements/recommendations for international students: Required—TOEFL. *Application deadline:* For fall admission, 4/1 for domestic students, 2/1 for international students; for spring admission, 11/1 for domestic students, 9/1 for international students. *Financial support:* Federal Work-Study, scholarships/grants, and tuition waivers (partial) available. Support available to part-time students. *Unit head:* Dr. Rick Belsky, Chair, 212-772-5480, E-mail: history@hunter.cuny.edu. *Application contact:* Barbara Welter, Graduate Advisor, 212-

772-5487, E-mail: bwelter@hunter.cuny.edu.
Website: http://www.hunter.cuny.edu/history/grad.shtml

Idaho State University, Office of Graduate Studies, College of Arts and Letters, Department of History, Pocatello, ID 83209-8079. Offers historical resources management (MA). Part-time programs available. *Degree requirements:* For master's, comprehensive exam, thesis optional, internship. *Entrance requirements:* For master's, GRE, 3 letters of recommendation, minimum of 18 upper division history credits. Additional exam requirements/recommendations for international students: Required—TOEFL (minimum score 550 paper-based; 80 iBT). Electronic applications accepted. *Faculty research:* Historical geographic information systems, historical and urban geography, environmental history and environmental policy, United States political history, womens' and gender history.

Illinois State University, Graduate School, College of Arts and Sciences, Department of History, Normal, IL 61790-2200. Offers MA, MS. *Degree requirements:* For master's, thesis or alternative. *Entrance requirements:* For master's, GRE General Test, minimum GPA of 2.6 in last 60 hours of course work.

Indiana State University, College of Graduate and Professional Studies, College of Arts and Sciences, Department of History, Terre Haute, IN 47809. Offers MA, MS. Part-time and evening/weekend programs available. *Degree requirements:* For master's, comprehensive exam (for some programs), thesis or alternative. *Entrance requirements:* For master's, equivalent of minor in geography or geology. Additional exam requirements/recommendations for international students: Required—TOEFL (minimum score 550 paper-based).

Indiana University Bloomington, University Graduate School, College of Arts and Sciences, Department of History, Bloomington, IN 47405. Offers MA, MAT, PhD, MA/MLS. *Faculty:* 44 full-time (12 women), 34 part-time/adjunct (15 women). *Students:* 109 full-time (57 women), 3 part-time (1 woman); includes 22 minority (9 Black or African American, non-Hispanic/Latino; 2 Asian, non-Hispanic/Latino; 9 Hispanic/Latino; 2 Two or more races, non-Hispanic/Latino), 6 international. Average age 31. 198 applicants, 14% accepted, 26 enrolled. In 2014, 18 master's, 11 doctorates awarded. Terminal master's awarded for partial completion of doctoral program. *Degree requirements:* For master's, one foreign language, thesis optional; for doctorate, variable foreign language requirement, comprehensive exam, thesis/dissertation. *Entrance requirements:* For master's and doctorate, GRE General Test. Additional exam requirements/recommendations for international students: Required—TOEFL. *Application deadline:* For fall admission, 12/1 for domestic students, 11/1 for international students. Application fee: $55 ($65 for international students). Electronic applications accepted. *Financial support:* In 2014–15, 80 students received support, including 16 fellowships with full tuition reimbursements available (averaging $17,000 per year), 3 research assistantships with full tuition reimbursements available (averaging $15,750 per year), 36 teaching assistantships with full tuition reimbursements available (averaging $15,750 per year); career-related internships or fieldwork, Federal Work-Study, institutionally sponsored loans, scholarships/grants, traineeships, health care benefits, and unspecified assistantships also available. Financial award application deadline: 12/1. *Faculty research:* Medieval and early modern Europe, Russia, Latin America, Middle East, Great Britain, United States, Africa, African Diaspora, Europe, eastern Europe, gender and sexuality. *Unit head:* Dr. Eric Sandweiss, Chairman, 812-855-3236, Fax: 812-855-3378, E-mail: sesandw@indiana.edu. *Application contact:* Sara Skinner, Admissions Secretary, 812-855-8233, Fax: 812-855-3378, E-mail: histadm@indiana.edu.
Website: http://www.indiana.edu/~histweb/

Indiana University of Pennsylvania, School of Graduate Studies and Research, College of Humanities and Social Sciences, Department of History, Program in History, Indiana, PA 15705-1087. Offers MA. Part-time programs available. *Faculty:* 8 full-time (4 women). *Students:* 14 full-time (3 women), 3 part-time (1 woman). Average age 26. 18 applicants, 83% accepted, 5 enrolled. In 2014, 8 master's awarded. *Degree requirements:* For master's, thesis optional. *Entrance requirements:* For master's, GRE, 2 letters of recommendation. Additional exam requirements/recommendations for international students: Required—TOEFL (minimum score 540 paper-based). *Application deadline:* Applications are processed on a rolling basis. Application fee: $50. Electronic applications accepted. *Financial support:* In 2014–15, 1 fellowship (averaging $1,000 per year), 5 research assistantships with full and partial tuition reimbursements (averaging $2,870 per year) were awarded; career-related internships or fieldwork, Federal Work-Study, scholarships/grants, and unspecified assistantships also available. Support available to part-time students. Financial award application deadline: 4/15; financial award applicants required to submit FAFSA. *Unit head:* Dr. Jeanine Mazak-Kahne, Graduate Coordinator, 724-357-2436, E-mail: j.mkahne@iup.edu.
Website: http://www.iup.edu/grad/history/default.aspx

Indiana University–Purdue University Indianapolis, School of Liberal Arts, Department of History, Indianapolis, IN 46202. Offers history (MA); public history (MA); MA/MLS. Part-time and evening/weekend programs available. *Faculty:* 14 full-time (6 women). *Students:* 12 full-time (6 women), 17 part-time (13 women); includes 2 minority (1 Black or African American, non-Hispanic/Latino; 1 Asian, non-Hispanic/Latino). Average age 33. 34 applicants, 32% accepted, 10 enrolled. In 2014, 15 master's awarded. *Degree requirements:* For master's, one foreign language, thesis. *Entrance requirements:* For master's, GRE General Test, minimum GPA of 3.0. *Application deadline:* For fall admission, 2/1 priority date for domestic and international students; for spring admission, 10/15 for domestic and international students. Application fee: $55 ($65 for international students). Electronic applications accepted. *Financial support:* In 2014–15, 19 students received support. Fellowships with full tuition reimbursements available, research assistantships with full tuition reimbursements available, teaching assistantships with full tuition reimbursements available, career-related internships or fieldwork, and health care benefits available. Financial award application deadline: 2/1. *Unit head:* Dr. Didier Gondola, Chair, 317-274-8160, Fax: 317-278-7800, E-mail: gondola@iupui.edu. *Application contact:* Amy Schramm, Office Coordinator, 317-274-5840, Fax: 317-278-7800, E-mail: ajschram@iupui.edu.
Website: http://liberalarts.iupui.edu/history/

Inter American University of Puerto Rico, Metropolitan Campus, Graduate Programs, Program in History, San Juan, PR 00919-1293. Offers American history (PhD); history (MA, PhD).

Inter American University of Puerto Rico, Metropolitan Campus, Graduate Programs, Program in History Education, San Juan, PR 00919-1293. Offers MA.

Iona College, School of Arts and Science, Department of History, New Rochelle, NY 10801-1890. Offers MA. Part-time and evening/weekend programs available. *Faculty:* 4 full-time (2 women). *Students:* 1 full-time (0 women), 3 part-time (1 woman), 1 international. Average age 26. 6 applicants, 83% accepted. In 2014, 5 master's awarded. *Degree requirements:* For master's, one foreign language, comprehensive exam, 27 credits of coursework and culminating project or 24 credits of coursework and thesis. *Entrance requirements:* For master's, undergraduate major in history or related field, minimum GPA of 3.0. Additional exam requirements/recommendations for international students: Required—TOEFL (minimum score 550 paper-based; 80 iBT), IELTS (minimum score 6.5). *Application deadline:* For fall admission, 8/1 priority date for domestic students, 5/1 priority date for international students; for spring admission, 1/1 priority date for domestic students, 8/1 priority date for international students. Applications are processed on a rolling basis. Application fee: $50. Electronic applications accepted. *Expenses: Tuition:* Part-time $985 per credit. *Required fees:* $245 per term. *Financial support:* Unspecified assistantships available. Financial award application deadline: 4/15; financial award applicants required to submit FAFSA. *Faculty research:* Military history, Asian economies, American diplomacy, Catholic education, Armenian history, the history of violence, French Revolution, medieval religion. *Unit head:* Daniel Thiery, PhD, Chairman, 914-633-2694, E-mail: dthiery@iona.edu. *Application contact:* Veronica Jarek-Prinz, Director, Graduate Admissions, 914-633-2420, Fax: 914-633-2277, E-mail: vjarekprinz@iona.edu.
Website: http://www.iona.edu/Academics/School-of-Arts-Science/Departments/History/Graduate-Programs.aspx

Iowa State University of Science and Technology, Department of History, Ames, IA 50011. Offers agricultural history and rural studies (PhD); history (MA); history of technology and science (MA, PhD). *Degree requirements:* For master's, thesis or alternative; for doctorate, thesis/dissertation. *Entrance requirements:* For master's and doctorate, GRE General Test. Additional exam requirements/recommendations for international students: Required—TOEFL (minimum score 600 paper-based; 79 iBT), IELTS (minimum score 7). Electronic applications accepted.

Jackson State University, Graduate School, College of Liberal Arts, Department of History and Philosophy, Jackson, MS 39217. Offers history (MA). Part-time and evening/weekend programs available. *Degree requirements:* For master's, comprehensive exam, thesis or alternative. *Entrance requirements:* For master's, GRE General Test. Additional exam requirements/recommendations for international students: Required—TOEFL (minimum score 520 paper-based; 67 iBT).

Jacksonville State University, College of Graduate Studies and Continuing Education, College of Arts and Sciences, Department of History, Jacksonville, AL 36265-1602. Offers MA. Part-time and evening/weekend programs available. *Faculty:* 9 full-time (2 women). *Students:* 1 full-time (0 women), 12 part-time (2 women); includes 1 minority (Black or African American, non-Hispanic/Latino), 1 international. Average age 33. 5 applicants, 80% accepted, 3 enrolled. In 2014, 10 master's awarded. *Degree requirements:* For master's, comprehensive exam, thesis (for some programs). *Entrance requirements:* For master's, GRE General Test or MAT. Additional exam requirements/recommendations for international students: Required—TOEFL (minimum score 500 paper-based; 61 iBT). *Application deadline:* Applications are processed on a rolling basis. Application fee: $35. Electronic applications accepted. *Financial support:* In 2014–15, 4 students received support. Available to part-time students. Application deadline: 4/1; applicants required to submit FAFSA. *Unit head:* Dr. Gordon Harvey, Head, 256-782-5622, E-mail: gharvey@jsu.edu. *Application contact:* Dr. Jean Pugliese, Associate Dean, 256-782-8278, Fax: 256-782-5321, E-mail: pugliese@jsu.edu.

James Madison University, The Graduate School, College of Arts and Letters, Department of History, Harrisonburg, VA 22807. Offers MA. Part-time programs available. *Faculty:* 31 full-time (9 women). *Students:* 22 full-time (11 women), 10 part-time (3 women); includes 2 minority (1 Black or African American, non-Hispanic/Latino; 1 Asian, non-Hispanic/Latino), 1 international. Average age 28. 32 applicants, 84% accepted, 13 enrolled. In 2014, 10 master's awarded. *Degree requirements:* For master's, one foreign language, comprehensive exam, thesis. *Application deadline:* For fall admission, 1/15 for domestic students. Application fee: $55. Electronic applications accepted. *Expenses:* Tuition, state resident: full-time $7812; part-time $434 per credit hour. Tuition, nonresident: full-time $20,430; part-time $1135 per credit hour. *Financial support:* In 2014–15, 15 students received support, including 4 fellowships, 3 teaching assistantships with full tuition reimbursements available (averaging $8,837 per year); Federal Work-Study also available. Financial award application deadline: 3/1; financial award applicants required to submit FAFSA. *Unit head:* Dr. Gabrielle Lanier, Department Head, 540-568-6132, E-mail: laniergm@jmu.edu. *Application contact:* Lynette D. Michael, Director of Graduate Admissions and Student Records, 540-568-6131 Ext. 6395, Fax: 540-568-7860, E-mail: michaeld@jmu.edu.
Website: http://www.jmu.edu/history

John Carroll University, Graduate School, Department of History, University Heights, OH 44118-4581. Offers MA. Part-time and evening/weekend programs available. *Degree requirements:* For master's, comprehensive exam, research essay or thesis. *Entrance requirements:* For master's, GRE General Test, minimum GPA of 2.5. Additional exam requirements/recommendations for international students: Required—TOEFL. Electronic applications accepted. *Faculty research:* Social history of Cleveland, early national Pennsylvania, modern Japanese journalism, Catholic Reformation.

Johns Hopkins University, Zanvyl Krieger School of Arts and Sciences, Department of History, Baltimore, MD 21218-2699. Offers PhD. *Degree requirements:* For doctorate, variable foreign language requirement, comprehensive exam, thesis/dissertation. *Entrance requirements:* For doctorate, GRE General Test. Additional exam requirements/recommendations for international students: Required—TOEFL (minimum score 600 paper-based; 100 iBT), IELTS. Electronic applications accepted. *Faculty research:* American, European, Latin American, East Asian, and African history.

Kansas State University, Graduate School, College of Arts and Sciences, Department of History, Manhattan, KS 66506. Offers MA, PhD. Part-time programs available. *Faculty:* 22 full-time (8 women). *Students:* 19 full-time (6 women), 27 part-time (8 women); includes 5 minority (1 Black or African American, non-Hispanic/Latino; 1 American Indian or Alaska Native, non-Hispanic/Latino; 1 Asian, non-Hispanic/Latino; 2 Two or more races, non-Hispanic/Latino), 1 international. Average age 36. 23 applicants, 57% accepted, 3 enrolled. In 2014, 3 master's, 3 doctorates awarded. *Degree requirements:* For master's, thesis (for some programs); for doctorate, one foreign language, thesis/dissertation, qualifying exam. *Entrance requirements:* For master's, GRE General Test, minimum undergraduate GPA of 3.0; for doctorate, GRE General Test. Additional exam requirements/recommendations for international students: Required—TOEFL (minimum score 600 paper-based). *Application deadline:* For fall admission, 3/1 priority date for domestic students, 1/1 priority date for international students; for spring admission, 10/15 priority date for domestic students, 8/1 priority date for international students. Application fee: $50 ($75 for international students). Electronic applications accepted. *Financial support:* In 2014–15, 1 research assistantship (averaging $9,800 per year), 14 teaching assistantships with full tuition reimbursements (averaging $11,637 per year) were awarded; career-related internships or fieldwork, Federal Work-Study, institutionally sponsored loans, and scholarships/grants also available. Support available to part-time students. Financial award application deadline: 3/1; financial award applicants required to submit FAFSA. *Faculty research:* Environmental history, religious history, American social history, history of war and society, history of international relations and diplomacy. *Total annual research expenditures:* $100,609. *Unit head:* Louise Breen, Associate Professor/Department Chair, 785-532-6730, Fax: 785-532-2045, E-mail: breen@ksu.edu. *Application contact:* Albert Hamscher, Professor/Director of Graduate Admissions, 785-532-0436, Fax: 785-532-2045, E-mail: aham@ksu.edu.
Website: http://www.k-state.edu/history/

History

Kent State University, College of Arts and Sciences, Department of History, Kent, OH 44242-0001. Offers history (PhD). Part-time programs available. *Faculty:* 13 full-time (4 women). *Students:* 34 full-time (13 women), 9 part-time (6 women); includes 3 minority (1 Black or African American, non-Hispanic/Latino; 1 Hispanic/Latino; 1 Two or more races, non-Hispanic/Latino), 1 international. Average age 32. 83 applicants, 55% accepted, 28 enrolled. In 2014, 5 master's, 2 doctorates awarded. *Degree requirements:* For master's, variable foreign language requirement, thesis; for doctorate, variable foreign language requirement, thesis/dissertation. *Entrance requirements:* For master's and doctorate, GRE General Test, GRE Subject Test, minimum GPA of 3.0, resume, statement of purpose, writing sample, 3 letters of recommendation. Additional exam requirements/recommendations for international students: Required—TOEFL (minimum score: paper-based 525, iBT 71), Michigan English Language Assessment Battery (minimum score of 75), IELTS (minimum score of 6.0), PTE Academic (minimum score of 48), or completion of ELS level 112 Intensive Program. *Application deadline:* For fall admission, 7/12 for domestic students; for spring admission, 11/29 for domestic students. Applications are processed on a rolling basis. Application fee: $45 ($70 for international students). Electronic applications accepted. *Expenses:* Tuition, state resident: full-time $8730; part-time $485 per credit hour. Tuition, nonresident: full-time $14,886; part-time $827 per credit hour. Tuition and fees vary according to campus/location and program. *Financial support:* In 2014–15, 21 students received support. Research assistantships with full tuition reimbursements available, teaching assistantships with full tuition reimbursements available, career-related internships or fieldwork, Federal Work-Study, scholarships/grants, and unspecified assistantships available. Financial award application deadline: 2/1. *Unit head:* Dr. Kenneth Bindas, Professor and Chair, 330-672-2882, E-mail: kbindas@kent.edu. *Application contact:* Dr. Timothy Scarnecchia, Professor and Graduate Coordinator, 330-672-2882, Fax: 330-672-2943, E-mail: history@kent.edu.
Website: http://www.kent.edu/stark/history

Lake Forest College, Graduate Program in Liberal Studies, Lake Forest, IL 60045. Offers American studies (MLS); environmental studies (MLS); history and freedom (MLS); writing (MLS). Part-time and evening/weekend programs available. *Faculty:* 11 full-time (5 women), 1 (woman) part-time/adjunct. *Students:* 42 part-time (22 women); includes 4 minority (2 Asian, non-Hispanic/Latino; 2 Hispanic/Latino). Average age 38. 26 applicants, 50% accepted, 9 enrolled. In 2014, 7 master's awarded. *Degree requirements:* For master's, thesis optional, 8 courses, including at least 3 interdisciplinary seminars. *Entrance requirements:* For master's, transcript, essay, interview. Additional exam requirements/recommendations for international students: Required—TOEFL (minimum score 550 paper-based; 83 iBT); Recommended—IELTS (minimum score 6.5). *Application deadline:* For fall admission, 7/15 priority date for domestic students, 6/1 priority date for international students; for winter admission, 12/15 for domestic students, 10/1 for international students; for spring admission, 12/1 priority date for domestic students, 10/1 priority date for international students. Applications are processed on a rolling basis. Application fee: $30. *Expenses:* Expenses: Contact institution. *Financial support:* In 2014–15, 4 students received support. Scholarships/grants and partial tuition grants (for full-time teachers) available. Financial award application deadline: 7/15. *Faculty research:* History of American political thought; American families; electron collisions with molecules; international relations, American foreign policy, and transparency in world politics; ethics and social justice; pacifism. *Unit head:* Prof. D. L. LeMahieu, Director, 847-735-5133, Fax: 847-735-6291, E-mail: lemahieu@lakeforest.edu. *Application contact:* Prof. Carol Gayle, Associate Director, 847-735-5083, Fax: 847-735-6291, E-mail: gayle@lakeforest.edu.
Website: http://www.lakeforest.edu/academics/programs/mls/

Lakehead University, Graduate Studies, Department of History, Thunder Bay, ON P7B 5E1, Canada. Offers gerontology (MA); history (MA); women's studies (MA). Part-time programs available. *Degree requirements:* For master's, one foreign language, thesis. *Entrance requirements:* For master's, minimum B average. Additional exam requirements/recommendations for international students: Required—TOEFL. *Faculty research:* Canadian history, British history, Russian/German history, women's studies.

Lamar University, College of Graduate Studies, College of Arts and Sciences, Department of History, Beaumont, TX 77710. Offers MA. Part-time programs available. *Faculty:* 3 full-time (1 woman). *Students:* 1 (woman) full-time, 10 part-time (6 women); includes 1 minority (Black or African American, non-Hispanic/Latino). Average age 29. 1 applicant, 100% accepted. In 2014, 1 master's awarded. *Degree requirements:* For master's, comprehensive exam (for some programs), thesis (for some programs). *Entrance requirements:* For master's, GRE General Test, minimum GPA of 2.5 in last 60 hours of undergraduate course work. Additional exam requirements/recommendations for international students: Required—TOEFL (minimum score 550 paper-based; 79 iBT), IELTS (minimum score 6.5). *Application deadline:* For fall admission, 8/11 for domestic students, 7/1 for international students; for spring admission, 1/5 for domestic students, 12/1 for international students. Applications are processed on a rolling basis. Application fee: $25 ($50 for international students). *Expenses:* Tuition, state resident: full-time $5724; part-time $1908 per semester. Tuition, nonresident: full-time $12,240; part-time $4080 per semester. *Required fees:* $1940; $318 per credit hour. *Financial support:* In 2014–15, fellowships (averaging $1,000 per year), teaching assistantships (averaging $2,000 per year) were awarded. Financial award application deadline: 4/1. *Faculty research:* Old South, nineteenth century reform, twentieth century U.S., religion in America's South, Renaissance/early modern Europe. *Unit head:* Dr. Mary L. Scheer, Chair, 409-880-8511, Fax: 409-880-8710. *Application contact:* Melissa Gallien, Director, Admissions and Academic Services, 409-880-8888, Fax: 409-880-7419, E-mail: gradmissions@lamar.edu.
Website: http://artsscience.lamar.edu/history

La Salle University, School of Arts and Sciences, Program in History, Philadelphia, PA 19141-1199. Offers American history (Certificate); European history (Certificate); history (MA); history for educators (MA); public history (MA); teaching advanced placement history (Certificate); world history (Certificate). Part-time programs available. *Degree requirements:* For master's, thesis or comprehensive exam. *Entrance requirements:* For master's, GRE or MAT, 18 hours of undergraduate coursework in history or a related discipline with minimum GPA of 3.0; two letters of recommendation; brief personal statement (250 to 500 words); writing sample (preferably from an undergraduate research paper). Additional exam requirements/recommendations for international students: Required—TOEFL. Electronic applications accepted. Application fee is waived when completed online.

Laurentian University, School of Graduate Studies and Research, Programme in History, Sudbury, ON P3E 2C6, Canada. Offers European history (MA); history of Northern Ontario (MA); North American history (MA). Part-time programs available. *Degree requirements:* For master's, thesis or alternative. *Entrance requirements:* For master's, honors degree with minimum second class. *Faculty research:* Franco-Ontarian history, northern Ontarian history, Canadian social history, European social history, Franco-Canadian history.

Lehigh University, College of Arts and Sciences, Department of History, Bethlehem, PA 18015. Offers Atlantic world (PhD); British history (PhD); history (MA); industrial and modern America (PhD); public history (MA). Part-time programs available. *Faculty:* 12 full-time (5 women). *Students:* 25 full-time (9 women), 23 part-time (7 women), 2 international. Average age 34. 28 applicants, 39% accepted, 7 enrolled. In 2014, 4 master's, 1 doctorate awarded. Terminal master's awarded for partial completion of doctoral program. *Degree requirements:* For master's, comprehensive exam (for some programs), comprehensive exam or thesis; for doctorate, comprehensive exam, thesis/dissertation. *Entrance requirements:* For master's, GRE General Test, recommendations, writing sample; for doctorate, GRE General Test, recommendations, writing samples. Additional exam requirements/recommendations for international students: Required—TOEFL. *Application deadline:* For fall admission, 4/15 for domestic and international students; for winter admission, 11/1 priority date for domestic students, 11/15 priority date for international students. Applications are processed on a rolling basis. Application fee: $75. Electronic applications accepted. *Expenses:* Expenses: $1,380 per credit hour. *Financial support:* In 2014–15, 2 fellowships with full tuition reimbursements (averaging $22,500 per year), 10 teaching assistantships with full and partial tuition reimbursements (averaging $19,700 per year) were awarded; research assistantships with full tuition reimbursements, institutionally sponsored loans, scholarships/grants, tuition waivers (full and partial), and unspecified assistantships also available. Support available to part-time students. Financial award application deadline: 1/15. *Faculty research:* Colonial America, modern America, history of technology, Atlantic world. *Total annual research expenditures:* $66,401. *Unit head:* Dr. John K. Smith, Chairman, 610-758-3360, Fax: 610-758-6554, E-mail: jks0@lehigh.edu. *Application contact:* Dr. Roger D. Simon, Graduate Coordinator, 610-758-3368, Fax: 610-758-6554, E-mail: rds2@lehigh.edu.
Website: http://history.cas2.lehigh.edu/

Lehman College of the City University of New York, Division of Arts and Humanities, Department of History, Bronx, NY 10468-1589. Offers MA. Part-time and evening/weekend programs available. *Degree requirements:* For master's, comprehensive exam, thesis. *Entrance requirements:* For master's, 18 undergraduate credits in history, minimum GPA of 2.7.

Liberty University, College of Arts and Sciences, Lynchburg, VA 24515. Offers English (MA); history (MA); philosophical studies (MA). *Accreditation:* AACN. Part-time programs available. Postbaccalaureate distance learning degree programs offered (minimal on-campus study). *Students:* 60 full-time (28 women), 14 part-time (4 women); includes 4 minority (1 Black or African American, non-Hispanic/Latino; 2 Hispanic/Latino; 1 Two or more races, non-Hispanic/Latino), 4 international. Average age 25. 66 applicants, 52% accepted, 23 enrolled. In 2014, 25 master's awarded. *Degree requirements:* For master's, comprehensive exam (for some programs), thesis (for some programs). *Entrance requirements:* For master's, GRE, minimum undergraduate GPA of 3.0, letters of recommendation, statement of purpose. Additional exam requirements/recommendations for international students: Required—TOEFL (minimum score 600 paper-based; 100 iBT). *Application deadline:* For fall admission, 6/1 for domestic students; for spring admission, 11/1 for domestic students. Applications are processed on a rolling basis. Application fee: $50. Electronic applications accepted. *Financial support:* Teaching assistantships with tuition reimbursements and Federal Work-Study available. *Faculty research:* God concept and adult attachment, building marital strength, image of God and gender, breastfeeding behavior among adolescent mothers, osteoporosis. *Unit head:* Dr. Roger Schultz, Dean, 434-592-4031, Fax: 434-522-0430, E-mail: rschultz@liberty.edu. *Application contact:* Dr. Terry Elam, Director of Graduate Admissions, 434-592-3966, Fax: 434-522-0430, E-mail: gradadmissions@liberty.edu.

Liberty University, School of Education, Lynchburg, VA 24515. Offers administration and supervision (M Ed); curriculum and instruction (Ed D, Ed S); early childhood education (M Ed); educational leadership (Ed D, Ed S); educational technology and online instruction (M Ed); elementary education (M Ed, MAT); English (M Ed); gifted education (M Ed, Certificate); history (M Ed); leadership (M Ed); math specialist (M Ed); middle grades (M Ed, MAT, Certificate); outdoor adventure sport (MS); preschool (Certificate); reading specialist (M Ed); school counseling (M Ed); school leadership (Certificate); secondary education (MAT); special education (M Ed, MAT); sport management (MS, Certificate), including administration (MS), outdoor recreation (MS), sport management (MS), tourism (MS); sports administration (MS); student service (M Ed); teaching and learning (M Ed); tourism (MS). *Accreditation:* NCATE. Part-time programs available. Postbaccalaureate distance learning degree programs offered (minimal on-campus study). *Students:* 2,200 full-time (1,590 women), 4,619 part-time (3,401 women); includes 1,660 minority (1,403 Black or African American, non-Hispanic/Latino; 33 American Indian or Alaska Native, non-Hispanic/Latino; 42 Asian, non-Hispanic/Latino; 42 Hispanic/Latino; 11 Native Hawaiian or other Pacific Islander, non-Hispanic/Latino; 129 Two or more races, non-Hispanic/Latino), 80 international. Average age 37. 6,006 applicants, 44% accepted, 1412 enrolled. In 2014, 1,199 master's, 118 doctorates, 539 other advanced degrees awarded. *Degree requirements:* For doctorate, comprehensive exam, thesis/dissertation. *Entrance requirements:* For master's, GRE General Test or MAT (if taken in or before 1999), 2 letters of recommendation, minimum undergraduate GPA of 3.0, curriculum vitae; for doctorate and other advanced degree, GRE General Test or MAT (if taken before 1999), minimum master's GPA of 3.0, 3 years of teaching experience. Additional exam requirements/recommendations for international students: Required—TOEFL (minimum score 600 paper-based; 100 iBT). *Application deadline:* For fall admission, 6/1 for domestic students; for spring admission, 11/1 for domestic students. Applications are processed on a rolling basis. Application fee: $50. Electronic applications accepted. *Expenses:* Expenses: Contact institution. *Financial support:* Federal Work-Study and tuition waivers (partial) available. *Faculty research:* Self-determination, character education, bibliotherapy, learning styles, distance education. *Unit head:* Dr. Karen L. Parker, Dean, 434-582-2195, Fax: 434-582-2468, E-mail: kparker@liberty.edu. *Application contact:* Jay Bridge, Director of Graduate Admissions, 800-424-9595, Fax: 800-628-7977, E-mail: gradadmissions@liberty.edu.
Website: http://www.liberty.edu/academics/education/graduate/

Lincoln University, Graduate Studies, Jefferson City, MO 65101. Offers business administration (MBA), including accounting, entrepreneurship, management, public administration and policy; educational leadership (Ed S), including elementary leadership, secondary leadership, superintendency; guidance and counseling (M Ed), including community/agency counseling, elementary school, secondary school; history (MA); school administration and supervision (M Ed), including elementary school administration, secondary school administration, special education administration; school teaching (M Ed), including elementary school teaching, secondary school teaching; sociology (MA); sociology/criminal justice (MA). Part-time and evening/weekend programs available. Postbaccalaureate distance learning degree programs offered (minimal on-campus study). *Students:* 57 full-time (35 women), 83 part-time (50 women); includes 64 minority (47 Black or African American, non-Hispanic/Latino; 1 American Indian or Alaska Native, non-Hispanic/Latino; 14 Asian, non-Hispanic/Latino; 1 Hispanic/Latino; 1 Two or more races, non-Hispanic/Latino), 9 international. Average age 33. 60 applicants, 68% accepted, 31 enrolled. In 2014, 52 master's, 2 other advanced degrees awarded. *Degree requirements:* For master's and Ed S, comprehensive exam, thesis optional. *Entrance requirements:* For master's and Ed S, GRE, MAT or GMAT, minimum GPA of 2.75 in major, 2.5 overall; 3 letters of recommendation; minimum C average in English composition; personal statement of purpose. Additional exam requirements/recommendations for international students: Required—TOEFL (minimum score 500 paper-based; 61 iBT). *Application deadline:* For fall admission, 8/1 priority date for domestic and international students; for spring

admission, 12/1 priority date for domestic and international students; for summer admission, 5/1 priority date for domestic and international students. Applications are processed on a rolling basis. Application fee: $30. *Expenses:* Tuition, state resident: full-time $6840; part-time $285 per credit hour. Tuition, nonresident: full-time $12,720; part-time $530 per credit hour. *Required fees:* $737; $737 per year. *Financial support:* In 2014–15, 1 fellowship with tuition reimbursement, 11 research assistantships with tuition reimbursements were awarded; Federal Work-Study and scholarships/grants also available. Support available to part-time students. Financial award application deadline: 3/1; financial award applicants required to submit FAFSA. *Unit head:* Dr. Linda S. Bickel, Dean, 573-681-5247, Fax: 573-681-5106, E-mail: gradschool@lincolnu.edu. *Application contact:* Irasema Steck, Administrative Assistant, 573-681-5247, Fax: 573-681-5106, E-mail: gradschool@lincolnu.edu.
Website: http://www.lincolnu.edu/web/graduate-studies/graduate-studies

Louisiana State University and Agricultural & Mechanical College, Graduate School, College of Humanities and Social Sciences, Department of History, Baton Rouge, LA 70803. Offers MA, PhD. Part-time programs available. *Faculty:* 29 full-time (13 women). *Students:* 47 full-time (18 women), 16 part-time (7 women); includes 7 minority (1 Black or African American, non-Hispanic/Latino; 4 Hispanic/Latino; 2 Two or more races, non-Hispanic/Latino). Average age 31. 61 applicants, 51% accepted, 10 enrolled. In 2014, 3 master's, 8 doctorates awarded. Terminal master's awarded for partial completion of doctoral program. *Degree requirements:* For master's, thesis (for some programs), oral exam; for doctorate, one foreign language, thesis/dissertation, comprehensive written and oral exams. *Entrance requirements:* For master's and doctorate, GRE General Test, minimum GPA of 3.0. Additional exam requirements/recommendations for international students: Required—TOEFL (minimum score 550 paper-based; 79 iBT), IELTS (minimum score 6.5), or PTE (minimum score 59). *Application deadline:* For fall admission, 1/1 priority date for domestic students, 5/15 for international students; for spring admission, 10/15 for domestic and international students; for summer admission, 5/15 for domestic and international students. Applications are processed on a rolling basis. Application fee: $50 ($70 for international students). Electronic applications accepted. *Financial support:* In 2014–15, 49 students received support, including 1 fellowship with full tuition reimbursement available (averaging $23,677 per year), 34 teaching assistantships with partial tuition reimbursements available (averaging $12,362 per year); research assistantships with partial tuition reimbursements available, career-related internships or fieldwork, Federal Work-Study, institutionally sponsored loans, health care benefits, and unspecified assistantships also available. Support available to part-time students. Financial award application deadline: 1/15; financial award applicants required to submit FAFSA. *Faculty research:* U.S. South, Civil War; modern Europe, British, medieval history. *Total annual research expenditures:* $41,749. *Unit head:* Dr. Victor Stater, Chair, 225-578-4471, Fax: 225-578-4909, E-mail: stater@lsu.edu. *Application contact:* Dr. Christine Kooi, Director of Graduate Studies, 225-578-4499, Fax: 225-578-4909, E-mail: ckooi1@lsu.edu.
Website: http://www.artsci.lsu.edu/hist/

Louisiana Tech University, Graduate School, College of Liberal Arts, Department of History, Ruston, LA 71272. Offers MA. Part-time programs available. *Degree requirements:* For master's, thesis or alternative. *Entrance requirements:* For master's, GRE General Test. *Application deadline:* For fall admission, 7/29 for domestic students; for spring admission, 2/3 for domestic students. Application fee: $40. *Financial support:* Fellowships available. Financial award application deadline: 2/1. *Unit head:* Dr. Jeffery R. Hankins, Interim Head, 318-257-2872, Fax: 318-257-3935, E-mail: jhankins@latech.edu. *Application contact:* Marilyn J. Robinson, Assistant to the Dean of the Graduate School, 318-257-2924, Fax: 318-257-4487.
Website: http://www.latech.edu/tech/liberal-arts/history/

Loyola University Chicago, Graduate School, Department of History, Chicago, IL 60660. Offers history (MA, PhD); public history (MA). Part-time and evening/weekend programs available. *Faculty:* 32 full-time (12 women), 7 part-time/adjunct (2 women). *Students:* 59 full-time (31 women), 13 part-time (6 women); includes 12 minority (5 Black or African American, non-Hispanic/Latino; 7 Hispanic/Latino), 1 international. Average age 31. 129 applicants, 44% accepted, 24 enrolled. In 2014, 14 master's, 7 doctorates awarded. Terminal master's awarded for partial completion of doctoral program. *Degree requirements:* For master's, one foreign language, comprehensive exam, thesis or alternative, Master's Essay/Thesis (Optional); Portfolio for Public History Program (Required); for doctorate, 2 foreign languages, comprehensive exam, thesis/dissertation. *Entrance requirements:* For master's, GRE General Test, Research paper/Writing Sample; for doctorate, GRE General Test, Seminar Paper or Master's Thesis. Additional exam requirements/recommendations for international students: Required—TOEFL (minimum score 550 paper-based), IELTS. *Application deadline:* For fall admission, 5/1 for domestic students; for spring admission, 10/1 for domestic students. Applications are processed on a rolling basis. Application fee: $50. Electronic applications accepted. Application fee is waived when completed online. *Expenses:* Expenses: Contact institution. *Financial support:* In 2014–15, 20 students received support, including 20 fellowships with full tuition reimbursements available (averaging $5,251 per year), 18 teaching assistantships with full tuition reimbursements available (averaging $17,722 per year); research assistantships with full tuition reimbursements available and Federal Work-Study also available. Financial award application deadline: 1/1; financial award applicants required to submit FAFSA. *Faculty research:* Medieval and Early Modern Europe, U.S. public history, U.S. urban history, gender history, Britain and Ireland, transnational history. *Unit head:* Dr. Robert O. Bucholz, Chair, 773-508-2232, Fax: 773-508-2153, E-mail: rbuchol@luc.edu. *Application contact:* Dr. Michelle Nickerson, Director, Graduate Programs, 773-508-2228, Fax: 773-508-2153, E-mail: mnickerson@luc.edu.
Website: http://www.luc.edu/history/

Lynchburg College, Graduate Studies, MA Program in History, Lynchburg, VA 24501-3199. Offers MA. Part-time and evening/weekend programs available. *Faculty:* 3 full-time (2 women). *Students:* 8 full-time (5 women), 5 part-time (all women); includes 2 minority (1 Black or African American, non-Hispanic/Latino; 1 Hispanic/Latino). Average age 34. In 2014, 7 master's awarded. *Degree requirements:* For master's, one foreign language, comprehensive exam, thesis or alternative. *Entrance requirements:* For master's, GRE, minimum GPA of 3.0 (preferred), official transcripts (bachelor's, others as relevant), three letters of recommendation, career goals statement. Additional exam requirements/recommendations for international students: Required—TOEFL (minimum score 550 paper-based; 79 iBT), IELTS (minimum score 6.5). *Application deadline:* For fall admission, 7/31 for domestic students, 6/1 for international students; for spring admission, 11/30 for domestic students, 10/15 for international students. Applications are processed on a rolling basis. Application fee: $30. Electronic applications accepted. Application fee is waived when completed online. *Financial support:* Fellowships, research assistantships, Federal Work-Study, scholarships/grants, health care benefits, and unspecified assistantships available. Support available to part-time students. Financial award application deadline: 7/31; financial award applicants required to submit FAFSA. *Unit head:* Dr. Nichole Sanders, Associate Professor/Director of MA in History, 434-544-8117, E-mail: sanders.n@lynchburg.edu. *Application contact:* Christine Priller, Executive Assistant, Graduate Studies, 434-544-8383, Fax: 434-544-8483, E-mail: gradstudies@lynchburg.edu.
Website: http://www.lynchburg.edu/graduate/master-of-arts-in-history/

Marquette University, Graduate School, College of Arts and Sciences, Department of History, Milwaukee, WI 53201-1881. Offers European history (MA, PhD); global studies (MA); United States history (MA, PhD). Part-time programs available. *Degree requirements:* For master's, comprehensive exam, essay, 2 classes of research seminars (6 hours); for doctorate, one foreign language, comprehensive exam, thesis/dissertation, 2 research seminars, dissertation seminar. *Entrance requirements:* For master's, GRE General Test, official transcripts from all current and previous colleges/universities except Marquette, one-page statement of purpose, three letters of recommendation from former teachers; for doctorate, GRE General Test, official transcripts from all current and previous colleges/universities except Marquette, one-page statement of purpose, three letters of recommendation from former teachers, writing sample. Additional exam requirements/recommendations for international students: Required—TOEFL (minimum score 530 paper-based). Electronic applications accepted. *Faculty research:* Children's history, Soviet and post-Soviet history, modern Ireland and Britain, Japan and martial arts, American Catholicism.

Marshall University, Academic Affairs Division, College of Liberal Arts, Department of History, Huntington, WV 25755. Offers MA, Certificate. *Students:* 16 full-time (5 women), 7 part-time (5 women); includes 1 minority (Two or more races, non-Hispanic/Latino). Average age 30. In 2014, 5 master's awarded. *Degree requirements:* For master's, thesis optional. *Entrance requirements:* For master's, GRE. Application fee: $40. *Unit head:* Dr. Dan Holbrook, Chair, 304-696-2417, Fax: 304-696-2957, E-mail: holbrook@marshall.edu. *Application contact:* Graduate Admissions, 304-746-1900, Fax: 304-746-1902, E-mail: services@marshall.edu.

McGill University, Faculty of Graduate and Postdoctoral Studies, Faculty of Arts, Department of History and Classical Studies, Montréal, QC H3A 2T5, Canada. Offers history (MA, PhD); history of medicine (MA).

McMaster University, School of Graduate Studies, Faculty of Humanities, Department of History, Hamilton, ON L8S 4M2, Canada. Offers MA, PhD. Part-time programs available. *Degree requirements:* For master's, one foreign language, thesis or alternative; for doctorate, one foreign language, comprehensive exam, thesis/dissertation. *Entrance requirements:* For master's, honors BA in history, minimum B+ average. Additional exam requirements/recommendations for international students: Required—TOEFL (minimum score 580 paper-based). *Faculty research:* Canadian, European, British, U.S. history; ancient history.

Memorial University of Newfoundland, School of Graduate Studies, Department of History, St. John's, NL A1C 5S7, Canada. Offers MA, PhD. Part-time programs available. *Degree requirements:* For master's, thesis or comprehensive exam; for doctorate, one foreign language, comprehensive exam, thesis/dissertation, oral defense of thesis. *Entrance requirements:* For master's, honors degree or equivalent; for doctorate, master's degree. Electronic applications accepted. *Faculty research:* Canadian history, maritime history, Newfoundland history, social history, labor history.

Miami University, College of Arts and Science, Department of History, Oxford, OH 45056. Offers MA. Part-time programs available. *Students:* 13 full-time (5 women), 1 (woman) part-time, 1 international. Average age 26. In 2014, 10 master's awarded. *Entrance requirements:* For master's, GRE General Test, minimum undergraduate cumulative GPA of 3.0, with higher grades in history courses; successful record of completion of undergraduate history courses; 2-3 page personal statement; 10-20 page academic writing sample; three letters of recommendation. Additional exam requirements/recommendations for international students: Recommended—TOEFL (minimum score 80 iBT), IELTS (minimum score 6.5), TSE (minimum score 54). *Application deadline:* For fall admission, 2/1 for domestic and international students. Application fee: $50. Electronic applications accepted. *Expenses:* Tuition, state resident: full-time $12,887; part-time $537 per credit hour. Tuition, nonresident: full-time $28,449; part-time $1186 per credit hour. *Required fees:* $530; $24 per credit hour. $30 per quarter. Part-time tuition and fees vary according to course load and program. *Financial support:* Fellowships with full and partial tuition reimbursements, research assistantships with full and partial tuition reimbursements, and teaching assistantships with full and partial tuition reimbursements available. Financial award application deadline: 2/1; financial award applicants required to submit FAFSA. *Unit head:* Dr. Weitse de Boer, Department Chair, 513-529-5121, E-mail: deboerwt@miamioh.edu. *Application contact:* Dr. Matthew Gordon, Director of Graduate Studies, 513-529-5128, E-mail: gordonms@miamioh.edu.
Website: http://www.MiamiOH.edu/history/

Michigan State University, The Graduate School, College of Social Science, Department of History, East Lansing, MI 48824. Offers history (MA, PhD); history-secondary school teaching (MA). *Entrance requirements:* Additional exam requirements/recommendations for international students: Required—TOEFL. Electronic applications accepted.

Middle Tennessee State University, College of Graduate Studies, College of Liberal Arts, Department of History, Program in History, Murfreesboro, TN 37132. Offers MA. Part-time and evening/weekend programs available. Postbaccalaureate distance learning degree programs offered. *Faculty:* 37 full-time (19 women), 1 part-time/adjunct (0 women). *Students:* 21 full-time (16 women), 48 part-time (32 women); includes 3 minority (2 Black or African American, non-Hispanic/Latino; 1 Two or more races, non-Hispanic/Latino). In 2014, 17 master's awarded. *Degree requirements:* For master's, one foreign language, comprehensive exam, thesis optional. *Entrance requirements:* For master's, GRE. Additional exam requirements/recommendations for international students: Required—TOEFL (minimum score 525 paper-based; 71 iBT) or IELTS (minimum score 6). *Application deadline:* For fall admission, 6/1 for domestic and international students. Applications are processed on a rolling basis. Application fee: $30. *Financial support:* In 2014–15, 22 students received support. Tuition waivers available. Support available to part-time students. Financial award application deadline: 4/1. *Unit head:* Dr. James Beeby, Chair, 615-898-2536, Fax: 615-898-5881, E-mail: james.beeby@mtsu.edu. *Application contact:* Dr. Michael D. Allen, Vice Provost for Research/Dean, 615-898-2840, Fax: 615-904-8020, E-mail: michael.allen@mtsu.edu.

Midwestern State University, Billie Doris McAda Graduate School, Prothro-Yeager College of Humanities and Social Sciences, Department of History, Wichita Falls, TX 76308. Offers MA. Part-time programs available. *Degree requirements:* For master's, one foreign language, thesis. *Entrance requirements:* For master's, GRE General Test. Additional exam requirements/recommendations for international students: Required—TOEFL (minimum score 550 paper-based). *Application deadline:* For fall admission, 7/1 priority date for domestic students, 4/1 for international students; for spring admission, 11/1 priority date for domestic students, 8/1 for international students. Applications are processed on a rolling basis. Application fee: $35 ($50 for international students). Electronic applications accepted. *Financial support:* Teaching assistantships with partial tuition reimbursements, career-related internships or fieldwork, Federal Work-Study, institutionally sponsored loans, scholarships/grants, and unspecified assistantships available. Support available to part-time students. Financial award application deadline: 3/1; financial award applicants required to submit FAFSA. *Faculty research:* Early modern England, Spanish borderlands, Jacksonian era, New Deal, Texas and the Southwest. *Unit head:* Dr. Harry P. Hewitt, Chair, 940-397-4152, E-mail: harry.hewitt@mwsu.edu. *Application contact:* Kay Hardin, Secretary, 940-397-4258,

Fax: 940-397-4899, E-mail: kay.hardin@mwsu.edu.
Website: http://www.mwsu.edu/academics/libarts/history/index

Millersville University of Pennsylvania, College of Graduate and Professional Studies, School of Humanities and Social Sciences, Department of History, Millersville, PA 17551-0302. Offers MA. Part-time and evening/weekend programs available. *Faculty:* 11 full-time (6 women), 1 part-time/adjunct (0 women). *Students:* 5 full-time (1 woman), 11 part-time (7 women); includes 2 minority (both Black or African American, non-Hispanic/Latino). Average age 29. 7 applicants, 100% accepted, 1 enrolled. In 2014, 8 master's awarded. *Degree requirements:* For master's, comprehensive exam, thesis optional. *Entrance requirements:* For master's, MAT or GRE (preferred) if GPA lower than 2.85, 3 letters of recommendation, writing sample, goal statement, official transcripts. Additional exam requirements/recommendations for international students: Required—TOEFL (minimum score 500 paper-based, 65 iBT) or IELTS (minimum score 6). *Application deadline:* For fall admission, 1/15 priority date for domestic and international students; for winter admission, 6/1 priority date for domestic and international students; for spring admission, 10/1 priority date for domestic and international students. Applications are processed on a rolling basis. Application fee: $40. Electronic applications accepted. *Expenses:* Tuition, state resident: full-time $8172. Tuition, nonresident: full-time $12,258. *Required fees:* $2300. Tuition and fees vary according to course load and program. *Financial support:* In 2014–15, 2 students received support, including 2 research assistantships with full tuition reimbursements available (averaging $3,950 per year); institutionally sponsored loans and unspecified assistantships also available. Support available to part-time students. Financial award application deadline: 3/15; financial award applicants required to submit FAFSA. *Faculty research:* United States, European, and African gender studies; military/diplomatic. *Total annual research expenditures:* $55,220. *Unit head:* Dr. Ronald B. Frankum, Graduate Coordinator, 717-871-7212, Fax: 717-871-7939, E-mail: ronald.frankum@millersville.edu. *Application contact:* Dr. Victor S. DeSantis, Dean of College of Graduate and Professional Studies/Associate Provost for Civic and Community Engagement, 717-871-7619, Fax: 717-871-7954, E-mail: victor.desantis@millersville.edu.
Website: http://www.millersville.edu/history/graduate-program.php

Minnesota State University Mankato, College of Graduate Studies, College of Social and Behavioral Sciences, Department of History, Mankato, MN 56001. Offers history (MA, MS); social studies (MAT). *Students:* 10 part-time (1 woman). *Degree requirements:* For master's, one foreign language, comprehensive exam, thesis or alternative. *Entrance requirements:* For master's, minimum GPA of 3.0 during previous 2 years. Additional exam requirements/recommendations for international students: Required—TOEFL. *Application deadline:* For fall admission, 7/1 priority date for domestic students; for spring admission, 11/1 for domestic students. Applications are processed on a rolling basis. Application fee: $40. Electronic applications accepted. *Financial support:* Research assistantships, teaching assistantships with full tuition reimbursements, career-related internships or fieldwork, Federal Work-Study, institutionally sponsored loans, and unspecified assistantships available. Support available to part-time students. Financial award application deadline: 3/15. *Faculty research:* Charivaris, Lindbergh in the U.S., Dutch trade to South America in the seventeenth and eighteenth centuries. *Unit head:* Dr. Melodie Andrews, Graduate Coordinator, 507-389-1618. *Application contact:* 507-389-2321, E-mail: grad@mnsu.edu.
Website: http://sbs.mnsu.edu/history/

Mississippi College, Graduate School, College of Arts and Sciences, School of Humanities and Social Sciences, Department of History, Political Science, Administration of Justice, and Paralegal Studies, Clinton, MS 39058. Offers administration of justice (MSS); history (M Ed, MA, MSS); paralegal studies (Certificate); political science (MSS); social sciences (M Ed, MSS). Part-time programs available. *Degree requirements:* For master's, one foreign language, comprehensive exam, thesis (for some programs). *Entrance requirements:* For master's, GRE or NTE, minimum GPA of 2.5. Additional exam requirements/recommendations for international students: Recommended—TOEFL, IELTS. Electronic applications accepted.

Mississippi State University, College of Arts and Sciences, Department of History, Mississippi State, MS 39762. Offers U.S. and European history (MA, PhD). Part-time programs available. *Faculty:* 22 full-time (9 women), 1 part-time/adjunct (0 women). *Students:* 46 full-time (17 women), 7 part-time (2 women); includes 5 minority (1 Black or African American, non-Hispanic/Latino; 1 American Indian or Alaska Native, non-Hispanic/Latino; 1 Asian, non-Hispanic/Latino; 1 Hispanic/Latino; 1 Two or more races, non-Hispanic/Latino), 4 international. Average age 29. 31 applicants, 65% accepted, 13 enrolled. In 2014, 7 master's, 2 doctorates awarded. *Degree requirements:* For master's, one foreign language, comprehensive exam, thesis optional; for doctorate, 2 foreign languages, thesis/dissertation, comprehensive oral and written exam. *Entrance requirements:* For master's, minimum GPA of 3.0 on last two years of undergraduate courses; for doctorate, GRE, writing sample, minimum graduate GPA of 3.0. Additional exam requirements/recommendations for international students: Required—TOEFL (minimum score 550 paper-based). *Application deadline:* For fall admission, 4/1 for domestic students, 5/1 for international students; for spring admission, 11/1 for domestic students, 9/1 for international students. Applications are processed on a rolling basis. Application fee: $60. Electronic applications accepted. *Expenses:* Tuition, state resident: full-time $7140; part-time $783 per credit hour. Tuition, nonresident: full-time $18,478; part-time $2043 per credit hour. *Financial support:* In 2014–15, 39 teaching assistantships with full tuition reimbursements (averaging $12,034 per year) were awarded; Federal Work-Study, institutionally sponsored loans, scholarships/grants, and unspecified assistantships also available. Financial award application deadline: 4/1; financial award applicants required to submit FAFSA. *Faculty research:* U.S. political, diplomatic, military, social, and cultural history; modern Europe; Latin America; Asian history; African history. *Unit head:* Dr. Alan I. Marcus, Head, 662-325-3604, Fax: 662-325-1139, E-mail: aim10@msstate.edu. *Application contact:* Dr. Stephen Brain, Graduate Coordinator, 662-325-3604, Fax: 662-325-1139, E-mail: correspondence@history.msstate.edu.
Website: http://www.history.msstate.edu

Missouri State University, Graduate College, College of Humanities and Public Affairs, Department of History, Springfield, MO 65897. Offers MA, MS Ed. Part-time programs available. *Faculty:* 18 full-time (7 women). *Students:* 14 full-time (5 women), 38 part-time (19 women); includes 2 minority (both Hispanic/Latino). Average age 34. 14 applicants, 100% accepted, 8 enrolled. In 2014, 1 master's awarded. *Degree requirements:* For master's, comprehensive exam, thesis or alternative. *Entrance requirements:* For master's, minimum GPA of 2.75, 24 hours of undergraduate course work in history (MA), 9-12 teaching certification (MS Ed). Additional exam requirements/recommendations for international students: Required—TOEFL (minimum score 550 paper-based; 79 iBT). *Application deadline:* For fall admission, 7/20 priority date for domestic students, 5/1 for international students; for spring admission, 12/20 priority date for domestic students, 9/1 for international students. Applications are processed on a rolling basis. Application fee: $35 ($50 for international students). Electronic applications accepted. *Expenses:* Tuition, state resident: full-time $2250; part-time $250 per credit hour. Tuition, nonresident: full-time $4509; part-time $501 per credit hour. Tuition and fees vary according to course level, course load and program. *Financial support:* Federal Work-Study, scholarships/grants, and unspecified assistantships available. Support available to part-time students. Financial award application deadline: 3/31; financial award applicants required to submit FAFSA. *Faculty research:* Early modern France, cultural history of modern Britain, Latin American history, women's history, American Civil War in Missouri. *Unit head:* Dr. Kathleen Kennedy, Head, 417-836-5511, Fax: 417-836-5523, E-mail: history@missouristate.edu. *Application contact:* Misty Stewart, Coordinator of Graduate Recruitment, 417-836-6079, Fax: 417-836-6200, E-mail: mistystewart@missouristate.edu.
Website: http://history.missouristate.edu/

Monmouth University, The Graduate School, Department of History, West Long Branch, NJ 07764-1898. Offers European history (MA); history of the United States (MA); world history (MA). Part-time and evening/weekend programs available. *Faculty:* 9 full-time (3 women). *Students:* 5 full-time (3 women), 37 part-time (14 women); includes 1 minority (Hispanic/Latino). Average age 35. 22 applicants, 100% accepted, 13 enrolled. In 2014, 16 master's awarded. *Degree requirements:* For master's, comprehensive exam (for some programs), thesis (for some programs). *Entrance requirements:* For master's, minimum GPA of 3.0 in major, 2.5 overall; two letters of recommendation; statement of interest areas and goals. Additional exam requirements/recommendations for international students: Required—TOEFL (minimum score 550 paper-based; 79 iBT), IELTS (minimum score 6) or Michigan English Language Assessment Battery (minimum score 77). *Application deadline:* For fall admission, 7/15 priority date for domestic students, 6/1 for international students; for spring admission, 11/15 priority date for domestic students, 11/1 for international students. Applications are processed on a rolling basis. Application fee: $50. Electronic applications accepted. *Expenses: Tuition:* Full-time $18,072; part-time $1004 per credit. *Required fees:* $157 per semester. *Financial support:* In 2014–15, 29 students received support, including 23 fellowships (averaging $2,264 per year), 4 research assistantships (averaging $7,796 per year); career-related internships or fieldwork, scholarships/grants, and unspecified assistantships also available. Support available to part-time students. Financial award applicants required to submit FAFSA. *Faculty research:* U.S. business; labor; British, German, and French Revolutions; Soviet Union; Africa. *Unit head:* Dr. Maryann Rhett, Program Director, 732-263-5768, Fax: 732-263-5112, E-mail: mrhett@monmouth.edu. *Application contact:* Andrea Thompson, Graduate Admission Counselor, 732-571-3452, Fax: 732-263-5123, E-mail: gradadm@monmouth.edu.
Website: http://www.monmouth.edu/school-of-humanities-social-sciences/ma-in-history.aspx

Montana State University, The Graduate School, College of Letters and Science, Department of History, Bozeman, MT 59717. Offers MA, PhD. Part-time programs available. *Degree requirements:* For master's, comprehensive exam; for doctorate, comprehensive exam, thesis/dissertation. *Entrance requirements:* For master's, GRE General Test, transcripts, 3 letters of recommendation, writing sample, statement of interest; for doctorate, GRE General Test, MA, transcripts, 3 letters of recommendation, writing sample, statement of interest. Additional exam requirements/recommendations for international students: Required—TOEFL (minimum score 550 paper-based). Electronic applications accepted. *Faculty research:* Science, environment, technology, American West, science and technology, environmental history, Asian studies.

Montclair State University, The Graduate School, College of Humanities and Social Sciences, MA Program in History, Montclair, NJ 07043-1624. Offers MA, Certificate. Part-time and evening/weekend programs available. *Students:* 1 full-time (0 women), 11 part-time (2 women); includes 3 minority (all Hispanic/Latino). Average age 32. 4 applicants, 75% accepted, 2 enrolled. In 2014, 5 master's awarded. *Degree requirements:* For master's, comprehensive exam. *Entrance requirements:* For master's, GRE General Test, 2 letters of recommendation, essay. Additional exam requirements/recommendations for international students: Required—TOEFL (minimum score 83 iBT) or IELTS (minimum score 6.5). *Application deadline:* For fall admission, 6/1 for international students; for spring admission, 11/1 for international students. Applications are processed on a rolling basis. Application fee: $60. Electronic applications accepted. *Expenses:* Tuition, state resident: full-time $9960; part-time $553.35 per credit. Tuition, nonresident: full-time $15,074; part-time $837.43 per credit. *Required fees:* $1595; $88.63 per credit. Tuition and fees vary according to degree level and program. *Financial support:* In 2014–15, 2 research assistantships with full tuition reimbursements (averaging $7,000 per year), 1 teaching assistantship (averaging $7,000 per year) were awarded; Federal Work-Study, scholarships/grants, and unspecified assistantships also available. Support available to part-time students. Financial award application deadline: 3/1; financial award applicants required to submit FAFSA. *Faculty research:* Social history, gender, war and memory, political economy, political history. *Unit head:* Dr. Michael Whelan, Chairperson, 973-655-7848. *Application contact:* Amy Aiello, Director of Admissions and Operations, 973-655-5147, Fax: 973-655-7869, E-mail: graduate.school@montclair.edu.

Morgan State University, School of Graduate Studies, College of Liberal Arts, Department of History and Geography, Baltimore, MD 21251. Offers African-American studies (MA); history (MA, PhD); museum studies and historic preservation (MA). Part-time and evening/weekend programs available. *Degree requirements:* For master's, comprehensive exam, thesis; for doctorate, comprehensive exam, thesis/dissertation. *Entrance requirements:* For master's, minimum GPA of 2.5; for doctorate, GRE or MAT. Additional exam requirements/recommendations for international students: Required—TOEFL (minimum score 550 paper-based). *Faculty research:* Women's history, African diaspora history, urban history.

Murray State University, College of Humanities and Fine Arts, Program in History, Murray, KY 42071. Offers MA. Part-time programs available. *Degree requirements:* For master's, one foreign language, comprehensive exam, thesis (for some programs). *Entrance requirements:* For master's, GRE General Test. Additional exam requirements/recommendations for international students: Required—TOEFL.

National University, Academic Affairs, College of Letters and Sciences, La Jolla, CA 92037-1011. Offers applied linguistics (MA); biology (MS); counseling psychology (MA), including licensed professional clinical counseling, marriage and family therapy; creative writing (MFA); English (MA), including Gothic studies, rhetoric; film studies (MA); forensic and crime science (Certificate); forensic studies (MFS), including criminalistics, investigation; history (MA); human behavior (MA); mathematics for educators (MS); performance psychology (MA); strategic communications (MA). Part-time and evening/weekend programs available. Postbaccalaureate distance learning degree programs offered (no on-campus study). *Faculty:* 69 full-time (34 women), 100 part-time/adjunct (55 women). *Students:* 727 full-time (532 women), 349 part-time (240 women); includes 505 minority (128 Black or African American, non-Hispanic/Latino; 5 American Indian or Alaska Native, non-Hispanic/Latino; 52 Asian, non-Hispanic/Latino; 260 Hispanic/Latino; 9 Native Hawaiian or other Pacific Islander, non-Hispanic/Latino; 51 Two or more races, non-Hispanic/Latino), 4 international. Average age 34. In 2014, 569 master's awarded. *Degree requirements:* For master's, thesis (for some programs). *Entrance requirements:* For master's, interview, minimum GPA of 2.5. Additional exam requirements/recommendations for international students: Required—TOEFL (minimum score 550 paper-based; 79 iBT), IELTS (minimum score 6). *Application deadline:* Applications are processed on a rolling basis. Application fee: $60 ($65 for international students).

Electronic applications accepted. *Expenses: Tuition:* Full-time $14,184; part-time $1773 per course. *Financial support:* Career-related internships or fieldwork, institutionally sponsored loans, scholarships/grants, and tuition waivers (partial) available. Support available to part-time students. Financial award application deadline: 6/30; financial award applicants required to submit FAFSA. *Unit head:* College of Letters and Sciences, 800-628-8648, E-mail: cols@nu.edu. *Application contact:* Frank Rojas, Interim Vice President for Enrollment Services, 800-628-8648, E-mail: advisor@nu.edu.
Website: http://www.nu.edu/OurPrograms/CollegeOfLettersAndSciences.html

Nebraska Wesleyan University, University College, Program in Historical Studies, Lincoln, NE 68504-2796. Offers MA. Part-time programs available. *Expenses:* Contact institution.

New Jersey Institute of Technology, College of Science and Liberal Arts, Newark, NJ 07102. Offers applied mathematics (MS); applied physics (M Sc, PhD); applied statistics (MS); biology (MS, PhD); biostatistics (MS); chemistry (MS, PhD); computational biology (MS); environmental science (MS, PhD); history (MA, MAT); materials science and engineering (MS, PhD); mathematical and computational finance (MS); mathematics science (PhD); pharmaceutical chemistry (MS); professional and technical communications (MS). Part-time and evening/weekend programs available. Terminal master's awarded for partial completion of doctoral program. *Degree requirements:* For master's, thesis optional; for doctorate, thesis/dissertation. *Entrance requirements:* For master's, GRE General Test; for doctorate, GRE General Test, minimum graduate GPA of 3.5. Additional exam requirements/recommendations for international students: Required—TOEFL (minimum score 550 paper-based; 79 iBT). Electronic applications accepted.

New Mexico Highlands University, Graduate Studies, College of Arts and Sciences, Department of History, Political Science, and Languages and Culture, Las Vegas, NM 87701. Offers public affairs (MA), including historical and cross-cultural perspectives, history/political science, political and governmental processes. *Faculty:* 9 full-time (3 women), 1 part-time/adjunct (0 women). *Students:* 13 full-time (6 women), 12 part-time (1 woman); includes 15 minority (all Hispanic/Latino), 5 international. Average age 34. 12 applicants, 100% accepted, 4 enrolled. In 2014, 1 master's awarded. *Degree requirements:* For master's, comprehensive exam, thesis or alternative. *Entrance requirements:* Additional exam requirements/recommendations for international students: Required—TOEFL (minimum score 540 paper-based). *Application deadline:* For fall admission, 8/1 priority date for domestic students. Applications are processed on a rolling basis. Application fee: $15. *Financial support:* In 2014–15, 11 teaching assistantships were awarded; research assistantships, career-related internships or fieldwork, Federal Work-Study, institutionally sponsored loans, scholarships/grants, traineeships, tuition waivers (full and partial), and unspecified assistantships also available. Support available to part-time students. Financial award application deadline: 3/1. *Unit head:* Dr. Steven Williams, Associate Professor, 505-454-3435. *Application contact:* Diane Trujillo, Administrative Assistant, Graduate Studies, 505-454-3266, Fax: 505-426-2117, E-mail: dtrujillo@nmhu.edu.
Website: http://www.nmhu.edu/current-students/graduate/arts-and-sciences/history-political-science-languages-and-culture/

New Mexico State University, College of Arts and Sciences, Department of History, Las Cruces, NM 88003. Offers history (MA); public history (MA). Part-time programs available. *Faculty:* 12 full-time (6 women), 1 part-time/adjunct (0 women). *Students:* 25 full-time (6 women), 19 part-time (8 women); includes 17 minority (1 Asian, non-Hispanic/Latino; 12 Hispanic/Latino; 4 Two or more races, non-Hispanic/Latino), 1 international. Average age 33. 19 applicants, 58% accepted, 8 enrolled. In 2014, 8 master's awarded. *Degree requirements:* For master's, one foreign language, comprehensive exam, thesis (for some programs). *Entrance requirements:* For master's, 12 undergraduate history credits, writing sample, minimum GPA of 3.0. Additional exam requirements/recommendations for international students: Required—TOEFL (minimum score 550 paper-based; 79 iBT), IELTS (minimum score 6.5). *Application deadline:* For fall admission, 7/1 priority date for domestic students; for spring admission, 11/1 for domestic students. Applications are processed on a rolling basis. Application fee: $40 ($50 for international students). Electronic applications accepted. *Expenses:* Tuition, state resident: full-time $3969; part-time $220.50 per credit hour. Tuition, nonresident: full-time $13,838; part-time $768.80 per credit hour. *Required fees:* $853; $47.40 per credit hour. *Financial support:* In 2014–15, 17 students received support, including 9 teaching assistantships (averaging $12,558 per year); career-related internships or fieldwork, Federal Work-Study, scholarships/grants, traineeships, health care benefits, and unspecified assistantships also available. Support available to part-time students. Financial award application deadline: 3/1. *Faculty research:* U.S. Southwestern and border history, Latin American history, U.S. women's history, European history, history of science, public history, East Asian history. *Total annual research expenditures:* $6,223. *Unit head:* Dr. Kenneth Hammond, Academic Department Head, 575-646-4601, Fax: 575-646-6096, E-mail: khammond@nmsu.edu. *Application contact:* Dr. Liz Horodowich, Director of Graduate Studies, 575-646-1515, Fax: 575-646-6096, E-mail: lizh@nmsu.edu.
Website: http://history.nmsu.edu

The New School, The New School for Social Research, Department in Historical Studies, New York, NY 10003. Offers MA, PhD. Part-time and evening/weekend programs available. Terminal master's awarded for partial completion of doctoral program. *Degree requirements:* For master's, thesis; for doctorate, comprehensive exam, thesis/dissertation, qualifying exam. *Entrance requirements:* For master's, GRE General Test; for doctorate, GRE General Test, MA. Additional exam requirements/recommendations for international students: Required—TOEFL (minimum score 600 paper-based; 100 iBT). Electronic applications accepted.

New York University, Graduate School of Arts and Science, Department of History, New York, NY 10012-1019. Offers African diaspora (PhD); African history (PhD); archival management (Advanced Certificate); Atlantic history (PhD); French studies/history (PhD); Hebrew and Judaic studies/history (PhD); history (MA, PhD), including Europe (PhD), Latin America and the Caribbean (PhD), United States (PhD), women's history (MA); Middle Eastern history (MA); Middle Eastern studies/history (PhD); public history (Advanced Certificate); world history (MA); JD/MA; MA/Advanced Certificate. Part-time programs available. *Faculty:* 43 full-time (19 women). *Students:* 120 full-time (72 women), 43 part-time (29 women); includes 33 minority (15 Black or African American, non-Hispanic/Latino; 1 American Indian or Alaska Native, non-Hispanic/Latino; 4 Asian, non-Hispanic/Latino; 9 Hispanic/Latino; 4 Two or more races, non-Hispanic/Latino), 41 international. Average age 29. 401 applicants, 31% accepted, 38 enrolled. In 2014, 24 master's, 16 doctorates awarded. Terminal master's awarded for partial completion of doctoral program. *Degree requirements:* For master's, seminar paper; for doctorate, one foreign language, thesis/dissertation, oral and written exams; for Advanced Certificate, internship. *Entrance requirements:* For master's, GRE General Test, minimum GPA of 3.0, writing sample; for doctorate, GRE. Additional exam requirements/recommendations for international students: Required—TOEFL. *Application deadline:* For fall admission, 12/18 for domestic and international students. Application fee: $100. *Financial support:* Fellowships with tuition reimbursements, research assistantships, teaching assistantships with tuition reimbursements, career-related internships or fieldwork, Federal Work-Study, institutionally sponsored loans, scholarships/grants, health care benefits, and unspecified assistantships available. Financial award application deadline: 12/18; financial award applicants required to submit FAFSA. *Faculty research:* African, East Asian, medieval, early modern, and modern European history; U.S. history; African and African diaspora; Latin American history; Atlantic world. *Unit head:* Barbara Weinstein, Chair, 212-998-8600, Fax: 212-995-4017, E-mail: history.admissions@nyu.edu. *Application contact:* Stepfanos Geroulanos, Director of Graduate Studies, 212-998-8600, Fax: 212-995-4017, E-mail: history.admissions@nyu.edu.
Website: http://history.as.nyu.edu/

New York University, Graduate School of Arts and Science, Institute for the Study of the Ancient World, New York, NY 10012-1019. Offers PhD. *Students:* 16 full-time (7 women); includes 3 minority (1 Asian, non-Hispanic/Latino; 1 Hispanic/Latino; 1 Two or more races, non-Hispanic/Latino), 10 international. Average age 31. 50 applicants, 10% accepted, 1 enrolled. *Degree requirements:* For doctorate, 4 foreign languages, comprehensive exam, thesis/dissertation, fieldwork, teaching experience. *Entrance requirements:* For doctorate, GRE General Test. *Application deadline:* For fall admission, 1/4 for domestic and international students. Application fee: $100. Electronic applications accepted. *Financial support:* Fellowships and stipends available. Financial award application deadline: 1/4; financial award applicants required to submit FAFSA. *Unit head:* Dr. Roger Bagnall, Director, 212-992-7843, Fax: 212-992-7809, E-mail: isaw@nyu.edu. *Application contact:* Marc Leblanc, Graduate Department Administrator, 212-992-7843, Fax: 212-992-7809, E-mail: isaw@nyu.edu.

North Carolina Central University, College of Liberal Arts, Department of History, Durham, NC 27707-3129. Offers MA. Part-time and evening/weekend programs available. *Degree requirements:* For master's, one foreign language, comprehensive exam, thesis. *Entrance requirements:* For master's, GRE, minimum GPA of 3.0 in major, 2.5 overall. Additional exam requirements/recommendations for international students: Required—TOEFL.

North Carolina State University, Graduate School, College of Humanities and Social Sciences, Department of History, Raleigh, NC 27695. Offers history (MA); public history (MA). Part-time and evening/weekend programs available. *Degree requirements:* For master's, thesis. *Entrance requirements:* For master's, GRE General Test. Electronic applications accepted. *Faculty research:* History of the United States, Europe, Asia Africa and the Middle East; history of science; intellectual, cultural, social, environmental and political history.

North Dakota State University, College of Graduate and Interdisciplinary Studies, College of Arts, Humanities and Social Sciences, Department of History, Fargo, ND 58108. Offers MA, MS, PhD. Part-time and evening/weekend programs available. *Degree requirements:* For master's, one foreign language, comprehensive exam, thesis optional; for doctorate, 2 foreign languages, comprehensive exam, thesis/dissertation. *Entrance requirements:* For master's and doctorate, GRE General Test. Additional exam requirements/recommendations for international students: Required—TOEFL (minimum score 600 paper-based; 100 iBT). Electronic applications accepted. *Faculty research:* Recent U.S., modern English, early modern European, North Dakota, Latin American, and Great Plains history.

Northeastern Illinois University, College of Graduate Studies and Research, College of Arts and Sciences, Program in History, Chicago, IL 60625-4699. Offers MA. Part-time and evening/weekend programs available. *Degree requirements:* For master's, comprehensive exam, thesis optional. *Entrance requirements:* For master's, 24 undergraduate hours in history, minimum GPA of 2.75. Additional exam requirements/recommendations for international students: Required—TOEFL (minimum score 550 paper-based; 79 iBT). Electronic applications accepted. *Faculty research:* Africa; East Asia; European medieval, early-modern, and modern history; U.S. social, cultural, and intellectual history.

Northeastern University, College of Social Sciences and Humanities, Boston, MA 02115. Offers criminology and criminal justice (MSCJ); criminology and justice policy (PhD); economics (MA, PhD); English (MA, PhD); law and public policy (MS, PhD); political science (MA, PhD); public administration (MPA); public history (MA); security and resilience studies (MS); sociology (MA, PhD); urban and regional policy (MS); world history (MA, PhD). *Degree requirements:* For doctorate, variable foreign language requirement, comprehensive exam, thesis/dissertation. *Entrance requirements:* For master's and doctorate, GRE. Additional exam requirements/recommendations for international students: Required—TOEFL, IELTS. Electronic applications accepted.

Northern Arizona University, Graduate College, College of Arts and Letters, Department of History, Flagstaff, AZ 86011. Offers MA. Part-time programs available. *Degree requirements:* For master's, thesis (for some programs), thesis or departmental qualifying exam. *Entrance requirements:* For master's, GRE General Test. Additional exam requirements/recommendations for international students: Required—TOEFL (minimum score 550 paper-based; 80 iBT), IELTS (minimum score 7). Electronic applications accepted. *Faculty research:* Twentieth-century United States, U.S. trans-Mississippi West, Arizona and the Southwest, women's history, U.S. intellectual history.

Northern Illinois University, Graduate School, College of Liberal Arts and Sciences, Department of History, De Kalb, IL 60115-2854. Offers MA, PhD. Part-time programs available. *Faculty:* 18 full-time (8 women), 2 part-time/adjunct (0 women). *Students:* 23 full-time (12 women), 29 part-time (11 women). Average age 33. 53 applicants, 58% accepted, 11 enrolled. In 2014, 9 master's, 6 doctorates awarded. Terminal master's awarded for partial completion of doctoral program. *Degree requirements:* For master's, variable foreign language requirement, comprehensive exam, thesis optional, research seminars; for doctorate, variable foreign language requirement, thesis/dissertation, candidacy exam, dissertation defense, research seminars. *Entrance requirements:* For master's, GRE General Test, minimum GPA of 2.75; for doctorate, GRE General Test, minimum undergraduate GPA of 2.75, graduate 3.2. Additional exam requirements/recommendations for international students: Required—TOEFL (minimum score 550 paper-based). *Application deadline:* For fall admission, 6/1 for domestic students, 5/1 for international students; for spring admission, 11/1 for domestic students, 10/1 for international students. Applications are processed on a rolling basis. Application fee: $40. Electronic applications accepted. *Financial support:* In 2014–15, 16 teaching assistantships with full tuition reimbursements were awarded; fellowships with full tuition reimbursements, research assistantships with full tuition reimbursements, career-related internships or fieldwork, Federal Work-Study, scholarships/grants, tuition waivers (full), and unspecified assistantships also available. Support available to part-time students. Financial award applicants required to submit FAFSA. *Faculty research:* History of the Carolingian empire, history of early modern Europe, modern Irish history, history of the Ming dynasty. *Unit head:* Dr. James Schmidt, Chair, 815-753-6810, Fax: 815-753-6302, E-mail: jschmidt@niu.edu. *Application contact:* Dr. Anne G. Hanley, Assistant Chair/Director of Graduate Studies, 815-753-6695, E-mail: ahanley@niu.edu.
Website: http://www.niu.edu/history/

Northwestern University, The Graduate School, Judd A. and Marjorie Weinberg College of Arts and Sciences, Department of History, Evanston, IL 60208. Offers PhD, JD/PhD. Admissions and degrees offered through The Graduate School. *Degree requirements:* For doctorate, variable foreign language requirement, thesis/dissertation, major and minor field exams. *Entrance requirements:* For doctorate, sample of written

work. Additional exam requirements/recommendations for international students: Required—TOEFL. Electronic applications accepted. *Faculty research:* Medieval and early modern Europe, Africa, race and slavery, Atlantic history, gender.

Northwestern University, School of Professional Studies, Program in Liberal Studies, Evanston, IL 60208. Offers American studies (MA); history (MA); religious and ethical studies (MA).

Northwest Missouri State University, Graduate School, College of Arts and Sciences, Department of History, Humanities, and Political Science, Maryville, MO 64468-6001. Offers geographic information systems (MS, Certificate); history (MA); teaching history (MS Ed). Part-time programs available. *Degree requirements:* For master's, comprehensive exam, thesis. *Entrance requirements:* For master's, GRE General Test, undergraduate major/minor in social studies/humanities, minimum undergraduate GPA of 2.5, writing sample. Additional exam requirements/recommendations for international students: Required—TOEFL (minimum score 550 paper-based). *Application deadline:* For fall admission, 7/1 for domestic and international students; for spring admission, 11/15 for domestic and international students. Applications are processed on a rolling basis. Application fee: $0 ($50 for international students). *Expenses:* Tuition, state resident: full-time $4464; part-time $346 per credit hour. Tuition, nonresident: full-time $8920; part-time $593 per credit hour. *Required fees:* $1763; $98 per credit hour. *Financial support:* Research assistantships with full tuition reimbursements and teaching assistantships with full tuition reimbursements available. Financial award application deadline: 4/1; financial award applicants required to submit FAFSA. *Unit head:* Dr. Joel Benson, Chair, 660-562-1288.
Website: http://www.nwmissouri.edu/socialsciences/

Norwich University, College of Graduate and Continuing Studies, Master of Arts in History Program, Northfield, VT 05663. Offers American history (MA); world history (MA). Evening/weekend programs available. Postbaccalaureate distance learning degree programs offered (minimal on-campus study). *Faculty:* 10 part-time/adjunct (2 women). *Students:* 61 full-time (29 women); includes 6 minority (1 Black or African American, non-Hispanic/Latino; 2 American Indian or Alaska Native, non-Hispanic/Latino; 1 Asian, non-Hispanic/Latino; 1 Native Hawaiian or other Pacific Islander, non-Hispanic/Latino; 1 Two or more races, non-Hispanic/Latino). Average age 38. 39 applicants, 95% accepted, 33 enrolled. In 2014, 3 master's awarded. *Degree requirements:* For master's, thesis optional. *Entrance requirements:* For master's, minimum undergraduate GPA of 2.75. Additional exam requirements/recommendations for international students: Required—TOEFL (minimum score 550 paper-based; 80 iBT), IELTS (minimum score 6.5). *Application deadline:* For fall admission, 8/8 for domestic and international students; for winter admission, 11/7 for domestic and international students; for spring admission, 2/16 for domestic and international students; for summer admission, 5/18 for domestic and international students. Applications are processed on a rolling basis. Electronic applications accepted. *Expenses:* Expenses: Contact institution. *Financial support:* In 2014–15, 21 students received support. Scholarships/grants available. Financial award applicants required to submit FAFSA. *Unit head:* Dr. James Ehrman, Program Director, 802-485-2885, Fax: 802-485-2533, E-mail: jehrman@norwich.edu. *Application contact:* Lars Nielsen, Associate Program Director, 802-485-2853, Fax: 802-485-2533, E-mail: lnielsen@norwich.edu.
Website: http://online.norwich.edu/degree-programs/masters/master-arts-history/overview

Oakland University, Graduate Study and Lifelong Learning, College of Arts and Sciences, Department of History, Rochester, MI 48309-4401. Offers MA. Part-time and evening/weekend programs available. *Entrance requirements:* For master's, minimum GPA of 3.0. Additional exam requirements/recommendations for international students: Required—TOEFL (minimum score 550 paper-based). Electronic applications accepted.

The Ohio State University, Graduate School, College of Arts and Sciences, Division of Arts and Humanities, Department of History, Columbus, OH 43210. Offers MA, PhD. *Faculty:* 67. *Students:* 120 full-time (49 women), 2 part-time (1 woman); includes 22 minority (8 Black or African American, non-Hispanic/Latino; 1 American Indian or Alaska Native, non-Hispanic/Latino; 4 Asian, non-Hispanic/Latino; 7 Hispanic/Latino; 2 Two or more races, non-Hispanic/Latino), 13 international. Average age 29. In 2014, 9 master's, 17 doctorates awarded. Terminal master's awarded for partial completion of doctoral program. *Degree requirements:* For master's, thesis optional; for doctorate, variable foreign language requirement, thesis/dissertation. *Entrance requirements:* For master's and doctorate, GRE General Test (for domestic applicants only; strongly recommended for international applicants). Additional exam requirements/recommendations for international students: Required—TOEFL (minimum score 550 paper-based; 79 iBT). *Application deadline:* For fall admission, 12/1 priority date for domestic students, 11/30 priority date for international students; for winter admission, 12/1 for domestic students, 11/1 for international students; for spring admission, 3/1 for domestic students, 2/1 for international students. Applications are processed on a rolling basis. Application fee: $60 ($70 for international students). Electronic applications accepted. *Financial support:* Fellowships with tuition reimbursements, research assistantships with tuition reimbursements, teaching assistantships with tuition reimbursements, Federal Work-Study, institutionally sponsored loans, and unspecified assistantships available. Support available to part-time students. *Unit head:* Dr. Peter L. Hahn, Chair, 614-292-3001, E-mail: hahn.29@osu.edu. *Application contact:* Graduate and Professional Admissions, 614-292-9444, Fax: 614-292-3895, E-mail: gpadmissions@osu.edu.
Website: http://history.osu.edu/

Ohio University, Graduate College, College of Arts and Sciences, Department of History, Athens, OH 45701-2979. Offers MA, PhD. *Degree requirements:* For master's, one foreign language, thesis optional; for doctorate, 2 foreign languages, comprehensive exam, thesis/dissertation. *Entrance requirements:* For master's, GRE, minimum GPA of 3.0; for doctorate, GRE, minimum GPA of 3.0, MA. Additional exam requirements/recommendations for international students: Required—TOEFL (minimum score 550 paper-based; 80 iBT) or IELTS (minimum score 6.5). Electronic applications accepted. *Faculty research:* U.S. foreign relations, modern Europe, Latin America, southeast Asia, U.S. women.

Oklahoma State University, College of Arts and Sciences, Department of History, Stillwater, OK 74078. Offers MA, PhD. *Faculty:* 25 full-time (7 women), 2 part-time/adjunct (1 woman). *Students:* 13 full-time (4 women), 46 part-time (15 women); includes 8 minority (1 Black or African American, non-Hispanic/Latino; 4 American Indian or Alaska Native, non-Hispanic/Latino; 1 Hispanic/Latino; 2 Two or more races, non-Hispanic/Latino), 1 international. Average age 34. 21 applicants, 71% accepted, 5 enrolled. In 2014, 9 master's, 6 doctorates awarded. *Degree requirements:* For master's, thesis; for doctorate, comprehensive exam, thesis/dissertation. *Entrance requirements:* For master's and doctorate, GRE. Additional exam requirements/recommendations for international students: Required—TOEFL (minimum score 550 paper-based; 79 iBT). *Application deadline:* For fall admission, 3/1 priority date for international students; for spring admission, 8/1 priority date for international students. Applications are processed on a rolling basis. Application fee: $40 ($75 for international students). Electronic applications accepted. *Expenses:* Tuition, state resident: full-time $4488; part-time $187 per credit hour. Tuition, nonresident: full-time $18,360; part-time $765 per credit hour. *Required fees:* $2413; $100.55 per credit hour. Tuition and fees vary according to campus/location. *Financial support:* In 2014–15, 23 teaching assistantships (averaging $15,992 per year) were awarded; career-related internships or fieldwork, Federal Work-Study, scholarships/grants, health care benefits, tuition waivers (partial), and unspecified assistantships also available. Support available to part-time students. Financial award application deadline: 3/1; financial award applicants required to submit FAFSA. *Faculty research:* U.S. history, the American West, Native American history, modern European history, women's history. *Unit head:* Dr. Laura Belmonte, Head, 405-744-8182, Fax: 405-744-5400, E-mail: laura.belmonte@okstate.edu. *Application contact:* Dr. David M. D'Andrea, Associate Professor and Director of Graduate Studies, 405-744-8195, Fax: 405-744-5400, E-mail: david.dandrea@okstate.edu.
Website: http://history.okstate.edu/

Old Dominion University, College of Arts and Letters, Program in History, Norfolk, VA 23529. Offers MA. Part-time and evening/weekend programs available. *Faculty:* 16 full-time (9 women), 1 part-time/adjunct (0 women). *Students:* 15 full-time (6 women), 26 part-time (6 women); includes 4 minority (2 Black or African American, non-Hispanic/Latino; 1 Hispanic/Latino; 1 Two or more races, non-Hispanic/Latino). Average age 33. 41 applicants, 80% accepted, 20 enrolled. In 2014, 11 master's awarded. *Degree requirements:* For master's, comprehensive exam, thesis optional. *Entrance requirements:* For master's, GRE General Test, 24 credits in history with minimum GPA of 3.0. Additional exam requirements/recommendations for international students: Recommended—TOEFL. *Application deadline:* For fall admission, 4/1 for domestic students; for spring admission, 11/1 for domestic students. Applications are processed on a rolling basis. Application fee: $50. Electronic applications accepted. *Expenses:* Tuition, state resident: full-time $10,488; part-time $437 per credit. Tuition, nonresident: full-time $26,136; part-time $1089 per credit. *Required fees:* $64 per semester. One-time fee: $50. *Financial support:* In 2014–15, 7 students received support, including 6 teaching assistantships (averaging $10,000 per year); career-related internships or fieldwork, scholarships/grants, and unspecified assistantships also available. Support available to part-time students. Financial award application deadline: 2/15; financial award applicants required to submit FAFSA. *Faculty research:* History: maritime, American, European, modern Asian, and African. *Unit head:* Dr. Michael C. Carhart, Graduate Program Director, 757-683-3949, Fax: 757-683-5644, E-mail: histgpd@odu.edu. *Application contact:* Dr. David C. Earnest, Associate Dean, 757-683-6077, Fax: 757-683-5746, E-mail: dearnest@odu.edu.
Website: http://al.odu.edu/history/

Penn State University Park, Graduate School, College of the Liberal Arts, Department of History, University Park, PA 16802. Offers MA, PhD. *Unit head:* Dr. Susan Welch, Dean, 814-865-7691, Fax: 814-863-2085, E-mail: swelch@psu.edu. *Application contact:* Lori A. Stania, Director, Graduate Student Services, 814-867-5278, Fax: 814-863-4627, E-mail: gswww@psu.edu.
Website: http://history.psu.edu/

Pittsburg State University, Graduate School, College of Arts and Sciences, Department of History, Pittsburg, KS 66762. Offers MA. *Degree requirements:* For master's, thesis or alternative.

Pontifical Catholic University of Puerto Rico, College of Arts and Humanities, Department of History, Ponce, PR 00717-0777. Offers MA. *Entrance requirements:* For master's, GRE General Test, minimum GPA of 2.75, 2 letters of recommendation.

Portland State University, Graduate Studies, College of Liberal Arts and Sciences, Department of History, Portland, OR 97207-0751. Offers MA. Part-time programs available. *Faculty:* 21 full-time (5 women), 6 part-time/adjunct (4 women). *Students:* 22 full-time (11 women), 21 part-time (12 women); includes 8 minority (2 American Indian or Alaska Native, non-Hispanic/Latino; 2 Asian, non-Hispanic/Latino; 3 Hispanic/Latino; 1 Two or more races, non-Hispanic/Latino). Average age 33. 35 applicants, 54% accepted, 13 enrolled. In 2014, 3 master's awarded. *Degree requirements:* For master's, one foreign language, comprehensive exam, thesis, oral and written exams. *Entrance requirements:* For master's, GRE General Test, minimum GPA of 3.5 in upper-division history courses, 2 letters of recommendation, BA/BS in history, statement of intent, writing samples. Additional exam requirements/recommendations for international students: Required—TOEFL (minimum score 550 paper-based; 80 iBT). *Application deadline:* For fall admission, 2/15 for domestic and international students; for winter admission, 9/1 for domestic students, 6/1 for international students; for spring admission, 11/1 for domestic and international students; for summer admission, 2/1 for domestic and international students. Application fee: $50. Electronic applications accepted. *Expenses:* Tuition, state resident: part-time $222 per credit. Tuition, nonresident: part-time $527 per credit. *Required fees:* $22 per contact hour. $100 per quarter. Tuition and fees vary according to program. *Financial support:* In 2014–15, 1 research assistantship with full tuition reimbursement (averaging $14,000 per year), 6 teaching assistantships with full and partial tuition reimbursements (averaging $2,190 per year) were awarded; career-related internships or fieldwork, Federal Work-Study, scholarships/grants, and unspecified assistantships also available. Support available to part-time students. Financial award application deadline: 3/1; financial award applicants required to submit FAFSA. *Faculty research:* Germany and modern Europe, early modern France and England, Mexico in the 1920's, eighteenth century France, Reformation, U.S. cultural history. *Total annual research expenditures:* $34,937. *Unit head:* Dr. Tim Garrison, Chair, 503-725-3978, Fax: 503-725-3953, E-mail: timgarrison@pdx.edu. *Application contact:* Dr. Richard Beyler, Graduate Coordinator, 503-725-3996, Fax: 503-725-3953, E-mail: r.beyler@pdx.edu.
Website: http://www.pdx.edu/history/

Princeton University, Graduate School, Department of Classics, Princeton, NJ 08544-1019. Offers classical and hellenic studies (PhD); classical philosophy (PhD); history (the ancient world) (PhD); literature and philology (PhD). *Degree requirements:* For doctorate, thesis/dissertation. *Entrance requirements:* For doctorate, GRE General Test, sample of written work. Additional exam requirements/recommendations for international students: Required—TOEFL (minimum score 600 paper-based). Electronic applications accepted.

Princeton University, Graduate School, Department of History, Princeton, NJ 08544-1019. Offers history (PhD); history of science (PhD). *Degree requirements:* For doctorate, variable foreign language requirement, comprehensive exam, thesis/dissertation. *Entrance requirements:* For doctorate, GRE General Test, sample of written work. Additional exam requirements/recommendations for international students: Required—TOEFL (minimum score 600 paper-based). Electronic applications accepted. *Faculty research:* World comparative, Europe-early modern, modern, late antique, medieval.

Providence College, Department of History, Providence, RI 02918. Offers American history (MA); modern European history (MA). Part-time and evening/weekend programs available. *Faculty:* 16 full-time (8 women), 2 part-time/adjunct (1 woman). *Students:* 15 full-time (6 women), 29 part-time (7 women); includes 2 minority (both Black or African American, non-Hispanic/Latino). 19 applicants, 100% accepted, 17 enrolled. In 2014, 18 master's awarded. *Degree requirements:* For master's, comprehensive exam, thesis optional. *Entrance requirements:* Additional exam requirements/recommendations for international students: Required—TOEFL (minimum score 577 paper-based; 90 iBT). *Application deadline:* For fall admission, 8/1 priority date for domestic and international students; for spring admission, 12/31 priority date for domestic students, 12/1 priority

date for international students. Applications are processed on a rolling basis. Application fee: $55. *Expenses: Tuition:* Part-time $390 per credit. *Financial support:* Career-related internships or fieldwork, institutionally sponsored loans, and unspecified assistantships available. Support available to part-time students. Financial award application deadline: 8/1; financial award applicants required to submit FAFSA. *Faculty research:* American history, Native American history, religion, slavery, Western civilization, labor movements, Japanese and Asian history, Early Modern Europe. *Unit head:* Dr. Paul O'Malley, Program Director, 401-865-2192, Fax: 401-865-1193, E-mail: pomalley@providence.edu. *Application contact:* Phyllis S. Cardullo, Senior Administrative Coordinator, 401-865-2193, Fax: 401-865-1193, E-mail: pcardull@providence.edu.
Website: http://www.providence.edu/history/

Purdue University, Graduate School, College of Liberal Arts, Department of History, West Lafayette, IN 47907. Offers MA, PhD. Part-time programs available. *Degree requirements:* For master's, thesis optional; for doctorate, one foreign language, thesis/dissertation. *Entrance requirements:* For master's, GRE General Test, minimum undergraduate GPA of 3.0 or equivalent; for doctorate, GRE General Test, minimum undergraduate GPA of 3.0 or equivalent; master's degree with minimum GPA of 3.0 or equivalent. Additional exam requirements/recommendations for international students: Required—TOEFL (minimum score 550 paper-based; 77 iBT), TWE. Electronic applications accepted. *Faculty research:* U.S. history, early modern and modern European history, global women's history, U.S. minority history, medieval history.

Purdue University Calumet, Graduate Studies Office, School of Liberal Arts and Social Sciences, Department of History and Political Science, Hammond, IN 46323-2094. Offers history (MA). Part-time and evening/weekend programs available. *Entrance requirements:* Additional exam requirements/recommendations for international students: Required—TOEFL. *Faculty research:* Mid-east, German history, U. S. regional history, U. S. social history, Holocaust.

Queens College of the City University of New York, Division of Graduate Studies, Social Science Division, Department of History, Flushing, NY 11367-1597. Offers MA. Part-time and evening/weekend programs available. *Degree requirements:* For master's, one foreign language, comprehensive exam, thesis. *Entrance requirements:* For master's, minimum GPA of 3.0. Additional exam requirements/recommendations for international students: Required—TOEFL.

Regent University, Graduate School, School of Divinity, Virginia Beach, VA 23464-9800. Offers leadership and renewal (D Min), including Christian leadership and renewal, clinical pastoral education, community transformation, military ministry, ministry leadership coaching; practical theology (M Div, MA), including Biblical studies (M Div, MTS, PhD), chaplain ministry (M Div), Christian theology (M Div, MTS, PhD), church and ministry, history of Christianity (M Div, MTS), inter-cultural studies, interdisciplinary studies (M Div, MA, MTS), worship and renewal; renewal studies (PhD), including Biblical studies (M Div, MTS, PhD), Christian theology (M Div, MTS, PhD), history of global Christianity; theological studies (MTS), including Biblical studies (M Div, MTS, PhD), Christian theology (M Div, MTS, PhD), history of Christianity (M Div, MTS), interdisciplinary studies (M Div, MA, MTS). *Accreditation:* ACIPE; ATS. Part-time programs available. Postbaccalaureate distance learning degree programs offered (minimal on-campus study). *Faculty:* 20 full-time (3 women), 29 part-time/adjunct (3 women). *Students:* 64 full-time (28 women), 616 part-time (258 women); includes 318 minority (269 Black or African American, non-Hispanic/Latino; 7 American Indian or Alaska Native, non-Hispanic/Latino; 16 Asian, non-Hispanic/Latino; 26 Hispanic/Latino), 37 international. Average age 43. 511 applicants, 52% accepted, 187 enrolled. In 2014, 121 master's, 24 doctorates awarded. *Degree requirements:* For master's, comprehensive exam, thesis or alternative, internship; for doctorate, thesis/dissertation or alternative. *Entrance requirements:* For master's, GRE General Test or MAT, minimum undergraduate GPA of 2.75, writing sample, clergy recommendation; for doctorate, M Div or theological master's degree; minimum graduate GPA of 3.5 (PhD), 3.0 (D Min); recommendations; writing sample; transcripts. Additional exam requirements/recommendations for international students: Required—TOEFL (minimum score 577 paper-based). *Application deadline:* For fall admission, 5/1 priority date for domestic students. Applications are processed on a rolling basis. Application fee: $50. Electronic applications accepted. *Expenses:* Expenses: Contact institution. *Financial support:* Fellowships with full and partial tuition reimbursements, career-related internships or fieldwork, scholarships/grants, tuition waivers (full and partial), and unspecified assistantships available. Support available to part-time students. Financial award application deadline: 9/1; financial award applicants required to submit FAFSA. *Faculty research:* Greek and Hebrew, theology, spiritual formation, global missions and world Christianity, women's studies. *Unit head:* Dr. Joseph Umidi, Interim Dean, 757-352-4401, Fax: 757-352-4597, E-mail: joseumi@regent.edu. *Application contact:* Matthew Chadwick, Director of Enrollment Support Services, 800-373-5504, Fax: 757-352-4381, E-mail: admissions@regent.edu.
Website: http://www.regent.edu/acad/schdiv/

Rhode Island College, School of Graduate Studies, Faculty of Arts and Sciences, Department of History, Providence, RI 02908-1991. Offers MA. Part-time and evening/weekend programs available. *Faculty:* 11 full-time (2 women). *Students:* 1 full-time (0 women), 3 part-time (2 women). Average age 36. *Degree requirements:* For master's, oral exam or thesis. *Entrance requirements:* For master's, GRE General and Subject Tests, 3 letters of recommendation, interview. Additional exam requirements/recommendations for international students: Recommended—TOEFL (minimum score 550 paper-based; 79 iBT). *Application deadline:* For fall admission, 3/1 for domestic students; for spring admission, 11/1 for domestic students. Applications are processed on a rolling basis. Application fee: $50. *Expenses:* Tuition, state resident: full-time $8928; part-time $372 per credit hour. Tuition, nonresident: full-time $17,376; part-time $724 per credit hour. *Required fees:* $602; $22 per credit. $72 per term. *Financial support:* In 2014–15, 1 teaching assistantship with full tuition reimbursement (averaging $3,500 per year) was awarded; Federal Work-Study, scholarships/grants, health care benefits, and unspecified assistantships also available. Support available to part-time students. Financial award application deadline: 5/15; financial award applicants required to submit FAFSA. *Unit head:* Dr. David Espinosa, Chair, 401-456-8039. *Application contact:* Graduate Studies, 401-456-8700.
Website: http://www.ric.edu/history/index.php

Rice University, Graduate Programs, School of Humanities, Department of History, Houston, TX 77251-1892. Offers MA, PhD. Terminal master's awarded for partial completion of doctoral program. *Degree requirements:* For doctorate, variable foreign language requirement, comprehensive exam, thesis/dissertation, 4 semesters of coursework. *Entrance requirements:* For doctorate, GRE, writing samples, letters of recommendation, personal statement, transcripts. Additional exam requirements/recommendations for international students: Required—TOEFL (minimum score 600 paper-based; 90 iBT) or IELTS (minimum score 7). Electronic applications accepted. *Faculty research:* U.S. Southern, Caribbean, African-American, world, Latin American.

Roosevelt University, Graduate Division, College of Arts and Sciences, Department of History, Art, and Philosophy, Chicago, IL 60605. Offers history (MA). Part-time and evening/weekend programs available. *Degree requirements:* For master's, thesis or

alternative. *Faculty research:* American social history, Holocaust, European history, African-American history, popular culture.

Rowan University, Graduate School, College of Humanities and Social Sciences, Department of History, Glassboro, NJ 08028-1701. Offers history (MA, CGS). *Faculty:* 4 full-time (2 women), 3 part-time/adjunct (2 women). *Students:* 4 full-time (3 women), 8 part-time (1 woman); includes 2 minority (1 Black or African American, non-Hispanic/Latino; 1 Hispanic/Latino). Average age 31. 7 applicants, 100% accepted, 6 enrolled. In 2014, 1 master's awarded. *Application deadline:* For fall admission, 8/1 for domestic and international students; for spring admission, 11/1 for domestic and international students; for summer admission, 4/1 for domestic and international students. Application fee: $65. *Expenses: Tuition, area resident:* Part-time $648 per credit. Tuition, state resident: part-time $648 per credit. Tuition, nonresident: part-time $648 per credit. *Required fees:* $145 per credit. Tuition and fees vary according to degree level, campus/location, program and student level. *Unit head:* Dr. Cindy Vitto, Dean, 856-256-5840, E-mail: vitto@rowan.edu. *Application contact:* Admissions and Enrollment Services, 856-256-4747, Fax: 856-256-5637, E-mail: globaladmissions@rowan.edu.

Rowan University, Graduate School, College of Humanities and Social Sciences, Program in History, Glassboro, NJ 08028-1701. Offers MA, CGS. *Faculty:* 4 full-time (2 women), 3 part-time/adjunct (2 women). *Students:* 4 full-time (3 women), 8 part-time (1 woman); includes 2 minority (1 Black or African American, non-Hispanic/Latino; 1 Hispanic/Latino). Average age 31. 7 applicants, 100% accepted, 6 enrolled. In 2014, 1 master's awarded. *Degree requirements:* For master's, thesis optional. *Entrance requirements:* For master's, GRE, statement of objectives; current resume; official transcript demonstrating that applicant has earned undergraduate degree from accredited institution with minimum GPA of 3.0; two letters of recommendation from undergraduate professors or other qualified professionals; writing sample. Additional exam requirements/recommendations for international students: Required—TOEFL (minimum score 90 iBT). *Application deadline:* For fall admission, 8/1 for domestic students, 5/1 for international students; for spring admission, 11/1 for domestic and international students; for summer admission, 4/1 for domestic students, 2/15 for international students. Applications are processed on a rolling basis. Application fee: $65. Electronic applications accepted. *Expenses: Tuition, area resident:* Part-time $648 per credit. Tuition, state resident: part-time $648 per credit. Tuition, nonresident: part-time $648 per credit. *Required fees:* $145 per credit. Tuition and fees vary according to degree level, campus/location, program and student level. *Unit head:* Dr. Cindy Vitto, Dean, 856-256-5840, E-mail: vitto@rowan.edu. *Application contact:* Admissions and Enrollment Services, 856-256-4747, Fax: 856-256-5637, E-mail: globaladmissions@rowan.edu.

Rutgers, The State University of New Jersey, Camden, Graduate School of Arts and Sciences, Program in American and Public History, Camden, NJ 08102. Offers MA. Part-time and evening/weekend programs available. *Degree requirements:* For master's, comprehensive exam, thesis optional, 30 credits. *Entrance requirements:* For master's, GRE General Test (for full-time applicants), 3 letters of recommendation; history or related undergraduate degree (preferred). Additional exam requirements/recommendations for international students: Required—TOEFL, IELTS. Electronic applications accepted. *Faculty research:* Women's history, military history, Afro-American history, urban history, history of technology.

Rutgers, The State University of New Jersey, Newark, Graduate School, Program in History, Newark, NJ 07102. Offers MA, MAT. MA, MAT offered jointly with New Jersey Institute of Technology. Part-time and evening/weekend programs available. *Degree requirements:* For master's, one foreign language, comprehensive exam, thesis optional. *Entrance requirements:* For master's, GRE, minimum undergraduate B average. *Faculty research:* Global history, American history, American diplomatic and legal history, women's history, history of technology, environment and medicine.

Rutgers, The State University of New Jersey, New Brunswick, Graduate School-New Brunswick, Program in History, Piscataway, NJ 08854-8097. Offers African-American history (PhD); early American history (PhD); early modern European history (PhD); east Asian history (PhD); global and comparative history (PhD); history (PhD); history of diplomacy and foreign relations (PhD); history of technology, environment and health (PhD); history of the Atlantic cultures and African diaspora (PhD); Latin American history (PhD); medieval history (PhD); modern European history (PhD); nineteenth and twentieth century American history (PhD); women's and gender history (PhD). *Degree requirements:* For doctorate, thesis/dissertation. *Entrance requirements:* For doctorate, GRE General Test, sample of written work. Electronic applications accepted. *Faculty research:* American history, European history, Afro-American history, women's history, Latin American history.

St. Cloud State University, School of Graduate Studies, College of Liberal Arts, Department of History, St. Cloud, MN 56301-4498. Offers MA, MS. Part-time programs available. *Degree requirements:* For master's, thesis or alternative. *Entrance requirements:* For master's, GRE General Test, GRE Subject Test, minimum GPA of 2.75. Additional exam requirements/recommendations for international students: Required—Michigan English Language Assessment Battery; Recommended—TOEFL (minimum score 550 paper-based), IELTS (minimum score 6.5).

St. John's University, St. John's College of Liberal Arts and Sciences, Department of History, Queens, NY 11439. Offers history (MA); modern world history (DA); public history (MA). Part-time and evening/weekend programs available. *Students:* 23 full-time (10 women), 49 part-time (20 women); includes 18 minority (6 Black or African American, non-Hispanic/Latino; 3 Asian, non-Hispanic/Latino; 8 Hispanic/Latino; 1 Two or more races, non-Hispanic/Latino), 10 international. Average age 33. 30 applicants, 90% accepted, 13 enrolled. In 2014, 16 master's, 3 doctorates awarded. *Degree requirements:* For master's, one foreign language, comprehensive exam, thesis optional, colloquia ; for doctorate, one foreign language, comprehensive exam, thesis/dissertation, internship, practicum. *Entrance requirements:* For master's, minimum GPA of 3.0, 24 undergraduate credits in history or related field, 2 letters of recommendation, personal statement; for doctorate, minimum GPA of 3.5 in history, 3.0 overall; writing sample, 3 letters of recommendation, personal essay, bachelor's degree, at least 24 undergraduate credits in history or related field. Additional exam requirements/recommendations for international students: Required—TOEFL (minimum score 600 paper-based; 100 iBT), IELTS (minimum score 7). *Application deadline:* For fall admission, 5/1 priority date for domestic and international students; for spring admission, 11/1 priority date for domestic and international students. Applications are processed on a rolling basis. Application fee: $70. Electronic applications accepted. *Expenses: Tuition:* Full-time $20,610; part-time $1145 per credit. *Required fees:* $170 per semester. *Financial support:* Fellowships, research assistantships, and scholarships/grants available. Support available to part-time students. Financial award application deadline: 3/1; financial award applicants required to submit FAFSA. *Faculty research:* World history, gender, transnationalism, history of technology, cultural history, social history. *Unit head:* Dr. Elaine Carey, Chair, 718-990-6228, E-mail: careye@stjohns.edu. *Application contact:* Robert Medrano, Director of Graduate Admission, 718-990-1601, Fax: 718-990-5686, E-mail: gradhelp@stjohns.edu.

Saint Louis University, Graduate Education, College of Arts and Sciences and Graduate Education, Department of History, St. Louis, MO 63103-2097. Offers MA, MA-

R, PhD. Part-time programs available. *Degree requirements:* For master's, one foreign language, comprehensive exam, thesis optional, comprehensive oral exam; for doctorate, 2 foreign languages, comprehensive exam, thesis/dissertation, preliminary oral and written exams. *Entrance requirements:* For master's, GRE General Test, letters of recommendation, resume, writing sample; for doctorate, GRE General Test, letters of recommendation, resumé, writing sample, goal statement, transcripts. Additional exam requirements/recommendations for international students: Required—TOEFL (minimum score 525 paper-based). Electronic applications accepted. *Faculty research:* Medieval Europe, Crusades, Byzantine Empire, U.S. West and Borderlands, Early Modern Europe.

Saint Mary's University, Faculty of Arts, Department of History, Halifax, NS B3H 3C3, Canada. Offers MA. Part-time programs available. *Degree requirements:* For master's, one foreign language, comprehensive exam, thesis. *Entrance requirements:* For master's, honors degree. *Expenses:* Contact institution. *Faculty research:* Atlantic Canada, British Empire, history of science, South Africa.

Salem State University, School of Graduate Studies, Program in History, Salem, MA 01970-5353. Offers MA, MAT. Part-time and evening/weekend programs available. *Entrance requirements:* For master's, GRE or MAT. Additional exam requirements/recommendations for international students: Required—TOEFL (minimum score 550 paper-based; 80 iBT) or IELTS (minimum score 5.5).

Salisbury University, Program in History, Salisbury, MD 21801-6837. Offers MA. Part-time and evening/weekend programs available. *Faculty:* 10 full-time (3 women), 1 part-time/adjunct (0 women). *Students:* 7 full-time (4 women), 9 part-time (4 women); includes 1 minority (Black or African American, non-Hispanic/Latino). Average age 29. 8 applicants, 100% accepted, 7 enrolled. In 2014, 9 master's awarded. *Degree requirements:* For master's, comprehensive exam, thesis optional. *Entrance requirements:* For master's, GRE, 3 letters of recommendation; undergraduate degree in history (or history equivalent) with minimum GPA of 3.0. Additional exam requirements/recommendations for international students: Required—TOEFL (minimum score 550 paper-based; 79 iBT), IELTS (minimum score 6.5). *Application deadline:* For fall admission, 4/1 priority date for domestic and international students; for spring admission, 10/15 priority date for domestic and international students. Applications are processed on a rolling basis. Application fee: $65. Electronic applications accepted. *Expenses:* Expenses: $358 per credit hour for residents; $647 for non-residents; $78 fees. *Financial support:* In 2014–15, 1 student received support. Institutionally sponsored loans and scholarships/grants available. Support available to part-time students. Financial award application deadline: 3/1; financial award applicants required to submit FAFSA. *Faculty research:* Chesapeake studies, U.S. history, Colonial and Revolutionary America, world history. *Unit head:* Dr. Richard Bowler, Graduate Program Director, History, 410-546-6003, Fax: 410-677-5038, E-mail: rcbowler@salisbury.edu. *Application contact:* -, Fax: -.
Website: http://www.salisbury.edu/gsr/gradstudies/HISTpage

Sam Houston State University, College of Humanities and Social Sciences, Department of History, Huntsville, TX 77341. Offers MA. Part-time and evening/weekend programs available. *Faculty:* 22 full-time (8 women), 1 part-time/adjunct (0 women). *Students:* 15 full-time (6 women), 87 part-time (34 women); includes 16 minority (3 Black or African American, non-Hispanic/Latino; 1 Asian, non-Hispanic/Latino; 10 Hispanic/Latino; 2 Two or more races, non-Hispanic/Latino). Average age 38. 55 applicants, 93% accepted, 45 enrolled. In 2014, 19 master's awarded. *Degree requirements:* For master's, comprehensive exam, thesis optional. *Entrance requirements:* For master's, GRE General Test. Additional exam requirements/recommendations for international students: Required—TOEFL (minimum score 550 paper-based; 79 iBT), IELTS (minimum score 6.5). *Application deadline:* For fall admission, 8/1 for domestic students, 6/25 for international students; for spring admission, 12/1 for domestic students, 11/12 for international students; for summer admission, 5/15 for domestic students, 4/9 for international students. Applications are processed on a rolling basis. Application fee: $45 ($75 for international students). Electronic applications accepted. *Expenses:* Tuition, state resident: full-time $2286; part-time $254 per credit hour. Tuition, nonresident: full-time $5544; part-time $616 per credit hour. *Required fees:* $440 per semester. Tuition and fees vary according to course load and campus/location. *Financial support:* In 2014–15, 10 research assistantships (averaging $8,213 per year) were awarded; career-related internships or fieldwork, Federal Work-Study, scholarships/grants, tuition waivers, and unspecified assistantships also available. Support available to part-time students. Financial award application deadline: 3/15; financial award applicants required to submit FAFSA. *Unit head:* Dr. Brian Domitrovic, Chair, 936-294-1474, Fax: 936-294-3938, E-mail: bfd001@shsu.edu. *Application contact:* Dr. Jeffrey L. Littlejohn, Director of Graduate Studies, 936-294-3853, E-mail: gradhistory@shsu.edu.
Website: http://www.shsu.edu/academics/history/

San Diego State University, Graduate and Research Affairs, College of Arts and Letters, Department of History, San Diego, CA 92182. Offers MA. *Degree requirements:* For master's, one foreign language. *Entrance requirements:* For master's, GRE General Test, bachelor's degree in related field. Additional exam requirements/recommendations for international students: Required—TOEFL. Electronic applications accepted. *Faculty research:* Latin American history, Filipino history.

San Francisco State University, Division of Graduate Studies, College of Liberal and Creative Arts, Department of History, San Francisco, CA 94132-1722. Offers MA. *Expenses:* Tuition, state resident: full-time $6738. Tuition, nonresident: full-time $17,898; part-time $372 per credit hour. *Required fees:* $498 per semester. *Unit head:* Dr. Philip Dreyfus, Chair, 415-338-1604, Fax: 415-338-7539, E-mail: pdreyfus@sfsu.edu. *Application contact:* Dr. Sarah Curtis, Graduate Coordinator, 415-338-2250, Fax: 415-338-7539, E-mail: scurtis@sfsu.edu.
Website: http://history.sfsu.edu/

San Jose State University, Graduate Studies and Research, College of Social Sciences, Department of History, San Jose, CA 95192-0001. Offers history (MA); history education (MA). *Degree requirements:* For master's, comprehensive exam, thesis or alternative. *Entrance requirements:* For master's, bachelor's degree or 15 units of course work in history, minimum GPA of 3.0. Electronic applications accepted.

Sarah Lawrence College, Graduate Studies, Program in Women's History, Bronxville, NY 10708-5999. Offers MA. Part-time programs available. *Degree requirements:* For master's, thesis. *Entrance requirements:* For master's, previous course work in history, minimum B average in undergraduate course work. Additional exam requirements/recommendations for international students: Required—TOEFL (minimum score 600 paper-based). Electronic applications accepted.

Seton Hall University, College of Arts and Sciences, Department of History, South Orange, NJ 07079-2697. Offers history (MA), including Catholic history, European history, global history, United States history. Part-time programs available. *Faculty:* 16 full-time (5 women). *Students:* 6 full-time (2 women), 12 part-time (4 women); includes 1 minority (Black or African American, non-Hispanic/Latino), 1 international. Average age 29. 10 applicants, 80% accepted, 5 enrolled. In 2014, 6 master's awarded. *Degree requirements:* For master's, thesis optional, thesis or comprehensive exam. *Entrance requirements:* For master's, GRE. Additional exam requirements/recommendations for international students: Required—TOEFL. *Application deadline:* For fall admission, 7/1 priority date for domestic and international students; for spring admission, 11/1 priority date for domestic and international students. Applications are processed on a rolling basis. Application fee: $75. Electronic applications accepted. *Financial support:* Research assistantships, career-related internships or fieldwork, Federal Work-Study, and unspecified assistantships available. Financial award applicants required to submit FAFSA. *Faculty research:* Catholic history, European history, global history, United States history, African-American history. *Unit head:* Dr. Nathaniel Knight, Chair, 973-275-2178, Fax: 973-761-7798, E-mail: knightna@shu.edu. *Application contact:* Dr. Dermot Quinn, Director of Graduate Studies, 973-275-5889, Fax: 973-761-7798, E-mail: dermot.quinn@shu.edu.
Website: http://www.shu.edu/academics/artsci/history/index.cfm

Shippensburg University of Pennsylvania, School of Graduate Studies, College of Arts and Sciences, Department of History and Philosophy, Shippensburg, PA 17257-2299. Offers MA. Part-time and evening/weekend programs available. *Faculty:* 7 full-time (3 women), 1 (woman) part-time/adjunct. *Students:* 8 full-time (6 women), 20 part-time (12 women); includes 3 minority (2 Black or African American, non-Hispanic/Latino; 1 Two or more races, non-Hispanic/Latino). Average age 29. 25 applicants, 68% accepted, 8 enrolled. In 2014, 10 master's awarded. *Degree requirements:* For master's, thesis, internship, or student teaching and professional practicum. *Entrance requirements:* For master's, 500-word statement of purpose; interview (if GPA is below 2.75). Additional exam requirements/recommendations for international students: Required—TOEFL (minimum score 580 paper-based); Recommended—IELTS (minimum score 6). *Application deadline:* For fall admission, 2/15 for domestic and international students; for spring admission, 9/15 for domestic and international students; for summer admission, 2/15 for domestic students. Applications are processed on a rolling basis. Application fee: $45. Electronic applications accepted. *Expenses: Tuition, area resident:* Part-time $454 per credit. Tuition, state resident: part-time $454 per credit. Tuition, nonresident: part-time $681 per credit. *Required fees:* $133 per credit. *Financial support:* In 2014–15, 7 research assistantships with full tuition reimbursements (averaging $5,000 per year) were awarded; career-related internships or fieldwork, scholarships/grants, unspecified assistantships, and resident hall director and student payroll positions also available. Support available to part-time students. Financial award application deadline: 3/1; financial award applicants required to submit FAFSA. *Unit head:* Dr. John D. Bloom, Program Coordinator, 717-477-1621, Fax: 717-477-4062, E-mail: jdbloo@ship.edu. *Application contact:* Jeremy R. Goshorn, Assistant Dean of Graduate Admissions, 717-477-1231, Fax: 717-477-4016, E-mail: jrgoshorn@ship.edu.
Website: http://www.ship.edu/history/

Shippensburg University of Pennsylvania, School of Graduate Studies, College of Education and Human Services, Department of Teacher Education, Shippensburg, PA 17257-2299. Offers curriculum and instruction (M Ed), including biology, early childhood education, elementary education, geography/earth science, history, mathematics, middle level education, modern languages; reading (M Ed). *Accreditation:* NCATE. Part-time and evening/weekend programs available. *Faculty:* 12 full-time (9 women), 3 part-time/adjunct (2 women). *Students:* 8 full-time (7 women), 66 part-time (53 women); includes 6 minority (2 Black or African American, non-Hispanic/Latino; 4 Hispanic/Latino), 1 international. Average age 30. 52 applicants, 75% accepted, 24 enrolled. In 2014, 29 master's awarded. *Degree requirements:* For master's, comprehensive exam (for some programs), thesis optional, practicum or internship; capstone seminar (for some programs). *Entrance requirements:* For master's, MAT or GRE (if GPA less than 2.75), interview, 3 letters of reference, questionnaire of teaching background and future goals, resume. Additional exam requirements/recommendations for international students: Required—TOEFL (minimum score 580 paper-based); Recommended—IELTS (minimum score 6). *Application deadline:* For fall admission, 6/1 priority date for domestic students, 4/30 for international students; for spring admission, 9/1 priority date for domestic students, 9/30 for international students; for summer admission, 2/1 priority date for domestic students. Applications are processed on a rolling basis. Application fee: $45. Electronic applications accepted. *Expenses: Tuition, area resident:* Part-time $454 per credit. Tuition, state resident: part-time $454 per credit. Tuition, nonresident: part-time $681 per credit. *Required fees:* $133 per credit. *Financial support:* In 2014–15, 1 research assistantship with full tuition reimbursement (averaging $5,000 per year) was awarded; career-related internships or fieldwork, scholarships/grants, unspecified assistantships, and resident hall director and student payroll positions also available. Support available to part-time students. Financial award application deadline: 3/1; financial award applicants required to submit FAFSA. *Unit head:* Dr. Christine A. Royce, Chairperson, 717-477-1688, Fax: 717-477-4046, E-mail: caroyc@ship.edu. *Application contact:* Jeremy R. Goshorn, Assistant Dean of Graduate Admissions, 717-477-1231, Fax: 717-477-4016, E-mail: jrgoshorn@ship.edu.
Website: http://www.ship.edu/teacher/

Simon Fraser University, Office of Graduate Studies, Faculty of Arts and Social Sciences, Department of History, Burnaby, BC V5A 1S6, Canada. Offers MA, PhD. *Degree requirements:* For master's, one foreign language, thesis, language exam; for doctorate, one foreign language, comprehensive exam, thesis/dissertation, language exam. *Entrance requirements:* For master's, minimum GPA of 3.0 (on scale of 4.33), or 3.33 based on last 60 credits of undergraduate courses; for doctorate, minimum GPA of 3.5 (on scale of 4.33). Additional exam requirements/recommendations for international students: Recommended—TOEFL (minimum score 580 paper-based; 93 iBT), IELTS (minimum score 7), TWE (minimum score 5). Electronic applications accepted. *Faculty research:* Colonialism and imperialism Asian history, labor history, race, gender and sexuality, political and social history, cultural and urban history.

Slippery Rock University of Pennsylvania, Graduate Studies (Recruitment), College of Education, Department of Secondary Education/Foundations of Education, Slippery Rock, PA 16057-1383. Offers educational leadership (M Ed); secondary education (M Ed), including English, math/science, social studies/history. *Accreditation:* NCATE. Part-time and evening/weekend programs available. *Faculty:* 7 full-time (4 women), 1 part-time/adjunct (0 women). *Students:* 53 full-time (31 women), 15 part-time (6 women); includes 3 minority (1 Black or African American, non-Hispanic/Latino; 2 Two or more races, non-Hispanic/Latino). Average age 27. 50 applicants, 84% accepted, 29 enrolled. In 2014, 28 master's awarded. *Degree requirements:* For master's, comprehensive exam, thesis (for some programs). *Entrance requirements:* For master's, minimum GPA of 2.8 or 3.0 (depending on program); copy of teaching certification and two letters of recommendation (for some programs). Additional exam requirements/recommendations for international students: Required—TOEFL (minimum score 550 paper-based; 80 iBT). *Application deadline:* For fall admission, 3/1 priority date for domestic students, 5/1 priority date for international students; for spring admission, 10/1 priority date for domestic students, 9/1 priority date for international students. Applications are processed on a rolling basis. Application fee: $25 ($30 for international students). Electronic applications accepted. *Expenses:* Tuition, state resident: full-time $8172; part-time $454 per credit. Tuition, nonresident: full-time $12,258; part-time $681 per credit. *Required fees:* $2326; $200 per credit. Tuition and fees vary according to degree level and program. *Financial support:* Career-related internships or fieldwork, Federal Work-Study, institutionally sponsored loans, scholarships/grants, tuition waivers (partial), and unspecified assistantships available. Support available to part-time

students. Financial award application deadline: 5/1; financial award applicants required to submit FAFSA. *Unit head:* Dr. Jeffrey Lehman, Graduate Coordinator, 724-738-2311, Fax: 724-738-4987, E-mail: jeffrey.lehman@sru.edu. *Application contact:* Brandi Weber-Mortimer, Director of Graduate Studies, 724-738-2051, Fax: 724-738-2146, E-mail: graduate.admissions@sru.edu.
Website: http://www.sru.edu/academics/colleges-and-departments/coe/departments/secondary-education-/-foundations-of-education

Smith College, Graduate and Special Programs, Department of History, Northampton, MA 01063. Offers MAT. *Faculty:* 10 full-time (5 women), 1 (woman) part-time/adjunct. *Students:* 1 (woman) part-time. Average age 31. 2 applicants, 50% accepted, 1 enrolled. *Entrance requirements:* Additional exam requirements/recommendations for international students: Required—TOEFL (minimum score 595 paper-based; 97 iBT). *Application deadline:* For fall admission, 4/15 for domestic students, 1/15 for international students; for spring admission, 12/1 for domestic students. Application fee: $60. *Expenses: Tuition:* Full-time $33,360; part-time $1390 per credit. *Financial support:* Career-related internships or fieldwork, institutionally sponsored loans, and scholarships/grants available. Support available to part-time students. Financial award application deadline: 1/15; financial award applicants required to submit CSS PROFILE or FAFSA. *Unit head:* Joshua Birk, Graduate Student Adviser, 413-585-3740, E-mail: jbirk@smith.edu. *Application contact:* Ruth Morgan, Program Assistant, 413-585-3050, Fax: 413-585-3054, E-mail: gradstdy@smith.edu.
Website: http://www.smith.edu/history/

Sonoma State University, School of Social Sciences, Department of History, Rohnert Park, CA 94928. Offers MA. Part-time programs available. *Degree requirements:* For master's, thesis or alternative. *Entrance requirements:* For master's, GRE General Test or GRE Subject Test, minimum GPA of 3.0. Additional exam requirements/recommendations for international students: Required—TOEFL (minimum score 500 paper-based).

Southeastern Louisiana University, College of Arts, Humanities and Social Sciences, Department of History and Political Science, Hammond, LA 70402. Offers history (MA). Part-time and evening/weekend programs available. *Faculty:* 10 full-time (2 women). *Students:* 13 full-time (3 women), 28 part-time (12 women); includes 5 minority (2 Black or African American, non-Hispanic/Latino; 2 Hispanic/Latino; 1 Two or more races, non-Hispanic/Latino). Average age 28. In 2014, 5 master's awarded. *Degree requirements:* For master's, comprehensive exam, thesis optional. *Entrance requirements:* For master's, GRE General Test (minimum score of 900), at least 30 undergraduate hours of history. Additional exam requirements/recommendations for international students: Required—TOEFL (minimum score 500 paper-based; 61 iBT). *Application deadline:* For fall admission, 7/15 priority date for domestic students, 6/1 priority date for international students; for spring admission, 12/1 priority date for domestic students, 10/1 priority date for international students. Applications are processed on a rolling basis. Application fee: $20 ($30 for international students). Electronic applications accepted. *Financial support:* In 2014–15, 7 research assistantships (averaging $8,314 per year), 9 teaching assistantships (averaging $9,366 per year) were awarded; career-related internships or fieldwork, Federal Work-Study, institutionally sponsored loans, scholarships/grants, and unspecified assistantships also available. Support available to part-time students. Financial award application deadline: 5/1; financial award applicants required to submit FAFSA. *Faculty research:* American, British and European, and Southern and Louisiana history; American and international politics; philosophy. *Unit head:* Dr. William Robison, Department Head, 985-549-2109, Fax: 985-549-2012, E-mail: wrobison@selu.edu. *Application contact:* Sandra Meyers, Graduate Admissions Analyst, 985-549-5620, Fax: 985-549-5632, E-mail: admissions@selu.edu.
Website: http://www.selu.edu/acad_research/depts/hist_ps

Southeast Missouri State University, School of Graduate Studies, Department of History, Cape Girardeau, MO 63701-4799. Offers heritage education (Certificate); historic preservation (Certificate); history (MA); public history (MA). Part-time and evening/weekend programs available. *Faculty:* 11 full-time (4 women). *Students:* 9 full-time (8 women), 12 part-time (3 women); includes 1 minority (Hispanic/Latino). Average age 30. 16 applicants, 81% accepted, 12 enrolled. In 2014, 11 master's awarded. *Degree requirements:* For master's, comprehensive exam (for some programs), thesis optional, thesis or exam, plus capstone project/paper (for history); thesis or internship, plus project in applied history and comprehensive exams (for public history). *Entrance requirements:* For master's and Certificate, minimum undergraduate GPA of 2.75; 2 letters of recommendation; writing sample; letter of intent; 24 semester hours of undergraduate history credit. Additional exam requirements/recommendations for international students: Required—TOEFL (minimum score 550 paper-based; 79 iBT), IELTS (minimum score 6), PTE (minimum score 53). *Application deadline:* For fall admission, 8/1 for domestic students, 6/1 for international students; for spring admission, 11/21 for domestic students, 10/1 for international students; for summer admission, 5/15 for domestic students. Applications are processed on a rolling basis. Application fee: $30 ($40 for international students). Electronic applications accepted. *Expenses:* Tuition, state resident: full-time $5256; part-time $292 per credit hour. Tuition, nonresident: full-time $9288; part-time $516 per credit hour. *Financial support:* In 2014–15, 8 students received support, including 1 research assistantship with full tuition reimbursement available (averaging $7,907 per year), 4 teaching assistantships with full tuition reimbursements available (averaging $7,907 per year); career-related internships or fieldwork, Federal Work-Study, scholarships/grants, traineeships, tuition waivers (full), and unspecified assistantships also available. Financial award application deadline: 6/30; financial award applicants required to submit FAFSA. *Faculty research:* Medieval Europe; modern Europe including Britain, Germany, France, Russia, and Spain; Colonial and nineteenth-century America; twentieth-century America and American West; public history and historic preservation; Latin America. *Unit head:* Dr. Wayne Bowen, Chairperson/Professor of History, 573-651-2179, Fax: 573-651-5114, E-mail: wbowen@semo.edu. *Application contact:* Dr. Erika Hosselkus, Graduate Coordinator/Assistant Professor of History, 573-651-2763, Fax: 573-651-5114, E-mail: ehosselkus@semo.edu.
Website: http://www.semo.edu/history/

Southern Connecticut State University, School of Graduate Studies, School of Arts and Sciences, Department of History, New Haven, CT 06515-1355. Offers MA, MS, MLS/MA. Part-time and evening/weekend programs available. *Degree requirements:* For master's, one foreign language, thesis. *Entrance requirements:* For master's, interview, undergraduate major or minor in history. Electronic applications accepted.

Southern Illinois University Carbondale, Graduate School, College of Liberal Arts, Department of History, Carbondale, IL 62901-4701. Offers MA, PhD. Part-time programs available. *Faculty:* 23 full-time (8 women). *Students:* 21 full-time (6 women), 21 part-time (7 women); includes 1 minority (Hispanic/Latino), 6 international. 18 applicants, 33% accepted, 4 enrolled. In 2014, 3 master's awarded. *Degree requirements:* For master's, one foreign language, research papers or thesis, written exams; for doctorate, 2 foreign languages, thesis/dissertation. *Entrance requirements:* For master's, GRE General Test, minimum GPA of 3.0; for doctorate, GRE General Test, minimum GPA of 3.25. Additional exam requirements/recommendations for international students: Required—TOEFL. *Application deadline:* For fall admission, 2/1 priority date for domestic students. Applications are processed on a rolling basis. Application fee: $50. *Expenses:* Tuition, state resident: full-time $10,176; part-time $1153 per credit. Tuition, nonresident: full-time $20,814; part-time $1744 per credit. *Required fees:* $7092; $394 per credit. $2364 per semester. *Financial support:* In 2014–15, 33 students received support, including 4 fellowships with full tuition reimbursements available, 5 research assistantships with full tuition reimbursements available, 18 teaching assistantships with full tuition reimbursements available; career-related internships or fieldwork, Federal Work-Study, institutionally sponsored loans, and tuition waivers (full) also available. Support available to part-time students. Financial award application deadline: 2/1. *Faculty research:* American, Asian, European, and Latin American history; global history. *Unit head:* Dr. Kay Carr, Chair, 618-453-7864, E-mail: kjcarr@siu.edu. *Application contact:* Chasity Shea, Administrative Clerk, 618-453-7863, E-mail: cshea@siu.edu.

Southern Illinois University Edwardsville, Graduate School, College of Arts and Sciences, Department of Historical Studies, Program in History, Edwardsville, IL 62026-0001. Offers MA. Part-time and evening/weekend programs available. *Faculty:* 17 full-time (9 women). *Students:* 11 full-time (7 women), 13 part-time (7 women); includes 4 minority (2 Black or African American, non-Hispanic/Latino; 1 Asian, non-Hispanic/Latino; 1 Hispanic/Latino). 10 applicants, 90% accepted. In 2014, 4 master's awarded. *Degree requirements:* For master's, one foreign language, thesis (for some programs), final exam. *Entrance requirements:* For master's, GRE. Additional exam requirements/recommendations for international students: Required—TOEFL (minimum score 550 paper-based; 79 iBT), IELTS (minimum score 6.5). *Application deadline:* For fall admission, 2/1 for domestic and international students; for spring admission, 10/1 for international students. Application fee: $30. Electronic applications accepted. *Expenses:* Tuition, state resident: full-time $5026. Tuition, nonresident: full-time $12,566. *International tuition:* $25,136 full-time. *Required fees:* $1682. Tuition and fees vary according to course load, campus/location and program. *Financial support:* In 2014–15, 10 students received support, including 10 teaching assistantships with full tuition reimbursements available; fellowships with full tuition reimbursements available, research assistantships with full tuition reimbursements available, career-related internships or fieldwork, institutionally sponsored loans, scholarships/grants, and unspecified assistantships also available. Financial award application deadline: 3/1; financial award applicants required to submit FAFSA. *Unit head:* Dr. Laura Fowler, Program Director, 618-650-2145, E-mail: lmilsk@siue.edu. *Application contact:* Melissa K. Mace, Assistant Director of Admissions for Graduate and International Recruitment, 618-650-2756, Fax: 618-650-3618, E-mail: mmace@siue.edu.
Website: http://www.siue.edu/artsandsciences/historicalstudies/

Southern Methodist University, Dedman College of Humanities and Sciences, Clements Department of History, Dallas, TX 75275. Offers classical/medieval history (MA); European history (MA); history (PhD); Ibero-American history (MA); United States history (MA). PhD offered jointly with the Clements Center for Southwest Studies. Part-time programs available. Terminal master's awarded for partial completion of doctoral program. *Degree requirements:* For master's, one foreign language, thesis, oral exam, thesis defense; for doctorate, one foreign language, thesis/dissertation, oral exam, dissertation defense. *Entrance requirements:* For master's and doctorate, GRE General Test, minimum GPA of 3.0, 12 undergraduate hours in advanced level history, writing sample. Additional exam requirements/recommendations for international students: Required—TOEFL. Electronic applications accepted. *Faculty research:* U.S. history, European history, Latin America, Africa/Middle East, China.

Southern University and Agricultural and Mechanical College, Graduate School, College of Arts and Humanities, Department of History, Baton Rouge, LA 70813. Offers social sciences (MA). Part-time programs available. *Degree requirements:* For master's, thesis. *Entrance requirements:* For master's, GRE General Test. Additional exam requirements/recommendations for international students: Required—TOEFL (minimum score 525 paper-based).

Southwestern Assemblies of God University, Thomas F. Harrison School of Graduate Studies, Program in History, Waxahachie, TX 75165-5735. Offers MA.

Spring Hill College, Graduate Programs, Program in Liberal Arts, Mobile, AL 36608-1791. Offers fine arts (MLA); history and social science (MLA); leadership and ethics (MLA, Postbaccalaureate Certificate); literature (MLA); studio art (Postbaccalaureate Certificate). Part-time and evening/weekend programs available. *Faculty:* 6 full-time (1 woman), 3 part-time/adjunct (all women). *Students:* 3 full-time (1 woman), 33 part-time (18 women); includes 9 minority (8 Black or African American, non-Hispanic/Latino; 1 American Indian or Alaska Native, non-Hispanic/Latino), 1 international. Average age 36. In 2014, 8 master's awarded. *Degree requirements:* For master's, capstone course, completion of program within 6 years of initial admittance. *Entrance requirements:* For master's, bachelor's degree with minimum undergraduate GPA of 3.0 or graduate/professional degree. Additional exam requirements/recommendations for international students: Required—TOEFL (minimum score 550 paper-based; 80 iBT), IELTS (minimum score 6.5), CPE or CAE (minimum score C), Michigan English Language Assessment Battery (minimum score 90). *Application deadline:* For fall admission, 8/1 priority date for domestic and international students; for spring admission, 12/1 priority date for domestic and international students. Applications are processed on a rolling basis. Application fee: $25 ($35 for international students). Electronic applications accepted. *Expenses:* Expenses: Contact institution. *Financial support:* Applicants required to submit FAFSA. *Unit head:* Dr. Thomas J. Hoffman, Director, 251-380-4184, Fax: 251-460-2115, E-mail: thoffman@shc.edu. *Application contact:* Robert Stewart, Vice President of Enrollment, 251-380-3030, Fax: 251-460-2186, E-mail: rstewart@shc.edu.
Website: http://ug.shc.edu/graduate-degrees/master-liberal-arts/

Stanford University, School of Humanities and Sciences, Department of History, Stanford, CA 94305-9991. Offers MA, PhD. Terminal master's awarded for partial completion of doctoral program. *Degree requirements:* For doctorate, variable foreign language requirement, thesis/dissertation, oral exam. *Entrance requirements:* For master's and doctorate, GRE General Test. Additional exam requirements/recommendations for international students: Required—TOEFL. Electronic applications accepted. *Expenses: Tuition:* Full-time $44,184; part-time $982 per credit hour. *Required fees:* $191.

State University of New York at Oswego, Graduate Studies, College of Liberal Arts and Sciences, Department of History, Oswego, NY 13126. Offers MA. Part-time programs available. *Degree requirements:* For master's, thesis optional. *Entrance requirements:* For master's, writing sample. Additional exam requirements/recommendations for international students: Required—TOEFL (minimum score 560 paper-based).

State University of New York College at Cortland, Graduate Studies, School of Arts and Sciences, Department of History, Cortland, NY 13045. Offers MA. Part-time and evening/weekend programs available. *Degree requirements:* For master's, one foreign language, comprehensive exam, thesis optional. *Entrance requirements:* Additional exam requirements/recommendations for international students: Required—TOEFL.

Stephen F. Austin State University, Graduate School, College of Liberal Arts, Department of History, Nacogdoches, TX 75962. Offers MA. Part-time and evening/weekend programs available. *Degree requirements:* For master's, comprehensive

exam. *Entrance requirements:* For master's, GRE General Test. Additional exam requirements/recommendations for international students: Required—TOEFL. *Faculty research:* U.S.-Third World foreign policy, racial attitudes of antebellum Southern whites, naval warfare in World War II, demography of East Texas, medieval sermons.

Stony Brook University, State University of New York, Graduate School, College of Arts and Sciences, Department of History, Stony Brook, NY 11794. Offers MA, PhD. Evening/weekend programs available. *Faculty:* 28 full-time (15 women), 5 part-time/adjunct (1 woman). *Students:* 61 full-time (27 women), 4 part-time (1 woman); includes 8 minority (3 Black or African American, non-Hispanic/Latino; 1 Asian, non-Hispanic/Latino; 3 Hispanic/Latino; 1 Two or more races, non-Hispanic/Latino), 12 international. Average age 34. 50 applicants, 58% accepted, 11 enrolled. In 2014, 6 master's, 9 doctorates awarded. *Degree requirements:* For doctorate, thesis/dissertation. *Entrance requirements:* For master's and doctorate, GRE General Test. Additional exam requirements/recommendations for international students: Required—TOEFL. *Application deadline:* For fall admission, 1/15 for domestic students; for spring admission, 10/1 for domestic students. Application fee: $100. *Expenses:* Tuition, state resident: full-time $10,370; part-time $432 per credit. Tuition, nonresident: full-time $20,190; part-time $841 per credit. *Required fees:* $1431. *Financial support:* In 2014–15, 2 fellowships, 28 teaching assistantships were awarded; research assistantships also available. *Faculty research:* American history, cultural history, political history. *Total annual research expenditures:* $44,425. *Unit head:* Prof. Gary Marker, Chair, 631-632-7510, Fax: 631-632-7367, E-mail: gary.marker@stonybrook.edu. *Application contact:* Roxanne Fernandez, Coordinator, 631-632-7490, Fax: 631-632-7367, E-mail: roxanne.fernandez@stonybrook.edu.
Website: http://www.sunysb.edu/history/

Sul Ross State University, School of Arts and Sciences, Department of Behavioral and Social Sciences, Program in History, Alpine, TX 79832. Offers MA. Part-time and evening/weekend programs available. *Degree requirements:* For master's, thesis optional. *Entrance requirements:* For master's, GRE General Test, minimum GPA of 2.5 in last 60 hours of undergraduate work. *Faculty research:* Borderland/Southwestern studies, British studies, women's history, Native American studies, local history.

Syracuse University, Maxwell School of Citizenship and Public Affairs, Program in History, Syracuse, NY 13244. Offers MA, PhD. Part-time programs available. *Students:* 45 full-time (18 women), 1 part-time (0 women); includes 3 minority (1 Black or African American, non-Hispanic/Latino; 1 Hispanic/Latino; 1 Two or more races, non-Hispanic/Latino), 7 international. Average age 34. 44 applicants, 2% accepted, 1 enrolled. In 2014, 8 master's, 1 doctorate awarded. Terminal master's awarded for partial completion of doctoral program. *Degree requirements:* For master's, comprehensive exam, thesis or alternative; for doctorate, 2 foreign languages, comprehensive exam, thesis/dissertation. *Entrance requirements:* For master's and doctorate, GRE General Test, sample of written work. Additional exam requirements/recommendations for international students: Required—TOEFL (minimum score 100 iBT). *Application deadline:* For fall admission, 1/1 priority date for domestic and international students. Application fee: $75. Electronic applications accepted. *Expenses: Tuition:* Part-time $1341 per credit. *Financial support:* Fellowships with full tuition reimbursements, research assistantships with full and partial tuition reimbursements, and teaching assistantships with full and partial tuition reimbursements available. Financial award application deadline: 1/1; financial award applicants required to submit FAFSA. *Faculty research:* American, medieval, European, South East Asian, and Russian history. *Unit head:* Dr. Susan Branson, Director of Graduate Studies, 315-443-4144, Fax: 315-443-5876, E-mail: branson@syr.edu. *Application contact:* Pat Bohrer, Information Contact, 315-443-2210, E-mail: pabohrer@syr.edu.
Website: http://www.maxwell.syr.edu/

Tarleton State University, College of Graduate Studies, College of Liberal and Fine Arts, Department of Social Sciences, Stephenville, TX 76402. Offers history (MA); political science (MA). Part-time and evening/weekend programs available. Postbaccalaureate distance learning degree programs offered (minimal on-campus study). *Degree requirements:* For master's, variable foreign language requirement, comprehensive exam, thesis optional. *Entrance requirements:* For master's, GRE General Test, minimum GPA of 3.0. Additional exam requirements/recommendations for international students: Required—TOEFL (minimum score 550 paper-based; 80 iBT). Electronic applications accepted.

Temple University, College of Liberal Arts, Department of History, Philadelphia, PA 19122-6096. Offers MA, PhD. Part-time and evening/weekend programs available. *Faculty:* 28 full-time (11 women), 3 part-time/adjunct (1 woman). *Students:* 83 full-time (25 women), 8 part-time (3 women); includes 10 minority (4 Black or African American, non-Hispanic/Latino; 1 Asian, non-Hispanic/Latino; 2 Hispanic/Latino; 3 Two or more races, non-Hispanic/Latino), 6 international. 119 applicants, 31% accepted, 13 enrolled. In 2014, 9 master's, 6 doctorates awarded. Terminal master's awarded for partial completion of doctoral program. *Degree requirements:* For doctorate, one foreign language, thesis/dissertation. *Entrance requirements:* For master's and doctorate, GRE General Test, minimum GPA of 3.0, 3 letters of recommendation. Additional exam requirements/recommendations for international students: Required—TOEFL (minimum score 550 paper-based; 79 iBT). *Application deadline:* For fall admission, 2/15 priority date for domestic students, 12/15 for international students; for spring admission, 10/15 for domestic students, 8/1 for international students. Application fee: $60. Electronic applications accepted. *Expenses:* Tuition, state resident: full-time $14,490; part-time $805 per credit hour. Tuition, nonresident: full-time $19,850; part-time $1103 per credit hour. *Required fees:* $690. Full-time tuition and fees vary according to class time, course load, degree level, campus/location and program. *Financial support:* Fellowships with tuition reimbursements, teaching assistantships with tuition reimbursements, career-related internships or fieldwork, and tuition waivers (partial) available. Support available to part-time students. Financial award application deadline: 1/15; financial award applicants required to submit FAFSA. *Faculty research:* American history, foreign relations, transnational and international history, military history, urban history, environmental history. *Unit head:* Dr. Andrew Isenberg, Graduate Director, 215-204-6176, Fax: 215-204-5891, E-mail: andrew.isenberg@temple.edu. *Application contact:* Vangeline Campbell, Coordinator, 215-204-7839, Fax: 215-204-5891, E-mail: vcampbel@temple.edu.
Website: http://www.cla.temple.edu/history/

Texas A&M International University, Office of Graduate Studies and Research, College of Arts and Sciences, Department of Humanities, Laredo, TX 78041-1900. Offers English (MA); Hispanic studies (PhD); history and political thought (MA); language, literature and translation (MA). *Degree requirements:* For master's, comprehensive exam (for some programs), thesis (for some programs). *Entrance requirements:* For master's, GRE General Test. Additional exam requirements/recommendations for international students: Required—TOEFL (minimum score 550 paper-based; 79 iBT).

Texas A&M International University, Office of Graduate Studies and Research, College of Arts and Sciences, Department of Public Affairs and Social Research, Laredo, TX 78041-1900. Offers criminal justice (MS); history and political thought (MA); political science (MA); public administration (MPA). *Degree requirements:* For master's, comprehensive exam (for some programs), thesis (for some programs). *Entrance requirements:* For master's, GRE General Test. Additional exam requirements/recommendations for international students: Required—TOEFL (minimum score 550 paper-based; 79 iBT).

Texas A&M University, College of Liberal Arts, Department of History, College Station, TX 77843. Offers MA, PhD. Part-time programs available. *Faculty:* 27. *Students:* 45 full-time (11 women), 20 part-time (9 women); includes 8 minority (7 Hispanic/Latino; 1 Two or more races, non-Hispanic/Latino), 2 international. Average age 34. 52 applicants, 38% accepted, 11 enrolled. In 2014, 3 master's, 7 doctorates awarded. Terminal master's awarded for partial completion of doctoral program. *Degree requirements:* For master's, one foreign language, thesis optional; for doctorate, 2 foreign languages, thesis/dissertation. *Entrance requirements:* For master's and doctorate, GRE General Test. Additional exam requirements/recommendations for international students: Required—TOEFL. *Application deadline:* For fall admission, 3/1 for domestic students. Application fee: $50 ($90 for international students). *Expenses:* Tuition, state resident: full-time $4078; part-time $226.55 per credit hour. Tuition, nonresident: full-time $10,594; part-time $577.55 per credit hour. *Required fees:* $2813; $237.70 per credit hour. $278.50 per semester. Tuition and fees vary according to degree level and student level. *Financial support:* In 2014–15, 48 students received support, including 10 fellowships with full and partial tuition reimbursements available (averaging $19,021 per year), 2 research assistantships with full and partial tuition reimbursements available (averaging $7,233 per year), 35 teaching assistantships with full and partial tuition reimbursements available (averaging $6,874 per year); career-related internships or fieldwork, institutionally sponsored loans, scholarships/grants, traineeships, health care benefits, tuition waivers (full and partial), and unspecified assistantships also available. Support available to part-time students. Financial award application deadline: 2/1; financial award applicants required to submit FAFSA. *Faculty research:* Recent U.S. history, Southwest, border studies, military history, Europe. *Unit head:* Dr. David Vaught, Department Head, 979-845-2571, Fax: 979-862-4314, E-mail: d-vaught@tamu.edu. *Application contact:* Adam Seipp, Director of Graduate Studies, 979-845-5996, Fax: 979-862-4314, E-mail: aseipp@tamu.edu.
Website: http://history.tamu.edu/

Texas A&M University–Central Texas, Graduate Studies and Research, Killeen, TX 76549. Offers accounting (MS); business administration (MBA); clinical mental health counseling (MS); criminal justice (MCJ); curriculum and instruction (M Ed); educational administration (M Ed); educational psychology - experimental psychology (MS); history (MA); human resource management (MS); information systems (MS); liberal studies (MS); management and leadership (MS); marriage and family therapy (MS); mathematics (MS); political science (MA); school counseling (M Ed); school psychology (Ed S).

Texas A&M University–Corpus Christi, College of Graduate Studies, College of Liberal Arts, Corpus Christi, TX 78412-5503. Offers communication (MA); English (MA); history (MA); psychology (MA); public administration (MPA); studio art (MA, MFA). Part-time and evening/weekend programs available. *Students:* 85 full-time (56 women), 100 part-time (68 women); includes 85 minority (3 Black or African American, non-Hispanic/Latino; 2 American Indian or Alaska Native, non-Hispanic/Latino; 4 Asian, non-Hispanic/Latino; 74 Hispanic/Latino; 2 Two or more races, non-Hispanic/Latino), 12 international. Average age 31. 206 applicants, 60% accepted, 83 enrolled. In 2014, 64 master's awarded. *Degree requirements:* For master's, comprehensive exam, thesis (for some programs). *Entrance requirements:* For master's, GRE General Test. Additional exam requirements/recommendations for international students: Required—TOEFL. *Application deadline:* For fall admission, 7/15 priority date for domestic students, 5/1 priority date for international students; for spring admission, 11/15 priority date for domestic students, 9/1 priority date for international students. Applications are processed on a rolling basis. Application fee: $50 ($70 for international students). Electronic applications accepted. *Financial support:* Research assistantships, teaching assistantships, career-related internships or fieldwork, Federal Work-Study, institutionally sponsored loans, scholarships/grants, health care benefits, and unspecified assistantships available. Support available to part-time students. Financial award application deadline: 3/15; financial award applicants required to submit FAFSA. *Unit head:* Dr. Mark Hartlaub, Interim Dean, 361-825-2659, Fax: 361-825-5844, E-mail: mark.hartlaub@tamucc.edu. *Application contact:* Graduate Admissions Coordinator, 361-825-2177, Fax: 361-825-2755, E-mail: gradweb@tamucc.edu.
Website: http://cla.tamucc.edu/

Texas A&M University–Kingsville, College of Graduate Studies, College of Arts and Sciences, Program in History and Political Science, Kingsville, TX 78363. Offers MA, MS. *Students:* 1 (woman) part-time; minority (Hispanic/Latino). Average age 32. In 2014, 3 master's awarded. *Degree requirements:* For master's, variable foreign language requirement, comprehensive exam, thesis (for some programs). *Entrance requirements:* For master's, GRE, MAT, GMAT. Additional exam requirements/recommendations for international students: Required—TOEFL (minimum score 550 paper-based; 79 iBT). *Application deadline:* For fall admission, 8/15 for domestic students, 6/1 for international students; for spring admission, 12/15 for domestic students, 10/1 for international students; for summer admission, 5/15 for domestic students, 4/1 for international students. Applications are processed on a rolling basis. Application fee: $35 ($50 for international students). Electronic applications accepted. *Financial support:* Career-related internships or fieldwork, Federal Work-Study, institutionally sponsored loans, scholarships/grants, health care benefits, tuition waivers (full and partial), and unspecified assistantships available. Support available to part-time students. Financial award application deadline: 5/15; financial award applicants required to submit FAFSA. *Unit head:* Dr. Shannon Baker, Department Chair, 361-593-3594, Fax: 361-593-3502, E-mail: shannon.baker@tamuk.edu. *Application contact:* Dr. Mohamed Abdelrahman, Dean of Graduate Studies, 361-593-2809, E-mail: mohamed.abdelrahman@tamuk.edu.

Texas Christian University, AddRan College of Liberal Arts, Department of History, Fort Worth, TX 76129. Offers United States (MA, PhD). *Faculty:* 14 full-time (3 women). *Students:* 52 full-time (22 women); includes 4 minority (3 Hispanic/Latino; 1 Two or more races, non-Hispanic/Latino), 1 international. Average age 32. 26 applicants, 54% accepted, 11 enrolled. In 2014, 4 master's, 7 doctorates awarded. Terminal master's awarded for partial completion of doctoral program. *Degree requirements:* For master's, comprehensive exam, thesis or alternative; for doctorate, one foreign language, comprehensive exam, thesis/dissertation. *Entrance requirements:* For master's and doctorate, GRE General Test. Additional exam requirements/recommendations for international students: Recommended—TOEFL. *Application deadline:* 2/1 for domestic and international students; for summer admission, 2/1 for domestic and international students. Applications are processed on a rolling basis. Application fee: $60. Electronic applications accepted. *Expenses: Tuition:* Full-time $22,860; part-time $1270 per credit hour. *Financial support:* In 2014–15, 50 students received support, including 3 fellowships with full tuition reimbursements available (averaging $20,000 per year), 15 research assistantships with full tuition reimbursements available (averaging $17,500 per year), 5 teaching assistantships with full tuition reimbursements available (averaging $17,500 per year); tuition waivers also available. Financial award application deadline: 2/1. *Faculty research:* Gender history, military history, popular culture, imperialism, American West. *Total annual research expenditures:* $48,000. *Unit head:* Dr. Jodi Campbell, Associate Professor, 817-257-5882, Fax: 817-257-5650, E-mail:

j.campbell@tcu.edu. *Application contact:* Dana Summers, Administrative Assistant, 817-257-7822, Fax: 817-257-5650, E-mail: d.summers@tcu.edu.
Website: http://www.his.tcu.edu/graduate.asp

Texas Southern University, College of Liberal Arts and Behavioral Sciences, Department of History and Geography, Houston, TX 77004-4584. Offers history (MA). Part-time and evening/weekend programs available. *Degree requirements:* For master's, comprehensive exam, thesis optional. *Entrance requirements:* For master's, GRE General Test, minimum GPA of 2.5. Additional exam requirements/ recommendations for international students: Required—TOEFL. Electronic applications accepted. *Faculty research:* American, Colonial, African, Asian, and African-American history.

Texas State University, The Graduate College, College of Liberal Arts, Program in History, San Marcos, TX 78666. Offers M Ed, MA. Part-time programs available. *Faculty:* 23 full-time (9 women), 1 (woman) part-time/adjunct. *Students:* 44 full-time (18 women), 44 part-time (20 women); includes 15 minority (2 Black or African American, non-Hispanic/Latino; 11 Hispanic/Latino; 1 Native Hawaiian or other Pacific Islander, non-Hispanic/Latino; 1 Two or more races, non-Hispanic/Latino). Average age 31. 41 applicants, 71% accepted, 19 enrolled. In 2014, 19 master's awarded. *Degree requirements:* For master's, comprehensive exam, thesis optional. *Entrance requirements:* For master's, GRE General Test (minimum preferred score 156 verbal reasoning/500 old test), baccalaureate degree from regionally-accredited university with minimum GPA of 2.75 on last 60 undergraduate semester hours. Additional exam requirements/recommendations for international students: Required—TOEFL (minimum score 550 paper-based; 78 iBT). *Application deadline:* For fall admission, 6/15 priority date for domestic students, 6/1 for international students; for spring admission, 10/15 priority date for domestic students, 10/1 for international students; for summer admission, 4/15 for domestic students, 3/15 for international students. Applications are processed on a rolling basis. Application fee: $40 ($90 for international students). Electronic applications accepted. *Expenses:* Expenses: $8,834 (tuition and fees combined). *Financial support:* In 2014–15, 42 students received support, including 7 research assistantships (averaging $11,359 per year), 31 teaching assistantships (averaging $12,306 per year); Federal Work-Study, institutionally sponsored loans, scholarships/grants, and unspecified assistantships also available. Support available to part-time students. Financial award application deadline: 4/1; financial award applicants required to submit FAFSA. *Faculty research:* Cattle ranching, revision of national history. *Total annual research expenditures:* $50,197. *Unit head:* Dr. Rebecca Montgomery, Graduate Advisor, 512-245-2116, Fax: 512-245-3043, E-mail: rm53@txstate.edu. *Application contact:* Dr. Andrea Golato, Dean of the Graduate College, 512-245-2581, E-mail: gradcollege@txstate.edu.
Website: http://www.txstate.edu/history/

Texas Tech University, Graduate School, College of Arts and Sciences, Department of History, Lubbock, TX 79409-1013. Offers MA, PhD. Part-time and evening/weekend programs available. *Faculty:* 33 full-time (10 women), 2 part-time/adjunct (0 women). *Students:* 64 full-time (23 women), 20 part-time (6 women); includes 17 minority (1 Black or African American, non-Hispanic/Latino; 1 American Indian or Alaska Native, non-Hispanic/Latino; 2 Asian, non-Hispanic/Latino; 11 Hispanic/Latino; 2 Two or more races, non-Hispanic/Latino), 4 international. Average age 33. 45 applicants, 62% accepted, 19 enrolled. In 2014, 10 master's, 4 doctorates awarded. *Degree requirements:* For master's, one foreign language, comprehensive exam (for some programs), thesis optional; for doctorate, one foreign language, comprehensive exam, thesis/dissertation. *Entrance requirements:* For master's and doctorate, GRE, statement of purpose, 3 letters of reference, writing sample. Additional exam requirements/recommendations for international students: Required—TOEFL (minimum score 550 paper-based; 79 iBT). *Application deadline:* For fall admission, 6/1 priority date for domestic students, 1/15 priority date for international students; for spring admission, 9/1 priority date for domestic students, 6/15 priority date for international students. Applications are processed on a rolling basis. Application fee: $60. Electronic applications accepted. *Expenses:* Tuition, state resident: full-time $6310; part-time $262.92 per credit hour. Tuition, nonresident: full-time $14,998; part-time $624.92 per credit hour. *Required fees:* $2701; $36.50 per credit. $912.50 per semester. Tuition and fees vary according to course load. *Financial support:* In 2014–15, 68 students received support, including 53 fellowships (averaging $2,861 per year), 1 research assistantship (averaging $15,667 per year), 59 teaching assistantships (averaging $12,221 per year); scholarships/grants, health care benefits, and unspecified assistantships also available. Financial award application deadline: 3/ 15; financial award applicants required to submit FAFSA. *Faculty research:* Global conflict and war, gender and identity, politics and social movements, nationalism, borderlands. *Total annual research expenditures:* $62,104. *Unit head:* Dr. Sean P. Cunningham, Interim Chair, 806-742-3744, Fax: 806-742-1060, E-mail: sean.cunningham@ttu.edu. *Application contact:* Dr. Laura Calkins, Director of Graduate Studies, 806-742-3744, Fax: 806-742-1060, E-mail: laura.calkins@ttu.edu.
Website: http://www.depts.ttu.edu/history/

Texas Woman's University, Graduate School, College of Arts and Sciences, Department of History and Government, Denton, TX 76201. Offers government (MA); history (MA). Part-time and evening/weekend programs available. *Degree requirements:* For master's, comprehensive exam, thesis. *Entrance requirements:* For master's, minimum GPA of 3.25, written statement of purpose; 2 letters of reference. Additional exam requirements/recommendations for international students: Required—TOEFL (minimum score 550 paper-based; 79 iBT). Electronic applications accepted. *Faculty research:* U.S. history, politics, and law; global history, politics, and law; Latin American and Caribbean history; legal studies; women in history, politics, and law.

Trinity Western University, School of Graduate Studies, Program in Interdisciplinary Humanities, Langley, BC V2Y 1Y1, Canada. Offers general humanities (MAIH); specialized (MAIH), including English, history, philosophy. Part-time programs available. *Degree requirements:* For master's, thesis or alternative, 36 semester hours. *Entrance requirements:* For master's, strong undergraduate degree in humanities or English, history or philosophy. Additional exam requirements/recommendations for international students: Recommended—TOEFL. Electronic applications accepted. *Faculty research:* Literary theory, gender, medieval and early modern literature, philosophy of religion, Thomas Merton's poetics.

Troy University, Graduate School, College of Arts and Sciences, Program in History, Troy, AL 36082. Offers American history (MA); European history (MA). Part-time and evening/weekend programs available. *Faculty:* 5 full-time (2 women). *Students:* 11 part-time (4 women). Average age 32. 28 applicants, 96% accepted, 5 enrolled. *Degree requirements:* For master's, variable foreign language requirement, comprehensive exam, thesis optional. *Entrance requirements:* For master's, GRE (minimum score of 850 on old exam or 290 on new exam), MAT (minimum score of 385), or GMAT (minimum score of 380), bachelor's degree, minimum undergraduate GPA of 2.5 or 3.0 on last 30 semester hours, letter of recommendation. Additional exam requirements/ recommendations for international students: Required—TOEFL (minimum score 523 paper-based; 70 iBT), IELTS (minimum score 6); Recommended—TWE. *Application deadline:* For fall admission, 6/1 for international students; for spring admission, 10/15 for international students. Applications are processed on a rolling basis. Application fee: $50. Electronic applications accepted. *Expenses:* Tuition, state resident: full-time $6570; part-time $365 per credit hour. Tuition, nonresident: full-time $13,140; part-time $730 per credit hour. *Required fees:* $365 per credit hour. *Unit head:* Dr. Allen E. Jones, Jr., Chairman, 334-340-3512, E-mail: ajones@troy.edu. *Application contact:* Jessica Campbell, Director of Graduate Admissions, 334-670-3178, Fax: 334-670-3733, E-mail: jacord@troy.edu.

Troy University, Graduate School, College of Education, Program in Secondary Education, Troy, AL 36082. Offers 5th year biology (MS); 5th year computer science (MS); 5th year history (MS); 5th year language arts (MS); 5th year mathematics (MS); 5th year social science (MS); traditional biology (MS); traditional computer science (MS); traditional history (MS); traditional language arts (MS); traditional mathematics (MS); traditional social science (MS). *Accreditation:* NCATE. Part-time and evening/weekend programs available. *Faculty:* 3 full-time (2 women). *Students:* 10 full-time (8 women), 15 part-time (11 women); includes 4 minority (all Black or African American, non-Hispanic/ Latino). Average age 29. 9 applicants, 100% accepted, 3 enrolled. In 2014, 12 master's awarded. *Degree requirements:* For master's, comprehensive exam, thesis. *Entrance requirements:* For master's, GRE (minimum score of 850 on old exam or 290 on new exam), GMAT (minimum score of 380), or MAT (minimum score of 385), bachelor's degree; minimum undergraduate GPA of 2.5 or 3.0 on last 30 semester hours, letter of recommendation. Additional exam requirements/recommendations for international students: Required—TOEFL (minimum score 523 paper-based; 70 iBT), IELTS (minimum score 6). *Application deadline:* Applications are processed on a rolling basis. Application fee: $50. Electronic applications accepted. *Expenses:* Tuition, state resident: full-time $6570; part-time $365 per credit hour. Tuition, nonresident: full-time $13,140; part-time $730 per credit hour. *Required fees:* $365 per credit hour. *Financial support:* Career-related internships or fieldwork available. Support available to part-time students. Financial award applicants required to submit FAFSA. *Unit head:* Dr. Jan Oliver, Associate Professor, 334-670-3444, Fax: 334-670-3548, E-mail: oliver@troy.edu. *Application contact:* Jessica A. Kimbro, Director of Graduate Admissions, 334-670-3178, E-mail: bcamp@troy.edu.

Tufts University, Graduate School of Arts and Sciences, Department of History, Medford, MA 02155. Offers history (MA, PhD); history and museum studies (MA). *Faculty:* 21 full-time (10 women). *Students:* 14 full-time (6 women), 4 part-time (3 women); includes 1 minority (Asian, non-Hispanic/Latino), 2 international. Average age 26. 54 applicants, 39% accepted, 5 enrolled. In 2014, 8 master's awarded. Terminal master's awarded for partial completion of doctoral program. *Degree requirements:* For master's, one foreign language; for doctorate, 2 foreign languages, thesis/dissertation. *Entrance requirements:* For master's and doctorate, GRE General Test, writing sample. Additional exam requirements/recommendations for international students: Required—TOEFL (minimum score 550 paper-based; 80 iBT), IELTS (minimum score 6.5). *Application deadline:* For fall admission, 1/15 for domestic and international students. Applications are processed on a rolling basis. Application fee: $75. Electronic applications accepted. *Expenses: Tuition:* Full-time $45,590; part-time $1161 per credit hour. *Required fees:* $782. Full-time tuition and fees vary according to degree level, program and student level. Part-time tuition and fees vary according to course load. *Financial support:* Teaching assistantships with full and partial tuition reimbursements, Federal Work-Study, scholarships/grants, tuition waivers (partial), and unspecified assistantships available. Financial award application deadline: 1/15. *Unit head:* Dr. Steven Marrone, Graduate Program Director. *Application contact:* Office of Graduate Admissions, 617-627-3395, E-mail: gradadmissions@tufts.edu.
Website: http://www.ase.tufts.edu/history/

Tulane University, School of Liberal Arts, Department of History, New Orleans, LA 70118-5669. Offers MA, PhD. *Degree requirements:* For master's, one foreign language, thesis; for doctorate, variable foreign language requirement, thesis/ dissertation. *Entrance requirements:* For master's, GRE General Test, minimum B average in undergraduate course work; for doctorate, GRE General Test. Additional exam requirements/recommendations for international students: Required—TOEFL. Electronic applications accepted. *Expenses: Tuition:* Full-time $46,326; part-time $2574 per credit hour. *Required fees:* $1980; $44.50 per credit hour. $550 per term. Tuition and fees vary according to course load and program.

Union Institute & University, Individualized Master of Arts Program, Cincinnati, OH 45206-1925. Offers creativity studies (MA); health and wellness (MA); history and culture (MA); leadership, public policy, and social issues (MA); literature and writing (MA). Part-time programs available. *Faculty:* 4 full-time (2 women), 3 part-time/adjunct (2 women). *Students:* 14 full-time (11 women), 107 part-time (75 women); includes 36 minority (29 Black or African American, non-Hispanic/Latino; 3 American Indian or Alaska Native, non-Hispanic/Latino; 3 Hispanic/Latino; 1 Two or more races, non-Hispanic/Latino). Average age 40. *Degree requirements:* For master's, thesis. *Entrance requirements:* For master's, transcript, essay, 3 letters of recommendation, resume. *Application deadline:* For spring admission, 3/13 for domestic students. Applications are processed on a rolling basis. Application fee: $50. Electronic applications accepted. *Expenses: Tuition:* Full-time $26,640; part-time $719 per credit hour. *Required fees:* $216; $54 per semester. Part-time tuition and fees vary according to course load, degree level and program. *Financial support:* Career-related internships or fieldwork and tuition waivers available. Financial award applicants required to submit FAFSA. *Unit head:* Andrea Scarpino, Program Director, 802-828-8777. *Application contact:* Director of Admissions, 800-861-6400.
Website: https://www.myunion.edu/academics/masters-programs/master-of-arts/

Université de Moncton, Faculty of Arts and Social Sciences, Department of History and Geography, Moncton, NB E1A 3E9, Canada. Offers history (MA). *Degree requirements:* For master's, thesis, proficiency in English and French. *Entrance requirements:* For master's, honors degree in history, minimum GPA of 2.7. Electronic applications accepted. *Faculty research:* Economic and social history (Canada, France, Acadia), sociocultural history, women's history, labor history, history of the press.

Université de Montréal, Faculty of Arts and Sciences, Department of History, Montréal, QC H3C 3J7, Canada. Offers MA, PhD. *Degree requirements:* For master's, thesis; for doctorate, thesis/dissertation, general exam. *Entrance requirements:* For doctorate, master's degree in related field. Electronic applications accepted. *Faculty research:* Preindustrial Quebec, Quebec working class, Quebec intellectual, diffusion of scientific thought, history of medicine.

Université de Sherbrooke, Faculty of Letters and Human Sciences, Department of Human Sciences, Sherbrooke, QC J1K 2R1, Canada. Offers history (MA); philosophy (MA). *Degree requirements:* For master's, thesis. *Entrance requirements:* For master's, minimum GPA of 2.75. *Faculty research:* Political, social, and urban history; history of women.

Université du Québec à Montréal, Graduate Programs, Program in History, Montréal, QC H3C 3P8, Canada. Offers MA, PhD. Part-time programs available. *Degree requirements:* For master's, thesis; for doctorate, thesis/dissertation. *Entrance requirements:* For master's, appropriate bachelor's degree or equivalent, proficiency in French; for doctorate, appropriate master's degree or equivalent, proficiency in French.

Université Laval, Faculty of Letters, Department of History, Programs in History, Québec, QC G1K 7P4, Canada. Offers MA, PhD. Terminal master's awarded for partial completion of doctoral program. *Degree requirements:* For master's, thesis (for some

programs); for doctorate, comprehensive exam, thesis/dissertation. *Entrance requirements:* For master's and doctorate, English exam (comprehension of written English), knowledge of French. Electronic applications accepted.

Université Laval, Faculty of Letters, Department of Literature, Programs in Ancient Civilization, Québec, QC G1K 7P4, Canada. Offers MA, PhD. Part-time programs available. Terminal master's awarded for partial completion of doctoral program. *Degree requirements:* For master's, thesis; for doctorate, comprehensive exam, thesis/dissertation. *Entrance requirements:* For master's and doctorate, English test (comprehension of written English), knowledge of French, knowledge of an ancient language. Electronic applications accepted.

University at Albany, State University of New York, College of Arts and Sciences, Department of History, Albany, NY 12222-0001. Offers history (MA, PhD); public history (Certificate). Part-time programs available. *Degree requirements:* For master's, variable foreign language requirement, exam, research paper or thesis; for doctorate, thesis/dissertation. *Entrance requirements:* For master's, minimum GPA of 3.0; for doctorate, GRE General Test, minimum GPA of 3.0. Additional exam requirements/recommendations for international students: Required—TOEFL (minimum score 550 paper-based). Electronic applications accepted. *Faculty research:* American history (all phases); public policy; European history (Medieval to modern); Asian, African, and Latin American history.

University at Buffalo, the State University of New York, Graduate School, College of Arts and Sciences, Department of History, Buffalo, NY 14260. Offers MA, PhD. Part-time programs available. *Faculty:* 24 full-time (10 women), 4 part-time/adjunct (1 woman). *Students:* 74 full-time (36 women), 11 part-time (5 women); includes 18 minority (4 Black or African American, non-Hispanic/Latino; 1 American Indian or Alaska Native, non-Hispanic/Latino; 10 Asian, non-Hispanic/Latino; 3 Hispanic/Latino), 3 international. Average age 29. 91 applicants, 24% accepted, 21 enrolled. In 2014, 16 master's, 1 doctorate awarded. Terminal master's awarded for partial completion of doctoral program. *Degree requirements:* For master's, project; for doctorate, variable foreign language requirement, thesis/dissertation, general exam. *Entrance requirements:* For master's and doctorate, GRE General Test. Additional exam requirements/recommendations for international students: Required—TOEFL (minimum score 79 iBT). *Application deadline:* For fall admission, 1/5 for domestic and international students; for spring admission, 10/1 priority date for domestic students, 10/1 for international students. Applications are processed on a rolling basis. Application fee: $75. Electronic applications accepted. *Financial support:* In 2014–15, 25 students received support, including 4 fellowships with full tuition reimbursements available (averaging $14,000 per year), 22 teaching assistantships with full tuition reimbursements available (averaging $15,000 per year); Federal Work-Study, institutionally sponsored loans, and unspecified assistantships also available. Financial award application deadline: 1/15; financial award applicants required to submit FAFSA. *Faculty research:* Geographical areas: Africa, Asia, early modern Europe, Latin America and Caribbean, modern Europe (Britain, France, Germany, Spain), North and South Atlantic, world, United States and Colonial America; thematic areas: African-American, gender, imperialism and colonialism, intellectual/cultural/religious, political, public history, medicine/disability/science/knowledge, slavery, transnational/international, urban. *Total annual research expenditures:* $35,000. *Unit head:* Dr. James Bono, Chair, 716-645-8423, Fax: 716-645-5954, E-mail: hischaos@buffalo.edu. *Application contact:* Dr. Jonathan Dewald, Director of Graduate Studies, 716-645-8406, Fax: 716-645-5954, E-mail: ubhistor@buffalo.edu.
Website: http://cas.buffalo.edu/depts/history

The University of Akron, Graduate School, Buchtel College of Arts and Sciences, Department of History, Akron, OH 44325. Offers MA, PhD. Part-time programs available. *Faculty:* 14 full-time (5 women), 2 part-time/adjunct (both women). *Students:* 22 full-time (9 women), 16 part-time (5 women); includes 4 minority (2 Black or African American, non-Hispanic/Latino; 1 American Indian or Alaska Native, non-Hispanic/Latino; 1 Two or more races, non-Hispanic/Latino). Average age 32. 24 applicants, 54% accepted, 11 enrolled. In 2014, 4 master's, 2 doctorates awarded. *Degree requirements:* For master's, one foreign language, thesis optional, written exams, seminars; for doctorate, 2 foreign languages, comprehensive exam, thesis/dissertation, written exams, oral exams. *Entrance requirements:* For master's, GRE General Test, minimum GPA of 3.0, writing sample, three letters of recommendation, letter of intent; for doctorate, GRE General Test, minimum GPA of 3.5, three letters of recommendation, personal statement, writing sample, evidence of reading knowledge in one foreign language. Additional exam requirements/recommendations for international students: Required—TOEFL (minimum score 580 paper-based; 92 iBT). *Application deadline:* For fall admission, 2/1 priority date for domestic and international students. Application fee: $45 ($70 for international students). Electronic applications accepted. *Expenses:* Tuition, state resident: full-time $7578; part-time $421 per credit hour. Tuition, nonresident: full-time $12,977; part-time $721 per credit hour. *Required fees:* $1388; $35 per credit hour. Tuition and fees vary according to course load. *Financial support:* In 2014–15, 1 fellowship, 15 teaching assistantships with full tuition reimbursements were awarded; unspecified assistantships also available. *Faculty research:* European, American, and world history. *Total annual research expenditures:* $126,338. *Unit head:* Dr. A. Martin Wainwright, Chair, 330-972-6512, E-mail: amartin@uakron.edu. *Application contact:* Dr. Martha Santos, Graduate Director, 330-972-2686, E-mail: santos@uakron.edu.
Website: http://www.uakron.edu/history/

The University of Alabama, Graduate School, College of Arts and Sciences, Department of History, Tuscaloosa, AL 35487. Offers MA, PhD. *Faculty:* 24 full-time (9 women). *Students:* 51 full-time (22 women), 7 part-time (0 women); includes 6 minority (1 Black or African American, non-Hispanic/Latino; 5 Hispanic/Latino), 4 international. Average age 30. 67 applicants, 43% accepted, 15 enrolled. In 2014, 13 master's, 6 doctorates awarded. Terminal master's awarded for partial completion of doctoral program. *Degree requirements:* For master's, one foreign language, thesis optional, oral exam; for doctorate, 2 foreign languages, comprehensive exam, thesis/dissertation, oral exams, written exam. *Entrance requirements:* For master's and doctorate, GRE General Test. *Application deadline:* For fall admission, 5/1 for domestic students. Applications are processed on a rolling basis. Application fee: $50 ($60 for international students). *Expenses:* Tuition, state resident: full-time $9826. Tuition, nonresident: full-time $24,950. *Financial support:* In 2014–15, 29 students received support, including 6 fellowships with full tuition reimbursements available (averaging $10,000 per year), research assistantships (averaging $10,000 per year), 23 teaching assistantships with full tuition reimbursements available (averaging $10,200 per year); institutionally sponsored loans and unspecified assistantships also available. Financial award application deadline: 1/15. *Faculty research:* United States, modern European, Latin American, military, and southern U.S. history. *Total annual research expenditures:* $67,900. *Unit head:* Dr. Michael Mendle, Chair, 205-348-7103. *Application contact:* Dr. Lisa Lindquist Dorr, Graduate Director, 205-348-1859, E-mail: ldorr@bama.ua.edu.

The University of Alabama at Birmingham, College of Arts and Sciences, Program in History, Birmingham, AL 35294. Offers MA. Part-time programs available. *Students:* 7 full-time (1 woman), 8 part-time (2 women); includes 2 minority (both Black or African American, non-Hispanic/Latino), 1 international. Average age 32. In 2014, 9 master's awarded. *Degree requirements:* For master's, variable foreign language requirement, thesis or alternative. *Entrance requirements:* For master's, GRE General Test. Additional exam requirements/recommendations for international students: Required—TOEFL, TWE. *Application deadline:* For fall admission, 7/1 for domestic students; for spring admission, 11/1 for domestic students. Applications are processed on a rolling basis. Application fee: $45 ($60 for international students). Electronic applications accepted. *Expenses:* Tuition, state resident: full-time $7090; part-time $370 per credit hour. Tuition, nonresident: full-time $16,072; part-time $869 per credit hour. Full-time tuition and fees vary according to course load and program. *Financial support:* Research assistantships, teaching assistantships, and institutionally sponsored loans available. *Faculty research:* History of Europe, United States, Latin America, American South. *Unit head:* Dr. John Van Sant, Program Director, 205-975-6520, E-mail: jvansant@uab.edu. *Application contact:* Susan Noblitt Banks, Director of Graduate School Operations, 205-934-8227, Fax: 205-934-8413, E-mail: gradschool@uab.edu.
Website: http://www.uab.edu/cas/history/graduate-program

The University of Alabama in Huntsville, School of Graduate Studies, College of Liberal Arts, Department of History, Huntsville, AL 35899. Offers education (MA); history (MA); social science (MA). Part-time and evening/weekend programs available. *Degree requirements:* For master's, one foreign language, comprehensive exam, thesis or alternative, oral and written exams. *Entrance requirements:* For master's, GRE General Test, minimum GPA of 3.0, bachelor's degree in history or related area. Additional exam requirements/recommendations for international students: Required—TOEFL (minimum score 500 paper-based; 80 iBT), IELTS (minimum score 6.5). Electronic applications accepted. *Faculty research:* Public history, history of the U.S. space program, military history, history of science and technology, women in history.

University of Alaska Fairbanks, College of Liberal Arts, Department of Northern Studies, Fairbanks, AK 99775-6460. Offers environmental politics and policy (MA); Northern history (MA). Part-time programs available. *Faculty:* 1 (woman) full-time. *Students:* 16 full-time (8 women), 17 part-time (13 women); includes 1 minority (Two or more races, non-Hispanic/Latino), 2 international. Average age 37. 15 applicants, 47% accepted, 7 enrolled. In 2014, 7 master's awarded. *Degree requirements:* For master's, comprehensive exam, oral defense of project or thesis. *Entrance requirements:* For master's, bachelor's degree from accredited institution with minimum cumulative undergraduate and major GPA of 3.0. Additional exam requirements/recommendations for international students: Required—TOEFL (minimum score 550 paper-based; 79 iBT), IELTS (minimum score 6.5). *Application deadline:* For fall admission, 6/1 for domestic students, 3/1 for international students; for spring admission, 10/15 for domestic students, 9/1 for international students. Applications are processed on a rolling basis. Application fee: $60. Electronic applications accepted. *Expenses:* Tuition, state resident: full-time $7614; part-time $423 per credit. Tuition, nonresident: full-time $15,552; part-time $864 per credit. Tuition and fees vary according to course level, course load and reciprocity agreements. *Financial support:* In 2014–15, 4 research assistantships with full tuition reimbursements (averaging $6,012 per year), 10 teaching assistantships with full tuition reimbursements (averaging $8,530 per year) were awarded; fellowships with full tuition reimbursements, career-related internships or fieldwork, Federal Work-Study, scholarships/grants, health care benefits, and unspecified assistantships also available. Support available to part-time students. Financial award application deadline: 1/1; financial award applicants required to submit FAFSA. *Unit head:* Mary Ehrlander, Director, 907-474-7126, Fax: 907-474-5817, E-mail: fynors@uaf.edu. *Application contact:* Mary Kreta, Director of Admissions, 907-474-7500, Fax: 907-474-7097, E-mail: admissions@uaf.edu.
Website: http://www.uaf.edu/northern/

University of Alberta, Faculty of Graduate Studies and Research, Department of History and Classics, Edmonton, AB T6G 2E1, Canada. Offers ancient history (PhD); classical archaeology (MA, PhD); classical literature (PhD); classics (MA); history (MA, PhD). Part-time and evening/weekend programs available. *Degree requirements:* For master's, one foreign language, thesis (for some programs); for doctorate, one foreign language, thesis/dissertation. *Entrance requirements:* For master's, minimum B+ average; for doctorate, minimum A- average. Additional exam requirements/recommendations for international students: Required—TOEFL (minimum score 580 paper-based). Electronic applications accepted. *Faculty research:* Western Canada, classical archaeology, Britain, Eastern Europe, East Asia.

The University of Arizona, College of Social and Behavioral Sciences, Department of History, Tucson, AZ 85721. Offers MA, PhD. Part-time programs available. Terminal master's awarded for partial completion of doctoral program. *Degree requirements:* For master's, one foreign language, comprehensive exam, thesis optional; for doctorate, 2 foreign languages, comprehensive exam, thesis/dissertation. *Entrance requirements:* For master's, GRE General Test, 3 letters of recommendation, writing sample; for doctorate, GRE General Test, 3 letters of recommendation, statement of purpose, 2 writing samples. Additional exam requirements/recommendations for international students: Required—TOEFL (minimum score 550 paper-based; 79 iBT). Electronic applications accepted. *Faculty research:* Latin American history, European history, U.S. history, women's history, global/environmental history.

University of Arkansas, Graduate School, J. William Fulbright College of Arts and Sciences, Department of History, Fayetteville, AR 72701-1201. Offers MA, PhD. Part-time programs available. *Degree requirements:* For master's, thesis optional; for doctorate, 2 foreign languages, thesis/dissertation. *Entrance requirements:* For master's, GRE General Test; for doctorate, GRE General Test, GRE Subject Test. Electronic applications accepted.

The University of British Columbia, Faculty of Arts, Department of History, Vancouver, BC V6T 1Z1, Canada. Offers MA, PhD. *Degree requirements:* For master's, one foreign language, thesis, six 3-credit courses; for doctorate, one foreign language, comprehensive exam, thesis/dissertation, four or five 3-credit courses. *Entrance requirements:* For master's, four-year bachelor's degree; for doctorate, master's degree (or equivalent) in history, first-class (A) standing in graduate courses, language relevant to dissertation research. Additional exam requirements/recommendations for international students: Required—TOEFL (minimum score 570 paper-based; 89 iBT). Electronic applications accepted. *Faculty research:* Canadian, British, European, modern Chinese and Japanese history; international relations.

University of Calgary, Faculty of Graduate Studies, Faculty of Arts, Department of History, Calgary, AB T2N 1N4, Canada. Offers MA, PhD. Part-time programs available. *Degree requirements:* For master's, one foreign language, thesis; for doctorate, one foreign language, thesis/dissertation, 3 written comprehensive exams, oral candidacy exam. *Entrance requirements:* For master's, minimum GPA of 3.4, writing sample; for doctorate, sample of written work, master's degree in history. Additional exam requirements/recommendations for international students: Recommended—TOEFL. Electronic applications accepted. *Faculty research:* Military history, Canadian history, Latin American history, gender/women's history, native history.

University of California, Berkeley, Graduate Division, College of Letters and Science, Department of History, Berkeley, CA 94720-2550. Offers PhD. *Degree requirements:* For doctorate, variable foreign language requirement, comprehensive exam, thesis/dissertation. *Entrance requirements:* For doctorate, GRE General Test, minimum GPA

of 3.0, 3 letters of recommendation, writing sample (not to exceed 10 pages), academic transcripts, 2 essays (statement of purpose, personal statement). Additional exam requirements/recommendations for international students: Required—TOEFL (minimum score 570 paper-based; 68 iBT). Electronic applications accepted. *Faculty research:* African, British, Byzantine, European (Ancient Greece and Rome, Medieval, Early Modern, Late Modern), Asian (China, Japan, South, Southeast), Jewish, Latin American, Middle Eastern, science, and United States history.

University of California, Berkeley, Graduate Division, College of Letters and Science, Group in Ancient History and Mediterranean Archaeology, Berkeley, CA 94720-1500. Offers MA, PhD. *Degree requirements:* For master's, one foreign language, exam or thesis; for doctorate, 2 foreign languages, thesis/dissertation, qualifying exam. *Entrance requirements:* For master's and doctorate, GRE General Test, minimum GPA of 3.0, 3 letters of recommendation. Additional exam requirements/recommendations for international students: Required—TOEFL (minimum score 570 paper-based), TWE.

University of California, Davis, Graduate Studies, Program in History, Davis, CA 95616. Offers MA, PhD. Terminal master's awarded for partial completion of doctoral program. *Degree requirements:* For master's, one foreign language, comprehensive exam (for some programs), thesis (for some programs); for doctorate, 2 foreign languages, thesis/dissertation. *Entrance requirements:* For master's, GRE General Test, minimum GPA of 3.0, writing sample; for doctorate, GRE General Test, master's degree, writing sample. Additional exam requirements/recommendations for international students: Required—TOEFL (minimum score 550 paper-based). Electronic applications accepted. *Faculty research:* American social, cultural, and western history; modern and early history; modern European, East Asian, and Latin American history; history of science and medicine; cross-cultural history of women.

University of California, Irvine, School of Humanities, Department of History, Irvine, CA 92697. Offers MA, PhD. *Students:* 50 full-time (25 women), 1 (woman) part-time; includes 18 minority (1 Black or African American, non-Hispanic/Latino; 1 Asian, non-Hispanic/Latino; 10 Hispanic/Latino; 6 Two or more races, non-Hispanic/Latino), 6 international. Average age 33. 89 applicants, 30% accepted, 13 enrolled. In 2014, 11 master's, 16 doctorates awarded. *Degree requirements:* For doctorate, thesis/dissertation. *Entrance requirements:* For master's and doctorate, GRE General Test, minimum GPA of 3.0. Additional exam requirements/recommendations for international students: Required—TOEFL (minimum score 550 paper-based). *Application deadline:* For fall admission, 1/2 priority date for domestic students, 1/2 for international students. Application fee: $90 ($110 for international students). Electronic applications accepted. *Financial support:* Fellowships, research assistantships with full tuition reimbursements, teaching assistantships, institutionally sponsored loans, traineeships, health care benefits, and unspecified assistantships available. Financial award application deadline: 3/1; financial award applicants required to submit FAFSA. *Faculty research:* European, U.S., Latin American, ancient, and East Asian history. *Unit head:* Prof. Emily Rosenberg, Chair, 949-824-9313, E-mail: erosenbe@uci.edu. *Application contact:* Arielle Hinojosa, Graduate Coordinator, 949-824-5891, E-mail: hinojosa@uci.edu.
Website: http://www.hnet.uci.edu/history/

University of California, Los Angeles, Graduate Division, College of Letters and Science, Department of History, Los Angeles, CA 90095. Offers MA, PhD, MLIS/MA. Terminal master's awarded for partial completion of doctoral program. *Degree requirements:* For master's, one foreign language, comprehensive exam; for doctorate, variable foreign language requirement, thesis/dissertation, oral and written qualifying exams. *Entrance requirements:* For doctorate, GRE General Test, bachelor's degree; minimum undergraduate GPA of 3.0, 3.5 graduate (or its equivalent if letter grade system not used). Additional exam requirements/recommendations for international students: Required—TOEFL. Electronic applications accepted.

University of California, Riverside, Graduate Division, Department of History, Riverside, CA 92521-0102. Offers archival management (MA); historic preservation (MA); history (MA, PhD); museum curatorship (MA). Part-time programs available. Terminal master's awarded for partial completion of doctoral program. *Degree requirements:* For master's, one foreign language, comprehensive exam, internship report and oral exams, or thesis; for doctorate, 2 foreign languages, thesis/dissertation, qualifying exams. *Entrance requirements:* For master's and doctorate, GRE General Test, minimum GPA of 3.2. Additional exam requirements/recommendations for international students: Required—TOEFL (minimum score 550 paper-based; 80 iBT). Electronic applications accepted. *Expenses:* Tuition, state resident: full-time $5399. Tuition, nonresident: full-time $10,433. *Faculty research:* Native American history, United States, public history, Europe, Latin America.

University of California, San Diego, Graduate Division, Department of History, La Jolla, CA 92093. Offers history (MA, PhD); Judaic studies (MA). *Students:* 91 full-time (36 women), 4 part-time (all women); includes 26 minority (3 Black or African American, non-Hispanic/Latino; 2 American Indian or Alaska Native, non-Hispanic/Latino; 2 Asian, non-Hispanic/Latino; 19 Hispanic/Latino), 18 international. 178 applicants, 17% accepted, 19 enrolled. In 2014, 5 master's, 9 doctorates awarded. *Degree requirements:* For master's, one foreign language, comprehensive exam; for doctorate, one foreign language, thesis/dissertation. *Entrance requirements:* For master's and doctorate, GRE General Test, minimum GPA of 3.0. Additional exam requirements/recommendations for international students: Required—TOEFL (minimum score 550 paper-based), IELTS. *Application deadline:* For fall admission, 1/5 for domestic students. Application fee: $90 ($110 for international students). Electronic applications accepted. *Expenses:* Tuition, state resident: full-time $11,220; part-time $5610 per quarter. Tuition, nonresident: full-time $26,322; part-time $13,161 per quarter. *Required fees:* $570 per quarter. Tuition and fees vary according to program. *Financial support:* Fellowships, research assistantships, teaching assistantships, career-related internships or fieldwork, scholarships/grants, and readerships available. Financial award applicants required to submit FAFSA. *Faculty research:* Ancient history, east Asian history, history of science, Judaic studies, Chinese studies. *Unit head:* David Gutierrez, Chair, 858-534-1996, E-mail: dggutierrez@ucsd.edu. *Application contact:* Amber Rieder, Graduate Coordinator, 858-822-0664, E-mail: arieder@ucsd.edu.
Website: http://history.ucsd.edu

University of California, Santa Barbara, Graduate Division, College of Letters and Sciences, Division of Humanities and Fine Arts, Department of History, Santa Barbara, CA 93106-9410. Offers European medieval studies (PhD); global studies (PhD); public historical studies (PhD); technology and society (PhD); women's studies (PhD); MA/PhD. *Degree requirements:* For doctorate, variable foreign language requirement, comprehensive exam, thesis/dissertation. *Entrance requirements:* For doctorate, GRE. Additional exam requirements/recommendations for international students: Required—TOEFL (minimum score 550 paper-based; 80 iBT), IELTS (minimum score 7). Electronic applications accepted. *Faculty research:* Europe, United States, Latin America, Africa, Middle East, East Asia.

University of California, Santa Cruz, Division of Graduate Studies, Division of Humanities, Department of History, Santa Cruz, CA 95064. Offers MA, PhD. *Degree requirements:* For doctorate, variable foreign language requirement, comprehensive exam, thesis/dissertation, qualifying exam. *Entrance requirements:* For master's and doctorate, GRE, writing sample of up to 30 pages. Additional exam requirements/recommendations for international students: Required—TOEFL (minimum score 550 paper-based; 83 iBT); Recommended—IELTS (minimum score 8). Electronic applications accepted. *Faculty research:* Comparative, interdisciplinary approach to history; the Americas, Asia, the Islamic world, and Europe since 1500; society history.

University of Central Arkansas, Graduate School, College of Liberal Arts, Department of History, Conway, AR 72035-0001. Offers MA. Part-time programs available. *Degree requirements:* For master's, one foreign language, comprehensive exam, thesis optional. *Entrance requirements:* For master's, GRE General Test, minimum GPA of 2.7. Additional exam requirements/recommendations for international students: Required—TOEFL (minimum score 550 paper-based). Electronic applications accepted. *Faculty research:* History Day, Russian culture.

University of Central Florida, College of Arts and Humanities, Department of History, Orlando, FL 32816. Offers MA. Part-time and evening/weekend programs available. *Faculty:* 30 full-time (14 women), 17 part-time/adjunct (6 women). *Students:* 31 full-time (11 women), 38 part-time (13 women); includes 11 minority (1 Asian, non-Hispanic/Latino; 9 Hispanic/Latino; 1 Two or more races, non-Hispanic/Latino). Average age 31. 38 applicants, 79% accepted, 15 enrolled. In 2014, 12 master's awarded. *Degree requirements:* For master's, thesis, written exam. *Entrance requirements:* For master's, GRE General Test, minimum GPA of 3.0 in last 60 hours. Additional exam requirements/recommendations for international students: Required—TOEFL. *Application deadline:* For fall admission, 7/15 for domestic students; for spring admission, 12/1 for domestic students. Electronic applications accepted. *Expenses:* Tuition, state resident: part-time $288.16 per credit hour. Tuition, nonresident: part-time $1073.31 per credit hour. *Financial support:* In 2014–15, 8 students received support, including 4 fellowships with partial tuition reimbursements available (averaging $1,800 per year), 1 research assistantship with partial tuition reimbursement available (averaging $10,600 per year), 7 teaching assistantships with partial tuition reimbursements available (averaging $6,700 per year); career-related internships or fieldwork, Federal Work-Study, institutionally sponsored loans, tuition waivers (partial), and unspecified assistantships also available. Financial award application deadline: 3/1; financial award applicants required to submit FAFSA. *Unit head:* Dr. John Sacher, Chair, 407-823-5501, E-mail: john.sacher@ucf.edu. *Application contact:* Barbara Rodriguez Lamas, Director, Admissions and Student Services, 407-823-2766, Fax: 407-823-6442, E-mail: gradadmissions@ucf.edu.
Website: http://history.cah.ucf.edu/

University of Central Missouri, The Graduate School, Warrensburg, MO 64093. Offers accountancy (MA); accounting (MBA); applied mathematics (MS); aviation safety (MA); biology (MS); business administration (MBA); career and technical education leadership (MS); college student personnel administration (MS); communication (MA); computer science (MS); counseling (MS); criminal justice (MS); educational leadership (Ed D); educational technology (MS); elementary and early childhood education (MSE); English (MA); environmental studies (MA); finance (MBA); history (MA); human services/educational technology (Ed S); human services/learning resources (Ed S); human services/professional counseling (Ed S); industrial hygiene (MS); industrial management (MS); information systems (MBA); information technology (MS); kinesiology (MS); library science and information services (MS); literacy education (MSE); marketing (MBA); mathematics (MS); music (MA); occupational safety management (MS); psychology (MS); rural family nursing (MS); school administration (MSE); social gerontology (MS); sociology (MA); special education (MSE); speech language pathology (MS); superintendency (Ed S); teaching (MAT); teaching English as a second language (MA); technology (MS); technology management (PhD); theatre (MA). Part-time programs available. *Faculty:* 314 full-time (137 women), 24 part-time/adjunct (14 women). *Students:* 1,624 full-time (542 women), 1,773 part-time (1,055 women); includes 194 minority (104 Black or African American, non-Hispanic/Latino; 6 American Indian or Alaska Native, non-Hispanic/Latino; 23 Asian, non-Hispanic/Latino; 41 Hispanic/Latino; 3 Native Hawaiian or other Pacific Islander, non-Hispanic/Latino; 17 Two or more races, non-Hispanic/Latino), 1,592 international. Average age 31. 2,800 applicants, 63% accepted, 1223 enrolled. In 2014, 796 master's, 81 other advanced degrees awarded. *Degree requirements:* For master's and Ed S, comprehensive exam (for some programs), thesis (for some programs). *Entrance requirements:* Additional exam requirements/recommendations for international students: Required—TOEFL (minimum score 550 paper-based; 79 iBT). *Application deadline:* For fall admission, 6/1 for domestic students; for spring admission, 10/1 for domestic and international students. Applications are processed on a rolling basis. Application fee: $30 ($75 for international students). Electronic applications accepted. *Expenses:* Tuition, state resident: full-time $6630; part-time $276.25 per credit hour. Tuition, nonresident: full-time $13,260; part-time $552.50 per credit hour. *Required fees:* $29 per credit hour. Tuition and fees vary according to campus/location. *Financial support:* In 2014–15, 118 students received support, including 271 research assistantships with full and partial tuition reimbursements available (averaging $7,500 per year), 109 teaching assistantships with full and partial tuition reimbursements available (averaging $7,500 per year); career-related internships or fieldwork, Federal Work-Study, scholarships/grants, and administrative and laboratory assistantships also available. Support available to part-time students. Financial award application deadline: 3/1; financial award applicants required to submit FAFSA. *Unit head:* Tina Church-Hockett, Director of Graduate School and International Admissions, 660-543-4621, Fax: 660-543-4778, E-mail: church@ucmo.edu. *Application contact:* Brittany Lawrence, Graduate Student Services Coordinator, 660-543-4621, Fax: 660-543-4778, E-mail: gradinfo@ucmo.edu.
Website: http://www.ucmo.edu/graduate/

University of Central Oklahoma, The Jackson College of Graduate Studies, College of Liberal Arts, Department of History, Edmond, OK 73034-5209. Offers history (MA); museum studies (MA). Part-time programs available. *Degree requirements:* For master's, one foreign language, comprehensive exam (for some programs), thesis (for some programs). *Entrance requirements:* For master's, GRE, writing sample, essay. Additional exam requirements/recommendations for international students: Required—TOEFL (minimum score 550 paper-based; 79 iBT), IELTS (minimum score 6.5). Electronic applications accepted. *Faculty research:* China, Russia, civil war, American naval logistics.

University of Chicago, Division of the Social Sciences, Department of History, Chicago, IL 60637. Offers PhD. *Students:* 177 full-time (73 women); includes 47 minority (10 Black or African American, non-Hispanic/Latino; 6 Asian, non-Hispanic/Latino; 19 Hispanic/Latino; 12 Two or more races, non-Hispanic/Latino), 35 international. 371 applicants, 13% accepted, 21 enrolled. In 2014, 28 doctorates awarded. *Degree requirements:* For doctorate, variable foreign language requirement, thesis/dissertation, oral exams in 3 fields. *Entrance requirements:* For doctorate, GRE General Test. Additional exam requirements/recommendations for international students: Required—TOEFL (minimum score 104 iBT), IELTS (minimum score 7). *Application deadline:* For fall admission, 12/15 for domestic and international students. Application fee: $90. Electronic applications accepted. *Expenses: Tuition:* Full-time $46,899. *Required fees:* $347. *Financial support:* In 2014–15, 21 students received support, including 21 fellowships with full tuition reimbursements available (averaging $23,000 per year); Federal Work-Study, institutionally sponsored loans, scholarships/grants, and health care benefits also available. Financial award application deadline: 12/15. *Unit head:*

History

Prof. Kenneth Pomeranz, Chair. *Application contact:* Office of the Dean of Students, 773-702-8415, E-mail: admissions@ssd.uchicago.edu.
Website: http://history.uchicago.edu

University of Cincinnati, Graduate School, McMicken College of Arts and Sciences, Department of History, Cincinnati, OH 45221. Offers MA, PhD. Terminal master's awarded for partial completion of doctoral program. *Degree requirements:* For master's, comprehensive exam, thesis optional; for doctorate, comprehensive exam, thesis/dissertation. *Entrance requirements:* For master's, GRE General Test, BA in history; for doctorate, GRE General Test, MA in history. Additional exam requirements/recommendations for international students: Required—TOEFL (minimum score 600 paper-based). Electronic applications accepted. *Faculty research:* U.S. cultural and social history, women's history, U.S. and British intellectual history, modern Europe.

University of Colorado Boulder, Graduate School, College of Arts and Sciences, Department of History, Boulder, CO 80309. Offers MA, PhD. *Faculty:* 35 full-time (15 women). *Students:* 55 full-time (28 women), 8 part-time (0 women); includes 8 minority (1 Black or African American, non-Hispanic/Latino; 1 American Indian or Alaska Native, non-Hispanic/Latino; 2 Asian, non-Hispanic/Latino; 3 Hispanic/Latino; 1 Two or more races, non-Hispanic/Latino), 3 international. Average age 33. 91 applicants, 32% accepted, 10 enrolled. In 2014, 6 master's, 7 doctorates awarded. Terminal master's awarded for partial completion of doctoral program. *Degree requirements:* For master's, comprehensive exam, thesis optional; for doctorate, one foreign language, thesis/dissertation. *Entrance requirements:* For master's, GRE General Test, minimum undergraduate GPA of 2.75; for doctorate, GRE General Test. *Application deadline:* For fall admission, 12/1 for domestic and international students. Application fee: $50 ($70 for international students). Electronic applications accepted. *Financial support:* In 2014–15, 112 students received support, including 25 fellowships (averaging $5,429 per year), 3 research assistantships with full and partial tuition reimbursements available (averaging $30,236 per year), 35 teaching assistantships with full and partial tuition reimbursements available (averaging $26,106 per year); institutionally sponsored loans, scholarships/grants, health care benefits, and unspecified assistantships also available. Financial award applicants required to submit FAFSA. *Faculty research:* History, social history, cultural history, American history, modern history. *Total annual research expenditures:* $449,654.
Website: http://www.colorado.edu/history/

University of Colorado Colorado Springs, College of Letters, Arts and Sciences, Department of History, Colorado Springs, CO 80933-7150. Offers MA. Part-time and evening/weekend programs available. *Faculty:* 9 full-time (3 women), 10 part-time/adjunct (8 women). *Students:* 5 full-time (3 women), 28 part-time (14 women); includes 3 minority (1 Black or African American, non-Hispanic/Latino; 2 Hispanic/Latino). Average age 36. 18 applicants, 83% accepted, 10 enrolled. In 2014, 11 master's awarded. *Degree requirements:* For master's, portfolio of 3-4 research projects, oral exam. *Entrance requirements:* For master's, minimum GPA of 3.0, writing sample. Additional exam requirements/recommendations for international students: Recommended—TOEFL (minimum score 550 paper-based; 80 iBT). *Application deadline:* For fall admission, 3/1 for domestic students; for spring admission, 10/15 for domestic students. Applications are processed on a rolling basis. Application fee: $60 ($100 for international students). *Expenses:* Tuition, state resident: full-time $9900; part-time $1892 per course. Tuition, nonresident: full-time $18,792; part-time $3375 per course. One-time fee: $100. Tuition and fees vary according to course load, program and reciprocity agreements. *Financial support:* In 2014–15, 10 students received support. Fellowships, research assistantships, teaching assistantships, Federal Work-Study, and scholarships/grants available. Support available to part-time students. Financial award application deadline: 3/1; financial award applicants required to submit FAFSA. *Faculty research:* Greek and Roman history; late antiquity; historiography; Greek and Latin languages/stylistics; ancient and Renaissance cultural history; early medieval history; Native American Indian ethnohistory east of the Mississippi; U.S. social history, 1865-1980; traditional West African (Yoruba) religion and syncretism; U.S. religious, political, economic, and cultural history; environmental history of modern India; Latin American history; Mexican history; history of cities, citizenship. *Total annual research expenditures:* $1,803. *Unit head:* Dr. Christina Jimenez, Chair, 719-255-4079, Fax: 719-255-4068, E-mail: cjimenez@uccs.edu. *Application contact:* Ian Smith, Administrative Assistant, 719-255-4069, Fax: 719-255-4068, E-mail: ismith2@uccs.edu.
Website: http://www.uccs.edu/~history/

University of Colorado Denver, College of Liberal Arts and Sciences, Department of History, Denver, CO 80217. Offers European history (MA); global history (MA); public history (MA); U.S. history (MA). Part-time and evening/weekend programs available. *Faculty:* 14 full-time (6 women), 1 part-time/adjunct (0 women). *Students:* 33 full-time (20 women), 20 part-time (11 women); includes 12 minority (1 Black or African American, non-Hispanic/Latino; 1 American Indian or Alaska Native, non-Hispanic/Latino; 1 Asian, non-Hispanic/Latino; 8 Hispanic/Latino; 1 Two or more races, non-Hispanic/Latino). Average age 34. 27 applicants, 59% accepted, 9 enrolled. In 2014, 9 master's awarded. *Degree requirements:* For master's, comprehensive exam, thesis optional, 36 semester hours (12 courses). *Entrance requirements:* For master's, GRE General Test, writing sample, minimum undergraduate GPA of 3.25, three letters of recommendation, statement of purpose addressing any weaknesses in academic record. Additional exam requirements/recommendations for international students: Required—TOEFL (minimum score 537 paper-based; 75 iBT); Recommended—IELTS (minimum score 6.5). *Application deadline:* For fall admission, 1/20 for domestic and international students; for spring admission, 10/1 for domestic and international students. Application fee: $50 ($75 for international students). Electronic applications accepted. *Financial support:* In 2014–15, 8 students received support. Fellowships, research assistantships, teaching assistantships, Federal Work-Study, institutionally sponsored loans, scholarships/grants, and traineeships available. Financial award application deadline: 4/1; financial award applicants required to submit FAFSA. *Faculty research:* Uses of pre-modern Islamic heritage in modern India; relationship between liberal understandings of democracy, crime, and police discretion; relationships between gender, class, health, and welfare in nineteenth and early twentieth century England; U.S. business cultures and their influences on marketing and personnel practices; intersection of business and political ideologies; social and environmental history of the Rocky Mountain West. *Unit head:* Dr. Pamela Laird, Associate Professor and Chair, 303-556-4497, E-mail: pamela.laird@ucdenver.edu. *Application contact:* Tabitha Fitzpatrick, Program Assistant, 303-315-1776, E-mail: tabitha.fitzpatrick@ucdenver.edu.
Website: http://www.ucdenver.edu/academics/colleges/CLAS/Departments/history/Programs/Masters/Pages/MasterofArts.aspx

University of Connecticut, Graduate School, College of Liberal Arts and Sciences, Department of History, Storrs, CT 06269. Offers MA, PhD. Terminal master's awarded for partial completion of doctoral program. *Degree requirements:* For master's, comprehensive exam; for doctorate, thesis/dissertation. *Entrance requirements:* For master's and doctorate, GRE General Test, GRE Subject Test. Additional exam requirements/recommendations for international students: Required—TOEFL (minimum score 550 paper-based). Electronic applications accepted.

University of Delaware, College of Arts and Sciences, Department of History, Hagley Program in the History of Technology and Industrialization, Newark, DE 19716. Offers MA, PhD. *Degree requirements:* For master's, thesis optional; for doctorate, comprehensive exam, thesis/dissertation. *Entrance requirements:* For master's and doctorate, interview. Electronic applications accepted.

University of Denver, University College, Denver, CO 80208. Offers geographic information systems (Certificate); global affairs (Certificate), including translation studies, world history and culture; information and communications technology (MCIS), including geographic information systems, information systems security, project management (MCIS, Certificate), software design and programming, technology management, telecommunications technology, Web design and development; leadership and organizations (Certificate), including human capital in organizations, philanthropic leadership, project management (MCIS, Certificate), strategic innovation and change; organizational and professional communication (MPS), including alternative dispute resolution, organizational communication, organizational development and training, public relations and marketing; security management (MAS, Certificate), including emergency planning and response, information security (MAS), organizational security. Part-time and evening/weekend programs available. Postbaccalaureate distance learning degree programs offered (no on-campus study). *Faculty:* 8 full-time (4 women), 133 part-time/adjunct (46 women). *Students:* 54 full-time (21 women), 1,327 part-time (775 women); includes 272 minority (106 Black or African American, non-Hispanic/Latino; 6 American Indian or Alaska Native, non-Hispanic/Latino; 26 Asian, non-Hispanic/Latino; 108 Hispanic/Latino; 1 Native Hawaiian or other Pacific Islander, non-Hispanic/Latino; 25 Two or more races, non-Hispanic/Latino), 116 international. Average age 35. 768 applicants, 95% accepted, 620 enrolled. In 2014, 391 master's, 196 other advanced degrees awarded. *Degree requirements:* For master's, capstone project. *Entrance requirements:* For master's, transcripts, two letters of recommendation, personal statement, resume. Additional exam requirements/recommendations for international students: Required—TOEFL (minimum score 550 paper-based; 80 iBT). *Application deadline:* For fall admission, 6/21 priority date for domestic students, 5/1 priority date for international students; for winter admission, 9/14 priority date for domestic students, 9/19 priority date for international students; for spring admission, 1/11 for domestic students, 12/12 for international students; for summer admission, 3/29 priority date for domestic students, 3/6 priority date for international students. Applications are processed on a rolling basis. Application fee: $75. Electronic applications accepted. *Expenses:* Expenses: $959 per credit hour. *Financial support:* In 2014–15, 19 students received support. Applicants required to submit FAFSA. *Unit head:* Dr. Michael McGuire, Interim Dean, 303-871-3518, E-mail: mmcguire@du.edu. *Application contact:* Information Contact, 303-871-2291, E-mail: ucoladm@du.edu.
Website: http://www.universitycollege.du.edu/

University of Florida, Graduate School, College of Liberal Arts and Sciences, Department of History, Gainesville, FL 32611. Offers historic preservation (MA, PhD); history (MA, PhD); Jewish studies (MA); women's and gender studies (PhD); JD/MA; JD/PhD. Part-time programs available. *Faculty:* 26 full-time (9 women), 9 part-time/adjunct (5 women). *Students:* 59 full-time (21 women), 14 part-time (6 women); includes 7 minority (4 Black or African American, non-Hispanic/Latino; 3 Hispanic/Latino), 6 international. 112 applicants, 21% accepted, 11 enrolled. In 2014, 6 master's, 14 doctorates awarded. Terminal master's awarded for partial completion of doctoral program. *Degree requirements:* For master's, variable foreign language requirement, thesis optional, 30 credit hours; for doctorate, variable foreign language requirement, comprehensive exam, thesis/dissertation, 90 credit hours. *Entrance requirements:* For master's and doctorate, GRE General Test, minimum GPA of 3.0. Additional exam requirements/recommendations for international students: Required—TOEFL (minimum score 550 paper-based; 80 iBT), IELTS (minimum score 6). *Application deadline:* For fall admission, 1/1 priority date for domestic students, 1/1 for international students. Applications are processed on a rolling basis. Application fee: $30. Electronic applications accepted. *Financial support:* In 2014–15, 15 fellowships, 9 research assistantships, 44 teaching assistantships were awarded; career-related internships or fieldwork and unspecified assistantships also available. Financial award application deadline: 1/15; financial award applicants required to submit FAFSA. *Faculty research:* Latin American and Caribbean history, nineteenth century U.S. history, medieval European history, African history and Atlantic world history. *Unit head:* Ida L. Altman, PhD, Professor and Chair, 352-392-6927, Fax: 352-392-6927, E-mail: ialtman@ufl.edu. *Application contact:* Elizabeth Dale, PhD, Graduate Coordinator, 352-273-3387, Fax: 352-392-6927, E-mail: edale@ufl.edu.
Website: http://www.history.ufl.edu/

University of Georgia, Franklin College of Arts and Sciences, Department of History, Athens, GA 30602. Offers MA, PhD. *Degree requirements:* For master's, one foreign language, thesis; for doctorate, one foreign language, thesis/dissertation. *Entrance requirements:* For master's and doctorate, GRE General Test. Electronic applications accepted.

University of Guelph, Graduate Studies, College of Arts, Department of History, Guelph, ON N1G 2W1, Canada. Offers MA, PhD. MA, PhD offered jointly with University of Waterloo, Wilfrid Laurier University. Part-time programs available. *Degree requirements:* For master's, one foreign language, thesis (for some programs); for doctorate, one foreign language, thesis/dissertation, 3 qualifying fields. *Entrance requirements:* For master's, minimum B+ average during previous 2 years of course work; for doctorate, minimum A- average in MA. Additional exam requirements/recommendations for international students: Required—TOEFL (minimum score 550 paper-based). Electronic applications accepted. *Faculty research:* Gender and family, Scottish history, rural and urban community studies, eighteenth century England, Canadian legal and social history, modern Europe.

University of Hawaii at Manoa, Graduate Division, College of Arts and Humanities, Department of History, Honolulu, HI 96822. Offers MA, PhD. Part-time programs available. *Degree requirements:* For master's, 2 foreign languages, thesis optional; for doctorate, 2 foreign languages, comprehensive exam, thesis/dissertation. *Entrance requirements:* For master's, GRE, minimum GPA of 3.0, writing sample; for doctorate, GRE, MA, sample of written work. Additional exam requirements/recommendations for international students: Required—TOEFL (minimum score 580 paper-based; 92 iBT), IELTS (minimum score 5). *Faculty research:* Asian, Pacific, world, American and European history.

University of Houston, College of Liberal Arts and Social Sciences, Department of History, Houston, TX 77204. Offers MA, PhD. Part-time programs available. Terminal master's awarded for partial completion of doctoral program. *Degree requirements:* For master's, one foreign language, thesis (for some programs); for doctorate, one foreign language, comprehensive exam, thesis/dissertation. *Entrance requirements:* For master's, GRE General Test, minimum GPA of 3.3; for doctorate, GRE General Test, minimum GPA of 3.67. Additional exam requirements/recommendations for international students: Required—TOEFL. Electronic applications accepted. *Faculty research:* U.S., Latin American, European, social, and women's history.

University of Houston–Clear Lake, School of Human Sciences and Humanities, Programs in Humanities and Fine Arts, Houston, TX 77058-1002. Offers history (MA); humanities (MA); literature (MA). Part-time and evening/weekend programs available. Postbaccalaureate distance learning degree programs offered (minimal on-campus study). *Degree requirements:* For master's, thesis or alternative. *Entrance requirements:*

For master's, GRE General Test. Additional exam requirements/recommendations for international students: Required—TOEFL (minimum score 550 paper-based). *Faculty research:* Digital media studies, Latin American history, labor history, Chaucer evolution versus creationism debate.

University of Idaho, College of Graduate Studies, College of Letters, Arts and Social Sciences, Department of History, Moscow, ID 83844-3175. Offers MA, PhD. *Faculty:* 6 full-time. *Students:* 8 full-time, 6 part-time. Average age 34. In 2014, 1 master's awarded. *Degree requirements:* For doctorate, thesis/dissertation. *Entrance requirements:* For master's, minimum GPA of 2.8; for doctorate, minimum undergraduate GPA of 2.8, 3.0 graduate. *Application deadline:* For fall admission, 8/1 for domestic students; for spring admission, 12/15 for domestic students. Applications are processed on a rolling basis. Application fee: $60. Electronic applications accepted. *Expenses:* Tuition, state resident: full-time $4784; part-time $280.50 per credit hour. Tuition, nonresident: full-time $18,314; part-time $957.50 per credit hour. *Required fees:* $2000; $58.50 per credit hour. Tuition and fees vary according to program. *Financial support:* Research assistantships and teaching assistantships available. Financial award applicants required to submit FAFSA. *Unit head:* Dr. Sean Quinlan, Chair, 208-885-6253, E-mail: history@uidaho.edu. *Application contact:* Sean Scoggin, Graduate Recruitment Coordinator, 208-885-4001, Fax: 208-885-4406, E-mail: graduateadmissions@uidaho.edu.
Website: http://www.uidaho.edu/class/history

University of Illinois at Chicago, Graduate College, College of Liberal Arts and Sciences, Department of History, Chicago, IL 60607-7128. Offers MA, MAT, PhD. Part-time and evening/weekend programs available. *Faculty:* 23 full-time (12 women), 12 part-time/adjunct (4 women). *Students:* 52 full-time (22 women), 15 part-time (7 women); includes 7 minority (1 Black or African American, non-Hispanic/Latino; 1 Asian, non-Hispanic/Latino; 5 Hispanic/Latino), 5 international. Average age 34. 104 applicants, 31% accepted, 15 enrolled. In 2014, 9 master's, 6 doctorates awarded. *Degree requirements:* For master's, one foreign language, comprehensive exam; for doctorate, 2 foreign languages, comprehensive exam, thesis/dissertation. *Entrance requirements:* For master's and doctorate, GRE General Test, previous course work in a foreign language, minimum GPA of 3.0. Additional exam requirements/recommendations for international students: Required—TOEFL. *Application deadline:* For fall admission, 1/1 priority date for domestic and international students; for spring admission, 10/1 for domestic students, 7/15 for international students. Applications are processed on a rolling basis. Application fee: $60. Electronic applications accepted. *Expenses:* Tuition, state resident: full-time $11,254; part-time $468 per credit hour. Tuition, nonresident: full-time $23,252; part-time $968 per credit hour. *Required fees:* $1217 per term. Part-time tuition and fees vary according to course load, degree level and program. *Financial support:* In 2014–15, 4 fellowships with full tuition reimbursements were awarded; research assistantships with full tuition reimbursements, teaching assistantships with full tuition reimbursements, Federal Work-Study, scholarships/grants, traineeships, tuition waivers (full), and unspecified assistantships also available. Financial award application deadline: 3/1; financial award applicants required to submit FAFSA. *Faculty research:* American urban and immigration history, early modern European history, Eastern European history. *Unit head:* Prof. Christopher Boyer, Chairperson, 312-996-2346, Fax: 312-996-6377, E-mail: crboyer@uic.edu. *Application contact:* Prof. Jeffrey Sklansky, Director of Graduate Studies, 312-996-3142, E-mail: sklanskj@uic.edu.
Website: http://history.las.uic.edu/

University of Illinois at Springfield, Graduate Programs, College of Liberal Arts and Sciences, Program in History, Springfield, IL 62703-5407. Offers MA. Part-time and evening/weekend programs available. *Faculty:* 4 full-time (2 women), 1 part-time/adjunct (0 women). *Students:* 13 full-time (7 women), 21 part-time (13 women); includes 1 minority (Black or African American, non-Hispanic/Latino), 1 international. Average age 33. 26 applicants, 62% accepted, 11 enrolled. In 2014, 9 master's awarded. *Degree requirements:* For master's, thesis, internship, or historiography. *Entrance requirements:* For master's, BA in history or related field, minimum undergraduate GPA of 2.5, writing sample. Additional exam requirements/recommendations for international students: Required—TOEFL (minimum score 500 paper-based; 61 iBT). *Application deadline:* Applications are processed on a rolling basis. Application fee: $60 ($75 for international students). Electronic applications accepted. *Expenses:* Tuition, state resident: full-time $7662; part-time $319.25 per credit hour. Tuition, nonresident: full-time $15,966; part-time $665.25 per credit hour. *Financial support:* In 2014–15, fellowships with full tuition reimbursements (averaging $9,900 per year), research assistantships with full tuition reimbursements (averaging $9,600 per year), teaching assistantships with full tuition reimbursements (averaging $9,600 per year) were awarded; career-related internships or fieldwork, Federal Work-Study, scholarships/grants, health care benefits, and unspecified assistantships also available. Support available to part-time students. Financial award application deadline: 11/15; financial award applicants required to submit FAFSA. *Unit head:* Dr. Peter Shapinsky, Program Administrator, 217-206-6595, Fax: 217-206-6217, E-mail: pshap2@uis.edu. *Application contact:* Dr. Lynn Pardie, Office of Graduate Studies, 800-252-8533, Fax: 217-206-7623, E-mail: lpard1@uis.edu.
Website: http://www.uis.edu/history/curriculum/ma/

University of Illinois at Urbana–Champaign, Graduate College, College of Liberal Arts and Sciences, Department of History, Champaign, IL 61820. Offers MA, PhD. *Students:* 91 (43 women). Application fee: $70 ($90 for international students). *Unit head:* Diane P. Koenker, Chair, 217-244-2077, Fax: 217-333-2297, E-mail: dkoenker@illinois.edu. *Application contact:* Shannon J. Croft, 217-244-2075, E-mail: shannon9@illinois.edu.
Website: http://www.history.illinois.edu/

University of Indianapolis, Graduate Programs, College of Arts and Sciences, Department of History and Political Science, Indianapolis, IN 46227-3697. Offers history (MA); international relations (MA). Part-time and evening/weekend programs available. *Faculty:* 6 full-time (1 woman). *Students:* 4 full-time (3 women), 19 part-time (7 women); includes 2 minority (1 Hispanic/Latino; 1 Two or more races, non-Hispanic/Latino), 6 international. Average age 29. In 2014, 5 master's awarded. *Degree requirements:* For master's, thesis optional. *Entrance requirements:* For master's, GRE Subject Test, minimum GPA of 3.0, 3 letters of recommendation. Additional exam requirements/recommendations for international students: Required—TOEFL (minimum score 550 paper-based). *Application deadline:* Applications are processed on a rolling basis. Application fee: $30. Electronic applications accepted. *Financial support:* Federal Work-Study, scholarships/grants, and tuition waivers (full and partial) available. Support available to part-time students. Financial award application deadline: 5/1; financial award applicants required to submit FAFSA. *Unit head:* Dr. Lawrence Sondhaus, Chairperson, 317-788-2196, Fax: 317-788-3480, E-mail: sondhaus@uindy.edu. *Application contact:* Linda Corn, Administrative Assistant, 317-788-3395, E-mail: lcorn@uindy.edu.
Website: http://history.uindy.edu/

The University of Iowa, Graduate College, College of Liberal Arts and Sciences, Department of History, Iowa City, IA 52242-1316. Offers MA, PhD. *Degree requirements:* For master's, thesis optional, exam; for doctorate, comprehensive exam, thesis/dissertation. *Entrance requirements:* For master's and doctorate, GRE General Test, minimum GPA of 3.0. Additional exam requirements/recommendations for international students: Required—TOEFL (minimum score 550 paper-based; 81 iBT). Electronic applications accepted.

The University of Kansas, Graduate Studies, College of Liberal Arts and Sciences, Department of History, Lawrence, KS 66045. Offers MA, PhD. Part-time programs available. *Faculty:* 35 full-time, 4 part-time/adjunct. *Students:* 66 full-time (23 women), 2 part-time (0 women); includes 6 minority (1 Asian, non-Hispanic/Latino; 5 Hispanic/Latino), 4 international. Average age 34. 81 applicants, 17% accepted, 6 enrolled. In 2014, 16 master's, 4 doctorates awarded. *Degree requirements:* For master's, variable foreign language requirement, 2 professional quality papers; for doctorate, variable foreign language requirement, comprehensive exam, thesis/dissertation. *Entrance requirements:* For master's and doctorate, GRE General Test, minimum GPA of 3.0. Additional exam requirements/recommendations for international students: Required—TOEFL. *Application deadline:* For fall admission, 12/1 for domestic students, 11/15 for international students. Application fee: $55 ($65 for international students). Electronic applications accepted. *Financial support:* In 2014–15, 6 fellowships with full tuition reimbursements, 31 teaching assistantships with full tuition reimbursements were awarded; research assistantships with full and partial tuition reimbursements and unspecified assistantships also available. Financial award application deadline: 12/1. *Faculty research:* Environmental history, early American history, modern European history. *Unit head:* Jeffrey P. Moran, Chair, 785-864-9461, E-mail: jefmoran@ku.edu. *Application contact:* Emily Lowrance-Floyd, Graduate Program Administrator, 785-864-9438, E-mail: lowrance@ku.edu.
Website: http://www.history.ku.edu/

University of Kentucky, Graduate School, College of Arts and Sciences, Program in History, Lexington, KY 40506-0032. Offers MA, PhD. Part-time programs available. *Degree requirements:* For master's, one foreign language, comprehensive exam, thesis optional; for doctorate, variable foreign language requirement, comprehensive exam, thesis/dissertation. *Entrance requirements:* For master's, GRE General Test, minimum undergraduate GPA of 2.75; for doctorate, GRE General Test, minimum graduate GPA of 3.0. Additional exam requirements/recommendations for international students: Required—TOEFL (minimum score 550 paper-based). Electronic applications accepted. *Faculty research:* English, British, European history; U.S. social, political and diplomatic history; U.S. early national history; U.S. Southern history; Native American and African-American history.

University of Louisiana at Lafayette, College of Liberal Arts, Department of History and Geography, Lafayette, LA 70504. Offers history (MA). Part-time programs available. *Degree requirements:* For master's, one foreign language, thesis or alternative. *Entrance requirements:* For master's, GRE General Test, minimum GPA of 2.75. Additional exam requirements/recommendations for international students: Required—TOEFL (minimum score 550 paper-based). Electronic applications accepted.

University of Louisiana at Monroe, Graduate School, College of Arts, Education, and Sciences, Department of History, Monroe, LA 71209-0001. Offers MA. Part-time and evening/weekend programs available. *Degree requirements:* For master's, thesis (for some programs). *Entrance requirements:* For master's, GRE General Test, minimum undergraduate GPA of 2.5. Additional exam requirements/recommendations for international students: Required—TOEFL (minimum score 500 paper-based; 61 iBT). Electronic applications accepted. *Faculty research:* Early Louisiana settlements, Soviet history, Anglo-American relations, U.S./East European relations.

University of Louisville, Graduate School, College of Arts and Sciences, Department of History, Louisville, KY 40292-0001. Offers history (MA); public history (Certificate). Part-time and evening/weekend programs available. *Students:* 19 full-time (8 women), 7 part-time (2 women); includes 2 minority (both Hispanic/Latino). Average age 27. 23 applicants, 78% accepted, 10 enrolled. In 2014, 4 master's, 1 other advanced degree awarded. *Degree requirements:* For master's, variable foreign language requirement, comprehensive exam (for some programs), thesis (for some programs). *Entrance requirements:* For master's, GRE General Test. Additional exam requirements/recommendations for international students: Required—TOEFL. *Application deadline:* For fall admission, 5/15 for domestic students, 5/1 priority date for international students; for spring admission, 12/1 for domestic students, 11/1 priority date for international students; for summer admission, 4/1 priority date for international students. Applications are processed on a rolling basis. Application fee: $60. Electronic applications accepted. *Expenses:* Tuition, state resident: full-time $11,326; part-time $630 per credit hour. Tuition, nonresident: full-time $23,568; part-time $1311 per credit hour. *Required fees:* $196. Tuition and fees vary according to program and reciprocity agreements. *Financial support:* Teaching assistantships available. Financial award applicants required to submit FAFSA. *Faculty research:* United States, British Empire, twentieth century women's history, Latin America, African diaspora. *Unit head:* Dr. Tracy Elaine K'Meyer, Chair, 502-852-6817, Fax: 502-852-0770, E-mail: tracyk@louisville.edu. *Application contact:* Libby Leggett, Director, Graduate Admissions, 502-852-3101, Fax: 502-852-6536, E-mail: gradadm@louisville.edu.
Website: http://louisville.edu/history/

University of Maine, Graduate School, College of Liberal Arts and Sciences, Department of History, Orono, ME 04469. Offers Asian studies (MA); Canadian studies (MA); European studies (MA). *Faculty:* 17 full-time (4 women). *Students:* 33 full-time (19 women), 12 part-time (4 women); includes 1 minority (Hispanic/Latino), 3 international. Average age 38. 31 applicants, 65% accepted, 6 enrolled. In 2014, 6 master's, 1 doctorate awarded. *Degree requirements:* For master's, variable foreign language requirement, thesis optional; for doctorate, one foreign language, comprehensive exam, thesis/dissertation. *Entrance requirements:* For master's and doctorate, GRE General Test. Additional exam requirements/recommendations for international students: Required—TOEFL. *Application deadline:* For fall admission, 1/15 priority date for domestic students; for spring admission, 10/15 for domestic students. Applications are processed on a rolling basis. Application fee: $65. Electronic applications accepted. *Expenses:* Tuition, state resident: part-time $658 per credit hour. Tuition, nonresident: part-time $1550 per credit hour. *Financial support:* In 2014–15, 26 students received support, including 4 fellowships (averaging $15,000 per year), 9 teaching assistantships with tuition reimbursements available (averaging $14,600 per year); career-related internships or fieldwork, Federal Work-Study, and tuition waivers (full and partial) also available. Support available to part-time students. Financial award application deadline: 3/1. *Faculty research:* Environmental history, gender history, nationalism, classical, popular culture, Napoleonic, globalization, peasant studies, diplomatic history, military, Native America, Colonial U.S. *Unit head:* Dr. Stephen Miller, Chair, 207-581-1905, Fax: 207-581-1817, E-mail: stephen.miller@maine.edu. *Application contact:* Scott G. Delcourt, Assistant Vice President for Graduate Studies and Senior Associate Dean, 207-581-3291, Fax: 207-581-3232, E-mail: graduate@maine.edu.
Website: http://www.umaine.edu/history/

The University of Manchester, School of Arts, Histories and Cultures, Manchester, United Kingdom. Offers anthropology, media and performance (PhD); applied theatre professional (PhD); archaeology (PhD); art history and visual studies (PhD); arts management and cultural policy (PhD); classics and ancient history (PhD); composition (PhD); creative writing (PhD); drama (PhD); economic and social history (PhD); electroacoustic composition (PhD); English and American studies (PhD); history (PhD);

History

humanitarianism and conflict response (PhD); museology (PhD); music (PhD); musicology (PhD); religions and theology (PhD).

University of Manitoba, Faculty of Graduate Studies, Faculty of Arts, Department of History, Winnipeg, MB R3T 2N2, Canada. Offers archival studies (MA); history (MA, PhD). MA offered jointly with The University of Winnipeg. *Degree requirements:* For master's, thesis; for doctorate, one foreign language, thesis/dissertation.

University of Maryland, Baltimore County, The Graduate School, College of Arts, Humanities and Social Sciences, Department of History, Program in Historical Studies, Baltimore, MD 21250. Offers MA. Part-time and evening/weekend programs available. *Faculty:* 15 full-time (9 women), 9 part-time/adjunct (3 women). *Students:* 22 full-time (16 women), 30 part-time (14 women); includes 3 minority (2 Black or African American, non-Hispanic/Latino; 1 Hispanic/Latino), 1 international. Average age 33. 26 applicants, 54% accepted, 12 enrolled. In 2014, 2 master's awarded. *Degree requirements:* For master's, thesis. *Entrance requirements:* For master's, GRE General Test, minimum GPA of 3.0. Additional exam requirements/recommendations for international students: Required—TOEFL. *Application deadline:* For fall admission, 2/15 priority date for domestic students, 1/1 for international students; for spring admission, 11/1 for domestic students, 5/1 for international students. Application fee: $50. Electronic applications accepted. *Expenses:* Tuition, state resident: part-time $557. Tuition, nonresident: part-time $922. *Required fees:* $122 per semester. One-time fee: $200 part-time. *Financial support:* In 2014–15, 9 students received support, including 1 research assistantship with full tuition reimbursement available (averaging $12,560 per year), 4 teaching assistantships with full and partial tuition reimbursements available (averaging $12,560 per year); career-related internships or fieldwork, health care benefits, tuition waivers (partial), and unspecified assistantships also available. Financial award application deadline: 2/15; financial award applicants required to submit FAFSA. *Faculty research:* U.S. history, European history, public history, community engagement. *Total annual research expenditures:* $50,000. *Unit head:* Dr. Michelle R. Scott, Graduate Program Director, 410-455-2035, Fax: 410-455-1045, E-mail: mscott@umbc.edu. *Application contact:* Carla S. Ison, Graduate Program Coordinator, 410-455-2049, Fax: 410-455-1045, E-mail: ison@umbc.edu.
Website: http://www.umbc.edu/history

University of Maryland, College Park, Academic Affairs, College of Arts and Humanities, Department of History, College Park, MD 20742. Offers MA, PhD. *Degree requirements:* For master's, comprehensive exam, thesis optional; for doctorate, one foreign language, thesis/dissertation, oral and written exams. *Entrance requirements:* For master's, GRE General Test, minimum GPA of 3.25, writing sample, 3 letters of recommendation, statements of goals and research interests and experiences; for doctorate, GRE General Test, minimum GPA of 3.5. Additional exam requirements/recommendations for international students: Required—TOEFL. Electronic applications accepted. *Faculty research:* Ancient, British, East Asian, Latin American, and diplomatic history; papers of Samuel Gompers; Freedman and Southern Society; Caesarea excavations; Folger Institute.

University of Maryland, College Park, Academic Affairs, Program in History, Library, and Information Services, College Park, MD 20742. Offers MA/MLS. *Entrance requirements:* Additional exam requirements/recommendations for international students: Required—TOEFL. Electronic applications accepted.

University of Massachusetts Amherst, Graduate School, College of Humanities and Fine Arts, Department of History, Amherst, MA 01003. Offers MA, PhD. Part-time programs available. *Faculty:* 49 full-time (21 women). *Students:* 53 full-time (32 women), 7 part-time (4 women); includes 5 minority (1 Black or African American, non-Hispanic/Latino; 2 Hispanic/Latino; 2 Two or more races, non-Hispanic/Latino), 2 international. Average age 32. 119 applicants, 39% accepted, 14 enrolled. In 2014, 7 master's, 3

doctorates awarded. Terminal master's awarded for partial completion of doctoral program. *Degree requirements:* For master's, one foreign language, thesis or alternative; for doctorate, one foreign language, comprehensive exam, thesis/dissertation. *Entrance requirements:* For master's and doctorate, GRE General Test, writing sample. Additional exam requirements/recommendations for international students: Required—TOEFL (minimum score 550 paper-based; 80 iBT), IELTS (minimum score 6.5). *Application deadline:* For fall admission, 1/2 for domestic and international students. Applications are processed on a rolling basis. Application fee: $75. Electronic applications accepted. *Expenses:* Tuition, state resident: full-time $1980; part-time $110 per credit. Tuition, nonresident: full-time $14,644; part-time $414 per credit. *Required fees:* $11,417. One-time fee: $357. *Financial support:* Fellowships with full and partial tuition reimbursements, research assistantships with full and partial tuition reimbursements, teaching assistantships with full and partial tuition reimbursements, career-related internships or fieldwork, Federal Work-Study, scholarships/grants, traineeships, health care benefits, tuition waivers (full and partial), and unspecified assistantships available. Support available to part-time students. Financial award application deadline: 1/2. *Faculty research:* Ancient and medieval history; global and comparative history; public history; history of science, technology, medicine and the environment; history of women, gender, sexuality and family. *Unit head:* Dr. Irene Krauthamer, Graduate Program Director, 413-545-6755, Fax: 413-545-6137. *Application contact:* Lindsay DeSantis, Supervisor of Admissions, 413-545-0722, Fax: 413-577-0010, E-mail: gradadm@grad.umass.edu.
Website: http://www.umass.edu/history/

University of Massachusetts Boston, College of Liberal Arts, Program in History, Boston, MA 02125-3393. Offers archival methods (MA); history (MA). Part-time and evening/weekend programs available. *Degree requirements:* For master's, thesis, oral exam. *Entrance requirements:* For master's, minimum GPA of 2.75. *Application deadline:* For fall admission, 3/1 for domestic students; for spring admission, 11/1 for domestic students. *Expenses:* Tuition, state resident: full-time $2590; part-time $108 per credit. Tuition, nonresident: full-time $9758; part-time $406.50 per credit. Tuition and fees vary according to course load and program. *Financial support:* Research assistantships with full tuition reimbursements, teaching assistantships with full tuition reimbursements, career-related internships or fieldwork, Federal Work-Study, and unspecified assistantships available. Support available to part-time students. Financial award application deadline: 3/1; financial award applicants required to submit FAFSA. *Faculty research:* European intellectual history, American labor and social history in nineteenth century, colonial American Revolution, Afro-American Cold War. *Unit head:* Dr. Spencer DiScala, Director, 617-287-6860, E-mail: spencer.discala@umb.edu. *Application contact:* Peggy Roldan Patel, Graduate Admissions Coordinator, 617-287-6400, Fax: 617-287-6236, E-mail: bos.gadm@dpc.umassp.edu.
See Display below and Close-Up on page 323.

University of Memphis, Graduate School, College of Arts and Sciences, Department of History, Memphis, TN 38152. Offers ancient Egyptian history (MA, PhD). Postbaccalaureate distance learning degree programs offered (no on-campus study). *Faculty:* 20 full-time (10 women), 1 (woman) part-time/adjunct. *Students:* 38 full-time (25 women), 47 part-time (23 women); includes 13 minority (12 Black or African American, non-Hispanic/Latino; 1 Hispanic/Latino), 3 international. Average age 36. 38 applicants, 32% accepted, 10 enrolled. In 2014, 13 master's, 5 doctorates awarded. *Degree requirements:* For master's, comprehensive exam, thesis optional; for doctorate, one foreign language, comprehensive exam, thesis/dissertation, 60 credits plus 12 dissertation credits, 2 research seminars. *Entrance requirements:* For master's, GRE General Test or MAT, 18 undergraduate hours of course work in history with minimum GPA of 3.0, 2 letters of recommendation, writing sample; for doctorate, GRE General

Test, GRE Subject Test, MA in history or related field, three letters of recommendation, writing sample, statement of purpose. Additional exam requirements/recommendations for international students: Required—TOEFL. *Application deadline:* For fall admission, 1/15 for domestic students; for spring admission, 9/15 for domestic students. Applications are processed on a rolling basis. Application fee: $35 ($60 for international students). Electronic applications accepted. *Financial support:* In 2014–15, 54 students received support. Research assistantships with full tuition reimbursements available, teaching assistantships with full tuition reimbursements available, career-related internships or fieldwork, Federal Work-Study, scholarships/grants, and unspecified assistantships available. Financial award application deadline: 2/15; financial award applicants required to submit FAFSA. *Faculty research:* African/African-American history; U.S. history; ancient Egyptian history; modern European history; women, gender, and family studies. *Unit head:* Dr. Aram Goudsouzian, Chairman, 901-678-2515, Fax: 901-678-2720, E-mail: agoudszn@memphis.edu. *Application contact:* Dr. Daniel Unowsky, Coordinator of Graduate Studies, 901-678-3385, Fax: 901-678-2720, E-mail: dunowsky@memphis.edu.
Website: http://history.memphis.edu/

University of Miami, Graduate School, College of Arts and Sciences, Department of History, Coral Gables, FL 33124. Offers MA, PhD. Part-time programs available. Terminal master's awarded for partial completion of doctoral program. *Degree requirements:* For master's, one foreign language, comprehensive exam, thesis optional; for doctorate, one foreign language, comprehensive exam, thesis/dissertation. *Entrance requirements:* For master's and doctorate, GRE General Test, GRE Subject Test. Additional exam requirements/recommendations for international students: Required—TOEFL (minimum score 550 paper-based; 59 iBT). Electronic applications accepted. *Faculty research:* Latin American, European, U.S., and public history.

University of Michigan, Horace H. Rackham School of Graduate Studies, College of Literature, Science, and the Arts, Department of History, Ann Arbor, MI 48109. Offers PhD. *Degree requirements:* For doctorate, 2 foreign languages, thesis/dissertation, oral defense of dissertation, preliminary exam. *Entrance requirements:* For doctorate, GRE General Test, writing sample. Additional exam requirements/recommendations for international students: Required—TOEFL. Electronic applications accepted. *Faculty research:* Europe, Latin America, Africa, Asia, Middle East/Near East, United States, world/global, science/medicine/technology, and topical/thematic history.

University of Michigan, Horace H. Rackham School of Graduate Studies, College of Literature, Science, and the Arts, Department of Women's Studies, Ann Arbor, MI 48109. Offers English and women's studies (PhD); history and women's studies (PhD); LGBTQ studies (Certificate); psychology and women's studies (PhD); women's studies (Certificate). *Faculty:* 36 full-time. *Students:* 58 full-time (48 women). 119 applicants, 8% accepted, 6 enrolled. In 2014, 7 doctorates, 4 other advanced degrees awarded. *Degree requirements:* For doctorate, variable foreign language requirement, comprehensive exam (for some programs), thesis/dissertation. *Entrance requirements:* For doctorate, GRE General Test, previous undergraduate coursework in women's studies. *Application deadline:* For fall admission, 12/1 for domestic and international students. Application fee: $75 ($90 for international students). Electronic applications accepted. *Financial support:* In 2014–15, fellowships with full tuition reimbursements (averaging $18,000 per year), research assistantships with full tuition reimbursements (averaging $18,000 per year), teaching assistantships with full tuition reimbursements (averaging $18,000 per year) were awarded; scholarships/grants, health care benefits, tuition waivers (full), and unspecified assistantships also available. *Faculty research:* LGBTQ studies, sexuality studies, feminist science studies, global feminism, health studies, international studies, cultural studies. *Unit head:* Lilia Cortina, Director of Graduate Studies, 734-763-2047, Fax: 734-647-4943, E-mail: lilia@umich.edu. *Application contact:* Aimee Germain, Graduate Program Coordinator, 734-763-2047, Fax: 734-647-4943, E-mail: wsdgradinquiry@umich.edu.
Website: http://www.lsa.umich.edu/women/

University of Michigan, Horace H. Rackham School of Graduate Studies, College of Literature, Science, and the Arts, Doctoral Program in Anthropology and History, Ann Arbor, MI 48109. Offers PhD. *Degree requirements:* For doctorate, 2 foreign languages, thesis/dissertation, oral defense of dissertation, preliminary exam. *Entrance requirements:* For doctorate, GRE General Test, writing sample. Additional exam requirements/recommendations for international students: Required—TOEFL. Electronic applications accepted. *Faculty research:* Historical anthropology.

University of Michigan, Horace H. Rackham School of Graduate Studies, College of Literature, Science, and the Arts, Interdepartmental Program in Greek and Roman History, Ann Arbor, MI 48109. Offers PhD, Certificate. Certificate program only open to students already studying in another PhD program at University of Michigan. *Faculty:* 6 full-time (2 women), 19 part-time/adjunct (12 women). *Students:* 12 full-time (5 women). Average age 28. 33 applicants, 6% accepted, 1 enrolled. In 2014, 2 doctorates awarded. *Degree requirements:* For doctorate, 4 foreign languages, comprehensive exam, thesis/dissertation, oral defense of dissertation, dissertation prospectus, preliminary exams, qualifying exams. *Entrance requirements:* For doctorate, GRE, strict minimum of 2 years each of classical Greek and Latin. Additional exam requirements/recommendations for international students: Required—TOEFL (minimum score 560 paper-based). *Application deadline:* For fall admission, 12/15 for domestic and international students. Application fee: $75 ($90 for international students). Electronic applications accepted. *Financial support:* In 2014–15, 12 students received support, including 4 fellowships with full tuition reimbursements available (averaging $23,000 per year), 8 teaching assistantships with full tuition reimbursements available (averaging $18,600 per year); career-related internships or fieldwork, Federal Work-Study, institutionally sponsored loans, scholarships/grants, traineeships, health care benefits, tuition waivers (full), and unspecified assistantships also available. Financial award application deadline: 4/15. *Faculty research:* Greek history, Roman history, history of ancient Mediterranean cultures. *Unit head:* Prof. David S. Potter, Professor, 734-936-2249, Fax: 734-763-4959, E-mail: dsp@umich.edu. *Application contact:* Molly Cravens, Student Services Coordinator, 734-615-3181, Fax: 734-763-4959, E-mail: mcravens@umich.edu.
Website: http://www.lsa.umich.edu/ipgrh

University of Minnesota, Twin Cities Campus, Graduate School, College of Liberal Arts, Department of Classical and Near Eastern Studies, Minneapolis, MN 55455-0213. Offers ancient and medieval art and archaeology (MA, PhD); classics (MA, PhD); Greek (MA, PhD); Latin (MA, PhD); religions in antiquity (MA). Part-time programs available. Terminal master's awarded for partial completion of doctoral program. *Degree requirements:* For master's, 2 foreign languages, comprehensive exam, thesis or alternative; for doctorate, variable foreign language requirement, comprehensive exam, thesis/dissertation. *Entrance requirements:* For master's and doctorate, GRE, 3 letters of recommendation, writing sample, copies of transcripts, personal statement. Additional exam requirements/recommendations for international students: Required—TOEFL. Electronic applications accepted. *Faculty research:* Greek and Latin literature, religions in antiquity, ancient Near East.

University of Minnesota, Twin Cities Campus, Graduate School, College of Liberal Arts, Department of History, Minneapolis, MN 55455-0213. Offers MA, PhD. *Degree requirements:* For master's, one foreign language, comprehensive exam, thesis or alternative; for doctorate, 2 foreign languages, comprehensive exam, thesis/dissertation. *Entrance requirements:* For doctorate, GRE General Test, writing sample, letters of recommendation. Additional exam requirements/recommendations for international students: Required—TOEFL (minimum score 550 paper-based). Electronic applications accepted. *Faculty research:* Early and modern United States; medieval, early modern and modern Europe; Africa; East and South Asia; Latin America.

University of Mississippi, Graduate School, College of Liberal Arts, Department of History, University, MS 38677. Offers MA, PhD. *Degree requirements:* For doctorate, thesis/dissertation. *Entrance requirements:* For master's, GRE General Test, GRE Subject Test, minimum GPA of 3.0; for doctorate, GRE General Test, GRE Subject Test. Additional exam requirements/recommendations for international students: Required—TOEFL. Electronic applications accepted.

University of Missouri, Office of Research and Graduate Studies, College of Arts and Science, Department of History, Columbia, MO 65211. Offers MA, PhD. *Faculty:* 16 full-time (5 women), 2 part-time/adjunct (0 women). *Students:* 57 full-time (20 women), 6 part-time (4 women); includes 2 minority (1 Asian, non-Hispanic/Latino; 1 Hispanic/Latino). Average age 31. 45 applicants, 33% accepted, 10 enrolled. In 2014, 3 master's, 3 doctorates awarded. *Degree requirements:* For master's, thesis; for doctorate, 2 foreign languages, comprehensive exam, thesis/dissertation. *Entrance requirements:* For master's, GRE General Test, minimum GPA of 3.0 in last 60 hours, 3.3 in undergraduate history courses; at least 18 hours in history; BA or BS; for doctorate, GRE General Test, minimum GPA of 3.0; MA in history (strongly preferred); master's thesis or research seminar paper. Additional exam requirements/recommendations for international students: Required—TOEFL (minimum score 500 paper-based; 61 iBT). *Application deadline:* For fall admission, 1/11 priority date for domestic and international students. Applications are processed on a rolling basis. Application fee: $55 ($75 for international students). Electronic applications accepted. *Financial support:* Fellowships with full tuition reimbursements, research assistantships with full tuition reimbursements, teaching assistantships with full tuition reimbursements, institutionally sponsored loans, health care benefits, and unspecified assistantships available. *Faculty research:* U.S. history, African-American history, ancient history, Latin American history, Asian history. *Unit head:* Dr. John H. Wigger, Department Chair, 573-882-2481, E-mail: wiggerj@missouri.edu. *Application contact:* Nancy Taube, Graduate Studies Administrator, 573-882-9461, E-mail: tauben@missouri.edu.
Website: http://history.missouri.edu/programs/grad.html

University of Missouri–Kansas City, College of Arts and Sciences, Department of History, Kansas City, MO 64110-2499. Offers MA, PhD. PhD (interdisciplinary) offered through the School of Graduate Studies. Part-time programs available. *Faculty:* 15 full-time (6 women), 2 part-time/adjunct (both women). *Students:* 2 full-time (1 woman), 29 part-time (9 women). Average age 35. 18 applicants, 100% accepted, 12 enrolled. In 2014, 10 master's awarded. *Degree requirements:* For master's, thesis optional; for doctorate, one foreign language, thesis/dissertation. *Entrance requirements:* For master's, GRE General Test, minimum GPA of 3.0, 2 writing samples, 3 letters of recommendation; for doctorate, GRE General Test. Additional exam requirements/recommendations for international students: Required—TOEFL (minimum score 550 paper-based; 80 iBT). *Application deadline:* For fall admission, 3/15 for domestic and international students; for spring admission, 10/1 priority date for domestic students, 10/1 for international students. Applications are processed on a rolling basis. Application fee: $45 ($50 for international students). Electronic applications accepted. *Financial support:* In 2014–15, 8 teaching assistantships with partial tuition reimbursements (averaging $11,675 per year) were awarded; career-related internships or fieldwork, Federal Work-Study, institutionally sponsored loans, and tuition waivers (full and partial) also available. Support available to part-time students. Financial award application deadline: 3/1; financial award applicants required to submit FAFSA. *Faculty research:* U.S. history, Europe, women and gender, religious studies, history of science. *Unit head:* Dr. John Herron, Chair, 816-235-2546, Fax: 816-235-5723, E-mail: herronj@umkc.edu. *Application contact:* Miriam Forman-Brunell, Master's Advisor, 816-235-5220, Fax: 816-235-5723, E-mail: forman-brunellm@umkc.edu.
Website: http://cas.umkc.edu/history/

The University of Montana, Graduate School, College of Humanities and Sciences, Department of History, Missoula, MT 59812-0002. Offers MA, PhD. *Degree requirements:* For master's, thesis or additional course work/professional paper. *Entrance requirements:* For master's, GRE General Test. Additional exam requirements/recommendations for international students: Required—TOEFL.

University of Nebraska at Kearney, Graduate Studies and Research, College of Natural and Social Sciences, Department of History, Kearney, NE 68849-0001. Offers MA. Part-time and evening/weekend programs available. Postbaccalaureate distance learning degree programs offered (no on-campus study). *Faculty:* 12 full-time (4 women). *Students:* 10 full-time (4 women), 153 part-time (64 women); includes 15 minority (2 Black or African American, non-Hispanic/Latino; 1 American Indian or Alaska Native, non-Hispanic/Latino; 7 Hispanic/Latino; 5 Two or more races, non-Hispanic/Latino). 81 applicants, 99% accepted, 55 enrolled. In 2014, 35 master's awarded. *Degree requirements:* For master's, comprehensive exam, thesis optional. *Entrance requirements:* For master's, letters of recommendation, writing sample, letter of interest. Additional exam requirements/recommendations for international students: Recommended—TOEFL (minimum score 550 paper-based; 79 iBT), IELTS (minimum score 6.5). *Application deadline:* For fall admission, 6/15 for domestic and international students; for spring admission, 10/15 for domestic and international students; for summer admission, 3/15 for domestic and international students. Application fee: $45. Electronic applications accepted. *Expenses:* Tuition, state resident: full-time $3897; part-time $216.50 per credit hour. Tuition, nonresident: full-time $8550; part-time $475 per credit hour. *Required fees:* $414; $23 per credit. $96.50 per semester. One-time fee: $45. Tuition and fees vary according to course load and program. *Financial support:* In 2014–15, 8 teaching assistantships with full tuition reimbursements (averaging $9,900 per year) were awarded; career-related internships or fieldwork, scholarships/grants, health care benefits, and unspecified assistantships also available. Support available to part-time students. Financial award application deadline: 2/28; financial award applicants required to submit FAFSA. *Faculty research:* Military history, labor history/labor and the law, state formation and nationalism, American intellectual history, Civil War and Reconstruction. *Unit head:* Dr. Mark Ellis, Chair, 308-865-8767, E-mail: ellismr@unk.edu. *Application contact:* Amber Alexander, Advisor, Graduate History Program, 308-865-8766, E-mail: alexanderaj@unk.edu.
Website: http://unkcms.unk.edu/academics/history/index.php

University of Nebraska at Omaha, Graduate Studies, College of Arts and Sciences, Department of History, Omaha, NE 68182. Offers MA. Part-time and evening/weekend programs available. *Faculty:* 12 full-time (6 women). *Students:* 9 full-time (5 women), 27 part-time (11 women); includes 3 minority (1 Black or African American, non-Hispanic/Latino; 1 Hispanic/Latino; 1 Two or more races, non-Hispanic/Latino), 1 international. Average age 33. 10 applicants, 50% accepted, 5 enrolled. In 2014, 9 master's awarded. *Degree requirements:* For master's, comprehensive exam, thesis (for some programs). *Entrance requirements:* For master's, minimum GPA of 3.0, 21 hours of course work in history, 2 letters of recommendation, resume, statement of purpose, writing sample, official transcripts. Additional exam requirements/recommendations for international students: Required—TOEFL, IELTS, PTE. *Application deadline:* For fall admission, 7/5

priority date for domestic and international students; for spring admission, 11/15 priority date for domestic and international students; for summer admission, 3/15 for domestic students. Applications are processed on a rolling basis. Application fee: $45. Electronic applications accepted. *Financial support:* In 2014–15, 6 students received support, including 6 teaching assistantships with tuition reimbursements available; fellowships, research assistantships with tuition reimbursements available, Federal Work-Study, institutionally sponsored loans, scholarships/grants, tuition waivers (partial), and unspecified assistantships also available. Support available to part-time students. Financial award application deadline: 3/1; financial award applicants required to submit FAFSA. *Unit head:* Dr. Mark Scherer, Chairperson, 402-554-2341, E-mail: graduate@unomaha.edu. *Application contact:* Dr. John Grigg, Graduate Program Chair, 402-554-2341, E-mail: graduate@unomaha.edu.

University of Nebraska–Lincoln, Graduate College, College of Arts and Sciences, Department of History, Lincoln, NE 68588. Offers MA, PhD. *Degree requirements:* For master's, thesis optional; for doctorate, one foreign language, comprehensive exam, thesis/dissertation. *Entrance requirements:* For master's and doctorate, GRE General Test, GRE Subject Test, writing sample. Additional exam requirements/recommendations for international students: Required—TOEFL (minimum score 575 paper-based). Electronic applications accepted. *Faculty research:* Military history, indigenous peoples, German history, American history (American West society and culture).

University of Nevada, Las Vegas, Graduate College, College of Liberal Arts, Department of History, Las Vegas, NV 89154-5020. Offers MA, PhD. Part-time programs available. *Faculty:* 17 full-time (6 women), 1 part-time/adjunct (0 women). *Students:* 25 full-time (12 women), 25 part-time (14 women); includes 8 minority (2 Black or African American, non-Hispanic/Latino; 1 American Indian or Alaska Native, non-Hispanic/Latino; 1 Hispanic/Latino; 4 Two or more races, non-Hispanic/Latino), 1 international. Average age 37. 26 applicants, 58% accepted, 6 enrolled. In 2014, 12 master's, 1 doctorate awarded. *Degree requirements:* For master's, one foreign language, comprehensive exam (for some programs), thesis (for some programs); for doctorate, 2 foreign languages, comprehensive exam, thesis/dissertation. *Entrance requirements:* For master's, minimum overall GPA of 3.0, 3.3 in history courses; for doctorate, GRE General Test, minimum overall GPA of 3.0, 3.3 in history courses. Additional exam requirements/recommendations for international students: Required—TOEFL (minimum score 550 paper-based; 80 iBT), IELTS (minimum score 7). *Application deadline:* For fall admission, 3/15 for domestic students, 5/1 for international students; for spring admission, 11/1 for domestic students, 10/1 for international students. Application fee: $60 ($95 for international students). Electronic applications accepted. *Financial support:* In 2014–15, 27 students received support, including 1 fellowship with full tuition reimbursement available (averaging $25,000 per year), 1 research assistantship with partial tuition reimbursement available (averaging $15,000 per year), 25 teaching assistantships with partial tuition reimbursements available (averaging $12,000 per year); institutionally sponsored loans, scholarships/grants, health care benefits, and unspecified assistantships also available. Financial award application deadline: 3/1. *Faculty research:* North American West, North American culture and society, European culture and society, American urban history, American gender and sexuality. *Total annual research expenditures:* $41,436. *Unit head:* Dr. Paul Werth, Chair/Professor, 702-895-3344, Fax: 702-895-1782, E-mail: paul.werth@unlv.edu. *Application contact:* Graduate College Admissions Evaluator, 702-895-3320, Fax: 702-895-4180, E-mail: gradcollege@unlv.edu.
Website: http://history.unlv.edu/graduate.html

University of Nevada, Reno, Graduate School, College of Liberal Arts, Department of History, Reno, NV 89557. Offers MA, PhD. Terminal master's awarded for partial completion of doctoral program. *Degree requirements:* For master's, thesis optional; for doctorate, one foreign language, thesis/dissertation. *Entrance requirements:* For master's, GRE General Test, minimum GPA of 2.75; for doctorate, GRE General Test, minimum GPA of 3.0. Additional exam requirements/recommendations for international students: Required—TOEFL (minimum score 500 paper-based; 61 iBT), IELTS (minimum score 6). Electronic applications accepted. *Faculty research:* History of medicine, science, environmental history, western America, social/cultural history.

University of New Brunswick Fredericton, School of Graduate Studies, Faculty of Arts, Department of History, Fredericton, NB E3B 5A3, Canada. Offers MA, PhD. Part-time programs available. *Faculty:* 12 full-time (3 women), 2 part-time/adjunct (both women). *Students:* 25 full-time (10 women), 9 part-time (2 women). In 2014, 5 master's, 2 doctorates awarded. *Degree requirements:* For master's, thesis; for doctorate, thesis/dissertation. *Entrance requirements:* For master's, minimum GPA of 3.0, resume, writing sample, statement of research interests, honors degree in history or equivalent; for doctorate, minimum GPA of 3.0, statement of research interests, writing sample, master's degree in history. Additional exam requirements/recommendations for international students: Required—TWE (minimum score 5.5), TOEFL (minimum paper-based score 600) or IELTS (minimum score 7). *Application deadline:* For fall admission, 3/1 for domestic students; for winter admission, 1/15 priority date for domestic and international students. Applications are processed on a rolling basis. Application fee: $50 Canadian dollars. Electronic applications accepted. *Financial support:* Fellowships, research assistantships, teaching assistantships, and scholarships/grants available. *Faculty research:* Atlantic Canada, military, early modern-modern Europe, colonial North America, women's and gender history, history of medicine. *Unit head:* Dr. David Charters, Director of Graduate Studies, 506-458-7740, Fax: 506-453-5068, E-mail: charters@unb.ca. *Application contact:* Elizabeth Arnold, Graduate Secretary, 506-458-7471, Fax: 506-453-5068, E-mail: eliz@unb.ca.
Website: http://go.unb.ca/gradprograms

University of New Hampshire, Graduate School, College of Liberal Arts, Department of History, Durham, NH 03824. Offers history (MA); museum studies (MA). Part-time programs available. *Faculty:* 21 full-time (11 women). *Students:* 27 full-time (12 women), 12 part-time (5 women); includes 1 minority (Two or more races, non-Hispanic/Latino), 2 international. Average age 34. 71 applicants, 51% accepted, 13 enrolled. In 2014, 10 master's, 3 doctorates awarded. *Degree requirements:* For master's, thesis or alternative; for doctorate, 2 foreign languages, thesis/dissertation. *Entrance requirements:* For master's and doctorate, GRE General Test. Additional exam requirements/recommendations for international students: Required—TOEFL (minimum score 550 paper-based; 80 iBT). *Application deadline:* For fall admission, 6/1 priority date for domestic students, 4/15 for international students; for spring admission, 12/1 for domestic students. Applications are processed on a rolling basis. Application fee: $65. Electronic applications accepted. *Expenses:* Tuition, state resident: full-time $13,500; part-time $750 per credit hour. Tuition, nonresident: full-time $26,460; part-time $1110 per credit hour. *Required fees:* $1788; $447 per semester. *Financial support:* In 2014–15, 18 students received support, including 1 fellowship, 14 teaching assistantships; research assistantships, career-related internships or fieldwork, Federal Work-Study, scholarships/grants, and tuition waivers (full and partial) also available. Support available to part-time students. Financial award application deadline: 2/15. *Unit head:* Dr. Eliga Gould, Chairperson, 603-862-3012. *Application contact:* Lara Demarest, Administrative Assistant, 603-862-1765, E-mail: history.grad@unh.edu.
Website: http://cola.unh.edu/history

University of New Mexico, Graduate School, College of Arts and Sciences, Program in History, Albuquerque, NM 87131-2039. Offers MA, PhD. Part-time programs available. *Faculty:* 20 full-time (11 women). *Students:* 39 full-time (17 women), 37 part-time (19 women); includes 19 minority (1 Black or African American, non-Hispanic/Latino; 7 American Indian or Alaska Native, non-Hispanic/Latino; 10 Hispanic/Latino; 1 Two or more races, non-Hispanic/Latino), 1 international. Average age 34. 58 applicants, 64% accepted, 14 enrolled. In 2014, 13 master's, 9 doctorates awarded. Terminal master's awarded for partial completion of doctoral program. *Degree requirements:* For master's, one foreign language, comprehensive exam, thesis optional; for doctorate, 2 foreign languages, comprehensive exam, thesis/dissertation. *Entrance requirements:* For master's, GRE, BA in history or equivalent; for doctorate, GRE, MA in history or equivalent. Additional exam requirements/recommendations for international students: Required—TOEFL. *Application deadline:* For fall admission, 12/15 for domestic students; for spring admission, 10/15 for domestic students. Application fee: $50. Electronic applications accepted. *Financial support:* In 2014–15, 23 students received support, including 2 fellowships (averaging $10,000 per year), 25 research assistantships (averaging $6,400 per year), 23 teaching assistantships with full tuition reimbursements available (averaging $13,700 per year); institutionally sponsored loans, scholarships/grants, and health care benefits also available. Financial award application deadline: 12/15. *Faculty research:* American Western history, Asian history, environmental history, European history, frontiers and borderlands, gender and sexuality, Latin American history, politics and economy, race and ethnicity, religion, United States history, war and society. *Unit head:* Dr. Charlie Steen, Chair, 505-277-2451, Fax: 505-277-6023, E-mail: csteen@unm.edu. *Application contact:* Yolanda Martinez, Department Administrator, 505-277-2451, Fax: 505-277-6023, E-mail: history@unm.edu.
Website: http://www.unm.edu/~hist/

University of New Orleans, Graduate School, College of Liberal Arts, Department of History, New Orleans, LA 70148. Offers MA. *Degree requirements:* For master's, one foreign language, thesis (for some programs). *Entrance requirements:* For master's, GRE General Test. Additional exam requirements/recommendations for international students: Required—TOEFL (minimum score 550 paper-based; 79 iBT), IELTS (minimum score 6.5). Electronic applications accepted. *Faculty research:* Recent U.S. political, military, urban, regional, and legal history.

University of North Alabama, College of Arts and Sciences, Department of History and Political Science, Florence, AL 35632-0001. Offers history (MA). Part-time and evening/weekend programs available. *Faculty:* 7 full-time (4 women), 1 (woman) part-time/adjunct. *Students:* 8 full-time (1 woman), 12 part-time (7 women); includes 1 minority (Black or African American, non-Hispanic/Latino). Average age 30. 12 applicants, 58% accepted, 7 enrolled. In 2014, 4 master's awarded. *Degree requirements:* For master's, comprehensive exam (for some programs), thesis optional. *Entrance requirements:* For master's, GRE, 3 letters of recommendation, essay, writing sample. Additional exam requirements/recommendations for international students: Required—TOEFL (minimum score 550 paper-based; 79 iBT), IELTS (minimum score 6). *Application deadline:* For fall admission, 7/1 for domestic and international students; for spring admission, 12/1 for domestic and international students. Applications are processed on a rolling basis. Application fee: $25 ($50 for international students). Electronic applications accepted. *Expenses:* Tuition, state resident: full-time $5166; part-time $1722 per semester. Tuition, nonresident: full-time $10,332; part-time $3444 per semester. *Required fees:* $393.50 per semester. *Financial support:* Applicants required to submit FAFSA. *Unit head:* Dr. Jeffrey Bibbee, Chair, 256-765-4306, E-mail: jrbibbee@una.edu. *Application contact:* Hillary N. Coats, Graduate Admissions Coordinator, 256-765-4447, E-mail: graduate@una.edu.
Website: http://www.una.edu/history/

The University of North Carolina at Chapel Hill, Graduate School, College of Arts and Sciences, Department of History, Chapel Hill, NC 27599. Offers MA, PhD. Terminal master's awarded for partial completion of doctoral program. *Degree requirements:* For master's, one foreign language, thesis, oral thesis defense; for doctorate, 2 foreign languages, comprehensive exam, thesis/dissertation, oral dissertation defense. *Entrance requirements:* For master's and doctorate, GRE General Test, minimum GPA of 3.0. Electronic applications accepted.

The University of North Carolina at Charlotte, College of Liberal Arts and Sciences, Department of History, Charlotte, NC 28223-0001. Offers MA. Part-time and evening/weekend programs available. *Faculty:* 25 full-time (11 women). *Students:* 19 full-time (8 women), 37 part-time (19 women); includes 11 minority (1 Black or African American, non-Hispanic/Latino; 9 Hispanic/Latino; 1 Two or more races, non-Hispanic/Latino), 4 international. Average age 32. 40 applicants, 90% accepted, 15 enrolled. In 2014, 23 master's awarded. *Degree requirements:* For master's, thesis or comprehensive exam. *Entrance requirements:* For master's, GRE General Test, minimum GPA of 3.0 in undergraduate major, 2.75 overall. Additional exam requirements/recommendations for international students: Required—TOEFL (minimum score 557 paper-based; 83 iBT). *Application deadline:* For fall admission, 2/1 for domestic and international students; for spring admission, 11/1 for domestic students, 10/1 for international students. Application fee: $75. Electronic applications accepted. *Expenses:* Tuition, state resident: full-time $4008. Tuition, nonresident: full-time $16,295. *Required fees:* $2755. Tuition and fees vary according to course load and program. *Financial support:* In 2014–15, 13 students received support, including 2 research assistantships (averaging $9,000 per year), 11 teaching assistantships (averaging $8,227 per year); career-related internships or fieldwork, Federal Work-Study, institutionally sponsored loans, scholarships/grants, unspecified assistantships, and administrative assistantships also available. Support available to part-time students. Financial award application deadline: 4/1; financial award applicants required to submit FAFSA. *Faculty research:* Southern United States history; Latin American history; race and gender history; urban history; history of science, medicine, technology. *Total annual research expenditures:* $157,840. *Unit head:* Dr. Jurgen Buchenau, Chair, 704-687-5136, Fax: 704-687-3218, E-mail: jbuchenau@uncc.edu. *Application contact:* Kathy B. Giddings, Director of Graduate Admissions, 704-687-5530, Fax: 704-687-1668, E-mail: gradadm@uncc.edu.
Website: https://history.uncc.edu/graduate-studies

The University of North Carolina at Greensboro, Graduate School, College of Arts and Sciences, Department of History, Greensboro, NC 27412-5001. Offers historic preservation (Certificate); history (MA); museum studies (Certificate); U.S. history (PhD). Part-time programs available. *Entrance requirements:* For master's, GRE General Test. Additional exam requirements/recommendations for international students: Required—TOEFL. Electronic applications accepted. *Faculty research:* Simultaneous discovery in science, progressive social reform, Robert Mayer.

The University of North Carolina Wilmington, College of Arts and Sciences, Department of History, Wilmington, NC 28403-3297. Offers MA. Part-time programs available. *Faculty:* 22 full-time (8 women). *Students:* 9 full-time (5 women), 34 part-time (17 women); includes 4 minority (2 Black or African American, non-Hispanic/Latino; 1 American Indian or Alaska Native, non-Hispanic/Latino; 1 Two or more races, non-Hispanic/Latino). 19 applicants, 79% accepted, 6 enrolled. In 2014, 13 master's awarded. *Degree requirements:* For master's, comprehensive exam, thesis. *Entrance requirements:* For master's, GRE General Test, minimum B average in undergraduate

major. Additional exam requirements/recommendations for international students: Required—TOEFL (minimum score 79 iBT), IELTS. *Application deadline:* For fall admission, 2/15 for domestic students. Applications are processed on a rolling basis. Application fee: $60. *Expenses:* Tuition, state resident: full-time $3240. Tuition, nonresident: full-time $9208. *Required fees:* $1967. *Financial support:* Career-related internships or fieldwork and Federal Work-Study available. Support available to part-time students. Financial award application deadline: 3/15; financial award applicants required to submit FAFSA. *Unit head:* Dr. Paul A. Townend, Chair, 910-962-3308, Fax: 910-962-7011, E-mail: townendp@uncw.edu. *Application contact:* Dr. W. Taylor Fain, Interim Graduate Coordinator, 910-962-3305, Fax: 910-962-7011, E-mail: fainwt@uncw.edu.
Website: http://www.uncw.edu/hst/graduate/index.html

University of North Dakota, Graduate School, College of Arts and Sciences, Department of History, Grand Forks, ND 58202. Offers MA, DA, PhD. Part-time programs available. *Degree requirements:* For master's, comprehensive exam (for some programs), thesis (for some programs), final exam; for doctorate, comprehensive exam, thesis/dissertation, final exam. *Entrance requirements:* For master's, minimum GPA of 3.0; for doctorate, minimum GPA of 3.5. Additional exam requirements/recommendations for international students: Required—TOEFL (minimum score 550 paper-based; 79 iBT), IELTS (minimum score 6.5). Electronic applications accepted. *Faculty research:* U.S. history, Latin America, Russia, modern Europe, women studies.

University of Northern British Columbia, Office of Graduate Studies, Prince George, BC V2N 4Z9, Canada. Offers business administration (Diploma); community health science (M Sc); disability management (MA); education (M Ed); first nations studies (MA); gender studies (MA); history (MA); interdisciplinary studies (MA); international studies (MA); mathematical, computer and physical sciences (M Sc); natural resources and environmental studies (M Sc, MA, MNRES, PhD); political science (MA); psychology (M Sc, PhD); social work (MSW). Part-time and evening/weekend programs available. Postbaccalaureate distance learning degree programs offered (no on-campus study). *Degree requirements:* For master's, thesis; for doctorate, thesis/dissertation. *Entrance requirements:* For master's, GRE, minimum B average in undergraduate course work; for doctorate, candidacy exam, minimum A average in graduate course work.

University of Northern Colorado, Graduate School, College of Humanities and Social Sciences, Program in History, Greeley, CO 80639. Offers MA. Part-time programs available. *Degree requirements:* For master's, comprehensive exam, thesis or alternative. *Entrance requirements:* For master's, GRE, 3 letters of recommendation. Electronic applications accepted.

University of Northern Colorado, Graduate School, College of Humanities and Social Sciences, School of History, Philosophy and Political Science, Greeley, CO 80639. Offers history (MA). Part-time programs available. *Degree requirements:* For master's, comprehensive exam, thesis or alternative. *Entrance requirements:* For master's, GRE, 3 letters of reference. Electronic applications accepted.

University of Northern Iowa, Graduate College, College of Social and Behavioral Sciences, Department of History, Cedar Falls, IA 50614. Offers history (MA); public history (MA). Part-time programs available. *Students:* 18 full-time (10 women), 15 part-time (7 women); includes 4 minority (1 Black or African American, non-Hispanic/Latino; 1 Asian, non-Hispanic/Latino; 2 Two or more races, non-Hispanic/Latino). 24 applicants, 67% accepted, 10 enrolled. In 2014, 11 master's awarded. *Degree requirements:* For master's, comprehensive exam (for some programs), thesis or alternative. *Entrance requirements:* For master's, minimum GPA of 3.2. Additional exam requirements/recommendations for international students: Required—TOEFL (minimum score 500 paper-based; 61 iBT). *Application deadline:* For fall admission, 8/1 priority date for domestic students. Applications are processed on a rolling basis. Application fee: $50 ($70 for international students). Electronic applications accepted. *Expenses:* Tuition, state resident: full-time $7912; part-time $880 per credit. Tuition, nonresident: full-time $17,906; part-time $880 per credit. *Required fees:* $1101; $325.50 per credit. $465.63 per semester. Tuition and fees vary according to course load and program. *Financial support:* Career-related internships or fieldwork, Federal Work-Study, scholarships/grants, and tuition waivers (full and partial) available. Support available to part-time students. Financial award application deadline: 2/1. *Unit head:* Dr. Robert Martin, Department Head, 319-273-2097, Fax: 319-273-5846, E-mail: robert.martin@uni.edu. *Application contact:* Laurie S. Russell, Record Analyst, 319-273-2623, Fax: 319-273-2885, E-mail: laurie.russell@uni.edu.
Website: http://www.uni.edu/history/

University of North Florida, College of Arts and Sciences, Department of History, Jacksonville, FL 32224. Offers European history (MA); U.S. history (MA). Part-time programs available. *Faculty:* 8 full-time (2 women). *Students:* 20 full-time (10 women), 20 part-time (9 women); includes 5 minority (1 Black or African American, non-Hispanic/Latino; 4 Hispanic/Latino). Average age 32. 24 applicants, 63% accepted, 13 enrolled. In 2014, 10 master's awarded. *Degree requirements:* For master's, comprehensive exam (for some programs), thesis optional. *Entrance requirements:* For master's, GRE General Test, 3 letters of recommendation, minimum GPA of 3.0 in last 60 hours of course work. Additional exam requirements/recommendations for international students: Required—TOEFL (minimum score 500 paper-based; 61 iBT). *Application deadline:* For fall admission, 7/1 priority date for domestic students, 5/1 for international students; for spring admission, 11/1 priority date for domestic students, 10/1 for international students. Application fee: $30. Electronic applications accepted. *Expenses:* Tuition, state resident: full-time $9794; part-time $408.10 per credit hour. Tuition, nonresident: full-time $22,383; part-time $932.61 per credit hour. *Required fees:* $2047; $85.29 per credit hour. Tuition and fees vary according to course load and program. *Financial support:* In 2014–15, 6 students received support, including 4 teaching assistantships (averaging $4,524 per year); career-related internships or fieldwork, Federal Work-Study, scholarships/grants, tuition waivers (partial), and unspecified assistantships also available. Financial award application deadline: 4/1; financial award applicants required to submit FAFSA. *Total annual research expenditures:* $21,515. *Unit head:* Dr. Charles Closmann, Chair, 904-620-1864, Fax: 904-620-1018, E-mail: cclosman@unf.edu. *Application contact:* Dr. Amanda Pascale, Director, The Graduate School, 904-620-1360, Fax: 904-620-1362, E-mail: graduateschool@unf.edu.
Website: http://www.unf.edu/coas/history/

University of North Georgia, Department of History and Philosophy, Dahlonega, GA 30597. Offers history (MA), including American history, military history, world history. Part-time and evening/weekend programs available. *Degree requirements:* For master's, thesis optional. *Entrance requirements:* For master's, GRE, 3 recommendations, writing sample, letter of intent, minimum GPA of 2.75. Additional exam requirements/recommendations for international students: Required—TOEFL (minimum score 550 paper-based; 79 iBT), IELTS (minimum score 6.5). Electronic applications accepted. *Faculty research:* Mongol empire, early modern Europe, late Antiquity, China and Korea from the seventeenth-century, the Reconstruction Era in the U.S., Middle East history, Spanish Florida, aviation, war and society in America.

University of North Texas, Robert B. Toulouse School of Graduate Studies, Denton, TX 76203-5459. Offers accounting (MS); applied anthropology (MA, MS); applied behavior analysis (Certificate); applied geography (MA); applied technology and performance improvement (M Ed, MS); art education (MA); art history (MA); art museum education (Certificate); arts leadership (Certificate); audiology (Au D); behavior analysis (MS); behavioral science (PhD); biochemistry and molecular biology (MS); biology (MA, MS); biomedical engineering (MS); business analysis (MS); chemistry (MS); clinical health psychology (PhD); communication studies (MA, MS); computer engineering (MS); computer science (MS); counseling (M Ed, MS), including clinical mental health counseling (MS), college and university counseling, elementary school counseling, secondary school counseling; creative writing (MA); criminal justice (MS); curriculum and instruction (M Ed); decision sciences (MBA); design (MA, MFA), including fashion design (MFA), innovation studies, interior design (MFA); early childhood studies (MS); economics (MS); educational leadership (M Ed, Ed D); educational psychology (MS, PhD), including family studies (MS), gifted and talented (MS), human development (MS), learning and cognition (MS), research, measurement and evaluation (MS); electrical engineering (MS); emergency management (MPA); engineering technology (MS); English (MA); English as a second language (MA); environmental science (MS); finance (MBA, MS); financial management (MPA); French (MA); health services management (MBA); higher education (M Ed, Ed D); history (MA, MS); hospitality management (MS); human resources management (MPA); information science (MS); information systems (PhD); information technologies (MBA); interdisciplinary studies (MA, MS); international studies (MA); international sustainable tourism (MS); jazz studies (MM); journalism (MA, MJ, Graduate Certificate), including interactive and virtual digital communication (Graduate Certificate), narrative journalism (Graduate Certificate), public relations (Graduate Certificate); kinesiology (MS); linguistics (MA); local government management (MPA); logistics (PhD); logistics and supply chain management (MBA); long-term care, senior housing, and aging services (MA); management (PhD); marketing (MBA); mathematics (MA, MS); mechanical and energy engineering (MS, PhD); music (MA), including ethnomusicology, music theory, musicology, performance; music composition (PhD); music education (MM Ed, PhD); nonprofit management (MPA); operations and supply chain management (MBA); performance (MM, DMA); philosophy (MA); political science (MA); professional and technical communication (MA); radio, television and film (MA, MFA); rehabilitation counseling (Certificate); sociology (MA); Spanish (MA); special education (M Ed); speech-language pathology (MA); strategic management (MBA); studio art (MFA); teaching (M Ed); MBA/MS. Part-time and evening/weekend programs available. Postbaccalaureate distance learning degree programs offered. *Faculty:* 651 full-time (215 women), 233 part-time/adjunct (139 women). *Students:* 3,040 full-time (1,598 women), 3,401 part-time (2,097 women); includes 1,740 minority (533 Black or African American, non-Hispanic/Latino; 15 American Indian or Alaska Native, non-Hispanic/Latino; 286 Asian, non-Hispanic/Latino; 746 Hispanic/Latino; 3 Native Hawaiian or other Pacific Islander, non-Hispanic/Latino; 157 Two or more races, non-Hispanic/Latino), 1,145 international. Terminal master's awarded for partial completion of doctoral program. *Degree requirements:* For master's, variable foreign language requirement, comprehensive exam (for some programs), thesis (for some programs); for doctorate, variable foreign language requirement, comprehensive exam (for some programs), thesis/dissertation; for other advanced degree, variable foreign language requirement, comprehensive exam (for some programs). *Entrance requirements:* For master's and doctorate, GRE, GMAT. Additional exam requirements/recommendations for international students: Required—TOEFL (minimum score 550 paper-based; 79 iBT). *Application deadline:* For fall admission, 7/15 for domestic students, 3/15 for international students; for spring admission, 11/15 for domestic students, 9/15 for international students; for summer admission, 5/1 for domestic students. Applications are processed on a rolling basis. Application fee: $60. Electronic applications accepted. *Expenses:* Tuition, state resident: full-time $5450; part-time $3633 per year. Tuition, nonresident: full-time $11,966; part-time $7977 per year. *Required fees:* $1301; $398 per credit hour. $685 per semester. Tuition and fees vary according to program and reciprocity agreements. *Financial support:* Fellowships with partial tuition reimbursements, research assistantships with partial tuition reimbursements, teaching assistantships, career-related internships or fieldwork, Federal Work-Study, institutionally sponsored loans, scholarships/grants, health care benefits, and library assistantships available. Support available to part-time students. Financial award applicants required to submit FAFSA. *Unit head:* Mark Wardell, Dean, 940-565-2383, E-mail: mark.wardell@unt.edu. *Application contact:* Toulouse School of Graduate Studies, 940-565-2383, Fax: 940-565-2141, E-mail: gradsch@unt.edu.
Website: http://tsgs.unt.edu/

University of Notre Dame, Graduate School, College of Arts and Letters, Division of Humanities, Department of History, Notre Dame, IN 46556. Offers MA, PhD. *Degree requirements:* For doctorate, one foreign language, thesis/dissertation, candidacy exam. *Entrance requirements:* For doctorate, GRE General Test. Additional exam requirements/recommendations for international students: Required—TOEFL (minimum score 600 paper-based; 80 iBT). Electronic applications accepted. *Faculty research:* U.S., modern European and medieval history; history of European and U.S. religions; U.S. and European intellectual and cultural history; history of Central Europe.

University of Oklahoma, College of Arts and Sciences, Department of History, Norman, OK 73019. Offers MA, PhD. *Faculty:* 38 full-time (13 women), 1 part-time/adjunct (0 women). *Students:* 34 full-time (13 women), 16 part-time (7 women); includes 7 minority (2 Black or African American, non-Hispanic/Latino; 5 Hispanic/Latino). Average age 30. 41 applicants, 66% accepted, 13 enrolled. In 2014, 4 master's, 7 doctorates awarded. *Degree requirements:* For master's, one foreign language, comprehensive exam (for some programs), thesis (for some programs), 30 hours of course work with minimum GPA of 3.0; for doctorate, one foreign language, comprehensive exam, thesis/dissertation, 90 hours of course work. *Entrance requirements:* For master's, GRE General Test, 3 letters of reference, statement of purpose, writing sample, minimum GPA of 3.5; for doctorate, GRE General Test, 3 letters of reference (preferably from applicant's professors), statement of purpose, writing sample, minimum GPA of 3.5. Additional exam requirements/recommendations for international students: Required—TOEFL (minimum score 79 iBT). *Application deadline:* For fall and spring admission, 12/1 for domestic and international students. Application fee: $50 ($100 for international students). Electronic applications accepted. *Expenses:* Tuition, state resident: full-time $4394; part-time $183.10 per credit hour. Tuition, nonresident: full-time $16,970; part-time $707.10 per credit hour. *Required fees:* $2892; $109.95 per credit hour. $126.50 per semester. *Financial support:* In 2014–15, 41 students received support, including 3 fellowships with full tuition reimbursements available (averaging $5,000 per year), 9 research assistantships with partial tuition reimbursements available (averaging $15,773 per year), 23 teaching assistantships with partial tuition reimbursements available (averaging $15,468 per year); scholarships/grants, health care benefits, and unspecified assistantships also available. Financial award application deadline: 6/1; financial award applicants required to submit FAFSA. *Faculty research:* American West, Native American, Latin American, environmental, and Judaic studies. *Unit head:* Dr. James Hart, Jr., Department Chair, 405-325-6305, Fax: 405-325-4503, E-mail: jshart@ou.edu. *Application contact:* Dr. Judith S. Lewis, Director of Graduate Studies, 405-325-6383, Fax: 405-325-4503, E-mail: judith.s.lewis-1@ou.edu.
Website: http://history.ou.edu

History

University of Oregon, Graduate School, College of Arts and Sciences, Department of History, Eugene, OR 97403. Offers MA, PhD. *Degree requirements:* For master's, one foreign language, thesis or alternative, written exam; for doctorate, 2 foreign languages, thesis/dissertation, oral and written exams. *Entrance requirements:* For master's and doctorate, GRE General Test, minimum GPA of 3.0. Additional exam requirements/recommendations for international students: Required—TOEFL. *Faculty research:* U.S., European, East and Southeast Asian, Latin American, and ancient history.

University of Ottawa, Faculty of Graduate and Postdoctoral Studies, Faculty of Arts, Department of History, Ottawa, ON K1N 6N5, Canada. Offers MA, PhD. *Degree requirements:* For master's, 2 foreign languages, thesis or alternative; for doctorate, 2 foreign languages, thesis/dissertation, oral exam. *Entrance requirements:* For master's, honors degree or equivalent, minimum B average; for doctorate, master's degree, minimum B+ average. Electronic applications accepted. *Faculty research:* Canadian history.

University of Pennsylvania, School of Arts and Sciences, Graduate Group in Ancient History, Philadelphia, PA 19104. Offers AM, PhD. *Faculty:* 26 full-time (10 women), 3 part-time/adjunct (0 women). *Students:* 11 full-time (3 women), 3 international. 30 applicants, 17% accepted, 3 enrolled. In 2014, 1 master's, 2 doctorates awarded. *Degree requirements:* For doctorate, 4 foreign languages, thesis/dissertation. *Application deadline:* For fall admission, 12/1 priority date for domestic students. Application fee: $70. Electronic applications accepted. *Financial support:* Institutionally sponsored loans, scholarships/grants, traineeships, health care benefits, and unspecified assistantships available. Financial award application deadline: 12/15. *Unit head:* Dr. Ralph M. Rosen, Associate Dean for Graduate Studies, 215-898-7156, Fax: 215-573-8068, E-mail: grad-dean@sas.upenn.edu. *Application contact:* Arts and Sciences Graduate Admissions, 215-573-5816, Fax: 215-573-8068, E-mail: gdasadmis@sas.upenn.edu.
Website: http://www.sas.upenn.edu/graduate-division

University of Pennsylvania, School of Arts and Sciences, Graduate Group in History, Philadelphia, PA 19104. Offers AM, PhD. *Faculty:* 50 full-time (21 women), 8 part-time/adjunct (3 women). *Students:* 91 full-time (50 women), 12 part-time (9 women); includes 15 minority (4 Black or African American, non-Hispanic/Latino; 2 Asian, non-Hispanic/Latino; 6 Hispanic/Latino; 3 Two or more races, non-Hispanic/Latino), 17 international. 327 applicants, 8% accepted, 18 enrolled. In 2014, 9 master's, 8 doctorates awarded. Terminal master's awarded for partial completion of doctoral program. *Degree requirements:* For master's, thesis; for doctorate, one foreign language, thesis/dissertation. *Entrance requirements:* For master's and doctorate, GRE General Test. Additional exam requirements/recommendations for international students: Required—TOEFL. *Application deadline:* For fall admission, 12/1 priority date for domestic students. Application fee: $70. Electronic applications accepted. *Financial support:* Institutionally sponsored loans, scholarships/grants, traineeships, health care benefits, and unspecified assistantships available. Financial award application deadline: 12/15. *Unit head:* Dr. Ralph M. Rosen, Associate Dean for Graduate Studies, 215-898-7156, Fax: 215-573-8068, E-mail: grad-dean@sas.upenn.edu. *Application contact:* Arts and Sciences Graduate Admissions, 215-573-5816, Fax: 215-573-8068, E-mail: gdasadmis@sas.upenn.edu.
Website: http://www.sas.upenn.edu/graduate-division

University of Pittsburgh, Dietrich School of Arts and Sciences, Department of History, Pittsburgh, PA 15260. Offers MA, PhD. *Faculty:* 27 full-time (9 women). *Students:* 42 full-time (16 women); includes 2 minority (both Hispanic/Latino), 13 international. 113 applicants, 12% accepted, 5 enrolled. In 2014, 5 master's, 4 doctorates awarded. *Degree requirements:* For master's, one foreign language, thesis, oral exam, seminar paper; for doctorate, 2 foreign languages, comprehensive exam, thesis/dissertation. *Entrance requirements:* For master's and doctorate, GRE General Test. Additional exam requirements/recommendations for international students: Required—TOEFL. *Application deadline:* For fall admission, 1/15 for domestic and international students. Application fee: $50. Electronic applications accepted. *Expenses:* Tuition, state resident: full-time $20,742; part-time $838 per credit. Tuition, nonresident: full-time $33,960; part-time $1389 per credit. *Required fees:* $800; $205 per term. Tuition and fees vary according to program. *Financial support:* In 2014–15, 35 students received support, including fellowships with full tuition reimbursements available (averaging $21,000 per year), 2 research assistantships with full tuition reimbursements available (averaging $17,000 per year), 18 teaching assistantships with full tuition reimbursements available; scholarships/grants and health care benefits also available. Financial award application deadline: 1/15. *Faculty research:* Europe, Latin America, Atlantic, United States, East Asia. *Unit head:* Prof. Lara Elisabeth Putnam, Chairperson, E-mail: lep12@pitt.edu. *Application contact:* Molly Dennis-Estes, Graduate Administrator, 412-648-7454, Fax: 412-648-9074, E-mail: wid2@pitt.edu.
Website: http://www.history.pitt.edu

University of Puerto Rico, Río Piedras Campus, College of Humanities, Department of History, San Juan, PR 00931-3300. Offers Caribbean history (PhD); history (MA); Puerto Rican history (PhD). Part-time programs available. *Degree requirements:* For master's, one foreign language, comprehensive exam, thesis; for doctorate, one foreign language, comprehensive exam, thesis/dissertation. *Entrance requirements:* For master's, PAEG or GRE, interview, minimum GPA of 3.0, 2 letters of recommendation; for doctorate, PAEG or GRE, interview, master's degree, minimum GPA of 3.0, 2 letters of recommendation.

University of Regina, Faculty of Graduate Studies and Research, Faculty of Arts, Department of History, Regina, SK S4S 0A2, Canada. Offers MA. Part-time programs available. *Faculty:* 11 full-time (4 women), 1 part-time/adjunct (0 women). *Students:* 6 full-time (5 women), 4 part-time (2 women). 7 applicants, 57% accepted. In 2014, 1 master's awarded. *Degree requirements:* For master's, thesis. *Entrance requirements:* Additional exam requirements/recommendations for international students: Required—TOEFL (minimum score 580 paper-based; 80 iBT), IELTS (minimum score 6.5), PTE (minimum score 59). *Application deadline:* For fall admission, 3/31 for domestic and international students. Application fee: $100. Electronic applications accepted. *Expenses: Tuition, area resident:* Full-time $4900 Canadian dollars; part-time $837.65 Canadian dollars per semester. *International tuition:* $7900 Canadian dollars full-time. *Required fees:* $396 Canadian dollars; $86.90 Canadian dollars per semester. *Financial support:* In 2014–15, 3 teaching assistantships (averaging $2,427 per year) were awarded; fellowships, research assistantships, and scholarships/grants also available. Financial award application deadline: 6/15. *Faculty research:* Canadian, European, Asian, British, and the Americas history. *Unit head:* Dr. Raymond Blake, Department Head, 306-585-5431, Fax: 306-585-4827, E-mail: raymond.blake@uregina.ca. *Application contact:* Dr. Philip Charrier, Graduate Program Coordinator, 306-585-4215, Fax: 306-585-4827, E-mail: philip.charrier@uregina.ca.
Website: http://www.uregina.ca/arts/history

University of Rhode Island, Graduate School, College of Arts and Sciences, Department of History, Kingston, RI 02881. Offers MA, MA/PhD, MLIS/MA. Part-time programs available. *Faculty:* 15 full-time (8 women), 1 part-time/adjunct (0 women). *Students:* 10 full-time (8 women), 5 part-time (3 women). In 2014, 3 master's awarded. *Degree requirements:* For master's, comprehensive exam (for some programs), thesis optional. *Entrance requirements:* For master's, GRE, 2 letters of recommendation. Additional exam requirements/recommendations for international students: Required—TOEFL (minimum score 550 paper-based). *Application deadline:* For fall admission, 7/15 for domestic students, 2/1 for international students; for spring admission, 11/15 for domestic students, 7/15 for international students. Application fee: $65. Electronic applications accepted. *Expenses:* Tuition, state resident: full-time $11,532; part-time $641 per credit. Tuition, nonresident: full-time $23,606; part-time $1311 per credit. *Required fees:* $1442; $39 per credit. $35 per semester. One-time fee: $155. *Financial support:* In 2014–15, 3 teaching assistantships with full and partial tuition reimbursements (averaging $15,844 per year) were awarded. Financial award application deadline: 2/1; financial award applicants required to submit FAFSA. *Unit head:* Dr. Timothy George, Chair, 401-874-4092, Fax: 401-874-2595, E-mail: tgeorge@uri.edu. *Application contact:* Dr. Evelyn Sterne, Director of Graduate Studies, 401-874-4074, Fax: 401-874-2595, E-mail: sterne@mail.uri.edu.
Website: http://www.uri.edu/artsci/his/

University of Rochester, School of Arts and Sciences, Department of History, Rochester, NY 14627. Offers American history (MA, PhD); European history (MA, PhD); global history (MA, PhD). *Faculty:* 18 full-time (4 women). *Students:* 30 full-time (8 women); includes 4 minority (1 Asian, non-Hispanic/Latino; 1 Hispanic/Latino; 2 Two or more races, non-Hispanic/Latino), 1 international. 32 applicants, 41% accepted, 7 enrolled. In 2014, 5 master's, 7 doctorates awarded. Terminal master's awarded for partial completion of doctoral program. *Degree requirements:* For master's, one foreign language, thesis or alternative; for doctorate, 2 foreign languages, thesis/dissertation, comprehensive oral exam, qualifying exam. *Entrance requirements:* For master's and doctorate, GRE General Test, sample of written work. Additional exam requirements/recommendations for international students: Required—TOEFL. *Application deadline:* For fall admission, 1/15 priority date for domestic students. Application fee: $60. Electronic applications accepted. *Expenses: Tuition:* Full-time $46,150; part-time $1442 per credit hour. *Required fees:* $504. *Financial support:* Fellowships, research assistantships, teaching assistantships, and tuition waivers (full and partial) available. Financial award application deadline: 1/15. *Unit head:* Matthew Lenoe, Chair, 585-275-9355. *Application contact:* Caleb Rood, Secretary, 585-275-2053.
Website: http://www.rochester.edu/College/HIS/

University of San Diego, College of Arts and Sciences, Program in History, San Diego, CA 92110-2492. Offers MA. Part-time and evening/weekend programs available. *Faculty:* 2 full-time (1 woman), 2 part-time/adjunct (1 woman). *Students:* 2 full-time (1 woman), 8 part-time (2 women); includes 3 minority (1 Black or African American, non-Hispanic/Latino; 2 Hispanic/Latino). Average age 30. 16 applicants, 69% accepted, 3 enrolled. In 2014, 8 master's awarded. *Degree requirements:* For master's, comprehensive exam, thesis or alternative. *Entrance requirements:* For master's, GRE General Test, minimum GPA of 3.0. Additional exam requirements/recommendations for international students: Required—TOEFL (minimum score 580 paper-based; 83 iBT), TWE. *Application deadline:* For fall admission, 8/1 for domestic and international students; for spring admission, 12/1 for domestic and international students. Applications are processed on a rolling basis. Application fee: $45. Electronic applications accepted. *Financial support:* In 2014–15, 8 students received support. Career-related internships or fieldwork, Federal Work-Study, institutionally sponsored loans, and unspecified assistantships available. Support available to part-time students. Financial award application deadline: 4/1; financial award applicants required to submit FAFSA. *Faculty research:* History of the American West, history of California, history of Mexico and Latin America, public history, environmental history. *Unit head:* Dr. Michael Gonzalez, Graduate Program Director, 619-260-4043, Fax: 619-260-2272, E-mail: mbyrnes@sandiego.edu. *Application contact:* Monica Mahon, Associate Director of Graduate Admissions, 619-260-4524, Fax: 619-260-4158, E-mail: grads@sandiego.edu.
Website: http://www.sandiego.edu/cas/history_ma/

University of Saskatchewan, College of Graduate Studies and Research, College of Arts and Science, Department of History, Saskatoon, SK S7N 5A2, Canada. Offers MA, PhD. Part-time programs available. *Degree requirements:* For master's, thesis; for doctorate, comprehensive exam (for some programs), thesis/dissertation. *Entrance requirements:* Additional exam requirements/recommendations for international students: Required—TOEFL (minimum score 80 iBT); Recommended—IELTS (minimum score 6.5). Electronic applications accepted.

University of South Africa, College of Human Sciences, Pretoria, South Africa. Offers adult education (M Ed); African languages (MA, PhD); African politics (MA, PhD); Afrikaans (MA, PhD); ancient history (MA, PhD); ancient Near Eastern studies (MA, PhD); anthropology (MA, PhD); applied linguistics (MA); Arabic (MA, PhD); archaeology (MA); art history (MA); Biblical archaeology (MA); Biblical studies (M Th, D Th, PhD); Christian spirituality (M Th, D Th); church history (M Th, D Th); classical studies (MA, PhD); clinical psychology (MA); communication (MA, PhD); comparative education (M Ed, Ed D); consulting psychology (D Admin, D Com, PhD); curriculum studies (M Ed, Ed D); development studies (M Admin, MA, D Admin, PhD); didactics (M Ed, Ed D); education (M Tech); education management (M Ed, Ed D); educational psychology (M Ed); English (MA); environmental education (M Ed); French (MA, PhD); German (MA, PhD); Greek (MA); guidance and counseling (M Ed); health studies (MA, PhD), including health sciences education (MA), health services management (MA), medical and surgical nursing science (critical care general) (MA), midwifery and neonatal nursing science (MA), trauma and emergency care (MA); history (MA, PhD); history of education (Ed D); inclusive education (M Ed, Ed D); information and communications technology policy and regulation (MA); information science (MA, MIS, PhD); international politics (MA, PhD); Islamic studies (MA, PhD); Italian (MA, PhD); Judaica (MA, PhD); linguistics (MA, PhD); mathematical education (M Ed); mathematics education (MA); missiology (M Th, D Th); modern Hebrew (MA, PhD); musicology (MA, MMus, D Mus, PhD); natural science education (M Ed); New Testament (M Th, D Th); Old Testament (D Th); pastoral therapy (M Th, D Th); philosophy (MA); philosophy of education (M Ed, Ed D); politics (MA, PhD); Portuguese (MA, PhD); practical theology (M Th, D Th); psychology (MA, MS, PhD); psychology of education (M Ed, Ed D); public health (MA); religious studies (MA, D Th, PhD); Romance languages (MA); Russian (MA, PhD); Semitic languages (MA, PhD); social behavior studies in HIV/AIDS (MA); social science (mental health) (MA); social science in development studies (MA); social science in psychology (MA); social science in social work (MA); social science in sociology (MA); social work (MSW, DSW, PhD); socio-education (M Ed, Ed D); sociolinguistics (MA); sociology (MA, PhD); Spanish (MA, PhD); systematic theology (M Th, D Th); TESOL (teaching English to speakers of other languages) (MA); theological ethics (M Th, D Th); theory of literature (MA, PhD); urban ministries (D Th); urban ministry (M Th).

University of South Alabama, College of Arts and Sciences, Department of History, Mobile, AL 36688. Offers MA. Part-time and evening/weekend programs available. *Faculty:* 9 full-time (4 women). *Students:* 13 full-time (6 women), 9 part-time (4 women); includes 3 minority (all Black or African American, non-Hispanic/Latino). Average age 31. 11 applicants, 73% accepted, 6 enrolled. In 2014, 1 master's awarded. *Degree requirements:* For master's, one foreign language, comprehensive exam, thesis optional, 33 credit hours of course work. *Entrance requirements:* For master's, GRE General Test, GRE Subject Test, 21 hours of course work in history, minimum GPA of 3.0. Additional exam requirements/recommendations for international students:

Required—TOEFL. *Application deadline:* For fall admission, 8/1 priority date for domestic students, 6/15 priority date for international students; for spring admission, 12/15 priority date for domestic students, 11/1 priority date for international students. Applications are processed on a rolling basis. Application fee: $35. Electronic applications accepted. *Expenses:* Tuition, state resident: full-time $9288; part-time $387 per credit hour. Tuition, nonresident: full-time $18,576; part-time $774 per credit hour. Part-time tuition and fees vary according to course load and program. *Financial support:* Fellowships, research assistantships, teaching assistantships, career-related internships or fieldwork, Federal Work-Study, institutionally sponsored loans, scholarships/grants, and unspecified assistantships available. Support available to part-time students. Financial award application deadline: 5/31; financial award applicants required to submit FAFSA. *Unit head:* Dr. Clarence Mohr, Chair, History, 251-460-6210, Fax: 251-460-6750, E-mail: cmohr@southalabama.edu. *Application contact:* Dr. Martha Brazy, Graduate Coordinator, History, 251-460-7540, E-mail: mjbrazy@southalabama.edu.
Website: http://www.southalabama.edu/history/pdf/gradbook.pdf

University of South Carolina, The Graduate School, College of Arts and Sciences, Department of History, Columbia, SC 29208. Offers history (MA, PhD); public history (MA, Certificate), including archive management (MA), historic preservation (MA), museum administration (MA), museum management (Certificate); MLIS/MA. IMA and MAT offered in cooperation with the College of Education. Part-time programs available. Terminal master's awarded for partial completion of doctoral program. *Degree requirements:* For master's, one foreign language, thesis; for doctorate, one foreign language, thesis/dissertation. *Entrance requirements:* For master's and doctorate, GRE General Test. Additional exam requirements/recommendations for international students: Required—TOEFL. Electronic applications accepted. *Faculty research:* U.S. history; European history; Latin American history; history of science and technology.

The University of South Dakota, Graduate School, College of Arts and Sciences, Department of History, Vermillion, SD 57069-2390. Offers MA, JD/MA. Part-time programs available. *Degree requirements:* For master's, thesis (for some programs). *Entrance requirements:* For master's, GRE General Test, minimum GPA of 2.7. Additional exam requirements/recommendations for international students: Required—TOEFL (minimum score 550 paper-based; 79 iBT). Electronic applications accepted.

University of Southern California, Graduate School, Dana and David Dornsife College of Letters, Arts and Sciences, Department of History, Los Angeles, CA 90089. Offers PhD. *Degree requirements:* For doctorate, 2 foreign languages, comprehensive exam, thesis/dissertation, 60 semester units of acceptable coursework. *Entrance requirements:* For doctorate, GRE General Test. Additional exam requirements/recommendations for international students: Recommended—TOEFL. Electronic applications accepted. *Faculty research:* U.S. North American and Latin American history, California and Western American history (including Borderlands), European history from the early Middle Ages to present, East Asian (Chinese, Japanese, Korean) history, early modern Atlantic world/world history.

University of Southern Mississippi, Graduate School, College of Arts and Letters, Department of History, Hattiesburg, MS 39406-0001. Offers MA, MS, PhD. Part-time programs available. *Degree requirements:* For master's, one foreign language, comprehensive exam, thesis (for some programs); for doctorate, 2 foreign languages, comprehensive exam, thesis/dissertation. *Entrance requirements:* For master's, GRE General Test, minimum GPA of 3.0 in field of study, 2.75 in last 2 years; for doctorate, GRE General Test, minimum GPA of 3.5. Additional exam requirements/recommendations for international students: Required—TOEFL, IELTS. *Faculty research:* Civil War, civil rights, modern European history, war history.

University of South Florida, College of Arts and Sciences, Department of History, Tampa, FL 33620-9951. Offers MA, PhD. Part-time and evening/weekend programs available. *Faculty:* 10 full-time (5 women). *Students:* 33 full-time (20 women), 14 part-time (4 women); includes 2 minority (both Hispanic/Latino), 1 international. Average age 33. 52 applicants, 44% accepted, 16 enrolled. In 2014, 10 master's awarded. *Degree requirements:* For master's, one foreign language, comprehensive exam, thesis optional; for doctorate, one foreign language, comprehensive exam, thesis/dissertation. *Entrance requirements:* For master's, GRE General Test (minimum preferred scores of 59th percentile (153) verbal, 18th percentile (144) quantitative, and 4.5 in writing), minimum GPA of 3.0, two letters of recommendation, 2-page statement of purpose, writing sample; for doctorate, GRE General Test (minimum preferred scores of 84th percentile (160) verbal, 18th percentile (144) quantitative, and 4.5 in writing), minimum GPA of 3.5 in master's degree coursework, three letters of recommendation, statement of purpose, writing sample, foreign language proficiency in the field of study. Additional exam requirements/recommendations for international students: Required—TOEFL (minimum score 550 paper-based; 79 iBT) or IELTS (minimum score 6.5). *Application deadline:* For fall admission, 1/15 priority date for domestic students, 1/15 for international students. Applications are processed on a rolling basis. Application fee: $30. Electronic applications accepted. *Financial support:* In 2014–15, 17 students received support, including 17 teaching assistantships with tuition reimbursements available (averaging $12,750 per year); unspecified assistantships also available. Financial award application deadline: 1/15. *Faculty research:* North American and U.S. history, European history, nineteenth and twentieth centuries/modern world, early modern world, ancient history, history of gender/sexuality, Latin American history, history of science and medicine. *Total annual research expenditures:* $223,828. *Unit head:* Dr. Fraser Ottanelli, Professor and Chair, 813-974-6209, Fax: 813-974-6228, E-mail: ottanelli@usf.edu. *Application contact:* Dr. Brian Connolly, Associate Professor and Graduate Program Director, 813-974-1087, Fax: 813-974-6228, E-mail: bconnelly@usf.edu.
Website: http://history.usf.edu

The University of Tennessee, Graduate School, College of Arts and Sciences, Department of History, Knoxville, TN 37996. Offers American history (PhD); European history (PhD); history (MA). Part-time programs available. *Degree requirements:* For master's, thesis or alternative; for doctorate, one foreign language, thesis/dissertation. *Entrance requirements:* For master's and doctorate, GRE General Test, minimum GPA of 2.7. Additional exam requirements/recommendations for international students: Required—TOEFL. Electronic applications accepted.

The University of Texas at Arlington, Graduate School, College of Liberal Arts, Department of History, Arlington, TX 76019. Offers history (MA); transatlantic history (PhD). Part-time and evening/weekend programs available. *Degree requirements:* For master's, one foreign language, comprehensive exam (for some programs), thesis (for some programs); for doctorate, one foreign language, comprehensive exam, thesis/dissertation. *Entrance requirements:* For master's, GRE General Test, minimum GPA of 3.0 in last 60 hours, 3 letters of recommendation; for doctorate, GRE General Test, minimum graduate GPA of 3.5, 3 letters of recommendation, academic writing sample. Additional exam requirements/recommendations for international students: Required—TOEFL (minimum score 550 paper-based). Electronic applications accepted.

The University of Texas at Austin, Graduate School, College of Liberal Arts, Department of History, Austin, TX 78712-1111. Offers MA, PhD. *Degree requirements:* For doctorate, thesis/dissertation. *Entrance requirements:* For master's and doctorate, GRE General Test. Electronic applications accepted. *Faculty research:* United States, Latin American, European, African, Asian, and Middle Eastern history.

The University of Texas at Brownsville, Graduate Studies, College of Liberal Arts, Department of History, Brownsville, TX 78520-4991. Offers MA. Part-time and evening/weekend programs available. *Degree requirements:* For master's, comprehensive exam (for some programs), thesis optional. *Entrance requirements:* For master's, GRE General Test, personal statement of at least 1,000 words; six undergraduate upper-division hours in history. Additional exam requirements/recommendations for international students: Required—TOEFL (minimum score 550 paper-based; 77 iBT). Electronic applications accepted.

The University of Texas at Dallas, School of Arts and Humanities, Program in Humanities, Richardson, TX 75080. Offers aesthetic studies (MA, PhD); history (MA); history of ideas (MA, PhD); humanities (MA, PhD); Latin American studies (MA); studies in literature (MA, PhD). *Faculty:* 35 full-time (11 women), 1 part-time/adjunct (0 women). *Students:* 148 full-time (94 women), 151 part-time (97 women); includes 78 minority (21 Black or African American, non-Hispanic/Latino; 4 American Indian or Alaska Native, non-Hispanic/Latino; 14 Asian, non-Hispanic/Latino; 28 Hispanic/Latino; 11 Two or more races, non-Hispanic/Latino), 16 international. Average age 39. 127 applicants, 46% accepted, 40 enrolled. In 2014, 40 master's, 15 doctorates awarded. *Degree requirements:* For master's, one foreign language, portfolio, thesis, or capstone project; for doctorate, one foreign language, thesis/dissertation. *Entrance requirements:* For master's, minimum GPA of 3.3 in upper-level coursework in field; for doctorate, field examinations, minimum GPA of 3.3 in upper-level coursework in field. Additional exam requirements/recommendations for international students: Required—TOEFL (minimum score 550 paper-based). *Application deadline:* For fall admission, 7/15 for domestic students, 5/1 priority date for international students; for spring admission, 11/15 for domestic students, 9/1 priority date for international students. Applications are processed on a rolling basis. Application fee: $50 ($100 for international students). Electronic applications accepted. *Expenses:* Tuition, state resident: full-time $11,940; part-time $663 per credit. Tuition, nonresident: full-time $22,282; part-time $1238 per credit. *Financial support:* In 2014–15, 161 students received support. Research assistantships with partial tuition reimbursements available, teaching assistantships with partial tuition reimbursements available, career-related internships or fieldwork, Federal Work-Study, institutionally sponsored loans, scholarships/grants, and unspecified assistantships available. Support available to part-time students. Financial award application deadline: 4/30; financial award applicants required to submit FAFSA. *Faculty research:* Holocaust studies, U.S./Mexico studies, translation studies, art history research, Chinese studies. *Unit head:* Dr. Michael Wilson, III, Associate Dean for Graduate Education, 972-883-2756, Fax: 972-883-2989, E-mail: mwilson@utdallas.edu. *Application contact:* Alice Salazar, Coordinator, 972-883-2756, Fax: 972-883-2989, E-mail: alice.salazar1@utdallas.edu.
Website: http://www.utdallas.edu/ah/programs/graduate

The University of Texas at El Paso, Graduate School, College of Liberal Arts, Department of History, El Paso, TX 79968-0001. Offers border history (MA); borderlands history (PhD); history (MA). Part-time programs available. *Degree requirements:* For master's, thesis optional; for doctorate, 2 foreign languages, thesis/dissertation. *Entrance requirements:* For master's, GRE, minimum GPA of 3.0, writing sample, letters of recommendation, transcripts; for doctorate, GRE, statement of purpose, writing sample, letters of recommendation, transcripts. Additional exam requirements/recommendations for international students: Required—TOEFL; Recommended—IELTS.

The University of Texas at San Antonio, College of Liberal and Fine Arts, Department of History, San Antonio, TX 78249-0617. Offers MA. Part-time programs available. *Faculty:* 11 full-time (6 women), 1 part-time/adjunct (0 women). *Students:* 13 full-time (5 women), 37 part-time (13 women); includes 27 minority (2 Black or African American, non-Hispanic/Latino; 23 Hispanic/Latino; 2 Two or more races, non-Hispanic/Latino). Average age 34. 15 applicants, 80% accepted, 11 enrolled. In 2014, 20 master's awarded. *Degree requirements:* For master's, comprehensive exam, thesis optional, minimum of 30 credit hours. *Entrance requirements:* For master's, GRE, bachelor's degree with 18 credit hours in field of study or in another appropriate field of study (12 of these hours must be at the upper-division level with minimum GPA of 3.0 in last 60 hours), statement of purpose. Additional exam requirements/recommendations for international students: Required—TOEFL (minimum score 550 paper-based; 79 iBT), IELTS (minimum score 6.5). *Application deadline:* For fall admission, 7/1 for domestic students, 4/1 for international students; for spring admission, 11/1 for domestic students, 9/1 for international students. Application fee: $45 ($80 for international students). Electronic applications accepted. *Expenses:* Expenses: Contact institution. *Financial support:* In 2014–15, 6 students received support, including 3 research assistantships (averaging $1,609 per year); Federal Work-Study also available. *Faculty research:* Borderlands and empires, Latin American history, early American history, Chinese history, Latina/o studies. *Total annual research expenditures:* $15,000. *Unit head:* Dr. Gregg Michel, Department Chair, 210-458-4033, Fax: 210-458-4796, E-mail: gregg.michel@utsa.edu. *Application contact:* Roschelle Kelly, Administrative Associate II, 210-458-5716, E-mail: roschelle.kelly@utsa.edu.
Website: http://colfa.utsa.edu/history/

The University of Texas at Tyler, College of Arts and Sciences, Department of History, Tyler, TX 75799-0001. Offers MA. Part-time and evening/weekend programs available. *Degree requirements:* For master's, one foreign language, comprehensive exam, thesis optional. *Entrance requirements:* For master's, GRE General Test, minimum GPA of 3.0. Additional exam requirements/recommendations for international students: Required—TOEFL. Electronic applications accepted. *Faculty research:* Early and modern U.S. history, early modern and modern European history.

The University of Texas of the Permian Basin, Office of Graduate Studies, College of Arts and Sciences, Department of History, Odessa, TX 79762-0001. Offers MA. Part-time and evening/weekend programs available. *Degree requirements:* For master's, comprehensive exam (for some programs), thesis (for some programs). *Entrance requirements:* For master's, GRE General Test. Additional exam requirements/recommendations for international students: Required—TOEFL (minimum score 550 paper-based).

The University of Texas–Pan American, College of Arts and Humanities, Department of History, Edinburg, TX 78539. Offers MA, MAIS. Part-time and evening/weekend programs available. *Degree requirements:* For master's, comprehensive exam, thesis or alternative. *Entrance requirements:* For master's, GRE General Test, minimum GPA of 3.0. *Expenses:* Tuition, state resident: full-time $4187; part-time $232.60 per credit hour. Tuition, nonresident: full-time $10,857; part-time $603.16 per credit hour. *Required fees:* $782; $27.50 per credit hour. $143.35 per semester. *Faculty research:* Texas-Mexican legacy, modern America, Southwest, labor, modern Europe.

The University of Toledo, College of Graduate Studies, College of Languages, Literature and Social Sciences, Department of History, Toledo, OH 43606-3390. Offers MA, PhD. Part-time programs available. *Degree requirements:* For master's, comprehensive exam (for some programs), thesis or comprehensive exam; for doctorate, thesis/dissertation, oral and written exams. *Entrance requirements:* For

master's and doctorate, GRE General Test, minimum cumulative point-hour ratio of 2.7 for all previous academic work, three letters of recommendation. Additional exam requirements/recommendations for international students: Required—TOEFL (minimum score 550 paper-based; 80 iBT). Electronic applications accepted. *Faculty research:* U.S. diplomatic history, U.S. history, urban history, public history, European history.

University of Toronto, School of Graduate Studies, Faculty of Arts and Science, Department of History, Toronto, ON M5S 2J7, Canada. Offers MA, PhD. Part-time programs available. *Degree requirements:* For master's, one foreign language, thesis or research essay, French language exam; for doctorate, comprehensive exam, thesis/dissertation, oral examination/thesis defense. *Entrance requirements:* For master's, minimum B+ average or GPA of 3.3, 6 full academic year history courses; for doctorate, MA in history, minimum A- average or GPA of 3.7. Additional exam requirements/recommendations for international students: Required—TOEFL (minimum score 580 paper-based; 93 iBT), TWE (minimum score 5). Electronic applications accepted.

The University of Tulsa, Graduate School, Kendall College of Arts and Sciences, Department of History, Tulsa, OK 74104-3189. Offers MA, MTA, JD/MA. Part-time programs available. *Faculty:* 9 full-time (3 women). *Students:* 6 full-time (2 women), 3 part-time (all women); includes 4 minority (3 American Indian or Alaska Native, non-Hispanic/Latino; 1 Two or more races, non-Hispanic/Latino). Average age 27. 6 applicants, 83% accepted, 5 enrolled. In 2014, 2 master's awarded. *Degree requirements:* For master's, one foreign language, public presentation or oral defense of thesis. *Entrance requirements:* For master's, GRE General Test, writing sample. Additional exam requirements/recommendations for international students: Required—TOEFL (minimum score 577 paper-based; 91 iBT), IELTS (minimum score 6.5). *Application deadline:* Applications are processed on a rolling basis. Application fee: $55. Electronic applications accepted. *Expenses: Tuition:* Full-time $20,160; part-time $1120 per credit hour. *Required fees:* $6 per credit hour. Tuition and fees vary according to course level and course load. *Financial support:* In 2014–15, 5 students received support, including 5 teaching assistantships with full and partial tuition reimbursements available (averaging $13,440 per year); fellowships, research assistantships, Federal Work-Study, scholarships/grants, health care benefits, tuition waivers (full and partial), and unspecified assistantships also available. Support available to part-time students. Financial award application deadline: 2/1; financial award applicants required to submit FAFSA. *Faculty research:* United States history, modern European history, Native American History, comparative history. *Total annual research expenditures:* $500. *Unit head:* Dr. Thomas Buoye, Chairperson, 918-631-2825, Fax: 918-631-2057, E-mail: thomas-buoye@utulsa.edu. *Application contact:* Dr. Christine Ruane, Adviser, 918-631-3814, Fax: 918-631-2057, E-mail: christine-ruane@utulsa.edu.
Website: http://artsandsciences.utulsa.edu/academics/departments-schools/history/

The University of Tulsa, Graduate School, Kendall College of Arts and Sciences, School of Education, Program in Teaching Arts, Tulsa, OK 74104-3189. Offers art (MTA); biology (MTA); English (MTA); history (MTA); mathematics (MTA). Part-time programs available. *Students:* 2 full-time (1 woman), 1 part-time (0 women); includes 1 minority (Black or African American, non-Hispanic/Latino). Average age 30. 2 applicants, 100% accepted, 1 enrolled. *Entrance requirements:* For master's, GRE General Test. Additional exam requirements/recommendations for international students: Required—TOEFL (minimum score 577 paper-based), IELTS (minimum score 6.5). *Application deadline:* Applications are processed on a rolling basis. Application fee: $55. Electronic applications accepted. *Expenses: Tuition:* Full-time $20,160; part-time $1120 per credit hour. *Required fees:* $6 per credit hour. Tuition and fees vary according to course level and course load. *Financial support:* In 2014–15, 2 students received support, including 1 research assistantship with full and partial tuition reimbursement available (averaging $13,148 per year), 1 teaching assistantship with full and partial tuition reimbursement available (averaging $13,148 per year); fellowships with full and partial tuition reimbursements available, career-related internships or fieldwork, Federal Work-Study, scholarships/grants, health care benefits, tuition waivers (full and partial), and unspecified assistantships also available. Support available to part-time students. Financial award application deadline: 2/1; financial award applicants required to submit FAFSA. *Unit head:* Dr. Kara Gae Neal, Chair, 918-631-2238, Fax: 918-631-3721, E-mail: karagae-neal@utulsa.edu. *Application contact:* Dr. David Brown, Advisor, 918-631-2719, Fax: 918-631-2133, E-mail: david-brown@utulsa.edu.

University of Utah, Graduate School, College of Humanities, Department of History, Salt Lake City, UT 84112. Offers MA, MS, PhD. Part-time and evening/weekend programs available. *Faculty:* 28 full-time (12 women), 8 part-time/adjunct (1 woman). *Students:* 28 full-time (17 women), 17 part-time (6 women); includes 3 minority (1 American Indian or Alaska Native, non-Hispanic/Latino; 2 Hispanic/Latino), 1 international. Average age 37. 47 applicants, 32% accepted, 13 enrolled. In 2014, 11 master's, 2 doctorates awarded. Terminal master's awarded for partial completion of doctoral program. *Degree requirements:* For master's, one foreign language, comprehensive exam (for some programs), thesis (for some programs); for doctorate, one foreign language, comprehensive exam, thesis/dissertation. *Entrance requirements:* For master's, GRE General Test, minimum GPA of 3.2; for doctorate, GRE General Test, minimum graduate GPA of 3.6. Additional exam requirements/recommendations for international students: Required—TOEFL (minimum score 500 paper-based). *Application deadline:* For fall admission, 1/15 for domestic and international students. Application fee: $55 ($65 for international students). Electronic applications accepted. *Financial support:* In 2014–15, 15 students received support, including 2 fellowships with full tuition reimbursements available (averaging $15,000 per year), 13 teaching assistantships with full tuition reimbursements available (averaging $14,000 per year); career-related internships or fieldwork also available. Financial award application deadline: 1/15. *Faculty research:* U.S. history, European history, Asian history, Middle East, Latin America. *Total annual research expenditures:* $20,744. *Unit head:* Prof. Isabel Moreira, Chair, 801-581-5685, Fax: 801-585-0580, E-mail: isabel.moreira@utah.edu. *Application contact:* Amarilys La Santa, Academic Advisor, 801-581-6121, Fax: 801-585-0580, E-mail: a.lasanta@utah.edu.
Website: http://history.utah.edu

University of Utah, Graduate School, College of Humanities, Program in Middle East Studies, Salt Lake City, UT 84112. Offers Arabic (MA, PhD); Hebrew (MA); history (MA, PhD); Persian (MA, PhD); political science (MA, PhD). *Students:* 1 full-time (0 women), 8 part-time (3 women); includes 1 minority (Asian, non-Hispanic/Latino), 3 international. Average age 40. In 2014, 5 master's, 1 doctorate awarded. Terminal master's awarded for partial completion of doctoral program. *Degree requirements:* For master's, 2 foreign languages, comprehensive exam, thesis optional; for doctorate, 3 foreign languages, comprehensive exam, thesis/dissertation. *Entrance requirements:* For master's, GRE General Test, minimum GPA of 3.2; for doctorate, GRE General Test, MA in Middle East studies or equivalent, minimum GPA of 3.2. Additional exam requirements/recommendations for international students: Required—TOEFL (minimum score 580 paper-based; 92 iBT); Recommended—IELTS (minimum score 7). *Application deadline:* For fall admission, 1/15 priority date for domestic and international students. Application fee: $55 ($65 for international students). Electronic applications accepted. *Financial support:* In 2014–15, 5 students received support, including 2 teaching assistantships with full tuition reimbursements available (averaging $13,500 per year); fellowships and unspecified assistantships also available. Financial award application deadline: 1/15. *Faculty research:* Islamic studies; Middle Eastern history; political science; Judaic studies; anthropology; Arabic, Persian, Hebrew, and Turkish language and literature. *Unit head:* Johanna Watzinger-Tharp, Director, 801-581-7148, Fax: 801-581-6105, E-mail: j.tharp@utah.edu. *Application contact:* Kellie Hubbard, Academic Advisor, 801-581-5362, Fax: 801-581-6105, E-mail: kellie.hubbard@utah.edu.
Website: http://www.mec.utah.edu

University of Vermont, Graduate College, College of Arts and Sciences, Department of History, Burlington, VT 05405. Offers MA. *Degree requirements:* For master's, thesis. *Entrance requirements:* For master's, GRE General Test, sample project. Additional exam requirements/recommendations for international students: Required—TOEFL (minimum score 550 paper-based; 80 iBT). Electronic applications accepted. *Faculty research:* American, European, and Asian history.

University of Victoria, Faculty of Graduate Studies, Faculty of Humanities, Department of History, Victoria, BC V8W 2Y2, Canada. Offers MA, PhD. Part-time programs available. *Degree requirements:* For master's, one foreign language, thesis; for doctorate, one foreign language, comprehensive exam, thesis/dissertation. *Entrance requirements:* Additional exam requirements/recommendations for international students: Required—TOEFL (minimum score 600 paper-based), TWE. Electronic applications accepted. *Faculty research:* Canadian social history, Canadian gender history, Canadian native history, Canadian military history, British Columbian history, Western history, medieval history, world history.

University of Virginia, College and Graduate School of Arts and Sciences, Department of History, Charlottesville, VA 22903. Offers MA, PhD, JD/MA. *Faculty:* 31 full-time (7 women), 3 part-time/adjunct (1 woman). *Students:* 74 full-time (34 women), 1 part-time (0 women); includes 5 minority (1 Asian, non-Hispanic/Latino; 3 Hispanic/Latino; 1 Two or more races, non-Hispanic/Latino), 10 international. Average age 28. 213 applicants, 10% accepted, 11 enrolled. In 2014, 16 master's, 19 doctorates awarded. *Degree requirements:* For master's, one foreign language, essay; for doctorate, variable foreign language requirement, comprehensive exam, thesis/dissertation. *Entrance requirements:* For master's and doctorate, GRE General Test, 2 or more letters of recommendation. Additional exam requirements/recommendations for international students: Required—TOEFL (minimum score 600 paper-based; 90 iBT), IELTS (minimum score 7). *Application deadline:* For fall admission, 12/1 for domestic and international students. Applications are processed on a rolling basis. Application fee: $60. Electronic applications accepted. *Expenses:* Tuition, state resident: full-time $14,164; part-time $349 per credit hour. Tuition, nonresident: full-time $23,722; part-time $1300 per credit hour. *Required fees:* $2514. *Financial support:* Fellowships and teaching assistantships available. Financial award application deadline: 12/1; financial award applicants required to submit FAFSA. *Unit head:* Paul Halliday, Chair, 434-924-6385, Fax: 434-924-7891, E-mail: history@virginia.edu. *Application contact:* S. Max Adelson, Director of Graduate Admissions, 434-924-6401, Fax: 434-924-7891, E-mail: edelson@virginia.edu.
Website: http://history.virginia.edu/

University of Washington, Graduate School, College of Arts and Sciences, Department of History, Seattle, WA 98195. Offers MA, PhD. Part-time programs available. *Degree requirements:* For master's, one foreign language, comprehensive exam, thesis optional; for doctorate, one foreign language, comprehensive exam, thesis/dissertation. *Entrance requirements:* For master's and doctorate, GRE, minimum GPA of 3.0. Additional exam requirements/recommendations for international students: Required—TOEFL. Electronic applications accepted. *Faculty research:* United States, Asia, Europe, comparative history.

University of Waterloo, Graduate Studies, Faculty of Arts, Department of Classical Studies, Waterloo, ON N2L 3G1, Canada. Offers ancient Mediterranean cultures (MA). *Degree requirements:* For master's, one foreign language. *Faculty research:* Ancient history, philosophy, anthropology, religion, culture.

University of Waterloo, Graduate Studies, Faculty of Arts, Department of History, Waterloo, ON N2L 3G1, Canada. Offers MA, PhD. PhD offered jointly with University of Guelph, Wilfrid Laurier University. Part-time and evening/weekend programs available. *Degree requirements:* For master's, one foreign language, thesis optional; for doctorate, one foreign language, thesis/dissertation. *Entrance requirements:* For master's, honors degree, minimum B+ average, resume; for doctorate, master's degree, minimum A average, resumé, writing sample. Additional exam requirements/recommendations for international students: Required—TOEFL, TWE. Electronic applications accepted. *Faculty research:* Canadian, British, international, modern, European, and U.S. history; women's history; imperialism and slavery.

The University of West Alabama, School of Graduate Studies, College of Education, Departments of Instructional Leadership and Support/Curriculum and Instruction, Program in Secondary Education, Livingston, AL 35470. Offers biology (MAT); English language arts (MAT); history (MAT); mathematics (MAT); science (MAT); secondary education (M Ed); social science (MAT). Part-time and evening/weekend programs available. Postbaccalaureate distance learning degree programs offered (no on-campus study). *Faculty:* 20 full-time (5 women), 6 part-time/adjunct (2 women). *Students:* 202 (131 women); includes 63 minority (57 Black or African American, non-Hispanic/Latino; 1 American Indian or Alaska Native, non-Hispanic/Latino; 2 Asian, non-Hispanic/Latino; 1 Hispanic/Latino; 2 Two or more races, non-Hispanic/Latino). Average age 31. 106 applicants, 79% accepted, 46 enrolled. In 2014, 52 master's awarded. *Degree requirements:* For master's, comprehensive exam, thesis optional. *Entrance requirements:* For master's, GRE General Test, MAT, minimum GPA of 2.75. Additional exam requirements/recommendations for international students: Required—TOEFL (minimum score 500 paper-based; 61 iBT). *Application deadline:* For fall admission, 8/12 for domestic students; for spring admission, 3/24 for domestic students. Applications are processed on a rolling basis. Application fee: $25. Electronic applications accepted. *Expenses:* Tuition, state resident: full-time $1902; part-time $317 per credit hour. Tuition, nonresident: full-time $3804; part-time $634 per credit hour. *Required fees:* $50 per semester. One-time fee: $65. Tuition and fees vary according to course load. *Financial support:* Teaching assistantships, career-related internships or fieldwork, Federal Work-Study, scholarships/grants, and unspecified assistantships available. Support available to part-time students. Financial award application deadline: 3/1; financial award applicants required to submit FAFSA. *Faculty research:* Integrated arts in the curriculum, moral development of children. *Unit head:* Dr. Jodie Winship, Chair of Curriculum and Instruction, 205-652-5415, Fax: 205-652-3706, E-mail: jwinship@uwa.edu. *Application contact:* Dr. Kathy Chandler, Dean of Graduate Studies, 205-652-3421, Fax: 205-652-3706, E-mail: kchandler@uwa.edu.
Website: http://www.uwa.edu/highschool612.aspx

The University of Western Ontario, Faculty of Graduate Studies, Social Sciences Division, Department of History, London, ON N6A 5B8, Canada. Offers MA, PhD. Part-time programs available. *Degree requirements:* For master's, one foreign language, thesis (for some programs); for doctorate, one foreign language, thesis/dissertation. *Entrance requirements:* For master's, minimum B+ average on last 10 senior courses; for doctorate, minimum A- average on MA or last year honors degree. Additional exam requirements/recommendations for international students: Required—TOEFL. *Faculty*

research: Canadian, U.S., Britain, Modern Europe, British Empire and Commonwealth Latin America.

University of West Florida, College of Arts and Sciences: Arts, Department of History, Pensacola, FL 32514-5750. Offers history (MA); military history (MA); public history (MA). Part-time and evening/weekend programs available. *Degree requirements:* For master's, thesis or alternative. *Entrance requirements:* For master's, GRE (minimum score: verbal 500, writing 3.5) or MAT (minimum score 415), minimum GPA of 3.0, minimum 15 hours of upper-level history courses; official transcripts; letter of intent; writing sample (undergraduate research paper preferred). Additional exam requirements/recommendations for international students: Required—TOEFL (minimum score 550 paper-based).

University of West Georgia, College of Arts and Humanities, Department of History, Carrollton, GA 30118. Offers history (MA); museum studies (Certificate); public history (Certificate). Part-time and evening/weekend programs available. *Faculty:* 15 full-time (6 women). *Students:* 24 full-time (12 women), 15 part-time (9 women); includes 6 minority (5 Black or African American, non-Hispanic/Latino; 1 Hispanic/Latino). Average age 35. 15 applicants, 87% accepted, 7 enrolled. In 2014, 12 master's, 5 other advanced degrees awarded. *Degree requirements:* For master's, one foreign language, comprehensive exam, thesis or alternative. *Entrance requirements:* For master's, GRE General Test (minimum score of 151 on verbal, 4.0 on analytical writing), undergraduate degree in history or related social studies, minimum GPA of 3.0; for Certificate, GRE General Test (minimum score 151 verbal, 4.0 writing), MA from another institution or enrolled in MA at UWG. Additional exam requirements/recommendations for international students: Required—TOEFL (minimum score 523 paper-based; 69 iBT); Recommended—IELTS (minimum score 6). *Application deadline:* For fall admission, 8/1 for domestic students, 6/1 for international students; for spring admission, 11/15 for domestic students, 10/15 for international students. Applications are processed on a rolling basis. Application fee: $40. Electronic applications accepted. *Financial support:* In 2014–15, 1 student received support, including 21 research assistantships with full tuition reimbursements available (averaging $6,000 per year), 2 teaching assistantships (averaging $5,000 per year); career-related internships or fieldwork, scholarships/grants, and unspecified assistantships also available. Support available to part-time students. Financial award application deadline: 4/1; financial award applicants required to submit FAFSA. *Faculty research:* Public history, United States, Europe, Atlantic, world war and society. *Unit head:* Dr. Howard Steven Goodson, Chair, 678-839-6042, E-mail: hgoodson@westga.edu. *Application contact:* Dr. Nadya Williams, Graduate Coordinator, 678-839-5453, E-mail: nwilliam@westga.edu.
Website: http://westga.edu/~history/

University of Windsor, Faculty of Graduate Studies, Faculty of Arts and Social Sciences, Department of History, Windsor, ON N9B 3P4, Canada. Offers MA. Part-time programs available. *Degree requirements:* For master's, thesis (for some programs). *Entrance requirements:* For master's, minimum B average. Additional exam requirements/recommendations for international students: Required—TOEFL (minimum score 600 paper-based). Electronic applications accepted. *Faculty research:* Gender history, social-history questions about class gender and national identity, divorce in France: 1792-1816, gender and sexuality in Western Europe during the high and later Middle Ages, U.S.-Canadian comparisons in women's history.

The University of Winnipeg, Graduate Studies, Department of History, Winnipeg, MB R3B 2E9, Canada. Offers MA. Program offered jointly with University of Manitoba. Part-time and evening/weekend programs available. *Degree requirements:* For master's, one foreign language, comprehensive exam or thesis. *Faculty research:* Canadian social history, European diplomacy, Indian history, colonial America, medieval history.

University of Wisconsin–Eau Claire, College of Arts and Sciences, Department of History, Eau Claire, WI 54702-4004. Offers public history (MA). Part-time programs available. *Degree requirements:* For master's, comprehensive exam, thesis optional, oral and written exams. *Entrance requirements:* For master's, minimum GPA of 3.15 during last 2 years, 3.3 in history, or 3.0 overall; research paper; bachelor's degree with minimum of 24 credits in history. Additional exam requirements/recommendations for international students: Required—TOEFL (minimum score 79 iBT).

University of Wisconsin–Madison, Graduate School, College of Letters and Science, Department of History, Madison, WI 53706-1380. Offers African history (MA, PhD); Central Asian history (MA, PhD); comparative world history (MA, PhD); East Asian history (MA, PhD); European history (MA, PhD); gender and women's history (MA, PhD); Latin American and Caribbean history (MA, PhD); Middle Eastern history (MA, PhD); South Asian history (MA, PhD); Southeast Asian history (MA, PhD); United States history (MA, PhD). Terminal master's awarded for partial completion of doctoral program. *Degree requirements:* For master's, thesis (for some programs); for doctorate, variable foreign language requirement, thesis/dissertation. *Entrance requirements:* For master's and doctorate, GRE General Test. Additional exam requirements/recommendations for international students: Required—Michigan English Language Assessment Battery or TOEFL. Electronic applications accepted. *Expenses:* Tuition, state resident: full-time $10,723; part-time $745 per credit. Tuition, nonresident: full-time $24,054; part-time $1578 per credit. *Required fees:* $374 per semester. Tuition and fees vary according to course load, program and reciprocity agreements. *Faculty research:* American, African, European, Asian, Latin American, and Middle Eastern history.

University of Wisconsin–Milwaukee, Graduate School, College of Letters and Sciences, Department of History, Milwaukee, WI 53201-0413. Offers global history (PhD); history (MA); modern studies (PhD); urban history (PhD). Part-time programs available. *Degree requirements:* For master's, comprehensive exam, thesis or alternative; for doctorate, thesis/dissertation. *Entrance requirements:* For master's and doctorate, GRE General Test. Additional exam requirements/recommendations for international students: Required—TOEFL (minimum score 550 paper-based; 79 iBT), IELTS (minimum score 6.5). Electronic applications accepted.

University of Wisconsin–Stevens Point, College of Letters and Science, Department of History, Stevens Point, WI 54481-3897. Offers MST. *Degree requirements:* For master's, thesis or alternative.

University of Wyoming, College of Arts and Sciences, Department of History, Laramie, WY 82071. Offers MA, MAT. Part-time programs available. *Degree requirements:* For master's, one foreign language, thesis (for some programs). *Entrance requirements:* For master's, GRE General Test, minimum GPA of 3.0, 12 semester hours of undergraduate course work in history. Additional exam requirements/recommendations for international students: Required—TOEFL. Electronic applications accepted. *Faculty research:* American West, Native American history, nineteenth and twentieth century U.S. history, European history, Asian studies.

Utah State University, School of Graduate Studies, College of Humanities, Arts and Social Sciences, Department of History, Logan, UT 84322. Offers MA, MS. Part-time and evening/weekend programs available. *Degree requirements:* For master's, one foreign language, thesis. *Entrance requirements:* For master's, GRE General Test, minimum GPA of 3.0. Additional exam requirements/recommendations for international students: Required—TOEFL. Electronic applications accepted. *Faculty research:* U.S. race and ethnicity, early modern and modern Europe, environmental history, western regional history.

Valdosta State University, Department of History, Valdosta, GA 31698. Offers MA. Part-time programs available. *Faculty:* 12 full-time (4 women). *Students:* 5 full-time (2 women), 4 part-time (1 woman); includes 2 minority (1 Hispanic/Latino; 1 Two or more races, non-Hispanic/Latino). Average age 23. 3 applicants, 33% accepted. In 2014, 1 master's awarded. *Degree requirements:* For master's, one foreign language, thesis optional, comprehensive written and/or oral exams. *Entrance requirements:* For master's, GRE General Test, minimum GPA of 2.5. Additional exam requirements/recommendations for international students: Required—TOEFL (minimum score 523 paper-based). *Application deadline:* For fall admission, 5/1 for domestic and international students; for spring admission, 11/15 for domestic and international students. Applications are processed on a rolling basis. Application fee: $35. Electronic applications accepted. *Expenses:* Tuition, state resident: part-time $236 per credit hour. Tuition, nonresident: part-time $850 per credit hour. *Required fees:* $1032 per semester. *Financial support:* In 2014–15, 4 students received support, including 5 research assistantships with full tuition reimbursements available (averaging $3,652 per year); scholarships/grants and unspecified assistantships also available. Support available to part-time students. Financial award application deadline: 7/1; financial award applicants required to submit FAFSA. *Faculty research:* Georgia history, U.S. history, Napoleonic France, American diplomatic history, English history, women's history. *Unit head:* Dr. Dixie Haggard, Head, 229-333-5947, Fax: 229-249-4865, E-mail: drhaggard@valdosta.edu. *Application contact:* Jessica Powers, Admissions Specialist, 229-333-5694, Fax: 229-245-3853, E-mail: jldevane@valdosta.edu.

Valparaiso University, Graduate School, Programs in Liberal Studies, Concentration in History, Valparaiso, IN 46383. Offers MALS, Post-Master's Certificate, JD/MALS. Part-time and evening/weekend programs available. *Students:* 1 full-time (0 women), 3 part-time (1 woman). Average age 32. In 2014, 3 master's awarded. *Entrance requirements:* For master's, minimum GPA of 3.0. Additional exam requirements/recommendations for international students: Required—TOEFL (minimum score 550 paper-based; 80 iBT), IELTS (minimum score 6). *Application deadline:* Applications are processed on a rolling basis. Application fee: $30 ($50 for international students). Electronic applications accepted. *Expenses: Tuition:* Full-time $10,710; part-time $595 per credit hour. *Required fees:* $378; $101 per term. Tuition and fees vary according to course load and program. *Financial support:* Available to part-time students. Applicants required to submit FAFSA. *Faculty research:* Regional Chinese history, British history, Martin Luther, Latin American history, African history. *Unit head:* Dr. Jennifer A. Ziegler, Dean, Graduate School and Continuing Education, 219-464-5313, Fax: 219-464-5381, E-mail: jennifer.ziegler@valpo.edu. *Application contact:* Jessica Choquette, Graduate Admissions Specialist, 219-464-5313, Fax: 219-464-5381, E-mail: jessica.choquette@valpo.edu.
Website: http://www.valpo.edu/grad/mals/history.php

Vanderbilt University, Graduate School, Department of History, Nashville, TN 37240-1001. Offers MA, MAT, PhD. *Faculty:* 35 full-time (10 women). *Students:* 58 full-time (34 women), 3 part-time (1 woman); includes 17 minority (4 Black or African American, non-Hispanic/Latino; 1 American Indian or Alaska Native, non-Hispanic/Latino; 1 Asian, non-Hispanic/Latino; 7 Hispanic/Latino; 4 Two or more races, non-Hispanic/Latino), 6 international. Average age 30. 207 applicants, 11% accepted, 11 enrolled. In 2014, 1 master's, 7 doctorates awarded. Terminal master's awarded for partial completion of doctoral program. *Degree requirements:* For doctorate, one foreign language, comprehensive exam, thesis/dissertation, final and qualifying exams. *Entrance requirements:* For doctorate, GRE General Test, sample of written work (recommended). Additional exam requirements/recommendations for international students: Required—TOEFL (minimum score 570 paper-based; 88 iBT). *Application deadline:* For fall admission, 1/15 for domestic and international students. Application fee: $0. Electronic applications accepted. *Expenses: Tuition:* Full-time $42,768; part-time $1782 per credit hour. *Required fees:* $422. One-time fee: $30 full-time. *Financial support:* Fellowships with full tuition reimbursements, teaching assistantships with full tuition reimbursements, Federal Work-Study, institutionally sponsored loans, scholarships/grants, and health care benefits available. Financial award application deadline: 1/15; financial award applicants required to submit CSS PROFILE or FAFSA. *Faculty research:* Southern American history, recent U.S. history, intellectual and cultural history, European history, Latin American history. *Unit head:* Dr. Matthew Ramsey, Director of Graduate Studies, 615-343-7769, Fax: 615-343-6002, E-mail: matthew.ramsey@vanderbilt.edu. *Application contact:* Jane Anderson, Program Coordinator, 615-322-2755, Fax: 615-343-6002, E-mail: jane.a.anderson@vanderbilt.edu.
Website: http://www.vanderbilt.edu/historydept/graduate.html

Villanova University, Graduate School of Liberal Arts and Sciences, Department of History, Villanova, PA 19085-1699. Offers MA. Part-time and evening/weekend programs available. *Faculty:* 8. *Students:* 38 full-time (19 women), 14 part-time (9 women); includes 3 minority (1 Black or African American, non-Hispanic/Latino; 2 Two or more races, non-Hispanic/Latino), 1 international. Average age 28. 37 applicants, 92% accepted, 17 enrolled. In 2014, 26 master's awarded. *Degree requirements:* For master's, comprehensive exam, thesis optional. *Entrance requirements:* For master's, GRE General Test, minimum GPA of 3.0, 3 letters of recommendation, personal statement. Additional exam requirements/recommendations for international students: Required—TOEFL. *Application deadline:* For fall admission, 3/1 for domestic students, 5/1 priority date for international students; for spring admission, 11/15 for domestic students, 10/15 priority date for international students; for summer admission, 5/1 for domestic students. Applications are processed on a rolling basis. Application fee: $50. Electronic applications accepted. *Financial support:* Research assistantships, Federal Work-Study, scholarships/grants, and unspecified assistantships available. Financial award applicants required to submit FAFSA. *Unit head:* Dr. Judith Giesberg, Director, 610-519-4668. *Application contact:* Dean, Graduate School of Liberal Arts and Sciences.
Website: http://www1.villanova.edu/villanova/artsci/history/academic-programs/graduate.html

Virginia Commonwealth University, Graduate School, College of Humanities and Sciences, Department of History, Richmond, VA 23284-9005. Offers MA. Part-time programs available. *Degree requirements:* For master's, thesis optional. *Entrance requirements:* For master's, GRE General Test, 30 undergraduate credits in history. Additional exam requirements/recommendations for international students: Required—TOEFL (minimum score 600 paper-based; 100 iBT); Recommended—IELTS (minimum score 6.5). Electronic applications accepted. *Faculty research:* United States history, history of the South, urban history, African American history, colonial American history, the Civil War, twentieth-century American history, European history, trans-Atlantic history.

Virginia Commonwealth University, Graduate School, School of the Arts, Department of Art History, Richmond, VA 23284-9005. Offers architectural history (MA); art history (MA, PhD); historical studies (MA); museum studies (MA). *Accreditation:* NASAD. *Degree requirements:* For master's, thesis; for doctorate, comprehensive exam, thesis/dissertation. *Entrance requirements:* For master's and doctorate, GRE General Test. Electronic applications accepted. *Faculty research:* Modern, nineteenth-century, Renaissance, American, and medieval art.

History

Virginia Polytechnic Institute and State University, Graduate School, College of Liberal Arts and Human Sciences, Blacksburg, VA 24061. Offers career and technical education (MS Ed, Ed D, PhD, Ed S); communication (MA); counselor education (MA Ed, Ed D, PhD, Ed S); creative writing (MFA); curriculum and instruction (MA Ed, Ed D, PhD, Ed S); educational leadership and policy studies (MA Ed, Ed D, PhD, Ed S); educational research and evaluation (PhD); English (MA); foreign languages, cultures, and literatures (MA); higher education and student affairs (MA Ed); history (MA); human development (MS, PhD); material culture and public humanities (MA); philosophy (MA); political science (MA); rhetoric and writing (PhD); science and technology studies (MS, PhD); social, political, ethical, and cultural thought (PhD); sociology (MS, PhD); theater arts (MFA). *Faculty:* 421 full-time (216 women), 2 part-time/adjunct (both women). *Students:* 642 full-time (437 women), 537 part-time (344 women); includes 235 minority (132 Black or African American, non-Hispanic/Latino; 2 American Indian or Alaska Native, non-Hispanic/Latino; 27 Asian, non-Hispanic/Latino; 52 Hispanic/Latino; 1 Native Hawaiian or other Pacific Islander, non-Hispanic/Latino; 21 Two or more races, non-Hispanic/Latino), 81 international. Average age 34. 890 applicants, 46% accepted, 303 enrolled. In 2014, 342 master's, 96 doctorates, 33 other advanced degrees awarded. *Degree requirements:* For master's, comprehensive exam (for some programs), thesis (for some programs); for doctorate, comprehensive exam (for some programs), thesis/dissertation (for some programs). *Entrance requirements:* For master's and doctorate, GRE/GMAT (may vary by department). Additional exam requirements/recommendations for international students: Required—TOEFL (minimum score 550 paper-based). *Application deadline:* For fall admission, 8/1 for domestic students, 4/1 for international students; for spring admission, 1/1 for domestic students, 9/1 for international students. Applications are processed on a rolling basis. Application fee: $75. Electronic applications accepted. *Expenses:* Tuition, state resident: full-time $11,656; part-time $647.50 per credit hour. Tuition, nonresident: full-time $23,351; part-time $1297.25 per credit hour. *Required fees:* $2533; $465.75 per semester. Tuition and fees vary according to course load, campus/location and program. *Financial support:* In 2014–15, 19 research assistantships with full tuition reimbursements (averaging $22,141 per year), 231 teaching assistantships with full tuition reimbursements (averaging $19,470 per year) were awarded. Financial award application deadline: 3/1; financial award applicants required to submit FAFSA. *Total annual research expenditures:* $6.5 million. *Unit head:* Elizabeth Spiller, Dean, 540-231-6779, Fax: 540-231-7157, E-mail: espiller@vt.edu. *Application contact:* Melissa Elliott, Executive Assistant, 540-231-6779, Fax: 540-231-7157, E-mail: elliott1@vt.edu.
Website: http://www.clahs.vt.edu/

Washington College, Graduate Programs, Department of History, Chestertown, MD 21620-1197. Offers MA. Part-time and evening/weekend programs available. *Degree requirements:* For master's, thesis optional. *Entrance requirements:* For master's, minimum undergradute GPA of 3.0; significant coursework in English at the undergraduate level.

Washington State University, College of Liberal Arts, Department of History, Pullman, WA 99164. Offers MA, PhD. Program applications must be made through the Pullman campus. Part-time programs available. *Students:* 23 full-time (6 women), 2 part-time (1 woman); includes 1 minority (Black or African American, non-Hispanic/Latino), 3 international. Average age 29. 26 applicants, 38% accepted, 8 enrolled. In 2014, 3 master's, 6 doctorates awarded. *Degree requirements:* For master's, comprehensive exam, thesis optional, oral exam; for doctorate, one foreign language, comprehensive exam, thesis/dissertation, oral and written exam. *Entrance requirements:* For master's and doctorate, GRE General Test, official transcripts from all universities attended; three letters of recommendation; statement of purpose; writing sample; Preferred Fields of Study form; Language Background form. Additional exam requirements/recommendations for international students: Required—TOEFL (minimum score 550 paper-based), IELTS. *Application deadline:* For fall admission, 1/10 priority date for domestic and international students; for spring admission, 7/1 for domestic and international students. Applications are processed on a rolling basis. Application fee: $75. Electronic applications accepted. *Expenses:* Tuition, state resident: full-time $11,768. Tuition, nonresident: full-time $25,200. *Required fees:* $960. Tuition and fees vary according to program. *Financial support:* In 2014–15, 1 research assistantship with full and partial tuition reimbursement (averaging $14,198 per year), 22 teaching assistantships with full and partial tuition reimbursements (averaging $13,825 per year) were awarded; career-related internships or fieldwork, Federal Work-Study, institutionally sponsored loans, scholarships/grants, and health care benefits also available. Financial award application deadline: 2/15; financial award applicants required to submit FAFSA. *Faculty research:* Public, world, environmental, women's and U.S. history. *Unit head:* Dr. Raymond Sun, Chair, 509-335-5139, Fax: 509-335-4171, E-mail: sunray@wsu.edu. *Application contact:* Dr. Steven Kale, Graduate Studies Director, 509-335-3059, Fax: 509-335-4171, E-mail: kale@wsu.edu.
Website: http://libarts.wsu.edu/history/

Washington University in St. Louis, Graduate School of Arts and Sciences, Department of History, St. Louis, MO 63130-4899. Offers PhD. *Degree requirements:* For doctorate, 2 foreign languages, thesis/dissertation. *Entrance requirements:* For doctorate, GRE General Test. Additional exam requirements/recommendations for international students: Required—TOEFL. Electronic applications accepted. *Faculty research:* African, American, civil rights history, China, gender, Japan, medieval Europe, Early Modern Britain, Central Europe.

Wayland Baptist University, Graduate Programs, Programs in Behavioral and Social Sciences, Plainview, TX 79072-6998. Offers counseling (MA); government administration (MPA); history (MA); homeland security (MPA); justice administration (MPA). Part-time and evening/weekend programs available. Postbaccalaureate distance learning degree programs offered. *Faculty:* 19 full-time (5 women), 18 part-time/adjunct (8 women). *Students:* 17 full-time (12 women), 428 part-time (264 women); includes 208 minority (66 Black or African American, non-Hispanic/Latino; 6 American Indian or Alaska Native, non-Hispanic/Latino; 14 Asian, non-Hispanic/Latino; 98 Hispanic/Latino; 4 Native Hawaiian or other Pacific Islander, non-Hispanic/Latino; 20 Two or more races, non-Hispanic/Latino). Average age 38. 152 applicants, 93% accepted, 67 enrolled. In 2014, 158 master's awarded. *Degree requirements:* For master's, comprehensive exam. *Entrance requirements:* For master's, GRE, MAT. Additional exam requirements/recommendations for international students: Required—TOEFL (minimum score 500 paper-based; 61 iBT). *Application deadline:* Applications are processed on a rolling basis. Application fee: $50. Electronic applications accepted. *Expenses: Tuition:* Full-time $8910; part-time $495 per credit hour. *Required fees:* $970; $495 per credit hour. $485 per semester. *Financial support:* Federal Work-Study, institutionally sponsored loans, and scholarships/grants available. Support available to part-time students. Financial award application deadline: 5/1; financial award applicants required to submit FAFSA. *Unit head:* Dr. Estelle Owens, Chairman, 806-291-1171, Fax: 806-291-1972, E-mail: owensest@wbu.edu. *Application contact:* Amanda Stanton, Graduate Studies, 806-291-3423, Fax: 806-291-1950, E-mail: stanton@wbu.edu.

Wayne State University, College of Liberal Arts and Sciences, Department of History, Detroit, MI 48202. Offers Africa (PhD); America (PhD); archival administration (Graduate Certificate); Europe (PhD); gender (PhD); history (MA); labor (PhD); science and technology (PhD); world history (PhD, Graduate Certificate); JD/MA; M Ed/MA; MLIS/MA. Doctoral programs admit for fall only. Evening/weekend programs available. *Faculty:* 22 full-time (9 women). *Students:* 32 full-time (14 women), 16 part-time (6 women); includes 4 minority (2 Black or African American, non-Hispanic/Latino; 2 Two or more races, non-Hispanic/Latino). Average age 39. 52 applicants, 37% accepted, 9 enrolled. In 2014, 5 master's awarded. *Degree requirements:* For master's, one foreign language, thesis (for some programs), final oral exam on thesis or essay and seminar; for doctorate, variable foreign language requirement, thesis/dissertation, qualifying exam in 4 fields of history. *Entrance requirements:* For master's, GRE General Test, minimum undergraduate GPA of 3.25 in history, 3.0 overall; at least 18 credits in history and related subjects at the advanced undergraduate level; foreign language; letter of intent; research paper; at least two letters of recommendation from former instructors; for doctorate, GRE General Test, minimum GPA of 3.0; letter of intent; research paper; at least three letters of recommendation from former professors; for Graduate Certificate, baccalaureate degree from accredited college or university; minimum GPA of 3.0, 3.25 in a minimum of eighteen semester credits in history and related subjects at the advanced undergraduate level. Additional exam requirements/recommendations for international students: Required—TOEFL (minimum score 550 paper-based; 79 iBT), TWE (minimum score 5.5), Michigan English Language Assessment Battery (minimum score 85); Recommended—IELTS (minimum score 6.5). *Application deadline:* For fall admission, 2/1 for domestic and international students; for winter admission, 11/1 for domestic students, 10/1 priority date for international students; for spring admission, 3/15 for domestic students, 1/1 priority date for international students. Applications are processed on a rolling basis. Application fee: $0. Electronic applications accepted. *Expenses:* Tuition, state resident: full-time $10,294; part-time $571.90 per credit hour. Tuition, nonresident: full-time $29,730; part-time $1238.75 per credit hour. *Required fees:* $1365; $43.50 per credit hour. $291.10 per semester. Tuition and fees vary according to course load and program. *Financial support:* In 2014–15, 19 students received support, including 1 fellowship with tuition reimbursement available (averaging $16,000 per year), 1 research assistantship with tuition reimbursement available (averaging $17,994 per year), 6 teaching assistantships with tuition reimbursements available (averaging $16,838 per year); scholarships/grants, health care benefits, and unspecified assistantships also available. Financial award application deadline: 3/31; financial award applicants required to submit FAFSA. *Faculty research:* Labor and working class history, urban history, citizenship and politics, gender and women's history. *Unit head:* Dr. Marc W. Kruman, Chair, 313-577-2525, Fax: 313-577-6987, E-mail: mkruman@wayne.edu. *Application contact:* Dr. Gayle McCreedy, Academic Service Officer, 313-577-2592, Fax: 313-577-6987, E-mail: g.mccreedy@wayne.edu.
Website: http://clas.wayne.edu/history/

West Chester University of Pennsylvania, College of Arts and Sciences, Department of History, West Chester, PA 19383. Offers history (M Ed, MA); Holocaust and genocide studies (MA, Certificate). Part-time and evening/weekend programs available. *Faculty:* 7 full-time (3 women). *Students:* 8 full-time (6 women), 30 part-time (13 women); includes 3 minority (1 Black or African American, non-Hispanic/Latino; 1 American Indian or Alaska Native, non-Hispanic/Latino; 1 Two or more races, non-Hispanic/Latino). Average age 29. 21 applicants, 95% accepted, 13 enrolled. In 2014, 17 master's awarded. *Degree requirements:* For master's, comprehensive exam (for MA in history and M Ed); thesis or comprehensive exam (for MA in Holocaust and genocide studies); for Certificate, 18 hours of coursework. *Entrance requirements:* For master's, statement of professional goals; writing sample, minimum GPA of 3.0 in history, and three letters of recommendation (for history); minimum GPA of 2.8 and two letters of recommendation (for Holocaust and genocide studies); for Certificate, statement of professional goals, two letters of recommendation, minimum GPA of 2.8. Additional exam requirements/recommendations for international students: Required—TOEFL (minimum score 550 paper-based; 80 iBT). *Application deadline:* For fall admission, 4/15 priority date for domestic students, 3/15 for international students; for spring admission, 10/15 priority date for domestic students, 9/1 for international students. Applications are processed on a rolling basis. Application fee: $45. Electronic applications accepted. *Expenses:* Tuition, state resident: full-time $8172; part-time $454 per credit. Tuition, nonresident: full-time $12,258; part-time $681 per credit. *Required fees:* $2231; $110.78 per credit. Tuition and fees vary according to campus/location and program. *Financial support:* Unspecified assistantships available. Support available to part-time students. Financial award application deadline: 2/15; financial award applicants required to submit FAFSA. *Unit head:* Dr. Wayne Hanley, Chair, 610-436-2201, E-mail: whanley@wcupa.edu. *Application contact:* Dr. Jonathan Friedman, Graduate Coordinator of Holocaust and Genocide Studies, 610-436-2972, E-mail: jfriedman@wcupa.edu.
Website: http://www.wcupa.edu/_academics/sch_cas.his/

Western Carolina University, Graduate School, College of Arts and Sciences, Department of History, Cullowhee, NC 28723. Offers MA. Part-time and evening/weekend programs available. *Degree requirements:* For master's, one foreign language, comprehensive exam, thesis or alternative. *Entrance requirements:* For master's, GRE General Test, appropriate undergraduate degree, 3 letters of recommendation. Additional exam requirements/recommendations for international students: Required—TOEFL (minimum score 550 paper-based; 79 iBT). *Faculty research:* Social and economic history of the American South, Islamic world history, German history, social and political protest, medieval social history.

Western Connecticut State University, Division of Graduate Studies, School of Arts and Sciences, Department of History, Danbury, CT 06810-6885. Offers MA. Part-time programs available. *Degree requirements:* For master's, thesis or research project, completion of program in 6 years. *Entrance requirements:* For master's, minimum GPA of 2.5. Additional exam requirements/recommendations for international students: Recommended—TOEFL (minimum score 550 paper-based; 79 iBT), IELTS (minimum score 6). *Faculty research:* History of jazz, music and leisure, African-American musicians.

Western Illinois University, School of Graduate Studies, College of Arts and Sciences, Department of History, Macomb, IL 61455-1390. Offers MA. Part-time programs available. *Students:* 15 full-time (7 women), 13 part-time (4 women); includes 1 minority (American Indian or Alaska Native, non-Hispanic/Latino). Average age 34. 18 applicants, 100% accepted, 12 enrolled. In 2014, 10 master's awarded. *Degree requirements:* For master's, thesis or alternative. *Entrance requirements:* Additional exam requirements/recommendations for international students: Required—TOEFL (minimum score 550 paper-based; 80 iBT). *Application deadline:* Applications are processed on a rolling basis. Application fee: $30. Electronic applications accepted. *Financial support:* In 2014–15, 9 students received support, including 9 teaching assistantships with full tuition reimbursements available (averaging $8,688 per year). Financial award applicants required to submit FAFSA. *Unit head:* Dr. Simon Cordery, Chairperson, 309-298-1053. *Application contact:* Dr. Nancy Parsons, Associate Provost and Director of Graduate Studies, 309-298-1806, Fax: 309-298-2345, E-mail: grad-office@wiu.edu.
Website: http://wiu.edu/history

Western Kentucky University, Graduate Studies, Potter College of Arts and Letters, Department of History, Bowling Green, KY 42101. Offers MA, MA Ed. Part-time and evening/weekend programs available. Postbaccalaureate distance learning degree programs offered. *Degree requirements:* For master's, comprehensive exam, thesis

optional, final exam. *Entrance requirements:* For master's, GRE General Test, minimum GPA of 2.75. Additional exam requirements/recommendations for international students: Required—TOEFL (minimum score 555 paper-based; 79 iBT). *Faculty research:* United States, Europe, China, India, Latin America.

Western Michigan University, Graduate College, College of Arts and Sciences, Department of History, Kalamazoo, MI 49008. Offers MA, PhD. *Degree requirements:* For master's, thesis optional; for doctorate, thesis/dissertation. *Application deadline:* For fall admission, 2/15 for domestic students. *Financial support:* Application deadline: 2/15. *Application contact:* Admissions and Orientation, 269-387-2000, Fax: 269-387-2096.

Western Washington University, Graduate School, College of Humanities and Social Sciences, Department of History, Bellingham, WA 98225-5996. Offers MA. Part-time programs available. *Degree requirements:* For master's, one foreign language, comprehensive exam, thesis (for some programs). *Entrance requirements:* For master's, GRE General Test, minimum GPA of 3.0 in last 60 semester hours or last 90 quarter hours. Additional exam requirements/recommendations for international students: Required—TOEFL (minimum score 567 paper-based). Electronic applications accepted.

Westfield State University, Division of Graduate and Continuing Education, Department of History, Westfield, MA 01086. Offers M Ed. Part-time and evening/weekend programs available. *Degree requirements:* For master's, thesis. *Entrance requirements:* For master's, GRE General Test or MAT, minimum undergraduate GPA of 2.7.

West Texas A&M University, College of Fine Arts and Humanities, Department of History, Canyon, TX 79016-0001. Offers MA. Part-time and evening/weekend programs available. *Degree requirements:* For master's, comprehensive exam, thesis optional. *Entrance requirements:* For master's, GRE General Test. Additional exam requirements/recommendations for international students: Required—TOEFL (minimum score 550 paper-based). Electronic applications accepted. *Faculty research:* Latin America, Middle and Far East, Southern Asia, Western Europe, United States.

West Virginia University, Eberly College of Arts and Sciences, Department of History, Morgantown, WV 26506. Offers African history (MA, PhD); African-American history (MA, PhD); American history (MA, PhD); Appalachian/regional history (MA, PhD); East Asian history (MA, PhD); European history (MA, PhD); history of science and technology (MA, PhD); Latin American history (MA). Part-time programs available. *Degree requirements:* For master's, one foreign language, thesis (for some programs), oral exam, thesis defense; for doctorate, one foreign language, comprehensive exam, thesis/dissertation, dissertation defense. *Entrance requirements:* For master's, GRE General Test, minimum GPA of 3.0; for doctorate, GRE General Test. Additional exam requirements/recommendations for international students: Required—TOEFL (minimum score 550 paper-based), IELTS (minimum score 6.5). Electronic applications accepted. *Faculty research:* United States, Appalachia, modern Europe, Africa, colonial and post-colonial societies.

Wichita State University, Graduate School, Fairmount College of Liberal Arts and Sciences, Department of History, Wichita, KS 67260. Offers MA. Part-time programs available. *Unit head:* Dr. Jay Price, Chair, 316-978-3150, Fax: 316-978-3473, E-mail: jay.price@wichita.edu. *Application contact:* Jordan Oleson, Admissions Coordinator, 316-978-3150, Fax: 316-978-3473, E-mail: jordan.oleson@wichita.edu.
Website: http://www.wichita.edu/history

Wilfrid Laurier University, Faculty of Graduate and Postdoctoral Studies, Faculty of Arts, Department of History, Waterloo, ON N2L 3C5, Canada. Offers MA, PhD. Part-time programs available. *Degree requirements:* For master's, thesis optional; for doctorate, thesis/dissertation. *Entrance requirements:* For master's, honors BA or the equivalent in history; minimum B+ average in undergraduate course work, exclusive of first year level courses; for doctorate, MA in history, minimum A- average. Additional exam requirements/recommendations for international students: Required—TOEFL (minimum score 89 iBT). Electronic applications accepted. *Faculty research:* Canadian, early modern European, modern European, Scottish, race, class, imperialism, slavery, British, urban and rural, science/medicine/technology, gender/women's/family, international, United States.

William Paterson University of New Jersey, College of Humanities and Social Sciences, Wayne, NJ 07470-8420. Offers applied sociology (MA); clinical and counseling psychology (MA); creative and professional writing (MFA); English (MA); history (MA); public policy and international affairs (MA). Part-time and evening/weekend programs available. *Faculty:* 32 full-time (16 women), 3 part-time/adjunct (1 woman). *Students:* 50 full-time (30 women), 114 part-time (88 women); includes 64 minority (7 Black or African American, non-Hispanic/Latino; 1 American Indian or Alaska Native, non-Hispanic/Latino; 4 Asian, non-Hispanic/Latino; 50 Hispanic/Latino; 2 Two or more races, non-Hispanic/Latino), 2 international. Average age 34. 115 applicants, 81% accepted, 65 enrolled. In 2014, 42 master's awarded. Terminal master's awarded for partial completion of doctoral program. *Degree requirements:* For master's, thesis (for some programs), internship (for some programs). *Entrance requirements:* For master's, GRE/MAT, minimum GPA of 3.0; 2 letters of recommendation; writing sample/personal statement. Additional exam requirements/recommendations for international students: Required—TOEFL (minimum score 550 paper-based; 79 iBT), IELTS (minimum score 6). *Application deadline:* For fall admission, 6/1 for domestic students, 3/1 for international students; for spring admission, 11/1 for domestic students, 10/1 for international students. Applications are processed on a rolling basis. Application fee: $50. Electronic applications accepted. *Expenses:* Tuition, state resident: full-time $12,413; part-time $564.21 per credit. Tuition, nonresident: full-time $20,487; part-time $931.21 per credit. *Required fees:* $2107; $95.79 per credit. $478.95 per semester. Tuition and fees vary according to course load and degree level. *Financial support:* Research assistantships with full tuition reimbursements, Federal Work-Study, scholarships/grants, and unspecified assistantships available. Support available to part-time students. Financial award application deadline: 4/1; financial award applicants required to submit FAFSA. *Faculty research:* Sexual violence, history of science in Muslim societies, bioethics, teaching writing for transfer, psychological impact of microagressions on minority communities. *Unit head:* Dr. Kara Rabbitt, Dean, 973-720-2731, Fax: 973-720-2955, E-mail: rabbittk@wpunj.edu. *Application contact:* Tinu Adeniran, Associate Director, Graduate Admissions, 973-720-2764, Fax: 973-720-2035, E-mail: adenirant@wpunj.edu.
Website: http://www.wpunj.edu/cohss

Winthrop University, College of Arts and Sciences, Department of History, Rock Hill, SC 29733. Offers MA. Part-time programs available. *Degree requirements:* For master's, one foreign language, thesis optional. *Entrance requirements:* For master's, GRE General Test or PRAXIS, 24 hours of history at the undergraduate level. Electronic applications accepted.

Worcester State University, Graduate Studies, Program in History, Worcester, MA 01602-2597. Offers MA. Part-time programs available. *Faculty:* 6 full-time (2 women), 1 part-time/adjunct (0 women). *Students:* 4 full-time (3 women), 33 part-time (17 women); includes 3 minority (1 Asian, non-Hispanic/Latino; 1 Hispanic/Latino; 1 Two or more races, non-Hispanic/Latino). Average age 33. 23 applicants, 83% accepted, 9 enrolled. In 2014, 7 master's awarded. *Degree requirements:* For master's, comprehensive exam (for some programs), thesis (for some programs), portfolio. *Entrance requirements:* For master's, GRE General Test or MAT, 18 undergraduate credits in history, including U.S. history and Western civilizations. Additional exam requirements/recommendations for international students: Required—TOEFL (minimum score 550 paper-based; 79 iBT). *Application deadline:* For fall admission, 6/15 for domestic and international students; for spring admission, 11/1 for domestic and international students; for summer admission, 4/1 for domestic and international students. Applications are processed on a rolling basis. Application fee: $50. Electronic applications accepted. *Expenses: Tuition, area resident:* Part-time $150 per credit. Tuition, state resident: part-time $150 per credit. Tuition, nonresident: part-time $150 per credit. *Financial support:* In 2014–15, 3 research assistantships with full tuition reimbursements (averaging $4,800 per year) were awarded; career-related internships or fieldwork, scholarships/grants, and unspecified assistantships also available. Financial award application deadline: 3/1; financial award applicants required to submit FAFSA. *Unit head:* Dr. Charlotte Haller, Coordinator, 508-929-8046, Fax: 508-929-8155, E-mail: challer1@worcester.edu. *Application contact:* Sara Grady, Acting Associate Dean of Graduate and Continuing Education, 508-929-8787, Fax: 508-929-8100, E-mail: sara.grady@worcester.edu.

Wright State University, School of Graduate Studies, College of Liberal Arts, Department of History, Dayton, OH 45435. Offers MA. *Degree requirements:* For master's, thesis optional. *Entrance requirements:* For master's, GRE General Test, minimum GPA of 3.0 in history, 2.7 overall. Additional exam requirements/recommendations for international students: Required—TOEFL. *Faculty research:* U.S. religions; women's, Southern, European, and archival history.

Yale University, Graduate School of Arts and Sciences, Department of History, New Haven, CT 06520. Offers history (M Phil, MA, PhD); history of science and medicine (MA, PhD). Terminal master's awarded for partial completion of doctoral program. *Degree requirements:* For master's, one foreign language; for doctorate, 2 foreign languages, thesis/dissertation. *Entrance requirements:* For doctorate, GRE General Test.

York University, Faculty of Graduate Studies, Faculty of Liberal Arts and Professional Studies, Program in History, Toronto, ON M3J 1P3, Canada. Offers MA, PhD. Part-time programs available. *Degree requirements:* For master's, thesis or alternative; for doctorate, one foreign language, comprehensive exam, thesis/dissertation, qualifying exam. Electronic applications accepted.

Youngstown State University, Graduate School, College of Liberal Arts and Social Sciences, Department of History, Youngstown, OH 44555-0001. Offers MA. Part-time programs available. *Degree requirements:* For master's, thesis optional, oral and written exams. *Entrance requirements:* For master's, minimum GPA of 2.75. Additional exam requirements/recommendations for international students: Required—TOEFL. *Faculty research:* Holocaust, Marxism, nineteenth- and twentieth-century United States, historic preservation, revolutionary France.

History of Medicine

McGill University, Faculty of Graduate and Postdoctoral Studies, Faculty of Arts, Department of History and Classical Studies, Montréal, QC H3A 2T5, Canada. Offers history (MA, PhD); history of medicine (MA).

McGill University, Faculty of Graduate and Postdoctoral Studies, Faculty of Medicine, Department of Social Studies in Medicine, Montréal, QC H3A 2T5, Canada. Offers medical anthropology (MA, PhD); medical history (MA, PhD); medical sociology (MA, PhD).

Rutgers, The State University of New Jersey, New Brunswick, Graduate School-New Brunswick, Program in History, Piscataway, NJ 08854-8097. Offers African-American history (PhD); early American history (PhD); early modern European history (PhD); east Asian history (PhD); global and comparative history (PhD); history (PhD); history of diplomacy and foreign relations (PhD); history of technology, environment and health (PhD); history of the Atlantic cultures and African diaspora (PhD); Latin American history (PhD); medieval history (PhD); modern European history (PhD); nineteenth and twentieth century American history (PhD); women's and gender history (PhD). *Degree requirements:* For doctorate, thesis/dissertation. *Entrance requirements:* For doctorate, GRE General Test, sample of written work. Electronic applications accepted. *Faculty research:* American history, European history, Afro-American history, women's history, Latin American history.

The University of Manchester, Faculty of Life Sciences, Manchester, United Kingdom. Offers adaptive organismal biology (M Phil, PhD); animal biology (M Phil, PhD); biochemistry (M Phil, PhD); bioinformatics (M Phil, PhD); biomolecular sciences (M Phil, PhD); biotechnology (M Phil, PhD); cell biology (M Phil, PhD); cell matrix research (M Phil, PhD); channels and transporters (M Phil, PhD); developmental biology (M Phil, PhD); Egyptology (M Phil, PhD); environmental biology (M Phil, PhD); evolutionary biology (M Phil, PhD); gene expression (M Phil, PhD); genetics (M Phil, PhD); history of science, technology and medicine (M Phil, PhD); immunology (M Phil, PhD); integrative neurobiology and behavior (M Phil, PhD); membrane trafficking (M Phil, PhD); microbiology (M Phil, PhD); molecular and cellular neuroscience (M Phil, PhD); molecular biology (M Phil, PhD); molecular cancer studies (M Phil, PhD); neuroscience (M Phil, PhD); ophthalmology (M Phil, PhD); optometry (M Phil, PhD); organelle function (M Phil, PhD); pharmacology (M Phil, PhD); physiology (M Phil, PhD); plant sciences (M Phil, PhD); stem cell research (M Phil, PhD); structural biology (M Phil, PhD); systems neuroscience (M Phil, PhD); toxicology (M Phil, PhD).

University of Minnesota, Twin Cities Campus, Graduate School, Program in the History of Science, Technology and Medicine, Minneapolis, MN 55455-0213. Offers MA, PhD. Part-time programs available. *Degree requirements:* For master's, one foreign language, thesis or alternative; for doctorate, 2 foreign languages, thesis/dissertation.

Entrance requirements: For master's and doctorate, GRE General Test. *Faculty research:* History of infectious diseases, history of public health, history of evolutionary biology, history of infertility, women in science.

Yale University, Graduate School of Arts and Sciences, Department of History, Program in the History of Science and Medicine, New Haven, CT 06520. Offers MS, PhD. *Degree requirements:* For doctorate, 2 foreign languages, thesis/dissertation. *Entrance requirements:* For doctorate, GRE General Test.

History of Science and Technology

Arizona State University at the Tempe campus, College of Liberal Arts and Sciences, School of Life Sciences, Tempe, AZ 85287-4601. Offers animal behavior (PhD); applied ethics (biomedical and health ethics) (MA); biology (MS, PhD), including biology, biology and society, complex adaptive systems science (PhD), plant biology and conservation (MS); environmental life sciences (PhD); evolutionary biology (PhD); history and philosophy of science (PhD); human and social dimensions of science and technology (PhD); microbiology (PhD); molecular and cellular biology (PhD); neuroscience (PhD). Terminal master's awarded for partial completion of doctoral program. *Degree requirements:* For master's, thesis (for some programs), interactive Program of Study (iPOS) submitted before completing 50 percent of required credit hours; for doctorate, variable foreign language requirement, comprehensive exam, thesis/dissertation, interactive Program of Study (iPOS) submitted before completing 50 percent of required credit hours. *Entrance requirements:* For master's and doctorate, GRE, minimum GPA of 3.0 or equivalent in last 2 years of work leading to bachelor's degree. Additional exam requirements/recommendations for international students: Required—TOEFL (minimum score 600 paper-based; 100 iBT). Electronic applications accepted.

Arizona State University at the Tempe campus, Graduate College, Program in Human and Social Dimensions of Science and Technology, Tempe, AZ 85287-5603. Offers PhD. *Degree requirements:* For doctorate, comprehensive exam, thesis/dissertation, interactive Program of Study (iPOS) submitted before completing 50 percent of required credit hours. *Entrance requirements:* For doctorate, GRE, minimum GPA of 3.0 in the last 2 years of work leading to the bachelor's degree, 3 letters of recommendation, statement of research interests and goals, curriculum vitae or resume, completed academic record form, 10-25 page writing sample. Additional exam requirements/recommendations for international students: Required—TOEFL (minimum score 550 paper-based; 80 iBT), IELTS (minimum score 6.5). Electronic applications accepted.

Brown University, Graduate School, Department of Egyptology and Ancient Western Asian Studies, Providence, RI 02912. Offers ancient western Asian studies (PhD); Egyptology (PhD); history of the exact sciences in antiquity (PhD). *Degree requirements:* For doctorate, 2 foreign languages, comprehensive exam, thesis/dissertation. *Entrance requirements:* For doctorate, GRE General Test.

Carnegie Mellon University, Dietrich College of Humanities and Social Sciences, Department of History, Pittsburgh, PA 15213-3891. Offers African and African-American diaspora (PhD); culture and power (PhD); labor, politics and social movements (PhD); technology, environment, science and health (PhD); women, gender and the family (PhD). Part-time programs available. *Degree requirements:* For doctorate, oral and written comprehensive exams, dissertation defense. *Entrance requirements:* For doctorate, GRE General Test. Additional exam requirements/recommendations for international students: Required—TOEFL. Electronic applications accepted. *Faculty research:* Anthropology and history, African-American history, technology/environment, cultural history analysis.

Cornell University, Graduate School, Graduate Fields of Arts and Sciences, Field of History, Ithaca, NY 14853-0001. Offers African history (MA, PhD); American history (MA, PhD); ancient Greek history (PhD); ancient history (MA, PhD); ancient Roman history (PhD); early modern European history (MA, PhD); English history (MA, PhD); French history (MA, PhD); German history (MA, PhD); history of science (MA, PhD); Korean history (PhD); Latin American history (MA, PhD); medieval Chinese history (MA, PhD); medieval history (MA, PhD); modern Chinese history (MA, PhD); modern European history (MA, PhD); modern Japanese history (MA, PhD); modern Middle Eastern history (PhD); premodern Islamic history (MA, PhD); premodern Japanese history (MA, PhD); Renaissance history (MA, PhD); Russian history (MA, PhD); South Asian history (PhD); Southeast Asian history (MA, PhD). Terminal master's awarded for partial completion of doctoral program. *Degree requirements:* For master's, thesis; for doctorate, 2 foreign languages, comprehensive exam, thesis/dissertation, 1 year of teaching experience. *Entrance requirements:* For master's and doctorate, GRE General Test, writing sample, 3 letters of recommendation. Additional exam requirements/recommendations for international students: Required—TOEFL (minimum score 550 paper-based; 77 iBT). Electronic applications accepted.

Cornell University, Graduate School, Graduate Fields of Arts and Sciences, Field of Science and Technology Studies, Ithaca, NY 14853-0001. Offers history and philosophy of science and technology (MA, PhD); social studies of science and technology (MA, PhD). Terminal master's awarded for partial completion of doctoral program. *Degree requirements:* For master's, one foreign language, thesis; for doctorate, one foreign language, comprehensive exam, thesis/dissertation. *Entrance requirements:* For master's and doctorate, GRE General Test, writing sample, 3 letters of recommendation. Additional exam requirements/recommendations for international students: Required—TOEFL (minimum score 550 paper-based; 77 iBT). Electronic applications accepted. *Faculty research:* History, philosophy, sociology, politics, and policy of science and technology; gender, legal order, environment, and communication.

Drexel University, College of Arts and Sciences, Department of History and Politics, Philadelphia, PA 19104-2875. Offers science, technology and society (MS). Part-time programs available. *Entrance requirements:* For master's, GRE. Additional exam requirements/recommendations for international students: Required—TOEFL. Electronic applications accepted.

Georgia Institute of Technology, Graduate Studies, Ivan Allen College of Liberal Arts, School of History, Technology, and Society, Atlanta, GA 30332-0001. Offers history and sociology of technology and science (MS, PhD). Part-time programs available. *Students:* 14 full-time (10 women), 11 part-time (4 women); includes 4 minority (1 Black or African American, non-Hispanic/Latino; 1 Asian, non-Hispanic/Latino; 2 Hispanic/Latino), 3 international. Average age 31. 35 applicants, 23% accepted, 4 enrolled. In 2014, 3 master's, 2 doctorates awarded. Terminal master's awarded for partial completion of doctoral program. *Degree requirements:* For master's, research paper; for doctorate, one foreign language, comprehensive exam, thesis/dissertation. *Entrance requirements:* For master's and doctorate, GRE, college transcripts, three letters of recommendation, biographical statement. Additional exam requirements/recommendations for international students: Required—TOEFL (minimum score 550 paper-based; 79 iBT). *Application deadline:* For fall admission, 2/1 priority date for domestic students, 3/1 for international students; for spring admission, 3/1 for domestic students. Applications are processed on a rolling basis. Application fee: $75. Electronic applications accepted. *Expenses:* Tuition, state resident: full-time $12,344; part-time $515 per credit hour. Tuition, nonresident: full-time $27,600; part-time $1150 per credit hour. *Required fees:* $1196 per term. Part-time tuition and fees vary according to course load. *Financial support:* Fellowships, research assistantships, teaching assistantships, career-related internships or fieldwork, Federal Work-Study, institutionally sponsored loans, tuition waivers (partial), and unspecified assistantships available. Support available to part-time students. Financial award application deadline: 5/1. *Faculty research:* Industrialization, labor history, modern Europe, social history, sociology of science. *Total annual research expenditures:* $171,570. *Unit head:* William Winders, Director, 404-894-8401, E-mail: bill.winders@gatech.edu. *Application contact:* LaDonna Bowen, Graduate Coordinator, 404-894-3198, E-mail: ladonna.bowen@hts.gatech.edu.
Website: http://www.hts.gatech.edu

Harvard University, Graduate School of Arts and Sciences, Department of the History of Science, Cambridge, MA 02138. Offers AM, PhD. Terminal master's awarded for partial completion of doctoral program. *Degree requirements:* For master's, one foreign language; for doctorate, 2 foreign languages, thesis/dissertation. *Entrance requirements:* For master's and doctorate, GRE General Test. Additional exam requirements/recommendations for international students: Required—TOEFL.

Indiana University Bloomington, University Graduate School, College of Arts and Sciences, Department of History and Philosophy of Science, Bloomington, IN 47405-7000. Offers MA, PhD, MLS/MA. Part-time programs available. *Faculty:* 8 full-time (2 women), 1 part-time/adjunct (0 women). *Students:* 31 full-time (9 women), 1 part-time (0 women); includes 2 minority (1 Hispanic/Latino; 1 Two or more races, non-Hispanic/Latino), 6 international. 25 applicants, 88% accepted, 7 enrolled. In 2014, 3 master's, 1 doctorate awarded. Terminal master's awarded for partial completion of doctoral program. *Degree requirements:* For master's, one foreign language, thesis optional; for doctorate, 2 foreign languages, thesis/dissertation. *Entrance requirements:* For master's and doctorate, GRE General Test. Additional exam requirements/recommendations for international students: Required—TOEFL. *Application deadline:* For fall admission, 1/15 priority date for domestic students, 12/1 for international students. Application fee: $55 ($65 for international students). Electronic applications accepted. *Financial support:* In 2014–15, 4 fellowships with full tuition reimbursements (averaging $19,500 per year), 3 research assistantships with full tuition reimbursements (averaging $15,750 per year), 8 teaching assistantships with full tuition reimbursements (averaging $15,750 per year) were awarded; Federal Work-Study, institutionally sponsored loans, scholarships/grants, health care benefits, and unspecified assistantships also available. Financial award application deadline: 3/1; financial award applicants required to submit FAFSA. *Faculty research:* History of scientific ideas, instruments, and institutions; foundations of physics; history of philosophy of science; history and philosophy of biology; early modern science and medicine. *Unit head:* Sander Gliboff, Chair, 812-856-7417, Fax: 812-855-3631, E-mail: sgliboff@indiana.edu. *Application contact:* Stephanei Bennett, Administrative Assistant, 812-855-3622, Fax: 812-855-3631, E-mail: hpscdept@indiana.edu.
Website: http://www.indiana.edu/~hpscdept/

Iowa State University of Science and Technology, Department of History, Ames, IA 50011. Offers agricultural history and rural studies (PhD); history (MA); history of technology and science (MA, PhD). *Degree requirements:* For master's, thesis or alternative; for doctorate, thesis/dissertation. *Entrance requirements:* For master's and doctorate, GRE General Test. Additional exam requirements/recommendations for international students: Required—TOEFL (minimum score 600 paper-based; 79 iBT), IELTS (minimum score 7). Electronic applications accepted.

Iowa State University of Science and Technology, Program in History of Technology and Science, Ames, IA 50011. Offers MS, PhD. *Entrance requirements:* For master's and doctorate, GRE General Test. Additional exam requirements/recommendations for international students: Required—TOEFL (minimum score 600 paper-based; 79 iBT), IELTS (minimum score 7). Electronic applications accepted.

Johns Hopkins University, Zanvyl Krieger School of Arts and Sciences, Department of the History of Science and Technology, Baltimore, MD 21218-2699. Offers MA, PhD. Terminal master's awarded for partial completion of doctoral program. *Degree requirements:* For master's, one foreign language, thesis; for doctorate, 2 foreign languages, thesis/dissertation. *Entrance requirements:* For doctorate, GRE General Test. Additional exam requirements/recommendations for international students: Required—TOEFL (minimum score 600 paper-based; 100 iBT), IELTS. Electronic applications accepted. *Faculty research:* History of physical and biological sciences, history of technology, history of medicine (sixteenth-twentieth centuries), environmental science (nineteenth-twentieth century).

Massachusetts Institute of Technology, School of Humanities, Arts, and Social Sciences, Program in Science, Technology, and Society, Cambridge, MA 02139. Offers history, anthropology, and science, technology and society (PhD). *Faculty:* 11 full-time (6 women). *Students:* 31 full-time (23 women); includes 7 minority (1 Black or African American, non-Hispanic/Latino; 2 American Indian or Alaska Native, non-Hispanic/Latino; 3 Asian, non-Hispanic/Latino; 1 Hispanic/Latino), 7 international. Average age 31. 145 applicants, 7% accepted, 3 enrolled. In 2014, 6 doctorates awarded. *Degree requirements:* For doctorate, comprehensive exam, thesis/dissertation. *Entrance requirements:* For doctorate, GRE General Test. Additional exam requirements/recommendations for international students: Required—TOEFL (minimum score 577 paper-based; 90 iBT), IELTS (minimum score 7). *Application deadline:* For fall admission, 12/15 for domestic and international students. Application fee: $75. Electronic applications accepted. *Expenses: Tuition:* Full-time $44,720; part-time $699 per unit. *Required fees:* $296. *Financial support:* In 2014–15, 29 students received support, including 19 fellowships (averaging $32,800 per year), 2 research assistantships (averaging $35,800 per year), 7 teaching assistantships (averaging $36,600 per year); Federal Work-Study, institutionally sponsored loans, scholarships/grants, health care benefits, and unspecified assistantships also available. Financial award application deadline: 4/15; financial award applicants required to submit FAFSA. *Faculty research:* History of science; history of technology; sociology of science and technology; anthropology of science and technology; science, technology, and society.

Total annual research expenditures: $64,000. *Unit head:* Prof. David Kaiser, Program Director, 617-253-4062, Fax: 617-258-8118, E-mail: stsprogram@mit.edu. *Application contact:* Academic Administrator, 617-253-9759, Fax: 617-258-8118, E-mail: hasts@mit.edu.
Website: http://web.mit.edu/sts/

Oregon State University, College of Liberal Arts, Program in History of Science, Corvallis, OR 97331. Offers MA, MS, PhD. Part-time programs available. *Faculty:* 13 full-time (4 women), 2 part-time/adjunct (1 woman). *Students:* 12 full-time (6 women), 2 part-time (1 woman), 2 international. Average age 40. 12 applicants, 58% accepted, 3 enrolled. In 2014, 2 master's, 1 doctorate awarded. *Entrance requirements:* For master's and doctorate, GRE. Additional exam requirements/recommendations for international students: Required—TOEFL (minimum score 80 iBT), IELTS (minimum score 6.5). *Application deadline:* For fall admission, 1/1 for domestic and international students. Application fee: $60. *Expenses:* Tuition, state resident: full-time $11,907; part-time $189 per credit hour. Tuition, nonresident: full-time $19,953; part-time $441 per credit hour. *Required fees:* $1472; $449 per term. One-time fee: $350. Tuition and fees vary according to course load and program. *Financial support:* Application deadline: 1/1. *Unit head:* Dr. Ben Mutschler, Director, 541-737-1268, E-mail: bmutschler@oregonstate.edu. *Application contact:* Dr. Allen Thompson, Director of Graduate Studies/Associate Professor, 541-737-5654, E-mail: allen.thompson@oregonstate.edu.
Website: http://liberalarts.oregonstate.edu/history/graduate-history-of-science

Princeton University, Graduate School, Department of History, Program in History of Science, Princeton, NJ 08544-1019. Offers PhD. *Degree requirements:* For doctorate, 2 foreign languages, thesis/dissertation. *Entrance requirements:* For doctorate, GRE General Test, sample of written work, 3 letters of recommendation. Additional exam requirements/recommendations for international students: Required—TOEFL (minimum score 600 paper-based). Electronic applications accepted. *Faculty research:* Early modern science, history of modern life sciences, history of physical sciences, history of modern technology, science and medicine in European expansion and colonialism.

Rensselaer Polytechnic Institute, Graduate School, School of Humanities, Arts, and Social Sciences, Program in Science and Technology Studies, Troy, NY 12180-3590. Offers MS, PhD. *Faculty:* 20 full-time (10 women). *Students:* 25 full-time (9 women), 3 part-time (1 woman); includes 5 minority (1 Black or African American, non-Hispanic/Latino; 2 Hispanic/Latino; 2 Two or more races, non-Hispanic/Latino), 4 international. Average age 32. 24 applicants, 33% accepted, 3 enrolled. In 2014, 3 master's, 1 doctorate awarded. Terminal master's awarded for partial completion of doctoral program. *Degree requirements:* For master's, thesis (for some programs); for doctorate, comprehensive exam, thesis/dissertation. *Entrance requirements:* For master's and doctorate, GRE. Additional exam requirements/recommendations for international students: Required—TOEFL (minimum score 600 paper-based; 100 iBT), IELTS (minimum score 7), PTE (minimum score 68). *Application deadline:* For fall admission, 1/1 priority date for domestic and international students; for spring admission, 8/15 priority date for domestic and international students. Applications are processed on a rolling basis. Application fee: $75. Electronic applications accepted. *Expenses: Tuition:* Full-time $46,700; part-time $1945 per credit. Tuition and fees vary according to course load. *Financial support:* In 2014–15, 25 students received support, including research assistantships (averaging $18,500 per year), teaching assistantships (averaging $18,500 per year); fellowships also available. Financial award application deadline: 1/1. *Faculty research:* Policy studies, science studies, technology studies. *Total annual research expenditures:* $5,000. *Unit head:* Dr. Abby Kinchy, Graduate Program Director, 518-276-6980, E-mail: kincha@rpi.edu. *Application contact:* Office of Graduate Admissions, 518-276-6216, E-mail: gradadmissions@rpi.edu.
Website: http://www.sts.rpi.edu/pl/graduate-programs-sts

Rutgers, The State University of New Jersey, New Brunswick, Graduate School-New Brunswick, Program in History, Piscataway, NJ 08854-8097. Offers African-American history (PhD); early American history (PhD); early modern European history (PhD); east Asian history (PhD); global and comparative history (PhD); history (PhD); history of diplomacy and foreign relations (PhD); history of technology, environment and health (PhD); history of the Atlantic cultures and African diaspora (PhD); Latin American history (PhD); medieval history (PhD); modern European history (PhD); nineteenth and twentieth century American history (PhD); women's and gender history (PhD). *Degree requirements:* For doctorate, thesis/dissertation. *Entrance requirements:* For doctorate, GRE General Test, sample of written work. Electronic applications accepted. *Faculty research:* American history, European history, Afro-American history, women's history, Latin American history.

University of California, Berkeley, Graduate Division, College of Letters and Science, Group in Logic and the Methodology of Science, Berkeley, CA 94720-1500. Offers PhD. *Degree requirements:* For doctorate, qualifying exam, oral defense of dissertation. *Entrance requirements:* For doctorate, GRE General Test, minimum GPA of 3.5, 3 letters of recommendation. *Faculty research:* Set theory, recursion theory, theoretical computer science, philosophy of mathematics, philosophy of language.

University of California, San Diego, Graduate Division, Program in Science Studies, La Jolla, CA 92093. Offers communication - science studies (PhD); history - science studies (PhD); philosophy - science studies (PhD); sociology - science studies (PhD). In 2014, 6 doctorates awarded. *Degree requirements:* For doctorate, one foreign language, thesis/dissertation, internship. *Entrance requirements:* For doctorate, GRE General Test, 3 letters of recommendation. Additional exam requirements/recommendations for international students: Required—TOEFL, IELTS. *Application deadline:* For fall admission, 12/14 for domestic students. Application fee: $90 ($110 for international students). Electronic applications accepted. *Expenses:* Tuition: state resident: full-time $11,220; part-time $5610 per quarter. Tuition, nonresident: full-time $26,322; part-time $13,161 per quarter. *Required fees:* $570 per quarter. Tuition and fees vary according to program. *Financial support:* Fellowships, research assistantships, teaching assistantships, and scholarships/grants available. Financial award applicants required to submit FAFSA. *Unit head:* Martha Lampland, Director, 858-534-5640, E-mail: mlampland@ucsd.edu. *Application contact:* Courtney Hibbard, Graduate Coordinator, 858-534-0491, E-mail: ssadmin@ucsd.edu.
Website: http://sciencestudies.ucsd.edu/

University of California, San Francisco, Graduate Division, Program in History of Health Sciences, San Francisco, CA 94143. Offers MA, PhD, MD/PhD. Program admits students biennially. Terminal master's awarded for partial completion of doctoral program. *Degree requirements:* For master's, 2 foreign languages, thesis; for doctorate, 2 foreign languages, thesis/dissertation. *Entrance requirements:* For master's and doctorate, GRE General Test.

University of Delaware, College of Arts and Sciences, Department of History, Hagley Program in the History of Technology and Industrialization, Newark, DE 19716. Offers MA, PhD. *Degree requirements:* For master's, thesis optional; for doctorate, comprehensive exam, thesis/dissertation. *Entrance requirements:* For master's and doctorate, interview. Electronic applications accepted.

The University of Manchester, Faculty of Life Sciences, Manchester, United Kingdom. Offers adaptive organismal biology (M Phil, PhD); animal biology (M Phil, PhD); biochemistry (M Phil, PhD); bioinformatics (M Phil, PhD); biomolecular sciences (M Phil, PhD); biotechnology (M Phil, PhD); cell biology (M Phil, PhD); cell matrix research (M Phil, PhD); channels and transporters (M Phil, PhD); developmental biology (M Phil, PhD); Egyptology (M Phil, PhD); environmental biology (M Phil, PhD); evolutionary biology (M Phil, PhD); gene expression (M Phil, PhD); genetics (M Phil, PhD); history of science, technology and medicine (M Phil, PhD); immunology (M Phil, PhD); integrative neurobiology and behavior (M Phil, PhD); membrane trafficking (M Phil, PhD); microbiology (M Phil, PhD); molecular and cellular neuroscience (M Phil, PhD); molecular biology (M Phil, PhD); molecular cancer studies (M Phil, PhD); neuroscience (M Phil, PhD); ophthalmology (M Phil, PhD); optometry (M Phil, PhD); organelle function (M Phil, PhD); pharmacology (M Phil, PhD); physiology (M Phil, PhD); plant sciences (M Phil, PhD); stem cell research (M Phil, PhD); structural biology (M Phil, PhD); systems neuroscience (M Phil, PhD); toxicology (M Phil, PhD).

University of Minnesota, Twin Cities Campus, College of Science and Engineering, Program in History of Science, Technology and Medicine, Minneapolis, MN 55455-0213. Offers MA, PhD. Terminal master's awarded for partial completion of doctoral program. *Degree requirements:* For master's, one foreign language; for doctorate, 2 foreign languages, thesis/dissertation. *Entrance requirements:* For master's and doctorate, GRE General Test. Additional exam requirements/recommendations for international students: Required—TOEFL. Electronic applications accepted. *Faculty research:* History of physical sciences, biological sciences, technology, and medicine.

University of Notre Dame, Graduate School, College of Arts and Letters, Division of Humanities, Program in History and Philosophy of Science, Notre Dame, IN 46556. Offers history and philosophy of science (MA, PhD); theology and science (PhD). *Degree requirements:* For doctorate, 2 foreign languages, comprehensive exam, thesis/dissertation, candidacy exam. *Entrance requirements:* For doctorate, GRE General Test. Additional exam requirements/recommendations for international students: Required—TOEFL (minimum score 600 paper-based; 80 iBT). Electronic applications accepted. *Faculty research:* Philosophy of physics, science and ethics, history and philosophy of biology, history of medicine and technology, history and philosophy of economics.

University of Oklahoma, College of Arts and Sciences, Department of History of Science, Norman, OK 73019. Offers history of science, technology and medicine (MA, PhD). *Faculty:* 12 full-time (4 women), 1 part-time/adjunct (0 women). *Students:* 14 full-time (7 women), 3 part-time (2 women); includes 3 minority (1 American Indian or Alaska Native, non-Hispanic/Latino; 2 Two or more races, non-Hispanic/Latino), 1 international. Average age 31. 9 applicants, 44% accepted, 2 enrolled. In 2014, 3 master's, 3 doctorates awarded. Terminal master's awarded for partial completion of doctoral program. *Degree requirements:* For master's, one foreign language, comprehensive exam (for some programs), thesis (for some programs); for doctorate, 2 foreign languages, comprehensive exam, thesis/dissertation. *Entrance requirements:* For master's, GRE General Test, BA from accredited institution; for doctorate, GRE General Test, MA in history of science or closely-related field. Additional exam requirements/recommendations for international students: Required—TOEFL (minimum score 79 iBT). *Application deadline:* For fall admission, 1/15 for domestic and international students; for spring admission, 11/1 for domestic students, 9/1 for international students. Application fee: $50 ($100 for international students). Electronic applications accepted. *Expenses:* Tuition, state resident: full-time $4394; part-time $183.10 per credit hour. Tuition, nonresident: full-time $16,970; part-time $707.10 per credit hour. *Required fees:* $2892; $109.95 per credit hour. $126.50 per semester. *Financial support:* In 2014–15, 16 students received support, including 2 fellowships with full tuition reimbursements available (averaging $5,000 per year), 4 research assistantships with partial tuition reimbursements available (averaging $15,125 per year), 9 teaching assistantships with partial tuition reimbursements available (averaging $16,114 per year); Federal Work-Study, institutionally sponsored loans, scholarships/grants, traineeships, health care benefits, and unspecified assistantships also available. Financial award application deadline: 6/1; financial award applicants required to submit FAFSA. *Faculty research:* Premodern science; biological, biomedical and the social sciences in the modern world; science and religion; history of technology; the public and popular culture in the modern era. *Total annual research expenditures:* $15,536. *Unit head:* Dr. Hunter Heyck, Department Chair, 405-325-2213, Fax: 405-325-2363, E-mail: hheyck@ou.edu. *Application contact:* Stella Graves Stuart, Graduate Studies Coordinator, 405-325-6026, Fax: 405-325-2363, E-mail: slgstuart@ou.edu.
Website: http://cas.ou.edu/hsci

University of Pennsylvania, School of Arts and Sciences, Graduate Group in the History and Sociology of Science, Philadelphia, PA 19104. Offers AM, PhD. *Faculty:* 26 full-time (12 women), 8 part-time/adjunct (5 women). *Students:* 29 full-time (20 women), 2 part-time (both women); includes 2 minority (both Asian, non-Hispanic/Latino), 6 international. 42 applicants, 29% accepted, 6 enrolled. In 2014, 3 master's, 1 doctorate awarded. *Degree requirements:* For master's, thesis or alternative; for doctorate, 2 foreign languages, thesis/dissertation. *Entrance requirements:* For master's and doctorate, GRE General Test. Additional exam requirements/recommendations for international students: Required—TOEFL. *Application deadline:* For fall admission, 12/1 priority date for domestic students. Application fee: $70. Electronic applications accepted. *Financial support:* Fellowships, research assistantships, teaching assistantships, institutionally sponsored loans, scholarships/grants, traineeships, health care benefits, and unspecified assistantships available. Financial award application deadline: 12/15. *Unit head:* Dr. Ralph M. Rosen, Associate Dean for Graduate Studies, 215-898-7156, Fax: 215-573-8068, E-mail: grad-dean@sas.upenn.edu. *Application contact:* Arts and Sciences Graduate Admissions, 215-573-5816, Fax: 215-573-8068, E-mail: gdasadmis@sas.upenn.edu.
Website: http://hss.sas.upenn.edu/hssc

University of Pittsburgh, Dietrich School of Arts and Sciences, Department of History and Philosophy of Science, Pittsburgh, PA 15260. Offers MA, PhD. *Faculty:* 9 full-time (2 women). *Students:* 28 full-time (13 women); includes 1 minority (Asian, non-Hispanic/Latino), 8 international. Average age 28. 53 applicants, 9% accepted, 4 enrolled. In 2014, 2 master's, 4 doctorates awarded. Terminal master's awarded for partial completion of doctoral program. *Degree requirements:* For master's, one foreign language, comprehensive exam, minimum of 24 credit hours; for doctorate, one foreign language, comprehensive exam, thesis/dissertation, minimum of 72 credit hours, proficiency in logic. *Entrance requirements:* For master's and doctorate, GRE General Test, curriculum vitae, statement of career objective, 3 letters of recommendation, sample of written work. Additional exam requirements/recommendations for international students: Required—TOEFL (minimum score 577 paper-based; 90 iBT). *Application deadline:* For fall admission, 1/10 for domestic and international students. Application fee: $50. Electronic applications accepted. *Expenses:* Tuition, state resident: full-time $20,742; part-time $838 per credit. Tuition, nonresident: full-time $33,960; part-time $1389 per credit. *Required fees:* $800; $205 per term. Tuition and fees vary according to program. *Financial support:* In 2014–15, 20 students received support, including 12 fellowships with full tuition reimbursements available (averaging $23,749 per year), 8 teaching assistantships with full tuition reimbursements available (averaging $23,749 per year); health care benefits also available. Financial award application deadline: 1/10. *Faculty research:* History and philosophy of biology, psychology, neuroscience; history and philosophy of physics; early modern science;

rhetoric of science; philosophy of social science. *Unit head:* Dr. James Lennox, Chairman, 412-624-5896, Fax: 412-624-6825, E-mail: jglennox@pitt.edu. *Application contact:* Joann McIntyre, Graduate Admissions Secretary, 412-624-5896, Fax: 412-624-6825, E-mail: vanna@pitt.edu.
Website: http://www.pitt.edu/~hpsdept/

University of Toronto, School of Graduate Studies, Faculty of Arts and Science, Institute for the History and Philosophy of Science and Technology, Toronto, ON M5S 2J7, Canada. Offers MA, PhD. Part-time programs available. *Degree requirements:* For master's, one foreign language, thesis optional, reading ability in French or German; for doctorate, 2 foreign languages, thesis/dissertation, reading knowledge examinations, thesis defense. *Entrance requirements:* For master's, 2 letters of reference, B+ in the final two years of undergraduate work; for doctorate, 2 letters of reference, MA in history and philosophy of science and technology, minimum A- average. Additional exam requirements/recommendations for international students: Required—TOEFL (minimum score 580 paper-based; 93 iBT), TWE (minimum score 5). Electronic applications accepted.

University of Wisconsin–Madison, Graduate School, College of Letters and Science, Department of History of Science, Madison, WI 53706-1380. Offers history of medicine (MA); history of science (MA, PhD). Terminal master's awarded for partial completion of doctoral program. *Degree requirements:* For master's, thesis; for doctorate, 2 foreign languages, thesis/dissertation. *Entrance requirements:* For master's and doctorate, GRE General Test. Electronic applications accepted. *Expenses:* Tuition, state resident: full-time $10,723; part-time $745 per credit. Tuition, nonresident: full-time $24,054; part-time $1578 per credit. *Required fees:* $374 per semester. Tuition and fees vary according to course load, program and reciprocity agreements. *Faculty research:* History of biology, physical sciences, technology, medicine.

Virginia Polytechnic Institute and State University, Graduate School, College of Liberal Arts and Human Sciences, Blacksburg, VA 24061. Offers career and technical education (MS Ed, Ed D, PhD, Ed S); communication (MA); counselor education (MA Ed, Ed D, PhD, Ed S); creative writing (MFA); curriculum and instruction (MA Ed, Ed D, PhD, Ed S); educational leadership and policy studies (MA Ed, Ed D, PhD, Ed S); educational research and evaluation (PhD); English (MA); foreign languages, cultures, and literatures (MA); higher education and student affairs (MA Ed); history (MA); human development (MS, PhD); material culture and public humanities (MA); philosophy (MA); political science (MA); rhetoric and writing (PhD); science and technology studies (MS, PhD); social, political, ethical, and cultural thought (PhD); sociology (MS, PhD); theater arts (MFA). *Faculty:* 421 full-time (216 women), 2 part-time/adjunct (both women). *Students:* 642 full-time (437 women), 537 part-time (344 women); includes 235 minority (132 Black or African American, non-Hispanic/Latino; 2 American Indian or Alaska Native, non-Hispanic/Latino; 27 Asian, non-Hispanic/Latino; 52 Hispanic/Latino; 1 Native Hawaiian or other Pacific Islander, non-Hispanic/Latino; 21 Two or more races, non-Hispanic/Latino), 81 international. Average age 34. 890 applicants, 46% accepted, 303 enrolled. In 2014, 342 master's, 96 doctorates, 33 other advanced degrees awarded. *Degree requirements:* For master's, comprehensive exam (for some programs), thesis (for some programs); for doctorate, comprehensive exam (for some programs), thesis/dissertation (for some programs). *Entrance requirements:* For master's and doctorate, GRE/GMAT (may vary by department). Additional exam requirements/recommendations for international students: Required—TOEFL (minimum score 550 paper-based). *Application deadline:* For fall admission, 8/1 for domestic students, 4/1 for international students; for spring admission, 1/1 for domestic students, 9/1 for international students. Applications are processed on a rolling basis. Application fee: $75. Electronic applications accepted. *Expenses:* Tuition, state resident: full-time $11,656; part-time $647.50 per credit hour. Tuition, nonresident: full-time $23,351; part-time $1297.25 per credit hour. *Required fees:* $2533; $465.75 per semester. Tuition and fees vary according to course load, campus/location and program. *Financial support:* In 2014–15, 19 research assistantships with full tuition reimbursements (averaging $22,141 per year), 231 teaching assistantships with full tuition reimbursements (averaging $19,470 per year) were awarded. Financial award application deadline: 3/1; financial award applicants required to submit FAFSA. *Total annual research expenditures:* $6.5 million. *Unit head:* Elizabeth Spiller, Dean, 540-231-6779, Fax: 540-231-7157, E-mail: espiller@vt.edu. *Application contact:* Melissa Elliott, Executive Assistant, 540-231-6779, Fax: 540-231-7157, E-mail: elliott1@vt.edu.
Website: http://www.clahs.vt.edu/

Wayne State University, College of Liberal Arts and Sciences, Department of History, Detroit, MI 48202. Offers Africa (PhD); America (PhD); archival administration (Graduate Certificate); Europe (PhD); gender (PhD); history (MA); labor (PhD); science and technology (PhD); world history (PhD, Graduate Certificate); JD/MA; M Ed/MA; MLIS/MA. Doctoral programs admit for fall only. Evening/weekend programs available. *Faculty:* 22 full-time (9 women). *Students:* 32 full-time (14 women), 16 part-time (6 women); includes 4 minority (2 Black or African American, non-Hispanic/Latino; 2 Two or more races, non-Hispanic/Latino). Average age 39. 52 applicants, 37% accepted, 9 enrolled. In 2014, 5 master's awarded. *Degree requirements:* For master's, one foreign language, thesis (for some programs), final oral exam on thesis or essay and seminar; for doctorate, variable foreign language requirement, thesis/dissertation, qualifying exam in 4 fields of history. *Entrance requirements:* For master's, GRE General Test, minimum undergraduate GPA of 3.25 in history, 3.0 overall; at least 18 credits in history and related subjects at the advanced undergraduate level; foreign language; letter of intent; research paper; at least two letters of recommendation from former instructors; for doctorate, GRE General Test, minimum GPA of 3.0; letter of intent; research paper; at least three letters of recommendation from former professors; for Graduate Certificate, baccalaureate degree from accredited college or university; minimum GPA of 3.0, 3.25 in a minimum of eighteen semester credits in history and related subjects at the advanced undergraduate level. Additional exam requirements/recommendations for international students: Required—TOEFL (minimum score 550 paper-based; 79 iBT), TWE (minimum score 5.5), Michigan English Language Assessment Battery (minimum score 85); Recommended—IELTS (minimum score 6.5). *Application deadline:* For fall admission, 2/1 for domestic and international students; for winter admission, 11/1 for domestic students, 10/1 priority date for international students; for spring admission, 3/15 for domestic students, 1/1 priority date for international students. Applications are processed on a rolling basis. Application fee: $0. Electronic applications accepted. *Expenses:* Tuition, state resident: full-time $10,294; part-time $571.90 per credit hour. Tuition, nonresident: full-time $29,730; part-time $1238.75 per credit hour. *Required fees:* $1365; $43.50 per credit hour. $291.10 per semester. Tuition and fees vary according to course load and program. *Financial support:* In 2014–15, 19 students received support, including 1 fellowship with tuition reimbursement available (averaging $16,000 per year), 1 research assistantship with tuition reimbursement available (averaging $17,994 per year), 6 teaching assistantships with tuition reimbursements available (averaging $16,838 per year); scholarships/grants, health care benefits, and unspecified assistantships also available. Financial award application deadline: 3/31; financial award applicants required to submit FAFSA. *Faculty research:* Labor and working class history, urban history, citizenship and politics, gender and women's history. *Unit head:* Dr. Marc W. Kruman, Chair, 313-577-2525, Fax: 313-577-6987, E-mail: mkruman@wayne.edu. *Application contact:* Dr. Gayle McCreedy, Academic Service Officer, 313-577-2592, Fax: 313-577-6987, E-mail: g.mccreedy@wayne.edu.
Website: http://clas.wayne.edu/history/

West Virginia University, Eberly College of Arts and Sciences, Department of History, Morgantown, WV 26506. Offers African history (MA, PhD); African-American history (MA, PhD); American history (MA, PhD); Appalachian/regional history (MA, PhD); East Asian history (MA, PhD); European history (MA, PhD); history of science and technology (MA, PhD); Latin American history (MA). Part-time programs available. *Degree requirements:* For master's, one foreign language, thesis (for some programs), oral exam, thesis defense; for doctorate, one foreign language, comprehensive exam, thesis/dissertation, dissertation defense. *Entrance requirements:* For master's, GRE General Test, minimum GPA of 3.0; for doctorate, GRE General Test. Additional exam requirements/recommendations for international students: Required—TOEFL (minimum score 550 paper-based), IELTS (minimum score 6.5). Electronic applications accepted. *Faculty research:* United States, Appalachia, modern Europe, Africa, colonial and post-colonial societies.

Yale University, Graduate School of Arts and Sciences, Department of History, Program in the History of Science and Medicine, New Haven, CT 06520. Offers MS, PhD. *Degree requirements:* For doctorate, 2 foreign languages, thesis/dissertation. *Entrance requirements:* For doctorate, GRE General Test.

Medieval and Renaissance Studies

Arizona State University at the Tempe campus, College of Liberal Arts and Sciences, Department of English, Tempe, AZ 85287-0302. Offers applied linguistics (PhD); creative writing (MFA); English (MA, PhD), including comparative literature (MA), linguistics (MA), literature, rhetoric and composition (MA), rhetoric, composition, and linguistics (PhD); film and media studies (MAS), including American media and popular culture; linguistics (Graduate Certificate); teaching English to speakers of other languages (MTESOL); translation studies (Graduate Certificate). Terminal master's awarded for partial completion of doctoral program. *Degree requirements:* For master's, variable foreign language requirement, comprehensive exam (for some programs), thesis (for some programs), interactive Program of Study (iPOS) submitted before completing 50 percent of required credit hours; for doctorate, variable foreign language requirement, comprehensive exam, thesis/dissertation, interactive Program of Study (iPOS) submitted before completing 50 percent of required credit hours. *Entrance requirements:* For master's and doctorate, GRE, minimum GPA of 3.0 or equivalent in last 2 years of work leading to bachelor's degree. Additional exam requirements/recommendations for international students: Required—TOEFL, IELTS, or PTE. Electronic applications accepted.

Arizona State University at the Tempe campus, College of Liberal Arts and Sciences, School of Historical, Philosophical and Religious Studies, Tempe, AZ 85287-4301. Offers European history (MA, PhD); medieval studies (Graduate Certificate); North American history (MA, PhD); philosophy (MA, PhD); public history (MA); religious studies (MA, PhD); Renaissance studies (Graduate Certificate); scholarly publishing (Graduate Certificate). Part-time programs available. Terminal master's awarded for partial completion of doctoral program. *Degree requirements:* For master's, thesis or alternative, interactive Program of Study (iPOS) submitted before completing 50 percent of required credit hours; for doctorate, variable foreign language requirement, comprehensive exam, thesis/dissertation, interactive Program of Study (iPOS) submitted before completing 50 percent of required credit hours. *Entrance requirements:* For master's and doctorate, GRE, minimum GPA of 3.0 or equivalent in last 2 years of work leading to bachelor's degree. Additional exam requirements/recommendations for international students: Required—TOEFL, IELTS, or PTE. Electronic applications accepted.

California State University, Long Beach, Graduate Studies, College of Liberal Arts, Department of History, Long Beach, CA 90840. Offers Africa and the Middle East (MA); ancient/medieval Europe (MA); Asia (MA); Latin America (MA); modern Europe (MA); United States (MA); world history (MA). Part-time and evening/weekend programs available. *Degree requirements:* For master's, one foreign language, comprehensive exam or thesis. Electronic applications accepted. *Faculty research:* All periods of European and American history, recent Asian and African history.

The Catholic University of America, School of Arts and Sciences, Department of History, Washington, DC 20064. Offers history (MA, PhD); religion and society in the late medieval and early modern world (MA); MA/JD; MSLS/MA. Part-time programs available. *Faculty:* 15 full-time (6 women). *Students:* 11 full-time (4 women), 23 part-time (11 women); includes 2 minority (both Two or more races, non-Hispanic/Latino), 2 international. Average age 31. 24 applicants, 58% accepted, 1 enrolled. In 2014, 3 master's, 4 doctorates awarded. *Degree requirements:* For master's, one foreign language, comprehensive exam, thesis optional; for doctorate, 2 foreign languages, comprehensive exam, thesis/dissertation. *Entrance requirements:* For master's and doctorate, GRE General Test, statement of purpose, official copies of academic transcripts, three letters of recommendation, writing sample. Additional exam requirements/recommendations for international students: Required—TOEFL (minimum score 580 paper-based). *Application deadline:* For fall admission, 7/15 priority date for domestic students, 7/1 for international students; for spring admission, 11/15 priority date for domestic students, 11/1 for international students. Applications are processed on a rolling basis. Application fee: $55. Electronic applications accepted. *Expenses:* Tuition: Full-time $40,200; part-time $1600 per credit hour. *Required fees:* $400; $195 per semester. One-time fee: $425. *Financial support:* Fellowships, research assistantships, teaching assistantships, Federal Work-Study, scholarships/grants, tuition waivers (full and partial), and unspecified assistantships available. Financial award application deadline: 2/1; financial award applicants required to submit FAFSA. *Faculty research:* Modern European intellectual history, history of mathematics and sciences, Renaissance, Catholic reformation, medieval women and gender. *Unit head:* Dr. Jerry Muller, Chair, 202-319-5484, Fax: 202-319-5569, E-mail: mullerj@cua.edu.

Application contact: Director of Graduate Admissions, 202-319-5057, Fax: 202-319-6533, E-mail: cua-admissions@cua.edu. Website: http://history.cua.edu/

The Catholic University of America, School of Arts and Sciences, Program in Medieval and Byzantine Studies, Washington, DC 20064. Offers MA, PhD, Certificate. Part-time programs available. *Students:* 6 full-time (1 woman), 3 part-time (1 woman). Average age 33. 11 applicants, 55% accepted, 4 enrolled. In 2014, 4 master's, 2 doctorates awarded. *Degree requirements:* For master's, one foreign language, comprehensive exam, thesis or alternative; for doctorate, 2 foreign languages, comprehensive exam, thesis/dissertation. *Entrance requirements:* For master's and doctorate, GRE General Test, statement of purpose, official copies of academic transcripts, three letters of recommendation. Additional exam requirements/recommendations for international students: Required—TOEFL (minimum score 580 paper-based). *Application deadline:* For fall admission, 7/15 priority date for domestic students, 7/1 for international students; for spring admission, 11/15 priority date for domestic students, 11/1 for international students. Applications are processed on a rolling basis. Application fee: $55. Electronic applications accepted. *Expenses: Tuition:* Full-time $40,200; part-time $1600 per credit hour. *Required fees:* $400; $195 per semester. One-time fee: $425. *Financial support:* Fellowships, research assistantships, teaching assistantships, Federal Work-Study, scholarships/grants, tuition waivers (full and partial), and unspecified assistantships available. Financial award application deadline: 2/1; financial award applicants required to submit FAFSA. *Faculty research:* Franciscan and medieval theology, history and medieval theology, medieval institutional history, medieval political theology, early medieval history. *Unit head:* Dr. Lilla Kopar, Director, 202-319-5794, Fax: 202-319-6609, E-mail: kopar@cua.edu. *Application contact:* Director of Graduate Admissions, 202-319-5057, Fax: 202-319-6533, E-mail: cua-admissions@cua.edu.
Website: http://mbs.cua.edu/

Central European University, Graduate Studies, Department of Medieval Studies, Budapest, Hungary. Offers comparative history: interdisciplinary Medieval studies (MA); Medieval studies (MA, PhD). *Faculty:* 13 full-time (4 women), 6 part-time/adjunct (3 women). *Students:* 79 full-time (41 women). Average age 28. 87 applicants, 47% accepted, 36 enrolled. In 2014, 23 master's, 5 doctorates awarded. *Degree requirements:* For master's, one foreign language, thesis; for doctorate, variable foreign language requirement, comprehensive exam, thesis/dissertation. *Entrance requirements:* For master's and doctorate, interview. Additional exam requirements/recommendations for international students: Required—TOEFL (minimum score 570 paper-based); Recommended—IELTS (minimum score 6.5). *Application deadline:* For fall admission, 1/24 for domestic and international students. Application fee: $40. Electronic applications accepted. *Expenses: Tuition:* Full-time 12,000 euros. *Required fees:* 200 euros. One-time fee: 500 euros full-time. *Financial support:* In 2014–15, 74 students received support, including 74 fellowships (averaging $6,100 per year); scholarships/grants, health care benefits, and tuition waivers (full and partial) also available. *Faculty research:* History and culture of the period between c.300 and c.1600. *Unit head:* Dr. Daniel Ziemann, Head, 36 1 327-3046, E-mail: ziemannd@ceu.edu. *Application contact:* Zsuzsanna Jaszberenyi, Admissions Officer, 361-324-3009, Fax: 367-327-3211, E-mail: admissions@ceu.hu.
Website: http://medievalstudies.ceu.hu/

Columbia University, Graduate School of Arts and Sciences, New York, NY 10027. Offers African-American studies (MA); American studies (MA); anthropology (MA, PhD); art history and archaeology (MA, PhD); astronomy (PhD); biological sciences (PhD); biotechnology (MA); chemical physics (PhD); chemistry (PhD); classical studies (MA, PhD); classics (MA, PhD); climate and society (MA); earth and environmental sciences (PhD); East Asia: regional studies (MA); East Asian languages and cultures (MA, PhD); ecology, evolution and environmental biology (MA), including conservation biology; ecology, evolution, and environmental biology (PhD), including ecology and evolutionary biology, evolutionary primatology; economics (PhD); English and comparative literature (MA, PhD); French and Romance philology (MA, PhD); Germanic languages (MA, PhD); global French studies (MA); Hispanic cultural studies (MA); history (PhD); history and literature (MA); human rights studies (MA); Islamic studies (MA); Italian (MA, PhD); Japanese pedagogy (MA); Jewish studies (MA); Latin America and the Caribbean: regional studies (MA); Latin American and Iberian cultures (PhD); mathematics (MA, PhD), including finance (MA); medieval and Renaissance studies (MA); Middle Eastern, South Asian, and African studies (MA, PhD); modern art: critical and curatorial studies (MA); modern European studies (MA); museum anthropology (MA); music (DMA, PhD); oral history (MA); philosophical foundations of physics (MA); philosophy (MA, PhD); physics (PhD); political science (MA, PhD); psychology (PhD); quantitative methods in the social sciences (MA); religion (MA, PhD); Russia, Eurasia and East Europe: regional studies (MA); Russian translation (MA); Slavic cultures (MA); Slavic languages (MA, PhD); sociology (MA, PhD); South Asian studies (MA); statistics (MA, PhD); theatre (PhD); JD/PhD; MA/MS; MD/PhD; MPA/MA. Dual-degree programs require admission to both Graduate School of Arts and Sciences and another Columbia school. Part-time and evening/weekend programs available. Terminal master's awarded for partial completion of doctoral program. *Degree requirements:* For master's, thesis (for some programs); for doctorate, comprehensive exam, thesis/dissertation. *Entrance requirements:* For master's and doctorate, GRE General Test, GRE Subject Test (for some programs). Electronic applications accepted. *Faculty research:* Humanities, natural sciences, social sciences.

Cornell University, Graduate School, Graduate Fields of Arts and Sciences, Field of Archaeology, Ithaca, NY 14853-0001. Offers environmental archaeology (MA); historical archaeology (MA); Latin American archaeology (MA); medieval archaeology (MA); Mediterranean and Near Eastern archaeology (MA); Stone Age archaeology (MA). *Degree requirements:* For master's, one foreign language, thesis. *Entrance requirements:* For master's, GRE General Test, 3 letters of recommendation, sample of written work. Additional exam requirements/recommendations for international students: Required—TOEFL (minimum score 550 paper-based; 77 iBT). Electronic applications accepted. *Faculty research:* Anatolia, Lydia, Sardis, classical and Hellenistic Greece, science in archaeology, North American Indians, Stone Age Africa, Mayan trade.

Cornell University, Graduate School, Graduate Fields of Arts and Sciences, Field of English Language and Literature, Ithaca, NY 14853-0001. Offers African-American literature (PhD); American literature after 1865 (PhD); American literature to 1865 (PhD); American studies (PhD); colonial and postcolonial literatures (PhD); creative writing (MFA); cultural studies (PhD); dramatic literature (PhD); English poetry (PhD); English Renaissance to 1660 (PhD); lesbian, bisexual, and gay literary studies (PhD); literary criticism and theory (PhD); Old and Middle English (PhD); prose fiction (PhD); Restoration and the eighteenth-century (PhD); the nineteenth century (PhD); the twentieth century (PhD); women's literature (PhD); MFA/PhD. Terminal master's awarded for partial completion of doctoral program. *Degree requirements:* For master's, one foreign language, thesis; for doctorate, one foreign language, comprehensive exam, thesis/dissertation, teaching experience. *Entrance requirements:* For master's, GRE General Test, 3 letters of recommendation, creative writing sample; for doctorate, GRE General Test, GRE Subject Test (English), 3 letters of recommendation, writing sample. Additional exam requirements/recommendations for international students: Required—TOEFL (minimum score 600 paper-based; 77 iBT). Electronic applications accepted. *Faculty research:* English and American literature, women's writing, ethnic and post-colonial literature, critical theory, medievalism.

Cornell University, Graduate School, Graduate Fields of Arts and Sciences, Field of History, Ithaca, NY 14853-0001. Offers African history (MA, PhD); American history (MA, PhD); ancient Greek history (PhD); ancient history (MA, PhD); ancient Roman history (PhD); early modern European history (MA, PhD); English history (MA, PhD); French history (MA, PhD); German history (MA, PhD); history of science (MA, PhD); Korean history (PhD); Latin American history (MA, PhD); medieval Chinese history (MA, PhD); medieval history (MA, PhD); modern Chinese history (MA, PhD); modern European history (MA, PhD); modern Japanese history (MA, PhD); modern Middle Eastern history (PhD); premodern Islamic history (MA, PhD); premodern Japanese history (MA, PhD); Renaissance history (MA, PhD); Russian history (MA, PhD); South Asian history (PhD); Southeast Asian history (MA, PhD). Terminal master's awarded for partial completion of doctoral program. *Degree requirements:* For master's, thesis; for doctorate, 2 foreign languages, comprehensive exam, thesis/dissertation, 1 year of teaching experience. *Entrance requirements:* For master's and doctorate, GRE General Test, writing sample, 3 letters of recommendation. Additional exam requirements/recommendations for international students: Required—TOEFL (minimum score 550 paper-based; 77 iBT). Electronic applications accepted.

Cornell University, Graduate School, Graduate Fields of Arts and Sciences, Field of History of Art, Archaeology and Visual Studies, Ithaca, NY 14853. Offers 19th century art (PhD); African, African American and African diaspora (PhD); American art (PhD); ancient art and archaeology (PhD); Asian American art (PhD); Baroque art (PhD); comparative modernities (PhD); digital art (PhD); East Asian art (PhD); history of photography (PhD); Islamic art (PhD); Latin American art (PhD); medieval art (PhD); modern art (PhD); Renaissance art (PhD); Southeast Asian art (PhD); theory and criticism (PhD); visual studies (PhD). *Degree requirements:* For doctorate, one foreign language, comprehensive exam, thesis/dissertation, general exams in 3 areas. *Entrance requirements:* For doctorate, GRE General Test, sample of written work, 3 letters of recommendation. Additional exam requirements/recommendations for international students: Required—TOEFL (minimum score 550 paper-based; 77 iBT). Electronic applications accepted.

Cornell University, Graduate School, Graduate Fields of Arts and Sciences, Field of Medieval Studies, Ithaca, NY 14853-0001. Offers medieval archaeology (PhD); medieval art (PhD); medieval history (PhD); medieval literature (PhD); medieval music (PhD); medieval philology and linguistics (PhD); medieval philosophy (PhD). *Degree requirements:* For doctorate, 3 foreign languages, comprehensive exam, thesis/dissertation, teaching experience. *Entrance requirements:* For doctorate, GRE General Test, 3 letters of recommendation, proficiency in Latin (recommended), 20-page writing sample on a Medieval topic. Additional exam requirements/recommendations for international students: Required—TOEFL (minimum score 600 paper-based; 77 iBT). Electronic applications accepted. *Faculty research:* Interdisciplinary study of medieval culture, languages, literatures, history, archaeology.

Fordham University, Graduate School of Arts and Sciences, Center for Medieval Studies, New York, NY 10458. Offers MA, Certificate. Part-time and evening/weekend programs available. *Students:* 11 full-time (5 women), 14 part-time (9 women), 2 international. Average age 27. 20 applicants, 80% accepted, 7 enrolled. In 2014, 7 master's awarded. *Degree requirements:* For master's, thesis. *Entrance requirements:* For master's, GRE General Test. Additional exam requirements/recommendations for international students: Required—TOEFL (minimum score 650 paper-based). *Application deadline:* For fall admission, 1/4 priority date for domestic students; for spring admission, 11/1 for domestic students. Application fee: $70. Electronic applications accepted. *Financial support:* In 2014–15, 4 students received support, including 6 research assistantships with full and partial tuition reimbursements available (averaging $22,240 per year); institutionally sponsored loans, tuition waivers (full and partial), and unspecified assistantships also available. Financial award application deadline: 1/4; financial award applicants required to submit FAFSA. *Faculty research:* Medieval literature, history, philosophy, theology, and fine arts; Anglo-Norman. *Unit head:* Dr. Susanne Hafner, Director, 718-817-4655, E-mail: hafner@fordham.edu. *Application contact:* Bernadette Valentino-Morrison, Director of Graduate Admissions, 718-817-4419, Fax: 718-817-3566, E-mail: valentinomor@fordham.edu.

Georgetown University, Graduate School of Arts and Sciences, School of Continuing Studies, Washington, DC 20057. Offers American studies (MALS); Catholic studies (MALS); classical civilizations (MALS); emergency and disaster management (MPS); ethics and the professions (MALS); hospitality management (MPS); human resources management (MPS); humanities (MALS); individualized study (MALS); international affairs (MALS); Islam and Muslim-Christian relations (MALS); journalism (MPS); liberal studies (DLS); literature and society (MALS); medieval and early modern European studies (MALS); public relations and corporate communications (MPS); real estate (MPS); religious studies (MALS); social and public policy (MALS); sports industry management (MPS); systems engineering management (MPS); technology management (MPS); the theory and practice of American democracy (MALS); urban and regional planning (MPS); visual culture (MALS). MPS in systems engineering management offered jointly with Stevens Institute of Technology. *Entrance requirements:* Additional exam requirements/recommendations for international students: Required—TOEFL.

The Graduate Center, City University of New York, Graduate Studies, Interdisciplinary Studies, New York, NY 10016-4039. Offers language in social context (PhD); medieval studies (PhD); public policy (MA, PhD); urban studies (MA, PhD); women's studies (MA, PhD). Terminal master's awarded for partial completion of doctoral program. *Degree requirements:* For master's, thesis; for doctorate, comprehensive exam, thesis/dissertation. *Entrance requirements:* For master's and doctorate, GRE General Test.

Harvard University, Graduate School of Arts and Sciences, Department of English and American Literature and Language, Cambridge, MA 02138. Offers critical theory (PhD); eighteenth-century literature (PhD); literature: nineteenth-century to the present (PhD); medieval literature and language (PhD); modern British and American literature (PhD); Renaissance literature (PhD). Terminal master's awarded for partial completion of doctoral program. *Degree requirements:* For doctorate, 2 foreign languages, thesis/dissertation, oral exam. *Entrance requirements:* For doctorate, GRE General Test, GRE Subject Test, writing sample. Additional exam requirements/recommendations for international students: Required—TOEFL. *Faculty research:* Old and Middle English language and literature, drama, creative writing, transition to Romanticism, history and theory of criticism.

Indiana University Bloomington, University Graduate School, College of Arts and Sciences, Department of Germanic Studies, Bloomington, IN 47405-7000. Offers German philology and linguistics (PhD); German studies (MA, PhD), including German (MA), German literature and culture (MA), German literature and linguistics (MA); medieval German studies (PhD); teaching German (MAT). *Faculty:* 13 full-time (4 women), 6 part-time/adjunct (2 women). *Students:* 29 full-time (16 women), 6 international. Average age 31. 22 applicants, 9% accepted, 2 enrolled. In 2014, 4 doctorates awarded. Terminal master's awarded for partial completion of doctoral

program. *Degree requirements:* For master's, one foreign language, project; for doctorate, one foreign language, comprehensive exam, thesis/dissertation. *Entrance requirements:* For master's, GRE General Test, BA in German or equivalent; for doctorate, GRE General Test, MA in German or equivalent. Additional exam requirements/recommendations for international students: Required—TOEFL. *Application deadline:* For fall admission, 1/15 priority date for domestic students, 12/1 for international students; for spring admission, 9/1 priority date for domestic students, 9/1 for international students. Applications are processed on a rolling basis. Application fee: $55 ($65 for international students). Electronic applications accepted. *Financial support:* Fellowships with full and partial tuition reimbursements, teaching assistantships with full tuition reimbursements, Federal Work-Study, institutionally sponsored loans, scholarships/grants, and unspecified assistantships available. Support available to part-time students. Financial award application deadline: 1/15; financial award applicants required to submit FAFSA. *Faculty research:* German and other European literature: medieval to modern/postmodern, German and culture studies, Germanic philology, literary theory, literature and the other arts. *Unit head:* Fritz Breithaupt, Department Chairman, 812-855-7947, Fax: 812-855-8292, E-mail: fbreitha@indiana.edu. *Application contact:* Michelle Dunbar, Graduate Secretary, 812-855-7947, E-mail: midunbar@indiana.edu.
Website: http://www.indiana.edu/~germanic/

Rutgers, The State University of New Jersey, New Brunswick, Graduate School-New Brunswick, Program in History, Piscataway, NJ 08854-8097. Offers African-American history (PhD); early American history (PhD); early modern European history (PhD); east Asian history (PhD); global and comparative history (PhD); history (PhD); history of diplomacy and foreign relations (PhD); history of technology, environment and health (PhD); history of the Atlantic cultures and African diaspora (PhD); Latin American history (PhD); medieval history (PhD); modern European history (PhD); nineteenth and twentieth century American history (PhD); women's and gender history (PhD). *Degree requirements:* For doctorate, thesis/dissertation. *Entrance requirements:* For doctorate, GRE General Test, sample of written work. Electronic applications accepted. *Faculty research:* American history, European history, Afro-American history, women's history, Latin American history.

Southern Methodist University, Dedman College of Humanities and Sciences, Program in Medieval Studies, Dallas, TX 75275. Offers MA. Part-time programs available. *Degree requirements:* For master's, 2 foreign languages, thesis. *Entrance requirements:* For master's, GRE General Test, minimum GPA of 3.0. Electronic applications accepted. *Faculty research:* Byzantine culture, medieval Europe, Arthurian literature, Chaucer, Romance.

University of California, Santa Barbara, Graduate Division, College of Letters and Sciences, Division of Humanities and Fine Arts, Department of English, Santa Barbara, CA 93106-3170. Offers English (PhD); European medieval studies (PhD); feminist studies (PhD); global studies (PhD); technology and society (PhD); translation studies (PhD); writing studies (PhD); MA/PhD. Terminal master's awarded for partial completion of doctoral program. *Degree requirements:* For doctorate, one foreign language, comprehensive exam, thesis/dissertation. *Entrance requirements:* For doctorate, GRE General Test, GRE Subject Test (English). Additional exam requirements/ recommendations for international students: Required—TOEFL (minimum score 550 paper-based; 80 iBT), IELTS (minimum score 7). Electronic applications accepted. *Faculty research:* Medieval, Romantic and Victorian studies; gender studies and feminist theory; literature and the mind; American literature; literature and new media/information culture.

University of California, Santa Barbara, Graduate Division, College of Letters and Sciences, Division of Humanities and Fine Arts, Department of History, Santa Barbara, CA 93106-9410. Offers European medieval studies (PhD); global studies (PhD); public historical studies (PhD); technology and society (PhD); women's studies (PhD); MA/ PhD. *Degree requirements:* For doctorate, variable foreign language requirement, comprehensive exam, thesis/dissertation. *Entrance requirements:* For doctorate, GRE. Additional exam requirements/recommendations for international students: Required—TOEFL (minimum score 550 paper-based; 80 iBT), IELTS (minimum score 7). Electronic applications accepted. *Faculty research:* Europe, United States, Latin America, Africa, Middle East, East Asia.

University of California, Santa Barbara, Graduate Division, College of Letters and Sciences, Division of Humanities and Fine Arts, Department of History of Art and Architecture, Santa Barbara, CA 93106-2014. Offers art history (PhD), including art history, European medieval studies, feminist studies; MA/PhD. Terminal master's awarded for partial completion of doctoral program. *Degree requirements:* For doctorate, 2 foreign languages, comprehensive exam, thesis/dissertation. *Entrance requirements:* For doctorate, GRE. Additional exam requirements/recommendations for international students: Required—TOEFL (minimum score 550 paper-based; 80 iBT), IELTS (minimum score 7). Electronic applications accepted. *Faculty research:* History of architecture, Renaissance-Italian, Baroque, American, Chinese, Japanese, contemporary, Northern Renaissance.

University of California, Santa Barbara, Graduate Division, College of Letters and Sciences, Division of Humanities and Fine Arts, Department of Religious Studies, Santa Barbara, CA 93106-3130. Offers ancient Mediterranean studies (PhD); cognitive science (PhD); European medieval studies (PhD); feminist studies (PhD); global studies (PhD); religious studies (MA, PhD); translation studies (PhD); MA/PhD. Terminal master's awarded for partial completion of doctoral program. *Degree requirements:* For master's, one foreign language, comprehensive exam (for some programs), thesis (for some programs), colloquium; for doctorate, 2 foreign languages, thesis/dissertation, methodology, colloquium. *Entrance requirements:* For master's and doctorate, GRE General Test. Additional exam requirements/recommendations for international students: Required—TOEFL (minimum score 550 paper-based; 80 iBT), IELTS (minimum score 7). Electronic applications accepted. *Faculty research:* Area studies; religious traditions; theory and method in the study of religion; religion, culture, and politics; spirituality and religious experience.

University of California, Santa Barbara, Graduate Division, College of Letters and Sciences, Division of Humanities and Fine Arts, Department of Spanish and Portuguese, Santa Barbara, CA 93106-4150. Offers Hispanic languages and literatures (PhD), including European medieval studies, feminist studies, Hispanic linguistics, Hispanic literature, Luso-Brazilian literature; Hispanic linguistics (MA); Luso-Brazilian literature (MA); Spanish or Spanish-American literature (MA); MA/PhD. Spanish Language Institute available during Summer session. Terminal master's awarded for partial completion of doctoral program. *Degree requirements:* For master's, 2 foreign languages, comprehensive exam (for some programs), thesis optional; for doctorate, 3 foreign languages, comprehensive exam, thesis/dissertation. *Entrance requirements:* For master's and doctorate, GRE. Additional exam requirements/recommendations for international students: Required—TOEFL (minimum score 550 paper-based; 80 iBT), IELTS (minimum score 7). Electronic applications accepted. *Faculty research:* Nineteenth-century Spanish and Portuguese literature, Spanish and Spanish-American literature, nineteenth- and twentieth-century Portuguese and Brazilian literatures, Hispanic linguistics, Catalan language and culture.

University of California, Santa Barbara, Graduate Division, College of Letters and Sciences, Division of Humanities and Fine Arts, Department of Theater and Dance, Santa Barbara, CA 93106-7060. Offers theater studies (MA, PhD), including European medieval studies (PhD), feminist studies (PhD), theatre studies (PhD); MA/PhD. Terminal master's awarded for partial completion of doctoral program. *Degree requirements:* For master's, comprehensive exam, thesis; for doctorate, one foreign language, comprehensive exam, thesis/dissertation. *Entrance requirements:* For master's and doctorate, GRE. Additional exam requirements/recommendations for international students: Required—TOEFL (minimum score 550 paper-based; 80 iBT), IELTS (minimum score 7). Electronic applications accepted. *Faculty research:* English and American theater and Ancient Greek; Spanish, Latin American and Caribbean performance; Renaissance and Baroque drama and intercultural theory; East Asian performance, gender and nationalism; Korean cultural studies, Russian literature, and Slavic folklore; history of German theater, Shakespeare, and European opera; postcolonialism, performance-based ethnography, globalism and national identity formation in Africa.

University of Connecticut, Graduate School, College of Liberal Arts and Sciences, Field of Medieval Studies, Storrs, CT 06269. Offers MA, PhD. Terminal master's awarded for partial completion of doctoral program. *Degree requirements:* For master's, comprehensive exam; for doctorate, 3 foreign languages, thesis/dissertation. *Entrance requirements:* For master's and doctorate, GRE General Test, GRE Subject Test. Additional exam requirements/recommendations for international students: Required—TOEFL (minimum score 550 paper-based). Electronic applications accepted.

University of Guelph, Graduate Studies, College of Arts, School of English and Theatre Studies, Joint Program in Literary Studies/Theatre Studies in English, Guelph, ON N1G 2W1, Canada. Offers PhD. Part-time programs available. *Degree requirements:* For doctorate, one foreign language, comprehensive exam, thesis/ dissertation. *Entrance requirements:* For doctorate, MA, 3 letters of reference, writing samples, resume, minimum A- average in graduate course work. Additional exam requirements/recommendations for international students: Required—TOEFL. Electronic applications accepted. *Faculty research:* Canadian studies, Early Modern studies, Postcolonial studies, studies in gender and genre, 19th Century studies.

University of Minnesota, Twin Cities Campus, Graduate School, College of Liberal Arts, Department of German, Scandinavian, and Dutch, Minneapolis, MN 55455. Offers Germanic studies (MA, PhD), including German, Germanic medieval studies, Scandinavian studies (MA). Part-time programs available. Terminal master's awarded for partial completion of doctoral program. *Degree requirements:* For doctorate, 2 foreign languages, thesis/dissertation. *Entrance requirements:* For master's, GRE General Test, BA in German, Scandinavian, or equivalent; for doctorate, MA in German, Scandinavian, or equivalent. Additional exam requirements/recommendations for international students: Required—TOEFL (minimum score 550 paper-based; 79 iBT). Electronic applications accepted. *Faculty research:* Cultural studies, literary theory, feminist criticism, film, Germanic medieval studies.

University of Notre Dame, Graduate School, College of Arts and Letters, Division of Humanities, Medieval Institute, Notre Dame, IN 46556. Offers MMS, PhD. Terminal master's awarded for partial completion of doctoral program. *Degree requirements:* For master's, 3 foreign languages, comprehensive exam; for doctorate, 3 foreign languages, thesis/dissertation, candidacy exam. *Entrance requirements:* For master's and doctorate, GRE General Test. Additional exam requirements/recommendations for international students: Required—TOEFL (minimum score 600 paper-based; 80 iBT). Electronic applications accepted. *Faculty research:* Medieval history, vernacular literatures, theology, philosophy, Ambrosiana manuscripts and drawings.

University of Pittsburgh, Dietrich School of Arts and Sciences, Program in Medieval and Renaissance Studies, Pittsburgh, PA 15260. Offers Certificate. Part-time programs available. *Faculty:* 42 full-time (18 women). *Students:* 7 full-time (5 women); includes 1 minority (Two or more races, non-Hispanic/Latino), 1 international. Average age 27. 1 applicant, 100% accepted, 1 enrolled. In 2014, 2 Certificates awarded. *Degree requirements:* For Certificate, thesis. *Entrance requirements:* For degree, minimum GPA of 3.0. *Application deadline:* Applications are processed on a rolling basis. *Expenses:* Tuition, state resident: full-time $20,742; part-time $838 per credit. Tuition, nonresident: full-time $33,960; part-time $1389 per credit. *Required fees:* $800; $205 per term. Tuition and fees vary according to program. *Faculty research:* Medieval historical writing, English Renaissance, Italian medieval/Renaissance architecture, medieval and early modern law and political thought, medieval music and music theory, religious history. *Unit head:* Dr. Jennifer Elizabeth Waldron, Program Director, 412-624-5225, Fax: 412-624-8505, E-mail: jwaldron@pitt.edu. *Application contact:* Lucy DiStazio, Program Administrator, 412-624-5225, Fax: 412-624-8505, E-mail: lud3@pitt.edu.
Website: http://www.medren.pitt.edu/

University of Toronto, School of Graduate Studies, Faculty of Arts and Science, Centre for Medieval Studies, Toronto, ON M5S 2J7, Canada. Offers MA, PhD. Part-time programs available. *Degree requirements:* For master's, one foreign language, 4 courses or 3 courses and thesis; for doctorate, 3 foreign languages, thesis/dissertation, proficiency in Latin, German and French. *Entrance requirements:* For master's, letters of reference, minimum B+ average, course work in the Medieval period; for doctorate, letters of reference. Additional exam requirements/recommendations for international students: Required—TOEFL (minimum score 580 paper-based; 93 iBT), TWE (minimum score 5). Electronic applications accepted.

Yale University, Graduate School of Arts and Sciences, Interdisciplinary Program in Medieval Studies, New Haven, CT 06520. Offers M Phil, PhD. *Entrance requirements:* For doctorate, GRE General Test.

Yale University, Graduate School of Arts and Sciences, Program in Renaissance Studies, New Haven, CT 06520. Offers PhD. *Degree requirements:* For doctorate, 3 foreign languages. *Entrance requirements:* For doctorate, GRE General Test.

Public History

American Public University System, AMU/APU Graduate Programs, Charles Town, WV 25414. Offers accounting (MBA, MS); criminal justice (MA), including business administration, emergency and disaster management, general (MA, MS); educational leadership (M Ed); emergency and disaster management (MA); entrepreneurship (MBA); environmental policy and management (MS), including environmental planning, environmental sustainability, fish and wildlife management, general (MA, MS), global environmental management; finance (MBA); general (MBA); global business management (MBA); history (MA), including American history, ancient and classical history, European history, global history, public history; homeland security (MA), including business administration, counter-terrorism studies, criminal justice, cyber, emergency management and public health, intelligence studies, transportation security; homeland security resource allocation (MBA); humanities (MA); information technology (MS), including digital forensics, enterprise software development, information assurance and security, IT project management; information technology management (MBA); intelligence studies (MA), including criminal intelligence, cyber, general (MA, MS), homeland security, intelligence analysis, intelligence collection, intelligence management, intelligence operations, terrorism studies; international relations and conflict resolution (MA), including comparative and security issues, conflict resolution, international and transnational security issues, peacekeeping; legal studies (MA); management (MA), including defense management, general (MA, MS), human resource management, organizational leadership, public administration; marketing (MBA); military history (MA), including American military history, American Revolution, civil war, war since 1945, World War II; military studies (MA), including joint warfare, strategic leadership; national security studies (MA), including general (MA, MS), homeland security, regional security studies, security and intelligence analysis, terrorism studies; nonprofit management (MBA); political science (MA), including American politics and government, comparative government and development, general (MA, MS), international relations, public policy; psychology (MA); public administration (MPA), including disaster management, environmental policy, health policy, human resources, national security, organizational management, security management; public health (MPH); reverse logistics management (MA); school counseling (M Ed); security management (MA); space studies (MS), including aerospace science, general (MA, MS), planetary science; sports and health sciences (MS); teaching (M Ed), including curriculum and instruction for elementary teachers, elementary reading, English language learners, instructional leadership, online learning, special education; transportation and logistics management (MA), including general (MA, MS), maritime engineering management, reverse logistics management. Programs offered via distance learning only. Part-time and evening/weekend programs available. Postbaccalaureate distance learning degree programs offered (no on-campus study). *Faculty:* 426 full-time (236 women), 1,864 part-time/adjunct (880 women). *Students:* 475 full-time (215 women), 10,067 part-time (4,085 women); includes 3,462 minority (1,863 Black or African American, non-Hispanic/Latino; 74 American Indian or Alaska Native, non-Hispanic/Latino; 273 Asian, non-Hispanic/Latino; 831 Hispanic/Latino; 78 Native Hawaiian or other Pacific Islander, non-Hispanic/Latino; 343 Two or more races, non-Hispanic/Latino), 131 international. Average age 36. In 2014, 3,740 master's awarded. *Degree requirements:* For master's, comprehensive exam or practicum. *Entrance requirements:* For master's, official transcript showing earned bachelor's degree from institution accredited by recognized accrediting body. Additional exam requirements/recommendations for international students: Required—TOEFL (minimum score 550 paper-based), IELTS (minimum score 6.5). *Application deadline:* Applications are processed on a rolling basis. Application fee: $0. Electronic applications accepted. *Financial support:* Applicants required to submit FAFSA. *Faculty research:* Military history, criminal justice, management performance, national security. *Unit head:* Dr. Karan Powell, Executive Vice President and Provost, 877-468-6268, Fax: 304-724-3780. *Application contact:* Terry Grant, Vice President of Enrollment Management, 877-468-6268, Fax: 304-724-3780, E-mail: info@apus.edu.
Website: http://www.apus.edu

Arizona State University at the Tempe campus, College of Liberal Arts and Sciences, School of Historical, Philosophical and Religious Studies, Tempe, AZ 85287-4301. Offers European history (MA, PhD); medieval studies (Graduate Certificate); North American history (MA, PhD); philosophy (MA, PhD); public history (MA); religious studies (MA, PhD); Renaissance studies (Graduate Certificate); scholarly publishing (Graduate Certificate). Part-time programs available. Terminal master's awarded for partial completion of doctoral program. *Degree requirements:* For master's, thesis or alternative, interactive Program of Study (iPOS) submitted before completing 50 percent of required credit hours; for doctorate, variable foreign language requirement, comprehensive exam, thesis/dissertation, interactive Program of Study (iPOS) submitted before completing 50 percent of required credit hours. *Entrance requirements:* For master's and doctorate, GRE, minimum GPA of 3.0 or equivalent in last 2 years of work leading to bachelor's degree. Additional exam requirements/recommendations for international students: Required—TOEFL, IELTS, or PTE. Electronic applications accepted.

Armstrong State University, School of Graduate Studies, Program in History, Savannah, GA 31419-1997. Offers American and European history (MA); public history (MA). Part-time and evening/weekend programs available. *Faculty:* 5 full-time (2 women), 1 (woman) part-time/adjunct. *Students:* 6 full-time (5 women), 7 part-time (4 women); includes 3 minority (1 Black or African American, non-Hispanic/Latino; 1 Asian, non-Hispanic/Latino; 1 Hispanic/Latino). Average age 32. 9 applicants, 67% accepted, 5 enrolled. In 2014, 9 master's awarded. *Degree requirements:* For master's, one foreign language, comprehensive exam (for some programs), thesis (for some programs), thesis, internship, or advanced fieldwork. *Entrance requirements:* For master's, GRE General Test, minimum GPA of 3.0, letters of recommendation, BA in history or equivalent. Additional exam requirements/recommendations for international students: Required—TOEFL (minimum score 523 paper-based). *Application deadline:* For fall admission, 6/30 priority date for domestic students, 5/1 priority date for international students; for spring admission, 11/15 priority date for domestic students, 9/15 priority date for international students; for summer admission, 4/15 priority date for domestic students, 9/15 for international students. Applications are processed on a rolling basis. Application fee: $30. Electronic applications accepted. *Expenses:* Tuition, state resident: part-time $206 per credit hour. Tuition, nonresident: part-time $763 per credit hour. *Required fees:* $612 per semester. Tuition and fees vary according to course load, campus/location and program. *Financial support:* In 2014–15, research assistantships with full tuition reimbursements (averaging $5,000 per year) were awarded; career-related internships or fieldwork, Federal Work-Study, and unspecified assistantships also available. Support available to part-time students. Financial award application deadline: 3/15; financial award applicants required to submit FAFSA. *Faculty research:* Public history; European, Latin American, African, and United States history. *Unit head:* Dr. Christopher Curtis, Department Head, 912-344-3051, Fax: 912-344-3451, E-mail: chris.curtis@armstrong.edu. *Application contact:* Kathy Ingram, Associate Director of Graduate/Adult and Nontraditional Students, 912-344-2503, Fax: 912-344-3417, E-mail: graduate@armstrong.edu.
Website: http://www.armstrong.edu/Liberal_Arts/history/history_graduate_program

California State University, East Bay, Office of Academic Programs and Graduate Studies, College of Letters, Arts, and Social Sciences, Department of History, Hayward, CA 94542-3000. Offers history (MA); public history (MA); teaching (MA). Part-time and evening/weekend programs available. *Degree requirements:* For master's, one foreign language, comprehensive exam, project, thesis, or exam. *Entrance requirements:* For master's, GRE (strongly recommended), minimum GPA of 3.0 in field, 3.3 in history; 2 letters of recommendation; writing sample. Additional exam requirements/recommendations for international students: Required—TOEFL (minimum score 550 paper-based). *Application deadline:* For fall admission, 5/16 for domestic and international students. Applications are processed on a rolling basis. Application fee: $55. Electronic applications accepted. *Expenses:* Tuition, state resident: full-time $7830; part-time $1302 per credit hour. Tuition, nonresident: full-time $16,368. *Required fees:* $327 per quarter. Tuition and fees vary according to course load and program. *Financial support:* Fellowships, teaching assistantships, career-related internships or fieldwork, Federal Work-Study, institutionally sponsored loans, and scholarships/grants available. Support available to part-time students. Financial award application deadline: 3/2; financial award applicants required to submit FAFSA. *Faculty research:* Digital history, American women, early America, Native Americans, medieval colonial India. *Unit head:* Dr. Linda L. Ivey, Chair, 510-885-4015, E-mail: linda.ivey@csueastbay.edu. *Application contact:* Dr. Khal Schneider, Graduate Coordinator, 510-885-3237, Fax: 510-885-4791, E-mail: khal.schneider@csueastbay.edu.
Website: http://www20.csueastbay.edu/class/departments/history/

California State University, Sacramento, Office of Graduate Studies, College of Arts and Letters, Department of History, Sacramento, CA 95819. Offers history (MA); public historical studies (PhD); public history (MA). PhD held jointly with University of California, Santa Barbara. Part-time programs available. *Degree requirements:* For master's, thesis, project or comprehensive exam; writing proficiency exam. *Entrance requirements:* For master's, GRE General Test, minimum GPA of 3.25 in history, 3.0 overall during previous 2 years; BA in history or equivalent. Additional exam requirements/recommendations for international students: Required—TOEFL. Electronic applications accepted.

Duquesne University, Graduate School of Liberal Arts, Department of History, Pittsburgh, PA 15282-0001. Offers historical studies (MA); public history (MA). Part-time and evening/weekend programs available. *Faculty:* 15 full-time (5 women), 5 part-time/adjunct (3 women). *Students:* 30 full-time (21 women), 7 part-time (2 women); includes 1 minority (Hispanic/Latino). Average age 28. 39 applicants, 69% accepted, 14 enrolled. In 2014, 19 master's awarded. *Degree requirements:* For master's, comprehensive exam (for some programs), thesis optional. *Entrance requirements:* For master's, GRE General Test, writing sample. Additional exam requirements/recommendations for international students: Required—TOEFL. *Application deadline:* For fall admission, 8/15 for domestic students, 5/1 for international students; for spring admission, 11/1 priority date for domestic students. Applications are processed on a rolling basis. Electronic applications accepted. *Expenses:* Tuition: Full-time $18,882; part-time $1049 per credit. *Required fees:* $1800; $100 per credit. Tuition and fees vary according to program. *Financial support:* In 2014–15, 4 teaching assistantships with full tuition reimbursements (averaging $6,000 per year) were awarded; career-related internships or fieldwork, Federal Work-Study, scholarships/grants, tuition waivers (full and partial), and unspecified assistantships also available. Support available to part-time students. Financial award application deadline: 5/1. *Faculty research:* American studies, immigration history, local social history, applied history, Eastern European history. *Unit head:* Dr. John Dwyer, Chair, 412-396-6470, E-mail: dwyer@duq.edu. *Application contact:* Linda Rendulic, Assistant to the Dean, 412-396-6400, E-mail: rendulic@duq.edu.
Website: http://www.duq.edu/academics/schools/liberal-arts/graduate-school/programs/history

East Carolina University, Graduate School, Thomas Harriot College of Arts and Sciences, Department of History, Greenville, NC 27858-4353. Offers American history (MA); Atlantic world (MA); European history (MA); history education (MA Ed); maritime studies (MA); military history (MA); public history (MA). Part-time and evening/weekend programs available. *Degree requirements:* For master's, one foreign language, comprehensive exam, thesis. *Entrance requirements:* For master's, GRE General Test, GRE Subject Test. Additional exam requirements/recommendations for international students: Required—TOEFL. *Expenses:* Tuition, state resident: full-time $4223. Tuition, nonresident: full-time $16,540. *Required fees:* $2184.

Eastern Illinois University, Graduate School, College of Arts and Humanities, Department of History, Charleston, IL 61920. Offers historical administration (MA); history (MA). Part-time and evening/weekend programs available. *Faculty:* 16. *Students:* 24 full-time (10 women), 27 part-time (15 women); includes 4 minority (2 Hispanic/Latino; 2 Two or more races, non-Hispanic/Latino). Average age 28. 42 applicants, 50% accepted, 17 enrolled. In 2014, 18 master's awarded. *Degree requirements:* For master's, comprehensive exam (for some programs), thesis (for some programs). *Entrance requirements:* For master's, GMAT or GRE. Additional exam requirements/recommendations for international students: Required—TOEFL (minimum score 500 paper-based; 61 iBT), IELTS (minimum score 6). *Application deadline:* For fall admission, 5/15 for domestic and international students; for spring admission, 10/15 for domestic and international students. Applications are processed on a rolling basis. Application fee: $30. Electronic applications accepted. *Expenses:* Tuition, state resident: full-time $3113; part-time $283 per credit hour. Tuition, nonresident: full-time $7469; part-time $679 per credit hour. *Required fees:* $2287; $96 per credit hour. Tuition and fees vary according to course load. *Financial support:* In 2014–15, 28 students received support, including 8 research assistantships with full tuition reimbursements available (averaging $8,820 per year); career-related internships or fieldwork, Federal Work-Study, and unspecified assistantships also available. Support available to part-time students. Financial award application deadline: 3/1; financial award applicants required to submit FAFSA. *Unit head:* Anita Shelton, Department Chair, 217-581-6989, Fax: 217-581-7233, E-mail: ashelton@eiu.edu. *Application contact:* Ed Wehrle, Graduate Coordinator, 217-581-3310, Fax: 217-581-7233, E-mail: efwehrle@eiu.edu.
Website: http://www.eiu.edu/history/

Florida State University, The Graduate School, College of Arts and Sciences, Department of History, Tallahassee, FL 32306. Offers historical administration and public history (MA); history (MA, MS, PhD). Part-time programs available. *Faculty:* 26

full-time (8 women). *Students:* 50 full-time (18 women), 47 part-time (18 women); includes 14 minority (3 Black or African American, non-Hispanic/Latino; 1 American Indian or Alaska Native, non-Hispanic/Latino; 2 Asian, non-Hispanic/Latino; 1 Hispanic/Latino; 7 Two or more races, non-Hispanic/Latino), 5 international. Average age 34. 53 applicants, 60% accepted, 15 enrolled. In 2014, 21 master's, 14 doctorates awarded. *Degree requirements:* For master's, one foreign language, comprehensive exam (for some programs), thesis (for some programs), internships; for doctorate, one foreign language, comprehensive exam, thesis/dissertation. *Entrance requirements:* For master's, GRE General Test, minimum GPA of 3.3, minimum 18 hours of course work in history; for doctorate, GRE General Test, master's degree, minimum graduate GPA of 3.65. Additional exam requirements/recommendations for international students: Required—TOEFL (minimum score 550 paper-based; 80 iBT). *Application deadline:* For fall admission, 12/1 for domestic and international students. Applications are processed on a rolling basis. Application fee: $30. Electronic applications accepted. *Expenses:* Tuition, state resident: part-time $403.51 per credit hour. Tuition, nonresident: part-time $1004.85 per credit hour. *Required fees:* $75.81 per credit hour. One-time fee: $20 part-time. Tuition and fees vary according to campus/location. *Financial support:* In 2014–15, 50 students received support, including 10 fellowships with full tuition reimbursements available (averaging $15,458 per year), 32 research assistantships with full tuition reimbursements available (averaging $13,127 per year), 8 teaching assistantships with full tuition reimbursements available (averaging $14,785 per year); Federal Work-Study, institutionally sponsored loans, scholarships/grants, tuition waivers (full and partial), and unspecified assistantships also available. Financial award application deadline: 12/1; financial award applicants required to submit FAFSA. *Faculty research:* Napoleon and the French Revolution, modern Europe, Latin America, U.S. intellectual and cultural history, modern Asia. *Unit head:* Dr. Edward Gray, Chair, 850-644-5888, Fax: 850-644-6402, E-mail: egray@fsu.edu. *Application contact:* Lisa VanMiddlesworth, Academic Program Assistant, 850-644-2610, E-mail: lvanmiddlesworth@fsu.edu.
Website: http://history.fsu.edu/

George Mason University, College of Humanities and Social Sciences, Department of History and Art History, Program in History, Fairfax, VA 22030. Offers history (MA); new media and information technology (PhD); public and applied history (PhD). *Faculty:* 45 full-time (18 women), 8 part-time/adjunct (4 women). *Students:* 66 full-time (32 women), 136 part-time (58 women); includes 19 minority (4 Black or African American, non-Hispanic/Latino; 3 Asian, non-Hispanic/Latino; 9 Hispanic/Latino; 3 Two or more races, non-Hispanic/Latino), 4 international. Average age 36. 145 applicants, 54% accepted, 42 enrolled. In 2014, 42 master's, 4 doctorates awarded. *Degree requirements:* For master's, comprehensive exam, translation language exam; for doctorate, comprehensive exam, thesis/dissertation. *Entrance requirements:* For master's, GRE (waived for students who received their undergraduate degree 10 or more years ago or hold another graduate degree), expanded goals statement; 2 letters of recommendation; resume; official transcript; for doctorate, GRE, expanded goals statement; 3 letters of recommendation; writing sample; official transcripts. Additional exam requirements/recommendations for international students: Required—TOEFL (minimum score 570 paper-based; 80 iBT), IELTS (minimum score 6.5), PTE. *Application deadline:* For fall admission, 3/15 priority date for domestic students; for spring admission, 11/1 priority date for domestic students. Application fee: $65 ($80 for international students). Electronic applications accepted. *Expenses:* Tuition, state resident: full-time $9794; part-time $408 per credit hour. Tuition, nonresident: full-time $26,978; part-time $1124 per credit hour. *Required fees:* $2820; $118 per credit hour. Tuition and fees vary according to course load and program. *Financial support:* In 2014–15, 31 students received support, including 2 fellowships with full tuition reimbursements available (averaging $7,151 per year), 16 research assistantships with full and partial tuition reimbursements available (averaging $17,210 per year), 14 teaching assistantships with full and partial tuition reimbursements available (averaging $14,330 per year); career-related internships or fieldwork, Federal Work-Study, scholarships/grants, unspecified assistantships, and health care benefits (for full-time research or teaching assistantship recipients) also available. Support available to part-time students. Financial award application deadline: 3/1; financial award applicants required to submit FAFSA. *Faculty research:* History and new media, American history (digital), building digital archives in the 1930's. *Unit head:* Randolph Scully, History Program Director, 703-993-1259, Fax: 703-993-1251, E-mail: rscully@gmu.edu. *Application contact:* Nicole Anne Roth, Graduate Program Coordinator, 703-993-1248, Fax: 703-993-1251, E-mail: nroth@gmu.edu.
Website: http://historyarthistory.gmu.edu/programs/la-ma-hist

Georgia College & State University, Graduate School, College of Arts and Sciences, Department of History, Geography and Philosophy, Milledgeville, GA 31061. Offers public history (MA); U. S., Europe and world (MA). Part-time and evening/weekend programs available. *Students:* 4 full-time (1 woman), 6 part-time (3 women); includes 2 minority (1 American Indian or Alaska Native, non-Hispanic/Latino; 1 Hispanic/Latino). Average age 32. 4 applicants, 100% accepted, 4 enrolled. In 2014, 3 master's awarded. *Degree requirements:* For master's, one foreign language, comprehensive exam (for some programs), thesis or alternative. *Entrance requirements:* For master's, GRE, 2 letters of reference, transcript, minimum GPA of 3.0, undergraduate degree in history or other major with substantial work in history, foreign language. Additional exam requirements/recommendations for international students: Recommended—TOEFL (minimum score 550 paper-based; 79 iBT). *Application deadline:* For fall admission, 4/15 for domestic and international students; for spring admission, 11/15 for domestic students, 9/1 for international students; for summer admission, 4/1 for domestic students. Application fee: $40. Electronic applications accepted. *Expenses: Tuition, area resident:* Part-time $283 per credit hour. Tuition, nonresident: part-time $1027 per credit hour. *Required fees:* $995 per semester. Full-time tuition and fees vary according to course load, degree level, campus/location and program. *Financial support:* In 2014–15, 6 research assistantships were awarded; unspecified assistantships also available. Support available to part-time students. Financial award applicants required to submit FAFSA. *Unit head:* Dr. Stephen Auerbach, Graduate Coordinator for MA in History, 478-445-8276, E-mail: stephen.auerbach@gcsu.edu. *Application contact:* Kate Marshall, Graduate Admissions Coordinator, 478-445-1184, Fax: 478-445-1336, E-mail: grad-admit@gcsu.edu.
Website: http://www.gcsu.edu/history/masters.htm

Georgia State University, College of Arts and Sciences, Department of History, Program in History, Atlanta, GA 30302-3083. Offers historic preservation (MA); history (PhD); public history (MA); world history (MA). Part-time and evening/weekend programs available. Terminal master's awarded for partial completion of doctoral program. *Degree requirements:* For master's, one foreign language, comprehensive exam, thesis optional, continuous enrollment; 6 hours of thesis credits; for doctorate, 2 foreign languages, comprehensive exam, thesis/dissertation, dissertation prospectus and prospectus defense; dissertation defense; residency; continuous enrollment; 6 hours of thesis credits. *Entrance requirements:* For master's, GRE, BA in history; statement of purpose; writing sample; three letters of recommendation; official transcripts; for doctorate, GRE, MA in history; master's thesis; statement of purpose; writing sample; three letters of recommendation; official transcripts; appropriate language skills. Additional exam requirements/recommendations for international students: Required—TOEFL (minimum score 550 paper-based; 80 iBT). *Application deadline:* For fall admission, 3/15 for domestic and international students; for spring admission, 10/15 for domestic and international students. Applications are processed on a rolling basis. Application fee: $50. Electronic applications accepted. *Expenses:* Tuition, state resident: full-time $6516; part-time $362 per credit hour. Tuition, nonresident: full-time $22,014; part-time $1223 per credit hour. *Required fees:* $2128 per semester. Tuition and fees vary according to course load and program. *Financial support:* Research assistantships with tuition reimbursements, teaching assistantships with tuition reimbursements, and scholarships/grants available. Financial award application deadline: 2/15. *Faculty research:* Nineteenth- and twentieth-century U.S. history, early modern European history, modern European history, world history, public history. *Unit head:* Dr. Michelle Brattain, Chair, 404-413-6352, Fax: 404-413-6384, E-mail: mbrattain@gsu.edu. *Application contact:* Dr. Joe Perry, Director of Graduate Studies, 404-413-6374, Fax: 404-413-6384, E-mail: jbperry@gsu.edu.
Website: http://www.gsu.edu/~wwwhis/

Indiana University of Pennsylvania, School of Graduate Studies and Research, College of Humanities and Social Sciences, Department of History, Indiana, PA 15705-1087. Offers history (MA); public history (MA). Part-time programs available. *Faculty:* 8 full-time (4 women). *Students:* 14 full-time (3 women), 3 part-time (1 woman). Average age 26. 18 applicants, 83% accepted, 5 enrolled. In 2014, 8 master's awarded. *Degree requirements:* For master's, thesis optional. *Entrance requirements:* For master's, GRE, 2 letters of recommendation. Additional exam requirements/recommendations for international students: Required—TOEFL (minimum score 540 paper-based). *Application deadline:* Applications are processed on a rolling basis. Application fee: $50. Electronic applications accepted. *Financial support:* In 2014–15, 1 fellowship with partial tuition reimbursement (averaging $1,000 per year), 5 research assistantships with full and partial tuition reimbursements (averaging $2,870 per year) were awarded; career-related internships or fieldwork, Federal Work-Study, scholarships/grants, and unspecified assistantships also available. Support available to part-time students. Financial award application deadline: 4/15; financial award applicants required to submit FAFSA. *Unit head:* Dr. R. Scott Moore, Chairperson, 724-357-2573, E-mail: rsmoore@iup.edu. *Application contact:* Dr. Jeanine Mazak-Kahne, Graduate Coordinator, 724-357-2436, E-mail: j.mkahne@iup.edu.
Website: http://www.iup.edu/history

Indiana University–Purdue University Indianapolis, School of Liberal Arts, Department of History, Indianapolis, IN 46202. Offers history (MA); public history (MA); MA/MLS. Part-time and evening/weekend programs available. *Faculty:* 14 full-time (6 women). *Students:* 12 full-time (6 women), 17 part-time (13 women); includes 2 minority (1 Black or African American, non-Hispanic/Latino; 1 Asian, non-Hispanic/Latino). Average age 33. 34 applicants, 32% accepted, 10 enrolled. In 2014, 15 master's awarded. *Degree requirements:* For master's, one foreign language, thesis. *Entrance requirements:* For master's, GRE General Test, minimum GPA of 3.0. *Application deadline:* For fall admission, 2/1 priority date for domestic and international students; for spring admission, 10/15 for domestic and international students. Application fee: $55 ($65 for international students). Electronic applications accepted. *Financial support:* In 2014–15, 19 students received support. Fellowships with full tuition reimbursements available, research assistantships with full tuition reimbursements available, teaching assistantships with full tuition reimbursements available, career-related internships or fieldwork, and health care benefits available. Financial award application deadline: 2/1. *Unit head:* Dr. Didier Gondola, Chair, 317-274-8160, Fax: 317-278-7800, E-mail: gondola@iupui.edu. *Application contact:* Amy Schramm, Office Coordinator, 317-274-5840, Fax: 317-278-7800, E-mail: ajschram@iupui.edu.
Website: http://liberalarts.iupui.edu/history/

La Salle University, School of Arts and Sciences, Program in History, Philadelphia, PA 19141-1199. Offers American history (Certificate); European history (Certificate); history (MA); history for educators (MA); public history (MA); teaching advanced placement history (Certificate); world history (Certificate). Part-time programs available. *Degree requirements:* For master's, thesis or comprehensive exam. *Entrance requirements:* For master's, GRE or MAT, 18 hours of undergraduate coursework in history or a related discipline with minimum GPA of 3.0; two letters of recommendation; brief personal statement (250 to 500 words); writing sample (preferably from an undergraduate research paper). Additional exam requirements/recommendations for international students: Required—TOEFL. Electronic applications accepted. Application fee is waived when completed online.

Lehigh University, College of Arts and Sciences, Department of History, Bethlehem, PA 18015. Offers Atlantic world (PhD); British history (PhD); history (MA); industrial and modern America (PhD); public history (MA). Part-time programs available. *Faculty:* 12 full-time (5 women). *Students:* 25 full-time (9 women), 23 part-time (7 women), 2 international. Average age 34. 28 applicants, 39% accepted, 7 enrolled. In 2014, 4 master's, 1 doctorate awarded. Terminal master's awarded for partial completion of doctoral program. *Degree requirements:* For master's, comprehensive exam (for some programs), comprehensive exam or thesis; for doctorate, comprehensive exam, thesis/dissertation. *Entrance requirements:* For master's, GRE General Test, recommendations, writing sample; for doctorate, GRE General Test, recommendations, writing samples. Additional exam requirements/recommendations for international students: Required—TOEFL. *Application deadline:* For fall admission, 4/15 for domestic and international students; for winter admission, 11/1 priority date for domestic students, 11/15 priority date for international students. Applications are processed on a rolling basis. Application fee: $75. Electronic applications accepted. *Expenses:* Expenses: $1,380 per credit hour. *Financial support:* In 2014–15, 2 fellowships with full tuition reimbursements (averaging $22,500 per year), 10 teaching assistantships with full and partial tuition reimbursements (averaging $19,700 per year) were awarded; research assistantships with full tuition reimbursements, institutionally sponsored loans, scholarships/grants, tuition waivers (full and partial), and unspecified assistantships also available. Support available to part-time students. Financial award application deadline: 1/15. *Faculty research:* Colonial America, modern America, history of technology, Atlantic world. *Total annual research expenditures:* $66,401. *Unit head:* Dr. John K. Smith, Chairman, 610-758-3360, Fax: 610-758-6554, E-mail: jks0@lehigh.edu. *Application contact:* Dr. Roger D. Simon, Graduate Coordinator, 610-758-3368, Fax: 610-758-6554, E-mail: rds2@lehigh.edu.
Website: http://history.cas2.lehigh.edu/

Loyola University Chicago, Graduate School, Department of History, Chicago, IL 60660. Offers history (MA, PhD); public history (MA). Part-time and evening/weekend programs available. *Faculty:* 32 full-time (12 women), 7 part-time/adjunct (2 women). *Students:* 59 full-time (31 women), 13 part-time (6 women); includes 12 minority (5 Black or African American, non-Hispanic/Latino; 7 Hispanic/Latino), 1 international. Average age 31. 129 applicants, 44% accepted, 24 enrolled. In 2014, 14 master's, 7 doctorates awarded. Terminal master's awarded for partial completion of doctoral program. *Degree requirements:* For master's, one foreign language, comprehensive exam, thesis or alternative, Master's Essay/Thesis (Optional); Portfolio for Public History Program (Required); for doctorate, 2 foreign languages, comprehensive exam, thesis/dissertation. *Entrance requirements:* For master's, GRE General Test, Research paper/Writing Sample; for doctorate, GRE General Test, Seminar Paper or Master's Thesis.

Additional exam requirements/recommendations for international students: Required—TOEFL (minimum score 550 paper-based), IELTS. *Application deadline:* For fall admission, 5/1 for domestic students; for spring admission, 10/1 for domestic students. Applications are processed on a rolling basis. Application fee: $50. Electronic applications accepted. Application fee is waived when completed online. *Expenses:* Expenses: Contact institution. *Financial support:* In 2014–15, 20 students received support, including 20 fellowships with full tuition reimbursements available (averaging $5,251 per year), 18 teaching assistantships with full tuition reimbursements available (averaging $17,722 per year); research assistantships with full tuition reimbursements available and Federal Work-Study also available. Financial award application deadline: 1/1; financial award applicants required to submit FAFSA. *Faculty research:* Medieval and Early Modern Europe, U.S. public history, U.S. urban history, gender history, Britain and Ireland, transnational history. *Unit head:* Dr. Robert O. Bucholz, Chair, 773-508-2232, Fax: 773-508-2153, E-mail: rbuchol@luc.edu. *Application contact:* Dr. Michelle Nickerson, Director, Graduate Programs, 773-508-2228, Fax: 773-508-2153, E-mail: mnickerson@luc.edu.
Website: http://www.luc.edu/history/

Middle Tennessee State University, College of Graduate Studies, College of Liberal Arts, Department of History, Program in Public History, Murfreesboro, TN 37132. Offers PhD. Part-time and evening/weekend programs available. Postbaccalaureate distance learning degree programs offered. *Faculty:* 37 full-time (19 women), 1 part-time/adjunct (0 women). *Students:* 9 full-time (6 women), 24 part-time (14 women); includes 6 minority (4 Black or African American, non-Hispanic/Latino; 2 Hispanic/Latino). *Degree requirements:* For doctorate, one foreign language, comprehensive exam, thesis/dissertation. *Entrance requirements:* For doctorate, GRE. Additional exam requirements/recommendations for international students: Required—TOEFL (minimum score 525 paper-based; 71 iBT) or IELTS (minimum score 6). *Application deadline:* For fall admission, 6/1 for domestic and international students. Applications are processed on a rolling basis. Application fee: $30. *Financial support:* In 2014–15, 23 students received support. Tuition waivers available. Support available to part-time students. Financial award application deadline: 4/1. *Unit head:* Dr. James Beeby, Chair, 615-898-2536, Fax: 615-898-5881, E-mail: james.beeby@mtsu.edu. *Application contact:* Dr. Michael D. Allen, Vice Provost for Research/Dean, 615-898-2840, Fax: 615-904-8020, E-mail: michael.allen@mtsu.edu.

New York University, Graduate School of Arts and Science, Department of History, New York, NY 10012-1019. Offers African diaspora (PhD); African history (PhD); archival management (Advanced Certificate); Atlantic history (PhD); French studies/history (PhD); Hebrew and Judaic studies/history (PhD); history (MA, PhD), including Europe (PhD), Latin America and the Caribbean (PhD), United States (PhD), women's history (MA); Middle Eastern history (MA); Middle Eastern studies/history (PhD); public history (Advanced Certificate); world history (MA); JD/MA; MA/Advanced Certificate. Part-time programs available. *Faculty:* 43 full-time (19 women). *Students:* 120 full-time (72 women), 43 part-time (29 women); includes 33 minority (15 Black or African American, non-Hispanic/Latino; 1 American Indian or Alaska Native, non-Hispanic/Latino; 4 Asian, non-Hispanic/Latino; 9 Hispanic/Latino; 4 Two or more races, non-Hispanic/Latino), 41 international. Average age 29. 401 applicants, 31% accepted, 38 enrolled. In 2014, 24 master's, 16 doctorates awarded. Terminal master's awarded for partial completion of doctoral program. *Degree requirements:* For master's, seminar paper; for doctorate, one foreign language, thesis/dissertation, oral and written exams; for Advanced Certificate, internship. *Entrance requirements:* For master's, GRE General Test, minimum GPA of 3.0, writing sample; for doctorate, GRE. Additional exam requirements/recommendations for international students: Required—TOEFL. *Application deadline:* For fall admission, 12/18 for domestic and international students. Application fee: $100. *Financial support:* Fellowships with tuition reimbursements, research assistantships, teaching assistantships with tuition reimbursements, career-related internships or fieldwork, Federal Work-Study, institutionally sponsored loans, scholarships/grants, health care benefits, and unspecified assistantships available. Financial award application deadline: 12/18; financial award applicants required to submit FAFSA. *Faculty research:* African, East Asian, medieval, early modern, and modern European history; U.S. history; African and African diaspora; Latin American history; Atlantic world. *Unit head:* Barbara Weinstein, Chair, 212-998-8600, Fax: 212-995-4017, E-mail: history.admissions@nyu.edu. *Application contact:* Stepfanos Geroulanos, Director of Graduate Studies, 212-998-8600, Fax: 212-995-4017, E-mail: history.admissions@nyu.edu.
Website: http://history.as.nyu.edu/

North Carolina State University, Graduate School, College of Humanities and Social Sciences, Department of History, Program in Public History, Raleigh, NC 27695. Offers MA. *Degree requirements:* For master's, thesis optional. *Entrance requirements:* For master's, GRE General Test. Electronic applications accepted.

Northeastern University, College of Social Sciences and Humanities, Boston, MA 02115. Offers criminology and criminal justice (MSCJ); criminology and justice policy (PhD); economics (MA, PhD); English (MA, PhD); law and public policy (MS, PhD); political science (MA, PhD); public administration (MPA); public history (MA); security and resilience studies (MS); sociology (MA, PhD); urban and regional policy (MS); world history (MA, PhD). *Degree requirements:* For doctorate, variable foreign language requirement, comprehensive exam, thesis/dissertation. *Entrance requirements:* For master's and doctorate, GRE. Additional exam requirements/recommendations for international students: Required—TOEFL, IELTS. Electronic applications accepted.

Northern Kentucky University, Office of Graduate Programs, College of Arts and Sciences, Program in Public History, Highland Heights, KY 41099. Offers MA. Part-time and evening/weekend programs available. *Faculty:* 5 full-time (1 woman), 1 part-time/adjunct (0 women). *Students:* 11 full-time (7 women), 18 part-time (9 women); includes 3 minority (1 Black or African American, non-Hispanic/Latino; 1 Asian, non-Hispanic/Latino; 1 Hispanic/Latino). Average age 39. In 2014, 13 master's awarded. *Degree requirements:* For master's, comprehensive exam, final capstone project. *Entrance requirements:* Additional exam requirements/recommendations for international students: Required—TOEFL (minimum score 550 paper-based; 79 iBT); Recommended—IELTS (minimum score 6.5). *Application deadline:* For fall admission, 8/1 priority date for domestic students, 6/1 priority date for international students; for spring admission, 12/1 priority date for domestic students, 10/1 priority date for international students; for summer admission, 5/1 priority date for domestic students, 4/1 priority date for international students. Application fee: $40. Electronic applications accepted. *Expenses: Tuition, area resident:* Part-time $518 per credit hour. Tuition, state resident: part-time $630 per credit hour. Tuition, nonresident: part-time $797 per credit hour. *Required fees:* $192 per semester. Tuition and fees vary according to course load, degree level, campus/location, program and reciprocity agreements. *Financial support:* In 2014–15, 11 students received support. Applicants required to submit FAFSA. *Faculty research:* Local history. *Unit head:* Dr. Brian Hackett, Director, Public History Program, 859-572-6072, E-mail: hackettb1@nku.edu. *Application contact:* Alison Swanson, Graduate Admissions Coordinator, 859-572-6971, E-mail: swansona1@nku.edu.
Website: http://hisgeo.nku.edu/programs/public/mapublic.php

Rutgers, The State University of New Jersey, Camden, Graduate School of Arts and Sciences, Program in American and Public History, Camden, NJ 08102. Offers MA. Part-time and evening/weekend programs available. *Degree requirements:* For master's, comprehensive exam, thesis optional, 30 credits. *Entrance requirements:* For master's, GRE General Test (for full-time applicants), 3 letters of recommendation; history or related undergraduate degree (preferred). Additional exam requirements/recommendations for international students: Required—TOEFL, IELTS. Electronic applications accepted. *Faculty research:* Women's history, military history, Afro-American history, urban history, history of technology.

St. John's University, St. John's College of Liberal Arts and Sciences, Department of History, Queens, NY 11439. Offers history (MA); modern world history (DA); public history (MA). Part-time and evening/weekend programs available. *Students:* 23 full-time (10 women), 49 part-time (20 women); includes 18 minority (6 Black or African American, non-Hispanic/Latino; 3 Asian, non-Hispanic/Latino; 8 Hispanic/Latino; 1 Two or more races, non-Hispanic/Latino), 10 international. Average age 33. 30 applicants, 90% accepted, 13 enrolled. In 2014, 16 master's, 3 doctorates awarded. *Degree requirements:* For master's, one foreign language, comprehensive exam, thesis optional, colloquia ; for doctorate, one foreign language, comprehensive exam, thesis/dissertation, internship, practicum. *Entrance requirements:* For master's, minimum GPA of 3.0, 24 undergraduate credits in history or related field, 2 letters of recommendation, personal statement; for doctorate, minimum GPA of 3.5 in history, 3.0 overall; writing sample, 3 letters of recommendation, personal essay, bachelor's degree, at least 24 undergraduate credits in history or related field. Additional exam requirements/recommendations for international students: Required—TOEFL (minimum score 600 paper-based; 100 iBT), IELTS (minimum score 7). *Application deadline:* For fall admission, 5/1 priority date for domestic and international students; for spring admission, 11/1 priority date for domestic and international students. Applications are processed on a rolling basis. Application fee: $70. Electronic applications accepted. *Expenses: Tuition:* Full-time $20,610; part-time $1145 per credit. *Required fees:* $170 per semester. *Financial support:* Fellowships, research assistantships, and scholarships/grants available. Support available to part-time students. Financial award application deadline: 3/1; financial award applicants required to submit FAFSA. *Faculty research:* World history, gender, transnationalism, history of technology, cultural history, social history. *Unit head:* Dr. Elaine Carey, Chair, 718-990-6228, E-mail: careye@stjohns.edu. *Application contact:* Robert Medrano, Director of Graduate Admission, 718-990-1601, Fax: 718-990-5686, E-mail: gradhelp@stjohns.edu.

Shippensburg University of Pennsylvania, School of Graduate Studies, College of Arts and Sciences, Department of Sociology and Anthropology, Shippensburg, PA 17257-2299. Offers organizational development and leadership (MS), including business, communications, environmental management, higher education structure and policy, historical administration, individual and organizational development, management information systems, public organizations, social structures and organizations. Part-time and evening/weekend programs available. *Faculty:* 4 full-time (all women). *Students:* 11 full-time (4 women), 42 part-time (26 women); includes 11 minority (7 Black or African American, non-Hispanic/Latino; 1 Asian, non-Hispanic/Latino; 2 Hispanic/Latino; 1 Two or more races, non-Hispanic/Latino), 2 international. Average age 30. 53 applicants, 60% accepted, 17 enrolled. In 2014, 21 master's awarded. *Degree requirements:* For master's, capstone experience including internship. *Entrance requirements:* For master's, interview (if GPA less than 2.75), resume, personal goals statement. Additional exam requirements/recommendations for international students: Required—TOEFL (minimum score 580 paper-based); Recommended—IELTS (minimum score 6). *Application deadline:* For fall admission, 4/30 for international students; for spring admission, 9/30 for international students. Applications are processed on a rolling basis. Application fee: $45. Electronic applications accepted. *Expenses: Tuition, area resident:* Part-time $454 per credit. Tuition, state resident: part-time $454 per credit. Tuition, nonresident: part-time $681 per credit. *Required fees:* $133 per credit. *Financial support:* In 2014–15, 15 research assistantships with full tuition reimbursements (averaging $5,000 per year) were awarded; career-related internships or fieldwork, scholarships/grants, unspecified assistantships, and resident hall director and student payroll positions also available. Support available to part-time students. Financial award applicants required to submit FAFSA. *Unit head:* Dr. Barbara Denison, Program Coordinator, 717-477-1735, Fax: 717-477-4011, E-mail: bjdeni@ship.edu. *Application contact:* Jeremy R. Goshorn, Assistant Dean of Graduate Admissions, 717-477-1231, Fax: 717-477-4016, E-mail: jrgoshorn@ship.edu.
Website: http://www.ship.edu/odl/

Sonoma State University, School of Social Sciences, Program in Cultural Resources Management, Rohnert Park, CA 94928. Offers MA. Part-time programs available. *Degree requirements:* For master's, thesis. *Entrance requirements:* For master's, minimum GPA of 3.0. Additional exam requirements/recommendations for international students: Required—TOEFL (minimum score 500 paper-based).

Southeast Missouri State University, School of Graduate Studies, Department of History, Cape Girardeau, MO 63701-4799. Offers heritage education (Certificate); historic preservation (Certificate); history (MA); public history (MA). Part-time and evening/weekend programs available. *Faculty:* 11 full-time (4 women). *Students:* 9 full-time (8 women), 12 part-time (3 women); includes 1 minority (Hispanic/Latino). Average age 30. 16 applicants, 81% accepted, 12 enrolled. In 2014, 11 master's awarded. *Degree requirements:* For master's, comprehensive exam (for some programs), thesis optional, thesis or exam, plus capstone project/paper (for history); thesis or internship, plus project in applied history and comprehensive exams (for public history). *Entrance requirements:* For master's and Certificate, minimum undergraduate GPA of 2.75; 2 letters of recommendation; writing sample; letter of intent; 24 semester hours of undergraduate history credit. Additional exam requirements/recommendations for international students: Required—TOEFL (minimum score 550 paper-based; 79 iBT), IELTS (minimum score 6), PTE (minimum score 53). *Application deadline:* For fall admission, 8/1 for domestic students, 6/1 for international students; for spring admission, 11/21 for domestic students, 10/1 for international students; for summer admission, 5/15 for domestic students. Applications are processed on a rolling basis. Application fee: $30 ($40 for international students). Electronic applications accepted. *Expenses:* Tuition, state resident: full-time $5256; part-time $292 per credit hour. Tuition, nonresident: full-time $9288; part-time $516 per credit hour. *Financial support:* In 2014–15, 8 students received support, including 1 research assistantship with full tuition reimbursement available (averaging $7,907 per year), 4 teaching assistantships with full tuition reimbursements available (averaging $7,907 per year); career-related internships or fieldwork, Federal Work-Study, scholarships/grants, traineeships, tuition waivers (full), and unspecified assistantships also available. Financial award application deadline: 6/30; financial award applicants required to submit FAFSA. *Faculty research:* Medieval Europe; modern Europe including Britain, Germany, France, Russia, and Spain; Colonial and nineteenth-century America; twentieth-century America and American West; public history and historic preservation; Latin America. *Unit head:* Dr. Wayne Bowen, Chairperson/Professor of History, 573-651-2179, Fax: 573-651-5114, E-mail: wbowen@semo.edu. *Application contact:* Dr. Erika Hosselkus, Graduate Coordinator/Assistant Professor of History, 573-651-2763, Fax: 573-651-5114, E-mail: ehosselkus@semo.edu. Website: http://www.semo.edu/history/

Public History

University at Albany, State University of New York, College of Arts and Sciences, Department of History, Albany, NY 12222-0001. Offers history (MA, PhD); public history (Certificate). Part-time programs available. *Degree requirements:* For master's, variable foreign language requirement, exam, research paper or thesis; for doctorate, thesis/dissertation. *Entrance requirements:* For master's, minimum GPA of 3.0; for doctorate, GRE General Test, minimum GPA of 3.0. Additional exam requirements/recommendations for international students: Required—TOEFL (minimum score 550 paper-based). Electronic applications accepted. *Faculty research:* American history (all phases); public policy; European history (Medieval to modern); Asian, African, and Latin American history.

University of Arkansas at Little Rock, Graduate School, College of Arts, Humanities, and Social Science, Department of History, Little Rock, AR 72204-1099. Offers public history (MA). Part-time programs available. *Degree requirements:* For master's, oral exam. *Entrance requirements:* For master's, GRE General Test, minimum GPA of 3.25 in history, 2.7 overall; 15 hours of undergraduate history; two letters of recommendation. *Application deadline:* Applications are processed on a rolling basis. *Expenses:* Tuition, state resident: full-time $6000; part-time $300 per credit hour. Tuition, nonresident: full-time $13,800; part-time $690 per credit hour. *Required fees:* $1126; $603 per term. One-time fee: $40 full-time. *Financial support:* Research assistantships with tuition reimbursements, teaching assistantships with tuition reimbursements, career-related internships or fieldwork, Federal Work-Study, institutionally sponsored loans, and unspecified assistantships available. Support available to part-time students. *Faculty research:* Historic preservation and restoration, museum studies, archives. *Unit head:* John A. Kirk, Chair, 501-569-3296, Fax: 501-569-8775. *Application contact:* Dr. Charles Romney, Graduate Coordinator, 501-569-8154, E-mail: cwromney@ualr.edu.
Website: http://ualr.edu/history/

University of California, Santa Barbara, Graduate Division, College of Letters and Sciences, Division of Humanities and Fine Arts, Department of History, Santa Barbara, CA 93106-9410. Offers European medieval studies (PhD); global studies (PhD); public historical studies (PhD); technology and society (PhD); women's studies (PhD); MA/PhD. *Degree requirements:* For doctorate, variable foreign language requirement, comprehensive exam, thesis/dissertation. *Entrance requirements:* For doctorate, GRE. Additional exam requirements/recommendations for international students: Required—TOEFL (minimum score 550 paper-based; 80 iBT), IELTS (minimum score 7). Electronic applications accepted. *Faculty research:* Europe, United States, Latin America, Africa, Middle East, East Asia.

University of Colorado Denver, College of Liberal Arts and Sciences, Department of History, Denver, CO 80217. Offers European history (MA); global history (MA); public history (MA); U.S. history (MA). Part-time and evening/weekend programs available. *Faculty:* 14 full-time (6 women), 1 part-time/adjunct (0 women). *Students:* 33 full-time (20 women), 20 part-time (11 women); includes 12 minority (1 Black or African American, non-Hispanic/Latino; 1 American Indian or Alaska Native, non-Hispanic/Latino; 1 Asian, non-Hispanic/Latino; 8 Hispanic/Latino; 1 Two or more races, non-Hispanic/Latino). Average age 34. 27 applicants, 59% accepted, 9 enrolled. In 2014, 9 master's awarded. *Degree requirements:* For master's, comprehensive exam, thesis optional, 36 semester hours (12 courses). *Entrance requirements:* For master's, GRE General Test, writing sample, minimum undergraduate GPA of 3.25, three letters of recommendation, statement of purpose addressing any weaknesses in academic record. Additional exam requirements/recommendations for international students: Required—TOEFL (minimum score 537 paper-based; 75 iBT); Recommended—IELTS (minimum score 6.5). *Application deadline:* For fall admission, 1/20 for domestic and international students; for spring admission, 10/1 for domestic and international students. Application fee: $50 ($75 for international students). Electronic applications accepted. *Financial support:* In 2014–15, 8 students received support. Fellowships, research assistantships, teaching assistantships, Federal Work-Study, institutionally sponsored loans, scholarships/grants, and traineeships available. Financial award application deadline: 4/1; financial award applicants required to submit FAFSA. *Faculty research:* Uses of pre-modern Islamic heritage in modern India; relationship between liberal understandings of democracy, crime, and police discretion; relationships between gender, class, health, and welfare in nineteenth and early twentieth century England; U.S. business cultures and their influences on marketing and personnel practices; intersection of business and political ideologies; social and environmental history of the Rocky Mountain West. *Unit head:* Dr. Pamela Laird, Associate Professor and Chair, 303-556-4497, E-mail: pamela.laird@ucdenver.edu. *Application contact:* Tabitha Fitzpatrick, Program Assistant, 303-315-1776, E-mail: tabitha.fitzpatrick@ucdenver.edu.
Website: http://www.ucdenver.edu/academics/colleges/CLAS/Departments/history/Programs/Masters/Pages/MasterofArts.aspx

University of Illinois at Springfield, Graduate Programs, College of Liberal Arts and Sciences, Program in History, Springfield, IL 62703-5407. Offers MA. Part-time and evening/weekend programs available. *Faculty:* 4 full-time (2 women), 1 part-time/adjunct (0 women). *Students:* 13 full-time (7 women), 21 part-time (13 women); includes 1 minority (Black or African American, non-Hispanic/Latino), 1 international. Average age 33. 26 applicants, 62% accepted, 11 enrolled. In 2014, 9 master's awarded. *Degree requirements:* For master's, thesis, internship, or historiography. *Entrance requirements:* For master's, BA in history or related field, minimum undergraduate GPA of 2.5, writing sample. Additional exam requirements/recommendations for international students: Required—TOEFL (minimum score 500 paper-based; 61 iBT). *Application deadline:* Applications are processed on a rolling basis. Application fee: $60 ($75 for international students). Electronic applications accepted. *Expenses:* Tuition, state resident: full-time $7662; part-time $319.25 per credit hour. Tuition, nonresident: full-time $15,966; part-time $665.25 per credit hour. *Financial support:* In 2014–15, fellowships with full tuition reimbursements (averaging $9,900 per year), research assistantships with full tuition reimbursements (averaging $9,600 per year), teaching assistantships with full tuition reimbursements (averaging $9,600 per year) were awarded; career-related internships or fieldwork, Federal Work-Study, scholarships/grants, health care benefits, and unspecified assistantships also available. Support available to part-time students. Financial award application deadline: 11/15; financial award applicants required to submit FAFSA. *Unit head:* Dr. Peter Shapinsky, Program Administrator, 217-206-6595, Fax: 217-206-6217, E-mail: pshap2@uis.edu. *Application contact:* Dr. Lynn Pardie, Office of Graduate Studies, 800-252-8533, Fax: 217-206-7623, E-mail: lpard1@uis.edu.
Website: http://www.uis.edu/history/curriculum/ma/

University of Louisville, Graduate School, College of Arts and Sciences, Department of History, Louisville, KY 40292-0001. Offers history (MA); public history (Certificate). Part-time and evening/weekend programs available. *Students:* 19 full-time (8 women), 7 part-time (2 women); includes 2 minority (both Hispanic/Latino). Average age 27. 23 applicants, 78% accepted, 10 enrolled. In 2014, 4 master's, 1 other advanced degree awarded. *Degree requirements:* For master's, variable foreign language requirement, comprehensive exam (for some programs), thesis (for some programs). *Entrance requirements:* For master's, GRE General Test. Additional exam requirements/recommendations for international students: Required—TOEFL. *Application deadline:* For fall admission, 5/15 for domestic students, 5/1 priority date for international students; for spring admission, 12/1 for domestic students, 11/1 priority date for international students; for summer admission, 4/1 priority date for international students. Applications are processed on a rolling basis. Application fee: $60. Electronic applications accepted. *Expenses:* Tuition, state resident: full-time $11,326; part-time $630 per credit hour. Tuition, nonresident: full-time $23,568; part-time $1311 per credit hour. *Required fees:* $196. Tuition and fees vary according to program and reciprocity agreements. *Financial support:* Teaching assistantships available. Financial award applicants required to submit FAFSA. *Faculty research:* United States, British Empire, twentieth century women's history, Latin America, African diaspora. *Unit head:* Dr. Tracy Elaine K'Meyer, Chair, 502-852-6817, Fax: 502-852-0770, E-mail: tracyk@louisville.edu. *Application contact:* Libby Leggett, Director, Graduate Admissions, 502-852-3101, Fax: 502-852-6536, E-mail: gradadm@louisville.edu.
Website: http://louisville.edu/history/

University of Maryland, Baltimore County, The Graduate School, College of Arts, Humanities and Social Sciences, Department of Public Policy, Program in Public Policy, Baltimore, MD 21250. Offers economics (PhD); educational policy (MPP); evaluation and analytical methods (MPP); health policy (MPP); policy history (PhD); public management (MPP, PhD); urban policy (MPP, PhD). Part-time and evening/weekend programs available. *Faculty:* 9 full-time (3 women), 1 part-time/adjunct (0 women). *Students:* 50 full-time (29 women), 68 part-time (39 women); includes 28 minority (15 Black or African American, non-Hispanic/Latino; 8 Asian, non-Hispanic/Latino; 3 Hispanic/Latino; 1 Native Hawaiian or other Pacific Islander, non-Hispanic/Latino; 1 Two or more races, non-Hispanic/Latino), 9 international. Average age 35. 71 applicants, 58% accepted, 25 enrolled. In 2014, 23 master's, 13 doctorates awarded. Terminal master's awarded for partial completion of doctoral program. *Degree requirements:* For master's, thesis optional, public analysis paper; for doctorate, comprehensive exam, thesis/dissertation, comprehensive and field qualifying exams. *Entrance requirements:* For master's and doctorate, GRE General Test, 3 academic letters of reference, transcripts, resume, research paper. Additional exam requirements/recommendations for international students: Required—TOEFL (minimum score 550 paper-based; 80 iBT). *Application deadline:* For fall admission, 1/15 priority date for domestic students, 1/1 priority date for international students; for spring admission, 11/1 priority date for domestic students, 5/1 priority date for international students. Applications are processed on a rolling basis. Application fee: $50. Electronic applications accepted. *Expenses:* Expenses: $679 per credit resident; $1,114 non-resident. *Financial support:* In 2014–15, 26 students received support, including 1 fellowship with full tuition reimbursement available (averaging $12,000 per year), 25 research assistantships with full tuition reimbursements available (averaging $20,000 per year); career-related internships or fieldwork, Federal Work-Study, scholarships/grants, health care benefits, and unspecified assistantships also available. Support available to part-time students. Financial award application deadline: 1/15; financial award applicants required to submit FAFSA. *Faculty research:* Health policy, education policy, urban policy, public management, evaluation and analytical methods. *Unit head:* Dr. Donald F. Norris, Director, 410-455-1455, E-mail: norris@umbc.edu. *Application contact:* Sally F. Helms, Administrator of Academic Affairs, 410-455-3202, Fax: 410-455-1172, E-mail: gradpubpol@umbc.edu.
Website: http://www.umbc.edu/pubpol

University of Northern Iowa, Graduate College, College of Social and Behavioral Sciences, Department of History, Cedar Falls, IA 50614. Offers history (MA); public history (MA). Part-time programs available. *Students:* 18 full-time (10 women), 15 part-time (7 women); includes 4 minority (1 Black or African American, non-Hispanic/Latino; 1 Asian, non-Hispanic/Latino; 2 Two or more races, non-Hispanic/Latino). 24 applicants, 67% accepted, 10 enrolled. In 2014, 11 master's awarded. *Degree requirements:* For master's, comprehensive exam (for some programs), thesis or alternative. *Entrance requirements:* For master's, minimum GPA of 3.2. Additional exam requirements/recommendations for international students: Required—TOEFL (minimum score 500 paper-based; 61 iBT). *Application deadline:* For fall admission, 8/1 priority date for domestic students. Applications are processed on a rolling basis. Application fee: $50 ($70 for international students). Electronic applications accepted. *Expenses:* Tuition, state resident: full-time $7912; part-time $880 per credit. Tuition, nonresident: full-time $17,906; part-time $880 per credit. *Required fees:* $1101; $325.50 per credit. $465.63 per semester. Tuition and fees vary according to course load and program. *Financial support:* Career-related internships or fieldwork, Federal Work-Study, scholarships/grants, and tuition waivers (full and partial) available. Support available to part-time students. Financial award application deadline: 2/1. *Unit head:* Dr. Robert Martin, Department Head, 319-273-2097, Fax: 319-273-5846, E-mail: robert.martin@uni.edu. *Application contact:* Laurie S. Russell, Record Analyst, 319-273-2623, Fax: 319-273-2885, E-mail: laurie.russell@uni.edu.
Website: http://www.uni.edu/history/

University of South Carolina, The Graduate School, College of Arts and Sciences, Department of History, Program in Public History, Columbia, SC 29208. Offers archive management (MA); historic preservation (MA); museum administration (MA); museum management (Certificate); MLIS/MA. *Degree requirements:* For master's, one foreign language, thesis, internship. *Entrance requirements:* For master's, GRE General Test, writing sample. Additional exam requirements/recommendations for international students: Required—TOEFL. Electronic applications accepted. *Faculty research:* Museum studies, historic preservation, archives administration.

The University of Texas at Austin, Graduate School, College of Liberal Arts, Department of Anthropology, Austin, TX 78712-1111. Offers archaeology (MA, PhD); cultural forms (MA, PhD); linguistic anthropology (MA, PhD); physical anthropology (MA, PhD); social anthropology (MA, PhD). Part-time programs available. Terminal master's awarded for partial completion of doctoral program. *Degree requirements:* For master's, thesis; for doctorate, one foreign language, thesis/dissertation. *Entrance requirements:* For master's and doctorate, GRE General Test. Additional exam requirements/recommendations for international students: Required—TOEFL. Electronic applications accepted.

University of West Florida, College of Arts and Sciences: Arts, Department of History, Pensacola, FL 32514-5750. Offers history (MA); military history (MA); public history (MA). Part-time and evening/weekend programs available. *Degree requirements:* For master's, thesis or alternative. *Entrance requirements:* For master's, GRE (minimum score: verbal 500, writing 3.5) or MAT (minimum score 415), minimum GPA of 3.0, minimum 15 hours of upper-level history courses; official transcripts; letter of intent; writing sample (undergraduate research paper preferred). Additional exam requirements/recommendations for international students: Required—TOEFL (minimum score 550 paper-based).

University of West Georgia, College of Arts and Humanities, Department of History, Carrollton, GA 30118. Offers history (MA); museum studies (Certificate); public history (Certificate). Part-time and evening/weekend programs available. *Faculty:* 15 full-time (6 women). *Students:* 24 full-time (12 women), 15 part-time (9 women); includes 6 minority (5 Black or African American, non-Hispanic/Latino; 1 Hispanic/Latino). Average age 35. 15 applicants, 87% accepted, 7 enrolled. In 2014, 12 master's, 5 other advanced degrees awarded. *Degree requirements:* For master's, one foreign language, comprehensive exam, thesis or alternative. *Entrance requirements:* For master's, GRE General Test (minimum score of 151 on verbal, 4.0 on analytical writing), undergraduate degree in history or related social studies, minimum GPA of 3.0; for Certificate, GRE

General Test (minimum score 151 verbal, 4.0 writing), MA from another institution or enrolled in MA at UWG. Additional exam requirements/recommendations for international students: Required—TOEFL (minimum score 523 paper-based; 69 iBT); Recommended—IELTS (minimum score 6). *Application deadline:* For fall admission, 8/1 for domestic students, 6/1 for international students; for spring admission, 11/15 for domestic students, 10/15 for international students. Applications are processed on a rolling basis. Application fee: $40. Electronic applications accepted. *Financial support:* In 2014–15, 1 student received support, including 21 research assistantships with full tuition reimbursements available (averaging $6,000 per year), 2 teaching assistantships (averaging $5,000 per year); career-related internships or fieldwork, scholarships/grants, and unspecified assistantships also available. Support available to part-time students. Financial award application deadline: 4/1; financial award applicants required to submit FAFSA. *Faculty research:* Public history, United States, Europe, Atlantic, world war and society. *Unit head:* Dr. Howard Steven Goodson, Chair, 678-839-6042, E-mail: hgoodson@westga.edu. *Application contact:* Dr. Nadya Williams, Graduate Coordinator, 678-839-5453, E-mail: nwilliam@westga.edu.
Website: http://westga.edu/~history/

UNIVERSITY OF MASSACHUSETTS BOSTON

Office of Graduate Studies
College of Liberal Arts
M.A. Program in History

UMASS BOSTON

Programs of Study

Students earning a Master of Arts (M.A.) in history from the University of Massachusetts (UMass) Boston have the option of choosing from the following three tracks: archives, history, and public history. The history department also offers an online M.A. program.

Archives: Training in historical methodology provides a crucial foundation for practicing archivists in the twenty-first century. Thus, archives students earn an M.A. in history with a concentration in archives, rather than an M.A. in library and informational science with a concentration in archives. Today, in an age in which information is created in various forms at exponential rates, archivists must learn to preserve and provide long-term access to materials and also learn to create, present, and archive history online. As technologies rapidly evolve, archivists must continually learn new technological skills throughout their career. Acquiring and mastering research and critical-thinking skills in history, rather than learning only technical skills, provides archivists with a vast and deep foundational knowledge and subject area expertise. This imbues them with an invaluable and transferable skill: the ability to assess and recognize the intrinsic research value to collections. Archives students also undertake semester-long internships at professional archives, working under the supervision of professionals in the field and gaining practical experience.

History: The history track offers a rigorous set of individually selected courses and supervised research and writing. Both demanding and flexible, the history track is designed for students who intend to pursue a Ph.D., secondary school teachers who wish to improve their knowledge of the field, and students who seek to test their capacity for graduate work. The program also accommodates teachers with a demanding schedule who wish to pursue their M.A. part time. All graduate courses consist of small seminars of no more than 15 students, these seminars provide students with individualized faculty attention and support. All students in the history track complete a master's thesis as a final project.

Public History: Public historians study the way we remember and interpret the past. They use historical methodologies to preserve, collect, present, and interpret history with and for public audiences. Public historians work with historic landscapes, sites, parks, and monuments; in museums and historic buildings; on film and the worldwide web; and with community groups and organizations, families, and institutions. They also study public awareness and consciousness of the past and how various actors, including public intellectuals and public interest groups, seek to raise historical consciousness and nurture historical thinking. Because of its urban mission, its close ties with public history institutions such as the John F. Kennedy Presidential Library and Museum, the Edward M. Kennedy Institute for the United States Senate, and the Massachusetts State Archives, and its faculty's interest in civic engagement, UMass Boston offers an ideal institutional setting for those graduate students who wish to study public history. Public history students must meet all the requirements of the traditional history degree, and also take courses in public history literature, theory, and methods. Public history students also undertake semester-long internships at historical organizations, gaining practical experience under the supervision of professionals in the field. The UMass Boston public history track also offers a solid foundation for Master of Arts (M.A.) students preparing for Ph.D. programs in history.

Online M.A.: As part of its M.A. program, the history department also offers an exclusively online M.A. degree. One of the few online History M.A. programs in the country, this program is both academically rigorous and flexible enough for students who are not able to enroll in a traditional face-to-face M.A. program because of work or personal obligations. All online courses are taught by full-time UMass Boston History faculty members. The program includes a wide array of required and elective courses, along with a supervised research and writing project. The requirements and expectations for the online M.A. program are identical to those of the regular M.A. program. Only the history track is available for online M.A. students. The public history and archives tracks are not currently available to online M.A. students.

Research Facilities

Students have access to neighboring institutions on Columbia Point: the John F. Kennedy Library and the Massachusetts State Archives and Commonwealth Museum. They also have access to nationally renowned repositories of historical materials in the Boston area, such as the Boston Public Library, the Boston Athenaeum, the Massachusetts Historical Society, the Schlesinger Library, and various other accessible research institutions.

Financial Aid

Financial support, which includes tuition waivers, scholarships, grants, or campus-funded graduate assistantships, is available on a competitive basis to a limited number of graduate students.

Cost of Study

Fall 2015 tuition and fees for students taking 12 credits and up is currently $8,058 per semester for state residents and $15,558 per semester for nonresidents. Students from the New England states entering the archives or public history tracks may be eligible for reduced tuition through the New England Regional Tuition Break Program.

Living and Housing Costs

While the University of Massachusetts Boston does not have on-campus housing facilities, the Office of Student Housing (OSH) is committed to assisting prospective students navigate the local housing market. For more information on local housing, please visit OSH at http://www.umb.edu/life_on_campus/housing.

The University

The University of Massachusetts Boston is nationally recognized as a model of excellence for urban public universities. The scenic waterfront campus, with easy access to downtown Boston, is located next to the John F. Kennedy Library and Presidential Museum and the Edward M. Kennedy Institute for the United States Senate. Part of the UMass system, UMass Boston combines a small-college experience with the vast resources of a major research university.

Ninety-three percent of full-time faculty members hold the highest degree in their fields. UMass Boston's academic excellence is reflected by a growing student body of more than 16,000 undergraduate and graduate students. The university's ten colleges

University of Massachusetts Boston

and schools offer more than 110 graduate programs. UMass Boston's diverse student body provides a global context for student learning, and its location in a major U.S. city provides connections to employers in industries such as finance, health care, technology, service, and education, offering students opportunities to gain valuable in-school experience via internships, clinicals, and other career-related placements.

Applying

Applicants for graduate study at UMass Boston must hold a bachelor's degree from a U.S. institution of recognized standing, or an international equivalent. The history department only accepts applicants for the fall semester. The application deadline for students interested in the graduate history program is January, 2016 for the 2016–17 academic year.

Correspondence and Information

For more information, students should contact:

Department Administrator: Maureen Dwyer
History Program
College of Liberal Arts
University of Massachusetts Boston
100 Morrissey Boulevard
Boston, Massachusetts 02125-3393
Phone: 617-287-6860
E-mail: Maureen.Dwyer@umb.edu
Website: http://www.umb.edu/academics/cla/history/grad

THE FACULTY

Paul Bookbinder, Associate Professor; Ph.D., Brandeis.
Jane Becker, Graduate Internship Coordinator, Ph.D., Boston University.
Maryann E. Brink, Lecturer; Ph.D., Brown.
Vincent J. Cannato, Graduate Program Director, Ph.D., Columbia.
Jonathan M. Chu, Professor; Ph.D., Washington (Seattle).
Spencer Di Scala, Professor; Ph.D., Columbia.
Timothy Hacsi, Department Chair and Associate Professor; Ph.D., Pennsylvania.
Sana Haroon, Assistant Professor; Ph.D., Yale.
David Hunt, Professor; Ph.D., Harvard.
Benjamin Johnson, Assistant Professor; Ph.D., Chicago.
Elizabeth McCahill, Associate Professor; Ph.D., Princeton.
Gary M. Miller, Lecturer; Ph.D., Yale.
Ruth A. Miller, Professor; Ph.D., Princeton.
Marilyn Morgan, Archives Director, Ph.D., Maine.
Monica Pelayo, Assistant Professor; Ph.D., USC.
Conevery B. Valencius, Associate Professor; Ph.D., Harvard.
Olivia Weisser, Assistant Professor; Ph.D., Princeton.
Julie P. Winch, Professor; Ph.D., Bryn Mawr.
Roberta L. Wollons, Professor, Ph.D., Chicago.
Weili Ye, Professor; Ph.D., Yale.

Section 8
Humanities

This section contains a directory of institutions offering graduate work in humanities, followed by an in-depth entry submitted by an institution that chose to prepare a detailed program description. Additional information about programs listed in the directory but not augmented by an in-depth entry may be obtained by writing directly to the dean of a graduate school or chair of a department at the address given in the directory.

For programs offering related work, see also in this book *Area and Cultural Studies, Geography, Interdisciplinary Studies, Philosophy, Political Science and International Affairs, Religious Studies,* and *Sociology, Anthropology, and Archaeology.*

CONTENTS

Program Directories

Displays and Close-Ups

Humanities

American Public University System, AMU/APU Graduate Programs, Charles Town, WV 25414. Offers accounting (MBA, MS); criminal justice (MA), including business administration, emergency management and disaster management, general (MA, MS); educational leadership (M Ed); emergency and disaster management (MA); entrepreneurship (MBA); environmental policy and management (MS), including environmental planning, environmental sustainability, fish and wildlife management, general (MA, MS), global environmental management; finance (MBA); general (MBA); global business management (MBA); history (MA), including American history, ancient and classical history, European history, global history, public history; homeland security (MA), including business administration, counter-terrorism studies, criminal justice, cyber, emergency management and public health, intelligence studies, transportation security; homeland security resource allocation (MBA); humanities (MA); information technology (MS), including digital forensics, enterprise software development, information assurance and security, IT project management; information technology management (MBA); intelligence studies (MA), including criminal intelligence, cyber, general (MA, MS), homeland security, intelligence analysis, intelligence collection, intelligence management, intelligence operations, terrorism studies; international relations and conflict resolution (MA), including comparative and security issues, conflict resolution, international and transnational security issues, peacekeeping; legal studies (MA); management (MA), including defense management, general (MA, MS), human resource management, organizational leadership, public administration; marketing (MBA); military history (MA), including American military history, American Revolution, civil war, war since 1945, World War II; military studies (MA), including joint warfare, strategic leadership; national security studies (MA), including general (MA, MS), homeland security, regional security studies, security and intelligence analysis, terrorism studies; nonprofit management (MBA); political science (MA), including American politics and government, comparative government and development, general (MA, MS), international relations, public policy; psychology (MA); public administration (MPA), including disaster management, environmental policy, health policy, human resources, national security, organizational management, security management; public health (MPH); reverse logistics management (MA); school counseling (M Ed); security management (MA); space studies (MS), including aerospace science, general (MA, MS), planetary science; sports and health sciences (MS); teaching (M Ed), including curriculum and instruction for elementary teachers, elementary reading, English language learners, instructional leadership, online learning, special education; transportation and logistics management (MA), including general (MA, MS), maritime engineering management, reverse logistics management. Programs offered via distance learning only. Part-time and evening/weekend programs available. Postbaccalaureate distance learning degree programs offered (no on-campus study). *Faculty:* 426 full-time (236 women), 1,864 part-time/adjunct (880 women). *Students:* 475 full-time (215 women), 10,067 part-time (4,085 women); includes 3,462 minority (1,863 Black or African American, non-Hispanic/Latino; 74 American Indian or Alaska Native, non-Hispanic/Latino; 273 Asian, non-Hispanic/Latino; 831 Hispanic/Latino; 78 Native Hawaiian or other Pacific Islander, non-Hispanic/Latino; 343 Two or more races, non-Hispanic/Latino), 131 international. Average age 36. In 2014, 3,740 master's awarded. *Degree requirements:* For master's, comprehensive exam or practicum. *Entrance requirements:* For master's, official transcript showing earned bachelor's degree from institution accredited by recognized accrediting body. Additional exam requirements/recommendations for international students: Required—TOEFL (minimum score 550 paper-based), IELTS (minimum score 6.5). *Application deadline:* Applications are processed on a rolling basis. Application fee: $0. Electronic applications accepted. *Financial support:* Applicants required to submit FAFSA. *Faculty research:* Military history, criminal justice, management performance, national security. *Unit head:* Dr. Karan Powell, Executive Vice President and Provost, 877-468-6268, Fax: 304-724-3780. *Application contact:* Terry Grant, Vice President of Enrollment Management, 877-468-6268, Fax: 304-724-3780, E-mail: info@apus.edu.
Website: http://www.apus.edu

Antioch University New England, Graduate School, Department of Education, Integrated Learning Program, Keene, NH 03431-3552. Offers early childhood education (M Ed); elementary education (M Ed), including arts and humanities, science and environmental education; special education (M Ed). *Degree requirements:* For master's, internship. *Entrance requirements:* For master's, previous course work or work experience in education. Additional exam requirements/recommendations for international students: Required—TOEFL (minimum score 550 paper-based). Electronic applications accepted. *Expenses:* Contact institution. *Faculty research:* Problem-based learning, place-based education, mathematics education, democratic classrooms, art education.

Arcadia University, Graduate Studies, Program in Humanities, Glenside, PA 19038-3295. Offers fine arts, theater, and music (MAH); history, philosophy, and religion (MAH); literature and language (MAH). Part-time programs available. *Degree requirements:* For master's, thesis or alternative. *Expenses:* Contact institution.

Brigham Young University, Graduate Studies, College of Humanities, Department of Humanities, Classics, and Comparative Literature, Provo, UT 84602. Offers comparative studies (MA). *Faculty:* 24 full-time (5 women). *Students:* 14 full-time (10 women), 8 part-time (5 women). Average age 26. 14 applicants, 50% accepted, 7 enrolled. In 2014, 6 master's awarded. *Degree requirements:* For master's, 2 foreign languages, thesis. *Entrance requirements:* For master's, GRE, minimum GPA of 3.0 in last 60 hours. Additional exam requirements/recommendations for international students: Required—TOEFL (minimum score 580 paper-based; 85 iBT), IELTS (minimum score 7). *Application deadline:* For fall admission, 3/1 for domestic and international students. Application fee: $50. Electronic applications accepted. *Expenses: Tuition:* Full-time $6310; part-time $371 per credit hour. Tuition and fees vary according to program and student's religious affiliation. *Financial support:* In 2014–15, 17 students received support, including 31 fellowships with partial tuition reimbursements available (averaging $1,604 per year), 4 research assistantships (averaging $1,500 per year), 29 teaching assistantships (averaging $2,503 per year); career-related internships or fieldwork, institutionally sponsored loans, scholarships/grants, tuition waivers (full and partial), and student instructorships also available. Support available to part-time students. *Unit head:* Dr. Carl Sederholm, Coordinator, 801-422-9078, Fax: 801-422-0305, E-mail: carl_sederholm@byu.edu. *Application contact:* Carolyn Hone, Graduate Secretary for Humanities and Comparative Literature, 801-422-4430, Fax: 801-422-0305, E-mail: carolyn_hone@byu.edu.

California Institute of Integral Studies, School of Consciousness and Transformation, San Francisco, CA 94103. Offers anthropology and social change (MA, PhD); creative inquiry/interdisciplinary arts (MFA); East-West psychology (MA, PhD); philosophy and religion (MA, PhD), including Asian and comparative studies, ecology, spirituality, and religion, philosophy, cosmology, and consciousness, women's spirituality; transformative leadership (MA); transformative studies (PhD); writing and consciousness (MFA). Part-time and evening/weekend programs available. Postbaccalaureate distance learning degree programs offered (no on-campus study). *Students:* 385 full-time (256 women), 102 part-time (71 women); includes 124 minority (31 Black or African American, non-Hispanic/Latino; 3 American Indian or Alaska Native, non-Hispanic/Latino; 19 Asian, non-Hispanic/Latino; 39 Hispanic/Latino; 1 Native Hawaiian or other Pacific Islander, non-Hispanic/Latino; 31 Two or more races, non-Hispanic/Latino), 53 international. Average age 43. 196 applicants, 92% accepted, 125 enrolled. In 2014, 75 master's, 41 doctorates awarded. Terminal master's awarded for partial completion of doctoral program. *Degree requirements:* For master's, thesis optional; for doctorate, comprehensive exam, thesis/dissertation, 1 foreign language (for Asian comparative studies). *Entrance requirements:* For master's, minimum GPA of 3.0, letters of recommendation, writing sample; for doctorate, master's degree, minimum GPA of 3.0, letters of recommendation, writing sample. Additional exam requirements/recommendations for international students: Required—TOEFL. *Application deadline:* For fall admission, 2/1 priority date for domestic and international students; for spring admission, 10/15 priority date for domestic and international students. Applications are processed on a rolling basis. Application fee: $65. Electronic applications accepted. *Expenses: Tuition:* Full-time $18,270; part-time $1015 per credit. *Required fees:* $85 per semester hour. *Financial support:* In 2014–15, 445 students received support, including 5 research assistantships (averaging $800 per year), 28 teaching assistantships (averaging $825 per year); career-related internships or fieldwork, Federal Work-Study, and scholarships/grants also available. Support available to part-time students. Financial award application deadline: 4/15; financial award applicants required to submit FAFSA. *Faculty research:* Ecology and sustainability, philosophy and religion, East-West psychology, integrative health, social and cultural anthropology, transformative leadership. *Application contact:* David Townes, Senior Admissions Counselor, 415-575-6152, Fax: 415-575-1268, E-mail: admissions@ciis.edu.
Website: http://www.ciis.edu/

California State University, Dominguez Hills, College of Arts and Humanities, Program in Arts and Humanities, Carson, CA 90747-0001. Offers MA. Part-time and evening/weekend programs available. *Faculty:* 2 full-time (both women). *Students:* 2 full-time (1 woman), 19 part-time (11 women); includes 14 minority (6 Black or African American, non-Hispanic/Latino; 7 Hispanic/Latino; 1 Two or more races, non-Hispanic/Latino). Average age 36. 10 applicants, 80% accepted, 5 enrolled. In 2014, 3 master's awarded. *Degree requirements:* For master's, thesis or alternative. *Entrance requirements:* For master's, minimum GPA of 3.0. Additional exam requirements/recommendations for international students: Required—TOEFL (minimum score 550 paper-based; 80 iBT). *Application deadline:* For fall admission, 6/1 for domestic students. Applications are processed on a rolling basis. Application fee: $55. *Expenses:* Tuition, state resident: full-time $6738; part-time $3960 per year. Tuition, nonresident: full-time $13,434; part-time $8370 per year. *Required fees:* $623; $623 per year. *Financial support:* Institutionally sponsored loans available. Support available to part-time students. Financial award application deadline: 8/1. *Faculty research:* African-American music, postmodernism, cities of antiquity, Faust, African studies. *Unit head:* Dr. Lorna Fitzsimmons, Coordinator, 310-243-3036, E-mail: lfitzsimmons@csudh.edu. *Application contact:* Brandy McLelland, Director of Student Information Services/Registrar, 310-243-3645, E-mail: bmclelland@csudh.edu.
Website: http://www4.csudh.edu/humanities/

California State University, Dominguez Hills, College of Extended and International Education, Humanities Program, Carson, CA 90747-0001. Offers MA. Part-time and evening/weekend programs available. Postbaccalaureate distance learning degree programs offered (no on-campus study). *Faculty:* 3 full-time (0 women), 30 part-time/adjunct (14 women). *Students:* 184 part-time (99 women); includes 31 minority (10 Black or African American, non-Hispanic/Latino; 3 Asian, non-Hispanic/Latino; 12 Hispanic/Latino; 6 Two or more races, non-Hispanic/Latino), 3 international. Average age 45. 41 applicants, 100% accepted, 21 enrolled. In 2014, 55 master's awarded. *Degree requirements:* For master's, thesis, advancement to candidacy essays. *Entrance requirements:* For master's, minimum GPA of 3.0 in last 60 undergraduate units. Additional exam requirements/recommendations for international students: Required—TOEFL. *Application deadline:* For fall admission, 6/1 for domestic and international students; for winter admission, 10/1 for domestic students, 11/1 for international students; for spring admission, 3/1 for domestic and international students. Application fee: $55. Electronic applications accepted. *Expenses:* Expenses: Contact institution. *Financial support:* Applicants required to submit FAFSA. *Faculty research:* Nineteenth- and twentieth-century literature, Arab history, Greek philosophy, ancient history, East Asian history, Soviet cultural history, Native American history and culture, feminist studies. *Unit head:* Dr. Emily Magruder, Coordinator, 310-243-3191, Fax: 310-516-4399, E-mail: emagruder@csudh.edu. *Application contact:* Nicole Ballard, Program Advisor, 310-243-3743, Fax: 310-516-4399, E-mail: nballard@csudh.edu.
Website: http://www.csudh.edu/hux/default.html

Central Michigan University, College of Graduate Studies, College of Humanities and Social and Behavioral Sciences, Program in Humanities, Mount Pleasant, MI 48859. Offers humanities (MA), including contemporary issues in the humanities: race, class, and gender, images and ideas of self, Native American issues in modern culture, popular culture studies, the rise of industrial society. Part-time and evening/weekend programs available. *Degree requirements:* For master's, thesis or alternative. Electronic applications accepted. *Faculty research:* Rise of industrial society; images and ideas of self; contemporary issues of race, class, and gender; popular culture; Native American issues in modern culture.

Claremont Graduate University, Graduate Programs, School of Arts and Humanities, Claremont, CA 91711-6160. Offers M Phil, MA, MFA, DCM, DMA, PhD, Certificate, MA/PhD, MBA/MA, MBA/PhD. Part-time programs available. *Faculty:* 29 full-time (13 women), 5 part-time/adjunct (0 women). *Students:* 400 full-time (206 women), 128 part-time (66 women); includes 137 minority (30 Black or African American, non-Hispanic/Latino; 4 American Indian or Alaska Native, non-Hispanic/Latino; 40 Asian, non-Hispanic/Latino; 47 Hispanic/Latino; 2 Native Hawaiian or other Pacific Islander, non-Hispanic/Latino; 14 Two or more races, non-Hispanic/Latino), 55 international. Average age 36. In 2014, 78 master's, 33 doctorates, 3 other advanced degrees awarded. *Degree requirements:* For doctorate, 2 foreign languages, comprehensive exam, thesis/dissertation, oral and written qualifying exams, oral defense of dissertation, recitals. *Entrance requirements:* For master's and doctorate, GRE General Test. Additional exam requirements/recommendations for international students: Required—TOEFL (minimum score 550 paper-based; 80 iBT). *Application deadline:* For fall admission, 2/1 priority date for domestic and international students. Applications are processed on a rolling basis. Application fee: $80. Electronic applications accepted. *Expenses: Tuition:* Full-time $41,784; part-time $1741 per credit. *Required fees:* $600; $300 per semester.

Financial support: Fellowships, research assistantships, teaching assistantships, Federal Work-Study, institutionally sponsored loans, and scholarships/grants available. Support available to part-time students. Financial award application deadline: 2/15; financial award applicants required to submit FAFSA. *Unit head:* Tammi Schneider, Dean/Professor, 909-607-3217, E-mail: tammi.schneider@cgu.edu. *Application contact:* Erma Cross, Admissions and Alumni Coordinator, 909-607-9843, Fax: 909-607-9587, E-mail: erminia.cross@cgu.edu.
Website: http://www.cgu.edu/pages/128.asp

Clemson University, Graduate School, Program in International Family and Community Studies, Clemson, SC 29634. Offers PhD. *Faculty:* 5 full-time (3 women), 5 part-time/adjunct (3 women). *Students:* 12 full-time (11 women), 22 part-time (18 women); includes 5 minority (1 Black or African American, non-Hispanic/Latino; 3 Asian, non-Hispanic/Latino; 1 Hispanic/Latino), 15 international. Average age 36. In 2014, 1 doctorate awarded. *Degree requirements:* For doctorate, thesis/dissertation. *Entrance requirements:* For doctorate, GRE General Test. Additional exam requirements/recommendations for international students: Required—TOEFL. *Application deadline:* Applications are processed on a rolling basis. Application fee: $70 ($80 for international students). Electronic applications accepted. *Expenses:* Expenses: Contact institution. *Financial support:* In 2014–15, 9 students received support, including 9 research assistantships with partial tuition reimbursements available (averaging $21,444 per year); fellowships with full and partial tuition reimbursements available, teaching assistantships, career-related internships or fieldwork, institutionally sponsored loans, scholarships/grants, health care benefits, and unspecified assistantships also available. Support available to part-time students. *Total annual research expenditures:* $728,285. *Unit head:* Dr. Mark Small, Director, 864-656-6286, E-mail: msmall@clemson.edu. *Application contact:* Information Contact, 864-656-3195, E-mail: gradapp@clemson.edu.
Website: http://www.grad.clemson.edu/programs/Family-Community-Studies/

The Colorado College, Education Department, Experienced Teacher Program, Colorado Springs, CO 80903-3294. Offers arts and humanities (MAT); integrated natural sciences (MAT); liberal arts (MAT); Southwest studies (MAT). Programs offered during summer only. Part-time programs available. *Degree requirements:* For master's, thesis, oral exam, 50-page paper. *Expenses:* Contact institution.

Concordia University, School of Graduate Studies, Faculty of Arts and Science, Program in Humanities, Montréal, QC H3G 1M8, Canada. Offers PhD. *Degree requirements:* For doctorate, one foreign language, comprehensive exam, thesis/dissertation.

Dominican University of California, School of Arts, Humanities and Social Sciences, Humanities Program, San Rafael, CA 94901-2298. Offers applied music (MA); art history (MA); creative writing (MA); history (MA); literature (MA); philosophy (MA); political theory (MA); religion (MA); women and gender studies (MA). Part-time programs available. *Faculty:* 11 full-time (5 women), 5 part-time/adjunct (2 women). *Students:* 2 full-time (1 woman), 25 part-time (16 women); includes 7 minority (1 Black or African American, non-Hispanic/Latino; 1 American Indian or Alaska Native, non-Hispanic/Latino; 3 Hispanic/Latino; 2 Two or more races, non-Hispanic/Latino). Average age 46. 12 applicants, 83% accepted, 7 enrolled. *Degree requirements:* For master's, thesis or alternative. *Entrance requirements:* For master's, minimum GPA of 3.0, interview. Additional exam requirements/recommendations for international students: Required—TOEFL (minimum score 550 paper-based; 80 iBT), IELTS (minimum score 6.5). *Application deadline:* For fall admission, 5/15 priority date for domestic and international students; for spring admission, 11/15 priority date for domestic and international students. Applications are processed on a rolling basis. Electronic applications accepted. Application fee is waived when completed online. *Expenses:* Expenses: $935 per unit. *Financial support:* Scholarships/grants available. Support available to part-time students. Financial award application deadline: 3/2; financial award applicants required to submit FAFSA. *Unit head:* Dr. Laura Stivers, Acting Dean, 415-458-3734, E-mail: laura.stivers@dominican.edu. *Application contact:* Ryan Purtill, Director, 415-458-3748, Fax: 415-485-3214, E-mail: ryan.purtill@dominican.edu.
Website: http://www.dominican.edu/academics/ahss/graduate-program/index_html

Drew University, Caspersen School of Graduate Studies, Program in Medical Humanities, Madison, NJ 07940-1493. Offers MMH, DMH, CMH. Programs conducted jointly with Saint Barnabas Medical Center. Part-time and evening/weekend programs available. *Degree requirements:* For master's, thesis; for doctorate, thesis/dissertation. *Entrance requirements:* For master's and doctorate, transcripts, writing sample, personal statement, recommendations. Additional exam requirements/recommendations for international students: Required—TOEFL (minimum score 585 paper-based; 95 iBT), TWE (minimum score 4). *Expenses:* Contact institution. *Faculty research:* Biomedical ethics, medical narrative, history of medicine, medicine and the arts.

Duke University, Graduate School, Program in Humanities, Durham, NC 27708. Offers AM, JD/AM. Part-time programs available. *Entrance requirements:* For master's, GRE General Test. Additional exam requirements/recommendations for international students: Required—TOEFL (minimum score 577 paper-based; 90 iBT) or IELTS (minimum score 7). Electronic applications accepted. *Expenses: Tuition:* Full-time $45,760; part-time $2765 per credit. *Required fees:* $978. Full-time tuition and fees vary according to program.

Georgetown University, Graduate School of Arts and Sciences, School of Continuing Studies, Washington, DC 20057. Offers American studies (MALS); Catholic studies (MALS); classical civilizations (MALS); emergency and disaster management (MPS); ethics and the professions (MALS); hospitality management (MPS); human resources management (MPS); humanities (MALS); individualized study (MALS); international affairs (MALS); Islam and Muslim-Christian relations (MALS); journalism (MPS); liberal studies (DLS); literature and society (MALS); medieval and early modern European studies (MALS); public relations and corporate communications (MPS); real estate (MPS); religious studies (MALS); social and public policy (MALS); sports industry management (MPS); systems engineering management (MPS); technology management (MPS); the theory and practice of American democracy (MALS); urban and regional planning (MPS); visual culture (MALS). MPS in systems engineering management offered jointly with Stevens Institute of Technology. *Entrance requirements:* Additional exam requirements/recommendations for international students: Required—TOEFL.

Harrison Middleton University, Graduate Program, Tempe, AZ 85282. Offers education (MA, Ed D); humanities (MA); imaginative literature (MA); interdisciplinary studies (DA); jurisprudence (MA); natural science (MA); philosophy and religion (MA); social science (MA). Part-time and evening/weekend programs available. Postbaccalaureate distance learning degree programs offered (no on-campus study). *Degree requirements:* For master's and doctorate, capstone project. *Entrance requirements:* For master's, interview; for doctorate, 2 academic letters of reference, interview, essay. Additional exam requirements/recommendations for international students: Required—TOEFL (minimum score 550 paper-based; 80 iBT). Electronic applications accepted. *Faculty research:* Japanese animation, educational leadership, war art, John Muir's wilderness.

Hofstra University, School of Education, Programs in Teacher Education, Hempstead, NY 11549. Offers bilingual education (MA), including biology (MA, MS Ed), geology; business education (MS Ed); early childhood and childhood education (MS Ed), including French; early childhood education (MA); education technology (Advanced Certificate); elementary education (MA), including math. science, technology (STEM); English education (MS Ed); fine arts education (MS Ed), including biology (MA, MS Ed); foreign language and TESOL (MS Ed); learning and teaching (Ed D), including applied linguistics, art education, arts and humanities, early childhood education, English education, human development, math education, math, science, and technology, multicultural education, physical education, science education, social studies education, special education; mathematics education (MA, MS Ed); secondary education (Advanced Certificate); social studies education (MA, MS Ed). Part-time and evening/weekend programs available. Postbaccalaureate distance learning degree programs offered (minimal on-campus study). *Students:* 141 full-time (111 women), 119 part-time (84 women); includes 58 minority (13 Black or African American, non-Hispanic/Latino; 14 Asian, non-Hispanic/Latino; 28 Hispanic/Latino; 1 Native Hawaiian or other Pacific Islander, non-Hispanic/Latino; 2 Two or more races, non-Hispanic/Latino), 18 international. Average age 30. 301 applicants, 87% accepted, 112 enrolled. In 2014, 133 master's, 5 doctorates, 28 other advanced degrees awarded. *Degree requirements:* For master's, comprehensive exam, thesis (for some programs), exit project, student teaching, fieldwork, electronic portfolio, curriculum project, minimum GPA of 3.0; for doctorate, thesis/dissertation; for Advanced Certificate, 3 foreign languages, comprehensive exam (for some programs), thesis project. *Entrance requirements:* For master's, 2 letters of recommendation, portfolio, teacher certification (MA), interview, essay; for doctorate, GMAT, GRE, LSAT, or MAT; for Advanced Certificate, 2 letters of recommendation, essay, interview and/or portfolio, teaching certificate. Additional exam requirements/recommendations for international students: Required—TOEFL (minimum score 550 paper-based; 80 iBT). *Application deadline:* Applications are processed on a rolling basis. Application fee: $70 ($75 for international students). Electronic applications accepted. *Expenses: Tuition:* Full-time $20,610; part-time $1145 per credit hour. *Required fees:* $970; $165 per term. Tuition and fees vary according to program. *Financial support:* In 2014–15, 153 students received support, including 60 fellowships with full and partial tuition reimbursements available (averaging $5,084 per year), 4 research assistantships with full and partial tuition reimbursements available (averaging $7,095 per year); Federal Work-Study, institutionally sponsored loans, scholarships/grants, health care benefits, and tuition waivers (full and partial) also available. Support available to part-time students. Financial award applicants required to submit FAFSA. *Faculty research:* Appropriate content in secondary school disciplines, lesson development across content, interdisciplinary curriculum, multicultural education. *Unit head:* Dr. Eustace Thompson, Chairperson, 516-463-5749, Fax: 516-463-6275, E-mail: edaegt@hofstra.edu. *Application contact:* Sunil Samuel, Assistant Vice President of Admissions, 516-463-4723, Fax: 516-463-4664, E-mail: graduateadmission@hofstra.edu.
Website: http://www.hofstra.edu/education/

Hollins University, Graduate Programs, Program in Liberal Studies, Roanoke, VA 24020. Offers humanities (MALS); interdisciplinary studies (MALS); leadership (MALS); liberal studies (CAS); social science (MALS); visual and performing arts (MALS). Part-time and evening/weekend programs available. *Students:* 3 full-time (all women), 37 part-time (32 women); includes 6 minority (4 Black or African American, non-Hispanic/Latino; 1 Hispanic/Latino; 1 Two or more races, non-Hispanic/Latino). Average age 44. 13 applicants, 100% accepted, 9 enrolled. In 2014, 15 master's awarded. *Degree requirements:* For master's, thesis. *Entrance requirements:* For master's, letters of recommendation, interview. Additional exam requirements/recommendations for international students: Required—TOEFL (minimum score 550 paper-based; 79 iBT). *Application deadline:* For fall admission, 7/1 priority date for domestic and international students; for spring admission, 12/10 priority date for domestic and international students. Applications are processed on a rolling basis. Application fee: $40. Electronic applications accepted. *Financial support:* In 2014–15, 7 students received support, including 7 fellowships (averaging $1,000 per year); scholarships/grants also available. Support available to part-time students. Financial award application deadline: 7/15; financial award applicants required to submit FAFSA. *Faculty research:* Diversity, gender and women's studies, political science, leadership. *Unit head:* Dr. Joe Leedom, Director, 540-362-6326, Fax: 540-362-6288, E-mail: jleedom@hollins.edu. *Application contact:* Cathy S. Koon, Manager of Graduate Services, 540-362-6326, Fax: 540-362-6288, E-mail: ckoon@hollins.edu.
Website: http://www.hollins.edu/

Hood College, Graduate School, Program in Humanities, Frederick, MD 21701-8575. Offers MA. Part-time and evening/weekend programs available. *Degree requirements:* For master's, capstone/research project. *Entrance requirements:* For master's, minimum GPA of 2.75. Additional exam requirements/recommendations for international students: Required—TOEFL (minimum score 575 paper-based; 89 iBT), IELTS (minimum score 6.5). Electronic applications accepted. Application fee is waived when completed online.

Illinois Institute of Technology, Graduate College, Lewis College of Human Sciences, Department of Humanities, Chicago, IL 60616. Offers information architecture (MS); technical communication (PhD); technical communication and information design (MS). Part-time programs available. *Faculty:* 17 full-time (10 women), 22 part-time/adjunct (14 women). *Students:* 11 full-time (6 women), 5 part-time (0 women); includes 5 minority (2 Black or African American, non-Hispanic/Latino; 1 Hispanic/Latino; 1 Native Hawaiian or other Pacific Islander, non-Hispanic/Latino; 1 Two or more races, non-Hispanic/Latino), 2 international. Average age 36. 29 applicants, 24% accepted, 5 enrolled. In 2014, 4 master's, 1 doctorate awarded. *Degree requirements:* For master's, comprehensive exam, thesis or alternative; for doctorate, comprehensive exam, thesis/dissertation. *Entrance requirements:* For master's, GRE General Test (minimum score 144 Quantitative, 153 Verbal, and 4.0 Analytical Writing), minimum undergraduate GPA of 3.0; 2 letters of recommendation from faculty or supervisors, professional statement discussing academic goals; for doctorate, GRE General Test (minimum score 144 Quantitative, 153 Verbal, and 4.0 Analytical Writing), Applicants must have completed a bachelor's or master's degree in a field that, in combination with the 27-credit hour technical core, would provide a solid basis for advanced academic work leading to original research in the field. 3 letters of recommendation from faculty or supervisors, professional statement discussing academic goals. Additional exam requirements/recommendations for international students: Required—TOEFL (minimum score 95 iBT); Recommended—IELTS (minimum score 7). *Application deadline:* For fall admission, 5/1 for domestic and international students; for spring admission, 10/15 for domestic and international students. Applications are processed on a rolling basis. Application fee: $50. Electronic applications accepted. *Expenses: Tuition:* Full-time $22,500; part-time $1250 per credit hour. *Required fees:* $30 per course. $260 per semester. One-time fee: $235. Tuition and fees vary according to course load and program. *Financial support:* Fellowships with partial tuition reimbursements, research assistantships with partial tuition reimbursements, teaching assistantships with partial tuition reimbursements, career-related internships or fieldwork, Federal Work-Study, institutionally sponsored loans, scholarships/grants, health care benefits, tuition waivers (partial), and unspecified assistantships available. Support available to part-time students. Financial award applicants required to submit FAFSA. *Faculty research:*

Humanities

Linguistics, punishment theory, political communication, gender and technology, philosophical and ethical issues in neuroscience. *Unit head:* Maureen Flanagan, Professor and Chair, 312-567-3563, Fax: 312-567-5187, E-mail: maureen.flanagan@iit.edu. *Application contact:* Rishab Malhotra, Director, Graduate Admission, 866-472-3448, Fax: 312-567-3138, E-mail: inquiry.grad@iit.edu.
Website: http://www.iit.edu/csl/hum/

Instituto Tecnologico de Santo Domingo, Graduate School, Area of Humanities and Social Sciences, Santo Domingo, Dominican Republic. Offers accounting (Certificate); adult education (Certificate); applied linguistics (MA); economics (MA); education (M Ed); educational psychology (MA, Certificate); gender and development (MA, Certificate); humanistic studies (MA); international marketing management (Certificate); international relations in the Caribbean basin (Certificate); intervention systems in family therapy (MA); linguistic and literary communication (Certificate); pedagogical support (MA); social science education (M Ed); sustainable human development (MA); terminal illness and death psychology (Certificate); youth and adult education (M Ed).

Instituto Tecnológico y de Estudios Superiores de Monterrey, Campus Central de Veracruz, Graduate Programs, Córdoba, Mexico. Offers administration (MA); administration of information technologies (MTI); computer sciences (MCC); education (MEE); educational institution administration (MAD); educational technology (MTE); electronic commerce (MCE); finance (MAF); humanistic studies (MEH); international business for Latin America (MNL); marketing (MMT); science (MCP). Part-time and evening/weekend programs available. Postbaccalaureate distance learning degree programs offered (minimal on-campus study). *Degree requirements:* For master's, thesis (for some programs). *Entrance requirements:* For master's, PAEP College Board. Electronic applications accepted.

Instituto Tecnológico y de Estudios Superiores de Monterrey, Campus Ciudad de México, Virtual University Division, Ciudad de Mexico, Mexico. Offers administration of information technologies (MA); computer sciences (MA); education (MA, PhD); educational technology (MA); environmental engineering (MA); environmental systems (MA); humanistic studies (MA); industrial engineering (MA); international business for Latin America (MA); quality systems (MA); quality systems and productivity (MA). Part-time and evening/weekend programs available. Postbaccalaureate distance learning degree programs offered (minimal on-campus study). *Entrance requirements:* For master's and doctorate, Instituto entrance exam. Additional exam requirements/recommendations for international students: Required—TOEFL.

Instituto Tecnológico y de Estudios Superiores de Monterrey, Campus Ciudad Juárez, Program in Humanistic Studies, Ciudad Juárez, Mexico. Offers MEH.

Instituto Tecnológico y de Estudios Superiores de Monterrey, Campus Estado de México, Professional and Graduate Division, Estado de Mexico, Mexico. Offers administration of information technologies (MITA); architecture (M Arch); business administration (GMBA, MBA); computer sciences (MCS, PhD); education (M Ed); educational institution administration (MAD); educational technology and innovation (PhD); electronic commerce (MEC); environmental systems (MS); finance (MAF); humanistic studies (MHS); information sciences and knowledge management (MISKM); information systems (MS); manufacturing systems (MS); marketing (MEM); quality systems and productivity (MS); science and materials engineering (PhD); telecommunications management (MTM). Part-time programs available. Postbaccalaureate distance learning degree programs offered (minimal on-campus study). *Degree requirements:* For master's, one foreign language, thesis (for some programs); for doctorate, one foreign language, thesis/dissertation. *Entrance requirements:* For master's, E-PAEP 500, interview; for doctorate, E-PAEP 500, research proposal. Additional exam requirements/recommendations for international students: Required—TOEFL (minimum score 550 paper-based). *Faculty research:* Surface treatments by plasmas, mechanical properties, robotics, graphical computing, mechatronics security protocols.

Instituto Tecnológico y de Estudios Superiores de Monterrey, Campus Irapuato, Graduate Programs, Irapuato, Mexico. Offers administration (MBA); administration of information technology (MAIT); administration of telecommunications (MAT); architecture (M Arch); computer science (MCS); education (M Ed); educational administration (MEA); educational innovation and technology (DEIT); educational technology (MET); electronic commerce (MBA); environmental administration and planning (MEAP); environmental systems (MES); finances (MBA); humanistic studies (MHS); international management for Latin American executives (MIMLAE); library and information science (MLIS); manufacturing quality management (MMQM); marketing research (MBA).

John Carroll University, Graduate School, Program in Humanities, University Heights, OH 44118-4581. Offers MA. Part-time and evening/weekend programs available. *Degree requirements:* For master's, thesis optional, comprehensive research essay. *Entrance requirements:* For master's, minimum GPA of 2.75, interview. Electronic applications accepted. *Faculty research:* Modern French history, modern American Catholic history.

Laurentian University, School of Graduate Studies and Research, Programme in Humanities: Interpretation and Values, Sudbury, ON P3E 2C6, Canada. Offers MA. Part-time programs available. *Faculty research:* Modern Canadian literature; aboriginal languages and cultures; relation between ethics, religion, and the arts; narrative conventions; Renaissance drama and Reformation literature, Biblical and philosophical hermeneutics.

Loyola University Chicago, Graduate School, Program in Digital Humanities, Chicago, IL 60660. Offers MA. Part-time programs available. *Students:* 3 full-time (2 women), 5 part-time (4 women); includes 2 minority (1 Black or African American, non-Hispanic/Latino; 1 Hispanic/Latino). Average age 38. 13 applicants, 92% accepted, 4 enrolled. In 2014, 5 master's awarded. *Entrance requirements:* For master's, GRE General Test, BS or BA, transcripts, 2 letters of recommendation, letter of intent. Application fee is waived when completed online. *Expenses: Tuition:* Full-time $17,370; part-time $965 per credit. *Required fees:* $138 per semester. *Unit head:* Dr. Samuel Attoh, Dean, 773-508-3459, Fax: 773-508-2460, E-mail: sattoh@luc.edu. *Application contact:* Ron Martin, Assistant Director of Enrollment Management, 312-915-8950, Fax: 312-915-8905, E-mail: gradapp@luc.edu.

Marshall University, Academic Affairs Division, College of Liberal Arts, Program in Humanities, Huntington, WV 25755. Offers MA, Certificate. Part-time and evening/weekend programs available. *Students:* 4 full-time (3 women), 5 part-time (3 women); includes 2 minority (1 Asian, non-Hispanic/Latino; 1 Two or more races, non-Hispanic/Latino). Average age 39. In 2014, 2 master's awarded. *Degree requirements:* For master's, thesis, comprehensive assessment. *Entrance requirements:* For master's, GRE General Test, MAT, bachelor's degree in humanities, minimum undergraduate GPA of 3.0. Application fee: $40. *Financial support:* Applicants required to submit FAFSA. *Unit head:* Dr. Luke Eric Lassiter, Chairperson, 304-746-1923, E-mail: lassiter@marshall.edu. *Application contact:* Information Contact, 304-746-1900, Fax: 304-746-1902, E-mail: services@marshall.edu.

Memorial University of Newfoundland, School of Graduate Studies, Interdisciplinary Programs in Humanities, St. John's, NL A1C 5S7, Canada. Offers M Phil. *Degree requirements:* For master's, comprehensive exam, journal. *Entrance requirements:* For master's, honors bachelor's degree. Electronic applications accepted. *Faculty research:* Western language, philosophy, literature, and history.

Mount Saint Mary's University, Graduate Division, Los Angeles, CA 90049-1599. Offers business administration (MBA); counseling psychology (MS); creative writing (MFA); education (MS, Certificate); film and television (MFA); health policy and management (MS); humanities (MA); nursing (MSN, Certificate); physical therapy (DPT); religious studies (MA). Part-time and evening/weekend programs available. *Faculty:* 15 full-time (11 women), 61 part-time/adjunct (33 women). *Students:* 462 full-time (345 women), 218 part-time (175 women); includes 417 minority (66 Black or African American, non-Hispanic/Latino; 3 American Indian or Alaska Native, non-Hispanic/Latino; 69 Asian, non-Hispanic/Latino; 254 Hispanic/Latino; 11 Native Hawaiian or other Pacific Islander, non-Hispanic/Latino; 14 Two or more races, non-Hispanic/Latino), 1 international. Average age 33. 1,086 applicants, 25% accepted, 241 enrolled. In 2014, 181 master's, 28 doctorates, 22 other advanced degrees awarded. *Entrance requirements:* Additional exam requirements/recommendations for international students: Required—TOEFL. *Application deadline:* For fall admission, 6/30 priority date for domestic and international students; for spring admission, 10/30 priority date for domestic and international students; for summer admission, 3/30 priority date for domestic and international students. Applications are processed on a rolling basis. Application fee: $50. Electronic applications accepted. *Expenses: Tuition:* Full-time $9756; part-time $813 per unit. One-time fee: $128. Tuition and fees vary according to degree level and program. *Financial support:* In 2014–15, 213 students received support. Career-related internships or fieldwork, Federal Work-Study, institutionally sponsored loans, and tuition waivers (full and partial) available. Support available to part-time students. Financial award application deadline: 3/15; financial award applicants required to submit FAFSA. *Unit head:* Dr. Linda Moody, Graduate Dean, 213-477-2800, E-mail: gradprograms@msmu.edu. *Application contact:* Tara Wessel, Senior Graduate Admission Counselor, 213-477-2800, E-mail: gradprograms@msmu.edu.
Website: http://www.msmu.edu/graduate-programs/admission/

New York University, Graduate School of Arts and Science, Draper Interdisciplinary Program in Humanities and Social Thought, New York, NY 10012-1019. Offers humanities and social thought (MA); religion (Advanced Certificate); social theory (Advanced Certificate). Part-time programs available. *Faculty:* 6 full-time (3 women). *Students:* 51 full-time (32 women), 69 part-time (44 women); includes 27 minority (8 Black or African American, non-Hispanic/Latino; 4 Asian, non-Hispanic/Latino; 11 Hispanic/Latino; 4 Two or more races, non-Hispanic/Latino), 17 international. Average age 29. 118 applicants, 67% accepted, 38 enrolled. In 2014, 50 master's awarded. *Degree requirements:* For master's, thesis, comprehensive exam or essay. *Entrance requirements:* For master's, GRE General Test; for Advanced Certificate, master's degree. Additional exam requirements/recommendations for international students: Required—TOEFL. *Application deadline:* For fall admission, 7/1 for domestic and international students; for spring admission, 12/1 for domestic and international students. Applications are processed on a rolling basis. Application fee: $100. *Financial support:* Teaching assistantships with tuition reimbursements, Federal Work-Study, institutionally sponsored loans, and tuition waivers (partial) available. Financial award application deadline: 7/1; financial award applicants required to submit FAFSA. *Faculty research:* Art world, gender politics, global histories, literary cultures, the city. *Unit head:* Robin Nagle, Director, 212-998-8070, Fax: 212-995-4691, E-mail: draper.program@nyu.edu. *Application contact:* Robert Dimit, Associate Director/Director of Graduate Studies, 212-998-8070, Fax: 212-995-4691, E-mail: draper.program@nyu.edu.
Website: http://www.nyu.edu/gsas/dept/draper/

New York University, Polytechnic School of Engineering, Department of Technology, Culture and Society, New York, NY 10012-1019. Offers integrated digital media (MS, Graduate Certificate). Part-time and evening/weekend programs available. *Faculty:* 17 full-time (5 women), 33 part-time/adjunct (14 women). *Students:* 45 full-time (25 women), 7 part-time (4 women); includes 16 minority (5 Black or African American, non-Hispanic/Latino; 6 Asian, non-Hispanic/Latino; 5 Hispanic/Latino), 24 international. Average age 26. 78 applicants, 42% accepted, 27 enrolled. In 2014, 16 master's awarded. *Degree requirements:* For master's, comprehensive exam (for some programs), thesis (for some programs). *Entrance requirements:* Additional exam requirements/recommendations for international students: Required—TOEFL (minimum score 550 paper-based; 80 iBT); Recommended—IELTS (minimum score 6.5). *Application deadline:* For fall admission, 2/15 priority date for domestic and international students; for spring admission, 11/1 priority date for domestic and international students. Applications are processed on a rolling basis. Application fee: $75. Electronic applications accepted. *Financial support:* Fellowships, research assistantships, teaching assistantships, career-related internships or fieldwork, institutionally sponsored loans, scholarships/grants, and unspecified assistantships available. Support available to part-time students. Financial award applicants required to submit FAFSA. *Faculty research:* Trade magazine journalism, technical writing, financial reporting, medical and science reporting, industrial advertising and public relations. *Total annual research expenditures:* $106,957. *Unit head:* Prof. Kristen Day, Head, 718-260-3999, E-mail: kday@poly.edu. *Application contact:* Raymond Lutzky, Director, Graduate Enrollment Management, 718-637-5984, Fax: 718-260-3624, E-mail: rlutzky@poly.edu.

Old Dominion University, College of Arts and Letters, Institute for the Humanities, Norfolk, VA 23529. Offers MA. Part-time and evening/weekend programs available. *Faculty:* 1 full-time (0 women), 1 part-time/adjunct (0 women). *Students:* 14 full-time (8 women), 16 part-time (7 women); includes 8 minority (2 Black or African American, non-Hispanic/Latino; 3 Hispanic/Latino; 1 Native Hawaiian or other Pacific Islander, non-Hispanic/Latino; 2 Two or more races, non-Hispanic/Latino), 1 international. Average age 41. 27 applicants, 96% accepted, 22 enrolled. In 2014, 7 master's awarded. *Degree requirements:* For master's, thesis optional, project. *Entrance requirements:* For master's, GRE General Test, minimum GPA of 3.25. *Application deadline:* For fall admission, 6/15 for domestic students; for spring admission, 11/15 for domestic students; for summer admission, 4/15 for domestic students. Applications are processed on a rolling basis. Application fee: $50. Electronic applications accepted. *Expenses:* Tuition, state resident: full-time $10,488; part-time $437 per credit. Tuition, nonresident: full-time $26,136; part-time $1089 per credit. *Required fees:* $64 per semester. One-time fee: $50. *Financial support:* In 2014–15, 3 students received support, including 5 research assistantships (averaging $10,000 per year); career-related internships or fieldwork, scholarships/grants, and unspecified assistantships also available. Financial award application deadline: 3/15; financial award applicants required to submit FAFSA. *Faculty research:* Media studies, cultural studies, gender studies, American literature, philosophy, art history, cultural geography. *Unit head:* Dr. Avi D. Santo, Graduate Program Director, 757-683-3719, Fax: 757-683-6191, E-mail: humgpd@odu.edu. *Application contact:* Dr. David C. Earnest, Associate Dean, 757-683-6077, Fax: 757-683-5746, E-mail: dearnest@odu.edu.
Website: http://al.odu.edu/hum/

Penn State Harrisburg, Graduate School, School of Humanities, Middletown, PA 17057-4898. Offers American studies (MA, PhD); communications (MA); folklore and ethnography (Certificate); heritage and museum practice (Certificate); humanities (MA);

writing instruction specialist (Certificate). Evening/weekend programs available. *Unit head:* Dr. Mukund S. Kulkarni, Chancellor, 717-948-6105, Fax: 717-948-6452, E-mail: msk5@psu.edu. *Application contact:* Robert W. Coffman, Jr., Director of Enrollment Management, Admissions, 717-948-6250, Fax: 717-948-6325, E-mail: ric1@psu.edu.
Website: http://harrisburg.psu.edu/humanities

Prescott College, Graduate Programs, Program in Humanities, Prescott, AZ 86301. Offers humanities (MA); social justice and human rights (MA); student-directed independent study (MA). Part-time programs available. Postbaccalaureate distance learning degree programs offered (minimal on-campus study). *Degree requirements:* For master's, thesis, fieldwork or internship, practicum. *Entrance requirements:* For master's, 2 letters of recommendation, resume, essay. Additional exam requirements/recommendations for international students: Required—TOEFL (minimum score 500 paper-based). Electronic applications accepted.

St. Edward's University, New College, Program in Liberal Arts, Austin, TX 78704. Offers global issues (MLA); humanities (MLA); liberal arts (Certificate); social justice (MLA); social sciences (MLA). Part-time and evening/weekend programs available. *Students:* 3 full-time (2 women), 49 part-time (36 women); includes 18 minority (2 Black or African American, non-Hispanic/Latino; 15 Hispanic/Latino; 1 Two or more races, non-Hispanic/Latino). Average age 35. 34 applicants, 68% accepted, 17 enrolled. In 2014, 23 master's awarded. *Degree requirements:* For master's, minimum of 24 resident hours. *Entrance requirements:* For master's, minimum GPA of 2.75 in last 60 hours of course work, interview. Additional exam requirements/recommendations for international students: Required—TOEFL (minimum score 79 iBT) or IELTS (minimum score 6). *Application deadline:* For fall admission, 6/1 priority date for domestic and international students; for spring admission, 10/1 priority date for domestic and international students; for summer admission, 3/1 priority date for domestic and international students. Applications are processed on a rolling basis. Application fee: $50. Electronic applications accepted. *Expenses: Tuition:* Full-time $22,448; part-time $1246 per credit hour. *Required fees:* $50 per trimester. Full-time tuition and fees vary according to course load and program. *Unit head:* Dr. H. Ramsey Fowler, Director, 512-448-8648, Fax: 512-448-8492, E-mail: ramseyf@stewards.edu. *Application contact:* Office of Admission, 512-448-8500, Fax: 512-464-8877, E-mail: seu.admit@stedwards.edu.
Website: http://www.stedwards.edu

Salve Regina University, Program in Humanities, Newport, RI 02840-4192. Offers humanitarian assistance (MA); humanities (PhD); public humanities (MA); religion, peace and justice (MA). Part-time and evening/weekend programs available. Postbaccalaureate distance learning degree programs offered (no on-campus study). *Faculty:* 1 full-time (0 women), 6 part-time/adjunct (2 women). *Students:* 3 full-time (0 women), 88 part-time (52 women); includes 9 minority (3 Black or African American, non-Hispanic/Latino; 2 Asian, non-Hispanic/Latino; 1 Hispanic/Latino; 1 Native Hawaiian or other Pacific Islander, non-Hispanic/Latino; 2 Two or more races, non-Hispanic/Latino), 2 international. Average age 48. 13 applicants, 85% accepted, 11 enrolled. In 2014, 3 master's, 3 doctorates awarded. *Degree requirements:* For master's, thesis optional; for doctorate, one foreign language, comprehensive exam, thesis/dissertation. *Entrance requirements:* For master's, GMAT, GRE General Test, or MAT; for doctorate, GRE General Test. Additional exam requirements/recommendations for international students: Required—TOEFL (minimum score 600 paper-based; 100 iBT) or IELTS. *Application deadline:* For fall admission, 3/15 priority date for domestic and international students; for spring admission, 9/15 priority date for domestic and international students. Applications are processed on a rolling basis. Application fee: $60. Electronic applications accepted. *Expenses: Tuition:* Full-time $8550; part-time $475 per credit. *Required fees:* $50 per term. Tuition and fees vary according to course level, course load and degree level. *Financial support:* Career-related internships or fieldwork and Federal Work-Study available. Support available to part-time students. Financial award application deadline: 3/1; financial award applicants required to submit FAFSA. *Unit head:* Dr. Michael Budd, Director, 401-341-3284, E-mail: michael.budd@salve.edu. *Application contact:* Kelly Alverson, Director of Graduate Admissions, 401-341-2153, Fax: 401-341-2973, E-mail: kelly.alverson@salve.edu.
Website: http://www.salve.edu/graduate-studies/humanities

Sam Houston State University, College of Humanities and Social Sciences, Huntsville, TX 77341. Offers MA, MFA, MPA, PhD, SSP. Part-time programs available. Postbaccalaureate distance learning degree programs offered (no on-campus study). *Faculty:* 120 full-time (50 women), 7 part-time/adjunct (1 woman). *Students:* 121 full-time (81 women), 251 part-time (134 women); includes 83 minority (19 Black or African American, non-Hispanic/Latino; 4 American Indian or Alaska Native, non-Hispanic/Latino; 4 Asian, non-Hispanic/Latino; 46 Hispanic/Latino; 10 Two or more races, non-Hispanic/Latino), 17 international. Average age 34. 310 applicants, 60% accepted, 143 enrolled. In 2014, 104 master's, 9 doctorates awarded. Terminal master's awarded for partial completion of doctoral program. *Degree requirements:* For master's, comprehensive exam (for some programs), thesis optional, internship, portfolio; for doctorate, comprehensive exam, thesis/dissertation. *Entrance requirements:* For master's, GRE General Test, personal essay, letters of recommendation, writing sample; for doctorate, GRE General Test, GRE Subject Test (advanced psychology), personal essay, letters of recommendation, resume. Additional exam requirements/recommendations for international students: Required—TOEFL (minimum score 550 paper-based; 79 iBT), IELTS (minimum score 6.5). *Application deadline:* For fall admission, 8/1 for domestic students, 6/25 for international students; for spring admission, 12/1 for domestic students, 11/12 for international students; for summer admission, 5/15 for domestic students, 4/9 for international students. Applications are processed on a rolling basis. Application fee: $45 ($75 for international students). Electronic applications accepted. *Expenses:* Tuition, state resident: full-time $2286; part-time $254 per credit hour. Tuition, nonresident: full-time $5544; part-time $616 per credit hour. *Required fees:* $440 per semester. Tuition and fees vary according to course load and campus/location. *Financial support:* In 2014–15, 101 research assistantships (averaging $7,474 per year), 20 teaching assistantships (averaging $7,648 per year) were awarded; career-related internships or fieldwork, Federal Work-Study, scholarships/grants, tuition waivers (partial), and unspecified assistantships also available. Support available to part-time students. Financial award application deadline: 3/15; financial award applicants required to submit FAFSA. *Unit head:* Dr. Abbey Zink, Dean, 936-294-2200, Fax: 936-294-2207, E-mail: alz007@shsu.edu. *Application contact:* Dr. Kandi Tayebi, Dean of Graduate Studies and Associate Vice President for Academic Affairs, 936-294-1971, Fax: 936-294-1271, E-mail: graduate@shsu.edu.
Website: http://www.shsu.edu/academics/humanities-and-social-sciences/

San Francisco State University, Division of Graduate Studies, College of Liberal and Creative Arts, Department of Humanities, San Francisco, CA 94132-1722. Offers MA. Part-time and evening/weekend programs available. *Expenses:* Tuition, state resident: full-time $6738. Tuition, nonresident: full-time $17,898; part-time $372 per credit hour. *Required fees:* $498 per semester. *Unit head:* Dr. Christina Ruotolo, Chair, 415-338-1830, E-mail: ruotolo@sfsu.edu. *Application contact:* Prof. Laura Garcia-Moreno, Graduate Coordinator, 415-338-1295, E-mail: lgmoreno@sfsu.edu.
Website: http://humanities.sfsu.edu/

Simon Fraser University, Office of Graduate Studies, Faculty of Arts and Social Sciences, Department of Humanities, Burnaby, BC V5A 1S6, Canada. Offers MA. *Degree requirements:* For master's, thesis. *Entrance requirements:* Additional exam requirements/recommendations for international students: Required—TOEFL (minimum score 580 paper-based; 93 iBT), IELTS (minimum score 7), TWE (minimum score 5). Electronic applications accepted. *Faculty research:* Classic and medieval studies, modern thought and culture, Renaissance humanism, Eastern and Western religions.

Tiffin University, Program in Humanities, Tiffin, OH 44883-2161. Offers art and visual media (MH); communication (MH); creative writing (MH); English (MH); film studies (MH); humanities (MH); individualized studies (MH). Part-time and evening/weekend programs available. Postbaccalaureate distance learning degree programs offered (no on-campus study). *Entrance requirements:* For master's, work experience. Additional exam requirements/recommendations for international students: Required—TOEFL (minimum score 550 paper-based; 79 iBT).

Towson University, Program in Humanities, Towson, MD 21252-0001. Offers MA. Part-time and evening/weekend programs available. *Students:* 1 (woman) full-time, 14 part-time (7 women); includes 1 minority (Two or more races, non-Hispanic/Latino). *Degree requirements:* For master's, thesis or alternative. *Entrance requirements:* For master's, bachelor's degree, 2 letters of recommendation, minimum GPA of 3.0, research paper, statement of intent. *Application deadline:* Applications are processed on a rolling basis. Application fee: $45. Electronic applications accepted. *Financial support:* Application deadline: 4/1. *Unit head:* Dr. Lana Portolano, Graduate Program Director, 410-704-3770, E-mail: mportolano@towson.edu. *Application contact:* Alicia Arkell-Kleis, Information Contact, 410-704-6004, E-mail: grads@towson.edu.
Website: http://grad.towson.edu/program/master/huma-ma/

Trinity Western University, School of Graduate Studies, Program in Interdisciplinary Humanities, Langley, BC V2Y 1Y1, Canada. Offers general humanities (MAIH); specialized (MAIH), including English, history, philosophy. Part-time programs available. *Degree requirements:* For master's, thesis or alternative, 36 semester hours. *Entrance requirements:* For master's, strong undergraduate degree in humanities or English, history or philosophy. Additional exam requirements/recommendations for international students: Recommended—TOEFL. Electronic applications accepted. *Faculty research:* Literary theory, gender, medieval and early modern literature, philosophy of religion, Thomas Merton's poetics.

Union Institute & University, PhD Program in Interdisciplinary Studies, Cincinnati, OH 45206-1925. Offers ethical and creative leadership (PhD), including Martin Luther King studies; humanities and culture (PhD), including Martin Luther King studies; public policy and social change (PhD), including Martin Luther King studies. Program requires participation in brief on-campus residencies twice each year (January and July). Postbaccalaureate distance learning degree programs offered (minimal on-campus study). *Faculty:* 6 full-time (4 women), 9 part-time/adjunct (7 women). *Students:* 92 full-time (51 women), 15 part-time (10 women); includes 37 minority (25 Black or African American, non-Hispanic/Latino; 4 American Indian or Alaska Native, non-Hispanic/Latino; 2 Asian, non-Hispanic/Latino; 3 Hispanic/Latino; 3 Native Hawaiian or other Pacific Islander, non-Hispanic/Latino), 1 international. Average age 46. *Degree requirements:* For doctorate, comprehensive exam, thesis/dissertation. *Entrance requirements:* For doctorate, master's degree, three letters of recommendation, statement of purpose. *Application deadline:* Applications are processed on a rolling basis. Application fee: $50. *Expenses: Tuition:* Full-time $26,640; part-time $719 per credit hour. *Required fees:* $216; $54 per semester. Part-time tuition and fees vary according to course load, degree level and program. *Financial support:* Federal Work-Study, scholarships/grants, and tuition waivers (partial) available. Financial award application deadline: 5/1; financial award applicants required to submit FAFSA. *Faculty research:* Social responsibility, ethical leadership, Martin Luther King studies. *Unit head:* Dr. Arlene Sacks, Dean, 513-861-6400, E-mail: arlene.sacks@myunion.edu. *Application contact:* Admissions Counselor, 800-486-3116.
Website: https://www.myunion.edu/academics/doctoral-programs/phd/

United Theological Seminary of the Twin Cities, Graduate Programs, New Brighton, MN 55112-2598. Offers advanced theological studies (Diploma); justice and peace studies (M Div, MA); leadership toward racial justice (M Div, MA, Certificate); Methodist studies (M Div, MA, Certificate); ministry (D Min); ministry renewal and professional development (Certificate); pastoral care and counseling (M Div, MA, MARL); religion and theology (MA); theological and religious studies (Certificate); theology and the arts (M Div, MA); urban ministry (M Div, MA, MARL); women's studies: religion, theology and ministry (M Div, MA). *Accreditation:* ACIPE; ATS. Part-time and evening/weekend programs available. *Degree requirements:* For master's, thesis; for doctorate, comprehensive exam, thesis/dissertation. *Entrance requirements:* For master's, minimum GPA of 2.75; strong analytical, reflective thinking and writing skills; vocational and academic goals compatible with those of Seminary; for doctorate, M Div or equivalent, minimum GPA of 3.0, 3 years experience in professional ministry; for other advanced degree, BA or equivalent life experience; strong analytical, reflective thinking and writing skills (Certificate); proficiency in English language, previous study of theology at a theological school, recommendation of student's denomination (Diploma). Additional exam requirements/recommendations for international students: Required—TOEFL (minimum score 550 paper-based).

University of California, Santa Cruz, Division of Graduate Studies, Division of Humanities, Program in the History of Consciousness, Santa Cruz, CA 95064. Offers PhD. *Degree requirements:* For doctorate, one foreign language, thesis/dissertation, qualifying exam. *Entrance requirements:* For doctorate, GRE General Test. Additional exam requirements/recommendations for international students: Required—TOEFL (minimum score 550 paper-based; 83 iBT); Recommended—IELTS (minimum score 8). Electronic applications accepted. *Faculty research:* Interdisciplinary humanities and social sciences, political theory, cultural theory, feminist studies, literary theory.

University of Chicago, Division of the Humanities, Master of Arts Program in the Humanities, Chicago, IL 60637. Offers art history (MA); classics (MA); comparative literature (MA); creative writing (MA); digital humanities (MA); English language and literature (MA); Germanic studies (MA); linguistics (MA); music (MA); philosophy (MA); Romance languages and literatures (MA); South Asian languages and civilizations (MA). *Students:* 83 full-time (41 women), 8 part-time (6 women); includes 14 minority (1 Black or African American, non-Hispanic/Latino; 6 Asian, non-Hispanic/Latino; 6 Hispanic/Latino; 1 Two or more races, non-Hispanic/Latino), 17 international. Average age 26. 153 applicants, 67% accepted, 80 enrolled. *Degree requirements:* For master's, thesis. *Entrance requirements:* For master's, GRE General Test. Additional exam requirements/recommendations for international students: Required—TOEFL (minimum score 600 paper-based; 104 iBT), IELTS (minimum score 7). *Application deadline:* For fall admission, 3/15 for domestic and international students. Application fee: $90. Electronic applications accepted. *Expenses: Tuition:* Full-time $46,899. *Required fees:* $347. *Financial support:* In 2014–15, 100 students received support, including 8 fellowships with partial tuition reimbursements available (averaging $12,000 per year); Federal Work-Study, institutionally sponsored loans, and tuition waivers (partial) also available. Financial award application deadline: 3/15; financial award applicants required to submit FAFSA. *Unit head:* Prof. David Wray, Director, 773-834-1201, E-mail: ma-humanities@uchicago.edu. *Application contact:* Program Coordinator, 773-834-1201,

Fax: 773-834-7526, E-mail: ma-humanities@uchicago.edu.
Website: http://maph.uchicago.edu/

University of Colorado Denver, College of Liberal Arts and Sciences, Program in Humanities, Denver, CO 80217. Offers community health science (MSS); humanities (MH); international studies (MSS); philosophy and theory (MH); social justice (MSS); society and the environment (MSS); visual studies (MH); women's and gender studies (MSS). Part-time and evening/weekend programs available. *Faculty:* 1 full-time (0 women), 1 (woman) part-time/adjunct. *Students:* 49 full-time (37 women), 26 part-time (19 women); includes 14 minority (3 Black or African American, non-Hispanic/Latino; 1 American Indian or Alaska Native, non-Hispanic/Latino; 1 Asian, non-Hispanic/Latino; 6 Hispanic/Latino; 3 Two or more races, non-Hispanic/Latino), 1 international. Average age 35. 27 applicants, 63% accepted, 11 enrolled. In 2014, 16 master's awarded. *Degree requirements:* For master's, 36 credit hours, project or thesis. *Entrance requirements:* For master's, writing sample, statement of purpose/letter of intent, three letters of recommendation. Additional exam requirements/recommendations for international students: Required—TOEFL (minimum score 537 paper-based; 75 iBT); Recommended—IELTS (minimum score 6.5). *Application deadline:* For fall admission, 5/15 for domestic students, 5/15 priority date for international students; for spring admission, 10/15 for domestic students, 10/15 priority date for international students; for summer admission, 3/15 for domestic and international students. Application fee: $50 ($75 for international students). Electronic applications accepted. *Financial support:* In 2014–15, 4 students received support. Fellowships, research assistantships, teaching assistantships, Federal Work-Study, institutionally sponsored loans, scholarships/grants, and traineeships available. Financial award application deadline: 4/1; financial award applicants required to submit FAFSA. *Faculty research:* Women and gender in the classical Mediterranean, communication theory and democracy, relationship between psychology and philosophy. *Unit head:* Margaret Woodhull, Director of Humanities, 303-315-3568, E-mail: margaret.woodhull@ucdenver.edu. *Application contact:* Angela Beale, Program Assistant, 303-315-3565, E-mail: angela.beale@ucdenver.edu.
Website: http://www.ucdenver.edu/academics/colleges/CLAS/Programs/HumanitiesSocialSciences/Programs/Pages/MasterofHumanities.aspx

University of Dallas, Braniff Graduate School of Liberal Arts, Program in Humanities, Irving, TX 75062-4736. Offers M Hum, MA. Part-time programs available. *Degree requirements:* For master's, one foreign language, comprehensive exam, thesis (for some programs). *Entrance requirements:* For master's, GRE General Test. Additional exam requirements/recommendations for international students: Required—TOEFL. *Faculty research:* Classical epic poetry, scholastic poetry, Renaissance drama, nineteenth and twentieth century Continental philosophy.

University of Houston–Clear Lake, School of Human Sciences and Humanities, Programs in Humanities and Fine Arts, Houston, TX 77058-1002. Offers history (MA); humanities (MA); literature (MA). Part-time and evening/weekend programs available. Postbaccalaureate distance learning degree programs offered (minimal on-campus study). *Degree requirements:* For master's, thesis or alternative. *Entrance requirements:* For master's, GRE General Test. Additional exam requirements/recommendations for international students: Required—TOEFL (minimum score 550 paper-based). *Faculty research:* Digital media studies, Latin American history, labor history, Chaucer evolution versus creationism debate.

University of Louisville, Graduate School, College of Arts and Sciences, Division of Humanities, Louisville, KY 40292-0001. Offers MA, PhD, MA/JD, MA/MBA. *Students:* 46 full-time (26 women), 25 part-time (12 women); includes 6 minority (2 Black or African American, non-Hispanic/Latino; 2 Asian, non-Hispanic/Latino; 2 Two or more races, non-Hispanic/Latino), 2 international. Average age 37. 23 applicants, 65% accepted, 16 enrolled. In 2014, 2 master's, 3 doctorates awarded. *Degree requirements:* For master's, one foreign language, comprehensive exam (for some programs), thesis (for some programs), directed study culminating project; for doctorate, 2 foreign languages, comprehensive exam, thesis/dissertation, internship. *Entrance requirements:* For master's, GRE General Test, letters of recommendation, transcripts; for doctorate, GRE General Test, letters of recommendation, transcripts, writing sample. Additional exam requirements/recommendations for international students: Required—TOEFL. *Application deadline:* For fall admission, 1/15 for domestic students, 5/1 priority date for international students; for spring admission, 11/1 priority date for international students; for summer admission, 4/1 priority date for international students. Application fee: $60. Electronic applications accepted. *Expenses:* Tuition, state resident: full-time $11,326; part-time $630 per credit hour. Tuition, nonresident: full-time $23,568; part-time $1311 per credit hour. *Required fees:* $196. Tuition and fees vary according to program and reciprocity agreements. *Financial support:* Fellowships, teaching assistantships, institutionally sponsored loans, scholarships/grants, and tuition waivers available. *Faculty research:* Studies in culture, aesthetics and creativity, religious studies, linguistics. *Unit head:* Prof. Elaine O. Wise, Chair, 502-852-7149, Fax: 502-852-0078, E-mail: elaine.wise@louisville.edu. *Application contact:* Libby Leggett, Director, Graduate Admissions, 502-852-3101, Fax: 502-852-6536, E-mail: gradadm@louisville.edu.
Website: http://louisville.edu/humanities/

University of South Florida, College of Arts and Sciences, Department of Humanities and Cultural Studies, Tampa, FL 33620-9951. Offers American studies (MA); liberal arts (MA), including Africana studies, film studies, humanities, social and political thought. Part-time and evening/weekend programs available. *Faculty:* 7 full-time (3 women). *Students:* 11 full-time (2 women), 8 part-time (2 women); includes 8 minority (4 Black or African American, non-Hispanic/Latino; 3 Hispanic/Latino; 1 Two or more races, non-Hispanic/Latino), 1 international. Average age 34. 9 applicants, 78% accepted, 5 enrolled. In 2014, 5 master's awarded. *Degree requirements:* For master's, comprehensive exam, thesis, language requirement (for humanities subconcentration). *Entrance requirements:* For master's, GRE General Test (minimum preferred score 59th percentile (153) verbal and 4.5 in analytical writing), minimum GPA of 3.0 in upper-division courses, personal statement, writing sample. Additional exam requirements/recommendations for international students: Required—TOEFL (minimum score 550 paper-based; 79 iBT) or IELTS (minimum score 6.5). *Application deadline:* For fall admission, 2/15 priority date for domestic students, 1/2 for international students; for spring admission, 10/15 priority date for domestic students, 6/1 for international students. Application fee: $30. *Financial support:* In 2014–15, 15 students received support, including 15 teaching assistantships with tuition reimbursements available (averaging $12,437 per year); scholarships/grants also available. Financial award application deadline: 4/1. *Faculty research:* American South, American autobiography, material culture, critical theory, cultural studies, film studies. *Unit head:* Dr. William Cummings, Professor and Chair, 813-974-9380, Fax: 813-974-9409, E-mail: wcummings@usf.edu. *Application contact:* Dr. Brook Sadler, Associate Professor and Graduate Program Director, 813-974-8841, Fax: 813-974-9409, E-mail: brooksadler@usf.edu.
Website: http://humanities.usf.edu/

The University of Texas at Dallas, School of Arts and Humanities, Program in Humanities, Richardson, TX 75080. Offers aesthetic studies (MA, PhD); history (MA); history of ideas (MA, PhD); humanities (MA, PhD); Latin American studies (MA); studies in literature (MA, PhD). *Faculty:* 35 full-time (11 women), 1 part-time/adjunct (0 women). *Students:* 148 full-time (94 women), 151 part-time (97 women); includes 78 minority (21 Black or African American, non-Hispanic/Latino; 4 American Indian or Alaska Native, non-Hispanic/Latino; 14 Asian, non-Hispanic/Latino; 28 Hispanic/Latino; 11 Two or more races, non-Hispanic/Latino), 16 international. Average age 39. 127 applicants, 46% accepted, 40 enrolled. In 2014, 40 master's, 15 doctorates awarded. *Degree requirements:* For master's, one foreign language, portfolio, thesis, or capstone project; for doctorate, one foreign language, thesis/dissertation. *Entrance requirements:* For master's, minimum GPA of 3.3 in upper-level coursework in field; for doctorate, field examinations, minimum GPA of 3.3 in upper-level coursework in field. Additional exam requirements/recommendations for international students: Required—TOEFL (minimum score 550 paper-based). *Application deadline:* For fall admission, 7/15 for domestic students, 5/1 priority date for international students; for spring admission, 11/15 for domestic students, 9/1 priority date for international students. Applications are processed on a rolling basis. Application fee: $50 ($100 for international students). Electronic applications accepted. *Expenses:* Tuition, state resident: full-time $11,940; part-time $663 per credit. Tuition, nonresident: full-time $22,282; part-time $1238 per credit. *Financial support:* In 2014–15, 161 students received support. Research assistantships with partial tuition reimbursements available, teaching assistantships with partial tuition reimbursements available, career-related internships or fieldwork, Federal Work-Study, institutionally sponsored loans, scholarships/grants, and unspecified assistantships available. Support available to part-time students. Financial award application deadline: 4/30; financial award applicants required to submit FAFSA. *Faculty research:* Holocaust studies, U.S./Mexico studies, translation studies, art history research, Chinese studies. *Unit head:* Dr. Michael Wilson, III, Associate Dean for Graduate Education, 972-883-2756, Fax: 972-883-2989, E-mail: mwilson@utdallas.edu. *Application contact:* Alice Salazar, Coordinator, 972-883-2756, Fax: 972-883-2989, E-mail: alice.salazar1@utdallas.edu.
Website: http://www.utdallas.edu/ah/programs/graduate

The University of Texas Medical Branch, Graduate School of Biomedical Sciences, Program in Medical Humanities, Galveston, TX 77555. Offers MA, PhD. *Degree requirements:* For master's, thesis; for doctorate, thesis/dissertation. *Entrance requirements:* For master's and doctorate, GRE General Test, writing sample. Additional exam requirements/recommendations for international students: Required—TOEFL (minimum score 550 paper-based). Electronic applications accepted.

University of Utah, Graduate School, College of Humanities, Environmental Humanities Graduate Program, Salt Lake City, UT 84112. Offers MA, MS. Postbaccalaureate distance learning degree programs offered. *Faculty:* 17 full-time (9 women), 1 (woman) part-time/adjunct. *Students:* 16 full-time (10 women), 6 part-time (3 women), 1 international. Average age 27. 22 applicants, 36% accepted, 7 enrolled. In 2014, 7 master's awarded. *Degree requirements:* For master's, one foreign language, comprehensive exam (for some programs), thesis (for some programs). *Entrance requirements:* For master's, GRE, minimum undergraduate GPA of 3.0; undergraduate degree. Additional exam requirements/recommendations for international students: Required—TOEFL (minimum score 500 paper-based; 80 iBT). *Application deadline:* For fall admission, 4/1 for domestic and international students; for winter admission, 2/1 priority date for domestic and international students; for spring admission, 11/1 for domestic and international students. Application fee: $55 ($65 for international students). Electronic applications accepted. *Financial support:* In 2014–15, 16 students received support, including 4 research assistantships with partial tuition reimbursements available (averaging $6,750 per year); fellowships with full tuition reimbursements available also available. Financial award application deadline: 2/1. *Faculty research:* Environmental writing, history/philosophy of science, environmental rhetoric and communication, the nuclear American West, American environmental history, urban environmentalism. *Unit head:* Jeffrey McCarthy, Director, 801-585-7052, Fax: 801-585-5190, E-mail: j.mccarthy@utah.edu. *Application contact:* Natasha Seegert, Graduate Advisor, 801-581-6889, E-mail: n.seegert@utah.edu.
Website: http://environmental-humanities.utah.edu

Virginia Commonwealth University, Graduate School, College of Humanities and Sciences, Richmond, VA 23284-9005. Offers MA, MFA, MPA, MS, MURP, PhD, CASR, CCJA, CPM, CURP, Certificate, Graduate Certificate, JD/MURP, MSW/Certificate. Part-time and evening/weekend programs available. *Entrance requirements:* Additional exam requirements/recommendations for international students: Required—TOEFL (minimum score 600 paper-based; 100 iBT) or IELTS (minimum score 6.5). Electronic applications accepted.

Virginia Polytechnic Institute and State University, Graduate School, College of Liberal Arts and Human Sciences, Blacksburg, VA 24061. Offers career and technical education (MS Ed, Ed D, PhD, Ed S); communication (MA); counselor education (MA Ed, Ed D, PhD, Ed S); creative writing (MFA); curriculum and instruction (MA Ed, Ed D, PhD, Ed S); educational leadership and policy studies (MA Ed, Ed D, PhD, Ed S); educational research and evaluation (PhD); English (MA); foreign languages, cultures, and literatures (MA); higher education and student affairs (MA Ed); history (MA); human development (MS, PhD); material culture and public humanities (MA); philosophy (MA); political science (MA); rhetoric and writing (PhD); science and technology studies (MS, PhD); social, political, ethical, and cultural thought (PhD); sociology (MS, PhD); theater arts (MFA). *Faculty:* 421 full-time (216 women), 2 part-time/adjunct (both women). *Students:* 642 full-time (437 women), 537 part-time (344 women); includes 235 minority (132 Black or African American, non-Hispanic/Latino; 2 American Indian or Alaska Native, non-Hispanic/Latino; 27 Asian, non-Hispanic/Latino; 52 Hispanic/Latino; 1 Native Hawaiian or other Pacific Islander, non-Hispanic/Latino; 21 Two or more races, non-Hispanic/Latino), 81 international. Average age 34. 890 applicants, 46% accepted, 303 enrolled. In 2014, 342 master's, 96 doctorates, 33 other advanced degrees awarded. *Degree requirements:* For master's, comprehensive exam (for some programs), thesis (for some programs); for doctorate, comprehensive exam (for some programs), thesis/dissertation (for some programs). *Entrance requirements:* For master's and doctorate, GRE/GMAT (may vary by department). Additional exam requirements/recommendations for international students: Required—TOEFL (minimum score 550 paper-based). *Application deadline:* For fall admission, 8/1 for domestic students, 4/1 for international students; for spring admission, 1/1 for domestic students, 9/1 for international students. Applications are processed on a rolling basis. Application fee: $75. Electronic applications accepted. *Expenses:* Tuition, state resident: full-time $11,656; part-time $647.50 per credit hour. Tuition, nonresident: full-time $23,351; part-time $1297.25 per credit hour. *Required fees:* $2533; $465.75 per semester. Tuition and fees vary according to course load, campus/location and program. *Financial support:* In 2014–15, 19 research assistantships with full tuition reimbursements (averaging $22,141 per year), 231 teaching assistantships with full tuition reimbursements (averaging $19,470 per year) were awarded. Financial award application deadline: 3/1; financial award applicants required to submit FAFSA. *Total annual research expenditures:* $6.5 million. *Unit head:* Elizabeth Spiller, Dean, 540-231-6779, Fax: 540-231-7157, E-mail: espiller@vt.edu. *Application contact:* Melissa Elliott, Executive Assistant, 540-231-6779, Fax: 540-231-7157, E-mail: elliott1@vt.edu.
Website: http://www.clahs.vt.edu/

Wright State University, School of Graduate Studies, College of Liberal Arts, Interdisciplinary Program in Humanities, Dayton, OH 45435. Offers M Hum. *Degree requirements:* For master's, thesis or alternative. *Entrance requirements:* Additional exam requirements/recommendations for international students: Required—TOEFL.

York University, Faculty of Graduate Studies, Faculty of Liberal Arts and Professional Studies, Program in Humanities, Toronto, ON M3J 1P3, Canada. Offers MA, PhD. Part-time programs available. *Degree requirements:* For master's, thesis or alternative; for doctorate, comprehensive exam, thesis/dissertation. *Entrance requirements:* Additional exam requirements/recommendations for international students: Required—TOEFL (minimum score 600 paper-based). Electronic applications accepted.

Liberal Studies

Abilene Christian University, Graduate School, College of Arts and Sciences, Interdisciplinary Program in the Liberal Arts, Abilene, TX 79699-9100. Offers MLA. Part-time programs available. *Students:* 1 (woman) part-time. 1 applicant, 100% accepted. In 2014, 2 master's awarded. *Degree requirements:* For master's, comprehensive exam, thesis or alternative. *Entrance requirements:* For master's, GRE General Test, MAT. Additional exam requirements/recommendations for international students: Required—TOEFL (minimum score 550 paper-based; 90 iBT), IELTS (minimum score 6.5), PTE. *Application deadline:* For fall admission, 4/1 priority date for domestic students; for spring admission, 11/1 for domestic students. Applications are processed on a rolling basis. Application fee: $50. Electronic applications accepted. *Expenses: Tuition:* Full-time $18,228; part-time $1016 per credit hour. *Financial support:* Federal Work-Study available. Support available to part-time students. Financial award application deadline: 4/1; financial award applicants required to submit FAFSA. *Unit head:* Dr. Joe Cardot, Graduate Director, 325-674-2136, Fax: 325-674-6966, E-mail: cardotj@acu.edu. *Application contact:* Corey Patterson, Director of Graduate Admission and Recruiting, 325-674-6566, Fax: 325-674-6717, E-mail: gradinfo@acu.edu.

Alaska Pacific University, Graduate Programs, Liberal Studies Department, Anchorage, AK 99508-4672. Offers self-designed study (MA).

Albertus Magnus College, Master of Arts in Liberal Studies Program, New Haven, CT 06511-1189. Offers MALS. Part-time and evening/weekend programs available. Postbaccalaureate distance learning degree programs offered (no on-campus study). *Faculty:* 10 full-time (3 women). *Students:* 1 (woman) full-time, 4 part-time (all women); includes 1 minority (Black or African American, non-Hispanic/Latino). Average age 44. *Degree requirements:* For master's, thesis, completion of all credits within six years from time when student begins program; minimum cumulative GPA of 3.9; final project. *Entrance requirements:* For master's, interview, 500-word essay detailing applicant's intellectual and professional interests, minimum GPA of 2.8, transcripts. Additional exam requirements/recommendations for international students: Required—TOEFL (minimum score 550 paper-based; 80 iBT). *Application deadline:* For fall admission, 8/31 for domestic students; for spring admission, 1/10 for domestic students. Applications are processed on a rolling basis. Application fee: $50. Electronic applications accepted. *Expenses:* Expenses: $1,878 per course; registration fee $10 per module; information technology fee $6 per credit. *Financial support:* Available to part-time students. Application deadline: 8/15. *Unit head:* Prof. Julia A. Coash, Director, Liberal Studies Program, 203-773-8993, Fax: 203-773-5257, E-mail: jcoash@albertus.edu. *Application contact:* Anthony Reich, Director of Admission, Division of Professional and Graduate Studies, 203-773-5032, Fax: 203-773-5257, E-mail: arreich@albertus.edu.

Alvernia University, Graduate Studies, Program in Liberal Studies, Reading, PA 19607-1799. Offers MALS. Part-time and evening/weekend programs available. *Degree requirements:* For master's, thesis optional. *Entrance requirements:* For master's, MAT or GRE (alumni excluded). Electronic applications accepted.

Antioch University Midwest, Graduate Programs, Individualized Liberal and Professional Studies Program, Yellow Springs, OH 45387-1609. Offers liberal and professional studies (MA), including counseling, creative writing, education, liberal studies, management, modern literature, psychology, visual arts. Part-time and evening/weekend programs available. Postbaccalaureate distance learning degree programs offered (minimal on-campus study). *Degree requirements:* For master's, thesis or alternative. *Entrance requirements:* For master's, resume, goal statement, interview. Electronic applications accepted. *Expenses:* Contact institution.

Arizona State University at the Tempe campus, College of Liberal Arts and Sciences, Program in Liberal Studies, Tempe, AZ 85287-6505. Offers MLS. Part-time and evening/weekend programs available. *Degree requirements:* For master's, thesis or alternative, integrated/capstone project, interactive Program of Study (iPOS) submitted before completing 50 percent of required credit hours. *Entrance requirements:* For master's, minimum GPA of 3.0 or equivalent in last 2 years of work leading to bachelor's degree, resume or biographical statement, personal letter expressing liberal studies concentration interest, official college transcripts, 2 letters of recommendation, interview with program director (recommended). Additional exam requirements/recommendations for international students: Required—TOEFL, IELTS, or PTE. Electronic applications accepted. *Expenses:* Contact institution.

Arkansas Tech University, College of Arts and Humanities, Russellville, AR 72801. Offers English (M Ed, MA); history (MA); liberal arts (MLA); multi-media journalism (MA); psychology (MS); teaching English as a second language (MA). Part-time programs available. *Students:* 70 full-time (39 women), 105 part-time (72 women); includes 20 minority (3 Black or African American, non-Hispanic/Latino; 2 American Indian or Alaska Native, non-Hispanic/Latino; 1 Asian, non-Hispanic/Latino; 10 Hispanic/Latino; 4 Two or more races, non-Hispanic/Latino), 51 international. Average age 30. In 2014, 63 master's awarded. *Degree requirements:* For master's, comprehensive exam (for some programs), thesis (for some programs), project. *Entrance requirements:* For master's, GRE General Test or GMAT. Additional exam requirements/recommendations for international students: Required—TOEFL (minimum score 550 paper-based; 79 iBT), IELTS (minimum score 6). *Application deadline:* For fall admission, 3/1 priority date for domestic students, 5/1 priority date for international students; for spring admission, 10/1 priority date for domestic and international students. Applications are processed on a rolling basis. Application fee: $25 ($75 for international students). Electronic applications accepted. *Expenses:* Tuition, state resident: full-time $6264; part-time $261 per credit hour. Tuition, nonresident: full-time $12,528; part-time $522 per credit hour. *Required fees:* $423 per semester. Tuition and fees vary according to course load. *Financial support:* In 2014–15, research assistantships with full tuition reimbursements (averaging $4,800 per year), teaching assistantships with full tuition reimbursements (averaging $4,800 per year) were awarded; career-related internships or fieldwork, Federal Work-Study, scholarships/grants, health care benefits, and unspecified assistantships also available. Support available to part-time students. Financial award application deadline: 4/15; financial award applicants required to submit FAFSA. *Unit head:* Dr. Jeffrey Woods, Dean, 479-968-0274, Fax: 479-964-0812, E-mail: jwoods@atu.edu. *Application contact:* Dr. Mary B. Gunter, Dean of Graduate College,

479-968-0398, Fax: 479-964-0542, E-mail: gradcollege@atu.edu. Website: http://www.atu.edu/humanities/

Auburn University at Montgomery, College of Public Policy and Justice, Montgomery, AL 36124-4023. Offers justice and public safety (MS, MSJPS, Certificate), including criminal studies (MSJPS), homeland security (MSJPS), homeland security and emergency management (MS), legal studies (MSJPS), organizational leadership (MSJPS), paralegal (Certificate); liberal arts (MLA); political science and public administration (MIR, MPA, MPS, PhD, Certificate), including international relations (MIR), nonprofit management and leadership (Certificate), political science (MPS), public administration (MPA), public administration and public policy (PhD), public health care administration and policy (Certificate); sociology (MA, MS). Part-time and evening/weekend programs available. *Faculty:* 31 full-time (13 women). *Students:* 24 full-time (15 women), 63 part-time (49 women); includes 20 minority (15 Black or African American, non-Hispanic/Latino; 2 American Indian or Alaska Native, non-Hispanic/Latino; 3 Two or more races, non-Hispanic/Latino), 4 international. Average age 34. 42 applicants, 90% accepted, 15 enrolled. In 2014, 8 master's, 1 other advanced degree awarded. *Degree requirements:* For master's, thesis. *Entrance requirements:* For master's, GRE or MAT. *Application deadline:* Applications are processed on a rolling basis. Electronic applications accepted. *Expenses:* Tuition, state resident: full-time $6264; part-time $348 per credit hour. Tuition, nonresident: full-time $14,094; part-time $783 per credit hour. *Financial support:* In 2014–15, 6 teaching assistantships were awarded; career-related internships or fieldwork and scholarships/grants also available. Support available to part-time students. Financial award application deadline: 3/1; financial award applicants required to submit FAFSA. *Unit head:* Dr. Michael Burger, Dean, 334-244-3380, Fax: 334-244-3740, E-mail: mburger1@aum.edu. *Application contact:* Dr. Eric Sterling, Director of the MLA Program, 334-244-3760, Fax: 334-244-3740, E-mail: esterlin@aum.edu. Website: http://www.aum.edu/schools/college-of-public-policy-justice

Averett University, Master in Education Program, Danville, VA 24541-3692. Offers administration and supervision (M Ed); art (M Ed); biology (M Ed); chemistry (M Ed); curriculum and instruction (M Ed); early childhood (M Ed); English (M Ed); English/theatre (M Ed); health/physical education (M Ed); history (M Ed); history/social science (M Ed); liberal studies (M Ed); mathematics (M Ed); middle grades (M Ed); physical science (M Ed); reading specialist (M Ed); special education (M Ed); special education learning disability (M Ed); theatre (M Ed). Program offered on Danville Campus only. Part-time and evening/weekend programs available. Postbaccalaureate distance learning degree programs offered (no on-campus study). *Faculty:* 7 full-time (4 women), 4 part-time/adjunct (2 women). *Students:* 25 full-time (20 women), 21 part-time (20 women); includes 10 minority (3 Black or African American, non-Hispanic/Latino; 6 American Indian or Alaska Native, non-Hispanic/Latino; 1 Hispanic/Latino). Average age 37. In 2014, 50 master's awarded. *Degree requirements:* For master's, 30-credit core curriculum, minimum GPA of 3.0 throughout program, completion of degree requirements within six years from start of program. *Entrance requirements:* For master's, PRAXIS I, GRE, or MAT; writing proficiency test, minimum cumulative GPA of 3.0 over the last 60 hours of undergraduate study toward a baccalaureate degree, three letters of recommendation, Virginia teaching license (or eligibility). Additional exam requirements/recommendations for international students: Required—TOEFL (minimum score 600 paper-based; 100 iBT). *Application deadline:* Applications are processed on a rolling basis. Application fee: $100. Electronic applications accepted. *Expenses:* Expenses: Contact institution. *Financial support:* Career-related internships or fieldwork and scholarships/grants available. Financial award application deadline: 4/1; financial award applicants required to submit FAFSA. *Unit head:* Dr. Sue Davis, Acting Education Chair, 434-791-5741, E-mail: suedavis@averett.edu. *Application contact:* Christy Pack, Associate Vice President for Client Relations, 804-887-8612, E-mail: dpack@averett.edu. Website: http://gps.averett.edu/programs/master-degrees/

Baker University, School of Professional and Graduate Studies, Program in Liberal Arts, Baldwin City, KS 66006-0065. Offers MLA. Program also offered in Overland Park, KS. Part-time and evening/weekend programs available. Postbaccalaureate distance learning degree programs offered (no on-campus study). *Students:* 24 full-time (19 women), 71 part-time (52 women); includes 27 minority (15 Black or African American, non-Hispanic/Latino; 3 American Indian or Alaska Native, non-Hispanic/Latino; 8 Hispanic/Latino; 1 Two or more races, non-Hispanic/Latino). Average age 37. In 2014, 37 master's awarded. *Degree requirements:* For master's, portfolio of learning. *Entrance requirements:* Additional exam requirements/recommendations for international students: Required—TOEFL (minimum score 600 paper-based; 100 iBT). *Application deadline:* Applications are processed on a rolling basis. Application fee: $45. *Financial support:* Applicants required to submit FAFSA. *Unit head:* Dr. Brian Posler, Provost and Dean of the School of Professional and Graduate Studies, 785-594-8312, E-mail: brian.posler@bakeru.edu. *Application contact:* Kelly Belk, Vice President of Enrollment Management, 913-491-4432, E-mail: kelly.belk@learn.bakeru.edu. Website: http://www.bakeru.edu/spgs-prospective-students/degrees-and-programs/mla

Barry University, College of Arts and Sciences, Interdisciplinary Program, Miami Shores, FL 33161-6695. Offers MA.

Brooklyn College of the City University of New York, School of Education, Program in Childhood Education, Brooklyn, NY 11210-2889. Offers bilingual education (MS Ed); liberal arts (MS Ed); mathematics (MS Ed); science and environmental education (MS Ed). Part-time and evening/weekend programs available. *Entrance requirements:* For master's, LAST, interview, previous course work in education, writing sample, resume, 2 letters of recommendation. Additional exam requirements/recommendations for international students: Required—TOEFL (minimum score 500 paper-based; 61 iBT). Electronic applications accepted. *Faculty research:* Emotional intelligence, multiculturalism, arts immersion, the Holocaust.

Cardinal Stritch University, College of Arts and Sciences, Milwaukee, WI 53217-3985. Offers MA, MM, MS. Part-time and evening/weekend programs available. *Degree requirements:* For master's, thesis.

Liberal Studies

Clayton State University, School of Graduate Studies, College of Arts and Sciences, Program in Liberal Studies, Morrow, GA 30260-0285. Offers MA. Part-time programs available. *Degree requirements:* For master's, thesis optional. *Entrance requirements:* For master's, GRE, 2 official transcripts, 3 letters of recommendation, statement of purpose, on-campus interview. Additional exam requirements/recommendations for international students: Required—TOEFL (minimum score 550 paper-based; 80 iBT). Electronic applications accepted.

The College at Brockport, State University of New York, General Education Division, Program in Liberal Studies, Brockport, NY 14420-2997. Offers MA. Part-time programs available. Postbaccalaureate distance learning degree programs offered (no on-campus study). *Faculty:* 2 part-time/adjunct (0 women). *Students:* 6 full-time (4 women), 20 part-time (12 women); includes 12 minority (6 Black or African American, non-Hispanic/Latino; 3 Asian, non-Hispanic/Latino; 2 Hispanic/Latino; 1 Two or more races, non-Hispanic/Latino). 12 applicants, 92% accepted, 10 enrolled. In 2014, 7 master's awarded. *Degree requirements:* For master's, portfolio. *Entrance requirements:* For master's, minimum GPA of 3.0, letters of recommendation. Additional exam requirements/recommendations for international students: Required—TOEFL (minimum score 550 paper-based; 79 iBT), IELTS (minimum score 6.5). *Application deadline:* For fall admission, 6/15 priority date for domestic and international students; for spring admission, 10/15 priority date for domestic and international students; for summer admission, 3/15 priority date for domestic and international students. Application fee: $50. Electronic applications accepted. *Financial support:* Federal Work-Study, scholarships/grants, and unspecified assistantships available. Support available to part-time students. Financial award application deadline: 3/15; financial award applicants required to submit FAFSA. *Unit head:* Dr. Kalathur Rajasethupathy, Director, 585-395-2262, Fax: 585-395-2172, E-mail: kraja@brockport.edu. *Application contact:* Danielle A. Welch, Graduate Admissions Counselor, 585-395-5465, Fax: 585-395-2515. Website: http://www.brockport.edu/graduate/

College of Staten Island of the City University of New York, Graduate Programs, Division of Humanities and Social Sciences, Program in Liberal Studies, Staten Island, NY 10314-6600. Offers MA. Evening/weekend programs available. *Faculty:* 3 full-time (0 women), 2 part-time/adjunct (0 women). *Students:* 22. Average age 38. 31 applicants, 58% accepted, 8 enrolled. In 2014, 8 master's awarded. *Degree requirements:* For master's, comprehensive exam, thesis, essay (extended reflection on a problem of contemporary social and/or cultural interest drawing on the intellectual tradition of the liberal arts and on the student's own values and analysis). *Entrance requirements:* For master's, BA or BS with minimum cumulative GPA of 3.0. Additional exam requirements/recommendations for international students: Required—TOEFL (minimum score 550 paper-based; 79 iBT), IELTS (minimum score 6.5). *Application deadline:* For fall admission, 6/1 priority date for domestic and international students. Applications are processed on a rolling basis. Application fee: $125. Electronic applications accepted. *Expenses:* Tuition, state resident: full-time $9650; part-time $405 per credit. Tuition, nonresident: full-time $17,880; part-time $745 per credit. *Required fees:* $141.10 per semester. Tuition and fees vary according to program. *Financial support:* In 2014–15, 12 students received support. Career-related internships or fieldwork, Federal Work-Study, and scholarships/grants available. Support available to part-time students. Financial award applicants required to submit FAFSA. *Unit head:* Dr. David Traboulay, Graduate Program Coordinator, 718-982-2877, Fax: 718-982-2864, E-mail: david.traboulay@csi.cuny.edu. *Application contact:* Sasha Spence, Assistant Director for Graduate Admissions, 718-982-2019, Fax: 718-982-2500, E-mail: sasha.spence@csi.cuny.edu. Website: http://www.csi.cuny.edu/catalog/graduate/master-of-arts-in-liberal-studies-ma.htm

The Colorado College, Education Department, Experienced Teacher Program, Colorado Springs, CO 80903-3294. Offers arts and humanities (MAT); integrated natural sciences (MAT); liberal arts (MAT); Southwest studies (MAT). Programs offered during summer only. Part-time programs available. *Degree requirements:* For master's, thesis, oral exam, 50-page paper. *Expenses:* Contact institution.

Concordia University Chicago, College of Graduate and Innovative Programs, Program in Liberal Studies, River Forest, IL 60305-1499. Offers MA. *Entrance requirements:* Additional exam requirements/recommendations for international students: Required—TOEFL (minimum score 550 paper-based). Electronic applications accepted.

Converse College, School of Education and Graduate Studies, Program in Liberal Arts, Spartanburg, SC 29302-0006. Offers English (MLA); history (MLA); political science (MLA). *Degree requirements:* For master's, capstone paper. *Entrance requirements:* For master's, minimum GPA of 3.0, 2 recommendations.

Dallas Baptist University, Liberal Arts Program, Dallas, TX 75211-9299. Offers arts (MLA); Christian ministry (MLA); East Asian studies (MLA); English (MLA); English as a second language (MLA); fine arts (MLA); history (MLA); missions (MLA); political science (MLA). Part-time and evening/weekend programs available. *Entrance requirements:* For master's, minimum GPA of 3.0. Additional exam requirements/recommendations for international students: Required—TOEFL. Electronic applications accepted. *Expenses: Tuition:* Full-time $14,130; part-time $785 per credit hour. *Required fees:* $200 per semester. Tuition and fees vary according to course level and course load. *Faculty research:* Milton and seventeenth-century Puritans, inter-Biblical years, nineteenth-century literature, Latin American and Texas history.

★ **Dartmouth College,** Arts and Sciences Graduate Programs, Master of Arts in Liberal Studies Program, Hanover, NH 03755. Offers MALS. Part-time programs available. *Faculty:* 14 full-time (4 women), 15 part-time/adjunct (7 women). *Students:* 45 full-time (29 women), 30 part-time (20 women); includes 14 minority (4 Black or African American, non-Hispanic/Latino; 2 Asian, non-Hispanic/Latino; 5 Hispanic/Latino; 3 Two or more races, non-Hispanic/Latino), 20 international. Average age 31. 104 applicants, 70% accepted, 48 enrolled. In 2014, 30 master's awarded. *Degree requirements:* For master's, thesis. *Entrance requirements:* Additional exam requirements/recommendations for international students: Required—TOEFL. *Application deadline:* For fall admission, 2/15 for domestic students; for winter admission, 7/15 for domestic students; for spring admission, 7/15 for domestic students. Application fee: $50. *Financial support:* Institutionally sponsored loans available. Financial award application deadline: 4/2. *Unit head:* Dr. Donald Pease, Chair, 603-646-3592. *Application contact:* Wole Ojurongbe, Director, 603-646-3592, Fax: 603-646-3590, E-mail: mals.program@dartmouth.edu. Website: http://www.dartmouth.edu/~mals/

See Display below and Close-Up on page 341.

Delta State University, Graduate Programs, College of Arts and Sciences, Program in Liberal Studies, Cleveland, MS 38733-0001. Offers evolving human voices (MALS); gender and diversity studies (MALS); globalization studies (MALS); Mississippi Delta studies (MALS); philosophy (MALS); religious studies (MALS). *Students:* 12 full-time (9 women), 7 part-time (5 women); includes 4 minority (all Black or African American, non-Hispanic/Latino). Average age 29. 6 applicants, 83% accepted, 4 enrolled. In 2014, 4 master's awarded. *Degree requirements:* For master's, oral and/or written comprehensive exam. *Application deadline:* For fall admission, 8/1 priority date for domestic students; for spring admission, 12/1 priority date for domestic students. Application fee: $30. *Expenses:* Tuition, state resident: full-time $6012; part-time $334 per credit hour. Tuition, nonresident: full-time $6012; part-time $334 per credit hour. Part-time tuition and fees vary according to course load. *Unit head:* Dr. Paul Hankins,

Dean, 662-846-4100, Fax: 662-846-4016, E-mail: phankins@deltastate.edu. *Application contact:* Dr. Beverly Moon, Dean of Graduate Studies, 662-846-4875, Fax: 662-846-4313, E-mail: grad-info@deltastate.edu.
Website: http://www.deltastate.edu/pages/4994.asp

DePaul University, College of Liberal Arts and Social Sciences, Chicago, IL 60614. Offers Arabic (MA); Chinese (MA); English (MA); French (MA); German (MA); history (MA); interdisciplinary studies (MA, MS); international public service (MS); international studies (MA); Italian (MA); Japanese (MA); leadership and policy studies (MS); liberal studies (MA); new media studies (MA); nonprofit management (MNM); public administration (MPA); public health (MPH); public service management (MS); social work (MSW); sociology (MA); Spanish (MA); sustainable urban development (MA); women and gender studies (MA); writing and publishing (MA); writing, rhetoric, and discourse (MA); MA/PhD. Part-time and evening/weekend programs available. Postbaccalaureate distance learning degree programs offered (no on-campus study). Terminal master's awarded for partial completion of doctoral program. *Degree requirements:* For master's, variable foreign language requirement, comprehensive exam (for some programs), thesis (for some programs). Electronic applications accepted.

Duke University, Graduate School, Program in Liberal Studies, Durham, NC 27708. Offers AM. Part-time and evening/weekend programs available. *Degree requirements:* For master's, thesis or alternative, final project. *Entrance requirements:* For master's, interview. Additional exam requirements/recommendations for international students: Required—IELTS (preferred) or TOEFL. Electronic applications accepted. *Expenses: Tuition:* Full-time $45,760; part-time $2765 per credit. *Required fees:* $978. Full-time tuition and fees vary according to program.

East Tennessee State University, School of Graduate Studies, School of Continuing Studies and Academic Outreach, Johnson City, TN 37614. Offers MALS, MPS, Postbaccalaureate Certificate. Part-time programs available. Postbaccalaureate distance learning degree programs offered (no on-campus study). *Faculty:* 12 full-time (6 women). *Students:* 10 full-time (6 women), 39 part-time (31 women); includes 10 minority (4 Black or African American, non-Hispanic/Latino; 1 American Indian or Alaska Native, non-Hispanic/Latino; 3 Hispanic/Latino; 2 Two or more races, non-Hispanic/Latino). Average age 38. 42 applicants, 50% accepted, 19 enrolled. In 2014, 10 master's, 5 other advanced degrees awarded. *Degree requirements:* For master's, comprehensive exam, thesis optional, professional project. *Entrance requirements:* For master's, GRE General Test, minimum GPA of 2.75, professional portfolio, three letters of recommendation, interview, writing sample; for Postbaccalaureate Certificate, minimum GPA of 2.5, three letters of recommendation, interview. Additional exam requirements/recommendations for international students: Required—TOEFL (minimum score 550 paper-based; 79 iBT). *Application deadline:* For fall admission, 6/1 for domestic students, 4/30 for international students; for spring admission, 11/1 for domestic students, 9/30 for international students. Application fee: $35 ($45 for international students). Electronic applications accepted. *Financial support:* In 2014–15, 14 students received support, including 7 research assistantships with full tuition reimbursements available (averaging $7,000 per year), 1 teaching assistantship with full tuition reimbursement available (averaging $6,000 per year); institutionally sponsored loans, scholarships/grants, tuition waivers, and unspecified assistantships also available. Financial award application deadline: 7/1; financial award applicants required to submit FAFSA. *Faculty research:* Appalachian studies, women's and gender studies, interdisciplinary theory, regional and Southern cultures. *Unit head:* Dr. Rick E. Osborn, Dean, 423-439-4223, Fax: 423-439-7091, E-mail: osbornr@etsu.edu. *Application contact:* Mary Duncan, Graduate Specialist, 423-439-4302, Fax: 423-439-5624, E-mail: duncanm@etsu.edu.
Website: http://www.etsu.edu/academicaffairs/scs/

Excelsior College, School of Liberal Arts, Albany, NY 12203-5159. Offers liberal studies (MA). Part-time and evening/weekend programs available. Postbaccalaureate distance learning degree programs offered (no on-campus study). *Faculty:* 28 part-time/adjunct (17 women). *Students:* 126 part-time (39 women); includes 53 minority (28 Black or African American, non-Hispanic/Latino; 3 American Indian or Alaska Native, non-Hispanic/Latino; 3 Asian, non-Hispanic/Latino; 12 Hispanic/Latino; 1 Native Hawaiian or other Pacific Islander, non-Hispanic/Latino; 6 Two or more races, non-Hispanic/Latino). Average age 47. In 2014, 43 master's awarded. *Degree requirements:* For master's, thesis or alternative. *Application deadline:* Applications are processed on a rolling basis. Application fee: $110. Electronic applications accepted. *Expenses: Tuition:* Part-time $620 per credit hour. *Financial support:* Scholarships/grants available. *Unit head:* Dr. Tracy Caldwell, Associate Dean, 518-464-8500, Fax: 518-464-8777, E-mail: mlsadmin@excelsior.edu. *Application contact:* Tanya Pratt, Administrative Assistant, 518-464-8500 Ext. 1323, Fax: 518-464-8777, E-mail: mls@excelsior.edu.
Website: http://www.excelsior.edu/programs/liberal-arts

Faulkner University, Alabama Christian College of Arts and Sciences, Department of Humanities, Montgomery, AL 36109-3398. Offers liberal arts (MLA).

Florida Atlantic University, Dorothy F. Schmidt College of Arts and Letters, Program in Liberal Studies, Boca Raton, FL 33431-0991. Offers MA. *Degree requirements:* For master's, thesis or alternative. *Expenses:* Tuition, state resident: full-time $7396; part-time $369.82 per credit hour. Tuition, nonresident: full-time $19,392; part-time $1024.81 per credit hour. Tuition and fees vary according to course load.

Florida International University, College of Arts and Sciences, Program in Liberal Studies, Miami, FL 33199. Offers MA. Part-time and evening/weekend programs available. *Degree requirements:* For master's, thesis optional. *Entrance requirements:* For master's, minimum GPA of 3.0, 2-3 letters of recommendation, writing sample, curriculum vitae. Additional exam requirements/recommendations for international students: Required—TOEFL (minimum score 550 paper-based; 80 iBT). Electronic applications accepted.

Fort Hays State University, Graduate School, College of Arts and Sciences, Center for Interdisciplinary Studies, Hays, KS 67601-4099. Offers liberal studies (MLS). Postbaccalaureate distance learning degree programs offered (minimal on-campus study). *Degree requirements:* For master's, comprehensive exam, thesis or alternative. *Entrance requirements:* Additional exam requirements/recommendations for international students: Required—TOEFL (minimum score 550 paper-based). Electronic applications accepted.

Georgetown University, Graduate School of Arts and Sciences, School of Continuing Studies, Washington, DC 20057. Offers American studies (MALS); Catholic studies (MALS); classical civilizations (MALS); emergency and disaster management (MPS); ethics and the professions (MALS); hospitality management (MPS); human resources management (MPS); humanities (MALS); individualized study (MALS); international affairs (MALS); Islam and Muslim-Christian relations (MALS); journalism (MPS); liberal studies (DLS); literature and society (MALS); medieval and early modern European studies (MALS); public relations and corporate communications (MPS); real estate (MPS); religious studies (MALS); social and public policy (MALS); sports industry management (MPS); systems engineering management (MPS); technology management (MPS); the theory and practice of American democracy (MALS); urban and regional planning (MPS); visual culture (MALS). MPS in systems engineering management offered jointly with Stevens Institute of Technology. *Entrance requirements:* Additional exam requirements/recommendations for international students: Required—TOEFL.

The Graduate Center, City University of New York, Graduate Studies, Program in Liberal Studies, New York, NY 10016-4039. Offers MA. *Degree requirements:* For master's, thesis. *Entrance requirements:* For master's, GRE General Test. Additional exam requirements/recommendations for international students: Required—TOEFL. Electronic applications accepted.

Hamline University, College of Liberal Arts, St. Paul, MN 55104-1284. Offers writing (MFA); writing for children and young adults (MFA); JD/MFA. Part-time and evening/weekend programs available. Postbaccalaureate distance learning degree programs offered (minimal on-campus study). *Faculty:* 4 full-time (all women), 22 part-time/adjunct (14 women). *Students:* 164 part-time (109 women); includes 5 minority (1 Black or African American, non-Hispanic/Latino; 1 Asian, non-Hispanic/Latino; 1 Hispanic/Latino; 2 Two or more races, non-Hispanic/Latino), 1 international. Average age 37. 60 applicants, 78% accepted, 24 enrolled. In 2014, 56 master's awarded. *Degree requirements:* For master's, thesis. *Entrance requirements:* For master's, official transcripts, 20-page writing sample (MFA), letters of recommendation, critical essay. Additional exam requirements/recommendations for international students: Required—TOEFL (minimum score 550 paper-based; 80 iBT). *Application deadline:* For fall admission, 2/1 for domestic students, 1/5 for international students; for spring admission, 9/1 for domestic and international students. Applications are processed on a rolling basis. Application fee: $0 ($100 for international students). Electronic applications accepted. *Expenses:* Expenses: Contact institution. *Financial support:* Federal Work-Study and scholarships/grants available. Support available to part-time students. Financial award applicants required to submit FAFSA. *Unit head:* Dr. John Matachek, Dean, 651-523-2206, Fax: 651-523-3055, E-mail: jmatachek@hamline.edu. *Application contact:* Shawn Skoog, Director of Graduate Recruitment and Admission, 651-523-2900, Fax: 651-523-3058, E-mail: sskoog03@hamline.edu.
Website: http://www.hamline.edu/cla/

Harvard University, Extension School, Cambridge, MA 02138-3722. Offers applied sciences (CAS); biotechnology (ALM); educational technologies (ALM); educational technology (CET); English for graduate and professional studies (DGP); environmental management (ALM, CEM); information technology (ALM); journalism (ALM); liberal arts (ALM); management (ALM, CM); mathematics for teaching (ALM); museum studies (ALM); premedical studies (Diploma); publication and communication (CPC). Part-time and evening/weekend programs available. *Degree requirements:* For master's, thesis. *Entrance requirements:* For master's, 3 completed graduate courses with grade of B or higher. Additional exam requirements/recommendations for international students: Required—TOEFL (minimum score 600 paper-based), TWE (minimum score 5). *Expenses:* Contact institution.

Henderson State University, Graduate Studies, Ellis College of Arts and Sciences, Arkadelphia, AR 71999-0001. Offers MLA. Part-time programs available. *Degree requirements:* For master's, thesis. *Entrance requirements:* For master's, MAT or GRE, minimum GPA of 2.7, interview, essay. Additional exam requirements/recommendations for international students: Required—TOEFL (minimum score 600 paper-based); Recommended—IELTS (minimum score 6.5).

Hollins University, Graduate Programs, Program in Liberal Studies, Roanoke, VA 24020. Offers humanities (MALS); interdisciplinary studies (MALS); leadership (MALS); liberal studies (CAS); social science (MALS); visual and performing arts (MALS). Part-time and evening/weekend programs available. *Students:* 3 full-time (all women), 37 part-time (32 women); includes 6 minority (4 Black or African American, non-Hispanic/Latino; 1 Hispanic/Latino; 1 Two or more races, non-Hispanic/Latino). Average age 44. 13 applicants, 100% accepted, 9 enrolled. In 2014, 15 master's awarded. *Degree requirements:* For master's, thesis. *Entrance requirements:* For master's, letters of recommendation, interview. Additional exam requirements/recommendations for international students: Required—TOEFL (minimum score 550 paper-based; 79 iBT). *Application deadline:* For fall admission, 7/1 priority date for domestic and international students; for spring admission, 12/10 priority date for domestic and international students. Applications are processed on a rolling basis. Application fee: $40. Electronic applications accepted. *Financial support:* In 2014–15, 7 students received support, including 7 fellowships (averaging $1,000 per year); scholarships/grants also available. Support available to part-time students. Financial award application deadline: 7/15; financial award applicants required to submit FAFSA. *Faculty research:* Diversity, gender and women's studies, political science, leadership. *Unit head:* Dr. Joe Leedom, Director, 540-362-6326, Fax: 540-362-6288, E-mail: jleedom@hollins.edu. *Application contact:* Cathy S. Koon, Manager of Graduate Services, 540-362-6326, Fax: 540-362-6288, E-mail: ckoon@hollins.edu.
Website: http://www.hollins.edu/

Houston Baptist University, Program in Liberal Arts, Houston, TX 77074-3298. Offers MLA. Part-time and evening/weekend programs available. *Students:* 7 full-time (4 women), 22 part-time (15 women); includes 11 minority (7 Black or African American, non-Hispanic/Latino; 1 American Indian or Alaska Native, non-Hispanic/Latino; 3 Hispanic/Latino). Average age 33. 41 applicants, 51% accepted, 15 enrolled. In 2014, 1 master's awarded. *Entrance requirements:* For master's, minimum GPA of 2.5, two recommendations, resume, bachelor's degree, transcript. Additional exam requirements/recommendations for international students: Required—TOEFL. *Application deadline:* For fall admission, 8/1 for domestic students, 6/1 for international students; for winter admission, 10/1 for domestic and international students; for spring admission, 12/1 for domestic students, 10/1 for international students; for summer admission, 5/1 for domestic students, 3/1 for international students. Applications are processed on a rolling basis. Application fee: $0. Electronic applications accepted. *Expenses:* Expenses: Contact institution. *Financial support:* Federal Work-Study and scholarships/grants available. Support available to part-time students. Financial award application deadline: 4/1; financial award applicants required to submit FAFSA. *Unit head:* Dr. Jodey Hinze, Dean, 281-649-3130, E-mail: jhinze@hbu.edu. *Application contact:* Kathy Holston, Administrative Assistant to the Dean, 281-649-3404, E-mail: kholston@hbu.edu.
Website: http://www.hbu.edu/mla

Indiana University Northwest, College of Arts and Sciences, Gary, IN 46408-1197. Offers clinical counseling (MS), including drug and alcohol counseling; liberal studies (MLS). *Students:* 7 full-time (5 women), 23 part-time (18 women); includes 15 minority (13 Black or African American, non-Hispanic/Latino; 2 Hispanic/Latino). 10 applicants, 80% accepted, 5 enrolled. In 2014, 2 master's awarded. *Unit head:* Robert Mucci, Graduate Program Director, 219-980-6607, E-mail: rmucci@iun.edu.
Website: http://www.iun.edu/coas/

Indiana University–Purdue University Fort Wayne, College of Arts and Sciences, Program in Liberal Studies, Fort Wayne, IN 46805-1499. Offers MLS. Part-time programs available. *Students:* 2 full-time (1 woman), 14 part-time (9 women); includes 2 minority (1 Black or African American, non-Hispanic/Latino; 1 American Indian or Alaska Native, non-Hispanic/Latino). Average age 45. 2 applicants, 100% accepted, 2 enrolled. In 2014, 11 master's awarded. *Entrance requirements:* For master's, minimum GPA of

3.0, major or minor in related area, three letters of recommendation. Additional exam requirements/recommendations for international students: Required—TOEFL (minimum score 550 paper-based; 79 iBT). *Application deadline:* For fall admission, 8/1 for domestic students; for spring admission, 12/1 for domestic students. Applications are processed on a rolling basis. Application fee: $50. *Financial support:* Scholarships/ grants available. Support available to part-time students. Financial award application deadline: 3/1; financial award applicants required to submit FAFSA. *Unit head:* Rachel Hile, Director, 260-481-6767, Fax: 260-481-6985, E-mail: hiler@ipfw.edu.

Indiana University–Purdue University Indianapolis, School of Liberal Arts, Indianapolis, IN 46202. Offers MA, MS, PhD, Certificate, JD/MA, MA/MA, MA/MLS, MD/ MA. *Students:* 117 full-time (53 women), 140 part-time (91 women); includes 30 minority (13 Black or African American, non-Hispanic/Latino; 5 Asian, non-Hispanic/Latino; 4 Hispanic/Latino; 8 Two or more races, non-Hispanic/Latino), 33 international. Average age 33. 234 applicants, 49% accepted, 84 enrolled. In 2014, 74 master's, 8 other advanced degrees awarded. Application fee: $55 ($65 for international students). *Unit head:* Dr. William Blomquist, Dean, School of Liberal Arts, 317-274-8448, E-mail: blomquis@iupui.edu. *Application contact:* Candice L. Smith, Coordinator of Academic and Graduate Programs, 317-274-8305, E-mail: canlsmit@iupui.edu.
Website: http://liberalarts.iupui.edu/

Indiana University South Bend, College of Liberal Arts and Sciences, South Bend, IN 46634-7111. Offers applied mathematics and computer science (MS); English (MA); liberal studies (MLS); public affairs (MPA). Part-time and evening/weekend programs available. *Faculty:* 79 full-time (33 women). *Students:* 41 full-time (26 women), 89 part-time (59 women); includes 24 minority (12 Black or African American, non-Hispanic/ Latino; 1 Asian, non-Hispanic/Latino; 3 Hispanic/Latino; 1 Native Hawaiian or other Pacific Islander, non-Hispanic/Latino; 7 Two or more races, non-Hispanic/Latino), 15 international. Average age 37. 58 applicants, 72% accepted, 33 enrolled. In 2014, 33 master's awarded. *Degree requirements:* For master's, thesis (for some programs). *Entrance requirements:* For master's, minimum GPA of 3.0. Additional exam requirements/recommendations for international students: Required—TOEFL. *Application deadline:* For fall admission, 7/31 priority date for domestic students, 7/1 priority date for international students; for spring admission, 3/31 priority date for domestic students, 11/1 priority date for international students. Applications are processed on a rolling basis. *Financial support:* In 2014–15, 5 teaching assistantships were awarded; Federal Work-Study also available. Support available to part-time students. *Faculty research:* Artificial intelligence, bioinformatics, English language and literature, creative writing, computer networks. *Total annual research expenditures:* $127,000. *Unit head:* Dr. Elizabeth E. Dunn, Dean, 574-520-4290, E-mail: elizdunn@iusb.edu. *Application contact:* Admissions Counselor, 574-520-4839, Fax: 574-520-4834, E-mail: graduate@iusb.edu.
Website: https://www.iusb.edu/clas/academics/index.php

Jacksonville State University, College of Graduate Studies and Continuing Education, College of Arts and Sciences, Department of Liberal Studies, Jacksonville, AL 36265-1602. Offers MA. Part-time and evening/weekend programs available. *Students:* 4 full-time (0 women), 31 part-time (17 women); includes 16 minority (15 Black or African American, non-Hispanic/Latino; 1 American Indian or Alaska Native, non-Hispanic/ Latino), 3 international. Average age 32. 21 applicants, 48% accepted, 10 enrolled. In 2014, 3 master's awarded. *Degree requirements:* For master's, comprehensive exam, thesis (for some programs). *Entrance requirements:* Additional exam requirements/ recommendations for international students: Required—TOEFL (minimum score 500 paper-based; 61 iBT). *Application deadline:* Applications are processed on a rolling basis. Application fee: $35. Electronic applications accepted. *Financial support:* In 2014–15, 12 students received support. Available to part-time students. Application deadline: 4/1; applicants required to submit FAFSA. *Unit head:* Dr. Earl Wade, Dean, 256-782-5649, E-mail: jwade@jsu.edu. *Application contact:* Dr. Jean Pugliese, Associate Dean, 256-782-8278, Fax: 256-782-5321, E-mail: pugliese@jsu.edu.

Johns Hopkins University, Zanvyl Krieger School of Arts and Sciences, Advanced Academic Programs, Program in Liberal Arts, Washington, DC 20036. Offers MA, Certificate. Part-time and evening/weekend programs available. Postbaccalaureate distance learning degree programs offered (minimal on-campus study). *Degree requirements:* For master's, thesis. *Entrance requirements:* For master's, minimum GPA of 3.0. Additional exam requirements/recommendations for international students: Required—TOEFL (minimum score 100 iBT). Electronic applications accepted.

Kent State University, College of Arts and Sciences, Center for Comparative and Integrative Programs, Kent, OH 44242-0001. Offers MLS. Part-time and evening/ weekend programs available. Postbaccalaureate distance learning degree programs offered. *Students:* 1 full-time (0 women), 16 part-time (13 women); includes 3 minority (2 Black or African American, non-Hispanic/Latino; 1 Asian, non-Hispanic/Latino). Average age 39. 27 applicants, 59% accepted, 11 enrolled. In 2014, 4 master's awarded. *Degree requirements:* For master's, thesis, capstone essay. *Entrance requirements:* For master's, minimum GPA of 3.0, transcript, goal statement, 3 letters of recommendation. Additional exam requirements/recommendations for international students: Required—TOEFL (minimum score: paper-based 525, iBT 71), Michigan English Language Assessment Battery (minimum score of 75), IELTS (minimum score of 6.0), PTE Academic (minimum score of 48), or completion of ELS level 112 Intensive Program. *Application deadline:* For fall admission, 5/1 for domestic students; for spring admission, 11/29 for domestic students. Applications are processed on a rolling basis. Application fee: $45 ($70 for international students). Electronic applications accepted. *Expenses:* Tuition, state resident: full-time $8730; part-time $485 per credit hour. Tuition, nonresident: full-time $14,886; part-time $827 per credit hour. Tuition and fees vary according to campus/location and program. *Financial support:* Career-related internships or fieldwork and Federal Work-Study available. *Unit head:* Dr. David W. Odell-Scott, Associate Dean, 330-672-0271, E-mail: dodellsc@kent.edu. *Application contact:* Richard M. Berrong, Director of Liberal Studies, E-mail: rberrong@kent.edu.
Website: http://www.kent.edu/ccip/graduate-degree-programs

Lake Forest College, Graduate Program in Liberal Studies, Lake Forest, IL 60045. Offers American studies (MLS); environmental studies (MLS); history and freedom (MLS); writing (MLS). Part-time and evening/weekend programs available. *Faculty:* 11 full-time (5 women), 1 (woman) part-time/adjunct. *Students:* 42 part-time (22 women); includes 4 minority (2 Asian, non-Hispanic/Latino; 2 Hispanic/Latino). Average age 38. 26 applicants, 50% accepted, 9 enrolled. In 2014, 7 master's awarded. *Degree requirements:* For master's, thesis optional, 8 courses, including at least 3 interdisciplinary seminars. *Entrance requirements:* For master's, transcript, essay, interview. Additional exam requirements/recommendations for international students: Required—TOEFL (minimum score 550 paper-based; 83 iBT); Recommended—IELTS (minimum score 6.5). *Application deadline:* For fall admission, 7/15 priority date for domestic students, 6/1 priority date for international students; for winter admission, 12/ 15 for domestic students, 10/1 for international students; for spring admission, 12/1 priority date for domestic students, 10/1 priority date for international students. Applications are processed on a rolling basis. Application fee: $30. *Expenses:* Expenses: Contact institution. *Financial support:* In 2014–15, 4 students received support. Scholarships/grants and partial tuition grants (for full-time teachers) available. Financial award application deadline: 7/15. *Faculty research:* History of American political thought; American families; electron collisions with molecules; international relations, American foreign policy, and transparency in world politics; ethics and social justice; pacifism. *Unit head:* Prof. D. L. LeMahieu, Director, 847-735-5133, Fax: 847-735-6291, E-mail: lemahieu@lakeforest.edu. *Application contact:* Prof. Carol Gayle, Associate Director, 847-735-5083, Fax: 847-735-6291, E-mail: gayle@lakeforest.edu.
Website: http://www.lakeforest.edu/academics/programs/mls/

Louisiana State University and Agricultural & Mechanical College, Graduate School, College of Humanities and Social Sciences, Interdepartmental Program in the Liberal Arts, Baton Rouge, LA 70803. Offers MALA. Part-time and evening/weekend programs available. *Students:* 11 full-time (5 women), 11 part-time (6 women); includes 5 minority (3 Black or African American, non-Hispanic/Latino; 2 Two or more races, non-Hispanic/Latino). Average age 32. 10 applicants, 100% accepted, 5 enrolled. In 2014, 9 master's awarded. *Degree requirements:* For master's, project or thesis. *Entrance requirements:* For master's, GRE General Test, minimum GPA of 3.0. Additional exam requirements/recommendations for international students: Required—TOEFL (minimum score 550 paper-based; 79 IBT), IELTS (minimum score 6.5), or PTE (minimum score 59). *Application deadline:* For fall admission, 1/1 priority date for domestic students, 5/15 for international students; for spring admission, 10/15 for domestic and international students; for summer admission, 5/15 for domestic and international students. Applications are processed on a rolling basis. Application fee: $50 ($70 for international students). Electronic applications accepted. *Financial support:* In 2014–15, 17 students received support. Fellowships with full tuition reimbursements available, research assistantships with partial tuition reimbursements available, teaching assistantships with partial tuition reimbursements available, Federal Work-Study, and health care benefits available. Financial award applicants required to submit FAFSA. *Total annual research expenditures:* $16,349. *Unit head:* Dr. William Clark, Director, 225-578-2549, Fax: 225-578-6447, E-mail: poclark@lsu.edu.
Website: http://www.artsci.lsu.edu/groups/MALA/MALAinfo.html

Louisiana State University in Shreveport, College of Arts and Sciences, Program in Liberal Arts, Shreveport, LA 71115-2399. Offers MA. Part-time and evening/weekend programs available. *Students:* 4 full-time (1 woman), 42 part-time (35 women); includes 9 minority (6 Black or African American, non-Hispanic/Latino; 1 Hispanic/Latino; 2 Two or more races, non-Hispanic/Latino), 2 international. Average age 36. 26 applicants, 100% accepted, 12 enrolled. In 2014, 12 master's awarded. *Degree requirements:* For master's, comprehensive exam, thesis or alternative. *Entrance requirements:* For master's, interview, minimum GPA of 3.0 during final 2 years of course work, statement of purpose. Additional exam requirements/recommendations for international students: Required—TOEFL (minimum score 550 paper-based; 61 iBT). *Application deadline:* For fall admission, 6/30 for domestic and international students; for spring admission, 11/30 for domestic and international students; for summer admission, 4/30 for domestic and international students. Applications are processed on a rolling basis. Application fee: $20 ($30 for international students). Electronic applications accepted. *Expenses:* Tuition, state resident: full-time $5234; part-time $290.80 per credit hour. Tuition, nonresident: full-time $16,774; part-time $879.61 per credit hour. *Required fees:* $52.28 per credit hour. *Financial support:* In 2014–15, 3 students received support, including 2 research assistantships (averaging $3,750 per year). *Unit head:* Dr. Helen Taylor, Program Director, 318-797-5211, Fax: 318-797-5358, E-mail: helen.taylor@lsus.edu. *Application contact:* Kimberly Thornton, Director of Admissions, 318-795-2405, Fax: 318-797-5286, E-mail: kimberly.thornton@lsus.edu.

Loyola University Maryland, Graduate Programs, Loyola College of Arts and Sciences, Department of Liberal Studies, Baltimore, MD 21210-2699. Offers MA. Part-time programs available. *Entrance requirements:* For master's, essay, 2 recommendations, transcripts, resume. Additional exam requirements/ recommendations for international students: Required—TOEFL. Electronic applications accepted.

Madonna University, Program in Liberal Studies, Livonia, MI 48150-1173. Offers MALS.

McDaniel College, Graduate and Professional Studies, Program in Liberal Arts, Westminster, MD 21157-4390. Offers MLA. Part-time and evening/weekend programs available. *Students:* 1 (woman) full-time, 21 part-time (17 women); includes 1 minority (Black or African American, non-Hispanic/Latino). *Degree requirements:* For master's, final project. *Entrance requirements:* For master's, 3 letters of reference. Additional exam requirements/recommendations for international students: Required—TOEFL (minimum score 79 iBT), IELTS (minimum score 6). *Application deadline:* Applications are processed on a rolling basis. Application fee: $75. Electronic applications accepted. *Financial support:* Application deadline: 3/1; applicants required to submit FAFSA. *Unit head:* Dr. Bryn Upton, Coordinator, 410-857-2416, E-mail: bupton@mcdaniel.edu. *Application contact:* Crystal L. Perry, Assistant Director, Graduate Enrollment Management, 410-857-2516, Fax: 410-857-2515, E-mail: cperry@mcdaniel.edu.

Metropolitan State University, College of Arts and Sciences, St. Paul, MN 55106-5000. Offers computer science (MS); liberal studies (MA); technical communication (MS). Part-time and evening/weekend programs available. *Entrance requirements:* For master's, minimum GPA of 2.75, resume. Additional exam requirements/ recommendations for international students: Required—TOEFL (minimum score 550 paper-based). Electronic applications accepted.

Mississippi College, Graduate School, Program in Liberal Studies, Clinton, MS 39058. Offers MLS. Part-time programs available. *Degree requirements:* For master's, comprehensive exam, thesis optional. *Entrance requirements:* For master's, GRE, minimum GPA of 2.5. Additional exam requirements/recommendations for international students: Recommended—TOEFL, IELTS.

Nazareth College of Rochester, Graduate Studies, Department of Liberal Studies, Rochester, NY 14618-3790. Offers MA. *Entrance requirements:* For master's, minimum GPA of 3.0.

The New School, The New School for Social Research, Department in Liberal Studies, New York, NY 10003. Offers MA. Part-time and evening/weekend programs available. *Degree requirements:* For master's, thesis. *Entrance requirements:* For master's, GRE General Test. Additional exam requirements/recommendations for international students: Required—TOEFL (minimum score 600 paper-based; 100 iBT). Electronic applications accepted.

North Carolina State University, Graduate School, College of Humanities and Social Sciences, Program in Liberal Studies, Raleigh, NC 27695. Offers MA. Part-time and evening/weekend programs available. *Degree requirements:* For master's, thesis optional. Electronic applications accepted. *Faculty research:* Humanities, social sciences, sciences.

North Central College, Graduate and Continuing Studies Programs, Program in Liberal Studies, Naperville, IL 60566-7063. Offers culture and society (MALS); ethics and public service (MALS); writing, editing, and publishing (MALS). Part-time and evening/weekend programs available. *Faculty:* 8 full-time (2 women), 4 part-time/adjunct (1 woman). *Students:* 2 full-time (1 woman), 24 part-time (14 women); includes 1 minority (Asian, non-Hispanic/Latino). Average age 36. 15 applicants, 73% accepted, 7 enrolled. In 2014, 6 master's awarded. *Degree requirements:* For master's, thesis optional, project.

Entrance requirements: For master's, interview. Additional exam requirements/recommendations for international students: Required—TOEFL (minimum score 550 paper-based; 80 iBT). *Application deadline:* For fall admission, 8/15 for domestic students, 7/15 for international students; for winter admission, 12/1 for domestic students, 11/1 for international students; for spring admission, 2/1 for domestic students, 12/1 for international students. Applications are processed on a rolling basis. Application fee: $25. Electronic applications accepted. Application fee is waived when completed online. *Expenses:* Expenses: Contact institution. *Financial support:* In 2014–15, 1 student received support. Scholarships/grants available. Support available to part-time students. Financial award applicants required to submit FAFSA. *Unit head:* Dr. Richard Guzman, Program Coordinator, Liberal Studies, 630-637-5285. *Application contact:* Wendy Kulpinski, Director of Graduate and Continuing Education Admission, 630-637-5808, Fax: 630-637-5844, E-mail: wekulpinski@noctrl.edu.
Website: http://northcentralcollege.edu/admission/liberal-studies

Northern Arizona University, Graduate College, College of Social and Behavioral Sciences, Program in Sustainable Communities, Flagstaff, AZ 86011. Offers MA. Part-time programs available. *Degree requirements:* For master's, thesis. *Entrance requirements:* For master's, minimum GPA of 3.0. Additional exam requirements/recommendations for international students: Required—TOEFL (minimum score 550 paper-based; 80 iBT), IELTS (minimum score 7). Electronic applications accepted.

Northern Kentucky University, Office of Graduate Programs, College of Arts and Sciences, Program in Integrative Studies, Highland Heights, KY 41099. Offers MA. Part-time and evening/weekend programs available. *Faculty:* 1 (woman) full-time. *Students:* 5 full-time (3 women), 25 part-time (21 women); includes 5 minority (2 Black or African American, non-Hispanic/Latino; 2 Asian, non-Hispanic/Latino; 1 Hispanic/Latino). Average age 35. In 2014, 10 master's awarded. *Degree requirements:* For master's, thesis or capstone. *Entrance requirements:* For master's, statement of purpose, three letters of reference, resume, minimum GPA of 3.0. Additional exam requirements/recommendations for international students: Required—TOEFL (minimum score 79 iBT); Recommended—IELTS (minimum score 6.5). *Application deadline:* For fall admission, 8/1 priority date for domestic students, 6/1 for international students; for spring admission, 12/1 priority date for domestic students, 10/1 for international students; for summer admission, 5/1 priority date for domestic students, 4/1 for international students. Application fee: $40. Electronic applications accepted. *Expenses: Tuition, area resident:* Part-time $518 per credit hour. Tuition, state resident: part-time $630 per credit hour. Tuition, nonresident: part-time $797 per credit hour. *Required fees:* $192 per semester. Tuition and fees vary according to course load, degree level, campus/location, program and reciprocity agreements. *Financial support:* In 2014–15, 15 students received support. Unspecified assistantships available. Financial award applicants required to submit FAFSA. *Faculty research:* Industrial/organizational psychology, truancy, athletic health training, motivation, compassion and stress. *Unit head:* Dr. Jennifer Webster, Interim Director of Integrative Studies, 859-572-1450, Fax: 859-572-6185, E-mail: websterj3@nku.edu. *Application contact:* Alison Swanson, Graduate Admissions Coordinator, 859-572-6971, E-mail: swansona1@nku.edu.
Website: http://artscience.nku.edu/departments/integrativestudies.html

Northwestern University, School of Professional Studies, Program in Liberal Studies, Evanston, IL 60208. Offers American studies (MA); history (MA); religious and ethical studies (MA).

Notre Dame of Maryland University, Graduate Studies, Program in Liberal Studies, Baltimore, MD 21210-2476. Offers MA. Part-time and evening/weekend programs available. *Degree requirements:* For master's, thesis or alternative. *Entrance requirements:* For master's, minimum GPA of 3.0. Additional exam requirements/recommendations for international students: Required—TOEFL (minimum score 500 paper-based; 61 iBT). Electronic applications accepted.

Oakland University, Graduate Study and Lifelong Learning, College of Arts and Sciences, Program in Liberal Studies, Rochester, MI 48309-4401. Offers MA. *Entrance requirements:* For master's, minimum GPA of 3.0. Additional exam requirements/recommendations for international students: Required—TOEFL (minimum score 550 paper-based). Electronic applications accepted.

Occidental College, Graduate Studies, Department of Education, Los Angeles, CA 90041-3314. Offers elementary education (MAT), including liberal studies; secondary education (MAT), including English and comparative literary studies, history, life science, mathematics, physical science, social science, Spanish. Part-time programs available. *Degree requirements:* For master's, comprehensive exam, synthesis paper. *Entrance requirements:* For master's, GRE General Test, minimum GPA of 3.0. Additional exam requirements/recommendations for international students: Required—TOEFL (minimum score 625 paper-based). *Expenses:* Contact institution. *Faculty research:* Preparing teacher-leaders, curriculum development.

Oklahoma City University, Petree College of Arts and Sciences, Program in Liberal Arts, Oklahoma City, OK 73106-1402. Offers MLA. Part-time and evening/weekend programs available. *Faculty:* 8 full-time (3 women), 2 part-time/adjunct (0 women). *Students:* 9 full-time (5 women), 4 part-time (all women); includes 2 minority (1 Black or African American, non-Hispanic/Latino; 1 Asian, non-Hispanic/Latino), 6 international. Average age 27. 8 applicants, 75% accepted, 4 enrolled. In 2014, 12 master's awarded. *Degree requirements:* For master's, comprehensive exam, thesis optional. *Entrance requirements:* For master's, bachelor's degree from accredited institution, minimum GPA of 3.0, essay, recommendation letters. Additional exam requirements/recommendations for international students: Required—TOEFL (minimum score 550 paper-based; 80 iBT). *Application deadline:* Applications are processed on a rolling basis. Application fee: $50. Electronic applications accepted. *Expenses: Tuition:* Part-time $936 per credit hour. *Required fees:* $115 per credit hour. One-time fee: $250. Tuition and fees vary according to course load, degree level, program and student's religious affiliation. *Financial support:* In 2014–15, 5 students received support. Career-related internships or fieldwork, Federal Work-Study, institutionally sponsored loans, scholarships/grants, and tuition waivers available. Support available to part-time students. Financial award application deadline: 6/1; financial award applicants required to submit FAFSA. *Unit head:* Dr. Regina Bennett, Director, 405-208-5178, Fax: 405-208-5451, E-mail: rbennett@okcu.edu. *Application contact:* Michael Harrington, Director, Graduate Admissions, 800-633-7242, Fax: 405-208-5916, E-mail: gadmissions@okcu.edu.
Website: http://www.okcu.edu/mla

Queens College of the City University of New York, Division of Graduate Studies, Social Science Division, Program in Liberal Studies, Flushing, NY 11367-1597. Offers MALS. Part-time and evening/weekend programs available. *Degree requirements:* For master's, thesis. *Entrance requirements:* For master's, minimum GPA of 3.0. Additional exam requirements/recommendations for international students: Required—TOEFL.

Ramapo College of New Jersey, Master of Arts in Liberal Studies Program, Mahwah, NJ 07430. Offers MA. Part-time and evening/weekend programs available. *Degree requirements:* For master's, thesis, capstone project may include a thesis or a project of an artistic or theatrical nature. *Entrance requirements:* For master's, official transcript; personal statement; 2 letters of recommendation; resume (recommended). Additional exam requirements/recommendations for international students: Required—TOEFL

(minimum score 550 paper-based; 79 iBT); Recommended—IELTS (minimum score 6). Electronic applications accepted. *Faculty research:* History of science, women's studies, Native American studies, theology, genocide studies.

Reed College, Graduate Program in Liberal Studies, Portland, OR 97202-8199. Offers MALS. Part-time and evening/weekend programs available. *Degree requirements:* For master's, thesis, oral defense of thesis. *Entrance requirements:* For master's, interview, letters of recommendation. Additional exam requirements/recommendations for international students: Recommended—TOEFL. Electronic applications accepted.

Regis University, College for Professional Studies, School of Humanities and Social Sciences, Master of Arts in Liberal Studies Program, Denver, CO 80221-1099. Offers MA. Program also offered in Henderson and Las Vegas (Summerlin), NV. Part-time and evening/weekend programs available. Postbaccalaureate distance learning degree programs offered (no on-campus study). *Faculty:* 11 full-time (4 women), 38 part-time/adjunct (25 women). *Students:* 73 full-time (62 women), 90 part-time (65 women); includes 42 minority (10 Black or African American, non-Hispanic/Latino; 1 American Indian or Alaska Native, non-Hispanic/Latino; 4 Asian, non-Hispanic/Latino; 24 Hispanic/Latino; 3 Two or more races, non-Hispanic/Latino), 3 international. Average age 41. 37 applicants, 84% accepted, 26 enrolled. In 2014, 77 master's awarded. *Degree requirements:* For master's, thesis, research project. *Entrance requirements:* For master's, official transcript reflecting baccalaureate degree awarded from regionally-accredited college or university, essays, letters of recommendation, resume, interview. Additional exam requirements/recommendations for international students: Required—TOEFL (minimum score 550 paper-based; 82 iBT). *Application deadline:* For fall admission, 8/13 for domestic students, 7/13 for international students; for winter admission, 10/8 for domestic students, 9/8 for international students; for spring admission, 12/17 for domestic students, 11/17 for international students. Applications are processed on a rolling basis. Application fee: $75. Electronic applications accepted. *Expenses:* Expenses: $460 per credit hour. *Financial support:* In 2014–15, 14 students received support. Federal Work-Study and scholarships/grants available. Financial award application deadline: 4/15; financial award applicants required to submit FAFSA. *Faculty research:* New methods and models, adult learning and the Capstone experience, goal setting, behavior of adult students, innovative studies for community colleges. *Unit head:* Franklin Medford, Chair, 303-964-3692, Fax: 303-964-5538, E-mail: fmedford@regis.edu. *Application contact:* Sarah Engel, Director of Admissions, 303-458-4900, Fax: 303-964-5534, E-mail: regisadm@regis.edu.
Website: http://regis.edu/CPS/Academics/Degrees-and-Programs/Graduate-Programs/Master-of-Arts.aspx

Rice University, Graduate Programs, Susanne M. Glasscock School of Continuing Studies, Houston, TX 77251-1892. Offers MLS. Part-time and evening/weekend programs available. *Degree requirements:* For master's, thesis or alternative, capstone paper/project. *Entrance requirements:* For master's, bachelor's degree from accredited institution; minimum GPA of 3.0; two letters of recommendation; personal statement; 3 writing samples; current resume. Additional exam requirements/recommendations for international students: Required—TOEFL (minimum score 600 paper-based; 90 iBT). *Expenses:* Contact institution.

Rollins College, Hamilton Holt School, Master of Liberal Studies Program, Winter Park, FL 32789. Offers MLS. Part-time and evening/weekend programs available. *Faculty:* 4 full-time (2 women), 2 part-time/adjunct (1 woman). *Students:* 2 full-time (1 woman), 45 part-time (27 women); includes 8 minority (1 Black or African American, non-Hispanic/Latino; 6 Hispanic/Latino; 1 Two or more races, non-Hispanic/Latino), 1 international. Average age 41. 9 applicants, 78% accepted, 7 enrolled. In 2014, 13 master's awarded. *Degree requirements:* For master's, thesis. *Entrance requirements:* For master's, official transcripts, two letters of recommendation, essay. Additional exam requirements/recommendations for international students: Required—TOEFL (minimum score 550 paper-based; 80 iBT). *Application deadline:* For fall admission, 4/1 for domestic students; for spring admission, 12/1 for domestic students. Application fee: $50. *Expenses:* Expenses: Contact institution. *Financial support:* In 2014–15, 23 students received support. Federal Work-Study, scholarships/grants, and unspecified assistantships available. Support available to part-time students. Financial award applicants required to submit FAFSA. *Unit head:* Dr. Patricia Lancaster, Faculty Director, 407-646-2237, Fax: 407-646-2363. *Application contact:* Carmen Rasnick, Graduate Coordinator, 407-646-2653, Fax: 407-646-1551, E-mail: crasnick@rollins.edu.
Website: http://www.rollins.edu/holt/graduate/mls.html

Rutgers, The State University of New Jersey, Camden, Graduate School of Arts and Sciences, Program in Liberal Studies, Camden, NJ 08102. Offers MALS. Part-time and evening/weekend programs available. *Degree requirements:* For master's, thesis, 30 credits. *Entrance requirements:* For master's, 2 letters of recommendation, writing sample, statement of personal, professional and academic goals. Additional exam requirements/recommendations for international students: Required—TOEFL, IELTS. Electronic applications accepted. *Faculty research:* Psychology, English, history, philosophy, religion.

St. Edward's University, New College, Program in Liberal Arts, Austin, TX 78704. Offers global issues (MLA); humanities (MLA); liberal arts (Certificate); social justice (MLA); social sciences (MLA). Part-time and evening/weekend programs available. *Students:* 3 full-time (2 women), 49 part-time (36 women); includes 18 minority (2 Black or African American, non-Hispanic/Latino; 15 Hispanic/Latino; 1 Two or more races, non-Hispanic/Latino). Average age 35. 34 applicants, 68% accepted, 17 enrolled. In 2014, 23 master's awarded. *Degree requirements:* For master's, minimum of 24 resident hours. *Entrance requirements:* For master's, minimum GPA of 2.75 in last 60 hours of course work, interview. Additional exam requirements/recommendations for international students: Required—TOEFL (minimum score 79 iBT) or IELTS (minimum score 6). *Application deadline:* For fall admission, 6/1 priority date for domestic and international students; for spring admission, 10/1 priority date for domestic and international students; for summer admission, 3/1 priority date for domestic and international students. Applications are processed on a rolling basis. Application fee: $50. Electronic applications accepted. *Expenses: Tuition:* Full-time $22,448; part-time $1246 per credit hour. *Required fees:* $50 per trimester. Full-time tuition and fees vary according to course load and program. *Unit head:* Dr. H. Ramsey Fowler, Director, 512-448-8648, Fax: 512-448-8492, E-mail: ramseyf@stewards.edu. *Application contact:* Office of Admission, 512-448-8500, Fax: 512-464-8877, E-mail: seu.admit@stedwards.edu.
Website: http://www.stedwards.edu

St. John's College, Graduate Institute, Annapolis, MD 21404. Offers MALA. Evening/weekend programs available. *Degree requirements:* For master's, thesis optional. *Entrance requirements:* For master's, bachelor's degree. Additional exam requirements/recommendations for international students: Required—TOEFL (minimum score 650 paper-based; 112 iBT), TWE (minimum score 5). Electronic applications accepted.

St. John's College, Graduate Institute in Liberal Education, Program in Liberal Arts, Santa Fe, NM 87505. Offers MA. Evening/weekend programs available. *Entrance requirements:* For master's, 2 letters of recommendation. Additional exam requirements/recommendations for international students: Required—TOEFL, TWE.

Liberal Studies

St. John's University, St. John's College of Liberal Arts and Sciences, Program in Liberal Studies, Queens, NY 11439. Offers MA. Part-time and evening/weekend programs available. *Students:* 6 full-time (4 women), 7 part-time (all women); includes 4 minority (2 Black or African American, non-Hispanic/Latino; 2 Hispanic/Latino; 1 international. Average age 35. 13 applicants, 92% accepted, 6 enrolled. In 2014, 5 master's awarded. *Degree requirements:* For master's, capstone project. *Entrance requirements:* For master's, minimum GPA of 3.0, personal essay, 2 letters of recommendation, 6 credit hours in area of concentration, bachelor's degree. Additional exam requirements/recommendations for international students: Required—TOEFL (minimum score 600 paper-based; 100 iBT), IELTS (minimum score 7). *Application deadline:* For fall admission, 5/1 priority date for domestic and international students; for spring admission, 11/1 priority date for domestic and international students. Applications are processed on a rolling basis. Application fee: $70. Electronic applications accepted. *Expenses: Tuition:* Full-time $20,610; part-time $1145 per credit. *Required fees:* $170 per semester. *Financial support:* Career-related internships or fieldwork and scholarships/grants available. Support available to part-time students. Financial award application deadline: 3/1; financial award applicants required to submit FAFSA. *Unit head:* Rev. Jean-Pierre Ruiz, Director, 718-990_5726, E-mail: ruizj@stjohns.edu. *Application contact:* Robert Medrano, Director of Graduate Admission, 718-990-1601, Fax: 718-990-5686, E-mail: gradhelp@stjohns.edu.

St. Norbert College, Program in Liberal Studies, De Pere, WI 54115-2099. Offers MA. Part-time and evening/weekend programs available. *Faculty:* 4 part-time/adjunct (1 woman). *Students:* 16 part-time (9 women); includes 3 minority (1 American Indian or Alaska Native, non-Hispanic/Latino; 2 Hispanic/Latino). Average age 40. 3 applicants, 100% accepted, 1 enrolled. In 2014, 5 master's awarded. *Degree requirements:* For master's, thesis. *Application deadline:* Applications are processed on a rolling basis. Application fee: $50. Electronic applications accepted. *Expenses: Tuition:* Part-time $472 per credit hour. *Unit head:* Dr. Howard Ebert, Director, 920-403-3956, Fax: 920-403-4086, E-mail: howard.ebert@snc.edu. *Application contact:* Dinah Grassel, Program Coordinator, 920-403-3957, Fax: 920-403-4086, E-mail: dinah.grassel@snc.edu. Website: http://www.snc.edu/mls/

San Diego State University, Graduate and Research Affairs, College of Arts and Letters, Program in Liberal Arts and Sciences, San Diego, CA 92182. Offers MA. Part-time and evening/weekend programs available. *Degree requirements:* For master's, thesis. *Entrance requirements:* For master's, GRE General Test. Additional exam requirements/recommendations for international students: Required—TOEFL. Electronic applications accepted.

Simon Fraser University, Office of Graduate Studies, Faculty of Arts and Social Sciences, Program in Liberal Studies, Vancouver, BC V6B 5K3, Canada. Offers MALS. Part-time and evening/weekend programs available. Postbaccalaureate distance learning degree programs offered (minimal on-campus study). *Degree requirements:* For master's, thesis or alternative. *Entrance requirements:* For master's, minimum GPA of 3.0 (on scale of 4.33), or 3.33 based on last 60 credits of undergraduate courses. Additional exam requirements/recommendations for international students: Recommended—TOEFL (minimum score 580 paper-based; 93 iBT), IELTS (minimum score 7), TWE (minimum score 5). Electronic applications accepted. *Faculty research:* Humanities, art history and culture, women's studies, literature, philosophy.

Skidmore College, Master of Arts in Liberal Studies Program, Saratoga Springs, NY 12866. Offers MA. Part-time programs available. Postbaccalaureate distance learning degree programs offered (minimal on-campus study). *Degree requirements:* For master's, thesis. Electronic applications accepted.

Southern Methodist University, Annette Caldwell Simmons School of Education and Human Development, Program in Liberal Studies, Dallas, TX 75275. Offers MLS.

Spring Hill College, Graduate Programs, Program in Liberal Arts, Mobile, AL 36608-1791. Offers fine arts (MLA); history and social science (MLA); leadership and ethics (MLA, Postbaccalaureate Certificate); literature (MLA); studio art (Postbaccalaureate Certificate). Part-time and evening/weekend programs available. *Faculty:* 6 full-time (1 woman), 3 part-time/adjunct (all women). *Students:* 3 full-time (1 woman), 33 part-time (18 women); includes 9 minority (8 Black or African American, non-Hispanic/Latino; 1 American Indian or Alaska Native, non-Hispanic/Latino), 1 international. Average age 36. In 2014, 8 master's awarded. *Degree requirements:* For master's, capstone course, completion of program within 6 years of initial admittance. *Entrance requirements:* For master's, bachelor's degree with minimum undergraduate GPA of 3.0 or graduate/professional degree. Additional exam requirements/recommendations for international students: Required—TOEFL (minimum score 550 paper-based; 80 iBT), IELTS (minimum score 6.5), CPE or CAE (minimum score C), Michigan English Language Assessment Battery (minimum score 90). *Application deadline:* For fall admission, 8/1 priority date for domestic and international students; for spring admission, 12/1 priority date for domestic and international students. Applications are processed on a rolling basis. Application fee: $25 ($35 for international students). Electronic applications accepted. *Expenses:* Expenses: Contact institution. *Financial support:* Applicants required to submit FAFSA. *Unit head:* Dr. Thomas J. Hoffman, Director, 251-380-4184, Fax: 251-460-2115, E-mail: thoffman@shc.edu. *Application contact:* Robert Stewart, Vice President of Enrollment, 251-380-3030, Fax: 251-460-2186, E-mail: rstewart@shc.edu. Website: http://ug.shc.edu/graduate-degrees/master-liberal-arts/

State University of New York Empire State College, School for Graduate Studies, Program in Liberal Studies, Saratoga Springs, NY 12866-4391. Offers MA. Part-time and evening/weekend programs available. Postbaccalaureate distance learning degree programs offered (minimal on-campus study). *Degree requirements:* For master's, thesis, final project. *Entrance requirements:* Additional exam requirements/recommendations for international students: Required—TOEFL (minimum score 600 paper-based). Electronic applications accepted.

Stony Brook University, State University of New York, School of Professional Development, Stony Brook, NY 11794. Offers biology (MAT); chemistry (MAT); coaching (Graduate Certificate); earth science (MAT); educational computing (Graduate Certificate); educational leadership (Advanced Certificate); English (MAT); environmental management (Graduate Certificate); French (MAT); German (MAT); higher education administration (MA, Certificate); human resource management (MS, Graduate Certificate); industrial management (Graduate Certificate); information systems management (Graduate Certificate); Italian (MAT); liberal studies (MA); mathematics (MAT); operations research (Graduate Certificate); physics (MAT); school district business leadership (Advanced Certificate); social science and the professions (MPS), including environmental management; social studies (MAT); Spanish (MAT). Part-time and evening/weekend programs available. Postbaccalaureate distance learning degree programs offered. *Faculty:* 100 part-time/adjunct (42 women). *Students:* 216 full-time (119 women), 905 part-time (624 women); includes 224 minority (63 Black or African American, non-Hispanic/Latino; 1 American Indian or Alaska Native, non-Hispanic/Latino; 33 Asian, non-Hispanic/Latino; 119 Hispanic/Latino; 1 Native Hawaiian or other Pacific Islander, non-Hispanic/Latino; 7 Two or more races, non-Hispanic/Latino), 7 international. Average age 28. 422 applicants, 88% accepted, 299 enrolled. In 2014, 362 master's, 146 other advanced degrees awarded. *Degree requirements:* For master's, one foreign language, thesis or alternative. *Application deadline:* For fall admission, 1/15 for domestic students; for spring admission, 10/1 for domestic students. Applications are processed on a rolling basis. Application fee: $100. *Expenses: Tuition,* state resident: full-time $10,370; part-time $432 per credit. Tuition, nonresident: full-time $20,190; part-time $841 per credit. *Required fees:* $1431. *Financial support:* Fellowships, research assistantships, teaching assistantships, and career-related internships or fieldwork available. Support available to part-time students. *Unit head:* Dr. Charles Taber, Vice Provost for Graduate and Professional Education, 631-632-7050, Fax: 631-632-9046, E-mail: charles.taber@stonybrook.edu. *Application contact:* 631-632-7050 Ext. 1, E-mail: spd@stonybrook.edu. Website: http://www.stonybrook.edu/spd/

Texas A&M University–Central Texas, Graduate Studies and Research, Killeen, TX 76549. Offers accounting (MS); business administration (MBA); clinical mental health counseling (MS); criminal justice (MCJ); curriculum and instruction (M Ed); educational administration (M Ed); educational psychology - experimental psychology (MS); history (MA); human resource management (MS); information systems (MS); liberal studies (MS); management and leadership (MS); marriage and family therapy (MS); mathematics (MS); political science (MA); school counseling (M Ed); school psychology (Ed S).

Texas Christian University, Master of Liberal Arts Program, Fort Worth, TX 76129. Offers MLA. Part-time and evening/weekend programs available. Postbaccalaureate distance learning degree programs offered (no on-campus study). *Faculty:* 10 part-time/adjunct (1 woman). *Students:* 50 full-time (23 women), 30 part-time (17 women); includes 21 minority (7 Black or African American, non-Hispanic/Latino; 1 American Indian or Alaska Native, non-Hispanic/Latino; 1 Asian, non-Hispanic/Latino; 8 Hispanic/Latino; 1 Native Hawaiian or other Pacific Islander, non-Hispanic/Latino; 3 Two or more races, non-Hispanic/Latino), 1 international. Average age 32. 48 applicants, 90% accepted, 29 enrolled. In 2014, 30 master's awarded. *Entrance requirements:* Additional exam requirements/recommendations for international students: Required—TOEFL (minimum score 550 paper-based; 80 iBT). *Application deadline:* For fall admission, 8/15 for domestic students, 8/1 for international students; for spring admission, 1/15 for domestic students, 1/1 for international students. Applications are processed on a rolling basis. Application fee: $60. Electronic applications accepted. *Expenses:* Expenses: Contact institution. *Financial support:* In 2014–15, 50 students received support. Scholarships/grants, unspecified assistantships, and employee tuition benefit available. Financial award applicants required to submit FAFSA. *Unit head:* Dr. Bonnie Melhart, Associate Provost/Dean of University Programs, 817-257-7104, Fax: 817-257-7484, E-mail: b.melhart@tcu.edu. *Application contact:* Anita Unger, Graduate Program Coordinator, 817-257-7515, Fax: 817-257-7484, E-mail: a.unger@tcu.edu. Website: http://www.mla.tcu.edu/

Thomas Edison State College, Heavin School of Arts and Sciences, Program in Liberal Studies, Trenton, NJ 08608-1176. Offers MALS. Part-time programs available. Postbaccalaureate distance learning degree programs offered (no on-campus study). *Degree requirements:* For master's, final project. *Entrance requirements:* For master's, bachelor's degree from a regionally-accredited college or university; minimum 2 letters of recommendation; 3-5 years of related working experience; current resume. Additional exam requirements/recommendations for international students: Required—TOEFL (minimum score 550 paper-based; 79 iBT). Electronic applications accepted.

Towson University, Program in Professional Studies, Towson, MD 21252-0001. Offers art history (MA); individualized plan (MA). Part-time and evening/weekend programs available. *Students:* 9 full-time (6 women), 27 part-time (21 women); includes 10 minority (7 Black or African American, non-Hispanic/Latino; 2 Asian, non-Hispanic/Latino; 1 Two or more races, non-Hispanic/Latino), 2 international. *Degree requirements:* For master's, thesis optional. *Entrance requirements:* For master's, minimum GPA of 3.0, essay. *Application deadline:* Applications are processed on a rolling basis. Application fee: $45. Electronic applications accepted. *Financial support:* Application deadline: 4/1. *Unit head:* Dr. James Smith, Graduate Program Director, 410-704-4620, E-mail: jmsmith@towson.edu. *Application contact:* Alicia Arkell-Kleis, Information Contact, 410-704-6004, E-mail: grads@towson.edu. Website: http://grad.towson.edu/program/master/lbps-ma/index.asp

Tulane University, Program in Liberal Arts, New Orleans, LA 70118-5669. Offers MLA. Part-time programs available. *Degree requirements:* For master's, thesis. *Entrance requirements:* For master's, GRE General Test, minimum B average in undergraduate course work. Additional exam requirements/recommendations for international students: Required—TOEFL. *Expenses: Tuition:* Full-time $46,326; part-time $2574 per credit hour. *Required fees:* $1980; $44.50 per credit hour. $550 per term. Tuition and fees vary according to course load and program.

University at Albany, State University of New York, College of Arts and Sciences, Liberal Studies Program, Albany, NY 12222-0001. Offers MALS. *Entrance requirements:* Additional exam requirements/recommendations for international students: Required—TOEFL (minimum score 550 paper-based). Electronic applications accepted.

University of Chicago, Graham School of Continuing Liberal and Professional Studies, Program in Liberal Arts, Chicago, IL 60637. Offers MLA. Part-time and evening/weekend programs available. *Students:* 4 full-time (2 women), 46 part-time (23 women); includes 13 minority (6 Black or African American, non-Hispanic/Latino; 6 Asian, non-Hispanic/Latino; 1 Hispanic/Latino), 3 international. 22 applicants, 82% accepted, 14 enrolled. *Entrance requirements:* Additional exam requirements/recommendations for international students: Required—TOEFL (minimum score 104 iBT), IELTS (minimum score 7). *Application deadline:* For fall admission, 8/3 for domestic and international students; for spring admission, 3/3 for domestic and international students. Application fee: $75. Electronic applications accepted. *Expenses: Tuition:* Full-time $46,899. *Required fees:* $347. *Unit head:* Jan Watson, Program Coordinator. *Application contact:* Bonni Van Eck, Admissions Coordinator, E-mail: mla@uchicago.edu. Website: https://grahamschool.uchicago.edu/credit/master-liberal-arts/index

University of Delaware, College of Arts and Sciences, Program in Liberal Studies, Newark, DE 19716. Offers MALS. Part-time and evening/weekend programs available. *Degree requirements:* For master's, thesis. Electronic applications accepted. *Faculty research:* British Raj, medical and scientific ethics, Jewish-American novelists, intellectual freedom.

University of Detroit Mercy, College of Liberal Arts and Education, Program in Liberal Studies, Detroit, MI 48221. Offers MALS. Part-time programs available.

University of Memphis, Graduate School, University College, Memphis, TN 38152. Offers liberal studies (MALS); merchandising and consumer science (MS), including consumer science and education; strategic leadership (MPS). Part-time and evening/weekend programs available. *Faculty:* 3 full-time (1 woman), 1 (woman) part-time/adjunct. *Students:* 24 full-time (10 women), 128 part-time (90 women); includes 94 minority (86 Black or African American, non-Hispanic/Latino; 1 Asian, non-Hispanic/Latino; 2 Hispanic/Latino; 5 Two or more races, non-Hispanic/Latino). Average age 39. 62 applicants, 82% accepted, 8 enrolled. In 2014, 52 master's awarded. *Degree requirements:* For master's, comprehensive exam, thesis (for some programs). *Entrance requirements:* For master's, MAT, GRE General Test (for MS), interview (MALS).

Additional exam requirements/recommendations for international students: Required—TOEFL (minimum score 550 paper-based). *Application deadline:* For fall admission, 7/1 for domestic students, 5/1 for international students; for spring admission, 11/1 for domestic students, 9/15 for international students. Applications are processed on a rolling basis. Application fee: $35 ($60 for international students). Electronic applications accepted. *Financial support:* In 2014–15, 123 students received support. Research assistantships with full tuition reimbursements available, teaching assistantships with tuition reimbursements available, Federal Work-Study, scholarships/grants, and unspecified assistantships available. Financial award application deadline: 2/15; financial award applicants required to submit FAFSA. *Faculty research:* Media ethics, history of psychiatry, public relations. *Unit head:* Dr. Dan Lattimore, Dean, 901-678-2991. *Application contact:* Dr. Herbert McCree, Coordinator of Graduate Studies, 901-678-4171, Fax: 901-678-3363, E-mail: hmccree@memphis.edu.
Website: http://www.memphis.edu/univcoll/

University of Miami, Graduate School, College of Arts and Sciences, Program in Liberal Studies, Coral Gables, FL 33124. Offers MALS. Part-time and evening/weekend programs available. *Degree requirements:* For master's, thesis or alternative. *Entrance requirements:* For master's, minimum GPA of 3.0. Additional exam requirements/recommendations for international students: Required—TOEFL. Electronic applications accepted. *Expenses:* Contact institution.

University of Minnesota, Duluth, Graduate School, College of Liberal Arts, Department of Sociology/Anthropology, Liberal Studies Program, Duluth, MN 55812-2496. Offers MLS. Part-time and evening/weekend programs available. *Faculty research:* Nature of knowledge, cultural studies, language, literature, sociology.

University of New Hampshire, Graduate School, College of Liberal Arts, Program in Liberal Studies, Durham, NH 03824. Offers MALS. *Students:* 1 full-time (0 women), 16 part-time (9 women); includes 1 minority (Hispanic/Latino). Average age 39. 2 applicants, 100% accepted, 2 enrolled. In 2014, 4 master's awarded. *Entrance requirements:* Additional exam requirements/recommendations for international students: Required—TOEFL (minimum score 550 paper-based; 80 iBT). *Application deadline:* For fall admission, 6/1 for domestic students, 4/1 for international students; for spring admission, 12/1 for domestic students. Applications are processed on a rolling basis. Application fee: $65. Electronic applications accepted. *Expenses:* Tuition, state resident: full-time $13,500; part-time $750 per credit hour. Tuition, nonresident: full-time $26,460; part-time $1110 per credit hour. *Required fees:* $1788; $447 per semester. *Financial support:* Fellowships, research assistantships, and teaching assistantships available. Financial award application deadline: 2/15. *Unit head:* Catherine Peebles, Chairperson, 603-862-3638, E-mail: liberal.studies@unh.edu. *Application contact:* Tama Andrews, Coordinator, 603-862-2321, E-mail: liberal.studies@unh.edu.
Website: http://www.cola.unh.edu/liberal-studies

University of North Carolina at Asheville, Graduate Studies, Asheville, NC 28804-3299. Offers MLA. Part-time and evening/weekend programs available. *Degree requirements:* For master's, thesis.

The University of North Carolina at Charlotte, College of Liberal Arts and Sciences, Interdisciplinary Liberal Arts and Sciences Programs, Charlotte, NC 28223-0001. Offers gerontology (MA, Graduate Certificate); Latin American studies (MA); liberal studies (MA); organizational psychology (PhD); public policy (PhD); women's studies (Graduate Certificate). *Faculty:* 6 full-time (3 women), 5 part-time/adjunct (all women). *Students:* 58 full-time (31 women), 55 part-time (45 women); includes 24 minority (15 Black or African American, non-Hispanic/Latino; 1 Asian, non-Hispanic/Latino; 6 Hispanic/Latino; 1 Native Hawaiian or other Pacific Islander, non-Hispanic/Latino; 1 Two or more races, non-Hispanic/Latino), 12 international. Average age 33. 96 applicants, 46% accepted, 29 enrolled. In 2014, 11 master's, 8 doctorates, 15 other advanced degrees awarded. Terminal master's awarded for partial completion of doctoral program. *Degree requirements:* For master's, thesis or alternative, comprehensive exam or project; for doctorate, thesis/dissertation. *Entrance requirements:* For master's, GRE General Test or MAT, minimum GPA of 3.0 during previous 2 years, 2.75 overall; for doctorate, GRE, letters of recommendation. Additional exam requirements/recommendations for international students: Required—TOEFL (minimum score 557 paper-based; 83 iBT). *Application deadline:* For fall admission, 5/1 priority date for domestic students, 5/1 for international students; for spring admission, 10/1 priority date for domestic students, 10/1 for international students. Applications are processed on a rolling basis. Application fee: $75. Electronic applications accepted. *Expenses:* Tuition, state resident: full-time $4008. Tuition, nonresident: full-time $16,295. *Required fees:* $2755. Tuition and fees vary according to course load and program. *Financial support:* In 2014–15, 24 students received support, including 20 research assistantships (averaging $10,400 per year), 4 teaching assistantships (averaging $8,250 per year); career-related internships or fieldwork, institutionally sponsored loans, scholarships/grants, and unspecified assistantships also available. Support available to part-time students. Financial award application deadline: 4/1; financial award applicants required to submit FAFSA. *Total annual research expenditures:* $15,045. *Unit head:* Dr. Nancy A. Gutierrez, Dean, 704-687-0081, Fax: 704-687-4347, E-mail: ngutierr@uncc.edu. *Application contact:* Kathy B. Giddings, Director of Graduate Admissions, 704-687-5503, Fax: 704-687-3279, E-mail: gradadm@uncc.edu.
Website: http://www.lbst.uncc.edu/

The University of North Carolina at Greensboro, Graduate School, Program in Liberal Studies, Greensboro, NC 27412-5001. Offers MALS. Electronic applications accepted.

The University of North Carolina Wilmington, College of Arts and Sciences, Graduate Liberal Studies Program, Wilmington, NC 28403-3297. Offers MA. Part-time programs available. *Faculty:* 1 (woman) full-time. *Students:* 5 full-time (3 women), 36 part-time (25 women); includes 8 minority (7 Black or African American, non-Hispanic/Latino; 1 Two or more races, non-Hispanic/Latino). 16 applicants, 100% accepted, 11 enrolled. In 2014, 15 master's awarded. *Degree requirements:* For master's, comprehensive exam, thesis or alternative, final project. *Entrance requirements:* For master's, minimum GPA of 3.0, writing sample. Additional exam requirements/recommendations for international students: Required—TOEFL (minimum score 79 iBT), IELTS. *Application deadline:* For fall admission, 6/13 for domestic students; for spring admission, 11/5 for domestic students; for summer admission, 3/14 for domestic students. Application fee: $60. *Expenses:* Tuition, state resident: full-time $3240. Tuition, nonresident: full-time $9208. *Required fees:* $1967. *Financial support:* Application deadline: 3/15; applicants required to submit FAFSA. *Unit head:* Dr. Patricia Turrisi, Director, 910-962-3299, Fax: 910-962-3542, E-mail: turrisip@uncw.edu. *Application contact:* Dr. Ashley Hudson, Assistant Director, 910-962-2427, Fax: 910-962-3542, E-mail: hudsona@uncw.edu.
Website: http://www.uncw.edu/gls/

University of Oklahoma, College of Liberal Studies, Norman, OK 73019. Offers administrative leadership (MA Ed); liberal studies (MA), including human and health services administration, museum studies; prevention science (MPS). Part-time programs available. Postbaccalaureate distance learning degree programs offered (no on-campus study). *Faculty:* 14 full-time (8 women), 3 part-time/adjunct (1 woman). *Students:* 65 full-time (33 women), 600 part-time (301 women); includes 184 minority (57 Black or African American, non-Hispanic/Latino; 37 American Indian or Alaska Native, non-Hispanic/Latino; 8 Asian, non-Hispanic/Latino; 44 Hispanic/Latino; 3 Native Hawaiian or other Pacific Islander, non-Hispanic/Latino; 35 Two or more races, non-Hispanic/Latino), 1 international. Average age 35. 217 applicants, 97% accepted, 141 enrolled. In 2014, 155 master's, 5 other advanced degrees awarded. Terminal master's awarded for partial completion of doctoral program. *Degree requirements:* For master's, comprehensive exam (for some programs), thesis optional, practicum (for museum studies only); for Graduate Certificate, comprehensive exam (for some programs), thesis optional. *Entrance requirements:* For master's and Graduate Certificate, minimum cumulative GPA of 3.0 in previous undergraduate/graduate coursework. Additional exam requirements/recommendations for international students: Required—TOEFL (minimum score 79 iBT). *Application deadline:* For fall admission, 7/1 for domestic and international students; for winter admission, 12/1 for domestic and international students; for spring admission, 5/1 for domestic and international students. Application fee: $50 ($100 for international students). Electronic applications accepted. *Expenses:* Tuition, state resident: full-time $4394; part-time $183.10 per credit hour. Tuition, nonresident: full-time $16,970; part-time $707.10 per credit hour. *Required fees:* $2892; $109.95 per credit hour. $126.50 per semester. *Financial support:* In 2014–15, 107 students received support. Career-related internships or fieldwork, Federal Work-Study, institutionally sponsored loans, scholarships/grants, health care benefits, and tuition waivers (partial) available. Support available to part-time students. Financial award application deadline: 6/1; financial award applicants required to submit FAFSA. *Faculty research:* Race, crime, and class inequality; human trafficking; textual analysis and early Christianity; drug policy implementation; professionalism in police practice; service-learning; Chinese cultural studies. *Unit head:* Dr. James Pappas, Dean/Vice President of OU Outreach, 405-325-6361, Fax: 405-325-7132, E-mail: jpappas@ou.edu. *Application contact:* Missy Heinze, Recruitment Coordinator, 405-325-0559, Fax: 405-325-7132, E-mail: mheinze@ou.edu.
Website: http://www.ou.edu/cls/

University of Pennsylvania, School of Arts and Sciences, College of Liberal and Professional Studies, Philadelphia, PA 19104. Offers applied geosciences (MSAG); applied positive psychology (MAP); chemical sciences (MCS); environmental studies (MES); individualized study (MLA); liberal arts (M Phil); medical physics (MMP); organization dynamics (M Phil). *Students:* 143 full-time (77 women), 322 part-time (179 women); includes 96 minority (33 Black or African American, non-Hispanic/Latino; 1 American Indian or Alaska Native, non-Hispanic/Latino; 24 Asian, non-Hispanic/Latino; 21 Hispanic/Latino; 17 Two or more races, non-Hispanic/Latino), 61 international. 461 applicants, 42% accepted, 132 enrolled. In 2014, 176 master's awarded. *Application deadline:* For fall admission, 12/1 priority date for domestic students. Application fee: $70. Electronic applications accepted. *Unit head:* Nora Lewis, Vice Dean, Professional and Liberal Education, 215-898-7326, E-mail: nlewis@sas.upenn.edu. *Application contact:* 215-898-7326, E-mail: lps@sas.upenn.edu.
Website: http://www.sas.upenn.edu/lps/graduate

University of St. Thomas, Program in Liberal Arts, Houston, TX 77006-4696. Offers MLA. Part-time and evening/weekend programs available. *Faculty:* 26 full-time (11 women), 14 part-time/adjunct (7 women). *Students:* 24 full-time (20 women), 86 part-time (59 women); includes 50 minority (15 Black or African American, non-Hispanic/Latino; 2 Asian, non-Hispanic/Latino; 26 Hispanic/Latino; 7 Two or more races, non-Hispanic/Latino), 13 international. Average age 34. 40 applicants, 98% accepted, 29 enrolled. In 2014, 49 master's awarded. *Degree requirements:* For master's, thesis optional, capstone, minimum cumulative GPA of 3.0. *Entrance requirements:* For master's, 4-year undergraduate degree with minimum GPA of 2.5, essay, 2 letters of recommendation, interview. Additional exam requirements/recommendations for international students: Required—TOEFL (minimum score 100 iBT). *Application deadline:* Applications are processed on a rolling basis. Application fee: $35. Electronic applications accepted. *Expenses: Tuition:* Full-time $20,124; part-time $1118 per credit hour. *Required fees:* $300; $82 per term. One-time fee: $100. Part-time tuition and fees vary according to course level, course load, campus/location and program. *Financial support:* In 2014–15, 18 students received support. Federal Work-Study, scholarships/grants, and state work-study, institutional employment available. Support available to part-time students. Financial award application deadline: 4/15; financial award applicants required to submit FAFSA. *Unit head:* Dr. Mark A. Newcomb, Director, 713-525-6951, Fax: 713-525-6924, E-mail: mla@stthom.edu. *Application contact:* Kate Henderson, Program Coordinator, 713-525-6951, Fax: 713-525-6924, E-mail: mla@stthom.edu.
Website: http://www.stthom.edu/Academics/School_of_Arts_and_Sciences/Graduate/Master_of_Liberal_Arts/Index.aqf

University of Southern Indiana, Graduate Studies, College of Liberal Arts, Program in Liberal Studies, Evansville, IN 47712-3590. Offers MA. Part-time and evening/weekend programs available. *Faculty:* 56 full-time (35 women), 7 part-time/adjunct (1 woman). *Students:* 2 full-time (1 woman), 7 part-time (5 women); includes 2 minority (1 American Indian or Alaska Native, non-Hispanic/Latino; 1 Two or more races, non-Hispanic/Latino). Average age 34. In 2014, 7 master's awarded. *Entrance requirements:* For master's, minimum GPA of 2.5, resume, interview. Additional exam requirements/recommendations for international students: Required—TOEFL (minimum score 550 paper-based; 79 iBT), IELTS (minimum score 6). *Application deadline:* For fall admission, 8/15 priority date for domestic students, 3/1 priority date for international students. Applications are processed on a rolling basis. Application fee: $40. Electronic applications accepted. *Financial support:* Federal Work-Study, scholarships/grants, tuition waivers (full and partial), and unspecified assistantships available. Financial award application deadline: 3/1; financial award applicants required to submit FAFSA. *Unit head:* Dr. Steven Zehr, Interim Director, 812-464-1981, E-mail: szehr@usi.edu. *Application contact:* Dr. Mayola Rowser, Director, Graduate Studies, 812-465-7016, E-mail: mrowser@usi.edu.
Website: http://www.usi.edu/liberalarts/master-of-arts-in-liberal-studies

University of South Florida, College of Arts and Sciences, Department of Humanities and Cultural Studies, Tampa, FL 33620-9951. Offers American studies (MA); liberal arts (MA), including Africana studies, film studies, humanities, social and political thought. Part-time and evening/weekend programs available. *Faculty:* 7 full-time (3 women). *Students:* 11 full-time (2 women), 8 part-time (2 women); includes 8 minority (4 Black or African American, non-Hispanic/Latino; 3 Hispanic/Latino; 1 Two or more races, non-Hispanic/Latino), 1 international. Average age 34. 9 applicants, 78% accepted, 5 enrolled. In 2014, 5 master's awarded. *Degree requirements:* For master's, comprehensive exam, thesis, language requirement (for humanities subconcentration). *Entrance requirements:* For master's, GRE General Test (minimum preferred score 59th percentile (153) verbal and 4.5 in analytical writing), minimum GPA of 3.0 in upper-division courses, personal statement, writing sample. Additional exam requirements/recommendations for international students: Required—TOEFL (minimum score 550 paper-based; 79 iBT) or IELTS (minimum score 6.5). *Application deadline:* For fall admission, 2/15 priority date for domestic students, 1/2 for international students; for spring admission, 10/15 priority date for domestic students, 6/1 for international students. Application fee: $30. *Financial support:* In 2014–15, 15 students received support, including 15 teaching assistantships with tuition reimbursements available (averaging $12,437 per year); scholarships/grants also available. Financial award

application deadline: 4/1. *Faculty research:* American South, American autobiography, material culture, critical theory, cultural studies, film studies. *Unit head:* Dr. William Cummings, Professor and Chair, 813-974-9380, Fax: 813-974-9409, E-mail: wcummings@usf.edu. *Application contact:* Dr. Brook Sadler, Associate Professor and Graduate Program Director, 813-974-8841, Fax: 813-974-9409, E-mail: brooksadler@usf.edu.
Website: http://humanities.usf.edu/

University of South Florida, St. Petersburg, College of Arts and Sciences, St. Petersburg, FL 33701. Offers digital journalism and design (MA); environmental science and policy (MA, MS); Florida studies (MLA); journalism and media studies (MA); liberal studies (MLA); psychology (MA). Part-time programs available. Postbaccalaureate distance learning degree programs offered (no on-campus study). *Degree requirements:* For master's, comprehensive exam, thesis or project. *Entrance requirements:* For master's, GRE, LSAT, MCAT (varies by program), letter of intent, 3 letters of recommendation, writing samples, bachelor's degree from regionally-accredited institution with minimum GPA of 3.0 overall or in upper two years. Additional exam requirements/recommendations for international students: Required—TOEFL (minimum score 550 paper-based; 79 iBT); Recommended—IELTS. Electronic applications accepted.

The University of Texas at El Paso, Graduate School, College of Liberal Arts, Master of Arts in Interdisciplinary Studies Program, El Paso, TX 79968-0001. Offers MAIS. Part-time and evening/weekend programs available. *Entrance requirements:* For master's, GRE, minimum GPA of 3.0, letters of recommendation. Additional exam requirements/recommendations for international students: Required—TOEFL; Recommended—IELTS. Electronic applications accepted.

The University of Toledo, College of Graduate Studies, College of Languages, Literature and Social Sciences, Master of Liberal Studies Program, Toledo, OH 43606-3390. Offers MLS. Part-time and evening/weekend programs available. *Degree requirements:* For master's, thesis. *Entrance requirements:* For master's, GRE if cumulative GPA is less than 3.0, minimum cumulative point-hour ratio of 2.7 for all previous academic work, three letters of recommendation, statement of purpose, transcripts from all prior institutions attended. Additional exam requirements/recommendations for international students: Required—TOEFL (minimum score 550 paper-based; 80 iBT). Electronic applications accepted.

University of Wisconsin–Milwaukee, Graduate School, College of Letters and Sciences, Interdepartmental Program in Liberal Studies, Milwaukee, WI 53201-0413. Offers MLS. *Entrance requirements:* For master's, interview, bachelor's degree. Additional exam requirements/recommendations for international students: Required—TOEFL (minimum score 600 paper-based; 79 iBT), IELTS (minimum score 7). Electronic applications accepted.

Ursuline College, School of Graduate Studies, Program in Liberal Studies, Pepper Pike, OH 44124-4398. Offers MALS. Part-time programs available. *Faculty:* 1 full-time (0 women). *Students:* 5 part-time (4 women); includes 4 minority (all Black or African American, non-Hispanic/Latino), 1 international. Average age 46. 4 applicants, 75% accepted, 3 enrolled. In 2014, 4 master's awarded. *Degree requirements:* For master's, thesis. *Entrance requirements:* For master's, minimum undergraduate GPA of 3.0. Additional exam requirements/recommendations for international students: Required—TOEFL (minimum score 500 paper-based). *Application deadline:* For fall admission, 8/1 priority date for domestic students. Applications are processed on a rolling basis. Application fee: $25. Electronic applications accepted. *Financial support:* In 2014–15, 1 student received support. Federal Work-Study available. Financial award application deadline: 3/1; financial award applicants required to submit FAFSA. *Unit head:* Dr. Tim Kinsella, Director, 440-646-8389, Fax: 440-684-6088, E-mail: tkinsell@ursuline.edu. *Application contact:* Stephanie Pratt, Graduate Admission Coordinator, 440-646-8119, Fax: 440-684-6138, E-mail: graduateadmissions@ursuline.edu.

Utica College, Liberal Studies Program, Utica, NY 13502-4892. Offers MS. Part-time and evening/weekend programs available. *Faculty:* 19 full-time (8 women). *Students:* 5 full-time (4 women), 29 part-time (23 women); includes 4 minority (1 Black or African American, non-Hispanic/Latino; 1 American Indian or Alaska Native, non-Hispanic/Latino; 1 Asian, non-Hispanic/Latino; 1 Two or more races, non-Hispanic/Latino). Average age 32. 62 applicants, 61% accepted, 37 enrolled. In 2014, 3 master's awarded. *Degree requirements:* For master's, comprehensive exam or thesis. *Entrance requirements:* For master's, GRE, minimum GPA of 3.0. Additional exam requirements/recommendations for international students: Required—TOEFL (minimum score 525 paper-based). *Application deadline:* Applications are processed on a rolling basis. Application fee: $50. Electronic applications accepted. *Expenses:* Expenses: Contact institution. *Financial support:* Career-related internships or fieldwork, scholarships/grants, tuition waivers (partial), and unspecified assistantships available. Support available to part-time students. Financial award application deadline: 3/15; financial award applicants required to submit FAFSA. *Unit head:* Prof. Polly Smith, Coordinator, 315-792-3124, E-mail: psmith@utica.edu. *Application contact:* John D. Rowe, Director of Graduate Admissions, 315-792-3824, Fax: 315-792-3003, E-mail: jrowe@utica.edu.

Valparaiso University, Graduate School, Programs in Liberal Studies, Concentration in Human Behavior and Society, Valparaiso, IN 46383. Offers MALS, Post-Master's Certificate, JD/MALS. Part-time and evening/weekend programs available. *Students:* 2 full-time (1 woman), 3 part-time (1 woman); includes 1 minority (Hispanic/Latino). Average age 33. In 2014, 6 master's awarded. *Entrance requirements:* For master's, minimum GPA of 3.0. Additional exam requirements/recommendations for international students: Required—TOEFL (minimum score 550 paper-based; 80 iBT), IELTS (minimum score 6). *Application deadline:* Applications are processed on a rolling basis. Application fee: $30 ($50 for international students). Electronic applications accepted. *Expenses: Tuition:* Full-time $10,710; part-time $595 per credit hour. *Required fees:* $378; $101 per term. Tuition and fees vary according to course load and program. *Financial support:* Available to part-time students. Applicants required to submit FAFSA. *Unit head:* Dr. Jennifer A. Ziegler, Dean, Graduate School and Continuing Education, 219-464-5313, Fax: 219-464-5381, E-mail: jennifer.ziegler@valpo.edu. *Application contact:* Jessica Choquette, Graduate Admissions Specialist, 219-464-5313, Fax: 219-464-5381, E-mail: jessica.choquette@valpo.edu.
Website: http://www.valpo.edu/grad/mals/hbs.php

Valparaiso University, Graduate School, Programs in Liberal Studies, Individualized Study Program, Valparaiso, IN 46383. Offers MALS, JD/MALS. Part-time and evening/weekend programs available. *Students:* 2 part-time (1 woman); includes 1 minority (Two or more races, non-Hispanic/Latino). Average age 46. In 2014, 2 master's awarded. *Entrance requirements:* For master's, minimum GPA of 3.0. Additional exam requirements/recommendations for international students: Required—TOEFL (minimum score 550 paper-based; 80 iBT), IELTS (minimum score 6). *Application deadline:* Applications are processed on a rolling basis. Application fee: $30 ($50 for international students). Electronic applications accepted. *Expenses: Tuition:* Full-time $10,710; part-time $595 per credit hour. *Required fees:* $378; $101 per term. Tuition and fees vary according to course load and program. *Financial support:* Available to part-time students. Applicants required to submit FAFSA. *Unit head:* Dr. Jennifer A. Ziegler, Dean, Graduate School and Continuing Education, 219-464-5313, Fax: 219-464-5381, E-mail:

jennifer.ziegler@valpo.edu. *Application contact:* Jessica Choquette, Graduate Admissions Specialist, 219-464-5313, Fax: 219-464-5381, E-mail: jessica.choquette@valpo.edu.
Website: http://www.valpo.edu/grad/mals/individ.php

Vanderbilt University, Graduate School, Program in Liberal Arts and Science, Nashville, TN 37240-1001. Offers MLAS. Part-time programs available. *Students:* 31 part-time (19 women); includes 6 minority (4 Black or African American, non-Hispanic/Latino; 2 Two or more races, non-Hispanic/Latino). Average age 42. 19 applicants, 79% accepted, 11 enrolled. In 2014, 9 master's awarded. *Degree requirements:* For master's, thesis optional. *Entrance requirements:* For master's, GRE General Test. Additional exam requirements/recommendations for international students: Required—TOEFL (minimum score 570 paper-based; 88 iBT). *Application deadline:* For fall admission, 1/15 priority date for domestic students, 1/15 for international students; for spring admission, 11/15 for domestic and international students. Applications are processed on a rolling basis. *Expenses: Tuition:* Full-time $42,768; part-time $1782 per credit hour. *Required fees:* $422. One-time fee: $30 full-time. *Financial support:* Institutionally sponsored loans and tuition waivers (partial) available. *Unit head:* Dr. Martin Rapisarda, Associate Dean and Director of Graduate Studies, 615-936-5964, Fax: 615-343-8702, E-mail: martin.rapisarda@vanderbilt.edu. *Application contact:* Nelly Gonzalez, Administrative Assistant, 615-343-3140, Fax: 615-343-8702, E-mail: nelly.gonzalez@vanderbilt.edu.
Website: http://www.vanderbilt.edu/mlas/

Villanova University, Graduate School of Liberal Arts and Sciences, Program in Liberal Studies, Villanova, PA 19085. Offers American studies (Certificate); ancient worlds (Certificate); great books (Certificate); interdisciplinary studies (Post-Master's Certificate); liberal studies (MA); peace and justice studies (Certificate). Part-time and evening/weekend programs available. *Faculty:* 4. *Students:* 10 full-time (7 women), 7 part-time (3 women); includes 1 minority (Black or African American, non-Hispanic/Latino), 3 international. Average age 36. 3 applicants, 100% accepted, 1 enrolled. In 2014, 6 master's awarded. *Degree requirements:* For master's, comprehensive exam. *Entrance requirements:* For master's, statement of goals, 2 recommendation letters. Additional exam requirements/recommendations for international students: Required—TOEFL. *Application deadline:* For fall admission, 3/1 for domestic students, 5/1 for international students; for spring admission, 11/15 for domestic students, 10/15 for international students; for summer admission, 5/1 for domestic students. Applications are processed on a rolling basis. Application fee: $50. Electronic applications accepted. *Financial support:* Research assistantships, scholarships/grants, and unspecified assistantships available. Financial award applicants required to submit FAFSA. *Unit head:* Dr. Marylu Hill, Director, Villanova Center for Liberal Education, 610-519-6936, E-mail: marylu.hill@villanova.edu. *Application contact:* Dean, Graduate School of Liberal Arts and Sciences.
Website: http://www1.villanova.edu/villanova/artsci/liberalstudies.html

Virginia Polytechnic Institute and State University, VT Online, Blacksburg, VA 24061. Offers advanced transportation systems (Certificate); aerospace engineering (MS); agricultural and life sciences (MSLFS); business information systems (Graduate Certificate); career and technical education (MS); civil engineering (MS); computer engineering (M Eng, MS); decision support systems (Graduate Certificate); eLearning leadership (MA); electrical engineering (M Eng, MS); engineering administration (MEA); environmental engineering (Certificate); environmental politics and policy (Graduate Certificate); environmental sciences and engineering (MS); foundations of political analysis (Graduate Certificate); health product risk management (Graduate Certificate); industrial and systems engineering (MS); information policy and society (Graduate Certificate); information security (Graduate Certificate); information technology (MIT); instructional technology (MA); integrative STEM education (MA Ed); liberal arts (Graduate Certificate); life sciences: health product risk management (MS); natural resources (MNR, Graduate Certificate); networking (Graduate Certificate); nonprofit and nongovernmental organization management (Graduate Certificate); ocean engineering (MS); political science (MA); security studies (Graduate Certificate); software development (Graduate Certificate). *Expenses:* Tuition, state resident: full-time $11,656; part-time $647.50 per credit hour. Tuition, nonresident: full-time $23,351; part-time $1297.25 per credit hour. *Required fees:* $2533; $465.75 per semester. Tuition and fees vary according to course load, campus/location and program.

Wake Forest University, Graduate School of Arts and Sciences, Liberal Studies Program, Winston-Salem, NC 27109. Offers MALS. Part-time programs available. *Degree requirements:* For master's, thesis. *Entrance requirements:* Additional exam requirements/recommendations for international students: Required—TOEFL (minimum score 79 iBT). Electronic applications accepted.

Washburn University, College of Arts and Sciences, Program in Liberal Studies, Topeka, KS 66621. Offers MLS. Part-time and evening/weekend programs available. *Students:* 1 full-time (0 women), 7 part-time (4 women). Average age 37. In 2014, 7 master's awarded. *Degree requirements:* For master's, thesis, 15 seminar hours. *Entrance requirements:* For master's, minimum GPA of 3.0 in the last 60 hours of undergraduate coursework. Additional exam requirements/recommendations for international students: Required—TOEFL (minimum score 80 iBT). *Application deadline:* For fall admission, 3/1 priority date for domestic students, 3/1 for international students; for spring admission, 10/1 priority date for domestic students, 10/1 for international students. Applications are processed on a rolling basis. *Expenses:* Tuition, state resident: full-time $6120; part-time $340 per credit hour. Tuition, nonresident: full-time $12,456; part-time $692 per credit hour. *Required fees:* $86; $43 per semester. Tuition and fees vary according to program. *Financial support:* Career-related internships or fieldwork, Federal Work-Study, and scholarships/grants available. Support available to part-time students. Financial award applicants required to submit FAFSA. *Faculty research:* European architecture/history, British cultural studies movement, American military strategy/history. *Unit head:* Dr. Bruce Mactavish, Associate Dean, College of Arts and Sciences/Program Director, 785-670-1636, Fax: 785-670-1297, E-mail: bruce.mactavish@washburn.edu. *Application contact:* Kris Klima, Director of Admissions, 785-670-1030, Fax: 785-670-1113, E-mail: admissions@washburn.edu.
Website: http://www.washburn.edu/academics/college-schools/arts-sciences/graduate/liberal-studies/

Wesleyan University, Graduate Liberal Studies Program, Middletown, CT 06459. Offers M Phil, MALS. Part-time and evening/weekend programs available. *Degree requirements:* For master's, thesis optional. *Entrance requirements:* For master's, essay, undergraduate transcripts, two letters of recommendation. Additional exam requirements/recommendations for international students: Required—TOEFL. *Expenses:* Contact institution. *Faculty research:* Interdisciplinary studies.

Western Illinois University, School of Graduate Studies, College of Arts and Sciences, Program in Liberal Arts and Sciences, Macomb, IL 61455-1390. Offers MLAS. Part-time programs available. *Students:* 7 full-time (6 women), 17 part-time (14 women); includes 6 minority (all Black or African American, non-Hispanic/Latino). Average age 36. 13 applicants, 100% accepted, 11 enrolled. In 2014, 15 master's awarded. *Degree requirements:* For master's, thesis or alternative. *Entrance requirements:* Additional exam requirements/recommendations for international students: Required—TOEFL (minimum score 550 paper-based; 80 iBT). *Application deadline:* Applications are processed on a rolling basis. Application fee: $30. Electronic applications accepted.

Financial support: In 2014–15, 6 students received support, including 6 teaching assistantships (averaging $8,688 per year). Financial award applicants required to submit FAFSA. *Unit head:* Dr. Amy Mossman, Program Director, 309-298-3025. *Application contact:* Dr. Nancy Parsons, Associate Provost and Director of Graduate Studies, 309-298-1806, Fax: 309-298-2345, E-mail: grad-office@wiu.edu. Website: http://wiu.edu/cas

West Virginia University, Eberly College of Arts and Sciences, Interdisciplinary Program in Liberal Studies, Morgantown, WV 26506. Offers MALS. Part-time programs available. *Degree requirements:* For master's, thesis or alternative. *Entrance requirements:* For master's, GRE General Test, minimum GPA of 3.0. Additional exam requirements/recommendations for international students: Required—TOEFL.

Wichita State University, Graduate School, Fairmount College of Liberal Arts and Sciences, Interdisciplinary Program in Liberal Studies, Wichita, KS 67260. Offers MA. Part-time programs available. *Unit head:* Dr. David Soles, Graduate Coordinator, 316-978-3125, E-mail: david.soles@wichita.edu. *Application contact:* Jordan Oleson, Admissions Coordinator, 316-978-3095, Fax: 316-978-3253, E-mail: jordan.oleson@wichita.edu. Website: http://www.wichita.edu/mals

Widener University, College of Arts and Sciences, Program in Liberal Studies, Chester, PA 19013-5792. Offers MA. Part-time and evening/weekend programs available. *Degree requirements:* For master's, thesis, project. *Entrance requirements:* For master's, interview, minimum undergraduate GPA of 3.0. *Expenses:* Contact institution. *Faculty research:* Contemporary analytical metaphysics, popular culture, British art, American literature, folklore.

Winthrop University, College of Arts and Sciences, Program in Liberal Arts, Rock Hill, SC 29733. Offers MLA. Part-time programs available. *Entrance requirements:* For master's, interview, minimum GPA of 3.0. Electronic applications accepted.

DARTMOUTH COLLEGE
Master of Arts in Liberal Studies

 For more information, visit http://petersons.to/dartmouthliberalstudies

Programs of Study

Interdisciplinary, Immersive, and Flexible Graduate-Level Study: The Master of Arts in Liberal Studies (MALS) program is part of Dartmouth's Graduate Arts and Sciences school, which offers nineteen graduate programs in the natural sciences, social sciences, and humanities.

MALS at Dartmouth is a highly selective, inclusive, and diverse program and awards the Master of Arts degree in the following concentrations:

- Cultural Studies
- Creative Writing
- Globalization Studies
- General Liberal Studies

Students enter MALS at Dartmouth from different stages in their academic or professional careers. They come from a wide array of backgrounds and include recent college graduates, scholars, doctors, business leaders, and artists, as well as military personnel, writers, educators, and lawyers.

MALS at Dartmouth is designed for individuals who want to engage in self-directed graduate study in the liberal arts at the Ivy League level. The program affords students full access to both Dartmouth's graduate and undergraduate schools in order to pursue comprehensive, interdisciplinary study. Students create an individualized plan-of-study that significantly enhances their academic and professional credentials. During the past few years, students have received prestigious awards such as the Fulbright Fellowship, the J.B. Reynolds Scholarship, and the MacArthur Genius Grant. The unique MALS at Dartmouth interdisciplinary experience prepares graduates to advance in their chosen field, pursue doctoral programs across all disciplines, as well as gain entrance into the professional schools of law, business, and medicine.

Candidates for the MALS at Dartmouth program may attend on a full-time, part-time, or summers-only basis (for teachers and other professionals) or in a combination of these patterns. The Dartmouth College academic year operates on a four-term/quarter system. The program generally takes six to eight terms (1½ to 2 years) with full-time attendance, including thesis research and writing; students have six years from the time of entry to complete the requirements and earn their degree.

The Application Process

The academic program at Dartmouth is intensive, so applications are evaluated carefully. A student's motivation, initiative, maturity, and ability to do graduate-level work are critical. The program typically enrolls 75 to 90 students during the academic year, and approximately 100 to 120 in the summer session.

The MALS at Dartmouth Admissions Committee requires the completion of an application form, three letters of professional/academic reference, a statement of purpose, and academic transcripts; GRE scores are not required. The application is available online through a link on the MALS at Dartmouth website.

An interview is required prior to the application deadline. Skype or telephone interviews are also acceptable for individuals living outside the immediate area. Application deadlines are February 15 (for summer or fall enrollment) and July 15 (for winter or spring entry). Successful applicants must enroll within the academic year of acceptance into the program.

Resources and History Provide Extraordinary Access

Dartmouth College's reach and reputation as a member of the Ivy League provides students opportunities to engage with the world's leaders and intellectuals. The College's extensive facilities are available to all graduate students year-round including the College library's collection of more than a million volumes, the Hopkins Center for the Performing Arts, the Hood Museum, Alumni Gym, and numerous other facilities and services.

Dartmouth also provides many other resources for students to engage in additional areas of academic and personal interest including community activism, international and public affairs, and intellectual forums with guest speakers, debates, discussion groups, and student organizations. Some of these resources include the Tucker Foundation, the John Sloan Dickey Center for International Affairs, the Nelson A. Rockefeller Center for Public Affairs, the Ethics Institute, the Humanities Center, and the Center for Women and Gender—among many others.

Cost of Study

For 2015–16, full-time tuition (2 credits) is $11,228 per term (3 months), plus activity and document fees of $110.

Room and board are estimated at $6,950 per term, while books and supplies are $350.

Faculty

For details on the extraordinary faculty members of MALS at Dartmouth, visit http://mals.dartmouth.edu/people.

Rural Setting Balances the Fast Pace of Academic Life

Dartmouth College is located in Hanover, New Hampshire, a small New England town dating back to a few years before the college's founding in 1769. Situated in the Upper Valley of the Connecticut River between the White Mountains of New Hampshire and the Green Mountains of Vermont, Hanover combines the advantages of a spectacular rural setting with the extraordinary resources of a university.

The Dartmouth College campus is approximately 2.5 hours by car from Boston and 3 hours from Montreal. Surrounding airports include Lebanon, Manchester (75 miles), Burlington (96 miles), Boston-Logan (126 miles) and Bradley International (150 miles) airports. There are Amtrak and Greyhound stations approximately 15 minutes from campus in White River Junction, Vermont. The Dartmouth Coach runs daily from Logan Airport and South Station to Hanover.

Correspondence and Information

Master of Arts in Liberal Studies
Graduate Studies Programs
Dartmouth College
116 Wentworth Hall, HB 6092
Hanover, New Hampshire 03755
United States
Phone: 603-646-3592
E-mail: mals.program@dartmouth.edu
Website: http://mals.dartmouth.edu/

MALS at Dartmouth College in Hanover, NH combines the advantages of a spectacular rural setting with the extraordinary resources of a university.

Section 9
Language and Literature

This section contains a directory of institutions offering graduate work in language and literature. Additional information about programs listed in the directory may be obtained by writing directly to the dean of a graduate school or chair of a department at the address given in the directory.

For programs offering related work, see also in this book *Area and Cultural Studies, Communication and Media, Political Science and International Affairs,* and *Sociology, Anthropology, and Archaeology.* In another guide in this series:

Graduate Programs in Business, Education, Information Studies, Law & Social Work
See *Special Focus* and *Subject Areas*

CONTENTS

Program Directories

Displays and Close-Ups

See:

Asian Languages

Cornell University, Graduate School, Graduate Fields of Arts and Sciences, Field of Linguistics, Ithaca, NY 14853-0001. Offers applied linguistics (MA, PhD); East Asian linguistics (MA, PhD); English linguistics (MA, PhD); general linguistics (MA, PhD); Germanic linguistics (MA, PhD); Indo-European linguistics (MA, PhD); phonetics (MA, PhD); phonological theory (MA, PhD); Romance linguistics (MA, PhD); second language acquisition (MA, PhD); semantics (MA, PhD); Slavic linguistics (MA, PhD); sociolinguistics (MA, PhD); South Asian linguistics (MA, PhD); Southeast Asian linguistics (MA, PhD); syntactic theory (MA, PhD). Terminal master's awarded for partial completion of doctoral program. *Degree requirements:* For master's, one foreign language, thesis; for doctorate, one foreign language, comprehensive exam, thesis/dissertation. *Entrance requirements:* For master's and doctorate, GRE General Test, 2 letters of recommendation. Additional exam requirements/recommendations for international students: Required—TOEFL (minimum score 600 paper-based; 77 iBT). Electronic applications accepted. *Faculty research:* Phonology and phonetics, syntax and semantics, historical linguistics, philosophy of language, language acquisition.

Harvard University, Graduate School of Arts and Sciences, Department of East Asian Languages and Civilizations, Cambridge, MA 02138. Offers Chinese (PhD); Japanese (PhD); Korean (PhD); Mongolian (PhD); Vietnamese (PhD). Terminal master's awarded for partial completion of doctoral program. *Degree requirements:* For doctorate, 3 foreign languages, thesis/dissertation, general exams. *Entrance requirements:* For doctorate, GRE General Test. Additional exam requirements/recommendations for international students: Required—TOEFL. *Faculty research:* Central Asian literature, religion, and premodern history.

Harvard University, Graduate School of Arts and Sciences, Department of Sanskrit and Indian Studies, Cambridge, MA 02138. Offers Indian philosophy (AM, PhD); Pali (AM, PhD); Sanskrit (AM, PhD); Tibetan (AM, PhD); Urdu (AM, PhD). Terminal master's awarded for partial completion of doctoral program. *Degree requirements:* For master's, 3 foreign languages; for doctorate, 3 foreign languages, thesis/dissertation. *Entrance requirements:* For master's, GRE General Test; for doctorate, GRE General Test, proficiency in French and German. Additional exam requirements/recommendations for international students: Required—TOEFL.

Indiana University Bloomington, University Graduate School, College of Arts and Sciences, School of Global and International Studies, Department of East Asian Languages and Cultures, Bloomington, IN 47408. Offers Chinese (MA, PhD); Chinese language pedagogy (MA); East Asian studies (MA); Japanese (MA, PhD); Japanese language pedagogy (MA). Part-time programs available. *Faculty:* 21 full-time (11 women), 14 part-time/adjunct (7 women). *Students:* 10 full-time (7 women), 20 part-time (12 women); includes 3 minority (2 Asian, non-Hispanic/Latino; 1 Hispanic/Latino), 15 international. 87 applicants, 31% accepted, 8 enrolled. In 2014, 5 master's awarded. *Degree requirements:* For master's, one foreign language, thesis; for doctorate, 2 foreign languages, comprehensive exam, thesis/dissertation. *Entrance requirements:* Additional exam requirements/recommendations for international students: Required—TOEFL (minimum score 93 iBT). *Application deadline:* For fall admission, 1/1 for domestic students, 12/1 for international students. Application fee: $55 ($65 for international students). Electronic applications accepted. *Financial support:* In 2014–15, 23 students received support, including fellowships with full tuition reimbursements available (averaging $18,000 per year), teaching assistantships with full tuition reimbursements available (averaging $15,750 per year). Financial award application deadline: 2/15. *Faculty research:* Modern East Asian history; politics and society; traditional Chinese thought and society; medieval and premodern Japanese history, literature and society; modern Chinese and Japanese film and literature; Chinese, Japanese, Korean language and linguistics. *Unit head:* Prof. Natsuko Tsujimura, Chair, 812-855-0856, Fax: 812-855-6402, E-mail: tsujimur@indiana.edu. *Application contact:* Stephen Thomas Johnson, Student Services Assistant, 812-856-4959, E-mail: johnsost@indiana.edu.
Website: http://www.indiana.edu/~ealc/index.shtml

Naropa University, Graduate Programs, Program in Indo-Tibetan Buddhism with Language, Boulder, CO 80302-6697. Offers MA. *Faculty:* 5 full-time (2 women), 10 part-time/adjunct (7 women). *Students:* 8 full-time (5 women), 2 part-time (0 women), 2 international. Average age 37. 7 applicants, 86% accepted, 4 enrolled. In 2014, 5 master's awarded. *Degree requirements:* For master's, comprehensive exam, thesis. *Entrance requirements:* For master's, interview (by phone or in-person), resume, letter of interest, 2 letters of recommendation. Additional exam requirements/recommendations for international students: Required—TOEFL (minimum score 600 paper-based; 80 iBT). *Application deadline:* For fall admission, 1/15 priority date for domestic and international students. Applications are processed on a rolling basis. Application fee: $60. Electronic applications accepted. *Expenses: Tuition:* Full-time $23,400; part-time $975 per credit. *Required fees:* $335 per semester. Tuition and fees vary according to course load. *Financial support:* In 2014–15, 2 students received support. Career-related internships or fieldwork, scholarships/grants, tuition waivers (partial), and unspecified assistantships available. Support available to part-time students. Financial award application deadline: 3/1; financial award applicants required to submit FAFSA. *Unit head:* Director, School of Humanities and Interdisciplinary Studies. *Application contact:* Office of Admissions, 303-546-3572, Fax: 303-546-3583, E-mail: admissions@naropa.edu.
Website: http://www.naropa.edu/academics/shis/grad/religious-studies-with-language-ma/index.php

The Ohio State University, Graduate School, College of Arts and Sciences, Division of Arts and Humanities, Department of East Asian Languages and Literatures, Columbus, OH 43210. Offers Chinese (MA, PhD); Japanese (MA, PhD). *Faculty:* 20. *Students:* 53 full-time (32 women), 3 part-time (2 women); includes 7 minority (1 Black or African American, non-Hispanic/Latino; 5 Asian, non-Hispanic/Latino; 1 Two or more races, non-Hispanic/Latino), 31 international. Average age 30. In 2014, 13 master's, 3 doctorates awarded. Terminal master's awarded for partial completion of doctoral program. *Degree requirements:* For master's, thesis optional; for doctorate, thesis/dissertation. *Entrance requirements:* For master's and doctorate, GRE General Test (if applying for financial aid). Additional exam requirements/recommendations for international students: Required—TOEFL (minimum score 577 paper-based; 90 iBT); Recommended—IELTS (minimum score 7.5). *Application deadline:* For fall admission, 11/30 priority date for domestic and international students; for winter admission, 12/1 for domestic students, 11/1 for international students; for spring admission, 3/1 for domestic students, 2/1 for international students. Applications are processed on a rolling basis. Application fee: $60 ($70 for international students). Electronic applications accepted. *Financial support:* Fellowships, research assistantships, teaching assistantships, Federal Work-Study, institutionally sponsored loans, and unspecified assistantships available. Support available to part-time students. *Unit head:* Mark Bender, PhD, Chair and Professor, 614-688-5737, E-mail: bender.4@osu.edu. *Application contact:* Graduate and Professional Admissions, 614-292-9444, Fax: 614-292-3895, E-mail: gpadmissions@osu.edu.
Website: http://deall.osu.edu/

St. John's College, Graduate Institute in Liberal Education, Program in Eastern Classics, Santa Fe, NM 87505. Offers MA. Part-time and evening/weekend programs available. *Entrance requirements:* For master's, 2 letters of recommendation. Additional exam requirements/recommendations for international students: Required—TOEFL, TWE. *Expenses:* Contact institution.

Stanford University, School of Humanities and Sciences, Department of East Asian Languages and Cultures, Stanford, CA 94305-9991. Offers Chinese (MA, PhD); Japanese (MA, PhD). Terminal master's awarded for partial completion of doctoral program. *Degree requirements:* For master's, one foreign language, thesis or an annotated translation of a literary or historical text; for doctorate, 2 foreign languages, thesis/dissertation, field exams. *Entrance requirements:* For master's and doctorate, GRE General Test. Additional exam requirements/recommendations for international students: Required—TOEFL. Electronic applications accepted. *Expenses: Tuition:* Full-time $44,184; part-time $982 per credit hour. *Required fees:* $191.

University of California, Berkeley, Graduate Division, College of Letters and Science, Department of South and Southeast Asian Studies, Berkeley, CA 94720-1500. Offers Hindi (MA, PhD); Indonesian (MA, PhD); Sanskrit (MA, PhD); Tamil (MA, PhD). Terminal master's awarded for partial completion of doctoral program. *Degree requirements:* For master's, 2 foreign languages, thesis; for doctorate, 2 foreign languages, thesis/dissertation, oral qualifying exam. *Entrance requirements:* For master's and doctorate, GRE General Test, minimum GPA of 3.0, 3 letters of recommendation. Electronic applications accepted.

University of California, Irvine, School of Humanities, Department of East Asian Languages and Literatures, Irvine, CA 92697. Offers Chinese (MA, PhD); East Asian languages and literatures (MA, PhD); Japanese (MA, PhD). *Students:* 12 full-time (10 women), 1 (woman) part-time; includes 4 minority (3 Asian, non-Hispanic/Latino; 1 Two or more races, non-Hispanic/Latino), 7 international. Average age 30. 40 applicants, 15% accepted, 3 enrolled. In 2014, 1 doctorate awarded. *Degree requirements:* For doctorate, thesis/dissertation. *Entrance requirements:* For master's and doctorate, GRE General Test, minimum GPA of 3.0. Additional exam requirements/recommendations for international students: Required—TOEFL (minimum score 550 paper-based). *Application deadline:* For fall admission, 1/15 priority date for domestic students, 1/15 for international students. Application fee: $90 ($110 for international students). Electronic applications accepted. *Financial support:* Fellowships with tuition reimbursements, research assistantships with full tuition reimbursements, teaching assistantships with partial tuition reimbursements, institutionally sponsored loans, traineeships, health care benefits, and unspecified assistantships available. Financial award application deadline: 3/1; financial award applicants required to submit FAFSA. *Faculty research:* Chinese, Japanese, and Korean literature and culture; language and textual analysis; historical, social, and cultural dimensions of literary study. *Unit head:* Michael A. Fuller, Chair, 949-824-2802 Ext. 2227, Fax: 949-824-3248, E-mail: mafuller@uci.edu. *Application contact:* Hu Ying, Graduate Faculty Advisor, 949-824-6312, Fax: 949-824-3248, E-mail: huying@uci.edu.
Website: http://www.hnet.uci.edu/eastasian/

University of California, Los Angeles, Graduate Division, College of Letters and Science, Department of Asian Languages and Cultures, Los Angeles, CA 90095. Offers MA, PhD. Terminal master's awarded for partial completion of doctoral program. *Degree requirements:* For master's, one foreign language, comprehensive exam or thesis; for doctorate, 2 foreign languages, thesis/dissertation, oral and written qualifying exams. *Entrance requirements:* For master's, GRE General Test, bachelor's degree; minimum undergraduate GPA of 3.0 (or its equivalent if letter grade system not used); writing sample; for doctorate, GRE General Test, master's degree; minimum undergraduate GPA of 3.0 (or its equivalent if letter grade system not used); writing sample. Additional exam requirements/recommendations for international students: Required—TOEFL. Electronic applications accepted.

University of California, Santa Barbara, Graduate Division, College of Letters and Sciences, Division of Humanities and Fine Arts, Department of East Asian Languages and Cultural Studies, Santa Barbara, CA 93106-7075. Offers applied linguistics (PhD); East Asian languages and cultural studies (MA, PhD); translation studies (PhD). *Degree requirements:* For master's, one foreign language, comprehensive exam (for some programs), thesis (for some programs); for doctorate, 2 foreign languages, thesis/dissertation, methodology. *Entrance requirements:* For master's and doctorate, GRE General Test. Additional exam requirements/recommendations for international students: Required—TOEFL (minimum score 550 paper-based; 80 iBT), IELTS (minimum score 7). Electronic applications accepted. *Faculty research:* Chinese literature, Chinese film, Japanese society, Japanese literature, East Asian cultural studies.

University of California, Santa Barbara, Graduate Division, College of Letters and Sciences, Division of Humanities and Fine Arts, Program in Comparative Literature, Santa Barbara, CA 93106-4130. Offers comparative literature (PhD); East Asian literatures (PhD); feminist studies (PhD); French (PhD); global studies (PhD); translation studies (PhD); MA/PhD. *Degree requirements:* For doctorate, 2 foreign languages, comprehensive exam, thesis/dissertation. *Entrance requirements:* For doctorate, GRE. Additional exam requirements/recommendations for international students: Required—TOEFL (minimum score 550 paper-based; 80 iBT), IELTS (minimum score 7). Electronic applications accepted. *Faculty research:* Comparative literary studies in global context, critical theory, translation studies, media technological studies, trauma studies.

University of Chicago, Division of the Humanities, Department of East Asian Languages and Civilizations, Chicago, IL 60637. Offers PhD. *Students:* 36 full-time (20 women); includes 3 minority (all Asian, non-Hispanic/Latino), 19 international. 91 applicants, 18% accepted, 4 enrolled. Terminal master's awarded for partial completion of doctoral program. *Degree requirements:* For doctorate, 2 foreign languages, thesis/dissertation. *Entrance requirements:* For doctorate, GRE General Test. Additional exam requirements/recommendations for international students: Required—TOEFL (minimum score 104 iBT), IELTS (minimum score 7). *Application deadline:* For fall admission, 12/15 for domestic and international students. Application fee: $90. Electronic applications accepted. *Expenses: Tuition:* Full-time $46,899. *Required fees:* $347. *Financial support:* Fellowships with full tuition reimbursements, teaching assistantships with tuition reimbursements, Federal Work-Study, institutionally sponsored loans, scholarships/grants, traineeships, and health care benefits available. Financial award application deadline: 12/15; financial award applicants required to submit FAFSA. *Unit head:* Dr. Michael Bourdaghs, Chair, 773-702-1255. *Application contact:* Braden Grams, Assistant

Dean of Students, Admissions and Fellowships, 773-702-1552, Fax: 773-834-9148, E-mail: humanitiesadmissions@uchicago.edu. Website: http://ealc.uchicago.edu/

University of Chicago, Division of the Humanities, Department of South Asian Languages and Civilizations, Chicago, IL 60637. Offers South Asian languages and civilizations (PhD), including Bengali, Hindi, Sanskrit, Tamil, Urdu. *Students:* 27 full-time (17 women); includes 5 minority (1 Black or African American, non-Hispanic/Latino; 2 Asian, non-Hispanic/Latino; 2 Two or more races, non-Hispanic/Latino), 12 international. 39 applicants, 31% accepted, 3 enrolled. Terminal master's awarded for partial completion of doctoral program. *Degree requirements:* For doctorate, 2 foreign languages, thesis/dissertation. *Entrance requirements:* For doctorate, GRE General Test. Additional exam requirements/recommendations for international students: Required—TOEFL (minimum score 104 iBT), IELTS (minimum score 7). *Application deadline:* For fall admission, 12/15 for domestic and international students. Application fee: $90. Electronic applications accepted. *Expenses: Tuition:* Full-time $46,899. *Required fees:* $347. *Financial support:* Fellowships with full tuition reimbursements, teaching assistantships with full tuition reimbursements, Federal Work-Study, institutionally sponsored loans, scholarships/grants, and health care benefits available. Financial award application deadline: 12/15; financial award applicants required to submit FAFSA. *Unit head:* Dr. Ulrike Stark, Chair. *Application contact:* Braden Grams, Assistant Dean of Students, Admissions and Fellowships, 773-702-1552, Fax: 773-834-9148, E-mail: humanitiesadmissions@uchicago.edu. Website: http://salc.uchicago.edu

University of Hawaii at Manoa, Graduate Division, College of Languages, Linguistics and Literature, Department of East Asian Languages and Literatures, Program in Korean, Honolulu, HI 96822. Offers MA, PhD. Part-time programs available. *Degree requirements:* For master's, 2 foreign languages, thesis optional; for doctorate, 2 foreign languages, comprehensive exam, thesis/dissertation. *Entrance requirements:* For master's and doctorate, GRE General Test. Additional exam requirements/recommendations for international students: Required—TOEFL (minimum score 560 paper-based; 83 iBT), IELTS (minimum score 5).

University of Illinois at Urbana–Champaign, Graduate College, College of Liberal Arts and Sciences, School of Literatures, Cultures and Linguistics, Department of East Asian Languages and Cultures, Champaign, IL 61820. Offers East Asian languages and cultures (PhD); East Asian studies (MA). *Students:* 16 (8 women). Application fee: $70 ($90 for international students). *Unit head:* Gary Gang Xu, Head, 217-244-4012, Fax: 217-244-2223, E-mail: garyxu@illinois.edu. *Application contact:* Lynn Stanke, Office Support Specialist, 217-333-6269, Fax: 217-244-3050, E-mail: stanke@illinois.edu. Website: http://www.ealc.illinois.edu/

The University of Iowa, Graduate College, College of Liberal Arts and Sciences, Program in Asian Civilizations, Iowa City, IA 52242-1316. Offers Chinese (MA); Hindi (MA); Sanskrit (MA); South Asian studies (MA). *Degree requirements:* For master's, thesis optional, exam. *Entrance requirements:* For master's, GRE General Test, minimum GPA of 3.0. Additional exam requirements/recommendations for international students: Required—TOEFL (minimum score 590 paper-based; 96 iBT). Electronic applications accepted.

The University of Kansas, Graduate Studies, College of Liberal Arts and Sciences, Department of East Asian Languages and Cultures, Lawrence, KS 66045. Offers MA, MBA/MA. Part-time programs available. *Faculty:* 9 full-time, 14 part-time/adjunct. *Students:* 9 full-time (7 women), 5 part-time (4 women), 5 international. Average age 28. 10 applicants, 50% accepted, 3 enrolled. In 2014, 6 master's awarded. *Degree requirements:* For master's, one foreign language, thesis. *Entrance requirements:* For master's, GRE, 3 letters of recommendation, writing sample, curriculum vitae, statement of purpose. Additional exam requirements/recommendations for international students: Required—TOEFL. *Application deadline:* For fall admission, 4/1 priority date for domestic students, 5/1 for international students; for spring admission, 12/1 priority date for domestic students, 12/1 for international students. Applications are processed on a rolling basis. Application fee: $55 ($65 for international students). Electronic applications accepted. *Financial support:* Fellowships, teaching assistantships with full and partial tuition reimbursements, and unspecified assistantships available. Financial award application deadline: 4/1. *Faculty research:* Gender relations in literature, ancient Chinese law, visual culture of modern Japan, Japanese language pedagogy, Chinese paleography, Korean shamanism, folklore, traditional Chinese and Japanese literature, Chinese linguistics and language pedagogy. *Unit head:* Dr. Margaret Childs, Chair, 785-864-9128, E-mail: mgchilds@ku.edu. *Application contact:* Cari Ann Kreienhop, Graduate Programs and Graduate Admissions Contact, 785-864-3665, E-mail: ckreienhop@ku.edu. Website: http://ealc.ku.edu/

University of Michigan, Horace H. Rackham School of Graduate Studies, College of Literature, Science, and the Arts, Department of Asian Languages and Cultures, Ann Arbor, MI 48104. Offers PhD. *Faculty:* 18 full-time (5 women). *Students:* 21 full-time; includes 8 minority (7 Asian, non-Hispanic/Latino; 1 Hispanic/Latino). Average age 32. 56 applicants, 9% accepted, 3 enrolled. In 2014, 3 doctorates awarded. Terminal master's awarded for partial completion of doctoral program. *Degree requirements:* For doctorate, 2 foreign languages, thesis/dissertation, preliminary exams, oral defense of dissertation. *Entrance requirements:* Additional exam requirements/recommendations for international students: Required—TOEFL (minimum score 600 paper-based; 106 iBT). *Application deadline:* For fall admission, 12/15 for domestic and international students. Application fee: $65 ($75 for international students). Electronic applications accepted. *Financial support:* In 2014–15, 24 students received support. Fellowships with full tuition reimbursements available, teaching assistantships with full tuition reimbursements available, scholarships/grants, and health care benefits available. Financial award application deadline: 12/15. *Faculty research:* Literature, religion, visual culture, history, modern culture. *Unit head:* Prof. Donald S. Lopez, Jr., Chair, 734-764-

8286, Fax: 734-647-0157, E-mail: um-alc@umich.edu. *Application contact:* Student Services, 734-734-8286, Fax: 734-647-0157, E-mail: alc-gradservices@umich.edu. Website: http://www.lsa.umich.edu/asian/

University of Minnesota, Twin Cities Campus, Graduate School, College of Liberal Arts, Department of Asian Languages and Literatures, Minneapolis, MN 55455-0213. Offers Asian literatures, cultures, and media (PhD). *Degree requirements:* For doctorate, comprehensive exam, thesis/dissertation. *Entrance requirements:* For doctorate, GRE, 3 letters of recommendation. Additional exam requirements/recommendations for international students: Required—TOEFL (minimum score 550 paper-based), IELTS (minimum score 6.5). Electronic applications accepted. *Faculty research:* Gender studies, post-colonial theory, poetics and poetic theory, film studies, post modernist thought.

University of Oregon, Graduate School, College of Arts and Sciences, Department of East Asian Languages and Literature, Eugene, OR 97403. Offers Chinese (MA, PhD); Japanese (MA, PhD). *Entrance requirements:* Additional exam requirements/recommendations for international students: Required—TOEFL. *Faculty research:* Linguistics, pedagogy.

University of Southern California, Graduate School, Dana and David Dornsife College of Letters, Arts and Sciences, Department of East Asian Languages and Cultures, Los Angeles, CA 90089. Offers classical Chinese literature (MA, PhD); classical Japanese literature (MA, PhD); linguistics (MA, PhD); modern Chinese literature (MA, PhD); modern Japanese literature (MA, PhD); modern Korean literature (MA, PhD). *Degree requirements:* For master's, thesis; for doctorate, 2 foreign languages, comprehensive exam, thesis/dissertation. *Entrance requirements:* For master's and doctorate, GRE, BA in relevant field. Additional exam requirements/recommendations for international students: Required—TOEFL. Electronic applications accepted. *Faculty research:* Gender, visual studies, multimedia, ecocriticism, second language acquisition.

University of Southern California, Graduate School, Dana and David Dornsife College of Letters, Arts and Sciences, Department of Linguistics, Los Angeles, CA 90089. Offers East Asian linguistics (PhD); Hispanic linguistics (PhD); linguistics (PhD); Slavic linguistics (PhD). *Degree requirements:* For doctorate, comprehensive exam, thesis/dissertation. *Entrance requirements:* For doctorate, GRE. Additional exam requirements/recommendations for international students: Required—TOEFL (minimum score 100 iBT). Electronic applications accepted. *Faculty research:* Syntax, phonology, phonetics, semantics, sociolinguistics, psycholinguistics.

The University of Texas at Austin, Graduate School, College of Liberal Arts, Department of Asian Studies, Austin, TX 78712-1111. Offers Asian cultures and languages (MA, PhD); Asian studies (MA). Part-time programs available. *Degree requirements:* For master's, thesis; for doctorate, 3 foreign languages, thesis/dissertation. *Entrance requirements:* For master's and doctorate, GRE General Test. Electronic applications accepted. *Faculty research:* Modern Taiwanese fiction, modern Japanese literature, religious studies in South Asia during classical period.

University of Washington, Graduate School, College of Arts and Sciences, Department of Asian Languages and Literature, Seattle, WA 98195. Offers Buddhist studies (MA, PhD); Chinese language and literature (MA, PhD); Japanese language and literature (MA, PhD); Korean language and literature (MA, PhD); South Asian language and literature (MA, PhD). *Degree requirements:* For master's, 2 foreign languages, general exam, thesis or 2 research papers; for doctorate, 3 foreign languages, thesis/dissertation, general exam. *Entrance requirements:* For master's, GRE, minimum GPA of 3.0; for doctorate, GRE, master's degree in related field, minimum GPA of 3.0. Additional exam requirements/recommendations for international students: Required—TOEFL. Electronic applications accepted. *Faculty research:* Textual, linguistic, philological, and literary study of languages and literatures of Asia.

University of Wisconsin–Madison, Graduate School, College of Letters and Science, Department of Languages and Cultures of Asia, Madison, WI 53706-1380. Offers civilizations and cultures (PhD); languages and cultures of Asia (MA); languages and literatures (PhD); religions of Asia (PhD). Part-time programs available. Terminal master's awarded for partial completion of doctoral program. *Degree requirements:* For master's, one foreign language, thesis or alternative; for doctorate, 2 foreign languages, thesis/dissertation. *Entrance requirements:* For master's, minimum GPA of 3.0; for doctorate, minimum GPA of 3.25, master's degree. Electronic applications accepted. *Expenses:* Tuition, state resident: full-time $10,723; part-time $745 per credit. Tuition, nonresident: full-time $24,054; part-time $1578 per credit. *Required fees:* $374 per semester. Tuition and fees vary according to course load, program and reciprocity agreements. *Faculty research:* Literature, folklore, religion.

Washington University in St. Louis, Graduate School of Arts and Sciences, Department of East Asian Languages and Cultures, St. Louis, MO 63130-4899. Offers Chinese (MA); Chinese and comparative literature (PhD); Chinese language and literature (PhD); East Asian studies (MA); Japanese (MA); Japanese and comparative literature (PhD); Japanese language and literature (PhD). Terminal master's awarded for partial completion of doctoral program. *Degree requirements:* For master's, thesis optional; for doctorate, thesis/dissertation. *Entrance requirements:* For master's and doctorate, GRE General Test. Additional exam requirements/recommendations for international students: Required—TOEFL. Electronic applications accepted. *Faculty research:* Chinese; Japanese; Chinese fiction, theater, poetry, modern literature; Japanese modern and classical fiction, translation theory; East Asian Studies.

Yale University, Graduate School of Arts and Sciences, Department of East Asian Languages and Literatures, New Haven, CT 06520. Offers East Asian languages and literatures (PhD); East Asian languages and literatures and film studies (PhD). *Degree requirements:* For doctorate, 2 foreign languages, thesis/dissertation. *Entrance requirements:* For doctorate, GRE General Test.

Celtic Languages

Harvard University, Graduate School of Arts and Sciences, Department of Celtic Languages and Literatures, Cambridge, MA 02138. Offers Irish (PhD); Welsh (PhD). *Degree requirements:* For doctorate, thesis/dissertation, proficiency in 2 Celtic languages; reading knowledge of French, German, and Latin. *Entrance requirements:* For doctorate, GRE General Test. Additional exam requirements/recommendations for international students: Required—TOEFL.

Chinese

Arizona State University at the Tempe campus, College of Liberal Arts and Sciences, School of International Letters and Cultures, Program in Chinese, Tempe, AZ 85287-0202. Offers Asian languages and civilizations: Chinese (MA); Chinese (PhD). Part-time and evening/weekend programs available. Terminal master's awarded for partial completion of doctoral program. *Degree requirements:* For master's, thesis, oral defense, interactive Program of Study (iPOS) submitted no later than beginning of third semester of study; for doctorate, comprehensive exam, thesis/dissertation, interactive Program of Study (iPOS) submitted before completing 50 percent of required credit hours. *Entrance requirements:* For master's, GRE, minimum GPA of 3.0 in the last two years of work leading to the bachelor's degree, BA in Chinese studies (preferred), personal statement, writing sample, 3 letters of recommendation; for doctorate, GRE, minimum GPA of 3.5 in the last two years of work leading to the bachelor's degree, completion of 3 years of modern Chinese and 1 year of classical Chinese, personal statement, writing sample, 3 letters of recommendation. Additional exam requirements/recommendations for international students: Required—TOEFL (minimum score 550 paper-based; 83 iBT), IELTS (minimum score 6.5). Electronic applications accepted.

DePaul University, College of Liberal Arts and Social Sciences, Chicago, IL 60614. Offers Arabic (MA); Chinese (MA); English (MA); French (MA); German (MA); history (MA); interdisciplinary studies (MA, MS); international public service (MS); international studies (MA); Italian (MA); Japanese (MA); leadership and policy studies (MS); liberal studies (MA); new media studies (MA); nonprofit management (MNM); public administration (MPA); public health (MPH); public service management (MS); social work (MSW); sociology (MA); Spanish (MA); sustainable urban development (MA); women and gender studies (MA); writing and publishing (MA); writing, rhetoric, and discourse (MA); MA/PhD. Part-time and evening/weekend programs available. Postbaccalaureate distance learning degree programs offered (no on-campus study). Terminal master's awarded for partial completion of doctoral program. *Degree requirements:* For master's, variable foreign language requirement, comprehensive exam (for some programs), thesis (for some programs). Electronic applications accepted.

Harvard University, Graduate School of Arts and Sciences, Department of East Asian Languages and Civilizations, Cambridge, MA 02138. Offers Chinese (PhD); Japanese (PhD); Korean (PhD); Mongolian (PhD); Vietnamese (PhD). Terminal master's awarded for partial completion of doctoral program. *Degree requirements:* For doctorate, 3 foreign languages, thesis/dissertation, general exams. *Entrance requirements:* For doctorate, GRE General Test. Additional exam requirements/recommendations for international students: Required—TOEFL. *Faculty research:* Central Asian literature, religion, and premodern history.

Hunter College of the City University of New York, Graduate School, School of Arts and Sciences, Department of Classical and Oriental Studies, New York, NY 10065-5085. Offers teaching Chinese (MA); teaching Latin (MA). Part-time and evening/weekend programs available. *Faculty:* 3 full-time (all women), 1 (woman) part-time/adjunct. *Degree requirements:* For master's, one foreign language, comprehensive exam. *Entrance requirements:* For master's, undergraduate major in Latin or equivalent with a minimum GPA of 3.0, 2.8 overall; interview, 2 letters of recommendation. Additional exam requirements/recommendations for international students: Required—TOEFL. *Application deadline:* For fall admission, 4/1 for domestic students; for spring admission, 11/1 for domestic students. *Financial support:* Federal Work-Study, scholarships/grants, and tuition waivers (partial) available. Support available to part-time students. Financial award application deadline: 4/15. *Faculty research:* Latin poetry, historiography, classical culture, archaeology. *Unit head:* Robert B. Koehl, Chairperson, 212-772-5061, E-mail: rkoehl@hunter.cuny.edu. *Application contact:* Milena Solo, Director of Admissions, 212-772-4480, E-mail: admissions@hunter.cuny.edu. Website: http://www.hunter.cuny.edu/classics/

Indiana University Bloomington, University Graduate School, College of Arts and Sciences, School of Global and International Studies, Department of East Asian Languages and Cultures, Bloomington, IN 47408. Offers Chinese (MA, PhD); Chinese language pedagogy (MA); East Asian studies (MA); Japanese (MA, PhD); Japanese language pedagogy (MA). Part-time programs available. *Faculty:* 21 full-time (11 women), 14 part-time/adjunct (7 women). *Students:* 10 full-time (7 women), 20 part-time (12 women); includes 3 minority (2 Asian, non-Hispanic/Latino; 1 Hispanic/Latino), 15 international. 87 applicants, 31% accepted, 8 enrolled. In 2014, 5 master's awarded. *Degree requirements:* For master's, one foreign language, thesis; for doctorate, 2 foreign languages, comprehensive exam, thesis/dissertation. *Entrance requirements:* Additional exam requirements/recommendations for international students: Required—TOEFL (minimum score 93 iBT). *Application deadline:* For fall admission, 1/1 for domestic students, 12/1 for international students. Application fee: $55 ($65 for international students). Electronic applications accepted. *Financial support:* In 2014–15, 23 students received support, including fellowships with full tuition reimbursements available (averaging $18,000 per year), teaching assistantships with full tuition reimbursements available (averaging $15,750 per year). Financial award application deadline: 2/15. *Faculty research:* Modern East Asian history; politics and society; traditional Chinese thought and society; medieval and premodern Japanese history, literature and society; modern Chinese and Japanese film and literature; Chinese, Japanese, Korean language and linguistics. *Unit head:* Prof. Natsuko Tsujimura, Chair, 812-855-0856, Fax: 812-855-6402, E-mail: tsujimur@indiana.edu. *Application contact:* Stephen Thomas Johnson, Student Services Assistant, 812-856-4959, E-mail: johnsost@indiana.edu. Website: http://www.indiana.edu/~ealc/index.shtml

Middlebury College, Language Schools, Chinese School, Middlebury, VT 05753-6002. Offers MA. *Faculty:* 34 full-time (24 women). *Students:* 37 full-time (29 women); includes 18 minority (1 American Indian or Alaska Native, non-Hispanic/Latino; 15 Asian, non-Hispanic/Latino; 2 Two or more races, non-Hispanic/Latino), 13 international. Average age 34. 57 applicants, 79% accepted, 37 enrolled. In 2014, 11 master's awarded. *Degree requirements:* For master's, one foreign language, teaching practicum. *Entrance requirements:* For master's, placement test, 3 letters of recommendation, writing sample, curriculum vitae, official transcripts of undergraduate coursework. Additional exam requirements/recommendations for international students: Required—TOEFL (minimum score 600 paper-based; 100 iBT), IELTS (minimum score 7.5). *Application deadline:* Applications are processed on a rolling basis. Application fee: $65. Electronic applications accepted. *Financial support:* Fellowships and scholarships/grants available. Financial award applicants required to submit FAFSA. *Unit head:* Dr. Jianhua Bai, Director, 802-443-5520, Fax: 802-443-2075, E-mail: jbai@middlebury.edu. *Application contact:* Anna Sun, Coordinator, 802-443-5520, Fax: 802-443-2075, E-mail: sun@middlebury.edu. Website: http://www.middlebury.edu/ls/grad_programs/chinese

New York University, Steinhardt School of Culture, Education, and Human Development, Department of Teaching and Learning, Program in Multilingual/Multicultural Studies, New York, NY 10003. Offers bilingual education (PhD); bilingual education for teachers (MA, Advanced Certificate); foreign language education (MA); teachers of English to speakers of other languages in college (PhD); teachers of French 7-12 (MA); teachers of Hebrew 7-12 (MA); teaching a foreign language 7-12 (MA), including teaching English to speakers of other languages, all grades; teaching English to speakers of other languages (MA); teaching foreign languages, 7-12 (MA), including Chinese, French, Italian, Japanese, Spanish; teaching French as a foreign language (MA), including teaching English to speakers of other languages; teaching Spanish as a foreign language and TESOL (MA). *Accreditation:* Teacher Education Accreditation Council. Part-time and evening/weekend programs available. *Faculty:* 6 full-time (4 women). *Students:* 118 full-time (94 women), 82 part-time (72 women); includes 40 minority (8 Black or African American, non-Hispanic/Latino; 18 Asian, non-Hispanic/Latino; 12 Hispanic/Latino; 2 Two or more races, non-Hispanic/Latino), 116 international. Average age 29. 431 applicants, 61% accepted, 92 enrolled. In 2014, 121 master's, 1 doctorate, 2 other advanced degrees awarded. *Degree requirements:* For master's, thesis (for some programs); for doctorate, thesis/dissertation. *Entrance requirements:* For doctorate, GRE General Test, interview; for Advanced Certificate, master's degree. Additional exam requirements/recommendations for international students: Required—TOEFL (minimum score 100 iBT). *Application deadline:* For fall admission, 12/1 priority date for domestic and international students; for spring admission, 10/1 for domestic and international students. Applications are processed on a rolling basis. Application fee: $75. Electronic applications accepted. *Financial support:* Fellowships with full and partial tuition reimbursements, career-related internships or fieldwork, Federal Work-Study, institutionally sponsored loans, scholarships/grants, and tuition waivers (partial) available. Support available to part-time students. Financial award application deadline: 2/1; financial award applicants required to submit FAFSA. *Faculty research:* Second language acquisition, cross-cultural communication, technology-enhanced language learning, language variation, action learning. *Unit head:* Prof. Shondel Nero, Director, 212-998-5757, E-mail: shondel.nero@nyu.edu. *Application contact:* 212-998-5030, Fax: 212-995-4328, E-mail: steinhardt.gradadmissions@nyu.edu. Website: http://steinhardt.nyu.edu/teachlearn/mms

The Ohio State University, Graduate School, College of Arts and Sciences, Division of Arts and Humanities, Department of East Asian Languages and Literatures, Columbus, OH 43210. Offers Chinese (MA, PhD); Japanese (MA, PhD). *Faculty:* 20. *Students:* 53 full-time (32 women), 3 part-time (2 women); includes 7 minority (1 Black or African American, non-Hispanic/Latino; 5 Asian, non-Hispanic/Latino; 1 Two or more races, non-Hispanic/Latino), 31 international. Average age 30. In 2014, 13 master's, 3 doctorates awarded. Terminal master's awarded for partial completion of doctoral program. *Degree requirements:* For master's, thesis optional; for doctorate, thesis/dissertation. *Entrance requirements:* For master's and doctorate, GRE General Test (if applying for financial aid). Additional exam requirements/recommendations for international students: Required—TOEFL (minimum score 577 paper-based; 90 iBT); Recommended—IELTS (minimum score 7.5). *Application deadline:* For fall admission, 11/30 priority date for domestic and international students; for winter admission, 12/1 for domestic students, 11/1 for international students; for spring admission, 3/1 for domestic students, 2/1 for international students. Applications are processed on a rolling basis. Application fee: $60 ($70 for international students). Electronic applications accepted. *Financial support:* Fellowships, research assistantships, teaching assistantships, Federal Work-Study, institutionally sponsored loans, and unspecified assistantships available. Support available to part-time students. *Unit head:* Mark Bender, PhD, Chair and Professor, 614-688-5737, E-mail: bender.4@osu.edu. *Application contact:* Graduate and Professional Admissions, 614-292-9444, Fax: 614-292-3895, E-mail: gpadmissions@osu.edu. Website: http://deall.osu.edu/

San Francisco State University, Division of Graduate Studies, College of Liberal and Creative Arts, Department of Foreign Languages and Literatures, Program in Chinese, San Francisco, CA 94132-1722. Offers MA. *Application deadline:* Applications are processed on a rolling basis. *Expenses:* Tuition, state resident: full-time $6738. Tuition, nonresident: full-time $17,898; part-time $372 per credit hour. *Required fees:* $498 per semester. *Unit head:* Dr. Mohammad Salama, Chair, 415-338-7413, Fax: 415-405-0588, E-mail: mrsalama@sfsu.edu. *Application contact:* Prof. Chris Wen-Chao Li, Graduate Advisor, 415-338-1034, Fax: 415-405-0588, E-mail: wenchao@sfsu.edu. Website: http://chinese.sfsu.edu/

Stanford University, School of Humanities and Sciences, Department of East Asian Languages and Cultures, Stanford, CA 94305-9991. Offers Chinese (MA, PhD); Japanese (MA, PhD). Terminal master's awarded for partial completion of doctoral program. *Degree requirements:* For master's, one foreign language, thesis or an annotated translation of a literary or historical text; for doctorate, 2 foreign languages, thesis/dissertation, field exams. *Entrance requirements:* For master's and doctorate, GRE General Test. Additional exam requirements/recommendations for international students: Required—TOEFL. Electronic applications accepted. *Expenses:* Tuition: Full-time $44,184; part-time $982 per credit hour. *Required fees:* $191.

Union Graduate College, School of Education, Schenectady, NY 12308-3107. Offers biology (MAT); chemistry (MAT); Chinese (MAT); earth science (MAT); English (MA, MAT); English and history (MA); French (MAT); general science (MAT); German (MAT); history (MA); Latin (MAT); life sciences (MS); mathematics (MAT); mathematics and computer technology (MS); mentoring and teacher leadership (AC); middle childhood extension (AC); national board certification and teacher leadership (AC); physical sciences (MS); physics (MAT); social studies (MAT); Spanish (MAT); technology (MAT). *Accreditation:* Teacher Education Accreditation Council. *Degree requirements:* For master's, thesis or project. *Entrance requirements:* For master's, minimum GPA of 3.0, letters of recommendation. Additional exam requirements/recommendations for international students: Required—TOEFL (minimum score 550 paper-based). Electronic applications accepted. *Expenses:* Contact institution. *Faculty research:* Transformative learning, science education, National Board Certification, teacher leadership, teacher quality.

University of Alberta, Faculty of Graduate Studies and Research, Department of East Asian Studies, Edmonton, AB T6G 2E1, Canada. Offers Chinese literature (MA); East Asian interdisciplinary studies (MA); Japanese literature (MA). Part-time programs available. *Degree requirements:* For master's, one foreign language, thesis. *Entrance requirements:* Additional exam requirements/recommendations for international students: Required—TOEFL. Electronic applications accepted. *Faculty research:* Classical Chinese poetry and poetics, Chinese philosophy, modern/contemporary Chinese literature, modern Japanese literature and culture, Japanese women's writing.

University of California, Berkeley, Graduate Division, College of Letters and Science, Department of East Asian Languages and Cultures, Berkeley, CA 94720-1500. Offers Chinese language (PhD); Japanese language (PhD). *Degree requirements:* For doctorate, one foreign language, thesis/dissertation, oral qualifying exam. *Entrance requirements:* For doctorate, GRE General Test, minimum GPA of 3.0, MA thesis, 3 letters of recommendation. Electronic applications accepted. *Faculty research:* Chinese and Japanese modern and classical texts, prose, and poetry; Chinese and Japanese linguistics.

University of California, Irvine, School of Humanities, Department of East Asian Languages and Literatures, Irvine, CA 92697. Offers Chinese (MA, PhD); East Asian languages and literatures (MA, PhD); Japanese (MA, PhD). *Students:* 12 full-time (10 women), 1 (woman) part-time; includes 4 minority (3 Asian, non-Hispanic/Latino; 1 Two or more races, non-Hispanic/Latino), 7 international. Average age 30. 40 applicants, 15% accepted, 3 enrolled. In 2014, 1 doctorate awarded. *Degree requirements:* For doctorate, thesis/dissertation. *Entrance requirements:* For master's and doctorate, GRE General Test, minimum GPA of 3.0. Additional exam requirements/recommendations for international students: Required—TOEFL (minimum score 550 paper-based). *Application deadline:* For fall admission, 1/15 priority date for domestic students, 1/15 for international students. Application fee: $90 ($110 for international students). Electronic applications accepted. *Financial support:* Fellowships with tuition reimbursements, research assistantships with full tuition reimbursements, teaching assistantships with partial tuition reimbursements, institutionally sponsored loans, traineeships, health care benefits, and unspecified assistantships available. Financial award application deadline: 3/1; financial award applicants required to submit FAFSA. *Faculty research:* Chinese, Japanese, and Korean literature and culture; language and textual analysis; historical, social, and cultural dimensions of literary study. *Unit head:* Michael A. Fuller, Chair, 949-824-2802 Ext. 2227, Fax: 949-824-3248, E-mail: mafuller@uci.edu. *Application contact:* Hu Ying, Graduate Faculty Advisor, 949-824-6312, Fax: 949-824-3248, E-mail: huying@uci.edu.
Website: http://www.hnet.uci.edu/eastasian/

University of Colorado Boulder, Graduate School, College of Arts and Sciences, Department of Asian Languages and Civilizations, Boulder, CO 80309. Offers Chinese (MA, PhD); Japanese (MA, PhD). *Faculty:* 11 full-time (4 women). *Students:* 24 full-time (12 women), 3 part-time (all women); includes 4 minority (2 Asian, non-Hispanic/Latino; 1 Hispanic/Latino; 1 Two or more races, non-Hispanic/Latino), 9 international. Average age 30. 55 applicants, 58% accepted, 12 enrolled. In 2014, 11 master's awarded. Terminal master's awarded for partial completion of doctoral program. *Degree requirements:* For master's, comprehensive exam. *Entrance requirements:* For master's, BA in Chinese or Japanese, minimum undergraduate GPA of 3.0. Additional exam requirements/recommendations for international students: Required—TOEFL. *Application deadline:* For fall admission, 1/1 for domestic students, 12/1 for international students; for spring admission, 10/1 for domestic students, 9/1 for international students. Applications are processed on a rolling basis. Application fee: $50 ($70 for international students). Electronic applications accepted. *Financial support:* In 2014–15, 63 students received support, including 11 fellowships (averaging $3,624 per year), 20 teaching assistantships with full and partial tuition reimbursements available (averaging $26,470 per year); institutionally sponsored loans, scholarships/grants, health care benefits, and unspecified assistantships also available. Financial award application deadline: 2/1; financial award applicants required to submit FAFSA. *Faculty research:* Asian languages/literature, Chinese language/literature, literary criticism, Japanese language/literature. *Total annual research expenditures:* $401,438.
Website: http://alc.colorado.edu/

University of Delaware, College of Arts and Sciences, Department of Foreign Languages and Literatures, Newark, DE 19716. Offers foreign languages and literatures (MA), including French, German, Spanish; foreign languages pedagogy (MA), including French, German, Spanish; technical Chinese translation (MA). *Degree requirements:* For master's, one foreign language, comprehensive exam, thesis optional. *Entrance requirements:* For master's, GRE General Test, letters of recommendation, writing sample. Additional exam requirements/recommendations for international students: Required—TOEFL. Electronic applications accepted. *Faculty research:* Medieval to Modern French and Spanish literature, twentieth-century German, French, Spanish literature by women, computer-assisted instruction.

University of Hawaii at Manoa, Graduate Division, College of Languages, Linguistics and Literature, Department of East Asian Languages and Literatures, Program in Chinese, Honolulu, HI 96822. Offers MA, PhD. Part-time programs available. *Degree requirements:* For master's, 2 foreign languages, thesis optional; for doctorate, 2 foreign languages, comprehensive exam, thesis/dissertation. *Entrance requirements:* For master's and doctorate, GRE General Test. Additional exam requirements/recommendations for international students: Required—TOEFL (minimum score 560 paper-based; 83 iBT), IELTS (minimum score 5).

University of Hawaii at Manoa, Graduate Division, School of Pacific and Asian Studies, Program in Asian Studies, Concentration in Chinese Studies, Honolulu, HI 96822. Offers Graduate Certificate. Part-time programs available. *Degree requirements:* For Graduate Certificate, one foreign language. *Entrance requirements:* For degree, GRE. Additional exam requirements/recommendations for international students: Required—TOEFL (minimum score 560 paper-based; 83 iBT), IELTS (minimum score 5).

The University of Iowa, Graduate College, College of Liberal Arts and Sciences, Program in Asian Civilizations, Iowa City, IA 52242-1316. Offers Chinese (MA); Hindi

(MA); Sanskrit (MA); South Asian studies (MA). *Degree requirements:* For master's, thesis optional, exam. *Entrance requirements:* For master's, GRE General Test, minimum GPA of 3.0. Additional exam requirements/recommendations for international students: Required—TOEFL (minimum score 590 paper-based; 96 iBT). Electronic applications accepted.

The University of Manchester, School of Languages, Linguistics and Cultures, Manchester, United Kingdom. Offers Arab world studies (PhD); Chinese studies (M Phil, PhD); East Asian studies (M Phil, PhD); English language (PhD); French studies (M Phil, PhD); German studies (M Phil, PhD); interpreting studies (PhD); Italian studies (M Phil, PhD); Japanese studies (M Phil, PhD); Latin American cultural studies (M Phil, PhD); linguistics (M Phil, PhD); Middle Eastern studies (M Phil, PhD); Polish studies (M Phil, PhD); Portuguese studies (M Phil, PhD); Russian studies (M Phil, PhD); Spanish studies (M Phil, PhD); translation and intercultural studies (M Phil, PhD).

University of Massachusetts Amherst, Graduate School, College of Humanities and Fine Arts, Department of Languages, Literatures, and Cultures, Programs in Asian Languages and Literatures, Amherst, MA 01003. Offers Chinese (MA); Japanese (MA). Part-time programs available. *Faculty:* 13 full-time (6 women). *Students:* 35 full-time (23 women), 6 part-time (4 women); includes 5 minority (all Asian, non-Hispanic/Latino), 22 international. Average age 28. 34 applicants, 50% accepted, 9 enrolled. In 2014, 6 master's awarded. *Degree requirements:* For master's, thesis, general exam. *Entrance requirements:* For master's, GRE General Test. Additional exam requirements/recommendations for international students: Required—TOEFL (minimum score 550 paper-based; 80 iBT), IELTS (minimum score 6.5). *Application deadline:* For fall admission, 2/1 for domestic and international students. Applications are processed on a rolling basis. Application fee: $75. Electronic applications accepted. *Expenses:* Tuition, state resident: full-time $1980; part-time $110 per credit. Tuition, nonresident: full-time $14,644; part-time $414 per credit. *Required fees:* $11,417. One-time fee: $357. *Financial support:* Fellowships with full and partial tuition reimbursements, research assistantships with full and partial tuition reimbursements, teaching assistantships with full and partial tuition reimbursements, career-related internships or fieldwork, Federal Work-Study, scholarships/grants, traineeships, health care benefits, tuition waivers (full and partial), and unspecified assistantships available. Support available to part-time students. Financial award application deadline: 2/1. *Unit head:* Dr. Stephen Miller, Department Head/Chair, 413-545-0886, Fax: 413-545-4975. *Application contact:* Lindsay DeSantis, Supervisor of Admissions, 413-545-0722, Fax: 413-577-0100, E-mail: gradadm@grad.umass.edu.
Website: http://www.umass.edu/asianlan/

University of Oregon, Graduate School, College of Arts and Sciences, Department of East Asian Languages and Literature, Eugene, OR 97403. Offers Chinese (MA, PhD); Japanese (MA, PhD). *Entrance requirements:* Additional exam requirements/recommendations for international students: Required—TOEFL. *Faculty research:* Linguistics, pedagogy.

University of Washington, Graduate School, College of Arts and Sciences, Department of Asian Languages and Literature, Seattle, WA 98195. Offers Buddhist studies (MA, PhD); Chinese language and literature (MA, PhD); Japanese language and literature (MA, PhD); Korean language and literature (MA, PhD); South Asian language and literature (MA, PhD). *Degree requirements:* For master's, 2 foreign languages, general exam, thesis or 2 research papers; for doctorate, 3 foreign languages, thesis/dissertation, general exam. *Entrance requirements:* For master's, GRE, minimum GPA of 3.0; for doctorate, GRE, master's degree in related field, minimum GPA of 3.0. Additional exam requirements/recommendations for international students: Required—TOEFL. Electronic applications accepted. *Faculty research:* Textual, linguistic, philological, and literary study of languages and literatures of Asia.

University of Wisconsin–Madison, Graduate School, College of Letters and Science, Department of East Asian Languages and Literature, Program in Chinese Literature, Madison, WI 53706-1380. Offers MA, PhD. Part-time programs available. Terminal master's awarded for partial completion of doctoral program. *Degree requirements:* For master's, one foreign language, seminars, written exam; for doctorate, 3 foreign languages, thesis/dissertation, seminars, preliminary exams, oral exam. *Entrance requirements:* For master's, bachelor's degree or equivalent in Chinese; for doctorate, master's degree or equivalent in Chinese. Electronic applications accepted. *Expenses:* Tuition, state resident: full-time $10,723; part-time $745 per credit. Tuition, nonresident: full-time $24,054; part-time $1578 per credit. *Required fees:* $374 per semester. Tuition and fees vary according to course load, program and reciprocity agreements. *Faculty research:* Chinese historical and modern linguistics, classical Chinese literary and cultural history, modern Chinese literary and cultural history, Chinese paleography.

Washington University in St. Louis, Graduate School of Arts and Sciences, Department of East Asian Languages and Cultures, St. Louis, MO 63130-4899. Offers Chinese (MA); Chinese and comparative literature (PhD); Chinese language and literature (PhD); East Asian studies (MA); Japanese (MA); Japanese and comparative literature (PhD); Japanese language and literature (PhD). Terminal master's awarded for partial completion of doctoral program. *Degree requirements:* For master's, thesis optional; for doctorate, thesis/dissertation. *Entrance requirements:* For master's and doctorate, GRE General Test. Additional exam requirements/recommendations for international students: Required—TOEFL. Electronic applications accepted. *Faculty research:* Chinese; Japanese; Chinese fiction, theater, poetry, modern literature; Japanese modern and classical fiction, translation theory; East Asian Studies.

Classics

American Public University System, AMU/APU Graduate Programs, Charles Town, WV 25414. Offers accounting (MBA, MS); criminal justice (MA), including business administration, emergency and disaster management, general (MA, MS); educational leadership (M Ed); emergency and disaster management (MA); entrepreneurship (MBA); environmental policy and management (MS), including environmental planning, environmental sustainability, fish and wildlife management, general (MA, MS), global environmental management; finance (MBA); general (MBA); global business management (MBA); history (MA), including American history, ancient and classical history, European history, global history, public history; homeland security (MA), including business administration, counter-terrorism studies, criminal justice, cyber, emergency management and public health, intelligence studies, transportation security; homeland security resource allocation (MBA); humanities (MA); information technology (MS), including digital forensics, enterprise software development, information assurance and security, IT project management; information technology management

(MBA); intelligence studies (MA), including criminal intelligence, cyber, general (MA, MS), homeland security, intelligence analysis, intelligence collection, intelligence management, intelligence operations, terrorism studies; international relations and conflict resolution (MA), including comparative and security issues, conflict resolution, international and transnational security issues, peacekeeping; legal studies (MA); management (MA), including defense management, general (MA, MS), human resource management, organizational leadership, public administration; marketing (MBA); military history (MA), including American military history, American Revolution, civil war, war since 1945, World War II; military studies (MA), including joint warfare, strategic leadership; national security studies (MA), including general (MA, MS), homeland security, regional security studies, security and intelligence analysis, terrorism studies; nonprofit management (MBA); political science (MA), including American politics and government, comparative government and development, general (MA, MS), international relations, public policy; psychology (MA); public administration (MPA),

including disaster management, environmental policy, health policy, human resources, national security, organizational management, security management; public health (MPH); reverse logistics management (MA); school counseling (M Ed); security management (MA); space studies (MS), including aerospace science, general (MA, MS), planetary science; sports and health sciences (MS); teaching (M Ed), including curriculum and instruction for elementary teachers, elementary reading, English language learners, instructional leadership, online learning, special education; transportation and logistics management (MA), including general (MA, MS), maritime engineering management, reverse logistics management. Programs offered via distance learning only. Part-time and evening/weekend programs available. Postbaccalaureate distance learning degree programs offered (no on-campus study). *Faculty:* 426 full-time (236 women), 1,864 part-time/adjunct (880 women). *Students:* 475 full-time (215 women), 10,067 part-time (4,085 women); includes 3,462 minority (1,863 Black or African American, non-Hispanic/Latino; 74 American Indian or Alaska Native, non-Hispanic/Latino; 273 Asian, non-Hispanic/Latino; 831 Hispanic/Latino; 78 Native Hawaiian or other Pacific Islander, non-Hispanic/Latino; 343 Two or more races, non-Hispanic/Latino), 131 international. Average age 36. In 2014, 3,740 master's awarded. *Degree requirements:* For master's, comprehensive exam or practicum. *Entrance requirements:* For master's, official transcript showing earned bachelor's degree from institution accredited by recognized accrediting body. Additional exam requirements/recommendations for international students: Required—TOEFL (minimum score 550 paper-based), IELTS (minimum score 6.5). *Application deadline:* Applications are processed on a rolling basis. Application fee: $0. Electronic applications accepted. *Financial support:* Applicants required to submit FAFSA. *Faculty research:* Military history, criminal justice, management performance, national security. *Unit head:* Dr. Karan Powell, Executive Vice President and Provost, 877-468-6268, Fax: 304-724-3780. *Application contact:* Terry Grant, Vice President of Enrollment Management, 877-468-6268, Fax: 304-724-3780, E-mail: info@apus.edu.
Website: http://www.apus.edu

Asbury University, School of Graduate and Professional Studies, Wilmore, KY 40390-1198. Offers biology: alternative certificate (MA Ed); chemistry: alternative certificate (MA Ed); English (MA Ed); English as a second language (MA Ed); ESL (MA Ed); French (MA Ed); Latin: alternative certificate (MA Ed); mathematics: alternative certificate (MA Ed); reading/writing endorsement (MA Ed); social studies (MA Ed); social work (MSW), including child and family services; Spanish (MA Ed); special education (MA Ed); special education: alternative certificate (MA Ed); teacher as leader endorsement (MA Ed). *Accreditation:* NCATE. Part-time programs available. *Degree requirements:* For master's, action research project, portfolio. *Entrance requirements:* For master's, PRAXIS/NTE, minimum GPA of 2.75, letters of recommendation. Additional exam requirements/recommendations for international students: Required—TOEFL (minimum score 550 paper-based). Electronic applications accepted.

Bethel Seminary, Graduate and Professional Programs, St. Paul, MN 55112-6998. Offers Anglican studies (Certificate); children's and family ministry (MA); Christian studies (Certificate); Christian thought (MA); Greek and Hebrew language (M Div); Greek language (M Div); Hebrew language (M Div); marriage and family therapy (MA, Certificate); ministry (D Min); ministry practice (MA, Certificate); theological studies (MA, Certificate); transformational leadership (MA); young life youth ministry (Certificate). *Accreditation:* ACIPE; ATS (one or more programs are accredited). Part-time and evening/weekend programs available. Postbaccalaureate distance learning degree programs offered (minimal on-campus study). *Faculty:* 15 full-time (3 women), 55 part-time/adjunct (27 women). *Students:* 422 full-time (167 women), 231 part-time (71 women); includes 165 minority (62 Black or African American, non-Hispanic/Latino; 58 Asian, non-Hispanic/Latino; 29 Hispanic/Latino; 1 Native Hawaiian or other Pacific Islander, non-Hispanic/Latino; 15 Two or more races, non-Hispanic/Latino), 16 international. Average age 37. 272 applicants, 77% accepted, 165 enrolled. In 2014, 147 master's, 13 doctorates, 8 other advanced degrees awarded. *Degree requirements:* For master's, variable foreign language requirement, thesis (for some programs); for doctorate, thesis/dissertation. *Entrance requirements:* For master's, letters of reference, transcripts, personal statement; for doctorate, M Div, letters of reference, organizational support; for Certificate, letters of reference, family essay, personal statement, and family of origin paper (for marriage and family therapy). Additional exam requirements/recommendations for international students: Required—TOEFL (minimum score 550 paper-based; 87 iBT). *Application deadline:* For fall admission, 8/1 priority date for domestic students, 8/1 for international students; for winter admission, 12/1 priority date for domestic students; for spring admission, 1/1 priority date for domestic students. Applications are processed on a rolling basis. Application fee: $0. Electronic applications accepted. *Financial support:* In 2014–15, 558 students received support, including 17 teaching assistantships; career-related internships or fieldwork, Federal Work-Study, and scholarships/grants also available. Financial award applicants required to submit FAFSA. *Faculty research:* Nature of theology, ethics, Biblical commentaries, nature of God, science and theology. *Unit head:* Dr. David Clark, Vice-President and Dean, Bethel Seminary, 651-638-6659. *Application contact:* Jen Niska, Director of Admissions, 651-638-6288, Fax: 651-638-6002, E-mail: bsem-admit@bethel.edu.

Boston College, Graduate School of Arts and Sciences, Department of Classics, Chestnut Hill, MA 02467-3800. Offers classics (MA); Greek (MA); Latin (MA). *Faculty:* 6 full-time. *Students:* 6 full-time. 15 applicants, 87% accepted, 3 enrolled. In 2014, 1 master's awarded. *Degree requirements:* For master's, one foreign language, thesis optional. *Entrance requirements:* For master's, GRE. Additional exam requirements/recommendations for international students: Required—TOEFL (minimum score 600 paper-based; 100 iBT), IELTS (minimum score 7). *Application deadline:* For fall admission, 2/1 for domestic and international students. Application fee: $75. Electronic applications accepted. *Financial support:* In 2014–15, 6 students received support, including teaching assistantships (averaging $9,000 per year); Federal Work-Study, scholarships/grants, and tuition waivers (full and partial) also available. Support available to part-time students. Financial award application deadline: 3/1; financial award applicants required to submit FAFSA. *Faculty research:* Latin, Greek, classical philology, ancient history, modern Greek. *Unit head:* Dr. Gail Hoffman, Chairperson, 617-552-2236, E-mail: hoffmaga@bc.edu. *Application contact:* Associate Dean, -, Fax: -.
Website: http://www.bc.edu/schools/cas/classics/

Boston University, Graduate School of Arts and Sciences, Department of Classical Studies, Boston, MA 02215. Offers MA, PhD, MA/PhD. *Faculty:* 14 full-time (6 women), 1 (woman) part-time/adjunct. *Students:* 18 full-time (9 women), 1 part-time (0 women); includes 2 minority (both Two or more races, non-Hispanic/Latino), 2 international. Average age 30. 31 applicants, 29% accepted, 3 enrolled. Terminal master's awarded for partial completion of doctoral program. *Degree requirements:* For master's, one foreign language, comprehensive exam; for doctorate, 2 foreign languages, comprehensive exam, thesis/dissertation. *Entrance requirements:* For master's, GRE General Test, 3 letters of recommendation, scholarly writing sample; for doctorate, GRE General Test, 3 letters of recommendation, scholarly writing sample, personal statement. Additional exam requirements/recommendations for international students: Required—TOEFL (minimum score 550 paper-based; 84 iBT). *Application deadline:* For fall admission, 1/15 for domestic and international students; for spring admission, 10/15 for domestic and international students. Application fee: $80. Electronic applications accepted. *Expenses: Tuition:* Full-time $45,686; part-time $1428 per credit hour. *Required fees:* $660; $60 per semester. Tuition and fees vary according to program. *Financial support:* In 2014–15, 19 students received support, including 4 fellowships with full tuition reimbursements available (averaging $20,500 per year), 1 research assistantship with full tuition reimbursement available (averaging $20,500 per year), 7 teaching assistantships with full tuition reimbursements available (averaging $20,500 per year); career-related internships or fieldwork, Federal Work-Study, institutionally sponsored loans, and health care benefits also available. Financial award application deadline: 1/15; financial award applicants required to submit FAFSA. *Faculty research:* Homer and Hesiod, tragedy and comedy, classical tradition, fifth century Athenian history, empire literature and history. *Unit head:* Ann Vasaly, Chairman, 617-353-2427, Fax: 617-353-1610, E-mail: vasaly@bu.edu. *Application contact:* Melissa Parno, Department Administrator, 617-353-2426, Fax: 617-353-1610, E-mail: josephmv@bu.edu.
Website: http://www.bu.edu/classics/

Brandeis University, Graduate School of Arts and Sciences, Department of Classical Studies, Waltham, MA 02454-9110. Offers MA, Certificate. Part-time programs available. *Degree requirements:* For master's, variable foreign language requirement, thesis or alternative, capstone course, paper. *Entrance requirements:* For master's and Certificate, 2 recommendation letters, curriculum vitae or resume, statement of purpose, official transcript(s). Additional exam requirements/recommendations for international students: Required—TOEFL (minimum score 600 paper-based; 100 iBT); Recommended—IELTS (minimum score 7). Electronic applications accepted.

Brigham Young University, Graduate Studies, College of Humanities, Department of Humanities, Classics, and Comparative Literature, Provo, UT 84602. Offers comparative studies (MA). *Faculty:* 24 full-time (5 women). *Students:* 14 full-time (10 women), 8 part-time (5 women). Average age 26. 14 applicants, 50% accepted, 7 enrolled. In 2014, 6 master's awarded. *Degree requirements:* For master's, 2 foreign languages, thesis. *Entrance requirements:* For master's, GRE, minimum GPA of 3.0 in last 60 hours. Additional exam requirements/recommendations for international students: Required—TOEFL (minimum score 580 paper-based; 85 iBT), IELTS (minimum score 7). *Application deadline:* For fall admission, 3/1 for domestic and international students. Application fee: $50. Electronic applications accepted. *Expenses: Tuition:* Full-time $6310; part-time $371 per credit hour. Tuition and fees vary according to program and student's religious affiliation. *Financial support:* In 2014–15, 17 students received support, including 31 fellowships with partial tuition reimbursements available (averaging $1,604 per year), 4 research assistantships (averaging $1,500 per year), 29 teaching assistantships (averaging $2,503 per year); career-related internships or fieldwork, institutionally sponsored loans, scholarships/grants, tuition waivers (full and partial), and student instructorships also available. Support available to part-time students. *Unit head:* Dr. Carl Sederholm, Coordinator, 801-422-9078, Fax: 801-422-0305, E-mail: carl_sederholm@byu.edu. *Application contact:* Carolyn Hone, Graduate Secretary for Humanities and Comparative Literature, 801-422-4430, Fax: 801-422-0305, E-mail: carolyn_hone@byu.edu.

Brock University, Faculty of Graduate Studies, Faculty of Humanities, Program in Classics, St. Catharines, ON L2S 3A1, Canada. Offers MA. Part-time programs available. *Degree requirements:* For master's, one foreign language, major research paper or thesis. *Entrance requirements:* For master's, honors degree, 3 letters of reference, written work (no more than 20 pages). Additional exam requirements/recommendations for international students: Required—TOEFL (minimum score 550 paper-based; 80 iBT), IELTS (minimum score 6.5), TWE (minimum score 4). Electronic applications accepted.

Brown University, Graduate School, Department of Classics, Providence, RI 02912. Offers MA, PhD. Terminal master's awarded for partial completion of doctoral program. *Degree requirements:* For master's, one foreign language, thesis; for doctorate, 2 foreign languages, thesis/dissertation. *Entrance requirements:* For master's and doctorate, GRE General Test. *Faculty research:* Philology, archaeology, Sanskrit.

Bryn Mawr College, Graduate School of Arts and Sciences, Department of Greek, Latin, and Classical Studies, Bryn Mawr, PA 19010-2899. Offers MA, PhD. Part-time programs available. *Faculty:* 6 full-time (3 women). *Students:* 14 full-time (10 women), 2 part-time (0 women); includes 1 minority (Asian, non-Hispanic/Latino). Average age 29. 21 applicants, 33% accepted, 3 enrolled. In 2014, 1 doctorate awarded. *Degree requirements:* For master's, 2 foreign languages, thesis; for doctorate, 3 foreign languages, comprehensive exam, thesis/dissertation. *Entrance requirements:* For master's and doctorate, GRE General Test. Additional exam requirements/recommendations for international students: Required—TOEFL (minimum score 600 paper-based). *Application deadline:* For fall admission, 1/3 for domestic and international students. Application fee: $50. *Expenses: Tuition:* Full-time $37,920. *Financial support:* In 2014–15, 10 fellowships with full tuition reimbursements (averaging $18,125 per year), 2 teaching assistantships with full tuition reimbursements (averaging $18,500 per year) were awarded; Federal Work-Study, scholarships/grants, and tuition waivers (full and partial) also available. Support available to part-time students. Financial award application deadline: 1/3. *Unit head:* Maria Dantis, Graduate Program Administrator, 610-526-5074, E-mail: gsas@brynmawr.edu.

The Catholic University of America, School of Arts and Sciences, Department of Greek and Latin, Washington, DC 20064. Offers Greek (Certificate); Greek and Latin (MA, PhD, Certificate); Latin (MA, Certificate). Part-time programs available. *Faculty:* 5 full-time (1 woman), 2 part-time/adjunct (1 woman). *Students:* 8 full-time (6 women), 14 part-time (3 women); includes 1 minority (Two or more races, non-Hispanic/Latino), 1 international. Average age 33. 23 applicants, 78% accepted, 5 enrolled. In 2014, 5 master's, 1 doctorate awarded. *Degree requirements:* For master's, one foreign language, comprehensive exam; for doctorate, 2 foreign languages, comprehensive exam, thesis/dissertation. *Entrance requirements:* For master's and doctorate, GRE General Test, statement of purpose, official copies of academic transcripts, three letters of recommendation; for Certificate, bachelor's degree. Additional exam requirements/recommendations for international students: Required—TOEFL (minimum score 580 paper-based). *Application deadline:* For fall admission, 7/15 priority date for domestic students, 7/1 for international students; for spring admission, 11/15 priority date for domestic students, 11/1 for international students. Applications are processed on a rolling basis. Application fee: $55. Electronic applications accepted. *Expenses: Tuition:* Full-time $40,200; part-time $1600 per credit hour. *Required fees:* $400; $195 per semester. One-time fee: $425. *Financial support:* Fellowships, research assistantships, teaching assistantships, Federal Work-Study, scholarships/grants, tuition waivers (full and partial), and unspecified assistantships available. Financial award application deadline: 2/1; financial award applicants required to submit FAFSA. *Faculty research:* Greek and Latin history and literature; classical, late antique and patristic history and literature. *Unit head:* Dr. William E. Klingshirn, Chair, 202-319-5216, Fax: 202-319-5297, E-mail: klingshirn@cua.edu. *Application contact:* Director of Graduate Admissions, 202-319-5057, Fax: 202-319-6533, E-mail: cua-admissions@cua.edu.
Website: http://greeklatin.cua.edu/

Columbia University, Graduate School of Arts and Sciences, New York, NY 10027. Offers African-American studies (MA); American studies (MA); anthropology (MA, PhD); art history and archaeology (MA, PhD); astronomy (PhD); biological sciences (PhD);

biotechnology (MA); chemical physics (PhD); chemistry (PhD); classical studies (MA, PhD); classics (MA, PhD); climate and society (MA); earth and environmental sciences (PhD); East Asia: regional studies (MA); East Asian languages and cultures (MA, PhD); ecology, evolution and environmental biology (MA), including conservation biology; ecology, evolution, and environmental biology (PhD), including ecology and evolutionary biology, evolutionary primatology; economics (PhD); English and comparative literature (MA, PhD); French and Romance philology (MA, PhD); Germanic languages (MA, PhD); global French studies (MA); Hispanic cultural studies (MA); history (PhD); history and literature (MA); human rights studies (MA); Islamic studies (MA); Italian (MA, PhD); Japanese pedagogy (MA); Jewish studies (MA); Latin America and the Caribbean: regional studies (MA); Latin American and Iberian cultures (PhD); mathematics (MA, PhD), including finance (MA); medieval and Renaissance studies (MA); Middle Eastern, South Asian, and African studies (MA, PhD); modern art: critical and curatorial studies (MA); modern European studies (MA); museum anthropology (MA); music (DMA, PhD); oral history (MA); philosophical foundations of physics (MA); philosophy (MA, PhD); physics (PhD); political science (MA, PhD); psychology (PhD); quantitative methods in the social sciences (MA); religion (MA, PhD); Russia, Eurasia and East Europe: regional studies (MA); Russian translation (MA); Slavic cultures (MA); Slavic languages (MA, PhD); sociology (MA, PhD); South Asian studies (MA); statistics (MA, PhD); theatre (PhD); JD/PhD; MA/MS; MD/PhD; MPA/MA. Dual-degree programs require admission to both Graduate School of Arts and Sciences and another Columbia school. Part-time and evening/weekend programs available. Terminal master's awarded for partial completion of doctoral program. *Degree requirements:* For master's, thesis (for some programs); for doctorate, comprehensive exam, thesis/dissertation. *Entrance requirements:* For master's and doctorate, GRE General Test, GRE Subject Test (for some programs). Electronic applications accepted. *Faculty research:* Humanities, natural sciences, social sciences.

Cornell University, Graduate School, Graduate Fields of Arts and Sciences, Field of Classics, Ithaca, NY 14853-0001. Offers ancient history (PhD); ancient philosophy (PhD); classical archaeology (PhD); classical literature and philology (PhD); classical myth (PhD); classical rhetoric (PhD); Greek and Latin language and linguistics (PhD); Indo-European linguistics (PhD); medieval and Renaissance Latin literature (PhD). *Degree requirements:* For doctorate, 2 foreign languages, comprehensive exam, thesis/dissertation. *Entrance requirements:* For doctorate, GRE General Test, 3 letters of recommendation, sample of written work. Additional exam requirements/recommendations for international students: Required—TOEFL (minimum score 550 paper-based; 77 iBT). Electronic applications accepted. *Faculty research:* Greek and Roman literature, ancient philosophy, Greek and Roman archaeology, ancient history, Indo-European linguistics.

Dalhousie University, Faculty of Arts and Social Science, Department of Classics, Halifax, NS B3H 4R2, Canada. Offers MA, PhD. *Entrance requirements:* Additional exam requirements/recommendations for international students: Required—TOEFL, IELTS, CANTEST, CAEL, or Michigan English Language Assessment Battery. Electronic applications accepted.

Duke University, Graduate School, Department of Classical Studies, Durham, NC 27708-0103. Offers PhD. *Degree requirements:* For doctorate, 2 foreign languages, thesis/dissertation. *Entrance requirements:* For doctorate, GRE General Test. Additional exam requirements/recommendations for international students: Required—TOEFL (minimum score 577 paper-based; 90 iBT) or IELTS (minimum score 7). Electronic applications accepted. *Expenses: Tuition:* Full-time $45,760; part-time $2765 per credit. *Required fees:* $978. Full-time tuition and fees vary according to program. *Faculty research:* Greek Bronze Age; classical and Roman archaeology; Pompeii and Hadrian; epigraphy, papyrology, and Latin paleography.

Duquesne University, School of Education, Department of Instruction and Leadership, Program in Secondary Education, Pittsburgh, PA 15282-0001. Offers biology (MS Ed); chemistry (MS Ed); English (MS Ed); K-12 education (MS Ed), including Latin; mathematics (MS Ed); physics (MS Ed); social studies (MS Ed). Part-time and evening/weekend programs available. *Faculty:* 5 full-time (4 women). *Students:* 32 full-time (23 women), 5 part-time (4 women); includes 4 minority (3 Black or African American, non-Hispanic/Latino; 1 Hispanic/Latino), 1 international. Average age 25. 44 applicants, 36% accepted, 16 enrolled. In 2014, 28 master's awarded. *Degree requirements:* For master's, thesis optional. *Entrance requirements:* For master's, letters of recommendation, letter of intent, interview, bachelor's degree. Additional exam requirements/recommendations for international students: Required—TOEFL (minimum score 550 paper-based), IELTS (minimum score 7). *Application deadline:* For fall admission, 9/1 for domestic students; for spring admission, 1/1 for domestic students. Applications are processed on a rolling basis. Application fee: $0. Electronic applications accepted. *Expenses: Tuition:* Full-time $18,882; part-time $1049 per credit. *Required fees:* $1800; $100 per credit. Tuition and fees vary according to program. *Financial support:* Research assistantships and Federal Work-Study available. Support available to part-time students. *Unit head:* Dr. Melissa Boston, Associate Professor and Director, 412-396-6109, E-mail: bostonm@duq.edu. *Application contact:* Michael Dolinger, Director of Student and Academic Services, 412-396-6647, Fax: 412-396-5585, E-mail: dolingerm@duq.edu.
Website: http://www.duq.edu/academics/schools/education/graduate-programs-education/ms-ed-secondary-education

Florida State University, The Graduate School, College of Arts and Sciences, Department of Classics, Tallahassee, FL 32306-1510. Offers ancient history (MA); classical archaeology (MA); classical civilization (MA); classics (MA, PhD), including classical archaeology (PhD); classics (PhD); Greek (MA); Greek and Latin (MA); Latin (MA). Part-time programs available. *Faculty:* 15 full-time (5 women). *Students:* 42 full-time (23 women); includes 2 minority (1 Black or African American, non-Hispanic/Latino; 1 Asian, non-Hispanic/Latino), 2 international. Average age 24. 61 applicants, 51% accepted, 10 enrolled. In 2014, 10 master's, 2 doctorates awarded. Terminal master's awarded for partial completion of doctoral program. *Degree requirements:* For master's, 2 foreign languages, comprehensive exam (for some programs), thesis or alternative; for doctorate, 4 foreign languages, comprehensive exam, thesis/dissertation. *Entrance requirements:* For master's, GRE General Test, minimum GPA of 3.0; for doctorate, GRE General Test, minimum GPA of 3.5. Additional exam requirements/recommendations for international students: Required—TOEFL. *Application deadline:* For fall admission, 1/15 priority date for domestic students, 2/15 for international students. Applications are processed on a rolling basis. Application fee: $30. Electronic applications accepted. *Expenses:* Tuition, state resident: part-time $403.51 per credit hour. Tuition, nonresident: part-time $1004.85 per credit hour. *Required fees:* $75.81 per credit hour. One-time fee: $20 part-time. Tuition and fees vary according to campus/location. *Financial support:* In 2014–15, 42 students received support, including 2 fellowships with full tuition reimbursements available (averaging $18,000 per year), research assistantships with full tuition reimbursements available (averaging $10,000 per year), 33 teaching assistantships with full tuition reimbursements available (averaging $10,000 per year); Federal Work-Study, institutionally sponsored loans, and tuition waivers (full and partial) also available. Support available to part-time students. Financial award application deadline: 1/15; financial award applicants required to submit FAFSA. *Faculty research:* Greek and Latin literature, classical archaeology, mythology,

ancient history, religion. *Total annual research expenditures:* $100,000. *Unit head:* Dr. Daniel J. Pullen, Chairman, 850-644-0304, Fax: 850-644-4073, E-mail: dpullen@fsu.edu. *Application contact:* Dr. Allen Romano, Admissions Director, 850-644-0305, Fax: 850-644-4073, E-mail: aromano@fsu.edu.
Website: http://classics.fsu.edu/

Fordham University, Graduate School of Arts and Sciences, Department of Classical Languages and Literatures, New York, NY 10458. Offers classical Greek and Latin literature (MA); classics (PhD). Part-time and evening/weekend programs available. *Faculty:* 7 full-time (1 woman). *Students:* 9 full-time (3 women), 5 part-time (3 women), 2 international. Average age 31. 11 applicants, 82% accepted, 3 enrolled. In 2014, 1 master's awarded. Terminal master's awarded for partial completion of doctoral program. *Degree requirements:* For master's, one foreign language, comprehensive exam; for doctorate, 2 foreign languages, comprehensive exam, thesis/dissertation. *Entrance requirements:* For master's and doctorate, GRE General Test. Additional exam requirements/recommendations for international students: Required—TOEFL (minimum score 650 paper-based). *Application deadline:* For fall admission, 1/4 priority date for domestic students; for spring admission, 11/1 for domestic students. Application fee: $70. Electronic applications accepted. *Financial support:* In 2014–15, 11 students received support, including 5 fellowships with full and partial tuition reimbursements available (averaging $27,000 per year), 8 teaching assistantships with full and partial tuition reimbursements available (averaging $21,000 per year); Federal Work-Study, institutionally sponsored loans, scholarships/grants, tuition waivers (full and partial), and unspecified assistantships also available. Support available to part-time students. Financial award application deadline: 1/4; financial award applicants required to submit FAFSA. *Unit head:* Dr. Christiana Sogno, Chair, 718-817-3135, Fax: 718-817-3134, E-mail: sogno@fordham.edu. *Application contact:* Bernadette Valentino-Morrison, Director of Graduate Admissions, 718-817-4419, Fax: 718-817-3566, E-mail: valentinomor@fordham.edu.

The Graduate Center, City University of New York, Graduate Studies, Program in Classics, New York, NY 10016-4039. Offers MA, PhD. *Degree requirements:* For master's, 2 foreign languages, thesis; for doctorate, 2 foreign languages, thesis/dissertation. *Entrance requirements:* For master's and doctorate, GRE General Test. Additional exam requirements/recommendations for international students: Required—TOEFL. Electronic applications accepted.

The Graduate Center, City University of New York, Graduate Studies, Program in Comparative Literature, New York, NY 10016-4039. Offers comparative literature (MA, PhD), including classics (PhD), German (PhD), Italian (PhD). PhD offered jointly with New York University. Terminal master's awarded for partial completion of doctoral program. *Degree requirements:* For master's, 2 foreign languages, comprehensive exam, thesis; for doctorate, 3 foreign languages, comprehensive exam, thesis/dissertation. *Entrance requirements:* For master's and doctorate, GRE General Test. Additional exam requirements/recommendations for international students: Required—TOEFL. Electronic applications accepted.

Harvard University, Graduate School of Arts and Sciences, Department of the Classics, Cambridge, MA 02138. Offers Byzantine Greek (PhD); classical archaeology (PhD); classical philology (PhD); classical philosophy (PhD); medieval Latin (PhD). *Degree requirements:* For doctorate, 4 foreign languages, thesis/dissertation, preliminary and special exams. *Entrance requirements:* For doctorate, GRE General Test. Additional exam requirements/recommendations for international students: Required—TOEFL.

Heritage Christian University, Graduate Programs, Florence, AL 35630. Offers counseling (MM); Greek (MA); ministry (MM); New Testament (MA). *Degree requirements:* For master's, practicum (MM), major research paper (MA). *Entrance requirements:* For master's, MAT or GRE, bachelor's degree in Bible from an accredited college or university, minimum GPA of 2.75, 3 letters of recommendation.

Hunter College of the City University of New York, Graduate School, School of Arts and Sciences, Department of Classical and Oriental Studies, Program in Teaching Latin, New York, NY 10065-5085. Offers MA. Part-time and evening/weekend programs available. *Faculty:* 3 full-time (all women), 1 (woman) part-time/adjunct. *Degree requirements:* For master's, one foreign language, comprehensive exam. *Entrance requirements:* For master's, undergraduate major in Latin or equivalent with a minimum GPA of 3.0, 2.8 overall; interview, 2 letters of recommendation. Additional exam requirements/recommendations for international students: Required—TOEFL. *Application deadline:* For fall admission, 4/28 for domestic students; for spring admission, 11/21 for domestic students. *Financial support:* Federal Work-Study, scholarships/grants, and tuition waivers (partial) available. Support available to part-time students. Financial award application deadline: 4/15. *Faculty research:* Late antique religion and social history, women in antiquity, Horace and lyric poetry, Roman comedy, Latin prose. *Unit head:* Robert B. Koehl, Chair, 212-772-5061, E-mail: rkoehl@hunter.cuny.edu. *Application contact:* Milena Solo, Director of Graduate Admissions, 212-772-4480, E-mail: admissions@hunter.cuny.edu.

Indiana University Bloomington, University Graduate School, College of Arts and Sciences, Department of Classical Studies, Bloomington, IN 47405. Offers MA, MAT, PhD. Part-time programs available. *Faculty:* 5 full-time (3 women). *Students:* 23 full-time (8 women); includes 4 minority (2 Hispanic/Latino; 2 Two or more races, non-Hispanic/Latino). Average age 28. 23 applicants, 22% accepted, 5 enrolled. In 2014, 2 master's, 2 doctorates awarded. *Degree requirements:* For master's, 2 foreign languages, comprehensive exam; for doctorate, 3 foreign languages, thesis/dissertation. *Entrance requirements:* For master's and doctorate, GRE, minimum GPA of 3.0. Additional exam requirements/recommendations for international students: Required—TOEFL. *Application deadline:* For fall admission, 1/15 priority date for domestic students, 12/1 for international students; for spring admission, 9/1 priority date for domestic students, 9/1 for international students. Applications are processed on a rolling basis. Application fee: $55 ($65 for international students). Electronic applications accepted. *Financial support:* Fellowships with full tuition reimbursements, teaching assistantships with full tuition reimbursements, and Federal Work-Study available. *Faculty research:* Roman literature (particularly Empire and late Latin), Greek drama, Homer, history of ideas, papyrology. *Unit head:* Prof. Matthew Christ, Chair, 812-855-6651. *Application contact:* Yvette Rollins, Graduate Secretary, 812-855-6651, E-mail: rollinsy@indiana.edu.
Website: http://www.indiana.edu/~classics/

Johns Hopkins University, Zanvyl Krieger School of Arts and Sciences, Department of Classics, Baltimore, MD 21218-2699. Offers PhD. Terminal master's awarded for partial completion of doctoral program. *Degree requirements:* For doctorate, 4 foreign languages, thesis/dissertation. *Entrance requirements:* For doctorate, GRE General Test. Additional exam requirements/recommendations for international students: Required—TOEFL (minimum score 600 paper-based), IELTS (minimum score 7). Electronic applications accepted. *Faculty research:* Greek culture and mythology, classical sculpture, Early Imperial Roman society.

Knox Theological Seminary, Graduate Programs, Master of Arts Programs, Fort Lauderdale, FL 33308. Offers Biblical and theological studies (MA); Christian and classical studies (MA). Part-time and evening/weekend programs available. *Entrance requirements:* Additional exam requirements/recommendations for international

students: Required—TOEFL (minimum score 520 paper-based; 83 iBT), TWE (minimum score 5).

Marshall University, Academic Affairs Division, College of Liberal Arts, Program in Latin, Huntington, WV 25755. Offers MA, Certificate. *Entrance requirements:* For master's, GRE General Test. *Unit head:* Dr. Del Chrol, Chair, 304-696-4323, E-mail: classical-studies@marshall.edu. *Application contact:* Information Contact, 304-746-1900, Fax: 304-746-1902, E-mail: services@marshall.edu.

McMaster University, School of Graduate Studies, Faculty of Humanities, Department of Classics, Hamilton, ON L8S 4M2, Canada. Offers MA, PhD. *Degree requirements:* For master's, one foreign language, thesis or alternative; for doctorate, 2 foreign languages, comprehensive exam, thesis/dissertation. *Entrance requirements:* For master's, honors degree, minimum B+ average. Additional exam requirements/recommendations for international students: Required—TOEFL (minimum score 580 paper-based). *Faculty research:* Ancient history, art and archaeology, Latin language and literature, Greek language and literature.

Memorial University of Newfoundland, School of Graduate Studies, Department of Classics, St. John's, NL A1C 5S7, Canada. Offers MA. Part-time programs available. *Degree requirements:* For master's, one foreign language, thesis, language exam, translation exam, research essay. *Entrance requirements:* For master's, honors degree in related field, course work in Greek and Latin. Electronic applications accepted. *Faculty research:* Ancient history, historiography, literature, drama, philosophy, paleography, epigraphy, and textual criticism.

New York University, Graduate School of Arts and Science, Department of Classics, New York, NY 10012-1019. Offers classics (MA, PhD); poetics and theory (Advanced Certificate). Part-time programs available. *Faculty:* 11 full-time (3 women). *Students:* 15 full-time (5 women), 3 part-time (2 women); includes 1 minority (Hispanic/Latino), 4 international. Average age 29. 47 applicants, 21% accepted, 6 enrolled. In 2014, 2 doctorates awarded. *Degree requirements:* For master's, 4 foreign languages, exam or specialized project; for doctorate, 4 foreign languages, thesis/dissertation, exams. *Entrance requirements:* For master's, GRE General Test, knowledge of Greek and Latin history and literature, proficiency in Greek and Latin translation; for doctorate, GRE General Test. Additional exam requirements/recommendations for international students: Required—TOEFL. *Application deadline:* For fall admission, 1/4 priority date for domestic students, 1/4 for international students. Application fee: $100. *Financial support:* Fellowships with tuition reimbursements, teaching assistantships with tuition reimbursements, Federal Work-Study, institutionally sponsored loans, scholarships/grants, health care benefits, and unspecified assistantships available. Financial award application deadline: 1/4; financial award applicants required to submit FAFSA. *Faculty research:* Greek and Latin literature, Greek and Roman history, epigraphy, Greek and Roman philosophy, classical archeology. *Unit head:* David Levene, Chair, 212-998-8590, Fax: 212-995-4209, E-mail: gsas.classic@nyu.edu. *Application contact:* Barbara Kowalzig, Director of Graduate Studies, 212-998-8590, Fax: 212-995-4209, E-mail: gsas.classics@nyu.edu.
Website: http://classics.as.nyu.edu/

The Ohio State University, Graduate School, College of Arts and Sciences, Division of Arts and Humanities, Department of Classics, Columbus, OH 43210. Offers Ancient Greek and Latin (MA, PhD); Greek studies (MA); Latin studies (MA, PhD); modern Greek (MA, PhD). *Faculty:* 16. *Students:* 28 full-time (13 women); includes 3 minority (2 Black or African American, non-Hispanic/Latino; 1 Hispanic/Latino), 1 international. Average age 28. In 2014, 1 master's, 5 doctorates awarded. *Degree requirements:* For master's, 2 foreign languages, thesis or alternative; for doctorate, 2 foreign languages, thesis/dissertation. *Entrance requirements:* For master's and doctorate, GRE General Test. Additional exam requirements/recommendations for international students: Required—TOEFL (minimum score 550 paper-based; 79 iBT), Michigan English Language Assessment Battery (minimum score 82); Recommended—IELTS (minimum score 7). *Application deadline:* For fall admission, 11/30 priority date for domestic and international students; for winter admission, 12/1 for domestic students, 11/1 for international students; for spring admission, 3/1 for domestic students, 2/1 for international students. Applications are processed on a rolling basis. Application fee: $60 ($70 for international students). Electronic applications accepted. *Financial support:* Fellowships with tuition reimbursements, research assistantships with tuition reimbursements, teaching assistantships with tuition reimbursements, Federal Work-Study, and institutionally sponsored loans available. Support available to part-time students. *Unit head:* Benjamin Acosta-Hughes, Chair, 614-292-2744, E-mail: acosta-hughes.1@osu.edu. *Application contact:* Graduate and Professional Admissions, 614-292-9444, Fax: 614-292-3895, E-mail: gpadmissions@osu.edu.
Website: http://classics.osu.edu/

Princeton University, Graduate School, Department of Classics, Princeton, NJ 08544-1019. Offers classical and hellenic studies (PhD); classical philosophy (PhD); history (the ancient world) (PhD); literature and philology (PhD). *Degree requirements:* For doctorate, thesis/dissertation. *Entrance requirements:* For doctorate, GRE General Test, sample of written work. Additional exam requirements/recommendations for international students: Required—TOEFL (minimum score 600 paper-based). Electronic applications accepted.

Queen's University at Kingston, School of Graduate Studies, Faculty of Arts and Sciences, Department of Classics, Kingston, ON K7L 3N6, Canada. Offers classics, Greek, Latin (MA). Part-time programs available. *Degree requirements:* For master's, one foreign language, thesis (for some programs). *Entrance requirements:* For master's, 3 years of Latin, 2 years of Greek. Additional exam requirements/recommendations for international students: Required—TOEFL. Electronic applications accepted. *Faculty research:* Greek and Latin literature, Greek and Roman history, ancient philosophy, Greek archaeology.

Rutgers, The State University of New Jersey, New Brunswick, Graduate School-New Brunswick, Department of Classics, Piscataway, NJ 08854-8097. Offers classics (MA, MAT, PhD); interdisciplinary classical studies and ancient history (MA, PhD). Part-time and evening/weekend programs available. Terminal master's awarded for partial completion of doctoral program. *Degree requirements:* For master's, 3 foreign languages, comprehensive exam, thesis or alternative; for doctorate, 3 foreign languages, comprehensive exam, thesis/dissertation. *Entrance requirements:* For master's and doctorate, GRE General Test. *Faculty research:* Greek and Latin literature, Greek and Roman social and political history, mythology, religion, ancient philosophy.

San Francisco State University, Division of Graduate Studies, College of Liberal and Creative Arts, Department of Classics, San Francisco, CA 94132-1722. Offers MA. Part-time programs available. *Application deadline:* Applications are processed on a rolling basis. *Expenses:* Tuition, state resident: full-time $6738. Tuition, nonresident: full-time $17,898; part-time $372 per credit hour. *Required fees:* $498 per semester. *Unit head:* Dr. David Leitao, Chair, 415-338-2068, E-mail: dleitao@sfsu.edu. *Application contact:* Dr. Michael A. Anderson, Graduate Coordinator, 415-338-3071, E-mail: maa35@sfsu.edu.
Website: http://classics.sfsu.edu/

Stanford University, School of Humanities and Sciences, Department of Classics, Stanford, CA 94305-9991. Offers MA, PhD. *Degree requirements:* For master's, 2 foreign languages, thesis or alternative; for doctorate, 4 foreign languages, thesis/dissertation, general exams. *Entrance requirements:* For master's and doctorate, GRE General Test. Additional exam requirements/recommendations for international students: Required—TOEFL. Electronic applications accepted. *Expenses: Tuition:* Full-time $44,184; part-time $982 per credit hour. *Required fees:* $191.

Texas Tech University, Graduate School, College of Arts and Sciences, Department of Classical and Modern Languages and Literatures, Lubbock, TX 79409-2071. Offers applied linguistics (MA); classics (MA); German (MA); languages and cultures (MA); Romance languages (MA); Spanish (PhD); MBA/MA. Part-time programs available. *Faculty:* 61 full-time (31 women), 7 part-time/adjunct (4 women). *Students:* 93 full-time (48 women), 15 part-time (10 women); includes 27 minority (1 Black or African American, non-Hispanic/Latino; 22 Hispanic/Latino; 4 Two or more races, non-Hispanic/Latino), 41 international. Average age 32. 60 applicants, 70% accepted, 26 enrolled. In 2014, 26 master's, 7 doctorates awarded. *Degree requirements:* For master's, comprehensive exam, thesis or alternative; for doctorate, comprehensive exam, thesis/dissertation. *Entrance requirements:* For master's and doctorate, GRE General Test. Additional exam requirements/recommendations for international students: Required—TOEFL (minimum score 550 paper-based; 79 iBT). *Application deadline:* For fall admission, 6/1 priority date for domestic students, 1/15 priority date for international students; for spring admission, 9/1 priority date for domestic students, 6/15 priority date for international students. Applications are processed on a rolling basis. Application fee: $60. Electronic applications accepted. *Expenses:* Tuition, state resident: full-time $6310; part-time $262.92 per credit hour. Tuition, nonresident: full-time $14,998; part-time $624.92 per credit hour. *Required fees:* $2701; $36.50 per credit. $912.50 per semester. Tuition and fees vary according to course load. *Financial support:* In 2014–15, 91 students received support, including 78 fellowships (averaging $2,724 per year), 4 research assistantships (averaging $17,800 per year), 82 teaching assistantships (averaging $11,423 per year); Federal Work-Study, scholarships/grants, and unspecified assistantships also available. Financial award application deadline: 4/15; financial award applicants required to submit FAFSA. *Faculty research:* Literature, comparative literature, linguistics, culture, applied linguistics. *Total annual research expenditures:* $1,380. *Unit head:* Dr. Erin Collopy, Chair and Associate Professor, 806-834-8497, Fax: 806-742-3306, E-mail: erin.collopy@ttu.edu. *Application contact:* Liz Hildebrand, Senior Advisor, 806-834-2463, Fax: 806-742-3306, E-mail: liz.hildebrand@ttu.edu.
Website: http://www.depts.ttu.edu/classic_modern/

Tufts University, Graduate School of Arts and Sciences, Department of Classics, Medford, MA 02155. Offers classical archaeology (MA); classics (MA); classics with teaching licensure (MA). Part-time programs available. *Faculty:* 7 full-time, 4 part-time/adjunct. *Students:* 11 full-time (4 women), 1 (woman) part-time. Average age 26. 38 applicants, 55% accepted, 6 enrolled. In 2014, 6 master's awarded. *Degree requirements:* For master's, 2 foreign languages, comprehensive exam, thesis or alternative. *Entrance requirements:* For master's, GRE General Test, writing sample. Additional exam requirements/recommendations for international students: Required—TOEFL (minimum score 550 paper-based; 80 iBT), IELTS (minimum score 6.5). *Application deadline:* For fall admission, 2/15 for domestic and international students; for spring admission, 10/15 for domestic and international students. Applications are processed on a rolling basis. Application fee: $75. Electronic applications accepted. *Expenses: Tuition:* Full-time $45,590; part-time $1161 per credit hour. *Required fees:* $782. Full-time tuition and fees vary according to degree level, program and student level. Part-time tuition and fees vary according to course load. *Financial support:* Teaching assistantships with full and partial tuition reimbursements, Federal Work-Study, scholarships/grants, tuition waivers (partial), and unspecified assistantships available. Financial award application deadline: 5/15; financial award applicants required to submit FAFSA. *Unit head:* Dr. Vickie Sullivan, Graduate Program Director. *Application contact:* Office of Graduate Admissions, 617-627-3395, E-mail: gradadmissions@tufts.edu.
Website: http://www.ase.tufts.edu/classics/

Tulane University, School of Liberal Arts, Department of Classical Studies, New Orleans, LA 70118-5669. Offers MA. *Degree requirements:* For master's, 2 foreign languages, thesis or alternative. *Entrance requirements:* For master's, GRE General Test, minimum B average in undergraduate course work. Additional exam requirements/recommendations for international students: Required—TOEFL. Electronic applications accepted. *Expenses: Tuition:* Full-time $46,326; part-time $2574 per credit hour. *Required fees:* $1980; $44.50 per credit hour. $550 per term. Tuition and fees vary according to course load and program.

Université de Montréal, Faculty of Arts and Sciences, Program in Classical Studies, Montréal, QC H3C 3J7, Canada. Offers MA. Electronic applications accepted.

University at Buffalo, the State University of New York, Graduate School, College of Arts and Sciences, Department of Classics, Buffalo, NY 14261. Offers MA, PhD. *Faculty:* 12 full-time (3 women), 1 (woman) part-time/adjunct. *Students:* 33 full-time (16 women), 4 international. Average age 25. 27 applicants, 33% accepted, 5 enrolled. In 2014, 2 doctorates awarded. Terminal master's awarded for partial completion of doctoral program. *Degree requirements:* For master's, 3 foreign languages, project; for doctorate, 4 foreign languages, comprehensive exam, thesis/dissertation, general and 2 special exams. *Entrance requirements:* For master's and doctorate, GRE General Test. Additional exam requirements/recommendations for international students: Required—TOEFL. *Application deadline:* For fall admission, 1/15 priority date for domestic and international students. Application fee: $75. Electronic applications accepted. *Expenses:* Expenses: Contact institution. *Financial support:* In 2014–15, 18 students received support, including 14 fellowships with full tuition reimbursements available (averaging $4,700 per year), 18 teaching assistantships with full tuition reimbursements available (averaging $13,560 per year); Federal Work-Study, institutionally sponsored loans, and unspecified assistantships also available. Financial award application deadline: 1/15. *Faculty research:* Greek and Latin literature, historiography, and epigraphy; Greek archaeology, mythology, and ancient philosophy; ancient and Roman religion and women's studies. *Total annual research expenditures:* $37,616. *Unit head:* Dr. Roger Woodard, Chairman, 716-645-0464, Fax: 716-645-2225, E-mail: rwoodard@buffalo.edu. *Application contact:* Dr. Bradley Ault, Director of Graduate Studies, 716-645-0458, Fax: 716-645-2225, E-mail: clarbrad@buffalo.edu.
Website: http://www.classics.buffalo.edu/

University at Buffalo, the State University of New York, Graduate School, Graduate School of Education, Department of Learning and Instruction, Buffalo, NY 14260. Offers biology education (Ed M, Certificate); chemistry education (Ed M, Certificate); childhood education (Ed M); childhood education with bilingual extension (Ed M); curriculum, instruction and the science of learning (PhD); early childhood education (Ed M); early childhood education with bilingual extension (birth-grade 2) (Ed M); earth science education (Ed M, Certificate); education studies (Ed M); educational technology and new literacies (Certificate); elementary education (Ed D); English education (Ed M, Certificate); English for speakers of other languages (Ed M); foreign and second language education (PhD); French education (Ed M, Certificate); German education (Ed M, Certificate); gifted education (Certificate); Latin education (Ed M, Certificate); literacy specialist (Ed M); literacy teaching and learning (Certificate); mathematics

education (Ed M, Certificate); music education (Ed M, Certificate); physics education (Ed M, Certificate); science and the public (Ed M); social studies education (Ed M, Certificate); Spanish education (Ed M, Certificate); special education (PhD); teaching English to speakers of other languages (Ed M). Part-time and evening/weekend programs available. Postbaccalaureate distance learning degree programs offered (no on-campus study). *Faculty:* 29 full-time (21 women), 64 part-time/adjunct (46 women). *Students:* 256 full-time (193 women), 303 part-time (222 women); includes 41 minority (21 Black or African American, non-Hispanic/Latino; 5 American Indian or Alaska Native, non-Hispanic/Latino; 13 Asian, non-Hispanic/Latino; 2 Hispanic/Latino), 84 international. Average age 30. 415 applicants, 84% accepted, 194 enrolled. In 2014, 160 master's, 20 doctorates, 32 other advanced degrees awarded. *Degree requirements:* For master's, comprehensive exam; for doctorate, thesis/dissertation, research analysis exam, research experience component. *Entrance requirements:* For master's, letters of reference; for doctorate, GRE General Test or MAT, interview, writing sample, letters of recommendation. Additional exam requirements/recommendations for international students: Required—TOEFL (minimum score 600 paper-based; 96 iBT). *Application deadline:* For fall admission, 2/1 priority date for domestic and international students; for spring admission, 11/15 priority date for domestic students, 10/1 for international students. Applications are processed on a rolling basis. Application fee: $50. Electronic applications accepted. *Financial support:* In 2014–15, 50 fellowships (averaging $12,110 per year), 32 research assistantships with tuition reimbursements (averaging $12,867 per year) were awarded; teaching assistantships, career-related internships or fieldwork, Federal Work-Study, institutionally sponsored loans, scholarships/grants, tuition waivers, and unspecified assistantships also available. Financial award application deadline: 2/28; financial award applicants required to submit FAFSA. *Faculty research:* Science assessment, foreign language teaching and learning, early learning, new literacies, gender and education. *Total annual research expenditures:* $1.3 million. *Unit head:* Dr. Suzanne Miller, Chair, 716-645-2455, Fax: 716-645-3161, E-mail: smiller@buffalo.edu. *Application contact:* Cathy Dimino, Admissions Assistant, 716-645-2110, Fax: 716-645-7937, E-mail: cadimino@buffalo.edu.
Website: http://gse.buffalo.edu/lai

University of Alberta, Faculty of Graduate Studies and Research, Department of History and Classics, Edmonton, AB T6G 2E1, Canada. Offers ancient history (PhD); classical archaeology (MA, PhD); classical literature (PhD); classics (MA); history (MA, PhD). Part-time and evening/weekend programs available. *Degree requirements:* For master's, one foreign language, thesis (for some programs); for doctorate, one foreign language, thesis/dissertation. *Entrance requirements:* For master's, minimum B+ average; for doctorate, minimum A- average. Additional exam requirements/recommendations for international students: Required—TOEFL (minimum score 580 paper-based). Electronic applications accepted. *Faculty research:* Western Canada, classical archaeology, Britain, Eastern Europe, East Asia.

The University of Arizona, College of Humanities, Department of Classics, Tucson, AZ 85721. Offers MA. Part-time programs available. *Degree requirements:* For master's, one foreign language, comprehensive exam, thesis. *Entrance requirements:* For master's, GRE General Test (minimum combined score of 1000 verbal and quantitative), 2 letters of recommendation. Additional exam requirements/recommendations for international students: Required—TOEFL (minimum score 550 paper-based; 79 iBT). Electronic applications accepted. *Faculty research:* Greek and Roman archaeology, ancient Greek, modern Greek, Latin, Greek and Roman religion, women in antiquity.

The University of British Columbia, Faculty of Arts and Faculty of Graduate Studies, Department of Classical, Near Eastern and Religious Studies, Programmes in Classics, Vancouver, BC V6T 1Z1, Canada. Offers ancient culture, religion, and ethnicity (MA); classical and near eastern archaeology (MA); classics (MA, PhD). Part-time programs available. *Degree requirements:* For master's, 2 foreign languages, thesis or comprehensive exam; for doctorate, 2 foreign languages, comprehensive exam, thesis/dissertation. *Entrance requirements:* For doctorate, MA. Additional exam requirements/recommendations for international students: Required—TOEFL (minimum score 600 paper-based), IELTS (minimum score 7.5). Electronic applications accepted. *Faculty research:* Classical archaeology, ancient historians, late antiquity, ancient prose fiction, epigraphy.

University of Calgary, Faculty of Graduate Studies, Faculty of Arts, Department of Greek and Roman Studies, Calgary, AB T2N 1N4, Canada. Offers MA, PhD. Part-time programs available. *Degree requirements:* For master's, one foreign language; for doctorate, 2 foreign languages, comprehensive exam, thesis/dissertation. *Entrance requirements:* For master's, BA in classics or related field, knowledge of Latin and/or Greek, minimum GPA of 3.7; for doctorate, MA in classics or related field, knowledge of Latin and Greek, GPA 3.7. Additional exam requirements/recommendations for international students: Required—TOEFL. Electronic applications accepted. *Faculty research:* Greek literature, Latin literature, Greek history, Roman history, classical archaeology.

University of California, Berkeley, Graduate Division, College of Letters and Science, Department of Classics, Berkeley, CA 94720-1500. Offers classical archaeology (MA, PhD); classics (MA, PhD); Greek (MA); Latin (MA). Terminal master's awarded for partial completion of doctoral program. *Degree requirements:* For master's, one foreign language, exams; for doctorate, 2 foreign languages, thesis/dissertation, qualifying exam. *Entrance requirements:* For master's and doctorate, GRE General Test, minimum GPA of 3.0, 3 letters of recommendation. Additional exam requirements/recommendations for international students: Required—TOEFL (minimum score 570 paper-based), TWE. *Faculty research:* Greek and Latin literature, textual criticism, history, archaeology and philosophy.

University of California, Irvine, School of Humanities, Department of Classics, Irvine, CA 92697. Offers MA, PhD. *Students:* 10 full-time (5 women); includes 1 minority (Two or more races, non-Hispanic/Latino). Average age 29. 11 applicants, 73% accepted, 2 enrolled. In 2014, 2 master's awarded. Terminal master's awarded for partial completion of doctoral program. *Degree requirements:* For master's, one foreign language, thesis or alternative; for doctorate, 2 foreign languages, thesis/dissertation. *Entrance requirements:* For master's and doctorate, GRE General Test, minimum GPA of 3.0. Additional exam requirements/recommendations for international students: Required—TOEFL (minimum score 550 paper-based). *Application deadline:* For fall admission, 1/15 priority date for domestic students, 1/15 for international students. Applications are processed on a rolling basis. Application fee: $90 ($110 for international students). Electronic applications accepted. *Financial support:* Fellowships, research assistantships with full tuition reimbursements, teaching assistantships, institutionally sponsored loans, traineeships, health care benefits, and unspecified assistantships available. Financial award application deadline: 3/1; financial award applicants required to submit FAFSA. *Faculty research:* Greek literature, computer application to Greek literature, Latin literature. *Unit head:* Susan Jarratt, Interim Chair, 949-824-6406, E-mail: sjarratt@uci.edu. *Application contact:* James Porter, Graduate Advisor, 949-824-8019, Fax: 949-824-1966, E-mail: james.porter@uci.edu.
Website: http://www.humanities.uci.edu/classics/

University of California, Los Angeles, Graduate Division, College of Letters and Science, Department of Classics, Los Angeles, CA 90095. Offers classics (MA, PhD); Greek (MA); Latin (MA). Terminal master's awarded for partial completion of doctoral

program. *Degree requirements:* For master's, 2 foreign languages, comprehensive exam; for doctorate, 2 foreign languages, thesis/dissertation, oral and written qualifying exams. *Entrance requirements:* For doctorate, GRE General Test, bachelor's degree; minimum undergraduate GPA of 3.0 (or its equivalent if letter grade system not used); Greek and Latin. Additional exam requirements/recommendations for international students: Required—TOEFL. Electronic applications accepted.

University of California, Riverside, Graduate Division, Tri-Campus Program in Classics, Riverside, CA 92521-0102. Offers PhD. Program offered jointly with University of California, Irvine and University of California, San Diego. *Degree requirements:* For doctorate, 3 foreign languages, comprehensive exam, thesis/dissertation. *Entrance requirements:* For doctorate, GRE, MA in classics. Additional exam requirements/recommendations for international students: Required—TOEFL (minimum score 550 paper-based; 80 iBT). Electronic applications accepted. *Expenses:* Tuition, state resident: full-time $5399. Tuition, nonresident: full-time $10,433. *Faculty research:* Rhetoric, Greek and Latin drama, Hellenistic poetry, Anglo-Latin literature, Greek and Latin prose.

University of California, Santa Barbara, Graduate Division, College of Letters and Sciences, Division of Humanities and Fine Arts, Department of Classics, Santa Barbara, CA 93106-2014. Offers ancient history (MA, PhD); classics (MA, PhD); literature and theory (PhD); MA/PhD. Terminal master's awarded for partial completion of doctoral program. *Degree requirements:* For master's, 3 foreign languages, comprehensive exam; for doctorate, 4 foreign languages, comprehensive exam, thesis/dissertation. *Entrance requirements:* For master's and doctorate, GRE. Additional exam requirements/recommendations for international students: Required—TOEFL (minimum score 550 paper-based; 80 iBT), IELTS (minimum score 7). Electronic applications accepted. *Faculty research:* Literary theory and cultural history, gender studies, Greek and Latin literature, Greek and Roman history, Greek and Roman drama and performance.

University of Chicago, Division of the Humanities, Department of Classics, Chicago, IL 60637. Offers ancient philosophy (PhD); classical archaeology (PhD); classical languages and literatures (PhD). *Students:* 32 full-time (15 women); includes 4 minority (2 Asian, non-Hispanic/Latino; 1 Hispanic/Latino; 1 Two or more races, non-Hispanic/Latino), 3 international. 74 applicants, 31% accepted, 6 enrolled. Terminal master's awarded for partial completion of doctoral program. *Degree requirements:* For doctorate, 2 foreign languages, thesis/dissertation. *Entrance requirements:* For doctorate, GRE General Test. Additional exam requirements/recommendations for international students: Required—TOEFL (minimum score 104 iBT), IELTS (minimum score 7). *Application deadline:* For fall admission, 12/15 for domestic and international students. Application fee: $90. Electronic applications accepted. *Expenses: Tuition:* Full-time $46,899. *Required fees:* $347. *Financial support:* Fellowships with full tuition reimbursements, teaching assistantships, Federal Work-Study, institutionally sponsored loans, scholarships/grants, and health care benefits available. Financial award application deadline: 12/15; financial award applicants required to submit FAFSA. *Unit head:* Dr. Mark Payne, Chair. *Application contact:* Braden Grams, Assistant Dean of Students, Admissions and Fellowships, 773-702-1552, Fax: 773-834-9148, E-mail: humanitiesadmissions@uchicago.edu.
Website: http://classics.uchicago.edu/

University of Chicago, Division of the Humanities, Master of Arts Program in the Humanities, Chicago, IL 60637. Offers art history (MA); classics (MA); comparative literature (MA); creative writing (MA); digital humanities (MA); English language and literature (MA); Germanic studies (MA); linguistics (MA); music (MA); philosophy (MA); Romance languages and literatures (MA); South Asian languages and civilizations (MA). *Students:* 83 full-time (41 women), 8 part-time (6 women); includes 14 minority (1 Black or African American, non-Hispanic/Latino; 6 Asian, non-Hispanic/Latino; 6 Hispanic/Latino; 1 Two or more races, non-Hispanic/Latino), 17 international. Average age 26. 153 applicants, 67% accepted, 80 enrolled. *Degree requirements:* For master's, thesis. *Entrance requirements:* For master's, GRE General Test. Additional exam requirements/recommendations for international students: Required—TOEFL (minimum score 600 paper-based; 104 iBT), IELTS (minimum score 7). *Application deadline:* For fall admission, 3/15 for domestic and international students. Application fee: $90. Electronic applications accepted. *Expenses: Tuition:* Full-time $46,899. *Required fees:* $347. *Financial support:* In 2014–15, 100 students received support, including 8 fellowships with partial tuition reimbursements available (averaging $12,000 per year); Federal Work-Study, institutionally sponsored loans, and tuition waivers (partial) also available. Financial award application deadline: 3/15; financial award applicants required to submit FAFSA. *Unit head:* Prof. David Wray, Director, 773-834-1201, E-mail: ma-humanities@uchicago.edu. *Application contact:* Program Coordinator, 773-834-1201, Fax: 773-834-7526, E-mail: ma-humanities@uchicago.edu.
Website: http://maph.uchicago.edu/

University of Cincinnati, Graduate School, McMicken College of Arts and Sciences, Department of Classics, Cincinnati, OH 45221. Offers MA, PhD. Part-time programs available. Terminal master's awarded for partial completion of doctoral program. *Degree requirements:* For master's, comprehensive exam (for some programs), thesis (for some programs); for doctorate, 2 foreign languages, comprehensive exam, thesis/dissertation. *Entrance requirements:* For master's and doctorate, GRE. Additional exam requirements/recommendations for international students: Required—TOEFL. Electronic applications accepted. *Faculty research:* Archaeology (bronze age and classical), philosophy (Greek and Latin), ancient history (Greek and Roman).

University of Colorado Boulder, Graduate School, College of Arts and Sciences, Department of Classics, Boulder, CO 80309. Offers MA, PhD. *Faculty:* 12 full-time (6 women). *Students:* 24 full-time (13 women), 1 part-time (0 women); includes 2 minority (both Hispanic/Latino). Average age 27. 68 applicants, 50% accepted, 11 enrolled. In 2014, 11 master's awarded. Terminal master's awarded for partial completion of doctoral program. *Degree requirements:* For master's, one foreign language, comprehensive exam, thesis or alternative, oral exam; for doctorate, 4 foreign languages, comprehensive exam, thesis/dissertation. *Entrance requirements:* For master's, minimum undergraduate GPA of 2.75; for doctorate, master's degree in classics or related field. *Application deadline:* For fall admission, 4/1 for domestic and international students; for spring admission, 11/1 for domestic students, 10/1 for international students. Applications are processed on a rolling basis. Application fee: $50 ($70 for international students). Electronic applications accepted. *Financial support:* In 2014–15, 50 students received support, including 5 fellowships (averaging $10,615 per year), 2 research assistantships with full and partial tuition reimbursements available (averaging $23,162 per year), 17 teaching assistantships with full and partial tuition reimbursements available (averaging $30,119 per year); institutionally sponsored loans, scholarships/grants, health care benefits, and unspecified assistantships also available. Financial award application deadline: 1/2; financial award applicants required to submit FAFSA. *Faculty research:* Classical Greek language/literature, classical Latin language/literature, ancient/classical history.
Website: http://www.colorado.edu/classics/

University of Florida, Graduate School, College of Liberal Arts and Sciences, Department of Classics, Gainesville, FL 32611. Offers classical studies (MA, PhD); Latin (MA, MAT, ML). Part-time programs available. Postbaccalaureate distance learning

degree programs offered. *Faculty:* 7 full-time (4 women), 2 part-time/adjunct (1 woman). *Students:* 8 full-time (3 women), 18 part-time (10 women); includes 2 minority (1 Black or African American, non-Hispanic/Latino; 1 Hispanic/Latino), 2 international. 8 applicants, 13% accepted. In 2014, 1 master's, 4 doctorates awarded. *Degree requirements:* For master's, one foreign language, thesis (for some programs); for doctorate, 2 foreign languages, comprehensive exam, thesis/dissertation. *Entrance requirements:* For master's, GRE General Test, minimum GPA of 3.0; for doctorate, GRE General Test, minimum GPA of 3.25 in graduate work, 3.25 in undergraduate work; MA in classical studies or equivalent. Additional exam requirements/recommendations for international students: Required—TOEFL (minimum score 550 paper-based; 80 iBT), IELTS (minimum score 6). *Application deadline:* For fall admission, 1/9 priority date for domestic students. Applications are processed on a rolling basis. Application fee: $30. Electronic applications accepted. *Financial support:* In 2014–15, 2 fellowships, 1 research assistantship, 7 teaching assistantships were awarded; unspecified assistantships also available. Financial award applicants required to submit FAFSA. *Faculty research:* Augustan Age Rome, ancient archaeology, Athenian democracy, Roman historiography and satire, Modern Greek studies. *Total annual research expenditures:* $15,450. *Unit head:* Victoria E. Pagan, PhD, Chair, 352-273-3696 Ext. 262, Fax: 352-846-0297, E-mail: vepagan@ufl.edu. *Application contact:* Jennifer Rea, PhD, Graduate Coordinator, 352-273-3797, Fax: 352-846-0297, E-mail: jrea@ufl.edu. Website: http://classics.ufl.edu/

University of Georgia, Franklin College of Arts and Sciences, Department of Classics, Athens, GA 30602. Offers classical languages (MA); Greek (MA); Latin (MA). *Degree requirements:* For master's, one foreign language, thesis. *Entrance requirements:* For master's, GRE General Test. Electronic applications accepted.

University of Illinois at Urbana–Champaign, Graduate College, College of Liberal Arts and Sciences, School of Literatures, Cultures and Linguistics, Department of the Classics, Champaign, IL 61820. Offers classical philology (PhD); classics (MA); teaching of Latin (MA). *Students:* 17 (6 women). Application fee: $70 ($90 for international students). *Unit head:* Ariana Traill, Head, 217-333-1008, Fax: 217-244-8430, E-mail: traill@illinois.edu. *Application contact:* Lynn Stanke, Office Support Specialist, 217-333-6269, Fax: 217-244-3050, E-mail: stanke@illinois.edu. Website: http://www.classics.illinois.edu/

The University of Iowa, Graduate College, College of Liberal Arts and Sciences, Department of Classics, Iowa City, IA 52242-1316. Offers classics (MA, PhD); Greek (MA); Latin (MA). *Degree requirements:* For master's, exam; for doctorate, comprehensive exam, thesis/dissertation. *Entrance requirements:* For master's and doctorate, GRE General Test, minimum GPA of 3.0. Additional exam requirements/recommendations for international students: Required—TOEFL (minimum score 550 paper-based; 81 iBT). Electronic applications accepted.

The University of Kansas, Graduate Studies, College of Liberal Arts and Sciences, Department of Classics, Lawrence, KS 66045. Offers MA. Part-time programs available. *Faculty:* 7 full-time, 1 part-time/adjunct. *Students:* 11 full-time (5 women), 1 (woman) part-time. Average age 25. 29 applicants, 41% accepted, 6 enrolled. In 2014, 4 master's awarded. *Degree requirements:* For master's, 3 foreign languages, comprehensive exam, thesis optional, 30 hours of coursework, 18 minimum in Greek and Latin (24 hours with thesis option). *Entrance requirements:* For master's, GRE (recommended), 15 junior/senior hours of course work in Latin and/or Greek (recommended). Additional exam requirements/recommendations for international students: Required—TOEFL. *Application deadline:* For fall admission, 1/15 priority date for domestic and international students; for spring admission, 1/15 for domestic students, 10/1 priority date for international students. Applications are processed on a rolling basis. Application fee: $55 ($65 for international students). Electronic applications accepted. *Financial support:* In 2014–15, 12 students received support, including 1 fellowship with full tuition reimbursement available (averaging $4,000 per year), 12 teaching assistantships with full and partial tuition reimbursements available; career-related internships or fieldwork, Federal Work-Study, scholarships/grants, traineeships, and unspecified assistantships also available. Support available to part-time students. Financial award application deadline: 1/15; financial award applicants required to submit FAFSA. *Faculty research:* Greek and Roman gender and sexuality, Roman literature (Cicero, Virgil, Horace, elegy, post-Virgilian epic), Greek literature (archaic epic, tragedy, Second Sophistic), Greek art and archaeology (the Bronze Age), Roman art and archaeology (imperial painting and architecture). *Unit head:* Prof. Tara Welch, Chair, 785-864-2395, E-mail: tswelch@ku.edu. *Application contact:* Emma Scioli, Graduate Admissions Contact, 785-864-2546, E-mail: scioli@ku.edu. Website: http://classics.drupal.ku.edu/

University of Kentucky, Graduate School, College of Arts and Sciences, Program in Modern and Classical Languages and Literatures, Lexington, KY 40506-0032. Offers MA. Part-time programs available. *Degree requirements:* For master's, one foreign language, comprehensive exam, thesis optional. *Entrance requirements:* For master's, GRE General Test, minimum undergraduate GPA of 2.75. Additional exam requirements/recommendations for international students: Required—TOEFL (minimum score 550 paper-based). Electronic applications accepted. *Faculty research:* Erasmus, Renaissance Latin, Greek and Roman epic, Greek biography, early Christian literature, classical philosophy.

The University of Manchester, School of Arts, Histories and Cultures, Manchester, United Kingdom. Offers anthropology, media and performance (PhD); applied theatre professional (PhD); archaeology (PhD); art history and visual studies (PhD); arts management and cultural policy (PhD); classics and ancient history (PhD); composition (PhD); creative writing (PhD); drama (PhD); economic and social history (PhD); electroacoustic composition (PhD); English and American studies (PhD); history (PhD); humanitarianism and conflict response (PhD); museology (PhD); music (PhD); musicology (PhD); religions and theology (PhD).

University of Manitoba, Faculty of Graduate Studies, Faculty of Arts, Department of Classics, Winnipeg, MB R3T 2N2, Canada. Offers MA. *Degree requirements:* For master's, thesis.

University of Maryland, College Park, Academic Affairs, College of Arts and Humanities, Department of Classics, College Park, MD 20742. Offers MA. *Degree requirements:* For master's, 2 foreign languages, thesis or alternative. *Entrance requirements:* For master's, writing sample, 3 letters of recommendation. Additional exam requirements/recommendations for international students: Required—TOEFL. Electronic applications accepted. *Faculty research:* Latin, Greek, and Roman culture.

University of Massachusetts Amherst, Graduate School, College of Humanities and Fine Arts, Department of Classics, Amherst, MA 01003. Offers Latin and classical humanities (MAT). Part-time programs available. *Faculty:* 9 full-time (4 women). *Students:* 12 full-time (7 women); includes 4 minority (2 Asian, non-Hispanic/Latino; 1 Hispanic/Latino; 1 Two or more races, non-Hispanic/Latino). Average age 24. 26 applicants, 31% accepted, 6 enrolled. In 2014, 7 master's awarded. *Degree requirements:* For master's, thesis or alternative. *Entrance requirements:* For master's, GRE General Test. Additional exam requirements/recommendations for international students: Required—TOEFL (minimum score 550 paper-based; 80 iBT), IELTS (minimum score 6.5). *Application deadline:* For fall admission, 2/1 for domestic and

international students. Applications are processed on a rolling basis. Application fee: $75. Electronic applications accepted. *Expenses:* Tuition, state resident: full-time $1980; part-time $110 per credit. Tuition, nonresident: full-time $14,644; part-time $414 per credit. *Required fees:* $11,417. One-time fee: $357. *Financial support:* Fellowships with full and partial tuition reimbursements, research assistantships with full and partial tuition reimbursements, teaching assistantships with full and partial tuition reimbursements, career-related internships or fieldwork, Federal Work-Study, scholarships/grants, traineeships, health care benefits, tuition waivers (full and partial), and unspecified assistantships available. Support available to part-time students. Financial award application deadline: 2/1. *Unit head:* Dr. Teresa Ramsby, Graduate Program Director, 413-545-0512, Fax: 413-545-6995. *Application contact:* Lindsay DeSantis, Supervisor of Admissions, 413-545-0722, Fax: 413-577-0100, E-mail: gradadm@grad.umass.edu. Website: http://www.umass.edu/classics/

University of Massachusetts Boston, College of Liberal Arts, Program in Latin and Classical Humanities, Boston, MA 02125-3393. Offers MA. *Expenses:* Tuition, state resident: full-time $2590; part-time $108 per credit. Tuition, nonresident: full-time $9758; part-time $406.50 per credit. Tuition and fees vary according to course load and program. *Unit head:* Dr. Donna Kuizenga, Dean, College of Liberal Arts, 617-287-6500, E-mail: donna.kuizenga@umb.edu. *Application contact:* Peggy Roldan Patel, Graduate Admissions Coordinator, 617-287-6400, Fax: 617-287-6236, E-mail: bos.gadm@dpc.umassp.edu.

University of Michigan, Horace H. Rackham School of Graduate Studies, College of Literature, Science, and the Arts, Department of Classical Studies, Ann Arbor, MI 48109. Offers classical studies (PhD); teaching Latin (MAT). *Faculty:* 18 full-time (9 women), 9 part-time/adjunct (3 women). *Students:* 25 full-time (11 women); includes 2 minority (both Hispanic/Latino), 3 international. Average age 27. 47 applicants, 13% accepted, 4 enrolled. In 2014, 7 master's, 2 doctorates awarded. Terminal master's awarded for partial completion of doctoral program. *Degree requirements:* For master's, one foreign language, comprehensive exam; for doctorate, 4 foreign languages, comprehensive exam, thesis/dissertation, oral defense of dissertation, preliminary exams, qualifying exams. *Entrance requirements:* For master's, GRE General Test, 2-3 years of Latin (for the Latin MAT); for doctorate, GRE General Test, strict minimum of 3 years of college-level Latin and 2 years of college-level Greek. Additional exam requirements/recommendations for international students: Required—TOEFL (minimum score 560 paper-based). *Application deadline:* For fall admission, 12/15 for domestic students, 1/5 for international students. Application fee: $75 ($90 for international students). Electronic applications accepted. *Financial support:* In 2014–15, 25 students received support, including 9 fellowships with full tuition reimbursements available (averaging $19,000 per year), 16 teaching assistantships with full tuition reimbursements available (averaging $18,600 per year); career-related internships or fieldwork, Federal Work-Study, institutionally sponsored loans, scholarships/grants, traineeships, tuition waivers (full), unspecified assistantships, and summer stipends, year-round health care also available. Financial award application deadline: 3/15. *Faculty research:* Greek and Latin literature, ancient history, papyrology, archaeology. *Unit head:* Prof. Sara Forsdyke, Chair and Professor, 734-764-0360, Fax: 734-763-4959, E-mail: classics@umich.edu. *Application contact:* Molly Cravens, Student Services Coordinator, 734-615-3181, Fax: 734-763-4959, E-mail: mcravens@umich.edu. Website: http://www.lsa.umich.edu/classics

University of Michigan, Horace H. Rackham School of Graduate Studies, College of Literature, Science, and the Arts, Interdepartmental Program in Greek and Roman History, Ann Arbor, MI 48109. Offers PhD, Certificate. Certificate program only open to students already studying in another PhD program at University of Michigan. *Faculty:* 6 full-time (2 women), 19 part-time/adjunct (12 women). *Students:* 12 full-time (5 women). Average age 28. 33 applicants, 6% accepted, 1 enrolled. In 2014, 2 doctorates awarded. *Degree requirements:* For doctorate, 4 foreign languages, comprehensive exam, thesis/dissertation, oral defense of dissertation, dissertation prospectus, preliminary exams, qualifying exams. *Entrance requirements:* For doctorate, GRE, strict minimum of 2 years each of classical Greek and Latin. Additional exam requirements/recommendations for international students: Required—TOEFL (minimum score 560 paper-based). *Application deadline:* For fall admission, 12/15 for domestic and international students. Application fee: $75 ($90 for international students). Electronic applications accepted. *Financial support:* In 2014–15, 12 students received support, including 4 fellowships with full tuition reimbursements available (averaging $23,000 per year), 8 teaching assistantships with full tuition reimbursements available (averaging $18,600 per year); career-related internships or fieldwork, Federal Work-Study, institutionally sponsored loans, scholarships/grants, traineeships, health care benefits, tuition waivers (full), and unspecified assistantships also available. Financial award application deadline: 4/15. *Faculty research:* Greek history, Roman history, history of ancient Mediterranean cultures. *Unit head:* Prof. David S. Potter, Professor, 734-936-2249, Fax: 734-763-4959, E-mail: dsp@umich.edu. *Application contact:* Molly Cravens, Student Services Coordinator, 734-615-3181, Fax: 734-763-4959, E-mail: mcravens@umich.edu. Website: http://www.lsa.umich.edu/ipgrh

University of Minnesota, Twin Cities Campus, Graduate School, College of Liberal Arts, Department of Classical and Near Eastern Studies, Minneapolis, MN 55455-0213. Offers ancient and medieval art and archaeology (MA, PhD); classics (MA, PhD); Greek (MA, PhD); Latin (MA, PhD); religions in antiquity (MA). Part-time programs available. Terminal master's awarded for partial completion of doctoral program. *Degree requirements:* For master's, 2 foreign languages, comprehensive exam, thesis or alternative; for doctorate, variable foreign language requirement, comprehensive exam, thesis/dissertation. *Entrance requirements:* For master's and doctorate, GRE, 3 letters of recommendation, writing sample, copies of transcripts, personal statement. Additional exam requirements/recommendations for international students: Required—TOEFL. Electronic applications accepted. *Faculty research:* Greek and Latin literature, religions in antiquity, ancient Near East.

University of Missouri, Office of Research and Graduate Studies, College of Arts and Science, Department of Classical Studies, Columbia, MO 65211. Offers classical languages (MA, PhD); classical studies (MA, PhD). *Faculty:* 9 full-time (2 women), 1 part-time/adjunct (0 women). *Students:* 21 full-time (9 women), 1 international. Average age 29. 8 applicants, 38% accepted, 3 enrolled. In 2014, 1 master's, 1 doctorate awarded. Terminal master's awarded for partial completion of doctoral program. *Degree requirements:* For master's, one foreign language; for doctorate, 2 foreign languages, comprehensive exam, thesis/dissertation. *Entrance requirements:* For master's, GRE General Test, minimum GPA of 3.0 during last 2 years; BA from accredited college/university; reading knowledge of Greek and/or Latin; for doctorate, GRE General Test, minimum GPA of 3.0; MA with major in Greek, Latin or classics or equivalent minimum of 21 hours of graduate work; reading knowledge of Greek, Latin, German, and French (or Italian). Additional exam requirements/recommendations for international students: Required—TOEFL (minimum score 500 paper-based; 61 iBT), IELTS (minimum score 5.5). *Application deadline:* For fall admission, 2/1 priority date for domestic and international students; for winter admission, 11/1 for domestic and international students. Applications are processed on a rolling basis. Application fee: $55 ($75 for international students). Electronic applications accepted. *Financial support:* In 2014–15,

4 fellowships with full tuition reimbursements, 1 research assistantship with full tuition reimbursement, 10 teaching assistantships with full tuition reimbursements were awarded; institutionally sponsored loans, traineeships, and health care benefits also available. *Faculty research:* Studies in the oral tradition, ancient Mediterranean religion, archaeology of the Ancient World, ancient political culture, late antiquity, rhetoric, the Classical Tradition. *Unit head:* Dr. Dennis Trout, Department Chair, 573-884-8593, E-mail: troutd@missouri.edu. *Application contact:* Debbie Strodtman, Administrative Assistant, 573-882-0679, E-mail: strodtmand@missouri.edu.
Website: http://classics.missouri.edu/grad/index.shtml

University of Nebraska–Lincoln, Graduate College, College of Arts and Sciences, Department of Classics and Religious Studies, Lincoln, NE 68588. Offers MA. *Degree requirements:* For master's, thesis optional. *Entrance requirements:* For master's, GRE. Additional exam requirements/recommendations for international students: Required—TOEFL (minimum score 550 paper-based). Electronic applications accepted. *Faculty research:* Greek and Latin poetry and prose, Greek and Latin linguistics, patristics, gnosticism, religion of late antiquity.

University of New Brunswick Fredericton, School of Graduate Studies, Faculty of Arts, Department of Classics and Ancient History, Fredericton, NB E3B 5A3, Canada. Offers classics (MA). Part-time programs available. *Faculty:* 4 full-time (1 woman), 2 part-time/adjunct (0 women). *Students:* 1 full-time (0 women). *Degree requirements:* For master's, thesis. *Entrance requirements:* For master's, minimum GPA of 3.0, minimum of 18 credit hours or equivalent in either Greek or Latin. Additional exam requirements/recommendations for international students: Required—TOEFL, TWE. *Application deadline:* For fall admission, 1/31 for domestic and international students; for winter admission, 1/15 priority date for domestic and international students; for spring admission, 1/31 for domestic and international students. Applications are processed on a rolling basis. Application fee: $50 Canadian dollars. Electronic applications accepted. *Financial support:* Teaching assistantships available. Financial award application deadline: 1/31. *Faculty research:* Roman history, Silver Age Latin poetry, stamped roof tiles, Plato, early Christianity, Greek and Roman archaeology, late Antiquity and Byzantium. *Unit head:* Prof. William Kerr, Director of Graduate Studies, 506-458-7507, Fax: 506-447-3072, E-mail: wkerr@unb.ca. *Application contact:* Joyce Smith, Graduate Secretary, 506-453-4762, Fax: 506-447-3072, E-mail: jsmith2@unb.ca.
Website: http://go.unb.ca/gradprograms

The University of North Carolina at Chapel Hill, Graduate School, College of Arts and Sciences, Department of Classics, Chapel Hill, NC 27599. Offers classical archaeology (MA, PhD); classics (MA, PhD). Terminal master's awarded for partial completion of doctoral program. *Degree requirements:* For master's, one foreign language, comprehensive exam, thesis; for doctorate, 2 foreign languages, comprehensive exam, thesis/dissertation. *Entrance requirements:* For master's and doctorate, GRE General Test, minimum GPA of 3.0. Electronic applications accepted.

The University of North Carolina at Greensboro, Graduate School, College of Arts and Sciences, Department of Classical Studies, Greensboro, NC 27412-5001. Offers Latin (M Ed). *Entrance requirements:* For master's, GRE General Test, MAT, or PRAXIS. Additional exam requirements/recommendations for international students: Required—TOEFL. Electronic applications accepted.

University of Oregon, Graduate School, College of Arts and Sciences, Department of Classics, Eugene, OR 97403. Offers classical civilization (MA); classics (MA), including Greek, Latin; Greek (MA); Latin (MA). Part-time programs available. *Degree requirements:* For master's, 2 foreign languages, thesis or alternative. *Entrance requirements:* For master's, GRE General Test, minimum GPA of 3.0. Additional exam requirements/recommendations for international students: Required—TOEFL. *Faculty research:* Roman religion, Greek philosophy, archaeology, Greek and Roman literature.

University of Ottawa, Faculty of Graduate and Postdoctoral Studies, Faculty of Arts, Department of Classics and Religious Studies, Ottawa, ON K1N 6N5, Canada. Offers classical studies (MA); religious studies (PhD). *Degree requirements:* For master's, comprehensive exam, thesis or alternative; for doctorate, comprehensive exam, thesis/dissertation. *Entrance requirements:* For master's, honors degree or equivalent, minimum B average; for doctorate, master's degree, minimum B+ average. Electronic applications accepted. *Faculty research:* Religions in Canada, including Amerindian and Inuit religions; religion and culture; late antiquity.

University of Pennsylvania, School of Arts and Sciences, Graduate Group in Classical Studies, Philadelphia, PA 19104. Offers AM, PhD. *Faculty:* 19 full-time (9 women), 1 part-time/adjunct (0 women). *Students:* 18 full-time (12 women), 1 (woman) part-time; includes 2 minority (both Two or more races, non-Hispanic/Latino), 3 international. 56 applicants, 14% accepted, 3 enrolled. In 2014, 1 master's, 5 doctorates awarded. Terminal master's awarded for partial completion of doctoral program. *Degree requirements:* For master's, 3 foreign languages, thesis or alternative; for doctorate, 4 foreign languages, thesis/dissertation. *Entrance requirements:* For master's and doctorate, GRE General Test, undergraduate course work in classical language and history. Additional exam requirements/recommendations for international students: Required—TOEFL. *Application deadline:* For fall admission, 12/1 priority date for domestic students. Application fee: $70. Electronic applications accepted. *Financial support:* Institutionally sponsored loans, scholarships/grants, traineeships, health care benefits, and unspecified assistantships available. Financial award application deadline: 12/15. *Unit head:* Dr. Ralph M. Rosen, Associate Dean for Graduate Studies, 215-898-7156, Fax: 215-573-8068, E-mail: grad-dean@sas.upenn.edu. *Application contact:* Arts and Sciences Graduate Admissions, 215-573-5816, Fax: 215-573-8068, E-mail: gdasadmis@sas.upenn.edu.

University of South Africa, College of Human Sciences, Pretoria, South Africa. Offers adult education (M Ed); African languages (MA, PhD); African politics (MA, PhD); Afrikaans (MA, PhD); ancient history (MA, PhD); ancient Near Eastern studies (MA, PhD); anthropology (MA, PhD); applied linguistics (MA); Arabic (MA, PhD); archaeology (MA); art history (MA); Biblical archaeology (MA); Biblical studies (M Th, D Th, PhD); Christian spirituality (M Th, D Th); church history (M Th, D Th); classical studies (MA, PhD); clinical psychology (MA); communication (MA, PhD); comparative education (M Ed, Ed D); consulting psychology (D Admin, D Com, PhD); curriculum studies (M Ed, Ed D); development studies (M Admin, MA, D Admin, PhD); didactics (M Ed, Ed D); education (M Tech); education management (M Ed, Ed D); educational psychology (M Ed); English (MA); environmental education (M Ed); French (MA, PhD); German (MA, PhD); Greek (MA); guidance and counseling (M Ed); health studies (MA, PhD), including health sciences education (MA), health services management (MA), medical and surgical nursing science (critical care general) (MA), midwifery and neonatal nursing science (MA), trauma and emergency care (MA); history (MA, PhD); history of education (Ed D); inclusive education (M Ed, Ed D); information and communications technology policy and regulation (MA); information science (MA, MIS, PhD); international politics (MA, PhD); Islamic studies (MA, PhD); Italian (MA, PhD); Judaica (MA, PhD); linguistics (MA, PhD); mathematical education (M Ed); mathematics education (MA); missiology (M Th, D Th); modern Hebrew (MA, PhD); musicology (MA, MMus, D Mus, PhD); natural science education (M Ed); New Testament (M Th, D Th); Old Testament (D Th); pastoral therapy (M Th, D Th); philosophy (MA); philosophy of education (M Ed, Ed D); politics (MA, PhD); Portuguese (MA, PhD); practical theology (M Th, D Th); psychology

(MA, MS, PhD); psychology of education (M Ed, Ed D); public health (MA); religious studies (MA, D Th, PhD); Romance languages (MA); Russian (MA, PhD); Semitic languages (MA, PhD); social behavior studies in HIV/AIDS (MA); social science (mental health) (MA); social science in development studies (MA); social science in psychology (MA); social science in social work (MA); social science in sociology (MA); social work (MSW, DSW, PhD); socio-education (M Ed, Ed D); sociolinguistics (MA); sociology (MA, PhD); Spanish (MA, PhD); systematic theology (M Th, D Th); TESOL (teaching English to speakers of other languages) (MA); theological ethics (M Th, D Th); theory of literature (MA, PhD); urban ministries (D Th); urban ministry (M Th).

University of Southern California, Graduate School, Dana and David Dornsife College of Letters, Arts and Sciences, Department of Classics, Los Angeles, CA 90089. Offers MA, PhD. Terminal master's awarded for partial completion of doctoral program. *Degree requirements:* For master's, 2 foreign languages, comprehensive exam, thesis or alternative, Greek and Latin; for doctorate, 2 foreign languages, comprehensive exam, thesis/dissertation, Greek and Latin. *Entrance requirements:* Additional exam requirements/recommendations for international students: Required—TOEFL. Electronic applications accepted. *Faculty research:* Roman literature, Roman history, Greek tragedy, ancient rhetoric and oratory, Greek philosophy.

The University of Texas at Austin, Graduate School, College of Liberal Arts, Department of Classics, Austin, TX 78712-1111. Offers MA, PhD. *Degree requirements:* For master's, 2 foreign languages, comprehensive exam, thesis; for doctorate, 4 foreign languages, comprehensive exam, thesis/dissertation. *Entrance requirements:* For master's, GRE General Test, proficiency in classics; for doctorate, GRE General Test, master's degree in classics. Electronic applications accepted.

University of Toronto, School of Graduate Studies, Faculty of Arts and Science, Department of Classics, Toronto, ON M5S 2J7, Canada. Offers MA, PhD. Part-time programs available. *Degree requirements:* For master's, qualifying examinations, sight translation exams in Greek and Latin; for doctorate, thesis/dissertation, qualifying examinations, sight translation exams in Greek and Latin. *Entrance requirements:* For master's, minimum B+ average in final year of an undergraduate program in classics, 3-4 years of course work in Greek and Latin; for doctorate, minimum B+ average with at least one A-; MA in classics. Electronic applications accepted.

University of Vermont, Graduate College, College of Arts and Sciences, Department of Classics, Burlington, VT 05405. Offers Greek (MA); Greek and Latin (MAT); Latin (MA). *Degree requirements:* For master's, one foreign language, thesis. *Entrance requirements:* For master's, GRE General Test. Additional exam requirements/recommendations for international students: Required—TOEFL (minimum score 550 paper-based; 80 iBT). Electronic applications accepted. *Faculty research:* Early Greek literature.

University of Victoria, Faculty of Graduate Studies, Faculty of Humanities, Department of Greek and Roman Studies, Victoria, BC V8W 2Y2, Canada. Offers MA, PhD. PhD offered by special arrangement. Part-time programs available. *Degree requirements:* For master's, 3 foreign languages, thesis. *Entrance requirements:* For master's, knowledge of Greek and Latin. Additional exam requirements/recommendations for international students: Required—TOEFL (minimum score 575 paper-based), IELTS (minimum score 7). Electronic applications accepted. *Faculty research:* Roman social history, Roman archaeology and technology, Roman literature, Greek literature, Homer and tragedy, Greek historiography.

University of Virginia, College and Graduate School of Arts and Sciences, Department of Classics, Charlottesville, VA 22903. Offers MA, PhD. *Faculty:* 9 full-time (3 women). *Students:* 22 full-time (9 women); includes 1 minority (Asian, non-Hispanic/Latino). Average age 29. 54 applicants, 11% accepted, 3 enrolled. In 2014, 1 master's, 3 doctorates awarded. *Degree requirements:* For master's, one foreign language, comprehensive exam, thesis, oral exam; for doctorate, 2 foreign languages, comprehensive exam, thesis/dissertation, oral exam. *Entrance requirements:* For master's and doctorate, GRE General Test, 2 letters of recommendation. Additional exam requirements/recommendations for international students: Required—TOEFL (minimum score 600 paper-based; 90 iBT), IELTS (minimum score 7). *Application deadline:* Applications are processed on a rolling basis. Application fee: $60. Electronic applications accepted. *Expenses:* Tuition, state resident: full-time $14,164; part-time $349 per credit hour. Tuition, nonresident: full-time $23,722; part-time $1300 per credit hour. *Required fees:* $2514. *Financial support:* Fellowships, teaching assistantships, and unspecified assistantships available. Financial award application deadline: 1/3; financial award applicants required to submit FAFSA. *Unit head:* K. Sara Myers, Chair, 434-924-3008, Fax: 434-924-3062, E-mail: classics@virginia.edu. *Application contact:* Coulter George, Director of Graduate Studies, 434-924-3008, Fax: 434-924-3062, E-mail: chg4n@virginia.edu.
Website: http://www.virginia.edu/classics/

University of Washington, Graduate School, College of Arts and Sciences, Department of Classics, Seattle, WA 98195. Offers MA, PhD. Part-time programs available. *Faculty:* 11 full-time (7 women). *Students:* 17 full-time (9 women); includes 7 minority (1 American Indian or Alaska Native, non-Hispanic/Latino; 3 Asian, non-Hispanic/Latino; 3 Hispanic/Latino), 2 international. Average age 30. 47 applicants, 38% accepted, 2 enrolled. In 2014, 4 master's, 3 doctorates awarded. Terminal master's awarded for partial completion of doctoral program. *Degree requirements:* For master's, one foreign language, thesis or alternative; for doctorate, 2 foreign languages, comprehensive exam, thesis/dissertation. *Entrance requirements:* For master's, GRE, bachelor's degree in classics, Greek, or Latin; minimum GPA of 3.0; for doctorate, GRE, minimum GPA of 3.0. Additional exam requirements/recommendations for international students: Required—TOEFL (minimum score 82 iBT). *Application deadline:* For fall admission, 1/5 for domestic students. Application fee: $75. Electronic applications accepted. *Financial support:* In 2014–15, 17 students received support, including 3 fellowships with full tuition reimbursements available (averaging $16,227 per year), research assistantships with full tuition reimbursements available (averaging $16,227 per year), 12 teaching assistantships with full tuition reimbursements available (averaging $16,227 per year); Federal Work-Study, institutionally sponsored loans, and tuition waivers (partial) also available. Financial award application deadline: 1/5; financial award applicants required to submit FAFSA. *Faculty research:* Greek and Latin poetry, Greek and Roman cultural institutions, Greek and Latin historiography, Greek tragedy. *Unit head:* Prof. Alain M. Gowing, Chair, 206-543-2266, Fax: 206-543-2267, E-mail: alain@uw.edu. *Application contact:* Prof. Kathryn Topper, Graduate Program Coordinator, 206-543-2526, Fax: 206-543-2267, E-mail: ktopper@uw.edu.
Website: http://depts.washington.edu/clasdept/

University of Washington, Graduate School, College of Arts and Sciences, Department of Philosophy, Seattle, WA 98195. Offers classics and philosophy (PhD); philosophy (MA, PhD). Terminal master's awarded for partial completion of doctoral program. *Degree requirements:* For master's, 3 papers; for doctorate, thesis/dissertation, general exam. *Entrance requirements:* For master's and doctorate, GRE, minimum GPA of 3.0. Additional exam requirements/recommendations for international students: Required—TOEFL. *Faculty research:* History and philosophy of science, epistemology, Aristotle's metaphysics, ethics and politics, causation in modern philosophy.

Classics

The University of Western Ontario, Faculty of Graduate Studies, Faculty of Arts and Humanities, Department of Classical Studies, London, ON N6A 5B8, Canada. Offers MA. Part-time programs available. *Degree requirements:* For master's, one foreign language. *Entrance requirements:* For master's, honors degree, minimum B+ average. Additional exam requirements/recommendations for international students: Required—TOEFL. *Faculty research:* Greek literature, Roman history and law, ancient sport, Byzantine literature, Bronze Age archaeology.

University of Wisconsin–Madison, Graduate School, College of Letters and Science, Department of Classics, Madison, WI 53706-1380. Offers classics (MA, PhD); Greek (MA); Latin (MA). Part-time programs available. Terminal master's awarded for partial completion of doctoral program. *Degree requirements:* For master's, 3 foreign languages, oral and written exams; for doctorate, 4 foreign languages, thesis/dissertation, written exams. *Entrance requirements:* For master's, GRE; for doctorate, master's degree. Electronic applications accepted. *Expenses:* Tuition, state resident: full-time $10,723; part-time $745 per credit. Tuition, nonresident: full-time $24,054; part-time $1578 per credit. *Required fees:* $374 per semester. Tuition and fees vary according to course load, program and reciprocity agreements. *Faculty research:* Greek tragedy, Latin elegy, historiography, Homer, Greek lyric poetry.

University of Wisconsin–Milwaukee, Graduate School, College of Letters and Sciences, Interdepartmental Program in Foreign Language and Literature, Milwaukee, WI 53201-0413. Offers classics and Hebrew studies (MAFLL); comparative literature (MAFLL); French and Italian (MAFLL); German (MAFLL); Slavic studies (MAFLL); translation (Certificate). Part-time programs available. *Degree requirements:* For master's, 2 foreign languages, thesis or alternative. *Entrance requirements:* Additional exam requirements/recommendations for international students: Required—TOEFL (minimum score 550 paper-based; 79 iBT), IELTS (minimum score 6.5). Electronic applications accepted.

Vanderbilt University, Graduate School, Department of Classical Studies, Nashville, TN 37240-1001. Offers classics (MA). *Faculty:* 4 full-time (2 women). *Students:* 2 full-time (1 woman). Average age 24. 1 applicant. In 2014, 4 master's awarded. *Degree requirements:* For master's, 2 foreign languages, thesis. *Entrance requirements:* For master's, GRE General Test. Additional exam requirements/recommendations for international students: Required—TOEFL (minimum score 570 paper-based; 88 iBT). *Application deadline:* For fall admission, 1/15 for domestic and international students. Electronic applications accepted. *Expenses: Tuition:* Full-time $42,768; part-time $1782 per credit hour. *Required fees:* $422. One-time fee: $30 full-time. *Financial support:* Fellowships with full and partial tuition reimbursements, teaching assistantships with full and partial tuition reimbursements, Federal Work-Study, institutionally sponsored loans, scholarships/grants, and health care benefits available. Financial award application deadline: 1/15; financial award applicants required to submit CSS PROFILE or FAFSA. *Faculty research:* Greek and Latin literature and language, Greek and Roman history, classical archaeology, philosophy, religion. *Unit head:* Dr. Joseph Rife, Director of Graduate Studies, 615-343-3177, Fax: 615-343-7261, E-mail: joseph.rife@vanderbilt.edu. *Application contact:* Tommye Corlew, Administrative Assistant, 615-322-2516, Fax: 615-343-7261, E-mail: tommye.j.corlew@vanderbilt.edu. Website: http://www.vanderbilt.edu/classics/

Villanova University, Graduate School of Liberal Arts and Sciences, Graduate Liberal Studies Program, Villanova, PA 19085-1699. Offers classical studies (MA). Part-time

and evening/weekend programs available. *Faculty:* 3. *Students:* 10 full-time (7 women), 7 part-time (3 women); includes 1 minority (Black or African American, non-Hispanic/Latino), 3 international. Average age 41. 3 applicants, 100% accepted, 1 enrolled. In 2014, 6 master's awarded. *Degree requirements:* For master's, comprehensive exam. *Entrance requirements:* For master's, GRE, statement of objectives, 2 letters of recommendation, writing sample. Additional exam requirements/recommendations for international students: Required—TOEFL. *Application deadline:* For fall admission, 5/1 priority date for international students; for spring admission, 10/15 priority date for international students. Applications are processed on a rolling basis. Application fee: $50. Electronic applications accepted. *Financial support:* Research assistantships, scholarships/grants, and unspecified assistantships available. Financial award applicants required to submit FAFSA. *Unit head:* Dr. Marylu Hill, Director, 610-519-7325. Website: http://www1.villanova.edu/villanova/artsci/liberalstudies.html

Washington University in St. Louis, Graduate School of Arts and Sciences, Department of Classics, St. Louis, MO 63130-4899. Offers MA. *Degree requirements:* For master's, thesis or alternative. *Entrance requirements:* For master's, GRE General Test. Additional exam requirements/recommendations for international students: Required—TOEFL. Electronic applications accepted. *Faculty research:* Greek and Latin language; Greek and Roman literature, philosophy, history, material culture.

Wayne State University, College of Liberal Arts and Sciences, Department of Classical and Modern Languages, Literatures, and Cultures, Program in Classics, Greek, and Latin, Detroit, MI 48202. Offers classics (MA), including ancient Greek and Latin, ancient studies, Latin. *Students:* 1 (woman) full-time, 1 part-time (0 women). In 2014, 1 master's awarded. *Degree requirements:* For master's, thesis optional. *Entrance requirements:* For master's, GRE, bachelor's degree in Latin, Greek, or classics; three letters of recommendation; writing sample; personal statement. Additional exam requirements/recommendations for international students: Required—TOEFL (minimum score 550 paper-based; 79 iBT), TWE (minimum score 6), Michigan English Language Assessment Battery (minimum score 85); Recommended—IELTS (minimum score 6.5). *Application deadline:* For fall admission, 6/1 priority date for domestic students, 5/1 priority date for international students; for winter admission, 10/1 priority date for domestic students, 9/1 priority date for international students; for spring admission, 2/1 priority date for domestic students, 1/1 priority date for international students. Applications are processed on a rolling basis. Application fee: $0. Electronic applications accepted. *Expenses:* Tuition, state resident: full-time $10,294; part-time $571.90 per credit hour. Tuition, nonresident: full-time $29,730; part-time $1238.75 per credit hour. *Required fees:* $1365; $43.50 per credit hour. $291.10 per semester. Tuition and fees vary according to course load and program. *Financial support:* Fellowships, teaching assistantships, scholarships/grants, and unspecified assistantships available. Financial award application deadline: 3/31; financial award applicants required to submit FAFSA. *Unit head:* Dr. Anne Duggan, Department Chair, E-mail: a.duggan@wayne.edu. *Application contact:* Dr. Joel Itzkowitz, Associate Professor and Graduate Director, 313-577-6591, E-mail: aa1529@wayne.edu. Website: http://clasweb.clas.wayne.edu/languages/Classics

Yale University, Graduate School of Arts and Sciences, Department of Classics, New Haven, CT 06520. Offers M Phil, MA, PhD. *Degree requirements:* For doctorate, 2 foreign languages, thesis/dissertation. *Entrance requirements:* For doctorate, GRE General Test.

Comparative Literature

The American University in Cairo, School of Humanities and Social Sciences, Department of English and Comparative Literature, Cairo, Egypt. Offers comparative literary studies (Graduate Diploma); English and comparative literature (MA). Part-time programs available. *Degree requirements:* For master's, thesis, proficiency in French or German. *Entrance requirements:* Additional exam requirements/recommendations for international students: Required—English entrance exam and/or TOEFL. Tuition and fees vary according to course load and program.

Antioch University Midwest, Graduate Programs, Individualized Liberal and Professional Studies Program, Yellow Springs, OH 45387-1609. Offers liberal and professional studies (MA), including counseling, creative writing, education, liberal studies, management, modern literature, psychology, visual arts. Part-time and evening/weekend programs available. Postbaccalaureate distance learning degree programs offered (minimal on-campus study). *Degree requirements:* For master's, thesis or alternative. *Entrance requirements:* For master's, resume, goal statement, interview. Electronic applications accepted. *Expenses:* Contact institution.

Arizona State University at the Tempe campus, College of Liberal Arts and Sciences, Department of English, Tempe, AZ 85287-0302. Offers applied linguistics (PhD); creative writing (MFA); English (MA, PhD), including comparative literature (MA), linguistics (MA), literature, rhetoric and composition (MA), rhetoric, composition, and linguistics (PhD); film and media studies (MAS), including American media and popular culture; linguistics (Graduate Certificate); teaching English to speakers of other languages (MTESOL); translation studies (Graduate Certificate). Terminal master's awarded for partial completion of doctoral program. *Degree requirements:* For master's, variable foreign language requirement, comprehensive exam (for some programs), thesis (for some programs), interactive Program of Study (iPOS) submitted before completing 50 percent of required credit hours; for doctorate, variable foreign language requirement, comprehensive exam, thesis/dissertation, interactive Program of Study (iPOS) submitted before completing 50 percent of required credit hours. *Entrance requirements:* For master's and doctorate, GRE, minimum GPA of 3.0 or equivalent in last 2 years of work leading to bachelor's degree. Additional exam requirements/recommendations for international students: Required—TOEFL, IELTS, or PTE. Electronic applications accepted.

Binghamton University, State University of New York, Graduate School, School of Arts and Sciences, Department of Comparative Literature, Vestal, NY 13850. Offers MA, PhD. Part-time programs available. *Faculty:* 7 full-time (5 women), 4 part-time/adjunct (1 woman). *Students:* 15 full-time (11 women), 46 part-time (27 women); includes 9 minority (2 Black or African American, non-Hispanic/Latino; 1 Asian, non-Hispanic/Latino; 4 Hispanic/Latino; 2 Native Hawaiian or other Pacific Islander, non-Hispanic/Latino), 32 international. Average age 34. 38 applicants, 79% accepted, 6 enrolled. In 2014, 8 master's, 4 doctorates awarded. Terminal master's awarded for partial completion of doctoral program. *Degree requirements:* For master's, 2 foreign languages, comprehensive exam, thesis or alternative; for doctorate, 2 foreign languages, comprehensive exam, thesis/dissertation. *Entrance requirements:* For master's and doctorate, GRE General Test, writing sample. Additional exam

requirements/recommendations for international students: Required—TOEFL (minimum score 550 paper-based; 80 iBT). *Application deadline:* For fall admission, 2/1 priority date for domestic and international students; for spring admission, 10/15 priority date for domestic and international students. Applications are processed on a rolling basis. Application fee: $75. Electronic applications accepted. *Expenses:* Tuition, state resident: full-time $7776; part-time $432 per credit. Tuition, nonresident: full-time $15,138; part-time $841 per credit. *Required fees:* $1754; $213 per credit. Tuition and fees vary according to degree level and program. *Financial support:* In 2014–15, 24 students received support, including 21 teaching assistantships with full tuition reimbursements available (averaging $14,500 per year); career-related internships or fieldwork, Federal Work-Study, institutionally sponsored loans, scholarships/grants, health care benefits, tuition waivers (full and partial), and unspecified assistantships also available. Financial award application deadline: 2/15; financial award applicants required to submit FAFSA. *Unit head:* Dr. Luiza Moreira, Chairperson, 607-777-3673, E-mail: lmoreira@binghamton.edu. *Application contact:* Kishan Zuber, Recruiting and Admissions Coordinator, 607-777-2151, Fax: 607-777-2501, E-mail: kzuber@binghamton.edu.

Brigham Young University, Graduate Studies, College of Humanities, Department of Humanities, Classics, and Comparative Literature, Provo, UT 84602. Offers comparative studies (MA). *Faculty:* 24 full-time (5 women). *Students:* 14 full-time (10 women), 8 part-time (5 women). Average age 26. 14 applicants, 50% accepted, 7 enrolled. In 2014, 6 master's awarded. *Degree requirements:* For master's, 2 foreign languages, thesis. *Entrance requirements:* For master's, GRE, minimum GPA of 3.0 in last 60 hours. Additional exam requirements/recommendations for international students: Required—TOEFL (minimum score 580 paper-based; 85 iBT), IELTS (minimum score 7). *Application deadline:* For fall admission, 3/1 for domestic and international students. Application fee: $50. Electronic applications accepted. *Expenses: Tuition:* Full-time $6310; part-time $371 per credit hour. Tuition and fees vary according to program and student's religious affiliation. *Financial support:* In 2014–15, 17 students received support, including 31 fellowships with partial tuition reimbursements available (averaging $1,604 per year), 4 research assistantships (averaging $1,500 per year), 29 teaching assistantships (averaging $2,503 per year); career-related internships or fieldwork, institutionally sponsored loans, scholarships/grants, tuition waivers (full and partial), and student instructorships also available. Support available to part-time students. *Unit head:* Dr. Carl Sederholm, Coordinator, 801-422-9078, Fax: 801-422-0305, E-mail: carl_sederholm@byu.edu. *Application contact:* Carolyn Hone, Graduate Secretary for Humanities and Comparative Literature, 801-422-4430, Fax: 801-422-0305, E-mail: carolyn_hone@byu.edu.

Brock University, Faculty of Graduate Studies, Faculty of Humanities, Program in Studies in Comparative Literatures and Arts, St. Catharines, ON L2S 3A1, Canada. Offers MA. *Degree requirements:* For master's, thesis optional. *Entrance requirements:* For master's, honors degree. Additional exam requirements/recommendations for international students: Required—TOEFL (minimum score 550 paper-based; 80 iBT), IELTS (minimum score 6.5), TWE (minimum score 4). Electronic applications accepted.

Brown University, Graduate School, Department of Comparative Literature, Providence, RI 02912. Offers PhD. *Degree requirements:* For doctorate, 2 foreign languages, thesis/dissertation, preliminary exam. *Entrance requirements:* For doctorate, GRE General Test, GRE Subject Test.

California State University, Northridge, Graduate Studies, College of Humanities, Department of English, Northridge, CA 91330. Offers creative writing (MA); literature (MA); rhetoric and composition theory (MA). Part-time and evening/weekend programs available. *Students:* 36 full-time (22 women), 84 part-time (53 women); includes 39 minority (3 Black or African American, non-Hispanic/Latino; 10 Asian, non-Hispanic/Latino; 22 Hispanic/Latino; 4 Two or more races, non-Hispanic/Latino), 1 international. Average age 32. *Degree requirements:* For master's, thesis or alternative. *Entrance requirements:* For master's, writing proficiency test, GRE General Test or minimum GPA of 3.0. Additional exam requirements/recommendations for international students: Required—TOEFL. *Application deadline:* For fall admission, 11/30 for domestic students. Application fee: $55. *Expenses: Required fees:* $12,402. *Financial support:* Teaching assistantships available. Financial award application deadline: 3/1. *Faculty research:* Reading improvement, professional writing, Dickens, Shaw, English as a second language. *Unit head:* Jackie Stallcup, Chair, 818-677-3434. *Application contact:* Dr. Marjie Seagoe, Graduate Studies Secretary, 818-677-3433.
Website: http://www.csun.edu/english/index.php

Carleton University, Faculty of Graduate Studies, Faculty of Arts and Social Sciences, School for Languages, Literatures, and Comparative Literary Studies, Ottawa, ON K1S 5B6, Canada. Offers cultural mediations (PhD). *Entrance requirements:* Additional exam requirements/recommendations for international students: Required—TOEFL. *Faculty research:* Literary history, theory of literature, cross-cultural studies, modernism/postmodernism, comparative Canadian literature.

Carnegie Mellon University, Dietrich College of Humanities and Social Sciences, Department of English, Pittsburgh, PA 15213-3891. Offers communication planning and design (M Des); literary and cultural studies (MA, PhD); professional writing (MAPW), including editing and publishing, policy and non-profit communication, public and media relations / corporate communications, science or healthcare communication, technical writing, writing for new media, writing for print media; rhetoric (MA, PhD). Part-time programs available. Terminal master's awarded for partial completion of doctoral program. *Degree requirements:* For doctorate, 2 foreign languages, comprehensive exam, thesis/dissertation. *Entrance requirements:* For master's and doctorate, GRE General Test. Additional exam requirements/recommendations for international students: Required—TOEFL, TWE. *Faculty research:* Cognitive processes in discourse with emphasis on writing, testing, and evaluation.

Case Western Reserve University, School of Graduate Studies, Department of Modern Languages and Literatures and Department of English, Program in World Literature, Cleveland, OH 44106. Offers MA. *Faculty:* 17 full-time (12 women). *Students:* 4 full-time (3 women). Average age 30. 2 applicants, 50% accepted, 1 enrolled. In 2014, 1 master's awarded. *Degree requirements:* For master's, 2 foreign languages, thesis, written exam. *Entrance requirements:* For master's, GRE General Test, sample of written work; project proposal. Additional exam requirements/recommendations for international students: Required—TOEFL (minimum score 577 paper-based; 90 iBT); Recommended—IELTS (minimum score 7). *Application deadline:* For fall admission, 3/1 priority date for domestic students. Applications are processed on a rolling basis. Application fee: $50. Electronic applications accepted. *Financial support:* Fellowships, career-related internships or fieldwork, institutionally sponsored loans, and tuition waivers (partial) available. Financial award application deadline: 3/1; financial award applicants required to submit CSS PROFILE or FAFSA. *Faculty research:* Literary theory and translation, Middle Ages, Renaissance, Baroque, Enlightenment, Romanticism, Modernism. *Unit head:* Prof. Stephen Haynesworth, Interim Chair, 216-368-3071, Fax: 216-368-2216. *Application contact:* Prof. Marie Landers, Director, Graduate Studies in French, 216-368-3071, Fax: 216-368-2216, E-mail: marie.landers@case.edu.
Website: http://artsci.case.edu/world-literature/

Claremont Graduate University, Graduate Programs, School of Arts and Humanities, Department of English, Claremont, CA 91711-6160. Offers American studies (MA, PhD); critical theory (MA, PhD); early modern studies (MA, PhD); English (M Phil, MA, PhD); literary theory (PhD); literature (MA, PhD); literature and creative writing (MA); literature and film (MA); MBA/MA; MBA/PhD. Part-time programs available. *Faculty:* 4 full-time (2 women), 2 part-time/adjunct (0 women). *Students:* 70 full-time (51 women), 27 part-time (17 women); includes 31 minority (4 Black or African American, non-Hispanic/Latino; 1 American Indian or Alaska Native, non-Hispanic/Latino; 12 Asian, non-Hispanic/Latino; 6 Hispanic/Latino; 8 Two or more races, non-Hispanic/Latino), 8 international. Average age 36. In 2014, 9 master's, 7 doctorates awarded. *Entrance requirements:* For master's and doctorate, GRE General Test. Additional exam requirements/recommendations for international students: Required—TOEFL (minimum score 550 paper-based; 80 iBT). *Application deadline:* For fall admission, 2/1 priority date for domestic and international students. Applications are processed on a rolling basis. Application fee: $80. Electronic applications accepted. *Expenses: Tuition:* Full-time $41,784; part-time $1741 per credit. *Required fees:* $600; $300 per semester. *Financial support:* Fellowships, Federal Work-Study, institutionally sponsored loans, and scholarships/grants available. Support available to part-time students. Financial award application deadline: 2/15; financial award applicants required to submit FAFSA. *Faculty research:* American, comparative, and English Renaissance literature; modernism; feminist literature and theory. *Unit head:* David Luis-Brown, Chair, E-mail: david.luis-brown@cgu.edu. *Application contact:* Erma Cross, Admissions and Alumni Coordinator, 909-607-9843, E-mail: erminia.cross@cgu.edu.
Website: http://www.cgu.edu/pages/568.asp

Columbia University, Graduate School of Arts and Sciences, New York, NY 10027. Offers African-American studies (MA); American studies (MA); anthropology (MA, PhD); art history and archaeology (MA, PhD); astronomy (PhD); biological sciences (PhD); biotechnology (MA); chemical physics (PhD); chemistry (PhD); classical studies (MA, PhD); classics (MA, PhD); climate and society (MA); earth and environmental sciences (PhD); East Asia: regional studies (MA); East Asian languages and cultures (MA, PhD); ecology, evolution and environmental biology (MA), including conservation biology; ecology, evolution, and environmental biology (PhD), including ecology and evolutionary biology, evolutionary primatology; economics (PhD); English and comparative literature (MA, PhD); French and Romance philology (MA, PhD); Germanic languages (MA, PhD); global French studies (MA); Hispanic cultural studies (MA); history (PhD); history and literature (MA); human rights studies (MA); Islamic studies (MA); Italian (MA, PhD); Japanese pedagogy (MA); Jewish studies (MA); Latin America and the Caribbean: regional studies (MA); Latin American and Iberian cultures (PhD); mathematics (MA, PhD), including finance (MA); medieval and Renaissance studies (MA); Middle Eastern, South Asian, and African studies (MA, PhD); modern art: critical and curatorial studies (MA); modern European studies (MA); museum anthropology (MA); music (DMA, PhD); oral history (MA); philosophical foundations of physics (MA); philosophy (MA, PhD); physics (PhD); political science (MA, PhD); psychology (PhD); quantitative methods in the social sciences (MA); religion (MA, PhD); Russia, Eurasia and East Europe: regional studies (MA); Russian translation (MA); Slavic cultures (MA); Slavic languages (MA, PhD); sociology (MA, PhD); South Asian studies (MA); statistics (MA, PhD); theatre (PhD); JD/PhD; MA/MS; MD/PhD; MPA/MA. Dual-degree programs require admission to both Graduate School of Arts and Sciences and another Columbia school. Part-time and evening/weekend programs available. Terminal master's awarded for partial completion of doctoral program. *Degree requirements:* For master's, thesis (for some programs); for doctorate, comprehensive exam, thesis/dissertation. *Entrance requirements:* For master's and doctorate, GRE General Test, GRE Subject Test (for some programs). Electronic applications accepted. *Faculty research:* Humanities, natural sciences, social sciences.

Cornell University, Graduate School, Graduate Fields of Arts and Sciences, Field of Comparative Literature, Ithaca, NY 14853-0001. Offers PhD. *Degree requirements:* For doctorate, 2 foreign languages, comprehensive exam, thesis/dissertation, teaching experience. *Entrance requirements:* For doctorate, GRE General Test, proficiency in 2 foreign literatures, writing sample, 3 letters of recommendation. Additional exam requirements/recommendations for international students: Required—TOEFL (minimum score 550 paper-based; 77 iBT). Electronic applications accepted. *Faculty research:* Critical theory, European studies, Latin American studies, Asian studies.

Dartmouth College, Arts and Sciences Graduate Programs, Comparative Literature Program, Hanover, NH 03755. Offers AM. *Faculty:* 30 full-time (18 women), 2 part-time/adjunct (both women). *Students:* 8 full-time (6 women); includes 5 minority (4 Hispanic/Latino; 1 Two or more races, non-Hispanic/Latino), 1 international. Average age 27. 29 applicants, 55% accepted, 9 enrolled. In 2014, 7 master's awarded. *Degree requirements:* For master's, final paper, oral exams. *Entrance requirements:* For master's, proficiency in 2 languages. Additional exam requirements/recommendations for international students: Required—TOEFL. *Application deadline:* For fall admission, 2/1 priority date for domestic students. Application fee: $30. Electronic applications accepted. *Financial support:* Fellowships with full tuition reimbursements, teaching assistantships with full tuition reimbursements, career-related internships or fieldwork, institutionally sponsored loans, scholarships/grants, and tuition waivers (full) available. Support available to part-time students. Financial award applicants required to submit CSS PROFILE. *Unit head:* Dr. Silvia Spitta, Chair, 603-646-2912. *Application contact:* Karen DeRosa, Program Administrator, 603-646-2912, Fax: 603-646-2912.
Website: http://www.dartmouth.edu/~complit/masters/

Duke University, Graduate School, Program in Literature, Durham, NC 27708. Offers PhD, JD/MA. *Degree requirements:* For doctorate, 2 foreign languages, thesis/dissertation. *Entrance requirements:* For doctorate, GRE General Test, writing sample. Additional exam requirements/recommendations for international students: Required—TOEFL (minimum score 577 paper-based; 90 iBT) or IELTS (minimum score 7). *Expenses: Tuition:* Full-time $45,760; part-time $2765 per credit. *Required fees:* $978. Full-time tuition and fees vary according to program.

East Carolina University, Graduate School, Thomas Harriot College of Arts and Sciences, Department of English, Greenville, NC 27858-4353. Offers creative writing (MA); English studies (MA); linguistics (MA); literature (MA); multicultural and transnational literatures (MA, Certificate); rhetoric and composition (MA); rhetoric, writing, and professional communication (PhD); teaching English in the two-year college (Certificate); teaching English to speakers of other languages (MA, Certificate); technical and professional communication (MA). Part-time and evening/weekend programs available. *Degree requirements:* For master's, one foreign language, comprehensive exam, thesis optional. *Entrance requirements:* For master's, GRE General Test, MAT (for MA Ed). Additional exam requirements/recommendations for international students: Required—TOEFL. *Expenses:* Tuition, state resident: full-time $4223. Tuition, nonresident: full-time $16,540. *Required fees:* $2184.

Emory University, Laney Graduate School, Department of Comparative Literature, Atlanta, GA 30322-1100. Offers comparative literature (PhD); philosophy (Certificate); psychoanalytic studies (PhD); women's studies (Certificate). *Degree requirements:* For doctorate, 2 foreign languages, comprehensive exam, thesis/dissertation. *Entrance requirements:* For doctorate, GRE General Test, minimum GPA of 3.0. Additional exam requirements/recommendations for international students: Required—TOEFL. Electronic applications accepted. *Faculty research:* Literary theory, psychoanalysis trauma and testimony, literature and religion, literature and technology, literature and philosophy, politics and global culture, literature and aesthetics.

Emory University, Laney Graduate School, Department of Spanish and Portuguese, Atlanta, GA 30322-1100. Offers comparative literature (Certificate); film studies (Certificate); Spanish (PhD); women's studies (Certificate). *Degree requirements:* For doctorate, 2 foreign languages, comprehensive exam, thesis/dissertation. *Entrance requirements:* For doctorate, GRE General Test. Additional exam requirements/recommendations for international students: Required—TOEFL. Electronic applications accepted. *Faculty research:* Spanish literature, Spanish American literature, literary theory, criticism, cultural studies.

Fairleigh Dickinson University, Metropolitan Campus, University College: Arts, Sciences, and Professional Studies, Department of English, Philosophy, and Humanities, Program in English and Literature, Teaneck, NJ 07666-1914. Offers MA.

Florida Atlantic University, Dorothy F. Schmidt College of Arts and Letters, Department of Languages, Linguistics, and Comparative Literature, Boca Raton, FL 33431-0991. Offers comparative literature (MA); French (MA); linguistics (MA); Spanish (MA). Part-time programs available. *Degree requirements:* For master's, one foreign language, comprehensive exam, thesis optional. *Entrance requirements:* For master's, GRE General Test, minimum GPA of 3.0. Additional exam requirements/recommendations for international students: Required—TOEFL (minimum score 500 paper-based; 61 iBT), IELTS (minimum score 6). *Expenses:* Tuition, state resident: full-time $7396; part-time $369.82 per credit hour. Tuition, nonresident: full-time $19,392; part-time $1024.81 per credit hour. Tuition and fees vary according to course load. *Faculty research:* Modern European studies, modern Latin America, medieval Europe.

Georgetown University, Graduate School of Arts and Sciences, School of Continuing Studies, Washington, DC 20057. Offers American studies (MALS); Catholic studies (MALS); classical civilizations (MALS); emergency and disaster management (MPS); ethics and the professions (MALS); hospitality management (MPS); human resources management (MPS); humanities (MALS); individualized study (MALS); international affairs (MALS); Islam and Muslim-Christian relations (MALS); journalism (MPS); liberal studies (DLS); literature and society (MALS); medieval and early modern European studies (MALS); public relations and corporate communications (MPS); real estate (MPS); religious studies (MALS); social and public policy (MALS); sports industry management (MPS); systems engineering management (MPS); technology management (MPS); the theory and practice of American democracy (MALS); urban and regional planning (MPS); visual culture (MALS). MPS in systems engineering management offered jointly with Stevens Institute of Technology. *Entrance requirements:* Additional exam requirements/recommendations for international students: Required—TOEFL.

The Graduate Center, City University of New York, Graduate Studies, Program in Comparative Literature, New York, NY 10016-4039. Offers comparative literature (MA, PhD), including classics (PhD), German (PhD), Italian (PhD). PhD offered jointly with New York University. Terminal master's awarded for partial completion of doctoral

program. *Degree requirements:* For master's, 2 foreign languages, comprehensive exam, thesis; for doctorate, 3 foreign languages, comprehensive exam, thesis/dissertation. *Entrance requirements:* For master's and doctorate, GRE General Test. Additional exam requirements/recommendations for international students: Required—TOEFL. Electronic applications accepted.

Harrison Middleton University, Graduate Program, Tempe, AZ 85282. Offers education (MA, Ed D); humanities (MA); imaginative literature (MA); interdisciplinary studies (DA); jurisprudence (MA); natural science (MA); philosophy and religion (MA); social science (MA). Part-time and evening/weekend programs available. Postbaccalaureate distance learning degree programs offered (no on-campus study). *Degree requirements:* For master's and doctorate, capstone project. *Entrance requirements:* For master's, interview; for doctorate, 2 academic letters of reference, interview, essay. Additional exam requirements/recommendations for international students: Required—TOEFL (minimum score 550 paper-based; 80 iBT). Electronic applications accepted. *Faculty research:* Japanese animation, educational leadership, war art, John Muir's wilderness.

Harvard University, Graduate School of Arts and Sciences, Department of Comparative Literature, Cambridge, MA 02138. Offers comparative literature (PhD); oral literature (PhD). *Degree requirements:* For doctorate, 4 foreign languages, thesis/dissertation, written and oral exams. *Entrance requirements:* For doctorate, GRE General Test, GRE Subject Test (recommended), sample of written work. Additional exam requirements/recommendations for international students: Required—TOEFL.

Indiana State University, College of Graduate and Professional Studies, College of Arts and Sciences, Department of English, Terre Haute, IN 47809. Offers English teaching (MA); history (MA); literature (MA). Part-time and evening/weekend programs available. *Degree requirements:* For master's, one foreign language, thesis optional. *Entrance requirements:* For master's, minimum GPA of 2.75 in all English courses above freshman level. Additional exam requirements/recommendations for international students: Required—TOEFL (minimum score 550 paper-based). Electronic applications accepted.

Indiana University Bloomington, University Graduate School, College of Arts and Sciences, Department of Comparative Literature, Bloomington, IN 47405. Offers MA, MAT, PhD. Part-time programs available. *Faculty:* 13 full-time (5 women), 24 part-time/adjunct (12 women). *Students:* 36 full-time (21 women); includes 4 minority (1 Asian, non-Hispanic/Latino; 3 Hispanic/Latino), 10 international. Average age 31. 36 applicants, 39% accepted, 7 enrolled. In 2014, 5 doctorates awarded. *Degree requirements:* For master's, 2 foreign languages, comprehensive exam (for some programs), thesis (for some programs); for doctorate, 3 foreign languages, comprehensive exam, thesis/dissertation. *Entrance requirements:* For master's, GRE, proficiency in 1 foreign language, 25-page writing sample, 3 letters of recommendation, transcripts, statement of purpose; for doctorate, GRE, proficiency in 2 foreign languages, 25-page writing sample, 3 letters of recommendation, transcripts, statement of purpose. Additional exam requirements/recommendations for international students: Required—TOEFL (minimum score 550 paper-based; 79 iBT). *Application deadline:* For fall admission, 1/15 priority date for domestic students, 12/1 priority date for international students. Application fee: $55 ($65 for international students). Electronic applications accepted. *Financial support:* Fellowships with full tuition reimbursements, research assistantships with partial tuition reimbursements, teaching assistantships with full tuition reimbursements, Federal Work-Study, tuition waivers (partial), and unspecified assistantships available. Financial award application deadline: 1/15. *Faculty research:* Literary theory, translation, African studies, medieval studies, comparative arts, East-West literary relations. *Unit head:* Prof. David Hertz, Chairperson, 812-855-8432, Fax: 812-855-2688, E-mail: hertzd@indiana.edu. *Application contact:* Mary Huskey, Graduate Secretary, 812-855-9602, Fax: 812-855-2688, E-mail: mphuskey@indiana.edu.
Website: http://www.indiana.edu/~complit/

Johns Hopkins University, Zanvyl Krieger School of Arts and Sciences, Humanities Center, Baltimore, MD 21218-2699. Offers comparative literature (PhD); intellectual history (PhD). *Degree requirements:* For doctorate, 2 foreign languages, thesis/dissertation. *Entrance requirements:* For doctorate, GRE General Test, samples of written work. Additional exam requirements/recommendations for international students: Required—TOEFL, IELTS. Electronic applications accepted.

La Salle University, School of Arts and Sciences, Program in English, Philadelphia, PA 19141-1199. Offers American studies (Certificate); English for educators (MA); English in literary and cultural studies (MA); global literature (Certificate); media studies and the performing and visual arts (Certificate); Philadelphia and regional studies (Certificate). Part-time and evening/weekend programs available. *Degree requirements:* For master's, critical-pedagogical project (for English for educators), thesis or comprehensive examination (for English in literary and cultural studies). *Entrance requirements:* For master's, GRE General Test or MAT, 18 hours of undergraduate course work in English or a related discipline with minimum GPA of 3.0; three letters of recommendation; brief personal statement; writing sample; for Certificate, undergraduate degree in English or a related discipline with minimum GPA of 3.0; 3 letters of recommendation. Additional exam requirements/recommendations for international students: Required—TOEFL. Electronic applications accepted. Application fee is waived when completed online.

Louisiana State University and Agricultural & Mechanical College, Graduate School, College of Humanities and Social Sciences, Interdepartmental Program in Comparative Literature, Baton Rouge, LA 70803. Offers MA, PhD. *Students:* 14 full-time (10 women), 4 part-time (3 women); includes 3 minority (all Hispanic/Latino), 6 international. Average age 32. 15 applicants, 47% accepted, 5 enrolled. Terminal master's awarded for partial completion of doctoral program. *Degree requirements:* For master's, 2 foreign languages, thesis optional; for doctorate, 2 foreign languages, thesis/dissertation. *Entrance requirements:* For master's and doctorate, GRE General Test, minimum GPA of 3.0. Additional exam requirements/recommendations for international students: Required—TOEFL (minimum score 550 paper-based; 79 IBT), IELTS (minimum score 6.5), or PTE (minimum score 59). *Application deadline:* For fall admission, 1/1 priority date for domestic students, 5/15 for international students; for spring admission, 10/15 for domestic and international students; for summer admission, 5/15 for domestic and international students. Applications are processed on a rolling basis. Application fee: $50 ($70 for international students). Electronic applications accepted. *Financial support:* In 2014–15, 14 students received support, including 2 research assistantships with full and partial tuition reimbursements available (averaging $14,000 per year), 11 teaching assistantships with full and partial tuition reimbursements available (averaging $14,282 per year); fellowships with full tuition reimbursements available, health care benefits, and unspecified assistantships also available. Financial award application deadline: 3/15; financial award applicants required to submit FAFSA. *Faculty research:* World literature, Islamic studies, Dante, Michel Foucault. *Total annual research expenditures:* $16,349. *Unit head:* Dr. Adelaide Russo, Director, 225-578-5172, Fax: 225-578-6670, E-mail: frruss@lsu.edu.
Website: http://uiswcmsweb.prod.lsu.edu/ArtSci/complit/

New York University, Graduate School of Arts and Science, Department of Comparative Literature, New York, NY 10012-1019. Offers MA, PhD. Part-time programs available. *Faculty:* 15 full-time (4 women). *Students:* 48 full-time (23 women); includes 7 minority (5 Hispanic/Latino; 2 Two or more races, non-Hispanic/Latino), 17 international. Average age 30. 175 applicants, 7% accepted, 7 enrolled. In 2014, 3 master's, 3 doctorates awarded. *Degree requirements:* For master's, 2 foreign languages, thesis; for doctorate, 3 foreign languages, thesis/dissertation. *Entrance requirements:* For master's and doctorate, GRE General Test. Additional exam requirements/recommendations for international students: Required—TOEFL. *Application deadline:* For fall admission, 12/18 for domestic and international students. Application fee: $100. *Financial support:* Fellowships with tuition reimbursements, teaching assistantships with tuition reimbursements, Federal Work-Study, institutionally sponsored loans, scholarships/grants, health care benefits, and unspecified assistantships available. Financial award application deadline: 12/18; financial award applicants required to submit FAFSA. *Faculty research:* European and non-European literature and culture, comparative poetics, cultural studies, Colonial and Post-Colonial literature and theory, philosophical issues and literary theory. *Unit head:* Avital Ronell, Acting Chair, 212-998-8790, Fax: 212-995-4377, E-mail: complit.grad.admissions@nyu.edu. *Application contact:* Richard Sieburth, Acting Director of Graduate Studies, 212-998-8790, Fax: 212-995-4377, E-mail: complit.grad.admissions@nyu.edu.
Website: http://www.nyu.edu/gsas/dept/complit/

Northwestern University, The Graduate School, Judd A. and Marjorie Weinberg College of Arts and Sciences, Program in Comparative Literary Studies, Evanston, IL 60208. Offers PhD. Admissions and degrees offered through The Graduate School. Part-time programs available. *Degree requirements:* For doctorate, 2 foreign languages, thesis/dissertation, preliminary exams. *Entrance requirements:* For doctorate, GRE General Test, sample of written work. Additional exam requirements/recommendations for international students: Required—TOEFL. *Faculty research:* The novel, modernism, post-colonial literature and theory, literature and the arts, Middle Ages and Renaissance, literature and philosophy.

Northwestern University, School of Professional Studies, Program in Literature, Evanston, IL 60208. Offers American literature (MA); British literature (MA); comparative and world literature (MA).

Penn State University Park, Graduate School, College of the Liberal Arts, Department of Comparative Literature, University Park, PA 16802. Offers comparative literature (MA, PhD); Russian and comparative literature (MA). *Unit head:* Dr. Susan Welch, Dean, 814-865-7691, Fax: 814-863-2085, E-mail: swelch@psu.edu. *Application contact:* Lori A. Stania, Director, Graduate Student Services, 814-867-5278, Fax: 814-863-4627, E-mail: gswww@psu.edu.
Website: http://complit.la.psu.edu/

Princeton University, Graduate School, Department of Comparative Literature, Princeton, NJ 08544-1019. Offers PhD. *Degree requirements:* For doctorate, variable foreign language requirement, thesis/dissertation. *Entrance requirements:* For doctorate, GRE General Test, GRE Subject Test, sample of written work. Additional exam requirements/recommendations for international students: Required—TOEFL (minimum score 600 paper-based). Electronic applications accepted.

Purdue University, Graduate School, College of Liberal Arts, Program in Comparative Literature, West Lafayette, IN 47907. Offers MA, PhD. Part-time programs available. *Degree requirements:* For master's, comprehensive exam (for some programs), thesis optional; for doctorate, comprehensive exam, thesis/dissertation. *Entrance requirements:* For master's, GRE General Test, minimum undergraduate GPA of 3.0 or equivalent; for doctorate, GRE General Test, minimum undergraduate GPA of 3.0 or equivalent; master's degree with minimum GPA of 3.0 or equivalent. Additional exam requirements/recommendations for international students: Required—TOEFL (minimum score 550 paper-based; 77 iBT); Recommended—TWE. Electronic applications accepted. *Faculty research:* Theory and criticism, philosophy and aesthetics, East Asian literature, postcolonial literature, classics.

Rutgers, The State University of New Jersey, New Brunswick, Graduate School-New Brunswick, Program in Comparative Literature, Piscataway, NJ 08854-8097. Offers MA, PhD. Part-time programs available. Terminal master's awarded for partial completion of doctoral program. *Degree requirements:* For master's, comprehensive exam; for doctorate, 3 foreign languages, thesis/dissertation, written and oral exams. *Entrance requirements:* For doctorate, GRE General Test, GRE Subject Test (recommended). Additional exam requirements/recommendations for international students: Required—TOEFL. Electronic applications accepted. *Faculty research:* Genres and periods, modern literary theory, psychoanalytic approaches to literature, literature and gender, cultural studies.

San Francisco State University, Division of Graduate Studies, College of Liberal and Creative Arts, Department of Comparative and World Literature, San Francisco, CA 94132-1722. Offers comparative literature (MA). Part-time programs available. *Degree requirements:* For master's, one foreign language. *Application deadline:* Applications are processed on a rolling basis. *Expenses:* Tuition, state resident: full-time $6738. Tuition, nonresident: full-time $17,898; part-time $372 per credit hour. *Required fees:* $498 per semester. *Unit head:* Dr. David Leitao, Chair, 415-338-2068, E-mail: dleitao@sfsu.edu. *Application contact:* Dr. Shirin Khanmohamadi, Graduate Coordinator, 415-338-7035, E-mail: shirin1@sfsu.edu.
Website: http://complit.sfsu.edu/

San Jose State University, Graduate Studies and Research, College of Humanities and the Arts, Department of English and Comparative Literature, San Jose, CA 95192-0001. Offers English (MFA); English literature (MA). *Degree requirements:* For master's, one foreign language, thesis or alternative. *Entrance requirements:* For master's, GRE. Additional exam requirements/recommendations for international students: Required—TOEFL. Electronic applications accepted.

Stanford University, School of Humanities and Sciences, Department of Comparative Literature, Stanford, CA 94305-9991. Offers PhD. *Degree requirements:* For doctorate, 3 foreign languages, thesis/dissertation, qualification procedures. *Entrance requirements:* For doctorate, GRE General Test, GRE Subject Test. Additional exam requirements/recommendations for international students: Required—TOEFL. Electronic applications accepted. *Expenses: Tuition:* Full-time $44,184; part-time $982 per credit hour. *Required fees:* $191.

Stanford University, School of Humanities and Sciences, Program in Modern Thought and Literature, Stanford, CA 94305-9991. Offers PhD. *Degree requirements:* For doctorate, 2 foreign languages, thesis/dissertation, qualifying paper, oral exam. *Entrance requirements:* For doctorate, GRE General Test. Additional exam requirements/recommendations for international students: Required—TOEFL. Electronic applications accepted. *Expenses: Tuition:* Full-time $44,184; part-time $982 per credit hour. *Required fees:* $191.

Stony Brook University, State University of New York, Graduate School, College of Arts and Sciences, Department of Cultural Analysis and Theory, Stony Brook, NY 11794. Offers comparative literature (MA, PhD); cultural studies (PhD, Certificate).

Evening/weekend programs available. *Faculty:* 19 full-time (9 women). *Students:* 43 full-time (30 women), 2 part-time (both women); includes 5 minority (2 Black or African American, non-Hispanic/Latino; 2 Asian, non-Hispanic/Latino; 1 Hispanic/Latino), 16 international. Average age 34. 79 applicants, 35% accepted, 10 enrolled. In 2014, 2 master's, 5 doctorates, 12 other advanced degrees awarded. Terminal master's awarded for partial completion of doctoral program. *Degree requirements:* For master's, 2 foreign languages, exam; for doctorate, 3 foreign languages, comprehensive exam, thesis/dissertation. *Entrance requirements:* For master's and doctorate, GRE General Test, minimum GPA of 3.5 in major, 3.0 overall. Additional exam requirements/recommendations for international students: Required—TOEFL. *Application deadline:* For fall admission, 1/15 for domestic students; for spring admission, 10/1 for domestic students. Application fee: $100. *Expenses:* Tuition, state resident: full-time $10,370; part-time $432 per credit. Tuition, nonresident: full-time $20,190; part-time $841 per credit. *Required fees:* $1431. *Financial support:* In 2014–15, 26 teaching assistantships were awarded; fellowships and research assistantships also available. *Faculty research:* Literary theory, interdisciplinary studies, literary history. *Unit head:* Prof. Robert Harvey, Chair, 631-632-7456, Fax: 631-632-5707, E-mail: robert.harvey@stonybrook.edu. *Application contact:* Mary Moran-Luba, Coordinator, 631-632-7460, Fax: 631-632-5707, E-mail: mary.moran-luba@stonybrook.edu. Website: http://www.stonybrook.edu/commcms/cat/index.html

Université de Montréal, Faculty of Arts and Sciences, Department of Comparative Literature, Montréal, QC H3C 3J7, Canada. Offers comparative literature (MA); literature (PhD). *Degree requirements:* For master's, 2 foreign languages, thesis; for doctorate, 3 foreign languages, thesis/dissertation, general exam. *Entrance requirements:* For doctorate, MA with minimum B+ average. Electronic applications accepted.

Université de Sherbrooke, Faculty of Letters and Human Sciences, Department of Letters and Communications, Sherbrooke, QC J1K 2R1, Canada. Offers comparative Canadian literature (MA, PhD); French literature (MA, PhD); linguistics (MA); theatre (MA). *Degree requirements:* For master's, thesis or alternative; for doctorate, thesis/dissertation. *Entrance requirements:* For master's, minimum GPA of 2.8; for doctorate, minimum GPA of 3.0.

Université du Québec à Chicoutimi, Graduate Programs, Program in Literary Studies, Chicoutimi, QC G7H 2B1, Canada. Offers MA. Program offered jointly with Université du Québec à Rimouski and Université du Québec à Trois-Rivières. Part-time programs available. *Degree requirements:* For master's, thesis optional. *Entrance requirements:* For master's, appropriate bachelor's degree, proficiency in French.

Université du Québec à Montréal, Graduate Programs, Program in Literary Studies, Montréal, QC H3C 3P8, Canada. Offers MA, PhD. Part-time programs available. *Degree requirements:* For master's, thesis; for doctorate, thesis/dissertation. *Entrance requirements:* For master's, appropriate bachelor's degree or equivalent, proficiency in French; for doctorate, appropriate master's degree or equivalent, proficiency in French.

Université du Québec à Montréal, Graduate Programs, Program in Semiology, Montréal, QC H3C 3P8, Canada. Offers PhD. Part-time programs available. *Degree requirements:* For doctorate, thesis/dissertation. *Entrance requirements:* For doctorate, appropriate master's degree or equivalent, proficiency in French.

Université du Québec à Rimouski, Graduate Programs, Program in Literary Studies, Rimouski, QC G5L 3A1, Canada. Offers MA, PhD. Programs offered jointly with Université du Québec à Chicoutimi and Université du Québec à Trois-Rivières. Part-time programs available. *Degree requirements:* For master's, thesis or alternative. *Entrance requirements:* For master's, appropriate bachelor's degree, proficiency in French.

Université du Québec à Trois-Rivières, Graduate Programs, Program in Literary Studies, Trois-Rivières, QC G9A 5H7, Canada. Offers MA. Program offered jointly with Université du Québec à Chicoutimi and Université du Québec à Rimouski. Part-time programs available. *Degree requirements:* For master's, thesis optional. *Entrance requirements:* For master's, appropriate bachelor's degree, proficiency in French.

Université Laval, Faculty of Letters, Department of Literature, Programs in Literary Studies, Québec, QC G1K 7P4, Canada. Offers MA, PhD. Part-time programs available. Terminal master's awarded for partial completion of doctoral program. *Degree requirements:* For master's, thesis; for doctorate, comprehensive exam, thesis/dissertation. *Entrance requirements:* For master's and doctorate, linguistics exams, knowledge of French, knowledge of a second language. Electronic applications accepted.

University at Buffalo, the State University of New York, Graduate School, College of Arts and Sciences, Department of Comparative Literature, Buffalo, NY 14260. Offers MA, PhD. Part-time programs available. *Faculty:* 9 full-time (2 women). *Students:* 33 full-time (18 women); includes 8 minority (6 Asian, non-Hispanic/Latino; 2 Hispanic/Latino), 14 international. Average age 25. 38 applicants, 55% accepted, 6 enrolled. In 2014, 5 master's, 2 doctorates awarded. Terminal master's awarded for partial completion of doctoral program. *Median time to degree:* Of those who began their doctoral program in fall 2006, 90% received their degree in 8 years or less. *Degree requirements:* For master's, one foreign language, exam or project; for doctorate, 2 foreign languages, comprehensive exam, thesis/dissertation. *Entrance requirements:* For master's and doctorate, GRE General Test, writing sample, 3 letters of recommendation, statement of purpose, undergraduate transcripts. Additional exam requirements/recommendations for international students: Required—TOEFL (minimum score 550 paper-based; 79 iBT). *Application deadline:* For fall admission, 1/15 for domestic and international students. Applications are processed on a rolling basis. Application fee: $75. Electronic applications accepted. *Financial support:* In 2014–15, 17 students received support, including 7 fellowships with full tuition reimbursements available (averaging $4,150 per year), 17 teaching assistantships with full tuition reimbursements available (averaging $13,600 per year); Federal Work-Study, institutionally sponsored loans, health care benefits, and unspecified assistantships also available. Financial award application deadline: 1/15; financial award applicants required to submit FAFSA. *Faculty research:* Theory; interaction between literature and philosophy; European, Francophone, African, American, and South American literature; postmodernism; postcolonialism. *Unit head:* Dr. Krzysztof Ziarek, Chair, 716-645-0858, Fax: 716-645-5979, E-mail: kziarek@buffalo.edu. *Application contact:* Dr. Shaun Irlam, Director of Graduate Studies, 716-645-0856, Fax: 716-645-5979, E-mail: irlam@buffalo.edu. Website: http://www.complit.buffalo.edu/

University of Arkansas, Graduate School, Interdisciplinary Program in Comparative Literature and Cultural Studies, Fayetteville, AR 72701-1201. Offers MA, PhD. *Degree requirements:* For doctorate, 2 foreign languages, comprehensive exam, thesis/dissertation optional. *Entrance requirements:* For doctorate, GRE General Test, official transcripts of all undergraduate and graduate work, three letters of recommendation, writing sample, statement of purpose. Additional exam requirements/recommendations for international students: Required—TOEFL (minimum score 550 paper-based; 80 iBT) or IELTS (minimum score 6.5). *Faculty research:* Literary and cultural theory, cultural studies, postcolonial theory, gender studies, world literature.

University of California, Berkeley, Graduate Division, College of Letters and Science, Department of Comparative Literature, Berkeley, CA 94720-1500. Offers PhD. *Degree requirements:* For doctorate, 3 foreign languages, thesis/dissertation, qualifying exam.

Entrance requirements: For doctorate, GRE General Test, fluency in 1 foreign language (2 preferred), minimum GPA of 3.0, writing sample, 3 letters of recommendation.

University of California, Davis, Graduate Studies, Graduate Group in Comparative Literature, Davis, CA 95616. Offers PhD. *Degree requirements:* For doctorate, 3 foreign languages, thesis/dissertation. *Entrance requirements:* For doctorate, GRE General Test, minimum GPA of 3.0. Additional exam requirements/recommendations for international students: Required—TOEFL (minimum score 550 paper-based). Electronic applications accepted. *Faculty research:* Literary criticism, literary theory, gender history and literature, genre.

University of California, Irvine, School of Humanities, Department of Comparative Literature, Irvine, CA 92697. Offers MA, PhD. *Students:* 27 full-time (13 women), 1 (woman) part-time; includes 4 minority (2 Asian, non-Hispanic/Latino; 2 Two or more races, non-Hispanic/Latino), 5 international. Average age 31. 53 applicants, 17% accepted, 6 enrolled. In 2014, 3 master's, 6 doctorates awarded. *Degree requirements:* For master's, one foreign language; for doctorate, 2 foreign languages, thesis/dissertation. *Entrance requirements:* For doctorate, GRE General Test, minimum GPA of 3.5, sample of written work, 3 letters of recommendation. Additional exam requirements/recommendations for international students: Required—TOEFL (minimum score 550 paper-based). *Application deadline:* For fall admission, 12/15 for domestic and international students. Application fee: $90 ($110 for international students). Electronic applications accepted. *Financial support:* Fellowships with full tuition reimbursements, research assistantships with full tuition reimbursements, teaching assistantships with partial tuition reimbursements, institutionally sponsored loans, and tuition waivers (partial) available. Financial award application deadline: 3/1; financial award applicants required to submit FAFSA. *Faculty research:* Critical theory, feminist studies, Asian-American studies. *Unit head:* Gabriele Schwab, Department Chair, 949-824-6406, Fax: 949-824-6416, E-mail: gmschwab@uci.edu. *Application contact:* Bindya Baliga, Graduate Coordinator, 949-824-7968, E-mail: bbaliga@uci.edu.

University of California, Los Angeles, Graduate Division, College of Letters and Science, Department of Comparative Literature, Los Angeles, CA 90095. Offers MA, PhD. Terminal master's awarded for partial completion of doctoral program. *Degree requirements:* For master's, 2 foreign languages; for doctorate, 2 foreign languages, thesis/dissertation, oral and written qualifying exams. *Entrance requirements:* For doctorate, GRE General Test, bachelor's degree; minimum undergraduate GPA of 3.0, 3.4 in upper-division literature courses (or its equivalent if letter grade system not used); literary proficiency in one foreign language and elementary knowledge of another; writing sample. Additional exam requirements/recommendations for international students: Required—TOEFL. Electronic applications accepted.

University of California, Riverside, Graduate Division, Department of Comparative Literature and Foreign Languages, Riverside, CA 92521-0102. Offers comparative literature (MA, PhD). Terminal master's awarded for partial completion of doctoral program. *Degree requirements:* For master's, 3 foreign languages, comprehensive exam; for doctorate, 3 foreign languages, thesis/dissertation, qualifying exams. *Entrance requirements:* For master's and doctorate, GRE General Test, minimum GPA of 3.0. Additional exam requirements/recommendations for international students: Required—TOEFL (minimum score 550 paper-based; 80 iBT). Electronic applications accepted. *Expenses:* Tuition, state resident: full-time $5399. Tuition, nonresident: full-time $10,433. *Faculty research:* French and German Enlightenment, modern drama and theatre, contemporary critical theory, East-West comparative studies, science fiction and fantasy.

University of California, Santa Barbara, Graduate Division, College of Letters and Sciences, Division of Humanities and Fine Arts, Program in Comparative Literature, Santa Barbara, CA 93106-4130. Offers comparative literature (PhD); East Asian literatures (PhD); feminist studies (PhD); French (PhD); global studies (PhD); translation studies (PhD); MA/PhD. *Degree requirements:* For doctorate, 2 foreign languages, comprehensive exam, thesis/dissertation. *Entrance requirements:* For doctorate, GRE. Additional exam requirements/recommendations for international students: Required—TOEFL (minimum score 550 paper-based; 80 iBT), IELTS (minimum score 7). Electronic applications accepted. *Faculty research:* Comparative literary studies in global context, critical theory, translation studies, media technological studies, trauma studies.

University of California, Santa Cruz, Division of Graduate Studies, Division of Humanities, Department of Literature, Santa Cruz, CA 95064. Offers MA, PhD. Terminal master's awarded for partial completion of doctoral program. *Degree requirements:* For master's, thesis; for doctorate, one foreign language, thesis/dissertation, qualifying exam. *Entrance requirements:* For master's, GRE General Test, writing sample, minimum GPA of 3.5; for doctorate, GRE General Test, minimum GPA of 3.5, writing sample. Additional exam requirements/recommendations for international students: Required—TOEFL (minimum score 550 paper-based; 83 iBT); Recommended—IELTS (minimum score 8). Electronic applications accepted. *Faculty research:* Technologies of narrative; trans/post/emergent nationalisms; poetics, poetry, and experimental writing; materialism and material culture; critical theories.

University of Chicago, Division of the Humanities, Department of Comparative Literature, Chicago, IL 60637. Offers PhD. *Students:* 27 full-time (15 women); includes 3 minority (1 Asian, non-Hispanic/Latino; 2 Hispanic/Latino), 6 international. 101 applicants, 30% accepted, 4 enrolled. Terminal master's awarded for partial completion of doctoral program. *Degree requirements:* For doctorate, 3 foreign languages, thesis/dissertation. *Entrance requirements:* For doctorate, GRE General Test. Additional exam requirements/recommendations for international students: Required—TOEFL (minimum score 104 iBT), IELTS (minimum score 7). *Application deadline:* For fall admission, 12/15 for domestic and international students. Application fee: $90. Electronic applications accepted. *Expenses: Tuition:* Full-time $46,899. *Required fees:* $347. *Financial support:* Fellowships with full tuition reimbursements, teaching assistantships with tuition reimbursements, Federal Work-Study, institutionally sponsored loans, scholarships/grants, and health care benefits available. Financial award application deadline: 12/15; financial award applicants required to submit FAFSA. *Unit head:* Dr. Thomas Pavel, Head, 773-702-8486. *Application contact:* Braden Grams, Assistant Dean of Students, Admissions and Fellowships, 773-702-1552, Fax: 773-834-9148, E-mail: humanitiesadmissions@uchicago.edu. Website: http://complit.uchicago.edu/

University of Chicago, Division of the Humanities, Master of Arts Program in the Humanities, Chicago, IL 60637. Offers art history (MA); classics (MA); comparative literature (MA); creative writing (MA); digital humanities (MA); English language and literature (MA); Germanic studies (MA); linguistics (MA); music (MA); philosophy (MA); Romance languages and literatures (MA); South Asian languages and civilizations (MA). *Students:* 83 full-time (41 women), 8 part-time (6 women); includes 14 minority (1 Black or African American, non-Hispanic/Latino; 6 Asian, non-Hispanic/Latino; 6 Hispanic/Latino; 1 Two or more races, non-Hispanic/Latino), 17 international. Average age 26. 153 applicants, 67% accepted, 80 enrolled. *Degree requirements:* For master's, thesis. *Entrance requirements:* For master's, GRE General Test. Additional exam requirements/recommendations for international students: Required—TOEFL (minimum score 600 paper-based; 104 iBT), IELTS (minimum score 7). *Application deadline:* For fall admission, 3/15 for domestic and international students. Application fee: $90. Electronic

applications accepted. *Expenses:* *Tuition:* Full-time $46,899. *Required fees:* $347. *Financial support:* In 2014–15, 100 students received support, including 8 fellowships with partial tuition reimbursements available (averaging $12,000 per year); Federal Work-Study, institutionally sponsored loans, and tuition waivers (partial) also available. Financial award application deadline: 3/15; financial award applicants required to submit FAFSA. *Unit head:* Prof. David Wray, Director, 773-834-1201, E-mail: ma-humanities@uchicago.edu. *Application contact:* Program Coordinator, 773-834-1201, Fax: 773-834-7526, E-mail: ma-humanities@uchicago.edu.
Website: http://maph.uchicago.edu/

University of Colorado Boulder, Graduate School, College of Arts and Sciences, Comparative Literature Program, Boulder, CO 80309. Offers MA, PhD. *Students:* 18 full-time (16 women), 1 part-time (0 women); includes 4 minority (3 Hispanic/Latino; 1 Two or more races, non-Hispanic/Latino), 1 international. Average age 29. 25 applicants, 60% accepted, 9 enrolled. In 2014, 3 master's, 3 doctorates awarded. Terminal master's awarded for partial completion of doctoral program. *Degree requirements:* For master's, 2 foreign languages, comprehensive exam, thesis or alternative; for doctorate, 3 foreign languages, comprehensive exam, thesis/dissertation. *Entrance requirements:* For master's, GRE General Test, minimum undergraduate GPA of 2.75; for doctorate, GRE General Test, MA in related field. *Application deadline:* For fall admission, 3/13 for domestic students, 12/1 for international students. Applications are processed on a rolling basis. Application fee: $50 ($70 for international students). Electronic applications accepted. *Financial support:* In 2014–15, 49 students received support, including 3 fellowships (averaging $1,033 per year), 3 research assistantships with full and partial tuition reimbursements available (averaging $36,458 per year), 15 teaching assistantships with full and partial tuition reimbursements available (averaging $36,839 per year); institutionally sponsored loans, scholarships/grants, health care benefits, and unspecified assistantships also available. Financial award application deadline: 1/1; financial award applicants required to submit FAFSA. *Faculty research:* Enlightenment to modern literature; literary theory and history; philosophy and literature; popular culture studies; reception, translation and interpretation; gender and sexual orientation; nationalism.
Website: http://complit.colorado.edu/

University of Connecticut, Graduate School, College of Liberal Arts and Sciences, Department of Modern and Classical Languages, Field of Comparative Literature and Cultural Studies, Storrs, CT 06269. Offers MA, PhD. Terminal master's awarded for partial completion of doctoral program. *Degree requirements:* For master's, comprehensive exam; for doctorate, thesis/dissertation. *Entrance requirements:* For master's and doctorate, GRE General Test, GRE Subject Test. Additional exam requirements/recommendations for international students: Required—TOEFL (minimum score 550 paper-based). Electronic applications accepted.

University of Dallas, Braniff Graduate School of Liberal Arts, Institute of Philosophic Studies, Program in Literature, Irving, TX 75062-4736. Offers PhD. *Degree requirements:* For doctorate, 2 foreign languages, comprehensive exam, thesis/dissertation, qualifying exams. *Entrance requirements:* For doctorate, GRE General Test. Additional exam requirements/recommendations for international students: Required—TOEFL. *Faculty research:* Medieval studies, modern literature, Renaissance, Shakespeare.

University of Georgia, Franklin College of Arts and Sciences, Department of Comparative Literature, Athens, GA 30602. Offers MA, PhD. *Degree requirements:* For master's, 2 foreign languages, thesis; for doctorate, one foreign language, thesis/dissertation. *Entrance requirements:* For master's and doctorate, GRE General Test. Electronic applications accepted.

University of Guelph, Graduate Studies, College of Arts, School of English and Theatre Studies, Joint Program in Literary Studies/Theatre Studies in English, Guelph, ON N1G 2W1, Canada. Offers PhD. Part-time programs available. *Degree requirements:* For doctorate, one foreign language, comprehensive exam, thesis/dissertation. *Entrance requirements:* For doctorate, MA, 3 letters of reference, writing samples, resume, minimum A- average in graduate course work. Additional exam requirements/recommendations for international students: Required—TOEFL. Electronic applications accepted. *Faculty research:* Canadian studies, Early Modern studies, Postcolonial studies, studies in gender and genre, 19th Century studies.

University of Houston, College of Liberal Arts and Social Sciences, Department of Modern and Classical Languages, Houston, TX 77204. Offers world cultures and literatures (MA). *Degree requirements:* For master's, one foreign language, thesis optional. *Entrance requirements:* For master's, GRE General Test, minimum GPA of 3.0 in last 60 hours of course work. Additional exam requirements/recommendations for international students: Required—TOEFL (minimum score 500 paper-based). Electronic applications accepted.

University of Illinois at Urbana–Champaign, Graduate College, College of Liberal Arts and Sciences, School of Literatures, Cultures and Linguistics, Program in Comparative and World Literature, Champaign, IL 61820. Offers comparative literature (MA, PhD). *Students:* 24 (18 women). *Entrance requirements:* For master's, minimum GPA of 3.0; writing sample. Application fee: $70 ($90 for international students). *Unit head:* Lilya Kaganovsky, Director, 217-333-4987, Fax: 217-244-4019, E-mail: lilya@illinois.edu. *Application contact:* Lynn Stanke, Office Support Specialist, 217-333-6269, Fax: 217-244-4019, E-mail: stanke@illinois.edu.
Website: http://www.complit.illinois.edu

University of Maryland, College Park, Academic Affairs, College of Arts and Humanities, Department of English, Program in Comparative Literature, College Park, MD 20742. Offers MA, PhD. *Degree requirements:* For master's, thesis, oral defense; for doctorate, 3 foreign languages, thesis/dissertation, comprehensive exams in 4 areas. *Entrance requirements:* For master's, GRE General Test, foreign language, writing sample, 3 letters of recommendation; for doctorate, GRE General Test, minimum GPA of 3.0, foreign language, writing sample. Additional exam requirements/recommendations for international students: Required—TOEFL. Electronic applications accepted. *Faculty research:* Renaissance studies, drama, modern literature, postcolonial studies, feminist scholarship.

University of Massachusetts Amherst, Graduate School, College of Humanities and Fine Arts, Department of Languages, Literatures, and Cultures, Program in Comparative Literature, Amherst, MA 01003. Offers MA, PhD. Part-time programs available. *Faculty:* 18 full-time (10 women). *Students:* 26 full-time (17 women), 17 part-time (11 women); includes 7 minority (1 Black or African American, non-Hispanic/Latino; 4 Hispanic/Latino; 2 Two or more races, non-Hispanic/Latino), 21 international. Average age 30. 57 applicants, 26% accepted, 8 enrolled. In 2014, 5 master's, 5 doctorates awarded. Terminal master's awarded for partial completion of doctoral program. *Degree requirements:* For master's, thesis or alternative; for doctorate, comprehensive exam, thesis/dissertation. *Entrance requirements:* For master's and doctorate, GRE General Test, writing samples. Additional exam requirements/recommendations for international students: Required—TOEFL (minimum score 550 paper-based; 80 iBT), IELTS (minimum score 6.5). *Application deadline:* For fall admission, 1/5 for domestic and international students. Applications are processed on a rolling basis. Application fee: $75. Electronic applications accepted. *Expenses:* Tuition, state resident: full-time $1980; part-time $110 per credit. Tuition, nonresident: full-time $14,644; part-time $414 per credit. *Required fees:* $11,417. One-time fee: $357. *Financial support:* Fellowships with full and partial tuition reimbursements, research assistantships with full and partial tuition reimbursements, teaching assistantships with full and partial tuition reimbursements, career-related internships or fieldwork, Federal Work-Study, scholarships/grants, traineeships, health care benefits, tuition waivers (full), and unspecified assistantships available. Support available to part-time students. Financial award application deadline: 1/5. *Unit head:* Dr. Maria Barbon, Graduate Program Director, 413-545-5808, Fax: 413-545-0908. *Application contact:* Lindsay DeSantis, Supervisor of Admissions, 413-545-0722, Fax: 413-577-0100, E-mail: gradadm@grad.umass.edu.
Website: http://www.umass.edu/complit/

University of Memphis, Graduate School, College of Arts and Sciences, Department of English, Memphis, TN 38152. Offers African-American literature (Graduate Certificate); applied linguistics (PhD); composition studies (PhD); creative writing (MFA); English as a second language (MA); linguistics (MA); literary and cultural studies (PhD), including African-American literature; literature (MA); professional writing (MA, PhD); teaching English as a second language (Graduate Certificate). Part-time and evening/weekend programs available. Postbaccalaureate distance learning degree programs offered (no on-campus study). *Faculty:* 30 full-time (15 women), 1 part-time/adjunct (0 women). *Students:* 89 full-time (45 women), 85 part-time (57 women); includes 35 minority (23 Black or African American, non-Hispanic/Latino; 6 Asian, non-Hispanic/Latino; 5 Hispanic/Latino; 1 Two or more races, non-Hispanic/Latino), 17 international. Average age 35. 83 applicants, 88% accepted, 19 enrolled. In 2014, 29 master's, 6 doctorates awarded. Terminal master's awarded for partial completion of doctoral program. *Degree requirements:* For master's, one foreign language, comprehensive exam, thesis optional; for doctorate, 2 foreign languages, comprehensive exam, thesis/dissertation. *Entrance requirements:* For master's and doctorate, GRE. Additional exam requirements/recommendations for international students: Required—TOEFL. *Application deadline:* For fall admission, 7/1 for domestic students; for spring admission, 10/15 for domestic students. Applications are processed on a rolling basis. Application fee: $35 ($60 for international students). Electronic applications accepted. *Financial support:* In 2014–15, 123 students received support. Research assistantships with full tuition reimbursements available, teaching assistantships with full tuition reimbursements available, Federal Work-Study, scholarships/grants, and unspecified assistantships available. Financial award application deadline: 2/15; financial award applicants required to submit FAFSA. *Faculty research:* Applied linguistics, British and American literature, professional writing, composition studies. *Unit head:* Dr. Joshua Phillips, Chair, 901-678-3067, Fax: 901-678-2226, E-mail: jsphllps@memphis.edu. *Application contact:* Dr. Jeffrey Scraba, Director, Graduate Studies, 901-678-3099, Fax: 901-678-2226, E-mail: jscraba@memphis.edu.
Website: http://www.memphis.edu/english

University of Michigan, Horace H. Rackham School of Graduate Studies, College of Literature, Science, and the Arts, Department of Comparative Literature, Ann Arbor, MI 48109. Offers PhD. *Faculty:* 18 full-time (9 women). *Students:* 32 full-time (17 women); includes 5 minority (1 Black or African American, non-Hispanic/Latino; 2 Asian, non-Hispanic/Latino; 2 Hispanic/Latino), 11 international. Average age 29. 66 applicants, 14% accepted, 5 enrolled. In 2014, 7 doctorates awarded. *Degree requirements:* For doctorate, thesis/dissertation, 2 languages at advanced level in addition to language of instruction, preliminary exam, topics paper, prospectus, oral defense of dissertation. *Entrance requirements:* For doctorate, GRE General Test. Additional exam requirements/recommendations for international students: Required—TOEFL (minimum score 560 paper-based; 84 iBT), Michigan English Language Assessment Battery, or IELTS (minimum score 6.5). *Application deadline:* For fall admission, 12/31 for domestic and international students. Application fee: $75 ($90 for international students). Electronic applications accepted. *Financial support:* In 2014–15, 31 students received support, including 28 fellowships with full tuition reimbursements available (averaging $43,365 per year), 2 research assistantships with full tuition reimbursements available (averaging $32,690 per year), 34 teaching assistantships with full tuition reimbursements available (averaging $43,510 per year); scholarships/grants, health care benefits, and unspecified assistantships also available. Financial award application deadline: 4/15. *Faculty research:* Postcolonial theory, cultural studies, critical translation studies, comparative poetics, classical reception studies, gender studies/queer theory. *Unit head:* Silke-Maria Weineck, Chair, 734-763-2351, Fax: 734-764-8503, E-mail: smwei@umich.edu. *Application contact:* Nancy E. W. Harris, Student Services Coordinator, 734-647-4894, Fax: 734-764-8503, E-mail: nwh@umich.edu.
Website: http://www.lsa.umich.edu/complit/

University of Minnesota, Twin Cities Campus, Graduate School, College of Liberal Arts, Department of Cultural Studies and Comparative Literature, Program in Comparative Literature, Minneapolis, MN 55455-0213. Offers PhD. *Degree requirements:* For doctorate, 3 foreign languages, comprehensive exam, thesis/dissertation. *Entrance requirements:* For doctorate, GRE General Test, sample of written work. Additional exam requirements/recommendations for international students: Required—TOEFL. *Faculty research:* Literary theory, emergent literatures, popular culture, postcolonial literature, gender and sexuality.

University of Missouri, Office of Research and Graduate Studies, College of Arts and Science, Department of Romance Languages and Literatures, Columbia, MO 65211. Offers French (MA, PhD); literature (MA); Spanish (MA, PhD); teaching (MA). *Faculty:* 25 full-time (12 women), 1 (woman) part-time/adjunct. *Students:* 28 full-time (19 women), 9 part-time (6 women); includes 9 minority (3 Black or African American, non-Hispanic/Latino; 4 Hispanic/Latino; 2 Two or more races, non-Hispanic/Latino), 15 international. Average age 36. 16 applicants, 69% accepted, 7 enrolled. In 2014, 3 master's, 1 doctorate awarded. Terminal master's awarded for partial completion of doctoral program. *Degree requirements:* For master's, one foreign language; for doctorate, 4 foreign languages, comprehensive exam, thesis/dissertation. *Entrance requirements:* For master's, GRE General Test, minimum GPA of 3.0 in field of major; bachelor's degree; for doctorate, GRE General Test, minimum GPA of 3.0 in field of major; master's degree. Additional exam requirements/recommendations for international students: Required—TOEFL (minimum score 500 paper-based; 61 iBT). *Application deadline:* For fall admission, 2/15 priority date for domestic students; for winter admission, 10/15 for domestic students. Applications are processed on a rolling basis. Application fee: $55 ($75 for international students). Electronic applications accepted. *Financial support:* Research assistantships, teaching assistantships with full tuition reimbursements, institutionally sponsored loans, health care benefits, and unspecified assistantships available. *Faculty research:* Afro-Romance studies. *Unit head:* Dr. Flore Zephir, Department Chair, 573-882-5048, E-mail: zephirf@missouri.edu. *Application contact:* Mary Harris, Administrative Assistant, 573-882-5039, E-mail: harrisma@missouri.edu.
Website: http://romancelanguages.missouri.edu/grad.shtml

University of Nebraska–Lincoln, Graduate College, College of Arts and Sciences, Department of English, Lincoln, NE 68588-0333. Offers composition and rhetoric (MA, PhD); creative writing (MA, PhD); literature studies (MA, PhD). *Degree requirements:* For master's, thesis optional; for doctorate, one foreign language, comprehensive exam,

thesis/dissertation. *Entrance requirements:* For master's, writing sample; for doctorate, GRE General Test, writing sample. Additional exam requirements/recommendations for international students: Required—TOEFL (minimum score 600 paper-based). Electronic applications accepted. *Faculty research:* Creative writing, composition and rhetoric, women's studies, North American literature, medieval/Renaissance studies.

University of New Hampshire, Graduate School, College of Liberal Arts, Department of English, Durham, NH 03824. Offers English (PhD); English education (MST); language and linguistics (MA); literature (MA). Part-time programs available. *Faculty:* 36 full-time (19 women). *Students:* 57 full-time (39 women), 38 part-time (22 women); includes 7 minority (2 Black or African American, non-Hispanic/Latino; 4 Hispanic/Latino; 1 Two or more races, non-Hispanic/Latino), 8 international. Average age 31. 194 applicants, 53% accepted, 32 enrolled. In 2014, 26 master's, 1 doctorate awarded. *Degree requirements:* For master's, one foreign language; for doctorate, 2 foreign languages, thesis/dissertation. *Entrance requirements:* For master's, GRE General Test, sample of written work; for doctorate, GRE General Test, GRE Subject Test, sample of written work. Additional exam requirements/recommendations for international students: Required—TOEFL (minimum score 550 paper-based; 80 iBT). *Application deadline:* For fall admission, 6/1 priority date for domestic students, 2/15 for international students; for spring admission, 12/1 for domestic students. Applications are processed on a rolling basis. Application fee: $65. Electronic applications accepted. *Expenses:* Tuition, state resident: full-time $13,500; part-time $750 per credit hour. Tuition, nonresident: full-time $26,460; part-time $1110 per credit hour. *Required fees:* $1788; $447 per semester. *Financial support:* In 2014–15, 56 students received support, including 2 fellowships, 42 teaching assistantships; research assistantships, career-related internships or fieldwork, Federal Work-Study, scholarships/grants, and tuition waivers (full and partial) also available. Support available to part-time students. Financial award application deadline: 2/15. *Unit head:* Dr. Rachel Trubowitz, Chairperson, 603-862-0254. *Application contact:* Janine Wilks, Administrative Assistant, 603-862-3963, E-mail: engl.grad@unh.edu. Website: http://cola.unh.edu/english

University of New Mexico, Graduate School, College of Arts and Sciences, Program in Foreign Languages and Literatures, Albuquerque, NM 87131-2039. Offers comparative literature and cultural studies (MA); French (MA); French studies (PhD); German studies (MA). Part-time programs available. *Faculty:* 12 full-time (8 women). *Students:* 25 full-time (17 women), 6 part-time (5 women); includes 3 minority (1 Black or African American, non-Hispanic/Latino; 2 Hispanic/Latino), 7 international. Average age 30. 22 applicants, 68% accepted, 10 enrolled. In 2014, 9 master's awarded. *Degree requirements:* For master's, one foreign language, thesis optional; for doctorate, 2 foreign languages, thesis/dissertation. *Entrance requirements:* For master's and doctorate, transcript, writing sample, 3 letters of recommendation. Additional exam requirements/recommendations for international students: Required—TOEFL. *Application deadline:* For fall admission, 2/1 priority date for domestic students; for spring admission, 10/1 priority date for domestic students. Application fee: $50. Electronic applications accepted. *Financial support:* In 2014–15, 28 students received support, including 1 research assistantship (averaging $4,730 per year), 23 teaching assistantships with tuition reimbursements available (averaging $10,300 per year); Federal Work-Study, health care benefits, and unspecified assistantships also available. Financial award application deadline: 3/1; financial award applicants required to submit FAFSA. *Faculty research:* German, Russian, Italian, Japanese, French, comparative literature, culture studies, classics. *Total annual research expenditures:* $4,750. *Unit head:* Dr. Walter Putnam, Chair, 505-277-4771, Fax: 505-277-3599, E-mail: wputnam@unm.edu. *Application contact:* Jacqueline Ochoa, Application and Graduation Advisor, 505-277-4471, Fax: 505-277-3599, E-mail: jochoa@unm.edu. Website: http://www.unm.edu/~fll/

University of Notre Dame, Graduate School, College of Arts and Letters, Division of Humanities, PhD Program in Literature, Notre Dame, IN 46556. Offers PhD. *Degree requirements:* For doctorate, 3 foreign languages, thesis/dissertation, candidacy exam. *Entrance requirements:* For doctorate, GRE General Test. Additional exam requirements/recommendations for international students: Required—TOEFL (minimum score 600 paper-based; 80 iBT). Electronic applications accepted. *Faculty research:* Interdisciplinary study of literature from a transitional and intercultural perspective; classics, East Asian, French, German, Irish, Italian, Iberian and Latin American (Portuguese, Spanish).

University of Oregon, Graduate School, College of Arts and Sciences, Program in Comparative Literature, Eugene, OR 97403. Offers MA, PhD. Part-time programs available. Terminal master's awarded for partial completion of doctoral program. *Degree requirements:* For master's, 2 foreign languages, field exam; for doctorate, 2 foreign languages, thesis/dissertation, field exam. *Entrance requirements:* For master's, previous course work in English and literature, proficiency in 3 foreign languages, writing sample; for doctorate, previous course work in English and literature, proficiency in 2 foreign languages, writing sample. Additional exam requirements/recommendations for international students: Required—TOEFL. *Faculty research:* Critical theory, historical periods, interdisciplinary approach, Feminist studies.

University of Pennsylvania, School of Arts and Sciences, Graduate Group in Comparative Literature and Literary Theory, Philadelphia, PA 19104. Offers comparative literature (AM, PhD); literary theory (AM, PhD). *Faculty:* 44 full-time (16 women), 6 part-time/adjunct (2 women). *Students:* 28 full-time (14 women), 1 (woman) part-time; includes 3 minority (1 Asian, non-Hispanic/Latino; 2 Hispanic/Latino), 9 international. 112 applicants, 11% accepted, 2 enrolled. In 2014, 5 master's, 4 doctorates awarded. *Degree requirements:* For master's, one foreign language, thesis; for doctorate, variable foreign language requirement, thesis/dissertation. *Entrance requirements:* For master's, GRE General Test, proficiency in 1 foreign language; for doctorate, GRE General Test, master's degree in a literature field, proficiency in 1 foreign language. Additional exam requirements/recommendations for international students: Required—TOEFL. *Application deadline:* For fall admission, 12/1 priority date for domestic students. Application fee: $70. Electronic applications accepted. *Financial support:* Institutionally sponsored loans, scholarships/grants, traineeships, health care benefits, and unspecified assistantships available. Financial award application deadline: 12/15. *Unit head:* Dr. Ralph M. Rosen, Associate Dean for Graduate Studies, 215-898-7156, Fax: 215-573-8068, E-mail: grad-dean@sas.upenn.edu. *Application contact:* Arts and Sciences Graduate Admissions, 215-573-5816, Fax: 215-573-8068, E-mail: gdasadmis@sas.upenn.edu. Website: http://ccat.sas.upenn.edu/Complit

University of Puerto Rico, Río Piedras Campus, College of Humanities, Department of Comparative Literature, San Juan, PR 00931-3300. Offers MA. Part-time programs available. *Degree requirements:* For master's, comprehensive exam, thesis. *Entrance requirements:* For master's, EXADEP, interview, minimum GPA of 3.0, letter of recommendation.

University of South Carolina, The Graduate School, College of Arts and Sciences, Department of Languages, Literatures, and Cultures, Columbia, SC 29208. Offers comparative literature (MA, PhD); foreign languages (MAT), including French, German, Spanish; French (MA); German (MA); Spanish (MA). MAT offered in cooperation with the College of Education. Part-time programs available. *Degree requirements:* For master's, one foreign language, comprehensive exam, thesis optional; for doctorate, 2

foreign languages, comprehensive exam, thesis/dissertation. *Entrance requirements:* For master's and doctorate, GRE General Test, writing sample. Additional exam requirements/recommendations for international students: Required—TOEFL (minimum score 75 iBT). Electronic applications accepted. *Faculty research:* Modern literature, linguistics, literature and culture, medieval literature, literary theory.

University of Southern California, Graduate School, Dana and David Dornsife College of Letters, Arts and Sciences, Comparative Studies in Literature and Culture Doctoral Program, Los Angeles, CA 90089. Offers comparative literature (PhD); comparative media and culture (PhD); Spanish and Latin American studies (PhD). *Degree requirements:* For doctorate, 2 foreign languages, comprehensive exam, thesis/dissertation. *Entrance requirements:* For doctorate, GRE, competence in language other than English (highly recommended). Additional exam requirements/recommendations for international students: Required—TOEFL. Electronic applications accepted. *Faculty research:* Literary theory, Japanese film and contemporary fiction, Francophone literature and cinema, Latin American and Caribbean literature, Spanish literature and film, nineteenth and twentieth century British and American literature.

University of South Florida, Innovative Education, Tampa, FL 33620-9951. *Unit head:* Kathy Barnes, Interdisciplinary Programs Coordinator, 813-974-8031, Fax: 813-974-7061, E-mail: barnesk@usf.edu. *Application contact:* Karen Tylinski, Metro Initiatives, 813-974-9943, Fax: 813-974-7061, E-mail: ktylinsk@usf.edu. Website: http://www.usf.edu/innovative-education/

The University of Texas at Austin, Graduate School, College of Liberal Arts, Program in Comparative Literature, Austin, TX 78712-1111. Offers MA, PhD. *Degree requirements:* For master's, 2 foreign languages, report or thesis; for doctorate, 3 foreign languages, thesis/dissertation. *Entrance requirements:* For master's and doctorate, GRE General Test. Electronic applications accepted.

The University of Texas at Dallas, School of Arts and Humanities, Program in Humanities, Richardson, TX 75080. Offers aesthetic studies (MA, PhD); history (MA); history of ideas (MA, PhD); humanities (MA, PhD); Latin American studies (MA); studies in literature (MA, PhD). *Faculty:* 35 full-time (11 women), 1 part-time/adjunct (0 women). *Students:* 148 full-time (94 women), 151 part-time (97 women); includes 78 minority (21 Black or African American, non-Hispanic/Latino; 4 American Indian or Alaska Native, non-Hispanic/Latino; 14 Asian, non-Hispanic/Latino; 28 Hispanic/Latino; 11 Two or more races, non-Hispanic/Latino), 16 international. Average age 39. 127 applicants, 46% accepted, 40 enrolled. In 2014, 40 master's, 15 doctorates awarded. *Degree requirements:* For master's, one foreign language, portfolio, thesis, or capstone project; for doctorate, one foreign language, thesis/dissertation. *Entrance requirements:* For master's, minimum GPA of 3.3 in upper-level coursework in field; for doctorate, field examinations, minimum GPA of 3.3 in upper-level coursework in field. Additional exam requirements/recommendations for international students: Required—TOEFL (minimum score 550 paper-based). *Application deadline:* For fall admission, 7/15 for domestic students, 5/1 priority date for international students; for spring admission, 11/15 for domestic students, 9/1 priority date for international students. Applications are processed on a rolling basis. Application fee: $50 ($100 for international students). Electronic applications accepted. *Expenses:* Tuition, state resident: full-time $11,940; part-time $663 per credit. Tuition, nonresident: full-time $22,282; part-time $1238 per credit. *Financial support:* In 2014–15, 161 students received support. Research assistantships with partial tuition reimbursements available, teaching assistantships with partial tuition reimbursements available, career-related internships or fieldwork, Federal Work-Study, institutionally sponsored loans, scholarships/grants, and unspecified assistantships available. Support available to part-time students. Financial award application deadline: 4/30; financial award applicants required to submit FAFSA. *Faculty research:* Holocaust studies, U.S./Mexico studies, translation studies, art history research, Chinese studies. *Unit head:* Dr. Michael Wilson, III, Associate Dean for Graduate Education, 972-883-2756, Fax: 972-883-2989, E-mail: mwilson@utdallas.edu. *Application contact:* Alice Salazar, Coordinator, 972-883-2756, Fax: 972-883-2989, E-mail: alice.salazar1@utdallas.edu. Website: http://www.utdallas.edu/ah/programs/graduate

University of Toronto, School of Graduate Studies, Faculty of Arts and Science, Centre for Comparative Literature, Toronto, ON M5S 2J7, Canada. Offers MA, PhD. Part-time programs available. *Degree requirements:* For doctorate, thesis/dissertation. *Entrance requirements:* For master's, 2 letters of recommendation, sample of work (short essay on a literary topic preferred), resume, bachelor's degree with a B+ average; for doctorate, 2 letters of recommendation, sample of work (short essay on a literary topic preferred), resume, master's degree with average grade of at least A-. Additional exam requirements/recommendations for international students: Required—TOEFL (minimum score 580 paper-based; 93 iBT), TWE (minimum score 5). Electronic applications accepted.

University of Utah, Graduate School, College of Humanities; Department of Languages and Literature, Salt Lake City, UT 84112. Offers comparative literary and cultural studies (MA, PhD); French (MA); Spanish (MA, MALP, PhD); world languages (MA). Part-time programs available. *Faculty:* 33 full-time (20 women), 14 part-time/adjunct (9 women). *Students:* 36 full-time (27 women), 6 part-time (5 women); includes 10 minority (1 Black or African American, non-Hispanic/Latino; 4 Asian, non-Hispanic/Latino; 5 Hispanic/Latino), 6 international. Average age 25. 23 applicants, 70% accepted. In 2014, 14 master's awarded. Terminal master's awarded for partial completion of doctoral program. *Degree requirements:* For master's, comprehensive exam (for some programs), thesis (for some programs), standard proficiency in 2 languages other than English; for doctorate, comprehensive exam, thesis/dissertation, standard proficiency in 2 languages other than English and language of study, advanced proficiency in 1 language other than English and language of study. *Entrance requirements:* For master's, GRE (except for French), bachelor's degree or strong undergraduate record in target languages, minimum GPA of 3.0; for doctorate, GRE, MA, advanced proficiency in a target language. Additional exam requirements/recommendations for international students: Required—TOEFL (minimum score 550 paper-based; 80 iBT). *Application deadline:* For fall admission, 1/15 priority date for domestic students, 12/15 priority date for international students. Application fee: $55 ($65 for international students). Electronic applications accepted. *Financial support:* In 2014–15, 27 teaching assistantships with full and partial tuition reimbursements (averaging $14,000 per year) were awarded; health care benefits and unspecified assistantships also available. Financial award application deadline: 1/15; financial award applicants required to submit FAFSA. *Faculty research:* Literary study, literary theory, linguistics, cultural studies, comparative studies. *Unit head:* Dr. Katharina Gerstenberger, Chair, 801-585-7908, Fax: 801-581-4768, E-mail: katharina.gerstenberger@utah.edu. *Application contact:* Marcie Leek, Academic Coordinator, 801-581-5401, Fax: 801-581-5401, E-mail: marcie.leek@utah.edu. Website: http://languages.utah.edu/

University of Washington, Graduate School, College of Arts and Sciences, Department of Comparative Literature, Seattle, WA 98195. Offers MA, PhD. Part-time programs available. Terminal master's awarded for partial completion of doctoral program. *Degree requirements:* For master's, 2 foreign languages, thesis optional; for doctorate, 3 foreign languages, thesis/dissertation. *Entrance requirements:* For master's, GRE General Test, BA in comparative literature or equivalent, minimum GPA of 3.0, proficiency in 1 foreign language; for doctorate, GRE General Test, MA in

comparative literature or equivalent, minimum GPA of 3.0, proficiency in 2 foreign languages. Additional exam requirements/recommendations for international students: Required—TOEFL. Electronic applications accepted. *Faculty research:* Literature and culture from classical antiquity to twentieth-century, literary theory and criticism.

The University of Western Ontario, Faculty of Graduate Studies, Faculty of Arts and Humanities, Department of Modern Languages and Literatures, London, ON N6A 5B8, Canada. Offers comparative literature (MA, PhD); Hispanic studies (MA, PhD). Part-time programs available. *Degree requirements:* For master's, 2 foreign languages, thesis (for some programs). *Entrance requirements:* For master's, honors degree in Spanish or equivalent, minimum B average. Additional exam requirements/recommendations for international students: Required—TOEFL (comparative literature). *Faculty research:* Spanish golden age, Latin-American, romance, medieval, film.

University of Wisconsin–Madison, Graduate School, College of Letters and Science, Department of Comparative Literature, Madison, WI 53706-1380. Offers MA, PhD. Part-time programs available. Terminal master's awarded for partial completion of doctoral program. *Degree requirements:* For master's, one foreign language, second-year exam; for doctorate, 3 foreign languages, thesis/dissertation, 3 preliminary exams. *Entrance requirements:* For master's, GRE General Test, writing sample; for doctorate, GRE General Test. Electronic applications accepted. *Expenses:* Tuition, state resident: full-time $10,723; part-time $745 per credit. Tuition, nonresident: full-time $24,054; part-time $1578 per credit. *Required fees:* $374 per semester. Tuition and fees vary according to course load, program and reciprocity agreements. *Faculty research:* Literary theory, cultural criticism, classics through early modern literature, postmodernity, gender studies.

University of Wisconsin–Madison, Graduate School, College of Letters and Science, Department of East Asian Languages and Literature, Program in Chinese Literature, Madison, WI 53706-1380. Offers MA, PhD. Part-time programs available. Terminal master's awarded for partial completion of doctoral program. *Degree requirements:* For master's, one foreign language, seminars, written exam; for doctorate, 3 foreign languages, thesis/dissertation, seminars, preliminary exams, oral exam. *Entrance requirements:* For master's, bachelor's degree or equivalent in Chinese; for doctorate, master's degree or equivalent in Chinese. Electronic applications accepted. *Expenses:* Tuition, state resident: full-time $10,723; part-time $745 per credit. Tuition, nonresident: full-time $24,054; part-time $1578 per credit. *Required fees:* $374 per semester. Tuition and fees vary according to course load, program and reciprocity agreements. *Faculty research:* Chinese historical and modern linguistics, classical Chinese literary and cultural history, modern Chinese literary and cultural history, Chinese paleography.

University of Wisconsin–Madison, Graduate School, College of Letters and Science, Department of Scandinavian Studies, Madison, WI 53706-1380. Offers area studies (MA); folklore (PhD); literature (MA, PhD); philology (PhD). Part-time programs available. *Degree requirements:* For master's, 2 foreign languages, exam; for doctorate, thesis/dissertation, exam. *Entrance requirements:* For master's, minimum GPA of 3.25; for doctorate, minimum GPA of 3.5. Electronic applications accepted. *Expenses:* Tuition, state resident: full-time $10,723; part-time $745 per credit. Tuition, nonresident: full-time $24,054; part-time $1578 per credit. *Required fees:* $374 per semester. Tuition and fees vary according to course load, program and reciprocity agreements. *Faculty research:* Historical fiction, Icelandic poetry, nineteenth-century literature, theater, gender studies, folklore.

University of Wisconsin–Milwaukee, Graduate School, College of Letters and Sciences, Department of English, Milwaukee, WI 53201-0413. Offers creative writing (PhD); English (MA); international technical communication (Certificate); linguistics (PhD); professional writing (PhD); professional writing and communication (Certificate); rhetoric and composition (PhD); MLIS/MA. *Degree requirements:* For master's, thesis or alternative; for doctorate, one foreign language, thesis/dissertation. *Entrance requirements:* For master's, GRE General Test, GRE Subject Test; for doctorate, GRE. Additional exam requirements/recommendations for international students: Required—TOEFL (minimum score 550 paper-based; 79 iBT), IELTS (minimum score 6.5). Electronic applications accepted.

University of Wisconsin–Milwaukee, Graduate School, College of Letters and Sciences, Interdepartmental Program in Foreign Language and Literature, Milwaukee, WI 53201-0413. Offers classics and Hebrew studies (MAFLL); comparative literature (MAFLL); French and Italian (MAFLL); German (MAFLL); Slavic studies (MAFLL); translation (Certificate). Part-time programs available. *Degree requirements:* For master's, 2 foreign languages, thesis or alternative. *Entrance requirements:* Additional exam requirements/recommendations for international students: Required—TOEFL (minimum score 550 paper-based; 79 iBT), IELTS (minimum score 6.5). Electronic applications accepted.

Washington University in St. Louis, Graduate School of Arts and Sciences, Department of East Asian Languages and Cultures, St. Louis, MO 63130-4899. Offers Chinese (MA); Chinese and comparative literature (PhD); Chinese language and literature (PhD); East Asian studies (MA); Japanese (MA); Japanese and comparative literature (PhD); Japanese language and literature (PhD). Terminal master's awarded for partial completion of doctoral program. *Degree requirements:* For master's, thesis optional; for doctorate, thesis/dissertation. *Entrance requirements:* For master's and doctorate, GRE General Test. Additional exam requirements/recommendations for international students: Required—TOEFL. Electronic applications accepted. *Faculty research:* Chinese; Japanese; Chinese fiction, theater, poetry, modern literature; Japanese modern and classical fiction, translation theory; East Asian Studies.

Washington University in St. Louis, Graduate School of Arts and Sciences, Department of Romance Languages and Literatures, Program in French, St. Louis, MO 63130-4899. Offers French (MA); French and comparative literature (PhD); French language and literature (PhD). Terminal master's awarded for partial completion of doctoral program. *Degree requirements:* For master's, thesis or alternative; for doctorate, thesis/dissertation. *Entrance requirements:* For master's and doctorate, GRE General Test. Additional exam requirements/recommendations for international students: Required—TOEFL. Electronic applications accepted. *Faculty research:* French language and literature.

Washington University in St. Louis, Graduate School of Arts and Sciences, Department of Romance Languages and Literatures, Program in Spanish, St. Louis, MO 63130-4899. Offers Hispanic languages and literatures (PhD); Spanish (MA); Spanish and comparative literature (PhD). Terminal master's awarded for partial completion of doctoral program. *Degree requirements:* For master's, thesis or alternative; for doctorate, thesis/dissertation. *Entrance requirements:* For master's and doctorate, GRE General Test. Additional exam requirements/recommendations for international students: Required—TOEFL. Electronic applications accepted. *Faculty research:* Latin American and Iberian literatures and languages, Spanish and comparative literature.

Washington University in St. Louis, Graduate School of Arts and Sciences, Program in Comparative Literature, St. Louis, MO 63130-4899. Offers PhD. Terminal master's awarded for partial completion of doctoral program. *Degree requirements:* For doctorate, thesis/dissertation. *Entrance requirements:* For doctorate, GRE General Test. Additional exam requirements/recommendations for international students: Required—TOEFL. Electronic applications accepted. *Faculty research:* World literature; literary theory; translation studies; global and multicultural theory; comparative drama; comparative arts; studies in literature, politics and society; narrative theory; media ecologies, histories, and poetics.

Wayne State University, College of Liberal Arts and Sciences, Department of English, Program in Comparative Literature, Detroit, MI 48202. Offers MA. *Students:* 1 (woman) full-time. Average age 39. 1 applicant. *Degree requirements:* For master's, one foreign language, essay or thesis. *Entrance requirements:* For master's, GRE General Test, minimum GPA of 3.25 in English, 3.0 overall. Additional exam requirements/recommendations for international students: Required—TOEFL (minimum score 550 paper-based); Recommended—TWE (minimum score 6). *Application deadline:* For fall admission, 7/1 for domestic students, 6/1 for international students; for winter admission, 10/1 for international students; for spring admission, 2/1 for international students. Application fee: $30 ($50 for international students). Electronic applications accepted. *Expenses:* Tuition, state resident: full-time $10,294; part-time $571.90 per credit hour. Tuition, nonresident: full-time $29,730; part-time $1238.75 per credit hour. *Required fees:* $1365; $43.50 per credit hour. $291.10 per semester. Tuition and fees vary according to course load and program. *Financial support:* Application deadline: 3/1. *Unit head:* Dr. Richard Grusin, Chair, 313-577-7692, Fax: 313-577-8618, E-mail: aj4671@wayne.edu. *Application contact:* Ross Pudaloff, Graduate Director, 313-577-7699, E-mail: r.pudaloff@wayne.edu.

Western Kentucky University, Graduate Studies, Potter College of Arts and Letters, Department of English, Bowling Green, KY 42101. Offers education (MA); English (MA Ed); literature (MA), including American literature, British literature, literary theory, women writers, world literature; teaching English as a second language (MA); writing (MA). Part-time and evening/weekend programs available. *Degree requirements:* For master's, comprehensive exam, thesis optional, final exam. *Entrance requirements:* For master's, GRE General Test, minimum GPA of 2.75. Additional exam requirements/recommendations for international students: Required—TOEFL (minimum score 555 paper-based; 79 iBT). *Faculty research:* Improving writing, linking teacher knowledge and performance, Victorian women writers, Kentucky women writers, Kentucky poets.

Yale University, Graduate School of Arts and Sciences, Department of Comparative Literature, New Haven, CT 06520. Offers PhD. *Degree requirements:* For doctorate, 2 foreign languages, thesis/dissertation. *Entrance requirements:* For doctorate, GRE General Test.

English

Abilene Christian University, Graduate School, College of Arts and Sciences, Department of English, Abilene, TX 79699-9100. Offers composition/rhetoric (MA); literature (MA); writing (MA). Part-time programs available. *Faculty:* 17 part-time/adjunct (7 women). *Students:* 12 full-time (6 women), 7 part-time (6 women); includes 2 minority (both Hispanic/Latino), 1 international. 20 applicants, 45% accepted, 7 enrolled. In 2014, 4 master's awarded. *Degree requirements:* For master's, one foreign language, comprehensive exam (for some programs), thesis (for some programs). *Entrance requirements:* For master's, GRE General Test. Additional exam requirements/recommendations for international students: Required—TOEFL (minimum score 550 paper-based; 90 iBT), IELTS (minimum score 6.5), PTE. *Application deadline:* For fall admission, 4/1 priority date for domestic students; for spring admission, 11/1 for domestic students. Applications are processed on a rolling basis. Application fee: $50. Electronic applications accepted. *Expenses: Tuition:* Full-time $18,228; part-time $1016 per credit hour. *Financial support:* In 2014–15, 14 students received support, including 6 teaching assistantships with partial tuition reimbursements available (averaging $5,800 per year); Federal Work-Study also available. Support available to part-time students. Financial award application deadline: 4/1; financial award applicants required to submit FAFSA. *Faculty research:* Feminism, Shakespearean dimensions of new literature, poetic consciousness, deconstruction myths. *Unit head:* Dr. Dana McMichael, Graduate Director, 325-674-2083, Fax: 325-674-2408, E-mail: dana.mcmichael@acu.edu. *Application contact:* Corey Patterson, Director of Graduate Admission and Recruiting, 325-674-6566, Fax: 325-674-6717, E-mail: gradinfo@acu.edu.

Acadia University, Faculty of Arts, Department of English, Wolfville, NS B4P 2R6, Canada. Offers MA. *Degree requirements:* For master's, thesis. *Entrance requirements:* For master's, honors degree in English, minimum A- average. Additional exam requirements/recommendations for international students: Required—TOEFL (minimum score 630 paper-based; 93 iBT), IELTS (minimum score 6.5). *Faculty research:* Renaissance, Canadian, medieval, Victorian, and Romantic literature.

The American University in Cairo, School of Humanities and Social Sciences, Department of English and Comparative Literature, Cairo, Egypt. Offers comparative literary studies (Graduate Diploma); English and comparative literature (MA). Part-time programs available. *Degree requirements:* For master's, thesis, proficiency in French or German. *Entrance requirements:* Additional exam requirements/recommendations for international students: Required—English entrance exam and/or TOEFL. Tuition and fees vary according to course load and program.

American University of Beirut, Graduate Programs, Faculty of Arts and Sciences, Beirut, Lebanon. Offers anthropology (MA); Arab and Middle Eastern history (PhD); Arabic language and literature (MA, PhD); archaeology (MA); biology (MS); cell and molecular biology (PhD); chemistry (MS); clinical psychology (MA); computational sciences (MS); computer science (MS); economics (MA); English language (MA); English literature (MA); environmental policy planning (MS); financial economics (MAFE); geology (MS); history (MA); mathematics (MA, MS); media studies (MA); Middle Eastern studies (MA); physics (MS); political studies (MA); psychology (MA); public administration (MA); sociology (MA); statistics (MA, MS); theoretical physics (PhD); transnational American studies (MA). Part-time programs available. *Faculty:* 107

full-time (32 women), 6 part-time/adjunct (2 women). *Students:* 230 full-time (161 women), 209 part-time (146 women). Average age 26. 261 applicants, 70% accepted, 83 enrolled. In 2014, 68 master's, 2 doctorates awarded. *Degree requirements:* For master's, one foreign language, comprehensive exam, thesis (for some programs); for doctorate, one foreign language, comprehensive exam, thesis/dissertation. *Entrance requirements:* For master's, GRE (for some MA/MS programs), letter of recommendation; for doctorate, GRE, letters of recommendation. Additional exam requirements/recommendations for international students: Required—TOEFL (minimum score 600 paper-based; 97 iBT), IELTS (minimum score 7). *Application deadline:* For fall admission, 4/1 for domestic and international students; for spring admission, 11/1 for domestic and international students. Application fee: $50. Electronic applications accepted. *Expenses: Tuition:* Full-time $15,462; part-time $859 per credit. *Required fees:* $692. Tuition and fees vary according to course load and program. *Financial support:* Research assistantships, career-related internships or fieldwork, institutionally sponsored loans, scholarships/grants, health care benefits, and unspecified assistantships available. Financial award application deadline: 2/4; financial award applicants required to submit FAFSA. *Faculty research:* Determinants of language proficiency among Arab learners of English as a foreign language; opinion mining, information retrieval, runtime verification, high performance computing; solar and fuel cells, self-organizing systems, heterocyclic chemistry, air and water chemistry; complex analysis, harmonic analysis, number theory; social and political psychology, clinical psychology; thin films physics and technology; theory of soft matter; religious and ethnic conflict; sports and politics. *Total annual research expenditures:* $966,000. *Unit head:* Dr. Patrick McGreevy, Dean, 961-1374374 Ext. 3800, Fax: 961-1744461, E-mail: pm07@aub.edu.lb. *Application contact:* Dr. Salim Kanaan, Director, Admissions Office, 961-1350000 Ext. 2590, Fax: 961-1750775, E-mail: sk00@aub.edu.lb.
Website: http://www.aub.edu.lb/fas/

Andrews University, School of Graduate Studies, College of Arts and Sciences, Department of English, Berrien Springs, MI 49104. Offers MA, MAT. Part-time programs available. *Faculty:* 12 full-time (5 women), 1 (woman) part-time/adjunct. *Students:* 3 full-time (2 women), 8 part-time (6 women); includes 1 minority (Hispanic/Latino), 2 international. Average age 32. 8 applicants, 63% accepted, 2 enrolled. In 2014, 7 master's awarded. *Degree requirements:* For master's, one foreign language, thesis optional. *Entrance requirements:* For master's, GRE Subject Test. Additional exam requirements/recommendations for international students: Required—TOEFL (minimum score 550 paper-based). *Application deadline:* For fall admission, 8/15 for domestic students. Applications are processed on a rolling basis. Application fee: $40. Tuition and fees vary according to course level. *Financial support:* Fellowships, research assistantships, teaching assistantships, career-related internships or fieldwork, and Federal Work-Study available. *Faculty research:* Christianity and literature, Victorian literature, social linguistics, rhetoric, American literature. *Unit head:* Dr. Douglas Jones, Chairperson, 269-471-3298. *Application contact:* Monica Wringer, Supervisor of Graduate Admission, 800-253-2874, Fax: 269-471-6321, E-mail: graduate@andrews.edu.

Angelo State University, College of Graduate Studies, College of Arts and Sciences, Department of English, San Angelo, TX 76909. Offers MA. Part-time and evening/weekend programs available. *Degree requirements:* For master's, comprehensive exam. *Entrance requirements:* For master's, essay. Additional exam requirements/recommendations for international students: Required—TOEFL or IELTS. Electronic applications accepted.

Appalachian State University, Cratis D. Williams Graduate School, Department of English, Boone, NC 28608. Offers English (MA); English education (MA). Part-time programs available. Postbaccalaureate distance learning degree programs offered (no on-campus study). *Degree requirements:* For master's, one foreign language, comprehensive exam, thesis (for some programs). *Entrance requirements:* For master's, GRE General Test, 3 letters of recommendation. Additional exam requirements/recommendations for international students: Required—TOEFL (minimum score 570 paper-based; 79 iBT), IELTS (minimum score 6.5). Electronic applications accepted. *Faculty research:* Contemporary Irish literature, Romantic psychology, cultural practices of everyday life, Gullah linguistics, Renaissance women's writing.

Arcadia University, Graduate Studies, Department of English, Glenside, PA 19038-3295. Offers MAE. Part-time and evening/weekend programs available. *Degree requirements:* For master's, thesis optional. *Expenses:* Contact institution.

Arizona State University at the Tempe campus, College of Liberal Arts and Sciences, Department of English, Tempe, AZ 85287-0302. Offers applied linguistics (PhD); creative writing (MFA); English (MA, PhD), including comparative literature (MA), linguistics (MA), literature, rhetoric and composition (MA), rhetoric, composition, and linguistics (PhD); film and media studies (MAS), including American media and popular culture; linguistics (Graduate Certificate); teaching English to speakers of other languages (MTESOL); translation studies (Graduate Certificate). Terminal master's awarded for partial completion of doctoral program. *Degree requirements:* For master's, variable foreign language requirement, comprehensive exam (for some programs), thesis (for some programs), interactive Program of Study (iPOS) submitted before completing 50 percent of required credit hours; for doctorate, variable foreign language requirement, comprehensive exam, thesis/dissertation, interactive Program of Study (iPOS) submitted before completing 50 percent of required credit hours. *Entrance requirements:* For master's and doctorate, GRE, minimum GPA of 3.0 or equivalent in last 2 years of work leading to bachelor's degree. Additional exam requirements/recommendations for international students: Required—TOEFL, IELTS, or PTE. Electronic applications accepted.

Arkansas State University, Graduate School, College of Humanities and Social Sciences, Department of English and Philosophy, State University, AR 72467. Offers English (MA); English education (MSE, SCCT). Part-time programs available. *Faculty:* 19 full-time (6 women). *Students:* 9 full-time (2 women), 19 part-time (11 women); includes 1 minority (Black or African American, non-Hispanic/Latino). Average age 28. 31 applicants, 65% accepted, 15 enrolled. In 2014, 9 master's awarded. *Degree requirements:* For master's, variable foreign language requirement, comprehensive exam, thesis or alternative, preliminary exam; for SCCT, comprehensive exam. *Entrance requirements:* For master's, GRE General Test or MAT, appropriate bachelor's degree, official transcript, valid teaching certificate (for MSE), immunization records; for SCCT, GRE General Test or MAT, interview, master's degree, official transcript, immunization records. Additional exam requirements/recommendations for international students: Required—TOEFL (minimum score 550 paper-based; 79 iBT), IELTS (minimum score 6), PTE (minimum score 56). *Application deadline:* For fall admission, 7/1 for domestic and international students; for spring admission, 11/15 for domestic students, 11/14 for international students. Applications are processed on a rolling basis. Application fee: $30 ($40 for international students). Electronic applications accepted. *Expenses:* Tuition, state resident: full-time $4392; part-time $244 per credit hour. Tuition, nonresident: full-time $8784; part-time $488 per credit hour. *International tuition:* $9484 full-time. *Required fees:* $1134; $63 per credit hour. $25 per term. Tuition and fees vary according to course load and program. *Financial support:* In 2014–15, 1 student received support. Teaching assistantships, career-related internships or fieldwork, scholarships/grants, and unspecified assistantships available. Financial award application deadline: 7/1; financial award applicants required to submit FAFSA. *Unit head:* Dr. Janelle Collins, Chair, 870-972-3043, Fax: 870-972-3045, E-mail: jcollins@astate.edu. *Application contact:* Vickey Ring, Graduate Admissions Coordinator, 870-972-3029, Fax: 870-972-3857, E-mail: vickeyring@astate.edu.
Website: http://www.astate.edu/college/humanities-and-social-sciences/departments/english-and-philosophy

Arkansas Tech University, College of Arts and Humanities, Russellville, AR 72801. Offers English (M Ed, MA); history (MA); liberal arts (MLA); multi-media journalism (MA); psychology (MS); teaching English as a second language (MA). Part-time programs available. *Students:* 70 full-time (39 women), 105 part-time (72 women); includes 20 minority (3 Black or African American, non-Hispanic/Latino; 2 American Indian or Alaska Native, non-Hispanic/Latino; 1 Asian, non-Hispanic/Latino; 10 Hispanic/Latino; 4 Two or more races, non-Hispanic/Latino), 51 international. Average age 30. In 2014, 63 master's awarded. *Degree requirements:* For master's, comprehensive exam (for some programs), thesis (for some programs), project. *Entrance requirements:* For master's, GRE General Test or GMAT. Additional exam requirements/recommendations for international students: Required—TOEFL (minimum score 550 paper-based; 79 iBT), IELTS (minimum score 6). *Application deadline:* For fall admission, 3/1 priority date for domestic students, 5/1 priority date for international students; for spring admission, 10/1 priority date for domestic and international students. Applications are processed on a rolling basis. Application fee: $25 ($75 for international students). Electronic applications accepted. *Expenses:* Tuition, state resident: full-time $6264; part-time $261 per credit hour. Tuition, nonresident: full-time $12,528; part-time $522 per credit hour. *Required fees:* $423 per semester. Tuition and fees vary according to course load. *Financial support:* In 2014–15, research assistantships with full tuition reimbursements (averaging $4,800 per year), teaching assistantships with full tuition reimbursements (averaging $4,800 per year) were awarded; career-related internships or fieldwork, Federal Work-Study, scholarships/grants, health care benefits, and unspecified assistantships also available. Support available to part-time students. Financial award application deadline: 4/15; financial award applicants required to submit FAFSA. *Unit head:* Dr. Jeffrey Woods, Dean, 479-968-0274, Fax: 479-964-0812, E-mail: jwoods@atu.edu. *Application contact:* Dr. Mary B. Gunter, Dean of Graduate College, 479-968-0398, Fax: 479-964-0542, E-mail: gradcollege@atu.edu.
Website: http://www.atu.edu/humanities/

Asbury University, School of Graduate and Professional Studies, Wilmore, KY 40390-1198. Offers biology: alternative certificate (MA Ed); chemistry: alternative certificate (MA Ed); English (MA Ed); English as a second language (MA Ed); ESL (MA Ed); French (MA Ed); Latin: alternative certificate (MA Ed); mathematics: alternative certificate (MA Ed); reading/writing endorsement (MA Ed); social studies (MA Ed); social work (MSW), including child and family services; Spanish (MA Ed); special education (MA Ed); special education: alternative certificate (MA Ed); teacher as leader endorsement (MA Ed). *Accreditation:* NCATE. Part-time programs available. *Degree requirements:* For master's, action research project, portfolio. *Entrance requirements:* For master's, PRAXIS/NTE, minimum GPA of 2.75, letters of recommendation. Additional exam requirements/recommendations for international students: Required—TOEFL (minimum score 550 paper-based). Electronic applications accepted.

Auburn University, Graduate School, College of Liberal Arts, Department of English, Auburn University, AL 36849. Offers English (MA, PhD); technical communication (MTPC). Part-time programs available. *Faculty:* 40 full-time (20 women), 24 part-time/adjunct (14 women). *Students:* 31 full-time (20 women), 45 part-time (30 women); includes 6 minority (5 Black or African American, non-Hispanic/Latino; 1 Hispanic/Latino). Average age 28. 90 applicants, 43% accepted, 18 enrolled. In 2014, 25 master's, 4 doctorates, 1 other advanced degree awarded. *Degree requirements:* For master's, one foreign language, thesis optional, written exam; for doctorate, 2 foreign languages, thesis/dissertation, oral and written exams. *Entrance requirements:* For master's, GRE General Test, sample of written work; for doctorate, GRE General Test, GRE Subject Test, sample of written work. *Application deadline:* For fall admission, 7/7 for domestic students; for spring admission, 11/24 for domestic students. Applications are processed on a rolling basis. Application fee: $50 ($60 for international students). Electronic applications accepted. *Expenses:* Tuition, state resident: full-time $8586; part-time $477 per credit hour. Tuition, nonresident: full-time $25,758; part-time $1431 per credit hour. *Required fees:* $804 per semester. Tuition and fees vary according to degree level and program. *Financial support:* Fellowships, teaching assistantships, and Federal Work-Study available. Support available to part-time students. Financial award application deadline: 3/15; financial award applicants required to submit FAFSA. *Faculty research:* English literature, American literature, linguistics, rhetoric and composition, literary theory. *Unit head:* Dr. Jeremy M. Downes, Chair, 334-844-9079. *Application contact:* Dr. George Flowers, Dean of the Graduate School, 334-844-2125.

Austin Peay State University, College of Graduate Studies, College of Arts and Letters, Department of Languages and Literature, Clarksville, TN 37044. Offers English (MA). Part-time programs available. Postbaccalaureate distance learning degree programs offered (minimal on-campus study). *Degree requirements:* For master's, comprehensive exam, thesis optional. *Entrance requirements:* For master's, GRE General Test, 3 letters of recommendation. Additional exam requirements/recommendations for international students: Required—TOEFL (minimum score 500 paper-based). Electronic applications accepted. *Faculty research:* American literature, British literature, linguistics, composition, technical writing.

Ball State University, Graduate School, College of Sciences and Humanities, Department of English, Muncie, IN 47306-1099. Offers English (MA, PhD), including composition, creative writing (MA), general (MA), literature; linguistics (MA, PhD), including English (PhD), linguistics (MA); linguistics and teaching English to speakers of other languages (MA); teaching English to speakers of other languages (MA). *Faculty:* 18 full-time (11 women). *Students:* 42 full-time (28 women), 31 part-time (18 women); includes 4 minority (1 Black or African American, non-Hispanic/Latino; 1 Hispanic/Latino; 2 Two or more races, non-Hispanic/Latino), 21 international. Average age 29. 98 applicants, 43% accepted, 24 enrolled. In 2014, 23 master's, 10 doctorates awarded. *Degree requirements:* For doctorate, variable foreign language requirement, thesis/dissertation. *Entrance requirements:* For master's, GRE General Test, writing sample; for doctorate, GRE General Test, GRE Subject Test, minimum graduate GPA of 3.2, writing sample. Application fee: $25 ($35 for international students). *Financial support:* In 2014–15, 58 students received support, including 3 research assistantships with partial tuition reimbursements available (averaging $10,858 per year), 34 teaching assistantships with partial tuition reimbursements available (averaging $15,539 per year); unspecified assistantships also available. Financial award application deadline: 3/1. *Faculty research:* American literature; literary editing; medieval, Renaissance, and eighteenth-century British literature; rhetoric. *Unit head:* Dr. Elizabeth Riddle, Chairperson, 765-285-8580, Fax: 765-285-3765, E-mail: emriddle@bsu.edu. *Application contact:* Dr. Jill Christman, Assistant Chair, 765-285-8415, E-mail: jcchristman@bsu.edu.
Website: http://www.bsu.edu/english/

Baylor University, Graduate School, College of Arts and Sciences, Department of English, Waco, TX 76798. Offers MA, PhD. Part-time programs available. Terminal master's awarded for partial completion of doctoral program. *Degree requirements:* For

master's, one foreign language, comprehensive exam, thesis (for some programs); for doctorate, 2 foreign languages, comprehensive exam, thesis/dissertation. *Entrance requirements:* For master's and doctorate, GRE General Test, 18 hours of upper-level course work in English. Additional exam requirements/recommendations for international students: Required—TOEFL. Electronic applications accepted. *Faculty research:* Nineteenth-century British literature, Renaissance studies, American studies, medieval studies, rhetoric and composition.

Belmont University, College of Liberal Arts and Social Sciences, Nashville, TN 37212-3757. Offers education (M Ed); English (MA); special education (MA); sport administration (MSA); teaching (MAT). Part-time and evening/weekend programs available. *Students:* 151 full-time (100 women), 65 part-time (53 women); includes 26 minority (9 Black or African American, non-Hispanic/Latino; 1 Asian, non-Hispanic/Latino; 8 Hispanic/Latino; 8 Two or more races, non-Hispanic/Latino), 3 international. Average age 29. *Degree requirements:* For master's, comprehensive exam (for some programs), thesis (for some programs). *Entrance requirements:* For master's, GRE, GMAT, MAT. Additional exam requirements/recommendations for international students: Required—TOEFL. *Application deadline:* For fall admission, 8/1 for domestic students; for spring admission, 12/1 for domestic students. Applications are processed on a rolling basis. Application fee: $50. Electronic applications accepted. *Expenses:* Expenses: Contact institution. *Financial support:* Fellowships with partial tuition reimbursements, teaching assistantships with partial tuition reimbursements, Federal Work-Study, institutionally sponsored loans, scholarships/grants, tuition waivers (partial), and unspecified assistantships available. Financial award application deadline: 4/15; financial award applicants required to submit FAFSA. *Unit head:* Dr. Bryce Sullivan, Dean, 615-460-6437, Fax: 615-385-5084, E-mail: bryce.sullivan@belmont.edu. *Application contact:* David Mee, Dean of Enrollment Services, 615-460-6785, Fax: 615-460-5434, E-mail: david.mee@belmont.edu.

Bemidji State University, School of Graduate Studies, Bemidji, MN 56601. Offers biology (MS); education (MS); English (MA, MS); environmental studies (MS); mathematics (MS); mathematics (elementary and middle level education) (MS); special education (M Sp Ed). Part-time programs available. Postbaccalaureate distance learning degree programs offered (no on-campus study). *Faculty:* 117 full-time (53 women), 20 part-time/adjunct (15 women). *Students:* 23 full-time (12 women), 144 part-time (92 women); includes 16 minority (2 Black or African American, non-Hispanic/Latino; 2 American Indian or Alaska Native, non-Hispanic/Latino; 4 Asian, non-Hispanic/Latino; 5 Hispanic/Latino; 3 Two or more races, non-Hispanic/Latino), 1 international. Average age 35. 103 applicants, 98% accepted, 69 enrolled. In 2014, 59 master's awarded. *Degree requirements:* For master's, comprehensive exam, thesis (for some programs). *Entrance requirements:* For master's, GRE; GMAT, letters of recommendation, letters of interest. Additional exam requirements/recommendations for international students: Required—TOEFL (minimum score 550 paper-based; 80 iBT). *Application deadline:* Applications are processed on a rolling basis. Application fee: $20. Electronic applications accepted. *Expenses:* Expenses: Contact institution. *Financial support:* In 2014–15, 16 research assistantships with partial tuition reimbursements (averaging $13,012 per year), 18 teaching assistantships with partial tuition reimbursements (averaging $13,012 per year) were awarded; scholarships/grants and unspecified assistantships also available. Financial award application deadline: 3/31; financial award applicants required to submit FAFSA. *Faculty research:* Human performance, sport, and health: physical education teacher education, continuum models, spiritual health, intellectual health, resiliency, health priorities; psychology: health psychology, college student drinking behavior, micro-aggressions, infant cognition, false memories, leadership assessment; biology: structure and dynamics of forest communities, aquatic and riverine ecology, interaction between animal populations and aquatic environments, cellular motility. *Unit head:* Dr. Martin Tadlock, Provost/Vice President of Academic Affairs, 218-755-2015, Fax: 218-755-2258, E-mail: mtadlock@bemidjistate.edu. *Application contact:* Joan Miller, Director, School of Graduate Studies, 218-755-2027, Fax: 218-755-2258, E-mail: jmiller@bemidjistate.edu.
Website: http://www.bemidjistate.edu/academics/graduate-studies/

Bennington College, Graduate Programs, The Bennington Writing Seminars, Bennington, VT 05201. Offers creative writing (MFA). Postbaccalaureate distance learning degree programs offered (minimal on-campus study). *Degree requirements:* For master's, thesis, collection of essays or poems, or collection of short stories and/or a novel. *Entrance requirements:* For master's, manuscript. *Expenses:* Contact institution.

Binghamton University, State University of New York, Graduate School, School of Arts and Sciences, Department of English, Vestal, NY 13850. Offers creative writing (MA); English (PhD); English/American literature (MA). Part-time programs available. *Faculty:* 28 full-time (16 women), 30 part-time/adjunct (18 women). *Students:* 39 full-time (22 women), 50 part-time (27 women); includes 11 minority (2 Black or African American, non-Hispanic/Latino; 1 Asian, non-Hispanic/Latino; 4 Hispanic/Latino; 4 Native Hawaiian or other Pacific Islander, non-Hispanic/Latino), 11 international. Average age 33. 90 applicants, 58% accepted, 19 enrolled. In 2014, 13 master's, 15 doctorates awarded. Terminal master's awarded for partial completion of doctoral program. *Degree requirements:* For master's, one foreign language, thesis; for doctorate, one foreign language, comprehensive exam, thesis/dissertation. *Entrance requirements:* For master's and doctorate, GRE General Test, writing sample. Additional exam requirements/recommendations for international students: Required—TOEFL (minimum score 550 paper-based; 80 iBT). *Application deadline:* For fall admission, 2/15 priority date for domestic and international students; for spring admission, 11/15 priority date for domestic and international students. Applications are processed on a rolling basis. Application fee: $75. Electronic applications accepted. *Expenses:* Tuition, state resident: full-time $7776; part-time $432 per credit. Tuition, nonresident: full-time $15,138; part-time $841 per credit. *Required fees:* $1754; $213 per credit. Tuition and fees vary according to degree level and program. *Financial support:* In 2014–15, 42 students received support, including 1 fellowship with full tuition reimbursement available (averaging $15,000 per year), 1 research assistantship (averaging $9,000 per year), 30 teaching assistantships with full tuition reimbursements available (averaging $15,000 per year); career-related internships or fieldwork, Federal Work-Study, institutionally sponsored loans, scholarships/grants, health care benefits, tuition waivers (full and partial), and unspecified assistantships also available. Financial award application deadline: 2/15; financial award applicants required to submit FAFSA. *Unit head:* Dr. Robert Micklus, Chairperson, 607-777-2169, E-mail: rmicklus@binghamton.edu. *Application contact:* Kishan Zuber, Recruiting and Admissions Coordinator, 607-777-2151, Fax: 607-777-2501, E-mail: kzuber@binghamton.edu.
Website: http://www2.binghamton.edu/english/

Bob Jones University, Graduate Programs, Greenville, SC 29614. Offers accountancy (MS); Bible (MA); Bible translation (MA); Biblical studies (Certificate); broadcast management (MS); business administration (MBA); church history (MA, PhD); church ministries (MA); church music (MM); cinema and video production (MA); counseling (MS); curriculum and instruction (Ed D); divinity (M Div); dramatic production (MA); educational leadership (MS, Ed D, Ed S); elementary education (M Ed, MAT); English (M Ed, MA, MAT); fine arts (MA); graphic design (MA); history (M Ed, MA); illustration (MA); interpretative speech (MA); mathematics (M Ed, MAT); medical missions (Certificate); ministry (MM, D Min); multi-categorical special education (M Ed, MAT); music (M Ed); New Testament interpretation (PhD); Old Testament interpretation (PhD); orchestral instrument performance (MM); organ performance (MM); pastoral studies (MA); personnel services (MS, Ed S); piano pedagogy (MM); piano performance (MM); platform arts (MA); radio and television broadcasting (MS); rhetoric and public address (MA); secondary education (M Ed); studio art (MA); teaching Bible (MA); theology (MA, PhD); voice performance (MM); youth ministries (MA); M Div/MM.

Boise State University, College of Arts and Sciences, Department of English, Boise, ID 83725-0399. Offers creative writing (MFA); English (MA); technical communication (MA). Part-time programs available. *Faculty:* 34 full-time, 14 part-time/adjunct. *Students:* 45 full-time (29 women), 29 part-time (17 women); includes 8 minority (1 Black or African American, non-Hispanic/Latino; 2 Asian, non-Hispanic/Latino; 5 Hispanic/Latino). Average age 37. 200 applicants, 97% accepted, 25 enrolled. In 2014, 30 master's awarded. *Degree requirements:* For master's, thesis. *Entrance requirements:* For master's, GRE, minimum GPA of 3.0. *Application deadline:* For fall admission, 7/17 priority date for domestic students; for spring admission, 12/5 priority date for domestic students. Applications are processed on a rolling basis. Application fee: $55. Electronic applications accepted. *Expenses:* Tuition, state resident: part-time $331 per credit hour. Tuition, nonresident: part-time $531 per credit hour. *Financial support:* In 2014–15, 31 teaching assistantships with full tuition reimbursements (averaging $9,368 per year) were awarded; research assistantships with full tuition reimbursements, career-related internships or fieldwork, Federal Work-Study, institutionally sponsored loans, and unspecified assistantships also available. Support available to part-time students. Financial award application deadline: 3/1. *Unit head:* Dr. Michelle Payne, Chair, 208-426-3426, Fax: 208-426-4373, E-mail: mpayne@boisestate.edu. *Application contact:* Linda Platt, Supervisor, Graduate Admission and Degree Services, 208-426-1074, E-mail: lplatt@boisestate.edu.
Website: http://english.boisestate.edu/graduate-programs/

Boston College, Graduate School of Arts and Sciences, Department of English, Chestnut Hill, MA 02467-3800. Offers MA, PhD. *Faculty:* 44 full-time. *Students:* 76 full-time (56 women); includes 6 minority (3 Asian, non-Hispanic/Latino; 2 Hispanic/Latino; 1 Two or more races, non-Hispanic/Latino), 6 international. 195 applicants, 52% accepted, 27 enrolled. In 2014, 23 master's, 6 doctorates awarded. Terminal master's awarded for partial completion of doctoral program. *Degree requirements:* For master's, one foreign language, thesis optional; for doctorate, 2 foreign languages, thesis/dissertation. *Entrance requirements:* For master's and doctorate, GRE General Test, GRE Subject Test. Additional exam requirements/recommendations for international students: Required—TOEFL (minimum score 600 paper-based; 100 iBT). *Application deadline:* For fall admission, 1/2 priority date for domestic students, 1/2 for international students. Application fee: $75. Electronic applications accepted. *Financial support:* In 2014–15, fellowships with full tuition reimbursements (averaging $20,500 per year), teaching assistantships with full tuition reimbursements (averaging $20,500 per year) were awarded; Federal Work-Study, scholarships/grants, health care benefits, tuition waivers (full and partial), and unspecified assistantships also available. Support available to part-time students. Financial award application deadline: 3/1; financial award applicants required to submit FAFSA. *Faculty research:* English and American literature, Irish literature, British literature, early modern and modern literature, critical theory. *Unit head:* Dr. Mary Crane, Chairperson, 617-552-3701, E-mail: mary.crane@bc.edu. *Application contact:* Dr. Min Song, Graduate Program Director, 617-552-3701, E-mail: min.song@bc.edu.
Website: http://www.bc.edu/english

Boston University, Graduate School of Arts and Sciences, Department of English, Boston, MA 02215. Offers MA, PhD. *Students:* 44 full-time (24 women), 2 part-time (both women); includes 5 minority (2 Asian, non-Hispanic/Latino; 3 Hispanic/Latino), 3 international. Average age 29. 257 applicants, 24% accepted, 10 enrolled. In 2014, 17 master's, 4 doctorates awarded. Terminal master's awarded for partial completion of doctoral program. *Degree requirements:* For master's, one foreign language, thesis; for doctorate, 2 foreign languages, comprehensive exam, thesis/dissertation, qualifying/oral exam. *Entrance requirements:* For master's and doctorate, GRE General Test, GRE Subject Test, sample of written work, 2 letters of recommendation. Additional exam requirements/recommendations for international students: Required—TOEFL (minimum score 550 paper-based; 84 iBT). *Application deadline:* For fall admission, 1/15 for domestic and international students. Application fee: $80. Electronic applications accepted. *Expenses: Tuition:* Full-time $45,686; part-time $1428 per credit hour. *Required fees:* $660; $60 per semester. Tuition and fees vary according to program. *Financial support:* In 2014–15, 43 students received support, including 5 fellowships with full tuition reimbursements available (averaging $20,500 per year), 24 teaching assistantships with full tuition reimbursements available (averaging $20,500 per year); research assistantships, Federal Work-Study, scholarships/grants, health care benefits, and unspecified assistantships also available. Financial award application deadline: 1/15. *Unit head:* Maurice Lee, Chairman, 617-353-2509, Fax: 617-353-3653, E-mail: molee@bu.edu. *Application contact:* Anne Austin, Administrative Assistant, 617-353-2509, Fax: 617-353-3653, E-mail: akaustin@bu.edu.
Website: http://www.bu.edu/english/

Bowie State University, Graduate Programs, Program in English, Bowie, MD 20715-9465. Offers MA. Part-time and evening/weekend programs available. *Faculty:* 9 full-time (4 women). *Students:* 8 full-time (3 women), 19 part-time (13 women); includes 20 minority (all Black or African American, non-Hispanic/Latino), 2 international. Average age 37. 8 applicants, 100% accepted, 5 enrolled. In 2014, 3 master's awarded. *Entrance requirements:* For master's, minimum GPA of 2.5, English degree. *Application deadline:* For fall admission, 4/1 priority date for domestic and international students; for spring admission, 11/1 priority date for domestic and international students. Applications are processed on a rolling basis. Electronic applications accepted. *Expenses:* Tuition, state resident: full-time $8928; part-time $372 per credit. Tuition, nonresident: full-time $16,176; part-time $674 per credit. *Required fees:* $2141. *Unit head:* Dr. Brenda DoHarris, Interim Chair, 301-860-3670, E-mail: bdoharris@bowiestate.edu. *Application contact:* Angela Issac, Information Contact, 301-860-4000.

Bowling Green State University, Graduate College, College of Arts and Sciences, Department of English, Program in English, Bowling Green, OH 43403. Offers English (MA, PhD); literature (MA); rhetoric and writing (PhD); scientific and technical communication (MA). Part-time programs available. *Degree requirements:* For master's, thesis or alternative; for doctorate, comprehensive exam, thesis/dissertation, foreign language or proficiency in Old English. *Entrance requirements:* For master's and doctorate, GRE General Test. Additional exam requirements/recommendations for international students: Required—TOEFL. Electronic applications accepted. *Faculty research:* Postmodern literary theory, rhetorical theory, ethnic American literature, literature and culture, composition pedagogy.

Bradley University, Graduate School, College of Liberal Arts and Sciences, Department of English, Peoria, IL 61625-0002. Offers MA. Part-time programs available. *Faculty:* 21 full-time (9 women). *Students:* 5 full-time (all women), 9 part-time (5 women); includes 2 minority (1 Black or African American, non-Hispanic/Latino; 1 Hispanic/Latino), 1 international. 18 applicants, 39% accepted, 5 enrolled. In 2014, 7 master's awarded. *Degree requirements:* For master's, comprehensive exam, thesis optional.

Entrance requirements: For master's, writing sample, 2 letters of recommendation. Additional exam requirements/recommendations for international students: Required—TOEFL (minimum score 550 paper-based; 79 iBT), IELTS (minimum score 6.5). *Application deadline:* For fall admission, 5/15 priority date for domestic and international students; for spring admission, 10/15 priority date for domestic and international students. Applications are processed on a rolling basis. Application fee: $40 ($50 for international students). Electronic applications accepted. *Expenses: Tuition:* Full-time $14,580; part-time $810 per credit. *Required fees:* $224. Full-time tuition and fees vary according to course load. *Financial support:* In 2014–15, 9 research assistantships with full and partial tuition reimbursements (averaging $9,820 per year) were awarded; teaching assistantships, scholarships/grants, tuition waivers (partial), and unspecified assistantships also available. Support available to part-time students. Financial award application deadline: 4/1. *Unit head:* Lee Newton, Chair, 309-677-2471, E-mail: lnewton@bradley.edu. *Application contact:* Kayla Carroll, Director of International Admissions and Student Services, 309-677-2375, E-mail: klcarroll@fsmail.bradley.edu.

Brandeis University, Graduate School of Arts and Sciences, Department of English, Waltham, MA 02454-9110. Offers English (MA, PhD); English and women's and gender studies (MA). Part-time programs available. *Degree requirements:* For master's, one foreign language, thesis or alternative; for doctorate, 2 foreign languages, thesis/dissertation, field exam, symposium presentation, prospectus defense. *Entrance requirements:* For master's and doctorate, resume, sample of work, 2 letters of recommendation, statement of purpose, transcript(s). Additional exam requirements/recommendations for international students: Required—TOEFL (minimum score 600 paper-based; 100 iBT); Recommended—IELTS (minimum score 7). Electronic applications accepted. *Faculty research:* Feminist and gender theory, American literature and post-Colonial theory, early modern (Renaissance) English literature, modernism, literature and science, literary theory and philosophy, contemporary poetry.

Bridgewater State University, College of Graduate Studies, School of Arts and Sciences, Department of English, Bridgewater, MA 02325-0001. Offers MA, MAT. Part-time and evening/weekend programs available. *Degree requirements:* For master's, one foreign language, comprehensive exam, thesis optional. *Entrance requirements:* For master's, GRE General Test.

Brigham Young University, Graduate Studies, College of Humanities, Department of English, Provo, UT 84602-1001. Offers creative writing (MFA); literature (MA); rhetoric/composition (MA). *Faculty:* 61 full-time (22 women). *Students:* 71 full-time (52 women), 5 part-time (all women). Average age 24. 71 applicants, 51% accepted, 31 enrolled. In 2014, 22 master's awarded. *Degree requirements:* For master's, thesis. *Entrance requirements:* For master's, GRE General Test, creative portfolio (for MFA). Additional exam requirements/recommendations for international students: Required—TOEFL (minimum score 213 paper-based). *Application deadline:* For fall admission, 1/15 for domestic and international students. Application fee: $50. Electronic applications accepted. *Expenses: Tuition:* Full-time $6310; part-time $371 per credit hour. Tuition and fees vary according to program and student's religious affiliation. *Financial support:* In 2014–15, 10 research assistantships (averaging $4,000 per year), 62 teaching assistantships (averaging $6,000 per year) were awarded; career-related internships or fieldwork, institutionally sponsored loans, scholarships/grants, and tuition waivers (partial) also available. Support available to part-time students. Financial award application deadline: 3/15. *Faculty research:* English literature, American literature, rhetoric, creative writing. *Unit head:* Prof. Phillip Snyder, Head, 801-422-2487, Fax: 801-422-0221, E-mail: phillip_snyder@byu.edu. *Application contact:* Lou Ann C. Crisler, Graduate Secretary, 801-422-8673, Fax: 801-422-0221, E-mail: louann_crisler@byu.edu.
Website: http://english.byu.edu/

Brock University, Faculty of Graduate Studies, Faculty of Humanities, Program in English, St. Catharines, ON L2S 3A1, Canada. Offers MA. Part-time programs available. *Degree requirements:* For master's, thesis optional. *Entrance requirements:* For master's, honours in English. Additional exam requirements/recommendations for international students: Required—TOEFL (minimum score 550 paper-based; 80 iBT), IELTS (minimum score 6.5), TWE (minimum score 4). Electronic applications accepted. *Faculty research:* Literary theory, Canadian literature, Milton and 17th century American literature, 19th century American literature, British Romantic literature and culture.

Brooklyn College of the City University of New York, School of Humanities and Social Sciences, Department of English, Brooklyn, NY 11210-2889. Offers creative writing (MFA), including fiction, playwriting, poetry; English (MA). Part-time and evening/weekend programs available. *Degree requirements:* For master's, one foreign language, comprehensive exam (for some programs), thesis (for some programs). *Entrance requirements:* For master's, advanced undergraduate courses in English, 2 letters of recommendation, writing sample, statement of purpose. Additional exam requirements/recommendations for international students: Required—TOEFL. Electronic applications accepted. *Faculty research:* Cultural studies, medieval literature, Virginia Woolf.

Brown University, Graduate School, Department of English, Providence, RI 02912. Offers English (PhD); literary arts (MFA). *Degree requirements:* For doctorate, thesis/dissertation. *Entrance requirements:* For master's and doctorate, GRE General Test, GRE Subject Test.

Bucknell University, Graduate Studies, College of Arts and Sciences, Department of English, Lewisburg, PA 17837. Offers MA. Part-time programs available. *Degree requirements:* For master's, one foreign language, thesis. *Entrance requirements:* For master's, GRE General Test, GRE Subject Test, minimum GPA of 3.0. Additional exam requirements/recommendations for international students: Required—TOEFL (minimum score 600 paper-based).

Buffalo State College, State University of New York, The Graduate School, Faculty of Arts and Humanities, Department of English, Buffalo, NY 14222-1095. Offers English (MA); secondary education (MS Ed), including English. Part-time and evening/weekend programs available. *Degree requirements:* For master's, thesis or project, 1 foreign language (MS Ed). *Entrance requirements:* For master's, minimum GPA of 2.75, 36 hours in English, New York teaching certificate (MS Ed). Additional exam requirements/recommendations for international students: Required—TOEFL (minimum score 550 paper-based).

Butler University, College of Liberal Arts and Sciences, Department of English, Indianapolis, IN 46208-3485. Offers creative writing (MFA); English (MA). Part-time and evening/weekend programs available. *Faculty:* 10 full-time (4 women), 2 part-time/adjunct (1 woman). *Students:* 6 full-time (3 women), 53 part-time (34 women); includes 6 minority (4 Black or African American, non-Hispanic/Latino; 1 Hispanic/Latino; 1 Two or more races, non-Hispanic/Latino), 2 international. Average age 36. 61 applicants, 61% accepted, 17 enrolled. In 2014, 16 master's awarded. *Entrance requirements:* For master's, GRE General Test, GRE Subject Test. Additional exam requirements/recommendations for international students: Required—TOEFL (minimum score 550 paper-based; 79 iBT), IELTS (minimum score 6). *Application deadline:* For fall admission, 8/15 priority date for domestic students. Applications are processed on a rolling basis. Application fee: $35. Electronic applications accepted. *Financial support:* Applicants required to submit FAFSA. *Unit head:* Dr. Lee Garver, Director of Graduate Studies, Department of English Language and Literature, 317-940-9859, E-mail:

lgarver@butler.edu. *Application contact:* Diane Dubord, Graduate Student Services Specialist, 317-940-8107, Fax: 317-940-8250, E-mail: ddubord@butler.edu.
Website: http://legacy.butler.edu/english/graduate-studies/ma-english/

California Baptist University, Program in English, Riverside, CA 92504-3206. Offers English pedagogy (MA); literature (MA); teaching English to speakers of other languages (TESOL) (MA). Part-time and evening/weekend programs available. *Faculty:* 9 full-time (5 women). *Students:* 2 full-time (both women), 18 part-time (14 women); includes 5 minority (1 Black or African American, non-Hispanic/Latino; 1 Asian, non-Hispanic/Latino; 3 Hispanic/Latino), 1 international. Average age 30. 8 applicants, 75% accepted, 4 enrolled. In 2014, 4 master's awarded. *Entrance requirements:* For master's, GRE for applicants with a GPA below 2.75 or CSET, minimum undergraduate GPA of 2.75; 18 semester hours of course work in English beyond freshman level; three recommendations; essay; demonstration of writing; interview. Additional exam requirements/recommendations for international students: Required—TOEFL (minimum score 80 iBT). *Application deadline:* For fall admission, 8/1 priority date for domestic students, 7/1 for international students; for spring admission, 12/1 priority date for domestic students, 11/1 for international students. Applications are processed on a rolling basis. Application fee: $45. Electronic applications accepted. *Expenses:* Expenses: Contact institution. *Financial support:* Institutionally sponsored loans available. Financial award applicants required to submit CSS PROFILE or FAFSA. *Faculty research:* Classical mythology and folklore, multicultural literature, genre studies, science fiction and fantasy literature, intercultural rhetoric. *Unit head:* Dr. Gayne Anacker, Dean, College of Arts and Sciences, 951-343-4682, E-mail: ganacker@calbaptist.edu. *Application contact:* Dr. Laura Veltman, Director, Master of Arts Program in English, 951-343-4276, Fax: 951-343-4661, E-mail: lveltman@calbaptist.edu.
Website: http://www.calbaptist.edu/maenglish/

California Polytechnic State University, San Luis Obispo, College of Liberal Arts, Department of English, San Luis Obispo, CA 93407. Offers MA. Part-time programs available. *Faculty:* 4 full-time (3 women). *Students:* 8 full-time (6 women), 14 part-time (9 women); includes 7 minority (1 Asian, non-Hispanic/Latino; 5 Hispanic/Latino; 1 Two or more races, non-Hispanic/Latino). Average age 27. 19 applicants, 84% accepted, 8 enrolled. In 2014, 9 master's awarded. *Degree requirements:* For master's, one foreign language, comprehensive exam. *Application deadline:* For fall admission, 6/1 for domestic students, 4/1 for international students; for winter admission, 11/1 for domestic students, 6/30 for international students; for spring admission, 2/1 for domestic students. Applications are processed on a rolling basis. Application fee: $55. *Expenses:* Tuition, state resident: full-time $6738; part-time $3906 per year. Tuition, nonresident: full-time $15,666; part-time $8370 per year. *Required fees:* $3447; $1001 per quarter. One-time fee: $3447 full-time; $3003 part-time. *Financial support:* Fellowships, teaching assistantships, career-related internships or fieldwork, Federal Work-Study, institutionally sponsored loans, and tutorships, writing laboratory assistantships available. Support available to part-time students. Financial award application deadline: 3/2; financial award applicants required to submit FAFSA. *Faculty research:* Feminist literary criticism, literary theory, British and American literature, linguistics, composition theory. *Unit head:* Dr. Paul Marchbanks, Graduate Coordinator, 805-756-2159, Fax: 805-756-6374, E-mail: pmarchba@calpoly.edu. *Application contact:* Dr. James Maraviglia, Associate Vice Provost for Marketing and Enrollment Development, 805-756-2311, Fax: 805-756-5400, E-mail: admissions@calpoly.edu.
Website: http://cla.calpoly.edu/engl.html

California State Polytechnic University, Pomona, Program in English, Pomona, CA 91768-2557. Offers MA. Part-time programs available. *Students:* 27 full-time (18 women), 46 part-time (36 women); includes 41 minority (2 Black or African American, non-Hispanic/Latino; 12 Asian, non-Hispanic/Latino; 25 Hispanic/Latino; 2 Two or more races, non-Hispanic/Latino), 3 international. Average age 30. 40 applicants, 83% accepted, 23 enrolled. In 2014, 15 master's awarded. *Degree requirements:* For master's, one foreign language, thesis or alternative. *Application deadline:* For fall admission, 5/1 priority date for domestic students; for winter admission, 10/15 priority date for domestic students; for spring admission, 1/20 priority date for domestic students. Applications are processed on a rolling basis. Application fee: $55. Electronic applications accepted. *Expenses:* Tuition, state resident: full-time $6738. Tuition, nonresident: full-time $12,300. *Required fees:* $1400. *Financial support:* In 2014–15, 2 fellowships were awarded; Federal Work-Study and institutionally sponsored loans also available. Support available to part-time students. Financial award application deadline: 3/2; financial award applicants required to submit FAFSA. *Unit head:* Dr. Aaron DeRosa, Graduate Coordinator, 909-869-3832, Fax: 909-869-4896, E-mail: amderosa@cpp.edu.
Website: http://www.cpp.edu/~efl/graduate.shtml

California State University, Bakersfield, Division of Graduate Studies, School of Arts and Humanities, Program in English, Bakersfield, CA 93311. Offers MA. *Degree requirements:* For master's, comprehensive exam or thesis. *Entrance requirements:* For master's, GRE General Test, GRE Subject Test (literature), minimum GPA of 2.5 for last 90 quarter units. Additional exam requirements/recommendations for international students: Required—TOEFL (minimum score 550 paper-based).

California State University, Chico, Office of Graduate Studies, College of Humanities and Fine Arts, English Department, Program in English, Chico, CA 95929-0722. Offers MA. *Faculty:* 11 full-time (5 women), 1 part-time/adjunct (0 women). *Students:* 14 full-time (8 women), 14 part-time (8 women); includes 4 minority (all Hispanic/Latino), 2 international. Average age 31. 12 applicants, 67% accepted, 8 enrolled. In 2014, 11 master's awarded. *Degree requirements:* For master's, thesis, project. *Entrance requirements:* For master's, GRE General Test, two letters of recommendation, statement of purpose, writing sample. Additional exam requirements/recommendations for international students: Required—TOEFL (minimum score 550 paper-based; 80 iBT), IELTS (minimum score 6.5), PTE (minimum score 59). *Application deadline:* For fall admission, 3/1 for domestic and international students; for spring admission, 9/15 for domestic and international students. Application fee: $55. Electronic applications accepted. *Expenses:* Tuition, state resident: full-time $7002. Tuition, nonresident: full-time $18,162. *Required fees:* $1530. Tuition and fees vary according to program. *Financial support:* Unspecified assistantships available. Financial award application deadline: 3/1; financial award applicants required to submit FAFSA. *Unit head:* Dr. Aiping Zhang, Chair, 530-898-5289, Fax: 530-898-4450, E-mail: engl@csuchico.edu. *Application contact:* Judy L. Rice, Graduate Admissions Coordinator, 530-898-5416, Fax: 530-898-3342, E-mail: jlrice@csuchico.edu.
Website: http://catalog.csuchico.edu/viewer/ENGL/ENGLNONEMA.html

California State University, Dominguez Hills, College of Arts and Humanities, Department of English, Carson, CA 90747-0001. Offers English (MA); rhetoric and composition (Certificate); teaching English as a second language (Certificate). Part-time and evening/weekend programs available. *Faculty:* 8 full-time (4 women). *Students:* 35 full-time (23 women), 42 part-time (24 women); includes 40 minority (10 Black or African American, non-Hispanic/Latino; 9 Asian, non-Hispanic/Latino; 20 Hispanic/Latino; 1 Two or more races, non-Hispanic/Latino), 11 international. Average age 35. 35 applicants, 77% accepted, 21 enrolled. In 2014, 29 master's awarded. *Degree requirements:* For master's, comprehensive exam (for some programs), thesis or alternative. *Entrance requirements:* For master's, minimum GPA of 3.0 in last 60 units. Additional exam

requirements/recommendations for international students: Required—TOEFL (minimum score 550 paper-based). *Application deadline:* Applications are processed on a rolling basis. Application fee: $55. Electronic applications accepted. *Expenses:* Tuition, state resident: full-time $6738; part-time $3960 per year. Tuition, nonresident: full-time $13,434; part-time $8370 per year. *Required fees:* $623; $623 per year. *Faculty research:* Gender studies, transnationalism, discourse analysis, visual culture, Shakespeare. *Unit head:* Dr. Timothy Chin, Chair, 310-243-3322, E-mail: english@csudh.edu. *Application contact:* Brandy McLelland, Director of Student Information Services/Registrar, 310-243-3645, E-mail: bmclelland@csudh.edu. Website: http://www4.csudh.edu/english/index

California State University, East Bay, Office of Academic Programs and Graduate Studies, College of Letters, Arts, and Social Sciences, Department of English, Hayward, CA 94542-3000. Offers creative writing (MA); literary studies (MA); teaching English to speakers of other languages (MA). Part-time programs available. *Degree requirements:* For master's, one foreign language, comprehensive exam, thesis optional. *Entrance requirements:* For master's, minimum GPA of 3.0 in field; 2 letters of recommendation; academic or professional writing sample; preferred teaching experience and some degree of bilingualism (for TESOL). Additional exam requirements/recommendations for international students: Required—TOEFL (minimum score 550 paper-based); Recommended—IELTS (minimum score 6.5). *Application deadline:* For fall admission, 6/30 for domestic and international students. Applications are processed on a rolling basis. Application fee: $55. Electronic applications accepted. *Expenses:* Tuition, state resident: full-time $7830; part-time $1302 per credit hour. Tuition, nonresident: full-time $16,368. *Required fees:* $327 per quarter. Tuition and fees vary according to course load and program. *Financial support:* Fellowships, teaching assistantships, career-related internships or fieldwork, Federal Work-Study, institutionally sponsored loans, and scholarships/grants available. Support available to part-time students. Financial award application deadline: 3/2; financial award applicants required to submit FAFSA. *Unit head:* Dr. Sarah Nielsen, Acting Chair, 510-885-3151, Fax: 510-885-4797. *Application contact:* Dr. Donna Wiley, Interim Associate Vice President for Academic Programs and Graduate Studies, 510-885-3716, Fax: 510-885-4777, E-mail: donna.wiley@csueastbay.edu. Website: http://www20.csueastbay.edu/class/departments/english/index.html

California State University, Fresno, Division of Graduate Studies, College of Arts and Humanities, Department of English, Fresno, CA 93740-8027. Offers composition theory (MA); creative writing (MFA); literature (MA). Part-time and evening/weekend programs available. *Degree requirements:* For master's, one foreign language, thesis. *Entrance requirements:* For master's, GRE General Test, minimum GPA of 3.0, writing sample. Additional exam requirements/recommendations for international students: Required—TOEFL. Electronic applications accepted. *Faculty research:* American literature, Renaissance literature, foreign literature.

California State University, Fullerton, Graduate Studies, College of Humanities and Social Sciences, Department of English, Comparative Literature, and Linguistics, Fullerton, CA 92834-9480. Offers English (MA); linguistics (MA). Part-time programs available. *Students:* 31 full-time (25 women), 45 part-time (30 women); includes 26 minority (1 American Indian or Alaska Native, non-Hispanic/Latino; 4 Asian, non-Hispanic/Latino; 19 Hispanic/Latino; 2 Two or more races, non-Hispanic/Latino), 1 international. Average age 28. 48 applicants, 63% accepted, 23 enrolled. In 2014, 26 master's awarded. *Degree requirements:* For master's, comprehensive exam, thesis or alternative. *Entrance requirements:* For master's, minimum GPA of 3.0 in major, 2.5 in last 60 hours. Application fee: $55. *Financial support:* Career-related internships or fieldwork, Federal Work-Study, institutionally sponsored loans, and scholarships/grants available. Support available to part-time students. Financial award application deadline: 3/1; financial award applicants required to submit FAFSA. *Unit head:* Lana L. Dalley, Chair, 657-278-2452. *Application contact:* Admissions/Applications, 657-278-2371.

California State University, Long Beach, Graduate Studies, College of Liberal Arts, Department of English, Long Beach, CA 90840. Offers creative writing (MFA); English (MA). Part-time programs available. *Degree requirements:* For master's, one foreign language, comprehensive exam or thesis. *Entrance requirements:* For master's, GRE Subject Test, minimum GPA of 3.0 in English. Electronic applications accepted. *Faculty research:* English and American literature, literary theory, linguistics, rhetoric and composition.

California State University, Los Angeles, Graduate Studies, College of Arts and Letters, Department of English, Los Angeles, CA 90032-8530. Offers MA. Part-time and evening/weekend programs available. *Degree requirements:* For master's, comprehensive exam or thesis. *Entrance requirements:* Additional exam requirements/recommendations for international students: Required—TOEFL (minimum score 500 paper-based). Electronic applications accepted. *Expenses:* Tuition, state resident: full-time $6738; part-time $3609 per year. Tuition, nonresident: full-time $15,666; part-time $8073 per year. Tuition and fees vary according to course load, degree level and program. *Faculty research:* English and American literature, linguistics, composition.

California State University, Northridge, Graduate Studies, College of Humanities, Department of English, Northridge, CA 91330. Offers creative writing (MA); literature (MA); rhetoric and composition theory (MA). Part-time and evening/weekend programs available. *Students:* 36 full-time (22 women), 84 part-time (53 women); includes 39 minority (3 Black or African American, non-Hispanic/Latino; 10 Asian, non-Hispanic/Latino; 22 Hispanic/Latino; 4 Two or more races, non-Hispanic/Latino), 1 international. Average age 32. *Degree requirements:* For master's, thesis or alternative. *Entrance requirements:* For master's, writing proficiency test, GRE General Test or minimum GPA of 3.0. Additional exam requirements/recommendations for international students: Required—TOEFL. *Application deadline:* For fall admission, 11/30 for domestic students. Application fee: $55. *Expenses: Required fees:* $12,402. *Financial support:* Teaching assistantships available. Financial award application deadline: 3/1. *Faculty research:* Reading improvement, professional writing, Dickens, Shaw, English as a second language. *Unit head:* Jackie Stallcup, Chair, 818-677-3434. *Application contact:* Dr. Marjie Seagoe, Graduate Studies Secretary, 818-677-3433. Website: http://www.csun.edu/english/index.php

California State University, Sacramento, Office of Graduate Studies, College of Arts and Letters, Department of English, Sacramento, CA 95819. Offers composition (MA); creative writing (MA); literature (MA); teaching English to speakers of other languages (MA). Part-time programs available. *Degree requirements:* For master's, thesis, project, or comprehensive exam; TESOL exam; writing proficiency exam. *Entrance requirements:* For master's, portfolio (creative writing); minimum GPA of 3.0 in English, 2.75 overall during previous 2 years. Additional exam requirements/recommendations for international students: Required—TOEFL. Electronic applications accepted. *Faculty research:* Teaching composition, remedial writing.

California State University, San Bernardino, Graduate Studies, College of Arts and Letters, Department of English, San Bernardino, CA 92407-2397. Offers creative writing (MFA), including fiction; English composition (MA), including composition. Part-time and evening/weekend programs available. *Students:* 31 full-time (17 women), 61 part-time (41 women); includes 46 minority (7 Black or African American, non-Hispanic/Latino; 1 Asian, non-Hispanic/Latino; 35 Hispanic/Latino; 3 Two or more races, non-Hispanic/

Latino), 2 international. Average age 27. 74 applicants, 53% accepted, 37 enrolled. In 2014, 45 master's awarded. *Degree requirements:* For master's, one foreign language, thesis. *Entrance requirements:* Additional exam requirements/recommendations for international students: Required—TOEFL. *Application deadline:* For fall admission, 7/17 for domestic students. Application fee: $55. *Expenses:* Tuition, state resident: full-time $6738; part-time $1302 per term. Tuition, nonresident: full-time $17,898; part-time $248 per unit. *Required fees:* $365 per quarter. Tuition and fees vary according to degree level and program. *Financial support:* Application deadline: 3/1. *Unit head:* Dr. Sunny Hyon, Chair, 909-537-5834, Fax: 909-537-7086, E-mail: shyon@csusb.edu. *Application contact:* Dr. Jeffrey Thompson, Dean of Graduate Studies, 909-537-5058, Fax: 909-537-5078, E-mail: jthompso@csusb.edu.

California State University, San Marcos, College of Humanities, Arts, Behavioral and Social Sciences, Program in Literature and Writing Studies, San Marcos, CA 92096-0001. Offers MA. Part-time and evening/weekend programs available. *Students:* 9 full-time (7 women), 8 part-time (5 women); includes 7 minority (2 Black or African American, non-Hispanic/Latino; 1 American Indian or Alaska Native, non-Hispanic/Latino; 1 Asian, non-Hispanic/Latino; 1 Hispanic/Latino; 2 Two or more races, non-Hispanic/Latino). Average age 33. *Degree requirements:* For master's, one foreign language, thesis. *Entrance requirements:* For master's, GRE General Test, minimum GPA of 3.0, writing sample. *Application deadline:* For fall admission, 3/15 priority date for domestic students; for spring admission, 11/15 for domestic students. Applications are processed on a rolling basis. Application fee: $55. *Expenses:* Tuition, state resident: full-time $6738. *Required fees:* $1692. Tuition and fees vary according to program. *Financial support:* Teaching assistantships with partial tuition reimbursements available. *Faculty research:* Postcolonialism, feminism rhetoric, cultural studies, creative writing, critical theory. *Unit head:* Prof. Salah Moukhlis, Chair, 760-750-8081, E-mail: smoukhli@csusm.edu. *Application contact:* Admissions, 760-750-4848, Fax: 760-750-3248, E-mail: apply@csusm.edu.

California State University, Stanislaus, College of Humanities and Social Sciences, Program in English (MA), Turlock, CA 95382. Offers literature (Certificate); rhetoric and teaching writing (MA); teaching English to speakers of other languages (MA). Part-time programs available. *Degree requirements:* For master's, comprehensive exam, thesis or alternative. *Entrance requirements:* For master's, GRE, minimum GPA of 3.0, 2 letters of reference, personal statement. Additional exam requirements/recommendations for international students: Required—TOEFL (minimum score 575 paper-based), TWE (minimum score 4). Electronic applications accepted. *Faculty research:* Transnational literacies, Renaissance and medieval literature, abolition writings and slave narratives, qualitative writing.

Carleton University, Faculty of Graduate Studies, Faculty of Arts and Social Sciences, Department of English Language and Literature, Ottawa, ON K1S 5B6, Canada. Offers MA, PhD. *Degree requirements:* For master's, thesis optional. *Entrance requirements:* For master's, honors degree. Additional exam requirements/recommendations for international students: Required—TOEFL. *Faculty research:* British, Canadian, American, and Commonwealth literatures; English language and writing; literary criticism; social and historical context of literature.

Carnegie Mellon University, Dietrich College of Humanities and Social Sciences, Department of English, Pittsburgh, PA 15213-3891. Offers communication planning and design (M Des); literary and cultural studies (MA, PhD); professional writing (MAPW), including editing and publishing, policy and non-profit communication, public and media relations / corporate communications, science or healthcare communication, technical writing, writing for new media, writing for print media; rhetoric (MA, PhD). Part-time programs available. Terminal master's awarded for partial completion of doctoral program. *Degree requirements:* For doctorate, 2 foreign languages, comprehensive exam, thesis/dissertation. *Entrance requirements:* For master's and doctorate, GRE General Test. Additional exam requirements/recommendations for international students: Required—TOEFL, TWE. *Faculty research:* Cognitive processes in discourse with emphasis on writing, testing, and evaluation.

Case Western Reserve University, School of Graduate Studies, Department of English, Cleveland, OH 44106. Offers MA, PhD. Part-time programs available. *Faculty:* 21 full-time (11 women). *Students:* 26 full-time (16 women), 8 part-time (3 women); includes 1 minority (Black or African American, non-Hispanic/Latino), 2 international. Average age 30. 78 applicants, 10% accepted, 8 enrolled. In 2014, 2 master's, 1 doctorate awarded. *Degree requirements:* For master's, one foreign language, comprehensive exam, thesis or alternative, written exam; for doctorate, one foreign language, thesis/dissertation, oral and written exams. *Entrance requirements:* For master's and doctorate, GRE General Test, sample of written work, letters of recommendation. Additional exam requirements/recommendations for international students: Required—TOEFL (minimum score 577 paper-based; 90 iBT); Recommended—IELTS (minimum score 7). *Application deadline:* For fall admission, 1/15 priority date for domestic students; for spring admission, 1/2 for domestic students. Applications are processed on a rolling basis. Application fee: $50. Electronic applications accepted. *Financial support:* Fellowships, teaching assistantships, Federal Work-Study, institutionally sponsored loans, and tuition waivers (partial) available. Financial award application deadline: 1/15; financial award applicants required to submit FAFSA. *Faculty research:* Sixteenth to twentieth century English literature, rhetorical and critical theory, women's studies, genre studies, Renaissance, America modernism, authorship. *Unit head:* Mary Grimm, Chair, 216-368-2355, Fax: 216-368-4681, E-mail: mary.grimm@case.edu. *Application contact:* Prof. Kurt Koenigsberger, Associate Professor and Graduate Director, 216-368-2362, Fax: 216-368-4367, E-mail: kurt.koenigsberger@case.edu. Website: http://english.case.edu/

The Catholic University of America, School of Arts and Sciences, Department of English Language and Literature, Washington, DC 20064. Offers English language and literature (MA, PhD); rhetoric (Certificate); MSLS/MA. Part-time programs available. *Faculty:* 15 full-time (5 women), 1 (woman) part-time/adjunct. *Students:* 19 full-time (11 women), 35 part-time (23 women); includes 5 minority (1 Black or African American, non-Hispanic/Latino; 3 Hispanic/Latino; 1 Two or more races, non-Hispanic/Latino), 3 international. Average age 29. 52 applicants, 48% accepted, 8 enrolled. In 2014, 7 master's, 5 doctorates awarded. *Degree requirements:* For master's, one foreign language, comprehensive exam; for doctorate, 2 foreign languages, comprehensive exam, thesis/dissertation. *Entrance requirements:* For master's and doctorate, GRE General Test, statement of purpose, official copies of academic transcripts, three letters of recommendation, writing sample. Additional exam requirements/recommendations for international students: Required—TOEFL (minimum score 580 paper-based). *Application deadline:* For fall admission, 7/15 priority date for domestic students, 7/1 for international students; for spring admission, 11/15 priority date for domestic students, 11/1 for international students. Applications are processed on a rolling basis. Application fee: $55. Electronic applications accepted. *Expenses:* Tuition: Full-time $40,200; part-time $1600 per credit hour. *Required fees:* $400; $195 per semester. One-time fee: $425. *Financial support:* Fellowships, research assistantships, teaching assistantships, Federal Work-Study, scholarships/grants, tuition waivers (full and partial), and unspecified assistantships available. Financial award application deadline: 2/1; financial award applicants required to submit FAFSA. *Faculty research:* Medieval literature,

theory and history of rhetoric, Renaissance literature, religion and literature, English and American drama. *Unit head:* Dr. Ernest Suarez, Chair, 202-319-5488, Fax: 202-319-4188, E-mail: suarez@cua.edu. *Application contact:* Director of Graduate Admissions, 202-319-5057, Fax: 202-319-6533, E-mail: cua-admissions@cua.edu. Website: http://english.cua.edu/.

Central Connecticut State University, School of Graduate Studies, College of Liberal Arts and Social Sciences, Department of English, Program in English, New Britain, CT 06050-4010. Offers MA, Certificate. Part-time and evening/weekend programs available. *Students:* 10 full-time (5 women), 19 part-time (16 women); includes 2 minority (1 Black or African American, non-Hispanic/Latino; 1 Asian, non-Hispanic/Latino). Average age 32. 13 applicants, 69% accepted, 6 enrolled. In 2014, 11 master's, 4 other advanced degrees awarded. *Degree requirements:* For master's, comprehensive exam, thesis or alternative; for Certificate, qualifying exam. *Entrance requirements:* For master's, minimum undergraduate GPA of 3.0, essay, writing sample, letters of recommendation. Additional exam requirements/recommendations for international students: Required—TOEFL (minimum score 550 paper-based; 79 iBT). *Application deadline:* For fall admission, 6/1 for domestic students, 5/1 for international students; for spring admission, 11/1 for domestic and international students. Applications are processed on a rolling basis. Application fee: $50. Electronic applications accepted. *Expenses: Tuition,* area resident: Full-time $5730; part-time $534 per credit. Tuition, state resident: full-time $8596; part-time $534 per credit. Tuition, nonresident: full-time $15,964; part-time $548 per credit. *Required fees:* $4211; $215 per credit. *Unit head:* Dr. Stephen Cohen, Chair, 860-832-2795, E-mail: cohens@mail.ccsu.edu. *Application contact:* Patricia Gardner, Associate Director of Graduate Studies, 860-832-2350, Fax: 860-832-2362, E-mail: graduateadmissions@ccsu.edu.

Central Michigan University, College of Graduate Studies, College of Humanities and Social and Behavioral Sciences, Department of English Language and Literature, Mount Pleasant, MI 48859. Offers English composition and communication (MA); English language and literature (MA), including children's and young adult literature, creative writing, English language and literature; TESOL: teaching English to speakers of other languages (MA). Part-time and evening/weekend programs available. *Degree requirements:* For master's, thesis or alternative. Electronic applications accepted. *Faculty research:* Composition theory, science fiction history and bibliography, children's and young adult literature, nineteenth century American literature, applied linguistics.

Central Washington University, Graduate Studies and Research, College of Arts and Humanities, Department of English, Ellensburg, WA 98926. Offers English (MA); teaching English as a second language (MA). Part-time programs available. *Degree requirements:* For master's, thesis or alternative. *Entrance requirements:* For master's, GRE General Test, minimum GPA of 3.0, writing sample. Additional exam requirements/recommendations for international students: Required—TOEFL (minimum score 550 paper-based; 79 iBT) or IELTS (minimum score 6.5). Electronic applications accepted.

Chapman University, Wilkinson College of Humanities and Social Sciences, Department of English, Orange, CA 92866. Offers creative writing (MFA); English (MA). Part-time and evening/weekend programs available. *Faculty:* 25 full-time (11 women), 37 part-time/adjunct (18 women). *Students:* 38 full-time (20 women), 23 part-time (19 women); includes 12 minority (1 Black or African American, non-Hispanic/Latino; 6 Hispanic/Latino; 1 Native Hawaiian or other Pacific Islander, non-Hispanic/Latino; 4 Two or more races, non-Hispanic/Latino). Average age 28. 66 applicants, 80% accepted, 21 enrolled. In 2014, 26 master's awarded. *Degree requirements:* For master's, comprehensive exam (for some programs), thesis (for some programs). *Entrance requirements:* For master's, GRE or MAT, minimum undergraduate GPA of 2.5. Additional exam requirements/recommendations for international students: Required—TOEFL (minimum score 550 paper-based; 80 iBT). *Application deadline:* For fall admission, 5/1 priority date for domestic students; for winter admission, 11/1 priority date for domestic students. Applications are processed on a rolling basis. Application fee: $60. Electronic applications accepted. *Expenses:* Expenses: Contact institution. *Financial support:* Fellowships, Federal Work-Study, and scholarships/grants available. Financial award applicants required to submit FAFSA. *Unit head:* Mark Axelrod, Director, 714-997-6586, E-mail: axelrod@chapman.edu. *Application contact:* Shannon McCance, Graduate Admission Counselor, 714-997-6711, E-mail: smccance@chapman.edu. Website: http://www.chapman.edu/wilkinson/english/

Chicago State University, School of Graduate and Professional Studies, College of Arts and Sciences, Department of English, Foreign Languages and Literatures, Chicago, IL 60628. Offers creative writing (MFA); English (MA). *Degree requirements:* For master's, comprehensive exam (for some programs), thesis (for some programs). *Entrance requirements:* For master's, minimum GPA of 3.0.

The Citadel, The Military College of South Carolina, Citadel Graduate College, Department of English, Charleston, SC 29409. Offers MA. Part-time and evening/weekend programs available. *Degree requirements:* For master's, one foreign language, comprehensive exam, thesis optional. *Entrance requirements:* For master's, GRE (minimum combined verbal and quantitative score of 300, 4 on writing assessment section) or MAT (minimum score of 400), minimum undergraduate GPA of 2.5 (3.0 in major); 2 letters of recommendation from former professors or recent supervisors; writing sample showing ability to perform literary analysis and to conduct research. Additional exam requirements/recommendations for international students: Required—TOEFL (minimum score 550 paper-based). Electronic applications accepted. *Faculty research:* Renaissance literature; eighteenth- and nineteenth-century British literature; eighteenth-, nineteenth-, and twentieth-century American literature.

City College of the City University of New York, Graduate School, College of Liberal Arts and Science, Division of the Humanities and Arts, Department of English, Program in English and American Literature, New York, NY 10031-9198. Offers MA. *Degree requirements:* For master's, one foreign language, comprehensive exam, thesis. *Entrance requirements:* For master's, minimum GPA of 3.0. Additional exam requirements/recommendations for international students: Required—TOEFL (minimum score 600 paper-based; 100 iBT). Electronic applications accepted.

Claremont Graduate University, Graduate Programs, School of Arts and Humanities, Department of English, Claremont, CA 91711-6160. Offers American studies (MA, PhD); critical theory (MA, PhD); early modern studies (MA, PhD); English (M Phil, MA, PhD); literary theory (PhD); literature (MA, PhD); literature and creative writing (MA); literature and film (MA); MBA/MA; MBA/PhD. Part-time programs available. *Faculty:* 4 full-time (2 women), 2 part-time/adjunct (0 women). *Students:* 70 full-time (51 women), 27 part-time (17 women); includes 31 minority (4 Black or African American, non-Hispanic/Latino; 1 American Indian or Alaska Native, non-Hispanic/Latino; 12 Asian, non-Hispanic/Latino; 6 Hispanic/Latino; 8 Two or more races, non-Hispanic/Latino), 8 international. Average age 36. In 2014, 9 master's, 7 doctorates awarded. *Entrance requirements:* For master's and doctorate, GRE General Test. Additional exam requirements/recommendations for international students: Required—TOEFL (minimum score 550 paper-based; 80 iBT). *Application deadline:* For fall admission, 2/1 priority date for domestic and international students. Applications are processed on a rolling basis. Application fee: $80. Electronic applications accepted. *Expenses: Tuition:* Full-time $41,784; part-time $1741 per credit.

Required fees: $600; $300 per semester. *Financial support:* Fellowships, Federal Work-Study, institutionally sponsored loans, and scholarships/grants available. Support available to part-time students. Financial award application deadline: 2/15; financial award applicants required to submit FAFSA. *Faculty research:* American, comparative, and English Renaissance literature; modernism; feminist literature and theory. *Unit head:* David Luis-Brown, Chair, E-mail: david.luis-brown@cgu.edu. *Application contact:* Erma Cross, Admissions and Alumni Coordinator, 909-607-9843, E-mail: erminia.cross@cgu.edu. Website: http://www.cgu.edu/pages/568.asp

Clark Atlanta University, School of Arts and Sciences, Department of English, Atlanta, GA 30314. Offers MA, DAH. Part-time programs available. *Faculty:* 5 full-time (2 women). *Students:* 5 full-time (all women), 20 part-time (12 women); includes 20 minority (all Black or African American, non-Hispanic/Latino), 2 international. Average age 31. 9 applicants, 89% accepted, 2 enrolled. In 2014, 1 doctorate awarded. *Degree requirements:* For master's, one foreign language, comprehensive exam, thesis; for doctorate, 2 foreign languages, comprehensive exam, thesis/dissertation. *Entrance requirements:* For master's, GRE General Test, minimum GPA of 2.5. Additional exam requirements/recommendations for international students: Required—TOEFL (minimum score 500 paper-based; 61 iBT). *Application deadline:* For fall admission, 4/1 for domestic and international students; for spring admission, 11/1 for domestic and international students. Applications are processed on a rolling basis. Application fee: $40 ($55 for international students). *Expenses: Tuition:* Full-time $14,904; part-time $828 per credit hour. *Required fees:* $746; $373 per semester. *Financial support:* Career-related internships or fieldwork, Federal Work-Study, scholarships/grants, and unspecified assistantships available. Support available to part-time students. Financial award application deadline: 4/30; financial award applicants required to submit FAFSA. *Unit head:* Dr. Susan Wright-McFadder, Chairperson, 404-880-6163, E-mail: smcfatt@cau.edu. *Application contact:* Michelle Clark-Davis, Graduate Program Admissions, 404-880-6605, E-mail: cauadmissions@cau.edu.

Clark University, Graduate School, Department of English, Worcester, MA 01610-1477. Offers MA. Part-time programs available. *Faculty:* 9 full-time (5 women), 11 part-time/adjunct (5 women). *Students:* 17 full-time (10 women), 4 part-time (3 women), 11 international. Average age 28. 17 applicants, 88% accepted, 8 enrolled. In 2014, 6 master's awarded. *Degree requirements:* For master's, thesis, oral exam. *Entrance requirements:* For master's, GRE Subject Test. Additional exam requirements/recommendations for international students: Required—TOEFL. *Application deadline:* For fall admission, 1/15 priority date for domestic students. Applications are processed on a rolling basis. Application fee: $75. *Expenses: Tuition:* Full-time $40,380; part-time $1262 per credit hour. *Required fees:* $30. *Financial support:* In 2014–15, research assistantships with full and partial tuition reimbursements (averaging $10,500 per year), 4 teaching assistantships with full and partial tuition reimbursements (averaging $10,500 per year) were awarded; fellowships, career-related internships or fieldwork, and tuition waivers (partial) also available. Support available to part-time students. Financial award application deadline: 2/15. *Faculty research:* Renaissance literature, American literature, medieval literature, Victorian literature. *Unit head:* Dr. Jay Elliott, Chair, 508-793-7152. *Application contact:* Terri Rutkiewicz, Program Assistant, 508-793-7630, Fax: 508-793-8892, E-mail: trutkiewicz@clarku.edu. Website: http://www.clarku.edu/departments/english/graduate/

Clemson University, Graduate School, College of Architecture, Arts, and Humanities, Department of English, Program in English, Clemson, SC 29634. Offers MA. Part-time programs available. *Students:* 22 full-time (17 women), 1 (woman) part-time; includes 2 minority (both Black or African American, non-Hispanic/Latino), 1 international. Average age 26. 24 applicants, 71% accepted, 12 enrolled. In 2014, 11 master's awarded. *Degree requirements:* For master's, one foreign language, thesis. *Entrance requirements:* For master's, GRE, 2 letters of recommendation, writing sample (at least 8-10 pages), statement of purpose, transcripts for all undergraduate work. Additional exam requirements/recommendations for international students: Required—TOEFL. *Application deadline:* For fall admission, 2/1 priority date for domestic and international students. Application fee: $70 ($80 for international students). Electronic applications accepted. *Financial support:* In 2014–15, 12 students received support, including 12 teaching assistantships with partial tuition reimbursements available (averaging $18,779 per year); fellowships with partial tuition reimbursements available, research assistantships with partial tuition reimbursements available, institutionally sponsored loans, scholarships/grants, and unspecified assistantships also available. Financial award application deadline: 2/1. *Faculty research:* Literature, literary theory, textual studies, new media, digital humanities. *Unit head:* Dr. Sean Williams, Chair, 864-656-3151, Fax: 864-656-1345, E-mail: lmorris@clemson.edu. *Application contact:* Dr. Kimberly Manganelli, Graduate Program Contact, 864-656-3151, Fax: 864-656-1345, E-mail: cpaul@clemson.edu. Website: http://www.clemson.edu/caah/english/graduate/ma_english/index.html

Cleveland State University, College of Graduate Studies, College of Liberal Arts and Social Sciences, Department of English, Cleveland, OH 44115. Offers creative writing (MFA); English (MA). Part-time and evening/weekend programs available. *Faculty:* 10 full-time (5 women), 3 part-time/adjunct (1 woman). *Students:* 21 full-time (13 women), 50 part-time (31 women); includes 11 minority (7 Black or African American, non-Hispanic/Latino; 1 American Indian or Alaska Native, non-Hispanic/Latino; 2 Hispanic/Latino; 1 Two or more races, non-Hispanic/Latino). Average age 34. 42 applicants, 71% accepted, 9 enrolled. In 2014, 21 master's awarded. *Degree requirements:* For master's, comprehensive exam, thesis. *Entrance requirements:* For master's, minimum GPA of 2.75, undergraduate concentration in English, writing sample, portfolio. Additional exam requirements/recommendations for international students: Required—TOEFL (minimum score 525 paper-based) or IELTS (minimum score 6). *Application deadline:* For fall admission, 7/15 priority date for domestic students, 5/15 for international students; for spring admission, 12/15 for domestic students, 11/1 for international students. Applications are processed on a rolling basis. Application fee: $30. Electronic applications accepted. *Expenses: Tuition,* state resident: full-time $9566; part-time $531 per credit hour. Tuition, nonresident: full-time $17,980; part-time $999 per credit hour. *Required fees:* $25 per semester. Tuition and fees vary according to degree level and program. *Financial support:* In 2014–15, 20 students received support, including 1 fellowship (averaging $1,000 per year), 5 research assistantships with full and partial tuition reimbursements available (averaging $3,480 per year), 7 teaching assistantships with full and partial tuition reimbursements available (averaging $3,480 per year); Federal Work-Study, institutionally sponsored loans, tuition waivers (full and partial), and unspecified assistantships also available. Support available to part-time students. Financial award application deadline: 2/1. *Faculty research:* Literary history and criticism, literature. Total annual research expenditures: $5,000. *Unit head:* Dr. John C. Gerlach, Interim Chairperson, 216-687-3951, Fax: 216-687-6943, E-mail: j.gerlach@csuohio.edu. *Application contact:* Dr. James J. Marino, Graduate Director, 216-687-6874, Fax: 216-687-6943, E-mail: j.marino22@csuohio.edu. Website: http://www.csuohio.edu/class/english/english

The College at Brockport, State University of New York, School of the Arts, Humanities and Social Sciences, Department of English, Brockport, NY 14420-2997. Offers creative writing (AGC); English (MA), including creative writing, literature. Part-

time programs available. *Faculty:* 12 full-time (7 women). *Students:* 13 full-time (11 women), 22 part-time (16 women); includes 5 minority (2 Black or African American, non-Hispanic/Latino; 2 Hispanic/Latino; 1 Two or more races, non-Hispanic/Latino). 20 applicants, 65% accepted, 8 enrolled. In 2014, 11 master's awarded. *Degree requirements:* For master's, thesis. *Entrance requirements:* For master's, minimum GPA of 3.0, letters of recommendation, writing sample. Additional exam requirements/recommendations for international students: Required—TOEFL (minimum score 550 paper-based; 79 iBT), IELTS (minimum score 6.5). *Application deadline:* For fall admission, 4/15 priority date for domestic and international students; for spring admission, 11/15 priority date for domestic and international students; for summer admission, 4/15 priority date for domestic and international students. Application fee: $50. Electronic applications accepted. *Financial support:* In 2014–15, 3 teaching assistantships with full tuition reimbursements (averaging $6,000 per year) were awarded; Federal Work-Study, scholarships/grants, and unspecified assistantships also available. Support available to part-time students. Financial award application deadline: 3/15; financial award applicants required to submit FAFSA. *Faculty research:* British and American literature, creative writing, film studies, children's literature, ancient and modern world literature. *Unit head:* Dr. Jennifer Haytock, Chairperson, 585-395-5832, Fax: 585-395-2391, E-mail: jhaytock@brockport.edu. *Application contact:* Dr. Janie Hinds, Graduate Program Director, 585-395-5712, Fax: 585-395-2391, E-mail: jhinds@brockport.edu.
Website: http://www.brockport.edu/english/graduate/

College of Charleston, Graduate School, School of Humanities and Social Sciences, Program in English, Charleston, SC 29424-0001. Offers MA. Program offered jointly with The Citadel, The Military College of South Carolina. Part-time and evening/weekend programs available. *Degree requirements:* For master's, one foreign language, comprehensive exam, thesis optional. *Entrance requirements:* For master's, GRE General Test or MAT, minimum GPA of 2.5 overall, 3.0 in major; 2 letters of recommendation; writing sample. Additional exam requirements/recommendations for international students: Required—TOEFL (minimum score 81 iBT). Electronic applications accepted.

The College of New Jersey, Graduate Studies, School of Humanities and Social Sciences, Department of English, Program in English, Ewing, NJ 08628. Offers MA. Part-time programs available. *Students:* 5 full-time (4 women), 26 part-time (21 women); includes 5 minority (2 Black or African American, non-Hispanic/Latino; 1 Asian, non-Hispanic/Latino; 1 Hispanic/Latino; 1 Two or more races, non-Hispanic/Latino). 10 applicants, 100% accepted, 7 enrolled. In 2014, 15 master's awarded. *Degree requirements:* For master's, comprehensive exam. *Entrance requirements:* For master's, GRE, minimum GPA of 3.0 in field or 2.75 overall. Additional exam requirements/recommendations for international students: Required—TOEFL. *Application deadline:* For fall admission, 2/1 priority date for domestic students; for spring admission, 10/1 priority date for domestic students. Application fee: $75. Electronic applications accepted. *Financial support:* Tuition waivers (partial) and unspecified assistantships available. Financial award application deadline: 5/1; financial award applicants required to submit FAFSA. *Unit head:* Dr. Lisa Ortiz, Coordinator, 609-771-3231, Fax: 609-637-5112, E-mail: ortiz@tcnj.edu. *Application contact:* Susan L. Hydro, Director of Graduate and Intersession Programs, 609-771-2300, Fax: 609-637-5105, E-mail: graduate@tcnj.edu.

The College of Saint Rose, Graduate Studies, School of Arts and Humanities, Department of English, Albany, NY 12203-1419. Offers MA. Part-time and evening/weekend programs available. *Degree requirements:* For master's, thesis optional, advanced project. *Entrance requirements:* For master's, 24 credits in English, minimum undergraduate GPA of 3.2, writing sample. Additional exam requirements/recommendations for international students: Required—TOEFL (minimum score 550 paper-based). Electronic applications accepted.

College of Staten Island of the City University of New York, Graduate Programs, Division of Humanities and Social Sciences, Program in English, Staten Island, NY 10314-6600. Offers MA. Part-time and evening/weekend programs available. *Faculty:* 1 (woman) full-time, 1 part-time/adjunct (0 women). *Students:* 12 part-time (7 women). Average age 28. 14 applicants, 36% accepted. In 2014, 7 master's awarded. *Degree requirements:* For master's, comprehensive exam, minimum overall GPA of 3.0, 34 credits (7 four-credit courses from either literature or rhetoric, 4 credits in education, and 2 credits of independent study), 2 papers, exam. *Entrance requirements:* For master's, BA with minimum GPA of 3.0 overall or in English courses, 32 undergraduate credits in English, two letters of recommendation, one- to two-page personal statement, minimum of 8-10 page paper written for an English course. Additional exam requirements/recommendations for international students: Required—TOEFL (minimum score 550 paper-based; 79 iBT), IELTS (minimum score 6.5). *Application deadline:* For fall admission, 7/15 for domestic and international students; for spring admission, 12/15 for domestic and international students. Application fee: $125. *Expenses:* Tuition, state resident: full-time $9650; part-time $405 per credit. Tuition, nonresident: full-time $17,880; part-time $745 per credit. *Required fees:* $141.10 per semester. Tuition and fees vary according to program. *Financial support:* In 2014–15, 1 student received support. Career-related internships or fieldwork, Federal Work-Study, and scholarships/grants available. Support available to part-time students. Financial award applicants required to submit FAFSA. *Unit head:* Dr. Katherine Goodland, Graduate Program Coordinator, 718-982-3639, E-mail: katherine.goodland@csi.cuny.edu. *Application contact:* Sasha Spence, Assistant Director for Graduate Admissions, 718-982-2019, Fax: 718-982-2500, E-mail: sasha.spence@csi.cuny.edu.
Website: http://www.csi.cuny.edu/catalog/graduate/master-of-arts-in-english-ma.htm

Colorado State University, Graduate School, College of Liberal Arts, Department of English, Fort Collins, CO 80523-1773. Offers creative writing (MFA); English (MA). Part-time programs available. *Faculty:* 30 full-time (19 women), 1 part-time/adjunct (0 women). *Students:* 75 full-time (53 women), 33 part-time (22 women); includes 12 minority (2 Asian, non-Hispanic/Latino; 4 Hispanic/Latino; 1 Native Hawaiian or other Pacific Islander, non-Hispanic/Latino; 5 Two or more races, non-Hispanic/Latino), 11 international. Average age 33. 247 applicants, 31% accepted, 33 enrolled. In 2014, 60 master's awarded. *Degree requirements:* For master's, variable foreign language requirement, thesis (for some programs), exams. *Entrance requirements:* For master's, GRE, writing sample, BA/BS with minimum GPA of 3.0, 3 letters of recommendation, transcripts, statement of purpose. Additional exam requirements/recommendations for international students: Required—TOEFL (minimum score 550 paper-based; 80 iBT). *Application deadline:* For fall admission, 4/1 priority date for domestic students; for spring admission, 9/1 priority date for domestic students. Applications are processed on a rolling basis. Application fee: $50. Electronic applications accepted. *Expenses:* Tuition, state resident: full-time $9348; part-time $519 per credit. Tuition, nonresident: full-time $22,916; part-time $1273 per credit. *Required fees:* $1584. *Financial support:* In 2014–15, 35 students received support, including 35 teaching assistantships with full tuition reimbursements available (averaging $13,875 per year); career-related internships or fieldwork, Federal Work-Study, institutionally sponsored loans, scholarships/grants, traineeships, and unspecified assistantships also available. Support available to part-time students. Financial award application deadline: 5/1; financial award applicants required to submit FAFSA. *Faculty research:* Computers and writing, environmental writing, cultural studies, new historicism, performance and identity. *Total annual research expenditures:* $136,378. *Unit head:* Dr. Louann Reid, Chair, 970-491-6428, Fax: 970-491-5601, E-mail: louann.reid@colostate.edu. *Application contact:* Marnie Leonard, Administrative Assistant, 970-491-2403, Fax: 970-491-7541, E-mail: marnie.leonard@colostate.edu.
Website: http://english.colostate.edu/

Columbia University, Graduate School of Arts and Sciences, New York, NY 10027. Offers African-American studies (MA); American studies (MA); anthropology (MA, PhD); art history and archaeology (MA, PhD); astronomy (PhD); biological sciences (PhD); biotechnology (MA); chemical physics (PhD); chemistry (PhD); classical studies (MA, PhD); classics (MA, PhD); climate and society (MA); earth and environmental sciences (PhD); East Asia: regional studies (MA); East Asian languages and cultures (MA, PhD); ecology, evolution and environmental biology (MA), including conservation biology; ecology, evolution, and environmental biology (PhD), including ecology and evolutionary biology, evolutionary primatology; economics (PhD); English and comparative literature (MA, PhD); French and Romance philology (MA, PhD); Germanic languages (MA, PhD); global French studies (MA); Hispanic cultural studies (MA); history (PhD); history and literature (MA); human rights studies (MA); Islamic studies (MA); Italian (MA, PhD); Japanese pedagogy (MA); Jewish studies (MA); Latin America and the Caribbean: regional studies (MA); Latin American and Iberian cultures (PhD); mathematics (MA, PhD), including finance (MA); medieval and Renaissance studies (MA); Middle Eastern, South Asian, and African studies (MA, PhD); modern art: critical and curatorial studies (MA); modern European studies (MA); museum anthropology (MA); music (DMA, PhD); oral history (MA); philosophical foundations of physics (MA); philosophy (MA, PhD); physics (PhD); political science (MA, PhD); psychology (PhD); quantitative methods in the social sciences (MA); religion (MA, PhD); Russia, Eurasia and East Europe: regional studies (MA); Russian translation (MA); Slavic cultures (MA); Slavic languages (MA, PhD); sociology (MA, PhD); South Asian studies (MA); statistics (MA, PhD); theatre (PhD); JD/PhD; MA/MS; MD/PhD; MPA/MA. Dual-degree programs require admission to both Graduate School of Arts and Sciences and another Columbia school. Part-time and evening/weekend programs available. Terminal master's awarded for partial completion of doctoral program. *Degree requirements:* For master's, thesis (for some programs); for doctorate, comprehensive exam, thesis/dissertation. *Entrance requirements:* For master's and doctorate, GRE General Test, GRE Subject Test (for some programs). Electronic applications accepted. *Faculty research:* Humanities, natural sciences, social sciences.

Concordia University, School of Graduate Studies, Faculty of Arts and Science, Department of English, Program in English, Montréal, QC H3G 1M8, Canada. Offers MA. *Degree requirements:* For master's, one foreign language, thesis optional. *Entrance requirements:* For master's, honors degree in English, minimum GPA of 3.3 in English literature.

Converse College, School of Education and Graduate Studies, Program in Liberal Arts, Spartanburg, SC 29302-0006. Offers English (MLA); history (MLA); political science (MLA). *Degree requirements:* For master's, capstone paper. *Entrance requirements:* For master's, minimum GPA of 3.0, 2 recommendations.

Converse College, School of Education and Graduate Studies, Program in Middle Level Education, Spartanburg, SC 29302-0006. Offers language arts/English (MAT); mathematics (MAT); middle level education (M Ed); science (MAT); social studies (MAT).

Cornell University, Graduate School, Graduate Fields of Arts and Sciences, Field of English Language and Literature, Ithaca, NY 14853-0001. Offers African-American literature (PhD); American literature after 1865 (PhD); American literature to 1865 (PhD); American studies (PhD); colonial and postcolonial literatures (PhD); creative writing (MFA); cultural studies (PhD); dramatic literature (PhD); English poetry (PhD); English Renaissance to 1660 (PhD); lesbian, bisexual, and gay literary studies (PhD); literary criticism and theory (PhD); Old and Middle English (PhD); prose fiction (PhD); Restoration and the eighteenth-century (PhD); the nineteenth century (PhD); the twentieth century (PhD); women's literature (PhD); MFA/PhD. Terminal master's awarded for partial completion of doctoral program. *Degree requirements:* For master's, one foreign language, thesis; for doctorate, one foreign language, comprehensive exam, thesis/dissertation, teaching experience. *Entrance requirements:* For master's, GRE General Test, 3 letters of recommendation, creative writing sample; for doctorate, GRE General Test, GRE Subject Test (English), 3 letters of recommendation, writing sample. Additional exam requirements/recommendations for international students: Required—TOEFL (minimum score 600 paper-based; 77 iBT). Electronic applications accepted. *Faculty research:* English and American literature, women's writing, ethnic and post-colonial literature, critical theory, medievalism.

Cornell University, Graduate School, Graduate Fields of Arts and Sciences, Field of Linguistics, Ithaca, NY 14853-0001. Offers applied linguistics (MA, PhD); East Asian linguistics (MA, PhD); English linguistics (MA, PhD); general linguistics (MA, PhD); Germanic linguistics (MA, PhD); Indo-European linguistics (MA, PhD); phonetics (MA, PhD); phonological theory (MA, PhD); Romance linguistics (MA, PhD); second language acquisition (MA, PhD); semantics (MA, PhD); Slavic linguistics (MA, PhD); sociolinguistics (MA, PhD); South Asian linguistics (MA, PhD); Southeast Asian linguistics (MA, PhD); syntactic theory (MA, PhD). Terminal master's awarded for partial completion of doctoral program. *Degree requirements:* For master's, one foreign language, thesis; for doctorate, one foreign language, comprehensive exam, thesis/dissertation. *Entrance requirements:* For master's and doctorate, GRE General Test, 2 letters of recommendation. Additional exam requirements/recommendations for international students: Required—TOEFL (minimum score 600 paper-based; 77 iBT). Electronic applications accepted. *Faculty research:* Phonology and phonetics, syntax and semantics, historical linguistics, philosophy of language, language acquisition.

Creighton University, Graduate School, College of Arts and Sciences, Department of English, Omaha, NE 68178-0001. Offers creative writing (MA, MFA). Part-time programs available. *Faculty:* 15 full-time (7 women). *Students:* 20 full-time (11 women), 6 part-time (3 women); includes 1 minority (Black or African American, non-Hispanic/Latino), 1 international. Average age 31. 26 applicants, 77% accepted, 7 enrolled. In 2014, 4 master's awarded. *Degree requirements:* For master's, thesis optional. *Entrance requirements:* For master's, GRE, 10-15 page writing sample, 3 letters of recommendation. Additional exam requirements/recommendations for international students: Required—TOEFL (minimum score 550 paper-based; 80 iBT). *Application deadline:* For fall admission, 3/15 priority date for domestic and international students. Application fee: $50. Electronic applications accepted. *Expenses:* *Tuition:* Full-time $14,040; part-time $780 per credit hour. *Required fees:* $153 per semester. Tuition and fees vary according to course load, campus/location, program, reciprocity agreements and student's religious affiliation. *Financial support:* In 2014–15, 5 fellowships with full and partial tuition reimbursements (averaging $11,240 per year) were awarded; tuition waivers (partial) and unspecified assistantships also available. Financial award applicants required to submit FAFSA. *Unit head:* Dr. Robert Whipple, Director, 402-280-2520, E-mail: whippl@creighton.edu. *Application contact:* Lindsay Johnson, Director of Graduate and Adult Recruitment, 402-280-2703, Fax: 402-280-2423, E-mail: gradschool@creighton.edu.

Dalhousie University, Faculty of Arts and Social Science, Department of English, Halifax, NS B3H 4R2, Canada. Offers MA, PhD. *Entrance requirements:* Additional exam requirements/recommendations for international students: Required—TOEFL, IELTS, CANTEST, CAEL, or Michigan English Language Assessment Battery. Electronic applications accepted. *Faculty research:* Victorian, Canadian, Renaissance, eighteenth-century, and modern literature.

DePaul University, College of Liberal Arts and Social Sciences, Chicago, IL 60614. Offers Arabic (MA); Chinese (MA); English (MA); French (MA); German (MA); history (MA); interdisciplinary studies (MA, MS); international public service (MS); international studies (MA); Italian (MA); Japanese (MA); leadership and policy studies (MS); liberal studies (MA); new media studies (MA); nonprofit management (MNM); public administration (MPA); public health (MPH); public service management (MS); social work (MSW); sociology (MA); Spanish (MA); sustainable urban development (MA); women and gender studies (MA); writing and publishing (MA); writing, rhetoric, and discourse (MA); MA/PhD. Part-time and evening/weekend programs available. Postbaccalaureate distance learning degree programs offered (no on-campus study). Terminal master's awarded for partial completion of doctoral program. *Degree requirements:* For master's, variable foreign language requirement, comprehensive exam (for some programs), thesis (for some programs). Electronic applications accepted.

Dominican University of California, School of Arts, Humanities and Social Sciences, Humanities Program, San Rafael, CA 94901-2298. Offers applied music (MA); art history (MA); creative writing (MA); history (MA); literature (MA); philosophy (MA); political theory (MA); religion (MA); women and gender studies (MA). Part-time programs available. *Faculty:* 11 full-time (5 women), 5 part-time/adjunct (2 women). *Students:* 2 full-time (1 woman), 25 part-time (16 women); includes 7 minority (1 Black or African American, non-Hispanic/Latino; 1 American Indian or Alaska Native, non-Hispanic/Latino; 3 Hispanic/Latino; 2 Two or more races, non-Hispanic/Latino). Average age 46. 12 applicants, 83% accepted, 7 enrolled. *Degree requirements:* For master's, thesis or alternative. *Entrance requirements:* For master's, minimum GPA of 3.0, interview. Additional exam requirements/recommendations for international students: Required—TOEFL (minimum score 550 paper-based; 80 iBT), IELTS (minimum score 6.5). *Application deadline:* For fall admission, 5/15 priority date for domestic and international students; for spring admission, 11/15 priority date for domestic and international students. Applications are processed on a rolling basis. Electronic applications accepted. Application fee is waived when completed online. *Expenses:* Expenses: $935 per unit. *Financial support:* Scholarships/grants available. Support available to part-time students. Financial award application deadline: 3/2; financial award applicants required to submit FAFSA. *Unit head:* Dr. Laura Stivers, Acting Dean, 415-458-3734, E-mail: laura.stivers@dominican.edu. *Application contact:* Ryan Purtill, Director, 415-458-3748, Fax: 415-485-3214, E-mail: ryan.purtill@dominican.edu.
Website: http://www.dominican.edu/academics/ahss/graduate-program/index_html

Drew University, Caspersen School of Graduate Studies, Program in Education, Madison, NJ 07940-1493. Offers biology (MAT); chemistry (MAT); English (MAT); French (MAT); Italian (MAT); math (MAT); physics (MAT); social studies (MAT); Spanish (MAT); theatre arts (MAT). *Accreditation:* Teacher Education Accreditation Council. Part-time programs available. *Degree requirements:* For master's, student teaching internship and seminar. *Entrance requirements:* For master's, transcripts, statement of purpose, three letters of recommendation. Additional exam requirements/recommendations for international students: Required—TOEFL. *Expenses:* Contact institution.

Duke University, Graduate School, Department of English, Durham, NC 27708. Offers PhD, JD/AM. *Degree requirements:* For doctorate, 2 foreign languages, thesis/dissertation. *Entrance requirements:* For doctorate, GRE General Test, writing sample. Additional exam requirements/recommendations for international students: Required—TOEFL (minimum score 577 paper-based; 90 iBT) or IELTS (minimum score 7). Electronic applications accepted. *Expenses: Tuition:* Full-time $45,760; part-time $2765 per credit. *Required fees:* $978. Full-time tuition and fees vary according to program.

Duquesne University, Graduate School of Liberal Arts, Department of English, Pittsburgh, PA 15282-0001. Offers MA, PhD. Part-time and evening/weekend programs available. *Faculty:* 16 full-time (10 women), 8 part-time/adjunct (4 women). *Students:* 61 full-time (41 women); includes 3 minority (2 Black or African American, non-Hispanic/Latino; 1 Asian, non-Hispanic/Latino), 1 international. Average age 29. 72 applicants, 57% accepted, 18 enrolled. In 2014, 17 master's, 5 doctorates awarded. *Degree requirements:* For master's, comprehensive exam, thesis or alternative; for doctorate, 2 foreign languages, comprehensive exam, thesis/dissertation. *Entrance requirements:* For master's and doctorate, GRE General Test, bachelor's degree in English, writing sample. Additional exam requirements/recommendations for international students: Required—TOEFL. *Application deadline:* For fall admission, 2/1 priority date for domestic and international students. Applications are processed on a rolling basis. Electronic applications accepted. *Expenses: Tuition:* Full-time $18,882; part-time $1049 per credit. *Required fees:* $1800; $100 per credit. Tuition and fees vary according to program. *Financial support:* In 2014–15, 6 research assistantships with full and partial tuition reimbursements (averaging $15,000 per year), 19 teaching assistantships with full tuition reimbursements (averaging $16,000 per year) were awarded; Federal Work-Study, scholarships/grants, tuition waivers (partial), and unspecified assistantships also available. Support available to part-time students. Financial award application deadline: 5/1. *Unit head:* Dr. Greg Barnhisel, Chair, 412-396-6420, E-mail: barnhiselg@duq.edu. *Application contact:* Linda Rendulic, Assistant to the Dean, 412-396-6400, E-mail: rendulic@duq.edu.
Website: http://www.duq.edu/academics/schools/liberal-arts/graduate-school/programs/english

East Carolina University, Graduate School, Thomas Harriot College of Arts and Sciences, Department of English, Greenville, NC 27858-4353. Offers creative writing (MA); English studies (MA); linguistics (MA); literature (MA); multicultural and transnational literatures (MA, Certificate); rhetoric and composition (MA); rhetoric, writing, and professional communication (PhD); teaching English in the two-year college (Certificate); teaching English to speakers of other languages (MA, Certificate); technical and professional communication (MA). Part-time and evening/weekend programs available. *Degree requirements:* For master's, one foreign language, comprehensive exam, thesis optional. *Entrance requirements:* For master's, GRE General Test, MAT (for MA Ed). Additional exam requirements/recommendations for international students: Required—TOEFL. *Expenses:* Tuition, state resident: full-time $4223. Tuition, nonresident: full-time $16,540. *Required fees:* $2184.

Eastern Illinois University, Graduate School, College of Arts and Humanities, Department of English, Charleston, IL 61920. Offers MA. Part-time and evening/weekend programs available. *Faculty:* 16. *Students:* 19 full-time (11 women), 11 part-time (9 women); includes 4 minority (3 Black or African American, non-Hispanic/Latino; 1 Hispanic/Latino), 1 international. Average age 31. 15 applicants, 80% accepted, 7 enrolled. In 2014, 18 master's awarded. *Degree requirements:* For master's, comprehensive exam (for some programs), thesis (for some programs). *Entrance requirements:* For master's, GMAT or GRE. Additional exam requirements/recommendations for international students: Required—TOEFL (minimum score 500 paper-based; 61 iBT), IELTS (minimum score 6). *Application deadline:* For fall admission, 5/15 for domestic and international students; for spring admission, 10/15 for domestic and international students. Applications are processed on a rolling basis. Application fee: $30. Electronic applications accepted. *Expenses:* Tuition, state resident: full-time $3113; part-time $283 per credit hour. Tuition, nonresident: full-time $7469; part-time $679 per credit hour. *Required fees:* $2287; $96 per credit hour. Tuition and fees vary according to course load. *Financial support:* In 2014–15, 32 students received support, including 16 teaching assistantships with full tuition reimbursements available (averaging $8,010 per year); career-related internships or fieldwork, Federal Work-Study, and unspecified assistantships also available. Support available to part-time students. Financial award application deadline: 3/1; financial award applicants required to submit FAFSA. *Unit head:* Dana Ringuette, Department Chair, 217-581-2428, Fax: 217-581-7209, E-mail: dringuette@eiu.edu. *Application contact:* Randall Beebe, Director of Graduate Studies, 217-581-2428, Fax: 217-581-7209, E-mail: rlbeebe@eiu.edu.
Website: http://www.eiu.edu/englishgrad/

Eastern Kentucky University, The Graduate School, College of Arts and Sciences, Department of English and Theatre, Richmond, KY 40475-3102. Offers creative writing (MFA); English (MA). Part-time and evening/weekend programs available. *Degree requirements:* For master's, thesis optional. *Entrance requirements:* For master's, GRE General Test, minimum GPA of 2.5, minor in English with 3.0 GPA. *Faculty research:* Old English, Victorian studies, women's studies, rhetoric, popular culture, novel studies.

Eastern Michigan University, Graduate School, College of Arts and Sciences, Department of English Language and Literature, Program in Children's Literature, Ypsilanti, MI 48197. Offers MA. Part-time and evening/weekend programs available. Postbaccalaureate distance learning degree programs offered (minimal on-campus study). *Students:* 3 full-time (all women), 8 part-time (5 women); includes 1 minority (Two or more races, non-Hispanic/Latino), 1 international. Average age 27. 9 applicants, 56% accepted, 2 enrolled. In 2014, 7 master's awarded. *Entrance requirements:* Additional exam requirements/recommendations for international students: Required—TOEFL. *Application deadline:* Applications are processed on a rolling basis. Application fee: $45. *Financial support:* Fellowships, research assistantships with full tuition reimbursements, teaching assistantships with full tuition reimbursements, and tuition waivers (partial) available. Financial award applicants required to submit FAFSA. *Application contact:* Dr. Ramona Caponegro, Program Coordinator, 734-487-0150, Fax: 734-483-9744, E-mail: rcaponeg@emich.edu.

Eastern Michigan University, Graduate School, College of Arts and Sciences, Department of English Language and Literature, Program in Literature, Ypsilanti, MI 48197. Offers MA. Part-time and evening/weekend programs available. Postbaccalaureate distance learning degree programs offered (minimal on-campus study). *Students:* 6 full-time (3 women), 15 part-time (11 women); includes 6 minority (4 Black or African American, non-Hispanic/Latino; 1 Asian, non-Hispanic/Latino; 1 Two or more races, non-Hispanic/Latino), 1 international. Average age 31. 21 applicants, 43% accepted, 6 enrolled. In 2014, 9 master's awarded. *Entrance requirements:* Additional exam requirements/recommendations for international students: Required—TOEFL. *Application deadline:* Applications are processed on a rolling basis. Application fee: $45. *Financial support:* Fellowships, research assistantships with full tuition reimbursements, teaching assistantships with full tuition reimbursements, career-related internships or fieldwork, Federal Work-Study, institutionally sponsored loans, scholarships/grants, tuition waivers (partial), and unspecified assistantships available. Support available to part-time students. Financial award applicants required to submit FAFSA. *Application contact:* Dr. Laura George, Program Coordinator, 734-487-2425, Fax: 734-483-9744, E-mail: lgeorge@emich.edu.

Eastern Michigan University, Graduate School, College of Arts and Sciences, Department of English Language and Literature, Programs in English Linguistics, Ypsilanti, MI 48197. Offers MA, Graduate Certificate. Part-time and evening/weekend programs available. Postbaccalaureate distance learning degree programs offered (minimal on-campus study). *Students:* 7 full-time (6 women), 14 part-time (11 women); includes 2 minority (both Black or African American, non-Hispanic/Latino), 5 international. Average age 30. 26 applicants, 42% accepted, 8 enrolled. In 2014, 3 master's awarded. *Degree requirements:* For master's, thesis (for some programs). *Entrance requirements:* Additional exam requirements/recommendations for international students: Required—TOEFL. *Application deadline:* Applications are processed on a rolling basis. Application fee: $45. *Financial support:* Fellowships with tuition reimbursements, research assistantships with full tuition reimbursements, teaching assistantships with full tuition reimbursements, career-related internships or fieldwork, Federal Work-Study, institutionally sponsored loans, scholarships/grants, tuition waivers (partial), and unspecified assistantships available. Support available to part-time students. Financial award applicants required to submit FAFSA. *Application contact:* Dr. Veronica Grondona, Program Advisor, 734-487-0968, Fax: 734-483-9744, E-mail: vgrondona@emich.edu.

Eastern New Mexico University, Graduate School, College of Liberal Arts and Sciences, Department of Languages and Literature, Portales, NM 88130. Offers English (MA), including English, literatures and cultures of migration. Part-time programs available. *Degree requirements:* For master's, one foreign language, thesis, oral and written comprehensive exams. *Entrance requirements:* For master's, minimum GPA of 3.0, foreign language proficiency, interview. Additional exam requirements/recommendations for international students: Required—TOEFL (minimum score 550 paper-based; 79 iBT), IELTS (minimum score 6). Electronic applications accepted.

Eastern Washington University, Graduate Studies, College of Arts, Letters and Education, Department of English, Cheney, WA 99004-2431. Offers literature (MA); rhetoric, composition, and technical communication (MA); teaching English as a second language (MA). *Degree requirements:* For master's, comprehensive exam, thesis or alternative. *Entrance requirements:* For master's, GRE General Test, minimum GPA of 3.0.

East Tennessee State University, School of Graduate Studies, College of Arts and Sciences, Department of Literature and Language, Johnson City, TN 37614. Offers MA, Postbaccalaureate Certificate. Part-time and evening/weekend programs available. *Faculty:* 31 full-time (12 women), 3 part-time/adjunct (1 woman). *Students:* 20 full-time (9 women), 4 part-time (3 women); includes 3 minority (2 Black or African American, non-Hispanic/Latino; 1 Two or more races, non-Hispanic/Latino), 2 international. Average age 27. 37 applicants, 24% accepted, 7 enrolled. In 2014, 7 master's, 11 other advanced degrees awarded. *Degree requirements:* For master's, comprehensive exam, thesis optional. *Entrance requirements:* For master's, GRE General Test, minimum undergraduate GPA of 3.0 in English, writing sample, three letters of recommendation; for Postbaccalaureate Certificate, GRE General Test, speaking and listening assessment, resume, three letters of recommendation. Additional exam requirements/recommendations for international students: Required—TOEFL (minimum score 550 paper-based; 79 iBT). *Application deadline:* For fall admission, 6/1 for domestic students, 4/30 for international students; for spring admission, 11/1 for domestic students, 9/30 for international students. Application fee: $35 ($45 for international students). Electronic applications accepted. *Financial support:* In 2014–15, 17 students received support, including 12 research assistantships with full tuition reimbursements

available (averaging $7,000 per year), 8 teaching assistantships with full tuition reimbursements available (averaging $7,000 per year); career-related internships or fieldwork, institutionally sponsored loans, scholarships/grants, and unspecified assistantships also available. Financial award application deadline: 7/1; financial award applicants required to submit FAFSA. *Faculty research:* Linguistics and dialectology, English education, critical literary theory, literary biography, environmental literature, modern and ancient languages. *Unit head:* Dr. Katherine Weiss, Chair, 423-439-4339, Fax: 423-439-7193, E-mail: weisk01@etsu.edu. *Application contact:* Kimberly Brockman, Graduate Specialist, 423-439-6165, Fax: 423-439-5624, E-mail: brockmank@etsu.edu.
Website: http://www.etsu.edu/cas/litlang/

Emory University, Laney Graduate School, Department of English, Atlanta, GA 30322-1100. Offers PhD, Graduate Certificate. *Degree requirements:* For doctorate, one foreign language, comprehensive exam, thesis/dissertation. *Entrance requirements:* For doctorate, GRE General Test, minimum GPA of 3.0. Additional exam requirements/recommendations for international students: Required—TOEFL. Electronic applications accepted. *Faculty research:* American literature, Renaissance literature, twentieth-century poetry, Irish literature, cultural studies.

Emporia State University, Program in English, Emporia, KS 66801-5415. Offers MA. Part-time programs available. *Faculty:* 18 full-time (8 women), 3 part-time/adjunct (2 women). *Students:* 11 full-time (6 women), 12 part-time (7 women); includes 4 minority (1 Black or African American, non-Hispanic/Latino; 1 American Indian or Alaska Native, non-Hispanic/Latino; 1 Hispanic/Latino; 1 Two or more races, non-Hispanic/Latino), 7 international. 11 applicants, 100% accepted, 7 enrolled. In 2014, 7 master's awarded. *Degree requirements:* For master's, comprehensive exam, thesis optional. *Entrance requirements:* For master's, minimum undergraduate GPA of 2.75 in last 60 hours. Additional exam requirements/recommendations for international students: Required—TOEFL (minimum score 550 paper-based; 68 iBT). *Application deadline:* For fall admission, 8/15 for domestic students. Application fee: $30 ($75 for international students). *Expenses:* Tuition, state resident: part-time $227 per credit hour. Tuition, nonresident: part-time $706 per credit hour. *Required fees:* $75 per credit hour. Tuition and fees vary according to campus/location. *Financial support:* In 2014–15, 14 teaching assistantships with full tuition reimbursements (averaging $8,244 per year) were awarded; Federal Work-Study, health care benefits, and unspecified assistantships also available. Financial award application deadline: 2/15; financial award applicants required to submit FAFSA. *Unit head:* Dr. Mel Storm, Interim Chair, 620-341-5216, E-mail: mstorm@emporia.edu. *Application contact:* Mary Sewell, Admissions Coordinator, 800-950-GRAD, Fax: 620-341-5909, E-mail: msewell@emporia.edu.
Website: http://www.emporia.edu/info/degrees-courses/grad/english

Fairleigh Dickinson University, Metropolitan Campus, University College: Arts, Sciences, and Professional Studies, Department of English, Philosophy, and Humanities, Program in English and Literature, Teaneck, NJ 07666-1914. Offers MA.

Fayetteville State University, Graduate School, Program in English, Fayetteville, NC 28301-4298. Offers MA. Part-time and evening/weekend programs available. *Faculty:* 11 full-time (7 women). *Students:* 1 part-time (0 women). Average age 29. In 2014, 2 master's awarded. *Degree requirements:* For master's, comprehensive exam, thesis, internship. *Entrance requirements:* For master's, GRE General Test. *Application deadline:* For fall admission, 4/15 for domestic students; for spring admission, 10/15 for domestic students. Applications are processed on a rolling basis. Application fee: $40. Electronic applications accepted. *Faculty research:* Medievalism: medieval political theory, medieval dream interpretation; animalism in modern literature; narrative tropes in medieval/early modern scientific texts; metacognitive reading strategies, twenty-first century literacy, critical reading and writing for underprepared students; popular culture; fat studies; rhetoric and rhetorical theory; composition and information literacy. *Unit head:* Dr. Trela Anderson, Chairperson, 910-672-1416, Fax: 910-672-1425, E-mail: emcshane@uncsfu.edu. *Application contact:* 910-672-1416, Fax: 910-672-1425, E-mail: emcshane@uncsfu.edu.

Fitchburg State University, Division of Graduate and Continuing Education, Programs in English and Teaching English (Secondary Level), Fitchburg, MA 01420-2697. Offers MA, MAT, Certificate. *Accreditation:* NCATE. Part-time and evening/weekend programs available. *Entrance requirements:* Additional exam requirements/recommendations for international students: Required—TOEFL (minimum score 550 paper-based; 79 iBT). Electronic applications accepted.

Florida Atlantic University, Dorothy F. Schmidt College of Arts and Letters, Department of English, Boca Raton, FL 33431-0991. Offers American literature (MA); British literature (MA); creative nonfiction (MFA); creative writing (MA); English (MAT); fiction (MFA); multicultural and world literacies (MA); poetry (MFA); rhetoric and composition (MA); science fiction and fantasy (MA). Part-time programs available. *Degree requirements:* For master's, one foreign language, thesis. *Entrance requirements:* For master's, GRE General Test, minimum GPA of 3.0, writing samples, 2 letters of recommendation. Additional exam requirements/recommendations for international students: Required—TOEFL (minimum score 500 paper-based; 61 iBT), IELTS (minimum score 6). Electronic applications accepted. *Expenses:* Tuition, state resident: full-time $7396; part-time $369.82 per credit hour. Tuition, nonresident: full-time $19,392; part-time $1024.81 per credit hour. Tuition and fees vary according to course load. *Faculty research:* African-American writers, critical theory, British-American, Asian-American.

Florida Gulf Coast University, College of Arts and Sciences, Program in English, Fort Myers, FL 33965-6565. Offers MA. Part-time programs available. *Faculty:* 230 full-time (93 women), 161 part-time/adjunct (75 women). *Students:* 7 full-time (4 women), 15 part-time (7 women). Average age 32. 24 applicants, 63% accepted. In 2014, 8 master's awarded. *Entrance requirements:* For master's, GRE General Test, minimum GPA of 3.0. Additional exam requirements/recommendations for international students: Required—TOEFL (minimum score 550 paper-based). *Application deadline:* For fall admission, 2/15 for domestic students. Application fee: $30. *Expenses:* Tuition, state resident: full-time $6974. Tuition, nonresident: full-time $28,170. *Required fees:* $1987. Tuition and fees vary according to course load. *Financial support:* In 2014–15, 2 students received support. Applicants required to submit FAFSA. *Unit head:* Kimberly Jackson, Interim Chair, 239-590-7423, E-mail: kjackson@fgcu.edu. *Application contact:* Patricia Rice, Executive Secretary, 239-590-7196, Fax: 239-590-7200, E-mail: price@fgcu.edu.

Florida International University, College of Arts and Sciences, Department of English, Program in English, Miami, FL 33199. Offers literature (MA). Part-time and evening/weekend programs available. *Degree requirements:* For master's, thesis. *Entrance requirements:* For master's, GRE General Test, minimum GPA of 3.0, letters of recommendation, letter of intent. Additional exam requirements/recommendations for international students: Required—TOEFL (minimum score 550 paper-based; 80 iBT). Electronic applications accepted.

Florida State University, The Graduate School, College of Arts and Sciences, Department of English, Tallahassee, FL 32312. Offers creative writing (MFA); English (PhD), including creative writing, literature, rhetoric and composition; literature (MA); rhetoric and composition (MA). Part-time programs available. *Faculty:* 47 full-time (24 women), 2 part-time/adjunct (1 woman). *Students:* 142 full-time (80 women), 31 part-time (23 women); includes 44 minority (17 Black or African American, non-Hispanic/Latino; 1 American Indian or Alaska Native, non-Hispanic/Latino; 12 Asian, non-Hispanic/Latino; 5 Hispanic/Latino; 9 Two or more races, non-Hispanic/Latino), 9 international. Average age 30. 307 applicants, 20% accepted, 38 enrolled. In 2014, 21 master's, 24 doctorates awarded. *Degree requirements:* For master's, one foreign language, thesis (for some programs), 33 hours of coursework including capstone essay, thesis or portfolio (MA); 45 hours of coursework including 9-12 thesis hours (MFA); for doctorate, comprehensive exam, thesis/dissertation, 27 hours of coursework, 24 hours of dissertation work. *Entrance requirements:* For master's and doctorate, GRE General Test, sample of written work, 3 letters of recommendation, resume. Additional exam requirements/recommendations for international students: Required—TOEFL. *Application deadline:* For fall admission, 1/1 priority date for domestic and international students. Application fee: $30. Electronic applications accepted. *Expenses:* Tuition, state resident: part-time $403.51 per credit hour. Tuition, nonresident: part-time $1004.85 per credit hour. *Required fees:* $75.81 per credit hour. One-time fee: $20 part-time. Tuition and fees vary according to campus/location. *Financial support:* In 2014–15, 132 students received support, including 5 fellowships with full and partial tuition reimbursements available, teaching assistantships with full and partial tuition reimbursements available (averaging $13,250 per year); career-related internships or fieldwork, Federal Work-Study, and institutionally sponsored loans also available. Financial award application deadline: 8/1; financial award applicants required to submit FAFSA. *Faculty research:* British and Irish literature, American literature, creative writing, rhetoric and composition, multiethnic transnational literature, history of text technology. *Unit head:* Dr. Eric Walker, Chairman, 850-644-4230, Fax: 850-644-0811, E-mail: ewalker@fsu.edu. *Application contact:* Ginger Martin, Senior Graduate Academic Coordinator, 850-644-1081, Fax: 850-644-9656, E-mail: vmartin@fsu.edu.
Website: http://english.fsu.edu/

Fordham University, Graduate School of Arts and Sciences, Department of English Language and Literature, New York, NY 10458. Offers MA, PhD. Part-time and evening/weekend programs available. *Faculty:* 37 full-time (23 women). *Students:* 73 full-time (50 women), 21 part-time (8 women); includes 7 minority (4 Black or African American, non-Hispanic/Latino; 1 Asian, non-Hispanic/Latino; 2 Hispanic/Latino), 6 international. Average age 31. 126 applicants, 58% accepted, 14 enrolled. In 2014, 28 master's, 10 doctorates awarded. Terminal master's awarded for partial completion of doctoral program. *Degree requirements:* For master's, one foreign language, comprehensive exam, thesis optional; for doctorate, 2 foreign languages, comprehensive exam, thesis/dissertation. *Entrance requirements:* For master's, GRE General Test; for doctorate, GRE General Test, GRE Subject Test. Additional exam requirements/recommendations for international students: Required—TOEFL (minimum score 650 paper-based). *Application deadline:* For fall admission, 1/4 priority date for domestic students; for spring admission, 11/1 for domestic students. Application fee: $70. Electronic applications accepted. *Financial support:* In 2014–15, 63 students received support, including 2 fellowships with full and partial tuition reimbursements available (averaging $20,580 per year), 65 teaching assistantships with full and partial tuition reimbursements available (averaging $20,586 per year); institutionally sponsored loans, tuition waivers (full and partial), and unspecified assistantships also available. Financial award application deadline: 1/4; financial award applicants required to submit FAFSA. *Faculty research:* Nineteenth century British and American literature, Shakespeare and early modern drama, Aesthetic Theory, Old Norse, poetics of race and gender, Anglo-Norman. *Unit head:* Dr. Edward Cahill, Director, Graduate Studies, 718-817-4017, Fax: 718-817-4010, E-mail: edcahill@fordham.edu. *Application contact:* Bernadette Valentino-Morrison, Director of Graduate Admissions, 718-817-4419, Fax: 718-817-3566, E-mail: valentinomor@fordham.edu.

Fort Hays State University, Graduate School, College of Arts and Sciences, Department of English, Hays, KS 67601-4099. Offers MA. *Degree requirements:* For master's, comprehensive exam, thesis or alternative. *Entrance requirements:* Additional exam requirements/recommendations for international students: Required—TOEFL (minimum score 550 paper-based). Electronic applications accepted. *Faculty research:* Eisenhower and Hansen papers, Celtic literature and culture, poetry of Robert Frost.

Gannon University, School of Graduate Studies, College of Humanities, Education, and Social Sciences, School of Humanities, Program in English, Erie, PA 16541-0001. Offers MA. Part-time and evening/weekend programs available. *Degree requirements:* For master's, thesis. *Entrance requirements:* For master's, GRE, interview. Additional exam requirements/recommendations for international students: Required—TOEFL (minimum score 79 iBT). Electronic applications accepted.

Gardner-Webb University, Graduate School, Department of English, Boiling Springs, NC 28017. Offers English (MA); English education (MA). Part-time and evening/weekend programs available. *Students:* 14 part-time (all women); includes 1 minority (American Indian or Alaska Native, non-Hispanic/Latino). Average age 32. 47 applicants, 36% accepted, 12 enrolled. In 2014, 1 master's awarded. *Degree requirements:* For master's, comprehensive exam. *Entrance requirements:* For master's, GRE General Test, MAT, or NTE; PRAXIS, minimum GPA of 2.5. *Application deadline:* For fall admission, 8/1 priority date for domestic students. Applications are processed on a rolling basis. Application fee: $40. Electronic applications accepted. *Expenses: Tuition:* Part-time $406 per credit hour. Tuition and fees vary according to program. *Financial support:* Unspecified assistantships available. *Unit head:* Dr. June Hobbs, Chair, 704-406-4412, Fax: 704-406-3921, E-mail: jhobbs@gardner-webb.edu. *Application contact:* Office of Graduate Admissions, 877-498-4723, Fax: 704-406-3895, E-mail: gradinfo@gardner-webb.edu.

George Mason University, College of Humanities and Social Sciences, Department of English, Fairfax, VA 22030. Offers creative writing (MFA), including fiction; English (MA, Certificate); linguistics (PhD); writing and rhetoric (PhD). *Faculty:* 78 full-time (45 women), 35 part-time/adjunct (21 women). *Students:* 103 full-time (71 women), 140 part-time (105 women); includes 36 minority (10 Black or African American, non-Hispanic/Latino; 8 Asian, non-Hispanic/Latino; 12 Hispanic/Latino; 6 Two or more races, non-Hispanic/Latino), 14 international. Average age 32. 267 applicants, 52% accepted, 67 enrolled. In 2014, 68 master's, 11 other advanced degrees awarded. *Degree requirements:* For master's, thesis (for some programs), proficiency in a foreign language by course work or translation test; for doctorate, thesis/dissertation, 2 graduating papers. *Entrance requirements:* For master's, official transcripts; expanded goals statement; writing sample; portfolio; 2 letters of recommendation; for doctorate, GRE, expanded goals statement; 3 letters of recommendation; writing sample; introductory course in linguistics; official transcripts; for Certificate, official transcripts; expanded goals statement; 3 letters of recommendation; portfolio and writing sample (for professional writing and rhetoric); resume and writing sample (for folklore). Additional exam requirements/recommendations for international students: Required—TOEFL (minimum score 570 paper-based; 80 iBT), IELTS (minimum score 6.5), PTE. *Application deadline:* For fall admission, 3/15 priority date for domestic students; for spring admission, 10/15 priority date for domestic students. Application fee: $65 ($80 for international students). Electronic applications accepted. *Expenses:* Tuition, state resident: full-time $9794; part-time $408 per credit hour. Tuition, nonresident: full-time $26,978; part-time $1124 per credit hour. *Required fees:* $2820; $118 per credit hour.

Tuition and fees vary according to course load and program. *Financial support:* In 2014–15, 72 students received support, including 3 fellowships (averaging $1,823 per year), 6 research assistantships with full and partial tuition reimbursements available (averaging $14,605 per year), 65 teaching assistantships with full and partial tuition reimbursements available (averaging $11,909 per year); career-related internships or fieldwork, Federal Work-Study, scholarships/grants, unspecified assistantships, and health care benefits (for full-time research or teaching assistantship recipients) also available. Support available to part-time students. Financial award application deadline: 3/1; financial award applicants required to submit FAFSA. *Faculty research:* Literature, professional writing and editing, writing of fiction or poetry. *Total annual research expenditures:* $84,493. *Unit head:* Debra Lattanzi-Shutika, Chair, 703-993-1170, Fax: 703-993-1161, E-mail: dshutika@gmu.edu. *Application contact:* Alex Walsh, Graduate Admissions Coordinator, 703-993-1185, Fax: 703-993-1161, E-mail: awalsh7@gmu.edu.
Website: http://english.gmu.edu

Georgetown University, Graduate School of Arts and Sciences, Department of English, Washington, DC 20057. Offers British and American literature (MA). *Degree requirements:* For master's, thesis or alternative, independent study, oral exam. *Entrance requirements:* For master's, GRE General Test. Additional exam requirements/recommendations for international students: Required—TOEFL.

The George Washington University, Columbian College of Arts and Sciences, Department of English, Washington, DC 20052. Offers MA, PhD. Part-time and evening/weekend programs available. *Faculty:* 38 full-time (17 women). *Students:* 30 full-time (22 women), 24 part-time (18 women); includes 5 minority (2 Black or African American, non-Hispanic/Latino; 1 Asian, non-Hispanic/Latino; 2 Hispanic/Latino), 8 international. Average age 29. 111 applicants, 32% accepted, 17 enrolled. In 2014, 9 master's, 5 doctorates awarded. Terminal master's awarded for partial completion of doctoral program. *Degree requirements:* For master's, one foreign language, comprehensive exam, thesis or alternative; for doctorate, 2 foreign languages, thesis/dissertation, general exam. *Entrance requirements:* For master's and doctorate, GRE General Test, GRE Subject Test, minimum GPA of 3.0, writing sample. Additional exam requirements/recommendations for international students: Required—TOEFL (minimum score 550 paper-based; 80 iBT). *Application deadline:* For fall admission, 1/15 priority date for domestic and international students; for spring admission, 10/1 priority date for domestic students, 9/1 priority date for international students. Applications are processed on a rolling basis. Application fee: $75. Electronic applications accepted. *Financial support:* In 2014–15, 18 students received support. Fellowships with tuition reimbursements available, teaching assistantships with tuition reimbursements available, and Federal Work-Study available. Financial award application deadline: 1/15. *Unit head:* Robert McRuer, Chair, 202-994-1461, E-mail: rmcruer@gwu.edu. *Application contact:* 202-994-6210, Fax: 202-994-6213, E-mail: askccas@gwu.edu.
Website: http://departments.columbian.gwu.edu/english/

Georgia College & State University, Graduate School, College of Arts and Sciences, Department of English and Rhetoric, Program in English, Milledgeville, GA 31061. Offers MA. Part-time and evening/weekend programs available. *Students:* 6 full-time (2 women), 4 part-time (3 women); includes 2 minority (both Black or African American, non-Hispanic/Latino). Average age 26. 5 applicants, 100% accepted, 4 enrolled. In 2014, 4 master's awarded. *Degree requirements:* For master's, one foreign language, comprehensive exam, thesis optional. *Entrance requirements:* For master's, GRE, undergraduate major in English, minimum GPA of 3.0, 2 letters of recommendation, writing samples. Additional exam requirements/recommendations for international students: Recommended—TOEFL (minimum score 550 paper-based; 79 iBT). *Application deadline:* For fall admission, 7/1 for domestic students, 4/1 for international students; for spring admission, 11/15 for domestic students, 9/1 for international students. Application fee: $40. Electronic applications accepted. *Expenses: Tuition, area resident:* Part-time $283 per credit hour. Tuition, nonresident: part-time $1027 per credit hour. *Required fees:* $995 per semester. Full-time tuition and fees vary according to course load, degree level, campus/location and program. *Financial support:* In 2014–15, 3 teaching assistantships were awarded; unspecified assistantships also available. Financial award applicants required to submit FAFSA. *Unit head:* Dr. Jennifer Flaherty, MA Program Coordinator, 478-445-3180, Fax: 478-445-4581, E-mail: jennifer.flaherty@gcsu.edu. *Application contact:* Kate Marshall, Graduate Admissions Coordinator, 478-445-1184, Fax: 478-445-1336, E-mail: grad-admit@gcsu.edu.
Website: http://www.gcsu.edu/english/maenglish.htm

Georgia Southern University, Jack N. Averitt College of Graduate Studies, College of Liberal Arts and Social Sciences, Program in English, Statesboro, GA 30460. Offers MA. Part-time programs available. *Students:* 13 full-time (all women), 3 part-time (2 women); includes 7 minority (2 Black or African American, non-Hispanic/Latino; 5 Hispanic/Latino), 1 international. Average age 28. 9 applicants, 89% accepted, 7 enrolled. In 2014, 6 master's awarded. *Degree requirements:* For master's, one foreign language, thesis optional, terminal exams. *Entrance requirements:* For master's, GRE General Test, minimum GPA of 3.0, letters of reference. Additional exam requirements/recommendations for international students: Required—TOEFL (minimum score 550 paper-based; 80 iBT), IELTS (minimum score 6). *Application deadline:* For fall admission, 3/1 priority date for domestic and international students; for spring admission, 10/1 priority date for domestic students, 10/1 for international students. Applications are processed on a rolling basis. Application fee: $50. Electronic applications accepted. *Expenses:* Tuition, state resident: full-time $7236; part-time $277 per semester hour. Tuition, nonresident: full-time $27,118; part-time $1105 per semester hour. *Required fees:* $2092. *Financial support:* In 2014–15, 11 students received support, including research assistantships with partial tuition reimbursements available (averaging $7,200 per year), teaching assistantships with partial tuition reimbursements available (averaging $7,200 per year); career-related internships or fieldwork, Federal Work-Study, scholarships/grants, tuition waivers (partial), and unspecified assistantships also available. Support available to part-time students. Financial award application deadline: 4/15; financial award applicants required to submit FAFSA. *Faculty research:* Irish literature, Gothic literature, modern British drama, American short story, children's literature. *Unit head:* Dr. Dustin Anderson, Graduate Program Director, 912-478-1354, E-mail: danderson@georgiasouthern.edu.
Website: http://class.georgiasouthern.edu/litphi/

Georgia State University, College of Arts and Sciences, Department of English, Atlanta, GA 30302-3083. Offers creative writing (MA, MFA, PhD), including creative writing (PhD), fiction (MA, MFA), poetry (MA, MFA); English (MA, PhD); literary studies (MA, PhD); rhetoric and composition (MA, PhD). Part-time programs available. *Faculty:* 46 full-time (21 women). *Students:* 119 full-time (79 women), 79 part-time (56 women); includes 22 minority (10 Black or African American, non-Hispanic/Latino; 8 Asian, non-Hispanic/Latino; 2 Hispanic/Latino; 2 Two or more races, non-Hispanic/Latino), 9 international. Average age 37. 203 applicants, 44% accepted, 32 enrolled. In 2014, 14 master's, 13 doctorates awarded. *Degree requirements:* For master's, one foreign language, thesis, 30 hours of coursework plus 6 hours of thesis credit; for doctorate, one foreign language, comprehensive exam, thesis/dissertation, second exam. *Entrance requirements:* For master's and doctorate, GRE. Additional exam requirements/recommendations for international students: Required—TOEFL (minimum score 550 paper-based; 80 iBT). *Application deadline:* For fall admission, 1/15 for domestic and international students. Application fee: $50. Electronic applications accepted. *Expenses:* Tuition, state resident: full-time $6516; part-time $362 per credit hour. Tuition, nonresident: full-time $22,014; part-time $1223 per credit hour. *Required fees:* $2128 per semester. Tuition and fees vary according to course load and program. *Financial support:* In 2014–15, research assistantships with full tuition reimbursements (averaging $6,000 per year), teaching assistantships with full tuition reimbursements (averaging $15,000 per year) were awarded; career-related internships or fieldwork, traineeships, and health care benefits also available. Financial award application deadline: 2/15. *Faculty research:* British and American literature and transnational literatures in English, literary theory and cultural studies, creative writing (fiction and poetry), rhetoric and composition, new media and digital humanities. *Unit head:* Dr. Calvin Thomas, Director of Graduate Studies in English, 404-413-5808, Fax: 404-413-5830, E-mail: cthomas@gsu.edu. *Application contact:* Amber Amari, Director, Graduate and Scheduling Services, 404-413-5037, E-mail: aamari@gsu.edu.
Website: http://www.english.gsu.edu

Governors State University, College of Arts and Sciences, Program in English, University Park, IL 60484. Offers MA. Part-time and evening/weekend programs available. *Degree requirements:* For master's, thesis or alternative. *Entrance requirements:* For master's, bachelor's degree in related field.

The Graduate Center, City University of New York, Graduate Studies, Program in English, New York, NY 10016-4039. Offers PhD. *Degree requirements:* For doctorate, 2 foreign languages, thesis/dissertation. *Entrance requirements:* For doctorate, GRE General Test, GRE Subject Test, writing sample, curriculum vitae. Additional exam requirements/recommendations for international students: Required—TOEFL. Electronic applications accepted.

Grambling State University, School of Graduate Studies and Research, College of Education, Department of Educational Leadership, Grambling, LA 71245. Offers developmental education (MS, Ed D, PMC), including curriculum and instructional design (Ed D), English (MS), guidance and counseling (MS), higher education administration and management (Ed D), mathematics (MS), reading (MS), science (MS), student development and personnel services (Ed D); educational leadership (M Ed). Part-time and evening/weekend programs available. *Degree requirements:* For master's, comprehensive exam, thesis (for some programs); for doctorate, comprehensive exam, thesis/dissertation. *Entrance requirements:* For master's, GRE, minimum GPA of 2.5 on last degree; for doctorate, GRE (minimum score 1000, 500 on Verbal), master's degree, minimum GPA of 3.0 on last degree. Additional exam requirements/recommendations for international students: Required—TOEFL (minimum score 500 paper-based; 62 iBT). Electronic applications accepted.

Grand Valley State University, College of Liberal Arts and Sciences, English Department, Allendale, MI 49401-9403. Offers MA. *Faculty:* 6 full-time (3 women). *Students:* 5 full-time (3 women), 26 part-time (17 women); includes 2 minority (both Hispanic/Latino). Average age 32. 14 applicants, 100% accepted, 6 enrolled. In 2014, 6 master's awarded. *Entrance requirements:* Additional exam requirements/recommendations for international students: Required—TOEFL. Application fee: $30. *Expenses:* Tuition, state resident: full-time $10,602; part-time $589 per credit hour. Tuition, nonresident: full-time $14,022; part-time $779 per credit hour. Tuition and fees vary according to degree level and program. *Financial support:* In 2014–15, 7 students received support, including 2 fellowships (averaging $1,125 per year), 5 research assistantships with full and partial tuition reimbursements available (averaging $4,819 per year). *Faculty research:* Literary history, philosophy and literature, feminist issues in literature. *Unit head:* Dr. Corinna McLeod, Chair, 616-331-8576, E-mail: mcleodc@gvsu.edu. *Application contact:* Dr. Jo Miller, Graduate Program Co-Director, 616-331-3552, E-mail: millerj@gvsu.edu.

Hardin-Simmons University, Graduate School, Cynthia Ann Parker College of Liberal Arts, Department of English, Abilene, TX 79698-0001. Offers MA. Part-time programs available. *Faculty:* 4 full-time (2 women), 1 (woman) part-time/adjunct. *Students:* 1 (woman) full-time, 2 part-time (1 woman). Average age 34. *Degree requirements:* For master's, one foreign language, comprehensive exam, thesis or alternative. *Entrance requirements:* For master's, minimum undergraduate GPA of 3.0 in English, 2.7 overall; writing sample; letters of recommendation; interview. Additional exam requirements/recommendations for international students: Required—TOEFL (minimum score 550 paper-based; 75 iBT). *Application deadline:* For fall admission, 8/15 priority date for domestic students, 4/1 for international students; for spring admission, 1/5 priority date for domestic students, 9/1 for international students. Applications are processed on a rolling basis. Application fee: $50. *Expenses: Tuition:* Full-time $12,060; part-time $670 per credit hour. *Required fees:* $325; $110 per semester. Tuition and fees vary according to program. *Financial support:* In 2014–15, 5 students received support. Fellowships and scholarships/grants available. Support available to part-time students. Financial award application deadline: 6/30; financial award applicants required to submit FAFSA. *Faculty research:* Milton, Tennyson, American Romantic period, Derek Walcott, women's literature. *Unit head:* Dr. Jason King, Program Director, 325-670-1303, Fax: 325-671-5764, E-mail: jking@hsutx.edu. *Application contact:* Dr. Nancy Kucinski, Dean of Graduate Studies, 325-670-1298, Fax: 325-670-1564, E-mail: gradoff@hsutx.edu.
Website: http://www.hsutx.edu/academics/cap/graduate/english

Harvard University, Extension School, Cambridge, MA 02138-3722. Offers applied sciences (CAS); biotechnology (ALM); educational technologies (ALM); educational technology (CET); English for graduate and professional studies (DGP); environmental management (ALM, CEM); information technology (ALM); journalism (ALM); liberal arts (ALM); management (ALM, CM); mathematics for teaching (ALM); museum studies (ALM); premedical studies (Diploma); publication and communication (CPC). Part-time and evening/weekend programs available. *Degree requirements:* For master's, thesis. *Entrance requirements:* For master's, 3 completed graduate courses with grade of B or higher. Additional exam requirements/recommendations for international students: Required—TOEFL (minimum score 600 paper-based), TWE (minimum score 5). *Expenses:* Contact institution.

Harvard University, Graduate School of Arts and Sciences, Department of English and American Literature and Language, Cambridge, MA 02138. Offers critical theory (PhD); eighteenth-century literature (PhD); literature: nineteenth-century to the present (PhD); medieval literature and language (PhD); modern British and American literature (PhD); Renaissance literature (PhD). Terminal master's awarded for partial completion of doctoral program. *Degree requirements:* For doctorate, 2 foreign languages, thesis/dissertation, oral exam. *Entrance requirements:* For doctorate, GRE General Test, GRE Subject Test, writing sample. Additional exam requirements/recommendations for international students: Required—TOEFL. *Faculty research:* Old and Middle English language and literature, drama, creative writing, transition to Romanticism, history and theory of criticism.

Heritage University, Graduate Programs in Education, Program in Professional Studies, Toppenish, WA 98948-9599. Offers bilingual education/ESL (M Ed); biology (M Ed); English and literature (M Ed); reading/literacy (M Ed); special education (M Ed). Part-time and evening/weekend programs available. *Degree requirements:* For master's, comprehensive exam (for some programs), thesis (for some programs).

English

Hofstra University, College of Liberal Arts and Sciences, Programs in English, Hempstead, NY 11549. Offers creative writing (MFA). Part-time programs available. *Students:* 14 full-time (8 women), 20 part-time (14 women); includes 6 minority (5 Black or African American, non-Hispanic/Latino; 1 Hispanic/Latino), 2 international. Average age 34. 32 applicants, 84% accepted, 12 enrolled. In 2014, 12 master's awarded. *Degree requirements:* For master's, thesis optional, minimum GPA of 3.0. *Entrance requirements:* For master's, writing sample, essay, minimum GPA of 3.0 in literature courses. Additional exam requirements/recommendations for international students: Required—TOEFL (minimum score 550 paper-based; 80 iBT). *Application deadline:* Applications are processed on a rolling basis. Application fee: $70 ($75 for international students). Electronic applications accepted. *Expenses:* Tuition: Full-time $20,610; part-time $1145 per credit hour. *Required fees:* $970; $165 per term. Tuition and fees vary according to program. *Financial support:* In 2014–15, 18 students received support, including 10 fellowships with full and partial tuition reimbursements available (averaging $4,530 per year), 1 research assistantship with full and partial tuition reimbursement available (averaging $9,013 per year); Federal Work-Study, institutionally sponsored loans, scholarships/grants, and tuition waivers (full and partial) also available. Support available to part-time students. Financial award applicants required to submit FAFSA. *Faculty research:* Poetry and novels, Chaucer, Shakespeare, Milton, Melville, Austen, Woolf, Morrision, British Modernism, medieval, Early Modern, Long Eighteenth Century, Victorian, literary criticism focusing on nineteenth century through twenty-first century American literature and culture, psychoanalysis, queer studies, disability studies, trauma theory, critical theory, Anglophone literatures, Post-colonial studies, digital studies. *Unit head:* Erik Brogger, Program Director, 516-463-5397, Fax: 516-463-6395, E-mail: engeab@hofstra.edu. *Application contact:* Sunil Samuel, Assistant Vice President of Admissions, 516-463-4723, Fax: 516-463-4664, E-mail: graduateadmission@hofstra.edu.
Website: http://www.hofstra.edu/hclas

Hollins University, Graduate Programs, Program in Children's Literature, Roanoke, VA 24020. Offers children's book writing and illustrating (MFA); children's literature (MA, MFA). Program offered during summer only. Part-time programs available. *Faculty:* 1 (woman) full-time, 9 part-time/adjunct (8 women). *Students:* 41 full-time (38 women), 11 part-time (all women); includes 4 minority (1 Asian, non-Hispanic/Latino; 3 Hispanic/Latino). Average age 34. 35 applicants, 100% accepted, 24 enrolled. In 2014, 11 degrees awarded. *Degree requirements:* For master's, one foreign language, comprehensive exam, thesis. *Entrance requirements:* For master's, letters of recommendation, portfolio. Additional exam requirements/recommendations for international students: Required—TOEFL (minimum score 550 paper-based; 79 iBT). *Application deadline:* For fall admission, 2/15 for domestic and international students. Application fee: $40. Electronic applications accepted. *Expenses:* Expenses: $775 per credit hour, technology fee $85. *Financial support:* In 2014–15, 23 students received support, including 23 fellowships (averaging $1,000 per year); Federal Work-Study and scholarships/grants also available. Support available to part-time students. Financial award application deadline: 2/15; financial award applicants required to submit FAFSA. *Faculty research:* Fantasy, children's film, young adult fiction, gender studies, mythology and folk tales, children's poetry, picture books. *Unit head:* Amanda Cockrell, Director, 540-362-6024, Fax: 540-362-6642, E-mail: acockrell@hollins.edu. *Application contact:* Cathy S. Koon, Manager of Graduate Services, 540-362-6326, Fax: 540-362-6288, E-mail: ckoon@hollins.edu.
Website: http://www.hollins.edu/

Howard University, Graduate School, Department of English, Washington, DC 20059-0002. Offers MA, PhD. Part-time programs available. *Degree requirements:* For master's, one foreign language, comprehensive exam, thesis; for doctorate, 2 foreign languages, comprehensive exam, thesis/dissertation, qualifying exam. *Entrance requirements:* For master's, GRE General Test, minimum GPA of 3.0; for doctorate, GRE General Test.

Humboldt State University, Academic Programs, College of Arts, Humanities, and Social Sciences, Department of English, Arcata, CA 95521-8299. Offers English (MA), including composition studies and pedagogy, literary and cultural studies, teaching English as a second language. *Students:* 9 full-time (6 women), 1 (woman) part-time; includes 2 minority (both Hispanic/Latino). Average age 26. 13 applicants, 38% accepted, 4 enrolled. In 2014, 8 master's awarded. *Degree requirements:* For master's, variable foreign language requirement, thesis or alternative, qualifying exam. *Entrance requirements:* For master's, GRE, minimum GPA of 3.0, 3 letters of recommendation, sample of writing. Additional exam requirements/recommendations for international students: Required—TOEFL (minimum score 500 paper-based). *Application deadline:* For fall admission, 3/1 for domestic students; for spring admission, 11/1 for domestic students. Applications are processed on a rolling basis. Application fee: $55. *Expenses:* Tuition, state resident: full-time $6738; part-time $3906 per year. Tuition, nonresident: full-time $13,434; part-time $6138 per year. *Required fees:* $1690; $1266 per year. Tuition and fees vary according to program. *Financial support:* Teaching assistantships, career-related internships or fieldwork, Federal Work-Study, and institutionally sponsored loans available. Financial award application deadline: 3/1; financial award applicants required to submit FAFSA. *Faculty research:* Teaching of writing, literature. *Unit head:* Mary Ann Creadon, Department Chair, 707-826-3758, E-mail: mac4@humboldt.edu. *Application contact:* Michael Eldridge, Professor, 707-826-5906, E-mail: me2@humboldt.edu.
Website: http://www.humboldt.edu/english/

Hunter College of the City University of New York, Graduate School, School of Arts and Sciences, Department of English, Program in British and American Literature, New York, NY 10065-5085. Offers MA. Part-time and evening/weekend programs available. *Students:* 44 part-time (25 women); includes 7 minority (3 Black or African American, non-Hispanic/Latino; 2 Asian, non-Hispanic/Latino; 2 Hispanic/Latino), 1 international. Average age 31. 23 applicants, 57% accepted, 7 enrolled. In 2014, 15 master's awarded. *Degree requirements:* For master's, one foreign language, comprehensive exam, thesis, essay. *Entrance requirements:* For master's, GRE General Test, minimum 18 credits of course work in English, excluding journalism and writing. Additional exam requirements/recommendations for international students: Required—TOEFL. *Application deadline:* For fall admission, 4/1 for domestic students, 2/1 for international students; for spring admission, 11/1 for domestic students, 9/1 for international students. *Financial support:* Federal Work-Study and tuition waivers (partial) available. Support available to part-time students. Financial award application deadline: 4/15. *Unit head:* Dr. Christina Alfar, Associate Professor, 212-772-5187, E-mail: calfar@hunter.cuny.edu. *Application contact:* David Carlson, Education Adviser, 212-772-5074, E-mail: dcarlson@hunter.cuny.edu.

Idaho State University, Office of Graduate Studies, College of Arts and Letters, Department of English, Pocatello, ID 83209-8056. Offers English (MA, DA); English and the teaching of English (PhD); TESOL (Post-Master's Certificate). Part-time programs available. *Degree requirements:* For master's, one foreign language, comprehensive exam, thesis optional; for doctorate, one foreign language, comprehensive exam, thesis/dissertation, 2 papers, 2 teaching internships; for Post-Master's Certificate, 6 credits of elective linguistics, practicum. *Entrance requirements:* For master's, GRE General Test (minimum 50th percentile verbal), general literature exam, minimum GPA of 3.0, 3

letters of recommendation, 5-page writing sample; for doctorate, GRE General Test, GRE Subject Test, minimum GPA of 3.5, writing examples, 3 letters of recommendation, master's degree in English; for Post-Master's Certificate, GRE (minimum 35th percentile on verbal section), bachelor's degree, minimum undergraduate GPA of 3.0 in last 2 years, 3 letters of recommendation, knowledge of second language. Additional exam requirements/recommendations for international students: Required—TOEFL (minimum score 550 paper-based; 80 iBT). Electronic applications accepted. *Faculty research:* American literature, Renaissance literature, composition and rhetoric, Intermountain West studies, ethics.

Illinois State University, Graduate School, College of Arts and Sciences, Department of English, Program in English, Normal, IL 61790-2200. Offers English (MA, MS); English studies (PhD). *Degree requirements:* For doctorate, thesis/dissertation, 2 terms of residency. *Entrance requirements:* For master's, GRE General Test, minimum GPA of 3.0 in last 60 hours; for doctorate, GRE General Test.

Indiana State University, College of Graduate and Professional Studies, College of Arts and Sciences, Department of English, Terre Haute, IN 47809. Offers English teaching (MA); history (MA); literature (MA). Part-time and evening/weekend programs available. *Degree requirements:* For master's, one foreign language, thesis optional. *Entrance requirements:* For master's, minimum GPA of 2.75 in all English courses above freshman level. Additional exam requirements/recommendations for international students: Required—TOEFL (minimum score 550 paper-based). Electronic applications accepted.

Indiana University Bloomington, University Graduate School, College of Arts and Sciences, Department of English, Bloomington, IN 47405. Offers composition, literacy, and culture (PhD); creative writing (MA, MFA), including fiction, poetry; language (MA); literature (MA, PhD); writing (MA). Part-time programs available. *Faculty:* 51 full-time (23 women). *Students:* 157 full-time (108 women), 7 part-time (4 women); includes 27 minority (5 Black or African American, non-Hispanic/Latino; 12 Asian, non-Hispanic/Latino; 4 Hispanic/Latino; 6 Two or more races, non-Hispanic/Latino), 6 international. Average age 30. 383 applicants, 5% accepted, 20 enrolled. In 2014, 20 master's, 12 doctorates awarded. Terminal master's awarded for partial completion of doctoral program. *Degree requirements:* For master's, 30-36 credit hours plus one language proficiency (for MA); 60 credit hours plus thesis (for MFA); for doctorate, thesis/dissertation, qualifying exam, 90 credit hours; 2nd language proficiency or one language only if acquired at in-depth level. *Entrance requirements:* For master's, GRE General Test, GRE Subject Test (for all but MFA and MA in creative writing), minimum GPA of 3.5; for doctorate, GRE General Test, GRE Subject Test, minimum GPA of 3.7. Additional exam requirements/recommendations for international students: Required—TOEFL. *Application deadline:* For fall admission, 1/1 priority date for domestic students, 12/1 for international students. Application fee: $55 ($65 for international students). Electronic applications accepted. *Financial support:* Fellowships with full and partial tuition reimbursements, research assistantships with partial tuition reimbursements, teaching assistantships with full tuition reimbursements, career-related internships or fieldwork, and health care benefits available. Financial award application deadline: 2/1. *Unit head:* Dr. Paul Gutjahr, Chair, 812-855-2147, Fax: 812-855-9535, E-mail: pgutjahr@indiana.edu. *Application contact:* Ellen MacKay, Director of Graduate Studies, 812-855-9536, Fax: 812-855-9535, E-mail: emackay@indiana.edu.
Website: http://www.indiana.edu/~engweb/

Indiana University of Pennsylvania, School of Graduate Studies and Research, College of Humanities and Social Sciences, Department of English, Program in Composition and Literature, Indiana, PA 15705-1087. Offers MA. *Faculty:* 29 full-time (13 women). *Students:* 7 full-time (all women), 1 (woman) part-time, 3 international. Average age 25. 17 applicants, 65% accepted, 4 enrolled. Application fee: $50. *Financial support:* In 2014–15, 2 research assistantships with full and partial tuition reimbursements (averaging $1,000 per year) were awarded. *Unit head:* Dr. Todd Thompson, Coordinator, 724-357-2267, E-mail: todd.thompson@iup.edu.
Website: http://www.iup.edu/english/grad/composition-literature-ma/

Indiana University of Pennsylvania, School of Graduate Studies and Research, College of Humanities and Social Sciences, Department of English, Program in Composition and Teaching English to Speakers of Other Languages, Indiana, PA 15705-1087. Offers PhD. Part-time programs available. *Faculty:* 29 full-time (13 women). *Students:* 25 full-time (15 women), 82 part-time (58 women); includes 11 minority (5 Black or African American, non-Hispanic/Latino; 3 Asian, non-Hispanic/Latino; 2 Hispanic/Latino; 1 Two or more races, non-Hispanic/Latino), 28 international. Average age 39. 175 applicants, 29% accepted, 12 enrolled. In 2014, 25 doctorates awarded. *Degree requirements:* For doctorate, one foreign language, comprehensive exam, thesis/dissertation. *Entrance requirements:* For doctorate, 2 letters of recommendation. Additional exam requirements/recommendations for international students: Required—TOEFL (minimum score 600 paper-based). *Application deadline:* For fall admission, 2/1 priority date for domestic students; for summer admission, 11/1 priority date for domestic students. Applications are processed on a rolling basis. Application fee: $50. Electronic applications accepted. *Financial support:* In 2014–15, 9 fellowships with full tuition reimbursements (averaging $727 per year), 17 research assistantships with full and partial tuition reimbursements (averaging $6,372 per year), 5 teaching assistantships with partial tuition reimbursements (averaging $23,305 per year) were awarded; career-related internships or fieldwork, Federal Work-Study, scholarships/grants, and unspecified assistantships also available. Support available to part-time students. Financial award application deadline: 4/15; financial award applicants required to submit FAFSA. *Unit head:* Dr. Sharon Deckert, Graduate Coordinator, 724-357-2261, E-mail: sharon.deckert@iup.edu.
Website: http://www.iup.edu/upper.aspx?id-49407

Indiana University of Pennsylvania, School of Graduate Studies and Research, College of Humanities and Social Sciences, Department of English, Program in English: Generalist, Indiana, PA 15705-1087. Offers MA. Part-time programs available. *Faculty:* 29 full-time (13 women). *Students:* 1 (woman) full-time. Average age 25. In 2014, 2 master's awarded. *Degree requirements:* For master's, thesis optional. *Entrance requirements:* Additional exam requirements/recommendations for international students: Required—TOEFL (minimum score 540 paper-based). *Application deadline:* Applications are processed on a rolling basis. Application fee: $50. Electronic applications accepted. *Financial support:* Research assistantships with full and partial tuition reimbursements, career-related internships or fieldwork, Federal Work-Study, scholarships/grants, and unspecified assistantships available. Financial award application deadline: 4/15; financial award applicants required to submit FAFSA. *Unit head:* Dr. Todd Thompson, Coordinator, 724-357-4931, E-mail: todd.thompson@iup.edu.
Website: http://www.iup.edu/grad/englishgeneralist/default.aspx

Indiana University of Pennsylvania, School of Graduate Studies and Research, College of Humanities and Social Sciences, Department of English, Program in English: Literature, Indiana, PA 15705-1087. Offers MA. Part-time programs available. *Faculty:* 29 full-time (13 women). *Students:* 17 full-time (11 women), 6 part-time (3 women), 10 international. Average age 27. 43 applicants, 60% accepted, 10 enrolled. In 2014, 7 master's awarded. *Degree requirements:* For master's, thesis optional. *Entrance requirements:* For master's, two letters of recommendation. Additional exam

requirements/recommendations for international students: Required—TOEFL (minimum score 540 paper-based). *Application deadline:* Applications are processed on a rolling basis. Application fee: $50. Electronic applications accepted. *Financial support:* In 2014–15, 1 research assistantship with full and partial tuition reimbursement (averaging $1,000 per year) was awarded; fellowships, teaching assistantships with tuition reimbursements, Federal Work-Study, scholarships/grants, and unspecified assistantships also available. Financial award application deadline: 4/15; financial award applicants required to submit FAFSA. *Unit head:* Dr. Todd Thompson, Coordinator, 724-357-4931, E-mail: todd.thompson@iup.edu.
Website: http://www.iup.edu/grad/literature/default.aspx

Indiana University of Pennsylvania, School of Graduate Studies and Research, College of Humanities and Social Sciences, Department of English, Program in Literature and Criticism, Indiana, PA 15705-1087. Offers PhD. Part-time programs available. *Faculty:* 29 full-time (13 women). *Students:* 27 full-time (12 women), 122 part-time (72 women); includes 22 minority (10 Black or African American, non-Hispanic/Latino; 2 Asian, non-Hispanic/Latino; 7 Hispanic/Latino; 3 Two or more races, non-Hispanic/Latino), 31 international. Average age 35. 57 applicants, 49% accepted, 13 enrolled. In 2014, 22 doctorates awarded. *Degree requirements:* For doctorate, one foreign language, comprehensive exam, thesis/dissertation. *Entrance requirements:* For doctorate, 2 letters of recommendation. Additional exam requirements/recommendations for international students: Required—TOEFL (minimum score 540 paper-based). *Application deadline:* Applications are processed on a rolling basis. Application fee: $50. Electronic applications accepted. *Financial support:* In 2014–15, 7 fellowships with full tuition reimbursements (averaging $1,027 per year), 16 research assistantships with full and partial tuition reimbursements (averaging $5,766 per year), 6 teaching assistantships with partial tuition reimbursements (averaging $23,305 per year) were awarded; career-related internships or fieldwork, Federal Work-Study, scholarships/grants, and unspecified assistantships also available. Support available to part-time students. Financial award application deadline: 4/15; financial award applicants required to submit FAFSA. *Unit head:* Dr. David Downing, Graduate Coordinator, 724-357-3963, E-mail: david.downing@iup.edu.
Website: http://www.iup.edu/upper.aspx?id-93418

Indiana University–Purdue University Fort Wayne, College of Arts and Sciences, Department of English and Linguistics, Fort Wayne, IN 46805-1499. Offers English (MA, MAT); TENL (teaching English as a new language) (Certificate). Part-time programs available. *Faculty:* 21 full-time (8 women), 1 part-time/adjunct (0 women). *Students:* 10 full-time (8 women), 17 part-time (10 women); includes 3 minority (1 Hispanic/Latino; 2 Two or more races, non-Hispanic/Latino), 1 international. Average age 32. 12 applicants, 100% accepted, 10 enrolled. In 2014, 14 master's awarded. *Degree requirements:* For master's, one foreign language, thesis (for some programs), teaching certificate (for MAT). *Entrance requirements:* For master's, GRE General Test, minimum GPA of 3.0, major or minor in English, 3 letters of recommendation; for Certificate, bachelor's degree with minimum GPA of 2.5. Additional exam requirements/recommendations for international students: Required—TOEFL (minimum score 600 paper-based; 79 iBT). *Application deadline:* For fall admission, 8/1 for domestic students; for spring admission, 10/15 for domestic students. Applications are processed on a rolling basis. Application fee: $50. *Financial support:* In 2014–15, 8 teaching assistantships with partial tuition reimbursements (averaging $13,522 per year) were awarded; career-related internships or fieldwork, scholarships/grants, and unspecified assistantships also available. Support available to part-time students. Financial award application deadline: 3/1; financial award applicants required to submit FAFSA. *Faculty research:* Hebrew names and the vernacular Savior in Anglo-Saxon England. *Total annual research expenditures:* $14,390. *Unit head:* Dr. Hardin Aasand, Chair/Professor, 260-481-6750, Fax: 260-481-6985, E-mail: aasandh@ipfw.edu. *Application contact:* Dr. Lewis Roberts, Graduate Program Director, 260-481-6754, Fax: 260-481-6985, E-mail: robertlc@ipfw.edu.
Website: http://www.ipfw.edu/english

Indiana University–Purdue University Indianapolis, School of Liberal Arts, Department of English, Indianapolis, IN 46202. Offers English (MA); teaching English to speakers of other languages (TESOL) (Certificate); teaching writing (Certificate). *Faculty:* 22 full-time (11 women). *Students:* 20 full-time (10 women), 24 part-time (16 women); includes 6 minority (1 Asian, non-Hispanic/Latino; 5 Two or more races, non-Hispanic/Latino). Average age 32. 36 applicants, 67% accepted, 19 enrolled. In 2014, 12 master's, 5 other advanced degrees awarded. *Entrance requirements:* For master's, GRE. Additional exam requirements/recommendations for international students: Required—TOEFL. *Application deadline:* For fall admission, 1/15 priority date for domestic and international students; for spring admission, 10/15 priority date for domestic and international students. Application fee: $55 ($65 for international students). *Financial support:* Fellowships, research assistantships, teaching assistantships, and career-related internships or fieldwork available. *Unit head:* Dr. Robert Rebein, Chair, 317-274-1405, E-mail: rrebein@iupui.edu.
Website: http://liberalarts.iupui.edu/english/

Indiana University South Bend, College of Liberal Arts and Sciences, South Bend, IN 46634-7111. Offers applied mathematics and computer science (MS); English (MA); liberal studies (MLS); public affairs (MPA). Part-time and evening/weekend programs available. *Faculty:* 79 full-time (33 women). *Students:* 41 full-time (26 women), 89 part-time (59 women); includes 24 minority (12 Black or African American, non-Hispanic/Latino; 1 Asian, non-Hispanic/Latino; 3 Hispanic/Latino; 1 Native Hawaiian or other Pacific Islander, non-Hispanic/Latino; 7 Two or more races, non-Hispanic/Latino), 15 international. Average age 37. 58 applicants, 72% accepted, 33 enrolled. In 2014, 33 master's awarded. *Degree requirements:* For master's, thesis (for some programs). *Entrance requirements:* For master's, minimum GPA of 3.0. Additional exam requirements/recommendations for international students: Required—TOEFL. *Application deadline:* For fall admission, 7/31 priority date for domestic students, 7/1 priority date for international students; for spring admission, 3/31 priority date for domestic students, 11/1 priority date for international students. Applications are processed on a rolling basis. *Financial support:* In 2014–15, 5 teaching assistantships were awarded; Federal Work-Study also available. Support available to part-time students. *Faculty research:* Artificial intelligence, bioinformatics, English language and literature, creative writing, computer networks. *Total annual research expenditures:* $127,000. *Unit head:* Dr. Elizabeth E. Dunn, Dean, 574-520-4290, E-mail: elizdunn@iusb.edu. *Application contact:* Admissions Counselor, 574-520-4839, Fax: 574-520-4834, E-mail: graduate@iusb.edu.
Website: https://www.iusb.edu/clas/academics/index.php

Inter American University of Puerto Rico, Metropolitan Campus, Graduate Programs, Program in English, San Juan, PR 00919-1293. Offers MA.

Iona College, School of Arts and Science, Department of English, New Rochelle, NY 10801-1890. Offers MA. Part-time programs available. *Faculty:* 4 full-time (all women). *Students:* 2 full-time (1 woman), 3 part-time (all women); includes 2 minority (both Hispanic/Latino). Average age 23. 3 applicants, 100% accepted, 1 enrolled. In 2014, 2 master's awarded. *Degree requirements:* For master's, one foreign language, thesis optional, foreign language competency for use in research. *Entrance requirements:* For master's, minimum GPA of 3.0. Additional exam requirements/recommendations for

international students: Required—TOEFL (minimum score 550 paper-based; 80 iBT), IELTS (minimum score 6.5). *Application deadline:* For fall admission, 8/1 priority date for domestic students, 5/1 priority date for international students; for spring admission, 1/1 priority date for domestic students, 9/1 priority date for international students. Applications are processed on a rolling basis. Application fee: $50. Electronic applications accepted. *Expenses: Tuition:* Part-time $985 per credit. *Required fees:* $245 per term. *Financial support:* Scholarships/grants, tuition waivers (partial), and unspecified assistantships available. Support available to part-time students. Financial award application deadline: 4/15; financial award applicants required to submit FAFSA. *Faculty research:* Victorian fiction, women's studies, nineteenth century American literature, Irish literature, Shakespeare. *Unit head:* Laura Shea, PhD, Chair, 914-637-2723, E-mail: lshea@iona.edu. *Application contact:* Krista Gottlieb, Graduate Admissions, 914-633-2420, Fax: 914-633-2277, E-mail: kgottlieb@iona.edu.
Website: http://www.iona.edu/Academics/School-of-Arts-Science/Departments/English/Graduate-Programs.aspx

Iowa State University of Science and Technology, Department of English, Ames, IA 50011. Offers creative writing (MFA); English (MA); rhetoric and professional communication (PhD). *Degree requirements:* For master's, thesis or alternative; for doctorate, thesis/dissertation. *Entrance requirements:* For master's, GRE General Test, sample of written work, resume, portfolio in creative writing; for doctorate, GRE General Test, sample of written work, resume. Additional exam requirements/recommendations for international students: Required—TOEFL (minimum score 600 paper-based; 100 iBT), IELTS (minimum score 7). Electronic applications accepted. *Faculty research:* Creative writing, literature, rhetoric, composition and professional communication, teaching English as a second language, applied linguistics.

Jackson State University, Graduate School, College of Liberal Arts, Department of English and Modern Foreign Languages, Jackson, MS 39217. Offers English (MA); teaching English (MAT). Part-time and evening/weekend programs available. *Degree requirements:* For master's, comprehensive exam, thesis or alternative. *Entrance requirements:* For master's, GRE General Test. Additional exam requirements/recommendations for international students: Required—TOEFL (minimum score 520 paper-based; 67 iBT).

Jacksonville State University, College of Graduate Studies and Continuing Education, College of Arts and Sciences, Department of English, Jacksonville, AL 36265-1602. Offers MA. Part-time and evening/weekend programs available. *Faculty:* 4 full-time (1 woman). *Students:* 2 full-time (both women), 13 part-time (10 women); includes 6 minority (all Black or African American, non-Hispanic/Latino). Average age 28. 6 applicants, 50% accepted, 3 enrolled. In 2014, 11 master's awarded. *Degree requirements:* For master's, comprehensive exam, thesis (for some programs). *Entrance requirements:* For master's, GRE General Test or MAT. Additional exam requirements/recommendations for international students: Required—TOEFL (minimum score 500 paper-based; 61 iBT). *Application deadline:* Applications are processed on a rolling basis. Application fee: $35. Electronic applications accepted. *Financial support:* In 2014–15, 4 students received support. Available to part-time students. Application deadline: 4/1; applicants required to submit FAFSA. *Unit head:* Dr. Robert Felgar, Head, 256-782-5413, E-mail: bfelgar@jsu.edu. *Application contact:* Dr. Jean Pugliese, Associate Dean, 256-782-8278, Fax: 256-782-5321, E-mail: pugliese@jsu.edu.

James Madison University, The Graduate School, College of Arts and Letters, Department of English, Harrisonburg, VA 22807. Offers MA. Part-time programs available. *Faculty:* 23 full-time (15 women), 1 (woman) part-time/adjunct. *Students:* 5 full-time (3 women), 3 part-time (0 women). Average age 28. 9 applicants, 78% accepted, 2 enrolled. In 2014, 4 master's awarded. *Degree requirements:* For master's, one foreign language, thesis. *Application deadline:* For fall admission, 2/10 for domestic students. Application fee: $55. Electronic applications accepted. *Expenses:* Tuition, state resident: full-time $7812; part-time $434 per credit hour. Tuition, nonresident: full-time $20,430; part-time $1135 per credit hour. *Financial support:* In 2014–15, 7 students received support, including 2 fellowships, 5 teaching assistantships with full tuition reimbursements available (averaging $12,129 per year); Federal Work-Study also available. Financial award application deadline: 3/1; financial award applicants required to submit FAFSA. *Unit head:* Dr. Dabney Bankert, Department Head, 540-568-6797, E-mail: bankerda@jmu.edu. *Application contact:* Lynette D. Michael, Director of Graduate Admissions and Student Records, 540-568-6131 Ext. 6395, Fax: 540-568-7860, E-mail: michaeld@jmu.edu.
Website: http://www.jmu.edu/english

John Carroll University, Graduate School, Department of English, University Heights, OH 44118-4581. Offers MA. Part-time and evening/weekend programs available. *Degree requirements:* For master's, comprehensive exam, research essay or thesis. *Entrance requirements:* For master's, GRE General Test, GRE Subject Test, minimum GPA of 3.0, writing sample. Additional exam requirements/recommendations for international students: Required—TOEFL. Electronic applications accepted. *Faculty research:* Post-colonial literature, African-American literature, Renaissance poetry, Anglo-Saxon literature, American literature.

Johns Hopkins University, Zanvyl Krieger School of Arts and Sciences, Department of English, Baltimore, MD 21218-2699. Offers English and American literature (PhD). *Degree requirements:* For doctorate, 2 foreign languages, comprehensive exam, thesis/dissertation, 10 seminars, 2 oral exams. *Entrance requirements:* Additional exam requirements/recommendations for international students: Required—TOEFL (minimum score 600 paper-based; 100 iBT), IELTS. Electronic applications accepted. *Faculty research:* Nineteenth-century British, eighteenth-century, Renaissance, American, and cultural studies.

Kansas State University, Graduate School, College of Arts and Sciences, Department of English, Manhattan, KS 66506. Offers MA, Graduate Certificate. Part-time programs available. *Faculty:* 25 full-time (15 women), 6 part-time/adjunct (1 woman). *Students:* 50 full-time (28 women), 9 part-time (5 women); includes 6 minority (4 Hispanic/Latino; 2 Two or more races, non-Hispanic/Latino), 5 international. Average age 25. 47 applicants, 87% accepted, 25 enrolled. In 2014, 28 master's, 2 other advanced degrees awarded. *Degree requirements:* For master's, one foreign language, thesis optional. *Entrance requirements:* For master's, GRE, minimum B average in English. Additional exam requirements/recommendations for international students: Required—TOEFL. *Application deadline:* For fall admission, 2/1 priority date for domestic and international students; for spring admission, 8/1 priority date for domestic and international students. Applications are processed on a rolling basis. Application fee: $50 ($75 for international students). Electronic applications accepted. *Financial support:* In 2014–15, 43 teaching assistantships with full tuition reimbursements (averaging $9,836 per year) were awarded; career-related internships or fieldwork, Federal Work-Study, institutionally sponsored loans, scholarships/grants, and tuition waivers (full) also available. Support available to part-time students. Financial award application deadline: 3/1; financial award applicants required to submit FAFSA. *Faculty research:* Cultural studies, children's literature, American literature, rhetorical and composition theory, British literature. *Unit head:* Karin Westman, Head, 785-532-2190, Fax: 785-532-2192, E-mail: westmank@ksu.edu. *Application contact:* Anne Longmuir, Director, 785-532-2169, Fax: 785-532-2192, E-mail: longmuir@ksu.edu.
Website: http://www.k-state.edu/english/

English

Kent State University, College of Arts and Sciences, Department of English, Kent, OH 44242-0001. Offers creative writing (MFA); English (PhD); English for teachers (MA); literature and writing (MA); rhetoric and composition (PhD); teaching English as a second language (MA); TESL/TEFL (Certificate). MFA program offered jointly with Cleveland State University, The University of Akron, and Youngstown State University. Part-time programs available. *Faculty:* 49 full-time (33 women). *Students:* 124 full-time (94 women), 25 part-time (17 women); includes 10 minority (1 Black or African American, non-Hispanic/Latino; 4 Asian, non-Hispanic/Latino; 2 Hispanic/Latino; 3 Two or more races, non-Hispanic/Latino), 30 international. Average age 32. 284 applicants, 61% accepted, 65 enrolled. In 2014, 42 master's, 9 doctorates, 1 other advanced degree awarded. Terminal master's awarded for partial completion of doctoral program. *Degree requirements:* For master's, one foreign language, thesis; for doctorate, one foreign language, comprehensive exam, thesis/dissertation. *Entrance requirements:* For master's and doctorate, GRE General Test, minimum GPA of 3.0, transcript, 8-15 page writing sample, resume, letter of intent, 3 letters of recommendation; for Certificate, minimum GPA of 3.0, transcripts. Additional exam requirements/recommendations for international students: Required—TOEFL (minimum score: paper-based 525, iBT 71), Michigan English Language Assessment Battery (minimum score of 75), IELTS (minimum score of 6.0), PTE Academic (minimum score of 48), or completion of ELS level 112 Intensive Program. *Application deadline:* For fall admission, 1/15 for domestic students, 2/1 for international students. Application fee: $45 ($70 for international students). Electronic applications accepted. *Expenses:* Tuition, state resident: full-time $8730; part-time $485 per credit hour. Tuition, nonresident: full-time $14,886; part-time $827 per credit hour. Tuition and fees vary according to campus/location and program. *Financial support:* Fellowships with full tuition reimbursements, research assistantships with full tuition reimbursements, teaching assistantships with full tuition reimbursements, career-related internships or fieldwork, Federal Work-Study, and unspecified assistantships available. Financial award application deadline: 2/1. *Unit head:* Dr. Robery Trogdon, Chair, 330-672-2676, E-mail: rcorthel@kent.edu. *Application contact:* Kevin Floyd, Graduate Student Coordinator, 330-672-2676, E-mail: english@kent.edu. Website: http://www.kent.edu/english/

Kutztown University of Pennsylvania, College of Liberal Arts and Sciences, Program in English, Kutztown, PA 19530-0730. Offers MA. Part-time and evening/weekend programs available. *Faculty:* 6 full-time (4 women). *Students:* 8 full-time (6 women), 11 part-time (9 women); includes 1 minority (Asian, non-Hispanic/Latino). Average age 29. 5 applicants, 100% accepted, 5 enrolled. In 2014, 6 master's awarded. *Degree requirements:* For master's, one foreign language, comprehensive exam, thesis optional. *Entrance requirements:* For master's, GRE General Test. Additional exam requirements/recommendations for international students: Required—TOEFL (minimum score 550 paper-based; 79 iBT). *Application deadline:* For fall admission, 8/1 priority date for domestic and international students; for spring admission, 12/1 priority date for domestic and international students. Applications are processed on a rolling basis. Application fee: $35. Electronic applications accepted. *Expenses: Tuition, area resident:* Part-time $454 per credit. Tuition, state resident: part-time $454 per credit. Tuition, nonresident: part-time $681 per credit. *Required fees:* $85 per credit. *Financial support:* Career-related internships or fieldwork, Federal Work-Study, scholarships/grants, and unspecified assistantships available. Financial award application deadline: 3/1; financial award applicants required to submit FAFSA. *Faculty research:* Women science fiction writers, Joyce Cary, myth and symbol, folklore, Victorian revision modes. *Unit head:* Dr. Andrew Vogel, Chairperson, 610-683-4353, Fax: 610-683-4355, E-mail: vogel@kutztown.edu. *Application contact:* Kelly Hish, Admissions Clerk, 610-683-4200, Fax: 610-683-1393, E-mail: graduate@kutztown.edu.

Lakehead University, Graduate Studies, Faculty of Social Sciences and Humanities, Department of English, Thunder Bay, ON P7B 5E1, Canada. Offers English (MA); women's studies (MA). Part-time and evening/weekend programs available. *Degree requirements:* For master's, one foreign language, thesis optional. *Entrance requirements:* For master's, minimum B average. Additional exam requirements/recommendations for international students: Required—TOEFL. *Faculty research:* Rhetoric and literary studies, children's literature, nineteenth- and twentieth-century American literature, modern literature, women's studies.

Lamar University, College of Graduate Studies, College of Arts and Sciences, Department of English and Foreign Languages, Beaumont, TX 77710. Offers English (MA). Part-time and evening/weekend programs available. *Faculty:* 8 full-time (3 women). *Students:* 8 full-time (7 women), 13 part-time (9 women); includes 2 minority (both Black or African American, non-Hispanic/Latino), 2 international. Average age 34. 6 applicants, 100% accepted, 3 enrolled. In 2014, 8 master's awarded. *Degree requirements:* For master's, one foreign language, thesis optional, practicum. *Entrance requirements:* For master's, GRE General Test, minimum GPA of 2.5 in last 60 hours of undergraduate course work. Additional exam requirements/recommendations for international students: Required—TOEFL (minimum score 550 paper-based; 79 iBT), IELTS (minimum score 6.5). *Application deadline:* For fall admission, 8/10 for domestic students, 7/1 for international students; for spring admission, 1/5 for domestic students, 12/1 for international students. Applications are processed on a rolling basis. Application fee: $25 ($50 for international students). *Expenses:* Tuition, state resident: full-time $5724; part-time $1908 per semester. Tuition, nonresident: full-time $12,240; part-time $4080 per semester. *Required fees:* $1940; $318 per credit hour. *Financial support:* In 2014–15, 6 students received support, including 4 teaching assistantships (averaging $8,000 per year); career-related internships or fieldwork, Federal Work-Study, and institutionally sponsored loans also available. Support available to part-time students. Financial award application deadline: 4/1. *Faculty research:* British, Renaissance, nineteenth century, and American literature; creative writing; modern literature; African-American literature. *Unit head:* Dr. Jim Sanderson, Chair, 409-880-8558, Fax: 409-880-8591. *Application contact:* Melissa Gallien, Director, Admissions and Academic Services, 409-880-8888, Fax: 409-880-7419, E-mail: gradmissions@lamar.edu. Website: http://artssciences.lamar.edu/english-and-modern-languages

La Salle University, School of Arts and Sciences, Program in Education, Philadelphia, PA 19141-1199. Offers American studies (MA); autism spectrum disorders (MA, Certificate); bilingual/bicultural studies (MA); classroom management (MA); dual early childhood and special education (MA); dual middle-level science and math and special education (MA); education (MA); English (MA); English as a second language (Certificate); history (MA); instructional coach (Certificate); instructional leadership (MA); reading specialist (MA, Certificate); secondary education (MA); special education (MA, Certificate). Part-time and evening/weekend programs available. *Degree requirements:* For master's, comprehensive exam. *Entrance requirements:* For master's and Certificate, MAT or GRE, 2 letters of recommendation. Additional exam requirements/recommendations for international students: Required—TOEFL. Electronic applications accepted. Application fee is waived when completed online. *Expenses:* Contact institution.

La Salle University, School of Arts and Sciences, Program in English, Philadelphia, PA 19141-1199. Offers American studies (Certificate); English for educators (MA); English in literary and cultural studies (MA); global literature (Certificate); media studies and the performing and visual arts (Certificate); Philadelphia and regional studies (Certificate). Part-time and evening/weekend programs available. *Degree requirements:* For master's, critical-pedagogical project (for English for educators), thesis or comprehensive examination (for English in literary and cultural studies). *Entrance requirements:* For master's, GRE General Test or MAT, 18 hours of undergraduate course work in English or a related discipline with minimum GPA of 3.0; three letters of recommendation; brief personal statement; writing sample; for Certificate, undergraduate degree in English or a related discipline with minimum GPA of 3.0; 3 letters of recommendation. Additional exam requirements/recommendations for international students: Required—TOEFL. Electronic applications accepted. Application fee is waived when completed online.

La Sierra University, College of Arts and Sciences, Department of English and Communication, Riverside, CA 92515. Offers communication (MA), including public relations/advertising, theory emphasis; English (MA), including literary emphasis, writing emphasis. Part-time programs available. *Degree requirements:* For master's, one foreign language. *Entrance requirements:* For master's, GRE General Test.

Lehigh University, College of Arts and Sciences, Department of English, Bethlehem, PA 18015. Offers MA, PhD. *Faculty:* 18 full-time (8 women). *Students:* 38 full-time (20 women), 6 part-time (4 women); includes 2 minority (1 American Indian or Alaska Native, non-Hispanic/Latino; 1 Asian, non-Hispanic/Latino). Average age 30. 36 applicants, 31% accepted, 4 enrolled. In 2014, 7 master's, 7 doctorates awarded. Terminal master's awarded for partial completion of doctoral program. *Degree requirements:* For master's, thesis optional; for doctorate, one foreign language, comprehensive exam, thesis/dissertation. *Entrance requirements:* For master's, GRE Subject Test (literature), GRE General Test, minimum GPA of 3.0 in undergraduate English courses; for doctorate, GRE General Test, minimum GPA of 3.5 in MA coursework. Additional exam requirements/recommendations for international students: Required—TOEFL (minimum score 620 paper-based; 96 iBT). *Application deadline:* For fall admission, 1/1 priority date for domestic and international students. Application fee: $75. Electronic applications accepted. *Expenses:* Expenses: $1,380 per credit. *Financial support:* In 2014–15, 6 students received support, including 3 fellowships with full tuition reimbursements available (averaging $23,833 per year), 33 teaching assistantships with full tuition reimbursements available (averaging $19,697 per year); scholarships/grants and tuition waivers (full and partial) also available. Support available to part-time students. Financial award application deadline: 1/1. *Faculty research:* British and American literature, literature and social justice, Transatlantic study, rhetoric and composition. *Unit head:* Dr. Scott P. Gordon, Chairperson, 610-758-3311, Fax: 610-758-6616, E-mail: spg4@lehigh.edu. *Application contact:* Dr. Dawn Keetley, Director of Graduate Studies, 610-758-5926, Fax: 610-758-6616, E-mail: dek7@lehigh.edu. Website: http://cas.lehigh.edu/casweb/English

Lehman College of the City University of New York, Division of Arts and Humanities, Department of English, Bronx, NY 10468-1589. Offers MA. *Degree requirements:* For master's, thesis. *Entrance requirements:* For master's, GRE, 18 upper-level credits in U. S. or English literature.

Liberty University, College of Arts and Sciences, Lynchburg, VA 24515. Offers English (MA); history (MA); philosophical studies (MA). *Accreditation:* AACN. Part-time programs available. Postbaccalaureate distance learning degree programs offered (minimal on-campus study). *Students:* 60 full-time (28 women), 14 part-time (4 women); includes 4 minority (1 Black or African American, non-Hispanic/Latino; 2 Hispanic/Latino; 1 Two or more races, non-Hispanic/Latino), 4 international. Average age 25. 66 applicants, 52% accepted, 23 enrolled. In 2014, 25 master's awarded. *Degree requirements:* For master's, comprehensive exam (for some programs), thesis (for some programs). *Entrance requirements:* For master's, GRE, minimum undergraduate GPA of 3.0, letters of recommendation, statement of purpose. Additional exam requirements/recommendations for international students: Required—TOEFL (minimum score 600 paper-based; 100 iBT). *Application deadline:* For fall admission, 6/1 for domestic students; for spring admission, 11/1 for domestic students. Applications are processed on a rolling basis. Application fee: $50. Electronic applications accepted. *Financial support:* Teaching assistantships with tuition reimbursements and Federal Work-Study available. *Faculty research:* God concept and adult attachment, building marital strength, image of God and gender, breastfeeding behavior among adolescent mothers, osteoporosis. *Unit head:* Dr. Roger Schultz, Dean, 434-592-4031, Fax: 434-522-0430, E-mail: rschultz@liberty.edu. *Application contact:* Dr. Terry Elam, Director of Graduate Admissions, 434-592-3966, Fax: 434-522-0430, E-mail: gradadmissions@liberty.edu.

Liberty University, School of Education, Lynchburg, VA 24515. Offers administration and supervision (M Ed); curriculum and instruction (Ed D, Ed S); early childhood education (M Ed); educational leadership (Ed D, Ed S); educational technology and online instruction (M Ed); elementary education (M Ed, MAT); English (M Ed); gifted education (M Ed, Certificate); history (M Ed); leadership (M Ed); math specialist (M Ed); middle grades (M Ed, MAT, Certificate); outdoor adventure sport (MS); preschool (Certificate); reading specialist (M Ed); school counseling (M Ed); school leadership (Certificate); secondary education (MAT); special education (M Ed, MAT); sport management (MS, Certificate), including administration (MS), outdoor recreation (MS), sport management (MS), tourism (MS); sports administration (MS); student service (M Ed); teaching and learning (M Ed); tourism (MS). *Accreditation:* NCATE. Part-time programs available. Postbaccalaureate distance learning degree programs offered (minimal on-campus study). *Students:* 2,200 full-time (1,590 women), 4,619 part-time (3,401 women); includes 1,660 minority (1,403 Black or African American, non-Hispanic/Latino; 33 American Indian or Alaska Native, non-Hispanic/Latino; 42 Asian, non-Hispanic/Latino; 42 Hispanic/Latino; 11 Native Hawaiian or other Pacific Islander, non-Hispanic/Latino; 129 Two or more races, non-Hispanic/Latino), 80 international. Average age 37. 6,006 applicants, 44% accepted, 1412 enrolled. In 2014, 1,199 master's, 118 doctorates, 539 other advanced degrees awarded. *Degree requirements:* For doctorate, comprehensive exam, thesis/dissertation. *Entrance requirements:* For master's, GRE General Test or MAT (if taken in or before 1999), 2 letters of recommendation, minimum undergraduate GPA of 3.0, curriculum vitae; for doctorate and other advanced degree, GRE General Test or MAT (if taken before 1999), minimum master's GPA of 3.0, 3 years of teaching experience. Additional exam requirements/recommendations for international students: Required—TOEFL (minimum score 600 paper-based; 100 iBT). *Application deadline:* For fall admission, 6/1 for domestic students; for spring admission, 11/1 for domestic students. Applications are processed on a rolling basis. Application fee: $50. Electronic applications accepted. *Expenses:* Expenses: Contact institution. *Financial support:* Federal Work-Study and tuition waivers (partial) available. *Faculty research:* Self-determination, character education, bibliotherapy, learning styles, distance education. *Unit head:* Dr. Karen L. Parker, Dean, 434-582-2195, Fax: 434-582-2468, E-mail: kparker@liberty.edu. *Application contact:* Jay Bridge, Director of Graduate Admissions, 800-424-9595, Fax: 800-628-7977, E-mail: gradadmissions@liberty.edu. Website: http://www.liberty.edu/academics/education/graduate/

Lipscomb University, Program in Education, Nashville, TN 37204-3951. Offers applied behavior analysis (MS, Certificate); collaborative professional learning (M Ed, Ed S); educational leadership (M Ed, Ed S); English language learning (M Ed, Ed S); instructional coaching (Certificate); instructional practice (M Ed); learning organizations and strategic change (Ed D); professional learning and coaching in mathematics (M Ed, Ed S); reading specialty (M Ed, Ed S); special education (M Ed); teaching, learning, and leading (M Ed); technology integration (M Ed); technology integration specialist

(Certificate). *Accreditation:* NCATE. Part-time and evening/weekend programs available. Postbaccalaureate distance learning degree programs offered (no on-campus study). *Faculty:* 22 full-time (16 women), 27 part-time/adjunct (17 women). *Students:* 168 full-time (128 women), 456 part-time (365 women); includes 114 minority (70 Black or African American, non-Hispanic/Latino; 1 American Indian or Alaska Native, non-Hispanic/Latino; 11 Asian, non-Hispanic/Latino; 25 Hispanic/Latino; 1 Native Hawaiian or other Pacific Islander, non-Hispanic/Latino; 6 Two or more races, non-Hispanic/Latino). Average age 32. In 2014, 195 master's, 34 doctorates, 80 other advanced degrees awarded. *Degree requirements:* For master's, comprehensive exam, portfolio, research project and presentation; for doctorate, practical capstone project in experiential setting. *Entrance requirements:* For master's, MAT (minimum score 31) or GRE General Test (minimum score 294), 2 reference letters, goals statement, writing sample, interview; for doctorate, MAT or GRE General Test, 3 reference letters, artifact of demonstrated academic excellence, written personal statements, interview. Additional exam requirements/recommendations for international students: Required—TOEFL (minimum score 570 paper-based; 80 iBT). *Application deadline:* For fall admission, 8/29 priority date for domestic students; for spring admission, 1/15 priority date for domestic students. Applications are processed on a rolling basis. Application fee: $50 ($75 for international students). *Expenses:* Expenses: $898 per credit hour. *Financial support:* Scholarships/grants, unspecified assistantships, and parterships with local school districts available. Financial award applicants required to submit FAFSA. *Faculty research:* Facilitative learning styles, leadership, student assessment, interactive multimedia inclusion, learning organizations and strategic change. *Unit head:* Dr. Deborah Boyd, Director of Graduate Studies, 615-966-6263, E-mail: deborah.boyd@lipscomb.edu. *Application contact:* Kristin Baese, Director of Enrollment and Outreach, 615-966-5173 Ext. 6081, E-mail: kristin.baese@lipscomb.edu. Website: http://www.lipscomb.edu/education/graduate-programs

Louisiana State University and Agricultural & Mechanical College, Graduate School, College of Humanities and Social Sciences, Department of English, Baton Rouge, LA 70803. Offers creative writing (MFA); English (MA, PhD). Part-time programs available. *Faculty:* 49 full-time (26 women). *Students:* 70 full-time (42 women), 11 part-time (7 women); includes 10 minority (2 Black or African American, non-Hispanic/Latino; 1 Asian, non-Hispanic/Latino; 5 Hispanic/Latino; 2 Two or more races, non-Hispanic/Latino), 6 international. Average age 30. 302 applicants, 7% accepted, 13 enrolled. In 2014, 8 master's, 11 doctorates awarded. Terminal master's awarded for partial completion of doctoral program. *Degree requirements:* For master's, comprehensive exam; for doctorate, one foreign language, comprehensive exam, thesis/dissertation. *Entrance requirements:* For master's, GRE General Test, minimum GPA of 3.0; for doctorate, GRE General Test, GRE Subject Test, minimum GPA of 3.0. Additional exam requirements/recommendations for international students: Required—TOEFL (minimum score 550 paper-based; 79 iBT), IELTS (minimum score 6.5), or PTE (minimum score 59). *Application deadline:* For fall admission, 5/15 priority date for domestic students, 5/15 for international students; for spring admission, 10/15 priority date for domestic students, 10/15 for international students. Applications are processed on a rolling basis. Application fee: $50 ($70 for international students). Electronic applications accepted. *Financial support:* In 2014–15, 76 students received support, including 1 fellowship with full tuition reimbursement available (averaging $16,163 per year), 1 research assistantship with partial tuition reimbursement available (averaging $25,000 per year), 67 teaching assistantships with partial tuition reimbursements available (averaging $16,813 per year); career-related internships or fieldwork, Federal Work-Study, traineeships, and health care benefits also available. Financial award application deadline: 2/1; financial award applicants required to submit FAFSA. *Faculty research:* American literature, British literature, cultural studies, rhetoric and composition, folklore. *Total annual research expenditures:* $64,887. *Unit head:* Dr. Elsie Michie, Chair, 225-578-4086, Fax: 225-578-4129, E-mail: enmich@lsu.edu. *Application contact:* Dr. Michelle Masse, Director of Graduate Studies, 225-578-7803, Fax: 225-578-4129, E-mail: egs@lsu.edu. Website: http://www.english.lsu.edu/

Louisiana Tech University, Graduate School, College of Liberal Arts, Department of English, Ruston, LA 71272. Offers English (MA); technical writing (Graduate Certificate). Part-time programs available. *Degree requirements:* For master's, thesis or alternative. *Entrance requirements:* For master's, GRE General Test. *Application deadline:* For fall admission, 7/29 for domestic students; for spring admission, 2/3 for domestic students. Applications are processed on a rolling basis. Application fee: $40. *Financial support:* Fellowships, research assistantships, teaching assistantships, and career-related internships or fieldwork available. Financial award application deadline: 2/1. *Unit head:* Dr. Susan Roach, Director, School of Literature and Language, 318-257-2718, Fax: 318-257-2719, E-mail: msroach@latech.edu. *Application contact:* Marilyn J. Robinson, Assistant to the Dean of the Graduate School, 318-257-2924, Fax: 318-257-4487. Website: http://www.latech.edu/tech/liberal-arts/english/html/literature/index.shtml

Loyola Marymount University, College of Liberal Arts, Department of English, Program in English, Los Angeles, CA 90045-2659. Offers MA. *Degree requirements:* For master's, comprehensive exam. *Entrance requirements:* For master's, GRE, 2 letters of recommendation, 2-page statement of ambition, writing sample (10-15 pages). Additional exam requirements/recommendations for international students: Required—TOEFL (minimum score 600 paper-based; 100 iBT).

Loyola University Chicago, Graduate School, Department of English, Chicago, IL 60660. Offers MA, PhD. Part-time and evening/weekend programs available. *Faculty:* 25 full-time (10 women). *Students:* 41 full-time (19 women), 6 part-time (5 women); includes 3 minority (1 Black or African American, non-Hispanic/Latino; 1 Asian, non-Hispanic/Latino; 1 Hispanic/Latino). Average age 26. 102 applicants, 50% accepted, 16 enrolled. In 2014, 19 master's, 1 doctorate awarded. Terminal master's awarded for partial completion of doctoral program. *Degree requirements:* For master's, comprehensive exam, thesis or alternative; for doctorate, one foreign language, comprehensive exam, thesis/dissertation. *Entrance requirements:* For master's, GRE General Test; for doctorate, GRE General Test, GRE Subject Test. Additional exam requirements/recommendations for international students: Required—TOEFL, IELTS. *Application deadline:* For fall admission, 6/1 for domestic students. Applications are processed on a rolling basis. Application fee: $0. Electronic applications accepted. *Expenses:* Tuition: Full-time $17,370; part-time $965 per credit. *Required fees:* $138 per semester. *Financial support:* In 2014–15, 26 students received support, including 5 fellowships with full tuition reimbursements available (averaging $16,000 per year), research assistantships with full tuition reimbursements available (averaging $10,000 per year), 21 teaching assistantships with full tuition reimbursements available (averaging $16,500 per year); Federal Work-Study, institutionally sponsored loans, tuition waivers (partial), and unspecified assistantships also available. Support available to part-time students. Financial award application deadline: 1/15; financial award applicants required to submit FAFSA. *Faculty research:* Medieval and Renaissance studies, Romantic period, Victorian literature, literary history and theory, American studies, modernism and postmodernism, Latino/a literature, postcolonialism, transnationalism, textual studies, digital humanities. *Unit head:* Dr. Pamela Caughie, Graduate Program Director, 773-508-2241, Fax: 773-508-8696, E-mail: pcaughi@luc.edu. *Application contact:* Stephen Heintz, Administrative Assistant, 773-

508-2241, Fax: 773-508-8696, E-mail: sheintz@luc.edu. Website: http://www.luc.edu/english/

Lynchburg College, Graduate Studies, MA Program in English, Lynchburg, VA 24501-3199. Offers MA. Part-time and evening/weekend programs available. *Faculty:* 2 full-time (1 woman). *Students:* 5 full-time (3 women), 7 part-time (5 women); includes 2 minority (1 Hispanic/Latino; 1 Two or more races, non-Hispanic/Latino). Average age 31. In 2014, 9 master's awarded. *Degree requirements:* For master's, thesis. *Entrance requirements:* For master's, GRE, official transcripts, personal essay, 3 letters of recommendation. Additional exam requirements/recommendations for international students: Required—TOEFL (minimum score 530 paper-based; 71 iBT), IELTS (minimum score 6.5). *Application deadline:* Applications are processed on a rolling basis. Electronic applications accepted. *Financial support:* Fellowships, research assistantships, Federal Work-Study, scholarships/grants, health care benefits, and unspecified assistantships available. Support available to part-time students. Financial award application deadline: 7/31; financial award applicants required to submit FAFSA. *Unit head:* Dr. Casey Clabough, Associate Professor, 434-544-8732, E-mail: clabough@lynchburg.edu. *Application contact:* Dr. Kim McCabe, Dean, School of Humanities and Social Sciences, 434-544-8129, E-mail: mccabe@lynchburg.edu. Website: http://www.lynchburg.edu/master-arts-english

Marquette University, Graduate School, College of Arts and Sciences, Department of English, Milwaukee, WI 53201-1881. Offers American literature (PhD); British and American literature (MA); British literature (PhD). Part-time programs available. Terminal master's awarded for partial completion of doctoral program. *Degree requirements:* For master's, comprehensive exam, thesis or alternative; for doctorate, one foreign language, thesis/dissertation, qualifying exam. *Entrance requirements:* For master's and doctorate, GRE General Test, GRE Subject Test, official transcripts from all current and previous colleges/universities except Marquette, three letters of recommendation, statement of purpose, one or two writing samples. Additional exam requirements/recommendations for international students: Required—TOEFL (minimum score 530 paper-based). Electronic applications accepted. *Faculty research:* Discourse analysis, American literature, British literature, textual criticism, literary history.

Marshall University, Academic Affairs Division, College of Liberal Arts, Department of English, Huntington, WV 25755. Offers MA, Graduate Certificate. *Students:* 37 full-time (22 women), 8 part-time (7 women); includes 4 minority (2 American Indian or Alaska Native, non-Hispanic/Latino; 1 Hispanic/Latino; 1 Two or more races, non-Hispanic/Latino), 12 international. Average age 28. In 2014, 22 master's awarded. *Degree requirements:* For master's, one foreign language, thesis optional. *Entrance requirements:* For master's, GRE General Test. Application fee: $40. *Unit head:* Dr. Jane Hill, Chair, 304-696-6638, E-mail: hillj@marshall.edu. *Application contact:* Dr. Kristen Lillvis, Information Contact, E-mail: lillvis@marshall.edu.

Mary Baldwin College, Graduate Studies, Program in Shakespeare and Renaissance Literature in Performance, Staunton, VA 24401-3610. Offers acting (M Litt); directing (M Litt); Shakespeare and Renaissance literature in performance (MFA); teaching (M Litt). *Entrance requirements:* For master's, GRE (M Litt).

Marygrove College, Graduate Division, Program in English, Detroit, MI 48221-2599. Offers MA.

Marymount University, School of Arts and Sciences, Program in English and the Humanities, Arlington, VA 22207-4299. Offers MA. Part-time and evening/weekend programs available. *Faculty:* 3 full-time (all women). *Students:* 2 full-time (both women), 10 part-time (7 women); includes 4 minority (3 Black or African American, non-Hispanic/Latino; 1 Two or more races, non-Hispanic/Latino). Average age 34. 7 applicants, 100% accepted, 4 enrolled. In 2014, 6 master's awarded. *Degree requirements:* For master's, thesis or alternative. *Entrance requirements:* For master's, 2 letters of recommendation, interview, minimum undergraduate GPA of 3.0 with major in English or other humanities discipline, writing sample. Additional exam requirements/recommendations for international students: Required—TOEFL (minimum score 600 paper-based; 96 iBT), IELTS (minimum score 6.5). *Application deadline:* Applications are processed on a rolling basis. Application fee: $40. Electronic applications accepted. *Expenses:* Tuition: Part-time $885 per credit. *Required fees:* $10 per credit. One-time fee: $220 part-time. Tuition and fees vary according to program. *Financial support:* In 2014–15, 6 students received support, including 4 research assistantships with full and partial tuition reimbursements available, 1 teaching assistantship with full and partial tuition reimbursement available; career-related internships or fieldwork, Federal Work-Study, scholarships/grants, and unspecified assistantships also available. Support available to part-time students. Financial award applicants required to submit FAFSA. *Unit head:* Dr. Tonya-Marie Howe, Director of Graduate Studies, 703-284-5762, Fax: 703-284-3859, E-mail: tonya-marie.howe@marymount.edu. *Application contact:* Francesca Reed, Director, Graduate Admissions, 703-284-5901, Fax: 703-527-3815, E-mail: grad.admissions@marymount.edu. Website: http://www.marymount.edu/Academics/School-of-Arts-Sciences/Graduate-Programs/English-Humanities-(M-A-)

McGill University, Faculty of Graduate and Postdoctoral Studies, Faculty of Arts, Department of English, Montréal, QC H3A 2T5, Canada. Offers MA, PhD. Electronic applications accepted.

McMaster University, School of Graduate Studies, Faculty of Humanities, Department of English and Cultural Studies, Hamilton, ON L8S 4M2, Canada. Offers cultural studies and critical theory (MA); English (MA, PhD). Part-time programs available. *Degree requirements:* For master's, one foreign language, thesis; for doctorate, one foreign language, comprehensive exam, thesis/dissertation. *Entrance requirements:* For master's, honors degree, minimum B+ average in at least 6 full courses of English beyond year 1; for doctorate, MA; minimum A- average in two of three courses. Additional exam requirements/recommendations for international students: Required—TOEFL (minimum score 580 paper-based). *Faculty research:* Literary theory, feminist theory, literature of migration, Bakhting globalization.

McNeese State University, Doré School of Graduate Studies, College of Liberal Arts, Department of English and Foreign Languages, Program in English, Lake Charles, LA 70609. Offers MA. Evening/weekend programs available. *Degree requirements:* For master's, one foreign language, thesis or alternative. *Entrance requirements:* For master's, GRE. *Faculty research:* Textual criticism, seventeenth century literature, American women writers, Romanticism and the origins of diplomacy.

Memorial University of Newfoundland, School of Graduate Studies, Department of English Language and Literature, St. John's, NL A1C 5S7, Canada. Offers MA, PhD. *Degree requirements:* For master's, thesis optional; for doctorate, one foreign language, comprehensive exam, thesis/dissertation, oral thesis defense, minimum 3 semesters of full-time study. *Entrance requirements:* For master's, honors degree. Electronic applications accepted. *Faculty research:* American, British, Canadian, and Anglo-Irish literature; Newfoundland literature.

Mercy College, School of Liberal Arts, Program in English Literature, Dobbs Ferry, NY 10522-1189. Offers MA. Part-time and evening/weekend programs available. Postbaccalaureate distance learning degree programs offered (no on-campus study). *Students:* 11 full-time (9 women), 47 part-time (32 women); includes 15 minority (9 Black

or African American, non-Hispanic/Latino; 1 Asian, non-Hispanic/Latino; 4 Hispanic/Latino; 1 Two or more races, non-Hispanic/Latino). Average age 35. 28 applicants, 68% accepted, 9 enrolled. In 2014, 27 master's awarded. *Degree requirements:* For master's, comprehensive exam, thesis. *Entrance requirements:* For master's, essay, 2 letters of recommendation, undergraduate transcripts. Additional exam requirements/recommendations for international students: Required—TOEFL (minimum score 600 paper-based; 100 iBT), IELTS (minimum score 8). *Application deadline:* For fall admission, 8/1 for international students. Applications are processed on a rolling basis. Application fee: $40. Electronic applications accepted. *Expenses: Tuition:* Full-time $14,952; part-time $814 per credit. *Required fees:* $600; $150 per semester. Tuition and fees vary according to course load, degree level and program. *Financial support:* Career-related internships or fieldwork, Federal Work-Study, scholarships/grants, and unspecified assistantships available. Support available to part-time students. Financial award applicants required to submit FAFSA. *Unit head:* Dr. Nagaraj Rao, Dean, School of Liberal Arts, 914-674-7593, E-mail: nrao@mercy.edu. *Application contact:* Allison Gurdineer, Senior Director of Admissions, 877-637-2946, Fax: 914-674-7382, E-mail: admissions@mercy.edu.
Website: https://www.mercy.edu/degrees-programs/ma-english-literature

Miami University, College of Arts and Science, Department of English, Oxford, OH 45056. Offers MA, MAT, PhD. Part-time programs available. *Students:* 71 full-time (43 women), 28 part-time (26 women); includes 12 minority (4 Black or African American, non-Hispanic/Latino; 2 Asian, non-Hispanic/Latino; 3 Hispanic/Latino; 3 Two or more races, non-Hispanic/Latino), 5 international. Average age 29. In 2014, 44 master's, 7 doctorates awarded. *Entrance requirements:* For master's and doctorate, 2-3 page personal statement; writing sample; three letters of recommendation. Additional exam requirements/recommendations for international students: Recommended—TOEFL (minimum score 80 iBT), IELTS (minimum score 6.5), TSE (minimum score 54). *Application deadline:* For fall admission, 1/2 for domestic and international students. Application fee: $50. Electronic applications accepted. *Expenses:* Tuition, state resident: full-time $12,887; part-time $537 per credit hour. Tuition, nonresident: full-time $28,449; part-time $1186 per credit hour. *Required fees:* $530; $24 per credit hour. $30 per quarter. Part-time tuition and fees vary according to course load and program. *Financial support:* Fellowships with full and partial tuition reimbursements, research assistantships with full and partial tuition reimbursements, and teaching assistantships with full and partial tuition reimbursements available. Financial award application deadline: 2/15; financial award applicants required to submit FAFSA. *Unit head:* Dr. LuMing Mao, Chair, 513-529-5221, Fax: 513-529-5221, E-mail: maolr@miamioh.edu. *Application contact:* Monica Baxter, Graduate Program Administrative Assistant, 513-529-7530, E-mail: baxterml@miamioh.edu.
Website: http://www.MiamiOH.edu/english/

Michigan State University, The Graduate School, College of Arts and Letters, Department of English, East Lansing, MI 48824. Offers English (PhD); literature in English (MA). *Entrance requirements:* For master's, GRE General Test, minimum GPA of 3.25, 2 years of foreign language or American Sign Language study, 3 letters of recommendation; for doctorate, GRE General Test, master's degree in English, 2 years of foreign language study, 3 letters of recommendation. Additional exam requirements/recommendations for international students: Required—TOEFL. Electronic applications accepted.

Middlebury College, Bread Loaf School of English, Middlebury, VT 05753. Offers M Litt, MA. Offered during summer only. Part-time programs available. *Faculty:* 47 full-time (21 women). *Students:* 404 full-time (270 women); includes 41 minority (10 Black or African American, non-Hispanic/Latino; 4 American Indian or Alaska Native, non-Hispanic/Latino; 11 Asian, non-Hispanic/Latino; 10 Hispanic/Latino; 1 Native Hawaiian or other Pacific Islander, non-Hispanic/Latino; 5 Two or more races, non-Hispanic/Latino), 17 international. Average age 34. 179 applicants, 83% accepted, 104 enrolled. In 2014, 86 master's awarded. *Entrance requirements:* For master's, 2 letters of recommendation; statement of purpose; official transcripts (both undergraduate and graduate); 3-to 10-page writing sample. *Application deadline:* Applications are processed on a rolling basis. Application fee: $65. Electronic applications accepted. *Financial support:* In 2014–15, 228 students received support, including 24 fellowships; scholarships/grants also available. Support available to part-time students. *Unit head:* Dr. Emily Bartels, Professor, 802-443-5418, Fax: 802-443-2060, E-mail: blse@breadnet.middlebury.edu. *Application contact:* Dana Olsen, Budget and Communications Manager/Director of Admissions, 802-443-5049, Fax: 802-443-2060, E-mail: dolsen@middlebury.edu.
Website: http://www.middlebury.edu/blse

Middle Tennessee State University, College of Graduate Studies, College of Liberal Arts, Department of English, Murfreesboro, TN 37132. Offers MA, PhD. Part-time and evening/weekend programs available. Postbaccalaureate distance learning degree programs offered. *Faculty:* 42 full-time (23 women), 2 part-time/adjunct (0 women). *Students:* 9 full-time (4 women), 82 part-time (53 women); includes 8 minority (1 Black or African American, non-Hispanic/Latino; 3 Asian, non-Hispanic/Latino; 3 Hispanic/Latino; 1 Two or more races, non-Hispanic/Latino), 6 international. 98 applicants, 61% accepted. In 2014, 6 master's, 11 doctorates awarded. *Degree requirements:* For master's, one foreign language, comprehensive exam, thesis optional; for doctorate, one foreign language, comprehensive exam, thesis/dissertation. *Entrance requirements:* For master's and doctorate, GRE. Additional exam requirements/recommendations for international students: Required—TOEFL (minimum score 525 paper-based; 71 iBT) or IELTS (minimum score 6). *Application deadline:* For fall admission, 6/1 for domestic and international students. Applications are processed on a rolling basis. Application fee: $30. Electronic applications accepted. *Financial support:* In 2014–15, 39 students received support. Institutionally sponsored loans and tuition waivers available. Support available to part-time students. Financial award application deadline: 4/1; financial award applicants required to submit FAFSA. *Unit head:* Dr. Tom Strawman, Chair, 615-898-2573, Fax: 615-898-5098, E-mail: tom.strawman@mtsu.edu. *Application contact:* Dr. Michael D. Allen, Vice Provost for Research/Dean, 615-898-2840, Fax: 615-904-8020, E-mail: michael.allen@mtsu.edu.

Midwestern State University, Billie Doris McAda Graduate School, Prothro-Yeager College of Humanities and Social Sciences, Department of English, Humanities, and Philosophy, Wichita Falls, TX 76308. Offers English (MA); philosophy (PhD). Part-time and evening/weekend programs available. *Degree requirements:* For master's, one foreign language, thesis optional. *Entrance requirements:* For master's, GRE General Test, MAT or GMAT. Additional exam requirements/recommendations for international students: Required—TOEFL (minimum score 550 paper-based). *Application deadline:* For fall admission, 7/1 priority date for domestic students, 4/1 for international students; for spring admission, 11/1 priority date for domestic students, 8/1 for international students. Applications are processed on a rolling basis. Application fee: $35 ($50 for international students). Electronic applications accepted. *Financial support:* Teaching assistantships with partial tuition reimbursements, career-related internships or fieldwork, Federal Work-Study, institutionally sponsored loans, scholarships/grants, tuition waivers (partial), and unspecified assistantships available. Support available to part-time students. Financial award application deadline: 3/1; financial award applicants required to submit FAFSA. *Faculty research:* Mythology, Shakespeare, Oscar Hahn,

origins of language, modern American literature. *Unit head:* Pam Marshall, Secretary, 940-397-4300, Fax: 940-397-4931, E-mail: pam.marshall@mwsu.edu.
Website: http://www.mwsu.edu/academics/libarts/english-humanities-philosophy/

Millersville University of Pennsylvania, College of Graduate and Professional Studies, School of Humanities and Social Sciences, Department of English, Millersville, PA 17551-0302. Offers M Ed, MA. Part-time programs available. *Faculty:* 22 full-time (13 women), 12 part-time/adjunct (7 women). *Students:* 9 full-time (5 women), 26 part-time (20 women); includes 5 minority (2 Black or African American, non-Hispanic/Latino; 2 Asian, non-Hispanic/Latino; 1 Native Hawaiian or other Pacific Islander, non-Hispanic/Latino). Average age 33. 13 applicants, 100% accepted, 6 enrolled. In 2014, 10 master's awarded. *Degree requirements:* For master's, one foreign language, thesis optional. *Entrance requirements:* For master's, GRE or MAT, 3 letters of recommendation, goal statement, official transcripts. Additional exam requirements/recommendations for international students: Required—TOEFL (minimum score 500 paper-based, 65 iBT) or IELTS (minimum score 6). *Application deadline:* For fall admission, 1/15 priority date for domestic and international students; for winter admission, 6/1 priority date for domestic and international students; for spring admission, 10/1 priority date for domestic and international students. Applications are processed on a rolling basis. Application fee: $40. Electronic applications accepted. *Expenses:* Tuition, state resident: full-time $8172. Tuition, nonresident: full-time $12,258. *Required fees:* $2300. Tuition and fees vary according to course load and program. *Financial support:* In 2014–15, 11 students received support, including 11 research assistantships with full tuition reimbursements available (averaging $3,745 per year); institutionally sponsored loans and unspecified assistantships also available. Support available to part-time students. Financial award application deadline: 3/15; financial award applicants required to submit FAFSA. *Faculty research:* American, early American, Contemporary American, African-American, British, comparative, medieval, and Victorian literature; film studies; critical theory; linguists; literacy; poetry and poetics; science fiction; writing pedagogy. *Unit head:* Dr. Jill R. Craven, Chair, 717-871-7384, Fax: 717-871-7933, E-mail: jill.craven@millersville.edu. *Application contact:* Dr. Victor S. DeSantis, Dean of College of Graduate and Professional Studies/Associate Provost for Civic and Community Engagement, 717-871-7619, Fax: 717-871-7954, E-mail: victor.desantis@millersville.edu.
Website: http://www.millersville.edu/english/graduate/index.php

Mills College, Graduate Studies, Department of English, Oakland, CA 94613-1000. Offers book art and creative writing (MFA); literature (MA); poetry (MFA); prose (MFA). Part-time programs available. *Faculty:* 12 full-time (10 women), 15 part-time/adjunct (13 women). *Students:* 60 full-time (50 women), 5 part-time (3 women); includes 24 minority (8 Black or African American, non-Hispanic/Latino; 1 American Indian or Alaska Native, non-Hispanic/Latino; 2 Asian, non-Hispanic/Latino; 8 Hispanic/Latino; 1 Native Hawaiian or other Pacific Islander, non-Hispanic/Latino; 4 Two or more races, non-Hispanic/Latino), 1 international. Average age 31. 128 applicants, 86% accepted, 32 enrolled. In 2014, 28 master's awarded. *Degree requirements:* For master's, comprehensive exam, thesis. *Entrance requirements:* For master's, 15-20 page writing sample. Additional exam requirements/recommendations for international students: Required—TOEFL (minimum score 600 paper-based; 100 iBT), IELTS (minimum score 7). *Application deadline:* For fall admission, 12/15 priority date for domestic students, 12/15 for international students. Applications are processed on a rolling basis. Application fee: $50. Electronic applications accepted. *Expenses:* Tuition: Full-time $31,620; part-time $7905 per course. *Required fees:* $1118. *Financial support:* In 2014–15, 70 students received support, including 60 fellowships (averaging $8,921 per year), 11 research assistantships (averaging $2,386 per year), 34 teaching assistantships with full and partial tuition reimbursements available (averaging $9,932 per year); scholarships/grants also available. Support available to part-time students. Financial award application deadline: 2/1; financial award applicants required to submit FAFSA. *Faculty research:* Creative writing, African-American literature, Victorian women writers, theories of sexuality, Shakespeare. *Unit head:* Dr. Ajuan Mance, Chair of the English Department, 510-430-2218, E-mail: dcady@mills.edu. *Application contact:* Shrim Bathey, Director of Graduate Admission, 510-430-3309, Fax: 510-430-2159, E-mail: grad-admission@mills.edu.
Website: http://www.mills.edu/english/

Minnesota State University Mankato, College of Graduate Studies, College of Arts and Humanities, Department of English, Mankato, MN 56001. Offers creative writing (MFA); English (MAT); English studies (MA); teaching English as a second language (MA, Certificate); technical communication (MA, Certificate). Part-time programs available. *Students:* 50 full-time (29 women), 108 part-time (78 women). *Degree requirements:* For master's, one foreign language, comprehensive exam, thesis or alternative. *Entrance requirements:* For master's, minimum GPA of 3.0 during previous 2 years, writing sample (MFA). Additional exam requirements/recommendations for international students: Required—TOEFL (minimum score 500 paper-based; 61 iBT). *Application deadline:* For fall admission, 7/1 for domestic students, 5/1 for international students. Applications are processed on a rolling basis. Application fee: $40. Electronic applications accepted. *Financial support:* Research assistantships with full tuition reimbursements, teaching assistantships with full tuition reimbursements, career-related internships or fieldwork, Federal Work-Study, and unspecified assistantships available. Financial award application deadline: 3/15; financial award applicants required to submit FAFSA. *Faculty research:* Keats and Christianity. *Unit head:* Dr. Nancy Drescher, Chairperson, 507-389-5504. *Application contact:* 507-389-2321, E-mail: grad@mnsu.edu.
Website: http://english.mnsu.edu/

Mississippi College, Graduate School, College of Arts and Sciences, School of Humanities and Social Sciences, Department of English, Clinton, MS 39058. Offers M Ed, MA. Part-time and evening/weekend programs available. *Degree requirements:* For master's, one foreign language, comprehensive exam, thesis or alternative. *Entrance requirements:* For master's, GRE or NTE, minimum GPA of 2.5. Additional exam requirements/recommendations for international students: Recommended—TOEFL, IELTS. Electronic applications accepted.

Mississippi State University, College of Arts and Sciences, Department of English, Mississippi State, MS 39762. Offers MA. Part-time programs available. *Faculty:* 26 full-time (14 women). *Students:* 19 full-time (12 women), 5 part-time (4 women); includes 5 minority (4 Black or African American, non-Hispanic/Latino; 1 Two or more races, non-Hispanic/Latino), 2 international. Average age 27. 20 applicants, 65% accepted, 8 enrolled. In 2014, 12 master's awarded. *Degree requirements:* For master's, thesis optional, comprehensive oral or written exam. *Entrance requirements:* For master's, GRE General Test, minimum GPA of 2.75 on last two years of undergraduate courses. Additional exam requirements/recommendations for international students: Required—TOEFL (minimum score 625 paper-based; 106 iBT); Recommended—IELTS (minimum score 8). *Application deadline:* For fall admission, 7/1 for domestic students, 5/1 for international students; for spring admission, 11/1 for domestic students, 9/1 for international students. Applications are processed on a rolling basis. Application fee: $60. Electronic applications accepted. *Expenses:* Tuition, state resident: full-time $7140; part-time $783 per credit hour. Tuition, nonresident: full-time $18,478; part-time $2043 per credit hour. *Financial support:* In 2014–15, 1 research assistantship

(averaging $9,520 per year), 18 teaching assistantships with partial tuition reimbursements (averaging $9,218 per year) were awarded; Federal Work-Study, institutionally sponsored loans, scholarships/grants, and unspecified assistantships also available. Financial award application deadline: 4/1; financial award applicants required to submit FAFSA. *Faculty research:* Literary criticism, linguistics, textual editing, editing &ITMississippi Quarterly&RO, Southern literature. *Unit head:* Dr. Richard Raymond, Department Head, 662-325-3606, Fax: 662-325-3645, E-mail: rr165@msstate.edu. *Application contact:* Dr. Shalyn Claggett, Interim Graduate Coordinator, 662-325-3644, Fax: 662-325-3645, E-mail: src173@msstate.edu.
Website: http://www.english.msstate.edu

Missouri State University, Graduate College, College of Arts and Letters, Department of English, Springfield, MO 65897. Offers English and writing (MA); secondary education (MS Ed), including English. Part-time and evening/weekend programs available. *Faculty:* 25 full-time (18 women), 5 part-time/adjunct (2 women). *Students:* 63 full-time (44 women), 48 part-time (33 women); includes 10 minority (1 Asian, non-Hispanic/Latino; 4 Hispanic/Latino; 5 Two or more races, non-Hispanic/Latino), 17 international. Average age 29. 44 applicants, 91% accepted, 26 enrolled. In 2014, 39 master's awarded. *Degree requirements:* For master's, one foreign language, comprehensive exam, thesis or alternative. *Entrance requirements:* For master's, GRE (MA), minimum GPA of 3.0 (MA), 9-12 teacher certification (MS Ed). Additional exam requirements/recommendations for international students: Required—TOEFL (minimum score 550 paper-based; 79 iBT). *Application deadline:* For fall admission, 7/20 for domestic students, 5/1 for international students; for spring admission, 12/20 for domestic students, 9/1 for international students. Applications are processed on a rolling basis. Application fee: $35 ($50 for international students). Electronic applications accepted. *Expenses:* Tuition, state resident: full-time $2250; part-time $250 per credit hour. Tuition, nonresident: full-time $4509; part-time $501 per credit hour. Tuition and fees vary according to course level, course load and program. *Financial support:* In 2014–15, 28 teaching assistantships with full tuition reimbursements (averaging $8,450 per year) were awarded; Federal Work-Study, institutionally sponsored loans, scholarships/grants, and unspecified assistantships also available. Support available to part-time students. Financial award application deadline: 3/31; financial award applicants required to submit FAFSA. *Faculty research:* History of rhetoric, modern poetry, African-American literature, digital writing, TESOL. *Unit head:* Dr. W. D. Blackmon, Head, 417-836-5107, Fax: 417-836-6940, E-mail: english@missouristate.edu. *Application contact:* Misty Stewart, Coordinator of Graduate Recruitment, 417-836-5331, Fax: 417-836-6888, E-mail: mistystewart@missouristate.edu.
Website: http://english.missouristate.edu/

Monmouth University, The Graduate School, Department of English, West Long Branch, NJ 07764-1898. Offers creative writing (MA); literature (MA); rhetoric and writing (MA). Part-time and evening/weekend programs available. *Faculty:* 11 full-time (7 women). *Students:* 9 full-time (6 women), 33 part-time (25 women); includes 2 minority (1 Black or African American, non-Hispanic/Latino; 1 Asian, non-Hispanic/Latino). Average age 30. 25 applicants, 88% accepted, 15 enrolled. In 2014, 18 master's awarded. *Degree requirements:* For master's, comprehensive exam (for some programs), thesis. *Entrance requirements:* For master's, minimum overall GPA of 2.75, fifteen or more credits in literature or related field, essay of 1,000 words describing interest and goals, two letters of recommendation, creative writing sample. Additional exam requirements/recommendations for international students: Required—TOEFL (minimum score 550 paper-based; 79 iBT), IELTS (minimum score 6), Michigan English Language Assessment Battery (minimum score 77). *Application deadline:* For fall admission, 7/15 for domestic students, 6/1 for international students; for spring admission, 11/15 for domestic students, 11/1 for international students. Application fee: $50. *Expenses:* Tuition: Full-time $18,072; part-time $1004 per credit. *Required fees:* $157 per semester. *Financial support:* In 2014–15, 30 students received support, including 26 fellowships (averaging $2,521 per year), 2 research assistantships (averaging $5,198 per year); career-related internships or fieldwork, scholarships/grants, and unspecified assistantships also available. Support available to part-time students. Financial award applicants required to submit FAFSA. *Faculty research:* Renaissance and medieval literature, nineteenth century American literature, eighteenth century British literature and women's studies, Old and Middle English, African diaspora and African post-colonial literature. *Unit head:* Dr. Jeffrey Jackson, Program Director, 732-571-3439, Fax: 732-263-5242, E-mail: jejackso@monmouth.edu. *Application contact:* Andrea Thompson, Graduate Admission Counselor, 732-571-3452, Fax: 732-263-5123, E-mail: gradadm@monmouth.edu.
Website: http://www.monmouth.edu/school-of-humanities-social-sciences/ma-english.aspx

Montana State University, The Graduate School, College of Letters and Science, Department of English, Bozeman, MT 59717. Offers MA. Part-time programs available. *Degree requirements:* For master's, comprehensive exam. *Entrance requirements:* For master's, GRE General Test, minimum GPA of 3.0, 3 recommendations. Additional exam requirements/recommendations for international students: Required—TOEFL (minimum score 550 paper-based). Electronic applications accepted. *Faculty research:* Writing studies, writing in the disciplines, contemporary literature, Renaissance, Shakespeare, American studies, global studies, urban studies, Victorian literature, popular culture gender and sexuality studies, pedagogy, queer theory, English education, literacy education, literary theory.

Montclair State University, The Graduate School, College of Humanities and Social Sciences, Program in English, Montclair, NJ 07043-1624. Offers MA. Part-time and evening/weekend programs available. *Students:* 15 full-time (10 women), 44 part-time (33 women); includes 2 minority (both Hispanic/Latino), 2 international. Average age 30. 42 applicants, 2% accepted, 1 enrolled. In 2014, 17 master's awarded. *Degree requirements:* For master's, thesis. *Entrance requirements:* For master's, GRE General Test, 2 letters of recommendation, essay. Additional exam requirements/recommendations for international students: Required—TOEFL (minimum score 83 iBT), IELTS (minimum score 6.5). *Application deadline:* Applications are processed on a rolling basis. Application fee: $60. Electronic applications accepted. *Expenses:* Tuition, state resident: full-time $9960; part-time $553.35 per credit. Tuition, nonresident: full-time $15,074; part-time $837.43 per credit. *Required fees:* $1595; $88.63 per credit. Tuition and fees vary according to degree level and program. *Financial support:* Federal Work-Study, scholarships/grants, and unspecified assistantships available. Support available to part-time students. Financial award application deadline: 3/1; financial award applicants required to submit FAFSA. *Faculty research:* Shakespeare and aging, nineteenth-century Gothic and Catholicism, African-American poetry and poetics, modern Irish and British culture, Darwin and literary modernism. *Unit head:* Dr. Dan Bronson, Chairperson, 973-655-4274. *Application contact:* Amy Aiello, Director of Graduate Admissions and Operations, 973-655-5147, Fax: 973-655-7869, E-mail: graduate.school@montclair.edu.
Website: http://chss.montclair.edu/english/programs/graduate/index.html

Morehead State University, Graduate Programs, Caudill College of Arts, Humanities and Social Sciences, Department of English, Morehead, KY 40351. Offers MA. Part-time and evening/weekend programs available. *Degree requirements:* For master's, comprehensive exam, thesis optional. *Entrance requirements:* For master's, GRE

General Test, minimum GPA of 3.0 in English; undergraduate major or minor in English. Additional exam requirements/recommendations for international students: Required—TOEFL (minimum score 500 paper-based). Electronic applications accepted. *Faculty research:* Nineteenth and twentieth century American literature, linguistics, Victorian literature, modern British literature, creative writing.

Morgan State University, School of Graduate Studies, College of Liberal Arts, Department of English, Baltimore, MD 21251. Offers MA, PhD. Part-time programs available. *Degree requirements:* For master's, comprehensive exam, thesis; for doctorate, comprehensive exam, thesis/dissertation. *Entrance requirements:* For master's, GRE, minimum GPA of 2.5; for doctorate, GRE. Additional exam requirements/recommendations for international students: Required—TOEFL (minimum score 550 paper-based). *Faculty research:* African and African-American studies, nineteenth century American literature, rhetoric, women's studies, children's literature.

Mount Mary University, Graduate Division, Program in English, Milwaukee, WI 53222-4597. Offers creative writing (MA); writing for social media (MA). Part-time and evening/weekend programs available. *Faculty:* 2 full-time (both women), 3 part-time/adjunct (1 woman). *Students:* 16 full-time (14 women), 15 part-time (14 women); includes 7 minority (4 Black or African American, non-Hispanic/Latino; 3 Two or more races, non-Hispanic/Latino), 1 international. Average age 39. 10 applicants, 60% accepted, 5 enrolled. In 2014, 17 master's awarded. *Degree requirements:* For master's, comprehensive exam, thesis or alternative. *Entrance requirements:* For master's, minimum GPA of 2.75. Additional exam requirements/recommendations for international students: Required—TOEFL (minimum score 550 paper-based, 80 iBT) or IELTS (minimum score 6.5). *Application deadline:* For fall admission, 8/1 for domestic and international students; for spring admission, 12/1 for domestic and international students; for summer admission, 5/1 for domestic and international students. Applications are processed on a rolling basis. Application fee: $50 ($0 for international students). Electronic applications accepted. *Expenses:* Expenses: Contact institution. *Financial support:* In 2014–15, 1 student received support. Career-related internships or fieldwork and Federal Work-Study available. Support available to part-time students. Financial award application deadline: 5/1; financial award applicants required to submit FAFSA. *Unit head:* Ann Angel, Graduate Program Chair, 414-258-4810, E-mail: angela@mtmary.edu. *Application contact:* Dr. Douglas J. Mickelson, Dean for Graduate Education, 414-256-1252, Fax: 414-256-0167, E-mail: mickelsd@mtmary.edu.
Website: http://www.mtmary.edu/majors-programs/graduate/english/index.html

Mount Saint Mary's University, Graduate Division, Los Angeles, CA 90049-1599. Offers business administration (MBA); counseling psychology (MS); creative writing (MFA); education (MS, Certificate); film and television (MFA); health policy and management (MS); humanities (MA); nursing (MSN, Certificate); physical therapy (DPT); religious studies (MA). Part-time and evening/weekend programs available. *Faculty:* 15 full-time (11 women), 61 part-time/adjunct (33 women). *Students:* 462 full-time (345 women), 218 part-time (175 women); includes 417 minority (66 Black or African American, non-Hispanic/Latino; 3 American Indian or Alaska Native, non-Hispanic/Latino; 69 Asian, non-Hispanic/Latino; 254 Hispanic/Latino; 11 Native Hawaiian or other Pacific Islander, non-Hispanic/Latino; 14 Two or more races, non-Hispanic/Latino), 1 international. Average age 33. 1,086 applicants, 25% accepted, 241 enrolled. In 2014, 181 master's, 28 doctorates, 22 other advanced degrees awarded. *Entrance requirements:* Additional exam requirements/recommendations for international students: Required—TOEFL. *Application deadline:* For fall admission, 6/30 priority date for domestic and international students; for spring admission, 10/30 priority date for domestic and international students; for summer admission, 3/30 priority date for domestic and international students. Applications are processed on a rolling basis. Application fee: $50. Electronic applications accepted. *Expenses:* Tuition: Full-time $9756; part-time $813 per unit. One-time fee: $128. Tuition and fees vary according to degree level and program. *Financial support:* In 2014–15, 213 students received support. Career-related internships or fieldwork, Federal Work-Study, institutionally sponsored loans, and tuition waivers (full and partial) available. Support available to part-time students. Financial award application deadline: 3/15; financial award applicants required to submit FAFSA. *Unit head:* Dr. Linda Moody, Graduate Dean, 213-477-2800, E-mail: gradprograms@msmu.edu. *Application contact:* Tara Wessel, Senior Graduate Admission Counselor, 213-477-2800, E-mail: gradprograms@msmu.edu.
Website: http://www.msmu.edu/graduate-programs/admission/

Murray State University, College of Humanities and Fine Arts, Department of English and Philosophy, Program in English, Murray, KY 42071. Offers MA. Part-time programs available. *Degree requirements:* For master's, comprehensive exam, thesis (for some programs).

National University, Academic Affairs, College of Letters and Sciences, La Jolla, CA 92037-1011. Offers applied linguistics (MA); biology (MS); counseling psychology (MA), including licensed professional clinical counseling, marriage and family therapy; creative writing (MFA); English (MA), including Gothic studies, rhetoric; film studies (MA); forensic and crime science (Certificate); forensic studies (MFS), including criminalistics, investigation; history (MA); human behavior (MA); mathematics for educators (MS); performance psychology (MA); strategic communications (MA). Part-time and evening/weekend programs available. Postbaccalaureate distance learning degree programs offered (no on-campus study). *Faculty:* 69 full-time (34 women), 100 part-time/adjunct (55 women). *Students:* 727 full-time (532 women), 349 part-time (240 women); includes 505 minority (128 Black or African American, non-Hispanic/Latino; 5 American Indian or Alaska Native, non-Hispanic/Latino; 52 Asian, non-Hispanic/Latino; 260 Hispanic/Latino; 9 Native Hawaiian or other Pacific Islander, non-Hispanic/Latino; 51 Two or more races, non-Hispanic/Latino), 4 international. Average age 34. In 2014, 569 master's awarded. *Degree requirements:* For master's, thesis (for some programs). *Entrance requirements:* For master's, interview, minimum GPA of 2.5. Additional exam requirements/recommendations for international students: Required—TOEFL (minimum score 550 paper-based; 79 iBT), IELTS (minimum score 6). *Application deadline:* Applications are processed on a rolling basis. Application fee: $60 ($65 for international students). Electronic applications accepted. *Expenses:* Tuition: Full-time $14,184; part-time $1773 per course. *Financial support:* Career-related internships or fieldwork, institutionally sponsored loans, scholarships/grants, and tuition waivers (partial) available. Support available to part-time students. Financial award application deadline: 6/30; financial award applicants required to submit FAFSA. *Unit head:* College of Letters and Sciences, 800-628-8648, E-mail: cols@nu.edu. *Application contact:* Frank Rojas, Interim Vice President for Enrollment Services, 800-628-8648, E-mail: advisor@nu.edu.
Website: http://www.nu.edu/OurPrograms/CollegeOfLettersAndSciences.html

New Mexico Highlands University, Graduate Studies, College of Arts and Sciences, Department of English, Las Vegas, NM 87701. Offers English (MA), including creative writing, language, rhetoric and composition, literature. *Faculty:* 3 full-time (2 women). *Students:* 11 full-time (5 women), 7 part-time (6 women); includes 7 minority (1 Black or African American, non-Hispanic/Latino; 1 American Indian or Alaska Native, non-Hispanic/Latino; 3 Hispanic/Latino; 2 Two or more races, non-Hispanic/Latino), 1 international. Average age 37. 6 applicants, 100% accepted, 4 enrolled. In 2014, 4 master's awarded. *Degree requirements:* For master's, comprehensive exam, thesis. *Entrance requirements:* For master's, minimum undergraduate GPA of 3.0. Additional exam requirements/recommendations for international students: Required—TOEFL

(minimum score 540 paper-based). *Application deadline:* For fall admission, 8/1 priority date for domestic students. Applications are processed on a rolling basis. Application fee: $15. *Financial support:* In 2014–15, 22 teaching assistantships were awarded; career-related internships or fieldwork, Federal Work-Study, institutionally sponsored loans, scholarships/grants, tuition waivers (full and partial), and unspecified assistantships also available. Support available to part-time students. Financial award application deadline: 3/1; financial award applicants required to submit FAFSA. *Faculty research:* Twentieth-century literature, life path writing in homeless shelters, native American philosophy, medieval intellectual and cultural history, creating pedagogical tools for teaching law. *Unit head:* Dr. Helen Blythe, Chair, 505-454-3329, E-mail: helenblythe@nmhu.edu. *Application contact:* Diane Trujillo, Administrative Assistant, Graduate Studies, 505-454-3266, Fax: 505-426-2117, E-mail: dtrujillo@nmhu.edu.

New Mexico State University, College of Arts and Sciences, Department of English, Las Cruces, NM 88003-8001. Offers creative writing (MA, MFA); English studies for teachers (MA); literature (MA); rhetoric and professional communication (MA, PhD). Part-time programs available. *Faculty:* 20 full-time (11 women), 3 part-time/adjunct (1 woman). *Students:* 65 full-time (41 women), 29 part-time (20 women); includes 30 minority (2 Black or African American, non-Hispanic/Latino; 2 American Indian or Alaska Native, non-Hispanic/Latino; 2 Asian, non-Hispanic/Latino; 22 Hispanic/Latino; 2 Two or more races, non-Hispanic/Latino), 4 international. Average age 33. 104 applicants, 19% accepted, 15 enrolled. In 2014, 18 master's, 2 doctorates awarded. *Degree requirements:* For master's, one foreign language, thesis (for some programs); for doctorate, comprehensive exam, thesis/dissertation, internship. *Entrance requirements:* For master's and doctorate, sample of written work. Additional exam requirements/recommendations for international students: Required—TOEFL (minimum score 550 paper-based; 79 iBT), IELTS (minimum score 6.5). *Application deadline:* For fall admission, 2/1 for domestic and international students. Application fee: $40 ($50 for international students). Electronic applications accepted. *Expenses:* Tuition, state resident: full-time $3969; part-time $220.50 per credit hour. Tuition, nonresident: full-time $13,838; part-time $768.80 per credit hour. *Required fees:* $853; $47.40 per credit hour. *Financial support:* In 2014–15, 61 students received support, including 17 fellowships (averaging $3,970 per year), 49 teaching assistantships (averaging $16,313 per year); career-related internships or fieldwork, Federal Work-Study, institutionally sponsored loans, scholarships/grants, traineeships, health care benefits, and unspecified assistantships also available. Support available to part-time students. Financial award application deadline: 3/1. *Faculty research:* Composition research, history and theory of rhetoric, technical/professional communication, creative writing, English and American literature. *Total annual research expenditures:* $5,069. *Unit head:* Dr. Barry L. Thatcher, Head, 575-646-2319, Fax: 575-646-7725, E-mail: bathatch@nmsu.edu. *Application contact:* Dr. Tracey Eileen Miller-Tomlinson, Director of Graduate Studies, 575-646-2213, Fax: 575-646-7725, E-mail: tomlin@nmsu.edu. Website: http://english.nmsu.edu

New York University, Graduate School of Arts and Science, Program in English and American Literature, New York, NY 10012-1019. Offers MA, PhD. *Students:* 77 full-time (40 women), 11 part-time (6 women); includes 17 minority (3 Black or African American, non-Hispanic/Latino; 1 American Indian or Alaska Native, non-Hispanic/Latino; 4 Asian, non-Hispanic/Latino; 6 Hispanic/Latino; 3 Two or more races, non-Hispanic/Latino), 16 international. Average age 28. 411 applicants, 26% accepted, 14 enrolled. In 2014, 20 master's, 9 doctorates awarded. *Degree requirements:* For master's, one foreign language, thesis or alternative, qualifying exams, special project; for doctorate, one foreign language, thesis/dissertation. *Entrance requirements:* For master's, GRE General Test; GRE Subject Test in English (recommended). Additional exam requirements/recommendations for international students: Required—TOEFL. *Application deadline:* For fall admission, 12/1 for domestic and international students. Application fee: $100. *Financial support:* Fellowships with tuition reimbursements, teaching assistantships with tuition reimbursements, Federal Work-Study, institutionally sponsored loans, scholarships/grants, health care benefits, and unspecified assistantships available. Financial award application deadline: 12/1; financial award applicants required to submit FAFSA. *Unit head:* Chris Cannon, Chair, 212-998-8800, Fax: 212-995-4019, E-mail: gsas.english.admissions@nyu.edu. *Application contact:* Crystal Parikh, Director of Graduate Studies, 212-998-8800, Fax: 212-995-4019, E-mail: gsas.english.admissions@nyu.edu.

North Carolina Agricultural and Technical State University, School of Graduate Studies, College of Arts and Sciences, Department of English, Greensboro, NC 27411. Offers English (MA); English and African-American literature (MA); English education (MAT, MS). Part-time and evening/weekend programs available. *Degree requirements:* For master's, comprehensive exam, qualifying exam. *Entrance requirements:* For master's, GRE General Test, minimum GPA of 3.0.

North Carolina Central University, College of Liberal Arts, Department of English and Mass Communication, Durham, NC 27707-3129. Offers English (MA). Part-time and evening/weekend programs available. *Degree requirements:* For master's, one foreign language, comprehensive exam, thesis. *Entrance requirements:* For master's, GRE, minimum GPA of 3.0 in major, 2.5 overall. Additional exam requirements/recommendations for international students: Required—TOEFL. *Faculty research:* Victorian literature, African-American literature, women's studies, literature and film, twentieth-century literature.

North Carolina State University, Graduate School, College of Humanities and Social Sciences, Department of English, Program in English, Raleigh, NC 27695. Offers MA. *Degree requirements:* For master's, thesis. *Entrance requirements:* For master's, GRE General Test. Electronic applications accepted. *Faculty research:* Creative writing, linguistics, rhetoric and composition, rhetoric and technical communication, film studies.

North Dakota State University, College of Graduate and Interdisciplinary Studies, College of Arts, Humanities and Social Sciences, Department of English, Fargo, ND 58108. Offers English (MA, MS); rhetoric, writing and culture (PhD). Part-time programs available. *Degree requirements:* For master's, one foreign language, thesis. *Entrance requirements:* Additional exam requirements/recommendations for international students: Required—TOEFL (minimum score 600 paper-based; 100 iBT), IELTS (minimum score 7). Electronic applications accepted. *Faculty research:* American and English literature, women's studies, language attitudes, composition practices, computers and composition.

See Display on page 753 and Close-Up on page 765.

Northeastern Illinois University, College of Graduate Studies and Research, College of Arts and Sciences, Programs in English, Chicago, IL 60625-4699. Offers composition/writing (MA); literature (MA). Part-time and evening/weekend programs available. *Degree requirements:* For master's, comprehensive exam, thesis optional. *Entrance requirements:* For master's, 30 hours of undergraduate course work in literature and composition (literature), BA in English or approval (composition/writing), minimum GPA of 2.75. Additional exam requirements/recommendations for international students: Required—TOEFL (minimum score 550 paper-based; 79 iBT). Electronic applications accepted. *Faculty research:* Arthurian literature, Southern American literature, rhetoric and theories of authorship.

Northeastern State University, College of Liberal Arts, Department of Languages and Literature, Tahlequah, OK 74464-2399. Offers English (MA), including literature, rhetoric/composition. *Faculty:* 10 full-time (4 women), 2 part-time/adjunct (1 woman). *Students:* 7 full-time (4 women), 33 part-time (22 women); includes 11 minority (7 American Indian or Alaska Native, non-Hispanic/Latino; 1 Hispanic/Latino; 3 Two or more races, non-Hispanic/Latino). Average age 35. In 2014, 8 master's awarded. *Degree requirements:* For master's, thesis. *Entrance requirements:* For master's, GRE or MAT, minimum GPA of 2.5. Additional exam requirements/recommendations for international students: Required—TOEFL. *Application deadline:* For fall admission, 6/1 priority date for domestic students. Applications are processed on a rolling basis. Application fee: $25. Electronic applications accepted. *Expenses:* Tuition, state resident: part-time $178.75 per credit hour. Tuition, nonresident: part-time $451.75 per credit hour. *Required fees:* $37.40 per credit hour. *Financial support:* Application deadline: 3/1. *Unit head:* Dr. Audell Shelburne, Chair, 918-456-3609, E-mail: shelburn@nsuok.edu. *Application contact:* Margie Railey, Administrative Assistant, 918-456-5511 Ext. 2093, Fax: 918-458-2061, E-mail: railey@nsouk.edu. Website: http://academics.nsuok.edu/languagesliterature/DegreePrograms/English,MA.aspx

Northeastern University, College of Social Sciences and Humanities, Boston, MA 02115. Offers criminology and criminal justice (MSCJ); criminology and justice policy (PhD); economics (MA, PhD); English (MA, PhD); law and public policy (MS, PhD); political science (MA, PhD); public administration (MPA); public history (MA); security and resilience studies (MS); sociology (MA, PhD); urban and regional policy (MS); world history (MA, PhD). *Degree requirements:* For doctorate, variable foreign language requirement, comprehensive exam, thesis/dissertation. *Entrance requirements:* For master's and doctorate, GRE. Additional exam requirements/recommendations for international students: Required—TOEFL, IELTS. Electronic applications accepted.

Northern Arizona University, Graduate College, College of Arts and Letters, Department of English, Flagstaff, AZ 86011. Offers applied linguistics (PhD); English (MA, MFA), including creative writing (MFA), general English studies (MA), literature (MA), rhetoric and the teaching of writing (MA), secondary English education (MA); professional writing (Certificate); teaching English as a second language (MA, Certificate). Part-time programs available. *Degree requirements:* For master's, comprehensive exam (for some programs), thesis (for some programs), departmental qualifying exam; for doctorate, comprehensive exam, thesis/dissertation, departmental qualifying exam. *Entrance requirements:* For master's, minimum GPA of 3.0 or GRE; for doctorate, GRE General Test. Additional exam requirements/recommendations for international students: Required—TOEFL (minimum score 550 paper-based; 80 iBT), IELTS (minimum score 7), TOEFL (minimum score 600 paper-based; 100 iBT) for PhD; TOEFL (minimum score 570 paper-based; 89 iBT) for MA. Electronic applications accepted.

Northern Illinois University, Graduate School, College of Liberal Arts and Sciences, Department of English, De Kalb, IL 60115-2854. Offers MA, PhD. Part-time programs available. *Faculty:* 32 full-time (13 women), 2 part-time/adjunct (both women). *Students:* 63 full-time (35 women), 49 part-time (28 women); includes 4 minority (1 Black or African American, non-Hispanic/Latino; 1 Asian, non-Hispanic/Latino; 2 Hispanic/Latino), 5 international. Average age 33. 77 applicants, 49% accepted, 18 enrolled. In 2014, 26 master's, 5 doctorates awarded. Terminal master's awarded for partial completion of doctoral program. *Degree requirements:* For master's, variable foreign language requirement, comprehensive exam, thesis optional; for doctorate, variable foreign language requirement, thesis/dissertation, candidacy exam, dissertation defense. *Entrance requirements:* For master's, GRE General Test, minimum GPA of 2.75; for doctorate, GRE General Test, minimum GPA of 2.75 (undergraduate), 3.2 (graduate). Additional exam requirements/recommendations for international students: Required—TOEFL (minimum score 550 paper-based). *Application deadline:* For fall admission, 6/1 for domestic students, 5/1 for international students; for spring admission, 11/1 for domestic students, 10/1 for international students. Applications are processed on a rolling basis. Application fee: $40. Electronic applications accepted. *Financial support:* In 2014–15, 3 research assistantships with full tuition reimbursements, 58 teaching assistantships with full tuition reimbursements were awarded; fellowships with full tuition reimbursements, career-related internships or fieldwork, Federal Work-Study, scholarships/grants, tuition waivers (full), and unspecified assistantships also available. Support available to part-time students. Financial award applicants required to submit FAFSA. *Faculty research:* Nineteenth-century English literature, linguistic programs, portfolio assembly, Mideast literature, old English folklore. *Unit head:* Dr. Amy Levin, Chair, 815-753-0615, Fax: 815-753-0606, E-mail: alevin@niu.edu. *Application contact:* Graduate School Office, 815-753-0395, E-mail: gradsch@niu.edu. Website: http://www.engl.niu.edu/

Northern Kentucky University, Office of Graduate Programs, College of Arts and Sciences, Program in English, Highland Heights, KY 41099. Offers composition and rhetoric (Certificate); creative writing (Certificate); cultural studies and discourses (Certificate); English (MA); professional writing (Certificate). Part-time and evening/weekend programs available. *Faculty:* 13 full-time (6 women), 6 part-time/adjunct (0 women). *Students:* 2 full-time (1 woman), 51 part-time (39 women); includes 3 minority (2 Black or African American, non-Hispanic/Latino; 1 Two or more races, non-Hispanic/Latino). Average age 36. In 2014, 10 master's, 9 other advanced degrees awarded. *Degree requirements:* For master's, comprehensive exam (for some programs), capstone (thesis, portfolio, project, or exams); 30 hours of credit; for Certificate, 18 hours of credit. *Entrance requirements:* For master's, bachelor's degree in English or related field from regionally-accredited institution with minimum GPA of 3.0 in major or cognate area coursework; official transcripts for all undergraduate and graduate work; two letters of reference; for Certificate, official transcripts for all undergraduate and graduate work; bachelor's degree from regionally-accredited institution; minimum undergraduate GPA of 2.5. Additional exam requirements/recommendations for international students: Required—TOEFL (minimum score 79 iBT); Recommended—IELTS (minimum score 6.5). *Application deadline:* For fall admission, 7/1 priority date for domestic students, 6/1 priority date for international students; for spring admission, 11/1 priority date for domestic students, 10/1 for international students. Application fee: $40. Electronic applications accepted. *Expenses: Tuition, area resident:* Part-time $518 per credit hour. Tuition, state resident: part-time $630 per credit hour. Tuition, nonresident: part-time $797 per credit hour. *Required fees:* $192 per semester. Tuition and fees vary according to course load, degree level, campus/location, program and reciprocity agreements. *Financial support:* In 2014–15, 8 students received support. Unspecified assistantships available. Financial award applicants required to submit FAFSA. *Unit head:* Dr. John Alberti, Director of English Graduate Studies, 859-572-5619, Fax: 859-572-6093, E-mail: alberti@nku.edu. *Application contact:* Alison Swanson, Graduate Admissions Coordinator, 859-572-6971, E-mail: swansona1@nku.edu. Website: http://english.nku.edu/gradprogram/

Northern Michigan University, Office of Graduate Education and Research, College of Arts and Sciences, Department of English, Marquette, MI 49855-5301. Offers creative writing (MFA); literature (MA); pedagogy (MA); teaching English to speakers of other languages (Graduate Certificate); theater (MA); writing (MA). Part-time and evening/weekend programs available. *Faculty:* 14 full-time (9 women). *Students:* 55 full-time (32

women), 11 part-time (7 women); includes 8 minority (1 Black or African American, non-Hispanic/Latino; 1 American Indian or Alaska Native, non-Hispanic/Latino; 2 Hispanic/Latino; 4 Two or more races, non-Hispanic/Latino). Average age 27. 135 applicants, 43% accepted, 28 enrolled. In 2014, 21 master's awarded. Terminal master's awarded for partial completion of doctoral program. *Degree requirements:* For master's, capstone project: thesis, practicum or portfolio (for MA); thesis (for MFA); for Graduate Certificate, one foreign language. *Entrance requirements:* For master's, minimum GPA of 3.0; bachelor's degree in English or minimum of 30 credit hours in undergraduate English; statement of purpose; resume; critical essay; 3 letters of recommendation; for Graduate Certificate, bachelor's degree. Additional exam requirements/recommendations for international students: Required—TOEFL (minimum score 550 paper-based; 79 iBT), IELTS (minimum score 6.5). *Application deadline:* For fall admission, 2/1 for domestic students; for winter admission, 2/1 for domestic students; for spring admission, 3/17 for domestic students. Applications are processed on a rolling basis. Application fee: $50. Electronic applications accepted. *Expenses:* Tuition, state resident: full-time $7716; part-time $441 per credit hour. Tuition, nonresident: full-time $10,812; part-time $634.50 per credit hour. *Required fees:* $31.88 per semester. Tuition and fees vary according to course load, degree level and program. *Financial support:* In 2014–15, research assistantships with full tuition reimbursements (averaging $8,898 per year), teaching assistantships with full tuition reimbursements (averaging $8,898 per year) were awarded; Federal Work-Study, institutionally sponsored loans, and unspecified assistantships also available. Support available to part-time students. Financial award application deadline: 3/1; financial award applicants required to submit FAFSA. *Faculty research:* Modern Arabic literature, British literature (medieval to contemporary), postcolonial literature, Native and African-American literature, creative writing, critical theory, pedagogy. *Unit head:* Prof. Russell Prather, PhD, Director of MA Program/Professor, 906-227-2857, E-mail: rprather@nmu.edu. *Application contact:* Prof. Russell Prather, PhD, Director of MA Program/Professor, 906-227-2857, E-mail: rprather@nmu.edu.
Website: http://www.nmu.edu/english/

Northwestern State University of Louisiana, Graduate Studies and Research, Department of Language and Communication, Natchitoches, LA 71497. Offers English (MA). *Degree requirements:* For master's, one foreign language, comprehensive exam, thesis or alternative. *Entrance requirements:* For master's, GRE General Test, minimum undergraduate GPA of 2.5. Additional exam requirements/recommendations for international students: Required—TOEFL. Electronic applications accepted.

Northwestern University, The Graduate School, Judd A. and Marjorie Weinberg College of Arts and Sciences, Department of English, Evanston, IL 60208. Offers MA, PhD. Admissions and degrees offered through The Graduate School. Terminal master's awarded for partial completion of doctoral program. *Degree requirements:* For master's, thesis; for doctorate, one foreign language, thesis/dissertation, oral and written qualifying exam. *Entrance requirements:* For master's and doctorate, GRE General Test, sample of written work. Additional exam requirements/recommendations for international students: Required—TOEFL. Electronic applications accepted. *Faculty research:* Renaissance literature, theatre and drama, American literature, modern European contemporary literature, poetry, cultural history.

Northwestern University, School of Professional Studies, Program in Literature, Evanston, IL 60208. Offers American literature (MA); British literature (MA); comparative and world literature (MA).

Northwest Missouri State University, Graduate School, College of Arts and Sciences, Department of English and Modern Languages, Maryville, MO 64468-6001. Offers English (MA, MS Ed); English with English pedagogy emphasis (MA). Part-time programs available. *Degree requirements:* For master's, comprehensive exam, thesis optional. *Entrance requirements:* For master's, GRE General Test (verbal and analytical writing portions), minimum undergraduate GPA of 3.0, writing sample. Additional exam requirements/recommendations for international students: Required—TOEFL (minimum score 550 paper-based). *Application deadline:* For fall admission, 7/1 for domestic and international students; for spring admission, 11/15 for domestic and international students. Applications are processed on a rolling basis. Application fee: $0 ($50 for international students). *Expenses:* Tuition, state resident: full-time $4464; part-time $346 per credit hour. Tuition, nonresident: full-time $8920; part-time $593 per credit hour. *Required fees:* $1763; $98 per credit hour. *Financial support:* Teaching assistantships with full tuition reimbursements available. Financial award application deadline: 4/1; financial award applicants required to submit FAFSA. *Unit head:* Dr. Michael Hobbs, Chair, 660-562-1285.
Website: http://www.nwmissouri.edu/languages/

Notre Dame de Namur University, Division of Academic Affairs, College of Arts and Sciences, Program in English, Belmont, CA 94002-1908. Offers English (MA); teaching English to speakers of other languages (Certificate). Part-time programs available. *Degree requirements:* For master's, thesis. *Entrance requirements:* For master's, minimum GPA of 2.5, writing sample. Additional exam requirements/recommendations for international students: Required—TOEFL (minimum score 550 paper-based; 79 iBT). Electronic applications accepted.

Oakland University, Graduate Study and Lifelong Learning, College of Arts and Sciences, Department of English, Rochester, MI 48309-4401. Offers MA. Part-time and evening/weekend programs available. *Entrance requirements:* For master's, minimum GPA of 3.0. Additional exam requirements/recommendations for international students: Required—TOEFL (minimum score 550 paper-based). Electronic applications accepted.

Ohio Dominican University, Graduate Programs, Division of Arts and Letters, Program in English, Columbus, OH 43219-2099. Offers MA. Part-time and evening/weekend programs available. Postbaccalaureate distance learning degree programs offered (no on-campus study). *Students:* 24 full-time (23 women), 4 part-time (2 women). *Degree requirements:* For master's, thesis or alternative. *Entrance requirements:* For master's, minimum undergraduate GPA of 3.0, 2 letters of recommendation, essay. Additional exam requirements/recommendations for international students: Required—TOEFL (minimum score 550 paper-based), IELTS (minimum score 6.5). *Application deadline:* For fall admission, 7/15 priority date for domestic and international students; for spring admission, 12/15 priority date for domestic and international students; for summer admission, 5/15 priority date for domestic and international students. Applications are processed on a rolling basis. Application fee: $25. Electronic applications accepted. *Expenses:* Tuition: Full-time $6792; part-time $566 per credit hour. *Required fees:* $200 per semester. Tuition and fees vary according to program and student's religious affiliation. *Financial support:* Applicants required to submit FAFSA. *Unit head:* Dr. Ann Hall, Director, 614-251-4673, E-mail: halla@ohiodominican.edu. *Application contact:* John W. Naughton, Director for Graduate Admissions, 614-251-4615, Fax: 614-251-6654, E-mail: grad@ohiodominican.edu.
Website: http://www.ohiodominican.edu/academics/graduate/ma-in-english

The Ohio State University, Graduate School, College of Arts and Sciences, Division of Arts and Humanities, Department of English, Columbus, OH 43210. Offers MA, MFA, PhD. *Faculty:* 96. *Students:* 152 full-time (96 women), 1 (woman) part-time; includes 31 minority (8 Black or African American, non-Hispanic/Latino; 7 Asian, non-Hispanic/Latino; 13 Hispanic/Latino; 1 Native Hawaiian or other Pacific Islander, non-Hispanic/

Latino; 2 Two or more races, non-Hispanic/Latino), 6 international. Average age 28. In 2014, 17 master's, 14 doctorates awarded. *Degree requirements:* For master's, one foreign language, thesis or written exam; for doctorate, one foreign language, thesis/dissertation. *Entrance requirements:* For master's and doctorate, GRE General Test. Additional exam requirements/recommendations for international students: Required—TOEFL (minimum score 600 paper-based; 100 iBT), IELTS (minimum score 8), Michigan English Language Assessment Battery (minimum score 86). *Application deadline:* For fall admission, 12/6 priority date for domestic students; 11/30 priority date for international students; for winter admission, 12/1 for domestic students, 11/1 for international students; for spring admission, 3/1 for domestic students, 2/1 for international students. Applications are processed on a rolling basis. Application fee: $60 ($70 for international students). Electronic applications accepted. *Financial support:* Fellowships with tuition reimbursements, research assistantships with tuition reimbursements, teaching assistantships with tuition reimbursements, Federal Work-Study, institutionally sponsored loans, and unspecified assistantships available. Support available to part-time students. *Unit head:* Debra Moddelmog, PhD, Chair, 614-292-6065, E-mail: moddelmog.1@osu.edu. *Application contact:* Graduate and Professional Admissions, 614-292-9444, Fax: 614-292-3895, E-mail: gpadmissions@osu.edu.
Website: http://english.osu.edu/

Ohio University, Graduate College, College of Arts and Sciences, Department of English Language and Literature, Athens, OH 45701-2979. Offers MA, PhD. Part-time programs available. *Degree requirements:* For master's, one foreign language, thesis or alternative; for doctorate, one foreign language, comprehensive exam, thesis/dissertation, oral exam, public lecture. *Entrance requirements:* For master's, GRE General Test, minimum GPA of 3.0, writing sample; for doctorate, GRE General Test, minimum GPA of 3.0, master's degree in English, writing sample. Additional exam requirements/recommendations for international students: Required—TOEFL (minimum score 550 paper-based; 80 iBT) or IELTS (minimum score 6.5). Electronic applications accepted. *Faculty research:* Environmental literature, post-colonial studies, print culture, film in popular culture, computers in pedagogy.

Oklahoma State University, College of Arts and Sciences, Department of English, Stillwater, OK 74078. Offers creative writing (MFA); English (MA, PhD). *Faculty:* 62 full-time (30 women), 2 part-time/adjunct (both women). *Students:* 7 full-time (6 women), 133 part-time (66 women); includes 19 minority (1 Black or African American, non-Hispanic/Latino; 2 American Indian or Alaska Native, non-Hispanic/Latino; 2 Asian, non-Hispanic/Latino; 2 Hispanic/Latino; 12 Two or more races, non-Hispanic/Latino), 20 international. Average age 33. 153 applicants, 27% accepted, 23 enrolled. In 2014, 18 master's, 8 doctorates awarded. *Degree requirements:* For master's, comprehensive exam, thesis; for doctorate, comprehensive exam, thesis/dissertation. *Entrance requirements:* For master's, GRE General Test, minimum GPA of 3.0, writing sample; for doctorate, GRE General Test, minimum GPA of 3.5, writing sample. Additional exam requirements/recommendations for international students: Required—TOEFL (minimum score 550 paper-based; 79 iBT). *Application deadline:* For fall admission, 3/1 priority date for international students; for spring admission, 8/1 priority date for international students. Applications are processed on a rolling basis. Application fee: $40 ($75 for international students). Electronic applications accepted. *Expenses:* Tuition, state resident: full-time $4488; part-time $187 per credit hour. Tuition, nonresident: full-time $18,360; part-time $765 per credit hour. *Required fees:* $2413; $100.55 per credit hour. Tuition and fees vary according to campus/location. *Financial support:* In 2014–15, 1 research assistantship (averaging $7,455 per year), 108 teaching assistantships (averaging $16,412 per year) were awarded; career-related internships or fieldwork, Federal Work-Study, scholarships/grants, health care benefits, tuition waivers (partial), and unspecified assistantships also available. Support available to part-time students. Financial award application deadline: 3/1; financial award applicants required to submit FAFSA. *Faculty research:* American and British novels, poetry, and autobiography; Native American languages and literature; institutional history of American film, history, and adaptations; rhetoric and theories of human communication; learning strategies of second language learners. *Unit head:* Dr. Richard Frohock, Department Head, 405-744-9474, Fax: 405-744-6326, E-mail: richard.frohock@okstate.edu.
Website: http://english.okstate.edu/

Old Dominion University, College of Arts and Letters, Doctoral Program in English, Norfolk, VA 23529. Offers PhD. Part-time and evening/weekend programs available. Postbaccalaureate distance learning degree programs offered (minimal on-campus study). *Faculty:* 25 full-time (15 women), 1 (woman) part-time/adjunct. *Students:* 8 full-time (6 women), 50 part-time (40 women); includes 9 minority (5 Black or African American, non-Hispanic/Latino; 1 Hispanic/Latino; 3 Two or more races, non-Hispanic/Latino). Average age 38. 79 applicants, 16% accepted, 11 enrolled. *Degree requirements:* For doctorate, comprehensive exam, thesis/dissertation, research competency in foreign language, statistics, or new media. *Entrance requirements:* For doctorate, GRE General Test, MA in English or related field with minimum GPA of 3.5, writing sample, resume, goals statement, letter of recommendation. Additional exam requirements/recommendations for international students: Required—TOEFL. *Application deadline:* For fall admission, 2/1 for domestic students. Application fee: $50. Electronic applications accepted. *Expenses:* Tuition, state resident: full-time $10,488; part-time $437 per credit. Tuition, nonresident: full-time $26,136; part-time $1089 per credit. *Required fees:* $64 per semester. One-time fee: $50. *Financial support:* In 2014–15, 13 students received support, including 3 fellowships with full tuition reimbursements available (averaging $15,000 per year), 1 research assistantship with full tuition reimbursement available (averaging $15,000 per year), 9 teaching assistantships with full tuition reimbursements available (averaging $15,000 per year); career-related internships or fieldwork, scholarships/grants, and unspecified assistantships also available. Support available to part-time students. Financial award application deadline: 2/15; financial award applicants required to submit FAFSA. *Faculty research:* New media studies, rhetorical history and theory, digital studies, writing studies, professional writing and document design, linguistics, textual studies, literary studies. *Unit head:* Dr. Kevin Eric DePew, Graduate Program Director, 757-683-4019, Fax: 757-683-3241, E-mail: kdepew@odu.edu. *Application contact:* Dr. David C. Earnest, Associate Dean, 757-683-6077, Fax: 757-683-5746, E-mail: dearnest@odu.edu.
Website: http://al.odu.edu/english/academics/phd/

Old Dominion University, College of Arts and Letters, Master's in English Program, Norfolk, VA 23529. Offers MA. Part-time and evening/weekend programs available. *Faculty:* 17 full-time (8 women). *Students:* 19 full-time (13 women), 22 part-time (19 women); includes 8 minority (1 Black or African American, non-Hispanic/Latino; 1 Asian, non-Hispanic/Latino; 5 Hispanic/Latino; 1 Two or more races, non-Hispanic/Latino). Average age 31. 56 applicants, 66% accepted, 30 enrolled. In 2014, 15 master's awarded. *Degree requirements:* For master's, comprehensive exam, thesis optional. *Entrance requirements:* For master's, GRE General Test, 24 hours in English, sample of written work, BA. Additional exam requirements/recommendations for international students: Required—TOEFL. *Application deadline:* For fall admission, 3/15 priority date for domestic and international students; for winter admission, 11/1 for domestic students, 10/1 for international students; for spring admission, 11/1 priority date for domestic students, 11/1 for international students. Application fee: $50. Electronic applications accepted. *Expenses:* Tuition, state resident: full-time $10,488; part-time $437 per credit. Tuition, nonresident: full-time $26,136; part-time $1089 per credit.

Required fees: $64 per semester. One-time fee: $50. *Financial support:* In 2014–15, 2 research assistantships (averaging $10,000 per year), 6 teaching assistantships (averaging $10,000 per year) were awarded; career-related internships or fieldwork and unspecified assistantships also available. Financial award application deadline: 2/15; financial award applicants required to submit FAFSA. *Faculty research:* Literary theory, composition theory, professional writing, rhetoric, British and American literature. *Total annual research expenditures:* $3,451. *Unit head:* Dr. Imtiaz Habib, Graduate Program Director, 757-683-3285, E-mail: ihabib@odu.edu. *Application contact:* Dr. David C. Earnest, Associate Dean, 757-683-6077, Fax: 757-683-5746, E-mail: dearnest@odu.edu.
Website: http://al.odu.edu/english/academics/ma/

Old Dominion University, Darden College of Education, Programs in Secondary Education, Norfolk, VA 23529. Offers chemistry (MS Ed); English (MS Ed); secondary education (MS Ed). *Accreditation:* NCATE. Part-time and evening/weekend programs available. Postbaccalaureate distance learning degree programs offered (minimal on-campus study). *Faculty:* 13 full-time (7 women), 10 part-time/adjunct (7 women). *Students:* 48 full-time (33 women), 71 part-time (49 women); includes 21 minority (10 Black or African American, non-Hispanic/Latino; 1 Asian, non-Hispanic/Latino; 4 Hispanic/Latino; 6 Two or more races, non-Hispanic/Latino). Average age 33. 75 applicants, 71% accepted, 53 enrolled. In 2014, 71 master's awarded. *Degree requirements:* For master's, comprehensive exam, thesis. *Entrance requirements:* For master's, GRE General Test or MAT, PRAXIS I (for licensure), minimum GPA of 2.8, teaching certificate. Additional exam requirements/recommendations for international students: Required—TOEFL. *Application deadline:* For fall admission, 6/1 for domestic and international students; for winter admission, 11/1 for domestic and international students; for spring admission, 3/1 for domestic and international students. Applications are processed on a rolling basis. Application fee: $50. Electronic applications accepted. *Expenses:* Tuition, state resident: full-time $10,488; part-time $437 per credit. Tuition, nonresident: full-time $26,136; part-time $1089 per credit. *Required fees:* $64 per semester. One-time fee: $50. *Financial support:* In 2014–15, 56 students received support, including fellowships (averaging $15,000 per year), research assistantships with tuition reimbursements available (averaging $9,000 per year), teaching assistantships with tuition reimbursements available (averaging $15,000 per year). Financial award application deadline: 2/15; financial award applicants required to submit FAFSA. *Faculty research:* Use of technology, writing project for teachers, geography teaching, reading. *Unit head:* Dr. Robert Lucking, Graduate Program Director, 757-683-5545, Fax: 757-683-5862, E-mail: rlucking@odu.edu. *Application contact:* William Heffelfinger, Director of Graduate Admissions, 757-683-5554, Fax: 757-683-3255, E-mail: gradadmit@odu.edu.
Website: http://education.odu.edu/eci/secondary/

Oregon State University, College of Liberal Arts, Program in English, Corvallis, OR 97331. Offers literature and culture (MA); rhetoric, writing and culture (MA). Part-time programs available. *Faculty:* 18 full-time (7 women), 4 part-time/adjunct (3 women). *Students:* 25 full-time (12 women), 2 part-time (both women); includes 3 minority (1 Asian, non-Hispanic/Latino; 1 Hispanic/Latino; 1 Two or more races, non-Hispanic/Latino), 1 international. Average age 27. 63 applicants, 40% accepted, 12 enrolled. In 2014, 14 master's awarded. *Degree requirements:* For master's, thesis. *Entrance requirements:* For master's, GRE (recommended). Additional exam requirements/recommendations for international students: Required—TOEFL (minimum score 80 iBT), IELTS (minimum score 6.5). *Application deadline:* For fall admission, 1/7 for domestic and international students. Application fee: $60. *Expenses:* Tuition, state resident: full-time $11,907; part-time $189 per credit hour. Tuition, nonresident: full-time $19,953; part-time $441 per credit hour. *Required fees:* $1472; $449 per term. One-time fee: $350. Tuition and fees vary according to course load and program. *Financial support:* Teaching assistantships and scholarships/grants available. Financial award application deadline: 1/7. *Unit head:* Dr. Anita Helle, Director, School of Writing, Literature, and Film. *Application contact:* Dr. Peter Betjemann, Associate Professor/Graduate Coordinator, 541-737-1651, E-mail: peter.betjemann@oregonstate.edu.
Website: http://liberalarts.oregonstate.edu/wlf/ma

Our Lady of the Lake University of San Antonio, College of Arts and Sciences, Program in English, San Antonio, TX 78207-4689. Offers English and communication arts (MA); English education (MA); English language and literature (MA); writing (MA); MA/MFA. Program offered jointly with University of the Incarnate Word and St. Mary's University. Part-time and evening/weekend programs available. *Degree requirements:* For master's, comprehensive exam, thesis optional. *Entrance requirements:* For master's, GRE General Test or MAT, minimum GPA of 3.0 in last 60 hours, 2.5 overall. Additional exam requirements/recommendations for international students: Required—TOEFL. Electronic applications accepted. *Faculty research:* Writing theory and research, contemporary Southern literature, popular culture, poetry, literature of the Southwest.

Penn State University Park, Graduate School, College of the Liberal Arts, Department of English, University Park, PA 16802. Offers MA, MFA, PhD. *Unit head:* Dr. Susan Welch, Dean, 814-865-7691, Fax: 814-863-2085, E-mail: swelch@psu.edu. *Application contact:* Lori A. Stania, Director, Graduate Student Services, 814-867-5278, Fax: 814-863-4627, E-mail: gswww@psu.edu.
Website: http://english.la.psu.edu/

Pittsburg State University, Graduate School, College of Arts and Sciences, Department of English, Pittsburg, KS 66762. Offers MA. *Degree requirements:* For master's, thesis or alternative. *Faculty research:* American fiction, American poetry, British fiction, British poetry, composition theory.

Portland State University, Graduate Studies, College of Liberal Arts and Sciences, Department of English, Portland, OR 97207-0751. Offers MA, MFA, MA/MS. Part-time and evening/weekend programs available. *Faculty:* 37 full-time (21 women), 34 part-time/adjunct (20 women). *Students:* 98 full-time (66 women), 51 part-time (34 women); includes 24 minority (3 Black or African American, non-Hispanic/Latino; 3 American Indian or Alaska Native, non-Hispanic/Latino; 3 Asian, non-Hispanic/Latino; 9 Hispanic/Latino; 1 Native Hawaiian or other Pacific Islander, non-Hispanic/Latino; 5 Two or more races, non-Hispanic/Latino), 1 international. Average age 32. 299 applicants, 26% accepted, 62 enrolled. In 2014, 47 master's awarded. *Degree requirements:* For master's, one foreign language, comprehensive exam (for some programs), thesis (for some programs), oral and written exams. *Entrance requirements:* For master's, GRE (for some programs), statement of purpose, 2 letters of recommendation, transcripts, writing samples. Additional exam requirements/recommendations for international students: Required—TOEFL (minimum score 600 paper-based; 100 iBT). *Application deadline:* For fall admission, 1/3 for domestic and international students; for winter admission, 9/1 for domestic and international students; for spring admission, 11/1 for domestic and international students. Application fee: $50. *Expenses:* Tuition, state resident: part-time $222 per credit. Tuition, nonresident: part-time $527 per credit. *Required fees:* $22 per contact hour. $100 per quarter. Tuition and fees vary according to program. *Financial support:* In 2014–15, 17 teaching assistantships with full tuition reimbursements (averaging $6,702 per year) were awarded; career-related internships or fieldwork, Federal Work-Study, scholarships/grants, and unspecified assistantships also available. Support available to part-time students. Financial award application

deadline: 3/1; financial award applicants required to submit FAFSA. *Faculty research:* American literature and cultural studies, medieval and British literature, writing prose fiction and poetry, rhetoric and composition, women's literature. *Total annual research expenditures:* $16,124. *Unit head:* Prof. Paul Collins, Chair, 503-725-3521, Fax: 503-725-3561, E-mail: pcollins@pdx.edu. *Application contact:* Matt Swetnam, Program Coordinator, 503-725-3623, Fax: 503-725-3561, E-mail: grdstudy@pdx.edu.
Website: http://www.pdx.edu/english/

Prairie View A&M University, College of Arts and Sciences, Department of Languages and Communication, Prairie View, TX 77446-0519. Offers English (MA). Part-time programs available. *Faculty:* 1 (woman) part-time/adjunct. In 2014, 8 master's awarded. *Degree requirements:* For master's, comprehensive exam, thesis, exit exam. *Entrance requirements:* For master's, GRE General Test, bachelor's degree in English or equivalent. Additional exam requirements/recommendations for international students: Required—TOEFL. *Application deadline:* For fall admission, 7/1 for domestic and international students; for winter admission, 4/1 for domestic students, 10/1 for international students; for spring admission, 11/1 for domestic and international students. Application fee: $50. *Expenses:* Tuition, state resident: full-time $4134; part-time $248.68 per credit hour. Tuition, nonresident: full-time $11,051; part-time $632.97 per credit hour. *Required fees:* $2552; $475.10 per credit hour. *Financial support:* In 2014–15, teaching assistantships (averaging $12,000 per year) were awarded; career-related internships or fieldwork, Federal Work-Study, institutionally sponsored loans, and tuition waivers (full and partial) also available. Support available to part-time students. Financial award application deadline: 4/1; financial award applicants required to submit FAFSA. *Faculty research:* Composition, rhetoric, technical writing, literature, communication, pedagogy in general and for literature, online teaching. *Unit head:* Dr. Dejun Liu, Head, 936-261-3731, Fax: 936-261-3209, E-mail: deliu@pvamu.edu. *Application contact:* Dr. William H. Parker, Office of Graduate Admissions, 936-261-3500, Fax: 936-261-3529, E-mail: whparker@pvamu.edu.

Princeton University, Graduate School, Department of English, Princeton, NJ 08544-1019. Offers PhD. *Degree requirements:* For doctorate, 2 foreign languages, thesis/dissertation. *Entrance requirements:* For doctorate, GRE General Test, GRE Subject Test, sample of written work. Additional exam requirements/recommendations for international students: Required—TOEFL (minimum score 600 paper-based). Electronic applications accepted.

Purdue University, Graduate School, College of Liberal Arts, Department of English, West Lafayette, IN 47907. Offers creative writing (MFA); literature (MA, PhD), including linguistics, literature and philosophy (PhD), rhetoric and composition, theory and cultural studies (PhD). Part-time programs available. *Degree requirements:* For master's, one foreign language, comprehensive exam (for some programs), thesis (for some programs); for doctorate, one foreign language, comprehensive exam, thesis/dissertation. *Entrance requirements:* For master's, GRE General Test; GRE Subject Test in English literature (recommended for students applying to literary studies), minimum undergraduate GPA of 3.0 or equivalent; for doctorate, GRE General Test; GRE Subject Test in English literature (recommended for students applying to literary studies), master's degree. Additional exam requirements/recommendations for international students: Required—TOEFL (minimum score 620 paper-based; 77 iBT). Electronic applications accepted. *Faculty research:* Cultural studies, postmodern narrative, contemporary women writers, composition theory, slave narratives.

Purdue University, Graduate School, Program in Philosophy and Literature, West Lafayette, IN 47907. Offers PhD. Program offered jointly with Department of English, School of Languages and Cultures, and Department of Philosophy. *Degree requirements:* For doctorate, one foreign language, comprehensive exam, thesis/dissertation. *Entrance requirements:* For doctorate, GRE, master's degree in either English, philosophy or foreign languages. Additional exam requirements/recommendations for international students: Required—TOEFL. Electronic applications accepted.

Purdue University Calumet, Graduate Studies Office, School of Liberal Arts and Social Sciences, Department of English and Philosophy, Hammond, IN 46323-2094. Offers English (MA). Part-time and evening/weekend programs available. Postbaccalaureate distance learning degree programs offered (minimal on-campus study). *Degree requirements:* For master's, comprehensive exam, thesis optional. *Entrance requirements:* Additional exam requirements/recommendations for international students: Required—TOEFL. Electronic applications accepted. *Faculty research:* English literature, American literature, critical theory, women's studies, historical philosophy.

Queens College of the City University of New York, Division of Graduate Studies, Arts and Humanities Division, Department of English, Flushing, NY 11367-1597. Offers creative writing (MA); English language and literature (MA). Part-time and evening/weekend programs available. *Degree requirements:* For master's, one foreign language, thesis (for some programs), oral exam (English language and literature). *Entrance requirements:* For master's, manuscript (creative writing), minimum GPA of 3.0. Additional exam requirements/recommendations for international students: Required—TOEFL.

Queen's University at Kingston, School of Graduate Studies, Faculty of Arts and Sciences, Department of English Language and Literature, Kingston, ON K7L 3N6, Canada. Offers MA, PhD. *Degree requirements:* For master's, one foreign language, thesis optional; for doctorate, 2 foreign languages, comprehensive exam, thesis/dissertation. *Entrance requirements:* For master's, B.A.H. upper 2nd class standing, 10 full courses in English; for doctorate, M.A. upper 2nd class standing. Additional exam requirements/recommendations for international students: Required—TOEFL, TWE. *Faculty research:* Renaissance, 18th century, post colonial, Canadian, 19th century.

Radford University, College of Graduate and Professional Studies, College of Humanities and Behavioral Sciences, Program in English, Radford, VA 24142. Offers MA, MS. Part-time programs available. *Faculty:* 14 full-time (6 women), 1 (woman) part-time/adjunct. *Students:* 31 full-time (20 women), 4 part-time (all women); includes 2 minority (1 Black or African American, non-Hispanic/Latino; 1 Asian, non-Hispanic/Latino). Average age 27. 18 applicants, 83% accepted, 14 enrolled. In 2014, 16 master's awarded. *Degree requirements:* For master's, comprehensive exam, thesis (for some programs). *Entrance requirements:* For master's, GRE, minimum GPA of 2.75; 2 letters of reference; sample of expository writing, resume, official transcripts. Additional exam requirements/recommendations for international students: Required—TOEFL (minimum score 550 paper-based; 79 iBT), IELTS (minimum score 6.5). *Application deadline:* For fall admission, 2/15 priority date for domestic students, 12/1 for international students; for spring admission, 7/1 for international students. Applications are processed on a rolling basis. Application fee: $50. Electronic applications accepted. *Expenses:* Tuition, state resident: full-time $7187; part-time $299 per credit hour. Tuition, nonresident: full-time $16,394; part-time $683 per credit hour. *Required fees:* $2974; $125 per credit hour. Tuition and fees vary according to course load and program. *Financial support:* In 2014–15, 27 students received support, including 7 research assistantships (averaging $6,429 per year), 20 teaching assistantships with partial tuition reimbursements available (averaging $10,500 per year); career-related internships or fieldwork, Federal Work-Study, institutionally sponsored loans, scholarships/grants, and unspecified

assistantships also available. Financial award application deadline: 3/1; financial award applicants required to submit FAFSA. *Faculty research:* The effect of translation on the works of James Joyce, the life and work of Olive Moore, the southern trajectory of the works of Phillis Wheatley after her death, the influence of French feminism on the poetry of Anne Bradstreet, postmodern theory and Native American fiction. *Unit head:* Dr. Paul Witkowsky, Coordinator, 540-831-5628, Fax: 540-831-6800, E-mail: english@radford.edu. *Application contact:* Rebecca Conner, Director, Graduate Enrollment, 540-831-6296, Fax: 540-831-6061, E-mail: gradcollege@radford.edu. Website: http://www.radford.edu/content/chbs/home/english.html

Rhode Island College, School of Graduate Studies, Faculty of Arts and Sciences, Department of English, Providence, RI 02908-1991. Offers creative writing (MA, CGS); English (MA); literature (CGS). Part-time and evening/weekend programs available. *Faculty:* 6 full-time (2 women). *Students:* 1 full-time (0 women), 10 part-time (6 women). Average age 33. In 2014, 5 master's awarded. *Degree requirements:* For master's, thesis (for some programs). *Entrance requirements:* For master's, GRE General Test, 3 letters of recommendation, interview. Additional exam requirements/recommendations for international students: Recommended—TOEFL (minimum score 550 paper-based; 79 iBT). *Application deadline:* For fall admission, 3/1 for domestic students; for spring admission, 11/1 for domestic students. Applications are processed on a rolling basis. Application fee: $50. *Expenses:* Tuition, state resident: full-time $8928; part-time $372 per credit hour. Tuition, nonresident: full-time $17,376; part-time $724 per credit hour. *Required fees:* $602; $22 per credit. $72 per term. *Financial support:* In 2014–15, 2 teaching assistantships with full tuition reimbursements (averaging $3,250 per year) were awarded; career-related internships or fieldwork, Federal Work-Study, scholarships/grants, health care benefits, and unspecified assistantships also available. Support available to part-time students. Financial award application deadline: 5/15; financial award applicants required to submit FAFSA. *Unit head:* Dr. Daniel Scott, III, Chair, 401-456-8028. *Application contact:* Graduate Studies, 401-456-8700. Website: http://www.ric.edu/english/index.php

Rice University, Graduate Programs, School of Humanities, Department of English, Houston, TX 77251-1892. Offers MA, PhD. Terminal master's awarded for partial completion of doctoral program. *Degree requirements:* For master's, comprehensive exam, thesis (for some programs); for doctorate, comprehensive exam, thesis/dissertation. *Entrance requirements:* For master's and doctorate, GRE General Test, minimum GPA of 3.0. Additional exam requirements/recommendations for international students: Required—TOEFL (minimum score 600 paper-based; 90 iBT). Electronic applications accepted. *Faculty research:* Traditional periods and genres (excluding Old English), literary criticism and theory, Victorian literature, feminist literature, Renaissance literature, American literature, African-American literature.

Rivier University, School of Graduate Studies, Department of English, Nashua, NH 03060. Offers English (MAT); writing and literature (MA). Part-time and evening/weekend programs available. *Degree requirements:* For master's, comprehensive exam (for some programs). *Entrance requirements:* For master's, GRE Subject Test.

Roosevelt University, Graduate Division, College of Arts and Sciences, Department of Literature and Languages, Program in English, Chicago, IL 60605. Offers MA. Part-time and evening/weekend programs available. *Degree requirements:* For master's, one foreign language, thesis or alternative. *Faculty research:* Eighteenth-century Victorian literature and culture, creative writing, eighteenth through twentieth century literature, American literature and culture.

Rutgers, The State University of New Jersey, Camden, Graduate School of Arts and Sciences, Program in English, Camden, NJ 08102. Offers MA. Part-time and evening/weekend programs available. *Degree requirements:* For master's, comprehensive exam, thesis optional, 30 credits. *Entrance requirements:* For master's, GRE General Test, 3 letters of recommendation, writing sample, statement of personal, professional, and academic goals. Additional exam requirements/recommendations for international students: Required—TOEFL, IELTS. Electronic applications accepted. *Faculty research:* British literature; American literature; women's studies; literary, poetic, and rhetorical theory; creative writing.

Rutgers, The State University of New Jersey, Newark, Graduate School, Program in English, Newark, NJ 07102. Offers MA. Part-time and evening/weekend programs available. *Degree requirements:* For master's, one foreign language, comprehensive exam, thesis optional. *Entrance requirements:* For master's, GRE, minimum undergraduate B average. Electronic applications accepted. *Faculty research:* British and American literature, cultural studies, literary theory, minority literatures.

Rutgers, The State University of New Jersey, New Brunswick, Graduate School-New Brunswick, Program of Literatures in English, Piscataway, NJ 08854-8097. Offers PhD. *Degree requirements:* For doctorate, one foreign language, thesis/dissertation, qualifying exam. *Entrance requirements:* For doctorate, GRE General Test, GRE Subject Test, writing sample, 3 letters of recommendation. Additional exam requirements/recommendations for international students: Required—TOEFL. Electronic applications accepted. *Faculty research:* Medieval literature; Renaissance; African American literature; 18th-century British literature; feminism, gender, and sexuality; postcolonial studies.

St. Bonaventure University, School of Graduate Studies, Department of English, St. Bonaventure, NY 14778-2284. Offers MA. Part-time programs available. *Faculty:* 4 full-time (2 women). *Students:* 7 full-time (3 women), 4 part-time (3 women); includes 1 minority (Black or African American, non-Hispanic/Latino), 2 international. Average age 27. 5 applicants, 100% accepted, 3 enrolled. In 2014, 7 master's awarded. *Degree requirements:* For master's, one foreign language, thesis, oral comprehensive examination. *Entrance requirements:* For master's, GRE General Test or 10-15 page writing sample, bachelor's degree; demonstrated competence in reading Latin, French, German or Spanish; recommendation letters; minimum of 24 hours of undergraduate English courses. Additional exam requirements/recommendations for international students: Required—TOEFL (minimum score 550 paper-based; 79 iBT). *Application deadline:* For fall admission, 6/15 priority date for domestic students, 2/1 priority date for international students; for spring admission, 11/15 priority date for domestic students, 7/1 priority date for international students. Applications are processed on a rolling basis. Application fee: $0. Electronic applications accepted. *Expenses:* Expenses: Contact institution. *Financial support:* In 2014–15, 7 fellowships were awarded; Federal Work-Study, scholarships/grants, health care benefits, and unspecified assistantships also available. Support available to part-time students. Financial award application deadline: 4/15; financial award applicants required to submit FAFSA. *Unit head:* Dr. Daniel Ellis, Program Director, 716-375-2452, Fax: 716-375-7665, E-mail: dellis@sbu.edu. *Application contact:* Bruce Campbell, Director of Graduate Admissions, 716-375-2429, Fax: 716-375-4015, E-mail: gradsch@sbu.edu. Website: http://www.sbu.edu/academics/schools/arts-and-sciences/graduate-degrees/master-of-arts-in-english

St. Cloud State University, School of Graduate Studies, College of Liberal Arts, Department of English, St. Cloud, MN 56301-4498. Offers English (MA, MS); teaching English as a second language (MA). Part-time programs available. *Degree requirements:* For master's, thesis or alternative. *Entrance requirements:* For master's, GRE General Test, minimum GPA of 2.75. Additional exam requirements/

recommendations for international students: Required—Michigan English Language Assessment Battery; Recommended—TOEFL (minimum score 550 paper-based), IELTS (minimum score 6.5). Electronic applications accepted.

St. John's University, St. John's College of Liberal Arts and Sciences, Department of English, Queens, NY 11439. Offers MA, DA. Part-time and evening/weekend programs available. *Students:* 40 full-time (10 women), 59 part-time (41 women); includes 27 minority (10 Black or African American, non-Hispanic/Latino; 6 Asian, non-Hispanic/Latino; 8 Hispanic/Latino; 3 Two or more races, non-Hispanic/Latino), 2 international. Average age 33. 41 applicants, 85% accepted, 25 enrolled. In 2014, 22 master's, 6 doctorates awarded. *Degree requirements:* For master's, comprehensive exam, thesis optional, portfolio; for doctorate, one foreign language, comprehensive exam, thesis/dissertation. *Entrance requirements:* For master's, GRE, minimum GPA of 3.0, 2 letters of recommendation, bachelor's degree; for doctorate, GRE, minimum GPA of 3.5 in literature, 3.0 overall; writing sample, 3 letters of recommendation, essay. Additional exam requirements/recommendations for international students: Required—TOEFL (minimum score 600 paper-based; 100 iBT), IELTS (minimum score 7). *Application deadline:* For fall admission, 5/1 priority date for domestic and international students; for spring admission, 11/1 priority date for domestic and international students. Applications are processed on a rolling basis. Application fee: $70. Electronic applications accepted. *Expenses: Tuition:* Full-time $20,610; part-time $1145 per credit. *Required fees:* $170 per semester. *Financial support:* Fellowships, research assistantships, and scholarships/grants available. Support available to part-time students. Financial award application deadline: 3/1; financial award applicants required to submit FAFSA. *Faculty research:* Modern comparative drama, literary theories and criticism, nineteenth and early twentieth century American literature, Chaucer, Elizabethan drama. *Unit head:* Dr. Stephen Sicari, Chair, 718-990-6390, E-mail: sicaris@stjohns.edu. *Application contact:* Robert Medrano, Director of Graduate Admission, 718-990-1601, Fax: 718-990-5686, E-mail: gradhelp@stjohns.edu.

Saint Louis University, Graduate Education, College of Arts and Sciences and Graduate Education, Department of English, St. Louis, MO 63103-2097. Offers MA, MA-R, PhD. Part-time programs available. *Degree requirements:* For master's, one foreign language, comprehensive exam, thesis optional, comprehensive oral exam; for doctorate, 2 foreign languages, comprehensive exam, thesis/dissertation, preliminary oral and written exams. *Entrance requirements:* For master's, GRE General Test, GRE Subject Test, letters of recommendation, resume, writing sample, interview; for doctorate, GRE General Test, GRE Subject Test, letters of recommendation, resumé, writing sample, interview, goal statement, writing sample. Additional exam requirements/recommendations for international students: Required—TOEFL (minimum score 550 paper-based). *Faculty research:* English literature, American literature, post-colonial literature, composition, literary theory.

Saint Louis University–Madrid Campus, Graduate Programs, Master of Arts in English Program, Madrid, Spain. Offers MA. Part-time programs available. *Faculty:* 8 full-time (5 women), 1 (woman) part-time/adjunct. *Students:* 4 full-time (all women), 8 part-time (7 women). Average age 28. 10 applicants, 90% accepted, 4 enrolled. In 2014, 3 master's awarded. *Degree requirements:* For master's, one foreign language, comprehensive exam, thesis optional. *Entrance requirements:* For master's, GRE General Test, transcripts, 3 letters of recommendation, writing sample, personal statement, curriculum vitae. Additional exam requirements/recommendations for international students: Required—TOEFL (minimum score 550 paper-based; 80 iBT). *Application deadline:* For fall admission, 3/1 priority date for domestic and international students; for spring admission, 9/1 priority date for domestic and international students. Applications are processed on a rolling basis. Application fee: $40. Electronic applications accepted. *Financial support:* In 2014–15, 5 students received support, including 2 fellowships with partial tuition reimbursements available, 3 teaching assistantships with full and partial tuition reimbursements available (averaging $1,350 per year); career-related internships or fieldwork, scholarships/grants, health care benefits, and unspecified assistantships also available. Support available to part-time students. Financial award application deadline: 3/1; financial award applicants required to submit FAFSA. *Faculty research:* English, Irish and American literature; literary theory; translation; linguistics. *Unit head:* Dr. Anne McCabe, Coordinator, English Department, 34-91-554-58-58 Ext. 237, Fax: 34-91-554-62-02, E-mail: mccabea@slu.edu. *Application contact:* Heidi Buffington, Admissions Counselor, 34-91-554-58-58, Fax: 34-91-554-62-02, E-mail: graduate_admissions-madrid@slu.edu. Website: http://spain.slu.edu/academics/degrees_&_programs/graduate_programs/MA_in_english/introduction.html

St. Mary's University, Graduate School, Department of Education, Program in Education, San Antonio, TX 78228-8507. Offers computer science (MA); education (MA); English literature and language (MA); international relations (MA); political science (MA). *Students:* 1 (woman) part-time; minority (Black or African American, non-Hispanic/Latino). Average age 28. 12 applicants, 17% accepted. In 2014, 3 master's awarded. *Entrance requirements:* For master's, GRE or MAT, 200 X GPA + Average GRE [(Verbal + Quantitative)/2]= 1050; or 10 X GPA + MAT = 68. *Expenses: Tuition:* Full-time $15,070; part-time $800 per credit hour. *Required fees:* $156 per semester. *Faculty research:* Bronfenbrenner's ecological systems theory: implications for education today. *Unit head:* Dr. Dan Higgins, Department Chair, 210-436-3121, E-mail: dhiggins@stmarytx.edu. Website: https://www.stmarytx.edu/academics/graduate/masters/education/

St. Mary's University, Graduate School, Department of English and Communication Studies, Program in English Literature and Language, San Antonio, TX 78228-8507. Offers MA, JD/MA. Part-time programs available. *Students:* 5 full-time (all women), 10 part-time (5 women); includes 8 minority (all Hispanic/Latino), 2 international. Average age 27. 7 applicants, 43% accepted, 4 enrolled. In 2014, 2 master's awarded. *Degree requirements:* For master's, comprehensive exam. *Entrance requirements:* For master's, GRE, Generally, the student is expected to score within the top 35% of the verbal section and the top 35% of the analytical section of the GRE as reported for the year in which it is taken. Students otherwise highly qualified, they may take the GRE during their first semester of enrollment, with further enrollment contingent upon receipt of test scores. Additional exam requirements/recommendations for international students: Required—TOEFL (minimum score 550 paper-based; 80 iBT). *Application deadline:* Applications are processed on a rolling basis. Application fee: $0. Electronic applications accepted. *Expenses: Tuition:* Full-time $15,070; part-time $800 per credit hour. *Required fees:* $156 per semester. *Financial support:* Application deadline: 3/31. *Unit head:* Dr. Gwendolyn Diaz, Director of English Literature and Language Graduate Program, 210-436-2007, E-mail: gdiaz@stmarytx.edu. Website: https://www.stmarytx.edu/academics/graduate/masters/english-literature/

Salem State University, School of Graduate Studies, Program in English, Salem, MA 01970-5353. Offers MA, MAT, MA/MAT. Part-time and evening/weekend programs available. *Entrance requirements:* For master's, GRE or MAT. Additional exam requirements/recommendations for international students: Required—TOEFL (minimum score 550 paper-based; 80 iBT) or IELTS (minimum score 5.5).

Salisbury University, Program in English, Salisbury, MD 21801-6837. Offers composition and rhetoric (MA); English (MA); literature (MA); TESOL (MA). Part-time and evening/weekend programs available. *Faculty:* 11 full-time (5 women). *Students:* 9

full-time (6 women), 24 part-time (19 women); includes 6 minority (3 Black or African American, non-Hispanic/Latino; 2 Hispanic/Latino; 1 Two or more races, non-Hispanic/Latino), 3 international. Average age 32. 11 applicants, 100% accepted, 11 enrolled. In 2014, 20 master's awarded. *Degree requirements:* For master's, comprehensive exam (for some programs), thesis optional. *Entrance requirements:* For master's, GRE, MAT, PRAXIS I, 2 letters of recommendation; personal statement. Additional exam requirements/recommendations for international students: Required—TOEFL (minimum score 550 paper-based; 79 iBT), IELTS (minimum score 6.5). *Application deadline:* For fall admission, 3/15 for domestic and international students; for spring admission, 10/1 for domestic and international students. Applications are processed on a rolling basis. Application fee: $65. Electronic applications accepted. *Expenses:* Expenses: $358 per credit hour for residents; $647 for non-residents; $78 fees. *Financial support:* In 2014–15, 12 teaching assistantships with full tuition reimbursements (averaging $9,498 per year) were awarded; career-related internships or fieldwork, institutionally sponsored loans, and unspecified assistantships also available. Support available to part-time students. Financial award application deadline: 3/1; financial award applicants required to submit FAFSA. *Faculty research:* American literature; British literature; linguistics, film, rhetoric and composition. *Unit head:* Dr. Christopher Vilmar, Graduate Program Director, English, 410-677-6511, Fax: -, E-mail: csvilmar@salisbury.edu.
Website: http://www.salisbury.edu/gsr/gradstudies/ENGpage.html

Sam Houston State University, College of Humanities and Social Sciences, Department of English, Huntsville, TX 77341. Offers creative writing, editing, and publishing (MFA); English (MA). Part-time programs available. *Faculty:* 25 full-time (13 women), 2 part-time/adjunct (0 women). *Students:* 12 full-time (6 women), 26 part-time (15 women); includes 7 minority (2 Black or African American, non-Hispanic/Latino; 2 American Indian or Alaska Native, non-Hispanic/Latino; 1 Hispanic/Latino; 2 Two or more races, non-Hispanic/Latino), 1 international. Average age 33. 17 applicants, 82% accepted, 12 enrolled. In 2014, 16 master's awarded. *Degree requirements:* For master's, comprehensive exam, thesis optional. *Entrance requirements:* For master's, GRE General Test, creative writing sample, letters of recommendation. Additional exam requirements/recommendations for international students: Required—TOEFL (minimum score 550 paper-based; 79 iBT), IELTS (minimum score 6.5). *Application deadline:* For fall admission, 3/15 priority date for domestic students, 6/25 for international students; for spring admission, 10/15 priority date for domestic students, 11/12 for international students. Applications are processed on a rolling basis. Application fee: $45 ($75 for international students). Electronic applications accepted. *Expenses:* Tuition, state resident: full-time $2286; part-time $254 per credit hour. Tuition, nonresident: full-time $5544; part-time $616 per credit hour. *Required fees:* $440 per semester. Tuition and fees vary according to course load and campus/location. *Financial support:* In 2014–15, 14 research assistantships (averaging $7,240 per year), 11 teaching assistantships (averaging $7,206 per year) were awarded; career-related internships or fieldwork, Federal Work-Study, scholarships/grants, tuition waivers (partial), and unspecified assistantships also available. Support available to part-time students. Financial award application deadline: 3/15; financial award applicants required to submit FAFSA. *Unit head:* Dr. Helena Halmari, Chair, 936-294-1404, Fax: 936-294-1408, E-mail: eng_shh@shsu.edu. *Application contact:* Dr. Paul Child, Advisor, 936-294-1412, Fax: 936-294-1408, E-mail: eng_pwc@shsu.edu.
Website: http://www.shsu.edu/~eng_www/

San Diego State University, Graduate and Research Affairs, College of Arts and Letters, Department of English and Comparative Literature, San Diego, CA 92182. Offers creative writing (MFA); English (MA). *Degree requirements:* For master's, one foreign language, comprehensive exam (for some programs), thesis (for some programs). *Entrance requirements:* For master's, GRE General Test, minimum GPA of 2.85, writing sample, 3 letters of recommendation. Additional exam requirements/recommendations for international students: Required—TOEFL. Electronic applications accepted.

San Francisco State University, Division of Graduate Studies, College of Liberal and Creative Arts, Department of English Language and Literature, Program in Composition, San Francisco, CA 94132-1722. Offers MA, Certificate. Part-time programs available. *Degree requirements:* For master's, comprehensive exam. *Entrance requirements:* Additional exam requirements/recommendations for international students: Required—TOEFL, TWE. *Application deadline:* Applications are processed on a rolling basis. *Expenses:* Tuition, state resident: full-time $6738. Tuition, nonresident: full-time $17,898; part-time $372 per credit hour. *Required fees:* $498 per semester. *Unit head:* Dr. Sugie Goen-Salter, Chair, 415-338-2660, E-mail: english@sfsu.edu. *Application contact:* Prof. Mark Roberge, Graduate Coordinator, 415-338-7457, E-mail: roberge@sfsu.edu.
Website: http://english.sfsu.edu/english/content/program-composition

San Francisco State University, Division of Graduate Studies, College of Liberal and Creative Arts, Department of English Language and Literature, Program in Literature, San Francisco, CA 94132-1722. Offers MA. Part-time programs available. *Application deadline:* Applications are processed on a rolling basis. *Expenses:* Tuition, state resident: full-time $6738. Tuition, nonresident: full-time $17,898; part-time $372 per credit hour. *Required fees:* $498 per semester. *Unit head:* Dr. Sugie Goen-Salter, Chair, 415-338-2660, E-mail: english@sfsu.edu. *Application contact:* Prof. Julie Paulson, Graduate Coordinator, 415-338-3107, E-mail: jpaulson@sfsu.edu.
Website: http://english.sfsu.edu/content/ma-programs

San Jose State University, Graduate Studies and Research, College of Humanities and the Arts, Department of English and Comparative Literature, San Jose, CA 95192-0001. Offers English (MFA); English literature (MA). *Degree requirements:* For master's, one foreign language, thesis or alternative. *Entrance requirements:* For master's, GRE. Additional exam requirements/recommendations for international students: Required—TOEFL. Electronic applications accepted.

Seton Hall University, College of Arts and Sciences, Department of English, South Orange, NJ 07079-2697. Offers literature (MA). Part-time and evening/weekend programs available. *Faculty:* 15 full-time (8 women). *Students:* 19 full-time (12 women), 18 part-time (13 women); includes 3 minority (2 Black or African American, non-Hispanic/Latino; 1 Asian, non-Hispanic/Latino), 1 international. Average age 27. 29 applicants, 86% accepted, 19 enrolled. In 2014, 9 master's awarded. *Degree requirements:* For master's, one foreign language, comprehensive exam, thesis (for some programs). *Entrance requirements:* For master's, GRE, minimum of 21 undergraduate credits in English. Additional exam requirements/recommendations for international students: Required—TOEFL. *Application deadline:* For fall admission, 7/1 priority date for domestic and international students; for spring admission, 11/1 priority date for domestic and international students. Applications are processed on a rolling basis. Application fee: $75. Electronic applications accepted. *Financial support:* Teaching assistantships with full tuition reimbursements, Federal Work-Study, and unspecified assistantships available. Financial award applicants required to submit FAFSA. *Faculty research:* The essay, modern poetry, the novel, medieval poetry, Renaissance drama. *Unit head:* Dr. Mary M. Balkun, Chair, 973-761-9388, Fax: 973-761-9596, E-mail: balkunma@shu.edu. *Application contact:* Dr. Angela Weisl, Director of Graduate Studies, 973-275-5889, Fax: 973-761-9596, E-mail: angela.weisl@shu.edu.
Website: http://www.shu.edu/academics/artsci/english/index.cfm

Sewanee: The University of the South, Sewanee School of Letters, Sewanee, TN 37383-1000. Offers American and English literature (MA); creative writing (MFA). Part-time programs available. *Faculty:* 2 full-time (1 woman), 8 part-time/adjunct (2 women). *Students:* 1 (woman) full-time, 49 part-time (30 women); includes 2 minority (1 Hispanic/Latino; 1 Two or more races, non-Hispanic/Latino). Average age 41. 18 applicants, 100% accepted, 12 enrolled. In 2014, 12 master's awarded. *Degree requirements:* For master's, thesis (for some programs). *Entrance requirements:* For master's, writing sample, 2 letters of recommendation. *Application deadline:* For summer admission, 2/1 priority date for domestic and international students. Applications are processed on a rolling basis. Application fee: $40. Electronic applications accepted. *Expenses:* Expenses: Contact institution. *Financial support:* Application deadline: 3/1; applicants required to submit FAFSA. *Unit head:* Dr. John M. Grammer, Director, 931-598-1483, Fax: 931-598-3303, E-mail: jgrammer@sewanee.edu. *Application contact:* April R. Alvarez, Coordinator, 931-598-1636, Fax: 931-598-3303.
Website: http://letters.sewanee.edu/

Simon Fraser University, Office of Graduate Studies, Faculty of Arts and Social Sciences, Department of English, Burnaby, BC V5A 1S6, Canada. Offers English (MA, PhD); teachers of English (MA). Part-time programs available. *Degree requirements:* For master's, one foreign language, thesis or alternative; for doctorate, one foreign language, thesis/dissertation, field exams. *Entrance requirements:* For master's, minimum GPA of 3.0 (on scale of 4.33), or 3.33 based on last 60 credits of undergraduate courses; for doctorate, minimum GPA of 3.5 (on scale of 4.33). Additional exam requirements/recommendations for international students: Recommended—TOEFL (minimum score 580 paper-based; 93 iBT), IELTS (minimum score 7), TWE (minimum score 5). Electronic applications accepted. *Faculty research:* Literary criticism, literature and psychoanalysis, Renaissance drama and poetry, Shakespeare, Canadian and American literature.

Sonoma State University, Department of English, Rohnert Park, CA 94928. Offers American literature (MA); creative writing (MA); English literature (MA); world literature (MA). Part-time and evening/weekend programs available. *Degree requirements:* For master's, one foreign language, thesis or alternative. *Entrance requirements:* For master's, minimum GPA of 2.5. Additional exam requirements/recommendations for international students: Required—TOEFL (minimum score 500 paper-based).

South Dakota State University, Graduate School, College of Arts and Science, Department of English, Brookings, SD 57007. Offers MA. Part-time programs available. *Degree requirements:* For master's, comprehensive exam (for some programs), thesis (for some programs), oral and written exams. *Entrance requirements:* For master's, minimum GPA of 2.75. Additional exam requirements/recommendations for international students: Required—TOEFL (minimum score 600 paper-based; 100 iBT). *Faculty research:* English and American literature topics, regional literature (Midwestern), women's literature, Lakota literature and culture, rhetoric and writing.

Southeastern Louisiana University, College of Arts, Humanities and Social Sciences, Department of English, Hammond, LA 70402. Offers creative writing (MA); language and theory (MA); professional writing (MA). Part-time programs available. *Faculty:* 19 full-time (8 women), 1 part-time/adjunct (0 women). *Students:* 12 full-time (8 women), 6 part-time (all women); includes 3 minority (1 Black or African American, non-Hispanic/Latino; 1 Asian, non-Hispanic/Latino; 1 Hispanic/Latino). Average age 27. In 2014, 6 master's awarded. *Degree requirements:* For master's, comprehensive exam, thesis optional. *Entrance requirements:* For master's, GRE General Test (minimum score of 850), bachelor's degree; minimum undergraduate GPA of 2.5; 24 hours of undergraduate English courses. Additional exam requirements/recommendations for international students: Required—TOEFL (minimum score 500 paper-based; 61 iBT), IELTS (minimum score 5.5). *Application deadline:* For fall admission, 7/15 priority date for domestic students, 6/1 priority date for international students; for spring admission, 12/1 priority date for domestic students, 10/1 priority date for international students. Applications are processed on a rolling basis. Application fee: $20 ($30 for international students). Electronic applications accepted. *Financial support:* In 2014–15, 21 research assistantships (averaging $7,842 per year), 1 teaching assistantship (averaging $9,000 per year) were awarded; career-related internships or fieldwork, Federal Work-Study, institutionally sponsored loans, scholarships/grants, and traineeships also available. Support available to part-time students. Financial award application deadline: 5/1; financial award applicants required to submit FAFSA. *Faculty research:* Creole studies, modernism, digital humanities, library studies, John Donne. *Total annual research expenditures:* $47,697. *Unit head:* Dr. David Hanson, Department Head, 985-549-2100, Fax: 985-549-5021, E-mail: dhanson@selu.edu. *Application contact:* Sandra Meyers, Graduate Admissions Analyst, 985-549-5620, Fax: 985-549-5632, E-mail: admissions@selu.edu.
Website: http://www.selu.edu/acad_research/depts/engl

Southeast Missouri State University, School of Graduate Studies, Department of English, Cape Girardeau, MO 63701-4799. Offers English (MA), including English studies, professional writing; teaching English to speakers of other languages (MA). Part-time and evening/weekend programs available. Postbaccalaureate distance learning degree programs offered (no on-campus study). *Faculty:* 15 full-time (8 women). *Students:* 49 full-time (37 women), 48 part-time (39 women); includes 5 minority (2 Black or African American, non-Hispanic/Latino; 1 Asian, non-Hispanic/Latino; 1 Hispanic/Latino; 1 Two or more races, non-Hispanic/Latino), 27 international. Average age 31. 58 applicants, 93% accepted, 44 enrolled. In 2014, 31 master's awarded. *Degree requirements:* For master's, comprehensive exam (for some programs), thesis optional. *Entrance requirements:* Additional exam requirements/recommendations for international students: Required—TOEFL (minimum score 550 paper-based; 79 iBT), IELTS (minimum score 6), PTE (minimum score 53). *Application deadline:* For fall admission, 8/1 for domestic students, 6/1 for international students; for spring admission, 11/21 for domestic students, 10/1 for international students; for summer admission, 5/15 for domestic students. Applications are processed on a rolling basis. Application fee: $30 ($40 for international students). Electronic applications accepted. *Expenses:* Tuition, state resident: full-time $5256; part-time $292 per credit hour. Tuition, nonresident: full-time $9288; part-time $516 per credit hour. *Financial support:* In 2014–15, 34 students received support, including 16 teaching assistantships with full tuition reimbursements available (averaging $7,907 per year); career-related internships or fieldwork, Federal Work-Study, scholarships/grants, traineeships, tuition waivers (full), and unspecified assistantships also available. Financial award application deadline: 6/30; financial award applicants required to submit FAFSA. *Faculty research:* Literature, creative writing, technical writing, secondary English education, teaching English as a second language. *Unit head:* Dr. Susan Kendrick, Department of English Chair, 573-651-2156, Fax: 573-651-5188, E-mail: skendrick@semo.edu.
Website: http://www.semo.edu/english/

Southern Connecticut State University, School of Graduate Studies, School of Arts and Sciences, Department of English, New Haven, CT 06515-1355. Offers MA, MS, MLS/MS. Part-time and evening/weekend programs available. *Degree requirements:* For master's, one foreign language, thesis or alternative. *Entrance requirements:* For master's, interview. Electronic applications accepted.

Southern Illinois University Carbondale, Graduate School, College of Liberal Arts, Department of English, Carbondale, IL 62901-4701. Offers composition (MA, PhD),

including composition, literature, rhetoric; creative writing (MFA). *Faculty:* 33 full-time (14 women), 1 (woman) part-time/adjunct. *Students:* 66 full-time (40 women), 34 part-time (20 women); includes 2 minority (both Hispanic/Latino), 7 international. 158 applicants, 22% accepted, 24 enrolled. In 2014, 18 master's, 9 doctorates awarded. *Degree requirements:* For master's, one foreign language, thesis; for doctorate, 2 foreign languages, thesis/dissertation. *Entrance requirements:* For master's, GRE General Test, GRE Subject Test, minimum GPA of 2.7; for doctorate, GRE General Test, GRE Subject Test, minimum GPA of 3.25. Additional exam requirements/recommendations for international students: Required—TOEFL. *Application deadline:* For fall admission, 2/15 for domestic students; for spring admission, 11/15 for domestic students. Applications are processed on a rolling basis. Application fee: $50. *Expenses:* Tuition, state resident: full-time $10,176; part-time $1153 per credit. Tuition, nonresident: full-time $20,814; part-time $1744 per credit. *Required fees:* $7092; $394 per credit. $2364 per semester. *Financial support:* In 2014–15, 2 fellowships with full tuition reimbursements, 5 research assistantships with full tuition reimbursements, 72 teaching assistantships with full tuition reimbursements were awarded; career-related internships or fieldwork, Federal Work-Study, institutionally sponsored loans, and tuition waivers (full) also available. Support available to part-time students. *Faculty research:* British literature, English literature, modern Continental literature, literary criticism and theory, film studies, Irish studies. *Unit head:* Dr. Ryan Netzley, Chair, 618-453-6894, E-mail: rnetzley@siu.edu. *Application contact:* Patty Norris, Administrative Clerk, 618-453-6894, Fax: 618-453-3253, E-mail: gradengl@siu.edu.
Website: http://english.siuc.edu/

Southern Illinois University Edwardsville, Graduate School, College of Arts and Sciences, Department of English Language and Literature, Program in American and English Literature, Edwardsville, IL 62026-0001. Offers MA, Postbaccalaureate Certificate. Part-time programs available. *Students:* 4 full-time (3 women), 17 part-time (11 women); includes 1 minority (Black or African American, non-Hispanic/Latino). 10 applicants, 80% accepted. In 2014, 2 master's awarded. *Degree requirements:* For master's, one foreign language, thesis (for some programs), written papers, oral examination. *Entrance requirements:* Additional exam requirements/recommendations for international students: Required—TOEFL (minimum score 550 paper-based, 79 iBT), IELTS (minimum score 6.5), Michigan Test of English Language Proficiency or PTE. *Application deadline:* For fall admission, 7/18 for domestic students, 6/1 for international students; for spring admission, 12/12 for domestic students, 10/1 for international students; for summer admission, 4/24 for domestic students, 3/1 for international students. Applications are processed on a rolling basis. Application fee: $30. Electronic applications accepted. *Expenses:* Tuition, state resident: full-time $5026. Tuition, nonresident: full-time $12,566. *International tuition:* $25,136 full-time. *Required fees:* $1682. Tuition and fees vary according to course load, campus/location and program. *Financial support:* Fellowships with full tuition reimbursements, research assistantships with full tuition reimbursements, teaching assistantships with full tuition reimbursements, institutionally sponsored loans, scholarships/grants, and unspecified assistantships available. Financial award application deadline: 3/1; financial award applicants required to submit FAFSA. *Unit head:* Dr. Jessica DeSpain, Program Director, 618-650-2151, E-mail: jdespai@siue.edu. *Application contact:* Melissa K. Mace, Assistant Director of Graduate and International Recruitment, 618-650-2756, Fax: 618-650-3618, E-mail: mmace@siue.edu.
Website: http://www.siue.edu/ENGLISH/Grad/grad_index.html

Southern Methodist University, Dedman College of Humanities and Sciences, Department of English, Dallas, TX 75275. Offers MA, PhD. Terminal master's awarded for partial completion of doctoral program. *Degree requirements:* For master's, one foreign language, comprehensive exam, thesis optional, oral exam; for doctorate, one foreign language, comprehensive exam, thesis/dissertation. *Entrance requirements:* For master's, GRE General Test, minimum GPA of 3.0; for doctorate, GRE General Test, minimum GPA of 3.5, BA in English or other appropriate field. Additional exam requirements/recommendations for international students: Required—TOEFL (minimum score 550 paper-based). Electronic applications accepted. *Faculty research:* British/American literature, critical theory, medieval studies, gender studies, book history.

Spring Hill College, Graduate Programs, Program in Liberal Arts, Mobile, AL 36608-1791. Offers fine arts (MLA); history and social science (MLA); leadership and ethics (MLA, Postbaccalaureate Certificate); literature (MLA); studio art (Postbaccalaureate Certificate). Part-time and evening/weekend programs available. *Faculty:* 6 full-time (1 woman), 3 part-time/adjunct (all women). *Students:* 3 full-time (1 woman), 33 part-time (18 women); includes 9 minority (8 Black or African American, non-Hispanic/Latino; 1 American Indian or Alaska Native, non-Hispanic/Latino), 1 international. Average age 36. In 2014, 8 master's awarded. *Degree requirements:* For master's, capstone course, completion of program within 6 years of initial admittance. *Entrance requirements:* For master's, bachelor's degree with minimum undergraduate GPA of 3.0 or graduate/professional degree. Additional exam requirements/recommendations for international students: Required—TOEFL (minimum score 550 paper-based; 80 iBT), IELTS (minimum score 6.5), CPE or CAE (minimum score C), Michigan English Language Assessment Battery (minimum score 90). *Application deadline:* For fall admission, 8/1 priority date for domestic and international students; for spring admission, 12/1 priority date for domestic and international students. Applications are processed on a rolling basis. Application fee: $25 ($35 for international students). Electronic applications accepted. *Expenses:* Expenses: Contact institution. *Financial support:* Applicants required to submit FAFSA. *Unit head:* Dr. Thomas J. Hoffman, Director, 251-380-4184, Fax: 251-460-2115, E-mail: thoffman@shc.edu. *Application contact:* Robert Stewart, Vice President of Enrollment, 251-380-3030, Fax: 251-460-2186, E-mail: rstewart@shc.edu.
Website: http://ug.shc.edu/graduate-degrees/master-liberal-arts/

Stanford University, School of Humanities and Sciences, Department of English, Stanford, CA 94305-9991. Offers MA, PhD. Terminal master's awarded for partial completion of doctoral program. *Degree requirements:* For master's, one foreign language, thesis (for some programs); for doctorate, 2 foreign languages, thesis/dissertation, oral exam. *Entrance requirements:* For master's and doctorate, GRE General Test, GRE Subject Test. Additional exam requirements/recommendations for international students: Required—TOEFL. Electronic applications accepted. *Expenses:* Tuition: Full-time $44,184; part-time $982 per credit hour. *Required fees:* $191.

State University of New York at New Paltz, Graduate School, School of Liberal Arts and Sciences, Department of English, New Paltz, NY 12561. Offers MA. Part-time and evening/weekend programs available. *Faculty:* 11 full-time (4 women). *Students:* 4 full-time (2 women), 33 part-time (17 women), 1 international. Average age 27. 15 applicants, 80% accepted, 9 enrolled. In 2014, 29 master's awarded. *Degree requirements:* For master's, comprehensive exam, thesis (for some programs), foreign language proficiency exam. *Entrance requirements:* For master's, minimum GPA of 3.0, 10-15 page writing sample. Additional exam requirements/recommendations for international students: Required—TOEFL (minimum score 563 paper-based; 85 iBT), IELTS (minimum score 7). *Application deadline:* For fall admission, 3/15 priority date for domestic students, 3/15 for international students; for spring admission, 10/15 for domestic and international students. Application fee: $50. Electronic applications accepted. *Financial support:* In 2014–15, 1 research assistantship with partial tuition reimbursement (averaging $5,000 per year), 17 teaching assistantships with partial tuition reimbursements (averaging $5,000 per year) were awarded. Financial award application deadline: 8/1. *Faculty research:* Twentieth-century British literature, Hemingway and modernism, British modernist fiction, Faulkner and the Southern Renaissance, revisionary approaches to early twentieth-century literature. *Unit head:* Dr. Nancy Johnson, Chair, 845-257-2720, E-mail: english@newpaltz.edu. *Application contact:* Dr. Thomas Festa, Graduate Coordinator, 845-257-2726, E-mail: festat@newpaltz.edu.
Website: http://www.newpaltz.edu/english/

State University of New York at Oswego, Graduate Studies, College of Liberal Arts and Sciences, Department of English, Oswego, NY 13126. Offers MA. Part-time programs available. *Degree requirements:* For master's, thesis optional. *Entrance requirements:* Additional exam requirements/recommendations for international students: Required—TOEFL (minimum score 560 paper-based).

State University of New York College at Cortland, Graduate Studies, School of Arts and Sciences, Department of English, Cortland, NY 13045. Offers MA. Part-time and evening/weekend programs available. *Degree requirements:* For master's, one foreign language, comprehensive exam, thesis. *Entrance requirements:* For master's, GRE General Test.

State University of New York College at Potsdam, School of Arts and Sciences, Department of English and Communication, Potsdam, NY 13676. Offers MA. Part-time and evening/weekend programs available. *Degree requirements:* For master's, one foreign language, thesis or alternative. *Entrance requirements:* For master's, minimum GPA of 3.0 in last 60 hours of undergraduate course work. Additional exam requirements/recommendations for international students: Required—TOEFL (minimum score 550 paper-based; 80 iBT), IELTS (minimum score 6). Electronic applications accepted.

Stephen F. Austin State University, Graduate School, College of Liberal Arts, Department of English and Philosophy, Nacogdoches, TX 75962. Offers English (MA). *Degree requirements:* For master's, comprehensive exam. *Entrance requirements:* For master's, GRE General Test. Additional exam requirements/recommendations for international students: Required—TOEFL. *Faculty research:* Creative writing, Latin American literature, modern American literature, modern British literature, literature for children.

Stony Brook University, State University of New York, Graduate School, College of Arts and Sciences, Department of Cultural Analysis and Theory, Stony Brook, NY 11794. Offers comparative literature (MA, PhD); cultural studies (PhD, Certificate). Evening/weekend programs available. *Faculty:* 19 full-time (9 women). *Students:* 43 full-time (30 women), 2 part-time (both women); includes 5 minority (2 Black or African American, non-Hispanic/Latino; 2 Asian, non-Hispanic/Latino; 1 Hispanic/Latino), 16 international. Average age 34. 79 applicants, 35% accepted, 10 enrolled. In 2014, 2 master's, 5 doctorates, 12 other advanced degrees awarded. Terminal master's awarded for partial completion of doctoral program. *Degree requirements:* For master's, 2 foreign languages, exam; for doctorate, 3 foreign languages, comprehensive exam, thesis/dissertation. *Entrance requirements:* For master's and doctorate, GRE General Test, minimum GPA of 3.5 in major, 3.0 overall. Additional exam requirements/recommendations for international students: Required—TOEFL. *Application deadline:* For fall admission, 1/15 for domestic students; for spring admission, 10/1 for domestic students. Application fee: $100. *Expenses:* Tuition, state resident: full-time $10,370; part-time $432 per credit. Tuition, nonresident: full-time $20,190; part-time $841 per credit. *Required fees:* $1431. *Financial support:* In 2014–15, 26 teaching assistantships were awarded; fellowships and research assistantships also available. *Faculty research:* Literary theory, interdisciplinary studies, literary history. *Unit head:* Prof. Robert Harvey, Chair, 631-632-7456, Fax: 631-632-5707, E-mail: robert.harvey@stonybrook.edu. *Application contact:* Mary Moran-Luba, Coordinator, 631-632-7460, Fax: 631-632-5707, E-mail: mary.moran-luba@stonybrook.edu.
Website: http://www.stonybrook.edu/commcms/cat/index.html

Stony Brook University, State University of New York, Graduate School, College of Arts and Sciences, Department of English, Stony Brook, NY 11794. Offers English (MA, PhD); English education (MAT). MAT offered through the School of Professional Development. Evening/weekend programs available. *Faculty:* 22 full-time (8 women), 3 part-time/adjunct (all women). *Students:* 64 full-time (37 women), 19 part-time (13 women); includes 12 minority (3 Asian, non-Hispanic/Latino; 5 Hispanic/Latino; 4 Two or more races, non-Hispanic/Latino), 8 international. Average age 32. 104 applicants, 36% accepted, 19 enrolled. In 2014, 7 master's, 7 doctorates awarded. Terminal master's awarded for partial completion of doctoral program. *Degree requirements:* For doctorate, thesis/dissertation. *Entrance requirements:* For master's and doctorate, GRE General Test. Additional exam requirements/recommendations for international students: Required—TOEFL. *Application deadline:* For fall admission, 1/15 for domestic students; for spring admission, 10/1 for domestic students. Application fee: $100. *Expenses:* Tuition, state resident: full-time $10,370; part-time $432 per credit. Tuition, nonresident: full-time $20,190; part-time $841 per credit. *Required fees:* $1431. *Financial support:* In 2014–15, 32 teaching assistantships were awarded; fellowships and research assistantships also available. *Faculty research:* American literature, British literature, literary critical theory, rhetoric and composition theory, women's studies. *Unit head:* Dr. Celia Marshik, Chair, 631-632-7415, E-mail: celia.marshik@stonybrook.edu. *Application contact:* Dorothy Mason, Director, 631-632-7373, Fax: 631-632-7568, E-mail: dorothy.mason@stonybrook.edu.
Website: http://www.stonybrook.edu/english/

Sul Ross State University, School of Arts and Sciences, Department of Languages and Literature, Alpine, TX 79832. Offers English (MA). Part-time and evening/weekend programs available. *Degree requirements:* For master's, thesis optional. *Entrance requirements:* For master's, GRE General Test, minimum GPA of 2.5 in last 60 hours of undergraduate work. *Faculty research:* Narrative theory, feminist literary criticism, autobiography studies, multiculturalism, biblical narrative.

Summit University, Graduate Studies, Clarks Summit, PA 18411-1297. Offers Bible (MA); counseling (MA, MS); curriculum and instruction (M Ed); educational administration (M Ed); intercultural studies (MA); literature (MA); missions (MA); organizational leadership (MA); reading specialist (M Ed); secondary English/communications (M Ed); social entrepreneurship (MA); worldview studies (MA). MA in missions program available only for Association of Baptists for World Evangelism missionary personnel. Part-time and evening/weekend programs available. Postbaccalaureate distance learning degree programs offered (no on-campus study). *Entrance requirements:* Additional exam requirements/recommendations for international students: Required—TOEFL (minimum score 500 paper-based).

Syracuse University, College of Arts and Sciences, Program in English, Syracuse, NY 13244. Offers MA, PhD. Part-time programs available. *Students:* 29 full-time (15 women); includes 6 minority (1 Asian, non-Hispanic/Latino; 2 Hispanic/Latino; 3 Two or more races, non-Hispanic/Latino), 3 international. Average age 27. 116 applicants, 23% accepted, 7 enrolled. In 2014, 4 master's, 4 doctorates awarded. *Degree requirements:* For doctorate, comprehensive exam, thesis/dissertation. *Entrance requirements:* For master's and doctorate, GRE General Test. Additional exam requirements/

recommendations for international students: Required—TOEFL (minimum score 100 iBT). *Application deadline:* For fall admission, 1/9 priority date for domestic and international students. Application fee: $75. Electronic applications accepted. *Expenses: Tuition:* Part-time $1341 per credit. *Financial support:* Fellowships with full tuition reimbursements and teaching assistantships with full tuition reimbursements available. Financial award application deadline: 1/1; financial award applicants required to submit FAFSA. *Unit head:* Prof. Claudia Klaver, Director of Graduate Studies, 315-443-6133. *Application contact:* Terri Zollo, Information Contact, 315-443-2174, E-mail: tazollo@syr.edu.
Website: http://english.syr.edu/

Tarleton State University, College of Graduate Studies, College of Liberal and Fine Arts, Department of English and Languages, Stephenville, TX 76402. Offers English (MA). Part-time and evening/weekend programs available. *Degree requirements:* For master's, comprehensive exam, thesis (for some programs). *Entrance requirements:* For master's, GRE General Test, minimum GPA of 3.0. Additional exam requirements/ recommendations for international students: Required—TOEFL (minimum score 550 paper-based; 80 iBT). Electronic applications accepted.

Temple University, College of Liberal Arts, Department of English, Philadelphia, PA 19122-6096. Offers creative writing (MFA); English (MA, PhD). Part-time programs available. *Faculty:* 38 full-time (20 women), 15 part-time/adjunct (7 women). *Students:* 56 full-time (38 women), 4 part-time (2 women); includes 7 minority (1 Black or African American, non-Hispanic/Latino; 5 Asian, non-Hispanic/Latino; 1 Hispanic/Latino), 1 international. 59 applicants, 66% accepted, 11 enrolled. In 2014, 5 master's, 10 doctorates awarded. *Degree requirements:* For doctorate, 2 foreign languages, thesis/ dissertation. *Entrance requirements:* For master's and doctorate, GRE General Test, minimum GPA of 3.0; 3 letters of recommendation. Additional exam requirements/ recommendations for international students: Required—TOEFL (minimum score 620 paper-based; 105 iBT). *Application deadline:* For fall admission, 12/15 for domestic and international students. Application fee: $60. Electronic applications accepted. *Expenses:* Tuition, state resident: full-time $14,490; part-time $805 per credit hour. Tuition, nonresident: full-time $19,850; part-time $1103 per credit hour. *Required fees:* $690. Full-time tuition and fees vary according to class time, course load, degree level, campus/location and program. *Financial support:* Fellowships, teaching assistantships, and Federal Work-Study available. Financial award application deadline: 1/15; financial award applicants required to submit FAFSA. *Faculty research:* Early modern British literature, American literature, modernism, critical theory, rhetoric, composition. *Unit head:* Dr. James Sue-Im Lee, Graduate Director, 215-204-1894, Fax: 215-204-9620, E-mail: leesi@temple.edu. *Application contact:* Sharon Logan, Coordinator, 215-204-1796, Fax: 215-204-9620, E-mail: logansd@temple.edu.
Website: http://www.temple.edu/english/

Tennessee Technological University, College of Graduate Studies, College of Arts and Sciences, Department of English, Cookeville, TN 38505. Offers MA. Part-time programs available. *Faculty:* 23 full-time (8 women). *Students:* 4 full-time (3 women), 4 part-time (2 women); includes 1 minority (Black or African American, non-Hispanic/ Latino). Average age 28. 3 applicants, 67% accepted, 2 enrolled. In 2014, 6 master's awarded. *Degree requirements:* For master's, comprehensive exam, thesis or alternative. *Entrance requirements:* For master's, GRE General Test. Additional exam requirements/recommendations for international students: Required—TOEFL (minimum score 527 paper-based; 71 iBT), IELTS (minimum score 5.5), PTE (minimum score 48), or TOEIC (Test of English as an International Communication). *Application deadline:* For fall admission, 8/1 for domestic students, 5/1 for international students; for spring admission, 12/1 for domestic students, 10/1 for international students. Applications are processed on a rolling basis. Application fee: $35 ($40 for international students). Electronic applications accepted. *Expenses:* Tuition, state resident: full-time $9783; part-time $492 per credit hour. Tuition, nonresident: full-time $24,071; part-time $1179 per credit hour. *Financial support:* In 2014–15, research assistantships (averaging $4,000 per year), 9 teaching assistantships (averaging $6,750 per year) were awarded; fellowships also available. Financial award application deadline: 4/1. *Unit head:* Dr. Ted Pelton, Chairperson, 931-372-3343, Fax: 931-372-6142, E-mail: tpelton@tntech.edu. *Application contact:* Shelia K. Kendrick, Coordinator of Graduate Studies, 931-372-3808, Fax: 931-372-3497, E-mail: skendrick@tntech.edu.

Texas A&M International University, Office of Graduate Studies and Research, College of Arts and Sciences, Department of Humanities, Laredo, TX 78041-1900. Offers English (MA); Hispanic studies (PhD); history and political thought (MA); language, literature and translation (MA). *Degree requirements:* For master's, comprehensive exam (for some programs), thesis (for some programs). *Entrance requirements:* For master's, GRE General Test. Additional exam requirements/ recommendations for international students: Required—TOEFL (minimum score 550 paper-based; 79 iBT).

Texas A&M University, College of Liberal Arts, Department of English, College Station, TX 77843. Offers MA, PhD. *Faculty:* 33. *Students:* 59 full-time (42 women), 25 part-time (13 women); includes 13 minority (3 Asian, non-Hispanic/Latino; 9 Hispanic/Latino; 1 Two or more races, non-Hispanic/Latino), 25 international. Average age 33. 39 applicants, 82% accepted, 17 enrolled. In 2014, 8 master's, 10 doctorates awarded. Terminal master's awarded for partial completion of doctoral program. *Degree requirements:* For master's, one foreign language, thesis optional; for doctorate, 2 foreign languages, thesis/dissertation. *Entrance requirements:* For master's and doctorate, GRE General Test, sample of written work. Additional exam requirements/ recommendations for international students: Required—TOEFL. *Application deadline:* For fall admission, 2/1 priority date for domestic and international students; for spring admission, 10/1 priority date for domestic and international students. Applications are processed on a rolling basis. Application fee: $50 ($90 for international students). Electronic applications accepted. *Expenses:* Tuition, state resident: full-time $4078; part-time $226.55 per credit hour. Tuition, nonresident: full-time $10,594; part-time $577.55 per credit hour. *Required fees:* $2813; $237.70 per credit hour. $278.50 per semester. Tuition and fees vary according to degree level and student level. *Financial support:* In 2014–15, 59 students received support, including 5 fellowships with full and partial tuition reimbursements available (averaging $16,172 per year), 13 research assistantships with full and partial tuition reimbursements available (averaging $5,175 per year), 48 teaching assistantships with full and partial tuition reimbursements available (averaging $6,246 per year); career-related internships or fieldwork, institutionally sponsored loans, scholarships/grants, traineeships, health care benefits, tuition waivers (full and partial), and unspecified assistantships also available. Support available to part-time students. Financial award application deadline: 4/1; financial award applicants required to submit FAFSA. *Faculty research:* American, Renaissance, medieval, textual, and discourse studies. *Unit head:* Dr. Nancy Warren, Head, 979-845-3890, E-mail: nwarren@tamu.edu. *Application contact:* Director of Graduate Studies, 979-845-9836, Fax: 979-862-2292, E-mail: grad-program@tamuenglish.org.
Website: http://www.english.tamu.edu/

Texas A&M University–Corpus Christi, College of Graduate Studies, College of Liberal Arts, Program in English, Corpus Christi, TX 78412-5503. Offers MA. Part-time and evening/weekend programs available. *Students:* 3 full-time (2 women), 30 part-time (23 women); includes 20 minority (1 Black or African American, non-Hispanic/Latino; 1 American Indian or Alaska Native, non-Hispanic/Latino; 18 Hispanic/Latino). Average age 32. 18 applicants, 61% accepted, 8 enrolled. In 2014, 7 master's awarded. *Degree requirements:* For master's, comprehensive exam, thesis optional, capstone. *Entrance requirements:* For master's, essay (500-1000 words), writing sample (minimum of 2000 words), 3 letters of recommendation. Additional exam requirements/recommendations for international students: Required—TOEFL (minimum score 550 paper-based; 79 iBT), IELTS (minimum score 6.5). *Application deadline:* For fall admission, 4/1 priority date for domestic and international students; for spring admission, 11/1 priority date for domestic students, 9/1 priority date for international students; for summer admission, 4/15 for domestic students. Applications are processed on a rolling basis. Application fee: $50 ($70 for international students). Electronic applications accepted. *Financial support:* In 2014–15, 5 students received support, including 1 research assistantship (averaging $8,545 per year); career-related internships or fieldwork, Federal Work-Study, institutionally sponsored loans, scholarships/grants, health care benefits, and unspecified assistantships also available. Support available to part-time students. Financial award application deadline: 3/15; financial award applicants required to submit FAFSA. *Unit head:* Dr. Molly Englehardt, Head, 361-825-3793, E-mail: molly.engelhardt@tamucc.edu. *Application contact:* Graduate Admissions Coordinator, 361-825-2177, Fax: 361-825-2755, E-mail: gradweb@tamucc.edu.
Website: http://cla.tamucc.edu/english/pages/graduate.html

Texas A&M University–Kingsville, College of Graduate Studies, College of Arts and Sciences, Department of Language and Literature, Program in English, Kingsville, TX 78363. Offers MA, MS. *Students:* 2 part-time (1 woman); includes 1 minority (Hispanic/ Latino). Average age 32. In 2014, 5 master's awarded. *Degree requirements:* For master's, variable foreign language requirement, comprehensive exam, thesis (for some programs). *Entrance requirements:* For master's, GRE, MAT, GMAT. Additional exam requirements/recommendations for international students: Required—TOEFL (minimum score 550 paper-based; 79 iBT). *Application deadline:* For fall admission, 8/15 for domestic students, 6/1 for international students; for spring admission, 12/15 for domestic students, 10/1 for international students; for summer admission, 5/15 for domestic students, 4/1 for international students. Applications are processed on a rolling basis. Application fee: $35 ($50 for international students). Electronic applications accepted. *Financial support:* In 2014–15, 1 teaching assistantship (averaging $3,766 per year) was awarded; career-related internships or fieldwork, Federal Work-Study, institutionally sponsored loans, scholarships/grants, health care benefits, tuition waivers (full and partial), and unspecified assistantships also available. Support available to part-time students. Financial award application deadline: 5/1; financial award applicants required to submit FAFSA. *Unit head:* Dr. Michelle Johnson-vela, Department Chair, 361-593-2597, E-mail: kfmrj00@tamuk.edu. *Application contact:* Dr. Mohamed Abdelrahman, Dean of Graduate Students, 361-593-2809, E-mail: mohamed.abdelrahman@tamuk.edu.

Texas A&M University–San Antonio, School of Arts and Sciences, San Antonio, TX 78224. Offers English (MA). Part-time and evening/weekend programs available. *Degree requirements:* For master's, comprehensive exam, thesis. *Entrance requirements:* For master's, GRE. Additional exam requirements/recommendations for international students: Required—TOEFL (minimum score 550 paper-based; 80 iBT), IELTS (minimum score 6). Electronic applications accepted. *Faculty research:* Twentieth-century British women's literature, twentieth-century American literature, visual studies, children's literature, multi-ethnic literatures.

Texas A&M University–Texarkana, Graduate Studies and Research, College of Education and Liberal Arts, Texarkana, TX 75505-5518. Offers adult education (MS); curriculum and instruction (M Ed); education (MS); educational administration (M Ed); English (MA); instructional technology (MS); interdisciplinary studies (MA, MS); special education (MS). Part-time and evening/weekend programs available. *Degree requirements:* For master's, comprehensive exam (for some programs), thesis optional. *Entrance requirements:* For master's, minimum GPA of 2.5 on last 60 hours of bachelor's degree. Additional exam requirements/recommendations for international students: Required—TOEFL. Electronic applications accepted.

Texas Christian University, AddRan College of Liberal Arts, Department of English, Fort Worth, TX 76129. Offers English (MA, PhD); rhetoric and composition (PhD). *Faculty:* 12 full-time (7 women), 1 (woman) part-time/adjunct. *Students:* 53 full-time (39 women); includes 8 minority (1 Black or African American, non-Hispanic/Latino; 4 Hispanic/Latino; 3 Two or more races, non-Hispanic/Latino), 1 international. Average age 30. 33 applicants, 48% accepted, 11 enrolled. In 2014, 4 master's, 2 doctorates awarded. *Degree requirements:* For master's, one foreign language, thesis; for doctorate, one foreign language, comprehensive exam, thesis/dissertation. *Entrance requirements:* For master's and doctorate, GRE General Test. Additional exam requirements/recommendations for international students: Recommended—TOEFL. *Application deadline:* For fall admission, 1/10 for domestic and international students; for winter admission, 1/10 for domestic and international students; for spring admission, 10/ 15 for domestic and international students. Application fee: $60. Electronic applications accepted. *Expenses: Tuition:* Full-time $22,860; part-time $1270 per credit hour. *Financial support:* In 2014–15, 51 students received support, including 4 fellowships with full tuition reimbursements available (averaging $21,000 per year), 4 research assistantships with full tuition reimbursements available, 24 teaching assistantships with full tuition reimbursements available (averaging $17,000 per year); Federal Work-Study, tuition waivers, and unspecified assistantships also available. Financial award application deadline: 1/10; financial award applicants required to submit FAFSA. *Faculty research:* Rhetoric, print culture and periodicals, new media writing, literary theory, women's studies. *Total annual research expenditures:* $6,500. *Unit head:* Dr. Mona Narain, Director of Graduate Studies, 817-257-7240, Fax: 817-257-6238, E-mail: m.narain@tcu.edu.
Website: http://www.eng.tcu.edu/

Texas Southern University, College of Liberal Arts and Behavioral Sciences, Department of English, Houston, TX 77004-4584. Offers MA. Part-time programs available. *Degree requirements:* For master's, one foreign language, comprehensive exam, thesis. *Entrance requirements:* For master's, GRE General Test, minimum GPA of 2.5. Additional exam requirements/recommendations for international students: Required—TOEFL. Electronic applications accepted. *Faculty research:* Linguistics, teaching of English, African-American literature, African literature, developmental English.

Texas State University, The Graduate College, College of Liberal Arts, Department of English, Program in Literature, San Marcos, TX 78666. Offers MA. Part-time and evening/weekend programs available. *Faculty:* 19 full-time (9 women). *Students:* 41 full-time (24 women), 23 part-time (16 women); includes 15 minority (3 Black or African American, non-Hispanic/Latino; 12 Hispanic/Latino). Average age 30. 47 applicants, 83% accepted, 30 enrolled. In 2014, 16 master's awarded. *Degree requirements:* For master's, comprehensive exam, thesis optional. *Entrance requirements:* For master's, GRE (preferred), baccalaureate degree from regionally-accredited university with minimum GPA of 2.75 on last 60 undergraduate semester hours, 3.25 in minimum of 24 hours of undergraduate English including at least 12 advanced hours; minimum of 6 hours in a foreign language. Additional exam requirements/recommendations for international students: Required—TOEFL (minimum score 550 paper-based; 78 iBT).

Application deadline: For fall admission, 6/15 priority date for domestic students, 6/1 for international students; for spring admission, 10/15 priority date for domestic students, 10/1 for international students; for summer admission, 4/15 for domestic students, 3/15 for international students. Applications are processed on a rolling basis. Application fee: $40 ($90 for international students). Electronic applications accepted. *Expenses:* Expenses: $8,834 (tuition and fees combined). *Financial support:* In 2014–15, 39 students received support, including 4 research assistantships (averaging $12,130 per year), 14 teaching assistantships (averaging $12,752 per year); Federal Work-Study and institutionally sponsored loans also available. Support available to part-time students. Financial award application deadline: 4/1; financial award applicants required to submit FAFSA. *Unit head:* Dr. Paul Cohen, Acting Graduate Adviser, 512-245-7685, Fax: 512-245-8546, E-mail: pc06@txstate.edu. *Application contact:* Dr. Andrea Golato, Dean of Graduate School, 512-245-2581, Fax: 512-245-8365, E-mail: gradcollege@txstate.edu.
Website: http://www.english.txstate.edu/

Texas Tech University, Graduate School, College of Arts and Sciences, Department of English, Lubbock, TX 79409-3091. Offers English (MA, PhD); technical communication (MA); technical communication and rhetoric (PhD). Part-time programs available. Postbaccalaureate distance learning degree programs offered (minimal on-campus study). *Faculty:* 62 full-time (35 women), 8 part-time/adjunct (4 women). *Students:* 92 full-time (55 women), 91 part-time (63 women); includes 24 minority (5 Black or African American, non-Hispanic/Latino; 2 American Indian or Alaska Native, non-Hispanic/Latino; 6 Asian, non-Hispanic/Latino; 6 Hispanic/Latino; 5 Two or more races, non-Hispanic/Latino), 9 international. Average age 34. 197 applicants, 36% accepted, 48 enrolled. In 2014, 12 master's, 14 doctorates awarded. Terminal master's awarded for partial completion of doctoral program. *Degree requirements:* For master's, variable foreign language requirement, comprehensive exam, thesis optional; for doctorate, variable foreign language requirement, comprehensive exam, thesis/dissertation. *Entrance requirements:* For master's and doctorate, GRE General Test. Additional exam requirements/recommendations for international students: Required—TOEFL (minimum score 550 paper-based; 79 iBT), IELTS (minimum score 6.5). *Application deadline:* For fall admission, 6/1 priority date for domestic students, 1/15 priority date for international students; for spring admission, 9/1 priority date for domestic students, 6/15 priority date for international students. Applications are processed on a rolling basis. Application fee: $60. Electronic applications accepted. *Expenses:* Tuition, state resident: full-time $6310; part-time $262.92 per credit hour. Tuition, nonresident: full-time $14,998; part-time $624.92 per credit hour. *Required fees:* $2701; $36.50 per credit. $912.50 per semester. Tuition and fees vary according to course load. *Financial support:* In 2014–15, 112 students received support, including 94 fellowships (averaging $2,592 per year), 8 research assistantships (averaging $19,331 per year), 89 teaching assistantships (averaging $14,644 per year); career-related internships or fieldwork, Federal Work-Study, scholarships/grants, and unspecified assistantships also available. Financial award application deadline: 12/15; financial award applicants required to submit FAFSA. *Faculty research:* American, British, and comparative literature; creative writing; linguistics; film; technical communication and rhetoric. *Total annual research expenditures:* $64,530. *Unit head:* Dr. Bruce Clarke, Professor, 806-742-2501, Fax: 806-742-0989, E-mail: bruce.clarke@ttu.edu. *Application contact:* Dr. Brian J. McFadden, Director of Graduate Studies, 806-742-2501 Ext. 246, Fax: 806-742-0989, E-mail: english.gradadvisor@ttu.edu.
Website: http://www.english.ttu.edu/

Texas Woman's University, Graduate School, College of Arts and Sciences, Department of English, Speech, and Foreign Languages, Denton, TX 76201. Offers English (MA); rhetoric (PhD). Part-time programs available. *Degree requirements:* For master's, comprehensive exam, thesis; for doctorate, comprehensive exam, thesis/dissertation. *Entrance requirements:* For master's, GRE General Test (preferred minimum score 153 [500 old version] verbal, 138 [350 old version] quantitative), 3 letters of reference, minimum GPA of 3.0 on previous upper-division and graduate work; for doctorate, GRE General Test (preferred minimum score 153 [500 old version] verbal, 138 [350 old version] quantitative), writing sample, 3 letters of reference, interview (for graduate assistants), minimum GPA of 3.0 on previous upper-division and graduate work. Additional exam requirements/recommendations for international students: Recommended—TOEFL (minimum score 600 paper-based; 100 iBT). Electronic applications accepted. *Faculty research:* British and American literature, rhetoric: historical and applied, composition studies and technology, literary theory and criticism, women's literature and feminist rhetoric.

Tiffin University, Program in Humanities, Tiffin, OH 44883-2161. Offers art and visual media (MH); communication (MH); creative writing (MH); English (MH); film studies (MH); humanities (MH); individualized studies (MH). Part-time and evening/weekend programs available. Postbaccalaureate distance learning degree programs offered (no on-campus study). *Entrance requirements:* For master's, work experience. Additional exam requirements/recommendations for international students: Required—TOEFL (minimum score 550 paper-based; 79 iBT).

Trinity College, Graduate Programs, Program in English, Hartford, CT 06106-3100. Offers literary studies (MA); writing, rhetoric, and media arts (MA). Part-time and evening/weekend programs available. *Degree requirements:* For master's, thesis (for some programs). *Entrance requirements:* For master's, minimum GPA of 3.0.

Trinity Western University, School of Graduate Studies, Program in Interdisciplinary Humanities, Langley, BC V2Y 1Y1, Canada. Offers general humanities (MAIH); specialized (MAIH), including English, history, philosophy. Part-time programs available. *Degree requirements:* For master's, thesis or alternative, 36 semester hours. *Entrance requirements:* For master's, strong undergraduate degree in humanities or English, history or philosophy. Additional exam requirements/recommendations for international students: Recommended—TOEFL. Electronic applications accepted. *Faculty research:* Literary theory, gender, medieval and early modern literature, philosophy of religion, Thomas Merton's poetics.

Truman State University, Graduate School, School of Arts and Letters, Program in English, Kirksville, MO 63501-4221. Offers MA. *Degree requirements:* For master's, thesis. *Entrance requirements:* For master's, GRE General Test, minimum GPA of 3.0. Additional exam requirements/recommendations for international students: Required—TOEFL (minimum score 550 paper-based). Electronic applications accepted.

Tufts University, Graduate School of Arts and Sciences, Department of English, Medford, MA 02155. Offers MA, PhD. *Faculty:* 15 full-time (6 women), 4 part-time/adjunct (3 women). *Students:* 62 full-time (33 women); includes 5 minority (2 Black or African American, non-Hispanic/Latino; 1 Asian, non-Hispanic/Latino; 1 Hispanic/Latino; 1 Two or more races, non-Hispanic/Latino), 4 international. Average age 31. 81 applicants, 27% accepted, 10 enrolled. In 2014, 7 master's, 9 doctorates awarded. Terminal master's awarded for partial completion of doctoral program. *Degree requirements:* For master's, one foreign language, thesis; for doctorate, 2 foreign languages, thesis/dissertation. *Entrance requirements:* For master's and doctorate, GRE General Test, GRE Subject Test, writing sample. Additional exam requirements/recommendations for international students: Required—TOEFL (minimum score 550 paper-based; 80 iBT), IELTS (minimum score 6.5). *Application deadline:* For fall admission, 1/15 for domestic and international students. Applications are processed on

a rolling basis. Application fee: $75. Electronic applications accepted. *Expenses: Tuition:* Full-time $45,590; part-time $1161 per credit hour. *Required fees:* $782. Full-time tuition and fees vary according to degree level, program and student level. Part-time tuition and fees vary according to course load. *Financial support:* Fellowships with full tuition reimbursements, teaching assistantships with full tuition reimbursements, Federal Work-Study, scholarships/grants, tuition waivers (full and partial), and unspecified assistantships available. Financial award application deadline: 1/15. *Unit head:* Dr. Judith Haber, Graduate Program Director. *Application contact:* Office of Graduate Admissions, 617-627-3395, E-mail: gradadmissions@tufts.edu.
Website: http://www.ase.tufts.edu/english/

Tulane University, School of Liberal Arts, Department of English, New Orleans, LA 70118-5669. Offers MA, PhD. *Degree requirements:* For master's, one foreign language, thesis or alternative; for doctorate, 2 foreign languages, thesis/dissertation. *Entrance requirements:* For master's, GRE General Test, minimum B average in undergraduate course work; for doctorate, GRE General Test. Additional exam requirements/recommendations for international students: Required—TOEFL. Electronic applications accepted. *Expenses: Tuition:* Full-time $46,326; part-time $2574 per credit hour. *Required fees:* $1980; $44.50 per credit hour. $550 per term. Tuition and fees vary according to course load and program.

Universidad de las Américas Puebla, Division of Graduate Studies, School of Humanities, Program in Literature, Puebla, Mexico. Offers MA. Part-time and evening/weekend programs available. *Degree requirements:* For master's, one foreign language, thesis. *Entrance requirements:* Additional exam requirements/recommendations for international students: Required—TOEFL. *Faculty research:* Women in literature, Mexican and Hispanic literature.

Université de Montréal, Faculty of Arts and Sciences, Department of English Studies, Montréal, QC H3C 3J7, Canada. Offers MA, PhD. *Degree requirements:* For doctorate, thesis/dissertation, general exam. *Entrance requirements:* For master's, BA in English with minimum B+ average; for doctorate, MA in English with minimum B+ average. Electronic applications accepted. *Faculty research:* British, Canadian, and American literature.

Université Laval, Faculty of Letters, Department of Literature, Programs in Ancient Civilization, Québec, QC G1K 7P4, Canada. Offers MA, PhD. Part-time programs available. Terminal master's awarded for partial completion of doctoral program. *Degree requirements:* For master's, thesis; for doctorate, comprehensive exam, thesis/dissertation. *Entrance requirements:* For master's and doctorate, English test (comprehension of written English), knowledge of French, knowledge of an ancient language. Electronic applications accepted.

Université Laval, Faculty of Letters, Department of Literature, Programs in English Literatures, Québec, QC G1K 7P4, Canada. Offers MA, PhD. Part-time programs available. Terminal master's awarded for partial completion of doctoral program. *Degree requirements:* For master's, thesis (for some programs); for doctorate, comprehensive exam, thesis/dissertation. *Entrance requirements:* For master's, French exam, knowledge of English; for doctorate, French exam, knowledge of English, knowledge of a third language. Electronic applications accepted.

University at Albany, State University of New York, College of Arts and Sciences, Department of English, Albany, NY 12222-0001. Offers MA, PhD. *Degree requirements:* For master's, one foreign language; for doctorate, one foreign language, comprehensive exam, thesis/dissertation, residency. *Entrance requirements:* For master's and doctorate, GRE General Test, GRE Subject Test. Additional exam requirements/recommendations for international students: Required—TOEFL (minimum score 550 paper-based). Electronic applications accepted. *Faculty research:* Women playwrights; critical literary theory; poetry and poetics; media history, writing and reporting; creative non-fiction.

University at Buffalo, the State University of New York, Graduate School, College of Arts and Sciences, Department of English, Buffalo, NY 14260. Offers MA, PhD. Part-time programs available. *Faculty:* 42 full-time (17 women). *Students:* 123 full-time (60 women), 3 part-time (1 woman); includes 26 minority (24 Asian, non-Hispanic/Latino; 2 Hispanic/Latino), 12 international. Average age 29. 257 applicants, 21% accepted, 20 enrolled. In 2014, 15 master's, 18 doctorates awarded. Terminal master's awarded for partial completion of doctoral program. *Degree requirements:* For master's, thesis or alternative; for doctorate, thesis/dissertation, departmental qualifying exam. *Entrance requirements:* For master's and doctorate, GRE General Test, sample of written work. Additional exam requirements/recommendations for international students: Required—TOEFL (minimum score 79 iBT). *Application deadline:* For fall admission, 12/15 for domestic and international students. Application fee: $75. Electronic applications accepted. *Financial support:* In 2014–15, 65 students received support, including 15 fellowships with full tuition reimbursements available (averaging $17,500 per year), 65 teaching assistantships with full tuition reimbursements available (averaging $13,900 per year); research assistantships, career-related internships or fieldwork, Federal Work-Study, institutionally sponsored loans, and unspecified assistantships also available. Financial award application deadline: 12/15; financial award applicants required to submit FAFSA. *Faculty research:* Psychoanalysis, early modern British literature, poetics, nineteenth century American literature, British and Irish Modernism. *Total annual research expenditures:* $38,000. *Unit head:* Dr. Graham Hammill, Chair, 716-645-0674, Fax: 716-645-5980, E-mail: ghammill@buffalo.edu. *Application contact:* Dr. Rachel Ablow, Director of Graduate Admissions, 716-645-2575, Fax: 716-645-5980, E-mail: eng-grad@buffalo.edu.
Website: http://www.buffalo.edu/cas/english.html

The University of Akron, Graduate School, Buchtel College of Arts and Sciences, Department of English, Akron, OH 44325. Offers composition (MA); creative writing (MFA); literature (MA). Part-time programs available. *Faculty:* 19 full-time (8 women), 1 part-time/adjunct (0 women). *Students:* 39 full-time (23 women), 30 part-time (25 women); includes 7 minority (4 Black or African American, non-Hispanic/Latino; 1 Asian, non-Hispanic/Latino; 1 Hispanic/Latino; 1 Two or more races, non-Hispanic/Latino), 6 international. Average age 32. 46 applicants, 87% accepted, 22 enrolled. In 2014, 25 master's awarded. *Degree requirements:* For master's, thesis optional. *Entrance requirements:* For master's, BA in English, minimum GPA of 2.75, statement of purpose. Additional exam requirements/recommendations for international students: Required—TOEFL (minimum score 580 paper-based; 92 iBT). *Application deadline:* Applications are processed on a rolling basis. Application fee: $45 ($70 for international students). Electronic applications accepted. *Expenses:* Tuition, state resident: full-time $7578; part-time $421 per credit hour. Tuition, nonresident: full-time $12,977; part-time $721 per credit hour. *Required fees:* $1388; $35 per credit hour. Tuition and fees vary according to course load. *Financial support:* In 2014–15, 1 research assistantship with full tuition reimbursement, 24 teaching assistantships with full tuition reimbursements were awarded. *Faculty research:* British and American literary studies, literary theory, creative writing, applied linguistics. *Total annual research expenditures:* $27,467. *Unit head:* Dr. William Thelin, Chair, 330-972-7472, E-mail: wthelin@uakron.edu. *Application contact:* Dr. Joseph Ceccio, Director of Graduate Studies, 330-972-7603, E-mail: jceccio@uakron.edu.
Website: http://www.uakron.edu/english/

English

The University of Alabama, Graduate School, College of Arts and Sciences, Department of English, Tuscaloosa, AL 35487. Offers applied linguistics (PhD); composition and rhetoric (PhD); creative writing (MFA), including fiction, poetry; literature (MA, PhD); rhetoric and composition (MA); teaching English as a second language (MATESOL). *Faculty:* 34 full-time (19 women). *Students:* 129 full-time (70 women), 9 part-time (8 women); includes 18 minority (9 Black or African American, non-Hispanic/Latino; 1 Asian, non-Hispanic/Latino; 5 Hispanic/Latino; 3 Two or more races, non-Hispanic/Latino), 7 international. Average age 28. 318 applicants, 18% accepted, 42 enrolled. In 2014, 39 master's, 2 doctorates awarded. *Degree requirements:* For master's, one foreign language, comprehensive exam, thesis optional; for doctorate, 2 foreign languages, comprehensive exam, thesis/dissertation. *Entrance requirements:* For master's, GRE (minimum score of 300, except for MFA), minimum GPA of 3.0, critical writing sample; for doctorate, GRE (minimum score of 300), minimum GPA of 3.5 on master's or equivalent graduate work, critical writing sample. Additional exam requirements/recommendations for international students: Required—TOEFL (minimum score 100 iBT). *Application deadline:* For fall admission, 12/31 priority date for domestic and international students. Application fee: $50 ($60 for international students). Electronic applications accepted. *Expenses:* Tuition, state resident: full-time $9826. Tuition, nonresident: full-time $24,950. *Financial support:* In 2014–15, 11 fellowships with full tuition reimbursements (averaging $15,000 per year), 1 research assistantship with full tuition reimbursement (averaging $12,366 per year), 112 teaching assistantships with full tuition reimbursements (averaging $12,366 per year) were awarded; career-related internships or fieldwork, scholarships/grants, health care benefits, and unspecified assistantships also available. Financial award application deadline: 12/31. *Faculty research:* American literature, British literature, composition/rhetoric, applied linguistics, creative writing. *Unit head:* Prof. Joel Brouwer, Department Chair, 205-348-9524, Fax: 205-348-1388, E-mail: joel.brouwer@ua.edu. *Application contact:* Jennifer Fuqua, Graduate Coordinator, 205-348-0766, Fax: 205-348-1388, E-mail: jfuqua@ua.edu.

The University of Alabama at Birmingham, College of Arts and Sciences, Program in English, Birmingham, AL 35294. Offers creative writing (MA); literature (MA); rhetoric and composition (MA). Part-time programs available. *Students:* 13 full-time (12 women), 12 part-time (4 women); includes 1 minority (Black or African American, non-Hispanic/Latino). Average age 29. In 2014, 11 master's awarded. *Degree requirements:* For master's, one foreign language, comprehensive exam, thesis or alternative. *Entrance requirements:* For master's, GRE General Test or MAT, minimum GPA of 2.75. *Application deadline:* For fall admission, 7/1 for domestic students; for spring admission, 11/1 for domestic students. Applications are processed on a rolling basis. Application fee: $45 ($60 for international students). Electronic applications accepted. *Expenses:* Tuition, state resident: full-time $7090; part-time $370 per credit hour. Tuition, nonresident: full-time $16,072; part-time $869 per credit hour. Full-time tuition and fees vary according to course load and program. *Financial support:* Teaching assistantships and career-related internships or fieldwork available. *Unit head:* Dr. Gale Temple, Program Director, 205-934-8593, Fax: 205-975-6610, E-mail: gtemple@uab.edu. *Application contact:* Susan Noblitt Banks, Director of Graduate School Operations, 205-934-8227, Fax: 205-934-8413, E-mail: gradschool@uab.edu. Website: http://www.uab.edu/cas/english/academic-programs

The University of Alabama in Huntsville, School of Graduate Studies, College of Liberal Arts, Department of English, Huntsville, AL 35899. Offers education (MA); English (MA); language arts (MA); reading specialist (MA); technical communications (Certificate). Part-time and evening/weekend programs available. *Degree requirements:* For master's, one foreign language, comprehensive exam, thesis or alternative, oral and written exams. *Entrance requirements:* For master's and Certificate, GRE General Test, minimum GPA of 3.0. Additional exam requirements/recommendations for international students: Required—TOEFL (minimum score 500 paper-based; 80 iBT), IELTS (minimum score 6.5). Electronic applications accepted. *Faculty research:* Fiction and identity, Shakespeare, science fiction, eighteenth-century literature, technical writing.

University of Alaska Anchorage, College of Arts and Sciences, Department of English, Anchorage, AK 99508. Offers MA. Part-time programs available. *Degree requirements:* For master's, comprehensive exam, thesis or alternative. *Entrance requirements:* For master's, GRE General Test, GRE Subject Test, portfolio, minimum GPA of 3.5, writing sample. Additional exam requirements/recommendations for international students: Required—TOEFL (minimum score 550 paper-based). *Faculty research:* The rhetoric of essays, American and American Indian literature, linguistics, Shakespeare, literature of war.

University of Alaska Fairbanks, College of Liberal Arts, Department of English, Fairbanks, AK 99775-5720. Offers creative writing (MFA); literature (MA); MA/MFA. Part-time programs available. *Faculty:* 15 full-time (5 women), 1 part-time/adjunct (0 women). *Students:* 31 full-time (20 women), 11 part-time (6 women); includes 5 minority (2 Asian, non-Hispanic/Latino; 3 Two or more races, non-Hispanic/Latino). Average age 31. 67 applicants, 34% accepted, 12 enrolled. In 2014, 7 master's awarded. *Degree requirements:* For master's, comprehensive exam, oral defense of project or thesis. *Entrance requirements:* For master's, GRE General Test, bachelor's degree from accredited institution with minimum cumulative undergraduate and major GPA of 3.0, academic writing sample. Additional exam requirements/recommendations for international students: Required—TOEFL (minimum score 550 paper-based; 79 iBT), IELTS (minimum score 6.5). *Application deadline:* For fall admission, 6/1 for domestic students, 3/1 for international students; for spring admission, 10/15 for domestic students, 9/1 for international students. Applications are processed on a rolling basis. Application fee: $60. Electronic applications accepted. *Expenses:* Tuition, state resident: full-time $7614; part-time $423 per credit. Tuition, nonresident: full-time $15,552; part-time $864 per credit. Tuition and fees vary according to course level, course load and reciprocity agreements. *Financial support:* In 2014–15, 27 teaching assistantships with full tuition reimbursements (averaging $11,241 per year) were awarded; fellowships with full tuition reimbursements, research assistantships with full tuition reimbursements, Federal Work-Study, scholarships/grants, health care benefits, and unspecified assistantships also available. Support available to part-time students. Financial award application deadline: 7/1; financial award applicants required to submit FAFSA. *Unit head:* Richard Carr, Department Chair, 907-474-7193, Fax: 907-474-5247, E-mail: uaf-english-dept@alaska.edu. *Application contact:* Mary Kreta, Director of Admissions, 907-474-7500, Fax: 907-474-7097, E-mail: admissions@uaf.edu. Website: http://www.uaf.edu/english

University of Alberta, Faculty of Graduate Studies and Research, Department of English and Film Studies, Edmonton, AB T6G 2E1, Canada. Offers English (MA, PhD). Part-time and evening/weekend programs available. *Degree requirements:* For master's, one foreign language, thesis optional; for doctorate, 2 foreign languages, thesis/dissertation. *Entrance requirements:* For master's, honors BA or equivalent; for doctorate, honors BA and MA. Additional exam requirements/recommendations for international students: Required—TOEFL (minimum score 600 paper-based). Electronic applications accepted. *Faculty research:* Women's writing, postcolonial theory, Victorian literature, Renaissance literature, Canadian literature.

The University of Arizona, College of Humanities, Department of English, English Language/Linguistics Program, Tucson, AZ 85721. Offers English (MA, PhD); ESL

(MA). *Entrance requirements:* Additional exam requirements/recommendations for international students: Required—TOEFL (minimum score 550 paper-based; 79 iBT); Recommended—IELTS (minimum score 7). Electronic applications accepted.

University of Arkansas, Graduate School, J. William Fulbright College of Arts and Sciences, Department of English, Program in English, Fayetteville, AR 72701-1201. Offers MA, PhD. *Degree requirements:* For master's, thesis; for doctorate, thesis/dissertation. *Entrance requirements:* For master's, GRE General Test; for doctorate, GRE General Test, GRE Subject Test. Electronic applications accepted. *Faculty research:* Creative writing, seventeenth century literature, twentieth century literature, American literature.

The University of British Columbia, Faculty of Arts and Faculty of Graduate Studies, Department of English, Vancouver, BC V6T 1Z1, Canada. Offers MA, PhD. *Degree requirements:* For master's, thesis or alternative; for doctorate, one foreign language, comprehensive exam, thesis/dissertation. *Entrance requirements:* For master's, BA or equivalent; for doctorate, MA. Additional exam requirements/recommendations for international students: Required—TOEFL (minimum score 615 paper-based; 104 iBT), IELTS (minimum score 8). Electronic applications accepted. *Faculty research:* English, American, Canadian, and Commonwealth post-colonial literature; English language; rhetoric.

The University of British Columbia, Faculty of Arts, School of Library, Archival and Information Studies, Master of Arts Program in Children's Literature, Vancouver, BC V6T 1Z1, Canada. Offers MA. Part-time programs available. *Degree requirements:* For master's, thesis. *Entrance requirements:* For master's, minimum GPA of 3.3 in undergraduate upper-division courses. Additional exam requirements/recommendations for international students: Required—TOEFL (minimum score 600 paper-based; 100 iBT). Electronic applications accepted. *Faculty research:* Children's and young adult literature; children's and young adult public library services; Canadian children's and young adult literature; publishing for youth.

University of Calgary, Faculty of Graduate Studies, Faculty of Arts, Department of English, Calgary, AB T2N 1N4, Canada. Offers MA, PhD. Part-time programs available. *Degree requirements:* For master's, one foreign language, comprehensive exam (for some programs), thesis; for doctorate, one foreign language, thesis/dissertation, candidacy exam. *Entrance requirements:* Additional exam requirements/recommendations for international students: Required—TOEFL (minimum score 600 paper-based). Electronic applications accepted. *Faculty research:* Various national and period literatures, creative writing, literary theory, gender and women's studies, postcolonial literatures.

University of California, Berkeley, Graduate Division, College of Letters and Science, Department of English, Berkeley, CA 94720-1500. Offers PhD. *Degree requirements:* For doctorate, 2 foreign languages, thesis/dissertation, qualifying exam. *Entrance requirements:* For doctorate, GRE General Test, GRE Subject Test, minimum GPA of 3.0, writing sample, 3 letters of recommendation.

University of California, Davis, Graduate Studies, Program in English, Davis, CA 95616. Offers creative writing (MA); English (MA, PhD). Terminal master's awarded for partial completion of doctoral program. *Degree requirements:* For master's, one foreign language, thesis optional; for doctorate, 2 foreign languages, thesis/dissertation. *Entrance requirements:* For master's and doctorate, GRE General Test, GRE Subject Test, minimum GPA of 3.0, writing sample. Additional exam requirements/recommendations for international students: Required—TOEFL (minimum score 550 paper-based). Electronic applications accepted. *Faculty research:* Feminist theory, ethnic literature, literary theory, history of literature, literature of nature.

University of California, Irvine, School of Humanities, Department of English, Program in English, Irvine, CA 92697. Offers English (MA); English and American literature (PhD). *Students:* 59 full-time (26 women); includes 12 minority (1 Black or African American, non-Hispanic/Latino; 4 Asian, non-Hispanic/Latino; 4 Hispanic/Latino; 3 Two or more races, non-Hispanic/Latino). Average age 31. 181 applicants, 10% accepted, 9 enrolled. In 2014, 29 master's, 10 doctorates awarded. Terminal master's awarded for partial completion of doctoral program. *Degree requirements:* For master's, one foreign language, comprehensive exam; for doctorate, 2 foreign languages, comprehensive exam, thesis/dissertation. *Entrance requirements:* For doctorate, GRE General Test, GRE Subject Test, minimum GPA of 3.5, sample of written work, 3 letters of recommendation. Additional exam requirements/recommendations for international students: Required—TOEFL (minimum score 550 paper-based). *Application deadline:* For fall admission, 12/1 for domestic and international students. Application fee: $80 ($100 for international students). Electronic applications accepted. *Financial support:* In 2014–15, 67 students received support. Fellowships with full tuition reimbursements available, research assistantships, teaching assistantships with partial tuition reimbursements available, institutionally sponsored loans, health care benefits, tuition waivers (full and partial), and unspecified assistantships available. Financial award application deadline: 3/1; financial award applicants required to submit FAFSA. *Faculty research:* Critical theory, literary history, cultural studies. *Unit head:* Martin Harries, Department Chair, 949-824-6715, Fax: 949-824-2916, E-mail: martin.harries@uci.edu. *Application contact:* Jerry Christensen, Graduate Faculty Advisor, 949-824-9046, Fax: 949-824-2916, E-mail: jchris@uci.edu.

University of California, Los Angeles, Graduate Division, College of Letters and Science, Department of English, Los Angeles, CA 90095. Offers MA, PhD. Terminal master's awarded for partial completion of doctoral program. *Degree requirements:* For master's, one foreign language, comprehensive exam, thesis; for doctorate, 2 foreign languages, thesis/dissertation, oral and written qualifying exams. *Entrance requirements:* For doctorate, GRE General Test, GRE Subject Test (literature), bachelor's degree; minimum undergraduate GPA of 3.0, 3.5 in upper-division English courses (or its equivalent if letter grade system not used), 3.7 in graduate courses for applicant with master's degree; writing sample. Additional exam requirements/recommendations for international students: Required—TOEFL. Electronic applications accepted.

University of California, Riverside, Graduate Division, Department of English, Riverside, CA 92521-0102. Offers MA, PhD. *Faculty:* 29 full-time (14 women). *Students:* 82 full-time (48 women); includes 19 minority (3 Black or African American, non-Hispanic/Latino; 1 American Indian or Alaska Native, non-Hispanic/Latino; 5 Asian, non-Hispanic/Latino; 10 Hispanic/Latino), 3 international. Average age 31. In 2014, 9 master's, 10 doctorates awarded. *Degree requirements:* For master's, one foreign language, comprehensive exam; for doctorate, 2 foreign languages, thesis/dissertation, qualifying exams. *Entrance requirements:* For doctorate, GRE General Test, minimum GPA of 3.5. Additional exam requirements/recommendations for international students: Required—TOEFL (minimum score 550 paper-based; 80 iBT). *Application deadline:* For fall admission, 12/10 for domestic and international students. Applications are processed on a rolling basis. Application fee: $60 ($75 for international students). Electronic applications accepted. *Expenses:* Tuition, state resident: full-time $5399. Tuition, nonresident: full-time $10,433. *Financial support:* In 2014–15, fellowships with full tuition reimbursements (averaging $15,000 per year), research assistantships (averaging $600 per year), teaching assistantships with partial tuition reimbursements (averaging $19,000 per year) were awarded; career-related internships or fieldwork,

Federal Work-Study, institutionally sponsored loans, and tuition waivers (full and partial) also available. Financial award application deadline: 12/10; financial award applicants required to submit FAFSA. *Faculty research:* Critical theory, cultural and film studies, lesbian and gay studies, minority and feminist discourses, rhetoric and composition. *Unit head:* Prof. George Haggerty, Chair, 951-827-1458, Fax: 951-827-3967, E-mail: george.haggerty@ucr.edu. *Application contact:* Tina M. Feldmann, Graduate Program Assistant, 951-827-1454, Fax: 951-827-3967, E-mail: english@ucr.edu.
Website: http://www.english.ucr.edu/

University of California, San Diego, Graduate Division, Department of Literature, La Jolla, CA 92093. Offers literature (PhD); writing (MFA). *Students:* 75 full-time (47 women); includes 36 minority (1 Black or African American, non-Hispanic/Latino; 2 American Indian or Alaska Native, non-Hispanic/Latino; 8 Asian, non-Hispanic/Latino; 25 Hispanic/Latino), 5 international. 285 applicants, 10% accepted, 16 enrolled. In 2014, 5 master's, 14 doctorates awarded. *Degree requirements:* For master's, thesis; for doctorate, comprehensive exam, thesis/dissertation, 3 quarters of teaching assistantship. *Entrance requirements:* For master's, writing sample; for doctorate, GRE General Test, writing sample. Additional exam requirements/recommendations for international students: Required—TOEFL (minimum score 550 paper-based; 80 iBT), IELTS. *Application deadline:* For fall admission, 12/1 for domestic students. Application fee: $90 ($110 for international students). Electronic applications accepted. *Expenses:* Tuition, state resident: full-time $11,220; part-time $5610 per quarter. Tuition, nonresident: full-time $26,322; part-time $13,161 per quarter. *Required fees:* $570 per quarter. Tuition and fees vary according to program. *Financial support:* Fellowships, research assistantships, teaching assistantships, scholarships/grants, and readerships available. Financial award applicants required to submit FAFSA. *Faculty research:* Chicano/a-Latino/a studies, European studies, film studies and visual culture, Latin American literary and cultural studies, medieval/early modern studies, transnational Africa/African diaspora studies, transnational Asia/Asian diaspora studies. *Unit head:* Stephanie Jed, Chair, 858-534-4618, E-mail: litchair@ucsd.edu. *Application contact:* Kristin Carnohan, PhD Coordinator, 858-534-3217, E-mail: litgrad@ucsd.edu.
Website: http://literature.ucsd.edu

University of California, Santa Barbara, Graduate Division, College of Letters and Sciences, Division of Humanities and Fine Arts, Department of English, Santa Barbara, CA 93106-3170. Offers English (PhD); European medieval studies (PhD); feminist studies (PhD); global studies (PhD); technology and society (PhD); translation studies (PhD); writing studies (PhD); MA/PhD. Terminal master's awarded for partial completion of doctoral program. *Degree requirements:* For doctorate, one foreign language, comprehensive exam, thesis/dissertation. *Entrance requirements:* For doctorate, GRE General Test, GRE Subject Test (English). Additional exam requirements/recommendations for international students: Required—TOEFL (minimum score 550 paper-based; 80 iBT), IELTS (minimum score 7). Electronic applications accepted. *Faculty research:* Medieval, Romantic and Victorian studies; gender studies and feminist theory; literature and the mind; American literature; literature and new media/information culture.

University of California, Santa Cruz, Division of Graduate Studies, Division of Humanities, Department of Literature, Santa Cruz, CA 95064. Offers MA, PhD. Terminal master's awarded for partial completion of doctoral program. *Degree requirements:* For master's, thesis; for doctorate, one foreign language, thesis/dissertation, qualifying exam. *Entrance requirements:* For master's, GRE General Test, writing sample, minimum GPA of 3.5; for doctorate, GRE General Test, minimum GPA of 3.5, writing sample. Additional exam requirements/recommendations for international students: Required—TOEFL (minimum score 550 paper-based; 83 iBT); Recommended—IELTS (minimum score 8). Electronic applications accepted. *Faculty research:* Technologies of narrative; trans/post/emergent nationalisms; poetics, poetry, and experimental writing; materialism and material culture; critical theories.

University of Central Arkansas, Graduate School, College of Liberal Arts, Department of English, Conway, AR 72035-0001. Offers MA. Part-time programs available. *Degree requirements:* For master's, comprehensive exam, thesis optional. *Entrance requirements:* For master's, GRE General Test, minimum GPA of 2.7. Additional exam requirements/recommendations for international students: Required—TOEFL (minimum score 550 paper-based). Electronic applications accepted. *Faculty research:* Writing project.

University of Central Florida, College of Arts and Humanities, Department of English, Orlando, FL 32816. Offers MA, MFA, PhD, Certificate. Part-time and evening/weekend programs available. *Faculty:* 42 full-time (23 women), 4 part-time/adjunct (2 women). *Students:* 79 full-time (46 women), 78 part-time (58 women); includes 20 minority (6 Black or African American, non-Hispanic/Latino; 11 Hispanic/Latino; 3 Two or more races, non-Hispanic/Latino), 1 international. Average age 34. 186 applicants, 42% accepted, 50 enrolled. In 2014, 33 master's, 2 doctorates, 6 other advanced degrees awarded. *Degree requirements:* For master's, one foreign language, thesis or alternative. *Entrance requirements:* For master's, GRE General Test, minimum GPA of 3.0 in last 60 hours of course work. Additional exam requirements/recommendations for international students: Required—TOEFL. *Application deadline:* For fall admission, 6/15 for domestic students; for spring admission, 12/1 for domestic students. Application fee: $30. Electronic applications accepted. *Expenses:* Tuition, state resident: part-time $288.16 per credit hour. Tuition, nonresident: part-time $1073.31 per credit hour. *Financial support:* In 2014–15, 45 students received support, including 12 fellowships with partial tuition reimbursements available (averaging $6,200 per year), 3 research assistantships with partial tuition reimbursements available (averaging $7,800 per year), 38 teaching assistantships with partial tuition reimbursements available (averaging $8,700 per year); career-related internships or fieldwork, Federal Work-Study, institutionally sponsored loans, tuition waivers (partial), and unspecified assistantships also available. Financial award application deadline: 3/1; financial award applicants required to submit FAFSA. *Unit head:* Dr. Patrick Murphy, Chair, 407-823-0989, E-mail: patrick.murphy@ucf.edu. *Application contact:* Barbara Rodriguez Lamas, Director, Admissions and Registration, 407-823-2766, Fax: 407-823-6442, E-mail: gradadmissions@ucf.edu.
Website: http://www.english.cah.ucf.edu/

University of Central Missouri, The Graduate School, Warrensburg, MO 64093. Offers accountancy (MA); accounting (MBA); applied mathematics (MS); aviation safety (MA); biology (MS); business administration (MBA); career and technical education leadership (MS); college student personnel administration (MS); communication (MA); computer science (MS); counseling (MS); criminal justice (MS); educational leadership (Ed D); educational technology (MS); elementary and early childhood education (MSE); English (MA); environmental studies (MA); finance (MBA); history (MA); human services/educational technology (Ed S); human services/learning resources (Ed S); human services/professional counseling (Ed S); industrial hygiene (MS); industrial management (MS); information systems (MBA); information technology (MS); kinesiology (MS); library science and information services (MS); literacy education (MSE); marketing (MBA); mathematics (MS); music (MA); occupational safety management (MS); psychology (MS); rural family nursing (MS); school administration (MSE); social gerontology (MS); sociology (MA); special education (MSE); speech language pathology (MS); superintendency (Ed S); teaching (MAT); teaching English as a second language (MA); technology (MS); technology management (PhD); theatre (MA). Part-time programs available. *Faculty:* 314 full-time (137 women), 24 part-time/adjunct (14 women). *Students:* 1,624 full-time (542 women), 1,773 part-time (1,055 women); includes 194 minority (104 Black or African American, non-Hispanic/Latino; 6 American Indian or Alaska Native, non-Hispanic/Latino; 23 Asian, non-Hispanic/Latino; 41 Hispanic/Latino; 3 Native Hawaiian or other Pacific Islander, non-Hispanic/Latino; 17 Two or more races, non-Hispanic/Latino), 1,592 international. Average age 31. 2,800 applicants, 63% accepted, 1223 enrolled. In 2014, 796 master's, 81 other advanced degrees awarded. *Degree requirements:* For master's and Ed S, comprehensive exam (for some programs), thesis (for some programs). *Entrance requirements:* Additional exam requirements/recommendations for international students: Required—TOEFL (minimum score 550 paper-based; 79 iBT). *Application deadline:* For fall admission, 6/1 for domestic students; for spring admission, 10/1 for domestic and international students. Applications are processed on a rolling basis. Application fee: $30 ($75 for international students). Electronic applications accepted. *Expenses:* Tuition, state resident: full-time $6630; part-time $276.25 per credit hour. Tuition, nonresident: full-time $13,260; part-time $552.50 per credit hour. *Required fees:* $29 per credit hour. Tuition and fees vary according to campus/location. *Financial support:* In 2014–15, 118 students received support, including 271 research assistantships with full and partial tuition reimbursements available (averaging $7,500 per year), 109 teaching assistantships with full and partial tuition reimbursements available (averaging $7,500 per year); career-related internships or fieldwork, Federal Work-Study, scholarships/grants, and administrative and laboratory assistantships also available. Support available to part-time students. Financial award application deadline: 3/1; financial award applicants required to submit FAFSA. *Unit head:* Tina Church-Hockett, Director of Graduate School and International Admissions, 660-543-4621, Fax: 660-543-4778, E-mail: church@ucmo.edu. *Application contact:* Brittany Lawrence, Graduate Student Services Coordinator, 660-543-4621, Fax: 660-543-4778, E-mail: gradinfo@ucmo.edu.
Website: http://www.ucmo.edu/graduate/

University of Central Oklahoma, The Jackson College of Graduate Studies, College of Liberal Arts, Department of English, Edmond, OK 73034-5209. Offers creative writing (MA, MFA); traditional studies (MA). Part-time programs available. *Degree requirements:* For master's, variable foreign language requirement, comprehensive exam (for some programs), thesis (for some programs), portfolio. *Entrance requirements:* For master's, GRE, 18-24 hours of course work in English language and literature; writing sample; essay. Additional exam requirements/recommendations for international students: Required—TOEFL (minimum score 550 paper-based; 79 iBT), IELTS (minimum score 6.5). Electronic applications accepted. *Faculty research:* John Milton, Harriet Beecher Stowe.

University of Chicago, Division of the Humanities, Department of English Language and Literature, Chicago, IL 60637. Offers PhD. *Students:* 89 full-time (37 women); includes 12 minority (1 Black or African American, non-Hispanic/Latino; 1 American Indian or Alaska Native, non-Hispanic/Latino; 4 Asian, non-Hispanic/Latino; 5 Hispanic/Latino; 1 Two or more races, non-Hispanic/Latino), 17 international. 523 applicants, 36% accepted, 16 enrolled. Terminal master's awarded for partial completion of doctoral program. *Degree requirements:* For doctorate, 2 foreign languages, thesis/dissertation. *Entrance requirements:* For doctorate, GRE General Test. Additional exam requirements/recommendations for international students: Required—TOEFL (minimum score 104 iBT), IELTS (minimum score 7). *Application deadline:* For fall admission, 12/15 for domestic and international students. Application fee: $90. Electronic applications accepted. *Expenses: Tuition:* Full-time $46,899. *Required fees:* $347. *Financial support:* Fellowships with full tuition reimbursements, teaching assistantships with full tuition reimbursements, Federal Work-Study, institutionally sponsored loans, scholarships/grants, and health care benefits available. Financial award application deadline: 12/15; financial award applicants required to submit FAFSA. *Unit head:* Dr. Frances Ferguson, Chair. *Application contact:* Braden Grams, Assistant Dean of Students, Admissions and Fellowships, 773-702-1552, Fax: 773-834-9148, E-mail: humanitiesadmissions@uchicago.edu.
Website: http://english.uchicago.edu/

University of Chicago, Division of the Humanities, Master of Arts Program in the Humanities, Chicago, IL 60637. Offers art history (MA); classics (MA); comparative literature (MA); creative writing (MA); digital humanities (MA); English language and literature (MA); Germanic studies (MA); linguistics (MA); music (MA); philosophy (MA); Romance languages and literatures (MA); South Asian languages and civilizations (MA). *Students:* 83 full-time (41 women), 8 part-time (6 women); includes 14 minority (1 Black or African American, non-Hispanic/Latino; 6 Asian, non-Hispanic/Latino; 6 Hispanic/Latino; 1 Two or more races, non-Hispanic/Latino), 17 international. Average age 26. 153 applicants, 67% accepted, 80 enrolled. *Degree requirements:* For master's, thesis. *Entrance requirements:* For master's, GRE General Test. Additional exam requirements/recommendations for international students: Required—TOEFL (minimum score 600 paper-based; 104 iBT), IELTS (minimum score 7). *Application deadline:* For fall admission, 3/15 for domestic and international students. Application fee: $90. Electronic applications accepted. *Expenses: Tuition:* Full-time $46,899. *Required fees:* $347. *Financial support:* In 2014–15, 100 students received support, including 8 fellowships with partial tuition reimbursements available (averaging $12,000 per year); Federal Work-Study, institutionally sponsored loans, and tuition waivers (partial) also available. Financial award application deadline: 3/15; financial award applicants required to submit FAFSA. *Unit head:* Prof. David Wray, Director, 773-834-1201, E-mail: ma-humanities@uchicago.edu. *Application contact:* Program Coordinator, 773-834-1201, Fax: 773-834-7526, E-mail: ma-humanities@uchicago.edu.
Website: http://maph.uchicago.edu/

University of Cincinnati, Graduate School, McMicken College of Arts and Sciences, Department of English and Comparative Literature, Cincinnati, OH 45221. Offers MA, MAT, PhD. Part-time programs available. Terminal master's awarded for partial completion of doctoral program. *Degree requirements:* For master's, one foreign language, thesis (for some programs); for doctorate, 2 foreign languages, thesis/dissertation. *Entrance requirements:* For master's, GRE General Test, letters of recommendation (3), writing samples; for doctorate, GRE General Test, GRE Subject Test, letters of recommendation (3), writing samples. Additional exam requirements/recommendations for international students: Required—TOEFL. Electronic applications accepted. *Faculty research:* Literature/theory, creative writing, composition, professional writing/editing, linguistics.

University of Colorado Boulder, Graduate School, College of Arts and Sciences, Department of English, Boulder, CO 80309. Offers literature (MA, PhD), including creative writing (MA). *Faculty:* 42 full-time (26 women). *Students:* 114 full-time (65 women), 7 part-time (5 women); includes 19 minority (2 Black or African American, non-Hispanic/Latino; 1 American Indian or Alaska Native, non-Hispanic/Latino; 2 Asian, non-Hispanic/Latino; 11 Hispanic/Latino; 3 Two or more races, non-Hispanic/Latino), 2 international. Average age 30. 508 applicants, 26% accepted, 35 enrolled. In 2014, 35 master's, 3 doctorates awarded. Terminal master's awarded for partial completion of doctoral program. *Degree requirements:* For master's, one foreign language, comprehensive exam, thesis or alternative; for doctorate, 2 foreign languages, comprehensive exam, thesis/dissertation. *Entrance requirements:* For master's, GRE

English

General Test, GRE Subject Test, minimum undergraduate GPA of 3.0; for doctorate, GRE General Test, GRE Subject Test. *Application deadline:* For fall admission, 2/1 for domestic students, 12/1 for international students. Application fee: $50 ($70 for international students). Electronic applications accepted. *Financial support:* In 2014–15, 236 students received support, including 26 fellowships (averaging $3,391 per year), 7 research assistantships with full and partial tuition reimbursements available (averaging $30,902 per year), 74 teaching assistantships with full and partial tuition reimbursements available (averaging $28,450 per year); institutionally sponsored loans, scholarships/grants, health care benefits, and unspecified assistantships also available. Financial award application deadline: 1/1; financial award applicants required to submit FAFSA. *Faculty research:* Literary criticism, English language/literature, modern language/literature, American literature, poetry. *Total annual research expenditures:* $3.9 million. Website: http://www.colorado.edu/English/

University of Colorado Boulder, Graduate School, College of Arts and Sciences, Department of Spanish and Portuguese, Boulder, CO 80309. Offers Hispanic linguistics (MA); medieval and early modern Hispanic literatures (PhD); Spanish and Spanish American literatures (MA, PhD). *Faculty:* 14 full-time (6 women). *Students:* 36 full-time (23 women), 1 (woman) part-time; includes 9 minority (1 American Indian or Alaska Native, non-Hispanic/Latino; 8 Hispanic/Latino), 12 international. Average age 31. 42 applicants, 17% accepted, 6 enrolled. In 2014, 7 master's, 2 doctorates awarded. Terminal master's awarded for partial completion of doctoral program. *Degree requirements:* For master's, one foreign language, comprehensive exam, thesis or alternative; for doctorate, 2 foreign languages, thesis/dissertation. *Entrance requirements:* For master's, minimum undergraduate GPA of 2.75. *Application deadline:* For fall admission, 12/19 for domestic and international students. Applications are processed on a rolling basis. Application fee: $50 ($70 for international students). Electronic applications accepted. *Financial support:* In 2014–15, 89 students received support, including 6 fellowships (averaging $948 per year), 33 teaching assistantships with full and partial tuition reimbursements available (averaging $38,597 per year); institutionally sponsored loans, scholarships/grants, health care benefits, and unspecified assistantships also available. Financial award application deadline: 12/15; financial award applicants required to submit FAFSA. *Faculty research:* Literary criticism, Spanish language literature, cultural history, Iberian studies. *Total annual research expenditures:* $37,611. Website: http://spanish.colorado.edu/

University of Colorado Denver, College of Liberal Arts and Sciences, Department of English, Denver, CO 80217. Offers applied linguistics (MA); literature (MA); rhetoric and teaching of writing (MA). Part-time and evening/weekend programs available. *Faculty:* 23 full-time (13 women), 1 (woman) part-time/adjunct. *Students:* 21 full-time (17 women), 16 part-time (10 women); includes 5 minority (1 Black or African American, non-Hispanic/Latino; 1 Asian, non-Hispanic/Latino; 3 Hispanic/Latino), 2 international. Average age 28. 19 applicants, 58% accepted, 4 enrolled. In 2014, 19 master's awarded. *Degree requirements:* For master's, variable foreign language requirement, comprehensive exam (for some programs), thesis (for some programs), minimum of 33 credit hours (for literature program), 30 (for rhetoric and teaching of writing and applied linguistics programs). *Entrance requirements:* For master's, GRE General Test, minimum GPA of 3.0 in undergraduate courses, critical writing sample, letters of recommendation, completion of 24 semester hours in English courses (at least 16 at the upper-division level), statement of purpose. Additional exam requirements/recommendations for international students: Required—TOEFL (minimum score 537 paper-based; 75 iBT); Recommended—IELTS (minimum score 6.5). *Application deadline:* For fall admission, 4/1 for domestic and international students; for spring admission, 10/1 for domestic and international students; for summer admission, 4/1 for domestic and international students. Application fee: $50 ($75 for international students). Electronic applications accepted. *Financial support:* In 2014–15, 9 students received support. Fellowships, research assistantships, teaching assistantships, Federal Work-Study, institutionally sponsored loans, scholarships/grants, traineeships, and unspecified assistantships available. Financial award application deadline: 4/1; financial award applicants required to submit FAFSA. *Faculty research:* Literature, rhetoric, teaching of writing, applied linguistics. *Unit head:* Prof. Nancy Ciccone, Chair, 303-556-8395, E-mail: nancy.ciccone@ucdenver.edu. *Application contact:* English Department, 303-556-2584, Fax: 303-556-2959.
Website: http://www.ucdenver.edu/academics/colleges/CLAS/Departments/english/Programs/Masters/Pages/Overview.aspx

University of Connecticut, Graduate School, College of Liberal Arts and Sciences, Department of English, Storrs, CT 06269. Offers MA, PhD. Terminal master's awarded for partial completion of doctoral program. *Degree requirements:* For master's, comprehensive exam; for doctorate, thesis/dissertation. *Entrance requirements:* For master's and doctorate, GRE General Test, GRE Subject Test. Additional exam requirements/recommendations for international students: Required—TOEFL (minimum score 550 paper-based). Electronic applications accepted.

University of Dallas, Braniff Graduate School of Liberal Arts, Program in English, Irving, TX 75062-4736. Offers MA. Part-time programs available. *Degree requirements:* For master's, one foreign language. *Entrance requirements:* For master's, GRE General Test. *Faculty research:* Modern literature, Renaissance, Shakespeare, medieval studies.

University of Dayton, Department of English, Dayton, OH 45469. Offers MA. Part-time and evening/weekend programs available. *Faculty:* 29 full-time (16 women). *Students:* 21 full-time (18 women), 8 part-time (6 women); includes 1 minority (Black or African American, non-Hispanic/Latino), 10 international. Average age 29. 44 applicants, 48% accepted, 6 enrolled. In 2014, 11 master's awarded. *Degree requirements:* For master's, thesis optional. *Entrance requirements:* For master's, minimum GPA of 3.0, 24 upper-level credit hours of course work in English. Additional exam requirements/recommendations for international students: Required—TOEFL (minimum score 550 paper-based; 80 iBT). *Application deadline:* For fall admission, 4/1 for domestic students, 5/1 for international students; for winter admission, 7/1 for international students; for spring admission, 11/1 for international students. Applications are processed on a rolling basis. Application fee: $0 ($50 for international students). Electronic applications accepted. *Expenses:* Tuition: Full-time $10,176; part-time $848 per credit. *Required fees:* $25; $25 per course. Part-time tuition and fees vary according to course level, course load, degree level and program. *Financial support:* In 2014–15, 9 teaching assistantships with full tuition reimbursements (averaging $10,589 per year) were awarded; institutionally sponsored loans, health care benefits, and unspecified assistantships also available. Financial award application deadline: 3/1; financial award applicants required to submit FAFSA. *Faculty research:* Religion and literature, rhetoric and composition, teaching literature and writing and creative writing. *Total annual research expenditures:* $6,000. *Unit head:* Dr. Andrew Slade, Chair, 937-229-3434, Fax: 937-229-3563, E-mail: aslade1@udayton.edu. *Application contact:* Dr. Tereza Szeghi, Director of Graduate Studies, 937-229-3443, E-mail: tszeghi1@udayton.edu.
Website: https://www.udayton.edu/artssciences/academics/english/welcome/index.php

University of Delaware, College of Arts and Sciences, Department of English, Newark, DE 19716. Offers English and American literature (MA, PhD); MA/PhD. Terminal master's awarded for partial completion of doctoral program. *Degree requirements:* For master's, one foreign language, thesis optional; for doctorate, 2 foreign languages, comprehensive exam, thesis/dissertation, specialty exam. *Entrance requirements:* For master's and doctorate, GRE General Test, GRE Subject Test. Additional exam requirements/recommendations for international students: Required—TOEFL (minimum score 550 paper-based). Electronic applications accepted. *Faculty research:* Significant strengths in American literature and culture, material cultural studies, Renaissance studies, archival studies.

University of Denver, Division of Arts, Humanities and Social Sciences, Department of English, Denver, CO 80208. Offers creative writing (PhD). Part-time programs available. *Faculty:* 19 full-time (8 women), 1 (woman) part-time/adjunct. *Students:* 28 full-time (21 women), 9 part-time (5 women); includes 9 minority (2 Asian, non-Hispanic/Latino; 3 Hispanic/Latino; 4 Two or more races, non-Hispanic/Latino), 3 international. Average age 32. 158 applicants, 20% accepted, 12 enrolled. In 2014, 4 master's, 9 doctorates awarded. *Degree requirements:* For master's, one foreign language, comprehensive exam, thesis; for doctorate, 2 foreign languages, comprehensive exam, thesis/dissertation. *Entrance requirements:* For master's, GRE General Test, GRE Subject Test (advanced literature), bachelor's degree, transcripts, academic essay, statement of intent, three letters of recommendation; for doctorate, GRE General Test, GRE Subject Test (advanced literature), master's degree, transcripts, academic essay, statement of intent, three letters of recommendation, and a writing sample (creative writing program only). Additional exam requirements/recommendations for international students: Required—TOEFL (minimum score 570 paper-based; 88 iBT). *Application deadline:* For fall admission, 1/1 priority date for domestic and international students. Applications are processed on a rolling basis. Application fee: $65. Electronic applications accepted. *Expenses:* Expenses: $1,199 per credit hour. *Financial support:* In 2014–15, 36 students received support, including 29 teaching assistantships with full and partial tuition reimbursements available (averaging $17,366 per year); Federal Work-Study, institutionally sponsored loans, scholarships/grants, and unspecified assistantships also available. Support available to part-time students. Financial award application deadline: 2/15; financial award applicants required to submit FAFSA. *Faculty research:* African diaspora semiotics, Susan Howe's poetics, Renaissance drama and emblematic culture, New England Colonial literature, postmodern literature. *Unit head:* Dr. Linda Bensel-Meyers, Chair, 303-871-2859, Fax: 303-871-2853, E-mail: lbenselm@du.edu. *Application contact:* Dr. Adam Rovner, Director of Graduate Studies, 303-871-2861, Fax: 303-871-2853, E-mail: adam.rovner@du.edu.
Website: http://www.du.edu/ahss/schools/english/

University of Florida, Graduate School, College of Liberal Arts and Sciences, Department of English, Gainesville, FL 32611. Offers creative writing (MFA); English (MA, PhD). *Faculty:* 39 full-time (14 women), 4 part-time/adjunct (all women). *Students:* 93 full-time (58 women), 12 part-time (8 women); includes 20 minority (7 Black or African American, non-Hispanic/Latino; 1 American Indian or Alaska Native, non-Hispanic/Latino; 1 Asian, non-Hispanic/Latino; 11 Hispanic/Latino), 15 international. 192 applicants, 8% accepted, 9 enrolled. In 2014, 7 master's, 11 doctorates awarded. *Degree requirements:* For master's, one foreign language, comprehensive exam, thesis or alternative; for doctorate, one foreign language, comprehensive exam, thesis/dissertation. *Entrance requirements:* For master's and doctorate, GRE General Test, minimum GPA of 3.0. Additional exam requirements/recommendations for international students: Required—TOEFL (minimum score 550 paper-based; 80 iBT), IELTS (minimum score 6). *Application deadline:* For fall admission, 1/15 for domestic and international students; for spring admission, 1/1 for domestic and international students. Application fee: $30. Electronic applications accepted. *Financial support:* In 2014–15, 66 fellowships, 22 research assistantships, 113 teaching assistantships were awarded; unspecified assistantships also available. Financial award application deadline: 1/15; financial award applicants required to submit FAFSA. *Faculty research:* Modern global literatures in English, film and media studies, cultural studies and critical theory, American literature, English literature. *Unit head:* Kenneth Kidd, PhD, Professor and Department Chair, 352-294-2807, Fax: 352-392-0860, E-mail: kbkidd@ufl.edu. *Application contact:* Sid Dobrin, PhD, Professor and Graduate Coordinator, 352-294-2868, Fax: 352-392-0860, E-mail: sdobrin@ufl.edu.
Website: http://web.english.ufl.edu/

University of Georgia, Franklin College of Arts and Sciences, Department of English, Athens, GA 30602. Offers creative writing (MFA, PhD); English (MA, MAT, PhD). *Degree requirements:* For master's, one foreign language, thesis (MA); for doctorate, 2 foreign languages, thesis/dissertation. *Entrance requirements:* For master's and doctorate, GRE General Test. Additional exam requirements/recommendations for international students: Required—TWE. Electronic applications accepted.

University of Guam, Office of Graduate Studies, College of Liberal Arts and Social Sciences, Department of English, Mangilao, GU 96923. Offers MA. *Entrance requirements:* For master's, GRE. Additional exam requirements/recommendations for international students: Required—TOEFL.

University of Guelph, Graduate Studies, College of Arts, School of English and Theatre Studies, Program in English, Guelph, ON N1G 2W1, Canada. Offers MA. Part-time programs available. *Degree requirements:* For master's, thesis (for some programs). *Entrance requirements:* For master's, letters of reference, 4-year honours undergraduate degree in English or drama. Additional exam requirements/recommendations for international students: Required—TOEFL. Electronic applications accepted. *Faculty research:* Post-colonial literature, Canadian literature, children's literature, Scottish literature, American literature, cultural studies.

University of Hawaii at Manoa, Graduate Division, College of Languages, Linguistics and Literature, Department of English, Honolulu, HI 96822. Offers MA, PhD. Part-time programs available. *Degree requirements:* For master's, 2 foreign languages, thesis optional; for doctorate, 2 foreign languages, comprehensive exam, thesis/dissertation. *Entrance requirements:* For master's, GRE General Test; for doctorate, GRE General Test, GRE Subject Test. Additional exam requirements/recommendations for international students: Required—TOEFL (minimum score 600 paper-based; 100 iBT), IELTS (minimum score 7). *Faculty research:* British and American literature, creative writing, cultural studies, rhetoric and composition.

University of Houston–Clear Lake, School of Human Sciences and Humanities, Programs in Humanities and Fine Arts, Houston, TX 77058-1002. Offers history (MA); humanities (MA); literature (MA). Part-time and evening/weekend programs available. Postbaccalaureate distance learning degree programs offered (minimal on-campus study). *Degree requirements:* For master's, thesis or alternative. *Entrance requirements:* For master's, GRE General Test. Additional exam requirements/recommendations for international students: Required—TOEFL (minimum score 550 paper-based). *Faculty research:* Digital media studies, Latin American history, labor history, Chaucer evolution versus creationism debate.

University of Houston–Downtown, College of Humanities and Social Sciences, Department of English, Houston, TX 77002. Offers rhetoric and composition (MA); technical communication (MS). Part-time and evening/weekend programs available. *Faculty:* 6 full-time (3 women), 1 (woman) part-time/adjunct. *Students:* 7 full-time (5 women), 30 part-time (22 women); includes 16 minority (12 Black or African American, non-Hispanic/Latino; 1 Asian, non-Hispanic/Latino; 2 Hispanic/Latino; 1 Two or more

races, non-Hispanic/Latino), 1 international. Average age 38. 28 applicants, 86% accepted, 16 enrolled. In 2014, 3 master's awarded. *Entrance requirements:* Additional exam requirements/recommendations for international students: Required—TOEFL. *Application deadline:* For fall admission, 4/1 for domestic and international students; for spring admission, 11/15 for domestic and international students. Application fee: $35 ($60 for international students). Electronic applications accepted. *Expenses:* Expenses: $260 per credit state resident, $572 nonresident. *Financial support:* Applicants required to submit FAFSA. *Faculty research:* Environmental rhetoric, instructional design, usability, assessment, presentation slides. *Unit head:* Dr. Michelle Moosally, Chair, 713-221-8254, Fax: 713-226-5205, E-mail: moosallym@uhd.edu. *Application contact:* Ceshia Love, Director of Graduate and International Admissions, 713-221-8093, Fax: 713-223-7408, E-mail: gradadmissions@uhd.edu.
Website: https://www.uhd.edu/academics/humanities/Pages/humanities-index.aspx

University of Idaho, College of Graduate Studies, College of Letters, Arts and Social Sciences, Department of English, Moscow, ID 83844-1102. Offers creative writing (MFA); English (MA, MAT); teaching English as a second language (MA). *Faculty:* 17 full-time. *Students:* 64 full-time, 8 part-time. Average age 31. In 2014, 27 master's awarded. *Entrance requirements:* For master's, minimum GPA of 2.8. Additional exam requirements/recommendations for international students: Required—TOEFL (minimum score 550 paper-based). *Application deadline:* For fall admission, 8/1 for domestic students; for spring admission, 12/15 for domestic students. Applications are processed on a rolling basis. Application fee: $60. Electronic applications accepted. *Expenses:* Tuition, state resident: full-time $4784; part-time $280.50 per credit hour. Tuition, nonresident: full-time $18,314; part-time $957.50 per credit hour. *Required fees:* $2000; $58.50 per credit hour. Tuition and fees vary according to program. *Financial support:* Research assistantships and teaching assistantships available. Financial award applicants required to submit FAFSA. *Unit head:* Dr. Scott Slovic, Chair, 208-883-6156, E-mail: englishdept@uidaho.edu. *Application contact:* Sean Scoggin, Graduate Recruitment Coordinator, 208-885-4001, Fax: 208-885-4406, E-mail: graduateadmissions@uidaho.edu.
Website: http://www.uidaho.edu/class/english

University of Illinois at Chicago, Graduate College, College of Liberal Arts and Sciences, Department of English, Chicago, IL 60607-7128. Offers MA, PhD. Part-time and evening/weekend programs available. *Faculty:* 63 full-time (30 women), 9 part-time/adjunct (6 women). *Students:* 76 full-time (38 women), 32 part-time (15 women); includes 15 minority (5 Black or African American, non-Hispanic/Latino; 3 Asian, non-Hispanic/Latino; 4 Hispanic/Latino; 3 Two or more races, non-Hispanic/Latino), 10 international. Average age 33. 266 applicants, 26% accepted, 23 enrolled. In 2014, 10 master's, 12 doctorates awarded. *Degree requirements:* For doctorate, variable foreign language requirement, thesis/dissertation, written and oral exams. *Entrance requirements:* For master's, GRE General Test, GRE Subject Test; for doctorate, GRE General Test, GRE Subject Test, minimum GPA of 2.0. Additional exam requirements/recommendations for international students: Required—TOEFL. *Application deadline:* For fall admission, 1/1 for domestic and international students. Applications are processed on a rolling basis. Application fee: $60. Electronic applications accepted. *Expenses:* Tuition, state resident: full-time $11,254; part-time $468 per credit hour. Tuition, nonresident: full-time $23,252; part-time $968 per credit hour. *Required fees:* $1217 per term. Part-time tuition and fees vary according to course load, degree level and program. *Financial support:* In 2014–15, 3 fellowships with full tuition reimbursements were awarded; research assistantships with full tuition reimbursements, teaching assistantships with full tuition reimbursements, career-related internships or fieldwork, Federal Work-Study, institutionally sponsored loans, scholarships/grants, traineeships, tuition waivers (full), and unspecified assistantships also available. Financial award application deadline: 3/1; financial award applicants required to submit FAFSA. *Faculty research:* Literary history and theory. *Unit head:* Prof. Walter Benn Michaels, Head, 312-413-2203, Fax: 312-413-1005, E-mail: wbm@uic.edu. *Application contact:* Prof. Lennard Davis, Director of Graduate Studies, 312-413-2239, Fax: 312-355-6516, E-mail: lendavis@uic.edu.
Website: http://www.uic.edu/depts/engl/

University of Illinois at Springfield, Graduate Programs, College of Liberal Arts and Sciences, Department of English and Modern Languages, Springfield, IL 62703-5407. Offers English (MA); teaching English (Graduate Certificate). Part-time and evening/weekend programs available. *Faculty:* 5 full-time (4 women). *Students:* 6 part-time (5 women); includes 1 minority (Asian, non-Hispanic/Latino). Average age 33. 2 applicants, 50% accepted, 1 enrolled. In 2014, 6 master's, 3 other advanced degrees awarded. *Degree requirements:* For master's, comprehensive exam, thesis, or project. *Entrance requirements:* For master's, GRE General Test, analytical writing sample, two letters of recommendation. Additional exam requirements/recommendations for international students: Required—TOEFL (minimum score 500 paper-based; 61 iBT). *Application deadline:* Applications are processed on a rolling basis. Application fee: $60 ($75 for international students). Electronic applications accepted. *Expenses:* Tuition, state resident: full-time $7662; part-time $319.25 per credit hour. Tuition, nonresident: full-time $15,966; part-time $665.25 per credit hour. *Financial support:* In 2014–15, fellowships with full tuition reimbursements (averaging $9,900 per year), research assistantships with full tuition reimbursements (averaging $9,600 per year), teaching assistantships with full tuition reimbursements (averaging $9,600 per year) were awarded; career-related internships or fieldwork, Federal Work-Study, scholarships/grants, health care benefits, and unspecified assistantships also available. Support available to part-time students. Financial award application deadline: 11/15; financial award applicants required to submit FAFSA. *Unit head:* Dr. Tena Helton, Program Administrator, 217-206-7441, Fax: 217-206-6217, E-mail: thelt2@uis.edu. *Application contact:* Dr. Lynn Pardie, Office of Graduate Studies, 800-252-8533, Fax: 217-206-7623, E-mail: lpard1@uis.edu.

University of Illinois at Urbana–Champaign, Graduate College, College of Liberal Arts and Sciences, Department of English, Champaign, IL 61820. Offers creative writing (MFA); English (MA, PhD). *Students:* 116 (76 women). Application fee: $70 ($90 for international students). *Unit head:* Michael Rothberg, Head, 217-333-2391, Fax: 217-333-4321, E-mail: mpr@illinois.edu. *Application contact:* Stephanie Shockey, Office Support Specialist, 217-244-1464, Fax: 217-333-4321, E-mail: shockey@illinois.edu.
Website: http://www.english.illinois.edu/

University of Indianapolis, Graduate Programs, College of Arts and Sciences, Department of English Language and Literature, Indianapolis, IN 46227-3697. Offers English (MA). Part-time and evening/weekend programs available. *Faculty:* 6 full-time (5 women), 1 part-time/adjunct (0 women). *Students:* 5 full-time (2 women), 5 part-time (3 women); includes 1 minority (Two or more races, non-Hispanic/Latino), 1 international. Average age 33. In 2014, 4 master's awarded. *Entrance requirements:* For master's, GRE Subject Test, minimum GPA of 2.5. Additional exam requirements/recommendations for international students: Required—TOEFL (minimum score 550 paper-based). *Application deadline:* Applications are processed on a rolling basis. Application fee: $30. Electronic applications accepted. *Financial support:* Federal Work-Study, scholarships/grants, and tuition waivers (full and partial) available. Support available to part-time students. Financial award application deadline: 5/1; financial award applicants required to submit FAFSA. *Unit head:* Dr. William R. Dynes, Chair, 317-788-2072, Fax: 317-788-3480. *Application contact:* Linda Corn, Administrative Assistant, 317-788-3395, E-mail: lcorn@uindy.edu.
Website: http://english.uindy.edu/

The University of Iowa, Graduate College, College of Liberal Arts and Sciences, Department of English, Iowa City, IA 52242-1316. Offers English (PhD); literary studies (MA); nonfiction writing (MFA). *Degree requirements:* For master's, thesis (for some programs), exam; for doctorate, comprehensive exam, thesis/dissertation. *Entrance requirements:* For master's and doctorate, GRE General Test, minimum GPA of 3.0. Additional exam requirements/recommendations for international students: Required—TOEFL (minimum score 640 paper-based; 111 iBT). Electronic applications accepted.

The University of Kansas, Graduate Studies, College of Liberal Arts and Sciences, Department of English, Lawrence, KS 66045. Offers creative writing (MFA); English (MA, PhD). Part-time programs available. *Faculty:* 31 full-time, 36 part-time/adjunct. *Students:* 80 full-time (51 women), 5 part-time (2 women); includes 17 minority (6 Black or African American, non-Hispanic/Latino; 1 Asian, non-Hispanic/Latino; 4 Hispanic/Latino; 6 Two or more races, non-Hispanic/Latino), 2 international. Average age 30. 202 applicants, 24% accepted, 25 enrolled. In 2014, 12 master's, 15 doctorates awarded. *Degree requirements:* For master's, one foreign language, comprehensive exam (for some programs), thesis or alternative; for doctorate, 2 foreign languages, comprehensive exam, thesis/dissertation. *Entrance requirements:* For master's and doctorate, GRE General Test, minimum GPA of 3.3. Additional exam requirements/recommendations for international students: Required—TOEFL. *Application deadline:* For fall admission, 12/31 for domestic and international students. Application fee: $55 ($65 for international students). Electronic applications accepted. *Financial support:* Fellowships with full tuition reimbursements, research assistantships with full and partial tuition reimbursements, teaching assistantships with full and partial tuition reimbursements, and unspecified assistantships available. Financial award application deadline: 12/31. *Faculty research:* Ecocriticism and science/science fiction writing; gender and sexuality studies; U.S. ethnic literatures, race, and diaspora studies; composition, rhetoric, and language studies; creative writing. *Unit head:* Anna Neill, Chair, 785-864-2521, E-mail: aneill@ku.edu. *Application contact:* Lydia Ash, Graduate Secretary, 785-864-2518, E-mail: lash@ku.edu.
Website: http://www.english.ku.edu

University of Kentucky, Graduate School, College of Arts and Sciences, Program in English, Lexington, KY 40506-0032. Offers MA, PhD. *Degree requirements:* For master's, one foreign language, comprehensive exam, thesis optional; for doctorate, one foreign language, comprehensive exam, thesis/dissertation. *Entrance requirements:* For master's, GRE General Test, minimum undergraduate GPA of 2.75; for doctorate, GRE General Test, minimum graduate GPA of 3.0. Additional exam requirements/recommendations for international students: Required—TOEFL (minimum score 550 paper-based). Electronic applications accepted.

University of Lethbridge, School of Graduate Studies, Lethbridge, AB T1K 3M4, Canada. Offers addictions counseling (M Sc); agricultural biotechnology (M Sc); agricultural studies (M Sc, MA); anthropology (MA); archaeology (M Sc, MA); art (MA, MFA); biochemistry (M Sc); biological sciences (M Sc); biomolecular science (PhD); biosystems and biodiversity (PhD); Canadian studies (MA); chemistry (M Sc); computer science (M Sc); computer science and geographical information science (M Sc); counseling (MC); counseling psychology (M Ed); dramatic arts (MA); earth, space, and physical science (PhD); economics (MA); education (MA); educational leadership (M Ed); English (MA); environmental science (M Sc); evolution and behavior (PhD); exercise science (M Sc); French (MA); French/German (MA); French/Spanish (MA); general education (M Ed); geography (M Sc, MA); German (MA); health sciences (M Sc); individualized multidisciplinary (M Sc, MA); kinesiology (M Sc, MA); management (M Sc), including accounting, finance, general management, human resource management and labor relations, information systems, international management, marketing, policy and strategy; mathematics (M Sc); modern languages (MA); music (M Mus, MA); Native American studies (MA); neuroscience (M Sc, PhD); new media (MA, MFA); nursing (M Sc, MN); philosophy (MA); physics (M Sc); political science (MA); psychology (M Sc, MA); religious studies (MA); sociology (MA); theatre and dramatic arts (MFA); theoretical and computational science (PhD); urban and regional studies (MA); women and gender studies (MA). Part-time and evening/weekend programs available. *Faculty:* 358. *Students:* 445 full-time (243 women), 116 part-time (72 women). Average age 31. 351 applicants, 26% accepted, 87 enrolled. In 2014, 129 master's, 13 doctorates awarded. *Degree requirements:* For master's, thesis (for some programs); for doctorate, comprehensive exam, thesis/dissertation. *Entrance requirements:* For master's, GMAT (for M Sc in management), bachelor's degree in related field, minimum GPA of 3.0 during previous 20 graded semester courses, 2 years' teaching or related experience (M Ed); for doctorate, master's degree, minimum graduate GPA of 3.5. Additional exam requirements/recommendations for international students: Required—TOEFL. Application fee: $100 Canadian dollars. *Financial support:* Fellowships, research assistantships, teaching assistantships, scholarships/grants, health care benefits, and unspecified assistantships available. *Faculty research:* Movement and brain plasticity, gibberellin physiology, photosynthesis, carbon cycling, molecular properties of main-group ring components. *Application contact:* School of Graduate Studies, 403-329-5194, E-mail: sgsinquiries@uleth.ca.
Website: http://www.uleth.ca/graduatestudies/

University of Louisiana at Lafayette, College of Liberal Arts, Department of English, Lafayette, LA 70504. Offers British and American literature (MA), including creative writing, folklore, rhetoric; creative writing (PhD); literature (PhD); rhetoric (PhD). Part-time programs available. Terminal master's awarded for partial completion of doctoral program. *Degree requirements:* For master's, one foreign language, thesis or alternative; for doctorate, 2 foreign languages, comprehensive exam, thesis/dissertation. *Entrance requirements:* For master's, GRE General Test, minimum GPA of 2.75; for doctorate, GRE General Test, minimum GPA of 3.0. Additional exam requirements/recommendations for international students: Required—TOEFL (minimum score 550 paper-based). Electronic applications accepted. *Faculty research:* Composition theory, Southern literature, medieval literature.

University of Louisiana at Monroe, Graduate School, College of Arts, Education, and Sciences, Department of English, Monroe, LA 71209-0001. Offers MA. Part-time and evening/weekend programs available. *Degree requirements:* For master's, one foreign language, thesis (for some programs). *Entrance requirements:* For master's, GRE General Test (minimum score 900 verbal and quantitative), minimum GPA of 3.0 in English, 2.5 overall. Additional exam requirements/recommendations for international students: Required—TOEFL (minimum score 500 paper-based; 61 iBT) or Michigan English Language Assessment Battery. Electronic applications accepted. *Faculty research:* Creative writing, American literature, British literature, multicultural literature, literary theory.

University of Louisville, Graduate School, College of Arts and Sciences, Department of English, Louisville, KY 40292. Offers English (MA), including creative writing, literature, rhetoric and composition (MA, PhD); English rhetoric and composition (PhD), including rhetoric and composition (MA, PhD). Part-time programs available. *Students:* 62 full-time (39 women), 20 part-time (10 women); includes 6 minority (2 Black or African American, non-Hispanic/Latino; 2 Hispanic/Latino; 2 Two or more races, non-Hispanic/

Latino), 2 international. Average age 29. 94 applicants, 53% accepted, 25 enrolled. In 2014, 18 master's, 4 doctorates awarded. *Degree requirements:* For master's, one foreign language, thesis or culminating project; for doctorate, 2 foreign languages, comprehensive exam, thesis/dissertation. *Entrance requirements:* For master's, GRE General Test, 2 academic letters of recommendation; for doctorate, GRE General Test, 15-20 page critical writing sample, 1000-word statement of professional goals, 3 academic letters of recommendation, transcripts of all college work. Additional exam requirements/recommendations for international students: Required—TOEFL (minimum score 600 paper-based; 100 iBT). *Application deadline:* For fall admission, 8/1 for domestic students, 5/1 priority date for international students; for spring admission, 12/1 for domestic students, 11/1 priority date for international students; for summer admission, 4/1 priority date for international students. Applications are processed on a rolling basis. Application fee: $60. Electronic applications accepted. *Expenses:* Tuition, state resident: full-time $11,326; part-time $630 per credit hour. Tuition, nonresident: full-time $23,568; part-time $1311 per credit hour. *Required fees:* $196. Tuition and fees vary according to program and reciprocity agreements. *Financial support:* Fellowships with full tuition reimbursements, teaching assistantships with full tuition reimbursements, health care benefits, and unspecified assistantships available. Financial award application deadline: 1/5. *Faculty research:* American and English literatures and cultures, rhetoric and composition, critical theory and cultural studies, creative writing. *Unit head:* Dr. Glynis Ridley, Chair, 502-852-6803, E-mail: glynis.ridley@louisville.edu. *Application contact:* Libby Leggett, Director, Graduate Admissions, 502-852-3101, Fax: 502-852-6536, E-mail: gradadm@louisville.edu.
Website: http://www.louisville.edu/english/graduate

University of Maine, Graduate School, College of Liberal Arts and Sciences, Department of English, Orono, ME 04469. Offers composition and pedagogy (MA); gender and literature (MA). Part-time and evening/weekend programs available. *Faculty:* 19 full-time (10 women). *Students:* 25 full-time (18 women), 3 part-time (2 women), 2 international. Average age 29. 41 applicants, 73% accepted, 14 enrolled. In 2014, 3 master's awarded. *Degree requirements:* For master's, one foreign language, thesis optional. *Entrance requirements:* For master's, GRE General Test, minimum GPA of 3.0. Additional exam requirements/recommendations for international students: Required—TOEFL. *Application deadline:* For fall admission, 1/15 priority date for domestic students. Applications are processed on a rolling basis. Application fee: $65. Electronic applications accepted. *Expenses:* Tuition, state resident: part-time $658 per credit hour. Tuition, nonresident: part-time $1550 per credit hour. *Financial support:* In 2014–15, 24 students received support, including 21 teaching assistantships with full tuition reimbursements available (averaging $14,600 per year); Federal Work-Study and tuition waivers (full and partial) also available. Financial award application deadline: 3/1. *Faculty research:* Poetry and poetics, critical studies, medieval studies, gender theory, nineteenth- and twentieth-century literature, Native American literature. *Unit head:* Dr. Richard Brucher, Chair, 207-581-3823, Fax: 207-581-1604. *Application contact:* Scott G. Delcourt, Assistant Vice President for Graduate Studies and Senior Associate Dean, 207-581-3291, Fax: 207-581-3232, E-mail: graduate@maine.edu.
Website: http://english.umaine.edu/

The University of Manchester, School of Arts, Histories and Cultures, Manchester, United Kingdom. Offers anthropology, media and performance (PhD); applied theatre professional (PhD); archaeology (PhD); art history and visual studies (PhD); arts management and cultural policy (PhD); classics and ancient history (PhD); composition (PhD); creative writing (PhD); drama (PhD); economic and social history (PhD); electroacoustic composition (PhD); English and American studies (PhD); history (PhD); humanitarianism and conflict response (PhD); museology (PhD); music (PhD); musicology (PhD); religions and theology (PhD).

University of Manitoba, Faculty of Graduate Studies, Faculty of Arts, Department of English, Film, and Theatre, Winnipeg, MB R3T 2N2, Canada. Offers English (MA, PhD). *Degree requirements:* For master's, one foreign language, thesis; for doctorate, one foreign language, thesis/dissertation.

University of Maryland, Baltimore County, The Graduate School, College of Arts, Humanities and Social Sciences, Program in English: Texts, Technologies, and Literature, Baltimore, MD 21250. Offers MA. Part-time programs available. *Faculty:* 10 full-time (8 women). *Students:* 3 full-time (all women), 10 part-time (6 women); includes 2 minority (1 Black or African American, non-Hispanic/Latino; 1 Hispanic/Latino). 9 applicants, 78% accepted, 5 enrolled. *Degree requirements:* For master's, thesis or portfolio. *Entrance requirements:* For master's, GRE. Additional exam requirements/recommendations for international students: Required—TOEFL. *Application deadline:* For fall admission, 5/1 for domestic students; for spring admission, 5/1 for domestic students. Applications are processed on a rolling basis. Electronic applications accepted. *Expenses:* Tuition, state resident: part-time $557. Tuition, nonresident: part-time $922. *Required fees:* $122 per semester. One-time fee: $200 part-time. *Financial support:* In 2014–15, 2 students received support, including 2 teaching assistantships (averaging $11,500 per year). Financial award application deadline: 5/1. *Unit head:* Dr. Orianne Smith, Graduate Program Director, 410-455-2384, Fax: 410-455-3010, E-mail: osmith@umbc.edu. *Application contact:* Dr. Lucille McCarthy, Graduate Program Director, 410-455-2384, Fax: 410-455-3010, E-mail: mccarthy@umbc.edu.
Website: http://www.umbc.edu/english/ma.html

University of Maryland, College Park, Academic Affairs, College of Arts and Humanities, Department of English, Program in English Language and Literature, College Park, MD 20742. Offers MA, PhD. *Degree requirements:* For master's, thesis optional; for doctorate, one foreign language, thesis/dissertation, oral and written exams. *Entrance requirements:* For master's, GRE General Test, minimum GPA of 3.5, writing sample, 3 letters of recommendation; for doctorate, GRE General Test, minimum GPA of 3.7, writing sample. Additional exam requirements/recommendations for international students: Required—TOEFL. Electronic applications accepted.

University of Massachusetts Amherst, Graduate School, College of Humanities and Fine Arts, Department of English, Amherst, MA 01003. Offers American studies (PhD); composition and rhetoric (PhD); creative writing (MFA); English and American literature (MA, PhD). Part-time programs available. *Faculty:* 49 full-time (24 women). *Students:* 100 full-time (60 women), 76 part-time (50 women); includes 29 minority (2 Black or African American, non-Hispanic/Latino; 6 Asian, non-Hispanic/Latino; 10 Hispanic/Latino; 1 Native Hawaiian or other Pacific Islander, non-Hispanic/Latino; 10 Two or more races, non-Hispanic/Latino), 17 international. Average age 30. 600 applicants, 12% accepted, 29 enrolled. In 2014, 26 master's, 10 doctorates awarded. Terminal master's awarded for partial completion of doctoral program. *Degree requirements:* For master's, one foreign language, thesis optional; for doctorate, one foreign language, comprehensive exam, thesis/dissertation. *Entrance requirements:* For master's, manuscript; for doctorate, GRE General Test, manuscript. Additional exam requirements/recommendations for international students: Required—TOEFL (minimum score 550 paper-based; 80 iBT), IELTS (minimum score 6.5). *Application deadline:* For fall admission, 12/15 for domestic and international students. Applications are processed on a rolling basis. Application fee: $75. Electronic applications accepted. *Expenses:* Tuition, state resident: full-time $1980; part-time $110 per credit. Tuition, nonresident: full-time $14,644; part-time $414 per credit. *Required fees:* $11,417. One-time fee: $357. *Financial support:* Fellowships with full and partial tuition reimbursements, research assistantships with full and partial tuition reimbursements, teaching assistantships with full and partial tuition reimbursements, career-related internships or fieldwork, Federal Work-Study, scholarships/grants, traineeships, health care benefits, tuition waivers (full and partial), and unspecified assistantships available. Support available to part-time students. Financial award application deadline: 12/15. *Unit head:* Dr. Jenny Spencer, Department Head, 413-545-2332, Fax: 413-545-3880. *Application contact:* Lindsay DeSantis, Supervisor of Admissions, 413-545-0722, Fax: 413-577-0010, E-mail: gradadm@grad.umass.edu.
Website: http://www.umass.edu/english/

University of Massachusetts Boston, College of Liberal Arts, Program in English, Boston, MA 02125-3393. Offers MA. Part-time and evening/weekend programs available. *Degree requirements:* For master's, one foreign language, final project. *Entrance requirements:* For master's, minimum GPA of 2.75. *Application deadline:* For fall admission, 3/1 for domestic students; for spring admission, 11/1 for domestic students. *Expenses:* Tuition, state resident: full-time $2590; part-time $108 per credit. Tuition, nonresident: full-time $9758; part-time $406.50 per credit. Tuition and fees vary according to course load and program. *Financial support:* Research assistantships with full tuition reimbursements, teaching assistantships with full tuition reimbursements, career-related internships or fieldwork, Federal Work-Study, and unspecified assistantships available. Support available to part-time students. Financial award application deadline: 3/1; financial award applicants required to submit FAFSA. *Faculty research:* Working class literature, women writers, British fiction, composition theory, modern American literature. *Unit head:* Dr. Pamela Annas, Director, 617-287-6700, E-mail: pamela.annas@umb.edu. *Application contact:* Peggy Roldan Patel, Graduate Admissions Coordinator, 617-287-6400, Fax: 617-287-6236, E-mail: bos.gadm@dpc.umassp.edu.

University of Memphis, Graduate School, College of Arts and Sciences, Department of English, Memphis, TN 38152. Offers African-American literature (Graduate Certificate); applied linguistics (PhD); composition studies (PhD); creative writing (MFA); English as a second language (MA); linguistics (MA); literary and cultural studies (PhD), including African-American literature; literature (MA); professional writing (MA, PhD); teaching English as a second language (Graduate Certificate). Part-time and evening/weekend programs available. Postbaccalaureate distance learning degree programs offered (no on-campus study). *Faculty:* 30 full-time (15 women), 1 part-time/adjunct (0 women). *Students:* 89 full-time (45 women), 85 part-time (57 women); includes 35 minority (23 Black or African American, non-Hispanic/Latino; 6 Asian, non-Hispanic/Latino; 5 Hispanic/Latino; 1 Two or more races, non-Hispanic/Latino), 17 international. Average age 35. 83 applicants, 88% accepted, 19 enrolled. In 2014, 29 master's, 6 doctorates awarded. Terminal master's awarded for partial completion of doctoral program. *Degree requirements:* For master's, one foreign language, comprehensive exam, thesis optional; for doctorate, 2 foreign languages, comprehensive exam, thesis/dissertation. *Entrance requirements:* For master's and doctorate, GRE. Additional exam requirements/recommendations for international students: Required—TOEFL. *Application deadline:* For fall admission, 7/1 for domestic students; for spring admission, 10/15 for domestic students. Applications are processed on a rolling basis. Application fee: $35 ($60 for international students). Electronic applications accepted. *Financial support:* In 2014–15, 123 students received support. Research assistantships with full tuition reimbursements available, teaching assistantships with full tuition reimbursements available, Federal Work-Study, scholarships/grants, and unspecified assistantships available. Financial award application deadline: 2/15; financial award applicants required to submit FAFSA. *Faculty research:* Applied linguistics, British and American literature, professional writing, composition studies. *Unit head:* Dr. Joshua Phillips, Chair, 901-678-3067, Fax: 901-678-2226, E-mail: jsphllps@memphis.edu. *Application contact:* Dr. Jeffrey Scraba, Director, Graduate Studies, 901-678-3099, Fax: 901-678-2226, E-mail: jscraba@memphis.edu.
Website: http://www.memphis.edu/english

University of Miami, Graduate School, College of Arts and Sciences, Department of English, Coral Gables, FL 33124. Offers creative writing (MFA); English (MA, PhD). Part-time programs available. Terminal master's awarded for partial completion of doctoral program. *Degree requirements:* For master's, one foreign language, thesis optional; for doctorate, one foreign language, thesis/dissertation. *Entrance requirements:* For master's and doctorate, GRE General Test. Electronic applications accepted. *Faculty research:* Anglo-Irish literature, feminist criticism and theory, Caribbean literature, early modern literature and culture, postcolonial and ethnic studies.

University of Michigan, Horace H. Rackham School of Graduate Studies, College of Literature, Science, and the Arts, Department of English Language and Literature, Ann Arbor, MI 48109. Offers creative writing (MFA); English and education (PhD); English and women's studies (PhD); English language and literature (PhD). *Faculty:* 50 full-time (28 women). *Students:* 74 full-time (49 women); includes 14 minority (4 Black or African American, non-Hispanic/Latino; 1 American Indian or Alaska Native, non-Hispanic/Latino; 5 Asian, non-Hispanic/Latino; 4 Hispanic/Latino), 2 international. 400 applicants, 6% accepted, 12 enrolled. *Degree requirements:* For doctorate, 2 foreign languages, comprehensive exam, thesis/dissertation, oral defense of dissertation, preliminary exam. *Entrance requirements:* For doctorate, GRE General Test, writing sample. Additional exam requirements/recommendations for international students: Required—TOEFL (minimum score 620 paper-based; 106 iBT). *Application deadline:* For fall admission, 12/15 for domestic and international students. Application fee: $75 ($90 for international students). Electronic applications accepted. *Financial support:* Fellowships with full tuition reimbursements, teaching assistantships with full tuition reimbursements, and health care benefits available. *Faculty research:* Post colonialism, modernism, early modern, American, British. *Application contact:* Graduate Admissions, 734-763-4139, Fax: 734-763-3128, E-mail: grad.eng.admis@um.cc.umich.edu.
Website: http://www.umich.edu/~engldept/

University of Michigan, Horace H. Rackham School of Graduate Studies, College of Literature, Science, and the Arts, Department of Women's Studies, Ann Arbor, MI 48109. Offers English and women's studies (PhD); history and women's studies (PhD); LGBTQ studies (Certificate); psychology and women's studies (PhD); women's studies (Certificate). *Faculty:* 36 full-time. *Students:* 58 full-time (48 women). 119 applicants, 8% accepted, 6 enrolled. In 2014, 7 doctorates, 4 other advanced degrees awarded. *Degree requirements:* For doctorate, variable foreign language requirement, comprehensive exam (for some programs), thesis/dissertation. *Entrance requirements:* For doctorate, GRE General Test, previous undergraduate coursework in women's studies. *Application deadline:* For fall admission, 12/1 for domestic and international students. Application fee: $75 ($90 for international students). Electronic applications accepted. *Financial support:* In 2014–15, fellowships with full tuition reimbursements (averaging $18,000 per year), research assistantships with full tuition reimbursements (averaging $18,000 per year), teaching assistantships with full tuition reimbursements (averaging $18,000 per year) were awarded; scholarships/grants, health care benefits, tuition waivers (full), and unspecified assistantships also available. *Faculty research:* LGBTQ studies, sexuality studies, feminist science studies, global feminism, health studies, international studies, cultural studies. *Unit head:* Lilia Cortina, Director of Graduate Studies, 734-763-2047, Fax: 734-647-4943, E-mail: lilia@umich.edu. *Application contact:* Aimee Germain,

Graduate Program Coordinator, 734-763-2047, Fax: 734-647-4943, E-mail: wsdgradinquiry@umich.edu. Website: http://www.lsa.umich.edu/women/

University of Michigan–Flint, College of Arts and Sciences, Program in English Language and Literature, Flint, MI 48502-1950. Offers literature (MA); writing and rhetoric (MA). Part-time programs available. *Faculty:* 28 full-time (18 women), 4 part-time/adjunct (2 women). *Students:* 3 full-time (2 women), 21 part-time (15 women); includes 3 minority (1 Black or African American, non-Hispanic/Latino; 1 Hispanic/Latino; 1 Two or more races, non-Hispanic/Latino), 2 international. Average age 36. 10 applicants, 70% accepted, 5 enrolled. In 2014, 20 master's awarded. *Entrance requirements:* For master's, minimum GPA of 3.0, bachelor's degree with major or significant coursework in English or related fields. Additional exam requirements/recommendations for international students: Required—TOEFL (minimum score 84 iBT), IELTS (minimum score 6.5). *Application deadline:* For fall admission, 8/1 for domestic students, 5/1 for international students; for winter admission, 11/15 for domestic students, 9/1 for international students; for spring admission, 3/15 for domestic students, 1/1 for international students; for summer admission, 5/15 for domestic students. Applications are processed on a rolling basis. Application fee: $55. Electronic applications accepted. *Expenses:* Expenses: Contact institution. *Financial support:* Federal Work-Study, scholarships/grants, and unspecified assistantships available. Support available to part-time students. Financial award application deadline: 3/1; financial award applicants required to submit FAFSA. *Unit head:* Dr. Kazuko Hiramatsu, Director, 810-762-3285, E-mail: kazukoh@umflint.edu. *Application contact:* Bradley T. Maki, Director of Graduate Admissions, 810-762-3171, Fax: 810-766-6789, E-mail: bmaki@umflint.edu.
Website: http://www.umflint.edu/graduateprograms/english-language-and-literature-ma

University of Minnesota, Duluth, Graduate School, College of Liberal Arts, Department of English, Duluth, MN 55812-2496. Offers MA. Part-time programs available. *Degree requirements:* For master's, one foreign language, comprehensive exam, 2 extended papers or projects. *Entrance requirements:* For master's, GRE General Test, minimum GPA of 3.0. Additional exam requirements/recommendations for international students: Required—TOEFL. *Faculty research:* British cultural studies, Irish literature, American studies, linguistics, information design.

University of Minnesota, Twin Cities Campus, Graduate School, College of Liberal Arts, Department of English, Minneapolis, MN 55455. Offers MA, PhD. Terminal master's awarded for partial completion of doctoral program. *Degree requirements:* For master's, one foreign language, thesis or alternative; for doctorate, 2 foreign languages, thesis/dissertation. *Entrance requirements:* For master's and doctorate, GRE General Test. Additional exam requirements/recommendations for international students: Required—TOEFL (minimum score 620 paper-based, 105 iBT) or IELTS (minimum score 7.5). Electronic applications accepted. *Faculty research:* British and American literature, medieval and early modern literature, postcolonial and contemporary literature, feminist studies, film and cultural studies.

University of Mississippi, Graduate School, College of Liberal Arts, Department of English, University, MS 38677. Offers MA, MFA, PhD. *Degree requirements:* For master's, one foreign language, thesis; for doctorate, 2 foreign languages, thesis/dissertation. *Entrance requirements:* For master's, GRE General Test, minimum GPA of 3.0; for doctorate, GRE General Test. Additional exam requirements/recommendations for international students: Required—TOEFL.

University of Missouri, Office of Research and Graduate Studies, College of Arts and Science, Department of English, Columbia, MO 65211. Offers MA, PhD. *Faculty:* 56 full-time (32 women), 5 part-time/adjunct (3 women). *Students:* 62 full-time (36 women), 26 part-time (14 women); includes 15 minority (6 Black or African American, non-Hispanic/Latino; 1 American Indian or Alaska Native, non-Hispanic/Latino; 3 Asian, non-Hispanic/Latino; 5 Hispanic/Latino), 7 international. Average age 32. 195 applicants, 14% accepted, 16 enrolled. In 2014, 6 master's, 10 doctorates awarded. Terminal master's awarded for partial completion of doctoral program. *Degree requirements:* For doctorate, 2 foreign languages, comprehensive exam, thesis/dissertation. *Entrance requirements:* For master's, GRE General Test, minimum GPA of 3.0; for doctorate, GRE General Test, minimum GPA of 3.0; MA in English or equivalent. Additional exam requirements/recommendations for international students: Required—TOEFL (minimum score 500 paper-based; 61 iBT). *Application deadline:* For fall admission, 1/1 priority date for domestic and international students. Applications are processed on a rolling basis. Application fee: $55 ($75 for international students). Electronic applications accepted. *Financial support:* Fellowships with full tuition reimbursements, research assistantships with full tuition reimbursements, teaching assistantships with full tuition reimbursements, institutionally sponsored loans, health care benefits, and unspecified assistantships available. *Faculty research:* British and American literature and culture, African Diaspora studies, creative writing, folklore, linguistics, rhetoric and composition. *Unit head:* Dr. David Read, Department Chair, 573-882-6066, E-mail: readd@missouri.edu. *Application contact:* Vickie Thorp, Senior Secretary, 573-882-4676, E-mail: thorpv@missouri.edu.
Website: http://english.missouri.edu/graduate.html

University of Missouri–Kansas City, College of Arts and Sciences, Department of English Language and Literature, Kansas City, MO 64110-2499. Offers creative writing and media arts (MFA); English (MA, PhD). PhD (interdisciplinary) offered through the School of Graduate Studies. Part-time and evening/weekend programs available. *Faculty:* 24 full-time (15 women), 8 part-time/adjunct (6 women). *Students:* 17 full-time (10 women), 34 part-time (21 women); includes 5 minority (2 Black or African American, non-Hispanic/Latino; 1 Asian, non-Hispanic/Latino; 1 Hispanic/Latino; 1 Two or more races, non-Hispanic/Latino). Average age 33. 58 applicants, 43% accepted, 14 enrolled. In 2014, 16 master's awarded. *Degree requirements:* For master's, one foreign language; for doctorate, 2 foreign languages, comprehensive exam, thesis/dissertation. *Entrance requirements:* For master's, GRE General Test, 3 letters of recommendation. Additional exam requirements/recommendations for international students: Required—TOEFL (minimum score 550 paper-based; 80 iBT). *Application deadline:* For fall admission, 1/15 for domestic students, 1/15 priority date for international students. Applications are processed on a rolling basis. Application fee: $45 ($50 for international students). Electronic applications accepted. *Financial support:* In 2014–15, 16 teaching assistantships (averaging $12,150 per year) were awarded; career-related internships or fieldwork, Federal Work-Study, and institutionally sponsored loans also available. Support available to part-time students. Financial award application deadline: 3/1; financial award applicants required to submit FAFSA. *Faculty research:* Creative writing: poetry and prose, computational linguistics, rhetoric and composition, African-American and British literature, print culture. *Unit head:* Dr. Virginia Blanton, Co-Chair, 816-235-2560, Fax: 816-235-1308, E-mail: blantonv@umkc.edu. *Application contact:* Dr. John Cyril Barton, Director of Graduate Studies, 816-235-5206, E-mail: bartonjc@umkc.edu.
Website: http://cas.umkc.edu/english/

University of Missouri–St. Louis, College of Arts and Sciences, Department of English, St. Louis, MO 63121. Offers MA, MFA. Part-time and evening/weekend programs available. *Faculty:* 19 full-time (6 women), 3 part-time/adjunct (all women). *Students:* 22 full-time (13 women), 52 part-time (33 women); includes 15 minority (3 Black or African American, non-Hispanic/Latino; 1 American Indian or Alaska Native, non-Hispanic/Latino; 2 Asian, non-Hispanic/Latino; 7 Hispanic/Latino; 2 Two or more races, non-Hispanic/Latino), 1 international. Average age 31. 65 applicants, 62% accepted, 17 enrolled. In 2014, 32 master's awarded. *Degree requirements:* For master's, thesis optional. *Entrance requirements:* For master's, two letters of recommendation; writing sample (MFA). Additional exam requirements/recommendations for international students: Required—TOEFL (minimum score 550 paper-based; 79 iBT), IELTS (minimum score 6.5). *Application deadline:* For fall admission, 7/1 priority date for domestic and international students; for spring admission, 12/1 priority date for domestic and international students. Applications are processed on a rolling basis. Application fee: $50 ($40 for international students). Electronic applications accepted. *Expenses:* Tuition, state resident: full-time $7364; part-time $409.10 per hour. Tuition, nonresident: full-time $18,153; part-time $1008.50 per hour. *Financial support:* In 2014–15, 6 teaching assistantships with full and partial tuition reimbursements (averaging $12,375 per year) were awarded. Financial award applicants required to submit FAFSA. *Faculty research:* Victorian literature, Shakespeare and Renaissance literature, eighteenth-century literature, composition theory. *Unit head:* Dr. Frank Grady, Director of Graduate Studies, 314-516-5541, Fax: 314-516-5781, E-mail: fgrady@umsl.edu. *Application contact:* 314-516-5458, Fax: 314-516-5310, E-mail: gradadm@umsl.edu.
Website: http://www.umsl.edu/~english/

The University of Montana, Graduate School, College of Humanities and Sciences, Department of English, Program in Literature, Missoula, MT 59812-0002. Offers MA. *Degree requirements:* For master's, thesis optional. *Entrance requirements:* For master's, GRE General Test, sample of written work. Additional exam requirements/recommendations for international students: Required—TOEFL. *Faculty research:* Literary history, cultural studies, criticism and theory, Western studies.

University of Montevallo, College of Arts and Sciences, Department of English, Montevallo, AL 35115. Offers English literature (MA). Part-time programs available. *Students:* 2 full-time (0 women), 6 part-time (2 women); includes 1 minority (Hispanic/Latino). In 2014, 9 master's awarded. *Degree requirements:* For master's, comprehensive exam, thesis optional. *Entrance requirements:* For master's, GRE General Test, MAT, minimum undergraduate GPA of 2.75 in last 60 hours or 2.5 overall, bachelor's degree in English or equivalent. Additional exam requirements/recommendations for international students: Required—TOEFL (minimum score 550 paper-based). *Application deadline:* For fall admission, 7/15 for domestic students; for spring admission, 11/15 for domestic students. Application fee: $25. *Financial support:* Federal Work-Study, scholarships/grants, and unspecified assistantships available. *Unit head:* Dr. Paul Mahaffey, Chair, 205-665-6420, E-mail: mahaffey@montevallo.edu. *Application contact:* Kevin Thornthwaite, Acting Director, Graduate Studies, 205-665-6350, E-mail: graduate@montevallo.edu.
Website: http://www.montevallo.edu/english/

University of Nebraska at Kearney, Graduate Studies and Research, College of Fine Arts and Humanities, Department of English, Kearney, NE 68849-0001. Offers creative writing (MA); literature (MA). Part-time and evening/weekend programs available. *Faculty:* 13 full-time (8 women). *Students:* 4 part-time (1 woman); includes 1 minority (Hispanic/Latino). 5 applicants, 80% accepted, 2 enrolled. *Degree requirements:* For master's, comprehensive exam (for some programs), thesis optional, thesis or exam (for literature option). *Entrance requirements:* For master's, GRE General Test, writing sample, three letters of recommendation, letter of interest. Additional exam requirements/recommendations for international students: Recommended—TOEFL (minimum score 550 paper-based; 79 iBT), IELTS (minimum score 6.5). *Application deadline:* For fall admission, 6/15 for domestic students, 5/15 for international students; for spring admission, 10/15 for domestic and international students; for summer admission, 3/15 for domestic and international students. Application fee: $45. Electronic applications accepted. *Expenses:* Tuition, state resident: full-time $3897; part-time $216.50 per credit hour. Tuition, nonresident: full-time $8550; part-time $475 per credit hour. *Required fees:* $414; $23 per credit. $96.50 per semester. One-time fee: $45. Tuition and fees vary according to course load and program. *Financial support:* In 2014–15, 2 teaching assistantships with full tuition reimbursements (averaging $9,900 per year) were awarded; research assistantships, career-related internships or fieldwork, scholarships/grants, and unspecified assistantships also available. Support available to part-time students. Financial award application deadline: 2/28; financial award applicants required to submit FAFSA. *Faculty research:* Narrative theory, popular culture, western and plains literature, women's studies, media studies. *Unit head:* Dr. Samuel J. Umland, Chair, 308-865-8299, E-mail: umlands@unk.edu. *Application contact:* Dr. Martha Kruse, Graduate Program Committee Chair, 308-865-8415, E-mail: krusem@unk.edu.
Website: http://www.unk.edu/academics/english/graduate_program.php

University of Nebraska at Omaha, Graduate Studies, College of Arts and Sciences, Department of English, Omaha, NE 68182. Offers advanced writing (Certificate); English (MA); teaching English to speakers of other languages (Certificate). Part-time and evening/weekend programs available. *Faculty:* 22 full-time (13 women). *Students:* 6 full-time (4 women), 51 part-time (31 women); includes 2 minority (1 Black or African American, non-Hispanic/Latino; 1 Two or more races, non-Hispanic/Latino). Average age 35. 26 applicants, 73% accepted, 12 enrolled. In 2014, 18 master's, 20 other advanced degrees awarded. *Degree requirements:* For master's, comprehensive exam, thesis (for some programs). *Entrance requirements:* For master's, GRE or MAT, minimum GPA of 3.0, transcripts, 3 letters of recommendation, statement of purpose, writing sample; for Certificate, minimum GPA of 3.0, transcripts, statement of purpose. Additional exam requirements/recommendations for international students: Required—TOEFL, IELTS, PTE. *Application deadline:* For fall admission, 8/1 for domestic students; for spring admission, 12/1 for domestic students. Applications are processed on a rolling basis. Application fee: $45. Electronic applications accepted. *Financial support:* In 2014–15, 16 students received support, including 2 research assistantships, 14 teaching assistantships with tuition reimbursements available; fellowships, Federal Work-Study, institutionally sponsored loans, scholarships/grants, tuition waivers (partial), and unspecified assistantships also available. Support available to part-time students. Financial award application deadline: 3/1; financial award applicants required to submit FAFSA. *Unit head:* Dr. Robert Darcy, Chairperson, 402-554-2341, E-mail: graduate@unomaha.edu. *Application contact:* Dr. Tracy Bridgeford, Graduate Program Chair, 402-554-2341, E-mail: graduate@unomaha.edu.

University of Nebraska–Lincoln, Graduate College, College of Arts and Sciences, Department of English, Lincoln, NE 68588-0333. Offers composition and rhetoric (MA, PhD); creative writing (MA, PhD); literature studies (MA, PhD). *Degree requirements:* For master's, thesis optional; for doctorate, one foreign language, comprehensive exam, thesis/dissertation. *Entrance requirements:* For master's, writing sample; for doctorate, GRE General Test, writing sample. Additional exam requirements/recommendations for international students: Required—TOEFL (minimum score 600 paper-based). Electronic applications accepted. *Faculty research:* Creative writing, composition and rhetoric, women's studies, North American literature, medieval/Renaissance studies.

University of Nevada, Las Vegas, Graduate College, College of Liberal Arts, Department of English, Las Vegas, NV 89154-5011. Offers creative writing (MFA); English (MA, PhD). Part-time programs available. *Faculty:* 25 full-time (12 women), 1 part-time/adjunct (0 women). *Students:* 61 full-time (31 women), 15 part-time (7 women);

includes 17 minority (1 Black or African American, non-Hispanic/Latino; 3 Asian, non-Hispanic/Latino; 5 Hispanic/Latino; 2 Native Hawaiian or other Pacific Islander, non-Hispanic/Latino; 6 Two or more races, non-Hispanic/Latino), 3 international. Average age 34. 192 applicants, 15% accepted, 18 enrolled. In 2014, 12 master's, 5 doctorates awarded. *Degree requirements:* For master's, one foreign language, comprehensive exam, thesis (for some programs); for doctorate, 2 foreign languages, comprehensive exam, thesis/dissertation. *Entrance requirements:* For master's, GRE General Test; for doctorate, GRE General Test, GRE Subject Test. Additional exam requirements/recommendations for international students: Required—TOEFL (minimum score 550 paper-based; 80 iBT), IELTS (minimum score 7). *Application deadline:* For fall admission, 1/15 for domestic students, 5/1 for international students; for spring admission, 11/1 for domestic students, 10/1 for international students. Application fee: $60 ($95 for international students). Electronic applications accepted. *Financial support:* In 2014–15, 57 students received support, including 57 teaching assistantships with partial tuition reimbursements available (averaging $13,088 per year); institutionally sponsored loans, scholarships/grants, health care benefits, and unspecified assistantships also available. Financial award application deadline: 3/1. *Faculty research:* Creative writing, poetry, fiction. *Unit head:* Dr. Richard Harp, Chair/Professor, 702-895-1258, Fax: 702-895-4801, E-mail: richard.harp@unlv.edu. *Application contact:* Graduate College Admissions Evaluator, 702-895-3320, Fax: 702-895-4180, E-mail: gradcollege@unlv.edu.
Website: http://english.unlv.edu/

University of Nevada, Reno, Graduate School, College of Liberal Arts, Department of English, Reno, NV 89557. Offers MA, MATE, PhD. Terminal master's awarded for partial completion of doctoral program. *Degree requirements:* For master's, variable foreign language requirement, thesis optional; for doctorate, variable foreign language requirement, thesis/dissertation. *Entrance requirements:* For master's, GRE General Test, minimum GPA of 2.75; for doctorate, GRE General Test, minimum GPA of 3.0. Additional exam requirements/recommendations for international students: Required—TOEFL (minimum score 500 paper-based; 61 iBT), IELTS (minimum score 6). Electronic applications accepted. *Faculty research:* Translating Persian/Iraqi literature, Shakespearean literature, modern American literature, composition and rhetoric.

University of New Brunswick Fredericton, School of Graduate Studies, Faculty of Arts, Department of English, Fredericton, NB E3B 5A3, Canada. Offers MA, PhD. Part-time programs available. *Faculty:* 20 full-time (10 women), 2 part-time/adjunct (0 women). *Students:* 27 full-time (16 women), 5 part-time (2 women). Average age 25. 62 applicants, 53% accepted, 15 enrolled. In 2014, 6 master's, 2 doctorates awarded. *Degree requirements:* For master's, thesis, 18 credit hours; for doctorate, one foreign language, comprehensive exam, thesis/dissertation. *Entrance requirements:* For master's, BA with minimum GPA of 3.5, honors English (preferred); for doctorate, minimum GPA of 3.7; MA in English. Additional exam requirements/recommendations for international students: Required—TWE (minimum score 4), TOEFL (minimum paper-based score 600) or IELTS (minimum score 7). *Application deadline:* For winter admission, 1/15 priority date for domestic and international students. Applications are processed on a rolling basis. Application fee: $50 Canadian dollars. Electronic applications accepted. *Financial support:* Fellowships, research assistantships with full tuition reimbursements, teaching assistantships with full tuition reimbursements, and health care benefits available. Financial award application deadline: 1/31. *Faculty research:* Creative writing, Canadian and maritime literature, post-Colonial/Commonwealth literature, early modern/Renaissance literature, scholarly editing and textual studies, American literature, British literature, film. *Unit head:* Dr. Edith Snook, Director of Graduate Studies, 506-458-7397, Fax: 506-453-5069, E-mail: esnook@unb.ca. *Application contact:* Theresa Keenan, Graduate Secretary, 506-451-6809, Fax: 506-453-5069, E-mail: tkeenan@unb.ca.
Website: http://go.unb.ca/gradprograms

University of New Hampshire, Graduate School, College of Liberal Arts, Department of English, Durham, NH 03824. Offers English (PhD); English education (MST); language and linguistics (MA); literature (MA). Part-time programs available. *Faculty:* 36 full-time (19 women). *Students:* 57 full-time (39 women), 38 part-time (22 women); includes 7 minority (2 Black or African American, non-Hispanic/Latino; 4 Hispanic/Latino; 1 Two or more races, non-Hispanic/Latino), 8 international. Average age 31. 194 applicants, 53% accepted, 32 enrolled. In 2014, 26 master's, 1 doctorate awarded. *Degree requirements:* For master's, one foreign language; for doctorate, 2 foreign languages, thesis/dissertation. *Entrance requirements:* For master's, GRE General Test, sample of written work; for doctorate, GRE General Test, GRE Subject Test, sample of written work. Additional exam requirements/recommendations for international students: Required—TOEFL (minimum score 550 paper-based; 80 iBT). *Application deadline:* For fall admission, 6/1 priority date for domestic students, 2/15 for international students; for spring admission, 12/1 for domestic students. Applications are processed on a rolling basis. Application fee: $65. Electronic applications accepted. *Expenses:* Tuition, state resident: full-time $13,500; part-time $750 per credit hour. Tuition, nonresident: full-time $26,460; part-time $1110 per credit hour. *Required fees:* $1788; $447 per semester. *Financial support:* In 2014–15, 56 students received support, including 2 fellowships, 42 teaching assistantships; research assistantships, career-related internships or fieldwork, Federal Work-Study, scholarships/grants, and tuition waivers (full and partial) also available. Support available to part-time students. Financial award application deadline: 2/15. *Unit head:* Dr. Rachel Trubowitz, Chairperson, 603-862-0254. *Application contact:* Janine Wilks, Administrative Assistant, 603-862-3963, E-mail: engl.grad@unh.edu.
Website: http://cola.unh.edu/english

University of New Mexico, Graduate School, College of Arts and Sciences, Program in English, Albuquerque, NM 87131. Offers MA, PhD. *Faculty:* 19 full-time (10 women), 2 part-time/adjunct (1 woman). *Students:* 54 full-time (40 women), 19 part-time (14 women); includes 12 minority (1 American Indian or Alaska Native, non-Hispanic/Latino; 9 Hispanic/Latino; 2 Two or more races, non-Hispanic/Latino), 3 international. Average age 34. 58 applicants, 62% accepted, 21 enrolled. In 2014, 16 master's, 7 doctorates awarded. *Degree requirements:* For master's, one foreign language, comprehensive exam (for some programs), thesis or alternative, portfolio; for doctorate, 2 foreign languages, comprehensive exam, thesis/dissertation. *Entrance requirements:* For master's, GRE General Test; for doctorate, GRE General Test, GRE Subject Test (literature). *Application deadline:* For fall admission, 1/15 for domestic and international students. Application fee: $50. Electronic applications accepted. *Financial support:* In 2014–15, 55 students received support, including 55 teaching assistantships with full tuition reimbursements available; health care benefits also available. Financial award application deadline: 1/15. *Faculty research:* American, Native American, Chicano, and British and Irish literature; rhetoric and writing; medieval studies. *Unit head:* Dr. Gail Turley Houston, Chair, 505-277-6347, Fax: 505-277-0021, E-mail: ghouston@unm.edu. *Application contact:* N. Ezra Meier, Graduate Advisor, 505-277-4437, Fax: 505-277-0021, E-mail: nezra@unm.edu.
Website: http://english.unm.edu/graduate/index.html

University of New Orleans, Graduate School, College of Liberal Arts, Department of English, Program in English, New Orleans, LA 70148. Offers MA. Part-time and evening/weekend programs available. *Degree requirements:* For master's, one foreign language, thesis (for some programs). *Entrance requirements:* For master's, GRE General Test. Additional exam requirements/recommendations for international students: Required—TOEFL (minimum score 550 paper-based; 79 iBT), IELTS (minimum score 6.5). Electronic applications accepted. *Faculty research:* British and American Literature, professional writing.

University of North Alabama, College of Arts and Sciences, Department of English, Florence, AL 35632-0001. Offers MA. Part-time and evening/weekend programs available. *Faculty:* 8 full-time (5 women), 1 part-time/adjunct (0 women). *Students:* 3 full-time (all women), 10 part-time (9 women); includes 2 minority (1 Black or African American, non-Hispanic/Latino; 1 Two or more races, non-Hispanic/Latino), 1 international. Average age 26. 8 applicants, 88% accepted, 6 enrolled. In 2014, 3 master's awarded. *Degree requirements:* For master's, comprehensive exam (for some programs), thesis optional. *Entrance requirements:* For master's, GRE, MAT. Additional exam requirements/recommendations for international students: Required—TOEFL (minimum score 550 paper-based; 79 iBT), IELTS (minimum score 6). *Application deadline:* For fall admission, 7/1 priority date for domestic students, 7/1 for international students; for spring admission, 12/1 for domestic and international students. Applications are processed on a rolling basis. Application fee: $25 ($50 for international students). Electronic applications accepted. *Expenses:* Tuition, state resident: full-time $5166; part-time $1722 per semester. Tuition, nonresident: full-time $10,332; part-time $3444 per semester. *Required fees:* $393.50 per semester. *Financial support:* Applicants required to submit FAFSA. *Unit head:* Dr. Larry W. Adams, Chair, 256-765-4487, E-mail: lwadams1@una.edu. *Application contact:* Hillary N. Coats, Graduate Admissions Coordinator, 256-765-4447, E-mail: graduate@una.edu.
Website: http://www.una.edu/english/

The University of North Carolina at Chapel Hill, Graduate School, College of Arts and Sciences, Department of English, Chapel Hill, NC 27599. Offers MA, PhD. *Degree requirements:* For master's, one foreign language, comprehensive exam, thesis; for doctorate, 2 foreign languages, comprehensive exam, thesis/dissertation. *Entrance requirements:* For master's and doctorate, GRE General Test, GRE Subject Test, minimum GPA of 3.0 for last 2 undergraduate years, writing sample. Additional exam requirements/recommendations for international students: Required—TOEFL. Electronic applications accepted. *Faculty research:* African-American, Southern, period, genre, critical theory/culture studies.

The University of North Carolina at Charlotte, College of Education, Department of Middle, Secondary and K-12 Education, Charlotte, NC 28223-0001. Offers curriculum and instruction (PhD); English education (MA); mathematics education (MA); middle grades education (MAT); secondary education (MAT); teaching English as a second language (M Ed). *Faculty:* 18 full-time (11 women), 3 part-time/adjunct (2 women). *Students:* 1 (woman) full-time, 35 part-time (32 women); includes 7 minority (4 Black or African American, non-Hispanic/Latino; 2 Hispanic/Latino; 1 Two or more races, non-Hispanic/Latino). Average age 31. 22 applicants, 95% accepted, 19 enrolled. In 2014, 27 master's awarded. *Degree requirements:* For master's, thesis. *Entrance requirements:* For master's, GRE or MAT. Additional exam requirements/recommendations for international students: Required—TOEFL (minimum score 557 paper-based; 83 iBT). *Application deadline:* For fall admission, 5/1 priority date for domestic students, 5/1 for international students; for spring admission, 10/1 priority date for domestic students, 10/1 for international students. Applications are processed on a rolling basis. Application fee: $75. Electronic applications accepted. *Expenses:* Tuition, state resident: full-time $4008. Tuition, nonresident: full-time $16,295. *Required fees:* $2755. Tuition and fees vary according to course load and program. *Financial support:* In 2014–15, 5 students received support, including 1 fellowship (averaging $35,417 per year), 4 research assistantships (averaging $11,750 per year); career-related internships or fieldwork, institutionally sponsored loans, scholarships/grants, and unspecified assistantships also available. Support available to part-time students. Financial award application deadline: 4/1; financial award applicants required to submit FAFSA. *Total annual research expenditures:* $117,786. *Unit head:* Dr. Warren DiBiase, Chair, 704-687-8881, Fax: 704-687-6430, E-mail: wjdibias@uncc.edu. *Application contact:* Kathy B. Giddings, Director of Graduate Admissions, 704-687-5503, Fax: 704-687-1668, E-mail: gradadm@uncc.edu.
Website: http://education.uncc.edu/mdsk

The University of North Carolina at Charlotte, College of Liberal Arts and Sciences, Department of English, Charlotte, NC 28223-0001. Offers English (MA); English education (MA); technical communication (Graduate Certificate). Part-time and evening/weekend programs available. *Faculty:* 31 full-time (16 women). *Students:* 30 full-time (22 women), 60 part-time (37 women); includes 16 minority (11 Black or African American, non-Hispanic/Latino; 1 American Indian or Alaska Native, non-Hispanic/Latino; 2 Hispanic/Latino; 1 Native Hawaiian or other Pacific Islander, non-Hispanic/Latino; 1 Two or more races, non-Hispanic/Latino), 4 international. Average age 31. 46 applicants, 83% accepted, 28 enrolled. In 2014, 13 master's, 4 other advanced degrees awarded. *Degree requirements:* For master's, comprehensive exam, thesis optional. *Entrance requirements:* For master's, GRE General Test, minimum undergraduate GPA of 3.0 in major, 2.75 overall. Additional exam requirements/recommendations for international students: Required—TOEFL (minimum score 557 paper-based; 83 iBT). *Application deadline:* For fall admission, 5/1 priority date for domestic students, 5/1 for international students; for spring admission, 10/1 priority date for domestic students, 10/1 for international students. Applications are processed on a rolling basis. Application fee: $75. Electronic applications accepted. *Expenses:* Tuition, state resident: full-time $4008. Tuition, nonresident: full-time $16,295. *Required fees:* $2755. Tuition and fees vary according to course load and program. *Financial support:* In 2014–15, 19 students received support, including 19 teaching assistantships (averaging $7,740 per year); career-related internships or fieldwork, institutionally sponsored loans, scholarships/grants, and unspecified assistantships also available. Support available to part-time students. Financial award application deadline: 4/1; financial award applicants required to submit FAFSA. *Faculty research:* Narrative, pragmatics and stance in medical discourse and Alzheimer's speech; online discourse and digital corpora of speech. *Total annual research expenditures:* $102,408. *Unit head:* Dr. Mark West, Interim Chair, 704-687-0618, Fax: 704-687-1401, E-mail: miwest@uncc.edu. *Application contact:* Kathy B. Giddings, Director of Graduate Admissions, 704-687-5503, Fax: 704-687-1668, E-mail: gradadm@uncc.edu.
Website: http://english.uncc.edu/MA-English/graduate-programs.html

The University of North Carolina at Greensboro, Graduate School, College of Arts and Sciences, Department of English, Program in English, Greensboro, NC 27412-5001. Offers American literature (PhD); English (M Ed, MA); English literature (PhD); rhetoric and composition (PhD). *Degree requirements:* For master's, comprehensive exam, thesis or alternative; for doctorate, variable foreign language requirement, thesis/dissertation, preliminary exam. *Entrance requirements:* For master's, GRE General Test, GRE Subject Test, minimum GPA of 3.0; for doctorate, GRE General Test, GRE Subject Test, critical writing sample, minimum GPA of 3.0. Additional exam requirements/recommendations for international students: Required—TOEFL. Electronic applications accepted.

The University of North Carolina Wilmington, College of Arts and Sciences, Department of English, Wilmington, NC 28403-3297. Offers MA. *Faculty:* 23 full-time (11 women). *Students:* 16 full-time (11 women), 6 part-time (all women); includes 2 minority

(1 Black or African American, non-Hispanic/Latino; 1 Two or more races, non-Hispanic/Latino). 25 applicants, 88% accepted, 12 enrolled. In 2014, 13 master's awarded. *Degree requirements:* For master's, comprehensive exam, thesis. *Entrance requirements:* For master's, GRE General Test, minimum B average in undergraduate major. Additional exam requirements/recommendations for international students: Required—TOEFL (minimum score 79 iBT), IELTS. *Application deadline:* For fall admission, 3/5 for domestic students; for spring admission, 11/1 for domestic students. Applications are processed on a rolling basis. Application fee: $60. *Expenses:* Tuition, state resident: full-time $3240. Tuition, nonresident: full-time $9208. *Required fees:* $1967. *Financial support:* Career-related internships or fieldwork and Federal Work-Study available. Support available to part-time students. Financial award application deadline: 3/15; financial award applicants required to submit FAFSA. *Unit head:* Dr. Katherine Montwieler, Chair, 910-962-3328, Fax: 910-962-7186, E-mail: montwielerk@uncw.edu. *Application contact:* Dr. Meghan Sweeney, Graduate Coordinator, 910-962-3054, Fax: 910-962-7186, E-mail: sweeneym@uncw.edu.
Website: http://www.uncw.edu/english/graduate/index.html

University of North Dakota, Graduate School, College of Arts and Sciences, Department of English, Grand Forks, ND 58202. Offers MA, PhD. *Degree requirements:* For master's, one foreign language, comprehensive exam, thesis or alternative; for doctorate, one foreign language, comprehensive exam, thesis/dissertation. *Entrance requirements:* For master's and doctorate, GRE General Test, minimum GPA of 3.0. Additional exam requirements/recommendations for international students: Required—TOEFL (minimum score 550 paper-based; 79 iBT), IELTS (minimum score 6.5). Electronic applications accepted. *Faculty research:* Creative writing, rhetorical theory, cinema, American literature, European literature.

University of Northern Colorado, Graduate School, College of Humanities and Social Sciences, School of English Language and Literature, Program in English, Greeley, CO 80639. Offers MA. Part-time programs available. *Degree requirements:* For master's, comprehensive exam. *Entrance requirements:* For master's, GRE General Test, 2 letters of recommendation. Electronic applications accepted.

University of Northern Iowa, Graduate College, College of Humanities, Arts and Sciences, Department of Languages and Literatures, MA Program in English, Cedar Falls, IA 50614. Offers creative writing (MA); English (MA); literature (MA). Part-time and evening/weekend programs available. *Students:* 14 full-time (9 women), 8 part-time (7 women); includes 2 minority (1 American Indian or Alaska Native, non-Hispanic/Latino; 1 Asian, non-Hispanic/Latino), 1 international. 17 applicants, 41% accepted, 6 enrolled. In 2014, 10 master's awarded. *Degree requirements:* For master's, one foreign language, comprehensive exam, thesis or alternative, portfolio. *Entrance requirements:* Additional exam requirements/recommendations for international students: Required—TOEFL (minimum score 600 paper-based; 100 iBT). *Application deadline:* For fall admission, 8/1 priority date for domestic students. Applications are processed on a rolling basis. Application fee: $50 ($70 for international students). Electronic applications accepted. *Expenses:* Tuition, state resident: full-time $7912; part-time $880 per credit. Tuition, nonresident: full-time $17,906; part-time $880 per credit. *Required fees:* $1101; $325.50 per credit. $465.63 per semester. Tuition and fees vary according to course load and program. *Financial support:* Career-related internships or fieldwork, Federal Work-Study, scholarships/grants, and tuition waivers (full and partial) available. Support available to part-time students. Financial award application deadline: 2/1. *Unit head:* Dr. Anne Myles, Coordinator, 319-273-6911, Fax: 319-273-5807, E-mail: anne.myles@uni.edu. *Application contact:* Laurie S. Russell, Record Analyst, 319-273-2623, Fax: 319-273-2885, E-mail: laurie.russell@uni.edu.
Website: http://www.uni.edu/langlit/

University of North Florida, College of Arts and Sciences, Department of English, Jacksonville, FL 32224. Offers MA. Part-time and evening/weekend programs available. *Faculty:* 9 full-time (4 women). *Students:* 13 full-time (5 women), 32 part-time (22 women); includes 3 minority (2 Hispanic/Latino; 1 Two or more races, non-Hispanic/Latino). Average age 31. 20 applicants, 70% accepted, 10 enrolled. In 2014, 22 master's awarded. *Degree requirements:* For master's, comprehensive exam, thesis optional. *Entrance requirements:* For master's, GRE General Test, minimum GPA of 3.0 in last 60 hours, writing sample. Additional exam requirements/recommendations for international students: Required—TOEFL (minimum score 500 paper-based; 61 iBT). *Application deadline:* For fall admission, 8/1 priority date for domestic students, 5/1 for international students; for spring admission, 12/1 priority date for domestic students, 10/1 for international students; for summer admission, 3/15 for domestic students. Applications are processed on a rolling basis. Application fee: $30. Electronic applications accepted. *Expenses:* Tuition, state resident: full-time $9794; part-time $408.10 per credit hour. Tuition, nonresident: full-time $22,383; part-time $932.61 per credit hour. *Required fees:* $2047; $85.29 per credit hour. Tuition and fees vary according to course load and program. *Financial support:* In 2014–15, 6 students received support. Research assistantships, teaching assistantships, Federal Work-Study, and scholarships/grants available. Financial award application deadline: 4/1; financial award applicants required to submit FAFSA. *Faculty research:* Genre, period, and individual author studies in British, American, and world literature; literary criticism and theory: psychological, new historical and cultural, deconstructive, feminist, narrative, mythic; film and popular culture; online poetry publishing. *Total annual research expenditures:* $45,461. *Unit head:* Dr. Brian A. Striar, Chair, 904-620-1245, Fax: 904-620-3940, E-mail: bstriar@unf.edu. *Application contact:* Dr. Amanda Pascale, Director, The Graduate School, 904-620-1360, Fax: 904-620-1362, E-mail: graduateschool@unf.edu.
Website: http://www.unf.edu/coas/english/

University of North Texas, Robert B. Toulouse School of Graduate Studies, Denton, TX 76203-5459. Offers accounting (MS); applied anthropology (MA, MS); applied behavior analysis (Certificate); applied geography (MA); applied technology and performance improvement (M Ed, MS); art education (MA); art history (MA); art museum education (Certificate); arts leadership (Certificate); audiology (Au D); behavior analysis (MS); behavioral science (PhD); biochemistry and molecular biology (MS); biology (MA, MS); biomedical engineering (MS); business analysis (MS); chemistry (MS); clinical health psychology (PhD); communication studies (MA, MS); computer engineering (MS); computer science (MS); counseling (M Ed, MS), including clinical mental health counseling (MS), college and university counseling, elementary school counseling, secondary school counseling; creative writing (MA); criminal justice (MS); curriculum and instruction (M Ed); decision sciences (MBA); design (MA, MFA), including fashion design (MFA), innovation studies, interior design (MFA); early childhood studies (MS); economics (MS); educational leadership (M Ed, Ed D); educational psychology (MS, PhD), including family studies (MS), gifted and talented (MS), human development (MS), learning and cognition (MS), research, measurement and evaluation (MS); electrical engineering (MS); emergency management (MPA); engineering technology (MS); English (MA); English as a second language (MA); environmental science (MS); finance (MBA, MS); financial management (MPA); French (MA); health services management (MBA); higher education (M Ed, Ed D); history (MA, MS); hospitality management (MS); human resources management (MPA); information science (MS); information systems (PhD); information technologies (MBA); interdisciplinary studies (MA, MS); international studies (MA); international sustainable tourism (MS); jazz studies (MM); journalism (MA, MJ, Graduate Certificate), including interactive and virtual digital communication (Graduate Certificate), narrative journalism (Graduate Certificate), public relations (Graduate Certificate); kinesiology (MS); linguistics (MA); local government management (MPA); logistics (PhD); logistics and supply chain management (MBA); long-term care, senior housing, and aging services (MA); management (PhD); marketing (MBA); mathematics (MA, MS); mechanical and energy engineering (MS, PhD); music (MA), including ethnomusicology, music theory, musicology, performance; music composition (PhD); music education (MM Ed, PhD); nonprofit management (MPA); operations and supply chain management (MBA); performance (MM, DMA); philosophy (MA); political science (MA); professional and technical communication (MA); radio, television and film (MA, MFA); rehabilitation counseling (Certificate); sociology (MA); Spanish (MA); special education (M Ed); speech-language pathology (MA); strategic management (MBA); studio art (MFA); teaching (M Ed); MBA/MS. Part-time and evening/weekend programs available. Postbaccalaureate distance learning degree programs offered. *Faculty:* 651 full-time (215 women), 233 part-time/adjunct (139 women). *Students:* 3,040 full-time (1,598 women), 3,401 part-time (2,097 women); includes 1,740 minority (533 Black or African American, non-Hispanic/Latino; 15 American Indian or Alaska Native, non-Hispanic/Latino; 286 Asian, non-Hispanic/Latino; 746 Hispanic/Latino; 3 Native Hawaiian or other Pacific Islander, non-Hispanic/Latino; 157 Two or more races, non-Hispanic/Latino), 1,145 international. Terminal master's awarded for partial completion of doctoral program. *Degree requirements:* For master's, variable foreign language requirement, comprehensive exam (for some programs), thesis (for some programs); for doctorate, variable foreign language requirement, comprehensive exam (for some programs), thesis/dissertation; for other advanced degree, variable foreign language requirement, comprehensive exam (for some programs). *Entrance requirements:* For master's and doctorate, GRE, GMAT. Additional exam requirements/recommendations for international students: Required—TOEFL (minimum score 550 paper-based; 79 iBT). *Application deadline:* For fall admission, 7/15 for domestic students, 3/15 for international students; for spring admission, 11/15 for domestic students, 9/15 for international students; for summer admission, 5/1 for domestic students. Applications are processed on a rolling basis. Application fee: $60. Electronic applications accepted. *Expenses:* Tuition, state resident: full-time $5450; part-time $3633 per year. Tuition, nonresident: full-time $11,966; part-time $7977 per year. *Required fees:* $1301; $398 per credit hour. $685 per semester. Tuition and fees vary according to program and reciprocity agreements. *Financial support:* Fellowships with partial tuition reimbursements, research assistantships with partial tuition reimbursements, teaching assistantships, career-related internships or fieldwork, Federal Work-Study, institutionally sponsored loans, scholarships/grants, health care benefits, and library assistantships available. Support available to part-time students. Financial award applicants required to submit FAFSA. *Unit head:* Mark Wardell, Dean, 940-565-2383, E-mail: mark.wardell@unt.edu. *Application contact:* Toulouse School of Graduate Studies, 940-565-2383, Fax: 940-565-2141, E-mail: gradsch@unt.edu.
Website: http://tsgs.unt.edu/

University of Notre Dame, Graduate School, College of Arts and Letters, Division of Humanities, Department of English, Notre Dame, IN 46556. Offers creative writing (MFA); English (MA, PhD). *Degree requirements:* For doctorate, one foreign language, thesis/dissertation, candidacy exam. *Entrance requirements:* For master's, GRE General Test, minimum GPA of 3.0; for doctorate, GRE General Test, GRE Subject Test, minimum GPA of 3.0. Additional exam requirements/recommendations for international students: Required—TOEFL (minimum score 600 paper-based; 80 iBT). Electronic applications accepted. *Faculty research:* Early modern studies (medieval/Renaissance), modern British studies (eighteenth-twentieth centuries), American Studies, literature and philosophy, Irish studies.

University of Oklahoma, College of Arts and Sciences, Department of English, Norman, OK 73019. Offers MA, PhD. *Faculty:* 26 full-time (13 women). *Students:* 46 full-time (27 women), 10 part-time (5 women); includes 10 minority (5 American Indian or Alaska Native, non-Hispanic/Latino; 2 Asian, non-Hispanic/Latino; 1 Hispanic/Latino; 2 Two or more races, non-Hispanic/Latino), 1 international. Average age 31. 50 applicants, 38% accepted, 10 enrolled. In 2014, 6 master's, 2 doctorates awarded. *Degree requirements:* For master's, one foreign language, comprehensive exam (for some programs), thesis (for some programs); for doctorate, one foreign language, comprehensive exam, thesis/dissertation. *Entrance requirements:* For master's and doctorate, GRE. Additional exam requirements/recommendations for international students: Required—TOEFL (minimum score 79 iBT). *Application deadline:* For fall admission, 1/5 for domestic and international students; for spring admission, 11/1 for domestic students, 9/1 for international students. Application fee: $50 ($100 for international students). Electronic applications accepted. *Expenses:* Tuition, state resident: full-time $4394; part-time $183.10 per credit hour. Tuition, nonresident: full-time $16,970; part-time $707.10 per credit hour. *Required fees:* $2892; $109.95 per credit hour. $126.50 per semester. *Financial support:* In 2014–15, 53 students received support, including 4 research assistantships with partial tuition reimbursements available (averaging $12,977 per year), 53 teaching assistantships with partial tuition reimbursements available (averaging $12,326 per year); scholarships/grants, health care benefits, tuition waivers (full), and unspecified assistantships also available. Financial award application deadline: 6/1; financial award applicants required to submit FAFSA. *Faculty research:* American literature, medieval/early modern literature, film and media studies, British literature, Native American literature. *Unit head:* Dr. Daniela Garofalo, Chair, 405-325-4661, Fax: 405-325-0831, E-mail: dg@ou.edu. *Application contact:* Sara Day, Graduate Programs Assistant, 405-325-0489, Fax: 405-325-0831, E-mail: redpanda@ou.edu.
Website: http://cas.ou.edu/english

University of Oregon, Graduate School, College of Arts and Sciences, Department of English, Eugene, OR 97403. Offers MA, PhD. Terminal master's awarded for partial completion of doctoral program. *Degree requirements:* For master's, one foreign language; for doctorate, 2 foreign languages, thesis/dissertation. *Entrance requirements:* For master's, GRE General Test; for doctorate, GRE Subject Test (English literature), minimum GPA of 3.5. Additional exam requirements/recommendations for international students: Required—TOEFL. *Faculty research:* Old and Middle English, women writers, critical theory, literature and the environment, rhetoric and composition.

University of Ottawa, Faculty of Graduate and Postdoctoral Studies, Faculty of Arts, Department of English, Ottawa, ON K1N 6N5, Canada. Offers MA, PhD. Part-time and evening/weekend programs available. *Degree requirements:* For master's, one foreign language, thesis optional; for doctorate, 2 foreign languages, comprehensive exam, thesis/dissertation. *Entrance requirements:* For master's, honors degree or equivalent, minimum B average; for doctorate, master's degree, minimum B+ average. Electronic applications accepted. *Faculty research:* Anglo-Saxon and medieval literature.

University of Pennsylvania, School of Arts and Sciences, Graduate Group in English, Philadelphia, PA 19104. Offers AM, PhD. *Faculty:* 43 full-time (19 women), 8 part-time/adjunct (4 women). *Students:* 63 full-time (43 women), 2 part-time (1 woman); includes 20 minority (7 Black or African American, non-Hispanic/Latino; 7 Asian, non-Hispanic/Latino; 3 Hispanic/Latino; 3 Two or more races, non-Hispanic/Latino), 10 international. 525 applicants, 4% accepted, 13 enrolled. In 2014, 8 master's, 5 doctorates awarded. Terminal master's awarded for partial completion of doctoral program. *Degree*

requirements: For master's, one foreign language; for doctorate, 2 foreign languages, thesis/dissertation, oral and written qualifying exams. *Entrance requirements:* For master's, GRE General Test, GRE Subject Test, sample of written work; for doctorate, GRE General Test, GRE Subject Test. Additional exam requirements/recommendations for international students: Required—TOEFL. *Application deadline:* For fall admission, 12/1 priority date for domestic students. Application fee: $70. Electronic applications accepted. *Financial support:* Fellowships, teaching assistantships, institutionally sponsored loans, scholarships/grants, traineeships, health care benefits, and unspecified assistantships available. Financial award application deadline: 12/15. *Faculty research:* Renaissance literature and intellectual theory, feminist studies, literary theory. *Unit head:* Dr. Ralph M. Rosen, Associate Dean for Graduate Studies, 215-898-7156, Fax: 215-573-8068, E-mail: grad-dean@sas.upenn.edu. *Application contact:* Arts and Sciences Graduate Admissions, 215-573-5816, Fax: 215-573-8068, E-mail: gdasadmis@sas.upenn.edu.
Website: http://www.english.upenn.edu

University of Pittsburgh, Dietrich School of Arts and Sciences, Department of English, Pittsburgh, PA 15260. Offers writing (MFA). *Faculty:* 53 full-time (25 women). *Students:* 141 full-time (94 women); includes 32 minority (8 Black or African American, non-Hispanic/Latino; 16 Asian, non-Hispanic/Latino; 8 Hispanic/Latino), 1 international. Average age 30. 309 applicants, 22% accepted, 20 enrolled. In 2014, 19 master's, 11 doctorates awarded. Terminal master's awarded for partial completion of doctoral program. *Degree requirements:* For master's, variable foreign language requirement, thesis; for doctorate, one foreign language, comprehensive exam, thesis/dissertation. *Entrance requirements:* For master's and doctorate, GRE General Test, writing sample. Additional exam requirements/recommendations for international students: Required—TOEFL (minimum score 550 paper-based; 90 iBT). *Application deadline:* For fall admission, 12/10 for domestic and international students. Application fee: $50. Electronic applications accepted. *Expenses:* Tuition, state resident: full-time $20,742; part-time $838 per credit. Tuition, nonresident: full-time $33,960; part-time $1389 per credit. *Required fees:* $800; $205 per term. Tuition and fees vary according to program. *Financial support:* In 2014–15, 106 students received support, including 32 fellowships with full tuition reimbursements available (averaging $21,262 per year), 14 research assistantships with full and partial tuition reimbursements available (averaging $13,980 per year), 60 teaching assistantships with full tuition reimbursements available (averaging $17,310 per year); Federal Work-Study, scholarships/grants, health care benefits, tuition waivers (full and partial), and unspecified assistantships also available. Financial award application deadline: 12/12. *Faculty research:* Cultural studies, literary history and theory, film, composition. *Unit head:* Dr. Don Bialostosky, Chair, 412-624-6509, Fax: 412-624-6639, E-mail: dhb2@pitt.edu. *Application contact:* Jesse Daugherty, Graduate Administrator, 412-624-6549, Fax: 412-624-6639, E-mail: engrad@pitt.edu.
Website: http://www.english.pitt.edu

University of Pittsburgh, School of Education, Department of Instruction and Learning, Program in Secondary Education, Pittsburgh, PA 15260. Offers English/communications education (M Ed, MAT); foreign languages education (MAT); language, literacy and culture education (Ed D, PhD); mathematics education (M Ed, MAT, Ed D); science education (M Ed, Ed D, PhD); secondary education (PhD); social studies education (M Ed, MAT); STEM education (Ed D). Part-time and evening/weekend programs available. *Faculty:* 27 full-time (17 women), 76 part-time/adjunct (57 women). *Students:* 114 full-time (74 women), 43 part-time (32 women); includes 16 minority (8 Black or African American, non-Hispanic/Latino; 1 Asian, non-Hispanic/Latino; 6 Hispanic/Latino; 1 Two or more races, non-Hispanic/Latino), 35 international. Average age 31. 213 applicants, 72% accepted, 101 enrolled. In 2014, 87 master's, 7 doctorates awarded. *Degree requirements:* For master's, thesis; for doctorate, thesis/dissertation. *Entrance requirements:* For master's, PRAXIS I; for doctorate, GRE General Test. Additional exam requirements/recommendations for international students: Required—TOEFL. *Application deadline:* For fall admission, 2/1 priority date for domestic students; for spring admission, 11/15 priority date for domestic students. Applications are processed on a rolling basis. Application fee: $50. Electronic applications accepted. *Expenses:* Tuition, state resident: full-time $20,742; part-time $838 per credit. Tuition, nonresident: full-time $33,960; part-time $1389 per credit. *Required fees:* $800; $205 per term. Tuition and fees vary according to program. *Financial support:* In 2014–15, fellowships with full and partial tuition reimbursements (averaging $20,500 per year), research assistantships with full and partial tuition reimbursements (averaging $17,800 per year), teaching assistantships with full and partial tuition reimbursements (averaging $17,800 per year) were awarded; career-related internships or fieldwork, Federal Work-Study, tuition waivers (partial), and unspecified assistantships also available. Support available to part-time students. Financial award application deadline: 3/15; financial award applicants required to submit FAFSA. *Unit head:* Dr. Richard Donato, Chairman, 412-624-7248, Fax: 412-648-7081, E-mail: donato@pitt.edu. *Application contact:* Marianne L. Budziszewski, Director of Admissions and Enrollment Services, 412-648-2230, Fax: 412-648-1899, E-mail: soeinfo@pitt.edu.
Website: http://www.education.pitt.edu/

University of Puerto Rico, Mayagüez Campus, Graduate Studies, College of Arts and Sciences, Department of English, Mayagüez, PR 00681-9000. Offers English education (MA). Part-time programs available. *Faculty:* 30 full-time (21 women), 3 part-time/adjunct (2 women). *Students:* 55 full-time (36 women), 1 (woman) part-time. 18 applicants, 83% accepted, 13 enrolled. In 2014, 15 master's awarded. *Degree requirements:* For master's, comprehensive exam, thesis optional. *Entrance requirements:* For master's, course work in linguistics or language, American literature, British literature, and structure/grammar or syntax. Additional exam requirements/recommendations for international students: Required—TOEFL (minimum score 550 paper-based). *Application deadline:* For fall admission, 2/15 for domestic and international students; for spring admission, 9/15 for domestic and international students. Applications are processed on a rolling basis. Application fee: $25. *Expenses: Tuition, area resident:* Full-time $2466; part-time $822 per credit. *International tuition:* $6371 full-time. *Required fees:* $1095; $1095 per year. Tuition and fees vary according to course level, course load and reciprocity agreements. *Financial support:* In 2014–15, 47 students received support, including 18 research assistantships (averaging $3,087 per year), 43 teaching assistantships (averaging $5,612 per year); fellowships with full tuition reimbursements available, Federal Work-Study, institutionally sponsored loans, and unspecified assistantships also available. *Faculty research:* Teaching English as a second language, linguistics, American literature, British literature. *Unit head:* Dr. Rosita Rivera, Director, 787-265-3847, Fax: 787-265-3847, E-mail: rosita.rivera1@upr.edu. *Application contact:* Dr. Nancy Vicente, Associate Director, 787-265-3847, E-mail: nancyv.vicente@upr.edu.
Website: http://www.uprm.edu./english/

University of Puerto Rico, Río Piedras Campus, College of Humanities, Department of English, San Juan, PR 00931-3300. Offers Caribbean linguistics (PhD); Caribbean literature (PhD); English (MA). Part-time programs available. *Degree requirements:* For master's, one foreign language, comprehensive exam, thesis; for doctorate, residency. *Entrance requirements:* For master's, PAEG or GRE, interview, minimum GPA of 3.0, 2 letters of recommendation; for doctorate, PAEG or GRE, minimum GPA of 3.0, 3 letters of recommendation, interview.

University of Regina, Faculty of Graduate Studies and Research, Faculty of Arts, Department of English, Regina, SK S4S 0A2, Canada. Offers creative writing and English (MA); English (MA). Part-time programs available. *Faculty:* 18 full-time (8 women), 1 (woman) part-time/adjunct. *Students:* 14 full-time (9 women), 8 part-time (5 women). 19 applicants, 47% accepted. In 2014, 2 master's awarded. *Degree requirements:* For master's, thesis (for some programs). *Entrance requirements:* For master's, writing sample and portfolio of creative material (creative writing and English). Additional exam requirements/recommendations for international students: Required—TOEFL (minimum score 600 paper-based; 100 iBT), IELTS (minimum score 7.5), PTE (minimum score 59). *Application deadline:* For fall admission, 4/15 for domestic and international students; for winter admission, 10/15 for domestic and international students; for spring admission, 2/15 for domestic and international students. Application fee: $100. Electronic applications accepted. *Expenses: Tuition, area resident:* Full-time $4900 Canadian dollars; part-time $837.65 Canadian dollars per semester. *International tuition:* $7900 Canadian dollars full-time. *Required fees:* $396 Canadian dollars; $86.90 Canadian dollars per semester. *Financial support:* In 2014–15, 1 fellowship (averaging $6,000 per year), 1 research assistantship (averaging $5,500 per year), 5 teaching assistantships (averaging $2,427 per year) were awarded; scholarships/grants also available. Financial award application deadline: 6/15. *Faculty research:* British, American, and Canadian literature; sixteenth-, eighteenth-, nineteenth-, and twentieth-century literature; literary theory. *Unit head:* Dr. Troni Grande, Department Head, 306-585-4570, Fax: 306-585-5429, E-mail: troni.grande@uregina.ca. *Application contact:* Dr. Susan Johnston, Graduate Chair, 306-585-4672, Fax: 306-585-5429, E-mail: susan.johnston@uregina.ca.
Website: http://www.uregina.ca/arts/english

University of Rhode Island, Graduate School, College of Arts and Sciences, Department of English, Kingston, RI 02881. Offers MA, PhD, MLIS/MA. Part-time programs available. *Faculty:* 19 full-time (12 women), 1 (woman) part-time/adjunct. *Students:* 39 full-time (31 women), 22 part-time (17 women); includes 6 minority (2 Black or African American, non-Hispanic/Latino; 1 Asian, non-Hispanic/Latino; 2 Hispanic/Latino; 1 Two or more races, non-Hispanic/Latino), 4 international. In 2014, 3 master's, 4 doctorates awarded. *Degree requirements:* For master's, comprehensive exam (for some programs), thesis optional; for doctorate, comprehensive exam, thesis/dissertation. *Entrance requirements:* For master's, 3 letters of recommendation, writing sample; for doctorate, GRE, 3 letters of recommendation, writing sample. Additional exam requirements/recommendations for international students: Required—TOEFL (minimum score 550 paper-based; 91 iBT). *Application deadline:* For fall admission, 1/15 for domestic and international students. Application fee: $65. Electronic applications accepted. *Expenses:* Tuition, state resident: full-time $11,532; part-time $641 per credit. Tuition, nonresident: full-time $23,606; part-time $1311 per credit. *Required fees:* $1442; $39 per credit. $35 per semester. One-time fee: $155. *Financial support:* In 2014–15, 30 teaching assistantships with full and partial tuition reimbursements (averaging $16,140 per year) were awarded. Financial award application deadline: 1/15; financial award applicants required to submit FAFSA. *Unit head:* Dr. Ryan S. Trimm, Chair, 401-874-5444, Fax: 401-874-2580, E-mail: engchair@gmail.com. *Application contact:* Dr. Kathleen Davis, Director of Graduate Studies, 401-874-2016, Fax: 401-874-2580, E-mail: kathleendavis@uri.edu.
Website: http://www.uri.edu/artsci/eng/

University of Rochester, School of Arts and Sciences, Department of English, Rochester, NY 14627. Offers MA, PhD. *Faculty:* 20 full-time (7 women). *Students:* 73 full-time (46 women), 2 part-time (both women); includes 14 minority (2 Black or African American, non-Hispanic/Latino; 4 Asian, non-Hispanic/Latino; 6 Hispanic/Latino; 2 Two or more races, non-Hispanic/Latino), 2 international. 154 applicants, 38% accepted, 27 enrolled. In 2014, 25 master's, 7 doctorates awarded. Terminal master's awarded for partial completion of doctoral program. *Degree requirements:* For doctorate, one foreign language, thesis/dissertation, qualifying exam. *Entrance requirements:* For master's and doctorate, GRE General Test. Additional exam requirements/recommendations for international students: Required—TOEFL. *Application deadline:* For fall admission, 1/15 priority date for domestic students. Application fee: $60. *Expenses: Tuition:* Full-time $46,150; part-time $1442 per credit hour. *Required fees:* $504. *Financial support:* Fellowships, research assistantships, teaching assistantships, and tuition waivers (full and partial) available. Financial award application deadline: 1/15. *Faculty research:* All periods and genres of English, American, and Anglophone literature, poetry, fiction, non-fiction, and drama. *Unit head:* John Michael, Chair, 585-275-4092. *Application contact:* Carrie Morriss, Graduate Secretary, 585-275-9256.
Website: http://www.rochester.edu/College/ENG/

University of St. Thomas, Graduate Studies, College of Arts and Sciences, Graduate Program in English, St. Paul, MN 55105-1096. Offers MA. Part-time and evening/weekend programs available. *Degree requirements:* For master's, essay. *Entrance requirements:* For master's, minimum GPA of 3.0, previous course work in literature, sample of written work. Additional exam requirements/recommendations for international students: Required—TOEFL. *Expenses:* Contact institution. *Faculty research:* Multicultural literature, literature and theory, regional writers.

University of Saskatchewan, College of Graduate Studies and Research, College of Arts and Science, Department of English, Saskatoon, SK S7N 5A2, Canada. Offers MA, PhD. *Degree requirements:* For master's, one foreign language, thesis; for doctorate, one foreign language, comprehensive exam (for some programs), thesis/dissertation. *Entrance requirements:* Additional exam requirements/recommendations for international students: Required—TOEFL (minimum score 80 iBT); Recommended—IELTS (minimum score 6.5). Electronic applications accepted.

University of South Africa, College of Human Sciences, Pretoria, South Africa. Offers adult education (M Ed); African languages (MA, PhD); African politics (MA, PhD); Afrikaans (MA, PhD); ancient history (MA, PhD); ancient Near Eastern studies (MA, PhD); anthropology (MA, PhD); applied linguistics (MA); Arabic (MA, PhD); archaeology (MA); art history (MA); Biblical archaeology (MA); Biblical studies (M Th, D Th, PhD); Christian spirituality (M Th, D Th); church history (M Th, D Th); classical studies (MA, PhD); clinical psychology (MA); communication (MA, PhD); comparative education (M Ed, Ed D); consulting psychology (D Admin, D Com, PhD); curriculum studies (M Ed, Ed D); development studies (M Admin, MA, D Admin, PhD); didactics (M Ed, Ed D); education (M Tech); education management (M Ed, Ed D); educational psychology (M Ed); English (MA); environmental education (M Ed); French (MA, PhD); German (MA, PhD); Greek (MA); guidance and counseling (M Ed); health studies (MA, PhD), including health sciences education (MA), health services management (MA), medical and surgical nursing science (critical care general) (MA), midwifery and neonatal nursing science (MA), trauma and emergency care (MA); history (MA, PhD); history of education (Ed D); inclusive education (M Ed, Ed D); information and communications technology policy and regulation (MA); information science (MA, MIS, PhD); international politics (MA, PhD); Islamic studies (MA, PhD); Italian (MA, PhD); Judaica (MA, PhD); linguistics (MA, PhD); mathematical education (M Ed); mathematics education (MA); missiology (M Th, D Th); modern Hebrew (MA, PhD); musicology (MA, MMus, D Mus, PhD); natural science education (M Ed); New Testament (M Th, D Th); Old Testament (D Th); pastoral therapy (M Th, D Th); philosophy (MA); philosophy of education (M Ed, Ed D); politics (MA, PhD); Portuguese (MA, PhD); practical theology (M Th, D Th); psychology

(MA, MS, PhD); psychology of education (M Ed, Ed D); public health (MA); religious studies (MA, D Th, PhD); Romance languages (MA); Russian (MA, PhD); Semitic languages (MA, PhD); social behavior studies in HIV/AIDS (MA); social science (mental health) (MA); social science in development studies (MA); social science in psychology (MA); social science in social work (MA); social science in sociology (MA); social work (MSW, DSW, PhD); socio-education (M Ed, Ed D); sociolinguistics (MA); sociology (MA, PhD); Spanish (MA, PhD); systematic theology (M Th, D Th); TESOL (teaching English to speakers of other languages) (MA); theological ethics (M Th, D Th); theory of literature (MA, PhD); urban ministries (D Th); urban ministry (M Th).

University of South Alabama, College of Arts and Sciences, Department of English, Mobile, AL 36688. Offers MA. Part-time and evening/weekend programs available. *Faculty:* 9 full-time (4 women), 1 (woman) part-time/adjunct. *Students:* 11 full-time (8 women), 14 part-time (11 women); includes 5 minority (3 Black or African American, non-Hispanic/Latino; 1 Hispanic/Latino; 1 Two or more races, non-Hispanic/Latino). Average age 30. 12 applicants, 50% accepted, 5 enrolled. In 2014, 4 master's awarded. *Degree requirements:* For master's, one foreign language, comprehensive exam, thesis optional. *Entrance requirements:* For master's, GRE General Test, BA in English or 30 hours of course work in English, minimum GPA of 3.0. Additional exam requirements/recommendations for international students: Required—TOEFL (minimum score 535 paper-based). *Application deadline:* For fall admission, 7/15 priority date for domestic students, 5/15 priority date for international students; for spring admission, 12/1 priority date for domestic students, 11/1 priority date for international students. Applications are processed on a rolling basis. Application fee: $35. Electronic applications accepted. *Expenses:* Tuition, state resident: full-time $9288; part-time $387 per credit hour. Tuition, nonresident: full-time $18,576; part-time $774 per credit hour. Part-time tuition and fees vary according to course load and program. *Financial support:* Fellowships, research assistantships, teaching assistantships, career-related internships or fieldwork, Federal Work-Study, institutionally sponsored loans, scholarships/grants, and unspecified assistantships available. Support available to part-time students. Financial award application deadline: 5/31; financial award applicants required to submit FAFSA. *Unit head:* Dr. Steven Trout, Chair, English, 251-460-6439, E-mail: strout@southalabama.edu. *Application contact:* Dr. Ellen Harrington, Graduate Coordinator, English, 251-460-7326, E-mail: eharrington@southalabama.edu. Website: http://www.southalabama.edu/colleges/artsandsci/english/

University of South Carolina, The Graduate School, College of Arts and Sciences, Department of English Language and Literature, Columbia, SC 29208. Offers creative writing (MFA); English (MA, PhD); English education (MAT); MLIS/MA. MAT offered in cooperation with the College of Education. Part-time programs available. *Degree requirements:* For master's, one foreign language, comprehensive exam, thesis; for doctorate, 2 foreign languages, comprehensive exam, thesis/dissertation. *Entrance requirements:* For master's, GRE General Test (MFA), GRE Subject Test (MA, MAT), sample of written work; for doctorate, GRE General Test, GRE Subject Test, sample of written work. Additional exam requirements/recommendations for international students: Required—TOEFL. Electronic applications accepted. *Faculty research:* American literature, British literature, composition and rhetoric, linguistics, speech communication.

The University of South Dakota, Graduate School, College of Arts and Sciences, Department of English, Vermillion, SD 57069-2390. Offers MA, PhD. *Degree requirements:* For master's, comprehensive exam (for some programs), thesis (for some programs); for doctorate, comprehensive exam, thesis/dissertation. *Entrance requirements:* For master's, minimum GPA of 3.0, writing sample; for doctorate, GRE, minimum GPA of 3.0, writing sample. Additional exam requirements/recommendations for international students: Required—TOEFL (minimum score 620 paper-based; 105 iBT). Electronic applications accepted.

University of Southern California, Graduate School, Dana and David Dornsife College of Letters, Arts and Sciences, Department of English, Los Angeles, CA 90089. Offers English (MA, PhD); literature and creative writing (PhD). Terminal master's awarded for partial completion of doctoral program. *Degree requirements:* For doctorate, one foreign language, comprehensive exam, thesis/dissertation. *Entrance requirements:* For doctorate, GRE General Test, GRE Subject Test (English literature). Additional exam requirements/recommendations for international students: Required—TOEFL. Electronic applications accepted. *Faculty research:* Creative writing and literature; early modern studies; gender and sexuality; narrative studies; poetry and poetics; media, film, and popular culture; studies in race and minority literature.

University of Southern Indiana, Graduate Studies, College of Liberal Arts, Program in English, Evansville, IN 47712-3590. Offers MA. *Unit head:* Michael L. Aakhus, Dean, 812-464-1853. *Application contact:* Dr. Mayola Rowser, Director, Graduate Studies, 812-465-7016, E-mail: mrowser@usi.edu.

University of Southern Mississippi, Graduate School, College of Arts and Letters, Department of English, Hattiesburg, MS 39406-0001. Offers creative writing (MA, PhD); English literature (MA, PhD). *Degree requirements:* For master's, one foreign language, comprehensive exam, thesis; for doctorate, 2 foreign languages, comprehensive exam, thesis/dissertation. *Entrance requirements:* For master's, GRE General Test, minimum GPA of 3.0 in field of study, 2.75 in last 2 years; for doctorate, GRE General Test, minimum GPA of 3.5. Additional exam requirements/recommendations for international students: Required—TOEFL, IELTS. Electronic applications accepted. *Faculty research:* English and American literature, critical theory and cultural studies, creative writing.

University of South Florida, College of Arts and Sciences, Department of English, Tampa, FL 33620-9951. Offers creative writing (MFA), including fiction, poetry; literature (MA, PhD); rhetoric and composition (MA, PhD). Part-time and evening/weekend programs available. *Faculty:* 24 full-time (12 women). *Students:* 73 full-time (52 women), 27 part-time (19 women); includes 16 minority (3 Black or African American, non-Hispanic/Latino; 4 Asian, non-Hispanic/Latino; 7 Hispanic/Latino; 2 Two or more races, non-Hispanic/Latino). Average age 32. 122 applicants, 44% accepted, 25 enrolled. In 2014, 26 master's, 5 doctorates awarded. *Degree requirements:* For master's, thesis (for MFA); thesis or comprehensive examination (for MA); for doctorate, one foreign language, comprehensive exam, thesis/dissertation. *Entrance requirements:* For master's, GRE General Test, minimum undergraduate GPA of 3.5 (for MA), 3.2 (for MFA); three letters of recommendation; personal statement; writing sample from 10 to 20 pages, depending on genre; for doctorate, GRE General Test, minimum graduate GPA of 3.7; three letters of recommendation; 2-3 page personal statement; 2500-word writing sample from English coursework. Additional exam requirements/recommendations for international students: Required—TOEFL (minimum score 550 paper-based; 79 iBT) or IELTS (minimum score 6.5) for MA and PhD; TOEFL (minimum score 600 paper-based) for MFA. *Application deadline:* For fall admission, 2/1 for domestic students, 1/2 for international students. Applications are processed on a rolling basis. Application fee: $30. Electronic applications accepted. *Financial support:* In 2014–15, 81 students received support, including 2 research assistantships (averaging $17,221 per year), 79 teaching assistantships with tuition reimbursements available (averaging $11,576 per year); unspecified assistantships also available. Financial award application deadline: 6/30; financial award applicants required to submit FAFSA. *Faculty research:* British and American literature, rhetoric and composition, world and comparative literatures, creative writing, gender and sexuality studies, women's literature, film and genre studies, literary theory, popular and visual culture, textual and

translation studies. *Total annual research expenditures:* $63,565. *Unit head:* Dr. Hunt Hawkins, Professor and Chairperson, 813-974-9492, Fax: 813-974-2270, E-mail: hhawkins@usf.edu. *Application contact:* Dr. Marty Gould, Associate Professor and Graduate Director, 813-974-9474, Fax: 813-974-2270, E-mail: mgould@usf.edu. Website: http://english.usf.edu/

University of South Florida, Innovative Education, Tampa, FL 33620-9951. *Unit head:* Kathy Barnes, Interdisciplinary Programs Coordinator, 813-974-8031, Fax: 813-974-7061, E-mail: barnesk@usf.edu. *Application contact:* Karen Tylinski, Metro Initiatives, 813-974-9943, Fax: 813-974-7061, E-mail: ktylinsk@usf.edu. Website: http://www.usf.edu/innovative-education/

The University of Tennessee, Graduate School, College of Arts and Sciences, Department of English, Knoxville, TN 37996. Offers MA, PhD. Part-time programs available. *Degree requirements:* For master's, one foreign language, thesis or alternative; for doctorate, one foreign language, thesis/dissertation. *Entrance requirements:* For master's, GRE General Test, minimum GPA of 2.7; for doctorate, GRE General Test, GRE Subject Test, minimum GPA of 2.7. Additional exam requirements/recommendations for international students: Required—TOEFL. Electronic applications accepted.

The University of Tennessee at Chattanooga, Program in English, Chattanooga, TN 37403. Offers creative writing (MA); literary study (MA); rhetoric and writing (MA, Graduate Certificate). Part-time and evening/weekend programs available. *Faculty:* 13 full-time (7 women). *Students:* 18 full-time (13 women), 20 part-time (13 women); includes 4 minority (1 Asian, non-Hispanic/Latino; 1 Hispanic/Latino; 2 Two or more races, non-Hispanic/Latino). Average age 28. 13 applicants, 85% accepted, 8 enrolled. In 2014, 17 master's awarded. *Degree requirements:* For master's, one foreign language, comprehensive exam, thesis. *Entrance requirements:* For master's, GRE General Test or GRE Subject Test (literature), minimum GPA of 3.0 in English. Additional exam requirements/recommendations for international students: Required—TOEFL (minimum score 550 paper-based; 79 iBT), IELTS (minimum score 6). *Application deadline:* For fall admission, 6/13 priority date for domestic students, 6/1 for international students; for spring admission, 10/15 priority date for domestic students, 10/1 for international students. Applications are processed on a rolling basis. Application fee: $30 ($35 for international students). Electronic applications accepted. *Expenses:* Tuition, state resident: full-time $7708; part-time $428 per credit hour. Tuition, nonresident: full-time $23,826; part-time $1323 per credit hour. *Required fees:* $1708; $252 per credit hour. *Financial support:* In 2014–15, 5 research assistantships with tuition reimbursements (averaging $6,445 per year), 6 teaching assistantships with tuition reimbursements (averaging $5,969 per year) were awarded; career-related internships or fieldwork, scholarships/grants, and unspecified assistantships also available. Support available to part-time students. Financial award applicants required to submit FAFSA. *Faculty research:* Technical writing, African-American literature, Milton, creative writing and poetry, American modernism and gender theory. *Total annual research expenditures:* $76,158. *Unit head:* Dr. Christopher Stuart, Department Head, 423-425-2140, Fax: 423-425-2282, E-mail: joe-wilferth@utc.edu. *Application contact:* Dr. J. Randy Walker, Interim Dean of Graduate Studies, 423-425-4478, Fax: 423-425-5223, E-mail: randy-walker@utc.edu. Website: http://www.utc.edu/Academic/English/

The University of Texas at Arlington, Graduate School, College of Liberal Arts, Department of English, Arlington, TX 76019. Offers English (MA); literature (PhD). Part-time and evening/weekend programs available. *Degree requirements:* For master's, thesis or comprehensive exam; for doctorate, one foreign language, comprehensive exam, thesis/dissertation. *Entrance requirements:* For master's, GRE General Test, minimum 5-page writing sample, minimum GPA of 3.0, 3 letters of recommendation; for doctorate, GRE General Test, minimum graduate GPA of 3.5, writing sample, 3 letters of recommendation. Additional exam requirements/recommendations for international students: Required—TOEFL (minimum score 550 paper-based). *Faculty research:* Rhetoric composition, American literature, British literature, cultural studies, women's studies.

The University of Texas at Austin, Graduate School, College of Liberal Arts, Department of English, Austin, TX 78712-1111. Offers creative writing (MFA); English (MA, PhD). Part-time programs available. Terminal master's awarded for partial completion of doctoral program. *Degree requirements:* For master's, 2 foreign languages; for doctorate, variable foreign language requirement. *Entrance requirements:* For master's and doctorate, GRE General Test. Electronic applications accepted.

The University of Texas at Brownsville, Graduate Studies, College of Liberal Arts, Department of English, Brownsville, TX 78520-4991. Offers MA. Part-time and evening/weekend programs available. Postbaccalaureate distance learning degree programs offered (minimal on-campus study). *Degree requirements:* For master's, comprehensive exam or thesis. *Entrance requirements:* For master's, GRE General Test, minimum GPA of 3.0 in 12 hours of upper-division English courses. Additional exam requirements/recommendations for international students: Required—TOEFL (minimum score 550 paper-based; 77 iBT). Electronic applications accepted. *Faculty research:* Sandra Cisneros, Nathaniel Hawthorne, Rodolfo Araya, Isabel Allende, linguistics.

The University of Texas at Dallas, School of Arts and Humanities, Program in Humanities, Richardson, TX 75080. Offers aesthetic studies (MA, PhD); history (MA); history of ideas (MA, PhD); humanities (MA, PhD); Latin American studies (MA); studies in literature (MA, PhD). *Faculty:* 35 full-time (11 women), 1 part-time/adjunct (0 women). *Students:* 148 full-time (94 women), 151 part-time (97 women); includes 78 minority (21 Black or African American, non-Hispanic/Latino; 4 American Indian or Alaska Native, non-Hispanic/Latino; 14 Asian, non-Hispanic/Latino; 28 Hispanic/Latino; 11 Two or more races, non-Hispanic/Latino), 16 international. Average age 39. 127 applicants, 46% accepted, 40 enrolled. In 2014, 40 master's, 15 doctorates awarded. *Degree requirements:* For master's, one foreign language, portfolio, thesis, or capstone project; for doctorate, one foreign language, thesis/dissertation. *Entrance requirements:* For master's, minimum GPA of 3.3 in upper-level coursework in field; for doctorate, field examinations, minimum GPA of 3.3 in upper-level coursework in field. Additional exam requirements/recommendations for international students: Required—TOEFL (minimum score 550 paper-based). *Application deadline:* For fall admission, 7/15 for domestic students, 5/1 priority date for international students; for spring admission, 11/15 for domestic students, 9/1 priority date for international students. Applications are processed on a rolling basis. Application fee: $50 ($100 for international students). Electronic applications accepted. *Expenses:* Tuition, state resident: full-time $11,940; part-time $663 per credit. Tuition, nonresident: full-time $22,282; part-time $1238 per credit. *Financial support:* In 2014–15, 161 students received support. Research assistantships with partial tuition reimbursements available, teaching assistantships with partial tuition reimbursements available, career-related internships or fieldwork, Federal Work-Study, institutionally sponsored loans, scholarships/grants, and unspecified assistantships available. Support available to part-time students. Financial award application deadline: 4/30; financial award applicants required to submit FAFSA. *Faculty research:* Holocaust studies, U.S./Mexico studies, translation studies, art history research, Chinese studies. *Unit head:* Dr. Michael Wilson, III, Associate Dean for Graduate Education, 972-883-2756, Fax: 972-883-2989, E-mail: mwilson@utdallas.edu.

Application contact: Alice Salazar, Coordinator, 972-883-2756, Fax: 972-883-2989, E-mail: alice.salazar1@utdallas.edu.
Website: http://www.utdallas.edu/ah/programs/graduate

The University of Texas at El Paso, Graduate School, College of Liberal Arts, Department of English, El Paso, TX 79968-0001. Offers bilingual professional writing (Certificate); English and American literature (MA); rhetoric and composition (PhD); rhetoric and writing studies (MA); teaching English (MAT). Part-time and evening/weekend programs available. *Degree requirements:* For master's, thesis optional. *Entrance requirements:* For master's, GRE General Test, minimum GPA of 3.0. Additional exam requirements/recommendations for international students: Required—TOEFL. Electronic applications accepted. *Faculty research:* Literature, creative writing, literary theory.

The University of Texas at San Antonio, College of Liberal and Fine Arts, Department of English, San Antonio, TX 78249-0617. Offers MA, PhD. Part-time and evening/weekend programs available. *Faculty:* 14 full-time (11 women), 1 (woman) part-time/adjunct. *Students:* 25 full-time (17 women), 36 part-time (23 women); includes 24 minority (21 Hispanic/Latino; 3 Two or more races, non-Hispanic/Latino). Average age 33. 36 applicants, 83% accepted, 19 enrolled. In 2014, 10 master's, 4 doctorates awarded. Terminal master's awarded for partial completion of doctoral program. *Degree requirements:* For master's, comprehensive exam, thesis optional; for doctorate, one foreign language, comprehensive exam, thesis/dissertation. *Entrance requirements:* For master's, GRE General Test, minimum GPA of 3.3 on all upper-division English courses, 18 hours of English of which 12 hours must be upper-division English literature; for doctorate, GRE General Test, GRE Subject Test (English literature), 18 hours of upper-division and/or graduate English, minimum GPA of 3.5, statement of purpose, writing sample, 3 letters of recommendation. Additional exam requirements/recommendations for international students: Required—TOEFL (minimum score 550 paper-based; 79 iBT), IELTS (minimum score 6.5). *Application deadline:* For fall admission, 7/1 for domestic students, 4/1 for international students; for spring admission, 11/1 for domestic students, 9/1 for international students. Applications are processed on a rolling basis. Application fee: $45 ($80 for international students). Electronic applications accepted. *Expenses:* Tuition, state resident: full-time $4671; part-time $260 per credit hour. Tuition, nonresident: full-time $18,022; part-time $1001 per credit hour. *Financial support:* Unspecified assistantships available. Financial award application deadline: 2/1. *Faculty research:* Transnational, cross-cultural studies in literature. *Unit head:* Dr. Mark Bayer, Department Chair, 210-458-6885, Fax: 210-458-5366, E-mail: mark.bayer@utsa.edu. *Application contact:* Dr. Bernadette Andrea, Master's Graduate Advisor of Record, 210-458-5339, Fax: 210-458-5366, E-mail: bernadette.andrea@utsa.edu.
Website: http://colfa.utsa.edu/English/

The University of Texas at Tyler, College of Arts and Sciences, Department of Literature and Languages, Tyler, TX 75799-0001. Offers English (MA); interdisciplinary studies (MAIS). Part-time and evening/weekend programs available. *Degree requirements:* For master's, one foreign language, comprehensive exam, thesis optional. *Entrance requirements:* For master's, GRE General Test, minimum GPA of 3.0; four semesters or the equivalent of one foreign language. Additional exam requirements/recommendations for international students: Required—TOEFL. Electronic applications accepted. *Faculty research:* Medieval and Tudor drama, Shakespeare, British Romanticism, British and Irish modernism, American realism, Greek drama, nineteenth-century American literature.

The University of Texas of the Permian Basin, Office of Graduate Studies, College of Arts and Sciences, Department of Literature and Languages, Program in English, Odessa, TX 79762-0001. Offers MA. Part-time and evening/weekend programs available. *Degree requirements:* For master's, comprehensive exam (for some programs), thesis (for some programs). *Entrance requirements:* For master's, GRE General Test. Additional exam requirements/recommendations for international students: Required—TOEFL (minimum score 550 paper-based).

The University of Texas–Pan American, College of Arts and Humanities, Department of English, Edinburg, TX 78539. Offers creative writing (MFA); English (MA, MAIS); English as a second language (MA). Part-time and evening/weekend programs available. *Degree requirements:* For master's, comprehensive exam, thesis optional. *Entrance requirements:* For master's, GRE General Test, minimum GPA of 3.0. *Expenses:* Tuition, state resident: full-time $4187; part-time $232.60 per credit hour. Tuition, nonresident: full-time $10,857; part-time $603.16 per credit hour. *Required fees:* $782; $27.50 per credit hour. $143.35 per semester. *Faculty research:* Oral vs. literary culture, Borderland literature, Mexican-American literature, topics in British and American literature, discourse analysis.

University of the District of Columbia, College of Arts and Sciences, Department of English, Program in English Composition and Rhetoric, Washington, DC 20008-1175. Offers MA. *Degree requirements:* For master's, comprehensive exam. *Entrance requirements:* For master's, writing proficiency exam.

The University of Toledo, College of Graduate Studies, College of Languages, Literature and Social Sciences, Department of English Language and Literature, Toledo, OH 43606-3390. Offers English as a second language (MA); teaching of writing (Certificate). Part-time programs available. *Degree requirements:* For master's, thesis. *Entrance requirements:* For master's, GRE if GPA is less than 3.0, minimum cumulative point-hour ratio of 2.7 for all previous academic work, three letters of recommendation, transcripts from all prior institutions attended, critical essay; for Certificate, statement of purpose, transcripts from all prior institutions attended, 2 letters of recommendation. Additional exam requirements/recommendations for international students: Required—TOEFL (minimum score 550 paper-based; 80 iBT). Electronic applications accepted. *Faculty research:* Literary criticism, linguistics, creative writing, folklore and cultural studies.

University of Toronto, School of Graduate Studies, Faculty of Arts and Science, Department of English, Toronto, ON M5S 2J7, Canada. Offers creative writing (MA); English (MA, PhD); JD/MA. Part-time programs available. *Degree requirements:* For master's, thesis optional; for doctorate, 2 foreign languages, thesis/dissertation. *Entrance requirements:* For master's, minimum B+ average, 2 letters of reference, portfolio (creative writing program); for doctorate, minimum A- average, 2 letters of reference, writing sample. Additional exam requirements/recommendations for international students: Required—TOEFL (minimum score 580 paper-based; 93 iBT), TWE (minimum score 5). Electronic applications accepted.

The University of Tulsa, Graduate School, Kendall College of Arts and Sciences, Department of English Language and Literature, Tulsa, OK 74104-3189. Offers MA, MTA, PhD, JD/MA. Part-time and evening/weekend programs available. *Faculty:* 13 full-time (4 women). *Students:* 26 full-time (15 women), 19 part-time (10 women); includes 4 minority (2 American Indian or Alaska Native, non-Hispanic/Latino; 2 Hispanic/Latino), 3 international. Average age 34. 41 applicants, 68% accepted, 10 enrolled. In 2014, 6 master's, 2 doctorates awarded. Terminal master's awarded for partial completion of doctoral program. *Degree requirements:* For master's, independent research project; for doctorate, one foreign language, comprehensive exam, thesis/dissertation. *Entrance requirements:* For master's, GRE General Test, writing sample; for doctorate, GRE General Test, writing sample, list of language proficiencies. Additional exam requirements/recommendations for international students: Required—TOEFL (minimum score 577 paper-based; 91 iBT), IELTS (minimum score 6.5). *Application deadline:* For fall admission, 1/15 priority date for domestic students, 1/15 for international students. Applications are processed on a rolling basis. Application fee: $55. Electronic applications accepted. *Expenses: Tuition:* Full-time $20,160; part-time $1120 per credit hour. *Required fees:* $6 per credit hour. Tuition and fees vary according to course level and course load. *Financial support:* In 2014–15, 34 students received support, including 14 fellowships with full and partial tuition reimbursements available (averaging $6,122 per year), 29 teaching assistantships with full and partial tuition reimbursements available (averaging $13,170 per year); career-related internships or fieldwork, Federal Work-Study, scholarships/grants, health care benefits, tuition waivers (full and partial), and unspecified assistantships also available. Support available to part-time students. Financial award application deadline: 1/15; financial award applicants required to submit FAFSA. *Faculty research:* Twentieth-century literature; modern and contemporary British, Irish, and American literatures; Victorian literature; American studies; cultural and gender studies; African-American literature; women's literature, nineteenth century American literature. *Total annual research expenditures:* $183,618. *Unit head:* Dr. Randall Fuller, Chairperson, 918-631-2812, Fax: 918-631-3033, E-mail: randall-fuller@utulsa.edu. *Application contact:* Dr. Robert Jackson, Advisor, 918-631-3736, Fax: 918-631-3033, E-mail: bob-jackson@utulsa.edu.
Website: http://artsandsciences.utulsa.edu/academics/departments-schools/english/

The University of Tulsa, Graduate School, Kendall College of Arts and Sciences, School of Education, Program in Teaching Arts, Tulsa, OK 74104-3189. Offers art (MTA); biology (MTA); English (MTA); history (MTA); mathematics (MTA). Part-time programs available. *Students:* 2 full-time (1 woman), 1 part-time (0 women); includes 1 minority (Black or African American, non-Hispanic/Latino). Average age 30. 2 applicants, 100% accepted, 1 enrolled. *Entrance requirements:* For master's, GRE General Test. Additional exam requirements/recommendations for international students: Required—TOEFL (minimum score 577 paper-based), IELTS (minimum score 6.5). *Application deadline:* Applications are processed on a rolling basis. Application fee: $55. Electronic applications accepted. *Expenses: Tuition:* Full-time $20,160; part-time $1120 per credit hour. *Required fees:* $6 per credit hour. Tuition and fees vary according to course level and course load. *Financial support:* In 2014–15, 2 students received support, including 1 research assistantship with full and partial tuition reimbursement available (averaging $13,148 per year), 1 teaching assistantship with full and partial tuition reimbursement available (averaging $13,148 per year); fellowships with full and partial tuition reimbursements available, career-related internships or fieldwork, Federal Work-Study, scholarships/grants, health care benefits, tuition waivers (full and partial), and unspecified assistantships also available. Support available to part-time students. Financial award application deadline: 2/1; financial award applicants required to submit FAFSA. *Unit head:* Dr. Kara Gae Neal, Chair, 918-631-2238, Fax: 918-631-3721, E-mail: karagae-neal@utulsa.edu. *Application contact:* Dr. David Brown, Advisor, 918-631-2719, Fax: 918-631-2133, E-mail: david-brown@utulsa.edu.

University of Utah, Graduate School, College of Humanities, Department of English, Salt Lake City, UT 84112. Offers American studies (MA, PhD); British and American literature (MA, PhD); creative writing (MFA, PhD), including fiction, non-fiction, poetry; rhetoric and composition (MA, PhD). *Faculty:* 27 full-time (10 women), 7 part-time/adjunct (2 women). *Students:* 47 full-time (27 women), 25 part-time (16 women); includes 5 minority (1 Black or African American, non-Hispanic/Latino; 2 Asian, non-Hispanic/Latino; 2 Two or more races, non-Hispanic/Latino), 3 international. Average age 35. 285 applicants, 12% accepted, 11 enrolled. In 2014, 7 master's, 7 doctorates awarded. Terminal master's awarded for partial completion of doctoral program. *Degree requirements:* For master's, one foreign language, comprehensive exam (for some programs), thesis (for some programs), 1 standard-level language; exam (for MA); thesis (for MFA); for doctorate, variable foreign language requirement, comprehensive exam, thesis/dissertation, 2 standard-level languages/1 advanced-level language. *Entrance requirements:* For master's and doctorate, GRE General Test, minimum GPA of 3.2. Additional exam requirements/recommendations for international students: Required—TOEFL (minimum score 650 paper-based; 115 iBT); Recommended—IELTS (minimum score 9). *Application deadline:* For fall admission, 12/15 for domestic and international students. Application fee: $55 ($65 for international students). Electronic applications accepted. *Financial support:* In 2014–15, 54 students received support, including 17 fellowships with full tuition reimbursements available (averaging $15,000 per year), 34 teaching assistantships with full tuition reimbursements available (averaging $14,000 per year); health care benefits also available. Financial award application deadline: 12/15; financial award applicants required to submit FAFSA. *Faculty research:* Creative writing including poetics and modern poetry, fiction, and experimental forms; nineteenth and twentieth century British and American literature; American studies, the American west, and environmental studies; critical theory and practice; race and gender studies. *Total annual research expenditures:* $126,500. *Unit head:* Prof. Barry L. Weller, Department Chair, 801-581-6168, E-mail: barry.weller@utah.edu. *Application contact:* Prof. Howard Horwitz, Director of Graduate Studies, 801-581-7353, E-mail: h.horwitz@english.utah.edu.
Website: http://www.hum.utah.edu/english/

University of Vermont, Graduate College, College of Arts and Sciences, Department of English, Burlington, VT 05405. Offers MA. *Degree requirements:* For master's, one foreign language, thesis. *Entrance requirements:* For master's, GRE General Test, writing sample. Additional exam requirements/recommendations for international students: Required—TOEFL (minimum score 550 paper-based; 80 iBT). Electronic applications accepted.

University of Victoria, Faculty of Graduate Studies, Faculty of Humanities, Department of English, Victoria, BC V8W 2Y2, Canada. Offers MA, PhD. Part-time programs available. *Degree requirements:* For master's, one foreign language, thesis (for some programs); for doctorate, 2 foreign languages, comprehensive exam, thesis/dissertation, candidacy exam. *Entrance requirements:* For master's, minimum A- average in last 2 years of undergraduate course work, writing sample, resume; for doctorate, minimum A- average in graduate course work, writing sample, resumé. Additional exam requirements/recommendations for international students: Required—TOEFL (minimum score 630 paper-based). Electronic applications accepted. *Faculty research:* Critical theory, nineteenth century literature, postcolonialism/multiculturalism, medieval and Renaissance literature, cultural theory.

University of Virginia, College and Graduate School of Arts and Sciences, Department of English Language and Literature, Program in English, Charlottesville, VA 22903. Offers MA, PhD, JD/MA. *Faculty:* 57 full-time (28 women), 5 part-time/adjunct (2 women). *Students:* 100 full-time (66 women), 2 part-time (both women); includes 15 minority (5 Black or African American, non-Hispanic/Latino; 6 Asian, non-Hispanic/Latino; 4 Two or more races, non-Hispanic/Latino), 6 international. Average age 27. 236 applicants, 23% accepted, 27 enrolled. In 2014, 22 master's, 18 doctorates awarded. *Degree requirements:* For master's, one foreign language, oral exam or thesis; for doctorate, 2 foreign languages, comprehensive exam, thesis/dissertation. *Entrance requirements:* For master's, GRE General Test, GRE Subject Test, 3 letters of recommendation, 2 writing samples; for doctorate, GRE General Test, GRE Subject Test, 3 letters of recommendation; 2 writing samples. Additional exam requirements/

recommendations for international students: Required—TOEFL (minimum score 600 paper-based; 90 iBT), IELTS (minimum score 7). *Application deadline:* For fall admission, 1/1 for domestic students, 1/2 for international students. Applications are processed on a rolling basis. Application fee: $60. Electronic applications accepted. *Expenses:* Tuition, state resident: full-time $14,164; part-time $349 per credit hour. Tuition, nonresident: full-time $23,722; part-time $1300 per credit hour. *Required fees:* $2514. *Financial support:* Fellowships and teaching assistantships available. Financial award applicants required to submit FAFSA. *Unit head:* Cynthia Wall, Chair, 434-924-7105, Fax: 434-924-1478, E-mail: wall@virginia.edu. *Application contact:* Clare Kinney, Director of Graduate Admissions, 434-924-6638, Fax: 434-924-1478, E-mail: crk4h@virginia.edu.
Website: http://www.engl.virginia.edu/

University of Virginia, Curry School of Education, Department of Curriculum, Instruction, and Special Education, Program in Curriculum and Instruction, Charlottesville, VA 22903. Offers curriculum and instruction (M Ed, Ed S); elementary education (M Ed, Ed D); English (M Ed, Ed D); foreign language education (M Ed); mathematics (M Ed, Ed D); reading (M Ed, Ed D, Ed S); science (Ed D); social studies (M Ed). *Students:* 47 full-time (39 women), 41 part-time (35 women); includes 6 minority (1 Asian, non-Hispanic/Latino; 3 Hispanic/Latino; 2 Two or more races, non-Hispanic/Latino), 6 international. Average age 32. 107 applicants, 64% accepted, 44 enrolled. In 2014, 62 master's, 3 doctorates, 9 other advanced degrees awarded. *Degree requirements:* For master's, comprehensive exam (for some programs); for doctorate, comprehensive exam, thesis/dissertation; for Ed S, comprehensive exam. *Entrance requirements:* For master's, doctorate, and Ed S, GRE General Test, 2 letters of recommendation. Additional exam requirements/recommendations for international students: Required—TOEFL (minimum score 600 paper-based; 90 iBT), IELTS (minimum score 7). *Application deadline:* Applications are processed on a rolling basis. Application fee: $60. Electronic applications accepted. *Expenses:* Tuition, state resident: full-time $14,164; part-time $349 per credit hour. Tuition, nonresident: full-time $23,722; part-time $1300 per credit hour. *Required fees:* $2514. *Financial support:* Fellowships with tuition reimbursements, research assistantships with tuition reimbursements, and teaching assistantships with tuition reimbursements available. Financial award application deadline: 1/5; financial award applicants required to submit FAFSA. *Unit head:* Stephanie van Hover, Chair, 434-924-0841, E-mail: sdv2w@virginia.edu. *Application contact:* Information Contact, E-mail: kgd9g@virginia.edu.
Website: http://curry.virginia.edu/academics/areas-of-study/curriculum-teaching-learning

University of Washington, Graduate School, College of Arts and Sciences, Department of English, Seattle, WA 98195. Offers creative writing (MFA); English as a second language (MAT); English literature and language (MA, MAT, PhD). Part-time programs available. Terminal master's awarded for partial completion of doctoral program. *Degree requirements:* For master's, one foreign language, thesis (for some programs); for doctorate, one foreign language, thesis/dissertation. *Entrance requirements:* For master's, GRE General Test, GRE Subject Test (MA and MAT in English), minimum GPA of 3.0; for doctorate, GRE General Test, GRE Subject Test. Additional exam requirements/recommendations for international students: Required—TOEFL. Electronic applications accepted. *Faculty research:* English and American literature, critical theory, creative writing, language theory.

University of Waterloo, Graduate Studies, Faculty of Arts, Department of English, Language and Literature, Waterloo, ON N2L 3G1, Canada. Offers English language and literature (PhD); literary studies (MA); rhetoric and communication design (MA). Part-time programs available. *Degree requirements:* For master's, one foreign language, thesis optional; for doctorate, 2 foreign languages, thesis/dissertation. *Entrance requirements:* For master's, honors degree, minimum B+ average; for doctorate, master's degree, minimum A- average. Additional exam requirements/recommendations for international students: Required—TOEFL, TWE. Electronic applications accepted. *Faculty research:* Shakespeare, American literature, rhetoric, Romantics, moderns.

The University of Western Ontario, Faculty of Graduate Studies, Faculty of Arts and Humanities, Department of English, London, ON N6A 5B8, Canada. Offers Canadian literature (MA); English (PhD); English literature (MA). *Degree requirements:* For master's, one foreign language, thesis or alternative; for doctorate, 2 foreign languages, thesis/dissertation, qualifying exam. *Entrance requirements:* For master's, minimum A average in appropriate field; for doctorate, MA or equivalent, minimum A average. Additional exam requirements/recommendations for international students: Required—TOEFL (minimum score 630 paper-based). *Faculty research:* Renaissance, nineteenth-century, modern, and postcolonial literature.

University of West Florida, College of Arts and Sciences: Arts, Department of English and Foreign Languages, Pensacola, FL 32514-5750. Offers creative writing (MA); literature (MA). Part-time and evening/weekend programs available. *Degree requirements:* For master's, thesis. *Entrance requirements:* For master's, GRE (minimum score: verbal 500, writing 4.5) or MAT (minimum score 413), official transcripts; two-page statement of purpose; writing sample (2,500 words of literary analysis for literature track or 2,500 words of fiction/non-fiction prose or 10 poems for creative writing track); three letters of recommendation from instructors; 20 hours upper-division undergraduate coursework in English. Additional exam requirements/recommendations for international students: Required—TOEFL (minimum score 550 paper-based). *Faculty research:* Faulkner, Shakespeare, American humor, women's studies, poetry.

University of West Georgia, College of Arts and Humanities, Department of English and Philosophy, Carrollton, GA 30118. Offers MA. Part-time and evening/weekend programs available. *Faculty:* 24 full-time (13 women). *Students:* 4 full-time (3 women), 24 part-time (14 women); includes 6 minority (3 Black or African American, non-Hispanic/Latino; 1 Hispanic/Latino; 2 Two or more races, non-Hispanic/Latino). Average age 28. 10 applicants, 80% accepted, 6 enrolled. In 2014, 11 master's awarded. *Degree requirements:* For master's, one foreign language, comprehensive exam, thesis optional. *Entrance requirements:* For master's, GRE General Test, NTE, undergraduate degree in English, minimum GPA of 3.2. Additional exam requirements/recommendations for international students: Required—TOEFL (minimum score 523 paper-based; 69 iBT); Recommended—IELTS (minimum score 6). *Application deadline:* For fall admission, 8/1 for domestic students, 6/1 for international students; for spring admission, 11/15 for domestic students, 10/15 for international students; for summer admission, 5/1 for domestic and international students. Applications are processed on a rolling basis. Application fee: $40. Electronic applications accepted. *Financial support:* In 2014–15, 6 students received support, including 10 research assistantships with full tuition reimbursements available (averaging $5,000 per year); career-related internships or fieldwork and unspecified assistantships also available. Support available to part-time students. Financial award application deadline: 4/1; financial award applicants required to submit FAFSA. *Faculty research:* British literature, American literature, African-American literature, creative writing, cultural studies. *Unit head:* Dr. Meg Pearson, Chair, 678-839-9892, Fax: 678-839-4849, E-mail: megp@westga.edu. *Application contact:* Kristy Gamble, Graduate Studies Associate, 678-839-5453, E-mail: kgamble@westga.edu. Website: http://www.westga.edu/english/

University of Windsor, Faculty of Graduate Studies, Faculty of Arts and Social Sciences, Department of English Language, Literature and Creative Writing, Windsor, ON N9B 3P4, Canada. Offers English: creative writing and language and literature (MA); English: language and literature (MA). Part-time programs available. *Degree requirements:* For master's, thesis. *Entrance requirements:* For master's, minimum B average, portfolio. Additional exam requirements/recommendations for international students: Required—TOEFL (minimum score 600 paper-based). Electronic applications accepted. *Faculty research:* Use of gender-related terms in popular culture; international and Aboriginal literatures: expression of cultural identity; critical analysis of authors: Pope, Munroe, Lady Morgan, Orwell, Thomas; the "feminine" voice in literature and contemporary culture.

University of Wisconsin–Eau Claire, College of Arts and Sciences, Program in English, Eau Claire, WI 54702-4004. Offers literature and textual interpretation (MA); writing (MA). Part-time programs available. *Degree requirements:* For master's, oral defense with thesis. *Entrance requirements:* For master's, minimum GPA of 3.25 in English, 3.0 overall; bachelor's degree with minimum of 24 credits in English. Additional exam requirements/recommendations for international students: Required—TOEFL (minimum score 79 iBT).

University of Wisconsin–Madison, Graduate School, College of Letters and Science, Department of English, Madison, WI 53706-1380. Offers applied English linguistics (MA); composition and rhetoric (PhD); creative writing (MFA); English language and linguistics (PhD); literary studies (MA, PhD). *Degree requirements:* For doctorate, thesis/dissertation. *Expenses:* Tuition, state resident: full-time $10,723; part-time $745 per credit. Tuition, nonresident: full-time $24,054; part-time $1578 per credit. *Required fees:* $374 per semester. Tuition and fees vary according to course load, program and reciprocity agreements.

University of Wisconsin–Milwaukee, Graduate School, College of Letters and Sciences, Department of English, Milwaukee, WI 53201-0413. Offers creative writing (PhD); English (MA); international technical communication (Certificate); linguistics (PhD); professional writing (PhD); professional writing and communication (Certificate); rhetoric and composition (PhD); MLIS/MA. *Degree requirements:* For master's, thesis or alternative; for doctorate, one foreign language, thesis/dissertation. *Entrance requirements:* For master's, GRE General Test, GRE Subject Test; for doctorate, GRE. Additional exam requirements/recommendations for international students: Required—TOEFL (minimum score 550 paper-based; 79 iBT), IELTS (minimum score 6.5). Electronic applications accepted.

University of Wisconsin–Oshkosh, Graduate Studies, College of Letters and Science, Department of English, Oshkosh, WI 54901. Offers MA. Part-time programs available. *Degree requirements:* For master's, thesis or alternative. *Entrance requirements:* For master's, GRE. Additional exam requirements/recommendations for international students: Required—TOEFL (minimum score 550 paper-based; 79 iBT). Electronic applications accepted.

University of Wisconsin–Stevens Point, College of Letters and Science, Department of English, Stevens Point, WI 54481-3897. Offers MST. *Degree requirements:* For master's, thesis or alternative.

University of Wyoming, College of Arts and Sciences, Department of English, Laramie, WY 82071. Offers creative writing (MFA); English (MA). Part-time programs available. *Degree requirements:* For master's, thesis or alternative, internship. *Entrance requirements:* For master's, GRE General Test, minimum GPA of 3.0. Electronic applications accepted. *Faculty research:* Literature and theory, creative writing, English as a second language, ethnic and women's studies, composition.

Utah State University, School of Graduate Studies, College of Humanities, Arts and Social Sciences, Department of English, Logan, UT 84322. Offers American studies (MA, MS), including folklore, western American literature and culture; English (MA, MS), including literature and writing, technical writing. Part-time and evening/weekend programs available. *Degree requirements:* For master's, thesis or alternative. *Entrance requirements:* For master's, GRE General Test or MAT, minimum GPA of 3.0, recommendation letters, writing samples. Additional exam requirements/recommendations for international students: Required—TOEFL. *Faculty research:* Scottish enlightenment, material culture, composition theory, creative nonfiction, literary criticism.

Valdosta State University, Department of English, Valdosta, GA 31698. Offers literature (MA); rhetoric and composition (MA); studies for language arts teachers (MA). Part-time programs available. *Faculty:* 12 full-time (9 women). *Students:* 6 full-time (5 women), 24 part-time (14 women); includes 2 minority (1 Black or African American, non-Hispanic/Latino; 1 Two or more races, non-Hispanic/Latino). Average age 24. 7 applicants, 71% accepted, 4 enrolled. *Degree requirements:* For master's, one foreign language, thesis, comprehensive written and/or oral exams. *Entrance requirements:* For master's, GRE General Test, minimum GPA of 3.0. Additional exam requirements/recommendations for international students: Required—TOEFL (minimum score 523 paper-based). *Application deadline:* For fall admission, 7/1 for domestic and international students; for spring admission, 11/1 for domestic and international students. Applications are processed on a rolling basis. Application fee: $35. Electronic applications accepted. *Expenses:* Tuition, state resident: part-time $236 per credit hour. Tuition, nonresident: part-time $850 per credit hour. *Required fees:* $1032 per semester. *Financial support:* In 2014–15, 11 students received support, including 6 research assistantships with full tuition reimbursements available (averaging $4,000 per year), 7 teaching assistantships with full tuition reimbursements available (averaging $8,000 per year); institutionally sponsored loans, scholarships/grants, and unspecified assistantships also available. Support available to part-time students. Financial award application deadline: 7/1; financial award applicants required to submit FAFSA. *Faculty research:* American literature, creative writing. *Unit head:* Dr. Mark Smith, Head, 229-333-5946, E-mail: marksmit@valdosta.edu. *Application contact:* Jessica Powers, Admissions Specialist, 229-333-5694, Fax: 229-245-3853, E-mail: jldevane@valdosta.edu.

Valparaiso University, Graduate School, Programs in Liberal Studies, Concentration in English, Valparaiso, IN 46383. Offers MALS, Post-Master's Certificate, JD/MALS. Part-time and evening/weekend programs available. *Students:* 2 full-time (1 woman), 1 part-time (0 women); includes 1 minority (Black or African American, non-Hispanic/Latino). Average age 36. In 2014, 1 master's awarded. *Entrance requirements:* For master's, minimum GPA of 3.0. Additional exam requirements/recommendations for international students: Required—TOEFL (minimum score 550 paper-based; 80 iBT), IELTS (minimum score 6). *Application deadline:* Applications are processed on a rolling basis. Application fee: $30 ($50 for international students). Electronic applications accepted. *Expenses:* Tuition: Full-time $10,710; part-time $595 per credit hour. *Required fees:* $378; $101 per term. Tuition and fees vary according to course load and program. *Financial support:* Available to part-time students. Applicants required to submit FAFSA. *Unit head:* Dr. Jennifer A. Ziegler, Dean, Graduate School and Continuing Education, 219-464-5313, Fax: 219-464-5381, E-mail: jennifer.ziegler@valpo.edu. *Application contact:* Jessica Choquette, Graduate Admissions Specialist, 219-464-5313, Fax: 219-464-5381, E-mail: jessica.choquette@valpo.edu.
Website: http://www.valpo.edu/grad/mals/eng.php

English

Vanderbilt University, Graduate School, Department of English, Nashville, TN 37240-1001. Offers MA, MAT, PhD. *Faculty:* 33 full-time (19 women). *Students:* 39 full-time (28 women); includes 15 minority (6 Black or African American, non-Hispanic/Latino; 4 Asian, non-Hispanic/Latino; 5 Hispanic/Latino), 3 international. Average age 28. 287 applicants, 6% accepted, 10 enrolled. In 2014, 7 master's, 9 doctorates awarded. *Degree requirements:* For master's, thesis; for doctorate, one foreign language, comprehensive exam, thesis/dissertation, final and qualifying exams. *Entrance requirements:* For master's and doctorate, GRE General Test, sample of written work. Additional exam requirements/recommendations for international students: Required—TOEFL (minimum score 570 paper-based; 88 iBT). *Application deadline:* For fall admission, 1/15 for domestic and international students. Electronic applications accepted. *Expenses: Tuition:* Full-time $42,768; part-time $1782 per credit hour. *Required fees:* $422. One-time fee: $30 full-time. *Financial support:* Fellowships with full and partial tuition reimbursements, research assistantships with full and partial tuition reimbursements, teaching assistantships with full tuition reimbursements, Federal Work-Study, institutionally sponsored loans, scholarships/grants, and health care benefits available. Financial award application deadline: 1/15; financial award applicants required to submit CSS PROFILE or FAFSA. *Faculty research:* British, American, and Anglophone literature, film, cultural studies, literary theory. *Unit head:* Dr. Dana Nelson, Director of Graduate Studies, 615-343-3185, Fax: 615-343-8028, E-mail: dana.d.nelson@vanderbilt.edu. *Application contact:* Donna Caplan, Administrative Assistant, 615-322-2541, Fax: 615-343-8028, E-mail: donna.caplan@vanderbilt.edu.
Website: http://as.vanderbilt.edu/english/graduate/

Villanova University, Graduate School of Liberal Arts and Sciences, Department of English, Villanova, PA 19085-1699. Offers MA. Part-time and evening/weekend programs available. *Faculty:* 6. *Students:* 30 full-time (20 women), 8 part-time (6 women); includes 4 minority (2 Black or African American, non-Hispanic/Latino; 1 American Indian or Alaska Native, non-Hispanic/Latino; 1 Hispanic/Latino), 1 international. Average age 27. 34 applicants, 82% accepted, 14 enrolled. In 2014, 14 master's awarded. *Degree requirements:* For master's, comprehensive exam, thesis optional. *Entrance requirements:* For master's, GRE General Test, minimum GPA of 3.0, writing sample, 3 recommendation letters. Additional exam requirements/recommendations for international students: Required—TOEFL. *Application deadline:* For fall admission, 3/1 priority date for domestic students, 5/1 for international students; for spring admission, 11/15 priority date for domestic students, 10/15 for international students; for summer admission, 5/1 for domestic students. Applications are processed on a rolling basis. Application fee: $50. Electronic applications accepted. *Financial support:* Research assistantships, Federal Work-Study, scholarships/grants, and unspecified assistantships available. Financial award applicants required to submit FAFSA. *Unit head:* Dr. Heather Hicks, Chairperson, 610-519-4645.
Website: http://www1.villanova.edu/villanova/artsci/english/gradenglish.html

Virginia Commonwealth University, Graduate School, College of Humanities and Sciences, Department of English, Program in English, Richmond, VA 23284-9005. Offers literature (MA); writing and rhetoric (MA). Part-time programs available. *Entrance requirements:* For master's, GRE General Test. Additional exam requirements/recommendations for international students: Required—TWE, TOEFL (minimum score 600 paper-based; 100 iBT) or IELTS (minimum score 6.5). Electronic applications accepted. *Faculty research:* Literature, writing, rhetoric.

Virginia Polytechnic Institute and State University, Graduate School, College of Liberal Arts and Human Sciences, Blacksburg, VA 24061. Offers career and technical education (MS Ed, Ed D, PhD, Ed S); communication (MA); counselor education (MA Ed, Ed D, PhD, Ed S); creative writing (MFA); curriculum and instruction (MA Ed, Ed D, PhD, Ed S); educational leadership and policy studies (MA Ed, Ed D, PhD, Ed S); educational research and evaluation (PhD); English (MA); foreign languages, cultures, and literatures (MA); higher education and student affairs (MA Ed); history (MA); human development (MS, PhD); material culture and public humanities (MA); philosophy (MA); political science (MA); rhetoric and writing (PhD); science and technology studies (MS, PhD); social, political, ethical, and cultural thought (PhD); sociology (MS, PhD); theater arts (MFA). *Faculty:* 421 full-time (216 women), 2 part-time/adjunct (both women). *Students:* 642 full-time (437 women), 537 part-time (344 women); includes 235 minority (132 Black or African American, non-Hispanic/Latino; 2 American Indian or Alaska Native, non-Hispanic/Latino; 27 Asian, non-Hispanic/Latino; 52 Hispanic/Latino; 1 Native Hawaiian or other Pacific Islander, non-Hispanic/Latino; 21 Two or more races, non-Hispanic/Latino), 81 international. Average age 34. 890 applicants, 46% accepted, 303 enrolled. In 2014, 342 master's, 96 doctorates, 33 other advanced degrees awarded. *Degree requirements:* For master's, comprehensive exam (for some programs), thesis (for some programs); for doctorate, comprehensive exam (for some programs), thesis/dissertation (for some programs). *Entrance requirements:* For master's and doctorate, GRE/GMAT (may vary by department). Additional exam requirements/recommendations for international students: Required—TOEFL (minimum score 550 paper-based). *Application deadline:* For fall admission, 8/1 for domestic students, 4/1 for international students; for spring admission, 1/1 for domestic students, 9/1 for international students. Applications are processed on a rolling basis. Application fee: $75. Electronic applications accepted. *Expenses:* Tuition, state resident: full-time $11,656; part-time $647.50 per credit hour. Tuition, nonresident: full-time $23,351; part-time $1297.25 per credit hour. *Required fees:* $2533; $465.75 per semester. Tuition and fees vary according to course load, campus/location and program. *Financial support:* In 2014–15, 19 research assistantships with full tuition reimbursements (averaging $22,141 per year), 231 teaching assistantships with full tuition reimbursements (averaging $19,470 per year) were awarded. Financial award application deadline: 3/1; financial award applicants required to submit FAFSA. *Total annual research expenditures:* $6.5 million. *Unit head:* Elizabeth Spiller, Dean, 540-231-6779, Fax: 540-231-7157, E-mail: espiller@vt.edu. *Application contact:* Melissa Elliott, Executive Assistant, 540-231-6779, Fax: 540-231-7157, E-mail: elliott1@vt.edu.
Website: http://www.clahs.vt.edu/

Virginia State University, College of Graduate Studies, College of Humanities and Social Sciences, Department of Languages and Literature, Petersburg, VA 23806-0001. Offers English (MA). Part-time and evening/weekend programs available. *Degree requirements:* For master's, one foreign language, thesis (for some programs). *Entrance requirements:* For master's, GRE General Test. *Faculty research:* Writing and learning instruction, high-risk students, twentieth-century literature.

Wake Forest University, Graduate School of Arts and Sciences, Department of English, Winston-Salem, NC 27109. Offers MA. Part-time programs available. *Degree requirements:* For master's, one foreign language, thesis. *Entrance requirements:* For master's, GRE General Test, writing sample. Additional exam requirements/recommendations for international students: Required—TOEFL (minimum score 79 iBT). Electronic applications accepted. *Faculty research:* Modern and contemporary poetry, feminist criticism and theory, Irish literature, British Commonwealth literature, medieval poetry.

Washington College, Graduate Programs, Department of English, Chestertown, MD 21620-1197. Offers MA. Part-time and evening/weekend programs available. *Degree requirements:* For master's, thesis optional.

Washington State University, College of Liberal Arts, Department of English, Pullman, WA 99164. Offers MA, PhD. Program applications must be made through the Pullman campus. *Students:* 41 full-time (29 women), 3 part-time (all women); includes 8 minority (1 Asian, non-Hispanic/Latino; 5 Hispanic/Latino; 2 Two or more races, non-Hispanic/Latino), 2 international. Average age 30. 66 applicants, 41% accepted, 15 enrolled. In 2014, 10 master's, 3 doctorates awarded. *Degree requirements:* For master's, one foreign language, comprehensive exam (for some programs), thesis (for some programs), oral exam; for doctorate, 2 foreign languages, comprehensive exam, thesis/dissertation, oral exam, written exam. *Entrance requirements:* For master's and doctorate, GRE General Test, GRE Subject Test, official transcripts; writing sample (approximately 10 pages); three letters of recommendation; statement of purpose (approximately 500 words); undergraduate major in English or other appropriate discipline. Additional exam requirements/recommendations for international students: Required—TOEFL, IELTS. *Application deadline:* For fall admission, 1/10 priority date for domestic students, 1/10 for international students. Applications are processed on a rolling basis. Application fee: $75. Electronic applications accepted. *Expenses:* Tuition, state resident: full-time $11,768. Tuition, nonresident: full-time $25,200. *Required fees:* $960. Tuition and fees vary according to program. *Financial support:* In 2014–15, 41 students received support, including 1 research assistantship with full and partial tuition reimbursement available (averaging $14,198 per year), 37 teaching assistantships with full and partial tuition reimbursements available (averaging $13,777 per year); career-related internships or fieldwork, Federal Work-Study, institutionally sponsored loans, scholarships/grants, health care benefits, and tuition waivers (partial) also available. Financial award application deadline: 2/10; financial award applicants required to submit FAFSA. *Faculty research:* Nationalism and gender in the American West, slavery and exploitation in nineteenth-century Britain, photography and the color line, D.H. Lawrence and Mexico, social movement cultures and the arts. *Unit head:* Dr. William Hamlin, Director, 509-335-7398, Fax: 509-335-2582, E-mail: whamlin@wsu.edu. *Application contact:* Graduate School Admissions, 800-GRADWSU, Fax: 509-335-1949, E-mail: gradsch@wsu.edu.
Website: http://libarts.wsu.edu/english/

Washington University in St. Louis, Graduate School of Arts and Sciences, Department of English, St. Louis, MO 63130-4899. Offers English and American literature (PhD); writing (MFAW). Terminal master's awarded for partial completion of doctoral program. *Degree requirements:* For master's, thesis or written exam; for doctorate, 2 foreign languages, thesis/dissertation. *Entrance requirements:* For master's and doctorate, GRE General Test, sample of written work. Additional exam requirements/recommendations for international students: Required—TOEFL. Electronic applications accepted. *Faculty research:* Medieval, early Modern, early American, eighteenth-century British, nineteenth-century British, nineteenth-century American, twentieth-century British, twentieth-century American, African-American literature and culture, Irish literature, Anglophone Postcolonial literature, gender and sexuality studies, Modernism, poetry and poetics, theory.

Wayne State University, College of Liberal Arts and Sciences, Department of English, Detroit, MI 48202. Offers comparative literature (MA); English (MA, PhD). Doctoral programs admit for fall only. *Students:* 61 full-time (37 women), 35 part-time (18 women); includes 16 minority (7 Black or African American, non-Hispanic/Latino; 5 Asian, non-Hispanic/Latino; 3 Hispanic/Latino; 1 Two or more races, non-Hispanic/Latino), 5 international. Average age 34. 136 applicants, 23% accepted, 15 enrolled. In 2014, 12 master's, 8 doctorates awarded. *Degree requirements:* For master's, variable foreign language requirement, essay or thesis; for doctorate, one foreign language, thesis/dissertation. *Entrance requirements:* For master's, statement of purpose; two academic letters of reference; sample essay from previous English course; for doctorate, GRE General Test, statement of purpose; two academic letters of reference; sample essay from previous English course. Additional exam requirements/recommendations for international students: Required—TOEFL (minimum score 550 paper-based; 79 iBT), TWE (minimum score 5.5), Michigan English Language Assessment Battery (minimum score 85); Recommended—IELTS (minimum score 6.5). *Application deadline:* For fall admission, 3/1 for domestic and international students; for winter admission, 11/1 for domestic and international students; for spring admission, 11/1 for domestic students. Application fee: $0. Electronic applications accepted. *Expenses:* Tuition, state resident: full-time $10,294; part-time $571.90 per credit hour. Tuition, nonresident: full-time $29,730; part-time $1238.75 per credit hour. *Required fees:* $1365; $43.50 per credit hour. $291.10 per semester. Tuition and fees vary according to course load and program. *Financial support:* In 2014–15, 56 students received support, including 4 fellowships with full and partial tuition reimbursements available (averaging $17,000 per year), 2 research assistantships with full and partial tuition reimbursements available (averaging $17,994 per year), 31 teaching assistantships with full and partial tuition reimbursements available (averaging $16,540 per year); scholarships/grants, health care benefits, and unspecified assistantships also available. Financial award application deadline: 3/31; financial award applicants required to submit FAFSA. *Faculty research:* English and American literature, cultural studies, composition, linguistics, film. *Unit head:* Dr. Ellen Barton, Professor and Department Chair, 313-577-7692, E-mail: ellen.barton@wayne.edu. *Application contact:* Dr. Carolin Maun, Interim Director of Graduate Studies, 313-577-7694, E-mail: caroline.maun@wayne.edu.
Website: http://clas.wayne.edu/english/

Weber State University, Telitha E. Lindquist College of Arts and Humanities, Program in English, Ogden, UT 84408-1001. Offers MA. Part-time and evening/weekend programs available. *Faculty:* 24 full-time (9 women). *Students:* 4 full-time (3 women), 49 part-time (35 women); includes 5 minority (1 Asian, non-Hispanic/Latino; 4 Hispanic/Latino), 1 international. Average age 36. In 2014, 22 master's awarded. *Degree requirements:* For master's, one foreign language. *Entrance requirements:* For master's, 3 letters of recommendation, 5- to 8-page writing sample. Additional exam requirements/recommendations for international students: Required—TOEFL (minimum score 550 paper-based; 79 iBT). *Application deadline:* For fall admission, 7/15 for domestic students; for spring admission, 10/15 for domestic students; for summer admission, 3/15 for domestic students. Applications are processed on a rolling basis. Application fee: $60 ($90 for international students). Electronic applications accepted. *Expenses:* Tuition, state resident: part-time $1638 per year. Tuition, nonresident: part-time $4912 per year. Tuition and fees vary according to course load and program. *Financial support:* In 2014–15, 17 students received support. Scholarships/grants available. Financial award application deadline: 4/1; financial award applicants required to submit FAFSA. *Unit head:* Dr. Gary Dohrer, Chair, 801-626-7318, Fax: 801-626-7760, E-mail: gdohrer@weber.edu. *Application contact:* Genevieve Bates, Office Specialist, 801-626-7179, Fax: 801-626-7760, E-mail: masterofenglish@weber.edu.
Website: http://weber.edu/maenglish

West Chester University of Pennsylvania, College of Arts and Sciences, Department of English, West Chester, PA 19383. Offers English (MA, Teaching Certificate); publishing (Certificate); TESL (MA). Part-time and evening/weekend programs available. *Faculty:* 11 full-time (8 women). *Students:* 31 full-time (18 women), 48 part-time (35 women); includes 11 minority (4 Black or African American, non-Hispanic/Latino; 1 Asian, non-Hispanic/Latino; 3 Hispanic/Latino; 3 Two or more races, non-Hispanic/Latino), 6 international. Average age 29. 45 applicants, 89% accepted, 21

enrolled. In 2014, 45 master's, 27 other advanced degrees awarded. *Degree requirements:* For master's, comprehensive exam (for some programs), thesis optional, capstone experience (for English); capstone review and teaching philosophy (for TESL). *Entrance requirements:* For master's, minimum GPA of 2.8, two letters of recommendation, and goals statement; writing sample and official transcripts (for English); introduction to linguistics coursework and experience in learning a second language (for TESL). Additional exam requirements/recommendations for international students: Required—TOEFL (minimum score 550 paper-based; 80 iBT). *Application deadline:* For fall admission, 4/15 priority date for domestic students, 3/15 for international students; for spring admission, 10/15 priority date for domestic students, 9/1 for international students. Applications are processed on a rolling basis. Application fee: $45. Electronic applications accepted. *Expenses:* Tuition, state resident: full-time $8172; part-time $454 per credit. Tuition, nonresident: full-time $12,258; part-time $681 per credit. *Required fees:* $2231; $110.78 per credit. Tuition and fees vary according to campus/location and program. *Financial support:* Unspecified assistantships available. Support available to part-time students. Financial award application deadline: 2/15; financial award applicants required to submit FAFSA. *Faculty research:* Critical theory, cultural studies, literature, composition, rhetoric, second language acquisition, language teacher development, language teaching methods, discourse analysis, computer-assisted language learning. *Unit head:* Dr. Jen Bacon, Chair, 610-436-2822, Fax: 610-738-0516, E-mail: jbacon@wcupa.edu. *Application contact:* Dr. Eric Dodson-Robinson, Graduate Coordinator for English, 610-738-0499, Fax: 610-738-0516, E-mail: edodsonrobinson@wcupa.edu.
Website: http://www.wcupa.edu/_academics/sch_cas.eng/

Western Carolina University, Graduate School, College of Arts and Sciences, Department of English, Cullowhee, NC 28723. Offers English (MA); teaching English as a second language or foreign language (MA). Part-time and evening/weekend programs available. *Degree requirements:* For master's, one foreign language, comprehensive exam, thesis (for some programs). *Entrance requirements:* For master's, GRE General Test, appropriate undergraduate degree, writing sample, 3 letters of recommendation. Additional exam requirements/recommendations for international students: Required—TOEFL (minimum score 550 paper-based; 79 iBT). *Faculty research:* Teaching English to speakers of other languages (TESOL), language assessment, applied linguistics, poetry, folk and fairy tales, post World War II British literature, Appalachian and southern literature.

Western Connecticut State University, Division of Graduate Studies, School of Arts and Sciences, Department of English, Danbury, CT 06810-6885. Offers English (MA); literature (MA); TESOL (MA); writing (MA). Part-time programs available. *Degree requirements:* For master's, thesis (for writing option), completion of program in 6 years. *Entrance requirements:* For master's, minimum GPA of 2.5, writing sample. Additional exam requirements/recommendations for international students: Recommended—TOEFL (minimum score 550 paper-based; 79 iBT), IELTS (minimum score 6). *Faculty research:* Developing inquiry in teachers and students, encouraging talent development, analyzing program development and assessment techniques, developing student learning outcomes, encouraging teachers as researchers, assessing the impact of computer technologies.

Western Illinois University, School of Graduate Studies, College of Arts and Sciences, Department of English and Journalism, Macomb, IL 61455-1390. Offers English (MA); literary studies (Certificate); professional writing (Certificate); teaching writing (Certificate). Part-time programs available. *Students:* 4 full-time (3 women), 36 part-time (24 women); includes 7 minority (1 Black or African American, non-Hispanic/Latino; 4 Hispanic/Latino; 2 Two or more races, non-Hispanic/Latino). Average age 30. 21 applicants, 95% accepted, 10 enrolled. In 2014, 16 master's, 6 other advanced degrees awarded. *Degree requirements:* For master's, thesis or alternative. *Entrance requirements:* Additional exam requirements/recommendations for international students: Required—TOEFL (minimum score 575 paper-based; 88 iBT). *Application deadline:* Applications are processed on a rolling basis. Application fee: $30. Electronic applications accepted. *Financial support:* In 2014–15, 14 students received support, including 14 teaching assistantships with full tuition reimbursements available (averaging $8,688 per year); research assistantships with full tuition reimbursements available also available. Financial award applicants required to submit FAFSA. *Unit head:* Dr. Mark Mossman, Chairperson, 309-298-1103. *Application contact:* Dr. Nancy Parsons, Associate Provost and Director of Graduate Studies, 309-298-1806, Fax: 309-298-2345, E-mail: grad-office@wiu.edu.
Website: http://wiu.edu/English

Western Kentucky University, Graduate Studies, Potter College of Arts and Letters, Department of English, Bowling Green, KY 42101. Offers education (MA); English (MA Ed); literature (MA), including American literature, British literature, literary theory, women writers, world literature; teaching English as a second language (MA); writing (MA). Part-time and evening/weekend programs available. *Degree requirements:* For master's, comprehensive exam, thesis optional, final exam. *Entrance requirements:* For master's, GRE General Test, minimum GPA of 2.75. Additional exam requirements/recommendations for international students: Required—TOEFL (minimum score 555 paper-based; 79 iBT). *Faculty research:* Improving writing, linking teacher knowledge and performance, Victorian women writers, Kentucky women writers, Kentucky poets.

Western Michigan University, Graduate College, College of Arts and Sciences, Department of English, Kalamazoo, MI 49008. Offers creative writing (MFA, PhD); English (MA, PhD); English teaching (MA). *Degree requirements:* For doctorate, one foreign language, thesis/dissertation. *Application deadline:* For fall admission, 2/1 for domestic students. *Financial support:* Application deadline: 2/15. *Application contact:* Admissions and Orientation, 269-387-2000, Fax: 269-387-2096.

Western Washington University, Graduate School, College of Humanities and Social Sciences, Department of English, Bellingham, WA 98225-5996. Offers MA. Part-time programs available. *Degree requirements:* For master's, one foreign language, comprehensive exam, thesis (for some programs). *Entrance requirements:* For master's, GRE General Test, writing sample, minimum GPA of 3.0 in last 60 semester hours or last 90 quarter hours of course work. Additional exam requirements/recommendations for international students: Required—TOEFL (minimum score 567 paper-based). Electronic applications accepted. *Faculty research:* Literature and technology, film, composition and rhetoric, technical writing, critical and cultural theory.

Westfield State University, Division of Graduate and Continuing Education, Department of English, Westfield, MA 01086. Offers MA. Part-time and evening/weekend programs available. *Degree requirements:* For master's, one foreign language, thesis. *Entrance requirements:* For master's, GRE General Test, MAT, minimum undergraduate GPA of 2.7, undergraduate course work in English.

West Texas A&M University, College of Fine Arts and Humanities, Department of English, Philosophy and Modern Languages, Canyon, TX 79016-0001. Offers English (MA). Part-time and evening/weekend programs available. *Degree requirements:* For master's, comprehensive exam, thesis optional. *Entrance requirements:* For master's, GRE General Test. Additional exam requirements/recommendations for international students: Required—TOEFL (minimum score 550 paper-based). Electronic applications accepted. *Faculty research:* Medieval studies, composition theory, literary criticism, Evelyn Scott, transformation of literacy in computer mediated communication.

West Virginia University, Eberly College of Arts and Sciences, Department of English, Morgantown, WV 26506. Offers creative writing (MFA); English (MA, PhD); literary/cultural studies (MA, PhD); writing (MA). Part-time and evening/weekend programs available. *Degree requirements:* For master's, one foreign language, thesis optional; for doctorate, one foreign language, thesis/dissertation, preliminary exam. *Entrance requirements:* For master's, GRE General Test, minimum GPA of 3.0; for doctorate, GRE General Test, GRE Subject Test, minimum GPA of 3.0. Additional exam requirements/recommendations for international students: Required—TOEFL. Electronic applications accepted. *Faculty research:* American studies, gender studies, media studies, cultural studies.

Wichita State University, Graduate School, Fairmount College of Liberal Arts and Sciences, Department of English, Wichita, KS 67260. Offers creative writing (MFA); English (MA). Part-time and evening/weekend programs available. *Entrance requirements:* For master's, writing sample (MFA). *Unit head:* Dr. Mary Waters, Chair, 316-978-3130, Fax: 316-978-3548, E-mail: mary.waters@wichita.edu. *Application contact:* Jordan Oleson, Admissions Coordinator, 316-978-3095, Fax: 316-978-3253, E-mail: jordan.oleson@wichita.edu.
Website: http://www.wichita.edu/english

Wilfrid Laurier University, Faculty of Graduate and Postdoctoral Studies, Faculty of Arts, Department of English and Film Studies, Waterloo, ON N2L 3C5, Canada. Offers English (MA); English and film (PhD). *Degree requirements:* For master's, thesis optional; for doctorate, thesis/dissertation. *Entrance requirements:* For master's, honours BA or the equivalent in English, minimum B+ in English courses above first year level; for doctorate, MA in English, minimum A- average in graduate work. Additional exam requirements/recommendations for international students: Recommended—TOEFL (minimum score 89 iBT). Electronic applications accepted. *Faculty research:* Gender and genre, Canadian studies, early modern studies, postcolonial studies, nineteenth century studies.

William Paterson University of New Jersey, College of Humanities and Social Sciences, Wayne, NJ 07470-8420. Offers applied sociology (MA); clinical and counseling psychology (MA); creative and professional writing (MFA); English (MA); history (MA); public policy and international affairs (MA). Part-time and evening/weekend programs available. *Faculty:* 32 full-time (16 women), 3 part-time/adjunct (1 woman). *Students:* 50 full-time (30 women), 114 part-time (88 women); includes 64 minority (7 Black or African American, non-Hispanic/Latino; 1 American Indian or Alaska Native, non-Hispanic/Latino; 4 Asian, non-Hispanic/Latino; 50 Hispanic/Latino; 2 Two or more races, non-Hispanic/Latino), 2 international. Average age 34. 115 applicants, 81% accepted, 65 enrolled. In 2014, 42 master's awarded. Terminal master's awarded for partial completion of doctoral program. *Degree requirements:* For master's, thesis (for some programs), internship (for some programs). *Entrance requirements:* For master's, GRE/MAT, minimum GPA of 3.0; 2 letters of recommendation; writing sample/personal statement. Additional exam requirements/recommendations for international students: Required—TOEFL (minimum score 550 paper-based; 79 iBT), IELTS (minimum score 6). *Application deadline:* For fall admission, 6/1 for domestic students, 3/1 for international students; for spring admission, 11/1 for domestic students, 10/1 for international students. Applications are processed on a rolling basis. Application fee: $50. Electronic applications accepted. *Expenses:* Tuition, state resident: full-time $12,413; part-time $564.21 per credit. Tuition, nonresident: full-time $20,487; part-time $931.21 per credit. *Required fees:* $2107; $95.79 per credit. $478.95 per semester. Tuition and fees vary according to course load and degree level. *Financial support:* Research assistantships with full tuition reimbursements, Federal Work-Study, scholarships/grants, and unspecified assistantships available. Support available to part-time students. Financial award application deadline: 4/1; financial award applicants required to submit FAFSA. *Faculty research:* Sexual violence, history of science in Muslim societies, bioethics, teaching writing for transfer, psychological impact of microagressions on minority communities. *Unit head:* Dr. Kara Rabbitt, Dean, 973-720-2731, Fax: 973-720-2955, E-mail: rabbittk@wpunj.edu. *Application contact:* Tinu Adeniran, Associate Director, Graduate Admissions, 973-720-2764, Fax: 973-720-2035, E-mail: adenirant@wpunj.edu.
Website: http://www.wpunj.edu/cohss

Winona State University, College of Liberal Arts, Department of English, Winona, MN 55987. Offers MA, MS. Part-time programs available. *Degree requirements:* For master's, thesis or alternative.

Winthrop University, College of Arts and Sciences, Department of English, Rock Hill, SC 29733. Offers MA. Part-time and evening/weekend programs available. *Degree requirements:* For master's, one foreign language, thesis optional. *Entrance requirements:* For master's, GRE General Test, MAT or PRAXIS, 24 undergraduate hours of course work in English. Electronic applications accepted.

Wright State University, School of Graduate Studies, College of Liberal Arts, Department of English Language and Literatures, Dayton, OH 45435. Offers composition and rhetoric (MA); English (MA); literature (MA); teaching English to speakers of other languages (MA). *Degree requirements:* For master's, thesis optional, portfolio. *Entrance requirements:* For master's, 20 hours in upper-level English. Additional exam requirements/recommendations for international students: Required—TOEFL. *Faculty research:* American literature, world literature in English, applied linguistics, writing theory and pedagogy.

Xavier University, College of Arts and Sciences, Department of English, Cincinnati, OH 45207. Offers MA. Part-time and evening/weekend programs available. *Faculty:* 3 full-time (0 women). *Students:* 2 full-time (1 woman), 7 part-time (4 women). Average age 33. 11 applicants, 64% accepted, 2 enrolled. In 2014, 12 master's awarded. *Degree requirements:* For master's, one foreign language, comprehensive exam, thesis optional. *Entrance requirements:* For master's, GRE, writing sample; minimum GPA of 3.2 in undergraduate English courses, 3.0 for all undergraduate coursework; official transcript; intent/purpose statement. Additional exam requirements/recommendations for international students: Required—TOEFL (minimum score 550 paper-based; 79 iBT). *Application deadline:* Applications are processed on a rolling basis. Application fee: $35. Electronic applications accepted. Application fee is waived when completed online. *Expenses:* Expenses: $600 per credit hour. *Financial support:* In 2014–15, 5 students received support. Applicants required to submit FAFSA. *Faculty research:* British literature, American literature, linguistics, literary theory, composition studies. *Unit head:* Dr. Tyrone Williams, Director of English Graduate Program, 513-745-2014, Fax: 513-745-3065, E-mail: williamt@xavier.edu. *Application contact:* Roger Bosse, Graduate Services Director, 513-745-3357, Fax: 513-745-1048, E-mail: bosse@xavier.edu.
Website: http://www.xavier.edu/english-ma/

Yale University, Graduate School of Arts and Sciences, Department of English Language and Literature, New Haven, CT 06520. Offers MA, PhD. Terminal master's awarded for partial completion of doctoral program. *Degree requirements:* For master's, 2 foreign languages; for doctorate, 3 foreign languages, thesis/dissertation. *Entrance requirements:* For master's and doctorate, GRE General Test, GRE Subject Test.

English

York University, Faculty of Graduate Studies, Faculty of Liberal Arts and Professional Studies, Program in English, Toronto, ON M3J 1P3, Canada. Offers MA, PhD. Part-time programs available. *Degree requirements:* For master's, thesis or alternative; for doctorate, one foreign language, comprehensive exam, thesis/dissertation. Electronic applications accepted.

Youngstown State University, Graduate School, College of Liberal Arts and Social Sciences, Department of English, Youngstown, OH 44555-0001. Offers MA. Part-time programs available. *Degree requirements:* For master's, portfolio. *Entrance requirements:* For master's, bachelor's degree in English, minimum GPA of 2.7. Additional exam requirements/recommendations for international students: Required—TOEFL. *Faculty research:* Technical communications, multicultural literacy, children's literature, women's literature, film study, linguistics.

French

Arizona State University at the Tempe campus, College of Liberal Arts and Sciences, School of International Letters and Cultures, Program in French, Tempe, AZ 85287-0202. Offers comparative literature (MA); linguistics (MA); literature (MA). Part-time and evening/weekend programs available. *Degree requirements:* For master's, thesis or applied project, interactive Program of Study (iPOS) submitted no later than beginning of third semester of study or before completing 50 percent of coursework towards completion of degree. *Entrance requirements:* For master's, GRE, minimum GPA of 3.25 in the last two years of work leading to the bachelor's degree in French major, personal statement, writing sample (preferably written in French), 3 letters of recommendation. Additional exam requirements/recommendations for international students: Required—TOEFL (minimum score 550 paper-based; 83 iBT), IELTS (minimum score 6.5). Electronic applications accepted.

Asbury University, School of Graduate and Professional Studies, Wilmore, KY 40390-1198. Offers biology: alternative certificate (MA Ed); chemistry: alternative certificate (MA Ed); English (MA Ed); English as a second language (MA Ed); ESL (MA Ed); French (MA Ed); Latin: alternative certificate (MA Ed); mathematics: alternative certificate (MA Ed); reading/writing endorsement (MA Ed); social studies (MA Ed); social work (MSW), including child and family services; Spanish (MA Ed); special education (MA Ed); special education: alternative certificate (MA Ed); teacher as leader endorsement (MA Ed). *Accreditation:* NCATE. Part-time programs available. *Degree requirements:* For master's, action research project, portfolio. *Entrance requirements:* For master's, PRAXIS/NTE, minimum GPA of 2.75, letters of recommendation. Additional exam requirements/recommendations for international students: Required—TOEFL (minimum score 550 paper-based). Electronic applications accepted.

Bennington College, Graduate Programs, MA in Teaching a Second Language Program, Bennington, VT 05201. Offers education (MATSL); foreign language education (MATSL); French (MATSL); Spanish (MATSL). Part-time programs available. *Degree requirements:* For master's, one foreign language, 2 major projects and presentations. *Entrance requirements:* For master's, Oral Proficiency Interview (OPI). Additional exam requirements/recommendations for international students: Required—TOEFL (minimum score 577 paper-based; 91 iBT). *Expenses:* Contact institution. *Faculty research:* Acquisition, evaluation, assessment, conceptual teaching and learning, content-driven communication, applied linguistics.

Binghamton University, State University of New York, Graduate School, School of Arts and Sciences, Department of Romance Languages and Literatures, Program in French, Vestal, NY 13850. Offers MA. *Students:* 2 part-time (0 women). Average age 28. 1 applicant, 100% accepted. *Degree requirements:* For master's, one foreign language, comprehensive exam, thesis or alternative. *Entrance requirements:* For master's, GRE General Test. Additional exam requirements/recommendations for international students: Required—TOEFL (minimum score 550 paper-based; 80 iBT). *Application deadline:* For fall admission, 2/15 priority date for domestic and international students; for spring admission, 11/15 priority date for domestic and international students. Applications are processed on a rolling basis. Application fee: $75. Electronic applications accepted. *Expenses:* Tuition, state resident: full-time $7776; part-time $432 per credit. Tuition, nonresident: full-time $15,138; part-time $841 per credit. *Required fees:* $1754; $213 per credit. Tuition and fees vary according to degree level and program. *Financial support:* Career-related internships or fieldwork, Federal Work-Study, institutionally sponsored loans, and unspecified assistantships available. Support available to part-time students. Financial award application deadline: 2/15. *Unit head:* Dr. Antonio Sobejano-Moran, Chairperson, 607-777-2548, E-mail: sobe@binghamton.edu. *Application contact:* Kishan Zuber, Recruiting and Admissions Coordinator, 607-777-2151, Fax: 607-777-2501, E-mail: kzuber@binghamton.edu.

Boston College, Graduate School of Arts and Sciences, Department of Romance Languages and Literatures, Chestnut Hill, MA 02467-3800. Offers French (MA); Italian (MA); Spanish (MA). Part-time programs available. *Faculty:* 21 full-time. *Students:* 34 full-time (30 women); includes 5 minority (2 Asian, non-Hispanic/Latino; 3 Hispanic/Latino), 8 international. 55 applicants, 33% accepted, 10 enrolled. In 2014, 9 master's awarded. Terminal master's awarded for partial completion of doctoral program. *Degree requirements:* For master's, one foreign language. *Entrance requirements:* Additional exam requirements/recommendations for international students: Required—TOEFL (minimum score 600 paper-based; 100 iBT), IELTS (minimum score 7). *Application deadline:* For fall admission, 1/2 for domestic and international students. Application fee: $75. Electronic applications accepted. *Financial support:* In 2014–15, fellowships with full tuition reimbursements (averaging $18,450 per year), teaching assistantships with full tuition reimbursements (averaging $18,450 per year) were awarded; Federal Work-Study, health care benefits, and unspecified assistantships also available. Support available to part-time students. Financial award application deadline: 3/1; financial award applicants required to submit FAFSA. *Faculty research:* Spanish-American literature, philology, medieval French romance and troubadour lyrics, Golden Age Peninsular literature, secondary language acquisition and pedagogy, Hispanic studies, French language and literature, Italian language and literature. *Unit head:* Dr. Franco Mormando, Chairperson, 617-552-6346, E-mail: franco.mormando@bc.edu. *Application contact:* Dr. Laurie Shepard, Associate Dean, 617-552-8269, Fax: 617-552-3700, E-mail: laurie.shepard@bc.edu.
Website: http://www.bc.edu/rll

Boston University, Graduate School of Arts and Sciences, Department of Romance Studies, Boston, MA 02215. Offers French language and literature (MA, PhD); Hispanic language and literatures (MA, PhD). *Students:* 39 full-time (29 women), 1 part-time (0 women); includes 5 minority (1 Black or African American, non-Hispanic/Latino; 4 Hispanic/Latino), 12 international. Average age 32. 81 applicants, 25% accepted, 10 enrolled. In 2014, 2 master's, 4 doctorates awarded. Terminal master's awarded for partial completion of doctoral program. *Degree requirements:* For master's, one foreign language, comprehensive exam; for doctorate, 2 foreign languages, comprehensive exam, thesis/dissertation. *Entrance requirements:* For master's and doctorate, GRE General Test, sample of written work, 3 letters of recommendation. Additional exam requirements/recommendations for international students: Required—TOEFL (minimum score 84 iBT). *Application deadline:* For fall admission, 1/15 for domestic and international students. Application fee: $80. Electronic applications accepted. *Expenses: Tuition:* Full-time $45,686; part-time $1428 per credit hour. *Required fees:* $660; $60 per semester. Tuition and fees vary according to program. *Financial support:* In 2014–15, 33 students received support, including 7 fellowships with full tuition reimbursements available (averaging $20,500 per year), 24 teaching assistantships with full tuition reimbursements available (averaging $20,500 per year); research assistantships, Federal Work-Study, scholarships/grants, and health care benefits also available. Support available to part-time students. Financial award application deadline: 1/15. *Unit head:* Nancy Harrowitz, Chairman, 617-353-6225, Fax: 617-353-6246, E-mail: nharrow@bu.edu. *Application contact:* Deanna Wong, Administrative Assistant, 617-353-2641, Fax: 617-353-6246, E-mail: dswong@bu.edu.
Website: http://www.bu.edu/rs/

Bowling Green State University, Graduate College, College of Arts and Sciences, Department of Romance and Classical Studies, Program in French, Bowling Green, OH 43403. Offers French (MA); French education (MAT). Part-time programs available. *Degree requirements:* For master's, one foreign language, thesis or alternative. *Entrance requirements:* For master's, GRE General Test. Additional exam requirements/recommendations for international students: Required—TOEFL. Electronic applications accepted. *Faculty research:* Francophone literature, French cinema, business French, nineteenth- and twentieth-century literature.

Brigham Young University, Graduate Studies, College of Humanities, Department of French and Italian, Provo, UT 84602. Offers French studies (MA). *Faculty:* 9 full-time (1 woman). *Students:* 2 full-time (1 woman), 3 part-time (2 women); includes 1 minority (Asian, non-Hispanic/Latino). Average age 28. 4 applicants, 100% accepted, 4 enrolled. In 2014, 3 master's awarded. *Degree requirements:* For master's, one foreign language, thesis. *Entrance requirements:* For master's, GRE General Test, BA in French. Additional exam requirements/recommendations for international students: Required—TOEFL. *Application deadline:* For fall admission, 2/28 for domestic and international students. Application fee: $50. Electronic applications accepted. *Expenses: Tuition:* Full-time $6310; part-time $371 per credit hour. Tuition and fees vary according to program and student's religious affiliation. *Financial support:* In 2014–15, 5 students received support, including 3 teaching assistantships (averaging $1,737 per year); research assistantships, career-related internships or fieldwork, institutionally sponsored loans, scholarships/grants, and tuition waivers (full and partial) also available. Support available to part-time students. *Faculty research:* Francophone studies, medieval literature, Provencal literature, existentialism, second language acquisition, cultural studies, the sacred, Renaissance poetry, satire. *Unit head:* Dr. Corry L. Cropper, Department Chair, 801-422-4484, Fax: 801-422-0260, E-mail: corrycropper@gmail.com. *Application contact:* Dr. Anca M. Sprenger, Graduate Coordinator, 801-422-2306, Fax: 801-422-0260, E-mail: anca_sprenger@byu.edu.
Website: http://frenital.byu.edu/department.html

Brooklyn College of the City University of New York, School of Humanities and Social Sciences, Department of Modern Languages and Literatures, Brooklyn, NY 11210-2889. Offers French (MA); Spanish (MA). *Degree requirements:* For master's, comprehensive exam or research paper. *Entrance requirements:* For master's, 18 credits in advanced courses in Spanish, 2 letters of recommendation. Additional exam requirements/recommendations for international students: Required—TOEFL (minimum score 500 paper-based; 61 iBT). Electronic applications accepted. *Faculty research:* Latin American contemporary novel, Caribbean female contemporary literature, nineteenth- and twentieth-century Spanish novel, twentieth-century Mexican poetry.

Brown University, Graduate School, Department of French Studies, Providence, RI 02912. Offers PhD. *Degree requirements:* For doctorate, variable foreign language requirement, thesis/dissertation, preliminary exam.

California State University, Fullerton, Graduate Studies, College of Humanities and Social Sciences, Department of Modern Languages and Literatures, Fullerton, CA 92834-9480. Offers French (MA); German (MA); Spanish (MA); teaching English to speakers of other languages (MS). Part-time programs available. *Students:* 36 full-time (26 women), 56 part-time (40 women); includes 57 minority (9 Asian, non-Hispanic/Latino; 46 Hispanic/Latino; 2 Two or more races, non-Hispanic/Latino), 19 international. Average age 32. 55 applicants, 69% accepted, 24 enrolled. In 2014, 30 master's awarded. *Degree requirements:* For master's, comprehensive exam, thesis or alternative. *Entrance requirements:* For master's, minimum GPA of 2.5 in last 60 hours of course work, undergraduate major in a language. Application fee: $55. *Financial support:* Career-related internships or fieldwork, Federal Work-Study, institutionally sponsored loans, and scholarships/grants available. Support available to part-time students. Financial award application deadline: 3/1; financial award applicants required to submit FAFSA. *Unit head:* Dr. Reyes Fidalgo, Chair, 657-278-4563. *Application contact:* Admissions/Applications, 657-278-2371.

California State University, Long Beach, Graduate Studies, College of Liberal Arts, Department of Romance, German, and Russian Languages and Literature, Program in French and Francophone Studies, Long Beach, CA 90840. Offers MA. Part-time programs available. *Degree requirements:* For master's, one foreign language, comprehensive exam, thesis optional. *Entrance requirements:* For master's, BA in French. Electronic applications accepted. *Faculty research:* Eighteenth-century encyclopedism, development of the novel, La Chanson de Roland.

California State University, Los Angeles, Graduate Studies, College of Arts and Letters, Department of Modern Languages and Literatures, Los Angeles, CA 90032-8530. Offers French (MA); Spanish (MA). Part-time and evening/weekend programs available. *Degree requirements:* For master's, comprehensive exam. *Entrance requirements:* Additional exam requirements/recommendations for international students: Required—TOEFL (minimum score 500 paper-based). Electronic applications accepted. *Expenses:* Tuition, state resident: full-time $6738; part-time $3609 per year. Tuition, nonresident: full-time $15,666; part-time $8073 per year. Tuition and fees vary according to course load, degree level and program. *Faculty research:* French literature,

language teaching and methodology, Spanish poetry, Spanish American fiction and poetry.

Carleton University, Faculty of Graduate Studies, Faculty of Arts and Social Sciences, Department of French, Ottawa, ON K1S 5B6, Canada. Offers MA. *Degree requirements:* For master's, thesis optional. *Entrance requirements:* For master's, honors degree. *Faculty research:* French, French Canadian and Acadian literatures and linguistics, Francophone studies, rhetorical studies.

Case Western Reserve University, School of Graduate Studies, Department of Modern Languages and Literatures, Program in French, Cleveland, OH 44106. Offers MA. Part-time programs available. *Faculty:* 5 full-time (3 women). *Students:* 2 part-time (both women); includes 1 minority (Two or more races, non-Hispanic/Latino). In 2014, 1 master's awarded. Terminal master's awarded for partial completion of doctoral program. *Degree requirements:* For master's, one foreign language, comprehensive exam, thesis or alternative. *Entrance requirements:* For master's, GRE General Test, writing sample, letters of recommendation. Additional exam requirements/recommendations for international students: Required—TOEFL (minimum score 577 paper-based; 90 iBT); Recommended—IELTS (minimum score 7). *Application deadline:* For fall admission, 3/1 priority date for domestic students; for spring admission, 11/1 priority date for domestic students. Applications are processed on a rolling basis. Application fee: $50. Electronic applications accepted. *Financial support:* Fellowships, institutionally sponsored loans, and tuition waivers (full) available. Financial award application deadline: 3/1; financial award applicants required to submit CSS PROFILE or FAFSA. *Faculty research:* Eighteenth and nineteenth century literature (novel, poetry, drama), literary theory, women's studies, cultural criticism. *Unit head:* Prof. Stephen Haynesworth, Interim Chair, 216-368-3071, Fax: 216-368-4681. *Application contact:* Prof. Marie Lathers, Director, Graduate Studies in French, 216-368-3071, Fax: 216-368-2216, E-mail: mhl5@case.edu.
Website: http://dmll.case.edu/graduate/

Central Connecticut State University, School of Graduate Studies, College of Liberal Arts and Social Sciences, Department of Modern Languages, Program in Modern Language, New Britain, CT 06050-4010. Offers French (MA, Certificate); German (Certificate); Italian (Certificate); modern language (MA); Spanish language and Hispanic culture (MA). Part-time and evening/weekend programs available. *Students:* 4 full-time (3 women), 28 part-time (22 women); includes 13 minority (1 Black or African American, non-Hispanic/Latino; 12 Hispanic/Latino), 1 international. Average age 34. 9 applicants, 100% accepted, 7 enrolled. In 2014, 8 master's, 5 other advanced degrees awarded. *Degree requirements:* For master's, one foreign language, comprehensive exam, thesis or alternative; for Certificate, qualifying exam. *Entrance requirements:* For master's, minimum undergraduate GPA of 2.7, 24 credits of undergraduate courses in each language in which graduate work will be undertaken. Additional exam requirements/recommendations for international students: Required—TOEFL (minimum score 550 paper-based; 79 iBT). *Application deadline:* For fall admission, 6/1 for domestic students, 5/1 for international students; for spring admission, 11/1 for domestic and international students. Applications are processed on a rolling basis. Application fee: $50. Electronic applications accepted. *Expenses: Tuition,* area resident: full-time $5730; part-time $534 per credit. Tuition, state resident: full-time $8596; part-time $534 per credit. Tuition, nonresident: full-time $15,964; part-time $548 per credit. *Required fees:* $4211; $215 per credit. *Faculty research:* Twentieth-century French theater, seventeenth-century French literature, French Middle Ages. *Unit head:* Dr. Lilian Uribe, Chair, 860-832-2875, E-mail: uribe@ccsu.edu. *Application contact:* Patricia Gardner, Associate Director of Graduate Studies, 860-832-2350, Fax: 860-832-2362, E-mail: graduateadmissions@ccsu.edu.

Cleveland State University, College of Graduate Studies, College of Liberal Arts and Social Sciences, Department of Modern Languages, Cleveland, OH 44115. Offers French (M Ed); Spanish (M Ed, MA), including language and linguistics (MA), Latin American studies (MA), peninsular studies (MA), Spanish (MA). Part-time and evening/weekend programs available. *Faculty:* 6 full-time (3 women), 1 (woman) part-time/adjunct. *Students:* 5 full-time (1 woman), 11 part-time (9 women); includes 7 minority (all Hispanic/Latino), 2 international. Average age 35. 7 applicants, 57% accepted, 2 enrolled. In 2014, 5 master's awarded. *Degree requirements:* For master's, one foreign language, comprehensive exam, thesis optional. *Entrance requirements:* For master's, undergraduate major in Spanish or equivalent, essay in Spanish, writing sample, 2 letters of reference, ACTFL "advanced low" oral proficiency rating. Additional exam requirements/recommendations for international students: Required—TOEFL (minimum score 525 paper-based; 65 iBT). *Application deadline:* For fall admission, 7/25 priority date for domestic students; for spring admission, 12/15 priority date for domestic students. Applications are processed on a rolling basis. Application fee: $30. Electronic applications accepted. *Expenses:* Tuition, state resident: full-time $9566; part-time $531 per credit hour. Tuition, nonresident: full-time $17,980; part-time $999 per credit hour. *Required fees:* $25 per semester. Tuition and fees vary according to degree level and program. *Financial support:* In 2014–15, 5 students received support, including 5 teaching assistantships with full tuition reimbursements available (averaging $8,000 per year); Federal Work-Study and unspecified assistantships also available. Financial award application deadline: 4/1. *Faculty research:* Peninsular poetry and prose, sociolinguistics, Latin American and Caribbean literature, Arabic diaspora in Latin America, border literature. *Unit head:* Dr. Antonio Medina-Rivera, Chairperson, 216-523-7175, Fax: 216-687-4650, E-mail: a.medinarivera@csuohio.edu. *Application contact:* Dr. Stephen Gingerich, Graduate Director, 216-687-4677, Fax: 216-687-4650, E-mail: s.gingerich@csuohio.edu.
Website: http://www.csuohio.edu/class/world-languages/world-languages

Columbia University, Graduate School of Arts and Sciences, New York, NY 10027. Offers African-American studies (MA); American studies (MA); anthropology (MA, PhD); art history and archaeology (MA, PhD); astronomy (PhD); biological sciences (PhD); biotechnology (MA); chemical physics (PhD); chemistry (PhD); classical studies (MA, PhD); classics (MA, PhD); climate and society (MA); earth and environmental sciences (PhD); East Asia: regional studies (MA); East Asian languages and cultures (MA, PhD); ecology, evolution and environmental biology (MA), including conservation biology; ecology, evolution, and environmental biology (PhD), including ecology and evolutionary biology, evolutionary primatology; economics (PhD); English and comparative literature (MA, PhD); French and Romance philology (MA, PhD); Germanic languages (MA, PhD); global French studies (MA); Hispanic cultural studies (MA); history (PhD); history and literature (MA); human rights studies (MA); Islamic studies (MA); Italian (MA, PhD); Japanese pedagogy (MA); Jewish studies (MA); Latin America and the Caribbean: regional studies (MA); Latin American and Iberian cultures (PhD); mathematics (MA, PhD), including finance (MA); medieval and Renaissance studies (MA); Middle Eastern, South Asian, and African studies (MA, PhD); modern art: critical and curatorial studies (MA); modern European studies (MA); museum anthropology (MA); music (DMA, PhD); oral history (MA); philosophical foundations of physics (MA); philosophy (MA, PhD); physics (PhD); political science (MA, PhD); psychology (PhD); quantitative methods in the social sciences (MA); religion (MA, PhD); Russia, Eurasia and East Europe: regional studies (MA); Russian translation (MA); Slavic cultures (MA); Slavic languages (MA, PhD); sociology (MA, PhD); South Asian studies (MA); statistics (MA, PhD); theatre (PhD); JD/PhD; MA/MS; MD/PhD; MPA/MA. Dual-degree programs require admission

to both Graduate School of Arts and Sciences and another Columbia school. Part-time and evening/weekend programs available. Terminal master's awarded for partial completion of doctoral program. *Degree requirements:* For master's, thesis (for some programs); for doctorate, comprehensive exam, thesis/dissertation. *Entrance requirements:* For master's and doctorate, GRE General Test, GRE Subject Test (for some programs). Electronic applications accepted. *Faculty research:* Humanities, natural sciences, social sciences.

Concordia University, School of Graduate Studies, Faculty of Arts and Science, Department of Études Franlfcaises, Montréal, QC H3G 1M8, Canada. Offers écriture (Certificate); anglais-franlfcais en langue et techniques de localisation (Certificate); littératures francophones et résonances médiatiques (MA); traductologie (MA); translation (Diploma). *Degree requirements:* For other advanced degree, one foreign language.

Cornell University, Graduate School, Graduate Fields of Arts and Sciences, Field of Romance Studies, Ithaca, NY 14853-0001. Offers French linguistics (PhD); French literature (PhD); Hispanic literature (PhD); Italian linguistics (PhD); Italian literature (PhD); Romance linguistics (PhD); Spanish linguistics (PhD). *Degree requirements:* For doctorate, 2 foreign languages, comprehensive exam, thesis/dissertation. *Entrance requirements:* For doctorate, GRE General Test, sample of written work, 3 letters of recommendation. Additional exam requirements/recommendations for international students: Required—TOEFL (minimum score 550 paper-based; 77 iBT). Electronic applications accepted. *Faculty research:* Literary theory, Hispanic studies, French studies, gender studies.

Dalhousie University, Faculty of Arts and Social Science, Department of French, Halifax, NS B3H 4R2, Canada. Offers MA, PhD. *Entrance requirements:* Additional exam requirements/recommendations for international students: Required—TOEFL, IELTS, CANTEST, CAEL, or Michigan English Language Assessment Battery. Electronic applications accepted. *Faculty research:* Literature, linguistics, French civilization, French and Francophone literature of all periods, translation and cultural studies.

DePaul University, College of Liberal Arts and Social Sciences, Chicago, IL 60614. Offers Arabic (MA); Chinese (MA); English (MA); French (MA); German (MA); history (MA); interdisciplinary studies (MA, MS); international public service (MS); international studies (MA); Italian (MA); Japanese (MA); leadership and policy studies (MS); liberal studies (MA); new media studies (MA); nonprofit management (MNM); public administration (MPA); public health (MPH); public service management (MS); social work (MSW); sociology (MA); Spanish (MA); sustainable urban development (MA); women and gender studies (MA); writing and publishing (MA); writing, rhetoric, and discourse (MA); MA/PhD. Part-time and evening/weekend programs available. Postbaccalaureate distance learning degree programs offered (no on-campus study). Terminal master's awarded for partial completion of doctoral program. *Degree requirements:* For master's, variable foreign language requirement, comprehensive exam (for some programs), thesis (for some programs). Electronic applications accepted.

Drew University, Caspersen School of Graduate Studies, Program in Education, Madison, NJ 07940-1493. Offers biology (MAT); chemistry (MAT); English (MAT); French (MAT); Italian (MAT); math (MAT); physics (MAT); social studies (MAT); Spanish (MAT); theatre arts (MAT). *Accreditation:* Teacher Education Accreditation Council. Part-time programs available. *Degree requirements:* For master's, student teaching internship and seminar. *Entrance requirements:* For master's, transcripts, statement of purpose, three letters of recommendation. Additional exam requirements/recommendations for international students: Required—TOEFL. *Expenses:* Contact institution.

Duke University, Graduate School, Department of Romance Studies, Durham, NC 27708. Offers French (PhD); Italian (PhD); Spanish (PhD); JD/AM. *Degree requirements:* For doctorate, 2 foreign languages, thesis/dissertation. *Entrance requirements:* For doctorate, GRE General Test. Additional exam requirements/recommendations for international students: Required—TOEFL (minimum score 577 paper-based; 90 iBT) or IELTS (minimum score 7). Electronic applications accepted. *Expenses: Tuition:* Full-time $45,760; part-time $2765 per credit. *Required fees:* $978. Full-time tuition and fees vary according to program.

Eastern Michigan University, Graduate School, College of Arts and Sciences, Department of World Languages, Ypsilanti, MI 48197. Offers foreign languages (MA, Graduate Certificate), including French (MA), German (MA), German for business (Graduate Certificate), Hispanic language and cultures (Graduate Certificate), Japanese business practices (Graduate Certificate), Spanish (MA). Part-time and evening/weekend programs available. Postbaccalaureate distance learning degree programs offered (minimal on-campus study). *Faculty:* 20 full-time (14 women). *Students:* 5 full-time (4 women), 46 part-time (35 women); includes 10 minority (2 Black or African American, non-Hispanic/Latino; 2 Asian, non-Hispanic/Latino; 6 Hispanic/Latino), 4 international. Average age 33. 46 applicants, 74% accepted, 21 enrolled. In 2014, 23 master's, 1 other advanced degree awarded. *Degree requirements:* For master's, one foreign language. *Entrance requirements:* Additional exam requirements/recommendations for international students: Required—TOEFL. *Application deadline:* Applications are processed on a rolling basis. Application fee: $45. *Financial support:* Fellowships, research assistantships with full tuition reimbursements, teaching assistantships with full tuition reimbursements, career-related internships or fieldwork, Federal Work-Study, institutionally sponsored loans, scholarships/grants, tuition waivers (partial), and unspecified assistantships available. Support available to part-time students. Financial award applicants required to submit FAFSA. *Unit head:* Dr. Rosemary Weston-Gil, Department Head, 734-487-0130, Fax: 734-487-3411, E-mail: rweston3@emich.edu.

Eastern University, Graduate Education Programs, St. Davids, PA 19087-3696. Offers ESL program specialist (K-12) (Certificate); general supervisor (PreK-12) (Certificate); health and physical education (K-12) (Certificate); middle level (4-8) (Certificate); multicultural education (M Ed); pre K-4 (Certificate); pre K-4 with special education (Certificate); reading (M Ed); reading specialist (K-12) (Certificate); reading supervisor (K-12) (Certificate); school health services (M Ed); school health supervisor (Certificate); school nurse (Certificate); school principalship (K-12) (Certificate); secondary biology education (7-12) (Certificate); secondary chemistry education (7-12) (Certificate); secondary communication education (7-12) (Certificate); secondary education (7-12) (Certificate); secondary English education (7-12) (Certificate); secondary math education (7-12) (Certificate); secondary social studies education (7-12) (Certificate); special education (M Ed); special education (7-12) (Certificate); special education (Pre K-8) (Certificate); special education supervisor (N-12) (Certificate); TESOL (M Ed); world language (Certificate), including French, Spanish. Part-time and evening/weekend programs available. Postbaccalaureate distance learning degree programs offered (no on-campus study). *Faculty:* 22 full-time (11 women), 26 part-time/adjunct (18 women). *Students:* 57 full-time (42 women), 241 part-time (174 women); includes 106 minority (80 Black or African American, non-Hispanic/Latino; 1 American Indian or Alaska Native, non-Hispanic/Latino; 6 Asian, non-Hispanic/Latino; 15 Hispanic/Latino; 1 Native Hawaiian or other Pacific Islander, non-Hispanic/Latino; 3 Two or more races, non-

Hispanic/Latino), 4 international. Average age 34. 109 applicants, 95% accepted, 85 enrolled. In 2014, 74 master's awarded. *Entrance requirements:* For master's, minimum GPA of 2.5; for Certificate, minimum GPA of 3.0. Additional exam requirements/recommendations for international students: Required—TOEFL. *Application deadline:* For fall admission, 8/14 for domestic students; for spring admission, 12/20 for domestic students. Applications are processed on a rolling basis. Application fee: $35. Application fee is waived when completed online. *Expenses: Tuition:* Full-time $15,600; part-time $650 per credit. *Required fees:* $30; $27.50 per semester. One-time fee: $50. Tuition and fees vary according to course load, degree level and program. *Financial support:* In 2014–15, 84 students received support, including 6 research assistantships with partial tuition reimbursements available (averaging $7,710 per year); scholarships/grants and unspecified assistantships also available. Financial award application deadline: 3/15; financial award applicants required to submit FAFSA. *Unit head:* Harry Gutelius, Associate Dean, 610-341-1729. *Application contact:* Michael Perpiglia, Associate Director of Enrollment, 610-341-5947, Fax: 484-581-1276, E-mail: mperpigl@eastern.edu.
Website: http://www.eastern.edu/academics/programs/loeb-school-education-0/graduateprograms

Emory University, Laney Graduate School, Department of French and Italian, Atlanta, GA 30322-1100. Offers French (PhD); French and educational studies (PhD). *Degree requirements:* For doctorate, one foreign language, comprehensive exam, thesis/dissertation. *Entrance requirements:* For doctorate, GRE General Test. Additional exam requirements/recommendations for international students: Recommended—TOEFL. Electronic applications accepted. *Faculty research:* French literature through multidisciplinary critical approaches, second language acquisition theory.

Florida Atlantic University, College of Education, Department of Teaching and Learning, Boca Raton, FL 33431-0991. Offers curriculum and instruction (M Ed), including art, biology, chemistry, English, French, German, mathematics, music, physics, Pre-K and primary education, reading, social sciences, Spanish; elementary education (M Ed); environmental education (M Ed); reading education (M Ed); social foundations of education (M Ed), including educational psychology, educational technology, multilingual education. *Accreditation:* NCATE. Part-time and evening/weekend programs available. *Entrance requirements:* For master's, GRE General Test, minimum GPA of 3.0 in last 2 years of undergraduate course work. Additional exam requirements/recommendations for international students: Required—TOEFL (minimum score 500 paper-based; 61 iBT), IELTS (minimum score 6). *Expenses:* Tuition, state resident: full-time $7396; part-time $369.82 per credit hour. Tuition, nonresident: full-time $19,392; part-time $1024.81 per credit hour. Tuition and fees vary according to course load. *Faculty research:* Technology, teaching English to speakers of other languages, math teaching, electronic portfolio assessment, global perspectives through social studies.

Florida Atlantic University, Dorothy F. Schmidt College of Arts and Letters, Department of Languages, Linguistics, and Comparative Literature, Boca Raton, FL 33431-0991. Offers comparative literature (MA); French (MA); linguistics (MA); Spanish (MA). Part-time programs available. *Degree requirements:* For master's, one foreign language, comprehensive exam, thesis optional. *Entrance requirements:* For master's, GRE General Test, minimum GPA of 3.0. Additional exam requirements/recommendations for international students: Required—TOEFL (minimum score 500 paper-based; 61 iBT), IELTS (minimum score 6). *Expenses:* Tuition, state resident: full-time $7396; part-time $369.82 per credit hour. Tuition, nonresident: full-time $19,392; part-time $1024.81 per credit hour. Tuition and fees vary according to course load. *Faculty research:* Modern European studies, modern Latin America, medieval Europe.

Florida State University, The Graduate School, College of Arts and Sciences, Department of Modern Languages, Program in French, Tallahassee, FL 32306. Offers MA, PhD. *Faculty:* 7 full-time (4 women), 4 part-time/adjunct (2 women). *Students:* 9 full-time (6 women); includes 2 minority (1 Black or African American, non-Hispanic/Latino; 1 Asian, non-Hispanic/Latino). Average age 25. 11 applicants, 73% accepted, 3 enrolled. In 2014, 3 master's, 1 doctorate awarded. Terminal master's awarded for partial completion of doctoral program. *Degree requirements:* For master's, thesis optional; for doctorate, thesis/dissertation, reading knowledge of French and 2 other languages. *Entrance requirements:* For master's and doctorate, GRE General Test, minimum GPA of 3.0. Additional exam requirements/recommendations for international students: Required—TOEFL (minimum score 550 paper-based). *Application deadline:* For fall admission, 2/1 for domestic and international students. Applications are processed on a rolling basis. Application fee: $30. Electronic applications accepted. *Expenses:* Tuition, state resident: part-time $403.51 per credit hour. Tuition, nonresident: part-time $1004.85 per credit hour. *Required fees:* $75.81 per credit hour. One-time fee: $20 part-time. Tuition and fees vary according to campus/location. *Financial support:* In 2014–15, fellowships with partial tuition reimbursements (averaging $16,500 per year), research assistantships with partial tuition reimbursements (averaging $9,500 per year), 9 teaching assistantships with partial tuition reimbursements (averaging $12,500 per year) were awarded. Financial award application deadline: 1/15; financial award applicants required to submit FAFSA. *Faculty research:* Twentieth century European novel, Renaissance and Middle Ages literature, second language acquisition. *Unit head:* Dr. Mark Pietralunga, Chair, 850-644-8600, Fax: 850-644-0524, E-mail: mpietralunga@fsu.edu. *Application contact:* Wendy E. Pigott, Graduate Academic Coordinator, 850-644-8397, Fax: 850-644-0524, E-mail: wpigott@fsu.edu.
Website: http://www.modlang.fsu.edu/Programs2/French/Graduate-Programs

George Mason University, College of Humanities and Social Sciences, Department of Modern and Classical Languages, Fairfax, VA 22030. Offers foreign languages (MA), including French. *Faculty:* 33 full-time (25 women), 41 part-time/adjunct (33 women). *Students:* 18 full-time (10 women), 15 part-time (13 women); includes 21 minority (3 Black or African American, non-Hispanic/Latino; 1 Asian, non-Hispanic/Latino; 15 Hispanic/Latino; 2 Two or more races, non-Hispanic/Latino), 1 international. Average age 36. 24 applicants, 75% accepted, 13 enrolled. In 2014, 9 master's awarded. *Degree requirements:* For master's, comprehensive exam, thesis optional. *Entrance requirements:* For master's, 3 letters of recommendation; official transcripts; goals statement; baccalaureate degree in French or Spanish with minimum GPA of 3.0 (recommended). Additional exam requirements/recommendations for international students: Required—TOEFL (minimum score 570 paper-based; 80 iBT), IELTS (minimum score 6.5), PTE. *Application deadline:* For fall admission, 5/15 priority date for domestic students; for spring admission, 11/1 priority date for domestic students. Application fee: $65 ($80 for international students). Electronic applications accepted. *Expenses:* Tuition, state resident: full-time $9794; part-time $408 per credit hour. Tuition, nonresident: full-time $26,978; part-time $1124 per credit hour. *Required fees:* $2820; $118 per credit hour. Tuition and fees vary according to course load and program. *Financial support:* In 2014–15, 7 students received support, including 7 teaching assistantships with full and partial tuition reimbursements available (averaging $10,066 per year); career-related internships or fieldwork, Federal Work-Study, scholarships/grants, unspecified assistantships, and health care benefits (for full-time research or teaching assistantship recipients) also available. Support available to part-time students. Financial award application deadline: 3/1; financial award applicants required to submit FAFSA. *Faculty research:* French Renaissance studies, early Modern (sixteenth-eighteenth centuries) literary and cultural studies, history, literature and philosophy, women's studies. *Total annual research expenditures:* $25,262. *Unit head:* Julie Christensen, Chair, 703-993-1230, Fax: 703-993-1245, E-mail: jchriste@gmu.edu. *Application contact:* Jen Barnard, Information Contact, 703-993-1230, Fax: 703-993-1245, E-mail: jbarnard@gmu.edu.
Website: http://mcl.gmu.edu/

Georgia State University, College of Arts and Sciences, Department of Modern and Classical Languages, Program in French, Atlanta, GA 30302-3083. Offers applied linguistics and pedagogy (MA); French studies (MA); literature and culture (MA). Part-time programs available. *Degree requirements:* For master's, one foreign language, comprehensive exam, thesis or alternative, Graduate Foreign Language Reading Exam. *Entrance requirements:* For master's, GRE, statement of purpose, writing sample in the target language, 2 letters of recommendation, official transcripts. Additional exam requirements/recommendations for international students: Required—TOEFL (minimum score 79 iBT). *Application deadline:* For fall admission, 3/15 priority date for domestic and international students; for spring admission, 11/15 priority date for domestic and international students. Application fee: $50. Electronic applications accepted. *Expenses:* Tuition, state resident: full-time $6516; part-time $362 per credit hour. Tuition, nonresident: full-time $22,014; part-time $1223 per credit hour. *Required fees:* $2128 per semester. Tuition and fees vary according to course load and program. *Financial support:* Institutionally sponsored loans available. Financial award applicants required to submit FAFSA. *Faculty research:* The nineteenth century novel, narratology, genetic criticism, poetics, semiotics, and intertextuality; Francophone and transnational studies; early modern travel literature; post/colonial and Diaspora studies; film studies; social and gender studies; eighteenth century French literature and history of ideas; history of civilization; Enlightenment, encyclopedism. *Unit head:* Dr. Fernando Reati, Department Chair, 404-413-5984, Fax: 404-413-5982, E-mail: freati@gsu.edu. *Application contact:* Lita Malveaux, Administrative Academic Specialist, 404-413-5046, Fax: 404-413-5036, E-mail: lmalveaux@gsu.edu.
Website: http://www.gsu.edu/~wwwmcl/

Georgia State University, College of Arts and Sciences, Department of Modern and Classical Languages, Program in Translation and Interpretation, Atlanta, GA 30302-3083. Offers interpretation (Certificate), including Spanish; translation (Certificate), including French, German, Spanish. Part-time programs available. *Entrance requirements:* For degree, entrance examination involving translating one passage from English to the target language and one passage from the target language to English, 3 letters of recommendation, resume/curriculum vitae, official transcripts. Additional exam requirements/recommendations for international students: Required—TOEFL (minimum score 79 iBT). *Application deadline:* For fall admission, 3/15 priority date for domestic and international students; for spring admission, 11/15 priority date for domestic and international students. Application fee: $50. Electronic applications accepted. *Expenses:* Tuition, state resident: full-time $6516; part-time $362 per credit hour. Tuition, nonresident: full-time $22,014; part-time $1223 per credit hour. *Required fees:* $2128 per semester. Tuition and fees vary according to course load and program. *Faculty research:* Romance linguistics and translation; theory and practice of translation; medical and legal interpretation. *Unit head:* Dr. Fernando Reati, Chair, 404-413-5984, Fax: 404-413-5982, E-mail: freati@gsu.edu. *Application contact:* Lita Malveaux, Administrative Academic Specialist, 404-413-5046, Fax: 404-413-5036, E-mail: lmalveaux@gsu.edu.
Website: http://wlc.gsu.edu/home/graduate/graduate-certificate/

The Graduate Center, City University of New York, Graduate Studies, Program in French, New York, NY 10016-4039. Offers PhD. *Degree requirements:* For doctorate, 2 foreign languages, thesis/dissertation. *Entrance requirements:* For doctorate, GRE General Test. Additional exam requirements/recommendations for international students: Required—TOEFL. Electronic applications accepted.

Harvard University, Graduate School of Arts and Sciences, Department of Romance Languages and Literatures, Cambridge, MA 02138. Offers French (AM, PhD); Italian (AM, PhD); Portuguese (AM, PhD); Spanish (AM, PhD). Terminal master's awarded for partial completion of doctoral program. *Degree requirements:* For master's, 2 foreign languages; for doctorate, 2 foreign languages, thesis/dissertation. *Entrance requirements:* For master's and doctorate, GRE General Test, sample of written work. Additional exam requirements/recommendations for international students: Required—TOEFL.

Hofstra University, School of Education, Programs in Teacher Education, Hempstead, NY 11549. Offers bilingual education (MA), including biology (MA, MS Ed), geology; business education (MS Ed); early childhood and childhood education (MS Ed), including French; early childhood education (MA); education technology (Advanced Certificate); elementary education (MA), including math. science, technology (STEM); English education (MS Ed); fine arts education (MS Ed), including biology (MA, MS Ed); foreign language and TESOL (MS Ed); learning and teaching (Ed D), including applied linguistics, art education, arts and humanities, early childhood education, English education, human development, math education, math, science, and technology, multicultural education, physical education, science education, social studies education, special education; mathematics education (MA, MS Ed); secondary education (Advanced Certificate); social studies education (MA, MS Ed). Part-time and evening/weekend programs available. Postbaccalaureate distance learning degree programs offered (minimal on-campus study). *Students:* 141 full-time (111 women), 119 part-time (84 women); includes 58 minority (13 Black or African American, non-Hispanic/Latino; 14 Asian, non-Hispanic/Latino; 28 Hispanic/Latino; 1 Native Hawaiian or other Pacific Islander, non-Hispanic/Latino; 2 Two or more races, non-Hispanic/Latino), 18 international. Average age 30. 301 applicants, 87% accepted, 112 enrolled. In 2014, 133 master's, 5 doctorates, 28 other advanced degrees awarded. *Degree requirements:* For master's, comprehensive exam, thesis (for some programs), exit project, student teaching, fieldwork, electronic portfolio, curriculum project, minimum GPA of 3.0; for doctorate, thesis/dissertation; for Advanced Certificate, 3 foreign languages, comprehensive exam (for some programs), thesis project. *Entrance requirements:* For master's, 2 letters of recommendation, portfolio, teacher certification (MA), interview, essay; for doctorate, GMAT, GRE, LSAT, or MAT; for Advanced Certificate, 2 letters of recommendation, essay, interview and/or portfolio, teaching certificate. Additional exam requirements/recommendations for international students: Required—TOEFL (minimum score 550 paper-based; 80 iBT). *Application deadline:* Applications are processed on a rolling basis. Application fee: $70 ($75 for international students). Electronic applications accepted. *Expenses: Tuition:* Full-time $20,610; part-time $1145 per credit hour. *Required fees:* $970; $165 per term. Tuition and fees vary according to program. *Financial support:* In 2014–15, 153 students received support, including 60 fellowships with full and partial tuition reimbursements available (averaging $5,084 per year), 4 research assistantships with full and partial tuition reimbursements available (averaging $7,095 per year); Federal Work-Study, institutionally sponsored loans, scholarships/grants, health care benefits, and tuition waivers (full and partial) also available. Support available to part-time students. Financial award applicants required to submit FAFSA. *Faculty research:* Appropriate content in secondary school disciplines, lesson development across content, interdisciplinary curriculum, multicultural education. *Unit*

head: Dr. Eustace Thompson, Chairperson, 516-463-5749, Fax: 516-463-6275, E-mail: edaegt@hofstra.edu. *Application contact:* Sunil Samuel, Assistant Vice President of Admissions, 516-463-4723, Fax: 516-463-4664, E-mail: graduateadmission@hofstra.edu.
Website: http://www.hofstra.edu/education/

Howard University, Graduate School, Department of Modern Languages and Literatures, Washington, DC 20059-0002. Offers French (MA); Spanish (MA). Part-time programs available. *Degree requirements:* For master's, one foreign language, comprehensive exam, thesis. *Entrance requirements:* For master's, GRE General Test, writing samples in English and French or Spanish. *Faculty research:* African literature in French, Spanish linguistics, Spanish Peninsular literature, Spanish sociolinguistics.

Hunter College of the City University of New York, Graduate School, School of Arts and Sciences, Department of Romance Languages, Program in French, New York, NY 10065-5085. Offers MA. Part-time and evening/weekend programs available. *Faculty:* 3 full-time (2 women). *Students:* 3 part-time (2 women), 1 international. Average age 41. 3 applicants, 33% accepted. In 2014, 2 master's awarded. *Degree requirements:* For master's, 2 foreign languages, comprehensive exam, thesis optional. *Entrance requirements:* For master's, GRE General Test, GRE Subject Test, ability to read, speak, and write French; interview. Additional exam requirements/recommendations for international students: Required—TOEFL. *Application deadline:* For fall admission, 4/1 for domestic students, 2/1 for international students; for spring admission, 11/1 for domestic students, 9/1 for international students. *Financial support:* Fellowships, Federal Work-Study, scholarships/grants, and tuition waivers (partial) available. Support available to part-time students. Financial award application deadline: 4/15. *Faculty research:* Contemporary French theater, Villiers de l 'Isle-Adam, Voltaire, medieval folklore, fin-de-siecle. *Unit head:* Prof. Marlene Barsoum, Graduate Advisor, 212-650-3511, E-mail: mbarsoum@hunter.cuny.edu. *Application contact:* Milena Solo, Director for Graduate Admissions, 212-772-4480, E-mail: milena.solo@hunter.cuny.edu.
Website: http://www.hunter.cuny.edu/romancelanguages/graduate/ma-requirements

Illinois State University, Graduate School, College of Arts and Sciences, Department of Foreign Languages, Literatures and Cultures, Normal, IL 61790-2200. Offers French (MA); French and German (MA); French and Spanish (MA); German (MA); German and Spanish (MA); Spanish (MA). *Degree requirements:* For master's, variable foreign language requirement, comprehensive exam, 1 term of residency. *Entrance requirements:* For master's, GRE General Test, minimum GPA of 2.8 in last 60 hours of course work.

Indiana University Bloomington, University Graduate School, College of Arts and Sciences, Department of French and Italian, Bloomington, IN 47405. Offers French (MA, PhD), including French instruction (MA), French linguistics, French literature; Italian (MA, PhD). Part-time programs available. *Faculty:* 21 full-time (7 women). *Students:* 61 full-time (35 women), 1 (woman) part-time; includes 4 minority (1 Black or African American, non-Hispanic/Latino; 1 Asian, non-Hispanic/Latino; 2 Hispanic/Latino), 23 international. Average age 30. 47 applicants, 47% accepted, 12 enrolled. In 2014, 21 master's, 5 doctorates awarded. Terminal master's awarded for partial completion of doctoral program. *Degree requirements:* For master's, variable foreign language requirement, comprehensive exam (for some programs), thesis optional; for doctorate, variable foreign language requirement, comprehensive exam, thesis/dissertation. *Entrance requirements:* For master's and doctorate, GRE General Test. Additional exam requirements/recommendations for international students: Required—TOEFL (minimum score 550 paper-based; 79 iBT). *Application deadline:* For fall admission, 1/15 priority date for domestic students, 12/1 priority date for international students; for spring admission, 9/1 priority date for domestic and international students. Application fee: $55 ($65 for international students). Electronic applications accepted. *Financial support:* In 2014–15, 46 students received support, including 7 fellowships with partial tuition reimbursements available (averaging $18,000 per year), 6 research assistantships with partial tuition reimbursements available (averaging $15,750 per year), 38 teaching assistantships with partial tuition reimbursements available (averaging $15,750 per year); health care benefits and unspecified assistantships also available. Financial award application deadline: 1/15. *Faculty research:* French and Italian literature, French linguistics, including the novel and political theory, literature and fine arts, literary theory, postcolonialism, French-Creole studies, French literature of Africa and its Diaspora, humanism, medieval folklore and mythology, humor in medieval and Renaissance literature, cinema Old Occitan and Old French, emigration, second language acquisition, syntax, sociolinguistics, phonology, lexicography. *Unit head:* Prof. Andrea Ciccarelli, Chair, 812-855-5458, Fax: 812-855-8877, E-mail: fritchr@indiana.edu. *Application contact:* Casey Green, Graduate Secretary, 812-855-1088, Fax: 812-855-8877, E-mail: fritgs@indiana.edu.
Website: http://www.indiana.edu/~frithome/

Johns Hopkins University, Zanvyl Krieger School of Arts and Sciences, Department of German and Romance Languages and Literatures, Baltimore, MD 21218-2699. Offers French (PhD); German (PhD); Italian (PhD); Spanish (PhD). *Degree requirements:* For doctorate, 2 foreign languages, thesis/dissertation. *Entrance requirements:* For doctorate, GRE General Test. Additional exam requirements/recommendations for international students: Required—TOEFL (minimum score 600 paper-based; 100 iBT), IELTS. Electronic applications accepted. *Faculty research:* Nineteenth-century French prose and poetry, genetic theory and criticism; twentieth-century Latin American literature and film; medieval and Renaissance Italian literature; gender and queer theory in German literature; the ideology of Baroque and Neobaroque aesthetics.

Lake Forest College, Master of Arts in Teaching Program, Lake Forest, IL 60045. Offers elementary education (MAT); K-12 French (MAT); K-12 music (MAT); K-12 Spanish (MAT); K-12 visual art (MAT); secondary biology (MAT); secondary chemistry (MAT); secondary English (MAT); secondary history (MAT); secondary mathematics (MAT). *Degree requirements:* For master's, comprehensive exam, portfolio. *Entrance requirements:* For master's, GRE.

Louisiana State University and Agricultural & Mechanical College, Graduate School, College of Humanities and Social Sciences, Department of French Studies, Baton Rouge, LA 70803. Offers French literature and linguistics (MA, PhD). *Faculty:* 13 full-time (5 women). *Students:* 19 full-time (12 women), 3 part-time (2 women), 7 international. Average age 32. 9 applicants, 67% accepted, 4 enrolled. In 2014, 5 master's, 2 doctorates awarded. Terminal master's awarded for partial completion of doctoral program. *Degree requirements:* For master's, thesis optional; for doctorate, 2 foreign languages, thesis/dissertation. *Entrance requirements:* For master's and doctorate, GRE General Test, minimum GPA of 3.0. Additional exam requirements/recommendations for international students: Required—TOEFL (minimum score 550 paper-based; 79 IBT), IELTS (minimum score 6.5), or PTE (minimum score 59). *Application deadline:* For fall admission, 1/1 priority date for domestic students, 5/15 for international students; for spring admission, 10/15 for domestic and international students; for summer admission, 5/15 for domestic students, 5/17 for international students. Applications are processed on a rolling basis. Application fee: $50 ($70 for international students). Electronic applications accepted. *Financial support:* In 2014–15, 21 students received support, including 3 research assistantships with partial tuition reimbursements available (averaging $16,333 per year), 15 teaching assistantships with partial tuition reimbursements available (averaging $17,347 per year); fellowships with full tuition reimbursements available, career-related internships or fieldwork, Federal Work-Study, institutionally sponsored loans, health care benefits, tuition waivers (full), and unspecified assistantships also available. Support available to part-time students. Financial award application deadline: 7/1; financial award applicants required to submit FAFSA. *Faculty research:* French literature of all periods, modern critical theory, linguistics, cinema, Francophonia. *Total annual research expenditures:* $133,794. *Unit head:* Dr. Greg Stone, Chair, 225-578-6627, Fax: 225-578-6628, E-mail: stone@lsu.edu. *Application contact:* Dr. Kate Jensen, Adviser, 225-578-6718, Fax: 225-578-6628, E-mail: kjensen@lsu.edu.
Website: http://uiswcmsweb.prod.lsu.edu/hss/french/

McGill University, Faculty of Graduate and Postdoctoral Studies, Faculty of Arts, Department of French Language and Literature, Montréal, QC H3A 2T5, Canada. Offers MA, PhD.

McMaster University, School of Graduate Studies, Faculty of Humanities, Department of French, Hamilton, ON L8S 4M2, Canada. Offers MA. Part-time and evening/weekend programs available. *Degree requirements:* For master's, thesis or alternative. *Entrance requirements:* For master's, honors degree in French, minimum B+ average. Additional exam requirements/recommendations for international students: Required—TOEFL (minimum score 580 paper-based). *Faculty research:* Medieval literature, eighteenth- and nineteenth-century literature, twentieth-century French and Francophone literature, linguistics.

Memorial University of Newfoundland, School of Graduate Studies, Department of French and Spanish, St. John's, NL A1C 5S7, Canada. Offers French studies (MA). Part-time programs available. *Degree requirements:* For master's, one foreign language, thesis. *Entrance requirements:* For master's, honors degree (minimum 2nd class standing). Electronic applications accepted. *Faculty research:* French and French-Canadian literature, literary theory, linguistics, philosophy, translation, Francophone culture.

Miami University, College of Arts and Science, Department of French and Italian, Oxford, OH 45056. Offers French (MA). Part-time programs available. *Students:* 7. *Entrance requirements:* For master's, GRE General Test (recommended), 5-15 page literary analysis sample in French; two letters of recommendation. Additional exam requirements/recommendations for international students: Recommended—TOEFL (minimum score 80 iBT), IELTS (minimum score 6.5), TSE (minimum score 54). *Application deadline:* For fall admission, 2/1 priority date for domestic and international students. Application fee: $50. Electronic applications accepted. *Expenses:* Tuition, state resident: full-time $12,887; part-time $537 per credit hour. Tuition, nonresident: full-time $28,449; part-time $1186 per credit hour. *Required fees:* $530; $24 per credit hour. $30 per quarter. Part-time tuition and fees vary according to course load and program. *Financial support:* Fellowships with full and partial tuition reimbursements, research assistantships, and teaching assistantships available. Financial award application deadline: 2/15; financial award applicants required to submit FAFSA. *Unit head:* Dr. Jonathan Strauss, Chair, 513-529-7508, E-mail: strausja@miamioh.edu. *Application contact:* Dr. Elisabeth Hodges, Graduate Director, 513-529-5809, E-mail: hodgesed@miamioh.edu.
Website: http://www.MiamiOH.edu/frenchitalian/

Michigan State University, The Graduate School, College of Arts and Letters, Department of French, Classics, and Italian, East Lansing, MI 48824. Offers French (MA); French language and literature (PhD). *Entrance requirements:* Additional exam requirements/recommendations for international students: Required—TOEFL. Electronic applications accepted.

Middlebury College, Language Schools, French School, Middlebury, VT 05753-6002. Offers MA, DML. *Faculty:* 37 full-time (16 women). *Students:* 99 full-time (72 women), 1 (woman) part-time; includes 19 minority (1 Black or African American, non-Hispanic/Latino; 1 Asian, non-Hispanic/Latino; 11 Hispanic/Latino; 6 Two or more races, non-Hispanic/Latino), 6 international. Average age 30. 163 applicants, 77% accepted, 100 enrolled. In 2014, 24 master's, 2 doctorates awarded. *Degree requirements:* For master's, one foreign language; for doctorate, 2 foreign languages, comprehensive exam, thesis/dissertation, residence abroad, teaching experience. *Entrance requirements:* For master's, online placement test, 3 letters of recommendation, critical essay, transcripts, personal statement; for doctorate, 1st and 2nd language online placement exam, 3 letters of recommendation, critical essay, transcripts, personal statement, MA in first language, oral interview. *Application deadline:* Applications are processed on a rolling basis. Application fee: $65. Electronic applications accepted. *Financial support:* Fellowships and scholarships/grants available. Financial award applicants required to submit FAFSA. *Unit head:* Dr. Phillipe France, Director, 802-443-5526, Fax: 802-443-2075. *Application contact:* Sheila Schwaneflugel, Coordinator, 802-443-5526, Fax: 802-443-2075, E-mail: sschwaneflugel@middlebury.edu.
Website: http://www.middlebury.edu/ls/grad_programs/french

Middle Tennessee State University, College of Graduate Studies, College of Liberal Arts, Department of Foreign Languages and Literatures, Murfreesboro, TN 37132. Offers foreign languages (MAT), including French, German, Spanish. Part-time and evening/weekend programs available. Postbaccalaureate distance learning degree programs offered. *Faculty:* 17 full-time (12 women), 1 part-time/adjunct (0 women). *Students:* 9 full-time (6 women), 11 part-time (5 women); includes 5 minority (2 Black or African American, non-Hispanic/Latino; 1 Asian, non-Hispanic/Latino; 1 Hispanic/Latino; 1 Two or more races, non-Hispanic/Latino), 1 international. 14 applicants, 86% accepted. In 2014, 8 master's awarded. *Degree requirements:* For master's, one foreign language, comprehensive exam, thesis optional. *Entrance requirements:* For master's, GRE. Additional exam requirements/recommendations for international students: Required—TOEFL (minimum score 525 paper-based; 71 iBT) or IELTS (minimum score 6). *Application deadline:* For fall admission, 6/1 for domestic and international students. Applications are processed on a rolling basis. Application fee: $30. Electronic applications accepted. *Financial support:* In 2014–15, 9 students received support. Tuition waivers available. Support available to part-time students. Financial award application deadline: 4/1; financial award applicants required to submit FAFSA. *Total annual research expenditures:* $135,499. *Unit head:* Dr. Joan McRae, Chair, 615-898-2981, Fax: 615-898-5735, E-mail: joan.mcrae@mtsu.edu. *Application contact:* Dr. Michael D. Allen, Vice Provost for Research/Dean, 615-898-2840, Fax: 615-904-8020, E-mail: michael.allen@mtsu.edu.

Millersville University of Pennsylvania, College of Graduate and Professional Studies, School of Humanities and Social Sciences, Department of Foreign Languages, Program in Languages and Cultures: French Option, Millersville, PA 17551-0302. Offers MA. Part-time programs available. *Faculty:* 8 full-time (4 women), 4 part-time/adjunct (3 women). *Degree requirements:* For master's, comprehensive exam, thesis optional. *Entrance requirements:* For master's, American Council on the Teaching of Foreign Languages Oral Proficiency Interview and Writing Proficiency Test, 3 letters of recommendation, goal statement, official transcripts. Additional exam requirements/recommendations for international students: Required—TOEFL (minimum score 500 paper-based, 65 iBT) or IELTS (minimum score 6). *Application deadline:* For fall admission, 1/15 priority date for domestic and international students; for winter admission, 6/1 priority date for domestic and international students; for spring

admission, 10/1 priority date for domestic and international students. Applications are processed on a rolling basis. Application fee: $40. Electronic applications accepted. *Expenses:* Tuition, state resident: full-time $8172. Tuition, nonresident: full-time $12,258. *Required fees:* $2300. Tuition and fees vary according to course load and program. *Financial support:* Research assistantships with full tuition reimbursements, institutionally sponsored loans, and unspecified assistantships available. Support available to part-time students. Financial award application deadline: 3/15; financial award applicants required to submit FAFSA. *Faculty research:* Detective fiction and women's literature. *Unit head:* Dr. Christine M. Gaudry-Hudson, Associate Professor and Program Contact, 717-871-7154, Fax: 717-871-7935, E-mail: christine.gaudry-hudson@millersville.edu. *Application contact:* Dr. Victor S. DeSantis, Dean of College of Graduate and Professional Studies/Associate Provost for Civic and Community Engagement, 717-871-7619, Fax: 717-871-7954, E-mail: victor.desantis@millersville.edu.
Website: http://www.millersville.edu/forlang/

Minnesota State University Mankato, College of Graduate Studies, College of Arts and Humanities, Department of Modern Languages, Program in French, Mankato, MN 56001. Offers MAT, MS. *Students:* 1 (woman) full-time, 2 part-time (1 woman), 1 international. *Degree requirements:* For master's, one foreign language, comprehensive exam, thesis or alternative. *Entrance requirements:* For master's, minimum GPA of 3.0 during previous 2 years. Additional exam requirements/recommendations for international students: Required—TOEFL. *Application deadline:* For fall admission, 7/1 priority date for domestic students; for spring admission, 11/1 for domestic students. Applications are processed on a rolling basis. Application fee: $40. Electronic applications accepted. *Financial support:* Research assistantships, teaching assistantships with full tuition reimbursements, and unspecified assistantships available. Financial award application deadline: 3/15; financial award applicants required to submit FAFSA. *Unit head:* Dr. Evan Bibbee, Graduate Coordinator, 507-389-6250. *Application contact:* 507-389-2321, E-mail: grad@mnsu.edu.

Mississippi State University, College of Arts and Sciences, Department of Classical and Modern Languages and Literatures, Mississippi State, MS 39762. Offers French (MA); German (MA); Spanish (MA). Part-time programs available. *Faculty:* 12 full-time (3 women). *Students:* 7 full-time (3 women); includes 2 minority (both Hispanic/Latino), 1 international. Average age 32. 7 applicants, 57% accepted, 3 enrolled. In 2014, 12 master's awarded. *Degree requirements:* For master's, one foreign language, thesis optional, comprehensive oral or written exam. *Entrance requirements:* For master's, minimum GPA of 2.75 on last two years of undergraduate courses. Additional exam requirements/recommendations for international students: Required—TOEFL (minimum score 525 paper-based; 70 iBT); Recommended—IELTS (minimum score 6). *Application deadline:* For fall admission, 7/1 for domestic students, 5/1 for international students; for spring admission, 11/1 for domestic students, 9/1 for international students. Applications are processed on a rolling basis. Application fee: $60. Electronic applications accepted. *Expenses:* Tuition, state resident: full-time $7140; part-time $783 per credit hour. Tuition, nonresident: full-time $18,478; part-time $2043 per credit hour. *Financial support:* Federal Work-Study, institutionally sponsored loans, and unspecified assistantships available. Financial award application deadline: 4/1; financial award applicants required to submit FAFSA. *Faculty research:* French, German, Spanish literature from medieval era to present; gender and cultural studies in French; Spanish-American literature; foreign language methodology; linguistics. *Unit head:* Dr. Lynn Holt, Professor and Interim Head, 662-325-3480, Fax: 662-325-8209, E-mail: lholt@cmll.msstate.edu. *Application contact:* Dr. Keith Moser, Graduate Coordinator, 662-325-3480, Fax: 662-325-8209, E-mail: kmoser@.msstate.edu.
Website: http://www.cmll.msstate.edu/

Montclair State University, The Graduate School, College of Education and Human Services, MAT Program in Teaching, Montclair, NJ 07043-1624. Offers art (MAT); biology (MAT); chemistry (MAT); earth science (MAT); English (MAT); French (MAT); health and physical education (MAT); health education (MAT); mathematics (MAT); music (MAT); physical education (MAT); physical science (MAT); social studies (MAT); Spanish (MAT); teacher of English as a second language (MAT). *Students:* 254 full-time (176 women), 205 part-time (167 women); includes 102 minority (50 Black or African American, non-Hispanic/Latino; 1 American Indian or Alaska Native, non-Hispanic/Latino; 17 Asian, non-Hispanic/Latino; 26 Hispanic/Latino; 8 Two or more races, non-Hispanic/Latino), 2 international. Average age 29. 181 applicants, 72% accepted, 120 enrolled. In 2014, 200 master's awarded. *Degree requirements:* For master's, comprehensive exam, thesis or alternative. *Entrance requirements:* For master's, GRE General Test, interview, 2 letters of recommendation. Additional exam requirements/recommendations for international students: Required—TOEFL (minimum score 83 iBT), IELTS (minimum score 6.5). *Application deadline:* Applications are processed on a rolling basis. Application fee: $60. Electronic applications accepted. *Expenses:* Tuition, state resident: full-time $9960; part-time $553.35 per credit. Tuition, nonresident: full-time $15,074; part-time $837.43 per credit. *Required fees:* $1595; $88.63 per credit. Tuition and fees vary according to degree level and program. *Financial support:* Federal Work-Study, scholarships/grants, and unspecified assistantships available. Support available to part-time students. Financial award application deadline: 3/1; financial award applicants required to submit FAFSA. *Unit head:* Dr. David Schwarzer, Chairperson, 973-655-5187. *Application contact:* Amy Aiello, Executive Director of The Graduate School, 973-655-5147, Fax: 973-655-7869, E-mail: graduate.school@montclair.edu.

Montclair State University, The Graduate School, College of Humanities and Social Sciences, Program in French, Montclair, NJ 07043-1624. Offers French literature (MA); French studies (MA). Part-time and evening/weekend programs available. *Students:* 3 full-time (2 women), 15 part-time (12 women); includes 7 minority (all Black or African American, non-Hispanic/Latino). Average age 38. 13 applicants, 69% accepted, 6 enrolled. In 2014, 6 master's awarded. *Degree requirements:* For master's, comprehensive exam, thesis optional. *Entrance requirements:* Additional exam requirements/recommendations for international students: Required—TOEFL (minimum score 83 iBT), IELTS (minimum score 6.5). *Application deadline:* Applications are processed on a rolling basis. Application fee: $60. Electronic applications accepted. *Expenses:* Tuition, state resident: full-time $9960; part-time $553.35 per credit. Tuition, nonresident: full-time $15,074; part-time $837.43 per credit. *Required fees:* $1595; $88.63 per credit. Tuition and fees vary according to degree level and program. *Financial support:* Federal Work-Study, scholarships/grants, and unspecified assistantships available. Support available to part-time students. Financial award application deadline: 3/1; financial award applicants required to submit FAFSA. *Faculty research:* Medieval to twentieth-century French literature, Francophone studies, critical theory, language pedagogy. *Unit head:* Dr. Lois Oppenheim, Chairperson, 973-655-4283. *Application contact:* Amy Aiello, Director of Graduate Admissions and Operations, 973-655-5147, Fax: 973-655-7869, E-mail: graduate.school@montclair.edu.

New York University, Graduate School of Arts and Science, Center for French Civilization and Culture, Department of French, New York, NY 10012-1019. Offers French (PhD); French language and civilization (MA); French literature (MA); Romance languages and literatures (MA). Part-time programs available. *Faculty:* 18 full-time (7 women), 2 part-time/adjunct (both women). *Students:* 52 full-time (36 women), 3 part-time (2 women); includes 10 minority (3 Black or African American, non-Hispanic/Latino; 2 Asian, non-Hispanic/Latino; 5 Hispanic/Latino), 12 international. Average age 29. 67 applicants, 58% accepted, 20 enrolled. In 2014, 15 master's, 15 doctorates awarded. Terminal master's awarded for partial completion of doctoral program. *Degree requirements:* For master's, one foreign language, thesis (for some programs); for doctorate, one foreign language, thesis/dissertation. *Entrance requirements:* For master's and doctorate, GRE General Test, proficiency in French. Additional exam requirements/recommendations for international students: Required—TOEFL. *Application deadline:* For fall admission, 1/4 for domestic and international students; for spring admission, 11/1 for domestic and international students. Application fee: $100. *Financial support:* Fellowships with tuition reimbursements, teaching assistantships with tuition reimbursements, Federal Work-Study, institutionally sponsored loans, scholarships/grants, traineeships, health care benefits, unspecified assistantships, and instructorships available. Financial award application deadline: 1/4; financial award applicants required to submit FAFSA. *Faculty research:* French and Francophone literature, literary theory, and history; rhetoric and poetics; cultural history; theater and cinema. *Unit head:* Lucien Nouis, Director of Graduate Studies, 212-998-8700, Fax: 212-995-4187, E-mail: french.grad@nyu.edu. *Application contact:* Erin Brau, Graduate Administrator, 212-998-8700, Fax: 212-995-4187, E-mail: french.grad@nyu.edu.
Website: http://www.nyu.edu/gsas/dept/french/

New York University, Graduate School of Arts and Science, Center for French Civilization and Culture, Institute of French Studies, New York, NY 10012-1019. Offers French civilization (PhD); French studies (MA, PhD, Advanced Certificate); French studies and anthropology (PhD); French studies and history (PhD); French studies and journalism (MA); French studies and sociology (PhD); JD/MA; MBA/MA. Part-time programs available. *Students:* 36 full-time (26 women), 4 part-time (2 women); includes 8 minority (2 Black or African American, non-Hispanic/Latino; 1 American Indian or Alaska Native, non-Hispanic/Latino; 1 Asian, non-Hispanic/Latino; 2 Hispanic/Latino; 2 Two or more races, non-Hispanic/Latino), 9 international. Average age 29. 56 applicants, 57% accepted, 19 enrolled. In 2014, 16 master's, 2 doctorates, 1 other advanced degree awarded. Terminal master's awarded for partial completion of doctoral program. *Degree requirements:* For master's, one foreign language, comprehensive exam; for doctorate, one foreign language, thesis/dissertation, qualifying exam. *Entrance requirements:* For master's and doctorate, GRE General Test, knowledge of French. Additional exam requirements/recommendations for international students: Required—TOEFL. *Application deadline:* For fall admission, 1/4 for domestic and international students. Application fee: $100. *Financial support:* Fellowships with tuition reimbursements, teaching assistantships with tuition reimbursements, Federal Work-Study, institutionally sponsored loans, scholarships/grants, health care benefits, and unspecified assistantships available. Financial award application deadline: 1/4; financial award applicants required to submit FAFSA. *Faculty research:* Contemporary French society, politics, economy, and culture; French history since 1789; French cultural studies, French colonialism and the post-colonial world; France and the European community. *Unit head:* Edward Berenson, Director, 212-988-8740, Fax: 212-995-4142, E-mail: institute.french@nyu.edu. *Application contact:* Frederic Viguier, Acting Director of Graduate Studies, 212-988-8740, Fax: 212-995-4142, E-mail: institute.french@nyu.edu.
Website: http://www.nyu.edu/fas/program/frenchstudies/

New York University, Steinhardt School of Culture, Education, and Human Development, Department of Teaching and Learning, Program in Multilingual/Multicultural Studies, New York, NY 10003. Offers bilingual education (PhD); bilingual education for teachers (MA, Advanced Certificate); foreign language education (MA); teachers of English to speakers of other languages in college (PhD); teachers of French 7-12 (MA); teachers of Hebrew 7-12 (MA); teaching a foreign language 7-12 (MA), including teaching English to speakers of other languages, all grades; teaching English to speakers of other languages (MA); teaching foreign languages, 7-12 (MA), including Chinese, French, Italian, Japanese, Spanish; teaching French as a foreign language (MA), including teaching English to speakers of other languages; teaching Spanish as a foreign language and TESOL (MA). *Accreditation:* Teacher Education Accreditation Council. Part-time and evening/weekend programs available. *Faculty:* 6 full-time (4 women). *Students:* 118 full-time (94 women), 82 part-time (72 women); includes 40 minority (8 Black or African American, non-Hispanic/Latino; 18 Asian, non-Hispanic/Latino; 12 Hispanic/Latino; 2 Two or more races, non-Hispanic/Latino), 116 international. Average age 29. 431 applicants, 61% accepted, 92 enrolled. In 2014, 121 master's, 1 doctorate, 2 other advanced degrees awarded. *Degree requirements:* For master's, thesis (for some programs); for doctorate, thesis/dissertation. *Entrance requirements:* For doctorate, GRE General Test, interview; for Advanced Certificate, master's degree. Additional exam requirements/recommendations for international students: Required—TOEFL (minimum score 100 iBT). *Application deadline:* For fall admission, 12/1 priority date for domestic and international students; for spring admission, 10/1 for domestic and international students. Applications are processed on a rolling basis. Application fee: $75. Electronic applications accepted. *Financial support:* Fellowships with full and partial tuition reimbursements, career-related internships or fieldwork, Federal Work-Study, institutionally sponsored loans, scholarships/grants, and tuition waivers (partial) available. Support available to part-time students. Financial award application deadline: 2/1; financial award applicants required to submit FAFSA. *Faculty research:* Second language acquisition, cross-cultural communication, technology-enhanced language learning, language variation, action learning. *Unit head:* Prof. Shondel Nero, Director, 212-998-5757, E-mail: shondel.nero@nyu.edu. *Application contact:* 212-998-5030, Fax: 212-995-4328, E-mail: steinhardt.gradadmissions@nyu.edu.
Website: http://steinhardt.nyu.edu/teachlearn/mms

North Carolina State University, Graduate School, College of Humanities and Social Sciences, Department of Foreign Languages and Literatures, Program in French Language and Literature, Raleigh, NC 27695. Offers MA. *Degree requirements:* For master's, thesis optional. *Entrance requirements:* For master's, fluency in French. Electronic applications accepted. *Faculty research:* 19th-century visual culture, translation, cinema, modern theater, linguistics.

Northern Illinois University, Graduate School, College of Liberal Arts and Sciences, Department of Foreign Languages and Literatures, De Kalb, IL 60115-2854. Offers French (MA); Spanish (MA). Part-time programs available. *Faculty:* 25 full-time (11 women). *Students:* 6 full-time (2 women), 12 part-time (8 women); includes 7 minority (1 Asian, non-Hispanic/Latino; 6 Hispanic/Latino), 1 international. Average age 32. 5 applicants, 80% accepted, 2 enrolled. In 2014, 6 master's awarded. *Degree requirements:* For master's, one foreign language, comprehensive exam, thesis or alternative, language proficiency exam. *Entrance requirements:* For master's, GRE General Test, interview, minimum GPA of 2.75, undergraduate major in French or Spanish. Additional exam requirements/recommendations for international students: Required—TOEFL (minimum score 550 paper-based). *Application deadline:* For fall admission, 6/1 for domestic students, 5/1 for international students; for spring admission, 11/1 for domestic students, 10/1 for international students. Applications are processed on a rolling basis. Application fee: $40. Electronic applications accepted. *Financial support:* In 2014–15, 11 teaching assistantships with full tuition reimbursements were awarded; fellowships with full tuition reimbursements, research

assistantships with full tuition reimbursements, career-related internships or fieldwork, Federal Work-Study, scholarships/grants, tuition waivers (full), and unspecified assistantships also available. Support available to part-time students. Financial award applicants required to submit FAFSA. *Faculty research:* Francophone women writers, prosodies of French and Italian, early Spanish drama, business German, history of Burmese literature. *Unit head:* Dr. Katharina Barbe, Chair, 815-753-1559, Fax: 815-753-5989, E-mail: kbarbe@niu.edu. *Application contact:* Graduate School Office, 815-753-0395, E-mail: gradsch@niu.edu.
Website: http://www.forlangs.net/

Northwestern University, The Graduate School, Judd A. and Marjorie Weinberg College of Arts and Sciences, Department of French and Italian, Evanston, IL 60208. Offers French/Francophone studies (PhD); Italian studies (Graduate Certificate). Admissions and degrees offered through The Graduate School. *Degree requirements:* For doctorate, one foreign language, thesis/dissertation, written and oral exams. *Entrance requirements:* For doctorate, GRE, writing sample, cassette recording. Additional exam requirements/recommendations for international students: Required—TOEFL. *Faculty research:* Francophone studies, eighteenth century contemporary theory.

The Ohio State University, Graduate School, College of Arts and Sciences, Division of Arts and Humanities, Department of French and Italian, Columbus, OH 43210. Offers French (MA, PhD); Italian (MA); Italian studies (PhD). *Faculty:* 12. *Students:* 28 full-time (19 women); includes 2 minority (1 Black or African American, non-Hispanic/Latino; 1 Two or more races, non-Hispanic/Latino), 5 international. Average age 30. In 2014, 5 master's, 1 doctorate awarded. Terminal master's awarded for partial completion of doctoral program. *Degree requirements:* For master's, variable foreign language requirement, thesis optional; for doctorate, variable foreign language requirement, thesis/dissertation. *Entrance requirements:* For master's and doctorate, GRE General Test. Additional exam requirements/recommendations for international students: Required—TOEFL (minimum score 550 paper-based; 79 iBT), IELTS (minimum score 7), Michigan English Language Assessment Battery (minimum score 82). *Application deadline:* For fall admission, 12/15 priority date for domestic students, 11/30 priority date for international students; for winter admission, 12/1 for domestic students, 11/1 for international students; for spring admission, 3/1 for domestic students, 2/1 for international students. Applications are processed on a rolling basis. Application fee: $60 ($70 for international students). Electronic applications accepted. *Financial support:* Fellowships with tuition reimbursements, research assistantships with tuition reimbursements, teaching assistantships with tuition reimbursements, Federal Work-Study, institutionally sponsored loans, and unspecified assistantships available. Support available to part-time students. *Faculty research:* Italian and Romance linguistics. *Unit head:* Dr. Jennifer Willging, Chair, 614-292-4938, E-mail: willging.1@osu.edu. *Application contact:* Graduate and Professional Admissions, 614-292-9444, Fax: 614-292-3895, E-mail: gpadmissions@osu.edu.
Website: http://frit.osu.edu/

Ohio University, Graduate College, College of Arts and Sciences, Department of Modern Languages, Athens, OH 45701-2979. Offers French (MA); Spanish (MA). Part-time programs available. *Degree requirements:* For master's, 2 foreign languages, comprehensive exam, thesis optional. *Entrance requirements:* For master's, oral and written samples. Additional exam requirements/recommendations for international students: Required—TOEFL (minimum score 550 paper-based; 80 iBT) or IELTS (minimum score 6.5). Electronic applications accepted. *Faculty research:* French and Spanish language and literature.

Penn State University Park, Graduate School, College of the Liberal Arts, Department of French and Francophone Studies, University Park, PA 16802. Offers MA, PhD. *Unit head:* Dr. Susan Welch, Dean, 814-865-7691, Fax: 814-863-2085, E-mail: swelch@psu.edu. *Application contact:* Lori A. Stania, Director, Graduate Student Services, 814-867-5278, Fax: 814-863-4627, E-mail: gswww@psu.edu.
Website: http://www.french.psu.edu/

Portland State University, Graduate Studies, College of Liberal Arts and Sciences, Department of World Languages and Literatures, Portland, OR 97207-0751. Offers foreign literature and language (MA); French (MA); German (MA); Japanese (MA); Spanish (MA). Part-time programs available. *Faculty:* 48 full-time (28 women), 33 part-time/adjunct (29 women). *Students:* 30 full-time (13 women), 8 part-time (3 women); includes 7 minority (2 Asian, non-Hispanic/Latino; 5 Hispanic/Latino), 13 international. Average age 30. 31 applicants, 65% accepted, 18 enrolled. In 2014, 9 master's awarded. *Degree requirements:* For master's, one foreign language, thesis (for some programs). *Entrance requirements:* Additional exam requirements/recommendations for international students: Required—TOEFL (minimum score 550 paper-based; 80 iBT), IELTS (minimum score 6.5). *Application deadline:* For fall admission, 4/1 for domestic students, 3/1 for international students; for winter admission, 9/1 for domestic students, 7/1 for international students; for spring admission, 11/1 for domestic and international students. Applications are processed on a rolling basis. Application fee: $50. *Expenses:* Tuition, state resident: part-time $222 per credit. Tuition, nonresident: part-time $527 per credit. *Required fees:* $22 per contact hour. $100 per quarter. Tuition and fees vary according to program. *Financial support:* In 2014–15, 29 teaching assistantships with full and partial tuition reimbursements (averaging $3,251 per year) were awarded; research assistantships with full tuition reimbursements, Federal Work-Study, scholarships/grants, and unspecified assistantships also available. Support available to part-time students. Financial award application deadline: 3/1; financial award applicants required to submit FAFSA. *Faculty research:* Foreign language pedagogy, applied and social linguistics, literary history and criticism. *Total annual research expenditures:* $412,070. *Unit head:* Dr. Jennifer Perlmutter, Chair, 503-725-8783, Fax: 503-725-5276, E-mail: jrp@pdx.edu.
Website: http://www.pdx.edu/wll/

Princeton University, Graduate School, Department of French and Italian, Princeton, NJ 08544-1019. Offers French language and literature (PhD). *Degree requirements:* For doctorate, variable foreign language requirement, thesis/dissertation. *Entrance requirements:* For doctorate, GRE General Test, sample of written work. Additional exam requirements/recommendations for international students: Required—TOEFL (minimum score 600 paper-based). Electronic applications accepted.

Purdue University, Graduate School, College of Liberal Arts, School of Languages and Cultures, West Lafayette, IN 47907. Offers French (MA, MAT, PhD), including French (MA, PhD), French education (MAT); German (MA, MAT, PhD), including German (MA, PhD), German education (MAT); Japanese pedagogy (MA); Spanish (MA, MAT, PhD), including Spanish (MA, PhD), Spanish education (MAT). Terminal master's awarded for partial completion of doctoral program. *Degree requirements:* For master's, one foreign language; for doctorate, 2 foreign languages, thesis/dissertation. *Entrance requirements:* For master's, GRE General Test (minimum score 600, 160 for new scoring), two writing samples, one in English, one in language (French, German, Japanese, or Spanish); sample recording of English and language of study; for doctorate, GRE General Test (minimum score 600, 160 for new scoring), master's degree with minimum GPA of 3.5 or equivalent; two writing samples, one in English, one in language (French, German, Japanese, or Spanish); sample recording of English and language of study. Additional exam requirements/recommendations for international students: Required—TOEFL (minimum score 550 paper-based; 77 iBT); Recommended—TWE. Electronic applications accepted. *Faculty research:* Linguistics, semiotics, literary criticism, pedagogy.

Queens College of the City University of New York, Division of Graduate Studies, Arts and Humanities Division, Department of European Languages and Literatures, Program in French, Flushing, NY 11367-1597. Offers MA. Part-time and evening/weekend programs available. *Degree requirements:* For master's, 2 foreign languages, comprehensive exam, thesis or alternative. *Entrance requirements:* For master's, minimum GPA of 3.0. Additional exam requirements/recommendations for international students: Required—TOEFL.

Queen's University at Kingston, School of Graduate Studies, Faculty of Arts and Sciences, Department of French Studies, Kingston, ON K7L 3N6, Canada. Offers MA, PhD. Part-time programs available. *Degree requirements:* For master's, thesis or 4 credits and oral exam; for doctorate, one foreign language, comprehensive exam, thesis/dissertation. *Entrance requirements:* For master's, minimum B+ average; for doctorate, minimum 80% average. Additional exam requirements/recommendations for international students: Required—TOEFL (minimum score 550 paper-based). Electronic applications accepted. *Faculty research:* Reception of Quebec literature in English Canada, autobiography and postcolonialism, irony in women's writing, critical editions of renaissance authors, aspectual systems and grammatical categories.

Rider University, Department of Graduate Education, Leadership and Counseling, Teacher Certification Program, Lawrenceville, NJ 08648-3001. Offers business education (Certificate); elementary education (Certificate); English as a second language (Certificate); English education (Certificate); mathematics education (Certificate); preschool to grade 3 (Certificate); science education (Certificate); social studies education (Certificate); world languages (Certificate), including French, German, Spanish. Part-time programs available. *Degree requirements:* For Certificate, internship, professional portfolio. *Entrance requirements:* For degree, PRAXIS, resume. Additional exam requirements/recommendations for international students: Required—TOEFL (minimum score 550 paper-based). Electronic applications accepted. *Faculty research:* Conceptual foundations for optimal development of creativity; creative theory, cognitive processes in mathematics learning, teacher collaboration.

Rutgers, The State University of New Jersey, New Brunswick, Graduate School-New Brunswick, Program in French, Piscataway, NJ 08854-8097. Offers French (MA, PhD); French studies (MAT). Part-time and evening/weekend programs available. Terminal master's awarded for partial completion of doctoral program. *Degree requirements:* For master's, one foreign language, written and oral exams (MA); for doctorate, 3 foreign languages, thesis/dissertation, qualifying exam. *Entrance requirements:* For master's and doctorate, GRE General Test. *Faculty research:* Literatures in French, literary history and theory, rhetoric and poetics.

Saint Louis University, Graduate Education, College of Arts and Sciences, Department of Modern and Classical Languages, St. Louis, MO 63103-2097. Offers French (MA); Spanish (MA). Part-time programs available. *Degree requirements:* For master's, one foreign language, comprehensive exam, thesis/dissertation (Spanish). *Entrance requirements:* For master's, GRE General Test or MAT, letters of recommendation, resume, interview. Additional exam requirements/recommendations for international students: Required—TOEFL (minimum score 525 paper-based). Electronic applications accepted. *Faculty research:* Culture studies, literature studies, foreign language acquisition.

San Francisco State University, Division of Graduate Studies, College of Liberal and Creative Arts, Department of Foreign Languages and Literatures, Program in French, San Francisco, CA 94132-1722. Offers MA. *Application deadline:* Applications are processed on a rolling basis. *Expenses:* Tuition, state resident: full-time $6738. Tuition, nonresident: full-time $17,898; part-time $372 per credit hour. *Required fees:* $498 per semester. *Unit head:* Dr. Anne Linton, Program Coordinator, 415-338-6061, Fax: 415-405-0588, E-mail: aelinton@sfsu.edu. *Application contact:* Dr. Berenice Le Marchand, Graduate Advisor, 415-338-7419, Fax: 415-405-0588, E-mail: blemarch@sfsu.edu.
Website: http://www.sfsu.edu/~french

San Jose State University, Graduate Studies and Research, College of Humanities and the Arts, Department of Foreign Languages, Program in French, San Jose, CA 95192-0001. Offers MA. *Degree requirements:* For master's, 2 foreign languages, thesis or comprehensive written and oral exam. *Entrance requirements:* Additional exam requirements/recommendations for international students: Required—TOEFL (minimum score 580 paper-based). Electronic applications accepted.

Simon Fraser University, Office of Graduate Studies, Faculty of Arts and Social Sciences, Department of French, Burnaby, BC V5A 1S6, Canada. Offers MA. *Degree requirements:* For master's, one foreign language, thesis or alternative. *Entrance requirements:* For master's, minimum GPA of 3.0 (on scale of 4.33), or 3.33 based on last 60 credits of undergraduate courses. Additional exam requirements/recommendations for international students: Recommended—TOEFL (minimum score 580 paper-based; 93 iBT), IELTS (minimum score 7), TWE (minimum score 5). Electronic applications accepted. *Faculty research:* French linguistics, Creole linguistics, French literature of the Middle Ages and Ancient Regime, modern and contemporary French literature, French Canadian language and literature.

Smith College, Graduate and Special Programs, Department of French Language and Literature, Northampton, MA 01063. Offers MAT. Part-time programs available. *Faculty:* 9 full-time (7 women). *Students:* 1 applicant, 100% accepted. *Degree requirements:* For master's, one foreign language. *Entrance requirements:* Additional exam requirements/recommendations for international students: Required—TOEFL (minimum score 595 paper-based; 97 iBT). *Application deadline:* For fall admission, 4/1 for domestic students, 1/15 for international students; for spring admission, 12/1 for domestic students. Application fee: $60. *Expenses: Tuition:* Full-time $33,360; part-time $1390 per credit. *Financial support:* Career-related internships or fieldwork, institutionally sponsored loans, and scholarships/grants available. Support available to part-time students. Financial award application deadline: 1/15; financial award applicants required to submit CSS PROFILE or FAFSA. *Unit head:* Helene Visentin, Chair, 413-585-3359, E-mail: hvisenti@smith.edu. *Application contact:* Ruth Morgan, Program Assistant, 413-585-3050, Fax: 413-585-3054, E-mail: gradstdy@smith.edu.
Website: http://www.smith.edu/french

Southern Oregon University, Graduate Studies, Department of Foreign Languages and Literatures, Ashland, OR 97520. Offers French language teaching (MA); Spanish language teaching (MA). Part-time programs available. Postbaccalaureate distance learning degree programs offered (minimal on-campus study). *Faculty:* 7 full-time (4 women), 6 part-time/adjunct (all women). *Students:* 49 full-time (38 women), 20 part-time (4 women); includes 15 minority (1 American Indian or Alaska Native, non-Hispanic/Latino; 1 Asian, non-Hispanic/Latino; 10 Hispanic/Latino; 3 Two or more races, non-Hispanic/Latino). Average age 36. 27 applicants, 89% accepted, 19 enrolled. In 2014, 21 master's awarded. *Degree requirements:* For master's, thesis (for some programs). *Entrance requirements:* For master's, GRE General Test, minimum cumulative GPA of 3.0 in the last 90 quarter credits (60 semester credits) of undergraduate coursework. Additional exam requirements/recommendations for international students: Required—TOEFL (minimum score 540 paper-based; 76 iBT),

IELTS (minimum score 6), ELPT (minimum score 964) or ELS (minimum score 112). *Application deadline:* For fall admission, 7/31 priority date for domestic and international students; for winter admission, 11/15 priority date for domestic and international students; for spring admission, 1/7 priority date for domestic and international students. Applications are processed on a rolling basis. Application fee: $50. Electronic applications accepted. *Expenses:* Tuition, state resident: full-time $10,225; part-time $1515 per quarter. Tuition, nonresident: full-time $12,782; part-time $1894 per quarter. *Required fees:* $1395; $261 per quarter. *Financial support:* Career-related internships or fieldwork, institutionally sponsored loans, scholarships/grants, and unspecified assistantships available. *Unit head:* Dr. Dan Morris, Graduate French Language Program Coordinator, 541-552-6740, E-mail: morris@sou.edu. *Application contact:* Dr. Anne Connor, Graduate Spanish Language Program Coordinator, 541-552-6743, E-mail: connora@sou.edu.
Website: http://www.sou.edu/language/

Stanford University, School of Humanities and Sciences, Department of French and Italian, Stanford, CA 94305-9991. Offers French (MA, PhD); Italian (MA, PhD). Terminal master's awarded for partial completion of doctoral program. *Degree requirements:* For master's, one foreign language, written exam; for doctorate, 2 foreign languages, thesis/dissertation, oral exam. *Entrance requirements:* For master's and doctorate, GRE General Test. Additional exam requirements/recommendations for international students: Required—TOEFL. Electronic applications accepted. *Expenses:* Tuition: Full-time $44,184; part-time $982 per credit hour. *Required fees:* $191.

State University of New York at New Paltz, Graduate School, School of Education, Department of Secondary Education, New Paltz, NY 12561. Offers adolescence education: biology (MAT, MS Ed); adolescence education: chemistry (MAT, MS Ed); adolescence education: earth science (MAT, MS Ed); adolescence education: English (MAT, MS Ed); adolescence education: French (MAT, MS Ed); adolescence education: social studies (MAT, MS Ed); adolescence education: Spanish (MAT, MS Ed); second language education (MS Ed, AC), including second language education (MS Ed); teaching English language learners (AC). *Accreditation:* NCATE. Part-time and evening/weekend programs available. *Faculty:* 11 full-time (7 women), 11 part-time/adjunct (6 women). *Students:* 66 full-time (36 women), 51 part-time (31 women); includes 24 minority (3 Black or African American, non-Hispanic/Latino; 1 American Indian or Alaska Native, non-Hispanic/Latino; 1 Asian, non-Hispanic/Latino; 16 Hispanic/Latino; 3 Two or more races, non-Hispanic/Latino), 2 international. Average age 30. 76 applicants, 83% accepted, 40 enrolled. In 2014, 55 master's awarded. *Degree requirements:* For master's, comprehensive exam (for some programs), portfolio. *Entrance requirements:* For master's, minimum GPA of 3.0, New York state teaching certificate (MS Ed). Additional exam requirements/recommendations for international students: Required—TOEFL (minimum score 550 paper-based; 80 iBT), IELTS (minimum score 6.5). *Application deadline:* For fall admission, 3/1 priority date for domestic students, 3/1 for international students; for spring admission, 10/1 priority date for domestic students, 10/1 for international students. Application fee: $50. Electronic applications accepted. *Financial support:* Application deadline: 8/1. *Unit head:* Dr. Laura Dull, Chair, 845-257-2849, E-mail: dullj@newpaltz.edu. *Application contact:* Vika Shock, Director of Graduate Admissions, 845-257-3285, Fax: 845-257-3284, E-mail: gradschool@newpaltz.edu.
Website: http://www.newpaltz.edu/secondaryed

Stony Brook University, State University of New York, Graduate School, College of Arts and Sciences, Department of European Languages, Literatures, and Cultures, Program in French, Stony Brook, NY 11794. Offers Romance languages (MA). Evening/weekend programs available. *Students:* 1 part-time (0 women). In 2014, 1 master's awarded. *Degree requirements:* For master's, one foreign language. *Entrance requirements:* For master's, GRE General Test. Additional exam requirements/recommendations for international students: Required—TOEFL. *Application deadline:* For fall admission, 1/15 for domestic students; for spring admission, 10/1 for domestic students. Application fee: $100. *Expenses:* Tuition, state resident: full-time $10,370; part-time $432 per credit. Tuition, nonresident: full-time $20,190; part-time $841 per credit. *Required fees:* $1431. *Unit head:* Prof. Nicholas Rzhevsky, Chair, 631-632-7440, Fax: 631-632-9612, E-mail: nicholas.rzhevsky@stonybrook.edu. *Application contact:* Mary Wilmarth, Coordinator, 631-632-7442, Fax: 631-632-9612, E-mail: mary.wilmarth@stonybrook.edu.

Syracuse University, College of Arts and Sciences, Program in French and Francophone Studies, Syracuse, NY 13244. Offers MA. Part-time programs available. *Students:* 6 full-time (5 women), 1 part-time (0 women), 2 international. Average age 27. 7 applicants, 71% accepted, 4 enrolled. In 2014, 3 master's awarded. *Degree requirements:* For master's, comprehensive exam, thesis or alternative. *Entrance requirements:* For master's, GRE General Test, writing sample in French. Additional exam requirements/recommendations for international students: Required—TOEFL (minimum score 100 iBT). *Application deadline:* For fall admission, 2/1 priority date for domestic and international students. Application fee: $75. Electronic applications accepted. *Expenses:* Tuition: Part-time $1341 per credit. *Financial support:* Fellowships with full tuition reimbursements, teaching assistantships with full and partial tuition reimbursements, and tuition waivers available. Financial award application deadline: 1/1; financial award applicants required to submit FAFSA. *Unit head:* Dr. Hope Glidden, Graduate Director, 315-443-2175, E-mail: hhglidde@syr.edu. *Application contact:* Collen Kepler, Information Contact, 315-443-2175, E-mail: cdkepler@syr.edu.
Website: http://lang.syr.edu/academics/French/MA-French.html

Tufts University, Graduate School of Arts and Sciences, Program in French, Medford, MA 02155. Offers MA. Part-time programs available. *Faculty:* 7 full-time (4 women). *Students:* 4 applicants, 75% accepted. In 2014, 3 master's awarded. *Degree requirements:* For master's, one foreign language. *Entrance requirements:* For master's, GRE General Test, writing sample. Additional exam requirements/recommendations for international students: Required—TOEFL (minimum score 550 paper-based; 80 iBT), IELTS (minimum score 6.5). *Application deadline:* For fall admission, 2/15 for domestic and international students; for spring admission, 10/15 for domestic and international students. Applications are processed on a rolling basis. Application fee: $75. Electronic applications accepted. *Expenses:* Tuition: Full-time $45,590; part-time $1161 per credit hour. *Required fees:* $782. Full-time tuition and fees vary according to degree level, program and student level. Part-time tuition and fees vary according to course load. *Financial support:* Federal Work-Study, scholarships/grants, and tuition waivers (partial) available. Support available to part-time students. Financial award application deadline: 3/1; financial award applicants required to submit FAFSA. *Unit head:* Dr. Gerard Gasarian, Graduate Program Director. *Application contact:* Office of Graduate Admissions, 617-627-3395, E-mail: gradadmissions@tufts.edu.

Tulane University, School of Liberal Arts, Department of French and Italian, New Orleans, LA 70118-5669. Offers French (MA, PhD). *Degree requirements:* For master's, one foreign language, thesis or alternative; for doctorate, 2 foreign languages, thesis/dissertation. *Entrance requirements:* For master's, GRE General Test, minimum B average in undergraduate course work; for doctorate, GRE General Test. Additional exam requirements/recommendations for international students: Required—TOEFL. Electronic applications accepted. *Expenses:* Tuition: Full-time $46,326; part-time $2574 per credit hour. *Required fees:* $1980; $44.50 per credit hour. $550 per term. Tuition and fees vary according to course load and program.

Université de Moncton, Faculty of Arts and Social Sciences, Department of French Studies, Moncton, NB E1A 3E9, Canada. Offers MA, PhD. Part-time programs available. Terminal master's awarded for partial completion of doctoral program. *Degree requirements:* For master's, thesis, proficiency in French; for doctorate, thesis/dissertation, proficiency in French. *Entrance requirements:* For master's, honors degree in French; for doctorate, MA in French. Electronic applications accepted. *Faculty research:* Language, linguistics, literature, ethnology, Acadian studies.

Université de Montréal, Faculty of Arts and Sciences, Department of French Literature, Montréal, QC H3C 3J7, Canada. Offers MA, PhD. *Degree requirements:* For master's, one foreign language, thesis; for doctorate, one foreign language, thesis/dissertation, general exam. Electronic applications accepted. *Faculty research:* Literary history, literary genres, critical edition, creative writing, Quebecois literature.

Université de Sherbrooke, Faculty of Letters and Human Sciences, Department of Letters and Communications, Sherbrooke, QC J1K 2R1, Canada. Offers comparative Canadian literature (MA, PhD); French literature (MA, PhD); linguistics (MA); theatre (MA). *Degree requirements:* For master's, thesis or alternative; for doctorate, thesis/dissertation. *Entrance requirements:* For master's, minimum GPA of 2.8; for doctorate, minimum GPA of 3.0.

Université du Québec à Chicoutimi, Graduate Programs, Program in Didactics of French-Mother Tongue, Chicoutimi, QC G7H 2B1, Canada. Offers Diploma. Part-time programs available. *Entrance requirements:* For degree, appropriate bachelor's degree, proficiency in French.

University at Buffalo, the State University of New York, Graduate School, College of Arts and Sciences, Department of Romance Languages and Literatures, Buffalo, NY 14260-4620. Offers French (MA, PhD); Spanish (MA, PhD). Part-time programs available. *Faculty:* 16 full-time (10 women), 6 part-time/adjunct (5 women). *Students:* 33 full-time (20 women), 4 part-time (2 women); includes 17 minority (2 Black or African American, non-Hispanic/Latino; 2 Asian, non-Hispanic/Latino; 9 Hispanic/Latino; 4 Two or more races, non-Hispanic/Latino), 11 international. 20 applicants, 85% accepted, 11 enrolled. In 2014, 3 master's, 7 doctorates awarded. Terminal master's awarded for partial completion of doctoral program. *Degree requirements:* For master's, one foreign language, comprehensive exam, thesis; for doctorate, 2 foreign languages, comprehensive exam, thesis/dissertation. *Entrance requirements:* For master's and doctorate, GRE. Additional exam requirements/recommendations for international students: Required—TOEFL (minimum score 550 paper-based; 79 iBT), IELTS (minimum score 6.5), PTE (minimum score 55). *Application deadline:* For fall admission, 1/15 priority date for domestic students, 1/1 for international students; for spring admission, 8/1 for international students. Applications are processed on a rolling basis. Application fee: $75. Electronic applications accepted. *Financial support:* In 2014–15, 24 students received support, including 3 fellowships (averaging $5,333 per year), 24 teaching assistantships with full tuition reimbursements available (averaging $13,454 per year); Federal Work-Study, institutionally sponsored loans, scholarships/grants, and health care benefits also available. Financial award application deadline: 1/1; financial award applicants required to submit FAFSA. *Faculty research:* Romance linguistics, cultural studies, literary studies, literature, philosophy and poetry. *Unit head:* Dr. David Castillo, Professor and Chair, 716-645-0869, Fax: 716-645-5981, E-mail: dc63@buffalo.edu. *Application contact:* Dr. Amy Graves-Monroe, Associate Professor and Director of Graduate Studies, 716-645-0880, Fax: 716-645-5981, E-mail: acgraves@buffalo.edu.
Website: http://rll.drupalgardens.com

University at Buffalo, the State University of New York, Graduate School, Graduate School of Education, Department of Learning and Instruction, Buffalo, NY 14260. Offers biology education (Ed M, Certificate); chemistry education (Ed M, Certificate); childhood education (Ed M); childhood education with bilingual extension (Ed M); curriculum, instruction and the science of learning (PhD); early childhood education (Ed M); early childhood education with bilingual extension (birth-grade 2) (Ed M); earth science education (Ed M, Certificate); education studies (Ed M); educational technology and new literacies (Certificate); elementary education (Ed D); English education (Ed M, Certificate); English for speakers of other languages (Ed M); foreign and second language education (PhD); French education (Ed M, Certificate); German education (Ed M, Certificate); gifted education (Certificate); Latin education (Ed M, Certificate); literacy specialist (Ed M); literacy teaching and learning (Certificate); mathematics education (Ed M, Certificate); music education (Ed M, Certificate); physics education (Ed M, Certificate); science and the public (Ed M); social studies education (Ed M, Certificate); Spanish education (Ed M, Certificate); special education (PhD); teaching English to speakers of other languages (Ed M). Part-time and evening/weekend programs available. Postbaccalaureate distance learning degree programs offered (no on-campus study). *Faculty:* 29 full-time (21 women), 64 part-time/adjunct (46 women). *Students:* 256 full-time (193 women), 303 part-time (222 women); includes 41 minority (21 Black or African American, non-Hispanic/Latino; 5 American Indian or Alaska Native, non-Hispanic/Latino; 13 Asian, non-Hispanic/Latino; 2 Hispanic/Latino), 84 international. Average age 30. 415 applicants, 84% accepted, 194 enrolled. In 2014, 160 master's, 20 doctorates, 32 other advanced degrees awarded. *Degree requirements:* For master's, comprehensive exam; for doctorate, thesis/dissertation, research analysis exam, research experience component. *Entrance requirements:* For master's, letters of reference; for doctorate, GRE General Test or MAT, interview, writing sample, letters of recommendation. Additional exam requirements/recommendations for international students: Required—TOEFL (minimum score 600 paper-based; 96 iBT). *Application deadline:* For fall admission, 2/1 priority date for domestic and international students; for spring admission, 11/15 priority date for domestic students, 10/1 for international students. Applications are processed on a rolling basis. Application fee: $50. Electronic applications accepted. *Financial support:* In 2014–15, 50 fellowships (averaging $12,110 per year), 32 research assistantships with tuition reimbursements (averaging $12,867 per year) were awarded; teaching assistantships, career-related internships or fieldwork, Federal Work-Study, institutionally sponsored loans, scholarships/grants, tuition waivers, and unspecified assistantships also available. Financial award application deadline: 2/28; financial award applicants required to submit FAFSA. *Faculty research:* Science assessment, foreign language teaching and learning, early learning, new literacies, gender and education. *Total annual research expenditures:* $1.3 million. *Unit head:* Dr. Suzanne Miller, Chair, 716-645-2455, Fax: 716-645-3161, E-mail: smiller@buffalo.edu. *Application contact:* Cathy Dimino, Admissions Assistant, 716-645-2110, Fax: 716-645-7937, E-mail: cadimino@buffalo.edu.
Website: http://gse.buffalo.edu/lai

The University of Alabama, Graduate School, College of Arts and Sciences, Department of Modern Languages and Classics, Tuscaloosa, AL 35487. Offers French (MA, PhD); French and Spanish (PhD); German (MA); Romance languages (MA, PhD); Spanish (MA, PhD). Part-time programs available. *Faculty:* 29 full-time (16 women). *Students:* 53 full-time (35 women), 10 part-time (6 women); includes 9 minority (3 Black or African American, non-Hispanic/Latino; 5 Hispanic/Latino; 1 Two or more races, non-Hispanic/Latino), 15 international. Average age 33. 24 applicants, 88% accepted, 14 enrolled. In 2014, 10 master's, 5 doctorates awarded. *Degree requirements:* For master's, comprehensive exam, thesis optional; for doctorate, one foreign language, thesis/dissertation, preliminary exam. *Entrance requirements:* For master's and

doctorate, minimum GPA of 3.0, writing sample. Additional exam requirements/recommendations for international students: Required—TOEFL or IELTS. *Application deadline:* For fall admission, 7/6 priority date for domestic students, 1/15 priority date for international students; for spring admission, 12/5 priority date for domestic students, 6/1 priority date for international students. Applications are processed on a rolling basis. Application fee: $50 ($60 for international students). Electronic applications accepted. *Expenses:* Tuition, state resident: full-time $9826. Tuition, nonresident: full-time $24,950. *Financial support:* In 2014–15, 7 students received support, including 1 fellowship, research assistantships with full tuition reimbursements available (averaging $10,291 per year), 6 teaching assistantships with full tuition reimbursements available (averaging $10,291 per year); career-related internships or fieldwork, Federal Work-Study, institutionally sponsored loans, and scholarships/grants also available. Financial award application deadline: 7/14. *Faculty research:* Non-English literature, linguistics, culture, film. *Unit head:* Dr. Michael Picone, Chair and Professor, 205-348-5054, Fax: 205-348-2042, E-mail: mpicone@bama.ua.edu. *Application contact:* Dr. K. Barbara Fischer, Graduate Director and Associate Professor, 205-348-8465, Fax: 205-348-2042, E-mail: bfischer@bama.ua.edu.
Website: http://bama.ua.edu/~mlc

University of Alberta, Faculty of Graduate Studies and Research, Department of Modern Languages and Cultural Studies, Edmonton, AB T6G 2E1, Canada. Offers applied linguistics (Germanic, Romance, Slavic) (MA); French language, literatures and linguistics (PhD); French language, literatures, and linguistics (MA); Germanic languages, literatures and linguistics (PhD); Germanic languages, literatures, and linguistics (MA); Italian studies (MA); Slavic languages and literatures (Russian, Ukrainian) (MA, PhD); Slavic linguistics (Russian, Ukrainian) (MA, PhD); Spanish and Latin American studies (MA, PhD); Ukrainian folklore (MA, PhD). Part-time programs available. *Degree requirements:* For master's, one foreign language, thesis; for doctorate, 2 foreign languages, comprehensive exam, thesis/dissertation. *Entrance requirements:* For master's and doctorate, 1 language other than English. Additional exam requirements/recommendations for international students: Required—Michigan English Language Assessment Battery or TOEFL (minimum score 550 paper-based). Electronic applications accepted. *Faculty research:* Russian/Ukrainian studies; German studies; contemporary Latin American, French and Francophone studies; Italian studies.

The University of Arizona, College of Humanities, Department of French and Italian, Tucson, AZ 85721. Offers French (MA). Part-time programs available. *Entrance requirements:* For master's, 3 letters of reference, writing sample in French, audio recording. Additional exam requirements/recommendations for international students: Required—TOEFL (minimum score 550 paper-based; 79 iBT). Electronic applications accepted. *Faculty research:* French literature (history, criticism, and theory), Francophone literature and culture, second language acquisition and teaching.

University of Arkansas, Graduate School, J. William Fulbright College of Arts and Sciences, Department of World Languages, Literature and Cultures, Program in French, Fayetteville, AR 72701-1201. Offers MA. *Degree requirements:* For master's, variable foreign language requirement. Electronic applications accepted.

The University of British Columbia, Faculty of Arts and Faculty of Graduate Studies, Department of French, Hispanic and Italian Studies, Vancouver, BC V6T 1Z1, Canada. Offers French (MA, PhD); Hispanic studies (MA, PhD). Part-time programs available. *Degree requirements:* For master's, thesis optional; for doctorate, 2 foreign languages, comprehensive exam, thesis/dissertation. *Entrance requirements:* For doctorate, MA. Additional exam requirements/recommendations for international students: Required—TOEFL (minimum score 550 paper-based; 80 iBT). Electronic applications accepted. *Faculty research:* Medieval and Renaissance literature, modern literature, romance philology and linguistics, cultural studies, women's literature.

University of Calgary, Faculty of Graduate Studies, Faculty of Arts, Department of French, Italian and Spanish, Calgary, AB T2N 1N4, Canada. Offers French (MA, PhD); Spanish (MA, PhD). PhD offered in special cases only. Part-time programs available. *Degree requirements:* For master's, one foreign language, thesis, exam; for doctorate, 2 foreign languages, comprehensive exam, thesis/dissertation, candidacy exam. *Entrance requirements:* Additional exam requirements/recommendations for international students: Required—TOEFL (minimum score 550 paper-based; 80 iBT) or IELTS (minimum score 7). Electronic applications accepted. *Faculty research:* French and French-Canadian language and literature, Hispanic language and literature, comparative literature, language instruction, literary theory.

University of California, Berkeley, Graduate Division, College of Letters and Science, Department of French, Berkeley, CA 94720-1500. Offers PhD. *Degree requirements:* For doctorate, one foreign language, thesis/dissertation, qualifying exam. *Entrance requirements:* For doctorate, minimum GPA of 3.0, 3 letters of recommendation.

University of California, Berkeley, Graduate Division, College of Letters and Science, Group in Romance Languages and Literature, Berkeley, CA 94720-1500. Offers French (PhD); Italian (PhD); Spanish (PhD). *Degree requirements:* For doctorate, thesis/dissertation, qualifying exam. *Entrance requirements:* For doctorate, GRE General Test, minimum GPA of 3.0, 3 letters of recommendation. Additional exam requirements/recommendations for international students: Required—TOEFL (minimum score 570 paper-based).

University of California, Davis, Graduate Studies, Program in French, Davis, CA 95616. Offers PhD. Part-time programs available. *Degree requirements:* For doctorate, thesis/dissertation. *Entrance requirements:* For doctorate, GRE General Test, minimum GPA of 3.0. Additional exam requirements/recommendations for international students: Required—TOEFL (minimum score 550 paper-based). Electronic applications accepted. *Faculty research:* Art and art criticism, Francophone literature, travel narrative, colonial and postcolonial studies and romance linguistics.

University of California, Irvine, School of Humanities, Department of European Languages and Studies, Irvine, CA 92697. Offers French (MA, PhD); German (MA, PhD). *Students:* 6 full-time (2 women); includes 1 minority (Two or more races, non-Hispanic/Latino). Average age 32. 4 applicants, 50% accepted, 1 enrolled. In 2014, 1 master's, 1 doctorate awarded. *Degree requirements:* For doctorate, thesis/dissertation. *Entrance requirements:* For master's and doctorate, GRE General Test, minimum GPA of 3.0. Additional exam requirements/recommendations for international students: Required—TOEFL (minimum score 550 paper-based). *Application deadline:* For fall admission, 1/15 for domestic and international students. Applications are processed on a rolling basis. Application fee: $90 ($110 for international students). Electronic applications accepted. *Financial support:* Fellowships, research assistantships with full tuition reimbursements, teaching assistantships, institutionally sponsored loans, traineeships, health care benefits, and unspecified assistantships available. Financial award application deadline: 3/1; financial award applicants required to submit FAFSA. *Faculty research:* Montaigne, psychoanalysis, feminism and the problem of repression, aesthetics of nationalism and the limits of culture. *Unit head:* Prof. Jane O. Newman, Chair, 949-824-6406, Fax: 949-824-1031, E-mail: jonewman@uci.edu. *Application contact:* Bindya Baliga, Graduate Program Coordinator, 949-824-7968, Fax: 949-824-6416, E-mail: bbaliga@uci.edu.
Website: http://www.humanities.uci.edu/els/

University of California, Los Angeles, Graduate Division, College of Letters and Science, Department of French and Francophone Studies, Los Angeles, CA 90095. Offers MA, PhD. Terminal master's awarded for partial completion of doctoral program. *Degree requirements:* For master's, one foreign language, comprehensive exam; for doctorate, 2 foreign languages, thesis/dissertation, oral and written qualifying exams. *Entrance requirements:* For doctorate, GRE General Test, bachelor's degree; minimum undergraduate GPA of 3.0 (or its equivalent if letter grade system not used); writing sample in French. Additional exam requirements/recommendations for international students: Required—TOEFL. Electronic applications accepted.

University of California, Santa Barbara, Graduate Division, College of Letters and Sciences, Division of Humanities and Fine Arts, Program in Comparative Literature, Santa Barbara, CA 93106-4130. Offers comparative literature (PhD); East Asian literatures (PhD); feminist studies (PhD); French (PhD); global studies (PhD); translation studies (PhD); MA/PhD. *Degree requirements:* For doctorate, 2 foreign languages, comprehensive exam, thesis/dissertation. *Entrance requirements:* For doctorate, GRE. Additional exam requirements/recommendations for international students: Required—TOEFL (minimum score 550 paper-based; 80 iBT), IELTS (minimum score 7). Electronic applications accepted. *Faculty research:* Comparative literary studies in global context, critical theory, translation studies, media technological studies, trauma studies.

University of Chicago, Division of the Humanities, Department of Romance Languages and Literatures, Chicago, IL 60637. Offers French (PhD); Italian (PhD); Spanish (PhD). *Students:* 44 full-time (28 women); includes 9 minority (1 Black or African American, non-Hispanic/Latino; 1 Asian, non-Hispanic/Latino; 6 Hispanic/Latino; 1 Two or more races, non-Hispanic/Latino), 13 international. 71 applicants, 39% accepted, 7 enrolled. Terminal master's awarded for partial completion of doctoral program. *Degree requirements:* For doctorate, 3 foreign languages, thesis/dissertation. *Entrance requirements:* For doctorate, GRE General Test. Additional exam requirements/recommendations for international students: Required—TOEFL (minimum score 104 iBT), IELTS (minimum score 7). *Application deadline:* For fall admission, 12/15 for domestic and international students. Application fee: $90. Electronic applications accepted. *Expenses: Tuition:* Full-time $46,899. *Required fees:* $347. *Financial support:* Fellowships with full tuition reimbursements, teaching assistantships with full tuition reimbursements, Federal Work-Study, institutionally sponsored loans, scholarships/grants, and health care benefits available. Financial award application deadline: 12/15; financial award applicants required to submit FAFSA. *Unit head:* Dr. Larry Norman, Chair. *Application contact:* Braden Grams, Assistant Dean of Students, Admissions and Fellowships, 773-702-1552, Fax: 773-834-9148, E-mail: humanitiesadmissions@uchicago.edu.
Website: http://rll.uchicago.edu

University of Cincinnati, Graduate School, McMicken College of Arts and Sciences, Department of Romance Languages and Literature, Program in French, Cincinnati, OH 45221. Offers MA, PhD. Terminal master's awarded for partial completion of doctoral program. *Degree requirements:* For master's, thesis optional; for doctorate, 2 foreign languages, thesis/dissertation. *Entrance requirements:* For master's, minimum GPA of 3.0. Electronic applications accepted.

University of Colorado Boulder, Graduate School, College of Arts and Sciences, Department of French and Italian, Boulder, CO 80309. Offers French (MA, PhD). *Faculty:* 7 full-time (4 women). *Students:* 23 full-time (17 women), 1 (woman) part-time; includes 2 minority (both Hispanic/Latino), 5 international. Average age 33. 20 applicants, 40% accepted, 5 enrolled. In 2014, 2 master's, 1 doctorate awarded. Terminal master's awarded for partial completion of doctoral program. *Degree requirements:* For master's, 2 foreign languages, comprehensive exam, thesis or alternative; for doctorate, 3 foreign languages, thesis/dissertation. *Entrance requirements:* For master's, GRE General Test, minimum undergraduate GPA of 3.0; for doctorate, GRE General Test. *Application deadline:* For fall admission, 1/5 for domestic students, 1/15 for international students. Applications are processed on a rolling basis. Application fee: $50 ($70 for international students). Electronic applications accepted. *Financial support:* In 2014–15, 54 students received support, including 5 fellowships (averaging $760 per year), 4 research assistantships with full and partial tuition reimbursements available (averaging $39,722 per year), 16 teaching assistantships with full and partial tuition reimbursements available (averaging $34,663 per year); institutionally sponsored loans, scholarships/grants, health care benefits, and unspecified assistantships also available. Financial award application deadline: 2/1; financial award applicants required to submit FAFSA. *Faculty research:* Literary criticism, French language/literature, arts/humanities/cultural activities, cinema/video.
Website: http://www.colorado.edu/FRIT/

University of Connecticut, Graduate School, College of Liberal Arts and Sciences, Department of Modern and Classical Languages, Field of French, Storrs, CT 06269. Offers MA, PhD. Terminal master's awarded for partial completion of doctoral program. *Degree requirements:* For master's, comprehensive exam; for doctorate, thesis/dissertation. *Entrance requirements:* For master's and doctorate, GRE General Test, GRE Subject Test. Additional exam requirements/recommendations for international students: Required—TOEFL (minimum score 550 paper-based). Electronic applications accepted.

University of Delaware, College of Arts and Sciences, Department of Foreign Languages and Literatures, Newark, DE 19716. Offers foreign languages and literatures (MA), including French, German, Spanish; foreign languages pedagogy (MA), including French, German, Spanish; technical Chinese translation (MA). *Degree requirements:* For master's, one foreign language, comprehensive exam, thesis optional. *Entrance requirements:* For master's, GRE General Test, letters of recommendation, writing sample. Additional exam requirements/recommendations for international students: Required—TOEFL. Electronic applications accepted. *Faculty research:* Medieval to Modern French and Spanish literature, twentieth-century German, French, Spanish literature by women, computer-assisted instruction.

University of Florida, Graduate School, College of Liberal Arts and Sciences, Department of Languages, Literatures and Cultures, Gainesville, FL 32611-5565. Offers French and Francophone studies (MA, PhD); German (MA, PhD), including women's and gender studies (PhD); romance languages (PhD), including French and Francophone studies. *Faculty:* 25 full-time (16 women), 3 part-time/adjunct (2 women). *Students:* 15 full-time (12 women), 1 (woman) part-time; includes 3 minority (1 Black or African American, non-Hispanic/Latino; 2 Hispanic/Latino), 6 international. 19 applicants, 68% accepted, 9 enrolled. In 2014, 5 master's awarded. *Degree requirements:* For master's, comprehensive exam, thesis optional; for doctorate, one foreign language, comprehensive exam, thesis/dissertation. *Entrance requirements:* For master's and doctorate, GRE General Test, minimum GPA of 3.0. Additional exam requirements/recommendations for international students: Required—TOEFL (minimum score 550 paper-based; 80 iBT), IELTS (minimum score 6). *Application deadline:* For fall admission, 6/1 priority date for domestic students. Applications are processed on a rolling basis. Application fee: $30. Electronic applications accepted. *Financial support:* In 2014–15, 15 teaching assistantships were awarded; associateships also available. Financial award applicants required to submit FAFSA. *Faculty research:* Medieval epic, romance, and allegory; Renaissance and Baroque poetry; the eighteenth century novel; nineteenth century prose, poetry, and poetics; the twentieth century novel, theater, and

poetry; the literatures of the Francophone world; French and Francophone film; the literatures in Breton and Occitan; criticism and critical theory; applied linguistics; the history of French; phonology; sociolinguistics; the structure of French; French and Haitian Creole linguistics. *Unit head:* Mary Watt, PhD, Associate Professor of Italian/Chair, 352-392-8149, Fax: 352-392-1443, E-mail: marywatt@ufl.edu. *Application contact:* Rori Bloom, PhD, French Studies Graduate Program Coordinator, 352-273-3769, E-mail: ribloom@ufl.edu.
Website: http://www.languages.ufl.edu/

University of Georgia, Franklin College of Arts and Sciences, Department of Romance Languages, Athens, GA 30602. Offers French (MA); Romance languages (MA, PhD); Spanish (MA). *Degree requirements:* For master's, one foreign language; for doctorate, 2 foreign languages, thesis/dissertation. *Entrance requirements:* For master's and doctorate, GRE General Test. Electronic applications accepted.

University of Guelph, Graduate Studies, College of Arts, School of Languages and Literatures, Guelph, ON N1G 2W1, Canada. Offers European studies (MA); French studies (MA). *Entrance requirements:* For master's, honours BA or equivalent. Electronic applications accepted. *Faculty research:* Sociolinguistics, poetics and politics of literature, language acquisition.

University of Hawaii at Manoa, Graduate Division, College of Languages, Linguistics and Literature, Department of Languages and Literatures of Europe and the Americas, Program in French, Honolulu, HI 96822. Offers MA. Part-time programs available. *Degree requirements:* For master's, one foreign language, thesis optional. *Entrance requirements:* Additional exam requirements/recommendations for international students: Required—TOEFL (minimum score 580 paper-based; 92 iBT), IELTS (minimum score 5).

University of Illinois at Chicago, Graduate College, College of Liberal Arts and Sciences, School of Literatures, Cultural Studies and Linguistics, Department of French and Francophone Studies, Chicago, IL 60607-7128. Offers MA. Part-time programs available. *Faculty:* 11 full-time (9 women), 2 part-time/adjunct (1 woman). *Students:* 4 full-time (3 women), 4 part-time (3 women); includes 2 minority (1 Black or African American, non-Hispanic/Latino; 1 Hispanic/Latino), 1 international. Average age 34. 9 applicants, 100% accepted, 5 enrolled. In 2014, 4 master's awarded. *Degree requirements:* For master's, one foreign language, thesis optional, exam. *Entrance requirements:* For master's, minimum GPA of 2.75. Additional exam requirements/recommendations for international students: Required—TOEFL. *Application deadline:* For fall admission, 1/1 priority date for domestic and international students; for spring admission, 10/1 for domestic students, 7/15 for international students. Applications are processed on a rolling basis. Application fee: $60. Electronic applications accepted. *Expenses:* Tuition, state resident: full-time $11,254; part-time $468 per credit hour. Tuition, nonresident: full-time $23,252; part-time $968 per credit hour. *Required fees:* $1217 per term. Part-time tuition and fees vary according to course load, degree level and program. *Financial support:* In 2014–15, 10 students received support, including 14 research assistantships with full tuition reimbursements available; fellowships with full tuition reimbursements available, teaching assistantships with full tuition reimbursements available, career-related internships or fieldwork, Federal Work-Study, scholarships/grants, traineeships, tuition waivers (full), and unspecified assistantships also available. Financial award application deadline: 3/1; financial award applicants required to submit FAFSA. *Faculty research:* French civilization, feminist theory, French theater, sociology of literature, narrative theory. *Unit head:* Prof. Ellen McClure, Head, French and Francophone Studies, 312-996-5076, E-mail: ellenmc@uic.edu. *Application contact:* Prof. Margaret Miner, Director of Graduate Studies, 312-996-3221, E-mail: mminer@uic.edu.
Website: http://lcsl.uic.edu/french

University of Illinois at Urbana–Champaign, Graduate College, College of Liberal Arts and Sciences, School of Literatures, Cultures and Linguistics, Department of French, Champaign, IL 61820. Offers MA, PhD. *Students:* 23 (12 women). Application fee: $70 ($90 for international students). *Unit head:* Marcus Keller, Head, 217-265-6476, Fax: 217-244-2223, E-mail: mkeller@illinois.edu. *Application contact:* Lynn Stanke, Office Support Specialist, 217-333-6269, Fax: 217-244-3050, E-mail: stanke@illinois.edu.
Website: http://www.french.illinois.edu/

The University of Iowa, Graduate College, College of Liberal Arts and Sciences, Department of French and Italian, Iowa City, IA 52242-1316. Offers French (MA, PhD). *Degree requirements:* For master's, thesis optional, exam; for doctorate, comprehensive exam, thesis/dissertation. *Entrance requirements:* For master's and doctorate, GRE General Test, minimum GPA of 3.0. Additional exam requirements/recommendations for international students: Required—TOEFL (minimum score 550 paper-based; 81 iBT). Electronic applications accepted.

The University of Kansas, Graduate Studies, College of Liberal Arts and Sciences, Department of French and Italian, Lawrence, KS 66045-7590. Offers French (MA, PhD). Part-time programs available. *Faculty:* 8 full-time, 14 part-time/adjunct. *Students:* 13 full-time (10 women), 2 part-time (both women), 2 international. Average age 30. 12 applicants, 75% accepted, 6 enrolled. In 2014, 5 master's, 4 doctorates awarded. *Degree requirements:* For master's, one foreign language, comprehensive exam, thesis optional; for doctorate, one foreign language, comprehensive exam, thesis/dissertation. *Entrance requirements:* For master's and doctorate, GRE. Additional exam requirements/recommendations for international students: Required—TOEFL (minimum score 23 iBT). *Application deadline:* For fall admission, 2/15 priority date for domestic students, 1/15 priority date for international students. Applications are processed on a rolling basis. Application fee: $55 ($65 for international students). Electronic applications accepted. *Financial support:* Fellowships, teaching assistantships with full tuition reimbursements, and unspecified assistantships available. Financial award applicants required to submit FAFSA. *Faculty research:* French literature and cultural studies; Francophone literature, film. *Unit head:* Dr. Caroline Jewers, Chair, 785-864-9076, E-mail: cjewers@ku.edu. *Application contact:* Cari Ann Kreienhop, Academic Advisor, 785-864-3665, E-mail: ckreienhop@ku.edu.
Website: http://www.frenchitalian.ku.edu/

University of Lethbridge, School of Graduate Studies, Lethbridge, AB T1K 3M4, Canada. Offers addictions counseling (M Sc); agricultural biotechnology (M Sc); agricultural studies (M Sc, MA); anthropology (MA); archaeology (M Sc, MA); art (MA, MFA); biochemistry (M Sc); biological sciences (M Sc); biomolecular science (PhD); biosystems and biodiversity (PhD); Canadian studies (MA); chemistry (M Sc); computer science (M Sc); computer science and geographical information science (M Sc); counseling (MC); counseling psychology (M Ed); dramatic arts (MA); earth, space, and physical science (PhD); economics (MA); education (MA); educational leadership (M Ed); English (MA); environmental science (M Sc); evolution and behavior (PhD); exercise science (M Sc); French (MA); French/German (MA); French/Spanish (MA); general education (M Ed); geography (M Sc, MA); German (MA); health sciences (M Sc); individualized multidisciplinary (M Sc, MA); kinesiology (M Sc, MA); management (M Sc), including accounting, finance, general management, human resource management and labor relations, information systems, international management, marketing, policy and strategy; mathematics (M Sc); modern languages (MA); music (M Mus, MA); Native American studies (MA); neuroscience (M Sc, PhD); new media (MA, MFA); nursing (M Sc, MN); philosophy (MA); physics (M Sc); political science (MA); psychology (M Sc, MA); religious studies (MA); sociology (MA); theatre and dramatic arts (MFA); theoretical and computational science (PhD); urban and regional studies (MA); women and gender studies (MA). Part-time and evening/weekend programs available. *Faculty:* 358. *Students:* 445 full-time (243 women), 116 part-time (72 women). Average age 31. 351 applicants, 26% accepted, 87 enrolled. In 2014, 129 master's, 13 doctorates awarded. *Degree requirements:* For master's, thesis (for some programs); for doctorate, comprehensive exam, thesis/dissertation. *Entrance requirements:* For master's, GMAT (for M Sc in management), bachelor's degree in related field, minimum GPA of 3.0 during previous 20 graded semester courses, 2 years' teaching or related experience (M Ed); for doctorate, master's degree, minimum graduate GPA of 3.5. Additional exam requirements/recommendations for international students: Required—TOEFL. Application fee: $100 Canadian dollars. *Financial support:* Fellowships, research assistantships, teaching assistantships, scholarships/grants, health care benefits, and unspecified assistantships available. *Faculty research:* Movement and brain plasticity, gibberellin physiology, photosynthesis, carbon cycling, molecular properties of main-group ring components. *Application contact:* School of Graduate Studies, 403-329-5194, E-mail: sgsinquiries@uleth.ca.
Website: http://www.uleth.ca/graduatestudies/

University of Louisiana at Lafayette, College of Liberal Arts, Department of Modern Languages, Program in Francophone Studies, Lafayette, LA 70504. Offers PhD. *Degree requirements:* For doctorate, 2 foreign languages, comprehensive exam, thesis/dissertation. *Entrance requirements:* For doctorate, GRE General Test, minimum GPA of 2.75. Additional exam requirements/recommendations for international students: Required—TOEFL (minimum score 550 paper-based). Electronic applications accepted. *Faculty research:* Louisiana folklore, eighteenth-century French literature, contemporary criticism.

University of Louisiana at Lafayette, College of Liberal Arts, Department of Modern Languages, Program in French, Lafayette, LA 70504. Offers MA. Part-time programs available. *Degree requirements:* For master's, 2 foreign languages, thesis or alternative. *Entrance requirements:* For master's, GRE General Test, minimum GPA of 2.75. Additional exam requirements/recommendations for international students: Required—TOEFL (minimum score 550 paper-based). Electronic applications accepted. *Faculty research:* Louisiana studies, nineteenth-century French literature, Francophone studies.

University of Louisville, Graduate School, College of Arts and Sciences, Department of Classical and Modern Languages, Louisville, KY 40292-0001. Offers French (MA); Spanish (MA). Part-time and evening/weekend programs available. *Students:* 22 full-time (16 women), 13 part-time (9 women); includes 11 minority (3 Black or African American, non-Hispanic/Latino; 1 Asian, non-Hispanic/Latino; 6 Hispanic/Latino; 1 Two or more races, non-Hispanic/Latino), 5 international. Average age 30. 25 applicants, 84% accepted, 14 enrolled. In 2014, 14 master's awarded. *Degree requirements:* For master's, one foreign language, thesis optional. *Entrance requirements:* For master's, GRE General Test (recommended). Additional exam requirements/recommendations for international students: Required—TOEFL (minimum score 550 paper-based). *Application deadline:* For fall admission, 5/1 priority date for international students; for spring admission, 11/1 priority date for international students; for summer admission, 4/1 priority date for international students. Applications are processed on a rolling basis. Application fee: $60. Electronic applications accepted. *Expenses:* Tuition, state resident: full-time $11,326; part-time $630 per credit hour. Tuition, nonresident: full-time $23,568; part-time $1311 per credit hour. *Required fees:* $196. Tuition and fees vary according to program and reciprocity agreements. *Financial support:* In 2014–15, 8 teaching assistantships with full tuition reimbursements were awarded; fellowships, institutionally sponsored loans, scholarships/grants, health care benefits, and unspecified assistantships also available. Financial award applicants required to submit FAFSA. *Faculty research:* Hispanic cultural studies, sociolinguistics, translation, contemporary France, medieval literature. *Unit head:* Dr. Augustus A. Mastri, Chair, 502-852-0403, Fax: 502-852-8885, E-mail: mastri@louisville.edu. *Application contact:* Libby Leggett, Director, Graduate Admissions, 502-852-3101, Fax: 502-852-6536, E-mail: gradadm@louisville.edu.
Website: http://louisville.edu/modernlanguages/

The University of Manchester, School of Languages, Linguistics and Cultures, Manchester, United Kingdom. Offers Arab world studies (PhD); Chinese studies (M Phil, PhD); East Asian studies (M Phil, PhD); English language (PhD); French studies (M Phil, PhD); German studies (M Phil, PhD); interpreting studies (PhD); Italian studies (M Phil, PhD); Japanese studies (M Phil, PhD); Latin American cultural studies (M Phil, PhD); linguistics (M Phil, PhD); Middle Eastern studies (M Phil, PhD); Polish studies (M Phil, PhD); Portuguese studies (M Phil, PhD); Russian studies (M Phil, PhD); Spanish studies (M Phil, PhD); translation and intercultural studies (M Phil, PhD).

University of Manitoba, Faculty of Graduate Studies, Faculty of Arts, Department of French, Spanish and Italian, Winnipeg, MB R3T 2N2, Canada. Offers French (MA, PhD). *Degree requirements:* For master's, one foreign language, thesis; for doctorate, 2 foreign languages, thesis/dissertation.

University of Maryland, College Park, Academic Affairs, College of Arts and Humanities, School of Languages, Literatures, and Cultures, Modern French Studies Program, College Park, MD 20742. Offers PhD. *Entrance requirements:* For doctorate, GRE, letters of recommendation, writing sample. Additional exam requirements/recommendations for international students: Required—TOEFL.

University of Maryland, College Park, Academic Affairs, College of Arts and Humanities, School of Languages, Literatures, and Cultures, Program in French Language and Literature, College Park, MD 20742. Offers MA. *Degree requirements:* For master's, one foreign language, comprehensive exam, thesis or alternative. *Entrance requirements:* For master's, GRE General Test, GRE Subject Test, minimum GPA of 3.0, 3 letters of recommendation. Additional exam requirements/recommendations for international students: Required—TOEFL. Electronic applications accepted.

University of Massachusetts Amherst, Graduate School, College of Humanities and Fine Arts, Department of Languages, Literatures, and Cultures, Program in French and Francophone Studies, Amherst, MA 01003. Offers French (MAT); French and Francophone studies (MA). Part-time programs available. *Students:* 5 full-time (4 women), 2 international. Average age 29. 6 applicants, 50% accepted, 1 enrolled. In 2014, 4 master's awarded. *Degree requirements:* For master's, thesis or alternative. *Entrance requirements:* For master's, GRE General Test. Additional exam requirements/recommendations for international students: Required—TOEFL (minimum score 550 paper-based; 80 iBT), IELTS (minimum score 6.5). *Application deadline:* For fall admission, 2/1 for domestic and international students; for spring admission, 10/1 for domestic and international students. Applications are processed on a rolling basis. Application fee: $75. Electronic applications accepted. *Expenses:* Tuition, state resident: full-time $1980; part-time $110 per credit. Tuition, nonresident: full-time $14,644; part-time $414 per credit. *Required fees:* $11,417. One-time fee: $357. *Financial support:* Fellowships with full and partial tuition reimbursements, research assistantships with full and partial tuition reimbursements, teaching assistantships with

full and partial tuition reimbursements, career-related internships or fieldwork, Federal Work-Study, scholarships/grants, traineeships, health care benefits, tuition waivers (full and partial), and unspecified assistantships available. Support available to part-time students. Financial award application deadline: 2/1. *Unit head:* Dr. Luke P. Bouvier, Graduate Program Director, 413-545-2314, Fax: 412-545-4778. *Application contact:* Lindsay DeSantis, Supervisor of Admissions, 413-545-0722, Fax: 413-577-0100, E-mail: gradadm@grad.umass.edu.
Website: http://www.umass.edu/french/

University of Memphis, Graduate School, College of Arts and Sciences, Department of Foreign Languages and Literatures, Memphis, TN 38152. Offers French (MA). Part-time programs available. *Faculty:* 8 full-time (4 women), 1 part-time/adjunct (0 women). *Students:* 15 full-time (14 women), 4 part-time (all women); includes 5 minority (all Hispanic/Latino). Average age 29. 12 applicants, 100% accepted, 2 enrolled. *Degree requirements:* For master's, 2 foreign languages, comprehensive exam. *Entrance requirements:* For master's, GRE, interview in language of concentration. Additional exam requirements/recommendations for international students: Required—TOEFL (minimum score 79 iBT). *Application deadline:* For fall admission, 5/15 for domestic students, 4/5 for international students; for spring admission, 11/30 for domestic students, 10/5 for international students. Applications are processed on a rolling basis. Application fee: $35 ($60 for international students). Electronic applications accepted. *Financial support:* In 2014–15, 11 students received support. Research assistantships with full tuition reimbursements available, teaching assistantships with full tuition reimbursements available, Federal Work-Study, scholarships/grants, and unspecified assistantships available. Financial award application deadline: 2/15; financial award applicants required to submit FAFSA. *Faculty research:* Latin American studies, Brazilian culture and literature, modernity and postmodernity, Hispanic studies, French studies, French and Hispanic culture and literature, Hispanic linguistics, applied linguistics. *Unit head:* Dr. Ralph Albanese, Professor and Chair, 901-678-2507, E-mail: ralbanes@memphis.edu. *Application contact:* Dr. Fernando Burgos, Professor and Coordinator of Graduate Studies, 901-678-3158, E-mail: fburgos@memphis.edu.
Website: http://www.memphis.edu/fl/

University of Miami, Graduate School, College of Arts and Sciences, Department of Modern Languages and Literatures, Coral Gables, FL 33124. Offers romance studies (PhD), including French, Spanish. *Degree requirements:* For doctorate, 2 foreign languages, thesis/dissertation, area exam, qualifying exam. *Entrance requirements:* For doctorate, 1 writing sample in English and 1 writing sample in French or Spanish, minimum GPA of 3.0, oral interview, letters of recommendation. Additional exam requirements/recommendations for international students: Required—TOEFL (minimum score 550 paper-based; 59 iBT). Electronic applications accepted. *Faculty research:* Transatlantic studies, Caribbean studies, comparative literature, gender theory, cultural studies.

University of Michigan, Horace H. Rackham School of Graduate Studies, College of Literature, Science, and the Arts, Department of Romance Languages and Literatures, Program in French, Ann Arbor, MI 48109. Offers PhD. *Faculty:* 8 full-time (4 women). *Students:* 8 full-time (4 women). Average age 25. 35 applicants, 11% accepted, 1 enrolled. In 2014, 2 doctorates awarded. *Degree requirements:* For doctorate, 2 foreign languages, thesis/dissertation, oral defense of dissertation, preliminary exams in essay format. *Entrance requirements:* Additional exam requirements/recommendations for international students: Required—TOEFL or Michigan English Language Assessment Battery. *Application deadline:* For fall admission, 12/18 for domestic and international students. Application fee: $65 ($75 for international students). Electronic applications accepted. *Financial support:* In 2014–15, 8 students received support. Fellowships with full tuition reimbursements available, teaching assistantships with full tuition reimbursements available, institutionally sponsored loans, scholarships/grants, health care benefits, and unspecified assistantships available. Financial award application deadline: 12/18. *Faculty research:* Comparative Romance studies, medieval and early modern studies, postcolonial and minority literatures, culture and materiality, reflection on the nature and function of scholarship. *Unit head:* Dr. Cristina Moreiras-Menor, Chair, 734-764-5344, Fax: 734-764-8163. *Application contact:* Katie Hayes, Graduate Assistant, 734-764-8164, Fax: 734-764-8163, E-mail: rll-admissions@umich.edu.
Website: http://www.lsa.umich.edu/rll

University of Minnesota, Twin Cities Campus, Graduate School, College of Liberal Arts, Department of French and Italian, Minneapolis, MN 55455-0213. Offers French (MA, PhD). Part-time programs available. *Degree requirements:* For master's, one foreign language, comprehensive exam, thesis optional; for doctorate, one foreign language, thesis/dissertation, individualized exam on topic areas. *Entrance requirements:* For master's and doctorate, GRE, minimum GPA of 3.25 (recommended). Additional exam requirements/recommendations for international students: Required—TOEFL (minimum score 550 paper-based). Electronic applications accepted. *Faculty research:* Francophone literature, cultural studies, feminism, critical theory, medieval studies.

University of Mississippi, Graduate School, College of Liberal Arts, Department of Modern Languages, University, MS 38677. Offers French (MA); German (MA); Spanish (MA). *Degree requirements:* For master's, thesis (for some programs). *Entrance requirements:* For master's, GRE General Test, minimum GPA of 3.0. Additional exam requirements/recommendations for international students: Required—TOEFL. Electronic applications accepted.

University of Missouri, Office of Research and Graduate Studies, College of Arts and Science, Department of Romance Languages and Literatures, Columbia, MO 65211. Offers French (MA, PhD); literature (MA); Spanish (MA, PhD); teaching (MA). *Faculty:* 25 full-time (12 women), 1 (woman) part-time/adjunct. *Students:* 28 full-time (19 women), 9 part-time (6 women); includes 9 minority (3 Black or African American, non-Hispanic/Latino; 4 Hispanic/Latino; 2 Two or more races, non-Hispanic/Latino), 15 international. Average age 36. 16 applicants, 69% accepted, 7 enrolled. In 2014, 3 master's, 1 doctorate awarded. Terminal master's awarded for partial completion of doctoral program. *Degree requirements:* For master's, one foreign language; for doctorate, 4 foreign languages, comprehensive exam, thesis/dissertation. *Entrance requirements:* For master's, GRE General Test, minimum GPA of 3.0 in field of major; bachelor's degree; for doctorate, GRE General Test, minimum GPA of 3.0 in field of major; master's degree. Additional exam requirements/recommendations for international students: Required—TOEFL (minimum score 500 paper-based; 61 iBT). *Application deadline:* For fall admission, 2/15 priority date for domestic students; for winter admission, 10/15 for domestic students. Applications are processed on a rolling basis. Application fee: $55 ($75 for international students). Electronic applications accepted. *Financial support:* Research assistantships, teaching assistantships with full tuition reimbursements, institutionally sponsored loans, health care benefits, and unspecified assistantships available. *Faculty research:* Afro-Romance studies. *Unit head:* Dr. Flore Zephir, Department Chair, 573-882-5048, E-mail: zephirf@missouri.edu. *Application contact:* Mary Harris, Administrative Assistant, 573-882-5039, E-mail: harrisma@missouri.edu.
Website: http://romancelanguages.missouri.edu/grad.shtml

University of Missouri–Kansas City, College of Arts and Sciences, Department of Foreign Languages and Literatures, Kansas City, MO 64110-2499. Offers romance languages and literatures (MA), including French, Spanish. Part-time programs available. *Faculty:* 15 full-time (8 women), 15 part-time/adjunct (12 women). *Students:* 3 full-time (2 women), 19 part-time (15 women); includes 11 minority (1 Black or African American, non-Hispanic/Latino; 10 Hispanic/Latino). Average age 32. 17 applicants, 59% accepted, 9 enrolled. In 2014, 8 master's awarded. *Degree requirements:* For master's, 2 foreign languages. *Entrance requirements:* For master's, GRE General Test, minimum GPA of 2.75, 2 letters of recommendation. Additional exam requirements/recommendations for international students: Required—TOEFL (minimum score 550 paper-based; 80 iBT). *Application deadline:* For fall admission, 4/1 priority date for domestic and international students; for spring admission, 11/1 priority date for domestic and international students. Applications are processed on a rolling basis. Application fee: $45 ($50 for international students). Electronic applications accepted. *Financial support:* In 2014–15, 1 teaching assistantship (averaging $12,600 per year) was awarded; Federal Work-Study, institutionally sponsored loans, and tuition waivers (full and partial) also available. Support available to part-time students. Financial award application deadline: 3/1; financial award applicants required to submit FAFSA. *Faculty research:* Literary analyses; psychology and literature; narrative techniques, poetic structure, and style; literature, politics, and society (especially in Latin America). *Unit head:* Dr. K. Scott Baker, Chair, 816-235-2823, Fax: 816-235-1312, E-mail: bakerks@umkc.edu. *Application contact:* 816-235-1311, Fax: 816-235-1312, E-mail: admit@umkc.edu.
Website: http://cas.umkc.edu/foreign

The University of Montana, Graduate School, College of Humanities and Sciences, Department of Modern and Classical Languages and Literatures, Missoula, MT 59812-0002. Offers French (MA); German (MA); Spanish (MA). *Degree requirements:* For master's, one foreign language. *Entrance requirements:* For master's, GRE General Test. Additional exam requirements/recommendations for international students: Required—TOEFL.

University of Nebraska–Lincoln, Graduate College, College of Arts and Sciences, Department of Modern Languages and Literatures, Lincoln, NE 68588. Offers French (MA, PhD); German (MA, PhD); Spanish (MA, PhD). *Degree requirements:* For master's, thesis optional; for doctorate, comprehensive exam, thesis/dissertation. *Entrance requirements:* For master's and doctorate, writing sample in target language. Additional exam requirements/recommendations for international students: Required—TOEFL (minimum score 550 paper-based). Electronic applications accepted. *Faculty research:* French, German, and Spanish language, literature, and culture.

University of Nevada, Reno, Graduate School, College of Liberal Arts, Department of Foreign Languages and Literatures, Reno, NV 89557. Offers French (MA); German (MA); Spanish (MA). *Degree requirements:* For master's, one foreign language, thesis optional. *Entrance requirements:* For master's, GRE General Test, minimum GPA of 2.75. Additional exam requirements/recommendations for international students: Required—TOEFL (minimum score 500 paper-based; 61 iBT), IELTS (minimum score 6). *Faculty research:* Thirteenth century mysticism, contemporary Spanish and Latin American poetry and theater, French interrelation between narration and photography, exile literature and Holocaust.

University of New Mexico, Graduate School, College of Arts and Sciences, Program in Foreign Languages and Literatures, Albuquerque, NM 87131-2039. Offers comparative literature and cultural studies (MA); French (MA); French studies (PhD); German studies (MA). Part-time programs available. *Faculty:* 12 full-time (8 women). *Students:* 25 full-time (17 women), 6 part-time (5 women); includes 3 minority (1 Black or African American, non-Hispanic/Latino; 2 Hispanic/Latino), 7 international. Average age 30. 22 applicants, 68% accepted, 10 enrolled. In 2014, 9 master's awarded. *Degree requirements:* For master's, one foreign language, thesis optional; for doctorate, 2 foreign languages, thesis/dissertation. *Entrance requirements:* For master's and doctorate, transcript, writing sample, 3 letters of recommendation. Additional exam requirements/recommendations for international students: Required—TOEFL. *Application deadline:* For fall admission, 2/1 priority date for domestic students; for spring admission, 10/1 priority date for domestic students. Application fee: $50. Electronic applications accepted. *Financial support:* In 2014–15, 28 students received support, including 1 research assistantship (averaging $4,730 per year), 23 teaching assistantships with tuition reimbursements available (averaging $10,300 per year); Federal Work-Study, health care benefits, and unspecified assistantships also available. Financial award application deadline: 3/1; financial award applicants required to submit FAFSA. *Faculty research:* German, Russian, Italian, Japanese, French, comparative literature, culture studies, classics. *Total annual research expenditures:* $4,750. *Unit head:* Dr. Walter Putnam, Chair, 505-277-4771, Fax: 505-277-3599, E-mail: wputnam@unm.edu. *Application contact:* Jacqueline Ochoa, Application and Graduation Advisor, 505-277-4471, Fax: 505-277-3599, E-mail: jochoa@unm.edu.
Website: http://www.unm.edu/~fll/

The University of North Carolina at Chapel Hill, Graduate School, College of Arts and Sciences, Department of Romance Languages and Literatures, Chapel Hill, NC 27599. Offers French (MA, PhD); Italian (MA, PhD); Portuguese (MA, PhD); Romance languages (MA, PhD); Romance philology (MA, PhD); Spanish (MA, PhD). *Degree requirements:* For master's, one foreign language, comprehensive exam, thesis; for doctorate, 2 foreign languages, comprehensive exam, thesis/dissertation. *Entrance requirements:* For master's and doctorate, GRE General Test, minimum GPA of 3.0. Additional exam requirements/recommendations for international students: Required—TOEFL (minimum score 550 paper-based). Electronic applications accepted.

The University of North Carolina at Greensboro, Graduate School, College of Arts and Sciences, Department of Languages, Literatures, and Cultures, Program in French, Greensboro, NC 27412-5001. Offers MA. *Degree requirements:* For master's, one foreign language, comprehensive exam, thesis or alternative. *Entrance requirements:* For master's, GRE General Test, 3-5 minute tape demonstrating foreign language proficiency, composition in French, sample paper in English. Additional exam requirements/recommendations for international students: Required—TOEFL. Electronic applications accepted.

University of North Texas, Robert B. Toulouse School of Graduate Studies, Denton, TX 76203-5459. Offers accounting (MS); applied anthropology (MA, MS); applied behavior analysis (Certificate); applied geography (MA); applied technology and performance improvement (M Ed, MS); art education (MA); art history (MA); art museum education (Certificate); arts leadership (Certificate); audiology (Au D); behavior analysis (MS); behavioral science (PhD); biochemistry and molecular biology (MS); biology (MA, MS); biomedical engineering (MS); business analysis (MS); chemistry (MS); clinical health psychology (PhD); communication studies (MA, MS); computer engineering (MS); computer science (MS); counseling (M Ed, MS), including clinical mental health counseling (MS), college and university counseling, elementary school counseling, secondary school counseling; creative writing (MA); criminal justice (MS); curriculum and instruction (M Ed); decision sciences (MBA); design (MA, MFA), including fashion design (MFA), innovation studies, interior design (MFA); early childhood studies (MS); economics (MS); educational leadership (M Ed, Ed D); educational psychology (MS, PhD), including family studies (MS), gifted and talented (MS), human development (MS), learning and cognition (MS), research, measurement and evaluation (MS); electrical engineering (MS); emergency management (MPA); engineering technology (MS);

English (MA); English as a second language (MA); environmental science (MS); finance (MBA, MS); financial management (MPA); French (MA); health services management (MBA); higher education (M Ed, Ed D); history (MA, MS); hospitality management (MS); human resources management (MPA); information science (MS); information systems (PhD); information technologies (MBA); interdisciplinary studies (MA, MS); international studies (MA); international sustainable tourism (MS); jazz studies (MM); journalism (MA, MJ, Graduate Certificate), including interactive and virtual digital communication (Graduate Certificate), narrative journalism (Graduate Certificate), public relations (Graduate Certificate); kinesiology (MS); linguistics (MA); local government management (MPA); logistics (PhD); logistics and supply chain management (MBA); long-term care, senior housing, and aging services (MA); management (PhD); marketing (MBA); mathematics (MA, MS); mechanical and energy engineering (MS, PhD); music (MA), including ethnomusicology, music theory, musicology, performance; music composition (PhD); music education (MM Ed, PhD); nonprofit management (MPA); operations and supply chain management (MBA); performance (MM, DMA); philosophy (MA); political science (MA); professional and technical communication (MA); radio, television and film (MA, MFA); rehabilitation counseling (Certificate); sociology (MA); Spanish (MA); special education (M Ed); speech-language pathology (MA); strategic management (MBA); studio art (MFA); teaching (M Ed); MBA/MS. Part-time and evening/weekend programs available. Postbaccalaureate distance learning degree programs offered. *Faculty:* 651 full-time (215 women), 233 part-time/adjunct (139 women). *Students:* 3,040 full-time (1,598 women), 3,401 part-time (2,097 women); includes 1,740 minority (533 Black or African American, non-Hispanic/Latino; 15 American Indian or Alaska Native, non-Hispanic/Latino; 286 Asian, non-Hispanic/Latino; 746 Hispanic/Latino; 3 Native Hawaiian or other Pacific Islander, non-Hispanic/Latino; 157 Two or more races, non-Hispanic/Latino), 1,145 international. Terminal master's awarded for partial completion of doctoral program. *Degree requirements:* For master's, variable foreign language requirement, comprehensive exam (for some programs), thesis (for some programs); for doctorate, variable foreign language requirement, comprehensive exam (for some programs), thesis/dissertation; for other advanced degree, variable foreign language requirement, comprehensive exam (for some programs). *Entrance requirements:* For master's and doctorate, GRE, GMAT. Additional exam requirements/recommendations for international students: Required—TOEFL (minimum score 550 paper-based; 79 iBT). *Application deadline:* For fall admission, 7/15 for domestic students, 3/15 for international students; for spring admission, 11/15 for domestic students, 9/15 for international students; for summer admission, 5/1 for domestic students. Applications are processed on a rolling basis. Application fee: $60. Electronic applications accepted. *Expenses:* Tuition, state resident: full-time $5450; part-time $3633 per year. Tuition, nonresident: full-time $11,966; part-time $7977 per year. *Required fees:* $1301; $398 per credit hour. $685 per semester. Tuition and fees vary according to program and reciprocity agreements. *Financial support:* Fellowships with partial tuition reimbursements, research assistantships with partial tuition reimbursements, teaching assistantships, career-related internships or fieldwork, Federal Work-Study, institutionally sponsored loans, scholarships/grants, health care benefits, and library assistantships available. Support available to part-time students. Financial award applicants required to submit FAFSA. *Unit head:* Mark Wardell, Dean, 940-565-2383, E-mail: mark.wardell@unt.edu. *Application contact:* Toulouse School of Graduate Studies, 940-565-2383, Fax: 940-565-2141, E-mail: gradsch@unt.edu.
Website: http://tsgs.unt.edu/

University of Notre Dame, Graduate School, College of Arts and Letters, Division of Humanities, Department of Romance Languages and Literatures, Notre Dame, IN 46556. Offers French and Francophone studies (MA); Iberian and Latin American studies (MA); Italian studies (MA); Romance literatures (MA). *Degree requirements:* For master's, 2 foreign languages, comprehensive exam, thesis optional. *Entrance requirements:* For master's, GRE General Test, BA in target language. Additional exam requirements/recommendations for international students: Required—TOEFL (minimum score 600 paper-based; 80 iBT). Electronic applications accepted. *Faculty research:* Literature of discovery and exploration, modern literature, literary criticism, medieval literature, feminist critical theory.

University of Oklahoma, College of Arts and Sciences, Department of Modern Languages, Program in French, Norman, OK 73019. Offers MA, PhD, MBA/MA. Part-time programs available. *Students:* 7 full-time (4 women), 4 part-time (all women), 3 international. Average age 34. 3 applicants, 100% accepted, 3 enrolled. In 2014, 1 master's awarded. Terminal master's awarded for partial completion of doctoral program. *Degree requirements:* For master's, comprehensive exam (for some programs), thesis optional, two languages (one must be French); for doctorate, comprehensive exam (for some programs), thesis/dissertation optional, two languages (one must be French). *Entrance requirements:* For master's, BA in French; for doctorate, MA in French. Additional exam requirements/recommendations for international students: Required—TOEFL (minimum score 79 iBT). *Application deadline:* For fall admission, 2/1 for domestic and international students; for spring admission, 10/1 for domestic and international students. Application fee: $50 ($100 for international students). Electronic applications accepted. *Expenses:* Tuition, state resident: full-time $4394; part-time $183.10 per credit hour. Tuition, nonresident: full-time $16,970; part-time $707.10 per credit hour. *Required fees:* $2892; $109.95 per credit hour. $126.50 per semester. *Financial support:* In 2014–15, 11 students received support. Scholarships/grants and unspecified assistantships available. Support available to part-time students. Financial award application deadline: 6/1; financial award applicants required to submit FAFSA. *Faculty research:* Medieval literature and culture, seventeenth-century literature, eighteenth-century literature and culture, nineteenth-century literature and culture, twentieth- to twenty-first century literature and culture. *Unit head:* Nancy LaGreca, Chair of Modern Languages, Literature and Linguistics, 405-325-6181, Fax: 405-325-0103, E-mail: lagreca@ou.edu. *Application contact:* Pamela Genova, Graduate Liaison, 405-325-6181, Fax: 405-325-0103, E-mail: genova@ou.edu.
Website: http://mlll.publishpath.com/french-ma

University of Oregon, Graduate School, College of Arts and Sciences, Department of Romance Languages, Program in French, Eugene, OR 97403. Offers MA. Part-time programs available. *Degree requirements:* For master's, one foreign language. *Entrance requirements:* For master's, GRE General Test, minimum GPA of 3.0. Additional exam requirements/recommendations for international students: Required—TOEFL.

University of Ottawa, Faculty of Graduate and Postdoctoral Studies, Faculty of Arts, Department of Lettres Franlfcaises, Ottawa, ON K1N 6N5, Canada. Offers MA, PhD. *Degree requirements:* For master's, thesis or alternative; for doctorate, thesis/dissertation, oral exam. *Entrance requirements:* For master's, honors degree or equivalent, minimum B average; for doctorate, master's degree, minimum B+ average. Electronic applications accepted. *Faculty research:* Littérature franlfcaise, du Moyen-lfQge á nos jours; littérature québécoise, des origines au XXe sie&,cle; création littéraire.

University of Pennsylvania, School of Arts and Sciences, Graduate Group in Romance Languages, Philadelphia, PA 19104. Offers French (AM, PhD); Italian (AM, PhD); Spanish (AM, PhD). *Faculty:* 44 full-time (16 women), 6 part-time/adjunct (2 women). *Students:* 61 full-time (29 women), 3 part-time (1 woman); includes 8 minority (all Hispanic/Latino), 34 international. 92 applicants, 23% accepted, 10 enrolled. In 2014, 11 master's, 9 doctorates awarded. Terminal master's awarded for partial completion of doctoral program. *Degree requirements:* For master's, one foreign language, thesis or alternative; for doctorate, 2 foreign languages, thesis/dissertation. *Entrance requirements:* For master's and doctorate, GRE General Test. Additional exam requirements/recommendations for international students: Required—TOEFL. *Application deadline:* For fall admission, 12/1 priority date for domestic students. Application fee: $70. Electronic applications accepted. *Financial support:* In 2014–15, 23 fellowships, 2 research assistantships, 39 teaching assistantships were awarded; institutionally sponsored loans, scholarships/grants, traineeships, health care benefits, and unspecified assistantships also available. Financial award application deadline: 12/15. *Faculty research:* Literary theory and criticism, cultural studies, history of Romance literatures, gender studies. *Unit head:* Dr. Ralph M. Rosen, Associate Dean for Graduate Studies, 215-898-7156, Fax: 215-573-8068, E-mail: grad-dean@sas.upenn.edu. *Application contact:* Arts and Sciences Graduate Admissions, 215-573-5816, Fax: 215-573-8068, E-mail: gdasadmis@sas.upenn.edu.
Website: http://www.sas.upenn.edu/graduate-division

University of Pittsburgh, Dietrich School of Arts and Sciences, Department of French and Italian, Program in French, Pittsburgh, PA 15260. Offers film studies (PhD); French (MA, PhD). Part-time programs available. *Faculty:* 7 full-time (3 women). *Students:* 20 full-time (11 women), 8 international. Average age 32. 12 applicants, 42% accepted, 3 enrolled. In 2014, 1 master's, 2 doctorates awarded. Terminal master's awarded for partial completion of doctoral program. *Degree requirements:* For master's, one foreign language, comprehensive exam, seminar paper; for doctorate, one foreign language, comprehensive exam, thesis/dissertation, dissertation defense. *Entrance requirements:* For master's, GRE General Test, phone interview, 2 writing samples (French and English); for doctorate, GRE General Test, phone interview, 2 writing samples (French and English), personal essay. Additional exam requirements/recommendations for international students: Required—TOEFL (minimum score 600 paper-based; 90 iBT). *Application deadline:* For fall admission, 1/10 priority date for domestic and international students. Application fee: $50. Electronic applications accepted. *Expenses:* Tuition, state resident: full-time $20,742; part-time $838 per credit. Tuition, nonresident: full-time $33,960; part-time $1389 per credit. *Required fees:* $800; $205 per term. Tuition and fees vary according to program. *Financial support:* In 2014–15, 16 students received support, including 3 fellowships with full tuition reimbursements available (averaging $19,615 per year), 12 teaching assistantships with full tuition reimbursements available (averaging $17,010 per year); career-related internships or fieldwork, Federal Work-Study, institutionally sponsored loans, scholarships/grants, traineeships, health care benefits, tuition waivers (partial), unspecified assistantships, and summer research stipends, summer teaching, teaching on study abroad program also available. Support available to part-time students. Financial award application deadline: 1/10. *Faculty research:* Literature and politics, constructs of the French nation, literary and cultural theory, French linguistics, gender and sexuality, French film, French and Francophone literature and culture of all periods. *Total annual research expenditures:* $3,200. *Unit head:* Dr. Lina Insana, Chair, 412-624-6269, Fax: 412-624-6263, E-mail: insana@pitt.edu. *Application contact:* Patrick Fogarty, Graduate Administrator, 412-624-5227, Fax: 412-624-6263, E-mail: pmf23@pitt.edu.
Website: http://www.frenchanditalian.pitt.edu/graduate/french/

University of Regina, Faculty of Graduate Studies and Research, Faculty of Arts, Department of French, Regina, SK S4S 0A2, Canada. Offers MA. Part-time programs available. *Faculty:* 4 full-time (0 women), 2 part-time/adjunct (1 woman). *Students:* 2 full-time (0 women). 4 applicants. In 2014, 4 master's awarded. *Degree requirements:* For master's, thesis, seminar presentation. *Entrance requirements:* Additional exam requirements/recommendations for international students: Required—TOEFL (minimum score 580 paper-based; 80 iBT), IELTS (minimum score 6.5), PTE (minimum score 59). *Application deadline:* Applications are processed on a rolling basis. Application fee: $100. Electronic applications accepted. *Expenses: Tuition, area resident:* Full-time $4900 Canadian dollars; part-time $837.65 Canadian dollars per semester. *International tuition:* $7900 Canadian dollars full-time. *Required fees:* $396 Canadian dollars; $86.90 Canadian dollars per semester. *Financial support:* In 2014–15, 2 teaching assistantships (averaging $2,427 per year) were awarded; fellowships, research assistantships, and scholarships/grants also available. Financial award application deadline: 6/15. *Faculty research:* French literature, French linguistics, rhetoric, translation and terminology, lexicography. *Unit head:* Dr. Emmanuel Aito, Department Head and Graduate Program Coordinator, 306-585-4323, Fax: 306-585-4827, E-mail: emmanuel.aito@uregina.ca.
Website: http://www.uregina.ca/arts/french

University of Saskatchewan, College of Graduate Studies and Research, College of Arts and Science, Department of Languages and Linguistics, Saskatoon, SK S7N 5A2, Canada. Offers MA. *Degree requirements:* For master's, 2 foreign languages, thesis. *Entrance requirements:* Additional exam requirements/recommendations for international students: Required—TOEFL (minimum score 80 iBT); Recommended—IELTS (minimum score 6.5). Electronic applications accepted.

University of South Africa, College of Human Sciences, Pretoria, South Africa. Offers adult education (M Ed); African languages (MA, PhD); African politics (MA, PhD); Afrikaans (MA, PhD); ancient history (MA, PhD); ancient Near Eastern studies (MA, PhD); anthropology (MA, PhD); applied linguistics (MA); Arabic (MA, PhD); archaeology (MA); art history (MA); Biblical archaeology (MA); Biblical studies (M Th, D Th, PhD); Christian spirituality (M Th, D Th); church history (M Th, D Th); classical studies (MA, PhD); clinical psychology (MA); communication (MA, PhD); comparative education (M Ed, Ed D); consulting psychology (D Admin, D Com, PhD); curriculum studies (M Ed, Ed D); development studies (M Admin, MA, D Admin, PhD); didactics (M Ed, Ed D); education (M Tech); education management (M Ed, Ed D); educational psychology (M Ed); English (MA); environmental education (M Ed); French (MA, PhD); German (MA, PhD); Greek (MA); guidance and counseling (M Ed); health studies (MA, PhD), including health sciences education (MA), health services management (MA), medical and surgical nursing science (critical care general) (MA), midwifery and neonatal nursing science (MA), trauma and emergency care (MA); history (MA, PhD); history of education (Ed D); inclusive education (M Ed, Ed D); information and communications technology policy and regulation (MA); information science (MA, MIS, PhD); international politics (MA, PhD); Islamic studies (MA, PhD); Italian (MA, PhD); Judaica (MA, PhD); linguistics (MA, PhD); mathematical education (M Ed); mathematics education (MA); missiology (M Th, D Th); modern Hebrew (MA, PhD); musicology (MA, MMus, D Mus, PhD); natural science education (M Ed); New Testament (M Th, D Th); Old Testament (D Th); pastoral therapy (M Th, D Th); philosophy (MA); philosophy of education (M Ed, Ed D); politics (MA, PhD); Portuguese (MA, PhD); practical theology (M Th, D Th); psychology (MA, MS, PhD); psychology of education (M Ed, Ed D); public health (MA); religious studies (MA, D Th, PhD); Romance languages (MA); Russian (MA, PhD); Semitic languages (MA, PhD); social behavior studies in HIV/AIDS (MA); social science (mental health) (MA); social science in development studies (MA); social science in psychology (MA); social science in social work (MA); social science in sociology (MA); social work (MSW, DSW, PhD); socio-education (M Ed, Ed D); sociolinguistics (MA); sociology (MA, PhD); Spanish (MA, PhD); systematic theology (M Th, D Th); TESOL (teaching English

to speakers of other languages) (MA); theological ethics (M Th, D Th); theory of literature (MA, PhD); urban ministries (D Th); urban ministry (M Th).

University of South Carolina, The Graduate School, College of Arts and Sciences, Department of Languages, Literatures, and Cultures, Columbia, SC 29208. Offers comparative literature (MA, PhD); foreign languages (MAT), including French, German, Spanish; French (MA); German (MA); Spanish (MA). MAT offered in cooperation with the College of Education. Part-time programs available. *Degree requirements:* For master's, one foreign language, comprehensive exam, thesis optional; for doctorate, 2 foreign languages, comprehensive exam, thesis/dissertation. *Entrance requirements:* For master's and doctorate, GRE General Test, writing sample. Additional exam requirements/recommendations for international students: Required—TOEFL (minimum score 75 iBT). Electronic applications accepted. *Faculty research:* Modern literature, linguistics, literature and culture, medieval literature, literary theory.

University of South Florida, College of Arts and Sciences, Department of World Languages, Tampa, FL 33620-9951. Offers applied linguistics: English as a second language (MA); French (MA); Spanish (MA). Part-time and evening/weekend programs available. *Faculty:* 21 full-time (14 women). *Students:* 44 full-time (29 women), 16 part-time (11 women); includes 23 minority (3 Black or African American, non-Hispanic/Latino; 1 Asian, non-Hispanic/Latino; 19 Hispanic/Latino), 8 international. Average age 35. 40 applicants, 60% accepted, 18 enrolled. In 2014, 18 master's awarded. *Degree requirements:* For master's, one foreign language, comprehensive exam, thesis optional. *Entrance requirements:* For master's, GRE General Test (minimum preferred scores of 41st percentile verbal and 4 in analytic writing, except for French program), minimum undergraduate GPA of 3.0; two-page statement of purpose (written in Spanish for Spanish program); oral interview (for Spanish and French programs); writing sample (for French program); 2-3 letters of recommendation. Additional exam requirements/recommendations for international students: Required—TOEFL (minimum score 600 paper-based; 80 iBT) or IELTS (minimum score 6.5) for MA; TOEFL (minimum score 550 paper-based; 80 iBT) or IELTS (minimum score 6.5) for PhD. *Application deadline:* For fall admission, 2/15 for domestic students, 1/2 for international students; for spring admission, 10/15 for domestic students, 6/1 for international students. Application fee: $30. Electronic applications accepted. *Financial support:* In 2014–15, 43 students received support, including 43 teaching assistantships with full and partial tuition reimbursements available (averaging $10,152 per year); tuition waivers (partial) and unspecified assistantships also available. Financial award application deadline: 6/30. *Faculty research:* Second language acquisition, instructional technology, foreign language education, ESOL, distance learning. *Total annual research expenditures:* $117,377. *Unit head:* Dr. Stephan Schindler, Chair and Professor, 813-974-2548, Fax: 813-905-9937, E-mail: skschindler@.usf.edu. *Application contact:* Patricia Garcia, Academic Program Specialist, 813-974-2548, Fax: 813-905-9937, E-mail: pgarcia@usf.edu.
Website: http://languages.usf.edu/

The University of Tennessee, Graduate School, College of Arts and Sciences, Department of Modern Foreign Languages and Literatures, Program in French, Knoxville, TN 37996. Offers MA. *Degree requirements:* For master's, one foreign language, thesis or alternative. *Entrance requirements:* For master's, minimum GPA of 2.7. Additional exam requirements/recommendations for international students: Required—TOEFL. Electronic applications accepted.

The University of Tennessee, Graduate School, College of Arts and Sciences, Department of Modern Foreign Languages and Literatures, Program in Modern Foreign Languages, Knoxville, TN 37996. Offers applied linguistics (PhD); French (PhD); German (PhD); Italian (PhD); Portuguese (PhD); Russian (PhD); Spanish (PhD). *Degree requirements:* For doctorate, 2 foreign languages, thesis/dissertation. *Entrance requirements:* For doctorate, minimum GPA of 2.7. Additional exam requirements/recommendations for international students: Required—TOEFL. Electronic applications accepted.

The University of Texas at Arlington, Graduate School, College of Liberal Arts, Department of Modern Languages, Arlington, TX 76019. Offers French (MA); Spanish (MA). Part-time and evening/weekend programs available. *Degree requirements:* For master's, 2 foreign languages, comprehensive exam, thesis optional. *Entrance requirements:* For master's, GRE General Test, minimum GPA of 3.0, 3 letters of recommendation. Additional exam requirements/recommendations for international students: Required—TOEFL (minimum score 550 paper-based).

The University of Texas at Austin, Graduate School, College of Liberal Arts, Department of French and Italian, Austin, TX 78712-1111. Offers French linguistics (MA, PhD); French studies (MA, PhD); Italian studies (MA, PhD); Romance linguistics (PhD). Part-time programs available. *Degree requirements:* For master's, one foreign language, thesis; for doctorate, 2 foreign languages, thesis/dissertation. *Entrance requirements:* For master's, GRE General Test, minimum GPA of 3.0, bachelor's degree in French or equivalent; for doctorate, GRE General Test, minimum GPA of 3.0, master's degree in French. Additional exam requirements/recommendations for international students: Required—TOEFL. Electronic applications accepted. *Faculty research:* Nineteenth-century Italian literature, Italian Renaissance, twentieth-century French literature, Francophone literature, fifteenth-century literature and culture.

The University of Toledo, College of Graduate Studies, College of Languages, Literature and Social Sciences, Department of Foreign Languages, Toledo, OH 43606-3390. Offers French (MA); German (MA); Spanish (MA). Part-time programs available. *Degree requirements:* For master's, one foreign language, comprehensive exam, comprehensive reading exam in 1 additional foreign language. *Entrance requirements:* For master's, minimum cumulative point-hour ratio of 2.7 for all previous academic work. Additional exam requirements/recommendations for international students: Required—TOEFL (minimum score 550 paper-based; 80 iBT). Electronic applications accepted.

University of Toronto, School of Graduate Studies, Faculty of Arts and Science, Department of French, Toronto, ON M5S 2J7, Canada. Offers French language and literature (MA, PhD). Part-time programs available. *Degree requirements:* For master's, research essay; for doctorate, one foreign language, thesis/dissertation, field exam. *Entrance requirements:* For master's, 2 letters of reference, writing sample, minimum B+ average overall and in French, undergraduate major in French; for doctorate, 7 courses in French language and literature, minimum A- average, writing sample. Additional exam requirements/recommendations for international students: Required—TOEFL (minimum score 580 paper-based; 93 iBT), TWE (minimum score 5). Electronic applications accepted.

University of Utah, Graduate School, College of Humanities, Department of Languages and Literature, Salt Lake City, UT 84112. Offers comparative literary and cultural studies (MA, PhD); French (MA); Spanish (MA, MALP, PhD); world languages (MA). Part-time programs available. *Faculty:* 33 full-time (20 women), 14 part-time/adjunct (9 women). *Students:* 36 full-time (27 women), 6 part-time (5 women); includes 10 minority (1 Black or African American, non-Hispanic/Latino; 4 Asian, non-Hispanic/Latino; 5 Hispanic/Latino), 6 international. Average age 25. 23 applicants, 70% accepted. In 2014, 14 master's awarded. Terminal master's awarded for partial completion of doctoral program. *Degree requirements:* For master's, comprehensive exam (for some programs), thesis (for some programs), standard proficiency in 2 languages other than

English; for doctorate, comprehensive exam, thesis/dissertation, standard proficiency in 2 languages other than English and language of study, advanced proficiency in 1 language other than English and language of study. *Entrance requirements:* For master's, GRE (except for French), bachelor's degree or strong undergraduate record in target languages, minimum GPA of 3.0; for doctorate, GRE, MA, advanced proficiency in a target language. Additional exam requirements/recommendations for international students: Required—TOEFL (minimum score 550 paper-based; 80 iBT). *Application deadline:* For fall admission, 1/15 priority date for domestic students, 12/15 priority date for international students. Application fee: $55 ($65 for international students). Electronic applications accepted. *Financial support:* In 2014–15, 27 teaching assistantships with full and partial tuition reimbursements (averaging $14,000 per year) were awarded; health care benefits and unspecified assistantships also available. Financial award application deadline: 1/15; financial award applicants required to submit FAFSA. *Faculty research:* Literary study, literary theory, linguistics, cultural studies, comparative studies. *Unit head:* Dr. Katharina Gerstenberger, Chair, 801-585-7908, Fax: 801-581-4768, E-mail: katharina.gerstenberger@utah.edu. *Application contact:* Marcie Leek, Academic Coordinator, 801-581-5401, Fax: 801-581-5401, E-mail: marcie.leek@utah.edu. Website: http://languages.utah.edu/

University of Vermont, Graduate College, College of Arts and Sciences, Department of Romance Languages, Burlington, VT 05405. Offers French (MA). *Degree requirements:* For master's, one foreign language. *Entrance requirements:* For master's, GRE General Test. Additional exam requirements/recommendations for international students: Required—TOEFL (minimum score 550 paper-based; 80 iBT). *Faculty research:* French, French-Canadian, and French-African literature.

University of Victoria, Faculty of Graduate Studies, Faculty of Humanities, Department of French, Victoria, BC V8W 2Y2, Canada. Offers literature (MA); teaching emphasis (MA). Part-time and evening/weekend programs available. *Degree requirements:* For master's, 2 foreign languages, thesis optional. *Entrance requirements:* For master's, BA in French. Additional exam requirements/recommendations for international students: Required—TOEFL (minimum score 575 paper-based), IELTS (minimum score 7). Electronic applications accepted. *Faculty research:* French-Canadian literature, stylistics, comparative literature, Francophone literature.

University of Virginia, College and Graduate School of Arts and Sciences, Department of French, Charlottesville, VA 22903. Offers MA, PhD. *Faculty:* 17 full-time (12 women), 3 part-time/adjunct (2 women). *Students:* 27 full-time (24 women); includes 3 minority (1 Asian, non-Hispanic/Latino; 2 Hispanic/Latino), 3 international. Average age 28. 26 applicants, 42% accepted, 6 enrolled. In 2014, 2 master's, 4 doctorates awarded. *Degree requirements:* For master's, one foreign language, comprehensive exam; for doctorate, one foreign language, comprehensive exam, thesis/dissertation. *Entrance requirements:* For master's and doctorate, GRE General Test, minimum GPA of 3.0 in major and overall; 2 letters of recommendation; writing sample. Additional exam requirements/recommendations for international students: Required—TOEFL (minimum score 600 paper-based; 90 iBT), IELTS (minimum score 7). *Application deadline:* For fall admission, 12/1 for domestic and international students. Applications are processed on a rolling basis. Application fee: $60. Electronic applications accepted. *Expenses:* Tuition, state resident: full-time $14,164; part-time $349 per credit hour. Tuition, nonresident: full-time $23,722; part-time $1300 per credit hour. *Required fees:* $2514. *Financial support:* Fellowships and teaching assistantships available. Financial award applicants required to submit FAFSA. *Unit head:* Ari Blatt, Chair, 434-924-7158, Fax: 434-924-7157, E-mail: ajb6f@virginia.edu. *Application contact:* Janet Horne, Director of Graduate Studies, 434-924-7158, Fax: 434-924-7157, E-mail: jrh9e@virginia.edu. Website: http://french.virginia.edu/

University of Washington, Graduate School, College of Arts and Sciences, Division of French and Italian Studies, Seattle, WA 98195. Offers French (MA, PhD); Italian (MA). Terminal master's awarded for partial completion of doctoral program. *Degree requirements:* For master's, 2 foreign languages, exam; for doctorate, 3 foreign languages, thesis/dissertation, exam. *Entrance requirements:* For master's and doctorate, GRE General Test, minimum GPA of 3.0. Additional exam requirements/recommendations for international students: Required—TOEFL. Electronic applications accepted. *Faculty research:* Interdisciplinary studies, literary theory and criticism, film, major periods of French and Italian literature, Francophonie.

University of Waterloo, Graduate Studies, Faculty of Arts, Department of French Studies, Waterloo, ON N2L 3G1, Canada. Offers French (MA, PhD). Part-time programs available. *Entrance requirements:* For master's, honors degree, minimum B average, course work and assignments in French, resume. Additional exam requirements/recommendations for international students: Required—TOEFL, TWE. Electronic applications accepted. *Faculty research:* French and Quebec literature: Middle Ages through twentieth century, phonology of Acadian dialect, computerized scholarly editions of medieval and Renaissance texts.

The University of Western Ontario, Faculty of Graduate Studies, Faculty of Arts and Humanities, Department of French Studies, London, ON N6A 5B8, Canada. Offers MA, PhD. *Degree requirements:* For master's, thesis or alternative; for doctorate, one foreign language, thesis/dissertation. *Entrance requirements:* For master's, minimum B average, honors degree, 2 years of teaching experience (MAT); for doctorate, MA or equivalent, minimum B average in French. Additional exam requirements/recommendations for international students: Required—TOEFL. Electronic applications accepted.

University of Wisconsin–Madison, Graduate School, College of Letters and Science, Department of French and Italian, Program in French, Madison, WI 53706-1380. Offers MA, PhD. Part-time programs available. *Degree requirements:* For master's, one foreign language; for doctorate, one foreign language, thesis/dissertation. *Entrance requirements:* For master's and doctorate, GRE. Electronic applications accepted. *Expenses:* Tuition, state resident: full-time $10,723; part-time $745 per credit. Tuition, nonresident: full-time $24,054; part-time $1578 per credit. *Required fees:* $374 per semester. Tuition and fees vary according to course load, program and reciprocity agreements. *Faculty research:* Francophone literature; French literature, culture, linguistics, and language pedagogy.

University of Wisconsin–Madison, Graduate School, College of Letters and Science, Department of French and Italian, Program in French Studies, Madison, WI 53706-1380. Offers MFS, Certificate. Part-time programs available. *Degree requirements:* For master's, one foreign language, thesis, internship; for Certificate, one foreign language, internship. *Entrance requirements:* For master's, GRE. Electronic applications accepted. *Expenses:* Tuition, state resident: full-time $10,723; part-time $745 per credit. Tuition, nonresident: full-time $24,054; part-time $1578 per credit. *Required fees:* $374 per semester. Tuition and fees vary according to course load, program and reciprocity agreements. *Faculty research:* International development, European citizenship, French and business, foreign language education, agricultural economics.

University of Wisconsin–Milwaukee, Graduate School, College of Letters and Sciences, Interdepartmental Program in Foreign Language and Literature, Milwaukee, WI 53201-0413. Offers classics and Hebrew studies (MAFLL); comparative literature (MAFLL); French and Italian (MAFLL); German (MAFLL); Slavic studies (MAFLL); translation (Certificate). Part-time programs available. *Degree requirements:* For

master's, 2 foreign languages, thesis or alternative. *Entrance requirements:* Additional exam requirements/recommendations for international students: Required—TOEFL (minimum score 550 paper-based; 79 iBT), IELTS (minimum score 6.5). Electronic applications accepted.

University of Wyoming, College of Arts and Sciences, Department of Modern and Classical Languages, Program in French, Laramie, WY 82071. Offers MA. Part-time programs available. *Degree requirements:* For master's, one foreign language, thesis or alternative. *Entrance requirements:* For master's, GRE General Test, minimum GPA of 3.0. *Faculty research:* Poetry, Asian literature, medieval literature, nineteenth- and twentieth century literature.

Vanderbilt University, Graduate School, Department of French and Italian, Nashville, TN 37240-1001. Offers French (MA, MAT, PhD). *Faculty:* 10 full-time (5 women). *Students:* 10 full-time (8 women), 4 international. Average age 30. 25 applicants, 32% accepted, 4 enrolled. In 2014, 1 master's, 2 doctorates awarded. Terminal master's awarded for partial completion of doctoral program. *Degree requirements:* For master's, one foreign language, comprehensive exam; for doctorate, 2 foreign languages, comprehensive exam, thesis/dissertation, final and qualifying exams. *Entrance requirements:* For master's and doctorate, GRE General Test. Additional exam requirements/recommendations for international students: Required—TOEFL (minimum score 570 paper-based; 88 iBT). *Application deadline:* For fall admission, 1/15 for domestic and international students. Electronic applications accepted. *Expenses: Tuition:* Full-time $42,768; part-time $1782 per credit hour. *Required fees:* $422. One-time fee: $30 full-time. *Financial support:* Fellowships with full and partial tuition reimbursements, teaching assistantships with full and partial tuition reimbursements, career-related internships or fieldwork, Federal Work-Study, institutionally sponsored loans, scholarships/grants, and health care benefits available. Financial award application deadline: 1/15; financial award applicants required to submit CSS PROFILE or FAFSA. *Faculty research:* Baudelaire, Rabelais, voyage literature, postcolonial literature, medieval epic. *Unit head:* Paul Miller, Director of Graduate Studies, 615-322-6906, Fax: 615-343-6909, E-mail: paul.b.miller@vanderbilt.edu. *Application contact:* Tamra Hicks, Department Administrator, 615-343-6900, Fax: 615-343-6909, E-mail: tamra.m.hicks@vanderbilt.edu.
Website: http://as.vanderbilt.edu/french-italian/

Washington University in St. Louis, Graduate School of Arts and Sciences, Department of Romance Languages and Literatures, Program in French, St. Louis, MO 63130-4899. Offers French (MA); French and comparative literature (PhD); French language and literature (PhD). Terminal master's awarded for partial completion of doctoral program. *Degree requirements:* For master's, thesis or alternative; for doctorate, thesis/dissertation. *Entrance requirements:* For master's and doctorate, GRE General Test. Additional exam requirements/recommendations for international students: Required—TOEFL. Electronic applications accepted. *Faculty research:* French language and literature.

Wayne State University, College of Liberal Arts and Sciences, Department of Classical and Modern Languages, Literatures, and Cultures, Program in Language Learning, Detroit, MI 48202. Offers Arabic (MALL); French (MALL); German (MALL); Italian (MALL); Spanish (MALL). *Students:* 1 (woman) full-time, 9 part-time (6 women); includes 2 minority (both Hispanic/Latino). Average age 34. In 2014, 2 master's awarded. *Degree requirements:* For master's, one foreign language, three-credit essay. *Entrance requirements:* For master's, GRE (recommended), target language proficiency, statement of purpose, three letters of recommendation, minimum GPA of 2.6 from accredited institution or 3.2 from non-accredited institution. Additional exam requirements/recommendations for international students: Required—TOEFL (minimum score 550 paper-based; 79 iBT), TWE (minimum score 5.5), Michigan English Language Assessment Battery (minimum score 85); Recommended—IELTS (minimum score 6.5). *Application deadline:* For fall admission, 6/1 priority date for domestic students, 5/1 for international students; for winter admission, 10/1 priority date for domestic students, 9/1 priority date for international students; for spring admission, 2/1 priority date for domestic students, 1/1 priority date for international students. Applications are processed on a rolling basis. Application fee: $0. Electronic applications accepted. *Expenses:* Tuition, state resident: full-time $10,294; part-time $571.90 per credit hour. Tuition, nonresident: full-time $29,730; part-time $1238.75 per credit hour. *Required fees:* $1365; $43.50 per credit hour. $291.10 per semester. Tuition and fees vary according to course load and program. *Financial support:* Scholarships/grants and unspecified assistantships available. Financial award application deadline: 3/31; financial award applicants required to submit FAFSA. *Unit head:* Dr. Anne Duggan, Department Chair, E-mail: a.duggan@wayne.edu.
Website: http://clas.wayne.edu/MALL/

Wayne State University, College of Liberal Arts and Sciences, Department of Classical and Modern Languages, Literatures, and Cultures, Program in Modern Languages, Detroit, MI 48202. Offers French (PhD); German (PhD); Spanish (PhD). *Students:* 15 full-time (13 women), 5 part-time (all women); includes 7 minority (1 Black or African American, non-Hispanic/Latino; 1 Asian, non-Hispanic/Latino; 5 Hispanic/Latino), 2 international. Average age 38. In 2014, 3 doctorates awarded. *Degree requirements:* For doctorate, 2 foreign languages, thesis/dissertation. *Entrance requirements:* For doctorate, master's degree in French, German, or Spanish, three letters of reccomendation, current curriculum vitae, writing sample such as term paper or thesis in language of specialization, statement of purpose (in English). Additional exam requirements/recommendations for international students: Required—TOEFL (minimum score 550 paper-based; 79 iBT), TWE (minimum score 5.5), Michigan English Language Assessment Battery (minimum score 85); Recommended—IELTS (minimum score 6.5). *Application deadline:* For fall admission, 6/1 priority date for domestic students, 5/1 priority date for international students; for winter admission, 10/1 priority date for domestic and international students; for spring admission, 2/1 priority date for domestic students, 1/1 priority date for international students. Applications are processed on a rolling basis. Application fee: $0. Electronic applications accepted. *Expenses:* Tuition, state resident: full-time $10,294; part-time $571.90 per credit hour. Tuition, nonresident: full-time $29,730; part-time $1238.75 per credit hour. *Required fees:* $1365; $43.50 per credit hour. $291.10 per semester. Tuition and fees vary according to course load and program. *Financial support:* In 2014–15, 12 students received support. Fellowships with tuition reimbursements available, teaching assistantships, scholarships/grants, health care benefits, and unspecified assistantships available. Financial award application deadline: 3/31; financial award applicants required to submit FAFSA. *Unit head:* Dr. Anne Duggan, Department Chair, E-mail: a.duggan@wayne.edu. *Application contact:* Dr. Michael Giordano, Professor and Graduate Director, 313-577-3002, E-mail: aa2144@wayne.edu.
Website: http://clasweb.clas.wayne.edu/languages/ModernLanguages(PhD)

Wayne State University, College of Liberal Arts and Sciences, Department of Classical and Modern Languages, Literatures, and Cultures, Program in Romance Languages, Detroit, MI 48202. Offers French (MA); Italian (MA); Spanish (MA). *Students:* 6 full-time (5 women), 22 part-time (15 women); includes 9 minority (4 Black or African American, non-Hispanic/Latino; 1 American Indian or Alaska Native, non-Hispanic/Latino; 1 Asian, non-Hispanic/Latino; 2 Hispanic/Latino; 1 Two or more races, non-Hispanic/Latino), 1 international. Average age 32. 13 applicants, 38% accepted, 5 enrolled. In 2014, 6 master's awarded. *Degree requirements:* For master's, one foreign language, thesis optional. *Entrance requirements:* For master's, GRE (strongly recommended), three letters of recommendation. Additional exam requirements/recommendations for international students: Required—TOEFL (minimum score 550 paper-based; 79 iBT), Michigan English Language Assessment Battery (minimum score 85); Recommended—IELTS (minimum score 6.5). *Application deadline:* For fall admission, 6/1 priority date for domestic students, 5/1 priority date for international students; for winter admission, 10/1 priority date for domestic students, 9/1 priority date for international students; for spring admission, 2/1 priority date for domestic students, 1/1 priority date for international students. Applications are processed on a rolling basis. Application fee: $0. Electronic applications accepted. *Expenses:* Tuition, state resident: full-time $10,294; part-time $571.90 per credit hour. Tuition, nonresident: full-time $29,730; part-time $1238.75 per credit hour. *Required fees:* $1365; $43.50 per credit hour. $291.10 per semester. Tuition and fees vary according to course load and program. *Financial support:* In 2014–15, 11 students received support. Fellowships, research assistantships, teaching assistantships, scholarships/grants, health care benefits, and unspecified assistantships available. Financial award application deadline: 3/31; financial award applicants required to submit FAFSA. *Unit head:* Dr. Anne Duggan, Department Chair, E-mail: a.duggan@wayne.edu. *Application contact:* Dr. Michael Giordano, Graduate Advisor, E-mail: aa2144@wayne.edu.
Website: http://clas.wayne.edu/languages/RomanceLanguagesLiteratures

West Chester University of Pennsylvania, College of Arts and Sciences, Department of Languages and Cultures, West Chester, PA 19383. Offers French (M Ed, MA, Teaching Certificate); Spanish (M Ed, MA, Teaching Certificate). Part-time and evening/weekend programs available. Postbaccalaureate distance learning degree programs offered. *Faculty:* 13 full-time (8 women). *Students:* 10 full-time (7 women), 21 part-time (19 women); includes 8 minority (4 Black or African American, non-Hispanic/Latino; 4 Hispanic/Latino). Average age 30. 22 applicants, 91% accepted, 11 enrolled. In 2014, 9 master's, 5 other advanced degrees awarded. *Degree requirements:* For master's, one foreign language, comprehensive exam, exit exam capstone project; thesis (for MA); for Teaching Certificate, one foreign language. *Entrance requirements:* For master's, undergraduate major in a language or native fluency. Additional exam requirements/recommendations for international students: Required—TOEFL (minimum score 550 paper-based; 80 iBT). *Application deadline:* For fall admission, 4/15 priority date for domestic students, 3/15 for international students; for spring admission, 10/15 priority date for domestic students, 9/1 for international students. Applications are processed on a rolling basis. Application fee: $45. Electronic applications accepted. *Expenses:* Tuition, state resident: full-time $8172; part-time $454 per credit. Tuition, nonresident: full-time $12,258; part-time $681 per credit. *Required fees:* $2231; $110.78 per credit. Tuition and fees vary according to campus/location and program. *Financial support:* Unspecified assistantships available. Support available to part-time students. Financial award application deadline: 2/15; financial award applicants required to submit FAFSA. *Faculty research:* Language structure, literature, film, culture, pedagogy, technology. *Unit head:* Dr. Jerome Williams, Chair, 610-436-2700, Fax: 610-436-3048, E-mail: jwilliams2@wcupa.edu. *Application contact:* Dr. Rebecca Pauly, Graduate Coordinator, 610-436-2382, Fax: 610-436-3048, E-mail: rpauly@wcupa.edu.
Website: http://www.wcupa.edu/_academics/sch_cas.flg/

Western Kentucky University, Graduate Studies, Potter College of Arts and Letters, Department of Modern Languages, Bowling Green, KY 42101. Offers French (MA Ed); German (MA Ed); Spanish (MA Ed).

West Virginia University, Eberly College of Arts and Sciences, Department of Foreign Languages, Morgantown, WV 26506. Offers French (MA); linguistics (MA); Spanish (MA); teaching English to speakers of other languages (MA). Part-time programs available. *Degree requirements:* For master's, one foreign language, comprehensive exam (for some programs), thesis optional. *Entrance requirements:* For master's, minimum GPA of 3.0. Electronic applications accepted. *Faculty research:* French, German, and Spanish literature; foreign language pedagogy; English as a second language; cultural studies; linguistics.

Yale University, Graduate School of Arts and Sciences, Department of French, New Haven, CT 06520. Offers M Phil, MA, PhD. *Degree requirements:* For doctorate, 3 foreign languages, thesis/dissertation. *Entrance requirements:* For doctorate, GRE General Test.

York University, Faculty of Graduate Studies, Glendon Campus, Program in French Studies, Toronto, ON M3J 1P3, Canada. Offers MA, PhD. *Degree requirements:* For master's, thesis or alternative. Electronic applications accepted.

German

Arizona State University at the Tempe campus, College of Liberal Arts and Sciences, School of International Letters and Cultures, Program in German, Tempe, AZ 85287-0202. Offers comparative literature (MA); language and culture (MA); literature (MA). *Degree requirements:* For master's, thesis, applied pedagogical project, or paper portfolio consisting of 2 seminar papers; interactive Program of Study (iPOS) submitted no later than beginning of third semester of study or before completing 50 percent of coursework. *Entrance requirements:* For master's, minimum GPA of 3.0 in the last two years of work leading to the bachelor's degree, personal statement, writing sample (preferably written in German), 3 letters of recommendation. Additional exam requirements/recommendations for international students: Required—TOEFL (minimum score 550 paper-based; 83 iBT), IELTS (minimum score 6.5). Electronic applications accepted.

Bowling Green State University, Graduate College, College of Arts and Sciences, Department of German, Russian, and East Asian Languages, Bowling Green, OH 43403. Offers German (MA, MAT); MA/MA. Part-time programs available. *Degree requirements:* For master's, one foreign language, thesis or alternative. *Entrance*

requirements: For master's, GRE General Test. Additional exam requirements/recommendations for international students: Required—TOEFL. Electronic applications accepted.

Brown University, Graduate School, Department of German Studies, Providence, RI 02912. Offers PhD. *Degree requirements:* For doctorate, 2 foreign languages, thesis/dissertation, preliminary exam. *Entrance requirements:* For doctorate, GRE General Test.

California State University, Fullerton, Graduate Studies, College of Humanities and Social Sciences, Department of Modern Languages and Literatures, Fullerton, CA 92834-9480. Offers French (MA); German (MA); Spanish (MA); teaching English to speakers of other languages (MS). Part-time programs available. *Students:* 36 full-time (26 women), 56 part-time (40 women); includes 57 minority (9 Asian, non-Hispanic/Latino; 46 Hispanic/Latino; 2 Two or more races, non-Hispanic/Latino), 19 international. Average age 32. 55 applicants, 69% accepted, 24 enrolled. In 2014, 30 master's awarded. *Degree requirements:* For master's, comprehensive exam, thesis or alternative. *Entrance requirements:* For master's, minimum GPA of 2.5 in last 60 hours of course work, undergraduate major in a language. Application fee: $55. *Financial support:* Career-related internships or fieldwork, Federal Work-Study, institutionally sponsored loans, and scholarships/grants available. Support available to part-time students. Financial award application deadline: 3/1; financial award applicants required to submit FAFSA. *Unit head:* Dr. Reyes Fidalgo, Chair, 657-278-4563. *Application contact:* Admissions/Applications, 657-278-2371.

California State University, Long Beach, Graduate Studies, College of Liberal Arts, Department of Romance, German, and Russian Languages and Literature, Program in German, Long Beach, CA 90840. Offers MA. Part-time programs available. *Degree requirements:* For master's, one foreign language, comprehensive exam or thesis. Electronic applications accepted. *Faculty research:* Contemporary German society, Baroque, Goethe, Wagner.

Central Connecticut State University, School of Graduate Studies, College of Liberal Arts and Social Sciences, Department of Modern Languages, Program in Modern Language, New Britain, CT 06050-4010. Offers French (MA, Certificate); German (Certificate); Italian (Certificate); modern language (MA); Spanish language and Hispanic culture (MA). Part-time and evening/weekend programs available. *Students:* 4 full-time (3 women), 28 part-time (22 women); includes 13 minority (1 Black or African American, non-Hispanic/Latino; 12 Hispanic/Latino), 1 international. Average age 34. 9 applicants, 100% accepted, 7 enrolled. In 2014, 8 master's, 5 other advanced degrees awarded. *Degree requirements:* For master's, one foreign language, comprehensive exam, thesis or alternative; for Certificate, qualifying exam. *Entrance requirements:* For master's, minimum undergraduate GPA of 2.7, 24 credits of undergraduate courses in each language in which graduate work will be undertaken. Additional exam requirements/recommendations for international students: Required—TOEFL (minimum score 550 paper-based; 79 iBT). *Application deadline:* For fall admission, 6/1 for domestic students, 5/1 for international students; for spring admission, 11/1 for domestic and international students. Applications are processed on a rolling basis. Application fee: $50. Electronic applications accepted. *Expenses: Tuition, area resident:* Full-time $5730; part-time $534 per credit. Tuition, state resident: full-time $8596; part-time $534 per credit. Tuition, nonresident: full-time $15,964; part-time $548 per credit. *Required fees:* $4211; $215 per credit. *Faculty research:* Twentieth-century French theater, seventeenth-century French literature, French Middle Ages. *Unit head:* Dr. Lilian Uribe, Chair, 860-832-2875, E-mail: uribe@ccsu.edu. *Application contact:* Patricia Gardner, Associate Director of Graduate Studies, 860-832-2350, Fax: 860-832-2362, E-mail: graduateadmissions@ccsu.edu.

Columbia University, Graduate School of Arts and Sciences, New York, NY 10027. Offers African-American studies (MA); American studies (MA); anthropology (MA, PhD); art history and archaeology (MA, PhD); astronomy (PhD); biological sciences (PhD); biotechnology (MA); chemical physics (PhD); chemistry (PhD); classical studies (MA, PhD); classics (MA, PhD); climate and society (MA); earth and environmental sciences (PhD); East Asia: regional studies (MA); East Asian languages and cultures (MA, PhD); ecology, evolution and environmental biology (MA), including conservation biology; ecology, evolution, and environmental biology (PhD), including ecology and evolutionary biology, evolutionary primatology; economics (PhD); English and comparative literature (MA, PhD); French and Romance philology (MA, PhD); Germanic languages (MA, PhD); global French studies (MA); Hispanic cultural studies (MA); history (PhD); history and literature (MA); human rights studies (MA); Islamic studies (MA); Italian (MA, PhD); Japanese pedagogy (MA); Jewish studies (MA); Latin America and the Caribbean: regional studies (MA); Latin American and Iberian cultures (PhD); mathematics (MA, PhD), including finance (MA); medieval and Renaissance studies (MA); Middle Eastern, South Asian, and African studies (MA, PhD); modern art: critical and curatorial studies (MA); modern European studies (MA); museum anthropology (MA); music (DMA, PhD); oral history (MA); philosophical foundations of physics (MA); philosophy (MA, PhD); physics (PhD); political science (MA, PhD); psychology (PhD); quantitative methods in the social sciences (MA); religion (MA, PhD); Russia, Eurasia and East Europe: regional studies (MA); Russian translation (MA); Slavic cultures (MA); Slavic languages (MA, PhD); sociology (MA, PhD); South Asian studies (MA); statistics (MA, PhD); theatre (PhD); JD/PhD; MA/MS; MD/PhD; MPA/MA. Dual-degree programs require admission to both Graduate School of Arts and Sciences and another Columbia school. Part-time and evening/weekend programs available. Terminal master's awarded for partial completion of doctoral program. *Degree requirements:* For master's, thesis (for some programs); for doctorate, comprehensive exam, thesis/dissertation. *Entrance requirements:* For master's and doctorate, GRE General Test, GRE Subject Test (for some programs). Electronic applications accepted. *Faculty research:* Humanities, natural sciences, social sciences.

Cornell University, Graduate School, Graduate Fields of Arts and Sciences, Field of Germanic Studies, Ithaca, NY 14853-0001. Offers German area studies (MA, PhD); German intellectual history (MA, PhD); Germanic linguistics (MA, PhD); Germanic literature (MA, PhD); old Norse (MA, PhD). Terminal master's awarded for partial completion of doctoral program. *Degree requirements:* For master's, one foreign language, thesis; for doctorate, 2 foreign languages, comprehensive exam, thesis/dissertation. *Entrance requirements:* For master's and doctorate, GRE General Test, fluency in German, writing sample, 2 letters of recommendation. Additional exam requirements/recommendations for international students: Required—TOEFL (minimum score 550 paper-based; 77 iBT). Electronic applications accepted. *Faculty research:* Women's studies, minority literature, literature and intellectual history, theater and film studies, Continental philosophy.

Cornell University, Graduate School, Graduate Fields of Arts and Sciences, Field of Linguistics, Ithaca, NY 14853-0001. Offers applied linguistics (MA, PhD); East Asian linguistics (MA, PhD); English linguistics (MA, PhD); general linguistics (MA, PhD); Germanic linguistics (MA, PhD); Indo-European linguistics (MA, PhD); phonetics (MA, PhD); phonological theory (MA, PhD); Romance linguistics (MA, PhD); second language acquisition (MA, PhD); semantics (MA, PhD); Slavic linguistics (MA, PhD); sociolinguistics (MA, PhD); South Asian linguistics (MA, PhD); Southeast Asian linguistics (MA, PhD); syntactic theory (MA, PhD). Terminal master's awarded for partial completion of doctoral program. *Degree requirements:* For master's, one foreign language, thesis; for doctorate, one foreign language, comprehensive exam, thesis/dissertation. *Entrance requirements:* For master's and doctorate, GRE General Test, 2 letters of recommendation. Additional exam requirements/recommendations for international students: Required—TOEFL (minimum score 600 paper-based; 77 iBT). Electronic applications accepted. *Faculty research:* Phonology and phonetics, syntax and semantics, historical linguistics, philosophy of language, language acquisition.

Dalhousie University, Faculty of Arts and Social Science, Department of German, Halifax, NS B3H 4R2, Canada. Offers MA. *Entrance requirements:* Additional exam requirements/recommendations for international students: Required—TOEFL, IELTS, CANTEST, CAEL, or Michigan English Language Assessment Battery. Electronic applications accepted. *Faculty research:* Baroque age in Germany, literature and philosophy of German idealism, twentieth-century German culture, aesthetics, reception of the Islamic Orient, reception of Greek and Roman antiquity, realism and ornament.

DePaul University, College of Liberal Arts and Social Sciences, Chicago, IL 60614. Offers Arabic (MA); Chinese (MA); English (MA); French (MA); German (MA); history (MA); interdisciplinary studies (MA, MS); international public service (MS); international studies (MA); Italian (MA); Japanese (MA); leadership and policy studies (MS); liberal studies (MA); new media studies (MA); nonprofit management (MNM); public administration (MPA); public health (MPH); public service management (MS); social work (MSW); sociology (MA); Spanish (MA); sustainable urban development (MA); women and gender studies (MA); writing and publishing (MA); writing, rhetoric, and discourse (MA); MA/PhD. Part-time and evening/weekend programs available. Postbaccalaureate distance learning degree programs offered (no on-campus study). Terminal master's awarded for partial completion of doctoral program. *Degree requirements:* For master's, variable foreign language requirement, comprehensive exam (for some programs), thesis (for some programs). Electronic applications accepted.

Duke University, Graduate School, Carolina-Duke Graduate Program in German Studies, Durham, NC 27708-0256. Offers PhD. Program offered jointly with The University of North Carolina Chapel Hill. Part-time programs available. *Degree requirements:* For doctorate, thesis/dissertation. *Entrance requirements:* For doctorate, GRE General Test, writing sample. Additional exam requirements/recommendations for international students: Required—TOEFL (minimum score 577 paper-based; 90 iBT) or IELTS (minimum score 7). Electronic applications accepted. *Expenses: Tuition:* Full-time $45,760; part-time $2765 per credit. *Required fees:* $978. Full-time tuition and fees vary according to program.

Eastern Michigan University, Graduate School, College of Arts and Sciences, Department of World Languages, Ypsilanti, MI 48197. Offers foreign languages (MA, Graduate Certificate), including French (MA), German (MA), German for business (Graduate Certificate), Hispanic language and cultures (Graduate Certificate), Japanese business practices (Graduate Certificate), Spanish (MA). Part-time and evening/weekend programs available. Postbaccalaureate distance learning degree programs offered (minimal on-campus study). *Faculty:* 20 full-time (14 women). *Students:* 5 full-time (4 women), 46 part-time (35 women); includes 10 minority (2 Black or African American, non-Hispanic/Latino; 2 Asian, non-Hispanic/Latino; 6 Hispanic/Latino), 4 international. Average age 33. 46 applicants, 74% accepted, 21 enrolled. In 2014, 23 master's, 1 other advanced degree awarded. *Degree requirements:* For master's, one foreign language. *Entrance requirements:* Additional exam requirements/recommendations for international students: Required—TOEFL. *Application deadline:* Applications are processed on a rolling basis. Application fee: $45. *Financial support:* Fellowships, research assistantships with full tuition reimbursements, teaching assistantships with full tuition reimbursements, career-related internships or fieldwork, Federal Work-Study, institutionally sponsored loans, scholarships/grants, tuition waivers (partial), and unspecified assistantships available. Support available to part-time students. Financial award applicants required to submit FAFSA. *Unit head:* Dr. Rosemary Weston-Gil, Department Head, 734-487-0130, Fax: 734-487-3411, E-mail: rweston3@emich.edu.

Florida Atlantic University, College of Education, Department of Teaching and Learning, Boca Raton, FL 33431-0991. Offers curriculum and instruction (M Ed), including art, biology, chemistry, English, French, German, mathematics, music, physics, Pre-K and primary education, reading, social sciences, Spanish; elementary education (M Ed); environmental education (M Ed); reading education (M Ed); social foundations of education (M Ed), including educational psychology, educational technology, multilingual education. *Accreditation:* NCATE. Part-time and evening/weekend programs available. *Entrance requirements:* For master's, GRE General Test, minimum GPA of 3.0 in last 2 years of undergraduate course work. Additional exam requirements/recommendations for international students: Required—TOEFL (minimum score 500 paper-based; 61 iBT), IELTS (minimum score 6). *Expenses:* Tuition, state resident: full-time $7396; part-time $369.82 per credit hour. Tuition, nonresident: full-time $19,392; part-time $1024.81 per credit hour. Tuition and fees vary according to course load. *Faculty research:* Technology, teaching English to speakers of other languages, math teaching, electronic portfolio assessment, global perspectives through social studies.

Florida State University, The Graduate School, College of Arts and Sciences, Department of Modern Languages, Program in German, Tallahassee, FL 32306. Offers MA. *Faculty:* 3 full-time (2 women), 2 part-time/adjunct (1 woman). *Students:* 11 full-time (7 women); includes 2 minority (1 Hispanic/Latino; 1 Two or more races, non-Hispanic/Latino). Average age 25. 8 applicants, 100% accepted, 8 enrolled. In 2014, 2 master's awarded. *Degree requirements:* For master's, thesis optional. *Entrance requirements:* For master's, GRE General Test, minimum GPA of 3.0. Additional exam requirements/recommendations for international students: Required—TOEFL (minimum score 550 paper-based). *Application deadline:* For fall admission, 2/15 for domestic and international students. Electronic applications accepted. *Expenses:* Tuition, state resident: part-time $403.51 per credit hour. Tuition, nonresident: part-time $1004.85 per credit hour. *Required fees:* $75.81 per credit hour. One-time fee: $20 part-time. Tuition and fees vary according to campus/location. *Financial support:* In 2014–15, 4 students received support, including research assistantships (averaging $12,000 per year), 10 teaching assistantships with partial tuition reimbursements available (averaging $11,500 per year). Financial award application deadline: 2/1; financial award applicants required to submit FAFSA. *Unit head:* Dr. Christian Weber, Divisional Coordinator, 850-644-8194, Fax: 850-644-0524, E-mail: eweber@fsu.edu. *Application contact:* Wendy E. Pigott, Graduate Academic Coordinator, 850-644-8397, Fax: 850-644-0524, E-mail: wpigott@fsu.edu.
Website: http://www.modlang.fsu.edu/Programs2/German/Graduate-program

Georgetown University, Graduate School of Arts and Sciences, Department of German, Washington, DC 20057. Offers MA, PhD, MA/PhD. *Degree requirements:* For master's, 2 foreign languages, research project; for doctorate, 3 foreign languages, thesis/dissertation. *Entrance requirements:* For master's, GRE General Test. Additional exam requirements/recommendations for international students: Required—TOEFL.

Georgetown University, Graduate School of Arts and Sciences, Edmund A. Walsh School of Foreign Service, BMW Center for German and European Studies, Washington, DC 20057. Offers MA, MA/JD, MA/PhD. *Degree requirements:* For

master's, 2 foreign languages, comprehensive exam. *Entrance requirements:* For master's, GRE General Test. Additional exam requirements/recommendations for international students: Required—TOEFL. Electronic applications accepted. *Faculty research:* Transatlantic relations, European Union, German and European Studies.

Georgia State University, College of Arts and Sciences, Department of Modern and Classical Languages, Program in Translation and Interpretation, Atlanta, GA 30302-3083. Offers interpretation (Certificate), including Spanish; translation (Certificate), including French, German, Spanish. Part-time programs available. *Entrance requirements:* For degree, entrance examination involving translating one passage from English to the target language and one passage from the target language to English, 3 letters of recommendation, resume/curriculum vitae, official transcripts. Additional exam requirements/recommendations for international students: Required—TOEFL (minimum score 79 iBT). *Application deadline:* For fall admission, 3/15 priority date for domestic and international students; for spring admission, 11/15 priority date for domestic and international students. Application fee: $50. Electronic applications accepted. *Expenses:* Tuition, state resident: full-time $6516; part-time $362 per credit hour. Tuition, nonresident: full-time $22,014; part-time $1223 per credit hour. *Required fees:* $2128 per semester. Tuition and fees vary according to course load and program. *Faculty research:* Romance linguistics and translation; theory and practice of translation; medical and legal interpretation. *Unit head:* Dr. Fernando Reati, Chair, 404-413-5984, Fax: 404-413-5982, E-mail: freati@gsu.edu. *Application contact:* Lita Malveaux, Administrative Academic Specialist, 404-413-5046, Fax: 404-413-5036, E-mail: lmalveaux@gsu.edu.
Website: http://wlc.gsu.edu/home/graduate/graduate-certificate/

The Graduate Center, City University of New York, Graduate Studies, Program in Comparative Literature, New York, NY 10016-4039. Offers comparative literature (MA, PhD), including classics (PhD), German (PhD), Italian (PhD). PhD offered jointly with New York University. Terminal master's awarded for partial completion of doctoral program. *Degree requirements:* For master's, 2 foreign languages, comprehensive exam, thesis; for doctorate, 3 foreign languages, comprehensive exam, thesis/dissertation. *Entrance requirements:* For master's and doctorate, GRE General Test. Additional exam requirements/recommendations for international students: Required—TOEFL. Electronic applications accepted.

The Graduate Center, City University of New York, Graduate Studies, Program in Germanic Languages and Literatures, New York, NY 10016-4039. Offers MA, PhD. *Degree requirements:* For master's, one foreign language, thesis; for doctorate, 2 foreign languages, thesis/dissertation. *Entrance requirements:* For master's and doctorate, GRE General Test.

Harvard University, Graduate School of Arts and Sciences, Department of Germanic Languages and Literatures, Cambridge, MA 02138. Offers German (PhD); Scandinavian (PhD). Terminal master's awarded for partial completion of doctoral program. *Degree requirements:* For doctorate, 2 foreign languages, thesis/dissertation, exams. *Entrance requirements:* For doctorate, GRE General Test, German writing sample. Additional exam requirements/recommendations for international students: Required—TOEFL.

Illinois State University, Graduate School, College of Arts and Sciences, Department of Foreign Languages, Literatures and Cultures, Normal, IL 61790-2200. Offers French (MA); French and German (MA); French and Spanish (MA); German (MA); German and Spanish (MA); Spanish (MA). *Degree requirements:* For master's, variable foreign language requirement, comprehensive exam, 1 term of residency. *Entrance requirements:* For master's, GRE General Test, minimum GPA of 2.8 in last 60 hours of course work.

Indiana University Bloomington, University Graduate School, College of Arts and Sciences, Department of Germanic Studies, Bloomington, IN 47405-7000. Offers German philology and linguistics (PhD); German studies (MA, PhD), including German (MA), German literature and culture (MA), German literature and linguistics (MA); medieval German studies (PhD); teaching German (MAT). *Faculty:* 13 full-time (4 women), 6 part-time/adjunct (2 women). *Students:* 29 full-time (16 women), 6 international. Average age 31. 22 applicants, 9% accepted, 2 enrolled. In 2014, 4 doctorates awarded. Terminal master's awarded for partial completion of doctoral program. *Degree requirements:* For master's, one foreign language, project; for doctorate, one foreign language, comprehensive exam, thesis/dissertation. *Entrance requirements:* For master's, GRE General Test, BA in German or equivalent; for doctorate, GRE General Test, MA in German or equivalent. Additional exam requirements/recommendations for international students: Required—TOEFL. *Application deadline:* For fall admission, 1/15 priority date for domestic students, 12/1 for international students; for spring admission, 9/1 priority date for domestic students, 9/1 for international students. Applications are processed on a rolling basis. Application fee: $55 ($65 for international students). Electronic applications accepted. *Financial support:* Fellowships with full and partial tuition reimbursements, teaching assistantships with full tuition reimbursements, Federal Work-Study, institutionally sponsored loans, scholarships/grants, and unspecified assistantships available. Support available to part-time students. Financial award application deadline: 1/15; financial award applicants required to submit FAFSA. *Faculty research:* German and other European literature: medieval to modern/postmodern, German and culture studies, Germanic philology, literary theory, literature and the other arts. *Unit head:* Fritz Breithaupt, Department Chairman, 812-855-7947, Fax: 812-855-8292, E-mail: fbreitha@indiana.edu. *Application contact:* Michelle Dunbar, Graduate Secretary, 812-855-7947, E-mail: midunbar@indiana.edu.
Website: http://www.indiana.edu/~germanic/

Johns Hopkins University, Zanvyl Krieger School of Arts and Sciences, Department of German and Romance Languages and Literatures, Baltimore, MD 21218-2699. Offers French (PhD); German (PhD); Italian (PhD); Spanish (PhD). *Degree requirements:* For doctorate, 2 foreign languages, thesis/dissertation. *Entrance requirements:* For doctorate, GRE General Test. Additional exam requirements/recommendations for international students: Required—TOEFL (minimum score 600 paper-based; 100 iBT), IELTS. Electronic applications accepted. *Faculty research:* Nineteenth-century French prose and poetry, genetic theory and criticism; twentieth-century Latin American literature and film; medieval and Renaissance Italian literature; gender and queer theory in German literature; the ideology of Baroque and Neobaroque aesthetics.

McGill University, Faculty of Graduate and Postdoctoral Studies, Faculty of Arts, Department of German Studies, Montréal, QC H3A 2T5, Canada. Offers MA, PhD.

Memorial University of Newfoundland, School of Graduate Studies, Department of German and Russian, St. John's, NL A1C 5S7, Canada. Offers German language and literature (M Phil, MA). Part-time programs available. *Degree requirements:* For master's, one foreign language, thesis (for some programs), comprehensive exam (M Phil). *Entrance requirements:* For master's, honors degree (minimum 2nd class standing). Electronic applications accepted. *Faculty research:* German literature from the Middle Ages to the twentieth century, German studies.

Michigan State University, The Graduate School, College of Arts and Letters, Department of Linguistics and Germanic, Slavic, Asian, and African Languages, East Lansing, MI 48824. Offers German studies (MA, PhD); linguistics (MA, PhD); teaching English to speakers of other languages (MA). Part-time and evening/weekend programs available. *Entrance requirements:* For master's, GRE General Test, minimum GPA of 3.2 in last 2 undergraduate years, 2 years of college-level foreign language, 3 letters of recommendation, portfolio (German studies); for doctorate, GRE General Test, minimum graduate GPA of 3.5, 3 letters of recommendation, master's degree or sufficient graduate course work in linguistics or language of study, master's thesis or major research paper. Additional exam requirements/recommendations for international students: Required—TOEFL. Electronic applications accepted.

Middlebury College, Language Schools, German School, Middlebury, VT 05753-6002. Offers MA, DML. *Faculty:* 21 full-time (11 women). *Students:* 12 full-time (6 women), 2 part-time (0 women); includes 3 minority (1 Black or African American, non-Hispanic/Latino; 2 Two or more races, non-Hispanic/Latino), 1 international. Average age 30. 21 applicants, 67% accepted, 14 enrolled. In 2014, 9 master's awarded. *Degree requirements:* For master's, one foreign language; for doctorate, 2 foreign languages, comprehensive exam, thesis/dissertation, residence abroad, teaching experience. *Entrance requirements:* For master's, placement exam, 3 letters of recommendation, transcripts, personal statement; for doctorate, 1st and 2nd language placement exams, 3 letters of recommendation, transcripts, personal statement, MA in German. *Application deadline:* Applications are processed on a rolling basis. Application fee: $65. Electronic applications accepted. *Financial support:* Scholarships/grants available. Financial award applicants required to submit FAFSA. *Unit head:* Dr. Bettina Matthias, Director, 802-443-3248, Fax: 802-443-2075, E-mail: bmatthia@middlebury.edu. *Application contact:* Christina Ellison, Coordinator, 802-443-5203, Fax: 802-443-2075, E-mail: ccartwri@middlebury.edu.
Website: http://www.middlebury.edu/ls/grad_programs/german

Middle Tennessee State University, College of Graduate Studies, College of Liberal Arts, Department of Foreign Languages and Literatures, Murfreesboro, TN 37132. Offers foreign languages (MAT), including French, German, Spanish. Part-time and evening/weekend programs available. Postbaccalaureate distance learning degree programs offered. *Faculty:* 17 full-time (12 women), 1 part-time/adjunct (0 women). *Students:* 9 full-time (6 women), 11 part-time (5 women); includes 5 minority (2 Black or African American, non-Hispanic/Latino; 1 Asian, non-Hispanic/Latino; 1 Hispanic/Latino; 1 Two or more races, non-Hispanic/Latino), 1 international. 14 applicants, 86% accepted. In 2014, 8 master's awarded. *Degree requirements:* For master's, one foreign language, comprehensive exam, thesis optional. *Entrance requirements:* For master's, GRE. Additional exam requirements/recommendations for international students: Required—TOEFL (minimum score 525 paper-based; 71 iBT) or IELTS (minimum score 6). *Application deadline:* For fall admission, 6/1 for domestic and international students. Applications are processed on a rolling basis. Application fee: $30. Electronic applications accepted. *Financial support:* In 2014–15, 9 students received support. Tuition waivers available. Support available to part-time students. Financial award application deadline: 4/1; financial award applicants required to submit FAFSA. *Total annual research expenditures:* $135,499. *Unit head:* Dr. Joan McRae, Chair, 615-898-2981, Fax: 615-898-5735, E-mail: joan.mcrae@mtsu.edu. *Application contact:* Dr. Michael D. Allen, Vice Provost for Research/Dean, 615-898-2840, Fax: 615-904-8020, E-mail: michael.allen@mtsu.edu.

Millersville University of Pennsylvania, College of Graduate and Professional Studies, School of Humanities and Social Sciences, Department of Foreign Languages, Program in Languages and Cultures: German Option, Millersville, PA 17551-0302. Offers MA. Part-time programs available. *Faculty:* 8 full-time (4 women), 4 part-time/adjunct (3 women). *Students:* 1 part-time (0 women). Average age 31. In 2014, 1 master's awarded. *Degree requirements:* For master's, comprehensive exam, thesis optional. *Entrance requirements:* For master's, American Council on the Teaching of Foreign Languages Oral Proficiency Interview and Writing Proficiency Test, 3 letters of recommendation, goal statement, official transcripts. Additional exam requirements/recommendations for international students: Required—TOEFL (minimum score 500 paper-based, 65 iBT) or IELTS (minimum score 6). *Application deadline:* For fall admission, 1/15 priority date for domestic and international students; for winter admission, 6/1 priority date for domestic and international students; for spring admission, 10/1 priority date for domestic and international students. Applications are processed on a rolling basis. Application fee: $40. Electronic applications accepted. *Expenses:* Tuition, state resident: full-time $8172. Tuition, nonresident: full-time $12,258. *Required fees:* $2300. Tuition and fees vary according to course load and program. *Financial support:* Research assistantships with full tuition reimbursements, institutionally sponsored loans, and unspecified assistantships available. Support available to part-time students. Financial award application deadline: 3/15; financial award applicants required to submit FAFSA. *Faculty research:* Language acquisition. *Unit head:* Dr. Susanne J. Nimmrichter, Associate Professor and Program Contact, 717-871-7154, Fax: 717-871-7935, E-mail: susanne.nimmrichter@millersville.edu. *Application contact:* Dr. Victor S. DeSantis, Dean of College of Graduate and Professional Studies/Associate Provost for Civic and Community Engagement, 717-871-7619, Fax: 717-871-7954, E-mail: victor.desantis@millersville.edu.
Website: http://www.millersville.edu/forlang/

Mississippi State University, College of Arts and Sciences, Department of Classical and Modern Languages and Literatures, Mississippi State, MS 39762. Offers French (MA); German (MA); Spanish (MA). Part-time programs available. *Faculty:* 12 full-time (3 women). *Students:* 7 full-time (3 women); includes 2 minority (both Hispanic/Latino), 1 international. Average age 32. 7 applicants, 57% accepted, 3 enrolled. In 2014, 12 master's awarded. *Degree requirements:* For master's, one foreign language, thesis optional, comprehensive oral or written exam. *Entrance requirements:* For master's, minimum GPA of 2.75 on last two years of undergraduate courses. Additional exam requirements/recommendations for international students: Required—TOEFL (minimum score 525 paper-based; 70 iBT); Recommended—IELTS (minimum score 6). *Application deadline:* For fall admission, 7/1 for domestic students, 5/1 for international students; for spring admission, 11/1 for domestic students, 9/1 for international students. Applications are processed on a rolling basis. Application fee: $60. Electronic applications accepted. *Expenses:* Tuition, state resident: full-time $7140; part-time $783 per credit hour. Tuition, nonresident: full-time $18,478; part-time $2043 per credit hour. *Financial support:* Federal Work-Study, institutionally sponsored loans, and unspecified assistantships available. Financial award application deadline: 4/1; financial award applicants required to submit FAFSA. *Faculty research:* French, German, Spanish literature from medieval era to present; gender and cultural studies in French; Spanish-American literature; foreign language methodology; linguistics. *Unit head:* Dr. Lynn Holt, Professor and Interim Head, 662-325-3480, Fax: 662-325-8209, E-mail: lholt@cmll.msstate.edu. *Application contact:* Dr. Keith Moser, Graduate Coordinator, 662-325-3480, Fax: 662-325-8209, E-mail: kmoser@.msstate.edu.
Website: http://www.cmll.msstate.edu/

New York University, Graduate School of Arts and Science, Department of German, New York, NY 10012-1019. Offers German studies and critical thought (MA, PhD). Part-time programs available. *Faculty:* 8 full-time (5 women), 5 part-time/adjunct (0 women). *Students:* 16 full-time (5 women); includes 2 minority (1 Black or African American, non-Hispanic/Latino; 1 Two or more races, non-Hispanic/Latino), 9 international. Average age 32. 15 applicants, 20% accepted, 2 enrolled. In 2014, 1 master's, 2 doctorates awarded. Terminal master's awarded for partial completion of doctoral program. *Degree*

requirements: For master's, one foreign language, thesis; for doctorate, 2 foreign languages, thesis/dissertation. *Entrance requirements:* For master's, GRE; for doctorate, GRE, sample of written work. Additional exam requirements/recommendations for international students: Required—TOEFL. *Application deadline:* For fall admission, 1/4 priority date for domestic students, 1/4 for international students. Application fee: $100. *Financial support:* Fellowships with tuition reimbursements, teaching assistantships with tuition reimbursements, Federal Work-Study, institutionally sponsored loans, scholarships/grants, health care benefits, and unspecified assistantships available. Financial award application deadline: 1/4; financial award applicants required to submit FAFSA. *Faculty research:* Eighteenth to twentieth century literature, culture and critical thought, film and visual culture, philosophy, critical theory. *Unit head:* Leif Weatherby, Director of Graduate Studies, 212-998-8650, Fax: 212-995-4823, E-mail: german.dept@nyu.edu. *Application contact:* Lindsay O'Connor, Department Administrator, 212-998-8650, Fax: 212-995-4823, E-mail: german.dept@nyu.edu.
Website: http://www.nyu.edu/gsas/dept/german/

Northwestern University, The Graduate School, Judd A. and Marjorie Weinberg College of Arts and Sciences, Department of German, Evanston, IL 60208. Offers German literature and critical thought (PhD). Admissions and degrees offered through The Graduate School. *Degree requirements:* For doctorate, one foreign language, thesis/dissertation. *Entrance requirements:* For doctorate, GRE General Test. Additional exam requirements/recommendations for international students: Required—TOEFL. Electronic applications accepted. *Faculty research:* Eighteenth through twentieth century German literature, comparative literature, theory, philosophy, language pedagogy.

The Ohio State University, Graduate School, College of Arts and Sciences, Division of Arts and Humanities, Department of Germanic Languages and Literatures, Columbus, OH 43210. Offers MA, PhD. *Faculty:* 14. *Students:* 22 full-time (14 women), 1 part-time (0 women); includes 1 minority (Two or more races, non-Hispanic/Latino), 10 international. Average age 27. In 2014, 2 master's, 2 doctorates awarded. *Degree requirements:* For master's, one foreign language, thesis optional; for doctorate, 2 foreign languages, thesis/dissertation. *Entrance requirements:* For master's and doctorate, GRE General Test. Additional exam requirements/recommendations for international students: Required—TOEFL (minimum score 550 paper-based; 79 iBT), Michigan English Language Assessment Battery (minimum score 82); Recommended—IELTS (minimum score 7). *Application deadline:* For fall admission, 12/13 priority date for domestic students, 11/30 priority date for international students; for winter admission, 12/1 for domestic students, 11/1 for international students; for spring admission, 3/1 for domestic students, 2/1 for international students. Applications are processed on a rolling basis. Application fee: $60 ($70 for international students). Electronic applications accepted. *Financial support:* Fellowships with tuition reimbursements, research assistantships with tuition reimbursements, teaching assistantships with tuition reimbursements, Federal Work-Study, and institutionally sponsored loans available. Support available to part-time students. *Faculty research:* German literature, Germanic philology, linguistics. *Unit head:* Dr. Robert C. Holub, Chair, Professor, and Ohio Eminent Scholar, 614-292-6985, E-mail: holub.5@osu.edu. *Application contact:* Graduate and Professional Admissions, 614-292-9444, Fax: 614-292-3895, E-mail: gpadmissions@osu.edu.
Website: http://germanic.osu.edu/

Penn State University Park, Graduate School, College of the Liberal Arts, Department of Germanic and Slavic Languages and Literatures, University Park, PA 16802. Offers MA, PhD. *Faculty research:* Literature, literary theory, culture, language pedagogy. *Unit head:* Dr. Susan Welch, Dean, 814-865-7691, Fax: 814-863-2085, E-mail: swelch@psu.edu. *Application contact:* Lori A. Stania, Director, Graduate Student Services, 814-867-5278, Fax: 814-863-4627, E-mail: gswww@psu.edu.
Website: http://german.la.psu.edu/

Portland State University, Graduate Studies, College of Liberal Arts and Sciences, Department of World Languages and Literatures, Portland, OR 97207-0751. Offers foreign literature and language (MA); French (MA); German (MA); Japanese (MA); Spanish (MA). Part-time programs available. *Faculty:* 48 full-time (28 women), 33 part-time/adjunct (29 women). *Students:* 30 full-time (13 women), 8 part-time (3 women); includes 7 minority (2 Asian, non-Hispanic/Latino; 5 Hispanic/Latino), 13 international. Average age 30. 31 applicants, 65% accepted, 18 enrolled. In 2014, 9 master's awarded. *Degree requirements:* For master's, one foreign language, thesis (for some programs). *Entrance requirements:* Additional exam requirements/recommendations for international students: Required—TOEFL (minimum score 550 paper-based; 80 iBT), IELTS (minimum score 6.5). *Application deadline:* For fall admission, 4/1 for domestic students, 3/1 for international students; for winter admission, 9/1 for domestic students, 7/1 for international students; for spring admission, 11/1 for domestic and international students. Applications are processed on a rolling basis. Application fee: $50. *Expenses:* Tuition, state resident: part-time $222 per credit. Tuition, nonresident: part-time $527 per credit. *Required fees:* $22 per contact hour. $100 per quarter. Tuition and fees vary according to program. *Financial support:* In 2014–15, 29 teaching assistantships with full and partial tuition reimbursements (averaging $3,251 per year) were awarded; research assistantships with full tuition reimbursements, Federal Work-Study, scholarships/grants, and unspecified assistantships also available. Support available to part-time students. Financial award application deadline: 3/1; financial award applicants required to submit FAFSA. *Faculty research:* Foreign language pedagogy, applied and social linguistics, literary history and criticism. *Total annual research expenditures:* $412,070. *Unit head:* Dr. Jennifer Perlmutter, Chair, 503-725-8783, Fax: 503-725-5276, E-mail: jrp@pdx.edu.
Website: http://www.pdx.edu/wll/

Princeton University, Graduate School, Department of German, Princeton, NJ 08544-1019. Offers PhD. *Degree requirements:* For doctorate, 2 foreign languages, thesis/dissertation. *Entrance requirements:* For doctorate, GRE General Test. Additional exam requirements/recommendations for international students: Required—TOEFL (minimum score 600 paper-based). Electronic applications accepted.

Purdue University, Graduate School, College of Liberal Arts, School of Languages and Cultures, West Lafayette, IN 47907. Offers French (MA, MAT, PhD), including French (MA, PhD), French education (MAT); German (MA, MAT, PhD), including German (MA, PhD), German education (MAT); Japanese pedagogy (MA); Spanish (MA, MAT, PhD), including Spanish (MA, PhD), Spanish education (MAT). Terminal master's awarded for partial completion of doctoral program. *Degree requirements:* For master's, one foreign language; for doctorate, 2 foreign languages, thesis/dissertation. *Entrance requirements:* For master's, GRE General Test (minimum score 600, 160 for new scoring), two writing samples, one in English, one in language (French, German, Japanese, or Spanish); sample recording of English and language of study; for doctorate, GRE General Test (minimum score 600, 160 for new scoring), master's degree with minimum GPA of 3.5 or equivalent; two writing samples, one in English, one in language (French, German, Japanese, or Spanish); sample recording of English and language of study. Additional exam requirements/recommendations for international students: Required—TOEFL (minimum score 550 paper-based; 77 iBT); Recommended—TWE. Electronic applications accepted. *Faculty research:* Linguistics, semiotics, literary criticism, pedagogy.

Queen's University at Kingston, School of Graduate Studies, Faculty of Arts and Sciences, Program in German, Kingston, ON K7L 3N6, Canada. Offers MA, PhD. Part-time programs available. *Degree requirements:* For master's, thesis optional; for doctorate, one foreign language, comprehensive exam, thesis/dissertation. *Entrance requirements:* For master's, 7 German courses, honors bachelor's degree in German; for doctorate, MA or equivalent in German. Additional exam requirements/recommendations for international students: Required—TOEFL. Electronic applications accepted. *Faculty research:* Goethe and Weimar classicism, Romanticism, nineteenth- and twentieth-century German literature.

Rider University, Department of Graduate Education, Leadership and Counseling, Teacher Certification Program, Lawrenceville, NJ 08648-3001. Offers business education (Certificate); elementary education (Certificate); English as a second language (Certificate); English education (Certificate); mathematics education (Certificate); preschool to grade 3 (Certificate); science education (Certificate); social studies education (Certificate); world languages (Certificate), including French, German, Spanish. Part-time programs available. *Degree requirements:* For Certificate, internship, professional portfolio. *Entrance requirements:* For degree, PRAXIS, resume. Additional exam requirements/recommendations for international students: Required—TOEFL (minimum score 550 paper-based). Electronic applications accepted. *Faculty research:* Conceptual foundations for optimal development of creativity; creative theory, cognitive processes in mathematics learning, teacher collaboration.

Rutgers, The State University of New Jersey, New Brunswick, Graduate School-New Brunswick, Program in German, Piscataway, NJ 08854-8097. Offers German (MAT, PhD); German literature (MA, PhD). Part-time and evening/weekend programs available. Terminal master's awarded for partial completion of doctoral program. *Degree requirements:* For master's, one foreign language, comprehensive exam, thesis or alternative; for doctorate, 2 foreign languages, comprehensive exam, thesis/dissertation. *Entrance requirements:* For master's and doctorate, GRE General Test. Additional exam requirements/recommendations for international students: Required—TOEFL. Electronic applications accepted. *Faculty research:* Literature and ideology; early German novella; narrative structures, mythology, psychology, and realist literature; German-American cultural history; literary theory and aesthetics; German film.

San Francisco State University, Division of Graduate Studies, College of Liberal and Creative Arts, Department of Foreign Languages and Literatures, Program in German, San Francisco, CA 94132-1722. Offers MA. *Application deadline:* Applications are processed on a rolling basis. *Expenses:* Tuition, state resident: full-time $6738. Tuition, nonresident: full-time $17,898; part-time $372 per credit hour. *Required fees:* $498 per semester. *Unit head:* Dr. Mohammad Salama, Chair, 415-338-7413, Fax: 415-405-0588, E-mail: mrsalama@sfsu.edu. *Application contact:* Dr. Llona Vandergriff, Graduate Advisor, 415-338-1106, Fax: 415-405-0588, E-mail: vdgriff@sfsu.edu.
Website: http://german.sfsu.edu/

Stanford University, School of Humanities and Sciences, Department of German Studies, Stanford, CA 94305-9991. Offers MA, PhD. *Degree requirements:* For master's, one foreign language, oral exam; for doctorate, 2 foreign languages, thesis/dissertation, oral exam, qualifying paper and exam. *Entrance requirements:* For master's and doctorate, GRE General Test. Additional exam requirements/recommendations for international students: Required—TOEFL. Electronic applications accepted. *Expenses: Tuition:* Full-time $44,184; part-time $982 per credit hour. *Required fees:* $191.

Texas Tech University, Graduate School, College of Arts and Sciences, Department of Classical and Modern Languages and Literatures, Lubbock, TX 79409-2071. Offers applied linguistics (MA); classics (MA); German (MA); languages and cultures (MA); Romance languages (MA); Spanish (PhD); MBA/MA. Part-time programs available. *Faculty:* 61 full-time (31 women), 7 part-time/adjunct (4 women). *Students:* 93 full-time (48 women), 15 part-time (10 women); includes 27 minority (1 Black or African American, non-Hispanic/Latino; 22 Hispanic/Latino; 4 Two or more races, non-Hispanic/Latino), 41 international. Average age 32. 60 applicants, 70% accepted, 26 enrolled. In 2014, 26 master's, 7 doctorates awarded. *Degree requirements:* For master's, comprehensive exam, thesis or alternative; for doctorate, comprehensive exam, thesis/dissertation. *Entrance requirements:* For master's and doctorate, GRE General Test. Additional exam requirements/recommendations for international students: Required—TOEFL (minimum score 550 paper-based; 79 iBT). *Application deadline:* For fall admission, 6/1 priority date for domestic students, 1/15 priority date for international students; for spring admission, 9/1 priority date for domestic students, 6/15 priority date for international students. Applications are processed on a rolling basis. Application fee: $60. Electronic applications accepted. *Expenses:* Tuition, state resident: full-time $6310; part-time $262.92 per credit hour. Tuition, nonresident: full-time $14,998; part-time $624.92 per credit hour. *Required fees:* $2701; $36.50 per credit. $912.50 per semester. Tuition and fees vary according to course load. *Financial support:* In 2014–15, 91 students received support, including 78 fellowships (averaging $2,724 per year), 4 research assistantships (averaging $17,800 per year), 82 teaching assistantships (averaging $11,423 per year); Federal Work-Study, scholarships/grants, and unspecified assistantships also available. Financial award application deadline: 4/15; financial award applicants required to submit FAFSA. *Faculty research:* Literature, comparative literature, linguistics, culture, applied linguistics. *Total annual research expenditures:* $1,380. *Unit head:* Dr. Erin Collopy, Chair and Associate Professor, 806-834-8497, Fax: 806-742-3306, E-mail: erin.collopy@ttu.edu. *Application contact:* Liz Hildebrand, Senior Advisor, 806-834-2463, Fax: 806-742-3306, E-mail: liz.hildebrand@ttu.edu.
Website: http://www.depts.ttu.edu/classic_modern/

Tufts University, Graduate School of Arts and Sciences, Department of Russian and German, Medford, MA 02155. Offers German (MA); German with teaching licensure (MA). Part-time programs available. *Students:* 1 (woman) full-time. Average age 24. 2 applicants, 100% accepted, 1 enrolled. In 2014, 3 master's awarded. *Degree requirements:* For master's, one foreign language, oral and written exam. *Entrance requirements:* For master's, GRE General Test. Additional exam requirements/recommendations for international students: Required—TOEFL (minimum score 550 paper-based; 80 iBT), IELTS (minimum score 6.5). *Application deadline:* For fall admission, 3/1 for domestic and international students; for spring admission, 10/15 for domestic and international students. Applications are processed on a rolling basis. Application fee: $75. Electronic applications accepted. *Expenses: Tuition:* Full-time $45,590; part-time $1161 per credit hour. *Required fees:* $782. Full-time tuition and fees vary according to degree level, program and student level. Part-time tuition and fees vary according to course load. *Financial support:* Federal Work-Study, scholarships/grants, and tuition waivers (partial) available. Support available to part-time students. Financial award application deadline: 3/1. *Unit head:* Dr. Markus Wilczek, Graduate Program Director. *Application contact:* Office of Graduate Admissions, 617-627-3395, E-mail: gradadmissions@tufts.edu.
Website: http://ase.tufts.edu/grall/

German

Université de Montréal, Faculty of Arts and Sciences, Department of Literatures and Modern Languages, Program in German Studies, Montréal, QC H3C 3J7, Canada. Offers MA. *Degree requirements:* For master's, 2 foreign languages, thesis. Electronic applications accepted.

University at Buffalo, the State University of New York, Graduate School, Graduate School of Education, Department of Learning and Instruction, Buffalo, NY 14260. Offers biology education (Ed M, Certificate); chemistry education (Ed M, Certificate); childhood education (Ed M); childhood education with bilingual extension (Ed M); curriculum, instruction and the science of learning (PhD); early childhood education (Ed M); early childhood education with bilingual extension (birth-grade 2) (Ed M); earth science education (Ed M, Certificate); education studies (Ed M); educational technology and new literacies (Certificate); elementary education (Ed D); English education (Ed M, Certificate); English for speakers of other languages (Ed M); foreign and second language education (PhD); French education (Ed M, Certificate); German education (Ed M, Certificate); gifted education (Certificate); Latin education (Ed M, Certificate); literacy specialist (Ed M); literacy teaching and learning (Certificate); mathematics education (Ed M, Certificate); music education (Ed M, Certificate); physics education (Ed M, Certificate); science and the public (Ed M); social studies education (Ed M, Certificate); Spanish education (Ed M, Certificate); special education (PhD); teaching English to speakers of other languages (Ed M). Part-time and evening/weekend programs available. Postbaccalaureate distance learning degree programs offered (no on-campus study). *Faculty:* 29 full-time (21 women), 64 part-time/adjunct (46 women). *Students:* 256 full-time (193 women), 303 part-time (222 women); includes 41 minority (21 Black or African American, non-Hispanic/Latino; 5 American Indian or Alaska Native, non-Hispanic/Latino; 13 Asian, non-Hispanic/Latino; 2 Hispanic/Latino), 84 international. Average age 30. 415 applicants, 84% accepted, 194 enrolled. In 2014, 160 master's, 20 doctorates, 32 other advanced degrees awarded. *Degree requirements:* For master's, comprehensive exam; for doctorate, thesis/dissertation, research analysis exam, research experience component. *Entrance requirements:* For master's, letters of reference; for doctorate, GRE General Test or MAT, interview, writing sample, letters of recommendation. Additional exam requirements/recommendations for international students: Required—TOEFL (minimum score 600 paper-based; 96 iBT). *Application deadline:* For fall admission, 2/1 priority date for domestic and international students; for spring admission, 11/15 priority date for domestic students, 10/1 for international students. Applications are processed on a rolling basis. Application fee: $50. Electronic applications accepted. *Financial support:* In 2014–15, 50 fellowships (averaging $12,110 per year), 32 research assistantships with tuition reimbursements (averaging $12,867 per year) were awarded; teaching assistantships, career-related internships or fieldwork, Federal Work-Study, institutionally sponsored loans, scholarships/grants, tuition waivers, and unspecified assistantships also available. Financial award application deadline: 2/28; financial award applicants required to submit FAFSA. *Faculty research:* Science assessment, foreign language teaching and learning, early learning, new literacies, gender and education. *Total annual research expenditures:* $1.3 million. *Unit head:* Dr. Suzanne Miller, Chair, 716-645-2455, Fax: 716-645-3161, E-mail: smiller@buffalo.edu. *Application contact:* Cathy Dimino, Admissions Assistant, 716-645-2110, Fax: 716-645-7937, E-mail: cadimino@buffalo.edu.
Website: http://gse.buffalo.edu/lai

The University of Alabama, Graduate School, College of Arts and Sciences, Department of Modern Languages and Classics, Tuscaloosa, AL 35487. Offers French (MA, PhD); French and Spanish (PhD); German (MA); Romance languages (MA, PhD); Spanish (MA, PhD). Part-time programs available. *Faculty:* 29 full-time (16 women). *Students:* 53 full-time (35 women), 10 part-time (6 women); includes 9 minority (3 Black or African American, non-Hispanic/Latino; 5 Hispanic/Latino; 1 Two or more races, non-Hispanic/Latino), 15 international. Average age 33. 24 applicants, 88% accepted, 14 enrolled. In 2014, 10 master's, 5 doctorates awarded. *Degree requirements:* For master's, comprehensive exam, thesis optional; for doctorate, one foreign language, thesis/dissertation, preliminary exam. *Entrance requirements:* For master's and doctorate, minimum GPA of 3.0, writing sample. Additional exam requirements/recommendations for international students: Required—TOEFL or IELTS. *Application deadline:* For fall admission, 7/6 priority date for domestic students, 1/15 priority date for international students; for spring admission, 12/5 priority date for domestic students, 6/1 priority date for international students. Applications are processed on a rolling basis. Application fee: $50 ($60 for international students). Electronic applications accepted. *Expenses:* Tuition, state resident: full-time $9826. Tuition, nonresident: full-time $24,950. *Financial support:* In 2014–15, 7 students received support, including 1 fellowship, research assistantships with full tuition reimbursements available (averaging $10,291 per year), 6 teaching assistantships with full tuition reimbursements available (averaging $10,291 per year); career-related internships or fieldwork, Federal Work-Study, institutionally sponsored loans, and scholarships/grants also available. Financial award application deadline: 7/14. *Faculty research:* Non-English literature, linguistics, culture, film. *Unit head:* Dr. Michael Picone, Chair and Professor, 205-348-5054, Fax: 205-348-2042, E-mail: mpicone@bama.ua.edu. *Application contact:* Dr. K. Barbara Fischer, Graduate Director and Associate Professor, 205-348-8465, Fax: 205-348-2042, E-mail: bfischer@bama.ua.edu.
Website: http://bama.ua.edu/~mlc

University of Alberta, Faculty of Graduate Studies and Research, Department of Modern Languages and Cultural Studies, Edmonton, AB T6G 2E1, Canada. Offers applied linguistics (Germanic, Romance, Slavic) (MA); French language, literatures and linguistics (PhD); French language, literatures, and linguistics (MA); Germanic languages, literatures and linguistics (PhD); Germanic languages, literatures, and linguistics (MA); Italian studies (MA); Slavic languages and literatures (Russian, Ukrainian) (MA, PhD); Slavic linguistics (Russian, Ukrainian) (MA, PhD); Spanish and Latin American studies (MA, PhD); Ukrainian folklore (MA, PhD). Part-time programs available. *Degree requirements:* For master's, one foreign language, thesis; for doctorate, 2 foreign languages, comprehensive exam, thesis/dissertation. *Entrance requirements:* For master's and doctorate, 1 language other than English. Additional exam requirements/recommendations for international students: Required—Michigan English Language Assessment Battery or TOEFL (minimum score 550 paper-based). Electronic applications accepted. *Faculty research:* Russian/Ukrainian studies; German studies; contemporary Latin American, French and Francophone studies; Italian studies.

The University of Arizona, College of Humanities, Department of German Studies, Tucson, AZ 85721. Offers German (MA); transcultural German (PhD). *Degree requirements:* For master's, one foreign language, comprehensive exam, oral exam; for doctorate, 2 foreign languages, comprehensive exam, thesis/dissertation, oral exam, oral defense. *Entrance requirements:* For master's, minimum major GPA of 3.3, 3 letters of recommendation, audio sample, curriculum vitae. Additional exam requirements/recommendations for international students: Required—TOEFL (minimum score 550 paper-based; 79 iBT). Electronic applications accepted. *Faculty research:* Literature, language, and foreign language pedagogy; computer-assisted text analysis.

University of Arkansas, Graduate School, J. William Fulbright College of Arts and Sciences, Department of World Languages, Literature and Cultures, Program in German, Fayetteville, AR 72701-1201. Offers MA. *Degree requirements:* For master's, variable foreign language requirement. Electronic applications accepted.

The University of British Columbia, Faculty of Arts and Faculty of Graduate Studies, Department of Central, Eastern and Northern European Studies, Vancouver, BC V6T2Z1, Canada. Offers Germanic studies (MA, PhD). Part-time programs available. *Degree requirements:* For master's, one foreign language, thesis optional, exam; for doctorate, one foreign language, comprehensive exam, thesis/dissertation. *Entrance requirements:* For master's, BA in German; for doctorate, MA in German. Additional exam requirements/recommendations for international students: Required—TOEFL (minimum score 550 paper-based; 80 iBT). Electronic applications accepted. *Faculty research:* Second language acquisition, media theory, performance theory, gender studies, cultural studies.

University of Calgary, Faculty of Graduate Studies, Faculty of Arts, Department of Linguistics, Languages and Culture, Calgary, AB T2N 1N4, Canada. Offers German (MA); linguistics (MA, PhD). *Degree requirements:* For master's, one foreign language, thesis; for doctorate, one foreign language, comprehensive exam, thesis/dissertation. *Entrance requirements:* For doctorate, MA. Additional exam requirements/recommendations for international students: Required—TOEFL (minimum score 560 paper-based). Electronic applications accepted. *Faculty research:* Theoretical linguistics, historical linguistics, language acquisition, Amerindian.

University of California, Berkeley, Graduate Division, College of Letters and Science, Department of German, Berkeley, CA 94720-1500. Offers PhD. *Degree requirements:* For doctorate, 2 foreign languages, thesis/dissertation, qualifying exam. *Entrance requirements:* For doctorate, GRE General Test, minimum GPA of 3.0, writing sample, 3 letters of recommendation. Electronic applications accepted. *Faculty research:* German literature/culture, film, Germanic linguistics, second-language acquisition.

University of California, Davis, Graduate Studies, Program in German, Davis, CA 95616. Offers MA, PhD. Terminal master's awarded for partial completion of doctoral program. *Degree requirements:* For master's, comprehensive exam (for some programs), thesis (for some programs); for doctorate, thesis/dissertation. *Entrance requirements:* For master's, GRE; for doctorate, GRE, master's degree or equivalent. Additional exam requirements/recommendations for international students: Required—TOEFL (minimum score 550 paper-based). Electronic applications accepted. *Faculty research:* Sixteenth to twentieth century medieval literature, critical theory, women's studies.

University of California, Irvine, School of Humanities, Department of European Languages and Studies, Irvine, CA 92697. Offers French (MA, PhD); German (MA, PhD). *Students:* 6 full-time (2 women); includes 1 minority (Two or more races, non-Hispanic/Latino). Average age 32. 4 applicants, 50% accepted, 1 enrolled. In 2014, 1 master's, 1 doctorate awarded. *Degree requirements:* For doctorate, thesis/dissertation. *Entrance requirements:* For master's and doctorate, GRE General Test, minimum GPA of 3.0. Additional exam requirements/recommendations for international students: Required—TOEFL (minimum score 550 paper-based). *Application deadline:* For fall admission, 1/15 for domestic and international students. Applications are processed on a rolling basis. Application fee: $90 ($110 for international students). Electronic applications accepted. *Financial support:* Fellowships, research assistantships with full tuition reimbursements, teaching assistantships, institutionally sponsored loans, traineeships, health care benefits, and unspecified assistantships available. Financial award application deadline: 3/1; financial award applicants required to submit FAFSA. *Faculty research:* Montaigne, psychoanalysis, feminism and the problem of repression, aesthetics of nationalism and the limits of culture. *Unit head:* Prof. Jane O. Newman, Chair, 949-824-6406, Fax: 949-824-1031, E-mail: jonewman@uci.edu. *Application contact:* Bindya Baliga, Graduate Program Coordinator, 949-824-7968, Fax: 949-824-6416, E-mail: bbaliga@uci.edu.
Website: http://www.humanities.uci.edu/els/

University of California, Los Angeles, Graduate Division, College of Letters and Science, Department of Germanic Languages, Program in Germanic Languages, Los Angeles, CA 90095. Offers MA, PhD. Terminal master's awarded for partial completion of doctoral program. *Degree requirements:* For master's, one foreign language, comprehensive exam or thesis; for doctorate, 2 foreign languages, thesis/dissertation, oral and written qualifying exams. *Entrance requirements:* For master's, GRE General Test, bachelor's degree; minimum undergraduate GPA of 3.0 (or its equivalent if letter grade system not used); for doctorate, GRE General Test, master's degree; minimum undergraduate GPA of 3.0 (or its equivalent if letter grade system not used). Additional exam requirements/recommendations for international students: Required—TOEFL. Electronic applications accepted.

University of Chicago, Division of the Humanities, Department of Germanic Languages and Literatures, Chicago, IL 60637. Offers PhD. *Students:* 24 full-time (10 women), 5 international. 22 applicants, 45% accepted, 2 enrolled. Terminal master's awarded for partial completion of doctoral program. *Degree requirements:* For doctorate, 2 foreign languages, thesis/dissertation. *Entrance requirements:* For doctorate, GRE General Test. Additional exam requirements/recommendations for international students: Required—TOEFL (minimum score 104 iBT), IELTS (minimum score 7). *Application deadline:* For fall admission, 12/15 for domestic and international students. Application fee: $90. Electronic applications accepted. *Expenses: Tuition:* Full-time $46,899. *Required fees:* $347. *Financial support:* Fellowships with full tuition reimbursements, teaching assistantships with full tuition reimbursements, Federal Work-Study, institutionally sponsored loans, scholarships/grants, traineeships, and health care benefits available. Financial award application deadline: 12/15; financial award applicants required to submit FAFSA. *Unit head:* Dr. David Wellberry, Chair, 773-702-8494. *Application contact:* Braden Grams, Assistant Dean of Students, Admissions and Fellowships, 773-702-1552, Fax: 773-834-9148, E-mail: humanitiesadmissions@uchicago.edu.
Website: http://german.uchicago.edu/

University of Chicago, Division of the Humanities, Master of Arts Program in the Humanities, Chicago, IL 60637. Offers art history (MA); classics (MA); comparative literature (MA); creative writing (MA); digital humanities (MA); English language and literature (MA); Germanic studies (MA); linguistics (MA); music (MA); philosophy (MA); Romance languages and literatures (MA); South Asian languages and civilizations (MA). *Students:* 83 full-time (41 women), 8 part-time (6 women); includes 14 minority (1 Black or African American, non-Hispanic/Latino; 6 Asian, non-Hispanic/Latino; 6 Hispanic/Latino; 1 Two or more races, non-Hispanic/Latino), 17 international. Average age 26. 153 applicants, 67% accepted, 80 enrolled. *Degree requirements:* For master's, thesis. *Entrance requirements:* For master's, GRE General Test. Additional exam requirements/recommendations for international students: Required—TOEFL (minimum score 600 paper-based; 104 iBT), IELTS (minimum score 7). *Application deadline:* For fall admission, 3/15 for domestic and international students. Application fee: $90. Electronic applications accepted. *Expenses: Tuition:* Full-time $46,899. *Required fees:* $347. *Financial support:* In 2014–15, 100 students received support, including 8 fellowships with partial tuition reimbursements available (averaging $12,000 per year); Federal Work-Study, institutionally sponsored loans, and tuition waivers (partial) also available. Financial award application deadline: 3/15; financial award applicants required to submit FAFSA. *Unit head:* Prof. David Wray, Director, 773-834-1201, E-mail: ma-humanities@uchicago.edu. *Application contact:* Program Coordinator, 773-834-1201,

Fax: 773-834-7526, E-mail: ma-humanities@uchicago.edu.
Website: http://maph.uchicago.edu/

University of Cincinnati, Graduate School, McMicken College of Arts and Sciences, Department of German Studies, Cincinnati, OH 45221. Offers MA, PhD. Part-time programs available. Terminal master's awarded for partial completion of doctoral program. *Degree requirements:* For master's, one foreign language, thesis or alternative; for doctorate, 3 foreign languages, thesis/dissertation. *Entrance requirements:* For master's, GRE General Test; for doctorate, GRE General Test, MA in German or equivalent. Additional exam requirements/recommendations for international students: Required—TOEFL (minimum score 560 paper-based). Electronic applications accepted. *Faculty research:* German literary culture, language and linguistics, medieval and early modern, German-Jewish literature, 20th and 21st century German literature and film.

University of Colorado Boulder, Graduate School, College of Arts and Sciences, Department of Germanic and Slavic Languages and Literature, Boulder, CO 80309. Offers German (MA). *Faculty:* 10 full-time (3 women). *Students:* 18 full-time (12 women), 1 part-time (0 women), 6 international. Average age 28. 13 applicants, 62% accepted, 7 enrolled. In 2014, 6 master's awarded. Terminal master's awarded for partial completion of doctoral program. *Degree requirements:* For master's, 2 foreign languages, comprehensive exam, thesis or alternative. *Entrance requirements:* For master's, minimum undergraduate GPA of 2.75. *Application deadline:* For fall admission, 2/1 for domestic and international students; for spring admission, 9/15 for domestic and international students. Application fee: $50 ($70 for international students). Electronic applications accepted. *Financial support:* In 2014–15, 51 students received support, including 7 fellowships (averaging $3,743 per year), 12 teaching assistantships with full and partial tuition reimbursements available (averaging $34,418 per year); institutionally sponsored loans, scholarships/grants, health care benefits, and unspecified assistantships also available. Financial award application deadline: 2/1; financial award applicants required to submit FAFSA. *Faculty research:* German language/literature, literary criticism, comparative literature language/literature, cultural history.
Website: http://gsll.colorado.edu/

University of Connecticut, Graduate School, College of Liberal Arts and Sciences, Department of Modern and Classical Languages, Field of German, Storrs, CT 06269. Offers MA, PhD. Terminal master's awarded for partial completion of doctoral program. *Degree requirements:* For master's, comprehensive exam; for doctorate, thesis/dissertation. *Entrance requirements:* For master's and doctorate, GRE General Test. Additional exam requirements/recommendations for international students: Required—TOEFL (minimum score 550 paper-based). Electronic applications accepted.

University of Delaware, College of Arts and Sciences, Department of Foreign Languages and Literatures, Newark, DE 19716. Offers foreign languages and literatures (MA), including French, German, Spanish; foreign languages pedagogy (MA), including French, German, Spanish; technical Chinese translation (MA). *Degree requirements:* For master's, one foreign language, comprehensive exam, thesis optional. *Entrance requirements:* For master's, GRE General Test, letters of recommendation, writing sample. Additional exam requirements/recommendations for international students: Required—TOEFL. Electronic applications accepted. *Faculty research:* Medieval to Modern French and Spanish literature, twentieth-century German, French, Spanish literature by women, computer-assisted instruction.

University of Florida, Graduate School, College of Liberal Arts and Sciences, Department of Languages, Literatures and Cultures, Gainesville, FL 32611-5565. Offers French and Francophone studies (MA, PhD); German (MA, PhD), including women's and gender studies (PhD); romance languages (PhD), including French and Francophone studies. *Faculty:* 25 full-time (16 women), 3 part-time/adjunct (2 women). *Students:* 15 full-time (12 women), 1 (woman) part-time; includes 3 minority (1 Black or African American, non-Hispanic/Latino; 2 Hispanic/Latino), 6 international. 19 applicants, 68% accepted, 9 enrolled. In 2014, 5 master's awarded. *Degree requirements:* For master's, comprehensive exam, thesis optional; for doctorate, one foreign language, comprehensive exam, thesis/dissertation. *Entrance requirements:* For master's and doctorate, GRE General Test, minimum GPA of 3.0. Additional exam requirements/recommendations for international students: Required—TOEFL (minimum score 550 paper-based; 80 iBT), IELTS (minimum score 6). *Application deadline:* For fall admission, 6/1 priority date for domestic students. Applications are processed on a rolling basis. Application fee: $30. Electronic applications accepted. *Financial support:* In 2014–15, 15 teaching assistantships were awarded; associateships also available. Financial award applicants required to submit FAFSA. *Faculty research:* Medieval epic, romance, and allegory; Renaissance and Baroque poetry; the eighteenth century novel; nineteenth century prose, poetry, and poetics; the twentieth century novel, theater, and poetry; the literatures of the Francophone world; French and Francophone film; the literatures in Breton and Occitan; criticism and critical theory; applied linguistics; the history of French; phonology; sociolinguistics; the structure of French; French and Haitian Creole linguistics. *Unit head:* Mary Watt, PhD, Associate Professor of Italian/Chair, 352-392-8149, Fax: 352-392-1443, E-mail: marywatt@ufl.edu. *Application contact:* Rori Bloom, PhD, French Studies Graduate Program Coordinator, 352-273-3769, E-mail: ribloom@ufl.edu.
Website: http://www.languages.ufl.edu/

University of Georgia, Franklin College of Arts and Sciences, Department of Germanic and Slavic Studies, Athens, GA 30602. Offers German (MA). *Degree requirements:* For master's, one foreign language, thesis. *Entrance requirements:* For master's, GRE General Test. Electronic applications accepted.

University of Illinois at Chicago, Graduate College, College of Liberal Arts and Sciences, School of Literatures, Cultural Studies and Linguistics, Department of Germanic Studies, Chicago, IL 60607-7128. Offers MA, PhD. PhD offered jointly with University of Illinois at Urbana–Champaign. Part-time programs available. *Faculty:* 10 full-time (9 women), 2 part-time/adjunct (both women). *Students:* 14 full-time (9 women), 5 part-time (3 women); includes 3 minority (2 Asian, non-Hispanic/Latino; 1 Two or more races, non-Hispanic/Latino), 4 international. Average age 29. 13 applicants, 77% accepted, 4 enrolled. In 2014, 3 master's, 1 doctorate awarded. Terminal master's awarded for partial completion of doctoral program. *Degree requirements:* For master's, thesis optional, exam; for doctorate, 2 foreign languages, thesis/dissertation. *Entrance requirements:* For master's and doctorate, GRE General Test, minimum GPA of 2.75. Additional exam requirements/recommendations for international students: Required—TOEFL. *Application deadline:* For fall admission, 1/1 priority date for domestic students, 1/10 priority date for international students; for spring admission, 1/1 priority date for domestic students, 7/15 for international students. Applications are processed on a rolling basis. Application fee: $60. Electronic applications accepted. *Expenses:* Tuition, state resident: full-time $11,254; part-time $468 per credit hour. Tuition, nonresident: full-time $23,252; part-time $968 per credit hour. *Required fees:* $1217 per term. Part-time tuition and fees vary according to course load, degree level and program. *Financial support:* In 2014–15, 3 fellowships with full tuition reimbursements were awarded; research assistantships with full tuition reimbursements, teaching assistantships with full tuition reimbursements, Federal Work-Study, institutionally sponsored loans, scholarships/grants, traineeships, tuition waivers (full), and unspecified assistantships also available. Support available to part-time students. Financial award application deadline: 3/1; financial award applicants required to submit FAFSA. *Faculty research:* German literature. *Unit head:* Prof. Elizabeth Loentz, Head and Director of Graduate Studies, 312-413-2370, E-mail: loentz@uic.edu.
Website: http://lcsl.las.uic.edu/germanic

University of Illinois at Urbana–Champaign, Graduate College, College of Liberal Arts and Sciences, School of Literatures, Cultures and Linguistics, Department of Germanic Languages and Literatures, Champaign, IL 61820. Offers German (MA, PhD). *Students:* 10 (7 women). Application fee: $70 ($90 for international students). *Unit head:* Craig Williams, Head, 217-333-6269, Fax: 217-244-2223, E-mail: cawllms@illinois.edu. *Application contact:* Lynn Stanke, Office Support Specialist, 217-333-6269, Fax: 217-244-3050, E-mail: stanke@illinois.edu.
Website: http://www.germanic.illinois.edu/

The University of Kansas, Graduate Studies, College of Liberal Arts and Sciences, Department of Germanic Languages and Literatures, Lawrence, KS 66045. Offers German (MA, PhD). *Faculty:* 7. *Students:* 7 full-time (5 women), 2 international. Average age 33. 2 applicants. In 2014, 2 master's, 2 doctorates awarded. *Degree requirements:* For master's, one foreign language, comprehensive exam, thesis optional, final oral exam; for doctorate, 2 foreign languages, comprehensive exam, thesis/dissertation, final oral exam. *Entrance requirements:* For master's, GRE (for fellowship funding consideration only), undergraduate major in German or equivalent; for doctorate, GRE (for fellowship funding consideration only), MA in German. Additional exam requirements/recommendations for international students: Required—TOEFL. *Application deadline:* For fall admission, 1/31 priority date for domestic students, 1/15 priority date for international students; for spring admission, 12/1 for domestic students. Applications are processed on a rolling basis. Application fee: $55 ($65 for international students). Electronic applications accepted. *Financial support:* Fellowships, research assistantships with full tuition reimbursements, teaching assistantships with full tuition reimbursements, Federal Work-Study, institutionally sponsored loans, and unspecified assistantships available. Support available to part-time students. Financial award application deadline: 1/31. *Faculty research:* Humanism, eighteenth to twentieth century literature, Germanic linguistics, German-American studies, German applied linguistics, German philology. *Unit head:* Paul Kelton, Chair, 785-864-9450, E-mail: pkelton@ku.edu. *Application contact:* Cari Ann Kreienhop, Academic Advisor, 785-864-3665, E-mail: ckreienhop@ku.edu.
Website: http://germanic.ku.edu/

University of Kentucky, Graduate School, College of Arts and Sciences, Program in German, Lexington, KY 40506-0032. Offers MA. *Degree requirements:* For master's, one foreign language, comprehensive exam, thesis optional. *Entrance requirements:* For master's, GRE General Test, minimum undergraduate GPA of 2.75. Additional exam requirements/recommendations for international students: Required—TOEFL (minimum score 550 paper-based). Electronic applications accepted. *Faculty research:* Medieval studies, literature from Enlightenment to present, literary theory, intellectual history, gender studies.

University of Lethbridge, School of Graduate Studies, Lethbridge, AB T1K 3M4, Canada. Offers addictions counseling (M Sc); agricultural biotechnology (M Sc); agricultural studies (M Sc, MA); anthropology (MA); archaeology (M Sc, MA); art (MA, MFA); biochemistry (M Sc); biological sciences (M Sc); biomolecular science (PhD); biosystems and biodiversity (PhD); Canadian studies (MA); chemistry (M Sc); computer science (M Sc); computer science and geographical information science (M Sc); counseling (MC); counseling psychology (M Ed); dramatic arts (MA); earth, space, and physical science (PhD); economics (MA); education (MA); educational leadership (M Ed); English (MA); environmental science (M Sc); evolution and behavior (PhD); exercise science (M Sc); French (MA); French/German (MA); French/Spanish (MA); general education (M Ed); geography (M Sc, MA); German (MA); health sciences (M Sc); individualized multidisciplinary (M Sc, MA); kinesiology (M Sc, MA); management (M Sc), including accounting, finance, general management, human resource management and labor relations, information systems, international management, marketing, policy and strategy; mathematics (M Sc); modern languages (MA); music (M Mus, MA); Native American studies (MA); neuroscience (M Sc, PhD); new media (MA, MFA); nursing (M Sc, MN); philosophy (MA); physics (M Sc); political science (MA); psychology (M Sc, MA); religious studies (MA); sociology (MA); theatre and dramatic arts (MFA); theoretical and computational science (PhD); urban and regional studies (MA); women and gender studies (MA). Part-time and evening/weekend programs available. *Faculty:* 358. *Students:* 445 full-time (243 women), 116 part-time (72 women). Average age 31. 351 applicants, 26% accepted, 87 enrolled. In 2014, 129 master's, 13 doctorates awarded. *Degree requirements:* For master's, thesis (for some programs); for doctorate, comprehensive exam, thesis/dissertation. *Entrance requirements:* For master's, GMAT (for M Sc in management), bachelor's degree in related field, minimum GPA of 3.0 during previous 20 graded semester courses, 2 years' teaching or related experience (M Ed); for doctorate, master's degree, minimum graduate GPA of 3.5. Additional exam requirements/recommendations for international students: Required—TOEFL. Application fee: $100 Canadian dollars. *Financial support:* Fellowships, research assistantships, teaching assistantships, scholarships/grants, health care benefits, and unspecified assistantships available. *Faculty research:* Movement and brain plasticity, gibberellin physiology, photosynthesis, carbon cycling, molecular properties of main-group ring components. *Application contact:* School of Graduate Studies, 403-329-5194, E-mail: sgsinquiries@uleth.ca.
Website: http://www.uleth.ca/graduatestudies/

The University of Manchester, School of Languages, Linguistics and Cultures, Manchester, United Kingdom. Offers Arab world studies (PhD); Chinese studies (M Phil, PhD); East Asian studies (M Phil, PhD); English language (PhD); French studies (M Phil, PhD); German studies (M Phil, PhD); interpreting studies (PhD); Italian studies (M Phil, PhD); Japanese studies (M Phil, PhD); Latin American cultural studies (M Phil, PhD); linguistics (M Phil, PhD); Middle Eastern studies (M Phil, PhD); Polish studies (M Phil, PhD); Portuguese studies (M Phil, PhD); Russian studies (M Phil, PhD); Spanish studies (M Phil, PhD); translation and intercultural studies (M Phil, PhD).

University of Manitoba, Faculty of Graduate Studies, Faculty of Arts, Department of German and Slavic Studies, Winnipeg, MB R3T 2N2, Canada. Offers German language and literature (MA); Slavic languages and literatures (MA). *Degree requirements:* For master's, one foreign language, thesis or alternative.

University of Maryland, College Park, Academic Affairs, College of Arts and Humanities, School of Languages, Literatures, and Cultures, Department of Germanic Studies, College Park, MD 20742. Offers Germanic language and literature (MA, PhD). *Degree requirements:* For master's, one foreign language, thesis optional, exams; for doctorate, 2 foreign languages, comprehensive exam, thesis/dissertation, reading exam, oral defense. *Entrance requirements:* For master's, writing sample, 3 letters of recommendation, interview; for doctorate, MA in German or related discipline. Additional exam requirements/recommendations for international students: Required—TOEFL. Electronic applications accepted. *Faculty research:* Language pedagogy, Germanic philology, medieval culture.

University of Massachusetts Amherst, Graduate School, College of Humanities and Fine Arts, Department of Languages, Literatures, and Cultures, Programs in German

and Scandinavian Studies, Amherst, MA 01003. Offers MA, PhD. Part-time programs available. *Faculty:* 11 full-time (4 women). *Students:* 13 full-time (9 women), 5 part-time (3 women); includes 3 minority (1 Black or African American, non-Hispanic/Latino; 1 Hispanic/Latino; 1 Two or more races, non-Hispanic/Latino), 3 international. Average age 34. 18 applicants, 44% accepted, 4 enrolled. In 2014, 5 master's awarded. Terminal master's awarded for partial completion of doctoral program. *Degree requirements:* For master's, thesis or alternative; for doctorate, one foreign language, comprehensive exam, thesis/dissertation. *Entrance requirements:* For master's and doctorate, writing sample in English and German. Additional exam requirements/recommendations for international students: Required—TOEFL (minimum score 550 paper-based; 80 iBT), IELTS (minimum score 6.5). *Application deadline:* For fall admission, 1/15 for domestic and international students; for spring admission, 10/1 for domestic and international students. Applications are processed on a rolling basis. Application fee: $75. Electronic applications accepted. *Expenses:* Tuition, state resident: full-time $1980; part-time $110 per credit. Tuition, nonresident: full-time $14,644; part-time $414 per credit. *Required fees:* $11,417. One-time fee: $357. *Financial support:* Fellowships with full and partial tuition reimbursements, research assistantships with full and partial tuition reimbursements, teaching assistantships with full and partial tuition reimbursements, career-related internships or fieldwork, Federal Work-Study, scholarships/grants, traineeships, health care benefits, tuition waivers (full and partial), and unspecified assistantships available. Support available to part-time students. Financial award application deadline: 2/1. *Unit head:* Dr. Frank Hugus, Acting Graduate Program Director, 413-545-2350, Fax: 413-545-6695. *Application contact:* Lindsay DeSantis, Supervisor of Admissions, 413-545-0722, Fax: 413-577-0010, E-mail: gradadm@grad.umass.edu.
Website: http://www.umass.edu/german/

University of Michigan, Horace H. Rackham School of Graduate Studies, College of Literature, Science, and the Arts, Department of Germanic Languages and Literatures, Ann Arbor, MI 48109. Offers German (AM, PhD). *Faculty:* 13 full-time (5 women), 4 part-time/adjunct (2 women). *Students:* 14 full-time (9 women); includes 2 minority (1 Hispanic/Latino; 1 Two or more races, non-Hispanic/Latino), 4 international. Average age 30. 13 applicants, 46% accepted, 2 enrolled. In 2014, 1 master's, 3 doctorates awarded. *Degree requirements:* For doctorate, one foreign language, comprehensive exam, thesis/dissertation, oral defense of dissertation, preliminary exam. *Entrance requirements:* For doctorate, GRE General Test. Additional exam requirements/recommendations for international students: Required—TOEFL (minimum score 560 paper-based). *Application deadline:* For fall and winter admission, 1/10 priority date for domestic and international students. Application fee: $75 ($90 for international students). Electronic applications accepted. *Financial support:* In 2014–15, 16 students received support, including 17 fellowships with full tuition reimbursements available (averaging $19,000 per year), 11 teaching assistantships with full tuition reimbursements available (averaging $18,971 per year); scholarships/grants, health care benefits, and tuition waivers (full) also available. *Faculty research:* German history, German literature, literary theory, film, political and social theory. *Unit head:* Prof. Johannes von Moltke, Chair, 734-764-8018, Fax: 734-763-6557, E-mail: moltke@umich.edu. *Application contact:* Jennifer White, Student Services Coordinator, 734-936-0150, Fax: 734-763-6557, E-mail: jenpatri@umich.edu.
Website: http://www.lsa.umich.edu/german

University of Minnesota, Twin Cities Campus, Graduate School, College of Liberal Arts, Department of German, Scandinavian, and Dutch, Minneapolis, MN 55455. Offers Germanic studies (MA, PhD), including German, Germanic medieval studies, Scandinavian studies (MA). Part-time programs available. Terminal master's awarded for partial completion of doctoral program. *Degree requirements:* For doctorate, 2 foreign languages, thesis/dissertation. *Entrance requirements:* For master's, GRE General Test, BA in German, Scandinavian, or equivalent; for doctorate, MA in German, Scandinavian, or equivalent. Additional exam requirements/recommendations for international students: Required—TOEFL (minimum score 550 paper-based; 79 iBT). Electronic applications accepted. *Faculty research:* Cultural studies, literary theory, feminist criticism, film, Germanic medieval studies.

University of Mississippi, Graduate School, College of Liberal Arts, Department of Modern Languages, University, MS 38677. Offers French (MA); German (MA); Spanish (MA). *Degree requirements:* For master's, thesis (for some programs). *Entrance requirements:* For master's, GRE General Test, minimum GPA of 3.0. Additional exam requirements/recommendations for international students: Required—TOEFL. Electronic applications accepted.

University of Missouri, Office of Research and Graduate Studies, College of Arts and Science, Department of German and Russian Studies, Columbia, MO 65211. Offers German (MA); Russian and Slavonic studies (MA). *Faculty:* 13 full-time (6 women), 1 part-time/adjunct (0 women). *Students:* 9 full-time (6 women), 6 part-time (3 women); includes 3 minority (2 Asian, non-Hispanic/Latino; 1 Two or more races, non-Hispanic/Latino), 6 international. Average age 25. 16 applicants, 75% accepted, 10 enrolled. In 2014, 4 master's awarded. *Entrance requirements:* For master's, GRE General Test, minimum GPA of 3.0. Additional exam requirements/recommendations for international students: Required—TOEFL (minimum score 500 paper-based; 61 iBT). *Application deadline:* For fall admission, 2/1 priority date for domestic and international students. Applications are processed on a rolling basis. Application fee: $55 ($75 for international students). Electronic applications accepted. *Financial support:* In 2014–15, 18 teaching assistantships with full tuition reimbursements were awarded; institutionally sponsored loans, health care benefits, and unspecified assistantships also available. *Faculty research:* German and Russian cultural studies including literature, film, media studies, philosophy, and the history of science. *Unit head:* Dr. Timothy Langen, Department Chair, 573-882-6167, E-mail: langent@missouri.edu. *Application contact:* Jennifer Arnold, Administrative Associate, 573-882-4328, E-mail: arnoldj@missouri.edu.
Website: http://german.missouri.edu/index.html

The University of Montana, Graduate School, College of Humanities and Sciences, Department of Modern and Classical Languages and Literatures, Missoula, MT 59812-0002. Offers French (MA); German (MA); Spanish (MA). *Degree requirements:* For master's, one foreign language. *Entrance requirements:* For master's, GRE General Test. Additional exam requirements/recommendations for international students: Required—TOEFL.

University of Nebraska–Lincoln, Graduate College, College of Arts and Sciences, Department of Modern Languages and Literatures, Lincoln, NE 68588. Offers French (MA, PhD); German (MA, PhD); Spanish (MA, PhD). *Degree requirements:* For master's, thesis optional; for doctorate, comprehensive exam, thesis/dissertation. *Entrance requirements:* For master's and doctorate, writing sample in target language. Additional exam requirements/recommendations for international students: Required—TOEFL (minimum score 550 paper-based). Electronic applications accepted. *Faculty research:* French, German, and Spanish language, literature, and culture.

University of Nevada, Reno, Graduate School, College of Liberal Arts, Department of Foreign Languages and Literatures, Reno, NV 89557. Offers French (MA); German (MA); Spanish (MA). *Degree requirements:* For master's, one foreign language, thesis optional. *Entrance requirements:* For master's, GRE General Test, minimum GPA of 2.75. Additional exam requirements/recommendations for international students: Required—TOEFL (minimum score 500 paper-based; 61 iBT), IELTS (minimum score 6). *Faculty research:* Thirteenth century mysticism, contemporary Spanish and Latin American poetry and theater, French interrelation between narration and photography, exile literature and Holocaust.

University of New Mexico, Graduate School, College of Arts and Sciences, Program in Foreign Languages and Literatures, Albuquerque, NM 87131-2039. Offers comparative literature and cultural studies (MA); French (MA); French studies (PhD); German studies (MA). Part-time programs available. *Faculty:* 12 full-time (8 women). *Students:* 25 full-time (17 women), 6 part-time (5 women); includes 3 minority (1 Black or African American, non-Hispanic/Latino; 2 Hispanic/Latino), 7 international. Average age 30. 22 applicants, 68% accepted, 10 enrolled. In 2014, 9 master's awarded. *Degree requirements:* For master's, one foreign language, thesis optional; for doctorate, 2 foreign languages, thesis/dissertation. *Entrance requirements:* For master's and doctorate, transcript, writing sample, 3 letters of recommendation. Additional exam requirements/recommendations for international students: Required—TOEFL. *Application deadline:* For fall admission, 2/1 priority date for domestic students; for spring admission, 10/1 priority date for domestic students. Application fee: $50. Electronic applications accepted. *Financial support:* In 2014–15, 28 students received support, including 1 research assistantship (averaging $4,730 per year), 23 teaching assistantships with tuition reimbursements available (averaging $10,300 per year); Federal Work-Study, health care benefits, and unspecified assistantships also available. Financial award application deadline: 3/1; financial award applicants required to submit FAFSA. *Faculty research:* German, Russian, Italian, Japanese, French, comparative literature, culture studies, classics. *Total annual research expenditures:* $4,750. *Unit head:* Dr. Walter Putnam, Chair, 505-277-4771, Fax: 505-277-3599, E-mail: wputnam@unm.edu. *Application contact:* Jacqueline Ochoa, Application and Graduation Advisor, 505-277-4471, Fax: 505-277-3599, E-mail: jochoa@unm.edu.
Website: http://www.unm.edu/~fll/

The University of North Carolina at Chapel Hill, Graduate School, College of Arts and Sciences, Department of Germanic Languages, Chapel Hill, NC 27599. Offers literature and linguistics (MA, PhD). Part-time programs available. Terminal master's awarded for partial completion of doctoral program. *Degree requirements:* For master's, comprehensive exam, thesis; for doctorate, one foreign language, comprehensive exam, thesis/dissertation. *Entrance requirements:* For master's and doctorate, GRE General Test, minimum GPA of 3.0. *Faculty research:* Gender and sexuality, literature and politics, German and Jewish culture, medieval through modern literature, Germanic linguistics.

University of Oklahoma, College of Arts and Sciences, Department of Modern Languages, Program in German, Norman, OK 73019. Offers MA, MBA/MA. Part-time programs available. *Students:* 5 full-time (4 women), 1 part-time (0 women). Average age 33. 1 applicant, 100% accepted, 1 enrolled. Terminal master's awarded for partial completion of doctoral program. *Degree requirements:* For master's, comprehensive exam (for some programs), thesis optional, two languages (one must be German). *Entrance requirements:* For master's, BA with major or minor in German. Additional exam requirements/recommendations for international students: Required—TOEFL (minimum score 79 iBT). *Application deadline:* For fall admission, 2/1 for domestic and international students; for spring admission, 10/1 for domestic and international students. Application fee: $50 ($100 for international students). Electronic applications accepted. *Expenses:* Tuition, state resident: full-time $4394; part-time $183.10 per credit hour. Tuition, nonresident: full-time $16,970; part-time $707.10 per credit hour. *Required fees:* $2892; $109.95 per credit hour. $126.50 per semester. *Financial support:* In 2014–15, 6 students received support. Scholarships/grants, health care benefits, and unspecified assistantships available. Financial award application deadline: 6/1; financial award applicants required to submit FAFSA. *Faculty research:* Goethe and German-Jewish studies, Arthurian romance, Kafka and turn-of-the-century Austria. *Unit head:* Karin Schutjer, Associate Professor and Section Head, 405-325-1907, E-mail: kschutjer@ou.edu. *Application contact:* Robert Lemon, Associate Professor, 405-325-1551, E-mail: rlemon@ou.edu.
Website: http://mlll.publishpath.com/german-ma

University of Oregon, Graduate School, College of Arts and Sciences, Department of Germanic Languages and Literatures, Eugene, OR 97403. Offers MA, PhD. *Degree requirements:* For master's, 2 foreign languages, thesis or alternative; for doctorate, 3 foreign languages, thesis/dissertation. *Entrance requirements:* For master's and doctorate, minimum GPA of 3.0. Additional exam requirements/recommendations for international students: Required—TOEFL. *Faculty research:* Medieval language and literature, eighteenth to twentieth century literature and philosophy, literary theory, feminist literature and theory, psychoanalysis and literature.

University of Pennsylvania, School of Arts and Sciences, Graduate Group in Germanic Languages, Philadelphia, PA 19104. Offers AM, PhD. *Faculty:* 19 full-time (5 women), 6 part-time/adjunct (1 woman). *Students:* 9 full-time (6 women), 2 international. 11 applicants, 45% accepted, 1 enrolled. In 2014, 3 master's, 1 doctorate awarded. Terminal master's awarded for partial completion of doctoral program. *Degree requirements:* For master's, one foreign language, thesis or alternative; for doctorate, one foreign language, comprehensive exam, thesis/dissertation. *Entrance requirements:* For master's and doctorate, GRE General Test. *Application deadline:* For fall admission, 12/1 priority date for domestic students. Application fee: $70. *Financial support:* Fellowships, teaching assistantships, institutionally sponsored loans, scholarships/grants, traineeships, health care benefits, and unspecified assistantships available. Financial award application deadline: 12/15. *Unit head:* Dr. Ralph M. Rosen, Associate Dean for Graduate Studies, 215-898-7156, Fax: 215-573-8068, E-mail: grad-dean@sas.upenn.edu. *Application contact:* Arts and Sciences Graduate Admissions, 215-573-5816, Fax: 215-573-8068, E-mail: gdasadmis@sas.upenn.edu.
Website: http://www.sas.upenn.edu/graduate-division

University of Saskatchewan, College of Graduate Studies and Research, College of Arts and Science, Department of Languages and Linguistics, Saskatoon, SK S7N 5A2, Canada. Offers MA. *Degree requirements:* For master's, 2 foreign languages, thesis. *Entrance requirements:* Additional exam requirements/recommendations for international students: Required—TOEFL (minimum score 80 iBT); Recommended—IELTS (minimum score 6.5). Electronic applications accepted.

University of South Africa, College of Human Sciences, Pretoria, South Africa. Offers adult education (M Ed); African languages (MA, PhD); African politics (MA, PhD); Afrikaans (MA, PhD); ancient history (MA, PhD); ancient Near Eastern studies (MA, PhD); anthropology (MA, PhD); applied linguistics (MA); Arabic (MA, PhD); archaeology (MA); art history (MA); Biblical archaeology (MA); Biblical studies (M Th, D Th, PhD); Christian spirituality (M Th, D Th); church history (M Th, D Th); classical studies (MA, PhD); clinical psychology (MA); communication (MA, PhD); comparative education (M Ed, Ed D); consulting psychology (D Admin, D Com, PhD); curriculum studies (M Ed, Ed D); development studies (M Admin, MA, D Admin, PhD); didactics (M Ed, Ed D); education (M Tech); education management (M Ed, Ed D); educational psychology (M Ed); English (MA); environmental education (M Ed); French (MA, PhD); German (MA, PhD); Greek (MA); guidance and counseling (M Ed); health studies (MA, PhD), including health sciences education (MA), health services management (MA), medical and surgical nursing science (critical care general) (MA), midwifery and neonatal nursing

science (MA), trauma and emergency care (MA); history (MA, PhD); history of education (Ed D); inclusive education (M Ed, Ed D); information and communications technology policy and regulation (MA); information science (MA, MIS, PhD); international politics (MA, PhD); Islamic studies (MA, PhD); Italian (MA, PhD); Judaica (MA, PhD); linguistics (MA, PhD); mathematical education (M Ed); mathematics education (MA); missiology (M Th, D Th); modern Hebrew (MA, PhD); musicology (MA, MMus, D Mus, PhD); natural science education (M Ed); New Testament (M Th, D Th); Old Testament (D Th); pastoral therapy (M Th, D Th); philosophy (MA); philosophy of education (M Ed, Ed D); politics (MA, PhD); Portuguese (MA, PhD); practical theology (M Th, D Th); psychology (MA, MS, PhD); psychology of education (M Ed, Ed D); public health (MA); religious studies (MA, D Th, PhD); Romance languages (MA); Russian (MA, PhD); Semitic languages (MA, PhD); social behavior studies in HIV/AIDS (MA); social science (mental health) (MA); social science in development studies (MA); social science in psychology (MA); social science in social work (MA); social science in sociology (MA); social work (MSW, DSW, PhD); socio-education (M Ed, Ed D); sociolinguistics (MA); sociology (MA, PhD); Spanish (MA, PhD); systematic theology (M Th, D Th); TESOL (teaching English to speakers of other languages) (MA); theological ethics (M Th, D Th); theory of literature (MA, PhD); urban ministries (D Th); urban ministry (M Th).

University of South Carolina, The Graduate School, College of Arts and Sciences, Department of Languages, Literatures, and Cultures, Columbia, SC 29208. Offers comparative literature (MA, PhD); foreign languages (MAT), including French, German, Spanish; French (MA); German (MA); Spanish (MA). MAT offered in cooperation with the College of Education. Part-time programs available. *Degree requirements:* For master's, one foreign language, comprehensive exam, thesis optional; for doctorate, 2 foreign languages, comprehensive exam, thesis/dissertation. *Entrance requirements:* For master's and doctorate, GRE General Test, writing sample. Additional exam requirements/recommendations for international students: Required—TOEFL (minimum score 75 iBT). Electronic applications accepted. *Faculty research:* Modern literature, linguistics, literature and culture, medieval literature, literary theory.

The University of Tennessee, Graduate School, College of Arts and Sciences, Department of Modern Foreign Languages and Literatures, Program in German, Knoxville, TN 37996. Offers MA. Part-time programs available. *Degree requirements:* For master's, one foreign language, thesis or alternative. *Entrance requirements:* For master's, minimum GPA of 2.7. Additional exam requirements/recommendations for international students: Required—TOEFL. Electronic applications accepted.

The University of Tennessee, Graduate School, College of Arts and Sciences, Department of Modern Foreign Languages and Literatures, Program in Modern Foreign Languages, Knoxville, TN 37996. Offers applied linguistics (PhD); French (PhD); German (PhD); Italian (PhD); Portuguese (PhD); Russian (PhD); Spanish (PhD). *Degree requirements:* For doctorate, 2 foreign languages, thesis/dissertation. *Entrance requirements:* For doctorate, minimum GPA of 2.7. Additional exam requirements/recommendations for international students: Required—TOEFL. Electronic applications accepted.

The University of Texas at Austin, Graduate School, College of Liberal Arts, Department of Germanic Studies, Austin, TX 78712-1111. Offers MA, PhD. *Degree requirements:* For master's, one foreign language, thesis or alternative; for doctorate, 2 foreign languages, thesis/dissertation. *Entrance requirements:* For master's and doctorate, GRE General Test. *Faculty research:* Germanic languages and culture (German, Austrian, Swiss, Dutch, Danish, Norwegian, Swedish, Yiddish), language pedagogy and linguistics.

The University of Toledo, College of Graduate Studies, College of Languages, Literature and Social Sciences, Department of Foreign Languages, Toledo, OH 43606-3390. Offers French (MA); German (MA); Spanish (MA). Part-time programs available. *Degree requirements:* For master's, one foreign language, comprehensive exam, comprehensive reading exam in 1 additional foreign language. *Entrance requirements:* For master's, minimum cumulative point-hour ratio of 2.7 for all previous academic work. Additional exam requirements/recommendations for international students: Required—TOEFL (minimum score 550 paper-based; 80 iBT). Electronic applications accepted.

University of Toronto, School of Graduate Studies, Faculty of Arts and Science, Department of Germanic Languages and Literatures, Toronto, ON M5S 2J7, Canada. Offers MA, PhD. Part-time programs available. *Degree requirements:* For master's, thesis optional, German language competence exam; for doctorate, thesis/dissertation, qualifying exam, thesis defense. *Entrance requirements:* For master's, 7 two-semester courses in German language and literature, 3 letters of recommendation; for doctorate, MA in German, minimum A- average, 3 letters of recommendation, writing sample, resume. Additional exam requirements/recommendations for international students: Required—TOEFL (minimum score 580 paper-based; 93 iBT), TWE (minimum score 5). Electronic applications accepted.

University of Vermont, Graduate College, College of Arts and Sciences, Department of German and Russian, Burlington, VT 05405. Offers German (MA). *Degree requirements:* For master's, one foreign language, thesis. *Entrance requirements:* For master's, GRE General Test. Additional exam requirements/recommendations for international students: Required—TOEFL (minimum score 550 paper-based; 80 iBT). Electronic applications accepted. *Faculty research:* Medieval, eighteenth, and nineteenth century literature; folklore.

University of Victoria, Faculty of Graduate Studies, Faculty of Humanities, Department of Germanic and Slavic Studies, Victoria, BC V8W 2Y2, Canada. Offers German studies (MA). Part-time programs available. *Degree requirements:* For master's, 2 foreign languages, oral defense of thesis. *Entrance requirements:* For master's, BA in German, minimum B+ average in undergraduate course work. Additional exam requirements/recommendations for international students: Required—TOEFL (minimum score 575 paper-based), IELTS (minimum score 7). Electronic applications accepted. *Faculty research:* Nineteenth and twentieth century German literature, literature and music, language acquisition, eighteenth and twentieth century drama and theater, military history.

University of Virginia, College and Graduate School of Arts and Sciences, Department of Germanic Languages and Literatures, Charlottesville, VA 22903. Offers German (MA, PhD). *Faculty:* 9 full-time (3 women), 1 (woman) part-time/adjunct. *Students:* 9 full-time (6 women), 2 international. Average age 28. 3 applicants. In 2014, 4 doctorates awarded. *Degree requirements:* For master's, one foreign language, comprehensive exam, thesis; for doctorate, one foreign language, comprehensive exam, thesis/dissertation. *Entrance requirements:* For master's, GRE General Test, 3 letters of recommendation, critical writing sample; for doctorate, GRE General Test, 3 letters of recommendation, critical writing sample. Additional exam requirements/recommendations for international students: Required—TOEFL (minimum score 600 paper-based; 90 iBT), IELTS (minimum score 7). *Application deadline:* For fall admission, 1/15 for domestic and international students. Applications are processed on a rolling basis. Application fee: $60. Electronic applications accepted. *Expenses:* Tuition, state resident: full-time $14,164; part-time $349 per credit hour. Tuition, nonresident: full-time $23,722; part-time $1300 per credit hour. *Required fees:* $2514. *Financial support:* Applicants required to submit FAFSA. *Unit head:* Jeffrey Grossman, Chair, 434-924-3530, Fax: 434-924-6700, E-mail: jg2t@virginia.edu. *Application*

contact: Benjamin Bennett, Graduate Admissions Contact, 434-924-3530, Fax: 434-924-6700, E-mail: bkb@virginia.edu.
Website: http://www.german.virginia.edu/

University of Washington, Graduate School, College of Arts and Sciences, Department of Germanics, Seattle, WA 98195. Offers MA, PhD. Part-time programs available. Terminal master's awarded for partial completion of doctoral program. *Degree requirements:* For master's, one foreign language, 2 research papers; for doctorate, 2 foreign languages, thesis/dissertation, 3 research papers. *Entrance requirements:* For master's and doctorate, GRE, minimum GPA of 3.0. Additional exam requirements/recommendations for international students: Required—TOEFL. Electronic applications accepted. *Faculty research:* Modern German literature, Germanic linguistics and philology, language pedagogy, literary theory, cinema studies.

University of Waterloo, Graduate Studies, Faculty of Arts, Department of Germanic and Slavic Studies, Waterloo, ON N2L 3G1, Canada. Offers German (MA, PhD); Russian (MA). Part-time and evening/weekend programs available. *Degree requirements:* For master's, one foreign language, thesis optional; for doctorate, 2 foreign languages, comprehensive exam, thesis/dissertation. *Entrance requirements:* For master's, honors degree, minimum B average; for doctorate, master's degree, minimum B average. Additional exam requirements/recommendations for international students: Required—TOEFL, TWE. Electronic applications accepted. *Faculty research:* Medieval theatre; history and literature; German and Russian literary relations; seventeenth, eighteenth, nineteenth, and twentieth century German literature.

University of Wisconsin–Madison, Graduate School, College of Letters and Science, Department of German, Madison, WI 53706-1380. Offers MA, PhD. Part-time programs available. Terminal master's awarded for partial completion of doctoral program. *Degree requirements:* For master's, one foreign language, comprehensive exam, thesis optional; for doctorate, 2 foreign languages, comprehensive exam, thesis/dissertation. *Entrance requirements:* For master's and doctorate, GRE. Electronic applications accepted. *Expenses:* Tuition, state resident: full-time $10,723; part-time $745 per credit. Tuition, nonresident: full-time $24,054; part-time $1578 per credit. *Required fees:* $374 per semester. Tuition and fees vary according to course load, program and reciprocity agreements. *Faculty research:* Literature, culture/linguistics, film, Dutch.

University of Wisconsin–Milwaukee, Graduate School, College of Letters and Sciences, Interdepartmental Program in Foreign Language and Literature, Milwaukee, WI 53201-0413. Offers classics and Hebrew studies (MAFLL); comparative literature (MAFLL); French and Italian (MAFLL); German (MAFLL); Slavic studies (MAFLL); translation (Certificate). Part-time programs available. *Degree requirements:* For master's, 2 foreign languages, thesis or alternative. *Entrance requirements:* Additional exam requirements/recommendations for international students: Required—TOEFL (minimum score 550 paper-based; 79 iBT), IELTS (minimum score 6.5). Electronic applications accepted.

University of Wyoming, College of Arts and Sciences, Department of Modern and Classical Languages, Program in German, Laramie, WY 82071. Offers MA. Part-time programs available. *Degree requirements:* For master's, one foreign language, thesis or alternative. *Entrance requirements:* For master's, GRE General Test, minimum GPA of 3.0. *Faculty research:* East German literature, German literature, theatre, poetry.

Vanderbilt University, Graduate School, Department of Germanic and Slavic Languages, Nashville, TN 37240-1001. Offers German (MA, MAT, PhD). *Faculty:* 6 full-time (3 women). *Students:* 23 full-time (18 women); includes 3 minority (2 Hispanic/Latino; 1 Two or more races, non-Hispanic/Latino), 9 international. Average age 32. 13 applicants, 38% accepted, 4 enrolled. In 2014, 1 master's, 2 doctorates awarded. Terminal master's awarded for partial completion of doctoral program. *Degree requirements:* For master's, one foreign language, comprehensive exam; for doctorate, 2 foreign languages, comprehensive exam, thesis/dissertation, qualifying and final exams. *Entrance requirements:* For master's and doctorate, GRE General Test, sample of written work. Additional exam requirements/recommendations for international students: Required—TOEFL (minimum score 570 paper-based; 88 iBT). *Application deadline:* For fall admission, 1/15 for domestic and international students. Electronic applications accepted. *Expenses:* Tuition: Full-time $42,768; part-time $1782 per credit hour. *Required fees:* $422. One-time fee: $30 full-time. *Financial support:* Fellowships with full and partial tuition reimbursements, teaching assistantships with full and partial tuition reimbursements, career-related internships or fieldwork, Federal Work-Study, institutionally sponsored loans, scholarships/grants, and health care benefits available. Financial award application deadline: 1/15; financial award applicants required to submit CSS PROFILE or FAFSA. *Faculty research:* 1750 to present, Middle Ages, Baroque, language pedagogy, linguistics. *Unit head:* Dr. Meike Werner, Director of Graduate Studies, 615-343-0404, Fax: 615-343-7258, E-mail: meike.werner@vanderbilt.edu. *Application contact:* Rose M. Dudney, Administrative Assistant, 615-322-2611, Fax: 615-343-7258, E-mail: rose.m.dudney@vanderbilt.edu.
Website: http://www.vanderbilt.edu/german/graduate/

Washington University in St. Louis, Graduate School of Arts and Sciences, Department of Germanic Languages and Literatures, St. Louis, MO 63130-4899. Offers PhD. Terminal master's awarded for partial completion of doctoral program. *Degree requirements:* For doctorate, thesis/dissertation. *Entrance requirements:* For doctorate, GRE General Test, sample of written work. Additional exam requirements/recommendations for international students: Required—TOEFL. Electronic applications accepted. *Faculty research:* German literature and culture from the Middle Ages through the twenty-first century, intellectual history, film and media studies, gender studies, Holocaust studies, history of the book, digital humanities.

Wayne State University, College of Liberal Arts and Sciences, Department of Classical and Modern Languages, Literatures, and Cultures, Program in German, Detroit, MI 48202. Offers MA. *Students:* 2 full-time (1 woman), 1 (woman) part-time. *Degree requirements:* For master's, one foreign language, comprehensive exam, thesis (for some programs), oral examination. *Entrance requirements:* Additional exam requirements/recommendations for international students: Required—TOEFL (minimum score 550 paper-based; 79 iBT), TWE (minimum score 5.5), Michigan English Language Assessment Battery (minimum score 85); Recommended—IELTS (minimum score 6.5). *Application deadline:* For fall admission, 6/1 priority date for domestic students, 5/1 priority date for international students; for winter admission, 10/1 priority date for domestic students, 9/1 priority date for international students; for spring admission, 2/1 priority date for domestic students, 1/1 priority date for international students. Applications are processed on a rolling basis. Electronic applications accepted. *Expenses:* Tuition, state resident: full-time $10,294; part-time $571.90 per credit hour. Tuition, nonresident: full-time $29,730; part-time $1238.75 per credit hour. *Required fees:* $1365; $43.50 per credit hour. $291.10 per semester. Tuition and fees vary according to course load and program. *Financial support:* Fellowships with tuition reimbursements, research assistantships, teaching assistantships with tuition reimbursements, scholarships/grants, health care benefits, tuition waivers (full and partial), and unspecified assistantships available. Financial award application deadline: 3/31; financial award applicants required to submit FAFSA. *Faculty research:* Exile and Holocaust, minority literature, gender studies, fairytale studies, sociolinguistics. *Unit head:* Dr. Anne Duggan, Chair, E-mail: a.duggan@wayne.edu. *Application contact:* Dr.

Anne Rothe, Professor/Advisor for MA in German Program, E-mail: rothe@wayne.edu.
Website: http://clas.wayne.edu/languages/German

Wayne State University, College of Liberal Arts and Sciences, Department of Classical and Modern Languages, Literatures, and Cultures, Program in Language Learning, Detroit, MI 48202. Offers Arabic (MALL); French (MALL); German (MALL); Italian (MALL); Spanish (MALL). *Students:* 1 (woman) full-time, 9 part-time (6 women); includes 2 minority (both Hispanic/Latino). Average age 34. In 2014, 2 master's awarded. *Degree requirements:* For master's, one foreign language, three-credit essay. *Entrance requirements:* For master's, GRE (recommended), target language proficiency, statement of purpose, three letters of recommendation, minimum GPA of 2.6 from accredited institution or 3.2 from non-accredited institution. Additional exam requirements/recommendations for international students: Required—TOEFL (minimum score 550 paper-based; 79 iBT), TWE (minimum score 5.5), Michigan English Language Assessment Battery (minimum score 85); Recommended—IELTS (minimum score 6.5). *Application deadline:* For fall admission, 6/1 priority date for domestic students, 5/1 for international students; for winter admission, 10/1 priority date for domestic students, 9/1 priority date for international students; for spring admission, 2/1 priority date for domestic students, 1/1 priority date for international students. Applications are processed on a rolling basis. Application fee: $0. Electronic applications accepted. *Expenses:* Tuition, state resident: full-time $10,294; part-time $571.90 per credit hour. Tuition, nonresident: full-time $29,730; part-time $1238.75 per credit hour. *Required fees:* $1365; $43.50 per credit hour. $291.10 per semester. Tuition and fees vary according to course load and program. *Financial support:* Scholarships/grants and unspecified assistantships available. Financial award application deadline: 3/31; financial award applicants required to submit FAFSA. *Unit head:* Dr. Anne Duggan, Department Chair, E-mail: a.duggan@wayne.edu.
Website: http://clas.wayne.edu/MALL/

Wayne State University, College of Liberal Arts and Sciences, Department of Classical and Modern Languages, Literatures, and Cultures, Program in Modern Languages, Detroit, MI 48202. Offers French (PhD); German (PhD); Spanish (PhD). *Students:* 15 full-time (13 women), 5 part-time (all women); includes 7 minority (1 Black or African American, non-Hispanic/Latino; 1 Asian, non-Hispanic/Latino; 5 Hispanic/Latino), 2 international. Average age 38. In 2014, 3 doctorates awarded. *Degree requirements:* For doctorate, 2 foreign languages, thesis/dissertation. *Entrance requirements:* For doctorate, master's degree in French, German, or Spanish, three letters of reccomendation, current curriculum vitae, writing sample such as term paper or thesis in language of specialization, statement of purpose (in English). Additional exam requirements/recommendations for international students: Required—TOEFL (minimum score 550 paper-based; 79 iBT), TWE (minimum score 5.5), Michigan English Language Assessment Battery (minimum score 85); Recommended—IELTS (minimum score 6.5). *Application deadline:* For fall admission, 6/1 priority date for domestic students, 5/1 priority date for international students; for winter admission, 10/1 priority date for domestic and international students; for spring admission, 2/1 priority date for domestic students, 1/1 priority date for international students. Applications are processed on a rolling basis. Application fee: $0. Electronic applications accepted. *Expenses:* Tuition, state resident: full-time $10,294; part-time $571.90 per credit hour. Tuition, nonresident: full-time $29,730; part-time $1238.75 per credit hour. *Required fees:* $1365; $43.50 per credit hour. $291.10 per semester. Tuition and fees vary according to course load and program. *Financial support:* In 2014–15, 12 students received support. Fellowships with tuition reimbursements available, teaching assistantships, scholarships/grants, health care benefits, and unspecified assistantships available. Financial award application deadline: 3/31; financial award applicants required to submit FAFSA. *Unit head:* Dr. Anne Duggan, Department Chair, E-mail: a.duggan@wayne.edu. *Application contact:* Dr. Michael Giordano, Professor and Graduate Director, 313-577-3002, E-mail: aa2144@wayne.edu.
Website: http://clasweb.clas.wayne.edu/languages/ModernLanguages(PhD)

Western Kentucky University, Graduate Studies, Potter College of Arts and Letters, Department of Modern Languages, Bowling Green, KY 42101. Offers French (MA Ed); German (MA Ed); Spanish (MA Ed).

Yale University, Graduate School of Arts and Sciences, Department of German, New Haven, CT 06520. Offers PhD. Terminal master's awarded for partial completion of doctoral program. *Degree requirements:* For doctorate, 3 foreign languages, thesis/dissertation. *Entrance requirements:* For doctorate, GRE General Test.

Hispanic and Latin American Languages

Boston University, Graduate School of Arts and Sciences, Department of Romance Studies, Boston, MA 02215. Offers French language and literature (MA, PhD); Hispanic language and literatures (MA, PhD). *Students:* 39 full-time (29 women), 1 part-time (0 women); includes 5 minority (1 Black or African American, non-Hispanic/Latino; 4 Hispanic/Latino), 12 international. Average age 32. 81 applicants, 25% accepted, 10 enrolled. In 2014, 2 master's, 4 doctorates awarded. Terminal master's awarded for partial completion of doctoral program. *Degree requirements:* For master's, one foreign language, comprehensive exam; for doctorate, 2 foreign languages, comprehensive exam, thesis/dissertation. *Entrance requirements:* For master's and doctorate, GRE General Test, sample of written work, 3 letters of recommendation. Additional exam requirements/recommendations for international students: Required—TOEFL (minimum score 84 iBT). *Application deadline:* For fall admission, 1/15 for domestic and international students. Application fee: $80. Electronic applications accepted. *Expenses: Tuition:* Full-time $45,686; part-time $1428 per credit hour. *Required fees:* $660; $60 per semester. Tuition and fees vary according to program. *Financial support:* In 2014–15, 33 students received support, including 7 fellowships with full tuition reimbursements available (averaging $20,500 per year), 24 teaching assistantships with full tuition reimbursements available (averaging $20,500 per year); research assistantships, Federal Work-Study, scholarships/grants, and health care benefits also available. Support available to part-time students. Financial award application deadline: 1/15. *Unit head:* Nancy Harrowitz, Chairman, 617-353-6225, Fax: 617-353-6246, E-mail: nharrow@bu.edu. *Application contact:* Deanna Wong, Administrative Assistant, 617-353-2641, Fax: 617-353-6246, E-mail: dswong@bu.edu.
Website: http://www.bu.edu/rs/

Brigham Young University, Graduate Studies, College of Humanities, Department of Spanish and Portuguese, Provo, UT 84602. Offers Portuguese (MA), including Luso-Brazilian literature, Portuguese linguistics, Portuguese pedagogy; Spanish (MA), including Hispanic linguistics, Hispanic literatures, Spanish pedagogy. *Faculty:* 29 full-time (5 women). *Students:* 16 full-time (6 women), 27 part-time (15 women); includes 16 minority (all Hispanic/Latino). Average age 34. 20 applicants, 55% accepted, 9 enrolled. In 2014, 15 master's awarded. *Degree requirements:* For master's, one foreign language, comprehensive exam, thesis, 1 semester of teaching. *Entrance requirements:* For master's, GRE, minimum GPA of 3.5 in Spanish or Portuguese, 3.3 overall. Additional exam requirements/recommendations for international students: Required—TOEFL (minimum score 580 paper-based; 85 iBT). *Application deadline:* For fall admission, 2/1 for domestic and international students. Application fee: $50. Electronic applications accepted. *Expenses: Tuition:* Full-time $6310; part-time $371 per credit hour. Tuition and fees vary according to program and student's religious affiliation. *Financial support:* In 2014–15, 25 students received support, including 4 research assistantships with partial tuition reimbursements available (averaging $2,500 per year), 69 teaching assistantships with partial tuition reimbursements available (averaging $3,500 per year); institutionally sponsored loans, scholarships/grants, tuition waivers (partial), and unspecified assistantships also available. Support available to part-time students. Financial award application deadline: 7/1. *Faculty research:* Mexican prose; Latin American theater, literature, phonetics, and phonology; pedagogy; classical Portuguese literature; Peninsular prose and theater. *Unit head:* Dr. David P. Laraway, Chair, 801-422-3807, Fax: 801-422-0628, E-mail: david_laraway@byu.edu. *Application contact:* Jessica C. Erickson, Graduate Secretary, 801-422-2196, Fax: 801-422-0628, E-mail: jessica_erickson@byu.edu.
Website: http://spanport.byu.edu/

California State University, San Marcos, College of Humanities, Arts, Behavioral and Social Sciences, Program in Spanish, San Marcos, CA 92096-0001. Offers Hispanic cultures and society (MA); Hispanic language and linguistics (MA); Hispanic literatures and literary theory (MA). Part-time and evening/weekend programs available. *Students:* 1 (woman) full-time, 14 part-time (all women); includes 12 minority (all Hispanic/Latino). Average age 35. *Degree requirements:* For master's, 2 foreign languages, exam. *Entrance requirements:* For master's, GRE General Test, minimum GPA of 3.0 overall and in upper-division Spanish courses, official transcripts, three letters of recommendation, 750-word statement of purpose (in English), academic writing sample (in Spanish). Additional exam requirements/recommendations for international students: Required—TOEFL (minimum score 500 paper-based), TWE (minimum score 4.5). *Application deadline:* For fall admission, 3/15 priority date for domestic students. Applications are processed on a rolling basis. Application fee: $55. Electronic applications accepted. *Expenses:* Tuition, state resident: full-time $6738. *Required fees:* $1692. Tuition and fees vary according to program. *Financial support:* Teaching assistantships available. *Faculty research:* Applied linguistics, Golden Age Spanish literature, Latin American literature, poetry, Chicano studies. *Unit head:* Dr. Michael Hughes, Department Chair, 760-750-8076, E-mail: mhughes@csusm.edu. *Application contact:* Admissions, 760-750-4848, Fax: 760-750-3248, E-mail: apply@csusm.edu.
Website: http://www.csusm.edu/modernlanguages/masters_degree/

Central Connecticut State University, School of Graduate Studies, College of Liberal Arts and Social Sciences, Department of Modern Languages, Program in Modern Language, New Britain, CT 06050-4010. Offers French (MA, Certificate); German (Certificate); Italian (Certificate); modern language (MA); Spanish language and Hispanic culture (MA). Part-time and evening/weekend programs available. *Students:* 4 full-time (3 women), 28 part-time (22 women); includes 13 minority (1 Black or African American, non-Hispanic/Latino; 12 Hispanic/Latino), 1 international. Average age 34. 9 applicants, 100% accepted, 7 enrolled. In 2014, 8 master's, 5 other advanced degrees awarded. *Degree requirements:* For master's, one foreign language, comprehensive exam, thesis or alternative; for Certificate, qualifying exam. *Entrance requirements:* For master's, minimum undergraduate GPA of 2.7, 24 credits of undergraduate courses in each language in which graduate work will be undertaken. Additional exam requirements/recommendations for international students: Required—TOEFL (minimum score 550 paper-based; 79 iBT). *Application deadline:* For fall admission, 6/1 for domestic students, 5/1 for international students; for spring admission, 11/1 for domestic and international students. Applications are processed on a rolling basis. Application fee: $50. Electronic applications accepted. *Expenses: Tuition, area resident:* Full-time $5730; part-time $534 per credit. Tuition, state resident: full-time $8596; part-time $534 per credit. Tuition, nonresident: full-time $15,964; part-time $548 per credit. *Required fees:* $4211; $215 per credit. *Faculty research:* Twentieth-century French theater, seventeenth-century French literature, French Middle Ages. *Unit head:* Dr. Lilian Uribe, Chair, 860-832-2875, E-mail: uribe@ccsu.edu. *Application contact:* Patricia Gardner, Associate Director of Graduate Studies, 860-832-2350, Fax: 860-832-2362, E-mail: graduateadmissions@ccsu.edu.

Cornell University, Graduate School, Graduate Fields of Arts and Sciences, Field of Romance Studies, Ithaca, NY 14853-0001. Offers French linguistics (PhD); French literature (PhD); Hispanic literature (PhD); Italian linguistics (PhD); Italian literature (PhD); Romance linguistics (PhD); Spanish linguistics (PhD). *Degree requirements:* For doctorate, 2 foreign languages, comprehensive exam, thesis/dissertation. *Entrance requirements:* For doctorate, GRE General Test, sample of written work, 3 letters of recommendation. Additional exam requirements/recommendations for international students: Required—TOEFL (minimum score 550 paper-based; 77 iBT). Electronic applications accepted. *Faculty research:* Literary theory, Hispanic studies, French studies, gender studies.

Eastern Michigan University, Graduate School, College of Arts and Sciences, Department of World Languages, Ypsilanti, MI 48197. Offers foreign languages (MA, Graduate Certificate), including French (MA), German (MA), German for business (Graduate Certificate), Hispanic language and cultures (Graduate Certificate), Japanese business practices (Graduate Certificate), Spanish (MA). Part-time and evening/weekend programs available. Postbaccalaureate distance learning degree programs offered (minimal on-campus study). *Faculty:* 20 full-time (14 women). *Students:* 5 full-time (4 women), 46 part-time (35 women); includes 10 minority (2 Black or African American, non-Hispanic/Latino; 2 Asian, non-Hispanic/Latino; 6 Hispanic/Latino), 4 international. Average age 33. 46 applicants, 74% accepted, 21 enrolled. In 2014, 23 master's, 1 other advanced degree awarded. *Degree requirements:* For master's, one foreign language. *Entrance requirements:* Additional exam requirements/recommendations for international students: Required—TOEFL. *Application deadline:* Applications are processed on a rolling basis. Application fee: $45. *Financial support:* Fellowships, research assistantships with full tuition reimbursements, teaching assistantships with full tuition reimbursements, career-related internships or fieldwork, Federal Work-Study, institutionally sponsored loans, scholarships/grants, tuition waivers (partial), and unspecified assistantships available. Support available to part-time

students. Financial award applicants required to submit FAFSA. *Unit head:* Dr. Rosemary Weston-Gil, Department Head, 734-487-0130, Fax: 734-487-3411, E-mail: rweston3@emich.edu.

The Graduate Center, City University of New York, Graduate Studies, Program in Hispanic and Luso-Brazilian Literatures and Languages, New York, NY 10016-4039. Offers PhD. *Degree requirements:* For doctorate, 2 foreign languages, thesis/dissertation. *Entrance requirements:* For doctorate, GRE General Test. Additional exam requirements/recommendations for international students: Required—TOEFL. Electronic applications accepted.

Indiana University Bloomington, University Graduate School, College of Arts and Sciences, Department of Spanish and Portuguese, Bloomington, IN 47405. Offers Portuguese (MA, PhD); Spanish (MA, PhD), including Hispanic linguistics, Hispanic literatures. *Faculty:* 22 full-time. *Students:* 86 full-time (53 women), 1 (woman) part-time; includes 20 minority (18 Hispanic/Latino; 2 Two or more races, non-Hispanic/Latino), 16 international. Average age 31. 64 applicants, 30% accepted, 15 enrolled. In 2014, 13 master's, 12 doctorates awarded. *Degree requirements:* For master's, one foreign language, comprehensive exam, thesis (optional for Portuguese); for doctorate, 2 foreign languages, comprehensive exam, thesis/dissertation. *Entrance requirements:* For master's, GRE General Test, bachelor's degree in Portuguese or Spanish, minimum GPA of 3.0; for doctorate, GRE General Test, master's degree in Portuguese or Spanish, minimum GPA of 3.0. Additional exam requirements/recommendations for international students: Required—TOEFL (minimum score 79 iBT). *Application deadline:* For fall admission, 1/15 priority date for domestic students, 12/1 priority date for international students. Application fee: $55 ($65 for international students). Electronic applications accepted. *Financial support:* Fellowships with full tuition reimbursements, research assistantships, teaching assistantships with full tuition reimbursements, scholarships/grants, health care benefits, and unspecified assistantships available. Financial award application deadline: 1/15. *Faculty research:* Spanish American literature, Spanish peninsular literature, Hispanic linguistics, Luso-Brazilian studies, Catalan studies. *Unit head:* Steven Wagschal, Chair, 812-855-8498, E-mail: swagscha@indiana.edu. *Application contact:* Patrick Dove, Director of Graduate Studies, 812-855-9194, E-mail: pdove@indiana.edu.
Website: http://www.indiana.edu/~spanport/

Indiana University of Pennsylvania, School of Graduate Studies and Research, College of Humanities and Social Sciences, Department of Foreign Languages, Program in Spanish/Hispanic Literatures and Cultures, Indiana, PA 15705-1087. Offers MA. *Faculty:* 4 full-time (0 women). *Students:* 5 applicants, 40% accepted, 1 enrolled. In 2014, 1 master's awarded. Application fee: $50. *Financial support:* Research assistantships with full and partial tuition reimbursements available. *Unit head:* Dr. Sean McDaniel, Chairperson, 724-357-7532, E-mail: mcdaniel@iup.edu.

Michigan State University, The Graduate School, College of Arts and Letters, Department of Spanish and Portuguese, East Lansing, MI 48824. Offers applied Spanish linguistics (MA); Hispanic cultural studies (PhD); Hispanic literatures (MA). *Entrance requirements:* Additional exam requirements/recommendations for international students: Required—TOEFL. Electronic applications accepted.

Queens College of the City University of New York, Division of Graduate Studies, Arts and Humanities Division, Department of Hispanic Languages and Literatures, Flushing, NY 11367-1597. Offers Spanish (MA). Part-time and evening/weekend programs available. *Degree requirements:* For master's, 2 foreign languages, comprehensive exam, thesis or alternative. *Entrance requirements:* For master's, minimum GPA of 3.0. Additional exam requirements/recommendations for international students: Required—TOEFL.

Stony Brook University, State University of New York, Graduate School, College of Arts and Sciences, Department of Hispanic Languages and Literature, Stony Brook, NY 11794. Offers MA, PhD. Evening/weekend programs available. *Faculty:* 13 full-time (8 women), 1 (woman) part-time/adjunct. *Students:* 37 full-time (25 women), 13 part-time (8 women); includes 26 minority (3 Black or African American, non-Hispanic/Latino; 23 Hispanic/Latino), 13 international. Average age 36. 40 applicants, 65% accepted, 7 enrolled. In 2014, 7 master's, 1 doctorate awarded. *Degree requirements:* For master's, one foreign language, thesis or alternative; for doctorate, 2 foreign languages, thesis/dissertation. *Entrance requirements:* For master's, GRE General Test, BA in Spanish; for doctorate, GRE General Test, MA in Spanish. Additional exam requirements/recommendations for international students: Required—TOEFL. *Application deadline:* For fall admission, 1/15 for domestic students; for spring admission, 10/1 for domestic students. Application fee: $100. *Expenses:* Expenses: Contact institution. *Financial support:* In 2014–15, 19 teaching assistantships were awarded; fellowships, research assistantships, tuition waivers, and unspecified assistantships also available. *Faculty research:* Spanish language and literature. *Unit head:* Dr. Kathleen M. Vernon, Chair, 631-632-9668, E-mail: roncero@oponline.net. *Application contact:* Joann Broderick, Director of Graduate Studies, 631-632-9669, Fax: 631-632-9724, E-mail: joann.broderick@stonybrook.edu.
Website: http://www.sunysb.edu/hispanic/

Université de Montréal, Faculty of Arts and Sciences, Department of Literatures and Modern Languages, Montréal, QC H3C 3J7, Canada. Offers German literature (PhD); German studies (MA); Hispanic literature (PhD); Hispanic studies (MA). Terminal master's awarded for partial completion of doctoral program. *Degree requirements:* For master's, 2 foreign languages, thesis; for doctorate, 2 foreign languages, thesis/dissertation, general exam. Electronic applications accepted.

University of California, Berkeley, Graduate Division, College of Letters and Science, Department of Hispanic Languages and Literature, Berkeley, CA 94720-1500. Offers PhD. *Degree requirements:* For doctorate, thesis/dissertation, qualifying exam. *Entrance requirements:* For doctorate, GRE General Test, minimum GPA of 3.0, 3 letters of recommendation. Additional exam requirements/recommendations for international students: Required—TOEFL (minimum score 570 paper-based).

University of California, Los Angeles, Graduate Division, College of Letters and Science, Department of Spanish and Portuguese, Program in Hispanic Languages and Literature, Los Angeles, CA 90095. Offers PhD. *Degree requirements:* For doctorate, 2 foreign languages, thesis/dissertation, oral and written qualifying exams. *Entrance requirements:* For doctorate, GRE General Test, master's degree; minimum undergraduate GPA of 3.0 (or its equivalent if letter grade system not used); writing sample. Additional exam requirements/recommendations for international students: Required—TOEFL. Electronic applications accepted.

University of California, Santa Barbara, Graduate Division, College of Letters and Sciences, Division of Humanities and Fine Arts, Department of Spanish and Portuguese, Santa Barbara, CA 93106-4150. Offers Hispanic languages and literatures (PhD), including European medieval studies, feminist studies, Hispanic linguistics, Hispanic literature, Luso-Brazilian literature; Hispanic linguistics (MA); Luso-Brazilian literature (MA); Spanish or Spanish-American literature (MA); MA/PhD. Spanish Language Institute available during Summer session. Terminal master's awarded for partial completion of doctoral program. *Degree requirements:* For master's, 2 foreign languages, comprehensive exam (for some programs), thesis optional; for doctorate, 3 foreign languages, comprehensive exam, thesis/dissertation. *Entrance requirements:*

For master's and doctorate, GRE. Additional exam requirements/recommendations for international students: Required—TOEFL (minimum score 550 paper-based; 80 iBT), IELTS (minimum score 7). Electronic applications accepted. *Faculty research:* Nineteenth-century Spanish and Portuguese literature, Spanish and Spanish-American literature, nineteenth- and twentieth-century Portuguese and Brazilian literatures, Hispanic linguistics, Catalan language and culture.

University of Colorado Boulder, Graduate School, College of Arts and Sciences, Department of Spanish and Portuguese, Boulder, CO 80309. Offers Hispanic linguistics (MA); medieval and early modern Hispanic literatures (PhD); Spanish and Spanish American literatures (MA, PhD). *Faculty:* 14 full-time (6 women). *Students:* 36 full-time (23 women), 1 (woman) part-time; includes 9 minority (1 American Indian or Alaska Native, non-Hispanic/Latino; 8 Hispanic/Latino), 12 international. Average age 31. 42 applicants, 17% accepted, 6 enrolled. In 2014, 7 master's, 2 doctorates awarded. Terminal master's awarded for partial completion of doctoral program. *Degree requirements:* For master's, one foreign language, comprehensive exam, thesis or alternative; for doctorate, 2 foreign languages, thesis/dissertation. *Entrance requirements:* For master's, minimum undergraduate GPA of 2.75. *Application deadline:* For fall admission, 12/19 for domestic and international students. Applications are processed on a rolling basis. Application fee: $50 ($70 for international students). Electronic applications accepted. *Financial support:* In 2014–15, 89 students received support, including 6 fellowships (averaging $948 per year), 33 teaching assistantships with full and partial tuition reimbursements available (averaging $38,597 per year); institutionally sponsored loans, scholarships/grants, health care benefits, and unspecified assistantships also available. Financial award application deadline: 12/15; financial award applicants required to submit FAFSA. *Faculty research:* Literary criticism, Spanish language literature, cultural history, Iberian studies. *Total annual research expenditures:* $37,611.
Website: http://spanish.colorado.edu/

University of Illinois at Chicago, Graduate College, College of Liberal Arts and Sciences, School of Literatures, Cultural Studies and Linguistics, Chicago, IL 60607-7128. Offers French and Francophone studies (MA); Germanic studies (MA); Hispanic and Italian studies (MAT, PhD), including Hispanic linguistics (PhD), Hispanic literary and cultural studies (PhD), teaching of Spanish (MAT); linguistics (MA), including teaching English to speakers of other languages/applied linguistics; Slavic and Baltic languages and literatures (MA), including Slavic studies (MA, PhD); Slavic and Baltic languages and literatures (PhD), including Slavic studies (MA, PhD). Part-time programs available. *Faculty:* 64 full-time (48 women), 80 part-time/adjunct (55 women). *Students:* 96 full-time (63 women), 31 part-time (18 women); includes 30 minority (1 Black or African American, non-Hispanic/Latino; 5 Asian, non-Hispanic/Latino; 22 Hispanic/Latino; 2 Two or more races, non-Hispanic/Latino), 38 international. Average age 31. 127 applicants, 64% accepted, 40 enrolled. In 2014, 31 master's, 4 doctorates awarded. Terminal master's awarded for partial completion of doctoral program. *Degree requirements:* For master's, one foreign language, exam. *Entrance requirements:* For master's, minimum GPA of 2.75. Additional exam requirements/recommendations for international students: Required—TOEFL. *Application deadline:* For fall admission, 1/1 priority date for domestic and international students. Applications are processed on a rolling basis. Application fee: $60. Electronic applications accepted. *Expenses:* Tuition, state resident: full-time $11,254; part-time $468 per credit hour. Tuition, nonresident: full-time $23,252; part-time $968 per credit hour. *Required fees:* $1217 per term. Part-time tuition and fees vary according to course load, degree level and program. *Financial support:* In 2014–15, 2 fellowships with full tuition reimbursements were awarded; research assistantships with full tuition reimbursements, teaching assistantships with full tuition reimbursements, career-related internships or fieldwork, Federal Work-Study, scholarships/grants, traineeships, tuition waivers (full), and unspecified assistantships also available. Financial award application deadline: 3/15; financial award applicants required to submit FAFSA. *Faculty research:* International studies, religious (Catholic, Jewish) studies, moving image arts. *Unit head:* Prof. Imke Meyer, Director, 312-413-2137, Fax: 312-413-1044, E-mail: ixmeyer@uic.edu.
Website: http://lcsl.las.uic.edu/lcsl

University of Massachusetts Amherst, Graduate School, College of Humanities and Fine Arts, Department of Languages, Literatures, and Cultures, Program in Spanish and Portuguese Studies, Amherst, MA 01003. Offers Hispanic literatures, cultures and linguistics (MA, PhD); teaching Spanish (MAT). Part-time programs available. *Faculty:* 13 full-time (5 women). *Students:* 30 full-time (23 women), 17 part-time (10 women); includes 11 minority (1 Black or African American, non-Hispanic/Latino; 1 Asian, non-Hispanic/Latino; 9 Hispanic/Latino), 25 international. Average age 33. 55 applicants, 29% accepted, 11 enrolled. In 2014, 7 master's, 3 doctorates awarded. Terminal master's awarded for partial completion of doctoral program. *Degree requirements:* For master's, one foreign language, thesis or alternative; for doctorate, 2 foreign languages, comprehensive exam, thesis/dissertation. *Entrance requirements:* For master's and doctorate, GRE General Test, sample academic term paper. Additional exam requirements/recommendations for international students: Required—TOEFL (minimum score 550 paper-based; 80 iBT), IELTS (minimum score 6.5). *Application deadline:* For fall admission, 2/1 for domestic and international students. Applications are processed on a rolling basis. Application fee: $75. Electronic applications accepted. *Expenses:* Tuition, state resident: full-time $1980; part-time $110 per credit. Tuition, nonresident: full-time $14,644; part-time $414 per credit. *Required fees:* $11,417. One-time fee: $357. *Financial support:* Fellowships with full and partial tuition reimbursements, research assistantships with full and partial tuition reimbursements, teaching assistantships with full and partial tuition reimbursements, career-related internships or fieldwork, Federal Work-Study, scholarships/grants, traineeships, health care benefits, tuition waivers (full and partial), and unspecified assistantships available. Support available to part-time students. Financial award application deadline: 2/1; financial award applicants required to submit FAFSA. *Unit head:* Dr. Albert Lloret, Graduate Program Director, 413-545-0544, Fax: 413-545-3178. *Application contact:* Lindsay DeSantis, Supervisor of Admissions, 413-545-0722, Fax: 413-577-0010, E-mail: gradadm@grad.umass.edu.
Website: http://www.umass.edu/spanport/

University of Minnesota, Twin Cities Campus, Graduate School, College of Liberal Arts, Department of Spanish and Portuguese Studies, Minneapolis, MN 55455-0213. Offers Hispanic and Lusophone literatures, cultures and linguistics (PhD); Hispanic linguistics (MA); Hispanic literature (MA); Lusophone literature (MA). *Degree requirements:* For master's, 2 foreign languages, comprehensive exam, thesis or alternative; for doctorate, 2 foreign languages, comprehensive exam, thesis/dissertation. *Entrance requirements:* For master's and doctorate, GRE General Test, samples of written work, 3 letters of recommendation, voice sample, statement of purpose. Additional exam requirements/recommendations for international students: Required—TOEFL (minimum score 550 paper-based; 79 iBT). Electronic applications accepted. *Faculty research:* Sociohistorical approaches to literature and culture, feminist studies, literary theory, ideologies and literature, pragmatics and sociolinguistics.

The University of North Carolina at Greensboro, Graduate School, College of Arts and Sciences, Department of Languages, Literatures, and Cultures, Program in Spanish, Greensboro, NC 27412-5001. Offers advanced Spanish language and

Hispanic cultural studies (Certificate); Spanish (MA). *Degree requirements:* For master's, one foreign language, comprehensive exam, thesis or alternative. *Entrance requirements:* For master's, GRE General Test, 3-5 minute tape demonstrating foreign language proficiency, composition in Spanish, sample paper in English. Additional exam requirements/recommendations for international students: Required—TOEFL. Electronic applications accepted.

University of Pittsburgh, Dietrich School of Arts and Sciences, Department of Hispanic Languages and Literatures, Pittsburgh, PA 15260. Offers MA, PhD. *Faculty:* 10 full-time (2 women). *Students:* 45 full-time (21 women); includes 9 minority (1 Black or African American, non-Hispanic/Latino; 8 Hispanic/Latino), 28 international. Average age 34. 48 applicants, 25% accepted, 6 enrolled. In 2014, 3 master's, 8 doctorates awarded. Terminal master's awarded for partial completion of doctoral program. *Degree requirements:* For master's, 2 foreign languages, comprehensive exam (for some programs), thesis or alternative, research paper; for doctorate, 2 foreign languages, comprehensive exam, thesis/dissertation. *Entrance requirements:* Additional exam requirements/recommendations for international students: Required—TOEFL (minimum score 600 paper-based; 90 iBT). *Application deadline:* For fall admission, 1/15 priority date for domestic and international students. Application fee: $50. Electronic applications accepted. *Expenses:* Tuition, state resident: full-time $20,742; part-time $838 per credit. Tuition, nonresident: full-time $33,960; part-time $1389 per credit. *Required fees:* $800; $205 per term. Tuition and fees vary according to program. *Financial support:* In 2014–15, 34 students received support, including 5 fellowships with full tuition reimbursements available (averaging $19,615 per year), 29 teaching assistantships with full tuition reimbursements available (averaging $17,010 per year); scholarships/grants, health care benefits, and tuition waivers (partial) also available. Financial award application deadline: 1/15. *Faculty research:* Latin American, Luso-Brazilian, and peninsular literature; cultural theory; cultural studies; race, ethnicity, and post-colonial studies; gender and sexuality studies; environment and literature; social conflict and violence, Chicano and U.S. Latino literature. *Unit head:* Dr. Daniel Balderston, Chair, 412-628-0279, Fax: 412-624-8505, E-mail: dbalder@pitt.edu. *Application contact:* Patrick Fogarty, Graduate Administrator, 412-624-5221, Fax: 412-624-6263, E-mail: pmf23@pitt.edu.
Website: http://www.hispanic.pitt.edu

The University of Texas at Austin, Graduate School, College of Liberal Arts, Department of Spanish and Portuguese, Austin, TX 78712-1111. Offers Hispanic linguistics (MA, PhD); Hispanic literature (MA, PhD); Ibero-romance philology and linguistics (PhD); Luso-Brazilian literature (MA, PhD). *Degree requirements:* For master's, 2 foreign languages, thesis or alternative; for doctorate, 3 foreign languages, thesis/dissertation. *Entrance requirements:* For master's and doctorate, GRE General Test. Electronic applications accepted.

University of Washington, Graduate School, College of Arts and Sciences, Division of Spanish and Portuguese Studies, Seattle, WA 98195. Offers Hispanic literary and cultural studies (MA). *Degree requirements:* For master's, 2 foreign languages, thesis optional, exam. *Entrance requirements:* For master's, GRE General Test, minimum GPA of 3.0. Additional exam requirements/recommendations for international students: Required—TOEFL. Electronic applications accepted. *Faculty research:* Medieval through modern Spanish literature and film, Latin American literature, poetry and essay, pan-Hispanic ballad, Hispanic cultural studies, second language acquisition and applied linguistics.

Italian

Binghamton University, State University of New York, Graduate School, School of Arts and Sciences, Department of Romance Languages and Literatures, Program in Italian, Vestal, NY 13850. Offers MA. *Students:* 1 (woman) full-time, 2 part-time (1 woman). Average age 38. 2 applicants, 100% accepted, 1 enrolled. *Degree requirements:* For master's, one foreign language, comprehensive exam, thesis or alternative. *Entrance requirements:* For master's, GRE General Test. Additional exam requirements/recommendations for international students: Required—TOEFL (minimum score 550 paper-based; 80 iBT). *Application deadline:* For fall admission, 2/15 priority date for domestic and international students; for spring admission, 11/15 priority date for domestic and international students. Applications are processed on a rolling basis. Application fee: $75. Electronic applications accepted. *Expenses:* Tuition, state resident: full-time $7776; part-time $432 per credit. Tuition, nonresident: full-time $15,138; part-time $841 per credit. *Required fees:* $1754; $213 per credit. Tuition and fees vary according to degree level and program. *Financial support:* Career-related internships or fieldwork, Federal Work-Study, institutionally sponsored loans, scholarships/grants, health care benefits, and unspecified assistantships available. Financial award application deadline: 2/15; financial award applicants required to submit FAFSA. *Unit head:* Dr. Antonio Sobejano-Moran, Chairperson, 607-777-2548, E-mail: sobe@binghamton.edu. *Application contact:* Kishan Zuber, Recruiting and Admissions Coordinator, 607-777-2151, Fax: 607-777-2501, E-mail: kzuber@binghamton.edu.

Boston College, Graduate School of Arts and Sciences, Department of Romance Languages and Literatures, Chestnut Hill, MA 02467-3800. Offers French (MA); Italian (MA); Spanish (MA). Part-time programs available. *Faculty:* 21 full-time. *Students:* 34 full-time (30 women); includes 5 minority (2 Asian, non-Hispanic/Latino; 3 Hispanic/Latino), 8 international. 55 applicants, 33% accepted, 10 enrolled. In 2014, 9 master's awarded. Terminal master's awarded for partial completion of doctoral program. *Degree requirements:* For master's, one foreign language. *Entrance requirements:* Additional exam requirements/recommendations for international students: Required—TOEFL (minimum score 600 paper-based; 100 iBT), IELTS (minimum score 7). *Application deadline:* For fall admission, 1/2 for domestic and international students. Application fee: $75. Electronic applications accepted. *Financial support:* In 2014–15, fellowships with full tuition reimbursements (averaging $18,450 per year), teaching assistantships with full tuition reimbursements (averaging $18,450 per year) were awarded; Federal Work-Study, health care benefits, and unspecified assistantships also available. Support available to part-time students. Financial award application deadline: 3/1; financial award applicants required to submit FAFSA. *Faculty research:* Spanish-American literature, philology, medieval French romance and troubadour lyrics, Golden Age Peninsular literature, secondary language acquisition and pedagogy, Hispanic studies, French language and literature, Italian language and literature. *Unit head:* Dr. Franco Mormando, Chairperson, 617-552-6346, E-mail: franco.mormando@bc.edu. *Application contact:* Dr. Laurie Shepard, Associate Dean, 617-552-8269, Fax: 617-552-3700, E-mail: laurie.shepard@bc.edu.
Website: http://www.bc.edu/rll

Brown University, Graduate School, Department of Italian Studies, Providence, RI 02912. Offers PhD. Terminal master's awarded for partial completion of doctoral program. *Degree requirements:* For doctorate, 2 foreign languages, thesis/dissertation, preliminary exam.

Central Connecticut State University, School of Graduate Studies, College of Liberal Arts and Social Sciences, Department of Modern Languages, Program in Modern Language, New Britain, CT 06050-4010. Offers French (MA, Certificate); German (Certificate); Italian (Certificate); modern language (MA); Spanish language and Hispanic culture (MA). Part-time and evening/weekend programs available. *Students:* 4 full-time (3 women), 28 part-time (22 women); includes 13 minority (1 Black or African American, non-Hispanic/Latino; 12 Hispanic/Latino), 1 international. Average age 34. 9 applicants, 100% accepted, 7 enrolled. In 2014, 8 master's, 5 other advanced degrees awarded. *Degree requirements:* For master's, one foreign language, comprehensive exam, thesis or alternative; for Certificate, qualifying exam. *Entrance requirements:* For master's, minimum undergraduate GPA of 2.7, 24 credits of undergraduate courses in each language in which graduate work will be undertaken. Additional exam requirements/recommendations for international students: Required—TOEFL (minimum score 550 paper-based; 79 iBT). *Application deadline:* For fall admission, 6/1 for domestic students, 5/1 for international students; for spring admission, 11/1 for domestic and international students. Applications are processed on a rolling basis. Application fee: $50. Electronic applications accepted. *Expenses: Tuition, area resident:* Full-time $5730; part-time $534 per credit. Tuition, state resident: full-time $8596; part-time $534 per credit. Tuition, nonresident: full-time $15,964; part-time $548 per credit. *Required fees:* $4211; $215 per credit. *Faculty research:* Twentieth-century French theater, seventeenth-century French literature, French Middle Ages. *Unit head:* Dr. Lilian Uribe, Chair, 860-832-2875, E-mail: uribe@ccsu.edu. *Application contact:* Patricia Gardner, Associate Director of Graduate Studies, 860-832-2350, Fax: 860-832-2362, E-mail: graduateadmissions@ccsu.edu.

Columbia University, Graduate School of Arts and Sciences, New York, NY 10027. Offers African-American studies (MA); American studies (MA); anthropology (MA, PhD); art history and archaeology (MA, PhD); astronomy (PhD); biological sciences (PhD); biotechnology (MA); chemical physics (PhD); chemistry (PhD); classical studies (MA, PhD); classics (MA, PhD); climate and society (MA); earth and environmental sciences (PhD); East Asia: regional studies (MA); East Asian languages and cultures (MA, PhD); ecology, evolution and environmental biology (MA), including conservation biology; ecology, evolution, and environmental biology (PhD), including ecology and evolutionary biology, evolutionary primatology; economics (PhD); English and comparative literature (MA, PhD); French and Romance philology (MA, PhD); Germanic languages (MA, PhD); global French studies (MA); Hispanic cultural studies (MA); history (PhD); history and literature (MA); human rights studies (MA); Islamic studies (MA); Italian (MA, PhD); Japanese pedagogy (MA); Jewish studies (MA); Latin America and the Caribbean: regional studies (MA); Latin American and Iberian cultures (PhD); mathematics (MA, PhD), including finance (MA); medieval and Renaissance studies (MA); Middle Eastern, South Asian, and African studies (MA, PhD); modern art: critical and curatorial studies (MA); modern European studies (MA); museum anthropology (MA); music (DMA, PhD); oral history (MA); philosophical foundations of physics (MA); philosophy (MA, PhD); physics (PhD); political science (MA, PhD); psychology (PhD); quantitative methods in the social sciences (MA); religion (MA, PhD); Russia, Eurasia and East Europe: regional studies (MA); Russian translation (MA); Slavic cultures (MA); Slavic languages (MA, PhD); sociology (MA, PhD); South Asian studies (MA); statistics (MA, PhD); theatre (PhD); JD/PhD; MA/MS; MD/PhD; MPA/MA. Dual-degree programs require admission to both Graduate School of Arts and Sciences and another Columbia school. Part-time and evening/weekend programs available. Terminal master's awarded for partial completion of doctoral program. *Degree requirements:* For master's, thesis (for some programs); for doctorate, comprehensive exam, thesis/dissertation. *Entrance requirements:* For master's and doctorate, GRE General Test, GRE Subject Test (for some programs). Electronic applications accepted. *Faculty research:* Humanities, natural sciences, social sciences.

Cornell University, Graduate School, Graduate Fields of Arts and Sciences, Field of Romance Studies, Ithaca, NY 14853-0001. Offers French linguistics (PhD); French literature (PhD); Hispanic literature (PhD); Italian linguistics (PhD); Italian literature (PhD); Romance linguistics (PhD); Spanish linguistics (PhD). *Degree requirements:* For doctorate, 2 foreign languages, comprehensive exam, thesis/dissertation. *Entrance requirements:* For doctorate, GRE General Test, sample of written work, 3 letters of recommendation. Additional exam requirements/recommendations for international students: Required—TOEFL (minimum score 550 paper-based; 77 iBT). Electronic applications accepted. *Faculty research:* Literary theory, Hispanic studies, French studies, gender studies.

DePaul University, College of Liberal Arts and Social Sciences, Chicago, IL 60614. Offers Arabic (MA); Chinese (MA); English (MA); French (MA); German (MA); history (MA); interdisciplinary studies (MA, MS); international public service (MS); international studies (MA); Italian (MA); Japanese (MA); leadership and policy studies (MS); liberal studies (MA); new media studies (MA); nonprofit management (MNM); public administration (MPA); public health (MPH); public service management (MS); social work (MSW); sociology (MA); Spanish (MA); sustainable urban development (MA); women and gender studies (MA); writing and publishing (MA); writing, rhetoric, and discourse (MA); MA/PhD. Part-time and evening/weekend programs available. Postbaccalaureate distance learning degree programs offered (no on-campus study). Terminal master's awarded for partial completion of doctoral program. *Degree requirements:* For master's, variable foreign language requirement, comprehensive exam (for some programs), thesis (for some programs). Electronic applications accepted.

Drew University, Caspersen School of Graduate Studies, Program in Education, Madison, NJ 07940-1493. Offers biology (MAT); chemistry (MAT); English (MAT); French (MAT); Italian (MAT); math (MAT); physics (MAT); social studies (MAT); Spanish (MAT); theatre arts (MAT). *Accreditation:* Teacher Education Accreditation Council. Part-time programs available. *Degree requirements:* For master's, student teaching internship and seminar. *Entrance requirements:* For master's, transcripts, statement of purpose, three letters of recommendation. Additional exam requirements/recommendations for international students: Required—TOEFL. *Expenses:* Contact institution.

Duke University, Graduate School, Department of Romance Studies, Durham, NC 27708. Offers French (PhD); Italian (PhD); Spanish (PhD); JD/AM. *Degree*

requirements: For doctorate, 2 foreign languages, thesis/dissertation. *Entrance requirements:* For doctorate, GRE General Test. Additional exam requirements/recommendations for international students: Required—TOEFL (minimum score 577 paper-based; 90 iBT) or IELTS (minimum score 7). Electronic applications accepted. *Expenses: Tuition:* Full-time $45,760; part-time $2765 per credit. *Required fees:* $978. Full-time tuition and fees vary according to program.

Florida State University, The Graduate School, College of Arts and Sciences, Department of Modern Languages, Program in Italian Studies, Tallahassee, FL 32306. Offers MA. *Faculty:* 7 full-time (4 women). *Students:* 10 full-time (8 women); includes 1 minority (Black or African American, non-Hispanic/Latino). Average age 24. 5 applicants, 80% accepted, 4 enrolled. In 2014, 2 master's awarded. *Entrance requirements:* For master's, GRE General Test, minimum GPA of 3.0. Additional exam requirements/recommendations for international students: Required—TOEFL (minimum score 550 paper-based). *Application deadline:* For fall admission, 2/15 for domestic and international students. Applications are processed on a rolling basis. Application fee: $30. Electronic applications accepted. *Expenses: Tuition:* state resident: part-time $403.51 per credit hour. Tuition, nonresident: part-time $1004.85 per credit hour. *Required fees:* $75.81 per credit hour. One-time fee: $20 part-time. Tuition and fees vary according to campus/location. *Financial support:* In 2014–15, 10 teaching assistantships with partial tuition reimbursements (averaging $11,500 per year) were awarded. Financial award application deadline: 2/15. *Unit head:* Dr. Mark Pietralunga, Coordinator, 850-644-8392, Fax: 850-644-0524, E-mail: mpietral@fsu.edu. *Application contact:* Wendy E. Pigott, Graduate Academic Coordinator, 850-644-8397, Fax: 850-644-0524, E-mail: wpigott@fsu.edu.
Website: http://modlang.ez.fsu.edu/Language-divisions-programs/Italian-Division/Graduate-Program

The Graduate Center, City University of New York, Graduate Studies, Program in Comparative Literature, New York, NY 10016-4039. Offers comparative literature (MA, PhD), including classics (PhD), German (PhD), Italian (PhD). PhD offered jointly with New York University. Terminal master's awarded for partial completion of doctoral program. *Degree requirements:* For master's, 2 foreign languages, comprehensive exam, thesis; for doctorate, 3 foreign languages, comprehensive exam, thesis/dissertation. *Entrance requirements:* For master's and doctorate, GRE General Test. Additional exam requirements/recommendations for international students: Required—TOEFL. Electronic applications accepted.

Harvard University, Graduate School of Arts and Sciences, Department of Romance Languages and Literatures, Cambridge, MA 02138. Offers French (AM, PhD); Italian (AM, PhD); Portuguese (AM, PhD); Spanish (AM, PhD). Terminal master's awarded for partial completion of doctoral program. *Degree requirements:* For master's, 2 foreign languages; for doctorate, 2 foreign languages, thesis/dissertation. *Entrance requirements:* For master's and doctorate, GRE General Test, sample of written work. Additional exam requirements/recommendations for international students: Required—TOEFL.

Hunter College of the City University of New York, Graduate School, School of Arts and Sciences, Department of Romance Languages, Program in Italian, New York, NY 10065-5085. Offers MA. *Faculty:* 3 full-time (2 women). *Students:* 7 part-time (5 women); includes 3 minority (all Hispanic/Latino). Average age 40. In 2014, 2 master's awarded. *Degree requirements:* For master's, 2 foreign languages, comprehensive exam, thesis optional. *Entrance requirements:* For master's, GRE General Test, GRE Subject Test, ability to read, speak, and write Italian; interview. Additional exam requirements/recommendations for international students: Required—TOEFL. *Application deadline:* For fall admission, 4/1 for domestic students, 2/1 for international students; for spring admission, 11/1 for domestic students, 9/1 for international students. *Financial support:* Federal Work-Study, scholarships/grants, and tuition waivers (partial) available. Support available to part-time students. Financial award application deadline: 4/15. *Faculty research:* Dante, Middle Ages, Renaissance, contemporary Italian novel and poetry, late Renaissance and Baroque. *Unit head:* Dr. Paolo Fasoli, Chairperson and Associate Professor, 212-772-5129, Fax: 212-772-5094, E-mail: pfasoli@hunter.cuny.edu. *Application contact:* Milena Solo, Director for Graduate Admissions, 212-772-4480, E-mail: milena.solo@hunter.cuny.edu.
Website: http://www.hunter.cuny.edu/romancelanguages/graduate/ma-requirements

Indiana University Bloomington, University Graduate School, College of Arts and Sciences, Department of French and Italian, Bloomington, IN 47405. Offers French (MA, PhD), including French instruction (MA), French linguistics, French literature; Italian (MA, PhD). Part-time programs available. *Faculty:* 21 full-time (7 women). *Students:* 61 full-time (35 women), 1 (woman) part-time; includes 4 minority (1 Black or African American, non-Hispanic/Latino; 1 Asian, non-Hispanic/Latino; 2 Hispanic/Latino), 23 international. Average age 30. 47 applicants, 47% accepted, 12 enrolled. In 2014, 21 master's, 5 doctorates awarded. Terminal master's awarded for partial completion of doctoral program. *Degree requirements:* For master's, variable foreign language requirement, comprehensive exam (for some programs), thesis optional; for doctorate, variable foreign language requirement, comprehensive exam, thesis/dissertation. *Entrance requirements:* For master's and doctorate, GRE General Test. Additional exam requirements/recommendations for international students: Required—TOEFL (minimum score 550 paper-based; 79 iBT). *Application deadline:* For fall admission, 1/15 priority date for domestic students, 12/1 priority date for international students; for spring admission, 9/1 priority date for domestic and international students. Application fee: $55 ($65 for international students). Electronic applications accepted. *Financial support:* In 2014–15, 46 students received support, including 7 fellowships with partial tuition reimbursements available (averaging $18,000 per year), 6 research assistantships with partial tuition reimbursements available (averaging $15,750 per year), 38 teaching assistantships with partial tuition reimbursements available (averaging $15,750 per year); health care benefits and unspecified assistantships also available. Financial award application deadline: 1/15. *Faculty research:* French and Italian literature, French linguistics, including the novel and political theory, literature and fine arts, literary theory, postcolonialism, French-Creole studies, French literature of Africa and its Diaspora, humanism, medieval folklore and mythology, humor in medieval and Renaissance literature, cinema Old Occitan and Old French, emigration, second language acquisition, syntax, sociolinguistics, phonology, lexicography. *Unit head:* Prof. Andrea Ciccarelli, Chair, 812-855-5458, Fax: 812-855-8877, E-mail: fritchr@indiana.edu. *Application contact:* Casey Green, Graduate Secretary, 812-855-1088, Fax: 812-855-8877, E-mail: fritgs@indiana.edu.
Website: http://www.indiana.edu/~frithome/

Johns Hopkins University, Zanvyl Krieger School of Arts and Sciences, Department of German and Romance Languages and Literatures, Baltimore, MD 21218-2699. Offers French (PhD); German (PhD); Italian (PhD); Spanish (PhD). *Degree requirements:* For doctorate, 2 foreign languages, thesis/dissertation. *Entrance requirements:* For doctorate, GRE General Test. Additional exam requirements/recommendations for international students: Required—TOEFL (minimum score 600 paper-based; 100 iBT), IELTS. Electronic applications accepted. *Faculty research:* Nineteenth-century French prose and poetry, genetic theory and criticism; twentieth-century Latin American literature and film; medieval and Renaissance Italian literature; gender and queer theory in German literature; the ideology of Baroque and Neobaroque aesthetics.

McGill University, Faculty of Graduate and Postdoctoral Studies, Faculty of Arts, Department of Italian Studies, Montréal, QC H3A 2T5, Canada. Offers MA, PhD.

Middlebury College, Language Schools, Italian School, Middlebury, VT 05753-6002. Offers MA, DML. *Faculty:* 19 full-time (12 women). *Students:* 47 full-time (38 women); includes 5 minority (1 Black or African American, non-Hispanic/Latino; 3 Hispanic/Latino; 1 Two or more races, non-Hispanic/Latino), 11 international. Average age 34. 66 applicants, 92% accepted, 47 enrolled. In 2014, 18 master's, 2 doctorates awarded. *Degree requirements:* For master's, one foreign language; for doctorate, 2 foreign languages, comprehensive exam, thesis/dissertation, residence abroad, teaching experience. *Entrance requirements:* For master's, online placement exam, 3 letters of recommendation, writing sample in Italian, transcripts, 200-word essay; for doctorate, 1st and 2nd language online placement exams, 3 letters of recommendation, writing sample in Italian, transcripts, 200-word essay. *Application deadline:* Applications are processed on a rolling basis. Application fee: $65. Electronic applications accepted. *Financial support:* Fellowships and scholarships/grants available. Financial award applicants required to submit FAFSA. *Unit head:* Dr. Antonio Vitti, Director, 802-443-5727, Fax: 802-443-2075, E-mail: acvitti@middlebury.edu. *Application contact:* Kara Gennarelli, Coordinator, 802-443-5727, Fax: 802-443-2075, E-mail: kgennar@middlebury.edu.
Website: http://www.middlebury.edu/ls/grad_programs/italian

New York University, Graduate School of Arts and Science, Department of Italian Studies, New York, NY 10012-1019. Offers Italian (MA, PhD), Italian studies (MA). Part-time programs available. *Faculty:* 6 full-time (3 women). *Students:* 33 full-time (21 women), 2 part-time (both women); includes 4 minority (3 Hispanic/Latino; 1 Two or more races, non-Hispanic/Latino), 8 international. Average age 35. 50 applicants, 60% accepted, 9 enrolled. In 2014, 7 master's, 3 doctorates awarded. Terminal master's awarded for partial completion of doctoral program. *Degree requirements:* For master's, one foreign language, thesis; for doctorate, 3 foreign languages, thesis/dissertation. *Entrance requirements:* For master's and doctorate, GRE General Test. Additional exam requirements/recommendations for international students: Required—TOEFL. *Application deadline:* For fall admission, 12/18 priority date for domestic students, 12/18 for international students. Application fee: $100. *Financial support:* Fellowships with tuition reimbursements, teaching assistantships with tuition reimbursements, Federal Work-Study, institutionally sponsored loans, scholarships/grants, and unspecified assistantships available. Financial award application deadline: 12/18; financial award applicants required to submit FAFSA. *Faculty research:* Dante, early modern literature, fascism and culture, contemporary literature, feminist theory. *Unit head:* Virginia Cox, Chair, 212-998-8730, Fax: 212-995-4012, E-mail: italian.dept@nyu.edu. *Application contact:* Maria Luisa Ardizzone, Acting Director of Graduate Studies, 212-998-8730, Fax: 212-995-4012, E-mail: italian.dept@nyu.edu.
Website: http://www.nyu.edu/gsas/dept/italian/

New York University, Steinhardt School of Culture, Education, and Human Development, Department of Teaching and Learning, Program in Multilingual/Multicultural Studies, New York, NY 10003. Offers bilingual education (PhD); bilingual education for teachers (MA, Advanced Certificate); foreign language education (MA); teachers of English to speakers of other languages in college (PhD); teachers of French 7-12 (MA); teachers of Hebrew 7-12 (MA); teaching a foreign language 7-12 (MA), including teaching English to speakers of other languages, all grades; teaching English to speakers of other languages (MA); teaching foreign languages, 7-12 (MA), including Chinese, French, Italian, Japanese, Spanish; teaching French as a foreign language (MA), including teaching English to speakers of other languages; teaching Spanish as a foreign language and TESOL (MA). *Accreditation:* Teacher Education Accreditation Council. Part-time and evening/weekend programs available. *Faculty:* 6 full-time (4 women). *Students:* 118 full-time (94 women), 82 part-time (72 women); includes 40 minority (8 Black or African American, non-Hispanic/Latino; 18 Asian, non-Hispanic/Latino; 12 Hispanic/Latino; 2 Two or more races, non-Hispanic/Latino), 116 international. Average age 29. 431 applicants, 61% accepted, 92 enrolled. In 2014, 121 master's, 1 doctorate, 2 other advanced degrees awarded. *Degree requirements:* For master's, thesis (for some programs); for doctorate, thesis/dissertation. *Entrance requirements:* For doctorate, GRE General Test, interview; for Advanced Certificate, master's degree. Additional exam requirements/recommendations for international students: Required—TOEFL (minimum score 100 iBT). *Application deadline:* For fall admission, 12/1 priority date for domestic and international students; for spring admission, 10/1 for domestic and international students. Applications are processed on a rolling basis. Application fee: $75. Electronic applications accepted. *Financial support:* Fellowships with full and partial tuition reimbursements, career-related internships or fieldwork, Federal Work-Study, institutionally sponsored loans, scholarships/grants, and tuition waivers (partial) available. Support available to part-time students. Financial award application deadline: 2/1; financial award applicants required to submit FAFSA. *Faculty research:* Second language acquisition, cross-cultural communication, technology-enhanced language learning, language variation, action learning. *Unit head:* Prof. Shondel Nero, Director, 212-998-5757, E-mail: shondel.nero@nyu.edu. *Application contact:* 212-998-5030, Fax: 212-995-4328, E-mail: steinhardt.gradadmissions@nyu.edu.
Website: http://steinhardt.nyu.edu/teachlearn/mms

Northwestern University, The Graduate School, Judd A. and Marjorie Weinberg College of Arts and Sciences, Department of French and Italian, Evanston, IL 60208. Offers French/Francophone studies (PhD); Italian studies (Graduate Certificate). Admissions and degrees offered through The Graduate School. *Degree requirements:* For doctorate, one foreign language, thesis/dissertation, written and oral exams. *Entrance requirements:* For doctorate, GRE, writing sample, cassette recording. Additional exam requirements/recommendations for international students: Required—TOEFL. *Faculty research:* Francophone studies, eighteenth century contemporary theory.

The Ohio State University, Graduate School, College of Arts and Sciences, Division of Arts and Humanities, Department of French and Italian, Columbus, OH 43210. Offers French (MA, PhD); Italian (MA); Italian studies (PhD). *Faculty:* 12. *Students:* 28 full-time (19 women); includes 2 minority (1 Black or African American, non-Hispanic/Latino; 1 Two or more races, non-Hispanic/Latino), 5 international. Average age 30. In 2014, 5 master's, 1 doctorate awarded. Terminal master's awarded for partial completion of doctoral program. *Degree requirements:* For master's, variable foreign language requirement, thesis optional; for doctorate, variable foreign language requirement, thesis/dissertation. *Entrance requirements:* For master's and doctorate, GRE General Test. Additional exam requirements/recommendations for international students: Required—TOEFL (minimum score 550 paper-based; 79 iBT), IELTS (minimum score 7), Michigan English Language Assessment Battery (minimum score 82). *Application deadline:* For fall admission, 12/15 priority date for domestic students, 11/30 priority date for international students; for winter admission, 12/1 for domestic students, 11/1 for international students; for spring admission, 3/1 for domestic students, 2/1 for international students. Applications are processed on a rolling basis. Application fee: $60 ($70 for international students). Electronic applications accepted. *Financial support:* Fellowships with tuition reimbursements, research assistantships with tuition reimbursements, teaching assistantships with tuition reimbursements, Federal Work-

Study, institutionally sponsored loans, and unspecified assistantships available. Support available to part-time students. *Faculty research:* Italian and Romance linguistics. *Unit head:* Dr. Jennifer Willging, Chair, 614-292-4938, E-mail: willging.1@osu.edu. *Application contact:* Graduate and Professional Admissions, 614-292-9444, Fax: 614-292-3895, E-mail: gpadmissions@osu.edu.
Website: http://frit.osu.edu/

Queens College of the City University of New York, Division of Graduate Studies, Arts and Humanities Division, Department of European Languages and Literatures, Program in Italian, Flushing, NY 11367-1597. Offers MA. Part-time and evening/weekend programs available. *Degree requirements:* For master's, 2 foreign languages, comprehensive exam, thesis or alternative. *Entrance requirements:* For master's, minimum GPA of 3.0. Additional exam requirements/recommendations for international students: Required—TOEFL.

Rutgers, The State University of New Jersey, New Brunswick, Graduate School-New Brunswick, Program in Italian, Piscataway, NJ 08854-8097. Offers Italian (MA, PhD); Italian literature and literary criticism (MA); language, literature and culture (MAT). Part-time and evening/weekend programs available. Terminal master's awarded for partial completion of doctoral program. *Degree requirements:* For master's, one foreign language, comprehensive exam (for some programs), thesis optional; for doctorate, 2 foreign languages, thesis/dissertation, qualifying exam. *Entrance requirements:* For master's and doctorate, GRE General Test. Additional exam requirements/recommendations for international students: Required—TOEFL. *Faculty research:* Literature.

San Francisco State University, Division of Graduate Studies, College of Liberal and Creative Arts, Department of Foreign Languages and Literatures, Program in Italian, San Francisco, CA 94132-1722. Offers MA. *Application deadline:* Applications are processed on a rolling basis. *Expenses:* Tuition, state resident: full-time $6738. Tuition, nonresident: full-time $17,898; part-time $372 per credit hour. *Required fees:* $498 per semester. *Unit head:* Dr. Mohammad Salama, Chair, 415-338-7413, Fax: 415-405-0588, E-mail: mrsalama@sfsu.edu. *Application contact:* Dr. Elisabetta Nelsen, Graduate Coordinator, 415-338-7418, Fax: 415-405-0588, E-mail: enelsen@sfsu.edu.
Website: http://italian.sfsu.edu/general-information

Stanford University, School of Humanities and Sciences, Department of French and Italian, Stanford, CA 94305-9991. Offers French (MA, PhD); Italian (MA, PhD). Terminal master's awarded for partial completion of doctoral program. *Degree requirements:* For master's, one foreign language, written exam; for doctorate, 2 foreign languages, thesis/dissertation, oral exam. *Entrance requirements:* For master's and doctorate, GRE General Test. Additional exam requirements/recommendations for international students: Required—TOEFL. Electronic applications accepted. *Expenses: Tuition:* Full-time $44,184; part-time $982 per credit hour. *Required fees:* $191.

Stony Brook University, State University of New York, Graduate School, College of Arts and Sciences, Department of European Languages, Literatures, and Cultures, Program in Italian, Stony Brook, NY 11794. Offers MA. Evening/weekend programs available. *Students:* 1 (woman) full-time, 4 part-time (all women); includes 1 minority (Hispanic/Latino). 4 applicants, 100% accepted, 2 enrolled. In 2014, 1 master's awarded. *Degree requirements:* For master's, one foreign language. *Entrance requirements:* For master's, GRE General Test. Additional exam requirements/recommendations for international students: Required—TOEFL. *Application deadline:* For fall admission, 1/15 for domestic students; for spring admission, 10/1 for domestic students. Application fee: $100. *Expenses:* Tuition, state resident: full-time $10,370; part-time $432 per credit. Tuition, nonresident: full-time $20,190; part-time $841 per credit. *Required fees:* $1431. *Unit head:* Prof. Nicholas Rzhevsky, Coordinator, 631-632-7440, Fax: 631-632-9612, E-mail: nicholas.rzhevsky@stonybrook.edu. *Application contact:* Mary Wilmarth, Coordinator, 631-632-7442, Fax: 631-632-9612, E-mail: mary.wilmarth@stonybrook.edu.

University of Alberta, Faculty of Graduate Studies and Research, Department of Modern Languages and Cultural Studies, Edmonton, AB T6G 2E1, Canada. Offers applied linguistics (Germanic, Romance, Slavic) (MA); French language, literatures and linguistics (PhD); French language, literatures, and linguistics (MA); Germanic languages, literatures and linguistics (PhD); Germanic languages, literatures, and linguistics (MA); Italian studies (MA); Slavic languages and literatures (Russian, Ukrainian) (MA, PhD); Slavic linguistics (Russian, Ukrainian) (MA, PhD); Spanish and Latin American studies (MA, PhD); Ukrainian folklore (MA, PhD). Part-time programs available. *Degree requirements:* For master's, one foreign language, thesis; for doctorate, 2 foreign languages, comprehensive exam, thesis/dissertation. *Entrance requirements:* For master's and doctorate, 1 language other than English. Additional exam requirements/recommendations for international students: Required—Michigan English Language Assessment Battery or TOEFL (minimum score 550 paper-based). Electronic applications accepted. *Faculty research:* Russian/Ukrainian studies; German studies; contemporary Latin American, French and Francophone studies; Italian studies.

University of California, Berkeley, Graduate Division, College of Letters and Science, Department of Italian Studies, Berkeley, CA 94720-1500. Offers PhD. *Degree requirements:* For doctorate, one foreign language, thesis/dissertation, oral and written qualifying exams. *Entrance requirements:* For doctorate, GRE General Test, minimum GPA of 3.0, 3 letters of recommendation. Additional exam requirements/recommendations for international students: Required—TOEFL (minimum score 570 paper-based). *Faculty research:* Literature and culture of Italy in Middle Ages and the Renaissance, literature and culture of Italy in nineteenth and twentieth centuries, Italian film studies, interdisciplinary cultural studies.

University of California, Berkeley, Graduate Division, College of Letters and Science, Group in Romance Languages and Literature, Berkeley, CA 94720-1500. Offers French (PhD); Italian (PhD); Spanish (PhD). *Degree requirements:* For doctorate, thesis/dissertation, qualifying exam. *Entrance requirements:* For doctorate, GRE General Test, minimum GPA of 3.0, 3 letters of recommendation. Additional exam requirements/recommendations for international students: Required—TOEFL (minimum score 570 paper-based).

University of California, Los Angeles, Graduate Division, College of Letters and Science, Department of Italian, Los Angeles, CA 90095. Offers MA, PhD. Terminal master's awarded for partial completion of doctoral program. *Degree requirements:* For master's, one foreign language, comprehensive exam or thesis; for doctorate, 2 foreign languages, thesis/dissertation, oral and written qualifying exams. *Entrance requirements:* For master's, GRE General Test, bachelor's degree; minimum undergraduate GPA of 3.0 (or its equivalent if letter grade system not used); for doctorate, GRE General Test, master's degree; minimum undergraduate GPA of 3.0 (or its equivalent if letter grade system not used). Additional exam requirements/recommendations for international students: Required—TOEFL. Electronic applications accepted.

University of Chicago, Division of the Humanities, Department of Romance Languages and Literatures, Chicago, IL 60637. Offers French (PhD); Italian (PhD); Spanish (PhD). *Students:* 44 full-time (28 women); includes 9 minority (1 Black or African American, non-Hispanic/Latino; 1 Asian, non-Hispanic/Latino; 6 Hispanic/Latino; 1 Two or more races, non-Hispanic/Latino), 13 international. 71 applicants, 39% accepted, 7 enrolled. Terminal master's awarded for partial completion of doctoral program. *Degree requirements:* For doctorate, 3 foreign languages, thesis/dissertation. *Entrance requirements:* For doctorate, GRE General Test. Additional exam requirements/recommendations for international students: Required—TOEFL (minimum score 104 iBT), IELTS (minimum score 7). *Application deadline:* For fall admission, 12/15 for domestic and international students. Application fee: $90. Electronic applications accepted. *Expenses: Tuition:* Full-time $46,899. *Required fees:* $347. *Financial support:* Fellowships with full tuition reimbursements, teaching assistantships with full tuition reimbursements, Federal Work-Study, institutionally sponsored loans, scholarships/grants, and health care benefits available. Financial award application deadline: 12/15; financial award applicants required to submit FAFSA. *Unit head:* Dr. Larry Norman, Chair. *Application contact:* Braden Grams, Assistant Dean of Students, Admissions and Fellowships, 773-702-1552, Fax: 773-834-9148, E-mail: humanitiesadmissions@uchicago.edu.
Website: http://rll.uchicago.edu

University of Connecticut, Graduate School, College of Liberal Arts and Sciences, Department of Modern and Classical Languages, Field of Italian, Storrs, CT 06269. Offers MA, PhD. Terminal master's awarded for partial completion of doctoral program. *Degree requirements:* For master's, comprehensive exam; for doctorate, thesis/dissertation. *Entrance requirements:* For master's, GRE General Test. Additional exam requirements/recommendations for international students: Required—TOEFL (minimum score 550 paper-based). Electronic applications accepted.

University of Illinois at Urbana–Champaign, Graduate College, College of Liberal Arts and Sciences, School of Literatures, Cultures and Linguistics, Department of Spanish, Italian and Portuguese, Champaign, IL 61820. Offers Italian (MA, PhD); Portuguese (MA, PhD); Spanish (MA, PhD). *Students:* 49 (37 women). Application fee: $70 ($90 for international students). *Financial support:* Tuition waivers available. *Unit head:* Silvina Montrul, Head, 217-333-1780, Fax: 217-244-8430, E-mail: montrul@illinois.edu. *Application contact:* Lynn Stanke, Office Support Specialist, 217-333-6269, Fax: 217-244-3050, E-mail: stanke@illinois.edu.
Website: http://www.sip.illinois.edu/

The University of Manchester, School of Languages, Linguistics and Cultures, Manchester, United Kingdom. Offers Arab world studies (PhD); Chinese studies (M Phil, PhD); East Asian studies (M Phil, PhD); English language (PhD); French studies (M Phil, PhD); German studies (M Phil, PhD); interpreting studies (PhD); Italian studies (M Phil, PhD); Japanese studies (M Phil, PhD); Latin American cultural studies (M Phil, PhD); linguistics (M Phil, PhD); Middle Eastern studies (M Phil, PhD); Polish studies (M Phil, PhD); Portuguese studies (M Phil, PhD); Russian studies (M Phil, PhD); Spanish studies (M Phil, PhD); translation and intercultural studies (M Phil, PhD).

University of Massachusetts Amherst, Graduate School, College of Humanities and Fine Arts, Department of Languages, Literatures, and Cultures, Program in Italian Studies, Amherst, MA 01003. Offers MAT. Part-time programs available. *Faculty:* 3 full-time (1 woman). *Students:* 1 (woman) full-time, 1 (woman) part-time, 1 international. Average age 30. 1 applicant, 100% accepted, 1 enrolled. *Degree requirements:* For master's, comprehensive exam, thesis or alternative. *Entrance requirements:* For master's, GRE General Test. Additional exam requirements/recommendations for international students: Required—TOEFL (minimum score 550 paper-based; 80 iBT), IELTS (minimum score 6.5). *Application deadline:* For fall admission, 2/1 for domestic and international students; for spring admission, 10/1 for domestic and international students. Applications are processed on a rolling basis. Application fee: $75. Electronic applications accepted. *Expenses:* Tuition, state resident: full-time $1980; part-time $110 per credit. Tuition, nonresident: full-time $14,644; part-time $414 per credit. *Required fees:* $11,417. One-time fee: $357. *Financial support:* Fellowships with full and partial tuition reimbursements, research assistantships with full and partial tuition reimbursements, teaching assistantships with full and partial tuition reimbursements, career-related internships or fieldwork, Federal Work-Study, scholarships/grants, traineeships, health care benefits, tuition waivers (full and partial), and unspecified assistantships available. Support available to part-time students. Financial award application deadline: 2/1. *Unit head:* Dr. Michael Papio, Graduate Program Director, 413-545-2314, Fax: 413-545-4778. *Application contact:* Lindsay DeSantis, Supervisor of Admissions, 413-545-0722, Fax: 413-577-0010, E-mail: gradadm@grad.umass.edu.
Website: http://www.umass.edu/italian/

University of Michigan, Horace H. Rackham School of Graduate Studies, College of Literature, Science, and the Arts, Department of Romance Languages and Literatures, Program in Italian, Ann Arbor, MI 48109. Offers PhD. *Faculty:* 4 full-time (2 women), 1 part-time/adjunct (0 women). *Students:* 9 full-time (3 women). Average age 26. 10 applicants, 30% accepted, 1 enrolled. *Degree requirements:* For doctorate, 2 foreign languages, thesis/dissertation, oral defense of dissertation, preliminary exams in essay format. *Entrance requirements:* Additional exam requirements/recommendations for international students: Required—TOEFL or Michigan English Language Assessment Battery. *Application deadline:* For fall admission, 12/18 for domestic and international students. Application fee: $65 ($75 for international students). Electronic applications accepted. *Financial support:* In 2014–15, 9 students received support. Fellowships with full tuition reimbursements available, teaching assistantships with full tuition reimbursements available, institutionally sponsored loans, scholarships/grants, health care benefits, and unspecified assistantships available. Financial award application deadline: 12/18. *Faculty research:* Cinema, transnational visual culture, nineteenth-twentieth century Italian literature, medieval and Renaissance literature, medieval Mediterranean literature. *Unit head:* Dr. Cristina Moreiras-Menor, Chair, 734-764-5344, Fax: 734-764-8163. *Application contact:* Katie Hayes, Graduate Assistant, 734-764-8164, Fax: 734-764-8163, E-mail: rll-admissions@umich.edu.
Website: http://www.lsa.umich.edu/rll/

The University of North Carolina at Chapel Hill, Graduate School, College of Arts and Sciences, Department of Romance Languages and Literatures, Chapel Hill, NC 27599. Offers French (MA, PhD); Italian (MA, PhD); Portuguese (MA, PhD); Romance languages (MA, PhD); Romance philology (MA, PhD); Spanish (MA, PhD). *Degree requirements:* For master's, one foreign language, comprehensive exam, thesis; for doctorate, 2 foreign languages, comprehensive exam, thesis/dissertation. *Entrance requirements:* For master's and doctorate, GRE General Test, minimum GPA of 3.0. Additional exam requirements/recommendations for international students: Required—TOEFL (minimum score 550 paper-based). Electronic applications accepted.

University of Notre Dame, Graduate School, College of Arts and Letters, Division of Humanities, Department of Romance Languages and Literatures, Notre Dame, IN 46556. Offers French and Francophone studies (MA); Iberian and Latin American studies (MA); Italian studies (MA); Romance literatures (MA). *Degree requirements:* For master's, 2 foreign languages, comprehensive exam, thesis optional. *Entrance requirements:* For master's, GRE General Test, BA in target language. Additional exam requirements/recommendations for international students: Required—TOEFL (minimum score 600 paper-based; 80 iBT). Electronic applications accepted. *Faculty research:* Literature of discovery and exploration, modern literature, literary criticism, medieval literature, feminist critical theory.

University of Oregon, Graduate School, College of Arts and Sciences, Department of Romance Languages, Program in Italian, Eugene, OR 97403. Offers MA. Part-time

programs available. *Degree requirements:* For master's, variable foreign language requirement. *Entrance requirements:* For master's, GRE General Test, minimum GPA of 3.0. Additional exam requirements/recommendations for international students: Required—TOEFL.

University of Pennsylvania, School of Arts and Sciences, Graduate Group in Romance Languages, Philadelphia, PA 19104. Offers French (AM, PhD); Italian (AM, PhD); Spanish (AM, PhD). *Faculty:* 44 full-time (16 women), 6 part-time/adjunct (2 women). *Students:* 61 full-time (29 women), 3 part-time (1 woman); includes 8 minority (all Hispanic/Latino), 34 international. 92 applicants, 23% accepted, 10 enrolled. In 2014, 11 master's, 9 doctorates awarded. Terminal master's awarded for partial completion of doctoral program. *Degree requirements:* For master's, one foreign language, thesis or alternative; for doctorate, 2 foreign languages, thesis/dissertation. *Entrance requirements:* For master's and doctorate, GRE General Test. Additional exam requirements/recommendations for international students: Required—TOEFL. *Application deadline:* For fall admission, 12/1 priority date for domestic students. Application fee: $70. Electronic applications accepted. *Financial support:* In 2014–15, 23 fellowships, 2 research assistantships, 39 teaching assistantships were awarded; institutionally sponsored loans, scholarships/grants, traineeships, health care benefits, and unspecified assistantships also available. Financial award application deadline: 12/15. *Faculty research:* Literary theory and criticism, cultural studies, history of Romance literatures, gender studies. *Unit head:* Dr. Ralph M. Rosen, Associate Dean for Graduate Studies, 215-898-7156, Fax: 215-573-8068, E-mail: grad-dean@sas.upenn.edu. *Application contact:* Arts and Sciences Graduate Admissions, 215-573-5816, Fax: 215-573-8068, E-mail: gdasadmis@sas.upenn.edu.
Website: http://www.sas.upenn.edu/graduate-division

University of Pittsburgh, Dietrich School of Arts and Sciences, Department of French and Italian, Program in Italian, Pittsburgh, PA 15260. Offers MA. Part-time programs available. *Faculty:* 3 full-time (2 women). *Students:* 4 full-time (all women); includes 1 minority (Two or more races, non-Hispanic/Latino), 1 international. Average age 27. 7 applicants, 57% accepted, 3 enrolled. In 2014, 3 master's awarded. *Degree requirements:* For master's, one foreign language, comprehensive exam, seminar paper/thesis. *Entrance requirements:* For master's, minimum GPA of 3.0, writing sample. Additional exam requirements/recommendations for international students: Required—TOEFL (minimum score 600 paper-based; 90 iBT). *Application deadline:* For fall admission, 2/1 priority date for domestic students, 2/1 for international students. Application fee: $50. Electronic applications accepted. *Expenses:* Tuition, state resident: full-time $20,742; part-time $838 per credit. Tuition, nonresident: full-time $33,960; part-time $1389 per credit. *Required fees:* $800; $205 per term. Tuition and fees vary according to program. *Financial support:* In 2014–15, 4 students received support, including 4 teaching assistantships with full tuition reimbursements available (averaging $17,130 per year); Federal Work-Study, institutionally sponsored loans, scholarships/grants, health care benefits, and tuition waivers (partial) also available. Support available to part-time students. Financial award application deadline: 2/1. *Faculty research:* Dante and his reception, humanism and Renaissance studies, seventeenth- and eighteenth-century Italian literature and culture, Italian theater, Holocaust literature and film, Sicilian literature and film, Italian-American studies. *Total annual research expenditures:* $2,000. *Unit head:* Dr. Lina Insana, Chair, 412-624-6269, Fax: 412-624-6263, E-mail: insana@pitt.edu. *Application contact:* Patrick Fogarty, Graduate Secretary, 412-624-5227, Fax: 412-624-6263, E-mail: pmf23@pitt.edu. Website: http://www.frenchanditalian.pitt.edu/graduate/italian

University of South Africa, College of Human Sciences, Pretoria, South Africa. Offers adult education (M Ed); African languages (MA, PhD); African politics (MA, PhD); Afrikaans (MA, PhD); ancient history (MA, PhD); ancient Near Eastern studies (MA, PhD); anthropology (MA, PhD); applied linguistics (MA); Arabic (MA, PhD); archaeology (MA); art history (MA); Biblical archaeology (MA); Biblical studies (M Th, D Th, PhD); Christian spirituality (M Th, D Th); church history (M Th, D Th); classical studies (MA, PhD); clinical psychology (MA); communication (MA, PhD); comparative education (M Ed, Ed D); consulting psychology (D Admin, D Com, PhD); curriculum studies (M Ed, Ed D); development studies (M Admin, MA, D Admin, PhD); didactics (M Ed, Ed D); education (M Tech); education management (M Ed, Ed D); educational psychology (M Ed); English (MA); environmental education (M Ed); French (MA, PhD); German (MA, PhD); Greek (MA); guidance and counseling (M Ed); health studies (MA, PhD), including health sciences education (MA), health services management (MA), medical and surgical nursing science (critical care general) (MA), midwifery and neonatal nursing science (MA), trauma and emergency care (MA); history (MA, PhD); history of education (Ed D); inclusive education (M Ed, Ed D); information and communications technology policy and regulation (MA); information science (MA, MIS, PhD); international politics (MA, PhD); Islamic studies (MA, PhD); Italian (MA, PhD); Judaica (MA, PhD); linguistics (MA, PhD); mathematical education (M Ed); mathematics education (MA); missiology (M Th, D Th); modern Hebrew (MA, PhD); musicology (MA, MMus, D Mus, PhD); natural science education (M Ed); New Testament (M Th, D Th); Old Testament (D Th); pastoral therapy (M Th, D Th); philosophy (MA); philosophy of education (M Ed, Ed D); politics (MA, PhD); Portuguese (MA, PhD); practical theology (M Th, D Th); psychology (MA, MS, PhD); psychology of education (M Ed, Ed D); public health (MA); religious studies (MA, D Th, PhD); Romance languages (MA); Russian (MA, PhD); Semitic languages (MA, PhD); social behavior studies in HIV/AIDS (MA); social science (mental health) (MA); social science in development studies (MA); social science in psychology (MA); social science in social work (MA); social science in sociology (MA); social work (MSW, DSW, PhD); socio-education (M Ed, Ed D); sociolinguistics (MA); sociology (MA, PhD); Spanish (MA, PhD); systematic theology (M Th, D Th); TESOL (teaching English to speakers of other languages) (MA); theological ethics (M Th, D Th); theory of literature (MA, PhD); urban ministries (D Th); urban ministry (M Th).

The University of Tennessee, Graduate School, College of Arts and Sciences, Department of Modern Foreign Languages and Literatures, Program in Modern Foreign Languages, Knoxville, TN 37996. Offers applied linguistics (PhD); French (PhD); German (PhD); Italian (PhD); Portuguese (PhD); Russian (PhD); Spanish (PhD). *Degree requirements:* For doctorate, 2 foreign languages, thesis/dissertation. *Entrance requirements:* For doctorate, minimum GPA of 2.7. Additional exam requirements/recommendations for international students: Required—TOEFL. Electronic applications accepted.

The University of Texas at Austin, Graduate School, College of Liberal Arts, Department of French and Italian, Austin, TX 78712-1111. Offers French linguistics (MA, PhD); French studies (MA, PhD); Italian studies (MA, PhD); Romance linguistics (PhD). Part-time programs available. *Degree requirements:* For master's, one foreign language, thesis; for doctorate, 2 foreign languages, thesis/dissertation. *Entrance requirements:* For master's, GRE General Test, minimum GPA of 3.0, bachelor's degree in French or equivalent; for doctorate, GRE General Test, minimum GPA of 3.0, master's degree in French. Additional exam requirements/recommendations for international students: Required—TOEFL. Electronic applications accepted. *Faculty research:* Nineteenth-century Italian literature, Italian Renaissance, twentieth-century French literature, Francophone literature, fifteenth-century literature and culture.

University of Toronto, School of Graduate Studies, Faculty of Arts and Science, Department of Italian Studies, Toronto, ON M5S 2J7, Canada. Offers MA, PhD. Part-

time programs available. *Degree requirements:* For doctorate, 2 foreign languages, comprehensive exam, thesis/dissertation, oral defense, language exam(s). *Entrance requirements:* For master's; minimum B average in last 2 years in Italian and in final year overall; 2 letters of recommendation; for doctorate, MA in Italian, minimum A- average. Electronic applications accepted.

University of Victoria, Faculty of Graduate Studies, Faculty of Humanities, Department of Hispanic and Italian Studies, Victoria, BC V8W 2Y2, Canada. Offers Hispanic and Italian studies (MA); Hispanic studies (MA). *Degree requirements:* For master's, one foreign language, comprehensive exam, thesis (for some programs). *Entrance requirements:* For master's, undergraduate major in Hispanic studies, minimum B+ average. Additional exam requirements/recommendations for international students: Required—TOEFL (minimum score 575 paper-based), IELTS (minimum score 7). Electronic applications accepted. *Faculty research:* Medieval/Renaissance Spanish and Italian literature, Golden Age literature, Latin American literature.

University of Virginia, College and Graduate School of Arts and Sciences, Department of Spanish, Italian and Portuguese, Program in Italian, Charlottesville, VA 22903. Offers MA. *Students:* 3 full-time (2 women); includes 1 minority (Hispanic/Latino), 1 international. Average age 25. 2 applicants. In 2014, 3 master's awarded. *Degree requirements:* For master's, one foreign language, comprehensive exam, thesis. *Entrance requirements:* For master's, GRE General Test, BA in Italian, 2 letters of recommendation. Additional exam requirements/recommendations for international students: Required—TOEFL (minimum score 600 paper-based; 90 iBT), IELTS (minimum score 7). *Application deadline:* For fall admission, 12/1 for domestic and international students. Applications are processed on a rolling basis. Application fee: $60. Electronic applications accepted. *Expenses:* Tuition, state resident: full-time $14,164; part-time $349 per credit hour. Tuition, nonresident: full-time $23,722; part-time $1300 per credit hour. *Required fees:* $2514. *Financial support:* Teaching assistantships available. Financial award applicants required to submit FAFSA. *Unit head:* Joel Rini, Chair, 434-924-7159, Fax: 434-924-7160, E-mail: sipinfo@virginia.edu. *Application contact:* Enrico Cesaretti, Director of Graduate Studies, Italian, 434-924-7159, Fax: 434-924-7160, E-mail: sipinfo@virginia.edu.
Website: http://spanitalport.virginia.edu/

University of Washington, Graduate School, College of Arts and Sciences, Division of French and Italian Studies, Seattle, WA 98195. Offers French (MA, PhD); Italian (MA). Terminal master's awarded for partial completion of doctoral program. *Degree requirements:* For master's, 2 foreign languages, exam; for doctorate, 3 foreign languages, thesis/dissertation, exam. *Entrance requirements:* For master's and doctorate, GRE General Test, minimum GPA of 3.0. Additional exam requirements/recommendations for international students: Required—TOEFL. Electronic applications accepted. *Faculty research:* Interdisciplinary studies, literary theory and criticism, film, major periods of French and Italian literature, Francophonie.

University of Wisconsin–Madison, Graduate School, College of Letters and Science, Department of French and Italian, Program in Italian, Madison, WI 53706-1380. Offers MA, PhD. Part-time programs available. *Degree requirements:* For master's, one foreign language; for doctorate, 2 foreign languages, thesis/dissertation. *Entrance requirements:* For master's and doctorate, GRE. Electronic applications accepted. *Expenses:* Tuition, state resident: full-time $10,723; part-time $745 per credit. Tuition, nonresident: full-time $24,054; part-time $1578 per credit. *Required fees:* $374 per semester. Tuition and fees vary according to course load, program and reciprocity agreements. *Faculty research:* Italian literature, culture, linguistics, cinema, and language.

University of Wisconsin–Milwaukee, Graduate School, College of Letters and Sciences, Interdepartmental Program in Foreign Language and Literature, Milwaukee, WI 53201-0413. Offers classics and Hebrew studies (MAFLL); comparative literature (MAFLL); French and Italian (MAFLL); German (MAFLL); Slavic studies (MAFLL); translation (Certificate). Part-time programs available. *Degree requirements:* For master's, 2 foreign languages, thesis or alternative. *Entrance requirements:* Additional exam requirements/recommendations for international students: Required—TOEFL (minimum score 550 paper-based; 79 iBT), IELTS (minimum score 6.5). Electronic applications accepted.

Wayne State University, College of Liberal Arts and Sciences, Department of Classical and Modern Languages, Literatures, and Cultures, Program in Language Learning, Detroit, MI 48202. Offers Arabic (MALL); French (MALL); German (MALL); Italian (MALL); Spanish (MALL). *Students:* 1 (woman) full-time, 9 part-time (6 women); includes 2 minority (both Hispanic/Latino). Average age 34. In 2014, 2 master's awarded. *Degree requirements:* For master's, one foreign language, three-credit essay. *Entrance requirements:* For master's, GRE (recommended), target language proficiency, statement of purpose, three letters of recommendation, minimum GPA of 2.6 from accredited institution or 3.2 from non-accredited institution. Additional exam requirements/recommendations for international students: Required—TOEFL (minimum score 550 paper-based; 79 iBT), TWE (minimum score 5.5), Michigan English Language Assessment Battery (minimum score 85); Recommended—IELTS (minimum score 6.5). *Application deadline:* For fall admission, 6/1 priority date for domestic students, 5/1 for international students; for winter admission, 10/1 priority date for domestic students, 9/1 priority date for international students; for spring admission, 2/1 priority date for domestic students, 1/1 priority date for international students. Applications are processed on a rolling basis. Application fee: $0. Electronic applications accepted. *Expenses:* Tuition, state resident: full-time $10,294; part-time $571.90 per credit hour. Tuition, nonresident: full-time $29,730; part-time $1238.75 per credit hour. *Required fees:* $1365; $43.50 per credit hour. $291.10 per semester. Tuition and fees vary according to course load and program. *Financial support:* Scholarships/grants and unspecified assistantships available. Financial award application deadline: 3/31; financial award applicants required to submit FAFSA. *Unit head:* Dr. Anne Duggan, Department Chair, E-mail: a.duggan@wayne.edu.
Website: http://clas.wayne.edu/MALL/

Wayne State University, College of Liberal Arts and Sciences, Department of Classical and Modern Languages, Literatures, and Cultures, Program in Romance Languages, Detroit, MI 48202. Offers French (MA); Italian (MA); Spanish (MA). *Students:* 6 full-time (5 women), 22 part-time (15 women); includes 9 minority (4 Black or African American, non-Hispanic/Latino; 1 American Indian or Alaska Native, non-Hispanic/Latino; 1 Asian, non-Hispanic/Latino; 2 Hispanic/Latino; 1 Two or more races, non-Hispanic/Latino), 1 international. Average age 32. 13 applicants, 38% accepted, 5 enrolled. In 2014, 6 master's awarded. *Degree requirements:* For master's, one foreign language, thesis optional. *Entrance requirements:* For master's, GRE (strongly recommended), three letters of recommendation. Additional exam requirements/recommendations for international students: Required—TOEFL (minimum score 550 paper-based; 79 iBT), Michigan English Language Assessment Battery (minimum score 85); Recommended—IELTS (minimum score 6.5). *Application deadline:* For fall admission, 6/1 priority date for domestic students, 5/1 priority date for international students; for winter admission, 10/1 priority date for domestic students, 9/1 priority date for international students; for spring admission, 2/1 priority date for domestic students, 1/1 priority date for international students. Applications are processed on a rolling basis. Application fee: $0. Electronic applications accepted. *Expenses:* Tuition, state resident: full-time $10,294; part-time

$571.90 per credit hour. Tuition, nonresident: full-time $29,730; part-time $1238.75 per credit hour. *Required fees:* $1365; $43.50 per credit hour. $291.10 per semester. Tuition and fees vary according to course load and program. *Financial support:* In 2014–15, 11 students received support. Fellowships, research assistantships, teaching assistantships, scholarships/grants, health care benefits, and unspecified assistantships available. Financial award application deadline: 3/31; financial award applicants required to submit FAFSA. *Unit head:* Dr. Anne Duggan, Department Chair, E-mail: a.duggan@wayne.edu. *Application contact:* Dr. Michael Giordano, Graduate Advisor, E-mail: aa2144@wayne.edu.
Website: http://clas.wayne.edu/languages/RomanceLanguagesLiteratures

Yale University, Graduate School of Arts and Sciences, Department of Italian Language and Literature, New Haven, CT 06520. Offers PhD. *Degree requirements:* For doctorate, 3 foreign languages, thesis/dissertation. *Entrance requirements:* For doctorate, GRE General Test.

Japanese

Arizona State University at the Tempe campus, College of Liberal Arts and Sciences, School of International Letters and Cultures, Program in Japanese, Tempe, AZ 85287-0202. Offers Asian languages and civilizations: Japanese (MA). Part-time and evening/weekend programs available. *Degree requirements:* For master's, thesis, oral defense, interactive Program of Study (iPOS) submitted no later than beginning of third semester of study. *Entrance requirements:* For master's, minimum GPA of 3.25 in the last two years of work leading to the bachelor's degree; BA in Japanese or at least 5 semesters of modern Japanese (preferred); personal statement; writing sample; 3 letters of recommendation. Additional exam requirements/recommendations for international students: Required—TOEFL (minimum score 550 paper-based; 83 iBT), IELTS (minimum score 6.5). Electronic applications accepted.

Columbia University, Graduate School of Arts and Sciences, New York, NY 10027. Offers African-American studies (MA); American studies (MA); anthropology (MA, PhD); art history and archaeology (MA, PhD); astronomy (PhD); biological sciences (PhD); biotechnology (MA); chemical physics (PhD); chemistry (PhD); classical studies (MA, PhD); classics (MA, PhD); climate and society (MA); earth and environmental sciences (PhD); East Asia: regional studies (MA); East Asian languages and cultures (MA, PhD); ecology, evolution and environmental biology (MA), including conservation biology; ecology, evolution, and environmental biology (PhD), including ecology and evolutionary biology, evolutionary primatology; economics (PhD); English and comparative literature (MA, PhD); French and Romance philology (MA, PhD); Germanic languages (MA, PhD); global French studies (MA); Hispanic cultural studies (MA); history (PhD); history and literature (MA); human rights studies (MA); Islamic studies (MA); Italian (MA, PhD); Japanese pedagogy (MA); Jewish studies (MA); Latin America and the Caribbean: regional studies (MA); Latin American and Iberian cultures (PhD); mathematics (MA, PhD), including finance (MA); medieval and Renaissance studies (MA); Middle Eastern, South Asian, and African studies (MA, PhD); modern art: critical and curatorial studies (MA); modern European studies (MA); museum anthropology (MA); music (DMA, PhD); oral history (MA); philosophical foundations of physics (MA); philosophy (MA, PhD); physics (PhD); political science (MA, PhD); psychology (PhD); quantitative methods in the social sciences (MA); religion (MA, PhD); Russia, Eurasia and East Europe: regional studies (MA); Russian translation (MA); Slavic cultures (MA); Slavic languages (MA, PhD); sociology (MA, PhD); South Asian studies (MA); statistics (MA, PhD); theatre (PhD); JD/PhD; MA/MS; MD/PhD; MPA/MA. Dual-degree programs require admission to both Graduate School of Arts and Sciences and another Columbia school. Part-time and evening/weekend programs available. Terminal master's awarded for partial completion of doctoral program. *Degree requirements:* For master's, thesis (for some programs); for doctorate, comprehensive exam, thesis/dissertation. *Entrance requirements:* For master's and doctorate, GRE General Test, GRE Subject Test (for some programs). Electronic applications accepted. *Faculty research:* Humanities, natural sciences, social sciences.

DePaul University, College of Liberal Arts and Social Sciences, Chicago, IL 60614. Offers Arabic (MA); Chinese (MA); English (MA); French (MA); German (MA); history (MA); interdisciplinary studies (MA, MS); international public service (MS); international studies (MA); Italian (MA); Japanese (MA); leadership and policy studies (MS); liberal studies (MA); new media studies (MA); nonprofit management (MNM); public administration (MPA); public health (MPH); public service management (MS); social work (MSW); sociology (MA); Spanish (MA); sustainable urban development (MA); women and gender studies (MA); writing and publishing (MA); writing, rhetoric, and discourse (MA); MA/PhD. Part-time and evening/weekend programs available. Postbaccalaureate distance learning degree programs offered (no on-campus study). Terminal master's awarded for partial completion of doctoral program. *Degree requirements:* For master's, variable foreign language requirement, comprehensive exam (for some programs), thesis (for some programs). Electronic applications accepted.

Eastern Michigan University, Graduate School, College of Arts and Sciences, Department of World Languages, Ypsilanti, MI 48197. Offers foreign languages (MA, Graduate Certificate), including French (MA), German (MA), German for business (Graduate Certificate), Hispanic language and cultures (Graduate Certificate), Japanese business practices (Graduate Certificate), Spanish (MA). Part-time and evening/weekend programs available. Postbaccalaureate distance learning degree programs offered (minimal on-campus study). *Faculty:* 20 full-time (14 women). *Students:* 5 full-time (4 women), 46 part-time (35 women); includes 10 minority (2 Black or African American, non-Hispanic/Latino; 2 Asian, non-Hispanic/Latino; 6 Hispanic/Latino), 4 international. Average age 33. 46 applicants, 74% accepted, 21 enrolled. In 2014, 23 master's, 1 other advanced degree awarded. *Degree requirements:* For master's, one foreign language. *Entrance requirements:* Additional exam requirements/recommendations for international students: Required—TOEFL. *Application deadline:* Applications are processed on a rolling basis. Application fee: $45. *Financial support:* Fellowships, research assistantships with full tuition reimbursements, teaching assistantships with full tuition reimbursements, career-related internships or fieldwork, Federal Work-Study, institutionally sponsored loans, scholarships/grants, tuition waivers (partial), and unspecified assistantships available. Support available to part-time students. Financial award applicants required to submit FAFSA. *Unit head:* Dr. Rosemary Weston-Gil, Department Head, 734-487-0130, Fax: 734-487-3411, E-mail: rweston3@emich.edu.

Harvard University, Graduate School of Arts and Sciences, Department of East Asian Languages and Civilizations, Cambridge, MA 02138. Offers Chinese (PhD); Japanese (PhD); Korean (PhD); Mongolian (PhD); Vietnamese (PhD). Terminal master's awarded for partial completion of doctoral program. *Degree requirements:* For doctorate, 3 foreign languages, thesis/dissertation, general exams. *Entrance requirements:* For doctorate, GRE General Test. Additional exam requirements/recommendations for international students: Required—TOEFL. *Faculty research:* Central Asian literature, religion, and premodern history.

Indiana University Bloomington, University Graduate School, College of Arts and Sciences, School of Global and International Studies, Department of East Asian Languages and Cultures, Bloomington, IN 47408. Offers Chinese (MA, PhD); Chinese language pedagogy (MA); East Asian studies (MA); Japanese (MA, PhD); Japanese language pedagogy (MA). Part-time programs available. *Faculty:* 21 full-time (11 women), 14 part-time/adjunct (7 women). *Students:* 10 full-time (7 women), 20 part-time (12 women); includes 3 minority (2 Asian, non-Hispanic/Latino; 1 Hispanic/Latino), 15 international. 87 applicants, 31% accepted, 8 enrolled. In 2014, 5 master's awarded. *Degree requirements:* For master's, one foreign language, thesis; for doctorate, 2 foreign languages, comprehensive exam, thesis/dissertation. *Entrance requirements:* Additional exam requirements/recommendations for international students: Required—TOEFL (minimum score 93 iBT). *Application deadline:* For fall admission, 1/1 for domestic students, 12/1 for international students. Application fee: $55 ($65 for international students). Electronic applications accepted. *Financial support:* In 2014–15, 23 students received support, including fellowships with full tuition reimbursements available (averaging $18,000 per year), teaching assistantships with full tuition reimbursements available (averaging $15,750 per year). Financial award application deadline: 2/15. *Faculty research:* Modern East Asian history; politics and society; traditional Chinese thought and society; medieval and premodern Japanese history, literature and society; modern Chinese and Japanese film and literature; Chinese, Japanese, Korean language and linguistics. *Unit head:* Prof. Natsuko Tsujimura, Chair, 812-855-0856, Fax: 812-855-6402, E-mail: tsujimur@indiana.edu. *Application contact:* Stephen Thomas Johnson, Student Services Assistant, 812-856-4959, E-mail: johnsost@indiana.edu.
Website: http://www.indiana.edu/~ealc/index.shtml

Kent State University, College of Arts and Sciences, Department of Modern and Classical Language Studies, Kent, OH 44242-0001. Offers translation (MA), including French, German, Japanese, Russian, Spanish; translation studies (PhD). Part-time programs available. *Faculty:* 36 full-time (22 women). *Students:* 89 full-time (56 women), 18 part-time (10 women); includes 12 minority (1 Black or African American, non-Hispanic/Latino; 3 Asian, non-Hispanic/Latino; 6 Hispanic/Latino; 2 Two or more races, non-Hispanic/Latino), 42 international. Average age 30. 228 applicants, 52% accepted, 90 enrolled. In 2014, 24 master's, 3 doctorates awarded. *Degree requirements:* For master's, variable foreign language requirement, comprehensive exam (for some programs), thesis (for some programs), case study (translation), language exam and interview (languages); for doctorate, variable foreign language requirement, comprehensive exam, thesis/dissertation. *Entrance requirements:* For master's, minimum GPA of 3.0, transcript, goal statement, conversational sample in two languages, written sample in second language, 3 letters of recommendation; for doctorate, minimum GPA of 3.0, transcript, goal statement, writing sample, professional credentials, 3 letters of recommendation. Additional exam requirements/recommendations for international students: Required—TOEFL (minimum score: paper-based 525, iBT 71), Michigan English Language Assessment Battery (minimum score of 75), IELTS (minimum score of 6.0), PTE Academic (minimum score of 48), or completion of ELS level 112 Intensive Program. *Application deadline:* For fall admission, 2/28 for domestic and international students. Applications are processed on a rolling basis. Application fee: $45 ($70 for international students). Electronic applications accepted. *Expenses:* Tuition, state resident: full-time $8730; part-time $485 per credit hour. Tuition, nonresident: full-time $14,886; part-time $827 per credit hour. Tuition and fees vary according to campus/location and program. *Financial support:* Research assistantships with full tuition reimbursements, teaching assistantships with full tuition reimbursements, Federal Work-Study, scholarships/grants, and unspecified assistantships available. Financial award application deadline: 2/1. *Unit head:* Keiran Dunne, Professor and Chair, 330-672-1805, E-mail: kdunne@kent.edu. *Application contact:* Brian James Baer, Professor and Graduate Coordinator, 330-672-2150, Fax: 330-672-4009, E-mail: bbaer@kent.edu.
Website: http://www.kent.edu/mcls/

New York University, Steinhardt School of Culture, Education, and Human Development, Department of Teaching and Learning, Program in Multilingual/Multicultural Studies, New York, NY 10003. Offers bilingual education (PhD); bilingual education for teachers (MA, Advanced Certificate); foreign language education (MA); teachers of English to speakers of other languages in college (PhD); teachers of French 7-12 (MA); teachers of Hebrew 7-12 (MA); teaching a foreign language 7-12 (MA), including teaching English to speakers of other languages, all grades; teaching English to speakers of other languages (MA); teaching foreign languages, 7-12 (MA), including Chinese, French, Italian, Japanese, Spanish; teaching French as a foreign language (MA), including teaching English to speakers of other languages; teaching Spanish as a foreign language and TESOL (MA). *Accreditation:* Teacher Education Accreditation Council. Part-time and evening/weekend programs available. *Faculty:* 6 full-time (4 women). *Students:* 118 full-time (94 women), 82 part-time (72 women); includes 40 minority (8 Black or African American, non-Hispanic/Latino; 18 Asian, non-Hispanic/Latino; 12 Hispanic/Latino; 2 Two or more races, non-Hispanic/Latino), 116 international. Average age 29. 431 applicants, 61% accepted, 92 enrolled. In 2014, 121 master's, 1 doctorate, 2 other advanced degrees awarded. *Degree requirements:* For master's, thesis (for some programs); for doctorate, thesis/dissertation. *Entrance requirements:* For doctorate, GRE General Test, interview; for Advanced Certificate, master's degree. Additional exam requirements/recommendations for international students: Required—TOEFL (minimum score 100 iBT). *Application deadline:* For fall admission, 12/1 priority date for domestic and international students; for spring admission, 10/1 for domestic and international students. Applications are processed on a rolling basis. Application fee: $75. Electronic applications accepted. *Financial support:* Fellowships with full and partial tuition reimbursements, career-related internships or fieldwork, Federal Work-Study, institutionally sponsored loans, scholarships/grants, and tuition waivers (partial) available. Support available to part-time students. Financial award application deadline: 2/1; financial award applicants required to submit FAFSA. *Faculty research:* Second language acquisition, cross-cultural communication,

technology-enhanced language learning, language variation, action learning. *Unit head:* Prof. Shondel Nero, Director, 212-998-5757, E-mail: shondel.nero@nyu.edu. *Application contact:* 212-998-5030, Fax: 212-995-4328, E-mail: steinhardt.gradadmissions@nyu.edu.
Website: http://steinhardt.nyu.edu/teachlearn/mms

The Ohio State University, Graduate School, College of Arts and Sciences, Division of Arts and Humanities, Department of East Asian Languages and Literatures, Columbus, OH 43210. Offers Chinese (MA, PhD); Japanese (MA, PhD). *Faculty:* 20. *Students:* 53 full-time (32 women), 3 part-time (2 women); includes 7 minority (1 Black or African American, non-Hispanic/Latino; 5 Asian, non-Hispanic/Latino; 1 Two or more races, non-Hispanic/Latino), 31 international. Average age 30. In 2014, 13 master's, 3 doctorates awarded. Terminal master's awarded for partial completion of doctoral program. *Degree requirements:* For master's, thesis optional; for doctorate, thesis/dissertation. *Entrance requirements:* For master's and doctorate, GRE General Test (if applying for financial aid). Additional exam requirements/recommendations for international students: Required—TOEFL (minimum score 577 paper-based; 90 iBT); Recommended—IELTS (minimum score 7.5). *Application deadline:* For fall admission, 11/30 priority date for domestic and international students; for winter admission, 12/1 for domestic students, 11/1 for international students; for spring admission, 3/1 for domestic students, 2/1 for international students. Applications are processed on a rolling basis. Application fee: $60 ($70 for international students). Electronic applications accepted. *Financial support:* Fellowships, research assistantships, teaching assistantships, Federal Work-Study, institutionally sponsored loans, and unspecified assistantships available. Support available to part-time students. *Unit head:* Mark Bender, PhD, Chair and Professor, 614-688-5737, E-mail: bender.4@osu.edu. *Application contact:* Graduate and Professional Admissions, 614-292-9444, Fax: 614-292-3895, E-mail: gpadmissions@osu.edu.
Website: http://deall.osu.edu/

Portland State University, Graduate Studies, College of Liberal Arts and Sciences, Department of World Languages and Literatures, Portland, OR 97207-0751. Offers foreign literature and language (MA); French (MA); German (MA); Japanese (MA); Spanish (MA). Part-time programs available. *Faculty:* 48 full-time (28 women), 33 part-time/adjunct (29 women). *Students:* 30 full-time (13 women), 8 part-time (3 women); includes 7 minority (2 Asian, non-Hispanic/Latino; 5 Hispanic/Latino), 13 international. Average age 30. 31 applicants, 65% accepted, 18 enrolled. In 2014, 9 master's awarded. *Degree requirements:* For master's, one foreign language, thesis (for some programs). *Entrance requirements:* Additional exam requirements/recommendations for international students: Required—TOEFL (minimum score 550 paper-based; 80 iBT), IELTS (minimum score 6.5). *Application deadline:* For fall admission, 4/1 for domestic students, 3/1 for international students; for winter admission, 9/1 for domestic students, 7/1 for international students; for spring admission, 11/1 for domestic and international students. Applications are processed on a rolling basis. Application fee: $50. *Expenses:* Tuition, state resident: part-time $222 per credit. Tuition, nonresident: part-time $527 per credit. *Required fees:* $22 per contact hour. $100 per quarter. Tuition and fees vary according to program. *Financial support:* In 2014–15, 29 teaching assistantships with full and partial tuition reimbursements (averaging $3,251 per year) were awarded; research assistantships with full tuition reimbursements, Federal Work-Study, scholarships/grants, and unspecified assistantships also available. Support available to part-time students. Financial award application deadline: 3/1; financial award applicants required to submit FAFSA. *Faculty research:* Foreign language pedagogy, applied and social linguistics, literary history and criticism. *Total annual research expenditures:* $412,070. *Unit head:* Dr. Jennifer Perlmutter, Chair, 503-725-8783, Fax: 503-725-5276, E-mail: jrp@pdx.edu.
Website: http://www.pdx.edu/wll/

Purdue University, Graduate School, College of Liberal Arts, School of Languages and Cultures, West Lafayette, IN 47907. Offers French (MA, MAT, PhD), including French (MA, PhD), French education (MAT); German (MA, MAT, PhD), including German (MA, PhD), German education (MAT); Japanese pedagogy (MA); Spanish (MA, MAT, PhD), including Spanish (MA, PhD), Spanish education (MAT). Terminal master's awarded for partial completion of doctoral program. *Degree requirements:* For master's, one foreign language; for doctorate, 2 foreign languages, thesis/dissertation. *Entrance requirements:* For master's, GRE General Test (minimum score 600, 160 for new scoring), two writing samples, one in English, one in language (French, German, Japanese, or Spanish); sample recording of English and language of study; for doctorate, GRE General Test (minimum score 600, 160 for new scoring), master's degree with minimum GPA of 3.5 or equivalent; two writing samples, one in English, one in language (French, German, Japanese, or Spanish); sample recording of English and language of study. Additional exam requirements/recommendations for international students: Required—TOEFL (minimum score 550 paper-based; 77 iBT); Recommended—TWE. Electronic applications accepted. *Faculty research:* Linguistics, semiotics, literary criticism, pedagogy.

San Francisco State University, Division of Graduate Studies, College of Liberal and Creative Arts, Department of Foreign Languages and Literatures, Program in Japanese, San Francisco, CA 94132-1722. Offers MA. Part-time programs available. *Application deadline:* Applications are processed on a rolling basis. *Expenses:* Tuition, state resident: full-time $6738. Tuition, nonresident: full-time $17,898; part-time $372 per credit hour. *Required fees:* $498 per semester. *Unit head:* Dr. Masahiko Minami, Program Coordinator, 415-338-7451, Fax: 415-405-0588, E-mail: mminami@sfsu.edu. *Application contact:* Dr. Makiko Asano, Graduate Advisor, 415-338-1131, Fax: 415-405-0588, E-mail: masano@sfsu.edu.
Website: http://japanese.sfsu.edu/

Stanford University, School of Humanities and Sciences, Department of East Asian Languages and Cultures, Stanford, CA 94305-9991. Offers Chinese (MA, PhD); Japanese (MA, PhD). Terminal master's awarded for partial completion of doctoral program. *Degree requirements:* For master's, one foreign language, thesis or an annotated translation of a literary or historical text; for doctorate, 2 foreign languages, thesis/dissertation, field exams. *Entrance requirements:* For master's and doctorate, GRE General Test. Additional exam requirements/recommendations for international students: Required—TOEFL. Electronic applications accepted. *Expenses:* Tuition: Full-time $44,184; part-time $982 per credit hour. *Required fees:* $191.

University of Alberta, Faculty of Graduate Studies and Research, Department of East Asian Studies, Edmonton, AB T6G 2E1, Canada. Offers Chinese literature (MA); East Asian interdisciplinary studies (MA); Japanese literature (MA). Part-time programs available. *Degree requirements:* For master's, one foreign language, thesis. *Entrance requirements:* Additional exam requirements/recommendations for international students: Required—TOEFL. Electronic applications accepted. *Faculty research:* Classical Chinese poetry and poetics, Chinese philosophy, modern/contemporary Chinese literature, modern Japanese literature and culture, Japanese women's writing.

University of California, Berkeley, Graduate Division, College of Letters and Science, Department of East Asian Languages and Cultures, Berkeley, CA 94720-1500. Offers Chinese language (PhD); Japanese language (PhD). *Degree requirements:* For doctorate, one foreign language, thesis/dissertation, oral qualifying exam. *Entrance requirements:* For doctorate, GRE General Test, minimum GPA of 3.0, MA thesis, 3

letters of recommendation. Electronic applications accepted. *Faculty research:* Chinese and Japanese modern and classical texts, prose, and poetry; Chinese and Japanese linguistics.

University of California, Irvine, School of Humanities, Department of East Asian Languages and Literatures, Irvine, CA 92697. Offers Chinese (MA, PhD); East Asian languages and literatures (MA, PhD); Japanese (MA, PhD). *Students:* 12 full-time (10 women), 1 (woman) part-time; includes 4 minority (3 Asian, non-Hispanic/Latino; 1 Two or more races, non-Hispanic/Latino), 7 international. Average age 30. 40 applicants, 15% accepted, 3 enrolled. In 2014, 1 doctorate awarded. *Degree requirements:* For doctorate, thesis/dissertation. *Entrance requirements:* For master's and doctorate, GRE General Test, minimum GPA of 3.0. Additional exam requirements/recommendations for international students: Required—TOEFL (minimum score 550 paper-based). *Application deadline:* For fall admission, 1/15 priority date for domestic students, 1/15 for international students. Application fee: $90 ($110 for international students). Electronic applications accepted. *Financial support:* Fellowships with tuition reimbursements, research assistantships with full tuition reimbursements, teaching assistantships with partial tuition reimbursements, institutionally sponsored loans, traineeships, health care benefits, and unspecified assistantships available. Financial award application deadline: 3/1; financial award applicants required to submit FAFSA. *Faculty research:* Chinese, Japanese, and Korean literature and culture; language and textual analysis; historical, social, and cultural dimensions of literary study. *Unit head:* Michael A. Fuller, Chair, 949-824-2802 Ext. 2227, Fax: 949-824-3248, E-mail: mafuller@uci.edu. *Application contact:* Hu Ying, Graduate Faculty Advisor, 949-824-6312, Fax: 949-824-3248, E-mail: huying@uci.edu.
Website: http://www.hnet.uci.edu/eastasian/

University of Colorado Boulder, Graduate School, College of Arts and Sciences, Department of Asian Languages and Civilizations, Boulder, CO 80309. Offers Chinese (MA, PhD); Japanese (MA, PhD). *Faculty:* 11 full-time (4 women). *Students:* 24 full-time (12 women), 3 part-time (all women); includes 4 minority (2 Asian, non-Hispanic/Latino; 1 Hispanic/Latino; 1 Two or more races, non-Hispanic/Latino), 9 international. Average age 30. 55 applicants, 58% accepted, 12 enrolled. In 2014, 11 master's awarded. Terminal master's awarded for partial completion of doctoral program. *Degree requirements:* For master's, comprehensive exam. *Entrance requirements:* For master's, BA in Chinese or Japanese, minimum undergraduate GPA of 3.0. Additional exam requirements/recommendations for international students: Required—TOEFL. *Application deadline:* For fall admission, 1/1 for domestic students, 12/1 for international students; for spring admission, 10/1 for domestic students, 9/1 for international students. Applications are processed on a rolling basis. Application fee: $50 ($70 for international students). Electronic applications accepted. *Financial support:* In 2014–15, 63 students received support, including 11 fellowships (averaging $3,624 per year), 20 teaching assistantships with full and partial tuition reimbursements available (averaging $26,470 per year); institutionally sponsored loans, scholarships/grants, health care benefits, and unspecified assistantships also available. Financial award application deadline: 2/1; financial award applicants required to submit FAFSA. *Faculty research:* Asian languages/literature, Chinese language/literature, literary criticism, Japanese language/literature. *Total annual research expenditures:* $401,438.
Website: http://alc.colorado.edu/

University of Hawaii at Manoa, Graduate Division, College of Languages, Linguistics and Literature, Department of East Asian Languages and Literatures, Program in Japanese, Honolulu, HI 96822. Offers MA, PhD. Part-time programs available. *Degree requirements:* For master's, 2 foreign languages, thesis optional; for doctorate, 2 foreign languages, comprehensive exam, thesis/dissertation. *Entrance requirements:* For master's and doctorate, GRE General Test. Additional exam requirements/recommendations for international students: Required—TOEFL (minimum score 560 paper-based; 83 iBT), IELTS (minimum score 5).

University of Hawaii at Manoa, Graduate Division, School of Pacific and Asian Studies, Program in Asian Studies, Concentration in Japanese Studies, Honolulu, HI 96822. Offers Graduate Certificate. Part-time programs available. *Degree requirements:* For Graduate Certificate, one foreign language. *Entrance requirements:* For degree, GRE. Additional exam requirements/recommendations for international students: Required—TOEFL (minimum score 560 paper-based; 83 iBT), IELTS (minimum score 5).

The University of Manchester, School of Languages, Linguistics and Cultures, Manchester, United Kingdom. Offers Arab world studies (PhD); Chinese studies (M Phil, PhD); East Asian studies (M Phil, PhD); English language (PhD); French studies (M Phil, PhD); German studies (M Phil, PhD); interpreting studies (PhD); Italian studies (M Phil, PhD); Japanese studies (M Phil, PhD); Latin American cultural studies (M Phil, PhD); linguistics (M Phil, PhD); Middle Eastern studies (M Phil, PhD); Polish studies (M Phil, PhD); Portuguese studies (M Phil, PhD); Russian studies (M Phil, PhD); Spanish studies (M Phil, PhD); translation and intercultural studies (M Phil, PhD).

University of Massachusetts Amherst, Graduate School, College of Humanities and Fine Arts, Department of Languages, Literatures, and Cultures, Programs in Asian Languages and Literatures, Amherst, MA 01003. Offers Chinese (MA); Japanese (MA). Part-time programs available. *Faculty:* 13 full-time (6 women). *Students:* 35 full-time (23 women), 6 part-time (4 women); includes 5 minority (all Asian, non-Hispanic/Latino), 22 international. Average age 28. 34 applicants, 50% accepted, 9 enrolled. In 2014, 6 master's awarded. *Degree requirements:* For master's, thesis, general exam. *Entrance requirements:* For master's, GRE General Test. Additional exam requirements/recommendations for international students: Required—TOEFL (minimum score 550 paper-based; 80 iBT), IELTS (minimum score 6.5). *Application deadline:* For fall admission, 2/1 for domestic and international students. Applications are processed on a rolling basis. Application fee: $75. Electronic applications accepted. *Expenses:* Tuition, state resident: full-time $1980; part-time $110 per credit. Tuition, nonresident: full-time $14,644; part-time $414 per credit. *Required fees:* $11,417. One-time fee: $357. *Financial support:* Fellowships with full and partial tuition reimbursements, research assistantships with full and partial tuition reimbursements, teaching assistantships with full and partial tuition reimbursements, career-related internships or fieldwork, Federal Work-Study, scholarships/grants, traineeships, health care benefits, tuition waivers (full and partial), and unspecified assistantships available. Support available to part-time students. Financial award application deadline: 2/1. *Unit head:* Dr. Stephen Miller, Department Head/Chair, 413-545-0886, Fax: 413-545-4975. *Application contact:* Lindsay DeSantis, Supervisor of Admissions, 413-545-0722, Fax: 413-577-0100, E-mail: gradadm@grad.umass.edu.
Website: http://www.umass.edu/asianlan/

University of Oregon, Graduate School, College of Arts and Sciences, Department of East Asian Languages and Literature, Eugene, OR 97403. Offers Chinese (MA, PhD); Japanese (MA, PhD). *Entrance requirements:* Additional exam requirements/recommendations for international students: Required—TOEFL. *Faculty research:* Linguistics, pedagogy.

University of Washington, Graduate School, College of Arts and Sciences, Department of Asian Languages and Literature, Seattle, WA 98195. Offers Buddhist studies (MA, PhD); Chinese language and literature (MA, PhD); Japanese language and

literature (MA, PhD); Korean language and literature (MA, PhD); South Asian language and literature (MA, PhD). *Degree requirements:* For master's, 2 foreign languages, general exam, thesis or 2 research papers; for doctorate, 3 foreign languages, thesis/dissertation, general exam. *Entrance requirements:* For master's, GRE, minimum GPA of 3.0; for doctorate, GRE, master's degree in related field, minimum GPA of 3.0. Additional exam requirements/recommendations for international students: Required—TOEFL. Electronic applications accepted. *Faculty research:* Textual, linguistic, philological, and literary study of languages and literatures of Asia.

University of Wisconsin–Madison, Graduate School, College of Letters and Science, Department of East Asian Languages and Literature, Program in Japanese Linguistics, Madison, WI 53706-1380. Offers MA, PhD. Part-time programs available. Terminal master's awarded for partial completion of doctoral program. *Degree requirements:* For master's, one foreign language, seminars, written exam; for doctorate, 3 foreign languages, thesis/dissertation, seminars, preliminary exams, oral exam. *Entrance requirements:* For master's, GRE General Test, bachelor's degree or equivalent in Japanese; for doctorate, GRE General Test, master's degree or equivalent in Japanese. Electronic applications accepted. *Expenses:* Tuition, state resident: full-time $10,723; part-time $745 per credit. Tuition, nonresident: full-time $24,054; part-time $1578 per credit. *Required fees:* $374 per semester. Tuition and fees vary according to course load, program and reciprocity agreements. *Faculty research:* Modern and historical Japanese linguistics, modern Japanese fiction and poetry, classical Japanese literature, language pedagogy.

Washington University in St. Louis, Graduate School of Arts and Sciences, Department of East Asian Languages and Cultures, St. Louis, MO 63130-4899. Offers Chinese (MA); Chinese and comparative literature (PhD); Chinese language and literature (PhD); East Asian studies (MA); Japanese (MA); Japanese and comparative literature (PhD); Japanese language and literature (PhD). Terminal master's awarded for partial completion of doctoral program. *Degree requirements:* For master's, thesis optional; for doctorate, thesis/dissertation. *Entrance requirements:* For master's and doctorate, GRE General Test. Additional exam requirements/recommendations for international students: Required—TOEFL. Electronic applications accepted. *Faculty research:* Chinese; Japanese; Chinese fiction, theater, poetry, modern literature; Japanese modern and classical fiction, translation theory; East Asian Studies.

Near and Middle Eastern Languages

The American University in Cairo, School of Humanities and Social Sciences, Department of Arab and Islamic Civilizations, Cairo, Egypt. Offers Arabic language and literature (MA); Islamic art and architecture (MA); Islamic studies (MA, Diploma); Middle Eastern history (MA). Part-time programs available. *Degree requirements:* For master's, thesis optional, proficiency in French or German. *Entrance requirements:* Additional exam requirements/recommendations for international students: Required—English entrance exam and/or TOEFL. Electronic applications accepted. Tuition and fees vary according to course load and program. *Faculty research:* History of early Islam, Ayyubid, and Mamluk periods; nineteenth- and twentieth-century Middle East Islamic jurisprudence; contemporary Arabic literary criticism.

American University of Beirut, Graduate Programs, Faculty of Arts and Sciences, Beirut, Lebanon. Offers anthropology (MA); Arab and Middle Eastern history (PhD); Arabic language and literature (MA, PhD); archaeology (MA); biology (MS); cell and molecular biology (PhD); chemistry (MS); clinical psychology (MA); computational sciences (MS); computer science (MS); economics (MA); English language (MA); English literature (MA); environmental policy planning (MS); financial economics (MAFE); geology (MS); history (MA); mathematics (MA, MS); media studies (MA); Middle Eastern studies (MA); physics (MS); political studies (MA); psychology (MA); public administration (MA); sociology (MA); statistics (MA, MS); theoretical physics (PhD); transnational American studies (MA). Part-time programs available. *Faculty:* 107 full-time (32 women), 6 part-time/adjunct (2 women). *Students:* 230 full-time (161 women), 209 part-time (146 women). Average age 26. 261 applicants, 70% accepted, 83 enrolled. In 2014, 68 master's, 2 doctorates awarded. *Degree requirements:* For master's, one foreign language, comprehensive exam, thesis (for some programs); for doctorate, one foreign language, comprehensive exam, thesis/dissertation. *Entrance requirements:* For master's, GRE (for some MA/MS programs), letter of recommendation; for doctorate, GRE, letters of recommendation. Additional exam requirements/recommendations for international students: Required—TOEFL (minimum score 600 paper-based; 97 iBT), IELTS (minimum score 7). *Application deadline:* For fall admission, 4/1 for domestic and international students; for spring admission, 11/1 for domestic and international students. Application fee: $50. Electronic applications accepted. *Expenses: Tuition:* Full-time $15,462; part-time $859 per credit. *Required fees:* $692. Tuition and fees vary according to course load and program. *Financial support:* Research assistantships, career-related internships or fieldwork, institutionally sponsored loans, scholarships/grants, health care benefits, and unspecified assistantships available. Financial award application deadline: 2/4; financial award applicants required to submit FAFSA. *Faculty research:* Determinants of language proficiency among Arab learners of English as a foreign language; opinion mining, information retrieval, runtime verification, high performance computing; solar and fuel cells, self-organizing systems, heterocyclic chemistry, air and water chemistry; complex analysis, harmonic analysis, number theory; social and political psychology, clinical psychology; thin films physics and technology; theory of soft matter; religious and ethnic conflict; sports and politics. *Total annual research expenditures:* $966,000. *Unit head:* Dr. Patrick McGreevy, Dean, 961-1374374 Ext. 3800, Fax: 961-1744461, E-mail: pm07@aub.edu.lb. *Application contact:* Dr. Salim Kanaan, Director, Admissions Office, 961-1350000 Ext. 2590, Fax: 961-1750775, E-mail: sk00@aub.edu.lb.
Website: http://www.aub.edu.lb/fas/

Bethel Seminary, Graduate and Professional Programs, St. Paul, MN 55112-6998. Offers Anglican studies (Certificate); children's and family ministry (MA); Christian studies (Certificate); Christian thought (MA); Greek and Hebrew language (M Div); Greek language (M Div); Hebrew language (M Div); marriage and family therapy (MA, Certificate); ministry (D Min); ministry practice (MA, Certificate); theological studies (MA, Certificate); transformational leadership (MA); young life youth ministry (Certificate). *Accreditation:* ACIPE; ATS (one or more programs are accredited). Part-time and evening/weekend programs available. Postbaccalaureate distance learning degree programs offered (minimal on-campus study). *Faculty:* 15 full-time (3 women), 55 part-time/adjunct (27 women). *Students:* 422 full-time (167 women), 231 part-time (71 women); includes 165 minority (62 Black or African American, non-Hispanic/Latino; 58 Asian, non-Hispanic/Latino; 29 Hispanic/Latino; 1 Native Hawaiian or other Pacific Islander, non-Hispanic/Latino; 15 Two or more races, non-Hispanic/Latino), 16 international. Average age 37. 272 applicants, 77% accepted, 165 enrolled. In 2014, 147 master's, 13 doctorates, 8 other advanced degrees awarded. *Degree requirements:* For master's, variable foreign language requirement, thesis (for some programs); for doctorate, thesis/dissertation. *Entrance requirements:* For master's, letters of reference, transcripts, personal statement; for doctorate, M Div, letters of reference, organizational support; for Certificate, letters of reference, family essay, personal statement, and family of origin paper (for marriage and family therapy). Additional exam requirements/recommendations for international students: Required—TOEFL (minimum score 550 paper-based; 87 iBT). *Application deadline:* For fall admission, 8/1 priority date for domestic students, 8/1 for international students; for winter admission, 12/1 priority date for domestic students; for spring admission, 1/1 priority date for domestic students. Applications are processed on a rolling basis. Application fee: $0. Electronic applications accepted. *Financial support:* In 2014–15, 558 students received support, including 17 teaching assistantships; career-related internships or fieldwork, Federal Work-Study, and scholarships/grants also available. Financial award applicants required to submit FAFSA. *Faculty research:* Nature of theology, ethics, Biblical commentaries, nature of God, science and theology. *Unit head:* Dr. David Clark, Vice-President and Dean, Bethel Seminary, 651-638-6659. *Application contact:* Jen Niska, Director of Admissions, 651-638-6288, Fax: 651-638-6002, E-mail: bsem-admit@bethel.edu.

Brandeis University, Graduate School of Arts and Sciences, Department of Near Eastern and Judaic Studies, Waltham, MA 02454-9110. Offers Near Eastern and Judaic studies (MA, PhD); Near Eastern and Judaic studies and sociology (PhD); Near Eastern and Judaic studies and women's and gender studies (MA); teaching of Hebrew (MAT). Part-time programs available. Terminal master's awarded for partial completion of doctoral program. *Degree requirements:* For master's, one foreign language, thesis or alternative, proseminar, capstone; for doctorate, variable foreign language requirement, comprehensive exam, thesis/dissertation. *Entrance requirements:* For master's and doctorate, 3 letters of recommendation, transcript(s), statement of purpose, writing sample, resume. Additional exam requirements/recommendations for international students: Required—TOEFL (minimum score 600 paper-based; 100 iBT), PTE (minimum score 68); Recommended—IELTS (minimum score 7). Electronic applications accepted. *Faculty research:* Ancient Near East and Bible, Judaic studies, Israel Studies, modern Middle East, Arabic and Islamic civilizations.

The Catholic University of America, School of Arts and Sciences, Department of Semitic and Egyptian Languages and Literatures, Washington, DC 20064. Offers Ancient Near East (Biblical Hebrew/Aramaic) (MA, PhD); Arabic (PhD); Christian Near East (Biblical Hebrew/Aramaic) (MA); Coptic (MA, PhD); Syriac (MA). Part-time programs available. *Faculty:* 3 full-time (0 women), 1 part-time/adjunct (0 women). *Students:* 10 full-time (2 women), 16 part-time (3 women); includes 3 minority (1 Hispanic/Latino; 2 Two or more races, non-Hispanic/Latino), 1 international. Average age 34. 11 applicants, 73% accepted, 4 enrolled. In 2014, 7 master's, 2 doctorates awarded. *Degree requirements:* For master's, one foreign language, comprehensive exam; for doctorate, 2 foreign languages, comprehensive exam, thesis/dissertation. *Entrance requirements:* For master's and doctorate, GRE General Test, statement of purpose, official copies of academic transcripts, three letters of recommendation. Additional exam requirements/recommendations for international students: Required—TOEFL (minimum score 580 paper-based). *Application deadline:* For fall admission, 7/15 priority date for domestic students, 7/1 for international students; for spring admission, 11/15 priority date for domestic students, 11/1 for international students. Applications are processed on a rolling basis. Application fee: $55. Electronic applications accepted. *Expenses: Tuition:* Full-time $40,200; part-time $1600 per credit hour. *Required fees:* $400; $195 per semester. One-time fee: $425. *Financial support:* Fellowships, research assistantships, teaching assistantships, Federal Work-Study, scholarships/grants, tuition waivers (full and partial), and unspecified assistantships available. Financial award application deadline: 2/1; financial award applicants required to submit FAFSA. *Faculty research:* Christian history and literature of the Near East, Biblical Hebrew, Arabic Christianity, Coptic, Syriac. *Unit head:* Dr. Edward M. Cook, Chair, 202-319-5083, Fax: 202-319-4735, E-mail: cooke@cua.edu. *Application contact:* Director of Graduate Admissions, 202-319-5057, Fax: 202-319-6533, E-mail: cua-admissions@cua.edu.
Website: http://semitics.cua.edu/

DePaul University, College of Liberal Arts and Social Sciences, Chicago, IL 60614. Offers Arabic (MA); Chinese (MA); English (MA); French (MA); German (MA); history (MA); interdisciplinary studies (MA, MS); international public service (MS); international studies (MA); Italian (MA); Japanese (MA); leadership and policy studies (MS); liberal studies (MA); new media studies (MA); nonprofit management (MNM); public administration (MPA); public health (MPH); public service management (MS); social work (MSW); sociology (MA); Spanish (MA); sustainable urban development (MA); women and gender studies (MA); writing and publishing (MA); writing, rhetoric, and discourse (MA); MA/PhD. Part-time and evening/weekend programs available. Postbaccalaureate distance learning degree programs offered (no on-campus study). Terminal master's awarded for partial completion of doctoral program. *Degree requirements:* For master's, variable foreign language requirement, comprehensive exam (for some programs), thesis (for some programs). Electronic applications accepted.

Georgetown University, Graduate School of Arts and Sciences, Edmund A. Walsh School of Foreign Service, The Center for Contemporary Arab Studies, Washington, DC 20057. Offers MA, Certificate, MA/JD, MA/PhD. *Degree requirements:* For master's, one foreign language, comprehensive exam, thesis or alternative, proficiency in Arabic. *Entrance requirements:* For master's, GRE, minimum GPA of 3.0. Additional exam requirements/recommendations for international students: Required—TOEFL (minimum score 600 paper-based; 100 iBT). Electronic applications accepted. *Faculty research:* Contemporary Arab world.

Harvard University, Graduate School of Arts and Sciences, Department of Near Eastern Languages and Civilizations, Cambridge, MA 02138. Offers Akkadian and Sumerian (AM, PhD); Arabic (AM, PhD); Armenian (AM, PhD); biblical history (AM, PhD); Hebrew (AM, PhD); Indo-Muslim culture (AM, PhD); Iranian (AM, PhD); Jewish history and literature (AM, PhD); Persian (AM, PhD); Semitic philology (AM, PhD); Syro-Palestinian archaeology (AM, PhD); Turkish (AM, PhD). *Degree requirements:* For doctorate, variable foreign language requirement, thesis/dissertation, general exams. *Entrance requirements:* For master's, GRE General Test; for doctorate, GRE General Test, proficiency in a Near Eastern language. Additional exam requirements/recommendations for international students: Required—TOEFL.

Hebrew Union College–Jewish Institute of Religion, School of Graduate Studies, Program in Hebrew Letters, New York, NY 10012-1186. Offers DHL. *Degree requirements:* For doctorate, one foreign language, thesis/dissertation. *Entrance requirements:* For doctorate, GRE. Additional exam requirements/recommendations for international students: Required—TOEFL. *Expenses:* Contact institution. *Faculty research:* Philosophy and theology, Bible, Hebrew, pastoral care, history and Rabbinics.

Indiana University Bloomington, University Graduate School, College of Arts and Sciences, School of Global and International Studies, Department of Near Eastern Languages and Cultures, Bloomington, IN 47405-7000. Offers MA, PhD. Part-time programs available. *Faculty:* 12 full-time (4 women). *Students:* 54 full-time (21 women), 4 part-time (1 woman); includes 3 minority (1 Black or African American, non-Hispanic/Latino; 1 Asian, non-Hispanic/Latino; 1 Two or more races, non-Hispanic/Latino), 33 international. Average age 32. 63 applicants, 43% accepted, 14 enrolled. In 2014, 9 master's, 5 doctorates awarded. Terminal master's awarded for partial completion of doctoral program. *Degree requirements:* For master's, 2 foreign languages, comprehensive exam, thesis or alternative; for doctorate, 3 foreign languages, comprehensive exam, thesis/dissertation. *Entrance requirements:* For master's and doctorate, GRE General Test. Additional exam requirements/recommendations for international students: Required—TOEFL. *Application deadline:* For fall admission, 1/15 priority date for domestic students, 12/15 for international students. Application fee: $55 ($65 for international students). Electronic applications accepted. *Financial support:* In 2014–15, 6 fellowships with full tuition reimbursements (averaging $18,000 per year), 2 research assistantships with full tuition reimbursements (averaging $15,750 per year), 14 teaching assistantships with full tuition reimbursements (averaging $7,875 per year) were awarded; Federal Work-Study, institutionally sponsored loans, and unspecified assistantships also available. Financial award application deadline: 1/1; financial award applicants required to submit FAFSA. *Faculty research:* Classical and modern Arabic literature and linguistics, Biblical and modern Hebrew studies, Persian language and literature, Islamic civilization, Iranian history and language. *Unit head:* Prof. Asma Afsaruddin, Chair, 812-855-5993, Fax: 812-855-7841. *Application contact:* Delgar Woodruff, Academic Secretary, 812-856-3711, Fax: 812-855-7841, E-mail: ubattulg@indiana.edu.
Website: http://www.indiana.edu/~nelc/

Johns Hopkins University, Zanvyl Krieger School of Arts and Sciences, Department of Near Eastern Studies, Baltimore, MD 21218-2699. Offers archaeology (PhD); Assyriology (PhD); Egyptology (PhD); Hebrew Bible/Northwest Semitics (PhD). *Degree requirements:* For doctorate, 2 foreign languages, comprehensive exam, thesis/dissertation. *Entrance requirements:* For doctorate, GRE. Additional exam requirements/recommendations for international students: Required—TOEFL (minimum score 600 paper-based; 100 iBT); Recommended—IELTS. Electronic applications accepted. *Faculty research:* Egyptology, Assyriology, Hebrew Bible/Northwest Semitic languages, Demotic Egyptian, archaeology.

Middlebury College, Language Schools, Arabic School, Middlebury, VT 05753-6002. Offers Arabic language pedagogy (MA); Arabic studies (MA). *Faculty:* 40 full-time (20 women). *Students:* 25 full-time (11 women); includes 3 minority (1 Asian, non-Hispanic/Latino; 1 Hispanic/Latino; 1 Two or more races, non-Hispanic/Latino), 9 international. Average age 32. 51 applicants, 61% accepted, 25 enrolled. *Degree requirements:* For master's, one foreign language. *Entrance requirements:* For master's, Arabic language oral and written proficiency tests, 3 letters of recommendation, personal statement, transcripts, writing sample in Arabic, Arabic course history, 4 years or equivalent of Arabic language study. Additional exam requirements/recommendations for international students: Required—TOEFL. *Application deadline:* Applications are processed on a rolling basis. Application fee: $65. Electronic applications accepted. *Financial support:* Scholarships/grants available. Financial award applicants required to submit FAFSA. *Unit head:* Dr. Mahmoud Abdalla, Director, 802-443-5230, Fax: 802-443-2075, E-mail: mabdalla@miis.edu. *Application contact:* Barbara Walter, Coordinator, 802-443-5230, Fax: 802-443-2075, E-mail: bwalter@middlebury.edu.
Website: http://www.middlebury.edu/ls/grad_programs/arabic

New York University, Steinhardt School of Culture, Education, and Human Development, Department of Teaching and Learning, Program in Multilingual/Multicultural Studies, New York, NY 10003. Offers bilingual education (PhD); bilingual education for teachers (MA, Advanced Certificate); foreign language education (MA); teachers of English to speakers of other languages in college (PhD); teachers of French 7-12 (MA); teachers of Hebrew 7-12 (MA); teaching a foreign language 7-12 (MA), including teaching English to speakers of other languages, all grades; teaching English to speakers of other languages (MA); teaching foreign languages, 7-12 (MA), including Chinese, French, Italian, Japanese, Spanish; teaching French as a foreign language (MA), including teaching English to speakers of other languages; teaching Spanish as a foreign language and TESOL (MA). *Accreditation:* Teacher Education Accreditation Council. Part-time and evening/weekend programs available. *Faculty:* 6 full-time (4 women). *Students:* 118 full-time (94 women), 82 part-time (72 women); includes 40 minority (8 Black or African American, non-Hispanic/Latino; 18 Asian, non-Hispanic/Latino; 12 Hispanic/Latino; 2 Two or more races, non-Hispanic/Latino), 116 international. Average age 29. 431 applicants, 61% accepted, 92 enrolled. In 2014, 121 master's, 1 doctorate, 2 other advanced degrees awarded. *Degree requirements:* For master's, thesis (for some programs); for doctorate, thesis/dissertation. *Entrance requirements:* For doctorate, GRE General Test, interview; for Advanced Certificate, master's degree. Additional exam requirements/recommendations for international students: Required—TOEFL (minimum score 100 iBT). *Application deadline:* For fall admission, 12/1 priority date for domestic and international students; for spring admission, 10/1 for domestic and international students. Applications are processed on a rolling basis. Application fee: $75. Electronic applications accepted. *Financial support:* Fellowships with full and partial tuition reimbursements, career-related internships or fieldwork, Federal Work-Study, institutionally sponsored loans, scholarships/grants, and tuition waivers (partial) available. Support available to part-time students. Financial award application deadline: 2/1; financial award applicants required to submit FAFSA. *Faculty research:* Second language acquisition, cross-cultural communication, technology-enhanced language learning, language variation, action learning. *Unit head:* Prof. Shondel Nero, Director, 212-998-5757, E-mail: shondel.nero@nyu.edu. *Application contact:* 212-998-5030, Fax: 212-995-4328, E-mail: steinhardt.gradadmissions@nyu.edu.
Website: http://steinhardt.nyu.edu/teachlearn/mms

The Ohio State University, Graduate School, College of Arts and Sciences, Division of Arts and Humanities, Department of Near Eastern Languages and Cultures, Columbus, OH 43210. Offers MA, PhD. *Faculty:* 15. *Students:* 22 full-time (6 women); includes 1 minority (Asian, non-Hispanic/Latino), 6 international. Average age 33. In 2014, 4 master's, 1 doctorate awarded. Terminal master's awarded for partial completion of doctoral program. *Degree requirements:* For master's, thesis optional. *Entrance requirements:* For master's and doctorate, GRE General Test, writing sample. Additional exam requirements/recommendations for international students: Required—TOEFL (minimum score 550 paper-based; 79 iBT), Michigan English Language Assessment Battery (minimum score 82); Recommended—IELTS (minimum score 7). *Application deadline:* For fall admission, 12/14 priority date for domestic students, 11/30 priority date

for international students; for winter admission, 12/1 for domestic students, 11/1 for international students; for spring admission, 3/1 for domestic students, 2/1 for international students. Applications are processed on a rolling basis. Application fee: $60 ($70 for international students). Electronic applications accepted. *Financial support:* Fellowships with tuition reimbursements, research assistantships with tuition reimbursements, teaching assistantships with tuition reimbursements, Federal Work-Study, and institutionally sponsored loans available. Support available to part-time students. *Unit head:* Dr. Kevin van Bladel, Chair, 614-292-5643, E-mail: vanbladel.2@osu.edu. *Application contact:* Graduate and Professionnal Admissions, 614-292-9444, Fax: 614-292-3895, E-mail: gpadmissions@osu.edu.
Website: http://nelc.osu.edu/

Oral Roberts University, School of Theology and Missions, Tulsa, OK 74171. Offers biblical literature (MA), including advanced languages, Judaic-Christian studies; Christian counseling (MA), including marriage and family therapy; divinity (M Div); missions (MA); practical theology (MA); theological/historical studies (MA); theology (D Min). *Accreditation:* ATS. Part-time programs available. Postbaccalaureate distance learning degree programs offered (minimal on-campus study). *Degree requirements:* For master's, thesis (for some programs), practicum/internship; for doctorate, thesis/dissertation, applied research project. *Entrance requirements:* For master's, GRE General Test or MAT, minimum GPA of 2.5; for doctorate, M Div, minimum GPA of 3.0, 3 years of full-time ministry experience. Additional exam requirements/recommendations for international students: Required—TOEFL (minimum score 550 paper-based; 79 iBT). Electronic applications accepted.

University of California, Los Angeles, Graduate Division, College of Letters and Science, Department of Near Eastern Languages and Cultures, Los Angeles, CA 90034. Offers MA, PhD. *Degree requirements:* For master's, one foreign language, comprehensive exam; for doctorate, 2 foreign languages, thesis/dissertation, oral and written qualifying exams. *Entrance requirements:* For master's, GRE General Test, bachelor's degree; minimum undergraduate GPA of 3.25 (or its equivalent if letter grade system not used); for doctorate, GRE General Test, master's degree; minimum undergraduate GPA of 3.25 (or its equivalent if letter grade system not used). Additional exam requirements/recommendations for international students: Required—TOEFL. Electronic applications accepted.

University of Chicago, Division of the Humanities, Department of Near Eastern Languages and Civilizations, Chicago, IL 60637. Offers PhD. *Students:* 126 full-time (47 women); includes 14 minority (4 Asian, non-Hispanic/Latino; 7 Hispanic/Latino; 3 Two or more races, non-Hispanic/Latino), 30 international. 143 applicants, 32% accepted, 14 enrolled. Terminal master's awarded for partial completion of doctoral program. *Degree requirements:* For doctorate, 2 foreign languages, comprehensive exam, thesis/dissertation. *Entrance requirements:* For doctorate, GRE General Test. Additional exam requirements/recommendations for international students: Required—TOEFL (minimum score 104 iBT), IELTS (minimum score 7). *Application deadline:* For fall admission, 12/15 for domestic and international students. Application fee: $90. Electronic applications accepted. *Expenses:* Tuition: Full-time $46,899. *Required fees:* $347. *Financial support:* Fellowships with full tuition reimbursements, teaching assistantships with full tuition reimbursements, Federal Work-Study, institutionally sponsored loans, scholarships/grants, and health care benefits available. Financial award application deadline: 12/15; financial award applicants required to submit FAFSA. *Unit head:* Dr. Theo van den Hout, Chair, 773-702-9512. *Application contact:* Braden Grams, Assistant Dean of Students, Admissions and Fellowships, 773-702-1552, Fax: 773-834-9148, E-mail: humanitiesadmissions@uchicago.edu.
Website: http://nelc.uchicago.edu/

The University of Manchester, School of Languages, Linguistics and Cultures, Manchester, United Kingdom. Offers Arab world studies (PhD); Chinese studies (M Phil, PhD); East Asian studies (M Phil, PhD); English language (PhD); French studies (M Phil, PhD); German studies (M Phil, PhD); interpreting studies (PhD); Italian studies (M Phil, PhD); Japanese studies (M Phil, PhD); Latin American cultural studies (M Phil, PhD); linguistics (M Phil, PhD); Middle Eastern studies (M Phil, PhD); Polish studies (M Phil, PhD); Portuguese studies (M Phil, PhD); Russian studies (M Phil, PhD); Spanish studies (M Phil, PhD); translation and intercultural studies (M Phil, PhD).

University of Michigan, Horace H. Rackham School of Graduate Studies, College of Literature, Science, and the Arts, Department of Near Eastern Studies, Ann Arbor, MI 49286. Offers ancient Near Eastern studies (AM, PhD); Arabic for professional purposes (AM); Arabic language and literature (AM, PhD); Armenian studies (AM, PhD); Christianity in late antiquity (AM, PhD); Egyptology (AM, PhD); Hebrew Bible and ancient Israel (AM, PhD); Hebrew literature (AM, PhD); Islamic studies (AM, PhD); Jewish cultural studies (AM, PhD); Jewish mysticism (AM, PhD); Persian and Iranian studies (AM, PhD); Rabbinic literature (AM, PhD); Second Temple Judaism (AM, PhD); teaching of Arabic as a foreign language (AM); Turkish studies (AM, PhD). *Faculty:* 22 full-time (5 women), 1 (woman) part-time/adjunct. *Students:* 37 full-time (16 women); includes 2 minority (both Asian, non-Hispanic/Latino), 11 international. Average age 32. 72 applicants, 19% accepted, 6 enrolled. In 2014, 7 master's, 3 doctorates awarded. Terminal master's awarded for partial completion of doctoral program. *Degree requirements:* For master's, 2 foreign languages; for doctorate, 4 foreign languages, comprehensive exam, thesis/dissertation, preliminary exams, oral defense of dissertation. *Entrance requirements:* Additional exam requirements/recommendations for international students: Required—TOEFL (minimum score 560 paper-based; 84 iBT). *Application deadline:* For fall admission, 12/15 for domestic and international students. Application fee: $65 ($75 for international students). Electronic applications accepted. *Financial support:* In 2014–15, 22 students received support. Fellowships with full tuition reimbursements available, teaching assistantships with full tuition reimbursements available, scholarships/grants, health care benefits, unspecified assistantships, and spring/summer stipends available. Financial award application deadline: 12/15. *Faculty research:* Middle and Near Eastern literatures, languages, cultures from ancient times to the present. *Unit head:* Prof. Gottfried Hagen, Chair, 734-764-0314, E-mail: ghagen@umich.edu. *Application contact:* Student Services, 734-764-0315, E-mail: nes-gradservices@umich.edu.
Website: http://www.umich.edu/~neareast/

University of South Africa, College of Human Sciences, Pretoria, South Africa. Offers adult education (M Ed); African languages (MA, PhD); African politics (MA, PhD); Afrikaans (MA, PhD); ancient history (MA, PhD); ancient Near Eastern studies (MA, PhD); anthropology (MA, PhD); applied linguistics (MA); Arabic (MA, PhD); archaeology (MA); art history (MA); Biblical archaeology (MA); Biblical studies (M Th, D Th, PhD); Christian spirituality (M Th, D Th); church history (M Th, D Th); classical studies (MA, PhD); clinical psychology (MA); communication (MA, PhD); comparative education (M Ed, Ed D); consulting psychology (D Admin, D Com, PhD); curriculum studies (M Ed, Ed D); development studies (M Admin, MA, D Admin, PhD); didactics (M Ed, Ed D); education (M Tech); education management (M Ed, Ed D); educational psychology (M Ed); English (MA); environmental education (M Ed); French (MA, PhD); German (MA, PhD); Greek (MA); guidance and counseling (M Ed); health studies (MA, PhD), including health sciences education (MA), health services management (MA), medical and surgical nursing science (critical care general) (MA), midwifery and neonatal nursing science (MA), trauma and emergency care (MA); history (MA, PhD); history of education

(Ed D); inclusive education (M Ed, Ed D); information and communications technology policy and regulation (MA); information science (MA, MIS, PhD); international politics (MA, PhD); Islamic studies (MA, PhD); Italian (MA, PhD); Judaica (MA, PhD); linguistics (MA, PhD); mathematical education (M Ed); mathematics education (MA); missiology (M Th, D Th); modern Hebrew (MA, PhD); musicology (MA, MMus, D Mus, PhD); natural science education (M Ed); New Testament (M Th, D Th); Old Testament (D Th); pastoral therapy (M Th, D Th); philosophy (MA); philosophy of education (M Ed, Ed D); politics (MA, PhD); Portuguese (MA, PhD); practical theology (M Th, D Th); psychology (MA, MS, PhD); psychology of education (M Ed, Ed D); public health (MA); religious studies (MA, D Th, PhD); Romance languages (MA); Russian (MA, PhD); Semitic languages (MA, PhD); social behavior studies in HIV/AIDS (MA); social science (mental health) (MA); social science in development studies (MA); social science in psychology (MA); social science in social work (MA); social science in sociology (MA); social work (MSW, DSW, PhD); socio-education (M Ed, Ed D); sociolinguistics (MA); sociology (MA, PhD); Spanish (MA, PhD); systematic theology (M Th, D Th); TESOL (teaching English to speakers of other languages) (MA); theological ethics (M Th, D Th); theory of literature (MA, PhD); urban ministries (D Th); urban ministry (M Th).

The University of Texas at Austin, Graduate School, College of Liberal Arts, Department of Middle Eastern Studies, Austin, TX 78712-1111. Offers Middle Eastern languages and cultures (MA, PhD); Middle Eastern studies (MA); JD/MA; MA/M Sc; MA/MA; MBA/MA; MPA/MA. *Degree requirements:* For master's, one foreign language, comprehensive exam, thesis; for doctorate, 2 foreign languages, comprehensive exam, thesis/dissertation. *Entrance requirements:* For master's and doctorate, GRE General Test. Additional exam requirements/recommendations for international students: Required—TOEFL. Electronic applications accepted. *Faculty research:* Islamic studies, Persian language and literature, Hebrew language, Jewish studies, Arabic literature and language.

University of Utah, Graduate School, College of Humanities, Program in Middle East Studies, Salt Lake City, UT 84112. Offers Arabic (MA, PhD); Hebrew (MA); history (MA, PhD); Persian (MA, PhD); political science (MA, PhD). *Students:* 1 full-time (0 women), 8 part-time (3 women); includes 1 minority (Asian, non-Hispanic/Latino), 3 international. Average age 40. In 2014, 5 master's, 1 doctorate awarded. Terminal master's awarded for partial completion of doctoral program. *Degree requirements:* For master's, 2 foreign languages, comprehensive exam, thesis optional; for doctorate, 3 foreign languages, comprehensive exam, thesis/dissertation. *Entrance requirements:* For master's, GRE General Test, minimum GPA of 3.2; for doctorate, GRE General Test, MA in Middle East studies or equivalent, minimum GPA of 3.2. Additional exam requirements/recommendations for international students: Required—TOEFL (minimum score 580 paper-based; 92 iBT); Recommended—IELTS (minimum score 7). *Application deadline:* For fall admission, 1/15 priority date for domestic and international students. Application fee: $55 ($65 for international students). Electronic applications accepted. *Financial support:* In 2014–15, 5 students received support, including 2 teaching assistantships with full tuition reimbursements available (averaging $13,500 per year); fellowships and unspecified assistantships also available. Financial award application deadline: 1/15. *Faculty research:* Islamic studies; Middle Eastern history; political science; Judaic studies; anthropology; Arabic, Persian, Hebrew, and Turkish language and literature. *Unit head:* Johanna Watzinger-Tharp, Director, 801-581-7148, Fax: 801-581-6105, E-mail: j.tharp@utah.edu. *Application contact:* Kellie Hubbard, Academic Advisor, 801-581-5362, Fax: 801-581-6105, E-mail: kellie.hubbard@utah.edu.
Website: http://www.mec.utah.edu

University of Wisconsin–Madison, Graduate School, College of Letters and Science, Department of Hebrew and Semitic Studies, Madison, WI 53706-1380. Offers MA, PhD. Terminal master's awarded for partial completion of doctoral program. *Degree requirements:* For master's, 2 foreign languages; for doctorate, thesis/dissertation. *Entrance requirements:* For master's and doctorate, GRE. Electronic applications accepted. *Expenses:* Tuition, state resident: full-time $10,723; part-time $745 per credit. Tuition, nonresident: full-time $24,054; part-time $1578 per credit. *Required fees:* $374 per semester. Tuition and fees vary according to course load, program and reciprocity agreements. *Faculty research:* Biblical language and literature, Northwest Semitic languages.

Wayne State University, College of Liberal Arts and Sciences, Department of Classical and Modern Languages, Literatures, and Cultures, Program in Language Learning, Detroit, MI 48202. Offers Arabic (MALL); French (MALL); German (MALL); Italian (MALL); Spanish (MALL). *Students:* 1 (woman) full-time, 9 part-time (6 women); includes 2 minority (both Hispanic/Latino). Average age 34. In 2014, 2 master's awarded. *Degree requirements:* For master's, one foreign language, three-credit essay. *Entrance requirements:* For master's, GRE (recommended), target language proficiency, statement of purpose, three letters of recommendation, minimum GPA of 2.6 from accredited institution or 3.2 from non-accredited institution. Additional exam requirements/recommendations for international students: Required—TOEFL (minimum score 550 paper-based; 79 iBT), TWE (minimum score 5.5), Michigan English Language Assessment Battery (minimum score 85); Recommended—IELTS (minimum score 6.5). *Application deadline:* For fall admission, 6/1 priority date for domestic students, 5/1 for international students; for winter admission, 10/1 priority date for domestic students, 9/1 priority date for international students; for spring admission, 2/1 priority date for domestic students, 1/1 priority date for international students. Applications are processed on a rolling basis. Application fee: $0. Electronic applications accepted. *Expenses:* Tuition, state resident: full-time $10,294; part-time $571.90 per credit hour. Tuition, nonresident: full-time $29,730; part-time $1238.75 per credit hour. *Required fees:* $1365; $43.50 per credit hour. $291.10 per semester. Tuition and fees vary according to course load and program. *Financial support:* Scholarships/grants and unspecified assistantships available. Financial award application deadline: 3/31; financial award applicants required to submit FAFSA. *Unit head:* Dr. Anne Duggan, Department Chair, E-mail: a.duggan@wayne.edu.
Website: http://clas.wayne.edu/MALL/

Wayne State University, College of Liberal Arts and Sciences, Department of Classical and Modern Languages, Literatures, and Cultures, Program in Near Eastern Languages, Detroit, MI 48202. Offers Arabic (MA); Hebrew (MA). *Students:* 5 full-time (2 women), 2 part-time (1 woman); includes 3 minority (1 Asian, non-Hispanic/Latino; 2 Two or more races, non-Hispanic/Latino). Average age 26. 10 applicants, 40% accepted, 1 enrolled. In 2014, 4 master's awarded. *Degree requirements:* For master's, one foreign language, thesis or essay. *Entrance requirements:* For master's, GRE (recommended), letter of intent, 5-7 page sample of writing in English, three confidential letters of recommendation, minimum undergraduate GPA of 3.0, two years of Arabic language with minimum GPA of 3.5 in Arabic courses, prior coursework in Islamic/Near Eastern studies (preferred), adequate knowledge of at least one Semitic language and Near Eastern culture. Additional exam requirements/recommendations for international students: Required—TOEFL (minimum score 550 paper-based; 79 iBT), TWE (minimum score 5.5), Michigan English Language Assessment Battery (minimum score 85); Recommended—IELTS (minimum score 6.5). *Application deadline:* For fall admission, 6/1 priority date for domestic students, 5/1 priority date for international students; for winter admission, 10/1 priority date for domestic students, 9/1 priority date for international students; for spring admission, 2/1 priority date for domestic students, 1/1 priority date for international students. Applications are processed on a rolling basis. Application fee: $0. Electronic applications accepted. *Expenses:* Tuition, state resident: full-time $10,294; part-time $571.90 per credit hour. Tuition, nonresident: full-time $29,730; part-time $1238.75 per credit hour. *Required fees:* $1365; $43.50 per credit hour. $291.10 per semester. Tuition and fees vary according to course load and program. *Financial support:* Fellowships, teaching assistantships with tuition reimbursements, scholarships/grants, health care benefits, and unspecified assistantships available. Support available to part-time students. Financial award application deadline: 3/31; financial award applicants required to submit FAFSA. *Faculty research:* Modern Middle East history, Arabic language and culture studies, Chinese linguistics, Islamic studies, Judaic studies. *Unit head:* Dr. Anne Duggan, Chair, E-mail: a.duggan@wayne.edu. *Application contact:* Vanessa DeGifis, Assistant Professor/Student Advisor, 313-577-0481, E-mail: vdegifis@wayne.edu.
Website: http://clas.wayne.edu/languages/manel

Yale University, Graduate School of Arts and Sciences, Department of Near Eastern Languages and Civilizations, New Haven, CT 06520. Offers Arabic and Islamic studies (MA, PhD); archaeology of the ancient Near East (MA, PhD); Assyriology (MA, PhD); Egyptology (MA, PhD); Graeco-Arabic studies (MA, PhD); Northwest Semitic, Bible, comparative Semitics (MA, PhD). *Degree requirements:* For doctorate, 2 foreign languages, thesis/dissertation. *Entrance requirements:* For doctorate, GRE General Test.

Portuguese

Brigham Young University, Graduate Studies, College of Humanities, Department of Spanish and Portuguese, Provo, UT 84602. Offers Portuguese (MA), including Luso-Brazilian literature, Portuguese linguistics, Portuguese pedagogy; Spanish (MA), including Hispanic linguistics, Hispanic literatures, Spanish pedagogy. *Faculty:* 29 full-time (5 women). *Students:* 16 full-time (6 women), 27 part-time (15 women); includes 16 minority (all Hispanic/Latino). Average age 34. 20 applicants, 55% accepted, 9 enrolled. In 2014, 15 master's awarded. *Degree requirements:* For master's, one foreign language, comprehensive exam, thesis, 1 semester of teaching. *Entrance requirements:* For master's, GRE, minimum GPA of 3.5 in Spanish or Portuguese, 3.3 overall. Additional exam requirements/recommendations for international students: Required—TOEFL (minimum score 580 paper-based; 85 iBT). *Application deadline:* For fall admission, 2/1 for domestic and international students. Application fee: $50. Electronic applications accepted. *Expenses: Tuition:* Full-time $6310; part-time $371 per credit hour. Tuition and fees vary according to program and student's religious affiliation. *Financial support:* In 2014–15, 25 students received support, including 4 research assistantships with partial tuition reimbursements available (averaging $2,500 per year), 69 teaching assistantships with partial tuition reimbursements available (averaging $3,500 per year); institutionally sponsored loans, scholarships/grants, tuition waivers (partial), and unspecified assistantships also available. Support available to part-time students. Financial award application deadline: 7/1. *Faculty research:* Mexican prose; Latin American theater, literature, phonetics, and phonology; pedagogy; classical Portuguese literature; Peninsular prose and theater. *Unit head:* Dr. David P. Laraway, Chair, 801-422-3807, Fax: 801-422-0628, E-mail: david_laraway@byu.edu. *Application contact:* Jessica C. Erickson, Graduate Secretary, 801-422-2196, Fax: 801-422-0628, E-mail: jessica_erickson@byu.edu.
Website: http://spanport.byu.edu/

Emory University, Laney Graduate School, Department of Spanish and Portuguese, Atlanta, GA 30322-1100. Offers comparative literature (Certificate); film studies (Certificate); Spanish (PhD); women's studies (Certificate). *Degree requirements:* For doctorate, 2 foreign languages, comprehensive exam, thesis/dissertation. *Entrance requirements:* For doctorate, GRE General Test. Additional exam requirements/recommendations for international students: Required—TOEFL. Electronic applications accepted. *Faculty research:* Spanish literature, Spanish American literature, literary theory, criticism, cultural studies.

Harvard University, Graduate School of Arts and Sciences, Department of Romance Languages and Literatures, Cambridge, MA 02138. Offers French (AM, PhD); Italian (AM, PhD); Portuguese (AM, PhD); Spanish (AM, PhD). Terminal master's awarded for partial completion of doctoral program. *Degree requirements:* For master's, 2 foreign languages; for doctorate, 2 foreign languages, thesis/dissertation. *Entrance requirements:* For master's and doctorate, GRE General Test, sample of written work. Additional exam requirements/recommendations for international students: Required—TOEFL.

Indiana University Bloomington, University Graduate School, College of Arts and Sciences, Department of Spanish and Portuguese, Bloomington, IN 47405. Offers Portuguese (MA, PhD); Spanish (MA, PhD), including Hispanic linguistics, Hispanic literatures. *Faculty:* 22 full-time. *Students:* 86 full-time (53 women), 1 (woman) part-time; includes 20 minority (18 Hispanic/Latino; 2 Two or more races, non-Hispanic/Latino), 16 international. Average age 31. 64 applicants, 30% accepted, 15 enrolled. In 2014, 13 master's, 12 doctorates awarded. *Degree requirements:* For master's, one foreign language, comprehensive exam, thesis (optional for Portuguese); for doctorate, 2 foreign languages, comprehensive exam, thesis/dissertation. *Entrance requirements:* For master's, GRE General Test, bachelor's degree in Portuguese or Spanish, minimum GPA of 3.0; for doctorate, GRE General Test, master's degree in Portuguese or Spanish, minimum GPA of 3.0. Additional exam requirements/recommendations for international students: Required—TOEFL (minimum score 79 iBT). *Application deadline:* For fall admission, 1/15 priority date for domestic students, 12/1 priority date for international students. Application fee: $55 ($65 for international students). Electronic applications accepted. *Financial support:* Fellowships with full tuition reimbursements, research assistantships, teaching assistantships with full tuition reimbursements, scholarships/grants, health care benefits, and unspecified assistantships available. Financial award application deadline: 1/15. *Faculty research:* Spanish American literature, Spanish peninsular literature, Hispanic linguistics, Luso-Brazilian studies,

Catalan studies. *Unit head:* Steven Wagschal, Chair, 812-855-8498, E-mail: swagscha@indiana.edu. *Application contact:* Patrick Dove, Director of Graduate Studies, 812-855-9194, E-mail: pdove@indiana.edu.
Website: http://www.indiana.edu/~spanport/

Michigan State University, The Graduate School, College of Arts and Letters, Department of Spanish and Portuguese, East Lansing, MI 48824. Offers applied Spanish linguistics (MA); Hispanic cultural studies (PhD); Hispanic literatures (MA). *Entrance requirements:* Additional exam requirements/recommendations for international students: Required—TOEFL. Electronic applications accepted.

New York University, Graduate School of Arts and Science, Department of Spanish and Portuguese Languages and Literatures, New York, NY 10012-1019. Offers Portuguese (MA, PhD); Spanish (PhD); Spanish and Latin American literatures and cultures (MA); Spanish language and translation (MA). Part-time programs available. *Students:* 82 full-time (39 women), 8 part-time (5 women); includes 21 minority (1 Black or African American, non-Hispanic/Latino; 2 Asian, non-Hispanic/Latino; 18 Hispanic/Latino), 56 international. Average age 32. 157 applicants, 43% accepted, 33 enrolled. In 2014, 29 master's, 5 doctorates awarded. *Degree requirements:* For master's, 2 foreign languages, thesis; for doctorate, 2 foreign languages, thesis/dissertation. *Entrance requirements:* For master's, GRE General Test; for doctorate, GRE General Test, master's degree. Additional exam requirements/recommendations for international students: Required—TOEFL. *Application deadline:* For fall admission, 1/4 priority date for domestic students, 1/4 for international students. Application fee: $100. *Financial support:* Fellowships with tuition reimbursements, teaching assistantships with tuition reimbursements, career-related internships or fieldwork, Federal Work-Study, institutionally sponsored loans, scholarships/grants, health care benefits, and unspecified assistantships available. Financial award application deadline: 1/4; financial award applicants required to submit FAFSA. *Faculty research:* Gender and sexuality, transatlantic studies, literacy and cultural theories, Colonial and Post-Colonial studies, autobiography and modern subjectivities. *Unit head:* Gigi Dopico-Black, Chair, 212-998-8770, Fax: 212-995-4149, E-mail: spanish.portuguese.info@nyu.edu. *Application contact:* James Fernandez, Director of Graduate Studies, 212-998-8770, Fax: 212-995-4149, E-mail: spanish.portuguese.info@nyu.edu.
Website: http://spanish.as.nyu.edu/

Northwestern University, The Graduate School, Judd A. and Marjorie Weinberg College of Arts and Sciences, Department of Spanish and Portuguese, Evanston, IL 60208. Offers PhD.

The Ohio State University, Graduate School, College of Arts and Sciences, Division of Arts and Humanities, Department of Spanish and Portuguese, Columbus, OH 43210. Offers MA, PhD. *Faculty:* 24. *Students:* 66 full-time (34 women), 3 part-time (all women); includes 13 minority (all Hispanic/Latino), 23 international. Average age 30. In 2014, 2 master's, 5 doctorates awarded. Terminal master's awarded for partial completion of doctoral program. *Degree requirements:* For master's, thesis optional; for doctorate, thesis/dissertation. *Entrance requirements:* For master's and doctorate, GRE General Test, sample of academic writing. Additional exam requirements/recommendations for international students: Required—TOEFL (minimum score 550 paper-based; 79 iBT), Michigan English Language Assessment Battery (minimum score 82); Recommended—IELTS (minimum score 7). *Application deadline:* For fall admission, 12/13 priority date for domestic students, 11/30 priority date for international students; for winter admission, 12/1 for domestic students, 11/1 for international students; for spring admission, 3/1 for domestic students, 2/1 for international students. Applications are processed on a rolling basis. Application fee: $60 ($70 for international students). Electronic applications accepted. *Financial support:* Fellowships, research assistantships, teaching assistantships, Federal Work-Study, institutionally sponsored loans, and unspecified assistantships available. Support available to part-time students. *Unit head:* Dr. Glenn A. Martinez, Chair and Professor, 614-292-4958, E-mail: spanport@osu.edu. *Application contact:* Graduate and Professional Admissions, 614-292-9444, Fax: 614-292-3895, E-mail: gpadmissions@osu.edu.
Website: http://sppo.osu.edu/

Princeton University, Graduate School, Department of Spanish and Portuguese Languages and Cultures, Princeton, NJ 08544-1019. Offers PhD. *Degree requirements:* For doctorate, variable foreign language requirement, thesis/dissertation. *Entrance requirements:* For doctorate, GRE General Test, sample of written work. Additional exam requirements/recommendations for international students: Required—TOEFL (minimum score 600 paper-based). Electronic applications accepted.

Tulane University, School of Liberal Arts, Department of Spanish and Portuguese, New Orleans, LA 70118-5669. Offers Portuguese (MA); Spanish (MA); Spanish and Portuguese (PhD). *Degree requirements:* For master's, 2 foreign languages; for doctorate, 2 foreign languages, thesis/dissertation. *Entrance requirements:* For master's, GRE General Test, minimum B average in undergraduate course work; for doctorate, GRE General Test. Additional exam requirements/recommendations for international students: Required—TOEFL. Electronic applications accepted. *Expenses: Tuition:* Full-time $46,326; part-time $2574 per credit hour. *Required fees:* $1980; $44.50 per credit hour. $550 per term. Tuition and fees vary according to course load and program.

University of California, Los Angeles, Graduate Division, College of Letters and Science, Department of Spanish and Portuguese, Program in Portuguese, Los Angeles, CA 90095. Offers MA. *Degree requirements:* For master's, one foreign language, comprehensive exam or thesis. *Entrance requirements:* For master's, GRE General Test, bachelor's degree; minimum undergraduate GPA of 3.0 (or its equivalent if letter grade system not used). Additional exam requirements/recommendations for international students: Required—TOEFL. Electronic applications accepted.

University of California, Santa Barbara, Graduate Division, College of Letters and Sciences, Division of Humanities and Fine Arts, Department of Spanish and Portuguese, Santa Barbara, CA 93106-4150. Offers Hispanic languages and literatures (PhD), including European medieval studies, feminist studies, Hispanic linguistics, Hispanic literature, Luso-Brazilian literature; Hispanic linguistics (MA); Luso-Brazilian literature (MA); Spanish or Spanish-American literature (MA); MA/PhD. Spanish Language Institute available during Summer session. Terminal master's awarded for partial completion of doctoral program. *Degree requirements:* For master's, 2 foreign languages, comprehensive exam (for some programs), thesis optional; for doctorate, 3 foreign languages, comprehensive exam, thesis/dissertation. *Entrance requirements:* For master's and doctorate, GRE. Additional exam requirements/recommendations for international students: Required—TOEFL (minimum score 550 paper-based; 80 iBT), IELTS (minimum score 7). Electronic applications accepted. *Faculty research:* Nineteenth-century Spanish and Portuguese literature, Spanish and Spanish-American literature, nineteenth- and twentieth-century Portuguese and Brazilian literatures, Hispanic linguistics, Catalan language and culture.

University of Illinois at Urbana–Champaign, Graduate College, College of Liberal Arts and Sciences, School of Literatures, Cultures and Linguistics, Department of Spanish, Italian and Portuguese, Champaign, IL 61820. Offers Italian (MA, PhD); Portuguese (MA, PhD); Spanish (MA, PhD). *Students:* 49 (37 women). Application fee: $70 ($90 for international students). *Financial support:* Tuition waivers available. *Unit head:* Silvina Montrul, Head, 217-333-1780, Fax: 217-244-8430, E-mail: montrul@illinois.edu. *Application contact:* Lynn Stanke, Office Support Specialist, 217-333-6269, Fax: 217-244-3050, E-mail: stanke@illinois.edu.
Website: http://www.sip.illinois.edu/

University of Maryland, College Park, Academic Affairs, College of Arts and Humanities, School of Languages, Literatures, and Cultures, Spanish Language and Literatures Program, College Park, MD 20742. Offers MA, PhD. *Degree requirements:* For master's, comprehensive exam, thesis optional, scholarly paper; for doctorate, 2 foreign languages, thesis/dissertation. *Entrance requirements:* For master's, minimum GPA of 3.0, interview, sample research paper, minimum of 12 credits in upper-level literature, 3 letters of recommendation; for doctorate, minimum GPA of 3.0, interview, sample research paper, minimum of 12 credits in upper-level literature. Additional exam requirements/recommendations for international students: Required—TOEFL. Electronic applications accepted.

University of Massachusetts Amherst, Graduate School, College of Humanities and Fine Arts, Department of Languages, Literatures, and Cultures, Program in Spanish and Portuguese Studies, Amherst, MA 01003. Offers Hispanic literatures, cultures and linguistics (MA, PhD); teaching Spanish (MAT). Part-time programs available. *Faculty:* 13 full-time (5 women). *Students:* 30 full-time (23 women), 17 part-time (10 women); includes 11 minority (1 Black or African American, non-Hispanic/Latino; 1 Asian, non-Hispanic/Latino; 9 Hispanic/Latino), 25 international. Average age 33. 55 applicants, 29% accepted, 11 enrolled. In 2014, 7 master's, 3 doctorates awarded. Terminal master's awarded for partial completion of doctoral program. *Degree requirements:* For master's, one foreign language, thesis or alternative; for doctorate, 2 foreign languages, comprehensive exam, thesis/dissertation. *Entrance requirements:* For master's and doctorate, GRE General Test, sample academic term paper. Additional exam requirements/recommendations for international students: Required—TOEFL (minimum score 550 paper-based; 80 iBT), IELTS (minimum score 6.5). *Application deadline:* For fall admission, 2/1 for domestic and international students. Applications are processed on a rolling basis. Application fee: $75. Electronic applications accepted. *Expenses:* Tuition, state resident: full-time $1980; part-time $110 per credit. Tuition, nonresident: full-time $14,644; part-time $414 per credit. *Required fees:* $11,417. One-time fee: $357. *Financial support:* Fellowships with full and partial tuition reimbursements, research assistantships with full and partial tuition reimbursements, teaching assistantships with full and partial tuition reimbursements, career-related internships or fieldwork, Federal Work-Study, scholarships/grants, traineeships, health care benefits, tuition waivers (full and partial), and unspecified assistantships available. Support available to part-time students. Financial award application deadline: 2/1; financial award applicants required to submit FAFSA. *Unit head:* Dr. Albert Lloret, Graduate Program Director, 413-545-0544, Fax: 413-545-3178. *Application contact:* Lindsay DeSantis, Supervisor of Admissions, 413-545-0722, Fax: 413-577-0010, E-mail: gradadm@grad.umass.edu.
Website: http://www.umass.edu/spanport/

University of Massachusetts Dartmouth, Graduate School, College of Arts and Sciences, Department of Portuguese, North Dartmouth, MA 02747-2300. Offers Luso-Afro Brazilian studies (PhD); Portuguese (MA). Part-time programs available. *Faculty:* 5 full-time (2 women), 2 part-time/adjunct (1 woman). *Students:* 9 full-time (7 women), 5 part-time (4 women); includes 7 minority (2 Black or African American, non-Hispanic/Latino; 5 Hispanic/Latino), 4 international. Average age 40. 9 applicants, 78% accepted, 4 enrolled. In 2014, 2 master's, 1 doctorate awarded. Terminal master's awarded for partial completion of doctoral program. *Degree requirements:* For master's, comprehensive exam (for some programs), written exam or research project; for doctorate, comprehensive exam, thesis/dissertation. *Entrance requirements:* For master's, GRE (recommended), statement of purpose (minimum of 300 words), resume, 3 letters of recommendation, official transcripts, writing samples in Portuguese (minimum of 10 pages); for doctorate, GRE (recommended), statement of purpose (minimum of 300 words), resume, 3 letters of recommendation, official transcripts, scholarly writing sample (minimum of 10 pages). Additional exam requirements/recommendations for international students: Required—TOEFL (minimum score 500 paper-based). *Application deadline:* For fall admission, 2/1 priority date for domestic students, 1/1 priority date for international students; for spring admission, 11/15 priority date for domestic students, 10/15 priority date for international students. Applications are processed on a rolling basis. Application fee: $60. Electronic applications accepted. *Expenses:* Tuition, state resident: full-time $2071; part-time $86.29 per credit. Tuition, nonresident: full-time $8099; part-time $337.46 per credit. *Required fees:* $16,520; $712.33 per credit. Tuition and fees vary according to course load and reciprocity agreements. *Financial support:* In 2014–15, 9 fellowships with full tuition reimbursements (averaging $18,295 per year) were awarded; Federal Work-Study and unspecified assistantships also available. Support available to part-time students. Financial award application deadline: 3/1; financial award applicants required to submit FAFSA. *Faculty research:* Translation studies, literature in Luso-Afro-Brazilian studies, literary and cultural theory, gender studies, studies in ethnicity and migration, bi-and multilingualism. *Total annual research expenditures:* $32,000. *Unit head:* Victor J. Mendes, Graduate Program Director, 508-999-8338, Fax: 508-910-9272, E-mail: vmendes@umassd.edu. *Application contact:* Steven Briggs, Director of Marketing and Recruitment for Graduate Studies, 508-999-8604, Fax: 508-999-8183, E-mail: graduate@umassd.edu.
Website: http://www.umassd.edu/cas/departmentsanddegreeprograms/portuguese/

University of Minnesota, Twin Cities Campus, Graduate School, College of Liberal Arts, Department of Spanish and Portuguese Studies, Minneapolis, MN 55455-0213. Offers Hispanic and Lusophone literatures, cultures and linguistics (PhD); Hispanic linguistics (MA); Hispanic literature (MA); Lusophone literature (MA). *Degree requirements:* For master's, 2 foreign languages, comprehensive exam, thesis or alternative; for doctorate, 2 foreign languages, comprehensive exam, thesis/dissertation. *Entrance requirements:* For master's and doctorate, GRE General Test, samples of written work, 3 letters of recommendation, voice sample, statement of purpose. Additional exam requirements/recommendations for international students: Required—TOEFL (minimum score 550 paper-based; 79 iBT). Electronic applications accepted. *Faculty research:* Sociohistorical approaches to literature and culture, feminist studies, literary theory, ideologies and literature, pragmatics and sociolinguistics.

University of New Mexico, Graduate School, College of Arts and Sciences, Program in Spanish and Portuguese, Albuquerque, NM 87131. Offers Portuguese (MA); Spanish (MA); Spanish and Portuguese (PhD). Part-time programs available. *Faculty:* 12 full-time (7 women), 1 part-time/adjunct (0 women). *Students:* 48 full-time (31 women), 10 part-time (7 women); includes 31 minority (all Hispanic/Latino), 10 international. Average age 33. 49 applicants, 59% accepted, 18 enrolled. In 2014, 13 master's, 3 doctorates awarded. *Degree requirements:* For master's, one foreign language, comprehensive exam, thesis optional; for doctorate, one foreign language, comprehensive exam, thesis/dissertation. *Entrance requirements:* For master's, BA in Spanish or Portuguese, 3 letters of recommendation, letter of intent; for doctorate, GRE, 3 letters of recommendation, letter of intent, sample research paper. Additional exam requirements/recommendations for international students: Required—TOEFL (minimum score 550 paper-based). *Application deadline:* For fall admission, 1/15 priority date for domestic

students; for spring admission, 11/15 for domestic students. Applications are processed on a rolling basis. Application fee: $50. Electronic applications accepted. *Financial support:* In 2014–15, 60 students received support, including 2 research assistantships (averaging $7,500 per year), 58 teaching assistantships with full and partial tuition reimbursements available (averaging $14,965 per year); Federal Work-Study, institutionally sponsored loans, scholarships/grants, health care benefits, and unspecified assistantships also available. Support available to part-time students. Financial award application deadline: 3/1; financial award applicants required to submit FAFSA. *Faculty research:* Languages and literatures from the Iberian Peninsula, Latin America and the American Southwest. *Unit head:* Dr. Anthony Cardenas, Chair, 505-277-5907, Fax: 505-277-3885, E-mail: ajcard@unm.edu. *Application contact:* Martha Hurd, Graduate Advisor, 505-277-2974, E-mail: marthah@unm.edu. Website: http://spanport.unm.edu

The University of North Carolina at Chapel Hill, Graduate School, College of Arts and Sciences, Department of Romance Languages and Literatures, Chapel Hill, NC 27599. Offers French (MA, PhD); Italian (MA, PhD); Portuguese (MA, PhD); Romance languages (MA, PhD); Romance philology (MA, PhD); Spanish (MA, PhD). *Degree requirements:* For master's, one foreign language, comprehensive exam, thesis; for doctorate, 2 foreign languages, comprehensive exam, thesis/dissertation. *Entrance requirements:* For master's and doctorate, GRE General Test, minimum GPA of 3.0. Additional exam requirements/recommendations for international students: Required—TOEFL (minimum score 550 paper-based). Electronic applications accepted.

University of South Africa, College of Human Sciences, Pretoria, South Africa. Offers adult education (M Ed); African languages (MA, PhD); African politics (MA, PhD); Afrikaans (MA, PhD); ancient history (MA, PhD); ancient Near Eastern studies (MA, PhD); anthropology (MA, PhD); applied linguistics (MA); Arabic (MA, PhD); archaeology (MA); art history (MA); Biblical archaeology (MA); Biblical studies (M Th, D Th, PhD); Christian spirituality (M Th, D Th); church history (M Th, D Th); classical studies (MA, PhD); clinical psychology (MA); communication (MA, PhD); comparative education (M Ed, Ed D); consulting psychology (D Admin, D Com, PhD); curriculum studies (M Ed, Ed D); development studies (M Admin, MA, D Admin, PhD); didactics (M Ed, Ed D); education (M Tech); education management (M Ed, Ed D); educational psychology (M Ed); English (MA); environmental education (M Ed); French (MA, PhD); German (MA, PhD); Greek (MA); guidance and counseling (M Ed); health studies (MA, PhD), including health sciences education (MA), health services management (MA), medical and surgical nursing science (critical care general) (MA), midwifery and neonatal nursing science (MA), trauma and emergency care (MA); history (MA, PhD); history of education (Ed D); inclusive education (M Ed, Ed D); information and communications technology policy and regulation (MA); information science (MA, MIS, PhD); international politics (MA, PhD); Islamic studies (MA, PhD); Italian (MA, PhD); Judaica (MA, PhD); linguistics (MA, PhD); mathematical education (M Ed); mathematics education (MA); missiology (M Th, D Th); modern Hebrew (MA, PhD); musicology (MA, MMus, D Mus, PhD); natural science education (M Ed); New Testament (M Th, D Th); Old Testament (D Th); pastoral therapy (M Th, D Th); philosophy (MA); philosophy of education (M Ed, Ed D); politics (MA, PhD); Portuguese (MA, PhD); practical theology (M Th, D Th); psychology (MA, MS, PhD); psychology of education (M Ed, Ed D); public health (MA); religious studies (MA, D Th, PhD); Romance languages (MA); Russian (MA, PhD); Semitic languages (MA, PhD); social behavior studies in HIV/AIDS (MA); social science (mental health) (MA); social science in development studies (MA); social science in psychology (MA); social science in social work (MA); social science in sociology (MA); social work (MSW, DSW, PhD); socio-education (M Ed, Ed D); sociolinguistics (MA); sociology (MA, PhD); Spanish (MA, PhD); systematic theology (M Th, D Th); TESOL (teaching English to speakers of other languages) (MA); theological ethics (M Th, D Th); theory of literature (MA, PhD); urban ministries (D Th); urban ministry (M Th).

The University of Tennessee, Graduate School, College of Arts and Sciences, Department of Modern Foreign Languages and Literatures, Program in Modern Foreign Languages, Knoxville, TN 37996. Offers applied linguistics (PhD); French (PhD); German (PhD); Italian (PhD); Portuguese (PhD); Russian (PhD); Spanish (PhD). *Degree requirements:* For doctorate, 2 foreign languages, thesis/dissertation. *Entrance requirements:* For doctorate, minimum GPA of 2.7. Additional exam requirements/recommendations for international students: Required—TOEFL. Electronic applications accepted.

The University of Texas at Austin, Graduate School, College of Liberal Arts, Department of Spanish and Portuguese, Austin, TX 78712-1111. Offers Hispanic linguistics (MA, PhD); Hispanic literature (MA, PhD); Ibero-romance philology and

linguistics (PhD); Luso-Brazilian literature (MA, PhD). *Degree requirements:* For master's, 2 foreign languages, thesis or alternative; for doctorate, 3 foreign languages, thesis/dissertation. *Entrance requirements:* For master's and doctorate, GRE General Test. Electronic applications accepted.

University of Toronto, School of Graduate Studies, Faculty of Arts and Science, Department of Spanish and Portuguese, Toronto, ON M5S 2J7, Canada. Offers MA, PhD. Part-time programs available. *Degree requirements:* For doctorate, thesis/dissertation. *Entrance requirements:* For master's, minimum B average in final year, 2 letters of reference; for doctorate, minimum A- average, 2 letters of reference, writing sample. Additional exam requirements/recommendations for international students: Required—TWE (minimum score 5), TOEFL, Michigan English Language Assessment Battery, IELTS, or COPE. Electronic applications accepted.

University of Washington, Graduate School, College of Arts and Sciences, Division of Spanish and Portuguese Studies, Seattle, WA 98195. Offers Hispanic literary and cultural studies (MA). *Degree requirements:* For master's, 2 foreign languages, thesis optional, exam. *Entrance requirements:* For master's, GRE General Test, minimum GPA of 3.0. Additional exam requirements/recommendations for international students: Required—TOEFL. Electronic applications accepted. *Faculty research:* Medieval through modern Spanish literature and film, Latin American literature, poetry and essay, pan-Hispanic ballad, Hispanic cultural studies, second language acquisition and applied linguistics.

University of Wisconsin–Madison, Graduate School, College of Letters and Science, Department of Spanish and Portuguese, Program in Portuguese, Madison, WI 53706-1380. Offers MA, PhD. *Degree requirements:* For master's, one foreign language; for doctorate, 2 foreign languages, thesis/dissertation. *Entrance requirements:* For master's, GRE (recommended), minimum GPA of 3.25 in Spanish or Portuguese; for doctorate, GRE (recommended), minimum graduate GPA of 3.4. Additional exam requirements/recommendations for international students: Required—TOEFL. Electronic applications accepted. *Expenses:* Tuition, state resident: full-time $10,723; part-time $745 per credit. Tuition, nonresident: full-time $24,054; part-time $1578 per credit. Required fees: $374 per semester. Tuition and fees vary according to course load, program and reciprocity agreements. *Faculty research:* Portuguese and Brazilian literature.

Vanderbilt University, Graduate School, Department of Spanish and Portuguese, Nashville, TN 37240-1001. Offers Portuguese (MA); Spanish (MA, MAT, PhD); Spanish and Portuguese (PhD). *Faculty:* 13 full-time (6 women). *Students:* 23 full-time (9 women), 1 part-time (0 women); includes 2 minority (1 Black or African American, non-Hispanic/Latino; 1 Hispanic/Latino), 11 international. Average age 31. 42 applicants, 31% accepted, 8 enrolled. In 2014, 3 master's, 4 doctorates awarded. *Degree requirements:* For master's, one foreign language, thesis; for doctorate, 2 foreign languages, thesis/dissertation, final and qualifying exams. *Entrance requirements:* For master's, GRE General Test; for doctorate, GRE General Test, writing sample in Spanish. Additional exam requirements/recommendations for international students: Required—TOEFL (minimum score 570 paper-based; 88 iBT). *Application deadline:* For fall admission, 1/15 for domestic and international students. Electronic applications accepted. *Expenses: Tuition:* Full-time $42,768; part-time $1782 per credit hour. *Required fees:* $422. One-time fee: $30 full-time. *Financial support:* Fellowships with full and partial tuition reimbursements, teaching assistantships with full tuition reimbursements, Federal Work-Study, institutionally sponsored loans, and health care benefits available. Financial award application deadline: 1/15; financial award applicants required to submit CSS PROFILE or FAFSA. *Faculty research:* Spanish, Portuguese, and Latin American literatures; foreign language pedagogy; Renaissance and Baroque poetry; nineteenth century Spanish novel. *Unit head:* Dr. Andres Zamora, Director of Graduate Studies, 615-322-6858, Fax: 615-343-7260, E-mail: andres.zamora@vanderbilt.edu. *Application contact:* Cindy Martinez, Administrative Assistant, 615-322-6930, Fax: 615-343-7260, E-mail: cindy.m.martinez@vanderbilt.edu. Website: http://as.vanderbilt.edu/spanish-portuguese/graduate/index.php

Yale University, Graduate School of Arts and Sciences, Department of Spanish and Portuguese, New Haven, CT 06520. Offers Latin American literature (PhD); Luso-Brazilian and Spanish/Spanish American literatures (PhD); Spanish peninsular literature (PhD). Terminal master's awarded for partial completion of doctoral program. *Degree requirements:* For doctorate, 3 foreign languages, thesis/dissertation. *Entrance requirements:* For doctorate, GRE General Test.

Romance Languages

Appalachian State University, Cratis D. Williams Graduate School, Department of Foreign Languages and Literatures, Boone, NC 28608. Offers romance languages (MA), including Spanish or French teaching. Part-time programs available. Postbaccalaureate distance learning degree programs offered (no on-campus study). *Degree requirements:* For master's, one foreign language, comprehensive exam, thesis optional. *Entrance requirements:* For master's, GRE General Test, 3 letters of recommendation. Additional exam requirements/recommendations for international students: Required—TOEFL (minimum score 570 paper-based; 79 iBT) or IELTS (minimum score 6.5). Electronic applications accepted. *Faculty research:* French and Spanish literature, Latin American culture, teaching foreign languages.

Boston University, Graduate School of Arts and Sciences, Department of Romance Studies, Boston, MA 02215. Offers French language and literature (MA, PhD); Hispanic language and literatures (MA, PhD). *Students:* 39 full-time (29 women), 1 part-time (0 women); includes 5 minority (1 Black or African American, non-Hispanic/Latino; 4 Hispanic/Latino), 12 international. Average age 32. 81 applicants, 25% accepted, 10 enrolled. In 2014, 2 master's, 4 doctorates awarded. Terminal master's awarded for partial completion of doctoral program. *Degree requirements:* For master's, one foreign language, comprehensive exam; for doctorate, 2 foreign languages, comprehensive exam, thesis/dissertation. *Entrance requirements:* For master's and doctorate, GRE General Test, sample of written work, 3 letters of recommendation. Additional exam requirements/recommendations for international students: Required—TOEFL (minimum score 84 iBT). *Application deadline:* For fall admission, 1/15 for domestic and international students. Application fee: $80. Electronic applications accepted. *Expenses: Tuition:* Full-time $45,686; part-time $1428 per credit hour. *Required fees:* $660; $60 per semester. Tuition and fees vary according to program. *Financial support:* In 2014–15, 33 students received support, including 7 fellowships with full tuition reimbursements available (averaging $20,500 per year), 24 teaching assistantships with full tuition reimbursements available (averaging $20,500 per year); research assistantships,

Federal Work-Study, scholarships/grants, and health care benefits also available. Support available to part-time students. Financial award application deadline: 1/15. *Unit head:* Nancy Harrowitz, Chairman, 617-353-6225, Fax: 617-353-6246, E-mail: nharrow@bu.edu. *Application contact:* Deanna Wong, Administrative Assistant, 617-353-2641, Fax: 617-353-6246, E-mail: dswong@bu.edu. Website: http://www.bu.edu/rs/

Clark Atlanta University, School of Arts and Sciences, Department of Foreign Languages, Atlanta, GA 30314. Offers Romance languages (MA, DAH). Part-time programs available. *Faculty:* 1 full-time (0 women), 1 part-time/adjunct (0 women). *Students:* 1 (woman) full-time, 1 (woman) part-time; both minorities (both Black or African American, non-Hispanic/Latino). Average age 40. 1 applicant, 100% accepted, 1 enrolled. *Degree requirements:* For master's, one foreign language, thesis; for doctorate, 2 foreign languages, comprehensive exam, thesis/dissertation. *Entrance requirements:* For master's, GRE General Test, minimum GPA of 2.5. Additional exam requirements/recommendations for international students: Required—TOEFL (minimum score 500 paper-based; 61 iBT). *Application deadline:* For fall admission, 4/1 for domestic and international students; for spring admission, 11/1 for domestic and international students. Applications are processed on a rolling basis. Application fee: $40 ($55 for international students). *Expenses: Tuition:* Full-time $14,904; part-time $828 per credit hour. *Required fees:* $746; $373 per semester. *Financial support:* Scholarships/grants and unspecified assistantships available. Financial award application deadline: 4/30; financial award applicants required to submit FAFSA. *Unit head:* Dr. Laurent Monye, Chairperson, 404-880-8547, E-mail: lmonye@cau.edu. *Application contact:* Michelle Clark-Davis, Graduate Program Admissions, 404-880-6605, E-mail: cauadmissions@cau.edu.

Columbia University, Graduate School of Arts and Sciences, New York, NY 10027. Offers African-American studies (MA); American studies (MA); anthropology (MA, PhD); art history and archaeology (MA, PhD); astronomy (PhD); biological sciences (PhD);

biotechnology (MA); chemical physics (PhD); chemistry (PhD); classical studies (MA, PhD); classics (MA, PhD); climate and society (MA); earth and environmental sciences (PhD); East Asia: regional studies (MA); East Asian languages and cultures (MA, PhD); ecology, evolution and environmental biology (MA), including conservation biology; ecology, evolution, and environmental biology (PhD), including ecology and evolutionary biology, evolutionary primatology; economics (PhD); English and comparative literature (MA, PhD); French and Romance philology (MA, PhD); Germanic languages (MA, PhD); global French studies (MA); Hispanic cultural studies (MA); history (PhD); history and literature (MA); human rights studies (MA); Islamic studies (MA); Italian (MA, PhD); Japanese pedagogy (MA); Jewish studies (MA); Latin America and the Caribbean: regional studies (MA); Latin American and Iberian cultures (PhD); mathematics (MA, PhD), including finance (MA); medieval and Renaissance studies (MA); Middle Eastern, South Asian, and African studies (MA, PhD); modern art: critical and curatorial studies (MA); modern European studies (MA); museum anthropology (MA); music (DMA, PhD); oral history (MA); philosophical foundations of physics (MA); philosophy (MA, PhD); physics (PhD); political science (MA, PhD); psychology (PhD); quantitative methods in the social sciences (MA); religion (MA, PhD); Russia, Eurasia and East Europe: regional studies (MA); Russian translation (MA); Slavic cultures (MA); Slavic languages (MA, PhD); sociology (MA, PhD); South Asian studies (MA); statistics (MA, PhD); theatre (PhD); JD/PhD; MA/MS; MD/PhD; MPA/MA. Dual-degree programs require admission to both Graduate School of Arts and Sciences and another Columbia school. Part-time and evening/weekend programs available. Terminal master's awarded for partial completion of doctoral program. *Degree requirements:* For master's, thesis (for some programs); for doctorate, comprehensive exam, thesis/dissertation. *Entrance requirements:* For master's and doctorate, GRE General Test, GRE Subject Test (for some programs). Electronic applications accepted. *Faculty research:* Humanities, natural sciences, social sciences.

Cornell University, Graduate School, Graduate Fields of Arts and Sciences, Field of Linguistics, Ithaca, NY 14853-0001. Offers applied linguistics (MA, PhD); East Asian linguistics (MA, PhD); English linguistics (MA, PhD); general linguistics (MA, PhD); Germanic linguistics (MA, PhD); Indo-European linguistics (MA, PhD); phonetics (MA, PhD); phonological theory (MA, PhD); Romance linguistics (MA, PhD); second language acquisition (MA, PhD); semantics (MA, PhD); Slavic linguistics (MA, PhD); sociolinguistics (MA, PhD); South Asian linguistics (MA, PhD); Southeast Asian linguistics (MA, PhD); syntactic theory (MA, PhD). Terminal master's awarded for partial completion of doctoral program. *Degree requirements:* For master's, one foreign language, thesis; for doctorate, one foreign language, comprehensive exam, thesis/dissertation. *Entrance requirements:* For master's and doctorate, GRE General Test, 2 letters of recommendation. Additional exam requirements/recommendations for international students: Required—TOEFL (minimum score 600 paper-based; 77 iBT). Electronic applications accepted. *Faculty research:* Phonology and phonetics, syntax and semantics, historical linguistics, philosophy of language, language acquisition.

Cornell University, Graduate School, Graduate Fields of Arts and Sciences, Field of Romance Studies, Ithaca, NY 14853-0001. Offers French linguistics (PhD); French literature (PhD); Hispanic literature (PhD); Italian linguistics (PhD); Italian literature (PhD); Romance linguistics (PhD); Spanish linguistics (PhD). *Degree requirements:* For doctorate, 2 foreign languages, comprehensive exam, thesis/dissertation. *Entrance requirements:* For doctorate, GRE General Test, sample of written work, 3 letters of recommendation. Additional exam requirements/recommendations for international students: Required—TOEFL (minimum score 550 paper-based; 77 iBT). Electronic applications accepted. *Faculty research:* Literary theory, Hispanic studies, French studies, gender studies.

Hunter College of the City University of New York, Graduate School, School of Arts and Sciences, Department of Romance Languages, New York, NY 10065-5085. Offers MA. Part-time and evening/weekend programs available. *Faculty:* 3 full-time (2 women). *Students:* 19 part-time (12 women); includes 4 minority (1 Black or African American, non-Hispanic/Latino; 3 Hispanic/Latino), 1 international. In 2014, 5 master's awarded. *Degree requirements:* For master's, 2 foreign languages, comprehensive exam, thesis optional. *Entrance requirements:* For master's, GRE General Test, GRE Subject Test, interview, proficiency in chosen language. Additional exam requirements/recommendations for international students: Required—TOEFL. *Application deadline:* For fall admission, 4/1 for domestic students, 2/1 for international students; for spring admission, 11/1 for domestic students, 9/1 for international students. *Financial support:* Fellowships, Federal Work-Study, scholarships/grants, and tuition waivers (partial) available. Support available to part-time students. Financial award application deadline: 4/15. *Unit head:* Dr. Giuseppe Carlo DiScipio, Chair, 212-772-5108, Fax: 212-772-5094, E-mail: gdiscipi@hunter.cuny.edu. *Application contact:* Milena Solo, Director for Graduate Admissions, 212-772-4480, E-mail: admissions@hunter.cuny.edu. Website: http://www.hunter.cuny.edu/romancelanguages

Johns Hopkins University, Zanvyl Krieger School of Arts and Sciences, Department of German and Romance Languages and Literatures, Baltimore, MD 21218-2699. Offers French (PhD); German (PhD); Italian (PhD); Spanish (PhD). *Degree requirements:* For doctorate, 2 foreign languages, thesis/dissertation. *Entrance requirements:* For doctorate, GRE General Test. Additional exam requirements/recommendations for international students: Required—TOEFL (minimum score 600 paper-based; 100 iBT), IELTS. Electronic applications accepted. *Faculty research:* Nineteenth-century French prose and poetry, genetic theory and criticism; twentieth-century Latin American literature and film; medieval and Renaissance Italian literature; gender and queer theory in German literature; the ideology of Baroque and Neobaroque aesthetics.

Michigan State University, The Graduate School, College of Arts and Letters, Department of French, Classics, and Italian, East Lansing, MI 48824. Offers French (MA); French language and literature (PhD). *Entrance requirements:* Additional exam requirements/recommendations for international students: Required—TOEFL. Electronic applications accepted.

New York University, Graduate School of Arts and Science, Center for French Civilization and Culture, Department of French, New York, NY 10012-1019. Offers French (PhD); French language and civilization (MA); French literature (MA); Romance languages and literatures (MA). Part-time programs available. *Faculty:* 18 full-time (7 women), 2 part-time/adjunct (both women). *Students:* 52 full-time (36 women), 3 part-time (2 women); includes 10 minority (3 Black or African American, non-Hispanic/Latino; 2 Asian, non-Hispanic/Latino; 5 Hispanic/Latino), 12 international. Average age 29. 67 applicants, 58% accepted, 20 enrolled. In 2014, 15 master's, 15 doctorates awarded. Terminal master's awarded for partial completion of doctoral program. *Degree requirements:* For master's, one foreign language, thesis (for some programs); for doctorate, one foreign language, thesis/dissertation. *Entrance requirements:* For master's and doctorate, GRE General Test, proficiency in French. Additional exam requirements/recommendations for international students: Required—TOEFL. *Application deadline:* For fall admission, 1/4 for domestic and international students; for spring admission, 11/1 for domestic and international students. Application fee: $100. *Financial support:* Fellowships with tuition reimbursements, teaching assistantships with tuition reimbursements, Federal Work-Study, institutionally sponsored loans, scholarships/grants, traineeships, health care benefits, unspecified assistantships, and instructorships available. Financial award application deadline: 1/4; financial award applicants required to submit FAFSA. *Faculty research:* French and Francophone literature, literary theory, and history; rhetoric and poetics; cultural history; theater and cinema. *Unit head:* Lucien Nouis, Director of Graduate Studies, 212-998-8700, Fax: 212-995-4187, E-mail: french.grad@nyu.edu. *Application contact:* Erin Brau, Graduate Administrator, 212-998-8700, Fax: 212-995-4187, E-mail: french.grad@nyu.edu. Website: http://www.nyu.edu/gsas/dept/french/

New York University, Graduate School of Arts and Science, Department of Spanish and Portuguese Languages and Literatures, New York, NY 10012-1019. Offers Portuguese (MA, PhD); Spanish (PhD); Spanish and Latin American literatures and cultures (MA); Spanish language and translation (MA). Part-time programs available. *Students:* 82 full-time (39 women), 8 part-time (5 women); includes 21 minority (1 Black or African American, non-Hispanic/Latino; 2 Asian, non-Hispanic/Latino; 18 Hispanic/Latino), 56 international. Average age 32. 157 applicants, 43% accepted, 33 enrolled. In 2014, 29 master's, 5 doctorates awarded. *Degree requirements:* For master's, 2 foreign languages, thesis; for doctorate, 2 foreign languages, thesis/dissertation. *Entrance requirements:* For master's, GRE General Test; for doctorate, GRE General Test, master's degree. Additional exam requirements/recommendations for international students: Required—TOEFL. *Application deadline:* For fall admission, 1/4 priority date for domestic students, 1/4 for international students. Application fee: $100. *Financial support:* Fellowships with tuition reimbursements, teaching assistantships with tuition reimbursements, career-related internships or fieldwork, Federal Work-Study, institutionally sponsored loans, scholarships/grants, health care benefits, and unspecified assistantships available. Financial award application deadline: 1/4; financial award applicants required to submit FAFSA. *Faculty research:* Gender and sexuality, transatlantic studies, literacy and cultural theories, Colonial and Post-Colonial studies, autobiography and modern subjectivities. *Unit head:* Gigi Dopico-Black, Chair, 212-998-8770, Fax: 212-995-4149, E-mail: spanish.portuguese.info@nyu.edu. *Application contact:* James Fernandez, Director of Graduate Studies, 212-998-8770, Fax: 212-995-4149, E-mail: spanish.portuguese.info@nyu.edu. Website: http://spanish.as.nyu.edu/

Northern Illinois University, Graduate School, College of Liberal Arts and Sciences, Department of Foreign Languages and Literatures, De Kalb, IL 60115-2854. Offers French (MA); Spanish (MA). Part-time programs available. *Faculty:* 25 full-time (11 women). *Students:* 6 full-time (2 women), 12 part-time (8 women); includes 7 minority (1 Asian, non-Hispanic/Latino; 6 Hispanic/Latino), 1 international. Average age 32. 5 applicants, 80% accepted, 2 enrolled. In 2014, 6 master's awarded. *Degree requirements:* For master's, one foreign language, comprehensive exam, thesis or alternative, language proficiency exam. *Entrance requirements:* For master's, GRE General Test, interview, minimum GPA of 2.75, undergraduate major in French or Spanish. Additional exam requirements/recommendations for international students: Required—TOEFL (minimum score 550 paper-based). *Application deadline:* For fall admission, 6/1 for domestic students, 5/1 for international students; for spring admission, 11/1 for domestic students, 10/1 for international students. Applications are processed on a rolling basis. Application fee: $40. Electronic applications accepted. *Financial support:* In 2014–15, 11 teaching assistantships with full tuition reimbursements were awarded; fellowships with full tuition reimbursements, research assistantships with full tuition reimbursements, career-related internships or fieldwork, Federal Work-Study, scholarships/grants, tuition waivers (full), and unspecified assistantships also available. Support available to part-time students. Financial award applicants required to submit FAFSA. *Faculty research:* Francophone women writers, prosodies of French and Italian, early Spanish drama, business German, history of Burmese literature. *Unit head:* Dr. Katharina Barbe, Chair, 815-753-1559, Fax: 815-753-5989; E-mail: kbarbe@niu.edu. *Application contact:* Graduate School Office, 815-753-0395, E-mail: gradsch@niu.edu. Website: http://www.forlangs.net/

Queens College of the City University of New York, Division of Graduate Studies, Arts and Humanities Division, Department of European Languages and Literatures, Flushing, NY 11367-1597. Offers French (MA); Italian (MA). Part-time and evening/weekend programs available. *Degree requirements:* For master's, 2 foreign languages, comprehensive exam, thesis or alternative. *Entrance requirements:* For master's, minimum GPA of 3.0. Additional exam requirements/recommendations for international students: Required—TOEFL.

San Diego State University, Graduate and Research Affairs, College of Arts and Letters, Department of European Studies, San Diego, CA 92182. Offers MA. *Degree requirements:* For master's, one foreign language. *Entrance requirements:* For master's, GRE General Test. Additional exam requirements/recommendations for international students: Required—TOEFL. Electronic applications accepted.

Stony Brook University, State University of New York, Graduate School, College of Arts and Sciences, Department of European Languages, Literatures, and Cultures, Program in French, Stony Brook, NY 11794. Offers Romance languages (MA). Evening/weekend programs available. *Students:* 1 part-time (0 women). In 2014, 1 master's awarded. *Degree requirements:* For master's, one foreign language. *Entrance requirements:* For master's, GRE General Test. Additional exam requirements/recommendations for international students: Required—TOEFL. *Application deadline:* For fall admission, 1/15 for domestic students; for spring admission, 10/1 for domestic students. Application fee: $100. *Expenses:* Tuition, state resident: full-time $10,370; part-time $432 per credit. Tuition, nonresident: full-time $20,190; part-time $841 per credit. *Required fees:* $1431. *Unit head:* Prof. Nicholas Rzhevsky, Chair, 631-632-7440, Fax: 631-632-9612, E-mail: nicholas.rzhevsky@stonybrook.edu. *Application contact:* Mary Wilmarth, Coordinator, 631-632-7442, Fax: 631-632-9612, E-mail: mary.wilmarth@stonybrook.edu.

Texas Tech University, Graduate School, College of Arts and Sciences, Department of Classical and Modern Languages and Literatures, Lubbock, TX 79409-2071. Offers applied linguistics (MA); classics (MA); German (MA); languages and cultures (MA); Romance languages (MA); Spanish (PhD); MBA/MA. Part-time programs available. *Faculty:* 61 full-time (31 women), 7 part-time/adjunct (4 women). *Students:* 93 full-time (48 women), 15 part-time (10 women); includes 27 minority (1 Black or African American, non-Hispanic/Latino; 22 Hispanic/Latino; 4 Two or more races, non-Hispanic/Latino), 41 international. Average age 32. 60 applicants, 70% accepted, 26 enrolled. In 2014, 26 master's, 7 doctorates awarded. *Degree requirements:* For master's, comprehensive exam, thesis or alternative; for doctorate, comprehensive exam, thesis/dissertation. *Entrance requirements:* For master's and doctorate, GRE General Test. Additional exam requirements/recommendations for international students: Required—TOEFL (minimum score 550 paper-based; 79 iBT). *Application deadline:* For fall admission, 6/1 priority date for domestic students, 1/15 priority date for international students; for spring admission, 9/1 priority date for domestic students, 6/15 priority date for international students. Applications are processed on a rolling basis. Application fee: $60. Electronic applications accepted. *Expenses:* Tuition, state resident: full-time $6310; part-time $262.92 per credit hour. Tuition, nonresident: full-time $14,998; part-time $624.92 per credit hour. *Required fees:* $2701; $36.50 per credit. $912.50 per semester. Tuition and fees vary according to course load. *Financial support:* In 2014–15, 91 students received support, including 78 fellowships (averaging $2,724 per year), 4 research assistantships (averaging $17,800 per year), 82 teaching assistantships

(averaging $11,423 per year); Federal Work-Study, scholarships/grants, and unspecified assistantships also available. Financial award application deadline: 4/15; financial award applicants required to submit FAFSA. *Faculty research:* Literature, comparative literature, linguistics, culture, applied linguistics. *Total annual research expenditures:* $1,380. *Unit head:* Dr. Erin Collopy, Chair and Associate Professor, 806-834-8497, Fax: 806-742-3306, E-mail: erin.collopy@ttu.edu. *Application contact:* Liz Hildebrand, Senior Advisor, 806-834-2463, Fax: 806-742-3306, E-mail: liz.hildebrand@ttu.edu.
Website: http://www.depts.ttu.edu/classic_modern/

University at Buffalo, the State University of New York, Graduate School, College of Arts and Sciences, Department of Romance Languages and Literatures, Buffalo, NY 14260-4620. Offers French (MA, PhD); Spanish (MA, PhD). Part-time programs available. *Faculty:* 16 full-time (10 women), 6 part-time/adjunct (5 women). *Students:* 33 full-time (20 women), 4 part-time (2 women); includes 17 minority (2 Black or African American, non-Hispanic/Latino; 2 Asian, non-Hispanic/Latino; 9 Hispanic/Latino; 4 Two or more races, non-Hispanic/Latino), 11 international. 20 applicants, 85% accepted, 11 enrolled. In 2014, 3 master's, 7 doctorates awarded. Terminal master's awarded for partial completion of doctoral program. *Degree requirements:* For master's, one foreign language, comprehensive exam, thesis; for doctorate, 2 foreign languages, comprehensive exam, thesis/dissertation. *Entrance requirements:* For master's and doctorate, GRE. Additional exam requirements/recommendations for international students: Required—TOEFL (minimum score 550 paper-based; 79 iBT), IELTS (minimum score 6.5), PTE (minimum score 55). *Application deadline:* For fall admission, 1/15 priority date for domestic students, 1/1 for international students; for spring admission, 8/1 for international students. Applications are processed on a rolling basis. Application fee: $75. Electronic applications accepted. *Financial support:* In 2014–15, 24 students received support, including 3 fellowships (averaging $5,333 per year), 24 teaching assistantships with full tuition reimbursements available (averaging $13,454 per year); Federal Work-Study, institutionally sponsored loans, scholarships/grants, and health care benefits also available. Financial award application deadline: 1/1; financial award applicants required to submit FAFSA. *Faculty research:* Romance linguistics, cultural studies, literary studies, literature, philosophy and poetry. *Unit head:* Dr. David Castillo, Professor and Chair, 716-645-0869, Fax: 716-645-5981, E-mail: dc63@buffalo.edu. *Application contact:* Dr. Amy Graves-Monroe, Associate Professor and Director of Graduate Studies, 716-645-0880, Fax: 716-645-5981, E-mail: acgraves@buffalo.edu.
Website: http://rll.drupalgardens.com

The University of Alabama, Graduate School, College of Arts and Sciences, Department of Modern Languages and Classics, Tuscaloosa, AL 35487. Offers French (MA, PhD); French and Spanish (PhD); German (MA); Romance languages (MA, PhD); Spanish (MA, PhD). Part-time programs available. *Faculty:* 29 full-time (16 women). *Students:* 53 full-time (35 women), 10 part-time (6 women); includes 9 minority (3 Black or African American, non-Hispanic/Latino; 5 Hispanic/Latino; 1 Two or more races, non-Hispanic/Latino), 15 international. Average age 33. 24 applicants, 88% accepted, 14 enrolled. In 2014, 10 master's, 5 doctorates awarded. *Degree requirements:* For master's, comprehensive exam, thesis optional; for doctorate, one foreign language, thesis/dissertation, preliminary exam. *Entrance requirements:* For master's and doctorate, minimum GPA of 3.0, writing sample. Additional exam requirements/recommendations for international students: Required—TOEFL or IELTS. *Application deadline:* For fall admission, 7/6 priority date for domestic students, 1/15 priority date for international students; for spring admission, 12/5 priority date for domestic students, 6/1 priority date for international students. Applications are processed on a rolling basis. Application fee: $50 ($60 for international students). Electronic applications accepted. *Expenses:* Tuition, state resident: full-time $9826. Tuition, nonresident: full-time $24,950. *Financial support:* In 2014–15, 7 students received support, including 1 fellowship, research assistantships with full tuition reimbursements available (averaging $10,291 per year), 6 teaching assistantships with full tuition reimbursements available (averaging $10,291 per year); career-related internships or fieldwork, Federal Work-Study, institutionally sponsored loans, and scholarships/grants also available. Financial award application deadline: 7/14. *Faculty research:* Non-English literature, linguistics, culture, film. *Unit head:* Dr. Michael Picone, Chair and Professor, 205-348-5054, Fax: 205-348-2042, E-mail: mpicone@bama.ua.edu. *Application contact:* Dr. K. Barbara Fischer, Graduate Director and Associate Professor, 205-348-8465, Fax: 205-348-2042, E-mail: bfischer@bama.ua.edu.
Website: http://bama.ua.edu/~mlc

University of California, Berkeley, Graduate Division, College of Letters and Science, Group in Romance Languages and Literature, Berkeley, CA 94720-1500. Offers French (PhD); Italian (PhD); Spanish (PhD). *Degree requirements:* For doctorate, thesis/dissertation, qualifying exam. *Entrance requirements:* For doctorate, GRE General Test, minimum GPA of 3.0, 3 letters of recommendation. Additional exam requirements/recommendations for international students: Required—TOEFL (minimum score 570 paper-based).

University of Chicago, Division of the Humanities, Department of Romance Languages and Literatures, Chicago, IL 60637. Offers French (PhD); Italian (PhD); Spanish (PhD). *Students:* 44 full-time (28 women); includes 9 minority (1 Black or African American, non-Hispanic/Latino; 1 Asian, non-Hispanic/Latino; 6 Hispanic/Latino; 1 Two or more races, non-Hispanic/Latino), 13 international. 71 applicants, 39% accepted, 7 enrolled. Terminal master's awarded for partial completion of doctoral program. *Degree requirements:* For doctorate, 3 foreign languages, thesis/dissertation. *Entrance requirements:* For doctorate, GRE General Test. Additional exam requirements/recommendations for international students: Required—TOEFL (minimum score 104 iBT), IELTS (minimum score 7). *Application deadline:* For fall admission, 12/15 for domestic and international students. Application fee: $90. Electronic applications accepted. *Expenses: Tuition:* Full-time $46,899. *Required fees:* $347. *Financial support:* Fellowships with full tuition reimbursements, teaching assistantships with full tuition reimbursements, Federal Work-Study, institutionally sponsored loans, scholarships/grants, and health care benefits available. Financial award application deadline: 12/15; financial award applicants required to submit FAFSA. *Unit head:* Dr. Larry Norman, Chair. *Application contact:* Braden Grams, Assistant Dean of Students, Admissions and Fellowships, 773-702-1552, Fax: 773-834-9148, E-mail: humanitiesadmissions@uchicago.edu.
Website: http://rll.uchicago.edu

University of Chicago, Division of the Humanities, Master of Arts Program in the Humanities, Chicago, IL 60637. Offers art history (MA); classics (MA); comparative literature (MA); creative writing (MA); digital humanities (MA); English language and literature (MA); Germanic studies (MA); linguistics (MA); music (MA); philosophy (MA); Romance languages and literatures (MA); South Asian languages and civilizations (MA). *Students:* 83 full-time (41 women), 8 part-time (6 women); includes 14 minority (1 Black or African American, non-Hispanic/Latino; 6 Asian, non-Hispanic/Latino; 6 Hispanic/Latino; 1 Two or more races, non-Hispanic/Latino), 17 international. Average age 26. 153 applicants, 67% accepted, 80 enrolled. *Degree requirements:* For master's, thesis. *Entrance requirements:* For master's, GRE General Test. Additional exam requirements/recommendations for international students: Required—TOEFL (minimum score 600 paper-based; 104 iBT), IELTS (minimum score 7). *Application deadline:* For fall admission, 3/15 for domestic and international students. Application fee: $90. Electronic applications accepted. *Expenses: Tuition:* Full-time $46,899. *Required fees:* $347. *Financial support:* In 2014–15, 100 students received support, including 8 fellowships with partial tuition reimbursements available (averaging $12,000 per year); Federal Work-Study, institutionally sponsored loans, and tuition waivers (partial) also available. Financial award application deadline: 3/15; financial award applicants required to submit FAFSA. *Unit head:* Prof. David Wray, Director, 773-834-1201, E-mail: ma-humanities@uchicago.edu. *Application contact:* Program Coordinator, 773-834-1201, Fax: 773-834-7526, E-mail: ma-humanities@uchicago.edu.
Website: http://maph.uchicago.edu/

University of Cincinnati, Graduate School, McMicken College of Arts and Sciences, Department of Romance Languages and Literature, Cincinnati, OH 45221. Offers French (MA, PhD); Romance languages and literatures (PhD); Spanish (MA, PhD). Terminal master's awarded for partial completion of doctoral program. *Degree requirements:* For master's, 2 foreign languages, comprehensive exam, thesis optional; for doctorate, 3 foreign languages, comprehensive exam, thesis/dissertation. *Entrance requirements:* For master's, minimum GPA of 3.0; for doctorate, MA or equivalent in French or Spanish language and literature. Additional exam requirements/recommendations for international students: Required—TOEFL (minimum score 520 paper-based). Electronic applications accepted. *Faculty research:* Teaching methods in Spanish, Spanish theater, Old French, Francophone studies, poetry.

University of Georgia, Franklin College of Arts and Sciences, Department of Romance Languages, Athens, GA 30602. Offers French (MA); Romance languages (MA, PhD); Spanish (MA). *Degree requirements:* For master's, one foreign language; for doctorate, 2 foreign languages, thesis/dissertation. *Entrance requirements:* For master's and doctorate, GRE General Test. Electronic applications accepted.

University of Illinois at Urbana–Champaign, Graduate College, College of Liberal Arts and Sciences, School of Literatures, Cultures and Linguistics, Program in Romance Linguistics, Champaign, IL 61820. Offers PhD. Application fee: $70 ($90 for international students). *Unit head:* Jean-Philippe Mathy, Director, 217-244-2718, Fax: 217-244-8430, E-mail: jmathy@illinois.edu. *Application contact:* Lynn Stanke, Office Support Specialist, 217-333-6269, Fax: 217-244-3050, E-mail: stanke@illinois.edu.

University of Miami, Graduate School, College of Arts and Sciences, Department of Modern Languages and Literatures, Coral Gables, FL 33124. Offers romance studies (PhD), including French, Spanish. *Degree requirements:* For doctorate, 2 foreign languages, thesis/dissertation, area exam, qualifying exam. *Entrance requirements:* For doctorate, 1 writing sample in English and 1 writing sample in French or Spanish, minimum GPA of 3.0, oral interview, letters of recommendation. Additional exam requirements/recommendations for international students: Required—TOEFL (minimum score 550 paper-based; 59 iBT). Electronic applications accepted. *Faculty research:* Transatlantic studies, Caribbean studies, comparative literature, gender theory, cultural studies.

University of Missouri, Office of Research and Graduate Studies, College of Arts and Science, Department of Romance Languages and Literatures, Columbia, MO 65211. Offers French (MA, PhD); literature (MA); Spanish (MA, PhD); teaching (MA). *Faculty:* 25 full-time (12 women), 1 (woman) part-time/adjunct. *Students:* 28 full-time (19 women), 9 part-time (6 women); includes 9 minority (3 Black or African American, non-Hispanic/Latino; 4 Hispanic/Latino; 2 Two or more races, non-Hispanic/Latino), 15 international. Average age 36. 16 applicants, 69% accepted, 7 enrolled. In 2014, 3 master's, 1 doctorate awarded. Terminal master's awarded for partial completion of doctoral program. *Degree requirements:* For master's, one foreign language; for doctorate, 4 foreign languages, comprehensive exam, thesis/dissertation. *Entrance requirements:* For master's, GRE General Test, minimum GPA of 3.0 in field of major; bachelor's degree; for doctorate, GRE General Test, minimum GPA of 3.0 in field of major; master's degree. Additional exam requirements/recommendations for international students: Required—TOEFL (minimum score 500 paper-based; 61 iBT). *Application deadline:* For fall admission, 2/15 priority date for domestic students; for winter admission, 10/15 for domestic students. Applications are processed on a rolling basis. Application fee: $55 ($75 for international students). Electronic applications accepted. *Financial support:* Research assistantships, teaching assistantships with full tuition reimbursements, institutionally sponsored loans, health care benefits, and unspecified assistantships available. *Faculty research:* Afro-Romance studies. *Unit head:* Dr. Flore Zephir, Department Chair, 573-882-5048, E-mail: zephirf@missouri.edu. *Application contact:* Mary Harris, Administrative Assistant, 573-882-5039, E-mail: harrisma@missouri.edu.
Website: http://romancelanguages.missouri.edu/grad.shtml

University of Missouri–Kansas City, College of Arts and Sciences, Department of Foreign Languages and Literatures, Kansas City, MO 64110-2499. Offers romance languages and literatures (MA), including French, Spanish. Part-time programs available. *Faculty:* 15 full-time (8 women), 15 part-time/adjunct (12 women). *Students:* 3 full-time (2 women), 19 part-time (15 women); includes 11 minority (1 Black or African American, non-Hispanic/Latino; 10 Hispanic/Latino). Average age 32. 17 applicants, 59% accepted, 9 enrolled. In 2014, 8 master's awarded. *Degree requirements:* For master's, 2 foreign languages. *Entrance requirements:* For master's, GRE General Test, minimum GPA of 2.75, 2 letters of recommendation. Additional exam requirements/recommendations for international students: Required—TOEFL (minimum score 550 paper-based; 80 iBT). *Application deadline:* For fall admission, 4/1 priority date for domestic and international students; for spring admission, 11/1 priority date for domestic and international students. Applications are processed on a rolling basis. Application fee: $45 ($50 for international students). Electronic applications accepted. *Financial support:* In 2014–15, 1 teaching assistantship (averaging $12,600 per year) was awarded; Federal Work-Study, institutionally sponsored loans, and tuition waivers (full and partial) also available. Support available to part-time students. Financial award application deadline: 3/1; financial award applicants required to submit FAFSA. *Faculty research:* Literary analyses; psychology and literature; narrative techniques, poetic structure, and style; literature, politics, and society (especially in Latin America). *Unit head:* Dr. K. Scott Baker, Chair, 816-235-2823, Fax: 816-235-1312, E-mail: bakerks@umkc.edu. *Application contact:* 816-235-1311, Fax: 816-235-1312, E-mail: admit@umkc.edu.
Website: http://cas.umkc.edu/foreign

University of New Orleans, Graduate School, College of Liberal Arts, Department of Foreign Languages, New Orleans, LA 70148. Offers MA. Part-time and evening/weekend programs available. *Degree requirements:* For master's, one foreign language, thesis optional. *Entrance requirements:* For master's, GRE General Test, minimum B average. Additional exam requirements/recommendations for international students: Required—TOEFL (minimum score 550 paper-based; 79 iBT), IELTS (minimum score 6.5). Electronic applications accepted. *Faculty research:* Translation studies, Michelet, Scève, Spanish canzoniero, theories of representation.

The University of North Carolina at Chapel Hill, Graduate School, College of Arts and Sciences, Department of Romance Languages and Literatures, Chapel Hill, NC 27599. Offers French (MA, PhD); Italian (MA, PhD); Portuguese (MA, PhD); Romance

languages (MA, PhD); Romance philology (MA, PhD); Spanish (MA, PhD). *Degree requirements:* For master's, one foreign language, comprehensive exam, thesis; for doctorate, 2 foreign languages, comprehensive exam, thesis/dissertation. *Entrance requirements:* For master's and doctorate, GRE General Test, minimum GPA of 3.0. Additional exam requirements/recommendations for international students: Required—TOEFL (minimum score 550 paper-based). Electronic applications accepted.

University of Notre Dame, Graduate School, College of Arts and Letters, Division of Humanities, Department of Romance Languages and Literatures, Notre Dame, IN 46556. Offers French and Francophone studies (MA); Iberian and Latin American studies (MA); Italian studies (MA); Romance literatures (MA). *Degree requirements:* For master's, 2 foreign languages, comprehensive exam, thesis optional. *Entrance requirements:* For master's, GRE General Test, BA in target language. Additional exam requirements/recommendations for international students: Required—TOEFL (minimum score 600 paper-based; 80 iBT). Electronic applications accepted. *Faculty research:* Literature of discovery and exploration, modern literature, literary criticism, medieval literature, feminist critical theory.

University of Oregon, Graduate School, College of Arts and Sciences, Department of Romance Languages, Program in Romance Languages, Eugene, OR 97403. Offers MA, PhD. Part-time programs available. *Degree requirements:* For master's, 2 foreign languages; for doctorate, 2 foreign languages, thesis/dissertation. *Entrance requirements:* For master's and doctorate, GRE General Test, minimum GPA of 3.0. Additional exam requirements/recommendations for international students: Required—TOEFL.

University of Pennsylvania, School of Arts and Sciences, Graduate Group in Romance Languages, Philadelphia, PA 19104. Offers French (AM, PhD); Italian (AM, PhD); Spanish (AM, PhD). *Faculty:* 44 full-time (16 women), 6 part-time/adjunct (2 women). *Students:* 61 full-time (29 women), 3 part-time (1 woman); includes 8 minority (all Hispanic/Latino), 34 international. 92 applicants, 23% accepted, 10 enrolled. In 2014, 11 master's, 9 doctorates awarded. Terminal master's awarded for partial completion of doctoral program. *Degree requirements:* For master's, one foreign language, thesis or alternative; for doctorate, 2 foreign languages, thesis/dissertation. *Entrance requirements:* For master's and doctorate, GRE General Test. Additional exam requirements/recommendations for international students: Required—TOEFL. *Application deadline:* For fall admission, 12/1 priority date for domestic students. Application fee: $70. Electronic applications accepted. *Financial support:* In 2014–15, 23 fellowships, 2 research assistantships, 39 teaching assistantships were awarded; institutionally sponsored loans, scholarships/grants, traineeships, health care benefits, and unspecified assistantships also available. Financial award application deadline: 12/15. *Faculty research:* Literary theory and criticism, cultural studies, history of Romance literatures, gender studies. *Unit head:* Dr. Ralph M. Rosen, Associate Dean for Graduate Studies, 215-898-7156, Fax: 215-573-8068, E-mail: grad-dean@sas.upenn.edu. *Application contact:* Arts and Sciences Graduate Admissions, 215-573-5816, Fax: 215-573-8068, E-mail: gdasadmis@sas.upenn.edu.
Website: http://www.sas.upenn.edu/graduate-division

University of South Africa, College of Human Sciences, Pretoria, South Africa. Offers adult education (M Ed); African languages (MA, PhD); African politics (MA, PhD); Afrikaans (MA, PhD); ancient history (MA, PhD); ancient Near Eastern studies (MA, PhD); anthropology (MA, PhD); applied linguistics (MA); Arabic (MA, PhD); archaeology (MA); art history (MA); Biblical archaeology (MA); Biblical studies (M Th, D Th, PhD); Christian spirituality (M Th, D Th); church history (M Th, D Th); classical studies (MA, PhD); clinical psychology (MA); communication (MA, PhD); comparative education (M Ed, Ed D); consulting psychology (D Admin, D Com, PhD); curriculum studies (M Ed, Ed D); development studies (M Admin, MA, D Admin, PhD); didactics (M Ed, Ed D); education (M Tech); education management (M Ed, Ed D); educational psychology (M Ed); English (MA); environmental education (M Ed); French (MA, PhD); German (MA, PhD); Greek (MA); guidance and counseling (M Ed); health studies (MA, PhD), including health sciences education (MA), health services management (MA), medical and surgical nursing science (critical care general) (MA), midwifery and neonatal nursing science (MA), trauma and emergency care (MA); history (MA, PhD); history of education (Ed D); inclusive education (M Ed, Ed D); information and communications technology policy and regulation (MA); information science (MA, MIS, PhD); international politics (MA, PhD); Islamic studies (MA, PhD); Italian (MA, PhD); Judaica (MA, PhD); linguistics (MA, PhD); mathematical education (M Ed); mathematics education (MA); missiology (M Th, D Th); modern Hebrew (MA, PhD); musicology (MA, MMus, D Mus, PhD); natural science education (M Ed); New Testament (M Th, D Th); Old Testament (D Th); pastoral therapy (M Th, D Th); philosophy (MA); philosophy of education (M Ed, Ed D); politics (MA, PhD); Portuguese (MA, PhD); practical theology (M Th, D Th); psychology (MA, MS, PhD); psychology of education (M Ed, Ed D); public health (MA); religious studies (MA, D Th, PhD); Romance languages (MA); Russian (MA, PhD); Semitic languages (MA, PhD); social behavior studies in HIV/AIDS (MA); social science (mental health) (MA); social science in development studies (MA); social science in psychology (MA); social science in social work (MA); social science in sociology (MA); social work (MSW, DSW, PhD); socio-education (M Ed, Ed D); sociolinguistics (MA); sociology (MA, PhD); Spanish (MA, PhD); systematic theology (M Th, D Th); TESOL (teaching English to speakers of other languages) (MA); theological ethics (M Th, D Th); theory of literature (MA, PhD); urban ministries (D Th); urban ministry (M Th).

The University of Texas at Austin, Graduate School, College of Liberal Arts, Department of French and Italian, Austin, TX 78712-1111. Offers French linguistics (MA, PhD); French studies (MA, PhD); Italian studies (MA, PhD); Romance linguistics (PhD). Part-time programs available. *Degree requirements:* For master's, one foreign language, thesis; for doctorate, 2 foreign languages, thesis/dissertation. *Entrance requirements:* For master's, GRE General Test, minimum GPA of 3.0, bachelor's degree in French or equivalent; for doctorate, GRE General Test, minimum GPA of 3.0, master's degree in French. Additional exam requirements/recommendations for international students: Required—TOEFL. Electronic applications accepted. *Faculty research:* Nineteenth-century Italian literature, Italian Renaissance, twentieth-century French literature, Francophone literature, fifteenth-century literature and culture.

University of Virginia, College and Graduate School of Arts and Sciences, Department of Spanish, Italian and Portuguese, Charlottesville, VA 22903. Offers Italian (MA); Spanish (MA, PhD). *Faculty:* 32 full-time (19 women). *Students:* 41 full-time (30 women); includes 7 minority (5 Hispanic/Latino; 2 Two or more races, non-Hispanic/Latino), 7 international. Average age 28. 38 applicants, 42% accepted, 10 enrolled. In 2014, 8 master's, 6 doctorates awarded. *Degree requirements:* For master's, comprehensive exam, thesis; for doctorate, one foreign language, comprehensive exam, thesis/dissertation. *Entrance requirements:* For master's and doctorate, GRE General Test, GRE Subject Test, 2 letters of recommendation. Additional exam requirements/recommendations for international students: Required—TOEFL (minimum score 600 paper-based; 90 iBT), IELTS (minimum score 7). *Application deadline:* For fall admission, 12/1 for domestic and international students. Applications are processed on a rolling basis. Application fee: $60. Electronic applications accepted. *Expenses:* Tuition, state resident: full-time $14,164; part-time $349 per credit hour. Tuition, nonresident: full-time $23,722; part-time $1300 per credit hour. *Required fees:* $2514. *Financial support:* Fellowships and teaching assistantships available. Financial award applicants required to submit FAFSA. *Unit head:* Joel Rini, Chair, 434-924-7159, Fax: 434-924-7160, E-mail: sipinfo@virginia.edu.
Website: http://spanitalport.virginia.edu/

Washington University in St. Louis, Graduate School of Arts and Sciences, Department of Romance Languages and Literatures, St. Louis, MO 63130-4899. Offers French (MA, PhD), including French (MA), French and comparative literature (PhD), French language and literature (PhD); Spanish (MA, PhD), including Hispanic languages and literatures (PhD), Spanish (MA), Spanish and comparative literature (PhD). Terminal master's awarded for partial completion of doctoral program. *Degree requirements:* For master's, thesis or alternative; for doctorate, thesis/dissertation. *Entrance requirements:* For doctorate, GRE General Test. Additional exam requirements/recommendations for international students: Required—TOEFL. Electronic applications accepted. *Faculty research:* French language and literature, Latin American and Iberian literatures and languages, Spanish and comparative literature.

Wayne State University, College of Liberal Arts and Sciences, Department of Classical and Modern Languages, Literatures, and Cultures, Program in Romance Languages, Detroit, MI 48202. Offers French (MA); Italian (MA); Spanish (MA). *Students:* 6 full-time (5 women), 22 part-time (15 women); includes 9 minority (4 Black or African American, non-Hispanic/Latino; 1 American Indian or Alaska Native, non-Hispanic/Latino; 1 Asian, non-Hispanic/Latino; 2 Hispanic/Latino; 1 Two or more races, non-Hispanic/Latino), 1 international. Average age 32. 13 applicants, 38% accepted, 5 enrolled. In 2014, 6 master's awarded. *Degree requirements:* For master's, one foreign language, thesis optional. *Entrance requirements:* For master's, GRE (strongly recommended), three letters of recommendation. Additional exam requirements/recommendations for international students: Required—TOEFL (minimum score 550 paper-based; 79 iBT), Michigan English Language Assessment Battery (minimum score 85); Recommended—IELTS (minimum score 6.5). *Application deadline:* For fall admission, 6/1 priority date for domestic students, 5/1 priority date for international students; for winter admission, 10/1 priority date for domestic students, 9/1 priority date for international students; for spring admission, 2/1 priority date for domestic students, 1/1 priority date for international students. Applications are processed on a rolling basis. Application fee: $0. Electronic applications accepted. *Expenses:* Tuition, state resident: full-time $10,294; part-time $571.90 per credit hour. Tuition, nonresident: full-time $29,730; part-time $1238.75 per credit hour. *Required fees:* $1365; $43.50 per credit hour. $291.10 per semester. Tuition and fees vary according to course load and program. *Financial support:* In 2014–15, 11 students received support. Fellowships, research assistantships, teaching assistantships, scholarships/grants, health care benefits, and unspecified assistantships available. Financial award application deadline: 3/31; financial award applicants required to submit FAFSA. *Unit head:* Dr. Anne Duggan, Department Chair, E-mail: a.duggan@wayne.edu. *Application contact:* Dr. Michael Giordano, Graduate Advisor, E-mail: aa2144@wayne.edu.
Website: http://clas.wayne.edu/languages/RomanceLanguagesLiteratures

Russian

Boston College, Graduate School of Arts and Sciences, Department of Slavic and Eastern Languages, Program in Russian and Slavic Languages and Literature, Chestnut Hill, MA 02467-3800. Offers MA, MA/JD, MBA/MA. *Degree requirements:* For master's, 3 foreign languages, comprehensive exam, thesis or alternative. *Entrance requirements:* Additional exam requirements/recommendations for international students: Required—TOEFL (minimum score 600 paper-based; 100 iBT), IELTS (minimum score 7). *Application deadline:* For fall admission, 2/1 for domestic and international students. Application fee: $75. Electronic applications accepted. *Financial support:* Teaching assistantships and Federal Work-Study available. Support available to part-time students. Financial award application deadline: 3/1; financial award applicants required to submit FAFSA. *Faculty research:* Structural analysis of language, poetry and semiotic systems. *Unit head:* Dr. Maxin Shrayer, Chairperson, 617-552-3910. *Application contact:* Dr. Michael Connolly, Graduate Program Director, 617-552-3912, E-mail: michael.connolly@bc.edu.
Website: http://www.bc.edu/sl

Brown University, Graduate School, Department of Slavic Languages, Providence, RI 02912. Offers Russian language and literature (AM); Slavic linguistics (AM); Slavic studies (PhD). *Degree requirements:* For master's, one foreign language; for doctorate, 2 foreign languages, thesis/dissertation, preliminary exam.

Columbia University, Graduate School of Arts and Sciences, New York, NY 10027. Offers African-American studies (MA); American studies (MA); anthropology (MA, PhD); art history and archaeology (MA, PhD); astronomy (PhD); biological sciences (PhD); biotechnology (MA); chemical physics (PhD); chemistry (PhD); classical studies (MA, PhD); classics (MA, PhD); climate and society (MA); earth and environmental sciences (PhD); East Asia: regional studies (MA); East Asian languages and cultures (MA, PhD); ecology, evolution and environmental biology (MA), including conservation biology; ecology, evolution, and environmental biology (PhD), including ecology and evolutionary biology, evolutionary primatology; economics (PhD); English and comparative literature (MA, PhD); French and Romance philology (MA, PhD); Germanic languages (MA, PhD); global French studies (MA); Hispanic cultural studies (MA); history (PhD); history and literature (MA); human rights studies (MA); Islamic studies (MA); Italian (MA, PhD); Japanese pedagogy (MA); Jewish studies (MA); Latin America and the Caribbean: regional studies (MA); Latin American and Iberian cultures (PhD); mathematics (MA, PhD), including finance (MA); medieval and Renaissance studies (MA); Middle Eastern, South Asian, and African studies (MA, PhD); modern art: critical and curatorial studies (MA); modern European studies (MA); museum anthropology (MA); music (DMA, PhD); oral history (MA); philosophical foundations of physics (MA); philosophy (MA, PhD); physics (PhD); political science (MA, PhD); psychology (PhD); quantitative methods in the social sciences (MA); religion (MA, PhD); Russia, Eurasia and East Europe: regional

studies (MA); Russian translation (MA); Slavic cultures (MA); Slavic languages (MA, PhD); sociology (MA, PhD); South Asian studies (MA); statistics (MA, PhD); theatre (PhD); JD/PhD; MA/MS; MD/PhD; MPA/MA. Dual-degree programs require admission to both Graduate School of Arts and Sciences and another Columbia school. Part-time and evening/weekend programs available. Terminal master's awarded for partial completion of doctoral program. *Degree requirements:* For master's, thesis (for some programs); for doctorate, comprehensive exam, thesis/dissertation. *Entrance requirements:* For master's and doctorate, GRE General Test, GRE Subject Test (for some programs). Electronic applications accepted. *Faculty research:* Humanities, natural sciences, social sciences.

Harvard University, Graduate School of Arts and Sciences, Department of Slavic Languages and Literatures, Cambridge, MA 02138. Offers Polish (PhD); Russian (PhD); Serbo-Croatian (PhD); Slavic philology (PhD); Ukrainian (PhD). *Degree requirements:* For doctorate, 4 foreign languages, thesis/dissertation. *Entrance requirements:* For doctorate, GRE General Test, writing sample. Additional exam requirements/recommendations for international students: Required—TOEFL.

Kent State University, College of Arts and Sciences, Department of Modern and Classical Language Studies, Kent, OH 44242-0001. Offers translation (MA), including French, German, Japanese, Russian, Spanish; translation studies (PhD). Part-time programs available. *Faculty:* 36 full-time (22 women). *Students:* 89 full-time (56 women), 18 part-time (10 women); includes 12 minority (1 Black or African American, non-Hispanic/Latino; 3 Asian, non-Hispanic/Latino; 6 Hispanic/Latino; 2 Two or more races, non-Hispanic/Latino), 42 international. Average age 30. 228 applicants, 52% accepted, 90 enrolled. In 2014, 24 master's, 3 doctorates awarded. *Degree requirements:* For master's, variable foreign language requirement, comprehensive exam (for some programs), thesis (for some programs), case study (translation), language exam and interview (languages); for doctorate, variable foreign language requirement, comprehensive exam, thesis/dissertation. *Entrance requirements:* For master's, minimum GPA of 3.0, transcript, goal statement, conversational sample in two languages, written sample in second language, 3 letters of recommendation; for doctorate, minimum GPA of 3.0, transcript, goal statement, writing sample, professional credentials, 3 letters of recommendation. Additional exam requirements/recommendations for international students: Required—TOEFL (minimum score: paper-based 525, iBT 71), Michigan English Language Assessment Battery (minimum score of 75), IELTS (minimum score of 6.0), PTE Academic (minimum score of 48), or completion of ELS level 112 Intensive Program. *Application deadline:* For fall admission, 2/28 for domestic and international students. Applications are processed on a rolling basis. Application fee: $45 ($70 for international students). Electronic applications accepted. *Expenses:* Tuition, state resident: full-time $8730; part-time $485 per credit hour. Tuition, nonresident: full-time $14,886; part-time $827 per credit hour. Tuition and fees vary according to campus/location and program. *Financial support:* Research assistantships with full tuition reimbursements, teaching assistantships with full tuition reimbursements, Federal Work-Study, scholarships/grants, and unspecified assistantships available. Financial award application deadline: 2/1. *Unit head:* Keiran Dunne, Professor and Chair, 330-672-1805, E-mail: kdunne@kent.edu. *Application contact:* Brian James Baer, Professor and Graduate Coordinator, 330-672-2150, Fax: 330-672-4009, E-mail: bbaer@kent.edu.
Website: http://www.kent.edu/mcls/

McGill University, Faculty of Graduate and Postdoctoral Studies, Faculty of Arts, Department of Russian and Slavic Studies, Montréal, QC H3A 2T5, Canada. Offers Russian literature (MA, PhD).

Middlebury College, Language Schools, Russian School, Middlebury, VT 05753-6002. Offers MA, DML. *Faculty:* 29 full-time (23 women). *Students:* 37 full-time (22 women); includes 5 minority (all Hispanic/Latino), 1 international. Average age 28. 49 applicants, 92% accepted, 37 enrolled. In 2014, 6 master's, 1 doctorate awarded. *Degree requirements:* For master's, one foreign language; for doctorate, 2 foreign languages, comprehensive exam, thesis/dissertation. *Entrance requirements:* For master's, language proficiency exam, placement exam, 3 letters of recommendation, writing sample in Russian, personal statement, transcripts; for doctorate, 1st and 2nd language exams, 3 letters of recommendation, writing sample in Russian, personal statement, transcripts. *Application deadline:* Applications are processed on a rolling basis. Application fee: $65. Electronic applications accepted. *Financial support:* Fellowships and scholarships/grants available. Financial award applicants required to submit FAFSA. *Unit head:* Dr. Jason Merrill, Director, 802-443-5230, Fax: 802-443-2075, E-mail: jmerrill@middlebury.edu. *Application contact:* Oliver Carling, Coordinator, 802-443-2006, Fax: 802-443-2075, E-mail: ocarling@middlebury.edu.
Website: http://www.middlebury.edu/ls/grad_programs/russian

New York University, Graduate School of Arts and Science, Department of Russian and Slavic Studies, New York, NY 10012-1019. Offers Russian literature (MA); Slavic literature (MA). Part-time programs available. *Faculty:* 8 full-time (3 women). *Students:* 4 full-time (3 women), 3 part-time (all women), 1 international. Average age 29. 14 applicants, 86% accepted, 4 enrolled. In 2014, 5 master's awarded. *Degree requirements:* For master's, one foreign language, comprehensive exam, thesis. *Entrance requirements:* For master's, GRE General Test, minimum 3 years of undergraduate Russian or equivalent. Additional exam requirements/recommendations for international students: Required—TOEFL. *Application deadline:* For fall admission, 4/15 for domestic and international students; for spring admission, 11/1 for domestic and international students. Application fee: $100. *Financial support:* Career-related internships or fieldwork, Federal Work-Study, and institutionally sponsored loans available. Financial award application deadline: 4/15; financial award applicants required to submit FAFSA. *Faculty research:* Modern Russian literature and art, contemporary Russian and East European literature, literary theory, Slavic linguistics, Russian journalism. *Unit head:* Anne Lounsbery, Chair, 212-998-8670, Fax: 212-995-4604, E-mail: gsas.russian.and.slavic@nyu.edu. *Application contact:* Michael Kunichika, Director of Graduate Studies, 212-998-8670, Fax: 212-995-4604, E-mail: gsas.russian.and.slavic@nyu.edu.
Website: http://russianslavic.as.nyu.edu/

Penn State University Park, Graduate School, College of the Liberal Arts, Department of Comparative Literature, University Park, PA 16802. Offers comparative literature (MA, PhD); Russian and comparative literature (MA). *Unit head:* Dr. Susan Welch, Dean, 814-865-7691, Fax: 814-863-2085, E-mail: swelch@psu.edu. *Application contact:* Lori A. Stania, Director, Graduate Student Services, 814-867-5278, Fax: 814-863-4627, E-mail: gswww@psu.edu.
Website: http://complit.la.psu.edu/

Princeton University, Graduate School, Department of Slavic Languages and Literatures, Princeton, NJ 08544-1019. Offers Russian and Slavic linguistics (PhD); Russian literature (PhD). *Degree requirements:* For doctorate, variable foreign language requirement, thesis/dissertation. *Entrance requirements:* For doctorate, GRE General Test. Additional exam requirements/recommendations for international students: Required—TOEFL (minimum score 600 paper-based). Electronic applications accepted.

The University of Arizona, College of Humanities, Department of Russian and Slavic Studies, Tucson, AZ 85721. Offers Russian (MA). Part-time programs available. *Degree requirements:* For master's, one foreign language, comprehensive exam (for some programs), thesis (for some programs). *Entrance requirements:* For master's, 3 letters of recommendation, audio sample. Additional exam requirements/recommendations for international students: Required—TOEFL (minimum score 550 paper-based; 79 iBT). Electronic applications accepted. *Faculty research:* Russian literature, language/pedagogy, linguistics, Russian culture.

University of California, Berkeley, Graduate Division, College of Letters and Science, Department of Slavic Languages and Literatures, Berkeley, CA 94720-1500. Offers Czech (PhD), including Czech linguistics, Czech literature; Polish (PhD), including Polish linguistics, Polish literature; Russian (PhD), including Russian linguistics, Russian literature; Serbo-Croatian (PhD), including Serbo-Croatian linguistics, Serbo-Croatian literature. Terminal master's awarded for partial completion of doctoral program. *Degree requirements:* For doctorate, thesis/dissertation, oral and written exams. *Entrance requirements:* For doctorate, GRE General Test, minimum GPA of 3.0, 3 letters of recommendation. Additional exam requirements/recommendations for international students: Required—TOEFL (minimum score 570 paper-based). Electronic applications accepted.

The University of Manchester, School of Languages, Linguistics and Cultures, Manchester, United Kingdom. Offers Arab world studies (PhD); Chinese studies (M Phil, PhD); East Asian studies (M Phil, PhD); English language (PhD); French studies (M Phil, PhD); German studies (M Phil, PhD); interpreting studies (PhD); Italian studies (M Phil, PhD); Japanese studies (M Phil, PhD); Latin American cultural studies (M Phil, PhD); linguistics (M Phil, PhD); Middle Eastern studies (M Phil, PhD); Polish studies (M Phil, PhD); Portuguese studies (M Phil, PhD); Russian studies (M Phil, PhD); Spanish studies (M Phil, PhD); translation and intercultural studies (M Phil, PhD).

University of Michigan, Horace H. Rackham School of Graduate Studies, College of Literature, Science, and the Arts, Department of Slavic Languages and Literatures, Ann Arbor, MI 48109-1275. Offers Russian (AM); Slavic languages and literatures (PhD). Terminal master's awarded for partial completion of doctoral program. *Degree requirements:* For doctorate, 3 foreign languages, comprehensive exam, thesis/dissertation, oral defense of dissertation, preliminary exam. *Entrance requirements:* For doctorate, GRE General Test. Additional exam requirements/recommendations for international students: Required—TOEFL (minimum score 560 paper-based). Electronic applications accepted. *Faculty research:* Russian literature (all periods), Polish literature, South Slavic literatures, Czech literature, Ukrainian literature.

University of Missouri, Office of Research and Graduate Studies, College of Arts and Science, Department of German and Russian Studies, Columbia, MO 65211. Offers German (MA); Russian and Slavonic studies (MA). *Faculty:* 13 full-time (6 women), 1 part-time/adjunct (0 women). *Students:* 9 full-time (6 women), 6 part-time (3 women); includes 3 minority (2 Asian, non-Hispanic/Latino; 1 Two or more races, non-Hispanic/Latino), 6 international. Average age 25. 16 applicants, 75% accepted, 10 enrolled. In 2014, 4 master's awarded. *Entrance requirements:* For master's, GRE General Test, minimum GPA of 3.0. Additional exam requirements/recommendations for international students: Required—TOEFL (minimum score 500 paper-based; 61 iBT). *Application deadline:* For fall admission, 2/1 priority date for domestic and international students. Applications are processed on a rolling basis. Application fee: $55 ($75 for international students). Electronic applications accepted. *Financial support:* In 2014–15, 18 teaching assistantships with full tuition reimbursements were awarded; institutionally sponsored loans, health care benefits, and unspecified assistantships also available. *Faculty research:* German and Russian cultural studies including literature, film, media studies, philosophy, and the history of science. *Unit head:* Dr. Timothy Langen, Department Chair, 573-882-6167, E-mail: langent@missouri.edu. *Application contact:* Jennifer Arnold, Administrative Associate, 573-882-4328, E-mail: arnoldj@missouri.edu.
Website: http://german.missouri.edu/index.html

The University of North Carolina at Chapel Hill, Graduate School, College of Arts and Sciences, Department of Slavic Languages and Literatures, Chapel Hill, NC 27599. Offers Polish literature (PhD); Russian and east European studies (MA); Russian literature (MA, PhD); Serbo-Croatian literature (PhD); Slavic linguistics (MA, PhD). Part-time programs available. Terminal master's awarded for partial completion of doctoral program. *Degree requirements:* For master's, 2 foreign languages, comprehensive exam, thesis; for doctorate, 4 foreign languages, comprehensive exam, thesis/dissertation. *Entrance requirements:* For master's and doctorate, GRE General Test, minimum GPA of 3.0. Electronic applications accepted. *Faculty research:* Russian cultural studies, literary translation, sociolinguistics, cognitive linguistics, ?migr? literature.

University of Oregon, Graduate School, College of Arts and Sciences, Program in Russian and East European Studies, Eugene, OR 97403. Offers MA. Part-time programs available. *Degree requirements:* For master's, 2 foreign languages, thesis. *Entrance requirements:* For master's, GRE General Test (recommended), minimum GPA of 3.0. Additional exam requirements/recommendations for international students: Required—TOEFL. *Faculty research:* L. N. Tolstoy's middle years, Russian folklore in eighteenth-century contexts, Bulgarian syntax, medieval Bulgarian texts, contemporary Russian culture film.

University of South Africa, College of Human Sciences, Pretoria, South Africa. Offers adult education (M Ed); African languages (MA, PhD); African politics (MA, PhD); Afrikaans (MA, PhD); ancient history (MA, PhD); ancient Near Eastern studies (MA, PhD); anthropology (MA, PhD); applied linguistics (MA); Arabic (MA, PhD); archaeology (MA); art history (MA); Biblical archaeology (MA); Biblical studies (M Th, D Th, PhD); Christian spirituality (M Th, D Th); church history (M Th, D Th); classical studies (MA, PhD); clinical psychology (MA); communication (MA, PhD); comparative education (M Ed, Ed D); consulting psychology (D Admin, D Com, PhD); curriculum studies (M Ed, Ed D); development studies (M Admin, MA, D Admin, PhD); didactics (M Ed, Ed D); education (M Tech); education management (M Ed, Ed D); educational psychology (M Ed); English (MA); environmental education (M Ed); French (MA, PhD); German (MA, PhD); Greek (MA); guidance and counseling (M Ed); health studies (MA, PhD), including health sciences education (MA), health services management (MA), medical and surgical nursing science (critical care general) (MA), midwifery and neonatal nursing science (MA), trauma and emergency care (MA); history (MA, PhD); history of education (Ed D); inclusive education (M Ed, Ed D); information and communications technology policy and regulation (MA); information science (MA, MIS, PhD); international politics (MA, PhD); Islamic studies (MA, PhD); Italian (MA, PhD); Judaica (MA, PhD); linguistics (MA, PhD); mathematical education (M Ed); mathematics education (MA); missiology (M Th, D Th); modern Hebrew (MA, PhD); musicology (MA, MMus, D Mus, PhD); natural science education (M Ed); New Testament (M Th, D Th); Old Testament (D Th); pastoral therapy (M Th, D Th); philosophy (MA); philosophy of education (M Ed, Ed D); politics (MA, PhD); Portuguese (MA, PhD); practical theology (M Th, D Th); psychology (MA, MS, PhD); psychology of education (M Ed, Ed D); public health (MA); religious studies (MA, D Th, PhD); Romance languages (MA); Russian (MA, PhD); Semitic languages (MA, PhD); social behavior studies in HIV/AIDS (MA); social science (mental health) (MA); social science in development studies (MA); social science in psychology (MA); social science in social work (MA); social science in sociology (MA); social work (MSW, DSW, PhD); socio-education (M Ed, Ed D); sociolinguistics (MA); sociology (MA, PhD); Spanish (MA, PhD); systematic theology (M Th, D Th); TESOL (teaching English

to speakers of other languages) (MA); theological ethics (M Th, D Th); theory of literature (MA, PhD); urban ministries (D Th); urban ministry (M Th).

The University of Tennessee, Graduate School, College of Arts and Sciences, Department of Modern Foreign Languages and Literatures, Program in Modern Foreign Languages, Knoxville, TN 37996. Offers applied linguistics (PhD); French (PhD); German (PhD); Italian (PhD); Portuguese (PhD); Russian (PhD); Spanish (PhD). *Degree requirements:* For doctorate, 2 foreign languages, thesis/dissertation. *Entrance requirements:* For doctorate, minimum GPA of 2.7. Additional exam requirements/recommendations for international students: Required—TOEFL. Electronic applications accepted.

University of Washington, Graduate School, College of Arts and Sciences, Department of Slavic Languages and Literatures, Seattle, WA 98195. Offers Russian literature (MA, PhD); Slavic linguistics (MA, PhD). *Degree requirements:* For master's, 2 foreign languages, thesis optional; for doctorate, 3 foreign languages, thesis/ dissertation. *Entrance requirements:* For master's and doctorate, GRE General Test, minimum GPA of 3.0. Additional exam requirements/recommendations for international students: Required—TOEFL. Electronic applications accepted. *Faculty research:* Modern and medieval East European languages and literatures, comparative literature,

Russian folk literature, Slavic literary theory and criticism, computerized morphology of Russian.

University of Waterloo, Graduate Studies, Faculty of Arts, Department of Germanic and Slavic Studies, Waterloo, ON N2L 3G1, Canada. Offers German (MA, PhD); Russian (MA). Part-time and evening/weekend programs available. *Degree requirements:* For master's, one foreign language, thesis optional; for doctorate, 2 foreign languages, comprehensive exam, thesis/dissertation. *Entrance requirements:* For master's, honors degree, minimum B average; for doctorate, master's degree, minimum B average. Additional exam requirements/recommendations for international students: Required—TOEFL, TWE. Electronic applications accepted. *Faculty research:* Medieval theatre; history and literature; German and Russian literary relations; seventeenth, eighteenth, nineteenth, and twentieth century German literature.

Yale University, Graduate School of Arts and Sciences, Department of Slavic Languages and Literatures, New Haven, CT 06520. Offers medieval Slavic literature and philology (PhD); Polish literature (PhD); Russian literature (PhD); Slavic languages and literatures and film studies (PhD). *Degree requirements:* For doctorate, 3 foreign languages, thesis/dissertation. *Entrance requirements:* For doctorate, GRE General Test.

Scandinavian Languages

Cornell University, Graduate School, Graduate Fields of Arts and Sciences, Field of Germanic Studies, Ithaca, NY 14853-0001. Offers German area studies (MA, PhD); German intellectual history (MA, PhD); Germanic linguistics (MA, PhD); Germanic literature (MA, PhD); old Norse (MA, PhD). Terminal master's awarded for partial completion of doctoral program. *Degree requirements:* For master's, one foreign language, thesis; for doctorate, 2 foreign languages, comprehensive exam, thesis/ dissertation. *Entrance requirements:* For master's and doctorate, GRE General Test, fluency in German, writing sample, 2 letters of recommendation. Additional exam requirements/recommendations for international students: Required—TOEFL (minimum score 550 paper-based; 77 iBT). Electronic applications accepted. *Faculty research:* Women's studies, minority literature, literature and intellectual history, theater and film studies, Continental philosophy.

Harvard University, Graduate School of Arts and Sciences, Department of Germanic Languages and Literatures, Cambridge, MA 02138. Offers German (PhD); Scandinavian (PhD). Terminal master's awarded for partial completion of doctoral program. *Degree requirements:* For doctorate, 2 foreign languages, thesis/dissertation, exams. *Entrance requirements:* For doctorate, GRE General Test, German writing sample. Additional exam requirements/recommendations for international students: Required—TOEFL.

University of California, Berkeley, Graduate Division, College of Letters and Science, Department of Scandinavian Languages and Literatures, Berkeley, CA 94720-1500. Offers PhD. *Degree requirements:* For doctorate, 2 foreign languages, thesis/ dissertation, 3 field papers, qualifying exam. *Entrance requirements:* For doctorate, GRE General Test, minimum GPA of 3.0, MA in Scandinavian language or equivalent, 3 letters of recommendation. Additional exam requirements/recommendations for international students: Required—TOEFL (minimum score 570 paper-based). *Faculty research:* Modern literatures, old Norse language and literatures, folklore, film.

University of California, Los Angeles, Graduate Division, College of Letters and Science, Department of Germanic Languages, Program in Scandinavian, Los Angeles, CA 90095. Offers MA. *Degree requirements:* For master's, 3 foreign languages, comprehensive exam. *Entrance requirements:* For master's, GRE General Test, bachelor's degree; minimum undergraduate GPA of 3.0 (or its equivalent if letter grade system not used); writing sample. Additional exam requirements/recommendations for international students: Required—TOEFL. Electronic applications accepted.

University of Massachusetts Amherst, Graduate School, College of Humanities and Fine Arts, Department of Languages, Literatures, and Cultures, Programs in German and Scandinavian Studies, Amherst, MA 01003. Offers MA, PhD. Part-time programs available. *Faculty:* 11 full-time (4 women). *Students:* 13 full-time (9 women), 5 part-time (3 women); includes 3 minority (1 Black or African American, non-Hispanic/Latino; 1 Hispanic/Latino; 1 Two or more races, non-Hispanic/Latino), 3 international. Average age 34. 18 applicants, 44% accepted, 4 enrolled. In 2014, 5 master's awarded. Terminal master's awarded for partial completion of doctoral program. *Degree requirements:* For master's, thesis or alternative; for doctorate, one foreign language, comprehensive exam, thesis/dissertation. *Entrance requirements:* For master's and doctorate, writing sample in English and German. Additional exam requirements/recommendations for international students: Required—TOEFL (minimum score 550 paper-based; 80 iBT), IELTS (minimum score 6.5). *Application deadline:* For fall admission, 1/15 for domestic

and international students; for spring admission, 10/1 for domestic and international students. Applications are processed on a rolling basis. Application fee: $75. Electronic applications accepted. *Expenses:* Tuition, state resident: full-time $1980; part-time $110 per credit. Tuition, nonresident: full-time $14,644; part-time $414 per credit. *Required fees:* $11,417. One-time fee: $357. *Financial support:* Fellowships with full and partial tuition reimbursements, research assistantships with full and partial tuition reimbursements, teaching assistantships with full and partial tuition reimbursements, career-related internships or fieldwork, Federal Work-Study, scholarships/grants, traineeships, health care benefits, tuition waivers (full and partial), and unspecified assistantships available. Support available to part-time students. Financial award application deadline: 2/1. *Unit head:* Dr. Frank Hugus, Acting Graduate Program Director, 413-545-2350, Fax: 413-545-6695. *Application contact:* Lindsay DeSantis, Supervisor of Admissions, 413-545-0722, Fax: 413-577-0010, E-mail: gradadm@grad.umass.edu.
Website: http://www.umass.edu/german/

University of Minnesota, Twin Cities Campus, Graduate School, College of Liberal Arts, Department of German, Scandinavian, and Dutch, Minneapolis, MN 55455. Offers Germanic studies (MA, PhD), including German, Germanic medieval studies, Scandinavian studies (MA). Part-time programs available. Terminal master's awarded for partial completion of doctoral program. *Degree requirements:* For doctorate, 2 foreign languages, thesis/dissertation. *Entrance requirements:* For master's, GRE General Test, BA in German, Scandinavian, or equivalent; for doctorate, MA in German, Scandinavian, or equivalent. Additional exam requirements/recommendations for international students: Required—TOEFL (minimum score 550 paper-based; 79 iBT). Electronic applications accepted. *Faculty research:* Cultural studies, literary theory, feminist criticism, film, Germanic medieval studies.

University of Washington, Graduate School, College of Arts and Sciences, Department of Scandinavian Studies, Seattle, WA 98195. Offers MA, PhD. *Degree requirements:* For master's, one foreign language, comprehensive exam, thesis optional; for doctorate, 2 foreign languages, comprehensive exam, thesis/dissertation. *Entrance requirements:* For master's, GRE, BA in Scandinavian or equivalent, minimum GPA of 3.0; for doctorate, GRE, master's degree, minimum GPA of 3.0. Additional exam requirements/recommendations for international students: Required—TOEFL. *Faculty research:* Scandinavian folklore, history, and politics; medieval to modern Scandinavian literature; Scandinavian fiction, poetry, drama, literary history, and theory.

University of Wisconsin–Madison, Graduate School, College of Letters and Science, Department of Scandinavian Studies, Madison, WI 53706-1380. Offers area studies (MA); folklore (PhD); literature (MA, PhD); philology (PhD). Part-time programs available. *Degree requirements:* For master's, 2 foreign languages, exam; for doctorate, thesis/dissertation, exam. *Entrance requirements:* For master's, minimum GPA of 3.25; for doctorate, minimum GPA of 3.5. Electronic applications accepted. *Expenses:* Tuition, state resident: full-time $10,723; part-time $745 per credit. Tuition, nonresident: full-time $24,054; part-time $1578 per credit. *Required fees:* $374 per semester. Tuition and fees vary according to course load, program and reciprocity agreements. *Faculty research:* Historical fiction, Icelandic poetry, nineteenth-century literature, theater, gender studies, folklore.

Slavic Languages

Brigham Young University, Graduate Studies, College of Family, Home, and Social Sciences, Department of Psychology, Provo, UT 84602. Offers behavioral neuroscience (PhD); clinical psychology (PhD); general psychology (MS). *Accreditation:* APA (one or more programs are accredited). *Faculty:* 29 full-time (6 women), 2 part-time/adjunct (1 woman). *Students:* 60 full-time (34 women); includes 6 minority (1 American Indian or Alaska Native, non-Hispanic/Latino; 3 Asian, non-Hispanic/Latino; 2 Hispanic/Latino), 3 international. Average age 26. 57 applicants, 25% accepted, 9 enrolled. In 2014, 6 master's, 17 doctorates awarded. *Degree requirements:* For master's, thesis; for doctorate, comprehensive exam, thesis/dissertation, publishable paper. *Entrance requirements:* For master's and doctorate, GRE General Test, minimum GPA of 3.0 in last 60 hours of upper-division course work. Additional exam requirements/ recommendations for international students: Required—TOEFL. *Application deadline:* For fall admission, 12/1 for domestic and international students. Application fee: $50. Electronic applications accepted. *Expenses: Tuition:* Full-time $6310; part-time $371 per credit hour. Tuition and fees vary according to program and student's religious affiliation. *Financial support:* In 2014–15, 43 students received support, including 27 research assistantships with partial tuition reimbursements available (averaging $10,000 per year), 11 teaching assistantships with partial tuition reimbursements available

(averaging $10,000 per year); fellowships, career-related internships or fieldwork, scholarships/grants, tuition waivers (partial), and unspecified assistantships also available. Financial award application deadline: 5/31. *Faculty research:* Psychotherapy process, Alzheimer's disease/dementia, psychology and law, health, psychology, developmental. *Total annual research expenditures:* $1 million. *Unit head:* Dr. Dawson Hedges, Chair, 801-422-6357, Fax: 801-422-0602, E-mail: dawson_hedges@byu.edu. *Application contact:* Leesa D. Scott, Coordinator of Student Programs, 801-422-4560, Fax: 801-422-0602, E-mail: leesa_scott@byu.edu.
Website: http://psychology.byu.edu/

Brown University, Graduate School, Department of Slavic Languages, Providence, RI 02912. Offers Russian language and literature (AM); Slavic linguistics (AM); Slavic studies (PhD). *Degree requirements:* For master's, one foreign language; for doctorate, 2 foreign languages, thesis/dissertation, preliminary exam.

Columbia University, Graduate School of Arts and Sciences, New York, NY 10027. Offers African-American studies (MA); American studies (MA); anthropology (MA, PhD); art history and archaeology (MA, PhD); astronomy (PhD); biological sciences (PhD); biotechnology (MA); chemical physics (PhD); chemistry (PhD); classical studies (MA, PhD); classics (MA, PhD); climate and society (MA); earth and environmental sciences

(PhD); East Asia: regional studies (MA); East Asian languages and cultures (MA, PhD); ecology, evolution and environmental biology (MA), including conservation biology; ecology, evolution, and environmental biology (PhD), including ecology and evolutionary biology, evolutionary primatology; economics (PhD); English and comparative literature (MA, PhD); French and Romance philology (MA, PhD); Germanic languages (MA, PhD); global French studies (MA); Hispanic cultural studies (MA); history (PhD); history and literature (MA); human rights studies (MA); Islamic studies (MA); Italian (MA, PhD); Japanese pedagogy (MA); Jewish studies (MA); Latin America and the Caribbean: regional studies (MA); Latin American and Iberian cultures (PhD); mathematics (MA, PhD), including finance (MA); medieval and Renaissance studies (MA); Middle Eastern, South Asian, and African studies (MA, PhD); modern art: critical and curatorial studies (MA); modern European studies (MA); museum anthropology (MA); music (DMA, PhD); oral history (MA); philosophical foundations of physics (MA); philosophy (MA, PhD); physics (PhD); political science (MA, PhD); psychology (PhD); quantitative methods in the social sciences (MA); religion (MA, PhD); Russia, Eurasia and East Europe: regional studies (MA); Russian translation (MA); Slavic cultures (MA); Slavic languages (MA, PhD); sociology (MA, PhD); South Asian studies (MA); statistics (MA, PhD); theatre (PhD); JD/PhD; MA/MS; MD/PhD; MPA/MA. Dual-degree programs require admission to both Graduate School of Arts and Sciences and another Columbia school. Part-time and evening/weekend programs available. Terminal master's awarded for partial completion of doctoral program. *Degree requirements:* For master's, thesis (for some programs); for doctorate, comprehensive exam, thesis/dissertation. *Entrance requirements:* For master's and doctorate, GRE General Test, GRE Subject Test (for some programs). Electronic applications accepted. *Faculty research:* Humanities, natural sciences, social sciences.

Cornell University, Graduate School, Graduate Fields of Arts and Sciences, Field of Linguistics, Ithaca, NY 14853-0001. Offers applied linguistics (MA, PhD); East Asian linguistics (MA, PhD); English linguistics (MA, PhD); general linguistics (MA, PhD); Germanic linguistics (MA, PhD); Indo-European linguistics (MA, PhD); phonetics (MA, PhD); phonological theory (MA, PhD); Romance linguistics (MA, PhD); second language acquisition (MA, PhD); semantics (MA, PhD); Slavic linguistics (MA, PhD); sociolinguistics (MA, PhD); South Asian linguistics (MA, PhD); Southeast Asian linguistics (MA, PhD); syntactic theory (MA, PhD). Terminal master's awarded for partial completion of doctoral program. *Degree requirements:* For master's, one foreign language, thesis; for doctorate, one foreign language, comprehensive exam, thesis/dissertation. *Entrance requirements:* For master's and doctorate, GRE General Test, 2 letters of recommendation. Additional exam requirements/recommendations for international students: Required—TOEFL (minimum score 600 paper-based; 77 iBT). Electronic applications accepted. *Faculty research:* Phonology and phonetics, syntax and semantics, historical linguistics, philosophy of language, language acquisition.

Duke University, Graduate School, Department of Slavic and Eurasian Studies, Durham, NC 27708. Offers AM, Certificate. Part-time programs available. *Entrance requirements:* For master's, GRE General Test, writing sample. Additional exam requirements/recommendations for international students: Required—TOEFL (minimum score 577 paper-based; 90 iBT) or IELTS (minimum score 7). Electronic applications accepted. *Expenses: Tuition:* Full-time $45,760; part-time $2765 per credit. *Required fees:* $978. Full-time tuition and fees vary according to program.

Florida State University, The Graduate School, College of Arts and Sciences, Department of Modern Languages, Program in Slavic Languages/Russian, Tallahassee, FL 32306. Offers Slavic languages and literatures (MA). *Faculty:* 4 full-time (3 women). *Students:* 6 full-time (3 women). Average age 24. 4 applicants, 100% accepted, 3 enrolled. *Degree requirements:* For master's, thesis optional. *Entrance requirements:* For master's, GRE General Test, minimum GPA of 3.0. Additional exam requirements/recommendations for international students: Required—TOEFL (minimum score 550 paper-based). *Application deadline:* For fall admission, 2/15 for domestic and international students. Applications are processed on a rolling basis. Application fee: $30. Electronic applications accepted. *Expenses:* Tuition, state resident: part-time $403.51 per credit hour. Tuition, nonresident: part-time $1004.85 per credit hour. *Required fees:* $75.81 per credit hour. One-time fee: $20 part-time. Tuition and fees vary according to campus/location. *Financial support:* In 2014–15, 3 students received support, including 5 teaching assistantships with partial tuition reimbursements available (averaging $11,500 per year); fellowships and institutionally sponsored loans also available. Financial award application deadline: 2/1; financial award applicants required to submit FAFSA. *Faculty research:* Contemporary literature, emigré literature, Old Russian word formation, political rhetoric, structure of modern Russian. *Total annual research expenditures:* $4,500. *Unit head:* Dr. Robert Romanchuk, Divisional Coordinator, 850-644-8198, Fax: 850-644-0524, E-mail: rromanch@fsu.edu. *Application contact:* Wendy E. Pigott, Graduate Academic Coordinator, 850-644-8397, Fax: 850-644-0524, E-mail: wpigott@fsu.edu.
Website: http://www.modlang.fsu.edu/Programs2/Slavic-Languages-Russian

Harvard University, Graduate School of Arts and Sciences, Department of Slavic Languages and Literatures, Cambridge, MA 02138. Offers Polish (PhD); Russian (PhD); Serbo-Croatian (PhD); Slavic philology (PhD); Ukrainian (PhD). *Degree requirements:* For doctorate, 4 foreign languages, thesis/dissertation. *Entrance requirements:* For doctorate, GRE General Test, writing sample. Additional exam requirements/recommendations for international students: Required—TOEFL.

Indiana University Bloomington, University Graduate School, College of Arts and Sciences, Department of Slavic Languages and Literatures, Bloomington, IN 47405. Offers MA, MAT, PhD. Part-time programs available. *Faculty:* 8 full-time (3 women). *Students:* 19 full-time (15 women), 2 international. Average age 29. 24 applicants, 21% accepted, 4 enrolled. In 2014, 4 master's awarded. Terminal master's awarded for partial completion of doctoral program. *Degree requirements:* For master's, variable foreign language requirement; for doctorate, variable foreign language requirement, comprehensive exam, thesis/dissertation. *Entrance requirements:* For master's, GRE General Test. Additional exam requirements/recommendations for international students: Required—TOEFL. *Application deadline:* For fall admission, 1/15 for domestic students, 12/1 for international students. Applications are processed on a rolling basis. Application fee: $55 ($65 for international students). Electronic applications accepted. *Financial support:* Fellowships with full tuition reimbursements, research assistantships with full tuition reimbursements, and teaching assistantships with full tuition reimbursements available. Financial award application deadline: 2/1. *Faculty research:* Russian stress, Slavic accentology and morphophonemics, Eastern European literature, Bible translation. *Unit head:* Dr. Russell Valentino, Chair, 812-855-2372, E-mail: russellv@indiana.edu. *Application contact:* Tricia Hodges, Graduate Secretary, 812-855-2608, Fax: 812-855-2107, E-mail: thodges@indiana.edu.
Website: http://www.indiana.edu/~iuslavic/

New York University, Graduate School of Arts and Science, Department of Russian and Slavic Studies, New York, NY 10012-1019. Offers Russian literature (MA); Slavic literature (MA). Part-time programs available. *Faculty:* 8 full-time (3 women). *Students:* 4 full-time (3 women), 3 part-time (all women), 1 international. Average age 29. 14 applicants, 86% accepted, 4 enrolled. In 2014, 5 master's awarded. *Degree requirements:* For master's, one foreign language, comprehensive exam, thesis. *Entrance requirements:* For master's, GRE General Test, minimum 3 years of undergraduate Russian or equivalent. Additional exam requirements/recommendations for international students: Required—TOEFL. *Application deadline:* For fall admission, 4/15 for domestic and international students; for spring admission, 11/1 for domestic and international students. Application fee: $100. *Financial support:* Career-related internships or fieldwork, Federal Work-Study, and institutionally sponsored loans available. Financial award application deadline: 4/15; financial award applicants required to submit FAFSA. *Faculty research:* Modern Russian literature and art, contemporary Russian and East European literature, literary theory, Slavic linguistics, Russian journalism. *Unit head:* Anne Lounsbery, Chair, 212-998-8670, Fax: 212-995-4604, E-mail: gsas.russian.and.slavic@nyu.edu. *Application contact:* Michael Kunichika, Director of Graduate Studies, 212-998-8670, Fax: 212-995-4604, E-mail: gsas.russian.and.slavic@nyu.edu.
Website: http://russianslavic.as.nyu.edu/

Northwestern University, The Graduate School, Judd A. and Marjorie Weinberg College of Arts and Sciences, Department of Slavic Languages and Literature, Evanston, IL 60208. Offers PhD. Admissions and degrees offered through The Graduate School. Part-time programs available. *Degree requirements:* For doctorate, 3 foreign languages, thesis/dissertation. *Entrance requirements:* For doctorate, GRE General Test. Additional exam requirements/recommendations for international students: Required—TOEFL. *Faculty research:* Russian poetry and prose, nineteenth through twentieth centuries, translation and Russian culture, Russian intellectual history, Slavic literature and nationalism, Polish poetry.

The Ohio State University, Graduate School, College of Arts and Sciences, Division of Arts and Humanities, Department of Slavic and East European Languages and Cultures, Columbus, OH 43210. Offers Slavic linguistics (MA, PhD); Slavic literature, film, and cultural studies (MA, PhD). *Faculty:* 10. *Students:* 15 full-time (9 women), 1 (woman) part-time; includes 1 minority (Hispanic/Latino), 2 international. Average age 30. In 2014, 2 master's, 5 doctorates awarded. Terminal master's awarded for partial completion of doctoral program. *Degree requirements:* For master's, variable foreign language requirement, thesis optional; for doctorate, variable foreign language requirement, thesis/dissertation. *Entrance requirements:* For master's and doctorate, GRE General Test, at least 3 years of Russian language study or equivalent. Additional exam requirements/recommendations for international students: Required—TOEFL (minimum score 550 paper-based; 79 iBT), Michigan English Language Assessment Battery (minimum score 82); Recommended—IELTS (minimum score 7). *Application deadline:* For fall admission, 12/12 priority date for domestic students, 11/30 priority date for international students; for winter admission, 12/1 for domestic students, 11/1 for international students; for spring admission, 3/1 for domestic students, 2/1 for international students. Applications are processed on a rolling basis. Application fee: $60 ($70 for international students). Electronic applications accepted. *Financial support:* Fellowships with tuition reimbursements, teaching assistantships with tuition reimbursements, Federal Work-Study, and institutionally sponsored loans available. Support available to part-time students. *Faculty research:* Polish literature. *Unit head:* Dr. Yana Hashamova, Chair and Professor, 614-292-6733, E-mail: hashamova.1@osu.edu. *Application contact:* Graduate and Professional Admissions, 614-292-9444, Fax: 614-292-3895, E-mail: gpadmissions@osu.edu.
Website: http://slavic.osu.edu/

Princeton University, Graduate School, Department of Slavic Languages and Literatures, Princeton, NJ 08544-1019. Offers Russian and Slavic linguistics (PhD); Russian literature (PhD). *Degree requirements:* For doctorate, variable foreign language requirement, thesis/dissertation. *Entrance requirements:* For doctorate, GRE General Test. Additional exam requirements/recommendations for international students: Required—TOEFL (minimum score 600 paper-based). Electronic applications accepted.

Stanford University, School of Humanities and Sciences, Department of Slavic Languages and Literatures, Stanford, CA 94305-9991. Offers MA, PhD. Terminal master's awarded for partial completion of doctoral program. *Degree requirements:* For master's, one foreign language, thesis or alternative; for doctorate, 3 foreign languages, thesis/dissertation. *Entrance requirements:* For master's and doctorate, GRE General Test. Additional exam requirements/recommendations for international students: Required—TOEFL. Electronic applications accepted. *Expenses: Tuition:* Full-time $44,184; part-time $982 per credit hour. *Required fees:* $191.

University of Alberta, Faculty of Graduate Studies and Research, Department of Modern Languages and Cultural Studies, Edmonton, AB T6G 2E1, Canada. Offers applied linguistics (Germanic, Romance, Slavic) (MA); French language, literatures and linguistics (PhD); French language, literatures, and linguistics (MA); Germanic languages, literatures and linguistics (PhD); Germanic languages, literatures, and linguistics (MA); Italian studies (MA); Slavic languages and literatures (Russian, Ukrainian) (MA, PhD); Slavic linguistics (Russian, Ukrainian) (MA, PhD); Spanish and Latin American studies (MA, PhD); Ukrainian folklore (MA, PhD). Part-time programs available. *Degree requirements:* For master's, one foreign language, thesis; for doctorate, 2 foreign languages, comprehensive exam, thesis/dissertation. *Entrance requirements:* For master's and doctorate, 1 language other than English. Additional exam requirements/recommendations for international students: Required—Michigan English Language Assessment Battery or TOEFL (minimum score 550 paper-based). Electronic applications accepted. *Faculty research:* Russian/Ukrainian studies; German studies; contemporary Latin American, French and Francophone studies; Italian studies.

University of California, Berkeley, Graduate Division, College of Letters and Science, Department of Slavic Languages and Literatures, Berkeley, CA 94720-1500. Offers Czech (PhD), including Czech linguistics, Czech literature; Polish (PhD), including Polish linguistics, Polish literature; Russian (PhD), including Russian linguistics, Russian literature; Serbo-Croatian (PhD), including Serbo-Croatian linguistics, Serbo-Croatian literature. Terminal master's awarded for partial completion of doctoral program. *Degree requirements:* For doctorate, thesis/dissertation, oral and written exams. *Entrance requirements:* For doctorate, GRE General Test, minimum GPA of 3.0, 3 letters of recommendation. Additional exam requirements/recommendations for international students: Required—TOEFL (minimum score 570 paper-based). Electronic applications accepted.

University of California, Los Angeles, Graduate Division, College of Letters and Science, Department of Slavic Languages and Literatures, Los Angeles, CA 90095. Offers MA, PhD. Terminal master's awarded for partial completion of doctoral program. *Degree requirements:* For master's, 2 foreign languages, comprehensive exam; for doctorate, 2 foreign languages, thesis/dissertation, oral and written qualifying exams. *Entrance requirements:* For master's and doctorate, GRE General Test (not required for applicants whose native language not English), bachelor's degree; minimum undergraduate GPA of 3.0 (or its equivalent if letter grade system not used); writing sample. Additional exam requirements/recommendations for international students: Required—TOEFL. Electronic applications accepted.

University of Illinois at Chicago, Graduate College, College of Liberal Arts and Sciences, School of Literatures, Cultural Studies and Linguistics, Department of Slavic and Baltic Languages and Literatures, Chicago, IL 60607-7128. Offers Slavic studies (MA, PhD). Evening/weekend programs available. *Faculty:* 7 full-time (4 women), 1 (woman) part-time/adjunct. *Students:* 8 full-time (4 women), 1 part-time (0 women), 6

international. Average age 31. 6 applicants, 33% accepted, 2 enrolled. In 2014, 1 doctorate awarded. Terminal master's awarded for partial completion of doctoral program. *Degree requirements:* For doctorate, one foreign language, thesis/dissertation. *Entrance requirements:* For master's and doctorate, GRE General Test, minimum GPA of 3.0. Additional exam requirements/recommendations for international students: Required—TOEFL. *Application deadline:* For fall admission, 1/1 priority date for domestic and international students; for spring admission, 11/1 for domestic students, 7/15 for international students. Application fee: $60. Electronic applications accepted. *Expenses:* Tuition, state resident: full-time $11,254; part-time $468 per credit hour. Tuition, nonresident: full-time $23,252; part-time $968 per credit hour. *Required fees:* $1217 per term. Part-time tuition and fees vary according to course load, degree level and program. *Financial support:* In 2014–15, 9 students received support. Fellowships with full tuition reimbursements available, research assistantships with full tuition reimbursements available, teaching assistantships with full tuition reimbursements available, institutionally sponsored loans, and tuition waivers (full) available. Financial award application deadline: 3/1; financial award applicants required to submit FAFSA. *Faculty research:* Twentieth-century Polish literature and culture, Russian and Polish modernisms, nineteenth- and twentieth-century Russian literature, Lithuanian language, Polish-Jewish culture and history, Yiddish literature and language. *Unit head:* Michal Pawel Markowski, Head, 312-996-5218, Fax: 312-413-1044, E-mail: markowsk@uic.edu.
Website: http://lcsl.las.uic.edu/slavic-baltic

University of Illinois at Urbana–Champaign, Graduate College, College of Liberal Arts and Sciences, School of Literatures, Cultures and Linguistics, Department of Slavic Languages and Literatures, Champaign, IL 61820. Offers MA, PhD. *Students:* 17 (14 women). Application fee: $70 ($90 for international students). *Unit head:* Michael C. Finke, Co-Acting Head, 217-333-2022, Fax: 217-333-7310, E-mail: mcfinke@illinois.edu. *Application contact:* Lynn Stanke, Office Support Specialist, 217-333-6269, Fax: 217-244-3050, E-mail: stanke@illinois.edu.
Website: http://www.slavic.illinois.edu/

The University of Kansas, Graduate Studies, College of Liberal Arts and Sciences, Department of Slavic Languages and Literatures, Lawrence, KS 66045. Offers MA, PhD. *Faculty:* 6 full-time, 3 part-time/adjunct. *Students:* 15 full-time (10 women); includes 2 minority (both Two or more races, non-Hispanic/Latino), 3 international. Average age 29. 10 applicants, 70% accepted, 4 enrolled. In 2014, 2 master's awarded. Terminal master's awarded for partial completion of doctoral program. *Degree requirements:* For master's, one foreign language, comprehensive exam, thesis or alternative; for doctorate, 3 foreign languages, comprehensive exam, thesis/dissertation, 2nd Slavic language. *Entrance requirements:* For master's, GRE, BA in Slavic languages and literatures or the equivalent; for doctorate, GRE, MA in Slavic languages and literatures. Additional exam requirements/recommendations for international students: Required—TOEFL. *Application deadline:* For fall admission, 1/31 priority date for domestic students; for winter admission, 1/31 priority date for international students. Applications are processed on a rolling basis. Application fee: $55 ($65 for international students). Electronic applications accepted. *Financial support:* Fellowships with tuition reimbursements, teaching assistantships with full and partial tuition reimbursements, Federal Work-Study, institutionally sponsored loans, scholarships/grants, and unspecified assistantships available. Financial award application deadline: 1/31. *Faculty research:* Russian and south Slavic linguistics, Polish and Russian literature, folklore, Russian intellectual history, Slavic culture. *Unit head:* Stephen M. Dickey, Chair, 785-864-2357, E-mail: smd@ku.edu. *Application contact:* Cari Ann Kreienhop, Senior Academic Advisor, Graduate Programs, 785-864-3665, E-mail: ckreienhop@ku.edu.
Website: https://slavic.ku.edu/

The University of Manchester, School of Languages, Linguistics and Cultures, Manchester, United Kingdom. Offers Arab world studies (PhD); Chinese studies (M Phil, PhD); East Asian studies (M Phil, PhD); English language (PhD); French studies (M Phil, PhD); German studies (M Phil, PhD); interpreting studies (PhD); Italian studies (M Phil, PhD); Japanese studies (M Phil, PhD); Latin American cultural studies (M Phil, PhD); linguistics (M Phil, PhD); Middle Eastern studies (M Phil, PhD); Polish studies (M Phil, PhD); Portuguese studies (M Phil, PhD); Russian studies (M Phil, PhD); Spanish studies (M Phil, PhD); translation and intercultural studies (M Phil, PhD).

University of Manitoba, Faculty of Graduate Studies, Faculty of Arts, Department of German and Slavic Studies, Winnipeg, MB R3T 2N2, Canada. Offers German language and literature (MA); Slavic languages and literatures (MA). *Degree requirements:* For master's, one foreign language, thesis or alternative.

University of Michigan, Horace H. Rackham School of Graduate Studies, College of Literature, Science, and the Arts, Department of Slavic Languages and Literatures, Ann Arbor, MI 48109-1275. Offers Russian (AM); Slavic languages and literatures (PhD). Terminal master's awarded for partial completion of doctoral program. *Degree requirements:* For doctorate, 3 foreign languages, comprehensive exam, thesis/dissertation, oral defense of dissertation, preliminary exam. *Entrance requirements:* For doctorate, GRE General Test. Additional exam requirements/recommendations for international students: Required—TOEFL (minimum score 560 paper-based). Electronic applications accepted. *Faculty research:* Russian literature (all periods), Polish literature, South Slavic literatures, Czech literature, Ukrainian literature.

The University of North Carolina at Chapel Hill, Graduate School, College of Arts and Sciences, Department of Slavic Languages and Literatures, Chapel Hill, NC 27599. Offers Polish literature (PhD); Russian and east European studies (MA); Russian literature (MA, PhD); Serbo-Croatian literature (PhD); Slavic linguistics (MA, PhD). Part-time programs available. Terminal master's awarded for partial completion of doctoral program. *Degree requirements:* For master's, 2 foreign languages, comprehensive exam, thesis; for doctorate, 4 foreign languages, comprehensive exam, thesis/dissertation. *Entrance requirements:* For master's and doctorate, GRE General Test, minimum GPA of 3.0. Electronic applications accepted. *Faculty research:* Russian cultural studies, literary translation, sociolinguistics, cognitive linguistics, ?migr? literature.

University of Pittsburgh, Dietrich School of Arts and Sciences, Department of Slavic Languages and Literatures, Pittsburgh, PA 15260. Offers MA, PhD. Part-time programs available. *Faculty:* 7 full-time (3 women), 2 part-time/adjunct (0 women). *Students:* 12 full-time (10 women), 8 international. Average age 27. 5 applicants, 40% accepted, 2 enrolled. In 2014, 1 master's, 1 doctorate awarded. Terminal master's awarded for partial completion of doctoral program. *Degree requirements:* For master's, 2 foreign languages, comprehensive exam; for doctorate, 3 foreign languages, comprehensive exam, thesis/dissertation. *Entrance requirements:* For master's and doctorate, GRE General Test. Additional exam requirements/recommendations for international students: Required—TOEFL. *Application deadline:* For fall admission, 1/15 priority date for domestic and international students. Application fee: $50. Electronic applications accepted. *Expenses:* Tuition, state resident: full-time $20,742; part-time $838 per credit. Tuition, nonresident: full-time $33,960; part-time $1389 per credit. *Required fees:* $800; $205 per term. Tuition and fees vary according to program. *Financial support:* In 2014–15, 11 students received support, including 3 fellowships with full tuition reimbursements available (averaging $19,800 per year), 7 teaching assistantships with full tuition reimbursements available (averaging $17,500 per year); Federal Work-Study, scholarships/grants, traineeships, and health care benefits also available. Support available to part-time students. Financial award application deadline: 1/15. *Faculty research:* Contemporary Russian literature and culture, Russian cinema. *Unit head:* Prof. David J. Birnbaum, Chair, 412-624-5712, Fax: 412-624-9714, E-mail: djbpitt@pitt.edu. *Application contact:* Patrick Fogarty, Graduate Administrator, 412-624-5221, Fax: 412-624-6263, E-mail: pmf23@pitt.edu.
Website: http://www.slavic.pitt.edu

University of Southern California, Graduate School, Dana and David Dornsife College of Letters, Arts and Sciences, Department of Linguistics, Los Angeles, CA 90089. Offers East Asian linguistics (PhD); Hispanic linguistics (PhD); linguistics (PhD); Slavic linguistics (PhD). *Degree requirements:* For doctorate, comprehensive exam, thesis/dissertation. *Entrance requirements:* For doctorate, GRE. Additional exam requirements/recommendations for international students: Required—TOEFL (minimum score 100 iBT). Electronic applications accepted. *Faculty research:* Syntax, phonology, phonetics, semantics, sociolinguistics, psycholinguistics.

University of Southern California, Graduate School, Dana and David Dornsife College of Letters, Arts and Sciences, Department of Slavic Languages and Literatures, Los Angeles, CA 90089. Offers MA, PhD. *Degree requirements:* For master's, one foreign language, comprehensive exam, thesis or alternative, 30 units; for doctorate, 3 foreign languages, comprehensive exam, thesis/dissertation, 60 units. *Entrance requirements:* For doctorate, GRE, BA in Russian literature or equivalent. Additional exam requirements/recommendations for international students: Required—TOEFL. Electronic applications accepted. *Faculty research:* Russian avant-garde art, intertextuality in Russian literature, eighteenth-century Russian culture, Russian poetry, Russian music history, twentieth-century Russian literature.

The University of Texas at Austin, Graduate School, College of Liberal Arts, Department of Slavic and Eurasian Studies, Austin, TX 78712-1111. Offers applied linguistics/pedagogy (PhD); literature and culture (PhD); Slavic languages (MA); Slavic linguistics (PhD). *Degree requirements:* For master's, 2 foreign languages, thesis; for doctorate, 3 foreign languages, thesis/dissertation. *Entrance requirements:* For master's and doctorate, GRE General Test. Electronic applications accepted. *Faculty research:* Slavic linguistics; applied linguistics; Russian, Czech, and Slavic literature and culture.

University of Toronto, School of Graduate Studies, Faculty of Arts and Science, Department of Slavic Languages and Literatures, Toronto, ON M5S 2J7, Canada. Offers MA, PhD. Part-time programs available. *Degree requirements:* For doctorate, comprehensive exam, thesis/dissertation. *Entrance requirements:* For master's, BA in related area; minimum A- average in Slavic courses taken in final year, writing sample, 2 letters of recommendation; for doctorate, MA in Slavic languages and literatures, minimum A- average, writing sample, 2 letters of recommendation. Additional exam requirements/recommendations for international students: Required—TOEFL (minimum score 580 paper-based; 93 iBT), TWE (minimum score 5). Electronic applications accepted.

University of Virginia, College and Graduate School of Arts and Sciences, Department of Slavic Languages and Literatures, Charlottesville, VA 22903. Offers MA, PhD. *Faculty:* 7 full-time (3 women), 1 part-time/adjunct (0 women). *Students:* 13 full-time (10 women), 2 international. Average age 26. 18 applicants, 67% accepted, 3 enrolled. In 2014, 1 master's awarded. *Degree requirements:* For master's, one foreign language, comprehensive exam, thesis (for some programs); for doctorate, one foreign language, comprehensive exam, thesis/dissertation. *Entrance requirements:* For master's, GRE General Test, 2 letters of recommendation, writing sample in English; for doctorate, GRE General Test, 2 letters of recommendation; writing sample in English. Additional exam requirements/recommendations for international students: Required—TOEFL (minimum score 600 paper-based; 90 iBT), IELTS (minimum score 7). *Application deadline:* Applications are processed on a rolling basis. Application fee: $60. Electronic applications accepted. *Expenses:* Tuition, state resident: full-time $14,164; part-time $349 per credit hour. Tuition, nonresident: full-time $23,722; part-time $1300 per credit hour. *Required fees:* $2514. *Financial support:* Teaching assistantships available. Financial award application deadline: 1/15; financial award applicants required to submit FAFSA. *Unit head:* David Herman, Chair, 434-924-3548, Fax: 434-982-2744, E-mail: herman@virginia.edu. *Application contact:* Edith Clowes, Director of Graduate Studies, 434-924-3548, Fax: 434-982-2744, E-mail: eec3c@virginia.edu.
Website: http://artsandsciences.virginia.edu/slavic/index.html

University of Washington, Graduate School, College of Arts and Sciences, Department of Slavic Languages and Literatures, Seattle, WA 98195. Offers Russian literature (MA, PhD); Slavic linguistics (MA, PhD). *Degree requirements:* For master's, 2 foreign languages, thesis optional; for doctorate, 3 foreign languages, thesis/dissertation. *Entrance requirements:* For master's and doctorate, GRE General Test, minimum GPA of 3.0. Additional exam requirements/recommendations for international students: Required—TOEFL. Electronic applications accepted. *Faculty research:* Modern and medieval East European languages and literatures, comparative literature, Russian folk literature, Slavic literary theory and criticism, computerized morphology of Russian.

University of Wisconsin–Madison, Graduate School, College of Letters and Science, Department of Slavic Languages and Literature, Madison, WI 53706-1380. Offers MA, PhD. Part-time programs available. Terminal master's awarded for partial completion of doctoral program. *Degree requirements:* For doctorate, thesis/dissertation. *Entrance requirements:* For master's and doctorate, GRE General Test. Additional exam requirements/recommendations for international students: Required—TOEFL. Electronic applications accepted. *Expenses:* Tuition, state resident: full-time $10,723; part-time $745 per credit. Tuition, nonresident: full-time $24,054; part-time $1578 per credit. *Required fees:* $374 per semester. Tuition and fees vary according to course load, program and reciprocity agreements. *Faculty research:* Polish literature, linguistics, South Slavic literature, second language acquisition, nineteenth- and twentieth-century Russian literature.

University of Wisconsin–Milwaukee, Graduate School, College of Letters and Sciences, Interdepartmental Program in Foreign Language and Literature, Milwaukee, WI 53201-0413. Offers classics and Hebrew studies (MAFLL); comparative literature (MAFLL); French and Italian (MAFLL); German (MAFLL); Slavic studies (MAFLL); translation (Certificate). Part-time programs available. *Degree requirements:* For master's, 2 foreign languages, thesis or alternative. *Entrance requirements:* Additional exam requirements/recommendations for international students: Required—TOEFL (minimum score 550 paper-based; 79 iBT), IELTS (minimum score 6.5). Electronic applications accepted.

Yale University, Graduate School of Arts and Sciences, Department of Slavic Languages and Literatures, New Haven, CT 06520. Offers medieval Slavic literature and philology (PhD); Polish literature (PhD); Russian literature (PhD); Slavic languages and literatures and film studies (PhD). *Degree requirements:* For doctorate, 3 foreign languages, thesis/dissertation. *Entrance requirements:* For doctorate, GRE General Test.

Spanish

Arizona State University at the Tempe campus, College of Liberal Arts and Sciences, School of International Letters and Cultures, Program in Spanish, Tempe, AZ 85287-0202. Offers cultural studies (PhD); linguistics (MA), including second language acquisition/applied linguistics, sociolinguistics; literature (PhD); literature and culture (MA). Part-time programs available. Terminal master's awarded for partial completion of doctoral program. *Degree requirements:* For master's, thesis, oral defense; written comprehensive exam (literature and culture); portfolio review (linguistics); interactive Program of Study (iPOS) submitted before completing 50 percent of required credit hours; for doctorate, comprehensive exam, thesis/dissertation, interactive Program of Study (iPOS) submitted before completing 50 percent of required credit hours. *Entrance requirements:* For master's, GRE (recommended), BA in Spanish or close equivalent from accredited institution with minimum GPA of 3.5, 3 letters of recommendation, personal statement, academic writing sample; for doctorate, GRE (recommended), MA in Spanish or equivalent from accredited institution with minimum GPA of 3.75, 3 letters of recommendation, personal statement, academic writing sample. Additional exam requirements/recommendations for international students: Required—TOEFL (minimum score 550 paper-based; 83 iBT), IELTS (minimum score 6.5). Electronic applications accepted.

Asbury University, School of Graduate and Professional Studies, Wilmore, KY 40390-1198. Offers biology: alternative certificate (MA Ed); chemistry: alternative certificate (MA Ed); English (MA Ed); English as a second language (MA Ed); ESL (MA Ed); French (MA Ed); Latin: alternative certificate (MA Ed); mathematics: alternative certificate (MA Ed); reading/writing endorsement (MA Ed); social studies (MA Ed); social work (MSW), including child and family services; Spanish (MA Ed); special education (MA Ed); special education: alternative certificate (MA Ed); teacher as leader endorsement (MA Ed). *Accreditation:* NCATE. Part-time programs available. *Degree requirements:* For master's, action research project, portfolio. *Entrance requirements:* For master's, PRAXIS/NTE, minimum GPA of 2.75, letters of recommendation. Additional exam requirements/recommendations for international students: Required—TOEFL (minimum score 550 paper-based). Electronic applications accepted.

Auburn University, Graduate School, College of Liberal Arts, Department of Foreign Languages and Literatures, Auburn University, AL 36849. Offers Spanish (MHS). Part-time programs available. *Faculty:* 30 full-time (19 women), 9 part-time/adjunct (7 women). *Students:* 15 full-time (5 women), 8 part-time (5 women); includes 5 minority (1 Black or African American, non-Hispanic/Latino; 4 Hispanic/Latino), 8 international. Average age 31. 11 applicants, 64% accepted, 7 enrolled. In 2014, 12 master's awarded. *Degree requirements:* For master's, one foreign language, comprehensive exam, thesis (for some programs). *Entrance requirements:* For master's, GRE General Test. *Application deadline:* For fall admission, 7/7 for domestic students; for spring admission, 11/24 for domestic students. Applications are processed on a rolling basis. Application fee: $50 ($60 for international students). Electronic applications accepted. *Expenses:* Tuition, state resident: full-time $8586; part-time $477 per credit hour. Tuition, nonresident: full-time $25,758; part-time $1431 per credit hour. *Required fees:* $804 per semester. Tuition and fees vary according to degree level and program. *Financial support:* Fellowships, teaching assistantships, and Federal Work-Study available. Support available to part-time students. Financial award application deadline: 3/15; financial award applicants required to submit FAFSA. *Unit head:* Dr. Lourdes Betanzos, Chair, 334-844-6350, Fax: 334-844-6378. *Application contact:* Dr. George Flowers, Dean of the Graduate School, 334-844-2125. Website: http://www.cla.auburn.edu/forlang/

Baylor University, Graduate School, College of Arts and Sciences, Department of Modern Languages and Cultures, Waco, TX 76798. Offers Spanish (MA). *Degree requirements:* For master's, 2 foreign languages, comprehensive exam, thesis optional. *Entrance requirements:* For master's, GRE General Test. Additional exam requirements/recommendations for international students: Required—TOEFL. Electronic applications accepted. *Faculty research:* Spanish post-civil war novel, Latin American detective fiction, nineteenth- and twentieth-century Hispanic women writers, semantics and pragmatics, Miguel de Unamuno.

Bennington College, Graduate Programs, MA in Teaching a Second Language Program, Bennington, VT 05201. Offers education (MATSL); foreign language education (MATSL); French (MATSL); Spanish (MATSL). Part-time programs available. *Degree requirements:* For master's, one foreign language, 2 major projects and presentations. *Entrance requirements:* For master's, Oral Proficiency Interview (OPI). Additional exam requirements/recommendations for international students: Required—TOEFL (minimum score 577 paper-based; 91 iBT). *Expenses:* Contact institution. *Faculty research:* Acquisition, evaluation, assessment, conceptual teaching and learning, content-driven communication, applied linguistics.

Binghamton University, State University of New York, Graduate School, School of Arts and Sciences, Department of Romance Languages and Literatures, Program in Spanish, Vestal, NY 13850. Offers MA. *Students:* 1 part-time (0 women). Average age 29. 2 applicants, 100% accepted. *Degree requirements:* For master's, one foreign language, comprehensive exam, thesis or alternative. *Entrance requirements:* For master's, GRE General Test. Additional exam requirements/recommendations for international students: Required—TOEFL (minimum score 550 paper-based; 80 iBT). *Application deadline:* For fall admission, 2/15 priority date for domestic and international students; for spring admission, 11/15 priority date for domestic and international students. Applications are processed on a rolling basis. Application fee: $75. Electronic applications accepted. *Expenses:* Tuition, state resident: full-time $7776; part-time $432 per credit. Tuition, nonresident: full-time $15,138; part-time $841 per credit. *Required fees:* $1754; $213 per credit. Tuition and fees vary according to degree level and program. *Financial support:* Career-related internships or fieldwork, Federal Work-Study, institutionally sponsored loans, scholarships/grants, health care benefits, and unspecified assistantships available. Financial award application deadline: 2/15; financial award applicants required to submit FAFSA. *Unit head:* Dr. Antonio Sobejano-Moran, Chairperson, 607-777-2548, E-mail: sobe@binghamton.edu. *Application contact:* Kishan Zuber, Recruiting and Admissions Coordinator, 607-777-2151, Fax: 607-777-2501, E-mail: kzuber@binghamton.edu.

Boston College, Graduate School of Arts and Sciences, Department of Romance Languages and Literatures, Chestnut Hill, MA 02467-3800. Offers French (MA); Italian (MA); Spanish (MA). Part-time programs available. *Faculty:* 21 full-time. *Students:* 34 full-time (30 women); includes 5 minority (2 Asian, non-Hispanic/Latino; 3 Hispanic/Latino), 8 international. 55 applicants, 33% accepted, 10 enrolled. In 2014, 9 master's awarded. Terminal master's awarded for partial completion of doctoral program. *Degree requirements:* For master's, one foreign language. *Entrance requirements:* Additional exam requirements/recommendations for international students: Required—TOEFL (minimum score 600 paper-based; 100 iBT), IELTS (minimum score 7). *Application deadline:* For fall admission, 1/2 for domestic and international students. Application fee: $75. Electronic applications accepted. *Financial support:* In 2014–15, fellowships with full tuition reimbursements (averaging $18,450 per year), teaching assistantships with full tuition reimbursements (averaging $18,450 per year) were awarded; Federal Work-Study, health care benefits, and unspecified assistantships also available. Support available to part-time students. Financial award application deadline: 3/1; financial award applicants required to submit FAFSA. *Faculty research:* Spanish-American literature, philology, medieval French romance and troubadour lyrics, Golden Age Peninsular literature, secondary language acquisition and pedagogy, Hispanic studies, French language and literature, Italian language and literature. *Unit head:* Dr. Franco Mormando, Chairperson, 617-552-6346, E-mail: franco.mormando@bc.edu. *Application contact:* Dr. Laurie Shepard, Associate Dean, 617-552-8269, Fax: 617-552-3700, E-mail: laurie.shepard@bc.edu. Website: http://www.bc.edu/rll

Bowling Green State University, Graduate College, College of Arts and Sciences, Department of Romance and Classical Studies, Program in Spanish, Bowling Green, OH 43403. Offers Spanish (MA); Spanish education (MAT). Part-time programs available. *Degree requirements:* For master's, one foreign language, thesis or alternative. *Entrance requirements:* For master's, GRE General Test. Additional exam requirements/recommendations for international students: Required—TOEFL. Electronic applications accepted. *Faculty research:* U.S. Latino literature and culture, Latin American film and popular culture, applied linguistics, Spanish popular culture.

Brigham Young University, Graduate Studies, College of Humanities, Department of Spanish and Portuguese, Provo, UT 84602. Offers Portuguese (MA), including Luso-Brazilian literature, Portuguese linguistics, Portuguese pedagogy; Spanish (MA), including Hispanic linguistics, Hispanic literatures, Spanish pedagogy. *Faculty:* 29 full-time (5 women). *Students:* 16 full-time (6 women), 27 part-time (15 women); includes 16 minority (all Hispanic/Latino). Average age 34. 20 applicants, 55% accepted, 9 enrolled. In 2014, 15 master's awarded. *Degree requirements:* For master's, one foreign language, comprehensive exam, thesis, 1 semester of teaching. *Entrance requirements:* For master's, GRE, minimum GPA of 3.5 in Spanish or Portuguese, 3.3 overall. Additional exam requirements/recommendations for international students: Required—TOEFL (minimum score 580 paper-based; 85 iBT). *Application deadline:* For fall admission, 2/1 for domestic and international students. Application fee: $50. Electronic applications accepted. *Expenses: Tuition:* Full-time $6310; part-time $371 per credit hour. Tuition and fees vary according to program and student's religious affiliation. *Financial support:* In 2014–15, 25 students received support, including 4 research assistantships with partial tuition reimbursements available (averaging $2,500 per year), 69 teaching assistantships with partial tuition reimbursements available (averaging $3,500 per year); institutionally sponsored loans, scholarships/grants, tuition waivers (partial), and unspecified assistantships also available. Support available to part-time students. Financial award application deadline: 7/1. *Faculty research:* Mexican prose; Latin American theater, literature, phonetics, and phonology; pedagogy; classical Portuguese literature; Peninsular prose and theater. *Unit head:* Dr. David P. Laraway, Chair, 801-422-3807, Fax: 801-422-0628, E-mail: david_laraway@byu.edu. *Application contact:* Jessica C. Erickson, Graduate Secretary, 801-422-2196, Fax: 801-422-0628, E-mail: jessica_erickson@byu.edu. Website: http://spanport.byu.edu/

Brooklyn College of the City University of New York, School of Humanities and Social Sciences, Department of Modern Languages and Literatures, Brooklyn, NY 11210-2889. Offers French (MA); Spanish (MA). *Degree requirements:* For master's, comprehensive exam or research paper. *Entrance requirements:* For master's, 18 credits in advanced courses in Spanish, 2 letters of recommendation. Additional exam requirements/recommendations for international students: Required—TOEFL (minimum score 500 paper-based; 61 iBT). Electronic applications accepted. *Faculty research:* Latin American contemporary novel, Caribbean female contemporary literature, nineteenth- and twentieth-century Spanish novel, twentieth-century Mexican poetry.

California State University, Bakersfield, Division of Graduate Studies, School of Arts and Humanities, Program in Spanish, Bakersfield, CA 93311. Offers MA. *Degree requirements:* For master's, capstone course.

California State University, Fresno, Division of Graduate Studies, College of Arts and Humanities, Department of Modern and Classical Languages and Literatures, Fresno, CA 93740-8027. Offers Spanish (MA). Part-time programs available. *Degree requirements:* For master's, one foreign language, thesis or alternative. *Entrance requirements:* For master's, GRE General Test, BA in Spanish, minimum GPA of 3.0. Additional exam requirements/recommendations for international students: Required—TOEFL. Electronic applications accepted.

California State University, Fullerton, Graduate Studies, College of Humanities and Social Sciences, Department of Modern Languages and Literatures, Fullerton, CA 92834-9480. Offers French (MA); German (MA); Spanish (MA); teaching English to speakers of other languages (MS). Part-time programs available. *Students:* 36 full-time (26 women), 56 part-time (40 women); includes 57 minority (9 Asian, non-Hispanic/Latino; 46 Hispanic/Latino; 2 Two or more races, non-Hispanic/Latino), 19 international. Average age 32. 55 applicants, 69% accepted, 24 enrolled. In 2014, 30 master's awarded. *Degree requirements:* For master's, comprehensive exam, thesis or alternative. *Entrance requirements:* For master's, minimum GPA of 2.5 in last 60 hours of course work, undergraduate major in a language. Application fee: $55. *Financial support:* Career-related internships or fieldwork, Federal Work-Study, institutionally sponsored loans, and scholarships/grants available. Support available to part-time students. Financial award application deadline: 3/1; financial award applicants required to submit FAFSA. *Unit head:* Dr. Reyes Fidalgo, Chair, 657-278-4563. *Application contact:* Admissions/Applications, 657-278-2371.

California State University, Long Beach, Graduate Studies, College of Liberal Arts, Department of Romance, German, and Russian Languages and Literature, Program in Spanish, Long Beach, CA 90840. Offers MA. Part-time programs available. *Degree requirements:* For master's, one foreign language, thesis or alternative, research paper. *Entrance requirements:* For master's, BA in Spanish. Electronic applications accepted. *Faculty research:* Literary translation, literature and politics, women writers, Latin American poetry, Latin American theatre.

California State University, Los Angeles, Graduate Studies, College of Arts and Letters, Department of Modern Languages and Literatures, Los Angeles, CA 90032-8530. Offers French (MA); Spanish (MA). Part-time and evening/weekend programs available. *Degree requirements:* For master's, comprehensive exam. *Entrance requirements:* Additional exam requirements/recommendations for international students: Required—TOEFL (minimum score 500 paper-based). Electronic applications accepted. *Expenses:* Tuition, state resident: full-time $6738; part-time $3609 per year.

Tuition, nonresident: full-time $15,666; part-time $8073 per year. Tuition and fees vary according to course load, degree level and program. *Faculty research:* French literature, language teaching and methodology, Spanish poetry, Spanish American fiction and poetry.

California State University, Northridge, Graduate Studies, College of Humanities, Department of Modern and Classical Languages and Literatures, Northridge, CA 91330. Offers Spanish (MA). Part-time and evening/weekend programs available. *Students:* 34 full-time (24 women), 29 part-time (24 women); includes 35 minority (1 Black or African American, non-Hispanic/Latino; 1 American Indian or Alaska Native, non-Hispanic/Latino; 2 Asian, non-Hispanic/Latino; 23 Hispanic/Latino; 8 Two or more races, non-Hispanic/Latino), 3 international. Average age 36. *Degree requirements:* For master's, one foreign language. *Entrance requirements:* For master's, GRE General Test or minimum GPA of 3.0. Additional exam requirements/recommendations for international students: Required—TOEFL. *Application deadline:* For fall admission, 11/30 for domestic students. Application fee: $55. *Expenses: Required fees:* $12,402. *Financial support:* Application deadline: 3/1. *Unit head:* Dr. Brian Castronovo, Chair, 818-677-3467, E-mail: brian.castronovo@csun.edu.
Website: http://www.csun.edu/mcll/

California State University, San Bernardino, Graduate Studies, College of Arts and Letters, Department of World Languages and Literatures, San Bernardino, CA 92407-2397. Offers Spanish (MA). Part-time and evening/weekend programs available. *Students:* 2 full-time (1 woman), 17 part-time (14 women); includes 17 minority (all Hispanic/Latino), 1 international. Average age 31. 8 applicants, 100% accepted, 7 enrolled. In 2014, 4 master's awarded. *Degree requirements:* For master's, comprehensive exam, advancement to candidacy. *Entrance requirements:* Additional exam requirements/recommendations for international students: Required—TOEFL. *Application deadline:* For fall admission, 7/17 for domestic students. Application fee: $55. *Expenses:* Tuition, state resident: full-time $6738; part-time $1302 per term. Tuition, nonresident: full-time $17,898; part-time $248 per unit. *Required fees:* $365 per quarter. Tuition and fees vary according to degree level and program. *Financial support:* Institutionally sponsored loans available. *Unit head:* Rafael Correa, Chair, 909-537-5849, Fax: 909-537-7091, E-mail: rafa@csusb.edu. *Application contact:* Dr. Jeffrey Thompson, Dean of Graduate Studies, 909-537-5058, E-mail: jthompso@csusb.edu.

California State University, San Marcos, College of Humanities, Arts, Behavioral and Social Sciences, Program in Spanish, San Marcos, CA 92096-0001. Offers Hispanic cultures and society (MA); Hispanic language and linguistics (MA); Hispanic literatures and literary theory (MA). Part-time and evening/weekend programs available. *Students:* 1 (woman) full-time, 14 part-time (all women); includes 12 minority (all Hispanic/Latino). Average age 35. *Degree requirements:* For master's, 2 foreign languages, exam. *Entrance requirements:* For master's, GRE General Test, minimum GPA of 3.0 overall and in upper-division Spanish courses, official transcripts, three letters of recommendation, 750-word statement of purpose (in English), academic writing sample (in Spanish). Additional exam requirements/recommendations for international students: Required—TOEFL (minimum score 500 paper-based), TWE (minimum score 4.5). *Application deadline:* For fall admission, 3/15 priority date for domestic students. Applications are processed on a rolling basis. Application fee: $55. Electronic applications accepted. *Expenses:* Tuition, state resident: full-time $6738. *Required fees:* $1692. Tuition and fees vary according to program. *Financial support:* Teaching assistantships available. *Faculty research:* Applied linguistics, Golden Age Spanish literature, Latin American literature, poetry, Chicano studies. *Unit head:* Dr. Michael Hughes, Department Chair, 760-750-8076, E-mail: mhughes@csusm.edu. *Application contact:* Admissions, 760-750-4848, Fax: 760-750-3248, E-mail: apply@csusm.edu.
Website: http://www.csusm.edu/modernlanguages/masters_degree/

The Catholic University of America, School of Arts and Sciences, Department of Modern Languages and Literatures, Washington, DC 20064. Offers Spanish (MA, PhD). Part-time programs available. *Faculty:* 18 full-time (13 women), 8 part-time/adjunct (6 women). *Students:* 6 full-time (3 women), 2 part-time (1 woman); includes 2 minority (both Hispanic/Latino), 4 international. Average age 34. 12 applicants, 67% accepted, 4 enrolled. In 2014, 1 master's, 2 doctorates awarded. *Degree requirements:* For master's, comprehensive exam; for doctorate, one foreign language, comprehensive exam, thesis/dissertation, final oral exam. *Entrance requirements:* For master's and doctorate, GRE General Test, statement of purpose, official copies of academic transcripts, three letters of recommendation. Additional exam requirements/recommendations for international students: Required—TOEFL (minimum score 580 paper-based). *Application deadline:* For fall admission, 7/15 priority date for domestic students, 7/1 for international students; for spring admission, 11/15 priority date for domestic students, 11/1 for international students. Applications are processed on a rolling basis. Application fee: $55. Electronic applications accepted. *Expenses: Tuition:* Full-time $40,200; part-time $1600 per credit hour. *Required fees:* $400; $195 per semester. One-time fee: $425. *Financial support:* Fellowships, research assistantships, teaching assistantships, Federal Work-Study, scholarships/grants, tuition waivers (full and partial), and unspecified assistantships available. Financial award application deadline: 2/1; financial award applicants required to submit FAFSA. *Faculty research:* Arthurian literature and medieval lyric, eighteenth-twentieth century Spanish literature, Latin American literature. *Total annual research expenditures:* $1,652. *Unit head:* Dr. Margaret Kassen, Interim Chair, 202-319-5240, Fax: 202-319-6077, E-mail: kassen@cua.edu. *Application contact:* Director of Graduate Admissions, 202-319-5057, Fax: 202-319-6533, E-mail: cua-admissions@cua.edu.
Website: http://modernlanguages.cua.edu/

Central Connecticut State University, School of Graduate Studies, College of Liberal Arts and Social Sciences, Department of Modern Languages, Program in Modern Language, New Britain, CT 06050-4010. Offers French (MA, Certificate); German (Certificate); Italian (Certificate); modern language (MA); Spanish language and Hispanic culture (MA). Part-time and evening/weekend programs available. *Students:* 4 full-time (3 women), 28 part-time (22 women); includes 13 minority (1 Black or African American, non-Hispanic/Latino; 12 Hispanic/Latino), 1 international. Average age 34. 9 applicants, 100% accepted, 7 enrolled. In 2014, 8 master's, 5 other advanced degrees awarded. *Degree requirements:* For master's, one foreign language, comprehensive exam, thesis or alternative; for Certificate, qualifying exam. *Entrance requirements:* For master's, minimum undergraduate GPA of 2.7, 24 credits of undergraduate courses in each language in which graduate work will be undertaken. Additional exam requirements/recommendations for international students: Required—TOEFL (minimum score 550 paper-based; 79 iBT). *Application deadline:* For fall admission, 6/1 for domestic students, 5/1 for international students; for spring admission, 11/1 for domestic and international students. Applications are processed on a rolling basis. Application fee: $50. Electronic applications accepted. *Expenses: Tuition, area resident:* Full-time $5730; part-time $534 per credit. Tuition, state resident: full-time $8596; part-time $534 per credit. Tuition, nonresident: full-time $15,964; part-time $548 per credit. *Required fees:* $4211; $215 per credit. *Faculty research:* Twentieth-century French theater, seventeenth-century French literature, French Middle Ages. *Unit head:* Dr. Lilian Uribe, Chair, 860-832-2875, E-mail: uribe@ccsu.edu. *Application contact:* Patricia Gardner, Associate Director of Graduate Studies, 860-832-2350, Fax: 860-832-2362, E-mail: graduateadmissions@ccsu.edu.

Central Connecticut State University, School of Graduate Studies, College of Liberal Arts and Social Sciences, Department of Modern Languages, Program in Spanish, New Britain, CT 06050-4010. Offers MS, Certificate. Part-time and evening/weekend programs available. *Students:* 1 applicant, 100% accepted. *Degree requirements:* For master's, one foreign language, comprehensive exam, thesis or alternative; for Certificate, qualifying exam. *Entrance requirements:* For master's, minimum undergraduate GPA of 2.7, 24 credits of undergraduate courses in each language in which graduate work will be undertaken. Additional exam requirements/recommendations for international students: Required—TOEFL (minimum score 550 paper-based; 79 iBT). *Application deadline:* For fall admission, 6/1 for domestic students, 5/1 for international students; for spring admission, 11/1 for domestic and international students. Applications are processed on a rolling basis. Application fee: $50. Electronic applications accepted. *Expenses: Tuition, area resident:* Full-time $5730; part-time $534 per credit. Tuition, state resident: full-time $8596; part-time $534 per credit. Tuition, nonresident: full-time $15,964; part-time $548 per credit. *Required fees:* $4211; $215 per credit. *Faculty research:* Linguistics, nineteenth- to twentieth-century Spanish literature, Spanish Golden Age prose/drama. *Unit head:* Dr. Lilian Uribe, Chair, 860-832-2875, E-mail: uribe@ccsu.edu. *Application contact:* Patricia Gardner, Associate Director of Graduate Studies, 860-832-2350, Fax: 860-832-2362, E-mail: graduateadmissions@ccsu.edu.

Central Michigan University, College of Graduate Studies, College of Humanities and Social and Behavioral Sciences, Department of Foreign Languages, Literatures, and Cultures, Mount Pleasant, MI 48859. Offers Spanish (MA). Part-time programs available. *Degree requirements:* For master's, thesis or alternative. Electronic applications accepted.

City College of the City University of New York, Graduate School, College of Liberal Arts and Science, Division of the Humanities and Arts, Department of Foreign Languages, New York, NY 10031-9198. Offers Spanish (MA). *Degree requirements:* For master's, one foreign language, comprehensive exam, thesis or alternative. *Entrance requirements:* For master's, minimum GPA of 3.0. Additional exam requirements/recommendations for international students: Required—TOEFL (minimum score 500 paper-based; 61 iBT). Electronic applications accepted.

Cleveland State University, College of Graduate Studies, College of Liberal Arts and Social Sciences, Department of Modern Languages, Cleveland, OH 44115. Offers French (M Ed); Spanish (M Ed, MA), including language and linguistics (MA), Latin American studies (MA), peninsular studies (MA), Spanish (MA). Part-time and evening/weekend programs available. *Faculty:* 6 full-time (3 women), 1 (woman) part-time/adjunct. *Students:* 5 full-time (1 woman), 11 part-time (9 women); includes 7 minority (all Hispanic/Latino), 2 international. Average age 35. 7 applicants, 57% accepted, 2 enrolled. In 2014, 5 master's awarded. *Degree requirements:* For master's, one foreign language, comprehensive exam, thesis optional. *Entrance requirements:* For master's, undergraduate major in Spanish or equivalent, essay in Spanish, writing sample, 2 letters of reference, ACTFL "advanced low" oral proficiency rating. Additional exam requirements/recommendations for international students: Required—TOEFL (minimum score 525 paper-based; 65 iBT). *Application deadline:* For fall admission, 7/25 priority date for domestic students; for spring admission, 12/15 priority date for domestic students. Applications are processed on a rolling basis. Application fee: $30. Electronic applications accepted. *Expenses:* Tuition, state resident: full-time $9566; part-time $531 per credit hour. Tuition, nonresident: full-time $17,980; part-time $999 per credit hour. *Required fees:* $25 per semester. Tuition and fees vary according to degree level and program. *Financial support:* In 2014–15, 5 students received support, including 5 teaching assistantships with full tuition reimbursements available (averaging $8,000 per year); Federal Work-Study and unspecified assistantships also available. Financial award application deadline: 4/1. *Faculty research:* Peninsular poetry and prose, sociolinguistics, Latin American and Caribbean literature, Arabic diaspora in Latin America, border literature. *Unit head:* Dr. Antonio Medina-Rivera, Chairperson, 216-523-7175, Fax: 216-687-4650, E-mail: a.medinarivera@csuohio.edu. *Application contact:* Dr. Stephen Gingerich, Graduate Director, 216-687-4677, Fax: 216-687-4650, E-mail: s.gingerich@csuohio.edu.
Website: http://www.csuohio.edu/class/world-languages/world-languages

Columbia University, Graduate School of Arts and Sciences, New York, NY 10027. Offers African-American studies (MA); American studies (MA); anthropology (MA, PhD); art history and archaeology (MA, PhD); astronomy (PhD); biological sciences (PhD); biotechnology (MA); chemical physics (PhD); chemistry (PhD); classical studies (MA, PhD); classics (MA, PhD); climate and society (MA); earth and environmental sciences (PhD); East Asia: regional studies (MA); East Asian languages and cultures (MA, PhD); ecology, evolution and environmental biology (MA), including conservation biology; ecology, evolution, and environmental biology (PhD), including ecology and evolutionary biology, evolutionary primatology; economics (PhD); English and comparative literature (MA, PhD); French and Romance philology (MA, PhD); Germanic languages (MA, PhD); global French studies (MA); Hispanic cultural studies (MA); history (PhD); history and literature (MA); human rights studies (MA); Islamic studies (MA); Italian (MA, PhD); Japanese pedagogy (MA); Jewish studies (MA); Latin America and the Caribbean: regional studies (MA); Latin American and Iberian cultures (PhD); mathematics (MA, PhD), including finance (MA); medieval and Renaissance studies (MA); Middle Eastern, South Asian, and African studies (MA, PhD); modern art: critical and curatorial studies (MA); modern European studies (MA); museum anthropology (MA); music (DMA, PhD); oral history (MA); philosophical foundations of physics (MA); philosophy (MA, PhD); physics (PhD); political science (MA, PhD); psychology (PhD); quantitative methods in the social sciences (MA); religion (MA, PhD); Russia, Eurasia and East Europe: regional studies (MA); Russian translation (MA); Slavic cultures (MA); Slavic languages (MA, PhD); sociology (MA, PhD); South Asian studies (MA); statistics (MA, PhD); theatre (PhD); JD/PhD; MA/MS; MD/PhD; MPA/MA. Dual-degree programs require admission to both Graduate School of Arts and Sciences and another Columbia school. Part-time and evening/weekend programs available. Terminal master's awarded for partial completion of doctoral program. *Degree requirements:* For master's, thesis (for some programs); for doctorate, comprehensive exam, thesis/dissertation. *Entrance requirements:* For master's and doctorate, GRE General Test, GRE Subject Test (for some programs). Electronic applications accepted. *Faculty research:* Humanities, natural sciences, social sciences.

Cornell University, Graduate School, Graduate Fields of Arts and Sciences, Field of Romance Studies, Ithaca, NY 14853-0001. Offers French linguistics (PhD); French literature (PhD); Hispanic literature (PhD); Italian linguistics (PhD); Italian literature (PhD); Romance linguistics (PhD); Spanish linguistics (PhD). *Degree requirements:* For doctorate, 2 foreign languages, comprehensive exam, thesis/dissertation. *Entrance requirements:* For doctorate, GRE General Test, sample of written work, 3 letters of recommendation. Additional exam requirements/recommendations for international students: Required—TOEFL (minimum score 550 paper-based; 77 iBT). Electronic applications accepted. *Faculty research:* Literary theory, Hispanic studies, French studies, gender studies.

DePaul University, College of Liberal Arts and Social Sciences, Chicago, IL 60614. Offers Arabic (MA); Chinese (MA); English (MA); French (MA); German (MA); history (MA); interdisciplinary studies (MA, MS); international public service (MS); international

studies (MA); Italian (MA); Japanese (MA); leadership and policy studies (MS); liberal studies (MA); new media studies (MA); nonprofit management (MNM); public administration (MPA); public health (MPH); public service management (MS); social work (MSW); sociology (MA); Spanish (MA); sustainable urban development (MA); women and gender studies (MA); writing and publishing (MA); writing, rhetoric, and discourse (MA); MA/PhD. Part-time and evening/weekend programs available. Postbaccalaureate distance learning degree programs offered (no on-campus study). Terminal master's awarded for partial completion of doctoral program. *Degree requirements:* For master's, variable foreign language requirement, comprehensive exam (for some programs), thesis (for some programs). Electronic applications accepted.

Drew University, Caspersen School of Graduate Studies, Program in Education, Madison, NJ 07940-1493. Offers biology (MAT); chemistry (MAT); English (MAT); French (MAT); Italian (MAT); math (MAT); physics (MAT); social studies (MAT); Spanish (MAT); theatre arts (MAT). *Accreditation:* Teacher Education Accreditation Council. Part-time programs available. *Degree requirements:* For master's, student teaching internship and seminar. *Entrance requirements:* For master's, transcripts, statement of purpose, three letters of recommendation. Additional exam requirements/ recommendations for international students: Required—TOEFL. *Expenses:* Contact institution.

Duke University, Graduate School, Department of Romance Studies, Durham, NC 27708. Offers French (PhD); Italian (PhD); Spanish (PhD); JD/AM. *Degree requirements:* For doctorate, 2 foreign languages, thesis/dissertation. *Entrance requirements:* For doctorate, GRE General Test. Additional exam requirements/ recommendations for international students: Required—TOEFL (minimum score 577 paper-based; 90 iBT) or IELTS (minimum score 7). Electronic applications accepted. *Expenses: Tuition:* Full-time $45,760; part-time $2765 per credit. *Required fees:* $978. Full-time tuition and fees vary according to program.

Eastern Michigan University, Graduate School, College of Arts and Sciences, Department of World Languages, Ypsilanti, MI 48197. Offers foreign languages (MA, Graduate Certificate), including French (MA), German (MA), German for business (Graduate Certificate), Hispanic language and cultures (Graduate Certificate), Japanese business practices (Graduate Certificate), Spanish (MA). Part-time and evening/ weekend programs available. Postbaccalaureate distance learning degree programs offered (minimal on-campus study). *Faculty:* 20 full-time (14 women). *Students:* 5 full-time (4 women), 46 part-time (35 women); includes 10 minority (2 Black or African American, non-Hispanic/Latino; 2 Asian, non-Hispanic/Latino; 6 Hispanic/Latino), 4 international. Average age 33. 46 applicants, 74% accepted, 21 enrolled. In 2014, 23 master's, 1 other advanced degree awarded. *Degree requirements:* For master's, one foreign language. *Entrance requirements:* Additional exam requirements/ recommendations for international students: Required—TOEFL. *Application deadline:* Applications are processed on a rolling basis. Application fee: $45. *Financial support:* Fellowships, research assistantships with full tuition reimbursements, teaching assistantships with full tuition reimbursements, career-related internships or fieldwork, Federal Work-Study, institutionally sponsored loans, scholarships/grants, tuition waivers (partial), and unspecified assistantships available. Support available to part-time students. Financial award applicants required to submit FAFSA. *Unit head:* Dr. Rosemary Weston-Gil, Department Head, 734-487-0130, Fax: 734-487-3411, E-mail: rweston3@emich.edu.

Eastern University, Graduate Education Programs, St. Davids, PA 19087-3696. Offers ESL program specialist (K-12) (Certificate); general supervisor (PreK-12) (Certificate); health and physical education (K-12) (Certificate); middle level (4-8) (Certificate); multicultural education (M Ed); pre K-4 (Certificate); pre K-4 with special education (Certificate); reading (M Ed); reading specialist (K-12) (Certificate); reading supervisor (K-12) (Certificate); school health services (M Ed); school health supervisor (Certificate); school nurse (Certificate); school principalship (K-12) (Certificate); secondary biology education (7-12) (Certificate); secondary chemistry education (7-12) (Certificate); secondary communication education (7-12) (Certificate); secondary education (7-12) (Certificate); secondary English education (7-12) (Certificate); secondary math education (7-12) (Certificate); secondary social studies education (7-12) (Certificate); special education (M Ed); special education (7-12) (Certificate); special education (Pre K-8) (Certificate); special education supervisor (N-12) (Certificate); TESOL (M Ed); world language (Certificate), including French, Spanish. Part-time and evening/weekend programs available. Postbaccalaureate distance learning degree programs offered (no on-campus study). *Faculty:* 22 full-time (11 women), 26 part-time/adjunct (18 women). *Students:* 57 full-time (42 women), 241 part-time (174 women); includes 106 minority (80 Black or African American, non-Hispanic/Latino; 1 American Indian or Alaska Native, non-Hispanic/Latino; 6 Asian, non-Hispanic/Latino; 15 Hispanic/Latino; 1 Native Hawaiian or other Pacific Islander, non-Hispanic/Latino; 3 Two or more races, non-Hispanic/Latino), 4 international. Average age 34. 109 applicants, 95% accepted, 85 enrolled. In 2014, 74 master's awarded. *Entrance requirements:* For master's, minimum GPA of 2.5; for Certificate, minimum GPA of 3.0. Additional exam requirements/ recommendations for international students: Required—TOEFL. *Application deadline:* For fall admission, 8/14 for domestic students; for spring admission, 12/20 for domestic students. Applications are processed on a rolling basis. Application fee: $35. Application fee is waived when completed online. *Expenses: Tuition:* Full-time $15,600; part-time $650 per credit. *Required fees:* $30; $27.50 per semester. One-time fee: $50. Tuition and fees vary according to course load, degree level and program. *Financial support:* In 2014–15, 84 students received support, including 6 research assistantships with partial tuition reimbursements available (averaging $7,710 per year); scholarships/grants and unspecified assistantships also available. Financial award application deadline: 3/15; financial award applicants required to submit FAFSA. *Unit head:* Harry Gutelius, Associate Dean, 610-341-1729. *Application contact:* Michael Perpiglia, Associate Director of Enrollment, 610-341-5947, Fax: 484-581-1276, E-mail: mperpigl@eastern.edu.
Website: http://www.eastern.edu/academics/programs/loeb-school-education-0/ graduateprograms

Emory University, Laney Graduate School, Department of Spanish and Portuguese, Atlanta, GA 30322-1100. Offers comparative literature (Certificate); film studies (Certificate); Spanish (PhD); women's studies (Certificate). *Degree requirements:* For doctorate, 2 foreign languages, comprehensive exam, thesis/dissertation. *Entrance requirements:* For doctorate, GRE General Test. Additional exam requirements/ recommendations for international students: Required—TOEFL. Electronic applications accepted. *Faculty research:* Spanish literature, Spanish American literature, literary theory, criticism, cultural studies.

Florida Atlantic University, College of Education, Department of Teaching and Learning, Boca Raton, FL 33431-0991. Offers curriculum and instruction (M Ed), including art, biology, chemistry, English, French, German, mathematics, music, physics, Pre-K and primary education, reading, social sciences, Spanish; elementary education (M Ed); environmental education (M Ed); reading education (M Ed); social foundations of education (M Ed), including educational psychology, educational technology, multilingual education. *Accreditation:* NCATE. Part-time and evening/ weekend programs available. *Entrance requirements:* For master's, GRE General Test, minimum GPA of 3.0 in last 2 years of undergraduate course work. Additional exam requirements/recommendations for international students: Required—TOEFL (minimum score 500 paper-based; 61 iBT), IELTS (minimum score 6). *Expenses:* Tuition, state resident: full-time $7396; part-time $369.82 per credit hour. Tuition, nonresident: full-time $19,392; part-time $1024.81 per credit hour. Tuition and fees vary according to course load. *Faculty research:* Technology, teaching English to speakers of other languages, math teaching, electronic portfolio assessment, global perspectives through social studies.

Florida Atlantic University, Dorothy F. Schmidt College of Arts and Letters, Department of Languages, Linguistics, and Comparative Literature, Boca Raton, FL 33431-0991. Offers comparative literature (MA); French (MA); linguistics (MA); Spanish (MA). Part-time programs available. *Degree requirements:* For master's, one foreign language, comprehensive exam, thesis optional. *Entrance requirements:* For master's, GRE General Test, minimum GPA of 3.0. Additional exam requirements/ recommendations for international students: Required—TOEFL (minimum score 500 paper-based; 61 iBT), IELTS (minimum score 6). *Expenses:* Tuition, state resident: full-time $7396; part-time $369.82 per credit hour. Tuition, nonresident: full-time $19,392; part-time $1024.81 per credit hour. Tuition and fees vary according to course load. *Faculty research:* Modern European studies, modern Latin America, medieval Europe.

Florida International University, College of Arts and Sciences, Department of Modern Languages, Miami, FL 33199. Offers Spanish (MA, PhD). Ph D program has fall admissions only. Part-time and evening/weekend programs available. *Degree requirements:* For master's, 2 foreign languages, comprehensive exam, thesis or 6 elective credits; for doctorate, 3 foreign languages, comprehensive exam, thesis/ dissertation. *Entrance requirements:* For master's, minimum GPA of 3.0, resume, writing sample in Spanish (6-7 pages minimum), 2 letters of recommendation; for doctorate, GRE General Test (minimum score of 1120) or EXADEP (minimum score of 500), minimum GPA of 3.0, letter of intent, resume, writing sample in Spanish (15 pages minimum), 2 letters of recommendation. Additional exam requirements/ recommendations for international students: Required—TOEFL (minimum score 550 paper-based; 80 iBT). Electronic applications accepted. *Faculty research:* Peninsular Spanish literature, Spanish-American literature, cultural studies, film studies, bilingualism.

Florida State University, The Graduate School, College of Arts and Sciences, Department of Modern Languages, Program in Spanish, Tallahassee, FL 32306. Offers MA, PhD. *Faculty:* 14 full-time (7 women), 2 part-time/adjunct (both women). *Students:* 27 full-time (20 women), 5 part-time (all women); includes 17 minority (2 Black or African American, non-Hispanic/Latino; 9 Hispanic/Latino; 6 Two or more races, non-Hispanic/ Latino). Average age 25. 29 applicants, 76% accepted, 8 enrolled. In 2014, 5 master's, 1 doctorate awarded. Terminal master's awarded for partial completion of doctoral program. *Degree requirements:* For master's, thesis optional; for doctorate, 2 foreign languages, thesis/dissertation. *Entrance requirements:* For master's and doctorate, GRE General Test, minimum GPA of 3.0. Additional exam requirements/ recommendations for international students: Required—TOEFL (minimum score 550 paper-based). *Application deadline:* For fall admission, 2/15 for domestic and international students. Applications are processed on a rolling basis. Application fee: $30. Electronic applications accepted. *Expenses:* Tuition, state resident: part-time $403.51 per credit hour. Tuition, nonresident: part-time $1004.85 per credit hour. *Required fees:* $75.81 per credit hour. One-time fee: $20 part-time. Tuition and fees vary according to campus/location. *Financial support:* In 2014–15, fellowships with partial tuition reimbursements (averaging $14,000 per year), research assistantships with partial tuition reimbursements (averaging $12,000 per year), 32 teaching assistantships with partial tuition reimbursements (averaging $14,400 per year) were awarded. Financial award application deadline: 2/1; financial award applicants required to submit FAFSA. *Faculty research:* Latin American theater, Hispanic literature of the United States, twentieth century Latin American poetry, Spanish-American colonial. *Unit head:* Dr. Gretchen Sunderman, Divisional Coordinator and Professor, 850-644-8186, Fax: 850-644-0524, E-mail: gsunderman@fsu.edu. *Application contact:* Wendy E. Pigott, Graduate Academic Coordinator, 850-644-8397, Fax: 850-644-0524, E-mail: wpigott@fsu.edu.
Website: http://modlang.fsu.edu/Programs2/Spanish/Graduate-program-in-Spanish

Framingham State University, Continuing Education, Program in Spanish, Framingham, MA 01701-9101. Offers M Ed.

Georgetown University, Graduate School of Arts and Sciences, Department of Spanish and Portuguese, Washington, DC 20057. Offers Spanish (MS, PhD), including Hispanic literature and cultural studies, Spanish linguistics, Spanish literature; MS/PhD. *Degree requirements:* For master's, one foreign language, research project; for doctorate, 3 foreign languages, thesis/dissertation. *Entrance requirements:* Additional exam requirements/recommendations for international students: Required—TOEFL.

Georgia Southern University, Jack N. Averitt College of Graduate Studies, College of Liberal Arts and Social Sciences, Program in Spanish, Statesboro, GA 30460. Offers MA. Part-time and evening/weekend programs available. *Students:* 12 full-time (9 women), 3 part-time (2 women); includes 12 minority (3 Black or African American, non-Hispanic/Latino; 9 Hispanic/Latino). Average age 29. 6 applicants, 83% accepted, 4 enrolled. In 2014, 7 master's awarded. *Degree requirements:* For master's, one foreign language, thesis optional. *Entrance requirements:* For master's, GRE, minimum GPA of 3.0, letters of reference. Additional exam requirements/recommendations for international students: Required—TOEFL (minimum score 550 paper-based; 80 iBT), IELTS (minimum score 6). *Application deadline:* For fall admission, 3/1 priority date for domestic and international students; for spring admission, 10/1 priority date for domestic students, 10/1 for international students. Applications are processed on a rolling basis. Application fee: $50. Electronic applications accepted. *Expenses:* Tuition, state resident: full-time $7236; part-time $277 per semester hour. Tuition, nonresident: full-time $27,118; part-time $1105 per semester hour. *Required fees:* $2092. *Financial support:* In 2014–15, 10 students received support, including research assistantships with partial tuition reimbursements available (averaging $7,200 per year), teaching assistantships with partial tuition reimbursements available (averaging $7,200 per year); career-related internships or fieldwork, Federal Work-Study, scholarships/grants, tuition waivers (partial), and unspecified assistantships also available. Support available to part-time students. Financial award application deadline: 4/15; financial award applicants required to submit FAFSA. *Faculty research:* Lettrism, twentieth-century France, Spanish medieval studies, Spanish Renaissance studies, Spanish-American colonial period, Mexican studies, Spanish linguistics, foreign language acquisition and education, drama and cinema of Spain and Latin America. *Unit head:* Dr. Eric Kartchner, Department Chair, 912-478-1381, Fax: 912-478-0652, E-mail: ekartchner@georgiasouthern.edu. *Application contact:* -, Fax: -.
Website: http://class.georgiasouthern.edu/fl

Georgia State University, College of Arts and Sciences, Department of Modern and Classical Languages, Program in Spanish, Atlanta, GA 30302-3083. Offers MA. *Degree requirements:* For master's, one foreign language, comprehensive exam, thesis or alternative, Graduate Foreign Language Reading Exam. *Entrance requirements:* For master's, GRE, statement of purpose, writing sample in the target language, 2 letters of recommendation, official transcripts. Additional exam requirements/recommendations

for international students: Required—TOEFL (minimum score 79 iBT). *Application deadline:* For fall admission, 3/15 priority date for domestic and international students; for spring admission, 11/15 priority date for domestic and international students. Application fee: $50. Electronic applications accepted. *Expenses:* Tuition, state resident: full-time $6516; part-time $362 per credit hour. Tuition, nonresident: full-time $22,014; part-time $1223 per credit hour. *Required fees:* $2128 per semester. Tuition and fees vary according to course load and program. *Financial support:* Institutionally sponsored loans available. *Faculty research:* History and literature of Colonial Latin America and the Early Modern Atlantic; contemporary Latin American poetry; interartistic and literary theory and culture; history of ideas in the Spanish Golden Age; interrelation between politics, cultural production in contemporary peninsular literature and film; second language acquisition; receptive skills as means to enhance language acquisition; acquisition of grammatical gender in Spanish as a foreign language. *Unit head:* Dr. Fernando Reati, Department Chair, 404-413-5984, Fax: 404-413-5982, E-mail: freati@gsu.edu. *Application contact:* Lita Malveaux, Administrative Academic Specialist, 404-413-5046, Fax: 404-413-5036, E-mail: lmalveaux@gsu.edu.
Website: http://www.gsu.edu/~wwwmcl/

Georgia State University, College of Arts and Sciences, Department of Modern and Classical Languages, Program in Translation and Interpretation, Atlanta, GA 30302-3083. Offers interpretation (Certificate), including Spanish; translation (Certificate), including French, German, Spanish. Part-time programs available. *Entrance requirements:* For degree, entrance examination involving translating one passage from English to the target language and one passage from the target language to English, 3 letters of recommendation, resume/curriculum vitae, official transcripts. Additional exam requirements/recommendations for international students: Required—TOEFL (minimum score 79 iBT). *Application deadline:* For fall admission, 3/15 priority date for domestic and international students; for spring admission, 11/15 priority date for domestic and international students. Application fee: $50. Electronic applications accepted. *Expenses:* Tuition, state resident: full-time $6516; part-time $362 per credit hour. Tuition, nonresident: full-time $22,014; part-time $1223 per credit hour. *Required fees:* $2128 per semester. Tuition and fees vary according to course load and program. *Faculty research:* Romance linguistics and translation; theory and practice of translation; medical and legal interpretation. *Unit head:* Dr. Fernando Reati, Chair, 404-413-5984, Fax: 404-413-5982, E-mail: freati@gsu.edu. *Application contact:* Lita Malveaux, Administrative Academic Specialist, 404-413-5046, Fax: 404-413-5036, E-mail: lmalveaux@gsu.edu.
Website: http://wlc.gsu.edu/home/graduate/graduate-certificate/

Harvard University, Graduate School of Arts and Sciences, Department of Romance Languages and Literatures, Cambridge, MA 02138. Offers French (AM, PhD); Italian (AM, PhD); Portuguese (AM, PhD); Spanish (AM, PhD). Terminal master's awarded for partial completion of doctoral program. *Degree requirements:* For master's, 2 foreign languages; for doctorate, 2 foreign languages, thesis/dissertation. *Entrance requirements:* For master's and doctorate, GRE General Test, sample of written work. Additional exam requirements/recommendations for international students: Required—TOEFL.

Howard University, Graduate School, Department of Modern Languages and Literatures, Washington, DC 20059-0002. Offers French (MA); Spanish (MA). Part-time programs available. *Degree requirements:* For master's, one foreign language, comprehensive exam, thesis. *Entrance requirements:* For master's, GRE General Test, writing samples in English and French or Spanish. *Faculty research:* African literature in French, Spanish linguistics, Spanish Peninsular literature, Spanish sociolinguistics.

Hunter College of the City University of New York, Graduate School, School of Arts and Sciences, Department of Romance Languages, Program in Spanish, New York, NY 10065-5085. Offers MA. Part-time and evening/weekend programs available. *Faculty:* 3 full-time (2 women). *Students:* 9 part-time (5 women); includes 6 minority (1 Black or African American, non-Hispanic/Latino; 5 Hispanic/Latino), 1 international. Average age 37. 4 applicants, 100% accepted, 3 enrolled. In 2014, 1 master's awarded. *Degree requirements:* For master's, 2 foreign languages, comprehensive exam, thesis optional. *Entrance requirements:* For master's, GRE General Test, GRE Subject Test, ability to read, speak, and write Spanish; interview. Additional exam requirements/recommendations for international students: Required—TOEFL. *Application deadline:* For fall admission, 4/1 for domestic students, 2/1 for international students; for spring admission, 11/1 for domestic students, 9/1 for international students. *Financial support:* Federal Work-Study and tuition waivers (partial) available. Support available to part-time students. Financial award application deadline: 4/15. *Faculty research:* Galician studies, contemporary Spanish poetry, Lope de Vega, comparative Hispanic literatures, contemporary Hispanic poetry. *Unit head:* Dr. Alicia O. Ramos, Associate Professor and Coordinator, 212-772-5130, E-mail: rosramos@hunter.cuny.edu. *Application contact:* Milena Solo, Director for Graduate Admissions, 212-772-4480, E-mail: admissions@hunter.cuny.edu.
Website: http://www.hunter.cuny.edu/romancelanguages/graduate/ma-requirements

Illinois State University, Graduate School, College of Arts and Sciences, Department of Foreign Languages, Literatures and Cultures, Normal, IL 61790-2200. Offers French (MA); French and German (MA); French and Spanish (MA); German (MA); German and Spanish (MA); Spanish (MA). *Degree requirements:* For master's, variable foreign language requirement, comprehensive exam, 1 term of residency. *Entrance requirements:* For master's, GRE General Test, minimum GPA of 2.8 in last 60 hours of course work.

Indiana University Bloomington, University Graduate School, College of Arts and Sciences, Department of Spanish and Portuguese, Bloomington, IN 47405. Offers Portuguese (MA, PhD); Spanish (MA, PhD), including Hispanic linguistics, Hispanic literatures. *Faculty:* 22 full-time. *Students:* 86 full-time (53 women), 1 (woman) part-time; includes 20 minority (18 Hispanic/Latino; 2 Two or more races, non-Hispanic/Latino), 16 international. Average age 31. 64 applicants, 30% accepted, 15 enrolled. In 2014, 13 master's, 12 doctorates awarded. *Degree requirements:* For master's, one foreign language, comprehensive exam, thesis (optional for Portuguese); for doctorate, 2 foreign languages, comprehensive exam, thesis/dissertation. *Entrance requirements:* For master's, GRE General Test, bachelor's degree in Portuguese or Spanish, minimum GPA of 3.0; for doctorate, GRE General Test, master's degree in Portuguese or Spanish, minimum GPA of 3.0. Additional exam requirements/recommendations for international students: Required—TOEFL (minimum score 79 iBT). *Application deadline:* For fall admission, 1/15 priority date for domestic students, 12/1 priority date for international students. Application fee: $55 ($65 for international students). Electronic applications accepted. *Financial support:* Fellowships with full tuition reimbursements, research assistantships, teaching assistantships with full tuition reimbursements, scholarships/grants, health care benefits, and unspecified assistantships available. Financial award application deadline: 1/15. *Faculty research:* Spanish American literature, Spanish peninsular literature, Hispanic linguistics, Luso-Brazilian studies, Catalan studies. *Unit head:* Steven Wagschal, Chair, 812-855-8498, E-mail: swagscha@indiana.edu. *Application contact:* Patrick Dove, Director of Graduate Studies, 812-855-9194, E-mail: pdove@indiana.edu.
Website: http://www.indiana.edu/~spanport/

Inter American University of Puerto Rico, Metropolitan Campus, Graduate Programs, Program in Spanish, San Juan, PR 00919-1293. Offers MA. Part-time and evening/weekend programs available. *Degree requirements:* For master's, one foreign language, comprehensive exam. *Entrance requirements:* For master's, GRE or EXADEP, interview, minimum GPA of 2.5, 6 credits each of Spanish literature and Hispanic-American literature. Electronic applications accepted.

Inter American University of Puerto Rico, Metropolitan Campus, Graduate Programs, Program in Spanish Education, San Juan, PR 00919-1293. Offers MA.

Inter American University of Puerto Rico, Ponce Campus, Graduate School, Mercedita, PR 00715-1602. Offers accounting (MBA); biology (M Ed); chemistry (M Ed); criminal justice (MA); elementary education (M Ed); English as a Second Language (M Ed); finance (MBA); history (M Ed); human resources (MBA); marketing (MBA); mathematics (M Ed); Spanish (M Ed). *Entrance requirements:* For master's, minimum GPA of 2.5.

Iona College, School of Arts and Science, Department of Education, New Rochelle, NY 10801-1890. Offers adolescence education: biology (MS Ed, MST); adolescence education: English (MS Ed); adolescence education: mathematics (MST); adolescence education: social studies (MS Ed, MST); adolescence education: Spanish (MS Ed); adolescence special education 5-12 (MST); childhood and special education (MST); early childhood and childhood (MST); educational leadership (MS Ed). *Accreditation:* NCATE. Part-time and evening/weekend programs available. *Faculty:* 8 full-time (6 women), 3 part-time/adjunct (2 women). *Students:* 26 full-time (21 women), 32 part-time (23 women); includes 7 minority (6 Hispanic/Latino; 1 Two or more races, non-Hispanic/Latino). Average age 25. 29 applicants, 90% accepted, 11 enrolled. In 2014, 59 master's awarded. *Degree requirements:* For master's, thesis or alternative. *Entrance requirements:* For master's, minimum GPA of 3.0, NY State teaching certificate and bachelor's degree (for MS Ed). Additional exam requirements/recommendations for international students: Required—TOEFL (minimum score 550 paper-based; 80 iBT), IELTS (minimum score 6.5). *Application deadline:* For fall admission, 8/1 priority date for domestic students, 5/1 priority date for international students; for spring admission, 1/1 priority date for domestic students, 9/1 priority date for international students. Applications are processed on a rolling basis. Application fee: $50. Electronic applications accepted. *Expenses: Tuition:* Part-time $985 per credit. *Required fees:* $245 per term. *Financial support:* In 2014–15, 15 students received support. Unspecified assistantships available. Support available to part-time students. Financial award application deadline: 4/15; financial award applicants required to submit FAFSA. *Faculty research:* Engaging teacher educators in scientific process, cross-national comparisons of mathematics teaching, questioning strategies in the classroom, research methods, literacy development. *Unit head:* Margaret Smith, PhD, Chair, 914-633-2210, Fax: 914-633-2608, E-mail: msmith@iona.edu. *Application contact:* Malissa Leipold, Graduate Director, Education Department, 914-633-2210, E-mail: mleipold@iona.edu.
Website: http://www.iona.edu/Academics/School-of-Arts-Science/Departments/Education/Graduate-Programs.aspx

Iona College, School of Arts and Science, Department of Foreign Languages, New Rochelle, NY 10801-1890. Offers Spanish literature (MA). Part-time and evening/weekend programs available. *Faculty:* 2 full-time (1 woman). *Students:* 4 part-time (3 women); includes 1 minority (Hispanic/Latino). Average age 37. 1 applicant, 100% accepted. In 2014, 1 master's awarded. *Degree requirements:* For master's, comprehensive exam (for some programs), thesis optional. *Entrance requirements:* For master's, minimum GPA of 3.0. Additional exam requirements/recommendations for international students: Required—TOEFL (minimum score 550 paper-based; 80 iBT), IELTS (minimum score 6.5). *Application deadline:* For fall admission, 8/1 priority date for domestic students, 5/1 priority date for international students; for spring admission, 1/1 priority date for domestic students, 9/1 priority date for international students. Applications are processed on a rolling basis. Application fee: $50. Electronic applications accepted. *Expenses: Tuition:* Part-time $985 per credit. *Required fees:* $245 per term. *Financial support:* Unspecified assistantships available. Support available to part-time students. Financial award application deadline: 4/15; financial award applicants required to submit FAFSA. *Faculty research:* Nineteenth- and twentieth-century Spanish theater, twentieth-century Spanish narrative, twentieth-century Latin American fiction, twentieth-century Latin American theater, Golden Age theater and narrative, feminist theory, literary history and narratology, transatlantic studies: Latin American literatures and cultures, colonial Spanish, British and French travel writing in Central American and the Caribbean areas, autobiographical testimonial literature, cultural studies, and theory. *Unit head:* Dr. Victoria L. Katz, Chair, 914-633-2425, E-mail: vketz@iona.edu. *Application contact:* Amanda St. Bernard, Assistant Director, Graduate Admissions, 914-633-2440, Fax: 914-633-2277, E-mail: astbernard@iona.edu.
Website: http://www.iona.edu/Academics/School-of-Arts-Science/Departments/Foreign-Languages/Graduate-Programs/Spanish.aspx

Johns Hopkins University, Zanvyl Krieger School of Arts and Sciences, Department of German and Romance Languages and Literatures, Baltimore, MD 21218-2699. Offers French (PhD); German (PhD); Italian (PhD); Spanish (PhD). *Degree requirements:* For doctorate, 2 foreign languages, thesis/dissertation. *Entrance requirements:* For doctorate, GRE General Test. Additional exam requirements/recommendations for international students: Required—TOEFL (minimum score 600 paper-based; 100 iBT), IELTS. Electronic applications accepted. *Faculty research:* Nineteenth-century French prose and poetry, genetic theory and criticism; twentieth-century Latin American literature and film; medieval and Renaissance Italian literature; gender and queer theory in German literature; the ideology of Baroque and Neobaroque aesthetics.

Kean University, College of Education, Program in Instruction and Curriculum, Union, NJ 07083. Offers bilingual/bicultural education (MA); classroom instruction (MA); earth science (MA); mathematics/science/computer education (MA); teaching (MA); teaching English as a second language (MA); world languages (Spanish) (MA). *Accreditation:* NCATE. Part-time programs available. *Faculty:* 22 full-time (13 women). *Students:* 11 full-time (6 women), 100 part-time (78 women); includes 72 minority (11 Black or African American, non-Hispanic/Latino; 61 Hispanic/Latino), 2 international. Average age 37. 51 applicants, 96% accepted, 39 enrolled. In 2014, 42 master's awarded. *Degree requirements:* For master's, comprehensive exam (for some programs), thesis optional, two-semester advanced seminar. *Entrance requirements:* For master's, GRE General Test or MAT; PRAXIS (for some programs), minimum GPA of 3.0, personal statement, professional resume/curriculum vitae, commitment to working with children, certification (for some programs), two letters of recommendation. Additional exam requirements/recommendations for international students: Required—TOEFL (minimum score 550 paper-based; 79 iBT). *Application deadline:* For fall admission, 6/1 for domestic and international students; for spring admission, 12/1 for domestic and international students. Applications are processed on a rolling basis. Application fee: $75 ($150 for international students). Electronic applications accepted. *Expenses:* Tuition, state resident: full-time $12,461; part-time $607 per credit. Tuition, nonresident: full-time $16,889; part-time $744 per credit. *Required fees:* $3141; $143 per credit. Tuition and fees vary according to course load, degree level and program. *Financial support:* In 2014–15, 3 research assistantships with full tuition reimbursements (averaging $3,742 per year) were awarded; scholarships/grants and unspecified assistantships also

available. Financial award applicants required to submit FAFSA. *Unit head:* Dr. Gail Verdi, Program Coordinator, 908-737-3908, E-mail: gverdi@kean.edu. *Application contact:* Ann-Marie Kay, Assistant Director for Graduate Admissions, 908-737-7132, Fax: 908-737-7135, E-mail: akay@kean.edu.
Website: http://grad.kean.edu/masters-programs/bilingualbicultural-education-instruction-and-curriculum

Lake Forest College, Master of Arts in Teaching Program, Lake Forest, IL 60045. Offers elementary education (MAT); K-12 French (MAT); K-12 music (MAT); K-12 Spanish (MAT); K-12 visual art (MAT); secondary biology (MAT); secondary chemistry (MAT); secondary English (MAT); secondary history (MAT); secondary mathematics (MAT). *Degree requirements:* For master's, comprehensive exam, portfolio. *Entrance requirements:* For master's, GRE.

Lehman College of the City University of New York, Division of Arts and Humanities, Department of Languages and Literatures, Bronx, NY 10468-1589. Offers Spanish (MA). Part-time and evening/weekend programs available. *Degree requirements:* For master's, one foreign language.

Loyola University Chicago, Graduate School, Department of Modern Languages and Literatures, Chicago, IL 60660. Offers Spanish (MA). Part-time and evening/weekend programs available. *Faculty:* 8 full-time (6 women), 1 part-time/adjunct (0 women). *Students:* 6 full-time (3 women), 1 (woman) part-time; includes 4 minority (3 Hispanic/Latino; 1 Two or more races, non-Hispanic/Latino). Average age 27. 18 applicants, 44% accepted, 3 enrolled. In 2014, 13 master's awarded. *Degree requirements:* For master's, 2 foreign languages, comprehensive exam, thesis or alternative. *Entrance requirements:* Additional exam requirements/recommendations for international students: Required—TOEFL, ACTFL (American Council on the Teaching of Foreign Languages) oral proficiency exam. *Application deadline:* For fall admission, 2/10 for domestic students; for spring admission, 12/1 for domestic students. Application fee: $50. *Expenses: Tuition:* Full-time $17,370; part-time $965 per credit. *Required fees:* $138 per semester. *Financial support:* In 2014–15, 6 students received support, including 3 teaching assistantships with full tuition reimbursements available (averaging $16,000 per year). Financial award applicants required to submit FAFSA. *Faculty research:* Linguistics, Latin American contemporary narrative, Latin American culture and civilization, Hispanic women's studies, twentieth century peninsular writing, Golden Age, Don Quixote. *Unit head:* Dr. Jacqueline Long, Chair, 773-508-2850, E-mail: jlong1@luc.edu. *Application contact:* Dr. D. Scott Hendrickson, SJ, Graduate Program Director, 773-508-2850, E-mail: dhendrickson@luc.edu.
Website: http://www.luc.edu/modernlang/

Marquette University, Graduate School, College of Arts and Sciences, Department of Foreign Languages and Literatures, Milwaukee, WI 53201-1881. Offers Spanish (MA). Part-time and evening/weekend programs available. *Degree requirements:* For master's, one foreign language, comprehensive exam. *Entrance requirements:* For master's, official transcripts from all current and previous colleges/universities except Marquette, three letters of recommendation, tape recording of foreign speaking voice. Additional exam requirements/recommendations for international students: Required—TOEFL (minimum score 530 paper-based). Electronic applications accepted. *Faculty research:* Latin American literature, Afro-Hispanic literature, descriptive Spanish linguistics, inter-American studies, foreign language education.

Marshall University, Academic Affairs Division, College of Liberal Arts, Program in Spanish, Huntington, WV 25755. Offers MA. *Students:* 1 (woman) part-time. Average age 32. *Entrance requirements:* For master's, GRE General Test. *Unit head:* Dr. Caroline A. Perkins, Department Chair, 304-696-2701, E-mail: perkins@marshall.edu. *Application contact:* Graduate Admissions, 304-746-1900, Fax: 304-746-1902, E-mail: services@marshall.edu.

Michigan State University, The Graduate School, College of Arts and Letters, Department of Spanish and Portuguese, East Lansing, MI 48824. Offers applied Spanish linguistics (MA); Hispanic cultural studies (PhD); Hispanic literatures (MA). *Entrance requirements:* Additional exam requirements/recommendations for international students: Required—TOEFL. Electronic applications accepted.

Middlebury College, Language Schools, Spanish School, Middlebury, VT 05753-6002. Offers MA, DML. *Faculty:* 57 full-time (35 women). *Students:* 169 full-time (122 women), 3 part-time (all women); includes 45 minority (3 Black or African American, non-Hispanic/Latino; 3 Asian, non-Hispanic/Latino; 37 Hispanic/Latino; 2 Two or more races, non-Hispanic/Latino), 4 international. Average age 31. 252 applicants, 87% accepted, 172 enrolled. In 2014, 52 master's, 2 doctorates awarded. *Degree requirements:* For master's, one foreign language; for doctorate, 2 foreign languages, comprehensive exam, thesis/dissertation, residence abroad, teaching experience. *Entrance requirements:* For master's, online placement exam, 3 letters of recommendation, personal statement, transcripts, Spanish essay; for doctorate, 1st and 2nd language placement exams, 3 letters of recommendation, personal statement, transcripts, MA in Spanish. *Application deadline:* Applications are processed on a rolling basis. Application fee: $65. Electronic applications accepted. *Financial support:* Fellowships and scholarships/grants available. Financial award applicants required to submit FAFSA. *Unit head:* Dr. Jacobo Sefami, Director, 802-443-5539, Fax: 802-443-2075, E-mail: jsefami@middlebury.edu. *Application contact:* Audrey LaRock, Coordinator, 802-443-5539, Fax: 802-443-2075, E-mail: larock@middlebury.edu.
Website: http://www.middlebury.edu/ls/grad_programs/spanish

Middle Tennessee State University, College of Graduate Studies, College of Liberal Arts, Department of Foreign Languages and Literatures, Murfreesboro, TN 37132. Offers foreign languages (MAT), including French, German, Spanish. Part-time and evening/weekend programs available. Postbaccalaureate distance learning degree programs offered. *Faculty:* 17 full-time (12 women), 1 part-time/adjunct (0 women). *Students:* 9 full-time (6 women), 11 part-time (5 women); includes 5 minority (2 Black or African American, non-Hispanic/Latino; 1 Asian, non-Hispanic/Latino; 1 Hispanic/Latino; 1 Two or more races, non-Hispanic/Latino), 1 international. 14 applicants, 86% accepted. In 2014, 8 master's awarded. *Degree requirements:* For master's, one foreign language, comprehensive exam, thesis optional. *Entrance requirements:* For master's, GRE. Additional exam requirements/recommendations for international students: Required—TOEFL (minimum score 525 paper-based; 71 iBT) or IELTS (minimum score 6). *Application deadline:* For fall admission, 6/1 for domestic and international students. Applications are processed on a rolling basis. Application fee: $30. Electronic applications accepted. *Financial support:* In 2014–15, 9 students received support. Tuition waivers available. Support available to part-time students. Financial award application deadline: 4/1; financial award applicants required to submit FAFSA. *Total annual research expenditures:* $135,499. *Unit head:* Dr. Joan McRae, Chair, 615-898-2981, Fax: 615-898-5735, E-mail: joan.mcrae@mtsu.edu. *Application contact:* Dr. Michael D. Allen, Vice Provost for Research/Dean, 615-898-2840, Fax: 615-904-8020, E-mail: michael.allen@mtsu.edu.

Millersville University of Pennsylvania, College of Graduate and Professional Studies, School of Humanities and Social Sciences, Department of Foreign Languages, Program in Languages and Cultures: Spanish Option, Millersville, PA 17551-0302. Offers MA. Part-time programs available. *Faculty:* 8 full-time (4 women), 4 part-time/adjunct (3 women). *Students:* 5 part-time (3 women); includes 1 minority (Hispanic/Latino). Average age 36. 2 applicants, 100% accepted. In 2014, 4 master's awarded. *Degree requirements:* For master's, comprehensive exam, thesis optional. *Entrance requirements:* For master's, American Council on the Teaching of Foreign Languages Oral Proficiency Interview and Writing Proficiency Test, 3 letters of recommendation, goal statement, official transcripts. Additional exam requirements/recommendations for international students: Required—TOEFL (minimum score 500 paper-based, 65 iBT) or IELTS (minimum score 6). *Application deadline:* For fall admission, 1/15 priority date for domestic and international students; for winter admission, 6/1 priority date for domestic and international students; for spring admission, 10/1 priority date for domestic and international students. Applications are processed on a rolling basis. Application fee: $40. Electronic applications accepted. *Expenses:* Tuition, state resident: full-time $8172. Tuition, nonresident: full-time $12,258. *Required fees:* $2300. Tuition and fees vary according to course load and program. *Financial support:* Research assistantships with full tuition reimbursements, institutionally sponsored loans, and unspecified assistantships available. Support available to part-time students. Financial award application deadline: 3/15; financial award applicants required to submit FAFSA. *Faculty research:* Twentieth-century Spanish and Latin American poetry, Latino music. *Unit head:* Dr. Marco A. Antolin, Associate Professor and Program Contact, 717-871-7154, Fax: 717-871-7935, E-mail: marco.antolin@millersville.edu. *Application contact:* Dr. Victor S. DeSantis, Dean of College of Graduate and Professional Studies/Associate Provost for Civic and Community Engagement, 717-871-7619, Fax: 717-871-7954, E-mail: victor.desantis@millersville.edu.
Website: http://www.millersville.edu/forlang/

Minnesota State University Mankato, College of Graduate Studies, College of Arts and Humanities, Department of Modern Languages, Program in Spanish, Mankato, MN 56001. Offers MAT, MS. *Students:* 7 full-time (4 women), 18 part-time (11 women). *Degree requirements:* For master's, one foreign language, comprehensive exam, thesis. *Entrance requirements:* For master's, minimum GPA of 3.0 during previous 2 years. *Application deadline:* For fall admission, 7/1 priority date for domestic students; for spring admission, 11/1 for domestic students. Applications are processed on a rolling basis. Application fee: $40. Electronic applications accepted. *Financial support:* Research assistantships with full tuition reimbursements, teaching assistantships with full tuition reimbursements, career-related internships or fieldwork, Federal Work-Study, institutionally sponsored loans, and unspecified assistantships available. Support available to part-time students. Financial award application deadline: 3/15. *Unit head:* Dr. Kimberly Contag, Graduate Coordinator, 507-389-2116. *Application contact:* 507-389-2321, E-mail: grad@mnsu.edu.

Mississippi State University, College of Arts and Sciences, Department of Classical and Modern Languages and Literatures, Mississippi State, MS 39762. Offers French (MA); German (MA); Spanish (MA). Part-time programs available. *Faculty:* 12 full-time (3 women). *Students:* 7 full-time (3 women); includes 2 minority (both Hispanic/Latino), 1 international. Average age 32. 7 applicants, 57% accepted, 3 enrolled. In 2014, 12 master's awarded. *Degree requirements:* For master's, one foreign language, thesis optional, comprehensive oral or written exam. *Entrance requirements:* For master's, minimum GPA of 2.75 on last two years of undergraduate courses. Additional exam requirements/recommendations for international students: Required—TOEFL (minimum score 525 paper-based; 70 iBT); Recommended—IELTS (minimum score 6). *Application deadline:* For fall admission, 7/1 for domestic students, 5/1 for international students; for spring admission, 11/1 for domestic students, 9/1 for international students. Applications are processed on a rolling basis. Application fee: $60. Electronic applications accepted. *Expenses:* Tuition, state resident: full-time $7140; part-time $783 per credit hour. Tuition, nonresident: full-time $18,478; part-time $2043 per credit hour. *Financial support:* Federal Work-Study, institutionally sponsored loans, and unspecified assistantships available. Financial award application deadline: 4/1; financial award applicants required to submit FAFSA. *Faculty research:* French, German, Spanish literature from medieval era to present; gender and cultural studies in French; Spanish-American literature; foreign language methodology; linguistics. *Unit head:* Dr. Lynn Holt, Professor and Interim Head, 662-325-3480, Fax: 662-325-8209, E-mail: lholt@cmll.msstate.edu. *Application contact:* Dr. Keith Moser, Graduate Coordinator, 662-325-3480, Fax: 662-325-8209, E-mail: kmoser@.msstate.edu.
Website: http://www.cmll.msstate.edu/

Montclair State University, The Graduate School, College of Education and Human Services, MAT Program in Teaching, Montclair, NJ 07043-1624. Offers art (MAT); biology (MAT); chemistry (MAT); earth science (MAT); English (MAT); French (MAT); health and physical education (MAT); health education (MAT); mathematics (MAT); music (MAT); physical education (MAT); physical science (MAT); social studies (MAT); Spanish (MAT); teacher of English as a second language (MAT). *Students:* 254 full-time (176 women), 205 part-time (167 women); includes 102 minority (50 Black or African American, non-Hispanic/Latino; 1 American Indian or Alaska Native, non-Hispanic/Latino; 17 Asian, non-Hispanic/Latino; 26 Hispanic/Latino; 8 Two or more races, non-Hispanic/Latino), 2 international. Average age 29. 181 applicants, 72% accepted, 120 enrolled. In 2014, 200 master's awarded. *Degree requirements:* For master's, comprehensive exam, thesis or alternative. *Entrance requirements:* For master's, GRE General Test, interview, 2 letters of recommendation. Additional exam requirements/recommendations for international students: Required—TOEFL (minimum score 83 iBT), IELTS (minimum score 6.5). *Application deadline:* Applications are processed on a rolling basis. Application fee: $60. Electronic applications accepted. *Expenses:* Tuition, state resident: full-time $9960; part-time $553.35 per credit. Tuition, nonresident: full-time $15,074; part-time $837.43 per credit. *Required fees:* $1595; $88.63 per credit. Tuition and fees vary according to degree level and program. *Financial support:* Federal Work-Study, scholarships/grants, and unspecified assistantships available. Support available to part-time students. Financial award application deadline: 3/1; financial award applicants required to submit FAFSA. *Unit head:* Dr. David Schwarzer, Chairperson, 973-655-5187. *Application contact:* Amy Aiello, Executive Director of The Graduate School, 973-655-5147, Fax: 973-655-7869, E-mail: graduate.school@montclair.edu.

Montclair State University, The Graduate School, College of Humanities and Social Sciences, Program in Spanish, Montclair, NJ 07043-1624. Offers MA. Part-time and evening/weekend programs available. *Students:* 2 full-time (1 woman), 13 part-time (10 women); includes 8 minority (all Hispanic/Latino). Average age 39. 7 applicants, 14% accepted, 1 enrolled. *Degree requirements:* For master's, comprehensive exam, thesis or alternative. *Entrance requirements:* For master's, GRE General Test, 2 letters of recommendation, essay. Additional exam requirements/recommendations for international students: Required—TOEFL (minimum score 83 iBT), IELTS (minimum score 6.5). *Application deadline:* Applications are processed on a rolling basis. Application fee: $60. Electronic applications accepted. *Expenses:* Tuition, state resident: full-time $9960; part-time $553.35 per credit. Tuition, nonresident: full-time $15,074; part-time $837.43 per credit. *Required fees:* $1595; $88.63 per credit. Tuition and fees vary according to degree level and program. *Financial support:* Federal Work-Study, scholarships/grants, and unspecified assistantships available. Support available to part-time students. Financial award application deadline: 3/1; financial award applicants required to submit FAFSA. *Faculty research:* Contemporary Spanish novel, Spanish poetry of the twentieth century, Golden Age drama, contemporary Spanish film, contemporary Latin American novel, nineteenth-century Latin American literature. *Unit*

head: Dr. Linda Gould Levine, Chairperson, 973-655-7506. *Application contact:* Amy Aiello, Executive Director of The Graduate School, 973-655-5147, Fax: 973-655-7869, E-mail: graduate.school@montclair.edu.
Website: http://www.montclair.edu/graduate/programs-of-study/spanish/

New Mexico State University, College of Arts and Sciences, Department of Languages and Linguistics, Las Cruces, NM 88003-8001. Offers MA. Part-time programs available. Postbaccalaureate distance learning degree programs offered (no on-campus study). *Faculty:* 12 full-time (5 women), 1 part-time/adjunct (0 women). *Students:* 23 full-time (20 women), 61 part-time (41 women); includes 43 minority (1 Black or African American, non-Hispanic/Latino; 42 Hispanic/Latino), 9 international. Average age 36. 44 applicants, 45% accepted, 12 enrolled. In 2014, 31 master's awarded. *Degree requirements:* For master's, one foreign language, comprehensive exam, thesis optional, oral and written exams. *Entrance requirements:* For master's, sample of written work in Spanish, 3 letters of reference, language evaluation form (or OPI score), letter of intent. Additional exam requirements/recommendations for international students: Required—TOEFL (minimum score 550 paper-based; 79 iBT), IELTS (minimum score 6.5). *Application deadline:* For fall admission, 2/15 for domestic students; for spring admission, 10/15 for domestic students. Applications are processed on a rolling basis. Application fee: $40 ($50 for international students). Electronic applications accepted. *Expenses:* Tuition, state resident: full-time $3969; part-time $220.50 per credit hour. Tuition, nonresident: full-time $13,838; part-time $768.80 per credit hour. *Required fees:* $853; $47.40 per credit hour. *Financial support:* In 2014–15, 17 students received support, including 15 teaching assistantships (averaging $16,278 per year); career-related internships or fieldwork, Federal Work-Study, institutionally sponsored loans, scholarships/grants, traineeships, health care benefits, and unspecified assistantships also available. Support available to part-time students. Financial award application deadline: 3/1. *Faculty research:* Spanish-American literature, U.S. Hispanic and Chicano literature and border culture, Hispanic linguistics. *Total annual research expenditures:* $12,419. *Unit head:* Dr. Glenn Fetzer, Academic Department Head, 575-646-3408, Fax: 575-646-7876, E-mail: gwfetzer@nmsu.edu. *Application contact:* Dr. Jeff Longwell, Graduate Program Director, 575-646-2726, Fax: 575-646-7876, E-mail: jelongw@nmsu.edu.
Website: http://www.nmsu.edu/~langling/

New York University, Graduate School of Arts and Science, Department of Spanish and Portuguese Languages and Literatures, New York, NY 10012-1019. Offers Portuguese (MA, PhD); Spanish (PhD); Spanish and Latin American literatures and cultures (MA); Spanish language and translation (MA). Part-time programs available. *Students:* 82 full-time (39 women), 8 part-time (5 women); includes 21 minority (1 Black or African American, non-Hispanic/Latino; 2 Asian, non-Hispanic/Latino; 18 Hispanic/Latino), 56 international. Average age 32. 157 applicants, 43% accepted, 33 enrolled. In 2014, 29 master's, 5 doctorates awarded. *Degree requirements:* For master's, 2 foreign languages, thesis; for doctorate, 2 foreign languages, thesis/dissertation. *Entrance requirements:* For master's, GRE General Test; for doctorate, GRE General Test, master's degree. Additional exam requirements/recommendations for international students: Required—TOEFL. *Application deadline:* For fall admission, 1/4 priority date for domestic students, 1/4 for international students. Application fee: $100. *Financial support:* Fellowships with tuition reimbursements, teaching assistantships with tuition reimbursements, career-related internships or fieldwork, Federal Work-Study, institutionally sponsored loans, scholarships/grants, health care benefits, and unspecified assistantships available. Financial award application deadline: 1/4; financial award applicants required to submit FAFSA. *Faculty research:* Gender and sexuality, transatlantic studies, literacy and cultural theories, Colonial and Post-Colonial studies, autobiography and modern subjectivities. *Unit head:* Gigi Dopico-Black, Chair, 212-998-8770, Fax: 212-995-4149, E-mail: spanish.portuguese.info@nyu.edu. *Application contact:* James Fernandez, Director of Graduate Studies, 212-998-8770, Fax: 212-995-4149, E-mail: spanish.portuguese.info@nyu.edu.
Website: http://spanish.as.nyu.edu/

New York University, Steinhardt School of Culture, Education, and Human Development, Department of Teaching and Learning, Program in Multilingual/Multicultural Studies, New York, NY 10003. Offers bilingual education (PhD); bilingual education for teachers (MA, Advanced Certificate); foreign language education (MA); teachers of English to speakers of other languages in college (PhD); teachers of French 7-12 (MA); teachers of Hebrew 7-12 (MA); teaching a foreign language 7-12 (MA), including teaching English to speakers of other languages, all grades; teaching English to speakers of other languages (MA); teaching foreign languages, 7-12 (MA), including Chinese, French, Italian, Japanese, Spanish; teaching French as a foreign language (MA), including teaching English to speakers of other languages; teaching Spanish as a foreign language and TESOL (MA). *Accreditation:* Teacher Education Accreditation Council. Part-time and evening/weekend programs available. *Faculty:* 6 full-time (4 women). *Students:* 118 full-time (94 women), 82 part-time (72 women); includes 40 minority (8 Black or African American, non-Hispanic/Latino; 18 Asian, non-Hispanic/Latino; 12 Hispanic/Latino; 2 Two or more races, non-Hispanic/Latino), 116 international. Average age 29. 431 applicants, 61% accepted, 92 enrolled. In 2014, 121 master's, 1 doctorate, 2 other advanced degrees awarded. *Degree requirements:* For master's, thesis (for some programs); for doctorate, thesis/dissertation. *Entrance requirements:* For doctorate, GRE General Test, interview; for Advanced Certificate, master's degree. Additional exam requirements/recommendations for international students: Required—TOEFL (minimum score 100 iBT). *Application deadline:* For fall admission, 12/1 priority date for domestic and international students; for spring admission, 10/1 for domestic and international students. Applications are processed on a rolling basis. Application fee: $75. Electronic applications accepted. *Financial support:* Fellowships with full and partial tuition reimbursements, career-related internships or fieldwork, Federal Work-Study, institutionally sponsored loans, scholarships/grants, and tuition waivers (partial) available. Support available to part-time students. Financial award application deadline: 2/1; financial award applicants required to submit FAFSA. *Faculty research:* Second language acquisition, cross-cultural communication, technology-enhanced language learning, language variation, action learning. *Unit head:* Prof. Shondel Nero, Director, 212-998-5757, E-mail: shondel.nero@nyu.edu. *Application contact:* 212-998-5030, Fax: 212-995-4328, E-mail: steinhardt.gradadmissions@nyu.edu.
Website: http://steinhardt.nyu.edu/teachlearn/mms

North Carolina State University, Graduate School, College of Humanities and Social Sciences, Department of Foreign Languages and Literatures, Program in Spanish Language and Literature, Raleigh, NC 27695. Offers MA. *Degree requirements:* For master's, thesis optional. *Entrance requirements:* For master's, fluency in Spanish. Electronic applications accepted. *Faculty research:* Applied linguistics, technology-assisted language instruction, Latin-American literature and culture, 20th and 21st Century Spanish narrative and film, children's literature.

Northern Arizona University, Graduate College, College of Arts and Letters, Department of Global Languages and Cultures, Flagstaff, AZ 86011. Offers Spanish teaching (MAT); Spanish teaching/Spanish education (MAT). Part-time programs available. *Degree requirements:* For master's, comprehensive exam, thesis optional. *Entrance requirements:* For master's, bachelor's degree in Spanish (coupled with preparation in general or foreign language education courses) or Spanish secondary education, or degree/experience in related field (e.g., bilingual education); minimum GPA of 3.0 or equivalent. Additional exam requirements/recommendations for international students: Required—TOEFL (minimum score 550 paper-based; 80 iBT), IELTS (minimum score 7). Electronic applications accepted.

Northern Illinois University, Graduate School, College of Liberal Arts and Sciences, Department of Foreign Languages and Literatures, De Kalb, IL 60115-2854. Offers French (MA); Spanish (MA). Part-time programs available. *Faculty:* 25 full-time (11 women). *Students:* 6 full-time (2 women), 12 part-time (8 women); includes 7 minority (1 Asian, non-Hispanic/Latino; 6 Hispanic/Latino), 1 international. Average age 32. 5 applicants, 80% accepted, 2 enrolled. In 2014, 6 master's awarded. *Degree requirements:* For master's, one foreign language, comprehensive exam, thesis or alternative, language proficiency exam. *Entrance requirements:* For master's, GRE General Test, interview, minimum GPA of 2.75, undergraduate major in French or Spanish. Additional exam requirements/recommendations for international students: Required—TOEFL (minimum score 550 paper-based). *Application deadline:* For fall admission, 6/1 for domestic students, 5/1 for international students; for spring admission, 11/1 for domestic students, 10/1 for international students. Applications are processed on a rolling basis. Application fee: $40. Electronic applications accepted. *Financial support:* In 2014–15, 11 teaching assistantships with full tuition reimbursements were awarded; fellowships with full tuition reimbursements, research assistantships with full tuition reimbursements, career-related internships or fieldwork, Federal Work-Study, scholarships/grants, tuition waivers (full), and unspecified assistantships also available. Support available to part-time students. Financial award applicants required to submit FAFSA. *Faculty research:* Francophone women writers, prosodies of French and Italian, early Spanish drama, business German, history of Burmese literature. *Unit head:* Dr. Katharina Barbe, Chair, 815-753-1559, Fax: 815-753-5989, E-mail: kbarbe@niu.edu. *Application contact:* Graduate School Office, 815-753-0395, E-mail: gradsch@niu.edu.
Website: http://www.forlangs.net/

Northwestern University, The Graduate School, Judd A. and Marjorie Weinberg College of Arts and Sciences, Department of Spanish and Portuguese, Evanston, IL 60208. Offers PhD.

The Ohio State University, Graduate School, College of Arts and Sciences, Division of Arts and Humanities, Department of Spanish and Portuguese, Columbus, OH 43210. Offers MA, PhD. *Faculty:* 24. *Students:* 66 full-time (34 women), 3 part-time (all women); includes 13 minority (all Hispanic/Latino), 23 international. Average age 30. In 2014, 2 master's, 5 doctorates awarded. Terminal master's awarded for partial completion of doctoral program. *Degree requirements:* For master's, thesis optional; for doctorate, thesis/dissertation. *Entrance requirements:* For master's and doctorate, GRE General Test, sample of academic writing. Additional exam requirements/recommendations for international students: Required—TOEFL (minimum score 550 paper-based; 79 iBT), Michigan English Language Assessment Battery (minimum score 82); Recommended—IELTS (minimum score 7). *Application deadline:* For fall admission, 12/13 priority date for domestic students, 11/30 priority date for international students; for winter admission, 12/1 for domestic students, 11/1 for international students; for spring admission, 3/1 for domestic students, 2/1 for international students. Applications are processed on a rolling basis. Application fee: $60 ($70 for international students). Electronic applications accepted. *Financial support:* Fellowships, research assistantships, teaching assistantships, Federal Work-Study, institutionally sponsored loans, and unspecified assistantships available. Support available to part-time students. *Unit head:* Dr. Glenn A. Martinez, Chair and Professor, 614-292-4958, E-mail: spanport@osu.edu. *Application contact:* Graduate and Professional Admissions, 614-292-9444, Fax: 614-292-3895, E-mail: gpadmissions@osu.edu.
Website: http://sppo.osu.edu/

Ohio University, Graduate College, College of Arts and Sciences, Department of Modern Languages, Athens, OH 45701-2979. Offers French (MA); Spanish (MA). Part-time programs available. *Degree requirements:* For master's, 2 foreign languages, comprehensive exam, thesis optional. *Entrance requirements:* For master's, oral and written samples. Additional exam requirements/recommendations for international students: Required—TOEFL (minimum score 550 paper-based; 80 iBT) or IELTS (minimum score 6.5). Electronic applications accepted. *Faculty research:* French and Spanish language and literature.

Penn State University Park, Graduate School, College of the Liberal Arts, Department of Spanish, Italian, and Portuguese, University Park, PA 16802. Offers MA, PhD. *Unit head:* Dr. Susan Welch, Dean, 814-865-7691, Fax: 814-863-2085, E-mail: swelch@psu.edu. *Application contact:* Lori A. Stania, Director, Graduate Student Services, 814-867-5278, Fax: 814-863-4627, E-mail: gswww@psu.edu.
Website: http://sip.la.psu.edu/

Pontifical Catholic University of Puerto Rico, College of Arts and Humanities, Department of Hispanic Studies, Ponce, PR 00717-0777. Offers grammar and writing (Professional Certificate); Hispanic studies (MA). Part-time and evening/weekend programs available. *Degree requirements:* For master's, variable foreign language requirement, comprehensive exam, thesis or alternative. *Entrance requirements:* For master's, GRE General Test, 2 letters of recommendation, interview, minimum GPA of 2.75. Electronic applications accepted.

Portland State University, Graduate Studies, College of Liberal Arts and Sciences, Department of World Languages and Literatures, Portland, OR 97207-0751. Offers foreign literature and language (MA); French (MA); German (MA); Japanese (MA); Spanish (MA). Part-time programs available. *Faculty:* 48 full-time (28 women), 33 part-time/adjunct (29 women). *Students:* 30 full-time (13 women), 8 part-time (3 women); includes 7 minority (2 Asian, non-Hispanic/Latino; 5 Hispanic/Latino), 13 international. Average age 30. 31 applicants, 65% accepted, 18 enrolled. In 2014, 9 master's awarded. *Degree requirements:* For master's, one foreign language, thesis (for some programs). *Entrance requirements:* Additional exam requirements/recommendations for international students: Required—TOEFL (minimum score 550 paper-based; 80 iBT), IELTS (minimum score 6.5). *Application deadline:* For fall admission, 4/1 for domestic students, 3/1 for international students; for winter admission, 9/1 for domestic students, 7/1 for international students; for spring admission, 11/1 for domestic and international students. Applications are processed on a rolling basis. Application fee: $50. *Expenses:* Tuition, state resident: part-time $222 per credit. Tuition, nonresident: part-time $527 per credit. *Required fees:* $22 per contact hour. $100 per quarter. Tuition and fees vary according to program. *Financial support:* In 2014–15, 29 teaching assistantships with full and partial tuition reimbursements (averaging $3,251 per year) were awarded; research assistantships with full tuition reimbursements, Federal Work-Study, scholarships/grants, and unspecified assistantships also available. Support available to part-time students. Financial award application deadline: 3/1; financial award applicants required to submit FAFSA. *Faculty research:* Foreign language pedagogy, applied and social linguistics, literary history and criticism. *Total annual research expenditures:* $412,070. *Unit head:* Dr. Jennifer Perlmutter, Chair, 503-725-8783, Fax: 503-725-5276, E-mail: jrp@pdx.edu.
Website: http://www.pdx.edu/wll/

Spanish

Princeton University, Graduate School, Department of Spanish and Portuguese Languages and Cultures, Princeton, NJ 08544-1019. Offers PhD. *Degree requirements:* For doctorate, variable foreign language requirement, thesis/dissertation. *Entrance requirements:* For doctorate, GRE General Test, sample of written work. Additional exam requirements/recommendations for international students: Required—TOEFL (minimum score 600 paper-based). Electronic applications accepted.

Purdue University, Graduate School, College of Liberal Arts, School of Languages and Cultures, West Lafayette, IN 47907. Offers French (MA, MAT, PhD), including French (MA, PhD), French education (MAT); German (MA, MAT, PhD), including German (MA, PhD), German education (MAT); Japanese pedagogy (MA); Spanish (MA, MAT, PhD), including Spanish (MA, PhD), Spanish education (MAT). Terminal master's awarded for partial completion of doctoral program. *Degree requirements:* For master's, one foreign language; for doctorate, 2 foreign languages, thesis/dissertation. *Entrance requirements:* For master's, GRE General Test (minimum score 600, 160 for new scoring), two writing samples, one in English, one in language (French, German, Japanese, or Spanish); sample recording of English and language of study; for doctorate, GRE General Test (minimum score 600, 160 for new scoring), master's degree with minimum GPA of 3.5 or equivalent; two writing samples, one in English, one in language (French, German, Japanese, or Spanish); sample recording of English and language of study. Additional exam requirements/recommendations for international students: Required—TOEFL (minimum score 550 paper-based; 77 iBT); Recommended—TWE. Electronic applications accepted. *Faculty research:* Linguistics, semiotics, literary criticism, pedagogy.

Queens College of the City University of New York, Division of Graduate Studies, Arts and Humanities Division, Department of Hispanic Languages and Literatures, Program in Spanish, Flushing, NY 11367-1597. Offers MA. Part-time and evening/weekend programs available. *Degree requirements:* For master's, 2 foreign languages, comprehensive exam, thesis or alternative. *Entrance requirements:* For master's, minimum GPA of 3.0. Additional exam requirements/recommendations for international students: Required—TOEFL.

Queen's University at Kingston, School of Graduate Studies, Faculty of Arts and Sciences, Department of Spanish and Italian, Kingston, ON K7L 3N6, Canada. Offers Spanish language and literature (MA). Part-time programs available. *Degree requirements:* For master's, one foreign language, thesis. *Entrance requirements:* Additional exam requirements/recommendations for international students: Required—TOEFL. Electronic applications accepted. *Faculty research:* Golden Age, nineteenth- and twentieth-century Peninsular novel, literary theory, colonial Latin America, nineteenth-and-twentieth century Latin America.

Rider University, Department of Graduate Education, Leadership and Counseling, Teacher Certification Program, Lawrenceville, NJ 08648-3001. Offers business education (Certificate); elementary education (Certificate); English as a second language (Certificate); English education (Certificate); mathematics education (Certificate); preschool to grade 3 (Certificate); science education (Certificate); social studies education (Certificate); world languages (Certificate), including French, German, Spanish. Part-time programs available. *Degree requirements:* For Certificate, internship, professional portfolio. *Entrance requirements:* For degree, PRAXIS, resume. Additional exam requirements/recommendations for international students: Required—TOEFL (minimum score 550 paper-based). Electronic applications accepted. *Faculty research:* Conceptual foundations for optimal development of creativity; creative theory, cognitive processes in mathematics learning, teacher collaboration.

Roosevelt University, Graduate Division, College of Arts and Sciences, Department of Literature and Languages, Program in Spanish, Chicago, IL 60605. Offers MA. Part-time and evening/weekend programs available. *Degree requirements:* For master's, variable foreign language requirement, thesis or alternative. *Entrance requirements:* For master's, BA in Spanish or the equivalent. *Faculty research:* Latin American narrative, feminism, Hispanic cultures, twentieth-century Hispanic literature, Latino studies.

Rutgers, The State University of New Jersey, New Brunswick, Graduate School-New Brunswick, Program in Spanish, Piscataway, NJ 08854-8097. Offers bilingualism and second language acquisition (MA, PhD); Spanish (MA, MAT, PhD); Spanish literature (MA, PhD); translation (MA). Part-time programs available. *Degree requirements:* For master's, comprehensive exam (for some programs), thesis (for some programs); for doctorate, 2 foreign languages, comprehensive exam, thesis/dissertation. *Entrance requirements:* For master's and doctorate, GRE General Test. Additional exam requirements/recommendations for international students: Required—TOEFL. Electronic applications accepted. *Faculty research:* Hispanic literature, Luso-Brazilian literature, Spanish linguistics, Spanish translation.

St. John's University, St. John's College of Liberal Arts and Sciences, Department of Languages and Literatures, Queens, NY 11439. Offers Spanish (MA). Part-time and evening/weekend programs available. *Students:* 5 full-time (4 women), 9 part-time (7 women); includes 12 minority (all Hispanic/Latino). Average age 36. 8 applicants, 88% accepted, 1 enrolled. In 2014, 6 master's awarded. *Degree requirements:* For master's, comprehensive exam, thesis optional. *Entrance requirements:* For master's, 24 credits of undergraduate course work in languages (18 credits in Spanish), minimum GPA of 3.0, bachelor's degree. Additional exam requirements/recommendations for international students: Required—TOEFL (minimum score 600 paper-based; 100 iBT), IELTS (minimum score 7). *Application deadline:* For fall admission, 5/1 priority date for domestic and international students; for spring admission, 11/1 priority date for domestic and international students. Applications are processed on a rolling basis. Application fee: $70. Electronic applications accepted. *Expenses: Tuition:* Full-time $20,610; part-time $1145 per credit. *Required fees:* $170 per semester. *Financial support:* Research assistantships and scholarships/grants available. Support available to part-time students. Financial award application deadline: 3/1; financial award applicants required to submit FAFSA. *Faculty research:* Paleography; early North American Spanish literature; medieval, Renaissance and Golden Century Spanish literature; journal and book editions. *Unit head:* Dr. Zoe Petropoulou, Chair, 718-990-5205, E-mail: petropouz@stjohns.edu. *Application contact:* Robert Medrano, Director of Graduate Admission, 718-990-1601, Fax: 718-990-5686, E-mail: gradhelp@stjohns.edu.

Saint Louis University, Graduate Education, College of Arts and Sciences, Department of Modern and Classical Languages, St. Louis, MO 63103-2097. Offers French (MA); Spanish (MA). Part-time programs available. *Degree requirements:* For master's, one foreign language, comprehensive exam, thesis/dissertation (Spanish). *Entrance requirements:* For master's, GRE General Test or MAT, letters of recommendation, resume, interview. Additional exam requirements/recommendations for international students: Required—TOEFL (minimum score 525 paper-based). Electronic applications accepted. *Faculty research:* Culture studies, literature studies, foreign language acquisition.

Saint Louis University–Madrid Campus, Graduate Programs, Master of Arts in Spanish Program, Madrid, Spain. Offers MA. Part-time programs available. *Faculty:* 5 full-time (all women), 4 part-time/adjunct (3 women). *Students:* 6 full-time (4 women), 11 part-time (7 women). Average age 28. 15 applicants, 87% accepted, 10 enrolled. In 2014, 14 master's awarded. *Degree requirements:* For master's, one foreign language, comprehensive exam, thesis optional. *Entrance requirements:* For master's, GRE General Test or MAT, 3 letters of recommendation, curriculum vitae, writing sample, interview. Additional exam requirements/recommendations for international students: Required—TOEFL. *Application deadline:* For fall admission, 3/1 priority date for domestic and international students; for spring admission, 8/1 priority date for domestic students, 9/1 priority date for international students; for summer admission, 5/31 for domestic and international students. Applications are processed on a rolling basis. Application fee: $40. Electronic applications accepted. *Financial support:* In 2014–15, 6 students received support, including 3 fellowships with partial tuition reimbursements available, 1 research assistantship with partial tuition reimbursement available, 2 teaching assistantships with partial tuition reimbursements available; career-related internships or fieldwork, scholarships/grants, health care benefits, and unspecified assistantships also available. Support available to part-time students. Financial award application deadline: 3/1; financial award applicants required to submit FAFSA. *Faculty research:* Spanish and Latin American literature, linguistics, cultural studies, gender studies. *Unit head:* Dr. Cristina Matute, Coordinator, Spanish Department, 34-91-554-58-58, Fax: 34-91-554-62-02, E-mail: cmatute@slu.edu. *Application contact:* Diego Rodriguez-Vila, Admissions Counselor, 34-91-554-58-58, Fax: 34-91-554-62-02, E-mail: graduate_admissions-madrid@slu.edu.
Website: http://spain.slu.edu/academics/degrees_&_programs/graduate_programs/MA_in_spanish/introduction.html

Saint Xavier University, Graduate Studies, School of Education, Chicago, IL 60655-3105. Offers counseling (MA); curriculum and instruction (MA); early childhood education (MA); educational administration (MA); elementary education (MA); individualized studies (MA), including educational technology, English as a second language (ESL), ISTEM (integrative science, technology, engineering, and math), science education; music education (MA); reading (MA); secondary education (MA); Spanish education (MA); special education (MA); teaching and leadership (MA). *Accreditation:* NCATE. Part-time and evening/weekend programs available. *Degree requirements:* For master's, thesis or project. *Entrance requirements:* For master's, minimum GPA of 3.0. *Expenses:* Contact institution.

Salem State University, School of Graduate Studies, Program in Spanish, Salem, MA 01970-5353. Offers MAT. Part-time and evening/weekend programs available. *Entrance requirements:* For master's, GRE or MAT. Additional exam requirements/recommendations for international students: Required—TOEFL (minimum score 550 paper-based; 80 iBT) or IELTS (minimum score 5.5).

Sam Houston State University, College of Humanities and Social Sciences, Department of Foreign Languages, Huntsville, TX 77341. Offers Spanish (MA). Part-time programs available. *Faculty:* 12 full-time (6 women), 1 part-time/adjunct (0 women). *Students:* 1 full-time (0 women), 24 part-time (16 women); includes 17 minority (all Hispanic/Latino), 4 international. Average age 40. 9 applicants, 100% accepted, 7 enrolled. In 2014, 7 master's awarded. *Degree requirements:* For master's, comprehensive exam, thesis (for some programs). *Entrance requirements:* For master's, GRE General Test, writing sample, letters of recommendation. Additional exam requirements/recommendations for international students: Required—TOEFL (minimum score 550 paper-based; 79 iBT), IELTS (minimum score 6.5). *Application deadline:* For fall admission, 8/1 for domestic students, 6/25 for international students; for spring admission, 12/1 for domestic students, 11/12 for international students; for summer admission, 5/15 for domestic students, 4/9 for international students. Applications are processed on a rolling basis. Application fee: $45 ($75 for international students). Electronic applications accepted. *Expenses:* Tuition, state resident: full-time $2286; part-time $254 per credit hour. Tuition, nonresident: full-time $5544; part-time $616 per credit hour. *Required fees:* $440 per semester. Tuition and fees vary according to course load and campus/location. *Financial support:* In 2014–15, 3 research assistantships (averaging $6,701 per year), 2 teaching assistantships (averaging $4,650 per year) were awarded; career-related internships or fieldwork, Federal Work-Study, scholarships/grants, tuition waivers (partial), and unspecified assistantships also available. Support available to part-time students. Financial award application deadline: 3/15; financial award applicants required to submit FAFSA. *Faculty research:* Pablo Picasso studies, Muslim women, Hispanic literature and art, sociolinguistics, language and the law, medical art and literature (Hispanic emphasis). *Unit head:* Dr. Debra D. Andrist, Chair, 936-294-1414, Fax: 936-294-4144, E-mail: andrist@shsu.edu. *Application contact:* Dr. Rafael E. Saumell, Academic Advisor, 936-294-1441, Fax: 936-294-4144, E-mail: fol_res@shsu.edu.
Website: http://www.shsu.edu/academics/foreign-languages/

San Diego State University, Graduate and Research Affairs, College of Arts and Letters, Department of Spanish and Portuguese, San Diego, CA 92182. Offers Spanish (MA). *Degree requirements:* For master's, one foreign language. *Entrance requirements:* For master's, GRE General Test, 3 letters of reference. Additional exam requirements/recommendations for international students: Required—TOEFL. Electronic applications accepted. *Faculty research:* New strategies for teaching foreign languages.

San Francisco State University, Division of Graduate Studies, College of Liberal and Creative Arts, Department of Foreign Languages and Literatures, Program in Spanish, San Francisco, CA 94132-1722. Offers MA. Part-time programs available. *Application deadline:* Applications are processed on a rolling basis. Electronic applications accepted. *Expenses:* Tuition, state resident: full-time $6738. Tuition, nonresident: full-time $17,898; part-time $372 per credit hour. *Required fees:* $498 per semester. *Financial support:* Unspecified assistantships available. *Unit head:* Prof. Michael Hammer, Program Coordinator, 415-338-1421, Fax: 415-405-0588, E-mail: mhammer@sfsu.edu. *Application contact:* Prof. Gustavo Calderon, Graduate Coordinator, 415-338-7426, Fax: 415-405-0588, E-mail: gusto@sfsu.edu.
Website: http://spanish.sfsu.edu/

San Jose State University, Graduate Studies and Research, College of Humanities and the Arts, Department of Foreign Languages, Program in Spanish, San Jose, CA 95192-0001. Offers MA. *Degree requirements:* For master's, 2 foreign languages, thesis or comprehensive exam. Electronic applications accepted.

Southern Oregon University, Graduate Studies, Department of Foreign Languages and Literatures, Ashland, OR 97520. Offers French language teaching (MA); Spanish language teaching (MA). Part-time programs available. Postbaccalaureate distance learning degree programs offered (minimal on-campus study). *Faculty:* 7 full-time (4 women), 6 part-time/adjunct (all women). *Students:* 49 full-time (38 women), 20 part-time (4 women); includes 15 minority (1 American Indian or Alaska Native, non-Hispanic/Latino; 1 Asian, non-Hispanic/Latino; 10 Hispanic/Latino; 3 Two or more races, non-Hispanic/Latino). Average age 36. 27 applicants, 89% accepted, 19 enrolled. In 2014, 21 master's awarded. *Degree requirements:* For master's, thesis (for some programs). *Entrance requirements:* For master's, GRE General Test, minimum cumulative GPA of 3.0 in the last 90 quarter credits (60 semester credits) of undergraduate coursework. Additional exam requirements/recommendations for international students: Required—TOEFL (minimum score 540 paper-based; 76 iBT), IELTS (minimum score 6), ELPT (minimum score 964) or ELS (minimum score 112). *Application deadline:* For fall admission, 7/31 priority date for domestic and international students; for winter admission, 11/15 priority date for domestic and international students; for spring admission, 1/7 priority date for domestic and international students.

Applications are processed on a rolling basis. Application fee: $50. Electronic applications accepted. *Expenses:* Tuition, state resident: full-time $10,225; part-time $1515 per quarter. Tuition, nonresident: full-time $12,782; part-time $1894 per quarter. *Required fees:* $1395; $261 per quarter. *Financial support:* Career-related internships or fieldwork, institutionally sponsored loans, scholarships/grants, and unspecified assistantships available. *Unit head:* Dr. Dan Morris, Graduate French Language Program Coordinator, 541-552-6740, E-mail: morris@sou.edu. *Application contact:* Dr. Anne Connor, Graduate Spanish Language Program Coordinator, 541-552-6743, E-mail: connora@sou.edu.
Website: http://www.sou.edu/language/

Stanford University, School of Humanities and Sciences, Division of Iberian and Latin American Cultures, Stanford, CA 94305-9991. Offers Spanish (MA, PhD). Terminal master's awarded for partial completion of doctoral program. *Degree requirements:* For master's, 2 foreign languages; for doctorate, 3 foreign languages, thesis/dissertation, oral exam. *Entrance requirements:* For master's and doctorate, GRE General Test. Additional exam requirements/recommendations for international students: Required—TOEFL. Electronic applications accepted. *Expenses: Tuition:* Full-time $44,184; part-time $982 per credit hour. *Required fees:* $191.

State University of New York at New Paltz, Graduate School, School of Education, Department of Secondary Education, New Paltz, NY 12561. Offers adolescence education: biology (MAT, MS Ed); adolescence education: chemistry (MAT, MS Ed); adolescence education: earth science (MAT, MS Ed); adolescence education: English (MAT, MS Ed); adolescence education: French (MAT, MS Ed); adolescence education: social studies (MAT, MS Ed); adolescence education: Spanish (MAT, MS Ed); second language education (MS Ed, AC), including second language education (MS Ed), teaching English language learners (AC). *Accreditation:* NCATE. Part-time and evening/weekend programs available. *Faculty:* 11 full-time (7 women), 11 part-time/adjunct (6 women). *Students:* 66 full-time (36 women), 51 part-time (31 women); includes 24 minority (3 Black or African American, non-Hispanic/Latino; 1 American Indian or Alaska Native, non-Hispanic/Latino; 1 Asian, non-Hispanic/Latino; 16 Hispanic/Latino; 3 Two or more races, non-Hispanic/Latino), 2 international. Average age 30. 76 applicants, 83% accepted, 40 enrolled. In 2014, 55 master's awarded. *Degree requirements:* For master's, comprehensive exam (for some programs), portfolio. *Entrance requirements:* For master's, minimum GPA of 3.0, New York state teaching certificate (MS Ed). Additional exam requirements/recommendations for international students: Required—TOEFL (minimum score 550 paper-based; 80 iBT), IELTS (minimum score 6.5). *Application deadline:* For fall admission, 3/1 priority date for domestic students, 3/1 for international students; for spring admission, 10/1 priority date for domestic students, 10/1 for international students. Application fee: $50. Electronic applications accepted. *Financial support:* Application deadline: 8/1. *Unit head:* Dr. Laura Dull, Chair, 845-257-2849, E-mail: dullj@newpaltz.edu. *Application contact:* Vika Shock, Director of Graduate Admissions, 845-257-3285, Fax: 845-257-3284, E-mail: gradschool@newpaltz.edu.
Website: http://www.newpaltz.edu/secondaryed/

Syracuse University, College of Arts and Sciences, Program in Spanish Language, Literature and Culture, Syracuse, NY 13244. Offers MA. Part-time programs available. *Students:* 5 full-time (all women), 1 (woman) part-time; includes 3 minority (all Hispanic/Latino), 1 international. Average age 26. 7 applicants, 86% accepted, 4 enrolled. In 2014, 6 master's awarded. *Degree requirements:* For master's, comprehensive exam, thesis (for some programs). *Entrance requirements:* For master's, GRE General Test. Additional exam requirements/recommendations for international students: Required—TOEFL (minimum score 100 iBT). *Application deadline:* For fall admission, 2/1 priority date for domestic and international students. Application fee: $75. Electronic applications accepted. *Expenses: Tuition:* Part-time $1341 per credit. *Financial support:* Fellowships with full tuition reimbursements, teaching assistantships with full and partial tuition reimbursements, and tuition waivers available. Financial award application deadline: 1/1; financial award applicants required to submit FAFSA. *Unit head:* Dr. Alicia Rios, Department Chair, 315-443-5379, Fax: 315-443-5376, E-mail: abrios@syr.edu. *Application contact:* Colleen Kepler, Information Contact, 315-443-2175, E-mail: cdkepler@syr.edu.
Website: http://lang.syr.edu/academics/Spanish/MA-Spanish.html

Temple University, College of Liberal Arts, Department of Spanish and Portuguese, Philadelphia, PA 19122-6096. Offers Spanish (MA, PhD). Part-time and evening/weekend programs available. *Faculty:* 17 full-time (7 women), 6 part-time/adjunct (5 women). *Students:* 31 full-time (17 women); includes 12 minority (2 Asian, non-Hispanic/Latino; 10 Hispanic/Latino), 5 international. 20 applicants, 70% accepted, 7 enrolled. In 2014, 3 master's, 4 doctorates awarded. Terminal master's awarded for partial completion of doctoral program. *Degree requirements:* For master's, one foreign language; for doctorate, 2 foreign languages, thesis/dissertation. *Entrance requirements:* For master's and doctorate, GRE General Test, minimum GPA of 3.0, 3 letters of recommendation. Additional exam requirements/recommendations for international students: Required—TOEFL. *Application deadline:* For fall admission, 1/15 for domestic students, 12/15 for international students; for spring admission, 9/30 for domestic students, 8/1 for international students. Applications are processed on a rolling basis. Application fee: $60. Electronic applications accepted. *Expenses:* Tuition, state resident: full-time $14,490; part-time $805 per credit hour. Tuition, nonresident: full-time $19,850; part-time $1103 per credit hour. *Required fees:* $690. Full-time tuition and fees vary according to class time, course load, degree level, campus/location and program. *Financial support:* Fellowships, teaching assistantships with full tuition reimbursements, and scholarships/grants available. Financial award application deadline: 1/15; financial award applicants required to submit FAFSA. *Faculty research:* Spanish literatures and cultures, Latin American literatures and cultures, Lusophone literatures and cultures, Spanish linguistics, literary and linguistic theory. *Unit head:* Dr. Sergio Franco, Associate Chair for Graduate Studies, 215-204-8285, Fax: 215-204-3731, E-mail: pereiro@temple.edu. *Application contact:* Annette Vega, Coordinator, 215-204-2877, Fax: 215-204-3731, E-mail: avega1@temple.edu.
Website: http://www.temple.edu/spanpor/

Texas A&M University, College of Liberal Arts, Department of Hispanic Studies, College Station, TX 77843. Offers Hispanic studies (MA, PhD); modern languages (MA), including Spanish. *Faculty:* 9. *Students:* 28 full-time (17 women), 16 part-time (13 women); includes 21 minority (all Hispanic/Latino), 13 international. Average age 41. 8 applicants, 100% accepted, 8 enrolled. In 2014, 1 master's, 3 doctorates awarded. Application fee: $50 ($90 for international students). *Expenses:* Tuition, state resident: full-time $4078; part-time $226.55 per credit hour. Tuition, nonresident: full-time $10,594; part-time $577.55 per credit hour. *Required fees:* $2813; $237.70 per credit hour. $278.50 per semester. Tuition and fees vary according to degree level and student level. *Financial support:* In 2014–15, 28 students received support, including 6 fellowships with full and partial tuition reimbursements available (averaging $18,410 per year), 9 research assistantships with full and partial tuition reimbursements available (averaging $5,424 per year), 19 teaching assistantships with full and partial tuition reimbursements available (averaging $7,110 per year); career-related internships or fieldwork, institutionally sponsored loans, scholarships/grants, traineeships, health care benefits, tuition waivers (full and partial), and unspecified assistantships also available. Support available to part-time students. Financial award applicants required to submit FAFSA. *Unit head:* Dr. Irene Moyna, Department Head, 979-845-2124, E-mail: moyna@tamu.edu. *Application contact:* Dr. Hilaire Kallendorf, Director of Graduate Studies, 979-458-0621, E-mail: h-kallendorf@tamu.edu.
Website: http://hispanicstudies.tamu.edu/graduate-program/

Texas A&M University–Kingsville, College of Graduate Studies, College of Arts and Sciences, Department of Language and Literature, Program in Spanish, Kingsville, TX 78363. Offers MA. In 2014, 1 master's awarded. *Degree requirements:* For master's, variable foreign language requirement, comprehensive exam, thesis (for some programs). *Entrance requirements:* For master's, GRE, MAT, GMAT. Additional exam requirements/recommendations for international students: Required—TOEFL (minimum score 550 paper-based; 79 iBT). *Application deadline:* For fall admission, 8/15 for domestic students, 6/1 for international students; for spring admission, 12/15 for domestic students, 10/1 for international students; for summer admission, 5/15 for domestic students, 4/1 for international students. Applications are processed on a rolling basis. Application fee: $35 ($50 for international students). Electronic applications accepted. *Financial support:* Career-related internships or fieldwork, Federal Work-Study, institutionally sponsored loans, scholarships/grants, health care benefits, tuition waivers (full and partial), and unspecified assistantships available. Support available to part-time students. Financial award application deadline: 5/1; financial award applicants required to submit FAFSA. *Unit head:* Dr. Michelle Johnson-Vela, Department Chair, 361-593-2597, E-mail: kfmrj00@tamuk.edu. *Application contact:* Roberto Vela, Graduate Coordinator, 361-593-4062, E-mail: roberto.vela@tamuk.edu.

Texas State University, The Graduate College, College of Liberal Arts, Program in Spanish, San Marcos, TX 78666. Offers MA. Part-time and evening/weekend programs available. *Faculty:* 7 full-time (5 women). *Students:* 13 full-time (9 women), 15 part-time (8 women); includes 20 minority (2 Black or African American, non-Hispanic/Latino; 18 Hispanic/Latino), 1 international. Average age 29. 15 applicants, 80% accepted, 7 enrolled. In 2014, 14 master's awarded. *Degree requirements:* For master's, one foreign language, comprehensive exam. *Entrance requirements:* For master's, GRE (preferred), baccalaureate degree from regionally-accredited university with minimum GPA of 2.75 on last 60 undergraduate semester hours. Additional exam requirements/recommendations for international students: Required—TOEFL (minimum score 550 paper-based; 78 iBT). *Application deadline:* For fall admission, 6/15 priority date for domestic students, 6/1 for international students; for spring admission, 10/15 priority date for domestic students, 10/1 for international students. Applications are processed on a rolling basis. Application fee: $40 ($90 for international students). Electronic applications accepted. *Expenses:* Expenses: $8,834 (tuition and fees combined). *Financial support:* In 2014–15, 17 students received support, including 8 teaching assistantships (averaging $13,165 per year); research assistantships, career-related internships or fieldwork, Federal Work-Study, institutionally sponsored loans, scholarships/grants, and unspecified assistantships also available. Support available to part-time students. Financial award application deadline: 4/1; financial award applicants required to submit FAFSA. *Unit head:* Dr. George Y. Porras, Graduate Advisor, 512-245-2360, Fax: 512-245-8298, E-mail: gradspanish@txstate.edu. *Application contact:* Dr. Andrea Golato, Dean of Graduate School, 512-245-2581, Fax: 512-245-8365, E-mail: gradcollege@txstate.edu.
Website: http://www.modlang.txstate.edu/

Texas Tech University, Graduate School, College of Arts and Sciences, Department of Classical and Modern Languages and Literatures, Lubbock, TX 79409-2071. Offers applied linguistics (MA); classics (MA); German (MA); languages and cultures (MA); Romance languages (MA); Spanish (PhD); MBA/MA. Part-time programs available. *Faculty:* 61 full-time (31 women), 7 part-time/adjunct (4 women). *Students:* 93 full-time (48 women), 15 part-time (10 women); includes 27 minority (1 Black or African American, non-Hispanic/Latino; 22 Hispanic/Latino; 4 Two or more races, non-Hispanic/Latino), 41 international. Average age 32. 60 applicants, 70% accepted, 26 enrolled. In 2014, 26 master's, 7 doctorates awarded. *Degree requirements:* For master's, comprehensive exam, thesis or alternative; for doctorate, comprehensive exam, thesis/dissertation. *Entrance requirements:* For master's and doctorate, GRE General Test. Additional exam requirements/recommendations for international students: Required—TOEFL (minimum score 550 paper-based; 79 iBT). *Application deadline:* For fall admission, 6/1 priority date for domestic students, 1/15 priority date for international students; for spring admission, 9/1 priority date for domestic students, 6/15 priority date for international students. Applications are processed on a rolling basis. Application fee: $60. Electronic applications accepted. *Expenses:* Tuition, state resident: full-time $6310; part-time $262.92 per credit hour. Tuition, nonresident: full-time $14,998; part-time $624.92 per credit hour. *Required fees:* $2701; $36.50 per credit. $912.50 per semester. Tuition and fees vary according to course load. *Financial support:* In 2014–15, 91 students received support, including 78 fellowships (averaging $2,724 per year), 4 research assistantships (averaging $17,800 per year), 82 teaching assistantships (averaging $11,423 per year); Federal Work-Study, scholarships/grants, and unspecified assistantships also available. Financial award application deadline: 4/15; financial award applicants required to submit FAFSA. *Faculty research:* Literature, comparative literature, linguistics, culture, applied linguistics. *Total annual research expenditures:* $1,380. *Unit head:* Dr. Erin Collopy, Chair and Associate Professor, 806-834-8497, Fax: 806-742-3306, E-mail: erin.collopy@ttu.edu. *Application contact:* Liz Hildebrand, Senior Advisor, 806-834-2463, Fax: 806-742-3306, E-mail: liz.hildebrand@ttu.edu.
Website: http://www.depts.ttu.edu/classic_modern/

Tulane University, School of Liberal Arts, Department of Spanish and Portuguese, New Orleans, LA 70118-5669. Offers Portuguese (MA); Spanish (MA); Spanish and Portuguese (PhD). *Degree requirements:* For master's, 2 foreign languages; for doctorate, 2 foreign languages, thesis/dissertation. *Entrance requirements:* For master's, GRE General Test, minimum B average in undergraduate course work; for doctorate, GRE General Test. Additional exam requirements/recommendations for international students: Required—TOEFL. Electronic applications accepted. *Expenses: Tuition:* Full-time $46,326; part-time $2574 per credit hour. *Required fees:* $1980; $44.50 per credit hour. $550 per term. Tuition and fees vary according to course load and program.

Universidad Autonoma de Guadalajara, Graduate Programs, Guadalajara, Mexico. Offers administrative law and justice (LL M); advertising and corporate communications (MA); architecture (M Arch); business (MBA); computational science (MCC); education (Ed M, Ed D); English-Spanish translation (MA); entrepreneurship and management (MBA); integrated management of digital animation (MA); international business (MIB); international corporate law (LL M); internet technologies (MS); manufacturing systems (MMS); occupational health (MS); philosophy (MA, PhD); power electronics (MS); quality systems (MQS); renewable energy (MS); social evaluation of projects (MBA); strategic market research (MBA); tax law (MA); teaching mathematics (MA).

Université de Montréal, Faculty of Arts and Sciences, Department of Literatures and Modern Languages, Program in Hispanic Studies, Montréal, QC H3C 3J7, Canada. Offers MA. *Degree requirements:* For master's, 2 foreign languages, thesis. Electronic applications accepted. *Faculty research:* Spanish literature and culture, Latin American literature and culture.

Spanish

Université Laval, Faculty of Letters, Department of Literature, Programs in Spanish Literatures, Québec, QC G1K 7P4, Canada. Offers MA, PhD. Part-time programs available. Terminal master's awarded for partial completion of doctoral program. *Degree requirements:* For master's, thesis; for doctorate, comprehensive exam, thesis/dissertation. *Entrance requirements:* For master's and doctorate, linguistics exams, knowledge of French and Spanish. Electronic applications accepted.

University at Albany, State University of New York, College of Arts and Sciences, Department of Languages, Literatures, and Cultures, Albany, NY 12222-0001. Offers Spanish (MA, PhD). *Degree requirements:* For doctorate, thesis/dissertation. *Entrance requirements:* Additional exam requirements/recommendations for international students: Required—TOEFL (minimum score 550 paper-based).

University at Buffalo, the State University of New York, Graduate School, College of Arts and Sciences, Department of Romance Languages and Literatures, Buffalo, NY 14260-4620. Offers French (MA, PhD); Spanish (MA, PhD). Part-time programs available. *Faculty:* 16 full-time (10 women), 6 part-time/adjunct (5 women). *Students:* 33 full-time (20 women), 4 part-time (2 women); includes 17 minority (2 Black or African American, non-Hispanic/Latino; 2 Asian, non-Hispanic/Latino; 9 Hispanic/Latino; 4 Two or more races, non-Hispanic/Latino), 11 international. 20 applicants, 85% accepted, 11 enrolled. In 2014, 3 master's, 7 doctorates awarded. Terminal master's awarded for partial completion of doctoral program. *Degree requirements:* For master's, one foreign language, comprehensive exam, thesis; for doctorate, 2 foreign languages, comprehensive exam, thesis/dissertation. *Entrance requirements:* For master's and doctorate, GRE. Additional exam requirements/recommendations for international students: Required—TOEFL (minimum score 550 paper-based; 79 iBT), IELTS (minimum score 6.5), PTE (minimum score 55). *Application deadline:* For fall admission, 1/15 priority date for domestic students, 1/1 for international students; for spring admission, 8/1 for international students. Applications are processed on a rolling basis. Application fee: $75. Electronic applications accepted. *Financial support:* In 2014–15, 24 students received support, including 3 fellowships (averaging $5,333 per year), 24 teaching assistantships with full tuition reimbursements available (averaging $13,454 per year); Federal Work-Study, institutionally sponsored loans, scholarships/grants, and health care benefits also available. Financial award application deadline: 1/1; financial award applicants required to submit FAFSA. *Faculty research:* Romance linguistics, cultural studies, literary studies, literature, philosophy and poetry. *Unit head:* Dr. David Castillo, Professor and Chair, 716-645-0869, Fax: 716-645-5981, E-mail: dc63@buffalo.edu. *Application contact:* Dr. Amy Graves-Monroe, Associate Professor and Director of Graduate Studies, 716-645-0880, Fax: 716-645-5981, E-mail: acgraves@buffalo.edu.
Website: http://rll.drupalgardens.com

University at Buffalo, the State University of New York, Graduate School, Graduate School of Education, Department of Learning and Instruction, Buffalo, NY 14260. Offers biology education (Ed M, Certificate); chemistry education (Ed M, Certificate); childhood education (Ed M); childhood education with bilingual extension (Ed M); curriculum, instruction and the science of learning (PhD); early childhood education (Ed M); early childhood education with bilingual extension (birth-grade 2) (Ed M); earth science education (Ed M, Certificate); education studies (Ed M); educational technology and new literacies (Certificate); elementary education (Ed D); English education (Ed M, Certificate); English for speakers of other languages (Ed M); foreign and second language education (PhD); French education (Ed M, Certificate); German education (Ed M, Certificate); gifted education (Certificate); Latin education (Ed M, Certificate); literacy specialist (Ed M); literacy teaching and learning (Certificate); mathematics education (Ed M, Certificate); music education (Ed M, Certificate); physics education (Ed M, Certificate); science and the public (Ed M); social studies education (Ed M, Certificate); Spanish education (Ed M, Certificate); special education (PhD); teaching English to speakers of other languages (Ed M). Part-time and evening/weekend programs available. Postbaccalaureate distance learning degree programs offered (no on-campus study). *Faculty:* 29 full-time (21 women), 64 part-time/adjunct (46 women). *Students:* 256 full-time (193 women), 303 part-time (222 women); includes 41 minority (21 Black or African American, non-Hispanic/Latino; 5 American Indian or Alaska Native, non-Hispanic/Latino; 13 Asian, non-Hispanic/Latino; 2 Hispanic/Latino), 84 international. Average age 30. 415 applicants, 84% accepted, 194 enrolled. In 2014, 160 master's, 20 doctorates, 32 other advanced degrees awarded. *Degree requirements:* For master's, comprehensive exam; for doctorate, thesis/dissertation, research analysis exam, research experience component. *Entrance requirements:* For master's, letters of reference; for doctorate, GRE General Test or MAT, interview, writing sample, letters of recommendation. Additional exam requirements/recommendations for international students: Required—TOEFL (minimum score 600 paper-based; 96 iBT). *Application deadline:* For fall admission, 2/1 priority date for domestic and international students; for spring admission, 11/15 priority date for domestic students, 10/1 for international students. Applications are processed on a rolling basis. Application fee: $50. Electronic applications accepted. *Financial support:* In 2014–15, 50 fellowships (averaging $12,110 per year), 32 research assistantships with tuition reimbursements (averaging $12,867 per year) were awarded; teaching assistantships, career-related internships or fieldwork, Federal Work-Study, institutionally sponsored loans, scholarships/grants, tuition waivers, and unspecified assistantships also available. Financial award application deadline: 2/28; financial award applicants required to submit FAFSA. *Faculty research:* Science assessment, foreign language teaching and learning, early learning, new literacies, gender and education. *Total annual research expenditures:* $1.3 million. *Unit head:* Dr. Suzanne Miller, Chair, 716-645-2455, Fax: 716-645-3161, E-mail: smiller@buffalo.edu. *Application contact:* Cathy Dimino, Admissions Assistant, 716-645-2110, Fax: 716-645-7937, E-mail: cadimino@buffalo.edu.
Website: http://gse.buffalo.edu/lai

The University of Akron, Graduate School, Buchtel College of Arts and Sciences, Department of Modern Languages, Akron, OH 44325. Offers Spanish (MA). Part-time and evening/weekend programs available. *Faculty:* 5 full-time (3 women). *Students:* 1 part-time (0 women); minority (Hispanic/Latino). Average age 38. *Degree requirements:* For master's, one foreign language, comprehensive exam, essay, oral exam, research paper. *Entrance requirements:* For master's, baccalaureate degree in Spanish, minimum GPA of 2.75, interview, proficiency in Spanish, three letters of recommendation, statement of purpose. Additional exam requirements/recommendations for international students: Required—TOEFL (minimum score 550 paper-based; 79 iBT), IELTS (minimum score 6.5). *Application deadline:* Applications are processed on a rolling basis. Application fee: $45 ($70 for international students). Electronic applications accepted. *Expenses:* Tuition, state resident: full-time $7578; part-time $421 per credit hour. Tuition, nonresident: full-time $12,977; part-time $721 per credit hour. *Required fees:* $1388; $35 per credit hour. Tuition and fees vary according to course load. *Financial support:* Institutionally sponsored loans available. *Faculty research:* Spanish literature and culture from the Golden Age to the present, contemporary Spanish cinema and the plastic arts, contemporary Latin America narrative and poetry, Spanish applied linguistics and pedagogy. *Unit head:* Dr. Maria Zanetta, Chair, 330-972-5872, E-mail: zanetta@uakron.edu. *Application contact:* Dr. Parizad Dejbord-Sawan, Director of Graduate Studies, 330-972-7824, E-mail: parizad@uakron.edu.
Website: http://www.uakron.edu/modlang/

The University of Alabama, Graduate School, College of Arts and Sciences, Department of Modern Languages and Classics, Tuscaloosa, AL 35487. Offers French (MA, PhD); French and Spanish (PhD); German (MA); Romance languages (MA, PhD); Spanish (MA, PhD). Part-time programs available. *Faculty:* 29 full-time (16 women). *Students:* 53 full-time (35 women), 10 part-time (6 women); includes 9 minority (3 Black or African American, non-Hispanic/Latino; 5 Hispanic/Latino; 1 Two or more races, non-Hispanic/Latino), 15 international. Average age 33. 24 applicants, 88% accepted, 14 enrolled. In 2014, 10 master's, 5 doctorates awarded. *Degree requirements:* For master's, comprehensive exam, thesis optional; for doctorate, one foreign language, thesis/dissertation, preliminary exam. *Entrance requirements:* For master's and doctorate, minimum GPA of 3.0, writing sample. Additional exam requirements/recommendations for international students: Required—TOEFL or IELTS. *Application deadline:* For fall admission, 7/6 priority date for domestic students, 1/15 priority date for international students; for spring admission, 12/5 priority date for domestic students, 6/1 priority date for international students. Applications are processed on a rolling basis. Application fee: $50 ($60 for international students). Electronic applications accepted. *Expenses:* Tuition, state resident: full-time $9826. Tuition, nonresident: full-time $24,950. *Financial support:* In 2014–15, 7 students received support, including 1 fellowship, research assistantships with full tuition reimbursements available (averaging $10,291 per year), 6 teaching assistantships with full tuition reimbursements available (averaging $10,291 per year); career-related internships or fieldwork, Federal Work-Study, institutionally sponsored loans, and scholarships/grants also available. Financial award application deadline: 7/14. *Faculty research:* Non-English literature, linguistics, culture, film. *Unit head:* Dr. Michael Picone, Chair and Professor, 205-348-5054, Fax: 205-348-2042, E-mail: mpicone@bama.ua.edu. *Application contact:* Dr. K. Barbara Fischer, Graduate Director and Associate Professor, 205-348-8465, Fax: 205-348-2042, E-mail: bfischer@bama.ua.edu.
Website: http://bama.ua.edu/~mlc

The University of Arizona, College of Humanities, Department of Spanish and Portuguese, Tucson, AZ 85721. Offers Spanish (MA, PhD). Terminal master's awarded for partial completion of doctoral program. *Degree requirements:* For master's, one foreign language, comprehensive exam, thesis optional; for doctorate, 3 foreign languages, comprehensive exam, thesis/dissertation. *Entrance requirements:* For master's, GRE General Test, minimum GPA of 3.3, writing sample, 3 letters of recommendation, audio sample; for doctorate, GRE General Test, minimum GPA of 3.4, 3 letters of recommendation, statement of purpose, writing sample, audio sample. Additional exam requirements/recommendations for international students: Required—TOEFL (minimum score 550 paper-based; 79 iBT). Electronic applications accepted. *Faculty research:* Spanish and Latin American literature and linguistics, literary theory.

University of Arkansas, Graduate School, J. William Fulbright College of Arts and Sciences, Department of World Languages, Literature and Cultures, Program in Spanish, Fayetteville, AR 72701-1201. Offers MA. *Degree requirements:* For master's, one foreign language, comprehensive exam, thesis optional. *Entrance requirements:* Additional exam requirements/recommendations for international students: Required—TOEFL (minimum score 550 paper-based), IELTS (minimum score 6.5). Electronic applications accepted. *Faculty research:* Medieval and Golden Age poetry, colonial Latin America, contemporary Latin America.

University of Calgary, Faculty of Graduate Studies, Faculty of Arts, Department of French, Italian and Spanish, Calgary, AB T2N 1N4, Canada. Offers French (MA, PhD); Spanish (MA, PhD). PhD offered in special cases only. Part-time programs available. *Degree requirements:* For master's, one foreign language, thesis, exam; for doctorate, 2 foreign languages, comprehensive exam, thesis/dissertation, candidacy exam. *Entrance requirements:* Additional exam requirements/recommendations for international students: Required—TOEFL (minimum score 550 paper-based; 80 iBT) or IELTS (minimum score 7). Electronic applications accepted. *Faculty research:* French and French-Canadian language and literature, Hispanic language and literature, comparative literature, language instruction, literary theory.

University of California, Berkeley, Graduate Division, College of Letters and Science, Group in Romance Languages and Literature, Berkeley, CA 94720-1500. Offers French (PhD); Italian (PhD); Spanish (PhD). *Degree requirements:* For doctorate, thesis/dissertation, qualifying exam. *Entrance requirements:* For doctorate, GRE General Test, minimum GPA of 3.0, 3 letters of recommendation. Additional exam requirements/recommendations for international students: Required—TOEFL (minimum score 570 paper-based).

University of California, Davis, Graduate Studies, Program in Spanish, Davis, CA 95616. Offers MA, PhD. Terminal master's awarded for partial completion of doctoral program. *Degree requirements:* For master's, comprehensive exam (for some programs), thesis (for some programs); for doctorate, 2 foreign languages, thesis/dissertation. *Entrance requirements:* For master's, GRE General Test, minimum GPA of 3.0; for doctorate, GRE General Test, master's degree, minimum GPA of 3.0. Additional exam requirements/recommendations for international students: Required—TOEFL (minimum score 550 paper-based). *Faculty research:* Medieval Spanish language and literature, Spanish linguistics, Latin American literature, nineteenth century Peninsular literature.

University of California, Irvine, School of Humanities, Department of Spanish and Portuguese, Irvine, CA 92697. Offers Spanish (MA, MAT, PhD). *Students:* 34 full-time (18 women), 1 (woman) part-time; includes 25 minority (all Hispanic/Latino). Average age 36. 23 applicants, 35% accepted, 5 enrolled. In 2014, 5 doctorates awarded. *Degree requirements:* For doctorate, thesis/dissertation. *Entrance requirements:* For master's and doctorate, GRE General Test, minimum GPA of 3.0. Additional exam requirements/recommendations for international students: Required—TOEFL (minimum score 550 paper-based). *Application deadline:* For fall admission, 1/2 priority date for domestic students, 1/2 for international students. Applications are processed on a rolling basis. Application fee: $90 ($110 for international students). Electronic applications accepted. *Financial support:* Fellowships, teaching assistantships, institutionally sponsored loans, traineeships, health care benefits, and unspecified assistantships available. Financial award application deadline: 3/1; financial award applicants required to submit FAFSA. *Faculty research:* Latin American literature, Spanish literature, Spanish linguistics in Creole studies, Hispanic literature in the U.S., Luso-Brazilian literature. *Unit head:* Luis Aviles, Department Chair, 949-824-7268, Fax: 949-824-2803, E-mail: laviles@uci.edu. *Application contact:* Linda Le, Department Manager, 949-824-7726, Fax: 949-824-2803, E-mail: ttle@uci.edu.
Website: http://www.hnet.uci.edu/spanishandportuguese/

University of California, Los Angeles, Graduate Division, College of Letters and Science, Department of Spanish and Portuguese, Program in Spanish, Los Angeles, CA 90095. Offers MA. *Degree requirements:* For master's, one foreign language, comprehensive exam or thesis. *Entrance requirements:* For master's, GRE General Test, bachelor's degree; minimum undergraduate GPA of 3.0 (or its equivalent if letter grade system not used). Additional exam requirements/recommendations for international students: Required—TOEFL. Electronic applications accepted.

University of California, Riverside, Graduate Division, Department of Hispanic Studies, Riverside, CA 92521-0102. Offers Spanish (MA, PhD). Terminal master's

awarded for partial completion of doctoral program. *Degree requirements:* For master's, one foreign language, comprehensive exam; for doctorate, one foreign language, thesis/dissertation, qualifying exams, 1 quarter of teaching experience. *Entrance requirements:* For master's and doctorate, GRE General Test, minimum GPA of 3.0. Additional exam requirements/recommendations for international students: Required—TOEFL (minimum score 550 paper-based; 80 iBT). Electronic applications accepted. *Expenses:* Tuition, state resident: full-time $5399. Tuition, nonresident: full-time $10,433. *Faculty research:* Spanish literature of the sixteenth-, seventeenth- and twentieth-century; pre-Columbian and colonial Latin American literature; nineteenth- and twentieth-century Latin American literature.

University of California, Santa Barbara, Graduate Division, College of Letters and Sciences, Division of Humanities and Fine Arts, Department of Spanish and Portuguese, Santa Barbara, CA 93106-4150. Offers Hispanic languages and literatures (PhD), including European medieval studies, feminist studies, Hispanic linguistics, Hispanic literature, Luso-Brazilian literature; Hispanic linguistics (MA); Luso-Brazilian literature (MA); Spanish or Spanish-American literature (MA); MA/PhD. Spanish Language Institute available during Summer session. Terminal master's awarded for partial completion of doctoral program. *Degree requirements:* For master's, 2 foreign languages, comprehensive exam (for some programs), thesis optional; for doctorate, 3 foreign languages, comprehensive exam, thesis/dissertation. *Entrance requirements:* For master's and doctorate, GRE. Additional exam requirements/recommendations for international students: Required—TOEFL (minimum score 550 paper-based; 80 iBT), IELTS (minimum score 7). Electronic applications accepted. *Faculty research:* Nineteenth-century Spanish and Portuguese literature, Spanish and Spanish-American literature, nineteenth- and twentieth-century Portuguese and Brazilian literatures, Hispanic linguistics, Catalan language and culture.

University of Central Florida, College of Arts and Humanities, Department of Modern Languages and Literatures, Program in Spanish, Orlando, FL 32816. Offers MA. Part-time and evening/weekend programs available. *Students:* 10 full-time (6 women), 7 part-time (4 women); includes 13 minority (all Hispanic/Latino). Average age 31. 9 applicants, 89% accepted, 6 enrolled. In 2014, 7 master's awarded. *Degree requirements:* For master's, one foreign language, comprehensive exam, thesis or alternative. *Entrance requirements:* For master's, GRE General Test, minimum GPA of 3.0 in last 60 hours. Additional exam requirements/recommendations for international students: Required—TOEFL. *Application deadline:* For fall admission, 6/1 for domestic students; for spring admission, 12/1 for domestic students. Application fee: $30. Electronic applications accepted. *Expenses:* Tuition, state resident: part-time $288.16 per credit hour. Tuition, nonresident: part-time $1073.31 per credit hour. *Financial support:* In 2014–15, 6 students received support, including 3 fellowships (averaging $5,500 per year), 5 teaching assistantships with partial tuition reimbursements available (averaging $7,850 per year); career-related internships or fieldwork, Federal Work-Study, institutionally sponsored loans, tuition waivers (partial), and unspecified assistantships also available. Financial award application deadline: 3/1; financial award applicants required to submit FAFSA. *Unit head:* Dr. Humberto Lopez Cruz, Chair, 407-823-3429, E-mail: hlopez@ucf.edu. *Application contact:* Barbara Rodriguez Lamas, Director, Admissions and Student Services, 407-823-2766, Fax: 407-823-6442, E-mail: gradadmissions@ucf.edu.
Website: http://mll.cah.ucf.edu/graduate/index.php#SpanishMA

University of Chicago, Division of the Humanities, Department of Romance Languages and Literatures, Chicago, IL 60637. Offers French (PhD); Italian (PhD); Spanish (PhD). *Students:* 44 full-time (28 women); includes 9 minority (1 Black or African American, non-Hispanic/Latino; 1 Asian, non-Hispanic/Latino; 6 Hispanic/Latino; 1 Two or more races, non-Hispanic/Latino), 13 international. 71 applicants, 39% accepted, 7 enrolled. Terminal master's awarded for partial completion of doctoral program. *Degree requirements:* For doctorate, 3 foreign languages, thesis/dissertation. *Entrance requirements:* For doctorate, GRE General Test. Additional exam requirements/recommendations for international students: Required—TOEFL (minimum score 104 iBT), IELTS (minimum score 7). *Application deadline:* For fall admission, 12/15 for domestic and international students. Application fee: $90. Electronic applications accepted. *Expenses: Tuition:* Full-time $46,899. *Required fees:* $347. *Financial support:* Fellowships with full tuition reimbursements, teaching assistantships with full tuition reimbursements, Federal Work-Study, institutionally sponsored loans, scholarships/grants, and health care benefits available. Financial award application deadline: 12/15; financial award applicants required to submit FAFSA. *Unit head:* Dr. Larry Norman, Chair. *Application contact:* Braden Grams, Assistant Dean of Students, Admissions and Fellowships, 773-702-1552, Fax: 773-834-9148, E-mail: humanitiesadmissions@uchicago.edu.
Website: http://rll.uchicago.edu

University of Cincinnati, Graduate School, McMicken College of Arts and Sciences, Department of Romance Languages and Literature, Program in Spanish, Cincinnati, OH 45221. Offers MA, PhD. Terminal master's awarded for partial completion of doctoral program. *Degree requirements:* For master's, thesis optional; for doctorate, 2 foreign languages, thesis/dissertation. *Entrance requirements:* For master's, minimum GPA of 3.0. Electronic applications accepted. *Faculty research:* Applied linguistics, Spanish essay, Latin American culture, women's studies, poetry.

University of Colorado Boulder, Graduate School, College of Arts and Sciences, Department of Spanish and Portuguese, Boulder, CO 80309. Offers Hispanic linguistics (MA); medieval and early modern Hispanic literatures (PhD); Spanish and Spanish American literatures (MA, PhD). *Faculty:* 14 full-time (6 women). *Students:* 36 full-time (23 women), 1 (woman) part-time; includes 9 minority (1 American Indian or Alaska Native, non-Hispanic/Latino; 8 Hispanic/Latino), 12 international. Average age 31. 42 applicants, 17% accepted, 6 enrolled. In 2014, 7 master's, 2 doctorates awarded. Terminal master's awarded for partial completion of doctoral program. *Degree requirements:* For master's, one foreign language, comprehensive exam, thesis or alternative; for doctorate, 2 foreign languages, thesis/dissertation. *Entrance requirements:* For master's, minimum undergraduate GPA of 2.75. *Application deadline:* For fall admission, 12/19 for domestic and international students. Applications are processed on a rolling basis. Application fee: $50 ($70 for international students). Electronic applications accepted. *Financial support:* In 2014–15, 89 students received support, including 6 fellowships (averaging $948 per year), 33 teaching assistantships with full and partial tuition reimbursements available (averaging $38,597 per year); institutionally sponsored loans, scholarships/grants, health care benefits, and unspecified assistantships also available. Financial award application deadline: 12/15; financial award applicants required to submit FAFSA. *Faculty research:* Literary criticism, Spanish language literature, cultural history, Iberian studies. *Total annual research expenditures:* $37,611.
Website: http://spanish.colorado.edu/

University of Colorado Denver, College of Liberal Arts and Sciences, Department of Modern Languages, Denver, CO 80217. Offers Spanish (MA). Part-time programs available. *Faculty:* 9 full-time (5 women). *Students:* 11 full-time (8 women), 9 part-time (8 women); includes 7 minority (all Hispanic/Latino). Average age 40. 7 applicants, 57% accepted, 3 enrolled. In 2014, 4 master's awarded. *Degree requirements:* For master's, comprehensive exam, thesis or alternative, 33 credit hours of course work. *Entrance requirements:* For master's, BA in Spanish from accredited institution, or BA in another discipline plus language skills that meet department's standards; minimum GPA of 2.5, 3.0 in all Spanish courses; written statement in Spanish; oral interview after the application has been submitted; three letters of recommendation. Additional exam requirements/recommendations for international students: Required—TOEFL (minimum score 550 paper-based; 80 iBT). *Application deadline:* For fall admission, 3/15 for domestic students, 2/15 for international students; for spring admission, 10/15 for domestic students, 9/15 for international students; for summer admission, 3/15 for domestic students, 2/15 for international students. Application fee: $50 ($75 for international students). Electronic applications accepted. *Financial support:* In 2014–15, 1 student received support. Fellowships, research assistantships, teaching assistantships, Federal Work-Study, institutionally sponsored loans, scholarships/grants, and traineeships available. Financial award application deadline: 4/1; financial award applicants required to submit FAFSA. *Faculty research:* Spanish American literature; sociolinguistics, bilingualism, phonology and historical linguistics; Spanish peninsular literature; applied linguistics, pragmatics and second language acquisition. *Unit head:* Dr. Devin Jenkins, Department Chair/Associate Professor of Spanish, 303-556-2848, E-mail: devin.jenkins@ucdenver.edu. *Application contact:* Dr. Michael Abeyta, Associate Professor of Spanish/Graduate Advisor, 303-556-4008, E-mail: michael.abeyta@ucdenver.edu.
Website: http://www.ucdenver.edu/academics/colleges/CLAS/Departments/ModernLanguages/Programs/SpanishMasters/Pages/MasterofArtsSpanish.aspx

University of Connecticut, Graduate School, College of Liberal Arts and Sciences, Department of Modern and Classical Languages, Field of Spanish, Storrs, CT 06269. Offers MA, PhD. Terminal master's awarded for partial completion of doctoral program. *Degree requirements:* For master's, one foreign language, comprehensive exam; for doctorate, 2 foreign languages, thesis/dissertation. *Entrance requirements:* For master's and doctorate, GRE General Test, GRE Subject Test. Additional exam requirements/recommendations for international students: Required—TOEFL (minimum score 550 paper-based). Electronic applications accepted.

University of Delaware, College of Arts and Sciences, Department of Foreign Languages and Literatures, Newark, DE 19716. Offers foreign languages and literatures (MA), including French, German, Spanish; foreign languages pedagogy (MA), including French, German, Spanish; technical Chinese translation (MA). *Degree requirements:* For master's, one foreign language, comprehensive exam, thesis optional. *Entrance requirements:* For master's, GRE General Test, letters of recommendation, writing sample. Additional exam requirements/recommendations for international students: Required—TOEFL. Electronic applications accepted. *Faculty research:* Medieval to Modern French and Spanish literature, twentieth-century German, French, Spanish literature by women, computer-assisted instruction.

University of Florida, Graduate School, College of Liberal Arts and Sciences, Department of Spanish and Portuguese Studies, Gainesville, FL 32611. Offers Spanish (MA, MAT, PhD). Part-time programs available. *Faculty:* 8 full-time (5 women), 3 part-time/adjunct (2 women). *Students:* 7 full-time (4 women), 1 international. 40 applicants, 40% accepted, 10 enrolled. In 2014, 3 doctorates awarded. Terminal master's awarded for partial completion of doctoral program. *Degree requirements:* For master's, one foreign language, comprehensive exam, thesis or extended research paper; for doctorate, 2 foreign languages, comprehensive exam, thesis/dissertation, qualifying exam. *Entrance requirements:* For master's and doctorate, GRE General Test, minimum GPA of 3.0. Additional exam requirements/recommendations for international students: Required—TOEFL (minimum score 550 paper-based; 80 iBT), IELTS (minimum score 6). *Application deadline:* For fall admission, 12/15 priority date for domestic and international students; for winter admission, 2/1 for domestic and international students. Applications are processed on a rolling basis. Application fee: $30. Electronic applications accepted. *Financial support:* In 2014–15, 10 fellowships, 5 research assistantships, 32 teaching assistantships were awarded. Financial award application deadline: 12/15; financial award applicants required to submit FAFSA. *Faculty research:* Spanish linguistics; second language acquisition and teaching; Spanish literature, film and culture; Latin American literature, film and culture; Portuguese literature, film and culture. *Total annual research expenditures:* $1,750. *Unit head:* Gillian Lord, PhD, Departmental Chair/Graduate Coordinator, 352-273-3749, Fax: 352-392-2017, E-mail: glord@ufl.edu. *Application contact:* Gillian Lord, PhD, Departmental Chair/Graduate Coordinator, 352-273-3749, Fax: 352-392-2017, E-mail: glord@ufl.edu.
Website: http://www.spanishandportuguese.ufl.edu/

University of Georgia, Franklin College of Arts and Sciences, Department of Romance Languages, Athens, GA 30602. Offers French (MA); Romance languages (MA, PhD); Spanish (MA). *Degree requirements:* For master's, one foreign language; for doctorate, 2 foreign languages, thesis/dissertation. *Entrance requirements:* For master's and doctorate, GRE General Test. Electronic applications accepted.

University of Hawaii at Manoa, Graduate Division, College of Languages, Linguistics and Literature, Department of Languages and Literatures of Europe and the Americas, Program in Spanish, Honolulu, HI 96822. Offers MA. Part-time programs available. *Degree requirements:* For master's, one foreign language, thesis optional. *Entrance requirements:* For master's, GRE General Test. Additional exam requirements/recommendations for international students: Required—TOEFL (minimum score 580 paper-based; 92 iBT), IELTS (minimum score 5).

University of Houston, College of Liberal Arts and Social Sciences, Department of Hispanic Studies, Houston, TX 77204. Offers Spanish (MA, PhD). Part-time programs available. *Degree requirements:* For master's, comprehensive exam, thesis optional; for doctorate, 2 foreign languages, comprehensive exam, thesis/dissertation. *Entrance requirements:* For master's and doctorate, GRE. Additional exam requirements/recommendations for international students: Required—TOEFL (minimum score 550 paper-based; 79 iBT); Recommended—IELTS (minimum score 6.5). Electronic applications accepted.

University of Houston, College of Liberal Arts and Social Sciences, Department of Modern and Classical Languages, Houston, TX 77204. Offers world cultures and literatures (MA). *Degree requirements:* For master's, one foreign language, thesis optional. *Entrance requirements:* For master's, GRE General Test, minimum GPA of 3.0 in last 60 hours of course work. Additional exam requirements/recommendations for international students: Required—TOEFL (minimum score 500 paper-based). Electronic applications accepted.

University of Illinois at Chicago, Graduate College, College of Liberal Arts and Sciences, School of Literatures, Cultural Studies and Linguistics, Department of Hispanic and Italian Studies, Chicago, IL 60607-7128. Offers Hispanic linguistics (PhD). Part-time programs available. *Faculty:* 23 full-time (19 women), 10 part-time/adjunct (7 women). *Students:* 45 full-time (32 women), 15 part-time (9 women); includes 19 minority (18 Hispanic/Latino; 1 Two or more races, non-Hispanic/Latino), 24 international. Average age 29. 50 applicants, 50% accepted, 13 enrolled. In 2014, 10 master's, 2 doctorates awarded. Terminal master's awarded for partial completion of doctoral program. *Degree requirements:* For master's, one foreign language, departmental qualifying exam. *Entrance requirements:* For master's, GRE General Test, minimum GPA of 2.75, undergraduate major in Spanish. Additional exam requirements/

recommendations for international students: Required—TOEFL. *Application deadline:* For fall admission, 2/1 for domestic and international students. Applications are processed on a rolling basis. Application fee: $60. Electronic applications accepted. *Expenses:* Tuition, state resident: full-time $11,254; part-time $468 per credit hour. Tuition, nonresident: full-time $23,252; part-time $968 per credit hour. *Required fees:* $1217 per term. Part-time tuition and fees vary according to course load, degree level and program. *Financial support:* In 2014–15, 2 fellowships with full tuition reimbursements were awarded; research assistantships with full tuition reimbursements, teaching assistantships with full tuition reimbursements, Federal Work-Study, scholarships/grants, traineeships, tuition waivers (full), and unspecified assistantships also available. Financial award application deadline: 3/1; financial award applicants required to submit FAFSA. *Faculty research:* Linguistic competence of bilingual speakers as a window to understanding the human faculty of language, neurocognitive processing of language among different speakers and learners, how languages are used within their social contexts. *Unit head:* Prof. Luis Lopez, Professor/Head of the Department of Hispanic and Italian Studies, 312-413-2646, E-mail: luislope@uic.edu. *Application contact:* Prof. Margarita Saona, Associate Professor and Director of Graduate Studies, 312-996-5222, E-mail: saona@uic.edu.
Website: http://lcsl.uic.edu/hispanic-italian

University of Illinois at Urbana–Champaign, Graduate College, College of Liberal Arts and Sciences, School of Literatures, Cultures and Linguistics, Department of Spanish, Italian and Portuguese, Champaign, IL 61820. Offers Italian (MA, PhD); Portuguese (MA, PhD); Spanish (MA, PhD). *Students:* 49 (37 women). Application fee: $70 ($90 for international students). *Financial support:* Tuition waivers available. *Unit head:* Silvina Montrul, Head, 217-333-1780, Fax: 217-244-8430, E-mail: montrul@illinois.edu. *Application contact:* Lynn Stanke, Office Support Specialist, 217-333-6269, Fax: 217-244-3050, E-mail: stanke@illinois.edu.
Website: http://www.sip.illinois.edu/

The University of Iowa, Graduate College, College of Liberal Arts and Sciences, Department of Spanish and Portuguese, Iowa City, IA 52242-1316. Offers Spanish (MA, PhD); Spanish creative writing (MFA). *Degree requirements:* For master's, thesis optional, exam; for doctorate, comprehensive exam, thesis/dissertation. *Entrance requirements:* For master's and doctorate, GRE General Test, minimum GPA of 3.0. Additional exam requirements/recommendations for international students: Required—TOEFL (minimum score 600 paper-based; 100 iBT). Electronic applications accepted.

The University of Kansas, Graduate Studies, College of Liberal Arts and Sciences, Department of Spanish and Portuguese, Lawrence, KS 66045. Offers Spanish (MA, PhD). *Faculty:* 15 full-time, 6 part-time/adjunct. *Students:* 39 full-time (23 women); includes 6 minority (1 American Indian or Alaska Native, non-Hispanic/Latino; 5 Hispanic/Latino), 11 international. Average age 30. 23 applicants, 43% accepted, 8 enrolled. In 2014, 3 master's, 2 doctorates awarded. *Degree requirements:* For master's, 2 foreign languages, comprehensive exam; for doctorate, 3 foreign languages, comprehensive exam, thesis/dissertation. *Entrance requirements:* For master's, BA, BS; for doctorate, master's degree. Additional exam requirements/recommendations for international students: Required—TOEFL. *Application deadline:* For fall admission, 5/15 priority date for domestic students, 12/15 priority date for international students; for spring admission, 10/15 priority date for domestic students, 5/15 priority date for international students. Applications are processed on a rolling basis. Application fee: $55 ($65 for international students). Electronic applications accepted. *Financial support:* Fellowships with tuition reimbursements, research assistantships with tuition reimbursements, teaching assistantships with full and partial tuition reimbursements, and unspecified assistantships available. Financial award application deadline: 1/15. *Faculty research:* Spanish and Latin American cultural studies, Spanish literature, Latin American literature, Hispanic linguistics. *Unit head:* Dr. Stuart A. Day, Chair, 785-864-3851, E-mail: day@ku.edu. *Application contact:* Jill Marietta Mignacca, Office Manager, Graduate Coordinator, 785-864-0279, E-mail: jmig@ku.edu.
Website: http://spanport.ku.edu/

University of Lethbridge, School of Graduate Studies, Lethbridge, AB T1K 3M4, Canada. Offers addictions counseling (M Sc); agricultural biotechnology (M Sc); agricultural studies (M Sc, MA); anthropology (MA); archaeology (M Sc, MA); art (MA, MFA); biochemistry (M Sc); biological sciences (M Sc); biomolecular science (PhD); biosystems and biodiversity (PhD); Canadian studies (MA); chemistry (M Sc); computer science (M Sc); computer science and geographical information science (M Sc); counseling (MC); counseling psychology (M Ed); dramatic arts (MA); earth, space, and physical science (PhD); economics (MA); education (MA); educational leadership (M Ed); English (MA); environmental science (M Sc); evolution and behavior (PhD); exercise science (M Sc); French (MA); French/German (MA); French/Spanish (MA); general education (M Ed); geography (M Sc, MA); German (MA); health sciences (M Sc); individualized multidisciplinary (M Sc, MA); kinesiology (M Sc, MA); management (M Sc), including accounting, finance, general management, human resource management and labor relations, information systems, international management, marketing, policy and strategy; mathematics (M Sc); modern languages (MA); music (M Mus, MA); Native American studies (MA); neuroscience (M Sc, PhD); new media (MA, MFA); nursing (M Sc, MN); philosophy (MA); physics (M Sc); political science (MA); psychology (M Sc, MA); religious studies (MA); sociology (MA); theatre and dramatic arts (MFA); theoretical and computational science (PhD); urban and regional studies (MA); women and gender studies (MA). Part-time and evening/weekend programs available. *Faculty:* 358. *Students:* 445 full-time (243 women), 116 part-time (72 women). Average age 31. 351 applicants, 26% accepted, 87 enrolled. In 2014, 129 master's, 13 doctorates awarded. *Degree requirements:* For master's, thesis (for some programs); for doctorate, comprehensive exam, thesis/dissertation. *Entrance requirements:* For master's, GMAT (for M Sc in management), bachelor's degree in related field, minimum GPA of 3.0 during previous 20 graded semester courses, 2 years' teaching or related experience (M Ed); for doctorate, master's degree, minimum graduate GPA of 3.5. Additional exam requirements/recommendations for international students: Required—TOEFL. Application fee: $100 Canadian dollars. *Financial support:* Fellowships, research assistantships, teaching assistantships, scholarships/grants, health care benefits, and unspecified assistantships available. *Faculty research:* Movement and brain plasticity, gibberellin physiology, photosynthesis, carbon cycling, molecular properties of main-group ring components. *Application contact:* School of Graduate Studies, 403-329-5194, E-mail: sgsinquiries@uleth.ca.
Website: http://www.uleth.ca/graduatestudies/

University of Louisville, Graduate School, College of Arts and Sciences, Department of Classical and Modern Languages, Louisville, KY 40292-0001. Offers French (MA); Spanish (MA). Part-time and evening/weekend programs available. *Students:* 22 full-time (16 women), 13 part-time (9 women); includes 11 minority (3 Black or African American, non-Hispanic/Latino; 1 Asian, non-Hispanic/Latino; 6 Hispanic/Latino; 1 Two or more races, non-Hispanic/Latino), 5 international. Average age 30. 25 applicants, 84% accepted, 14 enrolled. In 2014, 14 master's awarded. *Degree requirements:* For master's, one foreign language, thesis optional. *Entrance requirements:* For master's, GRE General Test (recommended). Additional exam requirements/recommendations for international students: Required—TOEFL (minimum score 550 paper-based). *Application deadline:* For fall admission, 5/1 priority date for international students; for spring admission, 11/1 priority date for international students; for summer admission, 4/1 priority date for international students. Applications are processed on a rolling basis. Application fee: $60. Electronic applications accepted. *Expenses:* Tuition, state resident: full-time $11,326; part-time $630 per credit hour. Tuition, nonresident: full-time $23,568; part-time $1311 per credit hour. *Required fees:* $196. Tuition and fees vary according to program and reciprocity agreements. *Financial support:* In 2014–15, 8 teaching assistantships with full tuition reimbursements were awarded; fellowships, institutionally sponsored loans, scholarships/grants, health care benefits, and unspecified assistantships also available. Financial award applicants required to submit FAFSA. *Faculty research:* Hispanic cultural studies, sociolinguistics, translation, contemporary France, medieval literature. *Unit head:* Dr. Augustus A. Mastri, Chair, 502-852-0403, Fax: 502-852-8885, E-mail: mastri@louisville.edu. *Application contact:* Libby Leggett, Director, Graduate Admissions, 502-852-3101, Fax: 502-852-6536, E-mail: gradadm@louisville.edu.
Website: http://louisville.edu/modernlanguages/

The University of Manchester, School of Languages, Linguistics and Cultures, Manchester, United Kingdom. Offers Arab world studies (PhD); Chinese studies (M Phil, PhD); East Asian studies (M Phil, PhD); English language (PhD); French studies (M Phil, PhD); German studies (M Phil, PhD); interpreting studies (PhD); Italian studies (M Phil, PhD); Japanese studies (M Phil, PhD); Latin American cultural studies (M Phil, PhD); linguistics (M Phil, PhD); Middle Eastern studies (M Phil, PhD); Polish studies (M Phil, PhD); Portuguese studies (M Phil, PhD); Russian studies (M Phil, PhD); Spanish studies (M Phil, PhD); translation and intercultural studies (M Phil, PhD).

University of Maryland, College Park, Academic Affairs, College of Arts and Humanities, School of Languages, Literatures, and Cultures, Spanish Language and Literatures Program, College Park, MD 20742. Offers MA, PhD. *Degree requirements:* For master's, comprehensive exam, thesis optional, scholarly paper; for doctorate, 2 foreign languages, thesis/dissertation. *Entrance requirements:* For master's, minimum GPA of 3.0, interview, sample research paper, minimum of 12 credits in upper-level literature, 3 letters of recommendation; for doctorate, minimum GPA of 3.0, interview, sample research paper, minimum of 12 credits in upper-level literature. Additional exam requirements/recommendations for international students: Required—TOEFL. Electronic applications accepted.

University of Massachusetts Amherst, Graduate School, College of Humanities and Fine Arts, Department of Languages, Literatures, and Cultures, Program in Spanish and Portuguese Studies, Amherst, MA 01003. Offers Hispanic literatures, cultures and linguistics (MA, PhD); teaching Spanish (MAT). Part-time programs available. *Faculty:* 13 full-time (5 women). *Students:* 30 full-time (23 women), 17 part-time (10 women); includes 11 minority (1 Black or African American, non-Hispanic/Latino; 1 Asian, non-Hispanic/Latino; 9 Hispanic/Latino), 25 international. Average age 33. 55 applicants, 29% accepted, 11 enrolled. In 2014, 7 master's, 3 doctorates awarded. Terminal master's awarded for partial completion of doctoral program. *Degree requirements:* For master's, one foreign language, thesis or alternative; for doctorate, 2 foreign languages, comprehensive exam, thesis/dissertation. *Entrance requirements:* For master's and doctorate, GRE General Test, sample academic term paper. Additional exam requirements/recommendations for international students: Required—TOEFL (minimum score 550 paper-based; 80 iBT), IELTS (minimum score 6.5). *Application deadline:* For fall admission, 2/1 for domestic and international students. Applications are processed on a rolling basis. Application fee: $75. Electronic applications accepted. *Expenses:* Tuition, state resident: full-time $1980; part-time $110 per credit. Tuition, nonresident: full-time $14,644; part-time $414 per credit. *Required fees:* $11,417. One-time fee: $357. *Financial support:* Fellowships with full and partial tuition reimbursements, research assistantships with full and partial tuition reimbursements, teaching assistantships with full and partial tuition reimbursements, career-related internships or fieldwork, Federal Work-Study, scholarships/grants, traineeships, health care benefits, tuition waivers (full and partial), and unspecified assistantships available. Support available to part-time students. Financial award application deadline: 2/1; financial award applicants required to submit FAFSA. *Unit head:* Dr. Albert Lloret, Graduate Program Director, 413-545-0544, Fax: 413-545-3178. *Application contact:* Lindsay DeSantis, Supervisor of Admissions, 413-545-0722, Fax: 413-577-0010, E-mail: gradadm@grad.umass.edu.
Website: http://www.umass.edu/spanport/

University of Miami, Graduate School, College of Arts and Sciences, Department of Modern Languages and Literatures, Coral Gables, FL 33124. Offers romance studies (PhD), including French, Spanish. *Degree requirements:* For doctorate, 2 foreign languages, thesis/dissertation, area exam, qualifying exam. *Entrance requirements:* For doctorate, 1 writing sample in English and 1 writing sample in French or Spanish, minimum GPA of 3.0, oral interview, letters of recommendation. Additional exam requirements/recommendations for international students: Required—TOEFL (minimum score 550 paper-based; 59 iBT). Electronic applications accepted. *Faculty research:* Transatlantic studies, Caribbean studies, comparative literature, gender theory, cultural studies.

University of Miami, Graduate School, School of Communication, Coral Gables, FL 33124. Offers communication (PhD); communication studies (MA); film studies (MA, PhD); motion pictures (MFA), including production, producing, and screenwriting; print journalism (MA); public relations (MA); Spanish language journalism (MA); television broadcast journalism (MA). Part-time programs available. *Degree requirements:* For master's, comprehensive exam (for some programs), thesis (for some programs); for doctorate, comprehensive exam, thesis/dissertation. *Entrance requirements:* For master's, GRE General Test; for doctorate, GRE General Test, master's thesis or scholarly research. Additional exam requirements/recommendations for international students: Required—TOEFL (minimum score 600 paper-based; 100 iBT). Electronic applications accepted. *Faculty research:* Communication studies, mass communication, international/interpersonal communication, film studies, journalism.

University of Michigan, Horace H. Rackham School of Graduate Studies, College of Literature, Science, and the Arts, Department of Romance Languages and Literatures, Program in Spanish, Ann Arbor, MI 48109. Offers PhD. *Faculty:* 19 full-time (7 women). *Students:* 38 full-time (24 women); includes 24 minority (1 Asian, non-Hispanic/Latino; 23 Hispanic/Latino). Average age 27. 63 applicants, 21% accepted, 7 enrolled. In 2014, 5 doctorates awarded. *Degree requirements:* For doctorate, 2 foreign languages, thesis/dissertation, oral defense of dissertation, preliminary exams in essay format. *Entrance requirements:* Additional exam requirements/recommendations for international students: Required—TOEFL or Michigan English Language Assessment Battery. *Application deadline:* For fall admission, 12/18 for domestic and international students. Application fee: $65 ($75 for international students). Electronic applications accepted. *Financial support:* In 2014–15, 38 students received support. Fellowships with full tuition reimbursements available, teaching assistantships with full tuition reimbursements available, institutionally sponsored loans, scholarships/grants, health care benefits, and unspecified assistantships available. Financial award application deadline: 12/18. *Faculty research:* Comparative Romance studies, medieval and early modern studies, postcolonial and minority literatures, culture and materiality, reflection on the nature and function of scholarship. *Unit head:* Dr. Cristina Moreiras-Menor, Chair, 734-764-5344, Fax: 734-764-8163. *Application contact:* Katie Hayes, Graduate

Assistant, 734-764-8164, Fax: 734-764-8163, E-mail: rll-admissions@umich.edu.
Website: http://www.lsa.umich.edu/rll

University of Minnesota, Twin Cities Campus, Graduate School, College of Liberal Arts, Department of Spanish and Portuguese Studies, Minneapolis, MN 55455-0213. Offers Hispanic and Lusophone literatures, cultures and linguistics (PhD); Hispanic linguistics (MA); Hispanic literature (MA); Lusophone literature (MA). *Degree requirements:* For master's, 2 foreign languages, comprehensive exam, thesis or alternative; for doctorate, 2 foreign languages, comprehensive exam, thesis/dissertation. *Entrance requirements:* For master's and doctorate, GRE General Test, samples of written work, 3 letters of recommendation, voice sample, statement of purpose. Additional exam requirements/recommendations for international students: Required—TOEFL (minimum score 550 paper-based; 79 iBT). Electronic applications accepted. *Faculty research:* Sociohistorical approaches to literature and culture, feminist studies, literary theory, ideologies and literature, pragmatics and sociolinguistics.

University of Mississippi, Graduate School, College of Liberal Arts, Department of Modern Languages, University, MS 38677. Offers French (MA); German (MA); Spanish (MA). *Degree requirements:* For master's, thesis (for some programs). *Entrance requirements:* For master's, GRE General Test, minimum GPA of 3.0. Additional exam requirements/recommendations for international students: Required—TOEFL. Electronic applications accepted.

University of Missouri, Office of Research and Graduate Studies, College of Arts and Science, Department of Romance Languages and Literatures, Columbia, MO 65211. Offers French (MA, PhD); literature (MA); Spanish (MA, PhD); teaching (MA). *Faculty:* 25 full-time (12 women), 1 (woman) part-time/adjunct. *Students:* 28 full-time (19 women), 9 part-time (6 women); includes 9 minority (3 Black or African American, non-Hispanic/Latino; 4 Hispanic/Latino; 2 Two or more races, non-Hispanic/Latino), 15 international. Average age 36. 16 applicants, 69% accepted, 7 enrolled. In 2014, 3 master's, 1 doctorate awarded. Terminal master's awarded for partial completion of doctoral program. *Degree requirements:* For master's, one foreign language; for doctorate, 4 foreign languages, comprehensive exam, thesis/dissertation. *Entrance requirements:* For master's, GRE General Test, minimum GPA of 3.0 in field of major; bachelor's degree; for doctorate, GRE General Test, minimum GPA of 3.0 in field of major; master's degree. Additional exam requirements/recommendations for international students: Required—TOEFL (minimum score 500 paper-based; 61 iBT). *Application deadline:* For fall admission, 2/15 priority date for domestic students; for winter admission, 10/15 for domestic students. Applications are processed on a rolling basis. Application fee: $55 ($75 for international students). Electronic applications accepted. *Financial support:* Research assistantships, teaching assistantships with full tuition reimbursements, institutionally sponsored loans, health care benefits, and unspecified assistantships available. *Faculty research:* Afro-Romance studies. *Unit head:* Dr. Flore Zephir, Department Chair, 573-882-5048, E-mail: zephirf@missouri.edu. *Application contact:* Mary Harris, Administrative Assistant, 573-882-5039, E-mail: harrisma@missouri.edu.
Website: http://romancelanguages.missouri.edu/grad.shtml

University of Missouri–Kansas City, College of Arts and Sciences, Department of Foreign Languages and Literatures, Kansas City, MO 64110-2499. Offers romance languages and literatures (MA), including French, Spanish. Part-time programs available. *Faculty:* 15 full-time (8 women), 15 part-time/adjunct (12 women). *Students:* 3 full-time (2 women), 19 part-time (15 women); includes 11 minority (1 Black or African American, non-Hispanic/Latino; 10 Hispanic/Latino). Average age 32. 17 applicants, 59% accepted, 9 enrolled. In 2014, 8 master's awarded. *Degree requirements:* For master's, 2 foreign languages. *Entrance requirements:* For master's, GRE General Test, minimum GPA of 2.75, 2 letters of recommendation. Additional exam requirements/recommendations for international students: Required—TOEFL (minimum score 550 paper-based; 80 iBT). *Application deadline:* For fall admission, 4/1 priority date for domestic and international students; for spring admission, 11/1 priority date for domestic and international students. Applications are processed on a rolling basis. Application fee: $45 ($50 for international students). Electronic applications accepted. *Financial support:* In 2014–15, 1 teaching assistantship (averaging $12,600 per year) was awarded; Federal Work-Study, institutionally sponsored loans, and tuition waivers (full and partial) also available. Support available to part-time students. Financial award application deadline: 3/1; financial award applicants required to submit FAFSA. *Faculty research:* Literary analyses; psychology and literature; narrative techniques, poetic structure, and style; literature, politics, and society (especially in Latin America). *Unit head:* Dr. K. Scott Baker, Chair, 816-235-2823, Fax: 816-235-1312, E-mail: bakerks@umkc.edu. *Application contact:* 816-235-1311, Fax: 816-235-1312, E-mail: admit@umkc.edu.
Website: http://cas.umkc.edu/foreign

The University of Montana, Graduate School, College of Humanities and Sciences, Department of Modern and Classical Languages and Literatures, Missoula, MT 59812-0002. Offers French (MA); German (MA); Spanish (MA). *Degree requirements:* For master's, one foreign language. *Entrance requirements:* For master's, GRE General Test. Additional exam requirements/recommendations for international students: Required—TOEFL.

University of Nebraska–Lincoln, Graduate College, College of Arts and Sciences, Department of Modern Languages and Literatures, Lincoln, NE 68588. Offers French (MA, PhD); German (MA, PhD); Spanish (MA, PhD). *Degree requirements:* For master's, thesis optional; for doctorate, comprehensive exam, thesis/dissertation. *Entrance requirements:* For master's and doctorate, writing sample in target language. Additional exam requirements/recommendations for international students: Required—TOEFL (minimum score 550 paper-based). Electronic applications accepted. *Faculty research:* French, German, and Spanish language, literature, and culture.

University of Nevada, Reno, Graduate School, College of Liberal Arts, Department of Foreign Languages and Literatures, Reno, NV 89557. Offers French (MA); German (MA); Spanish (MA). *Degree requirements:* For master's, one foreign language, thesis optional. *Entrance requirements:* For master's, GRE General Test, minimum GPA of 2.75. Additional exam requirements/recommendations for international students: Required—TOEFL (minimum score 500 paper-based; 61 iBT), IELTS (minimum score 6). *Faculty research:* Thirteenth century mysticism, contemporary Spanish and Latin American poetry and theater, French interrelation between narration and photography, exile literature and Holocaust.

University of New Hampshire, Graduate School, College of Liberal Arts, Program in Spanish, Durham, NH 03824. Offers MA. *Faculty:* 8 full-time (4 women). *Students:* 3 full-time (2 women), 4 part-time (3 women); includes 1 minority (Two or more races, non-Hispanic/Latino), 1 international. Average age 31. 10 applicants, 90% accepted, 3 enrolled. In 2014, 6 master's awarded. *Degree requirements:* For master's, one foreign language, thesis or alternative. *Entrance requirements:* Additional exam requirements/recommendations for international students: Required—TOEFL (minimum score 550 paper-based; 80 iBT). *Application deadline:* For fall admission, 6/1 priority date for domestic students, 4/1 for international students; for spring admission, 12/1 priority date for domestic students. Applications are processed on a rolling basis. Application fee: $65. Electronic applications accepted. *Expenses:* Tuition, state resident: full-time $13,500; part-time $750 per credit hour. Tuition, nonresident: full-time $26,460; part-time $1110 per credit hour. *Required fees:* $1788; $447 per semester. *Financial support:* In 2014–15, 3 students received support, including 3 teaching assistantships; fellowships, research assistantships, career-related internships or fieldwork, Federal Work-Study, scholarships/grants, and tuition waivers (full and partial) also available. Support available to part-time students. Financial award application deadline: 2/15. *Unit head:* Lina Lee, Chairperson, 603-862-3120. *Application contact:* Avary Thorne, Administrative Assistant, 603-862-4005, E-mail: spanish.master@unh.edu.
Website: http://cola.unh.edu/llc/program/spanish-ma

University of New Mexico, Graduate School, College of Arts and Sciences, Program in Spanish and Portuguese, Albuquerque, NM 87131. Offers Portuguese (MA); Spanish (MA); Spanish and Portuguese (PhD). Part-time programs available. *Faculty:* 12 full-time (7 women), 1 part-time/adjunct (0 women). *Students:* 48 full-time (31 women), 10 part-time (7 women); includes 31 minority (all Hispanic/Latino), 10 international. Average age 33. 49 applicants, 59% accepted, 18 enrolled. In 2014, 13 master's, 3 doctorates awarded. *Degree requirements:* For master's, one foreign language, comprehensive exam, thesis optional; for doctorate, one foreign language, comprehensive exam, thesis/dissertation. *Entrance requirements:* For master's, BA in Spanish or Portuguese, 3 letters of recommendation, letter of intent; for doctorate, GRE, 3 letters of recommendation, letter of intent, sample research paper. Additional exam requirements/recommendations for international students: Required—TOEFL (minimum score 550 paper-based). *Application deadline:* For fall admission, 1/15 priority date for domestic students; for spring admission, 11/15 for domestic students. Applications are processed on a rolling basis. Application fee: $50. Electronic applications accepted. *Financial support:* In 2014–15, 60 students received support, including 2 research assistantships (averaging $7,500 per year), 58 teaching assistantships with full and partial tuition reimbursements available (averaging $14,965 per year); Federal Work-Study, institutionally sponsored loans, scholarships/grants, health care benefits, and unspecified assistantships also available. Support available to part-time students. Financial award application deadline: 3/1; financial award applicants required to submit FAFSA. *Faculty research:* Languages and literatures from the Iberian Peninsula, Latin America and the American Southwest. *Unit head:* Dr. Anthony Cardenas, Chair, 505-277-5907, Fax: 505-277-3885, E-mail: ajcard@unm.edu. *Application contact:* Martha Hurd, Graduate Advisor, 505-277-2974, E-mail: marthah@unm.edu.
Website: http://spanport.unm.edu

The University of North Carolina at Chapel Hill, Graduate School, College of Arts and Sciences, Department of Romance Languages and Literatures, Chapel Hill, NC 27599. Offers French (MA, PhD); Italian (MA, PhD); Portuguese (MA, PhD); Romance languages (MA, PhD); Romance philology (MA, PhD); Spanish (MA, PhD). *Degree requirements:* For master's, one foreign language, comprehensive exam, thesis; for doctorate, 2 foreign languages, comprehensive exam, thesis/dissertation. *Entrance requirements:* For master's and doctorate, GRE General Test, minimum GPA of 3.0. Additional exam requirements/recommendations for international students: Required—TOEFL (minimum score 550 paper-based). Electronic applications accepted.

The University of North Carolina at Charlotte, College of Liberal Arts and Sciences, Department of Languages and Culture Studies, Charlotte, NC 28223-0001. Offers Spanish (MA); translating (Graduate Certificate). Part-time and evening/weekend programs available. *Faculty:* 19 full-time (10 women). *Students:* 14 full-time (13 women), 8 part-time (7 women); includes 10 minority (5 Black or African American, non-Hispanic/Latino; 4 Hispanic/Latino; 1 Two or more races, non-Hispanic/Latino), 1 international. Average age 30. 9 applicants, 89% accepted, 7 enrolled. In 2014, 7 master's, 5 other advanced degrees awarded. *Degree requirements:* For master's, thesis optional. *Entrance requirements:* For master's, GRE, 3 letters of reference, minimum GPA of 2.75. Additional exam requirements/recommendations for international students: Required—TOEFL (minimum score 557 paper-based; 83 iBT). *Application deadline:* For fall admission, 5/1 priority date for domestic students, 5/1 for international students; for spring admission, 10/1 priority date for domestic students, 10/1 for international students. Applications are processed on a rolling basis. Application fee: $75. Electronic applications accepted. *Expenses:* Tuition, state resident: full-time $4008. Tuition, nonresident: full-time $16,295. *Required fees:* $2755. Tuition and fees vary according to course load and program. *Financial support:* In 2014–15, 10 students received support, including 4 research assistantships (averaging $8,000 per year), 6 teaching assistantships (averaging $5,646 per year); career-related internships or fieldwork, institutionally sponsored loans, scholarships/grants, and unspecified assistantships also available. Support available to part-time students. Financial award application deadline: 4/1; financial award applicants required to submit FAFSA. *Faculty research:* Latin American literature, Spanish for business, Central American literature, Mexican literature, literature of the Southern Cone, language for specific purposes, Spanish for specific purposes. *Total annual research expenditures:* $187,912. *Unit head:* Dr. Sheri Spaine Long, Chair, 704-687-8754, Fax: 704-687-1653, E-mail: sheri.long@uncc.edu. *Application contact:* Kathy B. Giddings, Director of Graduate Admissions, 704-687-5503, Fax: 704-687-1668, E-mail: gradadm@uncc.edu.
Website: https://languages.uncc.edu/

The University of North Carolina at Greensboro, Graduate School, College of Arts and Sciences, Department of Languages, Literatures, and Cultures, Program in Spanish, Greensboro, NC 27412-5001. Offers advanced Spanish language and Hispanic cultural studies (Certificate); Spanish (MA). *Degree requirements:* For master's, one foreign language, comprehensive exam, thesis or alternative. *Entrance requirements:* For master's, GRE General Test, 3-5 minute tape demonstrating foreign language proficiency, composition in Spanish, sample paper in English. Additional exam requirements/recommendations for international students: Required—TOEFL. Electronic applications accepted.

The University of North Carolina Wilmington, College of Arts and Sciences, Department of Foreign Languages and Literatures, Wilmington, NC 28403-3297. Offers Hispanic studies (Graduate Certificate); Spanish (MA). Part-time programs available. Postbaccalaureate distance learning degree programs offered. *Faculty:* 14 full-time (7 women). *Students:* 3 full-time (all women), 11 part-time (8 women); includes 2 minority (both Hispanic/Latino). 8 applicants, 88% accepted, 7 enrolled. In 2014, 13 master's awarded. *Degree requirements:* For master's, one foreign language, comprehensive exam, thesis or alternative. *Entrance requirements:* For master's, GRE. Additional exam requirements/recommendations for international students: Required—TOEFL (minimum score 79 iBT), IELTS. *Application deadline:* For fall admission, 3/1 for domestic students; for spring admission, 11/1 for domestic students. Application fee: $60. *Expenses:* Tuition, state resident: full-time $3240. Tuition, nonresident: full-time $9208. *Required fees:* $1967. *Financial support:* Applicants required to submit FAFSA. *Unit head:* Dr. Michelle Scatton-Tessier, Chair, 910-962-4095, Fax: 910-962-7712, E-mail: scattonm@uncw.edu. *Application contact:* Dr. Brian Chandler, Graduate Coordinator, 910-962-2299, Fax: 910-962-7712, E-mail: chandlerb@uncw.edu.
Website: http://www.uncw.edu/fll/spanish/spngraduate.html

University of Northern Colorado, Graduate School, College of Humanities and Social Sciences, School of Modern Languages and Cultural Studies, Program in Foreign Languages, Greeley, CO 80639. Offers Spanish/teaching (MA). Part-time programs available. *Degree requirements:* For master's, comprehensive exam, thesis or

alternative. *Entrance requirements:* For master's, minimum undergraduate GPA of 3.0, BA in Spanish, 1 year of secondary teaching. Electronic applications accepted.

University of Northern Iowa, Graduate College, College of Humanities, Arts and Sciences, Department of Languages and Literatures, MA Program in Spanish, Cedar Falls, IA 50614. Offers Spanish (MA); Spanish teaching (MA). Part-time and evening/weekend programs available. *Students:* 4 full-time (3 women), 2 part-time (1 woman); includes 1 minority (Hispanic/Latino), 1 international. 7 applicants, 57% accepted, 3 enrolled. In 2014, 9 master's awarded. *Degree requirements:* For master's, one foreign language, comprehensive exam, thesis or alternative. *Entrance requirements:* For master's, minimum GPA of 3.0, valid teaching license, documentation of successful teaching experience. Additional exam requirements/recommendations for international students: Required—TOEFL (minimum score 600 paper-based; 100 iBT). *Application deadline:* For fall admission, 8/1 priority date for domestic students. Applications are processed on a rolling basis. Application fee: $50 ($70 for international students). Electronic applications accepted. *Expenses:* Tuition, state resident: full-time $7912; part-time $880 per credit. Tuition, nonresident: full-time $17,906; part-time $880 per credit. *Required fees:* $1101; $325.50 per credit. $465.63 per semester. Tuition and fees vary according to course load and program. *Financial support:* Career-related internships or fieldwork, Federal Work-Study, and tuition waivers (full and partial) available. Support available to part-time students. Financial award application deadline: 2/1. *Unit head:* Dr. Gabriela Olivares-Cuhat, Coordinator, 319-273-6102, Fax: 319-273-5807, E-mail: gabriela.olivares@uni.edu. *Application contact:* Laurie S. Russell, Record Analyst, 319-273-2623, Fax: 319-273-2885, E-mail: laurie.russell@uni.edu.
Website: http://www.uni.edu/langlit/

University of Northern Iowa, Graduate College, College of Humanities, Arts and Sciences, Department of Languages and Literatures, MA Program in TESOL/Spanish, Cedar Falls, IA 50614. Offers MA. *Students:* 6 full-time (5 women); includes 1 minority (Hispanic/Latino), 3 international. 3 applicants, 67% accepted, 2 enrolled. In 2014, 1 master's awarded. Application fee: $50 ($70 for international students). *Expenses:* Tuition, state resident: full-time $7912; part-time $880 per credit. Tuition, nonresident: full-time $17,906; part-time $880 per credit. *Required fees:* $1101; $325.50 per credit. $465.63 per semester. Tuition and fees vary according to course load and program. *Unit head:* Dr. Joyce Milambiling, Coordinator, 319-273-6099, Fax: 319-273-5807, E-mail: joyce.milambiling@uni.edu. *Application contact:* Laurie S. Russell, Record Analyst, 319-273-2623, Fax: 319-273-2885, E-mail: laurie.russell@uni.edu.

University of North Texas, Robert B. Toulouse School of Graduate Studies, Denton, TX 76203-5459. Offers accounting (MS); applied anthropology (MA, MS); applied behavior analysis (Certificate); applied geography (MA); applied technology and performance improvement (M Ed, MS); art education (MA); art history (MA); art museum education (Certificate); arts leadership (Certificate); audiology (Au D); behavior analysis (MS); behavioral science (PhD); biochemistry and molecular biology (MS); biology (MA, MS); biomedical engineering (MS); business analysis (MS); chemistry (MS); clinical health psychology (PhD); communication studies (MA, MS); computer engineering (MS); computer science (MS); counseling (M Ed, MS), including clinical mental health counseling (MS), college and university counseling, elementary school counseling, secondary school counseling; creative writing (MA); criminal justice (MS); curriculum and instruction (M Ed); decision sciences (MBA); design (MA, MFA), including fashion design (MFA), innovation studies, interior design (MFA); early childhood studies (MS); economics (MS); educational leadership (M Ed, Ed D); educational psychology (MS, PhD), including family studies (MS), gifted and talented (MS), human development (MS), learning and cognition (MS), research, measurement and evaluation (MS); electrical engineering (MS); emergency management (MPA); engineering technology (MS); English (MA); English as a second language (MA); environmental science (MS); finance (MBA, MS); financial management (MPA); French (MA); health services management (MBA); higher education (M Ed, Ed D); history (MA, MS); hospitality management (MS); human resources management (MPA); information science (MS); information systems (PhD); information technologies (MBA); interdisciplinary studies (MA, MS); international studies (MA); international sustainable tourism (MS); jazz studies (MM); journalism (MA, MJ, Graduate Certificate), including interactive and virtual digital communication (Graduate Certificate), narrative journalism (Graduate Certificate), public relations (Graduate Certificate); kinesiology (MS); linguistics (MA); local government management (MPA); logistics (PhD); logistics and supply chain management (MBA); long-term care, senior housing, and aging services (MA); management (PhD); marketing (MBA); mathematics (MA, MS); mechanical and energy engineering (MS, PhD); music (MA), including ethnomusicology, music theory, musicology, performance; music composition (PhD); music education (MM Ed, PhD); nonprofit management (MPA); operations and supply chain management (MBA); performance (MM, DMA); philosophy (MA); political science (MA); professional and technical communication (MA); radio, television and film (MA, MFA); rehabilitation counseling (Certificate); sociology (MA); Spanish (MA); special education (M Ed); speech-language pathology (MA); strategic management (MBA); studio art (MFA); teaching (M Ed); MBA/MS. Part-time and evening/weekend programs available. Postbaccalaureate distance learning degree programs offered. *Faculty:* 651 full-time (215 women), 233 part-time/adjunct (139 women). *Students:* 3,040 full-time (1,598 women), 3,401 part-time (2,097 women); includes 1,740 minority (533 Black or African American, non-Hispanic/Latino; 15 American Indian or Alaska Native, non-Hispanic/Latino; 286 Asian, non-Hispanic/Latino; 746 Hispanic/Latino; 3 Native Hawaiian or other Pacific Islander, non-Hispanic/Latino; 157 Two or more races, non-Hispanic/Latino), 1,145 international. Terminal master's awarded for partial completion of doctoral program. *Degree requirements:* For master's, variable foreign language requirement, comprehensive exam (for some programs), thesis (for some programs); for doctorate, variable foreign language requirement, comprehensive exam (for some programs), thesis/dissertation; for other advanced degree, variable foreign language requirement, comprehensive exam (for some programs). *Entrance requirements:* For master's and doctorate, GRE, GMAT. Additional exam requirements/recommendations for international students: Required—TOEFL (minimum score 550 paper-based; 79 iBT). *Application deadline:* For fall admission, 7/15 for domestic students, 3/15 for international students; for spring admission, 11/15 for domestic students, 9/15 for international students; for summer admission, 5/1 for domestic students. Applications are processed on a rolling basis. Application fee: $60. Electronic applications accepted. *Expenses:* Tuition, state resident: full-time $5450; part-time $3633 per year. Tuition, nonresident: full-time $11,966; part-time $7977 per year. *Required fees:* $1301; $398 per credit hour. $685 per semester. Tuition and fees vary according to program and reciprocity agreements. *Financial support:* Fellowships with partial tuition reimbursements, research assistantships with partial tuition reimbursements, teaching assistantships, career-related internships or fieldwork, Federal Work-Study, institutionally sponsored loans, scholarships/grants, health care benefits, and library assistantships available. Support available to part-time students. Financial award applicants required to submit FAFSA. *Unit head:* Mark Wardell, Dean, 940-565-2383, E-mail: mark.wardell@unt.edu. *Application contact:* Toulouse School of Graduate Studies, 940-565-2383, Fax: 940-565-2141, E-mail: gradsch@unt.edu.
Website: http://tsgs.unt.edu/

University of Notre Dame, Graduate School, College of Arts and Letters, Division of Humanities, Department of Romance Languages and Literatures, Notre Dame, IN 46556. Offers French and Francophone studies (MA); Iberian and Latin American studies (MA); Italian studies (MA); Romance literatures (MA). *Degree requirements:* For master's, 2 foreign languages, comprehensive exam, thesis optional. *Entrance requirements:* For master's, GRE General Test, BA in target language. Additional exam requirements/recommendations for international students: Required—TOEFL (minimum score 600 paper-based; 80 iBT). Electronic applications accepted. *Faculty research:* Literature of discovery and exploration, modern literature, literary criticism, medieval literature, feminist critical theory.

University of Oklahoma, College of Arts and Sciences, Department of Modern Languages, Program in Spanish, Norman, OK 73019. Offers MA, PhD, MBA/MA. Part-time programs available. *Students:* 9 full-time (5 women), 14 part-time (12 women); includes 6 minority (1 American Indian or Alaska Native, non-Hispanic/Latino; 1 Asian, non-Hispanic/Latino; 4 Hispanic/Latino), 8 international. Average age 36. 14 applicants, 64% accepted, 4 enrolled. In 2014, 3 master's awarded. Terminal master's awarded for partial completion of doctoral program. *Degree requirements:* For master's, 2 foreign languages, comprehensive exam, thesis optional; for doctorate, 2 foreign languages, comprehensive exam, thesis/dissertation. *Entrance requirements:* For master's, BA with at least 6 hours of Spanish literature; for doctorate, MA in any Spanish language-related literatures. Additional exam requirements/recommendations for international students: Required—TOEFL (minimum score 79 iBT). *Application deadline:* For fall admission, 2/1 for domestic and international students; for spring admission, 10/1 for domestic and international students. Application fee: $50 ($100 for international students). Electronic applications accepted. *Expenses:* Tuition, state resident: full-time $4394; part-time $183.10 per credit hour. Tuition, nonresident: full-time $16,970; part-time $707.10 per credit hour. *Required fees:* $2892; $109.95 per credit hour. $126.50 per semester. *Financial support:* In 2014–15, 22 students received support. Federal Work-Study, scholarships/grants, and unspecified assistantships available. Support available to part-time students. Financial award application deadline: 6/1; financial award applicants required to submit FAFSA. *Faculty research:* Twentieth- and twenty-first century Latin American literature, Colonial literature, nineteenth-century literature, Peninsular Golden Age literature, medieval literature, modern Peninsular literature. *Unit head:* Jose Juan Colin, Associate Professor, 405-325-1409, E-mail: josejuan@ou.edu. *Application contact:* Pamela Genova, Graduate Liaison, 405-325-6181, Fax: 405-325-0103, E-mail: genova@ou.edu.
Website: http://mlll.publishpath.com/spanish-ma

University of Oregon, Graduate School, College of Arts and Sciences, Department of Romance Languages, Program in Spanish, Eugene, OR 97403. Offers MA. Part-time programs available. *Degree requirements:* For master's, one foreign language. *Entrance requirements:* For master's, GRE General Test, minimum GPA of 3.0. Additional exam requirements/recommendations for international students: Required—TOEFL.

University of Ottawa, Faculty of Graduate and Postdoctoral Studies, Faculty of Arts, Department of Modern Languages and Literatures, Ottawa, ON K1N 6N5, Canada. Offers Spanish (MA, PhD). Part-time and evening/weekend programs available. *Degree requirements:* For master's, one foreign language, thesis or alternative; for doctorate, one foreign language, comprehensive exam, thesis/dissertation. *Entrance requirements:* For master's, BA with honors in Spanish, minimum B average; for doctorate, MA in Spanish or equivalent, minimum B average. Electronic applications accepted. *Faculty research:* Spanish American literature, Mexican literature and film studies, Spanish golden age literature, twentieth-century Spanish literature, Hispanic linguistics with special emphasis on linguistic theory.

University of Pennsylvania, School of Arts and Sciences, Graduate Group in Romance Languages, Philadelphia, PA 19104. Offers French (AM, PhD); Italian (AM, PhD); Spanish (AM, PhD). *Faculty:* 44 full-time (16 women), 6 part-time/adjunct (2 women). *Students:* 61 full-time (29 women), 3 part-time (1 woman); includes 8 minority (all Hispanic/Latino), 34 international. 92 applicants, 23% accepted, 10 enrolled. In 2014, 11 master's, 9 doctorates awarded. Terminal master's awarded for partial completion of doctoral program. *Degree requirements:* For master's, one foreign language, thesis or alternative; for doctorate, 2 foreign languages, thesis/dissertation. *Entrance requirements:* For master's and doctorate, GRE General Test. Additional exam requirements/recommendations for international students: Required—TOEFL. *Application deadline:* For fall admission, 12/1 priority date for domestic students. Application fee: $70. Electronic applications accepted. *Financial support:* In 2014–15, 23 fellowships, 2 research assistantships, 39 teaching assistantships were awarded; institutionally sponsored loans, scholarships/grants, traineeships, health care benefits, and unspecified assistantships also available. Financial award application deadline: 12/15. *Faculty research:* Literary theory and criticism, cultural studies, history of Romance literatures, gender studies. *Unit head:* Dr. Ralph M. Rosen, Associate Dean for Graduate Studies, 215-898-7156, Fax: 215-573-8068, E-mail: grad-dean@sas.upenn.edu. *Application contact:* Arts and Sciences Graduate Admissions, 215-573-5816, Fax: 215-573-8068, E-mail: gdasadmis@sas.upenn.edu.
Website: http://www.sas.upenn.edu/graduate-division

University of Pittsburgh, Dietrich School of Arts and Sciences, Program in Hispanic Linguistics, Pittsburgh, PA 15260. Offers MA, PhD. Part-time programs available. *Faculty:* 6 full-time (2 women). *Students:* 5 full-time (4 women), 2 part-time (both women); includes 1 minority (Hispanic/Latino), 4 international. Average age 26. 10 applicants, 20% accepted, 2 enrolled. In 2014, 2 master's, 1 doctorate awarded. Terminal master's awarded for partial completion of doctoral program. *Degree requirements:* For master's, one foreign language, thesis optional; for doctorate, 2 foreign languages, comprehensive exam, thesis/dissertation. *Entrance requirements:* For master's, GRE General Test; for doctorate, GRE General Test, MA in linguistics. Additional exam requirements/recommendations for international students: Required—TOEFL (minimum score 600 paper-based; 100 iBT). *Application deadline:* For fall admission, 12/15 for domestic and international students. Applications are processed on a rolling basis. Application fee: $50. Electronic applications accepted. *Expenses:* Tuition, state resident: full-time $20,742; part-time $838 per credit. Tuition, nonresident: full-time $33,960; part-time $1389 per credit. *Required fees:* $800; $205 per term. Tuition and fees vary according to program. *Financial support:* In 2014–15, 6 students received support, including 1 fellowship (averaging $21,261 per year), 4 teaching assistantships (averaging $17,800 per year); scholarships/grants, health care benefits, and unspecified assistantships also available. Financial award application deadline: 12/15. *Faculty research:* Hispanic linguistics. *Unit head:* Dr. Shelome Gooden, Chair, 412-624-5922, Fax: 412-624-5520, E-mail: sgooden@pitt.edu. *Application contact:* Connie Anne Markiw, Graduate Student Services Administrator, 412-624-6568, Fax: 412-624-6338, E-mail: cam177@pitt.edu.
Website: http://www.linguistics.pitt.edu

University of Rhode Island, Graduate School, College of Arts and Sciences, Department of Modern and Classical Languages and Literatures, Kingston, RI 02881. Offers Spanish (MA). Part-time programs available. *Faculty:* 27 full-time (15 women), 1 (woman) part-time/adjunct. *Students:* 3 full-time (all women), 8 part-time (6 women); includes 7 minority (all Hispanic/Latino), 1 international. In 2014, 3 master's awarded. *Degree requirements:* For master's, one foreign language, comprehensive exam, thesis optional. *Entrance requirements:* For master's, 2 letters of recommendation. Additional exam requirements/recommendations for international students: Required—TOEFL (minimum score 550 paper-based). *Application deadline:* For fall admission, 7/15 for

domestic students, 2/1 for international students; for spring admission, 11/15 for domestic students, 7/15 for international students. Application fee: $65. Electronic applications accepted. *Expenses:* Tuition, state resident: full-time $11,532; part-time $641 per credit. Tuition, nonresident: full-time $23,606; part-time $1311 per credit. *Required fees:* $1442; $39 per credit. $35 per semester. One-time fee: $155. *Financial support:* In 2014–15, 3 teaching assistantships with full and partial tuition reimbursements (averaging $13,203 per year) were awarded. Financial award application deadline: 2/1; financial award applicants required to submit FAFSA. *Total annual research expenditures:* $399,122. *Unit head:* Dr. Norbert Hedderich, Department Chair, 401-874-4710, Fax: 401-874-4694, E-mail: hedderich@uri.edu. *Application contact:* Graduate Admission, 401-874-2872, E-mail: gradadm@etal.uri.edu. Website: http://web.uri.edu/languages/

University of South Africa, College of Human Sciences, Pretoria, South Africa. Offers adult education (M Ed); African languages (MA, PhD); African politics (MA, PhD); Afrikaans (MA, PhD); ancient history (MA, PhD); ancient Near Eastern studies (MA, PhD); anthropology (MA, PhD); applied linguistics (MA); Arabic (MA, PhD); archaeology (MA); art history (MA); Biblical archaeology (MA); Biblical studies (M Th, D Th, PhD); Christian spirituality (M Th, D Th); church history (M Th, D Th); classical studies (MA, PhD); clinical psychology (MA); communication (MA, PhD); comparative education (M Ed, Ed D); consulting psychology (D Admin, D Com, PhD); curriculum studies (M Ed, Ed D); development studies (M Admin, MA, D Admin, PhD); didactics (M Ed, Ed D); education (M Tech); education management (M Ed, Ed D); educational psychology (M Ed); English (MA); environmental education (M Ed); French (MA, PhD); German (MA, PhD); Greek (MA); guidance and counseling (M Ed); health studies (MA, PhD), including health sciences education (MA), health services management (MA), medical and surgical nursing science (critical care general) (MA), midwifery and neonatal nursing science (MA), trauma and emergency care (MA); history (MA, PhD); history of education (Ed D); inclusive education (M Ed, Ed D); information and communications technology policy and regulation (MA); information science (MA, MIS, PhD); international politics (MA, PhD); Islamic studies (MA, PhD); Italian (MA, PhD); Judaica (MA, PhD); linguistics (MA, PhD); mathematical education (M Ed); mathematics education (MA); missiology (M Th, D Th); modern Hebrew (MA, PhD); musicology (MA, MMus, D Mus, PhD); natural science education (M Ed); New Testament (M Th, D Th); Old Testament (D Th); pastoral therapy (M Th, D Th); philosophy (MA); philosophy of education (M Ed, Ed D); politics (MA, PhD); Portuguese (MA, PhD); practical theology (M Th, D Th); psychology (MA, MS, PhD); psychology of education (M Ed, Ed D); public health (MA); religious studies (MA, D Th, PhD); Romance languages (MA); Russian (MA, PhD); Semitic languages (MA, PhD); social behavior studies in HIV/AIDS (MA); social science (mental health) (MA); social science in development studies (MA); social science in psychology (MA); social science in social work (MA); social science in sociology (MA); social work (MSW, DSW, PhD); socio-education (M Ed, Ed D); sociolinguistics (MA); sociology (MA, PhD); Spanish (MA, PhD); systematic theology (M Th, D Th); TESOL (teaching English to speakers of other languages) (MA); theological ethics (M Th, D Th); theory of literature (MA, PhD); urban ministries (D Th); urban ministry (M Th).

University of South Carolina, The Graduate School, College of Arts and Sciences, Department of Languages, Literatures, and Cultures, Columbia, SC 29208. Offers comparative literature (MA, PhD); foreign languages (MAT), including French, German, Spanish; French (MA); German (MA); Spanish (MA). MAT offered in cooperation with the College of Education. Part-time programs available. *Degree requirements:* For master's, one foreign language, comprehensive exam, thesis optional; for doctorate, 2 foreign languages, comprehensive exam, thesis/dissertation. *Entrance requirements:* For master's and doctorate, GRE General Test, writing sample. Additional exam requirements/recommendations for international students: Required—TOEFL (minimum score 75 iBT). Electronic applications accepted. *Faculty research:* Modern literature, linguistics, literature and culture, medieval literature, literary theory.

University of Southern California, Graduate School, Dana and David Dornsife College of Letters, Arts and Sciences, Comparative Studies in Literature and Culture Doctoral Program, Los Angeles, CA 90089. Offers comparative literature (PhD); comparative media and culture (PhD); Spanish and Latin American studies (PhD). *Degree requirements:* For doctorate, 2 foreign languages, comprehensive exam, thesis/dissertation. *Entrance requirements:* For doctorate, GRE, competence in language other than English (highly recommended). Additional exam requirements/recommendations for international students: Required—TOEFL. Electronic applications accepted. *Faculty research:* Literary theory, Japanese film and contemporary fiction, Francophone literature and cinema, Latin American and Caribbean literature, Spanish literature and film, nineteenth and twentieth century British and American literature.

University of South Florida, College of Arts and Sciences, Department of World Languages, Tampa, FL 33620-9951. Offers applied linguistics: English as a second language (MA); French (MA); Spanish (MA). Part-time and evening/weekend programs available. *Faculty:* 21 full-time (14 women). *Students:* 44 full-time (29 women), 16 part-time (11 women); includes 23 minority (3 Black or African American, non-Hispanic/Latino; 1 Asian, non-Hispanic/Latino; 19 Hispanic/Latino), 8 international. Average age 35. 40 applicants, 60% accepted, 18 enrolled. In 2014, 18 master's awarded. *Degree requirements:* For master's, one foreign language, comprehensive exam, thesis optional. *Entrance requirements:* For master's, GRE General Test (minimum preferred scores of 41st percentile verbal and 4 in analytic writing, except for French program), minimum undergraduate GPA of 3.0; two-page statement of purpose (written in Spanish for Spanish program); oral interview (for Spanish and French programs); writing sample (for French program); 2-3 letters of recommendation. Additional exam requirements/recommendations for international students: Required—TOEFL (minimum score 600 paper-based; 80 iBT) or IELTS (minimum score 6.5) for MA; TOEFL (minimum score 550 paper-based; 80 iBT) or IELTS (minimum score 6.5) for PhD. *Application deadline:* For fall admission, 2/15 for domestic students, 1/2 for international students; for spring admission, 10/15 for domestic students, 6/1 for international students. Application fee: $30. Electronic applications accepted. *Financial support:* In 2014–15, 43 students received support, including 43 teaching assistantships with full and partial tuition reimbursements available (averaging $10,152 per year); tuition waivers (partial) and unspecified assistantships also available. Financial award application deadline: 6/30. *Faculty research:* Second language acquisition, instructional technology, foreign language education, ESOL, distance learning. *Total annual research expenditures:* $117,377. *Unit head:* Dr. Stephan Schindler, Chair and Professor, 813-974-2548, Fax: 813-905-9937, E-mail: skschindler@usf.edu. *Application contact:* Patricia Garcia, Academic Program Specialist, 813-974-2548, Fax: 813-905-9937, E-mail: pgarcia@usf.edu. Website: http://languages.usf.edu/

The University of Tennessee, Graduate School, College of Arts and Sciences, Department of Modern Foreign Languages and Literatures, Program in Modern Foreign Languages, Knoxville, TN 37996. Offers applied linguistics (PhD); French (PhD); German (PhD); Italian (PhD); Portuguese (PhD); Russian (PhD); Spanish (PhD). *Degree requirements:* For doctorate, 2 foreign languages, thesis/dissertation. *Entrance requirements:* For doctorate, minimum GPA of 2.7. Additional exam requirements/recommendations for international students: Required—TOEFL. Electronic applications accepted.

The University of Tennessee, Graduate School, College of Arts and Sciences, Department of Modern Foreign Languages and Literatures, Program in Spanish, Knoxville, TN 37996. Offers MA. *Degree requirements:* For master's, one foreign language, thesis or alternative. *Entrance requirements:* For master's, minimum GPA of 2.7. Additional exam requirements/recommendations for international students: Required—TOEFL. Electronic applications accepted.

The University of Texas at Arlington, Graduate School, College of Liberal Arts, Department of Modern Languages, Arlington, TX 76019. Offers French (MA); Spanish (MA). Part-time and evening/weekend programs available. *Degree requirements:* For master's, 2 foreign languages, comprehensive exam, thesis optional. *Entrance requirements:* For master's, GRE General Test, minimum GPA of 3.0, 3 letters of recommendation. Additional exam requirements/recommendations for international students: Required—TOEFL (minimum score 550 paper-based).

The University of Texas at Austin, Graduate School, College of Liberal Arts, Department of Spanish and Portuguese, Austin, TX 78712-1111. Offers Hispanic linguistics (MA, PhD); Hispanic literature (MA, PhD); Ibero-romance philology and linguistics (PhD); Luso-Brazilian literature (MA, PhD). *Degree requirements:* For master's, 2 foreign languages, thesis or alternative; for doctorate, 3 foreign languages, thesis/dissertation. *Entrance requirements:* For master's and doctorate, GRE General Test. Electronic applications accepted.

The University of Texas at Brownsville, Graduate Studies, College of Liberal Arts, Department of Modern Languages, Brownsville, TX 78520-4991. Offers Spanish (MA); Spanish translation and interpreting (MA). Part-time and evening/weekend programs available. Postbaccalaureate distance learning degree programs offered (no on-campus study). *Degree requirements:* For master's, comprehensive exam (for some programs), thesis optional, project. *Entrance requirements:* For master's, GRE General Test, letters of recommendation, interview. Additional exam requirements/recommendations for international students: Required—TOEFL (minimum score 550 paper-based; 77 iBT). Electronic applications accepted. *Faculty research:* Children's literature, Hispanic folklore, translation.

The University of Texas at El Paso, Graduate School, College of Liberal Arts, Department of Creative Writing, El Paso, TX 79968-0001. Offers creative writing (MFA); creative writing of the Americas (MFA). Part-time and evening/weekend programs available. Postbaccalaureate distance learning degree programs offered (no on-campus study). *Degree requirements:* For master's, thesis. *Entrance requirements:* For master's, minimum GPA of 3.0, letters of recommendation, writing sample. Additional exam requirements/recommendations for international students: Recommended—TOEFL, IELTS. Electronic applications accepted.

The University of Texas at El Paso, Graduate School, College of Liberal Arts, Department of Languages and Linguistics, El Paso, TX 79968-0001. Offers linguistics (MA); Spanish (MA); teaching English to speakers of other languages (Certificate). Part-time and evening/weekend programs available. *Degree requirements:* For master's, thesis optional. *Entrance requirements:* For master's, GRE General Test, departmental exam, minimum GPA of 3.0, letters of recommendation. Additional exam requirements/recommendations for international students: Required—TOEFL; Recommended—IELTS. Electronic applications accepted.

The University of Texas at San Antonio, College of Liberal and Fine Arts, Department of Modern Languages and Literatures, San Antonio, TX 78249-0617. Offers Spanish (MA). Part-time programs available. *Faculty:* 7 full-time (4 women), 1 part-time/adjunct (0 women). *Students:* 5 full-time (3 women), 15 part-time (10 women); all minorities (all Hispanic/Latino). Average age 36. 14 applicants, 86% accepted, 5 enrolled. In 2014, 3 master's awarded. *Degree requirements:* For master's, one foreign language, comprehensive exam, thesis optional. *Entrance requirements:* For master's, minimum GPA of 3.0, sample of written and spoken work, letter of recommendation, statement of purpose. Additional exam requirements/recommendations for international students: Required—TOEFL (minimum score 550 paper-based; 79 iBT), IELTS (minimum score 6.5). *Application deadline:* For fall admission, 7/1 for domestic students, 4/1 for international students; for spring admission, 11/1 for domestic students, 9/1 for international students. Applications are processed on a rolling basis. Application fee: $45 ($80 for international students). Electronic applications accepted. *Expenses:* Tuition, state resident: full-time $4671; part-time $260 per credit hour. Tuition, nonresident: full-time $18,022; part-time $1001 per credit hour. *Financial support:* Scholarships/grants available. *Faculty research:* Film studies, religious studies, Spanish literature, Spanish culture, Spanish linguistics. *Unit head:* Dr. Marita Nummikosi, Department Chair, 210-458-4373, Fax: 210-458-5672, E-mail: marita.nummikoski@utsa.edu. *Application contact:* Dr. Malgorzata Oleszkiewicz-Peralba, Graduate Advisor of Record, 210-458-5214, Fax: 210-458-5223, E-mail: malgorzata.oleszkiewicz@utsa.edu. Website: http://colfa.utsa.edu/modern-languages/

The University of Texas of the Permian Basin, Office of Graduate Studies, College of Arts and Sciences, Department of Literature and Languages, Odessa, TX 79762-0001. Offers English (MA); Spanish (MA). *Degree requirements:* For master's, comprehensive exam (for some programs), thesis (for some programs). *Entrance requirements:* For master's, GRE General Test. Additional exam requirements/recommendations for international students: Required—TOEFL (minimum score 550 paper-based).

The University of Texas–Pan American, College of Arts and Humanities, Department of Modern Languages and Literatures, Edinburg, TX 78539. Offers Spanish (MA, PhD). PhD offered jointly with University of Houston. Part-time programs available. *Degree requirements:* For master's, comprehensive exam, thesis or alternative. *Entrance requirements:* For master's, GRE General Test, minimum GPA of 3.0. *Expenses:* Tuition, state resident: full-time $4187; part-time $232.60 per credit hour. Tuition, nonresident: full-time $10,857; part-time $603.16 per credit hour. *Required fees:* $782; $27.50 per credit hour. $143.35 per semester. *Faculty research:* Latin American literature, women's literature, Caribbean literature, Latina/o studies, sociolinguistics, applied linguistics, creative writing.

The University of Toledo, College of Graduate Studies, College of Languages, Literature and Social Sciences, Department of Foreign Languages, Toledo, OH 43606-3390. Offers French (MA); German (MA); Spanish (MA). Part-time programs available. *Degree requirements:* For master's, one foreign language, comprehensive exam, comprehensive reading exam in 1 additional foreign language. *Entrance requirements:* For master's, minimum cumulative point-hour ratio of 2.7 for all previous academic work. Additional exam requirements/recommendations for international students: Required—TOEFL (minimum score 550 paper-based; 80 iBT). Electronic applications accepted.

University of Toronto, School of Graduate Studies, Faculty of Arts and Science, Department of Spanish and Portuguese, Toronto, ON M5S 2J7, Canada. Offers MA, PhD. Part-time programs available. *Degree requirements:* For doctorate, thesis/dissertation. *Entrance requirements:* For master's, minimum B average in final year, 2 letters of reference; for doctorate, minimum A- average, 2 letters of reference, writing sample. Additional exam requirements/recommendations for international students: Required—TWE (minimum score 5), TOEFL, Michigan English Language Assessment Battery, IELTS, or COPE. Electronic applications accepted.

Spanish

University of Utah, Graduate School, College of Humanities, Department of Languages and Literature, Salt Lake City, UT 84112. Offers comparative literary and cultural studies (MA, PhD); French (MA); Spanish (MA, MALP, PhD); world languages (MA). Part-time programs available. *Faculty:* 33 full-time (20 women), 14 part-time/adjunct (9 women). *Students:* 36 full-time (27 women), 6 part-time (5 women); includes 10 minority (1 Black or African American, non-Hispanic/Latino; 4 Asian, non-Hispanic/Latino; 5 Hispanic/Latino), 6 international. Average age 25. 23 applicants, 70% accepted. In 2014, 14 master's awarded. Terminal master's awarded for partial completion of doctoral program. *Degree requirements:* For master's, comprehensive exam (for some programs), thesis (for some programs), standard proficiency in 2 languages other than English; for doctorate, comprehensive exam, thesis/dissertation, standard proficiency in 2 languages other than English and language of study, advanced proficiency in 1 language other than English and language of study. *Entrance requirements:* For master's, GRE (except for French), bachelor's degree or strong undergraduate record in target languages, minimum GPA of 3.0; for doctorate, GRE, MA, advanced proficiency in a target language. Additional exam requirements/recommendations for international students: Required—TOEFL (minimum score 550 paper-based; 80 iBT). *Application deadline:* For fall admission, 1/15 priority date for domestic students, 12/15 priority date for international students. Application fee: $55 ($65 for international students). Electronic applications accepted. *Financial support:* In 2014–15, 27 teaching assistantships with full and partial tuition reimbursements (averaging $14,000 per year) were awarded; health care benefits and unspecified assistantships also available. Financial award application deadline: 1/15; financial award applicants required to submit FAFSA. *Faculty research:* Literary study, literary theory, linguistics, cultural studies, comparative studies. *Unit head:* Dr. Katharina Gerstenberger, Chair, 801-585-7908, Fax: 801-581-4768, E-mail: katharina.gerstenberger@utah.edu. *Application contact:* Marcie Leek, Academic Coordinator, 801-581-5401, Fax: 801-581-5401, E-mail: marcie.leek@utah.edu.
Website: http://languages.utah.edu/

University of Virginia, College and Graduate School of Arts and Sciences, Department of Spanish, Italian and Portuguese, Program in Spanish, Charlottesville, VA 22903. Offers MA, PhD. *Students:* 38 full-time (28 women); includes 6 minority (4 Hispanic/Latino; 2 Two or more races, non-Hispanic/Latino), 6 international. Average age 27. 36 applicants, 44% accepted, 10 enrolled. In 2014, 5 master's, 6 doctorates awarded. *Degree requirements:* For master's, one foreign language, comprehensive exam, thesis; for doctorate, 2 foreign languages, comprehensive exam, thesis/dissertation. *Entrance requirements:* For master's, GRE General Test, GRE Subject Test, 2 letters of recommendation; for doctorate, GRE General Test, GRE Subject Test, 2 letters of recommendation, writing sample. Additional exam requirements/recommendations for international students: Required—TOEFL (minimum score 600 paper-based; 90 iBT), IELTS (minimum score 7). *Application deadline:* For fall admission, 12/1 for domestic and international students. Applications are processed on a rolling basis. Application fee: $60. Electronic applications accepted. *Expenses:* Tuition, state resident: full-time $14,164; part-time $349 per credit hour. Tuition, nonresident: full-time $23,722; part-time $1300 per credit hour. *Required fees:* $2514. *Financial support:* Fellowships and teaching assistantships available. Financial award applicants required to submit FAFSA. *Unit head:* Joel Rini, Chair, 434-924-7159, Fax: 434-924-7160, E-mail: sipinfo@virginia.edu. *Application contact:* Randolph Pope, Director of Graduate Studies, Spanish, 434-924-7159, Fax: 434-924-7160, E-mail: sipinfo@virginia.edu.
Website: http://spanitalport.virginia.edu/

University of Washington, Graduate School, College of Arts and Sciences, Division of Spanish and Portuguese Studies, Seattle, WA 98195. Offers Hispanic literary and cultural studies (MA). *Degree requirements:* For master's, 2 foreign languages, thesis optional, exam. *Entrance requirements:* For master's, GRE General Test, minimum GPA of 3.0. Additional exam requirements/recommendations for international students: Required—TOEFL. Electronic applications accepted. *Faculty research:* Medieval through modern Spanish literature and film, Latin American literature, poetry and essay, pan-Hispanic ballad, Hispanic cultural studies, second language acquisition and applied linguistics.

The University of Western Ontario, Faculty of Graduate Studies, Faculty of Arts and Humanities, Department of Modern Languages and Literatures, London, ON N6A 5B8, Canada. Offers comparative literature (MA, PhD); Hispanic studies (MA, PhD). Part-time programs available. *Degree requirements:* For master's, 2 foreign languages, thesis (for some programs). *Entrance requirements:* For master's, honors degree in Spanish or equivalent, minimum B average. Additional exam requirements/recommendations for international students: Required—TOEFL (comparative literature). *Faculty research:* Spanish golden age, Latin-American, romance, medieval, film.

University of Wisconsin–Madison, Graduate School, College of Letters and Science, Department of Spanish and Portuguese, Program in Spanish, Madison, WI 53706-1380. Offers MA, PhD. *Degree requirements:* For master's, one foreign language; for doctorate, 2 foreign languages, thesis/dissertation. *Entrance requirements:* For master's, GRE (recommended), minimum GPA of 3.25 in Spanish or Portuguese; for doctorate, GRE (recommended), minimum graduate GPA of 3.4, writing sample. Additional exam requirements/recommendations for international students: Required—TOEFL. Electronic applications accepted. *Expenses:* Tuition, state resident: full-time $10,723; part-time $745 per credit. Tuition, nonresident: full-time $24,054; part-time $1578 per credit. *Required fees:* $374 per semester. Tuition and fees vary according to course load, program and reciprocity agreements. *Faculty research:* Hispanic linguistics, Spanish and Spanish-American literature.

University of Wisconsin–Milwaukee, Graduate School, College of Letters and Sciences, Department of Spanish, Milwaukee, WI 53201-0413. Offers Spanish (MA); translation (Certificate). *Entrance requirements:* For master's, bachelor's degree. Electronic applications accepted. *Faculty research:* Sociolinguistics, Spanish-American literature, Spanish literature, Hispanic culture, Hispanic historiography.

University of Wyoming, College of Arts and Sciences, Department of Modern and Classical Languages, Program in Spanish, Laramie, WY 82071. Offers MA. Part-time programs available. *Degree requirements:* For master's, one foreign language, thesis or alternative. *Entrance requirements:* For master's, GRE General Test, minimum GPA of 3.0. *Faculty research:* Peninsular literature, Latin American literature, theatre, science and literature, linguistics.

Vanderbilt University, Graduate School, Department of Spanish and Portuguese, Nashville, TN 37240-1001. Offers Portuguese (MA); Spanish (MA, MAT, PhD); Spanish and Portuguese (PhD). *Faculty:* 13 full-time (6 women). *Students:* 23 full-time (9 women), 1 part-time (0 women); includes 2 minority (1 Black or African American, non-Hispanic/Latino; 1 Hispanic/Latino), 11 international. Average age 31. 42 applicants, 31% accepted, 8 enrolled. In 2014, 3 master's, 4 doctorates awarded. *Degree requirements:* For master's, one foreign language, thesis; for doctorate, 2 foreign languages, thesis/dissertation, final and qualifying exams. *Entrance requirements:* For master's, GRE General Test; for doctorate, GRE General Test, writing sample in Spanish. Additional exam requirements/recommendations for international students: Required—TOEFL (minimum score 570 paper-based; 88 iBT). *Application deadline:* For fall admission, 1/15 for domestic and international students. Electronic applications accepted. *Expenses: Tuition:* Full-time $42,768; part-time $1782 per credit hour. *Required fees:* $422. One-time fee: $30 full-time. *Financial support:* Fellowships with full and partial tuition reimbursements, teaching assistantships with full tuition reimbursements, Federal Work-Study, institutionally sponsored loans, and health care benefits available. Financial award application deadline: 1/15; financial award applicants required to submit CSS PROFILE or FAFSA. *Faculty research:* Spanish, Portuguese, and Latin American literatures; foreign language pedagogy; Renaissance and Baroque poetry; nineteenth century Spanish novel. *Unit head:* Dr. Andres Zamora, Director of Graduate Studies, 615-322-6858, Fax: 615-343-7260, E-mail: andres.zamora@vanderbilt.edu. *Application contact:* Cindy Martinez, Administrative Assistant, 615-322-6930, Fax: 615-343-7260, E-mail: cindy.m.martinez@vanderbilt.edu.
Website: http://as.vanderbilt.edu/spanish-portuguese/graduate/index.php

Washington University in St. Louis, Graduate School of Arts and Sciences, Department of Romance Languages and Literatures, Program in Spanish, St. Louis, MO 63130-4899. Offers Hispanic languages and literatures (PhD); Spanish (MA); Spanish and comparative literature (PhD). Terminal master's awarded for partial completion of doctoral program. *Degree requirements:* For master's, thesis or alternative; for doctorate, thesis/dissertation. *Entrance requirements:* For master's and doctorate, GRE General Test. Additional exam requirements/recommendations for international students: Required—TOEFL. Electronic applications accepted. *Faculty research:* Latin American and Iberian literatures and languages, Spanish and comparative literature.

Wayne State University, College of Liberal Arts and Sciences, Department of Classical and Modern Languages, Literatures, and Cultures, Program in Language Learning, Detroit, MI 48202. Offers Arabic (MALL); French (MALL); German (MALL); Italian (MALL); Spanish (MALL). *Students:* 1 (woman) full-time, 9 part-time (6 women); includes 2 minority (both Hispanic/Latino). Average age 34. In 2014, 2 master's awarded. *Degree requirements:* For master's, one foreign language, three-credit essay. *Entrance requirements:* For master's, GRE (recommended), target language proficiency, statement of purpose, three letters of recommendation, minimum GPA of 2.6 from accredited institution or 3.2 from non-accredited institution. Additional exam requirements/recommendations for international students: Required—TOEFL (minimum score 550 paper-based; 79 iBT), TWE (minimum score 5.5), Michigan English Language Assessment Battery (minimum score 85); Recommended—IELTS (minimum score 6.5). *Application deadline:* For fall admission, 6/1 priority date for domestic students, 5/1 for international students; for winter admission, 10/1 priority date for domestic students, 9/1 priority date for international students; for spring admission, 2/1 priority date for domestic students, 1/1 priority date for international students. Applications are processed on a rolling basis. Application fee: $0. Electronic applications accepted. *Expenses:* Tuition, state resident: full-time $10,294; part-time $571.90 per credit hour. Tuition, nonresident: full-time $29,730; part-time $1238.75 per credit hour. *Required fees:* $1365; $43.50 per credit hour. $291.10 per semester. Tuition and fees vary according to course load and program. *Financial support:* Scholarships/grants and unspecified assistantships available. Financial award application deadline: 3/31; financial award applicants required to submit FAFSA. *Unit head:* Dr. Anne Duggan, Department Chair, E-mail: a.duggan@wayne.edu.
Website: http://clas.wayne.edu/MALL/

Wayne State University, College of Liberal Arts and Sciences, Department of Classical and Modern Languages, Literatures, and Cultures, Program in Modern Languages, Detroit, MI 48202. Offers French (PhD); German (PhD); Spanish (PhD). *Students:* 15 full-time (13 women), 5 part-time (all women); includes 7 minority (1 Black or African American, non-Hispanic/Latino; 1 Asian, non-Hispanic/Latino; 5 Hispanic/Latino), 2 international. Average age 38. In 2014, 3 doctorates awarded. *Degree requirements:* For doctorate, 2 foreign languages, thesis/dissertation. *Entrance requirements:* For doctorate, master's degree in French, German, or Spanish, three letters of reccomendation, current curriculum vitae, writing sample such as term paper or thesis in language of specialization, statement of purpose (in English). Additional exam requirements/recommendations for international students: Required—TOEFL (minimum score 550 paper-based; 79 iBT), TWE (minimum score 5.5), Michigan English Language Assessment Battery (minimum score 85); Recommended—IELTS (minimum score 6.5). *Application deadline:* For fall admission, 6/1 priority date for domestic students, 5/1 priority date for international students; for winter admission, 10/1 priority date for domestic and international students; for spring admission, 2/1 priority date for domestic students, 1/1 priority date for international students. Applications are processed on a rolling basis. Application fee: $0. Electronic applications accepted. *Expenses:* Tuition, state resident: full-time $10,294; part-time $571.90 per credit hour. Tuition, nonresident: full-time $29,730; part-time $1238.75 per credit hour. *Required fees:* $1365; $43.50 per credit hour. $291.10 per semester. Tuition and fees vary according to course load and program. *Financial support:* In 2014–15, 12 students received support. Fellowships with tuition reimbursements available, teaching assistantships, scholarships/grants, health care benefits, and unspecified assistantships available. Financial award application deadline: 3/31; financial award applicants required to submit FAFSA. *Unit head:* Dr. Anne Duggan, Department Chair, E-mail: a.duggan@wayne.edu. *Application contact:* Dr. Michael Giordano, Professor and Graduate Director, 313-577-3002, E-mail: aa2144@wayne.edu.
Website: http://clasweb.clas.wayne.edu/languages/ModernLanguages(PhD)

Wayne State University, College of Liberal Arts and Sciences, Department of Classical and Modern Languages, Literatures, and Cultures, Program in Romance Languages, Detroit, MI 48202. Offers French (MA); Italian (MA); Spanish (MA). *Students:* 6 full-time (5 women), 22 part-time (15 women); includes 9 minority (4 Black or African American, non-Hispanic/Latino; 1 American Indian or Alaska Native, non-Hispanic/Latino; 1 Asian, non-Hispanic/Latino; 2 Hispanic/Latino; 1 Two or more races, non-Hispanic/Latino), 1 international. Average age 32. 13 applicants, 38% accepted, 5 enrolled. In 2014, 6 master's awarded. *Degree requirements:* For master's, one foreign language, thesis optional. *Entrance requirements:* For master's, GRE (strongly recommended), three letters of recommendation. Additional exam requirements/recommendations for international students: Required—TOEFL (minimum score 550 paper-based; 79 iBT), Michigan English Language Assessment Battery (minimum score 85); Recommended—IELTS (minimum score 6.5). *Application deadline:* For fall admission, 6/1 priority date for domestic students, 5/1 priority date for international students; for winter admission, 10/1 priority date for domestic students, 9/1 priority date for international students; for spring admission, 2/1 priority date for domestic students, 1/1 priority date for international students. Applications are processed on a rolling basis. Application fee: $0. Electronic applications accepted. *Expenses:* Tuition, state resident: full-time $10,294; part-time $571.90 per credit hour. Tuition, nonresident: full-time $29,730; part-time $1238.75 per credit hour. *Required fees:* $1365; $43.50 per credit hour. $291.10 per semester. Tuition and fees vary according to course load and program. *Financial support:* In 2014–15, 11 students received support. Fellowships, research assistantships, teaching assistantships, scholarships/grants, health care benefits, and unspecified assistantships available. Financial award application deadline: 3/31; financial award applicants required to submit FAFSA. *Unit head:* Dr. Anne Duggan, Department Chair, E-mail: a.duggan@wayne.edu. *Application contact:* Dr. Michael Giordano, Graduate Advisor, E-mail: aa2144@wayne.edu.
Website: http://clas.wayne.edu/languages/RomanceLanguagesLiteratures

West Chester University of Pennsylvania, College of Arts and Sciences, Department of Languages and Cultures, West Chester, PA 19383. Offers French (M Ed, MA,

Teaching Certificate); Spanish (M Ed, MA, Teaching Certificate). Part-time and evening/weekend programs available. Postbaccalaureate distance learning degree programs offered. *Faculty:* 13 full-time (8 women). *Students:* 10 full-time (7 women), 21 part-time (19 women); includes 8 minority (4 Black or African American, non-Hispanic/Latino; 4 Hispanic/Latino). Average age 30. 22 applicants, 91% accepted, 11 enrolled. In 2014, 9 master's, 5 other advanced degrees awarded. *Degree requirements:* For master's, one foreign language, comprehensive exam, exit exam capstone project; thesis (for MA); for Teaching Certificate, one foreign language. *Entrance requirements:* For master's, undergraduate major in a language or native fluency. Additional exam requirements/recommendations for international students: Required—TOEFL (minimum score 550 paper-based; 80 iBT). *Application deadline:* For fall admission, 4/15 priority date for domestic students, 3/15 for international students; for spring admission, 10/15 priority date for domestic students, 9/1 for international students. Applications are processed on a rolling basis. Application fee: $45. Electronic applications accepted. *Expenses:* Tuition, state resident: full-time $8172; part-time $454 per credit. Tuition, nonresident: full-time $12,258; part-time $681 per credit. *Required fees:* $2231; $110.78 per credit. Tuition and fees vary according to campus/location and program. *Financial support:* Unspecified assistantships available. Support available to part-time students. Financial award application deadline: 2/15; financial award applicants required to submit FAFSA. *Faculty research:* Language structure, literature, film, culture, pedagogy, technology. *Unit head:* Dr. Jerome Williams, Chair, 610-436-2700, Fax: 610-436-3048, E-mail: jwilliams2@wcupa.edu. *Application contact:* Dr. Rebecca Pauly, Graduate Coordinator, 610-436-2382, Fax: 610-436-3048, E-mail: rpauly@wcupa.edu. Website: http://www.wcupa.edu/_academics/sch_cas.flg/

Western Kentucky University, Graduate Studies, Potter College of Arts and Letters, Department of Modern Languages, Bowling Green, KY 42101. Offers French (MA Ed); German (MA Ed); Spanish (MA Ed).

Western Michigan University, Graduate College, College of Arts and Sciences, Department of Spanish, Kalamazoo, MI 49008. Offers MA, PhD. *Application deadline:* For fall admission, 2/15 for domestic students. *Financial support:* Application deadline: 2/15. *Application contact:* Admissions and Orientation, 269-387-2000, Fax: 269-387-2096.

West Virginia University, Eberly College of Arts and Sciences, Department of Foreign Languages, Morgantown, WV 26506. Offers French (MA); linguistics (MA); Spanish (MA); teaching English to speakers of other languages (MA). Part-time programs available. *Degree requirements:* For master's, one foreign language, comprehensive exam (for some programs), thesis optional. *Entrance requirements:* For master's, minimum GPA of 3.0. Electronic applications accepted. *Faculty research:* French, German, and Spanish literature; foreign language pedagogy; English as a second language; cultural studies; linguistics.

Wichita State University, Graduate School, Fairmount College of Liberal Arts and Sciences, Department of Modern and Classical Languages and Literatures, Wichita, KS 67260. Offers Spanish (MA). Part-time programs available. *Unit head:* Dr. Wilson Baldridge, Chair, 316-978-3180, Fax: 316-978-3293, E-mail: wilson.baldridge@wichita.edu. *Application contact:* Jordan Oleson, Admissions Coordinator, 316-978-3095, Fax: 316-978-3253, E-mail: jordan.oleson@wichita.edu. Website: http://www.wichita.edu/mcll

Winthrop University, College of Arts and Sciences, Program in Spanish, Rock Hill, SC 29733. Offers MA. Part-time programs available. *Entrance requirements:* For master's, GRE General Test and PRAXIS, minimum GPA of 3.0, 24 hours of undergraduate Spanish, or interview. Electronic applications accepted.

Worcester State University, Graduate Studies, Program in Spanish, Worcester, MA 01602-2597. Offers MA. Part-time programs available. *Faculty:* 3 full-time (1 woman). *Students:* 13 part-time (all women); includes 8 minority (all Hispanic/Latino). Average age 37. 7 applicants, 57% accepted, 3 enrolled. In 2014, 12 master's awarded. *Degree requirements:* For master's, one foreign language, thesis or comprehensive exam. *Entrance requirements:* For master's, GRE, MAT, BA in Spanish or related field and/or interview with faculty member. Additional exam requirements/recommendations for international students: Required—TOEFL (minimum score 550 paper-based; 79 iBT). *Application deadline:* For fall admission, 6/15 for domestic and international students; for spring admission, 11/1 for domestic and international students; for summer admission, 3/1 for domestic students, 4/1 for international students. Applications are processed on a rolling basis. Application fee: $50. Electronic applications accepted. *Expenses: Tuition, area resident:* Part-time $150 per credit. Tuition, state resident: part-time $150 per credit. Tuition, nonresident: part-time $150 per credit. *Financial support:* Career-related internships or fieldwork, scholarships/grants, and unspecified assistantships available. Financial award application deadline: 3/1; financial award applicants required to submit FAFSA. *Unit head:* Dr. Ana Perez-Manrique, Program Coordinator, 508-929-8577, E-mail: aperezmanrique@worcester.edu. *Application contact:* Sara Grady, Acting Associate Dean of Graduate and Continuing Education, 508-929-8787, Fax: 508-929-8100, E-mail: sara.grady@worcester.edu.

Yale University, Graduate School of Arts and Sciences, Department of Spanish and Portuguese, New Haven, CT 06520. Offers Latin American literature (PhD); Luso-Brazilian and Spanish/Spanish American literatures (PhD); Spanish peninsular literature (PhD). Terminal master's awarded for partial completion of doctoral program. *Degree requirements:* For doctorate, 3 foreign languages, thesis/dissertation. *Entrance requirements:* For doctorate, GRE General Test.

Section 10
Linguistic Studies

This section contains a directory of institutions offering graduate work in linguistic studies. Additional information about programs listed in the directory may be obtained by writing directly to the dean of a graduate school or chair of a department at the address given in the directory.

For programs offering related work, see also in this book *Area and Cultural Studies, Language and Literature,* and *Sociology, Anthropology, and Archaeology.*

CONTENTS

Program Directories

Linguistics

Arizona State University at the Tempe campus, College of Liberal Arts and Sciences, Department of English, Tempe, AZ 85287-0302. Offers applied linguistics (PhD); creative writing (MFA); English (MA, PhD), including comparative literature (MA), linguistics (MA), literature, rhetoric and composition (MA), rhetoric, composition, and linguistics (PhD); film and media studies (MAS), including American media and popular culture; linguistics (Graduate Certificate); teaching English to speakers of other languages (MTESOL); translation studies (Graduate Certificate). Terminal master's awarded for partial completion of doctoral program. *Degree requirements:* For master's, variable foreign language requirement, comprehensive exam (for some programs), thesis (for some programs), interactive Program of Study (iPOS) submitted before completing 50 percent of required credit hours; for doctorate, variable foreign language requirement, comprehensive exam, thesis/dissertation, interactive Program of Study (iPOS) submitted before completing 50 percent of required credit hours. *Entrance requirements:* For master's and doctorate, GRE, minimum GPA of 3.0 or equivalent in last 2 years of work leading to bachelor's degree. Additional exam requirements/recommendations for international students: Required—TOEFL, IELTS, or PTE. Electronic applications accepted.

Ball State University, Graduate School, College of Sciences and Humanities, Department of English, Program in Linguistics, Muncie, IN 47306-1099. Offers English (PhD), including applied linguistics; linguistics (MA). *Students:* 8 full-time (2 women), 5 part-time (3 women), 8 international. Average age 31. 31 applicants, 29% accepted, 4 enrolled. In 2014, 2 master's, 2 doctorates awarded. Application fee: $50. *Financial support:* In 2014–15, 1 research assistantship with partial tuition reimbursement (averaging $10,394 per year), 6 teaching assistantships with partial tuition reimbursements (averaging $16,540 per year) were awarded; career-related internships or fieldwork also available. Financial award application deadline: 3/1. *Faculty research:* Descriptive and theoretical linguistics. *Unit head:* Dr. Elizabeth Riddle, Director of Graduate Programs in English, 765-285-8580, Fax: 765-285-3765, E-mail: emriddle@bsu.edu. *Application contact:* Dr. Jill Christman, Assistant Chair, 765-285-8415, E-mail: jcchristman@bsu.edu.
Website: http://www.bsu.edu/english/

Biola University, Cook School of Intercultural Studies, La Mirada, CA 90639-0001. Offers anthropology (MA); applied linguistics (MA); intercultural education (PhD); intercultural studies (MA, PhD); linguistics (Certificate); linguistics and Biblical languages (MA); missions (MA); teaching English to speakers of other languages (MA, Certificate). Part-time programs available. *Faculty:* 19. *Students:* 86 full-time (41 women), 119 part-time (58 women); includes 68 minority (7 Black or African American, non-Hispanic/Latino; 1 American Indian or Alaska Native, non-Hispanic/Latino; 42 Asian, non-Hispanic/Latino; 14 Hispanic/Latino; 4 Two or more races, non-Hispanic/Latino), 29 international. In 2014, 29 master's, 16 doctorates awarded. *Entrance requirements:* For master's, minimum undergraduate GPA of 3.0; for doctorate, master's degree or equivalent, 3 years of cross-cultural experience, minimum graduate GPA of 3.3. Additional exam requirements/recommendations for international students: Required—TOEFL. *Application deadline:* For fall admission, 7/1 for domestic students, 6/1 for international students; for spring admission, 12/1 for domestic students; for summer admission, 5/1 for domestic students. Applications are processed on a rolling basis. Application fee: $65. Electronic applications accepted. *Financial support:* Scholarships/grants available. Support available to part-time students. Financial award applicants required to submit FAFSA. *Faculty research:* Linguistics, anthropology, intercultural studies, teaching English to speakers of other languages, missions, missiology. *Unit head:* Dr. Bulus Y. Galadima, Dean, 562-903-4844. *Application contact:* Graduate Admissions Office, 562-903-4752, E-mail: graduate.admissions@biola.edu.
Website: http://cook.biola.edu

Boston College, Graduate School of Arts and Sciences, Department of Slavic and Eastern Languages, Program in Linguistics, Chestnut Hill, MA 02467-3800. Offers MA, MA/JD, MBA/MA. *Degree requirements:* For master's, 3 foreign languages, comprehensive exam, thesis or alternative. *Application deadline:* For fall admission, 1/15 for domestic students. Application fee: $75. Electronic applications accepted. *Financial support:* Application deadline: 3/1. *Unit head:* Prof. Margaret Thomas, Chair, Department of Slavic and Eastern Languages and Literatures, 617-552-3910.
Website: http://www.bc.edu/sl

Boston University, Graduate School of Arts and Sciences, Program in Applied Linguistics, Boston, MA 02215. Offers MA, PhD. Part-time programs available. *Faculty:* 17 full-time (9 women). *Students:* 12 full-time (7 women), 7 part-time (6 women); includes 2 minority (both Two or more races, non-Hispanic/Latino), 2 international. Average age 31. 65 applicants, 20% accepted, 5 enrolled. Terminal master's awarded for partial completion of doctoral program. *Degree requirements:* For master's, one foreign language, project; for doctorate, 2 foreign languages, thesis/dissertation, 1 book review, 2 research papers, oral exam. *Entrance requirements:* For master's, GRE General Test, 3 letters of recommendation; for doctorate, GRE General Test, 3 letters of recommendation, scholarly writing sample. Additional exam requirements/recommendations for international students: Required—TOEFL. *Application deadline:* For fall admission, 2/1 priority date for domestic and international students. Applications are processed on a rolling basis. Application fee: $80. Electronic applications accepted. *Expenses: Tuition:* Full-time $45,686; part-time $1428 per credit hour. *Required fees:* $660; $60 per semester. Tuition and fees vary according to program. *Financial support:* In 2014–15, 12 students received support, including 1 research assistantship with full tuition reimbursement available (averaging $20,500 per year), 2 teaching assistantships with full tuition reimbursements available (averaging $20,500 per year); Federal Work-Study, scholarships/grants, health care benefits, and unspecified assistantships also available. Financial award application deadline: 1/15; financial award applicants required to submit FAFSA. *Faculty research:* Psycholinguistics, sociolinguistics, neurolinguistics, language acquisition, American Sign Language. *Total annual research expenditures:* $900,000. *Unit head:* Jonathan Barnes, Director, 617-353-6222, Fax: 617-358-2353, E-mail: mco@bu.edu. *Application contact:* Kendra Dickinson, Program Assistant, 617-353-6234, Fax: 617-353-2353, E-mail: linguist@bu.edu.
Website: http://www.bu.edu/applied-linguistics/

Brandeis University, Graduate School of Arts and Sciences, Program in Computational Linguistics, Waltham, MA 02454-9110. Offers MA. *Degree requirements:* For master's, internship in computational linguistics or thesis. *Entrance requirements:* For master's, GRE (recommended), statement of purpose, 2 letters of recommendation, official transcript(s), resume or curriculum vitae. Additional exam requirements/recommendations for international students: Required—TOEFL (minimum score 650 paper-based; 100 iBT), PTE (minimum score 68); Recommended—IELTS (minimum score 7). Electronic applications accepted.

Brigham Young University, Graduate Studies, College of Humanities, Department of Linguistics and English Language, Provo, UT 84602. Offers linguistics (MA); teaching English as a second language (MA). Part-time programs available. *Faculty:* 22 full-time (5 women), 1 part-time/adjunct (0 women). *Students:* 33 full-time (20 women), 28 part-time (17 women); includes 10 minority (5 Asian, non-Hispanic/Latino; 4 Hispanic/Latino; 1 Native Hawaiian or other Pacific Islander, non-Hispanic/Latino). Average age 30. 30 applicants, 77% accepted, 21 enrolled. In 2014, 16 master's awarded. *Degree requirements:* For master's, 2 foreign languages, thesis. *Entrance requirements:* For master's, GRE General Test, minimum GPA of 3.0 in last 60 hours of course work. Additional exam requirements/recommendations for international students: Required—TOEFL (minimum score 580 paper-based; 90 iBT), TWE. *Application deadline:* 1/15 for domestic and international students. Application fee: $50. Electronic applications accepted. *Expenses: Tuition:* Full-time $6310; part-time $371 per credit hour. Tuition and fees vary according to program and student's religious affiliation. *Financial support:* In 2014–15, 5 research assistantships with partial tuition reimbursements (averaging $1,140 per year), 12 teaching assistantships with partial tuition reimbursements (averaging $2,079 per year) were awarded; fellowships with partial tuition reimbursements, career-related internships or fieldwork, institutionally sponsored loans, scholarships/grants, tuition waivers (partial), unspecified assistantships, and student instructorships also available. Support available to part-time students. Financial award application deadline: 5/1. *Faculty research:* Teaching English to speakers of other languages, second language acquisition, computational linguistics, semiotics and semantics, computer-assisted language instruction, forensic linguistics. *Total annual research expenditures:* $27,000. *Unit head:* Dr. Diane Strong-Krause, Chair, 801-422-3970, Fax: 801-422-3970, E-mail: diane_strong-krause@byu.edu. *Application contact:* LoriAnne Spear, Secretary, 801-422-9010, Fax: 801-422-9010, E-mail: lorianne_spear@byu.edu.
Website: http://linguistics.byu.edu/

Brigham Young University, Graduate Studies, College of Humanities, Department of Spanish and Portuguese, Provo, UT 84602. Offers Portuguese (MA), including Luso-Brazilian literature, Portuguese linguistics, Portuguese pedagogy; Spanish (MA), including Hispanic linguistics, Hispanic literatures, Spanish pedagogy. *Faculty:* 29 full-time (5 women). *Students:* 16 full-time (6 women), 27 part-time (15 women); includes 16 minority (all Hispanic/Latino). Average age 34. 20 applicants, 55% accepted, 9 enrolled. In 2014, 15 master's awarded. *Degree requirements:* For master's, one foreign language, comprehensive exam, thesis, 1 semester of teaching. *Entrance requirements:* For master's, GRE, minimum GPA of 3.5 in Spanish or Portuguese, 3.3 overall. Additional exam requirements/recommendations for international students: Required—TOEFL (minimum score 580 paper-based; 85 iBT). *Application deadline:* For fall admission, 2/1 for domestic and international students. Application fee: $50. Electronic applications accepted. *Expenses: Tuition:* Full-time $6310; part-time $371 per credit hour. Tuition and fees vary according to program and student's religious affiliation. *Financial support:* In 2014–15, 25 students received support, including 4 research assistantships with partial tuition reimbursements available (averaging $2,500 per year), 69 teaching assistantships with partial tuition reimbursements available (averaging $3,500 per year); institutionally sponsored loans, scholarships/grants, tuition waivers (partial), and unspecified assistantships also available. Support available to part-time students. Financial award application deadline: 7/1. *Faculty research:* Mexican prose; Latin American theater, literature, phonetics, and phonology; pedagogy; classical Portuguese literature; Peninsular prose and theater. *Unit head:* Dr. David P. Laraway, Chair, 801-422-3807, Fax: 801-422-0628, E-mail: david_laraway@byu.edu. *Application contact:* Jessica C. Erickson, Graduate Secretary, 801-422-2196, Fax: 801-422-0628, E-mail: jessica_erickson@byu.edu.
Website: http://spanport.byu.edu/

Brown University, Graduate School, Department of Cognitive, Linguistic and Psychological Sciences, Providence, RI 02912. Offers cognitive science (Sc M, PhD); linguistics (AM, PhD); psychology (PhD). *Degree requirements:* For master's, one foreign language, thesis or alternative; for doctorate, 2 foreign languages, thesis/dissertation.

California State University, Fresno, Division of Graduate Studies, College of Arts and Humanities, Department of Linguistics, Fresno, CA 93740-8027. Offers linguistics (MA), including Teaching English as a second language. Part-time and evening/weekend programs available. *Degree requirements:* For master's, comprehensive exam. *Entrance requirements:* For master's, GRE General Test, minimum GPA of 3.0. Additional exam requirements/recommendations for international students: Required—TOEFL. Electronic applications accepted. *Faculty research:* Communication systems, bilingual education, animal communication, conflict resolution, literacy programs.

California State University, Fullerton, Graduate Studies, College of Humanities and Social Sciences, Department of English, Comparative Literature, and Linguistics, Fullerton, CA 92834-9480. Offers English (MA); linguistics (MA). Part-time programs available. *Students:* 31 full-time (25 women), 45 part-time (30 women); includes 26 minority (1 American Indian or Alaska Native, non-Hispanic/Latino; 4 Asian, non-Hispanic/Latino; 19 Hispanic/Latino; 2 Two or more races, non-Hispanic/Latino), 1 international. Average age 28. 48 applicants, 63% accepted, 23 enrolled. In 2014, 26 master's awarded. *Degree requirements:* For master's, comprehensive exam, thesis or alternative. *Entrance requirements:* For master's, minimum GPA of 3.0 in major, 2.5 in last 60 hours. Application fee: $55. *Financial support:* Career-related internships or fieldwork, Federal Work-Study, institutionally sponsored loans, and scholarships/grants available. Support available to part-time students. Financial award application deadline: 3/1; financial award applicants required to submit FAFSA. *Unit head:* Lana L. Dalley, Chair, 657-278-2452. *Application contact:* Admissions/Applications, 657-278-2371.

California State University, Fullerton, Graduate Studies, College of Humanities and Social Sciences, Program in Linguistics, Fullerton, CA 92834-9480. Offers analysis of specific language structures (MA); anthropological linguistics (MA); applied linguistics (MA); communication and semantics (MA); disorders of communication (MA); experimental phonetics (MA). Part-time programs available. *Students:* 45 full-time (28 women), 14 part-time (10 women); includes 11 minority (6 Asian, non-Hispanic/Latino; 5 Hispanic/Latino), 38 international. Average age 29. 36 applicants, 75% accepted, 21 enrolled. In 2014, 10 master's awarded. *Degree requirements:* For master's, one foreign language, thesis or alternative, project. *Entrance requirements:* For master's, minimum GPA of 3.0, undergraduate major in linguistics or related field. Application fee: $55. *Financial support:* Career-related internships or fieldwork, Federal Work-Study, institutionally sponsored loans, and scholarships/grants available. Support available to part-time students. Financial award application deadline: 3/1; financial award applicants required to submit FAFSA. *Unit head:* Dr. Franz Muller-Gotama, Adviser, 657-278-2441. *Application contact:* Admissions/Applications, 657-278-2371.

California State University, Long Beach, Graduate Studies, College of Liberal Arts, Department of Linguistics, Long Beach, CA 90840. Offers general linguistics (MA); language and culture (MA); special concentration (MA); teaching English to speakers of other languages (MA). Part-time and evening/weekend programs available. *Degree requirements:* For master's, one foreign language, comprehensive exam, thesis optional. Electronic applications accepted. *Faculty research:* Pedagogy of language instruction, role of language in society, Khmer language instruction.

California State University, Northridge, Graduate Studies, College of Humanities, Linguistics Program, Northridge, CA 91330. Offers MA. Part-time and evening/weekend programs available. *Students:* 19 full-time (11 women), 14 part-time (10 women); includes 10 minority (1 Black or African American, non-Hispanic/Latino; 1 American Indian or Alaska Native, non-Hispanic/Latino; 4 Asian, non-Hispanic/Latino; 4 Hispanic/Latino), 8 international. Average age 32. *Degree requirements:* For master's, one foreign language, comprehensive exam, thesis, or project. *Entrance requirements:* For master's, GRE General Test or minimum GPA of 3.0. Additional exam requirements/recommendations for international students: Required—TOEFL (minimum score 563 paper-based; 85 iBT). *Application deadline:* For fall admission, 11/30 for domestic students. Application fee: $55. *Expenses: Required fees:* $12,402. *Financial support:* Application deadline: 3/1. *Faculty research:* Ethnography of communication, stylistics, natural language processing, linguistics and humor, Otomanguean phonology and reconstruction. *Unit head:* Dr. Evelyn McClave, Coordinator, 818-677-5019, E-mail: emcclave@csun.edu. *Application contact:* 818-677-3755.
Website: http://www.csun.edu/linguistics/

Carleton University, Faculty of Graduate Studies, Faculty of Arts and Social Sciences, School of Linguistics and Applied Language Studies, Ottawa, ON K1S 5B6, Canada. Offers applied language studies (MA). *Degree requirements:* For master's, thesis optional. *Entrance requirements:* For master's, honors degree. Additional exam requirements/recommendations for international students: Required—TOEFL or CAEL. *Faculty research:* Language learning, acquisition and use of first and/or second languages in a variety of professional and academic contexts.

Carnegie Mellon University, Dietrich College of Humanities and Social Sciences, Department of Modern Languages, Pittsburgh, PA 15213-3891. Offers second language acquisition (MA, PhD). *Degree requirements:* For doctorate, one foreign language, comprehensive exam, thesis/dissertation. *Entrance requirements:* For doctorate, GRE General Test. Additional exam requirements/recommendations for international students: Required—TOEFL.

Case Western Reserve University, School of Graduate Studies, Department of Cognitive Science, Cleveland, OH 44106. Offers cognitive linguistics (MA). Part-time programs available. *Faculty:* 5 full-time (2 women), 3 part-time/adjunct (1 woman). *Students:* 7 full-time (4 women). Average age 27. 3 applicants, 100% accepted, 3 enrolled. In 2014, 2 master's awarded. *Degree requirements:* For master's, thesis. *Entrance requirements:* For master's, GRE, Statement of purpose, three letters of recommendation, writing sample. Additional exam requirements/recommendations for international students: Required—TOEFL (minimum score 577 paper-based; 90 iBT); Recommended—IELTS (minimum score 7). *Application deadline:* For fall admission, 5/1 priority date for domestic students. Application fee: $50. Electronic applications accepted. *Faculty research:* The workings of the human mind in design, art, and technology; the interaction of brain and culture in development and evolution; the origins of human higher-order cognition; the role of the body and social interaction in shaping human cognition; the operation of systems that human beings have invented to guide their thought and action individually and culturally. *Unit head:* Dr. Todd Oakley, Chair, 216-368-4753, E-mail: coglingadmission@case.edu. *Application contact:* Susan M. Benedict, Admissions Coordinator, 216-368-4400, Fax: 216-368-4250, E-mail: susan.benedict@case.edu.
Website: http://cognitivescience.case.edu/

Cleveland State University, College of Graduate Studies, College of Liberal Arts and Social Sciences, Department of Modern Languages, Cleveland, OH 44115. Offers French (M Ed); Spanish (M Ed, MA), including language and linguistics (MA), Latin American studies (MA), peninsular studies (MA), Spanish (MA). Part-time and evening/weekend programs available. *Faculty:* 6 full-time (3 women), 1 (woman) part-time/adjunct. *Students:* 5 full-time (1 woman), 11 part-time (9 women); includes 7 minority (all Hispanic/Latino), 2 international. Average age 35. 7 applicants, 57% accepted, 2 enrolled. In 2014, 5 master's awarded. *Degree requirements:* For master's, one foreign language, comprehensive exam, thesis optional. *Entrance requirements:* For master's, undergraduate major in Spanish or equivalent, essay in Spanish, writing sample, 2 letters of reference, ACTFL "advanced low" oral proficiency rating. Additional exam requirements/recommendations for international students: Required—TOEFL (minimum score 525 paper-based; 65 iBT). *Application deadline:* For fall admission, 7/25 priority date for domestic students; for spring admission, 12/15 priority date for domestic students. Applications are processed on a rolling basis. Application fee: $30. Electronic applications accepted. *Expenses:* Tuition, state resident: full-time $9566; part-time $531 per credit hour. Tuition, nonresident: full-time $17,980; part-time $999 per credit hour. *Required fees:* $25 per semester. Tuition and fees vary according to degree level and program. *Financial support:* In 2014–15, 5 students received support, including 5 teaching assistantships with full tuition reimbursements available (averaging $8,000 per year); Federal Work-Study and unspecified assistantships also available. Financial award application deadline: 4/1. *Faculty research:* Peninsular poetry and prose, sociolinguistics, Latin American and Caribbean literature, Arabic diaspora in Latin America, border literature. *Unit head:* Dr. Antonio Medina-Rivera, Chairperson, 216-523-7175, Fax: 216-687-4650, E-mail: a.medinarivera@csuohio.edu. *Application contact:* Dr. Stephen Gingerich, Graduate Director, 216-687-4677, Fax: 216-687-4650, E-mail: s.gingerich@csuohio.edu.
Website: http://www.csuohio.edu/class/world-languages/world-languages

Concordia University, School of Graduate Studies, Faculty of Arts and Science, Department of Education, Program in Applied Linguistics, Montréal, QC H3G 1M8, Canada. Offers applied linguistics (MA); teaching English as a second language (Certificate).

Cornell University, Graduate School, Graduate Fields of Arts and Sciences, Field of Asian Studies, Ithaca, NY 14853-0001. Offers East Asian linguistics (MA); East Asian studies (MA); South Asian linguistics (MA); South Asian studies (MA); Southeast Asian linguistics (MA); Southeast Asian studies (MA). *Degree requirements:* For master's, one foreign language, thesis. *Entrance requirements:* For master's, GRE General Test, 3 letters of recommendation. Additional exam requirements/recommendations for international students: Required—TOEFL (minimum score 550 paper-based; 77 iBT). Electronic applications accepted. *Faculty research:* East Asian studies, South Asian studies, Southeast Asian studies.

Cornell University, Graduate School, Graduate Fields of Arts and Sciences, Field of Linguistics, Ithaca, NY 14853-0001. Offers applied linguistics (MA, PhD); East Asian linguistics (MA, PhD); English linguistics (MA, PhD); general linguistics (MA, PhD); Germanic linguistics (MA, PhD); Indo-European linguistics (MA, PhD); phonetics (MA, PhD); phonological theory (MA, PhD); Romance linguistics (MA, PhD); second language acquisition (MA, PhD); semantics (MA, PhD); Slavic linguistics (MA, PhD);

sociolinguistics (MA, PhD); South Asian linguistics (MA, PhD); Southeast Asian linguistics (MA, PhD); syntactic theory (MA, PhD). Terminal master's awarded for partial completion of doctoral program. *Degree requirements:* For master's, one foreign language, thesis; for doctorate, one foreign language, comprehensive exam, thesis/dissertation. *Entrance requirements:* For master's and doctorate, GRE General Test, 2 letters of recommendation. Additional exam requirements/recommendations for international students: Required—TOEFL (minimum score 600 paper-based; 77 iBT). Electronic applications accepted. *Faculty research:* Phonology and phonetics, syntax and semantics, historical linguistics, philosophy of language, language acquisition.

East Carolina University, Graduate School, Thomas Harriot College of Arts and Sciences, Department of English, Greenville, NC 27858-4353. Offers creative writing (MA); English studies (MA); linguistics (MA); literature (MA); multicultural and transnational literatures (MA, Certificate); rhetoric and composition (MA); rhetoric, writing, and professional communication (PhD); teaching English in the two-year college (Certificate); teaching English to speakers of other languages (MA, Certificate); technical and professional communication (MA). Part-time and evening/weekend programs available. *Degree requirements:* For master's, one foreign language, comprehensive exam, thesis optional. *Entrance requirements:* For master's, GRE General Test, MAT (for MA Ed). Additional exam requirements/recommendations for international students: Required—TOEFL. *Expenses:* Tuition, state resident: full-time $4223. Tuition, nonresident: full-time $16,540. *Required fees:* $2184.

Eastern Michigan University, Graduate School, College of Arts and Sciences, Department of English Language and Literature, Programs in English Linguistics, Ypsilanti, MI 48197. Offers MA, Graduate Certificate. Part-time and evening/weekend programs available. Postbaccalaureate distance learning degree programs offered (minimal on-campus study). *Students:* 7 full-time (6 women), 14 part-time (11 women); includes 2 minority (both Black or African American, non-Hispanic/Latino), 5 international. Average age 30. 26 applicants, 42% accepted, 8 enrolled. In 2014, 3 master's awarded. *Degree requirements:* For master's, thesis (for some programs). *Entrance requirements:* Additional exam requirements/recommendations for international students: Required—TOEFL. *Application deadline:* Applications are processed on a rolling basis. Application fee: $45. *Financial support:* Fellowships with tuition reimbursements, research assistantships with full tuition reimbursements, teaching assistantships with full tuition reimbursements, career-related internships or fieldwork, Federal Work-Study, institutionally sponsored loans, scholarships/grants, tuition waivers (partial), and unspecified assistantships available. Support available to part-time students. Financial award applicants required to submit FAFSA. *Application contact:* Dr. Veronica Grondona, Program Advisor, 734-487-0968, Fax: 734-483-9744, E-mail: vgrondona@emich.edu.

Florida Atlantic University, Dorothy F. Schmidt College of Arts and Letters, Department of Languages, Linguistics, and Comparative Literature, Boca Raton, FL 33431-0991. Offers comparative literature (MA); French (MA); linguistics (MA); Spanish (MA). Part-time programs available. *Degree requirements:* For master's, one foreign language, comprehensive exam, thesis optional. *Entrance requirements:* For master's, GRE General Test, minimum GPA of 3.0. Additional exam requirements/recommendations for international students: Required—TOEFL (minimum score 500 paper-based; 61 iBT), IELTS (minimum score 6). *Expenses:* Tuition, state resident: full-time $7396; part-time $369.82 per credit hour. Tuition, nonresident: full-time $19,392; part-time $1024.81 per credit hour. Tuition and fees vary according to course load. *Faculty research:* Modern European studies, modern Latin America, medieval Europe.

Florida International University, College of Arts and Sciences, Department of English, Program in Linguistics, Miami, FL 33199. Offers MA. Part-time and evening/weekend programs available. *Degree requirements:* For master's, thesis or alternative. *Entrance requirements:* For master's, minimum GPA of 3.0, letter of intent, two letters of recommendation. Additional exam requirements/recommendations for international students: Required—TOEFL (minimum score 550 paper-based; 80 iBT). Electronic applications accepted.

Gallaudet University, The Graduate School, Washington, DC 20002-3625. Offers ASL/English bilingual early childhood education: birth to 5 (Certificate); audiology (Au D); clinical psychology (PhD); critical studies in the education of deaf learners (PhD); deaf and hard of hearing infants, toddlers, and their families (Certificate); deaf education (Ed S); deaf education: advanced studies (MA); deaf education: special programs (MA); deaf history (Certificate); deaf studies (MA, Certificate); educating deaf students with disabilities (Certificate); education: teacher preparation (MA), including deaf education, early childhood education and deaf education, elementary education and deaf education, secondary education and deaf education; educational neuroscience (PhD); hearing, speech and language sciences (MS, PhD); international development (MA); interpretation (MA, PhD), including combined interpreting practice and research (MA), interpreting research (MA); linguistics (MA, PhD); mental health counseling (MA); peer mentoring (Certificate); public administration (MPA); school counseling (MA); school psychology (Psy S); sign language teaching (MA); social work (MSW); speech-language pathology (MS). Part-time programs available. *Students:* 325 full-time (251 women), 118 part-time (90 women); includes 91 minority (41 Black or African American, non-Hispanic/Latino; 1 American Indian or Alaska Native, non-Hispanic/Latino; 14 Asian, non-Hispanic/Latino; 25 Hispanic/Latino; 10 Two or more races, non-Hispanic/Latino), 28 international. Average age 30. 617 applicants, 42% accepted, 171 enrolled. In 2014, 145 master's, 21 doctorates, 8 other advanced degrees awarded. Terminal master's awarded for partial completion of doctoral program. *Degree requirements:* For master's, comprehensive exam (for some programs), thesis optional; for doctorate, comprehensive exam, thesis/dissertation. *Entrance requirements:* For master's and doctorate, GRE General Test or MAT, letters of recommendation, interviews, goals statement, American Sign Language proficiency interview, written English competency. Additional exam requirements/recommendations for international students: Required—TOEFL. *Application deadline:* For fall admission, 2/15 for domestic students. Applications are processed on a rolling basis. Application fee: $75. Electronic applications accepted. *Expenses:* Tuition: Full-time $15,956; part-time $886.45 per credit hour. *Required fees:* $3404; $263 per semester. *Financial support:* Fellowships, research assistantships, teaching assistantships, career-related internships or fieldwork, Federal Work-Study, scholarships/grants, tuition waivers (partial), and unspecified assistantships available. Support available to part-time students. Financial award applicants required to submit FAFSA. *Faculty research:* Signing math dictionaries, telecommunications access, cancer genetics, linguistics, visual language and visual learning, integrated quantum materials, deaf legal discourse, advance recruitment and retention in geosciences. *Unit head:* Dr. Gaurav Mathur, Interim Dean, Graduate School and Continuing Studies, 202-250-2380, Fax: 202-651-5027, E-mail: gaurav.mathur@gallaudet.edu. *Application contact:* Wednesday Luria, Coordinator of Prospective Graduate Student Services, 202-651-5400, Fax: 202-651-5295, E-mail: graduate.school@gallaudet.edu.
Website: http://www.gallaudet.edu/x26696.xml

George Mason University, College of Humanities and Social Sciences, Department of English, Fairfax, VA 22030. Offers creative writing (MFA), including fiction; English (MA, Certificate); linguistics (PhD); writing and rhetoric (PhD). *Faculty:* 78 full-time (45 women), 35 part-time/adjunct (21 women). *Students:* 103 full-time (71 women), 140 part-

time (105 women); includes 36 minority (10 Black or African American, non-Hispanic/Latino; 8 Asian, non-Hispanic/Latino; 12 Hispanic/Latino; 6 Two or more races, non-Hispanic/Latino), 14 international. Average age 32. 267 applicants, 52% accepted, 67 enrolled. In 2014, 68 master's, 11 other advanced degrees awarded. *Degree requirements:* For master's, thesis (for some programs), proficiency in a foreign language by course work or translation test; for doctorate, thesis/dissertation, 2 graduating papers. *Entrance requirements:* For master's, official transcripts; expanded goals statement; writing sample; portfolio; 2 letters of recommendation; for doctorate, GRE, expanded goals statement; 3 letters of recommendation; writing sample; introductory course in linguistics; official transcripts; for Certificate, official transcripts; expanded goals statement; 3 letters of recommendation; portfolio and writing sample (for professional writing and rhetoric); resume and writing sample (for folklore). Additional exam requirements/recommendations for international students: Required—TOEFL (minimum score 570 paper-based; 80 iBT), IELTS (minimum score 6.5), PTE. *Application deadline:* For fall admission, 3/15 priority date for domestic students; for spring admission, 10/15 priority date for domestic students. Application fee: $65 ($80 for international students). Electronic applications accepted. *Expenses:* Tuition, state resident: full-time $9794; part-time $408 per credit hour. Tuition, nonresident: full-time $26,978; part-time $1124 per credit hour. *Required fees:* $2820; $118 per credit hour. Tuition and fees vary according to course load and program. *Financial support:* In 2014–15, 72 students received support, including 3 fellowships (averaging $1,823 per year), 6 research assistantships with full and partial tuition reimbursements available (averaging $14,605 per year), 65 teaching assistantships with full and partial tuition reimbursements available (averaging $11,909 per year); career-related internships or fieldwork, Federal Work-Study, scholarships/grants, unspecified assistantships, and health care benefits (for full-time research or teaching assistantship recipients) also available. Support available to part-time students. Financial award application deadline: 3/1; financial award applicants required to submit FAFSA. *Faculty research:* Literature, professional writing and editing, writing of fiction or poetry. *Total annual research expenditures:* $84,493. *Unit head:* Debra Lattanzi-Shutika, Chair, 703-993-1170, Fax: 703-993-1161, E-mail: dshutika@gmu.edu. *Application contact:* Alex Walsh, Graduate Admissions Coordinator, 703-993-1185, Fax: 703-993-1161, E-mail: awalsh7@gmu.edu.
Website: http://english.gmu.edu

Georgetown University, Graduate School of Arts and Sciences, Department of Linguistics, Washington, DC 20057. Offers language and communication (MA); linguistics (MS, PhD), including applied linguistics, computational linguistics, sociolinguistics, theoretical linguistics. Terminal master's awarded for partial completion of doctoral program. *Degree requirements:* For master's, one foreign language, comprehensive exam; for doctorate, 2 foreign languages, comprehensive exam, thesis/dissertation. *Entrance requirements:* For master's and doctorate, 18 undergraduate credits in a foreign language. Additional exam requirements/recommendations for international students: Required—TOEFL.

Georgia State University, College of Arts and Sciences, Department of Applied Linguistics and English as a Second Language, Atlanta, GA 30302-4099. Offers applied linguistics (MA, PhD). Part-time programs available. *Faculty:* 11 full-time (7 women). *Students:* 56 full-time (38 women), 10 part-time (6 women); includes 6 minority (2 Black or African American, non-Hispanic/Latino; 2 Asian, non-Hispanic/Latino; 1 Hispanic/Latino; 1 Two or more races, non-Hispanic/Latino), 16 international. Average age 32. 107 applicants, 31% accepted, 21 enrolled. In 2014, 23 master's, 3 doctorates awarded. *Degree requirements:* For master's, one foreign language, portfolio; for doctorate, one foreign language, comprehensive exam, thesis/dissertation, qualifying exam. *Entrance requirements:* For master's, GRE; for doctorate, GRE. Additional exam requirements/recommendations for international students: Required—TWE (minimum score 4), TOEFL (minimum score 600 paper-based; 97 iBT) or IELTS (minimum score 7). *Application deadline:* For fall admission, 1/15 for domestic and international students; for spring admission, 11/15 for domestic and international students. Applications are processed on a rolling basis. Application fee: $50. Electronic applications accepted. *Expenses:* Tuition, state resident: full-time $6516; part-time $362 per credit hour. Tuition, nonresident: full-time $22,014; part-time $1223 per credit hour. *Required fees:* $2128 per semester. Tuition and fees vary according to course load and program. *Financial support:* In 2014–15, fellowships with full tuition reimbursements (averaging $23,500 per year), research assistantships with full tuition reimbursements (averaging $5,000 per year), teaching assistantships with full tuition reimbursements (averaging $8,500 per year) were awarded; scholarships/grants and unspecified assistantships also available. Financial award application deadline: 6/1. *Faculty research:* Corpus linguistics, second language acquisition, second language literacy, assessment, teacher education. *Unit head:* Dr. Sara C. Weigle, Chair, 404-413-5192, Fax: 404-413-5201, E-mail: sweigle@gsu.edu. *Application contact:* Dr. Diane D. Belcher, Director of Graduate Studies, 404-413-5194, Fax: 404-413-5201, E-mail: dbelcher1@gsu.edu.
Website: http://www2.gsu.edu/~wwwesl/

Georgia State University, College of Arts and Sciences, Department of Modern and Classical Languages, Program in French, Atlanta, GA 30302-3083. Offers applied linguistics and pedagogy (MA); French studies (MA); literature and culture (MA). Part-time programs available. *Degree requirements:* For master's, one foreign language, comprehensive exam, thesis or alternative, Graduate Foreign Language Reading Exam. *Entrance requirements:* For master's, GRE, statement of purpose, writing sample in the target language, 2 letters of recommendation, official transcripts. Additional exam requirements/recommendations for international students: Required—TOEFL (minimum score 79 iBT). *Application deadline:* For fall admission, 3/15 priority date for domestic and international students; for spring admission, 11/15 priority date for domestic and international students. Application fee: $50. Electronic applications accepted. *Expenses:* Tuition, state resident: full-time $6516; part-time $362 per credit hour. Tuition, nonresident: full-time $22,014; part-time $1223 per credit hour. *Required fees:* $2128 per semester. Tuition and fees vary according to course load and program. *Financial support:* Institutionally sponsored loans available. Financial award applicants required to submit FAFSA. *Faculty research:* The nineteenth century novel, narratology, genetic criticism, poetics, semiotics, and intertextuality; Francophone and transnational studies; early modern travel literature; post/colonial and Diaspora studies; film studies; social and gender studies; eighteenth century French literature and history of ideas; history of civilization; Enlightenment, encyclopedism. *Unit head:* Dr. Fernando Reati, Department Chair, 404-413-5984, Fax: 404-413-5982, E-mail: freati@gsu.edu. *Application contact:* Lita Malveaux, Administrative Academic Specialist, 404-413-5046, Fax: 404-413-5036, E-mail: lmalveaux@gsu.edu.
Website: http://www.gsu.edu/~wwwmcl/

The Graduate Center, City University of New York, Graduate Studies, Program in Anthropology, New York, NY 10016-4039. Offers anthropological linguistics (PhD); archaeology (PhD); cultural anthropology (PhD); physical anthropology (PhD). *Degree requirements:* For doctorate, one foreign language, thesis/dissertation. *Entrance requirements:* For doctorate, GRE General Test. Additional exam requirements/recommendations for international students: Required—TOEFL. Electronic applications accepted.

The Graduate Center, City University of New York, Graduate Studies, Program in Linguistics, New York, NY 10016-4039. Offers MA, PhD. Terminal master's awarded for partial completion of doctoral program. *Degree requirements:* For master's, one foreign language, thesis; for doctorate, 2 foreign languages, thesis/dissertation. *Entrance requirements:* For master's and doctorate, GRE General Test. Additional exam requirements/recommendations for international students: Required—TOEFL. Electronic applications accepted.

Graduate Institute of Applied Linguistics, Graduate Programs, Dallas, TX 75236. Offers applied linguistics (MA, Certificate); language development (MA). Part-time programs available. *Degree requirements:* For master's, one foreign language, comprehensive exam (for some programs), thesis (for some programs). *Entrance requirements:* For master's, GRE. Additional exam requirements/recommendations for international students: Required—TOEFL (minimum score 577 paper-based; 90 iBT). Electronic applications accepted. *Faculty research:* Minority languages, endangered languages, language documentation.

Harvard University, Graduate School of Arts and Sciences, Department of Linguistics, Cambridge, MA 02138. Offers descriptive linguistics (PhD); historical linguistics (PhD); theoretical linguistics (PhD). *Degree requirements:* For doctorate, 4 foreign languages, thesis/dissertation, field exam, Indo-European language exam, research paper. *Entrance requirements:* For doctorate, GRE General Test. Additional exam requirements/recommendations for international students: Required—TOEFL.

Hofstra University, College of Liberal Arts and Sciences, Programs in Forensic Linguistics and Applied Linguistics, Hempstead, NY 11549. Offers applied linguistics (TESOL) (MA); linguistics (MA), including forensic linguistics. Part-time programs available. *Students:* 35 full-time (29 women), 4 part-time (all women); includes 6 minority (1 Black or African American, non-Hispanic/Latino; 1 Asian, non-Hispanic/Latino; 4 Hispanic/Latino), 6 international. Average age 27. 35 applicants, 83% accepted, 19 enrolled. In 2014, 21 master's awarded. *Degree requirements:* For master's, thesis, 36 credits, capstone, minimum GPA of 3.0. *Entrance requirements:* For master's, bachelor's degree in related area, interview, 2 letters of recommendation. Additional exam requirements/recommendations for international students: Required—TOEFL (minimum score 550 paper-based; 80 iBT). *Application deadline:* Applications are processed on a rolling basis. Application fee: $70 ($75 for international students). Electronic applications accepted. *Expenses: Tuition:* Full-time $20,610; part-time $1145 per credit hour. *Required fees:* $970; $165 per term. Tuition and fees vary according to program. *Financial support:* In 2014–15, 1 student received support, including 1 fellowship with full and partial tuition reimbursement available (averaging $13,500 per year); research assistantships with full and partial tuition reimbursements available, career-related internships or fieldwork, Federal Work-Study, institutionally sponsored loans, scholarships/grants, tuition waivers (full and partial), and unspecified assistantships also available. Support available to part-time students. Financial award applicants required to submit FAFSA. *Faculty research:* Application of linguistics to forensic data; interrogation techniques and invalid confessions; authorship analysis; forensic linguistically enhanced threat assessment; second language acquisition, second language writing. *Unit head:* Dr. Robert A. Leonard, Program Director, 516-463-5440, E-mail: cllral@hofstra.edu. *Application contact:* Sunil Samuel, Assistant Vice President of Admissions, 516-463-4723, Fax: 516-463-4664, E-mail: graduateadmission@hofstra.edu.
Website: http://www.hofstra.edu/hclas

Hofstra University, School of Education, Programs in Teacher Education, Hempstead, NY 11549. Offers bilingual education (MA), including biology (MA, MS Ed), geology; business education (MS Ed); early childhood and childhood education (MS Ed), including French; early childhood education (MA); education technology (Advanced Certificate); elementary education (MA), including math. science, technology (STEM); English education (MS Ed); fine arts education (MS Ed), including biology (MA, MS Ed); foreign language and TESOL (MS Ed); learning and teaching (Ed D), including applied linguistics, art education, arts and humanities, early childhood education, English education, human development, math education, math, science, and technology, multicultural education, physical education, science education, social studies education, special education; mathematics education (MA, MS Ed); secondary education (Advanced Certificate); social studies education (MA, MS Ed). Part-time and evening/weekend programs available. Postbaccalaureate distance learning degree programs offered (minimal on-campus study). *Students:* 141 full-time (111 women), 119 part-time (84 women); includes 58 minority (13 Black or African American, non-Hispanic/Latino; 14 Asian, non-Hispanic/Latino; 28 Hispanic/Latino; 1 Native Hawaiian or other Pacific Islander, non-Hispanic/Latino; 2 Two or more races, non-Hispanic/Latino), 18 international. Average age 30. 301 applicants, 87% accepted, 112 enrolled. In 2014, 133 master's, 5 doctorates, 28 other advanced degrees awarded. *Degree requirements:* For master's, comprehensive exam, thesis (for some programs), exit project, student teaching, fieldwork, electronic portfolio, curriculum project, minimum GPA of 3.0; for doctorate, thesis/dissertation; for Advanced Certificate, 3 foreign languages, comprehensive exam (for some programs), thesis project. *Entrance requirements:* For master's, 2 letters of recommendation, portfolio, teacher certification (MA), interview, essay; for doctorate, GMAT, GRE, LSAT, or MAT; for Advanced Certificate, 2 letters of recommendation, essay, interview and/or portfolio, teaching certificate. Additional exam requirements/recommendations for international students: Required—TOEFL (minimum score 550 paper-based; 80 iBT). *Application deadline:* Applications are processed on a rolling basis. Application fee: $70 ($75 for international students). Electronic applications accepted. *Expenses: Tuition:* Full-time $20,610; part-time $1145 per credit hour. *Required fees:* $970; $165 per term. Tuition and fees vary according to program. *Financial support:* In 2014–15, 153 students received support, including 60 fellowships with full and partial tuition reimbursements available (averaging $5,084 per year), 4 research assistantships with full and partial tuition reimbursements available (averaging $7,095 per year); Federal Work-Study, institutionally sponsored loans, scholarships/grants, health care benefits, and tuition waivers (full and partial) also available. Support available to part-time students. Financial award applicants required to submit FAFSA. *Faculty research:* Appropriate content in secondary school disciplines, lesson development across content, interdisciplinary curriculum, multicultural education. *Unit head:* Dr. Eustace Thompson, Chairperson, 516-463-5749, Fax: 516-463-6275, E-mail: edaegt@hofstra.edu. *Application contact:* Sunil Samuel, Assistant Vice President of Admissions, 516-463-4723, Fax: 516-463-4664, E-mail: graduateadmission@hofstra.edu.
Website: http://www.hofstra.edu/education/

Indiana State University, College of Graduate and Professional Studies, College of Arts and Sciences, Department of Languages, Literatures, and Linguistics, Terre Haute, IN 47809. Offers linguistics/teaching English as a second language (MA); TESL/TEFL (CAS). *Degree requirements:* For master's, comprehensive exam. Electronic applications accepted.

Indiana University Bloomington, University Graduate School, College of Arts and Sciences, Department of French and Italian, Bloomington, IN 47405. Offers French (MA, PhD), including French instruction (MA), French linguistics, French literature; Italian (MA, PhD). Part-time programs available. *Faculty:* 21 full-time (7 women). *Students:* 61 full-time (35 women), 1 (woman) part-time; includes 4 minority (1 Black or African

American, non-Hispanic/Latino; 1 Asian, non-Hispanic/Latino; 2 Hispanic/Latino), 23 international. Average age 30. 47 applicants, 47% accepted, 12 enrolled. In 2014, 21 master's, 5 doctorates awarded. Terminal master's awarded for partial completion of doctoral program. *Degree requirements:* For master's, variable foreign language requirement, comprehensive exam (for some programs), thesis optional; for doctorate, variable foreign language requirement, comprehensive exam, thesis/dissertation. *Entrance requirements:* For master's and doctorate, GRE General Test. Additional exam requirements/recommendations for international students: Required—TOEFL (minimum score 550 paper-based; 79 iBT). *Application deadline:* For fall admission, 1/15 priority date for domestic students, 12/1 priority date for international students; for spring admission, 9/1 priority date for domestic and international students. Application fee: $55 ($65 for international students). Electronic applications accepted. *Financial support:* In 2014–15, 46 students received support, including 7 fellowships with partial tuition reimbursements available (averaging $18,000 per year), 6 research assistantships with partial tuition reimbursements available (averaging $15,750 per year), 38 teaching assistantships with partial tuition reimbursements available (averaging $15,750 per year); health care benefits and unspecified assistantships also available. Financial award application deadline: 1/15. *Faculty research:* French and Italian literature, French linguistics, including the novel and political theory, literature and fine arts, literary theory, postcolonialism, French-Creole studies, French literature of Africa and its Diaspora, humanism, medieval folklore and mythology, humor in medieval and Renaissance literature, cinema Old Occitan and Old French, emigration, second language acquisition, syntax, sociolinguistics, phonology, lexicography. *Unit head:* Prof. Andrea Ciccarelli, Chair, 812-855-5458, Fax: 812-855-8877, E-mail: fritchr@indiana.edu. *Application contact:* Casey Green, Graduate Secretary, 812-855-1088, Fax: 812-855-8877, E-mail: fritgs@indiana.edu.
Website: http://www.indiana.edu/~frithome/

Indiana University Bloomington, University Graduate School, College of Arts and Sciences, Department of Germanic Studies, Bloomington, IN 47405-7000. Offers German philology and linguistics (PhD); German studies (MA, PhD), including German (MA), German literature and culture (MA), German literature and linguistics (MA); medieval German studies (PhD); teaching German (MAT). *Faculty:* 13 full-time (4 women), 6 part-time/adjunct (2 women). *Students:* 29 full-time (16 women), 6 international. Average age 31. 22 applicants, 9% accepted, 2 enrolled. In 2014, 4 doctorates awarded. Terminal master's awarded for partial completion of doctoral program. *Degree requirements:* For master's, one foreign language, project; for doctorate, one foreign language, comprehensive exam, thesis/dissertation. *Entrance requirements:* For master's, GRE General Test, BA in German or equivalent; for doctorate, GRE General Test, MA in German or equivalent. Additional exam requirements/recommendations for international students: Required—TOEFL. *Application deadline:* For fall admission, 1/15 priority date for domestic students, 12/1 for international students; for spring admission, 9/1 priority date for domestic students, 9/1 for international students. Applications are processed on a rolling basis. Application fee: $55 ($65 for international students). Electronic applications accepted. *Financial support:* Fellowships with full and partial tuition reimbursements, teaching assistantships with full tuition reimbursements, Federal Work-Study, institutionally sponsored loans, scholarships/grants, and unspecified assistantships available. Support available to part-time students. Financial award application deadline: 1/15; financial award applicants required to submit FAFSA. *Faculty research:* German and other European literature: medieval to modern/postmodern, German and culture studies, Germanic philology, literary theory, literature and the other arts. *Unit head:* Fritz Breithaupt, Department Chairman, 812-855-7947, Fax: 812-855-8292, E-mail: fbreitha@indiana.edu. *Application contact:* Michelle Dunbar, Graduate Secretary, 812-855-7947, E-mail: midunbar@indiana.edu.
Website: http://www.indiana.edu/~germanic/

Indiana University Bloomington, University Graduate School, College of Arts and Sciences, Department of Linguistics, Bloomington, IN 47405-7000. Offers African languages and linguistics (PhD); computational linguistics (MA, PhD); linguistics (MA, PhD). *Faculty:* 10 full-time (1 woman), 18 part-time/adjunct (7 women). *Students:* 64 full-time (34 women), 1 part-time (0 women); includes 4 minority (2 Black or African American, non-Hispanic/Latino; 1 Asian, non-Hispanic/Latino; 1 Two or more races, non-Hispanic/Latino), 24 international. Average age 32. 77 applicants, 35% accepted, 15 enrolled. In 2014, 6 master's, 8 doctorates awarded. Terminal master's awarded for partial completion of doctoral program. *Degree requirements:* For master's, one foreign language, thesis optional; for doctorate, one foreign language, comprehensive exam, thesis/dissertation, proficiency in research tool appropriate to research area. *Entrance requirements:* For master's and doctorate, GRE General Test. Additional exam requirements/recommendations for international students: Required—TOEFL (minimum score 580 paper-based; 92 iBT). *Application deadline:* For fall admission, 1/15 priority date for domestic students, 12/1 priority date for international students. Application fee: $55 ($65 for international students). Electronic applications accepted. *Financial support:* Fellowships with full tuition reimbursements, research assistantships with full tuition reimbursements, teaching assistantships with full tuition reimbursements, and unspecified assistantships available. *Faculty research:* African linguistics and language, semantics, phonology, syntactic theory, historical linguistics, phonetics-phonology, syntax, sociolinguistics, computational linguistics. *Total annual research expenditures:* $100,000. *Unit head:* Dr. Robert Botne, Chair, 812-855-6456, Fax: 812-855-3594, E-mail: botner@indiana.edu. *Application contact:* Margaret Anderson, Secretary, 812-855-6456, Fax: 812-855-5363, E-mail: maraande@indiana.edu.
Website: http://www.indiana.edu/~lingdept/

Instituto Tecnologico de Santo Domingo, Graduate School, Area of Humanities and Social Sciences, Santo Domingo, Dominican Republic. Offers accounting (Certificate); adult education (Certificate); applied linguistics (MA); economics (MA); education (M Ed); educational psychology (MA, Certificate); gender and development (MA, Certificate); humanistic studies (MA); international marketing management (Certificate); international relations in the Caribbean basin (Certificate); intervention systems in family therapy (MA); linguistic and literary communication (Certificate); pedagogical support (MA); social science education (M Ed); sustainable human development (MA); terminal illness and death psychology (Certificate); youth and adult education (M Ed).

Iowa State University of Science and Technology, Program in Applied Linguistics and Technology, Ames, IA 50011. Offers PhD. *Entrance requirements:* For doctorate, GRE, official academic transcripts, resume, three letters of recommendation, writing sample. Additional exam requirements/recommendations for international students: Required—TOEFL (minimum score 640 paper-based; 111 iBT), IELTS (minimum score 7.5). Electronic applications accepted.

Iowa State University of Science and Technology, Program in Teaching English as a Second Language/Applied Linguistics, Ames, IA 50011. Offers MA. *Entrance requirements:* For master's, GRE, official academic transcripts, resume, three letters of recommendation, statement of personal goals, writing sample. Additional exam requirements/recommendations for international students: Required—TOEFL (minimum score 600 paper-based; 100 iBT), IELTS (minimum score 7). Electronic applications accepted.

Massachusetts Institute of Technology, School of Humanities, Arts, and Social Sciences, Department of Linguistics and Philosophy, Linguistics Section, Cambridge, MA 02139. Offers PhD. *Faculty:* 13 full-time (3 women), 1 (woman) part-time/adjunct. *Students:* 44 full-time (19 women), 1 part-time (0 women); includes 4 minority (3 Asian, non-Hispanic/Latino; 1 Two or more races, non-Hispanic/Latino), 25 international. Average age 28. 172 applicants, 8% accepted, 11 enrolled. In 2014, 8 doctorates awarded. *Degree requirements:* For doctorate, one foreign language, comprehensive exam, thesis/dissertation, serve as Teaching Assistant during two semesters. *Entrance requirements:* Additional exam requirements/recommendations for international students: Required—TOEFL (minimum score 577 paper-based; 90 iBT), IELTS (minimum score 6.5). *Application deadline:* For fall admission, 1/2 for domestic and international students. Application fee: $75. Electronic applications accepted. *Expenses:* Tuition: Full-time $44,720; part-time $699 per unit. *Required fees:* $296. *Financial support:* In 2014–15, 14 fellowships (averaging $34,100 per year), 29 research assistantships (averaging $36,500 per year) were awarded; teaching assistantships also available. Financial award application deadline: 4/15; financial award applicants required to submit FAFSA. *Faculty research:* Phonology and phonetics, syntax and semantics, morphology, psycholinguistics, language acquisition. *Total annual research expenditures:* $332,000. *Unit head:* Prof. David Pesetsky, Linguistics Chair, 617-253-4141, Fax: 617-253-5017, E-mail: lp-admissions@mit.edu. *Application contact:* Graduate Admissions, 617-253-4141, Fax: 617-253-5017, E-mail: lp-admissions@mit.edu.
Website: http://web.mit.edu/linguistics/

McGill University, Faculty of Graduate and Postdoctoral Studies, Faculty of Arts, Department of Linguistics, Montréal, QC H3A 2T5, Canada. Offers language acquisition (PhD); linguistics (MA, PhD).

Memorial University of Newfoundland, School of Graduate Studies, Department of Linguistics, St. John's, NL A1C 5S7, Canada. Offers MA, PhD. *Degree requirements:* For master's, one foreign language, thesis or comprehensive exam; for doctorate, 2 foreign languages, comprehensive exam, thesis/dissertation, oral defense of thesis. *Entrance requirements:* For master's, BA in linguistics; for doctorate, master's degree in linguistics. Electronic applications accepted. *Faculty research:* Aboriginal languages of eastern North America, historical/comparative linguistics, languages and dialects of Newfoundland and Labrador.

Michigan State University, The Graduate School, College of Arts and Letters, Department of Linguistics and Germanic, Slavic, Asian, and African Languages, East Lansing, MI 48824. Offers German studies (MA, PhD); linguistics (MA, PhD); teaching English to speakers of other languages (MA). Part-time and evening/weekend programs available. *Entrance requirements:* For master's, GRE General Test, minimum GPA of 3.2 in last 2 undergraduate years, 2 years of college-level foreign language, 3 letters of recommendation, portfolio (German studies); for doctorate, GRE General Test, minimum graduate GPA of 3.5, 3 letters of recommendation, master's degree or sufficient graduate course work in linguistics or language of study, master's thesis or major research paper. Additional exam requirements/recommendations for international students: Required—TOEFL. Electronic applications accepted.

Michigan State University, The Graduate School, College of Arts and Letters, Department of Spanish and Portuguese, East Lansing, MI 48824. Offers applied Spanish linguistics (MA); Hispanic cultural studies (PhD); Hispanic literatures (MA). *Entrance requirements:* Additional exam requirements/recommendations for international students: Required—TOEFL. Electronic applications accepted.

Montclair State University, The Graduate School, College of Humanities and Social Sciences, Program in Applied Linguistics, Montclair, NJ 07043-1624. Offers MA. Part-time and evening/weekend programs available. *Students:* 14 full-time (11 women), 12 part-time (8 women); includes 4 minority (all Hispanic/Latino), 8 international. Average age 32. 25 applicants, 32% accepted, 6 enrolled. In 2014, 13 master's awarded. *Degree requirements:* For master's, comprehensive exam. *Entrance requirements:* For master's, GRE General Test, 2 letters of recommendation, essay. Additional exam requirements/recommendations for international students: Required—TOEFL (minimum score 83 iBT), IELTS (minimum score 6.5). *Application deadline:* Applications are processed on a rolling basis. Application fee: $60. Electronic applications accepted. *Expenses:* Tuition, state resident: full-time $9960; part-time $553.35 per credit. Tuition, nonresident: full-time $15,074; part-time $837.43 per credit. *Required fees:* $1595; $88.63 per credit. Tuition and fees vary according to degree level and program. *Financial support:* In 2014–15, 2 research assistantships with full tuition reimbursements (averaging $7,000 per year) were awarded; Federal Work-Study, scholarships/grants, and unspecified assistantships also available. Support available to part-time students. Financial award application deadline: 3/1; financial award applicants required to submit FAFSA. *Faculty research:* Research on short message service (SMS) text messaging; corpus building and research; research on online, hybrid, and mobile language learning; linguistic code switching and bilingual mental lexical, sentence comprehension; second language acquisition of American Sign Language; cognitive linguistics, phonetics, forensic. *Unit head:* Dr. Eileen Fitzpatrick, Chairperson, 973-655-4480. *Application contact:* Amy Aiello, Director of Graduate Admissions and Operations, 973-655-5147, E-mail: graduate.school@montclair.edu.

Montclair State University, The Graduate School, College of Humanities and Social Sciences, Program in Computational Linguistics, Montclair, NJ 07043-1624. Offers Certificate. Part-time and evening/weekend programs available. *Students:* 1 full-time (0 women); minority (Native Hawaiian or other Pacific Islander, non-Hispanic/Latino). Average age 22. 3 applicants, 67% accepted, 1 enrolled. In 2014, 2 Certificates awarded. *Entrance requirements:* For degree, 2 letters of recommendation, essay. Additional exam requirements/recommendations for international students: Required—TOEFL (minimum score 83 iBT), IELTS (minimum score 6.5). *Application deadline:* Applications are processed on a rolling basis. Application fee: $60. Electronic applications accepted. *Expenses:* Tuition, state resident: full-time $9960; part-time $553.35 per credit. Tuition, nonresident: full-time $15,074; part-time $837.43 per credit. *Required fees:* $1595; $88.63 per credit. Tuition and fees vary according to degree level and program. *Financial support:* Federal Work-Study, scholarships/grants, and unspecified assistantships available. Support available to part-time students. Financial award application deadline: 3/1; financial award applicants required to submit FAFSA. *Faculty research:* Resource light morphology, creativity, idiomatic sentence detection; computational approaches to deception detection; computational approaches to fusional morphology; computational approaches to figurative language. *Unit head:* Dr. Eileen Fitzpatrick, Chairperson, 973-655-4480. *Application contact:* Amy Aiello, Director of Graduate Admissions and Operations, 973-655-5147, Fax: 973-655-7869, E-mail: graduate.school@montclair.edu.

National University, Academic Affairs, College of Letters and Sciences, La Jolla, CA 92037-1011. Offers applied linguistics (MA); biology (MS); counseling psychology (MA), including licensed professional clinical counseling, marriage and family therapy; creative writing (MFA); English (MA), including Gothic studies, rhetoric; film studies (MA); forensic and crime science (Certificate); forensic studies (MFS), including criminalistics, investigation; history (MA); human behavior (MA); mathematics for educators (MS); performance psychology (MA); strategic communications (MA). Part-time and evening/weekend programs available. Postbaccalaureate distance learning degree programs

offered (no on-campus study). *Faculty:* 69 full-time (34 women), 100 part-time/adjunct (55 women). *Students:* 727 full-time (532 women), 349 part-time (240 women); includes 505 minority (128 Black or African American, non-Hispanic/Latino; 5 American Indian or Alaska Native, non-Hispanic/Latino; 52 Asian, non-Hispanic/Latino; 260 Hispanic/Latino; 9 Native Hawaiian or other Pacific Islander, non-Hispanic/Latino; 51 Two or more races, non-Hispanic/Latino), 4 international. Average age 34. In 2014, 569 master's awarded. *Degree requirements:* For master's, thesis (for some programs). *Entrance requirements:* For master's, interview, minimum GPA of 2.5. Additional exam requirements/recommendations for international students: Required—TOEFL (minimum score 550 paper-based; 79 iBT), IELTS (minimum score 6). *Application deadline:* Applications are processed on a rolling basis. Application fee: $60 ($65 for international students). Electronic applications accepted. *Expenses: Tuition:* Full-time $14,184; part-time $1773 per course. *Financial support:* Career-related internships or fieldwork, institutionally sponsored loans, scholarships/grants, and tuition waivers (partial) available. Support available to part-time students. Financial award application deadline: 6/30; financial award applicants required to submit FAFSA. *Unit head:* College of Letters and Sciences, 800-628-8648, E-mail: cols@nu.edu. *Application contact:* Frank Rojas, Interim Vice President for Enrollment Services, 800-628-8648, E-mail: advisor@nu.edu.
Website: http://www.nu.edu/OurPrograms/CollegeOfLettersAndSciences.html

New York University, Graduate School of Arts and Science, Department of Linguistics, New York, NY 10012-1019. Offers MA, PhD. Part-time programs available. *Faculty:* 8 full-time (2 women). *Students:* 39 full-time (22 women); includes 6 minority (1 Black or African American, non-Hispanic/Latino; 2 Asian, non-Hispanic/Latino; 3 Two or more races, non-Hispanic/Latino), 19 international. Average age 30. 124 applicants, 9% accepted, 4 enrolled. In 2014, 2 master's, 9 doctorates awarded. Terminal master's awarded for partial completion of doctoral program. *Degree requirements:* For master's, one foreign language, comprehensive exam, thesis optional; for doctorate, one foreign language, thesis/dissertation, 2 publishable papers. *Entrance requirements:* For master's and doctorate, GRE General Test. Additional exam requirements/recommendations for international students: Required—TOEFL. *Application deadline:* For fall admission, 1/4 priority date for domestic students, 1/4 for international students. Application fee: $100. *Financial support:* Fellowships with tuition reimbursements, teaching assistantships with tuition reimbursements, Federal Work-Study, institutionally sponsored loans, scholarships/grants, health care benefits, and unspecified assistantships available. Financial award application deadline: 1/4; financial award applicants required to submit FAFSA. *Faculty research:* Phonology, syntax, sociolinguistics, cognitive science. *Unit head:* Chris Barker, Chair, 212-998-7950, Fax: 212-995-4707, E-mail: linguistics@nyu.edu. *Application contact:* Lisa Davidson, Acting Director of Graduate Studies, 212-998-7950, Fax: 212-995-4707, E-mail: linguistics@nyu.edu.
Website: http://www.nyu.edu/gsas/dept/lingu/

New York University, Steinhardt School of Culture, Education, and Human Development, Department of Teaching and Learning, Program in English Education, New York, NY 10012-1019. Offers clinically-based English education, grades 7-12 (MA, Postbaccalaureate Certificate); English education (Advanced Certificate); English education secondary and college (PhD), including applied linguistics, English education secondary and college; teaching English 7-12 (MA). *Accreditation:* Teacher Education Accreditation Council. Part-time programs available. *Faculty:* 4 full-time (3 women). *Students:* 19 full-time (13 women), 34 part-time (19 women); includes 23 minority (13 Black or African American, non-Hispanic/Latino; 1 American Indian or Alaska Native, non-Hispanic/Latino; 3 Asian, non-Hispanic/Latino; 6 Hispanic/Latino), 2 international. Average age 33. 81 applicants, 78% accepted, 21 enrolled. In 2014, 27 master's, 6 doctorates awarded. *Degree requirements:* For master's, thesis (for some programs); for doctorate, thesis/dissertation. *Entrance requirements:* For doctorate, GRE General Test, interview; for other advanced degree, master's degree. Additional exam requirements/recommendations for international students: Required—TOEFL (minimum score 100 iBT). *Application deadline:* For fall admission, 12/1 priority date for domestic and international students; for spring admission, 10/1 for domestic and international students. Applications are processed on a rolling basis. Application fee: $75. Electronic applications accepted. *Financial support:* Fellowships with full and partial tuition reimbursements, teaching assistantships with full and partial tuition reimbursements, career-related internships or fieldwork, Federal Work-Study, institutionally sponsored loans, scholarships/grants, tuition waivers (partial), and unspecified assistantships available. Support available to part-time students. Financial award application deadline: 2/1; financial award applicants required to submit FAFSA. *Faculty research:* Making meaning of literature, teaching of literature, urban adolescent literacy and equity, literacy development and globalization, digital media and literacy. *Unit head:* Prof. Sarah W. Beck, Chairperson, 212-998-5473, Fax: 212-995-4049, E-mail: sarah.beck@nyu.edu. *Application contact:* 212-998-5030, Fax: 212-995-4328, E-mail: steinhardt.gradadmissions@nyu.edu.
Website: http://steinhardt.nyu.edu/teachlearn/english

Northeastern Illinois University, College of Graduate Studies and Research, College of Arts and Sciences, Program in Linguistics, Chicago, IL 60625-4699. Offers linguistics (MA); TESL (MA). Part-time and evening/weekend programs available. *Degree requirements:* For master's, one foreign language, comprehensive exam, thesis optional. *Entrance requirements:* For master's, 9 undergraduate hours in a foreign language or equivalent, minimum GPA of 2.75. Additional exam requirements/recommendations for international students: Required—TOEFL (minimum score 550 paper-based; 79 iBT). Electronic applications accepted. *Faculty research:* Acquisition of literacy, Mayan language, Rotuman language, English as a second language methodology, Farsi language.

Northern Arizona University, Graduate College, College of Arts and Letters, Department of English, Flagstaff, AZ 86011. Offers applied linguistics (PhD); English (MA, MFA), including creative writing (MFA), general English studies (MA), literature (MA), rhetoric and the teaching of writing (MA), secondary English education (MA); professional writing (Certificate); teaching English as a second language (MA, Certificate). Part-time programs available. *Degree requirements:* For master's, comprehensive exam (for some programs), thesis (for some programs), departmental qualifying exam; for doctorate, comprehensive exam, thesis/dissertation, departmental qualifying exam. *Entrance requirements:* For master's, minimum GPA of 3.0 or GRE; for doctorate, GRE General Test. Additional exam requirements/recommendations for international students: Required—TOEFL (minimum score 550 paper-based; 80 iBT), IELTS (minimum score 7), TOEFL (minimum score 600 paper-based; 100 iBT) for PhD; TOEFL (minimum score 570 paper-based; 89 iBT) for MA. Electronic applications accepted.

Northwestern University, The Graduate School, Judd A. and Marjorie Weinberg College of Arts and Sciences, Department of Linguistics, Evanston, IL 60208. Offers PhD, JD/PhD. Admissions and degrees offered through The Graduate School. Part-time programs available. Terminal master's awarded for partial completion of doctoral program. *Degree requirements:* For doctorate, 2 foreign languages, thesis/dissertation, 2 qualifying papers. *Entrance requirements:* For doctorate, GRE General Test. Additional exam requirements/recommendations for international students: Required—TOEFL. Electronic applications accepted. *Faculty research:* Theoretical linguistics, empirical approaches to the study of language, language and cognition.

Oakland University, Graduate Study and Lifelong Learning, College of Arts and Sciences, Department of Linguistics, Rochester, MI 48309-4401. Offers linguistics (MA); teaching English as a second language (Certificate). Part-time and evening/weekend programs available. *Entrance requirements:* For master's, minimum GPA of 3.0. Additional exam requirements/recommendations for international students: Required—TOEFL (minimum score 550 paper-based).

The Ohio State University, Graduate School, College of Arts and Sciences, Division of Arts and Humanities, Department of Linguistics, Columbus, OH 43210. Offers MA, PhD. *Faculty:* 16. *Students:* 36 full-time (12 women); includes 6 minority (1 Black or African American, non-Hispanic/Latino; 1 Asian, non-Hispanic/Latino; 1 Hispanic/Latino; 3 Two or more races, non-Hispanic/Latino), 7 international. Average age 28. In 2014, 5 master's, 8 doctorates awarded. Terminal master's awarded for partial completion of doctoral program. *Degree requirements:* For master's, one foreign language, exam or thesis; for doctorate, 2 foreign languages, thesis/dissertation, exam. *Entrance requirements:* For master's and doctorate, GRE General Test. Additional exam requirements/recommendations for international students: Required—TOEFL (minimum score 600 paper-based; 100 iBT), Michigan English Language Assessment Battery (minimum score 86); Recommended—IELTS (minimum score 8). *Application deadline:* For fall admission, 12/1 priority date for domestic students, 11/30 priority date for international students; for winter admission, 12/1 for domestic students, 11/1 for international students; for spring admission, 3/1 for domestic students, 2/1 for international students. Applications are processed on a rolling basis. Application fee: $60 ($70 for international students). Electronic applications accepted. *Financial support:* Fellowships with tuition reimbursements, research assistantships with tuition reimbursements, teaching assistantships with tuition reimbursements, Federal Work-Study, and institutionally sponsored loans available. Support available to part-time students. *Faculty research:* Experimental phonetics, nonlinear phonology, process morphology (synchronically and diachronically), syntactic theory, Montague semantics. *Unit head:* Dr. Shari R. Speer, Chair, 617-292-5389, E-mail: speer.21@osu.edu. *Application contact:* Graduate and Professional Admissions, 614-292-9444, Fax: 614-292-3895, E-mail: gpadmissions@osu.edu.
Website: http://linguistics.osu.edu/

The Ohio State University, Graduate School, College of Arts and Sciences, Division of Arts and Humanities, Department of Slavic and East European Languages and Cultures, Columbus, OH 43210. Offers Slavic linguistics (MA, PhD); Slavic literature, film, and cultural studies (MA, PhD). *Faculty:* 10. *Students:* 15 full-time (9 women), 1 (woman) part-time; includes 1 minority (Hispanic/Latino), 2 international. Average age 30. In 2014, 2 master's, 5 doctorates awarded. Terminal master's awarded for partial completion of doctoral program. *Degree requirements:* For master's, variable foreign language requirement, thesis optional; for doctorate, variable foreign language requirement, thesis/dissertation. *Entrance requirements:* For master's and doctorate, GRE General Test, at least 3 years of Russian language study or equivalent. Additional exam requirements/recommendations for international students: Required—TOEFL (minimum score 550 paper-based; 79 iBT), Michigan English Language Assessment Battery (minimum score 82); Recommended—IELTS (minimum score 7). *Application deadline:* For fall admission, 12/12 priority date for domestic students, 11/30 priority date for international students; for winter admission, 12/1 for domestic students, 11/1 for international students; for spring admission, 3/1 for domestic students, 2/1 for international students. Applications are processed on a rolling basis. Application fee: $60 ($70 for international students). Electronic applications accepted. *Financial support:* Fellowships with tuition reimbursements, teaching assistantships with tuition reimbursements, Federal Work-Study, and institutionally sponsored loans available. Support available to part-time students. *Faculty research:* Polish literature. *Unit head:* Dr. Yana Hashamova, Chair and Professor, 614-292-6733, E-mail: hashamova.1@osu.edu. *Application contact:* Graduate and Professional Admissions, 614-292-9444, Fax: 614-292-3895, E-mail: gpadmissions@osu.edu.
Website: http://slavic.osu.edu/

Ohio University, Graduate College, College of Arts and Sciences, Department of Linguistics, Athens, OH 45701-2979. Offers applied linguistics (MA). Part-time programs available. *Degree requirements:* For master's, one foreign language, thesis or alternative. *Entrance requirements:* For master's, minimum GPA of 3.0. Additional exam requirements/recommendations for international students: Required—TOEFL (minimum score 600 paper-based; 100 iBT) or IELTS (minimum score 7). Electronic applications accepted. *Faculty research:* Syntax, language learning, language teaching, computers for teaching, sociolinguistics.

Old Dominion University, College of Arts and Letters, Program in Applied Linguistics, Norfolk, VA 23529. Offers MA. Part-time programs available. *Faculty:* 4 full-time (all women). *Students:* 7 full-time (5 women), 19 part-time (15 women); includes 1 minority (Asian, non-Hispanic/Latino), 2 international. Average age 34. 23 applicants, 91% accepted, 11 enrolled. In 2014, 16 master's awarded. *Degree requirements:* For master's, one foreign language, comprehensive exam, thesis optional, program portfolio. *Entrance requirements:* For master's, GRE General Test, sample of written work; 12 hours in English, 9 on the upper-level; minimum B average; letters of recommendation; resume; essay. Additional exam requirements/recommendations for international students: Required—TOEFL (minimum score 570 paper-based; 88 iBT). *Application deadline:* For fall admission, 3/15 priority date for domestic and international students; for spring admission, 10/1 priority date for domestic and international students. Applications are processed on a rolling basis. Application fee: $50. Electronic applications accepted. *Expenses:* Tuition, state resident: full-time $10,488; part-time $437 per credit. Tuition, nonresident: full-time $26,136; part-time $1089 per credit. *Required fees:* $64 per semester. One-time fee: $50. *Financial support:* In 2014–15, 4 students received support, including 1 research assistantship (averaging $10,000 per year), 3 teaching assistantships (averaging $10,000 per year); career-related internships or fieldwork, institutionally sponsored loans, and unspecified assistantships also available. Financial award application deadline: 2/15. *Faculty research:* Discourse analysis, phonology, syntax, second language acquisition, gender, sociolinguistics. *Unit head:* Dr. Bridget Anderson, Graduate Program Director, 757-683-4020, Fax: 757-683-3241, E-mail: linggpd@odu.edu. *Application contact:* Dr. David C. Earnest, Associate Dean, 757-683-6077, Fax: 757-683-5746, E-mail: dearnest@odu.edu.
Website: http://al.odu.edu/english/academics/ma_linguistics.shtml

Penn State University Park, Graduate School, College of the Liberal Arts, Department of Applied Linguistics, University Park, PA 16802. Offers applied linguistics (PhD); teaching English as a second language (MA). *Unit head:* Dr. Susan Welch, Dean, 814-865-7691, Fax: 814-863-2085, E-mail: swelch@psu.edu. *Application contact:* Lori A. Stania, Director, Graduate Student Services, 814-867-5278, Fax: 814-863-4627, E-mail: gswww@psu.edu.
Website: http://aplng.la.psu.edu/

Purdue University, Graduate School, College of Health and Human Sciences, Department of Speech, Language, and Hearing Sciences, West Lafayette, IN 47907. Offers audiology clinic (MS, Au D, PhD); linguistics (MS, PhD); speech and hearing science (MS, PhD); speech-language pathology (MS, PhD). *Accreditation:* ASHA.

Degree requirements: For master's, comprehensive exam (for some programs), thesis optional; for doctorate, comprehensive exam, thesis/dissertation. *Entrance requirements:* For master's and doctorate, GRE General Test, minimum undergraduate GPA of 3.0 or equivalent. Additional exam requirements/recommendations for international students: Required—TOEFL (minimum score 77 iBT). Electronic applications accepted. *Faculty research:* Psychoacoustics, speech perception, speech physiology, stuttering, child language.

Purdue University, Graduate School, College of Liberal Arts, Department of English, West Lafayette, IN 47907. Offers creative writing (MFA); literature (MA, PhD), including linguistics, literature and philosophy (PhD), rhetoric and composition, theory and cultural studies (PhD). Part-time programs available. *Degree requirements:* For master's, one foreign language, comprehensive exam (for some programs), thesis (for some programs); for doctorate, one foreign language, comprehensive exam, thesis/dissertation. *Entrance requirements:* For master's, GRE General Test; GRE Subject Test in English literature (recommended for students applying to literary studies), minimum undergraduate GPA of 3.0 or equivalent; for doctorate, GRE General Test; GRE Subject Test in English literature (recommended for students applying to literary studies), master's degree. Additional exam requirements/recommendations for international students: Required—TOEFL (minimum score 620 paper-based; 77 iBT). Electronic applications accepted. *Faculty research:* Cultural studies, postmodern narrative, contemporary women writers, composition theory, slave narratives.

Purdue University, Graduate School, College of Liberal Arts, Program in Linguistics, West Lafayette, IN 47907. Offers MS, PhD. *Degree requirements:* For master's, one foreign language, thesis; for doctorate, 3 foreign languages, comprehensive exam, thesis/dissertation. *Entrance requirements:* For master's, GRE General Test (minimum score of 500 for verbal and quantitative respectively), minimum undergraduate GPA of 3.4; for doctorate, GRE General Test (minimum score of 500 for verbal and quantitative respectively), minimum undergraduate GPA of 3.4. Additional exam requirements/recommendations for international students: Required—TOEFL (minimum score 620 paper-based; 77 iBT), TWE. Electronic applications accepted. *Faculty research:* Sign languages, sociolinguistics and African American English, computational linguistics, indigenous languages, theoretical linguistics.

Queens College of the City University of New York, Division of Graduate Studies, Arts and Humanities Division, Department of Linguistics and Communication Disorders, Program in Applied Linguistics, Flushing, NY 11367-1597. Offers MA. Part-time and evening/weekend programs available. *Degree requirements:* For master's, thesis optional. *Entrance requirements:* For master's, minimum GPA of 3.0. Additional exam requirements/recommendations for international students: Required—TOEFL.

Rice University, Graduate Programs, School of Humanities, Department of Linguistics, Houston, TX 77251-1892. Offers MA, PhD. Terminal master's awarded for partial completion of doctoral program. *Degree requirements:* For master's, one foreign language, thesis; for doctorate, 2 foreign languages, thesis/dissertation, 3 research papers. *Entrance requirements:* For master's and doctorate, GRE General Test, minimum GPA of 3.0. Additional exam requirements/recommendations for international students: Required—TOEFL (minimum score 600 paper-based; 90 iBT). Electronic applications accepted. *Faculty research:* Typology, fieldwork and language description, cognitive grammar, historical linguistics, corpus linguistics.

Rutgers, The State University of New Jersey, New Brunswick, Graduate School-New Brunswick, Department of Linguistics, Piscataway, NJ 08854-8097. Offers PhD. *Degree requirements:* For doctorate, thesis/dissertation, 2 qualifying papers. *Entrance requirements:* For doctorate, GRE General Test, 3 letters of recommendation, writing sample. Additional exam requirements/recommendations for international students: Recommended—TOEFL. Electronic applications accepted. *Faculty research:* Theoretical linguistics, syntax, semantics, phonology, computational linguistics, phoenetics.

San Diego State University, Graduate and Research Affairs, College of Arts and Letters, Department of Linguistics and Oriental Languages, San Diego, CA 92182. Offers applied linguistics and English as a second language (CAL); computational linguistics (MA); English as a second language/applied linguistics (MA); general linguistics (MA). *Degree requirements:* For master's, one foreign language, comprehensive exam, thesis optional. *Entrance requirements:* For master's, GRE General Test, 2 letters of recommendation. Additional exam requirements/recommendations for international students: Required—TOEFL (minimum score 570 paper-based). Electronic applications accepted. *Faculty research:* Cross-cultural linguistic studies of semantics.

San Francisco State University, Division of Graduate Studies, College of Liberal and Creative Arts, Department of English Language and Literature, Program in Linguistics, San Francisco, CA 94132-1722. Offers MA. Part-time programs available. *Degree requirements:* For master's, 2 foreign languages, thesis (for some programs). *Application deadline:* Applications are processed on a rolling basis. *Expenses:* Tuition, state resident: full-time $6738. Tuition, nonresident: full-time $17,898; part-time $372 per credit hour. *Required fees:* $498 per semester. *Faculty research:* Mental lexicon, endangered languages, language and gender, linguistics, discourse analysis. *Unit head:* Dr. Sugie Goen-Salter, Chair, 415-338-2660, E-mail: english@sfsu.edu. *Application contact:* Prof. Troi Carleton, Graduate Coordinator, 415-338-3156, E-mail: troi@sfsu.edu.
Website: http://english.sfsu.edu/content/ma-linguistics

San Jose State University, Graduate Studies and Research, College of Humanities and the Arts, Department of Linguistics and Language Development, San Jose, CA 95192-0001. Offers computational linguistics (Certificate); linguistics (MA); teaching English to speakers of other languages (MA, Certificate). *Entrance requirements:* Additional exam requirements/recommendations for international students: Required—TOEFL (minimum score 570 paper-based). Electronic applications accepted.

Simon Fraser University, Office of Graduate Studies, Faculty of Arts and Social Sciences, Department of Linguistics, Burnaby, BC V5A 1S6, Canada. Offers MA, PhD. *Degree requirements:* For master's, one foreign language, thesis; for doctorate, 2 foreign languages, thesis/dissertation, qualifying papers. *Entrance requirements:* For master's, minimum GPA of 3.0 (on scale of 4.33), or 3.33 based on last 60 credits of undergraduate courses; for doctorate, minimum GPA of 3.5 (on scale of 4.33). Additional exam requirements/recommendations for international students: Recommended—TOEFL (minimum score 580 paper-based; 93 iBT), IELTS (minimum score 7), TWE (minimum score 5). Electronic applications accepted. *Faculty research:* History of linguistics, syntactic theory, relational grammar, experimental phonetics, pragmatics.

Southern Illinois University Carbondale, Graduate School, College of Liberal Arts, Department of Applied Linguistics, Carbondale, IL 62901-4701. Offers MA. *Faculty:* 9 full-time (6 women), 1 part-time/adjunct (0 women). *Students:* 70 full-time (38 women), 10 part-time (4 women); includes 3 minority (all Black or African American, non-Hispanic/Latino), 52 international. Average age 27. 93 applicants, 44% accepted, 18 enrolled. In 2014, 61 master's awarded. *Degree requirements:* For master's, one foreign language, thesis. *Entrance requirements:* For master's, minimum GPA of 3.0. Additional exam requirements/recommendations for international students: Required—TOEFL. *Application deadline:* For fall admission, 4/1 priority date for domestic students. Applications are processed on a rolling basis. Application fee: $50. *Expenses:* Tuition, state resident: full-time $10,176; part-time $1153 per credit. Tuition, nonresident: full-time $20,814; part-time $1744 per credit. *Required fees:* $7092; $394 per credit. $2364 per semester. *Financial support:* Fellowships with full tuition reimbursements, research assistantships with full tuition reimbursements, teaching assistantships with full tuition reimbursements, career-related internships or fieldwork, Federal Work-Study, institutionally sponsored loans, and tuition waivers (full) available. Support available to part-time students. Financial award application deadline: 4/1. *Faculty research:* Theory and methods, second language acquisition, pidgin and Creole languages, cognitive grammar. *Unit head:* Dr. Laura Halliday, Chair, 618-453-3385, E-mail: halliday@siu.edu. *Application contact:* Diane Korando, Departmental Secretary, 618-536-3385, Fax: 618-453-6527, E-mail: ling@siu.edu.
Website: http://www.linguistics.siuc.edu/

Stanford University, School of Humanities and Sciences, Department of Linguistics, Stanford, CA 94305-9991. Offers MA, PhD. *Degree requirements:* For master's, one foreign language, thesis; for doctorate, 2 foreign languages, thesis/dissertation, oral exam, qualifying papers. *Entrance requirements:* For master's and doctorate, GRE General Test. Additional exam requirements/recommendations for international students: Required—TOEFL. Electronic applications accepted. *Expenses: Tuition:* Full-time $44,184; part-time $982 per credit hour. *Required fees:* $191.

Stony Brook University, State University of New York, Graduate School, College of Arts and Sciences, Department of Linguistics, Program in Linguistics, Stony Brook, NY 11794. Offers MA, PhD. *Faculty:* 24 full-time (14 women), 9 part-time/adjunct (8 women). *Students:* 34 full-time (19 women), 1 part-time (0 women); includes 3 minority (2 Asian, non-Hispanic/Latino; 1 Hispanic/Latino), 21 international. Average age 31. 53 applicants, 40% accepted, 11 enrolled. In 2014, 2 master's awarded. *Application deadline:* For fall admission, 1/15 for domestic students; for spring admission, 10/1 for domestic students. Application fee: $100. *Expenses:* Tuition, state resident: full-time $10,370; part-time $432 per credit. Tuition, nonresident: full-time $20,190; part-time $841 per credit. *Required fees:* $1431. *Financial support:* Fellowships, research assistantships, and teaching assistantships available. *Unit head:* Dr. Richard Larson, Chair, 631-632-7774, Fax: 631-632-9789, E-mail: richard.larson@stonybrook.edu. *Application contact:* Michelle Carbone, Coordinator, 631-632-7774, Fax: 631-632-9789, E-mail: michelle.carbone@stonybrook.edu.

Syracuse University, College of Arts and Sciences, Program in Computational Linguistics, Syracuse, NY 13244. Offers MS. Program held jointly with School of Information Studies and the L.C. Smith College of Engineering and Computer Science. Part-time programs available. *Students:* 2 full-time (1 woman). Average age 27. 10 applicants, 80% accepted, 2 enrolled. *Degree requirements:* For master's, thesis or alternative, internship. *Entrance requirements:* For master's, GRE. Additional exam requirements/recommendations for international students: Required—TOEFL (minimum score 100 iBT). *Application deadline:* For fall admission, 2/1 for domestic students, 2/1 priority date for international students; for summer admission, 2/1 for domestic students, 2/1 priority date for international students. Application fee: $75. Electronic applications accepted. *Expenses: Tuition:* Part-time $1341 per credit. *Financial support:* Fellowships with full tuition reimbursements, research assistantships with full and partial tuition reimbursements, and teaching assistantships with full and partial tuition reimbursements available. Financial award application deadline: 1/1; financial award applicants required to submit FAFSA. *Unit head:* Dr. Jaklin Kornfilt, Professor of Linguistics, 315-443-2175, E-mail: kornfilt@syr.edu. *Application contact:* Coleen Kepler, Coordinator, 315-443-2175, E-mail: cdkepler@syr.edu.
Website: http://thecollege.syr.edu/

Syracuse University, College of Arts and Sciences, Program in Linguistic Studies, Syracuse, NY 13244. Offers MA. Part-time programs available. *Students:* 20 full-time (14 women), 11 international. Average age 25. 56 applicants, 59% accepted, 9 enrolled. In 2014, 16 master's awarded. *Degree requirements:* For master's, comprehensive exam, thesis or alternative. *Entrance requirements:* For master's, GRE General Test. Additional exam requirements/recommendations for international students: Required—TOEFL (minimum score 100 iBT). *Application deadline:* For fall admission, 1/10 priority date for domestic and international students. Application fee: $75. Electronic applications accepted. *Expenses: Tuition:* Part-time $1341 per credit. *Financial support:* Fellowships with full tuition reimbursements and teaching assistantships with full and partial tuition reimbursements available. Financial award application deadline: 1/1; financial award applicants required to submit FAFSA. *Unit head:* Dr. Jaklin Kornfilt, Director, 315-443-2175, Fax: 315-443-5376, E-mail: kornfilt@syr.edu. *Application contact:* Colleen Kepler, Recruiting Contact, 315-443-5906, E-mail: cdkepler@syr.edu.
Website: http://lang.syr.edu/academics/Linguistics/MA-Linguistics.html

Teachers College, Columbia University, Graduate Faculty of Education, Department of Arts and Humanities, Program in Applied Linguistics, New York, NY 10027. Offers Ed M, MA, Ed D. Part-time and evening/weekend programs available. *Faculty:* 9 full-time, 9 part-time/adjunct. *Students:* 10 full-time (8 women), 93 part-time (73 women); includes 27 minority (1 Black or African American, non-Hispanic/Latino; 21 Asian, non-Hispanic/Latino; 3 Hispanic/Latino; 2 Two or more races, non-Hispanic/Latino), 45 international. Average age 32. 95 applicants, 59% accepted, 19 enrolled. In 2014, 32 master's awarded. Terminal master's awarded for partial completion of doctoral program. *Degree requirements:* For master's, essay (for MA), project (for Ed M); for doctorate, comprehensive exam, thesis/dissertation. *Entrance requirements:* For master's, MA in applied linguistics, TESOL, or related field (for Ed M); for doctorate, MA in applied linguistics, TESOL, or related field. Additional exam requirements/recommendations for international students: Required—TOEFL (minimum score 600 paper-based; 102 iBT), IELTS (minimum score 7), TWE (minimum score 5). *Application deadline:* For fall admission, 1/15 priority date for domestic students; for spring admission, 11/1 for domestic students. Application fee: $65. Electronic applications accepted. *Expenses: Tuition:* Full-time $33,552; part-time $1398 per credit. *Required fees:* $418 per semester. *Financial support:* Fellowships, research assistantships, teaching assistantships, career-related internships or fieldwork, Federal Work-Study, institutionally sponsored loans, and tuition waivers (full and partial) available. Support available to part-time students. Financial award application deadline: 2/1. *Faculty research:* Linguistics applied to education and other professions, sociolinguistics and second language acquisition, rude speech and social rules of speaking. *Unit head:* Prof. ZhaoHong Han, Program Coordinator, 212-678-4051, E-mail: zhh2@columbia.edu. *Application contact:* Thomas P. Rock, Director of Admissions, 212-678-3083, Fax: 212-678-4171, E-mail: rock@tc.edu.
Website: http://www.tc.columbia.edu/tesolal/

Texas Tech University, Graduate School, College of Arts and Sciences, Department of Classical and Modern Languages and Literatures, Lubbock, TX 79409-2071. Offers applied linguistics (MA); classics (MA); German (MA); languages and cultures (MA); Romance languages (MA); Spanish (PhD); MBA/MA. Part-time programs available. *Faculty:* 61 full-time (31 women), 7 part-time/adjunct (4 women). *Students:* 93 full-time (48 women), 15 part-time (10 women); includes 27 minority (1 Black or African American, non-Hispanic/Latino; 22 Hispanic/Latino; 4 Two or more races, non-Hispanic/Latino), 41 international. Average age 32. 60 applicants, 70% accepted, 26 enrolled. In

2014, 26 master's, 7 doctorates awarded. *Degree requirements:* For master's, comprehensive exam, thesis or alternative; for doctorate, comprehensive exam, thesis/dissertation. *Entrance requirements:* For master's and doctorate, GRE General Test. Additional exam requirements/recommendations for international students: Required—TOEFL (minimum score 550 paper-based; 79 iBT). *Application deadline:* For fall admission, 6/1 priority date for domestic students, 1/15 priority date for international students; for spring admission, 9/1 priority date for domestic students, 6/15 priority date for international students. Applications are processed on a rolling basis. Application fee: $60. Electronic applications accepted. *Expenses:* Tuition, state resident: full-time $6310; part-time $262.92 per credit hour. Tuition, nonresident: full-time $14,998; part-time $624.92 per credit hour. *Required fees:* $2701; $36.50 per credit. $912.50 per semester. Tuition and fees vary according to course load. *Financial support:* In 2014–15, 91 students received support, including 78 fellowships (averaging $2,724 per year), 4 research assistantships (averaging $17,800 per year), 82 teaching assistantships (averaging $11,423 per year); Federal Work-Study, scholarships/grants, and unspecified assistantships also available. Financial award application deadline: 4/15; financial award applicants required to submit FAFSA. *Faculty research:* Literature, comparative literature, linguistics, culture, applied linguistics. *Total annual research expenditures:* $1,380. *Unit head:* Dr. Erin Collopy, Chair and Associate Professor, 806-834-8497, Fax: 806-742-3306, E-mail: erin.collopy@ttu.edu. *Application contact:* Liz Hildebrand, Senior Advisor, 806-834-2463, Fax: 806-742-3306, E-mail: liz.hildebrand@ttu.edu.
Website: http://www.depts.ttu.edu/classic_modern/

Trinity Western University, School of Graduate Studies, Program in Linguistics, Langley, BC V2Y 1Y1, Canada. Offers MA. *Degree requirements:* For master's, essay (for non-thesis students). *Entrance requirements:* For master's, minimum GPA of 2.7, 3.0 in last two years; 12 seminar hours; linguistic prerequisites; 1 foreign language. Additional exam requirements/recommendations for international students: Required—TOEFL (minimum score 600 paper-based). Electronic applications accepted. *Expenses:* Contact institution. *Faculty research:* Syntax, phonology, tone, historical and comparative, discourse analysis.

Universidad de las Américas Puebla, Division of Graduate Studies, School of Humanities, Program in Applied Linguistics, Puebla, Mexico. Offers linguistics (MA). Part-time and evening/weekend programs available. *Degree requirements:* For master's, one foreign language, thesis. *Entrance requirements:* Additional exam requirements/recommendations for international students: Required—TOEFL. *Faculty research:* English linguistics, teaching English to speakers of other languages.

Université de Montréal, Faculty of Arts and Sciences, Department of Linguistics and Translation, Montréal, QC H3C 3J7, Canada. Offers linguistics (MA, PhD); translation (MA, PhD, DESS). *Degree requirements:* For master's, thesis, general exam; for doctorate, thesis/dissertation, general exam. Electronic applications accepted.

Université de Sherbrooke, Faculty of Letters and Human Sciences, Department of Letters and Communications, Sherbrooke, QC J1K 2R1, Canada. Offers comparative Canadian literature (MA, PhD); French literature (MA, PhD); linguistics (MA); theatre (MA). *Degree requirements:* For master's, thesis or alternative; for doctorate, thesis/dissertation. *Entrance requirements:* For master's, minimum GPA of 2.8; for doctorate, minimum GPA of 3.0.

Université du Québec à Chicoutimi, Graduate Programs, Program in Linguistics, Chicoutimi, QC G7H 2B1, Canada. Offers MA. Part-time programs available. *Degree requirements:* For master's, thesis. *Entrance requirements:* For master's, appropriate bachelor's degree, proficiency in French.

Université du Québec à Montréal, Graduate Programs, Program in Linguistics, Montréal, QC H3C 3P8, Canada. Offers MA, PhD. Part-time programs available. *Degree requirements:* For master's, thesis optional; for doctorate, thesis/dissertation. *Entrance requirements:* For master's, appropriate bachelor's degree or equivalent, proficiency in French; for doctorate, appropriate master's degree or equivalent, proficiency in French.

Université Laval, Faculty of Letters, Department of Languages, Linguistics and Translations, Programs in Linguistics, Québec, QC G1K 7P4, Canada. Offers MA, PhD. Terminal master's awarded for partial completion of doctoral program. *Degree requirements:* For master's, thesis (for some programs); for doctorate, comprehensive exam, thesis/dissertation. *Entrance requirements:* For master's, English test (comprehension of written English), knowledge of French; for doctorate, English exam (comprehension of written English), knowledge of French. Electronic applications accepted.

University at Buffalo, the State University of New York, Graduate School, College of Arts and Sciences, Department of Linguistics, Buffalo, NY 14260. Offers MA, PhD. *Faculty:* 14 full-time (5 women). *Students:* 61 full-time (32 women), 5 part-time (3 women); includes 4 minority (1 Black or African American, non-Hispanic/Latino; 2 American Indian or Alaska Native, non-Hispanic/Latino; 1 Hispanic/Latino), 26 international. Average age 29. 53 applicants, 83% accepted, 14 enrolled. In 2014, 9 master's, 4 doctorates awarded. Terminal master's awarded for partial completion of doctoral program. *Degree requirements:* For master's, exam, project, or thesis; for doctorate, thesis/dissertation, qualifying paper. *Entrance requirements:* For master's and doctorate, GRE General Test. Additional exam requirements/recommendations for international students: Required—TOEFL (minimum score 600 paper-based; 100 iBT). *Application deadline:* For fall admission, 4/1 for domestic students, 3/1 for international students. Application fee: $75. Electronic applications accepted. *Financial support:* In 2014–15, 23 students received support, including 10 fellowships with full tuition reimbursements available (averaging $5,300 per year), 20 teaching assistantships with full tuition reimbursements available (averaging $13,695 per year); research assistantships, scholarships/grants, and unspecified assistantships also available. Financial award application deadline: 12/15; financial award applicants required to submit FAFSA. *Faculty research:* Typology, psycholinguistics/experimental linguistics, syntax, semantics, language documentation. *Unit head:* Dr. Jean-Pierre Koenig, Professor/Chair, 716-645-2177, Fax: 716-645-3825, E-mail: jpkoenig@buffalo.edu. *Application contact:* Jodi L. Reiner, Secretary, 716-645-3794, Fax: 716-645-3825, E-mail: jlreiner@buffalo.edu.
Website: http://www.linguistics.buffalo.edu

The University of Alabama, Graduate School, College of Arts and Sciences, Department of English, Tuscaloosa, AL 35487. Offers applied linguistics (PhD); composition and rhetoric (PhD); creative writing (MFA), including fiction, poetry; literature (MA, PhD); rhetoric and composition (MA); teaching English as a second language (MATESOL). *Faculty:* 34 full-time (19 women). *Students:* 129 full-time (70 women), 9 part-time (8 women); includes 18 minority (9 Black or African American, non-Hispanic/Latino; 1 Asian, non-Hispanic/Latino; 5 Hispanic/Latino; 3 Two or more races, non-Hispanic/Latino), 7 international. Average age 28. 318 applicants, 18% accepted, 42 enrolled. In 2014, 39 master's, 2 doctorates awarded. *Degree requirements:* For master's, one foreign language, comprehensive exam, thesis optional; for doctorate, 2 foreign languages, comprehensive exam, thesis/dissertation. *Entrance requirements:* For master's, GRE (minimum score of 300, except for MFA), minimum GPA of 3.0, critical writing sample; for doctorate, GRE (minimum score of 300), minimum GPA of 3.5 on master's or equivalent graduate work, critical writing sample. Additional exam requirements/recommendations for international students: Required—TOEFL (minimum score 100 iBT). *Application deadline:* For fall admission, 12/31 priority date for domestic and international students. Application fee: $50 ($60 for international students). Electronic applications accepted. *Expenses:* Tuition, state resident: full-time $9826. Tuition, nonresident: full-time $24,950. *Financial support:* In 2014–15, 11 fellowships with full tuition reimbursements (averaging $15,000 per year), 1 research assistantship with full tuition reimbursement (averaging $12,366 per year), 112 teaching assistantships with full tuition reimbursements (averaging $12,366 per year) were awarded; career-related internships or fieldwork, scholarships/grants, health care benefits, and unspecified assistantships also available. Financial award application deadline: 12/31. *Faculty research:* American literature, British literature, composition/rhetoric, applied linguistics, creative writing. *Unit head:* Prof. Joel Brouwer, Department Chair, 205-348-9524, Fax: 205-348-1388, E-mail: joel.brouwer@ua.edu. *Application contact:* Jennifer Fuqua, Graduate Coordinator, 205-348-0766, Fax: 205-348-1388, E-mail: jfuqua@ua.edu.

University of Alaska Fairbanks, College of Liberal Arts, Program in Linguistics, Fairbanks, AK 99775-6280. Offers applied linguistics (MA), including language documentation, second language acquisition teacher education. Part-time programs available. *Faculty:* 2 full-time (both women). *Students:* 4 full-time (2 women), 16 part-time (13 women); includes 10 minority (7 American Indian or Alaska Native, non-Hispanic/Latino; 3 Two or more races, non-Hispanic/Latino), 1 international. Average age 37. 7 applicants, 71% accepted, 4 enrolled. *Degree requirements:* For master's, one foreign language, comprehensive exam, oral defense of project or thesis. *Entrance requirements:* For master's, bachelor's degree from accredited institution with minimum cumulative undergraduate and major GPA of 3.0. Additional exam requirements/recommendations for international students: Required—TOEFL (minimum score 550 paper-based; 79 iBT), IELTS (minimum score 6.5). *Application deadline:* For fall admission, 6/1 for domestic students, 3/1 for international students; for spring admission, 10/15 for domestic students, 9/1 for international students. Applications are processed on a rolling basis. Application fee: $60. Electronic applications accepted. *Expenses:* Tuition, state resident: full-time $7614; part-time $423 per credit. Tuition, nonresident: full-time $15,552; part-time $864 per credit. Tuition and fees vary according to course level, course load and reciprocity agreements. *Financial support:* In 2014–15, 2 research assistantships with full tuition reimbursements (averaging $8,907 per year), 1 teaching assistantship with full tuition reimbursement (averaging $11,955 per year) were awarded; fellowships with full tuition reimbursements, career-related internships or fieldwork, Federal Work-Study, scholarships/grants, health care benefits, and unspecified assistantships also available. Support available to part-time students. Financial award application deadline: 7/1; financial award applicants required to submit FAFSA. *Faculty research:* Second language acquisition/teaching, Inupiaq, Athabaskan languages, language maintenance and shift, phonology, morphology. *Total annual research expenditures:* $21,000. *Unit head:* Dr. Siri Tuttle, Program Head, 907-474-7876, Fax: 907-474-6586, E-mail: fyling@uaf.edu. *Application contact:* Mary Kreta, Director of Admissions, 907-474-7500, Fax: 907-474-7097, E-mail: admissions@uaf.edu.
Website: http://www.uaf.edu/linguist/

University of Alberta, Faculty of Graduate Studies and Research, Department of Linguistics, Edmonton, AB T6G 2E1, Canada. Offers experimental linguistics (M Sc, PhD). *Degree requirements:* For master's, thesis (for some programs); for doctorate, thesis/dissertation. *Entrance requirements:* For master's, BA in linguistics; for doctorate, M Sc or MA in linguistics. Additional exam requirements/recommendations for international students: Required—TOEFL. *Faculty research:* Experimental phonetics, psycholinguistics, phonology, endangered languages, language acquisition.

University of Alberta, Faculty of Graduate Studies and Research, Department of Modern Languages and Cultural Studies, Edmonton, AB T6G 2E1, Canada. Offers applied linguistics (Germanic, Romance, Slavic) (MA); French language, literatures and linguistics (PhD); French language, literatures, and linguistics (MA); Germanic languages, literatures and linguistics (PhD); Germanic languages, literatures, and linguistics (MA); Italian studies (MA); Slavic languages and literatures (Russian, Ukrainian) (MA, PhD); Slavic linguistics (Russian, Ukrainian) (MA, PhD); Spanish and Latin American studies (MA, PhD); Ukrainian folklore (MA, PhD). Part-time programs available. *Degree requirements:* For master's, one foreign language, thesis; for doctorate, 2 foreign languages, comprehensive exam, thesis/dissertation. *Entrance requirements:* For master's and doctorate, 1 language other than English. Additional exam requirements/recommendations for international students: Required—Michigan English Language Assessment Battery or TOEFL (minimum score 550 paper-based). Electronic applications accepted. *Faculty research:* Russian/Ukrainian studies; German studies; contemporary Latin American, French and Francophone studies; Italian studies.

The University of Arizona, College of Social and Behavioral Sciences, Department of Linguistics, Tucson, AZ 85721. Offers human language technology (MS); linguistics and anthropology (PhD); Native American linguistics (MA); theoretical linguistics (PhD). PhD in linguistics and anthropology offered jointly with Department of Anthropology. Terminal master's awarded for partial completion of doctoral program. *Degree requirements:* For master's, one foreign language, thesis; for doctorate, one foreign language, comprehensive exam, thesis/dissertation. *Entrance requirements:* For master's, GRE General Test, 3 letters of recommendation, writing sample, resume; for doctorate, GRE General Test, 3 letters of recommendation, statement of purpose, writing sample, resume. Additional exam requirements/recommendations for international students: Required—TOEFL (minimum score 550 paper-based; 79 iBT). Electronic applications accepted. *Faculty research:* Semantic, syntactic, morphological, and phonological theories of natural languages; native languages of the American Southwest, psycholinguistics and computational linguistics.

The University of Arizona, College of Social and Behavioral Sciences, Program in Human Language Technology, Tucson, AZ 85721. Offers MS. *Entrance requirements:* Additional exam requirements/recommendations for international students: Required—TOEFL (minimum score 550 paper-based; 79 iBT), GRE.

The University of British Columbia, Faculty of Arts and Faculty of Graduate Studies, Department of Linguistics, Vancouver, BC V6T 1Z1, Canada. Offers MA, PhD. Part-time programs available. *Degree requirements:* For master's, one foreign language, thesis optional; for doctorate, 2 foreign languages, thesis/dissertation, 2 qualifying papers. *Entrance requirements:* Additional exam requirements/recommendations for international students: Required—TOEFL (minimum score 550 paper-based). Electronic applications accepted. *Faculty research:* Linguistic theory (phonology, syntax, semantics), Native American languages, African languages, first language acquisition, experimental phonetics.

University of Calgary, Faculty of Graduate Studies, Faculty of Arts, Department of Linguistics, Languages and Culture, Calgary, AB T2N 1N4, Canada. Offers German (MA); linguistics (MA, PhD). *Degree requirements:* For master's, one foreign language, thesis; for doctorate, one foreign language, comprehensive exam, thesis/dissertation. *Entrance requirements:* For doctorate, MA. Additional exam requirements/recommendations for international students: Required—TOEFL (minimum score 560 paper-based). Electronic applications accepted. *Faculty research:* Theoretical linguistics, historical linguistics, language acquisition, Amerindian.

University of California, Berkeley, Graduate Division, College of Letters and Science, Department of Linguistics, Berkeley, CA 94720-1500. Offers PhD. *Degree requirements:* For doctorate, thesis/dissertation, qualifying exam. *Entrance requirements:* For doctorate, GRE General Test, minimum GPA of 3.0, 3 letters of recommendation.

University of California, Davis, Graduate Studies, Graduate Group in Linguistics, Davis, CA 95616. Offers applied linguistics (MA, PhD); linguistics (MA). *Degree requirements:* For master's, one foreign language, comprehensive exam (for some programs), thesis (for some programs); for doctorate, thesis/dissertation. *Entrance requirements:* For master's and doctorate, GRE General Test, minimum GPA of 3.0. Additional exam requirements/recommendations for international students: Required—TOEFL (minimum score 550 paper-based). Electronic applications accepted. *Faculty research:* Grammatical analysis and theory, sociolinguistics, historical linguistics, Romance linguistics, neurolinguistics.

University of California, Los Angeles, Graduate Division, College of Letters and Science, Department of Applied Linguistics and Teaching English as a Second Language, Program in Applied Linguistics, Los Angeles, CA 90095. Offers MA, PhD. *Degree requirements:* For master's, one foreign language, thesis; for doctorate, one foreign language, thesis/dissertation, oral and written qualifying exams. *Entrance requirements:* For master's and doctorate, bachelor's degree; minimum undergraduate GPA of 3.0 (or its equivalent if letter grade system not used); research paper. Additional exam requirements/recommendations for international students: Required—TOEFL. Electronic applications accepted.

University of California, Los Angeles, Graduate Division, College of Letters and Science, Department of Linguistics, Los Angeles, CA 90095. Offers MA, PhD. Terminal master's awarded for partial completion of doctoral program. *Degree requirements:* For master's, one foreign language, comprehensive exam or thesis; for doctorate, thesis/dissertation, oral and written qualifying exams. *Entrance requirements:* For doctorate, bachelor's degree; minimum undergraduate GPA of 3.0 (or its equivalent if letter grade system not used); writing sample. Additional exam requirements/recommendations for international students: Required—TOEFL. Electronic applications accepted.

University of California, San Diego, Graduate Division, Department of Linguistics, La Jolla, CA 92093. Offers PhD. *Students:* 31 full-time (19 women), 1 (woman) part-time; includes 3 minority (2 Asian, non-Hispanic/Latino; 1 Hispanic/Latino), 12 international. 89 applicants, 20% accepted, 7 enrolled. In 2014, 2 doctorates awarded. *Degree requirements:* For doctorate, one foreign language, comprehensive exam, thesis/dissertation. *Entrance requirements:* For doctorate, GRE General Test. Additional exam requirements/recommendations for international students: Required—TOEFL (minimum score 550 paper-based; 80 iBT), IELTS. *Application deadline:* For fall admission, 12/2 for domestic students. Application fee: $90 ($110 for international students). Electronic applications accepted. *Expenses:* Tuition, state resident: full-time $11,220; part-time $5610 per quarter. Tuition, nonresident: full-time $26,322; part-time $13,161 per quarter. *Required fees:* $570 per quarter. Tuition and fees vary according to program. *Financial support:* Applicants required to submit FAFSA. *Faculty research:* Computational linguistics, computational psycholinguistics, experimental syntax, language acquisition and sign languages, language and the brain, speech production and perception. *Unit head:* Sharon Rose, Chair, 858-534-1159, E-mail: sxrose@ucsd.edu. *Application contact:* Alycia Randol, Graduate Coordinator, 858-534-1145, E-mail: arandol@ucsd.edu.
Website: http://ling.ucsd.edu

University of California, Santa Barbara, Graduate Division, College of Letters and Sciences, Division of Humanities and Fine Arts, Department of East Asian Languages and Cultural Studies, Santa Barbara, CA 93106-7075. Offers applied linguistics (PhD); East Asian languages and cultural studies (MA, PhD); translation studies (PhD). *Degree requirements:* For master's, one foreign language, comprehensive exam (for some programs), thesis (for some programs); for doctorate, 2 foreign languages, thesis/dissertation, methodology. *Entrance requirements:* For master's and doctorate, GRE General Test. Additional exam requirements/recommendations for international students: Required—TOEFL (minimum score 550 paper-based; 80 iBT), IELTS (minimum score 7). Electronic applications accepted. *Faculty research:* Chinese literature, Chinese film, Japanese society, Japanese literature, East Asian cultural studies.

University of California, Santa Barbara, Graduate Division, College of Letters and Sciences, Division of Humanities and Fine Arts, Department of Linguistics, Santa Barbara, CA 93106-9580. Offers PhD, MA/PhD. Terminal master's awarded for partial completion of doctoral program. *Degree requirements:* For doctorate, one foreign language, comprehensive exam, thesis/dissertation, qualifying paper. *Entrance requirements:* For doctorate, GRE. Additional exam requirements/recommendations for international students: Required—TOEFL (minimum score 550 paper-based; 80 iBT), IELTS (minimum score 7). Electronic applications accepted. *Faculty research:* Language documentation, discourse, typology, language and cognition, sociocultural linguistics.

University of California, Santa Barbara, Graduate Division, College of Letters and Sciences, Division of Humanities and Fine Arts, Department of Spanish and Portuguese, Santa Barbara, CA 93106-4150. Offers Hispanic languages and literatures (PhD), including European medieval studies, feminist studies, Hispanic linguistics, Hispanic literature, Luso-Brazilian literature; Hispanic linguistics (MA); Luso-Brazilian literature (MA); Spanish or Spanish-American literature (MA); MA/PhD. Spanish Language Institute available during Summer session. Terminal master's awarded for partial completion of doctoral program. *Degree requirements:* For master's, 2 foreign languages, comprehensive exam (for some programs), thesis optional; for doctorate, 3 foreign languages, comprehensive exam, thesis/dissertation. *Entrance requirements:* For master's and doctorate, GRE. Additional exam requirements/recommendations for international students: Required—TOEFL (minimum score 550 paper-based; 80 iBT), IELTS (minimum score 7). Electronic applications accepted. *Faculty research:* Nineteenth-century Spanish and Portuguese literature, Spanish and Spanish-American literature, nineteenth- and twentieth-century Portuguese and Brazilian literatures, Hispanic linguistics, Catalan language and culture.

University of California, Santa Cruz, Division of Graduate Studies, Division of Humanities, Department of Linguistics, Santa Cruz, CA 95064. Offers MA, PhD. Terminal master's awarded for partial completion of doctoral program. *Degree requirements:* For master's, one foreign language, research paper; for doctorate, one foreign language, thesis/dissertation, qualifying exam. *Entrance requirements:* For master's and doctorate, GRE General Test. Additional exam requirements/recommendations for international students: Required—TOEFL (minimum score 550 paper-based; 83 iBT); Recommended—IELTS (minimum score 8). Electronic applications accepted. *Faculty research:* Theoretical and descriptive linguistics: syntax, semantics and phonology.

University of Chicago, Division of the Humanities, Department of Linguistics, Chicago, IL 60637. Offers anthropology and linguistics (PhD); linguistics (PhD). *Students:* 41 full-time (21 women); includes 8 minority (1 American Indian or Alaska Native, non-Hispanic/Latino; 2 Asian, non-Hispanic/Latino; 5 Hispanic/Latino), 12 international. 133 applicants, 21% accepted, 3 enrolled. Terminal master's awarded for partial completion of doctoral program. *Degree requirements:* For doctorate, 2 foreign languages, thesis/dissertation. *Entrance requirements:* For doctorate, GRE General Test. Additional exam requirements/recommendations for international students: Required—TOEFL (minimum score 104 iBT), IELTS (minimum score 7). *Application deadline:* For fall admission, 12/15 for domestic and international students. Application fee: $90. Electronic applications accepted. *Expenses:* Tuition: Full-time $46,899. *Required fees:* $347. *Financial support:* Fellowships with full tuition reimbursements, teaching assistantships with full tuition reimbursements, Federal Work-Study, institutionally sponsored loans, scholarships/grants, and health care benefits available. Financial award application deadline: 12/15; financial award applicants required to submit FAFSA. *Unit head:* Dr. Chris Kennedy, Chair, 773-702-8522. *Application contact:* Braden Grams, Assistant Dean of Students, Admissions and Fellowships, 773-702-1552, Fax: 773-834-9148, E-mail: humanitiesadmissions@uchicago.edu.
Website: http://linguistics.uchicago.edu/

University of Chicago, Division of the Humanities, Master of Arts Program in the Humanities, Chicago, IL 60637. Offers art history (MA); classics (MA); comparative literature (MA); creative writing (MA); digital humanities (MA); English language and literature (MA); Germanic studies (MA); linguistics (MA); music (MA); philosophy (MA); Romance languages and literatures (MA); South Asian languages and civilizations (MA). *Students:* 83 full-time (41 women), 8 part-time (6 women); includes 14 minority (1 Black or African American, non-Hispanic/Latino; 6 Asian, non-Hispanic/Latino; 6 Hispanic/Latino; 1 Two or more races, non-Hispanic/Latino), 17 international. Average age 26. 153 applicants, 67% accepted, 80 enrolled. *Degree requirements:* For master's, thesis. *Entrance requirements:* For master's, GRE General Test. Additional exam requirements/recommendations for international students: Required—TOEFL (minimum score 600 paper-based; 104 iBT), IELTS (minimum score 7). *Application deadline:* For fall admission, 3/15 for domestic and international students. Application fee: $90. Electronic applications accepted. *Expenses:* Tuition: Full-time $46,899. *Required fees:* $347. *Financial support:* In 2014–15, 100 students received support, including 8 fellowships with partial tuition reimbursements available (averaging $12,000 per year); Federal Work-Study, institutionally sponsored loans, and tuition waivers (partial) also available. Financial award application deadline: 3/15; financial award applicants required to submit FAFSA. *Unit head:* Prof. David Wray, Director, 773-834-1201, E-mail: ma-humanities@uchicago.edu. *Application contact:* Program Coordinator, 773-834-1201, Fax: 773-834-7526, E-mail: ma-humanities@uchicago.edu.
Website: http://maph.uchicago.edu/

University of Colorado Boulder, Graduate School, College of Arts and Sciences, Department of Linguistics, Boulder, CO 80309. Offers MA, PhD. *Faculty:* 10 full-time (6 women). *Students:* 70 full-time (43 women), 7 part-time (4 women); includes 10 minority (1 Black or African American, non-Hispanic/Latino; 3 Asian, non-Hispanic/Latino; 5 Hispanic/Latino; 1 Two or more races, non-Hispanic/Latino), 19 international. Average age 29. 122 applicants, 39% accepted, 18 enrolled. In 2014, 15 master's, 2 doctorates awarded. Terminal master's awarded for partial completion of doctoral program. *Degree requirements:* For master's, comprehensive exam, thesis optional; for doctorate, one foreign language, thesis/dissertation. *Entrance requirements:* For master's, GRE General Test, minimum undergraduate GPA of 2.75; for doctorate, GRE General Test. *Application deadline:* For fall admission, 1/2 for domestic students, 12/1 for international students. Applications are processed on a rolling basis. Application fee: $50 ($70 for international students). Electronic applications accepted. *Financial support:* In 2014–15, 90 students received support, including 16 fellowships (averaging $3,400 per year), 6 research assistantships with full and partial tuition reimbursements available (averaging $29,613 per year), 21 teaching assistantships with full and partial tuition reimbursements available (averaging $29,659 per year); institutionally sponsored loans, scholarships/grants, health care benefits, and unspecified assistantships also available. Financial award application deadline: 1/15; financial award applicants required to submit FAFSA. *Faculty research:* Linguistics/philology, phonology, semantics, syntax, psycholinguistics. *Total annual research expenditures:* $1.1 million.
Website: http://www.colorado.edu/linguistics/

University of Colorado Denver, College of Liberal Arts and Sciences, Department of English, Denver, CO 80217. Offers applied linguistics (MA); literature (MA); rhetoric and teaching of writing (MA). Part-time and evening/weekend programs available. *Faculty:* 23 full-time (13 women), 1 (woman) part-time/adjunct. *Students:* 21 full-time (17 women), 16 part-time (10 women); includes 5 minority (1 Black or African American, non-Hispanic/Latino; 1 Asian, non-Hispanic/Latino; 3 Hispanic/Latino), 2 international. Average age 28. 19 applicants, 58% accepted, 4 enrolled. In 2014, 19 master's awarded. *Degree requirements:* For master's, variable foreign language requirement, comprehensive exam (for some programs), thesis (for some programs), minimum of 33 credit hours (for literature program), 30 (for rhetoric and teaching of writing and applied linguistics programs). *Entrance requirements:* For master's, GRE General Test, minimum GPA of 3.0 in undergraduate courses, critical writing sample, letters of recommendation, completion of 24 semester hours in English courses (at least 16 at the upper-division level), statement of purpose. Additional exam requirements/recommendations for international students: Required—TOEFL (minimum score 537 paper-based; 75 iBT); Recommended—IELTS (minimum score 6.5). *Application deadline:* For fall admission, 4/1 for domestic and international students; for spring admission, 10/1 for domestic and international students; for summer admission, 4/1 for domestic and international students. Application fee: $50 ($75 for international students). Electronic applications accepted. *Financial support:* In 2014–15, 9 students received support. Fellowships, research assistantships, teaching assistantships, Federal Work-Study, institutionally sponsored loans, scholarships/grants, traineeships, and unspecified assistantships available. Financial award application deadline: 4/1; financial award applicants required to submit FAFSA. *Faculty research:* Literature, rhetoric, teaching of writing, applied linguistics. *Unit head:* Prof. Nancy Ciccone, Chair, 303-556-8395, E-mail: nancy.ciccone@ucdenver.edu. *Application contact:* English Department, 303-556-2584, Fax: 303-556-2959.
Website: http://www.ucdenver.edu/academics/colleges/CLAS/Departments/english/Programs/Masters/Pages/Overview.aspx

University of Connecticut, Graduate School, College of Liberal Arts and Sciences, Department of Linguistics, Storrs, CT 06269. Offers MA, PhD. *Degree requirements:* For doctorate, thesis/dissertation. *Entrance requirements:* For doctorate, GRE General Test. Additional exam requirements/recommendations for international students: Required—TOEFL (minimum score 550 paper-based). Electronic applications accepted.

University of Delaware, College of Arts and Sciences, Department of Linguistics and Cognitive Science, Newark, DE 19716. Offers linguistics (PhD); linguistics and cognitive science (MA). *Degree requirements:* For doctorate, one foreign language, comprehensive exam, thesis/dissertation, publishable research papers. *Entrance requirements:* For master's, GRE General Test; for doctorate, GRE General Test, writing sample. Additional exam requirements/recommendations for international students: Required—TOEFL (minimum score 600 paper-based). Electronic applications accepted. *Faculty research:* East Asian, Austronesian and Romance languages, phonology, phonetics, syntax, cognitive science, semantics, psycholinguistics, language acquisition, endangered languages.

Linguistics

University of Florida, Graduate School, College of Liberal Arts and Sciences, Department of Linguistics, Gainesville, FL 32611. Offers linguistics (MA, PhD); teaching English as a second language (Certificate). Part-time programs available. *Faculty:* 14 full-time (11 women), 7 part-time/adjunct (4 women). *Students:* 44 full-time (27 women), 5 part-time (0 women); includes 8 minority (3 Black or African American, non-Hispanic/Latino; 2 American Indian or Alaska Native, non-Hispanic/Latino; 2 Asian, non-Hispanic/Latino; 1 Hispanic/Latino), 23 international. 75 applicants, 25% accepted, 8 enrolled. In 2014, 8 master's, 8 doctorates awarded. Terminal master's awarded for partial completion of doctoral program. *Degree requirements:* For master's, one foreign language, comprehensive exam, thesis (for some programs); for doctorate, 2 foreign languages, comprehensive exam, thesis/dissertation. *Entrance requirements:* For master's and doctorate, GRE General Test, minimum GPA of 3.0. Additional exam requirements/recommendations for international students: Required—TOEFL (minimum score 550 paper-based; 80 iBT), IELTS (minimum score 6). *Application deadline:* For fall admission, 12/15 priority date for domestic students, 12/15 for international students. Applications are processed on a rolling basis. Application fee: $30. Electronic applications accepted. *Financial support:* In 2014–15, 4 fellowships, 5 research assistantships, 25 teaching assistantships were awarded; institutionally sponsored loans and unspecified assistantships also available. Financial award application deadline: 12/15; financial award applicants required to submit FAFSA. *Faculty research:* Language documentation, psycholinguistics and neuro-linguistics, theoretical linguistics, sociolinguistics second language acquisition. *Total annual research expenditures:* $19,295. *Unit head:* Fiona McLaughlin, PhD, Chair, 352-392-4829, Fax: 352-392-8480, E-mail: fmcl@ufl.edu. *Application contact:* Eric Potsdam, PhD, Graduate Coordinator, 352-294-7456, Fax: 352-392-8480, E-mail: potsdam@ufl.edu.
Website: http://lin.ufl.edu/

University of Georgia, Franklin College of Arts and Sciences, Program in Linguistics, Athens, GA 30602. Offers MA, PhD. *Degree requirements:* For master's, one foreign language, thesis; for doctorate, 2 foreign languages, comprehensive exam, thesis/dissertation. *Entrance requirements:* For master's and doctorate, GRE General Test. Electronic applications accepted. *Expenses:* Contact institution. *Faculty research:* Applied linguistics, English linguistics, dialectology, lexicography, discourse analysis.

University of Hawaii at Manoa, Graduate Division, College of Languages, Linguistics and Literature, Department of Linguistics, Honolulu, HI 96822. Offers MA, PhD. Part-time programs available. Terminal master's awarded for partial completion of doctoral program. *Degree requirements:* For master's, 2 foreign languages, thesis optional; for doctorate, 2 foreign languages, comprehensive exam, thesis/dissertation. *Entrance requirements:* For master's and doctorate, GRE General Test. Additional exam requirements/recommendations for international students: Required—TOEFL (minimum score 600 paper-based; 100 iBT), IELTS (minimum score 7). *Faculty research:* Languages of the Pacific and Asia.

University of Houston, College of Liberal Arts and Social Sciences, Department of English, Houston, TX 77204. Offers applied English linguistics (MA); creative writing (MFA); creative writing and literature (MA, PhD); English (MA, PhD). *Degree requirements:* For master's, one foreign language, comprehensive exam (for some programs), thesis (MFA); for doctorate, 2 foreign languages, comprehensive exam, thesis/dissertation. *Entrance requirements:* For master's, GRE General Test, minimum GPA of 3.0 in last 60 hours of course work; for doctorate, GRE General Test, GRE Subject Test (literature), writing sample. Additional exam requirements/recommendations for international students: Required—TOEFL (minimum score 550 paper-based; 79 iBT). Electronic applications accepted.

University of Illinois at Chicago, Graduate College, College of Liberal Arts and Sciences, School of Literatures, Cultural Studies and Linguistics, Department of Linguistics, Chicago, IL 60607-7128. Offers MA. Part-time programs available. *Faculty:* 7 full-time (6 women), 1 (woman) part-time/adjunct. *Students:* 25 full-time (15 women), 6 part-time (3 women); includes 6 minority (3 Asian, non-Hispanic/Latino; 3 Hispanic/Latino), 3 international. Average age 33. 64 applicants, 59% accepted, 15 enrolled. In 2014, 14 master's awarded. *Degree requirements:* For master's, one foreign language, comprehensive exam, thesis (for some programs). *Entrance requirements:* For master's, minimum GPA of 3.0. Additional exam requirements/recommendations for international students: Required—TOEFL. *Application deadline:* For fall admission, 5/15 for domestic students, 2/15 for international students. Applications are processed on a rolling basis. Application fee: $60 ($0 for international students). Electronic applications accepted. *Expenses:* Tuition, state resident: full-time $11,254; part-time $468 per credit hour. Tuition, nonresident: full-time $23,252; part-time $968 per credit hour. *Required fees:* $1217 per term. Part-time tuition and fees vary according to course load, degree level and program. *Financial support:* Fellowships, research assistantships, teaching assistantships, career-related internships or fieldwork, Federal Work-Study, institutionally sponsored loans, and tuition waivers (full) available. Financial award application deadline: 3/1; financial award applicants required to submit FAFSA. *Faculty research:* Second language acquisition, methodology of second language teaching, lexicography, language, sex and gender. *Unit head:* Prof. Jessica Williams, Department Head/Professor of Linguistics/Director of Graduate Studies, 312-996-0259, Fax: 312-413-1005, E-mail: jessicaw@uic.edu.
Website: http://lcsl.uic.edu/linguistics

University of Illinois at Urbana–Champaign, Graduate College, College of Liberal Arts and Sciences, School of Literatures, Cultures and Linguistics, Department of Linguistics, Champaign, IL 61820. Offers linguistics (MA, PhD); teaching of English as a second language (MA). *Students:* 94 (66 women). Application fee: $70 ($90 for international students). *Unit head:* Hye Suk James Yoon, Acting Head, 217-244-3340, E-mail: jyoon@illinois.edu. *Application contact:* Lynn Stanke, Office Support Specialist, 217-333-6269, Fax: 217-244-3050, E-mail: stanke@illinois.edu.
Website: http://www.linguistics.illinois.edu/

University of Illinois at Urbana–Champaign, Graduate College, College of Liberal Arts and Sciences, School of Literatures, Cultures and Linguistics, Program in Romance Linguistics, Champaign, IL 61820. Offers PhD. Application fee: $70 ($90 for international students). *Unit head:* Jean-Philippe Mathy, Director, 217-244-2718, Fax: 217-244-8430, E-mail: jmathy@illinois.edu. *Application contact:* Lynn Stanke, Office Support Specialist, 217-333-6269, Fax: 217-244-3050, E-mail: stanke@illinois.edu.

The University of Iowa, Graduate College, College of Liberal Arts and Sciences, Department of Linguistics, Iowa City, IA 52242-1316. Offers MA, PhD. *Degree requirements:* For master's, thesis optional, exam; for doctorate, comprehensive exam, thesis/dissertation. *Entrance requirements:* For master's and doctorate, GRE General Test, minimum GPA of 3.0. Additional exam requirements/recommendations for international students: Required—TOEFL (minimum score 550 paper-based; 81 iBT). Electronic applications accepted.

The University of Kansas, Graduate Studies, College of Liberal Arts and Sciences, Department of Linguistics, Lawrence, KS 66045. Offers MA, PhD. *Faculty:* 11 full-time. *Students:* 29 full-time (15 women), 1 part-time (0 women), 20 international. Average age 29. 51 applicants, 25% accepted, 3 enrolled. In 2014, 10 master's, 2 doctorates awarded. Terminal master's awarded for partial completion of doctoral program. *Degree requirements:* For master's, one foreign language, thesis or alternative, 33 credit hours; for doctorate, one foreign language, comprehensive exam, thesis/dissertation, 24 credit hours, research skills, two qualifying papers. *Entrance requirements:* For master's and doctorate, GRE General Test, curriculum vitae, statement of purpose, 3 letters of recommendation. Additional exam requirements/recommendations for international students: Required—TOEFL (minimum score 53 paper-based; 20 iBT). *Application deadline:* For fall admission, 1/1 for domestic and international students. Application fee: $55 ($65 for international students). Electronic applications accepted. *Financial support:* Fellowships with full and partial tuition reimbursements, research assistantships with full and partial tuition reimbursements, teaching assistantships with full and partial tuition reimbursements, and scholarships/grants available. Financial award application deadline: 1/1. *Faculty research:* Phonetics and phonology, syntax and semantics, psycholinguistics, neurolinguistics, first and second language acquisition. *Unit head:* Allard Jongman, Chair, 785-864-2384, E-mail: jongman@ku.edu. *Application contact:* Corinna Johnson, Office Manager, 785-864-3450, E-mail: cljohns@ku.edu.
Website: http://www.linguistics.ku.edu/

The University of Manchester, School of Languages, Linguistics and Cultures, Manchester, United Kingdom. Offers Arab world studies (PhD); Chinese studies (M Phil, PhD); East Asian studies (M Phil, PhD); English language (PhD); French studies (M Phil, PhD); German studies (M Phil, PhD); interpreting studies (PhD); Italian studies (M Phil, PhD); Japanese studies (M Phil, PhD); Latin American cultural studies (M Phil, PhD); linguistics (M Phil, PhD); Middle Eastern studies (M Phil, PhD); Polish studies (M Phil, PhD); Portuguese studies (M Phil, PhD); Russian studies (M Phil, PhD); Spanish studies (M Phil, PhD); translation and intercultural studies (M Phil, PhD).

University of Manitoba, Faculty of Graduate Studies, Faculty of Arts, Department of Linguistics, Winnipeg, MB R3T 2N2, Canada. Offers MA, PhD.

University of Maryland, Baltimore County, The Graduate School, College of Arts, Humanities and Social Sciences, Department of Modern Languages and Linguistics, Program in Intercultural Communication, Baltimore, MD 21250. Offers MA. Part-time and evening/weekend programs available. *Faculty:* 17 full-time (9 women), 2 part-time/adjunct (1 woman). *Students:* 25 full-time (20 women), 7 part-time (5 women); includes 9 minority (8 Black or African American, non-Hispanic/Latino; 1 Hispanic/Latino), 13 international. 15 applicants, 87% accepted, 7 enrolled. In 2014, 10 master's awarded. *Degree requirements:* For master's, one foreign language, comprehensive exam (for some programs), thesis (for some programs). *Entrance requirements:* For master's, GRE General Test, minimum GPA of 3.0, 3 letters of recommendation, self-evaluation and statement of support, resume. Additional exam requirements/recommendations for international students: Required—TOEFL (minimum score 550 paper-based; 80 iBT). *Application deadline:* For fall admission, 1/31 for domestic and international students. Application fee: $50. Electronic applications accepted. *Expenses:* Tuition, state resident: part-time $557. Tuition, nonresident: part-time $922. *Required fees:* $122 per semester. One-time fee: $200 part-time. *Financial support:* In 2014–15, 8 students received support, including 6 teaching assistantships with full tuition reimbursements available (averaging $12,190 per year); Federal Work-Study, scholarships/grants, and tuition waivers (partial) also available. Financial award application deadline: 1/31; financial award applicants required to submit FAFSA. *Faculty research:* Comparative television research-cross-cultural; cultural studies; social developments in Latin America; intercultural communication; French civilization and cultural studies; language, gender and sexuality; sociolinguistics; African linguistics; immigrants in U.S. and Latin American societies. *Unit head:* Dr. Denis Provencher, Director, 410-455-2109 Ext. 52636, Fax: 410-455-2636, E-mail: provench@umbc.edu.
Website: http://www.umbc.edu/mll/incc/

University of Maryland, College Park, Academic Affairs, College of Arts and Humanities, Department of Linguistics, College Park, MD 20742. Offers MA, PhD. *Degree requirements:* For master's, thesis or alternative; for doctorate, thesis/dissertation. *Entrance requirements:* For master's, GRE General Test, minimum GPA of 3.0, sample of work, 3 letters of recommendation; for doctorate, GRE General Test, minimum GPA of 3.0, sample of work. Additional exam requirements/recommendations for international students: Required—TOEFL. Electronic applications accepted. *Faculty research:* Psycholinguistics, computational linguistics.

University of Massachusetts Amherst, Graduate School, College of Humanities and Fine Arts, Department of Linguistics, Amherst, MA 01003. Offers MA, PhD. Part-time programs available. *Faculty:* 20 full-time (9 women). *Students:* 30 full-time (15 women), 4 part-time (2 women); includes 3 minority (1 Black or African American, non-Hispanic/Latino; 2 Two or more races, non-Hispanic/Latino), 15 international. Average age 28. 134 applicants, 13% accepted, 5 enrolled. In 2014, 5 master's, 1 doctorate awarded. *Degree requirements:* For master's, thesis or alternative; for doctorate, comprehensive exam, thesis/dissertation. *Entrance requirements:* For doctorate, GRE General Test, writing sample. Additional exam requirements/recommendations for international students: Required—TOEFL (minimum score 550 paper-based; 80 iBT), IELTS (minimum score 6.5). *Application deadline:* For fall admission, 1/15 for domestic and international students. Applications are processed on a rolling basis. Application fee: $75. Electronic applications accepted. *Expenses:* Tuition, state resident: full-time $1980; part-time $110 per credit. Tuition, nonresident: full-time $14,644; part-time $414 per credit. *Required fees:* $11,417. One-time fee: $357. *Financial support:* Fellowships with full and partial tuition reimbursements, research assistantships with full and partial tuition reimbursements, teaching assistantships with full and partial tuition reimbursements, career-related internships or fieldwork, Federal Work-Study, scholarships/grants, traineeships, health care benefits, tuition waivers (full and partial), and unspecified assistantships available. Support available to part-time students. Financial award application deadline: 1/15. *Unit head:* Dr. Lisa Green, Graduate Program Director, 413-545-0889, Fax: 413-545-2792. *Application contact:* Lindsay DeSantis, Supervisor of Admissions, 413-545-0722, Fax: 413-577-0010, E-mail: gradadm@grad.umass.edu.
Website: http://www.umass.edu/linguist/

University of Massachusetts Boston, College of Liberal Arts, Program in Applied Linguistics, Boston, MA 02125-3393. Offers bilingual education (MA); English as a second language (MA); foreign language pedagogy (MA). Part-time and evening/weekend programs available. *Degree requirements:* For master's, one foreign language, comprehensive exam. *Entrance requirements:* For master's, minimum GPA of 2.75. *Application deadline:* For fall admission, 2/1 for domestic students; for spring admission, 10/15 for domestic students. *Expenses:* Tuition, state resident: full-time $2590; part-time $108 per credit. Tuition, nonresident: full-time $9758; part-time $406.50 per credit. Tuition and fees vary according to course load and program. *Financial support:* Research assistantships with full tuition reimbursements, teaching assistantships with full tuition reimbursements, career-related internships or fieldwork, Federal Work-Study, and unspecified assistantships available. Support available to part-time students. Financial award application deadline: 3/1; financial award applicants required to submit FAFSA. *Faculty research:* Multicultural theory and curriculum development, foreign language pedagogy, language and culture, applied psycholinguistics, bilingual education. *Unit head:* Dr. Donaldo Macedo, Director, 617-287-5760, E-mail: donalde.macedo@umb.edu. *Application contact:* Peggy Roldan Patel, Graduate Admissions Coordinator, 617-287-6400, Fax: 617-287-6236, E-mail: bos.gadm@dpc.umassp.edu.

University of Memphis, Graduate School, College of Arts and Sciences, Department of English, Memphis, TN 38152. Offers African-American literature (Graduate Certificate); applied linguistics (PhD); composition studies (PhD); creative writing (MFA); English as a second language (MA); linguistics (MA); literary and cultural studies (PhD), including African-American literature; literature (MA); professional writing (MA, PhD); teaching English as a second language (Graduate Certificate). Part-time and evening/weekend programs available. Postbaccalaureate distance learning degree programs offered (no on-campus study). *Faculty:* 30 full-time (15 women), 1 part-time/adjunct (0 women). *Students:* 89 full-time (45 women), 85 part-time (57 women); includes 35 minority (23 Black or African American, non-Hispanic/Latino; 6 Asian, non-Hispanic/Latino; 5 Hispanic/Latino; 1 Two or more races, non-Hispanic/Latino), 17 international. Average age 35. 83 applicants, 88% accepted, 19 enrolled. In 2014, 29 master's, 6 doctorates awarded. Terminal master's awarded for partial completion of doctoral program. *Degree requirements:* For master's, one foreign language, comprehensive exam, thesis optional; for doctorate, 2 foreign languages, comprehensive exam, thesis/dissertation. *Entrance requirements:* For master's and doctorate, GRE. Additional exam requirements/recommendations for international students: Required—TOEFL. *Application deadline:* For fall admission, 7/1 for domestic students; for spring admission, 10/15 for domestic students. Applications are processed on a rolling basis. Application fee: $35 ($60 for international students). Electronic applications accepted. *Financial support:* In 2014–15, 123 students received support. Research assistantships with full tuition reimbursements available, teaching assistantships with full tuition reimbursements available, Federal Work-Study, scholarships/grants, and unspecified assistantships available. Financial award application deadline: 2/15; financial award applicants required to submit FAFSA. *Faculty research:* Applied linguistics, British and American literature, professional writing, composition studies. *Unit head:* Dr. Joshua Phillips, Chair, 901-678-3067, Fax: 901-678-2226, E-mail: jsphllps@memphis.edu. *Application contact:* Dr. Jeffrey Scraba, Director, Graduate Studies, 901-678-3099, Fax: 901-678-2226, E-mail: jscraba@memphis.edu.
Website: http://www.memphis.edu/english

University of Michigan, Horace H. Rackham School of Graduate Studies, College of Literature, Science, and the Arts, Department of Anthropology, Ann Arbor, MI 48109-1107. Offers archaeological (PhD); biological (PhD); linguistic (PhD); sociocultural (PhD). *Faculty:* 40 full-time (18 women), 6 part-time/adjunct (3 women). *Students:* 99 full-time (59 women); includes 19 minority (1 Black or African American, non-Hispanic/Latino; 1 American Indian or Alaska Native, non-Hispanic/Latino; 6 Asian, non-Hispanic/Latino; 6 Hispanic/Latino; 5 Two or more races, non-Hispanic/Latino), 13 international. Average age 28. 206 applicants, 14% accepted, 15 enrolled. In 2014, 15 doctorates awarded. *Degree requirements:* For doctorate, one foreign language, comprehensive exam, thesis/dissertation, preliminary examination, oral defense of dissertation. *Entrance requirements:* For doctorate, GRE General Test. Additional exam requirements/recommendations for international students: Required—TOEFL (minimum score 560 paper-based; 84 iBT). *Application deadline:* For fall admission, 12/15 for domestic and international students. Application fee: $75 ($90 for international students). Electronic applications accepted. *Financial support:* In 2014–15, 67 students received support, including 47 fellowships with full tuition reimbursements available (averaging $19,350 per year), 4 research assistantships with full tuition reimbursements available (averaging $19,350 per year), 50 teaching assistantships with full tuition reimbursements available (averaging $19,350 per year); institutionally sponsored loans, scholarships/grants, traineeships, health care benefits, tuition waivers (full), and unspecified assistantships also available. Financial award application deadline: 3/1; financial award applicants required to submit FAFSA. *Faculty research:* Sociocultural, linguistic, biological and archaeological anthropology. *Unit head:* Dr. Thomas Fricke, Chair, 734-764-7274, Fax: 734-763-6077. *Application contact:* Katia Kitchen, Graduate Program Assistant, 734-936-7933, Fax: 734-763-6077, E-mail: kitchenk@umich.edu.
Website: http://www.lsa.umich.edu/anthro

University of Michigan, Horace H. Rackham School of Graduate Studies, College of Literature, Science, and the Arts, Department of Linguistics, Ann Arbor, MI 48109. Offers linguistics (PhD). *Faculty:* 18 full-time (8 women). *Students:* 24 full-time (12 women); includes 3 minority (2 Black or African American, non-Hispanic/Latino; 1 Asian, non-Hispanic/Latino), 8 international. Average age 29. 106 applicants, 8% accepted, 3 enrolled. In 2014, 4 doctorates awarded. *Degree requirements:* For doctorate, 2 foreign languages, thesis/dissertation, oral defense of dissertation. *Entrance requirements:* Additional exam requirements/recommendations for international students: Required—Michigan English Language Assessment Battery; Recommended—TOEFL (minimum score 620 paper-based; 95 iBT). *Application deadline:* For fall admission, 12/7 for domestic and international students. Application fee: $75 ($90 for international students). Electronic applications accepted. *Financial support:* In 2014–15, 23 students received support, including 7 fellowships with full tuition reimbursements available (averaging $18,971 per year), 1 research assistantship with full tuition reimbursement available (averaging $18,971 per year), 16 teaching assistantships with full tuition reimbursements available (averaging $18,971 per year); health care benefits and tuition waivers (full) also available. Financial award application deadline: 12/7. *Faculty research:* Broad-based approach to linguistics as a cognitive and social science including theoretical, experimental and computational approaches. *Unit head:* Prof. Robin Queen, Professor/Chair, 734-764-0353, Fax: 734-936-3406, E-mail: linguistics@umich.edu. *Application contact:* Dr. Jennifer Nguyen, Senior Student Services Assistant, 734-936-3403, Fax: 734-936-3406, E-mail: linggradadmissions@umich.edu.
Website: http://www.lsa.umich.edu/linguistics/

University of Minnesota, Twin Cities Campus, Graduate School, College of Liberal Arts, Institute of Linguistics, English as a Second Language, and Slavic Languages and Literatures (ILES), Program in Linguistics, Minneapolis, MN 55455-0213. Offers MA, PhD. Terminal master's awarded for partial completion of doctoral program. *Degree requirements:* For master's, one foreign language, comprehensive exam, thesis; for doctorate, 2 foreign languages, comprehensive exam, thesis/dissertation. *Entrance requirements:* For master's and doctorate, GRE General Test, 3 letters of recommendation, unit questionnaire. Additional exam requirements/recommendations for international students: Required—TOEFL (minimum score 550 paper-based; 79 iBT). Electronic applications accepted. *Faculty research:* Pragmatics and language processing, syntactic theory, language policy and planning, contact linguistics, language and cognition.

The University of Montana, Graduate School, College of Humanities and Sciences, Department of Anthropology, Missoula, MT 59812-0002. Offers anthropology (MA, PhD); applied anthropology (PhD); applied medical anthropology (MA); cultural heritage (MA, PhD); forensic anthropology (MA); linguistic anthropology (MA). *Degree requirements:* For master's, thesis (for some programs). *Entrance requirements:* For master's, GRE General Test. Additional exam requirements/recommendations for international students: Required—TOEFL. *Faculty research:* Historical preservation, plateau-plains archaeology and ethnohistory.

The University of Montana, Graduate School, College of Humanities and Sciences, Program in Linguistics, Missoula, MT 59812-0002. Offers MA. *Entrance requirements:*

For master's, GRE General Test. Additional exam requirements/recommendations for international students: Required—TOEFL.

University of New Hampshire, Graduate School, College of Liberal Arts, Department of English, Durham, NH 03824. Offers English (PhD); English education (MST); language and linguistics (MA); literature (MA). Part-time programs available. *Faculty:* 36 full-time (19 women). *Students:* 57 full-time (39 women), 38 part-time (22 women); includes 7 minority (2 Black or African American, non-Hispanic/Latino; 4 Hispanic/Latino; 1 Two or more races, non-Hispanic/Latino), 8 international. Average age 31. 194 applicants, 53% accepted, 32 enrolled. In 2014, 26 master's, 1 doctorate awarded. *Degree requirements:* For master's, one foreign language; for doctorate, 2 foreign languages, thesis/dissertation. *Entrance requirements:* For master's, GRE General Test, sample of written work; for doctorate, GRE General Test, GRE Subject Test, sample of written work. Additional exam requirements/recommendations for international students: Required—TOEFL (minimum score 550 paper-based; 80 iBT). *Application deadline:* For fall admission, 6/1 priority date for domestic students, 2/15 for international students; for spring admission, 12/1 for domestic students. Applications are processed on a rolling basis. Application fee: $65. Electronic applications accepted. *Expenses:* Tuition, state resident: full-time $13,500; part-time $750 per credit hour. Tuition, nonresident: full-time $26,460; part-time $1110 per credit hour. *Required fees:* $1788; $447 per semester. *Financial support:* In 2014–15, 56 students received support, including 2 fellowships, 42 teaching assistantships; research assistantships, career-related internships or fieldwork, Federal Work-Study, scholarships/grants, and tuition waivers (full and partial) also available. Support available to part-time students. Financial award application deadline: 2/15. *Unit head:* Dr. Rachel Trubowitz, Chairperson, 603-862-0254. *Application contact:* Janine Wilks, Administrative Assistant, 603-862-3963, E-mail: engl.grad@unh.edu.
Website: http://cola.unh.edu/english

University of New Mexico, Graduate School, College of Arts and Sciences, Program in Linguistics, Albuquerque, NM 87131-2039. Offers MA, PhD. Part-time programs available. *Faculty:* 8 full-time (6 women), 1 (woman) part-time/adjunct. *Students:* 43 full-time (26 women), 22 part-time (12 women); includes 11 minority (3 American Indian or Alaska Native, non-Hispanic/Latino; 1 Asian, non-Hispanic/Latino; 5 Hispanic/Latino; 2 Two or more races, non-Hispanic/Latino), 19 international. Average age 32. 58 applicants, 34% accepted, 14 enrolled. In 2014, 8 master's, 3 doctorates awarded. *Degree requirements:* For master's, comprehensive exam, thesis optional; for doctorate, one foreign language, comprehensive exam, thesis/dissertation, statistics through analysis of variance; knowledge of structure of a non-Indo European language. *Entrance requirements:* For master's, minimum GPA of 3.0, 3 letters of recommendation, letter of intent; for doctorate, MA in linguistics or equivalent, paper of publishable quality, 3 letters of recommendation, letter of intent. Additional exam requirements/recommendations for international students: Required—TOEFL (minimum score 550 paper-based; 79 iBT), IELTS (minimum score 7). *Application deadline:* For fall admission, 12/15 priority date for domestic and international students. Applications are processed on a rolling basis. Application fee: $50. Electronic applications accepted. *Financial support:* In 2014–15, 44 students received support, including 3 fellowships with full tuition reimbursements available (averaging $7,350 per year), 4 research assistantships (averaging $8,452 per year), 24 teaching assistantships with full and partial tuition reimbursements available (averaging $10,679 per year); Federal Work-Study, health care benefits, and tuition waivers (full and partial) also available. Financial award application deadline: 1/15; financial award applicants required to submit FAFSA. *Faculty research:* Cognitive-functional linguistics, signed language linguistics, Native American languages of the Southwest, language acquisition, language in interaction (discourse, prosody). *Total annual research expenditures:* $233,433. *Unit head:* Dr. Caroline Smith, Chair, 505-277-6353, Fax: 505-277-6355, E-mail: caroline@unm.edu. *Application contact:* Jessica Slocum, Administrative Assistant III, 505-277-6353, Fax: 505-277-6355, E-mail: jslocum@unm.edu.
Website: http://www.unm.edu/~linguist/

University of New Mexico, Graduate School, College of Education, Program in Educational Linguistics, Albuquerque, NM 87131-2039. Offers PhD. Part-time programs available. *Faculty:* 4 full-time (3 women). *Students:* 16 full-time (7 women), 6 part-time (5 women); includes 4 minority (1 American Indian or Alaska Native, non-Hispanic/Latino; 1 Asian, non-Hispanic/Latino; 1 Hispanic/Latino; 1 Two or more races, non-Hispanic/Latino), 9 international. Average age 46. 17 applicants, 47% accepted, 5 enrolled. In 2014, 2 doctorates awarded. *Degree requirements:* For doctorate, comprehensive exam, thesis/dissertation. *Entrance requirements:* For doctorate, master's degree in linguistics or complementary field (recommended). Additional exam requirements/recommendations for international students: Required—TOEFL (minimum score 550 paper-based; 79 iBT). *Application deadline:* For fall admission, 12/1 for domestic and international students. Application fee: $50. Electronic applications accepted. *Financial support:* In 2014–15, 6 students received support, including 2 teaching assistantships (averaging $6,384 per year); career-related internships or fieldwork, institutionally sponsored loans, scholarships/grants, and unspecified assistantships also available. Support available to part-time students. Financial award application deadline: 1/15; financial award applicants required to submit FAFSA. *Faculty research:* Bilingualism, language maintenance and loss, bilingual deaf education, Spanish dialectical studies, English as a second language, writing/composition, Native American language issues, language and thought, language policy studies, global English issues, assessment. *Unit head:* Dr. Holbrook Mahn, Graduate Director, 505-277-5887, Fax: 505-277-8362, E-mail: hmahn@unm.edu. *Application contact:* Mary Gurule Vernon, Administrator, 505-277-5282, Fax: 505-277-8362, E-mail: mgurule2@unm.edu.
Website: http://coe.unm.edu/departments/llss/ed-ling/

The University of North Carolina at Chapel Hill, Graduate School, College of Arts and Sciences, Department of Germanic Languages, Chapel Hill, NC 27599. Offers literature and linguistics (MA, PhD). Part-time programs available. Terminal master's awarded for partial completion of doctoral program. *Degree requirements:* For master's, comprehensive exam, thesis; for doctorate, one foreign language, comprehensive exam, thesis/dissertation. *Entrance requirements:* For master's and doctorate, GRE General Test, minimum GPA of 3.0. *Faculty research:* Gender and sexuality, literature and politics, German and Jewish culture, medieval through modern literature, Germanic linguistics.

The University of North Carolina at Chapel Hill, Graduate School, College of Arts and Sciences, Department of Linguistics, Chapel Hill, NC 27599. Offers MA. *Degree requirements:* For master's, one foreign language, comprehensive exam, thesis. *Entrance requirements:* For master's, GRE General Test, minimum GPA of 3.0. Additional exam requirements/recommendations for international students: Required—TOEFL (minimum score 79 iBT). Electronic applications accepted. *Faculty research:* Phonetics, phonology, morphology, syntax, semantics, historical linguistics, language acquisition, Mayan linguistics.

University of North Dakota, Graduate School, College of Arts and Sciences, Program in Linguistics, Grand Forks, ND 58202. Offers MA. *Degree requirements:* For master's, one foreign language, thesis, final examination. *Entrance requirements:* For master's, minimum GPA of 3.0. Additional exam requirements/recommendations for international students: Required—TOEFL (minimum score 550 paper-based; 79 iBT), IELTS

(minimum score 6.5). Electronic applications accepted. *Faculty research:* Practice-based field studies.

University of North Texas, Robert B. Toulouse School of Graduate Studies, Denton, TX 76203-5459. Offers accounting (MS); applied anthropology (MA, MS); applied behavior analysis (Certificate); applied geography (MA); applied technology and performance improvement (M Ed, MS); art education (MA); art history (MA); art museum education (Certificate); arts leadership (Certificate); audiology (Au D); behavior analysis (MS); behavioral science (PhD); biochemistry and molecular biology (MS); biology (MA, MS); biomedical engineering (MS); business analysis (MS); chemistry (MS); clinical health psychology (PhD); communication studies (MA, MS); computer engineering (MS); computer science (MS); counseling (M Ed, MS), including clinical mental health counseling (MS), college and university counseling, elementary school counseling, secondary school counseling; creative writing (MA); criminal justice (MS); curriculum and instruction (M Ed); decision sciences (MBA); design (MA, MFA), including fashion design (MFA), innovation studies, interior design (MFA); early childhood studies (MS); economics (MS); educational leadership (M Ed, Ed D); educational psychology (MS, PhD), including family studies (MS), gifted and talented (MS), human development (MS), learning and cognition (MS), research, measurement and evaluation (MS); electrical engineering (MS); emergency management (MPA); engineering technology (MS); English (MA); English as a second language (MA); environmental science (MS); finance (MBA, MS); financial management (MPA); French (MA); health services management (MBA); higher education (M Ed, Ed D); history (MA, MS); hospitality management (MS); human resources management (MPA); information science (MS); information systems (PhD); information technologies (MBA); interdisciplinary studies (MA, MS); international studies (MA); international sustainable tourism (MS); jazz studies (MM); journalism (MA, MJ, Graduate Certificate), including interactive and virtual digital communication (Graduate Certificate), narrative journalism (Graduate Certificate), public relations (Graduate Certificate); kinesiology (MS); linguistics (MA); local government management (MPA); logistics (PhD); logistics and supply chain management (MBA); long-term care, senior housing, and aging services (MA); management (PhD); marketing (MBA); mathematics (MA, MS); mechanical and energy engineering (MS, PhD); music (MA), including ethnomusicology, music theory, musicology, performance; music composition (PhD); music education (MM Ed, PhD); nonprofit management (MPA); operations and supply chain management (MBA); performance (MM, DMA); philosophy (MA); political science (MA); professional and technical communication (MA); radio, television and film (MA, MFA); rehabilitation counseling (Certificate); sociology (MA); Spanish (MA); special education (M Ed); speech-language pathology (MA); strategic management (MBA); studio art (MFA); teaching (M Ed); MBA/MS. Part-time and evening/weekend programs available. Postbaccalaureate distance learning degree programs offered. *Faculty:* 651 full-time (215 women), 233 part-time/adjunct (139 women). *Students:* 3,040 full-time (1,598 women), 3,401 part-time (2,097 women); includes 1,740 minority (533 Black or African American, non-Hispanic/Latino; 15 American Indian or Alaska Native, non-Hispanic/Latino; 286 Asian, non-Hispanic/Latino; 746 Hispanic/Latino; 3 Native Hawaiian or other Pacific Islander, non-Hispanic/Latino; 157 Two or more races, non-Hispanic/Latino), 1,145 international. Terminal master's awarded for partial completion of doctoral program. *Degree requirements:* For master's, variable foreign language requirement, comprehensive exam (for some programs), thesis (for some programs); for doctorate, variable foreign language requirement, comprehensive exam (for some programs), thesis/dissertation; for other advanced degree, variable foreign language requirement, comprehensive exam (for some programs). *Entrance requirements:* For master's and doctorate, GRE, GMAT. Additional exam requirements/recommendations for international students: Required—TOEFL (minimum score 550 paper-based; 79 iBT). *Application deadline:* For fall admission, 7/15 for domestic students, 3/15 for international students; for spring admission, 11/15 for domestic students, 9/15 for international students; for summer admission, 5/1 for domestic students. Applications are processed on a rolling basis. Application fee: $60. Electronic applications accepted. *Expenses:* Tuition, state resident: full-time $5450; part-time $3633 per year. Tuition, nonresident: full-time $11,966; part-time $7977 per year. *Required fees:* $1301; $398 per credit hour. $685 per semester. Tuition and fees vary according to program and reciprocity agreements. *Financial support:* Fellowships with partial tuition reimbursements, research assistantships with partial tuition reimbursements, teaching assistantships, career-related internships or fieldwork, Federal Work-Study, institutionally sponsored loans, scholarships/grants, health care benefits, and library assistantships available. Support available to part-time students. Financial award applicants required to submit FAFSA. *Unit head:* Mark Wardell, Dean, 940-565-2383, E-mail: mark.wardell@unt.edu. *Application contact:* Toulouse School of Graduate Studies, 940-565-2383, Fax: 940-565-2141, E-mail: gradsch@unt.edu.
Website: http://tsgs.unt.edu/

University of Oregon, Graduate School, College of Arts and Sciences, Department of Linguistics, Eugene, OR 97403. Offers MA, PhD. Terminal master's awarded for partial completion of doctoral program. *Degree requirements:* For master's, 2 foreign languages; for doctorate, thesis/dissertation. *Entrance requirements:* For master's and doctorate, GRE General Test, minimum GPA of 3.0. Additional exam requirements/recommendations for international students: Required—TOEFL. *Faculty research:* Functional syntax, discourse, empirical methods.

University of Ottawa, Faculty of Graduate and Postdoctoral Studies, Faculty of Arts, Department of Linguistics, Ottawa, ON K1N 6N5, Canada. Offers MA, PhD. *Degree requirements:* For master's, one foreign language, thesis or alternative; for doctorate, 2 foreign languages, comprehensive exam, thesis/dissertation. *Entrance requirements:* For master's, honors degree or equivalent, minimum B average; for doctorate, master's degree, minimum B+ average. Electronic applications accepted. *Faculty research:* Empirical linguistics, formal linguistics.

University of Pennsylvania, School of Arts and Sciences, Graduate Group in Linguistics, Philadelphia, PA 19104. Offers AM, PhD. *Faculty:* 8 full-time (1 woman), 5 part-time/adjunct (1 woman). *Students:* 34 full-time (19 women); includes 5 minority (1 Black or African American, non-Hispanic/Latino; 3 Asian, non-Hispanic/Latino; 1 Hispanic/Latino), 12 international. 138 applicants, 13% accepted, 8 enrolled. In 2014, 5 doctorates awarded. Terminal master's awarded for partial completion of doctoral program. *Degree requirements:* For master's, thesis; for doctorate, 2 foreign languages, thesis/dissertation. *Entrance requirements:* For master's and doctorate, GRE General Test. Additional exam requirements/recommendations for international students: Required—TOEFL. *Application deadline:* For fall admission, 12/1 priority date for domestic students. Application fee: $70. Electronic applications accepted. *Financial support:* Fellowships, research assistantships, teaching assistantships, institutionally sponsored loans, scholarships/grants, traineeships, health care benefits, and unspecified assistantships available. Financial award application deadline: 12/15. *Unit head:* Dr. Ralph M. Rosen, Associate Dean for Graduate Studies, 215-898-7156, Fax: 215-573-8068, E-mail: grad-dean@sas.upenn.edu. *Application contact:* Arts and Sciences Graduate Admissions, 215-573-5816, Fax: 215-573-8068, E-mail: gdasadmis@sas.upenn.edu.
Website: http://www.ling.upenn.edu/graduate/

University of Pittsburgh, Dietrich School of Arts and Sciences, Department of Linguistics, Pittsburgh, PA 15260. Offers MA, PhD. Part-time programs available. *Faculty:* 7 full-time (2 women). *Students:* 20 full-time (11 women), 8 part-time (6 women); includes 5 minority (2 Black or African American, non-Hispanic/Latino; 3 Asian, non-Hispanic/Latino), 8 international. Average age 29. 82 applicants, 26% accepted, 7 enrolled. In 2014, 1 master's awarded. Terminal master's awarded for partial completion of doctoral program. *Degree requirements:* For master's, one foreign language, thesis optional; for doctorate, 2 foreign languages, comprehensive exam, thesis/dissertation. *Entrance requirements:* For master's, GRE General Test; for doctorate, GRE General Test, MA in linguistics. Additional exam requirements/recommendations for international students: Required—TOEFL (minimum score 600 paper-based; 100 iBT). *Application deadline:* For fall admission, 12/15 priority date for domestic and international students. Applications are processed on a rolling basis. Application fee: $50. Electronic applications accepted. *Expenses:* Tuition, state resident: full-time $20,742; part-time $838 per credit. Tuition, nonresident: full-time $33,960; part-time $1389 per credit. *Required fees:* $800; $205 per term. Tuition and fees vary according to program. *Financial support:* In 2014–15, 14 students received support, including 3 fellowships with full and partial tuition reimbursements available (averaging $24,296 per year), 1 research assistantship with full and partial tuition reimbursement available (averaging $11,088 per year), 10 teaching assistantships with full and partial tuition reimbursements available (averaging $14,400 per year); scholarships/grants, health care benefits, and unspecified assistantships also available. Financial award application deadline: 12/15; financial award applicants required to submit FAFSA. *Faculty research:* Second language acquisition, phonetics, intonation, sociolinguistics, language contact. *Total annual research expenditures:* $161,750. *Unit head:* Dr. Shelome Gooden, Chair, 412-624-5922, Fax: 412-624-5520, E-mail: sgooden@pitt.edu. *Application contact:* Connie Anne Markiw, Graduate Student Services Administrator, 412-624-6568, Fax: 412-624-6338, E-mail: cam177@pitt.edu.
Website: http://www.linguistics.pitt.edu/

University of Puerto Rico, Río Piedras Campus, College of Humanities, Department of Hispanic Studies, San Juan, PR 00931-3300. Offers Hispanic linguistics (PhD); Hispanic studies (MA); Latin American literature (PhD); Puerto Rican literature (PhD); Spanish literature (PhD). Part-time programs available. *Degree requirements:* For master's, one foreign language, comprehensive exam, thesis; for doctorate, one foreign language, comprehensive exam, thesis/dissertation. *Entrance requirements:* For master's, PAEG or GRE, interview, minimum GPA of 3.0, letter of recommendation (2); for doctorate, PAEG or GRE, interview, master's degree, minimum GPA of 3.0, letter of recommendation (2). *Faculty research:* Poetry of Luis Palés Matos, short stories in Puerto Rico, language in the social process, "Decima Popular", Anglicism.

University of Puerto Rico, Río Piedras Campus, College of Humanities, Department of Linguistics, San Juan, PR 00931-3300. Offers MA. Part-time programs available. *Degree requirements:* For master's, one foreign language, comprehensive exam, thesis. *Entrance requirements:* For master's, PAEG or GRE, interview, minimum GPA of 3.0, letter of recommendation (2).

University of Regina, Faculty of Graduate Studies and Research, Faculty of Arts, Program in Linguistics, Regina, SK S4S 0A2, Canada. Offers MA. Offered as a special case program. Part-time programs available. *Students:* 1 (woman) full-time. 1 applicant. In 2014, 1 master's awarded. *Degree requirements:* For master's, thesis. *Entrance requirements:* Additional exam requirements/recommendations for international students: Required—TOEFL (minimum score 580 paper-based), IELTS (minimum score 6.5), PTE (minimum score 59). *Application deadline:* Applications are processed on a rolling basis. Application fee: $100. Electronic applications accepted. *Expenses: Tuition, area resident:* Full-time $4900 Canadian dollars; part-time $837.65 Canadian dollars per semester. *International tuition:* $7900 Canadian dollars full-time. *Required fees:* $396 Canadian dollars; $86.90 Canadian dollars per semester. *Financial support:* In 2014–15, 1 fellowship (averaging $6,000 per year) was awarded; research assistantships, teaching assistantships, and scholarships/grants also available. Financial award application deadline: 6/15. *Faculty research:* Advanced phonology, advanced morphology, advanced syntax, advanced semantics, diachronic linguistics. *Unit head:* Dr. Edward Doolittle, Department Head/Graduate Studies Advisor/Coordinator, 306-790-5950 Ext. 3260, Fax: 306-790-5994, E-mail: edoolittle@firstnationsuniversity.ca.

University of Rochester, School of Arts and Sciences, Department of Linguistics, Rochester, NY 14627. Offers MA. *Faculty:* 4 full-time (1 woman). *Students:* 2 full-time (1 woman), 1 part-time (0 women), 1 international. 11 applicants, 27% accepted, 2 enrolled. In 2014, 2 master's awarded. *Entrance requirements:* For master's, GRE, official transcripts, three letters of recommendation. Additional exam requirements/recommendations for international students: Required—TOEFL (minimum score 580 paper-based). *Application deadline:* For fall admission, 2/1 for domestic students. Application fee: $60. Electronic applications accepted. *Expenses: Tuition:* Full-time $46,150; part-time $1442 per credit hour. *Required fees:* $504. *Unit head:* Joyce McDonough, Chair, 585-273-2895. *Application contact:* Carla Gottschalk, Department Administrator, 585-275-8053.
Website: http://www.ling.rochester.edu/

University of South Africa, College of Human Sciences, Pretoria, South Africa. Offers adult education (M Ed); African languages (MA, PhD); African politics (MA, PhD); Afrikaans (MA, PhD); ancient history (MA, PhD); ancient Near Eastern studies (MA, PhD); anthropology (MA, PhD); applied linguistics (MA); Arabic (MA, PhD); archaeology (MA); art history (MA); Biblical archaeology (MA); Biblical studies (M Th, D Th, PhD); Christian spirituality (M Th, D Th); church history (M Th, D Th); classical studies (MA, PhD); clinical psychology (MA); communication (MA, PhD); comparative education (M Ed, Ed D); consulting psychology (D Admin, D Com, PhD); curriculum studies (M Ed, Ed D); development studies (M Admin, MA, D Admin, PhD); didactics (M Ed, Ed D); education (M Tech); education management (M Ed, Ed D); educational psychology (M Ed); English (MA); environmental education (M Ed); French (MA, PhD); German (MA, PhD); Greek (MA); guidance and counseling (M Ed); health studies (MA, PhD), including health sciences education (MA), health services management (MA), medical and surgical nursing science (critical care general) (MA), midwifery and neonatal nursing science (MA), trauma and emergency care (MA); history (MA, PhD); history of education (Ed D); inclusive education (M Ed, Ed D); information and communications technology policy and regulation (MA); information science (MA, MIS, PhD); international politics (MA, PhD); Islamic studies (MA, PhD); Italian (MA, PhD); Judaica (MA, PhD); linguistics (MA, PhD); mathematical education (M Ed); mathematics education (MA); missiology (M Th, D Th); modern Hebrew (MA, PhD); musicology (MA, MMus, D Mus, PhD); natural science education (M Ed); New Testament (M Th, D Th); Old Testament (D Th); pastoral therapy (M Th, D Th); philosophy (MA); philosophy of education (M Ed, Ed D); politics (MA, PhD); Portuguese (MA, PhD); practical theology (M Th, D Th); psychology (MA, MS, PhD); psychology of education (M Ed, Ed D); public health (MA); religious studies (MA, D Th, PhD); Romance languages (MA); Russian (MA, PhD); Semitic languages (MA, PhD); social behavior studies in HIV/AIDS (MA); social science (mental health) (MA); social science in development studies (MA); social science in psychology (MA); social science in social work (MA); social science in sociology (MA); social work (MSW, DSW, PhD); socio-education (M Ed, Ed D); sociolinguistics (MA); sociology (MA, PhD); Spanish (MA, PhD); systematic theology (M Th, D Th); TESOL (teaching English to speakers of other languages) (MA); theological ethics (M Th, D Th); theory of literature (MA, PhD); urban ministries (D Th); urban ministry (M Th).

University of South Carolina, The Graduate School, College of Arts and Sciences, Linguistics Program, Columbia, SC 29208. Offers linguistics (MA, PhD); teaching English to speakers of other languages (Certificate). Part-time programs available. Terminal master's awarded for partial completion of doctoral program. *Degree requirements:* For master's, one foreign language, comprehensive exam, thesis optional; for doctorate, 3 foreign languages, comprehensive exam, thesis/dissertation. *Entrance requirements:* For master's and Certificate, GRE General Test, minimum GPA of 3.0; for doctorate, GRE General Test, minimum GPA of 3.5. Additional exam requirements/recommendations for international students: Required—TOEFL. Electronic applications accepted. *Faculty research:* Second language acquisition, sociolinguistics, syntax, historical linguistics and phonology.

University of Southern California, Graduate School, Dana and David Dornsife College of Letters, Arts and Sciences, Department of East Asian Languages and Cultures, Los Angeles, CA 90089. Offers classical Chinese literature (MA, PhD); classical Japanese literature (MA, PhD); linguistics (MA, PhD); modern Chinese literature (MA, PhD); modern Japanese literature (MA, PhD); modern Korean literature (MA, PhD). *Degree requirements:* For master's, thesis; for doctorate, 2 foreign languages, comprehensive exam, thesis/dissertation. *Entrance requirements:* For master's and doctorate, GRE, BA in relevant field. Additional exam requirements/recommendations for international students: Required—TOEFL. Electronic applications accepted. *Faculty research:* Gender, visual studies, multimedia, ecocriticism, second language acquisition.

University of Southern California, Graduate School, Dana and David Dornsife College of Letters, Arts and Sciences, Department of Linguistics, Los Angeles, CA 90089. Offers East Asian linguistics (PhD); Hispanic linguistics (PhD); linguistics (PhD); Slavic linguistics (PhD). *Degree requirements:* For doctorate, comprehensive exam, thesis/dissertation. *Entrance requirements:* For doctorate, GRE. Additional exam requirements/recommendations for international students: Required—TOEFL (minimum score 100 iBT). Electronic applications accepted. *Faculty research:* Syntax, phonology, phonetics, semantics, sociolinguistics, psycholinguistics.

The University of Tennessee, Graduate School, College of Arts and Sciences, Department of Modern Foreign Languages and Literatures, Program in Modern Foreign Languages, Knoxville, TN 37996. Offers applied linguistics (PhD); French (PhD); German (PhD); Italian (PhD); Portuguese (PhD); Russian (PhD); Spanish (PhD). *Degree requirements:* For doctorate, 2 foreign languages, thesis/dissertation. *Entrance requirements:* For doctorate, minimum GPA of 2.7. Additional exam requirements/recommendations for international students: Required—TOEFL. Electronic applications accepted.

The University of Texas at Arlington, Graduate School, College of Liberal Arts, Department of Linguistics and TESOL, Program in Linguistics, Arlington, TX 76019. Offers MA, PhD. Part-time and evening/weekend programs available. Terminal master's awarded for partial completion of doctoral program. *Degree requirements:* For master's, one foreign language, comprehensive exam (for some programs), thesis optional; for doctorate, 2 foreign languages, comprehensive exam, thesis/dissertation, qualifying exam, dissertation proposal defense, professional development. *Entrance requirements:* For master's, GRE General Test, minimum undergraduate GPA of 3.0, 9 credits of undergraduate foundation courses; for doctorate, GRE General Test, 30 hours of graduate work in linguistics or a related discipline, minimum GPA of 3.5. Additional exam requirements/recommendations for international students: Required—TOEFL (minimum score 550 paper-based). Electronic applications accepted. *Faculty research:* Field linguistics, discourse analysis, text linguistics, phonology, teaching English as a second language.

The University of Texas at Austin, Graduate School, College of Liberal Arts, Department of French and Italian, Austin, TX 78712-1111. Offers French linguistics (MA, PhD); French studies (MA, PhD); Italian studies (MA, PhD); Romance linguistics (PhD). Part-time programs available. *Degree requirements:* For master's, one foreign language, thesis; for doctorate, 2 foreign languages, thesis/dissertation. *Entrance requirements:* For master's, GRE General Test, minimum GPA of 3.0, bachelor's degree in French or equivalent; for doctorate, GRE General Test, minimum GPA of 3.0, master's degree in French. Additional exam requirements/recommendations for international students: Required—TOEFL. Electronic applications accepted. *Faculty research:* Nineteenth-century Italian literature, Italian Renaissance, twentieth-century French literature, Francophone literature, fifteenth-century literature and culture.

The University of Texas at Austin, Graduate School, College of Liberal Arts, Department of Linguistics, Austin, TX 78712-1111. Offers MA, PhD. *Degree requirements:* For master's, one foreign language, thesis; for doctorate, 2 foreign languages, thesis/dissertation. *Entrance requirements:* For master's and doctorate, GRE General Test. Electronic applications accepted. *Faculty research:* Theoretical linguistics, sociolinguistics, documentary and descriptive linguistics, computational linguistics.

The University of Texas at Austin, Graduate School, College of Liberal Arts, Department of Slavic and Eurasian Studies, Austin, TX 78712-1111. Offers applied linguistics/pedagogy (PhD); literature and culture (PhD); Slavic languages (MA); Slavic linguistics (PhD). *Degree requirements:* For master's, 2 foreign languages, thesis; for doctorate, 3 foreign languages, thesis/dissertation. *Entrance requirements:* For master's and doctorate, GRE General Test. Electronic applications accepted. *Faculty research:* Slavic linguistics; applied linguistics; Russian, Czech, and Slavic literature and culture.

The University of Texas at Austin, Graduate School, College of Liberal Arts, Department of Spanish and Portuguese, Austin, TX 78712-1111. Offers Hispanic linguistics (MA, PhD); Hispanic literature (MA, PhD); Ibero-romance philology and linguistics (PhD); Luso-Brazilian literature (MA, PhD). *Degree requirements:* For master's, 2 foreign languages, thesis or alternative; for doctorate, 3 foreign languages, thesis/dissertation. *Entrance requirements:* For master's and doctorate, GRE General Test. Electronic applications accepted.

The University of Texas at El Paso, Graduate School, College of Liberal Arts, Department of Languages and Linguistics, El Paso, TX 79968-0001. Offers linguistics (MA); Spanish (MA); teaching English to speakers of other languages (Certificate). Part-time and evening/weekend programs available. *Degree requirements:* For master's, thesis optional. *Entrance requirements:* For master's, GRE General Test, departmental exam, minimum GPA of 3.0, letters of recommendation. Additional exam requirements/recommendations for international students: Required—TOEFL; Recommended—IELTS. Electronic applications accepted.

University of Toronto, School of Graduate Studies, Faculty of Arts and Science, Department of Linguistics, Toronto, ON M5S 2J7, Canada. Offers MA, PhD. Part-time programs available. *Degree requirements:* For master's, 2 foreign languages; for doctorate, thesis/dissertation, oral thesis proposal. *Entrance requirements:* For master's, BA in linguistics; for doctorate, MA in linguistics. Electronic applications accepted.

University of Utah, Graduate School, College of Humanities, Department of Linguistics, Salt Lake City, UT 84112-0492. Offers MA, PhD. *Faculty:* 10 full-time (5 women), 2 part-time/adjunct (1 woman). *Students:* 15 full-time (7 women), 11 part-time (7 women); includes 4 minority (1 Asian, non-Hispanic/Latino; 3 Hispanic/Latino), 5 international. Average age 31. 43 applicants, 19% accepted, 7 enrolled. In 2014, 3 master's, 3 doctorates awarded. *Degree requirements:* For master's, 2 foreign languages, comprehensive exam, thesis; for doctorate, 2 foreign languages, comprehensive exam, thesis/dissertation. *Entrance requirements:* For master's and doctorate, GRE General Test, minimum undergraduate GPA of 3.0. Additional exam requirements/recommendations for international students: Required—TOEFL (minimum score 600 paper-based; 100 iBT). *Application deadline:* For fall admission, 1/15 for domestic students, 12/1 for international students. Application fee: $55 ($65 for international students). Electronic applications accepted. *Financial support:* In 2014–15, 3 students received support, including 2 fellowships with full tuition reimbursements available (averaging $7,000 per year), 18 teaching assistantships with full tuition reimbursements available (averaging $12,139 per year); scholarships/grants, health care benefits, and unspecified assistantships also available. Financial award application deadline: 1/30. *Faculty research:* Phonology, second language acquisition, semantics, syntax, second language pedagogy. *Unit head:* Dr. Edward Rubin, Chair, 801-581-8047, Fax: 801-585-7351, E-mail: e.rubin@utah.edu. *Application contact:* Kacey Campbell, Academic Advisor, 801-581-3929, Fax: 801-585-7351, E-mail: kacey.campbell@utah.edu. Website: http://www.linguistics.utah.edu

University of Victoria, Faculty of Graduate Studies, Faculty of Humanities, Department of Linguistics, Victoria, BC V8W 2Y2, Canada. Offers applied linguistics (MA); linguistics (MA, PhD). Part-time programs available. *Degree requirements:* For master's, one foreign language, thesis, colloquium; for doctorate, 2 foreign languages, comprehensive exam, thesis/dissertation, candidacy exam. *Entrance requirements:* For master's, GRE; for doctorate, GRE, sample of written work. Additional exam requirements/recommendations for international students: Required—TOEFL. Electronic applications accepted. *Faculty research:* Grammatical theory, syntactic analysis, morphology, Western Amerindian languages; Salishan, applied linguistics.

University of Virginia, College and Graduate School of Arts and Sciences, Program in Linguistics, Charlottesville, VA 22903. Offers MA. *Students:* 10 full-time (7 women), 6 part-time (4 women); includes 3 minority (1 Hispanic/Latino; 2 Two or more races, non-Hispanic/Latino), 6 international. Average age 26. 17 applicants, 82% accepted, 7 enrolled. In 2014, 2 master's awarded. *Degree requirements:* For master's, one foreign language, comprehensive exam, thesis optional, reading knowledge of French or German. *Entrance requirements:* For master's, GRE General Test. Additional exam requirements/recommendations for international students: Required—TOEFL (minimum score 600 paper-based; 90 iBT), IELTS (minimum score 7). *Application deadline:* For fall admission, 2/15 for domestic and international students. Applications are processed on a rolling basis. Application fee: $60. Electronic applications accepted. *Expenses:* Tuition, state resident: full-time $14,164; part-time $349 per credit hour. Tuition, nonresident: full-time $23,722; part-time $1300 per credit hour. *Required fees:* $2514. *Financial support:* Teaching assistantships available. Financial award applicants required to submit FAFSA. *Unit head:* Lise Dobrin, Program Director, 434-924-7048, E-mail: ld4n@virginia.edu. Website: http://artsandsciences.virginia.edu/linguistics/

University of Washington, Graduate School, College of Arts and Sciences, Department of Linguistics, Seattle, WA 98195. Offers computational linguistics (MA); linguistics (MA, PhD); Romance linguistics (MA, PhD). Part-time programs available. Terminal master's awarded for partial completion of doctoral program. *Degree requirements:* For master's, one foreign language, thesis; for doctorate, 2 foreign languages, thesis/dissertation. *Entrance requirements:* For master's, GRE General Test, minimum GPA of 3.0; for doctorate, GRE, minimum GPA of 3.0. Additional exam requirements/recommendations for international students: Required—TOEFL. Electronic applications accepted. *Faculty research:* Syntax, phonology, semantics, phonetics, sociolinguistics.

University of Washington, Graduate School, College of Arts and Sciences, Department of Slavic Languages and Literatures, Seattle, WA 98195. Offers Russian literature (MA, PhD); Slavic linguistics (MA, PhD). *Degree requirements:* For master's, 2 foreign languages, thesis optional; for doctorate, 3 foreign languages, thesis/dissertation. *Entrance requirements:* For master's and doctorate, GRE General Test, minimum GPA of 3.0. Additional exam requirements/recommendations for international students: Required—TOEFL. Electronic applications accepted. *Faculty research:* Modern and medieval East European languages and literatures, comparative literature, Russian folk literature, Slavic literary theory and criticism, computerized morphology of Russian.

University of Wisconsin–Madison, Graduate School, College of Letters and Science, Department of East Asian Languages and Literature, Program in Japanese Linguistics, Madison, WI 53706-1380. Offers MA, PhD. Part-time programs available. Terminal master's awarded for partial completion of doctoral program. *Degree requirements:* For master's, one foreign language, seminars, written exam; for doctorate, 3 foreign languages, thesis/dissertation, seminars, preliminary exams, oral exam. *Entrance requirements:* For master's, GRE General Test, bachelor's degree or equivalent in Japanese; for doctorate, GRE General Test, master's degree or equivalent in Japanese. Electronic applications accepted. *Expenses:* Tuition, state resident: full-time $10,723; part-time $745 per credit. Tuition, nonresident: full-time $24,054; part-time $1578 per credit. *Required fees:* $374 per semester. Tuition and fees vary according to course load, program and reciprocity agreements. *Faculty research:* Modern and historical Japanese linguistics, modern Japanese fiction and poetry, classical Japanese literature, language pedagogy.

University of Wisconsin–Madison, Graduate School, College of Letters and Science, Department of English, Madison, WI 53706-1380. Offers applied English linguistics (MA); composition and rhetoric (PhD); creative writing (MFA); English language and linguistics (PhD); literary studies (MA, PhD). *Degree requirements:* For doctorate, thesis/dissertation. *Expenses:* Tuition, state resident: full-time $10,723; part-time $745 per credit. Tuition, nonresident: full-time $24,054; part-time $1578 per credit. *Required fees:* $374 per semester. Tuition and fees vary according to course load, program and reciprocity agreements.

University of Wisconsin–Madison, Graduate School, College of Letters and Science, Department of Linguistics, Madison, WI 53706-1380. Offers MA, PhD. Part-time programs available. Terminal master's awarded for partial completion of doctoral program. *Degree requirements:* For master's, 2 foreign languages; for doctorate, 3 foreign languages, thesis/dissertation. Electronic applications accepted. *Expenses:* Tuition, state resident: full-time $10,723; part-time $745 per credit. Tuition, nonresident: full-time $24,054; part-time $1578 per credit. *Required fees:* $374 per semester. Tuition and fees vary according to course load, program and reciprocity agreements. *Faculty research:* Formal linguistics, acoustic phonetics, American studies, Indo-European linguistics.

University of Wisconsin–Milwaukee, Graduate School, College of Letters and Sciences, Department of English, Milwaukee, WI 53201-0413. Offers creative writing (PhD); English (MA); international technical communication (Certificate); linguistics (PhD); professional writing (PhD); professional writing and communication (Certificate); rhetoric and composition (PhD); MLIS/MA. *Degree requirements:* For master's, thesis or alternative; for doctorate, one foreign language, thesis/dissertation. *Entrance requirements:* For master's, GRE General Test, GRE Subject Test; for doctorate, GRE.

Linguistics

Additional exam requirements/recommendations for international students: Required—TOEFL (minimum score 550 paper-based; 79 iBT), IELTS (minimum score 6.5). Electronic applications accepted.

University of Wisconsin–Milwaukee, Graduate School, College of Letters and Sciences, Department of Linguistics, Milwaukee, WI 53201-0413. Offers linguistics (MA, PhD); TESOL (Graduate Certificate).

Virginia International University, School of Education, Fairfax, VA 22030. Offers applied linguistics (MS); education (M Ed); teaching English to speakers of other languages (MA). Part-time programs available. Postbaccalaureate distance learning degree programs offered (no on-campus study). *Faculty:* 2 full-time (both women), 1 (woman) part-time/adjunct. *Students:* 4 full-time (3 women), 3 international. 23 applicants, 17% accepted, 3 enrolled. *Entrance requirements:* For master's, bachelor's degree. Additional exam requirements/recommendations for international students: Required—TOEFL (minimum score 550 paper-based; 80 iBT), IELTS (minimum score 6). *Application deadline:* For fall admission, 7/31 for domestic students, 7/13 for international students; for winter admission, 2/14 for international students; for spring admission, 12/18 for domestic students, 12/17 for international students; for summer admission, 4/28 for international students. Applications are processed on a rolling basis. Application fee: $150. Electronic applications accepted. *Expenses: Tuition:* Full-time $26,200. Full-time tuition and fees vary according to course load and program. *Financial support:* Scholarships/grants available. Financial award application deadline: 7/1. *Unit head:* Dr. Kimberly Daly, Dean, 703-591-7042, E-mail: kdaly@viu.edu. *Application contact:* Dr. Kimberly Daly, Dean, 703-591-7042, E-mail: kdaly@viu.edu.
Website: http://www.viu.edu/sed.html

Wayne State University, College of Liberal Arts and Sciences, Interdisciplinary Program in Linguistics, Detroit, MI 48202. Offers MA. *Faculty:* 20 full-time (11 women), 1 part-time/adjunct (0 women). *Students:* 10 full-time (5 women), 6 part-time (4 women); includes 1 minority (Black or African American, non-Hispanic/Latino), 6 international. Average age 29. 28 applicants, 43% accepted, 3 enrolled. In 2014, 5 master's awarded. *Degree requirements:* For master's, one foreign language, thesis, essay, oral defense. *Entrance requirements:* For master's, minimum one year of foreign language; at least one course in linguistics; statement of purpose. Additional exam requirements/recommendations for international students: Required—TOEFL (minimum score 550 paper-based; 79 iBT), TWE (minimum score 5.5), Michigan English Language Assessment Battery (minimum score 85); Recommended—IELTS (minimum score 6.5). *Application deadline:* For fall admission, 6/1 priority date for domestic students, 5/1 priority date for international students; for winter admission, 10/1 priority date for domestic students, 9/1 priority date for international students; for spring admission, 2/1 priority date for domestic students, 1/1 priority date for international students. Applications are processed on a rolling basis. Application fee: $0. Electronic applications accepted. *Expenses:* Tuition, state resident: full-time $10,294; part-time $571.90 per credit hour. Tuition, nonresident: full-time $29,730; part-time $1238.75 per credit hour. *Required fees:* $1365; $43.50 per credit hour. $291.10 per semester. Tuition and fees vary according to course load and program. *Financial support:* Scholarships/grants available. Financial award application deadline: 3/31; financial award applicants required to submit FAFSA. *Faculty research:* Phonology, syntax, sociolinguistics, historical linguistics, psycholinguistics. *Unit head:* Dr. Ljiljana Progovac, Professor/Director, Linguistics Program, 313-577-7553, E-mail: progovac@wayne.edu. *Application contact:* Dr. Martha Ratliff, Professor/Student Advisor, Linguistics Program, 313-577-7646, E-mail: ac6000@wayne.edu.
Website: http://clas.wayne.edu/linguistics/

Wesley Biblical Seminary, Graduate Programs, Jackson, MS 39206. Offers apologetics (MA); Biblical languages (M Div); Biblical literature (MA); Christian studies (MA); context and mission (M Div); honors research (M Div); interpretation (M Div); ministry (M Div); spiritual formation (M Div); teaching (M Div); theology (MA). *Accreditation:* ATS. Part-time programs available. *Degree requirements:* For master's, thesis. *Entrance requirements:* Additional exam requirements/recommendations for international students: Required—TOEFL. Electronic applications accepted. *Faculty research:* Patristics, missiology, culture, hermeneutics.

West Virginia University, Eberly College of Arts and Sciences, Department of Foreign Languages, Morgantown, WV 26506. Offers French (MA); linguistics (MA); Spanish (MA); teaching English to speakers of other languages (MA). Part-time programs available. *Degree requirements:* For master's, one foreign language, comprehensive exam (for some programs), thesis optional. *Entrance requirements:* For master's, minimum GPA of 3.0. Electronic applications accepted. *Faculty research:* French, German, and Spanish literature; foreign language pedagogy; English as a second language; cultural studies; linguistics.

Yale University, Graduate School of Arts and Sciences, Department of Linguistics, New Haven, CT 06520. Offers PhD. *Degree requirements:* For doctorate, 2 foreign languages, thesis/dissertation. *Entrance requirements:* For doctorate, GRE General Test.

York University, Faculty of Graduate Studies, Faculty of Liberal Arts and Professional Studies, Program in Linguistics and Applied Linguistics, Toronto, ON M3J 1P3, Canada. Offers MA, PhD. *Degree requirements:* For master's, thesis.

Translation and Interpretation

American University of Sharjah, Graduate Programs, Sharjah, United Arab Emirates. Offers accounting (MS); business (EMBA, MBA); chemical engineering (MS Ch E); civil engineering (MSCE); computer engineering (MS); electrical engineering (MSEE); engineering systems management (MS); mathematics (MS); mechanical engineering (MSME); mechatronics engineering (MS); teaching English to speakers of other languages (MA); translation and interpreting (MA); urban planning (MUP). Part-time and evening/weekend programs available. *Degree requirements:* For master's, thesis (for some programs). *Entrance requirements:* For master's, GMAT (for MBA). Additional exam requirements/recommendations for international students: Required—TOEFL (minimum score 550 paper-based; 80 iBT), TWE (minimum score 5); Recommended—IELTS (minimum score 6.5). Electronic applications accepted. *Faculty research:* Water pollution, management and waste water treatment, energy and sustainability, air pollution, Islamic finance, family business and small and medium enterprises.

Arizona State University at the Tempe campus, College of Liberal Arts and Sciences, Department of English, Tempe, AZ 85287-0302. Offers applied linguistics (PhD); creative writing (MFA); English (MA, PhD), including comparative literature (MA), linguistics (MA), literature, rhetoric and composition (MA), rhetoric, composition, and linguistics (PhD); film and media studies (MAS), including American media and popular culture; linguistics (Graduate Certificate); teaching English to speakers of other languages (MTESOL); translation studies (Graduate Certificate). Terminal master's awarded for partial completion of doctoral program. *Degree requirements:* For master's, variable foreign language requirement, comprehensive exam (for some programs), thesis (for some programs), interactive Program of Study (iPOS) submitted before completing 50 percent of required credit hours; for doctorate, variable foreign language requirement, comprehensive exam, thesis/dissertation, interactive Program of Study (iPOS) submitted before completing 50 percent of required credit hours. *Entrance requirements:* For master's and doctorate, GRE, minimum GPA of 3.0 or equivalent in last 2 years of work leading to bachelor's degree. Additional exam requirements/recommendations for international students: Required—TOEFL, IELTS, or PTE. Electronic applications accepted.

Babel University Professional School of Translation, Program in Translation, Honolulu, HI 96815-1302. Offers MS. Part-time and evening/weekend programs available. Postbaccalaureate distance learning degree programs offered (no on-campus study). *Degree requirements:* For master's, comprehensive exam, thesis. *Entrance requirements:* For master's, translation exam. Additional exam requirements/recommendations for international students: Recommended—TOEFL (minimum score 550 paper-based).

Binghamton University, State University of New York, Graduate School, School of Arts and Sciences, Translation Research and Instruction Program, Vestal, NY 13850. Offers PhD, Certificate. Part-time programs available. *Students:* 7 full-time (4 women), 21 part-time (14 women); includes 3 minority (all Hispanic/Latino), 19 international. Average age 34. 27 applicants, 59% accepted, 7 enrolled. In 2014, 4 doctorates, 6 other advanced degrees awarded. *Degree requirements:* For doctorate, one foreign language, comprehensive exam, thesis/dissertation; for Certificate, one foreign language, comprehensive exam. *Entrance requirements:* For doctorate and Certificate, GRE General Test. Additional exam requirements/recommendations for international students: Required—TOEFL (minimum score 550 paper-based; 80 iBT). *Application deadline:* For fall admission, 1/15 priority date for domestic and international students; for spring admission, 10/15 priority date for domestic and international students. Applications are processed on a rolling basis. Application fee: $75. Electronic applications accepted. *Expenses:* Tuition, state resident: full-time $7776; part-time $432 per credit. Tuition, nonresident: full-time $15,138; part-time $841 per credit. *Required fees:* $1754; $213 per credit. Tuition and fees vary according to degree level and program. *Financial support:* In 2014–15, 5 students received support, including 4 teaching assistantships with full tuition reimbursements available (averaging $14,500 per year); career-related internships or fieldwork, Federal Work-Study, institutionally sponsored loans, scholarships/grants, health care benefits, and unspecified assistantships also available. Financial award application deadline: 2/15; financial award applicants required to submit FAFSA. *Unit head:* Dr. Michael Pettid, Director, 607-777-3862, E-mail: mpettid@binghamton.edu. *Application contact:* Kishan Zuber, Recruiting and Admissions Coordinator, 607-777-2151, Fax: 607-777-2501, E-mail: kzuber@binghamton.edu.

Columbia University, Graduate School of Arts and Sciences, New York, NY 10027. Offers African-American studies (MA); American studies (MA); anthropology (MA, PhD); art history and archaeology (MA, PhD); astronomy (PhD); biological sciences (PhD); biotechnology (MA); chemical physics (PhD); chemistry (PhD); classical studies (MA, PhD); classics (MA, PhD); climate and society (MA); earth and environmental sciences (PhD); East Asia: regional studies (MA); East Asian languages and cultures (MA, PhD); ecology, evolution and environmental biology (MA), including conservation biology; ecology, evolution, and environmental biology (PhD), including ecology and evolutionary biology, evolutionary primatology; economics (PhD); English and comparative literature (MA, PhD); French and Romance philology (MA, PhD); Germanic languages (MA, PhD); global French studies (MA); Hispanic cultural studies (MA); history (PhD); history and literature (MA); human rights studies (MA); Islamic studies (MA); Italian (MA, PhD); Japanese pedagogy (MA); Jewish studies (MA); Latin America and the Caribbean: regional studies (MA); Latin American and Iberian cultures (PhD); mathematics (MA, PhD), including finance (MA); medieval and Renaissance studies (MA); Middle Eastern, South Asian, and African studies (MA, PhD); modern art: critical and curatorial studies (MA); modern European studies (MA); museum anthropology (MA); music (DMA, PhD); oral history (MA); philosophical foundations of physics (MA); philosophy (MA, PhD); physics (PhD); political science (MA, PhD); psychology (PhD); quantitative methods in the social sciences (MA); religion (MA, PhD); Russia, Eurasia and East Europe: regional studies (MA); Russian translation (MA); Slavic cultures (MA); Slavic languages (MA, PhD); sociology (MA, PhD); South Asian studies (MA); statistics (MA, PhD); theatre (PhD); JD/PhD; MA/MS; MD/PhD; MPA/MA. Dual-degree programs require admission to both Graduate School of Arts and Sciences and another Columbia school. Part-time and evening/weekend programs available. Terminal master's awarded for partial completion of doctoral program. *Degree requirements:* For master's, thesis (for some programs); for doctorate, comprehensive exam, thesis/dissertation. *Entrance requirements:* For master's and doctorate, GRE General Test, GRE Subject Test (for some programs). Electronic applications accepted. *Faculty research:* Humanities, natural sciences, social sciences.

Concordia University, School of Graduate Studies, Faculty of Arts and Science, Department of Études Franlfcaises, Montréal, QC H3G 1M8, Canada. Offers écriture (Certificate); anglais-franlfcais en langue et techniques de localisation (Certificate); littératures francophones et résonances médiatiques (MA); traductologie (MA); translation (Diploma). *Degree requirements:* For other advanced degree, one foreign language.

Drew University, Caspersen School of Graduate Studies, Program in Poetry, Madison, NJ 07940-1493. Offers poetry (MFA); poetry in translation (MFA). *Degree requirements:* For master's, thesis. *Entrance requirements:* For master's, transcripts, writing sample, recommendations. *Expenses:* Contact institution.

Gallaudet University, The Graduate School, Washington, DC 20002-3625. Offers ASL/English bilingual early childhood education: birth to 5 (Certificate); audiology (Au D); clinical psychology (PhD); critical studies in the education of deaf learners (PhD); deaf and hard of hearing infants, toddlers, and their families (Certificate); deaf education (Ed S); deaf education: advanced studies (MA); deaf education: special programs (MA); deaf history (Certificate); deaf studies (MA, Certificate); educating deaf students with disabilities (Certificate); education: teacher preparation (MA), including deaf education,

early childhood education and deaf education, elementary education and deaf education, secondary education and deaf education; educational neuroscience (PhD); hearing, speech and language sciences (MS, PhD); international development (MA); interpretation (MA, PhD), including combined interpreting practice and research (MA), interpreting research (MA); linguistics (MA, PhD); mental health counseling (MA); peer mentoring (Certificate); public administration (MPA); school counseling (MA); school psychology (Psy S); sign language teaching (MA); social work (MSW); speech-language pathology (MS). Part-time programs available. *Students:* 325 full-time (251 women), 118 part-time (90 women); includes 91 minority (41 Black or African American, non-Hispanic/Latino; 1 American Indian or Alaska Native, non-Hispanic/Latino; 14 Asian, non-Hispanic/Latino; 25 Hispanic/Latino; 10 Two or more races, non-Hispanic/Latino), 28 international. Average age 30. 617 applicants, 42% accepted, 171 enrolled. In 2014, 145 master's, 21 doctorates, 8 other advanced degrees awarded. Terminal master's awarded for partial completion of doctoral program. *Degree requirements:* For master's, comprehensive exam (for some programs), thesis optional; for doctorate, comprehensive exam, thesis/dissertation. *Entrance requirements:* For master's and doctorate, GRE General Test or MAT, letters of recommendation, interviews, goals statement, American Sign Language proficiency interview, written English competency. Additional exam requirements/recommendations for international students: Required—TOEFL. *Application deadline:* For fall admission, 2/15 for domestic students. Applications are processed on a rolling basis. Application fee: $75. Electronic applications accepted. *Expenses: Tuition:* Full-time $15,956; part-time $886.45 per credit hour. *Required fees:* $3404; $263 per semester. *Financial support:* Fellowships, research assistantships, teaching assistantships, career-related internships or fieldwork, Federal Work-Study, scholarships/grants, tuition waivers (partial), and unspecified assistantships available. Support available to part-time students. Financial award applicants required to submit FAFSA. *Faculty research:* Signing math dictionaries, telecommunications access, cancer genetics, linguistics, visual language and visual learning, integrated quantum materials, deaf legal discourse, advance recruitment and retention in geosciences. *Unit head:* Dr. Gaurav Mathur, Interim Dean, Graduate School and Continuing Studies, 202-250-2380, Fax: 202-651-5027, E-mail: gaurav.mathur@gallaudet.edu. *Application contact:* Wednesday Luria, Coordinator of Prospective Graduate Student Services, 202-651-5400, Fax: 202-651-5295, E-mail: graduate.school@gallaudet.edu.
Website: http://www.gallaudet.edu/x26696.xml

Georgia State University, College of Arts and Sciences, Department of Modern and Classical Languages, Program in Translation and Interpretation, Atlanta, GA 30302-3083. Offers interpretation (Certificate), including Spanish; translation (Certificate), including French, German, Spanish. Part-time programs available. *Entrance requirements:* For degree, entrance examination involving translating one passage from English to the target language and one passage from the target language to English, 3 letters of recommendation, resume/curriculum vitae, official transcripts. Additional exam requirements/recommendations for international students: Required—TOEFL (minimum score 79 iBT). *Application deadline:* For fall admission, 3/15 priority date for domestic and international students; for spring admission, 11/15 priority date for domestic and international students. Application fee: $50. Electronic applications accepted. *Expenses:* Tuition, state resident: full-time $6516; part-time $362 per credit hour. Tuition, nonresident: full-time $22,014; part-time $1223 per credit hour. *Required fees:* $2128 per semester. Tuition and fees vary according to course load and program. *Faculty research:* Romance linguistics and translation; theory and practice of translation; medical and legal interpretation. *Unit head:* Dr. Fernando Reati, Chair, 404-413-5984, Fax: 404-413-5982, E-mail: freati@gsu.edu. *Application contact:* Lita Malveaux, Administrative Academic Specialist, 404-413-5046, Fax: 404-413-5036, E-mail: lmalveaux@gsu.edu.
Website: http://wlc.gsu.edu/home/graduate/graduate-certificate/

Kent State University, College of Arts and Sciences, Department of Modern and Classical Language Studies, Kent, OH 44242-0001. Offers translation (MA), including French, German, Japanese, Russian, Spanish; translation studies (PhD). Part-time programs available. *Faculty:* 36 full-time (22 women). *Students:* 89 full-time (56 women), 18 part-time (10 women); includes 12 minority (1 Black or African American, non-Hispanic/Latino; 3 Asian, non-Hispanic/Latino; 6 Hispanic/Latino; 2 Two or more races, non-Hispanic/Latino), 42 international. Average age 30. 228 applicants, 52% accepted, 90 enrolled. In 2014, 24 master's, 3 doctorates awarded. *Degree requirements:* For master's, variable foreign language requirement, comprehensive exam (for some programs), thesis (for some programs), case study (translation), language exam and interview (languages); for doctorate, variable foreign language requirement, comprehensive exam, thesis/dissertation. *Entrance requirements:* For master's, minimum GPA of 3.0, transcript, goal statement, conversational sample in two languages, written sample in second language, 3 letters of recommendation; for doctorate, minimum GPA of 3.0, transcript, goal statement, writing sample, professional credentials, 3 letters of recommendation. Additional exam requirements/recommendations for international students: Required—TOEFL (minimum score: paper-based 525, iBT 71), Michigan English Language Assessment Battery (minimum score of 75), IELTS (minimum score of 6.0), PTE Academic (minimum score of 48), or completion of ELS level 112 Intensive Program. *Application deadline:* For fall admission, 2/28 for domestic and international students. Applications are processed on a rolling basis. Application fee: $45 ($70 for international students). Electronic applications accepted. *Expenses:* Tuition, state resident: full-time $8730; part-time $485 per credit hour. Tuition, nonresident: full-time $14,886; part-time $827 per credit hour. Tuition and fees vary according to campus/location and program. *Financial support:* Research assistantships with full tuition reimbursements, teaching assistantships with full tuition reimbursements, Federal Work-Study, scholarships/grants, and unspecified assistantships available. Financial award application deadline: 2/1. *Unit head:* Keiran Dunne, Professor and Chair, 330-672-1805, E-mail: kdunne@kent.edu. *Application contact:* Brian James Baer, Professor and Graduate Coordinator, 330-672-2150, Fax: 330-672-4009, E-mail: bbaer@kent.edu.
Website: http://www.kent.edu/mcls/

La Salle University, School of Arts and Sciences, Hispanic Institute, Philadelphia, PA 19141-1199. Offers bilingual/bicultural studies (MA); ESL specialist (Certificate); interpretation in English-Spanish/Spanish-English (Certificate); teaching English to speakers of other languages (MA); translation and interpretation (MA); translation English/Spanish-Spanish/English (Certificate). Part-time and evening/weekend programs available. *Degree requirements:* For master's, one foreign language, project or thesis. *Entrance requirements:* For master's, GRE, MAT, or GMAT, professional resume; two letters of recommendation; for Certificate, GRE, MAT, or GMAT, professional resume; two letters of recommendation; evidence of an advanced level in Spanish. Additional exam requirements/recommendations for international students: Required—TOEFL. Electronic applications accepted. Application fee is waived when completed online. *Expenses:* Contact institution. *Faculty research:* Puerto Rican literature, cross-cultural communication, English as a second language methodology, Spanish language.

Marygrove College, Graduate Division, Program in Modern Language Translation, Detroit, MI 48221-2599. Offers Certificate.

Middlebury Institute of International Studies, Graduate School of Translation, Interpretation and Language Education, Program in Translation and Interpretation, Monterey, CA 93940-2691. Offers conference interpretation (MA); translation (MA); translation and interpretation (MA); translation and localization management (MA). *Degree requirements:* For master's, one foreign language, thesis or alternative, exams. *Entrance requirements:* For master's, minimum GPA of 3.0, proficiency in a foreign language. Additional exam requirements/recommendations for international students: Required—TOEFL (minimum score 600 paper-based; 100 iBT). *Application deadline:* For fall admission, 3/15 priority date for domestic and international students; for spring admission, 10/1 priority date for domestic and international students. Applications are processed on a rolling basis. Application fee: $50. Electronic applications accepted. *Expenses: Tuition:* Full-time $36,020; part-time $1715 per credit. *Required fees:* $53 per semester. *Financial support:* Career-related internships or fieldwork, Federal Work-Study, institutionally sponsored loans, scholarships/grants, tuition waivers (partial), and unspecified assistantships available. Support available to part-time students. Financial award application deadline: 3/15; financial award applicants required to submit FAFSA. *Faculty research:* Assessment and testing in translation and interpretation, translation and interpretation pedagogy and curricula, integration of translation technology, language policy and planning. *Unit head:* Dr. Renee Jourdenais, Dean, 831-647-4185, Fax: 831-647-6650, E-mail: gstile@miis.edu. *Application contact:* 831-647-4123, Fax: 831-647-6405, E-mail: admit@miis.edu.
Website: http://www.miis.edu/academics/programs/gstile

Montclair State University, The Graduate School, College of Humanities and Social Sciences, Translation and Interpreting in Spanish Certificate Program, Montclair, NJ 07043-1624. Offers Certificate. *Students:* 1 (woman) full-time, 6 part-time (5 women); includes 3 minority (all Hispanic/Latino). Average age 41. 4 applicants, 75% accepted, 3 enrolled. In 2014, 1 Certificate awarded. *Expenses:* Tuition, state resident: full-time $9960; part-time $553.35 per credit. Tuition, nonresident: full-time $15,074; part-time $837.43 per credit. *Required fees:* $1595; $88.63 per credit. Tuition and fees vary according to degree level and program. *Unit head:* Dr. Linda Levine, Coordinator. *Application contact:* Amy Aiello, Executive Director of The Graduate School, 973-655-5147, Fax: 973-655-7869, E-mail: graduate.school@montclair.edu.

New York University, School of Continuing and Professional Studies, Center for Foreign Languages, Translation and Interpretation, New York, NY 10012-1019. Offers translation (MS), including English to Spanish, French to English, Spanish to English. Part-time and evening/weekend programs available. *Faculty:* 1 (woman) full-time, 18 part-time/adjunct (11 women). *Students:* 27 full-time (21 women), 32 part-time (24 women); includes 11 minority (3 Black or African American, non-Hispanic/Latino; 1 American Indian or Alaska Native, non-Hispanic/Latino; 2 Asian, non-Hispanic/Latino; 5 Hispanic/Latino), 19 international. Average age 29. 58 applicants, 64% accepted, 23 enrolled. In 2014, 16 master's awarded. *Degree requirements:* For master's, thesis. *Entrance requirements:* For master's, GRE or GMAT (only upon request), bachelor's degree, resume with relevant professional work, internship or volunteer experience, two letters of recommendation, statement of purpose. Additional exam requirements/recommendations for international students: Required—TOEFL (minimum score 600 paper-based; 100 iBT), IELTS (minimum score 7). *Application deadline:* For fall admission, 2/1 priority date for domestic and international students; for spring admission, 10/15 priority date for domestic students, 8/15 priority date for international students. Applications are processed on a rolling basis. Application fee: $150. Electronic applications accepted. *Financial support:* In 2014–15, 15 students received support, including 15 fellowships (averaging $1,896 per year); Federal Work-Study and scholarships/grants also available. Support available to part-time students. Financial award application deadline: 4/1; financial award applicants required to submit FAFSA. *Unit head:* Milena Savova, Academic Director and Clinical Professor, 212-998-7030. *Application contact:* Office of Admissions, 212-998-7100, E-mail: sps.gradadmissions@nyu.edu.
Website: http://www.sps.nyu.edu/areas-of-study/foreign-languages/

Rutgers, The State University of New Jersey, New Brunswick, Graduate School-New Brunswick, Program in Spanish, Piscataway, NJ 08854-8097. Offers bilingualism and second language acquisition (MA, PhD); Spanish (MA, MAT, PhD); Spanish literature (MA, PhD); translation (MA). Part-time programs available. *Degree requirements:* For master's, comprehensive exam (for some programs), thesis (for some programs); for doctorate, 2 foreign languages, comprehensive exam, thesis/dissertation. *Entrance requirements:* For master's and doctorate, GRE General Test. Additional exam requirements/recommendations for international students: Required—TOEFL. Electronic applications accepted. *Faculty research:* Hispanic literature, Luso-Brazilian literature, Spanish linguistics, Spanish translation.

Texas A&M International University, Office of Graduate Studies and Research, College of Arts and Sciences, Department of Humanities, Laredo, TX 78041-1900. Offers English (MA); Hispanic studies (PhD); history and political thought (MA); language, literature and translation (MA). *Degree requirements:* For master's, comprehensive exam (for some programs), thesis (for some programs). *Entrance requirements:* For master's, GRE General Test. Additional exam requirements/recommendations for international students: Required—TOEFL (minimum score 550 paper-based; 79 iBT).

Universidad Autonoma de Guadalajara, Graduate Programs, Guadalajara, Mexico. Offers administrative law and justice (LL M); advertising and corporate communications (MA); architecture (M Arch); business (MBA); computational science (MCC); education (Ed M, Ed D); English-Spanish translation (MA); entrepreneurship and management (MBA); integrated management of digital animation (MA); international business (MIB); international corporate law (LL M); internet technologies (MS); manufacturing systems (MMS); occupational health (MS); philosophy (MA, PhD); power electronics (MS); quality systems (MQS); renewable energy (MS); social evaluation of projects (MBA); strategic market research (MBA); tax law (MA); teaching mathematics (MA).

Université de Montréal, Faculty of Arts and Sciences, Department of Linguistics and Translation, Montréal, QC H3C 3J7, Canada. Offers linguistics (MA, PhD); translation (MA, PhD, DESS). *Degree requirements:* For master's, thesis, general exam; for doctorate, thesis/dissertation, general exam. Electronic applications accepted.

Université Laval, Faculty of Letters, Department of Languages, Linguistics and Translations, Programs in Terminology and Translation, Québec, QC G1K 7P4, Canada. Offers MA, Diploma. Part-time programs available. *Degree requirements:* For master's, thesis (for some programs). *Entrance requirements:* For master's and Diploma, knowledge of French and English. Electronic applications accepted.

University of California, Santa Barbara, Graduate Division, College of Letters and Sciences, Division of Humanities and Fine Arts, Department of East Asian Languages and Cultural Studies, Santa Barbara, CA 93106-7075. Offers applied linguistics (PhD); East Asian languages and cultural studies (MA, PhD); translation studies (PhD). *Degree requirements:* For master's, one foreign language, comprehensive exam (for some programs), thesis (for some programs); for doctorate, 2 foreign languages, thesis/dissertation, methodology. *Entrance requirements:* For master's and doctorate, GRE General Test. Additional exam requirements/recommendations for international students: Required—TOEFL (minimum score 550 paper-based; 80 iBT), IELTS

(minimum score 7). Electronic applications accepted. *Faculty research:* Chinese literature, Chinese film, Japanese society, Japanese literature, East Asian cultural studies.

University of California, Santa Barbara, Graduate Division, College of Letters and Sciences, Division of Humanities and Fine Arts, Department of English, Santa Barbara, CA 93106-3170. Offers English (PhD); European medieval studies (PhD); feminist studies (PhD); global studies (PhD); technology and society (PhD); translation studies (PhD); writing studies (PhD); MA/PhD. Terminal master's awarded for partial completion of doctoral program. *Degree requirements:* For doctorate, one foreign language, comprehensive exam, thesis/dissertation. *Entrance requirements:* For doctorate, GRE General Test, GRE Subject Test (English). Additional exam requirements/recommendations for international students: Required—TOEFL (minimum score 550 paper-based; 80 iBT), IELTS (minimum score 7). Electronic applications accepted. *Faculty research:* Medieval, Romantic and Victorian studies; gender studies and feminist theory; literature and the mind; American literature; literature and new media/information culture.

University of California, Santa Barbara, Graduate Division, College of Letters and Sciences, Division of Humanities and Fine Arts, Department of Religious Studies, Santa Barbara, CA 93106-3130. Offers ancient Mediterranean studies (PhD); cognitive science (PhD); European medieval studies (PhD); feminist studies (PhD); global studies (PhD); religious studies (MA, PhD); translation studies (PhD); MA/PhD. Terminal master's awarded for partial completion of doctoral program. *Degree requirements:* For master's, one foreign language, comprehensive exam (for some programs), thesis (for some programs), colloquium; for doctorate, 2 foreign languages, thesis/dissertation, methodology, colloquium. *Entrance requirements:* For master's and doctorate, GRE General Test. Additional exam requirements/recommendations for international students: Required—TOEFL (minimum score 550 paper-based; 80 iBT), IELTS (minimum score 7). Electronic applications accepted. *Faculty research:* Area studies; religious traditions; theory and method in the study of religion; religion, culture, and politics; spirituality and religious experience.

University of California, Santa Barbara, Graduate Division, College of Letters and Sciences, Division of Humanities and Fine Arts, Program in Comparative Literature, Santa Barbara, CA 93106-4130. Offers comparative literature (PhD); East Asian literatures (PhD); feminist studies (PhD); French (PhD); global studies (PhD); translation studies (PhD); MA/PhD. *Degree requirements:* For doctorate, 2 foreign languages, comprehensive exam, thesis/dissertation. *Entrance requirements:* For doctorate, GRE. Additional exam requirements/recommendations for international students: Required—TOEFL (minimum score 550 paper-based; 80 iBT), IELTS (minimum score 7). Electronic applications accepted. *Faculty research:* Comparative literary studies in global context, critical theory, translation studies, media technological studies, trauma studies.

University of Delaware, College of Arts and Sciences, Department of Foreign Languages and Literatures, Newark, DE 19716. Offers foreign languages and literatures (MA), including French, German, Spanish; foreign languages pedagogy (MA), including French, German, Spanish; technical Chinese translation (MA). *Degree requirements:* For master's, one foreign language, comprehensive exam, thesis optional. *Entrance requirements:* For master's, GRE General Test, letters of recommendation, writing sample. Additional exam requirements/recommendations for international students: Required—TOEFL. Electronic applications accepted. *Faculty research:* Medieval to Modern French and Spanish literature, twentieth-century German, French, Spanish literature by women, computer-assisted instruction.

University of Denver, University College, Denver, CO 80208. Offers geographic information systems (Certificate); global affairs (Certificate), including translation studies, world history and culture; information and communications technology (MCIS), including geographic information systems, information systems security, project management (MCIS, Certificate), software design and programming, technology management, telecommunications technology, Web design and development; leadership and organizations (Certificate), including human capital in organizations, philanthropic leadership, project management (MCIS, Certificate), strategic innovation and change; organizational and professional communication (MPS), including alternative dispute resolution, organizational communication, organizational development and training, public relations and marketing; security management (MAS, Certificate), including emergency planning and response, information security (MAS), organizational security. Part-time and evening/weekend programs available. Postbaccalaureate distance learning degree programs offered (no on-campus study). *Faculty:* 8 full-time (4 women), 133 part-time/adjunct (46 women). *Students:* 54 full-time (21 women), 1,327 part-time (775 women); includes 272 minority (106 Black or African American, non-Hispanic/Latino; 6 American Indian or Alaska Native, non-Hispanic/Latino; 26 Asian, non-Hispanic/Latino; 108 Hispanic/Latino; 1 Native Hawaiian or other Pacific Islander, non-Hispanic/Latino; 25 Two or more races, non-Hispanic/Latino), 116 international. Average age 35. 768 applicants, 95% accepted, 620 enrolled. In 2014, 391 master's, 196 other advanced degrees awarded. *Degree requirements:* For master's, capstone project. *Entrance requirements:* For master's, transcripts, two letters of recommendation, personal statement, resume. Additional exam requirements/recommendations for international students: Required—TOEFL (minimum score 550 paper-based; 80 iBT). *Application deadline:* For fall admission, 6/21 priority date for domestic students, 5/1 priority date for international students; for winter admission, 9/14 priority date for domestic students, 9/19 priority date for international students; for spring admission, 1/11 for domestic students, 12/12 for international students; for summer admission, 3/29 priority date for domestic students, 3/6 priority date for international students. Applications are processed on a rolling basis. Application fee: $75. Electronic applications accepted. *Expenses:* Expenses: $959 per credit hour. *Financial support:* In 2014–15, 19 students received support. Applicants required to submit FAFSA. *Unit head:* Dr. Michael McGuire, Interim Dean, 303-871-3518, E-mail: mmcguire@du.edu. *Application contact:* Information Contact, 303-871-2291, E-mail: ucoladm@du.edu.
Website: http://www.universitycollege.du.edu/

University of Illinois at Urbana–Champaign, Graduate College, College of Liberal Arts and Sciences, School of Literatures, Cultures and Linguistics, Center for Translation Studies, Champaign, IL 61820. Offers translation and interpreting (MA). Part-time programs available. Postbaccalaureate distance learning degree programs offered (no on-campus study). *Students:* 25 (19 women). *Entrance requirements:* For master's, BA or BS in languages, linguistics, international studies, area studies, or a related field; three letters of recommendation; resume or curriculum vitae; official transcripts. *Application deadline:* For fall admission, 6/15 for domestic students. Application fee: $70 ($90 for international students). *Unit head:* Elizabeth Lowe, Director, 217-300-1488, E-mail: elowe@illinois.edu. *Application contact:* Lynn Stanke, Office Support Specialist, 217-333-6269, Fax: 217-244-3050, E-mail: stanke@illinois.edu.
Website: http://www.translation.illinois.edu/

The University of Manchester, School of Languages, Linguistics and Cultures, Manchester, United Kingdom. Offers Arab world studies (PhD); Chinese studies (M Phil, PhD); East Asian studies (M Phil, PhD); English language (PhD); French studies (M Phil, PhD); German studies (M Phil, PhD); interpreting studies (PhD); Italian studies (M Phil, PhD); Japanese studies (M Phil, PhD); Latin American cultural studies (M Phil, PhD); linguistics (M Phil, PhD); Middle Eastern studies (M Phil, PhD); Polish studies (M Phil, PhD); Portuguese studies (M Phil, PhD); Russian studies (M Phil, PhD); Spanish studies (M Phil, PhD); translation and intercultural studies (M Phil, PhD).

The University of North Carolina at Charlotte, College of Liberal Arts and Sciences, Department of Languages and Culture Studies, Charlotte, NC 28223-0001. Offers Spanish (MA); translating (Graduate Certificate). Part-time and evening/weekend programs available. *Faculty:* 19 full-time (10 women). *Students:* 14 full-time (13 women), 8 part-time (7 women); includes 10 minority (5 Black or African American, non-Hispanic/Latino; 4 Hispanic/Latino; 1 Two or more races, non-Hispanic/Latino), 1 international. Average age 30. 9 applicants, 89% accepted, 7 enrolled. In 2014, 7 master's, 5 other advanced degrees awarded. *Degree requirements:* For master's, thesis optional. *Entrance requirements:* For master's, GRE, 3 letters of reference, minimum GPA of 2.75. Additional exam requirements/recommendations for international students: Required—TOEFL (minimum score 557 paper-based; 83 iBT). *Application deadline:* For fall admission, 5/1 priority date for domestic students, 5/1 for international students; for spring admission, 10/1 priority date for domestic students, 10/1 for international students. Applications are processed on a rolling basis. Application fee: $75. Electronic applications accepted. *Expenses:* Tuition, state resident: full-time $4008. Tuition, nonresident: full-time $16,295. *Required fees:* $2755. Tuition and fees vary according to course load and program. *Financial support:* In 2014–15, 10 students received support, including 4 research assistantships (averaging $8,000 per year), 6 teaching assistantships (averaging $5,646 per year); career-related internships or fieldwork, institutionally sponsored loans, scholarships/grants, and unspecified assistantships also available. Support available to part-time students. Financial award application deadline: 4/1; financial award applicants required to submit FAFSA. *Faculty research:* Latin American literature, Spanish for business, Central American literature, Mexican literature, literature of the Southern Cone, language for specific purposes, Spanish for specific purposes. *Total annual research expenditures:* $187,912. *Unit head:* Dr. Sheri Spaine Long, Chair, 704-687-8754, Fax: 704-687-1653, E-mail: sheri.long@uncc.edu. *Application contact:* Kathy B. Giddings, Director of Graduate Admissions, 704-687-5503, Fax: 704-687-1668, E-mail: gradadm@uncc.edu.
Website: https://languages.uncc.edu/

University of North Florida, College of Education and Human Services, Department of Exceptional, Deaf, and Interpreter Education, Jacksonville, FL 32224. Offers American Sign Language/English interpreting (M Ed); applied behavior analysis (M Ed); autism (M Ed); deaf education (M Ed); disability services (M Ed); exceptional student education (M Ed). *Accreditation:* NCATE. Part-time and evening/weekend programs available. *Faculty:* 11 full-time (9 women), 4 part-time/adjunct (all women). *Students:* 26 full-time (21 women), 52 part-time (44 women); includes 15 minority (9 Black or African American, non-Hispanic/Latino; 2 Asian, non-Hispanic/Latino; 3 Hispanic/Latino; 1 Two or more races, non-Hispanic/Latino), 2 international. Average age 32. 39 applicants, 51% accepted, 15 enrolled. In 2014, 51 master's awarded. *Entrance requirements:* For master's, GRE General Test, minimum GPA of 3.0 in last 60 hours, interview, 3 letters of recommendation. Additional exam requirements/recommendations for international students: Required—TOEFL (minimum score 500 paper-based). *Application deadline:* For fall admission, 7/1 priority date for domestic students, 5/1 for international students; for spring admission, 11/1 priority date for domestic students, 10/1 for international students. Application fee: $30. Electronic applications accepted. *Expenses:* Tuition, state resident: full-time $9794; part-time $408.10 per credit hour. Tuition, nonresident: full-time $22,383; part-time $932.61 per credit hour. *Required fees:* $2047; $85.29 per credit hour. Tuition and fees vary according to course load and program. *Financial support:* In 2014–15, 19 students received support, including 1 research assistantship (averaging $4,524 per year); teaching assistantships, career-related internships or fieldwork, Federal Work-Study, scholarships/grants, tuition waivers (partial), and unspecified assistantships also available. Support available to part-time students. Financial award application deadline: 4/1; financial award applicants required to submit FAFSA. *Faculty research:* Transition, integrating technology into teacher education, written language development, professional school development, learning strategies. *Total annual research expenditures:* $816,202. *Unit head:* Dr. Karen Patterson, Chair, 904-620-2930, Fax: 904-620-3895, E-mail: karen.patterson@unf.edu. *Application contact:* Dr. Amanda Pascale, Director, The Graduate School, 904-620-1360, Fax: 904-620-1362, E-mail: graduateschool@unf.edu.
Website: http://www.unf.edu/coehs/edie/

University of Ottawa, Faculty of Graduate and Postdoctoral Studies, Faculty of Arts, Institute of Canadian Studies, Ottawa, ON K1N 6N5, Canada. Offers economics (PhD); English (PhD); geography (PhD); history (PhD); lettres Franlfcaises (PhD); linguistics (PhD); philosophy (PhD); political science (PhD); psychology (PhD); religious studies (PhD); translation studies (PhD). *Degree requirements:* For doctorate, comprehensive exam, thesis/dissertation.

University of Ottawa, Faculty of Graduate and Postdoctoral Studies, Faculty of Arts, School of Translation and Interpretation, Ottawa, ON K1N 6N5, Canada. Offers interpreting (MA); Spanish translation (MA); translation (MA); translation studies (PhD). *Degree requirements:* For master's, one foreign language, thesis or alternative, research paper; for doctorate, thesis/dissertation, doctoral exam. *Entrance requirements:* For master's, school-administered exam, honors degree or equivalent, minimum B average; for doctorate, master's degree, minimum B+ average. Electronic applications accepted. *Faculty research:* Theory of translation, Spanish translation, conference interpreting, legal translation, translation-oriented lexicology and terminology.

University of Puerto Rico, Río Piedras Campus, College of Humanities, Program in Translation, San Juan, PR 00931-3300. Offers MA, Certificate. Part-time and evening/weekend programs available. *Degree requirements:* For master's, 2 foreign languages, comprehensive exam, thesis. *Entrance requirements:* For master's, PAEG, minimum GPA of 3.0, graduate-level knowledge of 2 languages (English, French, or Spanish), letter of recommendation.

University of Rochester, School of Arts and Sciences, Interdisciplinary Program in Literary Translation Studies, Rochester, NY 14627. Offers MA, Graduate Certificate. *Faculty:* 15 full-time (8 women). *Students:* 3 full-time (2 women), 1 (woman) part-time. 17 applicants, 59% accepted, 3 enrolled. In 2014, 5 master's awarded. *Degree requirements:* For master's, thesis. *Entrance requirements:* For master's, official transcripts, three letters of recommendation, personal statement. *Application deadline:* For fall admission, 2/15 for domestic students. Applications are processed on a rolling basis. Application fee: $60. Electronic applications accepted. *Expenses: Tuition:* Full-time $46,150; part-time $1442 per credit hour. *Required fees:* $504. *Unit head:* Prof. Claudia Schaefer, Advisor, 585-275-5569, E-mail: claudia.schaefer@rochester.edu. *Application contact:* Gretchen Briscoe, Recruiting and Marketing Manager, 585-275-5029, E-mail: graduate.admissions@rochester.edu.
Website: http://www.rochester.edu/college/translation/clts/

The University of Texas at Brownsville, Graduate Studies, College of Liberal Arts, Department of Modern Languages, Brownsville, TX 78520-4991. Offers Spanish (MA); Spanish translation and interpreting (MA). Part-time and evening/weekend programs available. Postbaccalaureate distance learning degree programs offered (no on-campus study). *Degree requirements:* For master's, comprehensive exam (for some programs), thesis optional, project. *Entrance requirements:* For master's, GRE General Test, letters

of recommendation, interview. Additional exam requirements/recommendations for international students: Required—TOEFL (minimum score 550 paper-based; 77 iBT). Electronic applications accepted. *Faculty research:* Children's literature, Hispanic folklore, translation.

University of Wisconsin–Milwaukee, Graduate School, College of Letters and Sciences, Department of Spanish, Milwaukee, WI 53201-0413. Offers Spanish (MA); translation (Certificate). *Entrance requirements:* For master's, bachelor's degree. Electronic applications accepted. *Faculty research:* Sociolinguistics, Spanish-American literature, Spanish literature, Hispanic culture, Hispanic historiography.

University of Wisconsin–Milwaukee, Graduate School, College of Letters and Sciences, Interdepartmental Program in Foreign Language and Literature, Milwaukee, WI 53201-0413. Offers classics and Hebrew studies (MAFLL); comparative literature (MAFLL); French and Italian (MAFLL); German (MAFLL); Slavic studies (MAFLL); translation (Certificate). Part-time programs available. *Degree requirements:* For master's, 2 foreign languages, thesis or alternative. *Entrance requirements:* Additional

exam requirements/recommendations for international students: Required—TOEFL (minimum score 550 paper-based; 79 iBT), IELTS (minimum score 6.5). Electronic applications accepted.

Wesley Biblical Seminary, Graduate Programs, Jackson, MS 39206. Offers apologetics (MA); Biblical languages (M Div); Biblical literature (MA); Christian studies (MA); context and mission (M Div); honors research (M Div); interpretation (M Div); ministry (M Div); spiritual formation (M Div); teaching (M Div); theology (MA). *Accreditation:* ATS. Part-time programs available. *Degree requirements:* For master's, thesis. *Entrance requirements:* Additional exam requirements/recommendations for international students: Required—TOEFL. Electronic applications accepted. *Faculty research:* Patristics, missiology, culture, hermeneutics.

York University, Faculty of Graduate Studies, Glendon Campus, Program in Translation, Toronto, ON M3J 1P3, Canada. Offers MA. *Degree requirements:* For master's, thesis or alternative. *Entrance requirements:* For master's, professional translating experience. Electronic applications accepted.

Section 11
Philosophy and Ethics

This section contains a directory of institutions offering graduate work in philosophy and ethics. Additional information about programs listed in the directory may be obtained by writing directly to the dean of a graduate school or chair of a department at the address given in the directory.

For programs offering related work, see also in this book *Area and Cultural Studies*, *History*, *Humanities*, *Religious Studies*, and *Social Sciences*.

CONTENTS

Program Directories

Ethics

American University, School of International Service, Washington, DC 20016-8071. Offers comparative and regional studies (Certificate); cross-cultural communication (Certificate); development management (MS); ethics, peace, and global affairs (MA); European studies (Certificate); global environmental policy (MA, Certificate); global information technology (Certificate); international affairs (MA), including comparative and international disability policy, comparative and regional studies, international economic relations, international politics, natural resources and sustainable development, U.S. foreign policy; international communication (MA, Certificate); international development (MA, Certificate); international economic policy (Certificate); international economic relations (Certificate); international media (MA); international peace and conflict resolution (MA, Certificate); international politics (Certificate); international relations (PhD); international service (MIS); peacebuilding (Certificate); social enterprise (MA); the Americas (Certificate); United States foreign policy (Certificate); JD/MA. Part-time and evening/weekend programs available. Postbaccalaureate distance learning degree programs offered (no on-campus study). *Faculty:* 112 full-time (43 women), 59 part-time/adjunct (27 women). *Students:* 545 full-time (335 women), 443 part-time (271 women); includes 231 minority (82 Black or African American, non-Hispanic/Latino; 8 American Indian or Alaska Native, non-Hispanic/Latino; 51 Asian, non-Hispanic/Latino; 81 Hispanic/Latino; 2 Native Hawaiian or other Pacific Islander, non-Hispanic/Latino; 7 Two or more races, non-Hispanic/Latino), 120 international. Average age 28. 1,991 applicants, 70% accepted, 365 enrolled. In 2014, 426 master's, 9 doctorates, 6 other advanced degrees awarded. Terminal master's awarded for partial completion of doctoral program. *Degree requirements:* For master's, one foreign language, comprehensive exam, thesis or alternative; for doctorate, one foreign language, comprehensive exam, thesis/dissertation. *Entrance requirements:* For master's, GRE, transcripts, resume, 2 letters of recommendation, statement of purpose; for doctorate, GRE, transcripts, resume, 3 letters of recommendation, statement of purpose. Additional exam requirements/recommendations for international students: Required—TOEFL (minimum score 600 paper-based; 100 iBT). *Application deadline:* For fall admission, 1/15 for domestic students; for spring admission, 10/1 for domestic students, 9/15 for international students. Application fee: $50. Electronic applications accepted. *Financial support:* Application deadline: 1/15. *Unit head:* Dr. James Goldgeier, Dean, 202-885-1603, Fax: 202-885-2494, E-mail: goldgeier@american.edu. *Application contact:* Jia Jiang, Associate Director, Graduate Education Enrollment, 202-885-1689, Fax: 202-885-1109, E-mail: jiang@american.edu.
Website: http://www.american.edu/sis/

Arizona State University at the Tempe campus, College of Liberal Arts and Sciences, School of Life Sciences, Tempe, AZ 85287-4601. Offers animal behavior (PhD); applied ethics (biomedical and health ethics) (MA); biology (MS, PhD), including biology, biology and society, complex adaptive systems science (PhD), plant biology and conservation (MS); environmental life sciences (PhD); evolutionary biology (PhD); history and philosophy of science (PhD); human and social dimensions of science and technology (PhD); microbiology (PhD); molecular and cellular biology (PhD); neuroscience (PhD). Terminal master's awarded for partial completion of doctoral program. *Degree requirements:* For master's, thesis (for some programs), interactive Program of Study (iPOS) submitted before completing 50 percent of required credit hours; for doctorate, variable foreign language requirement, comprehensive exam, thesis/dissertation, interactive Program of Study (iPOS) submitted before completing 50 percent of required credit hours. *Entrance requirements:* For master's and doctorate, GRE, minimum GPA of 3.0 or equivalent in last 2 years of work leading to bachelor's degree. Additional exam requirements/recommendations for international students: Required—TOEFL (minimum score 600 paper-based; 100 iBT). Electronic applications accepted.

Arizona State University at the Tempe campus, New College of Interdisciplinary Arts and Sciences, Phoenix, AZ 85069-7100. Offers applied ethics and the professions (MA); communication studies (MA); interdisciplinary studies (MA); psychology (MS); social justice and human rights (MA). Part-time and evening/weekend programs available. *Degree requirements:* For master's, thesis (for some programs), interactive Program of Study (iPOS) submitted before completing 50 percent of required credit hours. *Entrance requirements:* For master's, GRE, minimum GPA of 3.0 or equivalent in last 2 years of work leading to bachelor's degree. Additional exam requirements/recommendations for international students: Required—TOEFL, IELTS, or PTE. Electronic applications accepted.

Arizona State University at the Tempe campus, School of Letters and Sciences, Program in Applied Ethics, Tempe, AZ 85287-4503. Offers biomedical and health ethics (MA); ethics and emerging technologies (MA); public administration, policy and ethics (MA); science, technology and ethics (MA). Part-time and evening/weekend programs available. *Degree requirements:* For master's, thesis or alternative, applied project, interactive Program of Study (iPOS) submitted before completing 50 percent of required credit hours. *Entrance requirements:* For master's, GRE (for ethics and emerging technologies concentration), minimum GPA of 3.0 or equivalent in last 2 years of work leading to bachelor's degree, 2 letters of recommendation, resume, personal statement of interest and qualifications. Additional exam requirements/recommendations for international students: Required—TOEFL (minimum score 550 paper-based; 80 iBT). Electronic applications accepted.

Azusa Pacific University, Haggard Graduate School of Theology, Program in Theological Studies, Concentration in Religion: Theology and Ethics, Azusa, CA 91702-7000. Offers MA.

Chicago Theological Seminary, Graduate and Professional Programs, Chicago, IL 60637-1507. Offers preaching (D Min); religion and health (D Min); religious studies (MA); spirituality and spiritual direction (D Min); theology (M Div); theology, ethics and the human sciences (PhD); M Div/MSW. *Accreditation:* ACIPE; ATS. Part-time programs available. *Degree requirements:* For master's, thesis; for doctorate, 2 foreign languages, comprehensive exam, thesis/dissertation. *Entrance requirements:* For doctorate, GRE General Test. Additional exam requirements/recommendations for international students: Required—TOEFL. *Faculty research:* Bible, culture and hermeneutics, theology, gender and sexuality, black faith and life, spirituality and psychology, practical theology.

Claremont Graduate University, Graduate Programs, School of Arts and Humanities, Department of Religion, Claremont, CA 91711-6160. Offers Hebrew Bible (MA, PhD); history of Christianity and religions of North America (MA, PhD); New Testament (MA, PhD); philosophy of religion and theology (MA, PhD); theology, ethics and culture (MA, PhD); women's studies in religion (MA, PhD); MA/PhD; MBA/PhD. Part-time programs available. *Faculty:* 7 full-time (3 women), 2 part-time/adjunct (0 women). *Students:* 153 full-time (58 women), 31 part-time (16 women); includes 33 minority (12 Black or African American, non-Hispanic/Latino; 1 American Indian or Alaska Native, non-Hispanic/ Latino; 7 Asian, non-Hispanic/Latino; 10 Hispanic/Latino; 1 Native Hawaiian or other Pacific Islander, non-Hispanic/Latino; 2 Two or more races, non-Hispanic/Latino), 14 international. Average age 37. In 2014, 15 master's, 13 doctorates awarded. Terminal master's awarded for partial completion of doctoral program. *Entrance requirements:* For master's and doctorate, GRE General Test. Additional exam requirements/ recommendations for international students: Required—TOEFL (minimum score 550 paper-based; 80 iBT). *Application deadline:* For fall admission, 2/1 priority date for domestic and international students. Applications are processed on a rolling basis. Application fee: $80. Electronic applications accepted. *Expenses: Tuition:* Full-time $41,784; part-time $1741 per credit. *Required fees:* $600; $300 per semester. *Financial support:* Fellowships, research assistantships, teaching assistantships, Federal Work-Study, institutionally sponsored loans, and scholarships/grants available. Support available to part-time students. Financial award application deadline: 2/15; financial award applicants required to submit FAFSA. *Unit head:* Tammi Schneider, Chair, E-mail: tammi.schneider@cgu.edu. *Application contact:* Erma Cross, Admissions and Alumni Coordinator, 909-607-9843, E-mail: erminia.cross@cgu.edu.
Website: http://www.cgu.edu/pages/674.asp

Claremont School of Theology, Graduate and Professional Programs, Program in Religion, Claremont, CA 91711-3199. Offers practical theology (PhD), including religious education, spiritual care and counseling; religion (PhD), including Hebrew Bible, New Testament and Christian origins, process studies, religion, ethics, and society; religion and theology (MA); religious education (MARE). *Accreditation:* ACIPE; ATS. Terminal master's awarded for partial completion of doctoral program. *Degree requirements:* For master's, thesis; for doctorate, 2 foreign languages, thesis/dissertation. *Entrance requirements:* For doctorate, GRE General Test. Additional exam requirements/ recommendations for international students: Required—TOEFL. Electronic applications accepted.

Columbia University, Graduate School of Business, MBA Program, New York, NY 10027. Offers accounting (MBA); decision, risk, and operations (MBA); entrepreneurship (MBA); finance and economics (MBA); healthcare and pharmaceutical management (MBA); human resource management (MBA); international business (MBA); leadership and ethics (MBA); management (MBA); marketing (MBA); media (MBA); private equity (MBA); real estate (MBA); social enterprise (MBA); value investing (MBA); DDS/MBA; JD/MBA; MBA/MIA; MBA/MPH; MBA/MS; MD/MBA. *Entrance requirements:* For master's, GMAT, 2 letters of recommendation. Additional exam requirements/ recommendations for international students: Required—TOEFL. Electronic applications accepted. *Expenses:* Contact institution. *Faculty research:* Human decision making and behavioral research; real estate market and mortgage defaults; financial crisis and corporate governance; international business; security analysis and accounting.

Duke University, The Fuqua School of Business, The Duke MBA Daytime Program, Durham, NC 27708-0586. Offers academic excellence in finance (Certificate); business administration (MBA); decision sciences (MBA); energy and environment (MBA); energy finance (MBA); entrepreneurship and innovation (MBA); finance (MBA); financial analysis (MBA); health sector management (Certificate); leadership and ethics (MBA); management (MBA); marketing (MBA); operations management (MBA); social entrepreneurship (MBA); strategy (MBA). *Faculty:* 89 full-time (16 women), 51 part-time/ adjunct (10 women). *Students:* 889 full-time (295 women); includes 171 minority (28 Black or African American, non-Hispanic/Latino; 90 Asian, non-Hispanic/Latino; 45 Hispanic/Latino; 2 Native Hawaiian or other Pacific Islander, non-Hispanic/Latino; 6 Two or more races, non-Hispanic/Latino), 346 international. Average age 29. In 2014, 433 master's awarded. *Entrance requirements:* For master's, GMAT or GRE, transcripts, essays, resume, recommendation letters, interview. Additional exam requirements/ recommendations for international students: Required—TOEFL, IELTS, PTE. *Application deadline:* For fall admission, 9/17 for domestic and international students; for winter admission, 10/20 for domestic and international students; for spring admission, 1/ 5 for domestic and international students; for summer admission, 3/19 for domestic and international students. Application fee: $225. Electronic applications accepted. *Expenses:* Expenses: $58,000 (first-year tuition). *Financial support:* In 2014–15, 373 students received support. Institutionally sponsored loans and scholarships/grants available. Financial award applicants required to submit FAFSA. *Unit head:* Russ Morgan, Associate Dean for the Daytime MBA Program, 919-660-2931, Fax: 919-684-8742, E-mail: ruskin.morgan@duke.edu. *Application contact:* Liz Riley Hargrove, Associate Dean for Admissions, 919-660-7705, Fax: 919-681-8026, E-mail: admissions-info@fuqua.duke.edu.
Website: http://www.fuqua.duke.edu/daytime-mba/

Emory University, Candler School of Theology, Atlanta, GA 30322. Offers formation and witness (M Div); history, scripture and tradition (MTS); leadership in church and community (M Div); modern religious thought and experience (MTS); pastoral counseling (Th D); religion and race (M Div); religion, health and science (M Div); scripture and interpretation (M Div); society and personality (M Div); theology (Th M); theology and ethics (M Div); theology and the arts (M Div); traditions of the church (M Div); women and religion (M Div); JD/M Div; JD/MTS; M Div/MBA; M Div/MPH; MBA/ MTS; MTS/MPH. *Accreditation:* ACIPE; ATS. Part-time programs available. *Degree requirements:* For master's, thesis optional; for doctorate, comprehensive exam, thesis/ dissertation. *Entrance requirements:* For master's, minimum undergraduate GPA of 3.0; for doctorate, GRE, M Div, 8 units of course work in clinical pastoral education. Additional exam requirements/recommendations for international students: Required— TOEFL (minimum score 600 paper-based; 95 iBT). Electronic applications accepted. *Expenses:* Contact institution. *Faculty research:* Biblical studies, church history, ethics, ministry practice, pastoral care.

Fordham University, Graduate School of Arts and Sciences, Center for Ethics Education, New York, NY 10458. Offers ethics and society (MA); health care ethics (Certificate). Part-time programs available. *Students:* 8 full-time (6 women), 5 part-time (2 women); includes 2 minority (1 Black or African American, non-Hispanic/Latino; 1 Asian, non-Hispanic/Latino). Average age 34. 17 applicants, 71% accepted, 8 enrolled. In 2014, 7 master's awarded. *Entrance requirements:* Additional exam requirements/ recommendations for international students: Required—TOEFL. *Application deadline:* For fall admission, 1/4 priority date for domestic students; for spring admission, 10/31 for domestic students. Application fee: $70. Electronic applications accepted. *Financial support:* In 2014–15, 1 student received support, including 2 teaching assistantships (averaging $11,120 per year); Federal Work-Study, institutionally sponsored loans, scholarships/grants, tuition waivers (partial), and unspecified assistantships also available. Financial award application deadline: 1/4. *Unit head:* Dr. Adam Fried, Assistant Director, Fordham University Center for Ethics Education, 718-817-0926, Fax: 212-759-2009, E-mail: afried@fordham.edu. *Application contact:* Bernadette Valentino-Morrison, Director of Graduate Admissions, 718-817-4419, Fax: 718-817-3566, E-mail: valentinomor@fordham.edu.

Freed-Hardeman University, Program in Business Administration, Henderson, TN 38340-2399. Offers accounting (MBA); corporate responsibility (MBA); leadership (MBA). *Accreditation:* ACBSP. Part-time and evening/weekend programs available. Postbaccalaureate distance learning degree programs offered (no on-campus study). *Entrance requirements:* For master's, GMAT. Additional exam requirements/ recommendations for international students: Required—TOEFL (minimum score 500 paper-based).

George Mason University, College of Humanities and Social Sciences, Department of Philosophy, Fairfax, VA 22030. Offers ethics and public affairs (MA). *Faculty:* 11 full-time (3 women), 8 part-time/adjunct (1 woman). *Students:* 1 (woman) full-time, 12 part-time (1 woman); includes 2 minority (1 Black or African American, non-Hispanic/Latino; 1 Two or more races, non-Hispanic/Latino). Average age 39. 14 applicants, 57% accepted, 3 enrolled. In 2014, 2 master's awarded. *Degree requirements:* For master's, thesis optional. *Entrance requirements:* For master's, 3 letters of recommendation; official transcript; expanded goals statement; writing sample; resume. Additional exam requirements/recommendations for international students: Required—TOEFL (minimum score 570 paper-based; 80 iBT), IELTS (minimum score 6.5), PTE. *Application deadline:* For fall admission, 3/1 priority date for domestic students; for spring admission, 11/1 priority date for domestic students. Application fee: $65 ($80 for international students). Electronic applications accepted. *Expenses:* Tuition, state resident: full-time $9794; part-time $408 per credit hour. Tuition, nonresident: full-time $26,978; part-time $1124 per credit hour. *Required fees:* $2820; $118 per credit hour. Tuition and fees vary according to course load and program. *Financial support:* In 2014–15, 2 students received support, including 2 teaching assistantships (averaging $7,000 per year); career-related internships or fieldwork, Federal Work-Study, scholarships/grants, unspecified assistantships, and health care benefits (for full-time research or teaching assistantship recipients) also available. Financial award application deadline: 3/1; financial award applicants required to submit FAFSA. *Faculty research:* Cultural studies, political theory philosophy, social and political philosophy, feminist theory, analytical and Continental philosophy, philosophy of science. *Total annual research expenditures:* $6,841. *Unit head:* Ted Kinnaman, Chair/Associate Professor, 703-993-4328, Fax: 703-993-1297, E-mail: tkinnama@gmu.edu. *Application contact:* Rose Cherubin, Graduate Coordinator, 703-993-1332, Fax: 703-993-1297, E-mail: rcherubi@gmu.edu.
Website: http://philosophy.gmu.edu/

George Mason University, College of Humanities and Social Sciences, Interdisciplinary Studies Program, Fairfax, VA 22030. Offers community college teaching (MAIS); computational social science (MAIS); energy and sustainability (MAIS); film and video studies (MAIS); folklore studies (MAIS); higher education administration (MAIS); neuroethics (MAIS); religion, culture and values (MAIS); social entrepreneurship (MAIS); war and military in society (MAIS); women and gender studies (MAIS). *Faculty:* 11 full-time (3 women), 4 part-time/adjunct (all women). *Students:* 22 full-time (13 women), 87 part-time (51 women); includes 31 minority (21 Black or African American, non-Hispanic/Latino; 2 Asian, non-Hispanic/Latino; 6 Hispanic/Latino; 2 Two or more races, non-Hispanic/Latino), 6 international. Average age 32. 75 applicants, 75% accepted, 28 enrolled. In 2014, 31 master's awarded. *Degree requirements:* For master's, project or thesis. *Entrance requirements:* For master's, 3 letters of recommendation; writing sample; official transcript; resume. Additional exam requirements/recommendations for international students: Required—TOEFL (minimum score 570 paper-based; 80 iBT), IELTS (minimum score 6.5), PTE. *Application deadline:* For fall admission, 3/1 priority date for domestic students; for spring admission, 10/15 for domestic students. Application fee: $65 ($80 for international students). Electronic applications accepted. *Expenses:* Tuition, state resident: full-time $9794; part-time $408 per credit hour. Tuition, nonresident: full-time $26,978; part-time $1124 per credit hour. *Required fees:* $2820; $118 per credit hour. Tuition and fees vary according to course load and program. *Financial support:* In 2014–15, 10 students received support, including 1 fellowship (averaging $6,935 per year), 2 research assistantships with full and partial tuition reimbursements available (averaging $6,499 per year), 8 teaching assistantships with full and partial tuition reimbursements available (averaging $8,271 per year); career-related internships or fieldwork, Federal Work-Study, scholarships/ grants, unspecified assistantships, and health care benefits (for full-time research or teaching assistantship recipients) also available. Support available to part-time students. Financial award application deadline: 3/1; financial award applicants required to submit FAFSA. *Faculty research:* Combined English and folklore, religious and cultural studies (Christianity and Muslim society). *Unit head:* Meredith H. Lair, Director, 703-993-2159, Fax: 703-993-1251, E-mail: mlair@gmu.edu. *Application contact:* Lisa Struckmeyer, Administrative Coordinator, 703-993-8762, Fax: 703-993-5585, E-mail: lstruckm@gmu.edu.
Website: http://mais.gmu.edu

Georgetown University, Graduate School of Arts and Sciences, School of Continuing Studies, Washington, DC 20057. Offers American studies (MALS); Catholic studies (MALS); classical civilizations (MALS); emergency and disaster management (MPS); ethics and the professions (MALS); hospitality management (MPS); human resources management (MPS); humanities (MALS); individualized study (MALS); international affairs (MALS); Islam and Muslim-Christian relations (MALS); journalism (MPS); liberal studies (DLS); literature and society (MALS); medieval and early modern European studies (MALS); public relations and corporate communications (MPS); real estate (MPS); religious studies (MALS); social and public policy (MALS); sports industry management (MPS); systems engineering management (MPS); technology management (MPS); the theory and practice of American democracy (MALS); urban and regional planning (MPS); visual culture (MALS). MPS in systems engineering management offered jointly with Stevens Institute of Technology. *Entrance requirements:* Additional exam requirements/recommendations for international students: Required—TOEFL.

Graduate Theological Union, Graduate Programs, Berkeley, CA 94709-1212. Offers art and religion (MA, PhD, Th D); biblical languages (MA); biblical studies (MA); Biblical studies (PhD, Th D); Buddhist studies (MA); Christian spirituality (MA, PhD, Th D); cultural and historical studies of religions (MA, PhD, Th D); ethics and social theory (PhD, Th D); history (MA, PhD, Th D); homiletics (MA, PhD, Th D); interdisciplinary studies (PhD, Th D); Jewish studies (MA, PhD, Th D, Certificate); liturgical studies (MA, PhD, Th D); Near Eastern religions (PhD, Th D); Orthodox Christian studies (MA); religion and psychology (MA, PhD, Th D); religion and society/ethics and social theory (MA); systematic and philosophical theology (MA, PhD, Th D). PhD programs in Jewish studies and Near Eastern religions offered jointly with University of California, Berkeley. *Accreditation:* ATS. Terminal master's awarded for partial completion of doctoral program. *Degree requirements:* For master's, one foreign language, thesis; for doctorate, one foreign language, comprehensive exam, thesis/dissertation. *Entrance requirements:* For master's, GRE General Test; for doctorate, GRE General Test, MA or M Div. Additional exam requirements/recommendations for international students: Required—TOEFL. Electronic applications accepted.

Kennesaw State University, Siegel Institute for Leadership, Ethics and Character, Kennesaw, GA 30144. Offers leadership and ethics (Graduate Certificate). Part-time and evening/weekend programs available. Postbaccalaureate distance learning degree programs offered (no on-campus study). *Students:* 2 part-time (1 woman). Average age 55. 2 applicants, 50% accepted, 1 enrolled. In 2014, 13 Graduate Certificates awarded. *Entrance requirements:* Additional exam requirements/recommendations for international students: Required—TOEFL (minimum score 550 paper-based; 80 iBT), IELTS (minimum score 6.5). *Application deadline:* For fall admission, 6/1 for domestic and international students; for spring admission, 11/1 for domestic and international students; for summer admission, 5/1 for domestic and international students. Applications are processed on a rolling basis. Application fee: $60. Electronic applications accepted. *Expenses:* Tuition, state resident: part-time $275 per semester hour. Tuition, nonresident: part-time $990 per semester hour. *Financial support:* In 2014–15, 2 research assistantships with tuition reimbursements (averaging $8,000 per year) were awarded; unspecified assistantships also available. Financial award application deadline: 4/1; financial award applicants required to submit FAFSA. *Unit head:* Dr. Linda M. Johnston, Executive Director, 470-578-2000, E-mail: ljohnst9@kennesaw.edu. *Application contact:* Admissions Counselor, 470-578-4377, Fax: 470-578-9172, E-mail: ksugrad@kennesaw.edu.
Website: http://www.kennesaw.edu/siegelinstitute/

Lancaster Theological Seminary, Graduate and Professional Programs, Lancaster, PA 17603-2812. Offers biblical studies (MAR); Christian education (MAR); Christianity and the arts (MAR); church history (MAR); congregational life (MAR); lay leadership (Certificate); theological studies (M Div); theology (D Min); theology and ethics (MAR). *Accreditation:* ACIPE; ATS. *Degree requirements:* For doctorate, thesis/dissertation.

Loyola University Chicago, Graduate School of Business, MBA Programs, Chicago, IL 60611. Offers accounting (MBA); business ethics (MBA); derivative markets (MBA); economics (MBA); entrepreneurship (MBA); executive business administration (MBA); finance (MBA); healthcare management (MBA); human resources management (MBA); information systems management (MBA); intercontinental (MBA); international business (MBA); marketing (MBA); operations management (MBA); risk management (MBA); JD/ MBA; MBA/MSA; MBA/MSF; MBA/MSHR; MBA/MSN; MBA/MSP; MBA/MSSCM; MSIMC/MBA. Part-time and evening/weekend programs available. *Faculty:* 76 full-time (20 women), 10 part-time/adjunct (4 women). *Students:* 101 full-time (42 women), 335 part-time (159 women); includes 94 minority (26 Black or African American, non-Hispanic/Latino; 1 American Indian or Alaska Native, non-Hispanic/Latino; 35 Asian, non-Hispanic/Latino; 23 Hispanic/Latino; 9 Two or more races, non-Hispanic/Latino), 47 international. Average age 32. 490 applicants, 49% accepted, 127 enrolled. In 2014, 225 master's awarded. *Entrance requirements:* For master's, GMAT or GRE, a completed application, official transcripts, two letters of recommendation, a statement of purpose, resume. Additional exam requirements/recommendations for international students: Required—TOEFL (minimum score 90 iBT) or IELTS (minimum score 6.5). *Application deadline:* For fall admission, 7/15 for domestic and international students; for winter admission, 10/1 for domestic and international students; for spring admission, 1/15 for domestic and international students; for summer admission, 4/1 for domestic and international students. Applications are processed on a rolling basis. Application fee: $50. Electronic applications accepted. Application fee is waived when completed online. *Expenses: Tuition:* Full-time $17,370; part-time $965 per credit. *Required fees:* $138 per semester. *Financial support:* Scholarships/grants and unspecified assistantships available. *Faculty research:* Social enterprise and responsibility, emerging markets, supply chain management, risk management. *Unit head:* Katherine Acles, Assistant Dean for Graduate Programs, 312-915-6124, Fax: 312-915-7207, E-mail: kacles@luc.edu. *Application contact:* Lauren Griffin, Enrollment Advisor, Quinlan School of Business Graduate Programs, 312-915-6124, Fax: 312-915-7207, E-mail: lgriffin3@luc.edu.

Lutheran Theological Seminary Saskatoon, Graduate and Professional Programs, Saskatoon, SK S7N 0X3, Canada. Offers Biblical studies (MTS); church history (MTS); ethics/church and society (MTS); history of Christianity (STM); New Testament (STM); Old Testament (STM); pastoral studies (STM); pastoral theology (MTS); systematic theology (MTS); systematic theology and philosophy of religion (STM); theology (M Div, D Div). STM programs offered jointly with College of Emmanuel and St. Chad and St. Andrew's College. *Accreditation:* ATS. Part-time programs available. *Degree requirements:* For master's, thesis.

Marquette University, Graduate School, College of Arts and Sciences, Department of Philosophy, Milwaukee, WI 53201-1881. Offers ancient philosophy (PhD); British empiricism and analytic philosophy (PhD); Christian philosophy (PhD); early modern European philosophy (PhD); ethics (PhD); German philosophy (PhD); history of philosophy (MA); medieval philosophy (PhD); phenomenology and existentialism (PhD); philosophy of religion (PhD); social and applied philosophy (MA); JD/MA. Part-time programs available. Terminal master's awarded for partial completion of doctoral program. *Degree requirements:* For master's, variable foreign language requirement, comprehensive exam, thesis or alternative; for doctorate, 2 foreign languages, thesis/ dissertation, written and oral qualifying exams. *Entrance requirements:* For master's and doctorate, GRE General Test, official transcripts from all current and previous colleges/ universities except Marquette, statement of purpose, at least three letters of recommendation, sample of philosophical writing. Additional exam requirements/ recommendations for international students: Required—TOEFL (minimum score 530 paper-based). Electronic applications accepted. *Faculty research:* Aristotle, Augustine, Descartes, Hegel, Heidegger.

New England College of Business and Finance, Program in Business Ethics and Compliance, Boston, MA 02111-2645. Offers MS. Postbaccalaureate distance learning degree programs offered (no on-campus study).

North Central College, Graduate and Continuing Studies Programs, Program in Liberal Studies, Naperville, IL 60566-7063. Offers culture and society (MALS); ethics and public service (MALS); writing, editing, and publishing (MALS). Part-time and evening/weekend programs available. *Faculty:* 8 full-time (2 women), 4 part-time/adjunct (1 woman). *Students:* 2 full-time (1 woman), 24 part-time (14 women); includes 1 minority (Asian, non-Hispanic/Latino). Average age 36. 15 applicants, 73% accepted, 7 enrolled. In 2014, 6 master's awarded. *Degree requirements:* For master's, thesis optional, project. *Entrance requirements:* For master's, interview. Additional exam requirements/ recommendations for international students: Required—TOEFL (minimum score 550 paper-based; 80 iBT). *Application deadline:* For fall admission, 8/15 for domestic students, 7/15 for international students; for winter admission, 12/1 for domestic students, 11/1 for international students; for spring admission, 2/1 for domestic students, 12/1 for international students. Applications are processed on a rolling basis. Application fee: $25. Electronic applications accepted. Application fee is waived when completed online. *Expenses:* Expenses: Contact institution. *Financial support:* In 2014–15, 1 student received support. Scholarships/grants available. Support available to part-time students. Financial award applicants required to submit FAFSA. *Unit head:* Dr. Richard Guzman, Program Coordinator, Liberal Studies, 630-637-5285. *Application contact:* Wendy Kulpinski, Director of Graduate and Continuing Education Admission, 630-637-5808, Fax: 630-637-5844, E-mail: wekulpinski@noctrl.edu.
Website: http://northcentralcollege.edu/admission/liberal-studies

Northwestern University, School of Professional Studies, Program in Liberal Studies, Evanston, IL 60208. Offers American studies (MA); history (MA); religious and ethical studies (MA).

Ethics

Oregon State University, College of Liberal Arts, Program in Applied Ethics, Corvallis, OR 97331. Offers MA. Part-time programs available. *Faculty:* 10 full-time (3 women), 1 (woman) part-time/adjunct. *Students:* 8 full-time (3 women), 1 part-time (0 women); includes 4 minority (1 Black or African American, non-Hispanic/Latino; 3 Hispanic/Latino), 1 international. Average age 32. 8 applicants, 75% accepted, 4 enrolled. In 2014, 2 master's awarded. *Entrance requirements:* For master's, writing sample of 5-7 pages. Additional exam requirements/recommendations for international students: Required—TOEFL (minimum score 80 iBT), IELTS (minimum score 6.5). *Application deadline:* For fall admission, 1/15 for domestic and international students. Application fee: $60. *Expenses:* Tuition, state resident: full-time $11,907; part-time $189 per credit hour. Tuition, nonresident: full-time $19,953; part-time $441 per credit hour. *Required fees:* $1472; $449 per term. One-time fee: $350. Tuition and fees vary according to course load and program. *Financial support:* Application deadline: 3/15. *Unit head:* Dr. Ben Mutschler, Director. *Application contact:* Dr. Allen Thompson, Director of Graduate Studies, 541-737-5654, E-mail: allen.tompson@oregonstate.edu. Website: http://liberalarts.oregonstate.edu/shpr/philosophy

Phillips Theological Seminary, Programs in Theology, Tulsa, OK 74116. Offers administration of church agencies (M Div); campus ministry (M Div); church-related social work (M Div); college and seminary teaching (M Div); global mission work (M Div); institutional chaplaincy (M Div); ministerial vocations in Christian education (M Div); ministry (D Min), including parish ministry, pastoral counseling, practices of ministry; ministry and culture (MAMC), including Christian education, congregational leadership, history and practice of Christian spirituality, theology, ethics, and culture; ministry of music (M Div); pastoral care and counseling (M Div); pastoral ministry (M Div); theological studies (MTS). *Accreditation:* ATS. Part-time programs available. Postbaccalaureate distance learning degree programs offered (minimal on-campus study). *Degree requirements:* For master's, thesis (for some programs); for doctorate, thesis/dissertation. *Entrance requirements:* For master's, minimum GPA of 2.5; for doctorate, M Div, minimum GPA of 3.0. *Faculty research:* Biblical studies, historical studies, theology and culture, practical theology, theology and film.

St. Edward's University, Bill Munday School of Business, Program in Organizational Leadership and Ethics, Austin, TX 78704. Offers MS. Part-time and evening/weekend programs available. *Students:* 28 part-time (19 women); includes 12 minority (5 Black or African American, non-Hispanic/Latino; 7 Hispanic/Latino). Average age 40. 17 applicants, 94% accepted, 12 enrolled. In 2014, 15 master's awarded. *Degree requirements:* For master's, minimum of 24 hours in residence. *Entrance requirements:* For master's, GMAT or GRE General Test, minimum GPA of 2.75 in last 60 hours of course work. Additional exam requirements/recommendations for international students: Required—TOEFL (minimum score 79 iBT) or IELTS (minimum score 6). *Application deadline:* For fall admission, 6/1 priority date for domestic and international students; for spring admission, 10/1 priority date for domestic and international students; for summer admission, 3/1 priority date for domestic and international students. Applications are processed on a rolling basis. Application fee: $50. Electronic applications accepted. *Expenses:* Tuition: Full-time $22,448; part-time $1246 per credit hour. *Required fees:* $50 per trimester. Full-time tuition and fees vary according to course load and program. *Unit head:* Dr. Tom Sechrest, Director, 512-637-1954, Fax: 512-448-8492, E-mail: thomasl@stedwards.edu. *Application contact:* Office of Admission, 512-448-8500, Fax: 512-464-8877, E-mail: seu.admit@stedwards.edu. Website: http://www.stedwards.edu

Schreiner University, MBA Program, Kerrville, TX 78028-5697. Offers ethical leadership (MBA). Part-time programs available. Postbaccalaureate distance learning degree programs offered (no on-campus study). *Entrance requirements:* For master's, 3 recommendations; personal essay; transcripts; resume. Additional exam requirements/recommendations for international students: Required—TOEFL. Electronic applications accepted. *Expenses:* Contact institution.

Sonoma State University, School of Business and Economics, Rohnert Park, CA 94928-3609. Offers business administration (MBA), including contemporary business issues, international business and global issues, leadership and ethics; executive business administration (MBA); wine business (MBA), including contemporary business issues, international business and global issues, leadership and ethics. *Accreditation:* AACSB. Part-time and evening/weekend programs available. *Degree requirements:* For master's, thesis or alternative. *Entrance requirements:* For master's, GMAT. Additional exam requirements/recommendations for international students: Required—TOEFL (minimum score 500 paper-based).

Southeastern Baptist Theological Seminary, Graduate and Professional Programs, Wake Forest, NC 27588-1889. Offers advanced Biblical studies (M Div); Christian education (M Div, MACE); Christian ethics (PhD); Christian ministry (M Div); Christian planting (M Div); church music (MACM); counseling (MACO); evangelism (PhD); language (M Div); ministry (D Min); New Testament (PhD); Old Testament (PhD); philosophy (PhD); theology (Th M, PhD); women's studies (M Div). *Accreditation:* ACIPE; ATS (one or more programs are accredited). *Degree requirements:* For master's, thesis (for some programs), oral exam; for doctorate, thesis/dissertation, fieldwork. *Entrance requirements:* For master's, Cooperative English Test, minimum GPA of 2.0, M Div or equivalent (Th M); for doctorate, GRE General Test or MAT, Cooperative English Test, M Div or equivalent, 3 years of professional experience.

Southern Methodist University, Dedman College of Humanities and Sciences, Graduate Program in Religious Studies, Dallas, TX 75275-0133. Offers Hebrew Bible/Old Testament (PhD); history of the Christian tradition (PhD); New Testament (PhD); religion and culture (PhD); religious ethics (PhD); religious studies (MA); systematics theology (PhD). Terminal master's awarded for partial completion of doctoral program. *Degree requirements:* For master's, one foreign language, thesis, oral and written exams; for doctorate, variable foreign language requirement, thesis/dissertation, oral and written exams. *Entrance requirements:* For master's and doctorate, GRE General Test, minimum GPA of 3.0, course work in religion. Additional exam requirements/recommendations for international students: Required—TOEFL (minimum score 550 paper-based; 79 iBT). Electronic applications accepted. *Faculty research:* Theology, religious ethics, Biblical studies, history of Christianity, religion and culture.

Southern New Hampshire University, School of Business, Manchester, NH 03106-1045. Offers accounting (MBA, MS, Graduate Certificate); accounting finance (MS); accounting/auditing (MS); accounting/forensic accounting (MS); accounting/taxation (MS); athletic administration (MBA, Graduate Certificate); business administration (IMBA, MBA, Certificate, Graduate Certificate), including accounting (Certificate), business administration (MBA), business information systems (Graduate Certificate), human resource management (Certificate); corporate social responsibility (MBA); entrepreneurship (MBA); finance (MBA, MS, Graduate Certificate); finance/corporate finance (MS); finance/investments and securities (MS); forensic accounting (MBA); healthcare informatics (MBA); healthcare management (MBA); human resource management (Graduate Certificate); information technology (MS, Graduate Certificate); information technology management (MBA); international business (Graduate Certificate); international business and information technology (Graduate Certificate); international finance (Graduate Certificate); international sport management (Graduate Certificate); justice studies (MBA); leadership of nonprofit organizations (Graduate Certificate); marketing (MBA, MS, Graduate Certificate); operations and project

management (MS); operations and supply chain management (MBA, Graduate Certificate); organizational leadership (MS); project management (MBA, Graduate Certificate); Six Sigma (MBA); Six Sigma quality (Graduate Certificate); social media marketing (MBA); sport management (MBA, MS, Graduate Certificate); sustainability and environmental compliance (MBA); workplace conflict management (MBA); MBA/Certificate. *Accreditation:* ACBSP. Part-time and evening/weekend programs available. Postbaccalaureate distance learning degree programs offered (no on-campus study). Terminal master's awarded for partial completion of doctoral program. *Degree requirements:* For master's, one foreign language, comprehensive exam (for some programs), thesis or alternative. *Entrance requirements:* For master's, minimum GPA of 2.5. Additional exam requirements/recommendations for international students: Required—TOEFL (minimum score 500 paper-based). Electronic applications accepted.

Spring Hill College, Graduate Programs, Program in Liberal Arts, Mobile, AL 36608-1791. Offers fine arts (MLA); history and social science (MLA); leadership and ethics (MLA, Postbaccalaureate Certificate); literature (MLA); studio art (Postbaccalaureate Certificate). Part-time and evening/weekend programs available. *Faculty:* 6 full-time (1 woman), 3 part-time/adjunct (all women). *Students:* 3 full-time (1 woman), 33 part-time (18 women); includes 9 minority (8 Black or African American, non-Hispanic/Latino; 1 American Indian or Alaska Native, non-Hispanic/Latino), 1 international. Average age 36. In 2014, 8 master's awarded. *Degree requirements:* For master's, capstone course, completion of program within 6 years of initial admittance. *Entrance requirements:* For master's, bachelor's degree with minimum undergraduate GPA of 3.0 or graduate/professional degree. Additional exam requirements/recommendations for international students: Required—TOEFL (minimum score 550 paper-based; 80 iBT), IELTS (minimum score 6.5), CPE or CAE (minimum score C), Michigan English Language Assessment Battery (minimum score 90). *Application deadline:* For fall admission, 8/1 priority date for domestic and international students; for spring admission, 12/1 priority date for domestic and international students. Applications are processed on a rolling basis. Application fee: $25 ($35 for international students). Electronic applications accepted. *Expenses:* Expenses: Contact institution. *Financial support:* Applicants required to submit FAFSA. *Unit head:* Dr. Thomas J. Hoffman, Director, 251-380-4184, Fax: 251-460-2115, E-mail: thoffman@shc.edu. *Application contact:* Robert Stewart, Vice President of Enrollment, 251-380-3030, Fax: 251-460-2186, E-mail: rstewart@shc.edu.
Website: http://ug.shc.edu/graduate-degrees/master-liberal-arts/

Stevens Institute of Technology, Graduate School, College of Arts and Letters, Program in Technology, Policy, and Ethics, Hoboken, NJ 07030. Offers MA, Graduate Certificate.

Suffolk University, College of Arts and Sciences, Department of Philosophy, Boston, MA 02108-2770. Offers administration of higher education (M Ed, CAGS); ethics and public policy (MS). Part-time and evening/weekend programs available. *Faculty:* 5 full-time (1 woman), 1 part-time/adjunct (0 women). *Students:* 25 full-time (20 women), 34 part-time (25 women); includes 12 minority (1 Black or African American, non-Hispanic/Latino; 1 Asian, non-Hispanic/Latino; 9 Hispanic/Latino; 1 Two or more races, non-Hispanic/Latino), 3 international. Average age 28. 72 applicants, 63% accepted, 19 enrolled. In 2014, 30 master's awarded. *Degree requirements:* For master's, internship or thesis; practicum (for M Ed). *Entrance requirements:* For master's, GRE General Test, MAT, GMAT, statement of professional goals, official transcripts, 2 letters of recommendation, resume. Additional exam requirements/recommendations for international students: Required—TOEFL (minimum score 550 paper-based; 80 iBT). *Application deadline:* For fall and spring admission, 6/15 priority date for domestic and international students. Applications are processed on a rolling basis. Application fee: $50. Electronic applications accepted. *Expenses:* Expenses: Contact institution. *Financial support:* In 2014–15, 35 students received support, including 35 fellowships (averaging $8,008 per year); career-related internships or fieldwork, Federal Work-Study, institutionally sponsored loans, and unspecified assistantships also available. Support available to part-time students. Financial award application deadline: 4/1; financial award applicants required to submit FAFSA. *Faculty research:* Predicting competent Head Start preschoolers, cultural differences, school counseling technology, sibling attachment in divorce cases, consequences of ethical breaches by human resource professionals. *Unit head:* Dr. Greg Fried, Chair of Philosophy Department, 617-573-8109, E-mail: gfried@suffolk.edu. *Application contact:* Cory Meyers, Director of Graduate Admissions, 617-573-8302, Fax: 617-305-1733, E-mail: grad.admission@suffolk.edu.
Website: http://www.suffolk.edu/college/departments/9942.php

Texas State University, The Graduate College, College of Liberal Arts, Applied Philosophy and Ethics Program, San Marcos, TX 78666. Offers MA. *Faculty:* 9 full-time (3 women), 3 part-time/adjunct (2 women). *Students:* 14 full-time (2 women), 6 part-time (2 women); includes 6 minority (1 Black or African American, non-Hispanic/Latino; 4 Hispanic/Latino; 1 Two or more races, non-Hispanic/Latino). Average age 30. 13 applicants, 85% accepted, 4 enrolled. In 2014, 18 master's awarded. *Degree requirements:* For master's, comprehensive exam, thesis optional. *Entrance requirements:* For master's, GRE (preferred), baccalaureate degree from regionally-accredited university with minimum GPA of 3.0 on last 60 undergraduate semester hours. Additional exam requirements/recommendations for international students: Required—TOEFL (minimum score 550 paper-based; 78 iBT). *Application deadline:* For fall admission, 6/15 priority date for domestic students, 6/1 for international students; for spring admission, 10/15 priority date for domestic students, 10/1 for international students; for summer admission, 4/15 for domestic students, 3/15 for international students. Applications are processed on a rolling basis. Application fee: $40 ($90 for international students). *Financial support:* In 2014–15, 17 students received support, including 1 research assistantship (averaging $11,855 per year), 12 teaching assistantships (averaging $11,563 per year); scholarships/grants also available. Support available to part-time students. Financial award application deadline: 4/1; financial award applicants required to submit FAFSA. *Unit head:* Dr. Audrey Mckinney, Graduate Advisor, 512-245-2047, Fax: 512-245-8336, E-mail: am04@txstate.edu. *Application contact:* Dr. Andrea Golato, Dean of Graduate School, 512-245-2581, Fax: 512-245-8365, E-mail: gradcollege@txstate.edu.

Union Graduate College, Center for Bioethics and Clinical Leadership, Schenectady, NY 12308-3107. Offers bioethics (MS); clinical ethics (AC); clinical leadership in health management (MS); health, policy and law (AC); research ethics (AC). Part-time and evening/weekend programs available. Postbaccalaureate distance learning degree programs offered (minimal on-campus study). *Entrance requirements:* For master's, letters of recommendation. Additional exam requirements/recommendations for international students: Required—TOEFL (minimum score 550 paper-based). Electronic applications accepted. *Expenses:* Contact institution. *Faculty research:* Bioethics education, clinical ethics consultation, research ethics, history of biomedical ethics, international bioethics/research ethics.

Union Institute & University, PhD Program in Interdisciplinary Studies, Cincinnati, OH 45206-1925. Offers ethical and creative leadership (PhD), including Martin Luther King studies; humanities and culture (PhD), including Martin Luther King studies; public policy and social change (PhD), including Martin Luther King studies. Program requires participation in brief on-campus residencies twice each year (January and July).

Postbaccalaureate distance learning degree programs offered (minimal on-campus study). *Faculty:* 6 full-time (4 women), 9 part-time/adjunct (7 women). *Students:* 92 full-time (51 women), 15 part-time (10 women); includes 37 minority (25 Black or African American, non-Hispanic/Latino; 4 American Indian or Alaska Native, non-Hispanic/Latino; 2 Asian, non-Hispanic/Latino; 3 Hispanic/Latino; 3 Native Hawaiian or other Pacific Islander, non-Hispanic/Latino), 1 international. Average age 46. *Degree requirements:* For doctorate, comprehensive exam, thesis/dissertation. *Entrance requirements:* For doctorate, master's degree, three letters of recommendation, statement of purpose. *Application deadline:* Applications are processed on a rolling basis. Application fee: $50. *Expenses: Tuition:* Full-time $26,640; part-time $719 per credit hour. *Required fees:* $216; $54 per semester. Part-time tuition and fees vary according to course load, degree level and program. *Financial support:* Federal Work-Study, scholarships/grants, and tuition waivers (partial) available. Financial award application deadline: 5/1; financial award applicants required to submit FAFSA. *Faculty research:* Social responsibility, ethical leadership, Martin Luther King studies. *Unit head:* Dr. Arlene Sacks, Dean, 513-861-6400, E-mail: arlene.sacks@myunion.edu. *Application contact:* Admissions Counselor, 800-486-3116.
Website: https://www.myunion.edu/academics/doctoral-programs/phd/

Université de Sherbrooke, Faculty of Theology and Religious Studies, Sherbrooke, QC J1K 2R1, Canada. Offers applied ethics (Diploma); human science of religions (MA); intercultural training (Diploma); philosophy (MA, PhD); spiritual anthropology (Diploma); theology (MA, PhD, Diploma). Part-time and evening/weekend programs available. Postbaccalaureate distance learning degree programs offered. Terminal master's awarded for partial completion of doctoral program. *Entrance requirements:* For master's, bachelor's degree in related discipline; for doctorate, master's degree in related discipline. *Faculty research:* Faith and culture interrelation.

Université du Québec à Chicoutimi, Graduate Programs, Program in Ethics, Chicoutimi, QC G7H 2B1, Canada. Offers Diploma. *Entrance requirements:* For degree, appropriate bachelor's degree, proficiency in French.

Université du Québec à Rimouski, Graduate Programs, Program in Ethics, Rimouski, QC G5L 3A1, Canada. Offers MA, Diploma. Part-time programs available. *Degree requirements:* For master's, thesis. *Entrance requirements:* For master's, appropriate bachelor's degree, proficiency in French.

Université Laval, Faculty of Theology and Religious Sciences, Program in Applied Ethics, Québec, QC G1K 7P4, Canada. Offers DESS. Part-time programs available. *Entrance requirements:* For degree, knowledge of French. Electronic applications accepted.

University of Baltimore, Graduate School, Yale Gordon College of Arts and Sciences, Program in Legal and Ethical Studies, Baltimore, MD 21201-5779. Offers MA. Part-time and evening/weekend programs available. *Degree requirements:* For master's, thesis optional. *Entrance requirements:* For master's, minimum GPA of 3.0. Additional exam requirements/recommendations for international students: Required—TOEFL (minimum score 550 paper-based). Electronic applications accepted. *Faculty research:* Morality in law and economics, religion in lawmaking, comparative legal history, law and social change, critical issues in Constitutional law, theories of justice.

University of Chicago, Divinity School, PhD Program, Chicago, IL 60637. Offers anthropology and sociology of religions (PhD); bible (PhD); history of Christianity (PhD); history of Judaism (PhD); history of religions (PhD); Islamic studies (PhD); philosophy of religions (PhD); religion and literature (PhD); religions in America (PhD); religious ethics (PhD); theology (PhD). *Students:* 164 full-time (50 women); includes 18 minority (5 Black or African American, non-Hispanic/Latino; 8 Asian, non-Hispanic/Latino; 1 Hispanic/Latino; 4 Two or more races, non-Hispanic/Latino), 28 international. 185 applicants, 12% accepted, 18 enrolled. *Degree requirements:* For doctorate, 2 foreign languages, comprehensive exam, thesis/dissertation. *Entrance requirements:* For doctorate, GRE General Test. Additional exam requirements/recommendations for international students: Required—TOEFL (minimum score 600 paper-based; 104 iBT), IELTS (minimum score 7). *Application deadline:* For fall admission, 12/15 for domestic and international students. Application fee: $75. Electronic applications accepted. *Expenses: Tuition:* Full-time $46,899. *Required fees:* $347. *Financial support:* Fellowships, Federal Work-Study, institutionally sponsored loans, and scholarships/grants available. Financial award application deadline: 12/15; financial award applicants required to submit FAFSA. *Faculty research:* Anthropology and sociology of religions, history of religions, theology, religious ethics, philosophy of religions, Bible, history of Christianity/Judaism, Islamic studies, religions in America. *Unit head:* Dr. Margaret M. Mitchell, Dean/Professor of New Testament and Early Christian Literature, 773-702-8200. *Application contact:* John W. Howell, Coordinator for Recruiting and Admissions, 773-702-8249, Fax: 773-834-4581, E-mail: divinityadmissions@uchicago.edu.
Website: http://divinity.uchicago.edu/doctoral-program-phd

University of Maryland, Baltimore, Graduate School, Program in Research Ethics, Baltimore, MD 21201. Offers Certificate. Part-time programs available. Postbaccalaureate distance learning degree programs offered. *Students:* 10 part-time (9 women); includes 1 minority (Hispanic/Latino), 3 international. Average age 39. 15 applicants, 67% accepted, 7 enrolled. *Entrance requirements:* Additional exam requirements/recommendations for international students: Required—TOEFL (minimum score 550 paper-based; 80 iBT); Recommended—IELTS (minimum score 7). *Application deadline:* For fall admission, 7/10 priority date for domestic students, 1/15 for international students. Applications are processed on a rolling basis. Application fee: $75. Electronic applications accepted. *Unit head:* Dr. Bruce E. Jarrell, Chief Academic and Research Officer, 410-706-2304, Fax: 410-706-0500, E-mail: bjarrell@som.umaryland.edu. *Application contact:* Dr. Henry Silverman, Program Director, 410-328-4881, E-mail: hsilverm@medicine.umaryland.edu.
Website: http://www.graduate.umaryland.edu/research-ethics/

University of Missouri, Office of Research and Graduate Studies, Department of Health Management and Informatics, Columbia, MO 65211. Offers health administration (MHA); health ethics (Graduate Certificate); health informatics (MS, Graduate Certificate). *Accreditation:* CAHME. Part-time programs available. *Faculty:* 18 full-time (5 women), 2 part-time/adjunct (0 women). *Students:* 98 full-time (54 women), 27 part-time (14 women); includes 22 minority (8 Black or African American, non-Hispanic/Latino; 8 Asian, non-Hispanic/Latino; 3 Hispanic/Latino; 3 Two or more races, non-Hispanic/Latino), 20 international. Average age 30. 61 applicants, 56% accepted, 31 enrolled. In 2014, 53 master's, 10 other advanced degrees awarded. *Entrance requirements:* For master's, GRE General Test or GMAT, minimum GPA of 3.0. Additional exam requirements/recommendations for international students: Required—TOEFL (minimum score 500 paper-based; 61 iBT). *Application deadline:* Applications are processed on a rolling basis. Application fee: $55 ($75 for international students). Electronic applications accepted. *Financial support:* Fellowships, research assistantships, teaching assistantships, institutionally sponsored loans, scholarships/grants, traineeships, health care benefits, and unspecified assistantships available. Support available to part-time students. *Faculty research:* Application of informatics tools to day-to-day clinical operations, consumer health informatics, decision support, health literacy and numeracy, information interventions for persons with chronic illnesses, use of simulation in the education of health care professionals, statistical bioinformatics, classification, dimension reduction, ethics and end of life care, telehealth and tele-ethics, research ethics, health literacy, clinical informatics, human factors. *Unit head:* Dr. Suzanne Boren, Director of Graduate Studies, 573-882-1492, E-mail: borens@missouri.edu. *Application contact:* Veronica Kramer, Coordinator of Student Recruitment and Admissions, 573-884-0698, E-mail: kramerv@missouri.edu.
Website: http://www.hmi.missouri.edu/

University of New England, College of Arts and Sciences, Program in Education, Biddeford, ME 04005-9526. Offers advanced educational leadership (CAGS); career and technical education (MS Ed, CAGS); curriculum and instruction strategies (CAGS); curriculum and instruction strategy (MS Ed); educational leadership (MS Ed, CAGS); inclusion education (MS Ed); leadership, ethics and change (CAGS); literacy K-12 (MS Ed, CAGS); teaching methodologies (MS Ed). Part-time and evening/weekend programs available. Postbaccalaureate distance learning degree programs offered (no on-campus study). *Faculty:* 3 full-time (all women), 16 part-time/adjunct (7 women). *Students:* 212 full-time (164 women), 215 part-time (157 women); includes 24 minority (14 Black or African American, non-Hispanic/Latino; 2 American Indian or Alaska Native, non-Hispanic/Latino; 2 Asian, non-Hispanic/Latino; 3 Hispanic/Latino; 1 Native Hawaiian or other Pacific Islander, non-Hispanic/Latino; 2 Two or more races, non-Hispanic/Latino). Average age 37. 288 applicants, 77% accepted, 148 enrolled. In 2014, 183 master's, 130 CAGSs awarded. *Degree requirements:* For master's, collaborative action research project, integrative seminar portfolio. *Entrance requirements:* For master's, teaching certificate, 2 years of teaching experience. *Application deadline:* For fall admission, 9/15 for domestic students; for spring admission, 1/15 for domestic students. Applications are processed on a rolling basis. Application fee: $40. Electronic applications accepted. Tuition and fees vary according to degree level, program and student level. *Financial support:* Application deadline: 5/1; applicants required to submit FAFSA. *Faculty research:* Distance learning, effective teaching, transition planning, adult learning. *Unit head:* William Diehl, Chair, Education Department, 207-602-2681, E-mail: wdiehl@une.edu. *Application contact:* Scott Steinberg, Dean of University Admissions, 207-221-4225, Fax: 207-523-1925, E-mail: ssteinberg@une.edu.
Website: http://www.une.edu/cas/education/msonline.cfm

The University of North Carolina at Charlotte, College of Liberal Arts and Sciences, Department of Philosophy, Charlotte, NC 28223-0001. Offers applied ethics (Graduate Certificate); ethics and applied philosophy (MA). *Faculty:* 11 full-time (3 women). *Students:* 3 full-time (1 woman), 8 part-time (0 women); includes 2 minority (1 Black or African American, non-Hispanic/Latino; 1 Hispanic/Latino). Average age 29. 5 applicants, 100% accepted, 5 enrolled. In 2014, 7 master's, 2 other advanced degrees awarded. Terminal master's awarded for partial completion of doctoral program. *Degree requirements:* For master's, thesis or alternative, project. *Entrance requirements:* For master's, GRE or MAT, 3 letters of recommendation. Additional exam requirements/recommendations for international students: Required—TOEFL (minimum score 557 paper-based; 83 iBT). *Application deadline:* For fall admission, 5/1 for domestic and international students; for spring admission, 10/1 for domestic and international students. Applications are processed on a rolling basis. Application fee: $75. Electronic applications accepted. *Expenses:* Tuition, state resident: full-time $4008. Tuition, nonresident: full-time $16,295. *Required fees:* $2755. Tuition and fees vary according to course load and program. *Financial support:* In 2014–15, 5 students received support, including 1 research assistantship (averaging $3,000 per year), 4 teaching assistantships (averaging $6,125 per year); unspecified assistantships and administrative assistantships also available. Support available to part-time students. Financial award applicants required to submit FAFSA. *Faculty research:* Ethical issues in long-term care, cognitive enhancement and genetics, ethics and international affairs, political and aesthetic issues arising from contemporary American popular music, moral and legal issues made salient by emerging technologies. *Total annual research expenditures:* $1,547. *Unit head:* Dr. Shannon Sullivan, Chair, 704-687-5412, Fax: 704-687-2172. *Application contact:* Kathy B. Giddings, Director of Graduate Admissions, 704-687-5503, Fax: 704-687-1668, E-mail: gradadm@uncc.edu.
Website: http://philosophy.uncc.edu/

University of North Florida, College of Arts and Sciences, Department of Philosophy, Jacksonville, FL 32224. Offers applied ethics (Graduate Certificate); practical philosophy and applied ethics (MA). Part-time and evening/weekend programs available. *Faculty:* 9 full-time (5 women), 1 part-time/adjunct (0 women). *Students:* 8 full-time (3 women), 8 part-time (3 women); includes 2 minority (both Black or African American, non-Hispanic/Latino), 1 international. Average age 33. 14 applicants, 71% accepted, 5 enrolled. In 2014, 8 master's awarded. *Entrance requirements:* For master's, GRE General Test, minimum GPA of 3.0 in last 60 hours, 3 letters of recommendation, writing sample. Additional exam requirements/recommendations for international students: Required—TOEFL (minimum score 500 paper-based; 61 iBT). *Application deadline:* For fall admission, 7/1 priority date for domestic students, 5/1 for international students. Application fee: $30. Electronic applications accepted. *Expenses:* Tuition, state resident: full-time $9794; part-time $408.10 per credit hour. Tuition, nonresident: full-time $22,383; part-time $932.61 per credit hour. *Required fees:* $2047; $85.29 per credit hour. Tuition and fees vary according to course load and program. *Financial support:* In 2014–15, 3 students received support. Research assistantships, teaching assistantships, Federal Work-Study, scholarships/grants, tuition waivers, and unspecified assistantships available. Financial award application deadline: 4/1; financial award applicants required to submit FAFSA. *Faculty research:* Late modern philosophy, pragmatism, religion and American culture, hermeneutics, philosophy of mind. *Total annual research expenditures:* $34,367. *Unit head:* Dr. Hans-Herbert Koegler, Chair, 904-620-1330, Fax: 904-620-1840, E-mail: hkoegler@unf.edu. *Application contact:* Dr. Amanda Pascale, Director, The Graduate School, 904-620-1360, Fax: 904-620-1362, E-mail: graduateschool@unf.edu.
Website: http://www.unf.edu/coas/philosophy/

University of Pennsylvania, Wharton School, Legal Studies and Business Ethics Department, Philadelphia, PA 19104. Offers MBA, PhD.

University of St. Thomas, Graduate Studies, School of Law, Minneapolis, MN 55403-2015. Offers law (JD); organizational ethics and compliance (LL M, MSL); U.S. law (LL M); JD/MA; JD/MBA; JD/MSW. *Accreditation:* ABA. *Faculty:* 33 full-time (10 women), 76 part-time/adjunct (26 women). *Students:* 392 full-time (184 women), 15 part-time (7 women); includes 48 minority (11 Black or African American, non-Hispanic/Latino; 13 Asian, non-Hispanic/Latino; 12 Hispanic/Latino; 1 Native Hawaiian or other Pacific Islander, non-Hispanic/Latino; 11 Two or more races, non-Hispanic/Latino), 23 international. Average age 27. 716 applicants, 72% accepted, 114 enrolled. In 2014, 143 doctorates awarded. *Degree requirements:* For doctorate, mentor externship, public service. *Entrance requirements:* For doctorate, LSAT, 2 letters of recommendation. Additional exam requirements/recommendations for international students: Required—TOEFL (minimum score 550 paper-based), IELTS (minimum score 6.5), or Michigan English Language Assessment Battery (minimum score 80). *Application deadline:* For fall admission, 7/1 priority date for domestic and international students. Applications are processed on a rolling basis. Application fee: $0. Electronic applications accepted. *Financial support:* In 2014–15, 357 students received support. Scholarships/grants available. Financial award application deadline: 7/1; financial award applicants required to submit FAFSA. *Faculty research:* Constitutional law (executive powers and First

Amendment); banking, securities, and financial markets; law, religion, and jurisprudence; international law, development and dispute resolution; formation of professional identity, values, and skills. *Unit head:* Robert K. Vischer, Dean, 651-962-4880, Fax: 651-962-4881, E-mail: rkvischer@stthomas.edu. *Application contact:* Cari Haaland, Assistant Dean for Admissions and International Programs, 651-962-4895, Fax: 651-962-4876, E-mail: lawschool@stthomas.edu.
Website: http://www.stthomas.edu/law/

University of South Africa, College of Human Sciences, Pretoria, South Africa. Offers adult education (M Ed); African languages (MA, PhD); African politics (MA, PhD); Afrikaans (MA, PhD); ancient history (MA, PhD); ancient Near Eastern studies (MA, PhD); anthropology (MA, PhD); applied linguistics (MA); Arabic (MA, PhD); archaeology (MA); art history (MA); Biblical archaeology (MA); Biblical studies (M Th, D Th, PhD); Christian spirituality (M Th, D Th); church history (M Th, D Th); classical studies (MA, PhD); clinical psychology (MA); communication (MA, PhD); comparative education (M Ed, Ed D); consulting psychology (D Admin, D Com, PhD); curriculum studies (M Ed, Ed D); development studies (M Admin, MA, D Admin, PhD); didactics (M Ed, Ed D); education (M Tech); education management (M Ed, Ed D); educational psychology (M Ed); English (MA); environmental education (M Ed); French (MA, PhD); German (MA, PhD); Greek (MA); guidance and counseling (M Ed); health studies (MA, PhD), including health sciences education (MA), health services management (MA), medical and surgical nursing science (critical care general) (MA), midwifery and neonatal nursing science (MA), trauma and emergency care (MA); history (MA, PhD); history of education (Ed D); inclusive education (M Ed, Ed D); information and communications technology policy and regulation (MA); information science (MA, MIS, PhD); international politics (MA, PhD); Islamic studies (MA, PhD); Italian (MA, PhD); Judaica (MA, PhD); linguistics (MA, PhD); mathematical education (M Ed); mathematics education (MA); missiology (M Th, D Th); modern Hebrew (MA, PhD); musicology (MA, MMus, D Mus, PhD); natural science education (M Ed); New Testament (M Th, D Th); Old Testament (D Th); pastoral therapy (M Th, D Th); philosophy (MA); philosophy of education (M Ed, Ed D); politics (MA, PhD); Portuguese (MA, PhD); practical theology (M Th, D Th); psychology (MA, MS, PhD); psychology of education (M Ed, Ed D); public health (MA); religious studies (MA, D Th, PhD); Romance languages (MA); Russian (MA, PhD); Semitic languages (MA, PhD); social behavior studies in HIV/AIDS (MA); social science (mental health) (MA); social science in development studies (MA); social science in psychology (MA); social science in social work (MA); social science in sociology (MA); social work (MSW, DSW, PhD); socio-education (M Ed, Ed D); sociolinguistics (MA); sociology (MA, PhD); Spanish (MA, PhD); systematic theology (M Th, D Th); TESOL (teaching English to speakers of other languages) (MA); theological ethics (M Th, D Th); theory of literature (MA, PhD); urban ministries (D Th); urban ministry (M Th).

The University of Tennessee at Chattanooga, Department of Engineering Management, Chattanooga, TN 37403. Offers engineering management (MS); fundamentals of engineering management (Graduate Certificate); leadership and ethics (Graduate Certificate); logistics and supply chain management (Graduate Certificate); nuclear engineering (Graduate Certificate); power system protection (Graduate Certificate); power systems management (Graduate Certificate); project and value management (Graduate Certificate); quality management (Graduate Certificate); sustainable electric energy (Graduate Certificate). Postbaccalaureate distance learning degree programs offered (no on-campus study). *Faculty:* 5 full-time (1 woman). *Students:* 14 full-time (5 women), 67 part-time (14 women); includes 24 minority (13 Black or African American, non-Hispanic/Latino; 6 Asian, non-Hispanic/Latino; 4 Hispanic/Latino; 1 Two or more races, non-Hispanic/Latino), 6 international. Average age 31. 31 applicants, 45% accepted, 10 enrolled. In 2014, 31 master's, 17 other advanced degrees awarded. *Degree requirements:* For master's, thesis. *Entrance requirements:* For master's, GRE General Test, letters of recommendation; minimum undergraduate GPA of 2.5 overall or 3.0 in senior year. Additional exam requirements/recommendations for international students: Required—TOEFL (minimum score 550 paper-based; 79 iBT), IELTS (minimum score 6). *Application deadline:* For fall admission, 6/13 priority date for domestic students, 6/1 for international students; for spring admission, 10/15 priority date for domestic students, 10/1 for international students. Applications are processed on a rolling basis. Application fee: $30 ($35 for international students). Electronic applications accepted. *Expenses:* Tuition, state resident: full-time $7708; part-time $428 per credit hour. Tuition, nonresident: full-time $23,826; part-time $1323 per credit hour. *Required fees:* $1708; $252 per credit hour. *Financial support:* In 2014–15, 5 research assistantships (averaging $6,528 per year), 3 teaching assistantships (averaging $6,781 per year) were awarded; career-related internships or fieldwork, scholarships/grants, and unspecified assistantships also available. Support available to part-time students. Financial award applicants required to submit FAFSA. *Faculty research:* Plant layout design, lean manufacturing, Six Sigma, value management, product development. *Unit head:* Dr. Neslihan Alp, Department Head, 423-425-4032, Fax: 423-425-5229, E-mail: neslihan-alp@utc.edu. *Application contact:* Dr. J. Randy Walker, Interim Dean of Graduate Studies, 423-425-4478, Fax: 423-425-5223, E-mail: randy-walker@utc.edu.
Website: http://www.utc.edu/Departments/engrcs/engm/index.php

Valparaiso University, Graduate School, Programs in Humane Education, Valparaiso, IN 46383. Offers M Ed, MA, MALS, Graduate Certificate. Program offered in collaboration with Institute for Humane Education. Part-time and evening/weekend programs available. *Students:* 4 full-time (all women), 32 part-time (30 women); includes 1 minority (Two or more races, non-Hispanic/Latino), 1 international. Average age 37. In 2014, 5 master's, 4 other advanced degrees awarded. *Degree requirements:* For master's, thesis, project. *Entrance requirements:* For master's, minimum GPA of 3.0, two letters of reference, official transcripts, personal statement, interview. Additional exam requirements/recommendations for international students: Required—TOEFL (minimum score 550 paper-based; 80 iBT), IELTS (minimum score 6). *Application deadline:* Applications are processed on a rolling basis. Application fee: $30 ($50 for international students). Electronic applications accepted. *Expenses: Tuition:* Full-time $10,710; part-time $595 per credit hour. *Required fees:* $378; $101 per term. Tuition and fees vary according to course load and program. *Financial support:* Available to part-time students. Applicants required to submit FAFSA. *Unit head:* Dr. Jennifer A. Ziegler, Dean, Graduate School and Continuing Education, 219-464-5313, Fax: 219-464-5381, E-mail: jennifer.ziegler@valpo.edu. *Application contact:* Jessica Choquette, Graduate Admissions Specialist, 219-464-5313, Fax: 219-464-5381, E-mail: jessica.choquette@valpo.edu.
Website: http://www.valpo.edu/grad/humaneed/

Valparaiso University, Graduate School, Programs in Liberal Studies, Concentration in Ethics and Values, Valparaiso, IN 46383. Offers MALS, Post-Master's Certificate, JD/MALS. Part-time and evening/weekend programs available. *Students:* 1 (woman) full-time, 3 part-time (1 woman), 1 international. Average age 35. In 2014, 2 master's awarded. *Entrance requirements:* For master's, minimum GPA of 3.0. Additional exam requirements/recommendations for international students: Required—TOEFL (minimum score 550 paper-based; 80 iBT), IELTS (minimum score 6). *Application deadline:* Applications are processed on a rolling basis. Application fee: $30 ($50 for international students). Electronic applications accepted. *Expenses: Tuition:* Full-time $10,710; part-time $595 per credit hour. *Required fees:* $378; $101 per term. Tuition and fees vary according to course load and program. *Financial support:* Available to part-time students. Applicants required to submit FAFSA. *Unit head:* Dr. Jennifer A. Ziegler, Dean, Graduate School and Continuing Education, 219-464-5313, Fax: 219-464-5381, E-mail: jennifer.ziegler@valpo.edu. *Application contact:* Jessica Choquette, Graduate Admissions Specialist, 219-464-5313, Fax: 219-464-5381, E-mail: jessica.choquette@valpo.edu.
Website: http://www.valpo.edu/grad/mals/ethics.php

West Chester University of Pennsylvania, College of Arts and Sciences, Department of Philosophy, West Chester, PA 19383. Offers business ethics (Certificate); health care ethics (Certificate); philosophy (MA); philosophy: applied ethics (MA). Part-time and evening/weekend programs available. Postbaccalaureate distance learning degree programs offered (minimal on-campus study). *Faculty:* 7 full-time (2 women), 1 (woman) part-time/adjunct. *Students:* 6 full-time (0 women), 12 part-time (3 women); includes 3 minority (1 Black or African American, non-Hispanic/Latino; 1 American Indian or Alaska Native, non-Hispanic/Latino; 1 Hispanic/Latino). Average age 36. 13 applicants, 92% accepted, 9 enrolled. In 2014, 7 master's, 1 other advanced degree awarded. *Degree requirements:* For master's, at least one comprehensive exam plus either thesis or two additional comprehensive exams. *Entrance requirements:* For master's, GRE or writing sample, three letters of reference; for Certificate, BA transcripts. Additional exam requirements/recommendations for international students: Required—TOEFL (minimum score 550 paper-based; 80 iBT). *Application deadline:* For fall admission, 4/15 priority date for domestic students, 3/15 for international students; for spring admission, 10/15 priority date for domestic students, 9/1 for international students. Applications are processed on a rolling basis. Application fee: $45. Electronic applications accepted. *Expenses:* Tuition, state resident: full-time $8172; part-time $454 per credit. Tuition, nonresident: full-time $12,258; part-time $681 per credit. *Required fees:* $2231; $110.78 per credit. Tuition and fees vary according to campus/location and program. *Financial support:* Unspecified assistantships available. Support available to part-time students. Financial award application deadline: 2/15; financial award applicants required to submit FAFSA. *Faculty research:* Ethics: theory and application, social and political philosophy, feminist philosophy, continental philosophy, Asian philosophy. *Unit head:* Dr. Helen Daley Schroepfer, Chair and Graduate Coordinator, 610-436-2841, E-mail: hschroepfer@wcupa.edu.
Website: http://www.wcupa.edu/_academics/sch_cas.phi/

Xavier University, Williams College of Business, Master of Business Administration Program, Cincinnati, OH 45207. Offers business administration (Exec MBA, MBA); business intelligence (MBA); finance (MBA); health industry (MBA); international business (MBA); marketing (MBA); values-based leadership (MBA); MBA/MHSA; MSN/MBA. *Accreditation:* AACSB. Part-time and evening/weekend programs available. *Faculty:* 30 full-time (11 women), 12 part-time/adjunct (2 women). *Students:* 116 full-time (37 women), 393 part-time (119 women); includes 85 minority (29 Black or African American, non-Hispanic/Latino; 2 American Indian or Alaska Native, non-Hispanic/Latino; 31 Asian, non-Hispanic/Latino; 15 Hispanic/Latino; 8 Two or more races, non-Hispanic/Latino), 27 international. Average age 30. 213 applicants, 85% accepted, 106 enrolled. In 2014, 305 master's awarded. *Degree requirements:* For master's, capstone course. *Entrance requirements:* For master's, GMAT or GRE, official transcript; resume. Additional exam requirements/recommendations for international students: Required—TOEFL (minimum score 550 paper-based; 79 iBT). *Application deadline:* For fall admission, 8/1 priority date for domestic students, 5/1 for international students; for spring admission, 12/1 priority date for domestic students, 9/1 for international students. Applications are processed on a rolling basis. Application fee: $35. Electronic applications accepted. Application fee is waived when completed online. *Expenses:* Expenses: $780 per credit hour (for MBA), $860 (for MBA off-site), $1,225 (for executive MBA). *Financial support:* In 2014–15, 162 students received support. Scholarships/grants, tuition waivers (partial), and unspecified assistantships available. Financial award application deadline: 3/1; financial award applicants required to submit FAFSA. *Unit head:* Jennifer Bush, Assistant Dean of Graduate Programs, Williams College of Business, 513-745-3527, Fax: 513-745-2929, E-mail: bush@xavier.edu. *Application contact:* Lauren Parcell, MBA Advisor, 513-745-1014, Fax: 513-745-2929, E-mail: parcelll@xavier.edu.
Website: http://www.xavier.edu/williams/mba/

Philosophy

Acadia University, Faculty of Arts, Program in Social and Political Thought, Wolfville, NS B4P 2R6, Canada. Offers MA. *Degree requirements:* For master's, thesis. *Entrance requirements:* Additional exam requirements/recommendations for international students: Required—TOEFL (minimum score 580 paper-based; 93 iBT), IELTS (minimum score 6.5).

Arizona State University at the Tempe campus, College of Liberal Arts and Sciences, School of Historical, Philosophical and Religious Studies, Tempe, AZ 85287-4301. Offers European history (MA, PhD); medieval studies (Graduate Certificate); North American history (MA, PhD); philosophy (MA, PhD); public history (MA); religious studies (MA, PhD); Renaissance studies (Graduate Certificate); scholarly publishing (Graduate Certificate). Part-time programs available. Terminal master's awarded for partial completion of doctoral program. *Degree requirements:* For master's, thesis or alternative, interactive Program of Study (iPOS) submitted before completing 50 percent of required credit hours; for doctorate, variable foreign language requirement, comprehensive exam, thesis/dissertation, interactive Program of Study (iPOS) submitted before completing 50 percent of required credit hours. *Entrance requirements:* For master's and doctorate, GRE, minimum GPA of 3.0 or equivalent in last 2 years of work leading to bachelor's degree. Additional exam requirements/recommendations for international students: Required—TOEFL, IELTS, or PTE. Electronic applications accepted.

Baylor University, Graduate School, College of Arts and Sciences, Department of Philosophy, Waco, TX 76798. Offers MA, PhD. Terminal master's awarded for partial

completion of doctoral program. *Degree requirements:* For master's, comprehensive exam; for doctorate, comprehensive exam, thesis/dissertation, language or other research-related skill as needed. *Entrance requirements:* For master's and doctorate, GRE General Test. Additional exam requirements/recommendations for international students: Required—TOEFL. Electronic applications accepted. *Faculty research:* Epistemology, metaphysics, philosophy of religion, moral psychology, Kierkegaard.

Binghamton University, State University of New York, Graduate School, School of Arts and Sciences, Department of Philosophy, Vestal, NY 13850. Offers MA, PhD. *Faculty:* 14 full-time (5 women), 3 part-time/adjunct (1 woman). *Degree requirements:* For master's, 2 foreign languages, comprehensive exam (for some programs), thesis or alternative; for doctorate, one foreign language, thesis/dissertation. *Entrance requirements:* For master's and doctorate, GRE General Test, writing sample. Additional exam requirements/recommendations for international students: Required—TOEFL (minimum score 550 paper-based; 80 iBT). *Application deadline:* Applications are processed on a rolling basis. Application fee: $75. Electronic applications accepted. *Expenses:* Tuition, state resident: full-time $7776; part-time $432 per credit. Tuition, nonresident: full-time $15,138; part-time $841 per credit. *Required fees:* $1754; $213 per credit. Tuition and fees vary according to degree level and program. *Financial support:* Career-related internships or fieldwork, Federal Work-Study, institutionally sponsored loans, scholarships/grants, health care benefits, tuition waivers (full and partial), and unspecified assistantships available. Financial award application deadline: 2/15; financial award applicants required to submit FAFSA. *Unit head:* Dr. Maxim Pensky, Chairperson, 607-777-4163, E-mail: mpensky@binghamton.edu. *Application contact:* Kishan Zuber, Recruiting and Admissions Coordinator, 607-777-2151, Fax: 607-777-2501, E-mail: kzuber@binghamton.edu.
Website: http://www2.binghamton.edu/philosophy/

Binghamton University, State University of New York, Graduate School, School of Arts and Sciences, Philosophy, Interpretation and Culture Program, Vestal, NY 13850. Offers MA, PhD. *Faculty:* 1 part-time/adjunct (0 women). *Students:* 15 part-time (9 women); includes 3 minority (1 Black or African American, non-Hispanic/Latino; 1 Hispanic/Latino; 1 Native Hawaiian or other Pacific Islander, non-Hispanic/Latino), 8 international. Average age 41. In 2014, 6 doctorates awarded. *Degree requirements:* For doctorate, thesis/dissertation. *Entrance requirements:* Additional exam requirements/recommendations for international students: Required—TOEFL (minimum score 550 paper-based; 80 iBT). Application fee: $75. *Expenses:* Tuition, state resident: full-time $7776; part-time $432 per credit. Tuition, nonresident: full-time $15,138; part-time $841 per credit. *Required fees:* $1754; $213 per credit. Tuition and fees vary according to degree level and program. *Financial support:* In 2014–15, 1 student received support. Career-related internships or fieldwork, Federal Work-Study, institutionally sponsored loans, scholarships/grants, health care benefits, and unspecified assistantships available. Financial award application deadline: 2/15; financial award applicants required to submit FAFSA. *Unit head:* Dr. Nkiru Nzegwu, Coordinator, 607-777-3082, E-mail: panap@binghamton.edu. *Application contact:* Kishan Zuber, Recruiting and Admissions Coordinator, 607-777-2151, Fax: 607-777-2501, E-mail: kzuber@binghamton.edu.

Binghamton University, State University of New York, Graduate School, School of Arts and Sciences, Program in Social, Political, Ethical and Legal Philosophy, Vestal, NY 13850. Offers MA, PhD. *Students:* 18 full-time (10 women), 18 part-time (4 women); includes 8 minority (1 Black or African American, non-Hispanic/Latino; 6 Hispanic/Latino; 1 Native Hawaiian or other Pacific Islander, non-Hispanic/Latino), 5 international. Average age 31. 77 applicants, 30% accepted, 6 enrolled. In 2014, 2 master's, 3 doctorates awarded. *Degree requirements:* For master's, comprehensive exam, thesis or alternative; for doctorate, one foreign language, thesis/dissertation. *Entrance requirements:* For master's and doctorate, GRE General Test, writing sample. Additional exam requirements/recommendations for international students: Required—TOEFL (minimum score 550 paper-based; 80 iBT). Application fee: $75. *Expenses:* Tuition, state resident: full-time $7776; part-time $432 per credit. Tuition, nonresident: full-time $15,138; part-time $841 per credit. *Required fees:* $1754; $213 per credit. Tuition and fees vary according to degree level and program. *Financial support:* In 2014–15, 24 students received support, including 23 teaching assistantships with full tuition reimbursements available (averaging $15,000 per year); career-related internships or fieldwork, Federal Work-Study, institutionally sponsored loans, scholarships/grants, health care benefits, tuition waivers (full and partial), and unspecified assistantships also available. Financial award application deadline: 2/15; financial award applicants required to submit FAFSA. *Unit head:* Dr. Maxim Pensky, Chairperson, 607-777-4163, E-mail: mpensky@binghamton.edu. *Application contact:* Kishan Zuber, Recruiting and Admissions Coordinator, 607-777-2151, Fax: 607-777-2501, E-mail: kzuber@binghamton.edu.
Website: http://philosophy.binghamton.edu

Boston College, Graduate School of Arts and Sciences, Department of Philosophy, Chestnut Hill, MA 02467-3800. Offers MA, PhD. *Faculty:* 31 full-time. *Students:* 91 full-time (14 women); includes 12 minority (3 Asian, non-Hispanic/Latino; 5 Hispanic/Latino; 4 Two or more races, non-Hispanic/Latino), 19 international. 167 applicants, 44% accepted, 21 enrolled. In 2014, 22 master's, 7 doctorates awarded. Terminal master's awarded for partial completion of doctoral program. *Degree requirements:* For master's, one foreign language, thesis optional; for doctorate, 2 foreign languages, thesis/dissertation. *Entrance requirements:* For master's and doctorate, GRE General Test. Additional exam requirements/recommendations for international students: Required—TOEFL (minimum score 600 paper-based; 100 iBT). *Application deadline:* For fall admission, 1/2 for domestic and international students. Application fee: $75. *Financial support:* In 2014–15, fellowships with full tuition reimbursements (averaging $20,500 per year), teaching assistantships with full tuition reimbursements (averaging $20,500 per year) were awarded; Federal Work-Study, scholarships/grants, health care benefits, and unspecified assistantships also available. Support available to part-time students. Financial award application deadline: 3/1; financial award applicants required to submit FAFSA. *Faculty research:* History of philosophy, metaphysics, ethics, Continental philosophy, ancient philosophy, philosophy of science, social theory. *Unit head:* Dr. Arthur Madigan, Chairperson, 617-552-3847, E-mail: arhtur.madigan@bc.edu. *Application contact:* Dr. Gary Gurtler, Graduate Program Director, 617-552-3872, E-mail: gary.gurtler@bc.edu.
Website: http://www.bc.edu/philosophy

Boston University, Graduate School of Arts and Sciences, Department of Philosophy, Boston, MA 02215. Offers MA, PhD, JD/MA. *Students:* 44 full-time (13 women), 1 part-time (0 women); includes 5 minority (1 Asian, non-Hispanic/Latino; 3 Hispanic/Latino; 1 Two or more races, non-Hispanic/Latino), 9 international. Average age 29. 230 applicants, 9% accepted, 7 enrolled. In 2014, 13 master's, 3 doctorates awarded. Terminal master's awarded for partial completion of doctoral program. *Degree requirements:* For master's, one foreign language, thesis; for doctorate, one foreign language, comprehensive exam, thesis/dissertation. *Entrance requirements:* For master's and doctorate, GRE General Test, sample of written work, 3 letters of recommendation, scholarly writing sample. Additional exam requirements/recommendations for international students: Required—TOEFL (minimum score 550 paper-based; 84 iBT). *Application deadline:* For fall admission, 1/15 for domestic and international students. Application fee: $80. Electronic applications accepted. *Expenses:* *Tuition:* Full-time $45,686; part-time $1428 per credit hour. *Required fees:* $660; $60 per semester. Tuition and fees vary according to program. *Financial support:* In 2014–15, 38 students received support, including 14 fellowships with full tuition reimbursements available (averaging $20,500 per year), 1 research assistantship with full tuition reimbursement available (averaging $20,500 per year), 18 teaching assistantships with full tuition reimbursements available (averaging $20,500 per year); Federal Work-Study, scholarships/grants, and health care benefits also available. Financial award application deadline: 1/15. *Unit head:* C. Allen Speight, Chairman, 617-353-3067, Fax: 617-353-6805, E-mail: casp8@bu.edu. *Application contact:* Laura Hubbard, Senior Program Coordinator, 617-353-2571, Fax: 617-353-6805, E-mail: casphilo@bu.edu.
Website: http://www.bu.edu/philo/

Bowling Green State University, Graduate College, College of Arts and Sciences, Department of Philosophy, Bowling Green, OH 43403. Offers applied philosophy (PhD); institutional theory and history (PhD); philosophy (MA). Part-time programs available. Terminal master's awarded for partial completion of doctoral program. *Degree requirements:* For master's, thesis or alternative; for doctorate, comprehensive exam, thesis/dissertation, foreign language or research tool. *Entrance requirements:* For master's and doctorate, GRE General Test. Additional exam requirements/recommendations for international students: Required—TOEFL. Electronic applications accepted. *Faculty research:* Moral philosophy and ethics, political and social philosophy, decision theory, applied ethics, public policy.

Brandeis University, Graduate School of Arts and Sciences, Department of Philosophy, Waltham, MA 02454-9110. Offers MA. Part-time programs available. *Faculty:* 9 full-time (2 women). *Students:* 22 full-time (4 women); includes 1 minority (Black or African American, non-Hispanic/Latino), 2 international. 92 applicants, 27% accepted, 10 enrolled. In 2014, 9 master's awarded. *Degree requirements:* For master's, thesis or alternative, proseminar; symbolic logic; paper. *Entrance requirements:* For master's, GRE, official transcript(s), recommendation letters, resume, statement of purpose, writing sample. Additional exam requirements/recommendations for international students: Required—TOEFL (minimum score 600 paper-based; 100 iBT), PTE (minimum score 68); Recommended—IELTS (minimum score 7). *Application deadline:* For fall admission, 2/15 for domestic and international students. Application fee: $75. Electronic applications accepted. *Financial support:* In 2014–15, 24 teaching assistantships with partial tuition reimbursements (averaging $3,200 per year) were awarded; Federal Work-Study, scholarships/grants, and tuition waivers (partial) also available. Support available to part-time students. Financial award application deadline: 4/15; financial award applicants required to submit FAFSA. *Faculty research:* Metaphysics and epistemology, ethics, social and political philosophy, philosophy of language, logic, philosophy of mind and cognitive science, early modern philosophy, aesthetics, the philosophy of law. *Unit head:* Dr. Kate Moran, Director of Graduate Studies, 781-736-2789, Fax: 781-736-8562, E-mail: kmoran@brandeis.edu. *Application contact:* Julie Seeger, Department Administrator, 781-736-2789, Fax: 781-736-8562, E-mail: jseeger@brandeis.edu.
Website: http://www.brandeis.edu/departments/philosophy/

Brock University, Faculty of Graduate Studies, Faculty of Humanities, Program in Philosophy, St. Catharines, ON L2S 3A1, Canada. Offers MA. Part-time programs available. *Degree requirements:* For master's, thesis optional. *Entrance requirements:* For master's, honors BA in philosophy. Additional exam requirements/recommendations for international students: Required—TOEFL (minimum score 550 paper-based; 80 iBT), IELTS (minimum score 6.5), TWE (minimum score 4). Electronic applications accepted. *Faculty research:* Contemporary continental philosophy, Chinese and comparative philosophy, Indian philosophy, ethics.

Brown University, Graduate School, Department of Philosophy, Providence, RI 02912. Offers PhD. *Degree requirements:* For doctorate, variable foreign language requirement, thesis/dissertation. *Entrance requirements:* For doctorate, GRE General Test.

California Institute of Integral Studies, School of Consciousness and Transformation, San Francisco, CA 94103. Offers anthropology and social change (MA, PhD); creative inquiry/interdisciplinary arts (MFA); East-West psychology (MA, PhD); philosophy and religion (MA, PhD), including Asian and comparative studies, ecology, spirituality, and religion, philosophy, cosmology, and consciousness, women's spirituality; transformative leadership (MA); transformative studies (PhD); writing and consciousness (MFA). Part-time and evening/weekend programs available. Postbaccalaureate distance learning degree programs offered (no on-campus study). *Students:* 385 full-time (256 women), 102 part-time (71 women); includes 124 minority (31 Black or African American, non-Hispanic/Latino; 3 American Indian or Alaska Native, non-Hispanic/Latino; 19 Asian, non-Hispanic/Latino; 39 Hispanic/Latino; 1 Native Hawaiian or other Pacific Islander, non-Hispanic/Latino; 31 Two or more races, non-Hispanic/Latino), 53 international. Average age 43. 196 applicants, 92% accepted, 125 enrolled. In 2014, 75 master's, 41 doctorates awarded. Terminal master's awarded for partial completion of doctoral program. *Degree requirements:* For master's, thesis optional; for doctorate, comprehensive exam, thesis/dissertation, 1 foreign language (for Asian comparative studies). *Entrance requirements:* For master's, minimum GPA of 3.0, letters of recommendation, writing sample; for doctorate, master's degree, minimum GPA of 3.0, letters of recommendation, writing sample. Additional exam requirements/recommendations for international students: Required—TOEFL. *Application deadline:* For fall admission, 2/1 priority date for domestic and international students; for spring admission, 10/15 priority date for domestic and international students. Applications are processed on a rolling basis. Application fee: $65. Electronic applications accepted. *Expenses:* *Tuition:* Full-time $18,270; part-time $1015 per credit. *Required fees:* $85 per semester hour. *Financial support:* In 2014–15, 445 students received support, including 5 research assistantships (averaging $800 per year), 28 teaching assistantships (averaging $825 per year); career-related internships or fieldwork, Federal Work-Study, and scholarships/grants also available. Support available to part-time students. Financial award application deadline: 4/15; financial award applicants required to submit FAFSA. *Faculty research:* Ecology and sustainability, philosophy and religion, East-West psychology, integrative health, social and cultural anthropology, transformative leadership. *Application contact:* David Townes, Senior Admissions Counselor, 415-575-6152, Fax: 415-575-1268, E-mail: admissions@ciis.edu.
Website: http://www.ciis.edu/

California State University, Long Beach, Graduate Studies, College of Liberal Arts, Department of Philosophy, Long Beach, CA 90840. Offers MA. Part-time programs available. *Degree requirements:* For master's, comprehensive exam or thesis. Electronic applications accepted. *Faculty research:* Philosophy of science, ethics.

California State University, Los Angeles, Graduate Studies, College of Arts and Letters, Department of Philosophy, Los Angeles, CA 90032-8530. Offers MA. Part-time and evening/weekend programs available. *Degree requirements:* For master's, comprehensive exam. *Entrance requirements:* Additional exam requirements/recommendations for international students: Required—TOEFL (minimum score 500 paper-based). Electronic applications accepted. *Expenses:* Tuition, state resident: full-time $6738; part-time $3609 per year. Tuition, nonresident: full-time $15,666; part-time $8073 per year. Tuition and fees vary according to course load, degree level and program. *Faculty research:* Aesthetics, philosophy of language, ethics, philosophy of science, history of philosophy.

Philosophy

Carleton University, Faculty of Graduate Studies, Faculty of Arts and Social Sciences, Department of Philosophy, Ottawa, ON K1S 5B6, Canada. Offers MA. *Degree requirements:* For master's, thesis optional. *Entrance requirements:* For master's, honors degree. Additional exam requirements/recommendations for international students: Required—TOEFL. *Faculty research:* Application of philosophical theory to issues of current concern, history of philosophy, contemporary philosophy in North America and Europe.

Carnegie Mellon University, Dietrich College of Humanities and Social Sciences, Department of Philosophy, Pittsburgh, PA 15213-3891. Offers logic, computation and methodology (MS, PhD); philosophy (MA, PhD); pure and applied logic (PhD). Part-time programs available. *Degree requirements:* For master's, thesis; for doctorate, comprehensive exam, thesis/dissertation. *Entrance requirements:* For master's and doctorate, GRE General Test. Additional exam requirements/recommendations for international students: Required—TOEFL. Electronic applications accepted. *Faculty research:* Philosophy of science, artificial intelligence.

The Catholic University of America, School of Philosophy, Washington, DC 20064. Offers MA, PhD, Ph L, MA/JD. Part-time programs available. *Faculty:* 23 full-time (5 women), 4 part-time/adjunct (2 women). *Students:* 59 full-time (10 women), 87 part-time (13 women); includes 18 minority (2 Black or African American, non-Hispanic/Latino; 4 Asian, non-Hispanic/Latino; 7 Hispanic/Latino; 5 Two or more races, non-Hispanic/Latino), 7 international. Average age 32. 85 applicants, 67% accepted, 42 enrolled. In 2014, 24 master's, 4 doctorates awarded. *Degree requirements:* For master's, one foreign language, thesis, oral exam; for doctorate, 2 foreign languages, comprehensive exam, thesis/dissertation, oral exam. *Entrance requirements:* For master's, GRE General Test, statement of purpose, official copies of academic transcripts, three letters of recommendation, writing sample; for doctorate, GRE General Test, statement of purpose, official copies of academic transcripts, three letters of recommendation. Additional exam requirements/recommendations for international students: Required—TOEFL (minimum score 580 paper-based). *Application deadline:* For fall admission, 7/15 priority date for domestic students, 7/1 for international students; for spring admission, 11/15 priority date for domestic students, 11/1 for international students. Applications are processed on a rolling basis. Application fee: $55. Electronic applications accepted. *Expenses: Tuition:* Full-time $40,200; part-time $1600 per credit hour. *Required fees:* $400; $195 per semester. One-time fee: $425. *Financial support:* Fellowships, research assistantships, teaching assistantships, Federal Work-Study, scholarships/grants, tuition waivers (full and partial), and unspecified assistantships available. Financial award application deadline: 2/1; financial award applicants required to submit FAFSA. *Faculty research:* Ancient philosophy, modern philosophy, metaphysics, ethics, phenomenology. *Total annual research expenditures:* $14,697. *Unit head:* Dr. John McCarthy, Dean, 202-319-6649, Fax: 202-319-4731, E-mail: mccartjc@cua.edu. *Application contact:* Director of Graduate Admissions, 202-319-5057, Fax: 202-319-6533, E-mail: cua-admissions@cua.edu.
Website: http://philosophy.cua.edu/

Central European University, Graduate Studies, Department of Philosophy, Budapest, Hungary. Offers MA, PhD. *Faculty:* 10 full-time (3 women), 5 part-time/adjunct (2 women). *Students:* 54 full-time (17 women). Average age 29. 230 applicants, 46% accepted, 39 enrolled. In 2014, 15 master's, 4 doctorates awarded. *Degree requirements:* For master's, one foreign language, thesis; for doctorate, one foreign language, comprehensive exam, thesis/dissertation. *Entrance requirements:* For master's and doctorate, interview. Additional exam requirements/recommendations for international students: Required—TOEFL (minimum score 570 paper-based); Recommended—IELTS (minimum score 6.5). *Application deadline:* For fall admission, 1/24 for domestic and international students. Application fee: $40. Electronic applications accepted. *Expenses: Tuition:* Full-time 12,000 euros. *Required fees:* 200 euros. One-time fee: 500 euros full-time. *Financial support:* In 2014–15, 45 students received support, including 45 fellowships (averaging $6,100 per year); tuition waivers (full and partial) also available. *Faculty research:* Questions of metaphysics, both in a contemporary and historical perspective issues about the freedom of the will; ancient metaphysics and philosophy of nature modality in early modern philosophy; the philosophy of mind; perception; political philosophy; cognitive science; ethics and metaethics. *Unit head:* Dr. Hanoch Ben-Yami, Head of Department, 36 1 327-3806, Fax: 361-327-3072, E-mail: philosophy@ceu.hu. *Application contact:* Zsuzsanna Jaszberenyi, Admissions Officer, 361-324-3009, Fax: 367-327-3211, E-mail: admissions@ceu.hu.
Website: http://philosophy.ceu.hu/

Claremont Graduate University, Graduate Programs, School of Arts and Humanities, Department of Philosophy, Claremont, CA 91711-6160. Offers MA, PhD, MA/PhD, MBA/MA, MBA/PhD. Part-time programs available. *Faculty:* 3 full-time (1 woman). *Students:* 31 full-time (8 women), 7 part-time (2 women); includes 9 minority (5 Black or African American, non-Hispanic/Latino; 1 Asian, non-Hispanic/Latino; 3 Hispanic/Latino), 2 international. Average age 36. In 2014, 7 master's awarded. *Degree requirements:* For doctorate, research folio. *Entrance requirements:* For master's and doctorate, GRE General Test. Additional exam requirements/recommendations for international students: Required—TOEFL (minimum score 550 paper-based; 80 iBT). *Application deadline:* For fall admission, 2/1 priority date for domestic and international students. Applications are processed on a rolling basis. Application fee: $80. Electronic applications accepted. *Expenses: Tuition:* Full-time $41,784; part-time $1741 per credit. *Required fees:* $600; $300 per semester. *Financial support:* Fellowships, research assistantships, Federal Work-Study, institutionally sponsored loans, and scholarships/grants available. Support available to part-time students. Financial award application deadline: 2/15; financial award applicants required to submit FAFSA. *Faculty research:* Ancient philosophy, philosophy of science, probability theory, philosophical logic, philosophy of logic. *Unit head:* Masahiro Yamada, Chair, 909-607-0471, E-mail: masahiro.yamada@cgu.edu. *Application contact:* Erma Cross, Program Administrator, 909-607-3217, E-mail: erminia.cross@cgu.edu.
Website: http://www.cgu.edu/pages/370.asp

Cleveland State University, College of Graduate Studies, College of Liberal Arts and Social Sciences, Department of Philosophy and Comparative Religion, Cleveland, OH 44115. Offers bioethics (MA, Certificate), including bioethics (MA); philosophy (MA), including philosophy. Part-time and evening/weekend programs available. *Faculty:* 4 full-time (all women), 2 part-time/adjunct (1 woman). *Students:* 5 full-time (1 woman), 2 part-time (1 woman); includes 1 minority (Hispanic/Latino). Average age 37. 9 applicants, 100% accepted, 5 enrolled. In 2014, 6 master's, 1 other advanced degree awarded. *Degree requirements:* For master's, comprehensive exam, thesis optional, 32 credit hours of coursework; for Certificate, 12 credit hours of coursework. *Entrance requirements:* For master's and Certificate, BA, BS, or equivalent degree with minimum GPA of 2.75. Additional exam requirements/recommendations for international students: Required—TOEFL (minimum score 525 paper-based). *Application deadline:* For fall admission, 5/1 priority date for domestic and international students. Applications are processed on a rolling basis. Application fee: $30. *Expenses:* Tuition, state resident: full-time $9566; part-time $531 per credit hour. Tuition, nonresident: full-time $17,980; part-time $999 per credit hour. *Required fees:* $25 per semester. Tuition and fees vary according to degree level and program. *Financial support:* In 2014–15, 5 students received support, including 5 teaching assistantships with full tuition reimbursements available (averaging $4,000 per year); health care benefits, tuition waivers (full), and unspecified assistantships also available. Support available to part-time students. *Faculty research:* Ethics, early modern philosophy, bioethics, social and political philosophy, history of women philosophers. *Unit head:* Dr. Mary Ellen Waithe, Chairperson, 216-687-3900, Fax: 216-523-7482, E-mail: m.waithe@csuohio.edu. *Application contact:* Deborah L. Brown, Interim Assistant Director, Graduate Admissions, 216-523-7572, Fax: 216-687-5400, E-mail: d.l.brown@csuohio.edu.
Website: http://www.csuohio.edu/class/philosophy-religion/philosophy-religion

Collège Dominicain de Philosophie et de Théologie, Graduate Programs, Faculty of Philosophy, Ottawa, ON K1R 7G3, Canada. Offers MA Ph, PhD. *Degree requirements:* For master's, thesis; for doctorate, 2 foreign languages, thesis/dissertation, candidacy exam. *Entrance requirements:* For master's, honors degree in philosophy, minimum B average in undergraduate course work; for doctorate, master's degree in philosophy, minimum A average in graduate course work. *Faculty research:* Ethics, philosophy of Kant.

Colorado State University, Graduate School, College of Liberal Arts, Department of Philosophy, Fort Collins, CO 80523-1781. Offers MA. Part-time programs available. *Faculty:* 14 full-time (3 women), 1 part-time/adjunct (0 women). *Students:* 12 full-time (4 women), 8 part-time (5 women); includes 2 minority (both Hispanic/Latino). Average age 28. 42 applicants, 33% accepted, 8 enrolled. In 2014, 5 master's awarded. *Degree requirements:* For master's, variable foreign language requirement, comprehensive exam (for some programs), thesis (for some programs). *Entrance requirements:* For master's, GRE General Test, minimum GPA of 3.25, 3 letters of recommendation, writing sample, statement of purpose, transcripts. Additional exam requirements/recommendations for international students: Required—TOEFL. *Application deadline:* For fall admission, 2/15 priority date for domestic and international students; for spring admission, 8/1 priority date for domestic and international students. Applications are processed on a rolling basis. Application fee: $50. Electronic applications accepted. *Expenses:* Tuition, state resident: full-time $9348; part-time $519 per credit. Tuition, nonresident: full-time $22,916; part-time $1273 per credit. *Required fees:* $1584. *Financial support:* In 2014–15, 13 students received support, including 13 teaching assistantships with full tuition reimbursements available (averaging $13,410 per year); career-related internships or fieldwork, Federal Work-Study, institutionally sponsored loans, scholarships/grants, traineeships, and unspecified assistantships also available. Support available to part-time students. Financial award application deadline: 3/1; financial award applicants required to submit FAFSA. *Faculty research:* Animal ethics, environmental ethics, history of philosophy, comparative philosophy, epistemology. *Unit head:* Dr. Jane E. Kneller, Chair, 970-491-7614, Fax: 970-491-4900, E-mail: jane.kneller@colostate.edu. *Application contact:* Gaylene Wolfe, Graduate Contact, 970-491-3351, Fax: 970-491-4900, E-mail: gaylene.wolfe@colostate.edu.
Website: http://philosophy.colostate.edu/

Columbia University, Graduate School of Arts and Sciences, New York, NY 10027. Offers African-American studies (MA); American studies (MA); anthropology (MA, PhD); art history and archaeology (MA, PhD); astronomy (PhD); biological sciences (PhD); biotechnology (MA); chemical physics (PhD); chemistry (PhD); classical studies (MA, PhD); classics (MA, PhD); climate and society (MA); earth and environmental sciences (PhD); East Asia: regional studies (MA); East Asian languages and cultures (MA, PhD); ecology, evolution and environmental biology (MA), including conservation biology; ecology, evolution, and environmental biology (PhD), including ecology and evolutionary biology, evolutionary primatology; economics (PhD); English and comparative literature (MA, PhD); French and Romance philology (MA, PhD); Germanic languages (MA, PhD); global French studies (MA); Hispanic cultural studies (MA); history (PhD); history and literature (MA); human rights studies (MA); Islamic studies (MA); Italian (MA, PhD); Japanese pedagogy (MA); Jewish studies (MA); Latin America and the Caribbean: regional studies (MA); Latin American and Iberian cultures (PhD); mathematics (MA, PhD), including finance (MA); medieval and Renaissance studies (MA); Middle Eastern, South Asian, and African studies (MA, PhD); modern art: critical and curatorial studies (MA); modern European studies (MA); museum anthropology (MA); music (DMA, PhD); oral history (MA); philosophical foundations of physics (MA); philosophy (MA, PhD); physics (PhD); political science (MA, PhD); psychology (PhD); quantitative methods in the social sciences (MA); religion (MA, PhD); Russia, Eurasia and East Europe: regional studies (MA); Russian translation (MA); Slavic cultures (MA); Slavic languages (MA, PhD); sociology (MA, PhD); South Asian studies (MA); statistics (MA, PhD); theatre (PhD); JD/PhD; MA/MS; MD/PhD; MPA/MA. Dual-degree programs require admission to both Graduate School of Arts and Sciences and another Columbia school. Part-time and evening/weekend programs available. Terminal master's awarded for partial completion of doctoral program. *Degree requirements:* For master's, thesis (for some programs); for doctorate, comprehensive exam, thesis/dissertation. *Entrance requirements:* For master's and doctorate, GRE General Test, GRE Subject Test (for some programs). Electronic applications accepted. *Faculty research:* Humanities, natural sciences, social sciences.

Concordia University, School of Graduate Studies, Faculty of Arts and Science, Department of Philosophy, Montréal, QC H3G 1M8, Canada. Offers MA. *Degree requirements:* For master's, comprehensive exam, thesis or alternative. *Entrance requirements:* For master's, honors degree in philosophy or equivalent. *Faculty research:* Anglo-American analytic thought, Continental thought, pragmatic thought.

Cornell University, Graduate School, Graduate Fields of Arts and Sciences, Field of Philosophy, Ithaca, NY 14853-0001. Offers PhD. *Degree requirements:* For doctorate, comprehensive exam, thesis/dissertation, teaching experience. *Entrance requirements:* For doctorate, sample of written work in philosophy, 2 letters of recommendation. Additional exam requirements/recommendations for international students: Required—TOEFL (minimum score 550 paper-based; 77 iBT). Electronic applications accepted.

Dalhousie University, Faculty of Arts and Social Science, Department of Philosophy, Halifax, NS B3H 4R2, Canada. Offers MA, PhD. *Entrance requirements:* For doctorate, MA in philosophy. Additional exam requirements/recommendations for international students: Required—TOEFL, IELTS, CANTEST, CAEL, or Michigan English Language Assessment Battery. Electronic applications accepted. *Faculty research:* Ethical and political philosophy; epistemology; philosophy of language, history, and logic; bioethics; feminist theory.

Dallas Theological Seminary, Graduate Programs, Dallas, TX 75204-6499. Offers adult education (Th M); apologetics (Th M); Bible backgrounds (Th M); Bible translation (Th M); Biblical and theological studies (Certificate); biblical counseling (MA); biblical exegesis and linguistics (MA); biblical exposition (PhD); biblical studies (MA); Biblical theology (Th M); children's education (Th M); Christian education (MA, D Min); Christian leadership (MA); cross-cultural ministries (MA); educational administration (Th M); educational leadership (Th M); evangelism and discipleship (Th M); exposition of Biblical books (Th M); family life education (Th M); general studies (Th M); Hebrew and cognate studies (Th M); hermeneutics (Th M); historical theology (Th M); homiletics (Th M); intercultural ministries (Th M); Jesus studies (Th M); leadership studies (Th M); media and communication (MA); media arts (Th M); ministry (D Min); ministry with women (Th M); New Testament studies (Th M, PhD); Old Testament studies (Th M, PhD); parachurch ministries (Th M); pastoral care and counseling (Th M); pastoral theology

and practice (Th M); philosophy (Th M); sacred theology (STM); spiritual formation (Th M); systematic theology (Th M); teaching in Christian institutions (Th M); theological studies (PhD); urban ministries (Th M); worship studies (Th M); youth education (Th M). *Accreditation:* ATS (one or more programs are accredited). Part-time programs available. Postbaccalaureate distance learning degree programs offered (no on-campus study). *Degree requirements:* For master's, variable foreign language requirement, thesis (for some programs); for doctorate, 2 foreign languages, thesis/dissertation. *Entrance requirements:* For master's, GRE or MAT (if minimum undergraduate cumulative GPA is below 2.5 or undergraduate degree is unaccredited). Additional exam requirements/recommendations for international students: Required—TOEFL (minimum score 575 paper-based; 85 iBT), TWE. Electronic applications accepted.

Delta State University, Graduate Programs, College of Arts and Sciences, Program in Liberal Studies, Cleveland, MS 38733-0001. Offers evolving human voices (MALS); gender and diversity studies (MALS); globalization studies (MALS); Mississippi Delta studies (MALS); philosophy (MALS); religious studies (MALS). *Students:* 12 full-time (9 women), 7 part-time (5 women); includes 4 minority (all Black or African American, non-Hispanic/Latino). Average age 29. 6 applicants, 83% accepted, 4 enrolled. In 2014, 4 master's awarded. *Degree requirements:* For master's, oral and/or written comprehensive exam. *Application deadline:* For fall admission, 8/1 priority date for domestic students; for spring admission, 12/1 priority date for domestic students. Application fee: $30. *Expenses:* Tuition, state resident: full-time $6012; part-time $334 per credit hour. Tuition, nonresident: full-time $6012; part-time $334 per credit hour. Part-time tuition and fees vary according to course load. *Unit head:* Dr. Paul Hankins, Dean, 662-846-4100, Fax: 662-846-4016, E-mail: phankins@deltastate.edu. *Application contact:* Dr. Beverly Moon, Dean of Graduate Studies, 662-846-4875, Fax: 662-846-4313, E-mail: grad-info@deltastate.edu.
Website: http://www.deltastate.edu/pages/4994.asp

Dominican School of Philosophy and Theology, Graduate Programs, Berkeley, CA 94708. Offers philosophy (MA); theology (M Div, MA, MTS, Certificate); M Div/MA; MA/MA. Part-time programs available. *Faculty:* 12 full-time (3 women), 7 part-time/adjunct (0 women). *Students:* 40 full-time (7 women), 38 part-time (6 women); includes 24 minority (2 Black or African American, non-Hispanic/Latino; 1 American Indian or Alaska Native, non-Hispanic/Latino; 12 Asian, non-Hispanic/Latino; 5 Hispanic/Latino; 4 Two or more races, non-Hispanic/Latino), 3 international. *Degree requirements:* For master's, one foreign language, thesis. *Entrance requirements:* For master's, GRE General Test (for MA), minimum GPA of 3.0 (for MA), 2.3 (for M Div); academic writing sample (for MA); statement of purpose, official transcripts, letters of recommendation. Additional exam requirements/recommendations for international students: Required—TOEFL (minimum score 570 paper-based; 80 iBT), IELTS. *Application deadline:* For fall admission, 3/4 priority date for domestic and international students; for spring admission, 11/1 priority date for domestic and international students. Applications are processed on a rolling basis. Application fee: $50. Electronic applications accepted. *Expenses: Tuition:* Full-time $16,680; part-time $695 per unit. *Required fees:* $50; $50 per year. Tuition and fees vary according to course load. *Financial support:* Institutionally sponsored loans, scholarships/grants, and tuition waivers (partial) available. Financial award application deadline: 3/4. *Unit head:* Fr. Christopher Renz, OP, Academic Dean, 510-883-2084, Fax: 510-849-1372, E-mail: crenz@dspt.edu. *Application contact:* Jamie L. Martos, Director of Admissions and Recruitment, 510-883-2073, Fax: 510-849-1372, E-mail: admissions@dspt.edu.

Dominican University of California, School of Arts, Humanities and Social Sciences, Humanities Program, San Rafael, CA 94901-2298. Offers applied music (MA); art history (MA); creative writing (MA); history (MA); literature (MA); philosophy (MA); political theory (MA); religion (MA); women and gender studies (MA). Part-time programs available. *Faculty:* 11 full-time (5 women), 5 part-time/adjunct (2 women). *Students:* 2 full-time (1 woman), 25 part-time (16 women); includes 7 minority (1 Black or African American, non-Hispanic/Latino; 1 American Indian or Alaska Native, non-Hispanic/Latino; 3 Hispanic/Latino; 2 Two or more races, non-Hispanic/Latino). Average age 46. 12 applicants, 83% accepted, 7 enrolled. *Degree requirements:* For master's, thesis or alternative. *Entrance requirements:* For master's, minimum GPA of 3.0, interview. Additional exam requirements/recommendations for international students: Required—TOEFL (minimum score 550 paper-based; 80 iBT), IELTS (minimum score 6.5). *Application deadline:* For fall admission, 5/15 priority date for domestic and international students; for spring admission, 11/15 priority date for domestic and international students. Applications are processed on a rolling basis. Electronic applications accepted. Application fee is waived when completed online. *Expenses:* Expenses: $935 per unit. *Financial support:* Scholarships/grants available. Support available to part-time students. Financial award application deadline: 3/2; financial award applicants required to submit FAFSA. *Unit head:* Dr. Laura Stivers, Acting Dean, 415-458-3734, E-mail: laura.stivers@dominican.edu. *Application contact:* Ryan Purtill, Director, 415-458-3748, Fax: 415-485-3214, E-mail: ryan.purtill@dominican.edu.
Website: http://www.dominican.edu/academics/ahss/graduate-program/index_html

Duke University, Graduate School, Department of Philosophy, Durham, NC 27708. Offers PhD, JD/AM, JD/PhD. *Degree requirements:* For doctorate, one foreign language, thesis/dissertation. *Entrance requirements:* For doctorate, GRE General Test. Additional exam requirements/recommendations for international students: Required—TOEFL (minimum score 577 paper-based; 90 iBT) or IELTS (minimum score 7). Electronic applications accepted. *Expenses: Tuition:* Full-time $45,760; part-time $2765 per credit. *Required fees:* $978. Full-time tuition and fees vary according to program.

Duquesne University, Graduate School of Liberal Arts, Department of Philosophy, Pittsburgh, PA 15282-0001. Offers MA, PhD. Part-time and evening/weekend programs available. *Faculty:* 18 full-time (5 women), 4 part-time/adjunct (2 women). *Students:* 73 full-time (21 women), 3 part-time (0 women); includes 3 minority (1 Black or African American, non-Hispanic/Latino; 2 Hispanic/Latino), 12 international. Average age 31. 138 applicants, 26% accepted, 11 enrolled. In 2014, 9 master's, 9 doctorates awarded. Terminal master's awarded for partial completion of doctoral program. *Degree requirements:* For master's, one foreign language; for doctorate, 2 foreign languages, comprehensive exam, thesis/dissertation. *Entrance requirements:* For master's, GRE General Test, bachelor's degree in philosophy, minimum GPA of 3.5; for doctorate, GRE General Test, master's degree in philosophy, minimum GPA of 3.75. Additional exam requirements/recommendations for international students: Required—TOEFL. *Application deadline:* For fall admission, 2/15 for domestic and international students. Electronic applications accepted. *Expenses: Tuition:* Full-time $18,882; part-time $1049 per credit. *Required fees:* $1800; $100 per credit. Tuition and fees vary according to program. *Financial support:* In 2014–15, 18 teaching assistantships with full tuition reimbursements (averaging $17,000 per year) were awarded; Federal Work-Study, scholarships/grants, tuition waivers (partial), and unspecified assistantships also available. Financial award application deadline: 5/1. *Faculty research:* Phenomenology, twentieth century Continental philosophy, history of philosophy. *Unit head:* Dr. Ronald Polansky, Acting Chair, 412-396-6572, E-mail: polansky@duq.edu. *Application contact:* Linda Rendulic, Assistant to the Dean, 412-396-6400, E-mail: rendulic@duq.edu.
Website: http://www.duq.edu/academics/schools/liberal-arts/graduate-school/programs/philosophy

Eastern Michigan University, Graduate School, College of Arts and Sciences, Department of History and Philosophy, Program in Philosophy, Ypsilanti, MI 48197. Offers MA. Part-time and evening/weekend programs available. Postbaccalaureate distance learning degree programs offered (minimal on-campus study). *Students:* 2 full-time (1 woman), 2 part-time (0 women); includes 1 minority (Two or more races, non-Hispanic/Latino). Average age 25. 4 applicants, 100% accepted, 3 enrolled. *Degree requirements:* For master's, thesis optional. *Entrance requirements:* Additional exam requirements/recommendations for international students: Required—TOEFL. *Application deadline:* Applications are processed on a rolling basis. Application fee: $45. *Financial support:* Fellowships, research assistantships with full tuition reimbursements, teaching assistantships with full tuition reimbursements, career-related internships or fieldwork, Federal Work-Study, institutionally sponsored loans, traineeships, and unspecified assistantships available. Support available to part-time students. Financial award applicants required to submit FAFSA. *Application contact:* Dr. William John Koolage, Coordinator, 734-487-1018, Fax: 734-487-6835, E-mail: wkoolage@emich.edu.

Emory University, Laney Graduate School, Department of Comparative Literature, Atlanta, GA 30322-1100. Offers comparative literature (PhD); philosophy (Certificate); psychoanalytic studies (PhD); women's studies (Certificate). *Degree requirements:* For doctorate, 2 foreign languages, comprehensive exam, thesis/dissertation. *Entrance requirements:* For doctorate, GRE General Test, minimum GPA of 3.0. Additional exam requirements/recommendations for international students: Required—TOEFL. Electronic applications accepted. *Faculty research:* Literary theory, psychoanalysis trauma and testimony, literature and religion, literature and technology, literature and philosophy, politics and global culture, literature and aesthetics.

Emory University, Laney Graduate School, Department of Philosophy, Atlanta, GA 30322-1100. Offers PhD. *Degree requirements:* For doctorate, 2 foreign languages, comprehensive exam, thesis/dissertation. *Entrance requirements:* For doctorate, GRE General Test, minimum GPA of 3.0. Additional exam requirements/recommendations for international students: Required—TOEFL. Electronic applications accepted. *Faculty research:* History of philosophy, German idealism, twentieth century Continental philosophy, ethics, social theory.

Florida State University, The Graduate School, College of Arts and Sciences, Department of Philosophy, Tallahassee, FL 32306-1500. Offers history and philosophy of science (MA); philosophy (MA, PhD). *Faculty:* 15 full-time (3 women), 3 part-time/adjunct (2 women). *Students:* 37 full-time (7 women), 4 part-time (3 women); includes 7 minority (2 Black or African American, non-Hispanic/Latino; 1 Asian, non-Hispanic/Latino; 3 Hispanic/Latino; 1 Two or more races, non-Hispanic/Latino), 2 international. Average age 29. 50 applicants, 24% accepted, 6 enrolled. In 2014, 1 master's, 5 doctorates awarded. Terminal master's awarded for partial completion of doctoral program. *Degree requirements:* For master's, one foreign language, comprehensive exam, thesis or alternative; for doctorate, one foreign language, comprehensive exam, thesis/dissertation. *Entrance requirements:* For master's and doctorate, GRE General Test. Additional exam requirements/recommendations for international students: Required—TOEFL (minimum score 550 paper-based; 80 iBT). *Application deadline:* For fall admission, 3/31 priority date for domestic and international students; for winter admission, 10/19 for domestic and international students; for spring admission, 11/1 priority date for domestic and international students; for summer admission, 3/1 priority date for domestic and international students. Applications are processed on a rolling basis. Application fee: $30. Electronic applications accepted. *Expenses:* Tuition, state resident: part-time $403.51 per credit hour. Tuition, nonresident: part-time $1004.85 per credit hour. *Required fees:* $75.81 per credit hour. One-time fee: $20 part-time. Tuition and fees vary according to campus/location. *Financial support:* In 2014–15, 5 students received support, including 5 fellowships with full and partial tuition reimbursements available (averaging $30,000 per year), 28 teaching assistantships with partial tuition reimbursements available (averaging $16,000 per year); Federal Work-Study, scholarships/grants, and health care benefits also available. Financial award application deadline: 1/3; financial award applicants required to submit FAFSA. *Faculty research:* Philosophy of biology, Greek philosophy, ethics, action theory, philosophy of mind, metaphysics. *Unit head:* Dr. John Piers Rawling, Chairman, 850-644-1483, Fax: 850-644-3832, E-mail: prawling@fsu.edu. *Application contact:* Jeffrey Alexander Hinzmann, Academic Support Assistant, 850-644-1483, Fax: 850-644-3832, E-mail: philosophy@admin.fsu.edu.
Website: http://philosophy.fsu.edu/

Fordham University, Graduate School of Arts and Sciences, Department of Philosophy, New York, NY 10458. Offers philosophical resources (MA); philosophy (MA, PhD). Part-time and evening/weekend programs available. *Faculty:* 31 full-time (10 women). *Students:* 56 full-time (8 women), 15 part-time (1 woman); includes 1 minority (Hispanic/Latino), 1 international. Average age 30. 175 applicants, 13% accepted, 7 enrolled. In 2014, 11 master's, 5 doctorates awarded. Terminal master's awarded for partial completion of doctoral program. *Degree requirements:* For master's, one foreign language, comprehensive exam; for doctorate, 2 foreign languages, comprehensive exam, thesis/dissertation. *Entrance requirements:* For master's and doctorate, GRE General Test. Additional exam requirements/recommendations for international students: Required—TOEFL (minimum score 650 paper-based). *Application deadline:* For fall admission, 1/4 priority date for domestic students; for spring admission, 11/1 for domestic students. Application fee: $70. Electronic applications accepted. *Financial support:* In 2014–15, 45 students received support, including 3 fellowships with full and partial tuition reimbursements available (averaging $26,267 per year), 9 research assistantships with full and partial tuition reimbursements available (averaging $19,617 per year), 30 teaching assistantships with full and partial tuition reimbursements available (averaging $21,341 per year); institutionally sponsored loans, tuition waivers (full and partial), and unspecified assistantships also available. Support available to part-time students. Financial award application deadline: 1/4. *Faculty research:* Contemporary Continental philosophy (including German idealism), philosophy of religion, medieval philosophy, ethics, epistemology. *Unit head:* Dr. Jennifer Gosetti-Ferencei, Director, Graduate Studies, 718-817-2779, Fax: 718-817-3300, E-mail: gosetti@fordham.edu. *Application contact:* Bernadette Valentino-Morrison, Director of Graduate Admissions, 718-817-4419, Fax: 718-817-3566, E-mail: valentinomor@fordham.edu.

Franciscan University of Steubenville, Graduate Programs, Department of Philosophy, Steubenville, OH 43952-1763. Offers MA. Part-time programs available. *Faculty:* 3 part-time/adjunct (0 women). *Students:* 13 full-time (1 woman), 4 part-time (2 women); includes 2 minority (1 Hispanic/Latino; 1 Two or more races, non-Hispanic/Latino), 1 international. Average age 25. 17 applicants, 76% accepted, 7 enrolled. In 2014, 5 master's awarded. *Degree requirements:* For master's, one foreign language, thesis. *Entrance requirements:* For master's, minimum undergraduate GPA of 3.0. Additional exam requirements/recommendations for international students: Required—TOEFL. *Application deadline:* For fall admission, 7/1 for domestic students, 4/30 for international students; for spring admission, 12/15 for domestic students, 9/30 for international students. Applications are processed on a rolling basis. Application fee: $20. Electronic applications accepted. Application fee is waived when completed online. *Expenses: Tuition:* Full-time $12,330; part-time $685 per credit. *Required fees:* $288;

$16 per credit. One-time fee: $170 full-time. Tuition and fees vary according to course load and program. *Financial support:* Federal Work-Study and scholarships/grants available. Support available to part-time students. Financial award application deadline: 7/1; financial award applicants required to submit FAFSA. *Unit head:* Dr. John Crosby, Chairman and Program Director, 740-284-5349. *Application contact:* Mark McGuire, Director of Graduate Enrollment, 800-783-6220, Fax: 740-284-5456, E-mail: mmcguire@franciscan.edu.
Website: http://www.franciscan.edu/graduate-philosophy/

George Mason University, College of Humanities and Social Sciences, Department of Philosophy, Fairfax, VA 22030. Offers ethics and public affairs (MA). *Faculty:* 11 full-time (3 women), 8 part-time/adjunct (1 woman). *Students:* 1 (woman) full-time, 12 part-time (1 woman); includes 2 minority (1 Black or African American, non-Hispanic/Latino; 1 Two or more races, non-Hispanic/Latino). Average age 39. 14 applicants, 57% accepted, 3 enrolled. In 2014, 2 master's awarded. *Degree requirements:* For master's, thesis optional. *Entrance requirements:* For master's, 3 letters of recommendation; official transcript; expanded goals statement; writing sample; resume. Additional exam requirements/recommendations for international students: Required—TOEFL (minimum score 570 paper-based; 80 iBT), IELTS (minimum score 6.5), PTE. *Application deadline:* For fall admission, 3/1 priority date for domestic students; for spring admission, 11/1 priority date for domestic students. Application fee: $65 ($80 for international students). Electronic applications accepted. *Expenses:* Tuition, state resident: full-time $9794; part-time $408 per credit hour. Tuition, nonresident: full-time $26,978; part-time $1124 per credit hour. *Required fees:* $2820; $118 per credit hour. Tuition and fees vary according to course load and program. *Financial support:* In 2014–15, 2 students received support, including 2 teaching assistantships (averaging $7,000 per year); career-related internships or fieldwork, Federal Work-Study, scholarships/grants, unspecified assistantships, and health care benefits (for full-time research or teaching assistantship recipients) also available. Financial award application deadline: 3/1; financial award applicants required to submit FAFSA. *Faculty research:* Cultural studies, political theory philosophy, social and political philosophy, feminist theory, analytical and Continental philosophy, philosophy of science. *Total annual research expenditures:* $6,841. *Unit head:* Ted Kinnaman, Chair/Associate Professor, 703-993-4328, Fax: 703-993-1297, E-mail: tkinnama@gmu.edu. *Application contact:* Rose Cherubin, Graduate Coordinator, 703-993-1332, Fax: 703-993-1297, E-mail: rcherubi@gmu.edu.
Website: http://philosophy.gmu.edu/

Georgetown University, Graduate School of Arts and Sciences, Department of Philosophy, Washington, DC 20057. Offers bioethics (MA); philosophy (PhD); JD/MA; JD/PhD; MD/PhD. *Degree requirements:* For master's, thesis or alternative; for doctorate, 2 foreign languages, comprehensive exam, thesis/dissertation. *Entrance requirements:* For master's and doctorate, GRE General Test. Additional exam requirements/recommendations for international students: Required—TOEFL.

The George Washington University, Columbian College of Arts and Sciences, Department of Philosophy, Washington, DC 20052. Offers philosophy and social policy (MA). *Degree requirements:* For master's, comprehensive exam, thesis or alternative. *Entrance requirements:* For master's, GRE General Test, interview, minimum GPA of 3.0. Additional exam requirements/recommendations for international students: Required—TOEFL (minimum score 600 paper-based; 100 iBT). *Application deadline:* For fall admission, 4/1 priority date for domestic and international students; for spring admission, 10/1 priority date for domestic students, 9/1 priority date for international students. Applications are processed on a rolling basis. Application fee: $60. Electronic applications accepted. *Financial support:* In 2014–15, 2 students received support. Fellowships with tuition reimbursements available, Federal Work-Study, and institutionally sponsored loans available. Financial award application deadline: 1/15. *Unit head:* Dr. William B. Griffith, Academic Director, 202-994-8684, E-mail: wbg@gwu.edu. *Application contact:* Information Contact, 202-994-6265, Fax: 202-994-8683, E-mail: philosop@gwu.edu.
Website: http://departments.columbian.gwu.edu/philosophy

Georgia State University, College of Arts and Sciences, Department of Philosophy, Atlanta, GA 30302-4089. Offers MA, MA/JD. Part-time programs available. *Faculty:* 15 full-time (3 women). *Students:* 51 full-time (12 women), 3 part-time (0 women); includes 8 minority (3 Black or African American, non-Hispanic/Latino; 2 Asian, non-Hispanic/Latino; 3 Hispanic/Latino), 2 international. Average age 28. 160 applicants, 32% accepted, 23 enrolled. In 2014, 19 master's awarded. *Degree requirements:* For master's, thesis (for some programs). *Entrance requirements:* For master's, GRE, writing sample, 3 letters of recommendation. Additional exam requirements/recommendations for international students: Required—TOEFL (minimum score 550 paper-based; 80 iBT). *Application deadline:* For fall admission, 2/1 priority date for domestic and international students. Applications are processed on a rolling basis. Application fee: $50. Electronic applications accepted. *Expenses:* Tuition, state resident: full-time $6516; part-time $362 per credit hour. Tuition, nonresident: full-time $22,014; part-time $1223 per credit hour. *Required fees:* $2128 per semester. Tuition and fees vary according to course load and program. *Financial support:* In 2014–15, fellowships with full tuition reimbursements (averaging $15,000 per year), research assistantships with full tuition reimbursements (averaging $6,000 per year), teaching assistantships with full tuition reimbursements (averaging $10,000 per year) were awarded; health care benefits also available. Financial award application deadline: 8/1. *Faculty research:* Social and political philosophy, neurophilosophy (empirical philosophy of mind), Kant and post-Kantian German philosophy. *Unit head:* Dr. George Rainbolt, Chair, 404-413-6109, Fax: 404-413-6124, E-mail: grainbolt@gsu.edu. *Application contact:* Dr. Tim O'Keefe, Director of Graduate Studies, 404-413-6108, Fax: 404-413-6124, E-mail: tokeefe@gsu.edu.
Website: http://www2.gsu.edu/~wwwphi/

Gonzaga University, College of Arts and Sciences, Program in Philosophy, Spokane, WA 99258. Offers MA. Part-time programs available. *Faculty:* 6 full-time (0 women). *Students:* 12 part-time (5 women); includes 1 minority (Hispanic/Latino). Average age 28. 6 applicants, 100% accepted, 6 enrolled. *Degree requirements:* For master's, comprehensive exam. *Entrance requirements:* For master's, GRE General Test or MAT, minimum GPA of 3.0. Additional exam requirements/recommendations for international students: Required—TOEFL. *Application deadline:* For fall admission, 7/20 priority date for domestic students; for spring admission, 11/1 for domestic students. Applications are processed on a rolling basis. Application fee: $50. Electronic applications accepted. *Expenses: Tuition:* Full-time $18,000; part-time $900 per credit. *Required fees:* $245; $125 per semester. Tuition and fees vary according to course load, degree level and program. *Financial support:* In 2014–15, 8 students received support. Application deadline: 2/1; applicants required to submit FAFSA. *Unit head:* Dr. David Calhoun, Director of Graduate Studies, 509-313-6743, E-mail: calhoun@gem.gonzaga.edu. *Application contact:* Julie McCulloh, Dean of Admission, 509-313-6572, E-mail: mcculloh@gu.gonzaga.edu.

The Graduate Center, City University of New York, Graduate Studies, Program in Philosophy, New York, NY 10016-4039. Offers MA, PhD. Terminal master's awarded for partial completion of doctoral program. *Degree requirements:* For master's, thesis; for doctorate, one foreign language, comprehensive exam, thesis/dissertation. *Entrance requirements:* For master's, GRE General Test; for doctorate, GRE General Test, 3 letters of recommendation, writing sample. Additional exam requirements/recommendations for international students: Required—TOEFL. Electronic applications accepted.

Harrison Middleton University, Graduate Program, Tempe, AZ 85282. Offers education (MA, Ed D); humanities (MA); imaginative literature (MA); interdisciplinary studies (DA); jurisprudence (MA); natural science (MA); philosophy and religion (MA); social science (MA). Part-time and evening/weekend programs available. Postbaccalaureate distance learning degree programs offered (no on-campus study). *Degree requirements:* For master's and doctorate, capstone project. *Entrance requirements:* For master's, interview; for doctorate, 2 academic letters of reference, interview, essay. Additional exam requirements/recommendations for international students: Required—TOEFL (minimum score 550 paper-based; 80 iBT). Electronic applications accepted. *Faculty research:* Japanese animation, educational leadership, war art, John Muir's wilderness.

Harvard University, Graduate School of Arts and Sciences, Department of Philosophy, Cambridge, MA 02138. Offers classical philosophy (PhD); philosophy (PhD). *Degree requirements:* For doctorate, 2 foreign languages, thesis/dissertation, final exams. *Entrance requirements:* For doctorate, GRE General Test. Additional exam requirements/recommendations for international students: Required—TOEFL.

Harvard University, Graduate School of Arts and Sciences, Department of Sanskrit and Indian Studies, Cambridge, MA 02138. Offers Indian philosophy (AM, PhD); Pali (AM, PhD); Sanskrit (AM, PhD); Tibetan (AM, PhD); Urdu (AM, PhD). Terminal master's awarded for partial completion of doctoral program. *Degree requirements:* For master's, 3 foreign languages; for doctorate, 3 foreign languages, thesis/dissertation. *Entrance requirements:* For master's, GRE General Test; for doctorate, GRE General Test, proficiency in French and German. Additional exam requirements/recommendations for international students: Required—TOEFL.

Harvard University, Graduate School of Arts and Sciences, Department of the Classics, Cambridge, MA 02138. Offers Byzantine Greek (PhD); classical archaeology (PhD); classical philology (PhD); classical philosophy (PhD); medieval Latin (PhD). *Degree requirements:* For doctorate, 4 foreign languages, thesis/dissertation, preliminary and special exams. *Entrance requirements:* For doctorate, GRE General Test. Additional exam requirements/recommendations for international students: Required—TOEFL.

Houston Baptist University, School of Christian Thought, Houston, TX 77074-3298. Offers apologetics (MA); Biblical languages (MA); philosophy (MA); theological studies (MA). Part-time and evening/weekend programs available. *Faculty:* 19 full-time (2 women), 1 part-time/adjunct (0 women). *Students:* 21 full-time (9 women), 67 part-time (20 women); includes 42 minority (30 Black or African American, non-Hispanic/Latino; 3 Asian, non-Hispanic/Latino; 8 Hispanic/Latino; 1 Two or more races, non-Hispanic/Latino), 3 international. Average age 39. 94 applicants, 41% accepted, 20 enrolled. In 2014, 8 master's awarded. *Degree requirements:* For master's, comprehensive exam (for some programs), thesis optional. *Entrance requirements:* For master's, minimum GPA of 2.5, two recommendations (one must be pastoral for MABL and MATS), resume, bachelor's degree, transcript. Additional exam requirements/recommendations for international students: Required—TOEFL. *Application deadline:* For fall admission, 8/1 for domestic students, 6/1 for international students; for winter admission, 10/1 for domestic and international students; for spring admission, 12/1 for domestic students, 10/1 for international students; for summer admission, 5/1 for domestic students, 3/1 for international students. Applications are processed on a rolling basis. Application fee: $0. Electronic applications accepted. *Expenses:* Expenses: Contact institution. *Financial support:* Federal Work-Study and scholarships/grants available. Support available to part-time students. Financial award application deadline: 4/1; financial award applicants required to submit FAFSA. *Faculty research:* Apologetics, New Testament, Biblical languages, philosophy, theology. *Unit head:* Dr. Jeffrey Green, Dean, 281-649-3197, Fax: 281-649-3012, E-mail: jgreen@hbu.edu. *Application contact:* Celeste Risteski, Administrative Assistant to the Dean, 281-649-3383, Fax: 281-649-3012, E-mail: cristeski@hbu.edu.
Website: http://www.hbu.edu/sct

Howard University, Graduate School, Department of Philosophy, Washington, DC 20059-0002. Offers MA. Part-time programs available. *Degree requirements:* For master's, one foreign language, comprehensive exam, thesis. *Entrance requirements:* For master's, GRE General Test. Additional exam requirements/recommendations for international students: Required—TOEFL. *Faculty research:* African and African-American philosophy, social and political philosophy, ethics, philosophy of culture, applied philosophy.

Indiana University Bloomington, University Graduate School, College of Arts and Sciences, Department of Philosophy, Bloomington, IN 47405. Offers MA, PhD. *Faculty:* 17 full-time (5 women). *Students:* 36 full-time (9 women); includes 2 minority (1 Hispanic/Latino; 1 Two or more races, non-Hispanic/Latino), 6 international. Average age 31. 96 applicants, 6% accepted, 5 enrolled. In 2014, 1 master's, 4 doctorates awarded. Terminal master's awarded for partial completion of doctoral program. *Degree requirements:* For master's, variable foreign language requirement, thesis optional; for doctorate, comprehensive exam, thesis/dissertation, qualifying paper. *Entrance requirements:* For master's and doctorate, GRE General Test, writing sample. Additional exam requirements/recommendations for international students: Required—TOEFL. *Application deadline:* For fall admission, 12/15 priority date for domestic students, 12/1 for international students; for spring admission, 9/1 priority date for domestic students. Applications are processed on a rolling basis. Application fee: $55 ($65 for international students). Electronic applications accepted. *Financial support:* Fellowships with partial tuition reimbursements and teaching assistantships with partial tuition reimbursements available. Financial award application deadline: 4/15. *Faculty research:* Algebraic logic, cognitive science, history of modern philosophy, ancient and Jewish philosophy, medieval logic and semantics, epistemology, ethics, history, philosophy of mind, philosophy of language. *Unit head:* Gary Ebbs, Chair and Professor, 812-855-1093, Fax: 812-855-3777, E-mail: gebbs@indiana.edu. *Application contact:* Marge Clark, Administrative Secretary, 812-855-7088, Fax: 812-855-3777, E-mail: clarkma@indiana.edu.
Website: http://www.indiana.edu/~phil/

Indiana University–Purdue University Indianapolis, School of Liberal Arts, Department of Philosophy, Indianapolis, IN 46202. Offers American philosophy (Certificate); bioethics (Certificate); philosophy (MA); JD/MA; MD/MA. Part-time programs available. *Faculty:* 13 full-time (2 women), 1 part-time/adjunct (0 women). *Students:* 9 full-time (1 woman), 8 part-time (4 women); includes 1 minority (Two or more races, non-Hispanic/Latino), 1 international. Average age 32. 13 applicants, 85% accepted, 6 enrolled. In 2014, 5 master's, 2 other advanced degrees awarded. *Degree requirements:* For master's, thesis optional. *Entrance requirements:* For master's, GRE. Additional exam requirements/recommendations for international students: Required—TOEFL. *Application deadline:* For fall admission, 3/1 priority date for domestic and international students; for spring admission, 11/15 for domestic and international students. Applications are processed on a rolling basis. Application fee: $55 ($65 for international students). Electronic applications accepted. *Financial support:*

Fellowships, research assistantships with full tuition reimbursements, and teaching assistantships available. Financial award application deadline: 1/15; financial award applicants required to submit FAFSA. *Faculty research:* American philosophy, Peirce bioethics, metaphysics, ethical theory. *Unit head:* Dr. Timothy Lyons, Chair, 317-278-7768, E-mail: tdlyons@iupui.edu. *Application contact:* Dr. Chad Carmichael, Assistant Professor, 317-278-5825, E-mail: crcarmic@iupui.edu.
Website: http://liberalarts.iupui.edu/philosophy/index.php/programs/

Institute for Christian Studies, Graduate Programs, Toronto, ON M5T 1R4, Canada. Offers education (M Phil F, PhD); history of philosophy (M Phil F, PhD); philosophical aesthetics (M Phil F, PhD); philosophy of religion (M Phil F, PhD); political theory (M Phil F, PhD); systematic philosophy (M Phil F, PhD); theology (M Phil F, PhD); worldview studies (MWS). Part-time programs available. Postbaccalaureate distance learning degree programs offered (minimal on-campus study). *Degree requirements:* For master's, one foreign language, thesis; for doctorate, 2 foreign languages, thesis/dissertation. *Entrance requirements:* For master's and doctorate, philosophy background. Additional exam requirements/recommendations for international students: Required—TOEFL (minimum score 600 paper-based). *Faculty research:* Human rights, anthropology of self, medieval discourse, gender and body, post-modern thought; biblical hermeneutics, creational aesthetics, ecumenism, epistemology, political theory and public policy, relational psychotherapy.

Institute for Doctoral Studies in the Visual Arts, PhD Program in Visual Art: Philosophy, Aesthetics, and Art Theory, Portland, ME 04102. Offers aesthetics (PhD); art theory (PhD); philosophy (PhD). Postbaccalaureate distance learning degree programs offered (minimal on-campus study). *Faculty:* 3 full-time, 7 part-time/adjunct. *Students:* 56 full-time. *Degree requirements:* For doctorate, comprehensive exam, thesis/dissertation, dissertation defense. *Entrance requirements:* For doctorate, curriculum vitae, writing sample, portfolio, interview. *Application deadline:* Applications are processed on a rolling basis. Application fee: $56. Electronic applications accepted. Application fee is waived when completed online. *Financial support:* Fellowships and scholarships/grants available. Financial award applicants required to submit FAFSA. *Faculty research:* Visual culture, cultural studies, feminism, contemporary art. *Application contact:* Molly Davis, Co-Director of Admissions, 800-240-7357, E-mail: info@idsva.org.
Website: http://idsva.org

Johns Hopkins University, Zanvyl Krieger School of Arts and Sciences, Department of Philosophy, Baltimore, MD 21218-2699. Offers MA, PhD. *Degree requirements:* For doctorate, thesis/dissertation. *Entrance requirements:* For master's and doctorate, GRE General Test. Additional exam requirements/recommendations for international students: Required—TOEFL. Electronic applications accepted. *Faculty research:* Historical and analytical research on range of philosophical topics.

Kent State University, College of Arts and Sciences, Department of Philosophy, Kent, OH 44242-0001. Offers MA. Part-time programs available. *Faculty:* 9 full-time (3 women). *Students:* 11 full-time (3 women), 4 part-time (1 woman). Average age 26. 30 applicants, 93% accepted, 14 enrolled. In 2014, 7 master's awarded. *Degree requirements:* For master's, thesis or project. *Entrance requirements:* For master's, GRE General Test, minimum GPA of 3.0, transcript, resume, statement of purpose, 3 letters of recommendation. Additional exam requirements/recommendations for international students: Required—TOEFL (minimum score: paper-based 525, iBT 71), Michigan English Language Assessment Battery (minimum score of 75), IELTS (minimum score of 6.0), PTE Academic (minimum score of 48), or completion of ELS level 112 Intensive Program. *Application deadline:* For fall admission, 7/12 for domestic students; for spring admission, 11/29 for domestic students. Application fee: $45 ($70 for international students). Electronic applications accepted. *Expenses:* Tuition, state resident: full-time $8730; part-time $485 per credit hour. Tuition, nonresident: full-time $14,886; part-time $827 per credit hour. Tuition and fees vary according to campus/location and program. *Financial support:* Teaching assistantships with full tuition reimbursements, Federal Work-Study, and unspecified assistantships available. Financial award application deadline: 3/15; financial award applicants required to submit FAFSA. *Unit head:* Dr. Deborah Barnbaum, Professor and Chair, 330-672-4363, E-mail: dbarnbau@kent.edu. *Application contact:* Michael Byron, Associate Professor and Graduate Coordinator, 330-672-2315, E-mail: philo@kent.edu.
Website: http://www.kent.edu/philosophy

Liberty University, College of Arts and Sciences, Lynchburg, VA 24515. Offers English (MA); history (MA); philosophical studies (MA). *Accreditation:* AACN. Part-time programs available. Postbaccalaureate distance learning degree programs offered (minimal on-campus study). *Students:* 60 full-time (28 women), 14 part-time (4 women); includes 4 minority (1 Black or African American, non-Hispanic/Latino; 2 Hispanic/Latino; 1 Two or more races, non-Hispanic/Latino), 4 international. Average age 25. 66 applicants, 52% accepted, 23 enrolled. In 2014, 25 master's awarded. *Degree requirements:* For master's, comprehensive exam (for some programs), thesis (for some programs). *Entrance requirements:* For master's, GRE, minimum undergraduate GPA of 3.0, letters of recommendation, statement of purpose. Additional exam requirements/recommendations for international students: Required—TOEFL (minimum score 600 paper-based; 100 iBT). *Application deadline:* For fall admission, 6/1 for domestic students; for spring admission, 11/1 for domestic students. Applications are processed on a rolling basis. Application fee: $50. Electronic applications accepted. *Financial support:* Teaching assistantships with tuition reimbursements and Federal Work-Study available. *Faculty research:* God concept and adult attachment, building marital strength, image of God and gender, breastfeeding behavior among adolescent mothers, osteoporosis. *Unit head:* Dr. Roger Schultz, Dean, 434-592-4031, Fax: 434-522-0430, E-mail: rschultz@liberty.edu. *Application contact:* Dr. Terry Elam, Director of Graduate Admissions, 434-592-3966, Fax: 434-522-0430, E-mail: gradadmissions@liberty.edu.

Louisiana State University and Agricultural & Mechanical College, Graduate School, College of Humanities and Social Sciences, Department of Philosophy and Religious Studies, Baton Rouge, LA 70803. Offers philosophy (MA). Part-time programs available. *Faculty:* 17 full-time (4 women). *Students:* 7 full-time (1 woman), 1 international. Average age 27. 11 applicants, 91% accepted, 2 enrolled. In 2014, 5 master's awarded. *Degree requirements:* For master's, one foreign language, thesis (for some programs). *Entrance requirements:* For master's, GRE General Test, minimum GPA of 3.0. Additional exam requirements/recommendations for international students: Required—TOEFL (minimum score 550 paper-based; 79 IBT), IELTS (minimum score 6.5), or PTE (minimum score 59). *Application deadline:* For fall admission, 1/1 priority date for domestic students, 5/15 for international students; for spring admission, 10/15 for domestic and international students; for summer admission, 5/15 for domestic and international students. Applications are processed on a rolling basis. Application fee: $50 ($70 for international students). Electronic applications accepted. *Financial support:* In 2014–15, 7 students received support, including 7 teaching assistantships with partial tuition reimbursements available (averaging $9,773 per year); fellowships, research assistantships with partial tuition reimbursements available, Federal Work-Study, institutionally sponsored loans, scholarships/grants, health care benefits, and unspecified assistantships also available. Support available to part-time students. Financial award applicants required to submit FAFSA. *Faculty research:* Analytic philosophy, Continental philosophy, history of philosophy, philosophy and religion, existential value theory. *Total annual research expenditures:* $4,965. *Unit head:* Dr. Delbert Burkett, Chair, 225-578-2220, Fax: 225-578-4897, E-mail: dburket@lsu.edu. *Application contact:* Dr. Greg Schufreider, Professor, 225-578-2275, Fax: 225-578-4897, E-mail: gschufr@lsu.edu.
Website: http://www.artsci.lsu.edu/phil/

Loyola Marymount University, College of Liberal Arts, Department of Philosophy, Program in Philosophy, Los Angeles, CA 90045. Offers MA. *Degree requirements:* For master's, one foreign language, comprehensive exam. *Entrance requirements:* For master's, GRE, writing sample (10-15 pages), 2 letters of recommendation, personal statement (4 pages). Additional exam requirements/recommendations for international students: Required—TOEFL (minimum score 600 paper-based; 100 iBT).

Loyola University Chicago, Graduate School, Department of Philosophy, Chicago, IL 60626. Offers MA, PhD. Part-time and evening/weekend programs available. *Faculty:* 25 full-time (9 women). *Students:* 63 full-time (14 women), 4 part-time (0 women); includes 10 minority (1 Black or African American, non-Hispanic/Latino; 3 Asian, non-Hispanic/Latino; 6 Hispanic/Latino), 6 international. Average age 33. 168 applicants, 25% accepted, 12 enrolled. In 2014, 11 master's, 2 doctorates awarded. Terminal master's awarded for partial completion of doctoral program. *Degree requirements:* For master's, comprehensive exam (for some programs), thesis (for some programs), oral exam; for doctorate, one foreign language, thesis/dissertation, oral exam. *Entrance requirements:* For master's and doctorate, GRE General Test. Additional exam requirements/recommendations for international students: Required—TOEFL. *Application deadline:* For fall admission, 1/15 priority date for domestic and international students. Application fee: $50. Electronic applications accepted. Application fee is waived when completed online. *Expenses:* Tuition: Full-time $17,370; part-time $965 per credit. *Required fees:* $138 per semester. *Financial support:* In 2014–15, 23 students received support, including 4 fellowships with full tuition reimbursements available (averaging $16,000 per year), 19 teaching assistantships with full tuition reimbursements available (averaging $18,000 per year); institutionally sponsored loans, health care benefits, unspecified assistantships, and McNair Scholar Merit Funding also available. Financial award application deadline: 1/15; financial award applicants required to submit FAFSA. *Faculty research:* Social philosophy, ethics, bioethics, analytic philosophy, contemporary continental philosophy. *Unit head:* Dr. Mark Waymack, Chair, 773-508-2738, Fax: 773-508-2292, E-mail: mwaymac@luc.edu. *Application contact:* Dr. Victoria Wike, Graduate Program Director, 773-508-2735, Fax: 773-508-2292, E-mail: vwike@luc.edu.
Website: http://www.luc.edu/philosophy/

Marquette University, Graduate School, College of Arts and Sciences, Department of Philosophy, Milwaukee, WI 53201-1881. Offers ancient philosophy (PhD); British empiricism and analytic philosophy (PhD); Christian philosophy (PhD); early modern European philosophy (PhD); ethics (PhD); German philosophy (PhD); history of philosophy (MA); medieval philosophy (PhD); phenomenology and existentialism (PhD); philosophy of religion (PhD); social and applied philosophy (MA); JD/MA. Part-time programs available. Terminal master's awarded for partial completion of doctoral program. *Degree requirements:* For master's, variable foreign language requirement, comprehensive exam, thesis or alternative; for doctorate, 2 foreign languages, thesis/dissertation, written and oral qualifying exams. *Entrance requirements:* For master's and doctorate, GRE General Test, official transcripts from all current and previous colleges/universities except Marquette, statement of purpose, at least three letters of recommendation, sample of philosophical writing. Additional exam requirements/recommendations for international students: Required—TOEFL (minimum score 530 paper-based). Electronic applications accepted. *Faculty research:* Aristotle, Augustine, Descartes, Hegel, Heidegger.

Massachusetts Institute of Technology, School of Humanities, Arts, and Social Sciences, Department of Linguistics and Philosophy, Philosophy Section, Cambridge, MA 02139-4307. Offers PhD. *Faculty:* 11 full-time (1 woman), 1 part-time/adjunct (0 women). *Students:* 29 full-time (8 women), 2 part-time (1 woman); includes 7 minority (1 Black or African American, non-Hispanic/Latino; 5 Hispanic/Latino; 1 Two or more races, non-Hispanic/Latino), 8 international. Average age 27. 249 applicants, 4% accepted, 5 enrolled. In 2014, 4 doctorates awarded. *Degree requirements:* For doctorate, comprehensive exam, thesis/dissertation, teaching requirement. *Entrance requirements:* For doctorate, GRE General Test. Additional exam requirements/recommendations for international students: Required—TOEFL (minimum score 577 paper-based; 90 iBT), IELTS (minimum score 6.5). *Application deadline:* For fall admission, 1/2 for domestic and international students. Application fee: $75. Electronic applications accepted. *Expenses: Tuition:* Full-time $44,720; part-time $699 per unit. *Required fees:* $296. *Financial support:* In 2014–15, 7 fellowships (averaging $36,400 per year), 10 research assistantships (averaging $37,700 per year), 12 teaching assistantships (averaging $38,000 per year) were awarded. Financial award application deadline: 4/15; financial award applicants required to submit FAFSA. *Faculty research:* Metaphysics, philosophy of mind, philosophy of language, ethics, feminist philosophy. *Unit head:* Alex Byrne, Philosophy Chair, 617-253-4141, Fax: 617-253-5017. *Application contact:* Graduate Admissions, 617-253-4141, Fax: 617-253-5017, E-mail: lp-admissions@mit.edu.
Website: http://web.mit.edu/philos/www/

McGill University, Faculty of Graduate and Postdoctoral Studies, Faculty of Arts, Department of Philosophy, Montréal, QC H3A 2T5, Canada. Offers bioethics (MA); philosophy (PhD).

McMaster University, School of Graduate Studies, Faculty of Humanities, Department of Philosophy, Hamilton, ON L8S 4M2, Canada. Offers MA, PhD. Part-time programs available. *Degree requirements:* For master's, thesis; for doctorate, one foreign language, thesis/dissertation. *Entrance requirements:* For master's, honors degree in philosophy; minimum average B+; for doctorate, master's degree in philosophy. Additional exam requirements/recommendations for international students: Required—TOEFL (minimum score 580 paper-based). *Faculty research:* Twentieth-century European philosophy, twentieth-century Anglo-American philosophy, political philosophy, ethics, argumentation.

Memorial University of Newfoundland, School of Graduate Studies, Department of Philosophy, St. John's, NL A1C 5S7, Canada. Offers MA. Part-time programs available. *Degree requirements:* For master's, thesis. *Entrance requirements:* For master's, first-class undergraduate degree in philosophy. Electronic applications accepted. *Faculty research:* History of philosophy, philosophy of science, phenomenology and existentialism, contemporary metaphysics.

Miami University, College of Arts and Science, Department of Philosophy, Oxford, OH 45056. Offers MA. *Students:* 9. In 2014, 8 master's awarded. *Entrance requirements:* For master's, GRE, strong academic background and at least some demonstrated ability in philosophy, statement of purpose, 10-15 page writing sample, three letters of recommendation. Additional exam requirements/recommendations for international students: Recommended—TOEFL (minimum score 80 iBT), IELTS (minimum score 6.5), TSE (minimum score 54). *Application deadline:* For fall admission, 2/1 for domestic and international students. Application fee: $50. Electronic applications accepted. *Expenses:* Tuition, state resident: full-time $12,887; part-time $537 per credit hour. Tuition, nonresident: full-time $28,449; part-time $1186 per credit hour. *Required fees:*

$530; $24 per credit hour. $30 per quarter. Part-time tuition and fees vary according to course load and program. *Financial support:* Fellowships with full and partial tuition reimbursements, research assistantships with full and partial tuition reimbursements, and teaching assistantships with full and partial tuition reimbursements available. Financial award application deadline: 2/1; financial award applicants required to submit FAFSA. *Unit head:* Dr. Emily Zakin, Chair, 513-529-2428, E-mail: zakinea@miamioh.edu. *Application contact:* Dr. Pascal Massie, Associate Professor and Director of the Graduate Program, 513-529-2458, E-mail: massiep@miamioh.edu.
Website: http://www.MiamiOH.edu/philosophy/

Michigan State University, The Graduate School, College of Arts and Letters, Department of Philosophy, East Lansing, MI 48824. Offers MA, PhD. *Entrance requirements:* Additional exam requirements/recommendations for international students: Required—TOEFL. Electronic applications accepted.

Midwestern State University, Billie Doris McAda Graduate School, Prothro-Yeager College of Humanities and Social Sciences, Department of English, Humanities, and Philosophy, Wichita Falls, TX 76308. Offers English (MA); philosophy (PhD). Part-time and evening/weekend programs available. *Degree requirements:* For master's, one foreign language, thesis optional. *Entrance requirements:* For master's, GRE General Test, MAT or GMAT. Additional exam requirements/recommendations for international students: Required—TOEFL (minimum score 550 paper-based). *Application deadline:* For fall admission, 7/1 priority date for domestic students, 4/1 for international students; for spring admission, 11/1 priority date for domestic students, 8/1 for international students. Applications are processed on a rolling basis. Application fee: $35 ($50 for international students). Electronic applications accepted. *Financial support:* Teaching assistantships with partial tuition reimbursements, career-related internships or fieldwork, Federal Work-Study, institutionally sponsored loans, scholarships/grants, tuition waivers (partial), and unspecified assistantships available. Support available to part-time students. Financial award application deadline: 3/1; financial award applicants required to submit FAFSA. *Faculty research:* Mythology, Shakespeare, Oscar Hahn, origins of language, modern American literature. *Unit head:* Pam Marshall, Secretary, 940-397-4300, Fax: 940-397-4931, E-mail: pam.marshall@mwsu.edu.
Website: http://www.mwsu.edu/academics/libarts/english-humanities-philosophy/

Mount St. Mary's University, Program in Philosophical Studies, Emmitsburg, MD 21727-7799. Offers MA. Part-time programs available. *Faculty:* 6 full-time (2 women). In 2014, 6 master's awarded. *Degree requirements:* For master's, one foreign language, thesis. *Entrance requirements:* For master's, undergraduate degree, minimum cumulative undergraduate GPA of 3.0. Additional exam requirements/recommendations for international students: Required—TOEFL (minimum score 550 paper-based). *Expenses: Tuition:* Full-time $10,242; part-time $569 per credit hour. Tuition and fees vary according to program. *Financial support:* Unspecified assistantships available. Financial award applicants required to submit FAFSA. *Unit head:* Dr. Christopher Anadale, Director, 301-447-5368 Ext. 4307, E-mail: anadale@msmary.edu. *Application contact:* Joseph Lebherz, Director, Center for Professional and Continuing Studies, 301-682-8315, Fax: 301-682-5247, E-mail: lebherz@msmary.edu.
Website: http://www.msmary.edu/College_of_liberal_arts/philosophy/department-of-philosophy/masters-MAPS.html

The New School, The New School for Social Research, Department of Philosophy, New York, NY 10003. Offers MA, DS Sc, PhD. Part-time and evening/weekend programs available. Terminal master's awarded for partial completion of doctoral program. *Degree requirements:* For master's, one foreign language, exam or thesis; for doctorate, 2 foreign languages, comprehensive exam, thesis/dissertation, qualifying exam. *Entrance requirements:* For master's, GRE General Test; for doctorate, GRE General Test, MA. Additional exam requirements/recommendations for international students: Required—TOEFL (minimum score 600 paper-based; 100 iBT). Electronic applications accepted. *Faculty research:* Continental philosophy, history of philosophy, political philosophy, aesthetics, pragmatism.

New York University, Graduate School of Arts and Science, Department of Philosophy, New York, NY 10012-1019. Offers MA, PhD, JD/MA, JD/PhD, MD/MA. Part-time programs available. *Faculty:* 16 full-time (1 woman). *Students:* 46 full-time (14 women), 2 part-time (1 woman); includes 6 minority (5 Asian, non-Hispanic/Latino; 1 Hispanic/Latino), 15 international. Average age 28. 320 applicants, 6% accepted, 11 enrolled. In 2014, 3 master's, 16 doctorates awarded. *Degree requirements:* For master's, thesis or alternative; for doctorate, one foreign language, thesis/dissertation. *Entrance requirements:* For master's and doctorate, GRE General Test, sample of written work. Additional exam requirements/recommendations for international students: Required—TOEFL. *Application deadline:* For fall admission, 1/4 for domestic and international students. Application fee: $100. *Financial support:* Fellowships with tuition reimbursements, teaching assistantships with tuition reimbursements, Federal Work-Study, institutionally sponsored loans, scholarships/grants, health care benefits, and unspecified assistantships available. Financial award application deadline: 1/4; financial award applicants required to submit FAFSA. *Faculty research:* Philosophy of mind and language, metaphysics, ethics and political philosophy. *Unit head:* Don Garrett, Chair, 212-998-8320, Fax: 212-995-4179, E-mail: philosophy.admissions@nyu.edu. *Application contact:* David Chalmers, Director of Admissions, 212-998-8320, Fax: 212-995-4179, E-mail: philosophy.admissions@nyu.edu.
Website: http://www.nyu.edu/gsas/dept/philo/

Northern Illinois University, Graduate School, College of Liberal Arts and Sciences, Department of Philosophy, De Kalb, IL 60115-2854. Offers MA. Part-time programs available. *Faculty:* 12 full-time (2 women), 1 part-time/adjunct (0 women). *Students:* 24 full-time (6 women), 4 part-time (1 woman); includes 7 minority (1 Black or African American, non-Hispanic/Latino; 1 Hispanic/Latino; 5 Two or more races, non-Hispanic/Latino), 1 international. Average age 25. 132 applicants, 40% accepted, 15 enrolled. In 2014, 10 master's awarded. *Degree requirements:* For master's, comprehensive exam, thesis optional. *Entrance requirements:* For master's, GRE General Test, minimum GPA of 2.75, writing sample, major or minor in philosophy. Additional exam requirements/recommendations for international students: Required—TOEFL (minimum score 550 paper-based). *Application deadline:* For fall admission, 3/1 priority date for domestic students, 5/1 for international students; for spring admission, 11/1 for domestic students, 10/1 for international students. Applications are processed on a rolling basis. Application fee: $40. Electronic applications accepted. *Financial support:* In 2014–15, 14 teaching assistantships with full tuition reimbursements were awarded; fellowships with full tuition reimbursements, research assistantships with full tuition reimbursements, Federal Work-Study, scholarships/grants, tuition waivers (full), and unspecified assistantships also available. Support available to part-time students. Financial award applicants required to submit FAFSA. *Faculty research:* Epistemology, philosophy of biology, animal rights, philosophy of war, international ethics. *Unit head:* Dr. David J. Buller, Chair, 815-753-6299, Fax: 815-753-6302, E-mail: buller@niu.edu. *Application contact:* Dr. Geoffrey Pynn, Graduate Advisor, 815-753-6414, E-mail: askphilosophy@niu.edu.
Website: http://www.niu.edu/phil/

Northwestern University, The Graduate School, Judd A. and Marjorie Weinberg College of Arts and Sciences, Department of Philosophy, Evanston, IL 60208. Offers ancient philosophy (PhD); philosophy (PhD). Admissions and degrees offered through The Graduate School. *Degree requirements:* For doctorate, 2 foreign languages, thesis/dissertation. *Entrance requirements:* For doctorate, GRE General Test, sample of written work. Additional exam requirements/recommendations for international students: Required—TOEFL. Electronic applications accepted. *Faculty research:* Phenomenology, philosophy of science, history of philosophy, ethics, social and political philosophy, epistemology.

The Ohio State University, Graduate School, College of Arts and Sciences, Division of Arts and Humanities, Department of Philosophy, Columbus, OH 43210. Offers MA, PhD. *Faculty:* 17. *Students:* 35 full-time (9 women); includes 5 minority (1 Asian, non-Hispanic/Latino; 3 Hispanic/Latino; 1 Two or more races, non-Hispanic/Latino), 8 international. Average age 28. In 2014, 4 master's, 4 doctorates awarded. Terminal master's awarded for partial completion of doctoral program. *Degree requirements:* For master's, thesis optional; for doctorate, thesis/dissertation. *Entrance requirements:* For doctorate, GRE General Test, writing sample. Additional exam requirements/recommendations for international students: Required—TOEFL (minimum score 600 paper-based; 100 iBT); Recommended—IELTS (minimum score 8). *Application deadline:* For fall admission, 12/15 priority date for domestic students, 12/1 priority date for international students; for winter admission, 12/1 for domestic students, 11/1 for international students; for spring admission, 3/1 for domestic students, 2/1 for international students. Applications are processed on a rolling basis. Application fee: $60 ($70 for international students). Electronic applications accepted. *Financial support:* Fellowships with tuition reimbursements, research assistantships with tuition reimbursements, teaching assistantships with tuition reimbursements, Federal Work-Study, institutionally sponsored loans, and unspecified assistantships available. Support available to part-time students. *Unit head:* Dr. Justin D'Arms, Chair and Professor, 614-292-7914, E-mail: philosophy@osu.edu. *Application contact:* Graduate and Professional Admissions, 614-292-9444, Fax: 614-292-3895, E-mail: gpadmissions@osu.edu.
Website: http://philosophy.osu.edu/

Ohio University, Graduate College, College of Arts and Sciences, Department of Philosophy, Athens, OH 45701-2979. Offers MA. Part-time programs available. *Degree requirements:* For master's, thesis. *Entrance requirements:* For master's, 28 hours in philosophy including logic, ancient and modern philosophy; minimum GPA of 3.0; sample of philosophical writing. Additional exam requirements/recommendations for international students: Required—TOEFL (minimum score 550 paper-based; 80 iBT) or IELTS (minimum score 6.5). Electronic applications accepted. *Faculty research:* Ethics, phenomenology, applied ethics, Aristotle, Kant, epistemology.

Oklahoma State University, College of Arts and Sciences, Department of Philosophy, Stillwater, OK 74078. Offers MA. *Faculty:* 19 full-time (4 women), 1 part-time/adjunct (0 women). *Students:* 5 full-time (1 woman), 2 part-time (both women). Average age 28. 10 applicants, 70% accepted, 2 enrolled. In 2014, 5 master's awarded. *Degree requirements:* For master's, comprehensive exam, thesis. *Entrance requirements:* For master's, GRE, 2 letters of recommendation. Additional exam requirements/recommendations for international students: Required—TOEFL (minimum score 550 paper-based; 79 iBT). *Application deadline:* For fall admission, 3/1 priority date for international students; for spring admission, 8/1 priority date for international students. Applications are processed on a rolling basis. Application fee: $40 ($75 for international students). Electronic applications accepted. *Expenses:* Tuition, state resident: full-time $4488; part-time $187 per credit hour. Tuition, nonresident: full-time $18,360; part-time $765 per credit hour. *Required fees:* $2413; $100.55 per credit hour. Tuition and fees vary according to campus/location. *Financial support:* In 2014–15, 7 teaching assistantships (averaging $17,082 per year) were awarded; career-related internships or fieldwork, Federal Work-Study, scholarships/grants, health care benefits, tuition waivers (partial), and unspecified assistantships also available. Support available to part-time students. Financial award application deadline: 3/1; financial award applicants required to submit FAFSA. *Faculty research:* Theoretical and applied ethics, history and philosophy of science, east/west comparative philosophy, social/political/legal philosophy, truth and theory of knowledge. *Unit head:* Dr. Scott Gelfand, Department Head, 405-744-9238, Fax: 405-744-4635, E-mail: scott.gelfand@okstate.edu. *Application contact:* Dr. Eric Reitan, Professor and Graduate Advisor, 405-744-7753, E-mail: eric.reitan@okstate.edu.
Website: http://philosophy.okstate.edu

Penn State University Park, Graduate School, College of the Liberal Arts, Department of Philosophy, University Park, PA 16802. Offers MA, PhD. *Unit head:* Dr. Susan Welch, Dean, 814-865-7691, Fax: 814-863-2085, E-mail: swelch@psu.edu. *Application contact:* Lori A. Stania, Director, Graduate Student Services, 814-867-5278, Fax: 814-863-4627, E-mail: gswww@psu.edu.
Website: http://philosophy.la.psu.edu/

Princeton University, Graduate School, Department of Classics, Princeton, NJ 08544-1019. Offers classical and hellenic studies (PhD); classical philosophy (PhD); history (the ancient world) (PhD); literature and philology (PhD). *Degree requirements:* For doctorate, thesis/dissertation. *Entrance requirements:* For doctorate, GRE General Test, sample of written work. Additional exam requirements/recommendations for international students: Required—TOEFL (minimum score 600 paper-based). Electronic applications accepted.

Princeton University, Graduate School, Department of Philosophy, Princeton, NJ 08544-1019. Offers classical philosophy (PhD); philosophy (PhD); philosophy of science (PhD). *Degree requirements:* For doctorate, variable foreign language requirement, thesis/dissertation. *Entrance requirements:* For doctorate, GRE General Test, sample of written work. Additional exam requirements/recommendations for international students: Required—TOEFL (minimum score 600 paper-based). Electronic applications accepted.

Princeton University, Graduate School, Department of Politics, Princeton, NJ 08544-1019. Offers political philosophy (PhD); politics (PhD). *Degree requirements:* For doctorate, comprehensive exam, thesis/dissertation, teaching experience. *Entrance requirements:* For doctorate, GRE General Test, sample of written work, letters of recommendation. Additional exam requirements/recommendations for international students: Required—TOEFL (minimum score 600 paper-based). Electronic applications accepted. *Faculty research:* American politics, comparative politics, formal and quantitative methods, international relations, public law, political theory.

Purdue University, Graduate School, College of Liberal Arts, Department of Philosophy, West Lafayette, IN 47907. Offers MA, PhD. Part-time programs available. Terminal master's awarded for partial completion of doctoral program. *Degree requirements:* For master's, thesis optional; for doctorate, comprehensive exam, thesis/dissertation. *Entrance requirements:* For master's and doctorate, GRE General Test, minimum undergraduate GPA of 3.4 or equivalent. Additional exam requirements/recommendations for international students: Required—TOEFL (minimum score 550 paper-based; 100 iBT). Electronic applications accepted. *Faculty research:* Continental philosophy, ethics and social philosophy, analytic philosophy, history of philosophy, logic.

Purdue University, Graduate School, Program in Philosophy and Literature, West Lafayette, IN 47907. Offers PhD. Program offered jointly with Department of English, School of Languages and Cultures, and Department of Philosophy. *Degree requirements:* For doctorate, one foreign language, comprehensive exam, thesis/dissertation. *Entrance requirements:* For doctorate, GRE, master's degree in either

English, philosophy or foreign languages. Additional exam requirements/recommendations for international students: Required—TOEFL. Electronic applications accepted.

Queen's University at Kingston, School of Graduate Studies, Faculty of Arts and Sciences, Department of Philosophy, Kingston, ON K7L 3N6, Canada. Offers MA, PhD. Part-time programs available. *Degree requirements:* For master's, thesis; for doctorate, comprehensive exam, thesis/dissertation. *Entrance requirements:* Additional exam requirements/recommendations for international students: Required—TOEFL. Electronic applications accepted. *Faculty research:* Ethics, social and political philosophy, philosophy of language, epistemology, metaphysics.

Regis College, Graduate and Professional Programs, Toronto, ON M5S 2Z5, Canada. Offers eastern Christian studies (Certificate); Ignatian spirituality (Diploma); ministry (D Min); ministry and spirituality (MAMS); philosophical studies (Diploma); retreat direction (Certificate); sacred theology (STM, STD, STB, STL); spiritual direction (Diploma); theological studies (MTS, Diploma); theology (M Div, MA, Th M, PhD, Th D); M Div/MA. *Accreditation:* ATS (one or more programs are accredited). Terminal master's awarded for partial completion of doctoral program. *Degree requirements:* For master's, 2 foreign languages, thesis; for doctorate, 3 foreign languages, comprehensive exam, thesis/dissertation. *Entrance requirements:* For doctorate, minimum GPA of 3.7. Additional exam requirements/recommendations for international students: Required—TOEFL (minimum score 580 paper-based; 93 iBT), TWE (minimum score 5).

Rice University, Graduate Programs, School of Humanities, Department of Philosophy, Houston, TX 77251-1892. Offers MA, PhD. Terminal master's awarded for partial completion of doctoral program. *Degree requirements:* For master's, one foreign language; for doctorate, one foreign language, comprehensive exam, thesis/dissertation. *Entrance requirements:* For master's and doctorate, GRE General Test, minimum GPA of 3.0. Additional exam requirements/recommendations for international students: Required—TOEFL (minimum score 600 paper-based; 90 iBT). Electronic applications accepted. *Faculty research:* Metaphysics, philosophy of law, philosophy of science, medical ethics, philosophy of language.

Rutgers, The State University of New Jersey, New Brunswick, Graduate School-New Brunswick, Program in Philosophy, Piscataway, NJ 08854-8097. Offers PhD. *Degree requirements:* For doctorate, comprehensive exam, thesis/dissertation. *Entrance requirements:* For doctorate, GRE General Test, writing sample. Electronic applications accepted. *Faculty research:* Philosophy of mind, epistemology, philosophy of language, philosophy of science, metaphysics.

Saint Louis University, Graduate Education, College of Arts and Sciences and Graduate Education, Department of Philosophy, St. Louis, MO 63103-2097. Offers MA, MA-R, PhD. Part-time programs available. *Degree requirements:* For master's, one foreign language, thesis, comprehensive oral and written exams; for doctorate, 2 foreign languages, thesis/dissertation, preliminary exams, comprehensive oral and written exams. *Entrance requirements:* For master's, GRE General Test, letters of recommendation, resume, writing sample, interview; for doctorate, GRE General Test, letters of recommendation, resumé, writing sample, interview, goal statement, transcripts. Additional exam requirements/recommendations for international students: Required—TOEFL (minimum score 550 paper-based). Electronic applications accepted. *Faculty research:* Medieval philosophy, philosophy of religion, political philosophy, ethics, epistemology.

Saint Mary's University, Faculty of Arts, Department of Philosophy, Halifax, NS B3H 3C3, Canada. Offers MA. *Degree requirements:* For master's, thesis. *Entrance requirements:* For master's, 3 letters of recommendation, 2 samples of written work. Additional exam requirements/recommendations for international students: Required—TOEFL. *Faculty research:* History of philosophy, analytic philosophy, ethics, social philosophy, logic.

San Diego State University, Graduate and Research Affairs, College of Arts and Letters, Department of Philosophy, San Diego, CA 92182. Offers MA. Part-time programs available. *Entrance requirements:* For master's, GRE General Test. Additional exam requirements/recommendations for international students: Required—TOEFL. Electronic applications accepted. *Faculty research:* Ancient philosophy, modern philosophy, philosophy of technology, logic, philosophy of mind.

San Francisco State University, Division of Graduate Studies, College of Liberal and Creative Arts, Department of Philosophy, San Francisco, CA 94132-1722. Offers MA. Part-time programs available. *Application deadline:* Applications are processed on a rolling basis. *Expenses:* Tuition, state resident: full-time $6738. Tuition, nonresident: full-time $17,898; part-time $372 per credit hour. *Required fees:* $498 per semester. *Unit head:* Dr. Justin Tiwald, Acting Chair, 415-338-1598, E-mail: jtiwald@sfsu.edu. *Application contact:* Prof. David Landy, Graduate Coordinator, 415-338-1596, E-mail: landy@sfsu.edu.
Website: http://philosophy.sfsu.edu/

San Jose State University, Graduate Studies and Research, College of Humanities and the Arts, Department of Philosophy, San Jose, CA 95192-0001. Offers MA. *Degree requirements:* For master's, one foreign language, thesis or alternative. Electronic applications accepted.

Simon Fraser University, Office of Graduate Studies, Faculty of Arts and Social Sciences, Department of Philosophy, Burnaby, BC V5A 1S6, Canada. Offers MA, PhD. *Degree requirements:* For master's, thesis or alternative; for doctorate, comprehensive exam, thesis/dissertation. *Entrance requirements:* For master's, minimum GPA of 3.0 (on scale of 4.33), or 3.33 based on last 60 credits of undergraduate courses; for doctorate, minimum GPA of 3.5 (on scale of 4.33). Additional exam requirements/recommendations for international students: Recommended—TOEFL (minimum score 580 paper-based; 93 iBT), IELTS (minimum score 7), TWE (minimum score 5). Electronic applications accepted. *Faculty research:* Ethics; philosophy of mind; philosophy of science; epistemology and metaphysics; history of early modern, ancient, and analytic philosophy and logic.

Southeastern Baptist Theological Seminary, Graduate and Professional Programs, Wake Forest, NC 27588-1889. Offers advanced biblical studies (M Div); Christian education (M Div, MACE); Christian ethics (PhD); Christian ministry (M Div); Christian planting (M Div); church music (MACM); counseling (MACO); evangelism (PhD); language (M Div); ministry (D Min); New Testament (PhD); Old Testament (PhD); philosophy (PhD); theology (Th M, PhD); women's studies (M Div). *Accreditation:* ACIPE; ATS (one or more programs are accredited). *Degree requirements:* For master's, thesis (for some programs), oral exam; for doctorate, thesis/dissertation, fieldwork. *Entrance requirements:* For master's, Cooperative English Test, minimum GPA of 2.0, M Div or equivalent (Th M); for doctorate, GRE General Test or MAT, Cooperative English Test, M Div or equivalent, 3 years of professional experience.

Southern Baptist Theological Seminary, School of Theology, Louisville, KY 40280-0004. Offers applied theology (D Min); biblical and theological studies (M Div); biblical counseling (M Div, MA, D Min); biblical spirituality (D Min); Christian ministry (M Div); expository preaching (D Min); pastoral studies (M Div); theological studies (MA); theology (Th M, PhD); worldview and apologetics (M Div). *Accreditation:* ATS. Part-time

and evening/weekend programs available. Postbaccalaureate distance learning degree programs offered (minimal on-campus study). *Degree requirements:* For master's, 2 foreign languages, thesis; for doctorate, 4 foreign languages, thesis/dissertation. *Entrance requirements:* For master's, GRE General Test, MAT, M Div; for doctorate, GRE General Test, MAT, interview, M Div, field essay. Additional exam requirements/recommendations for international students: Required—TOEFL, TWE. *Faculty research:* Biblical studies, contemporary theology, church history, pastoral care, ministry/missions studies.

Southern Evangelical Seminary, Graduate Programs, Matthews, NC 28105. Offers apologetics (MA, D Min, Certificate); Christian education (MA); church ministry (MA, Certificate); divinity (Certificate), including apologetics (M Div, Certificate); Islamic studies (MA, Certificate); Jewish studies (MA); philosophy (MA); philosophy of religion (PhD); religion (MA); theology (M Div), including apologetics (M Div, Certificate), Biblical studies; youth ministry (MA). Part-time and evening/weekend programs available. Postbaccalaureate distance learning degree programs offered. *Degree requirements:* For master's, thesis (for some programs); for doctorate, 2 foreign languages, comprehensive exam (for some programs), thesis/dissertation. *Entrance requirements:* Additional exam requirements/recommendations for international students: Required—TOEFL (minimum score 600 paper-based).

Southern Illinois University Carbondale, Graduate School, College of Liberal Arts, Department of Philosophy, Carbondale, IL 62901-4701. Offers MA, PhD. *Faculty:* 11 full-time (2 women). *Students:* 25 full-time (7 women), 42 part-time (8 women); includes 4 minority (2 Black or African American, non-Hispanic/Latino; 1 Asian, non-Hispanic/Latino; 1 Hispanic/Latino), 10 international. Average age 25. 46 applicants, 30% accepted, 4 enrolled. In 2014, 6 master's, 7 doctorates awarded. *Degree requirements:* For master's, one foreign language, thesis; for doctorate, 2 foreign languages, thesis/dissertation. *Entrance requirements:* For master's, GRE General Test, minimum GPA of 2.7; for doctorate, GRE General Test, minimum GPA of 3.25. Additional exam requirements/recommendations for international students: Required—TOEFL. *Application deadline:* For fall admission, 2/1 for domestic students. Applications are processed on a rolling basis. Application fee: $50. *Expenses:* Tuition, state resident: full-time $10,176; part-time $1153 per credit. Tuition, nonresident: full-time $20,814; part-time $1744 per credit. *Required fees:* $7092; $394 per credit. $2364 per semester. *Financial support:* In 2014–15, 39 students received support, including 5 fellowships with full tuition reimbursements available, 10 research assistantships with full tuition reimbursements available, 12 teaching assistantships with full tuition reimbursements available; Federal Work-Study, institutionally sponsored loans, and tuition waivers (full) also available. Support available to part-time students. *Faculty research:* Continental philosophy, American philosophy, philosophy of mind, Asian philosophy. *Unit head:* Dr. Sara Beardsworth, Director of Graduate Studies, 618-453-7453, E-mail: beardswo@siu.edu. *Application contact:* Mary Kay Bledsoe, Administrative Assistant, 618-453-7432, E-mail: philgrad@siu.edu.

Stanford University, School of Humanities and Sciences, Department of Philosophy, Stanford, CA 94305-9991. Offers MA, PhD. Terminal master's awarded for partial completion of doctoral program. *Degree requirements:* For master's, oral exam; for doctorate, thesis/dissertation, oral exam. *Entrance requirements:* For master's and doctorate, GRE General Test. Additional exam requirements/recommendations for international students: Required—TOEFL. Electronic applications accepted. *Expenses:* Tuition: Full-time $44,184; part-time $982 per credit hour. *Required fees:* $191.

Stony Brook University, State University of New York, Graduate School, College of Arts and Sciences, Department of Philosophy, Stony Brook, NY 11794. Offers MA, PhD, Advanced Certificate. Evening/weekend programs available. *Faculty:* 19 full-time (5 women), 2 part-time/adjunct (both women). *Students:* 68 full-time (25 women), 10 part-time (3 women); includes 14 minority (2 Black or African American, non-Hispanic/Latino; 1 American Indian or Alaska Native, non-Hispanic/Latino; 1 Asian, non-Hispanic/Latino; 8 Hispanic/Latino; 2 Two or more races, non-Hispanic/Latino), 12 international. Average age 30. 177 applicants, 44% accepted, 15 enrolled. In 2014, 15 master's, 7 doctorates, 2 other advanced degrees awarded. *Degree requirements:* For doctorate, one foreign language, thesis/dissertation. *Entrance requirements:* For master's and doctorate, GRE General Test. Additional exam requirements/recommendations for international students: Required—TOEFL. *Application deadline:* For fall admission, 1/15 for domestic students; for spring admission, 10/1 for domestic students. Application fee: $100. *Expenses:* Tuition, state resident: full-time $10,370; part-time $432 per credit. Tuition, nonresident: full-time $20,190; part-time $841 per credit. *Required fees:* $1431. *Financial support:* In 2014–15, 1 fellowship, 35 teaching assistantships were awarded; research assistantships also available. *Faculty research:* Philosophy of science, philosophy of language, analytical philosophy, phenomenology, structuralism. *Total annual research expenditures:* $89,330. *Unit head:* Dr. Eduardo Mendieta, Chair, 631-632-7585, Fax: 631-632-7522, E-mail: eduardo.mendieta@stonybrook.edu. *Application contact:* Kathleen-Anna Amella, Coordinator, 631-632-7580, Fax: 631-632-7522, E-mail: kathleen-anna.amella@stonybrook.edu.
Website: http://www.sunysb.edu/philosophy/

Summit University, Graduate Studies, Clarks Summit, PA 18411-1297. Offers Bible (MA); counseling (MA, MS); curriculum and instruction (M Ed); educational administration (M Ed); intercultural studies (MA); literature (MA); missions (MA); organizational leadership (MA); reading specialist (M Ed); secondary English/communications (M Ed); social entrepreneurship (MA); worldview studies (MA). MA in missions program available only for Association of Baptists for World Evangelism missionary personnel. Part-time and evening/weekend programs available. Postbaccalaureate distance learning degree programs offered (no on-campus study). *Entrance requirements:* Additional exam requirements/recommendations for international students: Required—TOEFL (minimum score 500 paper-based).

Syracuse University, College of Arts and Sciences, Program in Philosophy, Syracuse, NY 13244. Offers MA, PhD. Part-time programs available. *Students:* 36 full-time (12 women), 4 part-time (1 woman); includes 7 minority (1 Black or African American, non-Hispanic/Latino; 3 Asian, non-Hispanic/Latino; 1 Hispanic/Latino; 1 Native Hawaiian or other Pacific Islander, non-Hispanic/Latino; 1 Two or more races, non-Hispanic/Latino), 8 international. Average age 30. 119 applicants, 12% accepted, 5 enrolled. In 2014, 1 master's, 5 doctorates awarded. *Degree requirements:* For master's, thesis or alternative; for doctorate, thesis/dissertation. *Entrance requirements:* For master's and doctorate, GRE, writing sample. Additional exam requirements/recommendations for international students: Required—TOEFL (minimum score 100 iBT). *Application deadline:* For fall admission, 1/15 priority date for domestic and international students. Application fee: $75. Electronic applications accepted. *Expenses:* Tuition: Part-time $1341 per credit. *Financial support:* Fellowships with full tuition reimbursements and teaching assistantships with full and partial tuition reimbursements available. Financial award application deadline: 1/1; financial award applicants required to submit FAFSA. *Faculty research:* Ethics, metaphysics, epistemology, philosophy of language. *Unit head:* Dr. Ben Bradley, Graduate Studies Director, 315-443-2245. *Application contact:* Lisa Farnsworth, Information Contact, 315-443-2245, E-mail: lfarmswo@syr.edu.
Website: http://philosophy.syr.edu/

Temple University, College of Liberal Arts, Department of Philosophy, Philadelphia, PA 19122-6096. Offers MA, PhD. Part-time programs available. *Faculty:* 13 full-time (4

women), 2 part-time/adjunct (1 woman). *Students:* 38 full-time (12 women), 4 part-time (0 women); includes 4 minority (2 Asian, non-Hispanic/Latino; 2 Hispanic/Latino), 1 international. 30 applicants, 73% accepted, 12 enrolled. In 2014, 2 master's, 4 doctorates awarded. Terminal master's awarded for partial completion of doctoral program. *Degree requirements:* For master's, thesis or alternative; for doctorate, one foreign language, thesis/dissertation. *Entrance requirements:* For master's and doctorate, GRE General Test, minimum GPA of 3.0, 3 letters of recommendation. Additional exam requirements/recommendations for international students: Required—TOEFL (minimum score 550 paper-based; 79 iBT). *Application deadline:* For fall admission, 1/1 for domestic students, 12/15 for international students; for spring admission, 10/1 for domestic students, 8/1 for international students. Applications are processed on a rolling basis. Application fee: $60. Electronic applications accepted. *Expenses:* Tuition, state resident: full-time $14,490; part-time $805 per credit hour. Tuition, nonresident: full-time $19,850; part-time $1103 per credit hour. *Required fees:* $690. Full-time tuition and fees vary according to class time, course load, degree level, campus/location and program. *Financial support:* Fellowships with full tuition reimbursements, teaching assistantships with full tuition reimbursements, institutionally sponsored loans, and tuition waivers (partial) available. Financial award application deadline: 1/15; financial award applicants required to submit FAFSA. *Faculty research:* History of philosophy, European philosophy, aesthetics, analytic philosophy, pragmatism. *Unit head:* Dr. Kristin Gjesdal, Graduate Director, 215-204-5673, Fax: 215-204-0200, E-mail: kristin.gjesdal@temple.edu. *Application contact:* Sonia Lawson, Coordinator, 215-204-1742, Fax: 215-204-0200, E-mail: slawson@temple.edu.
Website: http://www.cla.temple.edu/philosophy/

Texas A&M University, College of Liberal Arts, Department of Philosophy, College Station, TX 77843. Offers MA, PhD. Part-time programs available. *Faculty:* 13. *Students:* 30 full-time (11 women), 2 part-time (1 woman); includes 9 minority (1 Asian, non-Hispanic/Latino; 8 Hispanic/Latino), 2 international. Average age 30. 13 applicants, 100% accepted, 8 enrolled. In 2014, 1 master's, 2 doctorates awarded. Terminal master's awarded for partial completion of doctoral program. *Degree requirements:* For master's, thesis optional; for doctorate, comprehensive exam, thesis/dissertation. *Entrance requirements:* For master's, GRE General Test, letter of recommendation, resume, writing sample; for doctorate, GRE General Test, letters of recommendation, resume, writing sample. Additional exam requirements/recommendations for international students: Recommended—TOEFL. *Application deadline:* For fall admission, 1/15 for domestic students, 3/1 for international students; for winter admission, 8/1 for international students; for spring admission, 10/15 priority date for domestic students. Application fee: $50 ($90 for international students). Electronic applications accepted. *Expenses:* Tuition, state resident: full-time $4078; part-time $226.55 per credit hour. Tuition, nonresident: full-time $10,594; part-time $577.55 per credit hour. *Required fees:* $2813; $237.70 per credit hour. $278.50 per semester. Tuition and fees vary according to degree level and student level. *Financial support:* In 2014–15, 31 students received support, including 10 fellowships with full and partial tuition reimbursements available (averaging $23,055 per year), 4 research assistantships with full and partial tuition reimbursements available (averaging $6,889 per year), 24 teaching assistantships with full and partial tuition reimbursements available (averaging $6,748 per year); career-related internships or fieldwork, institutionally sponsored loans, scholarships/grants, traineeships, health care benefits, tuition waivers (full and partial), and unspecified assistantships also available. Support available to part-time students. Financial award application deadline: 1/15; financial award applicants required to submit FAFSA. *Faculty research:* American philosophy, applied ethics, philosophy of mind, philosophy of religion, history and philosophy of logic. *Unit head:* Dr. Theodore George, Interim Head, 979-845-5605, E-mail: t-george@tamu.edu. *Application contact:* Dr. Clare Palmer, Director of Graduate Program, 979-862-1435, E-mail: c.palmer@tamu.edu.
Website: http://philosophy.tamu.edu

Texas State University, The Graduate College, College of Liberal Arts, Applied Philosophy and Ethics Program, San Marcos, TX 78666. Offers MA. *Faculty:* 9 full-time (3 women), 3 part-time/adjunct (2 women). *Students:* 14 full-time (2 women), 6 part-time (2 women); includes 6 minority (1 Black or African American, non-Hispanic/Latino; 4 Hispanic/Latino; 1 Two or more races, non-Hispanic/Latino). Average age 30. 13 applicants, 85% accepted, 4 enrolled. In 2014, 18 master's awarded. *Degree requirements:* For master's, comprehensive exam, thesis optional. *Entrance requirements:* For master's, GRE (preferred), baccalaureate degree from regionally-accredited university with minimum GPA of 3.0 on last 60 undergraduate semester hours. Additional exam requirements/recommendations for international students: Required—TOEFL (minimum score 550 paper-based; 78 iBT). *Application deadline:* For fall admission, 6/15 priority date for domestic students, 6/1 for international students; for spring admission, 10/15 priority date for domestic students, 10/1 for international students; for summer admission, 4/15 for domestic students, 3/15 for international students. Applications are processed on a rolling basis. Application fee: $40 ($90 for international students). *Financial support:* In 2014–15, 17 students received support, including 1 research assistantship (averaging $11,855 per year), 12 teaching assistantships (averaging $11,563 per year); scholarships/grants also available. Support available to part-time students. Financial award application deadline: 4/1; financial award applicants required to submit FAFSA. *Unit head:* Dr. Audrey Mckinney, Graduate Advisor, 512-245-2047, Fax: 512-245-8336, E-mail: am04@txstate.edu. *Application contact:* Dr. Andrea Golato, Dean of Graduate School, 512-245-2581, Fax: 512-245-8365, E-mail: gradcollege@txstate.edu.

Texas Tech University, Graduate School, College of Arts and Sciences, Department of Philosophy, Lubbock, TX 79409-3092. Offers MA. Part-time programs available. *Faculty:* 11 full-time (2 women), 2 part-time/adjunct (0 women). *Students:* 29 full-time (6 women), 1 part-time (0 women); includes 3 minority (1 Hispanic/Latino; 2 Two or more races, non-Hispanic/Latino), 7 international. Average age 27. 42 applicants, 60% accepted, 12 enrolled. In 2014, 7 master's awarded. *Degree requirements:* For master's, thesis or alternative. *Entrance requirements:* For master's, GRE General Test. Additional exam requirements/recommendations for international students: Required—TOEFL (minimum score 550 paper-based; 79 iBT). *Application deadline:* For fall admission, 6/1 priority date for domestic students, 1/15 priority date for international students; for spring admission, 9/1 priority date for domestic students, 6/15 priority date for international students. Applications are processed on a rolling basis. Application fee: $60. Electronic applications accepted. *Expenses:* Tuition, state resident: full-time $6310; part-time $262.92 per credit hour. Tuition, nonresident: full-time $14,998; part-time $624.92 per credit hour. *Required fees:* $2701; $36.50 per credit. $912.50 per semester. Tuition and fees vary according to course load. *Financial support:* In 2014–15, 25 students received support, including 16 fellowships (averaging $4,986 per year), 1 research assistantship (averaging $13,000 per year), 23 teaching assistantships (averaging $12,696 per year). Financial award application deadline: 4/15; financial award applicants required to submit FAFSA. *Faculty research:* Aesthetics, ethics, history of philosophy, philosophy of mind, philosophy of science. *Total annual research expenditures:* $39,988. *Unit head:* Dr. Mark O. Webb, Professor and Chair, 806-742-3275, Fax: 806-742-0730, E-mail: mark.webb@ttu.edu. *Application contact:* Dr. Daniel O. Nathan, Director of Graduate Studies, 806-742-0373 Ext. 340, Fax: 806-742-0730, E-mail: daniel.nathan@ttu.edu. Website: http://www.philosophy.ttu.edu/

Trinity Western University, School of Graduate Studies, Program in Interdisciplinary Humanities, Langley, BC V2Y 1Y1, Canada. Offers general humanities (MAIH); specialized (MAIH), including English, history, philosophy. Part-time programs available. *Degree requirements:* For master's, thesis or alternative, 36 semester hours. *Entrance requirements:* For master's, strong undergraduate degree in humanities or English, history or philosophy. Additional exam requirements/recommendations for international students: Recommended—TOEFL. Electronic applications accepted. *Faculty research:* Literary theory, gender, medieval and early modern literature, philosophy of religion, Thomas Merton's poetics.

Tufts University, Graduate School of Arts and Sciences, Department of Philosophy, Medford, MA 02155. Offers MA. *Faculty:* 16 full-time (5 women), 1 (woman) part-time/adjunct. *Students:* 31 full-time (13 women), 3 part-time (1 woman); includes 5 minority (1 Black or African American, non-Hispanic/Latino; 4 Hispanic/Latino), 6 international. Average age 25. 130 applicants, 18% accepted, 14 enrolled. In 2014, 8 master's awarded. *Degree requirements:* For master's, one foreign language, comprehensive exam, departmental qualifying exam. *Entrance requirements:* For master's, GRE General Test, writing sample. Additional exam requirements/recommendations for international students: Required—TOEFL (minimum score 550 paper-based; 80 iBT), IELTS (minimum score 6.5). *Application deadline:* For fall admission, 1/15 for domestic and international students; for spring admission, 9/15 for domestic and international students. Applications are processed on a rolling basis. Application fee: $75. Electronic applications accepted. *Expenses: Tuition:* Full-time $45,590; part-time $1161 per credit hour. *Required fees:* $782. Full-time tuition and fees vary according to degree level, program and student level. Part-time tuition and fees vary according to course load. *Financial support:* Teaching assistantships with full and partial tuition reimbursements, Federal Work-Study, scholarships/grants, tuition waivers (partial), and unspecified assistantships available. Financial award application deadline: 1/15. *Unit head:* Dr. Patrick Forber, Graduate Program Director. *Application contact:* Office of Graduate Admissions, 617-627-3395, E-mail: gradadmissions@tufts.edu.
Website: http://ase.tufts.edu/philosophy/

Tulane University, School of Liberal Arts, Department of Philosophy, New Orleans, LA 70118-5669. Offers MA, PhD. *Degree requirements:* For master's, thesis or alternative; for doctorate, one foreign language, thesis/dissertation. *Entrance requirements:* For master's, GRE General Test, minimum B average in undergraduate course work; for doctorate, GRE General Test. Additional exam requirements/recommendations for international students: Required—TOEFL. Electronic applications accepted. *Expenses: Tuition:* Full-time $46,326; part-time $2574 per credit hour. *Required fees:* $1980; $44.50 per credit hour. $550 per term. Tuition and fees vary according to course load and program.

Universidad Autonoma de Guadalajara, Graduate Programs, Guadalajara, Mexico. Offers administrative law and justice (LL M); advertising and corporate communications (MA); architecture (M Arch); business (MBA); computational science (MCC); education (Ed M, Ed D); English-Spanish translation (MA); entrepreneurship and management (MBA); integrated management of digital animation (MA); international business (MIB); international corporate law (LL M); internet technologies (MS); manufacturing systems (MMS); occupational health (MS); philosophy (MA, PhD); power electronics (MS); quality systems (MQS); renewable energy (MS); social evaluation of projects (MBA); strategic market research (MBA); tax law (MA); teaching mathematics (MA).

Université de Montréal, Faculty of Arts and Sciences, Department of Philosophy, Montréal, QC H3C 3J7, Canada. Offers MA, PhD. *Degree requirements:* For master's, 2 foreign languages, thesis; for doctorate, thesis/dissertation, general exam. Electronic applications accepted. *Faculty research:* Ancient and modern philosophy; logic and philosophy of language, ethics, and politics; contemporary Continental philosophy.

Université de Sherbrooke, Faculty of Letters and Human Sciences, Department of Human Sciences, Sherbrooke, QC J1K 2R1, Canada. Offers history (MA); philosophy (MA). *Degree requirements:* For master's, thesis. *Entrance requirements:* For master's, minimum GPA of 2.75. *Faculty research:* Political, social, and urban history; history of women.

Université de Sherbrooke, Faculty of Theology and Religious Studies, Sherbrooke, QC J1K 2R1, Canada. Offers applied ethics (Diploma); human science of religions (MA); intercultural training (Diploma); philosophy (MA, PhD); spiritual anthropology (Diploma); theology (MA, PhD, Diploma). Part-time and evening/weekend programs available. Postbaccalaureate distance learning degree programs offered. Terminal master's awarded for partial completion of doctoral program. *Entrance requirements:* For master's, bachelor's degree in related discipline; for doctorate, master's degree in related discipline. *Faculty research:* Faith and culture interrelation.

Université du Québec à Montréal, Graduate Programs, Program in Philosophy, Montréal, QC H3C 3P8, Canada. Offers MA, PhD. PhD offered jointly with Université du Québec à Trois-Rivières. Part-time programs available. *Degree requirements:* For master's, thesis; for doctorate, thesis/dissertation. *Entrance requirements:* For master's, appropriate bachelor's degree or equivalent, proficiency in French; for doctorate, appropriate master's degree or equivalent, proficiency in French.

Université du Québec à Trois-Rivières, Graduate Programs, Program in Philosophy, Trois-Rivières, QC G9A 5H7, Canada. Offers MA, PhD. PhD offered jointly with Université du Québec à Montréal. Part-time programs available. *Degree requirements:* For master's, thesis; for doctorate, thesis/dissertation. *Entrance requirements:* For master's, appropriate bachelor's degree, proficiency in French; for doctorate, appropriate master's degree, proficiency in French.

Université Laval, Faculty of Philosophy, Programs in Philosophy, Québec, QC G1K 7P4, Canada. Offers MA, PhD. Terminal master's awarded for partial completion of doctoral program. *Degree requirements:* For master's, thesis; for doctorate, comprehensive exam, thesis/dissertation. *Entrance requirements:* For master's and doctorate, French exam. Electronic applications accepted.

University at Albany, State University of New York, College of Arts and Sciences, Department of Philosophy, Albany, NY 12222-0001. Offers MA, PhD. *Degree requirements:* For master's, one foreign language, thesis; for doctorate, thesis/dissertation. *Entrance requirements:* For master's and doctorate, GRE General Test. Additional exam requirements/recommendations for international students: Required—TOEFL (minimum score 550 paper-based). Electronic applications accepted. *Faculty research:* Philosophical logic, ethics, ancient philosophy/metaphysics, aesthetics, biomedical ethics.

University at Buffalo, the State University of New York, Graduate School, College of Arts and Sciences, Department of Philosophy, Buffalo, NY 14260. Offers MA, PhD. *Faculty:* 18 full-time (3 women), 2 part-time/adjunct (1 woman). *Students:* 20 full-time (1 woman), 27 part-time (4 women); includes 4 minority (3 Asian, non-Hispanic/Latino; 1 Hispanic/Latino), 13 international. Average age 31. 32 applicants, 94% accepted, 7 enrolled. In 2014, 5 master's, 8 doctorates awarded. Terminal master's awarded for partial completion of doctoral program. *Degree requirements:* For master's, variable foreign language requirement, thesis or alternative; for doctorate, variable foreign language requirement, comprehensive exam, thesis/dissertation. *Entrance requirements:* For master's and doctorate, GRE General Test, minimum GPA of 3.0.

Additional exam requirements/recommendations for international students: Required—TOEFL (minimum score 550 paper-based; 79 iBT). *Application deadline:* For fall admission, 1/2 for domestic and international students. Applications are processed on a rolling basis. Application fee: $75. Electronic applications accepted. *Financial support:* In 2014–15, 22 students received support, including 1 fellowship with full tuition reimbursement available (averaging $6,000 per year), 22 teaching assistantships with full tuition reimbursements available (averaging $13,250 per year); institutionally sponsored loans, tuition waivers, and unspecified assistantships also available. Financial award application deadline: 1/20; financial award applicants required to submit FAFSA. *Faculty research:* Logic, metaphysics (historical and contemporary), aesthetics, epistemology, ethics (historical and contemporary), ontology, social and political. *Total annual research expenditures:* $3.7 million. *Unit head:* Dr. David B. Hershenov, Chair, 716-645-0150, Fax: 716-645-6139, E-mail: dh25@buffalo.edu. *Application contact:* Dr. Neil Williams, Director of Graduate Studies, 716-645-0161, Fax: 716-645-6139, E-mail: new@buffalo.edu.
Website: http://wings.buffalo.edu/philosophy/

University of Alberta, Faculty of Graduate Studies and Research, Department of Philosophy, Edmonton, AB T6G 2E1, Canada. Offers MA, PhD. Part-time programs available. *Degree requirements:* For master's, thesis; for doctorate, thesis/dissertation. *Entrance requirements:* Additional exam requirements/recommendations for international students: Required—TOEFL (minimum score 550 paper-based). Electronic applications accepted. *Faculty research:* Philosophy of science, cognitive science, social and political philosophy, philosophy of language and logic, environmental aesthetics.

The University of Arizona, College of Social and Behavioral Sciences, Department of Philosophy, Tucson, AZ 85721. Offers MA, PhD, JD/PhD. Part-time programs available. Terminal master's awarded for partial completion of doctoral program. *Degree requirements:* For master's, exams, qualifying paper; for doctorate, thesis/dissertation, preliminary exams. *Entrance requirements:* For doctorate, GRE General Test, 3 letters of recommendation, writing sample. Additional exam requirements/recommendations for international students: Required—TOEFL (minimum score 550 paper-based; 79 iBT). Electronic applications accepted. *Faculty research:* Law, social, and political philosophy; epistemology; philosophy of mind; cognitive science.

University of Arkansas, Graduate School, J. William Fulbright College of Arts and Sciences, Department of Philosophy, Fayetteville, AR 72701-1201. Offers MA, PhD. Part-time programs available. *Degree requirements:* For master's, thesis; for doctorate, 2 foreign languages, thesis/dissertation. Electronic applications accepted.

The University of British Columbia, Faculty of Arts and Faculty of Graduate Studies, Department of Philosophy, Vancouver, BC V6T 1Z1, Canada. Offers MA, PhD. *Accreditation:* NCATE. Part-time programs available. *Degree requirements:* For master's, thesis (for some programs); for doctorate, comprehensive exam, thesis/dissertation. *Entrance requirements:* For master's, bachelor's degree with minimum average of 76% or minimum GPA of 3.0 in 3rd- and 4th-year coursework; 3 credits in formal logic; 6 credits at the upper-level in the history of philosophy and in metaphysics, epistemology, or philosophy; 3 credits at the upper-level in ethics or value theory; for doctorate, MA, honors BA with first class standing, or BA with first class standing in philosophy. Additional exam requirements/recommendations for international students: Required—TOEFL (minimum score 600 paper-based; 100 iBT), IELTS (minimum score 6.5), Michigan English Language Assessment Battery (minimum score 81). Electronic applications accepted. *Faculty research:* Ethics and applied ethics, metaphysics and epistemology, history of philosophy, philosophy of science, philosophy of biology, philosophy of mind, philosophy of cognitive science.

University of Calgary, Faculty of Graduate Studies, Faculty of Arts, Department of Philosophy, Calgary, AB T2N 1N4, Canada. Offers MA, PhD. Part-time programs available. *Degree requirements:* For master's, comprehensive exam (for some programs), thesis (for some programs); for doctorate, thesis/dissertation, candidacy exam. *Entrance requirements:* Additional exam requirements/recommendations for international students: Required—TOEFL (minimum score 550 paper-based). Electronic applications accepted. *Faculty research:* Ethics and political philosophy, metaphysics, philosophy of mind, philosophy of language.

University of California, Berkeley, Graduate Division, College of Letters and Science, Department of Philosophy, Berkeley, CA 94720-1500. Offers PhD. *Degree requirements:* For doctorate, thesis/dissertation, qualifying exam. *Entrance requirements:* For doctorate, GRE General Test, minimum GPA of 3.0, writing sample, 3 letters of recommendation.

University of California, Davis, Graduate Studies, Program in Philosophy, Davis, CA 95616. Offers MA, PhD. Terminal master's awarded for partial completion of doctoral program. *Degree requirements:* For doctorate, thesis/dissertation. *Entrance requirements:* For master's and doctorate, GRE General Test, minimum GPA of 3.0. Additional exam requirements/recommendations for international students: Required—TOEFL (minimum score 550 paper-based). Electronic applications accepted. *Faculty research:* Moral and political philosophy, philosophy of language, metaphysics, philosophy of science, history of philosophy.

University of California, Irvine, School of Humanities, Department of Philosophy, Irvine, CA 92697. Offers MA, PhD. *Students:* 25 full-time (7 women), 2 part-time (1 woman); includes 5 minority (1 Asian, non-Hispanic/Latino; 2 Hispanic/Latino; 2 Two or more races, non-Hispanic/Latino), 1 international. Average age 30. 42 applicants, 21% accepted, 5 enrolled. In 2014, 2 master's, 3 doctorates awarded. *Degree requirements:* For master's, thesis; for doctorate, thesis/dissertation. *Entrance requirements:* For master's and doctorate, GRE General Test, minimum GPA of 3.0. Additional exam requirements/recommendations for international students: Required—TOEFL (minimum score 550 paper-based). *Application deadline:* For fall admission, 1/15 priority date for domestic students, 1/15 for international students. Applications are processed on a rolling basis. Application fee: $90 ($110 for international students). Electronic applications accepted. *Financial support:* Fellowships with tuition reimbursements, teaching assistantships with partial tuition reimbursements, institutionally sponsored loans, traineeships, health care benefits, and unspecified assistantships available. Financial award application deadline: 3/1; financial award applicants required to submit FAFSA. *Faculty research:* Philosophy of action and decision theory, philosophy of language, philosophy of mathematics, virtue ethics, modern and contemporary Continental philosophy. *Unit head:* Aaron James, Department Chair, E-mail: aaron.james@uci.edu. *Application contact:* Kirsten S. Alonso, Department Coordinator, 949-824-6525, Fax: 949-824-6520, E-mail: kalonso@uci.edu.
Website: http://www.hnet.uci.edu/philosophy/

University of California, Irvine, School of Social Sciences, Department of Logic and Philosophy of Science, Irvine, CA 92697. Offers philosophy (PhD). *Students:* 17 full-time (5 women), 1 (woman) part-time, 2 international. Average age 26. 56 applicants, 36% accepted, 7 enrolled. In 2014, 1 doctorate awarded. *Entrance requirements:* For doctorate, GRE, minimum GPA of 3.0. Additional exam requirements/recommendations for international students: Required—TOEFL (minimum score 550 paper-based). *Application deadline:* For fall admission, 1/15 for domestic and international students. Application fee: $90 ($110 for international students). *Financial support:* Fellowships, research assistantships with full tuition reimbursements, teaching assistantships, institutionally sponsored loans, traineeships, health care benefits, and unspecified assistantships available. Financial award application deadline: 3/1. *Unit head:* P. Kyle Stanford, Chair, 949-824-6398, Fax: 949-824-8388, E-mail: stanford@uci.edu. *Application contact:* Kent Johnson, Graduate Advisor, 949-824-8968, Fax: 949-824-8388, E-mail: kent.johnson@uci.edu.

University of California, Los Angeles, Graduate Division, College of Letters and Science, Department of Philosophy, Los Angeles, CA 90095. Offers MA, PhD. Terminal master's awarded for partial completion of doctoral program. *Degree requirements:* For master's, one foreign language, comprehensive exam; for doctorate, one foreign language, thesis/dissertation, oral and written qualifying exams, 3 quarters of teaching experience. *Entrance requirements:* For doctorate, GRE General Test, bachelor's degree; minimum undergraduate GPA of 3.0 (or its equivalent if letter grade system not used); writing sample. Additional exam requirements/recommendations for international students: Required—TOEFL. Electronic applications accepted.

University of California, Riverside, Graduate Division, Department of Philosophy, Riverside, CA 92521-0102. Offers MA, PhD. Terminal master's awarded for partial completion of doctoral program. *Degree requirements:* For master's, logic exam, professional paper; for doctorate, one foreign language, thesis/dissertation, logic exam, proposition papers, qualifying exams. *Entrance requirements:* For master's, GRE General Test, minimum GPA of 3.2; for doctorate, GRE General Test, master's degree in philosophy, minimum GPA of 3.2. Additional exam requirements/recommendations for international students: Required—TOEFL (minimum score 550 paper-based; 80 iBT). Electronic applications accepted. *Expenses:* Tuition, state resident: full-time $5399. Tuition, nonresident: full-time $10,433. *Faculty research:* Moral philosophy, philosophy of science, history of philosophy, philosophy of language, Continental philosophy.

University of California, San Diego, Graduate Division, Department of Philosophy, La Jolla, CA 92093. Offers PhD. *Students:* 42 full-time (10 women); includes 4 minority (all Asian, non-Hispanic/Latino), 5 international. 202 applicants, 8% accepted, 2 enrolled. In 2014, 6 doctorates awarded. *Degree requirements:* For doctorate, thesis/dissertation, 3 quarters of teaching assistantship; original essay. *Entrance requirements:* For doctorate, GRE General Test. Additional exam requirements/recommendations for international students: Required—TOEFL (minimum score 550 paper-based; 80 iBT), IELTS (minimum score 7). *Application deadline:* For fall admission, 1/12 for domestic students. Application fee: $90 ($110 for international students). Electronic applications accepted. *Expenses:* Tuition, state resident: full-time $11,220; part-time $5610 per quarter. Tuition, nonresident: full-time $26,322; part-time $13,161 per quarter. *Required fees:* $570 per quarter. Tuition and fees vary according to program. *Financial support:* Fellowships, teaching assistantships, and scholarships/grants available. Financial award applicants required to submit FAFSA. *Faculty research:* Philosophy of science, ethics and political philosophy, history of philosophy, epistemology and metaphysics. *Unit head:* Donald Rutherford, Chair, 858-822-1655, E-mail: drutherford@ucsd.edu. *Application contact:* Catherine Asmann, Graduate Coordinator, 858-534-3076, E-mail: casmann@ucsd.edu.
Website: http://philosophy.ucsd.edu/

University of California, Santa Barbara, Graduate Division, College of Letters and Sciences, Division of Humanities and Fine Arts, Department of Philosophy, Santa Barbara, CA 93106-9580. Offers PhD, MA/PhD. Terminal master's awarded for partial completion of doctoral program. *Degree requirements:* For doctorate, thesis/dissertation. *Entrance requirements:* For doctorate, GRE. Additional exam requirements/recommendations for international students: Required—TOEFL (minimum score 550 paper-based; 80 iBT), IELTS (minimum score 7). Electronic applications accepted. *Faculty research:* Epistemology, philosophy of language, philosophy of mind, history of philosophy, logic.

University of California, Santa Cruz, Division of Graduate Studies, Division of Humanities, Department of Philosophy, Santa Cruz, CA 95064. Offers MA, PhD. *Degree requirements:* For doctorate, thesis/dissertation, qualifying exam. *Entrance requirements:* For master's, GRE, 3 letters of recommendation; for doctorate, GRE, official transcripts, 3 letters of recommendation. Additional exam requirements/recommendations for international students: Required—TOEFL (minimum score 550 paper-based; 83 iBT); Recommended—IELTS (minimum score 8). Electronic applications accepted. *Faculty research:* Philosophy of science.

University of Chicago, Division of the Humanities, Department of Philosophy, Chicago, IL 60637. Offers ancient philosophy (PhD); philosophy (PhD). *Students:* 51 full-time (13 women); includes 4 minority (2 Asian, non-Hispanic/Latino; 2 Hispanic/Latino), 22 international. 268 applicants, 41% accepted, 9 enrolled. Terminal master's awarded for partial completion of doctoral program. *Degree requirements:* For doctorate, one foreign language, thesis/dissertation. *Entrance requirements:* For doctorate, GRE General Test. Additional exam requirements/recommendations for international students: Required—TOEFL (minimum score 104 iBT), IELTS (minimum score 7). *Application deadline:* For fall admission, 12/15 for domestic and international students. Application fee: $90. Electronic applications accepted. *Expenses: Tuition:* Full-time $46,899. *Required fees:* $347. *Financial support:* Fellowships with full tuition reimbursements, teaching assistantships with full tuition reimbursements, Federal Work-Study, institutionally sponsored loans, scholarships/grants, and health care benefits available. Financial award application deadline: 12/15; financial award applicants required to submit FAFSA. *Unit head:* Dr. James Conant, Chair. *Application contact:* Braden Grams, Assistant Dean of Students, Admissions and Fellowships, 773-702-1552, Fax: 773-834-9148, E-mail: humanitiesadmissions@uchicago.edu.
Website: http://philosophy.uchicago.edu/

University of Chicago, Division of the Humanities, Master of Arts Program in the Humanities, Chicago, IL 60637. Offers art history (MA); classics (MA); comparative literature (MA); creative writing (MA); digital humanities (MA); English language and literature (MA); Germanic studies (MA); linguistics (MA); music (MA); philosophy (MA); Romance languages and literatures (MA); South Asian languages and civilizations (MA). *Students:* 83 full-time (41 women), 8 part-time (6 women); includes 14 minority (1 Black or African American, non-Hispanic/Latino; 6 Asian, non-Hispanic/Latino; 6 Hispanic/Latino; 1 Two or more races, non-Hispanic/Latino), 17 international. Average age 26. 153 applicants, 67% accepted, 80 enrolled. *Degree requirements:* For master's, thesis. *Entrance requirements:* For master's, GRE General Test. Additional exam requirements/recommendations for international students: Required—TOEFL (minimum score 600 paper-based; 104 iBT), IELTS (minimum score 7). *Application deadline:* For fall admission, 3/15 for domestic and international students. Application fee: $90. Electronic applications accepted. *Expenses: Tuition:* Full-time $46,899. *Required fees:* $347. *Financial support:* In 2014–15, 100 students received support, including 8 fellowships with partial tuition reimbursements available (averaging $12,000 per year); Federal Work-Study, institutionally sponsored loans, and tuition waivers (partial) also available. Financial award application deadline: 3/15; financial award applicants required to submit FAFSA. *Unit head:* Prof. David Wray, Director, 773-834-1201, E-mail: ma-humanities@uchicago.edu. *Application contact:* Program Coordinator, 773-834-1201, Fax: 773-834-7526, E-mail: ma-humanities@uchicago.edu.
Website: http://maph.uchicago.edu/

Philosophy

University of Cincinnati, Graduate School, McMicken College of Arts and Sciences, Department of Philosophy, Cincinnati, OH 45221. Offers MA, PhD. Terminal master's awarded for partial completion of doctoral program. *Degree requirements:* For master's, thesis; for doctorate, one foreign language, comprehensive exam, thesis/dissertation. *Entrance requirements:* For master's and doctorate, GRE General Test, BA in philosophy or equivalent experience. Additional exam requirements/recommendations for international students: Required—TOEFL. Electronic applications accepted.

University of Colorado Boulder, Graduate School, College of Arts and Sciences, Department of Philosophy, Boulder, CO 80309. Offers MA, PhD. *Faculty:* 21 full-time (4 women). *Students:* 39 full-time (6 women), 3 part-time (0 women); includes 5 minority (2 Black or African American, non-Hispanic/Latino; 1 Asian, non-Hispanic/Latino; 2 Hispanic/Latino), 3 international. Average age 29. 40 applicants, 5% accepted, 1 enrolled. In 2014, 6 master's, 5 doctorates awarded. Terminal master's awarded for partial completion of doctoral program. *Degree requirements:* For master's, comprehensive exam, thesis; for doctorate, one foreign language, thesis/dissertation, logic and qualifying papers, oral exam. *Entrance requirements:* For master's, GRE General Test, writing sample, minimum undergraduate GPA of 2.75; for doctorate, GRE General Test. *Application deadline:* For fall admission, 1/7 for domestic students, 12/1 for international students. Applications are processed on a rolling basis. Application fee: $50 ($70 for international students). Electronic applications accepted. *Financial support:* In 2014–15, 64 students received support, including 9 fellowships (averaging $4,211 per year), 1 research assistantship with full and partial tuition reimbursement available (averaging $9,866 per year), 26 teaching assistantships with full and partial tuition reimbursements available (averaging $33,860 per year); institutionally sponsored loans, scholarships/grants, health care benefits, and unspecified assistantships also available. Financial award application deadline: 1/17; financial award applicants required to submit FAFSA. *Faculty research:* Philosophy, ethics, history of philosophy, political philosophy, history of science and technology.
Website: http://www.colorado.edu/philosophy/

University of Connecticut, Graduate School, College of Liberal Arts and Sciences, Department of Philosophy, Storrs, CT 06269. Offers MA, PhD. Terminal master's awarded for partial completion of doctoral program. *Degree requirements:* For master's, comprehensive exam; for doctorate, 2 foreign languages, thesis/dissertation. *Entrance requirements:* For master's and doctorate, GRE General Test. Additional exam requirements/recommendations for international students: Required—TOEFL (minimum score 550 paper-based). Electronic applications accepted.

University of Dallas, Braniff Graduate School of Liberal Arts, Institute of Philosophic Studies, Doctoral Program in Philosophy, Irving, TX 75062-4736. Offers PhD. *Degree requirements:* For doctorate, 2 foreign languages, comprehensive exam, thesis/dissertation, qualifying exams. *Entrance requirements:* For doctorate, GRE General Test. *Faculty research:* Aesthetics, postmodernism, Hegel, ethics, Aristotle.

University of Dallas, Braniff Graduate School of Liberal Arts, Master's Program in Philosophy, Irving, TX 75062-4736. Offers MA. *Degree requirements:* For master's, one foreign language, comprehensive exam, thesis. *Entrance requirements:* For master's, GRE General Test. Additional exam requirements/recommendations for international students: Required—TOEFL. *Faculty research:* Aesthetics, postmodernism, Hegel, ethics, Aristotle.

University of Florida, Graduate School, College of Liberal Arts and Sciences, Department of Philosophy, Gainesville, FL 32611-8545. Offers MA, PhD. Part-time programs available. *Faculty:* 9 full-time (1 woman). *Students:* 12 full-time (3 women), 1 part-time (0 women); includes 2 minority (both Hispanic/Latino), 3 international. 14 applicants, 64% accepted, 5 enrolled. In 2014, 4 master's awarded. *Degree requirements:* For doctorate, one foreign language, comprehensive exam, thesis/dissertation. *Entrance requirements:* For master's and doctorate, GRE General Test, minimum GPA of 3.0. Additional exam requirements/recommendations for international students: Required—TOEFL (minimum score 550 paper-based; 80 iBT), IELTS (minimum score 6). *Application deadline:* For fall admission, 1/15 priority date for domestic students, 1/15 for international students. Applications are processed on a rolling basis. Application fee: $30. Electronic applications accepted. *Financial support:* In 2014–15, 10 teaching assistantships were awarded; unspecified assistantships also available. Financial award application deadline: 1/15; financial award applicants required to submit FAFSA. *Faculty research:* Philosophy of mind, metaphysics, philosophy of science, ancient philosophy, philosophical logic. *Unit head:* Gene Witmer, PhD, Chair, 352-273-1830, Fax: 352-392-5577, E-mail: gwitmer@ufl.edu. *Application contact:* Chuang Liu, PhD, Graduate Coordinator, 352-392-2084 Ext. 31811, Fax: 352-392-5577, E-mail: logics@ufl.edu.
Website: http://web.phil.ufl.edu/

University of Georgia, Franklin College of Arts and Sciences, Department of Philosophy, Athens, GA 30602. Offers MA, PhD. Part-time programs available. *Degree requirements:* For master's, one foreign language, thesis; for doctorate, one foreign language, thesis/dissertation. *Entrance requirements:* For master's and doctorate, GRE General Test. Additional exam requirements/recommendations for international students: Required—TOEFL. Electronic applications accepted.

University of Guelph, Graduate Studies, College of Arts, Department of Philosophy, Guelph, ON N1G 2W1, Canada. Offers MA, PhD. PhD offered jointly with McMaster University, Wilfrid Laurier University. Part-time programs available. *Degree requirements:* For master's, thesis (for some programs); for doctorate, one foreign language, thesis/dissertation. *Entrance requirements:* For master's, minimum B-average during previous 2 years of course work; for doctorate, minimum B average. Additional exam requirements/recommendations for international students: Required—TOEFL (minimum score 550 paper-based). Electronic applications accepted. *Faculty research:* Philosophy of science, ethics, modern philosophy, social philosophy, Continental philosophy.

University of Hawaii at Manoa, Graduate Division, College of Arts and Humanities, Department of Philosophy, Honolulu, HI 96822. Offers MA, PhD. Part-time programs available. *Degree requirements:* For master's, variable foreign language requirement, thesis optional, culminating exam; for doctorate, variable foreign language requirement, comprehensive exam, thesis/dissertation, final oral presentation. *Entrance requirements:* For master's and doctorate, GRE General Test. Additional exam requirements/recommendations for international students: Required—TOEFL (minimum score 600 paper-based; 100 iBT), IELTS (minimum score 7). *Faculty research:* Renaissance philosophy, Indian philosophy, logic, ethics, philosophy of science, philosophy of mathematics, Chinese philosophy.

University of Houston, College of Liberal Arts and Social Sciences, Department of Philosophy, Houston, TX 77204. Offers MA. *Degree requirements:* For master's, thesis (for some programs), thesis or additional course requirements. *Entrance requirements:* For master's, GRE General Test, minimum of 18 hours of course work in philosophy; minimum GPA of 3.3 in last 60 hours. Additional exam requirements/recommendations for international students: Required—TOEFL (minimum score 550 paper-based; 79 iBT). Electronic applications accepted. *Faculty research:* Skepticism, nominalism, history of philosophy, cognitive science.

University of Idaho, College of Graduate Studies, College of Letters, Arts and Social Sciences, The Martin School, Philosophy Department, Moscow, ID 83844-3173. Offers MA. *Faculty:* 2 full-time. In 2014, 1 master's awarded. *Expenses:* Tuition, state resident: full-time $4784; part-time $280.50 per credit hour. Tuition, nonresident: full-time $18,314; part-time $957.50 per credit hour. *Required fees:* $2000; $58.50 per credit hour. Tuition and fees vary according to program. *Unit head:* Dr. Douglas Lind, Professor, 208-885-7107, E-mail: phil@uidaho.edu. *Application contact:* Sean Scoggin, Graduate Recruitment Coordinator, 208-885-4001, E-mail: graduateadmissions@uidaho.edu.
Website: http://www.uidaho.edu/class/philosophy

University of Illinois at Chicago, Graduate College, College of Liberal Arts and Sciences, Department of Philosophy, Chicago, IL 60607-7128. Offers MA, PhD. *Faculty:* 16 full-time (5 women), 1 part-time/adjunct (0 women). *Students:* 31 full-time (9 women); includes 5 minority (1 Black or African American, non-Hispanic/Latino; 2 Asian, non-Hispanic/Latino; 2 Two or more races, non-Hispanic/Latino), 5 international. Average age 31. 86 applicants, 15% accepted, 5 enrolled. In 2014, 3 master's awarded. Terminal master's awarded for partial completion of doctoral program. *Degree requirements:* For doctorate, thesis/dissertation, preliminary exams. *Entrance requirements:* For master's and doctorate, minimum GPA of 2.75. Additional exam requirements/recommendations for international students: Required—TOEFL. *Application deadline:* For fall admission, 1/1 priority date for domestic and international students. Applications are processed on a rolling basis. Application fee: $60. Electronic applications accepted. *Expenses:* Tuition, state resident: full-time $11,254; part-time $468 per credit hour. Tuition, nonresident: full-time $23,252; part-time $968 per credit hour. *Required fees:* $1217 per term. Part-time tuition and fees vary according to course load, degree level and program. *Financial support:* In 2014–15, 5 students received support, including 1 fellowship with full tuition reimbursement available; research assistantships with full tuition reimbursements available, teaching assistantships with full tuition reimbursements available, Federal Work-Study, scholarships/grants, traineeships, tuition waivers (full), and unspecified assistantships also available. Financial award application deadline: 3/1; financial award applicants required to submit FAFSA. *Faculty research:* Philosophy of science, philosophy of language, epistemology and metaphysics, ethics, aesthetics. *Unit head:* Prof. Anthony Laden, Chair, 312-996-2658, Fax: 312-996-2480, E-mail: laden@uic.edu. *Application contact:* Prof. Nicholas Huggett, Director of Graduate Studies, 312-996-3022, E-mail: huggett@uic.edu.
Website: http://philosophy.las.uic.edu/

University of Illinois at Urbana–Champaign, Graduate College, College of Liberal Arts and Sciences, Department of Philosophy, Champaign, IL 61820. Offers MA, PhD, PhD/JD. *Students:* 19 (3 women). Application fee: $70 ($90 for international students). *Unit head:* Kirk Sanders, Chair, 217-333-2889, Fax: 217-244-8355, E-mail: ksanders@illinois.edu. *Application contact:* Erin Tarr, Office Support Specialist, 217-333-1950, Fax: 217-244-8355, E-mail: erintarr@illinois.edu.
Website: http://www.philosophy.illinois.edu/

The University of Iowa, Graduate College, College of Liberal Arts and Sciences, Department of Philosophy, Iowa City, IA 52242-1316. Offers PhD. *Degree requirements:* For doctorate, comprehensive exam, thesis/dissertation. *Entrance requirements:* For doctorate, GRE General Test, minimum GPA of 3.0. Additional exam requirements/recommendations for international students: Required—TOEFL (minimum score 550 paper-based; 81 iBT). Electronic applications accepted.

The University of Kansas, Graduate Studies, College of Liberal Arts and Sciences, Department of Philosophy, Lawrence, KS 66045. Offers MA, PhD, JD/MA. *Faculty:* 15. *Students:* 34 full-time (11 women), 1 part-time (0 women), 5 international. Average age 31. 31 applicants, 58% accepted, 6 enrolled. In 2014, 4 master's, 1 doctorate awarded. Terminal master's awarded for partial completion of doctoral program. *Degree requirements:* For master's, comprehensive exam, thesis optional; for doctorate, one foreign language, comprehensive exam, thesis/dissertation. *Entrance requirements:* For master's, GRE; for doctorate, GRE, MA in philosophy. Additional exam requirements/recommendations for international students: Required—TOEFL. *Application deadline:* For fall admission, 2/1 priority date for domestic students, 6/15 for international students. Applications are processed on a rolling basis. Application fee: $55 ($65 for international students). Electronic applications accepted. *Financial support:* Fellowships and teaching assistantships with full tuition reimbursements available. Financial award application deadline: 2/1. *Faculty research:* Theoretical and applied ethics, social and political philosophy, history of philosophy, analytic philosophy, philosophy of mind and language. *Unit head:* John Symons, Chair, 785-864-1948, E-mail: johnsymons@ku.edu. *Application contact:* Cari Ann Kreienhop, Graduate Program Coordinator, 785-864-3665, E-mail: ckreienhop@ku.edu.
Website: http://www.philosophy.ku.edu

University of Kentucky, Graduate School, College of Arts and Sciences, Program in Philosophy, Lexington, KY 40506-0032. Offers MA, PhD. *Degree requirements:* For master's, one foreign language, comprehensive exam, thesis; for doctorate, one foreign language, comprehensive exam, thesis/dissertation. *Entrance requirements:* For master's, GRE General Test, minimum undergraduate GPA of 2.75; for doctorate, GRE General Test, minimum graduate GPA of 3.0. Additional exam requirements/recommendations for international students: Required—TOEFL (minimum score 550 paper-based). Electronic applications accepted. *Faculty research:* History of philosophy, history and philosophy of science, ethics, social and political philosophy.

University of Lethbridge, School of Graduate Studies, Lethbridge, AB T1K 3M4, Canada. Offers addictions counseling (M Sc); agricultural biotechnology (M Sc); agricultural studies (M Sc, MA); anthropology (MA); archaeology (M Sc, MA); art (MA, MFA); biochemistry (M Sc); biological sciences (M Sc); biomolecular science (PhD); biosystems and biodiversity (PhD); Canadian studies (MA); chemistry (M Sc); computer science (M Sc); computer science and geographical information science (M Sc); counseling (MC); counseling psychology (M Ed); dramatic arts (MA); earth, space, and physical science (PhD); economics (MA); education (MA); educational leadership (M Ed); English (MA); environmental science (M Sc); evolution and behavior (PhD); exercise science (M Sc); French (MA); French/German (MA); French/Spanish (MA); general education (M Ed); geography (M Sc, MA); German (MA); health sciences (M Sc); individualized multidisciplinary (M Sc, MA); kinesiology (M Sc, MA); management (M Sc), including accounting, finance, general management, human resource management and labor relations, information systems, international management, marketing, policy and strategy; mathematics (M Sc); modern languages (MA); music (M Mus, MA); Native American studies (MA); neuroscience (M Sc, PhD); new media (MA, MFA); nursing (M Sc, MN); philosophy (MA); physics (M Sc); political science (MA); psychology (M Sc, MA); religious studies (MA); sociology (MA); theatre and dramatic arts (MFA); theoretical and computational science (PhD); urban and regional studies (MA); women and gender studies (MA). Part-time and evening/weekend programs available. *Faculty:* 358. *Students:* 445 full-time (243 women), 116 part-time (72 women). Average age 31. 351 applicants, 26% accepted, 87 enrolled. In 2014, 129 master's, 13 doctorates awarded. *Degree requirements:* For master's, thesis (for some programs); for doctorate, comprehensive exam, thesis/dissertation. *Entrance requirements:* For master's, GMAT (for M Sc in management), bachelor's degree in related field, minimum GPA of 3.0 during previous 20 graded semester courses, 2 years'

teaching or related experience (M Ed); for doctorate, master's degree, minimum graduate GPA of 3.5. Additional exam requirements/recommendations for international students: Required—TOEFL. Application fee: $100 Canadian dollars. *Financial support:* Fellowships, research assistantships, teaching assistantships, scholarships/grants, health care benefits, and unspecified assistantships available. *Faculty research:* Movement and brain plasticity, gibberellin physiology, photosynthesis, carbon cycling, molecular properties of main-group ring components. *Application contact:* School of Graduate Studies, 403-329-5194, E-mail: sgsinquiries@uleth.ca. Website: http://www.uleth.ca/graduatestudies/

University of Louisville, Graduate School, College of Arts and Sciences, Department of Philosophy, Louisville, KY 40292-0001. Offers humanities (MA). *Students:* 9 part-time (7 women); includes 4 minority (all Black or African American, non-Hispanic/Latino). Average age 34. *Degree requirements:* For master's, one foreign language, thesis or alternative. *Entrance requirements:* For master's, GRE General Test. Additional exam requirements/recommendations for international students: Required—TOEFL (minimum score 550 paper-based; 79 iBT). *Application deadline:* For fall admission, 5/1 priority date for international students; for spring admission, 11/1 priority date for international students; for summer admission, 4/1 priority date for international students. Applications are processed on a rolling basis. Application fee: $60. Electronic applications accepted. *Expenses:* Tuition, state resident: full-time $11,326; part-time $630 per credit hour. Tuition, nonresident: full-time $23,568; part-time $1311 per credit hour. *Required fees:* $196. Tuition and fees vary according to program and reciprocity agreements. *Unit head:* Dr. Robert Kimball, Chair, 502-852-0488, Fax: 502-852-0459, E-mail: robert.kimball@louisville.edu. *Application contact:* Libby Leggett, Director, Graduate Admissions, 502-852-3101, Fax: 502-852-6536, E-mail: gradadm@louisville.edu. Website: http://louisville.edu/philosophy

The University of Manchester, School of Social Sciences, Manchester, United Kingdom. Offers ethnographic documentary (M Phil); interdisciplinary study of culture (PhD); philosophy (PhD); politics (PhD); social anthropology (PhD); social anthropology with visual media (PhD); social change (PhD); social statistics (PhD); sociology (PhD); visual anthropology (M Phil).

University of Manitoba, Faculty of Graduate Studies, Faculty of Arts, Department of Philosophy, Winnipeg, MB R3T 2N2, Canada. Offers MA. *Degree requirements:* For master's, variable foreign language requirement, thesis or alternative.

University of Maryland, College Park, Academic Affairs, College of Arts and Humanities, Department of Philosophy, College Park, MD 20742. Offers MA, PhD. *Degree requirements:* For master's, thesis optional; for doctorate, thesis/dissertation, 2 semesters of undergraduate teaching, qualification in symbolic logic. *Entrance requirements:* For master's, GRE General Test, minimum GPA of 3.0, philosophy paper, writing sample, 3 letters of recommendation; for doctorate, GRE General Test, minimum GPA of 3.0, philosophy paper, writing sample. Electronic applications accepted. *Faculty research:* Contemporary British and American philosophy, the relationship between philosophy and other disciplines, ethical and conceptual issues in public policy.

University of Massachusetts Amherst, Graduate School, College of Humanities and Fine Arts, Department of Philosophy, Amherst, MA 01003. Offers MA, PhD. Part-time programs available. *Faculty:* 18 full-time (6 women). *Students:* 26 full-time (6 women), 19 part-time (6 women); includes 4 minority (1 Black or African American, non-Hispanic/Latino; 1 Asian, non-Hispanic/Latino; 1 Hispanic/Latino; 1 Two or more races, non-Hispanic/Latino), 9 international. Average age 30. 134 applicants, 18% accepted, 7 enrolled. In 2014, 1 master's, 3 doctorates awarded. Terminal master's awarded for partial completion of doctoral program. *Degree requirements:* For master's, thesis optional; for doctorate, comprehensive exam, thesis/dissertation. *Entrance requirements:* For master's and doctorate, GRE General Test, writing sample, 3 letters of recommendation. Additional exam requirements/recommendations for international students: Required—TOEFL (minimum score 550 paper-based; 80 iBT), IELTS (minimum score 6.5). *Application deadline:* For fall admission, 1/2 for domestic and international students. Applications are processed on a rolling basis. Application fee: $75. Electronic applications accepted. *Expenses:* Tuition, state resident: full-time $1980; part-time $110 per credit. Tuition, nonresident: full-time $14,644; part-time $414 per credit. *Required fees:* $11,417. One-time fee: $357. *Financial support:* Fellowships with full and partial tuition reimbursements, research assistantships with full and partial tuition reimbursements, teaching assistantships with full and partial tuition reimbursements, career-related internships or fieldwork, Federal Work-Study, scholarships/grants, traineeships, health care benefits, tuition waivers (full and partial), and unspecified assistantships available. Support available to part-time students. Financial award application deadline: 1/2. *Unit head:* Dr. Phillip Bricker, Graduate Program Director, 413-545-0836, Fax: 413-577-3800. *Application contact:* Lindsay DeSantis, Supervisor of Admissions, 413-545-0722, Fax: 413-577-0010, E-mail: gradadm@grad.umass.edu. Website: http://www.umass.edu/philosophy/

University of Memphis, Graduate School, College of Arts and Sciences, Department of Philosophy, Memphis, TN 38152. Offers MA, PhD. Part-time and evening/weekend programs available. *Faculty:* 9 full-time (3 women), 1 part-time/adjunct (0 women). *Students:* 25 full-time (6 women), 5 part-time (2 women); includes 10 minority (4 Black or African American, non-Hispanic/Latino; 3 Hispanic/Latino; 3 Two or more races, non-Hispanic/Latino), 5 international. Average age 30. 58 applicants, 41% accepted, 5 enrolled. In 2014, 7 master's, 4 doctorates awarded. Terminal master's awarded for partial completion of doctoral program. *Degree requirements:* For master's, comprehensive exam, thesis optional, 33 hours of class work; for doctorate, 2 foreign languages, comprehensive exam, thesis/dissertation, 72 hours of class work. *Entrance requirements:* For master's, GRE General Test, minimum GPA of 2.5, 18 hours of undergraduate course work in philosophy, 3 letters of recommendation, writing sample; for doctorate, GRE General Test, minimum GPA of 3.0, bachelor's degree in philosophy, 3 letters of recommendation, writing sample. Additional exam requirements/recommendations for international students: Required—TOEFL (minimum score 550 paper-based). *Application deadline:* For fall admission, 1/15 for domestic students. Application fee: $35 ($60 for international students). *Financial support:* In 2014–15, 9 students received support. Fellowships with full tuition reimbursements available, research assistantships with full tuition reimbursements available, teaching assistantships with full tuition reimbursements available, Federal Work-Study, scholarships/grants, tuition waivers (full), and unspecified assistantships available. Financial award application deadline: 2/15; financial award applicants required to submit FAFSA. *Faculty research:* Continental philosophy, ethics, analytic philosophy, feminist theory, Africana philosophy. *Unit head:* Dr. Deborah Tollefsen, Chair, 901-678-2535, Fax: 901-678-4365, E-mail: dtollfsn@memphis.edu. *Application contact:* Dr. Mary Beth Mader, Coordinator of Admission, 901-678-4526. Website: http://www.memphis.edu/philosophy/

University of Miami, Graduate School, College of Arts and Sciences, Department of Philosophy, Coral Gables, FL 33124. Offers MA, PhD. Part-time programs available. Terminal master's awarded for partial completion of doctoral program. *Degree requirements:* For master's, thesis or alternative; for doctorate, comprehensive exam, thesis/dissertation. *Entrance requirements:* For master's, GRE General Test; for doctorate, GRE General Test, minimum GPA of 3.0, 3 letters of recommendation, writing sample. Additional exam requirements/recommendations for international students: Required—TOEFL. Electronic applications accepted. *Faculty research:* Ethics, epistemology, pragmatism, philosophy of science, metaphysics.

University of Michigan, Horace H. Rackham School of Graduate Studies, College of Literature, Science, and the Arts, Department of Philosophy, Ann Arbor, MI 48109. Offers AM, PhD. *Faculty:* 23 full-time (6 women), 1 part-time/adjunct (0 women). *Students:* 38 full-time (13 women); includes 8 minority (6 Asian, non-Hispanic/Latino; 1 Hispanic/Latino; 1 Two or more races, non-Hispanic/Latino), 8 international. Average age 29. 259 applicants, 7% accepted, 4 enrolled. In 2014, 7 master's, 6 doctorates awarded. Terminal master's awarded for partial completion of doctoral program. *Degree requirements:* For doctorate, one foreign language, thesis/dissertation, oral defense of dissertation. *Entrance requirements:* For master's and doctorate, 3 letters of recommendation, writing sample. Additional exam requirements/recommendations for international students: Required—TOEFL (minimum score 560 paper-based; 84 iBT). *Application deadline:* For fall admission, 1/7 for domestic and international students. Application fee: $75 ($90 for international students). Electronic applications accepted. *Expenses:* Expenses: $40,892 pre-candidate tuition and fees. *Financial support:* In 2014–15, 38 students received support, including fellowships with full tuition reimbursements available (averaging $23,000 per year), teaching assistantships with full tuition reimbursements available (averaging $23,000 per year); health care benefits also available. Financial award application deadline: 1/7. *Faculty research:* Ethics, metaphysics, philosophy of language and mind, political and social philosophy, philosophy of science. *Unit head:* Elizabeth S. Anderson, Chair, 734-764-6285, Fax: 734-763-8071, E-mail: phil-chair@umich.edu. *Application contact:* Linda Shultes, Graduate Program Coordinator, 734-764-3260, Fax: 734-763-8071, E-mail: phil-admissions@umich.edu. Website: http://www.lsa.umich.edu/philosophy/

University of Minnesota, Twin Cities Campus, Graduate School, College of Liberal Arts, Department of Philosophy, Minneapolis, MN 55455-0213. Offers MA, PhD. Part-time programs available. Terminal master's awarded for partial completion of doctoral program. *Degree requirements:* For master's, comprehensive exam, thesis or 3 papers; oral exam; for doctorate, comprehensive exam, thesis/dissertation. *Entrance requirements:* For master's and doctorate, GRE. Additional exam requirements/recommendations for international students: Required—TOEFL (minimum score 550 paper-based), IELTS (minimum score 6.5), or Michigan English Language Assessment Battery (minimum score 80). Electronic applications accepted. *Faculty research:* Philosophy of science; ethics and social/political philosophy; logic, language, and mind.

University of Mississippi, Graduate School, College of Liberal Arts, Department of Philosophy and Religions, University, MS 38677. Offers philosophy (MA). *Degree requirements:* For master's, thesis. *Entrance requirements:* For master's, GRE General Test, minimum GPA of 3.0. Additional exam requirements/recommendations for international students: Required—TOEFL. Electronic applications accepted.

University of Missouri, Office of Research and Graduate Studies, College of Arts and Science, Department of Philosophy, Columbia, MO 65211. Offers MA, PhD. *Faculty:* 13 full-time (2 women), 4 part-time/adjunct (0 women). *Students:* 30 full-time (4 women); includes 2 minority (1 Black or African American, non-Hispanic/Latino; 1 Asian, non-Hispanic/Latino), 5 international. Average age 29. 42 applicants, 31% accepted, 7 enrolled. In 2014, 8 master's awarded. Terminal master's awarded for partial completion of doctoral program. *Degree requirements:* For doctorate, one foreign language, comprehensive exam, thesis/dissertation. *Entrance requirements:* For master's and doctorate, GRE General Test (minimum score 650 verbal, 700 quantitative), minimum GPA of 3.0, 3.9 in major. Additional exam requirements/recommendations for international students: Required—TOEFL (minimum score 500 paper-based; 61 iBT). *Application deadline:* For fall admission, 1/15 priority date for domestic and international students. Applications are processed on a rolling basis. Application fee: $55 ($75 for international students). Electronic applications accepted. *Financial support:* Fellowships with full tuition reimbursements, research assistantships with full tuition reimbursements, teaching assistantships with full tuition reimbursements, institutionally sponsored loans, health care benefits, and unspecified assistantships available. Financial award application deadline: 2/1. *Faculty research:* Epistemology, political philosophy, philosophy of biology, decision/game/rational choice theory, ethics, philosophy of mind and psychology, Indian philosophy, metaphysics, action theory. *Unit head:* Dr. Robert Johnson, Department Chair, 573-884-6210, E-mail: johnsonrn@missouri.edu. *Application contact:* Jonni Paxton, Administrative Assistant, 573-882-2871, E-mail: paxtonj@missouri.edu. Website: http://philosophy.missouri.edu/graduate.html

University of Missouri–St. Louis, College of Arts and Sciences, Department of Philosophy, St. Louis, MO 63121. Offers MA. Part-time and evening/weekend programs available. *Faculty:* 7 full-time (1 woman), 2 part-time/adjunct (1 woman). *Students:* 13 full-time (3 women), 7 part-time (1 woman); includes 3 minority (1 Black or African American, non-Hispanic/Latino; 2 Two or more races, non-Hispanic/Latino). Average age 29. 35 applicants, 63% accepted, 8 enrolled. In 2014, 10 master's awarded. *Entrance requirements:* For master's, writing sample, 3 letters of recommendation. Additional exam requirements/recommendations for international students: Required—TOEFL (minimum score 550 paper-based; 79 iBT), IELTS (minimum score 6.5). *Application deadline:* For fall admission, 6/1 priority date for domestic and international students; for spring admission, 12/1 priority date for domestic and international students. Applications are processed on a rolling basis. Application fee: $50 ($40 for international students). Electronic applications accepted. *Expenses:* Tuition, state resident: full-time $7364; part-time $409.10 per hour. Tuition, nonresident: full-time $18,153; part-time $1008.50 per hour. *Financial support:* In 2014–15, 2 research assistantships with full and partial tuition reimbursements (averaging $5,400 per year), 16 teaching assistantships with full and partial tuition reimbursements (averaging $6,510 per year) were awarded. Financial award applicants required to submit FAFSA. *Faculty research:* Ethics, philosophy and history of science, philosophical social science, aesthetics. *Unit head:* Dr. Eric Wiland, Graduate Program Director, 314-516-5495, Fax: 314-516-5816, E-mail: wiland@umsl.edu. *Application contact:* 314-516-5458, Fax: 314-516-6996, E-mail: gradadm@umsl.edu. Website: http://www.umsl.edu/~philo/

The University of Montana, Graduate School, College of Humanities and Sciences, Department of Philosophy, Missoula, MT 59812-0002. Offers MA. *Degree requirements:* For master's, thesis or additional course work/professional paper. *Entrance requirements:* For master's, GRE General Test. Additional exam requirements/recommendations for international students: Required—TOEFL (minimum score 525 paper-based). *Faculty research:* Philosophy of law, natural science, feminism, and technology; environmental, business, and medical ethics.

University of Nebraska–Lincoln, Graduate College, College of Arts and Sciences, Department of Philosophy, Lincoln, NE 68588. Offers MA, PhD. *Degree requirements:* For master's, thesis optional; for doctorate, comprehensive exam, thesis/dissertation. *Entrance requirements:* For master's and doctorate, GRE General Test, writing sample. Additional exam requirements/recommendations for international students: Required—TOEFL (minimum score 600 paper-based). Electronic applications accepted. *Faculty research:* Ethics, epistemology, metaphysics, cognitive science, history of philosophy.

Philosophy

University of Nevada, Reno, Graduate School, College of Liberal Arts, Department of Philosophy, Reno, NV 89557. Offers MA. *Degree requirements:* For master's, thesis optional. *Entrance requirements:* For master's, GRE General Test, minimum GPA of 2.75. Additional exam requirements/recommendations for international students: Required—TOEFL (minimum score 500 paper-based; 61 iBT), IELTS (minimum score 6). Electronic applications accepted. *Faculty research:* Ancient philosophy (Aristotle), ethics, political theory, violence, Continental philosophy.

University of New Mexico, Graduate School, College of Arts and Sciences, Program in Philosophy, Albuquerque, NM 87131-2039. Offers MA, PhD. Part-time programs available. *Faculty:* 8 full-time (3 women). *Students:* 23 full-time (4 women), 11 part-time (3 women); includes 4 minority (1 Black or African American, non-Hispanic/Latino; 1 Asian, non-Hispanic/Latino; 2 Two or more races, non-Hispanic/Latino), 2 international. Average age 32. 53 applicants, 32% accepted, 7 enrolled. In 2014, 5 master's, 5 doctorates awarded. Terminal master's awarded for partial completion of doctoral program. *Degree requirements:* For master's, thesis (for some programs); for doctorate, one foreign language, comprehensive exam, thesis/dissertation. *Entrance requirements:* For master's and doctorate, GRE. Additional exam requirements/recommendations for international students: Required—TOEFL. *Application deadline:* For fall admission, 3/1 for domestic and international students; for spring admission, 11/1 for domestic and international students. Application fee: $50. Electronic applications accepted. *Financial support:* In 2014–15, 13 students received support, including fellowships with tuition reimbursements available (averaging $7,818 per year), research assistantships (averaging $7,818 per year), 13 teaching assistantships with tuition reimbursements available (averaging $7,818 per year). Financial award application deadline: 3/1; financial award applicants required to submit FAFSA. *Faculty research:* Continental philosophy, Indian philosophy, history of philosophy, ethics, phenomenology and existentialism, philosophy of art and literature. *Unit head:* Dr. Richard Hayes, Chair, 505-277-2405, Fax: 505-277-6362, E-mail: rhayes@unm.edu. *Application contact:* Mercedes Nysus, Administrative Assistant II, 505-277-2405, Fax: 505-277-6362, E-mail: thinker@unm.edu.
Website: http://philosophy.unm.edu/

The University of North Carolina at Chapel Hill, Graduate School, College of Arts and Sciences, Department of Philosophy, Chapel Hill, NC 27599. Offers MA, PhD. *Degree requirements:* For master's, comprehensive exam, thesis; for doctorate, comprehensive exam, thesis/dissertation. *Entrance requirements:* For master's and doctorate, GRE General Test, minimum GPA of 3.0.

The University of North Carolina at Charlotte, College of Liberal Arts and Sciences, Department of Philosophy, Charlotte, NC 28223-0001. Offers applied ethics (Graduate Certificate); ethics and applied philosophy (MA). *Faculty:* 11 full-time (3 women). *Students:* 3 full-time (1 woman), 8 part-time (0 women); includes 2 minority (1 Black or African American, non-Hispanic/Latino; 1 Hispanic/Latino). Average age 29. 5 applicants, 100% accepted, 5 enrolled. In 2014, 7 master's, 2 other advanced degrees awarded. Terminal master's awarded for partial completion of doctoral program. *Degree requirements:* For master's, thesis or alternative, project. *Entrance requirements:* For master's, GRE or MAT, 3 letters of recommendation. Additional exam requirements/recommendations for international students: Required—TOEFL (minimum score 557 paper-based; 83 iBT). *Application deadline:* For fall admission, 5/1 for domestic and international students; for spring admission, 10/1 for domestic and international students. Applications are processed on a rolling basis. Application fee: $75. Electronic applications accepted. *Expenses:* Tuition, state resident: full-time $4008. Tuition, nonresident: full-time $16,295. *Required fees:* $2755. Tuition and fees vary according to course load and program. *Financial support:* In 2014–15, 5 students received support, including 1 research assistantship (averaging $3,000 per year), 4 teaching assistantships (averaging $6,125 per year); unspecified assistantships and administrative assistantships also available. Support available to part-time students. Financial award applicants required to submit FAFSA. *Faculty research:* Ethical issues in long-term care, cognitive enhancement and genetics, ethics and international affairs, political and aesthetic issues arising from contemporary American popular music, moral and legal issues made salient by emerging technologies. *Total annual research expenditures:* $1,547. *Unit head:* Dr. Shannon Sullivan, Chair, 704-687-5412, Fax: 704-687-2172. *Application contact:* Kathy B. Giddings, Director of Graduate Admissions, 704-687-5503, Fax: 704-687-1668, E-mail: gradadm@uncc.edu.
Website: http://philosophy.uncc.edu/

University of North Florida, College of Arts and Sciences, Department of Philosophy, Jacksonville, FL 32224. Offers applied ethics (Graduate Certificate); practical philosophy and applied ethics (MA). Part-time and evening/weekend programs available. *Faculty:* 9 full-time (5 women), 1 part-time/adjunct (0 women). *Students:* 8 full-time (3 women), 8 part-time (3 women); includes 2 minority (both Black or African American, non-Hispanic/Latino), 1 international. Average age 33. 14 applicants, 71% accepted, 5 enrolled. In 2014, 8 master's awarded. *Entrance requirements:* For master's, GRE General Test, minimum GPA of 3.0 in last 60 hours, 3 letters of recommendation, writing sample. Additional exam requirements/recommendations for international students: Required—TOEFL (minimum score 500 paper-based; 61 iBT). *Application deadline:* For fall admission, 7/1 priority date for domestic students, 5/1 for international students. Application fee: $30. Electronic applications accepted. *Expenses:* Tuition, state resident: full-time $9794; part-time $408.10 per credit hour. Tuition, nonresident: full-time $22,383; part-time $932.61 per credit hour. *Required fees:* $2047; $85.29 per credit hour. Tuition and fees vary according to course load and program. *Financial support:* In 2014–15, 3 students received support. Research assistantships, teaching assistantships, Federal Work-Study, scholarships/grants, tuition waivers, and unspecified assistantships available. Financial award application deadline: 4/1; financial award applicants required to submit FAFSA. *Faculty research:* Late modern philosophy, pragmatism, religion and American culture, hermeneutics, philosophy of mind. *Total annual research expenditures:* $34,367. *Unit head:* Dr. Hans-Herbert Koegler, Chair, 904-620-1330, Fax: 904-620-1840, E-mail: hkoegler@unf.edu. *Application contact:* Dr. Amanda Pascale, Director, The Graduate School, 904-620-1360, Fax: 904-620-1362, E-mail: graduateschool@unf.edu.
Website: http://www.unf.edu/coas/philosophy/

University of North Texas, Robert B. Toulouse School of Graduate Studies, Denton, TX 76203-5459. Offers accounting (MS); applied anthropology (MA, MS); applied behavior analysis (Certificate); applied geography (MA); applied technology and performance improvement (M Ed, MS); art education (MA); art history (MA); art museum education (Certificate); arts leadership (Certificate); audiology (Au D); behavior analysis (MS); behavioral science (PhD); biochemistry and molecular biology (MS); biology (MA, MS); biomedical engineering (MS); business analysis (MS); chemistry (MS); clinical health psychology (PhD); communication studies (MA, MS); computer engineering (MS); computer science (MS); counseling (M Ed, MS), including clinical mental health counseling (MS), college and university counseling, elementary school counseling, secondary school counseling; creative writing (MA); criminal justice (MS); curriculum and instruction (M Ed); decision sciences (MBA); design (MA, MFA), including fashion design (MFA), innovation studies, interior design (MFA); early childhood studies (MS); economics (MS); educational leadership (M Ed, Ed D); educational psychology (MS, PhD), including family studies (MS), gifted and talented (MS), human development (MS), learning and cognition (MS), research, measurement and evaluation (MS); electrical engineering (MS); emergency management (MPA); engineering technology (MS); English (MA); English as a second language (MA); environmental science (MS); finance (MBA, MS); financial management (MPA); French (MA); health services management (MBA); higher education (M Ed, Ed D); history (MA, MS); hospitality management (MS); human resources management (MPA); information science (MS); information systems (PhD); information technologies (MBA); interdisciplinary studies (MA, MS); international studies (MA); international sustainable tourism (MS); jazz studies (MM); journalism (MA, MJ, Graduate Certificate), including interactive and virtual digital communication (Graduate Certificate), narrative journalism (Graduate Certificate), public relations (Graduate Certificate); kinesiology (MS); linguistics (MA); local government management (MPA); logistics (PhD); logistics and supply chain management (MBA); long-term care, senior housing, and aging services (MA); management (PhD); marketing (MBA); mathematics (MA, MS); mechanical and energy engineering (MS, PhD); music (MA), including ethnomusicology, music theory, musicology, performance; music composition (PhD); music education (MM Ed, PhD); nonprofit management (MPA); operations and supply chain management (MBA); performance (MM, DMA); philosophy (MA); political science (MA); professional and technical communication (MA); radio, television and film (MA, MFA); rehabilitation counseling (Certificate); sociology (MA); Spanish (MA); special education (M Ed); speech-language pathology (MA); strategic management (MBA); studio art (MFA); teaching (M Ed); MBA/MS. Part-time and evening/weekend programs available. Postbaccalaureate distance learning degree programs offered. *Faculty:* 651 full-time (215 women), 233 part-time/adjunct (139 women). *Students:* 3,040 full-time (1,598 women), 3,401 part-time (2,097 women); includes 1,740 minority (533 Black or African American, non-Hispanic/Latino; 15 American Indian or Alaska Native, non-Hispanic/Latino; 286 Asian, non-Hispanic/Latino; 746 Hispanic/Latino; 3 Native Hawaiian or other Pacific Islander, non-Hispanic/Latino; 157 Two or more races, non-Hispanic/Latino), 1,145 international. Terminal master's awarded for partial completion of doctoral program. *Degree requirements:* For master's, variable foreign language requirement, comprehensive exam (for some programs), thesis (for some programs); for doctorate, variable foreign language requirement, comprehensive exam (for some programs), thesis/dissertation; for other advanced degree, variable foreign language requirement, comprehensive exam (for some programs). *Entrance requirements:* For master's and doctorate, GRE, GMAT. Additional exam requirements/recommendations for international students: Required—TOEFL (minimum score 550 paper-based; 79 iBT). *Application deadline:* For fall admission, 7/15 for domestic students, 3/15 for international students; for spring admission, 11/15 for domestic students, 9/15 for international students; for summer admission, 5/1 for domestic students. Applications are processed on a rolling basis. Application fee: $60. Electronic applications accepted. *Expenses:* Tuition, state resident: full-time $5450; part-time $3633 per year. Tuition, nonresident: full-time $11,966; part-time $7977 per year. *Required fees:* $1301; $398 per credit hour. $685 per semester. Tuition and fees vary according to program and reciprocity agreements. *Financial support:* Fellowships with partial tuition reimbursements, research assistantships with partial tuition reimbursements, teaching assistantships, career-related internships or fieldwork, Federal Work-Study, institutionally sponsored loans, scholarships/grants, health care benefits, and library assistantships available. Support available to part-time students. Financial award applicants required to submit FAFSA. *Unit head:* Mark Wardell, Dean, 940-565-2383, E-mail: mark.wardell@unt.edu. *Application contact:* Toulouse School of Graduate Studies, 940-565-2383, Fax: 940-565-2141, E-mail: gradsch@unt.edu.
Website: http://tsgs.unt.edu/

University of Notre Dame, Graduate School, College of Arts and Letters, Division of Humanities, Department of Philosophy, Notre Dame, IN 46556. Offers PhD. *Degree requirements:* For doctorate, 2 foreign languages, thesis/dissertation, candidacy exam. *Entrance requirements:* For doctorate, GRE General Test. Additional exam requirements/recommendations for international students: Required—TOEFL (minimum score 600 paper-based; 80 iBT). Electronic applications accepted. *Faculty research:* History of philosophy, ethics, philosophy of science and logic, philosophy of religion, Continental philosophy, metaphysics.

University of Oklahoma, College of Arts and Sciences, Department of Philosophy, Norman, OK 73019. Offers MA, PhD. Part-time and evening/weekend programs available. *Faculty:* 16 full-time (5 women). *Students:* 22 full-time (5 women), 11 part-time (2 women); includes 2 minority (1 Asian, non-Hispanic/Latino; 1 Hispanic/Latino), 4 international. Average age 29. 43 applicants, 56% accepted, 5 enrolled. In 2014, 2 master's awarded. Terminal master's awarded for partial completion of doctoral program. *Degree requirements:* For master's, thesis optional; for doctorate, comprehensive exam, thesis/dissertation, qualifying exam in second year. *Entrance requirements:* For master's and doctorate, GRE, BA in philosophy or related area. Additional exam requirements/recommendations for international students: Required—TOEFL (minimum score 79 iBT). *Application deadline:* For fall admission, 1/31 for domestic and international students; for spring admission, 10/15 for domestic and international students. Application fee: $50 ($100 for international students). Electronic applications accepted. *Expenses:* Tuition, state resident: full-time $4394; part-time $183.10 per credit hour. Tuition, nonresident: full-time $16,970; part-time $707.10 per credit hour. *Required fees:* $2892; $109.95 per credit hour. $126.50 per semester. *Financial support:* In 2014–15, 28 students received support, including 2 fellowships with full tuition reimbursements available (averaging $5,250 per year), 2 research assistantships with partial tuition reimbursements available (averaging $16,000 per year), 21 teaching assistantships with partial tuition reimbursements available (averaging $16,719 per year). Financial award application deadline: 6/1; financial award applicants required to submit FAFSA. *Faculty research:* Philosophy of religion, epistemology and metaphysics, history of philosophy, ethics and aesthetics, Chinese philosophy. *Total annual research expenditures:* $58,265. *Unit head:* Dr. Wayne Riggs, Associate Professor and Chair, 405-325-6324, Fax: 405-325-2660, E-mail: wriggs@ou.edu. *Application contact:* Shelley Konieczny, Department Secretary, 405-325-6324, Fax: 405-325-2660, E-mail: skonieczny@ou.edu.
Website: http://www.ou.edu/ouphil

University of Oregon, Graduate School, College of Arts and Sciences, Department of Philosophy, Eugene, OR 97403. Offers MA, PhD. Terminal master's awarded for partial completion of doctoral program. *Degree requirements:* For master's, one foreign language, thesis or alternative; for doctorate, one foreign language, thesis/dissertation. *Entrance requirements:* For master's and doctorate, GRE General Test. Additional exam requirements/recommendations for international students: Required—TOEFL. *Faculty research:* Social and political philosophy, feminist philosophy, American philosophy, aesthetics, philosophy of mind.

University of Ottawa, Faculty of Graduate and Postdoctoral Studies, Faculty of Arts, Department of Philosophy, Ottawa, ON K1N 6N5, Canada. Offers MA, PhD. *Degree requirements:* For master's, thesis or alternative; for doctorate, comprehensive exam, thesis/dissertation. *Entrance requirements:* For master's, honors degree or equivalent, minimum B average; for doctorate, master's degree, minimum B+ average. Electronic applications accepted. *Faculty research:* History of philosophy (ancient, medieval, modern and contemporary); metaphysics/epistemology; value theory: political philosophy, ethics.

University of Pennsylvania, School of Arts and Sciences, Graduate Group in Philosophy, Philadelphia, PA 19104. Offers AM, PhD, JD/PhD. *Faculty:* 12 full-time (3 women), 3 part-time/adjunct (1 woman). *Students:* 35 full-time (10 women), 1 part-time (0 women); includes 4 minority (1 Black or African American, non-Hispanic/Latino; 2 Hispanic/Latino; 1 Two or more races, non-Hispanic/Latino), 11 international. 96 applicants, 16% accepted, 6 enrolled. In 2014, 1 master's, 3 doctorates awarded. Terminal master's awarded for partial completion of doctoral program. *Degree requirements:* For master's, thesis; for doctorate, thesis/dissertation, 1 year of teaching experience. *Application deadline:* For fall admission, 12/1 priority date for domestic students. Application fee: $70. Electronic applications accepted. *Financial support:* Fellowships, teaching assistantships, institutionally sponsored loans, scholarships/grants, traineeships, health care benefits, and unspecified assistantships available. Financial award application deadline: 12/15. *Unit head:* Dr. Ralph M. Rosen, Associate Dean for Graduate Studies, 215-898-7156, Fax: 215-573-8068, E-mail: graddean@sas.upenn.edu. *Application contact:* Arts and Sciences Graduate Admissions, 215-573-5816, Fax: 215-573-8068, E-mail: gdasadmis@sas.upenn.edu.
Website: http://www.sas.upenn.edu/graduate-division

University of Pittsburgh, Dietrich School of Arts and Sciences, Department of History and Philosophy of Science, Pittsburgh, PA 15260. Offers MA, PhD. *Faculty:* 9 full-time (2 women). *Students:* 28 full-time (13 women); includes 1 minority (Asian, non-Hispanic/Latino), 8 international. Average age 28. 53 applicants, 9% accepted, 4 enrolled. In 2014, 2 master's, 4 doctorates awarded. Terminal master's awarded for partial completion of doctoral program. *Degree requirements:* For master's, one foreign language, comprehensive exam, minimum of 24 credit hours; for doctorate, one foreign language, comprehensive exam, thesis/dissertation, minimum of 72 credit hours, proficiency in logic. *Entrance requirements:* For master's and doctorate, GRE General Test, curriculum vitae, statement of career objective, 3 letters of recommendation, sample of written work. Additional exam requirements/recommendations for international students: Required—TOEFL (minimum score 577 paper-based; 90 iBT). *Application deadline:* For fall admission, 1/10 for domestic and international students. Application fee: $50. Electronic applications accepted. *Expenses:* Tuition, state resident: full-time $20,742; part-time $838 per credit. Tuition, nonresident: full-time $33,960; part-time $1389 per credit. *Required fees:* $800; $205 per term. Tuition and fees vary according to program. *Financial support:* In 2014–15, 20 students received support, including 12 fellowships with full tuition reimbursements available (averaging $23,749 per year), 8 teaching assistantships with full tuition reimbursements available (averaging $23,749 per year); health care benefits also available. Financial award application deadline: 1/10. *Faculty research:* History and philosophy of biology, psychology, neuroscience; history and philosophy of physics; early modern science; rhetoric of science; philosophy of social science. *Unit head:* Dr. James Lennox, Chairman, 412-624-5896, Fax: 412-624-6825, E-mail: jglennox@pitt.edu. *Application contact:* Joann McIntyre, Graduate Admissions Secretary, 412-624-5896, Fax: 412-624-6825, E-mail: vanna@pitt.edu.
Website: http://www.pitt.edu/~hpsdept/

University of Pittsburgh, Dietrich School of Arts and Sciences, Department of Philosophy, Pittsburgh, PA 15260. Offers MA, PhD. *Faculty:* 18 full-time (4 women). *Students:* 44 full-time (13 women); includes 7 minority (1 American Indian or Alaska Native, non-Hispanic/Latino; 4 Asian, non-Hispanic/Latino; 1 Hispanic/Latino; 1 Two or more races, non-Hispanic/Latino), 17 international. 192 applicants, 10% accepted, 6 enrolled. In 2014, 2 master's, 6 doctorates awarded. Terminal master's awarded for partial completion of doctoral program. *Degree requirements:* For master's, one foreign language; for doctorate, one foreign language, thesis/dissertation. *Entrance requirements:* For master's and doctorate, GRE General Test. Additional exam requirements/recommendations for international students: Required—TOEFL (minimum score 577 paper-based; 90 iBT), IELTS (minimum score 7). *Application deadline:* For fall admission, 1/10 for domestic and international students. Application fee: $50. Electronic applications accepted. *Expenses:* Tuition, state resident: full-time $20,742; part-time $838 per credit. Tuition, nonresident: full-time $33,960; part-time $1389 per credit. *Required fees:* $800; $205 per term. Tuition and fees vary according to program. *Financial support:* In 2014–15, 40 students received support, including 17 fellowships with full tuition reimbursements available (averaging $27,882 per year), 2 research assistantships with full tuition reimbursements available (averaging $21,268 per year), 21 teaching assistantships with full tuition reimbursements available (averaging $17,130 per year); Federal Work-Study, scholarships/grants, health care benefits, and tuition waivers (full and partial) also available. Financial award application deadline: 1/10. *Faculty research:* Metaphysics and epistemology, ethics, philosophy of science, history of philosophy, logic. *Unit head:* Dr. Anil Gupta, Chairman, 412-624-5768, Fax: 412-624-5377, E-mail: agupta@pitt.edu. *Application contact:* Kathy Rivet, Graduate Secretary, 412-624-5774, Fax: 412-624-5377, E-mail: krivet@pitt.edu.
Website: http://www.philosophy.pitt.edu/

University of Puerto Rico, Río Piedras Campus, College of Humanities, Department of Philosophy, San Juan, PR 00931-3300. Offers MA. Part-time programs available. *Degree requirements:* For master's, one foreign language, comprehensive exam, thesis. *Entrance requirements:* For master's, PAEG or GRE, interview, minimum GPA of 3.0, letter of recommendation (2).

University of Regina, Faculty of Graduate Studies and Research, Faculty of Arts, Department of Philosophy, Regina, SK S4S 0A2, Canada. Offers MA. Offered as a special case program. Part-time programs available. *Faculty:* 10 full-time (3 women). *Students:* 1 full-time (0 women). In 2014, 1 master's awarded. *Degree requirements:* For master's, thesis. *Entrance requirements:* Additional exam requirements/recommendations for international students: Required—TOEFL (minimum score 580 paper-based; 80 iBT), IELTS (minimum score 6.5), PTE (minimum score 59). *Application deadline:* Applications are processed on a rolling basis. Application fee: $100. Electronic applications accepted. *Expenses:* Tuition, area resident: Full-time $4900 Canadian dollars; part-time $837.65 Canadian dollars per semester. *International tuition:* $7900 Canadian dollars full-time. *Required fees:* $396 Canadian dollars; $86.90 Canadian dollars per semester. *Financial support:* In 2014–15, 1 fellowship (averaging $6,000 per year), 1 teaching assistantship (averaging $2,427 per year) were awarded; research assistantships and scholarships/grants also available. Financial award application deadline: 6/15. *Faculty research:* Ethics, politics, religion, history, critical thinking. *Unit head:* Dr. Eldon Soifer, Department Head, 306-585-4301, Fax: 306-585-4827, E-mail: eldon.soifer@uregina.ca.
Website: http://www.uregina.ca/arts/philosophy-classics

University of Regina, Faculty of Graduate Studies and Research, Faculty of Arts, Program in Social and Political Thought, Regina, SK S4S 0A2, Canada. Offers MA. Part-time programs available. *Students:* 2 full-time (0 women), 3 part-time (1 woman). 7 applicants, 57% accepted. In 2014, 1 master's awarded. *Degree requirements:* For master's, thesis. *Entrance requirements:* Additional exam requirements/recommendations for international students: Required—TOEFL (minimum score 580 paper-based; 80 iBT), IELTS (minimum score 6.5), PTE (minimum score 59). *Application deadline:* For fall admission, 3/30 for domestic and international students. Application fee: $100. Electronic applications accepted. *Expenses:* Tuition, area resident: Full-time $4900 Canadian dollars; part-time $837.65 Canadian dollars per

semester. *International tuition:* $7900 Canadian dollars full-time. *Required fees:* $396 Canadian dollars; $86.90 Canadian dollars per semester. *Financial support:* In 2014–15, 1 teaching assistantship (averaging $2,427 per year) was awarded; fellowships, research assistantships, and scholarships/grants also available. Financial award application deadline: 6/15. *Faculty research:* Liberalism and freedom, neo-conservatism, Aristotle's ethics, Kant's ethical theory and political philosophy, Hegel's philosophy of right. *Unit head:* Dr. Lee Ward, Graduate Coordinator, 306-359-1259, E-mail: lee.ward@uregina.ca. *Application contact:* Doreen Thompson, Administrative Assistant, 306-585-4332, E-mail: doreen.thompson@uregina.ca.

University of Rochester, School of Arts and Sciences, Department of Philosophy, Rochester, NY 14627. Offers MA, PhD. *Faculty:* 8 full-time (3 women). *Students:* 21 full-time (1 woman); includes 1 minority (Hispanic/Latino), 1 international. 59 applicants, 14% accepted, 2 enrolled. In 2014, 5 master's, 2 doctorates awarded. Terminal master's awarded for partial completion of doctoral program. *Degree requirements:* For doctorate, thesis/dissertation, qualifying exam. *Entrance requirements:* For master's, GRE General Test; for doctorate, GRE General Test, sample of written work. Additional exam requirements/recommendations for international students: Required—TOEFL. *Application deadline:* For fall admission, 1/15 priority date for domestic students. Application fee: $60. Electronic applications accepted. *Expenses:* Tuition: Full-time $46,150; part-time $1442 per credit hour. *Required fees:* $504. *Financial support:* Fellowships, research assistantships, teaching assistantships, and tuition waivers (full and partial) available. Financial award application deadline: 1/15. *Faculty research:* Epistemology, ethics, metaphysics, political philosophy, philosophy of science. *Unit head:* Deborah Modrak, Chair, 585-275-8111. *Application contact:* Amy Bray, Administrative Assistant, 585-275-4105.
Website: http://www.rochester.edu/College/PHL/

University of St. Thomas, Center for Thomistic Studies, Houston, TX 77006-4696. Offers philosophy (MA, PhD). Part-time programs available. *Faculty:* 5 full-time (1 woman). *Students:* 5 full-time (0 women), 27 part-time (5 women); includes 5 minority (all Hispanic/Latino), 1 international. Average age 39. 17 applicants, 59% accepted, 4 enrolled. In 2014, 2 master's, 3 doctorates awarded. Terminal master's awarded for partial completion of doctoral program. *Degree requirements:* For master's, one foreign language, comprehensive exam, thesis (for some programs); for doctorate, 2 foreign languages, comprehensive exam, thesis/dissertation. *Entrance requirements:* For master's, GRE, bachelor's degree with minimum GPA of 3.0 and at least 18 hours of undergraduate philosophy coursework, 3 letters of recommendation from professional educators, writing sample; for doctorate, GRE, MA in philosophy, 3 letters of recommendation from professional educators, writing sample, fulfillment of Latin language requirement (if not available at time of admission, must be completed no later than the third semester of doctoral study). Additional exam requirements/recommendations for international students: Required—TOEFL (minimum score 550 paper-based; 80 iBT). *Application deadline:* For fall admission, 2/1 priority date for domestic and international students. Applications are processed on a rolling basis. Application fee: $35. Electronic applications accepted. *Expenses:* Tuition: Full-time $20,124; part-time $1118 per credit hour. *Required fees:* $300; $82 per term. One-time fee: $100. Part-time tuition and fees vary according to course level, course load, campus/location and program. *Financial support:* In 2014–15, 17 students received support. Fellowships with tuition reimbursements available, teaching assistantships, Federal Work-Study, scholarships/grants, unspecified assistantships, and state work-study, institutional employment available. Support available to part-time students. Financial award application deadline: 2/1; financial award applicants required to submit FAFSA. *Faculty research:* Biomedical ethics, Islamic philosophy, metaphysics, virtue ethics, semiotics. *Unit head:* Dr. Thomas Osborne, Director, 713-942-3483, Fax: 713-942-3464, E-mail: osborntm@stthom.edu. *Application contact:* Valerie Hall, Administrative Assistant II, 713-525-3591, Fax: 713-942-3464, E-mail: hallvl@stthom.edu.
Website: http://www.stthom.edu/Academics/School_of_Arts_and_Sciences/Graduate/Philosophy/Philosophy_MA_PhD.aqf

University of Saskatchewan, College of Graduate Studies and Research, College of Arts and Science, Department of Philosophy, Saskatoon, SK S7N 5A2, Canada. Offers MA. *Degree requirements:* For master's, thesis. *Entrance requirements:* Additional exam requirements/recommendations for international students: Required—TOEFL (minimum score 80 iBT); Recommended—IELTS (minimum score 6.5). Electronic applications accepted.

University of South Africa, College of Human Sciences, Pretoria, South Africa. Offers adult education (M Ed); African languages (MA, PhD); African politics (MA, PhD); Afrikaans (MA, PhD); ancient history (MA, PhD); ancient Near Eastern studies (MA, PhD); anthropology (MA, PhD); applied linguistics (MA); Arabic (MA, PhD); archaeology (MA); art history (MA); Biblical archaeology (MA); Biblical studies (M Th, D Th, PhD); Christian spirituality (M Th, D Th); church history (M Th, D Th); classical studies (MA, PhD); clinical psychology (MA); communication (MA, PhD); comparative education (M Ed, Ed D); consulting psychology (D Admin, D Com, PhD); curriculum studies (M Ed, Ed D); development studies (M Admin, MA, D Admin, PhD); didactics (M Ed, Ed D); education (M Tech); education management (M Ed, Ed D); educational psychology (M Ed); English (MA); environmental education (M Ed); French (MA, PhD); German (MA, PhD); Greek (MA); guidance and counseling (M Ed); health studies (MA, PhD), including health sciences education (MA), health services management (MA), medical and surgical nursing science (critical care general) (MA), midwifery and neonatal nursing science (MA), trauma and emergency care (MA); history (MA, PhD); history of education (Ed D); inclusive education (M Ed, Ed D); information and communications technology policy and regulation (MA); information science (MA, MIS, PhD); international politics (MA, PhD); Islamic studies (MA, PhD); Italian (MA, PhD); Judaica (MA, PhD); linguistics (MA, PhD); mathematical education (M Ed); mathematics education (MA); missiology (M Th, D Th); modern Hebrew (MA, PhD); musicology (MA, MMus, D Mus, PhD); natural science education (M Ed); New Testament (M Th, D Th); Old Testament (D Th); pastoral therapy (M Th, D Th); philosophy (MA); philosophy of education (M Ed, Ed D); politics (MA, PhD); Portuguese (MA, PhD); practical theology (M Th, D Th); psychology (MA, MS, PhD); psychology of education (M Ed, Ed D); public health (MA); religious studies (MA, D Th, PhD); Romance languages (MA); Russian (MA, PhD); Semitic languages (MA, PhD); social behavior studies in HIV/AIDS (MA); social science (mental health) (MA); social science in development studies (MA); social science in psychology (MA); social science in social work (MA); social science in sociology (MA); social work (MSW, DSW, PhD); socio-education (M Ed, Ed D); sociolinguistics (MA); sociology (MA, PhD); Spanish (MA, PhD); systematic theology (M Th, D Th); TESOL (teaching English to speakers of other languages) (MA); theological ethics (M Th, D Th); theory of literature (MA, PhD); urban ministries (D Th); urban ministry (M Th).

University of South Carolina, The Graduate School, College of Arts and Sciences, Department of Philosophy, Columbia, SC 29208. Offers MA, PhD. Part-time programs available. *Degree requirements:* For master's, one foreign language, comprehensive exam, thesis optional; for doctorate, one foreign language, comprehensive exam, thesis/dissertation, candidacy exam. *Entrance requirements:* For master's and doctorate, GRE General Test, 18 hours in philosophy, 3 letters of recommendation, writing sample. Additional exam requirements/recommendations for international students: Required—

TOEFL (minimum score 590 paper-based). Electronic applications accepted. *Faculty research:* History of philosophy, ethics, philosophy of science, social philosophy.

University of Southern California, Graduate School, Dana and David Dornsife College of Letters, Arts and Sciences, School of Philosophy, Los Angeles, CA 90089. Offers MA, PhD, MA/JD. *Degree requirements:* For doctorate, one foreign language, thesis/dissertation, area exam, qualifying exam. *Entrance requirements:* For doctorate, GRE General Test. Additional exam requirements/recommendations for international students: Required—TOEFL. Electronic applications accepted. *Faculty research:* Logic, epistemology, ethics/metaethics, philosophy of language, philosophy of law.

University of South Florida, College of Arts and Sciences, Department of Humanities and Cultural Studies, Tampa, FL 33620-9951. Offers American studies (MA); liberal arts (MA), including Africana studies, film studies, humanities, social and political thought. Part-time and evening/weekend programs available. *Faculty:* 7 full-time (3 women). *Students:* 11 full-time (2 women), 8 part-time (2 women); includes 8 minority (4 Black or African American, non-Hispanic/Latino; 3 Hispanic/Latino; 1 Two or more races, non-Hispanic/Latino), 1 international. Average age 34. 9 applicants, 78% accepted, 5 enrolled. In 2014, 5 master's awarded. *Degree requirements:* For master's, comprehensive exam, thesis, language requirement (for humanities subconcentration). *Entrance requirements:* For master's, GRE General Test (minimum preferred score 59th percentile (153) verbal and 4.5 in analytical writing), minimum GPA of 3.0 in upper-division courses, personal statement, writing sample. Additional exam requirements/recommendations for international students: Required—TOEFL (minimum score 550 paper-based; 79 iBT) or IELTS (minimum score 6.5). *Application deadline:* For fall admission, 2/15 priority date for domestic students, 1/2 for international students; for spring admission, 10/15 priority date for domestic students, 6/1 for international students. Application fee: $30. *Financial support:* In 2014–15, 15 students received support, including 15 teaching assistantships with tuition reimbursements available (averaging $12,437 per year); scholarships/grants also available. Financial award application deadline: 4/1. *Faculty research:* American South, American autobiography, material culture, critical theory, cultural studies, film studies. *Unit head:* Dr. William Cummings, Professor and Chair, 813-974-9380, Fax: 813-974-9409, E-mail: wcummings@usf.edu. *Application contact:* Dr. Brook Sadler, Associate Professor and Graduate Program Director, 813-974-8841, Fax: 813-974-9409, E-mail: brooksadler@usf.edu. Website: http://humanities.usf.edu/

University of South Florida, College of Arts and Sciences, Department of Philosophy, Tampa, FL 33620-9951. Offers philosophy and religion (MA, PhD). Part-time and evening/weekend programs available. *Faculty:* 14 full-time (1 woman). *Students:* 48 full-time (10 women), 15 part-time (2 women); includes 10 minority (2 Black or African American, non-Hispanic/Latino; 3 Asian, non-Hispanic/Latino; 5 Hispanic/Latino), 1 international. Average age 31. 42 applicants, 67% accepted, 14 enrolled. In 2014, 9 master's, 7 doctorates awarded. Terminal master's awarded for partial completion of doctoral program. *Degree requirements:* For master's, comprehensive exam, thesis optional; for doctorate, comprehensive exam, thesis/dissertation. *Entrance requirements:* For master's and doctorate, GRE General Test, minimum GPA of 3.0, three letters of recommendation, 10-page philosophy writing sample, statement of philosophical interests. Additional exam requirements/recommendations for international students: Required—TOEFL (minimum score 550 paper-based; 79 iBT) or IELTS (minimum score 6.5). *Application deadline:* For fall admission, 2/15 for domestic and international students; for spring admission, 10/15 for domestic students, 8/1 for international students. Application fee: $30. Electronic applications accepted. *Financial support:* In 2014–15, 34 students received support, including 32 teaching assistantships with tuition reimbursements available (averaging $11,025 per year); unspecified assistantships also available. Financial award application deadline: 1/1. *Faculty research:* Medieval philosophy, early modern philosophy (seventeenth, eighteenth, and twentieth century Continental philosophy), feminist philosophy, social philosophy, ethics, philosophy of science. *Total annual research expenditures:* $128,071. *Unit head:* Dr. Roger Ariew, Professor and Chairperson, 813-974-8207, Fax: 813-974-5914, E-mail: rariew@usf.edu. *Application contact:* Dr. Joanne Waugh, Associate Professor, 813-974-5571, Fax: 813-974-5914, E-mail: jwaugh@usf.edu. Website: http://philosophy.usf.edu/

The University of Tennessee, Graduate School, College of Arts and Sciences, Department of Philosophy, Knoxville, TN 37996. Offers medical ethics (MA, PhD); philosophy (MA, PhD); religious studies (MA). Part-time programs available. *Degree requirements:* For master's, thesis or alternative; for doctorate, one foreign language, thesis/dissertation. *Entrance requirements:* For master's and doctorate, GRE General Test, minimum GPA of 2.7. Additional exam requirements/recommendations for international students: Required—TOEFL. Electronic applications accepted.

The University of Texas at Austin, Graduate School, College of Liberal Arts, Department of Philosophy, Austin, TX 78712-1111. Offers PhD. Part-time programs available. Terminal master's awarded for partial completion of doctoral program. *Degree requirements:* For doctorate, one foreign language, thesis/dissertation. *Entrance requirements:* For doctorate, GRE General Test. Electronic applications accepted. *Faculty research:* Ancient philosophy, cognitive science, Continental philosophy, history and philosophy of science.

The University of Texas at Dallas, School of Arts and Humanities, Program in Humanities, Richardson, TX 75080. Offers aesthetic studies (MA, PhD); history (MA); history of ideas (MA, PhD); humanities (MA, PhD); Latin American studies (MA); studies in literature (MA, PhD). *Faculty:* 35 full-time (11 women), 1 part-time/adjunct (0 women). *Students:* 148 full-time (94 women), 151 part-time (97 women); includes 78 minority (21 Black or African American, non-Hispanic/Latino; 4 American Indian or Alaska Native, non-Hispanic/Latino; 14 Asian, non-Hispanic/Latino; 28 Hispanic/Latino; 11 Two or more races, non-Hispanic/Latino), 16 international. Average age 39. 127 applicants, 46% accepted, 40 enrolled. In 2014, 40 master's, 15 doctorates awarded. *Degree requirements:* For master's, one foreign language, portfolio, thesis, or capstone project; for doctorate, one foreign language, thesis/dissertation. *Entrance requirements:* For master's, minimum GPA of 3.3 in upper-level coursework in field; for doctorate, field examinations, minimum GPA of 3.3 in upper-level coursework in field. Additional exam requirements/recommendations for international students: Required—TOEFL (minimum score 550 paper-based). *Application deadline:* For fall admission, 7/15 for domestic students, 5/1 priority date for international students; for spring admission, 11/15 for domestic students, 9/1 priority date for international students. Applications are processed on a rolling basis. Application fee: $50 ($100 for international students). Electronic applications accepted. *Expenses:* Tuition, state resident: full-time $11,940; part-time $663 per credit. Tuition, nonresident: full-time $22,282; part-time $1238 per credit. *Financial support:* In 2014–15, 161 students received support. Research assistantships with partial tuition reimbursements available, teaching assistantships with partial tuition reimbursements available, career-related internships or fieldwork, Federal Work-Study, institutionally sponsored loans, scholarships/grants, and unspecified assistantships available. Support available to part-time students. Financial award application deadline: 4/30; financial award applicants required to submit FAFSA. *Faculty research:* Holocaust studies, U.S./Mexico studies, translation studies, art history research, Chinese studies. *Unit head:* Dr. Michael Wilson, III, Associate Dean for

Graduate Education, 972-883-2756, Fax: 972-883-2989, E-mail: mwilson@utdallas.edu. *Application contact:* Alice Salazar, Coordinator, 972-883-2756, Fax: 972-883-2989, E-mail: alice.salazar1@utdallas.edu. Website: http://www.utdallas.edu/ah/programs/graduate

The University of Texas at El Paso, Graduate School, College of Liberal Arts, Department of Philosophy, El Paso, TX 79968-0001. Offers MA. *Degree requirements:* For master's, thesis, oral examination. *Entrance requirements:* For master's, GRE, 2 letters of recommendation.

The University of Texas at San Antonio, College of Liberal and Fine Arts, Department of Philosophy and Classics, San Antonio, TX 78249-0617. Offers MA. Part-time programs available. *Faculty:* 4 full-time (1 woman), 1 part-time/adjunct (0 women). *Students:* 5 full-time (3 women), 4 part-time (1 woman); includes 1 minority (Hispanic/Latino), 1 international. Average age 34. 9 applicants, 100% accepted, 5 enrolled. *Degree requirements:* For master's, comprehensive exam, thesis. *Entrance requirements:* For master's, GRE. Additional exam requirements/recommendations for international students: Required—TOEFL (minimum score 550 paper-based; 79 iBT). *Application deadline:* For fall admission, 7/1 for domestic students, 3/1 for international students; for spring admission, 11/1 for domestic students, 9/1 for international students. Application fee: $45 ($80 for international students). Electronic applications accepted. *Expenses:* Expenses: Contact institution. *Financial support:* In 2014–15, 6 students received support. Career-related internships or fieldwork, scholarships/grants, and unspecified assistantships available. Financial award applicants required to submit FAFSA. *Faculty research:* Metaphysics, epistemology, ethics, Continental, Ancient. *Total annual research expenditures:* $50,000. *Unit head:* Dr. Eva Browning, Department Chair, 210-458-6031, Fax: 210-458-6035, E-mail: eve.browning@utsa.edu. *Application contact:* Jill Hernandez, Graduate Advisor of Record, 210-458-6031, Fax: 210-458-6035, E-mail: jill.hernandez@utsa.edu.

The University of Toledo, College of Graduate Studies, College of Languages, Literature and Social Sciences, Department of Philosophy, Toledo, OH 43606-3390. Offers MA. Part-time programs available. *Degree requirements:* For master's, comprehensive exam, thesis, exam. *Entrance requirements:* For master's, minimum cumulative point-hour ratio of 2.7 for all previous academic work, three letters of recommendation. Additional exam requirements/recommendations for international students: Required—TOEFL (minimum score 550 paper-based; 80 iBT). Electronic applications accepted. *Faculty research:* History of philosophy, ethics, social/political philosophy, philosophy of science, European philosophy.

University of Toronto, School of Graduate Studies, Faculty of Arts and Science, Department of Philosophy, Toronto, ON M5S 2J7, Canada. Offers MA, PhD. Part-time programs available. *Degree requirements:* For doctorate, one foreign language, thesis/dissertation. *Entrance requirements:* For master's, GRE, 6 courses in philosophy; minimum A- average in philosophy courses, B overall; 2 letters of reference; writing sample; for doctorate, GRE, MA in philosophy, minimum A- average, 2 letters of reference, writing sample. Additional exam requirements/recommendations for international students: Required—TOEFL (minimum score 600 paper-based), TWE (minimum score 5). Electronic applications accepted.

University of Utah, Graduate School, College of Humanities, Department of Philosophy, Salt Lake City, UT 84112. Offers MA, MS, PhD. Part-time programs available. *Faculty:* 17 full-time (8 women), 3 part-time/adjunct (1 woman). *Students:* 15 full-time (4 women), 5 part-time (0 women), 1 international. Average age 32. 38 applicants, 11% accepted, 4 enrolled. In 2014, 3 master's, 5 doctorates awarded. *Degree requirements:* For master's, comprehensive exam, thesis or alternative; for doctorate, comprehensive exam, thesis/dissertation, qualifying oral exam. *Entrance requirements:* For master's, GRE General Test, minimum undergraduate GPA of 3.0; for doctorate, GRE General Test. Additional exam requirements/recommendations for international students: Required—TOEFL (minimum score 650 paper-based). *Application deadline:* For fall admission, 1/15 priority date for domestic and international students. Application fee: $55 ($65 for international students). Electronic applications accepted. *Financial support:* In 2014–15, 13 students received support, including 2 fellowships with full tuition reimbursements available (averaging $1,750 per year); teaching assistantships with full tuition reimbursements available, Federal Work-Study, institutionally sponsored loans, scholarships/grants, health care benefits, and unspecified assistantships also available. Financial award application deadline: 2/15; financial award applicants required to submit FAFSA. *Faculty research:* Philosophy of biology, philosophy of science, applied ethics, practical reasoning, political philosophy, philosophy of cognitive science. *Total annual research expenditures:* $15,000. *Unit head:* Dr. Stephen Matthew Downes, Chair, 801-581-6094, Fax: 801-585-5195, E-mail: s.downes@.utah.edu. *Application contact:* Connie Gladden Corbett, Academic Advisor, 801-581-8162, Fax: 801-585-5195, E-mail: c.corbett@utah.edu. Website: http://www.hum.utah.edu/philosophy/

University of Victoria, Faculty of Graduate Studies, Faculty of Humanities, Department of Philosophy, Victoria, BC V8W 2Y2, Canada. Offers MA. Part-time and evening/weekend programs available. *Degree requirements:* For master's, thesis. *Entrance requirements:* For master's, writing sample. Additional exam requirements/recommendations for international students: Required—TOEFL (minimum score 575 paper-based), IELTS (minimum score 7). *Faculty research:* Ethics, metaphysics, philosophy of mind, history of philosophy, political philosophy.

University of Virginia, College and Graduate School of Arts and Sciences, Department of Philosophy, Charlottesville, VA 22903. Offers MA, PhD, JD/MA. *Faculty:* 14 full-time (5 women). *Students:* 28 full-time (3 women); includes 2 minority (both Asian, non-Hispanic/Latino), 5 international. Average age 29. 127 applicants, 11% accepted, 5 enrolled. In 2014, 2 master's, 2 doctorates awarded. *Degree requirements:* For master's, 2 papers; for doctorate, thesis/dissertation, 2 papers. *Entrance requirements:* For master's, GRE General Test, GRE Subject Test, 3 letters of recommendation, writing sample; for doctorate, GRE General Test, GRE Subject Test, 3 letters of recommendation; writing sample. Additional exam requirements/recommendations for international students: Required—TOEFL (minimum score 600 paper-based; 90 iBT), IELTS. *Application deadline:* For fall admission, 1/1 for domestic students, 1/5 for international students. Applications are processed on a rolling basis. Application fee: $60. Electronic applications accepted. *Expenses:* Tuition, state resident: full-time $14,164; part-time $349 per credit hour. Tuition, nonresident: full-time $23,722; part-time $1300 per credit hour. *Required fees:* $2514. *Financial support:* Fellowships and teaching assistantships available. Financial award applicants required to submit FAFSA. *Unit head:* Talbot Brewer, Chair, 434-924-7701, Fax: 434-924-6927, E-mail: tbrewer@virginia.edu. *Application contact:* Antonia LoLordo, Director of Graduate Admissions, 434-924-7701, Fax: 434-924-6927, E-mail: lolordo@virginia.edu. Website: http://www.virginia.edu/philosophy/

University of Washington, Graduate School, College of Arts and Sciences, Department of Philosophy, Seattle, WA 98195. Offers classics and philosophy (PhD); philosophy (MA, PhD). Terminal master's awarded for partial completion of doctoral program. *Degree requirements:* For master's, 3 papers; for doctorate, thesis/dissertation, general exam. *Entrance requirements:* For master's and doctorate, GRE, minimum GPA of 3.0. Additional exam requirements/recommendations for international

students: Required—TOEFL. *Faculty research:* History and philosophy of science, epistemology, Aristotle's metaphysics, ethics and politics, causation in modern philosophy.

University of Waterloo, Graduate Studies, Faculty of Arts, Department of Philosophy, Waterloo, ON N2L 3G1, Canada. Offers MA, PhD. *Degree requirements:* For master's, thesis or alternative; for doctorate, one foreign language, thesis/dissertation. *Entrance requirements:* For master's, honors degree, minimum B+ average, writing sample, resume; for doctorate, master's degree, minimum A- average, resumé. Additional exam requirements/recommendations for international students: Required—TOEFL, TWE. Electronic applications accepted. *Faculty research:* Logic, ethics, social/political, cognitive science, philosophy of science.

The University of Western Ontario, Faculty of Graduate Studies, Faculty of Arts and Humanities, Department of Philosophy, London, ON N6A 5B8, Canada. Offers MA, PhD. *Degree requirements:* For master's, 1 competency exam; for doctorate, comprehensive exam, thesis/dissertation, 2 competency exams. *Entrance requirements:* For master's, honors degree. Additional exam requirements/recommendations for international students: Required—TOEFL (minimum score 600 paper-based). Electronic applications accepted. *Faculty research:* Philosophy of science, history of philosophy, philosophy of law, ethics, epistemology.

University of Windsor, Faculty of Graduate Studies, Faculty of Arts and Social Sciences, Department of Philosophy, Windsor, ON N9B 3P4, Canada. Offers MA. Part-time programs available. *Degree requirements:* For master's, thesis. *Entrance requirements:* For master's, minimum B average. Additional exam requirements/recommendations for international students: Required—TOEFL (minimum score 600 paper-based). Electronic applications accepted. *Faculty research:* Informal logic, contemporary Continental philosophy, epistemology.

University of Wisconsin–Madison, Graduate School, College of Letters and Science, Department of Philosophy, Madison, WI 53706-1380. Offers MA, PhD. Part-time programs available. Terminal master's awarded for partial completion of doctoral program. *Degree requirements:* For master's, thesis, preliminary exams; for doctorate, thesis/dissertation, preliminary exams. *Entrance requirements:* For doctorate, GRE, BA in philosophy or related area. Additional exam requirements/recommendations for international students: Required—TOEFL. Electronic applications accepted. *Expenses:* Tuition, state resident: full-time $10,723; part-time $745 per credit. Tuition, nonresident: full-time $24,054; part-time $1578 per credit. *Required fees:* $374 per semester. Tuition and fees vary according to course load, program and reciprocity agreements. *Faculty research:* History of philosophy, logic, philosophy of science, philosophy of mind, metaphysics.

University of Wisconsin–Milwaukee, Graduate School, College of Letters and Sciences, Department of Philosophy, Milwaukee, WI 53201-0413. Offers MA. Part-time programs available. *Degree requirements:* For master's, thesis or alternative. *Entrance requirements:* For master's, GRE General Test. Additional exam requirements/recommendations for international students: Required—TOEFL (minimum score 550 paper-based; 79 iBT), IELTS (minimum score 6.5). Electronic applications accepted.

University of Wyoming, College of Arts and Sciences, Department of Philosophy, Laramie, WY 82071. Offers MA. Part-time programs available. *Degree requirements:* For master's, thesis, logic proficiency, first-year paper. *Entrance requirements:* For master's, GRE General Test, minimum GPA of 3.0. Additional exam requirements/recommendations for international students: Required—TOEFL (minimum score 525 paper-based). Electronic applications accepted. *Faculty research:* Philosophy of science, political and ethical theory, philosophy of language, epistemology, philosophy of mind, early modern philosophy.

Vanderbilt University, Graduate School, Department of Philosophy, Nashville, TN 37240-1001. Offers MA, PhD. *Faculty:* 16 full-time (5 women), 1 part-time/adjunct (0 women). *Students:* 41 full-time (21 women); includes 7 minority (1 American Indian or Alaska Native, non-Hispanic/Latino; 1 Asian, non-Hispanic/Latino; 5 Hispanic/Latino), 2 international. Average age 32. 183 applicants, 4% accepted, 5 enrolled. In 2014, 3 master's, 5 doctorates awarded. Terminal master's awarded for partial completion of doctoral program. *Degree requirements:* For doctorate, one foreign language, comprehensive exam, thesis/dissertation, final and qualifying exams. *Entrance requirements:* For doctorate, GRE General Test, writing sample. Additional exam requirements/recommendations for international students: Required—TOEFL (minimum score 570 paper-based; 88 iBT). *Application deadline:* For fall admission, 1/15 for domestic and international students. Electronic applications accepted. *Expenses: Tuition:* Full-time $42,768; part-time $1782 per credit hour. *Required fees:* $422. One-time fee: $30 full-time. *Financial support:* Fellowships with full tuition reimbursements, teaching assistantships with full tuition reimbursements, Federal Work-Study, institutionally sponsored loans, scholarships/grants, and health care benefits available. Financial award application deadline: 1/15; financial award applicants required to submit CSS PROFILE or FAFSA. *Faculty research:* Ancient, medieval, and modern philosophy; philosophy of science; ethics; philosophy of language; philosophy of religion. *Unit head:* Dr. Robert B. Talisse, Director of Graduate Studies, 615-343-8671, Fax: 615-343-7259, E-mail: robert.talisse@vanderbilt.edu. *Application contact:* Rebecca Davenport, Administrative Assistant, 615-322-2637, Fax: 615-343-7259, E-mail: rebecca.davenport@vanderbilt.edu.
Website: http://www.vanderbilt.edu/AnS/philosophy/

Villanova University, Graduate School of Liberal Arts and Sciences, Department of Philosophy, Villanova, PA 19085-1699. Offers PhD. Part-time and evening/weekend programs available. *Faculty:* 5. *Students:* 55 full-time (22 women); includes 7 minority (1 Black or African American, non-Hispanic/Latino; 1 Asian, non-Hispanic/Latino; 4 Hispanic/Latino; 1 Two or more races, non-Hispanic/Latino), 6 international. Average age 31. 122 applicants, 6% accepted, 6 enrolled. In 2014, 6 doctorates awarded. *Degree requirements:* For doctorate, 2 foreign languages, comprehensive exam, thesis/dissertation. *Entrance requirements:* For doctorate, GRE, 3 recommendation letters, writing sample, curriculum vitae. Additional exam requirements/recommendations for international students: Required—TOEFL. *Application deadline:* For fall admission, 2/1 priority date for domestic and international students. Application fee: $50. *Financial support:* Research assistantships, teaching assistantships, scholarships/grants, and unspecified assistantships available. Financial award applicants required to submit FAFSA. *Unit head:* Dr. Annika Thiem, Director, 610-519-8997.
Website: http://www1.villanova.edu/villanova/artsci/philosophy/academic-programs/doctorate.html

Virginia Polytechnic Institute and State University, Graduate School, College of Liberal Arts and Human Sciences, Blacksburg, VA 24061. Offers career and technical education (MS Ed, Ed D, PhD, Ed S); communication (MA); counselor education (MA Ed, Ed D, PhD, Ed S); creative writing (MFA); curriculum and instruction (MA Ed, Ed D, PhD, Ed S); educational leadership and policy studies (MA Ed, Ed D, PhD, Ed S); educational research and evaluation (PhD); English (MA); foreign languages, cultures, and literatures (MA); higher education and student affairs (MA Ed); history (MA); human development (MS, PhD); material culture and public humanities (MA); philosophy (MA); political science (MA); rhetoric and writing (PhD); science and technology studies (MS, PhD); social, political, ethical, and cultural thought (PhD); sociology (MS, PhD); theater arts (MFA). *Faculty:* 421 full-time (216 women), 2 part-time/adjunct (both women). *Students:* 642 full-time (437 women), 537 part-time (344 women); includes 235 minority (132 Black or African American, non-Hispanic/Latino; 2 American Indian or Alaska Native, non-Hispanic/Latino; 27 Asian, non-Hispanic/Latino; 52 Hispanic/Latino; 1 Native Hawaiian or other Pacific Islander, non-Hispanic/Latino; 21 Two or more races, non-Hispanic/Latino), 81 international. Average age 34. 890 applicants, 46% accepted, 303 enrolled. In 2014, 342 master's, 96 doctorates, 33 other advanced degrees awarded. *Degree requirements:* For master's, comprehensive exam (for some programs), thesis (for some programs); for doctorate, comprehensive exam (for some programs), thesis/dissertation (for some programs). *Entrance requirements:* For master's and doctorate, GRE/GMAT (may vary by department). Additional exam requirements/recommendations for international students: Required—TOEFL (minimum score 550 paper-based). *Application deadline:* For fall admission, 8/1 for domestic students, 4/1 for international students; for spring admission, 1/1 for domestic students, 9/1 for international students. Applications are processed on a rolling basis. Application fee: $75. Electronic applications accepted. *Expenses:* Tuition, state resident: full-time $11,656; part-time $647.50 per credit hour. Tuition, nonresident: full-time $23,351; part-time $1297.25 per credit hour. *Required fees:* $2533; $465.75 per semester. Tuition and fees vary according to course load, campus/location and program. *Financial support:* In 2014–15, 19 research assistantships with full tuition reimbursements (averaging $22,141 per year), 231 teaching assistantships with full tuition reimbursements (averaging $19,470 per year) were awarded. Financial award application deadline: 3/1; financial award applicants required to submit FAFSA. *Total annual research expenditures:* $6.5 million. *Unit head:* Elizabeth Spiller, Dean, 540-231-6779, Fax: 540-231-7157, E-mail: espiller@vt.edu. *Application contact:* Melissa Elliott, Executive Assistant, 540-231-6779, Fax: 540-231-7157, E-mail: elliott1@vt.edu.
Website: http://www.clahs.vt.edu/

Washington University in St. Louis, Graduate School of Arts and Sciences, Department of Philosophy, St. Louis, MO 63130-4899. Offers philosophy (PhD); philosophy-neuroscience-psychology (PhD). *Degree requirements:* For doctorate, thesis/dissertation. *Entrance requirements:* For doctorate, GRE General Test, sample of written work. Additional exam requirements/recommendations for international students: Required—TOEFL. Electronic applications accepted. *Faculty research:* Ethics; social, political philosophy; history of philosophy; philosophy of law; philosophy of science, of mind and of language; theory of knowledge; aesthetics.

Wayne State University, College of Liberal Arts and Sciences, Department of Philosophy, Detroit, MI 48202. Offers MA, PhD. *Students:* 13 full-time (3 women), 5 part-time (1 woman); includes 2 minority (1 Asian, non-Hispanic/Latino; 1 Hispanic/Latino), 1 international. Average age 30. 57 applicants, 26% accepted, 1 enrolled. In 2014, 5 master's, 3 doctorates awarded. Terminal master's awarded for partial completion of doctoral program. *Degree requirements:* For master's, comprehensive exam (for some programs), thesis (for some programs); for doctorate, one foreign language, thesis/dissertation, oral exam, classroom lectures under supervision of Philosophy Department. *Entrance requirements:* For master's, GRE if upper-division GPA is below 2.75 (or 3.0 if from unaccredited college), writing sample, personal statement, three letters of recommendation; for doctorate, minimum undergraduate upper-division GPA of 3.0, undergraduate major or substantial work in philosophy, writing sample, personal statement, three letters of recommendation. Additional exam requirements/recommendations for international students: Required—TOEFL (minimum score 550 paper-based), TWE (minimum score 5.5), Michigan English Language Assessment Battery (minimum score 85); Recommended—IELTS (minimum score 6.5). *Application deadline:* For fall admission, 5/1 priority date for domestic and international students; for winter admission, 10/1 priority date for domestic students, 9/1 priority date for international students; for spring admission, 2/1 priority date for domestic students, 1/1 priority date for international students. Applications are processed on a rolling basis. Application fee: $0. Electronic applications accepted. *Expenses:* Tuition, state resident: full-time $10,294; part-time $571.90 per credit hour. Tuition, nonresident: full-time $29,730; part-time $1238.75 per credit hour. *Required fees:* $1365; $43.50 per credit hour. $291.10 per semester. Tuition and fees vary according to course load and program. *Financial support:* In 2014–15, 9 students received support, including 1 fellowship with tuition reimbursement available (averaging $16,000 per year), 6 teaching assistantships with tuition reimbursements available (averaging $17,040 per year); scholarships/grants, health care benefits, and unspecified assistantships also available. Financial award application deadline: 3/31; financial award applicants required to submit FAFSA. *Faculty research:* Metaphysics, ancient philosophy, philosophy of art, ethics, philosophy of science. *Unit head:* Dr. John Corvino, Chair, 313-577-6099, E-mail: j.corvino@wayne.edu. *Application contact:* Dr. Sean Stidd, Director of Graduate Admissions, E-mail: aj7365@wayne.edu.
Website: http://clas.wayne.edu/Philosophy

West Chester University of Pennsylvania, College of Arts and Sciences, Department of Philosophy, West Chester, PA 19383. Offers business ethics (Certificate); health care ethics (Certificate); philosophy (MA); philosophy: applied ethics (MA). Part-time and evening/weekend programs available. Postbaccalaureate distance learning degree programs offered (minimal on-campus study). *Faculty:* 7 full-time (2 women), 1 (woman) part-time/adjunct. *Students:* 6 full-time (0 women), 12 part-time (3 women); includes 3 minority (1 Black or African American, non-Hispanic/Latino; 1 American Indian or Alaska Native, non-Hispanic/Latino; 1 Hispanic/Latino). Average age 36. 13 applicants, 92% accepted, 9 enrolled. In 2014, 7 master's, 1 other advanced degree awarded. *Degree requirements:* For master's, at least one comprehensive exam plus either thesis or two additional comprehensive exams. *Entrance requirements:* For master's, GRE or writing sample, three letters of reference; for Certificate, BA transcripts. Additional exam requirements/recommendations for international students: Required—TOEFL (minimum score 550 paper-based; 80 iBT). *Application deadline:* For fall admission, 4/15 priority date for domestic students, 3/15 for international students; for spring admission, 10/15 priority date for domestic students, 9/1 for international students. Applications are processed on a rolling basis. Application fee: $45. Electronic applications accepted. *Expenses:* Tuition, state resident: full-time $8172; part-time $454 per credit. Tuition, nonresident: full-time $12,258; part-time $681 per credit. *Required fees:* $2231; $110.78 per credit. Tuition and fees vary according to campus/location and program. *Financial support:* Unspecified assistantships available. Support available to part-time students. Financial award application deadline: 2/15; financial award applicants required to submit FAFSA. *Faculty research:* Ethics: theory and application, social and political philosophy, feminist philosophy, continental philosophy, Asian philosophy. *Unit head:* Dr. Helen Daley Schroepfer, Chair and Graduate Coordinator, 610-436-2841, E-mail: hschroepfer@wcupa.edu.
Website: http://www.wcupa.edu/_academics/sch_cas.phi/

Western Michigan University, Graduate College, College of Arts and Sciences, Department of Philosophy, Kalamazoo, MI 49008. Offers MA. *Degree requirements:* For master's, thesis optional. *Application deadline:* For fall admission, 2/15 for domestic students. *Financial support:* Application deadline: 2/15. *Application contact:* Admissions and Orientation, 269-387-2000, Fax: 269-387-2096.

Wilfrid Laurier University, Faculty of Graduate and Postdoctoral Studies, Faculty of Arts, Department of Philosophy, Waterloo, ON N2L 3C5, Canada. Offers agency (MA);

Philosophy

community (MA); self (MA). *Entrance requirements:* For master's, honours BA in philosophy or equivalent with minimum B+ average in philosophy and in final year. Additional exam requirements/recommendations for international students: Required— TOEFL (minimum score 89 iBT). Electronic applications accepted. *Faculty research:* Self, agency, community.

Yale University, Graduate School of Arts and Sciences, Department of Philosophy, New Haven, CT 06520. Offers PhD. *Degree requirements:* For doctorate, 2 foreign languages, thesis/dissertation. *Entrance requirements:* For doctorate, GRE General Test.

York University, Faculty of Graduate Studies, Faculty of Liberal Arts and Professional Studies, Program in Philosophy, Toronto, ON M3J 1P3, Canada. Offers MA, PhD. Part-time programs available. *Degree requirements:* For master's, thesis or alternative; for doctorate, one foreign language, thesis/dissertation. Electronic applications accepted.

Section 12
Religious Studies

This section contains a directory of institutions offering graduate work in religious studies. Additional information about programs listed in the directory may be obtained by writing directly to the dean of a graduate school or chair of a department at the address given in the directory.

For programs offering related work, see also in this book *Area and Cultural Studies, History, Humanities,* and *Philosophy*. In another guide in this series:

Graduate Programs in Business, Education, Information Studies, Law & Social Work

See *Subject Areas (Religious Education)*

CONTENTS

Program Directories

Missions and Missiology

Abilene Christian University, Graduate School, College of Biblical Studies, Graduate School of Theology, Program in Global Service, Abilene, TX 79699-9100. Offers MAGS. Part-time programs available. *Students:* 1 full-time (0 women), 9 part-time (1 woman). 11 applicants, 45% accepted, 5 enrolled. In 2014, 2 degrees awarded. *Degree requirements:* For master's, comprehensive exam, thesis. *Entrance requirements:* Additional exam requirements/recommendations for international students: Required—TOEFL (minimum score 550 paper-based; 90 iBT), IELTS (minimum score 6.5), PTE. *Application deadline:* For fall admission, 4/1 priority date for domestic students; for spring admission, 11/1 for domestic students. Applications are processed on a rolling basis. Application fee: $50. Electronic applications accepted. *Expenses:* Expenses: Contact institution. *Financial support:* In 2014–15, 1 student received support. Teaching assistantships, career-related internships or fieldwork, and scholarships/grants available. Financial award application deadline: 4/1; financial award applicants required to submit FAFSA. *Faculty research:* Animism, contextualization, missions education. *Unit head:* Dr. Chris Flanders, Graduate Adviser, 325-674-3742, Fax: 325-674-6180, E-mail: chris.flanders@acu.edu. *Application contact:* Corey Patterson, Director of Graduate Admission and Recruiting, 325-674-6566, Fax: 325-674-6717, E-mail: gradinfo@acu.edu.

Anabaptist Mennonite Biblical Seminary, Graduate and Professional Programs, Elkhart, IN 46517-1999. Offers Christian formation (MA); divinity (M Div); mission and evangelism (MA); peace studies (MA); theological studies (MA, Certificate). *Accreditation:* ACIPE; ATS. Part-time programs available. *Degree requirements:* For master's, comprehensive exam, thesis optional. *Entrance requirements:* For master's and Certificate, 3 letters of reference. Additional exam requirements/recommendations for international students: Required—TOEFL (minimum score 550 paper-based). Electronic applications accepted. *Faculty research:* Biblical studies, theology, church history, church leadership.

Anderson University, School of Theology, Anderson, IN 46012-3495. Offers missions (MA); theology (M Div, MTS, D Min). *Accreditation:* ACIPE; ATS. Part-time programs available. *Degree requirements:* For master's, variable foreign language requirement, thesis (for some programs); for doctorate, thesis/dissertation. *Faculty research:* Small-church/bivocational ministry, women in ministry.

Andrews University, School of Graduate Studies, Seventh-day Adventist Theological Seminary, Program in Missiology, Berrien Springs, MI 49104. Offers D Miss. Tuition and fees vary according to course level. *Unit head:* Dr. Wagner Kuhn. *Application contact:* Monica Wringer, Director, 800-253-2874, Fax: 269-471-6321.

Asbury Theological Seminary, Graduate and Professional Programs, Wilmore, KY 40390-1199. Offers MA, MAAS, MACE, MACL, MACM, MACP, MAMFC, MAMHC, MAPC, MASF, MAYM, Th M, PhD, Certificate. *Accreditation:* ATS. Part-time programs available. Postbaccalaureate distance learning degree programs offered (minimal on-campus study). Terminal master's awarded for partial completion of doctoral program. *Degree requirements:* For master's, thesis (for some programs); for doctorate, thesis/dissertation, qualifying exam. *Entrance requirements:* For master's, minimum GPA of 2.75; for doctorate, minimum GPA of 3.0. Additional exam requirements/recommendations for international students: Required—TOEFL, IELTS. Electronic applications accepted.

Ashland Theological Seminary, Graduate Programs, Ashland, OH 44805. Offers biblical and theological studies (MAR); Biblical, historical and theological studies (MA), including Anabaptism and Pietism, Christian theology, church history, New Testament, Old Testament; Christian ministry (MAPT), including Black church studies (M Div, MAPT, D Min), chaplaincy (M Div, MAPT), Christian formation (M Div, MAPT), evangelism/church renewal and missions (M Div, MAPT), general ministry (M Div, MAPT), pastoral counseling and care (M Div, MAPT), specialized ministry, spiritual formation (M Div, MAPT, D Min); Christian studies (Diploma); clinical counseling (MACC); counseling (MAC); ministry (D Min), including Black church studies (M Div, MAPT, D Min), Canadian church studies, formational counseling, independent design, spiritual formation (M Div, MAPT, D Min), transformational leadership, Wesleyan practices; pastoral ministry (M Div), including Biblical studies - Old or New Testament, Black church studies (M Div, MAPT, D Min), chaplaincy (M Div, MAPT), Christian formation (M Div, MAPT), evangelism/church renewal and missions (M Div, MAPT), general Biblical studies, general ministry (M Div, MAPT), pastoral counseling and care (M Div, MAPT), spiritual formation (M Div, MAPT, D Min), theology or history. MAC program offered in Detroit, MI. *Accreditation:* ATS. Part-time programs available. *Degree requirements:* For master's, 2 foreign languages, comprehensive exam (for some programs), thesis (for some programs); for doctorate, thesis/dissertation. *Entrance requirements:* For master's, bachelor's degree from accredited institution with a minimum undergraduate GPA of 2.75; for doctorate, M Div, minimum undergraduate GPA of 3.0. Additional exam requirements/recommendations for international students: Required—TOEFL (minimum score 500 paper-based; 65 iBT). Electronic applications accepted. *Faculty research:* Semitic languages and linguistics, rhetorical and social-scientific criticism, Anabaptist studies, inner spiritual healing, African-American clergy in film and literature.

Assemblies of God Theological Seminary, Graduate and Professional Programs, Springfield, MO 65802. Offers Bible theology (PhD); Christian ministries (MA); counseling (MA); divinity (M Div); intercultural ministry (MA); intercultural studies (PhD); ministry (D Min); missiology (D Miss); theological studies (MA). *Accreditation:* ATS. Part-time and evening/weekend programs available. Postbaccalaureate distance learning degree programs offered (minimal on-campus study). *Degree requirements:* For master's, variable foreign language requirement; for doctorate, thesis/dissertation. *Entrance requirements:* For master's, minimum GPA of 2.5; for doctorate, GRE (for PhD in Bible theology), minimum GPA of 3.0. Additional exam requirements/recommendations for international students: Required—TOEFL (minimum score 550 paper-based; 80 iBT). Electronic applications accepted.

Biblical Theological Seminary, Graduate and Professional Programs, Hatfield, PA 19440-2499. Offers advanced missional leadership (D Min); advanced pastoral studies (Certificate); biblical counseling (Certificate); biblical studies (MA, Certificate); counseling (MA); ministry (M Div, MA); missional theology (MA). *Accreditation:* ATS. Part-time and evening/weekend programs available. *Faculty:* 9 full-time (0 women), 21 part-time/adjunct (4 women). *Students:* 139 full-time (41 women), 149 part-time (55 women); includes 103 minority (53 Black or African American, non-Hispanic/Latino; 42 Asian, non-Hispanic/Latino; 6 Hispanic/Latino; 2 Two or more races, non-Hispanic/Latino), 76 international. Average age 38. 91 applicants, 64% accepted, 56 enrolled. In 2014, 80 master's, 5 doctorates awarded. *Degree requirements:* For master's, variable foreign language requirement, thesis optional; for doctorate, thesis/dissertation. *Entrance requirements:* Additional exam requirements/recommendations for international students: Required—TOEFL (minimum score 550 paper-based; 80 iBT). *Application deadline:* Applications are processed on a rolling basis. Application fee: $30. Electronic applications accepted. *Expenses: Tuition:* Full-time $14,667; part-time $480 per credit. *Required fees:* $25 per trimester. One-time fee: $30. *Financial support:* In 2014–15, 192 students received support. Career-related internships or fieldwork, institutionally sponsored loans, and scholarships/grants available. Support available to part-time students. Financial award application deadline: 8/30; financial award applicants required to submit FAFSA. *Faculty research:* Theology, culture, Biblical interpretation. *Unit head:* Pamela Jean Smith, Vice President for Student Advancement, 215-368-5000 Ext. 122, Fax: 215-368-7002, E-mail: psmith@biblical.edu. *Application contact:* Dr. Malcolm Walls, Director of Recruitment and Student Services, 215-368-5000 Ext. 109, Fax: 215-368-7002, E-mail: mwalls@biblical.edu.
Website: http://www.biblical.edu/

Biola University, Cook School of Intercultural Studies, La Mirada, CA 90639-0001. Offers anthropology (MA); applied linguistics (MA); intercultural education (PhD); intercultural studies (MA, PhD); linguistics (Certificate); linguistics and Biblical languages (MA); missions (MA); teaching English to speakers of other languages (MA, Certificate). Part-time programs available. *Faculty:* 19. *Students:* 86 full-time (41 women), 119 part-time (58 women); includes 68 minority (7 Black or African American, non-Hispanic/Latino; 1 American Indian or Alaska Native, non-Hispanic/Latino; 42 Asian, non-Hispanic/Latino; 14 Hispanic/Latino; 4 Two or more races, non-Hispanic/Latino), 29 international. In 2014, 29 master's, 16 doctorates awarded. *Entrance requirements:* For master's, minimum undergraduate GPA of 3.0; for doctorate, master's degree or equivalent, 3 years of cross-cultural experience, minimum graduate GPA of 3.3. Additional exam requirements/recommendations for international students: Required—TOEFL. *Application deadline:* For fall admission, 7/1 for domestic students, 6/1 for international students; for spring admission, 12/1 for domestic students; for summer admission, 5/1 for domestic students. Applications are processed on a rolling basis. Application fee: $65. Electronic applications accepted. *Financial support:* Scholarships/grants available. Support available to part-time students. Financial award applicants required to submit FAFSA. *Faculty research:* Linguistics, anthropology, intercultural studies, teaching English to speakers of other languages, missions, missiology. *Unit head:* Dr. Bulus Y. Galadima, Dean, 562-903-4844. *Application contact:* Graduate Admissions Office, 562-903-4752, E-mail: graduate.admissions@biola.edu.
Website: http://cook.biola.edu

Biola University, Talbot School of Theology, La Mirada, CA 90639-0001. Offers adult/family ministry (MACE); Bible exposition (MA, Th M); Biblical and theological studies (MA); children's ministry (MACE); Christian education (M Div); cross-cultural education ministry (MACE); educational studies (Ed D, PhD); evangelism and discipleship (M Div); general Christian education (MACE); Messianic Jewish studies (M Div, Certificate); missions and intercultural studies (M Div); New Testament (MA, Th M); Old Testament (MA); Old Testament and Semitics (Th M); pastoral and general ministry (M Div); pastoral care and counseling (M Div); philosophy (MA); spiritual formation (M Div, Certificate); spiritual formation and soul care (MA); theology (Th M, D Min, Certificate); youth ministry (MACE). *Accreditation:* ATS. Part-time and evening/weekend programs available. *Faculty:* 77. *Students:* 581 full-time (140 women), 554 part-time (155 women); includes 522 minority (42 Black or African American, non-Hispanic/Latino; 3 American Indian or Alaska Native, non-Hispanic/Latino; 370 Asian, non-Hispanic/Latino; 78 Hispanic/Latino; 2 Native Hawaiian or other Pacific Islander, non-Hispanic/Latino; 27 Two or more races, non-Hispanic/Latino), 121 international. 437 applicants, 78% accepted, 241 enrolled. In 2014, 182 master's, 33 doctorates awarded. *Entrance requirements:* For master's, bachelor's degree from accredited college or university; minimum GPA of 2.6 (for M Div), 3.0 (for MA); for doctorate, M Div or MA. Additional exam requirements/recommendations for international students: Required—TOEFL (minimum score 600 paper-based; 88 iBT). *Application deadline:* For fall admission, 7/1 for domestic students, 6/1 for international students; for spring admission, 12/1 priority date for domestic students. Applications are processed on a rolling basis. Application fee: $65. Electronic applications accepted. *Financial support:* Scholarships/grants and unspecified assistantships available. Support available to part-time students. Financial award applicants required to submit FAFSA. *Faculty research:* New Testament, Old Testament, spiritual formation, Christian education, theological studies, Christian ministry, preaching and pastoral ministry, language and literature, bible exposition, Christian leadership. *Unit head:* Dr. Clint Arnold, Dean, 562-903-4816, Fax: 562-903-4748. *Application contact:* Graduate Admissions Office, 562-903-4752, E-mail: graduate.admissions@biola.edu.
Website: http://www.talbot.edu/

Briercrest Seminary, Graduate Programs, Program in Christian Ministries, Caronport, SK S0H 0S0, Canada. Offers leadership (MA); marriage and family counseling (MA); missions (MA); pastoral counseling (MA); worship (MA); youth and family ministry (MA). Part-time programs available. *Degree requirements:* For master's, comprehensive exam, thesis optional. *Entrance requirements:* Additional exam requirements/recommendations for international students: Required—TOEFL (minimum score 550 paper-based).

Calvin Theological Seminary, Graduate and Professional Programs, Grand Rapids, MI 49546-4387. Offers Bible and theology (MA); divinity (M Div), including ancient near eastern languages and literature, contextual ministry, evangelism and teaching, history of Christianity, new church development, New Testament, Old Testament, pastoral care and leadership, preaching and worship, theological studies, youth and family ministries; educational ministry (MA); historical theology (PhD); missions and evangelism (MA); pastoral care (MA); philosophical and moral theology (PhD); systematic theology (PhD); theological studies (MTS); theology (Th M); worship (MA); youth and family ministries (MA). *Accreditation:* ACIPE; ATS. Part-time programs available. *Degree requirements:* For master's, variable foreign language requirement, thesis (for some programs); for doctorate, 4 foreign languages, comprehensive exam, thesis/dissertation. *Entrance requirements:* For doctorate, GRE General Test, Hebrew, Greek, and a modern foreign language. Additional exam requirements/recommendations for international students: Required—TOEFL (minimum score 550 paper-based), TWE (minimum score 4). Electronic applications accepted. *Faculty research:* Recent Trinity theory, Christian anthropology, Proverbs, reformed confessions, Paul's view of law.

Catholic Theological Union, Graduate and Professional Programs, Chicago, IL 60615-5698. Offers biblical spirituality (Certificate); cross-cultural ministries (D Min); cross-cultural missions (Certificate); divinity (M Div); liturgical studies (Certificate); liturgy (D Min); pastoral studies (MAPS, Certificate); spiritual formation (Certificate); spirituality (D Min); theology (MA); M Div/MA; M Div/MSW; M Div/PhD. M Div/PhD offered jointly with University of Chicago; M Div/MSW with Loyola University Chicago and University of Chicago. *Accreditation:* ACIPE; ATS (one or more programs are accredited). Part-time and evening/weekend programs available. *Degree requirements:* For master's, one foreign language, comprehensive exam (for some programs), thesis (for some

programs); for doctorate, thesis/dissertation. *Entrance requirements:* For doctorate, master's degree, 5 years of active ministry. *Faculty research:* Doctrine, sacraments, ethics, Bible.

Central Baptist Theological Seminary, Graduate and Professional Programs, Shawnee, KS 66226. Offers missional church studies (MA); theological studies (MA); theology (M Div, Diploma). *Accreditation:* ACIPE; ATS (one or more programs are accredited). Part-time programs available. *Degree requirements:* For master's, thesis optional. *Entrance requirements:* Additional exam requirements/recommendations for international students: Required—TOEFL (minimum score 547 paper-based; 77 iBT). Electronic applications accepted.

Charlotte Christian College and Theological Seminary, Graduate Program, Charlotte, NC 28205. Offers urban Christian ministry (MA), including church planting, multi-cultural studies, sacred music, youth ministry. Part-time and evening/weekend programs available. *Faculty:* 5 full-time (1 woman), 9 part-time/adjunct (2 women). *Students:* 2 full-time (1 woman), 25 part-time (15 women); includes 18 minority (17 Black or African American, non-Hispanic/Latino; 1 Hispanic/Latino), 2 international. Average age 47. 2 applicants, 100% accepted, 2 enrolled. In 2014, 2 master's awarded. *Degree requirements:* For master's, thesis. *Entrance requirements:* For master's, MAT, writing sample/essay. Additional exam requirements/recommendations for international students: Required—TOEFL, IELTS. *Application deadline:* For fall admission, 7/24 for domestic students, 7/18 for international students; for spring admission, 12/11 for domestic students, 12/5 for international students; for summer admission, 4/18 for domestic and international students. Application fee: $50 ($140 for international students). Electronic applications accepted. *Expenses:* Expenses: 1 course: $1,200; 2 courses: $2,300; 3 courses: $3,300; 4 courses $3,900. *Financial support:* In 2014–15, 5 students received support. Federal Work-Study and scholarships/grants available. Financial award application deadline: 4/1; financial award applicants required to submit FAFSA. *Unit head:* Anne Witt, Registrar/Director of International Students, 704-344-6882 Ext. 103, Fax: 704-334-6885, E-mail: abwitt@charlottechristian.edu. *Application contact:* Constance Hemphill, Director of Admissions, 704-334-6882 Ext. 115, Fax: 704-334-6885, E-mail: chemphill@charlottechristian.edu.
Website: http://www.charlottechristian.edu

Columbia International University, Columbia Biblical Seminary and School of Ministry, Columbia, SC 29230-3122. Offers academic ministries (M Div); Bible and theology (Certificate); bible exposition (M Div, MABE); Biblical ministry (Certificate); chaplaincy (M Div); intercultural studies (MAIS); leadership (D Min); member care (D Min); missions (D Min); preaching (D Min); theological studies (MA). *Accreditation:* ATS (one or more programs are accredited). Part-time and evening/weekend programs available. *Faculty:* 14 full-time (1 woman), 9 part-time/adjunct (1 woman). *Students:* 180 full-time (59 women), 218 part-time (61 women); includes 81 minority (58 Black or African American, non-Hispanic/Latino; 1 American Indian or Alaska Native, non-Hispanic/Latino; 18 Asian, non-Hispanic/Latino; 4 Hispanic/Latino), 22 international. Average age 36. 277 applicants, 81% accepted, 117 enrolled. In 2014, 74 master's, 3 doctorates, 15 other advanced degrees awarded. *Degree requirements:* For doctorate, comprehensive exam, thesis/dissertation. *Entrance requirements:* For doctorate, 3 years of ministerial experience, M Div. Additional exam requirements/recommendations for international students: Required—TOEFL. *Application deadline:* For fall admission, 8/1 priority date for domestic and international students; for winter admission, 12/15 priority date for domestic and international students; for spring admission, 1/15 priority date for domestic and international students. Applications are processed on a rolling basis. Application fee: $45. Electronic applications accepted. *Expenses: Tuition:* Full-time $9540; part-time $530 per credit hour. *Required fees:* $480; $240 per semester. *Financial support:* In 2014–15, 120 students received support. Career-related internships or fieldwork, Federal Work-Study, institutionally sponsored loans, and scholarships/grants available. Financial award application deadline: 3/15; financial award applicants required to submit FAFSA. *Unit head:* Dr. Junias Venugopal, Dean, 803-754-4100 Ext. 5330, Fax: 803-786-4209, E-mail: jvenugopal@ciu.edu. *Application contact:* Michelle MacGregor, Director of Admissions, 800-777-2227 Ext. 5335, Fax: 803-786-4209, E-mail: yescbs@ciu.edu.
Website: http://www.ciu.edu/discover-ciu/who-we-are/academics/seminary-school-ministry

Dallas Baptist University, Gary Cook School of Leadership, Program in Christian Education, Dallas, TX 75211-9299. Offers adult ministry (MA); business ministry (MA); Christian studies (MA); collegiate ministry (MA); communication ministry (MA); counseling ministry (MA); family ministry (MA); general ministry (MA); leading the nonprofit organization (MA); missions ministry (MA); small group ministry (MA); student ministry (MA); worship ministry (MA); MA/MA. Part-time and evening/weekend programs available. *Entrance requirements:* For master's, minimum GPA of 3.0. Additional exam requirements/recommendations for international students: Required—TOEFL. Electronic applications accepted. *Expenses: Tuition:* Full-time $14,130; part-time $785 per credit hour. *Required fees:* $200 per semester. Tuition and fees vary according to course level and course load.

Dallas Baptist University, Gary Cook School of Leadership, Program in Global Leadership, Dallas, TX 75211-9299. Offers business communication (MA); East Asian studies (MA); ESL (MA); general studies (MA); global leadership (MA); global studies (MA); international business (MA); leading the nonprofit organization (MA); missions (MA); small group ministry (MA); MA/MA. Part-time and evening/weekend programs available. *Entrance requirements:* For master's, minimum GPA of 3.0. Additional exam requirements/recommendations for international students: Required—TOEFL, IELTS. *Expenses: Tuition:* Full-time $14,130; part-time $785 per credit hour. *Required fees:* $200 per semester. Tuition and fees vary according to course level and course load.

Dallas Baptist University, Liberal Arts Program, Dallas, TX 75211-9299. Offers arts (MLA); Christian ministry (MLA); East Asian studies (MLA); English (MLA); English as a second language (MLA); fine arts (MLA); history (MLA); missions (MLA); political science (MLA). Part-time and evening/weekend programs available. *Entrance requirements:* For master's, minimum GPA of 3.0. Additional exam requirements/recommendations for international students: Required—TOEFL. Electronic applications accepted. *Expenses: Tuition:* Full-time $14,130; part-time $785 per credit hour. *Required fees:* $200 per semester. Tuition and fees vary according to course level and course load. *Faculty research:* Milton and seventeenth-century Puritans, inter-Biblical years, nineteenth-century literature, Latin American and Texas history.

Dallas Baptist University, Professional Development Program, Dallas, TX 75211-9299. Offers business (MA); counseling (MA); criminal justice (MA); English as a second language (MA); higher education (MA); interdisciplinary (MA); leadership studies (MA); missions (MA); professional life coaching (MA); training and development (MA). Part-time and evening/weekend programs available. *Entrance requirements:* For master's, minimum GPA of 3.0. Additional exam requirements/recommendations for international students: Required—TOEFL, IELTS. *Expenses: Tuition:* Full-time $14,130; part-time $785 per credit hour. *Required fees:* $200 per semester. Tuition and fees vary according to course level and course load.

Dallas Theological Seminary, Graduate Programs, Dallas, TX 75204-6499. Offers adult education (Th M); apologetics (Th M); Bible backgrounds (Th M); Bible translation (Th M); Biblical and theological studies (Certificate); biblical counseling (MA); biblical exegesis and linguistics (MA); biblical exposition (PhD); biblical studies (MA); Biblical theology (Th M); children's education (Th M); Christian education (MA, D Min); Christian leadership (MA); cross-cultural ministries (MA); educational administration (Th M); educational leadership (Th M); evangelism and discipleship (Th M); exposition of Biblical books (Th M); family life education (Th M); general studies (Th M); Hebrew and cognate studies (Th M); hermeneutics (Th M); historical theology (Th M); homiletics (Th M); intercultural ministries (Th M); Jesus studies (Th M); leadership studies (Th M); media and communication (MA); media arts (Th M); ministry (D Min); ministry with women (Th M); New Testament studies (Th M, PhD); Old Testament studies (Th M, PhD); parachurch ministries (Th M); pastoral care and counseling (Th M); pastoral theology and practice (Th M); philosophy (Th M); sacred theology (STM); spiritual formation (Th M); systematic theology (Th M); teaching in Christian institutions (Th M); theological studies (PhD); urban ministries (Th M); worship studies (Th M); youth education (Th M). *Accreditation:* ATS (one or more programs are accredited). Part-time programs available. Postbaccalaureate distance learning degree programs offered (no on-campus study). *Degree requirements:* For master's, variable foreign language requirement, thesis (for some programs); for doctorate, 2 foreign languages, thesis/dissertation. *Entrance requirements:* For master's, GRE or MAT (if minimum undergraduate cumulative GPA is below 2.5 or undergraduate degree is unaccredited). Additional exam requirements/recommendations for international students: Required—TOEFL (minimum score 575 paper-based; 85 iBT), TWE. Electronic applications accepted.

Eastern University, Palmer Theological Seminary, King of Prussia, PA 19096-3430. Offers Biblical studies and theology (MTS); Christian counseling (MTS); Christian faith and public policy (MTS); divinity (M Div); general studies (MTS); leadership of missional church renewal (D Min); ministry (D Min), including marriage and family; M Div/MA; M Div/MBA; M Div/MSW. *Accreditation:* ACIPE; ATS; MSA/CIHE. Part-time programs available. Postbaccalaureate distance learning degree programs offered (minimal on-campus study). *Faculty:* 14 full-time (7 women), 17 part-time/adjunct (7 women). *Students:* 65 full-time (25 women), 185 part-time (102 women); includes 151 minority (145 Black or African American, non-Hispanic/Latino; 2 Asian, non-Hispanic/Latino; 3 Hispanic/Latino; 1 Two or more races, non-Hispanic/Latino), 3 international. Average age 47. 117 applicants, 56% accepted, 61 enrolled. In 2014, 53 master's, 17 doctorates awarded. *Degree requirements:* For master's, variable foreign language requirement, thesis (for some programs); for doctorate, thesis/dissertation. *Entrance requirements:* For master's, bachelor's degree from accredited institution; for doctorate, M Div or MA. Additional exam requirements/recommendations for international students: Required—TOEFL (minimum score 550 paper-based; 79 iBT). *Application deadline:* For fall admission, 8/1 priority date for domestic students, 3/31 for international students; for spring admission, 1/15 for domestic students, 10/31 for international students. Applications are processed on a rolling basis. Application fee: $30. Electronic applications accepted. Application fee is waived when completed online. *Expenses: Tuition:* Full-time $15,600; part-time $650 per credit. *Required fees:* $30; $27.50 per semester. One-time fee: $50. Tuition and fees vary according to course load, degree level and program. *Financial support:* In 2014–15, 130 students received support, including 2 fellowships (averaging $4,000 per year), 15 teaching assistantships (averaging $1,200 per year); career-related internships or fieldwork, Federal Work-Study, and scholarships/grants also available. Financial award application deadline: 8/1; financial award applicants required to submit FAFSA. *Faculty research:* Approaches to the spiritual formation of religious leaders; Latin, anti-Colonial, and constructive theologies; pastoral and ethical responses to human trafficking; inter-religious and political dimensions of peacemaking and social justice in Israel and the Palestinian Territories. *Unit head:* Dr. Edwin Aponte, Dean of the Seminary, 484-384-2935, E-mail: semdean@eastern.edu. *Application contact:* Tiffany S. Murphy, Director of Admissions, 610-896-5000 Ext. 2986, Fax: 484-654-3680, E-mail: semadmis@eastern.edu.
Website: http://www.palmerseminary.edu/

Emmanuel Christian Seminary, Graduate and Professional Programs, Johnson City, TN 37601-9438. Offers Christian care and counseling (M Div); Christian education (M Div); Christian ministries (MCM); Christian ministry (M Div); Christian theology (M Div, MAR); church history (MAR); church history/historical theology (M Div); general studies (M Div); ministry (D Min); New Testament (M Div, MAR); Old Testament (M Div, MAR); urban ministry (M Div); world missions (M Div). *Accreditation:* ACIPE; ATS. Part-time programs available. Postbaccalaureate distance learning degree programs offered (minimal on-campus study). *Degree requirements:* For master's, 2 foreign languages, thesis or alternative, portfolio; for doctorate, thesis/dissertation. *Entrance requirements:* For master's, bachelor's degree from accredited undergraduate institution; for doctorate, M Div or equivalent. Additional exam requirements/recommendations for international students: Required—TOEFL. Electronic applications accepted. *Faculty research:* Theology of Old Testament prophets, spiritual formation for Christian leaders, history of African churches and religions, social world of early Christianity, lay pastoral counseling, theology and art.

Evangelical Seminary, Graduate and Professional Programs, Myerstown, PA 17067-1212. Offers Biblical studies (MAR); congregational ministry (M Div); global and contextual studies (M Div, MAR); historical and theological studies (MAR); interdisciplinary studies (MAR); marriage and family counseling (M Div); marriage and family therapy (MA); New Testament (MAR); Old Testament (MAR); spiritual formation (MAR); teaching ministry (M Div); youth ministry (M Div). *Accreditation:* ATS (one or more programs are accredited). Part-time programs available. Postbaccalaureate distance learning degree programs offered (minimal on-campus study). *Degree requirements:* For master's, 2 foreign languages. *Entrance requirements:* For master's, minimum GPA of 2.5. Additional exam requirements/recommendations for international students: Required—TOEFL (minimum score 550 paper-based). *Faculty research:* Literary form and structure within the Hebrew and Greek scriptures, Wesley studies, esoteric biblical languages, the Mosaic law and the Christian, ethics.

Faulkner University, College of Biblical Studies, Montgomery, AL 36109-3398. Offers ministry (MABS); missions (MABS); New Testament (MABS); Old Testament (MABS); youth and family ministry (MABS).

Fresno Pacific University, Biblical Seminary, Program in Urban Mission, Fresno, CA 93702-4709. Offers MA. *Entrance requirements:* For master's, minimum GPA of 2.5. Application fee: $35. *Unit head:* Dr. Karen Crozier, Director, 559-453-2020, E-mail: karen.crozier@fresno.edu. *Application contact:* Amanda Krum-Stovall, Director of Graduate Admissions, 559-453-2016, E-mail: amanda.krum-stovall@fresno.edu.
Website: http://www.fresno.edu/programs-majors/biblical-seminary/urban-mission

Fuller Theological Seminary, Graduate Programs, Pasadena, CA 91182. Offers Christian leadership (MACL); clinical psychology (PhD, Psy D); family studies (MA); global leadership (MA); global ministries (D Min); global ministries (Korean language) (D Min); intercultural studies (MA, Th M, PhD); intercultural studies (Korean language) (MA); marital and family therapy (MS); marriage and family enrichment (Certificate); ministry (M Div, D Min); missiology (D Miss); missiology (Korean language) (Th M); theology (MA, Th M, PhD), including evangelism (MA), family life education (MA), pastoral ministry (MA), recovery ministry (MA), worship music ministry (MA), worship, theology, and the arts (MA), youth, family, and culture (MA); theology and ministry (MA).

Missions and Missiology

Gardner-Webb University, School of Divinity, Boiling Springs, NC 28017. Offers biblical studies (M Div); Christian education and formation (M Div); intercultural studies (M Div); ministry (D Min); missiology (M Div); pastoral care and counseling (M Div); pastoral care and counseling/member care for missionaries (D Min); pastoral studies (M Div); M Div/MA; M Div/MBA. *Accreditation:* ACIPE; ATS. Part-time programs available. *Faculty:* 10 full-time (2 women), 5 part-time/adjunct (1 woman). *Students:* 151 full-time (82 women), 76 part-time (22 women); includes 106 minority (92 Black or African American, non-Hispanic/Latino; 7 Asian, non-Hispanic/Latino; 7 Hispanic/Latino). Average age 41. 110 applicants, 53% accepted, 58 enrolled. *Entrance requirements:* For master's, minimum GPA of 2.6; for doctorate, minimum GPA of 2.75. Additional exam requirements/recommendations for international students: Required—TOEFL (minimum score 500 paper-based; 61 iBT). *Application deadline:* Applications are processed on a rolling basis. Application fee: $40. Electronic applications accepted. *Expenses:* Expenses: Contact institution. *Financial support:* Fellowships, institutionally sponsored loans, and unspecified assistantships available. Support available to part-time students. Financial award application deadline: 5/15. *Faculty research:* Jewish-Christian dialogue, Islam. *Unit head:* Dr. Robert W. Canoy, Sr., Dean, 704-406-4400, Fax: 704-406-3935, E-mail: rcanoy@gardner-webb.edu. *Application contact:* Kheresa Harmon, Director of Admissions, 704-406-3205, Fax: 704-406-3895, E-mail: kharmon@gardner-webb.edu.
Website: http://gardner-webb.edu/academic-programs-and-resources/colleges-and-schools/divinity/index

Georgia Christian University, School of Divinity, Atlanta, GA 30360. Offers Christian education (MA); divinity (M Div); ministry (D Min); mission studies and world Christianity (MA); theological studies (MA).

Global University, Graduate School of Theology, Springfield, MO 65804. Offers biblical studies (MA); divinity (M Div); ministerial studies (MA), including education, leadership, missions, New Testament, Old Testament. Part-time and evening/weekend programs available. Postbaccalaureate distance learning degree programs offered (no on-campus study). *Degree requirements:* For master's, thesis (for some programs). *Entrance requirements:* For master's, minimum undergraduate GPA of 3.0. Electronic applications accepted. *Faculty research:* Higher education, cross-cultural missions.

Gordon-Conwell Theological Seminary, Graduate and Professional Programs, South Hamilton, MA 01982. Offers Biblical languages (MABL); church history (MACH); counseling (MACO); ministry (D Min); missions/evangelism (MAME); New Testament (MANT); Old Testament (MAOT); religion (MAR); theology (M Div, MATH, Th M, Th D). *Accreditation:* ACIPE; ATS (one or more programs are accredited). Part-time and evening/weekend programs available. *Degree requirements:* For master's, one foreign language, thesis optional; for doctorate, 2 foreign languages, thesis/dissertation. *Entrance requirements:* For master's, minimum GPA of 2.5; for doctorate, minimum GPA of 3.0.

Grace Theological Seminary, Graduate and Professional Programs, Winona Lake, IN 46590-9907. Offers biblical studies (Certificate); camp administration (MA); counseling (M Div); exegetical studies (MA); intercultural studies (M Div, MA); local church studies (MA); pastoral studies (M Div); theological studies (MA); theology (D Min, Diploma). *Accreditation:* ATS. Part-time programs available. Postbaccalaureate distance learning degree programs offered (no on-campus study). *Degree requirements:* For master's, thesis optional; for doctorate, 2 foreign languages, thesis/dissertation. *Entrance requirements:* For master's, MAT, minimum GPA of 2.5. Electronic applications accepted. *Faculty research:* Biblical theology, language, and church ministries.

Grand Rapids Theological Seminary of Cornerstone University, Graduate Programs, Grand Rapids, MI 49525-5897. Offers biblical counseling (MA); Biblical counseling (M Div); chaplaincy (M Div); Christian education (M Div, MA); intercultural studies (M Div, MA); New Testament (MA, Th M); Old Testament (MA, Th M); pastoral studies (M Div); systematic theology (MA); theology (Th M). *Accreditation:* ATS. Part-time programs available. Postbaccalaureate distance learning degree programs offered (minimal on-campus study). *Entrance requirements:* Additional exam requirements/recommendations for international students: Required—TOEFL (minimum score 577 paper-based; 90 iBT). Electronic applications accepted.

Hope International University, School of Graduate and Professional Studies, Programs in Ministry, Fullerton, CA 92831-3138. Offers Christian leadership (MCM); church music (MA); church music (Korean track) (MCM); church planting (MCM); intercultural studies (MCM); worship (MCM). Part-time and evening/weekend programs available. Postbaccalaureate distance learning degree programs offered (minimal on-campus study). *Degree requirements:* For master's, thesis (for some programs), project. *Entrance requirements:* For master's, minimum GPA of 3.0, MCM program requires an undergraduate degree in music, 2 references. Additional exam requirements/recommendations for international students: Required—TOEFL (minimum score 550 paper-based; 86 iBT); Recommended—IELTS (minimum score 6.5). Electronic applications accepted. *Expenses:* Contact institution. *Faculty research:* Church dynamics, growth methodologies.

Huntington University, Graduate School, Huntington, IN 46750-1299. Offers counseling (MA), including licensed mental health counselor; early adolescent education (M Ed); education (M Ed); global missions leadership (MA); global youth ministry (MA); TESOL education (M Ed); youth ministry leadership (MA). Part-time programs available. Postbaccalaureate distance learning degree programs offered (minimal on-campus study). *Faculty:* 15 full-time (6 women), 17 part-time/adjunct (8 women). *Students:* 37 full-time (26 women), 94 part-time (62 women). 170 applicants, 47% accepted, 73 enrolled. In 2014, 25 master's awarded. *Degree requirements:* For master's, comprehensive exam (for some programs), thesis (for some programs). *Entrance requirements:* For master's, GRE (for counseling and education students only); for doctorate, GRE (for occupational therapy students). Additional exam requirements/recommendations for international students: Required—TOEFL (minimum score 85 iBT), IELTS (minimum score 6.5). *Application deadline:* For fall admission, 7/1 for domestic students, 5/1 for international students; for winter admission, 10/1 for domestic students, 9/1 for international students; for spring admission, 11/30 for domestic students, 10/30 for international students. Applications are processed on a rolling basis. Application fee: $30. Electronic applications accepted. *Expenses: Tuition:* Full-time $7965; part-time $531 per credit hour. Tuition and fees vary according to degree level and program. *Financial support:* In 2014–15, 30 students received support. Scholarships/grants and unspecified assistantships available. Support available to part-time students. Financial award application deadline: 8/1; financial award applicants required to submit FAFSA. *Faculty research:* Leadership, educational technology trends, evangelism, youth ministry, mental health. *Unit head:* Ann C. McPherren, EdD, VP for Strategy and Graduate and Professional Programs, 260-359-4225, Fax: 260-359-4126, E-mail: amcpherren@huntington.edu. *Application contact:* Becca Cline, Graduate Admissions Counselor, 260-359-4111, Fax: 260-359-4126, E-mail: bcline@huntington.edu.
Website: http://www.huntington.edu/graduate

Liberty University, Liberty Baptist Theological Seminary, Lynchburg, VA 24515. Offers Biblical studies (M Div, MAR, MTS, Th M); church history (M Div, MAR, MTS, Th M); discipleship (D Min); discipleship and church ministry (M Div, MAR, MCM); evangelism and church planting (M Div, MAR, MCM, D Min); global studies (M Div, MAR, MCM, MGS, Th M); homiletics (M Div, MAR, MCM, Th M, D Min); leadership (M Div, MAR, MCM, D Min); marketplace chaplaincy (M Div, MAR, MCM); ministry (D Min); pastoral counseling (M Div, MA, MAR, MCM, D Min), including addictions and recovery (MA), crisis response and trauma (MA), discipleship and church ministries (MA), leadership (MA), life coaching (MA), marketplace chaplaincy (MA), marriage and family (MA), military resilience (MA), pastoral counseling (MA); pastoral ministries (M Div, MAR, MCM); religious education (MRE); theology (M Div, MAR, MTS, Th M); theology and apologetics (PhD); worship (M Div, MAR, MCM, D Min). Part-time programs available. Postbaccalaureate distance learning degree programs offered (minimal on-campus study). *Students:* 2,865 full-time (781 women), 3,750 part-time (1,139 women); includes 1,742 minority (1,382 Black or African American, non-Hispanic/Latino; 22 American Indian or Alaska Native, non-Hispanic/Latino; 116 Asian, non-Hispanic/Latino; 105 Hispanic/Latino; 7 Native Hawaiian or other Pacific Islander, non-Hispanic/Latino; 110 Two or more races, non-Hispanic/Latino), 227 international. Average age 41. 5,446 applicants, 39% accepted, 1340 enrolled. In 2014, 1,969 master's, 126 doctorates, 75 other advanced degrees awarded. *Degree requirements:* For master's, 2 foreign languages, thesis (for some programs); for doctorate, 2 foreign languages, thesis/dissertation. *Entrance requirements:* For master's, minimum undergraduate GPA of 2.0; for doctorate, GRE General Test or MAT, minimum graduate GPA of 3.0. Additional exam requirements/recommendations for international students: Required—TOEFL (minimum score 600 paper-based; 100 iBT). *Application deadline:* For fall admission, 6/1 for domestic students; for spring admission, 11/1 for domestic students. Applications are processed on a rolling basis. Application fee: $50. Electronic applications accepted. *Expenses:* Expenses: Contact institution. *Financial support:* Teaching assistantships with tuition reimbursements, career-related internships or fieldwork, and Federal Work-Study available. Financial award applicants required to submit FAFSA. *Unit head:* Dr. David Hirschman, Acting Dean, 434-592-4140, Fax: 434-522-0415, E-mail: dwhirschman@liberty.edu. *Application contact:* Jay Bridge, Director of Graduate Admissions, 800-424-9595, Fax: 800-628-7977, E-mail: gradadmissions@liberty.edu.
Website: http://www.liberty.edu/seminary/

Liberty University, School of Music, Lynchburg, VA 24515. Offers ethnomusicology (MA); music and worship (MA); music education (MA); worship studies (MA, DWS), including church planting (MA), ethnomusicology (MA), leadership (MA). Part-time programs available. Postbaccalaureate distance learning degree programs offered (minimal on-campus study). *Students:* 57 full-time (19 women), 180 part-time (75 women); includes 48 minority (34 Black or African American, non-Hispanic/Latino; 1 American Indian or Alaska Native, non-Hispanic/Latino; 2 Asian, non-Hispanic/Latino; 2 Hispanic/Latino; 1 Native Hawaiian or other Pacific Islander, non-Hispanic/Latino; 8 Two or more races, non-Hispanic/Latino), 12 international. Average age 35. 330 applicants, 32% accepted, 57 enrolled. In 2014, 41 master's awarded. *Entrance requirements:* For master's, minimum GPA of 3.0; interview; letter of recommendation; statement of purpose; bachelor's/master's degree in music, worship, or related field, or 5 years of experience. Additional exam requirements/recommendations for international students: Required—TOEFL (minimum score 600 paper-based; 100 iBT). *Application deadline:* Applications are processed on a rolling basis. Application fee: $50. Electronic applications accepted. *Unit head:* Dr. Vernon Whaley, Dean, 434-592-3463, E-mail: vwhaley@liberty.edu. *Application contact:* Jay Bridge, Director of Admissions, 800-424-9595, Fax: 800-628-7977, E-mail: gradadmissions@liberty.edu.
Website: http://www.liberty.edu/academics/music/

Luther Seminary, Graduate and Professional Programs, St. Paul, MN 55108-1445. Offers aging and health (MA); Biblical preaching (D Min); children, youth and family (M Div, MA); congregational mission and leadership (M Th, MA, D Min); history of Christianity (M Th, MA); missions and world religions (M Th); New Testament (M Th, MA); Old Testament (M Th, MA); pastoral care: clinical pastoral theology (M Th); pastoral theology and ministry (M Th); systematic theology (M Th, MA). *Accreditation:* ACIPE; ATS. Part-time programs available. Postbaccalaureate distance learning degree programs offered (minimal on-campus study). *Faculty:* 25 full-time, 25 part-time/adjunct. *Students:* 401 full-time, 304 part-time, 31 international. Average age 30. 139 applicants, 96% accepted, 96 enrolled. In 2014, 140 master's, 23 doctorates awarded. *Degree requirements:* For master's, thesis or alternative; for doctorate, 2 foreign languages, thesis/dissertation. *Entrance requirements:* For master's, minimum GPA of 3.0; for doctorate, GRE General Test. Additional exam requirements/recommendations for international students: Required—TOEFL, IELTS. *Application deadline:* For fall admission, 7/1 priority date for domestic students, 4/30 for international students; for winter admission, 10/31 for international students; for spring admission, 10/31 for international students. Applications are processed on a rolling basis. Application fee: $0. Electronic applications accepted. *Financial support:* In 2014–15, 359 students received support. Career-related internships or fieldwork, Federal Work-Study, institutionally sponsored loans, and scholarships/grants available. Support available to part-time students. Financial award application deadline: 6/1; financial award applicants required to submit FAFSA. *Faculty research:* Theology, psychology (pastoral care), church history, Bible. *Unit head:* Dr. Craig Koester, Dean of Academic Affairs, 651-641-3471, Fax: 651-641-1609, E-mail: ckoester@luthersem.edu. *Application contact:* Jen Olsen Krengel, Director of Admissions, 651-641-3516, E-mail: jolsenkrengel001@luthersem.edu.
Website: http://www.luthersem.edu/

Nazarene Theological Seminary, Graduate and Professional Programs, Kansas City, MO 64131-1263. Offers Christian formation and discipleship (MA); intercultural studies (MA); theological studies (MA); theology (M Div, D Min). *Accreditation:* ACIPE; ATS. Part-time programs available. *Degree requirements:* For master's, comprehensive exam (for some programs), thesis (for some programs); for doctorate, thesis/dissertation. *Entrance requirements:* Additional exam requirements/recommendations for international students: Required—TOEFL. Electronic applications accepted.

Northern Baptist Theological Seminary, Graduate and Professional Programs, Lombard, IL 60148-5698. Offers Biblical studies (M Div); Christian ministries (MACM); missional leadership (D Min); spiritual transformation (D Min); theology (M Div). *Accreditation:* ATS. Part-time and evening/weekend programs available. *Faculty:* 6 full-time (1 woman), 33 part-time/adjunct (8 women). *Students:* 126 full-time (34 women), 80 part-time (32 women); includes 89 minority (73 Black or African American, non-Hispanic/Latino; 6 Asian, non-Hispanic/Latino; 8 Hispanic/Latino; 2 Two or more races, non-Hispanic/Latino), 3 international. Average age 44. *Degree requirements:* For doctorate, thesis/dissertation. *Entrance requirements:* For master's, all official transcripts, letter of reference from church, 3 letters of reference, autobiographical statement (400 words or more); for doctorate, M Div, 3 years in the ministry post-M Div, 3 letters of reference. Additional exam requirements/recommendations for international students: Required—TOEFL (minimum score 550 paper-based). *Application deadline:* For fall admission, 8/25 for domestic students, 2/1 for international students; for winter admission, 12/10 for domestic students, 2/1 for international students; for spring admission, 3/15 for domestic students, 2/1 for international students. Applications are processed on a rolling basis. Application fee: $35. Electronic applications accepted. *Expenses: Tuition:* Full-time $13,230; part-time $1470 per course. *Required fees:* $360; $120 per quarter. *Financial support:* Scholarships/grants available. Support available to part-time students. Financial award application deadline: 9/1; financial award applicants required to submit

FAFSA. *Faculty research:* Theology, worship studies, church history, evangelism, Christian ministry. *Unit head:* Dr. J. Alistair Brown, President, 630-620-2101, Fax: 630-620-2190. *Application contact:* Isaac Ampil, Director of Admissions, 630-620-2175, Fax: 630-620-2190, E-mail: admissions@seminary.edu.

Northwest Nazarene University, Graduate Studies, Program in Religion, Nampa, ID 83686-5897. Offers missional leadership (M Div, MA); pastoral ministry (MA); spiritual formation (M Div, MA); youth, children, and family ministry (M Div, MA). Part-time and evening/weekend programs available. Postbaccalaureate distance learning degree programs offered (no on-campus study). *Faculty:* 12 full-time (2 women), 15 part-time/adjunct (1 woman). *Students:* 91 full-time (27 women), 20 part-time (5 women); includes 11 minority (4 Black or African American, non-Hispanic/Latino; 1 American Indian or Alaska Native, non-Hispanic/Latino; 2 Asian, non-Hispanic/Latino; 3 Hispanic/Latino; 1 Native Hawaiian or other Pacific Islander, non-Hispanic/Latino), 1 international. Average age 39. 55 applicants, 65% accepted, 27 enrolled. In 2014, 40 master's awarded. *Entrance requirements:* For master's, minimum GPA of 2.5; 8 semester or 12 quarter credits of Bible, theology and/or Western philosophy. Additional exam requirements/recommendations for international students: Required—TOEFL. *Application deadline:* Applications are processed on a rolling basis. Application fee: $50. Electronic applications accepted. *Unit head:* Dr. Jay Akkerman, Director, Graduate Studies, 208-467-8437, Fax: 208-467-8252. *Application contact:* Vicki Funk, Program Coordinator, 208-467-8432, Fax: 208-467-8252, E-mail: vlfunk@nnu.edu.
Website: http://www.nnu.edu/ministry/

Northwest University, College of Ministry, Kirkland, WA 98033. Offers ministry (MIM); missional leadership (MA); theology and culture (MA). Part-time and evening/weekend programs available. Postbaccalaureate distance learning degree programs offered (no on-campus study). *Faculty:* 6 full-time (1 woman), 8 part-time/adjunct (1 woman). *Students:* 7 full-time (3 women), 81 part-time (19 women); includes 21 minority (2 Black or African American, non-Hispanic/Latino; 6 Asian, non-Hispanic/Latino; 3 Hispanic/Latino; 4 Native Hawaiian or other Pacific Islander, non-Hispanic/Latino; 6 Two or more races, non-Hispanic/Latino). Average age 43. 33 applicants, 97% accepted, 20 enrolled. In 2014, 33 master's awarded. *Degree requirements:* For master's, comprehensive exam (for some programs), thesis (for some programs). *Entrance requirements:* Additional exam requirements/recommendations for international students: Required—TOEFL (minimum score 550 paper-based; 75 iBT). *Application deadline:* For fall admission, 8/1 for domestic students, 4/1 for international students; for spring admission, 12/1 for domestic students, 8/1 for international students. Applications are processed on a rolling basis. Application fee: $50. Electronic applications accepted. *Expenses: Tuition:* Full-time $6894; part-time $684 per credit. *Required fees:* $12.50 per term. One-time fee: $98 full-time; $83 part-time. Tuition and fees vary according to course load, campus/location, program and reciprocity agreements. *Financial support:* In 2014–15, 10 students received support. Federal Work-Study available. *Unit head:* Dr. Wayde Goodall, Dean, 425-889-5211, E-mail: wayde.goodall@northwestu.edu. *Application contact:* Steven Curry, Graduate Enrollment Counselor, College of Ministry, 425-889-7795, E-mail: steven.curry@northwestu.edu.
Website: http://www.northwestu.edu/ministrygrad/

Nyack College, Alliance Theological Seminary, Nyack, NY 10960. Offers Biblical literature (MA), including New Testament, Old Testament; Christian ministry (MPS); intercultural studies (MA); ministry (D Min), including Christian leadership in the global context; theology and missions (M Div); urban ministry (MPS). *Accreditation:* ATS. Part-time and evening/weekend programs available. *Students:* 319 full-time (132 women), 439 part-time (214 women); includes 605 minority (230 Black or African American, non-Hispanic/Latino; 170 Asian, non-Hispanic/Latino; 195 Hispanic/Latino; 1 Native Hawaiian or other Pacific Islander, non-Hispanic/Latino; 9 Two or more races, non-Hispanic/Latino), 41 international. Average age 43. In 2014, 134 master's, 11 doctorates awarded. *Degree requirements:* For master's, comprehensive exam (for some programs), thesis optional, internship; for doctorate, thesis/dissertation. *Entrance requirements:* For master's, transcripts, Christian experience statement, personal goals statement, recommendations; for doctorate, transcripts, documented three years of ministry experience subsequent to 1st graduate theological degree, reference letters, formal academic paper. Additional exam requirements/recommendations for international students: Required—TOEFL (minimum score 83 iBT). *Application deadline:* Applications are processed on a rolling basis. Application fee: $30. Electronic applications accepted. *Expenses:* Expenses: Contact institution. *Financial support:* Career-related internships or fieldwork, Federal Work-Study, and scholarships/grants available. Financial award applicants required to submit FAFSA. *Unit head:* Dr. Ronald Walborn, Dean, 845-770-5715, Fax: 845-358-1663. *Application contact:* Julian Williams, ATS Associate Director of Admissions, 800-541-6891, Fax: 845-348-3912, E-mail: admissions.ats@nyack.edu.
Website: http://www.nyack.edu/ats

Oral Roberts University, School of Theology and Missions, Tulsa, OK 74171. Offers biblical literature (MA), including advanced languages, Judaic-Christian studies; Christian counseling (MA), including marriage and family therapy; divinity (M Div); missions (MA); practical theology (MA); theological/historical studies (MA); theology (D Min). *Accreditation:* ATS. Part-time programs available. Postbaccalaureate distance learning degree programs offered (minimal on-campus study). *Degree requirements:* For master's, thesis (for some programs), practicum/internship; for doctorate, thesis/dissertation, applied research project. *Entrance requirements:* For master's, GRE General Test or MAT, minimum GPA of 2.5; for doctorate, M Div, minimum GPA of 3.0, 3 years of full-time ministry experience. Additional exam requirements/recommendations for international students: Required—TOEFL (minimum score 550 paper-based; 79 iBT). Electronic applications accepted.

Phillips Theological Seminary, Programs in Theology, Tulsa, OK 74116. Offers administration of church agencies (M Div); campus ministry (M Div); church-related social work (M Div); college and seminary teaching (M Div); global mission work (M Div); institutional chaplaincy (M Div); ministerial vocations in Christian education (M Div); ministry (D Min), including parish ministry, pastoral counseling, practices of ministry; ministry and culture (MAMC), including Christian education, congregational leadership, history and practice of Christian spirituality, theology, ethics, and culture; ministry of music (M Div); pastoral care and counseling (M Div); pastoral ministry (M Div); theological studies (MTS). *Accreditation:* ATS. Part-time programs available. Postbaccalaureate distance learning degree programs offered (minimal on-campus study). *Degree requirements:* For master's, thesis (for some programs); for doctorate, thesis/dissertation. *Entrance requirements:* For master's, minimum GPA of 2.5; for doctorate, M Div, minimum GPA of 3.0. *Faculty research:* Biblical studies, historical studies, theology and culture, practical theology, theology and film.

Providence University College & Theological Seminary, Theological Seminary, Otterburne, MB R0A 1G0, Canada. Offers children's ministry (Certificate); Christian studies (MA, Certificate); counseling (MA); cross-cultural discipleship (Certificate); divinity (M Div); educational studies (MA), including counseling psychology, educational ministries, student development, teaching English to speakers of other languages, training teachers of English to speakers of other languages; global studies (MA); lay counseling (Diploma); ministry (D Min); teaching English to speakers of other languages (Certificate); theological studies (MA); training teacher of English to speakers of other languages (Certificate); youth ministry (Certificate). *Accreditation:* ATS. Part-time programs available. *Degree requirements:* For master's, variable foreign language requirement, thesis (for some programs); for doctorate, thesis/dissertation. *Entrance requirements:* Additional exam requirements/recommendations for international students: Recommended—TOEFL (minimum score 550 paper-based). *Faculty research:* Studies in Isaiah, theology of sin.

Reformed Theological Seminary–Jackson Campus, Graduate and Professional Programs, Jackson, MS 39209-3099. Offers Bible, theology, and missions (Certificate); Biblical exegesis (M Div); biblical studies (MA); Christian education (MA); counseling (M Div); marriage and family therapy (MA); ministry (D Min); missions (M Div, MA, D Min); theological studies (MA). *Accreditation:* AAMFT/COAMFTE (one or more programs are accredited); ATS (one or more programs are accredited). *Faculty:* 10 full-time (0 women), 1 (woman) part-time/adjunct. *Students:* 50 full-time (14 women), 86 part-time (19 women). *Degree requirements:* For master's, thesis (for some programs), fieldwork; for doctorate, 2 foreign languages, thesis/dissertation. *Entrance requirements:* For master's, minimum GPA of 2.6; for doctorate, minimum GPA of 3.0. Additional exam requirements/recommendations for international students: Required—TOEFL. *Application deadline:* Applications are processed on a rolling basis. Application fee: $35. *Financial support:* Research assistantships, career-related internships or fieldwork, scholarships/grants, and tuition waivers (full and partial) available. Financial award application deadline: 5/1. *Application contact:* Brian Gault, Director of Admissions, 601-923-1600, Fax: 601-923-1654.

Regent University, Graduate School, School of Divinity, Virginia Beach, VA 23464-9800. Offers leadership and renewal (D Min), including Christian leadership and renewal, clinical pastoral education, community transformation, military ministry, ministry leadership coaching; practical theology (M Div, MA), including Biblical studies (M Div, MTS, PhD), chaplain ministry (M Div), Christian theology (M Div, MTS, PhD), church and ministry, history of Christianity (M Div, MTS), inter-cultural studies, interdisciplinary studies (M Div, MA, MTS), worship and renewal; renewal studies (PhD), including Biblical studies (M Div, MTS, PhD), Christian theology (M Div, MTS, PhD), history of global Christianity; theological studies (MTS), including Biblical studies (M Div, MTS, PhD), Christian theology (M Div, MTS, PhD), history of Christianity (M Div, MTS), interdisciplinary studies (M Div, MA, MTS). *Accreditation:* ACIPE; ATS. Part-time programs available. Postbaccalaureate distance learning degree programs offered (minimal on-campus study). *Faculty:* 20 full-time (3 women), 29 part-time/adjunct (3 women). *Students:* 64 full-time (28 women), 616 part-time (258 women); includes 318 minority (269 Black or African American, non-Hispanic/Latino; 7 American Indian or Alaska Native, non-Hispanic/Latino; 16 Asian, non-Hispanic/Latino; 26 Hispanic/Latino), 37 international. Average age 43. 511 applicants, 52% accepted, 187 enrolled. In 2014, 121 master's, 24 doctorates awarded. *Degree requirements:* For master's, comprehensive exam, thesis or alternative, internship; for doctorate, thesis/dissertation or alternative. *Entrance requirements:* For master's, GRE General Test or MAT, minimum undergraduate GPA of 2.75, writing sample, clergy recommendation; for doctorate, M Div or theological master's degree; minimum graduate GPA of 3.5 (PhD), 3.0 (D Min); recommendations; writing sample; transcripts. Additional exam requirements/recommendations for international students: Required—TOEFL (minimum score 577 paper-based). *Application deadline:* For fall admission, 5/1 priority date for domestic students. Applications are processed on a rolling basis. Application fee: $50. Electronic applications accepted. *Expenses:* Expenses: Contact institution. *Financial support:* Fellowships with full and partial tuition reimbursements, career-related internships or fieldwork, scholarships/grants, tuition waivers (full and partial), and unspecified assistantships available. Support available to part-time students. Financial award application deadline: 9/1; financial award applicants required to submit FAFSA. *Faculty research:* Greek and Hebrew, theology, spiritual formation, global missions and world Christianity, women's studies. *Unit head:* Dr. Joseph Umidi, Interim Dean, 757-352-4401, Fax: 757-352-4597, E-mail: joseumi@regent.edu. *Application contact:* Matthew Chadwick, Director of Enrollment Support Services, 800-373-5504, Fax: 757-352-4381, E-mail: admissions@regent.edu.
Website: http://www.regent.edu/acad/schdiv/

Rochester College, Center for Missional Leadership, Rochester Hills, MI 48307-2764. Offers MRE.

Saint Paul University, Faculty of Human Sciences, Program in Mission and Interreligious Studies, Ottawa, ON K1S 1C4, Canada. Offers MA. *Degree requirements:* For master's, one foreign language, thesis. *Entrance requirements:* For master's, honors BA in mission, minimum B average. *Faculty research:* Theology of mission; mission and sociology; history of mission; faith, religion, and culture; world religions; practice of mission; religious anthropology; sociocultural anthropology.

Simpson University, A.W. Tozer Theological Seminary, Redding, CA 96003-8606. Offers intellectual leadership (MA). Part-time and evening/weekend programs available. Postbaccalaureate distance learning degree programs offered (minimal on-campus study). *Faculty:* 19 part-time/adjunct (4 women). *Students:* 4 full-time (2 women), 40 part-time (12 women); includes 10 minority (4 Black or African American, non-Hispanic/Latino; 3 Asian, non-Hispanic/Latino; 2 Hispanic/Latino; 1 Two or more races, non-Hispanic/Latino), 1 international. Average age 37. In 2014, 12 master's awarded. *Degree requirements:* For master's, student portfolio. *Entrance requirements:* For master's, GRE General Test (if undergraduate GPA less than 2.5), 2 letters of reference, Christian Experience statement. Additional exam requirements/recommendations for international students: Required—TOEFL. *Application deadline:* For fall admission, 9/4 priority date for domestic students, 9/4 for international students; for spring admission, 1/8 priority date for domestic students, 1/8 for international students. Applications are processed on a rolling basis. Application fee: $35. Electronic applications accepted. *Expenses:* Expenses: Contact institution. *Financial support:* Scholarships/grants available. Support available to part-time students. Financial award application deadline: 3/20; financial award applicants required to submit FAFSA. *Unit head:* Dr. Patrick Blewett, Dean, 530-226-4144, Fax: 530-226-4871, E-mail: pblewett@simpsonu.edu. *Application contact:* Kimberly Snow, Assistant Director of Graduate Studies Admissions, 530-226-4633, Fax: 530-226-4861, E-mail: admissions@simpsonu.edu.
Website: http://tozer.simpsonu.edu

Southeastern Baptist Theological Seminary, Graduate and Professional Programs, Wake Forest, NC 27588-1889. Offers advanced biblical studies (M Div); Christian education (M Div, MACE); Christian ethics (PhD); Christian ministry (M Div); Christian planting (M Div); church music (MACM); counseling (MACO); evangelism (PhD); language (M Div); ministry (D Min); New Testament (PhD); Old Testament (PhD); philosophy (PhD); theology (Th M, PhD); women's studies (M Div). *Accreditation:* ACIPE; ATS (one or more programs are accredited). *Degree requirements:* For master's, thesis (for some programs), oral exam; for doctorate, thesis/dissertation, fieldwork. *Entrance requirements:* For master's, Cooperative English Test, minimum GPA of 2.0, M Div or equivalent (Th M); for doctorate, GRE General Test or MAT, Cooperative English Test, M Div or equivalent, 3 years of professional experience.

Southern Adventist University, School of Religion, Collegedale, TN 37315-0370. Offers Biblical and theological studies (MA); church leadership and management (M Min); church ministry and homiletics (M Min); evangelism and world mission (M Min); religious studies (MA). Part-time programs available. *Degree requirements:* For

master's, comprehensive exam, thesis (for some programs). *Entrance requirements:* For master's, GRE. Additional exam requirements/recommendations for international students: Required—TOEFL (minimum score 600 paper-based). *Faculty research:* Biblical archaeology.

Southern Baptist Theological Seminary, Billy Graham School of Missions and Evangelism, Louisville, KY 40280-0004. Offers ministry (D Min); missiology (MA, D Miss); missions and evangelism (M Div, Th M, PhD); theological studies (MA). *Accreditation:* ATS. Part-time and evening/weekend programs available. Postbaccalaureate distance learning degree programs offered (minimal on-campus study). *Degree requirements:* For master's, 2 foreign languages; for doctorate, 4 foreign languages, thesis/dissertation. *Entrance requirements:* For doctorate, GRE General Test, MAT, M Div. Additional exam requirements/recommendations for international students: Required—TOEFL, TWE. *Faculty research:* Assimilation of church congregants, effective methodologies of evangelism, expectations of church members, spiritual warfare literature, formative church discipline.

Southern Baptist Theological Seminary, School of Church Ministries, Louisville, KY 40280-0004. Offers Biblical counseling (M Div, MA); children's and family ministry (M Div, MA); Christian education (MA); Christian worship (PhD); church ministries (M Div); church music (MCM); college ministry (M Div, MA); discipleship and family ministry (M Div, MA); education (Ed D); family ministry (D Min, PhD); higher education (PhD); leadership (M Div, MA, D Min, PhD); ministry (D Ed Min); missions and ethnodoxology (M Div); women's leadership (M Div, MA); worship leadership (M Div, MA); worship leadership and church ministry (MA); youth and family ministry (M Div, MA). Part-time programs available. Postbaccalaureate distance learning degree programs offered (minimal on-campus study). *Degree requirements:* For doctorate, thesis/dissertation. *Entrance requirements:* For doctorate, GRE General Test, interview, M Div or MACE. Additional exam requirements/recommendations for international students: Required—TWE. *Faculty research:* Gerontology, creative teaching methods, faith development in children, faith development in youth, transformational learning.

Southern Evangelical Seminary, Graduate Programs, Matthews, NC 28105. Offers apologetics (MA, D Min, Certificate); Christian education (MA); church ministry (MA, Certificate); divinity (Certificate), including apologetics (M Div, Certificate); Islamic studies (MA, Certificate); Jewish studies (MA); philosophy (MA); philosophy of religion (PhD); religion (MA); theology (M Div), including apologetics (M Div, Certificate), Biblical studies; youth ministry (MA). Part-time and evening/weekend programs available. Postbaccalaureate distance learning degree programs offered. *Degree requirements:* For master's, thesis (for some programs); for doctorate, 2 foreign languages, comprehensive exam (for some programs), thesis/dissertation. *Entrance requirements:* Additional exam requirements/recommendations for international students: Required—TOEFL (minimum score 600 paper-based).

Southwestern Assemblies of God University, Thomas F. Harrison School of Graduate Studies, Program in Theological Studies, Waxahachie, TX 75165-5735. Offers Bible and theology (MS); Biblical studies (M Div); counseling (M Div); cross cultural missions (M Div); practical theology (M Div); theological studies (M Div). Postbaccalaureate distance learning degree programs offered. *Degree requirements:* For master's, comprehensive written and oral exams. *Entrance requirements:* For master's, GRE General Test, minimum GPA of 2.5. Electronic applications accepted.

Southwestern Christian University, Program in Ministry, Bethany, OK 73008-0340. Offers church planting (M Min); church revitalization and renewal (M Min); intercultural studies (M Min); leadership (M Min); life coaching (M Min); pastoral ministries (M Min); work place ministries (M Min). Part-time programs available. *Degree requirements:* For master's, thesis. *Entrance requirements:* For master's, minimum GPA of 2.5. Additional exam requirements/recommendations for international students: Required—TOEFL (minimum score 500 paper-based). Electronic applications accepted.

Summit University, Baptist Bible Seminary, Clarks Summit, PA 18411-1297. Offers Biblical apologetics (MA); church education (M Div, M Min); church planting (M Div, M Min); global ministry (M Div, M Min); leadership in communication (D Min); leadership in counseling and spiritual development (D Min); leadership in global ministry (D Min); leadership in pastoral ministry (D Min); leadership in theological studies (D Min); military chaplaincy (M Div); ministry (PhD); organizational leadership (M Min); outreach pastor (M Div, M Min); pastoral counseling (M Div, M Min); pastoral leadership (M Div, M Min); theology (Th M); worship ministries leadership (M Div, M Min); youth pastor (M Div, M Min). Part-time and evening/weekend programs available. Postbaccalaureate distance learning degree programs offered (minimal on-campus study). Terminal master's awarded for partial completion of doctoral program. *Degree requirements:* For master's, 2 foreign languages, thesis, oral exam (for M Div); for doctorate, 2 foreign languages, comprehensive exam (for some programs), thesis/dissertation, oral exam. *Entrance requirements:* For doctorate, Greek and Hebrew entrance exams (for PhD). Electronic applications accepted.

Summit University, Graduate Studies, Clarks Summit, PA 18411-1297. Offers Bible (MA); counseling (MA, MS); curriculum and instruction (M Ed); educational administration (M Ed); intercultural studies (MA); literature (MA); missions (MA); organizational leadership (MA); reading specialist (M Ed); secondary English/communications (M Ed); social entrepreneurship (MA); worldview studies (MA). MA in missions program available only for Association of Baptists for World Evangelism missionary personnel. Part-time and evening/weekend programs available. Postbaccalaureate distance learning degree programs offered (no on-campus study). *Entrance requirements:* Additional exam requirements/recommendations for international students: Required—TOEFL (minimum score 500 paper-based).

Taylor College and Seminary, Graduate and Professional Programs, Edmonton, AB T6J 4T3, Canada. Offers Christian studies (Diploma); intercultural studies (MA, Diploma), including intercultural studies (Diploma), TESOL; theology (M Div, MTS). *Accreditation:* ATS. Part-time programs available. Postbaccalaureate distance learning degree programs offered (minimal on-campus study). *Degree requirements:* For master's, thesis optional. *Entrance requirements:* Additional exam requirements/recommendations for international students: Required—TOEFL (minimum score 550 paper-based; 80 iBT), IELTS (minimum score 6.5). *Faculty research:* Biblical studies, administration and organization, world religions, ethics, missiology.

Trinity International University, Trinity Evangelical Divinity School, Deerfield, IL 60015-1284. Offers Biblical and Near Eastern archaeology and languages (MA); Christian studies (MA, Certificate); Christian thought (MA); church history (MA, Th M); congregational ministry: pastor-teacher (M Div); congregational ministry: team ministry (M Div); counseling ministries (MA); counseling psychology (MA); cross-cultural ministry (M Div); educational studies (PhD); evangelism (MA); history of Christianity in America (MA); intercultural studies (MA, PhD); leadership and ministry management (D Min); military chaplaincy (D Min); ministry (MA); mission and evangelism (Th M); missions and evangelism (D Min); New Testament (MA, Th M); Old Testament (Th M); Old Testament and Semitic languages (MA); pastoral care (M Div); pastoral care and counseling (D Min); pastoral counseling and psychology (Th M); pastoral theology (Th M); philosophy of religion (MA); preaching (D Min); religion (MA); research ministry (M Div); systematic theology (Th M); theological studies (PhD); urban ministry (MA). *Accreditation:* ATS (one or more programs are accredited). Part-time programs available. Postbaccalaureate distance learning degree programs offered (minimal on-campus study). *Degree requirements:* For master's, comprehensive exam, thesis, fieldwork; for doctorate, comprehensive exam (for some programs), thesis/dissertation; for Certificate, comprehensive exam, integrative papers. *Entrance requirements:* For master's, GRE, MAT, minimum cumulative undergraduate GPA of 3.0; for doctorate, GRE, minimum cumulative graduate GPA of 3.2; for Certificate, GRE, MAT, minimum undergraduate GPA of 2.5. Additional exam requirements/recommendations for international students: Required—TOEFL (minimum score 580 paper-based), TWE (minimum score 4). Electronic applications accepted.

Trinity Lutheran Seminary, Graduate and Professional Programs, Columbus, OH 43209-2334. Offers African American studies (MTS); Biblical studies (MTS, STM); Christian education (MA); Christian spirituality (STM); church in the world (MTS); church music (MA); divinity (M Div); general theological studies (MTS); mission and evangelism (STM); pastoral leadership and practice (STM); youth and family ministry (MA); MSN/MTS; MTS/JD. *Accreditation:* ACIPE; ATS. Part-time programs available. *Faculty:* 11 full-time (5 women), 2 part-time/adjunct (both women). *Students:* 68 full-time (24 women), 43 part-time (18 women); includes 12 minority (10 Black or African American, non-Hispanic/Latino; 1 Asian, non-Hispanic/Latino; 1 Two or more races, non-Hispanic/Latino), 1 international. Average age 35. 45 applicants, 96% accepted, 34 enrolled. In 2014, 34 master's awarded. *Degree requirements:* For master's, variable foreign language requirement, comprehensive exam (for some programs), thesis (for some programs), field experience (for some programs). *Entrance requirements:* For master's, BA or equivalent (for MA, M Div, MTS); M Div, MTS, or equivalent (for STM); audition (for MACM). Additional exam requirements/recommendations for international students: Required—TOEFL. *Application deadline:* For fall admission, 7/15 priority date for domestic and international students. Applications are processed on a rolling basis. Application fee: $25. Electronic applications accepted. *Expenses:* Expenses: $13,760 tuition and fees for degree completion (for D Min). *Financial support:* In 2014–15, 72 students received support. Career-related internships or fieldwork, Federal Work-Study, and scholarships/grants available. Support available to part-time students. Financial award application deadline: 5/1; financial award applicants required to submit FAFSA. *Unit head:* Dr. Brad A. Binau, Academic Dean, 614-235-4136 Ext. 4674, Fax: 614-384-4635, E-mail: bbinau@tlsohio.edu. *Application contact:* Rev. Seth Bridger, Director of Admissions, 614-235-4136 Ext. 4650, Fax: 866-610-8572, E-mail: sbridger@tlsohio.edu.
Website: http://www.tlsohio.edu

Trinity School for Ministry, Graduate Programs, Ambridge, PA 15003-2397. Offers Anglican studies (Diploma); basic Christian studies (Diploma); divinity (M Div); ministry (D Min); mission and evangelism (MAME, Diploma); religion (MAR); youth ministry (Diploma). *Accreditation:* ATS (one or more programs are accredited). Part-time programs available. *Degree requirements:* For master's, thesis optional; for doctorate, thesis/dissertation. *Entrance requirements:* Additional exam requirements/recommendations for international students: Required—TOEFL. *Faculty research:* Pauline Epistles, contemporary theology, history of Anglican liturgy, book of Ruth, biblical theology.

Tyndale University College & Seminary, Graduate Programs, Toronto, ON M2M 4B3, Canada. Offers Biblical studies (M Div); Christian foundations (MTS); Christian studies (Diploma); counseling (M Div); educational ministry (M Div); missions (M Div, Diploma); pastoral and Chinese ministry (M Div); pastoral ministry (M Div); Pentecostal studies (MTS); spiritual formation (M Div, Diploma); theological studies (M Div); theology (Th M); worship and liturgy (M Div, MTS); youth and family ministry (M Div). *Accreditation:* ATS. Part-time programs available. Postbaccalaureate distance learning degree programs offered (no on-campus study). *Entrance requirements:* For master's and Diploma, minimum C+ average in undergraduate course work. Additional exam requirements/recommendations for international students: Required—TOEFL (minimum score 570 paper-based), TWE (minimum score 5). Electronic applications accepted. *Faculty research:* Canadian church history, Chinese church history, Old Testament, counseling ministries (narrative therapy), world religions.

University of South Africa, College of Human Sciences, Pretoria, South Africa. Offers adult education (M Ed); African languages (MA, PhD); African politics (MA, PhD); Afrikaans (MA, PhD); ancient history (MA, PhD); ancient Near Eastern studies (MA, PhD); anthropology (MA, PhD); applied linguistics (MA); Arabic (MA, PhD); archaeology (MA); art history (MA); Biblical archaeology (MA); Biblical studies (M Th, D Th, PhD); Christian spirituality (M Th, D Th); church history (M Th, D Th); classical studies (MA, PhD); clinical psychology (MA); communication (MA, PhD); comparative education (M Ed, Ed D); consulting psychology (D Admin, D Com, PhD); curriculum studies (M Ed, Ed D); development studies (M Admin, MA, D Admin, PhD); didactics (M Ed, Ed D); education (M Tech); education management (M Ed, Ed D); educational psychology (M Ed); English (MA); environmental education (M Ed); French (MA, PhD); German (MA, PhD); Greek (MA); guidance and counseling (M Ed); health studies (MA, PhD), including health sciences education (MA), health services management (MA), medical and surgical nursing science (critical care general) (MA), midwifery and neonatal nursing science (MA), trauma and emergency care (MA); history (MA, PhD); history of education (Ed D); inclusive education (M Ed, Ed D); information and communications technology policy and regulation (MA); information science (MA, MIS, PhD); international politics (MA, PhD); Islamic studies (MA, PhD); Italian (MA, PhD); Judaica (MA, PhD); linguistics (MA, PhD); mathematical education (M Ed); mathematics education (MA); missiology (M Th, D Th); modern Hebrew (MA, PhD); musicology (MA, MMus, D Mus, PhD); natural science education (M Ed); New Testament (M Th, D Th); Old Testament (D Th); pastoral therapy (M Th, D Th); philosophy (MA); philosophy of education (M Ed, Ed D); politics (MA, PhD); Portuguese (MA, PhD); practical theology (M Th, D Th); psychology (MA, MS, PhD); psychology of education (M Ed, Ed D); public health (MA); religious studies (MA, D Th, PhD); Romance languages (MA); Russian (MA, PhD); Semitic languages (MA, PhD); social behavior studies in HIV/AIDS (MA); social science (mental health) (MA); social science in development studies (MA); social science in psychology (MA); social science in social work (MA); social science in sociology (MA); social work (MSW, DSW, PhD); socio-education (M Ed, Ed D); sociolinguistics (MA); sociology (MA, PhD); Spanish (MA, PhD); systematic theology (M Th, D Th); TESOL (teaching English to speakers of other languages) (MA); theological ethics (M Th, D Th); theory of literature (MA, PhD); urban ministries (D Th); urban ministry (M Th).

Villanova University, Villanova School of Business, Master of Science in Church Management Program, Villanova, PA 19085. Offers MSCM. Part-time programs available. Postbaccalaureate distance learning degree programs offered (minimal on-campus study). *Faculty:* 101 full-time (33 women), 27 part-time/adjunct (6 women). *Students:* 20 part-time (10 women); includes 2 minority (both Black or African American, non-Hispanic/Latino). Average age 41. In 2014, 16 master's awarded. *Degree requirements:* For master's, minimum GPA of 3.0. *Entrance requirements:* Additional exam requirements/recommendations for international students: Required—TOEFL (minimum score 550 paper-based; 90 iBT). *Application deadline:* For fall admission, 5/10 for domestic and international students. Applications are processed on a rolling basis. Application fee: $50. Electronic applications accepted. *Expenses:* Expenses: Contact institution. *Financial support:* Scholarships/grants available. Support available to part-time students. Financial award application deadline: 6/30; financial award applicants

required to submit FAFSA. *Faculty research:* Business analytics; creativity, innovation and entrepreneurship; global leadership; real estate; church management; business ethics. *Unit head:* Dr. Charles Zech, Faculty Director, 610-519-4371, E-mail: charles.zech@villanova.edu. *Application contact:* James Gallo, Staff Director, 610-519-6015, E-mail: james.gallo@villanova.edu.
Website: http://www.villanova.edu/business/graduate/church/

Wesley Biblical Seminary, Graduate Programs, Jackson, MS 39206. Offers apologetics (MA); Biblical languages (M Div); Biblical literature (MA); Christian studies (MA); context and mission (M Div); honors research (M Div); interpretation (M Div); ministry (M Div); spiritual formation (M Div); teaching (M Div); theology (MA). *Accreditation:* ATS. Part-time programs available. *Degree requirements:* For master's, thesis. *Entrance requirements:* Additional exam requirements/recommendations for international students: Required—TOEFL. Electronic applications accepted. *Faculty research:* Patristics, missiology, culture, hermeneutics.

Westminster Theological Seminary, Graduate and Professional Programs, Philadelphia, PA 19118. Offers apologetics (Th M); Biblical and urban studies (Certificate); Biblical counseling (MA); biblical studies (MAR); Christian studies (Certificate); church history (Th M); counseling (M Div); general studies (M Div, MAR); hermeneutics and Bible interpretations (PhD); historical and theological studies (PhD); historical theology (Th M); New Testament (Th M); Old Testament (Th M); pastoral counseling (D Min); pastoral ministry (M Div, D Min); systematic theology (Th M); theological studies (MAR); urban missions (M Div, MA, MAR, D Min). *Accreditation:* ATS. Part-time programs available. Terminal master's awarded for partial completion of doctoral program. *Degree requirements:* For master's, thesis (for some programs); for doctorate, 4 foreign languages, comprehensive exam (for some programs), thesis/dissertation. *Entrance requirements:* For doctorate, GRE General Test. Additional exam requirements/recommendations for international students: Required—TOEFL, TWE.

Wheaton College, Graduate School, Department of Intercultural Studies, Wheaton, IL 60187-5593. Offers evangelism and leadership (MA); intercultural studies (MA); intercultural studies/teaching English as a second language (MA); missions (MA); teaching English as a second language (Certificate). Part-time programs available. *Students:* 33 full-time (19 women), 16 part-time (9 women); includes 10 minority (3 Black or African American, non-Hispanic/Latino; 6 Asian, non-Hispanic/Latino; 1 Hispanic/Latino), 13 international. Average age 33. 31 applicants, 90% accepted, 16 enrolled. In 2014, 53 master's, 1 other advanced degree awarded. *Degree requirements:* For master's, thesis or alternative. *Entrance requirements:* For master's, GRE General Test, MAT. Additional exam requirements/recommendations for international students: Required—TOEFL (minimum score 550 paper-based; 80 iBT), IELTS (minimum score 6.5), TOEFL (minimum score 600 paper-based; 90 iBT) or IELTS (minimum score 7.5) for MA in TESOL. *Application deadline:* For fall admission, 5/1 for domestic students, 1/1 for international students; for spring admission, 11/1 for domestic students. Applications are processed on a rolling basis. Application fee: $30. Electronic applications accepted. *Financial support:* Career-related internships or fieldwork, scholarships/grants, and unspecified assistantships available. Financial award application deadline: 3/1; financial award applicants required to submit FAFSA. *Unit head:* Dr. Robert Gallagher, Chair, 630-752-5948. *Application contact:* Dusty Di Santo, Director of Graduate Admissions, 630-752-5195, Fax: 630-752-5047, E-mail: graduate.admissions@wheaton.edu.
Website: http://www.wheaton.edu/academics/departments/intr

Pastoral Ministry and Counseling

Abilene Christian University, Graduate School, College of Biblical Studies, Graduate School of Theology, Program in Ministry, Abilene, TX 79699-9100. Offers D Min. Part-time programs available. *Students:* 1 full-time (0 women), 17 part-time (1 woman); includes 4 minority (2 Black or African American, non-Hispanic/Latino; 2 Hispanic/Latino), 1 international. 9 applicants, 89% accepted, 5 enrolled. In 2014, 8 doctorates awarded. *Degree requirements:* For doctorate, one foreign language, comprehensive exam, thesis/dissertation. *Entrance requirements:* Additional exam requirements/recommendations for international students: Required—TOEFL (minimum score 550 paper-based; 90 iBT), IELTS (minimum score 6.5), PTE. *Application deadline:* For fall admission, 4/1 priority date for domestic students; for spring admission, 11/1 for domestic students. Applications are processed on a rolling basis. Application fee: $50. *Expenses:* Expenses: Contact institution. *Financial support:* In 2014–15, 5 students received support. Scholarships/grants available. Financial award application deadline: 4/1; financial award applicants required to submit FAFSA. *Faculty research:* Church growth, ministry evaluation, leadership. *Unit head:* Dr. Carson Reed, Graduate Director, 325-674-3732, Fax: 325-674-6716, E-mail: carson.reed@acu.edu. *Application contact:* Corey Patterson, Director of Graduate Admission and Recruiting, 325-674-6566, Fax: 325-674-6717, E-mail: gradinfo@acu.edu.

Abilene Christian University, Graduate School, College of Biblical Studies, Graduate School of Theology, Programs in Christian Ministry, Abilene, TX 79699-9100. Offers MACM. Part-time programs available. Postbaccalaureate distance learning degree programs offered (minimal on-campus study). *Students:* 10 full-time (1 woman), 49 part-time (4 women); includes 15 minority (12 Black or African American, non-Hispanic/Latino; 2 Hispanic/Latino; 1 Two or more races, non-Hispanic/Latino), 2 international. 54 applicants, 69% accepted, 29 enrolled. In 2014, 9 master's awarded. *Degree requirements:* For master's, comprehensive exam, thesis. *Entrance requirements:* Additional exam requirements/recommendations for international students: Required—TOEFL (minimum score 550 paper-based; 90 iBT), IELTS (minimum score 6.5), PTE. *Application deadline:* For fall admission, 4/1 priority date for domestic students; for spring admission, 11/1 for domestic students. Applications are processed on a rolling basis. Application fee: $50. Electronic applications accepted. *Expenses:* Expenses: Contact institution. *Financial support:* In 2014–15, 7 students received support. Scholarships/grants available. Financial award application deadline: 4/1; financial award applicants required to submit FAFSA. *Faculty research:* Program innovation, instruments for educational evaluation. *Unit head:* Dr. Melinda Thompson, Graduate Advisor, 325-674-3706, Fax: 325-674-6180, E-mail: melinda.thomson@acu.edu. *Application contact:* Corey Patterson, Director of Graduate Admission and Recruiting, 325-674-6566, Fax: 325-674-6717, E-mail: gradinfo@acu.edu.

Ambrose University, Ambrose Seminary, Calgary, AB T3H 0L5, Canada. Offers Chinese ministries (Certificate); Christian studies (Certificate); intercultural ministries (M Div, Certificate); leadership and ministry (Diploma); pastoral ministries (M Div). *Accreditation:* ATS (one or more programs are accredited). Part-time programs available. Postbaccalaureate distance learning degree programs offered (minimal on-campus study). *Faculty:* 7 full-time (0 women), 24 part-time/adjunct (2 women). *Students:* 55 full-time (18 women), 128 part-time (64 women); includes 86 minority (3 Black or African American, non-Hispanic/Latino; 1 American Indian or Alaska Native, non-Hispanic/Latino; 82 Asian, non-Hispanic/Latino). Average age 41. *Degree requirements:* For master's, variable foreign language requirement, internship. *Entrance requirements:* For master's, undergraduate degree from other accredited university or bible college, minimum GPA of 2.0. Additional exam requirements/recommendations for international students: Required—TOEFL (minimum score 560 paper-based, 83 iBT) or IELTS (minimum score 6.5). *Application deadline:* For fall admission, 7/15 for domestic students, 3/1 for international students; for winter admission, 11/15 for domestic students, 7/1 for international students. Applications are processed on a rolling basis. Application fee: $70 ($100 for international students). Electronic applications accepted. *Financial support:* Career-related internships or fieldwork and scholarships/grants available. Support available to part-time students. Financial award application deadline: 3/30. *Faculty research:* Evangelicalism and sociology, missiological trends, chaplaincy, intertestamental studies, postmodernism. *Unit head:* Dr. Paul Spilsbury, Vice-President of Academic Affairs, 403-410-2917, Fax: 403-571-2556, E-mail: pspilsbury@ambrose.edu. *Application contact:* Kalie Eeles, Enrollment Advisor, 403-410-2954, Fax: 403-571-2556, E-mail: enrolment@ambrose.edu.
Website: https://ambrose.edu/seminary

American Baptist College of American Baptist Theological Seminary, Program in Pastoral Studies, Nashville, TN 37207. Offers MPS.

American Baptist Seminary of the West, Graduate and Professional Programs, Berkeley, CA 94704-3029. Offers community leadership (MA); theology (M Div, MA). MA program in theology offered jointly with Graduate Theological Union. *Accreditation:* ACIPE; ATS (one or more programs are accredited). Part-time and evening/weekend programs available. Postbaccalaureate distance learning degree programs offered (minimal on-campus study). *Entrance requirements:* Additional exam requirements/recommendations for international students: Required—TOEFL (minimum score 550 paper-based). Electronic applications accepted.

Amridge University, Graduate and Professional Programs, Montgomery, AL 36117. Offers behavioral leadership and management (MA); Biblical studies (MA, PhD); family therapy (D Min); leadership and management (MS); marriage and family therapy (M Div, MA, PhD); ministerial leadership (M Div, MS); pastoral counseling (M Div, MS); professional counseling (M Div, MA, PhD); theology (M Div, D Min). Part-time and evening/weekend programs available. Postbaccalaureate distance learning degree programs offered (no on-campus study). *Faculty:* 20 full-time (2 women), 7 part-time/adjunct (6 women). *Students:* 110 full-time (58 women), 224 part-time (139 women); includes 139 minority (133 Black or African American, non-Hispanic/Latino; 3 Asian, non-Hispanic/Latino; 3 Hispanic/Latino). Average age 35. 69 applicants, 75% accepted. In 2014, 72 master's, 11 doctorates awarded. *Degree requirements:* For master's, one foreign language, comprehensive exam (for some programs), thesis (for some programs); for doctorate, comprehensive exam (for some programs), thesis/dissertation (for some programs). *Entrance requirements:* For master's, official transcript showing an earned 4-year BA or BS from regionally- or nationally-accredited institution; for doctorate, official transcript showing earned graduate degree from regionally- or nationally-accredited institution; writing sample (e.g. career monograph, published journal article, term paper from master's degree or doctoral dissertation); interview. Additional exam requirements/recommendations for international students: Required—TOEFL. *Application deadline:* For fall admission, 9/1 priority date for domestic students; for spring admission, 1/1 priority date for domestic students. Applications are processed on a rolling basis. Application fee: $50. Electronic applications accepted. *Financial support:* In 2014–15, 102 students received support. Federal Work-Study and scholarships/grants available. Support available to part-time students. Financial award applicants required to submit FAFSA. *Faculty research:* Technology and mental healthcare, resilience in black families, theology and congregational ministry. *Unit head:* Brooks Housley, Student Affairs Coordinator, 888-790-8080 Ext. 2, Fax: 334-387-3878, E-mail: brookshousley@amridgeuniversity.edu. *Application contact:* Kristen Holcomb, Admissions Officer, 888-790-8080 Ext. 1, Fax: 334-387-3878, E-mail: admissions@amridgeuniversity.edu.

Anderson University, School of Christian Ministry, Anderson, SC 29621-4035. Offers M Min. Postbaccalaureate distance learning degree programs offered. *Degree requirements:* For master's, capstone course, ministry project. *Entrance requirements:* For master's, 3 references. *Financial support:* In 2014–15, 1 student received support. Tuition waivers available. Financial award application deadline: 3/1; financial award applicants required to submit FAFSA. *Unit head:* Dr. Michael Duduit, Dean, 800-542-3594, E-mail: ministry@andersonuniversity.edu. *Application contact:* Mallory Knight, Graduate Admission Counselor, 864-231-2182, Fax: 864-231-2115, E-mail: malloryknight@andersonuniversity.edu.

Andrews University, School of Graduate Studies, Seventh-day Adventist Theological Seminary, Berrien Springs, MI 49104. Offers ministry (M Div, D Min); missiology (D Miss); pastoral ministry (MA); religious education (MA, Ed D, PhD, Ed S); theology (M Th, Th D); youth ministry (MA). *Accreditation:* ATS. *Faculty:* 40 full-time (5 women), 5 part-time/adjunct (0 women). *Students:* 511 full-time (85 women), 446 part-time (75 women); includes 450 minority (247 Black or African American, non-Hispanic/Latino; 1 American Indian or Alaska Native, non-Hispanic/Latino; 41 Asian, non-Hispanic/Latino; 151 Hispanic/Latino; 3 Native Hawaiian or other Pacific Islander, non-Hispanic/Latino; 7 Two or more races, non-Hispanic/Latino), 240 international. Average age 40. 546 applicants, 46% accepted, 124 enrolled. In 2014, 145 master's, 40 doctorates awarded. *Degree requirements:* For master's, thesis optional; for doctorate, variable foreign language requirement, thesis/dissertation. *Entrance requirements:* For master's, GRE Subject Test, minimum GPA of 2.0. Additional exam requirements/recommendations for international students: Required—TOEFL (minimum score 550 paper-based). *Application deadline:* Applications are processed on a rolling basis. Application fee: $40. Tuition and fees vary according to course level. *Financial support:* Fellowships, research assistantships, teaching assistantships, career-related internships or fieldwork, Federal Work-Study, and institutionally sponsored loans available. *Unit head:* Dr. Jiri Moskala, Dean, 269-471-3537. *Application contact:* Monica Wringer, Director, 800-253-2874, Fax: 269-471-6321.

Anna Maria College, Graduate Division, Program in Pastoral Ministry, Paxton, MA 01612. Offers MA. Part-time and evening/weekend programs available. *Degree requirements:* For master's, pastoral project. *Entrance requirements:* For master's,

interview. Additional exam requirements/recommendations for international students: Required—TOEFL (minimum score 500 paper-based). Electronic applications accepted.

Appalachian Bible College, Graduate School, Bradley, WV 25818. Offers ministry (MA). Postbaccalaureate distance learning degree programs offered (no on-campus study). *Entrance requirements:* For master's, ABHE Bible Content Exam, bachelor's degree, 3 references, minimum undergraduate cumulative GPA of 2.75. Additional exam requirements/recommendations for international students: Required—TOEFL (minimum score 550 paper-based).

Aquinas Institute of Theology, Graduate and Professional Programs, St. Louis, MO 63108. Offers biblical studies (Certificate); church music (MM); health care mission (MAHCM); ministry (M Div); pastoral care (Certificate); pastoral ministry (MAPM); pastoral studies (MAPS); preaching (D Min); spiritual direction (Certificate); theology (M Div, MA); Thomistic studies (Certificate); M Div/MA; MA/PhD; MAPS/MSW. *Accreditation:* ATS (one or more programs are accredited). Part-time and evening/weekend programs available. Postbaccalaureate distance learning degree programs offered (minimal on-campus study). *Faculty:* 14 full-time (7 women), 24 part-time/adjunct (8 women). *Students:* 87 full-time (24 women), 59 part-time (37 women); includes 21 minority (9 Black or African American, non-Hispanic/Latino; 1 American Indian or Alaska Native, non-Hispanic/Latino; 4 Asian, non-Hispanic/Latino; 6 Hispanic/Latino; 1 Native Hawaiian or other Pacific Islander, non-Hispanic/Latino), 8 international. Average age 46. In 2014, 25 master's, 5 doctorates awarded. *Degree requirements:* For master's, variable foreign language requirement, comprehensive exam (for some programs), thesis (for some programs); for doctorate, thesis/dissertation. *Entrance requirements:* For master's and Certificate, MAT; for doctorate, 3 years of ministerial experience, 6 hours of graduate course work in homiletics, M Div or the equivalent, minimum GPA of 3.0. Additional exam requirements/recommendations for international students: Required—TOEFL. *Application deadline:* For fall admission, 3/15 priority date for domestic and international students; for spring admission, 11/15 priority date for domestic and international students. Applications are processed on a rolling basis. Application fee: $50. *Expenses:* Expenses: $680 per credit hour; $265 per semester in fees. *Financial support:* Scholarships/grants, health care benefits, and tuition waivers (partial) available. Support available to part-time students. Financial award application deadline: 3/15; financial award applicants required to submit CSS PROFILE or FAFSA. *Faculty research:* Theology of preaching, hermeneutics, lay ecclesial ministry, pastoral and practical theology. *Unit head:* Fr. Gregory Heille, Vice-President/Academic Dean, 314-256-8800, Fax: 314-256-8888, E-mail: heille@ai.edu. *Application contact:* David Werthmann, Director of Admissions, 314-256-8806, Fax: 314-256-8888, E-mail: admissions@ai.edu.
Website: http://www.ai.edu/

Argosy University, Sarasota, College of Psychology and Behavioral Sciences, Sarasota, FL 34235. Offers community counseling (MA); counseling psychology (Ed D); counselor education and supervision (Ed D); forensic psychology (MA); marriage and family therapy (MA); mental health counseling (MA); pastoral community counseling (Ed D).

Asbury Theological Seminary, Graduate and Professional Programs, Wilmore, KY 40390-1199. Offers MA, MAAS, MACE, MACL, MACM, MACP, MAMFC, MAMHC, MAPC, MASF, MAYM, Th M, PhD, Certificate. *Accreditation:* ATS. Part-time programs available. Postbaccalaureate distance learning degree programs offered (minimal on-campus study). Terminal master's awarded for partial completion of doctoral program. *Degree requirements:* For master's, thesis (for some programs); for doctorate, thesis/dissertation, qualifying exam. *Entrance requirements:* For master's, minimum GPA of 2.75; for doctorate, minimum GPA of 3.0. Additional exam requirements/recommendations for international students: Required—TOEFL, IELTS. Electronic applications accepted.

Ashland Theological Seminary, Graduate Programs, Ashland, OH 44805. Offers biblical and theological studies (MAR); Biblical, historical and theological studies (MA), including Anabaptism and Pietism, Christian theology, church history, New Testament, Old Testament; Christian ministry (MAPT), including Black church studies (M Div, MAPT, D Min), chaplaincy (M Div, MAPT), Christian formation (M Div, MAPT), evangelism/church renewal and missions (M Div, MAPT), general ministry (M Div, MAPT), pastoral counseling and care (M Div, MAPT), specialized ministry, spiritual formation (M Div, MAPT, D Min); Christian studies (Diploma); clinical counseling (MACC); counseling (MAC); ministry (D Min), including Black church studies (M Div, MAPT, D Min), Canadian church studies, formational counseling, independent design, spiritual formation (M Div, MAPT, D Min), transformational leadership, Wesleyan practices; pastoral ministry (M Div), including Biblical studies - Old or New Testament, Black church studies (M Div, MAPT, D Min), chaplaincy (M Div, MAPT), Christian formation (M Div, MAPT), evangelism/church renewal and missions (M Div, MAPT), general Biblical studies, general ministry (M Div, MAPT), pastoral counseling and care (M Div, MAPT), spiritual formation (M Div, MAPT, D Min), theology or history. MAC program offered in Detroit, MI. *Accreditation:* ATS. Part-time programs available. *Degree requirements:* For master's, 2 foreign languages, comprehensive exam (for some programs), thesis (for some programs); for doctorate, thesis/dissertation. *Entrance requirements:* For master's, bachelor's degree from accredited institution with a minimum undergraduate GPA of 2.75; for doctorate, M Div, minimum undergraduate GPA of 3.0. Additional exam requirements/recommendations for international students: Required—TOEFL (minimum score 500 paper-based; 65 iBT). Electronic applications accepted. *Faculty research:* Semitic languages and linguistics, rhetorical and social-scientific criticism, Anabaptist studies, inner spiritual healing, African-American clergy in film and literature.

Assemblies of God Theological Seminary, Graduate and Professional Programs, Springfield, MO 65802. Offers Bible theology (PhD); Christian ministries (MA); counseling (MA); divinity (M Div); intercultural ministry (MA); intercultural studies (PhD); ministry (D Min); missiology (D Miss); theological studies (MA). *Accreditation:* ATS. Part-time and evening/weekend programs available. Postbaccalaureate distance learning degree programs offered (minimal on-campus study). *Degree requirements:* For master's, variable foreign language requirement; for doctorate, thesis/dissertation. *Entrance requirements:* For master's, minimum GPA of 2.5; for doctorate, GRE (for PhD in Bible theology), minimum GPA of 3.0. Additional exam requirements/recommendations for international students: Required—TOEFL (minimum score 550 paper-based; 80 iBT). Electronic applications accepted.

The Athenaeum of Ohio, Graduate Programs, Cincinnati, OH 45230-5900. Offers biblical studies (MABS); divinity (M Div); lay ministry (Certificate); pastoral counseling (MAPC); pastoral ministry (MA); theology (MA Th); M Div/MA Th; M Div/MABS; M Div/MAPC. *Accreditation:* ATS (one or more programs are accredited). Part-time and evening/weekend programs available. *Degree requirements:* For master's, one foreign language, comprehensive exam (for some programs), thesis optional.

Atlantic School of Theology, Graduate and Professional Programs, Halifax, NS B3H 3B5, Canada. Offers ministry (M Div); theological studies (Graduate Certificate). *Accreditation:* ATS. Part-time programs available. Postbaccalaureate distance learning degree programs offered (minimal on-campus study). *Degree requirements:* For master's, thesis (for some programs). *Entrance requirements:* For master's and Graduate Certificate, minimum B average in undergraduate course work. *Faculty research:* Ethics and biology; death, dying and pastoral care; theology and the economy; adult education; John and anti-Judaism.

Atlantic University, Spiritual Guidance Mentor Program, Virginia Beach, VA 23451-2061. Offers Certificate. *Entrance requirements:* For degree, 500-word essay. Application fee: $35. *Expenses:* Expenses: Contact institution. *Application contact:* Rachel Alvidrez, Educational Services Manager, 757-631-8101, Fax: 757-631-8096, E-mail: info@atlanticuniv.edu.
Website: http://www.atlanticuniv.edu/spiritual_guidance_mentor_certificate.html

Austin Presbyterian Theological Seminary, Graduate and Professional Programs, Austin, TX 78705-5797. Offers divinity (M Div); ministry (D Min); ministry practice (MA); theological studies (MA); M Div/MSSW. M Div/MSSW offered in collaboration with The University of Texas at Austin School of Social Work. *Accreditation:* ACIPE; ATS. Part-time programs available. *Faculty:* 17 full-time (5 women), 7 part-time/adjunct (2 women). *Students:* 131 full-time (70 women), 66 part-time (35 women). *Degree requirements:* For master's, Greek, Hebrew (for M Div); for doctorate, thesis/dissertation. *Entrance requirements:* For master's, references (for M Div). Additional exam requirements/recommendations for international students: Required—TOEFL (minimum score 550 paper-based; 79 iBT). *Application deadline:* For fall admission, 5/1 for domestic students, 1/1 for international students; for spring admission, 9/1 for domestic students; for summer admission, 2/2 for domestic students. Applications are processed on a rolling basis. Application fee: $65. *Expenses: Tuition:* Full-time $12,600; part-time $210 per credit. *Required fees:* $220. One-time fee: $325 full-time; $85 part-time. *Financial support:* Fellowships, career-related internships or fieldwork, institutionally sponsored loans, scholarships/grants, and tutorships available. Support available to part-time students. Financial award application deadline: 3/1; financial award applicants required to submit FAFSA. *Faculty research:* Mystical theology, religious pluralism, narrative preaching, social ethics, pastoral care and healing. *Unit head:* Dr. David Jensen, Academic Dean, 512-404-4821, Fax: 512-479-0738, E-mail: dean@austinseminary.edu. *Application contact:* Dr. Jack Barden, Vice President for Admissions, 512-404-4827, Fax: 512-472-7089, E-mail: admissions@austinseminary.edu.

Ave Maria University, Graduate Programs, Ave Maria, FL 34142. Offers pastoral theology (MTS); theology (MA, PhD). Terminal master's awarded for partial completion of doctoral program. *Degree requirements:* For master's, one foreign language, thesis; for doctorate, 3 foreign languages, comprehensive exam, thesis/dissertation. *Entrance requirements:* For master's, GRE; for doctorate, GRE, M Div or equivalent; MA or MTS in religion, theology, or philosophy; bachelor's degree with strong background in religion, theology, and/or philosophy.

Azusa Pacific University, College of Liberal Arts and Sciences, Program in Transformational Urban Leadership, Azusa, CA 91702-7000. Offers MA.

Azusa Pacific University, Haggard Graduate School of Theology, Program in Divinity, Azusa, CA 91702-7000. Offers M Div.

Azusa Pacific University, Haggard Graduate School of Theology, Program in Pastoral Studies, Concentration in Church Leadership and Development, Azusa, CA 91702-7000. Offers MAPS.

Azusa Pacific University, Haggard Graduate School of Theology, Program in Pastoral Studies, Concentration in Worship Leadership, Azusa, CA 91702-7000. Offers MAPS.

Bakke Graduate University, Programs in Pastoral Ministry and Business, Seattle, WA 98104. Offers business administration (MBA); church and ministry multiplication (D Min); global urban leadership (MA); leadership (D Min); ministry in complex contexts (D Min); social and civic entrepreneurship (MA); theology of work (D Min); theology reflection (D Min); transformational leadership (DTL); urban youth ministry (D Min). Part-time programs available. Postbaccalaureate distance learning degree programs offered (minimal on-campus study). *Degree requirements:* For master's, thesis; for doctorate, thesis/dissertation. *Entrance requirements:* For master's, 2 years of ministry experience, BA in Biblical studies or theology; for doctorate, 3 years of ministry experience, M Div. Additional exam requirements/recommendations for international students: Required—TOEFL. Electronic applications accepted. *Faculty research:* Theological systems, church management, worship.

Baptist Bible College, Graduate School of Theology, Springfield, MO 65803-3498. Offers biblical counseling (MA); biblical studies (MA); church ministry (MA); intercultural studies (MA); theology (M Div). Part-time programs available. *Degree requirements:* For master's, 2 foreign languages, thesis (for some programs). Electronic applications accepted.

Baptist Theological Seminary at Richmond, Graduate and Professional Programs, Richmond, VA 23227. Offers Biblical interpretation (M Div); Christian education (M Div); Christian ministry (MCM); justice and peacebuilding (D Min); theological studies (MTS, Graduate Certificate); M Div/MS; M Div/MSW. *Accreditation:* ATS. Part-time programs available. Postbaccalaureate distance learning degree programs offered (minimal on-campus study). *Faculty:* 7 full-time (2 women), 14 part-time/adjunct (6 women). *Students:* 45 full-time (27 women), 40 part-time (24 women); includes 10 minority (9 Black or African American, non-Hispanic/Latino; 1 Hispanic/Latino), 3 international. *Degree requirements:* For doctorate, one foreign language, comprehensive exam, thesis/dissertation, field study, independent study. *Entrance requirements:* For master's, BA/BS, 2 references, resume, official transcripts; for doctorate, MAT, M Div, 3 years of full-time ministry experience, minimum GPA of 2.75, 3 references, resume, official transcripts, writing sample, personal statement. Additional exam requirements/recommendations for international students: Required—TOEFL (minimum score 550 paper-based). *Application deadline:* For fall admission, 7/1 for domestic students, 5/1 for international students; for winter admission, 12/15 for domestic students, 9/1 for international students; for spring admission, 1/15 for domestic students, 10/1 for international students. Applications are processed on a rolling basis. Application fee: $35. *Financial support:* Teaching assistantships, scholarships/grants, and tuition waivers (partial) available. Financial award application deadline: 2/1. *Faculty research:* Biblical studies, pastoral care, church history, theology, ministry. *Unit head:* Dr. Ronald W. Crawford, President, 804-204-1201, Fax: 804-355-8182, E-mail: rcrawford@btsr.edu. *Application contact:* Melissa Fallen, Director of Admissions and Recruitment, 804-204-1208, E-mail: admissions@btsr.edu.
Website: http://www.btsr.edu/programs/degree-programs/

Barry University, College of Arts and Sciences, Department of Theology and Philosophy, Miami Shores, FL 33161-6695. Offers ministry (D Min); pastoral ministry for Hispanics (MA); pastoral theology (MA); practical theology (MA). *Accreditation:* ATS. Part-time and evening/weekend programs available. *Degree requirements:* For master's, comprehensive exam, thesis optional; for doctorate, thesis/dissertation. *Entrance requirements:* For master's, GRE General Test or MAT, minimum GPA of 3.0. Electronic applications accepted. *Faculty research:* Fundamental morals, bioethics, social ethics, liturgical and sacramental theology, biblical studies.

Bethany Theological Seminary, Graduate and Professional Programs, Richmond, IN 47374-4019. Offers biblical studies (MA Th); ministry studies (M Div); peace studies (M Div, MA Th); theological studies (MA Th, CATS); youth ministry (M Div). *Accreditation:* ACIPE; ATS. Part-time programs available. Postbaccalaureate distance

learning degree programs offered (minimal on-campus study). *Degree requirements:* For master's, thesis (for some programs). *Entrance requirements:* For master's, letters of reference. Additional exam requirements/recommendations for international students: Required—TOEFL (minimum score 550 paper-based).

Bethel College, Adult and Graduate Programs, Program in Ministries, Mishawaka, IN 46545-5591. Offers M Min. Part-time and evening/weekend programs available. *Degree requirements:* For master's, thesis or alternative. *Entrance requirements:* Additional exam requirements/recommendations for international students: Required—TOEFL (minimum score 540 paper-based). Electronic applications accepted.

Bethel Seminary, Graduate and Professional Programs, St. Paul, MN 55112-6998. Offers Anglican studies (Certificate); children's and family ministry (MA); Christian studies (Certificate); Christian thought (MA); Greek and Hebrew language (M Div); Greek language (M Div); Hebrew language (M Div); marriage and family therapy (MA, Certificate); ministry (D Min); ministry practice (MA, Certificate); theological studies (MA, Certificate); transformational leadership (MA); young life youth ministry (Certificate). *Accreditation:* ACIPE; ATS (one or more programs are accredited). Part-time and evening/weekend programs available. Postbaccalaureate distance learning degree programs offered (minimal on-campus study). *Faculty:* 15 full-time (3 women), 55 part-time/adjunct (27 women). *Students:* 422 full-time (167 women), 231 part-time (71 women); includes 165 minority (62 Black or African American, non-Hispanic/Latino; 58 Asian, non-Hispanic/Latino; 29 Hispanic/Latino; 1 Native Hawaiian or other Pacific Islander, non-Hispanic/Latino; 15 Two or more races, non-Hispanic/Latino), 16 international. Average age 37. 272 applicants, 77% accepted, 165 enrolled. In 2014, 147 master's, 13 doctorates, 8 other advanced degrees awarded. *Degree requirements:* For master's, variable foreign language requirement, thesis (for some programs); for doctorate, thesis/dissertation. *Entrance requirements:* For master's, letters of reference, transcripts, personal statement; for doctorate, M Div, letters of reference, organizational support; for Certificate, letters of reference, family essay, personal statement, and family of origin paper (for marriage and family therapy). Additional exam requirements/recommendations for international students: Required—TOEFL (minimum score 550 paper-based; 87 iBT). *Application deadline:* For fall admission, 8/1 priority date for domestic students, 8/1 for international students; for winter admission, 12/1 priority date for domestic students; for spring admission, 1/1 priority date for domestic students. Applications are processed on a rolling basis. Application fee: $0. Electronic applications accepted. *Financial support:* In 2014–15, 558 students received support, including 17 teaching assistantships; career-related internships or fieldwork, Federal Work-Study, and scholarships/grants also available. Financial award applicants required to submit FAFSA. *Faculty research:* Nature of theology, ethics, Biblical commentaries, nature of God, science and theology. *Unit head:* Dr. David Clark, Vice-President and Dean, Bethel Seminary, 651-638-6659. *Application contact:* Jen Niska, Director of Admissions, 651-638-6288, Fax: 651-638-6002, E-mail: bsem-admit@bethel.edu.

Biblical Theological Seminary, Graduate and Professional Programs, Hatfield, PA 19440-2499. Offers advanced missional leadership (D Min); advanced pastoral studies (Certificate); biblical counseling (Certificate); biblical studies (MA, Certificate); counseling (MA); ministry (M Div, MA); missional theology (MA). *Accreditation:* ATS. Part-time and evening/weekend programs available. *Faculty:* 9 full-time (0 women), 21 part-time/adjunct (4 women). *Students:* 139 full-time (41 women), 149 part-time (55 women); includes 103 minority (53 Black or African American, non-Hispanic/Latino; 42 Asian, non-Hispanic/Latino; 6 Hispanic/Latino; 2 Two or more races, non-Hispanic/Latino), 76 international. Average age 38. 91 applicants, 64% accepted, 56 enrolled. In 2014, 80 master's, 5 doctorates awarded. *Degree requirements:* For master's, variable foreign language requirement, thesis optional; for doctorate, thesis/dissertation. *Entrance requirements:* Additional exam requirements/recommendations for international students: Required—TOEFL (minimum score 550 paper-based; 80 iBT). *Application deadline:* Applications are processed on a rolling basis. Application fee: $30. Electronic applications accepted. *Expenses: Tuition:* Full-time $14,667; part-time $480 per credit. *Required fees:* $25 per trimester. One-time fee: $30. *Financial support:* In 2014–15, 192 students received support. Career-related internships or fieldwork, institutionally sponsored loans, and scholarships/grants available. Support available to part-time students. Financial award application deadline: 8/30; financial award applicants required to submit FAFSA. *Faculty research:* Theology, culture, Biblical interpretation. *Unit head:* Pamela Jean Smith, Vice President for Student Advancement, 215-368-5000 Ext. 122, Fax: 215-368-7002, E-mail: psmith@biblical.edu. *Application contact:* Dr. Malcolm Walls, Director of Recruitment and Student Services, 215-368-5000 Ext. 109, Fax: 215-368-7002, E-mail: mwalls@biblical.edu.
Website: http://www.biblical.edu/

Biola University, Talbot School of Theology, La Mirada, CA 90639-0001. Offers adult/family ministry (MACE); Bible exposition (MA, Th M); Biblical and theological studies (MA); children's ministry (MACE); Christian education (M Div); cross-cultural education ministry (MACE); educational studies (Ed D, PhD); evangelism and discipleship (M Div); general Christian education (MACE); Messianic Jewish studies (M Div, Certificate); missions and intercultural studies (M Div); New Testament (MA, Th M); Old Testament (MA); Old Testament and Semitics (Th M); pastoral and general ministry (M Div); pastoral care and counseling (M Div); philosophy (MA); spiritual formation (M Div, Certificate); spiritual formation and soul care (MA); theology (Th M, D Min, Certificate); youth ministry (MACE). *Accreditation:* ATS. Part-time and evening/weekend programs available. *Faculty:* 77. *Students:* 581 full-time (140 women), 554 part-time (155 women); includes 522 minority (42 Black or African American, non-Hispanic/Latino; 3 American Indian or Alaska Native, non-Hispanic/Latino; 370 Asian, non-Hispanic/Latino; 78 Hispanic/Latino; 2 Native Hawaiian or other Pacific Islander, non-Hispanic/Latino; 27 Two or more races, non-Hispanic/Latino), 121 international. 437 applicants, 78% accepted, 241 enrolled. In 2014, 182 master's, 33 doctorates awarded. *Entrance requirements:* For master's, bachelor's degree from accredited college or university; minimum GPA of 2.6 (for M Div), 3.0 (for MA); for doctorate, M Div or MA. Additional exam requirements/recommendations for international students: Required—TOEFL (minimum score 600 paper-based; 88 iBT). *Application deadline:* For fall admission, 7/1 for domestic students, 6/1 for international students; for spring admission, 12/1 priority date for domestic students. Applications are processed on a rolling basis. Application fee: $65. Electronic applications accepted. *Financial support:* Scholarships/grants and unspecified assistantships available. Support available to part-time students. Financial award applicants required to submit FAFSA. *Faculty research:* New Testament, Old Testament, spiritual formation, Christian education, theological studies, Christian ministry, preaching and pastoral ministry, language and literature, bible exposition, Christian leadership. *Unit head:* Dr. Clint Arnold, Dean, 562-903-4816, Fax: 562-903-4748. *Application contact:* Graduate Admissions Office, 562-903-4752, E-mail: graduate.admissions@biola.edu.
Website: http://www.talbot.edu/

Bob Jones University, Graduate Programs, Greenville, SC 29614. Offers accountancy (MS); Bible (MA); Bible translation (MA); Biblical studies (Certificate); broadcast management (MS); business administration (MBA); church history (MA, PhD); church ministries (MA); church music (MM); cinema and video production (MA); counseling (MS); curriculum and instruction (Ed D); divinity (M Div); dramatic production (MA); educational leadership (MS, Ed D, Ed S); elementary education (M Ed, MAT); English

(M Ed, MA, MAT); fine arts (MA); graphic design (MA); history (M Ed, MA); illustration (MA); interpretative speech (MA); mathematics (M Ed, MAT); medical missions (Certificate); ministry (MM, D Min); multi-categorical special education (M Ed, MAT); music (M Ed); New Testament interpretation (PhD); Old Testament interpretation (PhD); orchestral instrument performance (MM); organ performance (MM); pastoral studies (MA); personnel services (MS, Ed S); piano pedagogy (MM); piano performance (MM); platform arts (MA); radio and television broadcasting (MS); rhetoric and public address (MA); secondary education (M Ed); studio art (MA); teaching Bible (MA); theology (MA, PhD); voice performance (MM); youth ministries (MA); M Div/MM.

Boston College, School of Theology and Ministry, Chestnut Hill, MA 02467-3800. Offers church leadership (MA); divinity (M Div); pastoral ministry (MA), including Hispanic ministry, liturgy and worship, pastoral care and counseling, spirituality; religious education (MA, PhD); sacred theology (STD, STL); social justice/social ministry (MA); spiritual direction (MA); theological studies (MTS); theology (Th M, PhD); youth ministry (MA); MA/MA; MS/MA; MSW/MA. *Accreditation:* Teacher Education Accreditation Council. Part-time programs available. *Degree requirements:* For doctorate, one foreign language, thesis/dissertation. *Entrance requirements:* For doctorate, GRE. Additional exam requirements/recommendations for international students: Required—TOEFL (minimum score 550 paper-based). Electronic applications accepted. *Faculty research:* Philosophy and practice of religious education, pastoral psychology, liturgical and spiritual theology, spiritual formation for the practice of ministry.

Briercrest Seminary, Graduate Programs, Program in Christian Ministries, Caronport, SK S0H 0S0, Canada. Offers leadership (MA); marriage and family counseling (MA); missions (MA); pastoral counseling (MA); worship (MA); youth and family ministry (MA). Part-time programs available. *Degree requirements:* For master's, comprehensive exam, thesis optional. *Entrance requirements:* Additional exam requirements/recommendations for international students: Required—TOEFL (minimum score 550 paper-based).

Briercrest Seminary, Graduate Programs, Program in Theology, Caronport, SK S0H 0S0, Canada. Offers Biblical studies (M Div); leadership and management (M Div); New Testament (MATS); Old Testament (MATS); pastoral counseling (M Div); pastoral ministry (M Div); theological studies (M Div); theology (MATS); worship (M Div); youth and family ministry (M Div). *Accreditation:* ATS. Part-time programs available. *Degree requirements:* For master's, comprehensive exam, thesis optional. *Entrance requirements:* Additional exam requirements/recommendations for international students: Required—TOEFL (minimum score 550 paper-based).

Cairn University, Department of Counseling, Langhorne, PA 19047-2990. Offers MS. Part-time and evening/weekend programs available. *Faculty:* 4 full-time (1 woman), 5 part-time/adjunct (2 women). *Students:* 20 full-time (16 women), 65 part-time (50 women); includes 33 minority (26 Black or African American, non-Hispanic/Latino; 2 Asian, non-Hispanic/Latino; 5 Hispanic/Latino), 4 international. Average age 34. 38 applicants, 61% accepted, 15 enrolled. In 2014, 33 master's awarded. *Entrance requirements:* Additional exam requirements/recommendations for international students: Required—TOEFL (minimum score 550 paper-based). *Application deadline:* Applications are processed on a rolling basis. Application fee: $25. Electronic applications accepted. Application fee is waived when completed online. *Expenses: Tuition:* Full-time $11,430; part-time $635 per credit. Tuition and fees vary according to program. *Financial support:* Scholarships/grants available. Support available to part-time students. Financial award applicants required to submit FAFSA. *Unit head:* Dr. Jeff Black, Chair, 215-702-4347, E-mail: jblack@cairn.edu. *Application contact:* Gwen Dorsey, Enrollment Counselor, Graduate Counseling, 800-572-2472, Fax: 215-702-4248, E-mail: gdorsey@cairn.edu.
Website: http://www.cairn.edu/academics/counseling

California Baptist University, Program in Counseling Ministry, Riverside, CA 92504-3206. Offers professional ministry (MA); research in counseling ministry (MA). Part-time and evening/weekend programs available. *Faculty:* 10 full-time (6 women), 4 part-time/adjunct (3 women). *Students:* 7 full-time (5 women), 6 part-time (4 women); includes 8 minority (4 Black or African American, non-Hispanic/Latino; 2 Hispanic/Latino; 1 Native Hawaiian or other Pacific Islander, non-Hispanic/Latino; 1 Two or more races, non-Hispanic/Latino). Average age 39. 11 applicants, 82% accepted, 4 enrolled. In 2014, 12 master's awarded. *Degree requirements:* For master's, comprehensive exam, additional professional ministry practicum or research thesis. *Entrance requirements:* For master's, GRE (minimum score of 300 for applicants with a GPA below 2.75), minimum undergraduate GPA of 2.75; official transcripts; three recommendations; comprehensive essay; interview; three prerequisite classes completed with minimum C grade. Additional exam requirements/recommendations for international students: Required—TOEFL (minimum score 80 iBT). *Application deadline:* For fall admission, 8/1 priority date for domestic students, 7/1 for international students; for spring admission, 12/1 priority date for domestic students, 11/1 for international students. Applications are processed on a rolling basis. Application fee: $45. Electronic applications accepted. *Expenses:* Expenses: Contact institution. *Financial support:* Institutionally sponsored loans available. Financial award applicants required to submit CSS PROFILE or FAFSA. *Faculty research:* Social psychology, clinical psychology, psychology of religion, child development, marriage and family therapy. *Unit head:* Dr. Jacqueline Gustafson, Dean, School of Behavioral Sciences, 951-343-4487, E-mail: jcraig@calbaptist.edu. *Application contact:* Dr. Nathan Lewis, Program Director of Counseling Ministry, 951-343-4348, E-mail: nlewis@calbaptist.edu.
Website: http://www.calbaptist.edu/macounseling

California Baptist University, Program in Counseling Ministry and Counseling Psychology (Dual Master's), Riverside, CA 92504-3206. Offers MA/MS. Part-time and evening/weekend programs available. *Faculty:* 17 full-time (10 women), 18 part-time/adjunct (10 women). *Students:* 9 full-time (7 women), 1 (woman) part-time; includes 6 minority (2 Asian, non-Hispanic/Latino; 4 Hispanic/Latino). Average age 34. 8 applicants, 25% accepted, 1 enrolled. *Entrance requirements:* Additional exam requirements/recommendations for international students: Required—TOEFL (minimum score 80 iBT). *Application deadline:* For fall admission, 8/1 priority date for domestic students, 7/1 for international students; for spring admission, 12/1 priority date for domestic students, 11/1 for international students. Applications are processed on a rolling basis. Application fee: $45. Electronic applications accepted. *Financial support:* Applicants required to submit CSS PROFILE or FAFSA. *Faculty research:* Law enforcement psychology, neurotheology, organizational neuroscience, integration of theology and behavioral science, cognitive development/cross-cultural psychology. *Unit head:* Dr. Jacqueline Gustafson, Dean, School of Behavioral Sciences, 951-343-4487, E-mail: jcraig@calbaptist.edu. *Application contact:* Dr. Angela Deulen, Director of Counseling Psychology Program, 951-343-4204, Fax: 877-228-8877, E-mail: adeulen@calbaptist.edu.
Website: http://www.calbaptist.edu/mft

Calvary Bible College and Theological Seminary, Calvary Theological Seminary, Kansas City, MO 64147-1341. Offers Bible and theology (MS); Biblical counseling (MA); Biblical studies (MA); Christian ministry (MA); Christian studies (MS); Christian theology (MA); New Testament (MA); Old Testament (MA); pastoral studies (M Div). Part-time and evening/weekend programs available. *Degree requirements:* For master's, variable foreign language requirement, comprehensive exam, thesis. *Entrance requirements:* For

master's, minimum GPA of 2.5, 50 semester hours of course work in liberal arts, BA or BS, doctrine agreement. Additional exam requirements/recommendations for international students: Required—TOEFL (minimum score 550 paper-based).

Calvin Theological Seminary, Graduate and Professional Programs, Grand Rapids, MI 49546-4387. Offers Bible and theology (MA); divinity (M Div), including ancient near eastern languages and literature, contextual ministry, evangelism and teaching, history of Christianity, new church development, New Testament, Old Testament, pastoral care and leadership, preaching and worship, theological studies, youth and family ministries; educational ministry (MA); historical theology (PhD); missions and evangelism (MA); pastoral care (MA); philosophical and moral theology (PhD); systematic theology (PhD); theological studies (MTS); theology (Th M); worship (MA); youth and family ministries (MA). *Accreditation:* ACIPE; ATS. Part-time programs available. *Degree requirements:* For master's, variable foreign language requirement, thesis (for some programs); for doctorate, 4 foreign languages, comprehensive exam, thesis/dissertation. *Entrance requirements:* For doctorate, GRE General Test, Hebrew, Greek, and a modern foreign language. Additional exam requirements/recommendations for international students: Required—TOEFL (minimum score 550 paper-based), TWE (minimum score 4). Electronic applications accepted. *Faculty research:* Recent Trinity theory, Christian anthropology, Proverbs, reformed confessions, Paul's view of law.

Campbell University, Graduate and Professional Programs, Divinity School, Buies Creek, NC 27506. Offers Christian ministry (MA); divinity (M Div); ministry (D Min); JD/M Div; M Div/MA; M Div/MBA. *Accreditation:* ATS. *Faculty:* 5 full-time, 7 part-time/adjunct. *Students:* 239 full-time (89 women), 28 part-time (13 women); includes 40 minority (35 Black or African American, non-Hispanic/Latino; 1 American Indian or Alaska Native, non-Hispanic/Latino; 4 Hispanic/Latino), 2 international. Average age 38. *Degree requirements:* For doctorate, final project. *Entrance requirements:* For master's, minimum GPA of 2.5; for doctorate, MAT, M Div, minimum graduate GPA of 3.0. Additional exam requirements/recommendations for international students: Required—TOEFL (minimum score 580 paper-based). *Application deadline:* For fall admission, 7/1 for domestic students; for spring admission, 11/15 for domestic students. Applications are processed on a rolling basis. Application fee: $20. *Expenses:* Expenses: Contact institution. *Financial support:* Fellowships, scholarships/grants, and unspecified assistantships available. Support available to part-time students. Financial award application deadline: 5/1. *Faculty research:* New Testament, theology, spiritual formation, Old Testament, Christian leadership. *Unit head:* Andrew H. Wakefield, Dean, 910-893-1830, Fax: 910-893-1835. *Application contact:* Amber H. Johnson, Director of Admissions, 800-760-9827 Ext. 4765, Fax: 910-893-1835, E-mail: ahjohnson@campbell.edu.
Website: http://divinity.campbell.edu/

Canadian Southern Baptist Seminary, Graduate Programs, Cochrane, AB T4C 2G1, Canada. Offers Biblical studies (MBS); Christian ministry (MCMin); ministry (M Div). *Accreditation:* ATS. Part-time programs available. Postbaccalaureate distance learning degree programs offered (no on-campus study). *Faculty:* 6 full-time (0 women), 3 part-time/adjunct (0 women). *Students:* 8 full-time (2 women), 29 part-time (9 women); includes 12 minority (2 Black or African American, non-Hispanic/Latino; 7 Asian, non-Hispanic/Latino; 3 Hispanic/Latino), 1 international. Average age 28. 12 applicants, 83% accepted, 7 enrolled. In 2014, 6 master's awarded. *Entrance requirements:* Additional exam requirements/recommendations for international students: Required—TOEFL (minimum score 560 paper-based; 83 iBT); Recommended—IELTS. *Application deadline:* For fall admission, 7/1 priority date for domestic and international students; for winter admission, 11/15 priority date for domestic and international students. Applications are processed on a rolling basis. Application fee: $50 ($150 for international students). *Expenses: Tuition:* Full-time $7200 Canadian dollars; part-time $300 Canadian dollars per credit hour. *Required fees:* $120 Canadian dollars. One-time fee: $50 Canadian dollars. *Financial support:* Scholarships/grants available. Financial award application deadline: 1/21. *Unit head:* Dr. Steve Booth, Academic Dean, 403-932-6622 Ext. 232, E-mail: steve.booth@csbs.ca. *Application contact:* Kathleen McNaughton, Registrar, 403-932-6622 Ext. 221, E-mail: kathleen.mcnaughton@csbs.ca.

Cardinal Stritch University, College of Arts and Sciences, Department of Religious Studies, Milwaukee, WI 53217-3985. Offers lay ministries (MA); ministry (MA); religious studies (MA). Part-time and evening/weekend programs available. *Degree requirements:* For master's, comprehensive exam, thesis, faculty recommendation, research project. *Entrance requirements:* For master's, interview, minimum GPA of 2.75.

Carolina Christian College, Program in Religious Education, Winston-Salem, NC 27102-0777. Offers Christian education (MRE); pastoral care (MRE). *Entrance requirements:* For master's, bachelor's degree from accredited institution, minimum undergraduate "B" average.

Carolina Evangelical Divinity School, Ministry Program, High Point, NC 27265. Offers D Min. *Degree requirements:* For doctorate, project. *Entrance requirements:* For doctorate, MAT, M Div or equivalent, minimum GPA of 3.0 on all previous graduate study, 3 years of ministry experience.

Carson-Newman University, Program in Applied Social Justice, Jefferson City, TN 37760. Offers MAASJ. *Faculty:* 1 full-time (0 women), 1 part-time/adjunct (0 women). *Students:* 1 full-time (0 women), 1 part-time (0 women). Average age 31. *Degree requirements:* For master's, completion of degree within five years of admissions into program. *Entrance requirements:* For master's, GRE (minimum score of 290), minimum GPA of 3.0. Additional exam requirements/recommendations for international students: Recommended—TOEFL (minimum score 210 paper-based; 79 iBT), IELTS (minimum score 6.5), TSE (minimum score 53). *Application deadline:* For fall admission, 7/15 for domestic students. Application fee: $50. *Expenses: Tuition:* Full-time $9680; part-time $440 per credit hour. *Required fees:* $300; $440 per credit hour. $150 per semester. *Unit head:* Dr. Laura Wadlington, Department Chair, 865-471-3270. *Application contact:* Graduate Admissions and Services Adviser, 865-471-3223, E-mail: adult@cn.edu.
Website: http://www.cn.edu/graduate-adult-studies/programs/applied-social-justice

Catholic Theological Union, Graduate and Professional Programs, Chicago, IL 60615-5698. Offers biblical spirituality (Certificate); cross-cultural ministries (D Min); cross-cultural missions (Certificate); divinity (M Div); liturgical studies (Certificate); liturgy (D Min); pastoral studies (MAPS, Certificate); spiritual formation (Certificate); spirituality (D Min); theology (MA); M Div/MA; M Div/MSW; M Div/PhD. M Div/PhD offered jointly with University of Chicago; M Div/MSW with Loyola University Chicago and University of Chicago. *Accreditation:* ACIPE; ATS (one or more programs are accredited). Part-time and evening/weekend programs available. *Degree requirements:* For master's, one foreign language, comprehensive exam (for some programs), thesis (for some programs); for doctorate, thesis/dissertation. *Entrance requirements:* For doctorate, master's degree, 5 years of active ministry. *Faculty research:* Doctrine, sacraments, ethics, Bible.

The Catholic University of America, School of Theology and Religious Studies, Washington, DC 20064. Offers M Div, MA, MRE, D Min, PhD, STD, Certificate, STB, STL, MSLS/MA. *Accreditation:* ATS (one or more programs are accredited). Part-time programs available. *Faculty:* 44 full-time (5 women), 8 part-time/adjunct (2 women). *Students:* 153 full-time (8 women), 206 part-time (51 women); includes 50 minority (8 Black or African American, non-Hispanic/Latino; 2 American Indian or Alaska Native,

non-Hispanic/Latino; 11 Asian, non-Hispanic/Latino; 16 Hispanic/Latino; 1 Native Hawaiian or other Pacific Islander, non-Hispanic/Latino; 12 Two or more races, non-Hispanic/Latino), 57 international. Average age 36. 197 applicants, 74% accepted, 69 enrolled. In 2014, 40 master's, 21 doctorates awarded. *Degree requirements:* For master's, variable foreign language requirement, comprehensive exam (for some programs), thesis (for some programs); for doctorate, variable foreign language requirement, comprehensive exam, thesis/dissertation. *Entrance requirements:* For master's and doctorate, GRE General Test, statement of purpose, official copies of academic transcripts, three letters of recommendation. Additional exam requirements/recommendations for international students: Required—TOEFL (minimum score 580 paper-based). *Application deadline:* For fall admission, 7/15 priority date for domestic students, 7/1 for international students; for spring admission, 11/15 priority date for domestic students, 11/1 for international students. Applications are processed on a rolling basis. Application fee: $55. Electronic applications accepted. *Expenses: Tuition:* Full-time $40,200; part-time $1600 per credit hour. *Required fees:* $400; $195 per semester. One-time fee: $425. *Financial support:* Fellowships, research assistantships, teaching assistantships, Federal Work-Study, scholarships/grants, tuition waivers (full and partial), and unspecified assistantships available. Financial award application deadline: 2/1; financial award applicants required to submit FAFSA. *Faculty research:* Historical and systematic theology, religious education and catechetics, moral theology and ethics, Biblical studies, liturgical studies and sacramental theology. *Unit head:* Msgr. Paul McPartlan, Acting Dean, 202-319-6515, Fax: 202-319-5704, E-mail: mcpartlan@cua.edu. *Application contact:* Director of Graduate Admissions, 202-319-5057, Fax: 202-319-6533, E-mail: cua-admissions@cua.edu.
Website: http://trs.cua.edu/

Chaminade University of Honolulu, Graduate Services, Program in Pastoral Theology, Honolulu, HI 96816-1578. Offers MPT. Part-time and evening/weekend programs available. Postbaccalaureate distance learning degree programs offered. *Degree requirements:* For master's, capstone course. *Entrance requirements:* For master's, 2 letters of recommendation. Additional exam requirements/recommendations for international students: Required—TOEFL (minimum score 550 paper-based). Electronic applications accepted.

Charlotte Christian College and Theological Seminary, Graduate Program, Charlotte, NC 28205. Offers urban Christian ministry (MA), including church planting, multi-cultural studies, sacred music, youth ministry. Part-time and evening/weekend programs available. *Faculty:* 5 full-time (1 woman), 9 part-time/adjunct (2 women). *Students:* 2 full-time (1 woman), 25 part-time (15 women); includes 18 minority (17 Black or African American, non-Hispanic/Latino; 1 Hispanic/Latino), 2 international. Average age 47. 2 applicants, 100% accepted, 2 enrolled. In 2014, 2 master's awarded. *Degree requirements:* For master's, thesis. *Entrance requirements:* For master's, MAT, writing sample/essay. Additional exam requirements/recommendations for international students: Required—TOEFL, IELTS. *Application deadline:* For fall admission, 7/24 for domestic students, 7/18 for international students; for spring admission, 12/11 for domestic students, 12/5 for international students; for summer admission, 4/18 for domestic and international students. Application fee: $50 ($140 for international students). Electronic applications accepted. *Expenses:* Expenses: 1 course: $1,200; 2 courses: $2,300; 3 courses: $3,300; 4 courses $3,900. *Financial support:* In 2014–15, 5 students received support. Federal Work-Study and scholarships/grants available. Financial award application deadline: 4/1; financial award applicants required to submit FAFSA. *Unit head:* Anne Witt, Registrar/Director of International Students, 704-344-6882 Ext. 103, Fax: 704-334-6885, E-mail: abwitt@charlottechristian.edu. *Application contact:* Constance Hemphill, Director of Admissions, 704-334-6882 Ext. 115, Fax: 704-334-6885, E-mail: chemphill@charlottechristian.edu.
Website: http://www.charlottechristian.edu

Chicago Theological Seminary, Graduate and Professional Programs, Chicago, IL 60637-1507. Offers preaching (D Min); religion and health (D Min); religious studies (MA); spirituality and spiritual direction (D Min); theology (M Div); theology, ethics and the human sciences (PhD); M Div/MSW. *Accreditation:* ACIPE; ATS. Part-time programs available. *Degree requirements:* For master's, thesis; for doctorate, 2 foreign languages, comprehensive exam, thesis/dissertation. *Entrance requirements:* For doctorate, GRE General Test. Additional exam requirements/recommendations for international students: Required—TOEFL. *Faculty research:* Bible, culture and hermeneutics, theology, gender and sexuality, black faith and life, spirituality and psychology, practical theology.

Christian Theological Seminary, Graduate and Professional Programs, Indianapolis, IN 46208-3301. Offers educational and arts ministries (MA); marriage and family therapy (MA); pastoral care and counseling (D Min); psychotherapy and faith (MA); theological studies (MTS); theology (M Div). *Accreditation:* AAMFT/COAMFTE (one or more programs are accredited); ACIPE; ATS. Part-time programs available. Terminal master's awarded for partial completion of doctoral program. *Degree requirements:* For master's, comprehensive exam (for some programs), thesis (for some programs), missionary and cross-cultural experience (for M Div); for doctorate, comprehensive exam, thesis/dissertation. *Entrance requirements:* For doctorate, M Div. Additional exam requirements/recommendations for international students: Recommended—TOEFL. Electronic applications accepted. *Faculty research:* Faith formation, peer learning post graduation.

Christ the King Seminary, Graduate and Professional Programs, East Aurora, NY 14052. Offers divinity (M Div); pastoral ministry (MA); theology (MA). *Accreditation:* ATS. Part-time and evening/weekend programs available. *Degree requirements:* For master's, comprehensive exam, thesis. *Entrance requirements:* For master's, previous course work in philosophy and religious studies.

Cincinnati Christian University, Graduate School, Program in Counseling, Cincinnati, OH 45204-3200. Offers MAC. *Degree requirements:* For master's, thesis or alternative, integration paper. *Entrance requirements:* For master's, GRE General Test, interview, minimum undergraduate GPA of 3.0. Additional exam requirements/recommendations for international students: Required—TOEFL. Electronic applications accepted. *Expenses:* Contact institution.

Claremont School of Theology, Graduate and Professional Programs, Program in Ministry, Claremont, CA 91711-3199. Offers D Min. *Accreditation:* ACIPE. *Degree requirements:* For doctorate, thesis/dissertation. *Entrance requirements:* For doctorate, GRE General Test. Additional exam requirements/recommendations for international students: Required—TOEFL. Electronic applications accepted.

Claremont School of Theology, Graduate and Professional Programs, Program in Religion, Claremont, CA 91711-3199. Offers practical theology (PhD), including religious education, spiritual care and counseling; religion (PhD), including Hebrew Bible, New Testament and Christian origins, process studies, religion, ethics, and society; religion and theology (MA); religious education (MARE). *Accreditation:* ACIPE; ATS. Terminal master's awarded for partial completion of doctoral program. *Degree requirements:* For master's, thesis; for doctorate, 2 foreign languages, thesis/dissertation. *Entrance requirements:* For doctorate, GRE General Test. Additional exam requirements/recommendations for international students: Required—TOEFL. Electronic applications accepted.

Columbia International University, Columbia Biblical Seminary and School of Ministry, Columbia, SC 29230-3122. Offers academic ministries (M Div); Bible and theology (Certificate); bible exposition (M Div, MABE); Biblical ministry (Certificate); chaplaincy (M Div); intercultural studies (MAIS); leadership (D Min); member care (D Min); missions (D Min); preaching (D Min); theological studies (MA). *Accreditation:* ATS (one or more programs are accredited). Part-time and evening/weekend programs available. *Faculty:* 14 full-time (1 woman), 9 part-time/adjunct (1 woman). *Students:* 180 full-time (59 women), 218 part-time (61 women); includes 81 minority (58 Black or African American, non-Hispanic/Latino; 1 American Indian or Alaska Native, non-Hispanic/Latino; 18 Asian, non-Hispanic/Latino; 4 Hispanic/Latino), 22 international. Average age 36. 277 applicants, 81% accepted, 117 enrolled. In 2014, 74 master's, 3 doctorates, 15 other advanced degrees awarded. *Degree requirements:* For doctorate, comprehensive exam, thesis/dissertation. *Entrance requirements:* For doctorate, 3 years of ministerial experience, M Div. Additional exam requirements/recommendations for international students: Required—TOEFL. *Application deadline:* For fall admission, 8/1 priority date for domestic and international students; for winter admission, 12/15 priority date for domestic and international students; for spring admission, 1/15 priority date for domestic and international students. Applications are processed on a rolling basis. Application fee: $45. Electronic applications accepted. *Expenses: Tuition:* Full-time $9540; part-time $530 per credit hour. *Required fees:* $480; $240 per semester. *Financial support:* In 2014–15, 120 students received support. Career-related internships or fieldwork, Federal Work-Study, institutionally sponsored loans, and scholarships/grants available. Financial award application deadline: 3/15; financial award applicants required to submit FAFSA. *Unit head:* Dr. Junias Venugopal, Dean, 803-754-4100 Ext. 5330, Fax: 803-786-4209, E-mail: jvenugopal@ciu.edu. *Application contact:* Michelle MacGregor, Director of Admissions, 800-777-2227 Ext. 5335, Fax: 803-786-4209, E-mail: yescbs@ciu.edu.
Website: http://www.ciu.edu/discover-ciu/who-we-are/academics/seminary-school-ministry

Columbia International University, Columbia Graduate School, Columbia, SC 29230-3122. Offers Bible teaching (MABT); Christian higher education leadership (PhD); Christian school leadership (PhD); counseling (MACN); curricular and instructional leadership (PhD); early childhood and elementary education (MAT); educational administration (M Ed); instruction and learning (M Ed); teaching English as a foreign language (Certificate); teaching English as a foreign language and intercultural studies (MATF). Part-time and evening/weekend programs available. Postbaccalaureate distance learning degree programs offered. *Faculty:* 11 full-time (4 women), 7 part-time/adjunct (5 women). *Students:* 231 full-time (127 women), 312 part-time (118 women); includes 167 minority (125 Black or African American, non-Hispanic/Latino; 1 American Indian or Alaska Native, non-Hispanic/Latino; 23 Asian, non-Hispanic/Latino; 8 Hispanic/Latino; 10 Two or more races, non-Hispanic/Latino), 43 international. Average age 35. 107 applicants, 56% accepted, 41 enrolled. In 2014, 62 degrees awarded. *Degree requirements:* For master's, internships, professional project. *Entrance requirements:* For master's, MAT; GRE (for some programs), minimum GPA of 2.7. Additional exam requirements/recommendations for international students: Required—TOEFL. *Application deadline:* For fall admission, 8/1 priority date for domestic and international students; for winter admission, 12/1 priority date for domestic students, 11/1 priority date for international students; for spring admission, 12/1 priority date for domestic students, 11/1 priority date for international students. Applications are processed on a rolling basis. Application fee: $45. Electronic applications accepted. *Expenses: Tuition:* Full-time $9540; part-time $530 per credit hour. *Required fees:* $480; $240 per semester. *Financial support:* In 2014–15, 35 students received support. Career-related internships or fieldwork, Federal Work-Study, institutionally sponsored loans, and scholarships/grants available. Financial award application deadline: 3/17; financial award applicants required to submit FAFSA. *Unit head:* Dr. John Harvey, Dean, 803-807-5363, Fax: 803-786-4209, E-mail: jharvey@ciu.edu. *Application contact:* Dori Beach, Associate Director of Graduate Admissions, 803-807-5088, Fax: 803-786-4209, E-mail: dbeach@ciu.edu.

Concordia University, Nebraska, Graduate Programs in Education, Program in Family Life Ministry, Seward, NE 68434-1556. Offers MS. Part-time and evening/weekend programs available. *Degree requirements:* For master's, thesis or alternative. *Entrance requirements:* For master's, GRE, MAT, or NTE, minimum GPA of 3.0, BS in education or equivalent.

Corban University, Graduate School, Program in Counseling, Salem, OR 97301-9392. Offers MA. *Degree requirements:* For master's, internship, practicum.

Corban University, Graduate School, School of Ministry, Salem, OR 97301-9392. Offers Biblical languages (M Div); Biblical leadership (Certificate); Christian leadership (MA); Church ministry (M Div); ministry (D Min). Part-time and evening/weekend programs available. *Degree requirements:* For master's, thesis. *Entrance requirements:* Additional exam requirements/recommendations for international students: Required—TOEFL (minimum score 550 paper-based), IELTS (minimum score 6).

Covenant Theological Seminary, Graduate and Professional Programs, St. Louis, MO 63141-8697. Offers M Div, MA, MAC, MAEM, Th M, D Min, Certificate. *Accreditation:* ATS (one or more programs are accredited). Part-time and evening/weekend programs available. Postbaccalaureate distance learning degree programs offered (no on-campus study). *Degree requirements:* For master's, 2 foreign languages, thesis (for some programs); for doctorate, 2 foreign languages, thesis/dissertation; for Certificate, 2 foreign languages. *Entrance requirements:* For doctorate and Certificate, M Div. Additional exam requirements/recommendations for international students: Required—TOEFL (minimum score 550 paper-based). *Application deadline:* Applications are processed on a rolling basis. Application fee: $50. Electronic applications accepted. *Financial support:* Career-related internships or fieldwork, institutionally sponsored loans, scholarships/grants, and tuition waivers (full and partial) available. Support available to part-time students. Financial award application deadline: 4/15; financial award applicants required to submit FAFSA. *Application contact:* John Patton, Director of Admissions, 314-434-4044, Fax: 314-434-4819, E-mail: admissions@covenantseminary.edu.
Website: http://www.covenantseminary.edu/academics/degrees/

The Criswell College, Graduate School of the Bible, Dallas, TX 75246-1537. Offers biblical studies (M Div); Christian leadership (MA); counseling (MA); Jewish studies (MA); ministry (MA); theological and biblical studies (MA). Part-time programs available. *Degree requirements:* For master's, 2 foreign languages, thesis optional. *Entrance requirements:* For master's, GRE General Test, minimum GPA of 2.5. Electronic applications accepted. *Faculty research:* Emphasis on biblical languages (Hebrew and Greek), expository preaching and evangelism in the local church.

Dallas Baptist University, Gary Cook School of Leadership, Program in Christian Education, Dallas, TX 75211-9299. Offers adult ministry (MA); business ministry (MA); Christian studies (MA); collegiate ministry (MA); communication ministry (MA); counseling ministry (MA); family ministry (MA); general ministry (MA); leading the nonprofit organization (MA); missions ministry (MA); small group ministry (MA); student ministry (MA); worship ministry (MA); MA/MA. Part-time and evening/weekend programs available. *Entrance requirements:* For master's, minimum GPA of 3.0. Additional exam requirements/recommendations for international students: Required—TOEFL. Electronic applications accepted. *Expenses: Tuition:* Full-time $14,130; part-time $785 per credit hour. *Required fees:* $200 per semester. Tuition and fees vary according to course level and course load.

Dallas Baptist University, Gary Cook School of Leadership, Program in Christian Education: Childhood Ministry, Dallas, TX 75211-9299. Offers MA, MA/MA. Part-time and evening/weekend programs available. *Entrance requirements:* For master's, minimum GPA of 3.0. Additional exam requirements/recommendations for international students: Required—TOEFL, IELTS. *Expenses: Tuition:* Full-time $14,130; part-time $785 per credit hour. *Required fees:* $200 per semester. Tuition and fees vary according to course level and course load.

Dallas Baptist University, Gary Cook School of Leadership, Program in Christian Education: Student Ministry, Dallas, TX 75211-9299. Offers MA, MA/MA. Part-time and evening/weekend programs available. *Entrance requirements:* For master's, minimum GPA of 3.0. Additional exam requirements/recommendations for international students: Required—TOEFL, IELTS. *Expenses: Tuition:* Full-time $14,130; part-time $785 per credit hour. *Required fees:* $200 per semester. Tuition and fees vary according to course level and course load.

Dallas Baptist University, Gary Cook School of Leadership, Program in Christian Ministry, Dallas, TX 75211-9299. Offers MA. Postbaccalaureate distance learning degree programs offered (no on-campus study). *Expenses: Tuition:* Full-time $14,130; part-time $785 per credit hour. *Required fees:* $200 per semester. Tuition and fees vary according to course level and course load.

Dallas Baptist University, Gary Cook School of Leadership, Program in Global Leadership, Dallas, TX 75211-9299. Offers business communication (MA); East Asian studies (MA); ESL (MA); general studies (MA); global leadership (MA); global studies (MA); international business (MA); leading the nonprofit organization (MA); missions (MA); small group ministry (MA); MA/MA. Part-time and evening/weekend programs available. *Entrance requirements:* For master's, minimum GPA of 3.0. Additional exam requirements/recommendations for international students: Required—TOEFL, IELTS. *Expenses: Tuition:* Full-time $14,130; part-time $785 per credit hour. *Required fees:* $200 per semester. Tuition and fees vary according to course level and course load.

Dallas Baptist University, Gary Cook School of Leadership, Program in Leadership Studies, Dallas, TX 75211-9299. Offers PhD. *Degree requirements:* For doctorate, thesis/dissertation. *Expenses: Tuition:* Full-time $14,130; part-time $785 per credit hour. *Required fees:* $200 per semester. Tuition and fees vary according to course level and course load.

Dallas Baptist University, Gary Cook School of Leadership, Program in Worship Leadership, Dallas, TX 75211-9299. Offers communication ministry (MA); worship leadership (MA); worship ministry (MA); worship music (MA); MA/MA. Part-time and evening/weekend programs available. *Entrance requirements:* For master's, minimum GPA of 3.0. Additional exam requirements/recommendations for international students: Required—TOEFL, IELTS. *Expenses: Tuition:* Full-time $14,130; part-time $785 per credit hour. *Required fees:* $200 per semester. Tuition and fees vary according to course level and course load.

Dallas Baptist University, Professional Development Program, Dallas, TX 75211-9299. Offers business (MA); counseling (MA); criminal justice (MA); English as a second language (MA); higher education (MA); interdisciplinary (MA); leadership studies (MA); missions (MA); professional life coaching (MA); training and development (MA). Part-time and evening/weekend programs available. *Entrance requirements:* For master's, minimum GPA of 3.0. Additional exam requirements/recommendations for international students: Required—TOEFL, IELTS. *Expenses: Tuition:* Full-time $14,130; part-time $785 per credit hour. *Required fees:* $200 per semester. Tuition and fees vary according to course level and course load.

Dallas Theological Seminary, Graduate Programs, Dallas, TX 75204-6499. Offers adult education (Th M); apologetics (Th M); Bible backgrounds (Th M); Bible translation (Th M); Biblical and theological studies (Certificate); biblical counseling (MA); biblical exegesis and linguistics (MA); biblical exposition (PhD); biblical studies (MA); Biblical theology (Th M); children's education (Th M); Christian education (MA, D Min); Christian leadership (MA); cross-cultural ministries (MA); educational administration (Th M); educational leadership (Th M); evangelism and discipleship (Th M); exposition of Biblical books (Th M); family life education (Th M); general studies (Th M); Hebrew and cognate studies (Th M); hermeneutics (Th M); historical theology (Th M); homiletics (Th M); intercultural ministries (Th M); Jesus studies (Th M); leadership studies (Th M); media and communication (MA); media arts (Th M); ministry (D Min); ministry with women (Th M); New Testament studies (Th M, PhD); Old Testament studies (Th M, PhD); parachurch ministries (Th M); pastoral care and counseling (Th M); pastoral theology and practice (Th M); philosophy (Th M); sacred theology (STM); spiritual formation (Th M); systematic theology (Th M); teaching in Christian institutions (Th M); theological studies (PhD); urban ministries (Th M); worship studies (Th M); youth education (Th M). *Accreditation:* ATS (one or more programs are accredited). Part-time programs available. Postbaccalaureate distance learning degree programs offered (no on-campus study). *Degree requirements:* For master's, variable foreign language requirement, thesis (for some programs); for doctorate, 2 foreign languages, thesis/dissertation. *Entrance requirements:* For master's, GRE or MAT (if minimum undergraduate cumulative GPA is below 2.5 or undergraduate degree is unaccredited). Additional exam requirements/recommendations for international students: Required—TOEFL (minimum score 575 paper-based; 85 iBT), TWE. Electronic applications accepted.

Denver Seminary, Graduate and Professional Programs, Littleton, CO 80120. Offers apologetics (Certificate); biblical studies (MA); Christian formation and soul care (MA, Certificate); Christian studies (MA, Certificate); church and parachurch leadership (D Min); counseling licensure (MA); counseling ministry (MA); intercultural ministry (Certificate); leadership (MA, Certificate); marriage and family counseling (D Min); pastoral ministry (D Min); philosophy of religion (MA); spiritual guidance (Certificate); theology (M Div, Certificate); worship (Certificate); youth and family ministry (MA). *Accreditation:* ACA; ACIPE; ATS (one or more programs are accredited). Part-time and evening/weekend programs available. Postbaccalaureate distance learning degree programs offered. *Degree requirements:* For master's, 2 foreign languages, thesis (for some programs); for doctorate, 2 foreign languages, thesis/dissertation. *Entrance requirements:* For doctorate, M Div, 3 years of ministry experience. Additional exam requirements/recommendations for international students: Required—TOEFL (minimum score 575 paper-based; 90 iBT). Electronic applications accepted.

Eastern Mennonite University, Eastern Mennonite Seminary, Harrisonburg, VA 22802-2462. Offers church leadership (MA); divinity (M Div); ministry studies (Certificate); religion (MA); theological studies (Certificate). *Accreditation:* ATS. Part-time programs available. *Degree requirements:* For master's, thesis (for some programs), supervised field education (for M Div). *Entrance requirements:* For master's, minimum GPA of 2.5. Additional exam requirements/recommendations for international students: Required—TOEFL (minimum score 550 paper-based). *Expenses:* Contact institution. *Faculty research:* Spiritual direction and culture of call, leadership coaching: an approach to leadership in a culture of call, clarity of call in the probationary process for United Methodist clergy in Virginia, EMS women's experiences of culture of call efforts, practices of excellent and fruitful Mennonite pastoral ministry.

Pastoral Ministry and Counseling

Eastern Mennonite University, Master of Arts in Counseling Program, Harrisonburg, VA 22802-2462. Offers MA, M Div/MA. *Accreditation:* ACA (one or more programs are accredited); ACIPE. Part-time programs available. *Degree requirements:* For master's, practicum, internship. *Entrance requirements:* For master's, minimum GPA of 3.0. Additional exam requirements/recommendations for international students: Required—TOEFL (minimum score 550 paper-based). Electronic applications accepted. *Expenses:* Contact institution. *Faculty research:* Career and gender, empathy and consciousness, emotion theory, education models.

Eastern University, Palmer Theological Seminary, King of Prussia, PA 19096-3430. Offers Biblical studies and theology (MTS); Christian counseling (MTS); Christian faith and public policy (MTS); divinity (M Div); general studies (MTS); leadership of missional church renewal (D Min); ministry (D Min), including marriage and family; M Div/MA; M Div/MBA; M Div/MSW. *Accreditation:* ACIPE; ATS; MSA/CIHE. Part-time programs available. Postbaccalaureate distance learning degree programs offered (minimal on-campus study). *Faculty:* 14 full-time (7 women), 17 part-time/adjunct (7 women). *Students:* 65 full-time (25 women), 185 part-time (102 women); includes 151 minority (145 Black or African American, non-Hispanic/Latino; 2 Asian, non-Hispanic/Latino; 3 Hispanic/Latino; 1 Two or more races, non-Hispanic/Latino), 3 international. Average age 47. 117 applicants, 56% accepted, 61 enrolled. In 2014, 53 master's, 17 doctorates awarded. *Degree requirements:* For master's, variable foreign language requirement, thesis (for some programs); for doctorate, thesis/dissertation. *Entrance requirements:* For master's, bachelor's degree from accredited institution; for doctorate, M Div or MA. Additional exam requirements/recommendations for international students: Required—TOEFL (minimum score 550 paper-based; 79 iBT). *Application deadline:* For fall admission, 8/1 priority date for domestic students, 3/31 for international students; for spring admission, 1/15 for domestic students, 10/31 for international students. Applications are processed on a rolling basis. Application fee: $30. Electronic applications accepted. Application fee is waived when completed online. *Expenses:* Tuition: Full-time $15,600; part-time $650 per credit. *Required fees:* $30; $27.50 per semester. One-time fee: $50. Tuition and fees vary according to course load, degree level and program. *Financial support:* In 2014–15, 130 students received support, including 2 fellowships (averaging $4,000 per year), 15 teaching assistantships (averaging $1,200 per year); career-related internships or fieldwork, Federal Work-Study, and scholarships/grants also available. Financial award application deadline: 8/1; financial award applicants required to submit FAFSA. *Faculty research:* Approaches to the spiritual formation of religious leaders; Latin, anti-Colonial, and constructive theologies; pastoral and ethical responses to human trafficking; inter-religious and political dimensions of peacemaking and social justice in Israel and the Palestinian Territories. *Unit head:* Dr. Edwin Aponte, Dean of the Seminary, 484-384-2935, E-mail: semdean@eastern.edu. *Application contact:* Tiffany S. Murphy, Director of Admissions, 610-896-5000 Ext. 2986, Fax: 484-654-3680, E-mail: semadmis@eastern.edu. Website: http://www.palmerseminary.edu/

East Texas Baptist University, School of Christian Studies, Marshall, TX 75670-1498. Offers Christian ministry (MACM); religion (MA). Part-time programs available. *Faculty:* 4 full-time (0 women). *Students:* 4 full-time (1 woman), 1 part-time (0 women); includes 2 minority (1 Black or African American, non-Hispanic/Latino; 1 Two or more races, non-Hispanic/Latino). Average age 31. 5 applicants, 80% accepted, 3 enrolled. In 2014, 3 master's awarded. *Degree requirements:* For master's, thesis optional. *Entrance requirements:* Additional exam requirements/recommendations for international students: Recommended—TOEFL (minimum score 550 paper-based; 79 iBT). *Application deadline:* For fall admission, 8/20 for domestic and international students; for spring admission, 1/7 for domestic and international students. Applications are processed on a rolling basis. Application fee: $50. Electronic applications accepted. *Expenses:* Expenses: Contact institution. *Financial support:* In 2014–15, 3 students received support. Federal Work-Study and scholarships/grants available. Financial award applicants required to submit FAFSA. *Unit head:* Dr. Warren Johnson, Director, 903-923-2180, Fax: 903-923-2077, E-mail: christianstudiesma@etbu.edu. *Application contact:* Den Murley, Graduate Services and Recruiting Coordinator, 903-923-2079, Fax: 903-934-8115, E-mail: dmurley@etbu.edu. Website: http://www.etbu.edu/christian-studies/masters-degrees/

Ecumenical Theological Seminary, Program in Ministry, Detroit, MI 48201. Offers D Min. *Accreditation:* ACIPE.

Emmanuel Christian Seminary, Graduate and Professional Programs, Johnson City, TN 37601-9438. Offers Christian care and counseling (M Div); Christian education (M Div); Christian ministries (MCM); Christian ministry (M Div); Christian theology (M Div, MAR); church history (MAR); church history/historical theology (M Div); general studies (M Div); ministry (D Min); New Testament (M Div, MAR); Old Testament (M Div, MAR); urban ministry (M Div); world missions (M Div). *Accreditation:* ACIPE; ATS. Part-time programs available. Postbaccalaureate distance learning degree programs offered (minimal on-campus study). *Degree requirements:* For master's, 2 foreign languages, thesis or alternative, portfolio; for doctorate, thesis/dissertation. *Entrance requirements:* For master's, bachelor's degree from accredited undergraduate institution; for doctorate, M Div or equivalent. Additional exam requirements/recommendations for international students: Required—TOEFL. Electronic applications accepted. *Faculty research:* Theology of Old Testament prophets, spiritual formation for Christian leaders, history of African churches and religions, social world of early Christianity, lay pastoral counseling, theology and art.

Emory University, Candler School of Theology, Atlanta, GA 30322. Offers formation and witness (M Div); history, scripture and tradition (MTS); leadership in church and community (M Div); modern religious thought and experience (MTS); pastoral counseling (Th D); religion and race (M Div); religion, health and science (M Div); scripture and interpretation (M Div); society and personality (M Div); theology (Th M); theology and ethics (M Div); theology and the arts (M Div); traditions of the church (M Div); women and religion (M Div); JD/M Div; JD/MTS; M Div/MBA; M Div/MPH; MBA/MTS; MTS/MPH. *Accreditation:* ACIPE; ATS. Part-time programs available. *Degree requirements:* For master's, thesis optional; for doctorate, comprehensive exam, thesis/dissertation. *Entrance requirements:* For master's, minimum undergraduate GPA of 3.0; for doctorate, GRE, M Div, 8 units of course work in clinical pastoral education. Additional exam requirements/recommendations for international students: Required—TOEFL (minimum score 600 paper-based; 95 iBT). Electronic applications accepted. *Expenses:* Contact institution. *Faculty research:* Biblical studies, church history, ethics, ministry practice, pastoral care.

Evangelical Seminary, Graduate and Professional Programs, Myerstown, PA 17067-1212. Offers Biblical studies (MAR); congregational ministry (M Div); global and contextual studies (M Div, MAR); historical and theological studies (MAR); interdisciplinary studies (MAR); marriage and family counseling (M Div); marriage and family therapy (MA); New Testament (MAR); Old Testament (MAR); spiritual formation (MAR); teaching ministry (M Div); youth ministry (M Div). *Accreditation:* ATS (one or more programs are accredited). Part-time programs available. Postbaccalaureate distance learning degree programs offered (minimal on-campus study). *Degree requirements:* For master's, 2 foreign languages. *Entrance requirements:* For master's, minimum GPA of 2.5. Additional exam requirements/recommendations for international students: Required—TOEFL (minimum score 550 paper-based). *Faculty research:*

Literary form and structure within the Hebrew and Greek scriptures, Wesley studies, esoteric biblical languages, the Mosaic law and the Christian, ethics.

Fairfield University, Graduate School of Education and Allied Professions, Fairfield, CT 06824. Offers applied behavior analysis (ATC); applied psychology (MA); clinical mental health counseling (MA, CAS); early childhood studies (ATC); educational technology (MA); elementary education (MA, CAS); family studies (MA); integration of spirituality and religion in counseling (ATC); marriage and family therapy (MA); school counseling (MA, CAS); school psychology (MA, CAS); school-based marriage and family therapy (ATC); secondary education (MA); special education (MA, CAS); substance abuse counseling (ATC); teaching (Certificate); teaching and foundations (MA, CAS); TESOL, world languages, and bilingual education (MA, CAS). *Accreditation:* NCATE. Part-time and evening/weekend programs available. *Faculty:* 23 full-time (19 women), 32 part-time/adjunct (25 women). *Students:* 148 full-time (131 women), 286 part-time (238 women); includes 81 minority (18 Black or African American, non-Hispanic/Latino; 1 American Indian or Alaska Native, non-Hispanic/Latino; 14 Asian, non-Hispanic/Latino; 39 Hispanic/Latino; 9 Two or more races, non-Hispanic/Latino), 13 international. Average age 34. 264 applicants, 54% accepted, 68 enrolled. In 2014, 142 master's awarded. *Degree requirements:* For master's, comprehensive exam. *Entrance requirements:* For master's, PRAXIS I (for certification programs), minimum GPA of 3.0, 2 recommendations, resume. Additional exam requirements/recommendations for international students: Required—TOEFL (minimum score 550 paper-based; 84 iBT) or IELTS (minimum score 7.5). *Application deadline:* For fall admission, 2/15 for international students; for spring admission, 10/1 for international students. Application fee: $60. Electronic applications accepted. *Expenses:* Expenses: $675 per credit hour. *Financial support:* In 2014–15, 55 students received support. Career-related internships or fieldwork and unspecified assistantships available. Financial award applicants required to submit FAFSA. *Faculty research:* Literacy, spirituality, special education, bilingual/multicultural education, mentoring and professional development. *Unit head:* Dr. Robert D. Hannafin, Dean, 203-254-4250, Fax: 203-254-4241, E-mail: rhannafin@fairfield.edu. *Application contact:* Marianne Gumpper, Director of Graduate and Continuing Studies Admission, 203-254-4184, Fax: 203-254-4073, E-mail: gradadmis@fairfield.edu. Website: http://www.fairfield.edu/academics/schoolscollegescenters/graduateschoolofeducationalliedprofessions/graduateprograms/

Faith Baptist Bible College and Theological Seminary, Graduate Program, Ankeny, IA 50023. Offers Biblical studies (MA); pastoral studies (M Div); pastoral training (MA); religion (MA); theological studies (MA). Part-time programs available. *Faculty:* 3 full-time (0 women), 4 part-time/adjunct (0 women). *Students:* 13 full-time (0 women), 32 part-time (8 women); includes 5 minority (1 Black or African American, non-Hispanic/Latino; 3 Asian, non-Hispanic/Latino; 1 Two or more races, non-Hispanic/Latino). Average age 30. In 2014, 9 master's awarded. *Degree requirements:* For master's, thesis or alternative. *Entrance requirements:* Additional exam requirements/recommendations for international students: Required—TOEFL (minimum score 550 paper-based). *Application deadline:* For fall admission, 8/1 priority date for domestic students, 8/1 for international students; for spring admission, 12/15 for domestic and international students. Applications are processed on a rolling basis. Application fee: $25. *Financial support:* Career-related internships or fieldwork and scholarships/grants available. Support available to part-time students. Financial award application deadline: 3/1; financial award applicants required to submit FAFSA. *Faculty research:* Baptist theology, American church history. *Unit head:* Dr. Ernest Schmidt, Interim President, 515-964-0601, E-mail: schmidte@faith.edu. *Application contact:* Stacy Lansdown, Admissions Administrative Assistant, 888-FAITH4U, Fax: 515-964-1638, E-mail: admissions@faith.edu. Website: http://www.faith.edu/

Faulkner University, College of Biblical Studies, Montgomery, AL 36109-3398. Offers ministry (MABS); missions (MABS); New Testament (MABS); Old Testament (MABS); youth and family ministry (MABS).

Fordham University, Graduate School of Religion and Religious Education, New York, NY 10458. Offers pastoral counseling and spiritual care (MA); pastoral ministry/spirituality/pastoral counseling (D Min); religion and religious education (MA); religious education (MS, PhD, PD); spiritual direction (Certificate). Part-time programs available. Terminal master's awarded for partial completion of doctoral program. *Degree requirements:* For master's, research paper; for doctorate, comprehensive exam, thesis/dissertation. *Entrance requirements:* For doctorate, MAT. Electronic applications accepted. *Expenses:* Contact institution. *Faculty research:* Spirituality and spiritual direction, pastoral care and counseling, adult family and community, growth and young adult.

Freed-Hardeman University, School of Biblical Studies, Program in Ministry, Henderson, TN 38340-2399. Offers M Min. Part-time programs available. *Degree requirements:* For master's, comprehensive exam, internship. *Entrance requirements:* For master's, GRE General Test or MAT. Additional exam requirements/recommendations for international students: Required—TOEFL (minimum score 500 paper-based).

Fresno Pacific University, Biblical Seminary, Program in Christian Ministry, Fresno, CA 93702-4709. Offers MA. Part-time programs available. *Entrance requirements:* For master's, minimum GPA of 2.5. Additional exam requirements/recommendations for international students: Required—TOEFL (minimum score 550 paper-based). *Application deadline:* For fall admission, 8/1 for domestic students; for spring admission, 12/1 for domestic students. Application fee: $35. *Expenses:* Expenses: $430 per unit. *Financial support:* Institutionally sponsored loans and scholarships/grants available. Support available to part-time students. Financial award application deadline: 5/1. *Unit head:* Dr. Brian Ross, Director, 559-453-2325, E-mail: brian.ross@fresno.edu. *Application contact:* Amanda Krum-Stovall, Director of Graduate Admissions, 559-453-2016, E-mail: amanda.krum-stovall@fresno.edu. Website: http://www.fresno.edu/programs-majors/biblical-seminary/christian-ministry

Fuller Theological Seminary, Graduate Programs, Pasadena, CA 91182. Offers Christian leadership (MACL); clinical psychology (PhD, Psy D); family studies (MA); global leadership (MA); global ministries (D Min); global ministries (Korean language) (D Min); intercultural studies (MA, Th M, PhD); intercultural studies (Korean language) (MA); marital and family therapy (MS); marriage and family enrichment (Certificate); ministry (M Div, D Min); missiology (D Miss); missiology (Korean language) (Th M); theology (MA, Th M, PhD), including evangelism (MA), family life education (MA), pastoral ministry (MA), recovery ministry (MA), worship music ministry (MA), worship, theology, and the arts (MA), youth, family, and culture (MA); theology and ministry (MA).

Gannon University, School of Graduate Studies, College of Humanities, Education, and Social Sciences, School of Humanities, Program in Pastoral Studies, Erie, PA 16541-0001. Offers pastoral studies (MA); theological studies (Certificate). Part-time and evening/weekend programs available. *Degree requirements:* For master's, comprehensive exam, thesis or alternative, research project, internship, written evaluation. *Entrance requirements:* For master's, GRE, interview; minimum 10 credits of course work in philosophy, religious studies, or theology. Additional exam requirements/

recommendations for international students: Required—TOEFL (minimum score 79 iBT). Electronic applications accepted.

Gardner-Webb University, School of Divinity, Boiling Springs, NC 28017. Offers biblical studies (M Div); Christian education and formation (M Div); intercultural studies (M Div); ministry (D Min); missiology (M Div); pastoral care and counseling (M Div); pastoral care and counseling/member care for missionaries (D Min); pastoral studies (M Div); M Div/MA; M Div/MBA. *Accreditation:* ACIPE; ATS. Part-time programs available. *Faculty:* 10 full-time (2 women), 5 part-time/adjunct (1 woman). *Students:* 151 full-time (82 women), 76 part-time (22 women); includes 106 minority (92 Black or African American, non-Hispanic/Latino; 7 Asian, non-Hispanic/Latino; 7 Hispanic/Latino). Average age 41. 110 applicants, 53% accepted, 58 enrolled. *Entrance requirements:* For master's, minimum GPA of 2.6; for doctorate, minimum GPA of 2.75. Additional exam requirements/recommendations for international students: Required— TOEFL (minimum score 500 paper-based; 61 iBT). *Application deadline:* Applications are processed on a rolling basis. Application fee: $40. Electronic applications accepted. *Expenses:* Expenses: Contact institution. *Financial support:* Fellowships, institutionally sponsored loans, and unspecified assistantships available. Support available to part-time students. Financial award application deadline: 5/15. *Faculty research:* Jewish-Christian dialogue, Islam. *Unit head:* Dr. Robert W. Canoy, Sr., Dean, 704-406-4400, Fax: 704-406-3935, E-mail: rcanoy@gardner-webb.edu. *Application contact:* Kheresa Harmon, Director of Admissions, 704-406-3205, Fax: 704-406-3895, E-mail: kharmon@gardner-webb.edu.
Website: http://gardner-webb.edu/academic-programs-and-resources/colleges-and-schools/divinity/index

Garrett-Evangelical Theological Seminary, Graduate and Professional Programs, Evanston, IL 60201-3298. Offers Bible and culture (PhD); Christian education (MA); Christian education and congregational studies (PhD); contemporary theology and culture (PhD); divinity (M Div); ethics, church, and society (MA); liturgical studies (PhD); ministry (D Min); music ministry (MA); pastoral care and counseling (MA); pastoral theology, personality, and culture (PhD); spiritual formation and evangelism (MA); theological studies (MTS); M Div/MSW. M Div/MSW offered jointly with Loyola University Chicago. *Accreditation:* ACIPE; ATS (one or more programs are accredited). Part-time programs available. *Degree requirements:* For master's, thesis (for some programs); for doctorate, thesis/dissertation. *Entrance requirements:* For doctorate, GRE (PhD). Additional exam requirements/recommendations for international students: Required—TOEFL (minimum score 560 paper-based). Electronic applications accepted.

General Theological Seminary, Graduate and Professional Programs, New York, NY 10011-4977. Offers Anglican studies (STM, Th D, Certificate); ascetical theology (Certificate); biblical studies (Certificate); congregational development (Certificate); divinity (M Div); historical and theological studies (Certificate); spiritual direction (MASD, STM, Certificate); theology (MA). *Accreditation:* ACIPE; ATS. Part-time and evening/weekend programs available. Terminal master's awarded for partial completion of doctoral program. *Degree requirements:* For master's, thesis; for doctorate, 2 foreign languages, thesis/dissertation. *Entrance requirements:* For master's, GRE General Test; for doctorate, GRE, M Div or MA. Additional exam requirements/recommendations for international students: Required—TOEFL. *Faculty research:* Liturgy, New Testament, ethics, history, ecumenical relations.

George Fox University, George Fox Evangelical Seminary, Newberg, OR 97132-2697. Offers Biblical studies (M Div); Christian earthkeeping (M Div); Christian history and theology (M Div); clinical pastoral education and hospital chaplaincy (M Div); leadership and spiritual formation (D Min); military chaplaincy (M Div); ministry leadership (MA); pastoral studies (M Div); semiotics and future studies (M Div); spiritual formation (MA, Certificate); spiritual formation and discipleship (M Div); theological studies (MA). *Accreditation:* ACIPE; ATS. Part-time and evening/weekend programs available. Postbaccalaureate distance learning degree programs offered (minimal on-campus study). *Degree requirements:* For master's, thesis optional, internship; for doctorate, comprehensive exam (for some programs), thesis/dissertation, internship. *Entrance requirements:* For master's, resume, three references (one pastoral, one academic or professional, one personal), one official transcript from each college or university attended; for doctorate, resume, 3 references (1 professional, 1 academic, 1 personal), one official transcript from each college or university attended. Additional exam requirements/recommendations for international students: Required—TOEFL (minimum score 577 paper-based; 90 iBT). Electronic applications accepted. *Expenses:* Contact institution.

Georgia Christian University, School of Divinity, Atlanta, GA 30360. Offers Christian education (MA); divinity (M Div); ministry (D Min); mission studies and world Christianity (MA); theological studies (MA).

Georgian Court University, School of Arts and Sciences, Lakewood, NJ 08701-2697. Offers applied behavior analysis (MA); Catholic school leadership (Certificate); clinical mental health counseling (MA); holistic health studies (MA, Certificate); homeland security (MS); parish administration (Certificate); pastoral ministry (Certificate); professional counseling (Certificate); religious education (Certificate); school psychology (MA, Certificate); theology (MA, Certificate). Part-time and evening/weekend programs available. *Faculty:* 19 full-time (9 women), 9 part-time/adjunct (4 women). *Students:* 87 full-time (74 women), 127 part-time (110 women); includes 47 minority (14 Black or African American, non-Hispanic/Latino; 2 Asian, non-Hispanic/Latino; 23 Hispanic/Latino; 8 Two or more races, non-Hispanic/Latino). Average age 34. In 2014, 68 master's, 11 other advanced degrees awarded. *Degree requirements:* For master's, comprehensive exam (for some programs), thesis (for some programs). *Entrance requirements:* For master's, GRE, MAT, or NTE/PRAXIS, 3 letters of recommendation. Additional exam requirements/recommendations for international students: Required— TOEFL (minimum score 550 paper-based). *Application deadline:* For fall admission, 8/1 priority date for domestic students, 4/1 for international students; for spring admission, 1/1 priority date for domestic students, 7/1 for international students. Applications are processed on a rolling basis. Application fee: $40. Electronic applications accepted. *Expenses:* Tuition: Full-time $19,752; part-time $823 per credit. *Required fees:* $948; $243 per semester hour. Tuition and fees vary according to campus/location and program. *Financial support:* Scholarships/grants, health care benefits, and unspecified assistantships available. Financial award application deadline: 4/15; financial award applicants required to submit FAFSA. *Unit head:* Dr. Rita Kipp, Dean, 732-987-2493, Fax: 732-987-2007, E-mail: rkipp@georgian.edu. *Application contact:* Patrick Givens, Interim Director of Enrollment Management, 732-987-2736, Fax: 732-987-2084, E-mail: graduateadmissions@georgian.edu.
Website: http://www.georgian.edu/arts_sciences/index.htm

Golden Gate Baptist Theological Seminary, Graduate and Professional Programs, Mill Valley, CA 94941-3197. Offers divinity (M Div); early childhood education (Certificate); education leadership (MAEL, Diploma); ministry (D Min); theological studies (MTS); theology (Th M); youth ministry (Certificate). *Accreditation:* ACIPE; ATS (one or more programs are accredited). Part-time and evening/weekend programs available. *Degree requirements:* For master's, thesis (for some programs); for doctorate, 2 foreign languages, thesis/dissertation. *Entrance requirements:* For doctorate, MAT. Additional exam requirements/recommendations for international students: Required— TOEFL (minimum score 550 paper-based). Electronic applications accepted.

Gordon-Conwell Theological Seminary, Graduate and Professional Programs, South Hamilton, MA 01982. Offers Biblical languages (MABL); church history (MACH); counseling (MACO); ministry (D Min); missions/evangelism (MAME); New Testament (MANT); Old Testament (MAOT); religion (MAR); theology (M Div, MATH, Th M, Th D). *Accreditation:* ACIPE; ATS (one or more programs are accredited). Part-time and evening/weekend programs available. *Degree requirements:* For master's, one foreign language, thesis optional; for doctorate, 2 foreign languages, thesis/dissertation. *Entrance requirements:* For master's, minimum GPA of 2.5; for doctorate, minimum GPA of 3.0.

Grace Theological Seminary, Graduate and Professional Programs, Winona Lake, IN 46590-9907. Offers biblical studies (Certificate); camp administration (MA); counseling (M Div); exegetical studies (MA); intercultural studies (M Div, MA); local church studies (MA); pastoral studies (M Div); theological studies (MA); theology (D Min, Diploma). *Accreditation:* ATS. Part-time programs available. Postbaccalaureate distance learning degree programs offered (no on-campus study). *Degree requirements:* For master's, thesis optional; for doctorate, 2 foreign languages, thesis/dissertation. *Entrance requirements:* For master's, MAT, minimum GPA of 2.5. Electronic applications accepted. *Faculty research:* Biblical theology, language, and church ministries.

Grace University, College of Graduate Studies, Counseling Program, Omaha, NE 68108. Offers MA. *Entrance requirements:* For master's, minimum undergraduate GPA of 3.0.

Grand Rapids Theological Seminary of Cornerstone University, Graduate Programs, Grand Rapids, MI 49525-5897. Offers biblical counseling (MA); Biblical counseling (M Div); chaplaincy (M Div); Christian education (M Div, MA); intercultural studies (M Div, MA); New Testament (MA, Th M); Old Testament (MA, Th M); pastoral studies (M Div); systematic theology (MA); theology (Th M). *Accreditation:* ATS. Part-time programs available. Postbaccalaureate distance learning degree programs offered (minimal on-campus study). *Entrance requirements:* Additional exam requirements/recommendations for international students: Required—TOEFL (minimum score 577 paper-based; 90 iBT). Electronic applications accepted.

Greenville College, Program in Leadership and Ministry, Greenville, IL 62246-0159. Offers MA. Part-time programs available. *Degree requirements:* For master's, 6 hours of research/practicum in applied ministry. *Entrance requirements:* For master's, 1 year of work experience in Christian ministry, interview. Additional exam requirements/recommendations for international students: Required—TOEFL (minimum score 525 paper-based). Electronic applications accepted.

Hampton University, School of Education and Human Development, Program in Counseling, Hampton, VA 23668. Offers college student development (MA); community agency counseling (MA); pastoral counseling (MA); school counseling (MA). *Accreditation:* NCATE. Part-time and evening/weekend programs available. Postbaccalaureate distance learning degree programs offered (minimal on-campus study). *Faculty:* 4 full-time (3 women), 2 part-time/adjunct (1 woman). *Students:* 21 full-time (15 women), 23 part-time (17 women); includes 43 minority (39 Black or African American, non-Hispanic/Latino; 2 American Indian or Alaska Native, non-Hispanic/Latino; 1 Asian, non-Hispanic/Latino; 1 Hispanic/Latino), 1 international. Average age 26. 19 applicants, 89% accepted, 12 enrolled. In 2014, 12 master's awarded. *Degree requirements:* For master's, comprehensive exam; for doctorate, comprehensive exam, thesis/dissertation. *Entrance requirements:* For master's, GRE General Test, TOEFL or IELTS, Personal statement and two letters of recommendation; for doctorate, GRE, Personal statement, writing sample, and three letters of recommendation; for Ed S, Personal statement and two letters of recommendation. Additional exam requirements/recommendations for international students: Required—TOEFL (minimum score 525 paper-based), IELTS (minimum score 6.5). *Application deadline:* For fall admission, 6/1 priority date for domestic students, 4/1 priority date for international students; for winter admission, 9/1 priority date for international students; for spring admission, 11/1 priority date for domestic students, 9/1 for international students; for summer admission, 4/1 priority date for domestic students, 2/1 priority date for international students. Applications are processed on a rolling basis. Application fee: $35. Electronic applications accepted. *Expenses: Tuition:* Full-time $20,526; part-time $522 per credit. *Required fees:* $100. *Financial support:* Fellowships, research assistantships, teaching assistantships, career-related internships or fieldwork, Federal Work-Study, institutionally sponsored loans, and scholarships/grants available. Support available to part-time students. Financial award application deadline: 6/30; financial award applicants required to submit FAFSA. *Faculty research:* Personality development, temperament, post-traumatic stress disorder, continuum of normal to abnormal personality. *Unit head:* Dr. Spencer R. Baker, Chair, 757-637-2232, E-mail: spencer.baker@hamptonu.edu.
Website: http://edhd.hamptonu.edu/counseling/

Harding School of Theology, Graduate Programs, Memphis, TN 38117-5499. Offers Christian ministry (MA); counseling (MA); ministry (M Div, D Min); religion (MA). *Accreditation:* ATS. Part-time programs available. Postbaccalaureate distance learning degree programs offered (minimal on-campus study). *Degree requirements:* For master's, variable foreign language requirement, thesis (for some programs); for doctorate, one foreign language, thesis/dissertation. *Entrance requirements:* For master's, minimum GPA of 2.7; for doctorate, minimum GPA of 3.0. Additional exam requirements/recommendations for international students: Required—TOEFL (minimum score 550 paper-based; 79 iBT). Electronic applications accepted.

Harding University, College of Bible and Ministry, Master of Ministry Program, Searcy, AR 72149-0001. Offers M Min. Part-time and evening/weekend programs available. Postbaccalaureate distance learning degree programs offered. *Faculty:* 14 part-time/adjunct (1 woman). *Students:* 19 part-time (1 woman); includes 2 minority (both Black or African American, non-Hispanic/Latino). Average age 39. 3 applicants, 100% accepted, 3 enrolled. In 2014, 12 master's awarded. *Degree requirements:* For master's, 3 practica (1 hour each), portfolio, capstone project. *Entrance requirements:* For master's, 16 hours of course work in Bible, minimum GPA of 2.75. *Application deadline:* For fall admission, 8/1 priority date for domestic and international students; for spring admission, 12/1 priority date for domestic students, 12/15 priority date for international students. Applications are processed on a rolling basis. Application fee: $25. Electronic applications accepted. *Expenses: Tuition:* Full-time $12,096; part-time $672 per credit hour. *Required fees:* $432; $24 per credit hour. Tuition and fees vary according to course load and degree level. *Financial support:* In 2014–15, 18 students received support. Scholarships/grants and unspecified assistantships available. *Unit head:* Dr. Bill Richardson, Director/Associate Professor, 501-279-4252, Fax: 501-279-4081, E-mail: mmin@harding.edu. *Application contact:* Amy Warren, Information Contact, 501-279-4252, E-mail: awarren3@harding.edu.

Hardin-Simmons University, Graduate School, Logsdon School of Theology, Logsdon Seminary, Seminary Program in Family Ministry, Abilene, TX 79698-0001. Offers MA. Part-time programs available. *Faculty:* 4 full-time (1 woman). *Students:* 16 full-time (9 women), 9 part-time (6 women); includes 6 minority (1 Black or African American, non-Hispanic/Latino; 1 Asian, non-Hispanic/Latino; 4 Hispanic/Latino), 2 international. Average age 35. In 2014, 4 master's awarded. *Degree requirements:* For master's, comprehensive exam, clinical experience, project. *Entrance requirements:* For master's,

minimum undergraduate GPA of 3.0 in major, 2.7 overall; 6 hours each of course work in psychology and Old and New Testament; interview; writing sample; references. Additional exam requirements/recommendations for international students: Required—TOEFL (minimum score 555 paper-based; 75 iBT). *Application deadline:* For fall admission, 8/15 priority date for domestic students, 4/1 for international students; for spring admission, 1/5 priority date for domestic students, 9/1 for international students. Applications are processed on a rolling basis. Application fee: $50. *Expenses: Tuition:* Full-time $12,060; part-time $670 per credit hour. *Required fees:* $325; $110 per semester. Tuition and fees vary according to program. *Financial support:* In 2014–15, 28 students received support. Fellowships, career-related internships or fieldwork, and scholarships/grants available. Support available to part-time students. Financial award application deadline: 6/30; financial award applicants required to submit FAFSA. *Unit head:* Dr. Randall Maurer, Director, 325-670-1599, Fax: 325-670-1406, E-mail: rmaurer@hsutx.edu. *Application contact:* Dr. Nancy Kucinski, Dean of Graduate Studies, 325-670-1298, Fax: 325-670-1564, E-mail: gradoff@hsutx.edu.
Website: http://www.logsdonseminary.org/index.php/academics/mafm

Hardin-Simmons University, Graduate School, Logsdon School of Theology, Logsdon Seminary, Seminary Program in Ministry, Abilene, TX 79698-0001. Offers D Min. Part-time programs available. *Faculty:* 6 full-time (0 women). *Students:* 34 part-time (2 women); includes 4 minority (3 Black or African American, non-Hispanic/Latino; 1 Hispanic/Latino). Average age 45. In 2014, 2 doctorates awarded. *Degree requirements:* For doctorate, ministry project. *Entrance requirements:* For doctorate, GRE or MAT, M Div or equivalent, minimum graduate GPA of 3.0, minimum 3 years' ministry experience, active current ministry involvement, interview, 4 letters of recommendation, church endorsement. *Application deadline:* For fall admission, 4/30 for domestic students. Application fee: $50. *Expenses: Tuition:* Full-time $12,060; part-time $670 per credit hour. *Required fees:* $325; $110 per semester. Tuition and fees vary according to program. *Financial support:* In 2014–15, 20 students received support. Application deadline: 6/30; applicants required to submit FAFSA. *Unit head:* Dr. Larry Baker, Director, 325-671-2110, Fax: 325-670-1406, E-mail: lbaker@hsutx.edu. *Application contact:* Dr. Nancy Kucinski, Dean of Graduate Studies, 325-670-1298, Fax: 325-670-1564, E-mail: gradoff@hsutx.edu.
Website: http://www.logsdonseminary.org/index.php/academics/doctor-of-ministry

Hartford Seminary, Graduate Programs, Hartford, CT 06105-2279. Offers Islamic studies (MA); ministry (D Min); religious studies (MA); spirituality (Certificate). *Accreditation:* ATS (one or more programs are accredited). Part-time and evening/weekend programs available. Postbaccalaureate distance learning degree programs offered (no on-campus study). *Degree requirements:* For master's, thesis optional, oral exam; for doctorate, thesis/dissertation, oral exam. *Entrance requirements:* For doctorate, experience in ministry, M Div. Additional exam requirements/recommendations for international students: Required—TOEFL (minimum score 550 paper-based; 80 iBT). *Faculty research:* Liturgy and social justice, professional leadership in ministry, congregational studies, Christian-Muslim relations, American religion.

Heritage Christian University, Graduate Programs, Florence, AL 35630. Offers counseling (MM); Greek (MA); ministry (MM); New Testament (MA). *Degree requirements:* For master's, practicum (MM), major research paper (MA). *Entrance requirements:* For master's, MAT or GRE, bachelor's degree in Bible from an accredited college or university, minimum GPA of 2.75, 3 letters of recommendation.

Hillsdale Free Will Baptist College, Department of Bible Studies, Moore, OK 73160-1208. Offers ministry (MA). Part-time and evening/weekend programs available. *Degree requirements:* For master's, thesis optional. *Entrance requirements:* Additional exam requirements/recommendations for international students: Recommended—TOEFL (minimum score 500 paper-based).

Holmes Institute, Graduate Program, Burbank, CA 91505. Offers consciousness studies (MS). Postbaccalaureate distance learning degree programs offered. *Faculty:* 50. *Students:* 100 part-time (72 women); includes 4 minority (all Black or African American, non-Hispanic/Latino). *Degree requirements:* For master's, comprehensive exam, 2 spiritual retreats per year, internship (1 per term), 2 spiritual conferences. *Entrance requirements:* For master's, 3 letters of recommendation, interview, background check, official transcripts of an accredited bachelor's degree. Additional exam requirements/recommendations for international students: Required—TOEFL. *Application deadline:* Applications are processed on a rolling basis. Application fee: $200. *Unit head:* Rev. Dr. Lynn Connolly, Director of Education, 720-279-8990, Fax: 303-526-0913, E-mail: lconnolly@religiousscience.org. *Application contact:* Maureen Thurston, Administrative Registrar, 720-279-8992, Fax: 303-526-0913, E-mail: mthurston@religiousscience.org.
Website: http://www.holmesinstitute.org

Holy Names University, Graduate Division, Department of Counseling Psychology, Oakland, CA 94619-1699. Offers counseling psychology (MA); forensic psychology (MA, Certificate); pastoral counseling (MA, Certificate). Part-time and evening/weekend programs available. *Faculty:* 15. *Students:* 43 full-time (42 women), 40 part-time (33 women); includes 60 minority (33 Black or African American, non-Hispanic/Latino; 4 Asian, non-Hispanic/Latino; 19 Hispanic/Latino; 3 Native Hawaiian or other Pacific Islander, non-Hispanic/Latino; 1 Two or more races, non-Hispanic/Latino). Average age 31. 42 applicants, 62% accepted, 15 enrolled. In 2014, 39 master's, 18 other advanced degrees awarded. *Degree requirements:* For master's, comprehensive paper, seminars. *Entrance requirements:* For master's, minimum undergraduate GPA of 2.6 overall, 3.0 in major. Additional exam requirements/recommendations for international students: Required—TOEFL (minimum score 550 paper-based; 79 iBT). *Application deadline:* For fall admission, 8/1 priority date for domestic students, 7/15 for international students; for spring admission, 12/1 priority date for domestic students, 12/1 for international students; for summer admission, 5/1 priority date for domestic students, 5/1 for international students. Applications are processed on a rolling basis. Application fee: $65. Electronic applications accepted. Application fee is waived when completed online. *Financial support:* Career-related internships or fieldwork, Federal Work-Study, scholarships/grants, and unspecified assistantships available. Support available to part-time students. Financial award application deadline: 3/2; financial award applicants required to submit FAFSA. *Faculty research:* Cognitive psychology, anger management, grief and grief counseling, post-modernism and psychotherapy, spirituality and psychology. *Unit head:* Dr. Helen Shoemaker, Program Director, 510-436-1543, E-mail: shoemaker@hnu.edu. *Application contact:* 800-430-1321, Fax: 510-436-1325, E-mail: graduateadmissions@hnu.edu.

Holy Names University, Graduate Division, Program in Pastoral Ministries, Oakland, CA 94619-1699. Offers MA, Certificate. Part-time programs available. Postbaccalaureate distance learning degree programs offered (no on-campus study). In 2014, 2 other advanced degrees awarded. *Degree requirements:* For master's, ministry project. *Entrance requirements:* Additional exam requirements/recommendations for international students: Required—TOEFL (minimum score 550 paper-based; 79 iBT). *Application deadline:* For fall admission, 8/1 priority date for domestic and international students; for spring admission, 12/1 priority date for domestic and international students; for summer admission, 5/1 priority date for domestic students, 5/1 for international students. Application fee: $0. *Financial support:* Application deadline: 3/2; applicants required to submit FAFSA. *Faculty research:* Ethics, cross-cultural management, faith development through liturgy, multi-cultural community building. *Unit head:* Dr. Robert Lassalle-Klein, Director, 510-436-1074. *Application contact:* Graduate Admissions Office, 800-430-1321, Fax: 510-436-1325, E-mail: graduateadmissions@hnu.edu.

Houston Baptist University, College of Education and Behavioral Sciences, Program in Christian Counseling, Houston, TX 77074-3298. Offers MACC. Part-time and evening/weekend programs available. *Faculty:* 5 full-time (4 women), 6 part-time/adjunct (all women). *Students:* 8 full-time (7 women), 21 part-time (18 women); includes 20 minority (8 Black or African American, non-Hispanic/Latino; 1 Asian, non-Hispanic/Latino; 11 Hispanic/Latino), 1 international. Average age 33. 48 applicants, 19% accepted, 7 enrolled. In 2014, 1 master's awarded. *Degree requirements:* For master's, comprehensive exam. *Entrance requirements:* For master's, GRE, official transcripts, two recommendation forms, resume, baccalaureate degree in psychology or equivalent, interview. Additional exam requirements/recommendations for international students: Required—TOEFL. *Application deadline:* For fall admission, 8/1 for domestic students, 6/1 for international students; for winter admission, 10/1 for domestic and international students; for spring admission, 12/1 for domestic students, 10/1 for international students; for summer admission, 5/1 for domestic students, 3/1 for international students. Applications are processed on a rolling basis. Application fee: $0. Electronic applications accepted. *Expenses:* Expenses: Contact institution. *Financial support:* In 2014–15, 2 students received support. Federal Work-Study and scholarships/grants available. Support available to part-time students. Financial award application deadline: 4/1; financial award applicants required to submit FAFSA. *Faculty research:* Psychology - church collaboration, trauma recovery. *Unit head:* Dr. Stephanie Ellis, Chair, 281-649-3608, Fax: 281-649-3361, E-mail: sellis@hbu.edu. *Application contact:* Grace Rosales, Administrative Assistant to the Dean, 281-649-3131, E-mail: grosales@hbu.edu.
Website: http://www.hbu.edu/macc

Houston Graduate School of Theology, Graduate Programs, Houston, TX 77092. Offers counseling (MA); pastoral ministry (M Div, D Min); theology (MA). *Accreditation:* ATS (one or more programs are accredited). Part-time and evening/weekend programs available. *Degree requirements:* For master's, thesis (for some programs); for doctorate, thesis/dissertation. *Entrance requirements:* For doctorate, GRE General Test or MAT, M Div or equivalent. Additional exam requirements/recommendations for international students: Required—TOEFL (minimum score 550 paper-based). *Faculty research:* Hermeneutics, spirituality, religion of Eastern Europe.

Howard Payne University, Program in Youth Ministry, Brownwood, TX 76801-2715. Offers MA. Part-time programs available. *Faculty:* 5 full-time (1 woman), 2 part-time/adjunct (1 woman). *Students:* 5 full-time (1 woman), 3 part-time (2 women); includes 2 minority (1 Black or African American, non-Hispanic/Latino; 1 Hispanic/Latino). Average age 27. In 2014, 2 master's awarded. *Degree requirements:* For master's, three 2-hour internships/mentorships. *Entrance requirements:* For master's, undergraduate degree from accredited university; leveling courses (for students who do not have undergraduate coursework in Old Testament, New Testament, and youth ministry). Additional exam requirements/recommendations for international students: Required—TOEFL (minimum score 79 iBT). *Application deadline:* For fall admission, 7/1 for domestic students; for spring admission, 12/1 for domestic students. Applications are processed on a rolling basis. Application fee: $0. Electronic applications accepted. *Financial support:* In 2014–15, 13 students received support. Application deadline: 3/15; applicants required to submit FAFSA. *Unit head:* Dr. Gary Gramling, Director, 325-649-8404, E-mail: ggramling@hputx.edu. *Application contact:* Leanne Bledsoe, Administrative Assistant for Christian Studies Graduate Programs, 325-649-8039, E-mail: lbledsoe@hputx.edu.
Website: http://www.hputx.edu/academics/schools/school-of-christian-studies/graduate-programs/ma-youth-ministry/

Huntington University, Graduate School, Huntington, IN 46750-1299. Offers counseling (MA), including licensed mental health counselor; early adolescent education (M Ed); education (M Ed); global missions leadership (MA); global youth ministry (MA); TESOL education (M Ed); youth ministry leadership (MA). Part-time programs available. Postbaccalaureate distance learning degree programs offered (minimal on-campus study). *Faculty:* 15 full-time (6 women), 17 part-time/adjunct (8 women). *Students:* 37 full-time (26 women), 94 part-time (62 women). 170 applicants, 47% accepted, 73 enrolled. In 2014, 25 master's awarded. *Degree requirements:* For master's, comprehensive exam (for some programs), thesis (for some programs). *Entrance requirements:* For master's, GRE (for counseling and education students only); for doctorate, GRE (for occupational therapy students). Additional exam requirements/recommendations for international students: Required—TOEFL (minimum score 85 iBT), IELTS (minimum score 6.5). *Application deadline:* For fall admission, 7/1 for domestic students, 5/1 for international students; for winter admission, 10/1 for domestic students, 9/1 for international students; for spring admission, 11/30 for domestic students, 10/30 for international students. Applications are processed on a rolling basis. Application fee: $30. Electronic applications accepted. *Expenses: Tuition:* Full-time $7965; part-time $531 per credit hour. Tuition and fees vary according to degree level and program. *Financial support:* In 2014–15, 30 students received support. Scholarships/grants and unspecified assistantships available. Support available to part-time students. Financial award application deadline: 8/1; financial award applicants required to submit FAFSA. *Faculty research:* Leadership, educational technology trends, evangelism, youth ministry, mental health. *Unit head:* Ann C. McPherren, EdD, VP for Strategy and Graduate and Professional Programs, 260-359-4225, Fax: 260-359-4126, E-mail: amcpherren@huntington.edu. *Application contact:* Becca Cline, Graduate Admissions Counselor, 260-359-4111, Fax: 260-359-4126, E-mail: bcline@huntington.edu.
Website: http://www.huntington.edu/graduate

Husson University, Graduate Programs in Counseling and Human Relations, Bangor, ME 04401-2999. Offers clinical mental health counseling (MS); human relations (MS); pastoral counseling (MS); school counseling (MS). Part-time and evening/weekend programs available. *Faculty:* 3 full-time (2 women), 2 part-time/adjunct (both women). *Students:* 39 full-time (33 women), 25 part-time (20 women); includes 3 minority (2 Black or African American, non-Hispanic/Latino; 1 Two or more races, non-Hispanic/Latino), 2 international. Average age 34. 55 applicants, 69% accepted, 32 enrolled. In 2014, 19 master's awarded. *Degree requirements:* For master's, comprehensive exam (for some programs), thesis optional. *Entrance requirements:* For master's, GRE or MAT, BS with minimum GPA of 3.0, letters of recommendation, interview. Additional exam requirements/recommendations for international students: Required—TOEFL (minimum score 550 paper-based; 80 iBT). *Application deadline:* For fall admission, 2/1 for domestic students. Applications are processed on a rolling basis. Application fee: $50. Electronic applications accepted. *Expenses:* Expenses: Contact institution. *Financial support:* In 2014–15, 1 student received support. Federal Work-Study, scholarships/grants, and unspecified assistantships available. Financial award application deadline: 4/15; financial award applicants required to submit FAFSA. *Faculty research:* Challenges and rewards of counseling practice in rural, small town and neighborhood settings. *Unit head:* Dr. Deborah Drew, Director, Graduate Counseling Programs, 207-992-4912, Fax: 207-992-4952, E-mail: drewd@husson.edu. *Application contact:* Kristen

Card, Director of Graduate Admissions, 207-404-5660, Fax: 207-941-7935, E-mail: cardk@husson.edu. Website: http://www.husson.edu/human-relations

Iliff School of Theology, Graduate and Professional Programs, Denver, CO 80210-4798. Offers biblical studies (MA); church history (MA); religion (MA); religion and social change (MA); specialized ministry (MASM), including justice and peace, pastoral theology and care, religions leadership; theology (M Div, MTS, D Min, PhD), including Biblical studies (PhD), religion and psychological studies (PhD), religion and social change (PhD), theology, philosophy and culture (PhD); theology/ethics (MA). PhD offered jointly with University of Denver. *Accreditation:* ACIPE; ATS. Part-time and evening/weekend programs available. *Degree requirements:* For master's, one foreign language, thesis (for some programs); for doctorate, 2 foreign languages, comprehensive exam, thesis/dissertation. *Entrance requirements:* For master's, minimum GPA of 3.0, writing sample, references; for doctorate, GRE General Test, minimum GPA of 3.0, writing sample, letters of recommendation. Additional exam requirements/recommendations for international students: Required—TOEFL (minimum score 550 paper-based). Electronic applications accepted. *Faculty research:* Pastoral care, history, church music, contemporary church, biblical studies.

Indiana Wesleyan University, Graduate School, Wesley Seminary, Program in Ministry, Marion, IN 46953-4974. Offers children, youth and family ministry (MA); ministerial leadership (MA). Part-time programs available. Postbaccalaureate distance learning degree programs offered (minimal on-campus study). *Degree requirements:* For master's, one foreign language, capstone practicum and/or project. *Entrance requirements:* Additional exam requirements/recommendations for international students: Required—TOEFL. Electronic applications accepted. *Expenses:* Contact institution. *Faculty research:* History of worship innovation, history of New Testament afterlife traditions, second century mantanism, cross-cultural ministry, church health and growth, leadership in Christian organizations, managing change in the church, effective youth ministry, women in ministry, Biblical hermeneutics.

Inter American University of Puerto Rico, Metropolitan Campus, Graduate Programs, Program in Pastoral Theology, San Juan, PR 00919-1293. Offers PhD.

International Baptist College and Seminary, Program in Ministry, Chandler, AZ 85286. Offers M Min, D Min.

Judson University, Graduate Programs, Master of Leadership in Ministry Program, Elgin, IL 60123-1498. Offers MLM. Evening/weekend programs available. Postbaccalaureate distance learning degree programs offered (minimal on-campus study). *Faculty:* 3 full-time (1 woman), 5 part-time/adjunct (2 women). *Students:* 9 full-time (5 women); includes 4 minority (all Black or African American, non-Hispanic/Latino). Average age 36. *Degree requirements:* For master's, thesis or alternative. *Entrance requirements:* For master's, Prior ministry experience whether professionally or volunteer. An undergraduate degree in a ministry related field is preferred but not required. *Application deadline:* Applications are processed on a rolling basis. Application fee: $35. Electronic applications accepted. *Expenses:* Expenses: Contact institution. *Financial support:* In 2014–15, 3 students received support. Scholarships/grants available. Financial award application deadline: 10/31; financial award applicants required to submit FAFSA. *Faculty research:* Volunteer development, ministry team development, ministry with military teams, intergenerational leadership. *Unit head:* Dr. Keith Krispin, Jr., Director, 847-628-1057, E-mail: kkrispin@judsonu.edu. *Application contact:* Debbie Sanders, Assistant - Department of Christian Ministries, 847-628-1124, E-mail: deborah.sanders@judsonu.edu.
Website: http://www.judsonu.edu/Graduate/Master_of_Leadership_in_Ministry/Overview/

King's University, Graduate and Professional Programs, Southlake, TX 76092. Offers Biblical studies (Graduate Certificate); Christian ministry (Graduate Certificate); ministry (M Div, MPT, D Min).

Kingswood University, Program in Pastoral Theology, Sussex, NB E4E 5L2, Canada. Offers MA.

Knox Theological Seminary, Graduate Programs, Program in Ministry, Fort Lauderdale, FL 33308. Offers D Min. Part-time programs available. *Degree requirements:* For doctorate, thesis/dissertation. *Entrance requirements:* For doctorate, M Div or equivalent. Additional exam requirements/recommendations for international students: Required—TOEFL, TWE (minimum score 5).

Lancaster Bible College, Capital Bible Seminary, Lancaster, PA 17601. Offers biblical studies (MA, Certificate); Christian counseling and discipleship (MA, Certificate); ministry (MA); theology (M Div). *Accreditation:* ATS (one or more programs are accredited). Part-time and evening/weekend programs available. *Degree requirements:* For master's, 2 foreign languages, comprehensive exam, thesis (for some programs). *Entrance requirements:* For master's, GRE General Test, Greek exam for those with 2 years of Greek, proficiency exam in theology, previous course work in Biblical studies. Additional exam requirements/recommendations for international students: Required—TOEFL (minimum score 550 paper-based). *Faculty research:* Dead Sea Scrolls, spiritual gifts, hermeneutics.

Lancaster Bible College, Graduate School, Lancaster, PA 17601-5036. Offers adult ministries (MA); Bible (MA); children and family ministry (MA); church planting (MA); consulting resource teacher (M Ed); elementary school counseling (M Ed); leadership (PhD); leadership studies (MA); marriage and family counseling (MA); mental health counseling (MA); pastoral studies (MA); secondary school counseling (M Ed); sports ministry (MA); student ministry (MA); town and country ministry (MA). Part-time and evening/weekend programs available. *Degree requirements:* For master's, comprehensive exam (for some programs), thesis (for some programs). *Entrance requirements:* For master's, bachelor's degree with a minimum of 30 credits of course work in Bible, minimum undergraduate GPA of 3.0, interview. Additional exam requirements/recommendations for international students: Required—TOEFL.

La Salle University, School of Arts and Sciences, Program in Counseling and Family Therapy, Philadelphia, PA 19141-1199. Offers industrial/organizational management and human resources (MA); marriage and family therapy (MA); pastoral counseling (MA); professional clinical counseling (MA). *Accreditation:* APA. Part-time and evening/weekend programs available. *Degree requirements:* For master's, comprehensive exam. *Entrance requirements:* For master's, GRE or MAT (waived for applicants that already possess a master's degree in any field or for applicants that have a cumulative GPA of 3.5 or higher), minimum of 15 hours in psychology, counseling, or marriage and family studies; minimum GPA of 3.0; three letters of recommendation; personal statement; work experience (paid or volunteer). Additional exam requirements/recommendations for international students: Required—TOEFL. Electronic applications accepted. Application fee is waived when completed online. *Expenses:* Contact institution. *Faculty research:* Cognitive therapy, attribution theory, work habits, single parent families, treatment of addictions.

La Salle University, School of Arts and Sciences, Program in Theological, Pastoral and Liturgical Studies, Philadelphia, PA 19141-1199. Offers Catholic studies (Th D); Christian spirituality (Th D); church ministry (Th D, Certificate); founder's studies (Th D); liturgy (Certificate); pastoral care (Certificate); pastoral studies (MA); religion (MA); religious education (Certificate); theological studies (MA, Certificate). Application

deadline for Th D is November 1. Part-time and evening/weekend programs available. Postbaccalaureate distance learning degree programs offered (minimal on-campus study). *Degree requirements:* For doctorate, one foreign language, thesis/dissertation, evidence of basic reading and/or speaking knowledge of one of the following languages: a modern language other than English, Hebrew (biblical), Greek (biblical), or Latin (classical). *Entrance requirements:* For master's and Certificate, 26 credits in humanistic subjects, religion, theology, or ministry-related work; 2 letters of recommendation; statement of purpose; for doctorate, master's degree in theology, religious studies, pastoral care, or similar field from accredited institution of higher education; professional resume; personal statement of interest in a doctoral degree; 2 letters of recommendation; personal on-campus interview. Additional exam requirements/recommendations for international students: Required—TOEFL (minimum score 550 paper-based). Electronic applications accepted. Application fee is waived when completed online.

La Sierra University, School of Religion, Riverside, CA 92515. Offers pastoral ministry (M Div); religion (MA); religious education (MA); religious studies (MA). Part-time programs available. *Degree requirements:* For master's, one foreign language, thesis or alternative. *Entrance requirements:* For master's, GRE General Test, minimum GPA of 3.0.

Lee University, Program in Religion, Cleveland, TN 37320-3450. Offers biblical studies (MA); ministry studies (MA); theological studies (MA); youth and family ministry (MA). Part-time programs available. *Faculty:* 12 full-time (3 women), 3 part-time/adjunct (0 women). *Students:* 49 full-time (19 women), 34 part-time (8 women); includes 17 minority (11 Black or African American, non-Hispanic/Latino; 1 American Indian or Alaska Native, non-Hispanic/Latino; 1 Asian, non-Hispanic/Latino; 4 Hispanic/Latino), 3 international. Average age 36. 18 applicants, 67% accepted, 11 enrolled. In 2014, 18 master's awarded. *Degree requirements:* For master's, variable foreign language requirement, comprehensive exam (for some programs), thesis (for some programs). *Entrance requirements:* For master's, GRE or MAT (for biblical/theological studies only), minimum GPA of 3.0, 2 letters of recommendation, interview, official transcripts, essay. Additional exam requirements/recommendations for international students: Required—TOEFL (minimum score 450 paper-based). *Application deadline:* For fall admission, 4/1 priority date for domestic and international students; for spring admission, 10/1 priority date for domestic and international students. Applications are processed on a rolling basis. Application fee: $25. *Expenses: Tuition:* Full-time $10,260; part-time $570 per credit hour. *Required fees:* $35 per semester. One-time fee: $25. Tuition and fees vary according to program. *Financial support:* In 2014–15, 33 students received support, including 1 teaching assistantship (averaging $1,000 per year); career-related internships or fieldwork, Federal Work-Study, institutionally sponsored loans, scholarships/grants, and unspecified assistantships also available. Financial award application deadline: 3/1; financial award applicants required to submit FAFSA. *Faculty research:* Book of Isaiah, Gospel of Mark, school of St. Victor of the twelfth century, spirit Christology, people groups of New Testament and work. *Unit head:* Dr. Bob Bayles, Director, 423-614-8338, E-mail: bbayles@leeuniversity.edu. *Application contact:* Vicki Glasscock, Graduate Admissions Director, 423-614-8059, E-mail: vglasscock@leeuniversity.edu.
Website: http://www.leeuniversity.edu/academics/graduate/religion

Liberty University, Liberty Baptist Theological Seminary, Lynchburg, VA 24515. Offers Biblical studies (M Div, MAR, MTS, Th M); church history (M Div, MAR, MTS, Th M); discipleship (D Min); discipleship and church ministry (M Div, MAR, MCM); evangelism and church planting (M Div, MAR, MCM, D Min); global studies (M Div, MAR, MCM, MGS, Th M); homiletics (M Div, MAR, MCM, Th M, D Min); leadership (M Div, MAR, MCM, D Min); marketplace chaplaincy (M Div, MAR, MCM); ministry (D Min); pastoral counseling (M Div, MA, MAR, MCM, D Min), including addictions and recovery (MA), crisis response and trauma (MA), discipleship and church ministries (MA), leadership (MA), life coaching (MA), marketplace chaplaincy (MA), marriage and family (MA), military resilience (MA), pastoral counseling (MA), pastoral ministries (M Div, MAR, MCM); religious education (MRE); theology (M Div, MAR, MTS, Th M); theology and apologetics (PhD); worship (M Div, MAR, MCM, D Min). Part-time programs available. Postbaccalaureate distance learning degree programs offered (minimal on-campus study). *Students:* 2,865 full-time (781 women), 3,750 part-time (1,139 women); includes 1,742 minority (1,382 Black or African American, non-Hispanic/Latino; 22 American Indian or Alaska Native, non-Hispanic/Latino; 116 Asian, non-Hispanic/Latino; 105 Hispanic/Latino; 7 Native Hawaiian or other Pacific Islander, non-Hispanic/Latino; 110 Two or more races, non-Hispanic/Latino), 227 international. Average age 41. 5,446 applicants, 39% accepted, 1340 enrolled. In 2014, 1,969 master's, 126 doctorates, 75 other advanced degrees awarded. *Degree requirements:* For master's, 2 foreign languages, thesis (for some programs); for doctorate, 2 foreign languages, thesis/dissertation. *Entrance requirements:* For master's, minimum undergraduate GPA of 2.0; for doctorate, GRE General Test or MAT, minimum graduate GPA of 3.0. Additional exam requirements/recommendations for international students: Required—TOEFL (minimum score 600 paper-based; 100 iBT). *Application deadline:* For fall admission, 6/1 for domestic students; for spring admission, 11/1 for domestic students. Applications are processed on a rolling basis. Application fee: $50. Electronic applications accepted. *Expenses:* Expenses: Contact institution. *Financial support:* Teaching assistantships with tuition reimbursements, career-related internships or fieldwork, and Federal Work-Study available. Financial award applicants required to submit FAFSA. *Unit head:* Dr. David Hirschman, Acting Dean, 434-592-4140, Fax: 434-522-0415, E-mail: dwhirschman@liberty.edu. *Application contact:* Jay Bridge, Director of Graduate Admissions, 800-424-9595, Fax: 800-628-7977, E-mail: gradadmissions@liberty.edu. Website: http://www.liberty.edu/seminary/

Liberty University, School of Behavioral Sciences, Lynchburg, VA 24515. Offers advanced clinical skills (PhD); clinical mental health counseling (MA); counselor education and supervision (PhD); human services counseling (MA), including addictions and recovery, business, child and family law, Christian ministries, criminal justice, crisis response and trauma, executive leadership, health and wellness, life coaching, marriage and family, military resilience; marriage and family therapy (MA); military resilience (Certificate); professional counseling (MA). Part-time programs available. Postbaccalaureate distance learning degree programs offered (minimal on-campus study). *Students:* 3,009 full-time (2,433 women), 6,251 part-time (4,981 women); includes 2,959 minority (2,520 Black or African American, non-Hispanic/Latino; 49 American Indian or Alaska Native, non-Hispanic/Latino; 51 Asian, non-Hispanic/Latino; 97 Hispanic/Latino; 9 Native Hawaiian or other Pacific Islander, non-Hispanic/Latino; 233 Two or more races, non-Hispanic/Latino), 153 international. Average age 38. 6,645 applicants, 55% accepted, 2039 enrolled. In 2014, 2,410 master's, 11 doctorates, 2 other advanced degrees awarded. *Application deadline:* Applications are processed on a rolling basis. Application fee: $50. Electronic applications accepted. *Financial support:* Applicants required to submit FAFSA. *Unit head:* Dr. Ronald Hawkins, Founding Dean, School of Behavioral Sciences. *Application contact:* Jay Bridge, Director of Admissions, 800-424-9595, Fax: 800-628-7977, E-mail: gradadmissions@liberty.edu.

Liberty University, School of Music, Lynchburg, VA 24515. Offers ethnomusicology (MA); music and worship (MA); music education (MA); worship studies (MA, DWS), including church planting (MA), ethnomusicology (MA), leadership (MA). Part-time

programs available. Postbaccalaureate distance learning degree programs offered (minimal on-campus study). *Students:* 57 full-time (19 women), 180 part-time (75 women); includes 48 minority (34 Black or African American, non-Hispanic/Latino; 1 American Indian or Alaska Native, non-Hispanic/Latino; 2 Asian, non-Hispanic/Latino; 2 Hispanic/Latino; 1 Native Hawaiian or other Pacific Islander, non-Hispanic/Latino; 8 Two or more races, non-Hispanic/Latino), 12 international. Average age 35. 330 applicants, 32% accepted, 57 enrolled. In 2014, 41 master's awarded. *Entrance requirements:* For master's, minimum GPA of 3.0; interview; letter of recommendation; statement of purpose; bachelor's/master's degree in music, worship, or related field, or 5 years of experience. Additional exam requirements/recommendations for international students: Required—TOEFL (minimum score 600 paper-based; 100 iBT). *Application deadline:* Applications are processed on a rolling basis. Application fee: $50. Electronic applications accepted. *Unit head:* Dr. Vernon Whaley, Dean, 434-592-3463, E-mail: vwhaley@liberty.edu. *Application contact:* Jay Bridge, Director of Admissions, 800-424-9595, Fax: 800-628-7977, E-mail: gradadmissions@liberty.edu.
Website: http://www.liberty.edu/academics/music/

Lincoln Christian Seminary, Graduate and Professional Programs, Lincoln, IL 62656-2167. Offers Bible and theology (MA); Christian ministries (MA); counseling (MA); divinity (M Div); leadership ministry (D Min); religious education (MRE). *Accreditation:* ACIPE; ATS. Part-time programs available. *Degree requirements:* For master's, 2 foreign languages, thesis; for doctorate, thesis/dissertation. *Entrance requirements:* For master's, minimum GPA of 2.5; for doctorate, M Div or equivalent. Additional exam requirements/recommendations for international students: Required—TOEFL (minimum score 550 paper-based). Electronic applications accepted.

Lipscomb University, Hazelip School of Theology, Nashville, TN 37204-3951. Offers Christian practice (MA); missional and spiritual formation (D Min); student ministry (Certificate); theology (M Div). *Accreditation:* ATS. Part-time and evening/weekend programs available. Postbaccalaureate distance learning degree programs offered (minimal on-campus study). *Faculty:* 11 full-time (1 woman), 4 part-time/adjunct (0 women). *Students:* 17 full-time (5 women), 96 part-time (25 women); includes 19 minority (17 Black or African American, non-Hispanic/Latino; 2 Hispanic/Latino). Average age 39. In 2014, 26 master's, 4 doctorates, 3 other advanced degrees awarded. *Degree requirements:* For master's, 2 foreign languages, comprehensive exam (for some programs), thesis optional; for doctorate, comprehensive exam, thesis/dissertation. *Entrance requirements:* For master's, 3 references, transcripts, goals statement; for doctorate, 3 references, transcripts, documentation of full-time participation in ministry, writing sample, interview. Additional exam requirements/recommendations for international students: Required—TOEFL (minimum score 570 paper-based; 80 iBT). *Application deadline:* For fall admission, 8/1 priority date for domestic students; for spring admission, 12/15 for domestic students. Applications are processed on a rolling basis. Application fee: $50 ($75 for international students). Electronic applications accepted. *Expenses:* Expenses: $898 per credit hour (for M Div, MACM, and MTS); $500 per credit hour (for MA); $333 per credit hour (for D Min). *Financial support:* Scholarships/grants and unspecified assistantships available. Financial award application deadline: 3/1; financial award applicants required to submit FAFSA. *Faculty research:* Status of Churches of Christ in foreign nations, Hebrew grammar, marriage and family. *Unit head:* Dr. Mark Black, Director, 615-966-5709, Fax: 615-966-6052, E-mail: mark.black@lipscomb.edu. *Application contact:* Kellye McCool, Coordinator of Student Services, 615-966-5458, Fax: 615-966-6052, E-mail: kellye.mccool@lipscomb.edu.
Website: http://www.lipscomb.edu/hst

Loma Linda University, Faculty of Religion, Program in Clinical Ministry, Loma Linda, CA 92350. Offers MA, Certificate. *Degree requirements:* For master's, comprehensive exam, thesis optional. *Entrance requirements:* For master's, minimum GPA of 3.0. Additional exam requirements/recommendations for international students: Required—TOEFL. Electronic applications accepted.

Loras College, Graduate Division, Program in Theology and Ministry, Dubuque, IA 52004-0178. Offers ministry (MA); theology (MA). Part-time and evening/weekend programs available. *Degree requirements:* For master's, comprehensive exam (for some programs), thesis (for some programs). *Entrance requirements:* For master's, bachelor's degree or undergraduate minor in religious studies or equivalent, minimum undergraduate GPA of 2.75.

Louisiana College, Caskey School of Divinity, Pineville, LA 71359-0001. Offers biblical and theological studies (MA); pastoral ministry (MA).

Loyola Marymount University, College of Liberal Arts, Department of Theological Studies, Program in Pastoral Theology, Los Angeles, CA 90045-8400. Offers MA. Part-time and evening/weekend programs available. *Degree requirements:* For master's, comprehensive exam, thesis or alternative. *Entrance requirements:* For master's, GRE General Test or MAT (recommended), 2 letters of recommendation, personal statement. Additional exam requirements/recommendations for international students: Required—TOEFL (minimum score 600 paper-based; 100 iBT). Electronic applications accepted.

Loyola University Chicago, Institute of Pastoral Studies, Master of Arts in Pastoral Counseling Program, Chicago, IL 60660. Offers pastoral studies (MA); social justice (MA); spirituality (MA). *Accreditation:* ACIPE. Part-time programs available. *Faculty:* 9 full-time (4 women), 12 part-time/adjunct (7 women). *Students:* 39 full-time (29 women), 55 part-time (29 women); includes 21 minority (10 Black or African American, non-Hispanic/Latino; 4 Asian, non-Hispanic/Latino; 6 Hispanic/Latino; 1 Two or more races, non-Hispanic/Latino), 11 international. Average age 40. 19 applicants, 74% accepted, 12 enrolled. In 2014, 8 master's awarded. *Degree requirements:* For master's, thesis or alternative, 100 hours of practicum, 700 hours of internship with clinical supervision, final integration project. *Entrance requirements:* Additional exam requirements/recommendations for international students: Required—TOEFL. *Application deadline:* For fall admission, 2/15 priority date for domestic students. Applications are processed on a rolling basis. Electronic applications accepted. *Expenses: Tuition:* Full-time $17,370; part-time $965 per credit. *Required fees:* $138 per semester. *Financial support:* In 2014–15, 33 students received support. Career-related internships or fieldwork, Federal Work-Study, institutionally sponsored loans, and scholarships/grants available. Support available to part-time students. Financial award application deadline: 3/1; financial award applicants required to submit FAFSA. *Faculty research:* Pastoral psychotherapy, enrichment outcome, marriage and family therapy, mindfulness, human relation skills, psychopathology, spirituality, gender and ethnicity issues, theological anthropology. *Unit head:* Dr. Brian J. Schmisek, Director, 312-915-7400, Fax: 312-915-7410, E-mail: bschmisek@luc.edu. *Application contact:* Dr. William Schmidt, Professor, 312-915-7478, Fax: 312-9157410, E-mail: wschmid@luc.edu.
Website: http://www.luc.edu/ips/academics/mapc/

Loyola University Chicago, Institute of Pastoral Studies, Master of Arts in Pastoral Studies Program, Chicago, IL 60660. Offers health care chaplaincy (MA); religious education (MA); youth ministry (MA). *Accreditation:* ACIPE. Part-time programs available. Postbaccalaureate distance learning degree programs offered (no on-campus study). *Faculty:* 9 full-time (4 women), 40 part-time/adjunct (20 women). *Students:* 13 full-time (10 women), 80 part-time (60 women); includes 12 minority (4 Black or African American, non-Hispanic/Latino; 1 Asian, non-Hispanic/Latino; 7 Hispanic/Latino), 2 international. Average age 46. 26 applicants, 73% accepted, 14 enrolled. In 2014, 20 master's awarded. *Degree requirements:* For master's, integration project. *Entrance requirements:* Additional exam requirements/recommendations for international students: Required—TOEFL. *Application deadline:* For fall admission, 8/1 priority date for domestic students; for spring admission, 12/1 for domestic students. Applications are processed on a rolling basis. Electronic applications accepted. *Expenses: Tuition:* Full-time $17,370; part-time $965 per credit. *Required fees:* $138 per semester. *Financial support:* In 2014–15, 36 students received support. Career-related internships or fieldwork, Federal Work-Study, institutionally sponsored loans, and scholarships/grants available. Support available to part-time students. Financial award application deadline: 3/1. *Faculty research:* Theology, pastoral ministry, ethics. *Unit head:* Dr. Brian J. Schmisek, Director, 312-915-7400, Fax: 312-915-7410, E-mail: bschmisek@luc.edu. *Application contact:* Dr. M. Therese Lysaught, Associate Director, 312-915-7485, Fax: 312-915-7410, E-mail: mlysaught@luc.edu.
Website: http://www.luc.edu/ips/academics/maps/index.shtml

Loyola University Maryland, Graduate Programs, Loyola College of Arts and Sciences, Department of Pastoral Counseling and Spiritual Care, Program in Pastoral Counseling, Baltimore, MD 21210-2699. Offers MA, MS, PhD, CAS, MS/PhD. *Accreditation:* ACA (one or more programs are accredited). Part-time and evening/weekend programs available. *Degree requirements:* For master's, comprehensive exam, thesis; for doctorate, comprehensive exam, thesis/dissertation. *Entrance requirements:* Additional exam requirements/recommendations for international students: Required—TOEFL (minimum score 550 paper-based). Electronic applications accepted.

Loyola University Maryland, Graduate Programs, Loyola College of Arts and Sciences, Department of Pastoral Counseling and Spiritual Care, Program in Spiritual and Pastoral Care, Baltimore, MD 21210-2699. Offers spiritual and pastoral care (MA); spirituality and trauma (Certificate). Part-time and evening/weekend programs available. *Degree requirements:* For master's and Certificate, comprehensive exam, thesis. *Entrance requirements:* Additional exam requirements/recommendations for international students: Required—TOEFL (minimum score 550 paper-based). Electronic applications accepted.

Lutheran School of Theology at Chicago, Graduate and Professional Programs, Chicago, IL 60615-5199. Offers ministry (MAM, D Min); theological studies (MATS, PhD); theology (M Div, Th M). *Accreditation:* ACIPE; ATS (one or more programs are accredited). Part-time programs available. Terminal master's awarded for partial completion of doctoral program. *Degree requirements:* For master's, variable foreign language requirement; for doctorate, variable foreign language requirement, comprehensive exam, thesis/dissertation. *Entrance requirements:* For master's, GRE (Th M), M Div or equivalent (Th M); for doctorate, GRE, M Div or equivalent, 3 years of professional experience (D Min). Additional exam requirements/recommendations for international students: Required—TOEFL (for Th M).

Lutheran Theological Seminary at Gettysburg, Graduate and Professional Programs, Gettysburg, PA 17325-1795. Offers divinity (M Div); ministerial studies (MAMS); outdoor ministry (MAR); parish ministry (D Min); theology (STM). *Accreditation:* ACIPE; ATS (one or more programs are accredited). Part-time programs available. Postbaccalaureate distance learning degree programs offered (no on-campus study). *Degree requirements:* For master's, thesis (for some programs). Electronic applications accepted.

The Lutheran Theological Seminary at Philadelphia, Graduate School, Philadelphia, PA 19119-1794. Offers divinity (M Div); ministry (D Min); public leadership (MA); religion (MAR); social ministry (Certificate); theology (STM, PhD). *Accreditation:* ACIPE; ATS. Part-time and evening/weekend programs available. *Faculty:* 20 full-time (5 women), 19 part-time/adjunct (6 women). *Students:* 106 full-time (50 women), 208 part-time (100 women); includes 92 minority (80 Black or African American, non-Hispanic/Latino; 2 Asian, non-Hispanic/Latino; 10 Hispanic/Latino), 14 international. *Degree requirements:* For master's, one foreign language, comprehensive exam (for some programs), thesis (for some programs); for doctorate, thesis/dissertation. *Entrance requirements:* For master's, minimum undergraduate GPA of 2.8; for doctorate, minimum GPA of 3.0. Additional exam requirements/recommendations for international students: Required—TOEFL (minimum score 550 paper-based), TWE. *Application deadline:* For fall admission, 6/1 priority date for domestic students. Applications are processed on a rolling basis. Application fee: $35. Electronic applications accepted. *Expenses: Tuition:* Full-time $14,310; part-time $1590 per course. *Required fees:* $175 per semester. Tuition and fees vary according to degree level and program. *Financial support:* Research assistantships with tuition reimbursements, teaching assistantships with tuition reimbursements, career-related internships or fieldwork, and Federal Work-Study available. Financial award application deadline: 7/1; financial award applicants required to submit FAFSA. *Unit head:* Rev. Dr. J. Jayakiran Sebastian, Dean, 215-248-6379, Fax: 215-248-4577, E-mail: jsebastian@ltsp.edu. *Application contact:* Matthew O'Rear, Associate Director of Admissions, 800-286-4616 Ext. 6304, Fax: 215-248-7315, E-mail: admissions@ltsp.edu.

Lutheran Theological Seminary Saskatoon, Graduate and Professional Programs, Saskatoon, SK S7N 0X3, Canada. Offers Biblical studies (MTS); church history (MTS); ethics/church and society (MTS); history of Christianity (STM); New Testament (STM); Old Testament (STM); pastoral studies (STM); pastoral theology (MTS); systematic theology (MTS); systematic theology and philosophy of religion (STM); theology (M Div, D Div). STM programs offered jointly with College of Emmanuel and St. Chad and St. Andrew's College. *Accreditation:* ATS. Part-time programs available. *Degree requirements:* For master's, thesis.

Luther Rice College & Seminary, Graduate Programs, Lithonia, GA 30038-2454. Offers apologetics (MA); Bible languages (M Div); Biblical counseling (MA); Christian ministry (M Div, D Min); Christian studies (MA); leadership (MA). Part-time and evening/weekend programs available. Postbaccalaureate distance learning degree programs offered (no on-campus study). *Faculty:* 14 full-time (2 women), 28 part-time/adjunct (8 women). *Students:* 250 full-time (50 women), 784 part-time (209 women); includes 476 minority (420 Black or African American, non-Hispanic/Latino; 7 American Indian or Alaska Native, non-Hispanic/Latino; 21 Asian, non-Hispanic/Latino; 21 Hispanic/Latino; 7 Two or more races, non-Hispanic/Latino). *Degree requirements:* For doctorate, thesis/dissertation. *Entrance requirements:* For master's, bachelor's degree or equivalent; for doctorate, M Div. Additional exam requirements/recommendations for international students: Required—TOEFL (minimum score 550 paper-based). *Application deadline:* Applications are processed on a rolling basis. Application fee: $50. Electronic applications accepted. *Expenses: Tuition:* Full-time $4266; part-time $237 per credit hour. *Required fees:* $330; $55 per course. *Financial support:* Scholarships/grants available. Financial award applicants required to submit FAFSA. *Unit head:* Dr. Brad Arnett, Graduate Dean, 770-484-1204 Ext. 5697, E-mail: barnett@lutherrice.edu. *Application contact:* Steve Pray, Enrollment Advisor, 770-484-1204 Ext. 5758, Fax: 770-484-1155, E-mail: admissions@lutherrice.edu.

Luther Seminary, Graduate and Professional Programs, St. Paul, MN 55108-1445. Offers aging and health (MA); Biblical preaching (D Min); children, youth and family (M Div, MA); congregational mission and leadership (M Th, MA, D Min); history of

Christianity (M Th, MA); missions and world religions (M Th); New Testament (M Th, MA); Old Testament (M Th, MA); pastoral care: clinical pastoral theology (M Th); pastoral theology and ministry (M Th); systematic theology (M Th, MA). *Accreditation:* ACIPE; ATS. Part-time programs available. Postbaccalaureate distance learning degree programs offered (minimal on-campus study). *Faculty:* 25 full-time, 25 part-time/adjunct. *Students:* 401 full-time, 304 part-time, 31 international. Average age 30. 139 applicants, 96% accepted, 96 enrolled. In 2014, 140 master's, 23 doctorates awarded. *Degree requirements:* For master's, thesis or alternative; for doctorate, 2 foreign languages, thesis/dissertation. *Entrance requirements:* For master's, minimum GPA of 3.0; for doctorate, GRE General Test. Additional exam requirements/recommendations for international students: Required—TOEFL, IELTS. *Application deadline:* For fall admission, 7/1 priority date for domestic students, 4/30 for international students; for winter admission, 10/31 for international students; for spring admission, 10/31 for international students. Applications are processed on a rolling basis. Application fee: $0. Electronic applications accepted. *Financial support:* In 2014–15, 359 students received support. Career-related internships or fieldwork, Federal Work-Study, institutionally sponsored loans, and scholarships/grants available. Support available to part-time students. Financial award application deadline: 6/1; financial award applicants required to submit FAFSA. *Faculty research:* Theology, psychology (pastoral care), church history, Bible. *Unit head:* Dr. Craig Koester, Dean of Academic Affairs, 651-641-3471, Fax: 651-641-1609, E-mail: ckoester@luthersem.edu. *Application contact:* Jen Olsen Krengel, Director of Admissions, 651-641-3516, E-mail: jolsenkrengel001@luthersem.edu.
Website: http://www.luthersem.edu/

Madonna University, Program in Religious Studies, Livonia, MI 48150-1173. Offers pastoral ministry (MA).

Maple Springs Baptist Bible College and Seminary, Graduate and Professional Programs, Capitol Heights, MD 20743. Offers biblical studies (MA, Certificate); Christian counseling (MA); church administration (MA); divinity (M Div); ministry (D Min); religious education (MRE).

Maranatha Baptist University, Program in Biblical Counseling, Watertown, WI 53094. Offers MA. Part-time programs available. *Faculty:* 4 full-time (0 women), 5 part-time/adjunct (0 women). *Students:* 2 full-time (1 woman), 10 part-time (2 women); includes 1 minority (Black or African American, non-Hispanic/Latino). Average age 30. 8 applicants, 88% accepted, 3 enrolled. In 2014, 6 master's awarded. *Entrance requirements:* Additional exam requirements/recommendations for international students: Recommended—TOEFL. *Application deadline:* Applications are processed on a rolling basis. Application fee: $50. *Expenses: Tuition:* Full-time $2655; part-time $295 per credit hour. *Required fees:* $25 per credit hour. Tuition and fees vary according to program. *Financial support:* In 2014–15, 2 students received support. Scholarships/grants and tuition waivers (full and partial) available. Support available to part-time students. Financial award applicants required to submit FAFSA. *Unit head:* Dr. Larry Oats, Dean of Maranatha Baptist Seminary, 920-206-2324, Fax: 920-261-9109, E-mail: larry.oats@mbu.edu. *Application contact:* Dr. Jim Harrison, Director of Admissions, 920-206-2327, Fax: 920-261-9109, E-mail: admissions@mbbc.edu.
Website: http://www.mbu.edu/academics/majors/biblical-counseling/

Martin University, Graduate School of Urban Ministry, Indianapolis, IN 46218-3867. Offers urban ministry studies (MA). Part-time and evening/weekend programs available. *Degree requirements:* For master's, Greek, oral and written comprehensive exam or thesis. *Faculty research:* How to bridge the gap between black theology and the black church.

Marymount University, School of Education and Human Services, Program in Counseling, Arlington, VA 22207-4299. Offers clinical mental health counseling (MA); counseling (Certificate); pastoral and spiritual care (MA); pastoral counseling (MA); school counseling (MA). *Accreditation:* ACA (one or more programs are accredited). Part-time and evening/weekend programs available. *Faculty:* 8 full-time (4 women), 7 part-time/adjunct (6 women). *Students:* 87 full-time (74 women), 44 part-time (37 women); includes 40 minority (14 Black or African American, non-Hispanic/Latino; 1 American Indian or Alaska Native, non-Hispanic/Latino; 6 Asian, non-Hispanic/Latino; 16 Hispanic/Latino; 3 Two or more races, non-Hispanic/Latino), 6 international. Average age 29. 87 applicants, 77% accepted, 42 enrolled. In 2014, 51 master's awarded. *Entrance requirements:* For master's, GRE, 2 letters of recommendation, interview, resume, personal statement; for Certificate, master's degree in counseling. Additional exam requirements/recommendations for international students: Required—TOEFL (minimum score 600 paper-based; 96 iBT), IELTS (minimum score 6.5). *Application deadline:* For fall admission, 2/3 priority date for domestic students, 7/1 for international students; for spring admission, 10/5 for domestic students. Application fee: $40. Electronic applications accepted. *Expenses: Tuition:* Part-time $885 per credit. *Required fees:* $10 per credit. One-time fee: $220 part-time. Tuition and fees vary according to program. *Financial support:* In 2014–15, 13 students received support, including 2 research assistantships with full and partial tuition reimbursements available, 1 teaching assistantship with full and partial tuition reimbursement available; career-related internships or fieldwork, Federal Work-Study, scholarships/grants, and unspecified assistantships also available. Support available to part-time students. Financial award applicants required to submit FAFSA. *Unit head:* Dr. Lisa Jackson-Cherry, Director, 703-284-1633, Fax: 703-284-5708, E-mail: lisa.jackson-cherry@marymount.edu. *Application contact:* Francesca Reed, Director, Graduate Admissions, 703-284-5901, Fax: 703-527-3815, E-mail: grad.admissions@marymount.edu.
Website: http://www.marymount.edu/Academics/School-of-Education-Human-Services/Graduate-Programs/Counseling-(M-A-)

The Master's College and Seminary, The Master's Seminary, Santa Clarita, CA 91321-1200. Offers biblical counseling (MABC); New Testament (Th D); Old Testament (Th D); preaching (D Min); theology (M Div, M Th, Th D). Part-time programs available. *Degree requirements:* For master's, 2 foreign languages, thesis; for doctorate, 4 foreign languages, thesis/dissertation. *Entrance requirements:* For master's, minimum GPA of 2.75; for doctorate, Th M, minimum GPA of 3.5. Additional exam requirements/recommendations for international students: Required—TOEFL (minimum score 550 paper-based).

McCormick Theological Seminary, Graduate and Professional Programs, Chicago, IL 60615. Offers ministry (D Min); theological studies (MATS, Certificate); theology (M Div); M Div/MSW. M Div/MSW offered jointly with Loyola University Chicago, University of Chicago, and University of Illinois at Chicago. *Accreditation:* ACIPE; ATS (one or more programs are accredited). Part-time and evening/weekend programs available. *Degree requirements:* For master's, thesis (for some programs); for doctorate, thesis/dissertation. *Entrance requirements:* For master's, minimum GPA of 3.0; for doctorate, M Div, minimum 3 years in pastorate. *Faculty research:* Faith formation, families, biblical literature, Dead Sea scrolls, women in antiquity.

McMaster University, McMaster Divinity College, Hamilton, ON L8S 4M2, Canada. Offers biblical studies (M Div); Biblical studies (MA, MTS, Diploma); Christian interpretation/history (M Div, MA, MTS, Diploma); Christian ministry (M Div, MA, MTS, Diploma); Christian Studies (Certificate); Christian theology (PhD). Affiliated with the Toronto School of Theology. *Accreditation:* ATS. Part-time programs available. *Degree requirements:* For master's, one foreign language, thesis optional; for doctorate, 3 foreign languages, comprehensive exam, thesis/dissertation; for other advanced degree, 2 foreign languages, thesis. *Entrance requirements:* For master's, minimum B average in undergraduate course work, 3 letters of reference; for doctorate, minimum B+ average in bachelor's and master's, appropriate modern/ancient language, interview; for other advanced degree, 6 units of related Biblical language, minimum B+ average in undergraduate course work, minimum 15 units of course work in related area of study, 3 letters of recommendation. Additional exam requirements/recommendations for international students: Required—TOEFL (minimum score 550 paper-based). *Faculty research:* Ethics, Biblical studies, language studies, church history, Christian ministry.

Meadville Lombard Theological School, Graduate and Professional Programs, Chicago, IL 60637-1602. Offers divinity (M Div); ministry (D Min); religion (MA); M Div/MSW. M Div/MSW offered jointly with University of Chicago. *Accreditation:* ACIPE; ATS. Part-time programs available. Postbaccalaureate distance learning degree programs offered (minimal on-campus study). *Entrance requirements:* For master's, bachelor's degree; for doctorate, bachelor's and masters degrees, 3 years of ministry.

Mercer University, Graduate Studies, Cecil B. Day Campus, James and Carolyn McAfee School of Theology, Atlanta, GA 30341. Offers Christian ministry (MACM); Christian spirituality (D Min); divinity (M Div); preaching (D Min); M Div/MBA; M Div/MM; M Div/MS. *Accreditation:* ATS. Part-time programs available. *Faculty:* 16 full-time (6 women), 8 part-time/adjunct (4 women). *Students:* 136 full-time (67 women), 66 part-time (32 women); includes 96 minority (88 Black or African American, non-Hispanic/Latino; 1 American Indian or Alaska Native, non-Hispanic/Latino; 6 Hispanic/Latino; 1 Two or more races, non-Hispanic/Latino), 5 international. Average age 35. 107 applicants, 71% accepted, 40 enrolled. In 2014, 47 master's, 8 doctorates awarded. *Degree requirements:* For doctorate, thesis/dissertation, fieldwork, seminars. *Entrance requirements:* For master's, bachelor's degree with liberal arts core from regionally-accredited college/university; for doctorate, MAT or GRE, minimum B+ average in undergraduate course work, letters of recommendation. Additional exam requirements/recommendations for international students: Required—TOEFL (minimum score 550 paper-based; 79 iBT). *Application deadline:* For fall admission, 7/1 for domestic students, 2/1 for international students; for spring admission, 1/4 for domestic students. Applications are processed on a rolling basis. Application fee: $35. Electronic applications accepted. *Expenses:* Expenses: $385 per credit hour (for M Div and MACM); $350 (for D Min). *Financial support:* In 2014–15, 30 students received support. Career-related internships or fieldwork, Federal Work-Study, institutionally sponsored loans, and merit-based scholarships available. Support available to part-time students. Financial award applicants required to submit FAFSA. *Faculty research:* Biblical studies, Baptist heritage, Christian heritage, theology, pastoral care, ethics, global missions, academic research. *Unit head:* Dr. R. Alan Culpepper, Dean, 678-547-6470, Fax: 678-547-6478, E-mail: culpepper_ra@mercer.edu. *Application contact:* Elizabeth P. Allen, Director of Admissions, 678-547-6357, Fax: 678-547-6478, E-mail: allen_l@mercer.edu.
Website: http://www.mercer.edu/theology

Mid-America Christian University, Program in Counseling, Oklahoma City, OK 73170-4504. Offers marital and family therapy (MS); pastoral/spiritual direction (MS); professional counselor (MS). *Entrance requirements:* For master's, MAT, bachelor's degree from a regionally accredited college or university, minimum overall cumulative GPA of 2.75 of bachelor course work. Additional exam requirements/recommendations for international students: Required—TOEFL (minimum score 550 paper-based).

Midwestern Baptist Theological Seminary, Graduate and Professional Programs, Kansas City, MO 64118-4697. Offers Christian education (MACE); Christian foundations (Graduate Certificate); church music (MCM); counseling (MA); ministry (D Ed Min, D Min); Old or New Testament studies (PhD); theology (M Div). *Accreditation:* ATS. Part-time programs available. Postbaccalaureate distance learning degree programs offered (minimal on-campus study). *Degree requirements:* For doctorate, thesis/dissertation. *Entrance requirements:* For doctorate, MAT. Electronic applications accepted. *Faculty research:* Ministerial studies, Biblical and theological studies, missions, counseling.

Missouri Baptist University, Graduate Programs, St. Louis, MO 63141-8660. Offers business administration (MBA); Christian ministries (MACM); counseling (MAC); education (MSE); education administration (MEA); educational leadership (MSE, Ed S); teaching (MAT).

Moody Bible Institute, Graduate School, Chicago, IL 60610-3284. Offers biblical studies (MABS, Graduate Certificate); intercultural studies (MAIS, Graduate Certificate); ministry (M Div, M Min); spiritual formation and discipleship (MASF, Graduate Certificate); urban studies (MA, Graduate Certificate). *Accreditation:* ATS. Part-time programs available. *Degree requirements:* For master's, 2 foreign languages, fieldwork (MABS); colloquium, field research project (MA Min). *Entrance requirements:* For master's, 30 hours in Bible/theology, 2 years of ministry experience (MA Min).

Mount Marty College, Graduate Studies Division, Yankton, SD 57078-3724. Offers business administration (MBA); nurse anesthesia (MS); nursing (MSN); pastoral ministries (MPM). *Accreditation:* AANA/CANAEP (one or more programs are accredited). *Degree requirements:* For master's, thesis or alternative. *Entrance requirements:* For master's, GRE General Test, minimum GPA of 3.0. Electronic applications accepted. *Faculty research:* Clinical anesthesia, professional characteristics, motivations of applicants.

Mount St. Joseph University, Graduate Program in Religious Studies, Cincinnati, OH 45233-1670. Offers pastoral administration (Certificate); religious studies (MA); spirituality and wellness (Certificate). Part-time and evening/weekend programs available. *Faculty:* 3 full-time (2 women). *Students:* 14 part-time (11 women); includes 1 minority (Black or African American, non-Hispanic/Latino). Average age 45. 6 applicants, 83% accepted, 4 enrolled. In 2014, 3 master's awarded. *Degree requirements:* For master's, integrating project, field experience. *Entrance requirements:* For master's, 3 letters of recommendation, interview, minimum GPA of 3.0, academic transcripts, essay. Additional exam requirements/recommendations for international students: Required—TOEFL (minimum score 560 paper-based; 83 iBT). *Application deadline:* Applications are processed on a rolling basis. Application fee: $50. Electronic applications accepted. *Expenses: Tuition:* Full-time $18,400; part-time $575 per credit hour. *Required fees:* $450; $450 per year. Part-time tuition and fees vary according to course load, degree level and program. *Financial support:* In 2014–15, 10 students received support. Scholarships/grants available. Financial award application deadline: 3/1; financial award applicants required to submit FAFSA. *Faculty research:* Contextual/cultural/systematic theology, historical/spiritual theology, business/economics ethics, social justice, Biblical/cultural/pastoral theology. *Unit head:* Dr. John Trokan, Chair of Religious/Pastoral Studies, 513-244-4272, Fax: 513-244-4222, E-mail: john.trokan@msj.edu. *Application contact:* Mary Brigham, Assistant Director of Graduate Recruitment, 513-244-4233, Fax: 513-244-4629, E-mail: mary.brigham@msj.edu.
Website: http://www.msj.edu/academics/graduate-programs/religious-studies-programs/

Neumann University, Program in Pastoral Counseling, Aston, PA 19014-1298. Offers pastoral counseling (MS, CAS); spiritual direction (CSD). Part-time and evening/weekend programs available. *Degree requirements:* For master's, clinical case study.

Pastoral Ministry and Counseling

Entrance requirements: Additional exam requirements/recommendations for international students: Required—TOEFL. Electronic applications accepted. *Faculty research:* Development of an integrated model of religion/psychology for remediation and prevention of emotional disturbance.

New Brunswick Theological Seminary, Graduate and Professional Programs, New Brunswick, NJ 08901-1196. Offers pastoral care and counseling (D Min). *Accreditation:* ACIPE; ATS. Part-time and evening/weekend programs available. *Faculty:* 10 full-time (3 women), 24 part-time/adjunct (7 women). *Students:* 35 full-time (19 women), 149 part-time (96 women); includes 146 minority (126 Black or African American, non-Hispanic/Latino; 11 Asian, non-Hispanic/Latino; 9 Hispanic/Latino), 3 international. Average age 35. 69 applicants, 62% accepted, 39 enrolled. In 2014, 24 master's, 1 doctorate awarded. *Degree requirements:* For master's, variable foreign language requirement, thesis (for some programs); for doctorate, thesis/dissertation. *Entrance requirements:* For master's, B.A./B.S. degree with a minimum of 3.0 for the M.A. or 2.5 for the Master of Divinity; for doctorate, M.Div. degree. Additional exam requirements/recommendations for international students: Required—TOEFL (minimum score 550 paper-based; 79 iBT); Recommended—IELTS (minimum score 6). *Application deadline:* For fall admission, 7/15 for domestic and international students; for spring admission, 11/15 for domestic and international students. Applications are processed on a rolling basis. Application fee: $50. Electronic applications accepted. *Expenses: Tuition:* Full-time $11,088; part-time $462 per credit. *Required fees:* $231 per semester. *Financial support:* In 2014–15, 75 students received support. Scholarships/grants and tuition waivers (full and partial) available. Financial award application deadline: 6/30; financial award applicants required to submit FAFSA. *Unit head:* Dr. Willard Ashley, Sr., Dean of the Seminary, 732-247-5241 Ext. 109, Fax: 732-249-5412, E-mail: washley@nbts.edu. *Application contact:* Dr. Beth L. Tanner, Chair, Admissions Committee, 732-247-5241 Ext. 116, Fax: 732-249-5412, E-mail: admissions@nbts.edu.

New Orleans Baptist Theological Seminary, Graduate and Professional Programs, Division of Pastoral Ministries, New Orleans, LA 70126-4858. Offers M Div, MAMFC, D Min, PhD. *Accreditation:* ACIPE. Postbaccalaureate distance learning degree programs offered. *Degree requirements:* For master's, 2 foreign languages, thesis (for some programs); for doctorate, 3 foreign languages, comprehensive exam, thesis/dissertation. *Entrance requirements:* For master's and doctorate, GRE General Test. Additional exam requirements/recommendations for international students: Required—TOEFL.

Northern Baptist Theological Seminary, Graduate and Professional Programs, Lombard, IL 60148-5698. Offers Biblical studies (M Div); Christian ministries (MACM); missional leadership (D Min); spiritual transformation (D Min); theology (M Div). *Accreditation:* ATS. Part-time and evening/weekend programs available. *Faculty:* 6 full-time (1 woman), 33 part-time/adjunct (8 women). *Students:* 126 full-time (34 women), 80 part-time (32 women); includes 89 minority (73 Black or African American, non-Hispanic/Latino; 6 Asian, non-Hispanic/Latino; 8 Hispanic/Latino; 2 Two or more races, non-Hispanic/Latino), 3 international. Average age 44. *Degree requirements:* For doctorate, thesis/dissertation. *Entrance requirements:* For master's, all official transcripts, letter of reference from church, 3 letters of reference, autobiographical statement (400 words or more); for doctorate, M Div, 3 years in the ministry post-M Div, 3 letters of reference. Additional exam requirements/recommendations for international students: Required—TOEFL (minimum score 550 paper-based). *Application deadline:* For fall admission, 8/25 for domestic students, 2/1 for international students; for winter admission, 12/10 for domestic students, 2/1 for international students; for spring admission, 3/15 for domestic students, 2/1 for international students. Applications are processed on a rolling basis. Application fee: $35. Electronic applications accepted. *Expenses: Tuition:* Full-time $13,230; part-time $1470 per course. *Required fees:* $360; $120 per quarter. *Financial support:* Scholarships/grants available. Support available to part-time students. Financial award application deadline: 9/1; financial award applicants required to submit FAFSA. *Faculty research:* Theology, worship studies, church history, evangelism, Christian ministry. *Unit head:* Dr. J. Alistair Brown, President, 630-620-2101, Fax: 630-620-2190. *Application contact:* Isaac Ampil, Director of Admissions, 630-620-2175, Fax: 630-620-2190, E-mail: admissions@seminary.edu.

North Greenville University, T. Walter Brashier Graduate School, Greer, SC 29651. Offers Christian ministry (MCM, D Min); education (M Ed, MAT); financial planning (MBA); human resources (MBA). Part-time and evening/weekend programs available. Postbaccalaureate distance learning degree programs offered (no on-campus study). *Faculty:* 10 full-time (2 women), 18 part-time/adjunct (5 women). *Students:* 165 full-time (66 women), 164 part-time (68 women); includes 47 minority (35 Black or African American, non-Hispanic/Latino; 3 Asian, non-Hispanic/Latino; 9 Hispanic/Latino). Average age 38. 207 applicants, 85% accepted, 176 enrolled. In 2014, 50 master's, 7 doctorates awarded. *Degree requirements:* For master's, comprehensive exam (for some programs), thesis or alternative, capstone course. *Entrance requirements:* For master's, minimum GPA of 2.25 overall, 2.5 in major; for doctorate, MAT. Additional exam requirements/recommendations for international students: Required—TOEFL (minimum score 550 paper-based). *Application deadline:* For fall admission, 8/1 for domestic students, 6/1 for international students; for winter admission, 1/1 for domestic students, 10/1 for international students; for spring admission, 3/1 for domestic students, 1/1 for international students. Applications are processed on a rolling basis. Application fee: $30. Electronic applications accepted. *Financial support:* In 2014–15, 23 students received support, including 1 research assistantship (averaging $2,000 per year); Federal Work-Study, institutionally sponsored loans, scholarships/grants, tuition waivers (partial), and unspecified assistantships also available. Support available to part-time students. Financial award applicants required to submit FAFSA. *Faculty research:* Organizational behavior, church growth, homiletics, human resources, business strategy. *Unit head:* Dr. Joseph Samuel Isgett, Jr., Vice President for Graduate Studies, 864-877-3052, Fax: 864-877-1653, E-mail: sisgett@ngu.edu. *Application contact:* Tawana P. Scott, EdD, Assistant Vice President of Graduate Academic Services, 864-877-1598, Fax: 864-877-1653, E-mail: tscott@ngu.edu. Website: http://www.ngu.edu/gradschool.php

North Park Theological Seminary, Graduate and Professional Programs, Program in Christian Ministry, Chicago, IL 60625-4895. Offers MACM, MA/MBA, MA/MM.

North Park Theological Seminary, Graduate and Professional Programs, Program in Christian Studies, Chicago, IL 60625-4895. Offers adult ministry (Certificate); camping and retreat ministry (Certificate); children and family ministry (Certificate); Christian formation (Certificate); faith and health (Certificate); intercultural studies (Certificate); justice ministry (Certificate); leadership and administration (Certificate); spiritual direction (Certificate); youth ministry (Certificate). *Accreditation:* ACIPE. Part-time programs available. *Entrance requirements:* For degree, minimum GPA of 2.5. Additional exam requirements/recommendations for international students: Required—TOEFL.

Northwest Nazarene University, Graduate Studies, Program in Religion, Nampa, ID 83686-5897. Offers missional leadership (M Div, MA); pastoral ministry (MA); spiritual formation (M Div, MA); youth, children, and family ministry (M Div, MA). Part-time and evening/weekend programs available. Postbaccalaureate distance learning degree programs offered (no on-campus study). *Faculty:* 12 full-time (2 women), 15 part-time/adjunct (1 woman). *Students:* 91 full-time (27 women), 20 part-time (5 women); includes 11 minority (4 Black or African American, non-Hispanic/Latino; 1 American Indian or Alaska Native, non-Hispanic/Latino; 2 Asian, non-Hispanic/Latino; 3 Hispanic/Latino; 1 Native Hawaiian or other Pacific Islander, non-Hispanic/Latino), 1 international. Average age 39. 55 applicants, 65% accepted, 27 enrolled. In 2014, 40 master's awarded. *Entrance requirements:* For master's, minimum GPA of 2.5; 8 semester or 12 quarter credits of Bible, theology and/or Western philosophy. Additional exam requirements/recommendations for international students: Required—TOEFL. *Application deadline:* Applications are processed on a rolling basis. Application fee: $50. Electronic applications accepted. *Unit head:* Dr. Jay Akkerman, Director, Graduate Studies, 208-467-8437, Fax: 208-467-8252. *Application contact:* Vicki Funk, Program Coordinator, 208-467-8432, Fax: 208-467-8252, E-mail: vlfunk@nnu.edu. Website: http://www.nnu.edu/ministry/

Northwest University, College of Ministry, Kirkland, WA 98033. Offers ministry (MIM); missional leadership (MA); theology and culture (MA). Part-time and evening/weekend programs available. Postbaccalaureate distance learning degree programs offered (no on-campus study). *Faculty:* 6 full-time (1 woman), 8 part-time/adjunct (1 woman). *Students:* 7 full-time (3 women), 81 part-time (19 women); includes 21 minority (2 Black or African American, non-Hispanic/Latino; 6 Asian, non-Hispanic/Latino; 3 Hispanic/Latino; 4 Native Hawaiian or other Pacific Islander, non-Hispanic/Latino; 6 Two or more races, non-Hispanic/Latino). Average age 43. 33 applicants, 97% accepted, 20 enrolled. In 2014, 33 master's awarded. *Degree requirements:* For master's, comprehensive exam (for some programs), thesis (for some programs). *Entrance requirements:* Additional exam requirements/recommendations for international students: Required—TOEFL (minimum score 550 paper-based; 75 iBT). *Application deadline:* For fall admission, 8/1 for domestic students, 4/1 for international students; for spring admission, 12/1 for domestic students, 8/1 for international students. Applications are processed on a rolling basis. Application fee: $50. Electronic applications accepted. *Expenses: Tuition:* Full-time $6894; part-time $684 per credit. *Required fees:* $12.50 per term. One-time fee: $98 full-time; $83 part-time. Tuition and fees vary according to course load, campus/location, program and reciprocity agreements. *Financial support:* In 2014–15, 10 students received support. Federal Work-Study available. *Unit head:* Dr. Wayde Goodall, Dean, 425-889-5211, E-mail: wayde.goodall@northwestu.edu. *Application contact:* Steven Curry, Graduate Enrollment Counselor, College of Ministry, 425-889-7795, E-mail: steven.curry@northwestu.edu. Website: http://www.northwestu.edu/ministrygrad/

Nyack College, Alliance Theological Seminary, Nyack, NY 10960. Offers Biblical literature (MA), including New Testament, Old Testament; Christian ministry (MPS); intercultural studies (MA); ministry (D Min), including Christian leadership in the global context; theology and missions (M Div); urban ministry (MPS). *Accreditation:* ATS. Part-time and evening/weekend programs available. *Students:* 319 full-time (132 women), 439 part-time (214 women); includes 605 minority (230 Black or African American, non-Hispanic/Latino; 170 Asian, non-Hispanic/Latino; 195 Hispanic/Latino; 1 Native Hawaiian or other Pacific Islander, non-Hispanic/Latino; 9 Two or more races, non-Hispanic/Latino), 41 international. Average age 43. In 2014, 134 master's, 11 doctorates awarded. *Degree requirements:* For master's, comprehensive exam (for some programs), thesis optional, internship; for doctorate, thesis/dissertation. *Entrance requirements:* For master's, transcripts, Christian experience statement, personal goals statement, recommendations; for doctorate, transcripts, documented three years of ministry experience subsequent to 1st graduate theological degree, reference letters, formal academic paper. Additional exam requirements/recommendations for international students: Required—TOEFL (minimum score 83 iBT). *Application deadline:* Applications are processed on a rolling basis. Application fee: $30. Electronic applications accepted. *Expenses:* Expenses: Contact institution. *Financial support:* Career-related internships or fieldwork, Federal Work-Study, and scholarships/grants available. Financial award applicants required to submit FAFSA. *Unit head:* Dr. Ronald Walborn, Dean, 845-770-5715, Fax: 845-358-1663. *Application contact:* Julian Williams, ATS Associate Director of Admissions, 800-541-6891, Fax: 845-348-3912, E-mail: admissions.ats@nyack.edu. Website: http://www.nyack.edu/ats

Oakwood University, Program in Pastoral Studies, Huntsville, AL 35896. Offers MA. *Entrance requirements:* For master's, Biblical Literacy Entrance Test (BLET), minimum cumulative GPA of 2.5, 2 letters of recommendation, current resume, 3 years of pastoral or local church leadership experience. Additional exam requirements/recommendations for international students: Required—TOEFL (minimum score 500 paper-based).

Oblate School of Theology, Graduate and Professional Programs, San Antonio, TX 78216-6693. Offers African-American pastoral leadership (D Min); divinity (M Div); pastoral leadership (D Min); pastoral ministry (MAP Min); pastoral studies (Certificate); spiritual formation in the local community (D Min); spirituality (MA Sp, PhD); spirituality and ministry (D Min); theology (MA Th); U.S. Hispanic/Latino ministry (D Min); M Div/MA Th. *Accreditation:* ACIPE; ATS (one or more programs are accredited). Part-time programs available. Postbaccalaureate distance learning degree programs offered (no on-campus study). *Faculty:* 23 full-time (8 women), 3 part-time/adjunct (0 women). *Students:* 59 full-time (6 women), 73 part-time (36 women); includes 56 minority (8 Black or African American, non-Hispanic/Latino; 9 Asian, non-Hispanic/Latino; 39 Hispanic/Latino), 41 international. Average age 40. 41 applicants, 88% accepted, 34 enrolled. In 2014, 31 master's, 3 doctorates awarded. *Degree requirements:* For master's, comprehensive exam (for some programs), thesis (for some programs), practicum; for doctorate, one foreign language, comprehensive exam, thesis/dissertation, paper, practicum. *Entrance requirements:* For master's, MAT, interview, course work in theology or religious studies, minimum GPA of 2.5; for doctorate, M Div, MA Th, or MA Sp. Additional exam requirements/recommendations for international students: Required—TOEFL (minimum score 71 iBT). *Application deadline:* For fall admission, 6/15 priority date for domestic and international students; for winter admission, 11/30 for domestic and international students; for spring admission, 11/30 for domestic and international students; for summer admission, 4/1 for domestic and international students. Applications are processed on a rolling basis. Application fee: $65. *Expenses:* Expenses: Contact institution. *Financial support:* In 2014–15, 25 students received support. Scholarships/grants available. Support available to part-time students. Financial award application deadline: 8/1; financial award applicants required to submit FAFSA. *Unit head:* Dr. R. Scott Woodward, Academic Dean, 210-341-1366, Fax: 210-341-4519, E-mail: rsw@ost.edu. *Application contact:* Mario A. Porter, Director of Admissions, 210-341-1366 Ext. 226, Fax: 210-341-4519, E-mail: registrar@ost.edu.

Oklahoma Christian University, Graduate School of Theology, Oklahoma City, OK 73136-1100. Offers family life ministry (MA); ministry (M Div, MA); youth ministry (MA). Part-time programs available. Postbaccalaureate distance learning degree programs offered (minimal on-campus study). *Degree requirements:* For master's, one foreign language, comprehensive exam, field experience. *Entrance requirements:* For master's, minimum undergraduate GPA of 3.0. Additional exam requirements/recommendations for international students: Required—TOEFL (minimum score 550 paper-based). Electronic applications accepted. *Faculty research:* Early marriage adjustment, new religions, Ethiopic language, church health, Hebrew rhetoric.

Oral Roberts University, School of Theology and Missions, Tulsa, OK 74171. Offers biblical literature (MA), including advanced languages, Judaic-Christian studies;

Christian counseling (MA), including marriage and family therapy; divinity (M Div); missions (MA); practical theology (MA); theological/historical studies (MA); theology (D Min). *Accreditation:* ATS. Part-time programs available. Postbaccalaureate distance learning degree programs offered (minimal on-campus study). *Degree requirements:* For master's, thesis (for some programs), practicum/internship; for doctorate, thesis/dissertation, applied research project. *Entrance requirements:* For master's, GRE General Test or MAT, minimum GPA of 2.5; for doctorate, M Div, minimum GPA of 3.0, 3 years of full-time ministry experience. Additional exam requirements/recommendations for international students: Required—TOEFL (minimum score 550 paper-based; 79 iBT). Electronic applications accepted.

Ottawa University, Graduate Studies-Arizona, Program in Professional Counseling, Ottawa, KS 66067-3399. Offers Christian counseling (MA); expressive arts therapy (MA); marriage and family therapy (MA); treatment of trauma, abuse and deprivation (MA). Programs offered in Mesa, Phoenix, Tempe and West Valley, AZ. Part-time and evening/weekend programs available. Postbaccalaureate distance learning degree programs offered. *Degree requirements:* For master's, comprehensive exam, thesis or alternative, field experience, practicum. *Entrance requirements:* For master's, minimum undergraduate GPA of 3.0; course work in theories of personality, abnormal psychology, and human growth and development. Additional exam requirements/recommendations for international students: Required—TOEFL (minimum score 550 paper-based).

Pentecostal Theological Seminary, Graduate and Professional Programs, Cleveland, TN 37320-3330. Offers biblical studies (MTS); church ministries (MA); counseling (MA); discipleship and Christian formation (MA); ministry (D Min); Pentecostal theology (MTS); theology (M Div). *Accreditation:* ACIPE; ATS. Part-time programs available. *Degree requirements:* For master's, variable foreign language requirement, thesis (for some programs), internship. *Faculty research:* Biblical exegesis.

Pepperdine University, Seaver College, Master of Science in Ministry Program, Malibu, CA 90263. Offers MS. *Students:* 1 (woman) part-time. *Entrance requirements:* For master's, GRE, letters of recommendation, writing sample. Additional exam requirements/recommendations for international students: Required—TOEFL. *Application deadline:* For fall admission, 2/1 priority date for domestic students. Applications are processed on a rolling basis. Application fee: $65. Electronic applications accepted. *Unit head:* Dr. Timothy Willis, Chair/Professor of Religion, 310-506-4352, E-mail: timothy.willis@pepperdine.edu. *Application contact:* Michael Truschke, Dean of Admission and Enrollment Management, 310-506-6165, Fax: 310-506-4861, E-mail: admission-seaver@pepperdine.edu.
Website: http://seaver.pepperdine.edu/religion/academics/msmin.htm

Phillips Theological Seminary, Programs in Theology, Doctor of Ministry Program, Tulsa, OK 74116. Offers parish ministry (D Min); pastoral counseling (D Min); practices of ministry (D Min). *Accreditation:* ATS. Part-time programs available. *Degree requirements:* For doctorate, thesis/dissertation. *Entrance requirements:* For doctorate, M Div, minimum GPA of 3.0, 3 years of post-M Div pastoral experience. *Expenses:* Contact institution. *Faculty research:* Politics and theology, media and theology, ecology and theology.

Phoenix Seminary, Graduate Programs, Phoenix, AZ 85018. Offers Biblical and theological studies (Graduate Diploma); Biblical communication (M Div); Biblical leadership (MA); Christian counseling (Graduate Diploma); counseling and family (M Div); leadership development (M Div); ministry (D Min); professional counseling (MA). *Accreditation:* ATS (one or more programs are accredited). Part-time and evening/weekend programs available. *Degree requirements:* For master's, 2 foreign languages, comprehensive exam; for doctorate, 2 foreign languages, thesis/dissertation. *Entrance requirements:* For master's, undergraduate degree with minimum GPA of 2.5; for doctorate, M Div (94 hours) with minimum GPA of 3.0. Additional exam requirements/recommendations for international students: Required—TOEFL (minimum score 587 paper-based; 92 iBT), TWE (minimum score 4.5).

Piedmont International University, Graduate School, Winston-Salem, NC 27101-5197. Offers Biblical studies (PhD); chaplaincy track (MABS); curriculum and instruction (M Ed); leadership (MA, PhD); ministry (MA Min); non-language track (MABS); PhD preparation track (MABS). Part-time programs available. Postbaccalaureate distance learning degree programs offered (no on-campus study). *Faculty:* 5 full-time (0 women), 8 part-time/adjunct (1 woman). *Students:* 84; includes 3 minority (2 Black or African American, non-Hispanic/Latino; 1 Asian, non-Hispanic/Latino). Average age 35. 12 applicants, 100% accepted. In 2014, 18 master's awarded. *Degree requirements:* For master's, 2 foreign languages, comprehensive exam, thesis or alternative; for doctorate, 2 foreign languages, comprehensive exam. *Entrance requirements:* For master's, GRE General Test; for doctorate, Hebrew and Greek proficiency, MA. *Application deadline:* For fall admission, 8/15 priority date for domestic students; for spring admission, 1/1 for domestic students. Applications are processed on a rolling basis. Application fee: $30. Electronic applications accepted. *Expenses: Tuition:* Part-time $295 per credit hour. Part-time tuition and fees vary according to degree level and program. *Financial support:* Career-related internships or fieldwork available. Support available to part-time students. Financial award applicants required to submit CSS PROFILE. *Faculty research:* Theological and Biblical studies. *Unit head:* Dr. Larry Tyler, Dean, 336-714-7989, Fax: 336-714-2715, E-mail: tylerl@piedmontu.edu. *Application contact:* Angela Hoover, Director of Graduate Admissions, 336-714-7927, Fax: 336-725-5522, E-mail: hoovera@piedmontu.edu.
Website: http://piedmontu.edu

Pittsburgh Theological Seminary, Graduate and Professional Programs, Pittsburgh, PA 15206-2596. Offers divinity (M Div); ministry (D Min); theology (MA, Th M); theology and ministry (MA); JD/M Div; M Div/MS; M Div/MSW. M Div/MSW offered jointly with University of Pittsburgh; JD/M Div with Duquesne University; M Div/MS with Carnegie Mellon University. *Accreditation:* ATS (one or more programs are accredited). Part-time and evening/weekend programs available. *Faculty:* 15 full-time (5 women), 7 part-time/adjunct (2 women). *Students:* 142 full-time (23 women), 77 part-time (27 women); includes 46 minority (35 Black or African American, non-Hispanic/Latino; 1 American Indian or Alaska Native, non-Hispanic/Latino; 3 Asian, non-Hispanic/Latino; 3 Hispanic/Latino; 1 Native Hawaiian or other Pacific Islander, non-Hispanic/Latino; 3 Two or more races, non-Hispanic/Latino), 7 international. Average age 35. 57 applicants, 93% accepted, 44 enrolled. In 2014, 39 master's, 11 doctorates awarded. *Degree requirements:* For master's, comprehensive exam (for some programs), thesis (for some programs); for doctorate, thesis/dissertation. *Entrance requirements:* For master's, bachelor's degree with minimum GPA of 2.7, interview, references; for doctorate, interview, references. Additional exam requirements/recommendations for international students: Required—TOEFL (minimum score 570 paper-based; 89 iBT). *Application deadline:* For fall admission, 6/30 priority date for domestic students, 12/1 for international students; for winter admission, 10/15 priority date for domestic students; for spring admission, 1/15 priority date for domestic students. Applications are processed on a rolling basis. Application fee: $50. *Expenses: Tuition:* Full-time $8640; part-time $320 per credit. *Financial support:* In 2014–15, 104 students received support. Career-related internships or fieldwork, scholarships/grants, and institutional work-study available. Financial award application deadline: 5/1; financial award applicants required to submit FAFSA. *Unit head:* Dr. Byron H. Jackson, Dean of Faculty and Vice President for Academic Affairs, 412-924-1374, Fax: 412-924-1774, E-mail: bjackson@pts.edu.

Application contact: Dr. James Downey, Vice President for Institutional Effectiveness, 412-924-1450, Fax: 412-924-1750, E-mail: jdowney@pts.edu.
Website: http://www.pts.edu/

Point Loma Nazarene University, School of Theology and Christian Ministry, San Diego, CA 92106-2899. Offers M Min. Part-time programs available. Postbaccalaureate distance learning degree programs offered (minimal on-campus study). *Faculty:* 9 part-time/adjunct (2 women). *Students:* 19 part-time (9 women); includes 4 minority (2 Black or African American, non-Hispanic/Latino; 2 Hispanic/Latino). Average age 41. 4 applicants, 75% accepted, 1 enrolled. In 2014, 8 master's awarded. *Degree requirements:* For master's, thesis optional. *Entrance requirements:* For master's, letters of recommendation, essay, transcripts, interview. Additional exam requirements/recommendations for international students: Recommended—TOEFL. *Application deadline:* For fall admission, 8/25 priority date for domestic students; for spring admission, 12/8 priority date for domestic students; for summer admission, 6/8 priority date for domestic students. Applications are processed on a rolling basis. Application fee: $0. Electronic applications accepted. *Expenses:* Expenses: $225 per unit, $90 per unit independent study fee, $100 graduation fee. *Financial support:* In 2014–15, 9 students received support. Scholarships/grants available. Financial award application deadline: 6/5; financial award applicants required to submit FAFSA. *Faculty research:* Theology, Christian education, church administration. *Unit head:* Dr. Ron Benefiel, Dean, 619-849-2935, E-mail: ronbenefiel@pointloma.edu. *Application contact:* Laura Leinweber, Director of Graduate Admissions, 866-692-4723, E-mail: lauraleinweber@pointloma.edu.
Website: http://www.pointloma.edu/experience/academics/schools-departments/school-theology-christian-ministry/programs/master-ministry

Providence University College & Theological Seminary, Theological Seminary, Otterburne, MB R0A 1G0, Canada. Offers children's ministry (Certificate); Christian studies (MA, Certificate); counseling (MA); cross-cultural discipleship (Certificate); divinity (M Div); educational studies (MA), including counseling psychology, educational ministries, student development, teaching English to speakers of other languages, training teachers of English to speakers of other languages; global studies (MA); lay counseling (Diploma); ministry (D Min); teaching English to speakers of other languages (Certificate); theological studies (MA); training teacher of English to speakers of other languages (Certificate); youth ministry (Certificate). *Accreditation:* ATS. Part-time programs available. *Degree requirements:* For master's, variable foreign language requirement, thesis (for some programs); for doctorate, thesis/dissertation. *Entrance requirements:* Additional exam requirements/recommendations for international students: Recommended—TOEFL (minimum score 550 paper-based). *Faculty research:* Studies in Isaiah, theology of sin.

Reformed Theological Seminary–Charlotte Campus, Graduate and Professional Programs, Charlotte, NC 28226-6318. Offers biblical studies (MA); ministry (D Min); pastoral ministry (M Div); theological studies (MA). Part-time programs available. *Degree requirements:* For master's, comprehensive exam; for doctorate, thesis/dissertation. *Entrance requirements:* For master's, minimum GPA of 2.6; for doctorate, minimum GPA of 3.0. Additional exam requirements/recommendations for international students: Required—TOEFL (minimum score 550 paper-based). Electronic applications accepted.

Reformed Theological Seminary–Jackson Campus, Graduate and Professional Programs, Jackson, MS 39209-3099. Offers Bible, theology, and missions (Certificate); Biblical exegesis (M Div); biblical studies (MA); Christian education (MA); counseling (M Div); marriage and family therapy (MA); ministry (D Min); missions (M Div, MA, D Min); theological studies (MA). *Accreditation:* AAMFT/COAMFTE (one or more programs are accredited); ATS (one or more programs are accredited). *Faculty:* 10 full-time (0 women), 1 (woman) part-time/adjunct. *Students:* 50 full-time (14 women), 86 part-time (19 women). *Degree requirements:* For master's, thesis (for some programs), fieldwork; for doctorate, 2 foreign languages, thesis/dissertation. *Entrance requirements:* For master's, minimum GPA of 2.6; for doctorate, minimum GPA of 3.0. Additional exam requirements/recommendations for international students: Required—TOEFL. *Application deadline:* Applications are processed on a rolling basis. Application fee: $35. *Financial support:* Research assistantships, career-related internships or fieldwork, scholarships/grants, and tuition waivers (full and partial) available. Financial award application deadline: 5/1. *Application contact:* Brian Gault, Director of Admissions, 601-923-1600, Fax: 601-923-1654.

Reformed Theological Seminary–Orlando Campus, Graduate Program, Oviedo, FL 32765-7197. Offers Bible (Certificate); biblical studies (MA); church planting (D Min); counseling (MA); general ministries (D Min); missions (Certificate); theological studies (MA); theology (M Div, Certificate). Part-time programs available. Postbaccalaureate distance learning degree programs offered (minimal on-campus study). *Faculty:* 11 full-time (0 women), 7 part-time/adjunct (1 woman). *Students:* 287. *Application deadline:* Applications are processed on a rolling basis. Application fee: $75. Electronic applications accepted. *Expenses: Tuition:* Full-time $15,900. *Required fees:* $160. *Unit head:* Dr. Don Sweeting, President, 407-278-4406, Fax: 407-366-9425. *Application contact:* Dr. Kevin Collins, Director of Admissions, Placement, and Marketing, 407-278-8824, Fax: 407-366-9425, E-mail: admissions.orlando@rts.edu.

Regent University, Graduate School, School of Divinity, Virginia Beach, VA 23464-9800. Offers leadership and renewal (D Min), including Christian leadership and renewal, clinical pastoral education, community transformation, military ministry, ministry leadership coaching; practical theology (M Div, MA), including Biblical studies (M Div, MTS, PhD), chaplain ministry (M Div), Christian theology (M Div, MTS, PhD), church and ministry, history of Christianity (M Div, MTS), inter-cultural studies, interdisciplinary studies (M Div, MA, MTS), worship and renewal; renewal studies (PhD), including Biblical studies (M Div, MTS, PhD), Christian theology (M Div, MTS, PhD), history of global Christianity; theological studies (MTS), including Biblical studies (M Div, MTS, PhD), Christian theology (M Div, MTS, PhD), history of Christianity (M Div, MTS), interdisciplinary studies (M Div, MA, MTS). *Accreditation:* ACIPE; ATS. Part-time programs available. Postbaccalaureate distance learning degree programs offered (minimal on-campus study). *Faculty:* 20 full-time (3 women), 29 part-time/adjunct (3 women). *Students:* 64 full-time (28 women), 616 part-time (258 women); includes 318 minority (269 Black or African American, non-Hispanic/Latino; 7 American Indian or Alaska Native, non-Hispanic/Latino; 16 Asian, non-Hispanic/Latino; 26 Hispanic/Latino), 37 international. Average age 43. 511 applicants, 52% accepted, 187 enrolled. In 2014, 121 master's, 24 doctorates awarded. *Degree requirements:* For master's, comprehensive exam, thesis or alternative, internship; for doctorate, thesis/dissertation or alternative. *Entrance requirements:* For master's, GRE General Test or MAT, minimum undergraduate GPA of 2.75, writing sample, clergy recommendation; for doctorate, M Div or theological master's degree; minimum graduate GPA of 3.5 (PhD), 3.0 (D Min); recommendations; writing sample; transcripts. Additional exam requirements/recommendations for international students: Required—TOEFL (minimum score 577 paper-based). *Application deadline:* For fall admission, 5/1 priority date for domestic students. Applications are processed on a rolling basis. Application fee: $50. Electronic applications accepted. *Expenses:* Expenses: Contact institution. *Financial support:* Fellowships with full and partial tuition reimbursements, career-related internships or fieldwork, scholarships/grants, tuition waivers (full and partial), and

unspecified assistantships available. Support available to part-time students. Financial award application deadline: 9/1; financial award applicants required to submit FAFSA. *Faculty research:* Greek and Hebrew, theology, spiritual formation, global missions and world Christianity, women's studies. *Unit head:* Dr. Joseph Umidi, Interim Dean, 757-352-4401, Fax: 757-352-4597, E-mail: joseumi@regent.edu. *Application contact:* Matthew Chadwick, Director of Enrollment Support Services, 800-373-5504, Fax: 757-352-4381, E-mail: admissions@regent.edu.
Website: http://www.regent.edu/acad/schdiv/

Regis College, Graduate and Professional Programs, Toronto, ON M5S 2Z5, Canada. Offers eastern Christian studies (Certificate); Ignatian spirituality (Diploma); ministry (D Min); ministry and spirituality (MAMS); philosophical studies (Diploma); retreat direction (Certificate); sacred theology (STM, STD, STB, STL); spiritual direction (Diploma); theological studies (MTS, Diploma); theology (M Div, MA, Th M, PhD, Th D); M Div/MA. *Accreditation:* ATS (one or more programs are accredited). Terminal master's awarded for partial completion of doctoral program. *Degree requirements:* For master's, 2 foreign languages, thesis; for doctorate, 3 foreign languages, comprehensive exam, thesis/dissertation. *Entrance requirements:* For doctorate, minimum GPA of 3.7. Additional exam requirements/recommendations for international students: Required—TOEFL (minimum score 580 paper-based; 93 iBT), TWE (minimum score 5).

Richmont Graduate University, School of Ministry, Atlanta, GA 30327. Offers MA. Evening/weekend programs available. *Degree requirements:* For master's, thesis optional. *Entrance requirements:* For master's, transcripts, 3 recommendations, personal statement, resume. Electronic applications accepted. *Faculty research:* Integration of Biblical/theological studies; personal and spiritual formation, leadership enrichment; Biblical interpretation; leadership; spiritual formation.

Sacred Heart Major Seminary, School of Theology, Detroit, MI 48206-1799. Offers pastoral studies (MAPS); theology (M Div, MA). *Accreditation:* ACIPE; ATS. Part-time and evening/weekend programs available. *Degree requirements:* For master's, one foreign language, thesis optional, integrating project. *Entrance requirements:* For master's, GRE, previous course work in philosophy and theology. *Faculty research:* Local church history, patristics, spirituality, religious education.

St. Ambrose University, College of Arts and Sciences, Program in Pastoral Theology, Davenport, IA 52803-2898. Offers MP Th. Part-time programs available. *Degree requirements:* For master's, integration project. *Entrance requirements:* For master's, minimum GPA of 2.6, prior pastoral experience, 9 credits of course work in theology. Additional exam requirements/recommendations for international students: Required—TOEFL. Electronic applications accepted. *Expenses:* Contact institution. *Faculty research:* Theological education, ecclesiology, spirituality and liturgy, medical ethics.

St. Augustine's Seminary of Toronto, Graduate and Professional Programs, Scarborough, ON M1M 1M3, Canada. Offers divinity (M Div); lay ministry (Diploma); religious education (MRE); theological studies (MTS, Diploma). *Accreditation:* ATS. Part-time and evening/weekend programs available. *Entrance requirements:* Additional exam requirements/recommendations for international students: Required—TOEFL (minimum score 580 paper-based), TWE (minimum score 5).

St. Bernard's School of Theology and Ministry, Graduate and Professional Programs, Rochester, NY 14618. Offers pastoral studies (MA, Certificate); theological studies (MA); theology (M Div). *Accreditation:* ATS (one or more programs are accredited). Part-time and evening/weekend programs available. *Degree requirements:* For master's, variable foreign language requirement, thesis (for some programs). *Entrance requirements:* For master's, minimum GPA of 2.5.

St. Catherine University, Graduate Programs, Program in Theology, St. Paul, MN 55105. Offers catechetical ministry (Certificate); pastoral ministry (Certificate); spiritual direction (Certificate); theology (MA). Part-time programs available. *Faculty:* 8 full-time (2 women). *Students:* 1 full-time (0 women), 31 part-time (26 women); includes 1 minority (Hispanic/Latino). Average age 50. 5 applicants, 60% accepted, 1 enrolled. In 2014, 3 master's awarded. *Degree requirements:* For master's, comprehensive exam, thesis (for some programs). *Entrance requirements:* For master's, MAT, minimum GPA of 3.0. Additional exam requirements/recommendations for international students: Required—Michigan English Language Assessment Battery or TOEFL (minimum score 600 paper-based; 100 iBT). *Application deadline:* For fall admission, 8/1 priority date for domestic students. Applications are processed on a rolling basis. Application fee: $35. *Expenses:* Expenses: $636 per credit. *Financial support:* In 2014–15, 12 students received support. Research assistantships, career-related internships or fieldwork, and institutionally sponsored loans available. Support available to part-time students. Financial award application deadline: 4/1; financial award applicants required to submit FAFSA. *Faculty research:* Feminist scholarship, historical theology, symbols, rites of purification, spirituality. *Unit head:* Dr. William McDonough, Director, 651-690-6072, Fax: 651-690-6024. *Application contact:* 651-690-6933, Fax: 651-690-6064.

St. John's Seminary, Graduate and Professional Programs, Camarillo, CA 93012-2598. Offers divinity (M Div); pastoral ministry (MAPM); theology (MA). *Accreditation:* ATS. Part-time programs available. *Degree requirements:* For master's, comprehensive exam (for some programs), thesis optional, comprehensive integration paper (MAPM). *Entrance requirements:* For master's, GRE General Test, minimum GPA of 3.5 (MA), 2.5 (MAPM). Additional exam requirements/recommendations for international students: Required—TOEFL (minimum score 550 paper-based; 79 iBT). Electronic applications accepted. *Faculty research:* Biblical studies, moral theology, church history, systematic theology, spiritual theology.

Saint John's University, Saint John's School of Theology and Seminary, Collegeville, MN 56321. Offers divinity (M Div); liturgical music (MA); liturgical studies (MA); pastoral ministry (MA); theology (MA), including church history, liturgy, monastic studies, scripture, spirituality, systematics; M Div/MA. *Accreditation:* ATS. Part-time programs available. Postbaccalaureate distance learning degree programs offered (no on-campus study). *Degree requirements:* For master's, one foreign language, comprehensive exam (for some programs), thesis (for some programs). *Entrance requirements:* For master's, GRE General Test or MAT. Electronic applications accepted. *Faculty research:* Religious education, biblical literature.

Saint Joseph's College of Maine, Master of Arts in Pastoral Theology Program, Standish, ME 04084. Offers MA. Part-time programs available. Postbaccalaureate distance learning degree programs offered (no on-campus study). *Entrance requirements:* For master's, baccalaureate degree with minimum cumulative GPA of 2.5.

St. Joseph's Seminary, Graduate and Professional Programs, Yonkers, NY 10704. Offers Catholic philosophical studies (MA); divinity (M Div); pastoral studies (MAPS); theology (MA). *Accreditation:* ATS. *Degree requirements:* For master's, one foreign language, thesis. *Entrance requirements:* For master's, 27 credits in philosophy and 9 in theology. *Financial support:* Scholarships/grants available. *Unit head:* Rev. Msgr. Peter I. Vaccari, Rector, 914-968-6200, Fax: 914-376-2019. *Application contact:* Fr. Thomas V. Berg, Director of Admissions, 914-968-6200, Fax: 914-376-2019.

Saint Leo University, Graduate Studies in Theology, Saint Leo, FL 33574-6665. Offers MA. Part-time and evening/weekend programs available. Postbaccalaureate distance learning degree programs offered (no on-campus study). *Faculty:* 12 full-time (1 woman), 4 part-time/adjunct (2 women). *Students:* 269 full-time (79 women); includes 51 minority (39 Black or African American, non-Hispanic/Latino; 1 Asian, non-Hispanic/Latino; 9 Hispanic/Latino; 2 Two or more races, non-Hispanic/Latino), 1 international. Average age 50. In 2014, 27 master's awarded. *Entrance requirements:* For master's, bachelor's degree with minimum GPA of 3.0 from regionally-accredited college or university, letter of recommendation. Additional exam requirements/recommendations for international students: Required—TOEFL (minimum score 550 paper-based; 80 iBT). *Application deadline:* For fall admission, 7/1 priority date for domestic and international students; for spring admission, 11/1 priority date for domestic and international students. Applications are processed on a rolling basis. Application fee: $80. Electronic applications accepted. *Expenses:* Expenses: Contact institution. *Financial support:* In 2014–15, 3 students received support. Scholarships/grants and health care benefits available. Financial award application deadline: 3/1; financial award applicants required to submit FAFSA. *Faculty research:* Ecclesiology and the Second Vatican Council, sacramental theology and the liturgical movement, Christian and Eastern religious traditions, ecumenism, ministry and technology. *Unit head:* Dr. Randall Woodard, Director, Graduate Theology, 352-588-8239, Fax: 352-588-8404, E-mail: randall.woodard@saintleo.edu. *Application contact:* Joshua Stagner, Director of Graduate Admission, 800-707-8846, Fax: 352-588-7873, E-mail: grad.admissions@saintleo.edu.
Website: http://www.saintleo.edu/academics/graduate/theology.aspx

Saint Mary-of-the-Woods College, Program in Pastoral Theology, Saint Mary of the Woods, IN 47876. Offers pastoral theology (MA); youth ministry (Graduate Certificate). Part-time and evening/weekend programs available. Postbaccalaureate distance learning degree programs offered (minimal on-campus study). *Degree requirements:* For master's, thesis, qualifying exam.

Saint Meinrad School of Theology, Master of Arts (Pastoral Theology) Program, Saint Meinrad, IN 47577. Offers MA. *Accreditation:* ATS. Part-time and evening/weekend programs available. *Faculty:* 22 full-time (2 women), 5 part-time/adjunct (1 woman). *Students:* 33 part-time (25 women). Average age 51. *Degree requirements:* For master's, thesis, three capstone essays, one research paper, or pastoral research project. *Entrance requirements:* Additional exam requirements/recommendations for international students: Required—TOEFL. *Application deadline:* For fall admission, 7/31 for domestic and international students; for winter admission, 11/15 for domestic and international students. Applications are processed on a rolling basis. Application fee: $30. *Expenses: Tuition:* Full-time $21,920; part-time $395 per credit hour. *Required fees:* $29 per course. *Financial support:* Federal Work-Study, institutionally sponsored loans, and scholarships/grants available. Support available to part-time students. Financial award application deadline: 7/31; financial award applicants required to submit FAFSA. *Unit head:* Dr. Robert Alvis, Academic Dean, 812-357-6543. *Application contact:* Sr. Jeana Visel, Director of Lay Degree Programs, 812-357-6678, Fax: 812-357-6462, E-mail: apply@saintmeinrad.edu.

Saint Paul University, Faculty of Canon Law, Ottawa, ON K1S 1C4, Canada. Offers canon law (MCL, JCD, PhD, Graduate Certificate, JCL); canonical practice (Graduate Certificate); ecclesiastical administration (Graduate Certificate). Part-time programs available. *Degree requirements:* For master's, one foreign language; for doctorate, one foreign language, comprehensive exam, thesis/dissertation; for other advanced degree, one foreign language, comprehensive exam and seminar paper (JCL). *Entrance requirements:* For master's, appropriate bachelor's degree, 18 credits in theology; for doctorate, JCL or MCL; for other advanced degree, B Th or equivalent (JCL), appropriate bachelor's degree, 18 credits in theology. *Faculty research:* Questions related to Church law.

Saint Paul University, Faculty of Human Sciences, Program in Counseling and Spirituality, Ottawa, ON K1S 1C4, Canada. Offers individual or marital/couple counseling (MA); spiritual care (MA). Part-time programs available. *Degree requirements:* For master's, research project or thesis. *Entrance requirements:* For master's, honors BA in human sciences, minimum B average, 12 theology credits.

Saints Cyril and Methodius Seminary, Graduate and Professional Programs, Orchard Lake, MI 48324. Offers pastoral ministry (MAPM); religious education (MARE); theology (M Div, MA). *Accreditation:* ATS. Part-time programs available.

St. Stephen's College, Programs in Theology, Edmonton, AB T6G 2J6, Canada. Offers ministry (D Min); pastoral counseling (MA); social transformation ministry (MA); spirituality and liturgy (MA); theological studies (MTS); theology (M Th). Part-time and evening/weekend programs available. Postbaccalaureate distance learning degree programs offered (minimal on-campus study). Terminal master's awarded for partial completion of doctoral program. *Degree requirements:* For master's, thesis; for doctorate, thesis/dissertation. *Entrance requirements:* Additional exam requirements/recommendations for international students: Required—TOEFL. Electronic applications accepted. *Faculty research:* Methodology for theological education, practice and supervision for ministry.

St. Thomas University, School of Theology and Ministry, Institute for Pastoral Ministries, Miami Gardens, FL 33054-6459. Offers pastoral ministries (MA, Certificate); practical theology (PhD). Part-time and evening/weekend programs available. *Degree requirements:* For master's, comprehensive exam; for doctorate, comprehensive exam, thesis/dissertation. *Entrance requirements:* For master's, interview, minimum GPA of 3.0 or GRE; for doctorate, GRE, MA in theology. Additional exam requirements/recommendations for international students: Required—TOEFL (minimum score 550 paper-based; 79 iBT). Electronic applications accepted.

Saint Vincent Seminary, School of Theology, Latrobe, PA 15650-2690. Offers ecclesial ministry (MA); ministry (M Div); monastic studies (MA); sacred scripture (MA); systematic theology (MA). *Accreditation:* ATS. Part-time and evening/weekend programs available. *Faculty:* 4 full-time (1 woman), 16 part-time/adjunct (1 woman). *Students:* 39 full-time (0 women), 4 part-time (0 women); includes 4 minority (2 Asian, non-Hispanic/Latino; 2 Hispanic/Latino), 10 international. Average age 36. 7 applicants, 100% accepted, 7 enrolled. In 2014, 14 master's awarded. *Degree requirements:* For master's, one foreign language, comprehensive exam, thesis optional, public presentation. *Entrance requirements:* For master's, minimum GPA of 2.5. Additional exam requirements/recommendations for international students: Required—TOEFL (minimum score 550 paper-based; 79 iBT). *Application deadline:* For fall admission, 8/15 priority date for domestic students, 8/15 for international students. Applications are processed on a rolling basis. Application fee: $34. *Expenses: Tuition:* Full-time $24,334; part-time $808 per credit. *Financial support:* In 2014–15, 43 students received support. Scholarships/grants available. Support available to part-time students. Financial award application deadline: 8/15. *Faculty research:* Church history, preaching, psychology of religion, Biblical studies, moral theology. *Unit head:* Very Rev. Timothy F. Whalen, President/Rector, 724-805-2592, Fax: 724-532-5052, E-mail: timothy.whalen@stvincent.edu. *Application contact:* Rev. Patrick T. Cronauer, OSB, Academic Dean, 724-805-2324, Fax: 724-805-2880, E-mail: patrick.cronauer@stvincent.edu.
Website: http://www.saintvincentseminary.edu

Santa Clara University, College of Arts and Sciences, Santa Clara, CA 95053. Offers pastoral ministry (MA). Part-time and evening/weekend programs available. *Faculty:* 5

full-time (1 woman), 1 part-time/adjunct (0 women). *Students:* 6 full-time (3 women), 52 part-time (31 women); includes 35 minority (1 Black or African American, non-Hispanic/Latino; 7 Asian, non-Hispanic/Latino; 26 Hispanic/Latino; 1 Two or more races, non-Hispanic/Latino), 4 international. Average age 45. 52 applicants, 96% accepted, 46 enrolled. In 2014, 8 master's awarded. *Degree requirements:* For master's, comprehensive exam, thesis optional. *Entrance requirements:* For master's, 3 letters of recommendation, resume, statement of purpose, transcripts. Additional exam requirements/recommendations for international students: Required—TOEFL. *Application deadline:* Applications are processed on a rolling basis. Application fee: $50. Electronic applications accepted. *Expenses:* Expenses: Contact institution. *Financial support:* In 2014–15, 85 students received support. Career-related internships or fieldwork, Federal Work-Study, institutionally sponsored loans, and scholarships/grants available. Support available to part-time students. Financial award applicants required to submit FAFSA. *Faculty research:* Scripture, spirituality, social justice. *Unit head:* Gary Macy, Director, Graduate Program in Pastoral Ministries, 408-554-2357, E-mail: gmacy@scu.edu. *Application contact:* Saralynn Ferrara, Senior Administrative Assistant, 408-554-4831, E-mail: sferrara@scu.edu.
Website: http://www.scu.edu/cas/pastoralministries/

Seattle University, School of Theology and Ministry, Program in Pastoral Counseling, Seattle, WA 98122-1090. Offers MAPC. Part-time and evening/weekend programs available. *Faculty:* 12 full-time (6 women), 9 part-time/adjunct (5 women). *Students:* 6 full-time (4 women), 30 part-time (19 women); includes 9 minority (3 Black or African American, non-Hispanic/Latino; 1 American Indian or Alaska Native, non-Hispanic/Latino; 4 Hispanic/Latino; 1 Two or more races, non-Hispanic/Latino). Average age 43. 12 applicants, 33% accepted, 3 enrolled. In 2014, 8 master's awarded. *Entrance requirements:* For master's, minimum GPA of 2.75 (3.0 for international students); two years of experience in some form of education, ministry, or service as a profession or volunteer; recommendations; interview with admissions committee. *Application deadline:* For fall admission, 7/1 for domestic students. *Financial support:* In 2014–15, 21 students received support. Scholarships/grants available. *Unit head:* Rev. Clinton McNair, Director, 206-296-6968. *Application contact:* Catherine Kehoe Fallon, Admissions Coordinator, 206-296-5333, Fax: 206-296-5329, E-mail: fallon@seattleu.edu.
Website: https://www.seattleu.edu/stm/degrees/marpt/

Seattle University, School of Theology and Ministry, Program in Pastoral Studies, Seattle, WA 98122-1090. Offers MAPS. Part-time and evening/weekend programs available. *Faculty:* 12 full-time (6 women), 9 part-time/adjunct (5 women). *Students:* 1 full-time (0 women), 27 part-time (20 women); includes 5 minority (2 Asian, non-Hispanic/Latino; 3 Hispanic/Latino). Average age 50. 15 applicants, 80% accepted, 10 enrolled. In 2014, 6 master's awarded. *Degree requirements:* For master's, project. *Entrance requirements:* For master's, minimum GPA of 2.75 (3.0 for international students); two years of experience in some form of education, ministry, or service as a profession or volunteer; recommendations; interview with admissions committee. *Application deadline:* For fall admission, 7/1 priority date for domestic students. Application fee: $55. *Financial support:* In 2014–15, 17 students received support. Application deadline: 4/1; applicants required to submit FAFSA. *Unit head:* Dr. Mark Markuly, Director, 206-296-5330, Fax: 206-296-5329, E-mail: markulym@seattleu.edu. *Application contact:* Catherine Kehoe Fallon, Admissions Coordinator, 206-296-5333, Fax: 206-296-5329, E-mail: fallon@seattleu.edu.
Website: https://www.seattleu.edu/stm/degrees/maps/

Seattle University, School of Theology and Ministry, Program in Transformational Leadership, Seattle, WA 98122-1090. Offers MATL. *Faculty:* 12 full-time (6 women), 9 part-time/adjunct (5 women). *Students:* 7 full-time (4 women), 22 part-time (15 women); includes 7 minority (2 Black or African American, non-Hispanic/Latino; 1 Asian, non-Hispanic/Latino; 1 Hispanic/Latino; 3 Two or more races, non-Hispanic/Latino), 2 international. Average age 38. 17 applicants, 65% accepted, 10 enrolled. In 2014, 6 master's awarded. *Degree requirements:* For master's, project. *Entrance requirements:* For master's, minimum GPA of 2.75 (3.0 for international students); two years of experience in some form of education, ministry, or service as a profession or volunteer; recommendations; interview with admissions committee. *Application deadline:* For fall admission, 7/1 priority date for domestic students. Application fee: $55. *Financial support:* In 2014–15, 21 students received support. Application deadline: 4/1; applicants required to submit FAFSA. *Unit head:* Dr. Mark Markuly, Dean, 206-296-5330, Fax: 206-296-5329, E-mail: stm@seattleu.edu. *Application contact:* Catherine Kehoe Fallon, Admissions Coordinator, 206-296-5333, Fax: 206-296-5329, E-mail: fallon@seattleu.edu.
Website: http://www.seattleu.edu/stm/degrees/matl/

Seminary of the Immaculate Conception, School of Theology, Huntington, NY 11743-1696. Offers pastoral studies (MA); theology (M Div, MA, D Min, Certificate). *Accreditation:* ATS (one or more programs are accredited). Part-time and evening/weekend programs available. *Degree requirements:* For master's, seminar and paper/thesis; for doctorate, thesis/dissertation. *Entrance requirements:* For master's, undergraduate degree; for doctorate, MA plus 30 credits or M Div; for Certificate, MA in theology.

Seton Hall University, Immaculate Conception Seminary School of Theology, South Orange, NJ 07079-2697. Offers Christian spirituality (Certificate); great spiritual books (Certificate); pastoral ministry (M Div, MA, Certificate); scripture studies (Certificate); Seminary's Theological Education for Parish Services (STEPS) (Certificate); theology (MA). *Accreditation:* ATS (one or more programs are accredited). Part-time and evening/weekend programs available. *Degree requirements:* For master's, comprehensive exam (for some programs), thesis (for some programs), final project (for some programs); 1 foreign language (for MA in theology research option). *Entrance requirements:* For master's, GRE General Test or MAT. Additional exam requirements/recommendations for international students: Required—TOEFL (minimum score 600 paper-based; 100 iBT). Electronic applications accepted. *Expenses:* Contact institution. *Faculty research:* Pauline literature, history of Biblical interpretation and theological exegesis, spirituality of St. Edith Stein, Thomism, history of Catholicism in America.

Shasta Bible College, Program in Biblical Counseling, Redding, CA 96002. Offers biblical counseling and Christian family life education (MA). Part-time programs available. *Degree requirements:* For master's, comprehensive exam (for some programs), thesis or alternative. *Entrance requirements:* For master's, minimum GPA of 2.5. Additional exam requirements/recommendations for international students: Required—TOEFL (minimum score 550 paper-based).

Shasta Bible College, Program in Christian Ministry, Redding, CA 96002. Offers MA. Part-time programs available. Postbaccalaureate distance learning degree programs offered (minimal on-campus study). *Entrance requirements:* Additional exam requirements/recommendations for international students: Required—TOEFL (minimum score 550 paper-based).

Shepherds Theological Seminary, Graduate Programs, Cary, NC 27518. Offers church ministry (MA); New Testament (M Div); Old Testament (M Div); theology (M Div). *Degree requirements:* For master's, thesis.

Shiloh University, Graduate Programs, Kalona, IA 52247. Offers Biblical and pastoral studies (MA); ministry (M Div). Part-time and evening/weekend programs available. Postbaccalaureate distance learning degree programs offered (no on-campus study). *Faculty:* 3 full-time (0 women), 6 part-time/adjunct (3 women). *Students:* 1 full-time (0 women), 26 part-time (5 women); includes 3 minority (1 Black or African American, non-Hispanic/Latino; 1 Hispanic/Latino; 1 Native Hawaiian or other Pacific Islander, non-Hispanic/Latino), 2 international. Average age 47. In 2014, 3 master's awarded. *Degree requirements:* For master's, thesis optional. *Entrance requirements:* For master's, bachelor's degree or educational equivalent from accredited school with minimum GPA of 2.75 on undergraduate work. Additional exam requirements/recommendations for international students: Recommended—TOEFL (minimum score 540 paper-based; 76 iBT), IELTS (minimum score 6.5). *Application deadline:* For fall admission, 7/6 for domestic and international students; for spring admission, 11/9 for domestic and international students; for summer admission, 3/7 for domestic and international students. Applications are processed on a rolling basis. Application fee: $0. Electronic applications accepted. *Expenses:* Expenses: $450 per credit. *Faculty research:* New testament theology, Pauline literature, relational theology. *Unit head:* Dr. Wesley Pinkham, Vice President of Academics, 319-656-2447 Ext. 2, Fax: 319-656-2448, E-mail: wess.pinkham@shilohuniversity.edu. *Application contact:* Andrew Thompson, Admissions Coordinator, 319-656-2447 Ext. 2, Fax: 319-656-2448, E-mail: admissions@shilohuniversity.edu.
Website: http://www.shilohuniversity.edu/academics/

Sioux Falls Seminary, Graduate and Professional Programs, Master of Divinity Program, Sioux Falls, SD 57105-1599. Offers marriage and family therapy (M Div); pastoral care and counseling (M Div). Program also offered in Omaha, NE. *Accreditation:* ACIPE. Part-time programs available. Postbaccalaureate distance learning degree programs offered (no on-campus study).

Sioux Falls Seminary, Graduate and Professional Programs, Program in Counseling, Sioux Falls, SD 57105-1599. Offers MA. Part-time programs available. *Entrance requirements:* For master's, minimum GPA of 2.5.

Sofia University, Hybrid: Face-to-Face/Online Programs, Palo Alto, CA 94303. Offers counseling psychology (MA); psychology (PhD), including transpersonal psychology; spiritual guidance (MA); transpersonal psychology (MA, Certificate); women's spirituality (MA, Certificate). Postbaccalaureate distance learning degree programs offered (minimal on-campus study). *Entrance requirements:* For master's, bachelor's degree; for doctorate, bachelor's degree; master's degree. Electronic applications accepted.

Southeastern University, College of Christian Ministries and Religion, Lakeland, FL 33801-6099. Offers ministerial leadership (MA). Evening/weekend programs available. Postbaccalaureate distance learning degree programs offered. *Degree requirements:* For master's, thesis/project.

Southern Baptist Theological Seminary, Billy Graham School of Missions and Evangelism, Louisville, KY 40280-0004. Offers ministry (D Min); missiology (MA, D Miss); missions and evangelism (M Div, Th M, PhD); theological studies (MA). *Accreditation:* ATS. Part-time and evening/weekend programs available. Postbaccalaureate distance learning degree programs offered (minimal on-campus study). *Degree requirements:* For master's, 2 foreign languages; for doctorate, 4 foreign languages, thesis/dissertation. *Entrance requirements:* For doctorate, GRE General Test, MAT, M Div. Additional exam requirements/recommendations for international students: Required—TOEFL, TWE. *Faculty research:* Assimilation of church congregants, effective methodologies of evangelism, expectations of church members, spiritual warfare literature, formative church discipline.

Southern Baptist Theological Seminary, School of Church Ministries, Louisville, KY 40280-0004. Offers Biblical counseling (M Div, MA); children's and family ministry (M Div, MA); Christian education (MA); Christian worship (PhD); church ministries (M Div); church music (MCM); college ministry (M Div, MA); discipleship and family ministry (M Div, MA); education (Ed D); family ministry (D Min, PhD); higher education (PhD); leadership (M Div, MA, D Min, PhD); ministry (D Ed Min); missions and ethnodoxology (M Div); women's leadership (M Div, MA); worship leadership (M Div, MA); worship leadership and church ministry (MA); youth and family ministry (M Div, MA). Part-time programs available. Postbaccalaureate distance learning degree programs offered (minimal on-campus study). *Degree requirements:* For doctorate, thesis/dissertation. *Entrance requirements:* For doctorate, GRE General Test, interview, M Div or MACE. Additional exam requirements/recommendations for international students: Required—TWE. *Faculty research:* Gerontology, creative teaching methods, faith development in children, faith development in youth, transformational learning.

Southern Baptist Theological Seminary, School of Theology, Louisville, KY 40280-0004. Offers applied theology (D Min); biblical and theological studies (M Div); biblical counseling (M Div, MA, D Min); biblical spirituality (D Min); Christian ministry (M Div); expository preaching (D Min); pastoral studies (M Div); theological studies (MA); theology (Th M, PhD); worldview and apologetics (M Div). *Accreditation:* ATS. Part-time and evening/weekend programs available. Postbaccalaureate distance learning degree programs offered (minimal on-campus study). *Degree requirements:* For master's, 2 foreign languages, thesis; for doctorate, 4 foreign languages, thesis/dissertation. *Entrance requirements:* For master's, GRE General Test, MAT, M Div; for doctorate, GRE General Test, MAT, interview, M Div, field essay. Additional exam requirements/recommendations for international students: Required—TOEFL, TWE. *Faculty research:* Biblical studies, contemporary theology, church history, pastoral care, ministry/missions studies.

Southern Evangelical Seminary, Graduate Programs, Matthews, NC 28105. Offers apologetics (MA, D Min, Certificate); Christian education (MA); church ministry (MA, Certificate); divinity (Certificate), including apologetics (M Div, Certificate); Islamic studies (MA, Certificate); Jewish studies (MA); philosophy (MA); philosophy of religion (PhD); religion (MA); theology (M Div), including apologetics (M Div, Certificate), Biblical studies; youth ministry (MA). Part-time and evening/weekend programs available. Postbaccalaureate distance learning degree programs offered. *Degree requirements:* For master's, thesis (for some programs); for doctorate, 2 foreign languages, comprehensive exam (for some programs), thesis/dissertation. *Entrance requirements:* Additional exam requirements/recommendations for international students: Required—TOEFL (minimum score 600 paper-based).

Southern Wesleyan University, Program in Christian Ministries, Central, SC 29630-1020. Offers M Min. Part-time and evening/weekend programs available. *Entrance requirements:* For master's, GRE General Test or MAT, biographical paper; 12 semester credit hours of undergraduate work in religion, Bible, or ethics; 2 years of full-time Christian ministry experience. Additional exam requirements/recommendations for international students: Required—TOEFL (minimum score 500 paper-based).

South University, Graduate Programs, Doctor of Ministry Program, Savannah, GA 31406. Offers D Min.

South University, Program in Ministry, Novi, MI 48377. Offers D Min.

Southwestern Assemblies of God University, Thomas F. Harrison School of Graduate Studies, Program in Theological Studies, Waxahachie, TX 75165-5735. Offers Bible and theology (MS); Biblical studies (M Div); counseling (M Div); cross cultural

missions (M Div); practical theology (M Div); theological studies (M Div). Postbaccalaureate distance learning degree programs offered. *Degree requirements:* For master's, comprehensive written and oral exams. *Entrance requirements:* For master's, GRE General Test, minimum GPA of 2.5. Electronic applications accepted.

Southwestern Baptist Theological Seminary, School of Theology, Fort Worth, TX 76122-0000. Offers ministry (D Min); theology (PhD). *Accreditation:* ACIPE; ATS (one or more programs are accredited). Part-time and evening/weekend programs available. Terminal master's awarded for partial completion of doctoral program. *Degree requirements:* For master's, 2 foreign languages, thesis (for some programs); for doctorate, 2 foreign languages, comprehensive exam, thesis/dissertation, oral exams. *Entrance requirements:* For doctorate, GRE, M Div or equivalent. Additional exam requirements/recommendations for international students: Required—TOEFL. *Application deadline:* For fall admission, 7/15 priority date for domestic students, 4/1 for international students; for spring admission, 12/15 priority date for domestic students, 10/1 for international students. Applications are processed on a rolling basis. Electronic applications accepted. *Financial support:* Teaching assistantships, career-related internships or fieldwork, institutionally sponsored loans, scholarships/grants, and tuition waivers (partial) available. Support available to part-time students. Financial award application deadline: 11/1. *Unit head:* Dr. David Allen, Dean, 817-923-1921 Ext. 4200, Fax: 817-921-8767, E-mail: dallen@swbts.edu. *Application contact:* Director of Admissions, 817-923-1921 Ext. 2700, Fax: 817-921-8757, E-mail: admissions@swbts.edu.
Website: http://swbts.edu/academics/schools-programs/theology/

Southwestern Christian University, Program in Ministry, Bethany, OK 73008-0340. Offers church planting (M Min); church revitalization and renewal (M Min); intercultural studies (M Min); leadership (M Min); life coaching (M Min); pastoral ministries (M Min); work place ministries (M Min). Part-time programs available. *Degree requirements:* For master's, thesis. *Entrance requirements:* For master's, minimum GPA of 2.5. Additional exam requirements/recommendations for international students: Required—TOEFL (minimum score 500 paper-based). Electronic applications accepted.

Spring Arbor University, School of Arts and Sciences, Spring Arbor, MI 49283-9799. Offers communication (MA); spiritual formation and leadership (MA). Part-time programs available. Postbaccalaureate distance learning degree programs offered (no on-campus study). *Degree requirements:* For master's, thesis (for some programs). *Entrance requirements:* For master's, GRE (minimum score of 40th percentile and taken within last 5 years), bachelor's degree from regionally-accredited college or university, minimum GPA of 3.0 for at least the last two years of the bachelor's degree, at least two recommendations from professional/academic individuals. Additional exam requirements/recommendations for international students: Required—TOEFL (minimum score 600 paper-based). *Expenses:* Contact institution.

Spring Hill College, Graduate Programs, Program in Theology, Mobile, AL 36608-1791. Offers faith companioning (Postbaccalaureate Certificate); pastoral ministry (Postbaccalaureate Certificate); pastoral studies (MPS); spiritual direction (Postbaccalaureate Certificate); theological studies (MTS); theology (MA). Part-time and evening/weekend programs available. *Faculty:* 5 full-time (0 women), 2 part-time/adjunct (both women). *Students:* 43 part-time (20 women); includes 3 minority (1 Black or African American, non-Hispanic/Latino; 2 Asian, non-Hispanic/Latino). Average age 47. In 2014, 8 master's, 4 other advanced degrees awarded. *Degree requirements:* For master's, variable foreign language requirement, comprehensive exam, thesis (for some programs), completion of program within 6 calendar years of initial enrollment (MTS, MPS); completion of program within 4 1/2 calendar years of formal acceptance (MA). *Entrance requirements:* For master's, bachelor's degree with minimum undergraduate GPA of 3.0; six hours of undergraduate theology, religious studies, or unquestioned equivalency. Additional exam requirements/recommendations for international students: Required—TOEFL (minimum score 550 paper-based; 80 iBT), IELTS (minimum score 6.5), CPE or CAE (minimum score C), Michigan English Language Assessment Battery (minimum score 90). *Application deadline:* For fall admission, 8/1 priority date for domestic and international students; for spring admission, 12/1 priority date for domestic and international students. Applications are processed on a rolling basis. Application fee: $25 ($35 for international students). Electronic applications accepted. *Expenses: Tuition:* Full-time $8820; part-time $490 per credit hour. Tuition and fees vary according to program. *Financial support:* Applicants required to submit FAFSA. *Unit head:* Dr. Timothy R. Carmody, Director, 251-380-4665, Fax: 251-460-2194, E-mail: carmody@shc.edu. *Application contact:* Robert Stewart, Vice President of Enrollment, 251-380-3030, Fax: 251-460-2186, E-mail: rstewart@shc.edu.
Website: http://ug.shc.edu/graduate-degrees/master-arts-theological-studies/

Summit University, Baptist Bible Seminary, Clarks Summit, PA 18411-1297. Offers Biblical apologetics (MA); church education (M Div, M Min); church planting (M Div, M Min); global ministry (M Div, M Min); leadership in communication (D Min); leadership in counseling and spiritual development (D Min); leadership in global ministry (D Min); leadership in pastoral ministry (D Min); leadership in theological studies (D Min); military chaplaincy (M Div); ministry (PhD); organizational leadership (M Min); outreach pastor (M Div, M Min); pastoral counseling (M Div, M Min); pastoral leadership (M Div, M Min); theology (Th M); worship ministries leadership (M Div, M Min); youth pastor (M Div, M Min). Part-time and evening/weekend programs available. Postbaccalaureate distance learning degree programs offered (minimal on-campus study). Terminal master's awarded for partial completion of doctoral program. *Degree requirements:* For master's, 2 foreign languages, thesis, oral exam (for M Div); for doctorate, 2 foreign languages, comprehensive exam (for some programs), thesis/dissertation, oral exam. *Entrance requirements:* For doctorate, Greek and Hebrew entrance exams (for PhD). Electronic applications accepted.

Trevecca Nazarene University, Graduate Religion Programs, Nashville, TN 37210-2877. Offers biblical studies (MA); pastoral arts (MA); preaching (MA); theological studies (MA). Part-time programs available. *Faculty:* 3 full-time (0 women), 1 part-time/adjunct (0 women). *Students:* 6 full-time (2 women), 7 part-time (1 woman); includes 3 minority (2 Black or African American, non-Hispanic/Latino; 1 Hispanic/Latino). Average age 36. In 2014, 14 master's awarded. *Degree requirements:* For master's, comprehensive exam, thesis. *Entrance requirements:* For master's, GRE General Test or MAT, minimum GPA of 2.7, official transcript from regionally-accredited institution, 2 letters of recommendation, philosophy of ministry statement. Additional exam requirements/recommendations for international students: Required—TOEFL (minimum score 550 paper-based). *Application deadline:* Applications are processed on a rolling basis. Application fee: $25. Electronic applications accepted. *Expenses:* Expenses: Contact institution. *Financial support:* Applicants required to submit FAFSA. *Unit head:* Dr. Tim Green, Dean, School of Religion and Philosophy/Director, Graduate Religion Program, 615-248-1378, Fax: 615-248-7417. *Application contact:* 615-248-1529, E-mail: cll@trevecca.edu.
Website: http://trevecca.edu/academics/program/religion

Trinity College, Faculty of Divinity, Toronto, ON M5S 1H8, Canada. Offers ministry (Diploma); ministry for church musicians (Diploma); theology (M Div, MA, MTS, Th M, D Min, PhD, Th D, Diploma, L Th); M Div/MA. *Accreditation:* ATS. Part-time programs available. *Degree requirements:* For master's, 2 foreign languages, thesis (for some programs); for doctorate, 3 foreign languages, comprehensive exam, thesis/dissertation; for other advanced degree, thesis (for some programs). *Entrance requirements:* For master's, 1 language (modern or ancient), interview; for doctorate, 2 languages (modern and ancient). Additional exam requirements/recommendations for international students: Required—TOEFL, TWE. *Faculty research:* Interreligious dialogue, feminist theology, systematic theology, philosophy of religion, pastoral theology.

Trinity International University, Trinity Evangelical Divinity School, Deerfield, IL 60015-1284. Offers Biblical and Near Eastern archaeology and languages (MA); Christian studies (MA, Certificate); Christian thought (MA); church history (MA, Th M); congregational ministry: pastor-teacher (M Div); congregational ministry: team ministry (M Div); counseling ministries (MA); counseling psychology (MA); cross-cultural ministry (M Div); educational studies (PhD); evangelism (MA); history of Christianity in America (MA); intercultural studies (MA, PhD); leadership and ministry management (D Min); military chaplaincy (D Min); ministry (MA); mission and evangelism (Th M); missions and evangelism (D Min); New Testament (MA, Th M); Old Testament (Th M); Old Testament and Semitic languages (MA); pastoral care (M Div); pastoral care and counseling (D Min); pastoral counseling and psychology (Th M); pastoral theology (Th M); philosophy of religion (MA); preaching (D Min); religion (MA); research ministry (M Div); systematic theology (Th M); theological studies (PhD); urban ministry (MA). *Accreditation:* ATS (one or more programs are accredited). Part-time programs available. Postbaccalaureate distance learning degree programs offered (minimal on-campus study). *Degree requirements:* For master's, comprehensive exam, thesis, fieldwork; for doctorate, comprehensive exam (for some programs), thesis/dissertation; for Certificate, comprehensive exam, integrative papers. *Entrance requirements:* For master's, GRE, MAT, minimum cumulative undergraduate GPA of 3.0; for doctorate, GRE, minimum cumulative graduate GPA of 3.2; for Certificate, GRE, MAT, minimum undergraduate GPA of 2.5. Additional exam requirements/recommendations for international students: Required—TOEFL (minimum score 580 paper-based), TWE (minimum score 4). Electronic applications accepted.

Trinity Lutheran Seminary, Graduate and Professional Programs, Columbus, OH 43209-2334. Offers African American studies (MTS); Biblical studies (MTS, STM); Christian education (MA); Christian spirituality (STM); church in the world (MTS); church music (MA); divinity (M Div); general theological studies (MTS); mission and evangelism (STM); pastoral leadership and practice (STM); youth and family ministry (MA); MSN/MTS; MTS/JD. *Accreditation:* ACIPE; ATS. Part-time programs available. *Faculty:* 11 full-time (5 women), 2 part-time/adjunct (both women). *Students:* 68 full-time (24 women), 43 part-time (18 women); includes 12 minority (10 Black or African American, non-Hispanic/Latino; 1 Asian, non-Hispanic/Latino; 1 Two or more races, non-Hispanic/Latino), 1 international. Average age 35. 45 applicants, 96% accepted, 34 enrolled. In 2014, 34 master's awarded. *Degree requirements:* For master's, variable foreign language requirement, comprehensive exam (for some programs), thesis (for some programs), field experience (for some programs). *Entrance requirements:* For master's, BA or equivalent (for MA, M Div, MTS); M Div, MTS, or equivalent (for STM); audition (for MACM). Additional exam requirements/recommendations for international students: Required—TOEFL. *Application deadline:* For fall admission, 7/15 priority date for domestic and international students. Applications are processed on a rolling basis. Application fee: $25. Electronic applications accepted. *Expenses:* Expenses: $13,760 tuition and fees for degree completion (for D Min). *Financial support:* In 2014–15, 72 students received support. Career-related internships or fieldwork, Federal Work-Study, and scholarships/grants available. Support available to part-time students. Financial award application deadline: 5/1; financial award applicants required to submit FAFSA. *Unit head:* Dr. Brad A. Binau, Academic Dean, 614-235-4136 Ext. 4674, Fax: 614-384-4635, E-mail: bbinau@tlsohio.edu. *Application contact:* Rev. Seth Bridger, Director of Admissions, 614-235-4136 Ext. 4650, Fax: 866-610-8572, E-mail: sbridger@tlsohio.edu.
Website: http://www.tlsohio.edu

Trinity School for Ministry, Graduate Programs, Ambridge, PA 15003-2397. Offers Anglican studies (Diploma); basic Christian studies (Diploma); divinity (M Div); ministry (D Min); mission and evangelism (MAME, Diploma); religion (MAR); youth ministry (Diploma). *Accreditation:* ATS (one or more programs are accredited). Part-time programs available. *Degree requirements:* For master's, thesis optional; for doctorate, thesis/dissertation. *Entrance requirements:* Additional exam requirements/recommendations for international students: Required—TOEFL. *Faculty research:* Pauline Epistles, contemporary theology, history of Anglican liturgy, book of Ruth, biblical theology.

Trinity Western University, ACTS Seminaries, Langley, BC V2Y 1Y1, Canada. Offers Christian studies (MA); cross cultural ministry (MA); theology (M Div, M Th, MAMFT, MLE, MTS, D Min). *Accreditation:* ATS. Part-time programs available. *Degree requirements:* For master's, thesis (for some programs), internship. *Entrance requirements:* For doctorate, MDiv or equivalent. Additional exam requirements/recommendations for international students: Required—TOEFL. *Expenses:* Contact institution. *Faculty research:* Theology of leadership.

Tyndale University College & Seminary, Graduate Programs, Toronto, ON M2M 4B3, Canada. Offers Biblical studies (M Div); Christian foundations (MTS); Christian studies (Diploma); counseling (M Div); educational ministry (M Div); missions (M Div, Diploma); pastoral and Chinese ministry (M Div); pastoral ministry (M Div); Pentecostal studies (MTS); spiritual formation (M Div, Diploma); theological studies (M Div); theology (Th M); worship and liturgy (M Div, MTS); youth and family ministry (M Div). *Accreditation:* ATS. Part-time programs available. Postbaccalaureate distance learning degree programs offered (no on-campus study). *Entrance requirements:* For master's and Diploma, minimum C+ average in undergraduate course work. Additional exam requirements/recommendations for international students: Required—TOEFL (minimum score 570 paper-based), TWE (minimum score 5). Electronic applications accepted. *Faculty research:* Canadian church history, Chinese church history, Old Testament, counseling ministries (narrative therapy), world religions.

Unification Theological Seminary, Graduate Program, Main Campus, Barrytown, NY 12507. Offers divinity (M Div); ministry (D Min); religious education (MRE); religious studies (MA). Part-time and evening/weekend programs available. *Faculty:* 1 full-time (0 women), 5 part-time/adjunct (1 woman). *Students:* 35 full-time (10 women); includes 21 minority (13 Black or African American, non-Hispanic/Latino; 5 Asian, non-Hispanic/Latino; 2 Hispanic/Latino; 1 Two or more races, non-Hispanic/Latino), 6 international. Average age 52. In 2014, 16 master's, 1 doctorate awarded. *Degree requirements:* For master's, variable foreign language requirement, thesis (for some programs); for doctorate, thesis/dissertation. *Entrance requirements:* For master's, bachelor's degree; for doctorate, M Div or equivalency. Additional exam requirements/recommendations for international students: Required—TOEFL (minimum score 450 paper-based; 45 iBT). *Application deadline:* For fall admission, 8/15 priority date for domestic students; for spring admission, 1/15 priority date for domestic students. Applications are processed on a rolling basis. Application fee: $30. Electronic applications accepted. *Expenses: Tuition:* Full-time $8280; part-time $460 per credit. *Required fees:* $125 per semester. Tuition and fees vary according to course load. *Financial support:* In 2014–15, 4 students received support. Scholarships/grants available. Financial award application deadline: 6/15; financial award applicants required to submit FAFSA. *Faculty research:* Church leadership, church history, world religions, ecumenism, interfaith peace building,

service-learning. *Unit head:* Dr. Kathy Winings, Vice-President for Academic Affairs, 845-752-3000 Ext. 228, Fax: 845-752-3014, E-mail: academics@uts.edu. *Application contact:* Henry Christopher, Director of Admissions, 845-752-3000 Ext. 244, Fax: 845-752-3014, E-mail: h.christopher@uts.edu.
Website: http://www.uts.edu

Union University, School of Theology and Missions, Jackson, TN 38305-3697. Offers Christian studies (MCS); expository preaching (D Min). Part-time and evening/weekend programs available. Postbaccalaureate distance learning degree programs offered (no on-campus study). *Students:* 143 full-time, 79 part-time. In 2014, 60 master's, 6 doctorates awarded. *Application deadline:* Applications are processed on a rolling basis. Application fee: $25. Electronic applications accepted. *Expenses: Tuition:* Full-time $6566; part-time $469 per credit hour. *Unit head:* Dr. James A. Patterson, Acting Dean, 731-661-5269, E-mail: jpatters@uu.edu. *Application contact:* Christy Lynn Young, Director of Adult and Professional Programs, 731-661-5987, Fax: 731-661-5987, E-mail: cyoung@uu.edu.

United Theological Seminary of the Twin Cities, Graduate Programs, New Brighton, MN 55112-2598. Offers advanced theological studies (Diploma); justice and peace studies (M Div, MA); leadership toward racial justice (M Div, MA, Certificate); Methodist studies (M Div, MA, Certificate); ministry (D Min); ministry renewal and professional development (Certificate); pastoral care and counseling (M Div, MA, MARL); religion and theology (MA); theological and religious studies (Certificate); theology and the arts (M Div, MA); urban ministry (M Div, MA, MARL); women's studies: religion, theology and ministry (M Div, MA). *Accreditation:* ACIPE; ATS. Part-time and evening/weekend programs available. *Degree requirements:* For master's, thesis; for doctorate, comprehensive exam, thesis/dissertation. *Entrance requirements:* For master's, minimum GPA of 2.75; strong analytical, reflective thinking and writing skills; vocational and academic goals compatible with those of Seminary; for doctorate, M Div or equivalent, minimum GPA of 3.0, 3 years experience in professional ministry; for other advanced degree, BA or equivalent life experience; strong analytical, reflective thinking and writing skills (Certificate); proficiency in English language, previous study of theology at a theological school, recommendation of student's denomination (Diploma). Additional exam requirements/recommendations for international students: Required—TOEFL (minimum score 550 paper-based).

University of Chicago, Divinity School, Program in Ministry, Chicago, IL 60637. Offers M Div. *Students:* 42 full-time (18 women), 1 (woman) part-time; includes 10 minority (8 Black or African American, non-Hispanic/Latino; 2 Asian, non-Hispanic/Latino), 2 international. 42 applicants, 81% accepted, 14 enrolled. *Degree requirements:* For master's, one foreign language, thesis, field education. *Entrance requirements:* For master's, GRE General Test. Additional exam requirements/recommendations for international students: Required—TOEFL (minimum score 600 paper-based; 104 iBT), IELTS (minimum score 7). *Application deadline:* For fall admission, 1/15 for domestic and international students. Application fee: $75. Electronic applications accepted. *Expenses: Tuition:* Full-time $46,899. *Required fees:* $347. *Financial support:* Career-related internships or fieldwork, Federal Work-Study, institutionally sponsored loans, and scholarships/grants available. Financial award application deadline: 1/15; financial award applicants required to submit FAFSA. *Unit head:* Cynthia G. Lindner, Director of Ministry Studies/Clinical Professor of Preaching and Pastoral Care, 773-702-8280, E-mail: clindner@uchicago.edu. *Application contact:* John W. Howell, Coordinator for Recruiting and Admissions, 773-702-8249, Fax: 773-834-4581, E-mail: divinityadmissions@uchicago.edu.
Website: http://divinity.uchicago.edu/ministry-program-mdiv

University of Dallas, Institute for Religious and Pastoral Studies, Irving, TX 75062-4736. Offers MCSL, MPM, MRE, MTS. *Accreditation:* ACIPE. Part-time and evening/weekend programs available. Postbaccalaureate distance learning degree programs offered (no on-campus study). *Faculty research:* Scripture, pastoral theology, ecclesiology, systematic theology, theological anthropology.

University of Dayton, Department of Religious Studies, Dayton, OH 45469. Offers pastoral ministry (MA); theological studies (MA); theology (PhD). Part-time and evening/weekend programs available. *Faculty:* 21 full-time (7 women), 9 part-time/adjunct (4 women). *Students:* 57 full-time (23 women), 7 part-time (3 women); includes 7 minority (1 Black or African American, non-Hispanic/Latino; 2 Asian, non-Hispanic/Latino; 2 Hispanic/Latino; 2 Two or more races, non-Hispanic/Latino), 2 international. Average age 34. 82 applicants, 52% accepted, 18 enrolled. In 2014, 13 master's, 7 doctorates awarded. Terminal master's awarded for partial completion of doctoral program. *Degree requirements:* For master's, thesis or alternative; for doctorate, 2 foreign languages, comprehensive exam, thesis/dissertation. *Entrance requirements:* For master's, minimum undergraduate GPA of 3.0, 3 letters of recommendation, personal statement, official transcript(s); for doctorate, GRE General Test (minimum score 600 verbal previous scale, 160 current scale), minimum GPA of 3.5, academic writing sample, 3 letters of recommendation, official transcript(s). Additional exam requirements/recommendations for international students: Required—TOEFL (minimum score 550 paper-based; 80 iBT). *Application deadline:* For fall admission, 3/1 priority date for domestic students, 5/1 priority date for international students; for winter admission, 7/1 for international students; for spring admission, 11/1 priority date for international students. Applications are processed on a rolling basis. Application fee: $0 ($50 for international students). Electronic applications accepted. *Expenses:* Expenses: Contact institution. *Financial support:* In 2014–15, 4 fellowships with full tuition reimbursements (averaging $17,600 per year), 7 research assistantships with full tuition reimbursements (averaging $10,413 per year), 16 teaching assistantships with full tuition reimbursements (averaging $17,600 per year) were awarded; career-related internships or fieldwork, institutionally sponsored loans, health care benefits, and unspecified assistantships also available. Financial award application deadline: 3/1; financial award applicants required to submit FAFSA. *Faculty research:* Practical/constructive theology, theological ethics, U.S. Catholic/Christian life and thought, methodologies in Biblical studies, religion and science. *Unit head:* Dr. Daniel Thompson, Chair, 937-229-4321, Fax: 937-229-4330. *Application contact:* Amy Doorley, Graduate Program Coordinator, 937-229-4321, Fax: 937-229-4330, E-mail: adoorley1@udayton.edu.
Website: http://www.udayton.edu/artssciences/academics/religiousstudies/welcome/index.php

University of Fort Lauderdale, Graduate Program, Lauderhill, FL 33313. Offers MS. *Degree requirements:* For master's, thesis.

University of Northwestern–St. Paul, Master of Divinity Program, St. Paul, MN 55113-1598. Offers M Div. Part-time and evening/weekend programs available. Postbaccalaureate distance learning degree programs offered (no on-campus study). *Application deadline:* Applications are processed on a rolling basis. Electronic applications accepted. *Expenses:* Expenses: $490 per credit. *Application contact:* College of Adult and Graduate Studies Admissions, 651-631-5200, E-mail: gradstudies@unwsp.edu.

University of Portland, Department of Theology, Portland, OR 97203-5798. Offers pastoral ministry (MA). Part-time programs available. *Faculty:* 4 full-time (1 woman). *Students:* 19 part-time (15 women); includes 6 minority (1 American Indian or Alaska Native, non-Hispanic/Latino; 2 Asian, non-Hispanic/Latino; 1 Hispanic/Latino; 2 Two or

more races, non-Hispanic/Latino). Average age 53. In 2014, 1 master's awarded. *Entrance requirements:* For master's, GRE or MAT, 3 letters of recommendation, minimum GPA of 3.0. Additional exam requirements/recommendations for international students: Required—TOEFL (minimum score 550 paper-based; 80 iBT), IELTS (minimum score 7). *Application deadline:* For fall admission, 7/15 priority date for domestic and international students. Application fee: $45. *Expenses: Tuition:* Full-time $19,260; part-time $1070 per credit hour. Tuition and fees vary according to program. *Financial support:* Federal Work-Study and scholarships/grants available. Financial award application deadline: 3/1; financial award applicants required to submit FAFSA. *Unit head:* Dr. Kathleen McManus, Director, 503-943-8879, E-mail: mapm@up.edu. *Application contact:* Allison Able, Graduate Program Coordinator, 503-943-7107, Fax: 503-943-7315, E-mail: able@up.edu.
Website: http://college.up.edu/theology/default.aspx?cid-2103&pid-195

University of Saint Francis, Graduate School, Department of Psychology and Counseling, Fort Wayne, IN 46808-3994. Offers clinical mental health counseling (MS, Post Master's Certificate); pastoral counseling (MS, Post Master's Certificate); psychology (MS); rehabilitation counseling (MS, Post Master's Certificate); school counseling (MS Ed). Part-time and evening/weekend programs available. *Faculty:* 3 full-time (1 woman). *Students:* 29 full-time (22 women), 20 part-time (all women); includes 10 minority (7 Black or African American, non-Hispanic/Latino; 2 Hispanic/Latino; 1 Two or more races, non-Hispanic/Latino), 1 international. Average age 32. 21 applicants, 90% accepted, 16 enrolled. In 2014, 23 master's awarded. *Entrance requirements:* For master's, minimum undergraduate GPA of 3.0; undergraduate coursework in psychology. Additional exam requirements/recommendations for international students: Required—TOEFL or IELTS. *Application deadline:* For fall admission, 7/1 for domestic students; for spring admission, 11/1 for domestic students. Applications are processed on a rolling basis. Application fee: $0. Electronic applications accepted. *Expenses:* Expenses: $830 per credit hour. *Financial support:* In 2014–15, 5 students received support. Federal Work-Study, scholarships/grants, and unspecified assistantships available. Support available to part-time students. Financial award application deadline: 3/10; financial award applicants required to submit FAFSA. *Unit head:* Dr. John Brinkman, Associate Professor/Chair, Department of Psychology and Counseling, 260-399-7700 Ext. 8425, Fax: 260-399-8170, E-mail: jbrinkman@sf.edu. *Application contact:* Kyle Richardson, Enrollment Specialist, 260-399-7700 Ext. 6310, Fax: 260-399-8152, E-mail: krichardson@sf.edu.
Website: http://psychology.sf.edu/

University of Saint Mary of the Lake–Mundelein Seminary, Graduate and Professional Programs, Mundelein, IL 60060. Offers liturgical studies (MA); ministry (D Min); pastoral studies (MA); theology (M Div). *Accreditation:* ATS (one or more programs are accredited). *Faculty:* 42 full-time (7 women), 19 part-time/adjunct (7 women). *Students:* 266 full-time (8 women); includes 10 minority (2 Black or African American, non-Hispanic/Latino; 3 Asian, non-Hispanic/Latino; 5 Hispanic/Latino), 78 international. *Degree requirements:* For doctorate, thesis/dissertation. *Entrance requirements:* For master's and doctorate, bachelor's degree. Additional exam requirements/recommendations for international students: Required—TOEFL. *Application deadline:* Applications are processed on a rolling basis. Application fee: $0. Electronic applications accepted. *Expenses: Tuition:* Full-time $23,520; part-time $940 per credit. *Required fees:* $300. One-time fee: $50 full-time. *Financial support:* Career-related internships or fieldwork available. *Unit head:* Very Rev. Thomas A. Baima, Dean of the Seminary and Graduate School, 847-566-6401. *Application contact:* Very Rev. Robert Barron, Rector-President, 847-566-6401, Fax: 847-566-7330.

University of St. Michael's College, Faculty of Theology, Toronto, ON M5S 1J4, Canada. Offers Catholic leadership (MA); eastern Christian studies (Diploma); religious education (Diploma); theological studies (Diploma); theology (M Div, MA, MRE, MTS, D Min, PhD, Th D); theology and Jewish studies (MA). Th D offered jointly with University of Toronto. *Accreditation:* ATS (one or more programs are accredited). Part-time programs available. *Degree requirements:* For master's, thesis (for some programs), 1 foreign language (MA), 2 foreign languages (Th M); for doctorate, 3 foreign languages, comprehensive exam, thesis/dissertation; for other advanced degree, thesis optional. *Entrance requirements:* For master's, M Div or BA, course work in an ancient or modern language, minimum GPA of 3.3; for doctorate, MA in theology, Th M, or M Div with thesis, minimum GPA of 3.7; for other advanced degree, minimum GPA of 2.7. Additional exam requirements/recommendations for international students: Required—TOEFL (minimum score 600 paper-based). Electronic applications accepted. *Expenses:* Contact institution. *Faculty research:* Patristics, eastern Christianity, ecology and theology, ecumenism, Jewish Christian studies.

University of St. Thomas, Graduate Studies, The Saint Paul Seminary School of Divinity, St. Paul, MN 55105. Offers pastoral ministry (MAPM); religious education (MARE); theology (MA). *Accreditation:* ACIPE; ATS. Part-time and evening/weekend programs available. *Degree requirements:* For master's, one foreign language, comprehensive exam (for some programs), thesis (for some programs). *Entrance requirements:* For master's, GRE, 3 letters of recommendation, interview. Additional exam requirements/recommendations for international students: Required—TOEFL (minimum score 550 paper-based). Electronic applications accepted. *Expenses:* Contact institution. *Faculty research:* Theological education.

University of St. Thomas, School of Theology, Houston, TX 77006. Offers divinity (M Div); pastoral studies (MAPS); theological studies (MA). *Accreditation:* ATS. Part-time programs available. *Faculty:* 8 full-time (4 women), 7 part-time/adjunct (1 woman). *Students:* 84 full-time (11 women), 86 part-time (26 women); includes 78 minority (7 Black or African American, non-Hispanic/Latino; 31 Asian, non-Hispanic/Latino; 36 Hispanic/Latino; 4 Two or more races, non-Hispanic/Latino), 15 international. Average age 35. 44 applicants, 100% accepted, 32 enrolled. In 2014, 57 master's awarded. *Degree requirements:* For master's, variable foreign language requirement, comprehensive exam. *Entrance requirements:* For master's, BA, BS or equivalent; personal essay (for some programs); undergraduate philosophy or theology courses; 2 letters of recommendation. Additional exam requirements/recommendations for international students: Required—TOEFL (minimum score 550 paper-based; 79 iBT). *Application deadline:* Applications are processed on a rolling basis. Application fee: $10. Electronic applications accepted. *Expenses:* Expenses: Contact institution. *Financial support:* In 2014–15, 14 students received support. Scholarships/grants available. Support available to part-time students. Financial award application deadline: 4/15; financial award applicants required to submit FAFSA. *Unit head:* Dr. Sandra C. Magie, Dean, 713-686-4345 Ext. 242, Fax: 713-683-8673, E-mail: smagie@stthom.edu. *Application contact:* Connie M. Henry, Office Manager, 713-686-4345 Ext. 231, Fax: 713-683-8673, E-mail: sms@stthom.edu.
Website: http://www.stthom.edu/Academics/School_of_Theology_at_St_Marys_Seminary/Index.aqf

University of South Africa, College of Human Sciences, Pretoria, South Africa. Offers adult education (M Ed); African languages (MA, PhD); African politics (MA, PhD); Afrikaans (MA, PhD); ancient history (MA, PhD); ancient Near Eastern studies (MA, PhD); anthropology (MA, PhD); applied linguistics (MA); Arabic (MA, PhD); archaeology (MA); art history (MA); Biblical archaeology (MA); Biblical studies (M Th, D Th, PhD); Christian spirituality (M Th, D Th); church history (M Th, D Th); classical studies (MA,

PhD); clinical psychology (MA); communication (MA, PhD); comparative education (M Ed, Ed D); consulting psychology (D Admin, D Com, PhD); curriculum studies (M Ed, Ed D); development studies (M Admin, MA, D Admin, PhD); didactics (M Ed, Ed D); education (M Tech); education management (M Ed, Ed D); educational psychology (M Ed); English (MA); environmental education (M Ed); French (MA, PhD); German (MA, PhD); Greek (MA); guidance and counseling (M Ed); health studies (MA, PhD), including health sciences education (MA), health services management (MA), medical and surgical nursing science (critical care general) (MA), midwifery and neonatal nursing science (MA), trauma and emergency care (MA); history (MA, PhD); history of education (Ed D); inclusive education (M Ed, Ed D); information and communications technology policy and regulation (MA); information science (MA, MIS, PhD); international politics (MA, PhD); Islamic studies (MA, PhD); Italian (MA, PhD); Judaica (MA, PhD); linguistics (MA, PhD); mathematical education (M Ed); mathematics education (MA); missiology (M Th, D Th); modern Hebrew (MA, PhD); musicology (MA, MMus, D Mus, PhD); natural science education (M Ed); New Testament (M Th, D Th); Old Testament (D Th); pastoral therapy (M Th, D Th); philosophy (MA); philosophy of education (M Ed, Ed D); politics (MA, PhD); Portuguese (MA, PhD); practical theology (M Th, D Th); psychology (MA, MS, PhD); psychology of education (M Ed, Ed D); public health (MA); religious studies (MA, D Th, PhD); Romance languages (MA); Russian (MA, PhD); Semitic languages (MA, PhD); social behavior studies in HIV/AIDS (MA); social science (mental health) (MA); social science in development studies (MA); social science in psychology (MA); social science in social work (MA); social science in sociology (MA); social work (MSW, DSW, PhD); socio-education (M Ed, Ed D); sociolinguistics (MA); sociology (MA, PhD); Spanish (MA, PhD); systematic theology (M Th, D Th); TESOL (teaching English to speakers of other languages) (MA); theological ethics (M Th, D Th); theory of literature (MA, PhD); urban ministries (D Th); urban ministry (M Th).

Valparaiso University, Graduate School, Program in Ministry Leadership and Administration, Valparaiso, IN 46383. Offers MMA. Part-time and evening/weekend programs available. *Students:* 1 full-time (0 women), 1 part-time (0 women); both minorities (both Black or African American, non-Hispanic/Latino). Average age 48. *Entrance requirements:* For master's, essay, two letters of recommendation, current resume, official transcripts. Additional exam requirements/recommendations for international students: Required—TOEFL (minimum score 550 paper-based; 80 iBT), IELTS (minimum score 6). *Application deadline:* Applications are processed on a rolling basis. Application fee: $30 ($50 for international students). Electronic applications accepted. *Expenses: Tuition:* Full-time $10,710; part-time $595 per credit hour. *Required fees:* $378; $101 per term. Tuition and fees vary according to course load and program. *Financial support:* Available to part-time students. Applicants required to submit FAFSA. *Unit head:* Dr. Jennifer A. Ziegler, Dean, Graduate School and Continuing Education, 219-464-5313, Fax: 219-464-5381, E-mail: jennifer.ziegler@valpo.edu. *Application contact:* Jessica Choquette, Graduate Admissions Specialist, 219-464-5313, Fax: 219-464-5381, E-mail: jessica.choquette@valpo.edu.
Website: http://www.valpo.edu/grad/appliedadmin/ministryadmin.php

Viterbo University, Master of Arts in Servant Leadership Program, La Crosse, WI 54601-4797. Offers MA. Part-time and evening/weekend programs available. *Faculty:* 2 full-time (0 women), 2 part-time/adjunct (1 woman). *Students:* 13 full-time (7 women), 37 part-time (25 women); includes 6 minority (5 Black or African American, non-Hispanic/ Latino; 1 Hispanic/Latino), 1 international. Average age 43. 13 applicants, 92% accepted, 8 enrolled. In 2014, 20 master's awarded. *Degree requirements:* For master's, 30 credits (15 credits of Servant Leadership core courses and any combination of 15 elective credits). *Entrance requirements:* For master's, letter of reference, statement of goals, baccalaureate degree, transcript, interview. Additional exam requirements/ recommendations for international students: Required—TOEFL (minimum score 525 paper-based). *Application deadline:* For fall admission, 8/1 for domestic students; for spring admission, 12/1 for domestic students; for summer admission, 5/1 for domestic students. Applications are processed on a rolling basis. Electronic applications accepted. *Expenses:* Expenses: $340 per credit. *Financial support:* In 2014–15, 12 students received support. Scholarships/grants available. Financial award application deadline: 2/1. *Faculty research:* Organizational culture, community building, ethical decision-making, leadership theory and practice. *Unit head:* Tom Thibodeau, Director, 608-796-3705, E-mail: tathibodeau@viterbo.edu. *Application contact:* Maureen Cooney, Administrative Assistant, 608-796-3082, E-mail: mjcooney@viterbo.edu.
Website: http://www.viterbo.edu/master-arts-servant-leadership

Walsh University, Graduate Studies, Master of Arts in Theology Program, North Canton, OH 44720-3396. Offers parish administration (MA); pastoral ministry (MA); religious education (MA). Part-time and evening/weekend programs available. *Faculty:* 3 full-time (0 women). *Students:* 4 full-time (0 women), 12 part-time (8 women); includes 1 minority (Black or African American, non-Hispanic/Latino), 3 international. Average age 44. 6 applicants, 50% accepted, 3 enrolled. In 2014, 4 master's awarded. *Degree requirements:* For master's, thesis or alternative, culminating assignment. *Entrance requirements:* For master's, MAT or GRE (minimum scores: Verbal 145, Quantitative 146, Combined 291, Writing 3.0), minimum GPA of 3.0. Additional exam requirements/ recommendations for international students: Required—TOEFL. *Application deadline:* For fall admission, 7/15 for domestic students. Applications are processed on a rolling basis. Application fee: $25. Electronic applications accepted. *Expenses: Tuition:* Full-time $11,250; part-time $625 per semester hour. Full-time tuition and fees vary according to program. *Financial support:* In 2014–15, 1 student received support, including 1 research assistantship (averaging $3,744 per year); scholarships/grants and unspecified assistantships also available. Financial award application deadline: 12/31; financial award applicants required to submit FAFSA. *Faculty research:* Historical theology, systematic theology, theological anthropology, existential phenomenology, Cardinal Newman, Second Temple Jerusalem, Mark's gospel, Deuterocanonical literature, Josephus, philosophical theology, phenomenology, hermeneutics, relationship between material and spiritual being, evolutionary theory, phenomenology of the sacrament, Edith Stein, Emmanuel Levinas, Paul Ricoeur, Jean-Luc Marion. *Unit head:* Dr. Chris Seeman, Chair, 330-244-4665, Fax: 330-244-4955, E-mail: cseeman@walsh.edu. *Application contact:* Audra Dice, Graduate Admissions Counselor, 330-490-7181, Fax: 330-244-4925, E-mail: adice@walsh.edu.

Wayland Baptist University, Graduate Programs, Programs in Religion, Plainview, TX 79072-6998. Offers Christian ministry (MCM); divinity (M Div); religion (MA). Part-time and evening/weekend programs available. Postbaccalaureate distance learning degree programs offered (no on-campus study). *Faculty:* 15 full-time (1 woman), 12 part-time/ adjunct (0 women). *Students:* 1 full-time (0 women), 99 part-time (23 women); includes 51 minority (25 Black or African American, non-Hispanic/Latino; 1 American Indian or Alaska Native, non-Hispanic/Latino; 4 Asian, non-Hispanic/Latino; 17 Hispanic/Latino; 1 Native Hawaiian or other Pacific Islander, non-Hispanic/Latino; 3 Two or more races, non-Hispanic/Latino). Average age 43. 45 applicants, 60% accepted, 12 enrolled. In 2014, 16 master's awarded. *Degree requirements:* For master's, comprehensive exam. *Entrance requirements:* For master's, GRE or MAT, minimum GPA of 3.0; letter of endorsement from Christian congregation, one academic and one personal letter of recommendation (for M Div). Additional exam requirements/recommendations for international students: Required—TOEFL (minimum score 500 paper-based; 61 iBT). *Application deadline:* Applications are processed on a rolling basis. Application fee: $50. Electronic applications accepted. *Expenses: Tuition:* Full-time $8910; part-time $495 per credit hour. *Required fees:* $970; $495 per credit hour. $485 per semester. *Financial support:* Federal Work-Study, institutionally sponsored loans, and scholarships/grants available. Support available to part-time students. Financial award application deadline: 5/1; financial award applicants required to submit FAFSA. *Unit head:* Dr. Paul Sadler, Chairman, 806-291-1160, Fax: 806-291-1969, E-mail: sadlerp@wbu.edu. *Application contact:* Amanda Stanton, Coordinator of Graduate Studies, 806-291-3423, Fax: 806-291-1950, E-mail: stanton@wbu.edu.

Wesley Biblical Seminary, Graduate Programs, Jackson, MS 39206. Offers apologetics (MA); Biblical languages (M Div); Biblical literature (MA); Christian studies (MA); context and mission (M Div); honors research (M Div); interpretation (M Div); ministry (M Div); spiritual formation (M Div); teaching (M Div); theology (MA). *Accreditation:* ATS. Part-time programs available. *Degree requirements:* For master's, thesis. *Entrance requirements:* Additional exam requirements/recommendations for international students: Required—TOEFL. Electronic applications accepted. *Faculty research:* Patristics, missiology, culture, hermeneutics.

Western Seminary, Graduate Programs, Program in Counseling, Portland, OR 97215-3367. Offers counseling (MA, Certificate); pastoral counseling (M Div); M Div/MA. Part-time and evening/weekend programs available. *Degree requirements:* For master's, practicum. *Entrance requirements:* Additional exam requirements/recommendations for international students: Required—TOEFL. *Expenses:* Contact institution.

Western Seminary, Graduate Programs, Program in Intercultural Studies, Portland, OR 97215-3367. Offers MA, D Miss, Certificate, G Dip. Part-time and evening/weekend programs available. *Degree requirements:* For master's, practicum; for doctorate, 2 foreign languages, thesis/dissertation. *Entrance requirements:* Additional exam requirements/recommendations for international students: Required—TOEFL.

Western Seminary, Graduate Programs, Program in Ministry and Leadership, Portland, OR 97215-3367. Offers chaplaincy (MA); coaching (MA); Jewish ministry (MA); pastoral care to women (MA); youth ministry (MA). *Degree requirements:* For master's, practicum. *Entrance requirements:* Additional exam requirements/recommendations for international students: Required—TOEFL.

Western Seminary–Sacramento Campus, Graduate Certificate Programs, Sacramento, CA 95821. Offers Bible (Graduate Certificate); coaching (Graduate Certificate); pastoral care to women (Graduate Certificate); theology (Graduate Certificate); youth and family (Graduate Certificate). Postbaccalaureate distance learning degree programs offered. *Entrance requirements:* For degree, essays, undergraduate transcripts, 4 recommendations. Additional exam requirements/ recommendations for international students: Required—TOEFL.

Western Seminary–Sacramento Campus, Graduate Diploma Programs, Sacramento, CA 95821. Offers Bible and theology (Graduate Diploma); ministry (Graduate Diploma); pastoral care to women (Graduate Diploma). *Entrance requirements:* For degree, essays, undergraduate transcripts, 4 recommendations. Additional exam requirements/ recommendations for international students: Required—TOEFL.

Western Seminary–Sacramento Campus, Program in Ministry and Leadership, Sacramento, CA 95821. Offers MA. *Entrance requirements:* For master's, essays, undergraduate transcripts, 4 recommendations. Additional exam requirements/ recommendations for international students: Required—TOEFL.

Western Seminary–San Jose Campus, Graduate Programs, Los Gatos, CA 95032-4520. Offers Bible and theology (Graduate Diploma); Bible, camp and conference ministry (CGS); Biblical and theological studies (MA), including exegetical track, theological track; coaching (CGS); expositional ministry (M Div); marital and family therapy (MA); ministry (Graduate Diploma); ministry and leadership (MA), including camp and conference ministry, coaching, pastoral care to women, youth ministry; pastoral care to women (CGS, Graduate Diploma); pastoral ministry (M Div); theology (CGS); youth and family (CGS). Part-time and evening/weekend programs available. Postbaccalaureate distance learning degree programs offered (minimal on-campus study). *Entrance requirements:* For master's, minimum GPA of 3.0. Electronic applications accepted.

Western Theological Seminary, Graduate and Professional Programs, Holland, MI 49423-3622. Offers Christian ministry (MACM); divinity (M Div); ministry (D Min); theology (M Th); urban pastoral ministry (Graduate Certificate); M Div/MSW. *Accreditation:* ACIPE; ATS. Part-time programs available. Postbaccalaureate distance learning degree programs offered (minimal on-campus study). *Faculty:* 17 full-time (4 women), 23 part-time/adjunct (4 women). *Students:* 187 full-time (58 women), 88 part-time (35 women); includes 32 minority (12 Black or African American, non-Hispanic/ Latino; 10 Asian, non-Hispanic/Latino; 7 Hispanic/Latino; 3 Two or more races, non-Hispanic/Latino), 11 international. In 2014, 35 master's, 1 doctorate awarded. *Degree requirements:* For doctorate, 2 foreign languages, thesis/dissertation. *Entrance requirements:* Additional exam requirements/recommendations for international students: Required—TOEFL. *Application deadline:* For fall admission, 4/1 priority date for domestic students. Applications are processed on a rolling basis. Application fee: $50. *Expenses: Tuition:* Full-time $13,120; part-time $410 per credit. *Required fees:* $90. One-time fee: $90 part-time. *Financial support:* Career-related internships or fieldwork, institutionally sponsored loans, and scholarships/grants available. Support available to part-time students. Financial award applicants required to submit FAFSA. *Unit head:* Dr. Timothy Brown, President, 616-392-8555 Ext. 137, Fax: 616-392-7717, E-mail: tim.brown@westernsem.edu. *Application contact:* Mark Poppen, Director of Admissions, 616-392-8555, Fax: 616-392-7717, E-mail: mark@westernsem.edu.
Website: http://www.westernsem.edu/

Westminster Theological Seminary, Graduate and Professional Programs, Philadelphia, PA 19118. Offers apologetics (Th M); Biblical and urban studies (Certificate); Biblical counseling (MA); biblical studies (MAR); Christian studies (Certificate); church history (Th M); counseling (M Div); general studies (M Div, MAR); hermeneutics and Bible interpretations (PhD); historical and theological studies (PhD); historical theology (Th M); New Testament (Th M); Old Testament (Th M); pastoral counseling (D Min); pastoral ministry (M Div, D Min); systematic theology (Th M); theological studies (MAR); urban missions (M Div, MA, MAR, D Min). *Accreditation:* ATS. Part-time programs available. Terminal master's awarded for partial completion of doctoral program. *Degree requirements:* For master's, thesis (for some programs); for doctorate, 4 foreign languages, comprehensive exam (for some programs), thesis/ dissertation. *Entrance requirements:* For doctorate, GRE General Test. Additional exam requirements/recommendations for international students: Required—TOEFL, TWE.

Wheaton College, Graduate School, Department of Psychology, Wheaton, IL 60187-5593. Offers clinical mental health counseling (MA); clinical psychology (MA, Psy D); counseling ministries (MA); marriage and family therapy (MA). *Accreditation:* APA (one or more programs are accredited). *Students:* 104 full-time (78 women), 22 part-time (14 women); includes 25 minority (13 Black or African American, non-Hispanic/Latino; 8 Asian, non-Hispanic/Latino; 2 Hispanic/Latino; 2 Two or more races, non-Hispanic/ Latino), 8 international. Average age 27. 141 applicants, 74% accepted, 64 enrolled. In 2014, 47 master's, 16 doctorates awarded. Terminal master's awarded for partial completion of doctoral program. *Degree requirements:* For master's, thesis or

alternative; for doctorate, thesis/dissertation, internship. *Entrance requirements:* For master's, GRE General Test, 18 hours of course work in psychology; for doctorate, GRE General Test. Additional exam requirements/recommendations for international students: Required—TOEFL (minimum score 550 paper-based; 80 iBT), IELTS (minimum score 6.5), TOEFL (minimum score 600 paper-based; 90 iBT) or IELTS (minimum score 7.5) for Psy D. *Application deadline:* For fall admission, 3/1 priority date for domestic students, 1/1 for international students. Applications are processed on a rolling basis. Application fee: $30. *Financial support:* In 2014–15, 3 research assistantships (averaging $4,800 per year) were awarded; career-related internships or fieldwork, Federal Work-Study, scholarships/grants, and unspecified assistantships also available. Financial award application deadline: 3/1; financial award applicants required to submit FAFSA. *Unit head:* Dr. Terri Watson, Associate Dean of Psychology, 630-752-5104. *Application contact:* Dusty Di Santo, Director of Graduate Admissions, 630-752-5195, Fax: 630-752-7047, E-mail: graduate.admissions@wheaton.edu.
Website: http://www.wheaton.edu/academics/departments/psychology

Wilfrid Laurier University, Waterloo Lutheran Seminary, Waterloo, ON N2L 3C5, Canada. Offers divinity (M Div); multifaith spiritual care and counseling (Diploma); pastoral leadership (D Min); spiritual care and counseling (D Min); theology (M Th, MTS); M Div/MTS/MSW. *Accreditation:* ATS. Part-time programs available. *Degree requirements:* For master's, one foreign language, thesis (for some programs); for doctorate, thesis/dissertation. *Entrance requirements:* For master's, two letters of reference; for doctorate, M Div, two letters of reference. Additional exam requirements/recommendations for international students: Required—TOEFL (minimum score 573 paper-based; 89 iBT), IELTS (minimum score 7). Electronic applications accepted. *Expenses:* Contact institution. *Faculty research:* Biblical study, church history, systematic theology.

Xavier University, College of Arts and Sciences, Department of Theology, Cincinnati, OH 45207. Offers health care mission integration (MA); theology (MA), including religious education, social and pastoral ministry, theology. Part-time and evening/weekend programs available. *Faculty:* 5 full-time (3 women), 1 part-time/adjunct (0 women). *Students:* 12 part-time (7 women), 1 international. Average age 43. 6 applicants, 100% accepted, 4 enrolled. In 2014, 3 master's awarded. *Degree requirements:* For master's, final paper (or thesis) and defense or comprehension exam. *Entrance requirements:* For master's, MAT or GRE, 2 letters of recommendation; statement of reasons and goals for enrolling in program (1,000-2,000 words); resume; transcript. Additional exam requirements/recommendations for international students: Required—TOEFL (minimum score 550 paper-based; 79 iBT). *Application deadline:* Applications are processed on a rolling basis. Application fee: $35. Electronic applications accepted. Application fee is waived when completed online. *Expenses:* Expenses: $600 per credit hour. *Financial support:* In 2014–15, 3 students received support. Scholarships/grants and unspecified assistantships available. Financial award applicants required to submit FAFSA. *Faculty research:* Scripture, ethics, constructive theology, historical theology. *Unit head:* Dr. Sarah Melcher, Chair, Theology Graduate Program, 513-745-2043, Fax: 513-745-3215, E-mail: melcher@xavier.edu. *Application contact:* Roger Bosse, Graduate Services Director, 513-745-3357, Fax: 513-745-1048, E-mail: bosse@xavier.edu.
Website: http://www.xavier.edu/theology-ma/

Xavier University of Louisiana, Graduate School, Institute for Black Catholic Studies, New Orleans, LA 70125-1098. Offers pastoral theology (Th M). Part-time programs available. *Degree requirements:* For master's, comprehensive exam, practicum. *Entrance requirements:* For master's, GRE General Test, MAT, minimum GPA of 2.5. Additional exam requirements/recommendations for international students: Required—TOEFL.

Religion

Abilene Christian University, Graduate School, College of Biblical Studies, Graduate School of Theology, Program in Ancient and Oriental Christianity, Abilene, TX 79699-9100. Offers MA. Part-time programs available. *Students:* 4 full-time (1 woman). 2 applicants, 50% accepted, 1 enrolled. *Degree requirements:* For master's, comprehensive exam, thesis. *Entrance requirements:* Additional exam requirements/recommendations for international students: Required—TOEFL (minimum score 550 paper-based; 90 iBT), IELTS (minimum score 6.5). *Application deadline:* For fall admission, 4/1 priority date for domestic students; for spring admission, 11/1 for domestic students. Application fee: $50. *Expenses:* Expenses: Contact institution. *Financial support:* Application deadline: 4/1; applicants required to submit FAFSA. *Unit head:* Dr. Jeff Childers, Graduate Advisor, 325-674-3797, Fax: 325-674-6180, E-mail: jeff.childers@acu.edu. *Application contact:* Corey Patterson, Director of Graduate Admission and Recruiting, 325-674-6566, Fax: 325-674-6717, E-mail: gradinfo@acu.edu.

Abilene Christian University, Graduate School, College of Biblical Studies, Graduate School of Theology, Program in Modern and American Christianity, Abilene, TX 79699-9100. Offers MA. Part-time programs available. *Students:* 1 full-time (0 women), 3 part-time (2 women). 1 applicant, 100% accepted, 1 enrolled. *Degree requirements:* For master's, comprehensive exam, thesis. *Entrance requirements:* Additional exam requirements/recommendations for international students: Required—TOEFL (minimum score 500 paper-based; 90 iBT), IELTS (minimum score 6.5), PTE. *Application deadline:* For fall admission, 4/1 priority date for domestic students; for spring admission, 11/1 for domestic students. Applications are processed on a rolling basis. Application fee: $50. Electronic applications accepted. *Expenses:* Expenses: Contact institution. *Financial support:* In 2014–15, 1 student received support. Application deadline: 4/1; applicants required to submit FAFSA. *Unit head:* Dr. Douglas Foster, Graduate Advisor, 325-674-3795, Fax: 325-674-6180, E-mail: doug.foster@acu.edu. *Application contact:* Corey Patterson, Director of Graduate Admission and Recruiting, 325-674-6566, Fax: 325-674-6717, E-mail: gradinfo@acu.edu.

Ambrose University, Ambrose Seminary, Calgary, AB T3H 0L5, Canada. Offers Chinese ministries (Certificate); Christian studies (Certificate); intercultural ministries (M Div, Certificate); leadership and ministry (Diploma); pastoral ministries (M Div). *Accreditation:* ATS (one or more programs are accredited). Part-time programs available. Postbaccalaureate distance learning degree programs offered (minimal on-campus study). *Faculty:* 7 full-time (0 women), 24 part-time/adjunct (2 women). *Students:* 55 full-time (18 women), 128 part-time (64 women); includes 86 minority (3 Black or African American, non-Hispanic/Latino; 1 American Indian or Alaska Native, non-Hispanic/Latino; 82 Asian, non-Hispanic/Latino). Average age 41. *Degree requirements:* For master's, variable foreign language requirement, internship. *Entrance requirements:* For master's, undergraduate degree from other accredited university or bible college, minimum GPA of 2.0. Additional exam requirements/recommendations for international students: Required—TOEFL (minimum score 560 paper-based, 83 iBT) or IELTS (minimum score 6.5). *Application deadline:* For fall admission, 7/15 for domestic students, 3/1 for international students; for winter admission, 11/15 for domestic students, 7/1 for international students. Applications are processed on a rolling basis. Application fee: $70 ($100 for international students). Electronic applications accepted. *Financial support:* Career-related internships or fieldwork and scholarships/grants available. Support available to part-time students. Financial award application deadline: 3/30. *Faculty research:* Evangelicalism and sociology, missiological trends, chaplaincy, intertestamental studies, postmodernism. *Unit head:* Dr. Paul Spilsbury, Vice-President of Academic Affairs, 403-410-2917, Fax: 403-571-2556, E-mail: pspilsbury@ambrose.edu. *Application contact:* Kalie Eeles, Enrollment Advisor, 403-410-2954, Fax: 403-571-2556, E-mail: enrolment@ambrose.edu.
Website: https://ambrose.edu/seminary

The American University of Rome, Graduate School, Rome, Italy. Offers religious studies (MA); sustainable cultural heritage (MA). *Faculty:* 1 (woman) full-time, 13 part-time/adjunct (3 women). *Students:* 4 full-time (2 women). Average age 37. 8 applicants, 75% accepted, 4 enrolled. *Degree requirements:* For master's, thesis, internship. *Entrance requirements:* For master's, bachelor's degree in the liberal arts, humanities or social sciences; minimum GPA of 2.75. Additional exam requirements/recommendations for international students: Required—TOEFL (minimum score 550 paper-based; 80 iBT), IELTS (minimum score 6.5). *Application deadline:* For fall admission, 5/1 for domestic and international students. Applications are processed on a rolling basis. Application fee: $60. Electronic applications accepted. *Expenses: Tuition:* Full-time 13,000 euros. *Faculty research:* Sustainable cultural heritage, archaeology in Europe and Italy. *Unit head:* Dr. Maria Grazia Quieti, Dean of Graduate Studies, 39 06 5833 0919 Ext. 711, E-mail: m.quieti@aur.edu. *Application contact:* Arianna D'Amico, Director of Admissions and Financial Aid, 39 06-5833-0919, E-mail: admissions@aur.edu.
Website: http://www.aur.edu/gradschool

Amridge University, Graduate and Professional Programs, Montgomery, AL 36117. Offers behavioral leadership and management (MA); Biblical studies (MA, PhD); family therapy (D Min); leadership and management (MS); marriage and family therapy (M Div, MA, PhD); ministerial leadership (M Div, MS); pastoral counseling (M Div, MS); professional counseling (M Div, MA, PhD); theology (M Div, D Min). Part-time and evening/weekend programs available. Postbaccalaureate distance learning degree programs offered (no on-campus study). *Faculty:* 20 full-time (2 women), 7 part-time/adjunct (6 women). *Students:* 110 full-time (58 women), 224 part-time (139 women); includes 139 minority (133 Black or African American, non-Hispanic/Latino; 3 Asian, non-Hispanic/Latino; 3 Hispanic/Latino). Average age 35. 69 applicants, 75% accepted. In 2014, 72 master's, 11 doctorates awarded. *Degree requirements:* For master's, one foreign language, comprehensive exam (for some programs), thesis (for some programs); for doctorate, comprehensive exam (for some programs), thesis/dissertation (for some programs). *Entrance requirements:* For master's, official transcript showing an earned 4-year BA or BS from regionally- or nationally-accredited institution; for doctorate, official transcript showing earned graduate degree from regionally- or nationally-accredited institution; writing sample (e.g. career monograph, published journal article, term paper from master's degree or doctoral dissertation); interview. Additional exam requirements/recommendations for international students: Required—TOEFL. *Application deadline:* For fall admission, 9/1 priority date for domestic students; for spring admission, 1/1 priority date for domestic students. Applications are processed on a rolling basis. Application fee: $50. Electronic applications accepted. *Financial support:* In 2014–15, 102 students received support. Federal Work-Study and scholarships/grants available. Support available to part-time students. Financial award applicants required to submit FAFSA. *Faculty research:* Technology and mental healthcare, resilience in black families, theology and congregational ministry. *Unit head:* Brooks Housley, Student Affairs Coordinator, 888-790-8080 Ext. 2, Fax: 334-387-3878, E-mail: brookshousley@amridgeuniversity.edu. *Application contact:* Kristen Holcomb, Admissions Officer, 888-790-8080 Ext. 1, Fax: 334-387-3878, E-mail: admissions@amridgeuniversity.edu.

Arizona State University at the Tempe campus, College of Liberal Arts and Sciences, School of Historical, Philosophical and Religious Studies, Tempe, AZ 85287-4301. Offers European history (MA, PhD); medieval studies (Graduate Certificate); North American history (MA, PhD); philosophy (MA, PhD); public history (MA); religious studies (MA, PhD); Renaissance studies (Graduate Certificate); scholarly publishing (Graduate Certificate). Part-time programs available. Terminal master's awarded for partial completion of doctoral program. *Degree requirements:* For master's, thesis or alternative, interactive Program of Study (iPOS) submitted before completing 50 percent of required credit hours; for doctorate, variable foreign language requirement, comprehensive exam, thesis/dissertation, interactive Program of Study (iPOS) submitted before completing 50 percent of required credit hours. *Entrance requirements:* For master's and doctorate, GRE, minimum GPA of 3.0 or equivalent in last 2 years of work leading to bachelor's degree. Additional exam requirements/recommendations for international students: Required—TOEFL, IELTS, or PTE. Electronic applications accepted.

Baptist Theological Seminary at Richmond, Graduate and Professional Programs, Richmond, VA 23227. Offers Biblical interpretation (M Div); Christian education (M Div); Christian ministry (MCM); justice and peacebuilding (D Min); theological studies (MTS, Graduate Certificate); M Div/MS; M Div/MSW. *Accreditation:* ATS. Part-time programs available. Postbaccalaureate distance learning degree programs offered (minimal on-campus study). *Faculty:* 7 full-time (2 women), 14 part-time/adjunct (6 women). *Students:* 45 full-time (27 women), 40 part-time (24 women); includes 10 minority (9 Black or African American, non-Hispanic/Latino; 1 Hispanic/Latino), 3 international. *Degree requirements:* For doctorate, one foreign language, comprehensive exam, thesis/dissertation, field study, independent study. *Entrance requirements:* For master's, BA/BS, 2 references, resume, official transcripts; for doctorate, MAT, M Div, 3 years of full-time ministry experience, minimum GPA of 2.75, 3 references, resume, official transcripts, writing sample, personal statement. Additional exam requirements/recommendations for international students: Required—TOEFL (minimum score 550 paper-based). *Application deadline:* For fall admission, 7/1 for domestic students, 5/1 for international students; for winter admission, 12/15 for domestic students, 9/1 for international students; for spring admission, 1/15 for domestic students, 10/1 for

international students. Applications are processed on a rolling basis. Application fee: $35. *Financial support:* Teaching assistantships, scholarships/grants, and tuition waivers (partial) available. Financial award application deadline: 2/1. *Faculty research:* Biblical studies, pastoral care, church history, theology, ministry. *Unit head:* Dr. Ronald W. Crawford, President, 804-204-1201, Fax: 804-355-8182, E-mail: rcrawford@btsr.edu. *Application contact:* Melissa Fallen, Director of Admissions and Recruitment, 804-204-1208, E-mail: admissions@btsr.edu.
Website: http://www.btsr.edu/programs/degree-programs/

Baylor University, Graduate School, College of Arts and Sciences, Department of History, Waco, TX 76798. Offers history (MA); religion and culture (PhD); U.S. and Britain (PhD). Part-time programs available. Terminal master's awarded for partial completion of doctoral program. *Degree requirements:* For master's, one foreign language, comprehensive exam, thesis; for doctorate, one foreign language, comprehensive exam, thesis/dissertation. *Entrance requirements:* For master's and doctorate, GRE General Test, 18 semester hours in history. Additional exam requirements/recommendations for international students: Required—TOEFL. *Faculty research:* American religion and culture, medieval women and religion, U.S. women's history, Chinese missions, late nineteenth-century Germany, twentieth-century urban United States.

Baylor University, Graduate School, College of Arts and Sciences, Department of Religion, Waco, TX 76798. Offers MA, PhD. Terminal master's awarded for partial completion of doctoral program. *Degree requirements:* For master's, one foreign language, thesis; for doctorate, 2 foreign languages, thesis/dissertation. *Entrance requirements:* For master's and doctorate, GRE General Test. Additional exam requirements/recommendations for international students: Required—TOEFL.

Bellarmine University, Bellarmine College (Arts and Sciences), Louisville, KY 40205-0671. Offers spirituality (MA). Part-time programs available. *Faculty:* 3 part-time/adjunct (0 women). *Students:* 10 part-time (9 women). Average age 50. *Entrance requirements:* For master's, minimum GPA of 2.8, letter of recommendation, spirituality autobiography. Additional exam requirements/recommendations for international students: Required—TOEFL (minimum score 550 paper-based; 80 iBT). *Application deadline:* For spring admission, 3/15 for domestic students. Application fee: $25. *Expenses:* Expenses: Contact institution. *Faculty research:* Early Christianity, Catholic social teaching, Christian spirituality, social justice. *Unit head:* Dr. Gregory Hillis, Program Director, 502-272-3800, E-mail: ghillis@bellarmine.edu. *Application contact:* Dr. Sara Pettingill, Dean of Graduate Admission, 502-272-8401, E-mail: spettingill@bellarmine.edu.
Website: http://www.bellarmine.edu/cas/

Bethany Theological Seminary, Graduate and Professional Programs, Richmond, IN 47374-4019. Offers biblical studies (MA Th); ministry studies (M Div); peace studies (M Div, MA Th); theological studies (MA Th, CATS); youth ministry (M Div). *Accreditation:* ACIPE; ATS. Part-time programs available. Postbaccalaureate distance learning degree programs offered (minimal on-campus study). *Degree requirements:* For master's, thesis (for some programs). *Entrance requirements:* For master's, letters of reference. Additional exam requirements/recommendations for international students: Required—TOEFL (minimum score 550 paper-based).

Bethel Seminary, Graduate and Professional Programs, St. Paul, MN 55112-6998. Offers Anglican studies (Certificate); children's and family ministry (MA); Christian studies (Certificate); Christian thought (MA); Greek and Hebrew language (M Div); Greek language (M Div); Hebrew language (M Div); marriage and family therapy (MA, Certificate); ministry (D Min); ministry practice (MA, Certificate); theological studies (MA, Certificate); transformational leadership (MA); young life youth ministry (Certificate). *Accreditation:* ACIPE; ATS (one or more programs are accredited). Part-time and evening/weekend programs available. Postbaccalaureate distance learning degree programs offered (minimal on-campus study). *Faculty:* 15 full-time (3 women), 55 part-time/adjunct (27 women). *Students:* 422 full-time (167 women), 231 part-time (71 women); includes 165 minority (62 Black or African American, non-Hispanic/Latino; 58 Asian, non-Hispanic/Latino; 29 Hispanic/Latino; 1 Native Hawaiian or other Pacific Islander, non-Hispanic/Latino; 15 Two or more races, non-Hispanic/Latino), 16 international. Average age 37. 272 applicants, 77% accepted, 165 enrolled. In 2014, 147 master's, 13 doctorates, 8 other advanced degrees awarded. *Degree requirements:* For master's, variable foreign language requirement, thesis (for some programs); for doctorate, thesis/dissertation. *Entrance requirements:* For master's, letters of reference, transcripts, personal statement; for doctorate, M Div, letters of reference, organizational support; for Certificate, letters of reference, family essay, personal statement, and family of origin paper (for marriage and family therapy). Additional exam requirements/recommendations for international students: Required—TOEFL (minimum score 550 paper-based; 87 iBT). *Application deadline:* For fall admission, 8/1 priority date for domestic students, 8/1 for international students; for winter admission, 12/1 priority date for domestic students; for spring admission, 1/1 priority date for domestic students. Applications are processed on a rolling basis. Application fee: $0. Electronic applications accepted. *Financial support:* In 2014–15, 558 students received support, including 17 teaching assistantships; career-related internships or fieldwork, Federal Work-Study, and scholarships/grants also available. Financial award applicants required to submit FAFSA. *Faculty research:* Nature of theology, ethics, Biblical commentaries, nature of God, science and theology. *Unit head:* Dr. David Clark, Vice-President and Dean, Bethel Seminary, 651-638-6659. *Application contact:* Jen Niska, Director of Admissions, 651-638-6288, Fax: 651-638-6002, E-mail: bsem-admit@bethel.edu.

Bethesda University, Graduate and Professional Programs, Anaheim, CA 92801. Offers biblical studies (MA); music (MA); theology (M Div). *Entrance requirements:* For master's, interview. Additional exam requirements/recommendations for international students: Recommended—TOEFL.

Beulah Heights University, Graduate School, Atlanta, GA 30316. Offers biblical studies (MA); leadership studies (MA). *Entrance requirements:* Additional exam requirements/recommendations for international students: Required—TOEFL (minimum score 500 paper-based). Electronic applications accepted.

Biola University, School of Arts and Sciences, La Mirada, CA 90639-0001. Offers Christian apologetics (MA, Certificate); science and religion (MA). Part-time and evening/weekend programs available. Postbaccalaureate distance learning degree programs offered (minimal on-campus study). *Faculty:* 20. *Students:* 20 full-time (2 women), 256 part-time (45 women); includes 57 minority (14 Black or African American, non-Hispanic/Latino; 2 American Indian or Alaska Native, non-Hispanic/Latino; 20 Asian, non-Hispanic/Latino; 14 Hispanic/Latino; 7 Two or more races, non-Hispanic/Latino), 14 international. 168 applicants, 70% accepted, 77 enrolled. In 2014, 53 master's awarded. *Entrance requirements:* For master's, minimum GPA of 3.0, bachelor's degree from accredited college or university (in science-related field for science and religion program). Additional exam requirements/recommendations for international students: Required—TOEFL (minimum score 600 paper-based; 100 iBT). *Application deadline:* For fall admission, 7/1 for domestic students, 6/1 for international students; for spring admission, 12/1 for domestic students. Applications are processed on a rolling basis. Application fee: $65. Electronic applications accepted. *Financial support:* Scholarships/grants and unspecified assistantships available. Support available to part-time students. Financial award applicants required to submit FAFSA. *Faculty research:* Apologetics, science and religion, intelligent design. *Application contact:* Graduate Admissions Office, 562-903-4752, E-mail: graduate.admissions@biola.edu.
Website: http://www.biola.edu/academics/sas/

Biola University, Talbot School of Theology, La Mirada, CA 90639-0001. Offers adult/family ministry (MACE); Bible exposition (MA, Th M); Biblical and theological studies (MA); children's ministry (MACE); Christian education (M Div); cross-cultural education ministry (MACE); educational studies (Ed D, PhD); evangelism and discipleship (M Div); general Christian education (MACE); Messianic Jewish studies (M Div, Certificate); missions and intercultural studies (M Div); New Testament (MA, Th M); Old Testament (MA); Old Testament and Semitics (Th M); pastoral and general ministry (M Div); pastoral care and counseling (M Div); philosophy (MA); spiritual formation (M Div, Certificate); spiritual formation and soul care (MA); theology (Th M, D Min, Certificate); youth ministry (MACE). *Accreditation:* ATS. Part-time and evening/weekend programs available. *Faculty:* 77. *Students:* 581 full-time (140 women), 554 part-time (155 women); includes 522 minority (42 Black or African American, non-Hispanic/Latino; 3 American Indian or Alaska Native, non-Hispanic/Latino; 370 Asian, non-Hispanic/Latino; 78 Hispanic/Latino; 2 Native Hawaiian or other Pacific Islander, non-Hispanic/Latino; 27 Two or more races, non-Hispanic/Latino), 121 international. 437 applicants, 78% accepted, 241 enrolled. In 2014, 182 master's, 33 doctorates awarded. *Entrance requirements:* For master's, bachelor's degree from accredited college or university; minimum GPA of 2.6 (for M Div), 3.0 (for MA); for doctorate, M Div or MA. Additional exam requirements/recommendations for international students: Required—TOEFL (minimum score 600 paper-based; 88 iBT). *Application deadline:* For fall admission, 7/1 for domestic students, 6/1 for international students; for spring admission, 12/1 priority date for domestic students. Applications are processed on a rolling basis. Application fee: $65. Electronic applications accepted. *Financial support:* Scholarships/grants and unspecified assistantships available. Support available to part-time students. Financial award applicants required to submit FAFSA. *Faculty research:* New Testament, Old Testament, spiritual formation, Christian education, theological studies, Christian ministry, preaching and pastoral ministry, language and literature, bible exposition, Christian leadership. *Unit head:* Dr. Clint Arnold, Dean, 562-903-4816, Fax: 562-903-4748. *Application contact:* Graduate Admissions Office, 562-903-4752, E-mail: graduate.admissions@biola.edu.
Website: http://www.talbot.edu/

Bob Jones University, Graduate Programs, Greenville, SC 29614. Offers accountancy (MS); Bible (MA); Bible translation (MA); Biblical studies (Certificate); broadcast management (MS); business administration (MBA); church history (MA, PhD); church ministries (MA); church music (MM); cinema and video production (MA); counseling (MS); curriculum and instruction (Ed D); divinity (M Div); dramatic production (MA); educational leadership (MS, Ed D, Ed S); elementary education (M Ed, MAT); English (M Ed, MA, MAT); fine arts (MA); graphic design (MA); history (M Ed, MA); illustration (MA); interpretative speech (MA); mathematics (M Ed, MAT); medical missions (Certificate); ministry (MM, D Min); multi-categorical special education (M Ed, MAT); music (M Ed); New Testament interpretation (PhD); Old Testament interpretation (PhD); orchestral instrument performance (MM); organ performance (MM); pastoral studies (MA); personnel services (MS, Ed S); piano pedagogy (MM); piano performance (MM); platform arts (MA); radio and television broadcasting (MS); rhetoric and public address (MA); secondary education (M Ed); studio art (MA); teaching Bible (MA); theology (MA, PhD); voice performance (MM); youth ministries (MA); M Div/MM.

Boston University, Graduate School of Arts and Sciences, Frederick S. Pardee School of Global Studies, Boston, MA 02215. Offers international affairs (MA); international relations and environmental policy (MA); international relations and international communication (MA); international relations and religion (MA); international relations, mid-career (MA); Latin American studies (MA); MA/JD; MBA/MA. *Faculty:* 33 full-time (8 women), 10 part-time/adjunct (4 women). *Students:* 78 full-time (50 women), 15 part-time (11 women); includes 12 minority (3 Black or African American, non-Hispanic/Latino; 5 Asian, non-Hispanic/Latino; 3 Hispanic/Latino; 1 Two or more races, non-Hispanic/Latino), 26 international. Average age 25. 338 applicants, 68% accepted, 36 enrolled. In 2014, 51 master's awarded. *Degree requirements:* For master's, one foreign language, capstone. *Entrance requirements:* For master's, GRE General Test, 3 letters of recommendation, transcript of all prior college coursework, statement of purpose. Additional exam requirements/recommendations for international students: Required—TOEFL (minimum score 600 paper-based; 94 iBT). *Application deadline:* For fall admission, 4/15 for domestic and international students; for spring admission, 10/15 for domestic and international students. Applications are processed on a rolling basis. Application fee: $80. Electronic applications accepted. *Expenses: Tuition:* Full-time $45,686; part-time $1428 per credit hour. *Required fees:* $660; $60 per semester. Tuition and fees vary according to program. *Financial support:* In 2014–15, 21 students received support. Federal Work-Study, scholarships/grants, and unspecified assistantships available. Financial award application deadline: 1/3; financial award applicants required to submit FAFSA. *Faculty research:* International relations, area studies, political economy, global development policy, global climate. *Unit head:* Adil Najam, Dean, 617-353-9279, Fax: 617-353-9290, E-mail: psgs@bu.edu. *Application contact:* Michael Williams, Graduate Program Administrator, 617-353-9349, Fax: 617-353-9290, E-mail: psgsgrad@bu.edu.
Website: http://www.bu.edu/PardeeSchool

Boston University, Graduate School of Arts and Sciences, Graduate Division of Religious Studies, Boston, MA 02215. Offers MA, PhD. *Students:* 52 full-time (20 women), 11 part-time (3 women); includes 10 minority (2 Black or African American, non-Hispanic/Latino; 4 Asian, non-Hispanic/Latino; 2 Hispanic/Latino; 2 Two or more races, non-Hispanic/Latino), 10 international. Average age 32. 106 applicants, 12% accepted, 8 enrolled. In 2014, 13 master's, 5 doctorates awarded. Terminal master's awarded for partial completion of doctoral program. *Degree requirements:* For master's, one foreign language, comprehensive exam, thesis; for doctorate, 2 foreign languages, comprehensive exam, thesis/dissertation. *Entrance requirements:* For master's and doctorate, GRE General Test, 3 letters of recommendation, academic writing sample. Additional exam requirements/recommendations for international students: Required—TOEFL (minimum score 550 paper-based; 84 iBT). *Application deadline:* For fall admission, 1/15 for domestic and international students. Application fee: $80. Electronic applications accepted. *Expenses: Tuition:* Full-time $45,686; part-time $1428 per credit hour. *Required fees:* $660; $60 per semester. Tuition and fees vary according to program. *Financial support:* In 2014–15, 60 students received support, including 13 fellowships with full tuition reimbursements available (averaging $20,500 per year), 1 research assistantship with full tuition reimbursement available (averaging $20,500 per year), 6 teaching assistantships with full tuition reimbursements available (averaging $20,500 per year); career-related internships or fieldwork, Federal Work-Study, scholarships/grants, health care benefits, and unspecified assistantships also available. Financial award application deadline: 1/15. *Unit head:* Nancy Ammerman, Director, 617-358-0634, Fax: 617-353-5441, E-mail: nta@bu.edu. *Application contact:* Karen Nardella, Department Administrator, 617-353-2636, Fax: 617-353-5441, E-mail: kcn@bu.edu.
Website: http://www.bu.edu/rs/

Briercrest Seminary, Graduate Programs, Program in Christian Ministries, Caronport, SK S0H 0S0, Canada. Offers leadership (MA); marriage and family counseling (MA); missions (MA); pastoral counseling (MA); worship (MA); youth and family ministry (MA). Part-time programs available. *Degree requirements:* For master's, comprehensive exam, thesis optional. *Entrance requirements:* Additional exam requirements/recommendations for international students: Required—TOEFL (minimum score 550 paper-based).

Briercrest Seminary, Graduate Programs, Program in Theology, Caronport, SK S0H 0S0, Canada. Offers Biblical studies (M Div); leadership and management (M Div); New Testament (MATS); Old Testament (MATS); pastoral counseling (M Div); pastoral ministry (M Div); theological studies (M Div); theology (MATS); worship (M Div); youth and family ministry (M Div). *Accreditation:* ATS. Part-time programs available. *Degree requirements:* For master's, comprehensive exam, thesis optional. *Entrance requirements:* Additional exam requirements/recommendations for international students: Required—TOEFL (minimum score 550 paper-based).

Brown University, Graduate School, Department of Religious Studies, Providence, RI 02912. Offers Asian religious traditions (PhD); religion and critical thought (PhD); religions of the ancient Mediterranean (PhD). *Degree requirements:* For doctorate, 2 foreign languages, thesis/dissertation. *Entrance requirements:* For doctorate, GRE General Test.

Bryn Athyn College of the New Church, Academy of the New Church Theological School, Bryn Athyn, PA 19009-0717. Offers divinity (M Div); religious studies (MA). Part-time programs available. Postbaccalaureate distance learning degree programs offered (minimal on-campus study). *Degree requirements:* For master's, variable foreign language requirement, thesis. *Entrance requirements:* Additional exam requirements/recommendations for international students: Required—TOEFL.

Cairn University, School of Divinity, Langhorne, PA 19047-2990. Offers divinity (M Div); religion (MA). Part-time and evening/weekend programs available. *Faculty:* 6 full-time (0 women), 2 part-time/adjunct (0 women). *Students:* 22 full-time (1 woman), 56 part-time (21 women); includes 39 minority (34 Black or African American, non-Hispanic/Latino; 3 Asian, non-Hispanic/Latino; 2 Hispanic/Latino). Average age 40. 36 applicants, 83% accepted, 25 enrolled. In 2014, 17 master's awarded. *Entrance requirements:* Additional exam requirements/recommendations for international students: Required—TOEFL (minimum score 550 paper-based). *Application deadline:* Applications are processed on a rolling basis. Application fee: $25. Electronic applications accepted. Application fee is waived when completed online. *Expenses: Tuition:* Full-time $11,430; part-time $635 per credit. Tuition and fees vary according to program. *Financial support:* Scholarships/grants available. Support available to part-time students. Financial award applicants required to submit FAFSA. *Unit head:* Dr. Jonathan L. Master, Dean, 215-702-4358, Fax: 215-702-4359, E-mail: divinity@cairn.edu. *Application contact:* Abigail Sattler, Assistant Director, Graduate Admissions, 800-572-2472, Fax: 215-702-4248, E-mail: asattler@cairn.edu.
Website: http://www.cairn.edu/academics/divinity

California Institute of Integral Studies, School of Consciousness and Transformation, San Francisco, CA 94103. Offers anthropology and social change (MA, PhD); creative inquiry/interdisciplinary arts (MFA); East-West psychology (MA, PhD); philosophy and religion (MA, PhD), including Asian and comparative studies, ecology, spirituality, and religion, philosophy, cosmology, and consciousness, women's spirituality; transformative leadership (MA); transformative studies (PhD); writing and consciousness (MFA). Part-time and evening/weekend programs available. Postbaccalaureate distance learning degree programs offered (no on-campus study). *Students:* 385 full-time (256 women), 102 part-time (71 women); includes 124 minority (31 Black or African American, non-Hispanic/Latino; 3 American Indian or Alaska Native, non-Hispanic/Latino; 19 Asian, non-Hispanic/Latino; 39 Hispanic/Latino; 1 Native Hawaiian or other Pacific Islander, non-Hispanic/Latino; 31 Two or more races, non-Hispanic/Latino; 53 international. Average age 43. 196 applicants, 92% accepted, 125 enrolled. In 2014, 75 master's, 41 doctorates awarded. Terminal master's awarded for partial completion of doctoral program. *Degree requirements:* For master's, thesis optional; for doctorate, comprehensive exam, thesis/dissertation, 1 foreign language (for Asian comparative studies). *Entrance requirements:* For master's, minimum GPA of 3.0, letters of recommendation, writing sample; for doctorate, master's degree, minimum GPA of 3.0, letters of recommendation, writing sample. Additional exam requirements/recommendations for international students: Required—TOEFL. *Application deadline:* For fall admission, 2/1 priority date for domestic and international students; for spring admission, 10/15 priority date for domestic and international students. Applications are processed on a rolling basis. Application fee: $65. Electronic applications accepted. *Expenses: Tuition:* Full-time $18,270; part-time $1015 per credit. *Required fees:* $85 per semester hour. *Financial support:* In 2014–15, 445 students received support, including 5 research assistantships (averaging $800 per year), 28 teaching assistantships (averaging $825 per year); career-related internships or fieldwork, Federal Work-Study, and scholarships/grants also available. Support available to part-time students. Financial award application deadline: 4/15; financial award applicants required to submit FAFSA. *Faculty research:* Ecology and sustainability, philosophy and religion, East-West psychology, integrative health, social and cultural anthropology, transformative leadership. *Application contact:* David Townes, Senior Admissions Counselor, 415-575-6152, Fax: 415-575-1268, E-mail: admissions@ciis.edu.
Website: http://www.ciis.edu/

California State University, Long Beach, Graduate Studies, College of Liberal Arts, Department of Religious Studies, Long Beach, CA 90840. Offers MA. Part-time and evening/weekend programs available. *Entrance requirements:* Additional exam requirements/recommendations for international students: Required—TOEFL. Electronic applications accepted.

Calvin Theological Seminary, Graduate and Professional Programs, Grand Rapids, MI 49546-4387. Offers Bible and theology (MA); divinity (M Div), including ancient near eastern languages and literature, contextual ministry, evangelism and teaching, history of Christianity, new church development, New Testament, Old Testament, pastoral care and leadership, preaching and worship, theological studies, youth and family ministries; educational ministry (MA); historical theology (PhD); missions and evangelism (MA); pastoral care (MA); philosophical and moral theology (PhD); systematic theology (PhD); theological studies (MTS); theology (Th M); worship (MA); youth and family ministries (MA). *Accreditation:* ACIPE; ATS. Part-time programs available. *Degree requirements:* For master's, variable foreign language requirement, thesis (for some programs); for doctorate, 4 foreign languages, comprehensive exam, thesis/dissertation. *Entrance requirements:* For doctorate, GRE General Test, Hebrew, Greek, and a modern foreign language. Additional exam requirements/recommendations for international students: Required—TOEFL (minimum score 550 paper-based), TWE (minimum score 4). Electronic applications accepted. *Faculty research:* Recent Trinity theory, Christian anthropology, Proverbs, reformed confessions, Paul's view of law.

Canadian Southern Baptist Seminary, Graduate Programs, Cochrane, AB T4C 2G1, Canada. Offers Biblical studies (MBS); Christian ministry (MCMin); ministry (M Div). *Accreditation:* ATS. Part-time programs available. Postbaccalaureate distance learning degree programs offered (no on-campus study). *Faculty:* 6 full-time (0 women), 3 part-time/adjunct (0 women). *Students:* 8 full-time (2 women), 29 part-time (9 women); includes 12 minority (2 Black or African American, non-Hispanic/Latino; 7 Asian, non-Hispanic/Latino; 3 Hispanic/Latino), 1 international. Average age 28. 12 applicants, 83% accepted, 7 enrolled. In 2014, 6 master's awarded. *Entrance requirements:* Additional exam requirements/recommendations for international students: Required—TOEFL (minimum score 560 paper-based; 83 iBT); Recommended—IELTS. *Application deadline:* For fall admission, 7/1 priority date for domestic and international students; for winter admission, 11/15 priority date for domestic and international students. Applications are processed on a rolling basis. Application fee: $50 ($150 for international students). *Expenses: Tuition:* Full-time $7200 Canadian dollars; part-time $300 Canadian dollars per credit hour. *Required fees:* $120 Canadian dollars. One-time fee: $50 Canadian dollars. *Financial support:* Scholarships/grants available. Financial award application deadline: 1/21. *Unit head:* Dr. Steve Booth, Academic Dean, 403-932-6622 Ext. 232, E-mail: steve.booth@csbs.ca. *Application contact:* Kathleen McNaughton, Registrar, 403-932-6622 Ext. 221, E-mail: kathleen.mcnaughton@csbs.ca.

Cardinal Stritch University, College of Arts and Sciences, Department of Religious Studies, Milwaukee, WI 53217-3985. Offers lay ministries (MA); ministry (MA); religious studies (MA). Part-time and evening/weekend programs available. *Degree requirements:* For master's, comprehensive exam, thesis, faculty recommendation, research project. *Entrance requirements:* For master's, interview, minimum GPA of 2.75.

The Catholic University of America, School of Arts and Sciences, Program in Early Christian Studies, Washington, DC 20064. Offers MA, PhD. Part-time programs available. *Faculty:* 1 full-time (0 women). *Students:* 2 full-time (1 woman), 5 part-time (2 women), 1 international. Average age 32. 7 applicants, 29% accepted, 1 enrolled. In 2014, 1 doctorate awarded. *Degree requirements:* For master's, one foreign language, comprehensive exam; for doctorate, 2 foreign languages, comprehensive exam, thesis/dissertation. *Entrance requirements:* For master's and doctorate, GRE General Test, statement of purpose, official copies of academic transcripts, three letters of recommendation. Additional exam requirements/recommendations for international students: Required—TOEFL (minimum score 580 paper-based). *Application deadline:* For fall admission, 7/15 priority date for domestic students, 7/1 for international students; for spring admission, 11/15 priority date for domestic students, 11/1 for international students. Applications are processed on a rolling basis. Application fee: $55. Electronic applications accepted. *Expenses: Tuition:* Full-time $40,200; part-time $1600 per credit hour. *Required fees:* $400; $195 per semester. One-time fee: $425. *Financial support:* Fellowships, research assistantships, teaching assistantships, Federal Work-Study, scholarships/grants, tuition waivers (full and partial), and unspecified assistantships available. Financial award application deadline: 2/1; financial award applicants required to submit FAFSA. *Faculty research:* Languages and literatures of the Christian Near East, systematic and fundamental theology, Greek and Latin patristics, early Christian poetry and hagiography, ancient philosophy. *Unit head:* Dr. Philip Rousseau, Director, 202-319-6217, Fax: 202-319-6609, E-mail: rousseau@cua.edu. *Application contact:* Director of Graduate Admissions, 202-319-5057, Fax: 202-319-6533, E-mail: cua-admissions@cua.edu.
Website: http://earlychristianity.cua.edu/

The Catholic University of America, School of Theology and Religious Studies, Washington, DC 20064. Offers M Div, MA, MRE, D Min, PhD, STD, Certificate, STB, STL, MSLS/MA. *Accreditation:* ATS (one or more programs are accredited). Part-time programs available. *Faculty:* 44 full-time (5 women), 8 part-time/adjunct (2 women). *Students:* 153 full-time (8 women), 206 part-time (51 women); includes 50 minority (8 Black or African American, non-Hispanic/Latino; 2 American Indian or Alaska Native, non-Hispanic/Latino; 11 Asian, non-Hispanic/Latino; 16 Hispanic/Latino; 1 Native Hawaiian or other Pacific Islander, non-Hispanic/Latino; 12 Two or more races, non-Hispanic/Latino), 57 international. Average age 36. 197 applicants, 74% accepted, 69 enrolled. In 2014, 40 master's, 21 doctorates awarded. *Degree requirements:* For master's, variable foreign language requirement, comprehensive exam (for some programs), thesis (for some programs); for doctorate, variable foreign language requirement, comprehensive exam, thesis/dissertation. *Entrance requirements:* For master's and doctorate, GRE General Test, statement of purpose, official copies of academic transcripts, three letters of recommendation. Additional exam requirements/recommendations for international students: Required—TOEFL (minimum score 580 paper-based). *Application deadline:* For fall admission, 7/15 priority date for domestic students, 7/1 for international students; for spring admission, 11/15 priority date for domestic students, 11/1 for international students. Applications are processed on a rolling basis. Application fee: $55. Electronic applications accepted. *Expenses: Tuition:* Full-time $40,200; part-time $1600 per credit hour. *Required fees:* $400; $195 per semester. One-time fee: $425. *Financial support:* Fellowships, research assistantships, teaching assistantships, Federal Work-Study, scholarships/grants, tuition waivers (full and partial), and unspecified assistantships available. Financial award application deadline: 2/1; financial award applicants required to submit FAFSA. *Faculty research:* Historical and systematic theology, religious education and catechetics, moral theology and ethics, Biblical studies, liturgical studies and sacramental theology. *Unit head:* Msgr. Paul McPartlan, Acting Dean, 202-319-6515, Fax: 202-319-5704, E-mail: mcpartlan@cua.edu. *Application contact:* Director of Graduate Admissions, 202-319-5057, Fax: 202-319-6533, E-mail: cua-admissions@cua.edu.
Website: http://trs.cua.edu/

Charlotte Christian College and Theological Seminary, Graduate Program, Charlotte, NC 28205. Offers urban Christian ministry (MA), including church planting, multi-cultural studies, sacred music, youth ministry. Part-time and evening/weekend programs available. *Faculty:* 5 full-time (1 woman), 9 part-time/adjunct (2 women). *Students:* 2 full-time (1 woman), 25 part-time (15 women); includes 18 minority (17 Black or African American, non-Hispanic/Latino; 1 Hispanic/Latino), 2 international. Average age 47. 2 applicants, 100% accepted, 2 enrolled. In 2014, 2 master's awarded. *Degree requirements:* For master's, thesis. *Entrance requirements:* For master's, MAT, writing sample/essay. Additional exam requirements/recommendations for international students: Required—TOEFL, IELTS. *Application deadline:* For fall admission, 7/24 for domestic students, 7/18 for international students; for spring admission, 12/11 for domestic students, 12/5 for international students; for summer admission, 4/18 for domestic and international students. Application fee: $50 ($140 for international students). Electronic applications accepted. *Expenses:* Expenses: 1 course: $1,200; 2 courses: $2,300; 3 courses: $3,300; 4 courses $3,900. *Financial support:* In 2014–15, 5 students received support. Federal Work-Study and scholarships/grants available. Financial award application deadline: 4/1; financial award applicants required to submit FAFSA. *Unit head:* Anne Witt, Registrar/Director of International Students, 704-344-6882 Ext. 103, Fax: 704-334-6885, E-mail: abwitt@charlottechristian.edu. *Application contact:* Constance Hemphill, Director of Admissions, 704-334-6882 Ext. 115, Fax: 704-334-6885, E-mail: chemphill@charlottechristian.edu.
Website: http://www.charlottechristian.edu

Chicago Theological Seminary, Graduate and Professional Programs, Chicago, IL 60637-1507. Offers preaching (D Min); religion and health (D Min); religious studies (MA); spirituality and spiritual direction (D Min); theology (M Div); theology, ethics and the human sciences (PhD); M Div/MSW. *Accreditation:* ACIPE; ATS. Part-time programs available. *Degree requirements:* For master's, thesis; for doctorate, 2 foreign languages,

comprehensive exam, thesis/dissertation. *Entrance requirements:* For doctorate, GRE General Test. Additional exam requirements/recommendations for international students: Required—TOEFL. *Faculty research:* Bible, culture and hermeneutics, theology, gender and sexuality, black faith and life, spirituality and psychology, practical theology.

Christian Brothers University, School of Arts, Memphis, TN 38104-5581. Offers Catholic studies (MACS); educational leadership (MSEL); teacher-leadership (M Ed); teaching (MAT). Part-time and evening/weekend programs available. *Entrance requirements:* For master's, GRE, GMAT, PRAXIS II. *Expenses:* Contact institution.

Christian Theological Seminary, Graduate and Professional Programs, Indianapolis, IN 46208-3301. Offers educational and arts ministries (MA); marriage and family therapy (MA); pastoral care and counseling (D Min); psychotherapy and faith (MA); theological studies (MTS); theology (M Div). *Accreditation:* AAMFT/COAMFTE (one or more programs are accredited); ACIPE; ATS. Part-time programs available. Terminal master's awarded for partial completion of doctoral program. *Degree requirements:* For master's, comprehensive exam (for some programs), thesis (for some programs), missionary and cross-cultural experience (for M Div); for doctorate, comprehensive exam, thesis/dissertation. *Entrance requirements:* For doctorate, M Div. Additional exam requirements/recommendations for international students: Recommended—TOEFL. Electronic applications accepted. *Faculty research:* Faith formation, peer learning post graduation.

Cincinnati Christian University, Graduate School, Cincinnati, OH 45204-3200. Offers biblical studies (MA); church history (MA); counseling (MAC); divinity (M Div); ministry (M Min); practical ministries (MA); theological studies (MA). *Accreditation:* ATS. Part-time programs available. *Degree requirements:* For master's, variable foreign language requirement, thesis (for some programs), oral exam (for M Div). *Entrance requirements:* Additional exam requirements/recommendations for international students: Required—TOEFL. Electronic applications accepted.

Claremont Graduate University, Graduate Programs, School of Arts and Humanities, Department of Religion, Claremont, CA 91711-6160. Offers Hebrew Bible (MA, PhD); history of Christianity and religions of North America (MA, PhD); New Testament (MA, PhD); philosophy of religion and theology (MA, PhD); theology, ethics and culture (MA, PhD); women's studies in religion (MA, PhD); MA/PhD; MBA/PhD. Part-time programs available. *Faculty:* 7 full-time (3 women), 2 part-time/adjunct (0 women). *Students:* 153 full-time (58 women), 31 part-time (16 women); includes 33 minority (12 Black or African American, non-Hispanic/Latino; 1 American Indian or Alaska Native, non-Hispanic/Latino; 7 Asian, non-Hispanic/Latino; 10 Hispanic/Latino; 1 Native Hawaiian or other Pacific Islander, non-Hispanic/Latino; 2 Two or more races, non-Hispanic/Latino), 14 international. Average age 37. In 2014, 15 master's, 13 doctorates awarded. Terminal master's awarded for partial completion of doctoral program. *Entrance requirements:* For master's and doctorate, GRE General Test. Additional exam requirements/recommendations for international students: Required—TOEFL (minimum score 550 paper-based; 80 iBT). *Application deadline:* For fall admission, 2/1 priority date for domestic and international students. Applications are processed on a rolling basis. Application fee: $80. Electronic applications accepted. *Expenses: Tuition:* Full-time $41,784; part-time $1741 per credit. *Required fees:* $600; $300 per semester. *Financial support:* Fellowships, research assistantships, teaching assistantships, Federal Work-Study, institutionally sponsored loans, and scholarships/grants available. Support available to part-time students. Financial award application deadline: 2/15; financial award applicants required to submit FAFSA. *Unit head:* Tammi Schneider, Chair, E-mail: tammi.schneider@cgu.edu. *Application contact:* Erma Cross, Admissions and Alumni Coordinator, 909-607-9843, E-mail: erminia.cross@cgu.edu.
Website: http://www.cgu.edu/pages/674.asp

Claremont School of Theology, Graduate and Professional Programs, Program in Religion, Claremont, CA 91711-3199. Offers practical theology (PhD), including religious education, spiritual care and counseling; religion (PhD), including Hebrew Bible, New Testament and Christian origins, process studies, religion, ethics, and society; religion and theology (MA); religious education (MARE). *Accreditation:* ACIPE; ATS. Terminal master's awarded for partial completion of doctoral program. *Degree requirements:* For master's, thesis; for doctorate, 2 foreign languages, thesis/dissertation. *Entrance requirements:* For doctorate, GRE General Test. Additional exam requirements/recommendations for international students: Required—TOEFL. Electronic applications accepted.

Columbia University, Graduate School of Arts and Sciences, New York, NY 10027. Offers African-American studies (MA); American studies (MA); anthropology (MA, PhD); art history and archaeology (MA, PhD); astronomy (PhD); biological sciences (PhD); biotechnology (MA); chemical physics (PhD); chemistry (PhD); classical studies (MA, PhD); classics (MA, PhD); climate and society (MA); earth and environmental sciences (PhD); East Asia: regional studies (MA); East Asian languages and cultures (MA, PhD); ecology, evolution and environmental biology (MA), including conservation biology; ecology, evolution, and environmental biology (PhD), including ecology and evolutionary biology, evolutionary primatology; economics (PhD); English and comparative literature (MA, PhD); French and Romance philology (MA, PhD); Germanic languages (MA, PhD); global French studies (MA); Hispanic cultural studies (MA); history (PhD); history and literature (MA); human rights studies (MA); Islamic studies (MA); Italian (MA, PhD); Japanese pedagogy (MA); Jewish studies (MA); Latin America and the Caribbean: regional studies (MA); Latin American and Iberian cultures (PhD); mathematics (MA, PhD), including finance (MA); medieval and Renaissance studies (MA); Middle Eastern, South Asian, and African studies (MA, PhD); modern art: critical and curatorial studies (MA); modern European studies (MA); museum anthropology (MA); music (DMA, PhD); oral history (MA); philosophical foundations of physics (MA); philosophy (MA, PhD); physics (PhD); political science (MA, PhD); psychology (PhD); quantitative methods in the social sciences (MA); religion (MA, PhD); Russia, Eurasia and East Europe: regional studies (MA); Russian translation (MA); Slavic cultures (MA); Slavic languages (MA, PhD); sociology (MA, PhD); South Asian studies (MA); statistics (MA, PhD); theatre (PhD); JD/PhD; MA/MS; MD/PhD; MPA/MA. Dual-degree programs require admission to both Graduate School of Arts and Sciences and another Columbia school. Part-time and evening/weekend programs available. Terminal master's awarded for partial completion of doctoral program. *Degree requirements:* For master's, thesis (for some programs); for doctorate, comprehensive exam, thesis/dissertation. *Entrance requirements:* For master's and doctorate, GRE General Test, GRE Subject Test (for some programs). Electronic applications accepted. *Faculty research:* Humanities, natural sciences, social sciences.

Concordia University, School of Graduate Studies, Faculty of Arts and Science, Department of Religion, Program in History and Philosophy of Religion, Montréal, QC H3G 1M8, Canada. Offers MA. *Degree requirements:* For master's, comprehensive exam, thesis optional. *Entrance requirements:* For master's, honors degree in religion or equivalent. *Faculty research:* Comparative ethics, social theory and political society, Judaic studies.

Concordia University, School of Graduate Studies, Faculty of Arts and Science, Department of Religion, Program in Religion, Montréal, QC H3G 1M8, Canada. Offers PhD. Program offered jointly with Université du Québec à Montréal. *Degree requirements:* For doctorate, one foreign language, comprehensive exam, thesis/dissertation.

Concordia University, School of Theology, Irvine, CA 92612-3299. Offers Christian leadership (MA); research in theology (MA); theology and culture (MA). Part-time and evening/weekend programs available. *Degree requirements:* For master's, project/thesis or vicarage. *Entrance requirements:* For master's, official college transcript(s), statement of intent, 2 references, interview. Additional exam requirements/recommendations for international students: Required—TOEFL. Electronic applications accepted. *Expenses:* Contact institution.

Concordia University Chicago, College of Graduate and Innovative Programs, Program in Religion, River Forest, IL 60305-1499. Offers MA. Part-time and evening/weekend programs available. *Degree requirements:* For master's, comprehensive exam, thesis. *Entrance requirements:* For master's, minimum GPA of 2.9. Additional exam requirements/recommendations for international students: Required—TOEFL (minimum score 550 paper-based). Electronic applications accepted. *Faculty research:* Dead Sea Scrolls, cultural construction of gender in early modern Europe, Luther, Luther's theology of the cross, gospels of Mark and John.

Concordia University College of Alberta, Program in Biblical and Christian Studies, Edmonton, AB T5B 4E4, Canada. Offers MA.

Cornell University, Graduate School, Graduate Fields of Arts and Sciences, Field of Asian Literature, Religion and Culture, Ithaca, NY 14853-0001. Offers Asian religions (MA, PhD); Chinese philosophy (PhD); classical Chinese literature (PhD); classical Japanese literature (PhD); East Asian literature and culture (PhD); Korean literature (PhD); modern Chinese literature (PhD); modern Japanese literature (PhD); South Asian literature and culture (PhD); Southeast Asian literature and culture (PhD). *Degree requirements:* For doctorate, comprehensive exam, thesis/dissertation. *Entrance requirements:* For doctorate, GRE General Test, academic writing sample, 3 letters of recommendation. Additional exam requirements/recommendations for international students: Required—TOEFL (minimum score 600 paper-based; 77 iBT). Electronic applications accepted.

Dallas Baptist University, Gary Cook School of Leadership, Program in Christian Education, Dallas, TX 75211-9299. Offers adult ministry (MA); business ministry (MA); Christian studies (MA); collegiate ministry (MA); communication ministry (MA); counseling ministry (MA); family ministry (MA); general ministry (MA); leading the nonprofit organization (MA); missions ministry (MA); small group ministry (MA); student ministry (MA); worship ministry (MA); MA/MA. Part-time and evening/weekend programs available. *Entrance requirements:* For master's, minimum GPA of 3.0. Additional exam requirements/recommendations for international students: Required—TOEFL. Electronic applications accepted. *Expenses: Tuition:* Full-time $14,130; part-time $785 per credit hour. *Required fees:* $200 per semester. Tuition and fees vary according to course level and course load.

Dallas Theological Seminary, Graduate Programs, Dallas, TX 75204-6499. Offers adult education (Th M); apologetics (Th M); Bible backgrounds (Th M); Bible translation (Th M); Biblical and theological studies (Certificate); biblical counseling (MA); biblical exegesis and linguistics (MA); biblical exposition (PhD); biblical studies (MA); Biblical theology (Th M); children's education (Th M); Christian education (MA, D Min); Christian leadership (MA); cross-cultural ministries (MA); educational administration (Th M); educational leadership (Th M); evangelism and discipleship (Th M); exposition of Biblical books (Th M); family life education (Th M); general studies (Th M); Hebrew and cognate studies (Th M); hermeneutics (Th M); historical theology (Th M); homiletics (Th M); intercultural ministries (Th M); Jesus studies (Th M); leadership studies (Th M); media and communication (MA); media arts (Th M); ministry (D Min); ministry with women (Th M); New Testament studies (Th M, PhD); Old Testament studies (Th M, PhD); parachurch ministries (Th M); pastoral care and counseling (Th M); pastoral theology and practice (Th M); philosophy (Th M); sacred theology (STM); spiritual formation (Th M); systematic theology (Th M); teaching in Christian institutions (Th M); theological studies (PhD); urban ministries (Th M); worship studies (Th M); youth education (Th M). *Accreditation:* ATS (one or more programs are accredited). Part-time programs available. Postbaccalaureate distance learning degree programs offered (no on-campus study). *Degree requirements:* For master's, variable foreign language requirement, thesis (for some programs); for doctorate, 2 foreign languages, thesis/dissertation. *Entrance requirements:* For master's, GRE or MAT (if minimum undergraduate cumulative GPA is below 2.5 or undergraduate degree is unaccredited). Additional exam requirements/recommendations for international students: Required—TOEFL (minimum score 575 paper-based; 85 iBT), TWE. Electronic applications accepted.

Delta State University, Graduate Programs, College of Arts and Sciences, Program in Liberal Studies, Cleveland, MS 38733-0001. Offers evolving human voices (MALS); gender and diversity studies (MALS); globalization studies (MALS); Mississippi Delta studies (MALS); philosophy (MALS); religious studies (MALS). *Students:* 12 full-time (9 women), 7 part-time (5 women); includes 4 minority (all Black or African American, non-Hispanic/Latino). Average age 29. 6 applicants, 83% accepted, 4 enrolled. In 2014, 4 master's awarded. *Degree requirements:* For master's, oral and/or written comprehensive exam. *Application deadline:* For fall admission, 8/1 priority date for domestic students; for spring admission, 12/1 priority date for domestic students. Application fee: $30. *Expenses:* Tuition, state resident: full-time $6012; part-time $334 per credit hour. Tuition, nonresident: full-time $6012; part-time $334 per credit hour. Part-time tuition and fees vary according to course load. *Unit head:* Dr. Paul Hankins, Dean, 662-846-4100, Fax: 662-846-4016, E-mail: phankins@deltastate.edu. *Application contact:* Dr. Beverly Moon, Dean of Graduate Studies, 662-846-4875, Fax: 662-846-4313, E-mail: grad-info@deltastate.edu.
Website: http://www.deltastate.edu/pages/4994.asp

Denver Seminary, Graduate and Professional Programs, Littleton, CO 80120. Offers apologetics (Certificate); biblical studies (MA); Christian formation and soul care (MA, Certificate); Christian studies (MA, Certificate); church and parachurch leadership (D Min); counseling licensure (MA); counseling ministry (MA); intercultural ministry (Certificate); leadership (MA, Certificate); marriage and family counseling (D Min); pastoral ministry (D Min); philosophy of religion (MA); spiritual guidance (Certificate); theology (M Div, Certificate); worship (Certificate); youth and family ministry (MA). *Accreditation:* ACA; ACIPE; ATS (one or more programs are accredited). Part-time and evening/weekend programs available. Postbaccalaureate distance learning degree programs offered. *Degree requirements:* For master's, 2 foreign languages, thesis (for some programs); for doctorate, 2 foreign languages, thesis/dissertation. *Entrance requirements:* For doctorate, M Div, 3 years of ministry experience. Additional exam requirements/recommendations for international students: Required—TOEFL (minimum score 575 paper-based; 90 iBT). Electronic applications accepted.

Dominican University of California, School of Arts, Humanities and Social Sciences, Humanities Program, San Rafael, CA 94901-2298. Offers applied music (MA); art history (MA); creative writing (MA); history (MA); literature (MA); philosophy (MA); political theory (MA); religion (MA); women and gender studies (MA). Part-time programs available. *Faculty:* 11 full-time (5 women), 5 part-time/adjunct (2 women). *Students:* 2 full-time (1 woman), 25 part-time (16 women); includes 7 minority (1 Black or African American, non-Hispanic/Latino; 1 American Indian or Alaska Native, non-

Hispanic/Latino; 3 Hispanic/Latino; 2 Two or more races, non-Hispanic/Latino). Average age 46. 12 applicants, 83% accepted, 7 enrolled. *Degree requirements:* For master's, thesis or alternative. *Entrance requirements:* For master's, minimum GPA of 3.0, interview. Additional exam requirements/recommendations for international students: Required—TOEFL (minimum score 550 paper-based; 80 iBT), IELTS (minimum score 6.5). *Application deadline:* For fall admission, 5/15 priority date for domestic and international students; for spring admission, 11/15 priority date for domestic and international students. Applications are processed on a rolling basis. Electronic applications accepted. Application fee is waived when completed online. *Expenses:* Expenses: $935 per unit. *Financial support:* Scholarships/grants available. Support available to part-time students. Financial award application deadline: 3/2; financial award applicants required to submit FAFSA. *Unit head:* Dr. Laura Stivers, Acting Dean, 415-458-3734, E-mail: laura.stivers@dominican.edu. *Application contact:* Ryan Purtill, Director, 415-458-3748, Fax: 415-485-3214, E-mail: ryan.purtill@dominican.edu. Website: http://www.dominican.edu/academics/ahss/graduate-program/index_html

Duke University, Graduate School, Department of Religion, Durham, NC 27708. Offers MA, PhD, JD/MA. Part-time programs available. Terminal master's awarded for partial completion of doctoral program. *Degree requirements:* For master's, one foreign language, thesis or alternative; for doctorate, 2 foreign languages, thesis/dissertation. *Entrance requirements:* For master's and doctorate, GRE General Test. Additional exam requirements/recommendations for international students: Required—TOEFL (minimum score 577 paper-based; 90 iBT) or IELTS (minimum score 7). Electronic applications accepted. *Expenses: Tuition:* Full-time $45,760; part-time $2765 per credit. *Required fees:* $978. Full-time tuition and fees vary according to program.

Earlham School of Religion, Graduate Programs, Richmond, IN 47374-5360. Offers religion (MA); theology (M Div, M Min). *Accreditation:* ACIPE; ATS. Part-time programs available. Postbaccalaureate distance learning degree programs offered (minimal on-campus study). *Faculty:* 8 full-time (3 women), 4 part-time/adjunct (2 women). *Students:* 30 full-time (18 women), 23 part-time (17 women). *Degree requirements:* For master's, variable foreign language requirement, comprehensive exam (for some programs), thesis (for some programs), internship (M Div). *Entrance requirements:* For master's, 3 references. Additional exam requirements/recommendations for international students: Required—TOEFL (minimum score 550 paper-based; 82 iBT), IELTS. *Application deadline:* For fall admission, 7/15 priority date for domestic students; for winter admission, 12/15 priority date for domestic students. Applications are processed on a rolling basis. Application fee: $35. Electronic applications accepted. *Expenses: Tuition:* Full-time $11,502; part-time $426 per credit. *Financial support:* Scholarships/grants and tuition waivers (full and partial) available. Financial award application deadline: 4/15; financial award applicants required to submit FAFSA. *Faculty research:* Digitizing Quaker texts, vital Quaker ministry, research in Quaker studies and other seminary areas. *Unit head:* Jay W. Marshall, Dean, 800-432-1377, Fax: 765-983-1688, E-mail: marshja@earlham.edu. *Application contact:* Matthew Hisrich, Director of Recruitment and Admissions, 765-983-1523, Fax: 765-983-1688, E-mail: hisrima@earlham.edu. Website: http://www.esr.earlham.edu/academics-programs/degree-programs

Eastern Mennonite University, Eastern Mennonite Seminary, Harrisonburg, VA 22802-2462. Offers church leadership (MA); divinity (M Div); ministry studies (Certificate); religion (MA); theological studies (Certificate). *Accreditation:* ATS. Part-time programs available. *Degree requirements:* For master's, thesis (for some programs), supervised field education (for M Div). *Entrance requirements:* For master's, minimum GPA of 2.5. Additional exam requirements/recommendations for international students: Required—TOEFL (minimum score 550 paper-based). *Expenses:* Contact institution. *Faculty research:* Spiritual direction and culture of call, leadership coaching: an approach to leadership in a culture of call, clarity of call in the probationary process for United Methodist clergy in Virginia, EMS women's experiences of culture of call efforts, practices of excellent and fruitful Mennonite pastoral ministry.

East Texas Baptist University, School of Christian Studies, Marshall, TX 75670-1498. Offers Christian ministry (MACM); religion (MA). Part-time programs available. *Faculty:* 4 full-time (0 women). *Students:* 4 full-time (1 woman), 1 part-time (0 women); includes 2 minority (1 Black or African American, non-Hispanic/Latino; 1 Two or more races, non-Hispanic/Latino). Average age 31. 5 applicants, 80% accepted, 3 enrolled. In 2014, 3 master's awarded. *Degree requirements:* For master's, thesis optional. *Entrance requirements:* Additional exam requirements/recommendations for international students: Recommended—TOEFL (minimum score 550 paper-based; 79 iBT). *Application deadline:* For fall admission, 8/20 for domestic and international students; for spring admission, 1/7 for domestic and international students. Applications are processed on a rolling basis. Application fee: $50. Electronic applications accepted. *Expenses:* Expenses: Contact institution. *Financial support:* In 2014–15, 3 students received support. Federal Work-Study and scholarships/grants available. Financial award applicants required to submit FAFSA. *Unit head:* Dr. Warren Johnson, Director, 903-923-2180, Fax: 903-923-2077, E-mail: christianstudiesma@etbu.edu. *Application contact:* Den Murley, Graduate Services and Recruiting Coordinator, 903-923-2079, Fax: 903-934-8115, E-mail: dmurley@etbu.edu. Website: http://www.etbu.edu/christian-studies/masters-degrees/

Elms College, Religious Studies Department, Chicopee, MA 01013-2839. Offers MAAT. Part-time and evening/weekend programs available. *Faculty:* 2 full-time (0 women), 5 part-time/adjunct (2 women). *Students:* 2 full-time (0 women), 3 part-time (0 women); includes 1 minority (Black or African American, non-Hispanic/Latino). Average age 51. 2 applicants, 100% accepted, 2 enrolled. In 2014, 3 master's awarded. *Degree requirements:* For master's, thesis. *Entrance requirements:* For master's, minimum GPA of 3.0. Additional exam requirements/recommendations for international students: Required—TOEFL. *Application deadline:* For fall admission, 7/1 priority date for domestic students; for spring admission, 11/1 priority date for domestic students. Applications are processed on a rolling basis. Application fee: $30. *Financial support:* Tuition waivers (partial) available. Financial award applicants required to submit FAFSA. *Unit head:* Dr. Martin Pion, Director of Religious Studies, 413-265-3581, Fax: 413-594-3951, E-mail: pionm@elms.edu. *Application contact:* Dr. Elizabeth Teahan Hukowicz, Dean, School of Graduate and Professional Studies, 413-265-2360, Fax: 413-265-2459, E-mail: hukowicze@elms.edu.

Emmanuel Christian Seminary, Graduate and Professional Programs, Johnson City, TN 37601-9438. Offers Christian care and counseling (M Div); Christian education (M Div); Christian ministries (MCM); Christian ministry (M Div); Christian theology (M Div, MAR); church history (MAR); church history/historical theology (M Div); general studies (M Div); ministry (D Min); New Testament (M Div, MAR); Old Testament (M Div, MAR); urban ministry (M Div); world missions (M Div). *Accreditation:* ACIPE; ATS. Part-time programs available. Postbaccalaureate distance learning degree programs offered (minimal on-campus study). *Degree requirements:* For master's, 2 foreign languages, thesis or alternative, portfolio; for doctorate, thesis/dissertation. *Entrance requirements:* For master's, bachelor's degree from accredited undergraduate institution; for doctorate, M Div or equivalent. Additional exam requirements/recommendations for international students: Required—TOEFL. Electronic applications accepted. *Faculty research:* Theology of Old Testament prophets, spiritual formation for Christian leaders, history of African churches and religions, social world of early Christianity, lay pastoral counseling, theology and art.

Emory University, Laney Graduate School, Division of Religion, Atlanta, GA 30322-1100. Offers PhD. *Degree requirements:* For doctorate, 2 foreign languages, comprehensive exam, thesis/dissertation. *Entrance requirements:* For doctorate, GRE General Test, minimum GPA of 3.0. Additional exam requirements/recommendations for international students: Required—TOEFL. Electronic applications accepted. *Faculty research:* Systematic and historical theology, Biblical studies.

Faith Baptist Bible College and Theological Seminary, Graduate Program, Ankeny, IA 50023. Offers Biblical studies (MA); pastoral studies (M Div); pastoral training (MA); religion (MA); theological studies (MA). Part-time programs available. *Faculty:* 3 full-time (0 women), 4 part-time/adjunct (0 women). *Students:* 13 full-time (0 women), 32 part-time (8 women); includes 5 minority (1 Black or African American, non-Hispanic/Latino; 3 Asian, non-Hispanic/Latino; 1 Two or more races, non-Hispanic/Latino). Average age 30. In 2014, 9 master's awarded. *Degree requirements:* For master's, thesis or alternative. *Entrance requirements:* Additional exam requirements/recommendations for international students: Required—TOEFL (minimum score 550 paper-based). *Application deadline:* For fall admission, 8/1 priority date for domestic students, 8/1 for international students; for spring admission, 12/15 for domestic and international students. Applications are processed on a rolling basis. Application fee: $25. *Financial support:* Career-related internships or fieldwork and scholarships/grants available. Support available to part-time students. Financial award application deadline: 3/1; financial award applicants required to submit FAFSA. *Faculty research:* Baptist theology, American church history. *Unit head:* Dr. Ernest Schmidt, Interim President, 515-964-0601, E-mail: schmidte@faith.edu. *Application contact:* Stacy Lansdown, Admissions Administrative Assistant, 888-FAITH4U, Fax: 515-964-1638, E-mail: admissions@faith.edu. Website: http://www.faith.edu/

Florida International University, College of Arts and Sciences, Department of Religious Studies, Miami, FL 33199. Offers MA, MA/PhD. Part-time and evening/weekend programs available. *Degree requirements:* For master's, thesis or alternative. *Entrance requirements:* For master's, minimum GPA of 3.0, 2 letters of recommendation. Additional exam requirements/recommendations for international students: Required—TOEFL (minimum score 550 paper-based; 80 iBT). Electronic applications accepted.

Florida State University, The Graduate School, College of Arts and Sciences, Department of Religion, Tallahassee, FL 32306-1520. Offers humanities (PhD), including religion; religion (MA, PhD). *Faculty:* 18 full-time (5 women), 1 (woman) part-time/adjunct. *Students:* 61 full-time (17 women), 5 part-time (2 women); includes 6 minority (2 Black or African American, non-Hispanic/Latino; 1 American Indian or Alaska Native, non-Hispanic/Latino; 2 Asian, non-Hispanic/Latino; 1 Hispanic/Latino). Average age 26. 54 applicants, 35% accepted, 12 enrolled. In 2014, 5 master's, 3 doctorates awarded. Terminal master's awarded for partial completion of doctoral program. *Degree requirements:* For master's, one foreign language, comprehensive exam (for some programs), thesis (for some programs); for doctorate, 2 foreign languages, thesis/dissertation. *Entrance requirements:* For master's, GRE General Test, minimum GPA of 3.0; for doctorate, GRE General Test, MA in religion. Additional exam requirements/recommendations for international students: Required—TOEFL. *Application deadline:* For fall admission, 12/15 for domestic and international students. Application fee: $30. Electronic applications accepted. *Expenses:* Tuition, state resident: part-time $403.51 per credit hour. Tuition, nonresident: part-time $1004.85 per credit hour. *Required fees:* $75.81 per credit hour. One-time fee: $20 part-time. Tuition and fees vary according to campus/location. *Financial support:* In 2014–15, 61 students received support, including 3 fellowships with partial tuition reimbursements available (averaging $15,000 per year), 21 research assistantships with partial tuition reimbursements available (averaging $10,500 per year), 32 teaching assistantships with partial tuition reimbursements available (averaging $12,000 per year); institutionally sponsored loans and unspecified assistantships also available. Financial award application deadline: 3/15; financial award applicants required to submit FAFSA. *Faculty research:* American religious history, comparative religious ethics, religions of Western antiquity, Asian religions and culture, history and ethnography of religion. *Unit head:* Dr. John Kelsay, Chair, 850-644-1020, Fax: 850-644-7225, E-mail: jkelsay@fsu.edu. *Application contact:* Dr. Nicole Kelley, Director of Graduate Studies, 850-644-1020, Fax: 850-644-7225, E-mail: nkelley@fsu.edu. Website: http://www.religion.fsu.edu

Fordham University, Graduate School of Religion and Religious Education, New York, NY 10458. Offers pastoral counseling and spiritual care (MA); pastoral ministry/spirituality/pastoral counseling (D Min); religion and religious education (MA); religious education (MS, PhD, PD); spiritual direction (Certificate). Part-time programs available. Terminal master's awarded for partial completion of doctoral program. *Degree requirements:* For master's, research paper; for doctorate, comprehensive exam, thesis/dissertation. *Entrance requirements:* For doctorate, MAT. Electronic applications accepted. *Expenses:* Contact institution. *Faculty research:* Spirituality and spiritual direction, pastoral care and counseling, adult family and community, growth and young adult.

General Theological Seminary, Graduate and Professional Programs, New York, NY 10011-4977. Offers Anglican studies (STM, Th D, Certificate); ascetical theology (Certificate); biblical studies (Certificate); congregational development (Certificate); divinity (M Div); historical and theological studies (Certificate); spiritual direction (MASD, STM, Certificate); theology (MA). *Accreditation:* ACIPE; ATS. Part-time and evening/weekend programs available. Terminal master's awarded for partial completion of doctoral program. *Degree requirements:* For master's, thesis; for doctorate, 2 foreign languages, thesis/dissertation. *Entrance requirements:* For master's, GRE General Test; for doctorate, GRE, M Div or MA. Additional exam requirements/recommendations for international students: Required—TOEFL. *Faculty research:* Liturgy, New Testament, ethics, history, ecumenical relations.

George Mason University, College of Humanities and Social Sciences, Interdisciplinary Studies Program, Fairfax, VA 22030. Offers community college teaching (MAIS); computational social science (MAIS); energy and sustainability (MAIS); film and video studies (MAIS); folklore studies (MAIS); higher education administration (MAIS); neuroethics (MAIS); religion, culture and values (MAIS); social entrepreneurship (MAIS); war and military in society (MAIS); women and gender studies (MAIS). *Faculty:* 11 full-time (3 women), 4 part-time/adjunct (all women). *Students:* 22 full-time (13 women), 87 part-time (51 women); includes 31 minority (21 Black or African American, non-Hispanic/Latino; 2 Asian, non-Hispanic/Latino; 6 Hispanic/Latino; 2 Two or more races, non-Hispanic/Latino), 6 international. Average age 32. 75 applicants, 75% accepted, 28 enrolled. In 2014, 31 master's awarded. *Degree requirements:* For master's, project or thesis. *Entrance requirements:* For master's, 3 letters of recommendation; writing sample; official transcript; resume. Additional exam requirements/recommendations for international students: Required—TOEFL (minimum score 570 paper-based; 80 iBT), IELTS (minimum score 6.5), PTE. *Application deadline:* For fall admission, 3/1 priority date for domestic students; for spring admission, 10/15 for domestic students. Application fee: $65 ($80 for international students). Electronic applications accepted. *Expenses:* Tuition, state resident: full-time $9794; part-time $408 per credit hour. Tuition, nonresident: full-time $26,978; part-time $1124 per credit hour.

Required fees: $2820; $118 per credit hour. Tuition and fees vary according to course load and program. *Financial support:* In 2014–15, 10 students received support, including 1 fellowship (averaging $6,935 per year), 2 research assistantships with full and partial tuition reimbursements available (averaging $6,499 per year), 8 teaching assistantships with full and partial tuition reimbursements available (averaging $8,271 per year); career-related internships or fieldwork, Federal Work-Study, scholarships/grants, unspecified assistantships, and health care benefits (for full-time research or teaching assistantship recipients) also available. Support available to part-time students. Financial award application deadline: 3/1; financial award applicants required to submit FAFSA. *Faculty research:* Combined English and folklore, religious and cultural studies (Christianity and Muslim society). *Unit head:* Meredith H. Lair, Director, 703-993-2159, Fax: 703-993-1251, E-mail: mlair@gmu.edu. *Application contact:* Lisa Struckmeyer, Administrative Coordinator, 703-993-8762, Fax: 703-993-5585, E-mail: lstruckm@gmu.edu.
Website: http://mais.gmu.edu

Georgetown University, Graduate School of Arts and Sciences, School of Continuing Studies, Washington, DC 20057. Offers American studies (MALS); Catholic studies (MALS); classical civilizations (MALS); emergency and disaster management (MPS); ethics and the professions (MALS); hospitality management (MPS); human resources management (MPS); humanities (MALS); individualized study (MALS); international affairs (MALS); Islam and Muslim-Christian relations (MALS); journalism (MPS); liberal studies (DLS); literature and society (MALS); medieval and early modern European studies (MALS); public relations and corporate communications (MPS); real estate (MPS); religious studies (MALS); social and public policy (MALS); sports industry management (MPS); systems engineering management (MPS); technology management (MPS); the theory and practice of American democracy (MALS); urban and regional planning (MPS); visual culture (MALS). MPS in systems engineering management offered jointly with Stevens Institute of Technology. *Entrance requirements:* Additional exam requirements/recommendations for international students: Required—TOEFL.

The George Washington University, Columbian College of Arts and Sciences, Department of Religion, Washington, DC 20052. Offers Islam (MA), including Hinduism and Islam. Part-time and evening/weekend programs available. *Faculty:* 8 full-time (3 women). *Students:* 8 full-time (4 women); includes 4 minority (3 Asian, non-Hispanic/Latino; 1 Hispanic/Latino), 3 international. Average age 27. 12 applicants, 83% accepted, 4 enrolled. In 2014, 2 master's awarded. *Degree requirements:* For master's, one foreign language, comprehensive exam, thesis. *Entrance requirements:* For master's, GRE General Test, interview, minimum GPA of 3.0. Additional exam requirements/recommendations for international students: Required—TOEFL (minimum score 550 paper-based; 80 iBT). *Application deadline:* For fall admission, 4/1 priority date for domestic students, 1/15 priority date for international students; for spring admission, 10/1 priority date for domestic students, 9/1 priority date for international students. Applications are processed on a rolling basis. Application fee: $75. Electronic applications accepted. *Financial support:* In 2014–15, 1 student received support. Federal Work-Study and tuition waivers available. *Unit head:* Dr. Robert Eisen, Chair, 202-994-4780, Fax: 202-994-9379, E-mail: eisen@gwu.edu. *Application contact:* Information Contact, 202-994-6325, Fax: 202-994-9379, E-mail: religion@gwu.edu.
Website: http://www.gwu.edu/~religion/

Georgia State University, College of Arts and Sciences, Department of Religious Studies, Atlanta, GA 30302-4089. Offers MA. Part-time programs available. *Faculty:* 9 full-time (4 women). *Students:* 19 full-time (13 women), 4 part-time (3 women); includes 9 minority (6 Black or African American, non-Hispanic/Latino; 1 Asian, non-Hispanic/Latino; 1 Hispanic/Latino; 1 Two or more races, non-Hispanic/Latino). Average age 42. 15 applicants, 73% accepted, 8 enrolled. In 2014, 9 master's awarded. *Degree requirements:* For master's, thesis optional. *Entrance requirements:* For master's, GRE. Additional exam requirements/recommendations for international students: Required—TOEFL (minimum score 79 iBT). *Application deadline:* For fall admission, 2/1 priority date for domestic and international students. Application fee: $50. Electronic applications accepted. *Expenses:* Tuition, state resident: full-time $6516; part-time $362 per credit hour. Tuition, nonresident: full-time $22,014; part-time $1223 per credit hour. *Required fees:* $2128 per semester. Tuition and fees vary according to course load and program. *Financial support:* In 2014–15, research assistantships with full tuition reimbursements (averaging $5,000 per year), teaching assistantships with full tuition reimbursements (averaging $6,000 per year) were awarded; career-related internships or fieldwork, health care benefits, and unspecified assistantships also available. Financial award application deadline: 2/1; financial award applicants required to submit FAFSA. *Faculty research:* Comparative/world religions; religion in the Americas; religion, gender and sexuality; religion and public policy/non-profit management; religion, ethics and politics. *Unit head:* Dr. Kathryn McClymond, Chairperson, 404-413-6119, Fax: 404-413-6124, E-mail: kmcclymond@gsu.edu. *Application contact:* Dr. Molly Bassett, Director of Graduate Studies, 404-413-6134, E-mail: mbassett@gsu.edu.
Website: http://religiousstudies.gsu.edu/graduate/

Gordon-Conwell Theological Seminary, Graduate and Professional Programs, South Hamilton, MA 01982. Offers Biblical languages (MABL); church history (MACH); counseling (MACO); ministry (D Min); missions/evangelism (MAME); New Testament (MANT); Old Testament (MAOT); religion (MAR); theology (M Div, MATH, Th M, Th D). *Accreditation:* ACIPE; ATS (one or more programs are accredited). Part-time and evening/weekend programs available. *Degree requirements:* For master's, one foreign language, thesis optional; for doctorate, 2 foreign languages, thesis/dissertation. *Entrance requirements:* For master's, minimum GPA of 2.5; for doctorate, minimum GPA of 3.0.

Graceland University, Community of Christ Seminary, Independence, MO 64050. Offers MAR. Part-time programs available. Postbaccalaureate distance learning degree programs offered (minimal on-campus study). *Faculty:* 2 full-time (1 woman), 5 part-time/adjunct (0 women). *Students:* 23 full-time (15 women); includes 2 minority (1 Asian, non-Hispanic/Latino; 1 Native Hawaiian or other Pacific Islander, non-Hispanic/Latino), 5 international. Average age 43. 6 applicants, 100% accepted, 6 enrolled. In 2014, 2 master's awarded. *Degree requirements:* For master's, thesis optional, portfolio. *Entrance requirements:* For master's, minimum cumulative GPA of 3.0. Additional exam requirements/recommendations for international students: Required—TOEFL. *Application deadline:* For fall admission, 8/15 priority date for domestic students; for winter admission, 10/15 priority date for domestic students; for spring admission, 4/15 priority date for domestic students. Applications are processed on a rolling basis. Application fee: $50. *Expenses:* Expenses: Contact institution. *Financial support:* Scholarships/grants available. Financial award application deadline: 12/15; financial award applicants required to submit FAFSA. *Faculty research:* Theology, scripture. *Unit head:* Dr. Stassi Cramm, Dean, 816-521-3034, Fax: 816-521-3034, E-mail: scramm@graceland.edu. *Application contact:* Sharon Ward, Administrative Assistant, 816-423-4676, Fax: 816-423-4753, E-mail: ward@graceland.edu.
Website: http://www.graceland.edu/seminary

Graduate Theological Union, Graduate Programs, Berkeley, CA 94709-1212. Offers art and religion (MA, PhD, Th D); biblical languages (MA); biblical studies (MA); Biblical studies (PhD, Th D); Buddhist studies (MA); Christian spirituality (MA, PhD, Th D); cultural and historical studies of religions (MA, PhD, Th D); ethics and social theory (PhD, Th D); history (MA, PhD, Th D); homiletics (MA, PhD, Th D); interdisciplinary studies (PhD, Th D); Jewish studies (MA, PhD, Th D, Certificate); liturgical studies (MA, PhD, Th D); Near Eastern religions (PhD, Th D); Orthodox Christian studies (MA); religion and psychology (MA, PhD, Th D); religion and society/ethics and social theory (MA); systematic and philosophical theology (MA, PhD, Th D). PhD programs in Jewish studies and Near Eastern religions offered jointly with University of California, Berkeley. *Accreditation:* ATS. Terminal master's awarded for partial completion of doctoral program. *Degree requirements:* For master's, one foreign language, thesis; for doctorate, one foreign language, comprehensive exam, thesis/dissertation. *Entrance requirements:* For master's, GRE General Test; for doctorate, GRE General Test, MA or M Div. Additional exam requirements/recommendations for international students: Required—TOEFL. Electronic applications accepted.

Grand Rapids Theological Seminary of Cornerstone University, Graduate Programs, Grand Rapids, MI 49525-5897. Offers biblical counseling (MA); Biblical counseling (M Div); chaplaincy (M Div); Christian education (M Div, MA); intercultural studies (M Div, MA); New Testament (MA, Th M); Old Testament (MA, Th M); pastoral studies (M Div); systematic theology (MA); theology (Th M). *Accreditation:* ATS. Part-time programs available. Postbaccalaureate distance learning degree programs offered (minimal on-campus study). *Entrance requirements:* Additional exam requirements/recommendations for international students: Required—TOEFL (minimum score 577 paper-based; 90 iBT). Electronic applications accepted.

Harding School of Theology, Graduate Programs, Memphis, TN 38117-5499. Offers Christian ministry (MA); counseling (MA); ministry (M Div, D Min); religion (MA). *Accreditation:* ATS. Part-time programs available. Postbaccalaureate distance learning degree programs offered (minimal on-campus study). *Degree requirements:* For master's, variable foreign language requirement, thesis (for some programs); for doctorate, one foreign language, thesis/dissertation. *Entrance requirements:* For master's, minimum GPA of 2.7; for doctorate, minimum GPA of 3.0. Additional exam requirements/recommendations for international students: Required—TOEFL (minimum score 550 paper-based; 79 iBT). Electronic applications accepted.

Hardin-Simmons University, Graduate School, Logsdon School of Theology, Program in Religion, Abilene, TX 79698-0001. Offers MA. Part-time programs available. *Faculty:* 17 full-time (3 women), 16 part-time/adjunct (1 woman). *Students:* 1 full-time (0 women), 3 part-time (1 woman). Average age 27. *Degree requirements:* For master's, one foreign language, comprehensive exam, thesis or alternative. *Entrance requirements:* For master's, minimum undergraduate GPA of 3.0 in major, 2.7 overall, 18 hours of course work in religious studies, interview. Additional exam requirements/recommendations for international students: Required—TOEFL (minimum score 550 paper-based; 75 iBT). *Application deadline:* For fall admission, 8/15 priority date for domestic students, 4/1 for international students; for spring admission, 1/5 priority date for domestic students, 9/1 for international students. Applications are processed on a rolling basis. Application fee: $50. *Expenses: Tuition:* Full-time $12,060; part-time $670 per credit hour. *Required fees:* $325; $110 per semester. Tuition and fees vary according to program. *Financial support:* In 2014–15, 3 students received support. Fellowships and scholarships/grants available. Support available to part-time students. Financial award application deadline: 6/30; financial award applicants required to submit FAFSA. *Faculty research:* Archaeology research in Christian origins, Hebrew grammar, history of Christian education, training of ministers into the twenty-first century, role of women in the Old Testament, contemporary ethical issues. *Unit head:* Dr. Dan Stiver, Program Director, 325-670-1398, Fax: 325-670-1406, E-mail: dstiver@hsutx.edu. *Application contact:* Dr. Nancy Kucinski, Dean of Graduate Studies, 325-670-1298, Fax: 325-670-1564, E-mail: gradoff@hsutx.edu.
Website: http://www.logsdonseminary.org/academics/religion/

Harrison Middleton University, Graduate Program, Tempe, AZ 85282. Offers education (MA, Ed D); humanities (MA); imaginative literature (MA); interdisciplinary studies (DA); jurisprudence (MA); natural science (MA); philosophy and religion (MA); social science (MA). Part-time and evening/weekend programs available. Postbaccalaureate distance learning degree programs offered (no on-campus study). *Degree requirements:* For master's and doctorate, capstone project. *Entrance requirements:* For master's, interview; for doctorate, 2 academic letters of reference, interview, essay. Additional exam requirements/recommendations for international students: Required—TOEFL (minimum score 550 paper-based; 80 iBT). Electronic applications accepted. *Faculty research:* Japanese animation, educational leadership, war art, John Muir's wilderness.

Hartford Seminary, Graduate Programs, Hartford, CT 06105-2279. Offers Islamic studies (MA); ministry (D Min); religious studies (MA); spirituality (Certificate). *Accreditation:* ATS (one or more programs are accredited). Part-time and evening/weekend programs available. Postbaccalaureate distance learning degree programs offered (no on-campus study). *Degree requirements:* For master's, thesis optional, oral exam; for doctorate, thesis/dissertation, oral exam. *Entrance requirements:* For doctorate, experience in ministry, M Div. Additional exam requirements/recommendations for international students: Required—TOEFL (minimum score 550 paper-based; 80 iBT). *Faculty research:* Liturgy and social justice, professional leadership in ministry, congregational studies, Christian-Muslim relations, American religion.

Harvard University, Graduate School of Arts and Sciences, Committee on the Study of Religion, Cambridge, MA 02138. Offers PhD. Program offered jointly with Harvard Divinity School. *Degree requirements:* For doctorate, 2 foreign languages, thesis/dissertation. *Entrance requirements:* For doctorate, GRE General Test. Additional exam requirements/recommendations for international students: Required—TOEFL.

Heritage Christian University, Graduate Programs, Florence, AL 35630. Offers counseling (MM); Greek (MA); ministry (MM); New Testament (MA). *Degree requirements:* For master's, practicum (MM), major research paper (MA). *Entrance requirements:* For master's, MAT or GRE, bachelor's degree in Bible from an accredited college or university, minimum GPA of 2.75, 3 letters of recommendation.

Holy Names University, Graduate Division, Sophia Center in Culture and Spirituality, Oakland, CA 94619-1699. Offers MA, Certificate. *Faculty:* 7. *Students:* 6 full-time (4 women), 21 part-time (19 women); includes 12 minority (10 Black or African American, non-Hispanic/Latino; 2 Hispanic/Latino), 1 international. Average age 35. 13 applicants, 46% accepted, 5 enrolled. In 2014, 6 master's, 3 other advanced degrees awarded. *Degree requirements:* For master's, thesis or alternative. *Entrance requirements:* For master's, minimum undergraduate GPA of 2.6 overall, 3.0 in major. Additional exam requirements/recommendations for international students: Required—TOEFL (minimum score 500 paper-based; 79 iBT). *Application deadline:* For fall admission, 8/1 priority date for domestic students, 7/15 for international students; for spring admission, 12/1 priority date for domestic students, 12/1 for international students; for summer admission, 5/1 priority date for domestic students, 5/1 for international students. Applications are processed on a rolling basis. Application fee: $65. Electronic applications accepted. Application fee is waived when completed online. *Financial support:* Available to part-time students. Application deadline: 3/2; applicants required to submit FAFSA. *Faculty research:* Medieval mystics, environmental justice, work and

spirituality. *Unit head:* Dr. James Conlon, Professor and Chair of Culture and Spirituality, 510-436-1427, E-mail: conlon@hnu.edu. *Application contact:* Graduate Admission Office, 800-430-1321, Fax: 510-436-1325, E-mail: graduateadmissions@hnu.edu.

Hope International University, School of Graduate and Professional Studies, Programs in Ministry, Fullerton, CA 92831-3138. Offers Christian leadership (MCM); church music (MA); church music (Korean track) (MCM); church planting (MCM); intercultural studies (MCM); worship (MCM). Part-time and evening/weekend programs available. Postbaccalaureate distance learning degree programs offered (minimal on-campus study). *Degree requirements:* For master's, thesis (for some programs), project. *Entrance requirements:* For master's, minimum GPA of 3.0, MCM program requires an undergraduate degree in music, 2 references. Additional exam requirements/recommendations for international students: Required—TOEFL (minimum score 550 paper-based; 86 iBT); Recommended—IELTS (minimum score 6.5). Electronic applications accepted. *Expenses:* Contact institution. *Faculty research:* Church dynamics, growth methodologies.

Iliff School of Theology, Graduate and Professional Programs, Denver, CO 80210-4798. Offers biblical studies (MA); church history (MA); religion (MA); religion and social change (MA); specialized ministry (MASM), including justice and peace, pastoral theology and care, religions leadership; theology (M Div, MTS, D Min, PhD), including Biblical studies (PhD), religion and psychological studies (PhD), religion and social change (PhD), theology, philosophy and culture (PhD); theology/ethics (MA). PhD offered jointly with University of Denver. *Accreditation:* ACIPE; ATS. Part-time and evening/weekend programs available. *Degree requirements:* For master's, one foreign language, thesis (for some programs); for doctorate, 2 foreign languages, comprehensive exam, thesis/dissertation. *Entrance requirements:* For master's, minimum GPA of 3.0, writing sample, references; for doctorate, GRE General Test, minimum GPA of 3.0, writing sample, letters of recommendation. Additional exam requirements/recommendations for international students: Required—TOEFL (minimum score 550 paper-based). Electronic applications accepted. *Faculty research:* Pastoral care, history, church music, contemporary church, biblical studies.

Indiana University Bloomington, University Graduate School, College of Arts and Sciences, Department of Religious Studies, Bloomington, IN 47405-7005. Offers MA, PhD. Part-time programs available. *Faculty:* 19 full-time (9 women). *Students:* 27 full-time (13 women); includes 5 minority (2 Black or African American, non-Hispanic/Latino; 1 Asian, non-Hispanic/Latino; 1 Hispanic/Latino; 1 Two or more races, non-Hispanic/Latino), 4 international. Average age 32. 104 applicants, 12% accepted, 4 enrolled. In 2014, 1 doctorate awarded. Terminal master's awarded for partial completion of doctoral program. *Degree requirements:* For master's, variable foreign language requirement, thesis or alternative; for doctorate, 2 foreign languages, thesis/dissertation. *Entrance requirements:* For master's, GRE General Test; for doctorate, GRE, MA, writing sample. Additional exam requirements/recommendations for international students: Required—TOEFL. *Application deadline:* For fall admission, 12/15 priority date for domestic students, 12/1 priority date for international students. Application fee: $55 ($65 for international students). Electronic applications accepted. *Financial support:* In 2014–15, 7 fellowships with full tuition reimbursements (averaging $18,700 per year), 16 teaching assistantships with full tuition reimbursements (averaging $15,750 per year) were awarded; research assistantships with full tuition reimbursements, Federal Work-Study, institutionally sponsored loans, and health care benefits also available. Financial award application deadline: 2/1. *Unit head:* Prof. Winnifred Sullivan, Chair, 812-855-3531, Fax: 812-855-4687, E-mail: wfsulliv@indiana.edu. *Application contact:* Debra Melsheimer, Graduate Secretary, 812-855-3531, Fax: 812-855-4687, E-mail: dmelshei@indiana.edu. Website: http://www.indiana.edu/~relstud/

The Jewish Theological Seminary, The Graduate School, New York, NY 10027-4649. Offers ancient Judaism (MA, DHL, PhD); Bible and ancient Semitic languages (MA, DHL, PhD); interdepartmental studies (MA); Jewish art and visual culture (MA); Jewish gender and women's studies (MA); Jewish history (MA, DHL, PhD); Jewish literature (MA, DHL, PhD); Jewish philosophy (DHL); Jewish thought (MA, PhD); liturgy (MA, DHL, PhD); medieval Jewish studies (MA, DHL, PhD); Midrash (DHL); Midrash and scriptural interpretation (MA, PhD); modern Jewish studies (MA, DHL, PhD); Talmud and rabbinics (MA, DHL, PhD); MA/MSW. MA/MSW offered jointly with Columbia University. *Accreditation:* ACIPE. Part-time programs available. Terminal master's awarded for partial completion of doctoral program. *Degree requirements:* For master's, one foreign language, comprehensive exam (for some programs), thesis (for some programs); for doctorate, 3 foreign languages, comprehensive exam (for some programs), thesis/dissertation. *Entrance requirements:* For master's, GRE or MAT, 3 letters of recommendation, writing sample; for doctorate, GRE or MAT, 3 letters of recommendation, writing research sample. Additional exam requirements/recommendations for international students: Required—TOEFL.

John Carroll University, Graduate School, Department of Religious Studies, University Heights, OH 44118-4581. Offers MA. Part-time and evening/weekend programs available. *Degree requirements:* For master's, comprehensive exam, research essay or thesis, foreign language proficiency. *Entrance requirements:* For master's, GRE General Test or MAT, minimum GPA of 2.5. Additional exam requirements/recommendations for international students: Required—TOEFL. Electronic applications accepted. *Faculty research:* Ethics, women's studies, contemporary theology, Bible studies, Latin American theology.

Kentucky Christian University, Graduate School, Grayson, KY 41143-2205. Offers Biblical studies (MA); Christian leadership (MA). Part-time programs available. *Degree requirements:* For master's, comprehensive exam (for some programs), thesis optional. *Entrance requirements:* For master's, minimum cumulative GPA of 2.75 in major or 2.5 overall; 6 additional hours in Bible (for non-Biblical undergraduate majors). Additional exam requirements/recommendations for international students: Required—TOEFL (minimum score 550 paper-based). Electronic applications accepted.

Knox Theological Seminary, Graduate Programs, Master of Arts Programs, Fort Lauderdale, FL 33308. Offers Biblical and theological studies (MA); Christian and classical studies (MA). Part-time and evening/weekend programs available. *Entrance requirements:* Additional exam requirements/recommendations for international students: Required—TOEFL (minimum score 520 paper-based; 83 iBT), TWE (minimum score 5).

Lancaster Theological Seminary, Graduate and Professional Programs, Lancaster, PA 17603-2812. Offers biblical studies (MAR); Christian education (MAR); Christianity and the arts (MAR); church history (MAR); congregational life (MAR); lay leadership (Certificate); theological studies (M Div); theology (D Min); theology and ethics (MAR). *Accreditation:* ACIPE; ATS. *Degree requirements:* For doctorate, thesis/dissertation.

La Salle University, School of Arts and Sciences, Program in Theological, Pastoral and Liturgical Studies, Philadelphia, PA 19141-1199. Offers Catholic studies (Th D); Christian spirituality (Th D); church ministry (Th D, Certificate); founder's studies (Th D); liturgy (Certificate); pastoral care (Certificate); pastoral studies (MA); religion (MA); religious education (Certificate); theological studies (MA, Certificate). Application deadline for Th D is November 1. Part-time and evening/weekend programs available. Postbaccalaureate distance learning degree programs offered (minimal on-campus study). *Degree requirements:* For doctorate, one foreign language, thesis/dissertation, evidence of basic reading and/or speaking knowledge of one of the following languages: a modern language other than English, Hebrew (biblical), Greek (biblical), or Latin (classical). *Entrance requirements:* For master's and Certificate, 26 credits in humanistic subjects, religion, theology, or ministry-related work; 2 letters of recommendation; statement of purpose; for doctorate, master's degree in theology, religious studies, pastoral care, or similar field from accredited institution of higher education; professional resume; personal statement of interest in a doctoral degree; 2 letters of recommendation; personal on-campus interview. Additional exam requirements/recommendations for international students: Required—TOEFL (minimum score 550 paper-based). Electronic applications accepted. Application fee is waived when completed online.

La Sierra University, School of Religion, Riverside, CA 92515. Offers pastoral ministry (M Div); religion (MA); religious education (MA); religious studies (MA). Part-time programs available. *Degree requirements:* For master's, one foreign language, thesis or alternative. *Entrance requirements:* For master's, GRE General Test, minimum GPA of 3.0.

Lee University, Program in Religion, Cleveland, TN 37320-3450. Offers biblical studies (MA); ministry studies (MA); theological studies (MA); youth and family ministry (MA). Part-time programs available. *Faculty:* 12 full-time (3 women), 3 part-time/adjunct (0 women). *Students:* 49 full-time (19 women), 34 part-time (8 women); includes 17 minority (11 Black or African American, non-Hispanic/Latino; 1 American Indian or Alaska Native, non-Hispanic/Latino; 1 Asian, non-Hispanic/Latino; 4 Hispanic/Latino), 3 international. Average age 36. 18 applicants, 67% accepted, 11 enrolled. In 2014, 18 master's awarded. *Degree requirements:* For master's, variable foreign language requirement, comprehensive exam (for some programs), thesis (for some programs). *Entrance requirements:* For master's, GRE or MAT (for biblical/theological studies only), minimum GPA of 3.0, 2 letters of recommendation, interview, official transcripts, essay. Additional exam requirements/recommendations for international students: Required—TOEFL (minimum score 450 paper-based). *Application deadline:* For fall admission, 4/1 priority date for domestic and international students; for spring admission, 10/1 priority date for domestic and international students. Applications are processed on a rolling basis. Application fee: $25. *Expenses: Tuition:* Full-time $10,260; part-time $570 per credit hour. *Required fees:* $35 per semester. One-time fee: $25. Tuition and fees vary according to program. *Financial support:* In 2014–15, 33 students received support, including 1 teaching assistantship (averaging $1,000 per year); career-related internships or fieldwork, Federal Work-Study, institutionally sponsored loans, scholarships/grants, and unspecified assistantships also available. Financial award application deadline: 3/1; financial award applicants required to submit FAFSA. *Faculty research:* Book of Isaiah, Gospel of Mark, school of St. Victor of the twelfth century, spirit Christology, people groups of New Testament and work. *Unit head:* Dr. Bob Bayles, Director, 423-614-8338, E-mail: bbayles@leeuniversity.edu. *Application contact:* Vicki Glasscock, Graduate Admissions Director, 423-614-8059, E-mail: vglasscock@leeuniversity.edu.
Website: http://www.leeuniversity.edu/academics/graduate/religion

Liberty University, Liberty Baptist Theological Seminary, Lynchburg, VA 24515. Offers Biblical studies (M Div, MAR, MTS, Th M); church history (M Div, MAR, MTS, Th M); discipleship (D Min); discipleship and church ministry (M Div, MAR, MCM); evangelism and church planting (M Div, MAR, MCM, D Min); global studies (M Div, MAR, MCM, MGS, Th M); homiletics (M Div, MAR, MCM, Th M, D Min); leadership (M Div, MAR, MCM, D Min); marketplace chaplaincy (M Div, MAR, MCM); ministry (D Min); pastoral counseling (M Div, MA, MAR, MCM, D Min), including addictions and recovery (MA), crisis response and trauma (MA), discipleship and church ministries (MA), leadership (MA), life coaching (MA), marketplace chaplaincy (MA), marriage and family (MA), military resilience (MA), pastoral counseling (MA); pastoral ministries (M Div, MAR, MCM); religious education (MRE); theology (M Div, MAR, MTS, Th M); theology and apologetics (PhD); worship (M Div, MAR, MCM, D Min). Part-time programs available. Postbaccalaureate distance learning degree programs offered (minimal on-campus study). *Students:* 2,865 full-time (781 women), 3,750 part-time (1,139 women); includes 1,742 minority (1,382 Black or African American, non-Hispanic/Latino; 22 American Indian or Alaska Native, non-Hispanic/Latino; 116 Asian, non-Hispanic/Latino; 105 Hispanic/Latino; 7 Native Hawaiian or other Pacific Islander, non-Hispanic/Latino; 110 Two or more races, non-Hispanic/Latino), 227 international. Average age 41. 5,446 applicants, 39% accepted, 1340 enrolled. In 2014, 1,969 master's, 126 doctorates, 75 other advanced degrees awarded. *Degree requirements:* For master's, 2 foreign languages, thesis (for some programs); for doctorate, 2 foreign languages, thesis/dissertation. *Entrance requirements:* For master's, minimum undergraduate GPA of 2.0; for doctorate, GRE General Test or MAT, minimum graduate GPA of 3.0. Additional exam requirements/recommendations for international students: Required—TOEFL (minimum score 600 paper-based; 100 iBT). *Application deadline:* For fall admission, 6/1 for domestic students; for spring admission, 11/1 for domestic students. Applications are processed on a rolling basis. Application fee: $50. Electronic applications accepted. *Expenses:* Expenses: Contact institution. *Financial support:* Teaching assistantships with tuition reimbursements, career-related internships or fieldwork, and Federal Work-Study available. Financial award applicants required to submit FAFSA. *Unit head:* Dr. David Hirschman, Acting Dean, 434-592-4140, Fax: 434-522-0415, E-mail: dwhirschman@liberty.edu. *Application contact:* Jay Bridge, Director of Graduate Admissions, 800-424-9595, Fax: 800-628-7977, E-mail: gradadmissions@liberty.edu.
Website: http://www.liberty.edu/seminary/

Loma Linda University, Faculty of Religion, Program in Religion and Science, Loma Linda, CA 92350. Offers MA. *Degree requirements:* For master's, comprehensive exam, thesis optional. *Entrance requirements:* Additional exam requirements/recommendations for international students: Required—TOEFL. Electronic applications accepted.

Louisville Presbyterian Theological Seminary, Graduate and Professional Programs, Louisville, KY 40205-1798. Offers Bible (MAR); divinity (M Div); ministry (D Min); religious thought (MAR); JD/M Div; M Div/MBA; M Div/MSSW. JD/M Div, M Div/MBA, and M Div/MSSW offered jointly with University of Louisville. *Accreditation:* AAMFT/COAMFTE (one or more programs are accredited); ACIPE; ATS (one or more programs are accredited). Part-time programs available. *Faculty:* 17 full-time (7 women), 20 part-time/adjunct (9 women). *Students:* 105 full-time (65 women), 64 part-time (33 women); includes 44 minority (33 Black or African American, non-Hispanic/Latino; 1 American Indian or Alaska Native, non-Hispanic/Latino; 5 Asian, non-Hispanic/Latino; 5 Hispanic/Latino), 2 international. Average age 40. *Degree requirements:* For master's, 2 foreign languages, thesis (for some programs); for doctorate, thesis/dissertation. *Entrance requirements:* For doctorate, M Div. Additional exam requirements/recommendations for international students: Required—TOEFL (minimum score 550 paper-based). *Application deadline:* For fall admission, 6/15 priority date for domestic students, 2/1 priority date for international students; for spring admission, 11/15 priority date for domestic students, 11/15 for international students. Applications are processed on a rolling basis. Application fee: $50. Electronic applications accepted. *Expenses: Tuition:* Full-time $10,260; part-time $342 per credit hour. *Required fees:* $143 per term. *Financial support:* Career-related internships or fieldwork, Federal Work-Study, institutionally sponsored loans, and scholarships/grants available. Financial award

application deadline: 2/1; financial award applicants required to submit FAFSA. *Unit head:* Dr. Susan R. Garrett, Dean, 502-895-3411, Fax: 502-895-1096, E-mail: sgarrett@lpts.edu. *Application contact:* Grant Crusor, Director of Admissions, 502-895-3411, Fax: 502-895-1096, E-mail: gcrusor@lpts.edu.
Website: http://www.lpts.edu/

Lutheran Theological Seminary at Gettysburg, Graduate and Professional Programs, Gettysburg, PA 17325-1795. Offers divinity (M Div); ministerial studies (MAMS); outdoor ministry (MAR); parish ministry (D Min); theology (STM). *Accreditation:* ACIPE; ATS (one or more programs are accredited). Part-time programs available. Postbaccalaureate distance learning degree programs offered (no on-campus study). *Degree requirements:* For master's, thesis (for some programs). Electronic applications accepted.

The Lutheran Theological Seminary at Philadelphia, Graduate School, Philadelphia, PA 19119-1794. Offers divinity (M Div); ministry (D Min); public leadership (MA); religion (MAR); social ministry (Certificate); theology (STM, PhD). *Accreditation:* ACIPE; ATS. Part-time and evening/weekend programs available. *Faculty:* 20 full-time (5 women), 19 part-time/adjunct (6 women). *Students:* 106 full-time (50 women), 208 part-time (100 women); includes 92 minority (80 Black or African American, non-Hispanic/Latino; 2 Asian, non-Hispanic/Latino; 10 Hispanic/Latino), 14 international. *Degree requirements:* For master's, one foreign language, comprehensive exam (for some programs), thesis (for some programs); for doctorate, thesis/dissertation. *Entrance requirements:* For master's, minimum undergraduate GPA of 2.8; for doctorate, minimum GPA of 3.0. Additional exam requirements/recommendations for international students: Required—TOEFL (minimum score 550 paper-based), TWE. *Application deadline:* For fall admission, 6/1 priority date for domestic students. Applications are processed on a rolling basis. Application fee: $35. Electronic applications accepted. *Expenses: Tuition:* Full-time $14,310; part-time $1590 per course. *Required fees:* $175 per semester. Tuition and fees vary according to degree level and program. *Financial support:* Research assistantships with tuition reimbursements, teaching assistantships with tuition reimbursements, career-related internships or fieldwork, and Federal Work-Study available. Financial award application deadline: 7/1; financial award applicants required to submit FAFSA. *Unit head:* Rev. Dr. J. Jayakiran Sebastian, Dean, 215-248-6379, Fax: 215-248-4577, E-mail: jsebastian@ltsp.edu. *Application contact:* Matthew O'Rear, Associate Director of Admissions, 800-286-4616 Ext. 6304, Fax: 215-248-7315, E-mail: admissions@ltsp.edu.

Lutheran Theological Seminary Saskatoon, Graduate and Professional Programs, Saskatoon, SK S7N 0X3, Canada. Offers Biblical studies (MTS); church history (MTS); ethics/church and society (MTS); history of Christianity (STM); New Testament (STM); Old Testament (STM); pastoral studies (STM); pastoral theology (MTS); systematic theology (MTS); systematic theology and philosophy of religion (STM); theology (M Div, D Div). STM programs offered jointly with College of Emmanuel and St. Chad and St. Andrew's College. *Accreditation:* ATS. Part-time programs available. *Degree requirements:* For master's, thesis.

Luther Rice College & Seminary, Graduate Programs, Lithonia, GA 30038-2454. Offers apologetics (MA); Bible languages (M Div); Biblical counseling (MA); Christian ministry (M Div, D Min); Christian studies (MA); leadership (MA). Part-time and evening/weekend programs available. Postbaccalaureate distance learning degree programs offered (no on-campus study). *Faculty:* 14 full-time (2 women), 28 part-time/adjunct (8 women). *Students:* 250 full-time (50 women), 784 part-time (209 women); includes 476 minority (420 Black or African American, non-Hispanic/Latino; 7 American Indian or Alaska Native, non-Hispanic/Latino; 21 Asian, non-Hispanic/Latino; 21 Hispanic/Latino; 7 Two or more races, non-Hispanic/Latino). *Degree requirements:* For doctorate, thesis/dissertation. *Entrance requirements:* For master's, bachelor's degree or equivalent; for doctorate, M Div. Additional exam requirements/recommendations for international students: Required—TOEFL (minimum score 550 paper-based). *Application deadline:* Applications are processed on a rolling basis. Application fee: $50. Electronic applications accepted. *Expenses: Tuition:* Full-time $4266; part-time $237 per credit hour. *Required fees:* $330; $55 per course. *Financial support:* Scholarships/grants available. Financial award applicants required to submit FAFSA. *Unit head:* Dr. Brad Arnett, Graduate Dean, 770-484-1204 Ext. 5697, E-mail: barnett@lutherrice.edu. *Application contact:* Steve Pray, Enrollment Advisor, 770-484-1204 Ext. 5758, Fax: 770-484-1155, E-mail: admissions@lutherrice.edu.

Maranatha Baptist University, Master of Arts in English Bible Program, Watertown, WI 53094. Offers MA. Part-time programs available. Postbaccalaureate distance learning degree programs offered (no on-campus study). *Faculty:* 4 full-time (0 women), 5 part-time/adjunct (0 women). *Students:* 2 full-time (1 woman), 22 part-time (1 woman); includes 3 minority (1 Asian, non-Hispanic/Latino; 2 Hispanic/Latino), 3 international. Average age 39. 7 applicants, 57% accepted, 4 enrolled. In 2014, 2 degrees awarded. Application fee: $50. *Expenses: Tuition:* Full-time $2655; part-time $295 per credit hour. *Required fees:* $25 per credit hour. Tuition and fees vary according to program. *Unit head:* Dr. Larry Oats, Dean of Maranatha Baptist Seminary, 920-206-2324, Fax: 920-261-9109, E-mail: larry.oats@mbu.edu. *Application contact:* Dr. Jim Harrison, Director of Admissions, 920-206-2327, Fax: 920-261-9109, E-mail: admissions@mbu.edu.

McGill University, Faculty of Graduate and Postdoctoral Studies, Faculty of Religious Studies, Montréal, QC H3A 2T5, Canada. Offers MA, STM, PhD. *Accreditation:* ATS.

McMaster University, School of Graduate Studies, Faculty of Social Sciences, Department of Religious Studies, Hamilton, ON L8S 4M2, Canada. Offers MA, PhD. Part-time programs available. *Degree requirements:* For master's, one foreign language, thesis; for doctorate, 2 foreign languages, comprehensive exam, thesis/dissertation. *Entrance requirements:* For master's, minimum B+ average. Additional exam requirements/recommendations for international students: Required—TOEFL (minimum score 580 paper-based). *Faculty research:* Hellenistic Judaism, religious biographies in Asia, medieval India, synoptic gospels, ritual and belief systems.

Memorial University of Newfoundland, School of Graduate Studies, Department of Religious Studies, St. John's, NL A1C 5S7, Canada. Offers MA. Part-time programs available. *Degree requirements:* For master's, one foreign language, thesis. *Entrance requirements:* For master's, honors degree in religious studies or equivalent. Electronic applications accepted. *Faculty research:* Biblical studies, Christian thought and history, world religions, ethics, contemporary spirituality.

Missouri State University, Graduate College, College of Humanities and Public Affairs, Department of Religious Studies, Springfield, MO 65897. Offers MA. Part-time programs available. *Faculty:* 11 full-time (3 women). *Students:* 8 full-time (1 woman), 10 part-time (2 women); includes 1 minority (Two or more races, non-Hispanic/Latino), 1 international. Average age 29. 12 applicants, 92% accepted, 8 enrolled. In 2014, 5 master's awarded. *Degree requirements:* For master's, one foreign language, comprehensive exam, thesis or alternative. *Entrance requirements:* For master's, GRE, minimum GPA of 3.2. Additional exam requirements/recommendations for international students: Required—TOEFL (minimum score 550 paper-based; 79 iBT). *Application deadline:* For fall admission, 7/20 priority date for domestic students, 5/1 for international students; for spring admission, 12/20 priority date for domestic students, 9/1 for international students. Applications are processed on a rolling basis. Application fee: $35 ($50 for international students). Electronic applications accepted. *Expenses:* Tuition, state resident: full-time $2250; part-time $250 per credit hour. Tuition, nonresident: full-time $4509; part-time $501 per credit hour. Tuition and fees vary according to course level, course load and program. *Financial support:* Federal Work-Study, institutionally sponsored loans, scholarships/grants, and unspecified assistantships available. Financial award application deadline: 3/31; financial award applicants required to submit FAFSA. *Faculty research:* Apocalyptic literature, Protestantism in American society, contemporary Hinduism, Christian history. *Unit head:* Dr. Stephen Berkwitz, Department Head, 417-836-4147, Fax: 417-836-4757, E-mail: religiousstudies@missouristate.edu. *Application contact:* Misty Stewart, Coordinator of Graduate Recruitment, 417-836-6079, Fax: 417-836-6200, E-mail: mistystewart@missouristate.edu.
Website: http://www.missouristate.edu/relst/

Moody Theological Seminary?Michigan, Graduate Programs, Plymouth, MI 48170. Offers Bible (Graduate Certificate); Christian education (MA); counseling psychology (MA); divinity (M Div); theological studies (MA). *Accreditation:* ATS. Part-time and evening/weekend programs available. *Degree requirements:* For master's, one foreign language, thesis. *Faculty research:* Judaism, cults, world religions.

Mount St. Joseph University, Graduate Program in Religious Studies, Cincinnati, OH 45233-1670. Offers pastoral administration (Certificate); religious studies (MA); spirituality and wellness (Certificate). Part-time and evening/weekend programs available. *Faculty:* 3 full-time (2 women). *Students:* 14 part-time (11 women); includes 1 minority (Black or African American, non-Hispanic/Latino). Average age 45. 6 applicants, 83% accepted, 4 enrolled. In 2014, 3 master's awarded. *Degree requirements:* For master's, integrating project, field experience. *Entrance requirements:* For master's, 3 letters of recommendation, interview, minimum GPA of 3.0, academic transcripts, essay. Additional exam requirements/recommendations for international students: Required—TOEFL (minimum score 560 paper-based; 83 iBT). *Application deadline:* Applications are processed on a rolling basis. Application fee: $50. Electronic applications accepted. *Expenses: Tuition:* Full-time $18,400; part-time $575 per credit hour. *Required fees:* $450; $450 per year. Part-time tuition and fees vary according to course load, degree level and program. *Financial support:* In 2014–15, 10 students received support. Scholarships/grants available. Financial award application deadline: 3/1; financial award applicants required to submit FAFSA. *Faculty research:* Contextual/cultural/systematic theology, historical/spiritual theology, business/economics ethics, social justice, Biblical/cultural/pastoral theology. *Unit head:* Dr. John Trokan, Chair of Religious/Pastoral Studies, 513-244-4272, Fax: 513-244-4222, E-mail: john.trokan@msj.edu. *Application contact:* Mary Brigham, Assistant Director of Graduate Recruitment, 513-244-4233, Fax: 513-244-4629, E-mail: mary.brigham@msj.edu.
Website: http://www.msj.edu/academics/graduate-programs/religious-studies-programs/

Mount Saint Mary's University, Graduate Division, Los Angeles, CA 90049-1599. Offers business administration (MBA); counseling psychology (MS); creative writing (MFA); education (MS, Certificate); film and television (MFA); health policy and management (MS); humanities (MA); nursing (MSN, Certificate); physical therapy (DPT); religious studies (MA). Part-time and evening/weekend programs available. *Faculty:* 15 full-time (11 women), 61 part-time/adjunct (33 women). *Students:* 462 full-time (345 women), 218 part-time (175 women); includes 417 minority (66 Black or African American, non-Hispanic/Latino; 3 American Indian or Alaska Native, non-Hispanic/Latino; 69 Asian, non-Hispanic/Latino; 254 Hispanic/Latino; 11 Native Hawaiian or other Pacific Islander, non-Hispanic/Latino; 14 Two or more races, non-Hispanic/Latino), 1 international. Average age 33. 1,086 applicants, 25% accepted, 241 enrolled. In 2014, 181 master's, 28 doctorates, 22 other advanced degrees awarded. *Entrance requirements:* Additional exam requirements/recommendations for international students: Required—TOEFL. *Application deadline:* For fall admission, 6/30 priority date for domestic and international students; for spring admission, 10/30 priority date for domestic and international students; for summer admission, 3/30 priority date for domestic and international students. Applications are processed on a rolling basis. Application fee: $50. Electronic applications accepted. *Expenses: Tuition:* Full-time $9756; part-time $813 per unit. One-time fee: $128. Tuition and fees vary according to degree level and program. *Financial support:* In 2014–15, 213 students received support. Career-related internships or fieldwork, Federal Work-Study, institutionally sponsored loans, and tuition waivers (full and partial) available. Support available to part-time students. Financial award application deadline: 3/15; financial award applicants required to submit FAFSA. *Unit head:* Dr. Linda Moody, Graduate Dean, 213-477-2800, E-mail: gradprograms@msmu.edu. *Application contact:* Tara Wessel, Senior Graduate Admission Counselor, 213-477-2800, E-mail: gradprograms@msmu.edu.
Website: http://www.msmu.edu/graduate-programs/admission/

Naropa University, Graduate Programs, Program in Indo-Tibetan Buddhism, Boulder, CO 80302-6697. Offers MA. *Faculty:* 5 full-time (2 women), 10 part-time/adjunct (7 women). *Students:* 3 full-time (0 women), 3 part-time (1 woman), 1 international. Average age 30. 2 applicants, 100% accepted, 2 enrolled. In 2014, 3 master's awarded. *Degree requirements:* For master's, comprehensive exam, thesis. *Entrance requirements:* For master's, interview (by phone or in-person), 3 letters of recommendation, letter of interest, resume. Additional exam requirements/recommendations for international students: Required—TOEFL (minimum score 600 paper-based; 80 iBT). *Application deadline:* For fall admission, 1/15 priority date for domestic and international students. Applications are processed on a rolling basis. Application fee: $60. Electronic applications accepted. *Expenses: Tuition:* Full-time $23,400; part-time $975 per credit. *Required fees:* $335 per semester. Tuition and fees vary according to course load. *Financial support:* In 2014–15, 1 student received support. Career-related internships or fieldwork, scholarships/grants, tuition waivers (partial), and unspecified assistantships available. Support available to part-time students. Financial award application deadline: 3/1; financial award applicants required to submit FAFSA. *Unit head:* Director, School of Humanities and Interdisciplinary Studies. *Application contact:* Office of Admissions, 303-546-3572, Fax: 303-546-3583, E-mail: admissions@naropa.edu.
Website: http://www.naropa.edu/academics/shis/grad/religious-studies-ma/index.php

Naropa University, Graduate Programs, Program in Indo-Tibetan Buddhism with Language, Boulder, CO 80302-6697. Offers MA. *Faculty:* 5 full-time (2 women), 10 part-time/adjunct (7 women). *Students:* 8 full-time (5 women), 2 part-time (0 women), 2 international. Average age 37. 7 applicants, 86% accepted, 4 enrolled. In 2014, 5 master's awarded. *Degree requirements:* For master's, comprehensive exam, thesis. *Entrance requirements:* For master's, interview (by phone or in-person), resume, letter of interest, 2 letters of recommendation. Additional exam requirements/recommendations for international students: Required—TOEFL (minimum score 600 paper-based; 80 iBT). *Application deadline:* For fall admission, 1/15 priority date for domestic and international students. Applications are processed on a rolling basis. Application fee: $60. Electronic applications accepted. *Expenses: Tuition:* Full-time $23,400; part-time $975 per credit. *Required fees:* $335 per semester. Tuition and fees vary according to course load. *Financial support:* In 2014–15, 2 students received support. Career-related internships or fieldwork, scholarships/grants, tuition waivers (partial), and unspecified assistantships available. Support available to part-time students. Financial award application deadline: 3/1; financial award applicants required

to submit FAFSA. *Unit head:* Director, School of Humanities and Interdisciplinary Studies. *Application contact:* Office of Admissions, 303-546-3572, Fax: 303-546-3583, E-mail: admissions@naropa.edu.
Website: http://www.naropa.edu/academics/shis/grad/religious-studies-with-language-ma/index.php

Naropa University, Graduate Programs, Program in Religious Studies, Boulder, CO 80302-6697. Offers MA. *Faculty:* 5 full-time (2 women), 10 part-time/adjunct (7 women). *Students:* 6 full-time (3 women), 2 part-time (both women). Average age 37. 7 applicants, 43% accepted, 3 enrolled. In 2014, 3 master's awarded. *Degree requirements:* For master's, comprehensive exam, thesis. *Entrance requirements:* For master's, interview (by phone or in-person), transcripts, letter of interest, resume, 2 letters of recommendation. Additional exam requirements/recommendations for international students: Required—TOEFL (minimum score 600 paper-based; 80 iBT). *Application deadline:* For fall admission, 1/15 priority date for domestic and international students. Applications are processed on a rolling basis. Application fee: $60. Electronic applications accepted. *Expenses: Tuition:* Full-time $23,400; part-time $975 per credit. *Required fees:* $335 per semester. Tuition and fees vary according to course load. *Financial support:* In 2014–15, 6 students received support, including 1 research assistantship with partial tuition reimbursement available (averaging $7,000 per year); career-related internships or fieldwork, scholarships/grants, tuition waivers (partial), and unspecified assistantships also available. Support available to part-time students. Financial award application deadline: 3/1; financial award applicants required to submit FAFSA. *Application contact:* Office of Admissions, 303-546-3572, Fax: 303-546-3583, E-mail: admissions@naropa.edu.
Website: http://www.naropa.edu/academics/shis/grad/religious-studies-ma/index.php

Naropa University, Graduate Programs, Program in Religious Studies with Language, Boulder, CO 80302-6697. Offers MA. *Faculty:* 5 full-time (2 women), 10 part-time/adjunct (7 women). *Students:* 8 full-time (3 women), 1 part-time (0 women); includes 1 minority (Two or more races, non-Hispanic/Latino). Average age 31. 5 applicants, 60% accepted, 1 enrolled. *Degree requirements:* For master's, comprehensive exam, thesis. *Entrance requirements:* For master's, interview, transcripts, resume, 2 letters of recommendation, letter of interest. Additional exam requirements/recommendations for international students: Required—TOEFL (minimum score 600 paper-based; 80 iBT). *Application deadline:* For fall admission, 1/15 priority date for domestic and international students. Applications are processed on a rolling basis. Application fee: $60. Electronic applications accepted. *Expenses: Tuition:* Full-time $23,400; part-time $975 per credit. *Required fees:* $335 per semester. Tuition and fees vary according to course load. *Financial support:* In 2014–15, 6 students received support, including 3 research assistantships with partial tuition reimbursements available (averaging $4,333 per year); career-related internships or fieldwork, scholarships/grants, tuition waivers (partial), and unspecified assistantships also available. Support available to part-time students. Financial award application deadline: 3/1; financial award applicants required to submit FAFSA. *Application contact:* Office of Admissions, 303-546-3572, Fax: 303-546-3583, E-mail: admissions@naropa.edu.
Website: http://www.naropa.edu/academics/shis/grad/religious-studies-with-language-ma/index.php

New Saint Andrews College, Graduate School, Moscow, ID 83843. Offers classical Christian studies (Graduate Certificate); theology and letters (MA). Part-time programs available. *Faculty:* 12 part-time/adjunct (0 women). *Students:* 7 full-time (3 women), 6 part-time (3 women); includes 3 minority (1 Asian, non-Hispanic/Latino; 2 Two or more races, non-Hispanic/Latino). 11 applicants, 45% accepted, 4 enrolled. In 2014, 5 master's awarded. *Degree requirements:* For master's, thesis (for some programs), final oral exam. *Entrance requirements:* For master's, GRE, 2 letters of recommendation; for Graduate Certificate, GRE, bachelor's degree, essays, 2 letters of recommendation. *Application deadline:* For fall admission, 12/1 for domestic students. Application fee: $50. Electronic applications accepted. *Expenses: Tuition:* Full-time $7600; part-time $475 per credit. *Unit head:* Benjamin Merkle, Academic Dean, 208-882-1566 Ext. 104, E-mail: bmerkle@nsa.edu. *Application contact:* Brenda Schlect, Director of Admissions, 208-882-1566 Ext. 113, Fax: 208-882-4293, E-mail: admissions@nsa.edu.
Website: http://www.nsa.edu/academics/graduate-school/

New York University, Graduate School of Arts and Science, Draper Interdisciplinary Program in Humanities and Social Thought, New York, NY 10012-1019. Offers humanities and social thought (MA); religion (Advanced Certificate); social theory (Advanced Certificate). Part-time programs available. *Faculty:* 6 full-time (3 women). *Students:* 51 full-time (32 women), 69 part-time (44 women); includes 27 minority (8 Black or African American, non-Hispanic/Latino; 4 Asian, non-Hispanic/Latino; 11 Hispanic/Latino; 4 Two or more races, non-Hispanic/Latino), 17 international. Average age 29. 118 applicants, 67% accepted, 38 enrolled. In 2014, 50 master's awarded. *Degree requirements:* For master's, thesis, comprehensive exam or essay. *Entrance requirements:* For master's, GRE General Test; for Advanced Certificate, master's degree. Additional exam requirements/recommendations for international students: Required—TOEFL. *Application deadline:* For fall admission, 7/1 for domestic and international students; for spring admission, 12/1 for domestic and international students. Applications are processed on a rolling basis. Application fee: $100. *Financial support:* Teaching assistantships with tuition reimbursements, Federal Work-Study, institutionally sponsored loans, and tuition waivers (partial) available. Financial award application deadline: 7/1; financial award applicants required to submit FAFSA. *Faculty research:* Art world, gender politics, global histories, literary cultures, the city. *Unit head:* Robin Nagle, Director, 212-998-8070, Fax: 212-995-4691, E-mail: draper.program@nyu.edu. *Application contact:* Robert Dimit, Associate Director/Director of Graduate Studies, 212-998-8070, Fax: 212-995-4691, E-mail: draper.program@nyu.edu.
Website: http://www.nyu.edu/gsas/dept/draper/

New York University, Graduate School of Arts and Science, Program in Religious Studies, New York, NY 10012-1019. Offers MA. Part-time programs available. *Students:* 2 full-time (1 woman), 3 part-time (1 woman); includes 1 minority (Hispanic/Latino), 1 international. Average age 25. 14 applicants, 57% accepted, 2 enrolled. In 2014, 3 master's awarded. *Degree requirements:* For master's, one foreign language, thesis. *Entrance requirements:* For master's, GRE General Test. Additional exam requirements/recommendations for international students: Required—TOEFL. *Application deadline:* For fall admission, 1/4 priority date for domestic students, 1/4 for international students. Application fee: $100. *Financial support:* Teaching assistantships with tuition reimbursements, Federal Work-Study, and institutionally sponsored loans available. Financial award application deadline: 1/4; financial award applicants required to submit FAFSA. *Faculty research:* Biblical and rabbinic Judaism, New Testament and early Christianity, comparative mysticism, gender and embodiment, East Asian religions. *Unit head:* Adam Becker, Director/Director Graduate Studies, 212-998-3756, Fax: 212-995-4827, E-mail: religious.studies@nyu.edu. *Application contact:* Janine Paolucci, Program Administrator, 212-998-3756, Fax: 212-995-4827, E-mail: religious.studies@nyu.edu.
Website: http://religiousstudies.as.nyu.edu/page/home

Northwestern University, The Graduate School, Judd A. and Marjorie Weinberg College of Arts and Sciences, Department of Religious Studies, Evanston, IL 60208. Offers PhD.

Northwestern University, School of Professional Studies, Program in Liberal Studies, Evanston, IL 60208. Offers American studies (MA); history (MA); religious and ethical studies (MA).

Northwest Nazarene University, Graduate Studies, Program in Religion, Nampa, ID 83686-5897. Offers missional leadership (M Div, MA); pastoral ministry (MA); spiritual formation (M Div, MA); youth, children, and family ministry (M Div, MA). Part-time and evening/weekend programs available. Postbaccalaureate distance learning degree programs offered (no on-campus study). *Faculty:* 12 full-time (2 women), 15 part-time/adjunct (1 woman). *Students:* 91 full-time (27 women), 20 part-time (5 women); includes 11 minority (4 Black or African American, non-Hispanic/Latino; 1 American Indian or Alaska Native, non-Hispanic/Latino; 2 Asian, non-Hispanic/Latino; 3 Hispanic/Latino; 1 Native Hawaiian or other Pacific Islander, non-Hispanic/Latino), 1 international. Average age 39. 55 applicants, 65% accepted, 27 enrolled. In 2014, 40 master's awarded. *Entrance requirements:* For master's, minimum GPA of 2.5; 8 semester or 12 quarter credits of Bible, theology and/or Western philosophy. Additional exam requirements/recommendations for international students: Required—TOEFL. *Application deadline:* Applications are processed on a rolling basis. Application fee: $50. Electronic applications accepted. *Unit head:* Dr. Jay Akkerman, Director, Graduate Studies, 208-467-8437, Fax: 208-467-8252. *Application contact:* Vicki Funk, Program Coordinator, 208-467-8432, Fax: 208-467-8252, E-mail: vlfunk@nnu.edu.
Website: http://www.nnu.edu/ministry/

Nyack College, College of Bible and Christian Ministry, Nyack, NY 10960. Offers ancient Judaism and Christian origins (MA). Part-time and evening/weekend programs available. *Students:* 4 full-time (1 woman), 5 part-time (1 woman); includes 4 minority (1 Black or African American, non-Hispanic/Latino; 3 Hispanic/Latino), 1 international. Average age 33. *Degree requirements:* For master's, 2 foreign languages, comprehensive exam. *Entrance requirements:* For master's, GRE, proficiency exam in Biblical Hebrew, essay, Christian experience statement, pastoral reference, academic references, writing sample. Additional exam requirements/recommendations for international students: Required—TOEFL (minimum score 83 iBT). *Application deadline:* Applications are processed on a rolling basis. Application fee: $30. Electronic applications accepted. *Expenses:* Expenses: Contact institution. *Financial support:* Applicants required to submit FAFSA. *Unit head:* Dr. Steven Notley, Director, 646-378-6148. *Application contact:* 800-541-6891, Fax: 845-348-3912, E-mail: admissions.grad@nyack.edu.

Oblate School of Theology, Graduate and Professional Programs, San Antonio, TX 78216-6693. Offers African-American pastoral leadership (D Min); divinity (M Div); pastoral leadership (D Min); pastoral ministry (MAP Min); pastoral studies (Certificate); spiritual formation in the local community (D Min); spirituality (MA Sp, PhD); spirituality and ministry (D Min); theology (MA Th); U.S. Hispanic/Latino ministry (D Min); M Div/MA Th. *Accreditation:* ACIPE; ATS (one or more programs are accredited). Part-time programs available. Postbaccalaureate distance learning degree programs offered (no on-campus study). *Faculty:* 23 full-time (8 women), 3 part-time/adjunct (0 women). *Students:* 59 full-time (6 women), 73 part-time (36 women); includes 56 minority (8 Black or African American, non-Hispanic/Latino; 9 Asian, non-Hispanic/Latino; 39 Hispanic/Latino), 41 international. Average age 40. 41 applicants, 88% accepted, 34 enrolled. In 2014, 31 master's, 3 doctorates awarded. *Degree requirements:* For master's, comprehensive exam (for some programs), thesis (for some programs), practicum; for doctorate, one foreign language, comprehensive exam, thesis/dissertation, paper, practicum. *Entrance requirements:* For master's, MAT, interview, course work in theology or religious studies, minimum GPA of 2.5; for doctorate, M Div, MA Th, or MA Sp. Additional exam requirements/recommendations for international students: Required—TOEFL (minimum score 71 iBT). *Application deadline:* For fall admission, 6/15 priority date for domestic and international students; for winter admission, 11/30 for domestic and international students; for spring admission, 11/30 for domestic and international students; for summer admission, 4/1 for domestic and international students. Applications are processed on a rolling basis. Application fee: $65. *Expenses:* Expenses: Contact institution. *Financial support:* In 2014–15, 25 students received support. Scholarships/grants available. Support available to part-time students. Financial award application deadline: 8/1; financial award applicants required to submit FAFSA. *Unit head:* Dr. R. Scott Woodward, Academic Dean, 210-341-1366, Fax: 210-341-4519, E-mail: rsw@ost.edu. *Application contact:* Mario A. Porter, Director of Admissions, 210-341-1366 Ext. 226, Fax: 210-341-4519, E-mail: registrar@ost.edu.

Oklahoma City University, Petree College of Arts and Sciences, Wimberly School of Religion, Oklahoma City, OK 73106-1402. Offers M Rel. Part-time and evening/weekend programs available. *Faculty:* 2 full-time (1 woman). *Students:* 1 (woman) part-time, all international. Average age 43. 1 applicant, 100% accepted, 1 enrolled. *Entrance requirements:* For master's, minimum GPA of 3.0. Additional exam requirements/recommendations for international students: Required—TOEFL (minimum score 550 paper-based; 80 iBT). *Application deadline:* Applications are processed on a rolling basis. Application fee: $50 ($70 for international students). Electronic applications accepted. *Expenses: Tuition:* Part-time $936 per credit hour. *Required fees:* $115 per credit hour. One-time fee: $250. Tuition and fees vary according to course load, degree level, program and student's religious affiliation. *Financial support:* Career-related internships or fieldwork, Federal Work-Study, and tuition waivers available. Support available to part-time students. Financial award applicants required to submit FAFSA. *Faculty research:* Biblical studies, church history, social ethics, world religions. *Unit head:* Dr. Sharon Betsworth, Director, 405-208-5602, Fax: 405-208-6046, E-mail: sbetsworth@okcu.edu. *Application contact:* Michelle Cook, Director, Admissions, 800-633-7242, Fax: 405-208-5916, E-mail: gadmissions@okcu.edu.
Website: http://www.okcu.edu/religion/

Olivet Nazarene University, Graduate School, Division of Religion, Bourbonnais, IL 60914. Offers biblical literature (MA); religion (MA); theology (MA). Part-time programs available. *Degree requirements:* For master's, thesis or alternative.

Oxford Graduate School, Graduate Programs, Dayton, TN 37321-6736. Offers family life education (M Litt); organizational leadership (M Litt); sociological integration of religion and society (D Phil).

Pacific School of Religion, Graduate and Professional Programs, Berkeley, CA 94709-1323. Offers M Div, MA, MTS, D Min, PhD, Th D, CAPS, CMS, CSS, CTS. MA, PhD, Th D offered jointly with Graduate Theological Union; D Min with Church Divinity School of the Pacific. *Accreditation:* ACIPE; ATS (one or more programs are accredited). Part-time programs available. *Degree requirements:* For master's, one foreign language, thesis (for some programs); for doctorate, thesis/dissertation. *Entrance requirements:* For master's, minimum GPA of 3.0; for doctorate, M Div, minimum GPA of 3.0 (D Min); for other advanced degree, M Div, minimum GPA of 3.0 (CAPS). Additional exam requirements/recommendations for international students: Required—TOEFL (minimum score 550 paper-based). Electronic applications accepted. *Faculty research:* Medical ethics, gay/lesbian studies in religion, Asian-American religion, race, culture and theology, theology in context.

Pepperdine University, Seaver College, Master of Arts in Religion Program, Malibu, CA 90263. Offers MA. Part-time and evening/weekend programs available. *Students:* 2 full-time (1 woman), 9 part-time (4 women). In 2014, 1 master's awarded. *Entrance*

requirements: For master's, GRE General Test, letters of recommendation, writing sample. Additional exam requirements/recommendations for international students: Required—TOEFL. *Application deadline:* For fall admission, 2/1 priority date for domestic students. Applications are processed on a rolling basis. Application fee: $65. Electronic applications accepted. *Financial support:* Applicants required to submit FAFSA. *Unit head:* Dr. Timothy Willis, Chair/Professor, 310-506-4352, Fax: 310-506-7271, E-mail: timothy.willis@pepperdine.edu. *Application contact:* Michael Truschke, Dean of Admission and Enrollment Management, 310-506-6165, Fax: 310-506-4861, E-mail: admission-seaver@pepperdine.edu.
Website: http://seaver.pepperdine.edu/religion/graduate/mareligion/

Point Loma Nazarene University, School of Theology and Christian Ministry, San Diego, CA 92106-2899. Offers M Min. Part-time programs available. Postbaccalaureate distance learning degree programs offered (minimal on-campus study). *Faculty:* 9 part-time/adjunct (2 women). *Students:* 19 part-time (9 women); includes 4 minority (2 Black or African American, non-Hispanic/Latino; 2 Hispanic/Latino). Average age 41. 4 applicants, 75% accepted, 1 enrolled. In 2014, 8 master's awarded. *Degree requirements:* For master's, thesis optional. *Entrance requirements:* For master's, letters of recommendation, essay, transcripts, interview. Additional exam requirements/recommendations for international students: Recommended—TOEFL. *Application deadline:* For fall admission, 8/25 priority date for domestic students; for spring admission, 12/8 priority date for domestic students; for summer admission, 6/8 priority date for domestic students. Applications are processed on a rolling basis. Application fee: $0. Electronic applications accepted. *Expenses:* Expenses: $225 per unit, $90 per unit independent study fee, $100 graduation fee. *Financial support:* In 2014–15, 9 students received support. Scholarships/grants available. Financial award application deadline: 6/5; financial award applicants required to submit FAFSA. *Faculty research:* Theology, Christian education, church administration. *Unit head:* Dr. Ron Benefiel, Dean, 619-849-2935, E-mail: ronbenefiel@pointloma.edu. *Application contact:* Laura Leinweber, Director of Graduate Admissions, 866-692-4723, E-mail: lauraleinweber@pointloma.edu.
Website: http://www.pointloma.edu/experience/academics/schools-departments/school-theology-christian-ministry/programs/master-ministry

Princeton Theological Seminary, Graduate and Professional Programs, Princeton, NJ 08542-0803. Offers M Div, MA, Th M, D Min, PhD. *Accreditation:* ACIPE; ATS. Part-time programs available. Terminal master's awarded for partial completion of doctoral program. *Degree requirements:* For doctorate, 2 foreign languages, thesis/dissertation, comprehensive exam (PhD), French and German. *Entrance requirements:* For doctorate, GRE General Test. Additional exam requirements/recommendations for international students: Required—TOEFL. Electronic applications accepted.

Princeton University, Graduate School, Department of Religion, Princeton, NJ 08544-1019. Offers PhD. *Degree requirements:* For doctorate, variable foreign language requirement, comprehensive exam, thesis/dissertation. *Entrance requirements:* For doctorate, GRE General Test. Additional exam requirements/recommendations for international students: Required—TOEFL (minimum score 600 paper-based). Electronic applications accepted.

Providence College, Department of Religious Studies, Providence, RI 02918. Offers Biblical studies (MA); theology (MA, MTS). Part-time and evening/weekend programs available. *Faculty:* 8 full-time (2 women), 1 part-time/adjunct (0 women). *Students:* 8 full-time (2 women), 10 part-time (2 women), 3 international. Average age 34. 17 applicants, 100% accepted, 6 enrolled. In 2014, 5 master's awarded. *Degree requirements:* For master's, comprehensive exam, thesis. *Entrance requirements:* For master's, GRE (for MA). Additional exam requirements/recommendations for international students: Required—TOEFL (minimum score 550 paper-based; 90 iBT). *Application deadline:* For fall admission, 8/1 priority date for domestic and international students; for spring admission, 12/1 priority date for domestic and international students. Applications are processed on a rolling basis. Application fee: $55. *Expenses: Tuition:* Part-time $390 per credit. *Financial support:* Career-related internships or fieldwork and unspecified assistantships available. Support available to part-time students. Financial award application deadline: 8/1; financial award applicants required to submit FAFSA. *Unit head:* Dr. Robert J. Barry, Director, 401-865-2274, Fax: 401-865-2274, E-mail: rbarry@providence.edu. *Application contact:* Rev. Mark D. Nowel, Dean of Undergraduate and Graduate Studies, 401-865-2649, Fax: 401-865-1496, E-mail: mnowel@providence.edu.
Website: http://www.providence.edu/theology/Pages/default.aspx

Queen's University at Kingston, School of Graduate Studies, Faculty of Arts and Sciences, Department of Religious Studies, Kingston, ON K7L 3N6, Canada. Offers MA. *Degree requirements:* For master's, one foreign language, essay. *Entrance requirements:* For master's, honors BA in religious studies or equivalent. Additional exam requirements/recommendations for international students: Required—TOEFL (minimum score 600 paper-based). *Faculty research:* Modernity, culture, feminism, world religions, traditions.

Reformed Theological Seminary–Charlotte Campus, Graduate and Professional Programs, Charlotte, NC 28226-6318. Offers biblical studies (MA); ministry (D Min); pastoral ministry (M Div); theological studies (MA). Part-time programs available. *Degree requirements:* For master's, comprehensive exam; for doctorate, thesis/dissertation. *Entrance requirements:* For master's, minimum GPA of 2.6; for doctorate, minimum GPA of 3.0. Additional exam requirements/recommendations for international students: Required—TOEFL (minimum score 550 paper-based). Electronic applications accepted.

Reformed Theological Seminary–Houston Campus, Graduate Program, Houston, TX 77024. Offers MA. *Faculty:* 5 part-time/adjunct (0 women). *Students:* 75 part-time (4 women). *Application deadline:* Applications are processed on a rolling basis. Electronic applications accepted. *Expenses: Tuition:* Part-time $475 per credit hour. *Financial support:* Scholarships/grants available. *Application contact:* Matt Stahl, Admissions Counselor/Administrative Assistant to the Executive Director, 832-786-3530, E-mail: mstahl@rts.edu.
Website: http://www.rts.edu/site/academics/degree_programs/mar/houstonc.aspx

Reformed Theological Seminary–Jackson Campus, Graduate and Professional Programs, Jackson, MS 39209-3099. Offers Bible, theology, and missions (Certificate); Biblical exegesis (M Div); biblical studies (MA); Christian education (MA); counseling (M Div); marriage and family therapy (MA); ministry (D Min); missions (M Div, MA, D Min); theological studies (MA). *Accreditation:* AAMFT/COAMFTE (one or more programs are accredited); ATS (one or more programs are accredited). *Faculty:* 10 full-time (0 women), 1 (woman) part-time/adjunct. *Students:* 50 full-time (14 women), 86 part-time (19 women). *Degree requirements:* For master's, thesis (for some programs), fieldwork; for doctorate, 2 foreign languages, thesis/dissertation. *Entrance requirements:* For master's, minimum GPA of 2.6; for doctorate, minimum GPA of 3.0. Additional exam requirements/recommendations for international students: Required—TOEFL. *Application deadline:* Applications are processed on a rolling basis. Application fee: $35. *Financial support:* Research assistantships, career-related internships or fieldwork, scholarships/grants, and tuition waivers (full and partial) available. Financial award application deadline: 5/1. *Application contact:* Brian Gault, Director of Admissions, 601-923-1600, Fax: 601-923-1654.

Reformed Theological Seminary–Washington D.C., Graduate and Professional Programs, McLean, VA 22102. Offers Bible (M Div); practical theology (M Div); religion (MA); theology (M Div). Part-time and evening/weekend programs available. *Faculty:* 3 full-time (0 women), 11 part-time/adjunct (1 woman). *Students:* 9 full-time (0 women), 104 part-time (7 women); includes 41 minority (14 Black or African American, non-Hispanic/Latino; 24 Asian, non-Hispanic/Latino; 3 Hispanic/Latino). Average age 35. 43 applicants, 91% accepted, 27 enrolled. In 2014, 9 master's awarded. *Degree requirements:* For master's, integrative paper. *Entrance requirements:* For master's, minimum undergraduate GPA of 2.6. Additional exam requirements/recommendations for international students: Required—TOEFL (minimum score 550 paper-based), TWE. *Application deadline:* Applications are processed on a rolling basis. Application fee: $75. Electronic applications accepted. *Expenses:* Expenses: Contact institution. *Financial support:* In 2014–15, 121 students received support. Scholarships/grants and tuition waivers (partial) available. Support available to part-time students. Financial award application deadline: 5/1. *Faculty research:* Theology, Biblical studies, cultural studies. *Unit head:* Dr. John S. Redd, Jr., President, 703-448-3393 Ext. 107, E-mail: sredd@rts.edu. *Application contact:* Geoff M. Sackett, Director of Admissions, 703-448-3393 Ext. 104, E-mail: gsackett@rts.edu.
Website: http://www.rts.edu/

Regent University, Graduate School, School of Divinity, Virginia Beach, VA 23464-9800. Offers leadership and renewal (D Min), including Christian leadership and renewal, clinical pastoral education, community transformation, military ministry, ministry leadership coaching; practical theology (M Div, MA), including Biblical studies (M Div, MTS, PhD), chaplain ministry (M Div), Christian theology (M Div, MTS, PhD), church and ministry, history of Christianity (M Div, MTS), inter-cultural studies, interdisciplinary studies (M Div, MA, MTS), worship and renewal; renewal studies (PhD), including Biblical studies (M Div, MTS, PhD), Christian theology (M Div, MTS, PhD), history of global Christianity; theological studies (MTS), including Biblical studies (M Div, MTS, PhD), Christian theology (M Div, MTS, PhD), history of Christianity (M Div, MTS), interdisciplinary studies (M Div, MA, MTS). *Accreditation:* ACIPE; ATS. Part-time programs available. Postbaccalaureate distance learning degree programs offered (minimal on-campus study). *Faculty:* 20 full-time (3 women), 29 part-time/adjunct (3 women). *Students:* 64 full-time (28 women), 616 part-time (258 women); includes 318 minority (269 Black or African American, non-Hispanic/Latino; 7 American Indian or Alaska Native, non-Hispanic/Latino; 16 Asian, non-Hispanic/Latino; 26 Hispanic/Latino), 37 international. Average age 43. 511 applicants, 52% accepted, 187 enrolled. In 2014, 121 master's, 24 doctorates awarded. *Degree requirements:* For master's, comprehensive exam, thesis or alternative, internship; for doctorate, thesis/dissertation or alternative. *Entrance requirements:* For master's, GRE General Test or MAT, minimum undergraduate GPA of 2.75, writing sample, clergy recommendation; for doctorate, M Div or theological master's degree; minimum graduate GPA of 3.5 (PhD), 3.0 (D Min); recommendations; writing sample; transcripts. Additional exam requirements/recommendations for international students: Required—TOEFL (minimum score 577 paper-based). *Application deadline:* For fall admission, 5/1 priority date for domestic students. Applications are processed on a rolling basis. Application fee: $50. Electronic applications accepted. *Expenses:* Expenses: Contact institution. *Financial support:* Fellowships with full and partial tuition reimbursements, career-related internships or fieldwork, scholarships/grants, tuition waivers (full and partial), and unspecified assistantships available. Support available to part-time students. Financial award application deadline: 9/1; financial award applicants required to submit FAFSA. *Faculty research:* Greek and Hebrew, theology, spiritual formation, global missions and world Christianity, women's studies. *Unit head:* Dr. Joseph Umidi, Interim Dean, 757-352-4401, Fax: 757-352-4597, E-mail: joseumi@regent.edu. *Application contact:* Matthew Chadwick, Director of Enrollment Support Services, 800-373-5504, Fax: 757-352-4381, E-mail: admissions@regent.edu.
Website: http://www.regent.edu/acad/schdiv/

Rice University, Graduate Programs, School of Humanities, Department of Religious Studies, Houston, TX 77251-1892. Offers African religions (PhD); African-American religions (PhD); contemplative studies (PhD); ghosticism, esotericism, mysticism (PhD); Islam (PhD); Jewish thought and philosophy (PhD); modern Christianity in thought and popular culture (PhD); psychology of religion (PhD); the Bible and beyond (PhD). *Degree requirements:* For doctorate, 2 foreign languages, comprehensive exam, thesis/dissertation. *Entrance requirements:* For doctorate, GRE, letters of recommendation, writing sample. Additional exam requirements/recommendations for international students: Required—TOEFL (minimum score 600 paper-based; 90 iBT). Electronic applications accepted. *Faculty research:* Origins and historical development of Islam, history of Christianity, the study of comparative religion, African-American religion, religion and culture.

The Robert E. Webber Institute for Worship Studies, Doctor of Worship Studies Program, Orange Park, FL 32073. Offers DWS. *Degree requirements:* For doctorate, thesis/dissertation, practicum.

The Robert E. Webber Institute for Worship Studies, Master of Worship Studies Program, Orange Park, FL 32073. Offers MWS. *Degree requirements:* For master's, internship.

Rutgers, The State University of New Jersey, New Brunswick, Graduate School-New Brunswick, Department of Religion, Piscataway, NJ 08854-8097. Offers religious studies (MA, Graduate Certificate). *Entrance requirements:* For master's and Graduate Certificate, GRE, personal statement, two letters of recommendation, official transcripts. Electronic applications accepted.

Sacred Heart University, Graduate Programs, College of Arts and Sciences, Department of Theology and Religious Studies, Fairfield, CT 06825-1000. Offers religious studies (MA). Part-time programs available. *Faculty:* 2 full-time (0 women). *Students:* 1 full-time (0 women), 3 part-time (1 woman). Average age 30. In 2014, 2 master's awarded. *Degree requirements:* For master's, comprehensive exam. *Entrance requirements:* For master's, GRE, bachelor's degree in humanities or social sciences. Additional exam requirements/recommendations for international students: Required—PTE; Recommended—TOEFL (minimum score 570 paper-based; 80 iBT), IELTS (minimum score 6.5). *Application deadline:* Applications are processed on a rolling basis. Application fee: $60. Electronic applications accepted. *Expenses:* Expenses: Contact institution. *Financial support:* Unspecified assistantships available. Financial award applicants required to submit FAFSA. *Unit head:* Dr. Brian Stiltner, Chair/Assistant Professor, 203-365-7557, E-mail: dyilynrtb@sacredheart.edu. *Application contact:* Kathy Dilks, Executive Director of Graduate Admissions, 203-365-7619, Fax: 203-365-4732, E-mail: gradstudies@sacredheart.edu.
Website: http://www.sacredheart.edu/academics/collegeofartssciences/academicdepartments/philosophytheologyreligiousstudies/

St. Bonaventure University, School of Graduate Studies, School of Franciscan Studies, St. Bonaventure, NY 14778-2284. Offers MA. Part-time programs available. In 2014, 1 master's awarded. *Degree requirements:* For master's, comprehensive exam, thesis optional. *Entrance requirements:* For master's, letter of intent, bachelor's degree,

transcripts, letters of recommendation. Additional exam requirements/recommendations for international students: Required—TOEFL (minimum score 550 paper-based; 79 iBT). *Application deadline:* For fall admission, 3/15 priority date for domestic students, 2/1 priority date for international students. Applications are processed on a rolling basis. Application fee: $0. Electronic applications accepted. *Expenses: Required fees:* $711 per credit hour. One-time fee: $100 part-time. *Financial support:* Research assistantships, Federal Work-Study, scholarships/grants, health care benefits, tuition waivers (full and partial), and unspecified assistantships available. Support available to part-time students. Financial award application deadline: 4/15; financial award applicants required to submit FAFSA. *Unit head:* Fr. David Couturier, OFM, Dean, 716-375-2160, E-mail: dcouturi@sbu.edu. *Application contact:* Bruce Campbell, Director of Graduate Admissions, 716-375-2429, Fax: 716-375-4015, E-mail: gradsch@sbu.edu.
Website: http://www.sbu.edu/

Saint Charles Borromeo Seminary, Overbrook, Graduate and Professional Programs, Program of Catholic Studies, Wynnewood, PA 19096. Offers MA. Part-time and evening/weekend programs available. *Degree requirements:* For master's, comprehensive exam. *Entrance requirements:* For master's, 18 undergraduate credits in theology and/or philosophy or the equivalent. Additional exam requirements/recommendations for international students: Required—TOEFL.

Saint John's Seminary, Graduate Programs, Brighton, MA 02135. Offers M Div, MA Th, MAM. *Accreditation:* ATS.

St. Joseph's Seminary, Graduate and Professional Programs, Yonkers, NY 10704. Offers Catholic philosophical studies (MA); divinity (M Div); pastoral studies (MAPS); theology (MA). *Accreditation:* ATS. *Degree requirements:* For master's, one foreign language, thesis. *Entrance requirements:* For master's, 27 credits in philosophy and 9 in theology. *Financial support:* Scholarships/grants available. *Unit head:* Rev. Msgr. Peter I. Vaccari, Rector, 914-968-6200, Fax: 914-376-2019. *Application contact:* Fr. Thomas V. Berg, Director of Admissions, 914-968-6200, Fax: 914-376-2019.

Saint Mary's University, Faculty of Arts, Department of Religious Studies, Halifax, NS B3H 3C3, Canada. Offers theology and religious studies (MA).

Salve Regina University, Program in Humanities, Newport, RI 02840-4192. Offers humanitarian assistance (MA); humanities (PhD); public humanities (MA); religion, peace and justice (MA). Part-time and evening/weekend programs available. Postbaccalaureate distance learning degree programs offered (no on-campus study). *Faculty:* 1 full-time (0 women), 6 part-time/adjunct (2 women). *Students:* 3 full-time (0 women), 88 part-time (52 women); includes 9 minority (3 Black or African American, non-Hispanic/Latino; 2 Asian, non-Hispanic/Latino; 1 Hispanic/Latino; 1 Native Hawaiian or other Pacific Islander, non-Hispanic/Latino; 2 Two or more races, non-Hispanic/Latino), 2 international. Average age 48. 13 applicants, 85% accepted, 11 enrolled. In 2014, 3 master's, 3 doctorates awarded. *Degree requirements:* For master's, thesis optional; for doctorate, one foreign language, comprehensive exam, thesis/dissertation. *Entrance requirements:* For master's, GMAT, GRE General Test, or MAT; for doctorate, GRE General Test. Additional exam requirements/recommendations for international students: Required—TOEFL (minimum score 600 paper-based; 100 iBT) or IELTS. *Application deadline:* For fall admission, 3/15 priority date for domestic and international students; for spring admission, 9/15 priority date for domestic and international students. Applications are processed on a rolling basis. Application fee: $60. Electronic applications accepted. *Expenses: Tuition:* Full-time $8550; part-time $475 per credit. *Required fees:* $50 per term. Tuition and fees vary according to course level, course load and degree level. *Financial support:* Career-related internships or fieldwork and Federal Work-Study available. Support available to part-time students. Financial award application deadline: 3/1; financial award applicants required to submit FAFSA. *Unit head:* Dr. Michael Budd, Director, 401-341-3284, E-mail: michael.budd@salve.edu. *Application contact:* Kelly Alverson, Director of Graduate Admissions, 401-341-2153, Fax: 401-341-2973, E-mail: kelly.alverson@salve.edu.
Website: http://www.salve.edu/graduate-studies/humanities

The Seattle School of Theology and Psychology, Graduate Programs, Seattle, WA 98121. Offers Christian studies (MA); counseling psychology (MA); divinity (M Div). Part-time programs available. *Entrance requirements:* For master's, MAT.

Seton Hall University, College of Arts and Sciences, Department of Religion, South Orange, NJ 07079-2697. Offers Jewish-Christian Studies (MA). Part-time and evening/weekend programs available. *Faculty:* 4 full-time (0 women). *Students:* 9 full-time (5 women), 8 part-time (5 women); includes 6 minority (1 Asian, non-Hispanic/Latino; 2 Hispanic/Latino; 3 Native Hawaiian or other Pacific Islander, non-Hispanic/Latino), 1 international. Average age 45. 6 applicants, 100% accepted, 5 enrolled. In 2014, 1 master's awarded. *Degree requirements:* For master's, thesis optional. *Entrance requirements:* For master's, interview or suitable correspondence with department chair. Additional exam requirements/recommendations for international students: Required—TOEFL. *Application deadline:* For fall admission, 7/1 priority date for domestic and international students; for spring admission, 11/1 priority date for domestic and international students. Applications are processed on a rolling basis. Application fee: $75. Electronic applications accepted. *Financial support:* Fellowships, research assistantships, career-related internships or fieldwork, Federal Work-Study, scholarships/grants, tuition waivers (full and partial), and unspecified assistantships available. Support available to part-time students. Financial award application deadline: 8/31; financial award applicants required to submit FAFSA. *Faculty research:* Jewish-Christian issues, Biblical studies, Holocaust studies. *Unit head:* Prof. KC Choi, Chair, 973-761-9462, E-mail: kijoo.choi@shu.edu. *Application contact:* Fr. Lawrence Frizzell, Program Chair, 973-761-9751, Fax: 973-761-9596, E-mail: lawrence.frizzell@shu.edu.
Website: http://www.shu.edu/academics/artsci/religion/

Seton Hall University, Immaculate Conception Seminary School of Theology, South Orange, NJ 07079-2697. Offers Christian spirituality (Certificate); great spiritual books (Certificate); pastoral ministry (M Div, MA, Certificate); scripture studies (Certificate); Seminary's Theological Education for Parish Services (STEPS) (Certificate); theology (MA). *Accreditation:* ATS (one or more programs are accredited). Part-time and evening/weekend programs available. *Degree requirements:* For master's, comprehensive exam (for some programs), thesis (for some programs), final project (for some programs); 1 foreign language (for MA in theology research option). *Entrance requirements:* For master's, GRE General Test or MAT. Additional exam requirements/recommendations for international students: Required—TOEFL (minimum score 600 paper-based; 100 iBT). Electronic applications accepted. *Expenses:* Contact institution. *Faculty research:* Pauline literature, history of Biblical interpretation and theological exegesis, spirituality of St. Edith Stein, Thomism, history of Catholicism in America.

Sioux Falls Seminary, Graduate and Professional Programs, Program in Christian Leadership, Sioux Falls, SD 57105-1599. Offers MA. Postbaccalaureate distance learning degree programs offered (no on-campus study).

Southern Adventist University, School of Religion, Collegedale, TN 37315-0370. Offers Biblical and theological studies (MA); church leadership and management (M Min); church ministry and homiletics (M Min); evangelism and world mission (M Min); religious studies (MA). Part-time programs available. *Degree requirements:* For master's, comprehensive exam, thesis (for some programs). *Entrance requirements:* For master's, GRE. Additional exam requirements/recommendations for international students: Required—TOEFL (minimum score 600 paper-based). *Faculty research:* Biblical archaeology.

Southern Baptist Theological Seminary, School of Church Ministries, Louisville, KY 40280-0004. Offers Biblical counseling (M Div, MA); children's and family ministry (M Div, MA); Christian education (MA); Christian worship (PhD); church ministries (M Div); church music (MCM); college ministry (M Div, MA); discipleship and family ministry (M Div, MA); education (Ed D); family ministry (D Min, PhD); higher education (PhD); leadership (M Div, MA, D Min, PhD); ministry (D Ed Min); missions and ethnodoxology (M Div); women's leadership (M Div, MA); worship leadership (M Div, MA); worship leadership and church ministry (MA); youth and family ministry (M Div, MA). Part-time programs available. Postbaccalaureate distance learning degree programs offered (minimal on-campus study). *Degree requirements:* For doctorate, thesis/dissertation. *Entrance requirements:* For doctorate, GRE General Test, interview, M Div or MACE. Additional exam requirements/recommendations for international students: Required—TWE. *Faculty research:* Gerontology, creative teaching methods, faith development in children, faith development in youth, transformational learning.

Southern Baptist Theological Seminary, School of Theology, Louisville, KY 40280-0004. Offers applied theology (D Min); biblical and theological studies (M Div); biblical counseling (M Div, MA, D Min); biblical spirituality (D Min); Christian ministry (M Div); expository preaching (D Min); pastoral studies (M Div); theological studies (MA); theology (Th M, PhD); worldview and apologetics (M Div). *Accreditation:* ATS. Part-time and evening/weekend programs available. Postbaccalaureate distance learning degree programs offered (minimal on-campus study). *Degree requirements:* For master's, 2 foreign languages, thesis; for doctorate, 4 foreign languages, thesis/dissertation. *Entrance requirements:* For master's, GRE General Test, MAT, M Div; for doctorate, GRE General Test, MAT, interview, M Div, field essay. Additional exam requirements/recommendations for international students: Required—TOEFL, TWE. *Faculty research:* Biblical studies, contemporary theology, church history, pastoral care, ministry/missions studies.

Southern California Seminary, Graduate and Professional Programs, El Cajon, CA 92019. Offers Biblical studies (MABS); counseling psychology (MACP); marriage and family therapy (MAMFT); psychology (Psy D); religious studies (MRS); theology (M Div). Part-time and evening/weekend programs available. Postbaccalaureate distance learning degree programs offered (minimal on-campus study). *Degree requirements:* For master's, thesis (for some programs); for doctorate, thesis/dissertation. *Entrance requirements:* For doctorate, master's degree in psychology. Additional exam requirements/recommendations for international students: Required—TOEFL (minimum score 550 paper-based). Electronic applications accepted.

Southern Evangelical Seminary, Graduate Programs, Matthews, NC 28105. Offers apologetics (MA, D Min, Certificate); Christian education (MA); church ministry (MA, Certificate); divinity (Certificate), including apologetics (M Div, Certificate); Islamic studies (MA, Certificate); Jewish studies (MA); philosophy (MA); philosophy of religion (PhD); religion (MA); theology (M Div), including apologetics (M Div, Certificate), Biblical studies; youth ministry (MA). Part-time and evening/weekend programs available. Postbaccalaureate distance learning degree programs offered. *Degree requirements:* For master's, thesis (for some programs); for doctorate, 2 foreign languages, comprehensive exam (for some programs), thesis/dissertation. *Entrance requirements:* Additional exam requirements/recommendations for international students: Required—TOEFL (minimum score 600 paper-based).

Southern Methodist University, Dedman College of Humanities and Sciences, Graduate Program in Religious Studies, Dallas, TX 75275-0133. Offers Hebrew Bible/Old Testament (PhD); history of the Christian tradition (PhD); New Testament (PhD); religion and culture (PhD); religious ethics (PhD); religious studies (MA); systematics theology (PhD). Terminal master's awarded for partial completion of doctoral program. *Degree requirements:* For master's, one foreign language, thesis, oral and written exams; for doctorate, variable foreign language requirement, thesis/dissertation, oral and written exams. *Entrance requirements:* For master's and doctorate, GRE General Test, minimum GPA of 3.0, course work in religion. Additional exam requirements/recommendations for international students: Required—TOEFL (minimum score 550 paper-based; 79 iBT). Electronic applications accepted. *Faculty research:* Theology, religious ethics, Biblical studies, history of Christianity, religion and culture.

Southwestern Assemblies of God University, Thomas F. Harrison School of Graduate Studies, Program in Theological Studies, Waxahachie, TX 75165-5735. Offers Bible and theology (MS); Biblical studies (M Div); counseling (M Div); cross cultural missions (M Div); practical theology (M Div); theological studies (M Div). Postbaccalaureate distance learning degree programs offered. *Degree requirements:* For master's, comprehensive written and oral exams. *Entrance requirements:* For master's, GRE General Test, minimum GPA of 2.5. Electronic applications accepted.

Stanford University, School of Humanities and Sciences, Department of Religious Studies, Stanford, CA 94305-9991. Offers MA, PhD. Terminal master's awarded for partial completion of doctoral program. *Degree requirements:* For master's, one foreign language, thesis optional; for doctorate, 2 foreign languages, thesis/dissertation, qualifying exam. *Entrance requirements:* For master's and doctorate, GRE General Test. Additional exam requirements/recommendations for international students: Required—TOEFL. Electronic applications accepted. *Expenses: Tuition:* Full-time $44,184; part-time $982 per credit hour. *Required fees:* $191.

Summit University, Baptist Bible Seminary, Clarks Summit, PA 18411-1297. Offers Biblical apologetics (MA); church education (M Div, M Min); church planting (M Div, M Min); global ministry (M Div, M Min); leadership in communication (D Min); leadership in counseling and spiritual development (D Min); leadership in global ministry (D Min); leadership in pastoral ministry (D Min); leadership in theological studies (D Min); military chaplaincy (M Div); ministry (PhD); organizational leadership (M Min); outreach pastor (M Div, M Min); pastoral counseling (M Div, M Min); pastoral leadership (M Div, M Min); theology (Th M); worship ministries leadership (M Div, M Min); youth pastor (M Div, M Min). Part-time and evening/weekend programs available. Postbaccalaureate distance learning degree programs offered (minimal on-campus study). Terminal master's awarded for partial completion of doctoral program. *Degree requirements:* For master's, 2 foreign languages, thesis, oral exam (for M Div); for doctorate, 2 foreign languages, comprehensive exam (for some programs), thesis/dissertation, oral exam. *Entrance requirements:* For doctorate, Greek and Hebrew entrance exams (for PhD). Electronic applications accepted.

Syracuse University, College of Arts and Sciences, Program in Religion, Syracuse, NY 13244. Offers MA, PhD. Part-time programs available. *Students:* 30 full-time (21 women), 6 part-time (2 women); includes 2 minority (1 Asian, non-Hispanic/Latino; 1 Hispanic/Latino), 4 international. Average age 33. 63 applicants, 17% accepted, 3 enrolled. In 2014, 4 master's, 2 doctorates awarded. Terminal master's awarded for partial completion of doctoral program. *Degree requirements:* For master's, one foreign language, comprehensive exam, thesis optional; for doctorate, 2 foreign languages, comprehensive exam, thesis/dissertation. *Entrance requirements:* For master's and doctorate, GRE General Test. Additional exam requirements/recommendations for international students: Required—TOEFL (minimum score 100 iBT). *Application deadline:* For fall admission, 1/10 priority date for domestic and international students.

Application fee: $75. Electronic applications accepted. *Expenses: Tuition:* Part-time $1341 per credit. *Financial support:* Fellowships with full tuition reimbursements, teaching assistantships with full and partial tuition reimbursements, and tuition waivers available. Financial award application deadline: 1/1; financial award applicants required to submit FAFSA. *Unit head:* Dr. M. Gail Hammer, Director of Graduate Studies, 315-443-3861, Fax: 315-443-3958, E-mail: jpwaghor@syr.edu. *Application contact:* Jackie Borowre, Recruiting Contact, 315-443-3861, E-mail: jborowre@syr.edu.
Website: http://religion.syr.edu/

Temple Baptist Seminary, Program in Theology, Chattanooga, TN 37404-3530. Offers biblical languages (M Div); Biblical studies (MABS); Christian education (MACE); English Bible ? language tools (M Div); theology (MM, D Min). Part-time and evening/weekend programs available. Postbaccalaureate distance learning degree programs offered (minimal on-campus study). *Degree requirements:* For doctorate, thesis/dissertation. *Entrance requirements:* For doctorate, minimum GPA of 3.0, M Div.

Temple University, College of Liberal Arts, Department of Religion, Philadelphia, PA 19122-6096. Offers MA, PhD. Part-time programs available. *Faculty:* 12 full-time (4 women), 2 part-time/adjunct (1 woman). *Students:* 55 full-time (23 women), 4 part-time (1 woman); includes 14 minority (3 Black or African American, non-Hispanic/Latino; 5 Asian, non-Hispanic/Latino; 4 Hispanic/Latino; 2 Two or more races, non-Hispanic/Latino), 4 international. 34 applicants, 59% accepted, 6 enrolled. In 2014, 2 master's, 4 doctorates awarded. *Degree requirements:* For doctorate, variable foreign language requirement, thesis/dissertation. *Entrance requirements:* For master's and doctorate, GRE General Test, minimum GPA of 3.0, 3 letters of recommendation. Additional exam requirements/recommendations for international students: Required—TOEFL (minimum score 600 paper-based; 100 iBT). *Application deadline:* For fall admission, 1/15 for domestic students, 12/15 for international students. Application fee: $60. Electronic applications accepted. *Expenses:* Tuition, state resident: full-time $14,490; part-time $805 per credit hour. Tuition, nonresident: full-time $19,850; part-time $1103 per credit hour. *Required fees:* $690. Full-time tuition and fees vary according to class time, course load, degree level, campus/location and program. *Financial support:* Fellowships, teaching assistantships, Federal Work-Study, institutionally sponsored loans, and tuition waivers (full and partial) available. Financial award application deadline: 1/15; financial award applicants required to submit FAFSA. *Faculty research:* Buddhism, gender/sexuality, Hebrew Bible, Islam, world religions. *Unit head:* Dr. Jeremy Schipper, Graduate Director, 215-204-7973, Fax: 215-204-2535, E-mail: jeremy.schipper@temple.edu. *Application contact:* Linda Jenkins, Coordinator, 215-204-7973, Fax: 215-204-2535, E-mail: jenkinsl@temple.edu.
Website: http://www.cla.temple.edu/religion/

Trevecca Nazarene University, Graduate Religion Programs, Nashville, TN 37210-2877. Offers biblical studies (MA); pastoral arts (MA); preaching (MA); theological studies (MA). Part-time programs available. *Faculty:* 3 full-time (0 women), 1 part-time/adjunct (0 women). *Students:* 6 full-time (2 women), 7 part-time (1 woman); includes 3 minority (2 Black or African American, non-Hispanic/Latino; 1 Hispanic/Latino). Average age 36. In 2014, 14 master's awarded. *Degree requirements:* For master's, comprehensive exam, thesis. *Entrance requirements:* For master's, GRE General Test or MAT, minimum GPA of 2.7, official transcript from regionally-accredited institution, 2 letters of recommendation, philosophy of ministry statement. Additional exam requirements/recommendations for international students: Required—TOEFL (minimum score 550 paper-based). *Application deadline:* Applications are processed on a rolling basis. Application fee: $25. Electronic applications accepted. *Expenses:* Expenses: Contact institution. *Financial support:* Applicants required to submit FAFSA. *Unit head:* Dr. Tim Green, Dean, School of Religion and Philosophy/Director, Graduate Religion Program, 615-248-1378, Fax: 615-248-7417. *Application contact:* 615-248-1529, E-mail: cll@trevecca.edu.
Website: http://trevecca.edu/academics/program/religion

Trinity International University, South Florida Campus, Divinity School, Davie, FL 33324. Offers MA, Certificate.

Trinity School for Ministry, Graduate Programs, Ambridge, PA 15003-2397. Offers Anglican studies (Diploma); basic Christian studies (Diploma); divinity (M Div); ministry (D Min); mission and evangelism (MAME, Diploma); religion (MAR); youth ministry (Diploma). *Accreditation:* ATS (one or more programs are accredited). Part-time programs available. *Degree requirements:* For master's, thesis optional; for doctorate, thesis/dissertation. *Entrance requirements:* Additional exam requirements/recommendations for international students: Required—TOEFL. *Faculty research:* Pauline Epistles, contemporary theology, history of Anglican liturgy, book of Ruth, biblical theology.

Unification Theological Seminary, Graduate Program, Main Campus, Barrytown, NY 12507. Offers divinity (M Div); ministry (D Min); religious education (MRE); religious studies (MA). Part-time and evening/weekend programs available. *Faculty:* 1 full-time (0 women), 5 part-time/adjunct (1 woman). *Students:* 35 full-time (10 women); includes 21 minority (13 Black or African American, non-Hispanic/Latino; 5 Asian, non-Hispanic/Latino; 2 Hispanic/Latino; 1 Two or more races, non-Hispanic/Latino), 6 international. Average age 52. In 2014, 16 master's, 1 doctorate awarded. *Degree requirements:* For master's, variable foreign language requirement, thesis (for some programs); for doctorate, thesis/dissertation. *Entrance requirements:* For master's, bachelor's degree; for doctorate, M Div or equivalency. Additional exam requirements/recommendations for international students: Required—TOEFL (minimum score 450 paper-based; 45 iBT). *Application deadline:* For fall admission, 8/15 priority date for domestic students; for spring admission, 1/15 priority date for domestic students. Applications are processed on a rolling basis. Application fee: $30. Electronic applications accepted. *Expenses: Tuition:* Full-time $8280; part-time $460 per credit. *Required fees:* $125 per semester. Tuition and fees vary according to course load. *Financial support:* In 2014–15, 4 students received support. Scholarships/grants available. Financial award application deadline: 6/15; financial award applicants required to submit FAFSA. *Faculty research:* Church leadership, church history, world religions, ecumenism, interfaith peace building, service-learning. *Unit head:* Dr. Kathy Winings, Vice-President for Academic Affairs, 845-752-3000 Ext. 228, Fax: 845-752-3014, E-mail: academics@uts.edu. *Application contact:* Henry Christopher, Director of Admissions, 845-752-3000 Ext. 244, Fax: 845-752-3014, E-mail: h.christopher@uts.edu.
Website: http://www.uts.edu

Unification Theological Seminary, Graduate Program, New York Extension, New York, NY 10036. Offers divinity (M Div); religious education (MRE); religious studies (MA). Part-time and evening/weekend programs available. *Faculty:* 1 full-time (0 women), 8 part-time/adjunct (2 women). *Students:* 28 full-time (9 women), 22 part-time (9 women); includes 22 minority (15 Black or African American, non-Hispanic/Latino; 4 Asian, non-Hispanic/Latino; 2 Hispanic/Latino; 1 Two or more races, non-Hispanic/Latino), 23 international. Average age 45. *Degree requirements:* For master's, variable foreign language requirement, thesis (for some programs). *Entrance requirements:* For master's, bachelor's degree. Additional exam requirements/recommendations for international students: Required—TOEFL (minimum score 450 paper-based; 45 iBT). *Application deadline:* For fall admission, 8/15 priority date for domestic students; for spring admission, 1/15 priority date for domestic students. Applications are processed on a rolling basis. Application fee: $30. Electronic applications accepted. *Expenses: Tuition:* Full-time $8280; part-time $460 per credit. *Required fees:* $125 per semester. Tuition and fees vary according to course load. *Financial support:* In 2014–15, 50 students received support. Career-related internships or fieldwork, institutionally sponsored loans, scholarships/grants, and tuition waivers (partial) available. Support available to part-time students. Financial award application deadline: 6/15; financial award applicants required to submit FAFSA. *Faculty research:* Church history, world religions, ecumenism, interfaith peace building, service-learning. *Unit head:* Dr. Kathy Winings, Vice-President for Academic Affairs, 212-563-6647 Ext. 101, Fax: 212-563-6431, E-mail: academics@uts.edu. *Application contact:* Joy Theriot, Recruiter, 212-563-6647, Fax: 212-563-6431, E-mail: j.theriot@uts.edu.
Website: http://www.uts.edu

Union University, School of Theology and Missions, Jackson, TN 38305-3697. Offers Christian studies (MCS); expository preaching (D Min). Part-time and evening/weekend programs available. Postbaccalaureate distance learning degree programs offered (no on-campus study). *Students:* 143 full-time, 79 part-time. In 2014, 60 master's, 6 doctorates awarded. *Application deadline:* Applications are processed on a rolling basis. Application fee: $25. Electronic applications accepted. *Expenses: Tuition:* Full-time $6566; part-time $469 per credit hour. *Unit head:* Dr. James A. Patterson, Acting Dean, 731-661-5269, E-mail: jpatters@uu.edu. *Application contact:* Christy Lynn Young, Director of Adult and Professional Programs, 731-661-5987, Fax: 731-661-5987, E-mail: cyoung@uu.edu.

United Theological Seminary of the Twin Cities, Graduate Programs, New Brighton, MN 55112-2598. Offers advanced theological studies (Diploma); justice and peace studies (M Div, MA); leadership toward racial justice (M Div, MA, Certificate); Methodist studies (M Div, MA, Certificate); ministry (D Min); ministry renewal and professional development (Certificate); pastoral care and counseling (M Div, MA, MARL); religion and theology (MA); theological and religious studies (Certificate); theology and the arts (M Div, MA); urban ministry (M Div, MA, MARL); women's studies: religion, theology and ministry (M Div, MA). *Accreditation:* ACIPE; ATS. Part-time and evening/weekend programs available. *Degree requirements:* For master's, thesis; for doctorate, comprehensive exam, thesis/dissertation. *Entrance requirements:* For master's, minimum GPA of 2.75; strong analytical, reflective thinking and writing skills; vocational and academic goals compatible with those of Seminary; for doctorate, M Div or equivalent, minimum GPA of 3.0, 3 years experience in professional ministry; for other advanced degree, BA or equivalent life experience; strong analytical, reflective thinking and writing skills (Certificate); proficiency in English language, previous study of theology at a theological school, recommendation of student's denomination (Diploma). Additional exam requirements/recommendations for international students: Required—TOEFL (minimum score 550 paper-based).

Université de Montréal, Faculty of Theology and Sciences of Religions, Montréal, QC H3C 3J7, Canada. Offers health, spirituality and bioethics (DESS); practical theology (MA, PhD); religious sciences (MA, PhD); theology (MA, D Th, PhD, L Th); theology-Biblical studies (PhD). *Degree requirements:* For master's, one foreign language; for doctorate, 2 foreign languages, thesis/dissertation, general exam. Electronic applications accepted.

Université de Sherbrooke, Faculty of Theology and Religious Studies, Sherbrooke, QC J1K 2R1, Canada. Offers applied ethics (Diploma); human science of religions (MA); intercultural training (Diploma); philosophy (MA, PhD); spiritual anthropology (Diploma); theology (MA, PhD, Diploma). Part-time and evening/weekend programs available. Postbaccalaureate distance learning degree programs offered. Terminal master's awarded for partial completion of doctoral program. *Entrance requirements:* For master's, bachelor's degree in related discipline; for doctorate, master's degree in related discipline. *Faculty research:* Faith and culture interrelation.

Université du Québec à Montréal, Graduate Programs, Program in Religious Sciences, Montréal, QC H3C 3P8, Canada. Offers MA, PhD. MA offered jointly with Concordia University. Part-time programs available. *Degree requirements:* For master's, thesis; for doctorate, thesis/dissertation. *Entrance requirements:* For master's, appropriate bachelor's degree or equivalent, proficiency in French; for doctorate, appropriate master's degree or equivalent, proficiency in French.

Université Laval, Faculty of Theology and Religious Sciences, Programs in Human Sciences of Religion, Québec, QC G1K 7P4, Canada. Offers MA, PhD. Terminal master's awarded for partial completion of doctoral program. *Degree requirements:* For master's, thesis (for some programs); for doctorate, comprehensive exam, thesis/dissertation. *Entrance requirements:* For master's, knowledge of French, comprehension of a second language; for doctorate, knowledge of French and English. Electronic applications accepted.

The University of British Columbia, Faculty of Arts and Faculty of Graduate Studies, Department of Classical, Near Eastern and Religious Studies, Program in Religious Studies, Vancouver, BC V6T 1Z1, Canada. Offers MA, PhD. Part-time programs available. *Degree requirements:* For master's, 2 foreign languages, comprehensive exam, thesis optional; for doctorate, 2 foreign languages, comprehensive exam, thesis/dissertation. *Entrance requirements:* For doctorate, MA. Additional exam requirements/recommendations for international students: Required—TOEFL (minimum score 600 paper-based), IELTS. Electronic applications accepted. *Faculty research:* Hebrew Bible in ancient Near Eastern context, Christian scriptures in Greco-Roman context, mystical aspects of religion, the feminine in western traditions, modern Jewish experience.

The University of British Columbia, Faculty of Arts and Faculty of Graduate Studies, Department of Classical, Near Eastern and Religious Studies, Programmes in Classics, Vancouver, BC V6T 1Z1, Canada. Offers ancient culture, religion, and ethnicity (MA); classical and near eastern archaeology (MA); classics (MA, PhD). Part-time programs available. *Degree requirements:* For master's, 2 foreign languages, thesis or comprehensive exam; for doctorate, 2 foreign languages, comprehensive exam, thesis/dissertation. *Entrance requirements:* For doctorate, MA. Additional exam requirements/recommendations for international students: Required—TOEFL (minimum score 600 paper-based), IELTS (minimum score 7.5). Electronic applications accepted. *Faculty research:* Classical archaeology, ancient historians, late antiquity, ancient prose fiction, epigraphy.

University of Calgary, Faculty of Graduate Studies, Faculty of Arts, Department of Religious Studies, Calgary, AB T2N 1N4, Canada. Offers MA, PhD. Part-time programs available. *Degree requirements:* For master's, one foreign language, thesis; for doctorate, 2 foreign languages, thesis/dissertation, candidacy exam. *Entrance requirements:* For master's, minimum GPA of 3.3; for doctorate, minimum GPA of 3.5. Additional exam requirements/recommendations for international students: Required—TOEFL (minimum score 550 paper-based). *Faculty research:* Eastern religions, Western religions, nature of religion.

University of California, Berkeley, Graduate Division, College of Letters and Science, Department of Near Eastern Studies, Group in Near Eastern Religions, Berkeley, CA 94720-1500. Offers PhD. Program offered jointly with Graduate Theological Union. *Degree requirements:* For doctorate, 2 foreign languages, thesis/dissertation, qualifying exam. *Entrance requirements:* For doctorate, GRE General Test, MA or equivalent in Near Eastern studies or related field; minimum GPA of 3.0, 3 letters of recommendation.

University of California, Berkeley, Graduate Division, College of Letters and Science, Group in Buddhist Studies, Berkeley, CA 94720-1500. Offers PhD. *Degree requirements:* For doctorate, 4 foreign languages, thesis/dissertation, dissertation defense, qualifying exam. *Entrance requirements:* For doctorate, GRE General Test, MA in Japanese, Chinese, or Sanskrit; minimum GPA of 3.0, 3 letters of recommendation. Electronic applications accepted.

University of California, Riverside, Graduate Division, Department of Religious Studies, Riverside, CA 92521. Offers PhD. *Faculty:* 8 full-time (2 women). *Students:* 20 full-time (8 women); includes 2 minority (both Asian, non-Hispanic/Latino). Average age 34. 11 applicants, 55% accepted, 4 enrolled. Terminal master's awarded for partial completion of doctoral program. *Degree requirements:* For doctorate, 2 foreign languages, comprehensive exam. *Entrance requirements:* For doctorate, GRE General Test, 3 letters of recommendation from academic references, a statement of purpose, and personal history; basic and advanced courses in religious studies, beginning work in foreign language and ability to work across methods, traditions, and disciplines. Additional exam requirements/recommendations for international students: Required—TOEFL (minimum score 550 paper-based; 80 iBT), Individual section score on IELTS must not be less than 6 in any area; Recommended—IELTS (minimum score 7). *Application deadline:* For fall admission, 1/5 priority date for domestic and international students. Applications are processed on a rolling basis. Application fee: $80 ($100 for international students). Electronic applications accepted. *Expenses:* Tuition, state resident: full-time $5399. Tuition, nonresident: full-time $10,433. *Financial support:* In 2014–15, 18 students received support, including 7 fellowships with full tuition reimbursements available (averaging $11,000 per year), 13 teaching assistantships with full tuition reimbursements available (averaging $18,000 per year); scholarships/grants and unspecified assistantships also available. Financial award application deadline: 1/5; financial award applicants required to submit FAFSA. *Faculty research:* American religions, southeast asian religions, transnational buddhism, modern hinduism, gender theory, sikh studies. *Unit head:* Dr. Pashaura Singh, Chair, 951-827-1251, E-mail: pashaura.singh@ucr.edu. *Application contact:* Trina B. Elerts, Graduate Program Coordinator, 951-827-1584, Fax: 951-827-2237, E-mail: trina.elerts@ucr.edu.
Website: http://religiousstudies.ucr.edu/

University of California, Santa Barbara, Graduate Division, College of Letters and Sciences, Division of Humanities and Fine Arts, Department of Religious Studies, Santa Barbara, CA 93106-3130. Offers ancient Mediterranean studies (PhD); cognitive science (PhD); European medieval studies (PhD); feminist studies (PhD); global studies (PhD); religious studies (MA, PhD); translation studies (PhD); MA/PhD. Terminal master's awarded for partial completion of doctoral program. *Degree requirements:* For master's, one foreign language, comprehensive exam (for some programs), thesis (for some programs), colloquium; for doctorate, 2 foreign languages, thesis/dissertation, methodology, colloquium. *Entrance requirements:* For master's and doctorate, GRE General Test. Additional exam requirements/recommendations for international students: Required—TOEFL (minimum score 550 paper-based; 80 iBT), IELTS (minimum score 7). Electronic applications accepted. *Faculty research:* Area studies; religious traditions; theory and method in the study of religion; religion, culture, and politics; spirituality and religious experience.

University of California, Santa Barbara, Graduate Division, College of Letters and Sciences, Division of Social Sciences, Department of Global and International Studies, Santa Barbara, CA 93106-7065. Offers global culture, ideology, and religion (MA); global government, civil society, and human rights (MA); global studies (PhD); political economy, sustainable development, and the environment (MA). *Degree requirements:* For master's, one foreign language, thesis, 2 years of a second language. *Entrance requirements:* For master's, GRE, 2 years of a second language with minimum B grade in the final term, 3 letters of recommendation, resume/curriculum vitae, personal statement, writing sample. Additional exam requirements/recommendations for international students: Required—TOEFL (minimum score 600 paper-based; 94 iBT), IELTS (minimum score 7). Electronic applications accepted. *Faculty research:* Global culture, ideology, and religion; global governance, civil society, and human rights; political economy, sustainable development and the environment.

University of Chicago, Divinity School, Master of Arts in Religious Studies Program, Chicago, IL 60637. Offers MA. Part-time programs available. *Students:* 7 full-time (5 women), 4 part-time (1 woman); includes 1 minority (Black or African American, non-Hispanic/Latino), 3 international. 12 applicants, 100% accepted, 8 enrolled. *Degree requirements:* For master's, oral examination, one year of coursework. *Entrance requirements:* For master's, GRE General Test. Additional exam requirements/recommendations for international students: Required—TOEFL (minimum score 600 paper-based; 104 iBT), IELTS (minimum score 7). *Application deadline:* For fall admission, 7/1 for domestic and international students; for winter admission, 10/15 for domestic and international students; for spring admission, 1/15 for domestic and international students. Applications are processed on a rolling basis. Application fee: $75. Electronic applications accepted. *Expenses: Tuition:* Full-time $46,899. *Required fees:* $347. *Financial support:* Federal Work-Study, institutionally sponsored loans, and scholarships/grants available. Financial award applicants required to submit FAFSA. *Unit head:* Dr. Margaret M. Mitchell, Dean/Professor of New Testament and Early Christian Literature, 773-702-8221. *Application contact:* John W. Howell, Coordinator for Recruiting and Admissions, 773-702-8249, Fax: 773-834-4581, E-mail: divinityadmissions@uchicago.edu.
Website: http://divinity.uchicago.edu/master-arts-religious-studies-amrs

University of Chicago, Divinity School, Master of Arts Program, Chicago, IL 60637. Offers MA. *Students:* 92 full-time (46 women), 6 part-time (3 women); includes 12 minority (3 Black or African American, non-Hispanic/Latino; 6 Asian, non-Hispanic/Latino; 3 Hispanic/Latino), 11 international. 142 applicants, 89% accepted, 53 enrolled. *Degree requirements:* For master's, one foreign language, 2 years of study. *Entrance requirements:* For master's, GRE General Test. Additional exam requirements/recommendations for international students: Required—TOEFL (minimum score 600 paper-based; 104 iBT), IELTS (minimum score 7). *Application deadline:* For fall admission, 12/15 for domestic and international students. Application fee: $75. Electronic applications accepted. *Expenses: Tuition:* Full-time $46,899. *Required fees:* $347. *Financial support:* Federal Work-Study, institutionally sponsored loans, and scholarships/grants available. Financial award application deadline: 12/15; financial award applicants required to submit FAFSA. *Unit head:* Dr. Margaret M. Mitchell, Dean/Professor of New Testament and Early Christian Literature, 773-702-8200. *Application contact:* John W. Howell, Coordinator for Recruiting and Admissions, 773-702-8249, Fax: 773-834-4581, E-mail: divinityadmissions@uchicago.edu.
Website: http://divinity.uchicago.edu/master-arts-ma

University of Chicago, Divinity School, PhD Program, Chicago, IL 60637. Offers anthropology and sociology of religions (PhD); bible (PhD); history of Christianity (PhD); history of Judaism (PhD); history of religions (PhD); Islamic studies (PhD); philosophy of religions (PhD); religion and literature (PhD); religions in America (PhD); religious ethics (PhD); theology (PhD). *Students:* 164 full-time (50 women); includes 18 minority (5 Black or African American, non-Hispanic/Latino; 8 Asian, non-Hispanic/Latino; 1 Hispanic/Latino; 4 Two or more races, non-Hispanic/Latino), 28 international. 185 applicants, 12% accepted, 18 enrolled. *Degree requirements:* For doctorate, 2 foreign languages, comprehensive exam, thesis/dissertation. *Entrance requirements:* For doctorate, GRE General Test. Additional exam requirements/recommendations for international students: Required—TOEFL (minimum score 600 paper-based; 104 iBT), IELTS (minimum score 7). *Application deadline:* For fall admission, 12/15 for domestic and international students. Application fee: $75. Electronic applications accepted. *Expenses: Tuition:* Full-time $46,899. *Required fees:* $347. *Financial support:* Fellowships, Federal Work-Study, institutionally sponsored loans, and scholarships/grants available. Financial award application deadline: 12/15; financial award applicants required to submit FAFSA. *Faculty research:* Anthropology and sociology of religions, history of religions, theology, religious ethics, philosophy of religions, Bible, history of Christianity/Judaism, Islamic studies, religions in America. *Unit head:* Dr. Margaret M. Mitchell, Dean/Professor of New Testament and Early Christian Literature, 773-702-8200. *Application contact:* John W. Howell, Coordinator for Recruiting and Admissions, 773-702-8249, Fax: 773-834-4581, E-mail: divinityadmissions@uchicago.edu.
Website: http://divinity.uchicago.edu/doctoral-program-phd

University of Colorado Boulder, Graduate School, College of Arts and Sciences, Department of Religious Studies, Boulder, CO 80309. Offers MA. *Faculty:* 8 full-time (3 women). *Students:* 21 full-time (7 women), 1 (woman) part-time; includes 1 minority (Two or more races, non-Hispanic/Latino), 2 international. Average age 28. 35 applicants, 60% accepted, 12 enrolled. In 2014, 3 master's awarded. Terminal master's awarded for partial completion of doctoral program. *Degree requirements:* For master's, one foreign language, comprehensive exam, thesis. *Entrance requirements:* For master's, minimum undergraduate GPA of 2.75. *Application deadline:* For fall admission, 1/15 for domestic students, 12/15 for international students; for spring admission, 10/15 for domestic students, 9/15 for international students. Applications are processed on a rolling basis. Application fee: $50 ($70 for international students). Electronic applications accepted. *Financial support:* In 2014–15, 52 students received support, including 7 fellowships (averaging $3,726 per year), 18 teaching assistantships with full and partial tuition reimbursements available (averaging $22,305 per year); institutionally sponsored loans, scholarships/grants, health care benefits, and unspecified assistantships also available. Financial award application deadline: 1/15; financial award applicants required to submit FAFSA. *Faculty research:* Religious studies, comparative religion, area studies (arts/humanities), arts/humanities/cultural activities.
Website: http://www.colorado.edu/ReligiousStudies

University of Denver, Division of Arts, Humanities and Social Sciences, Department of Religious Studies, Denver, CO 80208. Offers MA. *Faculty:* 6 full-time (3 women), 1 part-time/adjunct (0 women). *Students:* 1 full-time (0 women), 11 part-time (4 women); includes 1 minority (Hispanic/Latino), 1 international. Average age 28. 10 applicants, 90% accepted, 4 enrolled. In 2014, 6 master's awarded. *Degree requirements:* For master's, variable foreign language requirement, comprehensive exam, thesis. *Entrance requirements:* For master's, GRE General Test, bachelor's degree, transcripts, personal statement, writing sample, three letters of recommendation. Additional exam requirements/recommendations for international students: Required—TOEFL (minimum score 550 paper-based; 80 iBT). *Application deadline:* For fall admission, 2/15 priority date for domestic and international students. Applications are processed on a rolling basis. Application fee: $65. Electronic applications accepted. *Expenses:* Expenses: $1,199 per credit hour. *Financial support:* In 2014–15, 9 students received support. Federal Work-Study, scholarships/grants, and unspecified assistantships available. Financial award application deadline: 2/15; financial award applicants required to submit FAFSA. *Unit head:* Dr. Greg Robbins, Chair, 303-871-2751, Fax: 303-871-2750, E-mail: grobbins@du.edu. *Application contact:* Dr. Carl Raschke, Professor and Graduate Advisor, 303-871-3117, Fax: 303-871-2750, E-mail: rlgs@du.edu.
Website: http://www.du.edu/ahss/religiousstudies/index.html

University of Denver, DU-Iliff Joint PhD Program in Religious and Theological Studies, Denver, CO 80208. Offers PhD. Program jointly offered with Iliff School of Theology. Part-time programs available. *Faculty:* 13 full-time (6 women). *Students:* 34 full-time (16 women), 31 part-time (13 women); includes 13 minority (4 Black or African American, non-Hispanic/Latino; 1 American Indian or Alaska Native, non-Hispanic/Latino; 1 Asian, non-Hispanic/Latino; 5 Hispanic/Latino; 2 Two or more races, non-Hispanic/Latino). Average age 40. 39 applicants, 38% accepted, 9 enrolled. In 2014, 5 doctorates awarded. *Degree requirements:* For doctorate, one foreign language, comprehensive exam, thesis/dissertation. *Entrance requirements:* For doctorate, GRE General Test, transcripts, three letters of recommendation, personal statement, writing sample, research paper. Additional exam requirements/recommendations for international students: Required—TOEFL (minimum score 550 paper-based; 80 iBT). *Application deadline:* For fall admission, 1/1 priority date for domestic students. Application fee: $65. Electronic applications accepted. *Expenses:* Expenses: $826 per credit. *Financial support:* In 2014–15, 32 students received support, including 10 teaching assistantships with full and partial tuition reimbursements available (averaging $3,000 per year); scholarships/grants and unspecified assistantships also available. *Faculty research:* Religion and social change, theology, philosophy and cultural theory (including comparative religious study), Biblical interpretation. *Unit head:* Dr. Greg Robbins, Director, 303-765-3232. *Application contact:* Information Contact, 303-765-3117, E-mail: jointphd@iliff.edu.
Website: http://www.du.edu/duiliffjoint/

University of Detroit Mercy, College of Liberal Arts and Education, Department of Religious Studies, Detroit, MI 48221. Offers MA. *Degree requirements:* For master's, thesis or alternative. *Entrance requirements:* For master's, minimum GPA of 3.0. *Faculty research:* History of religions, textual studies (Old and New Testaments), ethical and cultural studies.

University of Florida, Graduate School, College of Liberal Arts and Sciences, Department of Religion, Gainesville, FL 32611-7410. Offers Jewish studies (MA); religion (MA, PhD); tropical conservation and development (MA, PhD); women's and gender studies (MA, PhD). Part-time programs available. *Faculty:* 10 full-time (3 women), 15 part-time/adjunct (7 women). *Students:* 21 full-time (13 women), 2 part-time (1 woman); includes 4 minority (3 Asian, non-Hispanic/Latino; 1 Hispanic/Latino), 3 international. Average age 33. 29 applicants, 48% accepted, 3 enrolled. In 2014, 3 master's, 2 doctorates awarded. *Degree requirements:* For master's, one foreign language, thesis optional; for doctorate, one foreign language, comprehensive exam, thesis/dissertation. *Entrance requirements:* For master's, GRE General Test, minimum GPA of 3.0. Additional exam requirements/recommendations for international students: Required—TOEFL (minimum score 550 paper-based; 80 iBT), IELTS (minimum score 6). *Application deadline:* For fall admission, 6/1 priority date for domestic students. Applications are processed on a rolling basis. Electronic applications accepted. *Financial support:* In 2014–15, 6 fellowships, 3 research assistantships, 18 teaching assistantships were awarded; Federal Work-Study and unspecified assistantships also available. Financial award applicants required to submit FAFSA. *Faculty research:* Religion in America, Christian thought, Islam, religions of India, comparative religion. *Unit head:* Manuel A. Vasquez, PhD, Professor and Chair, 352-392-1625, Fax: 352-392-7395, E-mail: manuelv@ufl.edu. *Application contact:* Terje Ostebo, PhD, Director of Graduate Studies, 352-392-2175, Fax: 352-392-7395, E-mail: manuelv@ufl.edu.
Website: http://religion.ufl.edu/

Religion

University of Georgia, Franklin College of Arts and Sciences, Department of Religion, Athens, GA 30602. Offers MA. *Degree requirements:* For master's, one foreign language, thesis. *Entrance requirements:* For master's, GRE General Test. Electronic applications accepted.

University of Hawaii at Manoa, Graduate Division, College of Arts and Humanities, Department of Religion, Honolulu, HI 96822. Offers MA. Part-time programs available. *Degree requirements:* For master's, one foreign language, thesis optional. *Entrance requirements:* For master's, GRE General Test. Additional exam requirements/recommendations for international students: Required—TOEFL (minimum score 600 paper-based; 100 iBT), IELTS (minimum score 7). *Faculty research:* Buddhism, East Asian religion, South Asian religion, Polynesian religion, Western religions.

University of Illinois at Urbana–Champaign, Graduate College, College of Liberal Arts and Sciences, School of Literatures, Cultures and Linguistics, Department of Religion, Champaign, IL 61820. Offers religious studies (MA). *Students:* 14 (3 women). *Degree requirements:* For master's, one foreign language, comprehensive exam, thesis optional. *Application deadline:* For fall admission, 1/1 for domestic students. Application fee: $70 ($90 for international students). *Unit head:* David Price, Head, 217-265-6199, E-mail: dhprice@illinois.edu. *Application contact:* Lynn Stanke, Office Support Specialist, 217-333-6269, E-mail: stanke@illinois.edu.
Website: http://www.religion.illinois.edu/

The University of Iowa, Graduate College, College of Liberal Arts and Sciences, Department of Religious Studies, Iowa City, IA 52242-1316. Offers MA, PhD. Terminal master's awarded for partial completion of doctoral program. *Degree requirements:* For master's, thesis optional, exam; for doctorate, comprehensive exam, thesis/dissertation. *Entrance requirements:* For master's and doctorate, GRE General Test, minimum GPA of 3.0. Additional exam requirements/recommendations for international students: Required—TOEFL (minimum score 550 paper-based; 81 iBT). Electronic applications accepted. *Faculty research:* Eastern and Western religion.

The University of Kansas, Graduate Studies, College of Liberal Arts and Sciences, Department of Religious Studies, Lawrence, KS 66045. Offers MA. Part-time programs available. *Faculty:* 11. *Students:* 10 full-time (5 women), 2 part-time; includes 4 minority (1 Black or African American, non-Hispanic/Latino; 1 American Indian or Alaska Native, non-Hispanic/Latino; 2 Two or more races, non-Hispanic/Latino), 2 international. Average age 28. 18 applicants, 44% accepted, 6 enrolled. In 2014, 7 master's awarded. *Degree requirements:* For master's, comprehensive exam, thesis optional. *Entrance requirements:* For master's, minimum GPA of 3.0. Additional exam requirements/recommendations for international students: Required—TOEFL. *Application deadline:* For fall admission, 2/1 for domestic and international students; for spring admission, 3/1 priority date for domestic and international students. Application fee: $55 ($65 for international students). Electronic applications accepted. *Financial support:* Fellowships, teaching assistantships with full tuition reimbursements, scholarships/grants, and unspecified assistantships available. Financial award application deadline: 1/1. *Faculty research:* Hinduism, Chinese Buddhism, Islam, Biblical literatures, American and indigenous people's religion. *Unit head:* Daniel B. Stevenson, Chair, 785-864-7258, E-mail: dbsteve@ku.edu. *Application contact:* Patricia Baudino, Administrative Associate, 785-864-4341, E-mail: pbaudino@ku.edu.
Website: https://religiousstudies.ku.edu/

University of Lethbridge, School of Graduate Studies, Lethbridge, AB T1K 3M4, Canada. Offers addictions counseling (M Sc); agricultural biotechnology (M Sc); agricultural studies (M Sc, MA); anthropology (MA); archaeology (M Sc, MA); art (MA, MFA); biochemistry (M Sc); biological sciences (M Sc); biomolecular science (PhD); biosystems and biodiversity (PhD); Canadian studies (MA); chemistry (M Sc); computer science (M Sc); computer science and geographical information science (M Sc); counseling (MC); counseling psychology (M Ed); dramatic arts (MA); earth, space, and physical science (PhD); economics (MA); education (MA); educational leadership (M Ed); English (MA); environmental science (M Sc); evolution and behavior (PhD); exercise science (M Sc); French (MA); French/German (MA); French/Spanish (MA); general education (M Ed); geography (M Sc, MA); German (MA); health sciences (M Sc); individualized multidisciplinary (M Sc, MA); kinesiology (M Sc, MA); management (M Sc), including accounting, finance, general management, human resource management and labor relations, information systems, international management, marketing, policy and strategy; mathematics (M Sc); modern languages (MA); music (M Mus, MA); Native American studies (MA); neuroscience (M Sc, PhD); new media (MA, MFA); nursing (M Sc, MN); philosophy (MA); physics (M Sc); political science (MA); psychology (M Sc, MA); religious studies (MA); sociology (MA); theatre and dramatic arts (MFA); theoretical and computational science (PhD); urban and regional studies (MA); women and gender studies (MA). Part-time and evening/weekend programs available. *Faculty:* 358. *Students:* 445 full-time (243 women), 116 part-time (72 women). Average age 31. 351 applicants, 26% accepted, 87 enrolled. In 2014, 129 master's, 13 doctorates awarded. *Degree requirements:* For master's, thesis (for some programs); for doctorate, comprehensive exam, thesis/dissertation. *Entrance requirements:* For master's, GMAT (for M Sc in management), bachelor's degree in related field, minimum GPA of 3.0 during previous 20 graded semester courses, 2 years' teaching or related experience (M Ed); for doctorate, master's degree, minimum graduate GPA of 3.5. Additional exam requirements/recommendations for international students: Required—TOEFL. Application fee: $100 Canadian dollars. *Financial support:* Fellowships, research assistantships, teaching assistantships, scholarships/grants, health care benefits, and unspecified assistantships available. *Faculty research:* Movement and brain plasticity, gibberellin physiology, photosynthesis, carbon cycling, molecular properties of main-group ring components. *Application contact:* School of Graduate Studies, 403-329-5194, E-mail: sgsinquiries@uleth.ca.
Website: http://www.uleth.ca/graduatestudies/

The University of Manchester, School of Arts, Histories and Cultures, Manchester, United Kingdom. Offers anthropology, media and performance (PhD); applied theatre professional (PhD); archaeology (PhD); art history and visual studies (PhD); arts management and cultural policy (PhD); classics and ancient history (PhD); composition (PhD); creative writing (PhD); drama (PhD); economic and social history (PhD); electroacoustic composition (PhD); English and American studies (PhD); history (PhD); humanitarianism and conflict response (PhD); museology (PhD); music (PhD); musicology (PhD); religions and theology (PhD).

University of Manitoba, Faculty of Graduate Studies, Faculty of Arts, Department of Religion, Winnipeg, MB R3T 2N2, Canada. Offers MA, PhD. MA offered jointly with The University of Winnipeg. *Degree requirements:* For master's, one foreign language, thesis or alternative.

University of Michigan, Horace H. Rackham School of Graduate Studies, College of Literature, Science, and the Arts, Department of Near Eastern Studies, Ann Arbor, MI 49286. Offers ancient Near Eastern studies (AM, PhD); Arabic for professional purposes (AM); Arabic language and literature (AM, PhD); Armenian studies (AM, PhD); Christianity in late antiquity (AM, PhD); Egyptology (AM, PhD); Hebrew Bible and ancient Israel (AM, PhD); Hebrew literature (AM, PhD); Islamic studies (AM, PhD); Jewish cultural studies (AM, PhD); Jewish mysticism (AM, PhD); Persian and Iranian studies (AM, PhD); Rabbinic literature (AM, PhD); Second Temple Judaism (AM, PhD); teaching of Arabic as a foreign language (AM); Turkish studies (AM, PhD). *Faculty:* 22 full-time (5 women), 1 (woman) part-time/adjunct. *Students:* 37 full-time (16 women); includes 2 minority (both Asian, non-Hispanic/Latino), 11 international. Average age 32. 72 applicants, 19% accepted, 6 enrolled. In 2014, 7 master's, 3 doctorates awarded. Terminal master's awarded for partial completion of doctoral program. *Degree requirements:* For master's, 2 foreign languages; for doctorate, 4 foreign languages, comprehensive exam, thesis/dissertation, preliminary exams, oral defense of dissertation. *Entrance requirements:* Additional exam requirements/recommendations for international students: Required—TOEFL (minimum score 560 paper-based; 84 iBT). *Application deadline:* For fall admission, 12/15 for domestic and international students. Application fee: $65 ($75 for international students). Electronic applications accepted. *Financial support:* In 2014–15, 22 students received support. Fellowships with full tuition reimbursements available, teaching assistantships with full tuition reimbursements available, scholarships/grants, health care benefits, unspecified assistantships, and spring/summer stipends available. Financial award application deadline: 12/15. *Faculty research:* Middle and Near Eastern literatures, languages, cultures from ancient times to the present. *Unit head:* Prof. Gottfried Hagen, Chair, 734-764-0314, E-mail: ghagen@umich.edu. *Application contact:* Student Services, 734-764-0315, E-mail: nes-gradservices@umich.edu.
Website: http://www.umich.edu/~neareast/

University of Minnesota, Twin Cities Campus, Graduate School, College of Liberal Arts, Department of Classical and Near Eastern Studies, Minneapolis, MN 55455-0213. Offers ancient and medieval art and archaeology (MA, PhD); classics (MA, PhD); Greek (MA, PhD); Latin (MA, PhD); religions in antiquity (MA). Part-time programs available. Terminal master's awarded for partial completion of doctoral program. *Degree requirements:* For master's, 2 foreign languages, comprehensive exam, thesis or alternative; for doctorate, variable foreign language requirement, comprehensive exam, thesis/dissertation. *Entrance requirements:* For master's and doctorate, GRE, 3 letters of recommendation, writing sample, copies of transcripts, personal statement. Additional exam requirements/recommendations for international students: Required—TOEFL. Electronic applications accepted. *Faculty research:* Greek and Latin literature, religions in antiquity, ancient Near East.

University of Missouri, Office of Research and Graduate Studies, College of Arts and Science, Department of Religious Studies, Columbia, MO 65211. Offers MA. *Faculty:* 9 full-time (2 women). *Students:* 7 full-time (2 women), 2 part-time (0 women); includes 2 minority (both Hispanic/Latino). Average age 27. 11 applicants, 45% accepted, 5 enrolled. In 2014, 6 master's awarded. *Entrance requirements:* For master's, GRE General Test, minimum GPA of 3.0. Additional exam requirements/recommendations for international students: Required—TOEFL (minimum score 550 paper-based; 79 iBT). *Application deadline:* For fall admission, 2/1 priority date for domestic students. Application fee: $55 ($75 for international students). Electronic applications accepted. *Financial support:* Fellowships with full tuition reimbursements, research assistantships, teaching assistantships with full tuition reimbursements, institutionally sponsored loans, health care benefits, and unspecified assistantships available. *Faculty research:* American religious history, Biblical studies, history of Christianity, religion and society, religions of East Asia, religions of indigenous peoples, religions of South Asia, women and religion. *Unit head:* Dr. Richard Callahan, Department Chair, 573-882-0060, E-mail: callahanrj@missouri.edu. *Application contact:* Dr. Signe Cohen, Director of Graduate Studies, 573-882-4769, E-mail: cohens@missouri.edu.
Website: http://religiousstudies.missouri.edu/programs/grad/

The University of North Carolina at Chapel Hill, Graduate School, College of Arts and Sciences, Department of Religious Studies, Chapel Hill, NC 27599. Offers MA, PhD. Terminal master's awarded for partial completion of doctoral program. *Degree requirements:* For master's, one foreign language, comprehensive exam, thesis; for doctorate, 2 foreign languages, comprehensive exam, thesis/dissertation. *Entrance requirements:* For master's and doctorate, GRE General Test, minimum GPA of 3.0. Additional exam requirements/recommendations for international students: Required—TOEFL. Electronic applications accepted. *Faculty research:* Religion.

The University of North Carolina at Charlotte, College of Liberal Arts and Sciences, Department of Religious Studies, Charlotte, NC 28223-0001. Offers MA. *Faculty:* 10 full-time (3 women). *Students:* 2 full-time (both women), 14 part-time (2 women); includes 1 minority (Black or African American, non-Hispanic/Latino). Average age 32. 6 applicants, 100% accepted, 3 enrolled. In 2014, 5 master's awarded. *Degree requirements:* For master's, comprehensive exam, thesis or alternative, portfolio. *Entrance requirements:* For master's, GRE or MAT, minimum GPA of 3.0, letters of reference. Additional exam requirements/recommendations for international students: Required—TOEFL (minimum score 557 paper-based; 83 iBT). *Application deadline:* For fall admission, 6/15 for domestic students, 5/1 for international students; for spring admission, 10/1 for domestic and international students. Application fee: $75. Electronic applications accepted. *Expenses:* Tuition, state resident: full-time $4008. Tuition, nonresident: full-time $16,295. *Required fees:* $2755. Tuition and fees vary according to course load and program. *Financial support:* In 2014–15, 4 students received support, including 4 teaching assistantships (averaging $9,500 per year); career-related internships or fieldwork, institutionally sponsored loans, scholarships/grants, and unspecified assistantships also available. Support available to part-time students. Financial award application deadline: 4/1; financial award applicants required to submit FAFSA. *Total annual research expenditures:* $4,160. *Unit head:* Dr. James D. Tabor, Chair, 704-687-5188, Fax: 704-687-3002, E-mail: jdtabor@uncc.edu. *Application contact:* Kathy B. Giddings, Director of Graduate Admissions, 704-687-5503, Fax: 704-687-1668, E-mail: gradadm@uncc.edu.
Website: http://www.religiousstudies.uncc.edu/

University of Notre Dame, Graduate School, College of Arts and Letters, Division of Humanities, Program in Early Christian Studies, Notre Dame, IN 46556. Offers MA. *Degree requirements:* For master's, 3 foreign languages, comprehensive exam. *Entrance requirements:* For master's, GRE General Test. Additional exam requirements/recommendations for international students: Required—TOEFL (minimum score 600 paper-based; 80 iBT). Electronic applications accepted. *Faculty research:* Early Christian theology, worship and scriptural interpretation; late antique and Byzantine history; art and culture; Greek and Latin literature.

University of Ottawa, Faculty of Graduate and Postdoctoral Studies, Faculty of Arts, Department of Classics and Religious Studies, Ottawa, ON K1N 6N5, Canada. Offers classical studies (MA); religious studies (PhD). *Degree requirements:* For master's, comprehensive exam, thesis or alternative; for doctorate, comprehensive exam, thesis/dissertation. *Entrance requirements:* For master's, honors degree or equivalent, minimum B average; for doctorate, master's degree, minimum B+ average. Electronic applications accepted. *Faculty research:* Religions in Canada, including Amerindian and Inuit religions; religion and culture; late antiquity.

University of Pennsylvania, School of Arts and Sciences, Graduate Group in Religious Studies, Philadelphia, PA 19104. Offers PhD. *Faculty:* 19 full-time (10 women), 9 part-time/adjunct (2 women). *Students:* 18 full-time (4 women), 5 part-time (3 women); includes 5 minority (3 Asian, non-Hispanic/Latino; 1 Hispanic/Latino; 1 Two or more races, non-Hispanic/Latino), 7 international. 38 applicants, 8% accepted, 2 enrolled. In 2014, 4 doctorates awarded. *Degree requirements:* For doctorate, thesis/dissertation,

approved specialty languages, preliminary and final exams. *Entrance requirements:* For doctorate, GRE. Additional exam requirements/recommendations for international students: Required—TOEFL. *Application deadline:* For fall admission, 12/1 priority date for domestic students. Application fee: $70. Electronic applications accepted. *Financial support:* In 2014–15, 10 students received support, including 2 fellowships, 1 research assistantship, 3 teaching assistantships; institutionally sponsored loans, scholarships/grants, traineeships, health care benefits, and unspecified assistantships also available. Financial award application deadline: 12/15. *Faculty research:* Judaism and Christianity (ancient, medieval, modern), Islam, Hinduism, Buddhism, modern religious thought. *Unit head:* Dr. Ralph M. Rosen, Associate Dean for Graduate Studies, 215-898-7156, Fax: 215-573-8068, E-mail: grad-dean@sas.upenn.edu. *Application contact:* Arts and Sciences Graduate Admissions, 215-573-5816, Fax: 215-573-8068, E-mail: gdasadmis@sas.upenn.edu.
Website: http://www.sas.upenn.edu/religious_studies/graduate

University of Regina, Faculty of Graduate Studies and Research, Faculty of Arts, Department of Religious Studies, Regina, SK S4S 0A2, Canada. Offers MA. Part-time programs available. *Faculty:* 10 full-time (4 women), 1 part-time/adjunct (0 women). *Students:* 3 full-time (2 women), 1 part-time (0 women). *Degree requirements:* For master's, thesis. *Entrance requirements:* Additional exam requirements/recommendations for international students: Required—TOEFL (minimum score 580 paper-based; 80 iBT), IELTS (minimum score 6.5), PTE (minimum score 59). *Application deadline:* Applications are processed on a rolling basis. Application fee: $100. Electronic applications accepted. *Expenses: Tuition, area resident:* Full-time $4900 Canadian dollars; part-time $837.65 Canadian dollars per semester. *International tuition:* $7900 Canadian dollars full-time. *Required fees:* $396 Canadian dollars; $86.90 Canadian dollars per semester. *Financial support:* In 2014–15, 1 fellowship (averaging $6,000 per year) was awarded; research assistantships, teaching assistantships, and scholarships/grants also available. Financial award application deadline: 6/15. *Faculty research:* Comparative religion; religious traditions; thematic and methodological studies; advanced studies in Christianity, Islam, and ancient religions. *Unit head:* Dr. William Arnal, Department Head, 306-585-5680, Fax: 306-585-4815, E-mail: william.arnal@uregina.ca.
Website: http://www.uregina.ca/arts/religious-studies

University of St. Thomas, Center for Faith and Culture, Houston, TX 77006-4696. Offers MA. Part-time programs available. *Faculty:* 5 full-time (1 woman), 3 part-time/adjunct (0 women). *Students:* 4 full-time (2 women), 24 part-time (17 women); includes 10 minority (4 Black or African American, non-Hispanic/Latino; 2 Asian, non-Hispanic/Latino; 3 Hispanic/Latino; 1 Two or more races, non-Hispanic/Latino). Average age 43. 6 applicants, 100% accepted, 6 enrolled. In 2014, 2 master's awarded. *Degree requirements:* For master's, service learning and leadership practicum, integrating presentation. *Entrance requirements:* For master's, bachelor's degree with minimum GPA of 2.75 or advanced degree; 3 letters of recommendation (professional or academic only); essay on student goals and expectations; interview with CFC admissions committee; writing sample; favorable review by admissions committee. Additional exam requirements/recommendations for international students: Required—TOEFL (minimum score 550 paper-based; 100 iBT), IELTS (minimum score 6.5). *Application deadline:* For fall admission, 7/1 for domestic students, 6/1 for international students; for spring admission, 11/1 for domestic students, 10/1 for international students. Applications are processed on a rolling basis. Application fee: $35. Electronic applications accepted. *Expenses: Tuition:* Full-time $20,124; part-time $1118 per credit hour. *Required fees:* $300; $82 per term. One-time fee: $100. Part-time tuition and fees vary according to course level, course load, campus/location and program. *Financial support:* In 2014–15, 16 students received support. Federal Work-Study, scholarships/grants, and state work-study, institutional employment available. Support available to part-time students. Financial award application deadline: 4/15; financial award applicants required to submit FAFSA. *Unit head:* Fr. Donald S. Nesti, Director, 713-942-5066, E-mail: cfc@stthom.edu. *Application contact:* Dr. Adam Martinez, Program Director, 713-942-5066, E-mail: cfc@stthom.edu.
Website: http://www.stthom.edu/Academics/Centers_of_Excellence/Center_for_Faith_Culture/Index.aqf

University of St. Thomas, Graduate Studies, College of Arts and Sciences, Master of Arts Program in Catholic Studies, St. Paul, MN 55105-1096. Offers MA. Part-time and evening/weekend programs available. *Degree requirements:* For master's, thesis. *Entrance requirements:* For master's, bachelor's degree with minimum GPA of 3.0, writing sample, personal statement, 3 letters of recommendation. Additional exam requirements/recommendations for international students: Required—TOEFL (minimum score 550 paper-based). Electronic applications accepted. Application fee is waived when completed online.

University of Saskatchewan, College of Graduate Studies and Research, College of Arts and Science, Department of Religion and Culture, Saskatoon, SK S7N 5A2, Canada. Offers MA. *Degree requirements:* For master's, thesis. *Entrance requirements:* Additional exam requirements/recommendations for international students: Required—TOEFL (minimum score 80 iBT); Recommended—IELTS (minimum score 6.5). Electronic applications accepted.

University of South Africa, College of Human Sciences, Pretoria, South Africa. Offers adult education (M Ed); African languages (MA, PhD); African politics (MA, PhD); Afrikaans (MA, PhD); ancient history (MA, PhD); ancient Near Eastern studies (MA, PhD); anthropology (MA, PhD); applied linguistics (MA); Arabic (MA, PhD); archaeology (MA); art history (MA); Biblical archaeology (MA); Biblical studies (M Th, D Th, PhD); Christian spirituality (M Th, D Th); church history (M Th, D Th); classical studies (MA, PhD); clinical psychology (MA); communication (MA, PhD); comparative education (M Ed, Ed D); consulting psychology (D Admin, D Com, PhD); curriculum studies (M Ed, Ed D); development studies (M Admin, MA, D Admin, PhD); didactics (M Ed, Ed D); education (M Tech); education management (M Ed, Ed D); educational psychology (M Ed); English (MA); environmental education (M Ed); French (MA, PhD); German (MA, PhD); Greek (MA); guidance and counseling (M Ed); health studies (MA, PhD), including health sciences education (MA), health services management (MA), medical and surgical nursing science (critical care general) (MA), midwifery and neonatal nursing science (MA), trauma and emergency care (MA); history (MA, PhD); history of education (Ed D); inclusive education (M Ed, Ed D); information and communications technology policy and regulation (MA); information science (MA, MIS, PhD); international politics (MA, PhD); Islamic studies (MA, PhD); Italian (MA, PhD); Judaica (MA, PhD); linguistics (MA, PhD); mathematical education (M Ed); mathematics education (MA); missiology (M Th, D Th); modern Hebrew (MA, PhD); musicology (MA, MMus, D Mus, PhD); natural science education (M Ed); New Testament (M Th, D Th); Old Testament (D Th); pastoral therapy (M Th, D Th); philosophy (MA); philosophy of education (M Ed, Ed D); politics (MA, PhD); Portuguese (MA, PhD); practical theology (M Th, D Th); psychology (MA, MS, PhD); psychology of education (M Ed, Ed D); public health (MA); religious studies (MA, D Th, PhD); Romance languages (MA); Russian (MA, PhD); Semitic languages (MA, PhD); social behavior studies in HIV/AIDS (MA); social science (mental health) (MA); social science in development studies (MA); social science in psychology (MA); social science in social work (MA); social science in sociology (MA); social work (MSW, DSW, PhD); socio-education (M Ed, Ed D); sociolinguistics (MA); sociology (MA, PhD); Spanish (MA, PhD); systematic theology (M Th, D Th); TESOL (teaching English to speakers of other languages) (MA); theological ethics (M Th, D Th); theory of literature (MA, PhD); urban ministries (D Th); urban ministry (M Th).

University of South Carolina, The Graduate School, College of Arts and Sciences, Department of Religious Studies, Columbia, SC 29208. Offers MA. Part-time programs available. *Degree requirements:* For master's, one foreign language, comprehensive exam, thesis. *Entrance requirements:* For master's, GRE General Test or MAT. Additional exam requirements/recommendations for international students: Required—TOEFL. Electronic applications accepted. *Faculty research:* Biblical and Near Eastern studies, theology and religious thought, religion and culture, South Asian religions, Islamic studies.

University of South Florida, College of Arts and Sciences, Department of Philosophy, Tampa, FL 33620-9951. Offers philosophy and religion (MA, PhD). Part-time and evening/weekend programs available. *Faculty:* 14 full-time (1 woman). *Students:* 48 full-time (10 women), 15 part-time (2 women); includes 10 minority (2 Black or African American, non-Hispanic/Latino; 3 Asian, non-Hispanic/Latino; 5 Hispanic/Latino), 1 international. Average age 31. 42 applicants, 67% accepted, 14 enrolled. In 2014, 9 master's, 7 doctorates awarded. Terminal master's awarded for partial completion of doctoral program. *Degree requirements:* For master's, comprehensive exam, thesis optional; for doctorate, comprehensive exam, thesis/dissertation. *Entrance requirements:* For master's and doctorate, GRE General Test, minimum GPA of 3.0, three letters of recommendation, 10-page philosophy writing sample, statement of philosophical interests. Additional exam requirements/recommendations for international students: Required—TOEFL (minimum score 550 paper-based; 79 iBT) or IELTS (minimum score 6.5). *Application deadline:* For fall admission, 2/15 for domestic and international students; for spring admission, 10/15 for domestic students, 8/1 for international students. Application fee: $30. Electronic applications accepted. *Financial support:* In 2014–15, 34 students received support, including 32 teaching assistantships with tuition reimbursements available (averaging $11,025 per year); unspecified assistantships also available. Financial award application deadline: 1/1. *Faculty research:* Medieval philosophy, early modern philosophy (seventeenth, eighteenth, and twentieth century Continental philosophy), feminist philosophy, social philosophy, ethics, philosophy of science. *Total annual research expenditures:* $128,071. *Unit head:* Dr. Roger Ariew, Professor and Chairperson, 813-974-8207, Fax: 813-974-5914, E-mail: rariew@usf.edu. *Application contact:* Dr. Joanne Waugh, Associate Professor, 813-974-5571, Fax: 813-974-5914, E-mail: jwaugh@usf.edu.
Website: http://philosophy.usf.edu/

University of South Florida, College of Arts and Sciences, Department of Religious Studies, Tampa, FL 33620-9951. Offers MA. Part-time and evening/weekend programs available. *Faculty:* 5 full-time (0 women). *Students:* 8 full-time (3 women), 1 (woman) part-time; includes 3 minority (1 Black or African American, non-Hispanic/Latino; 2 Hispanic/Latino), 1 international. Average age 36. 10 applicants, 60% accepted, 4 enrolled. In 2014, 3 master's awarded. *Degree requirements:* For master's, comprehensive exam, thesis optional. *Entrance requirements:* For master's, GRE General Test, minimum GPA of 3.0, three letters of recommendation, 1-3 page personal statement of intellectual interest, writing sample. Additional exam requirements/recommendations for international students: Required—TOEFL (minimum score 550 paper-based; 79 iBT) or IELTS (minimum score 6.5). *Application deadline:* For fall admission, 2/15 priority date for domestic students, 1/2 priority date for international students; for spring admission, 10/15 priority date for domestic students, 6/1 priority date for international students. Applications are processed on a rolling basis. Application fee: $30. Electronic applications accepted. *Financial support:* In 2014–15, 7 students received support, including 7 teaching assistantships with tuition reimbursements available (averaging $9,751 per year); unspecified assistantships also available. Financial award applicants required to submit FAFSA. *Faculty research:* Biblical studies, Biblical archaeology, Christianity, Judaism, Mysticism, philosophy of religion, Buddhism, Daoism, Confucianism, Hinduism, Chinese medicine, Vedic religion, Hinduism, religion in culture and society, African religion, African-American religion, Afro-Caribbean religion. *Total annual research expenditures:* $12,889. *Unit head:* Dr. James Cavendish, Professor and Interim Chairperson, 813-974-2758, Fax: 813-974-1853, E-mail: jcavendi@usf.edu. *Application contact:* Dr. Cass Fisher, Associate Professor and Graduate Program Director, 813-974-0445, Fax: 813-974-1853, E-mail: cass@usf.edu.
Website: http://religious-studies.usf.edu/

The University of Tennessee, Graduate School, College of Arts and Sciences, Department of Philosophy, Knoxville, TN 37996. Offers medical ethics (MA, PhD); philosophy (MA, PhD); religious studies (MA). Part-time programs available. *Degree requirements:* For master's, thesis or alternative; for doctorate, one foreign language, thesis/dissertation. *Entrance requirements:* For master's and doctorate, GRE General Test, minimum GPA of 2.7. Additional exam requirements/recommendations for international students: Required—TOEFL. Electronic applications accepted.

University of the Cumberlands, Program in Christian Studies, Williamsburg, KY 40769-1372. Offers MA. Part-time and evening/weekend programs available. Postbaccalaureate distance learning degree programs offered (no on-campus study). *Entrance requirements:* For master's, GRE or MAT. Additional exam requirements/recommendations for international students: Required—TOEFL. Electronic applications accepted.

University of the Incarnate Word, School of Graduate Studies and Research, College of Humanities, Arts, and Social Sciences, Pastoral Institute, San Antonio, TX 78209-6397. Offers MA. Part-time programs available. *Faculty:* 3 full-time (2 women). *Students:* 10 part-time (8 women); includes 6 minority (all Hispanic/Latino). Average age 49. 3 applicants, 67% accepted, 1 enrolled. In 2014, 2 master's awarded. *Degree requirements:* For master's, pastoral project. *Entrance requirements:* For master's, recommendation letters, 12 credit hours of related undergraduate coursework. Additional exam requirements/recommendations for international students: Required—TOEFL (minimum score 560 paper-based; 83 iBT). *Application deadline:* Applications are processed on a rolling basis. Application fee: $20. Electronic applications accepted. *Expenses: Tuition:* Part-time $815 per credit hour. *Required fees:* $86 per credit hour. *Financial support:* Federal Work-Study, scholarships/grants, and tuition waivers (partial) available. Financial award applicants required to submit FAFSA. *Unit head:* Sr. Eilish Ryan, Chair, 210-829-3871, Fax: 210-829-3880, E-mail: eryan@uiwtx.edu. *Application contact:* Andrea Cyterski-Acosta, Dean of Enrollment, 210-829-6005, Fax: 210-829-3921, E-mail: admis@uiwtx.edu.
Website: http://www.uiw.edu/pastoral/index.htm

University of the West, Department of Psychology, Rosemead, CA 91770. Offers Buddhist psychology (MA); multicultural counseling (MA). Part-time and evening/weekend programs available. *Degree requirements:* For master's, fieldwork; comprehensive exam or thesis.

University of the West, Department of Religious Studies, Rosemead, CA 91770. Offers Buddhism (PhD); Buddhist studies (MA); comparative religions (PhD); comparative religious studies (MA); religious studies (PhD). Part-time and evening/weekend programs available. *Degree requirements:* For master's, thesis or comprehensive exam, competency in language associated with Buddhist Canon literature; for doctorate, 2

foreign languages, comprehensive exam, thesis/dissertation. *Entrance requirements:* For master's and doctorate, BA in religious studies, theology, philosophy or equivalent from an accredited university; official transcript; three letters of recommendation; essay. Additional exam requirements/recommendations for international students: Required—TOEFL, IELTS.

University of Toronto, School of Graduate Studies, Faculty of Arts and Science, Centre for the Study of Religion, Toronto, ON M5S 2J7, Canada. Offers MA, PhD. Part-time programs available. *Degree requirements:* For master's, one foreign language, research paper, language examination; for doctorate, 2 foreign languages, thesis/dissertation, language examinations, general examinations, oral examination. *Entrance requirements:* For master's, BA in religion or a related field; minimum A- average in final year, 3 letters of recommendation, resume; for doctorate, MA in religion, minimum average of A- in MA courses with no individual grade below a B, 3 letters of recommendation, resume, brief writing sample. Additional exam requirements/recommendations for international students: Required—TOEFL (minimum score 580 paper-based; 93 iBT), TWE (minimum score 5). Electronic applications accepted.

University of Valley Forge, Program in Christian Leadership, Phoenixville, PA 19460. Offers MA. *Degree requirements:* For master's, project.

University of Valley Forge, Program in Worship Studies, Phoenixville, PA 19460. Offers MA.

University of Virginia, College and Graduate School of Arts and Sciences, Department of Religious Studies, Charlottesville, VA 22903. Offers MA, PhD. *Faculty:* 31 full-time (10 women). *Students:* 78 full-time (27 women), 2 part-time (1 woman); includes 6 minority (2 Black or African American, non-Hispanic/Latino; 2 Asian, non-Hispanic/Latino; 2 Hispanic/Latino), 11 international. Average age 32. 168 applicants, 29% accepted, 15 enrolled. In 2014, 16 master's, 14 doctorates awarded. *Degree requirements:* For master's, one foreign language, thesis optional; for doctorate, 2 foreign languages, comprehensive exam, thesis/dissertation. *Entrance requirements:* For master's and doctorate, GRE General Test, 3 letters of recommendation. Additional exam requirements/recommendations for international students: Required—TOEFL (minimum score 600 paper-based; 90 iBT), IELTS (minimum score 7). *Application deadline:* For fall admission, 12/1 for domestic students, 12/3 for international students. Applications are processed on a rolling basis. Application fee: $60. Electronic applications accepted. *Expenses:* Tuition, state resident: full-time $14,164; part-time $349 per credit hour. Tuition, nonresident: full-time $23,722; part-time $1300 per credit hour. *Required fees:* $2514. *Financial support:* Fellowships and teaching assistantships available. Financial award applicants required to submit FAFSA. *Unit head:* Kurtis Schaeffer, Chair, 434-924-6705, Fax: 434-924-1467, E-mail: ks6bb@virginia.edu. *Application contact:* Willis Jenkins, Director of Graduate Program, 434-924-6705, Fax: 434-924-1467, E-mail: wjj2c@virginia.edu.
Website: http://religiousstudies.virginia.edu/

University of Washington, Graduate School, College of Arts and Sciences, Department of Asian Languages and Literature, Seattle, WA 98195. Offers Buddhist studies (MA, PhD); Chinese language and literature (MA, PhD); Japanese language and literature (MA, PhD); Korean language and literature (MA, PhD); South Asian language and literature (MA, PhD). *Degree requirements:* For master's, 2 foreign languages, general exam, thesis or 2 research papers; for doctorate, 3 foreign languages, thesis/dissertation, general exam. *Entrance requirements:* For master's, GRE, minimum GPA of 3.0; for doctorate, GRE, master's degree in related field, minimum GPA of 3.0. Additional exam requirements/recommendations for international students: Required—TOEFL. Electronic applications accepted. *Faculty research:* Textual, linguistic, philological, and literary study of languages and literatures of Asia.

University of Washington, Graduate School, College of Arts and Sciences, Henry M. Jackson School of International Studies, Comparative Religion Program, Seattle, WA 98195. Offers MAIS. *Degree requirements:* For master's, 2 foreign languages. *Entrance requirements:* For master's, GRE General Test, minimum GPA of 3.0 in last two years. Additional exam requirements/recommendations for international students: Required—TOEFL (minimum score 500 paper-based; 92 iBT), IELTS (minimum score 7). Electronic applications accepted.

University of Waterloo, Graduate Studies, Faculty of Arts, Department of Religious Studies, Waterloo, ON N2L 3G1, Canada. Offers religious diversity in North America (PhD). *Degree requirements:* For doctorate, thesis/dissertation. *Entrance requirements:* Additional exam requirements/recommendations for international students: Required—TOEFL. Electronic applications accepted. *Faculty research:* Religious diversity in North America.

The University of Winnipeg, Graduate Studies, Department of Religious Studies, Winnipeg, MB R3B 2E9, Canada. Offers MA. Program offered jointly with University of Manitoba. Part-time programs available. *Faculty research:* Religion and culture, social ethics, religious liberalism, history of Canaanite and Israelite religion, literary criticism of the Hebrew Bible.

Vancouver School of Theology, Graduate and Professional Programs, Vancouver, BC V6T 1L4, Canada. Offers indigenous and inter-religious studies (MA, Th M); theological studies (MATS, Diploma); theology (M Div, Th M). *Accreditation:* ATS. Part-time programs available. Postbaccalaureate distance learning degree programs offered (minimal on-campus study). *Degree requirements:* For master's, comprehensive exam (for some programs), thesis (for some programs); for Diploma, one foreign language, thesis. *Entrance requirements:* Additional exam requirements/recommendations for international students: Required—TOEFL (minimum score 80 paper-based); Recommended—IELTS (minimum score 6.5). Electronic applications accepted. *Faculty research:* Old Testament studies, pastoral theology, New Testament studies, field education, church history, systematic theology, spirituality.

Vanderbilt University, Graduate School, Department of Religion, Nashville, TN 37240-1001. Offers MA, PhD. *Faculty:* 7 full-time (3 women). *Students:* 83 full-time (37 women); includes 18 minority (12 Black or African American, non-Hispanic/Latino; 4 Asian, non-Hispanic/Latino; 2 Hispanic/Latino), 9 international. Average age 34. 160 applicants, 9% accepted, 10 enrolled. In 2014, 7 master's, 10 doctorates awarded. *Degree requirements:* For master's, one foreign language, thesis; for doctorate, 2 foreign languages, thesis/dissertation, final and qualifying exams. *Entrance requirements:* For master's and doctorate, GRE General Test. Additional exam requirements/recommendations for international students: Required—TOEFL (minimum score 570 paper-based; 88 iBT). *Application deadline:* For fall admission, 1/15 for domestic and international students. Electronic applications accepted. *Expenses: Tuition:* Full-time $42,768; part-time $1782 per credit hour. *Required fees:* $422. One-time fee: $30 full-time. *Financial support:* Fellowships with full and partial tuition reimbursements, teaching assistantships with full and partial tuition reimbursements, Federal Work-Study, institutionally sponsored loans, health care benefits, and tuition waivers (full and partial) available. Support available to part-time students. Financial award application deadline: 1/15; financial award applicants required to submit CSS PROFILE or FAFSA. *Faculty research:* Hebrew Bible, New Testament, church history, theology, ethics. *Unit head:* Dr. Jimmy Byrd, Director of Graduate Studies/Assistant Dean, 615-343-3976, Fax: 615-343-9957, E-mail: james.p.byrd@vanderbilt.edu. *Application contact:* Marie McEntire, Administrative Assistant, 615-322-2776, Fax: 615-343-9957, E-mail: marie.mcentire@vanderbilt.edu.
Website: http://divinity.vanderbilt.edu/degrees/graduate/index.php

Vanguard University of Southern California, Graduate Programs in Religion, Costa Mesa, CA 92626-9601. Offers leadership studies (MA); theological studies (MTS). Part-time and evening/weekend programs available. *Degree requirements:* For master's, comprehensive exam (for some programs), thesis (for some programs). *Entrance requirements:* For master's, minimum GPA of 3.0 (MA), 2.5 (MTS). Additional exam requirements/recommendations for international students: Required—TOEFL (minimum score 550 paper-based; 79 iBT). Electronic applications accepted. *Expenses:* Contact institution. *Faculty research:* Narrative theology, ecumenism and Pentecost, leadership studies.

Virginia University of Lynchburg, Graduate Programs, Lynchburg, VA 24501-6417. Offers Christian ministry (M Div).

Wake Forest University, Graduate School of Arts and Sciences, Department of Religion, Winston-Salem, NC 27109. Offers MA. *Accreditation:* ACIPE. Part-time programs available. *Degree requirements:* For master's, one foreign language, thesis. *Entrance requirements:* For master's, GRE General Test. Additional exam requirements/recommendations for international students: Required—TOEFL (minimum score 79 iBT). Electronic applications accepted. *Faculty research:* Christian origins, biblical archaeology, psychology and religion, religion and literature.

Washington Adventist University, Program in Religion, Takoma Park, MD 20912. Offers MAR. Part-time programs available. *Entrance requirements:* Additional exam requirements/recommendations for international students: Required—TOEFL (minimum score 550 paper-based), IELTS (minimum score 5).

Washington University in St. Louis, Graduate School of Arts and Sciences, Department of Jewish, Islamic, and Near Eastern Languages and Cultures, St. Louis, MO 63130-4899. Offers Islamic and Near Eastern studies (MA); Jewish studies (MA). *Degree requirements:* For master's, one foreign language, thesis (for some programs). *Entrance requirements:* For master's, GRE General Test. Additional exam requirements/recommendations for international students: Required—TOEFL. Electronic applications accepted. *Faculty research:* Islamic and Near Eastern studies (Islamic history, Arabic language and literature, modern Middle East history), Jewish studies (Hebrew Bible, Rabbinic literature, Jewish history, modern Hebrew literature).

Wayland Baptist University, Graduate Programs, Programs in Religion, Plainview, TX 79072-6998. Offers Christian ministry (MCM); divinity (M Div); religion (MA). Part-time and evening/weekend programs available. Postbaccalaureate distance learning degree programs offered (no on-campus study). *Faculty:* 15 full-time (1 woman), 12 part-time/adjunct (0 women). *Students:* 1 full-time (0 women), 99 part-time (23 women); includes 51 minority (25 Black or African American, non-Hispanic/Latino; 1 American Indian or Alaska Native, non-Hispanic/Latino; 4 Asian, non-Hispanic/Latino; 17 Hispanic/Latino; 1 Native Hawaiian or other Pacific Islander, non-Hispanic/Latino; 3 Two or more races, non-Hispanic/Latino). Average age 43. 45 applicants, 60% accepted, 12 enrolled. In 2014, 16 master's awarded. *Degree requirements:* For master's, comprehensive exam. *Entrance requirements:* For master's, GRE or MAT, minimum GPA of 3.0; letter of endorsement from Christian congregation, one academic and one personal letter of recommendation (for M Div). Additional exam requirements/recommendations for international students: Required—TOEFL (minimum score 500 paper-based; 61 iBT). *Application deadline:* Applications are processed on a rolling basis. Application fee: $50. Electronic applications accepted. *Expenses: Tuition:* Full-time $8910; part-time $495 per credit hour. *Required fees:* $970; $495 per credit hour. $485 per semester. *Financial support:* Federal Work-Study, institutionally sponsored loans, and scholarships/grants available. Support available to part-time students. Financial award application deadline: 5/1; financial award applicants required to submit FAFSA. *Unit head:* Dr. Paul Sadler, Chairman, 806-291-1160, Fax: 806-291-1969, E-mail: sadlerp@wbu.edu. *Application contact:* Amanda Stanton, Coordinator of Graduate Studies, 806-291-3423, Fax: 806-291-1950, E-mail: stanton@wbu.edu.

Wesley Biblical Seminary, Graduate Programs, Jackson, MS 39206. Offers apologetics (MA); Biblical languages (M Div); Biblical literature (MA); Christian studies (MA); context and mission (M Div); honors research (M Div); interpretation (M Div); ministry (M Div); spiritual formation (M Div); teaching (M Div); theology (MA). *Accreditation:* ATS. Part-time programs available. *Degree requirements:* For master's, thesis. *Entrance requirements:* Additional exam requirements/recommendations for international students: Required—TOEFL. Electronic applications accepted. *Faculty research:* Patristics, missiology, culture, hermeneutics.

Western Michigan University, Graduate College, College of Arts and Sciences, Department of Comparative Religion, Kalamazoo, MI 49008. Offers MA, Graduate Certificate. *Degree requirements:* For master's, one foreign language, thesis optional. *Application deadline:* For fall admission, 2/15 for domestic students. *Financial support:* Application deadline: 2/15. *Application contact:* Admissions and Orientation, 269-387-2000, Fax: 269-387-2096.

Western Seminary, Graduate Programs, Program in Biblical and Theological Studies, Portland, OR 97215-3367. Offers biblical and theological studies (MA, G Dip); biblical studies (Certificate); theology (Th M). *Accreditation:* ATS. Part-time and evening/weekend programs available. *Degree requirements:* For master's, thesis or alternative, practicum. *Entrance requirements:* Additional exam requirements/recommendations for international students: Required—TOEFL.

Westminster Seminary California, Programs in Theology, Escondido, CA 92027-4128. Offers Biblical studies (MA); historical theology (MA); theological studies (M Div, MA). *Accreditation:* ATS. Part-time and evening/weekend programs available. *Degree requirements:* For master's, 2 foreign languages, thesis (for some programs). *Entrance requirements:* For master's, 2 letters of reference. Additional exam requirements/recommendations for international students: Required—TOEFL (minimum score 570 paper-based; 89 iBT), TWE (minimum score 4.5). *Faculty research:* Neo-paganism, New Testament background, eschatology, Protestant scholasticism, Ezekiel.

Westminster Theological Seminary, Graduate and Professional Programs, Philadelphia, PA 19118. Offers apologetics (Th M); Biblical and urban studies (Certificate); Biblical counseling (MA); biblical studies (MAR); Christian studies (Certificate); church history (Th M); counseling (M Div); general studies (M Div, MAR); hermeneutics and Bible interpretations (PhD); historical and theological studies (PhD); historical theology (Th M); New Testament (Th M); Old Testament (Th M); pastoral counseling (D Min); pastoral ministry (M Div, D Min); systematic theology (Th M); theological studies (MAR); urban missions (M Div, MA, MAR, D Min). *Accreditation:* ATS. Part-time programs available. Terminal master's awarded for partial completion of doctoral program. *Degree requirements:* For master's, thesis (for some programs); for doctorate, 4 foreign languages, comprehensive exam (for some programs), thesis/dissertation. *Entrance requirements:* For doctorate, GRE General Test. Additional exam requirements/recommendations for international students: Required—TOEFL, TWE.

Wilfrid Laurier University, Faculty of Graduate and Postdoctoral Studies, Faculty of Arts, Department of Religion and Culture, Waterloo, ON N2L 3C5, Canada. Offers religion and culture (MA); religious diversity of North America (PhD). Part-time programs available. *Degree requirements:* For master's, thesis optional; for doctorate, thesis/

dissertation. *Entrance requirements:* For master's, honors BA or the equivalent in religious studies or other interdisciplinary social science or humanities program, minimum B average in overall undergraduate course work, B+ average in the undergraduate major; for doctorate, MA in religious studies, minimum A- average. Additional exam requirements/recommendations for international students: Required—TOEFL (minimum score 89 iBT). Electronic applications accepted. *Faculty research:* Religious diversity in North America.

WON Institute of Graduate Studies, Applied Meditation Studies Program, Glenside, PA 19038. Offers MAMS, Certificate. Part-time and evening/weekend programs available. *Faculty:* 2 full-time (1 woman), 1 (woman) part-time/adjunct. *Students:* 3 full-time (1 woman), 7 part-time (4 women); includes 2 minority (both Black or African American, non-Hispanic/Latino), 2 international. 3 applicants, 100% accepted, 2 enrolled. In 2014, 1 master's awarded. *Degree requirements:* For master's, project. *Entrance requirements:* For master's, bachelor's degree; for Certificate, master's or bachelor's degree with significant professional experience. *Application deadline:* For fall admission, 6/15 for domestic students, 2/15 for international students. Applications are processed on a rolling basis. Application fee: $75. *Unit head:* Dr. Glenn Wallis, Chair, 215-884-8942, Fax: 215-884-9002, E-mail: glenn.wallis@woninstitute.edu. *Application contact:* Jennifer Cake, Enrollment Management Counselor, 215-884-8942 Ext. 219, E-mail: jennifer.cake@woninstitute.edu.
Website: http://woninstitute.edu/index.php?page-applied-meditation-studies

WON Institute of Graduate Studies, Won Buddhist Studies Program, Glenside, PA 19038. Offers MA. Part-time programs available. *Faculty:* 3 full-time (2 women). *Students:* 4 full-time (2 women), 4 part-time (2 women); includes 2 minority (both Black or African American, non-Hispanic/Latino), 5 international. Average age 36. 4 applicants, 75% accepted, 3 enrolled. In 2014, 2 master's awarded. *Degree requirements:* For master's, comprehensive exam, comprehensive ordination exam or thesis. *Entrance requirements:* For master's, bachelor's degree or one-year preparatory course in Won Buddhist studies. Additional exam requirements/recommendations for international students: Required—TOEFL (minimum score 550 paper-based; 79 iBT). *Application deadline:* For fall admission, 6/15 for domestic students, 2/15 for

international students. Applications are processed on a rolling basis. Application fee: $75. *Financial support:* In 2014–15, 7 students received support. Application deadline: 8/1. *Faculty research:* Environmental ethics, the concept of religion. *Unit head:* Rev. Dr. Sanghyeon Cheon, Chair, 215-884-8942, E-mail: sanghyeon.cheon@woninstitute.edu. *Application contact:* Jennifer Cake, Enrollment Management Counselor, 215-884-8942 Ext. 219, E-mail: jennifer.cake@woninstitute.edu.
Website: http://woninstitute.edu/index.php?page-won-buddist-studies

Wycliffe College, Division of Advanced Degree Studies, Toronto, ON M5S 1H7, Canada. Offers MA, Th M, D Min, PhD, Th D. PhD, D Min, MA offered jointly with Toronto School of Theology; Th D, Th M with University of Toronto. *Accreditation:* ATS (one or more programs are accredited). Part-time programs available. Terminal master's awarded for partial completion of doctoral program. *Degree requirements:* For master's, 2 foreign languages, thesis (for some programs); for doctorate, 3 foreign languages, thesis/dissertation. *Entrance requirements:* Additional exam requirements/recommendations for international students: Required—TOEFL (minimum score 600 paper-based). *Expenses:* Contact institution. *Faculty research:* Old and New Testament, doctrine, ethics, philosophy, history.

Wycliffe College, Division of Basic Degree Studies, Toronto, ON M5S 1H7, Canada. Offers Christian Studies (Diploma); theology (M Div, M Rel, MTS). M Div, M Rel, MTS offered jointly with University of Toronto. *Accreditation:* ATS. Part-time programs available. *Degree requirements:* For master's, one foreign language, thesis. *Entrance requirements:* Additional exam requirements/recommendations for international students: Required—TOEFL (minimum score 580 paper-based).

Yale University, Graduate School of Arts and Sciences, Department of Religious Studies, New Haven, CT 06520. Offers PhD. *Degree requirements:* For doctorate, 2 foreign languages, thesis/dissertation. *Entrance requirements:* For doctorate, GRE General Test.

Yeshiva Derech Chaim, Graduate Program, Brooklyn, NY 11218. Offers PhD. *Accreditation:* AARTS.

Theology

Abilene Christian University, Graduate School, College of Biblical Studies, Graduate School of Theology, Program in Divinity, Abilene, TX 79699-9100. Offers M Div. *Accreditation:* ATS. Part-time and evening/weekend programs available. *Students:* 21 full-time (6 women), 19 part-time (3 women); includes 4 minority (2 Black or African American, non-Hispanic/Latino; 2 Hispanic/Latino), 3 international. 28 applicants, 43% accepted, 7 enrolled. In 2014, 5 master's awarded. *Degree requirements:* For master's, comprehensive exam, e-portfolio review. *Entrance requirements:* Additional exam requirements/recommendations for international students: Required—TOEFL (minimum score 550 paper-based; 90 iBT), IELTS (minimum score 6.5), PTE. *Application deadline:* For fall admission, 4/1 priority date for domestic students; for spring admission, 11/1 for domestic students. Applications are processed on a rolling basis. Application fee: $50. Electronic applications accepted. *Expenses:* Expenses: Contact institution. *Financial support:* In 2014–15, 6 students received support. Scholarships/grants available. Financial award applicants required to submit FAFSA. *Unit head:* Dr. Tim Sensing, Graduate Advisor, 325-674-3792, Fax: 325-674-6716, E-mail: sensingt@acu.edu. *Application contact:* Corey Patterson, Director of Graduate Admission and Recruiting, 325-674-6566, Fax: 325-674-6717, E-mail: gradinfo@acu.edu.

Abilene Christian University, Graduate School, College of Biblical Studies, Graduate School of Theology, Program in New Testament, Abilene, TX 79699-9100. Offers MA. *Accreditation:* ATS. Part-time programs available. *Students:* 3 full-time (0 women). 4 applicants, 25% accepted. In 2014, 1 master's awarded. *Degree requirements:* For master's, comprehensive exam, thesis. *Entrance requirements:* Additional exam requirements/recommendations for international students: Required—TOEFL (minimum score 550 paper-based; 90 iBT), IELTS (minimum score 6.5), PTE. *Application deadline:* For fall admission, 4/1 priority date for domestic students; for spring admission, 11/1 for domestic students. Applications are processed on a rolling basis. Application fee: $50. Electronic applications accepted. *Expenses:* Expenses: Contact institution. *Financial support:* In 2014–15, 1 student received support. Application deadline: 4/1; applicants required to submit FAFSA. *Unit head:* Dr. James Thompson, Graduate Advisor, 325-674-3781, Fax: 325-674-6180, E-mail: thompsonja@acu.edu. *Application contact:* Corey Patterson, Director of Graduate Admission and Recruiting, 325-674-6566, Fax: 325-674-6717, E-mail: gradinfo@acu.edu.

Abilene Christian University, Graduate School, College of Biblical Studies, Graduate School of Theology, Program in Old Testament, Abilene, TX 79699-9100. Offers MA. Part-time programs available. *Students:* 1 full-time (0 women), 3 part-time (1 woman). 2 applicants, 50% accepted, 1 enrolled. In 2014, 1 master's awarded. *Degree requirements:* For master's, comprehensive exam, thesis. *Entrance requirements:* Additional exam requirements/recommendations for international students: Required—TOEFL (minimum score 550 paper-based; 90 iBT), IELTS (minimum score 6.5), PTE. *Application deadline:* For fall admission, 4/1 priority date for domestic students; for spring admission, 11/1 for domestic students. Applications are processed on a rolling basis. Application fee: $50. Electronic applications accepted. *Expenses:* Expenses: Contact institution. *Financial support:* Scholarships/grants available. Financial award application deadline: 4/1; financial award applicants required to submit FAFSA. *Unit head:* Dr. Mark Hamilton, Graduate Advisor, 325-674-3765, Fax: 325-674-6180, E-mail: wmh00c@acu.edu. *Application contact:* Corey Patterson, Director of Graduate Admission and Recruiting, 325-674-6566, Fax: 325-674-6717, E-mail: gradinfo@acu.edu.

Abilene Christian University, Graduate School, College of Biblical Studies, Graduate School of Theology, Program in Theology, Abilene, TX 79699-9100. Offers MA. Part-time programs available. *Students:* 7 full-time (2 women), 7 part-time (2 women); includes 3 minority (1 Black or African American, non-Hispanic/Latino; 1 Asian, non-Hispanic/Latino; 1 Hispanic/Latino), 1 international. 10 applicants, 40% accepted, 4 enrolled. In 2014, 1 master's awarded. *Degree requirements:* For master's, comprehensive exam, thesis. *Entrance requirements:* Additional exam requirements/recommendations for international students: Required—TOEFL (minimum score 550 paper-based; 90 iBT), IELTS (minimum score 6.5), PTE. *Application deadline:* For fall admission, 4/1 priority date for domestic students; for spring admission, 11/1 for domestic students. Applications are processed on a rolling basis. Application fee: $50. Electronic applications accepted. *Expenses:* Expenses: Contact institution. *Financial support:* Application deadline: 4/1; applicants required to submit FAFSA. *Unit head:* Dr. Frederick Aquino, Graduate Advisor, 325-674-3730, Fax: 325-674-6180, E-mail:

frederick.aquino@acu.edu. *Application contact:* Corey Patterson, Director of Graduate Admission and Recruiting, 325-674-6566, Fax: 325-674-6717, E-mail: gradinfo@acu.edu.

Acadia University, Divinity College, Wolfville, NS B4P 2R6, Canada. Offers divinity (M Div); theology (MA, D Min), including Biblical studies (MA), church history (MA), theology (MA). *Accreditation:* ATS. Part-time programs available. *Degree requirements:* For master's, variable foreign language requirement, thesis (for some programs); for doctorate, one foreign language, comprehensive exam, thesis/dissertation. *Entrance requirements:* For doctorate, minimum GPA of 3.0, 3 years ministry experience. Additional exam requirements/recommendations for international students: Required—TOEFL. *Expenses:* Contact institution. *Faculty research:* Biblical canon, Jesus, Dead Sea Scrolls, Baptist studies, Old Testament-Septuagint.

Ambrose University, Ambrose Seminary, Calgary, AB T3H 0L5, Canada. Offers Chinese ministries (Certificate); Christian studies (Certificate); intercultural ministries (M Div, Certificate); leadership and ministry (Diploma); pastoral ministries (M Div). *Accreditation:* ATS (one or more programs are accredited). Part-time programs available. Postbaccalaureate distance learning degree programs offered (minimal on-campus study). *Faculty:* 7 full-time (0 women), 24 part-time/adjunct (2 women). *Students:* 55 full-time (18 women), 128 part-time (64 women); includes 86 minority (3 Black or African American, non-Hispanic/Latino; 1 American Indian or Alaska Native, non-Hispanic/Latino; 82 Asian, non-Hispanic/Latino). Average age 41. *Degree requirements:* For master's, variable foreign language requirement, internship. *Entrance requirements:* For master's, undergraduate degree from other accredited university or bible college, minimum GPA of 2.0. Additional exam requirements/recommendations for international students: Required—TOEFL (minimum score 560 paper-based, 83 iBT) or IELTS (minimum score 6.5). *Application deadline:* For fall admission, 7/15 for domestic students, 3/1 for international students; for winter admission, 11/15 for domestic students, 7/1 for international students. Applications are processed on a rolling basis. Application fee: $70 ($100 for international students). Electronic applications accepted. *Financial support:* Career-related internships or fieldwork and scholarships/grants available. Support available to part-time students. Financial award application deadline: 3/30. *Faculty research:* Evangelicalism and sociology, missiological trends, chaplaincy, intertestamental studies, postmodernism. *Unit head:* Dr. Paul Spilsbury, Vice-President of Academic Affairs, 403-410-2917, Fax: 403-571-2556, E-mail: pspilsbury@ambrose.edu. *Application contact:* Kalie Eeles, Enrollment Advisor, 403-410-2954, Fax: 403-571-2556, E-mail: enrolment@ambrose.edu.
Website: https://ambrose.edu/seminary

American Baptist Seminary of the West, Graduate and Professional Programs, Berkeley, CA 94704-3029. Offers community leadership (MA); theology (M Div, MA). MA program in theology offered jointly with Graduate Theological Union. *Accreditation:* ACIPE; ATS (one or more programs are accredited). Part-time and evening/weekend programs available. Postbaccalaureate distance learning degree programs offered (minimal on-campus study). *Entrance requirements:* Additional exam requirements/recommendations for international students: Required—TOEFL (minimum score 550 paper-based). Electronic applications accepted.

American Jewish University, Ziegler School of Rabbinic Studies, Bel Air, CA 90077-1599. Offers MARS. *Degree requirements:* For master's, one foreign language. *Entrance requirements:* For master's, GRE General Test, interview. Additional exam requirements/recommendations for international students: Required—TOEFL.

Amridge University, Graduate and Professional Programs, Montgomery, AL 36117. Offers behavioral leadership and management (MA); Biblical studies (MA, PhD); family therapy (D Min); leadership and management (MS); marriage and family therapy (M Div, MA, PhD); ministerial leadership (M Div, MS); pastoral counseling (M Div, MS); professional counseling (M Div, MA, PhD); theology (M Div, D Min). Part-time and evening/weekend programs available. Postbaccalaureate distance learning degree programs offered (no on-campus study). *Faculty:* 20 full-time (2 women), 7 part-time/adjunct (6 women). *Students:* 110 full-time (58 women), 224 part-time (139 women); includes 139 minority (133 Black or African American, non-Hispanic/Latino; 3 Asian, non-Hispanic/Latino; 3 Hispanic/Latino). Average age 35. 69 applicants, 75% accepted. In 2014, 72 master's, 11 doctorates awarded. *Degree requirements:* For master's, one foreign language, comprehensive exam (for some programs), thesis (for some

programs); for doctorate, comprehensive exam (for some programs), thesis/dissertation (for some programs). *Entrance requirements:* For master's, official transcript showing an earned 4-year BA or BS from regionally- or nationally-accredited institution; for doctorate, official transcript showing earned graduate degree from regionally- or nationally-accredited institution; writing sample (e.g. career monograph, published journal article, term paper from master's degree or doctoral dissertation); interview. Additional exam requirements/recommendations for international students: Required—TOEFL. *Application deadline:* For fall admission, 9/1 priority date for domestic students; for spring admission, 1/1 priority date for domestic students. Applications are processed on a rolling basis. Application fee: $50. Electronic applications accepted. *Financial support:* In 2014–15, 102 students received support. Federal Work-Study and scholarships/grants available. Support available to part-time students. Financial award applicants required to submit FAFSA. *Faculty research:* Technology and mental healthcare, resilience in black families, theology and congregational ministry. *Unit head:* Brooks Housley, Student Affairs Coordinator, 888-790-8080 Ext. 2, Fax: 334-387-3878, E-mail: brookshousley@amridgeuniversity.edu. *Application contact:* Kristen Holcomb, Admissions Officer, 888-790-8080 Ext. 1, Fax: 334-387-3878, E-mail: admissions@amridgeuniversity.edu.

Anabaptist Mennonite Biblical Seminary, Graduate and Professional Programs, Elkhart, IN 46517-1999. Offers Christian formation (MA); divinity (M Div); mission and evangelism (MA); peace studies (MA); theological studies (MA, Certificate). *Accreditation:* ACIPE; ATS. Part-time programs available. *Degree requirements:* For master's, comprehensive exam, thesis optional. *Entrance requirements:* For master's and Certificate, 3 letters of reference. Additional exam requirements/recommendations for international students: Required—TOEFL (minimum score 550 paper-based). Electronic applications accepted. *Faculty research:* Biblical studies, theology, church history, church leadership.

Anderson University, School of Theology, Anderson, IN 46012-3495. Offers missions (MA); theology (M Div, MTS, D Min). *Accreditation:* ACIPE; ATS. Part-time programs available. *Degree requirements:* For master's, variable foreign language requirement, thesis (for some programs); for doctorate, thesis/dissertation. *Faculty research:* Small-church/bivocational ministry, women in ministry.

Andover Newton Theological School, Graduate and Professional Programs, Newton Centre, MA 02459-2243. Offers divinity (M Div); theological research (MA); theological studies (MA); theology (D Min). *Accreditation:* ACIPE; ATS. Part-time programs available. *Faculty:* 15 full-time (7 women), 28 part-time/adjunct (14 women). *Students:* 52 full-time (28 women), 210 part-time (131 women). In 2014, 54 master's, 9 doctorates awarded. *Degree requirements:* For master's, comprehensive exam (for some programs), thesis (for some programs); for doctorate, comprehensive exam, thesis/dissertation. *Entrance requirements:* For doctorate, M Div or equivalent. Additional exam requirements/recommendations for international students: Required—TOEFL (minimum score 550 paper-based). *Application deadline:* For fall admission, 4/1 priority date for domestic students, 4/1 for international students; for winter admission, 9/1 for domestic students; for spring admission, 10/1 priority date for domestic students. Applications are processed on a rolling basis. Application fee: $50. Electronic applications accepted. *Financial support:* Career-related internships or fieldwork and scholarships/grants available. Support available to part-time students. Financial award application deadline: 4/15; financial award applicants required to submit FAFSA. *Unit head:* Martin Copenhaver, President, 617-964-1100 Ext. 2410, Fax: 617-965-9756, E-mail: mcopenhaver@ants.edu. *Application contact:* Margaret L. Carroll, Director of Enrollment, 800-964-2687 Ext. 2428, Fax: 617-558-9785, E-mail: admissions@ants.edu.
Website: http://www.ants.edu/

Andrews University, School of Graduate Studies, Seventh-day Adventist Theological Seminary, Berrien Springs, MI 49104. Offers ministry (M Div, D Min); missiology (D Miss); pastoral ministry (MA); religious education (MA, Ed D, PhD, Ed S); theology (M Th, Th D); youth ministry (MA). *Accreditation:* ATS. *Faculty:* 40 full-time (5 women), 5 part-time/adjunct (0 women). *Students:* 511 full-time (85 women), 446 part-time (75 women); includes 450 minority (247 Black or African American, non-Hispanic/Latino; 1 American Indian or Alaska Native, non-Hispanic/Latino; 41 Asian, non-Hispanic/Latino; 151 Hispanic/Latino; 3 Native Hawaiian or other Pacific Islander, non-Hispanic/Latino; 7 Two or more races, non-Hispanic/Latino), 240 international. Average age 40. 546 applicants, 46% accepted, 124 enrolled. In 2014, 145 master's, 40 doctorates awarded. *Degree requirements:* For master's, thesis optional; for doctorate, variable foreign language requirement, thesis/dissertation. *Entrance requirements:* For master's, GRE Subject Test, minimum GPA of 2.0. Additional exam requirements/recommendations for international students: Required—TOEFL (minimum score 550 paper-based). *Application deadline:* Applications are processed on a rolling basis. Application fee: $40. Tuition and fees vary according to course level. *Financial support:* Fellowships, research assistantships, teaching assistantships, career-related internships or fieldwork, Federal Work-Study, and institutionally sponsored loans available. *Unit head:* Dr. Jiri Moskala, Dean, 269-471-3537. *Application contact:* Monica Wringer, Director, 800-253-2874, Fax: 269-471-6321.

Apex School of Theology, Graduate Programs, Durham, NC 27703. Offers M Div, MACC, MCE, D Min. *Faculty research:* Sociology, educational sciences, economics.

Aquinas Institute of Theology, Graduate and Professional Programs, St. Louis, MO 63108. Offers biblical studies (Certificate); church music (MM); health care mission (MAHCM); ministry (M Div); pastoral care (Certificate); pastoral ministry (MAPM); pastoral studies (MAPS); preaching (D Min); spiritual direction (Certificate); theology (M Div, MA); Thomistic studies (Certificate); M Div/MA; MA/PhD; MAPS/MSW. *Accreditation:* ATS (one or more programs are accredited). Part-time and evening/weekend programs available. Postbaccalaureate distance learning degree programs offered (minimal on-campus study). *Faculty:* 14 full-time (7 women), 24 part-time/adjunct (8 women). *Students:* 87 full-time (24 women), 59 part-time (37 women); includes 21 minority (9 Black or African American, non-Hispanic/Latino; 1 American Indian or Alaska Native, non-Hispanic/Latino; 4 Asian, non-Hispanic/Latino; 6 Hispanic/Latino; 1 Native Hawaiian or other Pacific Islander, non-Hispanic/Latino), 8 international. Average age 46. In 2014, 25 master's, 5 doctorates awarded. *Degree requirements:* For master's, variable foreign language requirement, comprehensive exam (for some programs), thesis (for some programs); for doctorate, thesis/dissertation. *Entrance requirements:* For master's and Certificate, MAT; for doctorate, 3 years of ministerial experience, 6 hours of graduate course work in homiletics, M Div or the equivalent, minimum GPA of 3.0. Additional exam requirements/recommendations for international students: Required—TOEFL. *Application deadline:* For fall admission, 3/15 priority date for domestic and international students; for spring admission, 11/15 priority date for domestic and international students. Applications are processed on a rolling basis. Application fee: $50. *Expenses:* Expenses: $680 per credit hour; $265 per semester in fees. *Financial support:* Scholarships/grants, health care benefits, and tuition waivers (partial) available. Support available to part-time students. Financial award application deadline: 3/15; financial award applicants required to submit CSS PROFILE or FAFSA. *Faculty research:* Theology of preaching, hermeneutics, lay ecclesial ministry, pastoral and practical theology. *Unit head:* Fr. Gregory Heille, Vice-President/Academic Dean, 314-256-8800, Fax: 314-256-8888, E-mail: heille@ai.edu. *Application contact:* David Werthmann, Director of Admissions, 314-256-8806, Fax: 314-256-8888, E-mail: admissions@ai.edu.
Website: http://www.ai.edu/

Arlington Baptist College, Program in Biblical and Theological Studies, Arlington, TX 76012-3425. Offers MA. *Entrance requirements:* For master's, official transcript, letter of reference from pastor, two letters of recommendation, essay. Additional exam requirements/recommendations for international students: Required—TOEFL. Electronic applications accepted.

Asbury Theological Seminary, Graduate and Professional Programs, Wilmore, KY 40390-1199. Offers MA, MAAS, MACE, MACL, MACM, MACP, MAMFC, MAMHC, MAPC, MASF, MAYM, Th M, PhD, Certificate. *Accreditation:* ATS. Part-time programs available. Postbaccalaureate distance learning degree programs offered (minimal on-campus study). Terminal master's awarded for partial completion of doctoral program. *Degree requirements:* For master's, thesis (for some programs); for doctorate, thesis/dissertation, qualifying exam. *Entrance requirements:* For master's, minimum GPA of 2.75; for doctorate, minimum GPA of 3.0. Additional exam requirements/recommendations for international students: Required—TOEFL, IELTS. Electronic applications accepted.

Ashland Theological Seminary, Graduate Programs, Ashland, OH 44805. Offers biblical and theological studies (MAR); Biblical, historical and theological studies (MA), including Anabaptism and Pietism, Christian theology, church history, New Testament, Old Testament; Christian ministry (MAPT), including Black church studies (M Div, MAPT, D Min), chaplaincy (M Div, MAPT), Christian formation (M Div, MAPT), evangelism/church renewal and missions (M Div, MAPT), general ministry (M Div, MAPT), pastoral counseling and care (M Div, MAPT), specialized ministry, spiritual formation (M Div, MAPT, D Min); Christian studies (Diploma); clinical counseling (MACC); counseling (MAC); ministry (D Min), including Black church studies (M Div, MAPT, D Min), Canadian church studies, formational counseling, independent design, spiritual formation (M Div, MAPT, D Min), transformational leadership, Wesleyan practices; pastoral ministry (M Div), including Biblical studies - Old or New Testament, Black church studies (M Div, MAPT, D Min), chaplaincy (M Div, MAPT), Christian formation (M Div, MAPT), evangelism/church renewal and missions (M Div, MAPT), general Biblical studies, general ministry (M Div, MAPT), pastoral counseling and care (M Div, MAPT), spiritual formation (M Div, MAPT, D Min), theology or history. MAC program offered in Detroit, MI. *Accreditation:* ATS. Part-time programs available. *Degree requirements:* For master's, 2 foreign languages, comprehensive exam (for some programs), thesis (for some programs); for doctorate, thesis/dissertation. *Entrance requirements:* For master's, bachelor's degree from accredited institution with a minimum undergraduate GPA of 2.75; for doctorate, M Div, minimum undergraduate GPA of 3.0. Additional exam requirements/recommendations for international students: Required—TOEFL (minimum score 500 paper-based; 65 iBT). Electronic applications accepted. *Faculty research:* Semitic languages and linguistics, rhetorical and social-scientific criticism, Anabaptist studies, inner spiritual healing, African-American clergy in film and literature.

Assemblies of God Theological Seminary, Graduate and Professional Programs, Springfield, MO 65802. Offers Bible theology (PhD); Christian ministries (MA); counseling (MA); divinity (M Div); intercultural ministry (MA); intercultural studies (PhD); ministry (D Min); missiology (D Miss); theological studies (MA). *Accreditation:* ATS. Part-time and evening/weekend programs available. Postbaccalaureate distance learning degree programs offered (minimal on-campus study). *Degree requirements:* For master's, variable foreign language requirement; for doctorate, thesis/dissertation. *Entrance requirements:* For master's, minimum GPA of 2.5; for doctorate, GRE (for PhD in Bible theology), minimum GPA of 3.0. Additional exam requirements/recommendations for international students: Required—TOEFL (minimum score 550 paper-based; 80 iBT). Electronic applications accepted.

The Athenaeum of Ohio, Graduate Programs, Cincinnati, OH 45230-5900. Offers biblical studies (MABS); divinity (M Div); lay ministry (Certificate); pastoral counseling (MAPC); pastoral ministry (MA); theology (MA Th); M Div/MA Th; M Div/MABS; M Div/MAPC. *Accreditation:* ATS (one or more programs are accredited). Part-time and evening/weekend programs available. *Degree requirements:* For master's, one foreign language, comprehensive exam (for some programs), thesis optional.

Atlantic School of Theology, Graduate and Professional Programs, Halifax, NS B3H 3B5, Canada. Offers ministry (M Div); theological studies (Graduate Certificate). *Accreditation:* ATS. Part-time programs available. Postbaccalaureate distance learning degree programs offered (minimal on-campus study). *Degree requirements:* For master's, thesis (for some programs). *Entrance requirements:* For master's and Graduate Certificate, minimum B average in undergraduate course work. *Faculty research:* Ethics and biology; death, dying and pastoral care; theology and the economy; adult education; John and anti-Judaism.

Austin Graduate School of Theology, Program in Theological Studies, Austin, TX 78752. Offers MATS. Part-time programs available. *Degree requirements:* For master's, 2 foreign languages, comprehensive exam, faculty forums. *Entrance requirements:* For master's, 3 letters of reference. Additional exam requirements/recommendations for international students: Required—TOEFL (minimum score 530 paper-based). *Faculty research:* Revelation, synoptic problem, Acadian, Biblical archaeology, worship.

Austin Presbyterian Theological Seminary, Graduate and Professional Programs, Austin, TX 78705-5797. Offers divinity (M Div); ministry (D Min); ministry practice (MA); theological studies (MA); M Div/MSSW. M Div/MSSW offered in collaboration with The University of Texas at Austin School of Social Work. *Accreditation:* ACIPE; ATS. Part-time programs available. *Faculty:* 17 full-time (5 women), 7 part-time/adjunct (2 women). *Students:* 131 full-time (70 women), 66 part-time (35 women). *Degree requirements:* For master's, Greek, Hebrew (for M Div); for doctorate, thesis/dissertation. *Entrance requirements:* For master's, references (for M Div). Additional exam requirements/recommendations for international students: Required—TOEFL (minimum score 550 paper-based; 79 iBT). *Application deadline:* For fall admission, 5/1 for domestic students, 1/1 for international students; for spring admission, 9/1 for domestic students; for summer admission, 2/2 for domestic students. Applications are processed on a rolling basis. Application fee: $65. *Expenses: Tuition:* Full-time $12,600; part-time $210 per credit. *Required fees:* $220. One-time fee: $325 full-time; $85 part-time. *Financial support:* Fellowships, career-related internships or fieldwork, institutionally sponsored loans, scholarships/grants, and tutorships available. Support available to part-time students. Financial award application deadline: 3/1; financial award applicants required to submit FAFSA. *Faculty research:* Mystical theology, religious pluralism, narrative preaching, social ethics, pastoral care and healing. *Unit head:* Dr. David Jensen, Academic Dean, 512-404-4821, Fax: 512-479-0738, E-mail: dean@austinseminary.edu. *Application contact:* Dr. Jack Barden, Vice President for Admissions, 512-404-4827, Fax: 512-472-7089, E-mail: admissions@austinseminary.edu.

Ave Maria University, Graduate Programs, Ave Maria, FL 34142. Offers pastoral theology (MTS); theology (MA, PhD). Terminal master's awarded for partial completion of doctoral program. *Degree requirements:* For master's, one foreign language, thesis; for doctorate, 3 foreign languages, comprehensive exam, thesis/dissertation. *Entrance requirements:* For master's, GRE; for doctorate, GRE, M Div or equivalent; MA or MTS

in religion, theology, or philosophy; bachelor's degree with strong background in religion, theology, and/or philosophy.

Azusa Pacific University, Haggard Graduate School of Theology, Program in Ministry, Azusa, CA 91702-7000. Offers D Min.

Azusa Pacific University, Haggard Graduate School of Theology, Program in Theological Studies, Concentration in Religion: Biblical Studies, Azusa, CA 91702-7000. Offers MAR.

Azusa Pacific University, Haggard Graduate School of Theology, Program in Theological Studies, Concentration in Religion: Theology and Ethics, Azusa, CA 91702-7000. Offers MA.

Bakke Graduate University, Programs in Pastoral Ministry and Business, Seattle, WA 98104. Offers business administration (MBA); church and ministry multiplication (D Min); global urban leadership (MA); leadership (D Min); ministry in complex contexts (D Min); social and civic entrepreneurship (MA); theology of work (D Min); theology reflection (D Min); transformational leadership (DTL); urban youth ministry (D Min). Part-time programs available. Postbaccalaureate distance learning degree programs offered (minimal on-campus study). *Degree requirements:* For master's, thesis; for doctorate, thesis/dissertation. *Entrance requirements:* For master's, 2 years of ministry experience, BA in Biblical studies or theology; for doctorate, 3 years of ministry experience, M Div. Additional exam requirements/recommendations for international students: Required—TOEFL. Electronic applications accepted. *Faculty research:* Theological systems, church management, worship.

Baptist Bible College, Graduate School of Theology, Springfield, MO 65803-3498. Offers biblical counseling (MA); biblical studies (MA); church ministry (MA); intercultural studies (MA); theology (M Div). Part-time programs available. *Degree requirements:* For master's, 2 foreign languages, thesis (for some programs). Electronic applications accepted.

The Baptist College of Florida, Graduate Programs, Graceville, FL 32440-1898. Offers Christian studies (MA); music and worship leadership (MA). Part-time programs available. Postbaccalaureate distance learning degree programs offered (no on-campus study). *Faculty:* 12 full-time (0 women). *Students:* 33 full-time (6 women); includes 2 minority (1 Black or African American, non-Hispanic/Latino; 1 Hispanic/Latino). Average age 28. 10 applicants, 100% accepted, 10 enrolled. *Degree requirements:* For master's, variable foreign language requirement, comprehensive exam (for some programs), thesis (for some programs). *Entrance requirements:* For master's, regionally-accredited undergraduate degree, undergraduate courses in field, minimum GPA of 2.5. Additional exam requirements/recommendations for international students: Required—TOEFL. *Application deadline:* For fall admission, 8/15 for domestic students; for spring admission, 1/15 for domestic students. Applications are processed on a rolling basis. Application fee: $25. Electronic applications accepted. *Expenses:* Expenses: $310 per hour. *Financial support:* In 2014–15, 2 students received support. *Faculty research:* Biblical studies, ministry studies. *Unit head:* Dr. Ed Scott, Chair of the Graduate Division, 850-263-3261 Ext. 488, E-mail: eescott@baptistcollege.edu. *Application contact:* Sandra Richards, Director of Admissions, 850-263-3261 Ext. 415.

Baptist Missionary Association Theological Seminary, Graduate and Professional Programs, Jacksonville, TX 75766-5407. Offers M Div, MAR. Part-time programs available. *Degree requirements:* For master's, variable foreign language requirement, thesis optional. *Entrance requirements:* Additional exam requirements/recommendations for international students: Required—TOEFL (minimum score 550 paper-based). Electronic applications accepted. *Faculty research:* Education, Biblical studies.

Baptist Theological Seminary at Richmond, Graduate and Professional Programs, Richmond, VA 23227. Offers Biblical interpretation (M Div); Christian education (M Div); Christian ministry (MCM); justice and peacebuilding (D Min); theological studies (MTS, Graduate Certificate); M Div/MS; M Div/MSW. *Accreditation:* ATS. Part-time programs available. Postbaccalaureate distance learning degree programs offered (minimal on-campus study). *Faculty:* 7 full-time (2 women), 14 part-time/adjunct (6 women). *Students:* 45 full-time (27 women), 40 part-time (24 women); includes 10 minority (9 Black or African American, non-Hispanic/Latino; 1 Hispanic/Latino), 3 international. *Degree requirements:* For doctorate, one foreign language, comprehensive exam, thesis/dissertation, field study, independent study. *Entrance requirements:* For master's, BA/BS, 2 references, resume, official transcripts; for doctorate, MAT, M Div, 3 years of full-time ministry experience, minimum GPA of 2.75, 3 references, resume, official transcripts, writing sample, personal statement. Additional exam requirements/recommendations for international students: Required—TOEFL (minimum score 550 paper-based). *Application deadline:* For fall admission, 7/1 for domestic students, 5/1 for international students; for winter admission, 12/15 for domestic students, 9/1 for international students; for spring admission, 1/15 for domestic students, 10/1 for international students. Applications are processed on a rolling basis. Application fee: $35. *Financial support:* Teaching assistantships, scholarships/grants, and tuition waivers (partial) available. Financial award application deadline: 2/1. *Faculty research:* Biblical studies, pastoral care, church history, theology, ministry. *Unit head:* Dr. Ronald W. Crawford, President, 804-204-1201, Fax: 804-355-8182, E-mail: rcrawford@btsr.edu. *Application contact:* Melissa Fallen, Director of Admissions and Recruitment, 804-204-1208, E-mail: admissions@btsr.edu. Website: http://www.btsr.edu/programs/degree-programs/

Barclay College, Master of Arts Program, Haviland, KS 67059-0288. Offers MA. Postbaccalaureate distance learning degree programs offered (minimal on-campus study). *Faculty:* 3 full-time (0 women), 15 part-time/adjunct (0 women). *Students:* 30 full-time (4 women); includes 2 minority (both Black or African American, non-Hispanic/Latino), 2 international. Average age 38. 16 applicants, 75% accepted, 10 enrolled. In 2014, 14 master's awarded. *Degree requirements:* For master's, comprehensive exam, capstone project. *Entrance requirements:* Additional exam requirements/recommendations for international students: Required—TOEFL. *Application deadline:* For fall admission, 7/20 for domestic and international students; for spring admission, 12/1 for domestic and international students. Applications are processed on a rolling basis. Application fee: $0. Electronic applications accepted. *Expenses:* Tuition: Part-time $3555 per semester. *Required fees:* $300 per semester. *Financial support:* In 2014–15, 20 students received support. Scholarships/grants available. Financial award application deadline: 7/20; financial award applicants required to submit FAFSA. *Unit head:* Dr. Jim Le Shana, Vice President for Graduate Studies, 800-862-0226, E-mail: jim.leshana@barclaycollege.edu. *Application contact:* Dr. David Kingrey, Chair, Quaker Studies and Spiritual Formation, 800-862-0226, E-mail: dave.kingrey@barclaycollege.edu.

Barry University, College of Arts and Sciences, Department of Theology and Philosophy, Miami Shores, FL 33161-6695. Offers ministry (D Min); pastoral ministry for Hispanics (MA); pastoral theology (MA); practical theology (MA). *Accreditation:* ATS. Part-time and evening/weekend programs available. *Degree requirements:* For master's, comprehensive exam, thesis optional; for doctorate, thesis/dissertation. *Entrance requirements:* For master's, GRE General Test or MAT, minimum GPA of 3.0. Electronic applications accepted. *Faculty research:* Fundamental morals, bioethics, social ethics, liturgical and sacramental theology, biblical studies.

Baylor University, George W. Truett Theological Seminary, Waco, TX 76798. Offers M Div, MACM, MTS, D Min, M Div/MBA, M Div/MM, M Div/MSW, MTS/MSW. M Div/MBA offered jointly with Hankamer School of Business. *Accreditation:* ATS. Part-time programs available. *Entrance requirements:* For master's, 4-year college degree; for doctorate, 4 recommendations, 3 writing assignments, equivalent to Truett's 93-hour M Div. Additional exam requirements/recommendations for international students: Required—TOEFL (minimum score 80 iBT). Electronic applications accepted. Application fee is waived when completed online.

Bethany Theological Seminary, Graduate and Professional Programs, Richmond, IN 47374-4019. Offers biblical studies (MA Th); ministry studies (M Div); peace studies (M Div, MA Th); theological studies (MA Th, CATS); youth ministry (M Div). *Accreditation:* ACIPE; ATS. Part-time programs available. Postbaccalaureate distance learning degree programs offered (minimal on-campus study). *Degree requirements:* For master's, thesis (for some programs). *Entrance requirements:* For master's, letters of reference. Additional exam requirements/recommendations for international students: Required—TOEFL (minimum score 550 paper-based).

Bethel College, Adult and Graduate Programs, Program in Theological Studies, Mishawaka, IN 46545-5591. Offers MATS. Part-time and evening/weekend programs available. *Entrance requirements:* Additional exam requirements/recommendations for international students: Required—TOEFL (minimum score 540 paper-based). Electronic applications accepted.

Bethel Seminary, Graduate and Professional Programs, St. Paul, MN 55112-6998. Offers Anglican studies (Certificate); children's and family ministry (MA); Christian studies (Certificate); Christian thought (MA); Greek and Hebrew language (M Div); Greek language (M Div); Hebrew language (M Div); marriage and family therapy (MA, Certificate); ministry (D Min); ministry practice (MA, Certificate); theological studies (MA, Certificate); transformational leadership (MA); young life youth ministry (Certificate). *Accreditation:* ACIPE; ATS (one or more programs are accredited). Part-time and evening/weekend programs available. Postbaccalaureate distance learning degree programs offered (minimal on-campus study). *Faculty:* 15 full-time (3 women), 55 part-time/adjunct (27 women). *Students:* 422 full-time (167 women), 231 part-time (71 women); includes 165 minority (62 Black or African American, non-Hispanic/Latino; 58 Asian, non-Hispanic/Latino; 29 Hispanic/Latino; 1 Native Hawaiian or other Pacific Islander, non-Hispanic/Latino; 15 Two or more races, non-Hispanic/Latino), 16 international. Average age 37. 272 applicants, 77% accepted, 165 enrolled. In 2014, 147 master's, 13 doctorates, 8 other advanced degrees awarded. *Degree requirements:* For master's, variable foreign language requirement, thesis (for some programs); for doctorate, thesis/dissertation. *Entrance requirements:* For master's, letters of reference, transcripts, personal statement; for doctorate, M Div, letters of reference, organizational support; for Certificate, letters of reference, family essay, personal statement, and family of origin paper (for marriage and family therapy). Additional exam requirements/recommendations for international students: Required—TOEFL (minimum score 550 paper-based; 87 iBT). *Application deadline:* For fall admission, 8/1 priority date for domestic students, 8/1 for international students; for winter admission, 12/1 priority date for domestic students; for spring admission, 1/1 priority date for domestic students. Applications are processed on a rolling basis. Application fee: $0. Electronic applications accepted. *Financial support:* In 2014–15, 558 students received support, including 17 teaching assistantships; career-related internships or fieldwork, Federal Work-Study, and scholarships/grants also available. Financial award applicants required to submit FAFSA. *Faculty research:* Nature of theology, ethics, Biblical commentaries, nature of God, science and theology. *Unit head:* Dr. David Clark, Vice-President and Dean, Bethel Seminary, 651-638-6659. *Application contact:* Jen Niska, Director of Admissions, 651-638-6288, Fax: 651-638-6002, E-mail: bsem-admit@bethel.edu.

Bethesda University, Graduate and Professional Programs, Anaheim, CA 92801. Offers biblical studies (MA); music (MA); theology (M Div). *Entrance requirements:* For master's, interview. Additional exam requirements/recommendations for international students: Recommended—TOEFL.

Beth HaMedrash Shaarei Yosher Institute, Graduate Programs, Brooklyn, NY 11204. *Accreditation:* AARTS.

Beth Hatalmud Rabbinical College, Graduate Programs, Brooklyn, NY 11214. *Accreditation:* AARTS.

Beth Medrash Govoha, Graduate Programs, Lakewood, NJ 08701-2797. *Accreditation:* AARTS.

Bethune-Cookman University, School of Graduate Studies, Daytona Beach, FL 32114-3099. Offers transformative leadership (MS). Postbaccalaureate distance learning degree programs offered (minimal on-campus study). *Degree requirements:* For master's, thesis. *Entrance requirements:* For master's, GRE or MAT, minimum GPA of 2.75 in the last 60 semester hours; 3 letters of recommendation. Additional exam requirements/recommendations for international students: Required—TOEFL (minimum score 550 paper-based). Electronic applications accepted. *Faculty research:* Civic engagement, communication ethics, service learning in higher education women in leadership.

Bexley Hall Episcopal Seminary, Graduate Programs, Columbus, OH 43209-2325. Offers M Div, MA. *Accreditation:* ATS.

Biblical Theological Seminary, Graduate and Professional Programs, Hatfield, PA 19440-2499. Offers advanced missional leadership (D Min); advanced pastoral studies (Certificate); biblical counseling (Certificate); biblical studies (MA, Certificate); counseling (MA); ministry (M Div, MA); missional theology (MA). *Accreditation:* ATS. Part-time and evening/weekend programs available. *Faculty:* 9 full-time (0 women), 21 part-time/adjunct (4 women). *Students:* 139 full-time (41 women), 149 part-time (55 women); includes 103 minority (53 Black or African American, non-Hispanic/Latino; 42 Asian, non-Hispanic/Latino; 6 Hispanic/Latino; 2 Two or more races, non-Hispanic/Latino), 76 international. Average age 38. 91 applicants, 64% accepted, 56 enrolled. In 2014, 80 master's, 5 doctorates awarded. *Degree requirements:* For master's, variable foreign language requirement, thesis optional; for doctorate, thesis/dissertation. *Entrance requirements:* Additional exam requirements/recommendations for international students: Required—TOEFL (minimum score 550 paper-based; 80 iBT). *Application deadline:* Applications are processed on a rolling basis. Application fee: $30. Electronic applications accepted. *Expenses:* Tuition: Full-time $14,667; part-time $480 per credit. *Required fees:* $25 per trimester. One-time fee: $30. *Financial support:* In 2014–15, 192 students received support. Career-related internships or fieldwork, institutionally sponsored loans, and scholarships/grants available. Support available to part-time students. Financial award application deadline: 8/30; financial award applicants required to submit FAFSA. *Faculty research:* Theology, culture, Biblical interpretation. *Unit head:* Pamela Jean Smith, Vice President for Student Advancement, 215-368-5000 Ext. 122, Fax: 215-368-7002, E-mail: psmith@biblical.edu. *Application contact:* Dr. Malcolm Walls, Director of Recruitment and Student Services, 215-368-5000 Ext. 109, Fax: 215-368-7002, E-mail: mwalls@biblical.edu. Website: http://www.biblical.edu/

Biola University, Talbot School of Theology, La Mirada, CA 90639-0001. Offers adult/family ministry (MACE); Bible exposition (MA, Th M); Biblical and theological studies

(MA); children's ministry (MACE); Christian education (M Div); cross-cultural education ministry (MACE); educational studies (Ed D, PhD); evangelism and discipleship (M Div); general Christian education (MACE); Messianic Jewish studies (M Div, Certificate); missions and intercultural studies (M Div); New Testament (MA, Th M); Old Testament (MA); Old Testament and Semitics (Th M); pastoral and general ministry (M Div); pastoral care and counseling (M Div); philosophy (MA); spiritual formation (M Div, Certificate); spiritual formation and soul care (MA); theology (Th M, D Min, Certificate); youth ministry (MACE). *Accreditation:* ATS. Part-time and evening/weekend programs available. *Faculty:* 77. *Students:* 581 full-time (140 women), 554 part-time (155 women); includes 522 minority (42 Black or African American, non-Hispanic/Latino; 3 American Indian or Alaska Native, non-Hispanic/Latino; 370 Asian, non-Hispanic/Latino; 78 Hispanic/Latino; 2 Native Hawaiian or other Pacific Islander, non-Hispanic/Latino; 27 Two or more races, non-Hispanic/Latino), 121 international. 437 applicants, 78% accepted, 241 enrolled. In 2014, 182 master's, 33 doctorates awarded. *Entrance requirements:* For master's, bachelor's degree from accredited college or university; minimum GPA of 2.6 (for M Div), 3.0 (for MA); for doctorate, M Div or MA. Additional exam requirements/recommendations for international students: Required—TOEFL (minimum score 600 paper-based; 88 iBT). *Application deadline:* For fall admission, 7/1 for domestic students, 6/1 for international students; for spring admission, 12/1 priority date for domestic students. Applications are processed on a rolling basis. Application fee: $65. Electronic applications accepted. *Financial support:* Scholarships/grants and unspecified assistantships available. Support available to part-time students. Financial award applicants required to submit FAFSA. *Faculty research:* New Testament, Old Testament, spiritual formation, Christian education, theological studies, Christian ministry, preaching and pastoral ministry, language and literature, bible exposition, Christian leadership. *Unit head:* Dr. Clint Arnold, Dean, 562-903-4816, Fax: 562-903-4748. *Application contact:* Graduate Admissions Office, 562-903-4752, E-mail: graduate.admissions@biola.edu.
Website: http://www.talbot.edu/

Bob Jones University, Graduate Programs, Greenville, SC 29614. Offers accountancy (MS); Bible (MA); Bible translation (MA); Biblical studies (Certificate); broadcast management (MS); business administration (MBA); church history (MA, PhD); church ministries (MA); church music (MM); cinema and video production (MA); counseling (MS); curriculum and instruction (Ed D); divinity (M Div); dramatic production (MA); educational leadership (MS, Ed D, Ed S); elementary education (M Ed, MAT); English (M Ed, MA, MAT); fine arts (MA); graphic design (MA); history (M Ed, MA); illustration (MA); interpretative speech (MA); mathematics (M Ed, MAT); medical missions (Certificate); ministry (MM, D Min); multi-categorical special education (M Ed, MAT); music (M Ed); New Testament interpretation (PhD); Old Testament interpretation (PhD); orchestral instrument performance (MM); organ performance (MM); pastoral studies (MA); personnel services (MS, Ed S); piano pedagogy (MM); piano performance (MM); platform arts (MA); radio and television broadcasting (MS); rhetoric and public address (MA); secondary education (M Ed); studio art (MA); teaching Bible (MA); theology (MA, PhD); voice performance (MM); youth ministries (MA); M Div/MM.

Boston College, Graduate School of Arts and Sciences, Department of Theology, Chestnut Hill, MA 02467-3800. Offers PhD. *Accreditation:* ATS. *Faculty:* 34 full-time. *Students:* 82 full-time. 114 applicants, 26% accepted, 16 enrolled. In 2014, 11 doctorates awarded. Terminal master's awarded for partial completion of doctoral program. *Degree requirements:* For doctorate, thesis/dissertation. *Entrance requirements:* For doctorate, GRE General Test. Additional exam requirements/recommendations for international students: Required—TOEFL (minimum score 600 paper-based; 100 iBT), IELTS (minimum score 7). *Application deadline:* For fall admission, 1/2 for domestic and international students. Application fee: $75. Electronic applications accepted. *Financial support:* In 2014–15, fellowships with full tuition reimbursements (averaging $21,000 per year), research assistantships with full tuition reimbursements (averaging $21,000 per year), teaching assistantships with full tuition reimbursements (averaging $21,000 per year) were awarded; Federal Work-Study, scholarships/grants, and health care benefits also available. Support available to part-time students. Financial award application deadline: 3/1; financial award applicants required to submit FAFSA. *Faculty research:* Historical theology, history of Christianity, systematic theology, Biblical studies, theological ethics, comparative theology. *Unit head:* Dr. Kenneth Himes, Chairperson, 617-552-8440, E-mail: kenneth.himes@bc.edu. *Application contact:* Dr. Richard Gaillardetz, Graduate Program Director, 617-552-3873, E-mail: gaillard@bc.edu.
Website: http://www.bc.edu/theology

Boston College, School of Theology and Ministry, Chestnut Hill, MA 02467-3800. Offers church leadership (MA); divinity (M Div); pastoral ministry (MA), including Hispanic ministry, liturgy and worship, pastoral care and counseling, spirituality; religious education (MA, PhD); sacred theology (STD, STL); social justice/social ministry (MA); spiritual direction (MA); theological studies (MTS); theology (Th M, PhD); youth ministry (MA); MA/MA; MS/MA; MSW/MA. *Accreditation:* Teacher Education Accreditation Council. Part-time programs available. *Degree requirements:* For doctorate, one foreign language, thesis/dissertation. *Entrance requirements:* For doctorate, GRE. Additional exam requirements/recommendations for international students: Required—TOEFL (minimum score 550 paper-based). Electronic applications accepted. *Faculty research:* Philosophy and practice of religious education, pastoral psychology, liturgical and spiritual theology, spiritual formation for the practice of ministry.

Boston University, School of Theology, Boston, MA 02215. Offers M Div, MSM, MTS, STM, D Min, PhD, Th D, D Min/MSW, M Div/MSM, M Div/MSW, MTS/MSW. *Accreditation:* ACIPE; ATS. Part-time programs available. *Faculty:* 30 full-time (15 women), 19 part-time/adjunct (4 women). *Students:* 279 full-time (133 women), 29 part-time (11 women); includes 52 minority (25 Black or African American, non-Hispanic/Latino; 1 American Indian or Alaska Native, non-Hispanic/Latino; 6 Asian, non-Hispanic/Latino; 16 Hispanic/Latino; 4 Two or more races, non-Hispanic/Latino), 51 international. Average age 34. 252 applicants, 59% accepted, 82 enrolled. In 2014, 39 master's, 41 doctorates awarded. *Degree requirements:* For master's, comprehensive exam (for some programs), contextual education; for doctorate, 2 foreign languages, comprehensive exam, thesis/dissertation. *Entrance requirements:* For master's, minimum GPA of 3.0; for doctorate, GRE General Test, minimum GPA of 3.3. Additional exam requirements/recommendations for international students: Required—TOEFL (minimum score 570 paper-based; 89 iBT). *Application deadline:* For fall admission, 2/15 priority date for domestic students, 3/15 priority date for international students; for spring admission, 9/15 priority date for domestic and international students. Applications are processed on a rolling basis. Application fee: $70. Electronic applications accepted. *Expenses:* Expenses: $18,900 plus $660 fees. *Financial support:* In 2014–15, 258 students received support, including 73 fellowships (averaging $12,000 per year), 66 research assistantships (averaging $3,000 per year), 49 teaching assistantships (averaging $4,000 per year); Federal Work-Study, institutionally sponsored loans, and scholarships/grants also available. Support available to part-time students. Financial award application deadline: 7/15; financial award applicants required to submit FAFSA. *Faculty research:* Practical theology, Biblical literature in its social and cultural context, history of Christianity, social ethics, theological studies. *Unit head:* Rev. Dr. Mary Elizabeth Moore, Dean, 617-353-3050, Fax: 617-353-3061. *Application contact:* Rev. Anastasia Kidd, Director of Admissions, 617-353-3036, Fax: 617-358-0140, E-mail: sthadmis@bu.edu. Website: http://www.bu.edu/sth

Briercrest Seminary, Graduate Programs, Program in Theology, Caronport, SK S0H 0S0, Canada. Offers Biblical studies (M Div); leadership and management (M Div); New Testament (MATS); Old Testament (MATS); pastoral counseling (M Div); pastoral ministry (M Div); theological studies (M Div); theology (MATS); worship (M Div); youth and family ministry (M Div). *Accreditation:* ATS. Part-time programs available. *Degree requirements:* For master's, comprehensive exam, thesis optional. *Entrance requirements:* Additional exam requirements/recommendations for international students: Required—TOEFL (minimum score 550 paper-based).

Bryn Athyn College of the New Church, Academy of the New Church Theological School, Bryn Athyn, PA 19009-0717. Offers divinity (M Div); religious studies (MA). Part-time programs available. Postbaccalaureate distance learning degree programs offered (minimal on-campus study). *Degree requirements:* For master's, variable foreign language requirement, thesis. *Entrance requirements:* Additional exam requirements/recommendations for international students: Required—TOEFL.

Cairn University, School of Divinity, Langhorne, PA 19047-2990. Offers divinity (M Div); religion (MA). Part-time and evening/weekend programs available. *Faculty:* 6 full-time (0 women), 2 part-time/adjunct (0 women). *Students:* 22 full-time (1 woman), 56 part-time (21 women); includes 39 minority (34 Black or African American, non-Hispanic/Latino; 3 Asian, non-Hispanic/Latino; 2 Hispanic/Latino). Average age 40. 36 applicants, 83% accepted, 25 enrolled. In 2014, 17 master's awarded. *Entrance requirements:* Additional exam requirements/recommendations for international students: Required—TOEFL (minimum score 550 paper-based). *Application deadline:* Applications are processed on a rolling basis. Application fee: $25. Electronic applications accepted. Application fee is waived when completed online. *Expenses: Tuition:* Full-time $11,430; part-time $635 per credit. Tuition and fees vary according to program. *Financial support:* Scholarships/grants available. Support available to part-time students. Financial award applicants required to submit FAFSA. *Unit head:* Dr. Jonathan L. Master, Dean, 215-702-4358, Fax: 215-702-4359, E-mail: divinity@cairn.edu. *Application contact:* Abigail Sattler, Assistant Director, Graduate Admissions, 800-572-2472, Fax: 215-702-4248, E-mail: asattler@cairn.edu.
Website: http://www.cairn.edu/academics/divinity

California Institute of Integral Studies, School of Consciousness and Transformation, San Francisco, CA 94103. Offers anthropology and social change (MA, PhD); creative inquiry/interdisciplinary arts (MFA); East-West psychology (MA, PhD); philosophy and religion (MA, PhD), including Asian and comparative studies, ecology, spirituality, and religion, philosophy, cosmology, and consciousness, women's spirituality; transformative leadership (MA); transformative studies (PhD); writing and consciousness (MFA). Part-time and evening/weekend programs available. Postbaccalaureate distance learning degree programs offered (no on-campus study). *Students:* 385 full-time (256 women), 102 part-time (71 women); includes 124 minority (31 Black or African American, non-Hispanic/Latino; 3 American Indian or Alaska Native, non-Hispanic/Latino; 19 Asian, non-Hispanic/Latino; 39 Hispanic/Latino; 1 Native Hawaiian or other Pacific Islander, non-Hispanic/Latino; 31 Two or more races, non-Hispanic/Latino), 53 international. Average age 43. 196 applicants, 92% accepted, 125 enrolled. In 2014, 75 master's, 41 doctorates awarded. Terminal master's awarded for partial completion of doctoral program. *Degree requirements:* For master's, thesis optional; for doctorate, comprehensive exam, thesis/dissertation, 1 foreign language (for Asian comparative studies). *Entrance requirements:* For master's, minimum GPA of 3.0, letters of recommendation, writing sample; for doctorate, master's degree, minimum GPA of 3.0, letters of recommendation, writing sample. Additional exam requirements/recommendations for international students: Required—TOEFL. *Application deadline:* For fall admission, 2/1 priority date for domestic and international students; for spring admission, 10/15 priority date for domestic and international students. Applications are processed on a rolling basis. Application fee: $65. Electronic applications accepted. *Expenses: Tuition:* Full-time $18,270; part-time $1015 per credit. *Required fees:* $85 per semester hour. *Financial support:* In 2014–15, 445 students received support, including 5 research assistantships (averaging $800 per year), 28 teaching assistantships (averaging $825 per year); career-related internships or fieldwork, Federal Work-Study, and scholarships/grants also available. Support available to part-time students. Financial award application deadline: 4/15; financial award applicants required to submit FAFSA. *Faculty research:* Ecology and sustainability, philosophy and religion, East-West psychology, integrative health, social and cultural anthropology, transformative leadership. *Application contact:* David Townes, Senior Admissions Counselor, 415-575-6152, Fax: 415-575-1268, E-mail: admissions@ciis.edu.
Website: http://www.ciis.edu/

California Lutheran University, Graduate Studies, Pacific Lutheran Theological Seminary, Thousand Oaks, CA 91360-2787. Offers M Div, MA, MCM, MTS, PhD, Th D, Certificate, M Div/MA. MA, Th D, PhD offered jointly with Graduate Theological Union; PhD with University of California, Berkeley. *Accreditation:* ACIPE; ATS (one or more programs are accredited). Part-time programs available. *Degree requirements:* For master's, variable foreign language requirement, thesis or alternative. *Faculty research:* Theology and genetics, power and prayer, liturgy and ethics, Christianity and Confucianism, religion and abuse.

Calvary Bible College and Theological Seminary, Calvary Theological Seminary, Kansas City, MO 64147-1341. Offers Bible and theology (MS); Biblical counseling (MA); Biblical studies (MA); Christian ministry (MA); Christian studies (MS); Christian theology (MA); New Testament (MA); Old Testament (MA); pastoral studies (M Div). Part-time and evening/weekend programs available. *Degree requirements:* For master's, variable foreign language requirement, comprehensive exam, thesis. *Entrance requirements:* For master's, minimum GPA of 2.5, 50 semester hours of course work in liberal arts, BA or BS, doctrine agreement. Additional exam requirements/recommendations for international students: Required—TOEFL (minimum score 550 paper-based).

Calvin Theological Seminary, Graduate and Professional Programs, Grand Rapids, MI 49546-4387. Offers Bible and theology (MA); divinity (M Div), including ancient near eastern languages and literature, contextual ministry, evangelism and teaching, history of Christianity, new church development, New Testament, Old Testament, pastoral care and leadership, preaching and worship, theological studies, youth and family ministries; educational ministry (MA); historical theology (PhD); missions and evangelism (MA); pastoral care (MA); philosophical and moral theology (PhD); systematic theology (PhD); theological studies (MTS); theology (Th M); worship (MA); youth and family ministries (MA). *Accreditation:* ACIPE; ATS. Part-time programs available. *Degree requirements:* For master's, variable foreign language requirement, thesis (for some programs); for doctorate, 4 foreign languages, comprehensive exam, thesis/dissertation. *Entrance requirements:* For doctorate, GRE General Test, Hebrew, Greek, and a modern foreign language. Additional exam requirements/recommendations for international students: Required—TOEFL (minimum score 550 paper-based), TWE (minimum score 4). Electronic applications accepted. *Faculty research:* Recent Trinity theory, Christian anthropology, Proverbs, reformed confessions, Paul's view of law.

Campbellsville University, School of Theology, Campbellsville, KY 42718-2799. Offers theology (M Th). Part-time programs available. *Students:* 16 full-time (4 women), 29

part-time (6 women); includes 20 minority (all Black or African American, non-Hispanic/Latino). Average age 43. In 2014, 14 master's awarded. *Degree requirements:* For master's, comprehensive exam, thesis optional. *Entrance requirements:* For master's, GRE General Test, minimum GPA of 3.0 in major, 2.75 overall; 18 hours of undergraduate coursework in Christian studies. *Application deadline:* For fall admission, 8/25 priority date for domestic students; for spring admission, 1/25 for domestic students. Applications are processed on a rolling basis. Application fee: $25. Electronic applications accepted. *Financial support:* In 2014–15, 26 students received support, including 2 fellowships (averaging $1,500 per year); institutionally sponsored loans and scholarships/grants also available. Financial award application deadline: 6/1; financial award applicants required to submit FAFSA. *Faculty research:* Clergy needing graduate theology education, trinity and Christian faith, Old Testament David narratives, leadership principles on Christian university integration of Christian principles in counseling process. *Unit head:* Dr. John E. Hurtgen, Dean, 270-789-5077, Fax: 270-789-5050, E-mail: jehurtgen@campbellsville.edu. *Application contact:* Monica Bamwine, Assistant Director of Admissions, 270-789-5221, Fax: 270-789-5071, E-mail: mkbamwine@campbellsville.edu.
Website: http://www.campbellsville.edu/

Campbell University, Graduate and Professional Programs, Divinity School, Buies Creek, NC 27506. Offers Christian ministry (MA); divinity (M Div); ministry (D Min); JD/M Div; M Div/MA; M Div/MBA. *Accreditation:* ATS. *Faculty:* 5 full-time, 7 part-time/adjunct. *Students:* 239 full-time (89 women), 28 part-time (13 women); includes 40 minority (35 Black or African American, non-Hispanic/Latino; 1 American Indian or Alaska Native, non-Hispanic/Latino; 4 Hispanic/Latino), 2 international. Average age 38. *Degree requirements:* For doctorate, final project. *Entrance requirements:* For master's, minimum GPA of 2.5; for doctorate, MAT, M Div, minimum graduate GPA of 3.0. Additional exam requirements/recommendations for international students: Required—TOEFL (minimum score 580 paper-based). *Application deadline:* For fall admission, 7/1 for domestic students; for spring admission, 11/15 for domestic students. Applications are processed on a rolling basis. Application fee: $20. *Expenses:* Expenses: Contact institution. *Financial support:* Fellowships, scholarships/grants, and unspecified assistantships available. Support available to part-time students. Financial award application deadline: 5/1. *Faculty research:* New Testament, theology, spiritual formation, Old Testament, Christian leadership. *Unit head:* Andrew H. Wakefield, Dean, 910-893-1830, Fax: 910-893-1835. *Application contact:* Amber H. Johnson, Director of Admissions, 800-760-9827 Ext. 4765, Fax: 910-893-1835, E-mail: ahjohnson@campbell.edu.
Website: http://divinity.campbell.edu/

Canadian Southern Baptist Seminary, Graduate Programs, Cochrane, AB T4C 2G1, Canada. Offers Biblical studies (MBS); Christian ministry (MCMin); ministry (M Div). *Accreditation:* ATS. Part-time programs available. Postbaccalaureate distance learning degree programs offered (no on-campus study). *Faculty:* 6 full-time (0 women), 3 part-time/adjunct (0 women). *Students:* 8 full-time (2 women), 29 part-time (9 women); includes 12 minority (2 Black or African American, non-Hispanic/Latino; 7 Asian, non-Hispanic/Latino; 3 Hispanic/Latino), 1 international. Average age 28. 12 applicants, 83% accepted, 7 enrolled. In 2014, 6 master's awarded. *Entrance requirements:* Additional exam requirements/recommendations for international students: Required—TOEFL (minimum score 560 paper-based; 83 iBT); Recommended—IELTS. *Application deadline:* For fall admission, 7/1 priority date for domestic and international students; for winter admission, 11/15 priority date for domestic and international students. Applications are processed on a rolling basis. Application fee: $50 ($150 for international students). *Expenses: Tuition:* Full-time $7200 Canadian dollars; part-time $300 Canadian dollars per credit hour. *Required fees:* $120 Canadian dollars. One-time fee: $50 Canadian dollars. *Financial support:* Scholarships/grants available. Financial award application deadline: 1/21. *Unit head:* Dr. Steve Booth, Academic Dean, 403-932-6622 Ext. 232, E-mail: steve.booth@csbs.ca. *Application contact:* Kathleen McNaughton, Registrar, 403-932-6622 Ext. 221, E-mail: kathleen.mcnaughton@csbs.ca.

Carey Theological College, Graduate Programs, Vancouver, BC V6T 1J6, Canada. Offers M Div, MASF, D Min. *Accreditation:* ATS. Part-time programs available. *Degree requirements:* For doctorate, thesis/dissertation. *Entrance requirements:* For master's, undergraduate degree with minimum GPA of 2.7; for doctorate, M Div with minimum GPA of 3.5. Additional exam requirements/recommendations for international students: Required—TOEFL (minimum score 577 paper-based; 90 iBT). Electronic applications accepted. *Faculty research:* Missional church, new monasticism, women in leadership, spiritual formation, applied theology.

Carolina Evangelical Divinity School, Divinity Program, High Point, NC 27265. Offers M Div. *Accreditation:* ATS.

Carolina Evangelical Divinity School, Program in Theological Studies, High Point, NC 27265. Offers MA. *Accreditation:* ATS.

Carson-Newman University, Program in Applied Theology, Jefferson City, TN 37760. Offers MAAT. *Faculty:* 2 full-time (0 women). *Students:* 2 part-time (1 woman). Average age 35. In 2014, 1 master's awarded. *Degree requirements:* For master's, thesis optional, completetion of degree within five years of admission into program. *Entrance requirements:* For master's, GRE (minimum score of 290), minimum GPA of 3.0. Additional exam requirements/recommendations for international students: Recommended—TOEFL (minimum score 210 paper-based; 79 iBT), IELTS (minimum score 6.5), TSE (minimum score 53). *Application deadline:* For fall admission, 7/15 priority date for domestic students. Applications are processed on a rolling basis. Application fee: $50. *Expenses: Tuition:* Full-time $9680; part-time $440 per credit hour. *Required fees:* $300; $440 per credit hour. $150 per semester. *Unit head:* Dr. David E. Crutchley, Dean, School of Religion, 865-471-3277, E-mail: dcruthley@cn.edu. *Application contact:* Graduate Admissions and Services Adviser, 865-473-3468, Fax: 865-472-3475.
Website: http://www.cn.edu/graduate-adult-studies/programs/religion-graduate

Catholic Distance University, Graduate Programs, Hamilton, VA 20158. Offers religious studies (MRS); theology (MA). Part-time and evening/weekend programs available. Postbaccalaureate distance learning degree programs offered (no on-campus study). *Degree requirements:* For master's, comprehensive exam, capstone paper or project.

Catholic Theological Union, Graduate and Professional Programs, Chicago, IL 60615-5698. Offers biblical spirituality (Certificate); cross-cultural ministries (D Min); cross-cultural missions (Certificate); divinity (M Div); liturgical studies (Certificate); liturgy (D Min); pastoral studies (MAPS, Certificate); spiritual formation (Certificate); spirituality (D Min); theology (MA); M Div/MA; M Div/MSW; M Div/PhD. M Div/PhD offered jointly with University of Chicago; M Div/MSW with Loyola University Chicago and University of Chicago. *Accreditation:* ACIPE; ATS (one or more programs are accredited). Part-time and evening/weekend programs available. *Degree requirements:* For master's, one foreign language, comprehensive exam (for some programs), thesis (for some programs); for doctorate, thesis/dissertation. *Entrance requirements:* For doctorate, master's degree, 5 years of active ministry. *Faculty research:* Doctrine, sacraments, ethics, Bible.

The Catholic University of America, School of Canon Law, Washington, DC 20064. Offers JCD, JCL, JD/JCL. Part-time programs available. *Faculty:* 6 full-time (1 woman), 1 part-time/adjunct (0 women). *Students:* 40 full-time (4 women), 46 part-time (7 women); includes 9 minority (1 Black or African American, non-Hispanic/Latino; 2 Asian, non-Hispanic/Latino; 3 Hispanic/Latino; 3 Two or more races, non-Hispanic/Latino), 10 international. Average age 38. 34 applicants, 91% accepted, 22 enrolled. In 2014, 1 doctorate awarded. *Degree requirements:* For doctorate, 2 foreign languages, thesis/dissertation, fluency in canonical Latin. *Entrance requirements:* For doctorate, GRE General Test, minimum A- average, JCL. Additional exam requirements/recommendations for international students: Required—TOEFL (minimum score 580 paper-based). *Application deadline:* For fall admission, 7/15 priority date for domestic students, 7/1 for international students; for spring admission, 11/15 priority date for domestic students, 11/1 for international students. Applications are processed on a rolling basis. Application fee: $55. Electronic applications accepted. *Expenses: Tuition:* Full-time $40,200; part-time $1600 per credit hour. *Required fees:* $400; $195 per semester. One-time fee: $425. *Financial support:* Fellowships, research assistantships, teaching assistantships, Federal Work-Study, scholarships/grants, tuition waivers (full and partial), and unspecified assistantships available. Financial award application deadline: 2/1; financial award applicants required to submit FAFSA. *Faculty research:* Ecclesiology and the Sacrament of Orders, procedural law, temporal goods, matrimonial jurisprudence, sacramental and liturgical law. *Unit head:* Rev. Robert Kaslyn, SJ, Dean, 202-319-5492, Fax: 202-319-4187, E-mail: cua-canonlaw@cua.edu. *Application contact:* Director of Graduate Admissions, 202-319-5057, Fax: 202-319-6533, E-mail: cua-admissions@cua.edu.
Website: http://canonlaw.cua.edu

The Catholic University of America, School of Theology and Religious Studies, Washington, DC 20064. Offers M Div, MA, MRE, D Min, PhD, STD, Certificate, STB, STL, MSLS/MA. *Accreditation:* ATS (one or more programs are accredited). Part-time programs available. *Faculty:* 44 full-time (5 women), 8 part-time/adjunct (2 women). *Students:* 153 full-time (8 women), 206 part-time (51 women); includes 50 minority (8 Black or African American, non-Hispanic/Latino; 2 American Indian or Alaska Native, non-Hispanic/Latino; 11 Asian, non-Hispanic/Latino; 16 Hispanic/Latino; 1 Native Hawaiian or other Pacific Islander, non-Hispanic/Latino; 12 Two or more races, non-Hispanic/Latino), 57 international. Average age 36. 197 applicants, 74% accepted, 69 enrolled. In 2014, 40 master's, 21 doctorates awarded. *Degree requirements:* For master's, variable foreign language requirement, comprehensive exam (for some programs), thesis (for some programs); for doctorate, variable foreign language requirement, comprehensive exam, thesis/dissertation. *Entrance requirements:* For master's and doctorate, GRE General Test, statement of purpose, official copies of academic transcripts, three letters of recommendation. Additional exam requirements/recommendations for international students: Required—TOEFL (minimum score 580 paper-based). *Application deadline:* For fall admission, 7/15 priority date for domestic students, 7/1 for international students; for spring admission, 11/15 priority date for domestic students, 11/1 for international students. Applications are processed on a rolling basis. Application fee: $55. Electronic applications accepted. *Expenses: Tuition:* Full-time $40,200; part-time $1600 per credit hour. *Required fees:* $400; $195 per semester. One-time fee: $425. *Financial support:* Fellowships, research assistantships, teaching assistantships, Federal Work-Study, scholarships/grants, tuition waivers (full and partial), and unspecified assistantships available. Financial award application deadline: 2/1; financial award applicants required to submit FAFSA. *Faculty research:* Historical and systematic theology, religious education and catechetics, moral theology and ethics, Biblical studies, liturgical studies and sacramental theology. *Unit head:* Msgr. Paul McPartlan, Acting Dean, 202-319-6515, Fax: 202-319-5704, E-mail: mcpartlan@cua.edu. *Application contact:* Director of Graduate Admissions, 202-319-5057, Fax: 202-319-6533, E-mail: cua-admissions@cua.edu.
Website: http://trs.cua.edu/

Central Baptist Theological Seminary, Graduate and Professional Programs, Shawnee, KS 66226. Offers missional church studies (MA); theological studies (MA); theology (M Div, Diploma). *Accreditation:* ACIPE; ATS (one or more programs are accredited). Part-time programs available. *Degree requirements:* For master's, thesis optional. *Entrance requirements:* Additional exam requirements/recommendations for international students: Required—TOEFL (minimum score 547 paper-based; 77 iBT). Electronic applications accepted.

Central Yeshiva Tomchei Tmimim-Lubavitch, Graduate Programs, Brooklyn, NY 11230. Offers Jewish/Judaic studies (MA); Talmudic studies (MA). *Accreditation:* AARTS.

Chaminade University of Honolulu, Graduate Services, Program in Pastoral Theology, Honolulu, HI 96816-1578. Offers MPT. Part-time and evening/weekend programs available. Postbaccalaureate distance learning degree programs offered. *Degree requirements:* For master's, capstone course. *Entrance requirements:* For master's, 2 letters of recommendation. Additional exam requirements/recommendations for international students: Required—TOEFL (minimum score 550 paper-based). Electronic applications accepted.

Charlotte Christian College and Theological Seminary, Graduate Program, Charlotte, NC 28205. Offers urban Christian ministry (MA), including church planting, multi-cultural studies, sacred music, youth ministry. Part-time and evening/weekend programs available. *Faculty:* 5 full-time (1 woman), 9 part-time/adjunct (2 women). *Students:* 2 full-time (1 woman), 25 part-time (15 women); includes 18 minority (17 Black or African American, non-Hispanic/Latino; 1 Hispanic/Latino), 2 international. Average age 47. 2 applicants, 100% accepted, 2 enrolled. In 2014, 2 master's awarded. *Degree requirements:* For master's, thesis. *Entrance requirements:* For master's, MAT, writing sample/essay. Additional exam requirements/recommendations for international students: Required—TOEFL, IELTS. *Application deadline:* For fall admission, 7/24 for domestic students, 7/18 for international students; for spring admission, 12/11 for domestic students, 12/5 for international students; for summer admission, 4/18 for domestic and international students. Application fee: $50 ($140 for international students). Electronic applications accepted. *Expenses:* Expenses: 1 course: $1,200; 2 courses: $2,300; 3 courses: $3,300; 4 courses $3,900. *Financial support:* In 2014–15, 5 students received support. Federal Work-Study and scholarships/grants available. Financial award application deadline: 4/1; financial award applicants required to submit FAFSA. *Unit head:* Anne Witt, Registrar/Director of International Students, 704-344-6882 Ext. 103, Fax: 704-334-6885, E-mail: abwitt@charlottechristian.edu. *Application contact:* Constance Hemphill, Director of Admissions, 704-334-6882 Ext. 115, Fax: 704-334-6885, E-mail: chemphill@charlottechristian.edu.
Website: http://www.charlottechristian.edu

Chicago Theological Seminary, Graduate and Professional Programs, Chicago, IL 60637-1507. Offers preaching (D Min); religion and health (D Min); religious studies (MA); spirituality and spiritual direction (D Min); theology (M Div); theology, ethics and the human sciences (PhD); M Div/MSW. *Accreditation:* ACIPE; ATS. Part-time programs available. *Degree requirements:* For master's, thesis; for doctorate, 2 foreign languages, comprehensive exam, thesis/dissertation. *Entrance requirements:* For doctorate, GRE General Test. Additional exam requirements/recommendations for international students: Required—TOEFL. *Faculty research:* Bible, culture and hermeneutics,

theology, gender and sexuality, black faith and life, spirituality and psychology, practical theology.

Christendom College, Notre Dame Graduate School, Alexandria, VA 22312. Offers theological studies (MA), including catechetics, moral theology, systematic theology. Part-time and evening/weekend programs available. Postbaccalaureate distance learning degree programs offered (no on-campus study). *Degree requirements:* For master's, one foreign language, comprehensive exam, thesis or alternative. Electronic applications accepted.

Christian Theological Seminary, Graduate and Professional Programs, Indianapolis, IN 46208-3301. Offers educational and arts ministries (MA); marriage and family therapy (MA); pastoral care and counseling (D Min); psychotherapy and faith (MA); theological studies (MTS); theology (M Div). *Accreditation:* AAMFT/COAMFTE (one or more programs are accredited); ACIPE; ATS. Part-time programs available. Terminal master's awarded for partial completion of doctoral program. *Degree requirements:* For master's, comprehensive exam (for some programs), thesis (for some programs), missionary and cross-cultural experience (for M Div); for doctorate, comprehensive exam, thesis/dissertation. *Entrance requirements:* For doctorate, M Div. Additional exam requirements/recommendations for international students: Recommended—TOEFL. Electronic applications accepted. *Faculty research:* Faith formation, peer learning post graduation.

Christ the King Seminary, Graduate and Professional Programs, East Aurora, NY 14052. Offers divinity (M Div); pastoral ministry (MA); theology (MA). *Accreditation:* ATS. Part-time and evening/weekend programs available. *Degree requirements:* For master's, comprehensive exam, thesis. *Entrance requirements:* For master's, previous course work in philosophy and religious studies.

Church Divinity School of the Pacific, Graduate and Professional Programs, Berkeley, CA 94709-1217. Offers M Div, MA, MTS, D Min, Certificate. MA program offered jointly with Graduate Theological Union. *Accreditation:* ACIPE; ATS (one or more programs are accredited). Part-time programs available. *Degree requirements:* For master's, one foreign language, thesis (for some programs); for doctorate, thesis/dissertation. *Entrance requirements:* For master's and Certificate, GRE General Test, letters of reference; for doctorate, letters of reference. Additional exam requirements/recommendations for international students: Required—TOEFL. Electronic applications accepted.

Cincinnati Christian University, Graduate School, Cincinnati, OH 45204-3200. Offers biblical studies (MA); church history (MA); counseling (MAC); divinity (M Div); ministry (M Min); practical ministries (MA); theological studies (MA). *Accreditation:* ATS. Part-time programs available. *Degree requirements:* For master's, variable foreign language requirement, thesis (for some programs), oral exam (for M Div). *Entrance requirements:* Additional exam requirements/recommendations for international students: Required—TOEFL. Electronic applications accepted.

Claremont Graduate University, Graduate Programs, School of Arts and Humanities, Department of Religion, Claremont, CA 91711-6160. Offers Hebrew Bible (MA, PhD); history of Christianity and religions of North America (MA, PhD); New Testament (MA, PhD); philosophy of religion and theology (MA, PhD); theology, ethics and culture (MA, PhD); women's studies in religion (MA, PhD); MA/PhD; MBA/PhD. Part-time programs available. *Faculty:* 7 full-time (3 women), 2 part-time/adjunct (0 women). *Students:* 153 full-time (58 women), 31 part-time (16 women); includes 33 minority (12 Black or African American, non-Hispanic/Latino; 1 American Indian or Alaska Native, non-Hispanic/Latino; 7 Asian, non-Hispanic/Latino; 10 Hispanic/Latino; 1 Native Hawaiian or other Pacific Islander, non-Hispanic/Latino; 2 Two or more races, non-Hispanic/Latino), 14 international. Average age 37. In 2014, 15 master's, 13 doctorates awarded. Terminal master's awarded for partial completion of doctoral program. *Entrance requirements:* For master's and doctorate, GRE General Test. Additional exam requirements/recommendations for international students: Required—TOEFL (minimum score 550 paper-based; 80 iBT). *Application deadline:* For fall admission, 2/1 priority date for domestic and international students. Applications are processed on a rolling basis. Application fee: $80. Electronic applications accepted. *Expenses: Tuition:* Full-time $41,784; part-time $1741 per credit. *Required fees:* $600; $300 per semester. *Financial support:* Fellowships, research assistantships, teaching assistantships, Federal Work-Study, institutionally sponsored loans, and scholarships/grants available. Support available to part-time students. Financial award application deadline: 2/15; financial award applicants required to submit FAFSA. *Unit head:* Tammi Schneider, Chair, E-mail: tammi.schneider@cgu.edu. *Application contact:* Erma Cross, Admissions and Alumni Coordinator, 909-607-9843, E-mail: erminia.cross@cgu.edu.
Website: http://www.cgu.edu/pages/674.asp

Claremont School of Theology, Graduate and Professional Programs, Master of Divinity Program, Claremont, CA 91711-3199. Offers M Div. *Accreditation:* ACIPE; ATS. Part-time programs available. *Entrance requirements:* Additional exam requirements/recommendations for international students: Required—TOEFL. Electronic applications accepted.

Claremont School of Theology, Graduate and Professional Programs, Program in Religion, Claremont, CA 91711-3199. Offers practical theology (PhD), including religious education, spiritual care and counseling; religion (PhD), including Hebrew Bible, New Testament and Christian origins, process studies, religion, ethics, and society; religion and theology (MA); religious education (MARE). *Accreditation:* ACIPE; ATS. Terminal master's awarded for partial completion of doctoral program. *Degree requirements:* For master's, thesis; for doctorate, 2 foreign languages, thesis/dissertation. *Entrance requirements:* For doctorate, GRE General Test. Additional exam requirements/recommendations for international students: Required—TOEFL. Electronic applications accepted.

Colgate Rochester Crozer Divinity School, Graduate and Professional Programs, Rochester, NY 14620-2530. Offers M Div, MA, D Min, Certificate. *Accreditation:* ACIPE; ATS (one or more programs are accredited). Part-time programs available. Postbaccalaureate distance learning degree programs offered (minimal on-campus study). *Faculty:* 7 full-time (3 women), 12 part-time/adjunct (7 women). *Students:* 65 full-time, 42 part-time; includes 45 minority (42 Black or African American, non-Hispanic/Latino; 1 Asian, non-Hispanic/Latino; 1 Hispanic/Latino; 1 Two or more races, non-Hispanic/Latino), 2 international. Average age 42. 39 applicants, 67% accepted, 23 enrolled. In 2014, 16 master's, 2 doctorates awarded. *Degree requirements:* For master's, thesis (for some programs), supervised ministry year (for M Div); for doctorate, thesis/dissertation. *Entrance requirements:* For master's, BA/BS, personal statement, 4 recommendations; for doctorate, M Div, 3 years' professional experience, writing sample, personal statement, curriculum vitae, 4 recommendations. Additional exam requirements/recommendations for international students: Required—TOEFL (minimum score 600 paper-based; 93 iBT). *Application deadline:* For fall admission, 7/1 priority date for domestic students, 3/1 for international students; for spring admission, 12/1 priority date for domestic students, 9/1 for international students. Applications are processed on a rolling basis. Application fee: $35. Electronic applications accepted. *Expenses: Tuition:* Full-time $10,590; part-time $1765 per course. *Required fees:* $255; $35 per course. One-time fee: $225. Tuition and fees vary according to course load, degree level and reciprocity agreements. *Financial support:* Scholarships/grants available. Financial award application deadline: 9/1; financial award applicants required to submit FAFSA. *Faculty research:* Old Testament, New Testament, Christian ethics, black church studies, woman and gender studies. *Unit head:* Rev. Marvin A. McMickle, PhD, President, 585-271-1320 Ext. 680, Fax: 585-271-8013. *Application contact:* Melissa M. Morral, Vice President for Enrollment Services, 585-340-9633, Fax: 585-340-9644, E-mail: mmorral@crcds.edu.
Website: http://www.crcds.edu

Collège Dominicain de Philosophie et de Théologie, Graduate Programs, Faculty of Theology, Ottawa, ON K1R 7G3, Canada. Offers M Th, MA Th, PhD, Th D, L Th. Part-time and evening/weekend programs available. *Degree requirements:* For master's, 2 foreign languages, research paper; for doctorate, 2 foreign languages, thesis/dissertation, candidacy exam. *Entrance requirements:* For master's, B Th or equivalent, minimum A- average in undergraduate course work; for doctorate, MA Th or equivalent, minimum A- average in graduate course work. *Faculty research:* Exegese, bioethics, history of church, New Testament.

College of Emmanuel and St. Chad, Bachelor of Theology Program, Saskatoon, SK S7N 0W6, Canada. Offers B Th. Part-time programs available. Postbaccalaureate distance learning degree programs offered (minimal on-campus study). *Degree requirements:* For B Th, internship. *Entrance requirements:* For degree, 1 year of university-level work or equivalent. Additional exam requirements/recommendations for international students: Required—TOEFL. *Faculty research:* Pauline studies, New Testament, ethics, congregational development, trauma and spirituality.

College of Emmanuel and St. Chad, Graduate Programs, Saskatoon, SK S7N 0W6, Canada. Offers M Div, MTS, STM, L Th. STM program offered jointly with Lutheran Theological Seminary and St. Andrew's College. Part-time programs available. *Degree requirements:* For master's, thesis optional. *Entrance requirements:* For master's, M Div or MTS (STM). Additional exam requirements/recommendations for international students: Required—TOEFL. *Faculty research:* New Testament, systematics, Christian education, theology, ethics.

College of Saint Elizabeth, Department of Theology and Philosophy, Morristown, NJ 07960-6989. Offers MA. Part-time programs available. *Degree requirements:* For master's, thesis or alternative. *Entrance requirements:* For master's, minimum GPA of 3.0, personal interview with coordinator and another faculty member. Additional exam requirements/recommendations for international students: Required—TOEFL. Electronic applications accepted.

Columbia International University, Columbia Biblical Seminary and School of Ministry, Columbia, SC 29230-3122. Offers academic ministries (M Div); Bible and theology (Certificate); bible exposition (M Div, MABE); Biblical ministry (Certificate); chaplaincy (M Div); intercultural studies (MAIS); leadership (D Min); member care (D Min); missions (D Min); preaching (D Min); theological studies (MA). *Accreditation:* ATS (one or more programs are accredited). Part-time and evening/weekend programs available. *Faculty:* 14 full-time (1 woman), 9 part-time/adjunct (1 woman). *Students:* 180 full-time (59 women), 218 part-time (61 women); includes 81 minority (58 Black or African American, non-Hispanic/Latino; 1 American Indian or Alaska Native, non-Hispanic/Latino; 18 Asian, non-Hispanic/Latino; 4 Hispanic/Latino), 22 international. Average age 36. 277 applicants, 81% accepted, 117 enrolled. In 2014, 74 master's, 3 doctorates, 15 other advanced degrees awarded. *Degree requirements:* For doctorate, comprehensive exam, thesis/dissertation. *Entrance requirements:* For doctorate, 3 years of ministerial experience, M Div. Additional exam requirements/recommendations for international students: Required—TOEFL. *Application deadline:* For fall admission, 8/1 priority date for domestic and international students; for winter admission, 12/15 priority date for domestic and international students; for spring admission, 1/15 priority date for domestic and international students. Applications are processed on a rolling basis. Application fee: $45. Electronic applications accepted. *Expenses: Tuition:* Full-time $9540; part-time $530 per credit hour. *Required fees:* $480; $240 per semester. *Financial support:* In 2014–15, 120 students received support. Career-related internships or fieldwork, Federal Work-Study, institutionally sponsored loans, and scholarships/grants available. Financial award application deadline: 3/15; financial award applicants required to submit FAFSA. *Unit head:* Dr. Junias Venugopal, Dean, 803-754-4100 Ext. 5330, Fax: 803-786-4209, E-mail: jvenugopal@ciu.edu. *Application contact:* Michelle MacGregor, Director of Admissions, 800-777-2227 Ext. 5335, Fax: 803-786-4209, E-mail: yescbs@ciu.edu.
Website: http://www.ciu.edu/discover-ciu/who-we-are/academics/seminary-school-ministry

Columbia Theological Seminary, Graduate and Professional Programs, Decatur, GA 30031-0520. Offers M Div, MATS, Th M, D Min, Th D. Th D program offered jointly with Emory University; D Min with Interdenominational Theological Center. *Accreditation:* ACIPE; ATS (one or more programs are accredited). Terminal master's awarded for partial completion of doctoral program. *Degree requirements:* For master's, variable foreign language requirement, thesis (for some programs); for doctorate, one foreign language, thesis/dissertation. *Entrance requirements:* For doctorate, M Div or equivalent, 3 years practice of ministry. Additional exam requirements/recommendations for international students: Required—TOEFL.

Concordia Lutheran Seminary, Graduate and Professional Programs, Edmonton, AB T5B 4E3, Canada. Offers M Div, Graduate Certificate. *Accreditation:* ATS (one or more programs are accredited). Part-time programs available. *Degree requirements:* For master's, thesis or alternative. *Entrance requirements:* For master's, GRE General Test. Additional exam requirements/recommendations for international students: Required—TOEFL. *Faculty research:* Lutheran Pietism, Christianity and culture, missiology, Christian worship, homiletics.

Concordia Seminary, Graduate Programs, St. Louis, MO 63105-3199. Offers M Div, MA, STM, D Min, PhD, Certificate. *Accreditation:* ACIPE; ATS (one or more programs are accredited). Terminal master's awarded for partial completion of doctoral program. *Degree requirements:* For master's, variable foreign language requirement, comprehensive exam (for some programs), thesis (for some programs); for doctorate, 4 foreign languages, thesis/dissertation. *Entrance requirements:* For master's, GRE General Test, previous course work in public speaking, Greek, Hebrew, Old Testament, New Testament, and Christian Doctrine (for M Div); for doctorate, GRE General Test, theological essay in English (foreign students only). Additional exam requirements/recommendations for international students: Required—TOEFL. *Faculty research:* Family counseling, educational administration, contemporary theology, pastoral office, humanism and education.

Concordia Theological Seminary, Graduate and Professional Programs, Fort Wayne, IN 46825-4996. Offers M Div, MA, STM, D Min, PhD. *Accreditation:* ATS. Part-time programs available. *Degree requirements:* For master's, variable foreign language requirement, thesis (for some programs); for doctorate, comprehensive exam, thesis/dissertation, oral exam. *Entrance requirements:* For master's, GRE General Test (for M Div), minimum GPA of 2.25 (for M Div).

Concordia University, School of Graduate Studies, Faculty of Arts and Science, Department of Theological Studies, Montréal, QC H3G 1M8, Canada. Offers MA. *Degree requirements:* For master's, one foreign language, research papers or thesis.

Entrance requirements: For master's, minimum B average in theology. *Faculty research:* Interpretation theory, theological methodology.

Concordia University, School of Theology, Irvine, CA 92612-3299. Offers Christian leadership (MA); research in theology (MA); theology and culture (MA). Part-time and evening/weekend programs available. *Degree requirements:* For master's, project/thesis or vicarage. *Entrance requirements:* For master's, official college transcript(s), statement of intent, 2 references, interview. Additional exam requirements/recommendations for international students: Required—TOEFL. Electronic applications accepted. *Expenses:* Contact institution.

Concordia University College of Alberta, Program in Biblical and Christian Studies, Edmonton, AB T5B 4E4, Canada. Offers MA.

Corban University, Graduate School, School of Ministry, Salem, OR 97301-9392. Offers Biblical languages (M Div); Biblical leadership (Certificate); Christian leadership (MA); Church ministry (M Div); ministry (D Min). Part-time and evening/weekend programs available. *Degree requirements:* For master's, thesis. *Entrance requirements:* Additional exam requirements/recommendations for international students: Required—TOEFL (minimum score 550 paper-based), IELTS (minimum score 6).

Covenant Theological Seminary, Graduate and Professional Programs, St. Louis, MO 63141-8697. Offers M Div, MA, MAC, MAEM, Th M, D Min, Certificate. *Accreditation:* ATS (one or more programs are accredited). Part-time and evening/weekend programs available. Postbaccalaureate distance learning degree programs offered (no on-campus study). *Degree requirements:* For master's, 2 foreign languages, thesis (for some programs); for doctorate, 2 foreign languages, thesis/dissertation; for Certificate, 2 foreign languages. *Entrance requirements:* For doctorate and Certificate, M Div. Additional exam requirements/recommendations for international students: Required—TOEFL (minimum score 550 paper-based). *Application deadline:* Applications are processed on a rolling basis. Application fee: $50. Electronic applications accepted. *Financial support:* Career-related internships or fieldwork, institutionally sponsored loans, scholarships/grants, and tuition waivers (full and partial) available. Support available to part-time students. Financial award application deadline: 4/15; financial award applicants required to submit FAFSA. *Application contact:* John Patton, Director of Admissions, 314-434-4044, Fax: 314-434-4819, E-mail: admissions@covenantseminary.edu.
Website: http://www.covenantseminary.edu/academics/degrees/

Creighton University, Graduate School, College of Arts and Sciences, Department of Theology, Omaha, NE 68178-0001. Offers MA. Part-time and evening/weekend programs available. Postbaccalaureate distance learning degree programs offered (minimal on-campus study). *Faculty:* 21 full-time (6 women). *Students:* 2 full-time (1 woman), 21 part-time (12 women); includes 2 minority (1 Black or African American, non-Hispanic/Latino; 1 American Indian or Alaska Native, non-Hispanic/Latino), 1 international. Average age 43. 6 applicants, 50% accepted, 3 enrolled. In 2014, 20 master's awarded. *Degree requirements:* For master's, thesis (for some programs). *Entrance requirements:* For master's, GRE General Test, 9 hours of theology course work, 3 letters of recommendation. Additional exam requirements/recommendations for international students: Required—TOEFL (minimum score 550 paper-based; 80 iBT). *Application deadline:* For fall admission, 3/1 for domestic and international students; for winter admission, 10/1 for domestic students, 5/1 for international students; for spring admission, 4/1 for domestic students, 10/1 for international students; for summer admission, 3/1 for domestic and international students. Applications are processed on a rolling basis. Application fee: $50. Electronic applications accepted. *Expenses: Tuition:* Full-time $14,040; part-time $780 per credit hour. *Required fees:* $153 per semester. Tuition and fees vary according to course load, campus/location, program, reciprocity agreements and student's religious affiliation. *Financial support:* Scholarships/grants and tuition waivers (partial) available. Support available to part-time students. Financial award applicants required to submit FAFSA. *Unit head:* Dr. Richard Miller, Director, 402-280-3618, E-mail: richardmiller@creighton.edu. *Application contact:* Lindsay Johnson, Director of Graduate and Adult Recruitment, 402-280-2703, Fax: 402-280-2423, E-mail: gradschool@creighton.edu.

The Criswell College, Graduate School of the Bible, Dallas, TX 75246-1537. Offers biblical studies (M Div); Christian leadership (MA); counseling (MA); Jewish studies (MA); ministry (MA); theological and biblical studies (MA). Part-time programs available. *Degree requirements:* For master's, 2 foreign languages, thesis optional. *Entrance requirements:* For master's, GRE General Test, minimum GPA of 2.5. Electronic applications accepted. *Faculty research:* Emphasis on biblical languages (Hebrew and Greek), expository preaching and evangelism in the local church.

Crown College, Adult and Graduate Studies, St. Bonifacius, MN 55375-9001. Offers Christian studies (MA); instructional leadership (MA); international leadership (MA); ministry leadership (MA); organizational leadership (MA). Part-time and evening/weekend programs available. Postbaccalaureate distance learning degree programs offered (no on-campus study). *Degree requirements:* For master's, thesis optional. *Entrance requirements:* For master's, 12 credits in foundational studies, minimum GPA of 2.5 and bachelor's degree from regionally-accredited college. Additional exam requirements/recommendations for international students: Required—TOEFL (minimum score 550 paper-based; 80 iBT). Electronic applications accepted.

Dallas Baptist University, Gary Cook School of Leadership, Program in Theological Studies, Dallas, TX 75211-9299. Offers MATS. *Expenses: Tuition:* Full-time $14,130; part-time $785 per credit hour. *Required fees:* $200 per semester. Tuition and fees vary according to course level and course load.

Dallas Theological Seminary, Graduate Programs, Dallas, TX 75204-6499. Offers adult education (Th M); apologetics (Th M); Bible backgrounds (Th M); Bible translation (Th M); Biblical and theological studies (Certificate); biblical counseling (MA); biblical exegesis and linguistics (MA); biblical exposition (PhD); biblical studies (MA); Biblical theology (Th M); children's education (Th M); Christian education (MA, D Min); Christian leadership (MA); cross-cultural ministries (MA); educational administration (Th M); educational leadership (Th M); evangelism and discipleship (Th M); exposition of Biblical books (Th M); family life education (Th M); general studies (Th M); Hebrew and cognate studies (Th M); hermeneutics (Th M); historical theology (Th M); homiletics (Th M); intercultural ministries (Th M); Jesus studies (Th M); leadership studies (Th M); media and communication (MA); media arts (Th M); ministry (D Min); ministry with women (Th M); New Testament studies (Th M, PhD); Old Testament studies (Th M, PhD); parachurch ministries (Th M); pastoral care and counseling (Th M); pastoral theology and practice (Th M); philosophy (Th M); sacred theology (STM); spiritual formation (Th M); systematic theology (Th M); teaching in Christian institutions (Th M); theological studies (PhD); urban ministries (Th M); worship studies (Th M); youth education (Th M). *Accreditation:* ATS (one or more programs are accredited). Part-time programs available. Postbaccalaureate distance learning degree programs offered (no on-campus study). *Degree requirements:* For master's, variable foreign language requirement, thesis (for some programs); for doctorate, 2 foreign languages, thesis/dissertation. *Entrance requirements:* For master's, GRE or MAT (if minimum undergraduate cumulative GPA is below 2.5 or undergraduate degree is unaccredited). Additional exam requirements/recommendations for international students: Required—TOEFL (minimum score 575 paper-based; 85 iBT), TWE. Electronic applications accepted.

Denver Seminary, Graduate and Professional Programs, Littleton, CO 80120. Offers apologetics (Certificate); biblical studies (MA); Christian formation and soul care (MA, Certificate); Christian studies (MA, Certificate); church and parachurch leadership (D Min); counseling licensure (MA); counseling ministry (MA); intercultural ministry (Certificate); leadership (MA, Certificate); marriage and family counseling (D Min); pastoral ministry (D Min); philosophy of religion (MA); spiritual guidance (Certificate); theology (M Div, Certificate); worship (Certificate); youth and family ministry (MA). *Accreditation:* ACA; ACIPE; ATS (one or more programs are accredited). Part-time and evening/weekend programs available. Postbaccalaureate distance learning degree programs offered. *Degree requirements:* For master's, 2 foreign languages, thesis (for some programs); for doctorate, 2 foreign languages, thesis/dissertation. *Entrance requirements:* For doctorate, M Div, 3 years of ministry experience. Additional exam requirements/recommendations for international students: Required—TOEFL (minimum score 575 paper-based; 90 iBT). Electronic applications accepted.

Dominican House of Studies, Pontifical Faculty of the Immaculate Conception, Graduate and Professional Programs in Theology, Washington, DC 20017-1585. Offers moral theology (STL); sacred scripture (STL); systematic theology (STL); theology (M Div, MA, STB); Thomistic studies (MA, STD, STL). *Accreditation:* ATS (one or more programs are accredited). Part-time programs available. *Faculty:* 16 full-time (1 woman), 9 part-time/adjunct (3 women). *Students:* 71 full-time (1 woman), 16 part-time (4 women); includes 5 minority (2 Asian, non-Hispanic/Latino; 3 Hispanic/Latino), 13 international. Average age 33. *Degree requirements:* For master's, thesis, thesis defense; for other advanced degree, comprehensive exam (for some programs), thesis (for some programs), lecture. *Entrance requirements:* For master's, 18 credits of philosophy, reading knowledge of Latin, BA with a minimum GPA of 3.0; for other advanced degree, 36 credits of philosophy, BA with minimum GPA of 3.25 (for STB). Additional exam requirements/recommendations for international students: Required—TOEFL (minimum score 550 paper-based; 79 iBT). *Application deadline:* For fall admission, 7/1 for domestic and international students; for spring admission, 12/1 for domestic and international students. Applications are processed on a rolling basis. Application fee: $50. *Expenses: Tuition:* Full-time $16,080; part-time $670 per credit. *Financial support:* Career-related internships or fieldwork and Federal Work-Study available. Support available to part-time students. Financial award application deadline: 6/30; financial award applicants required to submit FAFSA. *Faculty research:* Sacred scripture, moral theology, systematic theology, philosophy, languages. *Unit head:* Rev. Thomas Petri, OP, Vice-President/Academic Dean, 202-495-3832, Fax: 202-495-3873, E-mail: dean@dhs.edu. *Application contact:* Rev. Albert Trudel, OP, Registrar, 202-495-3836, Fax: 202-495-3873, E-mail: registrar@dhs.edu.

Dominican School of Philosophy and Theology, Graduate Programs, Berkeley, CA 94708. Offers philosophy (MA); theology (M Div, MA, MTS, Certificate); M Div/MA; MA/MA. Part-time programs available. *Faculty:* 12 full-time (3 women), 7 part-time/adjunct (0 women). *Students:* 40 full-time (7 women), 38 part-time (6 women); includes 24 minority (2 Black or African American, non-Hispanic/Latino; 1 American Indian or Alaska Native, non-Hispanic/Latino; 12 Asian, non-Hispanic/Latino; 5 Hispanic/Latino; 4 Two or more races, non-Hispanic/Latino), 3 international. *Degree requirements:* For master's, one foreign language, thesis. *Entrance requirements:* For master's, GRE General Test (for MA), minimum GPA of 3.0 (for MA), 2.3 (for M Div); academic writing sample (for MA); statement of purpose, official transcripts, letters of recommendation. Additional exam requirements/recommendations for international students: Required—TOEFL (minimum score 570 paper-based; 80 iBT), IELTS. *Application deadline:* For fall admission, 3/4 priority date for domestic and international students; for spring admission, 11/1 priority date for domestic and international students. Applications are processed on a rolling basis. Application fee: $50. Electronic applications accepted. *Expenses: Tuition:* Full-time $16,680; part-time $695 per unit. *Required fees:* $50; $50 per year. Tuition and fees vary according to course load. *Financial support:* Institutionally sponsored loans, scholarships/grants, and tuition waivers (partial) available. Financial award application deadline: 3/4. *Unit head:* Fr. Christopher Renz, OP, Academic Dean, 510-883-2084, Fax: 510-849-1372, E-mail: crenz@dspt.edu. *Application contact:* Jamie L. Martos, Director of Admissions and Recruitment, 510-883-2073, Fax: 510-849-1372, E-mail: admissions@dspt.edu.

Drew University, Theological School, Madison, NJ 07940-1493. Offers M Div, MA, MA Min, STM, D Min, PhD, Certificate. *Accreditation:* ACIPE; ATS. Part-time programs available. Postbaccalaureate distance learning degree programs offered (minimal on-campus study). *Degree requirements:* For doctorate, thesis/dissertation. *Entrance requirements:* Additional exam requirements/recommendations for international students: Required—TOEFL (minimum score 580 paper-based; 88 iBT), TWE. Electronic applications accepted. *Expenses:* Contact institution. *Faculty research:* Biblical studies, constructive theology, ecology and religion, gender and religion, race/ethnicity and religion.

Duke University, Divinity School, Durham, NC 27708-0586. Offers M Div, MACP, MACS, MTS, Th M, D Min, Th D, JD/MTS, M Div/MSW. *Accreditation:* ACIPE; ATS. Part-time programs available. Postbaccalaureate distance learning degree programs offered (minimal on-campus study). Terminal master's awarded for partial completion of doctoral program. *Degree requirements:* For master's, thesis (for some programs); for doctorate, 2 foreign languages, comprehensive exam (for some programs), thesis/dissertation. *Entrance requirements:* For master's, 5 letters of reference, bachelor's degree from regionally-accredited college or university prior to intended date of enrollment, minimum GPA of 2.75, committment to some form of ordained or lay ministry; for doctorate, GRE, M Div, MTS or comparable master's degree from institution accredited by ATS; bachelor's degree from regionally-accredited college or university prior to intended date of enrollment; 4 letters of reference; 2-page statement of purpose; one sample of academic writing. Additional exam requirements/recommendations for international students: Required—TOEFL (minimum score 580 paper-based; 93 iBT). Electronic applications accepted. *Expenses:* Contact institution. *Faculty research:* Biblical studies, historical church studies, theological studies, church ministry studies.

Duquesne University, Graduate School of Liberal Arts, Department of Theology, Pittsburgh, PA 15282-0001. Offers pastoral ministry (MA); religious education (MA); systematic theology (PhD); theology (MA). Part-time and evening/weekend programs available. *Faculty:* 17 full-time (6 women). *Students:* 57 full-time (16 women), 13 part-time (all women); includes 9 minority (4 Black or African American, non-Hispanic/Latino; 1 Asian, non-Hispanic/Latino; 2 Hispanic/Latino; 2 Two or more races, non-Hispanic/Latino), 16 international. Average age 40. 33 applicants, 42% accepted, 13 enrolled. In 2014, 55 master's, 6 doctorates awarded. *Degree requirements:* For master's, comprehensive exam; for doctorate, 2 foreign languages, comprehensive exam, thesis/dissertation. *Entrance requirements:* For master's and doctorate, GRE General Test. Additional exam requirements/recommendations for international students: Required—TOEFL. *Application deadline:* For fall admission, 2/1 for domestic and international students. Electronic applications accepted. *Expenses: Tuition:* Full-time $18,882; part-time $1049 per credit. *Required fees:* $1800; $100 per credit. Tuition and fees vary according to program. *Financial support:* In 2014–15, 13 teaching assistantships with full tuition reimbursements (averaging $17,000 per year) were awarded; career-related internships or fieldwork, scholarships/grants, tuition waivers (partial), and unspecified assistantships also available. Support available to part-time students. Financial award

application deadline: 5/1. *Unit head:* Dr. Maureen O'Brien, Chair, 412-396-6530, E-mail: obrien@duq.edu. *Application contact:* Linda Rendulic, Assistant to the Dean, 412-396-6400, E-mail: rendulic@duq.edu.
Website: http://www.duq.edu/academics/schools/liberal-arts/graduate-school/programs/theology

Earlham School of Religion, Graduate Programs, Richmond, IN 47374-5360. Offers religion (MA); theology (M Div, M Min). *Accreditation:* ACIPE; ATS. Part-time programs available. Postbaccalaureate distance learning degree programs offered (minimal on-campus study). *Faculty:* 8 full-time (3 women), 4 part-time/adjunct (2 women). *Students:* 30 full-time (18 women), 23 part-time (17 women). *Degree requirements:* For master's, variable foreign language requirement, comprehensive exam (for some programs), thesis (for some programs), internship (M Div). *Entrance requirements:* For master's, 3 references. Additional exam requirements/recommendations for international students: Required—TOEFL (minimum score 550 paper-based; 82 iBT), IELTS. *Application deadline:* For fall admission, 7/15 priority date for domestic students; for winter admission, 12/15 priority date for domestic students. Applications are processed on a rolling basis. Application fee: $35. Electronic applications accepted. *Expenses: Tuition:* Full-time $11,502; part-time $426 per credit. *Financial support:* Scholarships/grants and tuition waivers (full and partial) available. Financial award application deadline: 4/15; financial award applicants required to submit FAFSA. *Faculty research:* Digitizing Quaker texts, vital Quaker ministry, research in Quaker studies and other seminary areas. *Unit head:* Jay W. Marshall, Dean, 800-432-1377, Fax: 765-983-1688, E-mail: marshja@earlham.edu. *Application contact:* Matthew Hisrich, Director of Recruitment and Admissions, 765-983-1523, Fax: 765-983-1688, E-mail: hisrima@earlham.edu.
Website: http://www.esr.earlham.edu/academics-programs/degree-programs

Eastern Mennonite University, Eastern Mennonite Seminary, Harrisonburg, VA 22802-2462. Offers church leadership (MA); divinity (M Div); ministry studies (Certificate); religion (MA); theological studies (Certificate). *Accreditation:* ATS. Part-time programs available. *Degree requirements:* For master's, thesis (for some programs), supervised field education (for M Div). *Entrance requirements:* For master's, minimum GPA of 2.5. Additional exam requirements/recommendations for international students: Required—TOEFL (minimum score 550 paper-based). *Expenses:* Contact institution. *Faculty research:* Spiritual direction and culture of call, leadership coaching: an approach to leadership in a culture of call, clarity of call in the probationary process for United Methodist clergy in Virginia, EMS women's experiences of culture of call efforts, practices of excellent and fruitful Mennonite pastoral ministry.

Eastern University, Palmer Theological Seminary, King of Prussia, PA 19096-3430. Offers Biblical studies and theology (MTS); Christian counseling (MTS); Christian faith and public policy (MTS); divinity (M Div); general studies (MTS); leadership of missional church renewal (D Min); ministry (D Min), including marriage and family; M Div/MA; M Div/MBA; M Div/MSW. *Accreditation:* ACIPE; ATS; MSA/CIHE. Part-time programs available. Postbaccalaureate distance learning degree programs offered (minimal on-campus study). *Faculty:* 14 full-time (7 women), 17 part-time/adjunct (7 women). *Students:* 65 full-time (25 women), 185 part-time (102 women); includes 151 minority (145 Black or African American, non-Hispanic/Latino; 2 Asian, non-Hispanic/Latino; 3 Hispanic/Latino; 1 Two or more races, non-Hispanic/Latino), 3 international. Average age 47. 117 applicants, 56% accepted, 61 enrolled. In 2014, 53 master's, 17 doctorates awarded. *Degree requirements:* For master's, variable foreign language requirement, thesis (for some programs); for doctorate, thesis/dissertation. *Entrance requirements:* For master's, bachelor's degree from accredited institution; for doctorate, M Div or MA. Additional exam requirements/recommendations for international students: Required—TOEFL (minimum score 550 paper-based; 79 iBT). *Application deadline:* For fall admission, 8/1 priority date for domestic students, 3/31 for international students; for spring admission, 1/15 for domestic students, 10/31 for international students. Applications are processed on a rolling basis. Application fee: $30. Electronic applications accepted. Application fee is waived when completed online. *Expenses: Tuition:* Full-time $15,600; part-time $650 per credit. *Required fees:* $30; $27.50 per semester. One-time fee: $50. Tuition and fees vary according to course load, degree level and program. *Financial support:* In 2014–15, 130 students received support, including 2 fellowships (averaging $4,000 per year), 15 teaching assistantships (averaging $1,200 per year); career-related internships or fieldwork, Federal Work-Study, and scholarships/grants also available. Financial award application deadline: 8/1; financial award applicants required to submit FAFSA. *Faculty research:* Approaches to the spiritual formation of religious leaders; Latin, anti-Colonial, and constructive theologies; pastoral and ethical responses to human trafficking; inter-religious and political dimensions of peacemaking and social justice in Israel and the Palestinian Territories. *Unit head:* Dr. Edwin Aponte, Dean of the Seminary, 484-384-2935, E-mail: semdean@eastern.edu. *Application contact:* Tiffany S. Murphy, Director of Admissions, 610-896-5000 Ext. 2986, Fax: 484-654-3680, E-mail: semadmis@eastern.edu.
Website: http://www.palmerseminary.edu/

Ecumenical Theological Seminary, Professional Program, Detroit, MI 48201. Offers M Div. *Accreditation:* ACIPE; ATS.

Eden Theological Seminary, Graduate and Professional Programs, St. Louis, MO 63119-3192. Offers M Div, MAPS, MTS, D Min. *Accreditation:* ACIPE; ATS. *Faculty:* 10 full-time (6 women), 7 part-time/adjunct (2 women). *Students:* 98 full-time (48 women), 52 part-time (28 women); includes 28 minority (all Black or African American, non-Hispanic/Latino), 8 international. *Degree requirements:* For master's, comprehensive exam (for some programs), thesis (for some programs), 2 oral exams; for doctorate, professional essay, supervised in-service projects. *Entrance requirements:* For master's, interview, minimum GPA of 2.7; for doctorate, interview, minimum GPA of 3.0. Additional exam requirements/recommendations for international students: Required—TOEFL (minimum score 550 paper-based). *Application deadline:* For fall admission, 8/1 for domestic students, 11/15 for international students; for winter admission, 12/1 for domestic students; for spring admission, 1/1 for domestic students. Applications are processed on a rolling basis. Application fee: $25. Electronic applications accepted. *Expenses: Tuition:* Full-time $12,500; part-time $12,500 per year. *Required fees:* $30 per semester. Tuition and fees vary according to degree level. *Financial support:* Career-related internships or fieldwork and scholarships/grants available. Financial award application deadline: 6/15; financial award applicants required to submit FAFSA. *Faculty research:* Psalms, pastoral ethics, historical Jesus, leadership roles, congregational life. *Unit head:* Dr. David M. Greenhaw, President, 314-961-2620. *Application contact:* Tiffany Pittman, Admissions Office, 314-918-2501, Fax: 314-918-2640, E-mail: tpittman@eden.edu.

Emmanuel Christian Seminary, Graduate and Professional Programs, Johnson City, TN 37601-9438. Offers Christian care and counseling (M Div); Christian education (M Div); Christian ministries (MCM); Christian ministry (M Div); Christian theology (M Div, MAR); church history (MAR); church history/historical theology (M Div); general studies (M Div); ministry (D Min); New Testament (M Div, MAR); Old Testament (M Div, MAR); urban ministry (M Div); world missions (M Div). *Accreditation:* ACIPE; ATS. Part-time programs available. Postbaccalaureate distance learning degree programs offered (minimal on-campus study). *Degree requirements:* For master's, 2 foreign languages, thesis or alternative, portfolio; for doctorate, thesis/dissertation. *Entrance requirements:* For master's, bachelor's degree from accredited undergraduate institution; for doctorate,

M Div or equivalent. Additional exam requirements/recommendations for international students: Required—TOEFL. Electronic applications accepted. *Faculty research:* Theology of Old Testament prophets, spiritual formation for Christian leaders, history of African churches and religions, social world of early Christianity, lay pastoral counseling, theology and art.

Emory University, Candler School of Theology, Atlanta, GA 30322. Offers formation and witness (M Div); history, scripture and tradition (MTS); leadership in church and community (M Div); modern religious thought and experience (MTS); pastoral counseling (Th D); religion and race (M Div); religion, health and science (M Div); scripture and interpretation (M Div); society and personality (M Div); theology (Th M); theology and ethics (M Div); theology and the arts (M Div); traditions of the church (M Div); women and religion (M Div); JD/M Div; JD/MTS; M Div/MBA; M Div/MPH; MBA/MTS; MTS/MPH. *Accreditation:* ACIPE; ATS. Part-time programs available. *Degree requirements:* For master's, thesis optional; for doctorate, comprehensive exam, thesis/dissertation. *Entrance requirements:* For master's, minimum undergraduate GPA of 3.0; for doctorate, GRE, M Div, 8 units of course work in clinical pastoral education. Additional exam requirements/recommendations for international students: Required—TOEFL (minimum score 600 paper-based; 95 iBT). Electronic applications accepted. *Expenses:* Contact institution. *Faculty research:* Biblical studies, church history, ethics, ministry practice, pastoral care.

Episcopal Divinity School, Graduate and Professional Programs, Cambridge, MA 02138-3494. Offers M Div, MATS, D Min, CTS. *Accreditation:* ACIPE; ATS (one or more programs are accredited). Part-time programs available. *Degree requirements:* For master's, thesis optional; for doctorate, thesis/dissertation, project. *Entrance requirements:* For master's, GRE General Test or MAT, 2 interviews, 4 letters of recommendation, 1500-word autobiographical statement; for doctorate, interview, M Div or equivalent, 3 letters of recommendation, 1500-word autobiographical statement; for CTS, GRE General Test, MAT, or advanced degree; interview; 2 letters of recommendation, 1000-word autobiographical statement. Additional exam requirements/recommendations for international students: Required—TOEFL. *Faculty research:* Anglican, global, and ecumenical studies; congregational studies; feminist liberation theologies.

Erskine Theological Seminary, Graduate and Professional Programs, Due West, SC 29639-0668. Offers M Div, MAPM, MATS, Th M, D Min. *Accreditation:* ATS. Part-time and evening/weekend programs available. *Degree requirements:* For doctorate, thesis/dissertation. *Entrance requirements:* For master's, Myers-Briggs Type Indicator, Taylor Johnson Temperament Analysis, Ministry Specialties Test (MACM), minimum GPA of 3.0, interview with committee (MACM); for doctorate, minimum GPA of 3.0 during M Div. Additional exam requirements/recommendations for international students: Required—TOEFL (minimum score 550 paper-based). Electronic applications accepted. *Faculty research:* Church administration, biblical studies.

Evangelical Seminary, Graduate and Professional Programs, Myerstown, PA 17067-1212. Offers Biblical studies (MAR); congregational ministry (M Div); global and contextual studies (M Div, MAR); historical and theological studies (MAR); interdisciplinary studies (MAR); marriage and family counseling (M Div); marriage and family therapy (MA); New Testament (MAR); Old Testament (MAR); spiritual formation (MAR); teaching ministry (M Div); youth ministry (M Div). *Accreditation:* ATS (one or more programs are accredited). Part-time programs available. Postbaccalaureate distance learning degree programs offered (minimal on-campus study). *Degree requirements:* For master's, 2 foreign languages. *Entrance requirements:* For master's, minimum GPA of 2.5. Additional exam requirements/recommendations for international students: Required—TOEFL (minimum score 550 paper-based). *Faculty research:* Literary form and structure within the Hebrew and Greek scriptures, Wesley studies, esoteric biblical languages, the Mosaic law and the Christian, ethics.

Evangelical Seminary of Puerto Rico, Graduate and Professional Programs, San Juan, PR 00925-2207. Offers M Div, MAR, D Min. *Accreditation:* ATS. Part-time programs available. *Degree requirements:* For master's, comprehensive exam. *Entrance requirements:* For doctorate, 3 years experience in ministry service. Additional exam requirements/recommendations for international students: Required—TOEFL. *Faculty research:* Protestantism in Puerto Rico.

Faith Baptist Bible College and Theological Seminary, Graduate Program, Ankeny, IA 50023. Offers Biblical studies (MA); pastoral studies (M Div); pastoral training (MA); religion (MA); theological studies (MA). Part-time programs available. *Faculty:* 3 full-time (0 women), 4 part-time/adjunct (0 women). *Students:* 13 full-time (0 women), 32 part-time (8 women); includes 5 minority (1 Black or African American, non-Hispanic/Latino; 3 Asian, non-Hispanic/Latino; 1 Two or more races, non-Hispanic/Latino). Average age 30. In 2014, 9 master's awarded. *Degree requirements:* For master's, thesis or alternative. *Entrance requirements:* Additional exam requirements/recommendations for international students: Required—TOEFL (minimum score 550 paper-based). *Application deadline:* For fall admission, 8/1 priority date for domestic students, 8/1 for international students; for spring admission, 12/15 for domestic and international students. Applications are processed on a rolling basis. Application fee: $25. *Financial support:* Career-related internships or fieldwork and scholarships/grants available. Support available to part-time students. Financial award application deadline: 3/1; financial award applicants required to submit FAFSA. *Faculty research:* Baptist theology, American church history. *Unit head:* Dr. Ernest Schmidt, Interim President, 515-964-0601, E-mail: schmidte@faith.edu. *Application contact:* Stacy Lansdown, Admissions Administrative Assistant, 888-FAITH4U, Fax: 515-964-1638, E-mail: admissions@faith.edu.
Website: http://www.faith.edu/

Faith Evangelical College & Seminary, Graduate and Professional Programs, Tacoma, WA 98407. Offers M Div, MACM, MTS, D Min. Part-time and evening/weekend programs available. Postbaccalaureate distance learning degree programs offered (minimal on-campus study). *Degree requirements:* For master's, thesis optional; for doctorate, thesis/dissertation. *Entrance requirements:* For master's, minimum undergraduate GPA of 2.7; for doctorate, minimum graduate GPA of 3.0. Additional exam requirements/recommendations for international students: Required—TOEFL (minimum score 550 paper-based).

Faith Theological Seminary, Graduate Programs, Baltimore, MD 21212. Offers M Div, D Min, Th D.

Faulkner University, College of Biblical Studies, Montgomery, AL 36109-3398. Offers ministry (MABS); missions (MABS); New Testament (MABS); Old Testament (MABS); youth and family ministry (MABS).

Fordham University, Graduate School of Arts and Sciences, Department of Theology, New York, NY 10458. Offers MA, PhD. Part-time and evening/weekend programs available. *Faculty:* 22 full-time (7 women). *Students:* 51 full-time (20 women), 9 part-time (2 women); includes 7 minority (2 Black or African American, non-Hispanic/Latino; 1 American Indian or Alaska Native, non-Hispanic/Latino; 2 Asian, non-Hispanic/Latino; 2 Hispanic/Latino), 1 international. Average age 37. 69 applicants, 33% accepted, 8 enrolled. In 2014, 11 master's, 5 doctorates awarded. Terminal master's awarded for partial completion of doctoral program. *Degree requirements:* For master's, one foreign language, comprehensive exam; for doctorate, 2 foreign languages, comprehensive

exam, thesis/dissertation. *Entrance requirements:* For master's and doctorate, GRE General Test. Additional exam requirements/recommendations for international students: Required—TOEFL (minimum score 650 paper-based). *Application deadline:* For fall admission, 1/4 priority date for domestic students; for spring admission, 11/1 for domestic students. Application fee: $70. Electronic applications accepted. *Financial support:* In 2014–15, 28 students received support, including 2 fellowships with full and partial tuition reimbursements available (averaging $25,755 per year), 7 teaching assistantships with full and partial tuition reimbursements available (averaging $18,143 per year); institutionally sponsored loans, tuition waivers (full and partial), and unspecified assistantships also available. Support available to part-time students. Financial award application deadline: 1/4. *Faculty research:* History of Christian tradition, contemporary systematic theology, theological/feminist ethics, American Catholicism, Biblical exegesis and theology. *Unit head:* Dr. Patrick Hornbeck, Chair, 718-817-3240, E-mail: ttilley@fordham.edu. *Application contact:* Bernadette Valentino-Morrison, Director of Graduate Admissions, 718-817-4419, Fax: 718-817-3566, E-mail: valentinomor@fordham.edu.

Franciscan School of Theology, Graduate and Professional Programs, Berkeley, CA 94709-1294. Offers M Div, MA, MAMC, MTS. *Accreditation:* ATS (one or more programs are accredited). Part-time programs available. *Degree requirements:* For master's, one foreign language, thesis. *Entrance requirements:* For master's, GRE General Test (MA). Additional exam requirements/recommendations for international students: Required—TOEFL (minimum score 550 paper-based). *Faculty research:* Church history, multicultural ministries, ethics and morality, catechesis, biblical studies.

Franciscan University of Steubenville, Graduate Programs, Department of Theology, Steubenville, OH 43952-1763. Offers theology and Christian ministry (MA). Part-time programs available. Postbaccalaureate distance learning degree programs offered (minimal on-campus study). *Faculty:* 8 full-time (1 woman), 6 part-time/adjunct (0 women). *Students:* 62 full-time (28 women), 224 part-time (107 women); includes 42 minority (1 Black or African American, non-Hispanic/Latino; 8 Asian, non-Hispanic/Latino; 27 Hispanic/Latino; 6 Two or more races, non-Hispanic/Latino), 10 international. Average age 38. 194 applicants, 88% accepted, 121 enrolled. In 2014, 49 master's awarded. *Degree requirements:* For master's, comprehensive exam. *Entrance requirements:* For master's, minimum undergraduate GPA of 3.0. Additional exam requirements/recommendations for international students: Required—TOEFL. *Application deadline:* For fall admission, 7/1 for domestic students, 4/30 for international students; for spring admission, 12/15 for domestic students, 9/30 for international students. Applications are processed on a rolling basis. Application fee: $20. Electronic applications accepted. Application fee is waived when completed online. *Expenses: Tuition:* Full-time $12,330; part-time $685 per credit. *Required fees:* $288; $16 per credit. One-time fee: $170 full-time. Tuition and fees vary according to course load and program. *Financial support:* Federal Work-Study and scholarships/grants available. Support available to part-time students. Financial award application deadline: 7/1; financial award applicants required to submit FAFSA. *Unit head:* Dr. Stephen Hildebrand, Program Director, 740-284-5313, E-mail: dhildebrand@franciscan.edu. *Application contact:* Mark McGuire, Director of Graduate Enrollment, 800-783-6220, Fax: 740-284-5456, E-mail: mmcguire@franciscan.edu.
Website: http://www.franciscan.edu/departments/theology/

Freed-Hardeman University, School of Biblical Studies, Program in Divinity, Henderson, TN 38340-2399. Offers M Div. Part-time programs available. *Degree requirements:* For master's, comprehensive exam. *Entrance requirements:* For master's, GRE General Test or MAT. Additional exam requirements/recommendations for international students: Required—TOEFL (minimum score 500 paper-based).

Freed-Hardeman University, School of Biblical Studies, Program in New Testament, Henderson, TN 38340-2399. Offers MA. Part-time programs available. *Degree requirements:* For master's, one foreign language, comprehensive exam, thesis. *Entrance requirements:* For master's, GRE General Test or MAT. Additional exam requirements/recommendations for international students: Required—TOEFL (minimum score 500 paper-based).

Fresno Pacific University, Biblical Seminary, Program in Divinity, Fresno, CA 93702-4709. Offers M Div. *Accreditation:* ATS. *Entrance requirements:* For master's, minimum GPA of 2.5. *Application deadline:* For fall admission, 8/1 for domestic students; for spring admission, 12/1 for domestic students. Application fee: $35. *Expenses:* Expenses: $430 per unit. *Financial support:* Application deadline: 5/1. *Unit head:* Dr. Brian Ross, Director, 559-453-2325, E-mail: brian.ross@fresno.edu. *Application contact:* Amanda Krum-Stovall, Director of Graduate Admissions, 559-453-2016, E-mail: amanda.krum-stovall@fresno.edu.
Website: http://www.fresno.edu/programs-majors/biblical-seminary/master-divinity

Fresno Pacific University, Biblical Seminary, Programs in New Testament, Old Testament, and Theology, Fresno, CA 93702-4709. Offers New Testament (MA); Old Testament (MA); theology (MA). Part-time programs available. *Entrance requirements:* Additional exam requirements/recommendations for international students: Required—TOEFL (minimum score 550 paper-based). *Application deadline:* For fall admission, 8/1 for domestic students; for spring admission, 12/1 for domestic students. Application fee: $35. *Financial support:* Application deadline: 5/1. *Unit head:* Tim Geddert, Professor, 559-453-2316, E-mail: tim.geddert@fresno.edu. *Application contact:* Amanda Krum-Stovall, Director of Graduate Admissions, 559-453-2016, E-mail: amanda.krum-stovall@fresno.edu.

Friends University, Graduate School, Wichita, KS 67213. Offers business law (MBL); Christian ministry (MACM); family therapy (MSFT); global (MBA), including accounting, business law, change management, health care leadership, management information systems, supply chain management and logistics; health care leadership (MHCL); management information systems (MMIS); operations management (MSOM); professional (MBA), including accounting, business law, change management, health care leadership, management information systems, supply chain management and logistics; teaching (MAT). Part-time and evening/weekend programs available. Postbaccalaureate distance learning degree programs offered (no on-campus study). *Degree requirements:* For master's, research project. *Entrance requirements:* For master's, bachelor's degree from accredited institution, official transcripts, interview with program director, letter(s) of recommendation. Additional exam requirements/recommendations for international students: Required—TOEFL (minimum score 560 paper-based). Electronic applications accepted.

Fuller Theological Seminary, Graduate Programs, Pasadena, CA 91182. Offers Christian leadership (MACL); clinical psychology (PhD, Psy D); family studies (MA); global leadership (MA); global ministries (D Min); global ministries (Korean language) (D Min); intercultural studies (MA, Th M, PhD); intercultural studies (Korean language) (MA); marital and family therapy (MS); marriage and family enrichment (Certificate); ministry (M Div, D Min); missiology (D Miss); missiology (Korean language) (Th M); theology (MA, Th M, PhD), including evangelism (MA), family life education (MA), pastoral ministry (MA), recovery ministry (MA), worship music ministry (MA), worship, theology, and the arts (MA), youth, family, and culture (MA); theology and ministry (MA).

Gannon University, School of Graduate Studies, College of Humanities, Education, and Social Sciences, School of Humanities, Program in Pastoral Studies, Erie, PA 16541-0001. Offers pastoral studies (MA); theological studies (Certificate). Part-time and evening/weekend programs available. *Degree requirements:* For master's, comprehensive exam, thesis or alternative, research project, internship, written evaluation. *Entrance requirements:* For master's, GRE, interview; minimum 10 credits of course work in philosophy, religious studies, or theology. Additional exam requirements/recommendations for international students: Required—TOEFL (minimum score 79 iBT). Electronic applications accepted.

Gardner-Webb University, School of Divinity, Boiling Springs, NC 28017. Offers biblical studies (M Div); Christian education and formation (M Div); intercultural studies (M Div); ministry (D Min); missiology (M Div); pastoral care and counseling (M Div); pastoral care and counseling/member care for missionaries (D Min); pastoral studies (M Div); M Div/MA; M Div/MBA. *Accreditation:* ACIPE; ATS. Part-time programs available. *Faculty:* 10 full-time (2 women), 5 part-time/adjunct (1 woman). *Students:* 151 full-time (82 women), 76 part-time (22 women); includes 106 minority (92 Black or African American, non-Hispanic/Latino; 7 Asian, non-Hispanic/Latino; 7 Hispanic/Latino). Average age 41. 110 applicants, 53% accepted, 58 enrolled. *Entrance requirements:* For master's, minimum GPA of 2.6; for doctorate, minimum GPA of 2.75. Additional exam requirements/recommendations for international students: Required—TOEFL (minimum score 500 paper-based; 61 iBT). *Application deadline:* Applications are processed on a rolling basis. Application fee: $40. Electronic applications accepted. *Expenses:* Expenses: Contact institution. *Financial support:* Fellowships, institutionally sponsored loans, and unspecified assistantships available. Support available to part-time students. Financial award application deadline: 5/15. *Faculty research:* Jewish-Christian dialogue, Islam. *Unit head:* Dr. Robert W. Canoy, Sr., Dean, 704-406-4400, Fax: 704-406-3935, E-mail: rcanoy@gardner-webb.edu. *Application contact:* Kheresa Harmon, Director of Admissions, 704-406-3205, Fax: 704-406-3895, E-mail: kharmon@gardner-webb.edu.
Website: http://gardner-webb.edu/academic-programs-and-resources/colleges-and-schools/divinity/index

Garrett-Evangelical Theological Seminary, Graduate and Professional Programs, Evanston, IL 60201-3298. Offers Bible and culture (PhD); Christian education (MA); Christian education and congregational studies (PhD); contemporary theology and culture (PhD); divinity (M Div); ethics, church, and society (MA); liturgical studies (PhD); ministry (D Min); music ministry (MA); pastoral care and counseling (MA); pastoral theology, personality, and culture (PhD); spiritual formation and evangelism (MA); theological studies (MTS); M Div/MSW. M Div/MSW offered jointly with Loyola University Chicago. *Accreditation:* ACIPE; ATS (one or more programs are accredited). Part-time programs available. *Degree requirements:* For master's, thesis (for some programs); for doctorate, thesis/dissertation. *Entrance requirements:* For doctorate, GRE (PhD). Additional exam requirements/recommendations for international students: Required—TOEFL (minimum score 560 paper-based). Electronic applications accepted.

General Theological Seminary, Graduate and Professional Programs, New York, NY 10011-4977. Offers Anglican studies (STM, Th D, Certificate); ascetical theology (Certificate); biblical studies (Certificate); congregational development (Certificate); divinity (M Div); historical and theological studies (Certificate); spiritual direction (MASD, STM, Certificate); theology (MA). *Accreditation:* ACIPE; ATS. Part-time and evening/weekend programs available. Terminal master's awarded for partial completion of doctoral program. *Degree requirements:* For master's, thesis; for doctorate, 2 foreign languages, thesis/dissertation. *Entrance requirements:* For master's, GRE General Test; for doctorate, GRE, M Div or MA. Additional exam requirements/recommendations for international students: Required—TOEFL. *Faculty research:* Liturgy, New Testament, ethics, history, ecumenical relations.

George Fox University, George Fox Evangelical Seminary, Newberg, OR 97132-2697. Offers Biblical studies (M Div); Christian earthkeeping (M Div); Christian history and theology (M Div); clinical pastoral education and hospital chaplaincy (M Div); leadership and spiritual formation (D Min); military chaplaincy (M Div); ministry leadership (MA); pastoral studies (M Div); semiotics and future studies (M Div); spiritual formation (MA, Certificate); spiritual formation and discipleship (M Div); theological studies (MA). *Accreditation:* ACIPE; ATS. Part-time and evening/weekend programs available. Postbaccalaureate distance learning degree programs offered (minimal on-campus study). *Degree requirements:* For master's, thesis optional, internship; for doctorate, comprehensive exam (for some programs), thesis/dissertation, internship. *Entrance requirements:* For master's, resume, three references (one pastoral, one academic or professional, one personal), one official transcript from each college or university attended; for doctorate, resume, 3 references (1 professional, 1 academic, 1 personal), one official transcript from each college or university attended. Additional exam requirements/recommendations for international students: Required—TOEFL (minimum score 577 paper-based; 90 iBT). Electronic applications accepted. *Expenses:* Contact institution.

Georgetown University, Graduate School of Arts and Sciences, Department of Theology, Washington, DC 20057. Offers PhD.

Georgia Christian University, School of Divinity, Atlanta, GA 30360. Offers Christian education (MA); divinity (M Div); ministry (D Min); mission studies and world Christianity (MA); theological studies (MA).

Georgian Court University, School of Arts and Sciences, Lakewood, NJ 08701-2697. Offers applied behavior analysis (MA); Catholic school leadership (Certificate); clinical mental health counseling (MA); holistic health studies (MA, Certificate); homeland security (MS); parish administration (Certificate); pastoral ministry (Certificate); professional counseling (Certificate); religious education (Certificate); school psychology (MA, Certificate); theology (MA, Certificate). Part-time and evening/weekend programs available. *Faculty:* 19 full-time (9 women), 9 part-time/adjunct (4 women). *Students:* 87 full-time (74 women), 127 part-time (110 women); includes 47 minority (14 Black or African American, non-Hispanic/Latino; 2 Asian, non-Hispanic/Latino; 23 Hispanic/Latino; 8 Two or more races, non-Hispanic/Latino). Average age 34. In 2014, 68 master's, 11 other advanced degrees awarded. *Degree requirements:* For master's, comprehensive exam (for some programs), thesis (for some programs). *Entrance requirements:* For master's, GRE, MAT, or NTE/PRAXIS, 3 letters of recommendation. Additional exam requirements/recommendations for international students: Required—TOEFL (minimum score 550 paper-based). *Application deadline:* For fall admission, 8/1 priority date for domestic students, 4/1 for international students; for spring admission, 1/1 priority date for domestic students, 7/1 for international students. Applications are processed on a rolling basis. Application fee: $40. Electronic applications accepted. *Expenses: Tuition:* Full-time $19,752; part-time $823 per credit. *Required fees:* $948; $243 per semester hour. Tuition and fees vary according to campus/location and program. *Financial support:* Scholarships/grants, health care benefits, and unspecified assistantships available. Financial award application deadline: 4/15; financial award applicants required to submit FAFSA. *Unit head:* Dr. Rita Kipp, Dean, 732-987-2493, Fax: 732-987-2007, E-mail: rkipp@georgian.edu. *Application contact:* Patrick Givens, Interim Director of Enrollment Management, 732-987-2736, Fax: 732-987-2084, E-mail: graduateadmissions@georgian.edu.
Website: http://www.georgian.edu/arts_sciences/index.htm

Theology

Global University, Graduate School of Theology, Springfield, MO 65804. Offers biblical studies (MA); divinity (M Div); ministerial studies (MA), including education, leadership, missions, New Testament, Old Testament. Part-time and evening/weekend programs available. Postbaccalaureate distance learning degree programs offered (no on-campus study). *Degree requirements:* For master's, thesis (for some programs). *Entrance requirements:* For master's, minimum undergraduate GPA of 3.0. Electronic applications accepted. *Faculty research:* Higher education, cross-cultural missions.

Golden Gate Baptist Theological Seminary, Graduate and Professional Programs, Mill Valley, CA 94941-3197. Offers divinity (M Div); early childhood education (Certificate); education leadership (MAEL, Diploma); ministry (D Min); theological studies (MTS); theology (Th M); youth ministry (Certificate). *Accreditation:* ACIPE; ATS (one or more programs are accredited). Part-time and evening/weekend programs available. *Degree requirements:* For master's, thesis (for some programs); for doctorate, 2 foreign languages, thesis/dissertation. *Entrance requirements:* For doctorate, MAT. Additional exam requirements/recommendations for international students: Required—TOEFL (minimum score 550 paper-based). Electronic applications accepted.

Gordon-Conwell Theological Seminary, Graduate and Professional Programs, South Hamilton, MA 01982. Offers Biblical languages (MABL); church history (MACH); counseling (MACO); ministry (D Min); missions/evangelism (MAME); New Testament (MANT); Old Testament (MAOT); religion (MAR); theology (M Div, MATH, Th M, Th D). *Accreditation:* ACIPE; ATS (one or more programs are accredited). Part-time and evening/weekend programs available. *Degree requirements:* For master's, one foreign language, thesis optional; for doctorate, 2 foreign languages, thesis/dissertation. *Entrance requirements:* For master's, minimum GPA of 2.5; for doctorate, minimum GPA of 3.0.

Graceland University, Community of Christ Seminary, Independence, MO 64050. Offers MAR. Part-time programs available. Postbaccalaureate distance learning degree programs offered (minimal on-campus study). *Faculty:* 2 full-time (1 woman), 5 part-time/adjunct (0 women). *Students:* 23 full-time (15 women); includes 2 minority (1 Asian, non-Hispanic/Latino; 1 Native Hawaiian or other Pacific Islander, non-Hispanic/Latino), 5 international. Average age 43. 6 applicants, 100% accepted, 6 enrolled. In 2014, 2 master's awarded. *Degree requirements:* For master's, thesis optional, portfolio. *Entrance requirements:* For master's, minimum cumulative GPA of 3.0. Additional exam requirements/recommendations for international students: Required—TOEFL. *Application deadline:* For fall admission, 8/15 priority date for domestic students; for winter admission, 10/15 priority date for domestic students; for spring admission, 4/15 priority date for domestic students. Applications are processed on a rolling basis. Application fee: $50. *Expenses:* Expenses: Contact institution. *Financial support:* Scholarships/grants available. Financial award application deadline: 12/15; financial award applicants required to submit FAFSA. *Faculty research:* Theology, scripture. *Unit head:* Dr. Stassi Cramm, Dean, 816-521-3034, Fax: 816-521-3034, E-mail: scramm@graceland.edu. *Application contact:* Sharon Ward, Administrative Assistant, 816-423-4676, Fax: 816-423-4753, E-mail: ward@graceland.edu.
Website: http://www.graceland.edu/seminary

Grace Theological Seminary, Graduate and Professional Programs, Winona Lake, IN 46590-9907. Offers biblical studies (Certificate); camp administration (MA); counseling (M Div); exegetical studies (MA); intercultural studies (M Div, MA); local church studies (MA); pastoral studies (M Div); theological studies (MA); theology (D Min, Diploma). *Accreditation:* ATS. Part-time programs available. Postbaccalaureate distance learning degree programs offered (no on-campus study). *Degree requirements:* For master's, thesis optional; for doctorate, 2 foreign languages, thesis/dissertation. *Entrance requirements:* For master's, MAT, minimum GPA of 2.5. Electronic applications accepted. *Faculty research:* Biblical theology, language, and church ministries.

Grace University, College of Graduate Studies, Bible Department, Omaha, NE 68108. Offers MA. *Degree requirements:* For master's, thesis optional. *Entrance requirements:* For master's, minimum undergraduate GPA of 3.0. Electronic applications accepted.

Graduate Theological Union, Graduate Programs, Berkeley, CA 94709-1212. Offers art and religion (MA, PhD, Th D); biblical languages (MA); biblical studies (MA); Biblical studies (PhD, Th D); Buddhist studies (MA); Christian spirituality (MA, PhD, Th D); cultural and historical studies of religions (MA, PhD, Th D); ethics and social theory (PhD, Th D); history (MA, PhD, Th D); homiletics (MA, PhD, Th D); interdisciplinary studies (PhD, Th D); Jewish studies (MA, PhD, Th D, Certificate); liturgical studies (MA, PhD, Th D); Near Eastern religions (PhD, Th D); Orthodox Christian studies (MA); religion and psychology (MA, PhD, Th D); religion and society/ethics and social theory (MA); systematic and philosophical theology (MA, PhD, Th D). PhD programs in Jewish studies and Near Eastern religions offered jointly with University of California, Berkeley. *Accreditation:* ATS. Terminal master's awarded for partial completion of doctoral program. *Degree requirements:* For master's, one foreign language, thesis; for doctorate, one foreign language, comprehensive exam, thesis/dissertation. *Entrance requirements:* For master's, GRE General Test; for doctorate, GRE General Test, MA or M Div. Additional exam requirements/recommendations for international students: Required—TOEFL. Electronic applications accepted.

Grand Rapids Theological Seminary of Cornerstone University, Graduate Programs, Grand Rapids, MI 49525-5897. Offers biblical counseling (MA); Biblical counseling (M Div); chaplaincy (M Div); Christian education (M Div, MA); intercultural studies (M Div, MA); New Testament (MA, Th M); Old Testament (MA, Th M); pastoral studies (M Div); systematic theology (MA); theology (Th M). *Accreditation:* ATS. Part-time programs available. Postbaccalaureate distance learning degree programs offered (minimal on-campus study). *Entrance requirements:* Additional exam requirements/recommendations for international students: Required—TOEFL (minimum score 577 paper-based; 90 iBT). Electronic applications accepted.

Harding School of Theology, Graduate Programs, Memphis, TN 38117-5499. Offers Christian ministry (MA); counseling (MA); ministry (M Div, D Min); religion (MA). *Accreditation:* ATS. Part-time programs available. Postbaccalaureate distance learning degree programs offered (minimal on-campus study). *Degree requirements:* For master's, variable foreign language requirement, thesis (for some programs); for doctorate, one foreign language, thesis/dissertation. *Entrance requirements:* For master's, minimum GPA of 2.7; for doctorate, minimum GPA of 3.0. Additional exam requirements/recommendations for international students: Required—TOEFL (minimum score 550 paper-based; 79 iBT). Electronic applications accepted.

Hardin-Simmons University, Graduate School, Logsdon School of Theology, Abilene, TX 79698-0001. Offers M Div, MA, D Min. Part-time and evening/weekend programs available. *Faculty:* 27 full-time (4 women), 16 part-time/adjunct (1 woman). *Students:* 58 full-time (20 women), 90 part-time (21 women); includes 44 minority (15 Black or African American, non-Hispanic/Latino; 1 American Indian or Alaska Native, non-Hispanic/Latino; 2 Asian, non-Hispanic/Latino; 25 Hispanic/Latino; 1 Two or more races, non-Hispanic/Latino), 2 international. Average age 33. In 2014, 18 master's, 2 doctorates awarded. *Entrance requirements:* Additional exam requirements/recommendations for international students: Required—TOEFL (minimum score 550 paper-based; 75 iBT). *Application deadline:* For fall admission, 8/15 priority date for domestic students, 4/1 for international students; for spring admission, 1/5 priority date for domestic students, 9/1 for international students. Applications are processed on a rolling basis. Application fee: $50. *Expenses: Tuition:* Full-time $12,060; part-time $670 per credit hour. *Required fees:* $325; $110 per semester. Tuition and fees vary according to program. *Financial support:* In 2014–15, 129 students received support. Fellowships and scholarships/grants available. Support available to part-time students. Financial award application deadline: 6/30; financial award applicants required to submit FAFSA. *Unit head:* Dr. Don Williford, Dean, 325-670-1491, Fax: 325-671-2157, E-mail: willifrd@hsutx.edu. *Application contact:* Dr. Nancy Kucinski, Dean of Graduate Studies, 325-670-1298, Fax: 325-670-1564, E-mail: gradoff@hsutx.edu.
Website: http://www.hsutx.edu/academics/logsdon

Hardin-Simmons University, Graduate School, Logsdon School of Theology, Logsdon Seminary, Seminary Program in Theology, Abilene, TX 79698-0001. Offers M Div. *Accreditation:* ATS. Part-time programs available. *Faculty:* 17 full-time (3 women), 16 part-time/adjunct (1 woman). *Students:* 41 full-time (11 women), 44 part-time (12 women); includes 34 minority (11 Black or African American, non-Hispanic/Latino; 1 American Indian or Alaska Native, non-Hispanic/Latino; 1 Asian, non-Hispanic/Latino; 20 Hispanic/Latino; 1 Two or more races, non-Hispanic/Latino). Average age 36. In 2014, 14 master's awarded. *Entrance requirements:* Additional exam requirements/recommendations for international students: Required—TOEFL (minimum score 550 paper-based; 75 iBT). *Application deadline:* For fall admission, 8/15 priority date for domestic students, 4/1 for international students; for spring admission, 1/5 priority date for domestic students, 9/1 for international students. Applications are processed on a rolling basis. Application fee: $50. *Expenses: Tuition:* Full-time $12,060; part-time $670 per credit hour. *Required fees:* $325; $110 per semester. Tuition and fees vary according to program. *Financial support:* In 2014–15, 78 students received support. Fellowships, career-related internships or fieldwork, and scholarships/grants available. Support available to part-time students. Financial award application deadline: 6/30; financial award applicants required to submit FAFSA. *Faculty research:* Hebrew grammar, history of Christian education, training of ministers into the twenty-first century, role of women in the Old Testament, contemporary ethical issues, Ricouer in contemporary theology. *Unit head:* Dr. Robert Ellis, Director, 325-670-5841, Fax: 325-670-1406, E-mail: rellis@hsutx.edu. *Application contact:* Dr. Nancy Kucinski, Dean of Graduate Studies, 325-670-1298, Fax: 325-670-1564, E-mail: gradoff@hsutx.edu.
Website: http://www.logsdonseminary.org/index.php/academics/mdiv

Hartford Seminary, Graduate Programs, Hartford, CT 06105-2279. Offers Islamic studies (MA); ministry (D Min); religious studies (MA); spirituality (Certificate). *Accreditation:* ATS (one or more programs are accredited). Part-time and evening/weekend programs available. Postbaccalaureate distance learning degree programs offered (no on-campus study). *Degree requirements:* For master's, thesis optional, oral exam; for doctorate, thesis/dissertation, oral exam. *Entrance requirements:* For doctorate, experience in ministry, M Div. Additional exam requirements/recommendations for international students: Required—TOEFL (minimum score 550 paper-based; 80 iBT). *Faculty research:* Liturgy and social justice, professional leadership in ministry, congregational studies, Christian-Muslim relations, American religion.

Harvard University, Harvard Divinity School, Cambridge, MA 02138. Offers M Div, MTS, Th M. *Accreditation:* ACIPE; ATS. *Faculty:* 45 full-time (20 women), 65 part-time/adjunct (25 women). *Students:* 323 full-time (179 women), 6 part-time (4 women). Average age 29. In 2014, 106 master's awarded. *Degree requirements:* For master's, one foreign language, thesis (for some programs). *Entrance requirements:* For master's, GRE General Test. Additional exam requirements/recommendations for international students: Required—TOEFL. *Application deadline:* For fall admission, 1/15 for domestic and international students. Application fee: $75. Electronic applications accepted. *Expenses:* Expenses: Contact institution. *Financial support:* In 2014–15, 290 students received support, including 289 fellowships with tuition reimbursements available (averaging $24,389 per year); teaching assistantships, career-related internships or fieldwork, Federal Work-Study, and scholarships/grants also available. Support available to part-time students. Financial award application deadline: 2/4; financial award applicants required to submit FAFSA. *Faculty research:* Theology, women's studies, history, comparative religion, ministry studies. *Unit head:* David N. Hempton, Dean/Professor of Evangelical Theological Studies and Divinity, 617-495-4513, Fax: 617-496-8026. *Application contact:* Prudence Goss, Director of Admissions, 617-495-5796, Fax: 617-495-0345, E-mail: admissions@hds.harvard.edu.
Website: http://hds.harvard.edu/

Hebrew College, Rabbinical School, Newton Centre, MA 02459. Offers MA. *Entrance requirements:* For master's, interview. Additional exam requirements/recommendations for international students: Required—TOEFL.

Hebrew Union College–Jewish Institute of Religion, Rabbinical School, New York, NY 10012-1186. Offers MAHL. *Degree requirements:* For master's, one foreign language. *Entrance requirements:* For master's, GRE, language exam, minimum GPA of 3.0, minimum 2 years of college-level Hebrew. Additional exam requirements/recommendations for international students: Required—TOEFL. *Faculty research:* Philosophy and theology, Bible, Hebrew, pastoral care, history and Rabbinics.

Hebrew Union College–Jewish Institute of Religion, School of Graduate Studies, Program in Pastoral Counseling, New York, NY 10012-1186. Offers D Min. *Accreditation:* ACIPE. *Degree requirements:* For doctorate, thesis/dissertation. *Entrance requirements:* For doctorate, M Div (or higher), ordination/certification for ministry. Additional exam requirements/recommendations for international students: Required—TOEFL. *Expenses:* Contact institution. *Faculty research:* Philosophy and theology, Bible, Hebrew, pastoral care, history and Rabbinics.

Heritage College and Seminary, Graduate and Professional Programs, Cambridge, ON N3C 3T2, Canada. Offers general (M Div); intercultural studies (M Div); pastoral (M Div); research (M Div); theological studies (MTS, CTS). *Accreditation:* ATS.

Holy Apostles College and Seminary, Department of Theology, Cromwell, CT 06416-2005. Offers bioethics (MA, Certificate, Post Master's Certificate); church history (MA, Certificate, Post Master's Certificate); dogmatic theology (MA, Certificate, Post Master's Certificate); liturgical music (MA, Certificate, Post Master's Certificate); liturgy (MA, Certificate, Post Master's Certificate); moral theology (MA, Certificate, Post Master's Certificate); philosophical theology (MA, Certificate, Post Master's Certificate); religious education (MA, Certificate, Post Master's Certificate); sacred scripture (MA, Post Master's Certificate); sacred scriptures (Certificate); theology (M Div). Part-time and evening/weekend programs available. Postbaccalaureate distance learning degree programs offered (no on-campus study). *Degree requirements:* For master's, one foreign language, comprehensive exam, thesis optional; for other advanced degree, culminating paper. *Entrance requirements:* For master's, minimum undergraduate GPA of 3.0; for other advanced degree, minimum graduate GPA of 3.0. Electronic applications accepted. *Faculty research:* Roman Catholic theology, philosophy.

Holy Cross Greek Orthodox School of Theology, Theological Programs, Brookline, MA 02445-7496. Offers M Div, MTS, Th M. *Accreditation:* ATS. Part-time programs available. *Degree requirements:* For master's, 2 foreign languages, thesis (for some programs). *Entrance requirements:* For master's, GRE General Test, interview, official transcripts, letters of recommendation, health report and immunization verification. Additional exam requirements/recommendations for international students: Required—

TOEFL (minimum score 550 paper-based; 80 iBT). *Faculty research:* Spirituality, liturgies, ecumenism, church history.

Hood Theological Seminary, Graduate and Professional Programs, Salisbury, NC 28144. Offers M Div, MTS, D Min. *Accreditation:* ATS. Part-time and evening/weekend programs available. Postbaccalaureate distance learning degree programs offered (minimal on-campus study). *Degree requirements:* For master's, thesis optional; for doctorate, thesis/dissertation. *Faculty research:* Old Testament human sexuality, preaching and the vulnerable, socio-historical issues, Pauline studies, multiculturalism/African-American studies.

Houston Baptist University, School of Christian Thought, Houston, TX 77074-3298. Offers apologetics (MA); Biblical languages (MA); philosophy (MA); theological studies (MA). Part-time and evening/weekend programs available. *Faculty:* 19 full-time (2 women), 1 part-time/adjunct (0 women). *Students:* 21 full-time (9 women), 67 part-time (20 women); includes 42 minority (30 Black or African American, non-Hispanic/Latino; 3 Asian, non-Hispanic/Latino; 8 Hispanic/Latino; 1 Two or more races, non-Hispanic/Latino), 3 international. Average age 39. 94 applicants, 41% accepted, 20 enrolled. In 2014, 8 master's awarded. *Degree requirements:* For master's, comprehensive exam (for some programs), thesis optional. *Entrance requirements:* For master's, minimum GPA of 2.5, two recommendations (one must be pastoral for MABL and MATS), resume, bachelor's degree, transcript. Additional exam requirements/recommendations for international students: Required—TOEFL. *Application deadline:* For fall admission, 8/1 for domestic students, 6/1 for international students; for winter admission, 10/1 for domestic and international students; for spring admission, 12/1 for domestic students, 10/1 for international students; for summer admission, 5/1 for domestic students, 3/1 for international students. Applications are processed on a rolling basis. Application fee: $0. Electronic applications accepted. *Expenses:* Expenses: Contact institution. *Financial support:* Federal Work-Study and scholarships/grants available. Support available to part-time students. Financial award application deadline: 4/1; financial award applicants required to submit FAFSA. *Faculty research:* Apologetics, New Testament, Biblical languages, philosophy, theology. *Unit head:* Dr. Jeffrey Green, Dean, 281-649-3197, Fax: 281-649-3012, E-mail: jgreen@hbu.edu. *Application contact:* Celeste Risteski, Administrative Assistant to the Dean, 281-649-3383, Fax: 281-649-3012, E-mail: cristeski@hbu.edu.
Website: http://www.hbu.edu/sct

Houston Graduate School of Theology, Graduate Programs, Houston, TX 77092. Offers counseling (MA); pastoral ministry (M Div, D Min); theology (MA). *Accreditation:* ATS (one or more programs are accredited). Part-time and evening/weekend programs available. *Degree requirements:* For master's, thesis (for some programs); for doctorate, thesis/dissertation. *Entrance requirements:* For doctorate, GRE General Test or MAT, M Div or equivalent. Additional exam requirements/recommendations for international students: Required—TOEFL (minimum score 550 paper-based). *Faculty research:* Hermeneutics, spirituality, religion of Eastern Europe.

Howard Payne University, Program in Theology and Ministry, Brownwood, TX 76801-2715. Offers MA. Part-time programs available. *Faculty:* 6 full-time (0 women), 2 part-time/adjunct (1 woman). *Students:* 3 full-time (0 women), 9 part-time (1 woman); includes 2 minority (1 Hispanic/Latino; 1 Two or more races, non-Hispanic/Latino). Average age 30. 1 applicant, 100% accepted, 1 enrolled. *Degree requirements:* For master's, three 2-hour internships/mentorships. *Entrance requirements:* For master's, undergraduate degree from accredited university; leveling courses (for students without undergraduate coursework in Old Testament, New Testament, and theology). Additional exam requirements/recommendations for international students: Required—TOEFL (minimum score 79 iBT). *Application deadline:* For fall admission, 7/1 for domestic students; for spring admission, 12/1 for domestic students. Applications are processed on a rolling basis. Application fee: $0. Electronic applications accepted. *Unit head:* Dr. Gary Gramling, Director of Graduate Programs/Professor of Christian Studies, 325-649-8404, E-mail: ggramling@hputx.edu. *Application contact:* Leanne Bledsoe, Administrative Assistant for Christian Studies Graduate Programs, 325-649-8039, E-mail: lbledsoe@hputx.edu.
Website: http://www.hputx.edu/academics/schools/school-of-christian-studies/graduate-programs/ma-theology-and-ministry/

Howard University, School of Divinity, Washington, DC 20017. Offers M Div, MARS, D Min. *Accreditation:* ACIPE; ATS. Part-time and evening/weekend programs available. *Degree requirements:* For master's, thesis; for doctorate, thesis/dissertation. *Entrance requirements:* For master's and doctorate, minimum GPA of 3.0. Electronic applications accepted. *Faculty research:* African-American religious experience, women in ministry, ecumenics, biblical studies.

Iliff School of Theology, Graduate and Professional Programs, Denver, CO 80210-4798. Offers biblical studies (MA); church history (MA); religion (MA); religion and social change (MA); specialized ministry (MASM), including justice and peace, pastoral theology and care, religions leadership; theology (M Div, MTS, D Min, PhD), including Biblical studies (PhD), religion and psychological studies (PhD), religion and social change (PhD), theology, philosophy and culture (PhD); theology/ethics (MA). PhD offered jointly with University of Denver. *Accreditation:* ACIPE; ATS. Part-time and evening/weekend programs available. *Degree requirements:* For master's, one foreign language, thesis (for some programs); for doctorate, 2 foreign languages, comprehensive exam, thesis/dissertation. *Entrance requirements:* For master's, minimum GPA of 3.0, writing sample, references; for doctorate, GRE General Test, minimum GPA of 3.0, writing sample, letters of recommendation. Additional exam requirements/recommendations for international students: Required—TOEFL (minimum score 550 paper-based). Electronic applications accepted. *Faculty research:* Pastoral care, history, church music, contemporary church, biblical studies.

Indiana Wesleyan University, Graduate School, Wesley Seminary, Master of Divinity Program, Marion, IN 46953-4974. Offers M Div. Postbaccalaureate distance learning degree programs offered (minimal on-campus study).

Institute for Christian Studies, Graduate Programs, Toronto, ON M5T 1R4, Canada. Offers education (M Phil F, PhD); history of philosophy (M Phil F, PhD); philosophical aesthetics (M Phil F, PhD); philosophy of religion (M Phil F, PhD); political theory (M Phil F, PhD); systematic philosophy (M Phil F, PhD); theology (M Phil F, PhD); worldview studies (MWS). Part-time programs available. Postbaccalaureate distance learning degree programs offered (minimal on-campus study). *Degree requirements:* For master's, one foreign language, thesis; for doctorate, 2 foreign languages, thesis/dissertation. *Entrance requirements:* For master's and doctorate, philosophy background. Additional exam requirements/recommendations for international students: Required—TOEFL (minimum score 600 paper-based). *Faculty research:* Human rights, anthropology of self, medieval discourse, gender and body, post-modern thought; biblical hermeneutics, creational aesthetics, ecumenism, epistemology, political theory and public policy, relational psychotherapy.

Institute for Creation Research, School of Biblical Apologetics, Dallas, TX 75229. Offers biblical education and apologetics (MCE); Christian school teaching (MCE); creation research (MCE); Genesis studies (MCE); sacred humanities (MCE). Part-time programs available. *Degree requirements:* For master's, comprehensive exam (for some programs), thesis (for some programs). *Entrance requirements:* For master's, minimum undergraduate GPA of 3.0, bachelor's degree in science or science education. *Faculty research:* Age of the earth, limits of variation, catastrophe, optimum methods for teaching.

Inter American University of Puerto Rico, Metropolitan Campus, Graduate Programs, Program in Theological Studies, San Juan, PR 00919-1293. Offers PhD.

Interdenominational Theological Center, Graduate and Professional Programs, Atlanta, GA 30314-4112. Offers M Div, MACE, MACM, D Min, Th D, M Div/MACE, M Div/MACM, MACM/MACE. D Min and Th D programs offered in collaboration with the Atlanta Theological Association. *Accreditation:* ACIPE; ATS (one or more programs are accredited). Part-time and evening/weekend programs available. Postbaccalaureate distance learning degree programs offered (minimal on-campus study). *Faculty:* 17 full-time (8 women), 10 part-time/adjunct (4 women). *Students:* 153 full-time (65 women), 153 part-time (70 women). *Degree requirements:* For doctorate, thesis/dissertation. *Entrance requirements:* For doctorate, master's degree. *Application deadline:* For fall admission, 7/1 for domestic and international students; for spring admission, 10/1 for domestic and international students. Applications are processed on a rolling basis. Application fee: $50. *Expenses: Tuition:* Full-time $12,370; part-time $740 per credit hour. *Required fees:* $477; $476.50 per degree program. *Financial support:* Research assistantships, career-related internships or fieldwork, and Federal Work-Study available. Support available to part-time students. Financial award application deadline: 6/15; financial award applicants required to submit FAFSA. *Unit head:* Edward Lorenza Wheeler, President, 404-527-7702, Fax: 404-527-7770. *Application contact:* Michelle Davis, Office of Admission and Recruitment, 404-527-7793, E-mail: lmdavis@itc.edu.
Website: http://www.itc.edu/

International Baptist College and Seminary, Program in Biblical Studies, Chandler, AZ 85286. Offers MA.

The Jewish Theological Seminary, The Graduate School, New York, NY 10027-4649. Offers ancient Judaism (MA, DHL, PhD); Bible and ancient Semitic languages (MA, DHL, PhD); interdepartmental studies (MA); Jewish art and visual culture (MA); Jewish gender and women's studies (MA); Jewish history (MA, DHL, PhD); Jewish literature (MA, DHL, PhD); Jewish philosophy (DHL); Jewish thought (MA, PhD); liturgy (MA, DHL, PhD); medieval Jewish studies (MA, DHL, PhD); Midrash (DHL); Midrash and scriptural interpretation (MA, PhD); modern Jewish studies (MA, DHL, PhD); Talmud and rabbinics (MA, DHL, PhD); MA/MSW. MA/MSW offered jointly with Columbia University. *Accreditation:* ACIPE. Part-time programs available. Terminal master's awarded for partial completion of doctoral program. *Degree requirements:* For master's, one foreign language, comprehensive exam (for some programs), thesis (for some programs); for doctorate, 3 foreign languages, comprehensive exam (for some programs), thesis/dissertation. *Entrance requirements:* For master's, GRE or MAT, 3 letters of recommendation, writing sample; for doctorate, GRE or MAT, 3 letters of recommendation, writing research sample. Additional exam requirements/recommendations for international students: Required—TOEFL.

The Jewish Theological Seminary, The Rabbinical School, New York, NY 10027-4649. Offers MA, Rabbi. *Accreditation:* ACIPE. *Degree requirements:* For master's and Rabbi, one foreign language, competency exams. *Entrance requirements:* For master's and Rabbi, GRE, interview, writing sample. Additional exam requirements/recommendations for international students: Required—TOEFL. *Expenses:* Contact institution.

John Paul the Great Catholic University, School of Theology, Escondido, CA 92025. Offers biblical theology (MA).

Johnson University, Graduate and Professional Programs, Knoxville, TN 37998-1001. Offers educational technology (MA); intercultural studies (MA); leadership studies (PhD); marriage and family therapy/professional counseling (MA); New Testament (MA); school counseling (MA); teacher education (MA). Part-time and evening/weekend programs available. Postbaccalaureate distance learning degree programs offered (no on-campus study). *Faculty:* 18 full-time (3 women), 39 part-time/adjunct (12 women). *Students:* 112 full-time (46 women), 117 part-time (45 women); includes 22 minority (10 Black or African American, non-Hispanic/Latino; 1 American Indian or Alaska Native, non-Hispanic/Latino; 2 Asian, non-Hispanic/Latino; 5 Hispanic/Latino; 4 Two or more races, non-Hispanic/Latino), 20 international. Average age 30. In 2014, 39 master's awarded. *Degree requirements:* For master's, variable foreign language requirement, comprehensive exam, thesis (for some programs), internships; for doctorate, variable foreign language requirement, comprehensive exam, thesis/dissertation, internships. *Entrance requirements:* For master's, doctorate, and Graduate Certificate, interview, 3 references, transcripts, essay, minimum GPA of 3.0. Additional exam requirements/recommendations for international students: Required—TOEFL. *Application deadline:* For fall admission, 7/1 for domestic students; for spring admission, 11/1 for domestic students. Application fee: $50. Electronic applications accepted. *Expenses:* Expenses: $16,800; $11,625 (online master's degree); $32,310 (online doctoral degree). *Financial support:* Scholarships/grants available. Financial award application deadline: 4/15; financial award applicants required to submit FAFSA. *Unit head:* Tim Wingfield, VP for Enrollment Services, 865-573-4517. *Application contact:* Stacy Abernathy, Director of Graduate and Non-traditional Admissions, 865-573-4517.

Kehilath Yakov Rabbinical Seminary, Graduate Programs, Ossining, NY 10562. *Accreditation:* AARTS.

Kenrick-Glennon Seminary, Graduate and Professional Programs, St. Louis, MO 63119-4330. Offers M Div, MA. *Accreditation:* ATS. *Degree requirements:* For master's, thesis optional.

Kentucky Christian University, Graduate School, Grayson, KY 41143-2205. Offers Biblical studies (MA); Christian leadership (MA). Part-time programs available. *Degree requirements:* For master's, comprehensive exam (for some programs), thesis optional. *Entrance requirements:* For master's, minimum cumulative GPA of 2.75 in major or 2.5 overall; 6 additional hours in Bible (for non-Biblical undergraduate majors). Additional exam requirements/recommendations for international students: Required—TOEFL (minimum score 550 paper-based). Electronic applications accepted.

King's University, Graduate and Professional Programs, Southlake, TX 76092. Offers Biblical studies (Graduate Certificate); Christian ministry (Graduate Certificate); ministry (M Div, MPT, D Min).

Kingswood University, Program in Pastoral Theology, Sussex, NB E4E 5L2, Canada. Offers MA.

Knox College, College of Theology, Toronto, ON M5S 2E6, Canada. Offers M Div, MRE, MTS, Th M, D Min, Th D. Applicants for D Min, Th M, and Th D must apply to Toronto School of Theology; MRE, M Div, MTS, Th D, and Th M programs offered jointly with University of Toronto. *Accreditation:* ATS. Part-time programs available. *Degree requirements:* For master's, one foreign language, thesis (for some programs); for doctorate, 2 foreign languages, thesis/dissertation. *Entrance requirements:* For doctorate, M Div. Additional exam requirements/recommendations for international students: Required—TOEFL (minimum score 580 paper-based), TWE (minimum score 5). *Faculty research:* Nineteenth century theologians.

Theology

Knox Theological Seminary, Graduate Programs, Master of Arts Programs, Fort Lauderdale, FL 33308. Offers Biblical and theological studies (MA); Christian and classical studies (MA). Part-time and evening/weekend programs available. *Entrance requirements:* Additional exam requirements/recommendations for international students: Required—TOEFL (minimum score 520 paper-based; 83 iBT), TWE (minimum score 5).

Knox Theological Seminary, Graduate Programs, Program in Divinity, Fort Lauderdale, FL 33308. Offers M Div. *Accreditation:* ATS. Part-time and evening/ weekend programs available. *Entrance requirements:* Additional exam requirements/ recommendations for international students: Required—TOEFL (minimum score 520 paper-based; 83 iBT), TWE (minimum score 5).

Lakeland College, Graduate Studies Division, Program in Theology, Sheboygan, WI 53082-0359. Offers MAT.

Lancaster Bible College, Capital Bible Seminary, Lancaster, PA 17601. Offers biblical studies (MA, Certificate); Christian counseling and discipleship (MA, Certificate); ministry (MA); theology (M Div). *Accreditation:* ATS (one or more programs are accredited). Part-time and evening/weekend programs available. *Degree requirements:* For master's, 2 foreign languages, comprehensive exam, thesis (for some programs). *Entrance requirements:* For master's, GRE General Test, Greek exam for those with 2 years of Greek, proficiency exam in theology, previous course work in Biblical studies. Additional exam requirements/recommendations for international students: Required— TOEFL (minimum score 550 paper-based). *Faculty research:* Dead Sea Scrolls, spiritual gifts, hermeneutics.

Lancaster Bible College, Graduate School, Lancaster, PA 17601-5036. Offers adult ministries (MA); Bible (MA); children and family ministry (MA); church planting (MA); consulting resource teacher (M Ed); elementary school counseling (M Ed); leadership (PhD); leadership studies (MA); marriage and family counseling (MA); mental health counseling (MA); pastoral studies (MA); secondary school counseling (M Ed); sports ministry (MA); student ministry (MA); town and country ministry (MA). Part-time and evening/weekend programs available. *Degree requirements:* For master's, comprehensive exam (for some programs), thesis (for some programs). *Entrance requirements:* For master's, bachelor's degree with a minimum of 30 credits of course work in Bible, minimum undergraduate GPA of 3.0, interview. Additional exam requirements/recommendations for international students: Required—TOEFL.

Lancaster Theological Seminary, Graduate and Professional Programs, Lancaster, PA 17603-2812. Offers biblical studies (MAR); Christian education (MAR); Christianity and the arts (MAR); church history (MAR); congregational life (MAR); lay leadership (Certificate); theological studies (M Div); theology (D Min); theology and ethics (MAR). *Accreditation:* ACIPE; ATS. *Degree requirements:* For doctorate, thesis/dissertation.

La Salle University, School of Arts and Sciences, Program in Theological, Pastoral and Liturgical Studies, Philadelphia, PA 19141-1199. Offers Catholic studies (Th D); Christian spirituality (Th D); church ministry (Th D, Certificate); founder's studies (Th D); liturgy (Certificate); pastoral care (Certificate); pastoral studies (MA); religion (MA); religious education (Certificate); theological studies (MA, Certificate). Application deadline for Th D is November 1. Part-time and evening/weekend programs available. Postbaccalaureate distance learning degree programs offered (minimal on-campus study). *Degree requirements:* For doctorate, one foreign language, thesis/dissertation, evidence of basic reading and/or speaking knowledge of one of the following languages: a modern language other than English, Hebrew (biblical), Greek (biblical), or Latin (classical). *Entrance requirements:* For master's and Certificate, 26 credits in humanistic subjects, religion, theology, or ministry-related work; 2 letters of recommendation; statement of purpose; for doctorate, master's degree in theology, religious studies, pastoral care, or similar field from accredited institution of higher education; professional resume; personal statement of interest in a doctoral degree; 2 letters of recommendation; personal on-campus interview. Additional exam requirements/ recommendations for international students: Required—TOEFL (minimum score 550 paper-based). Electronic applications accepted. Application fee is waived when completed online.

Lee University, Program in Religion, Cleveland, TN 37320-3450. Offers biblical studies (MA); ministry studies (MA); theological studies (MA); youth and family ministry (MA). Part-time programs available. *Faculty:* 12 full-time (3 women), 3 part-time/adjunct (0 women). *Students:* 49 full-time (19 women), 34 part-time (8 women); includes 17 minority (11 Black or African American, non-Hispanic/Latino; 1 American Indian or Alaska Native, non-Hispanic/Latino; 1 Asian, non-Hispanic/Latino; 4 Hispanic/Latino), 3 international. Average age 36. 18 applicants, 67% accepted, 11 enrolled. In 2014, 18 master's awarded. *Degree requirements:* For master's, variable foreign language requirement, comprehensive exam (for some programs), thesis (for some programs). *Entrance requirements:* For master's, GRE or MAT (for biblical/theological studies only), minimum GPA of 3.0, 2 letters of recommendation, interview, official transcripts, essay. Additional exam requirements/recommendations for international students: Required— TOEFL (minimum score 450 paper-based). *Application deadline:* For fall admission, 4/1 priority date for domestic and international students; for spring admission, 10/1 priority date for domestic and international students. Applications are processed on a rolling basis. Application fee: $25. *Expenses: Tuition:* Full-time $10,260; part-time $570 per credit hour. *Required fees:* $35 per semester. One-time fee: $25. Tuition and fees vary according to program. *Financial support:* In 2014–15, 33 students received support, including 1 teaching assistantship (averaging $1,000 per year); career-related internships or fieldwork, Federal Work-Study, institutionally sponsored loans, scholarships/grants, and unspecified assistantships also available. Financial award application deadline: 3/1; financial award applicants required to submit FAFSA. *Faculty research:* Book of Isaiah, Gospel of Mark, school of St. Victor of the twelfth century, spirit Christology, people groups of New Testament and work. *Unit head:* Dr. Bob Bayles, Director, 423-614-8338, E-mail: bbayles@leeuniversity.edu. *Application contact:* Vicki Glasscock, Graduate Admissions Director, 423-614-8059, E-mail: vglasscock@leeuniversity.edu.
Website: http://www.leeuniversity.edu/academics/graduate/religion

Lexington Theological Seminary, Graduate and Professional Programs, Lexington, KY 40508-3218. Offers M Div, MA, MAPS, D Min, M Div/MSW. M Div/MSW offered jointly with University of Kentucky. *Accreditation:* ACIPE; ATS. Part-time and evening/ weekend programs available. *Degree requirements:* For master's, thesis; for doctorate, thesis/dissertation. *Entrance requirements:* Additional exam requirements/ recommendations for international students: Required—TOEFL (minimum score 600 paper-based). *Faculty research:* History of biblical interpretation, biblical apocalyptic, psalms, history of Stone-Campbell traditions.

Liberty University, Liberty Baptist Theological Seminary, Lynchburg, VA 24515. Offers Biblical studies (M Div, MAR, MTS, Th M); church history (M Div, MAR, MTS, Th M); discipleship (D Min); discipleship and church ministry (M Div, MAR, MCM); evangelism and church planting (M Div, MAR, MCM, D Min); global studies (M Div, MAR, MCM, MGS, Th M); homiletics (M Div, MAR, MCM, Th M, D Min); leadership (M Div, MAR, MCM, D Min); marketplace chaplaincy (M Div, MAR, MCM); ministry (D Min); pastoral counseling (M Div, MA, MAR, MCM, D Min), including addictions and recovery (MA), crisis response and trauma (MA), discipleship and church ministries (MA), leadership

(MA), life coaching (MA), marketplace chaplaincy (MA), marriage and family (MA), military resilience (MA), pastoral counseling (MA); pastoral ministries (M Div, MAR, MCM); religious education (MRE); theology (M Div, MAR, MTS, Th M); theology and apologetics (PhD); worship (M Div, MAR, MCM, D Min). Part-time programs available. Postbaccalaureate distance learning degree programs offered (minimal on-campus study). *Students:* 2,865 full-time (781 women), 3,750 part-time (1,139 women); includes 1,742 minority (1,382 Black or African American, non-Hispanic/Latino; 22 American Indian or Alaska Native, non-Hispanic/Latino; 116 Asian, non-Hispanic/Latino; 105 Hispanic/Latino; 7 Native Hawaiian or other Pacific Islander, non-Hispanic/Latino; 110 Two or more races, non-Hispanic/Latino), 227 international. Average age 41. 5,446 applicants, 39% accepted, 1340 enrolled. In 2014, 1,969 master's, 126 doctorates, 75 other advanced degrees awarded. *Degree requirements:* For master's, 2 foreign languages, thesis (for some programs); for doctorate, 2 foreign languages, thesis/ dissertation. *Entrance requirements:* For master's, minimum undergraduate GPA of 2.0; for doctorate, GRE General Test or MAT, minimum graduate GPA of 3.0. Additional exam requirements/recommendations for international students: Required—TOEFL (minimum score 600 paper-based; 100 iBT). *Application deadline:* For fall admission, 6/ 1 for domestic students; for spring admission, 11/1 for domestic students. Applications are processed on a rolling basis. Application fee: $50. Electronic applications accepted. *Expenses:* Expenses: Contact institution. *Financial support:* Teaching assistantships with tuition reimbursements, career-related internships or fieldwork, and Federal Work-Study available. Financial award applicants required to submit FAFSA. *Unit head:* Dr. David Hirschman, Acting Dean, 434-592-4140, Fax: 434-522-0415, E-mail: dwhirschman@liberty.edu. *Application contact:* Jay Bridge, Director of Graduate Admissions, 800-424-9595, Fax: 800-628-7977, E-mail: gradadmissions@liberty.edu. Website: http://www.liberty.edu/seminary/

Lincoln Christian Seminary, Graduate and Professional Programs, Lincoln, IL 62656-2167. Offers Bible and theology (MA); Christian ministries (MA); counseling (MA); divinity (M Div); leadership ministry (D Min); religious education (MRE). *Accreditation:* ACIPE; ATS. Part-time programs available. *Degree requirements:* For master's, 2 foreign languages, thesis; for doctorate, thesis/dissertation. *Entrance requirements:* For master's, minimum GPA of 2.5; for doctorate, M Div or equivalent. Additional exam requirements/recommendations for international students: Required—TOEFL (minimum score 550 paper-based). Electronic applications accepted.

Lincoln Christian University, Hargrove School of Adult and Graduate Studies, Lincoln, IL 62656-2167. Offers bible and theology (MA); intercultural studies (MA); marriage and family therapy (MA); organizational leadership (MA); spiritual formation (MA); TESOL (MA). MA in marriage and family therapy offered in Las Vegas, NV; MA in spiritual formation program offered in Bloomington-Normal, IL. Postbaccalaureate distance learning degree programs offered (no on-campus study). *Faculty:* 6 full-time (3 women), 20 part-time/adjunct (3 women). *Students:* 5 full-time (4 women), 137 part-time (53 women); includes 33 minority (19 Black or African American, non-Hispanic/Latino; 3 American Indian or Alaska Native, non-Hispanic/Latino; 1 Asian, non-Hispanic/Latino; 7 Hispanic/Latino; 3 Two or more races, non-Hispanic/Latino), 7 international. Average age 39. 114 applicants, 68% accepted, 62 enrolled. In 2014, 53 master's awarded. *Degree requirements:* For master's, 2.5 cumulative GPA in Undergraduate Degree studies. *Entrance requirements:* For master's, If undergrad cum GPA is lower than 2.5 (on a 4.0 scale) applicant may be required to complete the Miller Analogies Test at an authorized center. Additional exam requirements/recommendations for international students: Required—TOEFL (minimum score 550 paper-based); Recommended— IELTS (minimum score 6). *Application deadline:* For fall admission, 8/1 for domestic students, 3/1 for international students; for spring admission, 11/15 for domestic students, 11/1 for international students. Application fee: $25 ($50 for international students). Application fee is waived when completed online. *Expenses: Tuition:* Full-time $7524; part-time $418 per credit hour. One-time fee: $144. Tuition and fees vary according to campus/location and program. *Financial support:* Applicants required to submit FAFSA.

Lipscomb University, Hazelip School of Theology, Nashville, TN 37204-3951. Offers Christian practice (MA); missional and spiritual formation (D Min); student ministry (Certificate); theology (M Div). *Accreditation:* ATS. Part-time and evening/weekend programs available. Postbaccalaureate distance learning degree programs offered (minimal on-campus study). *Faculty:* 11 full-time (1 woman), 4 part-time/adjunct (0 women). *Students:* 17 full-time (5 women), 96 part-time (25 women); includes 19 minority (17 Black or African American, non-Hispanic/Latino; 2 Hispanic/Latino). Average age 39. In 2014, 26 master's, 4 doctorates, 3 other advanced degrees awarded. *Degree requirements:* For master's, 2 foreign languages, comprehensive exam (for some programs), thesis optional; for doctorate, comprehensive exam, thesis/ dissertation. *Entrance requirements:* For master's, 3 references, transcripts, goals statement; for doctorate, 3 references, transcripts, documentation of full-time participation in ministry, writing sample, interview. Additional exam requirements/ recommendations for international students: Required—TOEFL (minimum score 570 paper-based; 80 iBT). *Application deadline:* For fall admission, 8/1 priority date for domestic students; for spring admission, 12/15 for domestic students. Applications are processed on a rolling basis. Application fee: $50 ($75 for international students). Electronic applications accepted. *Expenses:* Expenses: $898 per credit hour (for M Div, MACM, and MTS); $500 per credit hour (for MA); $333 per credit hour (for D Min). *Financial support:* Scholarships/grants and unspecified assistantships available. Financial award application deadline: 3/1; financial award applicants required to submit FAFSA. *Faculty research:* Status of Churches of Christ in foreign nations, Hebrew grammar, marriage and family. *Unit head:* Dr. Mark Black, Director, 615-966-5709, Fax: 615-966-6052, E-mail: mark.black@lipscomb.edu. *Application contact:* Kellye McCool, Coordinator of Student Services, 615-966-5458, Fax: 615-966-6052, E-mail: kellye.mccool@lipscomb.edu.
Website: http://www.lipscomb.edu/hst

Logos Evangelical Seminary, Graduate Programs, El Monte, CA 91731. Offers M Div, MA, Th M, D Min. *Accreditation:* ATS (one or more programs are accredited). Part-time programs available. Postbaccalaureate distance learning degree programs offered (minimal on-campus study). *Faculty:* 14 full-time (6 women), 7 part-time/adjunct (1 woman). *Students:* 77 full-time (30 women), 77 part-time (32 women); includes 93 minority (all Asian, non-Hispanic/Latino), 61 international. Average age 48. 49 applicants, 86% accepted, 32 enrolled. In 2014, 21 master's, 5 doctorates awarded. *Degree requirements:* For master's, 2 foreign languages, comprehensive exam, thesis; for doctorate, thesis/dissertation. *Entrance requirements:* For master's, MA in Biblical studies with minimum GPA of 3.33, 1.5 years of a Biblical language, 2 recommendations, 1 research paper; for doctorate, M Div with minimum GPA of 3.0, 3 years of ministry experience, 2 recommendations. Additional exam requirements/ recommendations for international students: Required—TOEFL (minimum score 450 paper-based; 45 iBT), IELTS (minimum score 5). *Application deadline:* For fall admission, 7/15 for domestic students, 5/15 for international students; for spring admission, 12/15 for domestic students, 10/15 for international students. Applications are processed on a rolling basis. Application fee: $75. Electronic applications accepted. *Expenses: Tuition:* Full-time $6840; part-time $285 per unit. One-time fee: $200. *Financial support:* Application deadline: 3/1. *Faculty research:* Asian-American hermeneutics, narrative theology, Biblical studies, pastors' mental health. *Unit head:*

Rev. Ekron Chen, PhD, Academic Dean, 626-571-5110 Ext. 120, Fax: 626-571-5119, E-mail: ekron@les.edu. *Application contact:* Becky Perng, Admission Specialist, 626-571-5110 Ext. 112, Fax: 626-571-5119, E-mail: admission@les.edu.
Website: http://www.les.edu

Loras College, Graduate Division, Program in Theology and Ministry, Dubuque, IA 52004-0178. Offers ministry (MA); theology (MA). Part-time and evening/weekend programs available. *Degree requirements:* For master's, comprehensive exam (for some programs), thesis (for some programs). *Entrance requirements:* For master's, bachelor's degree or undergraduate minor in religious studies or equivalent, minimum undergraduate GPA of 2.75.

Louisiana College, Caskey School of Divinity, Pineville, LA 71359-0001. Offers biblical and theological studies (MA); pastoral ministry (MA).

Louisville Presbyterian Theological Seminary, Graduate and Professional Programs, Louisville, KY 40205-1798. Offers Bible (MAR); divinity (M Div); ministry (D Min); religious thought (MAR); JD/M Div; M Div/MBA; M Div/MSSW. JD/M Div, M Div/MBA, and M Div/MSSW offered jointly with University of Louisville. *Accreditation:* AAMFT/COAMFTE (one or more programs are accredited); ACIPE; ATS (one or more programs are accredited). Part-time programs available. *Faculty:* 17 full-time (7 women), 20 part-time/adjunct (9 women). *Students:* 105 full-time (65 women), 64 part-time (33 women); includes 44 minority (33 Black or African American, non-Hispanic/Latino; 1 American Indian or Alaska Native, non-Hispanic/Latino; 5 Asian, non-Hispanic/Latino; 5 Hispanic/Latino), 2 international. Average age 40. *Degree requirements:* For master's, 2 foreign languages, thesis (for some programs); for doctorate, thesis/dissertation. *Entrance requirements:* For doctorate, M Div. Additional exam requirements/recommendations for international students: Required—TOEFL (minimum score 550 paper-based). *Application deadline:* For fall admission, 6/15 priority date for domestic students, 2/1 priority date for international students; for spring admission, 11/15 priority date for domestic students, 11/15 for international students. Applications are processed on a rolling basis. Application fee: $50. Electronic applications accepted. *Expenses: Tuition:* Full-time $10,260; part-time $342 per credit hour. *Required fees:* $143 per term. *Financial support:* Career-related internships or fieldwork, Federal Work-Study, institutionally sponsored loans, and scholarships/grants available. Financial award application deadline: 2/1; financial award applicants required to submit FAFSA. *Unit head:* Dr. Susan R. Garrett, Dean, 502-895-3411, Fax: 502-895-1096, E-mail: sgarrett@lpts.edu. *Application contact:* Grant Crusor, Director of Admissions, 502-895-3411, Fax: 502-895-1096, E-mail: gcrusor@lpts.edu.
Website: http://www.lpts.edu/

Lourdes University, Graduate School, Sylvania, OH 43560-2898. Offers business (MBA); leadership (M Ed); nurse anesthesia (MSN); nurse educator (MSN); nurse leader (MSN); organizational leadership (MOL); reading (M Ed); teaching and curriculum (M Ed); theology (MA). Evening/weekend programs available. *Entrance requirements:* Additional exam requirements/recommendations for international students: Required—TOEFL.

Loyola Marymount University, College of Liberal Arts, Department of Theological Studies, Program in Theology, Los Angeles, CA 90045-8400. Offers MA. *Accreditation:* ATS. *Degree requirements:* For master's, comprehensive exam, thesis or alternative. *Entrance requirements:* For master's, GRE or MAT (recommended), 2 letters of recommendation, personal statement. Additional exam requirements/recommendations for international students: Required—TOEFL (minimum score 600 paper-based; 100 iBT). Electronic applications accepted.

Loyola University Chicago, Graduate School, Department of Theology, Chicago, IL 60660. Offers MA, PhD. Part-time and evening/weekend programs available. *Faculty:* 23 full-time (9 women). *Students:* 56 full-time (19 women), 2 part-time (0 women); includes 9 minority (5 Black or African American, non-Hispanic/Latino; 3 Hispanic/Latino; 1 Native Hawaiian or other Pacific Islander, non-Hispanic/Latino), 5 international. Average age 33. 50 applicants, 48% accepted, 11 enrolled. In 2014, 4 master's, 8 doctorates awarded. Terminal master's awarded for partial completion of doctoral program. *Degree requirements:* For master's, comprehensive exam; for doctorate, 2 foreign languages, comprehensive exam, thesis/dissertation. *Entrance requirements:* For master's, GRE General Test, minimum GPA of 3.0, 9 hours of course work in theology; for doctorate, GRE General Test, minimum GPA of 3.0, master's degree or equivalent. Additional exam requirements/recommendations for international students: Required—TOEFL, IELTS. *Application deadline:* For fall admission, 1/15 for domestic and international students; for spring admission, 12/1 for domestic and international students. Application fee: $50. Electronic applications accepted. Application fee is waived when completed online. *Expenses: Tuition:* Full-time $17,370; part-time $965 per credit. *Required fees:* $138 per semester. *Financial support:* In 2014–15, 12 students received support, including 12 research assistantships (averaging $18,000 per year); fellowships, teaching assistantships, and institutionally sponsored loans also available. Financial award application deadline: 1/15; financial award applicants required to submit FAFSA. *Faculty research:* Systematics, historical theology, constructive theology, scripture, theological ethics. *Unit head:* Dr. Wendy J. Cotter, Department Chair, 773-508-8457, Fax: 773-508-2386, E-mail: wcotter@luc.edu. *Application contact:* Ron Martin, Assistant Director of Enrollment Management, 312-915-8950, Fax: 312-915-8905, E-mail: gradapp@luc.edu.
Website: http://luc.edu/theology/

Loyola University Chicago, Institute of Pastoral Studies, Master of Arts in Pastoral Counseling Program, Chicago, IL 60660. Offers pastoral studies (MA); social justice (MA); spirituality (MA). *Accreditation:* ACIPE. Part-time programs available. *Faculty:* 9 full-time (4 women), 12 part-time/adjunct (7 women). *Students:* 39 full-time (29 women), 55 part-time (29 women); includes 21 minority (10 Black or African American, non-Hispanic/Latino; 4 Asian, non-Hispanic/Latino; 6 Hispanic/Latino; 1 Two or more races, non-Hispanic/Latino), 11 international. Average age 40. 19 applicants, 74% accepted, 12 enrolled. In 2014, 8 master's awarded. *Degree requirements:* For master's, thesis or alternative, 100 hours of practicum, 700 hours of internship with clinical supervision, final integration project. *Entrance requirements:* Additional exam requirements/recommendations for international students: Required—TOEFL. *Application deadline:* For fall admission, 2/15 priority date for domestic students. Applications are processed on a rolling basis. Electronic applications accepted. *Expenses: Tuition:* Full-time $17,370; part-time $965 per credit. *Required fees:* $138 per semester. *Financial support:* In 2014–15, 33 students received support. Career-related internships or fieldwork, Federal Work-Study, institutionally sponsored loans, and scholarships/grants available. Support available to part-time students. Financial award application deadline: 3/1; financial award applicants required to submit FAFSA. *Faculty research:* Pastoral psychotherapy, enrichment outcome, marriage and family therapy, mindfulness, human relation skills, psychopathology, spirituality, gender and ethnicity issues, theological anthropology. *Unit head:* Dr. Brian J. Schmisek, Director, 312-915-7400, Fax: 312-915-7410, E-mail: bschmisek@luc.edu. *Application contact:* Dr. William Schmidt, Professor, 312-915-7478, Fax: 312-9157410, E-mail: wschmid@luc.edu.
Website: http://www.luc.edu/ips/academics/mapc/

Loyola University Chicago, Institute of Pastoral Studies, Master of Arts in Spirituality Program, Chicago, IL 60660. Offers contemporary spirituality (MA); spiritual direction (MA, Certificate). *Faculty:* 9 full-time (4 women), 7 part-time/adjunct (6 women). *Students:* 37 full-time (24 women). Average age 43. 22 applicants, 64% accepted, 10 enrolled. In 2014, 12 master's, 4 other advanced degrees awarded. *Entrance requirements:* Additional exam requirements/recommendations for international students: Required—TOEFL. *Application deadline:* Applications are processed on a rolling basis. Electronic applications accepted. *Expenses: Tuition:* Full-time $17,370; part-time $965 per credit. *Required fees:* $138 per semester. *Financial support:* In 2014–15, 14 students received support. Career-related internships or fieldwork, Federal Work-Study, and scholarships/grants available. *Faculty research:* Spiritual accompaniment, Ignatian exercises. *Unit head:* Dr. Brian J. Schmisek, Director, 312-915-7400, Fax: 312-915-7410, E-mail: bschmisek@luc.edu. *Application contact:* Dr. M. Therese Lysaught, Associate Director, 312-915-7485, Fax: 312-915-7410, E-mail: mlysaught@luc.edu.
Website: http://www.luc.edu/ips/academics/massd/

Loyola University Chicago, Institute of Pastoral Studies, Master of Divinity Program, Chicago, IL 60660. Offers M Div, M Div/MA, M Div/MSN, M Div/MSW. *Accreditation:* ACIPE. Part-time programs available. *Faculty:* 9 full-time (4 women), 40 part-time/adjunct (20 women). *Students:* 6 full-time (4 women), 16 part-time (11 women); includes 4 minority (2 Black or African American, non-Hispanic/Latino; 1 Asian, non-Hispanic/Latino; 1 Hispanic/Latino). Average age 43. 13 applicants, 69% accepted, 3 enrolled. In 2014, 7 master's awarded. *Degree requirements:* For master's, final integration project. *Entrance requirements:* Additional exam requirements/recommendations for international students: Required—TOEFL (minimum score 550 paper-based; 79 iBT). *Application deadline:* For fall admission, 8/1 priority date for domestic students; for spring admission, 12/1 priority date for domestic students. Applications are processed on a rolling basis. Electronic applications accepted. Application fee is waived when completed online. *Expenses:* Expenses: Contact institution. *Financial support:* In 2014–15, 22 students received support. Career-related internships or fieldwork, Federal Work-Study, institutionally sponsored loans, and scholarships/grants available. Financial award application deadline: 2/1; financial award applicants required to submit FAFSA. *Faculty research:* Healthcare ethics, Christian anthropology, spirituality, justice, science and religion. *Unit head:* Dr. Brian J. Schmisek, Director, 312-915-7400, Fax: 312-915-7410, E-mail: bschmisek@luc.edu. *Application contact:* Dr. Heidi Russell, Assistant Professor, 312-915-7476, Fax: 312-915-7410, E-mail: hrussell@luc.edu.
Website: http://www.luc.edu/ips

Loyola University Maryland, Graduate Programs, Loyola College of Arts and Sciences, Department of Theology, Baltimore, MD 21210-2699. Offers MTS.

Loyola University New Orleans, College of Social Sciences, Loyola Institute for Ministry, New Orleans, LA 70118-6195. Offers pastoral studies (MPS); religious education (MRE); theology and ministry (Certificate). Part-time and evening/weekend programs available. Postbaccalaureate distance learning degree programs offered (no on-campus study). *Faculty:* 3 full-time (1 woman), 4 part-time/adjunct (2 women). *Students:* 18 full-time (11 women), 141 part-time (88 women); includes 19 minority (6 Black or African American, non-Hispanic/Latino; 1 American Indian or Alaska Native, non-Hispanic/Latino; 2 Asian, non-Hispanic/Latino; 8 Hispanic/Latino; 2 Two or more races, non-Hispanic/Latino). Average age 48. 35 applicants, 89% accepted, 31 enrolled. In 2014, 58 master's, 1 other advanced degree awarded. *Entrance requirements:* For master's, minimum GPA of 2.5, resume, 2 letters of recommendation, work experience, 3-page statement of purpose. Additional exam requirements/recommendations for international students: Required—TOEFL (minimum score 550 paper-based). *Application deadline:* Applications are processed on a rolling basis. Application fee: $20. Electronic applications accepted. Application fee is waived when completed online. *Financial support:* Career-related internships or fieldwork, scholarships/grants, health care benefits, and tuition waivers (partial) available. Support available to part-time students. Financial award application deadline: 5/1; financial award applicants required to submit FAFSA. *Faculty research:* Practical theology, ministry education, small Christian communities, religion and ecology, Christian spirituality. *Unit head:* Dr. Tom Ryan, Director, 504-865-2069, Fax: 504-865-2066, E-mail: tfryan@loyno.edu. *Application contact:* Diane Blair, Manager of Admissions, 504-865-3728, Fax: 504-865-2066, E-mail: lim@loyno.edu.
Website: http://lim.loyno.edu/

Lubbock Christian University, Graduate Biblical Studies, Lubbock, TX 79407-2099. Offers Bible and ministry (MS); biblical interpretation (MA). Part-time programs available. *Degree requirements:* For master's, one foreign language, thesis (for some programs). *Entrance requirements:* For master's, GRE General Test or MAT. *Faculty research:* Commentary on John, commentary on First and Second Thessalonians, mission teams, church leadership, family systems.

Lutheran School of Theology at Chicago, Graduate and Professional Programs, Chicago, IL 60615-5199. Offers ministry (MAM, D Min); theological studies (MATS, PhD); theology (M Div, Th M). *Accreditation:* ACIPE; ATS (one or more programs are accredited). Part-time programs available. Terminal master's awarded for partial completion of doctoral program. *Degree requirements:* For master's, variable foreign language requirement; for doctorate, variable foreign language requirement, comprehensive exam, thesis/dissertation. *Entrance requirements:* For master's, GRE (Th M), M Div or equivalent (Th M); for doctorate, GRE, M Div or equivalent, 3 years of professional experience (D Min). Additional exam requirements/recommendations for international students: Required—TOEFL (for Th M).

Lutheran Theological Seminary at Gettysburg, Graduate and Professional Programs, Gettysburg, PA 17325-1795. Offers divinity (M Div); ministerial studies (MAMS); outdoor ministry (MAR); parish ministry (D Min); theology (STM). *Accreditation:* ACIPE; ATS (one or more programs are accredited). Part-time programs available. Postbaccalaureate distance learning degree programs offered (no on-campus study). *Degree requirements:* For master's, thesis (for some programs). Electronic applications accepted.

The Lutheran Theological Seminary at Philadelphia, Graduate School, Philadelphia, PA 19119-1794. Offers divinity (M Div); ministry (D Min); public leadership (MA); religion (MAR); social ministry (Certificate); theology (STM, PhD). *Accreditation:* ACIPE; ATS. Part-time and evening/weekend programs available. *Faculty:* 20 full-time (5 women), 19 part-time/adjunct (6 women). *Students:* 106 full-time (50 women), 208 part-time (100 women); includes 92 minority (80 Black or African American, non-Hispanic/Latino; 2 Asian, non-Hispanic/Latino; 10 Hispanic/Latino), 14 international. *Degree requirements:* For master's, one foreign language, comprehensive exam (for some programs), thesis (for some programs); for doctorate, thesis/dissertation. *Entrance requirements:* For master's, minimum undergraduate GPA of 2.8; for doctorate, minimum GPA of 3.0. Additional exam requirements/recommendations for international students: Required—TOEFL (minimum score 550 paper-based), TWE. *Application deadline:* For fall admission, 6/1 priority date for domestic students. Applications are processed on a rolling basis. Application fee: $35. Electronic applications accepted. *Expenses: Tuition:* Full-time $14,310; part-time $1590 per course. *Required fees:* $175 per semester. Tuition and fees vary according to degree level and program. *Financial support:* Research assistantships with tuition reimbursements, teaching assistantships with tuition reimbursements, career-related internships or fieldwork, and Federal Work-Study available. Financial award application deadline: 7/1; financial award applicants required

to submit FAFSA. *Unit head:* Rev. Dr. J. Jayakiran Sebastian, Dean, 215-248-6379, Fax: 215-248-4577, E-mail: jsebastian@ltsp.edu. *Application contact:* Matthew O'Rear, Associate Director of Admissions, 800-286-4616 Ext. 6304, Fax: 215-248-7315, E-mail: admissions@ltsp.edu.

Lutheran Theological Seminary Saskatoon, Graduate and Professional Programs, Saskatoon, SK S7N 0X3, Canada. Offers Biblical studies (MTS); church history (MTS); ethics/church and society (MTS); history of Christianity (STM); New Testament (STM); Old Testament (STM); pastoral studies (STM); pastoral theology (MTS); systematic theology (MTS); systematic theology and philosophy of religion (STM); theology (M Div, D Div). STM programs offered jointly with College of Emmanuel and St. Chad and St. Andrew's College. *Accreditation:* ATS. Part-time programs available. *Degree requirements:* For master's, thesis.

Lutheran Theological Southern Seminary, Graduate and Professional Programs, Columbia, SC 29203. Offers M Div, MAR, STM, D Min. *Accreditation:* ACIPE; ATS. Part-time programs available. *Degree requirements:* For master's, comprehensive exam (for some programs), thesis (for some programs). *Entrance requirements:* Additional exam requirements/recommendations for international students: Recommended—TOEFL. *Faculty research:* Theology in the twenty-first century, Biblical interpretation.

Luther Rice College & Seminary, Graduate Programs, Lithonia, GA 30038-2454. Offers apologetics (MA); Bible languages (M Div); Biblical counseling (MA); Christian ministry (M Div, D Min); Christian studies (MA); leadership (MA). Part-time and evening/weekend programs available. Postbaccalaureate distance learning degree programs offered (no on-campus study). *Faculty:* 14 full-time (2 women), 28 part-time/adjunct (8 women). *Students:* 250 full-time (50 women), 784 part-time (209 women); includes 476 minority (420 Black or African American, non-Hispanic/Latino; 7 American Indian or Alaska Native, non-Hispanic/Latino; 21 Asian, non-Hispanic/Latino; 21 Hispanic/Latino; 7 Two or more races, non-Hispanic/Latino). *Degree requirements:* For doctorate, thesis/dissertation. *Entrance requirements:* For master's, bachelor's degree or equivalent; for doctorate, M Div. Additional exam requirements/recommendations for international students: Required—TOEFL (minimum score 550 paper-based). *Application deadline:* Applications are processed on a rolling basis. Application fee: $50. Electronic applications accepted. *Expenses: Tuition:* Full-time $4266; part-time $237 per credit hour. *Required fees:* $330; $55 per course. *Financial support:* Scholarships/grants available. Financial award applicants required to submit FAFSA. *Unit head:* Dr. Brad Arnett, Graduate Dean, 770-484-1204 Ext. 5697, E-mail: barnett@lutherrice.edu. *Application contact:* Steve Pray, Enrollment Advisor, 770-484-1204 Ext. 5758, Fax: 770-484-1155, E-mail: admissions@lutherrice.edu.

Luther Seminary, Graduate and Professional Programs, St. Paul, MN 55108-1445. Offers aging and health (MA); Biblical preaching (D Min); children, youth and family (M Div, MA); congregational mission and leadership (M Th, MA, D Min); history of Christianity (M Th, MA); missions and world religions (M Th); New Testament (M Th, MA); Old Testament (M Th, MA); pastoral care: clinical pastoral theology (M Th); pastoral theology and ministry (M Th); systematic theology (M Th, MA). *Accreditation:* ACIPE; ATS. Part-time programs available. Postbaccalaureate distance learning degree programs offered (minimal on-campus study). *Faculty:* 25 full-time, 25 part-time/adjunct. *Students:* 401 full-time, 304 part-time, 31 international. Average age 30. 139 applicants, 96% accepted, 96 enrolled. In 2014, 140 master's, 23 doctorates awarded. *Degree requirements:* For master's, thesis or alternative; for doctorate, 2 foreign languages, thesis/dissertation. *Entrance requirements:* For master's, minimum GPA of 3.0; for doctorate, GRE General Test. Additional exam requirements/recommendations for international students: Required—TOEFL, IELTS. *Application deadline:* For fall admission, 7/1 priority date for domestic students, 4/30 for international students; for winter admission, 10/31 for international students; for spring admission, 10/31 for international students. Applications are processed on a rolling basis. Application fee: $0. Electronic applications accepted. *Financial support:* In 2014–15, 359 students received support. Career-related internships or fieldwork, Federal Work-Study, institutionally sponsored loans, and scholarships/grants available. Support available to part-time students. Financial award application deadline: 6/1; financial award applicants required to submit FAFSA. *Faculty research:* Theology, psychology (pastoral care), church history, Bible. *Unit head:* Dr. Craig Koester, Dean of Academic Affairs, 651-641-3471, Fax: 651-641-1609, E-mail: ckoester@luthersem.edu. *Application contact:* Jen Olsen Krengel, Director of Admissions, 651-641-3516, E-mail: jolsenkrengel001@luthersem.edu.
Website: http://www.luthersem.edu/

Machzikei Hadath Rabbinical College, Graduate Programs, Brooklyn, NY 11204-1805. Offers First Talmudic Degree. *Accreditation:* AARTS.

Madonna University, Program in Religious Studies, Livonia, MI 48150-1173. Offers pastoral ministry (MA).

Malone University, Graduate Program in Theological Studies, Canton, OH 44709. Offers MA. Part-time and evening/weekend programs available. *Entrance requirements:* For master's, minimum GPA of 3.0. Additional exam requirements/recommendations for international students: Required—TOEFL (minimum score 550 paper-based; 79 iBT). *Expenses:* Contact institution. *Faculty research:* Sacramental nature of the Biblical canon, theological anthropology, narrative criticism of the New Testament, Old Testament prophets, rhetorical criticism of the New Testament.

Maple Springs Baptist Bible College and Seminary, Graduate and Professional Programs, Capitol Heights, MD 20743. Offers biblical studies (MA, Certificate); Christian counseling (MA); church administration (MA); divinity (M Div); ministry (D Min); religious education (MRE).

Maranatha Baptist University, Master of Divinity Program, Watertown, WI 53094. Offers M Div. Part-time programs available. *Faculty:* 4 full-time (0 women), 5 part-time/adjunct (0 women). *Students:* 11 full-time (0 women), 21 part-time (0 women); includes 3 minority (1 Hispanic/Latino; 2 Two or more races, non-Hispanic/Latino), 1 international. Average age 29. 13 applicants, 92% accepted, 9 enrolled. In 2014, 3 master's awarded. *Degree requirements:* For master's, 2 foreign languages. *Entrance requirements:* Additional exam requirements/recommendations for international students: Required—TOEFL. *Application deadline:* Applications are processed on a rolling basis. Application fee: $50. *Expenses: Tuition:* Full-time $2655; part-time $295 per credit hour. *Required fees:* $25 per credit hour. Tuition and fees vary according to program. *Financial support:* Scholarships/grants and tuition waivers (full and partial) available. Support available to part-time students. *Faculty research:* Church history, counseling techniques, Bible structure, ancient language. *Unit head:* Dr. Larry Oats, Dean of Maranatha Baptist Seminary, 920-206-2324, Fax: 920-261-9109, E-mail: larry.oats@mbu.edu. *Application contact:* Dr. Jim Harrison, Director of Admissions, 920-206-2327, Fax: 920-261-9109, E-mail: admissions@mbu.edu.
Website: http://www.mbu.edu/seminary/academics/programs/master-of-divinity/

Maranatha Baptist University, Program in Biblical Studies, Watertown, WI 53094. Offers MA. Part-time programs available. *Faculty:* 4 full-time (0 women), 5 part-time/adjunct (0 women). *Students:* 2 full-time (0 women), 7 part-time (1 woman); includes 1 minority (Black or African American, non-Hispanic/Latino). Average age 31. 1 applicant, 100% accepted, 1 enrolled. In 2014, 8 master's awarded. *Degree requirements:* For master's, one foreign language. *Application deadline:* Applications are processed on a rolling basis. Application fee: $50. *Expenses: Tuition:* Full-time $2655; part-time $295 per credit hour. *Required fees:* $25 per credit hour. Tuition and fees vary according to program. *Financial support:* In 2014–15, 7 students received support. Scholarships/grants and tuition waivers (full and partial) available. Support available to part-time students. *Faculty research:* Bible structure, counseling techniques, church history. *Unit head:* Dr. Larry Oats, Dean of Maranatha Baptist Seminary, 920-206-2324, Fax: 920-261-9109, E-mail: larry.oats@mbu.edu. *Application contact:* Dr. Jim Harrison, Director of Admissions, 920-206-2327, Fax: 920-261-9109, E-mail: admissions@mbu.edu.
Website: http://www.mbu.edu/seminary/academics/programs/biblical-studies/

Marquette University, Graduate School, College of Arts and Sciences, Department of Theology, Milwaukee, WI 53201-1881. Offers MA, PhD. Part-time and evening/weekend programs available. Terminal master's awarded for partial completion of doctoral program. *Degree requirements:* For master's, one foreign language, comprehensive exam, thesis or alternative; for doctorate, 2 foreign languages, comprehensive exam, thesis/dissertation. *Entrance requirements:* For master's, GRE General Test, official transcripts from all current and previous colleges/universities except Marquette, three letters of recommendation, short personal statement; for doctorate, GRE General Test, official transcripts from all current and previous colleges/universities except Marquette, three letters of recommendation, short personal statement, academic writing sample. Additional exam requirements/recommendations for international students: Required—TOEFL (minimum score 530 paper-based). Electronic applications accepted. *Faculty research:* Old Testament theology, New Testament theology, church history, Christian ethics.

Marylhurst University, Applied Pastoral Theology Program, Marylhurst, OR 97036-0261. Offers MA. Part-time and evening/weekend programs available. *Students:* 1 (woman) full-time, 5 part-time (3 women). Average age 49. In 2014, 2 master's awarded. *Degree requirements:* For master's, thesis. *Entrance requirements:* For master's, MAT, transcripts from all universities attended, 3 letters of recommendation, resume, personal statement, autobiography, interview. Additional exam requirements/recommendations for international students: Required—TOEFL (minimum score 550 paper-based; 79 iBT), IELTS (minimum score 6.5), PTE (minimum score 53). *Application deadline:* For fall admission, 6/30 priority date for domestic students, 6/30 for international students; for winter admission, 11/30 priority date for domestic students, 11/30 for international students; for spring admission, 3/30 priority date for domestic students, 3/30 for international students. Applications are processed on a rolling basis. Application fee: $50. Electronic applications accepted. *Expenses: Tuition:* Full-time $21,096; part-time $586 per credit. Tuition and fees vary according to course load, campus/location and program. *Financial support:* Scholarships/grants available. Support available to part-time students. Financial award applicants required to submit FAFSA. *Faculty research:* Pastoral care, scripture, world religions. *Unit head:* Dr. Jerry Roussell, Jr., Chair, 503-636-8141, Fax: 503-697-5597, E-mail: jroussell@marylhurst.edu. *Application contact:* Maruksa Lynch, Graduate Admissions Counselor, 800-634-9982 Ext. 6322, Fax: 503-699-6320, E-mail: admissions@marylhurst.edu.
Website: http://www.marylhurst.edu

Marylhurst University, Divinity Program, Marylhurst, OR 97036-0261. Offers M Div. Part-time and evening/weekend programs available. *Students:* 8 full-time (5 women), 16 part-time (10 women); includes 2 minority (1 Black or African American, non-Hispanic/Latino; 1 Two or more races, non-Hispanic/Latino). In 2014, 4 master's awarded. *Degree requirements:* For master's, project. *Entrance requirements:* For master's, MAT, official transcripts from all previous institutions, letters of recommendation, personal statement, autobiography, interview. Additional exam requirements/recommendations for international students: Required—TOEFL (minimum score 550 paper-based; 79 iBT), IELTS (minimum score 6.5), PTE (minimum score 53). *Application deadline:* For fall admission, 6/30 for domestic students; for winter admission, 11/30 for domestic students; for spring admission, 3/30 for domestic students. Applications are processed on a rolling basis. Application fee: $50. Electronic applications accepted. *Expenses: Tuition:* Full-time $21,096; part-time $586 per credit. Tuition and fees vary according to course load, campus/location and program. *Financial support:* Scholarships/grants available. Support available to part-time students. Financial award applicants required to submit FAFSA. *Faculty research:* Scripture-Biblical studies, theology, history, ministry, spirituality. *Unit head:* Dr. Jerry Roussell, Jr., Chair, 503-636-8141, Fax: 503-697-5597, E-mail: jroussell@marylhurst.edu. *Application contact:* Maruska Lynch, Graduate Admissions Counselor, 800-634-9982 Ext. 6322, Fax: 503-699-6320, E-mail: admissions@marylhurst.edu.
Website: http://www.marylhurst.edu

The Master's College and Seminary, The Master's Seminary, Santa Clarita, CA 91321-1200. Offers biblical counseling (MABC); New Testament (Th D); Old Testament (Th D); preaching (D Min); theology (M Div, M Th, Th D). Part-time programs available. *Degree requirements:* For master's, 2 foreign languages, thesis; for doctorate, 4 foreign languages, thesis/dissertation. *Entrance requirements:* For master's, minimum GPA of 2.75; for doctorate, Th M, minimum GPA of 3.5. Additional exam requirements/recommendations for international students: Required—TOEFL (minimum score 550 paper-based).

McCormick Theological Seminary, Graduate and Professional Programs, Chicago, IL 60615. Offers ministry (D Min); theological studies (MATS, Certificate); theology (M Div); M Div/MSW. M Div/MSW offered jointly with Loyola University Chicago, University of Chicago, and University of Illinois at Chicago. *Accreditation:* ACIPE; ATS (one or more programs are accredited). Part-time and evening/weekend programs available. *Degree requirements:* For master's, thesis (for some programs); for doctorate, thesis/dissertation. *Entrance requirements:* For master's, minimum GPA of 3.0; for doctorate, M Div, minimum 3 years in pastorate. *Faculty research:* Faith formation, families, biblical literature, Dead Sea scrolls, women in antiquity.

McGill University, Faculty of Graduate and Postdoctoral Studies, Faculty of Religious Studies, Montréal, QC H3A 2T5, Canada. Offers MA, STM, PhD. *Accreditation:* ATS.

McMaster University, McMaster Divinity College, Hamilton, ON L8S 4M2, Canada. Offers biblical studies (M Div); Biblical studies (MA, MTS, Diploma); Christian interpretation/history (M Div, MA, MTS, Diploma); Christian ministry (M Div, MA, MTS, Diploma); Christian Studies (Certificate); Christian theology (PhD). Affiliated with the Toronto School of Theology. *Accreditation:* ATS. Part-time programs available. *Degree requirements:* For master's, one foreign language, thesis optional; for doctorate, 3 foreign languages, comprehensive exam, thesis/dissertation; for other advanced degree, 2 foreign languages, thesis. *Entrance requirements:* For master's, minimum B average in undergraduate course work, 3 letters of reference; for doctorate, minimum B+ average in bachelor's and master's, appropriate modern/ancient language, interview; for other advanced degree, 6 units of related Biblical language, minimum B+ average in undergraduate course work, minimum 15 units of course work in related area of study, 3 letters of recommendation. Additional exam requirements/recommendations for international students: Required—TOEFL (minimum score 550 paper-based). *Faculty research:* Ethics, Biblical studies, language studies, church history, Christian ministry.

Meadville Lombard Theological School, Graduate and Professional Programs, Chicago, IL 60637-1602. Offers divinity (M Div); ministry (D Min); religion (MA); M Div/MSW. M Div/MSW offered jointly with University of Chicago. *Accreditation:* ACIPE; ATS.

Part-time programs available. Postbaccalaureate distance learning degree programs offered (minimal on-campus study). *Entrance requirements:* For master's, bachelor's degree; for doctorate, bachelor's and masters degrees, 3 years of ministry.

Memphis Theological Seminary, Graduate and Professional Programs, Memphis, TN 38104-4395. Offers M Div, MAR, D Min. *Accreditation:* ATS. Part-time programs available. *Degree requirements:* For doctorate, thesis/dissertation. *Entrance requirements:* For doctorate, M Div, 3 years in ministry.

Mercer University, Graduate Studies, Cecil B. Day Campus, James and Carolyn McAfee School of Theology, Atlanta, GA 30341. Offers Christian ministry (MACM); Christian spirituality (D Min); divinity (M Div); preaching (D Min); M Div/MBA; M Div/MM; M Div/MS. *Accreditation:* ATS. Part-time programs available. *Faculty:* 16 full-time (6 women), 8 part-time/adjunct (4 women). *Students:* 136 full-time (67 women), 66 part-time (32 women); includes 96 minority (88 Black or African American, non-Hispanic/Latino; 1 American Indian or Alaska Native, non-Hispanic/Latino; 6 Hispanic/Latino; 1 Two or more races, non-Hispanic/Latino), 5 international. Average age 35. 107 applicants, 71% accepted, 40 enrolled. In 2014, 47 master's, 8 doctorates awarded. *Degree requirements:* For doctorate, thesis/dissertation, fieldwork, seminars. *Entrance requirements:* For master's, bachelor's degree with liberal arts core from regionally-accredited college/university; for doctorate, MAT or GRE, minimum B+ average in undergraduate course work, letters of recommendation. Additional exam requirements/recommendations for international students: Required—TOEFL (minimum score 550 paper-based; 79 iBT). *Application deadline:* For fall admission, 7/1 for domestic students, 2/1 for international students; for spring admission, 1/4 for domestic students. Applications are processed on a rolling basis. Application fee: $35. Electronic applications accepted. *Expenses:* Expenses: $385 per credit hour (for M Div and MACM); $350 (for D Min). *Financial support:* In 2014–15, 30 students received support. Career-related internships or fieldwork, Federal Work-Study, institutionally sponsored loans, and merit-based scholarships available. Support available to part-time students. Financial award applicants required to submit FAFSA. *Faculty research:* Biblical studies, Baptist heritage, Christian heritage, theology, pastoral care, ethics, global missions, academic research. *Unit head:* Dr. R. Alan Culpepper, Dean, 678-547-6470, Fax: 678-547-6478, E-mail: culpepper_ra@mercer.edu. *Application contact:* Elizabeth P. Allen, Director of Admissions, 678-547-6357, Fax: 678-547-6478, E-mail: allen_l@mercer.edu. Website: http://www.mercer.edu/theology

Mesivta of Eastern Parkway–Yeshiva Zichron Meilech, Graduate Programs, Brooklyn, NY 11218-5559. *Accreditation:* AARTS.

Mesivta Torah Vodaath Rabbinical Seminary, Graduate Programs, Brooklyn, NY 11218-5299. *Accreditation:* AARTS.

Mesivtha Tifereth Jerusalem of America, Graduate Programs, New York, NY 10002-6301. *Accreditation:* AARTS.

Methodist Theological School in Ohio, Graduate and Professional Programs, Delaware, OH 43015-8004. Offers M Div, MACE, MACM, MTS, D Min. *Accreditation:* ACIPE; ATS. Part-time programs available. *Entrance requirements:* For master's, 3 letters of recommendation. Additional exam requirements/recommendations for international students: Required—TOEFL (minimum score 577 paper-based; 90 iBT).

Mid-America Baptist Theological Seminary, Graduate and Professional Programs, Cordova, TN 38016. Offers M Div, MACE, MCE, MM, D Min, PhD. *Degree requirements:* For doctorate, 4 foreign languages, thesis/dissertation. *Entrance requirements:* For doctorate, MAT. Additional exam requirements/recommendations for international students: Required—TOEFL (minimum score 600 paper-based). Electronic applications accepted.

Mid-America Baptist Theological Seminary Northeast Branch, Program in Theology, Schenectady, NY 12303-3463. Offers M Div. Part-time and evening/weekend programs available. *Entrance requirements:* Additional exam requirements/recommendations for international students: Required—TOEFL. Electronic applications accepted.

Mid-America Reformed Seminary, Graduate Programs, Dyer, IN 46311. Offers M Div, MTS. *Entrance requirements:* Additional exam requirements/recommendations for international students: Required—TOEFL (minimum score 550 paper-based).

Midwestern Baptist Theological Seminary, Graduate and Professional Programs, Kansas City, MO 64118-4697. Offers Christian education (MACE); Christian foundations (Graduate Certificate); church music (MCM); counseling (MA); ministry (D Ed Min, D Min); Old or New Testament studies (PhD); theology (M Div). *Accreditation:* ATS. Part-time programs available. Postbaccalaureate distance learning degree programs offered (minimal on-campus study). *Degree requirements:* For doctorate, thesis/dissertation. *Entrance requirements:* For doctorate, MAT. Electronic applications accepted. *Faculty research:* Ministerial studies, Biblical and theological studies, missions, counseling.

Mirrer Yeshiva, Graduate Programs, Brooklyn, NY 11223-2010. *Accreditation:* AARTS.

Moody Bible Institute, Graduate School, Chicago, IL 60610-3284. Offers biblical studies (MABS, Graduate Certificate); intercultural studies (MAIS, Graduate Certificate); ministry (M Div, M Min); spiritual formation and discipleship (MASF, Graduate Certificate); urban studies (MA, Graduate Certificate). *Accreditation:* ATS. Part-time programs available. *Degree requirements:* For master's, 2 foreign languages, fieldwork (MABS); colloquium, field research project (MA Min). *Entrance requirements:* For master's, 30 hours in Bible/theology, 2 years of ministry experience (MA Min).

Moody Theological Seminary?Michigan, Graduate Programs, Plymouth, MI 48170. Offers Bible (Graduate Certificate); Christian education (MA); counseling psychology (MA); divinity (M Div); theological studies (MA). *Accreditation:* ATS. Part-time and evening/weekend programs available. *Degree requirements:* For master's, one foreign language, thesis. *Faculty research:* Judaism, cults, world religions.

Moravian Theological Seminary, Graduate and Certificate Programs, Bethlehem, PA 18018-6614. Offers divinity (M Div); formative spirituality (M Div, MATS, Graduate Certificate); spiritual direction (Graduate Certificate). *Accreditation:* ACIPE; ATS (one or more programs are accredited). Part-time programs available. *Faculty:* 6 full-time (2 women), 13 part-time/adjunct (6 women). *Students:* 27 full-time (12 women), 49 part-time (30 women); includes 15 minority (8 Black or African American, non-Hispanic/Latino; 1 American Indian or Alaska Native, non-Hispanic/Latino; 4 Hispanic/Latino; 2 Two or more races, non-Hispanic/Latino), 4 international. Average age 46. In 2014, 12 master's, 8 other advanced degrees awarded. *Degree requirements:* For master's, thesis (for some programs). *Entrance requirements:* For master's, reference forms, essay, denominational endorsement (M Div); for Graduate Certificate, reference forms, essay. Additional exam requirements/recommendations for international students: Required—TOEFL (minimum score 550 paper-based; 60 iBT). *Application deadline:* For fall admission, 4/1 priority date for international students; for spring admission, 9/1 priority date for international students. Applications are processed on a rolling basis. Application fee: $50. Electronic applications accepted. *Expenses:* Tuition: Full-time $12,432; part-time $576 per credit hour. *Required fees:* $215 per semester. One-time fee: $100. *Financial support:* In 2014–15, 71 students received support. Career-related internships or fieldwork, Federal Work-Study, and scholarships/grants available. Support available to part-time students. Financial award application deadline: 5/1; financial award applicants required to submit FAFSA. *Faculty research:* Pastoral counseling in post-modern age, history of Moravian Church, ordination of Moravian women, evangelism, interfaith studies. *Unit head:* Rev. Dr. Frank L. Crouch, Dean and Vice President, 610-861-1516, E-mail: crouchf@moravian.edu. *Application contact:* Dr. David H. DeRemer, Director of Enrollment, 610-861-1512, Fax: 610-861-1569, E-mail: deremerd@moravian.edu. Website: http://moravianseminary.edu

Mount Angel Seminary, Program in Theology, Saint Benedict, OR 97373. Offers M Div, MA. *Accreditation:* ACIPE; ATS. Part-time programs available. *Degree requirements:* For master's, thesis optional.

Mount St. Joseph University, Graduate Program in Religious Studies, Cincinnati, OH 45233-1670. Offers pastoral administration (Certificate); religious studies (MA); spirituality and wellness (Certificate). Part-time and evening/weekend programs available. *Faculty:* 3 full-time (2 women). *Students:* 14 part-time (11 women); includes 1 minority (Black or African American, non-Hispanic/Latino). Average age 45. 6 applicants, 83% accepted, 4 enrolled. In 2014, 3 master's awarded. *Degree requirements:* For master's, integrating project, field experience. *Entrance requirements:* For master's, 3 letters of recommendation, interview, minimum GPA of 3.0, academic transcripts, essay. Additional exam requirements/recommendations for international students: Required—TOEFL (minimum score 560 paper-based; 83 iBT). *Application deadline:* Applications are processed on a rolling basis. Application fee: $50. Electronic applications accepted. *Expenses:* Tuition: Full-time $18,400; part-time $575 per credit hour. *Required fees:* $450; $450 per year. Part-time tuition and fees vary according to course load, degree level and program. *Financial support:* In 2014–15, 10 students received support. Scholarships/grants available. Financial award application deadline: 3/1; financial award applicants required to submit FAFSA. *Faculty research:* Contextual/cultural/systematic theology, historical/spiritual theology, business/economics ethics, social justice, Biblical/cultural/pastoral theology. *Unit head:* Dr. John Trokan, Chair of Religious/Pastoral Studies, 513-244-4272, Fax: 513-244-4222, E-mail: john.trokan@msj.edu. *Application contact:* Mary Brigham, Assistant Director of Graduate Recruitment, 513-244-4233, Fax: 513-244-4629, E-mail: mary.brigham@msj.edu. Website: http://www.msj.edu/academics/graduate-programs/religious-studies-programs/

Mount St. Mary's University, Graduate Seminary, Emmitsburg, MD 21727-7799. Offers M Div, MA. *Accreditation:* ATS. *Faculty:* 10 full-time (1 woman), 3 part-time/adjunct (1 woman). *Students:* 157 full-time (0 women); includes 7 minority (2 Asian, non-Hispanic/Latino; 5 Hispanic/Latino), 12 international. Average age 28. 38 applicants, 100% accepted, 35 enrolled. In 2014, 28 master's awarded. *Degree requirements:* For master's, one foreign language, comprehensive exam, thesis, language proficiency exams. *Entrance requirements:* For master's, 18 credits of course work in philosophy. Additional exam requirements/recommendations for international students: Required—TOEFL (minimum score 550 paper-based). *Application deadline:* For fall admission, 8/1 for domestic and international students. Application fee: $0. *Expenses:* Expenses: Contact institution. *Financial support:* In 2014–15, 37 students received support. Career-related internships or fieldwork and scholarships/grants available. Financial award applicants required to submit FAFSA. *Faculty research:* Priestly spirituality, religious liberty, Hispanic ministry, Pope Francis, spiritual reading. *Unit head:* Rev. Steven P. Rohlfs, Vice President/Rector, 301-447-5295, Fax: 301-447-5636, E-mail: rohlfs@msmary.edu. *Application contact:* Susan Nield, Seminary Admissions, 301-447-7423, Fax: 301-447-7402, E-mail: nield@msmary.edu. Website: http://www.msmary.edu/seminary

Mount Vernon Nazarene University, Program in Ministry, Mount Vernon, OH 43050-9500. Offers M Min. Part-time and evening/weekend programs available. *Degree requirements:* For master's, project. *Faculty research:* Pastoral effectiveness and professional development.

Multnomah University, Multnomah Biblical Seminary, Portland, OR 97220-5898. Offers M Div, MABS, MACL, MATS, Th M, D Min. *Accreditation:* ATS. Part-time programs available. *Faculty:* 6 full-time (2 women), 12 part-time/adjunct (2 women). *Students:* 121 full-time (28 women), 60 part-time (13 women); includes 30 minority (6 Black or African American, non-Hispanic/Latino; 2 American Indian or Alaska Native, non-Hispanic/Latino; 3 Asian, non-Hispanic/Latino; 11 Hispanic/Latino; 2 Native Hawaiian or other Pacific Islander, non-Hispanic/Latino; 6 Two or more races, non-Hispanic/Latino), 3 international. Average age 35. 80 applicants, 75% accepted, 47 enrolled. In 2014, 42 master's awarded. *Degree requirements:* For master's, variable foreign language requirement, thesis (for some programs). *Entrance requirements:* For master's, interview; for doctorate, interview, M Div equivalency. Additional exam requirements/recommendations for international students: Required—TOEFL (minimum score 550 paper-based). *Application deadline:* For fall and spring admission, 12/1 priority date for domestic and international students. Applications are processed on a rolling basis. Application fee: $40. *Expenses:* Tuition: Part-time $525 per semester hour. *Required fees:* $50 per semester. Tuition and fees vary according to course level, course load and program. *Financial support:* Career-related internships or fieldwork and scholarships/grants available. Support available to part-time students. Financial award application deadline: 7/1; financial award applicants required to submit FAFSA. *Faculty research:* Grief theology, intercultural studies, New Testament, theology and culture, historical theology, Biblical theology. *Unit head:* Dr. Roy Andrews, Dean, 503-252-6731, Fax: 503-251-6444, E-mail: randrews@multnomah.edu. *Application contact:* Armae Johnson, Seminary Admissions Counselor, 503-251-6487, Fax: 503-254-1268, E-mail: admiss@multnomah.edu.

Naropa University, Graduate Programs, Program in Divinity, Boulder, CO 80302-6697. Offers M Div. *Faculty:* 5 full-time (2 women), 10 part-time/adjunct (7 women). *Students:* 20 full-time (8 women), 11 part-time (4 women); includes 8 minority (1 Asian, non-Hispanic/Latino; 3 Hispanic/Latino; 4 Two or more races, non-Hispanic/Latino), 2 international. Average age 37. 16 applicants, 94% accepted, 10 enrolled. In 2014, 6 master's awarded. *Degree requirements:* For master's, thesis, internship, field work. *Entrance requirements:* For master's, resume, 2 letters of recommendation, letter of interest, transcripts, on-site or phone interview. Additional exam requirements/recommendations for international students: Required—TOEFL (minimum score 600 paper-based; 80 iBT). *Application deadline:* For fall admission, 1/15 priority date for domestic and international students. Applications are processed on a rolling basis. Application fee: $60. Electronic applications accepted. *Expenses:* Tuition: Full-time $23,400; part-time $975 per credit. *Required fees:* $335 per semester. Tuition and fees vary according to course load. *Financial support:* In 2014–15, 15 students received support, including 2 research assistantships with partial tuition reimbursements available (averaging $5,250 per year); career-related internships or fieldwork, scholarships/grants, tuition waivers (partial), and unspecified assistantships also available. Support available to part-time students. Financial award application deadline: 3/1; financial award applicants required to submit FAFSA. *Application contact:* Office of Admissions, 303-546-3572, Fax: 303-546-3583, E-mail: admissions@naropa.edu. Website: http://www.naropa.edu/academics/shis/grad/master-of-divinity/index.php

Nashotah House, Theological Seminary, Nashotah, WI 53058-9793. Offers M Div, MA Min, MTS, STM, D Min, Certificate. *Accreditation:* ACIPE; ATS (one or more

programs are accredited). Part-time programs available. *Faculty:* 8 full-time (0 women), 4 part-time/adjunct (0 women). *Students:* 78 full-time (14 women), 5 part-time (2 women); includes 3 minority (2 Black or African American, non-Hispanic/Latino; 1 Asian, non-Hispanic/Latino). Average age 37. *Degree requirements:* For master's, thesis optional. *Entrance requirements:* For master's and Certificate, GRE General Test or MAT, interview. Additional exam requirements/recommendations for international students: Required—TOEFL. *Application deadline:* For fall admission, 7/1 priority date for domestic students. Applications are processed on a rolling basis. Application fee: $0. *Financial support:* Teaching assistantships, career-related internships or fieldwork, scholarships/grants, and tuition waivers (partial) available. Support available to part-time students. Financial award application deadline: 9/15; financial award applicants required to submit FAFSA. *Faculty research:* Formation for parochial ministry, ancient Semitic epigraphy. *Unit head:* Dr. Steven A. Peay, Dean/President, 262-646-6512, Fax: 262-646-6504, E-mail: speay@nashotah.edu. *Application contact:* Alane Evans, Registrar, 262-646-6516, Fax: 262-646-6504, E-mail: aevans@nashotah.edu.
Website: http://www.nashotah.edu/

Nazarene Theological Seminary, Graduate and Professional Programs, Kansas City, MO 64131-1263. Offers Christian formation and discipleship (MA); intercultural studies (MA); theological studies (MA); theology (M Div, D Min). *Accreditation:* ACIPE; ATS. Part-time programs available. *Degree requirements:* For master's, comprehensive exam (for some programs), thesis (for some programs); for doctorate, thesis/dissertation. *Entrance requirements:* Additional exam requirements/recommendations for international students: Required—TOEFL. Electronic applications accepted.

Ner Israel Rabbinical College, Graduate Programs, Baltimore, MD 21208. Offers MTL, DTL, Professional Certificate. *Accreditation:* AARTS.

Ner Israel Yeshiva College of Toronto, Graduate Programs, Thornhill, ON L4J 8A7, Canada. *Accreditation:* AARTS.

New Brunswick Theological Seminary, Graduate and Professional Programs, New Brunswick, NJ 08901-1196. Offers pastoral care and counseling (D Min). *Accreditation:* ACIPE; ATS. Part-time and evening/weekend programs available. *Faculty:* 10 full-time (3 women), 24 part-time/adjunct (7 women). *Students:* 35 full-time (19 women), 149 part-time (96 women); includes 146 minority (126 Black or African American, non-Hispanic/Latino; 11 Asian, non-Hispanic/Latino; 9 Hispanic/Latino), 3 international. Average age 35. 69 applicants, 62% accepted, 39 enrolled. In 2014, 24 master's, 1 doctorate awarded. *Degree requirements:* For master's, variable foreign language requirement, thesis (for some programs); for doctorate, thesis/dissertation. *Entrance requirements:* For master's, B.A/.B.S. degree with a minimum of 3.0 for the M.A. or 2.5 for the Master of Divinity; for doctorate, M.Div. degree. Additional exam requirements/recommendations for international students: Required—TOEFL (minimum score 550 paper-based; 79 iBT); Recommended—IELTS (minimum score 6). *Application deadline:* For fall admission, 7/15 for domestic and international students; for spring admission, 11/15 for domestic and international students. Applications are processed on a rolling basis. Application fee: $50. Electronic applications accepted. *Expenses: Tuition:* Full-time $11,088; part-time $462 per credit. *Required fees:* $231 per semester. *Financial support:* In 2014–15, 75 students received support. Scholarships/grants and tuition waivers (full and partial) available. Financial award application deadline: 6/30; financial award applicants required to submit FAFSA. *Unit head:* Dr. Willard Ashley, Sr., Dean of the Seminary, 732-247-5241 Ext. 109, Fax: 732-249-5412, E-mail: washley@nbts.edu. *Application contact:* Dr. Beth L. Tanner, Chair, Admissions Committee, 732-247-5241 Ext. 116, Fax: 732-249-5412, E-mail: admissions@nbts.edu.

Newman Theological College, Theology Programs, Edmonton, AB T6V 1H3, Canada. Offers M Div, M Th, MTS. *Accreditation:* ATS. Part-time programs available. *Faculty:* 7 full-time (0 women), 12 part-time/adjunct (2 women). *Students:* 26 full-time (3 women), 9 part-time (6 women). *Degree requirements:* For master's, comprehensive exam, thesis. *Entrance requirements:* For master's, bachelor's degree. Additional exam requirements/recommendations for international students: Required—TOEFL (minimum score 560 paper-based; 86 iBT), IELTS (minimum score 6.5), TWE (minimum score 5). *Application deadline:* For fall admission, 8/4 priority date for domestic students; for winter admission, 1/2 priority date for domestic students; for spring admission, 5/6 priority date for domestic students. Applications are processed on a rolling basis. Application fee: $45 ($250 for international students). *Expenses: Tuition:* Full-time $7492 Canadian dollars; part-time $639 Canadian dollars per course. Tuition and fees vary according to campus/location. *Financial support:* Tuition bursaries available. Support available to part-time students. Financial award application deadline: 5/31. *Unit head:* Dr. Jason West, Academic Dean and President, 780-392-2450 Ext. 5222, Fax: 780-462-4013, E-mail: jason.west@newman.edu. *Application contact:* Maria Saulnier, Registrar, 780-392-2451, Fax: 780-462-4013, E-mail: registrar@newman.edu.
Website: http://www.newman.edu/

Newman University, Graduate Theology Program, Wichita, KS 67213-2097. Offers theological studies (MTS); theology (MA). Part-time programs available. Postbaccalaureate distance learning degree programs offered (minimal on-campus study). *Faculty:* 2 full-time (0 women), 1 part-time/adjunct (0 women). *Students:* 27 part-time (16 women); includes 4 minority (2 Black or African American, non-Hispanic/Latino; 2 Hispanic/Latino). Average age 46. 18 applicants, 72% accepted, 13 enrolled. In 2014, 17 master's awarded. *Degree requirements:* For master's, 2 foreign languages, comprehensive exam (for some programs), thesis (for some programs). *Entrance requirements:* For master's, letter of recommendation from pastor; bachelor's degree in theology or related field (MA), in any field (MTS). Additional exam requirements/recommendations for international students: Required—TOEFL (minimum score 600 paper-based; 100 iBT). *Application deadline:* For fall admission, 8/1 priority date for domestic students. Application fee: $25 ($40 for international students). *Expenses:* Expenses: Contact institution. *Financial support:* In 2014–15, 35 students received support. Scholarships/grants available. Financial award application deadline: 8/15; financial award applicants required to submit FAFSA. *Unit head:* Fr. Joseph Gile, Assistant Professor of Theology/Director of Graduate Theology Program, 316-942-4291 Ext. 2861, Fax: 316-942-4483, E-mail: gilej@newmanu.edu. *Application contact:* Kimberly Wilkerson, Director of Graduate Admissions, 316-942-4291 Ext. 2437, E-mail: wilkersonk@newmanu.edu.
Website: http://www.newmanu.edu/studynu/graduate/theology/master-arts-theology

New Orleans Baptist Theological Seminary, Graduate and Professional Programs, Division of Biblical Studies, New Orleans, LA 70126-4858. Offers M Div, MA, PhD. *Accreditation:* ACIPE; ATS (one or more programs are accredited). *Degree requirements:* For master's, 2 foreign languages, comprehensive exam (for some programs), thesis (for some programs); for doctorate, 4 foreign languages, comprehensive exam, thesis/dissertation. *Entrance requirements:* For doctorate, GRE General Test.

New Orleans Baptist Theological Seminary, Graduate and Professional Programs, Division of Theological and Historical Studies, New Orleans, LA 70126-4858. Offers M Div, MA, D Min, PhD. *Accreditation:* ACIPE; ATS (one or more programs are accredited). Postbaccalaureate distance learning degree programs offered (minimal on-campus study). *Degree requirements:* For master's, 2 foreign languages, comprehensive exam (for some programs), thesis (for some programs); for doctorate, 3 foreign languages, comprehensive exam, thesis/dissertation. *Entrance requirements:* For doctorate, GRE General Test. Additional exam requirements/recommendations for international students: Required—TOEFL.

New Saint Andrews College, Graduate School, Moscow, ID 83843. Offers classical Christian studies (Graduate Certificate); theology and letters (MA). Part-time programs available. *Faculty:* 12 part-time/adjunct (0 women). *Students:* 7 full-time (3 women), 6 part-time (3 women); includes 3 minority (1 Asian, non-Hispanic/Latino; 2 Two or more races, non-Hispanic/Latino). 11 applicants, 45% accepted, 4 enrolled. In 2014, 5 master's awarded. *Degree requirements:* For master's, thesis (for some programs), final oral exam. *Entrance requirements:* For master's, GRE, 2 letters of recommendation; for Graduate Certificate, GRE, bachelor's degree, essays, 2 letters of recommendation. *Application deadline:* For fall admission, 12/1 for domestic students. Application fee: $50. Electronic applications accepted. *Expenses: Tuition:* Full-time $7600; part-time $475 per credit. *Unit head:* Benjamin Merkle, Academic Dean, 208-882-1566 Ext. 104, E-mail: bmerkle@nsa.edu. *Application contact:* Brenda Schlect, Director of Admissions, 208-882-1566 Ext. 113, Fax: 208-882-4293, E-mail: admissions@nsa.edu.
Website: http://www.nsa.edu/academics/graduate-school/

New York Theological Seminary, Graduate and Professional Programs, New York, NY 10115. Offers M Div, MPS, MSW, D Min. MSW offered jointly with Fordham University. *Accreditation:* ACIPE; ATS (one or more programs are accredited). Part-time programs available. *Degree requirements:* For doctorate, thesis/dissertation. *Entrance requirements:* For doctorate, M Div, 3 years of ministry experience, interview. Additional exam requirements/recommendations for international students: Required—TOEFL. *Faculty research:* Women in leadership; crime and punishment; church history; culture, politics and theology.

Northeastern Seminary at Roberts Wesleyan College, Graduate and Professional Programs, Rochester, NY 14624. Offers ministry (D Min); theological studies (MA); theology (M Div); M Div/MSW. M Div/MSW offered jointly with Roberts Wesleyan College. *Accreditation:* ATS. Evening/weekend programs available. *Degree requirements:* For master's, thesis (for some programs); for doctorate, one foreign language, thesis/dissertation. *Entrance requirements:* For doctorate, M Div, 3 years of full-time ministry experience. Additional exam requirements/recommendations for international students: Required—TOEFL (minimum score 550 paper-based). Electronic applications accepted. *Faculty research:* Historical theology, spiritual formation, biblical theology, counseling education.

Northern Baptist Theological Seminary, Graduate and Professional Programs, Lombard, IL 60148-5698. Offers Biblical studies (M Div); Christian ministries (MACM); missional leadership (D Min); spiritual transformation (D Min); theology (M Div). *Accreditation:* ATS. Part-time and evening/weekend programs available. *Faculty:* 6 full-time (1 woman), 33 part-time/adjunct (8 women). *Students:* 126 full-time (34 women), 80 part-time (32 women); includes 89 minority (73 Black or African American, non-Hispanic/Latino; 6 Asian, non-Hispanic/Latino; 8 Hispanic/Latino; 2 Two or more races, non-Hispanic/Latino), 3 international. Average age 44. *Degree requirements:* For doctorate, thesis/dissertation. *Entrance requirements:* For master's, all official transcripts, letter of reference from church, 3 letters of reference, autobiographical statement (400 words or more); for doctorate, M Div, 3 years in the ministry post-M Div, 3 letters of reference. Additional exam requirements/recommendations for international students: Required—TOEFL (minimum score 550 paper-based). *Application deadline:* For fall admission, 8/25 for domestic students, 2/1 for international students; for winter admission, 12/10 for domestic students, 2/1 for international students; for spring admission, 3/15 for domestic students, 2/1 for international students. Applications are processed on a rolling basis. Application fee: $35. Electronic applications accepted. *Expenses: Tuition:* Full-time $13,230; part-time $1470 per course. *Required fees:* $360; $120 per quarter. *Financial support:* Scholarships/grants available. Support available to part-time students. Financial award application deadline: 9/1; financial award applicants required to submit FAFSA. *Faculty research:* Theology, worship studies, church history, evangelism, Christian ministry. *Unit head:* Dr. J. Alistair Brown, President, 630-620-2101, Fax: 630-620-2190. *Application contact:* Isaac Ampil, Director of Admissions, 630-620-2175, Fax: 630-620-2190, E-mail: admissions@seminary.edu.

North Park Theological Seminary, Graduate and Professional Programs, Professional Program, Chicago, IL 60625-4895. Offers M Div, M Div/MBA, M Div/MM. M Div/MBA offered jointly with North Park University. *Accreditation:* ACIPE; ATS. Part-time programs available. *Entrance requirements:* Additional exam requirements/recommendations for international students: Required—TOEFL.

North Park Theological Seminary, Graduate and Professional Programs, Program in Christian Formation, Chicago, IL 60625-4895. Offers MA, MA/MM.

North Park Theological Seminary, Graduate and Professional Programs, Program in Preaching, Chicago, IL 60625-4895. Offers D Min. Program offered jointly with Chicago Theological Seminary, Lutheran School of Theology at Chicago, McCormick Theological Seminary, Seabury-Western Theological Seminary. *Accreditation:* ACIPE; ATS. *Degree requirements:* For doctorate, thesis/dissertation. *Entrance requirements:* For doctorate, 3 years of preaching experience.

North Park Theological Seminary, Graduate and Professional Programs, Program in Theological Studies, Chicago, IL 60625-4895. Offers MATS, MATS/MBA, MATS/MM. MATS/MBA offered jointly with North Park University. *Accreditation:* ACIPE; ATS. Part-time programs available. *Degree requirements:* For master's, comprehensive exam or thesis. *Entrance requirements:* For master's, minimum GPA of 2.5. Additional exam requirements/recommendations for international students: Required—TOEFL.

Northwest Nazarene University, Graduate Studies, Program in Religion, Nampa, ID 83686-5897. Offers missional leadership (M Div, MA); pastoral ministry (MA); spiritual formation (M Div, MA); youth, children, and family ministry (M Div, MA). Part-time and evening/weekend programs available. Postbaccalaureate distance learning degree programs offered (no on-campus study). *Faculty:* 12 full-time (2 women), 15 part-time/adjunct (1 woman). *Students:* 91 full-time (27 women), 20 part-time (5 women); includes 11 minority (4 Black or African American, non-Hispanic/Latino; 1 American Indian or Alaska Native, non-Hispanic/Latino; 2 Asian, non-Hispanic/Latino; 3 Hispanic/Latino; 1 Native Hawaiian or other Pacific Islander, non-Hispanic/Latino), 1 international. Average age 39. 55 applicants, 65% accepted, 27 enrolled. In 2014, 40 master's awarded. *Entrance requirements:* For master's, minimum GPA of 2.5; 8 semester or 12 quarter credits of Bible, theology and/or Western philosophy. Additional exam requirements/recommendations for international students: Required—TOEFL. *Application deadline:* Applications are processed on a rolling basis. Application fee: $50. Electronic applications accepted. *Unit head:* Dr. Jay Akkerman, Director, Graduate Studies, 208-467-8437, Fax: 208-467-8252. *Application contact:* Vicki Funk, Program Coordinator, 208-467-8432, Fax: 208-467-8252, E-mail: vlfunk@nnu.edu.
Website: http://www.nnu.edu/ministry/

Northwest University, College of Ministry, Kirkland, WA 98033. Offers ministry (MIM); missional leadership (MA); theology and culture (MA). Part-time and evening/weekend programs available. Postbaccalaureate distance learning degree programs offered (no on-campus study). *Faculty:* 6 full-time (1 woman), 8 part-time/adjunct (1 woman). *Students:* 7 full-time (3 women), 81 part-time (19 women); includes 21 minority (2 Black or African American, non-Hispanic/Latino; 6 Asian, non-Hispanic/Latino; 3 Hispanic/

Latino; 4 Native Hawaiian or other Pacific Islander, non-Hispanic/Latino; 6 Two or more races, non-Hispanic/Latino). Average age 43. 33 applicants, 97% accepted, 20 enrolled. In 2014, 33 master's awarded. *Degree requirements:* For master's, comprehensive exam (for some programs), thesis (for some programs). *Entrance requirements:* Additional exam requirements/recommendations for international students: Required— TOEFL (minimum score 550 paper-based; 75 iBT). *Application deadline:* For fall admission, 8/1 for domestic students, 4/1 for international students; for spring admission, 12/1 for domestic students, 8/1 for international students. Applications are processed on a rolling basis. Application fee: $50. Electronic applications accepted. *Expenses: Tuition:* Full-time $6894; part-time $684 per credit. *Required fees:* $12.50 per term. One-time fee: $98 full-time; $83 part-time. Tuition and fees vary according to course load, campus/location, program and reciprocity agreements. *Financial support:* In 2014–15, 10 students received support. Federal Work-Study available. *Unit head:* Dr. Wayde Goodall, Dean, 425-889-5211, E-mail: wayde.goodall@northwestu.edu. *Application contact:* Steven Curry, Graduate Enrollment Counselor, College of Ministry, 425-889-7795, E-mail: steven.curry@northwestu.edu.
Website: http://www.northwestu.edu/ministrygrad/

Notre Dame Seminary, Graduate School of Theology, New Orleans, LA 70118-4391. Offers M Div, MA. *Accreditation:* ACIPE; ATS. Part-time programs available. *Degree requirements:* For master's, one foreign language, comprehensive exam, thesis. *Entrance requirements:* For master's, GRE. Additional exam requirements/ recommendations for international students: Required—TOEFL.

Nyack College, Alliance Theological Seminary, Nyack, NY 10960. Offers Biblical literature (MA), including New Testament, Old Testament; Christian ministry (MPS); intercultural studies (MA); ministry (D Min), including Christian leadership in the global context; theology and missions (M Div); urban ministry (MPS). *Accreditation:* ATS. Part-time and evening/weekend programs available. *Students:* 319 full-time (132 women), 439 part-time (214 women); includes 605 minority (230 Black or African American, non-Hispanic/Latino; 170 Asian, non-Hispanic/Latino; 195 Hispanic/Latino; 1 Native Hawaiian or other Pacific Islander, non-Hispanic/Latino; 9 Two or more races, non-Hispanic/Latino), 41 international. Average age 43. In 2014, 134 master's, 11 doctorates awarded. *Degree requirements:* For master's, comprehensive exam (for some programs), thesis optional, internship; for doctorate, thesis/dissertation. *Entrance requirements:* For master's, transcripts, Christian experience statement, personal goals statement, recommendations; for doctorate, transcripts, documented three years of ministry experience subsequent to 1st graduate theological degree, reference letters, formal academic paper. Additional exam requirements/recommendations for international students: Required—TOEFL (minimum score 83 iBT). *Application deadline:* Applications are processed on a rolling basis. Application fee: $30. Electronic applications accepted. *Expenses:* Expenses: Contact institution. *Financial support:* Career-related internships or fieldwork, Federal Work-Study, and scholarships/grants available. Financial award applicants required to submit FAFSA. *Unit head:* Dr. Ronald Walborn, Dean, 845-770-5715, Fax: 845-358-1663. *Application contact:* Julian Williams, ATS Associate Director of Admissions, 800-541-6891, Fax: 845-348-3912, E-mail: admissions.ats@nyack.edu.
Website: http://www.nyack.edu/ats

Oakland City University, Chapman Seminary, Oakland City, IN 47660-1099. Offers M Div, D Min. *Accreditation:* ATS. Part-time programs available. *Degree requirements:* For doctorate, thesis/dissertation. *Entrance requirements:* For doctorate, GRE, MAT, letters of recommendation. Additional exam requirements/recommendations for international students: Required—TOEFL. *Expenses:* Contact institution. *Faculty research:* Pastoral ministry, Christian education, missions.

Oblate School of Theology, Graduate and Professional Programs, San Antonio, TX 78216-6693. Offers African-American pastoral leadership (D Min); divinity (M Div); pastoral leadership (D Min); pastoral ministry (MAP Min); pastoral studies (Certificate); spiritual formation in the local community (D Min); spirituality (MA Sp, PhD); spirituality and ministry (D Min); theology (MA Th); U.S. Hispanic/Latino ministry (D Min); M Div/ MA Th. *Accreditation:* ACIPE; ATS (one or more programs are accredited). Part-time programs available. Postbaccalaureate distance learning degree programs offered (no on-campus study). *Faculty:* 23 full-time (8 women), 3 part-time/adjunct (0 women). *Students:* 59 full-time (6 women), 73 part-time (36 women); includes 56 minority (8 Black or African American, non-Hispanic/Latino; 9 Asian, non-Hispanic/Latino; 39 Hispanic/ Latino), 41 international. Average age 40. 41 applicants, 88% accepted, 34 enrolled. In 2014, 31 master's, 3 doctorates awarded. *Degree requirements:* For master's, comprehensive exam (for some programs), thesis (for some programs), practicum; for doctorate, one foreign language, comprehensive exam, thesis/dissertation, paper, practicum. *Entrance requirements:* For master's, MAT, interview, course work in theology or religious studies, minimum GPA of 2.5; for doctorate, M Div, MA Th, or MA Sp. Additional exam requirements/recommendations for international students: Required—TOEFL (minimum score 71 iBT). *Application deadline:* For fall admission, 6/ 15 priority date for domestic and international students; for winter admission, 11/30 for domestic and international students; for spring admission, 11/30 for domestic and international students; for summer admission, 4/1 for domestic and international students. Applications are processed on a rolling basis. Application fee: $65. *Expenses:* Expenses: Contact institution. *Financial support:* In 2014–15, 25 students received support. Scholarships/grants available. Support available to part-time students. Financial award application deadline: 8/1; financial award applicants required to submit FAFSA. *Unit head:* Dr. R. Scott Woodward, Academic Dean, 210-341-1366, Fax: 210-341-4519, E-mail: rsw@ost.edu. *Application contact:* Mario A. Porter, Director of Admissions, 210-341-1366 Ext. 226, Fax: 210-341-4519, E-mail: registrar@ost.edu.

Ohio Dominican University, Graduate Programs, Division of Arts and Letters, Program in Theology, Columbus, OH 43219-2099. Offers MA. Part-time and evening/weekend programs available. *Students:* 3 full-time (2 women), 13 part-time (5 women). *Degree requirements:* For master's, thesis optional. *Entrance requirements:* For master's, 20 undergraduate semester hours of theology or the equivalent, 2 letters of recommendation, interview. Additional exam requirements/recommendations for international students: Required—TOEFL (minimum score 550 paper-based), IELTS (minimum score 6.5). *Application deadline:* For fall admission, 7/15 priority date for domestic and international students; for spring admission, 12/15 priority date for domestic and international students. Applications are processed on a rolling basis. Application fee: $25. Electronic applications accepted. *Expenses: Tuition:* Full-time $6792; part-time $566 per credit hour. *Required fees:* $200 per semester. Tuition and fees vary according to program and student's religious affiliation. *Financial support:* Applicants required to submit FAFSA. *Unit head:* Dr. Leo Madden, Program Director, 614-251-4720, E-mail: maddenl@ohiodominican.edu. *Application contact:* John W. Naughton, Director for Graduate Admissions, 614-251-4615, Fax: 614-251-6654, E-mail: grad@ohiodominican.edu.

Ohr Hameir Theological Seminary, Graduate Programs, Cortlandt Manor, NY 10567. *Accreditation:* AARTS.

Oklahoma Christian University, Graduate School of Theology, Oklahoma City, OK 73136-1100. Offers family life ministry (MA); ministry (M Div, MA); youth ministry (MA). Part-time programs available. Postbaccalaureate distance learning degree programs offered (minimal on-campus study). *Degree requirements:* For master's, one foreign

language, comprehensive exam, field experience. *Entrance requirements:* For master's, minimum undergraduate GPA of 3.0. Additional exam requirements/recommendations for international students: Required—TOEFL (minimum score 550 paper-based). Electronic applications accepted. *Faculty research:* Early marriage adjustment, new religions, Ethiopic language, church health, Hebrew rhetoric.

Oklahoma Wesleyan University, Professional Studies Division, Bartlesville, OK 74006-6299. Offers nursing administration (MSN); nursing education (MSN); strategic leadership (MS); theology and apologetics (MA).

Olivet Nazarene University, Graduate School, Department of Practical Ministries, Bourbonnais, IL 60914. Offers MPM. Part-time programs available. *Degree requirements:* For master's, thesis or alternative.

Olivet Nazarene University, Graduate School, Division of Religion, Bourbonnais, IL 60914. Offers biblical literature (MA); religion (MA); theology (MA). Part-time programs available. *Degree requirements:* For master's, thesis or alternative.

Oral Roberts University, School of Theology and Missions, Tulsa, OK 74171. Offers biblical literature (MA), including advanced languages, Judaic-Christian studies; Christian counseling (MA), including marriage and family therapy; divinity (M Div); missions (MA); practical theology (MA); theological/historical studies (MA); theology (D Min). *Accreditation:* ATS. Part-time programs available. Postbaccalaureate distance learning degree programs offered (minimal on-campus study). *Degree requirements:* For master's, thesis (for some programs), practicum/internship; for doctorate, thesis/ dissertation, applied research project. *Entrance requirements:* For master's, GRE General Test or MAT, minimum GPA of 2.5; for doctorate, M Div, minimum GPA of 3.0, 3 years of full-time ministry experience. Additional exam requirements/ recommendations for international students: Required—TOEFL (minimum score 550 paper-based; 79 iBT). Electronic applications accepted.

Pacific School of Religion, Graduate and Professional Programs, Berkeley, CA 94709-1323. Offers M Div, MA, MTS, D Min, PhD, Th D, CAPS, CMS, CSS, CTS. MA, PhD, Th D offered jointly with Graduate Theological Union; D Min with Church Divinity School of the Pacific. *Accreditation:* ACIPE; ATS (one or more programs are accredited). Part-time programs available. *Degree requirements:* For master's, one foreign language, thesis (for some programs); for doctorate, thesis/dissertation. *Entrance requirements:* For master's, minimum GPA of 3.0; for doctorate, M Div, minimum GPA of 3.0 (D Min); for other advanced degree, M Div, minimum GPA of 3.0 (CAPS). Additional exam requirements/recommendations for international students: Required—TOEFL (minimum score 550 paper-based). Electronic applications accepted. *Faculty research:* Medical ethics, gay/lesbian studies in religion, Asian-American religion, race, culture and theology, theology in context.

Palm Beach Atlantic University, School of Ministry, West Palm Beach, FL 33416-4708. Offers M Div. Part-time programs available. *Faculty:* 1 full-time (0 women), 9 part-time/adjunct (1 woman). *Students:* 29 full-time (3 women); includes 10 minority (3 Black or African American, non-Hispanic/Latino; 1 Asian, non-Hispanic/Latino; 5 Hispanic/ Latino; 1 Two or more races, non-Hispanic/Latino), 1 international. Average age 28. 19 applicants, 84% accepted, 12 enrolled. *Entrance requirements:* For master's, GRE General Test, minimum GPA of 3.0 in last 60 hours. Additional exam requirements/ recommendations for international students: Required—TOEFL (minimum score 550 paper-based). *Application deadline:* For fall admission, 7/15 priority date for domestic students; for spring admission, 11/15 priority date for domestic students. Applications are processed on a rolling basis. Application fee: $50. Electronic applications accepted. *Expenses: Tuition:* Part-time $510 per credit hour. *Financial support:* In 2014–15, 16 students received support. Tuition waivers, unspecified assistantships, and Employee Education grants available. Financial award application deadline: 5/1; financial award applicants required to submit FAFSA. *Unit head:* Dr. Randy Richards, Dean, 561-803-2295. *Application contact:* Julie Ziaja, Assistant Director of Graduate and Evening Admissions, 888-468-6722, Fax: 561-803-2115, E-mail: grad@pba.edu.
Website: http://www.pba.edu/school-of-ministry

Payne Theological Seminary, Program in Theology, Wilberforce, OH 45384-3474. Offers M Div. *Accreditation:* ACIPE; ATS. Part-time and evening/weekend programs available. Postbaccalaureate distance learning degree programs offered (minimal on-campus study).

Pentecostal Theological Seminary, Graduate and Professional Programs, Cleveland, TN 37320-3330. Offers biblical studies (MTS); church ministries (MA); counseling (MA); discipleship and Christian formation (MA); ministry (D Min); Pentecostal theology (MTS); theology (M Div). *Accreditation:* ACIPE; ATS. Part-time programs available. *Degree requirements:* For master's, variable foreign language requirement, thesis (for some programs), internship. *Faculty research:* Biblical exegesis.

Pepperdine University, Seaver College, Master of Divinity Program, Malibu, CA 90263. Offers M Div. *Students:* 1 full-time (0 women), 6 part-time (2 women); includes 2 minority (1 Black or African American, non-Hispanic/Latino; 1 Asian, non-Hispanic/Latino). In 2014, 2 master's awarded. *Entrance requirements:* For master's, GRE, letters of recommendation, writing sample. Additional exam requirements/recommendations for international students: Required—TOEFL. *Application deadline:* For fall admission, 2/1 priority date for domestic students. Applications are processed on a rolling basis. Application fee: $65. Electronic applications accepted. *Financial support:* Applicants required to submit FAFSA. *Unit head:* Dr. Timothy Willis, Chair/Professor of Religion, 310-506-4352, E-mail: timothy.willis@pepperdine.edu. *Application contact:* Michael Truschke, Dean of Admission and Enrollment Management, 310-506-6165, Fax: 310-506-4861, E-mail: admission-seaver@pepperdine.edu.
Website: http://seaver.pepperdine.edu/religion/academics/mdiv.htm

Pfeiffer University, Program in Practical Theology, Misenheimer, NC 28109-0960. Offers MA. Part-time and evening/weekend programs available. *Entrance requirements:* For master's, minimum GPA of 2.75.

Phillips Theological Seminary, Programs in Theology, Tulsa, OK 74116. Offers administration of church agencies (M Div); campus ministry (M Div); church-related social work (M Div); college and seminary teaching (M Div); global mission work (M Div); institutional chaplaincy (M Div); ministerial vocations in Christian education (M Div); ministry (D Min), including parish ministry, pastoral counseling, practices of ministry; ministry and culture (MAMC), including Christian education, congregational leadership, history and practice of Christian spirituality, theology, ethics, and culture; ministry of music (M Div); pastoral care and counseling (M Div); pastoral ministry (M Div); theological studies (MTS). *Accreditation:* ATS. Part-time programs available. Postbaccalaureate distance learning degree programs offered (minimal on-campus study). *Degree requirements:* For master's, thesis (for some programs); for doctorate, thesis/dissertation. *Entrance requirements:* For master's, minimum GPA of 2.5; for doctorate, M Div, minimum GPA of 3.0. *Faculty research:* Biblical studies, historical studies, theology and culture, practical theology, theology and film.

Phoenix Seminary, Graduate Programs, Phoenix, AZ 85018. Offers Biblical and theological studies (Graduate Diploma); Biblical communication (M Div); Biblical leadership (MA); Christian counseling (Graduate Diploma); counseling and family (M Div); leadership development (M Div); ministry (D Min); professional counseling (MA). *Accreditation:* ATS (one or more programs are accredited). Part-time and evening/

weekend programs available. *Degree requirements:* For master's, 2 foreign languages, comprehensive exam; for doctorate, 2 foreign languages, thesis/dissertation. *Entrance requirements:* For master's, undergraduate degree with minimum GPA of 2.5; for doctorate, M Div (94 hours) with minimum GPA of 3.0. Additional exam requirements/recommendations for international students: Required—TOEFL (minimum score 587 paper-based; 92 iBT), TWE (minimum score 4.5).

Piedmont International University, Graduate School, Winston-Salem, NC 27101-5197. Offers Biblical studies (PhD); chaplaincy track (MABS); curriculum and instruction (M Ed); leadership (MA, PhD); ministry (MA Min); non-language track (MABS); PhD preparation track (MABS). Part-time programs available. Postbaccalaureate distance learning degree programs offered (no on-campus study). *Faculty:* 5 full-time (0 women), 8 part-time/adjunct (1 woman). *Students:* 84; includes 3 minority (2 Black or African American, non-Hispanic/Latino; 1 Asian, non-Hispanic/Latino). Average age 35. 12 applicants, 100% accepted. In 2014, 18 master's awarded. *Degree requirements:* For master's, 2 foreign languages, comprehensive exam, thesis or alternative; for doctorate, 2 foreign languages, comprehensive exam. *Entrance requirements:* For master's, GRE General Test; for doctorate, Hebrew and Greek proficiency, MA. *Application deadline:* For fall admission, 8/15 priority date for domestic students; for spring admission, 1/1 for domestic students. Applications are processed on a rolling basis. Application fee: $30. Electronic applications accepted. *Expenses: Tuition:* Part-time $295 per credit hour. Part-time tuition and fees vary according to degree level and program. *Financial support:* Career-related internships or fieldwork available. Support available to part-time students. Financial award applicants required to submit CSS PROFILE. *Faculty research:* Theological and Biblical studies. *Unit head:* Dr. Larry Tyler, Dean, 336-714-7989, Fax: 336-714-2715, E-mail: tylerl@piedmontu.edu. *Application contact:* Angela Hoover, Director of Graduate Admissions, 336-714-7927, Fax: 336-725-5522, E-mail: hoovera@piedmontu.edu.
Website: http://piedmontu.edu

Pittsburgh Theological Seminary, Graduate and Professional Programs, Pittsburgh, PA 15206-2596. Offers divinity (M Div); ministry (D Min); theology (MA, Th M); theology and ministry (MA); JD/M Div; M Div/MS; M Div/MSW. M Div/MSW offered jointly with University of Pittsburgh; JD/M Div with Duquesne University; M Div/MS with Carnegie Mellon University. *Accreditation:* ATS (one or more programs are accredited). Part-time and evening/weekend programs available. *Faculty:* 15 full-time (5 women), 7 part-time/adjunct (2 women). *Students:* 142 full-time (23 women), 77 part-time (27 women); includes 46 minority (35 Black or African American, non-Hispanic/Latino; 1 American Indian or Alaska Native, non-Hispanic/Latino; 3 Asian, non-Hispanic/Latino; 3 Hispanic/Latino; 1 Native Hawaiian or other Pacific Islander, non-Hispanic/Latino; 3 Two or more races, non-Hispanic/Latino), 7 international. Average age 35. 57 applicants, 93% accepted, 44 enrolled. In 2014, 39 master's, 11 doctorates awarded. *Degree requirements:* For master's, comprehensive exam (for some programs), thesis (for some programs); for doctorate, thesis/dissertation. *Entrance requirements:* For master's, bachelor's degree with minimum GPA of 2.7, interview, references; for doctorate, interview, references. Additional exam requirements/recommendations for international students: Required—TOEFL (minimum score 570 paper-based; 89 iBT). *Application deadline:* For fall admission, 6/30 priority date for domestic students, 12/1 for international students; for winter admission, 10/15 priority date for domestic students; for spring admission, 1/15 priority date for domestic students. Applications are processed on a rolling basis. Application fee: $50. *Expenses: Tuition:* Full-time $8640; part-time $320 per credit. *Financial support:* In 2014–15, 104 students received support. Career-related internships or fieldwork, scholarships/grants, and institutional work-study available. Financial award application deadline: 5/1; financial award applicants required to submit FAFSA. *Unit head:* Dr. Byron H. Jackson, Dean of Faculty and Vice President for Academic Affairs, 412-924-1374, Fax: 412-924-1774, E-mail: bjackson@pts.edu. *Application contact:* Dr. James Downey, Vice President for Institutional Effectiveness, 412-924-1450, Fax: 412-924-1750, E-mail: jdowney@pts.edu.
Website: http://www.pts.edu/

Pontifical Catholic University of Puerto Rico, College of Arts and Humanities, Department of Theology and Philosophy, Ponce, PR 00717-0777. Offers M Div.

Pontifical College Josephinum, School of Theology, Columbus, OH 43235. Offers M Div, MA. *Accreditation:* ATS. Part-time programs available. *Degree requirements:* For master's, 3 foreign languages, comprehensive exam, thesis. *Entrance requirements:* For master's, GRE General Test, 15 credit hours of course work in philosophy, 6 credit hours of course work in scripture. Additional exam requirements/recommendations for international students: Required—TOEFL (minimum score 600 paper-based).

Pope St. John XXIII National Seminary, Graduate Program, Weston, MA 02493-2618. Offers M Div. *Accreditation:* ATS. *Application deadline:* For fall admission, 7/15 priority date for domestic students. Applications are processed on a rolling basis. Application fee: $0. *Financial support:* Career-related internships or fieldwork available. *Unit head:* Rev. William B. Palardy, Rector/President, 781-899-5500, Fax: 781-891-9057.

Princeton Theological Seminary, Graduate and Professional Programs, Princeton, NJ 08542-0803. Offers M Div, MA, Th M, D Min, PhD. *Accreditation:* ACIPE; ATS. Part-time programs available. Terminal master's awarded for partial completion of doctoral program. *Degree requirements:* For doctorate, 2 foreign languages, thesis/dissertation, comprehensive exam (PhD), French and German. *Entrance requirements:* For doctorate, GRE General Test. Additional exam requirements/recommendations for international students: Required—TOEFL. Electronic applications accepted.

Providence College, Department of Religious Studies, Providence, RI 02918. Offers Biblical studies (MA); theology (MA, MTS). Part-time and evening/weekend programs available. *Faculty:* 8 full-time (2 women), 1 part-time/adjunct (0 women). *Students:* 8 full-time (2 women), 10 part-time (2 women), 3 international. Average age 34. 17 applicants, 100% accepted, 6 enrolled. In 2014, 5 master's awarded. *Degree requirements:* For master's, comprehensive exam, thesis. *Entrance requirements:* For master's, GRE (for MA). Additional exam requirements/recommendations for international students: Required—TOEFL (minimum score 550 paper-based; 90 iBT). *Application deadline:* For fall admission, 8/1 priority date for domestic and international students; for spring admission, 12/1 priority date for domestic and international students. Applications are processed on a rolling basis. Application fee: $55. *Expenses: Tuition:* Part-time $390 per credit. *Financial support:* Career-related internships or fieldwork and unspecified assistantships available. Support available to part-time students. Financial award application deadline: 8/1; financial award applicants required to submit FAFSA. *Unit head:* Dr. Robert J. Barry, Director, 401-865-2274, Fax: 401-865-2274, E-mail: rbarry@providence.edu. *Application contact:* Rev. Mark D. Nowel, Dean of Undergraduate and Graduate Studies, 401-865-2649, Fax: 401-865-1496, E-mail: mnowel@providence.edu.
Website: http://www.providence.edu/theology/Pages/default.aspx

Providence University College & Theological Seminary, Theological Seminary, Otterburne, MB R0A 1G0, Canada. Offers children's ministry (Certificate); Christian studies (MA, Certificate); counseling (MA); cross-cultural discipleship (Certificate); divinity (M Div); educational studies (MA), including counseling psychology, educational ministries, student development, teaching English to speakers of other languages, training teachers of English to speakers of other languages; global studies (MA); lay counseling (Diploma); ministry (D Min); teaching English to speakers of other languages (Certificate); theological studies (MA); training teacher of English to speakers of other languages (Certificate); youth ministry (Certificate). *Accreditation:* ATS. Part-time programs available. *Degree requirements:* For master's, variable foreign language requirement, thesis (for some programs); for doctorate, thesis/dissertation. *Entrance requirements:* Additional exam requirements/recommendations for international students: Recommended—TOEFL (minimum score 550 paper-based). *Faculty research:* Studies in Isaiah, theology of sin.

Queen's University at Kingston, Queen's School of Religion, Kingston, ON K7L 3N6, Canada. Offers M Div, MTS, Certificate. *Accreditation:* ATS. Part-time programs available. *Degree requirements:* For master's, thesis (for some programs). *Entrance requirements:* For master's, minimum undergraduate B average. Additional exam requirements/recommendations for international students: Required—TOEFL (minimum score 580 paper-based). *Faculty research:* Early Christian group formations, pastoral care and spiritual direction, feminist theology, public religion, interpretation of Biblical texts using psychologies of shame and trauma.

Rabbi Isaac Elchanan Theological Seminary, Graduate Program, New York, NY 10033-1807. Offers Certificate of Advanced Ordination, Certificate of Ordination. *Degree requirements:* For other advanced degree, one foreign language, comprehensive exam. *Entrance requirements:* For degree, oral exam, 2 interview, undergraduate major in Jewish studies or equivalent. *Faculty research:* Talmud, rabbinics.

Rabbinical Academy Mesivta Rabbi Chaim Berlin, Graduate Program, Brooklyn, NY 11230-4715. Offers Advanced Talmudic Degree, Second Talmudic Degree. *Accreditation:* AARTS. *Degree requirements:* For other advanced degree, 2 foreign languages. *Entrance requirements:* For degree, must be a graduate of a rabbinical school.

Rabbinical College Beth Shraga, Graduate Programs, Monsey, NY 10952-3035. *Accreditation:* AARTS.

Rabbinical College Bobover Yeshiva B'nei Zion, Graduate Programs, Brooklyn, NY 11219. *Accreditation:* AARTS.

Rabbinical College Ch'san Sofer, Graduate Programs, Brooklyn, NY 11204. *Accreditation:* AARTS.

Rabbinical College of Long Island, Graduate Programs, Long Beach, NY 11561-3305. *Accreditation:* AARTS.

Rabbinical Seminary of America, Graduate Programs, Flushing, NY 11367. School offers a master's and first professional degree. *Accreditation:* AARTS.

Reconstructionist Rabbinical College, Graduate Programs, Wyncote, PA 19095-1898. Offers Jewish studies (MAJS); rabbinics (MAHL, DHL); women's studies (Certificate). Certificate offered jointly with Temple University. Part-time programs available. *Degree requirements:* For master's, one foreign language, thesis (MAJS), completion of rabbinical program (MAHL); for doctorate, one foreign language. *Entrance requirements:* For master's, GRE General Test; placement examinations in Hebrew and Judaism (MAHL); for doctorate, GRE General Test, placement examinations in Hebrew and Judaism. *Faculty research:* Bible, Hebrew Semitic texts, contemporary Judaism.

Reformed Episcopal Seminary, Graduate Program, Blue Bell, PA 19422. Offers M Div. *Students:* 18 full-time (3 women), 21 part-time (8 women). *Entrance requirements:* For master's, personal reference letter, pastor's reference letter, transcript. *Application contact:* David A. France, Director of Admissions and Recruiting, 610-292-9852 Ext. 104, Fax: 610-292-9853, E-mail: admissions@reseminary.edu.

Reformed Presbyterian Theological Seminary, Graduate and Professional Programs, Pittsburgh, PA 15208-2594. Offers M Div, MTS, D Min. *Accreditation:* ATS. Part-time and evening/weekend programs available. Electronic applications accepted. *Faculty research:* Prayer.

Reformed Theological Seminary–Atlanta Campus, Graduate Programs, Marietta, GA 30067. Offers M Div, MABS, MAR, D Min, Certificate.

Reformed Theological Seminary–Charlotte Campus, Graduate and Professional Programs, Charlotte, NC 28226-6318. Offers biblical studies (MA); ministry (D Min); pastoral ministry (M Div); theological studies (MA). Part-time programs available. *Degree requirements:* For master's, comprehensive exam; for doctorate, thesis/dissertation. *Entrance requirements:* For master's, minimum GPA of 2.6; for doctorate, minimum GPA of 3.0. Additional exam requirements/recommendations for international students: Required—TOEFL (minimum score 550 paper-based). Electronic applications accepted.

Reformed Theological Seminary–Jackson Campus, Graduate and Professional Programs, Jackson, MS 39209-3099. Offers Bible, theology, and missions (Certificate); Biblical exegesis (M Div); biblical studies (MA); Christian education (MA); counseling (M Div); marriage and family therapy (MA); ministry (D Min); missions (M Div, MA, D Min); theological studies (MA). *Accreditation:* AAMFT/COAMFTE (one or more programs are accredited); ATS (one or more programs are accredited). *Faculty:* 10 full-time (0 women), 1 (woman) part-time/adjunct. *Students:* 50 full-time (14 women), 86 part-time (19 women). *Degree requirements:* For master's, thesis (for some programs), fieldwork; for doctorate, 2 foreign languages, thesis/dissertation. *Entrance requirements:* For master's, minimum GPA of 2.6; for doctorate, minimum GPA of 3.0. Additional exam requirements/recommendations for international students: Required—TOEFL. *Application deadline:* Applications are processed on a rolling basis. Application fee: $35. *Financial support:* Research assistantships, career-related internships or fieldwork, scholarships/grants, and tuition waivers (full and partial) available. Financial award application deadline: 5/1. *Application contact:* Brian Gault, Director of Admissions, 601-923-1600, Fax: 601-923-1654.

Reformed Theological Seminary–Orlando Campus, Graduate Program, Oviedo, FL 32765-7197. Offers Bible (Certificate); biblical studies (MA); church planting (D Min); counseling (MA); general ministries (D Min); missions (Certificate); theological studies (MA); theology (M Div, Certificate). Part-time programs available. Postbaccalaureate distance learning degree programs offered (minimal on-campus study). *Faculty:* 11 full-time (0 women), 7 part-time/adjunct (1 woman). *Students:* 287. *Application deadline:* Applications are processed on a rolling basis. Application fee: $75. Electronic applications accepted. *Expenses: Tuition:* Full-time $15,900. *Required fees:* $160. *Unit head:* Dr. Don Sweeting, President, 407-278-4406, Fax: 407-366-9425. *Application contact:* Dr. Kevin Collins, Director of Admissions, Placement, and Marketing, 407-278-8824, Fax: 407-366-9425, E-mail: admissions.orlando@rts.edu.

Reformed Theological Seminary–Washington D.C., Graduate and Professional Programs, McLean, VA 22102. Offers Bible (M Div); practical theology (M Div); religion (MA); theology (M Div). Part-time and evening/weekend programs available. *Faculty:* 3 full-time (0 women), 11 part-time/adjunct (1 woman). *Students:* 9 full-time (0 women), 104 part-time (7 women); includes 41 minority (14 Black or African American, non-Hispanic/Latino; 24 Asian, non-Hispanic/Latino; 3 Hispanic/Latino). Average age 35. 43 applicants, 91% accepted, 27 enrolled. In 2014, 9 master's awarded. *Degree requirements:* For master's, integrative paper. *Entrance requirements:* For master's, minimum undergraduate GPA of 2.6. Additional exam requirements/recommendations for international students: Required—TOEFL (minimum score 550 paper-based), TWE.

Application deadline: Applications are processed on a rolling basis. Application fee: $75. Electronic applications accepted. *Expenses:* Expenses: Contact institution. *Financial support:* In 2014–15, 121 students received support. Scholarships/grants and tuition waivers (partial) available. Support available to part-time students. Financial award application deadline: 5/1. *Faculty research:* Theology, Biblical studies, cultural studies. *Unit head:* Dr. John S. Redd, Jr., President, 703-448-3393 Ext. 107, E-mail: sredd@rts.edu. *Application contact:* Geoff M. Sackett, Director of Admissions, 703-448-3393 Ext. 104, E-mail: gsackett@rts.edu. Website: http://www.rts.edu/

Regent College, Program in Theology, Vancouver, BC V6T 2E4, Canada. Offers M Div, MATS, Th M, Dip CS. *Accreditation:* ATS (one or more programs are accredited). Part-time programs available. *Degree requirements:* For master's, thesis (for some programs). *Entrance requirements:* For master's, minimum GPA of 2.8 (MCS), 3.5 (Th M); for Dip CS, minimum GPA of 2.8. Additional exam requirements/recommendations for international students: Required—TOEFL (minimum score 575 paper-based; 90 iBT). Electronic applications accepted. *Faculty research:* Integration of theology with secular life, Biblical studies.

Regent University, Graduate School, School of Divinity, Virginia Beach, VA 23464-9800. Offers leadership and renewal (D Min), including Christian leadership and renewal, clinical pastoral education, community transformation, military ministry, ministry leadership coaching; practical theology (M Div, MA), including Biblical studies (M Div, MTS, PhD), chaplain ministry (M Div), Christian theology (M Div, MTS, PhD), church and ministry, history of Christianity (M Div, MTS), inter-cultural studies, interdisciplinary studies (M Div, MA, MTS), worship and renewal; renewal studies (PhD), including Biblical studies (M Div, MTS, PhD), Christian theology (M Div, MTS, PhD), history of global Christianity; theological studies (MTS), including Biblical studies (M Div, MTS, PhD), Christian theology (M Div, MTS, PhD), history of Christianity (M Div, MTS), interdisciplinary studies (M Div, MA, MTS). *Accreditation:* ACIPE; ATS. Part-time programs available. Postbaccalaureate distance learning degree programs offered (minimal on-campus study). *Faculty:* 20 full-time (3 women), 29 part-time/adjunct (3 women). *Students:* 64 full-time (28 women), 616 part-time (258 women); includes 318 minority (269 Black or African American, non-Hispanic/Latino; 7 American Indian or Alaska Native, non-Hispanic/Latino; 16 Asian, non-Hispanic/Latino; 26 Hispanic/Latino), 37 international. Average age 43. 511 applicants, 52% accepted, 187 enrolled. In 2014, 121 master's, 24 doctorates awarded. *Degree requirements:* For master's, comprehensive exam, thesis or alternative, internship; for doctorate, thesis/dissertation or alternative. *Entrance requirements:* For master's, GRE General Test or MAT, minimum undergraduate GPA of 2.75, writing sample, clergy recommendation; for doctorate, M Div or theological master's degree; minimum graduate GPA of 3.5 (PhD), 3.0 (D Min); recommendations; writing sample; transcripts. Additional exam requirements/recommendations for international students: Required—TOEFL (minimum score 577 paper-based). *Application deadline:* For fall admission, 5/1 priority date for domestic students. Applications are processed on a rolling basis. Application fee: $50. Electronic applications accepted. *Expenses:* Expenses: Contact institution. *Financial support:* Fellowships with full and partial tuition reimbursements, career-related internships or fieldwork, scholarships/grants, tuition waivers (full and partial), and unspecified assistantships available. Support available to part-time students. Financial award application deadline: 9/1; financial award applicants required to submit FAFSA. *Faculty research:* Greek and Hebrew, theology, spiritual formation, global missions and world Christianity, women's studies. *Unit head:* Dr. Joseph Umidi, Interim Dean, 757-352-4401, Fax: 757-352-4597, E-mail: joseumi@regent.edu. *Application contact:* Matthew Chadwick, Director of Enrollment Support Services, 800-373-5504, Fax: 757-352-4381, E-mail: admissions@regent.edu. Website: http://www.regent.edu/acad/schdiv/

Regis College, Graduate and Professional Programs, Toronto, ON M5S 2Z5, Canada. Offers eastern Christian studies (Certificate); Ignatian spirituality (Diploma); ministry (D Min); ministry and spirituality (MAMS); philosophical studies (Diploma); retreat direction (Certificate); sacred theology (STM, STD, STB, STL); spiritual direction (Diploma); theological studies (MTS, Diploma); theology (M Div, MA, Th M, PhD, Th D); M Div/MA. *Accreditation:* ATS (one or more programs are accredited). Terminal master's awarded for partial completion of doctoral program. *Degree requirements:* For master's, 2 foreign languages, thesis; for doctorate, 3 foreign languages, comprehensive exam, thesis/dissertation. *Entrance requirements:* For doctorate, minimum GPA of 3.7. Additional exam requirements/recommendations for international students: Required—TOEFL (minimum score 580 paper-based; 93 iBT), TWE (minimum score 5).

Sacred Heart Major Seminary, School of Theology, Detroit, MI 48206-1799. Offers pastoral studies (MAPS); theology (M Div, MA). *Accreditation:* ACIPE; ATS. Part-time and evening/weekend programs available. *Degree requirements:* For master's, one foreign language, thesis optional, integrating project. *Entrance requirements:* For master's, GRE, previous course work in philosophy and theology. *Faculty research:* Local church history, patristics, spirituality, religious education.

Sacred Heart School of Theology, Graduate and Professional Programs, Hales Corners, WI 53130-0429. Offers priestly formation (Certificate); theology (M Div, MA). *Accreditation:* ACIPE; ATS. Part-time programs available. *Degree requirements:* For master's, essay or comprehensive exam. *Entrance requirements:* For master's, MAT, 6 hours of course work each in philosophy and theology, letter of recommendation. Additional exam requirements/recommendations for international students: Required—TOEFL.

St. Andrew's College, Graduate Programs in Theology, Saskatoon, SK S7N 0W3, Canada. Offers M Div, MTS, STM, D Min, Diploma. *Accreditation:* ATS. *Faculty:* 4 full-time (3 women), 2 part-time/adjunct (both women). *Students:* 14 full-time (9 women), 14 part-time (7 women). *Entrance requirements:* Additional exam requirements/recommendations for international students: Required—TOEFL. Application fee: $75. *Expenses: Tuition:* Full-time $6750 Canadian dollars; part-time $675 Canadian dollars per course. *Required fees:* $50 Canadian dollars; $28 Canadian dollars per term. Tuition and fees vary according to course level and degree level. *Application contact:* Colleen Walker, Registrar, 306-966-5244, Fax: 306-966-8981, E-mail: standrews.registrar@usask.ca.

St. Andrew's College in Winnipeg, Graduate Programs, Winnipeg, MB R3T 2M7, Canada. Offers M Div. *Faculty research:* Church history, doctrine, liturgical theology.

St. Augustine's Seminary of Toronto, Graduate and Professional Programs, Scarborough, ON M1M 1M3, Canada. Offers divinity (M Div); lay ministry (Diploma); religious education (MRE); theological studies (MTS, Diploma). *Accreditation:* ATS. Part-time and evening/weekend programs available. *Entrance requirements:* Additional exam requirements/recommendations for international students: Required—TOEFL (minimum score 580 paper-based), TWE (minimum score 5).

St. Bernard's School of Theology and Ministry, Graduate and Professional Programs, Rochester, NY 14618. Offers pastoral studies (MA, Certificate); theological studies (MA); theology (M Div). *Accreditation:* ATS (one or more programs are accredited). Part-time and evening/weekend programs available. *Degree requirements:*

For master's, variable foreign language requirement, thesis (for some programs). *Entrance requirements:* For master's, minimum GPA of 2.5.

St. Catherine University, Graduate Programs, Program in Theology, St. Paul, MN 55105. Offers catechetical ministry (Certificate); pastoral ministry (Certificate); spiritual direction (Certificate); theology (MA). Part-time programs available. *Faculty:* 8 full-time (2 women). *Students:* 1 full-time (0 women), 31 part-time (26 women); includes 1 minority (Hispanic/Latino). Average age 50. 5 applicants, 60% accepted, 1 enrolled. In 2014, 3 master's awarded. *Degree requirements:* For master's, comprehensive exam, thesis (for some programs). *Entrance requirements:* For master's, MAT, minimum GPA of 3.0. Additional exam requirements/recommendations for international students: Required—Michigan English Language Assessment Battery or TOEFL (minimum score 600 paper-based; 100 iBT). *Application deadline:* For fall admission, 8/1 priority date for domestic students. Applications are processed on a rolling basis. Application fee: $35. *Expenses:* Expenses: $636 per credit. *Financial support:* In 2014–15, 12 students received support. Research assistantships, career-related internships or fieldwork, and institutionally sponsored loans available. Support available to part-time students. Financial award application deadline: 4/1; financial award applicants required to submit FAFSA. *Faculty research:* Feminist scholarship, historical theology, symbols, rites of purification, spirituality. *Unit head:* Dr. William McDonough, Director, 651-690-6072, Fax: 651-690-6024. *Application contact:* 651-690-6933, Fax: 651-690-6064.

Saint Charles Borromeo Seminary, Overbrook, Graduate and Professional Programs, Division of Theology, Wynnewood, PA 19096. Offers M Div, MA. *Accreditation:* ATS. *Degree requirements:* For master's, comprehensive exam, research papers. *Entrance requirements:* For master's, M Div. Additional exam requirements/recommendations for international students: Required—TOEFL.

St. John's Seminary, Graduate and Professional Programs, Camarillo, CA 93012-2598. Offers divinity (M Div); pastoral ministry (MAPM); theology (MA). *Accreditation:* ATS. Part-time programs available. *Degree requirements:* For master's, comprehensive exam (for some programs), thesis optional, comprehensive integration paper (MAPM). *Entrance requirements:* For master's, GRE General Test, minimum GPA of 3.5 (MA), 2.5 (MAPM). Additional exam requirements/recommendations for international students: Required—TOEFL (minimum score 550 paper-based; 79 iBT). Electronic applications accepted. *Faculty research:* Biblical studies, moral theology, church history, systematic theology, spiritual theology.

Saint John's Seminary, Graduate Programs, Brighton, MA 02135. Offers M Div, MA Th, MAM. *Accreditation:* ATS.

St. John's University, St. John's College of Liberal Arts and Sciences, Department of Theology and Religious Studies, Queens, NY 11439. Offers theology (MA). *Accreditation:* ACIPE. Part-time and evening/weekend programs available. *Students:* 11 full-time (2 women), 26 part-time (15 women); includes 16 minority (7 Black or African American, non-Hispanic/Latino; 1 Asian, non-Hispanic/Latino; 8 Hispanic/Latino), 7 international. Average age 41. 17 applicants, 76% accepted, 10 enrolled. In 2014, 15 master's awarded. *Degree requirements:* For master's, comprehensive exam, thesis optional, portfolio. *Entrance requirements:* For master's, minimum GPA of 3.0, bachelor's degree in related area, 12 undergraduate credits in theology, philosophy or related subjects. Additional exam requirements/recommendations for international students: Required—TOEFL (minimum score 600 paper-based; 100 iBT), IELTS (minimum score 7). *Application deadline:* For fall admission, 5/1 priority date for domestic and international students; for spring admission, 11/1 priority date for domestic and international students. Applications are processed on a rolling basis. Application fee: $70. Electronic applications accepted. *Expenses: Tuition:* Full-time $20,610; part-time $1145 per credit. *Required fees:* $170 per semester. *Financial support:* Research assistantships and scholarships/grants available. Support available to part-time students. Financial award application deadline: 3/1; financial award applicants required to submit FAFSA. *Faculty research:* Systematic theology, moral theory, Biblical studies, pastoral theology, church history. *Unit head:* Dr. Christopher Vogt, Chair, 718-990-1556, E-mail: vogtc@stjohns.edu. *Application contact:* Robert Medrano, Director of Graduate Admission, 718-990-1601, Fax: 718-990-5686, E-mail: gradhelp@stjohns.edu.

Saint John's University, Saint John's School of Theology and Seminary, Collegeville, MN 56321. Offers divinity (M Div); liturgical music (MA); liturgical studies (MA); pastoral ministry (MA); theology (MA), including church history, liturgy, monastic studies, scripture, spirituality, systematics; M Div/MA. *Accreditation:* ATS. Part-time programs available. Postbaccalaureate distance learning degree programs offered (no on-campus study). *Degree requirements:* For master's, one foreign language, comprehensive exam (for some programs), thesis (for some programs). *Entrance requirements:* For master's, GRE General Test or MAT. Electronic applications accepted. *Faculty research:* Religious education, biblical literature.

St. Joseph's Seminary, Graduate and Professional Programs, Yonkers, NY 10704. Offers Catholic philosophical studies (MA); divinity (M Div); pastoral studies (MAPS); theology (MA). *Accreditation:* ATS. *Degree requirements:* For master's, one foreign language, thesis. *Entrance requirements:* For master's, 27 credits in philosophy and 9 in theology. *Financial support:* Scholarships/grants available. *Unit head:* Rev. Msgr. Peter I. Vaccari, Rector, 914-968-6200, Fax: 914-376-2019. *Application contact:* Fr. Thomas V. Berg, Director of Admissions, 914-968-6200, Fax: 914-376-2019.

Saint Louis University, Graduate Education, College of Arts and Sciences, Department of Theological Studies, St. Louis, MO 63103-2097. Offers historical theology (MA, PhD); theology (MA). Part-time programs available. *Degree requirements:* For master's, comprehensive exam; for doctorate, 4 foreign languages, comprehensive exam, thesis/dissertation, preliminary exams. *Entrance requirements:* For master's, GRE General Test, letters of recommendation, resume; for doctorate, GRE General Test, letters of recommendation, resumé, interview, transcripts, goal statement. Additional exam requirements/recommendations for international students: Required—TOEFL (minimum score 550 paper-based). Electronic applications accepted. *Faculty research:* Biblical and early church studies, medieval and renaissance studies, modern and American Christianity, comparative and interreligious studies, moral and ethical theology.

Saint Mary-of-the-Woods College, Program in Pastoral Theology, Saint Mary of the Woods, IN 47876. Offers pastoral theology (MA); youth ministry (Graduate Certificate). Part-time and evening/weekend programs available. Postbaccalaureate distance learning degree programs offered (minimal on-campus study). *Degree requirements:* For master's, thesis, qualifying exam.

Saint Mary Seminary and Graduate School of Theology, Graduate and Professional Programs, Wickliffe, OH 44092-2527. Offers M Div, MA, D Min. *Accreditation:* ATS. Part-time programs available. *Degree requirements:* For master's, comprehensive exam, symposium; for doctorate, thesis/dissertation, final project, symposium. *Entrance requirements:* For master's, GRE General Test, previous course work in religion; for doctorate, M Div or equivalent, 3 years in full-time ministry, interviews, ministry profile report. *Faculty research:* Pastoral ministry, theology of ministry, ecclesiology, American Catholics.

St. Mary's Seminary and University, Ecumenical Institute of Theology, Baltimore, MD 21210-1994. Offers church ministries (MA); theology (MA Th, Certificate). *Accreditation:*

ATS. Part-time and evening/weekend programs available. *Degree requirements:* For master's, thesis or alternative, comprehensive exam or colloquium. *Expenses:* Contact institution. *Faculty research:* Scripture and ethics, theology and literature, early Christianity and Judaism, medical and social ethics.

St. Mary's Seminary and University, School of Theology, Baltimore, MD 21210-1994. Offers M Div, MA Th, STD, STB, STL. *Accreditation:* ATS (one or more programs are accredited). Part-time programs available. Terminal master's awarded for partial completion of doctoral program. *Degree requirements:* For master's, comprehensive exam; for other advanced degree, one foreign language, thesis. *Entrance requirements:* For master's, Computerized Adaptive Placement Assessment and Support System.

Saint Mary's University, Faculty of Arts, Department of Religious Studies, Halifax, NS B3H 3C3, Canada. Offers theology and religious studies (MA).

St. Mary's University, Graduate School, Department of Theology, San Antonio, TX 78228-8507. Offers theological studies (PGC); JD/MA. Part-time and evening/weekend programs available. Postbaccalaureate distance learning degree programs offered (no on-campus study). *Faculty:* 4 full-time (0 women), 2 part-time/adjunct (0 women). *Students:* 3 full-time (all women), 20 part-time (15 women); includes 10 minority (1 Black or African American, non-Hispanic/Latino; 1 Asian, non-Hispanic/Latino; 8 Hispanic/Latino), 2 international. Average age 43. 6 applicants, 67% accepted, 3 enrolled. In 2014, 5 master's awarded. *Degree requirements:* For master's, comprehensive exam, thesis optional, 10 clock hours (Graduate Learning Community Experience). *Entrance requirements:* For master's, GRE, Undergraduate transcripts, departmental writing sample. For those without a prior degree in theology, must earn at least an A- in 3 prerequisite courses (9 hours) in Undergraduate Theology from StMU. Additional exam requirements/recommendations for international students: Required—TOEFL (minimum score 550 paper-based; 80 iBT). *Application deadline:* For fall admission, 8/1 for domestic students. Applications are processed on a rolling basis. Application fee: $0. Electronic applications accepted. *Expenses: Tuition:* Full-time $15,070; part-time $800 per credit hour. *Required fees:* $156 per semester. *Financial support:* In 2014–15, 1 research assistantship (averaging $12,000 per year) was awarded; career-related internships or fieldwork, Federal Work-Study, institutionally sponsored loans, scholarships/grants, health care benefits, and unspecified assistantships also available. Financial award application deadline: 3/31; financial award applicants required to submit FAFSA. *Faculty research:* Theological anthropology, medical ethics, peace and justice studies, The Book of Jubilees, Old Testament. *Unit head:* Dr. Andrew Getz, Graduate Theology Program Director, 210-436-3011, E-mail: agetz@stmarytx.edu. *Application contact:* Dean of the Graduate School.
Website: https://www.stmarytx.edu/academics/graduate/masters/theology/

Saint Meinrad School of Theology, Master of Arts (Catholic Philosophical Studies) Program, Saint Meinrad, IN 47577. Offers MA. *Faculty:* 21 full-time (2 women), 6 part-time/adjunct. *Students:* 22 full-time (0 women); includes 1 minority (Hispanic/Latino), 2 international. Average age 32. In 2014, 18 master's awarded. *Degree requirements:* For master's, thesis. *Entrance requirements:* Additional exam requirements/recommendations for international students: Required—TOEFL. *Application deadline:* For fall admission, 7/31 for domestic and international students; for winter admission, 11/15 for domestic and international students. Applications are processed on a rolling basis. *Expenses: Tuition:* Full-time $21,920; part-time $395 per credit hour. *Required fees:* $29 per course. *Unit head:* Dr. Robert Alvis, Academic Dean, 812-357-6543, Fax: 812-357-6816, E-mail: ralvis@saintmeinrad.edu. *Application contact:* Fr. Luke Waugh, OSB, Director of Enrollment, 812-357-6422, Fax: 812-357-6462, E-mail: lwaugh@saintmeinrad.edu.
Website: http://www.saintmeinrad.edu/priesthood-formation/academic-formation/pre-theologyma/

Saint Meinrad School of Theology, Master of Arts (Pastoral Theology) Program, Saint Meinrad, IN 47577. Offers MA. *Accreditation:* ATS. Part-time and evening/weekend programs available. *Faculty:* 22 full-time (2 women), 5 part-time/adjunct (1 woman). *Students:* 33 part-time (25 women). Average age 51. *Degree requirements:* For master's, thesis, three capstone essays, one research paper, or pastoral research project. *Entrance requirements:* Additional exam requirements/recommendations for international students: Required—TOEFL. *Application deadline:* For fall admission, 7/31 for domestic and international students; for winter admission, 11/15 for domestic and international students. Applications are processed on a rolling basis. Application fee: $30. *Expenses: Tuition:* Full-time $21,920; part-time $395 per credit hour. *Required fees:* $29 per course. *Financial support:* Federal Work-Study, institutionally sponsored loans, and scholarships/grants available. Support available to part-time students. Financial award application deadline: 7/31; financial award applicants required to submit FAFSA. *Unit head:* Dr. Robert Alvis, Academic Dean, 812-357-6543. *Application contact:* Sr. Jeana Visel, Director of Lay Degree Programs, 812-357-6678, Fax: 812-357-6462, E-mail: apply@saintmeinrad.edu.

Saint Meinrad School of Theology, Master of Arts (Theology) Program, Saint Meinrad, IN 47577. Offers MA. *Accreditation:* ATS. Part-time and evening/weekend programs available. *Faculty:* 22 full-time (2 women), 5 part-time/adjunct (1 woman). *Students:* 1 full-time (0 women), 45 part-time (15 women). Average age 45. *Degree requirements:* For master's, comprehensive exam, three capstone essays or one research paper. *Entrance requirements:* Additional exam requirements/recommendations for international students: Required—TOEFL. *Application deadline:* For fall admission, 7/31 for domestic and international students; for winter admission, 11/15 for domestic and international students. Applications are processed on a rolling basis. Application fee: $30. *Expenses: Tuition:* Full-time $21,920; part-time $395 per credit hour. *Required fees:* $29 per course. *Financial support:* Federal Work-Study, institutionally sponsored loans, and scholarships/grants available. Support available to part-time students. Financial award application deadline: 7/31; financial award applicants required to submit FAFSA. *Unit head:* Sr. Jeana Visel, OSB, Director of Lay Degree Programs, 812-357-6678, Fax: 812-357-6462. *Application contact:* Fr. Luke Waugh, OSB, Director of Enrollment, 812-357-6422, Fax: 812-357-6462, E-mail: lwaugh@saintmeinrad.edu.

Saint Meinrad School of Theology, Master of Divinity Program, Saint Meinrad, IN 47577. Offers M Div. *Accreditation:* ATS. *Faculty:* 22 full-time (2 women), 5 part-time/adjunct (1 woman). *Students:* 98 full-time (0 women). *Entrance requirements:* Additional exam requirements/recommendations for international students: Required—TOEFL. *Application deadline:* For fall admission, 7/31 for domestic and international students; for winter admission, 11/15 for domestic and international students. Applications are processed on a rolling basis. Application fee: $0. *Expenses: Tuition:* Full-time $21,920; part-time $395 per credit hour. *Required fees:* $29 per course. *Financial support:* Federal Work-Study, institutionally sponsored loans, and scholarships/grants available. Support available to part-time students. Financial award application deadline: 7/31; financial award applicants required to submit FAFSA. *Unit head:* Dr. Robert Alvis, Academic Dean, 812-357-6543, Fax: 812-357-6816, E-mail: ralvis@saintmeinrad.edu. *Application contact:* Fr. Luke Waugh, OSB, Director of Enrollment, 812-357-6422, Fax: 812-357-6462, E-mail: lwaugh@saintmeinrad.edu.
Website: http://www.saintmeinrad.edu/priesthood-formation/academic-formation/master-of-divinity/

St. Norbert College, Program in Theological Studies, De Pere, WI 54115-2099. Offers MTS. Part-time and evening/weekend programs available. *Faculty:* 10 part-time/adjunct (3 women). *Students:* 58 part-time (37 women); includes 10 minority (1 Black or African American, non-Hispanic/Latino; 1 Asian, non-Hispanic/Latino; 7 Hispanic/Latino; 1 Two or more races, non-Hispanic/Latino). Average age 53. 4 applicants, 100% accepted, 4 enrolled. In 2014, 6 master's awarded. *Degree requirements:* For master's, comprehensive exam, thesis. *Entrance requirements:* For master's, minimum of 8 credits of course work in theology/religious studies, BA from accredited institution. *Application deadline:* Applications are processed on a rolling basis. Application fee: $50. Electronic applications accepted. *Expenses: Tuition:* Part-time $472 per credit hour. *Financial support:* In 2014–15, 14 students received support. Scholarships/grants available. Support available to part-time students. *Faculty research:* Practical theology, Holocaust, Karl Rahner, women in the Bible and Christian ethics. *Unit head:* Dr. Howard Ebert, Director, 920-403-3956, Fax: 920-403-4086, E-mail: howard.ebert@snc.edu. *Application contact:* Dinah Grassel, Program Coordinator, 920-403-3957, Fax: 920-403-4086, E-mail: dinah.grassel@snc.edu.
Website: http://www.snc.edu/mts/

St. Patrick's Seminary & University, School of Theology, Menlo Park, CA 94025-3596. Offers M Div, MA, STB. STB offered jointly with St. Mary's Seminary and University. *Accreditation:* ATS (one or more programs are accredited). Part-time programs available. *Degree requirements:* For master's, comprehensive exam, thesis or alternative. *Entrance requirements:* For master's, GRE General Test, minimum GPA of 3.0, interview. Additional exam requirements/recommendations for international students: Required—TOEFL (minimum score 550 paper-based; 80 iBT), TWE. *Faculty research:* Systematic theology, sacred scripture, moral theology, liturgy.

Saint Paul School of Theology, Graduate and Professional Programs, Overland Park, KS 66211. Offers M Div, MA, MTS, D Min. *Accreditation:* ACIPE; ATS. Part-time programs available. *Degree requirements:* For doctorate, thesis/dissertation. *Entrance requirements:* For master's, minimum GPA of 2.75; for doctorate, minimum GPA of 3.0. Additional exam requirements/recommendations for international students: Required—TOEFL. *Faculty research:* Religion and aging; leadership development; feminist, African-American, and liberation theology; rural ministry; worship and the arts.

Saint Paul University, Faculty of Canon Law, Ottawa, ON K1S 1C4, Canada. Offers canon law (MCL, JCD, PhD, Graduate Certificate, JCL); canonical practice (Graduate Certificate); ecclesiastical administration (Graduate Certificate). Part-time programs available. *Degree requirements:* For master's, one foreign language; for doctorate, one foreign language, comprehensive exam, thesis/dissertation; for other advanced degree, one foreign language, comprehensive exam and seminar paper (JCL). *Entrance requirements:* For master's, appropriate bachelor's degree, 18 credits in theology; for doctorate, JCL or MCL; for other advanced degree, B Th or equivalent (JCL), appropriate bachelor's degree, 18 credits in theology. *Faculty research:* Questions related to Church law.

Saint Paul University, Faculty of Human Sciences, Program in Counseling and Spirituality, Ottawa, ON K1S 1C4, Canada. Offers individual or marital/couple counseling (MA); spiritual care (MA). Part-time programs available. *Degree requirements:* For master's, research project or thesis. *Entrance requirements:* For master's, honors BA in human sciences, minimum B average, 12 theology credits.

Saint Paul University, Faculty of Theology, Ottawa, ON K1S 1C4, Canada. Offers MA Th, MP Th, MRE, D Min, D Th, PhD, L Th. *Degree requirements:* For master's and L Th, one foreign language; for doctorate, one foreign language, comprehensive exam, thesis/dissertation. *Entrance requirements:* For master's, B Th; for doctorate, MA Th, L Th, MP Th, M Div. *Faculty research:* Biblical studies, systematic and historical theology, ethics, spirituality, Eastern Christian studies, applied theology.

St. Peter's Seminary, Department of Theology, London, ON N6A 3Y1, Canada. Offers M Div, MTS. *Accreditation:* ATS.

Saints Cyril and Methodius Seminary, Graduate and Professional Programs, Orchard Lake, MI 48324. Offers pastoral ministry (MAPM); religious education (MARE); theology (M Div, MA). *Accreditation:* ATS. Part-time programs available.

St. Stephen's College, Programs in Theology, Edmonton, AB T6G 2J6, Canada. Offers ministry (D Min); pastoral counseling (MA); social transformation ministry (MA); spirituality and liturgy (MA); theological studies (MTS); theology (M Th). Part-time and evening/weekend programs available. Postbaccalaureate distance learning degree programs offered (minimal on-campus study). Terminal master's awarded for partial completion of doctoral program. *Degree requirements:* For master's, thesis; for doctorate, thesis/dissertation. *Entrance requirements:* Additional exam requirements/recommendations for international students: Required—TOEFL. Electronic applications accepted. *Faculty research:* Methodology for theological education, practice and supervision for ministry.

St. Thomas University, School of Theology and Ministry, Institute for Pastoral Ministries, Miami Gardens, FL 33054-6459. Offers pastoral ministries (MA, Certificate); practical theology (PhD). Part-time and evening/weekend programs available. *Degree requirements:* For master's, comprehensive exam; for doctorate, comprehensive exam, thesis/dissertation. *Entrance requirements:* For master's, interview, minimum GPA of 3.0 or GRE; for doctorate, GRE, MA in theology. Additional exam requirements/recommendations for international students: Required—TOEFL (minimum score 550 paper-based; 79 iBT). Electronic applications accepted.

St. Tikhon's Orthodox Theological Seminary, Divinity Program, South Canaan, PA 18459. Offers M Div. *Accreditation:* ATS. *Entrance requirements:* For master's, reference letter, official transcripts. Additional exam requirements/recommendations for international students: Required—TOEFL (minimum score 87 iBT). *Faculty research:* Church history, patristics, scripture, spirituality.

St. Vincent de Paul Regional Seminary, Graduate and Professional Programs, Boynton Beach, FL 33436-4899. Offers theology (M Div, MA Th). *Accreditation:* ATS. Part-time programs available. *Degree requirements:* For master's, comprehensive exam (for some programs), thesis optional. *Entrance requirements:* For master's, GRE General Test, MAT. Additional exam requirements/recommendations for international students: Required—TOEFL.

Saint Vincent Seminary, School of Theology, Latrobe, PA 15650-2690. Offers ecclesial ministry (MA); ministry (M Div); monastic studies (MA); sacred scripture (MA); systematic theology (MA). *Accreditation:* ATS. Part-time and evening/weekend programs available. *Faculty:* 4 full-time (1 woman), 16 part-time/adjunct (1 woman). *Students:* 39 full-time (0 women), 4 part-time (0 women); includes 4 minority (2 Asian, non-Hispanic/Latino; 2 Hispanic/Latino), 10 international. Average age 36. 7 applicants, 100% accepted, 7 enrolled. In 2014, 14 master's awarded. *Degree requirements:* For master's, one foreign language, comprehensive exam, thesis optional, public presentation. *Entrance requirements:* For master's, minimum GPA of 2.5. Additional exam requirements/recommendations for international students: Required—TOEFL (minimum score 550 paper-based; 79 iBT). *Application deadline:* For fall admission, 8/15 priority date for domestic students, 8/15 for international students. Applications are processed on a rolling basis. Application fee: $34. *Expenses: Tuition:* Full-time $24,334; part-time $808 per credit. *Financial support:* In 2014–15, 43 students received support.

Scholarships/grants available. Support available to part-time students. Financial award application deadline: 8/15. *Faculty research:* Church history, preaching, psychology of religion, Biblical studies, moral theology. *Unit head:* Very Rev. Timothy F. Whalen, President/Rector, 724-805-2592, Fax: 724-532-5052, E-mail: timothy.whalen@stvincent.edu. *Application contact:* Rev. Patrick T. Cronauer, OSB, Academic Dean, 724-805-2324, Fax: 724-805-2880, E-mail: patrick.cronauer@stvincent.edu. Website: http://www.saintvincentseminary.edu

St. Vladimir's Orthodox Theological Seminary, Graduate School of Theology, Crestwood, NY 10707-1699. Offers general theological studies (MA); liturgical music (MA); religious education (MA); theology (M Div, M Th, D Min); M Div/MA. MA in general theological studies, M Div offered jointly with St. Nersess Seminary. *Accreditation:* ATS. Part-time programs available. *Degree requirements:* For master's, one foreign language, thesis, fieldwork; for doctorate, thesis/dissertation, fieldwork. *Entrance requirements:* For doctorate, M Div, minimum GPA of 3.0. Additional exam requirements/recommendations for international students: Required—TOEFL.

Samford University, Beeson School of Divinity, Birmingham, AL 35229. Offers M Div, MATS, D Min, JD/M Div, JD/MATS, M Div/M Ed, M Div/MBA, M Div/MM. *Accreditation:* ATS. Part-time programs available. *Faculty:* 14 full-time (2 women), 1 part-time/adjunct (0 women). *Students:* 169 full-time (34 women), 15 part-time (7 women); includes 31 minority (24 Black or African American, non-Hispanic/Latino; 1 American Indian or Alaska Native, non-Hispanic/Latino; 3 Asian, non-Hispanic/Latino; 2 Hispanic/Latino; 1 Two or more races, non-Hispanic/Latino), 3 international. Average age 30. 53 applicants, 85% accepted, 37 enrolled. In 2014, 36 master's, 4 doctorates awarded. *Degree requirements:* For master's, one foreign language, thesis optional; for doctorate, thesis/dissertation. *Entrance requirements:* For master's, minimum GPA of 2.5; for doctorate, minimum GPA of 3.0. Additional exam requirements/recommendations for international students: Required—TOEFL (minimum score 550 paper-based; 80 iBT). *Application deadline:* For fall admission, 2/15 for domestic and international students; for spring admission, 10/1 for domestic and international students. Application fee: $35. Electronic applications accepted. *Expenses:* Expenses: $2,774 tuition and fees (for D Min), $12,362 (for M Div). *Financial support:* In 2014–15, 144 students received support. Federal Work-Study, institutionally sponsored loans, scholarships/grants, and tuition waivers (full and partial) available. Financial award application deadline: 3/1; financial award applicants required to submit FAFSA. *Faculty research:* New Testament theology, exegesis of Psalms, doctrinal preaching, history of Anglicanism, racial reconciliation. *Unit head:* Dr. Timothy George, Dean, 205-726-2632, E-mail: tfgeorge@samford.edu. *Application contact:* Sherri Spurling Brown, Director of Admission, 205-726-2066, Fax: 205-726-4120, E-mail: sbrown5@samford.edu. Website: http://www.beesondivinity.com/

San Francisco Theological Seminary, Graduate and Professional Programs, San Anselmo, CA 94960-2997. Offers M Div, MA, MATS, D Min, PhD, Th D, M Div/MA. MA, Th D, PhD, M Div/MA offered jointly with Graduate Theological Union. *Accreditation:* ACIPE; ATS (one or more programs are accredited). Part-time programs available. *Degree requirements:* For master's, one foreign language, thesis (for some programs); for doctorate, thesis/dissertation. *Entrance requirements:* For master's, minimum GPA of 3.0; for doctorate, M Div. Additional exam requirements/recommendations for international students: Required—TOEFL.

Santa Clara University, Jesuit School of Theology, Berkeley, CA 94709. Offers M Div, MA, MABL, MTS, Th M, STD, STB, STL, M Div/MA. *Accreditation:* ATS. Part-time and evening/weekend programs available. *Faculty:* 17 full-time (4 women), 8 part-time/adjunct (4 women). *Students:* 127 full-time (33 women), 14 part-time (5 women); includes 72 minority (18 Black or African American, non-Hispanic/Latino; 1 American Indian or Alaska Native, non-Hispanic/Latino; 36 Asian, non-Hispanic/Latino; 13 Hispanic/Latino; 4 Two or more races, non-Hispanic/Latino). Average age 36. 102 applicants, 95% accepted, 69 enrolled. In 2014, 38 master's, 1 doctorate awarded. *Degree requirements:* For doctorate, thesis/dissertation (for some programs). *Entrance requirements:* For master's, GRE; for doctorate, GRE, master's degree or equivalent. Additional exam requirements/recommendations for international students: Required—TOEFL (minimum score 550 paper-based; 79 iBT). *Application deadline:* For fall admission, 3/1 for domestic and international students; for spring admission, 10/1 for domestic and international students. Applications are processed on a rolling basis. Application fee: $50 ($0 for international students). Electronic applications accepted. *Expenses:* Expenses: Contact institution. *Financial support:* Career-related internships or fieldwork, Federal Work-Study, and scholarships/grants available. Support available to part-time students. Financial award application deadline: 3/2; financial award applicants required to submit FAFSA. *Faculty research:* Psalms and wisdom literature/women in Old Testament, liberation theology and the contributions of Jesuit martyr Ignazio Ellacuria, Catholic social teaching and recent Vatican teachings on environment, pastoral and applied theology in diverse cultural contexts, sociological analysis of American Catholicism. *Unit head:* Alison Benders, Associate Academic Dean, 510-549-5055, E-mail: abenders@jstb.edu. *Application contact:* Maureen Beckman, Assistant Dean of Enrollment Management, 510-549-5013, Fax: 510-841-8536, E-mail: mbeckman@jstb.edu. Website: http://www.scu.edu/jst/

Seabury-Western Theological Seminary, School of Theology, Evanston, IL 60201-2976. Offers advanced theological studies (Certificate); church music and liturgy (MTS); congregational development (D Min); preaching (D Min); theological studies (MA); theology (M Div, L Th). D Min in congregational development offered in summer only; D Min in preaching offered jointly with Chicago Theological Seminary, Lutheran School of Theology at Chicago, McCormick Theological Seminary, and Northern Baptist Theological Seminary. *Accreditation:* ACIPE; ATS (one or more programs are accredited). Part-time programs available. *Degree requirements:* For master's, thesis; for doctorate, thesis/dissertation; for other advanced degree, thesis (for some programs). *Entrance requirements:* For master's, interview, sample of written work. *Faculty research:* Liturgical interpretations of baptism, trinitarian theology, congregational development, post modern biblical criticism-Matthew.

Seattle Pacific University, Master of Arts (MA) in Theology Program, Seattle, WA 98119-1997. Offers Christian studies (Graduate Certificate); theology (MA). *Students:* 10 full-time (3 women), 10 part-time (4 women); includes 5 minority (4 Black or African American, non-Hispanic/Latino; 1 Two or more races, non-Hispanic/Latino), 1 international. Average age 31. 18 applicants, 44% accepted, 8 enrolled. In 2014, 5 master's awarded. *Degree requirements:* For master's, internship or thesis. *Entrance requirements:* For master's, two letters of recommendation; personal statement; bachelor's degree from regionally-accredited college or university or its equivalent; official copy of transcripts from college or university that granted the bachelor's degree and any institution attended since that time; minimum GPA of 3.0. Additional exam requirements/recommendations for international students: Required—TOEFL (minimum score 550 paper-based). *Application deadline:* For fall admission, 7/1 for domestic students, 6/15 for international students. Applications are processed on a rolling basis. Application fee: $50. Electronic applications accepted. *Financial support:* Application deadline: 4/1; applicants required to submit FAFSA. *Unit head:* Dr. Doug Strong, Dean, 206-281-2473, E-mail: dstrong@spu.edu. *Application contact:* John Glancy, Director,

Graduate Admissions and Marketing, 206-281-2325, Fax: 206-281-2877, E-mail: jglancy@spu.edu. Website: http://spu.edu/academics/school-of-theology/seattle-pacific-seminary/seminary-degrees/ma-theology

Seattle Pacific University, The Master of Divinity Program, Seattle, WA 98119-1997. Offers M Div. *Students:* 19 full-time (9 women), 18 part-time (8 women); includes 10 minority (2 Black or African American, non-Hispanic/Latino; 6 Asian, non-Hispanic/Latino; 2 Two or more races, non-Hispanic/Latino). Average age 31. 27 applicants, 52% accepted, 14 enrolled. In 2014, 4 master's awarded. *Entrance requirements:* For master's, two letters of recommendation; personal statement; BA; official transcript; minimum GPA of 3.0. Additional exam requirements/recommendations for international students: Required—TOEFL (minimum score 550 paper-based). *Application deadline:* For fall admission, 7/1 for domestic students. Application fee: $50. *Financial support:* Scholarships/grants available. Financial award applicants required to submit FAFSA. *Unit head:* Dr. Doug Strong, Dean, 206-281-2473, E-mail: dstrong@spu.edu. Website: http://spu.edu/academics/school-of-theology/seattle-pacific-seminary/seminary-degrees/ma-divinity

The Seattle School of Theology and Psychology, Graduate Programs, Seattle, WA 98121. Offers Christian studies (MA); counseling psychology (MA); divinity (M Div). Part-time programs available. *Entrance requirements:* For master's, MAT.

Seattle University, School of Theology and Ministry, Program in Divinity, Seattle, WA 98122-1090. Offers M Div. *Accreditation:* ATS. Part-time and evening/weekend programs available. *Faculty:* 12 full-time (6 women), 9 part-time/adjunct (5 women). *Students:* 25 full-time (18 women), 40 part-time (29 women); includes 13 minority (8 Black or African American, non-Hispanic/Latino; 2 Asian, non-Hispanic/Latino; 2 Hispanic/Latino; 1 Two or more races, non-Hispanic/Latino), 1 international. Average age 46. 28 applicants, 57% accepted, 11 enrolled. In 2014, 10 master's awarded. *Entrance requirements:* For master's, minimum GPA of 2.75 (3.0 for international students); two years of experience in some form of education, ministry, or service as a profession or volunteer; recommendations; interview with admissions committee. *Application deadline:* For fall admission, 7/1 priority date for domestic students. *Financial support:* In 2014–15, 44 students received support. Career-related internships or fieldwork and Federal Work-Study available. Support available to part-time students. Financial award applicants required to submit FAFSA. *Unit head:* Dr. Mark Markuly, Dean, 206-296-5330, Fax: 206-296-5329, E-mail: markulym@seattleu.edu. *Application contact:* Catherine Kehoe Fallon, Admissions Coordinator, 206-296-5333, Fax: 206-296-5329, E-mail: fallon@seattleu.edu. Website: https://www.seattleu.edu/stm/degrees/mdiv/

Seattle University, School of Theology and Ministry, Program in Transforming Spirituality, Seattle, WA 98122-1090. Offers MATS, Certificate. *Accreditation:* ATS. Part-time and evening/weekend programs available. *Faculty:* 12 full-time (6 women), 9 part-time/adjunct (5 women). *Students:* 2 full-time (1 woman), 13 part-time (9 women); includes 7 minority (4 Black or African American, non-Hispanic/Latino; 2 Hispanic/Latino; 1 Two or more races, non-Hispanic/Latino), 1 international. Average age 45. 4 applicants, 50% accepted, 2 enrolled. In 2014, 2 master's awarded. *Degree requirements:* For master's, project. *Entrance requirements:* For master's, minimum GPA of 2.75 (3.0 for international students); two years of experience in some form of education, ministry, or service as a profession or volunteer; recommendations; interview with admissions committee. *Application deadline:* For fall admission, 7/1 for domestic students. Application fee: $55. *Financial support:* In 2014–15, 11 students received support. Career-related internships or fieldwork and Federal Work-Study available. Support available to part-time students. Financial award application deadline: 4/1; financial award applicants required to submit FAFSA. *Unit head:* Dr. Mark Markuly, Director, 206-296-5330, Fax: 206-296-5329, E-mail: markulym@seattleu.edu. *Application contact:* Catherine Kehoe Fallon, Admissions Coordinator, 206-296-5333, Fax: 206-296-5329, E-mail: fallon@seattleu.edu. Website: http://www.seattleu.edu/stm/degrees/mats/

Seminary of the Immaculate Conception, School of Theology, Huntington, NY 11743-1696. Offers pastoral studies (MA); theology (M Div, MA, D Min, Certificate). *Accreditation:* ATS (one or more programs are accredited). Part-time and evening/weekend programs available. *Degree requirements:* For master's, seminar and paper/thesis; for doctorate, thesis/dissertation. *Entrance requirements:* For master's, undergraduate degree; for doctorate, MA plus 30 credits or M Div; for Certificate, MA in theology.

Seminary of the Southwest, Graduate and Professional Programs, Austin, TX 78768-2247. Offers M Div, MAC, MAR, MCPC, MSF, Advanced Diploma. *Accreditation:* ACIPE; ATS (one or more programs are accredited). Part-time and evening/weekend programs available. *Faculty:* 10 full-time (3 women), 9 part-time/adjunct (4 women). *Students:* 46 full-time (19 women), 52 part-time (41 women); includes 18 minority (6 Black or African American, non-Hispanic/Latino; 1 American Indian or Alaska Native, non-Hispanic/Latino; 6 Hispanic/Latino; 5 Two or more races, non-Hispanic/Latino). Average age 49. 48 applicants, 65% accepted, 26 enrolled. In 2014, 31 master's, 1 other advanced degree awarded. *Degree requirements:* For master's, thesis (for some programs). *Entrance requirements:* For master's, GRE, MAT, interview; for Advanced Diploma, interview. Additional exam requirements/recommendations for international students: Recommended—TOEFL. *Application deadline:* For fall admission, 6/30 priority date for domestic and international students; for spring admission, 12/1 priority date for domestic and international students. Applications are processed on a rolling basis. Application fee: $50. *Expenses:* Tuition: Full-time $13,152; part-time $548 per credit hour. One-time fee: $75 full-time; $20 part-time. Tuition and fees vary according to class time. *Financial support:* In 2014–15, 30 students received support. Career-related internships or fieldwork and scholarships/grants available. Support available to part-time students. Financial award application deadline: 6/15. *Unit head:* Rev. Dr. Cynthia Briggs Kittredge, Dean and President, 512-472-4133 Ext. 332, Fax: 512-472-3098, E-mail: cynthia.kittredge@ssw.edu. *Application contact:* Jennielle Strother, Vice President of Enrollment Management, 512-472-4133 Ext. 375, Fax: 512-472-3098, E-mail: jennielle.strother@ssw.edu.

Seton Hall University, Immaculate Conception Seminary School of Theology, South Orange, NJ 07079-2697. Offers Christian spirituality (Certificate); great spiritual books (Certificate); pastoral ministry (M Div, MA, Certificate); scripture studies (Certificate); Seminary's Theological Education for Parish Services (STEPS) (Certificate); theology (MA). *Accreditation:* ATS (one or more programs are accredited). Part-time and evening/weekend programs available. *Degree requirements:* For master's, comprehensive exam (for some programs), thesis (for some programs), final project (for some programs); 1 foreign language (for MA in theology research option). *Entrance requirements:* For master's, GRE General Test or MAT. Additional exam requirements/recommendations for international students: Required—TOEFL (minimum score 600 paper-based; 100 iBT). Electronic applications accepted. *Expenses:* Contact institution. *Faculty research:* Pauline literature, history of Biblical interpretation and theological exegesis, spirituality of St. Edith Stein, Thomism, history of Catholicism in America.

Sewanee: The University of the South, School of Theology, Sewanee, TN 37383. Offers M Div, MA, STM, D Min. *Accreditation:* ACIPE; ATS. Part-time programs

available. *Faculty:* 10 full-time, 9 part-time/adjunct. *Students:* 76 full-time (35 women), 2 part-time (1 woman); includes 4 minority (1 Black or African American, non-Hispanic/Latino; 1 American Indian or Alaska Native, non-Hispanic/Latino; 2 Two or more races, non-Hispanic/Latino), 3 international. Average age 44. 52 applicants, 87% accepted, 34 enrolled. In 2014, 22 master's, 5 doctorates awarded. *Degree requirements:* For master's, thesis (for some programs); for doctorate, thesis/dissertation. *Entrance requirements:* For master's, M Div (for STM); for doctorate, M Div. Additional exam requirements/recommendations for international students: Required—TOEFL (minimum score 550 paper-based). *Application deadline:* For fall admission, 4/1 priority date for domestic students, 4/1 for international students. Applications are processed on a rolling basis. Application fee: $0. *Financial support:* Institutionally sponsored loans and scholarships/grants available. Support available to part-time students. Financial award application deadline: 3/8. *Unit head:* Very Rev. Dr. J. Neil Alexander, Dean, 931-598-1288, Fax: 931-598-1412, E-mail: deansot@sewanee.edu. *Application contact:* Rev. Annwn H. Myers, Associate Dean for Recruiting and Admission, 931-598-1373, E-mail: amyers@sewanee.edu.
Website: http://theology.sewanee.edu/

Shaw University, Divinity School, Raleigh, NC 27601-2399. Offers M Div, MACE. *Accreditation:* ATS. Part-time and evening/weekend programs available. *Faculty:* 11 full-time (4 women), 8 part-time/adjunct (1 woman). *Students:* 70 full-time (33 women), 35 part-time (24 women); includes 95 minority (all Black or African American, non-Hispanic/Latino). Average age 49. 40 applicants, 98% accepted, 29 enrolled. In 2014, 18 master's awarded. *Degree requirements:* For master's, thesis. *Entrance requirements:* For master's, official undergraduate transcripts, letters of reference, essay, interview. *Application deadline:* For fall admission, 7/30 priority date for domestic students, 1/30 priority date for international students; for spring admission, 11/30 priority date for domestic students, 8/30 priority date for international students. Applications are processed on a rolling basis. Application fee: $50. Electronic applications accepted. *Expenses: Tuition:* Full-time $10,404; part-time $578 per semester hour. *Required fees:* $2784. *Financial support:* In 2014–15, 35 students received support. Federal Work-Study, scholarships/grants, and tuition waivers (full) available. Support available to part-time students. Financial award applicants required to submit FAFSA. *Faculty research:* Health disparities and the African-American Church, Christian community development, teaching for social change, technology and theological education, best practices in historically black theological schools. *Unit head:* Dr. David Forbes, Interim Dean, 919-546-8574, Fax: 919-546-8571, E-mail: dforbes@shawu.edu. *Application contact:* Stella Goldston, Secretary, 919-546-3570, Fax: 919-546-8271, E-mail: sgoldston@shawu.edu.
Website: http://www.shawu.edu/suds/

Shepherds Theological Seminary, Graduate Programs, Cary, NC 27518. Offers church ministry (MA); New Testament (M Div); Old Testament (M Div); theology (M Div). *Degree requirements:* For master's, thesis.

Shepherd University, School of Theology, Los Angeles, CA 90065. Offers M Div, D Min.

Shiloh University, Graduate Programs, Kalona, IA 52247. Offers Biblical and pastoral studies (MA); ministry (M Div). Part-time and evening/weekend programs available. Postbaccalaureate distance learning degree programs offered (no on-campus study). *Faculty:* 3 full-time (0 women), 6 part-time/adjunct (3 women). *Students:* 1 full-time (0 women), 26 part-time (5 women); includes 3 minority (1 Black or African American, non-Hispanic/Latino; 1 Hispanic/Latino; 1 Native Hawaiian or other Pacific Islander, non-Hispanic/Latino), 2 international. Average age 47. In 2014, 3 master's awarded. *Degree requirements:* For master's, thesis optional. *Entrance requirements:* For master's, bachelor's degree or educational equivalent from accredited school with minimum GPA of 2.75 on undergraduate work. Additional exam requirements/recommendations for international students: Recommended—TOEFL (minimum score 540 paper-based; 76 iBT), IELTS (minimum score 6.5). *Application deadline:* For fall admission, 7/6 for domestic and international students; for spring admission, 11/9 for domestic and international students; for summer admission, 3/7 for domestic and international students. Applications are processed on a rolling basis. Application fee: $0. Electronic applications accepted. *Expenses:* Expenses: $450 per credit. *Faculty research:* New testament theology, Pauline literature, relational theology. *Unit head:* Dr. Wesley Pinkham, Vice President of Academics, 319-656-2447 Ext. 2, Fax: 319-656-2448, E-mail: wess.pinkham@shilohuniversity.edu. *Application contact:* Andrew Thompson, Admissions Coordinator, 319-656-2447 Ext. 2, Fax: 319-656-2448, E-mail: admissions@shilohuniversity.edu.
Website: http://www.shilohuniversity.edu/academics/

Sh'or Yoshuv Rabbinical College, Graduate Programs, Far Rockaway, NY 11691-4002. *Accreditation:* AARTS.

Sioux Falls Seminary, Graduate and Professional Programs, Master of Divinity Program, Sioux Falls, SD 57105-1599. Offers marriage and family therapy (M Div); pastoral care and counseling (M Div). Program also offered in Omaha, NE. *Accreditation:* ACIPE. Part-time programs available. Postbaccalaureate distance learning degree programs offered (no on-campus study).

Sioux Falls Seminary, Graduate and Professional Programs, Program in Bible and Theology, Sioux Falls, SD 57105-1599. Offers MA. *Accreditation:* ACIPE; ATS. Part-time programs available. *Degree requirements:* For master's, 2 foreign languages, thesis or alternative. *Entrance requirements:* For master's, minimum GPA of 2.5.

Sioux Falls Seminary, Graduate and Professional Programs, Program in Ministry, Sioux Falls, SD 57105-1599. Offers D Min. *Accreditation:* ACIPE. Part-time programs available. *Degree requirements:* For doctorate, thesis/dissertation. *Entrance requirements:* For doctorate, M Div, 3 years of ministry.

Sioux Falls Seminary, Graduate and Professional Programs, Program in Theological Studies, Sioux Falls, SD 57105-1599. Offers Certificate.

Southeastern Baptist Theological Seminary, Graduate and Professional Programs, Wake Forest, NC 27588-1889. Offers advanced biblical studies (M Div); Christian education (M Div, MACE); Christian ethics (PhD); Christian ministry (M Div); Christian planting (M Div); church music (MACM); counseling (MACO); evangelism (PhD); language (M Div); ministry (D Min); New Testament (PhD); Old Testament (PhD); philosophy (PhD); theology (Th M, PhD); women's studies (M Div). *Accreditation:* ACIPE; ATS (one or more programs are accredited). *Degree requirements:* For master's, thesis (for some programs), oral exam; for doctorate, thesis/dissertation, fieldwork. *Entrance requirements:* For master's, Cooperative English Test, minimum GPA of 2.0, M Div or equivalent (Th M); for doctorate, GRE General Test or MAT, Cooperative English Test, M Div or equivalent, 3 years of professional experience.

Southern Adventist University, School of Religion, Collegedale, TN 37315-0370. Offers Biblical and theological studies (MA); church leadership and management (M Min); church ministry and homiletics (M Min); evangelism and world mission (M Min); religious studies (MA). Part-time programs available. *Degree requirements:* For master's, comprehensive exam, thesis (for some programs). *Entrance requirements:* For master's, GRE. Additional exam requirements/recommendations for international students: Required—TOEFL (minimum score 600 paper-based). *Faculty research:* Biblical archaeology.

Southern Baptist Theological Seminary, Billy Graham School of Missions and Evangelism, Louisville, KY 40280-0004. Offers ministry (D Min); missiology (MA, D Miss); missions and evangelism (M Div, Th M, PhD); theological studies (MA). *Accreditation:* ATS. Part-time and evening/weekend programs available. Postbaccalaureate distance learning degree programs offered (minimal on-campus study). *Degree requirements:* For master's, 2 foreign languages; for doctorate, 4 foreign languages, thesis/dissertation. *Entrance requirements:* For doctorate, GRE General Test, MAT, M Div. Additional exam requirements/recommendations for international students: Required—TOEFL, TWE. *Faculty research:* Assimilation of church congregants, effective methodologies of evangelism, expectations of church members, spiritual warfare literature, formative church discipline.

Southern Baptist Theological Seminary, School of Theology, Louisville, KY 40280-0004. Offers applied theology (D Min); biblical and theological studies (M Div); biblical counseling (M Div, MA, D Min); biblical spirituality (D Min); Christian ministry (M Div); expository preaching (D Min); pastoral studies (M Div); theological studies (MA); theology (Th M, PhD); worldview and apologetics (M Div). *Accreditation:* ATS. Part-time and evening/weekend programs available. Postbaccalaureate distance learning degree programs offered (minimal on-campus study). *Degree requirements:* For master's, 2 foreign languages, thesis; for doctorate, 4 foreign languages, thesis/dissertation. *Entrance requirements:* For master's, GRE General Test, MAT, M Div; for doctorate, GRE General Test, MAT, interview, M Div, field essay. Additional exam requirements/recommendations for international students: Required—TOEFL, TWE. *Faculty research:* Biblical studies, contemporary theology, church history, pastoral care, ministry/missions studies.

Southern California Seminary, Graduate and Professional Programs, El Cajon, CA 92019. Offers Biblical studies (MABS); counseling psychology (MACP); marriage and family therapy (MAMFT); psychology (Psy D); religious studies (MRS); theology (M Div). Part-time and evening/weekend programs available. Postbaccalaureate distance learning degree programs offered (minimal on-campus study). *Degree requirements:* For master's, thesis (for some programs); for doctorate, thesis/dissertation. *Entrance requirements:* For doctorate, master's degree in psychology. Additional exam requirements/recommendations for international students: Required—TOEFL (minimum score 550 paper-based). Electronic applications accepted.

Southern Evangelical Seminary, Graduate Programs, Matthews, NC 28105. Offers apologetics (MA, D Min, Certificate); Christian education (MA); church ministry (MA, Certificate); divinity (Certificate), including apologetics (M Div, Certificate); Islamic studies (MA, Certificate); Jewish studies (MA); philosophy (MA); philosophy of religion (PhD); religion (MA); theology (M Div), including apologetics (M Div, Certificate), Biblical studies; youth ministry (MA). Part-time and evening/weekend programs available. Postbaccalaureate distance learning degree programs offered. *Degree requirements:* For master's, thesis (for some programs); for doctorate, 2 foreign languages, comprehensive exam (for some programs), thesis/dissertation. *Entrance requirements:* Additional exam requirements/recommendations for international students: Required—TOEFL (minimum score 600 paper-based).

Southern Methodist University, Dedman College of Humanities and Sciences, Graduate Program in Religious Studies, Dallas, TX 75275-0133. Offers Hebrew Bible/Old Testament (PhD); history of the Christian tradition (PhD); New Testament (PhD); religion and culture (PhD); religious ethics (PhD); religious studies (MA); systematics theology (PhD). Terminal master's awarded for partial completion of doctoral program. *Degree requirements:* For master's, one foreign language, thesis, oral and written exams; for doctorate, variable foreign language requirement, thesis/dissertation, oral and written exams. *Entrance requirements:* For master's and doctorate, GRE General Test, minimum GPA of 3.0, course work in religion. Additional exam requirements/recommendations for international students: Required—TOEFL (minimum score 550 paper-based; 79 iBT). Electronic applications accepted. *Faculty research:* Theology, religious ethics, Biblical studies, history of Christianity, religion and culture.

Southern Methodist University, Perkins School of Theology, Dallas, TX 75275. Offers CMM, M Div, MSM, MTS, D Min. *Accreditation:* ACIPE; ATS. Part-time programs available. *Degree requirements:* For master's, thesis (for some programs), internship; for doctorate, internship, oral exam, professional project. *Entrance requirements:* For master's, minimum GPA of 2.75; for doctorate, minimum graduate GPA of 3.0, M Div or equivalent, 3 years of ministry experience. Additional exam requirements/recommendations for international students: Required—TOEFL (minimum score 600 paper-based; 100 iBT), TWE. *Expenses:* Contact institution.

Southwestern Assemblies of God University, Thomas F. Harrison School of Graduate Studies, Program in Theological Studies, Waxahachie, TX 75165-5735. Offers Bible and theology (MS); Biblical studies (M Div); counseling (M Div); cross cultural missions (M Div); practical theology (M Div); theological studies (M Div). Postbaccalaureate distance learning degree programs offered. *Degree requirements:* For master's, comprehensive written and oral exams. *Entrance requirements:* For master's, GRE General Test, minimum GPA of 2.5. Electronic applications accepted.

Southwestern Baptist Theological Seminary, School of Theology, Fort Worth, TX 76122-0000. Offers ministry (D Min); theology (PhD). *Accreditation:* ACIPE; ATS (one or more programs are accredited). Part-time and evening/weekend programs available. Terminal master's awarded for partial completion of doctoral program. *Degree requirements:* For master's, 2 foreign languages, thesis (for some programs); for doctorate, 2 foreign languages, comprehensive exam, thesis/dissertation, oral exams. *Entrance requirements:* For doctorate, GRE, M Div or equivalent. Additional exam requirements/recommendations for international students: Required—TOEFL. *Application deadline:* For fall admission, 7/15 priority date for domestic students, 4/1 for international students; for spring admission, 12/15 priority date for domestic students, 10/1 for international students. Applications are processed on a rolling basis. Electronic applications accepted. *Financial support:* Teaching assistantships, career-related internships or fieldwork, institutionally sponsored loans, scholarships/grants, and tuition waivers (partial) available. Support available to part-time students. Financial award application deadline: 11/1. *Unit head:* Dr. David Allen, Dean, 817-923-1921 Ext. 4200, Fax: 817-921-8767, E-mail: dallen@swbts.edu. *Application contact:* Director of Admissions, 817-923-1921 Ext. 2700, Fax: 817-921-8757, E-mail: admissions@swbts.edu.
Website: http://swbts.edu/academics/schools-programs/theology/

Southwestern College, Professional Studies Programs, Wichita, KS 67207. Offers accountancy (MA); business administration (MBA); leadership (MS); management (MS); security administration (MS); specialized ministries (MA); theological studies (MA). Part-time and evening/weekend programs available. Postbaccalaureate distance learning degree programs offered (minimal on-campus study). *Faculty:* 34 part-time/adjunct (11 women). *Students:* 100 part-time (37 women); includes 24 minority (10 Black or African American, non-Hispanic/Latino; 3 Asian, non-Hispanic/Latino; 6 Hispanic/Latino; 5 Two or more races, non-Hispanic/Latino). Average age 37. 75 applicants, 71% accepted, 22 enrolled. In 2014, 78 master's awarded. *Degree requirements:* For master's, practicum/capstone project. *Entrance requirements:* For master's, baccalaureate degree; minimum GPA of 2.5 (for MA and MS), 3.0 (for MBA). Additional exam requirements/recommendations for international students: Required—TOEFL (minimum score 550

paper-based). *Application deadline:* For fall admission, 8/1 for domestic students; for spring admission, 12/1 for domestic students. Applications are processed on a rolling basis. Application fee: $0. Electronic applications accepted. *Expenses:* Expenses: $10,836. *Financial support:* In 2014–15, 5 students received support. Federal Work-Study, tuition waivers (partial), and unspecified assistantships available. Financial award application deadline: 4/1; financial award applicants required to submit FAFSA. *Unit head:* Susan Backofen, Vice President for Enrollment Management, 888-684-5335 Ext. 214, Fax: 316-688-5218, E-mail: susan.backofen@sckans.edu. *Application contact:* 888-684-5335, Fax: 316-688-5218, E-mail: enrollment@sckans.edu.
Website: http://www.southwesterncollege.org

Spring Arbor University, School of Arts and Sciences, Spring Arbor, MI 49283-9799. Offers communication (MA); spiritual formation and leadership (MA). Part-time programs available. Postbaccalaureate distance learning degree programs offered (no on-campus study). *Degree requirements:* For master's, thesis (for some programs). *Entrance requirements:* For master's, GRE (minimum score of 40th percentile and taken within last 5 years), bachelor's degree from regionally-accredited college or university, minimum GPA of 3.0 for at least the last two years of the bachelor's degree, at least two recommendations from professional/academic individuals. Additional exam requirements/recommendations for international students: Required—TOEFL (minimum score 600 paper-based). *Expenses:* Contact institution.

Spring Hill College, Graduate Programs, Program in Theology, Mobile, AL 36608-1791. Offers faith companioning (Postbaccalaureate Certificate); pastoral ministry (Postbaccalaureate Certificate); pastoral studies (MPS); spiritual direction (Postbaccalaureate Certificate); theological studies (MTS); theology (MA). Part-time and evening/weekend programs available. *Faculty:* 5 full-time (0 women), 2 part-time/adjunct (both women). *Students:* 43 part-time (20 women); includes 3 minority (1 Black or African American, non-Hispanic/Latino; 2 Asian, non-Hispanic/Latino). Average age 47. In 2014, 8 master's, 4 other advanced degrees awarded. *Degree requirements:* For master's, variable foreign language requirement, comprehensive exam, thesis (for some programs), completion of program within 6 calendar years of initial enrollment (MTS, MPS); completion of program within 4 1/2 calendar years of formal acceptance (MA). *Entrance requirements:* For master's, bachelor's degree with minimum undergraduate GPA of 3.0; six hours of undergraduate theology, religious studies, or unquestioned equivalency. Additional exam requirements/recommendations for international students: Required—TOEFL (minimum score 550 paper-based; 80 iBT), IELTS (minimum score 6.5), CPE or CAE (minimum score C), Michigan English Language Assessment Battery (minimum score 90). *Application deadline:* For fall admission, 8/1 priority date for domestic and international students; for spring admission, 12/1 priority date for domestic and international students. Applications are processed on a rolling basis. Application fee: $25 ($35 for international students). Electronic applications accepted. *Expenses:* Tuition: Full-time $8820; part-time $490 per credit hour. Tuition and fees vary according to program. *Financial support:* Applicants required to submit FAFSA. *Unit head:* Dr. Timothy R. Carmody, Director, 251-380-4665, Fax: 251-460-2194, E-mail: carmody@shc.edu. *Application contact:* Robert Stewart, Vice President of Enrollment, 251-380-3030, Fax: 251-460-2186, E-mail: rstewart@shc.edu.
Website: http://ug.shc.edu/graduate-degrees/master-arts-theological-studies/

Starr King School for the Ministry, Professional Program, Berkeley, CA 94709-1209. Offers M Div. *Accreditation:* ACIPE; ATS.

Summit University, Baptist Bible Seminary, Clarks Summit, PA 18411-1297. Offers Biblical apologetics (MA); church education (M Div, M Min); church planting (M Div, M Min); global ministry (M Div, M Min); leadership in communication (D Min); leadership in counseling and spiritual development (D Min); leadership in global ministry (D Min); leadership in pastoral ministry (D Min); leadership in theological studies (D Min); military chaplaincy (M Div); ministry (PhD); organizational leadership (M Min); outreach pastor (M Div, M Min); pastoral counseling (M Div, M Min); pastoral leadership (M Div, M Min); theology (Th M); worship ministries leadership (M Div, M Min); youth pastor (M Div, M Min). Part-time and evening/weekend programs available. Postbaccalaureate distance learning degree programs offered (minimal on-campus study). Terminal master's awarded for partial completion of doctoral program. *Degree requirements:* For master's, 2 foreign languages, thesis, oral exam (for M Div); for doctorate, 2 foreign languages, comprehensive exam (for some programs), thesis/dissertation, oral exam. *Entrance requirements:* For doctorate, Greek and Hebrew entrance exams (for PhD). Electronic applications accepted.

Summit University, Graduate Studies, Clarks Summit, PA 18411-1297. Offers Bible (MA); counseling (MA, MS); curriculum and instruction (M Ed); educational administration (M Ed); intercultural studies (MA); literature (MA); missions (MA); organizational leadership (MA); reading specialist (M Ed); secondary English/communications (M Ed); social entrepreneurship (MA); worldview studies (MA). MA in missions program available only for Association of Baptists for World Evangelism missionary personnel. Part-time and evening/weekend programs available. Postbaccalaureate distance learning degree programs offered (no on-campus study). *Entrance requirements:* Additional exam requirements/recommendations for international students: Required—TOEFL (minimum score 500 paper-based).

Talmudic College of Florida, Program in Talmudic Law, Miami Beach, FL 33139. Offers MRE. *Accreditation:* AARTS. *Degree requirements:* For master's, 2 foreign languages. *Entrance requirements:* For master's, oral exam, undergraduate Judaic studies degree.

Taylor College and Seminary, Graduate and Professional Programs, Edmonton, AB T6J 4T3, Canada. Offers Christian studies (Diploma); intercultural studies (MA, Diploma), including intercultural studies (Diploma), TESOL; theology (M Div, MTS). *Accreditation:* ATS. Part-time programs available. Postbaccalaureate distance learning degree programs offered (minimal on-campus study). *Degree requirements:* For master's, thesis optional. *Entrance requirements:* Additional exam requirements/recommendations for international students: Required—TOEFL (minimum score 550 paper-based; 80 iBT), IELTS (minimum score 6.5). *Faculty research:* Biblical studies, administration and organization, world religions, ethics, missiology.

Temple Baptist Seminary, Program in Theology, Chattanooga, TN 37404-3530. Offers biblical languages (M Div); Biblical studies (MABS); Christian education (MACE); English Bible ? language tools (M Div); theology (MM, D Min). Part-time and evening/weekend programs available. Postbaccalaureate distance learning degree programs offered (minimal on-campus study). *Degree requirements:* For doctorate, thesis/dissertation. *Entrance requirements:* For doctorate, minimum GPA of 3.0, M Div.

Toronto School of Theology, Graduate Programs, Toronto, ON M5S 2C3, Canada. Offers M Div, M Mus, M Rel, MA, MAMS, MPS, MRE, MTS, Th M, D Min, PhD, Th D. *Accreditation:* ATS. Postbaccalaureate distance learning degree programs offered (minimal on-campus study). Terminal master's awarded for partial completion of doctoral program. *Degree requirements:* For master's, 2 foreign languages, thesis; for doctorate, 3 foreign languages, comprehensive exam, thesis/dissertation. *Entrance requirements:* For master's, language exams, minimum B+ average in undergraduate course work; for doctorate, language exams, first-class standing in master's program. Additional exam requirements/recommendations for international students: Required—TOEFL. Electronic applications accepted.

Trevecca Nazarene University, Graduate Religion Programs, Nashville, TN 37210-2877. Offers biblical studies (MA); pastoral arts (MA); preaching (MA); theological studies (MA). Part-time programs available. *Faculty:* 3 full-time (0 women), 1 part-time/adjunct (0 women). *Students:* 6 full-time (2 women), 7 part-time (1 woman); includes 3 minority (2 Black or African American, non-Hispanic/Latino; 1 Hispanic/Latino). Average age 36. In 2014, 14 master's awarded. *Degree requirements:* For master's, comprehensive exam, thesis. *Entrance requirements:* For master's, GRE General Test or MAT, minimum GPA of 2.7, official transcript from regionally-accredited institution, 2 letters of recommendation, philosophy of ministry statement. Additional exam requirements/recommendations for international students: Required—TOEFL (minimum score 550 paper-based). *Application deadline:* Applications are processed on a rolling basis. Application fee: $25. Electronic applications accepted. *Expenses:* Expenses: Contact institution. *Financial support:* Applicants required to submit FAFSA. *Unit head:* Dr. Tim Green, Dean, School of Religion and Philosophy/Director, Graduate Religion Program, 615-248-1378, Fax: 615-248-7417. *Application contact:* 615-248-1529, E-mail: cll@trevecca.edu.
Website: http://trevecca.edu/academics/program/religion

Trinity College, Faculty of Divinity, Toronto, ON M5S 1H8, Canada. Offers ministry (Diploma); ministry for church musicians (Diploma); theology (M Div, MA, MTS, Th M, D Min, PhD, Th D, Diploma, L Th); M Div/MA. *Accreditation:* ATS. Part-time programs available. *Degree requirements:* For master's, 2 foreign languages, thesis (for some programs); for doctorate, 3 foreign languages, comprehensive exam, thesis/dissertation; for other advanced degree, thesis (for some programs). *Entrance requirements:* For master's, 1 language (modern or ancient), interview; for doctorate, 2 languages (modern and ancient). Additional exam requirements/recommendations for international students: Required—TOEFL, TWE. *Faculty research:* Interreligious dialogue, feminist theology, systematic theology, philosophy of religion, pastoral theology.

Trinity International University, Trinity Evangelical Divinity School, Deerfield, IL 60015-1284. Offers Biblical and Near Eastern archaeology and languages (MA); Christian studies (MA, Certificate); Christian thought (MA); church history (MA, Th M); congregational ministry: pastor-teacher (M Div); congregational ministry: team ministry (M Div); counseling ministries (MA); counseling psychology (MA); cross-cultural ministry (M Div); educational studies (PhD); evangelism (MA); history of Christianity in America (MA); intercultural studies (MA, PhD); leadership and ministry management (D Min); military chaplaincy (D Min); ministry (MA); mission and evangelism (Th M); missions and evangelism (D Min); New Testament (MA, Th M); Old Testament (Th M); Old Testament and Semitic languages (MA); pastoral care (M Div); pastoral care and counseling (D Min); pastoral counseling and psychology (Th M); pastoral theology (Th M); philosophy of religion (MA); preaching (D Min); religion (MA); research ministry (M Div); systematic theology (Th M); theological studies (PhD); urban ministry (MA). *Accreditation:* ATS (one or more programs are accredited). Part-time programs available. Postbaccalaureate distance learning degree programs offered (minimal on-campus study). *Degree requirements:* For master's, comprehensive exam, thesis, fieldwork; for doctorate, comprehensive exam (for some programs), thesis/dissertation; for Certificate, comprehensive exam, integrative papers. *Entrance requirements:* For master's, GRE, MAT, minimum cumulative undergraduate GPA of 3.0; for doctorate, GRE, minimum cumulative graduate GPA of 3.2; for Certificate, GRE, MAT, minimum undergraduate GPA of 2.5. Additional exam requirements/recommendations for international students: Required—TOEFL (minimum score 580 paper-based), TWE (minimum score 4). Electronic applications accepted.

Trinity Lutheran Seminary, Graduate and Professional Programs, Columbus, OH 43209-2334. Offers African American studies (MTS); Biblical studies (MTS, STM); Christian education (MA); Christian spirituality (STM); church in the world (MTS); church music (MA); divinity (M Div); general theological studies (MTS); mission and evangelism (STM); pastoral leadership and practice (STM); youth and family ministry (MA); MSN/MTS; MTS/JD. *Accreditation:* ACIPE; ATS. Part-time programs available. *Faculty:* 11 full-time (5 women), 2 part-time/adjunct (both women). *Students:* 68 full-time (24 women), 43 part-time (18 women); includes 12 minority (10 Black or African American, non-Hispanic/Latino; 1 Asian, non-Hispanic/Latino; 1 Two or more races, non-Hispanic/Latino), 1 international. Average age 35. 45 applicants, 96% accepted, 34 enrolled. In 2014, 34 master's awarded. *Degree requirements:* For master's, variable foreign language requirement, comprehensive exam (for some programs), thesis (for some programs), field experience (for some programs). *Entrance requirements:* For master's, BA or equivalent (for MA, M Div, MTS); M Div, MTS, or equivalent (for STM); audition (for MACM). Additional exam requirements/recommendations for international students: Required—TOEFL. *Application deadline:* For fall admission, 7/15 priority date for domestic and international students. Applications are processed on a rolling basis. Application fee: $25. Electronic applications accepted. *Expenses:* Expenses: $13,760 tuition and fees for degree completion (for D Min). *Financial support:* In 2014–15, 72 students received support. Career-related internships or fieldwork, Federal Work-Study, and scholarships/grants available. Support available to part-time students. Financial award application deadline: 5/1; financial award applicants required to submit FAFSA. *Unit head:* Dr. Brad A. Binau, Academic Dean, 614-235-4136 Ext. 4674, Fax: 614-384-4635, E-mail: bbinau@tlsohio.edu. *Application contact:* Rev. Seth Bridger, Director of Admissions, 614-235-4136 Ext. 4650, Fax: 866-610-8572, E-mail: sbridger@tlsohio.edu.
Website: http://www.tlsohio.edu

Trinity School for Ministry, Graduate Programs, Ambridge, PA 15003-2397. Offers Anglican studies (Diploma); basic Christian studies (Diploma); divinity (M Div); ministry (D Min); mission and evangelism (MAME, Diploma); religion (MAR); youth ministry (Diploma). *Accreditation:* ATS (one or more programs are accredited). Part-time programs available. *Degree requirements:* For master's, thesis optional; for doctorate, thesis/dissertation. *Entrance requirements:* Additional exam requirements/recommendations for international students: Required—TOEFL. *Faculty research:* Pauline Epistles, contemporary theology, history of Anglican liturgy, book of Ruth, biblical theology.

Trinity Western University, ACTS Seminaries, Langley, BC V2Y 1Y1, Canada. Offers Christian studies (MA); cross cultural ministry (MA); theology (M Div, M Th, MAMFT, MLE, MTS, D Min). *Accreditation:* ATS. Part-time programs available. *Degree requirements:* For master's, thesis (for some programs), internship. *Entrance requirements:* For doctorate, MDiv or equivalent. Additional exam requirements/recommendations for international students: Required—TOEFL. *Expenses:* Contact institution. *Faculty research:* Theology of leadership.

Trinity Western University, School of Graduate Studies, Program in Biblical Studies, Langley, BC V2Y 1Y1, Canada. Offers MA. *Accreditation:* ATS. Part-time programs available. *Degree requirements:* For master's, 2 foreign languages, thesis, 2 years Greek, 2 years Hebrew. *Entrance requirements:* For master's, minimum GPA of 3.0, degree in biblical studies, master of divinity or 42 hours Biblical Study credit. Additional exam requirements/recommendations for international students: Required—TOEFL (minimum score 600 paper-based). Electronic applications accepted. *Faculty research:* Intertestamental literature, Dead Sea Scrolls, Biblical literature, history of Jesus, ancient languages.

Theology

Tri-State Bible College, Graduate Program, South Point, OH 45680-8402. Offers MA. *Entrance requirements:* For master's, bachelor's degree, minimum undergraduate GPA of 2.75, autobiographical statement, two letters of recommendation. Electronic applications accepted.

Tyndale University College & Seminary, Graduate Programs, Toronto, ON M2M 4B3, Canada. Offers Biblical studies (M Div); Christian foundations (MTS); Christian studies (Diploma); counseling (M Div); educational ministry (M Div); missions (M Div, Diploma); pastoral and Chinese ministry (M Div); pastoral ministry (M Div); Pentecostal studies (MTS); spiritual formation (M Div, Diploma); theological studies (M Div); theology (Th M); worship and liturgy (M Div, MTS); youth and family ministry (M Div). *Accreditation:* ATS. Part-time programs available. Postbaccalaureate distance learning degree programs offered (no on-campus study). *Entrance requirements:* For master's and Diploma, minimum C+ average in undergraduate course work. Additional exam requirements/recommendations for international students: Required—TOEFL (minimum score 570 paper-based), TWE (minimum score 5). Electronic applications accepted. *Faculty research:* Canadian church history, Chinese church history, Old Testament, counseling ministries (narrative therapy), world religions.

Unification Theological Seminary, Graduate Program, Main Campus, Barrytown, NY 12507. Offers divinity (M Div); ministry (D Min); religious education (MRE); religious studies (MA). Part-time and evening/weekend programs available. *Faculty:* 1 full-time (0 women), 5 part-time/adjunct (1 woman). *Students:* 35 full-time (10 women); includes 21 minority (13 Black or African American, non-Hispanic/Latino; 5 Asian, non-Hispanic/Latino; 2 Hispanic/Latino; 1 Two or more races, non-Hispanic/Latino), 6 international. Average age 52. In 2014, 16 master's, 1 doctorate awarded. *Degree requirements:* For master's, variable foreign language requirement, thesis (for some programs); for doctorate, thesis/dissertation. *Entrance requirements:* For master's, bachelor's degree; for doctorate, M Div or equivalency. Additional exam requirements/recommendations for international students: Required—TOEFL (minimum score 450 paper-based; 45 iBT). *Application deadline:* For fall admission, 8/15 priority date for domestic students; for spring admission, 1/15 priority date for domestic students. Applications are processed on a rolling basis. Application fee: $30. Electronic applications accepted. *Expenses: Tuition:* Full-time $8280; part-time $460 per credit. *Required fees:* $125 per semester. Tuition and fees vary according to course load. *Financial support:* In 2014–15, 4 students received support. Scholarships/grants available. Financial award application deadline: 6/15; financial award applicants required to submit FAFSA. *Faculty research:* Church leadership, church history, world religions, ecumenism, interfaith peace building, service-learning. *Unit head:* Dr. Kathy Winings, Vice-President for Academic Affairs, 845-752-3000 Ext. 228, Fax: 845-752-3014, E-mail: academics@uts.edu. *Application contact:* Henry Christopher, Director of Admissions, 845-752-3000 Ext. 244, Fax: 845-752-3014, E-mail: h.christopher@uts.edu.
Website: http://www.uts.edu

Unification Theological Seminary, Graduate Program, New York Extension, New York, NY 10036. Offers divinity (M Div); religious education (MRE); religious studies (MA). Part-time and evening/weekend programs available. *Faculty:* 1 full-time (0 women), 8 part-time/adjunct (2 women). *Students:* 28 full-time (9 women), 22 part-time (9 women); includes 22 minority (15 Black or African American, non-Hispanic/Latino; 4 Asian, non-Hispanic/Latino; 2 Hispanic/Latino; 1 Two or more races, non-Hispanic/Latino), 23 international. Average age 45. *Degree requirements:* For master's, variable foreign language requirement, thesis (for some programs). *Entrance requirements:* For master's, bachelor's degree. Additional exam requirements/recommendations for international students: Required—TOEFL (minimum score 450 paper-based; 45 iBT). *Application deadline:* For fall admission, 8/15 priority date for domestic students; for spring admission, 1/15 priority date for domestic students. Applications are processed on a rolling basis. Application fee: $30. Electronic applications accepted. *Expenses: Tuition:* Full-time $8280; part-time $460 per credit. *Required fees:* $125 per semester. Tuition and fees vary according to course load. *Financial support:* In 2014–15, 50 students received support. Career-related internships or fieldwork, institutionally sponsored loans, scholarships/grants, and tuition waivers (partial) available. Support available to part-time students. Financial award application deadline: 6/15; financial award applicants required to submit FAFSA. *Faculty research:* Church history, world religions, ecumenism, interfaith peace building, service-learning. *Unit head:* Dr. Kathy Winings, Vice-President for Academic Affairs, 212-563-6647 Ext. 101, Fax: 212-563-6431, E-mail: academics@uts.edu. *Application contact:* Joy Theriot, Recruiter, 212-563-6647, Fax: 212-563-6431, E-mail: j.theriot@uts.edu.
Website: http://www.uts.edu

Union Theological Seminary in the City of New York, Graduate and Professional Programs, New York, NY 10027-5710. Offers M Div, MA, STM, Ed D, PhD, M Div/MSSW. Ed D offered jointly with Teachers College, Columbia University; M Div/MSSW with Columbia University. *Accreditation:* ACIPE; ATS (one or more programs are accredited). Part-time programs available. *Degree requirements:* For master's, one foreign language, thesis; for doctorate, 2 foreign languages, thesis/dissertation. *Entrance requirements:* For doctorate, GRE General Test, sample of written work. *Faculty research:* American religious history, psychiatry and religion, Christian ethics, New Testament.

United Talmudical Seminary, Graduate Programs, Brooklyn, NY 11211. *Accreditation:* AARTS.

United Theological Seminary, Graduate and Professional Programs, Dayton, OH 45426. Offers M Div, MA, MATS, D Min, M Div/MA. *Accreditation:* ATS. Part-time and evening/weekend programs available. Postbaccalaureate distance learning degree programs offered (minimal on-campus study). *Degree requirements:* For master's, thesis (for some programs); for doctorate, thesis/dissertation, final exam. *Entrance requirements:* For master's, minimum GPA of 2.5, interview, 5 letters of recommendation; for doctorate, minimum GPA of 3.0, 2 letters of recommendation, interview. Additional exam requirements/recommendations for international students: Required—TOEFL (minimum score 550 paper-based). Electronic applications accepted.

United Theological Seminary of the Twin Cities, Graduate Programs, New Brighton, MN 55112-2598. Offers advanced theological studies (Diploma); justice and peace studies (M Div, MA); leadership toward racial justice (M Div, MA, Certificate); Methodist studies (M Div, MA, Certificate); ministry (D Min); ministry renewal and professional development (Certificate); pastoral care and counseling (M Div, MA, MARL); religion and theology (MA); theological and religious studies (Certificate); theology and the arts (M Div, MA); urban ministry (M Div, MA, MARL); women's studies: religion, theology and ministry (M Div, MA). *Accreditation:* ACIPE; ATS. Part-time and evening/weekend programs available. *Degree requirements:* For master's, thesis; for doctorate, comprehensive exam, thesis/dissertation. *Entrance requirements:* For master's, minimum GPA of 2.75; strong analytical, reflective thinking and writing skills; vocational and academic goals compatible with those of Seminary; for doctorate, M Div or equivalent, minimum GPA of 3.0, 3 years experience in professional ministry; for other advanced degree, BA or equivalent life experience; strong analytical, reflective thinking and writing skills (Certificate); proficiency in English language, previous study of theology at a theological school, recommendation of student's denomination (Diploma). Additional exam requirements/recommendations for international students: Required—TOEFL (minimum score 550 paper-based).

Université de Montréal, Faculty of Theology and Sciences of Religions, Montréal, QC H3C 3J7, Canada. Offers health, spirituality and bioethics (DESS); practical theology (MA, PhD); religious sciences (MA, PhD); theology (MA, D Th, PhD, L Th); theology-Biblical studies (PhD). *Degree requirements:* For master's, one foreign language; for doctorate, 2 foreign languages, thesis/dissertation, general exam. Electronic applications accepted.

Université de Sherbrooke, Faculty of Theology and Religious Studies, Sherbrooke, QC J1K 2R1, Canada. Offers applied ethics (Diploma); human science of religions (MA); intercultural training (Diploma); philosophy (MA, PhD); spiritual anthropology (Diploma); theology (MA, PhD, Diploma). Part-time and evening/weekend programs available. Postbaccalaureate distance learning degree programs offered. Terminal master's awarded for partial completion of doctoral program. *Entrance requirements:* For master's, bachelor's degree in related discipline; for doctorate, master's degree in related discipline. *Faculty research:* Faith and culture interrelation.

Université du Québec à Chicoutimi, Graduate Programs, Program in Theology (Pastoral Studies), Chicoutimi, QC G7H 2B1, Canada. Offers MA, PhD. Programs offered jointly with Université de Montréal. Part-time programs available. *Degree requirements:* For doctorate, thesis/dissertation. *Entrance requirements:* For master's, appropriate bachelor's degree, proficiency in French; for doctorate, appropriate master's degree, proficiency in French.

Université Laval, Faculty of Theology and Religious Sciences, Program in Practical Theology, Québec, QC G1K 7P4, Canada. Offers D Th P. Part-time programs available. *Degree requirements:* For doctorate, comprehensive exam, thesis/dissertation. *Entrance requirements:* For doctorate, knowledge of French and English. Electronic applications accepted.

Université Laval, Faculty of Theology and Religious Sciences, Programs in Theology, Québec, QC G1K 7P4, Canada. Offers MA, PhD. Terminal master's awarded for partial completion of doctoral program. *Degree requirements:* For master's, thesis (for some programs); for doctorate, comprehensive exam, thesis/dissertation. *Entrance requirements:* For master's and doctorate, knowledge of French, comprehension of written English. Electronic applications accepted.

University of Chicago, Divinity School, PhD Program, Chicago, IL 60637. Offers anthropology and sociology of religions (PhD); bible (PhD); history of Christianity (PhD); history of Judaism (PhD); history of religions (PhD); Islamic studies (PhD); philosophy of religions (PhD); religion and literature (PhD); religions in America (PhD); religious ethics (PhD); theology (PhD). *Students:* 164 full-time (50 women); includes 18 minority (5 Black or African American, non-Hispanic/Latino; 8 Asian, non-Hispanic/Latino; 1 Hispanic/Latino; 4 Two or more races, non-Hispanic/Latino), 28 international. 185 applicants, 12% accepted, 18 enrolled. *Degree requirements:* For doctorate, 2 foreign languages, comprehensive exam, thesis/dissertation. *Entrance requirements:* For doctorate, GRE General Test. Additional exam requirements/recommendations for international students: Required—TOEFL (minimum score 600 paper-based; 104 iBT), IELTS (minimum score 7). *Application deadline:* For fall admission, 12/15 for domestic and international students. Application fee: $75. Electronic applications accepted. *Expenses: Tuition:* Full-time $46,899. *Required fees:* $347. *Financial support:* Fellowships, Federal Work-Study, institutionally sponsored loans, and scholarships/grants available. Financial award application deadline: 12/15; financial award applicants required to submit FAFSA. *Faculty research:* Anthropology and sociology of religions, history of religions, theology, religious ethics, philosophy of religions, Bible, history of Christianity/Judaism, Islamic studies, religions in America. *Unit head:* Dr. Margaret M. Mitchell, Dean/Professor of New Testament and Early Christian Literature, 773-702-8200. *Application contact:* John W. Howell, Coordinator for Recruiting and Admissions, 773-702-8249, Fax: 773-834-4581, E-mail: divinityadmissions@uchicago.edu.
Website: http://divinity.uchicago.edu/doctoral-program-phd

University of Dallas, Braniff Graduate School of Liberal Arts, Department of Theology, Irving, TX 75062-4736. Offers M Th, MA. Part-time programs available. *Degree requirements:* For master's, one foreign language, comprehensive exam, thesis (for some programs). *Entrance requirements:* For master's, GRE General Test. *Faculty research:* Patristics, justice in the Old and New Testament, Pauline literature, Christology, theology of the Trinity.

University of Dayton, Department of Religious Studies, Dayton, OH 45469. Offers pastoral ministry (MA); theological studies (MA); theology (PhD). Part-time and evening/weekend programs available. *Faculty:* 21 full-time (7 women), 9 part-time/adjunct (4 women). *Students:* 57 full-time (23 women), 7 part-time (3 women); includes 7 minority (1 Black or African American, non-Hispanic/Latino; 2 Asian, non-Hispanic/Latino; 2 Hispanic/Latino; 2 Two or more races, non-Hispanic/Latino), 2 international. Average age 34. 82 applicants, 52% accepted, 18 enrolled. In 2014, 13 master's, 7 doctorates awarded. Terminal master's awarded for partial completion of doctoral program. *Degree requirements:* For master's, thesis or alternative; for doctorate, 2 foreign languages, comprehensive exam, thesis/dissertation. *Entrance requirements:* For master's, minimum undergraduate GPA of 3.0, 3 letters of recommendation, personal statement, official transcript(s); for doctorate, GRE General Test (minimum score 600 verbal previous scale, 160 current scale), minimum GPA of 3.5, academic writing sample, 3 letters of recommendation, official transcript(s). Additional exam requirements/recommendations for international students: Required—TOEFL (minimum score 550 paper-based; 80 iBT). *Application deadline:* For fall admission, 3/1 priority date for domestic students, 5/1 priority date for international students; for winter admission, 7/1 for international students; for spring admission, 11/1 priority date for international students. Applications are processed on a rolling basis. Application fee: $0 ($50 for international students). Electronic applications accepted. *Expenses:* Expenses: Contact institution. *Financial support:* In 2014–15, 4 fellowships with full tuition reimbursements (averaging $17,600 per year), 7 research assistantships with full tuition reimbursements (averaging $10,413 per year), 16 teaching assistantships with full tuition reimbursements (averaging $17,600 per year) were awarded; career-related internships or fieldwork, institutionally sponsored loans, health care benefits, and unspecified assistantships also available. Financial award application deadline: 3/1; financial award applicants required to submit FAFSA. *Faculty research:* Practical/constructive theology, theological ethics, U.S. Catholic/Christian life and thought, methodologies in Biblical studies, religion and science. *Unit head:* Dr. Daniel Thompson, Chair, 937-229-4321, Fax: 937-229-4330. *Application contact:* Amy Doorley, Graduate Program Coordinator, 937-229-4321, Fax: 937-229-4330, E-mail: adoorley1@udayton.edu.
Website: http://www.udayton.edu/artssciences/academics/religiousstudies/welcome/index.php

University of Denver, DU-Iliff Joint PhD Program in Religious and Theological Studies, Denver, CO 80208. Offers PhD. Program jointly offered with Iliff School of Theology. Part-time programs available. *Faculty:* 13 full-time (6 women). *Students:* 34 full-time (16 women), 31 part-time (13 women); includes 13 minority (4 Black or African American, non-Hispanic/Latino; 1 American Indian or Alaska Native, non-Hispanic/Latino; 1 Asian, non-Hispanic/Latino; 5 Hispanic/Latino; 2 Two or more races, non-Hispanic/Latino). Average age 40. 39 applicants, 38% accepted, 9 enrolled. In 2014, 5 doctorates awarded. *Degree requirements:* For doctorate, one foreign language, comprehensive exam, thesis/dissertation. *Entrance requirements:* For doctorate, GRE General Test,

transcripts, three letters of recommendation, personal statement, writing sample, research paper. Additional exam requirements/recommendations for international students: Required—TOEFL (minimum score 550 paper-based; 80 iBT). *Application deadline:* For fall admission, 1/1 priority date for domestic students. Application fee: $65. Electronic applications accepted. *Expenses:* Expenses: $826 per credit. *Financial support:* In 2014–15, 32 students received support, including 10 teaching assistantships with full and partial tuition reimbursements available (averaging $3,000 per year); scholarships/grants and unspecified assistantships also available. *Faculty research:* Religion and social change, theology, philosophy and cultural theory (including comparative religious study), Biblical interpretation. *Unit head:* Dr. Greg Robbins, Director, 303-765-3232. *Application contact:* Information Contact, 303-765-3117, E-mail: jointphd@iliff.edu.
Website: http://www.du.edu/duiliffjoint/

University of Dubuque, University of Dubuque Theological Seminary, Dubuque, IA 52001. Offers M Div, MAMC, D Min. *Accreditation:* ACIPE; ATS. Postbaccalaureate distance learning degree programs offered (minimal on-campus study). *Degree requirements:* For doctorate, thesis/dissertation. *Entrance requirements:* Additional exam requirements/recommendations for international students: Recommended—TOEFL (minimum score 550 paper-based; 80 iBT). *Faculty research:* Biblical theology, reformed history and theology, pastoral theology, homiletics.

The University of Manchester, School of Arts, Histories and Cultures, Manchester, United Kingdom. Offers anthropology, media and performance (PhD); applied theatre professional (PhD); archaeology (PhD); art history and visual studies (PhD); arts management and cultural policy (PhD); classics and ancient history (PhD); composition (PhD); creative writing (PhD); drama (PhD); economic and social history (PhD); electroacoustic composition (PhD); English and American studies (PhD); history (PhD); humanitarianism and conflict response (PhD); museology (PhD); music (PhD); musicology (PhD); religions and theology (PhD).

University of Northwestern–St. Paul, Master of Arts in Theological Studies Program, St. Paul, MN 55113-1598. Offers MATS. Part-time and evening/weekend programs available. Postbaccalaureate distance learning degree programs offered (no on-campus study). *Application deadline:* Applications are processed on a rolling basis. Electronic applications accepted. *Expenses:* Expenses: $490 per credit.
Website: https://www.unwsp.edu/web/graduate-studies/master-of-arts-in-theological-studies

University of Northwestern–St. Paul, Master of Divinity Program, St. Paul, MN 55113-1598. Offers M Div. Part-time and evening/weekend programs available. Postbaccalaureate distance learning degree programs offered (no on-campus study). *Application deadline:* Applications are processed on a rolling basis. Electronic applications accepted. *Expenses:* Expenses: $490 per credit. *Application contact:* College of Adult and Graduate Studies Admissions, 651-631-5200, E-mail: gradstudies@unwsp.edu.

University of Notre Dame, Graduate School, College of Arts and Letters, Division of Humanities, Department of Theology, Notre Dame, IN 46556. Offers M Div, MA, MSM, MTS, PhD. *Accreditation:* ACIPE; ATS. Terminal master's awarded for partial completion of doctoral program. *Degree requirements:* For master's, one foreign language, comprehensive exam, thesis or alternative; for doctorate, 3 foreign languages, comprehensive exam, thesis/dissertation, candidacy exam. *Entrance requirements:* For master's and doctorate, GRE General Test. Additional exam requirements/recommendations for international students: Required—TOEFL (minimum score 600 paper-based; 80 iBT). Electronic applications accepted. *Faculty research:* Liturgy, ethics, historical studies, Biblical studies, systematic theology.

University of Notre Dame, Graduate School, College of Arts and Letters, Division of Humanities, Program in History and Philosophy of Science, Notre Dame, IN 46556. Offers history and philosophy of science (MA, PhD); theology and science (PhD). *Degree requirements:* For doctorate, 2 foreign languages, comprehensive exam, thesis/dissertation, candidacy exam. *Entrance requirements:* For doctorate, GRE General Test. Additional exam requirements/recommendations for international students: Required—TOEFL (minimum score 600 paper-based; 80 iBT). Electronic applications accepted. *Faculty research:* Philosophy of physics, science and ethics, history and philosophy of biology, history of medicine and technology, history and philosophy of economics.

University of Philosophical Research, Master's in Consciousness Studies Program, Los Angeles, CA 90027. Offers MA. *Degree requirements:* For master's, thesis. Electronic applications accepted.

University of Philosophical Research, Master's in Transformational Psychology Program, Los Angeles, CA 90027. Offers MA. *Degree requirements:* For master's, thesis. Electronic applications accepted.

University of Saint Francis, Graduate School, Department of Philosophy and Theology, Fort Wayne, IN 46808-3994. Offers theology (MA). Part-time and evening/weekend programs available. *Faculty:* 3 full-time (0 women), 1 (woman) part-time/adjunct. *Students:* 5 part-time (2 women); includes 1 minority (Hispanic/Latino). Average age 48. 2 applicants, 100% accepted, 1 enrolled. In 2014, 2 master's awarded. *Degree requirements:* For master's, comprehensive exam, thesis or alternative. *Entrance requirements:* For master's, GRE, theology placement exam, minimum undergraduate GPA of 3.0, writing sample, interview with program director. Additional exam requirements/recommendations for international students: Required—TOEFL or IELTS. *Application deadline:* For fall admission, 7/1 for domestic students; for spring admission, 11/1 for domestic students. Applications are processed on a rolling basis. Application fee: $0. Electronic applications accepted. *Expenses:* Expenses: $830 per credit hour. *Financial support:* In 2014–15, 1 student received support. Federal Work-Study, scholarships/grants, and unspecified assistantships available. Support available to part-time students. Financial award application deadline: 3/10; financial award applicants required to submit FAFSA. *Unit head:* Dr. Adam DeVille, Associate Professor/Chair of Department of Philosophy and Theology, 260-399-7700 Ext. 8120, Fax: 260-399-8172, E-mail: adeville@sf.edu. *Application contact:* Kyle Richardson, Enrollment Specialist, 260-399-7700 Ext. 6310, Fax: 260-399-8152, E-mail: krichardson@sf.edu.
Website: http://philosophy.sf.edu/

University of Saint Mary of the Lake–Mundelein Seminary, Graduate and Professional Programs, Mundelein, IL 60060. Offers liturgical studies (MA); ministry (D Min); pastoral studies (MA); theology (M Div). *Accreditation:* ATS (one or more programs are accredited). *Faculty:* 42 full-time (7 women), 19 part-time/adjunct (7 women). *Students:* 266 full-time (8 women); includes 10 minority (2 Black or African American, non-Hispanic/Latino; 3 Asian, non-Hispanic/Latino; 5 Hispanic/Latino), 78 international. *Degree requirements:* For doctorate, thesis/dissertation. *Entrance requirements:* For master's and doctorate, bachelor's degree. Additional exam requirements/recommendations for international students: Required—TOEFL. *Application deadline:* Applications are processed on a rolling basis. Application fee: $0. Electronic applications accepted. *Expenses:* *Tuition:* Full-time $23,520; part-time $940 per credit. *Required fees:* $300. One-time fee: $50 full-time. *Financial support:* Career-related internships or fieldwork available. *Unit head:* Very Rev. Thomas A. Baima, Dean of the Seminary and Graduate School, 847-566-6401. *Application contact:* Very Rev. Robert Barron, Rector-President, 847-566-6401, Fax: 847-566-7330.

University of St. Michael's College, Faculty of Theology, Toronto, ON M5S 1J4, Canada. Offers Catholic leadership (MA); eastern Christian studies (Diploma); religious education (Diploma); theological studies (Diploma); theology (M Div, MA, MRE, MTS, D Min, PhD, Th D); theology and Jewish studies (MA). Th D offered jointly with University of Toronto. *Accreditation:* ATS (one or more programs are accredited). Part-time programs available. *Degree requirements:* For master's, thesis (for some programs), 1 foreign language (MA), 2 foreign languages (Th M); for doctorate, 3 foreign languages, comprehensive exam, thesis/dissertation; for other advanced degree, thesis optional. *Entrance requirements:* For master's, M Div or BA, course work in an ancient or modern language, minimum GPA of 3.3; for doctorate, MA in theology, Th M, or M Div with thesis, minimum GPA of 3.7; for other advanced degree, minimum GPA of 2.7. Additional exam requirements/recommendations for international students: Required—TOEFL (minimum score 600 paper-based). Electronic applications accepted. *Expenses:* Contact institution. *Faculty research:* Patristics, eastern Christianity, ecology and theology, ecumenism, Jewish Christian studies.

University of St. Thomas, Graduate Studies, The Saint Paul Seminary School of Divinity, St. Paul, MN 55105. Offers pastoral ministry (MAPM); religious education (MARE); theology (MA). *Accreditation:* ACIPE; ATS. Part-time and evening/weekend programs available. *Degree requirements:* For master's, one foreign language, comprehensive exam (for some programs), thesis (for some programs). *Entrance requirements:* For master's, GRE, 3 letters of recommendation, interview. Additional exam requirements/recommendations for international students: Required—TOEFL (minimum score 550 paper-based). Electronic applications accepted. *Expenses:* Contact institution. *Faculty research:* Theological education.

University of St. Thomas, School of Theology, Houston, TX 77006. Offers divinity (M Div); pastoral studies (MAPS); theological studies (MA). *Accreditation:* ATS. Part-time programs available. *Faculty:* 8 full-time (4 women), 7 part-time/adjunct (1 woman). *Students:* 84 full-time (11 women), 86 part-time (26 women); includes 78 minority (7 Black or African American, non-Hispanic/Latino; 31 Asian, non-Hispanic/Latino; 36 Hispanic/Latino; 4 Two or more races, non-Hispanic/Latino), 15 international. Average age 35. 44 applicants, 100% accepted, 32 enrolled. In 2014, 57 master's awarded. *Degree requirements:* For master's, variable foreign language requirement, comprehensive exam. *Entrance requirements:* For master's, BA, BS or equivalent; personal essay (for some programs); undergraduate philosophy or theology courses; 2 letters of recommendation. Additional exam requirements/recommendations for international students: Required—TOEFL (minimum score 550 paper-based; 79 iBT). *Application deadline:* Applications are processed on a rolling basis. Application fee: $10. Electronic applications accepted. *Expenses:* Expenses: Contact institution. *Financial support:* In 2014–15, 14 students received support. Scholarships/grants available. Support available to part-time students. Financial award application deadline: 4/15; financial award applicants required to submit FAFSA. *Unit head:* Dr. Sandra C. Magie, Dean, 713-686-4345 Ext. 242, Fax: 713-683-8673, E-mail: smagie@stthom.edu. *Application contact:* Connie M. Henry, Office Manager, 713-686-4345 Ext. 231, Fax: 713-683-8673, E-mail: sms@stthom.edu.
Website: http://www.stthom.edu/Academics/School_of_Theology_at_St_Marys_Seminary/Index.aqf

The University of Scranton, College of Graduate and Continuing Education, Program in Theology, Scranton, PA 18510. Offers MA. Part-time and evening/weekend programs available. *Faculty:* 14 full-time (5 women). *Students:* 5 full-time (2 women), 3 part-time (0 women). Average age 32. 5 applicants, 60% accepted. In 2014, 4 master's awarded. *Degree requirements:* For master's, thesis (for some programs), capstone experience. *Entrance requirements:* For master's, minimum GPA of 3.0. Additional exam requirements/recommendations for international students: Required—TOEFL (minimum score 500 paper-based), IELTS (minimum score 6). *Application deadline:* Applications are processed on a rolling basis. Application fee: $0. *Expenses:* Expenses: Contact institution. *Financial support:* In 2014–15, 2 students received support, including 2 teaching assistantships with partial tuition reimbursements available (averaging $4,400 per year); career-related internships or fieldwork, Federal Work-Study, and unspecified assistantships also available. Support available to part-time students. Financial award application deadline: 3/1. *Unit head:* Dr. Charles R. Pinches, Chair, 570-941-4302, Fax: 570-941-6369, E-mail: pinchesc1@scranton.edu. *Application contact:* Joseph M. Roback, Director of Admissions, 570-941-4385, Fax: 570-941-5928, E-mail: robackj2@scranton.edu.
Website: http://www.scranton.edu/academics/cas/theology/masters-program.shtml

University of South Africa, College of Human Sciences, Pretoria, South Africa. Offers adult education (M Ed); African languages (MA, PhD); African politics (MA, PhD); Afrikaans (MA, PhD); ancient history (MA, PhD); ancient Near Eastern studies (MA, PhD); anthropology (MA, PhD); applied linguistics (MA); Arabic (MA, PhD); archaeology (MA); art history (MA); Biblical archaeology (MA); Biblical studies (M Th, D Th, PhD); Christian spirituality (M Th, D Th); church history (M Th, D Th); classical studies (MA, PhD); clinical psychology (MA); communication (MA, PhD); comparative education (M Ed, Ed D); consulting psychology (D Admin, D Com, PhD); curriculum studies (M Ed, Ed D); development studies (M Admin, MA, D Admin, PhD); didactics (M Ed, Ed D); education (M Tech); education management (M Ed, Ed D); educational psychology (M Ed); English (MA); environmental education (M Ed); French (MA, PhD); German (MA, PhD); Greek (MA); guidance and counseling (M Ed); health studies (MA, PhD), including health sciences education (MA), health services management (MA), medical and surgical nursing science (critical care general) (MA), midwifery and neonatal nursing science (MA), trauma and emergency care (MA); history (MA, PhD); history of education (Ed D); inclusive education (M Ed, Ed D); information and communications technology policy and regulation (MA); information science (MA, MIS, PhD); international politics (MA, PhD); Islamic studies (MA, PhD); Italian (MA, PhD); Judaica (MA, PhD); linguistics (MA, PhD); mathematical education (M Ed); mathematics education (MA); missiology (M Th, D Th); modern Hebrew (MA, PhD); musicology (MA, MMus, D Mus, PhD); natural science education (M Ed); New Testament (M Th, D Th); Old Testament (D Th); pastoral therapy (M Th, D Th); philosophy (MA); philosophy of education (M Ed, Ed D); politics (MA, PhD); Portuguese (MA, PhD); practical theology (M Th, D Th); psychology (MA, MS, PhD); psychology of education (M Ed, Ed D); public health (MA); religious studies (MA, D Th, PhD); Romance languages (MA); Russian (MA, PhD); Semitic languages (MA, PhD); social behavior studies in HIV/AIDS (MA); social science (mental health) (MA); social science in development studies (MA); social science in psychology (MA); social science in social work (MA); social science in sociology (MA); social work (MSW, DSW, PhD); socio-education (M Ed, Ed D); sociolinguistics (MA); sociology (MA, PhD); Spanish (MA, PhD); systematic theology (M Th, D Th); TESOL (teaching English to speakers of other languages) (MA); theological ethics (M Th, D Th); theory of literature (MA, PhD); urban ministries (D Th); urban ministry (M Th).

University of the West, Program in Buddhist Chaplaincy, Rosemead, CA 91770. Offers M Div. *Entrance requirements:* Additional exam requirements/recommendations for international students: Required—TOEFL (minimum score 550 paper-based; 79 iBT); Recommended—IELTS.

Theology

University of Valley Forge, Program in Theology, Phoenixville, PA 19460. Offers MA. *Degree requirements:* For master's, project.

The University of Winnipeg, Faculty of Theology, Winnipeg, MB R3B 2E9, Canada. Offers marriage and family therapy (MMFT, Certificate); sacred theology (STM); theology (M Div). *Accreditation:* AAMFT/COAMFTE; ATS. Part-time programs available.

Urshan Graduate School of Theology, Graduate Programs, Florissant, MO 63031. Offers M Div, MACM, MTS. Postbaccalaureate distance learning degree programs offered (minimal on-campus study). *Degree requirements:* For master's, capstone project (for MACM and MTS); portfolio (for M Div).

Ursuline College, School of Graduate Studies, Graduate Program in Ministry, Pepper Pike, OH 44124-4398. Offers MA. Part-time programs available. *Faculty:* 3 full-time (all women). *Students:* 11 part-time (10 women); includes 2 minority (both Black or African American, non-Hispanic/Latino). Average age 50. 9 applicants, 67% accepted, 5 enrolled. In 2014, 4 master's awarded. *Degree requirements:* For master's, thesis. *Entrance requirements:* For master's, minimum undergraduate GPA of 3.0, interview. Additional exam requirements/recommendations for international students: Required—TOEFL (minimum score 500 paper-based). *Application deadline:* For fall admission, 8/1 priority date for domestic students. Applications are processed on a rolling basis. Application fee: $25. *Expenses:* Expenses: Contact institution. *Financial support:* In 2014–15, 11 students received support. Federal Work-Study available. Financial award application deadline: 3/1; financial award applicants required to submit FAFSA. *Unit head:* Dr. Linda Martin, Co-Director, 440-646-8191, Fax: 440-684-6088, E-mail: lmartin@ursuline.edu. *Application contact:* Stephanie Pratt, Graduate Admission Coordinator, 440-646-8119, Fax: 440-684-6138, E-mail: graduateadmissions@ursuline.edu.

Valparaiso University, Graduate School, Programs in Liberal Studies, Concentration in Theology, Valparaiso, IN 46383. Offers MALS, Post-Master's Certificate, JD/MALS. Part-time and evening/weekend programs available. *Students:* 2 full-time (both women), 1 part-time (0 women). Average age 26. *Entrance requirements:* For master's, minimum GPA of 3.0. Additional exam requirements/recommendations for international students: Required—TOEFL (minimum score 550 paper-based; 80 iBT), IELTS (minimum score 6). *Application deadline:* Applications are processed on a rolling basis. Application fee: $30 ($50 for international students). Electronic applications accepted. *Expenses:* Tuition: Full-time $10,710; part-time $595 per credit hour. *Required fees:* $378; $101 per term. Tuition and fees vary according to course load and program. *Financial support:* Available to part-time students. Applicants required to submit FAFSA. *Unit head:* Dr. Jennifer A. Ziegler, Dean, Graduate School and Continuing Education, 219-464-5313, Fax: 219-464-5381, E-mail: jennifer.ziegler@valpo.edu. *Application contact:* Jessica Choquette, Graduate Admissions Specialist, 219-464-5313, Fax: 219-464-5381, E-mail: jessica.choquette@valpo.edu. Website: http://www.valpo.edu/grad/mals/theo.php

Valparaiso University, Graduate School, Programs in Liberal Studies, Concentration in Theology and Ministry, Valparaiso, IN 46383. Offers MALS, Post-Master's Certificate. Part-time and evening/weekend programs available. *Entrance requirements:* For master's, minimum GPA of 3.0. Additional exam requirements/recommendations for international students: Required—TOEFL (minimum score 550 paper-based; 80 iBT), IELTS (minimum score 6). *Application deadline:* Applications are processed on a rolling basis. Application fee: $30 ($50 for international students). Electronic applications accepted. *Expenses:* Tuition: Full-time $10,710; part-time $595 per credit hour. *Required fees:* $378; $101 per term. Tuition and fees vary according to course load and program. *Financial support:* Available to part-time students. Applicants required to submit FAFSA. *Unit head:* Dr. Jennifer A. Ziegler, Dean, Graduate School and Continuing Education, 219-464-5313, Fax: 219-464-5381, E-mail: jennifer.ziegler@valpo.edu. *Application contact:* Jessica Choquette, Graduate Admissions Specialist, 219-464-5313, Fax: 219-464-5381, E-mail: jessica.choquette@valpo.edu. Website: http://www.valpo.edu/grad/mals/theo.php

Vancouver School of Theology, Graduate and Professional Programs, Vancouver, BC V6T 1L4, Canada. Offers indigenous and inter-religious studies (MA, Th M); theological studies (MATS, Diploma); theology (M Div, Th M). *Accreditation:* ATS. Part-time programs available. Postbaccalaureate distance learning degree programs offered (minimal on-campus study). *Degree requirements:* For master's, comprehensive exam (for some programs), thesis (for some programs); for Diploma, one foreign language, thesis. *Entrance requirements:* Additional exam requirements/recommendations for international students: Required—TOEFL (minimum score 80 paper-based); Recommended—IELTS (minimum score 6.5). Electronic applications accepted. *Faculty research:* Old Testament studies, pastoral theology, New Testament studies, field education, church history, systematic theology, spirituality.

Vanderbilt University, Divinity School, Nashville, TN 37240. Offers M Div, MTS, JD/M Div, JD/MTS, MBA/M Div, MBA/MTS, MD/M Div, MD/MTS, MSN/M Div, MSN/MTS. *Accreditation:* ACIPE; ATS. Part-time programs available. *Entrance requirements:* Additional exam requirements/recommendations for international students: Required—TOEFL (minimum score 600 paper-based; 95 iBT), IELTS (minimum score 7). Electronic applications accepted. *Expenses:* Tuition: Full-time $42,768; part-time $1782 per credit hour. *Required fees:* $422. One-time fee: $30 full-time.

Vanguard University of Southern California, Graduate Programs in Religion, Costa Mesa, CA 92626-9601. Offers leadership studies (MA); theological studies (MTS). Part-time and evening/weekend programs available. *Degree requirements:* For master's, comprehensive exam (for some programs), thesis (for some programs). *Entrance requirements:* For master's, minimum GPA of 3.0 (MA), 2.5 (MTS). Additional exam requirements/recommendations for international students: Required—TOEFL (minimum score 550 paper-based; 79 iBT). Electronic applications accepted. *Expenses:* Contact institution. *Faculty research:* Narrative theology, ecumenism and Pentecost, leadership studies.

Victoria University, Emmanuel College, Toronto, ON M5S 1K7, Canada. Offers M Div, MA, MPS, MRE, MSMus, MTS, Th M, D Min, PhD, Th D, Certificate, Diploma, L Th, M Div/MA, M Div/MPS, M Div/MRE. M Div, MRE, Th M, Th D, M Div/MA, M Div/MRE, M Div/MPS offered jointly with University of Toronto; MA, PhD with University of St. Michael's College. *Accreditation:* ATS. Terminal master's awarded for partial completion of doctoral program. *Degree requirements:* For master's, variable foreign language requirement, thesis (for some programs); for doctorate, 2 foreign languages, thesis/dissertation. *Entrance requirements:* For master's and other advanced degree, BA, BSc; for doctorate, MDiv, MA, MTS, ThM. Additional exam requirements/recommendations for international students: Required—TOEFL (minimum score 600 paper-based; 100 iBT), IELTS (minimum score 7), TWE (minimum score 5). Electronic applications accepted. *Faculty research:* New Testament and Old Testament hermeneutics, religious symbolism, Reformation, liberation theology, Canadian church history.

Villanova University, Graduate School of Liberal Arts and Sciences, Department of Theology, Villanova, PA 19085-1699. Offers MA. Part-time and evening/weekend programs available. *Faculty:* 13. *Students:* 25 full-time (11 women), 13 part-time (3 women); includes 3 minority (all Hispanic/Latino), 3 international. Average age 37. 14 applicants, 93% accepted, 9 enrolled. In 2014, 14 master's awarded. *Degree requirements:* For master's, one foreign language, comprehensive exam, thesis optional. *Entrance requirements:* For master's, GRE, minimum GPA of 3.0, statement of goals, 3 recommendation letters. Additional exam requirements/recommendations for international students: Required—TOEFL. *Application deadline:* For fall admission, 3/1 for domestic students, 5/1 priority date for international students; for spring admission, 11/15 for domestic students, 10/15 for international students; for summer admission, 5/1 for domestic students. Applications are processed on a rolling basis. Application fee: $50. Electronic applications accepted. *Financial support:* Research assistantships, teaching assistantships, scholarships/grants, and unspecified assistantships available. Financial award applicants required to submit FAFSA. *Unit head:* Dr. Timothy Brunk, Director, 610-519-3052. Website: http://www1.villanova.edu/villanova/artsci/theology/graduate.html

Virginia Beach Theological Seminary, Graduate Programs, Virginia Beach, VA 23464. Offers M Div, MBS, Th M. *Entrance requirements:* For master's, GRE, interview, minimum cumulative GPA of 2.4, church endorsement, 4 recommendations. Electronic applications accepted.

Virginia Theological Seminary, Graduate and Professional Programs, Alexandria, VA 22304. Offers M Div, MACE, MTS, D Min. *Accreditation:* ATS. Part-time programs available. *Degree requirements:* For master's, 2 foreign languages, thesis; for doctorate, thesis/dissertation. *Entrance requirements:* For master's and doctorate, GRE General Test.

Virginia Union University, Samuel DeWitt Proctor School of Theology, Richmond, VA 23220-1170. Offers M Div, D Min. *Accreditation:* ACIPE; ATS. Part-time and evening/weekend programs available. *Entrance requirements:* Additional exam requirements/recommendations for international students: Required—TOEFL.

Walsh University, Graduate Studies, Master of Arts in Theology Program, North Canton, OH 44720-3396. Offers parish administration (MA); pastoral ministry (MA); religious education (MA). Part-time and evening/weekend programs available. *Faculty:* 3 full-time (0 women). *Students:* 4 full-time (0 women), 12 part-time (8 women); includes 1 minority (Black or African American, non-Hispanic/Latino), 3 international. Average age 44. 6 applicants, 50% accepted, 3 enrolled. In 2014, 4 master's awarded. *Degree requirements:* For master's, thesis or alternative, culminating assignment. *Entrance requirements:* For master's, MAT or GRE (minimum scores: Verbal 145, Quantitative 146, Combined 291, Writing 3.0), minimum GPA of 3.0. Additional exam requirements/recommendations for international students: Required—TOEFL. *Application deadline:* For fall admission, 7/15 for domestic students. Applications are processed on a rolling basis. Application fee: $25. Electronic applications accepted. *Expenses:* Tuition: Full-time $11,250; part-time $625 per semester hour. Full-time tuition and fees vary according to program. *Financial support:* In 2014–15, 1 student received support, including 1 research assistantship (averaging $3,744 per year); scholarships/grants and unspecified assistantships also available. Financial award application deadline: 12/31; financial award applicants required to submit FAFSA. *Faculty research:* Historical theology, systematic theology, theological anthropology, existential phenomenology, Cardinal Newman, Second Temple Jerusalem, Mark's gospel, Deuterocanonical literature, Josephus, philosophical theology, phenomenology, hermeneutics, relationship between material and spiritual being, evolutionary theory, phenomenology of the sacrament, Edith Stein, Emmanual Levinas, Paul Ricoeur, Jean-Luc Marion. *Unit head:* Dr. Chris Seeman, Chair, 330-244-4665, Fax: 330-244-4955, E-mail: cseeman@walsh.edu. *Application contact:* Audra Dice, Graduate Admissions Counselor, 330-490-7181, Fax: 330-244-4925, E-mail: adice@walsh.edu.

Wartburg Theological Seminary, Graduate and Professional Programs, Dubuque, IA 52004-5004. Offers diaconal ministry (MA); ministry (M Div); theology (MA). *Accreditation:* ACIPE; ATS. Postbaccalaureate distance learning degree programs offered (minimal on-campus study). *Faculty:* 14 full-time (5 women), 9 part-time/adjunct (4 women). *Students:* 116 full-time (64 women), 7 part-time (4 women); includes 14 minority (5 Black or African American, non-Hispanic/Latino; 1 American Indian or Alaska Native, non-Hispanic/Latino; 1 Asian, non-Hispanic/Latino; 2 Hispanic/Latino; 5 Two or more races, non-Hispanic/Latino), 1 international. Average age 38. 35 applicants, 89% accepted, 25 enrolled. In 2014, 30 master's awarded. *Degree requirements:* For master's, thesis (for some programs). *Entrance requirements:* For master's, minimum GPA of 3.0 (STM). Additional exam requirements/recommendations for international students: Required—TOEFL (minimum score 500 paper-based; 80 iBT). *Application deadline:* For fall admission, 5/15 priority date for domestic students, 10/1 priority date for international students; for winter admission, 10/1 for international students; for spring admission, 12/15 priority date for domestic students, 10/1 for international students. Applications are processed on a rolling basis. Application fee: $0. Electronic applications accepted. *Expenses:* Tuition: Full-time $15,400; part-time $735 per semester hour. *Required fees:* $554; $50 per semester. Tuition and fees vary according to course load. *Financial support:* In 2014–15, 87 students received support, including 12 research assistantships (averaging $1,238 per year); career-related internships or fieldwork, Federal Work-Study, institutionally sponsored loans, and scholarships/grants also available. Support available to part-time students. Financial award application deadline: 6/15; financial award applicants required to submit FAFSA. *Unit head:* Rev. Dr. Craig L. Nessan, Academic Dean, 563-589-0207, Fax: 563-589-0333. *Application contact:* Rev. Karla Wildberger, Director of Admissions, 563-589-0203, Fax: 563-589-0333, E-mail: admissions@wartburgseminary.edu. Website: http://www.wartburgseminary.edu/

Wayland Baptist University, Graduate Programs, Programs in Religion, Plainview, TX 79072-6998. Offers Christian ministry (MCM); divinity (M Div); religion (MA). Part-time and evening/weekend programs available. Postbaccalaureate distance learning degree programs offered (no on-campus study). *Faculty:* 15 full-time (1 woman), 12 part-time/adjunct (0 women). *Students:* 1 full-time (0 women), 99 part-time (23 women); includes 51 minority (25 Black or African American, non-Hispanic/Latino; 1 American Indian or Alaska Native, non-Hispanic/Latino; 4 Asian, non-Hispanic/Latino; 17 Hispanic/Latino; 1 Native Hawaiian or other Pacific Islander, non-Hispanic/Latino; 3 Two or more races, non-Hispanic/Latino). Average age 43. 45 applicants, 60% accepted, 12 enrolled. In 2014, 16 master's awarded. *Degree requirements:* For master's, comprehensive exam. *Entrance requirements:* For master's, GRE or MAT, minimum GPA of 3.0; letter of endorsement from Christian congregation, one academic and one personal letter of recommendation (for M Div). Additional exam requirements/recommendations for international students: Required—TOEFL (minimum score 500 paper-based; 61 iBT). *Application deadline:* Applications are processed on a rolling basis. Application fee: $50. Electronic applications accepted. *Expenses:* Tuition: Full-time $8910; part-time $495 per credit hour. *Required fees:* $970; $495 per credit hour. $485 per semester. *Financial support:* Federal Work-Study, institutionally sponsored loans, and scholarships/grants available. Support available to part-time students. Financial award application deadline: 5/1; financial award applicants required to submit FAFSA. *Unit head:* Dr. Paul Sadler, Chairman, 806-291-1160, Fax: 806-291-1969, E-mail: sadlerp@wbu.edu. *Application contact:* Amanda Stanton, Coordinator of Graduate Studies, 806-291-3423, Fax: 806-291-1950, E-mail: stanton@wbu.edu.

Wesley Biblical Seminary, Graduate Programs, Jackson, MS 39206. Offers apologetics (MA); Biblical languages (M Div); Biblical literature (MA); Christian studies (MA); context and mission (M Div); honors research (M Div); interpretation (M Div);

ministry (M Div); spiritual formation (M Div); teaching (M Div); theology (MA). *Accreditation:* ATS. Part-time programs available. *Degree requirements:* For master's, thesis. *Entrance requirements:* Additional exam requirements/recommendations for international students: Required—TOEFL. Electronic applications accepted. *Faculty research:* Patristics, missiology, culture, hermeneutics.

Wesley Theological Seminary, Graduate and Professional Programs, Washington, DC 20016-5690. Offers M Div, MA, MTS, D Min, M Div/MA, M Div/MTS. *Accreditation:* ACIPE; ATS. Part-time programs available. *Degree requirements:* For master's, thesis; for doctorate, thesis/dissertation. *Entrance requirements:* For master's, minimum GPA of 2.7; for doctorate, minimum GPA of 3.0.

Western Seminary, Graduate Programs, Master of Divinity Program, Portland, OR 97215-3367. Offers M Div. *Entrance requirements:* Additional exam requirements/ recommendations for international students: Required—TOEFL.

Western Seminary, Graduate Programs, Program in Biblical and Theological Studies, Portland, OR 97215-3367. Offers biblical and theological studies (MA, G Dip); biblical studies (Certificate); theology (Th M). *Accreditation:* ATS. Part-time and evening/ weekend programs available. *Degree requirements:* For master's, thesis or alternative, practicum. *Entrance requirements:* Additional exam requirements/recommendations for international students: Required—TOEFL.

Western Seminary–Sacramento Campus, Graduate Certificate Programs, Sacramento, CA 95821. Offers Bible (Graduate Certificate); coaching (Graduate Certificate); pastoral care to women (Graduate Certificate); theology (Graduate Certificate); youth and family (Graduate Certificate). Postbaccalaureate distance learning degree programs offered. *Entrance requirements:* For degree, essays, undergraduate transcripts, 4 recommendations. Additional exam requirements/ recommendations for international students: Required—TOEFL.

Western Seminary–Sacramento Campus, Graduate Diploma Programs, Sacramento, CA 95821. Offers Bible and theology (Graduate Diploma); ministry (Graduate Diploma); pastoral care to women (Graduate Diploma). *Entrance requirements:* For degree, essays, undergraduate transcripts, 4 recommendations. Additional exam requirements/ recommendations for international students: Required—TOEFL.

Western Seminary–Sacramento Campus, Master of Divinity Program, Sacramento, CA 95821. Offers M Div. *Entrance requirements:* Additional exam requirements/ recommendations for international students: Required—TOEFL.

Western Seminary–Sacramento Campus, Program in Biblical and Theological Studies, Sacramento, CA 95821. Offers MA. *Entrance requirements:* For master's, essays, undergraduate transcripts, 4 recommendations. Additional exam requirements/ recommendations for international students: Required—TOEFL.

Western Seminary–San Jose Campus, Graduate Programs, Los Gatos, CA 95032-4520. Offers Bible and theology (Graduate Diploma); Bible, camp and conference ministry (CGS); Biblical and theological studies (MA), including exegetical track, theological track; coaching (CGS); expositional ministry (M Div); marital and family therapy (MA); ministry (Graduate Diploma); ministry and leadership (MA), including camp and conference ministry, coaching, pastoral care to women, youth ministry; pastoral care to women (CGS, Graduate Diploma); pastoral ministry (M Div); theology (CGS); youth and family (CGS). Part-time and evening/weekend programs available. Postbaccalaureate distance learning degree programs offered (minimal on-campus study). *Entrance requirements:* For master's, minimum GPA of 3.0. Electronic applications accepted.

Western Theological Seminary, Graduate and Professional Programs, Holland, MI 49423-3622. Offers Christian ministry (MACM); divinity (M Div); ministry (D Min); theology (M Th); urban pastoral ministry (Graduate Certificate); M Div/MSW. *Accreditation:* ACIPE; ATS. Part-time programs available. Postbaccalaureate distance learning degree programs offered (minimal on-campus study). *Faculty:* 17 full-time (4 women), 23 part-time/adjunct (4 women). *Students:* 187 full-time (58 women), 88 part-time (35 women); includes 32 minority (12 Black or African American, non-Hispanic/ Latino; 10 Asian, non-Hispanic/Latino; 7 Hispanic/Latino; 3 Two or more races, non-Hispanic/Latino), 11 international. In 2014, 35 master's, 1 doctorate awarded. *Degree requirements:* For doctorate, 2 foreign languages, thesis/dissertation. *Entrance requirements:* Additional exam requirements/recommendations for international students: Required—TOEFL. *Application deadline:* For fall admission, 4/1 priority date for domestic students. Applications are processed on a rolling basis. Application fee: $50. *Expenses: Tuition:* Full-time $13,120; part-time $410 per credit. *Required fees:* $90. One-time fee: $90 part-time. *Financial support:* Career-related internships or fieldwork, institutionally sponsored loans, and scholarships/grants available. Support available to part-time students. Financial award applicants required to submit FAFSA. *Unit head:* Dr. Timothy Brown, President, 616-392-8555 Ext. 137, Fax: 616-392-7717, E-mail: tim.brown@westernsem.edu. *Application contact:* Mark Poppen, Director of Admissions, 616-392-8555, Fax: 616-392-7717, E-mail: mark@westernsem.edu.
Website: http://www.westernsem.edu/

Westminster Seminary California, Programs in Theology, Escondido, CA 92027-4128. Offers Biblical studies (MA); historical theology (MA); theological studies (M Div, MA). *Accreditation:* ATS. Part-time and evening/weekend programs available. *Degree requirements:* For master's, 2 foreign languages, thesis (for some programs). *Entrance requirements:* For master's, 2 letters of reference. Additional exam requirements/ recommendations for international students: Required—TOEFL (minimum score 570 paper-based; 89 iBT), TWE (minimum score 4.5). *Faculty research:* Neo-paganism, New Testament background, eschatology, Protestant scholasticism, Ezekiel.

Westminster Theological Seminary, Graduate and Professional Programs, Philadelphia, PA 19118. Offers apologetics (Th M); Biblical and urban studies (Certificate); Biblical counseling (MA); biblical studies (MAR); Christian studies (Certificate); church history (Th M); counseling (M Div); general studies (M Div, MAR); hermeneutics and Bible interpretations (PhD); historical and theological studies (PhD); historical theology (Th M); New Testament (Th M); Old Testament (Th M); pastoral counseling (D Min); pastoral ministry (M Div, D Min); systematic theology (Th M); theological studies (MAR); urban missions (M Div, MA, MAR, D Min). *Accreditation:* ATS. Part-time programs available. Terminal master's awarded for partial completion of doctoral program. *Degree requirements:* For master's, thesis (for some programs); for doctorate, 4 foreign languages, comprehensive exam (for some programs), thesis/ dissertation. *Entrance requirements:* For doctorate, GRE General Test. Additional exam requirements/recommendations for international students: Required—TOEFL, TWE.

Wheaton College, Graduate School, Department of Biblical and Theological Studies, Wheaton, IL 60187-5593. Offers Biblical and theological studies (PhD); Biblical archaeology (MA); Biblical exegesis (MA); Biblical studies (MA); general theological studies (MA); historical and systematic theology (MA), including biblical and theological studies; history of Christianity (MA), including Biblical and theological studies. Part-time programs available. *Students:* 64 full-time (13 women), 64 part-time (28 women); includes 10 minority (6 Asian, non-Hispanic/Latino; 3 Hispanic/Latino; 1 Two or more races, non-Hispanic/Latino), 12 international. Average age 33. 159 applicants, 72% accepted, 68 enrolled. In 2014, 48 master's, 9 doctorates awarded. *Degree requirements:* For doctorate, thesis/dissertation. *Entrance requirements:* For master's, GRE General Test. Additional exam requirements/recommendations for international students: Required—TOEFL (minimum score 550 paper-based; 80 iBT), IELTS (minimum score 6.5), TOEFL (minimum score 600 paper-based; 90 iBT) or IELTS (minimum score 7.5) for PhD. *Application deadline:* For fall admission, 1/1 priority date for domestic students, 1/1 for international students; for spring admission, 11/1 for domestic students. Applications are processed on a rolling basis. Application fee: $30. Electronic applications accepted. *Financial support:* Scholarships/grants and unspecified assistantships available. Financial award application deadline: 3/1; financial award applicants required to submit FAFSA. *Unit head:* Dr. Jeffrey Bingham, Associate Dean, 630-752-5905, E-mail: jeffrey.p.greenman@wheaton.edu. *Application contact:* Dusty Di Santo, Director of Graduate Admissions, 630-752-5195, Fax: 630-752-7047, E-mail: graduate.admissions@wheaton.edu.
Website: http://www.wheaton.edu/academics/departments/theology

Whitworth University, Master of Arts in Theology Program, Spokane, WA 99251-0001. Offers MA. Part-time and evening/weekend programs available. *Faculty:* 16. *Students:* 49 part-time (24 women); includes 3 minority (2 Black or African American, non-Hispanic/Latino; 1 Hispanic/Latino). Average age 37. Tuition and fees vary according to course load, campus/location and program. *Financial support:* In 2014–15, 16 students received support. Application deadline: 8/10; applicants required to submit FAFSA. *Unit head:* Dr. Jeremy Wynne, Director, 509-777-3222, E-mail: graduateandcsadmissions@whitworth.edu. *Application contact:* Kathy Benson, Graduate Admissions, 509-777-3222, E-mail: graduateandcsadmissions@whitworth.edu.

Wilfrid Laurier University, Waterloo Lutheran Seminary, Waterloo, ON N2L 3C5, Canada. Offers divinity (M Div); multifaith spiritual care and counseling (Diploma); pastoral leadership (D Min); spiritual care and counseling (D Min); theology (M Th, MTS); M Div/MTS/MSW. *Accreditation:* ATS. Part-time programs available. *Degree requirements:* For master's, one foreign language, thesis (for some programs); for doctorate, thesis/dissertation. *Entrance requirements:* For master's, two letters of reference; for doctorate, M Div, two letters of reference. Additional exam requirements/ recommendations for international students: Required—TOEFL (minimum score 573 paper-based; 89 iBT), IELTS (minimum score 7). Electronic applications accepted. *Expenses:* Contact institution. *Faculty research:* Biblical study, church history, systematic theology.

Winebrenner Theological Seminary, Graduate Programs, Findlay, OH 45840. Offers clinical counseling (MA); family ministry (MA); practical theology (MA); theological studies (MA); theological/ministerial studies (D Min); theology/ministerial studies (M Div). *Accreditation:* ATS (one or more programs are accredited). Part-time programs available. Postbaccalaureate distance learning degree programs offered (minimal on-campus study). *Faculty:* 5 full-time (1 woman), 9 part-time/adjunct (2 women). *Students:* 26 full-time (11 women), 38 part-time (21 women); includes 8 minority (6 Black or African American, non-Hispanic/Latino; 2 Asian, non-Hispanic/Latino), 4 international. Average age 44. 24 applicants, 100% accepted, 19 enrolled. In 2014, 4 master's, 3 doctorates awarded. *Degree requirements:* For master's, variable foreign language requirement, thesis (for some programs), supervised ministry; for doctorate, thesis/dissertation, research project. *Entrance requirements:* For doctorate, 3 years of post-M Div full-time ministry. Additional exam requirements/recommendations for international students: Required—TOEFL (minimum score 550 paper-based; 80 iBT). *Application deadline:* For fall admission, 8/15 priority date for domestic students, 7/15 priority date for international students; for winter admission, 12/15 priority date for domestic students, 11/15 priority date for international students; for spring admission, 4/15 priority date for domestic students, 3/15 priority date for international students. Applications are processed on a rolling basis. Application fee: $30. Electronic applications accepted. *Expenses: Tuition:* Full-time $12,555; part-time $465 per credit. *Required fees:* $135 per term. Tuition and fees vary according to degree level. *Financial support:* In 2014–15, 34 students received support, including 3 research assistantships with partial tuition reimbursements available (averaging $1,335 per year), teaching assistantships with partial tuition reimbursements available (averaging $1,335 per year); institutionally sponsored loans, scholarships/grants, tuition waivers (partial), unspecified assistantships, and denominational discounts also available. Financial award applicants required to submit FAFSA. *Faculty research:* Discipleship/spiritual growth, limbic system and pastoral care/ counseling, Kingdom of God as central theological motif, series of 10 electronic articles in Logos software for print publication, classic texts of the Old Testament. *Unit head:* Dr. Joel W. Cocklin, Academic Dean, 419-434-4250, Fax: 419-434-4267, E-mail: jcocklin@winebrenner.edu. *Application contact:* Jim Wilder, Coordinator of Admissions, Marketing, and Church Relations, 419-434-4220, Fax: 419-434-4267, E-mail: admissions@winebrenner.edu.
Website: http://www.winebrenner.edu

Wycliffe College, Division of Advanced Degree Studies, Toronto, ON M5S 1H7, Canada. Offers MA, Th M, D Min, PhD, Th D, PhD, D Min, MA offered jointly with Toronto School of Theology; Th D, Th M with University of Toronto. *Accreditation:* ATS (one or more programs are accredited). Part-time programs available. Terminal master's awarded for partial completion of doctoral program. *Degree requirements:* For master's, 2 foreign languages, thesis (for some programs); for doctorate, 3 foreign languages, thesis/dissertation. *Entrance requirements:* Additional exam requirements/ recommendations for international students: Required—TOEFL (minimum score 600 paper-based). *Expenses:* Contact institution. *Faculty research:* Old and New Testament, doctrine, ethics, philosophy, history.

Wycliffe College, Division of Basic Degree Studies, Toronto, ON M5S 1H7, Canada. Offers Christian Studies (Diploma); theology (M Div, M Rel, MTS). M Div, M Rel, MTS offered jointly with University of Toronto. *Accreditation:* ATS. Part-time programs available. *Degree requirements:* For master's, one foreign language, thesis. *Entrance requirements:* Additional exam requirements/recommendations for international students: Required—TOEFL (minimum score 580 paper-based).

Xavier University, College of Arts and Sciences, Department of Theology, Cincinnati, OH 45207. Offers health care mission integration (MA); theology (MA), including religious education, social and pastoral ministry, theology. Part-time and evening/ weekend programs available. *Faculty:* 5 full-time (3 women), 1 part-time/adjunct (0 women). *Students:* 12 part-time (7 women), 1 international. Average age 43. 6 applicants, 100% accepted, 4 enrolled. In 2014, 3 master's awarded. *Degree requirements:* For master's, final paper (or thesis) and defense or comprehension exam. *Entrance requirements:* For master's, MAT or GRE, 2 letters of recommendation; statement of reasons and goals for enrolling in program (1,000-2,000 words); resume; transcript. Additional exam requirements/recommendations for international students: Required—TOEFL (minimum score 550 paper-based; 79 iBT). *Application deadline:* Applications are processed on a rolling basis. Application fee: $35. Electronic applications accepted. Application fee is waived when completed online. *Expenses:* Expenses: $600 per credit hour. *Financial support:* In 2014–15, 3 students received support. Scholarships/grants and unspecified assistantships available. Financial award applicants required to submit FAFSA. *Faculty research:* Scripture, ethics, constructive theology, historical theology. *Unit head:* Dr. Sarah Melcher, Chair, Theology Graduate Program, 513-745-2043, Fax: 513-745-3215, E-mail: melcher@xavier.edu. *Application*

contact: Roger Bosse, Graduate Services Director, 513-745-3357, Fax: 513-745-1048, E-mail: bosse@xavier.edu. Website: http://www.xavier.edu/theology-ma/

Xavier University of Louisiana, Graduate School, Institute for Black Catholic Studies, New Orleans, LA 70125-1098. Offers pastoral theology (Th M). Part-time programs available. *Degree requirements:* For master's, comprehensive exam, practicum. *Entrance requirements:* For master's, GRE General Test, MAT, minimum GPA of 2.5. Additional exam requirements/recommendations for international students: Required—TOEFL.

Yale University, Divinity School, New Haven, CT 06511. Offers M Div, MAR, STM, JD/M Div, JD/MAR, M Div/MBA, M Div/MF, M Div/MSN, M Div/MSW, MAR/MSN, MAR/MSW, MD/M Div, MD/MAR. *Accreditation:* ACIPE; ATS. Part-time programs available. *Entrance requirements:* Additional exam requirements/recommendations for international students: Required—IELTS (minimum score 7). Electronic applications accepted. *Expenses:* Contact institution.

Yeshiva Beth Moshe, Graduate Programs, Scranton, PA 18505-2124. Offers Second Talmudical Degree, Talmudic Fellow Degree. *Accreditation:* AARTS.

Yeshiva Karlin Stolin Rabbinical Institute, Graduate Programs, Brooklyn, NY 11204. Offers Advanced Rabbinical Degree. *Accreditation:* AARTS.

Yeshiva of Nitra Rabbinical College, Graduate Programs, Mount Kisco, NY 10549. *Accreditation:* AARTS.

Yeshiva Shaar Hatorah Talmudic Research Institute, Graduate Programs, Kew Gardens, NY 11418-1469. *Accreditation:* AARTS.

Yeshivath Zichron Moshe, Graduate Programs, South Fallsburg, NY 12779. Offers Advanced Talmudic Degree, Talmudic Scholar Degree. *Accreditation:* AARTS. Part-time programs available.

Yeshiva Toras Chaim Talmudical Seminary, Graduate Programs, Denver, CO 80204-1415.

Section 13
Writing

This section contains a directory of institutions offering graduate work in writing, followed by an in-depth entry submitted by an institution that chose to prepare a detailed program description. Additional information about programs listed in the directory but not augmented by an in-depth entry may be obtained by writing directly to the dean of a graduate school or chair of a department at the address given in the directory.

For programs offering related work, see also in this book *Communication and Media* and *Language and Literature.*

CONTENTS

Technical Writing

Carnegie Mellon University, Dietrich College of Humanities and Social Sciences, Department of English, Program in Professional Writing, Pittsburgh, PA 15213-3891. Offers editing and publishing (MAPW); policy and non-profit communication (MAPW); public and media relations/corporate communications (MAPW); science or healthcare communication (MAPW); technical writing (MAPW); writing for new media (MAPW); writing for print media (MAPW). Part-time programs available. *Entrance requirements:* For master's, GRE General Test. Additional exam requirements/recommendations for international students: Required—TOEFL, TWE.

Colorado State University, Graduate School, College of Liberal Arts, Department of Journalism and Technical Communication, Fort Collins, CO 80523-1785. Offers public communication and technology (MS, PhD); technical communication (MS). Part-time programs available. *Faculty:* 16 full-time (8 women). *Students:* 31 full-time (23 women), 37 part-time (26 women); includes 9 minority (2 Black or African American, non-Hispanic/Latino; 1 American Indian or Alaska Native, non-Hispanic/Latino; 4 Hispanic/Latino; 2 Two or more races, non-Hispanic/Latino), 6 international. Average age 33. 36 applicants, 67% accepted, 20 enrolled. In 2014, 6 master's, 2 doctorates awarded. *Degree requirements:* For master's, variable foreign language requirement, comprehensive exam (for some programs), thesis (for some programs); for doctorate, variable foreign language requirement, comprehensive exam (for some programs), thesis/dissertation (for some programs). *Entrance requirements:* For master's, GRE General Test, samples of written work, letters of recommendation, resume or curriculum vitae, 3 writing/communication projects, statement of purpose, transcripts; for doctorate, GRE General Test, master's degree, minimum GPA of 3.0, scholarly/professional work, letters of recommendation, statement of career plans, resume, transcripts. Additional exam requirements/recommendations for international students: Required—TOEFL (minimum score 550 paper-based; 80 iBT). *Application deadline:* For fall admission, 2/15 priority date for domestic students, 12/15 priority date for international students; for spring admission, 6/15 priority date for domestic students. Applications are processed on a rolling basis. Application fee: $50. Electronic applications accepted. *Expenses:* Tuition, state resident: full-time $9348; part-time $519 per credit. Tuition, nonresident: full-time $22,916; part-time $1273 per credit. *Required fees:* $1584. *Financial support:* In 2014–15, 36 students received support, including 4 research assistantships with full and partial tuition reimbursements available (averaging $14,586 per year), 32 teaching assistantships with partial tuition reimbursements available (averaging $14,327 per year); career-related internships or fieldwork, Federal Work-Study, institutionally sponsored loans, scholarships/grants, traineeships, and unspecified assistantships also available. Support available to part-time students. Financial award application deadline: 3/1; financial award applicants required to submit FAFSA. *Faculty research:* Technical/science communication, public relations, health/risk communication, Web/new media technologies, environmental communication. *Total annual research expenditures:* $1.1 million. *Unit head:* Dr. Greg Luft, Chair, 970-491-1979, Fax: 970-491-2908, E-mail: greg.luft@colostate.edu. *Application contact:* Dr. Linda Kidder, Graduate Program Coordinator, 970-491-5132, Fax: 970-491-2908, E-mail: linda.kidder@colostate.edu.
Website: http://journalism.colostate.edu/

Drexel University, College of Arts and Sciences, Department of Culture and Communication, Philadelphia, PA 19104-2875. Offers communication (MS), including public communication, science communication, technical communication; publication management (MS). Part-time and evening/weekend programs available. *Degree requirements:* For master's, internship, professional portfolio. *Entrance requirements:* Additional exam requirements/recommendations for international students: Required—TOEFL. Electronic applications accepted. *Faculty research:* Science information and attitudes, science influence on literature, process of technical writing, document design, software documentation.

Fitchburg State University, Division of Graduate and Continuing Education, Program in Applied Communications, Fitchburg, MA 01420-2697. Offers applied communications (MS, Certificate); health communication (MS); library media (MS); technical and professional writing (MS). Part-time and evening/weekend programs available. *Entrance requirements:* Additional exam requirements/recommendations for international students: Required—TOEFL (minimum score 550 paper-based; 79 iBT). Electronic applications accepted.

Illinois Institute of Technology, Graduate College, Lewis College of Human Sciences, Department of Humanities, Chicago, IL 60616. Offers information architecture (MS); technical communication (PhD); technical communication and information design (MS). Part-time programs available. *Faculty:* 17 full-time (10 women), 22 part-time/adjunct (14 women). *Students:* 11 full-time (6 women), 5 part-time (0 women); includes 5 minority (2 Black or African American, non-Hispanic/Latino; 1 Hispanic/Latino; 1 Native Hawaiian or other Pacific Islander, non-Hispanic/Latino; 1 Two or more races, non-Hispanic/Latino), 2 international. Average age 36. 29 applicants, 24% accepted, 5 enrolled. In 2014, 4 master's, 1 doctorate awarded. *Degree requirements:* For master's, comprehensive exam, thesis or alternative; for doctorate, comprehensive exam, thesis/dissertation. *Entrance requirements:* For master's, GRE General Test (minimum score 144 Quantitative, 153 Verbal, and 4.0 Analytical Writing), minimum undergraduate GPA of 3.0; 2 letters of recommendation from faculty or supervisors, professional statement discussing academic goals; for doctorate, GRE General Test (minimum score 144 Quantitative, 153 Verbal, and 4.0 Analytical Writing), Applicants must have completed a bachelor's or master's degree in a field that, in combination with the 27-credit hour technical core, would provide a solid basis for advanced academic work leading to original research in the field. 3 letters of recommendation from faculty or supervisors, professional statement discussing academic goals. Additional exam requirements/recommendations for international students: Required—TOEFL (minimum score 95 iBT); Recommended—IELTS (minimum score 7). *Application deadline:* For fall admission, 5/1 for domestic and international students; for spring admission, 10/15 for domestic and international students. Applications are processed on a rolling basis. Application fee: $50. Electronic applications accepted. *Expenses: Tuition:* Full-time $22,500; part-time $1250 per credit hour. *Required fees:* $30 per course. $260 per semester. One-time fee: $235. Tuition and fees vary according to course load and program. *Financial support:* Fellowships with partial tuition reimbursements, research assistantships with partial tuition reimbursements, teaching assistantships with partial tuition reimbursements, career-related internships or fieldwork, Federal Work-Study, institutionally sponsored loans, scholarships/grants, health care benefits, tuition waivers (partial), and unspecified assistantships available. Support available to part-time students. Financial award applicants required to submit FAFSA. *Faculty research:* Linguistics, punishment theory, political communication, gender and technology, philosophical and ethical issues in neuroscience. *Unit head:* Maureen Flanagan, Professor and Chair, 312-567-3563, Fax: 312-567-5187, E-mail: maureen.flanagan@iit.edu. *Application contact:* Rishab Malhotra, Director, Graduate Admission, 866-472-3448, Fax: 312-567-3138, E-mail: inquiry.grad@iit.edu.
Website: http://www.iit.edu/csl/hum/

James Madison University, The Graduate School, College of Arts and Letters, School of Writing, Rhetoric, and Technical Communication, Harrisonburg, VA 22807. Offers MA, MS. Part-time programs available. *Faculty:* 20 full-time (11 women), 1 (woman) part-time/adjunct. *Students:* 13 full-time (10 women), 3 part-time (2 women); includes 3 minority (1 Black or African American, non-Hispanic/Latino; 1 Asian, non-Hispanic/Latino; 1 Hispanic/Latino). Average age 28. 12 applicants, 83% accepted, 8 enrolled. In 2014, 8 master's awarded. *Degree requirements:* For master's, one foreign language, thesis. *Application deadline:* For fall admission, 5/31 for domestic students; for spring admission, 8/31 for domestic students. Application fee: $55. Electronic applications accepted. *Expenses:* Tuition, state resident: full-time $7812; part-time $434 per credit hour. Tuition, nonresident: full-time $20,430; part-time $1135 per credit hour. *Financial support:* In 2014–15, 12 students received support, including 1 fellowship, 2 teaching assistantships with full tuition reimbursements available (averaging $8,837 per year); career-related internships or fieldwork, Federal Work-Study, and 9 assistantships (averaging $7112) also available. Financial award application deadline: 3/1; financial award applicants required to submit FAFSA. *Unit head:* Dr. Traci A. Zimmerman, Director of the School of Writing, Rhetoric and Technical Communication, 540-568-2334, E-mail: zimmerta@jmu.edu. *Application contact:* Lynette D. Michael, Director of Graduate Admissions and Student Records, 540-568-6131 Ext. 6395, Fax: 540-568-7860, E-mail: michaeld@jmu.edu.
Website: http://www.jmu.edu/wrtc/

Johns Hopkins University, Zanvyl Krieger School of Arts and Sciences, Advanced Academic Programs, Program in Writing, Washington, DC 20036. Offers science writing (MA, Certificate); writing (MA). Part-time and evening/weekend programs available. *Degree requirements:* For master's, thesis. *Entrance requirements:* For master's, minimum GPA of 3.0, writing samples. Additional exam requirements/recommendations for international students: Required—TOEFL (minimum score 600 paper-based; 100 iBT). Electronic applications accepted.

Laurentian University, School of Graduate Studies and Research, Programme in Science Communication, Sudbury, ON P3E 2C6, Canada. Offers G Dip.

Louisiana Tech University, Graduate School, College of Liberal Arts, Department of English, Ruston, LA 71272. Offers English (MA); technical writing (Graduate Certificate). Part-time programs available. *Degree requirements:* For master's, thesis or alternative. *Entrance requirements:* For master's, GRE General Test. *Application deadline:* For fall admission, 7/29 for domestic students; for spring admission, 2/3 for domestic students. Applications are processed on a rolling basis. Application fee: $40. *Financial support:* Fellowships, research assistantships, teaching assistantships, and career-related internships or fieldwork available. Financial award application deadline: 2/1. *Unit head:* Dr. Susan Roach, Director, School of Literature and Language, 318-257-2718, Fax: 318-257-2719, E-mail: msroach@latech.edu. *Application contact:* Marilyn J. Robinson, Assistant to the Dean of the Graduate School, 318-257-2924, Fax: 318-257-4487.
Website: http://www.latech.edu/tech/liberal-arts/english/html/literature/index.shtml

Massachusetts Institute of Technology, School of Humanities, Arts, and Social Sciences, Programs in Comparative Media/Science writing, Graduate Program in Science Writing, Cambridge, MA 02139. Offers SM. *Faculty:* 6 full-time (1 woman). *Students:* 8 full-time (6 women); all minorities (all Black or African American, non-Hispanic/Latino). Average age 26. 61 applicants, 20% accepted, 8 enrolled. In 2014, 9 master's awarded. *Degree requirements:* For master's, thesis. *Entrance requirements:* For master's, GRE General Test. Additional exam requirements/recommendations for international students: Required—TOEFL (minimum score 600 paper-based), IELTS (minimum score 7.5). *Application deadline:* For fall admission, 1/15 for domestic and international students. Application fee: $75. Electronic applications accepted. *Expenses: Tuition:* Full-time $44,720; part-time $699 per unit. *Required fees:* $296. *Financial support:* In 2014–15, 7 students received support, including 8 fellowships (averaging $8,400 per year); research assistantships, teaching assistantships, Federal Work-Study, institutionally sponsored loans, scholarships/grants, health care benefits, and unspecified assistantships also available. Financial award application deadline: 4/15; financial award applicants required to submit FAFSA. *Faculty research:* Communicating science to the public. *Unit head:* Prof. Thomas Levenson, Program Head, 617-253-6668, Fax: 617-452-5100, E-mail: sciwrite-www@mit.edu. *Application contact:* Science Writing Graduate Admissions, 617-253-6668, Fax: 617-452-5100, E-mail: sciwrite-www@mit.edu.
Website: http://cmsw.mit.edu/education/writing/science-writing/

Metropolitan State University, College of Arts and Sciences, St. Paul, MN 55106-5000. Offers computer science (MS); liberal studies (MA); technical communication (MS). Part-time and evening/weekend programs available. *Entrance requirements:* For master's, minimum GPA of 2.75, resume. Additional exam requirements/recommendations for international students: Required—TOEFL (minimum score 550 paper-based). Electronic applications accepted.

Texas Tech University, Graduate School, College of Arts and Sciences, Department of English, Lubbock, TX 79409-3091. Offers English (MA, PhD); technical communication (MA); technical communication and rhetoric (PhD). Part-time programs available. Postbaccalaureate distance learning degree programs offered (minimal on-campus study). *Faculty:* 62 full-time (35 women), 8 part-time/adjunct (4 women). *Students:* 92 full-time (55 women), 91 part-time (63 women); includes 24 minority (5 Black or African American, non-Hispanic/Latino; 2 American Indian or Alaska Native, non-Hispanic/Latino; 6 Asian, non-Hispanic/Latino; 6 Hispanic/Latino; 5 Two or more races, non-Hispanic/Latino), 9 international. Average age 34. 197 applicants, 36% accepted, 48 enrolled. In 2014, 12 master's, 14 doctorates awarded. Terminal master's awarded for partial completion of doctoral program. *Degree requirements:* For master's, variable foreign language requirement, comprehensive exam, thesis optional; for doctorate, variable foreign language requirement, comprehensive exam, thesis/dissertation. *Entrance requirements:* For master's and doctorate, GRE General Test. Additional exam requirements/recommendations for international students: Required—TOEFL (minimum score 550 paper-based; 79 iBT), IELTS (minimum score 6.5). *Application deadline:* For fall admission, 6/1 priority date for domestic students, 1/15 priority date for international students; for spring admission, 9/1 priority date for domestic students, 6/15 priority date for international students. Applications are processed on a rolling basis. Application fee: $60. Electronic applications accepted. *Expenses:* Tuition, state resident: full-time $6310; part-time $262.92 per credit hour. Tuition, nonresident: full-time $14,998; part-time $624.92 per credit hour. *Required fees:* $2701; $36.50 per credit. $912.50 per semester. Tuition and fees vary according to course load. *Financial support:* In 2014–15, 112 students received support, including 94 fellowships (averaging $2,592 per year), 8 research assistantships (averaging $19,331 per year), 89 teaching assistantships

(averaging $14,644 per year); career-related internships or fieldwork, Federal Work-Study, scholarships/grants, and unspecified assistantships also available. Financial award application deadline: 12/15; financial award applicants required to submit FAFSA. *Faculty research:* American, British, and comparative literature; creative writing; linguistics; film; technical communication and rhetoric. *Total annual research expenditures:* $64,530. *Unit head:* Dr. Bruce Clarke, Professor, 806-742-2501, Fax: 806-742-0989, E-mail: bruce.clarke@ttu.edu. *Application contact:* Dr. Brian J. McFadden, Director of Graduate Studies, 806-742-2501 Ext. 246, Fax: 806-742-0989, E-mail: english.gradadvisor@ttu.edu.
Website: http://www.english.ttu.edu/

The University of Alabama in Huntsville, School of Graduate Studies, College of Liberal Arts, Department of English, Huntsville, AL 35899. Offers education (MA); English (MA); language arts (MA); reading specialist (MA); technical communications (Certificate). Part-time and evening/weekend programs available. *Degree requirements:* For master's, one foreign language, comprehensive exam, thesis or alternative, oral and written exams. *Entrance requirements:* For master's and Certificate, GRE General Test, minimum GPA of 3.0. Additional exam requirements/recommendations for international students: Required—TOEFL (minimum score 500 paper-based; 80 iBT), IELTS (minimum score 6.5). Electronic applications accepted. *Faculty research:* Fiction and identity, Shakespeare, science fiction, eighteenth-century literature, technical writing.

University of Arkansas at Little Rock, Graduate School, College of Social Sciences and Communication, Department of Rhetoric and Writing, Little Rock, AR 72204-1099. Offers professional and technical writing (MA). Part-time and evening/weekend programs available. *Degree requirements:* For master's, thesis or alternative, oral defense of final project. *Entrance requirements:* For master's, GRE, minimum GPA of 3.0, writing portfolio. *Application deadline:* Applications are processed on a rolling basis. *Expenses:* Tuition, state resident: full-time $6000; part-time $300 per credit hour. Tuition, nonresident: full-time $13,800; part-time $690 per credit hour. *Required fees:* $1126; $603 per term. One-time fee: $40 full-time. *Financial support:* Research assistantships with tuition reimbursements, teaching assistantships with tuition reimbursements, career-related internships or fieldwork, Federal Work-Study, institutionally sponsored loans, and unspecified assistantships available. Support available to part-time students. *Faculty research:* Writing for industry, science,

business, and government; composition and rhetorical theory; writing nonfiction; teaching of writing. *Unit head:* Dr. George H. Jensen, Chairperson, 501-569-3160, E-mail: ghjensen@ualr.edu. *Application contact:* Dr. Cynthia A. Nahrwold, Coordinator, 501-569-3316, Fax: 501-569-8279, E-mail: canahrwold@ualr.edu.
Website: http://ualr.edu/rhetoric/

The University of North Carolina at Greensboro, Graduate School, College of Arts and Sciences, Department of English, Greensboro, NC 27412-5001. Offers creative writing (MFA); English (M Ed, MA, PhD, Certificate), including American literature (PhD), English (M Ed, MA), English literature (PhD), rhetoric and composition (PhD), technical writing (Certificate), women's studies (Certificate). *Degree requirements:* For master's, comprehensive exam; for doctorate, variable foreign language requirement, thesis/dissertation, preliminary exam. *Entrance requirements:* For master's, GRE General Test, minimum GPA of 3.0; for doctorate, GRE General Test, GRE Subject Test, critical writing sample, minimum GPA of 3.0. Additional exam requirements/recommendations for international students: Required—TOEFL. Electronic applications accepted.

University of the Sciences, College of Graduate Studies, Program in Biomedical Writing, Philadelphia, PA 19104-4495. Offers biomedical writing (MS); medical marketing writing (Certificate); regulatory affairs writing (Certificate). Part-time and evening/weekend programs available. Postbaccalaureate distance learning degree programs offered (minimal on-campus study). *Entrance requirements:* For master's, GRE General Test. Additional exam requirements/recommendations for international students: Required—TOEFL, TWE. *Expenses:* Contact institution. *Faculty research:* History of medical writing and publishing, compliance, regulatory.

University of Waterloo, Graduate Studies, Faculty of Arts, Department of English, Language and Literature, Waterloo, ON N2L 3G1, Canada. Offers English language and literature (PhD); literary studies (MA); rhetoric and communication design (MA). Part-time programs available. *Degree requirements:* For master's, one foreign language, thesis optional; for doctorate, 2 foreign languages, thesis/dissertation. *Entrance requirements:* For master's, honors degree, minimum B+ average; for doctorate, master's degree, minimum A- average. Additional exam requirements/recommendations for international students: Required—TOEFL, TWE. Electronic applications accepted. *Faculty research:* Shakespeare, American literature, rhetoric, Romantics, moderns.

Writing

Abilene Christian University, Graduate School, College of Arts and Sciences, Department of English, Abilene, TX 79699-9100. Offers composition/rhetoric (MA); literature (MA); writing (MA). Part-time programs available. *Faculty:* 17 part-time/adjunct (7 women). *Students:* 12 full-time (6 women), 7 part-time (6 women); includes 2 minority (both Hispanic/Latino), 1 international. 20 applicants, 45% accepted, 7 enrolled. In 2014, 4 master's awarded. *Degree requirements:* For master's, one foreign language, comprehensive exam (for some programs), thesis (for some programs). *Entrance requirements:* For master's, GRE General Test. Additional exam requirements/recommendations for international students: Required—TOEFL (minimum score 550 paper-based; 90 iBT), IELTS (minimum score 6.5), PTE. *Application deadline:* For fall admission, 4/1 priority date for domestic students; for spring admission, 11/1 for domestic students. Applications are processed on a rolling basis. Application fee: $50. Electronic applications accepted. *Expenses:* Tuition: Full-time $18,228; part-time $1016 per credit hour. *Financial support:* In 2014–15, 14 students received support, including 6 teaching assistantships with partial tuition reimbursements available (averaging $5,800 per year); Federal Work-Study also available. Support available to part-time students. Financial award application deadline: 4/1; financial award applicants required to submit FAFSA. *Faculty research:* Feminism, Shakespearean dimensions of new literature, poetic consciousness, deconstruction myths. *Unit head:* Dr. Dana McMichael, Graduate Director, 325-674-2083, Fax: 325-674-2408, E-mail: dana.mcmichael@acu.edu. *Application contact:* Corey Patterson, Director of Graduate Admission and Recruiting, 325-674-6566, Fax: 325-674-6717, E-mail: gradinfo@acu.edu.

Academy of Art University, Graduate Program, School of Writing for Film, Television and Digital Media, San Francisco, CA 94105-3410. Offers MFA. Part-time programs available. Postbaccalaureate distance learning degree programs offered (no on-campus study). *Faculty:* 1 full-time (0 women). *Students:* 1 (woman) full-time; minority (Black or African American, non-Hispanic/Latino). Average age 24. *Degree requirements:* For master's, final review. *Entrance requirements:* For master's, statement of intent; resume; portfolio/reel; official college transcripts. *Application deadline:* Applications are processed on a rolling basis. Application fee: $100. Electronic applications accepted. *Expenses:* Tuition: Part-time $910 per unit. *Financial support:* Career-related internships or fieldwork and Federal Work-Study available. Support available to part-time students. Financial award application deadline: 8/10; financial award applicants required to submit FAFSA. *Unit head:* 800-544-ARTS, E-mail: info@academyart.edu. *Application contact:* 800-544-ARTS, E-mail: info@academyart.edu.
Website: http://www.academyart.edu/academics/writing-film-television-digital-media

Adelphi University, College of Arts and Sciences, Program in Creative Writing, Garden City, NY 11530-0701. Offers MFA. Part-time and evening/weekend programs available. *Students:* 11 full-time (4 women), 5 part-time (3 women); includes 2 minority (both Hispanic/Latino), 3 international. Average age 25. In 2014, 6 master's awarded. *Degree requirements:* For master's, thesis. *Entrance requirements:* For master's, 2 letters of reference, manuscript in chosen genre (poetry, fiction, playwriting), personal statement essay, college transcript. Additional exam requirements/recommendations for international students: Required—TOEFL (minimum score 550 paper-based; 80 iBT). *Application deadline:* For fall admission, 5/1 priority date for international students; for spring admission, 11/1 priority date for international students. Applications are processed on a rolling basis. Application fee: $50. Electronic applications accepted. *Financial support:* Fellowships and Federal Work-Study available. *Unit head:* Judith Baumel, Director, 516-877-4031, E-mail: baumel@adelphi.edu. *Application contact:* Christine Murphy, Director of Admissions, 516-877-3050, Fax: 516-877-3039, E-mail: graduateadmissions@adelphi.edu.
Website: http://academics.adelphi.edu/artsci/creativewriting/

See Display on next page and Close-Up on page 591.

Albertus Magnus College, Master of Fine Arts in Creative Writing Program, New Haven, CT 06511-1189. Offers MFA. Part-time and evening/weekend programs available. Postbaccalaureate distance learning degree programs offered (minimal on-campus study). *Faculty:* 5 full-time (1 woman), 1 part-time/adjunct (0 women). *Students:* 3 full-time (0 women), 6 part-time (all women); includes 2 minority (both Black or African American, non-Hispanic/Latino). Average age 38. In 2014, 4 master's awarded. *Degree*

requirements: For master's, thesis, project, minimum cumulative GPA of 3.0, completion of all requirements within seven years of matriculation. *Entrance requirements:* Additional exam requirements/recommendations for international students: Recommended—TOEFL (minimum score 550 paper-based). *Application deadline:* For fall admission, 8/15 for domestic students; for spring admission, 1/15 for domestic students. Applications are processed on a rolling basis. Application fee: $50. Electronic applications accepted. *Expenses:* Expenses: $4,120 per four-credit course; registration fee $25 per semester, information technology fee $6 per credit. *Unit head:* Charles Rafferty, Co-Director, 203-773-6901, Fax: 203-777-3701, E-mail: crafferty@albertus.edu. *Application contact:* Prof. Sarah Harris Wallman, Co-Director, 203-777-4473, Fax: 203-777-3701, E-mail: swallman@albertus.edu.
Website: http://www.albertus.edu/masters-degrees/mfa/

Antioch University Los Angeles, Graduate Programs, Program in Creative Writing, Culver City, CA 90230. Offers creative writing (MFA); pedagogy of creative writing (Certificate). Postbaccalaureate distance learning degree programs offered (minimal on-campus study). *Degree requirements:* For master's, thesis. *Entrance requirements:* For master's, sample of written work. Additional exam requirements/recommendations for international students: Required—TOEFL. *Faculty research:* Creative nonfiction, fiction, poetry.

Antioch University Midwest, Graduate Programs, Individualized Liberal and Professional Studies Program, Yellow Springs, OH 45387-1609. Offers liberal and professional studies (MA), including counseling, creative writing, education, liberal studies, management, modern literature, psychology, visual arts. Part-time and evening/weekend programs available. Postbaccalaureate distance learning degree programs offered (minimal on-campus study). *Degree requirements:* For master's, thesis or alternative. *Entrance requirements:* For master's, resume, goal statement, interview. Electronic applications accepted. *Expenses:* Contact institution.

Arizona State University at the Tempe campus, College of Liberal Arts and Sciences, Department of English, Interdisciplinary Program in Creative Writing, Tempe, AZ 85287-0302. Offers MFA. *Degree requirements:* For master's, thesis, practicum (9 hours). *Entrance requirements:* For master's, undergraduate major in English or creative writing (preferred), minimum GPA of 3.0, 3 letters of recommendation, resume or curriculum vitae, personal statement, official transcripts, 3 copies of manuscript sample (20 pages of poetry, 30 pages of prose, or both). Additional exam requirements/recommendations for international students: Required—TOEFL, IELTS, or PTE. Electronic applications accepted.

Arizona State University at the Tempe campus, Herberger Institute for Design and the Arts, School of Film, Dance and Theatre, Tempe, AZ 85287-2002. Offers dance (MFA), including dance, interdisciplinary digital media and performance; theatre (MA, MFA, PhD), including arts entrepreneurship and management (MFA), directing (MFA), dramatic writing (MFA), interdisciplinary digital media and performance (MFA), performance (MFA), performance design (MFA), theatre (MFA), theatre and performance of the Americas (PhD), theatre for youth (MFA, PhD). Terminal master's awarded for partial completion of doctoral program. *Degree requirements:* For master's, comprehensive exam (for some programs), thesis (for some programs), applied project (for some programs); interactive Program of Study (iPOS) submitted before completing 50 percent of required credit hours; for doctorate, comprehensive exam, thesis/dissertation, interactive Program of Study (iPOS) submitted before completing 50 percent of required credit hours. *Entrance requirements:* For master's, GRE or MAT, minimum GPA of 3.0 in last 2 years of work leading to bachelor's degree (depending on program); for doctorate, GRE, minimum GPA of 3.0 or equivalent in last 2 years of work leading to bachelor's degree, 3 letters of recommendation, resume, scholarly writing sample, statement of purpose. Additional exam requirements/recommendations for international students: Required—TOEFL, IELTS, or PTE. Electronic applications accepted.

Armstrong State University, School of Graduate Studies, Program in Professional Communication and Leadership, Savannah, GA 31419-1997. Offers MA, Certificate. Part-time and evening/weekend programs available. *Faculty:* 13 full-time (6 women), 4 part-time/adjunct (3 women). *Students:* 22 full-time (16 women), 46 part-time (29

women); includes 28 minority (24 Black or African American, non-Hispanic/Latino; 1 Asian, non-Hispanic/Latino; 3 Hispanic/Latino). Average age 34. 32 applicants, 81% accepted, 23 enrolled. In 2014, 10 master's awarded. *Degree requirements:* For master's, comprehensive exam, project. *Entrance requirements:* For master's, minimum GPA of 2.5, letters of recommendation, letter of intent, resume. Additional exam requirements/recommendations for international students: Required—TOEFL (minimum score 523 paper-based). *Application deadline:* For fall admission, 6/1 priority date for domestic students, 5/1 priority date for international students; for spring admission, 11/15 priority date for domestic students, 9/15 priority date for international students; for summer admission, 4/15 for domestic students, 9/15 priority date for international students. Application fee: $30. *Expenses:* Tuition, state resident: part-time $206 per credit hour. Tuition, nonresident: part-time $763 per credit hour. *Required fees:* $612 per semester. Tuition and fees vary according to course load, campus/location and program. *Financial support:* In 2014–15, research assistantships with full tuition reimbursements (averaging $5,000 per year) were awarded; scholarships/grants and unspecified assistantships also available. Financial award application deadline: 3/15; financial award applicants required to submit FAFSA. *Faculty research:* Organizational communication, conflict resolution and mediation, rhetoric and language identity, brand identity and marketing, communication theory. *Unit head:* Dr. Chris Hendricks, Program Coordinator, 912-344-2725, E-mail: chris.hendricks@armstrong.edu. *Application contact:* Kathy Ingram, Associate Director of Graduate/Adult and Nontraditional Students, 912-344-2503, Fax: 912-344-3417, E-mail: graduate@armstrong.edu. Website: http://www.armstrong.edu/Majors/degree/master_professional_communication_leadership

Asbury University, School of Graduate and Professional Studies, Wilmore, KY 40390-1198. Offers biology: alternative certificate (MA Ed); chemistry: alternative certificate (MA Ed); English (MA Ed); English as a second language (MA Ed); ESL (MA Ed); French (MA Ed); Latin: alternative certificate (MA Ed); mathematics: alternative certificate (MA Ed); reading/writing endorsement (MA Ed); social studies (MA Ed); social work (MSW), including child and family services; Spanish (MA Ed); special education (MA Ed); special education: alternative certificate (MA Ed); teacher as leader endorsement (MA Ed). *Accreditation:* NCATE. Part-time programs available. *Degree requirements:* For master's, action research project, portfolio. *Entrance requirements:* For master's, PRAXIS/NTE, minimum GPA of 2.75, letters of recommendation. Additional exam requirements/recommendations for international students: Required—TOEFL (minimum score 550 paper-based). Electronic applications accepted.

Ashland University, College of Arts and Sciences, Program in Creative Writing, Ashland, OH 44805-3702. Offers MFA. Postbaccalaureate distance learning degree programs offered (minimal on-campus study). *Degree requirements:* For master's, thesis. *Entrance requirements:* For master's, writing sample, minimum GPA of 2.75. Electronic applications accepted. *Expenses:* Contact institution.

Ball State University, Graduate School, College of Sciences and Humanities, Department of English, Muncie, IN 47306-1099. Offers English (MA, PhD), including composition, creative writing (MA), general (MA), literature; linguistics (MA, PhD), including English (PhD), linguistics (MA); linguistics and teaching English to speakers of other languages (MA); teaching English to speakers of other languages (MA). *Faculty:* 18 full-time (11 women). *Students:* 42 full-time (28 women), 31 part-time (18 women); includes 4 minority (1 Black or African American, non-Hispanic/Latino; 1 Hispanic/Latino; 2 Two or more races, non-Hispanic/Latino), 21 international. Average age 29. 98 applicants, 43% accepted, 24 enrolled. In 2014, 23 master's, 10 doctorates awarded. *Degree requirements:* For doctorate, variable foreign language requirement, thesis/dissertation. *Entrance requirements:* For master's, GRE General Test, writing sample; for doctorate, GRE General Test, GRE Subject Test, minimum graduate GPA of 3.2, writing sample. Application fee: $25 ($35 for international students). *Financial support:*

In 2014–15, 58 students received support, including 3 research assistantships with partial tuition reimbursements available (averaging $10,858 per year), 34 teaching assistantships with partial tuition reimbursements available (averaging $15,539 per year); unspecified assistantships also available. Financial award application deadline: 3/1. *Faculty research:* American literature; literary editing; medieval, Renaissance, and eighteenth-century British literature; rhetoric. *Unit head:* Dr. Elizabeth Riddle, Chairperson, 765-285-8580, Fax: 765-285-3765, E-mail: emriddle@bsu.edu. *Application contact:* Dr. Jill Christman, Assistant Chair, 765-285-8415, E-mail: jcchristman@bsu.edu. Website: http://www.bsu.edu/english/

Bay Path University, Program in Creative Nonfiction, Longmeadow, MA 01106-2292. Offers MFA. Part-time and evening/weekend programs available. Postbaccalaureate distance learning degree programs offered (no on-campus study). *Students:* 6 full-time (5 women), 15 part-time (all women); includes 2 minority (1 Black or African American, non-Hispanic/Latino; 1 Hispanic/Latino). Average age 46. 29 applicants, 93% accepted, 21 enrolled. *Entrance requirements:* For master's, minimum GPA of 3.0 or grades at the B level or higher in English and/or writing classes. *Application deadline:* Applications are processed on a rolling basis. Application fee: $45. Electronic applications accepted. Application fee is waived when completed online. *Financial support:* In 2014–15, 6 students received support. Applicants required to submit FAFSA. *Unit head:* Leanne James Blackwell, Director, 413-565-1232, E-mail: ljblackwell@baypath.edu. *Application contact:* Diane Ranaldi, Dean of Graduate Admissions, 413-565-1332, Fax: 413-565-1250, E-mail: dranaldi@baypath.edu. Website: http://graduate.baypath.edu/graduate-programs/programs-online/mfa-program/creative-nonfiction

Bennington College, Graduate Programs, The Bennington Writing Seminars, Bennington, VT 05201. Offers creative writing (MFA). Postbaccalaureate distance learning degree programs offered (minimal on-campus study). *Degree requirements:* For master's, thesis, collection of essays or poems, or collection of short stories and/or a novel. *Entrance requirements:* For master's, manuscript. *Expenses:* Contact institution.

Binghamton University, State University of New York, Graduate School, School of Arts and Sciences, Department of English, Vestal, NY 13850. Offers creative writing (MA); English (PhD); English/American literature (MA). Part-time programs available. *Faculty:* 28 full-time (16 women), 30 part-time/adjunct (18 women). *Students:* 39 full-time (22 women), 50 part-time (27 women); includes 11 minority (2 Black or African American, non-Hispanic/Latino; 1 Asian, non-Hispanic/Latino; 4 Hispanic/Latino; 4 Native Hawaiian or other Pacific Islander, non-Hispanic/Latino), 11 international. Average age 33. 90 applicants, 58% accepted, 19 enrolled. In 2014, 13 master's, 15 doctorates awarded. Terminal master's awarded for partial completion of doctoral program. *Degree requirements:* For master's, one foreign language, thesis; for doctorate, one foreign language, comprehensive exam, thesis/dissertation. *Entrance requirements:* For master's and doctorate, GRE General Test, writing sample. Additional exam requirements/recommendations for international students: Required—TOEFL (minimum score 550 paper-based; 80 iBT). *Application deadline:* For fall admission, 2/15 priority date for domestic and international students; for spring admission, 11/15 priority date for domestic and international students. Applications are processed on a rolling basis. Application fee: $75. Electronic applications accepted. *Expenses:* Tuition, state resident: full-time $7776; part-time $432 per credit. Tuition, nonresident: full-time $15,138; part-time $841 per credit. *Required fees:* $1754; $213 per credit. Tuition and fees vary according to degree level and program. *Financial support:* In 2014–15, 42 students received support, including 1 fellowship with full tuition reimbursement available (averaging $15,000 per year), 1 research assistantship (averaging $9,000 per year), 30 teaching assistantships with full tuition reimbursements available (averaging $15,000 per year); career-related internships or fieldwork, Federal Work-Study,

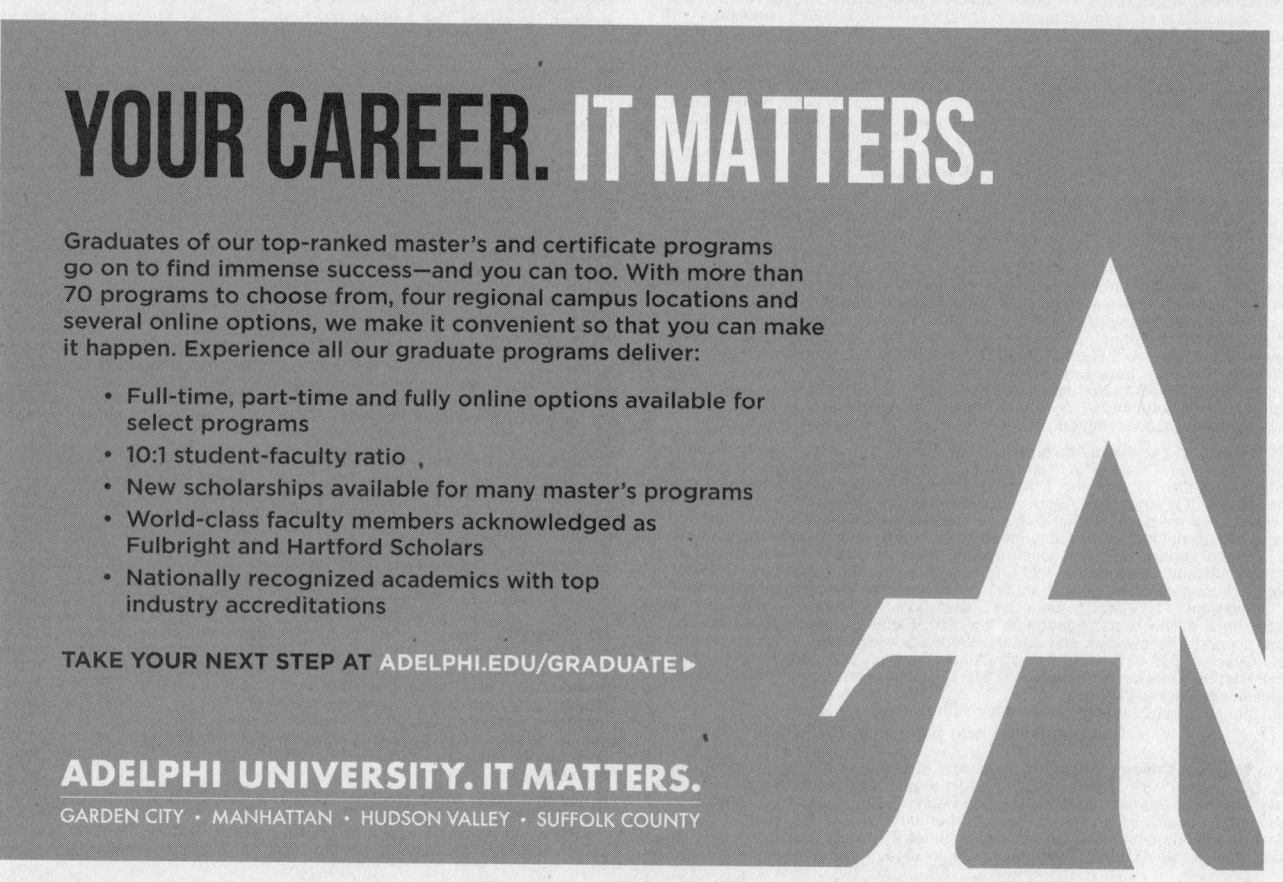

institutionally sponsored loans, scholarships/grants, health care benefits, tuition waivers (full and partial), and unspecified assistantships also available. Financial award application deadline: 2/15; financial award applicants required to submit FAFSA. *Unit head:* Dr. Robert Micklus, Chairperson, 607-777-2169, E-mail: rmicklus@binghamton.edu. *Application contact:* Kishan Zuber, Recruiting and Admissions Coordinator, 607-777-2151, Fax: 607-777-2501, E-mail: kzuber@binghamton.edu.
Website: http://www2.binghamton.edu/english/

Boise State University, College of Arts and Sciences, Department of English, Boise, ID 83725-0399. Offers creative writing (MFA); English (MA); technical communication (MA). Part-time programs available. *Faculty:* 34 full-time, 14 part-time/adjunct. *Students:* 45 full-time (29 women), 29 part-time (17 women); includes 8 minority (1 Black or African American, non-Hispanic/Latino; 2 Asian, non-Hispanic/Latino; 5 Hispanic/Latino). Average age 37. 200 applicants, 97% accepted, 25 enrolled. In 2014, 30 master's awarded. *Degree requirements:* For master's, thesis. *Entrance requirements:* For master's, GRE, minimum GPA of 3.0. *Application deadline:* For fall admission, 7/17 priority date for domestic students; for spring admission, 12/5 priority date for domestic students. Applications are processed on a rolling basis. Application fee: $55. Electronic applications accepted. *Expenses:* Tuition, state resident: part-time $331 per credit hour. Tuition, nonresident: part-time $531 per credit hour. *Financial support:* In 2014–15, 31 teaching assistantships with full tuition reimbursements (averaging $9,368 per year) were awarded; research assistantships with full tuition reimbursements, career-related internships or fieldwork, Federal Work-Study, institutionally sponsored loans, and unspecified assistantships also available. Support available to part-time students. Financial award application deadline: 3/1. *Unit head:* Dr. Michelle Payne, Chair, 208-426-3426, Fax: 208-426-4373, E-mail: mpayne@boisestate.edu. *Application contact:* Linda Platt, Supervisor, Graduate Admission and Degree Services, 208-426-1074, E-mail: lplatt@boisestate.edu.
Website: http://english.boisestate.edu/graduate-programs/

Boston University, Graduate School of Arts and Sciences, Creative Writing Program, Boston, MA 02215. Offers MFA. *Students:* 19 full-time (12 women), 8 part-time (4 women); includes 8 minority (5 Asian, non-Hispanic/Latino; 3 Hispanic/Latino), 1 international. Average age 27. 351 applicants, 5% accepted, 17 enrolled. In 2014, 18 master's awarded. *Entrance requirements:* Additional exam requirements/recommendations for international students: Required—TOEFL. *Application deadline:* For fall admission, 3/1 for domestic and international students. Application fee: $80. Electronic applications accepted. *Expenses:* Tuition: Full-time $45,686; part-time $1428 per credit hour. *Required fees:* $660; $60 per semester. Tuition and fees vary according to program. *Financial support:* In 2014–15, 17 students received support, including teaching assistantships with partial tuition reimbursements available (averaging $10,250 per year); Federal Work-Study and unspecified assistantships also available. Support available to part-time students. Financial award application deadline: 3/1. *Unit head:* Karl Kirchwey, Director, 617-353-2510, Fax: 617-353-3653, E-mail: kirchwey@bu.edu. *Application contact:* Catherine Con, Administrative Coordinator, 617-353-2510, Fax: 617-353-3653, E-mail: crwr@bu.edu.
Website: http://www.bu.edu/writing/

Boston University, Graduate School of Arts and Sciences, Editorial Institute, Boston, MA 02215. Offers MA, PhD. *Students:* 15 full-time (9 women), 5 part-time (4 women); includes 3 minority (all Hispanic/Latino), 1 international. Average age 35. 7 applicants, 86% accepted, 5 enrolled. *Degree requirements:* For master's, one foreign language, thesis; for doctorate, one foreign language, comprehensive exam, thesis/dissertation. *Entrance requirements:* For master's and doctorate, GRE General Test, thesis proposal, 3 letters of recommendation. Additional exam requirements/recommendations for international students: Required—TOEFL (minimum score 550 paper-based; 84 iBT). *Application deadline:* For fall admission, 4/15 for domestic and international students. Application fee: $80. Electronic applications accepted. *Expenses:* Tuition: Full-time $45,686; part-time $1428 per credit hour. *Required fees:* $660; $60 per semester. Tuition and fees vary according to program. *Financial support:* In 2014–15, 15 students received support, including 4 fellowships with full tuition reimbursements available (averaging $20,500 per year), 3 teaching assistantships with full tuition reimbursements available (averaging $20,500 per year); Federal Work-Study, scholarships/grants, health care benefits, and unspecified assistantships also available. Financial award application deadline: 1/15. *Unit head:* Archie Burnett, Co-Director, 617-353-6631, E-mail: burnetta@bu.edu. *Application contact:* Allison Vanouse, Administrative Assistant, 617-358-1937, Fax: 617-353-6917, E-mail: editinst@bu.edu.
Website: http://www.bu.edu/editinst/

Boston University, Graduate School of Arts and Sciences, Playwriting Program, Boston, MA 02215. Offers MFA. Program offered jointly with College of Fine Arts; program admits students in even-numbered years. *Students:* 7 full-time (4 women), 3 part-time (2 women); includes 1 minority (Asian, non-Hispanic/Latino), 1 international. Average age 29. 28 applicants, 21% accepted, 5 enrolled. *Entrance requirements:* For master's, GRE, 3 letters of recommendation, one original full-length play or two one-act plays. Additional exam requirements/recommendations for international students: Required—TOEFL (minimum score 550 paper-based; 84 iBT). *Application deadline:* For fall admission, 3/15 for domestic and international students. Application fee: $80. Electronic applications accepted. *Expenses:* Tuition: Full-time $45,686; part-time $1428 per credit hour. *Required fees:* $660; $60 per semester. Tuition and fees vary according to program. *Financial support:* In 2014–15, 4 students received support, including 2 teaching assistantships with full and partial tuition reimbursements available (averaging $10,250 per year); Federal Work-Study, scholarships/grants, health care benefits, and unspecified assistantships also available. Financial award application deadline: 3/15. *Unit head:* Katherine Snodgrass, Artistic Director, 617-353-5104, Fax: 617-353-6196, E-mail: ksnodgra@bu.edu. *Application contact:* Martin Gastmann, Assistant Director of Admissions and Financial Aid, 617-353-2696, Fax: 617-358-5492, E-mail: grs@bu.edu.
Website: http://www.bu.edu/bpt/playwriting-program.html

Bowling Green State University, Graduate College, College of Arts and Sciences, Department of English, Program in Creative Writing, Bowling Green, OH 43403. Offers fiction (MFA); poetry (MFA). Part-time programs available. *Degree requirements:* For master's, thesis or alternative. *Entrance requirements:* For master's, GRE General Test. Additional exam requirements/recommendations for international students: Required—TOEFL. Electronic applications accepted. *Faculty research:* Poetry, criticism, novels, translation, travel writing.

Bowling Green State University, Graduate College, College of Arts and Sciences, Department of English, Program in English, Bowling Green, OH 43403. Offers English (MA, PhD); literature (MA); rhetoric and writing (PhD); scientific and technical communication (MA). Part-time programs available. *Degree requirements:* For master's, thesis or alternative; for doctorate, comprehensive exam, thesis/dissertation, foreign language or proficiency in Old English. *Entrance requirements:* For master's and doctorate, GRE General Test. Additional exam requirements/recommendations for international students: Required—TOEFL. Electronic applications accepted. *Faculty research:* Postmodern literary theory, rhetorical theory, ethnic American literature, literature and culture, composition pedagogy.

Brigham Young University, Graduate Studies, College of Humanities, Department of English, Provo, UT 84602-1001. Offers creative writing (MFA); literature (MA); rhetoric/composition (MA). *Faculty:* 61 full-time (22 women). *Students:* 71 full-time (52 women), 5 part-time (all women). Average age 24. 71 applicants, 51% accepted, 31 enrolled. In 2014, 22 master's awarded. *Degree requirements:* For master's, thesis. *Entrance requirements:* For master's, GRE General Test, creative portfolio (for MFA). Additional exam requirements/recommendations for international students: Required—TOEFL (minimum score 213 paper-based). *Application deadline:* For fall admission, 1/15 for domestic and international students. Application fee: $50. Electronic applications accepted. *Expenses:* Tuition: Full-time $6310; part-time $371 per credit hour. Tuition and fees vary according to program and student's religious affiliation. *Financial support:* In 2014–15, 10 research assistantships (averaging $4,000 per year), 62 teaching assistantships (averaging $6,000 per year) were awarded; career-related internships or fieldwork, institutionally sponsored loans, scholarships/grants, and tuition waivers (partial) also available. Support available to part-time students. Financial award application deadline: 3/15. *Faculty research:* English literature, American literature, rhetoric, creative writing. *Unit head:* Prof. Phillip Snyder, Head, 801-422-2487, Fax: 801-422-0221, E-mail: phillip_snyder@byu.edu. *Application contact:* Lou Ann C. Crisler, Graduate Secretary, 801-422-8673, Fax: 801-422-0221, E-mail: louann_crisler@byu.edu.
Website: http://english.byu.edu/

Brooklyn College of the City University of New York, School of Humanities and Social Sciences, Department of English, Brooklyn, NY 11210-2889. Offers creative writing (MFA), including fiction, playwriting, poetry; English (MA). Part-time and evening/weekend programs available. *Degree requirements:* For master's, one foreign language, comprehensive exam (for some programs), thesis (for some programs). *Entrance requirements:* For master's, advanced undergraduate courses in English, 2 letters of recommendation, writing sample, statement of purpose. Additional exam requirements/recommendations for international students: Required—TOEFL. Electronic applications accepted. *Faculty research:* Cultural studies, medieval literature, Virginia Woolf.

Brown University, Graduate School, Department of English, Providence, RI 02912. Offers English (PhD); literary arts (MFA). *Degree requirements:* For doctorate, thesis/dissertation. *Entrance requirements:* For master's and doctorate, GRE General Test, GRE Subject Test.

Butler University, College of Liberal Arts and Sciences, Department of English, Indianapolis, IN 46208-3485. Offers creative writing (MFA); English (MA). Part-time and evening/weekend programs available. *Faculty:* 10 full-time (4 women), 2 part-time/adjunct (1 woman). *Students:* 6 full-time (3 women), 53 part-time (34 women); includes 6 minority (4 Black or African American, non-Hispanic/Latino; 1 Hispanic/Latino; 1 Two or more races, non-Hispanic/Latino), 2 international. Average age 36. 61 applicants, 61% accepted, 17 enrolled. In 2014, 16 master's awarded. *Entrance requirements:* For master's, GRE General Test, GRE Subject Test. Additional exam requirements/recommendations for international students: Required—TOEFL (minimum score 550 paper-based; 79 iBT), IELTS (minimum score 6). *Application deadline:* For fall admission, 8/15 priority date for domestic students. Applications are processed on a rolling basis. Application fee: $35. Electronic applications accepted. *Financial support:* Applicants required to submit FAFSA. *Unit head:* Dr. Lee Garver, Director of Graduate Studies, Department of English Language and Literature, 317-940-9859, E-mail: lgarver@butler.edu. *Application contact:* Diane Dubord, Graduate Student Services Specialist, 317-940-8107, Fax: 317-940-8250, E-mail: ddubord@butler.edu.
Website: http://legacy.butler.edu/english/graduate-studies/ma-english/

California College of the Arts, Graduate Programs, MFA in Writing Program, San Francisco, CA 94107. Offers creative non-fiction (MFA); fiction (MFA); poetry (MFA). *Degree requirements:* For master's, thesis. *Entrance requirements:* For master's, appropriate bachelor's degree, portfolio, transcripts, letters of recommendation. Additional exam requirements/recommendations for international students: Required—TOEFL (minimum score 600 paper-based; 100 iBT). Electronic applications accepted.

California Institute of Integral Studies, School of Consciousness and Transformation, San Francisco, CA 94103. Offers anthropology and social change (MA, PhD); creative inquiry/interdisciplinary arts (MFA); East-West psychology (MA, PhD); philosophy and religion (MA, PhD), including Asian and comparative studies, ecology, spirituality, and religion, philosophy, cosmology, and consciousness, women's spirituality; transformative leadership (MA); transformative studies (PhD); writing and consciousness (MFA). Part-time and evening/weekend programs available. Postbaccalaureate distance learning degree programs offered (no on-campus study). *Students:* 385 full-time (256 women), 102 part-time (71 women); includes 124 minority (31 Black or African American, non-Hispanic/Latino; 3 American Indian or Alaska Native, non-Hispanic/Latino; 19 Asian, non-Hispanic/Latino; 39 Hispanic/Latino; 1 Native Hawaiian or other Pacific Islander, non-Hispanic/Latino; 31 Two or more races, non-Hispanic/Latino), 53 international. Average age 43. 196 applicants, 92% accepted, 125 enrolled. In 2014, 75 master's, 41 doctorates awarded. Terminal master's awarded for partial completion of doctoral program. *Degree requirements:* For master's, thesis optional; for doctorate, comprehensive exam, thesis/dissertation, 1 foreign language (for Asian comparative studies). *Entrance requirements:* For master's, minimum GPA of 3.0, letters of recommendation, writing sample; for doctorate, master's degree, minimum GPA of 3.0, letters of recommendation, writing sample. Additional exam requirements/recommendations for international students: Required—TOEFL. *Application deadline:* For fall admission, 2/1 priority date for domestic and international students; for spring admission, 10/15 priority date for domestic and international students. Applications are processed on a rolling basis. Application fee: $65. Electronic applications accepted. *Expenses:* Tuition: Full-time $18,270; part-time $1015 per credit. *Required fees:* $85 per semester hour. *Financial support:* In 2014–15, 445 students received support, including 5 research assistantships (averaging $800 per year), 28 teaching assistantships (averaging $825 per year); career-related internships or fieldwork, Federal Work-Study, and scholarships/grants also available. Support available to part-time students. Financial award application deadline: 4/15; financial award applicants required to submit FAFSA. *Faculty research:* Ecology and sustainability, philosophy and religion, East-West psychology, integrative health, social and cultural anthropology, transformative leadership. *Application contact:* David Townes, Senior Admissions Counselor, 415-575-6152, Fax: 415-575-1268, E-mail: admissions@ciis.edu.
Website: http://www.ciis.edu/

California Institute of the Arts, School of Critical Studies, Valencia, CA 91355-2340. Offers writing (MFA, Adv C). *Entrance requirements:* For master's, portfolio. Additional exam requirements/recommendations for international students: Required—TOEFL.

California Institute of the Arts, School of Theatre, Valencia, CA 91355-2340. Offers acting (MFA, Adv C); design and technology (Adv C); directing (MFA); performing arts design and technology (MFA); theater management (MFA, Adv C); writing for performance (MFA). *Degree requirements:* For master's, thesis (for some programs), faculty review, performance or portfolio. *Entrance requirements:* For master's, audition or portfolio, interview. Additional exam requirements/recommendations for international students: Required—TOEFL. Electronic applications accepted.

Writing

California State University, East Bay, Office of Academic Programs and Graduate Studies, College of Letters, Arts, and Social Sciences, Department of English, Hayward, CA 94542-3000. Offers creative writing (MA); literary studies (MA); teaching English to speakers of other languages (MA). Part-time programs available. *Degree requirements:* For master's, one foreign language, comprehensive exam, thesis optional. *Entrance requirements:* For master's, minimum GPA of 3.0 in field; 2 letters of recommendation; academic or professional writing sample; preferred teaching experience and some degree of bilingualism (for TESOL). Additional exam requirements/recommendations for international students: Required—TOEFL (minimum score 550 paper-based); Recommended—IELTS (minimum score 6.5). *Application deadline:* For fall admission, 6/30 for domestic and international students. Applications are processed on a rolling basis. Application fee: $55. Electronic applications accepted. *Expenses:* Tuition, state resident: full-time $7830; part-time $1302 per credit hour. Tuition, nonresident: full-time $16,368. *Required fees:* $327 per quarter. Tuition and fees vary according to course load and program. *Financial support:* Fellowships, teaching assistantships, career-related internships or fieldwork, Federal Work-Study, institutionally sponsored loans, and scholarships/grants available. Support available to part-time students. Financial award application deadline: 3/2; financial award applicants required to submit FAFSA. *Unit head:* Dr. Sarah Nielsen, Acting Chair, 510-885-3151, Fax: 510-885-4797. *Application contact:* Dr. Donna Wiley, Interim Associate Vice President for Academic Programs and Graduate Studies, 510-885-3716, Fax: 510-885-4777, E-mail: donna.wiley@csueastbay.edu.
Website: http://www20.csueastbay.edu/class/departments/english/index.html

California State University, Fresno, Division of Graduate Studies, College of Arts and Humanities, Department of English, Fresno, CA 93740-8027. Offers composition theory (MA); creative writing (MFA); literature (MA). Part-time and evening/weekend programs available. *Degree requirements:* For master's, one foreign language, thesis. *Entrance requirements:* For master's, GRE General Test, minimum GPA of 3.0, writing sample. Additional exam requirements/recommendations for international students: Required—TOEFL. Electronic applications accepted. *Faculty research:* American literature, Renaissance literature, foreign literature.

California State University, Long Beach, Graduate Studies, College of Liberal Arts, Department of English, Long Beach, CA 90840. Offers creative writing (MFA); English (MA). Part-time programs available. *Degree requirements:* For master's, one foreign language, comprehensive exam or thesis. *Entrance requirements:* For master's, GRE Subject Test, minimum GPA of 3.0 in English. Electronic applications accepted. *Faculty research:* English and American literature, literary theory, linguistics, rhetoric and composition.

California State University, Northridge, Graduate Studies, College of Humanities, Department of English, Northridge, CA 91330. Offers creative writing (MA); literature (MA); rhetoric and composition theory (MA). Part-time and evening/weekend programs available. *Students:* 36 full-time (22 women), 84 part-time (53 women); includes 39 minority (3 Black or African American, non-Hispanic/Latino; 10 Asian, non-Hispanic/Latino; 22 Hispanic/Latino; 4 Two or more races, non-Hispanic/Latino), 1 international. Average age 32. *Degree requirements:* For master's, thesis or alternative. *Entrance requirements:* For master's, writing proficiency test, GRE General Test or minimum GPA of 3.0. Additional exam requirements/recommendations for international students: Required—TOEFL. *Application deadline:* For fall admission, 11/30 for domestic students. Application fee: $55. *Expenses: Required fees:* $12,402. *Financial support:* Teaching assistantships available. Financial award application deadline: 3/1. *Faculty research:* Reading improvement, professional writing, Dickens, Shaw, English as a second language. *Unit head:* Jackie Stallcup, Chair, 818-677-3434. *Application contact:* Dr. Marjie Seagoe, Graduate Studies Secretary, 818-677-3433.
Website: http://www.csun.edu/english/index.php

California State University, Sacramento, Office of Graduate Studies, College of Arts and Letters, Department of English, Sacramento, CA 95819. Offers composition (MA); creative writing (MA); literature (MA); teaching English to speakers of other languages (MA). Part-time programs available. *Degree requirements:* For master's, thesis, project, or comprehensive exam; TESOL exam; writing proficiency exam. *Entrance requirements:* For master's, portfolio (creative writing); minimum GPA of 3.0 in English, 2.75 overall during previous 2 years. Additional exam requirements/recommendations for international students: Required—TOEFL. Electronic applications accepted. *Faculty research:* Teaching composition, remedial writing.

California State University, San Bernardino, Graduate Studies, College of Arts and Letters, Department of English, San Bernardino, CA 92407-2397. Offers creative writing (MFA), including fiction; English composition (MA), including composition. Part-time and evening/weekend programs available. *Students:* 31 full-time (17 women), 61 part-time (41 women); includes 46 minority (7 Black or African American, non-Hispanic/Latino; 1 Asian, non-Hispanic/Latino; 35 Hispanic/Latino; 3 Two or more races, non-Hispanic/Latino), 2 international. Average age 27. 74 applicants, 53% accepted, 37 enrolled. In 2014, 45 master's awarded. *Degree requirements:* For master's, one foreign language, thesis. *Entrance requirements:* Additional exam requirements/recommendations for international students: Required—TOEFL. *Application deadline:* For fall admission, 7/17 for domestic students. Application fee: $55. *Expenses:* Tuition, state resident: full-time $6738; part-time $1302 per term. Tuition, nonresident: full-time $17,898; part-time $248 per unit. *Required fees:* $365 per quarter. Tuition and fees vary according to degree level and program. *Financial support:* Application deadline: 3/1. *Unit head:* Dr. Sunny Hyon, Chair, 909-537-5834, Fax: 909-537-7086, E-mail: shyon@csusb.edu. *Application contact:* Dr. Jeffrey Thompson, Dean of Graduate Studies, 909-537-5058, Fax: 909-537-5078, E-mail: jthompso@csusb.edu.

California State University, San Marcos, College of Humanities, Arts, Behavioral and Social Sciences, Program in Literature and Writing Studies, San Marcos, CA 92096-0001. Offers MA. Part-time and evening/weekend programs available. *Students:* 9 full-time (7 women), 8 part-time (5 women); includes 7 minority (2 Black or African American, non-Hispanic/Latino; 1 American Indian or Alaska Native, non-Hispanic/Latino; 1 Asian, non-Hispanic/Latino; 1 Hispanic/Latino; 2 Two or more races, non-Hispanic/Latino). Average age 33. *Degree requirements:* For master's, one foreign language, thesis. *Entrance requirements:* For master's, GRE General Test, minimum GPA of 3.0, writing sample. *Application deadline:* For fall admission, 3/15 priority date for domestic students; for spring admission, 11/15 for domestic students. Applications are processed on a rolling basis. Application fee: $55. *Expenses:* Tuition, state resident: full-time $6738. *Required fees:* $1692. Tuition and fees vary according to program. *Financial support:* Teaching assistantships with partial tuition reimbursements available. *Faculty research:* Postcolonialism, feminism rhetoric, cultural studies, creative writing, critical theory. *Unit head:* Prof. Salah Moukhlis, Chair, 760-750-8081, E-mail: smoukhli@csusm.edu. *Application contact:* Admissions, 760-750-4848, Fax: 760-750-3248, E-mail: apply@csusm.edu.

California State University, Stanislaus, College of Humanities and Social Sciences, Program in English (MA), Turlock, CA 95382. Offers literature (Certificate); rhetoric and teaching writing (MA); teaching English to speakers of other languages (MA). Part-time programs available. *Degree requirements:* For master's, comprehensive exam, thesis or alternative. *Entrance requirements:* For master's, GRE, minimum GPA of 3.0, 2 letters of reference, personal statement. Additional exam requirements/recommendations for international students: Required—TOEFL (minimum score 575 paper-based), TWE (minimum score 4). Electronic applications accepted. *Faculty research:* Transnational literacies, Renaissance and medieval literature, abolition writings and slave narratives, qualitative writing.

Carlow University, College of Learning and Innovation, Program in Creative Writing, Pittsburgh, PA 15213-3165. Offers fiction (MFA); non-fiction (MFA); poetry (MFA). Part-time and evening/weekend programs available. Postbaccalaureate distance learning degree programs offered (minimal on-campus study). *Students:* 27 part-time (21 women); includes 3 minority (2 Black or African American, non-Hispanic/Latino; 1 Hispanic/Latino). Average age 36. In 2014, 10 master's awarded. *Degree requirements:* For master's, manuscript. *Application deadline:* Applications are processed on a rolling basis. *Expenses: Tuition:* Full-time $9750; part-time $785 per credit. Part-time tuition and fees vary according to degree level and program. *Unit head:* Dr. Jan Beatty, Program Director, Creative Writing, 412-578-6081, Fax: 412-578-8816, E-mail: jpbeatty@carlow.edu. *Application contact:* Stephanie Wytovich, Counselor, Graduate Enrollment Management, 412-578-6363, E-mail: smwytovich@carlow.edu.
Website: http://www.carlow.edu/Master_of_Fine_Arts_in_Creative_Writing.aspx

Carnegie Mellon University, Dietrich College of Humanities and Social Sciences, Department of English, Program in Professional Writing, Pittsburgh, PA 15213-3891. Offers editing and publishing (MAPW); policy and non-profit communication (MAPW); public and media relations/corporate communications (MAPW); science or healthcare communication (MAPW); technical writing (MAPW); writing for new media (MAPW); writing for print media (MAPW). Part-time programs available. *Entrance requirements:* For master's, GRE General Test. Additional exam requirements/recommendations for international students: Required—TOEFL, TWE.

Cedar Crest College, Program in Creative Writing, Allentown, PA 18104-6196. Offers MFA. Postbaccalaureate distance learning degree programs offered (no on-campus study). *Faculty:* 6 part-time/adjunct (1 woman). *Students:* 19 part-time (all women). Average age 39. *Degree requirements:* For master's, final book-length creative thesis. *Unit head:* Dr. Robert Wilson, Director of Writing Program, 610-606-4666 Ext. 3474, E-mail: rawilson@cedarcrest.edu. *Application contact:* Mary Ellen Hickes, Director of School of Adult and Graduate Education, 610-437-4471, E-mail: sage@cedarcrest.edu.
Website: http://sage.cedarcrest.edu/graduate/mfa/

Central Michigan University, College of Graduate Studies, College of Humanities and Social and Behavioral Sciences, Department of English Language and Literature, Mount Pleasant, MI 48859. Offers English composition and communication (MA); English language and literature (MA), including children's and young adult literature, creative writing, English language and literature; TESOL: teaching English to speakers of other languages (MA). Part-time and evening/weekend programs available. *Degree requirements:* For master's, thesis or alternative. Electronic applications accepted. *Faculty research:* Composition theory, science fiction history and bibliography, children's and young adult literature, nineteenth century American literature, applied linguistics.

Chapman University, Wilkinson College of Humanities and Social Sciences, Department of English, Orange, CA 92866. Offers creative writing (MFA); English (MA). Part-time and evening/weekend programs available. *Faculty:* 25 full-time (11 women), 37 part-time/adjunct (18 women). *Students:* 38 full-time (20 women), 23 part-time (19 women); includes 12 minority (1 Black or African American, non-Hispanic/Latino; 6 Hispanic/Latino; 1 Native Hawaiian or other Pacific Islander, non-Hispanic/Latino; 4 Two or more races, non-Hispanic/Latino). Average age 28. 66 applicants, 80% accepted, 21 enrolled. In 2014, 26 master's awarded. *Degree requirements:* For master's, comprehensive exam (for some programs), thesis (for some programs). *Entrance requirements:* For master's, GRE or MAT, minimum undergraduate GPA of 2.5. Additional exam requirements/recommendations for international students: Required—TOEFL (minimum score 550 paper-based; 80 iBT). *Application deadline:* For fall admission, 5/1 priority date for domestic students; for winter admission, 11/1 priority date for domestic students. Applications are processed on a rolling basis. Application fee: $60. Electronic applications accepted. *Expenses:* Expenses: Contact institution. *Financial support:* Fellowships, Federal Work-Study, and scholarships/grants available. Financial award applicants required to submit FAFSA. *Unit head:* Mark Axelrod, Director, 714-997-6586, E-mail: axelrod@chapman.edu. *Application contact:* Shannon McCance, Graduate Admission Counselor, 714-997-6711, E-mail: smccance@chapman.edu.
Website: http://www.chapman.edu/wilkinson/english/

Chatham University, Program in Writing, Pittsburgh, PA 15232-2826. Offers children's writing (MFA); fiction (MFA); non-fiction (MFA); poetry (MFA); professional writing (MPW); screenwriting (MFA). Part-time and evening/weekend programs available. Postbaccalaureate distance learning degree programs offered (minimal on-campus study). *Faculty:* 3 full-time (2 women), 36 part-time/adjunct (29 women). *Students:* 51 full-time (39 women), 69 part-time (63 women); includes 11 minority (3 Black or African American, non-Hispanic/Latino; 5 Hispanic/Latino; 3 Two or more races, non-Hispanic/Latino), 3 international. Average age 32. 134 applicants, 85% accepted, 52 enrolled. In 2014, 54 master's awarded. *Entrance requirements:* For master's, minimum GPA of 3.0, writing sample, recommendation letters. Additional exam requirements/recommendations for international students: Required—TOEFL (minimum score 600 paper-based; 100 iBT), IELTS (minimum score 7), TWE. *Application deadline:* For fall admission, 1/15 priority date for domestic and international students; for spring admission, 11/1 priority date for domestic students, 10/1 priority date for international students. Applications are processed on a rolling basis. Application fee: $45. Electronic applications accepted. Application fee is waived when completed online. *Expenses: Tuition:* Full-time $15,318; part-time $851 per credit hour. *Required fees:* $440; $24 per credit hour. Tuition and fees vary according to course load, program and reciprocity agreements. *Financial support:* Career-related internships or fieldwork available. Financial award applicants required to submit FAFSA. *Faculty research:* Ecopoetics; environment and culture; wilderness and literature; literature of exploration, exile, and home. *Unit head:* Dr. Sheryl St. Germain, Director, 412-365-1190, Fax: 412-365-1505, E-mail: sstgermain@chatham.edu. *Application contact:* Katie Noel, Assistant Director of Graduate Admission, 412-365-2758, Fax: 412-365-1609, E-mail: gradadmissions@chatham.edu.
Website: http://www.chatham.edu/mfa

Chicago State University, School of Graduate and Professional Studies, College of Arts and Sciences, Department of English, Foreign Languages and Literatures, Chicago, IL 60628. Offers creative writing (MFA); English (MA). *Degree requirements:* For master's, comprehensive exam (for some programs), thesis (for some programs). *Entrance requirements:* For master's, minimum GPA of 3.0.

City College of the City University of New York, Graduate School, College of Liberal Arts and Science, Division of the Humanities and Arts, Department of English, Program in Creative Writing, New York, NY 10031-9198. Offers MA, MFA. *Degree requirements:* For master's, one foreign language, comprehensive exam, thesis. *Entrance requirements:* For master's, minimum GPA of 3.0, 10-15 poems or 30-50 pages of fiction (short stories or novel excerpt). Additional exam requirements/recommendations for international students: Required—TOEFL (minimum score 600 paper-based; 100 iBT). Electronic applications accepted.

Claremont Graduate University, Graduate Programs, School of Arts and Humanities, Department of English, Claremont, CA 91711-6160. Offers American studies (MA, PhD); critical theory (MA, PhD); early modern studies (MA, PhD); English (M Phil, MA, PhD); literary theory (PhD); literature (MA, PhD); literature and creative writing (MA); literature and film (MA); MBA/MA; MBA/PhD. Part-time programs available. *Faculty:* 4 full-time (2 women), 2 part-time/adjunct (0 women). *Students:* 70 full-time (51 women), 27 part-time (17 women); includes 31 minority (4 Black or African American, non-Hispanic/Latino; 1 American Indian or Alaska Native, non-Hispanic/Latino; 12 Asian, non-Hispanic/Latino; 6 Hispanic/Latino; 8 Two or more races, non-Hispanic/Latino), 8 international. Average age 36. In 2014, 9 master's, 7 doctorates awarded. *Entrance requirements:* For master's and doctorate, GRE General Test. Additional exam requirements/recommendations for international students: Required—TOEFL (minimum score 550 paper-based; 80 iBT). *Application deadline:* For fall admission, 2/1 priority date for domestic and international students. Applications are processed on a rolling basis. Application fee: $80. Electronic applications accepted. *Expenses:* Tuition: Full-time $41,784; part-time $1741 per credit. *Required fees:* $600; $300 per semester. *Financial support:* Fellowships, Federal Work-Study, institutionally sponsored loans, and scholarships/grants available. Support available to part-time students. Financial award application deadline: 2/15; financial award applicants required to submit FAFSA. *Faculty research:* American, comparative, and English Renaissance literature; modernism; feminist literature and theory. *Unit head:* David Luis-Brown, Chair, E-mail: david.luis-brown@cgu.edu. *Application contact:* Erma Cross, Admissions and Alumni Coordinator, 909-607-9843, E-mail: erminia.cross@cgu.edu.
Website: http://www.cgu.edu/pages/568.asp

Clemson University, Graduate School, College of Architecture, Arts, and Humanities, Department of English, Program in Professional Communication, Clemson, SC 29634. Offers MA. Part-time programs available. *Students:* 24 full-time (16 women), 5 part-time (all women); includes 8 minority (3 Black or African American, non-Hispanic/Latino; 3 Hispanic/Latino; 2 Two or more races, non-Hispanic/Latino). Average age 27. 24 applicants, 71% accepted, 12 enrolled. In 2014, 8 master's awarded. *Degree requirements:* For master's, one foreign language, thesis or alternative, oral exam. *Entrance requirements:* For master's, GRE General Test, minimum GPA of 3.0. Additional exam requirements/recommendations for international students: Required—TOEFL, IELTS. *Application deadline:* For fall admission, 2/1 priority date for domestic students, 2/1 for international students; for spring admission, 11/1 priority date for domestic students, 11/1 for international students. Applications are processed on a rolling basis. Application fee: $70 ($80 for international students). Electronic applications accepted. *Financial support:* In 2014–15, 10 students received support, including 10 teaching assistantships with partial tuition reimbursements available (averaging $18,839 per year); fellowships with full and partial tuition reimbursements available, research assistantships with partial tuition reimbursements available, career-related internships or fieldwork, institutionally sponsored loans, scholarships/grants, health care benefits, and unspecified assistantships also available. Support available to part-time students. Financial award application deadline: 4/1; financial award applicants required to submit FAFSA. *Faculty research:* Usability and user experience design, rhetoric, intercultural communication, digital publishing, social media authoring, technical writing. *Unit head:* Dr. Sean Williams, Chair, 864-656-3151, Fax: 864-656-1345, E-mail: sean@clemson.edu. *Application contact:* Dr. Tharon Howard, Graduate Coordinator, 864-656-6689, Fax: 864-656-1345, E-mail: tharon@clemson.edu.
Website: http://www.clemson.edu/caah/english/graduate/mapc/index.html

Cleveland State University, College of Graduate Studies, College of Liberal Arts and Social Sciences, Department of English, Cleveland, OH 44115. Offers creative writing (MFA); English (MA). Part-time and evening/weekend programs available. *Faculty:* 10 full-time (5 women), 3 part-time/adjunct (1 woman). *Students:* 21 full-time (13 women), 50 part-time (31 women); includes 11 minority (7 Black or African American, non-Hispanic/Latino; 1 American Indian or Alaska Native, non-Hispanic/Latino; 2 Hispanic/Latino; 1 Two or more races, non-Hispanic/Latino). Average age 34. 42 applicants, 71% accepted, 9 enrolled. In 2014, 21 master's awarded. *Degree requirements:* For master's, comprehensive exam, thesis. *Entrance requirements:* For master's, minimum GPA of 2.75, undergraduate concentration in English, writing sample, portfolio. Additional exam requirements/recommendations for international students: Required—TOEFL (minimum score 525 paper-based) or IELTS (minimum score 6). *Application deadline:* For fall admission, 7/15 priority date for domestic students, 5/15 for international students; for spring admission, 12/15 for domestic students, 11/1 for international students. Applications are processed on a rolling basis. Application fee: $30. Electronic applications accepted. *Expenses:* Tuition, state resident: full-time $9566; part-time $531 per credit hour. Tuition, nonresident: full-time $17,980; part-time $999 per credit hour. *Required fees:* $25 per semester. Tuition and fees vary according to degree level and program. *Financial support:* In 2014–15, 20 students received support, including 1 fellowship (averaging $1,000 per year), 5 research assistantships with full and partial tuition reimbursements available (averaging $3,480 per year), 7 teaching assistantships with full and partial tuition reimbursements available (averaging $3,480 per year); Federal Work-Study, institutionally sponsored loans, tuition waivers (full and partial), and unspecified assistantships also available. Support available to part-time students. Financial award application deadline: 2/1. *Faculty research:* Literary history and criticism, literature. *Total annual research expenditures:* $5,000. *Unit head:* Dr. John C. Gerlach, Interim Chairperson, 216-687-3951, Fax: 216-687-6943, E-mail: j.gerlach@csuohio.edu. *Application contact:* Dr. James J. Marino, Graduate Director, 216-687-6874, Fax: 216-687-6943, E-mail: j.marino22@csuohio.edu.
Website: http://www.csuohio.edu/class/english/english

Coastal Carolina University, Thomas W. and Robin W. Edwards College of Humanities and Fine Arts, Conway, SC 29528-6054. Offers writing (MA). Part-time and evening/weekend programs available. *Faculty:* 9 full-time (5 women). *Students:* 19 full-time (10 women), 11 part-time (7 women); includes 2 minority (1 Black or African American, non-Hispanic/Latino; 1 Hispanic/Latino). Average age 34. 31 applicants, 77% accepted, 21 enrolled. In 2014, 13 master's awarded. *Degree requirements:* For master's, thesis. *Entrance requirements:* For master's, GRE, official transcripts, 3 letters of recommendation, writing sample, minimum GPA of 3.3 in 18 hours of coursework in English or related discipline. Additional exam requirements/recommendations for international students: Required—TOEFL (minimum score 550 paper-based; 79 iBT). *Application deadline:* For fall admission, 5/15 priority date for domestic and international students; for spring admission, 11/15 priority date for domestic and international students. Applications are processed on a rolling basis. Application fee: $45. Electronic applications accepted. *Expenses:* Tuition, state resident: full-time $12,384; part-time $516 per credit hour. Tuition, nonresident: full-time $22,560; part-time $940 per credit hour. *Required fees:* $5 per credit hour. *Financial support:* Fellowships, research assistantships, and unspecified assistantships available. Support available to part-time students. Financial award application deadline: 3/1; financial award applicants required to submit FAFSA. *Unit head:* Jennifer E. Boyle, Associate Professor/Director of the MA in Writing, 843-349-6654, E-mail: jboyle@coastal.edu. *Application contact:* Dr. James O. Luken, Associate Provost/Director of Graduate Studies, 843-349-2235, Fax: 843-349-6444, E-mail: joluken@coastal.edu.
Website: http://www.coastal.edu/humanities/index.html

The College at Brockport, State University of New York, School of the Arts, Humanities and Social Sciences, Department of English, Brockport, NY 14420-2997. Offers creative writing (AGC); English (MA), including creative writing, literature. Part-time programs available. *Faculty:* 12 full-time (7 women). *Students:* 13 full-time (11 women), 22 part-time (16 women); includes 5 minority (2 Black or African American, non-Hispanic/Latino; 2 Hispanic/Latino; 1 Two or more races, non-Hispanic/Latino). 20 applicants, 65% accepted, 8 enrolled. In 2014, 11 master's awarded. *Degree requirements:* For master's, thesis. *Entrance requirements:* For master's, minimum GPA of 3.0, letters of recommendation, writing sample. Additional exam requirements/recommendations for international students: Required—TOEFL (minimum score 550 paper-based; 79 iBT), IELTS (minimum score 6.5). *Application deadline:* For fall admission, 4/15 priority date for domestic and international students; for spring admission, 11/15 priority date for domestic and international students; for summer admission, 4/15 priority date for domestic and international students. Application fee: $50. Electronic applications accepted. *Financial support:* In 2014–15, 3 teaching assistantships with full tuition reimbursements (averaging $6,000 per year) were awarded; Federal Work-Study, scholarships/grants, and unspecified assistantships also available. Support available to part-time students. Financial award application deadline: 3/15; financial award applicants required to submit FAFSA. *Faculty research:* British and American literature, creative writing, film studies, children's literature, ancient and modern world literature. *Unit head:* Dr. Jennifer Haytock, Chairperson, 585-395-5832, Fax: 585-395-2391, E-mail: jhaytock@brockport.edu. *Application contact:* Dr. Janie Hinds, Graduate Program Director, 585-395-5712, Fax: 585-395-2391, E-mail: jhinds@brockport.edu.
Website: http://www.brockport.edu/english/graduate/

Colorado State University, Graduate School, College of Liberal Arts, Department of English, Fort Collins, CO 80523-1773. Offers creative writing (MFA); English (MA). Part-time programs available. *Faculty:* 30 full-time (19 women), 1 part-time/adjunct (0 women). *Students:* 75 full-time (53 women), 33 part-time (22 women); includes 12 minority (2 Asian, non-Hispanic/Latino; 4 Hispanic/Latino; 1 Native Hawaiian or other Pacific Islander, non-Hispanic/Latino; 5 Two or more races, non-Hispanic/Latino), 11 international. Average age 33. 247 applicants, 31% accepted, 33 enrolled. In 2014, 60 master's awarded. *Degree requirements:* For master's, variable foreign language requirement, thesis (for some programs), exams. *Entrance requirements:* For master's, GRE, writing sample, BA/BS with minimum GPA of 3.0, 3 letters of recommendation, transcripts, statement of purpose. Additional exam requirements/recommendations for international students: Required—TOEFL (minimum score 550 paper-based; 80 iBT). *Application deadline:* For fall admission, 4/1 priority date for domestic students; for spring admission, 9/1 priority date for domestic students. Applications are processed on a rolling basis. Application fee: $50. Electronic applications accepted. *Expenses:* Tuition, state resident: full-time $9348; part-time $519 per credit. Tuition, nonresident: full-time $22,916; part-time $1273 per credit. *Required fees:* $1584. *Financial support:* In 2014–15, 35 students received support, including 35 teaching assistantships with full tuition reimbursements available (averaging $13,875 per year); career-related internships or fieldwork, Federal Work-Study, institutionally sponsored loans, scholarships/grants, traineeships, and unspecified assistantships also available. Support available to part-time students. Financial award application deadline: 5/1; financial award applicants required to submit FAFSA. *Faculty research:* Computers and writing, environmental writing, cultural studies, new historicism, performance and identity. *Total annual research expenditures:* $136,378. *Unit head:* Dr. Louann Reid, Chair, 970-491-6428, Fax: 970-491-5601, E-mail: louann.reid@colostate.edu. *Application contact:* Marnie Leonard, Administrative Assistant, 970-491-2403, Fax: 970-491-7541, E-mail: marnie.leonard@colostate.edu.
Website: http://english.colostate.edu/

Columbia College Chicago, Graduate School, Department of Creative Writing, Chicago, IL 60605-1996. Offers fiction (MFA); nonfiction (MFA); poetry (MFA). Part-time programs available. *Faculty:* 20 full-time (8 women), 28 part-time/adjunct (12 women). *Students:* 109 full-time (65 women); includes 21 minority (11 Black or African American, non-Hispanic/Latino; 4 Asian, non-Hispanic/Latino; 6 Hispanic/Latino). Average age 30. *Degree requirements:* For master's, thesis. *Entrance requirements:* For master's, self-assessment essay, work samples, letters of recommendation. Additional exam requirements/recommendations for international students: Required—TOEFL (minimum score 600 paper-based; 100 iBT). *Application deadline:* For fall admission, 1/15 for domestic and international students. Application fee: $55 ($100 for international students). Electronic applications accepted. *Financial support:* In 2014–15, 18 students received support, including 12 fellowships, 6 research assistantships, 45 teaching assistantships; career-related internships or fieldwork, Federal Work-Study, scholarships/grants, and unspecified assistantships also available. Support available to part-time students. Financial award application deadline: 8/15; financial award applicants required to submit FAFSA. *Unit head:* Matthew Shenoda, Interim Chair, Creative Writing, 312-369-7263, E-mail: mshenoda@colum.edu. *Application contact:* Kara Leffler, Associate Director of Graduate Admissions, 312-369-7262, Fax: 312-369-8024, E-mail: kleffler@colum.edu.
Website: http://www.colum.edu/Admissions/Graduate/index.php

Columbia University, School of the Arts, Writing Program, New York, NY 10027. Offers fiction (MFA); nonfiction (MFA); poetry (MFA). *Degree requirements:* For master's, thesis. *Entrance requirements:* For master's, 3 letters of recommendation, writing sample. Additional exam requirements/recommendations for international students: Required—TOEFL (minimum score 600 paper-based). Electronic applications accepted.
See Display on page 257 and Close-Up on page 273.

Concordia University, School of Graduate Studies, Faculty of Arts and Science, Department of English, Program in Creative Writing, Montréal, QC H3G 1M8, Canada. Offers MA. *Degree requirements:* For master's, one foreign language, thesis. *Entrance requirements:* For master's, honors degree in English, minimum GPA of 3.3 in English literature, portfolio. *Faculty research:* Fiction, poetry, prose, drama.

Cornell University, Graduate School, Graduate Fields of Arts and Sciences, Field of English Language and Literature, Ithaca, NY 14853-0001. Offers African-American literature (PhD); American literature after 1865 (PhD); American literature to 1865 (PhD); American studies (PhD); colonial and postcolonial literatures (PhD); creative writing (MFA); cultural studies (PhD); dramatic literature (PhD); English poetry (PhD); English Renaissance to 1660 (PhD); lesbian, bisexual, and gay literary studies (PhD); literary criticism and theory (PhD); Old and Middle English (PhD); prose fiction (PhD); Restoration and the eighteenth-century (PhD); the nineteenth century (PhD); the twentieth century (PhD); women's literature (PhD); MFA/PhD. Terminal master's awarded for partial completion of doctoral program. *Degree requirements:* For master's, one foreign language, thesis; for doctorate, one foreign language, comprehensive exam, thesis/dissertation, teaching experience. *Entrance requirements:* For master's, GRE General Test, 3 letters of recommendation, creative writing sample; for doctorate, GRE General Test, GRE Subject Test (English), 3 letters of recommendation, writing sample. Additional exam requirements/recommendations for international students: Required—TOEFL (minimum score 600 paper-based; 77 iBT). Electronic applications accepted. *Faculty research:* English and American literature, women's writing, ethnic and post-colonial literature, critical theory, medievalism.

Writing

Creighton University, Graduate School, College of Arts and Sciences, Department of English, Omaha, NE 68178-0001. Offers creative writing (MA, MFA). Part-time programs available. *Faculty:* 15 full-time (7 women). *Students:* 20 full-time (11 women), 6 part-time (3 women); includes 1 minority (Black or African American, non-Hispanic/Latino), 1 international. Average age 31. 26 applicants, 77% accepted, 7 enrolled. In 2014, 4 master's awarded. *Degree requirements:* For master's, thesis optional. *Entrance requirements:* For master's, GRE, 10-15 page writing sample, 3 letters of recommendation. Additional exam requirements/recommendations for international students: Required—TOEFL (minimum score 550 paper-based; 80 iBT). *Application deadline:* For fall admission, 3/15 priority date for domestic and international students. Application fee: $50. Electronic applications accepted. *Expenses: Tuition:* Full-time $14,040; part-time $780 per credit hour. *Required fees:* $153 per semester. Tuition and fees vary according to course load, campus/location, program, reciprocity agreements and student's religious affiliation. *Financial support:* In 2014–15, 5 fellowships with full and partial tuition reimbursements (averaging $11,240 per year) were awarded; tuition waivers (partial) and unspecified assistantships also available. Financial award applicants required to submit FAFSA. *Unit head:* Dr. Robert Whipple, Director, 402-280-2520, E-mail: whippl@creighton.edu. *Application contact:* Lindsay Johnson, Director of Graduate and Adult Recruitment, 402-280-2703, Fax: 402-280-2423, E-mail: gradschool@creighton.edu.

DePaul University, College of Liberal Arts and Social Sciences, Chicago, IL 60614. Offers Arabic (MA); Chinese (MA); English (MA); French (MA); German (MA); history (MA); interdisciplinary studies (MA, MS); international public service (MS); international studies (MA); Italian (MA); Japanese (MA); leadership and policy studies (MS); liberal studies (MA); new media studies (MA); nonprofit management (MNM); public administration (MPA); public health (MPH); public service management (MS); social work (MSW); sociology (MA); Spanish (MA); sustainable urban development (MA); women and gender studies (MA); writing and publishing (MA); writing, rhetoric, and discourse (MA); MA/PhD. Part-time and evening/weekend programs available. Postbaccalaureate distance learning degree programs offered (no on-campus study). Terminal master's awarded for partial completion of doctoral program. *Degree requirements:* For master's, variable foreign language requirement, comprehensive exam (for some programs), thesis (for some programs). Electronic applications accepted.

Dominican University of California, School of Arts, Humanities and Social Sciences, Humanities Program, San Rafael, CA 94901-2298. Offers applied music (MA); art history (MA); creative writing (MA); history (MA); literature (MA); philosophy (MA); political theory (MA); religion (MA); women and gender studies (MA). Part-time programs available. *Faculty:* 11 full-time (5 women), 5 part-time/adjunct (2 women). *Students:* 2 full-time (1 woman), 25 part-time (16 women); includes 7 minority (1 Black or African American, non-Hispanic/Latino; 1 American Indian or Alaska Native, non-Hispanic/Latino; 3 Hispanic/Latino; 2 Two or more races, non-Hispanic/Latino). Average age 46. 12 applicants, 83% accepted, 7 enrolled. *Degree requirements:* For master's, thesis or alternative. *Entrance requirements:* For master's, minimum GPA of 3.0, interview. Additional exam requirements/recommendations for international students: Required—TOEFL (minimum score 550 paper-based; 80 iBT), IELTS (minimum score 6.5). *Application deadline:* For fall admission, 5/15 priority date for domestic and international students; for spring admission, 11/15 priority date for domestic and international students. Applications are processed on a rolling basis. Electronic applications accepted. Application fee is waived when completed online. *Expenses:* Expenses: $935 per unit. *Financial support:* Scholarships/grants available. Support available to part-time students. Financial award application deadline: 3/2; financial award applicants required to submit FAFSA. *Unit head:* Dr. Laura Stivers, Acting Dean, 415-458-3734, E-mail: laura.stivers@dominican.edu. *Application contact:* Ryan Purtill, Director, 415-458-3748, Fax: 415-485-3214, E-mail: ryan.purtill@dominican.edu. Website: http://www.dominican.edu/academics/ahss/graduate-program/index_html

Drew University, Caspersen School of Graduate Studies, Program in Poetry, Madison, NJ 07940-1493. Offers poetry (MFA); poetry in translation (MFA). *Degree requirements:* For master's, thesis. *Entrance requirements:* For master's, transcripts, writing sample, recommendations. *Expenses:* Contact institution.

East Carolina University, Graduate School, Thomas Harriot College of Arts and Sciences, Department of English, Greenville, NC 27858-4353. Offers creative writing (MA); English studies (MA); linguistics (MA); literature (MA); multicultural and transnational literatures (MA, Certificate); rhetoric and composition (MA); rhetoric, writing, and professional communication (PhD); teaching English in the two-year college (Certificate); teaching English to speakers of other languages (MA, Certificate); technical and professional communication (MA). Part-time and evening/weekend programs available. *Degree requirements:* For master's, one foreign language, comprehensive exam, thesis optional. *Entrance requirements:* For master's, GRE General Test, MAT (for MA Ed). Additional exam requirements/recommendations for international students: Required—TOEFL. *Expenses:* Tuition, state resident: full-time $4223. Tuition, nonresident: full-time $16,540. *Required fees:* $2184.

Eastern Kentucky University, The Graduate School, College of Arts and Sciences, Department of English and Theatre, Richmond, KY 40475-3102. Offers creative writing (MFA); English (MA). Part-time and evening/weekend programs available. *Degree requirements:* For master's, thesis optional. *Entrance requirements:* For master's, GRE General Test, minimum GPA of 2.5, minor in English with 3.0 GPA. *Faculty research:* Old English, Victorian studies, women's studies, rhetoric, popular culture, novel studies.

Eastern Michigan University, Graduate School, College of Arts and Sciences, Department of English Language and Literature, Program in Creative Writing, Ypsilanti, MI 48197. Offers MA. Part-time and evening/weekend programs available. Postbaccalaureate distance learning degree programs offered (minimal on-campus study). *Students:* 2 full-time (0 women), 14 part-time (7 women); includes 2 minority (1 Black or African American, non-Hispanic/Latino; 1 Hispanic/Latino), 1 international. Average age 29. 24 applicants, 58% accepted, 7 enrolled. In 2014, 1 master's awarded. *Entrance requirements:* Additional exam requirements/recommendations for international students: Required—TOEFL. *Application deadline:* Applications are processed on a rolling basis. Application fee: $45. *Financial support:* Fellowships, research assistantships with full tuition reimbursements, teaching assistantships with full tuition reimbursements, career-related internships or fieldwork, Federal Work-Study, institutionally sponsored loans, scholarships/grants, tuition waivers (partial), and unspecified assistantships available. Support available to part-time students. Financial award applicants required to submit FAFSA. *Application contact:* Carla Harryman, Graduate Coordinator, 734-487-3173, Fax: 734-483-9744, E-mail: charryma@emich.edu.

Eastern Michigan University, Graduate School, College of Arts and Sciences, Department of English Language and Literature, Programs in Written Communication, Ypsilanti, MI 48197. Offers technical communications (MA, Graduate Certificate); written communications (MA). Part-time and evening/weekend programs available. Postbaccalaureate distance learning degree programs offered (minimal on-campus study). *Students:* 2 full-time (both women), 15 part-time (9 women); includes 1 minority (Two or more races, non-Hispanic/Latino). Average age 34. 12 applicants, 42% accepted, 3 enrolled. In 2014, 11 master's, 1 other advanced degree awarded. *Entrance*

requirements: Additional exam requirements/recommendations for international students: Required—TOEFL. *Application deadline:* Applications are processed on a rolling basis. Application fee: $45. *Financial support:* Fellowships, research assistantships with full tuition reimbursements, teaching assistantships with full tuition reimbursements, career-related internships or fieldwork, Federal Work-Study, institutionally sponsored loans, scholarships/grants, tuition waivers (partial), and unspecified assistantships available. Support available to part-time students. Financial award applicants required to submit FAFSA. *Application contact:* Dr. Steve Benninghoff, Program Coordinator, 734-487-2075, Fax: 734-483-9744, E-mail: steve.benninghoff@emich.edu.

Eastern Washington University, Graduate Studies, College of Arts, Letters and Education, Inland Northwest Center for Writers, Cheney, WA 99004-2431. Offers MFA. *Degree requirements:* For master's, comprehensive exam, thesis. *Entrance requirements:* For master's, GRE General Test, minimum GPA of 3.0, sample of written work.

Emerson College, Graduate Studies, School of the Arts, Department of Writing, Literature and Publishing, Program in Creative Writing, Boston, MA 02116-4624. Offers MFA. Part-time and evening/weekend programs available. *Students:* 111 full-time (65 women), 8 part-time (all women); includes 26 minority (7 Black or African American, non-Hispanic/Latino; 2 Asian, non-Hispanic/Latino; 11 Hispanic/Latino; 6 Two or more races, non-Hispanic/Latino), 3 international. Average age 28. 310 applicants, 41% accepted, 39 enrolled. In 2014, 42 master's awarded. *Entrance requirements:* For master's, GRE General Test, 15-page writing sample. Additional exam requirements/recommendations for international students: Required—TOEFL (minimum score 550 paper-based; 80 iBT), IELTS (minimum score 6.5). *Application deadline:* For fall admission, 2/15 for domestic and international students. Applications are processed on a rolling basis. Application fee: $60 ($75 for international students). Electronic applications accepted. *Expenses: Tuition:* Part-time $1145 per credit. *Financial support:* In 2014–15, 29 students received support, including 29 fellowships with full and partial tuition reimbursements available (averaging $14,243 per year); research assistantships with partial tuition reimbursements available, Federal Work-Study, scholarships/grants, and unspecified assistantships also available. Financial award application deadline: 2/15; financial award applicants required to submit FAFSA. *Unit head:* Prof. Pablo Medina, Graduate Program Director, 617-824-8750, E-mail: pablo_medina@emerson.edu. *Application contact:* Leanda Ferland, Office of Graduate Admission, 617-824-8610, Fax: 617-824-8614, E-mail: gradapp@emerson.edu. Website: http://www.emerson.edu/graduate_admission

Emerson College, Graduate Studies, School of the Arts, Department of Writing, Literature and Publishing, Program in Publishing and Writing, Boston, MA 02116-4624. Offers MA. Part-time and evening/weekend programs available. *Students:* 105 full-time (92 women), 13 part-time (11 women); includes 24 minority (5 Black or African American, non-Hispanic/Latino; 2 Asian, non-Hispanic/Latino; 16 Hispanic/Latino; 1 Two or more races, non-Hispanic/Latino), 7 international. Average age 25. 180 applicants, 59% accepted, 48 enrolled. In 2014, 43 master's awarded. *Degree requirements:* For master's, thesis or alternative. *Entrance requirements:* For master's, GRE General Test, 15-page writing sample. Additional exam requirements/recommendations for international students: Required—TOEFL (minimum score 550 paper-based; 80 iBT), IELTS (minimum score 6.5). *Application deadline:* For fall admission, 3/1 priority date for domestic and international students. Applications are processed on a rolling basis. Application fee: $60 ($75 for international students). Electronic applications accepted. *Expenses: Tuition:* Part-time $1145 per credit. *Financial support:* In 2014–15, 23 students received support, including 23 fellowships with partial tuition reimbursements available (averaging $8,696 per year); research assistantships with partial tuition reimbursements available, Federal Work-Study, scholarships/grants, and unspecified assistantships also available. Financial award application deadline: 3/1; financial award applicants required to submit FAFSA. *Faculty research:* Publishing. *Unit head:* Prof. Lisa Diercks, Graduate Program Director, 617-824-8750, E-mail: lisa_diercks@emerson.edu. *Application contact:* Leanda Ferland, Office of Graduate Admission, 617-824-8610, Fax: 617-824-8614, E-mail: gradapp@emerson.edu. Website: http://www.emerson.edu/graduate_admission

Fairfield University, College of Arts and Sciences, Fairfield, CT 06824. Offers American studies (MA); communication (MA); creative writing (MFA); mathematics (MS); public administration (MPA). Part-time and evening/weekend programs available. Postbaccalaureate distance learning degree programs offered (minimal on-campus study). *Faculty:* 35 full-time (20 women), 5 part-time/adjunct (1 woman). *Students:* 54 full-time (35 women), 65 part-time (37 women); includes 18 minority (4 Black or African American, non-Hispanic/Latino; 4 Asian, non-Hispanic/Latino; 6 Hispanic/Latino; 1 Native Hawaiian or other Pacific Islander, non-Hispanic/Latino; 3 Two or more races, non-Hispanic/Latino), 6 international. Average age 35. 77 applicants, 69% accepted, 27 enrolled. In 2014, 51 master's awarded. *Degree requirements:* For master's, capstone research course. *Entrance requirements:* For master's, minimum GPA of 3.0, 2 letters of recommendation, resume. Additional exam requirements/recommendations for international students: Required—TOEFL (minimum score 550 paper-based; 80 iBT) or IELTS (minimum score 6.5). *Application deadline:* For fall admission, 5/14 for international students; for spring admission, 10/15 for international students. Applications are processed on a rolling basis. Application fee: $60. Electronic applications accepted. *Expenses: Tuition:* Part-time $695 per credit hour. Full-time tuition and fees vary according to degree level and program. *Financial support:* In 2014–15, 41 students received support. Scholarships/grants and unspecified assistantships available. Financial award applicants required to submit FAFSA. *Faculty research:* Ethical theory, media industries, community-based teaching and learning, non commutative algebra and partial differential equations, cancer research in biology and physics. *Unit head:* Dr. James Simon, Dean, 203-254-4000 Ext. 2221, Fax: 203-254-4119, E-mail: jsimon@fairfield.edu. *Application contact:* Marianne Gumpper, Director of Graduate and Continuing Studies Admission, 203-254-4184, Fax: 203-254-4073, E-mail: gradadmis@fairfield.edu. Website: http://www.fairfield.edu/academics/schoolscollegescenters/collegeofartssciences/graduateprograms/

Fairleigh Dickinson University, College at Florham, Maxwell Becton College of Arts and Sciences, Department of English, Communication and Philosophy, Program in Creative Writing, Madison, NJ 07940-1099. Offers MFA.

Fairleigh Dickinson University, College at Florham, Maxwell Becton College of Arts and Sciences, Department of English, Communication and Philosophy, Program in Creative Writing and Literature for Educators, Madison, NJ 07940-1099. Offers MA.

Florida Atlantic University, Dorothy F. Schmidt College of Arts and Letters, Department of English, Boca Raton, FL 33431-0991. Offers American literature (MA); British literature (MA); creative nonfiction (MFA); creative writing (MA); English (MAT); fiction (MFA); multicultural and world literacies (MA); poetry (MFA); rhetoric and composition (MA); science fiction and fantasy (MA). Part-time programs available. *Degree requirements:* For master's, one foreign language, thesis. *Entrance requirements:* For master's, GRE General Test, minimum GPA of 3.0, writing samples, 2 letters of recommendation. Additional exam requirements/recommendations for international students: Required—TOEFL (minimum score 500 paper-based; 61 iBT),

IELTS (minimum score 6). Electronic applications accepted. *Expenses:* Tuition, state resident: full-time $7396; part-time $369.82 per credit hour. Tuition, nonresident: full-time $19,392; part-time $1024.81 per credit hour. Tuition and fees vary according to course load. *Faculty research:* African-American writers, critical theory, British-American, Asian-American.

Florida International University, College of Arts and Sciences, Department of English, Program in Creative Writing, Miami, FL 33199. Offers MFA. Part-time and evening/weekend programs available. *Degree requirements:* For master's, comprehensive exam. *Entrance requirements:* For master's, GRE General Test, minimum undergraduate GPA of 3.0, writing sample, 2 letters of recommendation. Additional exam requirements/recommendations for international students: Required—TOEFL (minimum score 550 paper-based; 80 iBT). Electronic applications accepted.

Florida State University, The Graduate School, College of Arts and Sciences, Department of English, Tallahassee, FL 32312. Offers creative writing (MFA); English (PhD), including creative writing, literature, rhetoric and composition; literature (MA); rhetoric and composition (MA). Part-time programs available. *Faculty:* 47 full-time (24 women), 2 part-time/adjunct (1 woman). *Students:* 142 full-time (80 women), 31 part-time (23 women); includes 44 minority (17 Black or African American, non-Hispanic/Latino; 1 American Indian or Alaska Native, non-Hispanic/Latino; 12 Asian, non-Hispanic/Latino; 5 Hispanic/Latino; 9 Two or more races, non-Hispanic/Latino), 9 international. Average age 30. 307 applicants, 20% accepted, 38 enrolled. In 2014, 21 master's, 24 doctorates awarded. *Degree requirements:* For master's, one foreign language, thesis (for some programs), 33 hours of coursework including capstone essay, thesis or portfolio (MA); 45 hours of coursework including 9-12 thesis hours (MFA); for doctorate, comprehensive exam, thesis/dissertation, 27 hours of coursework, 24 hours of dissertation work. *Entrance requirements:* For master's and doctorate, GRE General Test, sample of written work, 3 letters of recommendation, resume. Additional exam requirements/recommendations for international students: Required—TOEFL. *Application deadline:* For fall admission, 1/1 priority date for domestic and international students. Application fee: $30. Electronic applications accepted. *Expenses:* Tuition, state resident: part-time $403.51 per credit hour. Tuition, nonresident: part-time $1004.85 per credit hour. *Required fees:* $75.81 per credit hour. One-time fee: $20 part-time. Tuition and fees vary according to campus/location. *Financial support:* In 2014–15, 132 students received support, including 5 fellowships with full and partial tuition reimbursements available, teaching assistantships with full and partial tuition reimbursements available (averaging $13,250 per year); career-related internships or fieldwork, Federal Work-Study, and institutionally sponsored loans also available. Financial award application deadline: 8/1; financial award applicants required to submit FAFSA. *Faculty research:* British and Irish literature, American literature, creative writing, rhetoric and composition, multiethnic transnational literature, history of text technology. *Unit head:* Dr. Eric Walker, Chairman, 850-644-4230, Fax: 850-644-0811, E-mail: ewalker@fsu.edu. *Application contact:* Ginger Martin, Senior Graduate Academic Coordinator, 850-644-1081, Fax: 850-644-9656, E-mail: vmartin@fsu.edu.
Website: http://english.fsu.edu/

Florida State University, The Graduate School, College of Motion Picture Arts, Tallahassee, FL 32306-2350. Offers film production (MFA); screenwriting (MFA). *Faculty:* 24 full-time (9 women), 3 part-time/adjunct (1 woman). *Students:* 53 full-time (24 women); includes 22 minority (10 Black or African American, non-Hispanic/Latino; 7 Asian, non-Hispanic/Latino; 4 Hispanic/Latino; 1 Two or more races, non-Hispanic/Latino). Average age 25. 189 applicants, 16% accepted, 30 enrolled. In 2014, 30 master's awarded. *Degree requirements:* For master's, thesis, thesis film project. *Entrance requirements:* For master's, GRE (for MFA in writing), minimum GPA of 3.0, application documents (resume, statement of purpose, writing sample, 3 letters of recommendation, creative portfolio). Additional exam requirements/recommendations for international students: Required—TOEFL (minimum score 550 paper-based; 80 iBT). *Application deadline:* For fall admission, 12/1 for domestic and international students. Application fee: $30. Electronic applications accepted. *Expenses:* Tuition, state resident: part-time $403.51 per credit hour. Tuition, nonresident: part-time $1004.85 per credit hour. *Required fees:* $75.81 per credit hour. One-time fee: $20 part-time. Tuition and fees vary according to campus/location. *Financial support:* In 2014–15, 20 students received support, including 20 teaching assistantships with partial tuition reimbursements available (averaging $5,500 per year); institutionally sponsored loans and unspecified assistantships also available. Financial award application deadline: 12/1; financial award applicants required to submit FAFSA. *Faculty research:* Producing, screenwriting, directing, cinematography, editing. *Unit head:* Frank Patterson, Dean, 850-644-0453, Fax: 850-644-2626. *Application contact:* Emily Burgess, Director of Student Services, 850-644-4927, Fax: 850-644-2626, E-mail: eburgess@film.fsu.edu.
Website: http://film.fsu.edu/

Full Sail University, Creative Writing Master of Fine Arts Program - Online, Winter Park, FL 32792-7437. Offers MFA. Postbaccalaureate distance learning degree programs offered (no on-campus study).

George Mason University, College of Humanities and Social Sciences, Department of English, Program in Creative Writing, Fairfax, VA 22030. Offers MFA. *Faculty:* 10 full-time (4 women), 1 (woman) part-time/adjunct. *Students:* 57 full-time (37 women), 31 part-time (21 women); includes 15 minority (4 Black or African American, non-Hispanic/Latino; 2 Asian, non-Hispanic/Latino; 5 Hispanic/Latino; 4 Two or more races, non-Hispanic/Latino), 1 international. Average age 31. 117 applicants, 53% accepted, 24 enrolled. In 2014, 25 master's awarded. *Degree requirements:* For master's, one foreign language, thesis, exam or project. *Entrance requirements:* For master's, expanded goals statement; 2 letters of recommendation; portfolio; official transcripts. Additional exam requirements/recommendations for international students: Required—TOEFL (minimum score 570 paper-based; 80 iBT), IELTS (minimum score 6.5), PTE. *Application deadline:* For fall admission, 1/2 priority date for domestic students. Application fee: $65 ($80 for international students). Electronic applications accepted. *Expenses:* Tuition, state resident: full-time $9794; part-time $408 per credit hour. Tuition, nonresident: full-time $26,978; part-time $1124 per credit hour. *Required fees:* $2820; $118 per credit hour. Tuition and fees vary according to course load and program. *Financial support:* In 2014–15, 49 students received support, including 1 fellowship with tuition reimbursement available (averaging $3,468 per year), 3 research assistantships with full and partial tuition reimbursements available (averaging $12,733 per year), 47 teaching assistantships with full and partial tuition reimbursements available (averaging $11,945 per year); career-related internships or fieldwork, Federal Work-Study, scholarships/grants, unspecified assistantships, and health care benefits (for full-time research or teaching assistantship recipients) also available. Support available to part-time students. Financial award application deadline: 3/1; financial award applicants required to submit FAFSA. *Faculty research:* British Romantic poetry and literary celebrity, Arab feminist novelists in the West, masculinity and African-American culture, public rhetoric and the South African Truth Commission, the origins of children's literature in eighteenth and nineteenth century Britain. *Unit head:* William Miller, Director, 703-993-2763, Fax: 703-993-1161, E-mail: wmiller@gmu.edu. *Application contact:* Jay Patel, Graduate Coordinator, 703-993-1180, Fax: 703-993-1161, E-mail: jpatel2@gmu.edu.
Website: http://creativewriting.gmu.edu/

Georgia College & State University, Graduate School, College of Arts and Sciences, Department of English and Rhetoric, Program in Creative Writing, Milledgeville, GA 31061. Offers MFA. Part-time and evening/weekend programs available. *Students:* 5 full-time (2 women), 25 part-time (20 women); includes 8 minority (3 Black or African American, non-Hispanic/Latino; 2 Hispanic/Latino; 3 Two or more races, non-Hispanic/Latino). Average age 33. 87 applicants, 22% accepted, 9 enrolled. In 2014, 10 master's awarded. *Degree requirements:* For master's, one foreign language, thesis, complete program in no more than 4 years. *Entrance requirements:* For master's, GRE or MAT, writing portfolio, letters of recommendation, statement of purpose, transcript. Additional exam requirements/recommendations for international students: Recommended—TOEFL (minimum score 550 paper-based; 79 iBT). *Application deadline:* For fall admission, 2/1 for domestic students. Application fee: $40. Electronic applications accepted. *Expenses: Tuition, area resident:* Part-time $283 per credit hour. Tuition, nonresident: part-time $1027 per credit hour. *Required fees:* $995 per semester. Full-time tuition and fees vary according to course load, degree level, campus/location and program. *Financial support:* In 2014–15, 27 teaching assistantships with full tuition reimbursements were awarded; unspecified assistantships also available. Financial award applicants required to submit FAFSA. *Unit head:* Dr. Martin Lammon, Coordinator, 478-445-3508, E-mail: mfa@gcsu.edu. *Application contact:* Kate Marshall, Graduate Admissions Coordinator, 478-445-1184, Fax: 478-445-1336, E-mail: grad-admit@gcsu.edu.
Website: http://www.gcsu.edu/english/macreativewriting.htm

Georgia State University, College of Arts and Sciences, Department of English, Program in Creative Writing, Atlanta, GA 30302-3083. Offers creative writing (PhD); fiction (MA, MFA); poetry (MA, MFA). Part-time programs available. *Degree requirements:* For master's, one foreign language, comprehensive exam, thesis, 27 hours of coursework plus 6 hours of thesis credit; for doctorate, one foreign language, comprehensive exam, thesis/dissertation, 30-39 hours of coursework plus 20 hours of thesis credit. *Entrance requirements:* For master's and doctorate, GRE. Additional exam requirements/recommendations for international students: Required—TOEFL (minimum score 550 paper-based; 80 iBT). *Application deadline:* For fall admission, 1/15 for domestic and international students. Application fee: $50. Electronic applications accepted. *Expenses:* Tuition, state resident: full-time $6516; part-time $362 per credit hour. Tuition, nonresident: full-time $22,014; part-time $1223 per credit hour. *Required fees:* $2128 per semester. Tuition and fees vary according to course load and program. *Financial support:* In 2014–15, research assistantships with full tuition reimbursements (averaging $6,000 per year), teaching assistantships with full tuition reimbursements (averaging $15,000 per year) were awarded; unspecified assistantships also available. *Faculty research:* Poetry writing, fiction writing, contemporary poetry, contemporary fiction, form and theory of fiction and poetry. *Unit head:* Dr. Josh Russell, Co-Director of the Creative Writing Program, 404-413-5800, Fax: 404-413-5830, E-mail: josh@gsu.edu. *Application contact:* Dr. Heather Russel, Assistant to the Directors of Creative Writing, 404-413-5806, Fax: 404-413-5830, E-mail: heather@gsu.edu.
Website: http://www.english.gsu.edu

Goddard College, Graduate Division, Master of Fine Arts in Creative Writing Program, Plainfield, VT 05667-9432. Offers MFA. Program residency available in Plainfield, VT or Port Townsend, WA. Postbaccalaureate distance learning degree programs offered (minimal on-campus study). *Faculty:* 1 (woman) full-time, 23 part-time/adjunct (16 women). *Students:* 109 full-time. Average age 38. 142 applicants, 55% accepted, 41 enrolled. In 2014, 57 master's awarded. *Degree requirements:* For master's, thesis, completed full-length manuscript, teaching practicum, 3 critical papers, annotations of 45 to 60 literary works. *Entrance requirements:* For master's, statement of purpose, preliminary bibliography, creative portfolio, three letters of recommendation. *Application deadline:* Applications are processed on a rolling basis. Application fee: $40. Electronic applications accepted. *Expenses:* Expenses: Contact institution. *Financial support:* Scholarships/grants and tuition waivers (full and partial) available. Financial award applicants required to submit FAFSA. *Unit head:* Paul Selig, Director, 802-454-8311, Fax: 802-454-7835, E-mail: paul.selig@goddard.edu. *Application contact:* David DeLucca, Senior Admissions Counselor, 800-906-8312 Ext. 248, Fax: 802-454-1029, E-mail: david.delucca@goddard.edu.
Website: http://www.goddard.edu/academics/master-fine-arts-creative-writing-2/

Goucher College, MA and MFA Programs, Baltimore, MD 21204-2794. Offers arts administration (MA); creative nonfiction (MFA); cultural sustainability (MA); digital arts (MFA); environmental studies (MA); historic preservation (MA); management (MA). Part-time and evening/weekend programs available. Postbaccalaureate distance learning degree programs offered (minimal on-campus study). *Faculty:* 83 part-time/adjunct (42 women). *Students:* 72 full-time (58 women), 65 part-time (54 women); includes 39 minority (15 Black or African American, non-Hispanic/Latino; 16 American Indian or Alaska Native, non-Hispanic/Latino; 2 Asian, non-Hispanic/Latino; 4 Hispanic/Latino; 2 Two or more races, non-Hispanic/Latino), 4 international. 120 applicants, 95% accepted, 50 enrolled. In 2014, 63 master's awarded. *Degree requirements:* For master's, thesis, e-portfolio completion. *Entrance requirements:* Additional exam requirements/recommendations for international students: Required—TOEFL (minimum score 550 paper-based; 80 iBT), IELTS (minimum score 7). *Application deadline:* Applications are processed on a rolling basis. Application fee: $75. *Expenses:* Expenses: $825 per credit; fees vary according to program. *Financial support:* Unspecified assistantships available. Financial award application deadline: 4/15; financial award applicants required to submit FAFSA. *Unit head:* Lynne Lochte, Vice President for New Ventures and Business Strategies, 410-337-6572, E-mail: lynne.lochte@goucher.edu. *Application contact:* Hanora Barron, Admissions Coordinator, 410-337-6200, Fax: 410-337-6085, E-mail: hanora.barron@goucher.edu.
Website: http://www.goucher.edu/grad

Hamline University, College of Liberal Arts, St. Paul, MN 55104-1284. Offers writing (MFA); writing for children and young adults (MFA); JD/MFA. Part-time and evening/weekend programs available. Postbaccalaureate distance learning degree programs offered (minimal on-campus study). *Faculty:* 4 full-time (all women), 22 part-time/adjunct (14 women). *Students:* 164 part-time (109 women); includes 5 minority (1 Black or African American, non-Hispanic/Latino; 1 Asian, non-Hispanic/Latino; 1 Hispanic/Latino; 2 Two or more races, non-Hispanic/Latino), 1 international. Average age 37. 60 applicants, 78% accepted, 24 enrolled. In 2014, 56 master's awarded. *Degree requirements:* For master's, thesis. *Entrance requirements:* For master's, official transcripts, 20-page writing sample (MFA), letters of recommendation, critical essay. Additional exam requirements/recommendations for international students: Required—TOEFL (minimum score 550 paper-based; 80 iBT). *Application deadline:* For fall admission, 2/1 for domestic students, 1/5 for international students; for spring admission, 9/1 for domestic and international students. Applications are processed on a rolling basis. Application fee: $0 ($100 for international students). Electronic applications accepted. *Expenses:* Expenses: Contact institution. *Financial support:* Federal Work-Study and scholarships/grants available. Support available to part-time students. Financial award applicants required to submit FAFSA. *Unit head:* Dr. John Matachek, Dean, 651-523-2206, Fax: 651-523-3055, E-mail: jmatachek@hamline.edu. *Application contact:* Shawn Skoog, Director of Graduate Recruitment and Admission, 651-523-2900, Fax: 651-523-3058, E-mail: sskoog03@hamline.edu.
Website: http://www.hamline.edu/cla/

Writing

Hofstra University, College of Liberal Arts and Sciences, Programs in English, Hempstead, NY 11549. Offers creative writing (MFA). Part-time programs available. *Students:* 14 full-time (8 women), 20 part-time (14 women); includes 6 minority (5 Black or African American, non-Hispanic/Latino; 1 Hispanic/Latino), 2 international. Average age 34. 32 applicants, 84% accepted, 12 enrolled. In 2014, 12 master's awarded. *Degree requirements:* For master's, thesis optional, minimum GPA of 3.0. *Entrance requirements:* For master's, writing sample, essay, minimum GPA of 3.0 in literature courses. Additional exam requirements/recommendations for international students: Required—TOEFL (minimum score 550 paper-based; 80 iBT). *Application deadline:* Applications are processed on a rolling basis. Application fee: $70 ($75 for international students). Electronic applications accepted. *Expenses:* Tuition: Full-time $20,610; part-time $1145 per credit hour. *Required fees:* $970; $165 per term. Tuition and fees vary according to program. *Financial support:* In 2014–15, 18 students received support, including 10 fellowships with full and partial tuition reimbursements available (averaging $4,530 per year), 1 research assistantship with full and partial tuition reimbursement available (averaging $9,013 per year); Federal Work-Study, institutionally sponsored loans, scholarships/grants, and tuition waivers (full and partial) also available. Support available to part-time students. Financial award applicants required to submit FAFSA. *Faculty research:* Poetry and novels, Chaucer, Shakespeare, Milton, Melville, Austen, Woolf, Morrision, British Modernism, medieval, Early Modern, Long Eighteenth Century, Victorian, literary criticism focusing on nineteenth century through twenty-first century American literature and culture, psychoanalysis, queer studies, disability studies, trauma theory, critical theory, Anglophone literatures, Post-colonial studies, digital studies. *Unit head:* Erik Brogger, Program Director, 516-463-5397, Fax: 516-463-6395, E-mail: engeab@hofstra.edu. *Application contact:* Sunil Samuel, Assistant Vice President of Admissions, 516-463-4723, Fax: 516-463-4664, E-mail: graduateadmission@hofstra.edu.
Website: http://www.hofstra.edu/hclas

Hollins University, Graduate Programs, Program in Children's Literature, Roanoke, VA 24020. Offers children's book writing and illustrating (MFA); children's literature (MA, MFA). Program offered during summer only. Part-time programs available. *Faculty:* 1 (woman) full-time, 9 part-time/adjunct (8 women). *Students:* 41 full-time (38 women), 11 part-time (all women); includes 4 minority (1 Asian, non-Hispanic/Latino; 3 Hispanic/Latino). Average age 34. 35 applicants, 100% accepted, 24 enrolled. In 2014, 11 degrees awarded. *Degree requirements:* For master's, one foreign language, comprehensive exam, thesis. *Entrance requirements:* For master's, letters of recommendation, portfolio. Additional exam requirements/recommendations for international students: Required—TOEFL (minimum score 550 paper-based; 79 iBT). *Application deadline:* For fall admission, 2/15 for domestic and international students. Application fee: $40. Electronic applications accepted. *Expenses:* Expenses: $775 per credit hour, technology fee $85. *Financial support:* In 2014–15, 23 students received support, including 23 fellowships (averaging $1,000 per year); Federal Work-Study and scholarships/grants also available. Support available to part-time students. Financial award application deadline: 2/15; financial award applicants required to submit FAFSA. *Faculty research:* Fantasy, children's film, young adult fiction, gender studies, mythology and folk tales, children's poetry, picture books. *Unit head:* Amanda Cockrell, Director, 540-362-6024, Fax: 540-362-6642, E-mail: acockrell@hollins.edu. *Application contact:* Cathy S. Koon, Manager of Graduate Services, 540-362-6326, Fax: 540-362-6288, E-mail: ckoon@hollins.edu.
Website: http://www.hollins.edu/

Hollins University, Graduate Programs, Program in Creative Writing, Roanoke, VA 24020. Offers MFA. *Faculty:* 7 full-time (4 women), 1 (woman) part-time/adjunct. *Students:* 24 full-time (19 women); includes 3 minority (1 Black or African American, non-Hispanic/Latino; 1 Hispanic/Latino; 1 Two or more races, non-Hispanic/Latino). Average age 27. 175 applicants, 16% accepted, 12 enrolled. In 2014, 12 master's awarded. *Degree requirements:* For master's, comprehensive exam, thesis. *Entrance requirements:* For master's, manuscripts, 3 letters of recommendation. Additional exam requirements/recommendations for international students: Required—TOEFL (minimum score 550 paper-based; 79 iBT). *Application deadline:* For fall admission, 1/6 for domestic and international students. Application fee: $40. Electronic applications accepted. *Expenses:* Expenses: $19,868 for tuition, $325 for technology fee, $350 health services. *Financial support:* In 2014–15, 24 students received support, including 24 fellowships with full and partial tuition reimbursements available, 4 teaching assistantships (averaging $7,000 per year); scholarships/grants and unspecified assistantships also available. Support available to part-time students. Financial award application deadline: 2/2; financial award applicants required to submit FAFSA. *Faculty research:* Poetry, fiction, creative nonfiction, literary criticism, literary theory. *Unit head:* Thorpe Moeckel, Director, 540-362-6317, Fax: 540-362-6097, E-mail: creative.writing@hollins.edu. *Application contact:* Cathy S. Koon, Manager of Graduate Services, 540-362-6326, Fax: 540-362-6288, E-mail: ckoon@hollins.edu.

Hollins University, Graduate Programs, Program in Playwriting, Roanoke, VA 24020. Offers new play direction (Certificate); new play performance (Certificate); playwriting (MFA). Part-time programs available. *Faculty:* 1 full-time (0 women), 5 part-time/adjunct (3 women). *Students:* 29 full-time (21 women), 1 part-time (0 women); includes 4 minority (3 Black or African American, non-Hispanic/Latino; 1 American Indian or Alaska Native, non-Hispanic/Latino). Average age 40. 19 applicants, 89% accepted, 12 enrolled. In 2014, 6 master's awarded. *Degree requirements:* For master's, comprehensive exam, thesis. *Entrance requirements:* For master's, letters of recommendation, writing samples. Additional exam requirements/recommendations for international students: Required—TOEFL (minimum score 550 paper-based; 79 iBT). *Application deadline:* For summer admission, 2/15 priority date for domestic students. Application fee: $40. *Expenses:* Expenses: $775 per credit hour, $85 technology fee. *Financial support:* In 2014–15, 20 students received support, including 20 fellowships (averaging $1,000 per year). Financial award application deadline: 2/15. *Unit head:* Todd Ristau, Director, 540-362-6386, E-mail: tristau@hollins.edu. *Application contact:* Cathy S. Koon, Manager of Graduate Services, 540-362-6326, Fax: 540-362-6288, E-mail: ckoon@hollins.edu.
Website: http://www.hollins.edu/grad/playwriting/index.html

Hollins University, Graduate Programs, Program in Screenwriting and Film Studies, Roanoke, VA 24020. Offers screenwriting (MFA); screenwriting and film studies (MA). Program offered during summer only. Part-time programs available. *Faculty:* 1 (woman) full-time, 5 part-time/adjunct (0 women). *Students:* 30 full-time (7 women), 5 part-time (all women); includes 8 minority (5 Black or African American, non-Hispanic/Latino; 2 Asian, non-Hispanic/Latino; 1 Two or more races, non-Hispanic/Latino). Average age 39. 18 applicants, 100% accepted, 12 enrolled. In 2014, 5 master's awarded. *Degree requirements:* For master's, one foreign language, comprehensive exam, thesis. *Entrance requirements:* For master's, letters of recommendation, portfolio. Additional exam requirements/recommendations for international students: Required—TOEFL (minimum score 550 paper-based; 79 iBT). *Application deadline:* For fall admission, 2/15 for domestic and international students. Application fee: $40. Electronic applications accepted. *Expenses:* Expenses: $775 per credit hour, $85 technology fee. *Financial support:* In 2014–15, 18 students received support, including 18 fellowships (averaging $1,000 per year); Federal Work-Study and scholarships/grants also available. Support available to part-time students. Financial award application deadline: 2/15; financial

award applicants required to submit FAFSA. *Faculty research:* Censorship, minorities in film, writing for television, new media. *Unit head:* Dr. Tim Albaugh, Director, 540-362-6326, E-mail: albaughtt@hollins.edu. *Application contact:* Cathy S. Koon, Manager of Graduate Services, 540-362-6326, Fax: 540-362-6288, E-mail: ckoon@hollins.edu.
Website: http://www.hollins.edu/

Holy Names University, Graduate Division, Master of Arts in English: The Writer's Craft Program, Oakland, CA 94619-1699. Offers MA. *Faculty:* 3. *Students:* 3 part-time (2 women); includes 1 minority (Hispanic/Latino). Average age 42. 2 applicants. In 2014, 6 master's awarded. *Entrance requirements:* For master's, two recommendations, writing sample. Additional exam requirements/recommendations for international students: Required—TOEFL (minimum score 550 paper-based; 79 iBT). *Application deadline:* For fall admission, 8/1 priority date for domestic students, 7/15 for international students; for spring admission, 12/1 priority date for domestic students, 12/1 for international students; for summer admission, 5/5 for international students. Applications are processed on a rolling basis. Application fee: $65. Electronic applications accepted. Application fee is waived when completed online. *Financial support:* Career-related internships or fieldwork, Federal Work-Study, scholarships/grants, and unspecified assistantships available. Financial award application deadline: 3/2; financial award applicants required to submit FAFSA. *Unit head:* Dr. Daniel Schmidt, Associate Professor of English, 510-436-1507, E-mail: schmidt@hnu.edu. *Application contact:* Graduate Admissions Office, 800-430-1321, Fax: 510-436-1325, E-mail: graduateadmissions@hnu.edu.
Website: http://www.hnu.edu/academics/graduatePrograms/english.html

Hunter College of the City University of New York, Graduate School, School of Arts and Sciences, Department of English, Program in Creative Writing, New York, NY 10065-5085. Offers fiction (MFA); memoir (MFA); poetry (MFA). Part-time and evening/weekend programs available. *Faculty:* 5 full-time (3 women), 1 (woman) part-time/adjunct. *Students:* 2 full-time (1 woman), 38 part-time (28 women); includes 10 minority (2 Black or African American, non-Hispanic/Latino; 4 Asian, non-Hispanic/Latino; 4 Hispanic/Latino). Average age 31. 518 applicants, 4% accepted, 19 enrolled. In 2014, 13 master's awarded. *Degree requirements:* For master's, thesis. *Entrance requirements:* For master's, creative writing manuscript (up to 10 pages of poetry or 25-30 pages of fiction or nonfiction), nonfiction proposal (for nonfiction applicants only). *Application deadline:* For fall admission, 2/1 for domestic and international students. *Financial support:* In 2014–15, 18 students received support, including 12 fellowships (averaging $5,000 per year); Federal Work-Study and tuition waivers (partial) also available. Support available to part-time students. Financial award application deadline: 4/15. *Unit head:* Peter Carey, Executive Director, 212-772-5074, E-mail: pcarey@hunter.cuny.edu. *Application contact:* Elena Georgiou, Coordinator, 212-772-5164, Fax: 212-772-5076, E-mail: egeorgio@hunter.cuny.edu.
Website: http://www.hunter.cuny.edu/creativewriting

Hunter College of the City University of New York, Graduate School, School of Arts and Sciences, Department of Theatre, Program in Playwriting, New York, NY 10065-5085. Offers MFA. *Faculty:* 5 full-time (3 women), 1 (woman) part-time/adjunct. *Students:* 8 part-time (5 women); includes 1 minority (Black or African American, non-Hispanic/Latino). Average age 34. 19 applicants, 21% accepted, 4 enrolled. In 2014, 4 master's awarded. *Entrance requirements:* For master's, bachelor's degree, two letters of recommendation, full-length or one-act play of at least 40 pages (both hard copy and PDF attachment). *Application deadline:* For fall admission, 4/1 for domestic students. *Unit head:* Tina Howe, Playwright-in-Residence, 212-362-0219, E-mail: thowe@hunter.cuny.edu. *Application contact:* Milena Solo, Graduate Admissions Director, 212-772-4480, E-mail: admissions@hunter.cuny.edu.
Website: http://www.hunter.cuny.edu/theatre/graduate-program/m.f.a.-in-playwriting

Illinois State University, Graduate School, College of Arts and Sciences, Department of English, Program in Writing, Normal, IL 61790-2200. Offers MA, MS. *Degree requirements:* For master's, comprehensive exam, internship or practicum. *Entrance requirements:* For master's, GRE General Test, minimum GPA of 3.0 in last 60 hours.

Indiana State University, College of Graduate and Professional Studies, College of Arts and Sciences, Department of English, Terre Haute, IN 47809. Offers English teaching (MA); history (MA); literature (MA). Part-time and evening/weekend programs available. *Degree requirements:* For master's, one foreign language, thesis optional. *Entrance requirements:* For master's, minimum GPA of 2.75 in all English courses above freshman level. Additional exam requirements/recommendations for international students: Required—TOEFL (minimum score 550 paper-based). Electronic applications accepted.

Indiana University Bloomington, University Graduate School, College of Arts and Sciences, Department of English, Bloomington, IN 47405. Offers composition, literacy, and culture (PhD); creative writing (MA, MFA), including fiction, poetry; language (MA); literature (MA, PhD); writing (MA). Part-time programs available. *Faculty:* 51 full-time (23 women). *Students:* 157 full-time (108 women), 7 part-time (4 women); includes 27 minority (5 Black or African American, non-Hispanic/Latino; 12 Asian, non-Hispanic/Latino; 4 Hispanic/Latino; 6 Two or more races, non-Hispanic/Latino), 6 international. Average age 30. 383 applicants, 5% accepted, 20 enrolled. In 2014, 20 master's, 12 doctorates awarded. Terminal master's awarded for partial completion of doctoral program. *Degree requirements:* For master's, 30-36 credit hours plus one language proficiency (for MA); 60 credit hours plus thesis (for MFA); for doctorate, thesis/dissertation, qualifying exam, 90 credit hours; 2nd language proficiency or one language only if acquired at in-depth level. *Entrance requirements:* For master's, GRE General Test, GRE Subject Test (for all but MFA and MA in creative writing), minimum GPA of 3.5; for doctorate, GRE General Test, GRE Subject Test, minimum GPA of 3.7. Additional exam requirements/recommendations for international students: Required—TOEFL. *Application deadline:* For fall admission, 1/1 priority date for domestic students, 12/1 for international students. Application fee: $55 ($65 for international students). Electronic applications accepted. *Financial support:* Fellowships with full and partial tuition reimbursements, research assistantships with partial tuition reimbursements, teaching assistantships with full tuition reimbursements, career-related internships or fieldwork, and health care benefits available. Financial award application deadline: 2/1. *Unit head:* Dr. Paul Gutjahr, Chair, 812-855-2147, Fax: 812-855-9535, E-mail: pgutjahr@indiana.edu. *Application contact:* Ellen MacKay, Director of Graduate Studies, 812-855-9536, Fax: 812-855-9535, E-mail: emackay@indiana.edu.
Website: http://www.indiana.edu/~engweb/

Indiana University–Purdue University Indianapolis, School of Liberal Arts, Department of English, Indianapolis, IN 46202. Offers English (MA); teaching English to speakers of other languages (TESOL) (Certificate); teaching writing (Certificate). *Faculty:* 22 full-time (11 women). *Students:* 20 full-time (10 women), 24 part-time (16 women); includes 6 minority (1 Asian, non-Hispanic/Latino; 5 Two or more races, non-Hispanic/Latino). Average age 32. 36 applicants, 67% accepted, 19 enrolled. In 2014, 12 master's, 5 other advanced degrees awarded. *Entrance requirements:* For master's, GRE. Additional exam requirements/recommendations for international students: Required—TOEFL. *Application deadline:* For fall admission, 1/15 priority date for domestic and international students; for spring admission, 10/15 priority date for domestic and international students. Application fee: $55 ($65 for international students). *Financial support:* Fellowships, research assistantships, teaching

assistantships, and career-related internships or fieldwork available. *Unit head:* Dr. Robert Rebein, Chair, 317-274-1405, E-mail: rrebein@iupui.edu. Website: http://liberalarts.iupui.edu/english/

Institute of American Indian Arts, Low Residency MFA in Creative Writing Program, Santa Fe, NM 87508. Offers MFA. Postbaccalaureate distance learning degree programs offered (minimal on-campus study). *Students:* 52 full-time (33 women), 9 part-time (6 women). *Entrance requirements:* For master's, sample of creative work, essay, sample craft or scholarly essay, two letters of recommendation, all official college transcripts. *Application deadline:* For fall admission, 1/31 for domestic and international students. Application fee: $25. Electronic applications accepted. *Expenses:* Tuition, state resident: full-time $9360. Tuition, nonresident: full-time $9360. *Required fees:* $600. *Financial support:* Scholarships/grants available. Financial award application deadline: 1/31; financial award applicants required to submit FAFSA. *Unit head:* Jon Davis, Director, Low Residency MFA in Creative Writing, 505-424-2365, Fax: 505-424-3030, E-mail: mfa@iaia.edu. Website: http://www.iaia.edu/academics/mfa-in-creative-writing/

Iowa State University of Science and Technology, Department of English, Ames, IA 50011. Offers creative writing (MFA); English (MA); rhetoric and professional communication (PhD). *Degree requirements:* For master's, thesis or alternative; for doctorate, thesis/dissertation. *Entrance requirements:* For master's, GRE General Test, sample of written work, resume, portfolio in creative writing; for doctorate, GRE General Test, sample of written work, resume. Additional exam requirements/recommendations for international students: Required—TOEFL (minimum score 600 paper-based; 100 iBT), IELTS (minimum score 7). Electronic applications accepted. *Faculty research:* Creative writing, literature, rhetoric, composition and professional communication, teaching English as a second language, applied linguistics.

Iowa State University of Science and Technology, Program in Creative Writing and Environment, Ames, IA 50011. Offers MFA. *Entrance requirements:* For master's, GRE, official academic transcripts, resume, three letters of recommendation, statement of personal goals, writing samples. Additional exam requirements/recommendations for international students: Required—TOEFL (minimum score 600 paper-based; 100 iBT), IELTS (minimum score 7). Electronic applications accepted.

James Madison University, The Graduate School, College of Arts and Letters, School of Writing, Rhetoric, and Technical Communication, Harrisonburg, VA 22807. Offers MA, MS. Part-time programs available. *Faculty:* 20 full-time (11 women), 1 (woman) part-time/adjunct. *Students:* 13 full-time (10 women), 3 part-time (2 women); includes 3 minority (1 Black or African American, non-Hispanic/Latino; 1 Asian, non-Hispanic/Latino; 1 Hispanic/Latino). Average age 28. 12 applicants, 83% accepted, 8 enrolled. In 2014, 8 master's awarded. *Degree requirements:* For master's, one foreign language, thesis. *Application deadline:* For fall admission, 5/31 for domestic students; for spring admission, 8/31 for domestic students. Application fee: $55. Electronic applications accepted. *Expenses:* Tuition, state resident: full-time $7812; part-time $434 per credit hour. Tuition, nonresident: full-time $20,430; part-time $1135 per credit hour. *Financial support:* In 2014–15, 12 students received support, including 1 fellowship, 2 teaching assistantships with full tuition reimbursements available (averaging $8,837 per year); career-related internships or fieldwork, Federal Work-Study, and 9 assistantships (averaging $7112) also available. Financial award application deadline: 3/1; financial award applicants required to submit FAFSA. *Unit head:* Dr. Traci A. Zimmerman, Director of the School of Writing, Rhetoric and Technical Communication, 540-568-2334, E-mail: zimmerta@jmu.edu. *Application contact:* Lynette D. Michael, Director of Graduate Admissions and Student Records, 540-568-6131 Ext. 6395, Fax: 540-568-7860, E-mail: michaeld@jmu.edu. Website: http://www.jmu.edu/wrtc/

Johns Hopkins University, Zanvyl Krieger School of Arts and Sciences, Advanced Academic Programs, Program in Writing, Washington, DC 20036. Offers science writing (MA, Certificate); writing (MA). Part-time and evening/weekend programs available. *Degree requirements:* For master's, thesis. *Entrance requirements:* For master's, minimum GPA of 3.0, writing samples. Additional exam requirements/recommendations for international students: Required—TOEFL (minimum score 600 paper-based; 100 iBT). Electronic applications accepted.

Johns Hopkins University, Zanvyl Krieger School of Arts and Sciences, The Writing Seminars, Baltimore, MD 21218-2699. Offers fiction writing (MFA); poetry (MFA). *Degree requirements:* For master's, one foreign language, thesis, foreign language exam (MFA). *Entrance requirements:* For master's, GRE General Test, GRE Subject Test (recommended), foreign language exam, sample of written work, 3 letters of recommendation, transcripts of all college/university course work. Additional exam requirements/recommendations for international students: Required—TOEFL (minimum score 600 paper-based; 100 iBT). Electronic applications accepted. *Faculty research:* Contemporary fiction and poetry, film history, literary criticism, psychoanalysis.

Kean University, College of Humanities and Social Sciences, Program in English Writing Studies, Union, NJ 07083. Offers MA. Part-time programs available. *Faculty:* 18 full-time (9 women). *Students:* 6 full-time (4 women), 12 part-time (8 women); includes 6 minority (2 Black or African American, non-Hispanic/Latino; 4 Hispanic/Latino). Average age 34. 7 applicants, 100% accepted, 4 enrolled. In 2014, 9 master's awarded. *Degree requirements:* For master's, thesis. *Entrance requirements:* For master's, GRE General Test, minimum GPA of 3.0, official transcripts from all institutions attended, two letters of recommendation, personal statement, professional resume/curriculum vitae. Additional exam requirements/recommendations for international students: Required—TOEFL (minimum score 550 paper-based; 79 iBT). *Application deadline:* For fall admission, 6/1 for domestic and international students; for spring admission, 12/8 for domestic and international students. Applications are processed on a rolling basis. Application fee: $75 ($150 for international students). Electronic applications accepted. *Expenses:* Tuition, state resident: full-time $12,461; part-time $607 per credit. Tuition, nonresident: full-time $16,889; part-time $744 per credit. *Required fees:* $3141; $143 per credit. Tuition and fees vary according to course load, degree level and program. *Financial support:* In 2014–15, 5 research assistantships with full tuition reimbursements (averaging $3,742 per year) were awarded; scholarships/grants and unspecified assistantships also available. Financial award applicants required to submit FAFSA. *Unit head:* Dr. Mia Zamora, Program Coordinator, 908-737-0385, E-mail: schandler@kean.edu. *Application contact:* Ann-Marie Kay, Assistant Director of Graduate Admissions, 908-737-7132, Fax: 908-737-7135, E-mail: akay@kean.edu. Website: http://grad.kean.edu/masters-programs/english-writing-studies

Kennesaw State University, College of Humanities and Social Sciences, Program in Professional Writing, Kennesaw, GA 30144. Offers MAPW. Part-time and evening/weekend programs available. *Students:* 15 full-time (10 women), 30 part-time (27 women); includes 3 minority (2 Black or African American, non-Hispanic/Latino; 1 Hispanic/Latino). Average age 36. 26 applicants, 73% accepted, 13 enrolled. In 2014, 24 master's awarded. *Degree requirements:* For master's, thesis optional. *Entrance requirements:* For master's, GRE General Test, minimum GPA of 2.5, writing sample. Additional exam requirements/recommendations for international students: Required—TOEFL (minimum score 550 paper-based; 80 iBT), IELTS (minimum score 6.5). *Application deadline:* For fall admission, 2/1 for domestic and international students.

Application fee: $60. Electronic applications accepted. *Expenses:* Tuition, state resident: part-time $275 per semester hour. Tuition, nonresident: part-time $990 per semester hour. *Financial support:* In 2014–15, 2 research assistantships with full tuition reimbursements (averaging $8,000 per year), 2 teaching assistantships with full tuition reimbursements (averaging $8,000 per year) were awarded; Federal Work-Study and unspecified assistantships also available. Support available to part-time students. Financial award application deadline: 4/1; financial award applicants required to submit FAFSA. *Unit head:* Dr. Jim Elledge, Director, 470-578-2039, E-mail: jellege1@kennesaw.edu. *Application contact:* Terri Brennen, Admissions Counselor, 470-578-3335, Fax: 470-578-9172, E-mail: ksugrad@kennesaw.edu. Website: http://www.ksu-mapw.com/

Kent State University, College of Arts and Sciences, Department of English, Kent, OH 44242-0001. Offers creative writing (MFA); English (PhD); English for teachers (MA); literature and writing (MA); rhetoric and composition (PhD); teaching English as a second language (MA); TESL/TEFL (Certificate). MFA program offered jointly with Cleveland State University, The University of Akron, and Youngstown State University. Part-time programs available. *Faculty:* 49 full-time (33 women). *Students:* 124 full-time (94 women), 25 part-time (17 women); includes 10 minority (1 Black or African American, non-Hispanic/Latino; 4 Asian, non-Hispanic/Latino; 2 Hispanic/Latino; 3 Two or more races, non-Hispanic/Latino), 30 international. Average age 32. 284 applicants, 61% accepted, 65 enrolled. In 2014, 42 master's, 9 doctorates, 1 other advanced degree awarded. Terminal master's awarded for partial completion of doctoral program. *Degree requirements:* For master's, one foreign language, thesis; for doctorate, one foreign language, comprehensive exam, thesis/dissertation. *Entrance requirements:* For master's and doctorate, GRE General Test, minimum GPA of 3.0, transcript, 8-15 page writing sample, resume, letter of intent, 3 letters of recommendation; for Certificate, minimum GPA of 3.0, transcripts. Additional exam requirements/recommendations for international students: Required—TOEFL (minimum score: paper-based 525, iBT 71), Michigan English Language Assessment Battery (minimum score of 75), IELTS (minimum score of 6.0), PTE Academic (minimum score of 48), or completion of ELS level 112 Intensive Program. *Application deadline:* For fall admission, 1/15 for domestic students, 2/1 for international students. Application fee: $45 ($70 for international students). Electronic applications accepted. *Expenses:* Tuition, state resident: full-time $8730; part-time $485 per credit hour. Tuition, nonresident: full-time $14,886; part-time $827 per credit hour. Tuition and fees vary according to campus/location and program. *Financial support:* Fellowships with full tuition reimbursements, research assistantships with full tuition reimbursements, teaching assistantships with full tuition reimbursements, career-related internships or fieldwork, Federal Work-Study, and unspecified assistantships available. Financial award application deadline: 2/1. *Unit head:* Dr. Robery Trogdon, Chair, 330-672-2676, E-mail: rcorthel@kent.edu. *Application contact:* Kevin Floyd, Graduate Student Coordinator, 330-672-2676, E-mail: english@kent.edu. Website: http://www.kent.edu/english/

Lake Forest College, Graduate Program in Liberal Studies, Lake Forest, IL 60045. Offers American studies (MLS); environmental studies (MLS); history and freedom (MLS); writing (MLS). Part-time and evening/weekend programs available. *Faculty:* 11 full-time (5 women), 1 (woman) part-time/adjunct. *Students:* 42 part-time (22 women); includes 4 minority (2 Asian, non-Hispanic/Latino; 2 Hispanic/Latino). Average age 38. 26 applicants, 50% accepted, 9 enrolled. In 2014, 7 master's awarded. *Degree requirements:* For master's, thesis optional, 8 courses, including at least 3 interdisciplinary seminars. *Entrance requirements:* For master's, transcript, essay, interview. Additional exam requirements/recommendations for international students: Required—TOEFL (minimum score 550 paper-based; 83 iBT); Recommended—IELTS (minimum score 6.5). *Application deadline:* For fall admission, 7/15 priority date for domestic students, 6/1 priority date for international students; for winter admission, 12/15 for domestic students, 10/1 for international students; for spring admission, 12/1 priority date for domestic students, 10/1 priority date for international students. Applications are processed on a rolling basis. Application fee: $30. *Expenses:* Expenses: Contact institution. *Financial support:* In 2014–15, 4 students received support. Scholarships/grants and partial tuition grants (for full-time teachers) available. Financial award application deadline: 7/15. *Faculty research:* History of American political thought; American families; electron collisions with molecules; international relations, American foreign policy, and transparency in world politics; ethics and social justice; pacifism. *Unit head:* Prof. D. L. LeMahieu, Director, 847-735-5133, Fax: 847-735-6291, E-mail: lemahieu@lakeforest.edu. *Application contact:* Prof. Carol Gayle, Associate Director, 847-735-5083, Fax: 847-735-6291, E-mail: gayle@lakeforest.edu. Website: http://www.lakeforest.edu/academics/programs/mls/

La Sierra University, College of Arts and Sciences, Department of English and Communication, Riverside, CA 92515. Offers communication (MA), including public relations/advertising, theory emphasis; English (MA), including literary emphasis, writing emphasis. Part-time programs available. *Degree requirements:* For master's, one foreign language. *Entrance requirements:* For master's, GRE General Test.

Lenoir-Rhyne University, Graduate Programs, School of Arts and Letters, Program in Writing, Hickory, NC 28601. Offers MA. *Faculty:* 1 (woman) full-time. *Students:* 2 full-time (both women), 13 part-time (10 women); includes 1 minority (Hispanic/Latino). Average age 39. *Entrance requirements:* For master's, GRE General Test or MAT, essay; resume; minimum GPA of 2.7 undergraduate, 3.0 graduate. Additional exam requirements/recommendations for international students: Required—TOEFL (minimum score 600 paper-based). Application fee: $35. Electronic applications accepted. *Expenses:* Tuition: Full-time $9000; part-time $500 per credit hour. Tuition and fees vary according to program. *Unit head:* Dr. Amy Wood, Assistant Provost & Dean of Graduate Studies, 828-328-7728, Fax: 828-328-7368, E-mail: amy.wood@lr.edu. *Application contact:* Mary Ann Gosnell, Associate Director of Enrollment Management Graduate Studies and Adult Learners, 828-328-7300, E-mail: admission@lr.edu. Website: http://www.lr.edu/academics/programs/writing

Lesley University, Graduate School of Arts and Social Sciences, Cambridge, MA 02138-2790. Offers clinical mental health counseling (MA), including holistic counseling, school and community counseling, trauma studies; counseling psychology (MA, CAGS), including professional counseling (MA), school counseling (MA); creative writing (MFA); expressive therapies (MA, PhD, CAGS), including art (MA), clinical mental health counseling (MA), dance (MA), expressive therapies (MA), music (MA); independent studies (CAGS); independent study (MA); intercultural relations (MA, CAGS); interdisciplinary studies (MA), including individualized studies, integrative holistic health, mindfulness studies, peace and conflict transformation, trauma sensitive assessment, intervention, and consultation, women's studies; urban environmental leadership (MA). Part-time programs available. Postbaccalaureate distance learning degree programs offered (no on-campus study). *Faculty:* 35 full-time (25 women), 115 part-time/adjunct (90 women). *Students:* 420 full-time (379 women), 514 part-time (414 women); includes 142 minority (50 Black or African American, non-Hispanic/Latino; 5 American Indian or Alaska Native, non-Hispanic/Latino; 16 Asian, non-Hispanic/Latino; 48 Hispanic/Latino; 23 Two or more races, non-Hispanic/Latino), 46 international. Average age 33. In 2014, 475 master's, 11 doctorates, 4 other advanced degrees awarded. *Degree requirements:* For master's, internship, practicum, thesis (for expressive therapies); for doctorate, thesis/dissertation, arts apprenticeship, field placement; for CAGS, thesis, internship (for

counseling psychology, expressive therapies). *Entrance requirements:* For master's, MAT (counseling psychology), interview, writing samples, art portfolio; for doctorate, GRE or MAT, interview, master's degree; for CAGS, interview, master's degree. Additional exam requirements/recommendations for international students: Required—TOEFL (minimum score 550 paper-based; 80 iBT). *Application deadline:* Applications are processed on a rolling basis. Application fee: $50. Electronic applications accepted. *Financial support:* Fellowships, career-related internships or fieldwork, Federal Work-Study, scholarships/grants, tuition waivers, and unspecified assistantships available. Financial award applicants required to submit FAFSA. *Faculty research:* Psychotherapy and culture; psychotherapy and psychological trauma; women's issues in art, teaching and psychotherapy; community-based art, psycho-spiritual inquiry. *Unit head:* Dr. Catherine Koverola, Dean, 617-349-8317, Fax: 617-349-8366, E-mail: koverola@lesley.edu. *Application contact:* Martha Sheehan, Director, Graduate Admissions, 888-LESLEYU, Fax: 617-349-8313, E-mail: info@lesley.edu.
Website: http://www.lesley.edu/graduate-school-of-arts-and-social-sciences/

Lindenwood University, Graduate Programs, School of Accelerated Degree Programs, St. Charles, MO 63301-1695. Offers administration (MSA); business administration (MBA); communications (MA); criminal justice and administration (MS); gerontology (MA); healthcare administration (MS); human resource management (MS); information technology (Certificate); managing information technology (MS); writing (MFA). Part-time and evening/weekend programs available. Postbaccalaureate distance learning degree programs offered (no on-campus study). *Faculty:* 22 full-time (9 women), 96 part-time/adjunct (34 women). *Students:* 811 full-time (488 women), 169 part-time (113 women); includes 374 minority (312 Black or African American, non-Hispanic/Latino; 6 American Indian or Alaska Native, non-Hispanic/Latino; 8 Asian, non-Hispanic/Latino; 26 Hispanic/Latino; 22 Two or more races, non-Hispanic/Latino), 25 international. Average age 35. 891 applicants, 65% accepted, 513 enrolled. In 2014, 498 master's awarded. *Degree requirements:* For master's, thesis (for some programs), minimum cumulative GPA of 3.0. *Entrance requirements:* For master's, interview, minimum GPA of 3.0. Additional exam requirements/recommendations for international students: Required—TOEFL (minimum score 550 paper-based; 80 iBT). *Application deadline:* For fall admission, 10/3 priority date for domestic and international students; for winter admission, 1/4 priority date for domestic and international students; for spring admission, 4/5 priority date for domestic and international students. Applications are processed on a rolling basis. Application fee: $30 ($100 for international students). Electronic applications accepted. *Expenses: Tuition:* Full-time $15,230; part-time $440 per credit hour. *Required fees:* $205 per semester. Tuition and fees vary according to course level, course load and degree level. *Financial support:* In 2014–15, 479 students received support. Career-related internships or fieldwork, institutionally sponsored loans, scholarships/grants, tuition waivers (partial), and unspecified assistantships available. Financial award application deadline: 6/30; financial award applicants required to submit FAFSA. *Unit head:* Dr. Gina Ganahl, Dean, 636-949-4501, Fax: 636-949-4505, E-mail: gganahl@lindenwood.edu. *Application contact:* Tyler Kostich, Director of Evening and Graduate Admissions, 636-949-4138, Fax: 636-949-4109, E-mail: adultadmissions@lindenwood.edu.
Website: http://www.lindenwood.edu/lead/

Louisiana State University and Agricultural & Mechanical College, Graduate School, College of Humanities and Social Sciences, Department of English, Baton Rouge, LA 70803. Offers creative writing (MFA); English (MA, PhD). Part-time programs available. *Faculty:* 49 full-time (26 women). *Students:* 70 full-time (42 women), 11 part-time (7 women); includes 10 minority (2 Black or African American, non-Hispanic/Latino; 1 Asian, non-Hispanic/Latino; 5 Hispanic/Latino; 2 Two or more races, non-Hispanic/Latino), 6 international. Average age 30. 302 applicants, 7% accepted, 13 enrolled. In 2014, 8 master's, 11 doctorates awarded. Terminal master's awarded for partial completion of doctoral program. *Degree requirements:* For master's, comprehensive exam; for doctorate, one foreign language, comprehensive exam, thesis/dissertation. *Entrance requirements:* For master's, GRE General Test, minimum GPA of 3.0; for doctorate, GRE General Test, GRE Subject Test, minimum GPA of 3.0. Additional exam requirements/recommendations for international students: Required—TOEFL (minimum score 550 paper-based; 79 IBT), IELTS (minimum score 6.5), or PTE (minimum score 59). *Application deadline:* For fall admission, 5/15 priority date for domestic students, 5/15 for international students; for spring admission, 10/15 priority date for domestic students, 10/15 for international students. Applications are processed on a rolling basis. Application fee: $50 ($70 for international students). Electronic applications accepted. *Financial support:* In 2014–15, 76 students received support, including 1 fellowship with full tuition reimbursement available (averaging $16,163 per year), 1 research assistantship with partial tuition reimbursement available (averaging $25,000 per year), 67 teaching assistantships with partial tuition reimbursements available (averaging $16,813 per year); career-related internships or fieldwork, Federal Work-Study, traineeships, and health care benefits also available. Financial award application deadline: 2/1; financial award applicants required to submit FAFSA. *Faculty research:* American literature, British literature, cultural studies, rhetoric and composition, folklore. *Total annual research expenditures:* $64,887. *Unit head:* Dr. Elsie Michie, Chair, 225-578-4086, Fax: 225-578-4129, E-mail: enmich@lsu.edu. *Application contact:* Dr. Michelle Masse, Director of Graduate Studies, 225-578-7803, Fax: 225-578-4129, E-mail: egs@lsu.edu.
Website: http://www.english.lsu.edu/

Loyola Marymount University, School of Film and Television, Department of Screenwriting, Program in Feature Film Screenwriting, Los Angeles, CA 90045-8347. Offers MFA. *Degree requirements:* For master's, thesis, project or script. *Entrance requirements:* For master's, GRE, writing sample, 2 letters of recommendation, personal statement. Additional exam requirements/recommendations for international students: Required—TOEFL (minimum score 600 paper-based; 100 iBT). Electronic applications accepted.

Manhattanville College, Program in Creative Writing, Purchase, NY 10577-2132. Offers MFA. Part-time and evening/weekend programs available. *Degree requirements:* For master's, thesis. *Entrance requirements:* For master's, 2 letters of recommendation, 2-3 page autobiographical essay, 10-12 page writing sample, official transcripts. Additional exam requirements/recommendations for international students: Required—TOEFL. *Application deadline:* Applications are processed on a rolling basis. Application fee: $75. Electronic applications accepted. Application fee is waived when completed online. *Expenses: Tuition:* Full-time $16,110; part-time $895 per credit. *Required fees:* $60 per semester. Part-time tuition and fees vary according to course load and program. *Financial support:* Career-related internships or fieldwork, Federal Work-Study, institutionally sponsored loans, scholarships/grants, and unspecified assistantships available. Financial award application deadline: 4/1; financial award applicants required to submit FAFSA. *Unit head:* Mark Nowak, Director, 914-323-7157, Fax: 914-694-2200, E-mail: mark.nowak@mville.edu.
Website: http://mvillemfa.com

Massachusetts Institute of Technology, School of Humanities, Arts, and Social Sciences, Programs in Comparative Media/Science writing, Graduate Program in Science Writing, Cambridge, MA 02139. Offers SM. *Faculty:* 6 full-time (1 woman). *Students:* 8 full-time (6 women); all minorities (all Black or African American, non-Hispanic/Latino). Average age 26. 61 applicants, 20% accepted, 8 enrolled. In 2014, 9 master's awarded. *Degree requirements:* For master's, thesis. *Entrance requirements:* For master's, GRE General Test. Additional exam requirements/recommendations for international students: Required—TOEFL (minimum score 600 paper-based), IELTS (minimum score 7.5). *Application deadline:* For fall admission, 1/15 for domestic and international students. Application fee: $75. Electronic applications accepted. *Expenses: Tuition:* Full-time $44,720; part-time $699 per unit. *Required fees:* $296. *Financial support:* In 2014–15, 7 students received support, including 8 fellowships (averaging $8,400 per year); research assistantships, teaching assistantships, Federal Work-Study, institutionally sponsored loans, scholarships/grants, health care benefits, and unspecified assistantships also available. Financial award application deadline: 4/15; financial award applicants required to submit FAFSA. *Faculty research:* Communicating science to the public. *Unit head:* Prof. Thomas Levenson, Program Head, 617-253-6668, Fax: 617-452-5100, E-mail: sciwrite-www@mit.edu. *Application contact:* Science Writing Graduate Admissions, 617-253-6668, Fax: 617-452-5100, E-mail: sciwrite-www@mit.edu.
Website: http://cmsw.mit.edu/education/writing/science-writing/

McNeese State University, Doré School of Graduate Studies, College of Liberal Arts, Department of English and Foreign Languages, Program in Creative Writing, Lake Charles, LA 70609. Offers MFA. Evening/weekend programs available. *Degree requirements:* For master's, thesis, public reading. *Entrance requirements:* For master's, GRE, writing sample.

Michigan State University, The Graduate School, College of Arts and Letters, Program in Rhetoric and Writing, East Lansing, MI 48824. Offers critical studies in literacy and pedagogy (MA); digital rhetoric and professional writing (MA); rhetoric and writing (PhD). *Entrance requirements:* Additional exam requirements/recommendations for international students: Required—TOEFL. Electronic applications accepted. *Faculty research:* Rhetoric, writing and communication studies; media studies; technical communication, writing for digital environments.

Mills College, Graduate Studies, Department of English, Oakland, CA 94613-1000. Offers book art and creative writing (MFA); literature (MA); poetry (MFA); prose (MFA). Part-time programs available. *Faculty:* 12 full-time (10 women), 15 part-time/adjunct (13 women). *Students:* 60 full-time (50 women), 5 part-time (3 women); includes 24 minority (8 Black or African American, non-Hispanic/Latino; 1 American Indian or Alaska Native, non-Hispanic/Latino; 2 Asian, non-Hispanic/Latino; 8 Hispanic/Latino; 1 Native Hawaiian or other Pacific Islander, non-Hispanic/Latino; 4 Two or more races, non-Hispanic/Latino), 1 international. Average age 31. 128 applicants, 86% accepted, 32 enrolled. In 2014, 28 master's awarded. *Degree requirements:* For master's, comprehensive exam, thesis. *Entrance requirements:* For master's, 15-20 page writing sample. Additional exam requirements/recommendations for international students: Required—TOEFL (minimum score 600 paper-based; 100 iBT), IELTS (minimum score 7). *Application deadline:* For fall admission, 12/15 priority date for domestic students, 12/15 for international students. Applications are processed on a rolling basis. Application fee: $50. Electronic applications accepted. *Expenses: Tuition:* Full-time $31,620; part-time $7905 per course. *Required fees:* $1118. *Financial support:* In 2014–15, 70 students received support, including 60 fellowships (averaging $8,921 per year), 11 research assistantships (averaging $2,386 per year), 34 teaching assistantships with full and partial tuition reimbursements available (averaging $9,932 per year); scholarships/grants also available. Support available to part-time students. Financial award application deadline: 2/1; financial award applicants required to submit FAFSA. *Faculty research:* Creative writing, African-American literature, Victorian women writers, theories of sexuality, Shakespeare. *Unit head:* Dr. Ajuan Mance, Chair of the English Department, 510-430-2218, E-mail: dcady@mills.edu. *Application contact:* Shrim Bathey, Director of Graduate Admission, 510-430-3309, Fax: 510-430-2159, E-mail: grad-admission@mills.edu.
Website: http://www.mills.edu/english/

Mills College, Graduate Studies, Program in Book Art and Creative Writing, Oakland, CA 94613-1000. Offers MFA. *Faculty:* 1 (woman) full-time, 1 (woman) part-time/adjunct. *Students:* 9 full-time (8 women), 2 part-time (both women); includes 4 minority (1 Black or African American, non-Hispanic/Latino; 1 Hispanic/Latino; 2 Two or more races, non-Hispanic/Latino). Average age 28. 20 applicants, 60% accepted, 4 enrolled. In 2014, 2 master's awarded. *Degree requirements:* For master's, thesis project. *Entrance requirements:* For master's, visual portfolio of 15-25 images, written portfolio sample (for creative writing program). Additional exam requirements/recommendations for international students: Required—TOEFL (minimum score 600 paper-based; 100 iBT), IELTS (minimum score 7). *Application deadline:* For fall admission, 12/15 priority date for domestic students, 12/15 for international students. Application fee: $50. *Expenses: Tuition:* Full-time $31,620; part-time $7905 per course. *Required fees:* $1118. *Financial support:* In 2014–15, 10 students received support, including 11 fellowships with full and partial tuition reimbursements available (averaging $8,035 per year), 4 teaching assistantships with full and partial tuition reimbursements available (averaging $3,625 per year). Financial award application deadline: 2/1; financial award applicants required to submit FAFSA. *Unit head:* Kathleen Walkup, Professor of Book Arts, 510-430-2001, Fax: 510-430-2159, E-mail: kwalk@mills.edu. *Application contact:* Shrim Bathey, Director of Graduate Admission, 510-430-3309, Fax: 510-430-2159, E-mail: grad-admission@mills.edu.
Website: http://www.mills.edu/academics/graduate/eng/programs/MFA_in_bookart.php

Minnesota State University Mankato, College of Graduate Studies, College of Arts and Humanities, Department of English, Mankato, MN 56001. Offers creative writing (MFA); English (MAT); English studies (MA); teaching English as a second language (MA, Certificate); technical communication (MA, Certificate). Part-time programs available. *Students:* 50 full-time (29 women), 108 part-time (78 women). *Degree requirements:* For master's, one foreign language, comprehensive exam, thesis or alternative. *Entrance requirements:* For master's, minimum GPA of 3.0 during previous 2 years, writing sample (MFA). Additional exam requirements/recommendations for international students: Required—TOEFL (minimum score 500 paper-based; 61 iBT). *Application deadline:* For fall admission, 7/1 for domestic students, 5/1 for international students. Applications are processed on a rolling basis. Application fee: $40. Electronic applications accepted. *Financial support:* Research assistantships with full tuition reimbursements, teaching assistantships with full tuition reimbursements, career-related internships or fieldwork, Federal Work-Study, and unspecified assistantships available. Financial award application deadline: 3/15; financial award applicants required to submit FAFSA. *Faculty research:* Keats and Christianity. *Unit head:* Dr. Nancy Drescher, Chairperson, 507-389-5504. *Application contact:* 507-389-2321, E-mail: grad@mnsu.edu.
Website: http://english.mnsu.edu/

Missouri Western State University, Program in Written Communication, St. Joseph, MO 64507-2294. Offers technical communication (MAA); writing studies (MAA). Part-time programs available. *Students:* 3 full-time (all women), 12 part-time (9 women); includes 2 minority (1 American Indian or Alaska Native, non-Hispanic/Latino; 1 Two or more races, non-Hispanic/Latino), 3 international. Average age 32. 8 applicants, 100% accepted, 7 enrolled. In 2014, 2 degrees awarded. *Entrance requirements:* For master's, minimum GPA of 3.0, essay, letters of reference, portfolio. Additional exam

requirements/recommendations for international students: Recommended—TOEFL (minimum score 70 iBT), IELTS (minimum score 6). *Application deadline:* For fall admission, 7/15 for domestic and international students; for spring admission, 11/1 for domestic students, 10/15 for international students; for summer admission, 4/29 for domestic students. Applications are processed on a rolling basis. Application fee: $45 ($50 for international students). Electronic applications accepted. *Expenses:* Tuition, state resident: full-time $5506; part-time $305.91 per credit hour. Tuition, nonresident: full-time $10,075; part-time $559.71 per credit hour. *Required fees:* $504; $99 per credit hour. $176 per semester. Tuition and fees vary according to course load and program. *Financial support:* Scholarships/grants and unspecified assistantships available. Support available to part-time students. *Unit head:* Dr. Michael Charlton, Associate Professor/Director of Graduate Studies, 816-271-4323, E-mail: mcharlton@missouriwestern.edu. *Application contact:* Dr. Benjamin D. Caldwell, Dean of the Graduate School, 816-271-4394, Fax: 816-271-4525, E-mail: graduate@missouriwestern.edu.
Website: https://www.missouriwestern.edu/eml/maawc/

Monmouth University, The Graduate School, Department of English, West Long Branch, NJ 07764-1898. Offers creative writing (MA); literature (MA); rhetoric and writing (MA). Part-time and evening/weekend programs available. *Faculty:* 11 full-time (7 women). *Students:* 9 full-time (6 women), 33 part-time (25 women); includes 2 minority (1 Black or African American, non-Hispanic/Latino; 1 Asian, non-Hispanic/Latino). Average age 30. 25 applicants, 88% accepted, 15 enrolled. In 2014, 18 master's awarded. *Degree requirements:* For master's, comprehensive exam (for some programs), thesis. *Entrance requirements:* For master's, minimum overall GPA of 2.75, fifteen or more credits in literature or related field, essay of 1,000 words describing interest and goals, two letters of recommendation, creative writing sample. Additional exam requirements/recommendations for international students: Required—TOEFL (minimum score 550 paper-based; 79 iBT), IELTS (minimum score 6), Michigan English Language Assessment Battery (minimum score 77). *Application deadline:* For fall admission, 7/15 for domestic students, 6/1 for international students; for spring admission, 11/15 for domestic students, 11/1 for international students. Application fee: $50. *Expenses: Tuition:* Full-time $18,072; part-time $1004 per credit. *Required fees:* $157 per semester. *Financial support:* In 2014–15, 30 students received support, including 26 fellowships (averaging $2,521 per year), 2 research assistantships (averaging $5,198 per year); career-related internships or fieldwork, scholarships/grants, and unspecified assistantships also available. Support available to part-time students. Financial award applicants required to submit FAFSA. *Faculty research:* Renaissance and medieval literature, nineteenth century American literature, eighteenth century British literature and women's studies, Old and Middle English, African diaspora and African post-colonial literature. *Unit head:* Dr. Jeffrey Jackson, Program Director, 732-571-3439, Fax: 732-263-5242, E-mail: jejackso@monmouth.edu. *Application contact:* Andrea Thompson, Graduate Admission Counselor, 732-571-3452, Fax: 732-263-5123, E-mail: gradadm@monmouth.edu.
Website: http://www.monmouth.edu/school-of-humanities-social-sciences/ma-english.aspx

Montclair State University, The Graduate School, College of Humanities and Social Sciences, Teaching Writing Certificate Program, Montclair, NJ 07043-1624. Offers Certificate. Part-time and evening/weekend programs available. *Students:* 5 part-time (4 women). Average age 33. 8 applicants, 63% accepted, 1 enrolled. In 2014, 1 Certificate awarded. *Entrance requirements:* For degree, 2 letters of recommendation, essay. Additional exam requirements/recommendations for international students: Required—TOEFL (minimum score 83 iBT), IELTS (minimum score 6.5). *Application deadline:* Applications are processed on a rolling basis. Application fee: $60. Electronic applications accepted. *Expenses:* Tuition, state resident: full-time $9960; part-time $553.35 per credit. Tuition, nonresident: full-time $15,074; part-time $837.43 per credit. *Required fees:* $1595; $88.63 per credit. Tuition and fees vary according to degree level and program. *Financial support:* Federal Work-Study, scholarships/grants, and unspecified assistantships available. Support available to part-time students. Financial award application deadline: 3/1; financial award applicants required to submit FAFSA. *Faculty research:* Pedagogy in writing. *Unit head:* Dr. Dan Bronson, Chairperson, 973-655-4274. *Application contact:* Amy Aiello, Director of Graduate Admissions and Operations, 973-655-5147, Fax: 973-655-7869, E-mail: graduate.school@montclair.edu.
Website: http://www.montclair.edu/catalog/view_requirements.php?CurriculumID=3131

Mount Mary University, Graduate Division, Program in English, Milwaukee, WI 53222-4597. Offers creative writing (MA); writing for social media (MA). Part-time and evening/weekend programs available. *Faculty:* 2 full-time (both women), 3 part-time/adjunct (1 woman). *Students:* 16 full-time (14 women), 15 part-time (14 women); includes 7 minority (4 Black or African American, non-Hispanic/Latino; 3 Two or more races, non-Hispanic/Latino), 1 international. Average age 39. 10 applicants, 60% accepted, 5 enrolled. In 2014, 17 master's awarded. *Degree requirements:* For master's, comprehensive exam, thesis or alternative. *Entrance requirements:* For master's, minimum GPA of 2.75. Additional exam requirements/recommendations for international students: Required—TOEFL (minimum score 550 paper-based, 80 iBT) or IELTS (minimum score 6.5). *Application deadline:* For fall admission, 8/1 for domestic and international students; for spring admission, 12/1 for domestic and international students; for summer admission, 5/1 for domestic and international students. Applications are processed on a rolling basis. Application fee: $50 ($0 for international students). Electronic applications accepted. *Expenses:* Expenses: Contact institution. *Financial support:* In 2014–15, 1 student received support. Career-related internships or fieldwork and Federal Work-Study available. Support available to part-time students. Financial award application deadline: 5/1; financial award applicants required to submit FAFSA. *Unit head:* Ann Angel, Graduate Program Chair, 414-258-4810, E-mail: angela@mtmary.edu. *Application contact:* Dr. Douglas J. Mickelson, Dean for Graduate Education, 414-256-1252, Fax: 414-256-0167, E-mail: mickelsd@mtmary.edu.
Website: http://www.mtmary.edu/majors-programs/graduate/english/index.html

Mount Saint Mary's University, Graduate Division, Los Angeles, CA 90049-1599. Offers business administration (MBA); counseling psychology (MS); creative writing (MFA); education (MS, Certificate); film and television (MFA); health policy and management (MS); humanities (MA); nursing (MSN, Certificate); physical therapy (DPT); religious studies (MA). Part-time and evening/weekend programs available. *Faculty:* 15 full-time (11 women), 61 part-time/adjunct (33 women). *Students:* 462 full-time (345 women), 218 part-time (175 women); includes 417 minority (66 Black or African American, non-Hispanic/Latino; 3 American Indian or Alaska Native, non-Hispanic/Latino; 69 Asian, non-Hispanic/Latino; 254 Hispanic/Latino; 11 Native Hawaiian or other Pacific Islander, non-Hispanic/Latino; 14 Two or more races, non-Hispanic/Latino), 1 international. Average age 33. 1,086 applicants, 25% accepted, 241 enrolled. In 2014, 181 master's, 28 doctorates, 22 other advanced degrees awarded. *Entrance requirements:* Additional exam requirements/recommendations for international students: Required—TOEFL. *Application deadline:* For fall admission, 6/30 priority date for domestic and international students; for spring admission, 10/30 priority date for domestic and international students; for summer admission, 3/30 priority date for domestic and international students. Applications are processed on a rolling basis. Application fee: $50. Electronic applications accepted. *Expenses: Tuition:* Full-time

$9756; part-time $813 per unit. One-time fee: $128. Tuition and fees vary according to degree level and program. *Financial support:* In 2014–15, 213 students received support. Career-related internships or fieldwork, Federal Work-Study, institutionally sponsored loans, and tuition waivers (full and partial) available. Support available to part-time students. Financial award application deadline: 3/15; financial award applicants required to submit FAFSA. *Unit head:* Dr. Linda Moody, Graduate Dean, 213-477-2800, E-mail: gradprograms@msmu.edu. *Application contact:* Tara Wessel, Senior Graduate Admission Counselor, 213-477-2800, E-mail: gradprograms@msmu.edu.
Website: http://www.msmu.edu/graduate-programs/admission/

Murray State University, College of Humanities and Fine Arts, Department of English and Philosophy, Program in Creative Writing, Murray, KY 42071. Offers MFA.

Naropa University, Graduate Programs, Program in Creative Writing, Boulder, CO 80302-6697. Offers MFA. Program is offered online only. Part-time and evening/weekend programs available. Postbaccalaureate distance learning degree programs offered (no on-campus study). *Faculty:* 3 part-time/adjunct (all women). *Students:* 1 (woman) full-time, 12 part-time (7 women); includes 2 minority (1 Black or African American, non-Hispanic/Latino; 1 American Indian or Alaska Native, non-Hispanic/Latino). Average age 39. In 2014, 9 master's awarded. *Degree requirements:* For master's, manuscript. *Entrance requirements:* For master's, manuscript/writing sample, resume, transcripts, 2 letters of recommendation, letter of interest, technology check list. Additional exam requirements/recommendations for international students: Required—TOEFL (minimum score 600 paper-based; 80 iBT). *Application deadline:* For fall admission, 1/13 priority date for domestic students, 1/15 priority date for international students; for spring admission, 10/15 for domestic students, 10/15 priority date for international students. Applications are processed on a rolling basis. Application fee: $60. Electronic applications accepted. *Expenses: Tuition:* Full-time $23,400; part-time $975 per credit. *Required fees:* $335 per semester. Tuition and fees vary according to course load. *Financial support:* In 2014–15, 2 students received support. Career-related internships or fieldwork, Federal Work-Study, scholarships/grants, tuition waivers (partial), and unspecified assistantships available. Support available to part-time students. Financial award application deadline: 3/1; financial award applicants required to submit FAFSA. *Unit head:* Michelle Naka Pierce, Director, Jack Kerouac School of Disembodied Poetics, 303-245-4808, E-mail: michelle@naropa.edu. *Application contact:* Office of Admissions, 303-546-3572, Fax: 303-546-3583, E-mail: admissions@naropa.edu.
Website: http://www.naropa.edu/academics/jks/grad/creative-writing-low-residency-mfa/index.php

Naropa University, Graduate Programs, Program in Creative Writing and Poetics, Boulder, CO 80302-6697. Offers MFA. *Faculty:* 6 full-time (4 women), 4 part-time/adjunct (3 women). *Students:* 24 full-time (13 women), 11 part-time (6 women); includes 9 minority (1 Black or African American, non-Hispanic/Latino; 6 Hispanic/Latino; 2 Two or more races, non-Hispanic/Latino), 1 international. Average age 31. 57 applicants, 63% accepted, 13 enrolled. In 2014, 22 master's awarded. *Degree requirements:* For master's, thesis. *Entrance requirements:* For master's, resume, 2 letters of recommendation, transcripts, statement of interest, 10-15 page writing sample, phone interview. Additional exam requirements/recommendations for international students: Required—TOEFL (minimum score 600 paper-based; 80 iBT). *Application deadline:* For fall admission, 1/15 priority date for domestic and international students; for spring admission, 10/15 priority date for domestic and international students. Applications are processed on a rolling basis. Application fee: $60. Electronic applications accepted. *Expenses: Tuition:* Full-time $23,400; part-time $975 per credit. *Required fees:* $335 per semester. Tuition and fees vary according to course load. *Financial support:* In 2014–15, 21 students received support, including 3 fellowships with full tuition reimbursements available (averaging $28,088 per year), 14 research assistantships with partial tuition reimbursements available (averaging $4,571 per year); teaching assistantships, career-related internships or fieldwork, scholarships/grants, tuition waivers (partial), and unspecified assistantships also available. Support available to part-time students. Financial award application deadline: 3/1; financial award applicants required to submit FAFSA. *Unit head:* Bhanu Kapil, Dean, Jack Kerouac School of Disembodied Poetics, 303-245-4629, E-mail: bkapil@naropa.edu. *Application contact:* Office of Admissions, 303-546-3572, Fax: 303-546-3583, E-mail: admissions@naropa.edu.
Website: http://www.naropa.edu/academics/jks/grad/writing-and-poetics-mfa/index.php

National Louis University, College of Arts and Sciences, Chicago, IL 60603. Offers adult education (Ed D); counseling and human services (MS); language and academic development (M Ed, Certificate); psychology (MA, PhD, Certificate); public policy (MA); written communication (MS, Certificate). Part-time and evening/weekend programs available. Postbaccalaureate distance learning degree programs offered (minimal on-campus study). *Degree requirements:* For master's and Certificate, comprehensive exam (for some programs), thesis (for some programs); for doctorate, thesis/dissertation. *Entrance requirements:* For master's, MAT or GRE, 3 professional or academic references, interview, minimum GPA of 3.0; for doctorate, GRE General Test, MAT, or Watson-Glaser Critical Thinking Appraisal, three professional or academic references, statement of academic and professional goals, 3 years of experience in field, interview, master's degree, resume, writing sample; for Certificate, GRE, MAT, or Watson-Glaser Critical Thinking Appraisal, three professional or academic references, statement of academic and professional goals, interview, minimum GPA of 3.0. Additional exam requirements/recommendations for international students: Required—Department of Language Studies Assessment or TOEFL (minimum score 550 paper-based; 79 iBT). Electronic applications accepted.

National University, Academic Affairs, College of Letters and Sciences, La Jolla, CA 92037-1011. Offers applied linguistics (MA); biology (MS); counseling psychology (MA), including licensed professional clinical counseling, marriage and family therapy; creative writing (MFA); English (MA), including Gothic studies, rhetoric; film studies (MA); forensic and crime science (Certificate); forensic studies (MFS), including criminalistics, investigation; history (MA); human behavior (MA); mathematics for educators (MS); performance psychology (MA); strategic communications (MA). Part-time and evening/weekend programs available. Postbaccalaureate distance learning degree programs offered (no on-campus study). *Faculty:* 69 full-time (34 women), 100 part-time/adjunct (55 women). *Students:* 727 full-time (532 women), 349 part-time (240 women); includes 505 minority (128 Black or African American, non-Hispanic/Latino; 5 American Indian or Alaska Native, non-Hispanic/Latino; 52 Asian, non-Hispanic/Latino; 260 Hispanic/Latino; 9 Native Hawaiian or other Pacific Islander, non-Hispanic/Latino; 51 Two or more races, non-Hispanic/Latino), 4 international. Average age 34. In 2014, 569 master's awarded. *Degree requirements:* For master's, thesis (for some programs). *Entrance requirements:* For master's, interview, minimum GPA of 2.5. Additional exam requirements/recommendations for international students: Required—TOEFL (minimum score 550 paper-based; 79 iBT), IELTS (minimum score 6). *Application deadline:* Applications are processed on a rolling basis. Application fee: $60 ($65 for international students). Electronic applications accepted. *Expenses: Tuition:* Full-time $14,184; part-time $1773 per course. *Financial support:* Career-related internships or fieldwork, institutionally sponsored loans, scholarships/grants, and tuition waivers (partial) available. Support available to part-time students. Financial award application deadline: 6/30; financial award applicants required to submit FAFSA. *Unit head:* College of Letters and Sciences,

800-628-8648, E-mail: cols@nu.edu. *Application contact:* Frank Rojas, Interim Vice President for Enrollment Services, 800-628-8648, E-mail: advisor@nu.edu.
Website: http://www.nu.edu/OurPrograms/CollegeOfLettersAndSciences.html

National University, Academic Affairs, School of Professional Studies, La Jolla, CA 92037-1011. Offers criminal justice (MCJ); digital cinema (MFA); digital journalism (MA); juvenile justice (MS); professional screen writing (MFA); public administration (MPA), including human resource management, organizational leadership, public finance. Part-time and evening/weekend programs available. Postbaccalaureate distance learning degree programs offered (no on-campus study). *Faculty:* 19 full-time (8 women), 28 part-time/adjunct (7 women). *Students:* 277 full-time (141 women), 140 part-time (80 women); includes 248 minority (102 Black or African American, non-Hispanic/Latino; 23 Asian, non-Hispanic/Latino; 102 Hispanic/Latino; 5 Native Hawaiian or other Pacific Islander, non-Hispanic/Latino; 16 Two or more races, non-Hispanic/Latino), 8 international. Average age 37. *Degree requirements:* For master's, thesis (for some programs). *Entrance requirements:* For master's, interview, minimum GPA of 2.5. Additional exam requirements/recommendations for international students: Required—TOEFL (minimum score 550 paper-based; 79 iBT), IELTS (minimum score 6). *Application deadline:* Applications are processed on a rolling basis. Application fee: $60 ($65 for international students). Electronic applications accepted. *Expenses: Tuition:* Full-time $14,184; part-time $1773 per course. *Financial support:* Career-related internships or fieldwork, institutionally sponsored loans, scholarships/grants, and tuition waivers (partial) available. Support available to part-time students. Financial award application deadline: 6/30; financial award applicants required to submit FAFSA. *Unit head:* School of Professional Studies, 800-628-8648, E-mail: sops@nu.edu. *Application contact:* Frank Rojas, Vice President for Enrollment Services, 800-628-8648, E-mail: advisor@nu.edu.
Website: http://www.nu.edu/OurPrograms/School-of-Professional-Studies.html

New England College, Programs in Writing, Henniker, NH 03242-3293. Offers poetry (MFA); professional writing (MA). Part-time and evening/weekend programs available. Electronic applications accepted. *Faculty research:* Poetry collections.

New Hampshire Institute of Art, Graduate Programs, Manchester, NH 03104. Offers art education (MA); creative writing (MFA); photography (MFA); visual arts (MFA); writing for stage and screen (MFA). Part-time programs available. *Faculty:* 31 part-time/adjunct (14 women). *Students:* 43 full-time (25 women), 20 part-time (17 women). Average age 44. 36 applicants, 72% accepted, 24 enrolled. *Degree requirements:* For master's, thesis. *Entrance requirements:* For master's, writing sample or visual art portfolio; curriculum vitae; transcripts; letters of recommendation. Additional exam requirements/recommendations for international students: Required—TOEFL (minimum score 530 paper-based; 71 iBT). *Application deadline:* For fall admission, 5/15 for domestic students; for spring admission, 10/1 for domestic students. Applications are processed on a rolling basis. Application fee: $50. Electronic applications accepted. *Expenses:* Expenses: $9,500 per semester plus $495 residency fee (for MFA in visual arts or photography); $9,000 per semester plus $495 residency fee (for MFA in creative writing or writing for stage and screen); $7,155 per semester for full-time student (for MA in art education). *Financial support:* In 2014–15, 54 students received support, including 8 teaching assistantships with partial tuition reimbursements available; scholarships/grants and unspecified assistantships also available. Support available to part-time students. *Unit head:* Alison Williams, Dean of Graduate Studies, 603-836 2522, E-mail: alisonwilliams@nhia.edu. *Application contact:* Graduate Admissions, 603-836 2122, E-mail: gradadmissions@nhia.edu.

New Mexico Highlands University, Graduate Studies, College of Arts and Sciences, Department of English, Las Vegas, NM 87701. Offers English (MA), including creative writing, language, rhetoric and composition, literature. *Faculty:* 3 full-time (2 women). *Students:* 11 full-time (5 women), 7 part-time (6 women); includes 7 minority (1 Black or African American, non-Hispanic/Latino; 1 American Indian or Alaska Native, non-Hispanic/Latino; 3 Hispanic/Latino; 2 Two or more races, non-Hispanic/Latino), 1 international. Average age 37. 6 applicants, 100% accepted, 4 enrolled. In 2014, 4 master's awarded. *Degree requirements:* For master's, comprehensive exam, thesis. *Entrance requirements:* For master's, minimum undergraduate GPA of 3.0. Additional exam requirements/recommendations for international students: Required—TOEFL (minimum score 540 paper-based). *Application deadline:* For fall admission, 8/1 priority date for domestic students. Applications are processed on a rolling basis. Application fee: $15. *Financial support:* In 2014–15, 22 teaching assistantships were awarded; career-related internships or fieldwork, Federal Work-Study, institutionally sponsored loans, scholarships/grants, tuition waivers (full and partial), and unspecified assistantships also available. Support available to part-time students. Financial award application deadline: 3/1; financial award applicants required to submit FAFSA. *Faculty research:* Twentieth-century literature, life path writing in homeless shelters, native American philosophy, medieval intellectual and cultural history, creating pedagogical tools for teaching law. *Unit head:* Dr. Helen Blythe, Chair, 505-454-3329, E-mail: helenblythe@nmhu.edu. *Application contact:* Diane Trujillo, Administrative Assistant, Graduate Studies, 505-454-3266, Fax: 505-426-2117, E-mail: dtrujillo@nmhu.edu.

New Mexico State University, College of Arts and Sciences, Department of English, Las Cruces, NM 88003-8001. Offers creative writing (MA, MFA); English studies for teachers (MA); literature (MA); rhetoric and professional communication (MA, PhD). Part-time programs available. *Faculty:* 20 full-time (11 women), 3 part-time/adjunct (1 woman). *Students:* 65 full-time (41 women), 29 part-time (20 women); includes 30 minority (2 Black or African American, non-Hispanic/Latino; 2 American Indian or Alaska Native, non-Hispanic/Latino; 2 Asian, non-Hispanic/Latino; 22 Hispanic/Latino; 2 Two or more races, non-Hispanic/Latino), 4 international. Average age 33. 104 applicants, 19% accepted, 15 enrolled. In 2014, 18 master's, 2 doctorates awarded. *Degree requirements:* For master's, one foreign language, thesis (for some programs); for doctorate, comprehensive exam, thesis/dissertation, internship. *Entrance requirements:* For master's and doctorate, sample of written work. Additional exam requirements/recommendations for international students: Required—TOEFL (minimum score 550 paper-based; 79 iBT), IELTS (minimum score 6.5). *Application deadline:* For fall admission, 2/1 for domestic and international students. Application fee: $40 ($50 for international students). Electronic applications accepted. *Expenses:* Tuition, state resident: full-time $3969; part-time $220.50 per credit hour. Tuition, nonresident: full-time $13,838; part-time $768.80 per credit hour. *Required fees:* $853; $47.40 per credit hour. *Financial support:* In 2014–15, 61 students received support, including 17 fellowships (averaging $3,970 per year), 49 teaching assistantships (averaging $16,313 per year); career-related internships or fieldwork, Federal Work-Study, institutionally sponsored loans, scholarships/grants, traineeships, health care benefits, and unspecified assistantships also available. Support available to part-time students. Financial award application deadline: 3/1. *Faculty research:* Composition research, history and theory of rhetoric, technical/professional communication, creative writing, English and American literature. *Total annual research expenditures:* $5,069. *Unit head:* Dr. Barry L. Thatcher, Head, 575-646-2319, Fax: 575-646-7725, E-mail: bathatch@nmsu.edu. *Application contact:* Dr. Tracey Eileen Miller-Tomlinson, Director of Graduate Studies, 575-646-2213, Fax: 575-646-7725, E-mail: tomlin@nmsu.edu.
Website: http://english.nmsu.edu

The New School, The New School for Public Engagement, Program in Creative Writing, New York, NY 10011. Offers MFA. Evening/weekend programs available. *Degree requirements:* For master's, thesis, literature project. *Entrance requirements:* For master's, portfolio. Additional exam requirements/recommendations for international students: Required—TOEFL (minimum score 600 paper-based; 100 iBT). Electronic applications accepted. *Expenses:* Contact institution.

New York University, Graduate School of Arts and Science, Program in Creative Writing, New York, NY 10012-1019. Offers MA, MFA. Part-time and evening/weekend programs available. *Students:* 116 full-time (72 women), 18 part-time (13 women); includes 36 minority (9 Black or African American, non-Hispanic/Latino; 7 Asian, non-Hispanic/Latino; 13 Hispanic/Latino; 7 Two or more races, non-Hispanic/Latino), 13 international. Average age 31. 553 applicants, 21% accepted, 68 enrolled. In 2014, 60 master's awarded. *Degree requirements:* For master's, one foreign language, thesis or alternative. *Entrance requirements:* For master's, GRE General Test, sample of written work. Additional exam requirements/recommendations for international students: Required—TOEFL. *Application deadline:* For fall admission, 12/18 for domestic and international students. Application fee: $100. *Financial support:* Fellowships with tuition reimbursements, teaching assistantships with tuition reimbursements, Federal Work-Study, institutionally sponsored loans, scholarships/grants, health care benefits, tuition waivers (full and partial), and unspecified assistantships available. Financial award application deadline: 12/18; financial award applicants required to submit FAFSA. *Faculty research:* Fiction, poetry. *Unit head:* Deborah Landau, Director, 212-998-8816, Fax: 212-995-4864, E-mail: creative.writing@nyu.edu. *Application contact:* Zachary Sussman, Graduate Program Manager, 212-998-8816, Fax: 212-995-4864, E-mail: creative.writing@nyu.edu.
Website: http://www.nyu.edu/gsas/program/cwp/

New York University, School of Continuing and Professional Studies, Division of Humanities, Arts, and Writing, New York, NY 10012-1019. Offers professional writing (MS). Part-time and evening/weekend programs available. Postbaccalaureate distance learning degree programs offered (no on-campus study). *Faculty:* 1 full-time (0 women), 5 part-time/adjunct (4 women). *Students:* 4 full-time (3 women), 17 part-time (16 women); includes 9 minority (7 Black or African American, non-Hispanic/Latino; 2 Hispanic/Latino), 1 international. Average age 32. 24 applicants, 63% accepted, 12 enrolled. *Degree requirements:* For master's, thesis. *Entrance requirements:* For master's, GRE or GMAT (only upon request), bachelor's degree, resume with relevant professional work, internship or volunteer experience, two letters of recommendation, statement of purpose. Additional exam requirements/recommendations for international students: Required—TOEFL (minimum score 600 paper-based; 100 iBT), IELTS (minimum score 7). *Application deadline:* For fall admission, 2/1 priority date for domestic and international students; for spring admission, 10/15 priority date for domestic students, 8/15 priority date for international students. Applications are processed on a rolling basis. Application fee: $150. Electronic applications accepted. *Financial support:* In 2014–15, 5 students received support, including 5 fellowships (averaging $2,300 per year); Federal Work-Study and scholarships/grants also available. Support available to part-time students. Financial award application deadline: 4/1; financial award applicants required to submit FAFSA. *Unit head:* Terry Shtob, Academic Director and Clinical Associate Professor, 212-998-7289. *Application contact:* Office of Admissions, 212-998-7100, E-mail: sps.gradadmissions@nyu.edu.
Website: http://www.sps.nyu.edu/academics/departments/humanities-arts-and-writing.html

New York University, Tisch School of the Arts, Rita and Burton Goldberg Department of Dramatic Writing, New York, NY 10012-1019. Offers MFA. *Faculty:* 15 full-time, 16 part-time/adjunct. *Students:* 50 full-time (26 women); includes 11 minority (8 Black or African American, non-Hispanic/Latino; 1 Asian, non-Hispanic/Latino; 2 Hispanic/Latino), 12 international. Average age 30. 223 applicants, 21% accepted, 29 enrolled. In 2014, 20 master's awarded. *Degree requirements:* For master's, thesis, play or screenplay, internship. *Entrance requirements:* For master's, writing sample. Additional exam requirements/recommendations for international students: Required—TOEFL or IELTS. *Application deadline:* For fall admission, 12/1 for domestic and international students. Application fee: $60. Electronic applications accepted. *Financial support:* In 2014–15, 19 students received support, including 5 fellowships with full and partial tuition reimbursements available; career-related internships or fieldwork, Federal Work-Study, institutionally sponsored loans, and scholarships/grants also available. Financial award application deadline: 2/15; financial award applicants required to submit FAFSA. *Faculty research:* Craft of screenwriting film story analysis, production elements in film and theatre. *Unit head:* Dr. Sheril D. Antonio, Chair, 212-998-1940, Fax: 212-995-4069. *Application contact:* Dan Sandford, Director of Graduate Admissions, 212-998-1918, Fax: 212-995-4060, E-mail: tisch.gradadmissions@nyu.edu.
Website: http://www.ddw.tisch.nyu.edu/

North Carolina State University, Graduate School, College of Humanities and Social Sciences, Department of English, Program in Creative Writing, Raleigh, NC 27695. Offers MFA. *Degree requirements:* For master's, thesis optional. *Entrance requirements:* For master's, GRE. Electronic applications accepted. *Faculty research:* Science fiction, Asian poetry, translation, Southern writers, satiric fiction.

North Central College, Graduate and Continuing Studies Programs, Program in Liberal Studies, Naperville, IL 60566-7063. Offers culture and society (MALS); ethics and public service (MALS); writing, editing, and publishing (MALS). Part-time and evening/weekend programs available. *Faculty:* 8 full-time (2 women), 4 part-time/adjunct (1 woman). *Students:* 2 full-time (1 woman), 24 part-time (14 women); includes 1 minority (Asian, non-Hispanic/Latino). Average age 36. 15 applicants, 73% accepted, 7 enrolled. In 2014, 6 master's awarded. *Degree requirements:* For master's, thesis optional, project. *Entrance requirements:* For master's, interview. Additional exam requirements/recommendations for international students: Required—TOEFL (minimum score 550 paper-based; 80 iBT). *Application deadline:* For fall admission, 8/15 for domestic students, 7/15 for international students; for winter admission, 12/1 for domestic students, 11/1 for international students; for spring admission, 2/1 for domestic students, 12/1 for international students. Applications are processed on a rolling basis. Application fee: $25. Electronic applications accepted. Application fee is waived when completed online. *Expenses:* Expenses: Contact institution. *Financial support:* In 2014–15, 1 student received support. Scholarships/grants available. Support available to part-time students. Financial award applicants required to submit FAFSA. *Unit head:* Dr. Richard Guzman, Program Coordinator, Liberal Studies, 630-637-5285. *Application contact:* Wendy Kulpinski, Director of Graduate and Continuing Education Admission, 630-637-5808, Fax: 630-637-5844, E-mail: wekulpinski@noctrl.edu.
Website: http://northcentralcollege.edu/admission/liberal-studies

North Dakota State University, College of Graduate and Interdisciplinary Studies, College of Arts, Humanities and Social Sciences, Department of English, Fargo, ND 58108. Offers English (MA, MS); rhetoric, writing and culture (PhD). Part-time programs available. *Degree requirements:* For master's, one foreign language, thesis. *Entrance requirements:* Additional exam requirements/recommendations for international students: Required—TOEFL (minimum score 600 paper-based; 100 iBT), IELTS (minimum score 7). Electronic applications accepted. *Faculty research:* American and

English literature, women's studies, language attitudes, composition practices, computers and composition.

See Display on page 753 and Close-Up on page 765.

Northeastern Illinois University, College of Graduate Studies and Research, College of Arts and Sciences, Programs in English, Chicago, IL 60625-4699. Offers composition/writing (MA); literature (MA). Part-time and evening/weekend programs available. *Degree requirements:* For master's, comprehensive exam, thesis optional. *Entrance requirements:* For master's, 30 hours of undergraduate course work in literature and composition (literature), BA in English or approval (composition/writing), minimum GPA of 2.75. Additional exam requirements/recommendations for international students: Required—TOEFL (minimum score 550 paper-based; 79 iBT). Electronic applications accepted. *Faculty research:* Arthurian literature, Southern American literature, rhetoric and theories of authorship.

Northern Arizona University, Graduate College, College of Arts and Letters, Department of English, Flagstaff, AZ 86011. Offers applied linguistics (PhD); English (MA, MFA), including creative writing (MFA), general English studies (MA), literature (MA), rhetoric and the teaching of writing (MA), secondary English education (MA); professional writing (Certificate); teaching English as a second language (MA, Certificate). Part-time programs available. *Degree requirements:* For master's, comprehensive exam (for some programs), thesis (for some programs), departmental qualifying exam; for doctorate, comprehensive exam, thesis/dissertation, departmental qualifying exam. *Entrance requirements:* For master's, minimum GPA of 3.0 or GRE; for doctorate, GRE General Test. Additional exam requirements/recommendations for international students: Required—TOEFL (minimum score 550 paper-based; 80 iBT), IELTS (minimum score 7), TOEFL (minimum score 600 paper-based; 100 iBT) for PhD; TOEFL (minimum score 570 paper-based; 89 iBT) for MA. Electronic applications accepted.

Northern Kentucky University, Office of Graduate Programs, College of Arts and Sciences, Program in English, Highland Heights, KY 41099. Offers composition and rhetoric (Certificate); creative writing (Certificate); cultural studies and discourses (Certificate); English (MA); professional writing (Certificate). Part-time and evening/weekend programs available. *Faculty:* 13 full-time (6 women), 6 part-time/adjunct (0 women). *Students:* 2 full-time (1 woman), 51 part-time (39 women); includes 3 minority (2 Black or African American, non-Hispanic/Latino; 1 Two or more races, non-Hispanic/Latino). Average age 36. In 2014, 10 master's, 9 other advanced degrees awarded. *Degree requirements:* For master's, comprehensive exam (for some programs), capstone (thesis, portfolio, project, or exams); 30 hours of credit; for Certificate, 18 hours of credit. *Entrance requirements:* For master's, bachelor's degree in English or related field from regionally-accredited institution with minimum GPA of 3.0 in major or cognate area coursework; official transcripts for all undergraduate and graduate work; two letters of reference; for Certificate, official transcripts for all undergraduate and graduate work; bachelor's degree from regionally-accredited institution; minimum undergraduate GPA of 2.5. Additional exam requirements/recommendations for international students: Required—TOEFL (minimum score 79 iBT); Recommended—IELTS (minimum score 6.5). *Application deadline:* For fall admission, 7/1 priority date for domestic students, 6/1 priority date for international students; for spring admission, 11/1 priority date for domestic students, 10/1 for international students. Application fee: $40. Electronic applications accepted. *Expenses: Tuition, area resident:* Part-time $518 per credit hour. Tuition, state resident: part-time $630 per credit hour. Tuition, nonresident: part-time $797 per credit hour. *Required fees:* $192 per semester. Tuition and fees vary according to course load, degree level, campus/location, program and reciprocity agreements. *Financial support:* In 2014–15, 8 students received support. Unspecified assistantships available. Financial award applicants required to submit FAFSA. *Unit head:* Dr. John Alberti, Director of English Graduate Studies, 859-572-5619, Fax: 859-572-6093, E-mail: alberti@nku.edu. *Application contact:* Alison Swanson, Graduate Admissions Coordinator, 859-572-6971, E-mail: swansona1@nku.edu.
Website: http://english.nku.edu/gradprogram/

Northern Michigan University, Office of Graduate Education and Research, College of Arts and Sciences, Department of English, Marquette, MI 49855-5301. Offers creative writing (MFA); literature (MA); pedagogy (MA); teaching English to speakers of other languages (Graduate Certificate); theater (MA); writing (MA). Part-time and evening/weekend programs available. *Faculty:* 14 full-time (9 women). *Students:* 55 full-time (32 women), 11 part-time (7 women); includes 8 minority (1 Black or African American, non-Hispanic/Latino; 1 American Indian or Alaska Native, non-Hispanic/Latino; 2 Hispanic/Latino; 4 Two or more races, non-Hispanic/Latino). Average age 27. 135 applicants, 43% accepted, 28 enrolled. In 2014, 21 master's awarded. Terminal master's awarded for partial completion of doctoral program. *Degree requirements:* For master's, capstone project: thesis, practicum or portfolio (for MA); thesis (for MFA); for Graduate Certificate, one foreign language. *Entrance requirements:* For master's, minimum GPA of 3.0; bachelor's degree in English or minimum of 30 credit hours in undergraduate English; statement of purpose; resume; critical essay; 3 letters of recommendation; for Graduate Certificate, bachelor's degree. Additional exam requirements/recommendations for international students: Required—TOEFL (minimum score 550 paper-based; 79 iBT), IELTS (minimum score 6.5). *Application deadline:* For fall admission, 2/1 for domestic students; for winter admission, 2/1 for domestic students; for spring admission, 3/17 for domestic students. Applications are processed on a rolling basis. Application fee: $50. Electronic applications accepted. *Expenses:* Tuition, state resident: full-time $7716; part-time $441 per credit hour. Tuition, nonresident: full-time $10,812; part-time $634.50 per credit hour. *Required fees:* $31.88 per semester. Tuition and fees vary according to course load, degree level and program. *Financial support:* In 2014–15, research assistantships with full tuition reimbursements (averaging $8,898 per year), teaching assistantships with full tuition reimbursements (averaging $8,898 per year) were awarded; Federal Work-Study, institutionally sponsored loans, and unspecified assistantships also available. Support available to part-time students. Financial award application deadline: 3/1; financial award applicants required to submit FAFSA. *Faculty research:* Modern Arabic literature, British literature (medieval to contemporary), postcolonial literature, Native and African-American literature, creative writing, critical theory, pedagogy. *Unit head:* Prof. Russell Prather, PhD, Director of MA Program/Professor, 906-227-2857, E-mail: rprather@nmu.edu. *Application contact:* Prof. Russell Prather, PhD, Director of MA Program/Professor, 906-227-2857, E-mail: rprather@nmu.edu.
Website: http://www.nmu.edu/english/

Northwestern University, Medill School of Journalism, Media, and Integrated Marketing Communications, Evanston, IL 60208. Offers integrated marketing communications (MSIMC), including brand strategy, content marketing, direct and interactive marketing, marketing analytics, strategic communications; interactive publishing (MSJ); magazine writing/editing (MSJ); reporting (MSJ); video/broadcast (MSJ). *Accreditation:* ACEJMC (one or more programs are accredited). *Entrance requirements:* For master's, GRE General Test, GMAT or LSAT (for MSJ). Additional exam requirements/recommendations for international students: Required—TOEFL. Electronic applications accepted. *Expenses:* Contact institution. *Faculty research:* Web business journalism, cultural stereotypes, voter apathy, digital television.

Northwestern University, School of Professional Studies, Program in Creative Writing, Evanston, IL 60208. Offers MA, MFA.

Northwest Institute of Literary Arts, Master of Fine Arts in Creative Writing Program, Freeland, WA 98249. Offers fiction (MFA); nonfiction (MFA); poetry (MFA); writing for children and young adults (MFA). Part-time programs available. Postbaccalaureate distance learning degree programs offered (minimal on-campus study). *Faculty:* 8 part-time/adjunct (4 women). *Students:* 39 full-time (33 women), 12 part-time (10 women), 4 international. 12 applicants, 67% accepted, 2 enrolled. In 2014, 10 master's awarded. *Entrance requirements:* For master's, manuscript of original work, personal essay, college transcripts, 3 letters of recommendation. Additional exam requirements/recommendations for international students: Required—TOEFL. *Application deadline:* For fall admission, 3/15 for domestic students; for spring admission, 10/1 for domestic students. Applications are processed on a rolling basis. Application fee: $50. Electronic applications accepted. *Expenses: Tuition:* Full-time $11,550; part-time $2100 per course. *Required fees:* $1100. One-time fee: $150 full-time. Tuition and fees vary according to class time and degree level. *Financial support:* In 2014–15, 2 students received support. Scholarships/grants available. Financial award application deadline: 3/15; financial award applicants required to submit FAFSA. *Unit head:* Wayne Ude, MFA Program Director, 360-331-0307, E-mail: ude@nila.edu. *Application contact:* Susan Janow, Director of Admission, 360-331-0307, E-mail: mfa@nila.edu.
Website: http://www.nila.edu/mfa/

Nova Southeastern University, Farquhar College of Arts and Sciences, Program in Writing, Fort Lauderdale, FL 33314-7796. Offers MA. Part-time and evening/weekend programs available. *Faculty:* 13 full-time (9 women). *Students:* 13 full-time (10 women); includes 7 minority (1 Black or African American, non-Hispanic/Latino; 5 Hispanic/Latino; 1 Two or more races, non-Hispanic/Latino). Average age 33. 12 applicants, 25% accepted, 2 enrolled. In 2014, 5 master's awarded. *Degree requirements:* For master's, thesis. *Entrance requirements:* For master's, GRE, 3 letters of recommendation, official transcripts, 25-page portfolio, 500-word essay. Additional exam requirements/recommendations for international students: Required—TOEFL (minimum score 550 paper-based; 79 iBT). *Application deadline:* For fall admission, 6/1 for domestic and international students; for winter admission, 10/15 for domestic and international students. Application fee: $50. Electronic applications accepted. *Expenses:* Expenses: $560 per credit; $25 registration fee (per semester); Student Services Fees: $150 (per semester) for 1-3 credits, $300 (per semester) for 4 or more credits. *Financial support:* Application deadline: 6/30; applicants required to submit FAFSA. *Faculty research:* Gender studies, fiction and poetry, music history, mystery and detective fiction, ancient philosophy, technical writing. *Unit head:* Dr. Star Vanguri, Assistant Professor, 954-262-7680, E-mail: sm1850@nova.edu. *Application contact:* Isabelle De Castro, Graduate Program Enrollment Coordinator, 954-262-8361, E-mail: id7@nova.edu.
Website: http://www.fcas.nova.edu/programs/graduate/writing/index.cfm

Oklahoma State University, College of Arts and Sciences, Department of English, Stillwater, OK 74078. Offers creative writing (MFA); English (MA, PhD). *Faculty:* 62 full-time (30 women), 2 part-time/adjunct (both women). *Students:* 7 full-time (6 women), 133 part-time (66 women); includes 19 minority (1 Black or African American, non-Hispanic/Latino; 2 American Indian or Alaska Native, non-Hispanic/Latino; 2 Asian, non-Hispanic/Latino; 2 Hispanic/Latino; 12 Two or more races, non-Hispanic/Latino), 20 international. Average age 33. 153 applicants, 27% accepted, 23 enrolled. In 2014, 18 master's, 8 doctorates awarded. *Degree requirements:* For master's, comprehensive exam, thesis; for doctorate, comprehensive exam, thesis/dissertation. *Entrance requirements:* For master's, GRE General Test, minimum GPA of 3.0, writing sample; for doctorate, GRE General Test, minimum GPA of 3.5, writing sample. Additional exam requirements/recommendations for international students: Required—TOEFL (minimum score 550 paper-based; 79 iBT). *Application deadline:* For fall admission, 3/1 priority date for international students; for spring admission, 8/1 priority date for international students. Applications are processed on a rolling basis. Application fee: $40 ($75 for international students). Electronic applications accepted. *Expenses:* Tuition, state resident: full-time $4488; part-time $187 per credit hour. Tuition, nonresident: full-time $18,360; part-time $765 per credit hour. *Required fees:* $2413; $100.55 per credit hour. Tuition and fees vary according to campus/location. *Financial support:* In 2014–15, 1 research assistantship (averaging $7,455 per year), 108 teaching assistantships (averaging $16,412 per year) were awarded; career-related internships or fieldwork, Federal Work-Study, scholarships/grants, health care benefits, tuition waivers (partial), and unspecified assistantships also available. Support available to part-time students. Financial award application deadline: 3/1; financial award applicants required to submit FAFSA. *Faculty research:* American and British novels, poetry, and autobiography; Native American languages and literature; institutional history of American film, history, and adaptations; rhetoric and theories of human communication; learning strategies of second language learners. *Unit head:* Dr. Richard Frohock, Department Head, 405-744-9474, Fax: 405-744-6326, E-mail: richard.frohock@okstate.edu.
Website: http://english.okstate.edu/

Old Dominion University, College of Arts and Letters, MFA Program in Creative Writing, Norfolk, VA 23529. Offers MFA. Part-time programs available. *Faculty:* 7 full-time (3 women), 5 part-time/adjunct (all women). *Students:* 25 full-time (11 women), 6 part-time (4 women); includes 7 minority (4 Black or African American, non-Hispanic/Latino; 1 Hispanic/Latino; 2 Two or more races, non-Hispanic/Latino). Average age 31. 60 applicants, 30% accepted, 12 enrolled. In 2014, 9 master's awarded. *Degree requirements:* For master's, comprehensive exam, thesis. *Entrance requirements:* For master's, GRE General Test, 24 hours of previous course work in English, sample of written work. Additional exam requirements/recommendations for international students: Required—TOEFL. *Application deadline:* For fall admission, 2/1 for domestic students. Application fee: $50. Electronic applications accepted. *Expenses:* Tuition, state resident: full-time $10,488; part-time $437 per credit. Tuition, nonresident: full-time $26,136; part-time $1089 per credit. *Required fees:* $64 per semester. One-time fee: $50. *Financial support:* In 2014–15, 17 students received support, including 2 fellowships with full tuition reimbursements available (averaging $11,000 per year), 3 research assistantships with full tuition reimbursements available (averaging $10,000 per year), 6 teaching assistantships with full tuition reimbursements available (averaging $10,000 per year); scholarships/grants and unspecified assistantships also available. Financial award application deadline: 2/1. *Faculty research:* Literary fiction, nonfiction, poetry. *Total annual research expenditures:* $35,000. *Unit head:* Dr. Luisa Igloria, Graduate Program Director, 757-683-3929, Fax: 757-683-3241, E-mail: cwgpd@odu.edu. *Application contact:* Dr. David C. Earnest, Associate Dean, 757-683-6077, Fax: 757-683-5746, E-mail: dearnest@odu.edu.
Website: http://al.odu.edu/english/mfacw/

Oregon State University, College of Liberal Arts, Program in Creative Writing, Corvallis, OR 97331. Offers MFA. Part-time programs available. *Faculty:* 19 full-time (8 women), 8 part-time/adjunct (6 women). *Students:* 47 full-time (31 women), 1 part-time (0 women); includes 6 minority (1 Asian, non-Hispanic/Latino; 4 Hispanic/Latino; 1 Two or more races, non-Hispanic/Latino). Average age 31. 372 applicants, 10% accepted, 25 enrolled. In 2014, 13 master's awarded. *Entrance requirements:* Additional exam requirements/recommendations for international students: Required—TOEFL (minimum score 80 iBT), IELTS (minimum score 6.5). *Application deadline:* For fall admission, 1/7

for domestic and international students. Application fee: $60. *Expenses:* Tuition, state resident: full-time $11,907; part-time $189 per credit hour. Tuition, nonresident: full-time $19,953; part-time $441 per credit hour. *Required fees:* $1472; $449 per term. One-time fee: $350. Tuition and fees vary according to course load and program. *Financial support:* Fellowships and teaching assistantships available. Financial award application deadline: 1/7. *Unit head:* Dr. Karen Homberg, MFA Director, Creative Writing, 541-737-1661, E-mail: karen.holmberg@oregonstate.edu.
Website: http://oregonstate.edu/cla/wlf/mfa

Otis College of Art and Design, Program in Writing, Los Angeles, CA 90045-9785. Offers MFA. *Degree requirements:* For master's, thesis. *Entrance requirements:* For master's, writing sample. Electronic applications accepted.

Our Lady of the Lake University of San Antonio, College of Arts and Sciences, Program in English, San Antonio, TX 78207-4689. Offers English and communication arts (MA); English education (MA); English language and literature (MA); writing (MA); MA/MFA. Program offered jointly with University of the Incarnate Word and St. Mary's University. Part-time and evening/weekend programs available. *Degree requirements:* For master's, comprehensive exam, thesis optional. *Entrance requirements:* For master's, GRE General Test or MAT, minimum GPA of 3.0 in last 60 hours, 2.5 overall. Additional exam requirements/recommendations for international students: Required—TOEFL. Electronic applications accepted. *Faculty research:* Writing theory and research, contemporary Southern literature, popular culture, poetry, literature of the Southwest.

Pacific Lutheran University, Graduate Programs and Continuing Education, Division of Humanities, Tacoma, WA 98447. Offers creative writing (MFA). Part-time programs available. Postbaccalaureate distance learning degree programs offered (minimal on-campus study). *Faculty:* 1 full-time (0 women). *Students:* 51 part-time (38 women); includes 1 minority (Hispanic/Latino). Average age 43. 54 applicants, 46% accepted, 15 enrolled. In 2014, 16 master's awarded. *Degree requirements:* For master's, thesis, final residency including teaching class. *Entrance requirements:* For master's, portfolio, book review. Additional exam requirements/recommendations for international students: Required—TOEFL. *Application deadline:* For fall admission, 11/30 for domestic and international students; for summer admission, 2/15 for domestic and international students. Applications are processed on a rolling basis. Application fee: $40. Electronic applications accepted. Application fee is waived when completed online. *Expenses:* Expenses: Contact institution. *Financial support:* In 2014–15, 25 students received support, including 10 fellowships (averaging $1,000 per year); scholarships/grants, health care benefits, and unspecified assistantships also available. Support available to part-time students. Financial award application deadline: 3/1; financial award applicants required to submit FAFSA. *Unit head:* Dr. James Albrecht, Dean, 253-535-7698, Fax: 253-535-7321, E-mail: albrecjm@plu.edu. *Application contact:* Rick Barot, Director of MFA in Creative Writing Program, 253-535-7318, E-mail: mfa@plu.edu.
Website: http://www.plu.edu/mfa/

Pacific University, Program in Writing, Forest Grove, OR 97116-1797. Offers MFA. Part-time programs available.

Park University, School of Graduate and Professional Studies, Kansas City, MO 54105. Offers adult education (M Ed); business and government leadership (Graduate Certificate); business, government, and global society (MPA); communication and leadership (MA); creative and life writing (Graduate Certificate); disaster and emergency management (MPA, Graduate Certificate); educational leadership (M Ed); finance (MBA, Graduate Certificate); general business (MBA); global business (Graduate Certificate); healthcare administration (MHA); healthcare services management and leadership (Graduate Certificate); international business (MBA); language and literacy (M Ed), including English for speakers of other languages, special reading teacher/literacy coach; leadership of international healthcare organizations (Graduate Certificate); management information systems (MBA, Graduate Certificate); music performance (ADP, Graduate Certificate), including cello (MM, ADP), piano (MM, ADP), viola (MM, ADP), violin (MM, ADP); nonprofit and community services management (MPA); nonprofit leadership (Graduate Certificate); performance (MM), including cello (MM, ADP), piano (MM, ADP), viola (MM, ADP), violin (MM, ADP); public management (MPA); social work (MSW); teacher leadership (M Ed), including curriculum and assessment, instructional leader. Part-time and evening/weekend programs available. Postbaccalaureate distance learning degree programs offered (no on-campus study). *Degree requirements:* For master's, comprehensive exam (for some programs), thesis (for some programs), internship (for some programs); exam (for some programs). *Entrance requirements:* For master's, GRE or GMAT (for some programs), teacher certification (for some M Ed programs), letters of recommendation, essay, resume (for some programs). Additional exam requirements/recommendations for international students: Required—TOEFL (minimum score 550 paper-based; 79 iBT), IELTS (minimum score 6). Electronic applications accepted.

Penn State Harrisburg, Graduate School, School of Humanities, Middletown, PA 17057-4898. Offers American studies (MA, PhD); communications (MA); folklore and ethnography (Certificate); heritage and museum practice (Certificate); humanities (MA); writing instruction specialist (Certificate). Evening/weekend programs available. *Unit head:* Dr. Mukund S. Kulkarni, Chancellor, 717-948-6105, Fax: 717-948-6452, E-mail: msk5@psu.edu. *Application contact:* Robert W. Coffman, Jr., Director of Enrollment Management, Admissions, 717-948-6250, Fax: 717-948-6325, E-mail: ric1@psu.edu.
Website: http://harrisburg.psu.edu/humanities

Penn State University Park, Graduate School, College of the Liberal Arts, Department of English, University Park, PA 16802. Offers MA, MFA, PhD. *Unit head:* Dr. Susan Welch, Dean, 814-865-7691, Fax: 814-863-2085, E-mail: swelch@psu.edu. *Application contact:* Lori A. Stania, Director, Graduate Student Services, 814-867-5278, Fax: 814-863-4627, E-mail: gswww@psu.edu.
Website: http://english.la.psu.edu/

Pepperdine University, Seaver College, Master of Fine Arts Program in Writing for Screen and Television, Malibu, CA 90263. Offers MFA. *Students:* 7 full-time (5 women), 22 part-time (12 women); includes 4 minority (2 Black or African American, non-Hispanic/Latino; 1 Asian, non-Hispanic/Latino; 1 Hispanic/Latino). In 2014, 7 master's awarded. *Entrance requirements:* For master's, GRE General Test, statement of purpose and intent for writing as a vocation, script writing sample, letters of recommendation. Additional exam requirements/recommendations for international students: Required—TOEFL. *Application deadline:* For fall admission, 2/1 priority date for domestic students. Application fee: $55. Electronic applications accepted. *Unit head:* Dr. Maire Mullins, Chair/Professor of English, Humanities and Teacher Education Division, 310-506-4894, E-mail: maire.mullins@pepperdine.edu. *Application contact:* Michael Truschke, Dean of Admission and Enrollment Management, 310-506-6165, Fax: 310-506-4861, E-mail: admission-seaver@pepperdine.edu.
Website: http://seaver.pepperdine.edu/humanities/academics/ma-screenwriting.htm

Pratt Institute, School of Liberal Arts and Sciences, Program in Writing, Brooklyn, NY 11205-3899. Offers MFA. *Students:* 11 full-time (8 women); includes 7 minority (5 Black or African American, non-Hispanic/Latino; 2 Hispanic/Latino). 56 applicants, 59% accepted, 11 enrolled. *Application deadline:* For fall admission, 1/5 for domestic and international students; for spring admission, 10/1 for domestic and international students. Application fee: $50 ($90 for international students). Electronic applications accepted. *Financial support:* Application deadline: 2/1; applicants required to submit FAFSA. *Unit head:* Maria Damon, Chairperson, 718-636-3790, E-mail: mdamon@pratt.edu. *Application contact:* Young Hah, Director of Graduate Admissions, 718-636-3683, Fax: 718-399-4242, E-mail: yhah@pratt.edu.
Website: https://www.pratt.edu/academics/liberal-arts-and-sciences/graduate-writing/

Purdue University, Graduate School, College of Liberal Arts, Department of English, West Lafayette, IN 47907. Offers creative writing (MFA); literature (MA, PhD), including linguistics, literature and philosophy (PhD), rhetoric and composition, theory and cultural studies (PhD). Part-time programs available. *Degree requirements:* For master's, one foreign language, comprehensive exam (for some programs), thesis (for some programs); for doctorate, one foreign language, comprehensive exam, thesis/dissertation. *Entrance requirements:* For master's, GRE General Test; GRE Subject Test in English literature (recommended for students applying to literary studies), minimum undergraduate GPA of 3.0 or equivalent; for doctorate, GRE General Test; GRE Subject Test in English literature (recommended for students applying to literary studies), master's degree. Additional exam requirements/recommendations for international students: Required—TOEFL (minimum score 620 paper-based; 77 iBT). Electronic applications accepted. *Faculty research:* Cultural studies, postmodern narrative, contemporary women writers, composition theory, slave narratives.

Queens College of the City University of New York, Division of Graduate Studies, Arts and Humanities Division, Department of English, Flushing, NY 11367-1597. Offers creative writing (MA); English language and literature (MA). Part-time and evening/weekend programs available. *Degree requirements:* For master's, one foreign language, thesis (for some programs), oral exam (English language and literature). *Entrance requirements:* For master's, manuscript (creative writing), minimum GPA of 3.0. Additional exam requirements/recommendations for international students: Required—TOEFL.

Queens University of Charlotte, College of Arts and Sciences, Charlotte, NC 28274-0002. Offers creative writing (MFA). Part-time programs available. Postbaccalaureate distance learning degree programs offered (minimal on-campus study). Electronic applications accepted.

Regent University, Graduate School, School of Communication and the Arts, Virginia Beach, VA 23464-9800. Offers acting (MFA); communication (MA, PhD), including political communication (MA), strategic communication (MA); directing for cinema/television (MFA); film and TV (MA), including producing, production, script writing; journalism (MA); producing for cinema/television (MFA); script and screenwriting (MFA); theatre (MA). Part-time programs available. Postbaccalaureate distance learning degree programs offered (minimal on-campus study). *Faculty:* 20 full-time (3 women), 26 part-time/adjunct (7 women). *Students:* 89 full-time (49 women), 211 part-time (125 women); includes 92 minority (69 Black or African American, non-Hispanic/Latino; 2 American Indian or Alaska Native, non-Hispanic/Latino; 2 Asian, non-Hispanic/Latino; 19 Hispanic/Latino), 10 international. Average age 35. 199 applicants, 53% accepted, 77 enrolled. In 2014, 48 master's, 8 doctorates awarded. *Degree requirements:* For master's, thesis or alternative; for doctorate, thesis/dissertation. *Entrance requirements:* For master's, GRE General Test or MAT, minimum undergraduate GPA of 3.0, writing sample, computer literacy survey, recommendation, resume, interview, audition (for MFA programs); for doctorate, GRE General Test, minimum graduate GPA of 3.0, writing sample, computer literacy survey, recommendation, interview, transcripts. Additional exam requirements/recommendations for international students: Required—TOEFL (minimum score 577 paper-based). *Application deadline:* For fall admission, 3/1 priority date for domestic students; for spring admission, 10/1 priority date for domestic students. Applications are processed on a rolling basis. Application fee: $50. Electronic applications accepted. *Expenses:* Expenses: Contact institution. *Financial support:* Fellowships with full and partial tuition reimbursements, career-related internships or fieldwork, scholarships/grants, tuition waivers (full and partial), and unspecified assistantships available. Support available to part-time students. Financial award application deadline: 9/1; financial award applicants required to submit FAFSA. *Faculty research:* Southern gospel music, education and entertainment, celebrities and the media, journalism and ethics, C.S. Lewis. *Unit head:* Dr. Mitch Land, Dean, 757-352-4916, Fax: 757-352-4291, E-mail: mland@regent.edu. *Application contact:* Matthew Chadwick, Director of Enrollment Support Services, 800-373-5504, Fax: 757-352-4381, E-mail: admissions@regent.edu.
Website: http://www.regent.edu/acad/schcom/

Regis College, Program in Professional Writing for New Media, Weston, MA 02493. Offers MA, Certificate.

Rhode Island College, School of Graduate Studies, Faculty of Arts and Sciences, Department of English, Providence, RI 02908-1991. Offers creative writing (MA, CGS); English (MA); literature (CGS). Part-time and evening/weekend programs available. *Faculty:* 6 full-time (2 women). *Students:* 1 full-time (0 women), 10 part-time (6 women). Average age 33. In 2014, 5 master's awarded. *Degree requirements:* For master's, thesis (for some programs). *Entrance requirements:* For master's, GRE General Test, 3 letters of recommendation, interview. Additional exam requirements/recommendations for international students: Recommended—TOEFL (minimum score 550 paper-based; 79 iBT). *Application deadline:* For fall admission, 3/1 for domestic students; for spring admission, 11/1 for domestic students. Applications are processed on a rolling basis. Application fee: $50. *Expenses:* Tuition, state resident: full-time $8928; part-time $372 per credit hour. Tuition, nonresident: full-time $17,376; part-time $724 per credit hour. *Required fees:* $602; $22 per credit. $72 per term. *Financial support:* In 2014–15, 2 teaching assistantships with full tuition reimbursements (averaging $3,250 per year) were awarded; career-related internships or fieldwork, Federal Work-Study, scholarships/grants, health care benefits, and unspecified assistantships also available. Support available to part-time students. Financial award application deadline: 5/15; financial award applicants required to submit FAFSA. *Unit head:* Dr. Daniel Scott, III, Chair, 401-456-8028. *Application contact:* Graduate Studies, 401-456-8700.
Website: http://www.ric.edu/english/index.php

Rivier University, School of Graduate Studies, Department of English, Nashua, NH 03060. Offers English (MAT); writing and literature (MA). Part-time and evening/weekend programs available. *Degree requirements:* For master's, comprehensive exam (for some programs). *Entrance requirements:* For master's, GRE Subject Test.

Roosevelt University, Graduate Division, College of Arts and Sciences, Department of Literature and Languages, Program in Creative Writing, Chicago, IL 60605. Offers MFA. Part-time and evening/weekend programs available. *Faculty research:* Poetry, fiction, nonfiction, script writing.

Rosemont College, Schools of Graduate and Professional Studies, Creative Writing Program, Rosemont, PA 19010-1699. Offers MFA. Part-time and evening/weekend programs available. *Faculty:* 8 part-time/adjunct (6 women). *Students:* 9 full-time (3 women), 52 part-time (43 women); includes 10 minority (6 Black or African American, non-Hispanic/Latino; 1 Asian, non-Hispanic/Latino; 1 Hispanic/Latino; 2 Two or more races, non-Hispanic/Latino). Average age 38. 38 applicants, 68% accepted, 14 enrolled. In 2014, 12 master's awarded. *Degree requirements:* For master's, comprehensive exam, thesis. *Entrance requirements:* For master's, 3 letters of recommendation, baccalaureate degree with minimum GPA of 3.0, writing sample. Additional exam

requirements/recommendations for international students: Required—TOEFL. *Application deadline:* Applications are processed on a rolling basis. Application fee: $50. Electronic applications accepted. Application fee is waived when completed online. *Financial support:* Career-related internships or fieldwork and unspecified assistantships available. Financial award applicants required to submit FAFSA. *Unit head:* Prof. Carla J. Spataro, Director, 610-527-0200 Ext. 2346, Fax: 610-526-2964, E-mail: cspataro@rosemont.edu. *Application contact:* Graduate Admissions Counselor, 610-527-0200 Ext. 2596, Fax: 610-520-4399, E-mail: sgpsadmissions@rosemont.edu.
Website: http://www.rosemont.edu/gp/creative-writing-poetry-or-fiction/index.aspx

Rowan University, Graduate School, College of Communication and Creative Arts, Program in Writing, Glassboro, NJ 08028-1701. Offers MA. Part-time and evening/weekend programs available. *Faculty:* 4 full-time (3 women). *Students:* 1 full-time (0 women), 19 part-time (16 women); includes 2 minority (1 Black or African American, non-Hispanic/Latino; 1 Hispanic/Latino). Average age 35. 12 applicants, 67% accepted, 7 enrolled. In 2014, 7 master's awarded. *Degree requirements:* For master's, thesis. *Entrance requirements:* For master's, GRE General Test. Additional exam requirements/recommendations for international students: Required—TOEFL. *Application deadline:* For fall admission, 8/1 for domestic students; for spring admission, 11/1 for domestic students. Applications are processed on a rolling basis. Application fee: $65. Electronic applications accepted. *Expenses: Tuition, area resident:* Part-time $648 per credit. Tuition, state resident: part-time $648 per credit. Tuition, nonresident: part-time $648 per credit. *Required fees:* $145 per credit. Tuition and fees vary according to degree level, campus/location, program and student level. *Financial support:* Career-related internships or fieldwork, scholarships/grants, and health care benefits available. Support available to part-time students. *Unit head:* Dr. Horacio Sosa, Vice President, Global Learning and Partnerships, 856-256-4747, Fax: 856-256-5638, E-mail: sosa@rowan.edu. *Application contact:* Admissions and Enrollment Services, 856-256-4747, Fax: 856-256-5637, E-mail: globaladmissions@rowan.edu.

Rowan University, Graduate School, College of Communication and Creative Arts, Writing, Composition, and Rhetoric Certificate of Graduate Study Program, Glassboro, NJ 08028-1701. Offers CGS. *Expenses: Tuition, area resident:* Part-time $648 per credit. Tuition, state resident: part-time $648 per credit. Tuition, nonresident: part-time $648 per credit. *Required fees:* $145 per credit. Tuition and fees vary according to degree level, campus/location, program and student level. *Unit head:* Dr. Horacio Sosa, Vice President, Global Learning and Partnerships, 856-256-4747, Fax: 856-256-5638, E-mail: sosa@rowan.edu. *Application contact:* Admissions and Enrollment Services, 856-256-4747, Fax: 856-256-5637, E-mail: globaladmissions@rowan.edu.

Rutgers, The State University of New Jersey, Camden, Graduate School of Arts and Sciences, Program in Creative Writing, Camden, NJ 08102. Offers MFA. Part-time and evening/weekend programs available. *Degree requirements:* For master's, thesis, 42 credits. *Entrance requirements:* For master's, GRE (for assistantships), 2 letters of recommendation, writing sample, statement of personal, professional, and academic goals. Additional exam requirements/recommendations for international students: Required—TOEFL, IELTS. Electronic applications accepted. *Faculty research:* Poetry, fiction, nonfiction.

Rutgers, The State University of New Jersey, Newark, Graduate School, Program in Creative Writing, Newark, NJ 07102. Offers MFA. *Entrance requirements:* For master's, GRE, minimum undergraduate B average.

Rutgers, The State University of New Jersey, New Brunswick, Mason Gross School of the Arts, Theater Arts Department, New Brunswick, NJ 08901. Offers acting (MFA); design (MFA); directing (MFA); playwriting (MFA); stage management (MFA). *Degree requirements:* For master's, thesis (for some programs), performance project. *Entrance requirements:* For master's, audition, interview, portfolio. Additional exam requirements/recommendations for international students: Required—TOEFL (minimum score 550 paper-based), IELTS (minimum score 7). Electronic applications accepted. *Faculty research:* Faculty of working professional.

St. Joseph's College, New York, Graduate Programs, Program in Creative Writing, Brooklyn, NY 11205-3688. Offers MFA. *Faculty:* 1 full-time (0 women). *Students:* 30 full-time (20 women), 3 part-time (2 women); includes 2 minority (1 Asian, non-Hispanic/Latino; 1 Hispanic/Latino). Average age 36. 18 applicants, 100% accepted, 16 enrolled. *Expenses: Tuition:* Full-time $14,040; part-time $780 per credit hour. *Required fees:* $133 per semester. *Unit head:* Ted Hamm, Associate Professor/Chair, 718-940-5307, E-mail: thamm@sjcny.edu.
Website: http://www.sjcny.edu

Saint Joseph's University, College of Arts and Sciences, Program in Writing Studies, Philadelphia, PA 19131-1395. Offers MA. Part-time and evening/weekend programs available. *Faculty:* 7 full-time (4 women), 1 (woman) part-time/adjunct. *Students:* 7 full-time (3 women), 27 part-time (12 women); includes 10 minority (7 Black or African American, non-Hispanic/Latino; 2 Hispanic/Latino; 1 Two or more races, non-Hispanic/Latino), 1 international. Average age 34. 18 applicants, 67% accepted, 12 enrolled. In 2014, 9 master's awarded. *Entrance requirements:* For master's, 2 letters of recommendation, resume, 2 writing samples. Additional exam requirements/recommendations for international students: Required—TOEFL (minimum score 550 paper-based; 80 iBT). *Application deadline:* For fall admission, 7/15 priority date for domestic students, 4/15 priority date for international students; for winter admission, 1/15 priority date for international students; for spring admission, 11/15 priority date for domestic students, 10/15 priority date for international students. Applications are processed on a rolling basis. Application fee: $35. Electronic applications accepted. *Financial support:* In 2014–15, 2 students received support. Unspecified assistantships available. Financial award applicants required to submit FAFSA. *Unit head:* Dr. Tenaya Darlington, Director, 610-660-3131, E-mail: gradstudies@sju.edu. *Application contact:* Elisabeth Woodward, Director of Marketing and Admissions, Graduate Arts and Sciences, 610-660-3131, Fax: 610-660-3230, E-mail: gradstudies@sju.edu.
Website: http://sju.edu/writingstudies

Saint Mary's College of California, School of Liberal Arts, MFA Program in Creative Writing, Moraga, CA 94575. Offers MFA. *Degree requirements:* For master's, thesis. *Entrance requirements:* For master's, sample of written work. Electronic applications accepted. *Faculty research:* Poetry, fiction, nonfiction.

Sam Houston State University, College of Humanities and Social Sciences, Department of English, Huntsville, TX 77341. Offers creative writing, editing, and publishing (MFA); English (MA). Part-time programs available. *Faculty:* 25 full-time (13 women), 2 part-time/adjunct (0 women). *Students:* 12 full-time (6 women), 26 part-time (15 women); includes 7 minority (2 Black or African American, non-Hispanic/Latino; 2 American Indian or Alaska Native, non-Hispanic/Latino; 1 Hispanic/Latino; 2 Two or more races, non-Hispanic/Latino), 1 international. Average age 33. 17 applicants, 82% accepted, 12 enrolled. In 2014, 16 master's awarded. *Degree requirements:* For master's, comprehensive exam, thesis optional. *Entrance requirements:* For master's, GRE General Test, creative writing sample, letters of recommendation. Additional exam requirements/recommendations for international students: Required—TOEFL (minimum score 550 paper-based; 79 iBT), IELTS (minimum score 6.5). *Application deadline:* For fall admission, 3/15 priority date for domestic students, 6/25 for international students; for spring admission, 10/15 priority date for domestic students, 11/12 for international students. Applications are processed on a rolling basis. Application fee: $45 ($75 for international students). Electronic applications accepted. *Expenses:* Tuition, state resident: full-time $2286; part-time $254 per credit hour. Tuition, nonresident: full-time $5544; part-time $616 per credit hour. *Required fees:* $440 per semester. Tuition and fees vary according to course load and campus/location. *Financial support:* In 2014–15, 14 research assistantships (averaging $7,240 per year), 11 teaching assistantships (averaging $7,206 per year) were awarded; career-related internships or fieldwork, Federal Work-Study, scholarships/grants, tuition waivers (partial), and unspecified assistantships also available. Support available to part-time students. Financial award application deadline: 3/15; financial award applicants required to submit FAFSA. *Unit head:* Dr. Helena Halmari, Chair, 936-294-1404, Fax: 936-294-1408, E-mail: eng_shh@shsu.edu. *Application contact:* Dr. Paul Child, Advisor, 936-294-1412, Fax: 936-294-1408, E-mail: eng_pwc@shsu.edu.
Website: http://www.shsu.edu/~eng_www/

San Diego State University, Graduate and Research Affairs, College of Arts and Letters, Department of English and Comparative Literature, San Diego, CA 92182. Offers creative writing (MFA); English (MA). *Degree requirements:* For master's, one foreign language, comprehensive exam (for some programs), thesis (for some programs). *Entrance requirements:* For master's, GRE General Test, minimum GPA of 2.85, writing sample, 3 letters of recommendation. Additional exam requirements/recommendations for international students: Required—TOEFL. Electronic applications accepted.

San Diego State University, Graduate and Research Affairs, College of Arts and Letters, Department of Rhetoric and Writing Studies, San Diego, CA 92182. Offers MA. Part-time programs available. *Degree requirements:* For master's, thesis. *Entrance requirements:* For master's, GRE General Test, writing sample, 3 letters of reference. Additional exam requirements/recommendations for international students: Required—TOEFL. Electronic applications accepted.

San Francisco State University, Division of Graduate Studies, College of Liberal and Creative Arts, Department of Creative Writing, San Francisco, CA 94132-1722. Offers MA, MFA. Part-time programs available. *Degree requirements:* For master's, thesis. *Expenses:* Tuition, state resident: full-time $6738. Tuition, nonresident: full-time $17,898; part-time $372 per credit hour. *Required fees:* $498 per semester. *Financial support:* Career-related internships or fieldwork and Federal Work-Study available. *Unit head:* Prof. Maxine Chernoff, Chair, 415-338-1891, Fax: 415-405-2142, E-mail: cwriting@sfsu.edu. *Application contact:* Prof. Nona Caspers, Graduate Advisor, 415-338-1118, E-mail: ncaspers@sfsu.edu.
Website: http://creativewriting.sfsu.edu/

Sarah Lawrence College, Graduate Studies, Program in Writing, Bronxville, NY 10708-5999. Offers creative non-fiction (MFA); fiction (MFA); poetry (MFA). Part-time programs available. *Degree requirements:* For master's, thesis. *Entrance requirements:* For master's, sample of creative writing, minimum B average in undergraduate course work. Additional exam requirements/recommendations for international students: Required—TOEFL (minimum score 600 paper-based).

Savannah College of Art and Design, Graduate School, Program in Dramatic Writing, Savannah, GA 31402-3146. Offers MFA. Part-time programs available. *Faculty:* 1 full-time (0 women). *Students:* 14 full-time (6 women), 2 part-time (both women), 5 international. Average age 25. 14 applicants, 43% accepted, 4 enrolled. In 2014, 10 master's awarded. *Degree requirements:* For master's, thesis, internship. *Entrance requirements:* For master's, portfolio. Additional exam requirements/recommendations for international students: Required—TOEFL (minimum score 550 paper-based, 85 iBT), IELTS (minimum score 6.5), or ACTFL. *Application deadline:* For fall admission, 4/1 for domestic and international students. Applications are processed on a rolling basis. Application fee: $40. Electronic applications accepted. *Expenses: Tuition:* Full-time $34,605; part-time $3845 per course. One-time fee: $500. Tuition and fees vary according to course load. *Financial support:* Fellowships, career-related internships or fieldwork, Federal Work-Study, and scholarships/grants available. Financial award application deadline: 4/1; financial award applicants required to submit FAFSA. *Unit head:* Averie Storck, Program Coordinator. *Application contact:* Jenny Jaquillard, Executive Director of Admissions, Recruitment and Events, 912-525-5100, Fax: 912-525-5985, E-mail: admission@scad.edu.
Website: http://www.scad.edu/academics/programs/dramatic-writing

Savannah College of Art and Design, Graduate School, Program in Writing, Savannah, GA 31402-3146. Offers MFA. Part-time programs available. *Faculty:* 5 full-time (2 women), 1 part-time/adjunct (0 women). *Students:* 36 full-time (31 women), 13 part-time (11 women); includes 21 minority (19 Black or African American, non-Hispanic/Latino; 2 Hispanic/Latino). Average age 30. 33 applicants, 45% accepted, 10 enrolled. In 2014, 19 master's awarded. *Degree requirements:* For master's, thesis, internship. *Entrance requirements:* For master's, portfolio. Additional exam requirements/recommendations for international students: Required—TOEFL (minimum score 550 paper-based, 85 iBT), IELTS (minimum score 6.5), or ACTFL. *Application deadline:* For fall admission, 4/1 for domestic and international students. Applications are processed on a rolling basis. Application fee: $40. Electronic applications accepted. *Expenses: Tuition:* Full-time $34,605; part-time $3845 per course. One-time fee: $500. Tuition and fees vary according to course load. *Financial support:* Fellowships, career-related internships or fieldwork, Federal Work-Study, and scholarships/grants available. Financial award application deadline: 4/1; financial award applicants required to submit FAFSA. *Unit head:* Dr. Beth Concepcion, Dean. *Application contact:* Jenny Jaquillard, Executive Director of Admissions, Recruitment and Events, 912-525-5100, Fax: 912-525-5985, E-mail: admission@scad.edu.
Website: http://www.scad.edu/academics/programs/writing

School of the Art Institute of Chicago, Graduate Division, Program in Writing, Chicago, IL 60603-3103. Offers MFA, Certificate. *Entrance requirements:* Additional exam requirements/recommendations for international students: Required—TOEFL.

School of Visual Arts, Graduate Programs, Program in Visual Narrative, New York, NY 10010-3994. Offers MFA. Summer admission only. *Degree requirements:* For master's, thesis, 60 credits, including all required courses. *Entrance requirements:* For master's, portfolio, statement of purpose; unique and complete short story/visual narrative (minimum 2-5 pages/images, or 2-5 minutes for video or animation submissions). Additional exam requirements/recommendations for international students: Required—TOEFL (minimum score 550 paper-based; 79 iBT). Electronic applications accepted. *Faculty research:* Storytelling, animation, design, illustration, art history, painting, printmaking, writing, graphic novels.

Seattle Pacific University, Master of Fine Arts in Creative Writing Program, Seattle, WA 98119-1997. Offers MFA. Part-time programs available. *Students:* 1 full-time (0 women), 24 part-time (14 women); includes 1 minority (Hispanic/Latino). Average age 35. In 2014, 14 master's awarded. *Degree requirements:* For master's, thesis. *Entrance requirements:* For master's, 10 pages of poetry or 25 to 30 double-spaced pages of prose, whether of fiction or creative nonfiction, in the student's chosen genre; three- to four-page (double-spaced) personal essay describing development as writer and as person of faith; three recommendations; bachelor's degree; official transcripts from previous schools attended. *Application deadline:* For winter admission, 11/15 for

domestic students; for summer admission, 5/15 for domestic students. Application fee: $50. Electronic applications accepted. *Financial support:* Applicants required to submit FAFSA. *Unit head:* Dr. Gregory Wolfe, Director, 206-281-2109, E-mail: gwolfe@spu.edu. *Application contact:* The Graduate Center, 206-281-2091.
Website: http://www.spu.edu/prospects/grad/academics/mfa/index.asp

Seton Hill University, Program in Writing Popular Fiction, Greensburg, PA 15601. Offers MFA, Certificate. Part-time programs available. *Faculty:* 4 full-time (2 women), 18 part-time/adjunct (10 women). *Students:* 77 full-time (52 women), 26 part-time (18 women); includes 19 minority (8 Black or African American, non-Hispanic/Latino; 5 Hispanic/Latino; 6 Two or more races, non-Hispanic/Latino). Average age 35. 41 applicants, 59% accepted, 12 enrolled. In 2014, 43 master's awarded. *Entrance requirements:* For master's, 10-page writing sample, 3 letters of recommendation, resume, letter of intent, official transcripts. Additional exam requirements/recommendations for international students: Required—TOEFL (minimum score 650 paper-based; 114 iBT), IELTS (minimum score 7). *Application deadline:* For spring admission, 4/5 for domestic students. Application fee: $35. Application fee is waived when completed online. *Expenses: Tuition:* Full-time $7362; part-time $818 per credit. *Required fees:* $34 per credit. *Financial support:* In 2014–15, 66 students received support. Scholarships/grants and tuition discounts available. Financial award application deadline: 8/15; financial award applicants required to submit FAFSA. *Faculty research:* Writing pedagogy; Appalachian themes; horror and the uncanny in film, fiction and culture; methods of description in popular fiction; paranormal fiction. *Unit head:* Dr. Nicole Peeler, Director, 724-552-2967, E-mail: peeler@setonhill.edu. *Application contact:* Ellen Monnich, Assistant Director, Graduate and Adult Studies, 724-838-4221, E-mail: monnich@setonhill.edu.
Website: http://www.setonhill.edu/academics/graduate_programs/fiction

Sewanee: The University of the South, Sewanee School of Letters, Sewanee, TN 37383-1000. Offers American and English literature (MA); creative writing (MFA). Part-time programs available. *Faculty:* 2 full-time (1 woman), 8 part-time/adjunct (2 women). *Students:* 1 (woman) full-time, 49 part-time (30 women); includes 2 minority (1 Hispanic/Latino; 1 Two or more races, non-Hispanic/Latino). Average age 41. 18 applicants, 100% accepted, 12 enrolled. In 2014, 12 master's awarded. *Degree requirements:* For master's, thesis (for some programs). *Entrance requirements:* For master's, writing sample, 2 letters of recommendation. *Application deadline:* For summer admission, 2/1 priority date for domestic and international students. Applications are processed on a rolling basis. Application fee: $40. Electronic applications accepted. *Expenses:* Expenses: Contact institution. *Financial support:* Application deadline: 3/1; applicants required to submit FAFSA. *Unit head:* Dr. John M. Grammer, Director, 931-598-1483, Fax: 931-598-3303, E-mail: jgrammer@sewanee.edu. *Application contact:* April R. Alvarez, Coordinator, 931-598-1636, Fax: 931-598-3303.
Website: http://letters.sewanee.edu/

Sonoma State University, Department of English, Rohnert Park, CA 94928. Offers American literature (MA); creative writing (MA); English literature (MA); world literature (MA). Part-time and evening/weekend programs available. *Degree requirements:* For master's, one foreign language, thesis or alternative. *Entrance requirements:* For master's, minimum GPA of 2.5. Additional exam requirements/recommendations for international students: Required—TOEFL (minimum score 500 paper-based).

Southeastern Louisiana University, College of Arts, Humanities and Social Sciences, Department of English, Hammond, LA 70402. Offers creative writing (MA); language and theory (MA); professional writing (MA). Part-time programs available. *Faculty:* 19 full-time (8 women), 1 part-time/adjunct (0 women). *Students:* 12 full-time (8 women), 6 part-time (all women); includes 3 minority (1 Black or African American, non-Hispanic/Latino; 1 Asian, non-Hispanic/Latino; 1 Hispanic/Latino). Average age 27. In 2014, 6 master's awarded. *Degree requirements:* For master's, comprehensive exam, thesis optional. *Entrance requirements:* For master's, GRE General Test (minimum score of 850), bachelor's degree; minimum undergraduate GPA of 2.5; 24 hours of undergraduate English courses. Additional exam requirements/recommendations for international students: Required—TOEFL (minimum score 500 paper-based; 61 iBT), IELTS (minimum score 5.5). *Application deadline:* For fall admission, 7/15 priority date for domestic students, 6/1 priority date for international students; for spring admission, 12/1 priority date for domestic students, 10/1 priority date for international students. Applications are processed on a rolling basis. Application fee: $20 ($30 for international students). Electronic applications accepted. *Financial support:* In 2014–15, 21 research assistantships (averaging $7,842 per year), 1 teaching assistantship (averaging $9,000 per year) were awarded; career-related internships or fieldwork, Federal Work-Study, institutionally sponsored loans, scholarships/grants, and traineeships also available. Support available to part-time students. Financial award application deadline: 5/1; financial award applicants required to submit FAFSA. *Faculty research:* Creole studies, modernism, digital humanities, library studies, John Donne. *Total annual research expenditures:* $47,697. *Unit head:* Dr. David Hanson, Department Head, 985-549-2100, Fax: 985-549-5021, E-mail: dhanson@selu.edu. *Application contact:* Sandra Meyers, Graduate Admissions Analyst, 985-549-5620, Fax: 985-549-5632, E-mail: admissions@selu.edu.
Website: http://www.selu.edu/acad_research/depts/engl

Southeast Missouri State University, School of Graduate Studies, Department of English, Cape Girardeau, MO 63701-4799. Offers English (MA), including English studies, professional writing; teaching English to speakers of other languages (MA). Part-time and evening/weekend programs available. Postbaccalaureate distance learning degree programs offered (no on-campus study). *Faculty:* 15 full-time (8 women). *Students:* 49 full-time (37 women), 48 part-time (39 women); includes 5 minority (2 Black or African American, non-Hispanic/Latino; 1 Asian, non-Hispanic/Latino; 1 Hispanic/Latino; 1 Two or more races, non-Hispanic/Latino), 27 international. Average age 31. 58 applicants, 93% accepted, 44 enrolled. In 2014, 31 master's awarded. *Degree requirements:* For master's, comprehensive exam (for some programs), thesis optional. *Entrance requirements:* Additional exam requirements/recommendations for international students: Required—TOEFL (minimum score 550 paper-based; 79 iBT), IELTS (minimum score 6), PTE (minimum score 53). *Application deadline:* For fall admission, 8/1 for domestic students, 6/1 for international students; for spring admission, 11/21 for domestic students, 10/1 for international students; for summer admission, 5/15 for domestic students. Applications are processed on a rolling basis. Application fee: $30 ($40 for international students). Electronic applications accepted. *Expenses:* Tuition, state resident: full-time $5256; part-time $292 per credit hour. Tuition, nonresident: full-time $9288; part-time $516 per credit hour. *Financial support:* In 2014–15, 34 students received support, including 16 teaching assistantships with full tuition reimbursements available (averaging $7,907 per year); career-related internships or fieldwork, Federal Work-Study, scholarships/grants, traineeships, tuition waivers (full), and unspecified assistantships also available. Financial award application deadline: 6/30; financial award applicants required to submit FAFSA. *Faculty research:* Literature, creative writing, technical writing, secondary English education, teaching English as a second language. *Unit head:* Dr. Susan Kendrick, Department of English Chair, 573-651-2156, Fax: 573-651-5188, E-mail: skendrick@semo.edu.
Website: http://www.semo.edu/english/

Southern Illinois University Carbondale, Graduate School, College of Liberal Arts, Department of English, Program in Creative Writing, Carbondale, IL 62901-4701. Offers MFA. *Faculty:* 5 full-time (3 women). *Students:* 33 full-time (18 women), 2 part-time (both women). 132 applicants, 12% accepted, 13 enrolled. In 2014, 9 master's awarded. *Degree requirements:* For master's, one foreign language, thesis. *Entrance requirements:* For master's, GRE General Test, GRE Subject Test, minimum GPA of 2.7. Additional exam requirements/recommendations for international students: Required—TOEFL. *Application deadline:* For fall admission, 2/15 for domestic students; for spring admission, 11/15 for domestic students. Applications are processed on a rolling basis. Application fee: $50. *Expenses:* Tuition, state resident: full-time $10,176; part-time $1153 per credit. Tuition, nonresident: full-time $20,814; part-time $1744 per credit. *Required fees:* $7092; $394 per credit. $2364 per semester. *Financial support:* In 2014–15, 28 students received support, including 1 fellowship with full tuition reimbursement available, 1 research assistantship with full tuition reimbursement available, 24 teaching assistantships with full tuition reimbursements available; career-related internships or fieldwork, Federal Work-Study, institutionally sponsored loans, and tuition waivers (full) also available. Support available to part-time students. *Unit head:* Dr. Ryan Netzley, Chair, 618-453-6894, E-mail: rnetzley@siu.edu. *Application contact:* Patty Norris, Administrative Clerk, 618-453-6894, Fax: 618-453-3253, E-mail: gradengl@siu.edu.
Website: http://cola.siu.edu/english/graduate/index.php

Southern Illinois University Edwardsville, Graduate School, College of Arts and Sciences, Department of English Language and Literature, Program in Creative Writing, Edwardsville, IL 62026-0001. Offers MA. Part-time programs available. *Students:* 3 full-time (0 women), 3 part-time (2 women). 4 applicants, 75% accepted. In 2014, 10 master's awarded. *Degree requirements:* For master's, one foreign language, thesis. *Entrance requirements:* Additional exam requirements/recommendations for international students: Required—TOEFL (minimum score 550 paper-based, 79 iBT), IELTS (minimum score 6.5), Michigan Test of English Language Proficiency or PTE. *Application deadline:* For fall admission, 7/18 for domestic students, 6/1 for international students; for spring admission, 12/12 for domestic students, 10/1 for international students; for summer admission, 4/24 for domestic students, 3/1 for international students. Applications are processed on a rolling basis. Application fee: $30. Electronic applications accepted. *Expenses:* Tuition, state resident: full-time $5026. Tuition, nonresident: full-time $12,566. *International tuition:* $25,136 full-time. *Required fees:* $1682. Tuition and fees vary according to course load, campus/location and program. *Financial support:* Fellowships with full tuition reimbursements, research assistantships with full tuition reimbursements, teaching assistantships with full tuition reimbursements, scholarships/grants, and unspecified assistantships available. Financial award application deadline: 3/1; financial award applicants required to submit FAFSA. *Unit head:* Dr. Jessica DeSpain, Program Director, 618-650-2151, E-mail: jdespai@siue.edu. *Application contact:* Melissa K. Mace, Assistant Director of Graduate and International Recruitment, 618-650-2756, Fax: 618-650-3618, E-mail: mmace@siue.edu.
Website: http://www.siue.edu/ENGLISH/CW/

Southern New Hampshire University, School of Arts and Sciences, Manchester, NH 03106-1045. Offers community mental health (Graduate Certificate); community mental health and mental health counseling (MS); fiction and nonfiction (MFA); teaching English as a foreign language (MS). Part-time and evening/weekend programs available. *Degree requirements:* For master's, one foreign language, thesis. *Entrance requirements:* For master's, minimum GPA of 2.75 (for MS in teaching English as a foreign language), 3.0 (for MFA). Additional exam requirements/recommendations for international students: Required—TOEFL (minimum score 550 paper-based; 79 iBT), IELTS (minimum score 6.5), TWE (minimum score 5). Electronic applications accepted. *Expenses:* Contact institution. *Faculty research:* Action research, state of the art practice in behavioral health services, wraparound approaches to working with youth, learning styles.

Spalding University, Graduate Studies, College of Social Sciences and Humanities, Master of Fine Arts in Writing Program, Louisville, KY 40203-2188. Offers MFA. Postbaccalaureate distance learning degree programs offered (minimal on-campus study). *Faculty:* 1 (woman) full-time, 33 part-time/adjunct (20 women). *Students:* 113 full-time (86 women), 20 part-time (12 women); includes 12 minority (7 Black or African American, non-Hispanic/Latino; 3 Asian, non-Hispanic/Latino; 2 Two or more races, non-Hispanic/Latino). Average age 42. 54 applicants, 57% accepted, 28 enrolled. In 2014, 47 master's awarded. *Degree requirements:* For master's, thesis. *Entrance requirements:* For master's, writing sample, letters of recommendation, personal essays. Additional exam requirements/recommendations for international students: Required—TOEFL (minimum score 535 paper-based). *Application deadline:* For fall admission, 8/1 priority date for domestic students, 7/1 for international students; for spring admission, 2/1 priority date for domestic students, 1/15 for international students. Application fee: $30. *Financial support:* Scholarships/grants and unspecified assistantships available. Financial award application deadline: 3/30; financial award applicants required to submit FAFSA. *Faculty research:* Fiction, creative nonfiction, poetry, writing for children, playwriting/screenwriting. *Unit head:* Dr. Sena Jeter Naslund, Director, 502-873-4401, Fax: 502-585-7158, E-mail: snaslund@spalding.edu. *Application contact:* Karen J. Mann, Administrative Director, 502-873-4399, Fax: 502-585-7158, E-mail: kmann@spalding.edu.
Website: http://www.spalding.edu/mfa

Stony Brook University, State University of New York, Graduate School, College of Arts and Sciences, Program in Writing and Rhetoric, Stony Brook, NY 11794. Offers teaching writing (Graduate Certificate). *Students:* 1 (woman) full-time, all international. 1 applicant. In 2014, 6 Graduate Certificates awarded. *Degree requirements:* For Graduate Certificate, practicum. *Application deadline:* For fall admission, 1/15 for domestic students. *Expenses:* Tuition, state resident: full-time $10,370; part-time $432 per credit. Tuition, nonresident: full-time $20,190; part-time $841 per credit. *Required fees:* $1431. *Financial support:* In 2014–15, 4 teaching assistantships were awarded. *Unit head:* Dr. Eugene Hammond, Director, 631-632-7390, E-mail: eugene.hammond@stonybrook.edu. *Application contact:* Melissa Jordan, Assistant Dean for Records and Admission, 631-632-9712, Fax: 631-632-7243, E-mail: gradadmissions@stonybrook.edu.
Website: http://www.stonybrook.edu/commcms/writrhet//

Stony Brook University, State University of New York, Stony Brook Southampton, Program in Writing and Literature, Stony Brook, NY 11794. Offers fiction (MFA); poetry (MFA); scientific writing (MFA), including environmental, medical, technological; scriptwriting (MFA). *Faculty:* 6 full-time (3 women), 32 part-time/adjunct (17 women). *Students:* 36 full-time (24 women), 65 part-time (44 women); includes 11 minority (1 Black or African American, non-Hispanic/Latino; 3 Asian, non-Hispanic/Latino; 4 Hispanic/Latino; 3 Two or more races, non-Hispanic/Latino), 5 international. 63 applicants, 70% accepted, 25 enrolled. In 2014, 14 master's awarded. *Application deadline:* For fall admission, 1/15 for domestic students; for spring admission, 10/1 for domestic students. Application fee: $100. *Expenses:* Tuition, state resident: full-time $10,370; part-time $432 per credit. Tuition, nonresident: full-time $20,190; part-time $841 per credit. *Required fees:* $1431. *Financial support:* Teaching assistantships available. *Unit head:* Dr. Robert Reeves, Director, 631-632-5030, Fax: 631-632-2576,

E-mail: robert.reeves@stonybrook.edu. *Application contact:* Prof. Julie Sheehan, Program Director, 631-632-5030, Fax: 631-632-2576, E-mail: southamptonarts@stonybrook.edu.

Syracuse University, College of Arts and Sciences, Program in Composition and Cultural Rhetoric, Syracuse, NY 13244. Offers PhD. *Students:* 29 full-time (19 women), 2 part-time (1 woman); includes 9 minority (3 Black or African American, non-Hispanic/Latino; 5 Hispanic/Latino; 1 Two or more races, non-Hispanic/Latino). Average age 33. 47 applicants, 11% accepted, 4 enrolled. In 2014, 5 doctorates awarded. *Degree requirements:* For doctorate, comprehensive exam, thesis/dissertation. *Entrance requirements:* For doctorate, GRE. Additional exam requirements/recommendations for international students: Required—TOEFL (minimum score 100 iBT). *Application deadline:* For fall admission, 1/15 priority date for domestic and international students. Application fee: $75. Electronic applications accepted. *Expenses: Tuition:* Part-time $1341 per credit. *Financial support:* Fellowships with full and partial tuition reimbursements and teaching assistantships with full and partial tuition reimbursements available. Financial award application deadline: 1/1; financial award applicants required to submit FAFSA. *Unit head:* Prof. Eileen Schell, Graduate Chair, 315-443-5146, E-mail: eeschell@syr.edu. *Application contact:* Kristen Krause, Office Coordinator III, 315-443-5146, E-mail: kkrause@syr.edu.
Website: http://ccr.syr.edu/

Syracuse University, College of Arts and Sciences, Program in Creative Writing, Syracuse, NY 13244. Offers MFA. *Students:* 36 full-time (15 women); includes 8 minority (4 Black or African American, non-Hispanic/Latino; 3 Asian, non-Hispanic/Latino; 1 Hispanic/Latino), 2 international. Average age 29. 779 applicants, 2% accepted, 12 enrolled. In 2014, 12 master's awarded. *Degree requirements:* For master's, thesis. *Entrance requirements:* For master's, GRE General Test, sample of written work. Additional exam requirements/recommendations for international students: Required—TOEFL (minimum score 100 iBT). *Application deadline:* For fall admission, 1/9 priority date for domestic and international students. Application fee: $75. Electronic applications accepted. *Expenses: Tuition:* Part-time $1341 per credit. *Financial support:* Fellowships with full tuition reimbursements and teaching assistantships with full and partial tuition reimbursements available. Financial award application deadline: 1/1; financial award applicants required to submit FAFSA. *Unit head:* Prof. Sarah Harwell, Associate Director, 315-443-9480, E-mail: harwel@syr.edu. *Application contact:* Terri Zollo, Information Contact, 315-443-2174, E-mail: tazollo@syr.edu.
Website: http://english.syr.edu/creative_writing/index.html

Temple University, Center for the Arts, Division of Theater, Film and Media Arts, Department of Theater, Philadelphia, PA 19122. Offers acting (MFA); design (MFA); directing (MFA); playwriting (MFA). *Accreditation:* NAST. Part-time programs available. *Faculty:* 13 full-time (4 women), 18 part-time/adjunct (15 women). *Students:* 19 full-time (9 women), 4 part-time (1 woman); includes 4 minority (1 Black or African American, non-Hispanic/Latino; 3 Two or more races, non-Hispanic/Latino), 1 international. 10 applicants, 50% accepted, 4 enrolled. In 2014, 4 master's awarded. *Degree requirements:* For master's, thesis (for some programs). *Entrance requirements:* For master's, minimum GPA of 3.0; audition/interview, portfolio, or samples of written work. Additional exam requirements/recommendations for international students: Required—TOEFL (minimum score 550 paper-based; 79 iBT). *Application deadline:* For fall admission, 12/15 for international students. Application fee: $60. Electronic applications accepted. *Expenses:* Expenses: Contact institution. *Financial support:* Teaching assistantships with full tuition reimbursements, Federal Work-Study, institutionally sponsored loans, and unspecified assistantships available. Financial award application deadline: 3/1; financial award applicants required to submit FAFSA. *Faculty research:* Acting/voice/speech/movement, theatrical design and production, musical theater, directing, playwriting. *Unit head:* Dr. Douglas Wager, Associate Dean, 215-204-6127, E-mail: theater@temple.edu. *Application contact:* Leah Dempsey, Assistant Director for Administration, 215-204-8791, E-mail: leahdempsey@temple.edu.
Website: http://www.temple.edu/theater/

Temple University, College of Liberal Arts, Department of English, Philadelphia, PA 19122-6096. Offers creative writing (MFA); English (MA, PhD). Part-time programs available. *Faculty:* 38 full-time (20 women), 15 part-time/adjunct (7 women). *Students:* 56 full-time (38 women), 4 part-time (2 women); includes 7 minority (1 Black or African American, non-Hispanic/Latino; 5 Asian, non-Hispanic/Latino; 1 Hispanic/Latino), 1 international. 59 applicants, 66% accepted, 11 enrolled. In 2014, 5 master's, 10 doctorates awarded. *Degree requirements:* For doctorate, 2 foreign languages, thesis/dissertation. *Entrance requirements:* For master's and doctorate, GRE General Test, minimum GPA of 3.0; 3 letters of recommendation. Additional exam requirements/recommendations for international students: Required—TOEFL (minimum score 620 paper-based; 105 iBT). *Application deadline:* For fall admission, 12/15 for domestic and international students. Application fee: $60. Electronic applications accepted. *Expenses:* Tuition, state resident: full-time $14,490; part-time $805 per credit hour. Tuition, nonresident: full-time $19,850; part-time $1103 per credit hour. *Required fees:* $690. Full-time tuition and fees vary according to class time, course load, degree level, campus/location and program. *Financial support:* Fellowships, teaching assistantships, and Federal Work-Study available. Financial award application deadline: 1/15; financial award applicants required to submit FAFSA. *Faculty research:* Early modern British literature, American literature, modernism, critical theory, rhetoric, composition. *Unit head:* Dr. James Sue-Im Lee, Graduate Director, 215-204-1894, Fax: 215-204-9620, E-mail: leesi@temple.edu. *Application contact:* Sharon Logan, Coordinator, 215-204-1796, Fax: 215-204-9620, E-mail: logansd@temple.edu.
Website: http://www.temple.edu/english/

Texas State University, The Graduate College, College of Fine Arts and Communication, Department of Theatre Arts and Dance, Program in Theatre Arts, San Marcos, TX 78666. Offers directing (MFA); playwriting (MA); theatre history, dramatic criticism and dramaturgy (MA). Part-time and evening/weekend programs available. *Faculty:* 6 full-time (2 women), 2 part-time/adjunct (0 women). *Students:* 14 full-time (4 women); includes 5 minority (1 Black or African American, non-Hispanic/Latino; 4 Hispanic/Latino). Average age 34. 19 applicants, 63% accepted, 6 enrolled. In 2014, 6 master's awarded. *Degree requirements:* For master's, comprehensive exam, thesis (for some programs). *Entrance requirements:* For master's, GRE General Test (minimum preferred score of 300), baccalaureate degree from regionally-accredited institution with minimum GPA of 2.75 in last 60 hours of undergraduate course work. Additional exam requirements/recommendations for international students: Required—TOEFL (minimum score 550 paper-based; 78 iBT). *Application deadline:* For fall admission, 3/15 priority date for domestic students, 3/15 for international students. Applications are processed on a rolling basis. Application fee: $40 ($90 for international students). Electronic applications accepted. *Expenses:* Expenses: $8,834 (tuition and fees combined). *Financial support:* In 2014-15, 13 students received support, including 2 research assistantships (averaging $12,152 per year), 12 teaching assistantships (averaging $11,953 per year); Federal Work-Study, institutionally sponsored loans, scholarships/grants, and unspecified assistantships also available. Support available to part-time students. Financial award application deadline: 4/1; financial award applicants required to submit FAFSA. *Faculty research:* Theatre history (especially nineteenth century American theatre), stage productions, playwriting. *Unit head:* Dr. Sandra Mayo,

Graduate Advisor, 512-245-2061, Fax: 512-245-8440, E-mail: sm37@txstate.edu. *Application contact:* Dr. Andrea Golato, Dean of Graduate School, 512-245-2581, Fax: 512-245-8365, E-mail: gradcollege@txstate.edu.
Website: http://www.theatreanddance.txstate.edu/

Texas State University, The Graduate College, College of Liberal Arts, Department of English, Program in Creative Writing, San Marcos, TX 78666. Offers MFA. Part-time and evening/weekend programs available. *Faculty:* 9 full-time (3 women). *Students:* 54 full-time (28 women), 9 part-time (8 women); includes 15 minority (1 Black or African American, non-Hispanic/Latino; 1 Asian, non-Hispanic/Latino; 12 Hispanic/Latino; 1 Native Hawaiian or other Pacific Islander, non-Hispanic/Latino), 1 international. Average age 29. 145 applicants, 38% accepted, 23 enrolled. In 2014, 30 master's awarded. *Degree requirements:* For master's, comprehensive exam, thesis. *Entrance requirements:* For master's, GRE (preferred), baccalaureate degree from regionally-accredited university with minimum GPA of 2.75 on last 60 undergraduate semester hours. Additional exam requirements/recommendations for international students: Required—TOEFL (minimum score 550 paper-based; 78 iBT). *Application deadline:* For fall admission, 1/15 priority date for domestic students, 1/15 for international students; for spring admission, 11/1 priority date for domestic students, 11/1 for international students. Applications are processed on a rolling basis. Application fee: $40 ($90 for international students). Electronic applications accepted. *Expenses:* Expenses: $8,834 (tuition and fees combined). *Financial support:* In 2014-15, 44 students received support, including 4 research assistantships (averaging $14,087 per year), 39 teaching assistantships (averaging $14,222 per year); Federal Work-Study and institutionally sponsored loans also available. Support available to part-time students. Financial award application deadline: 4/1; financial award applicants required to submit FAFSA. *Unit head:* Tom Grimes, Graduate Adviser, 512-245-7681, Fax: 512-245-8546, E-mail: tg02@txstate.edu. *Application contact:* Dr. Andrea Golato, Dean of Graduate School, 512-245-2581, Fax: 512-245-8365, E-mail: gradcollege@txstate.edu.
Website: http://www.english.txstate.edu/

Tiffin University, Program in Humanities, Tiffin, OH 44883-2161. Offers art and visual media (MH); communication (MH); creative writing (MH); English (MH); film studies (MH); humanities (MH); individualized studies (MH). Part-time and evening/weekend programs available. Postbaccalaureate distance learning degree programs offered (no on-campus study). *Entrance requirements:* For master's, work experience. Additional exam requirements/recommendations for international students: Required—TOEFL (minimum score 550 paper-based; 79 iBT).

Towson University, Program in Professional Writing, Towson, MD 21252-0001. Offers MS. Part-time and evening/weekend programs available. *Students:* 14 full-time (10 women), 38 part-time (35 women); includes 16 minority (10 Black or African American, non-Hispanic/Latino; 2 Asian, non-Hispanic/Latino; 3 Hispanic/Latino; 1 Two or more races, non-Hispanic/Latino). *Degree requirements:* For master's, thesis optional. *Entrance requirements:* For master's, sample of written work, minimum GPA of 3.0, 2 letters of recommendation, essay. *Application deadline:* For fall admission, 3/1 for domestic students; for spring admission, 10/1 for domestic students. Applications are processed on a rolling basis. Application fee: $45. Electronic applications accepted. *Financial support:* Application deadline: 4/1. *Unit head:* Prof. Goeffrey Becker, Graduate Program Director, 410-704-5196, E-mail: gbecker@towson.edu. *Application contact:* Alicia Arkell-Kleis, Information Contact, 410-704-6004, E-mail: grads@towson.edu.
Website: http://grad.towson.edu/program/master/prwr-ms/

Trinity College, Graduate Programs, Program in English, Hartford, CT 06106-3100. Offers literary studies (MA); writing, rhetoric, and media arts (MA). Part-time and evening/weekend programs available. *Degree requirements:* For master's, thesis (for some programs). *Entrance requirements:* For master's, minimum GPA of 3.0.

Union Institute & University, Individualized Master of Arts Program, Cincinnati, OH 45206-1925. Offers creativity studies (MA); health and wellness (MA); history and culture (MA); leadership, public policy, and social issues (MA); literature and writing (MA). Part-time programs available. *Faculty:* 4 full-time (2 women), 3 part-time/adjunct (2 women). *Students:* 14 full-time (11 women), 107 part-time (75 women); includes 36 minority (29 Black or African American, non-Hispanic/Latino; 3 American Indian or Alaska Native, non-Hispanic/Latino; 3 Hispanic/Latino; 1 Two or more races, non-Hispanic/Latino). Average age 40. *Degree requirements:* For master's, thesis. *Entrance requirements:* For master's, transcript, essay, 3 letters of recommendation, resume. *Application deadline:* For spring admission, 3/13 for domestic students. Applications are processed on a rolling basis. Application fee: $50. Electronic applications accepted. *Expenses: Tuition:* Full-time $26,640; part-time $719 per credit hour. *Required fees:* $216; $54 per semester. Part-time tuition and fees vary according to course load, degree level and program. *Financial support:* Career-related internships or fieldwork and tuition waivers available. Financial award applicants required to submit FAFSA. *Unit head:* Andrea Scarpino, Program Director, 802-828-8777. *Application contact:* Director of Admissions, 800-861-6400.
Website: https://www.myunion.edu/academics/masters-programs/master-of-arts/

The University of Akron, Graduate School, Buchtel College of Arts and Sciences, Department of English, Akron, OH 44325. Offers composition (MA); creative writing (MFA); literature (MA). Part-time programs available. *Faculty:* 19 full-time (8 women), 1 part-time/adjunct (0 women). *Students:* 39 full-time (23 women), 30 part-time (25 women); includes 7 minority (4 Black or African American, non-Hispanic/Latino; 1 Asian, non-Hispanic/Latino; 1 Hispanic/Latino; 1 Two or more races, non-Hispanic/Latino), 6 international. Average age 32. 46 applicants, 87% accepted, 22 enrolled. In 2014, 25 master's awarded. *Degree requirements:* For master's, thesis optional. *Entrance requirements:* For master's, BA in English, minimum GPA of 2.75, statement of purpose. Additional exam requirements/recommendations for international students: Required—TOEFL (minimum score 580 paper-based; 92 iBT). *Application deadline:* Applications are processed on a rolling basis. Application fee: $45 ($70 for international students). Electronic applications accepted. *Expenses:* Tuition, state resident: full-time $7578; part-time $421 per credit hour. Tuition, nonresident: full-time $12,977; part-time $721 per credit hour. *Required fees:* $1388; $35 per credit hour. Tuition and fees vary according to course load. *Financial support:* In 2014-15, 1 research assistantship with full tuition reimbursement, 24 teaching assistantships with full tuition reimbursements were awarded. *Faculty research:* British and American literary studies, literary theory, creative writing, applied linguistics. *Total annual research expenditures:* $27,467. *Unit head:* Dr. William Thelin, Chair, 330-972-7472, E-mail: wthelin@uakron.edu. *Application contact:* Dr. Joseph Ceccio, Director of Graduate Studies, 330-972-7603, E-mail: jceccio@uakron.edu.
Website: http://www.uakron.edu/english/

The University of Alabama, Graduate School, College of Arts and Sciences, Department of English, Tuscaloosa, AL 35487. Offers applied linguistics (PhD); composition and rhetoric (PhD); creative writing (MFA), including fiction, poetry; literature (MA, PhD); rhetoric and composition (MA); teaching English as a second language (MATESOL). *Faculty:* 34 full-time (19 women). *Students:* 129 full-time (70 women), 9 part-time (8 women); includes 18 minority (9 Black or African American, non-Hispanic/Latino; 1 Asian, non-Hispanic/Latino; 5 Hispanic/Latino; 3 Two or more races, non-Hispanic/Latino), 7 international. Average age 28. 318 applicants, 18% accepted, 42 enrolled. In 2014, 39 master's, 2 doctorates awarded. *Degree requirements:* For

master's, one foreign language, comprehensive exam, thesis optional; for doctorate, 2 foreign languages, comprehensive exam, thesis/dissertation. *Entrance requirements:* For master's, GRE (minimum score of 300, except for MFA), minimum GPA of 3.0, critical writing sample; for doctorate, GRE (minimum score of 300), minimum GPA of 3.5 on master's or equivalent graduate work, critical writing sample. Additional exam requirements/recommendations for international students: Required—TOEFL (minimum score 100 iBT). *Application deadline:* For fall admission, 12/31 priority date for domestic and international students. Application fee: $50 ($60 for international students). Electronic applications accepted. *Expenses:* Tuition, state resident: full-time $9826. Tuition, nonresident: full-time $24,950. *Financial support:* In 2014–15, 11 fellowships with full tuition reimbursements (averaging $15,000 per year), 1 research assistantship with full tuition reimbursement (averaging $12,366 per year), 112 teaching assistantships with full tuition reimbursements (averaging $12,366 per year) were awarded; career-related internships or fieldwork, scholarships/grants, health care benefits, and unspecified assistantships also available. Financial award application deadline: 12/31. *Faculty research:* American literature, British literature, composition/rhetoric, applied linguistics, creative writing. *Unit head:* Prof. Joel Brouwer, Department Chair, 205-348-9524, Fax: 205-348-1388, E-mail: joel.brouwer@ua.edu. *Application contact:* Jennifer Fuqua, Graduate Coordinator, 205-348-0766, Fax: 205-348-1388, E-mail: jfuqua@ua.edu.

The University of Alabama at Birmingham, College of Arts and Sciences, Program in English, Birmingham, AL 35294. Offers creative writing (MA); literature (MA); rhetoric and composition (MA). Part-time programs available. *Students:* 13 full-time (12 women), 12 part-time (4 women); includes 1 minority (Black or African American, non-Hispanic/Latino). Average age 29. In 2014, 11 master's awarded. *Degree requirements:* For master's, one foreign language, comprehensive exam, thesis or alternative. *Entrance requirements:* For master's, GRE General Test or MAT, minimum GPA of 2.75. *Application deadline:* For fall admission, 7/1 for domestic students; for spring admission, 11/1 for domestic students. Applications are processed on a rolling basis. Application fee: $45 ($60 for international students). Electronic applications accepted. *Expenses:* Tuition, state resident: full-time $7090; part-time $370 per credit hour. Tuition, nonresident: full-time $16,072; part-time $869 per credit hour. Full-time tuition and fees vary according to course load and program. *Financial support:* Teaching assistantships and career-related internships or fieldwork available. *Unit head:* Dr. Gale Temple, Program Director, 205-934-8593, Fax: 205-975-6610, E-mail: gtemple@uab.edu. *Application contact:* Susan Noblitt Banks, Director of Graduate School Operations, 205-934-8227, Fax: 205-934-8413, E-mail: gradschool@uab.edu.
Website: http://www.uab.edu/cas/english/academic-programs

University of Alaska Anchorage, College of Arts and Sciences, Program in Creative Writing and Literary Arts, Anchorage, AK 99508. Offers MFA. Part-time programs available. *Degree requirements:* For master's, comprehensive exam, thesis or alternative. *Entrance requirements:* For master's, portfolio, minimum GPA of 3.0. Additional exam requirements/recommendations for international students: Required—TOEFL (minimum score 550 paper-based). *Faculty research:* Alaska Quarterly Review publications, feminist studies, ecocriticism and native writing, poetry.

University of Alaska Fairbanks, College of Liberal Arts, Department of English, Fairbanks, AK 99775-5720. Offers creative writing (MFA); literature (MA); MA/MFA. Part-time programs available. *Faculty:* 15 full-time (5 women), 1 part-time/adjunct (0 women). *Students:* 31 full-time (20 women), 11 part-time (6 women); includes 5 minority (2 Asian, non-Hispanic/Latino; 3 Two or more races, non-Hispanic/Latino). Average age 31. 67 applicants, 34% accepted, 12 enrolled. In 2014, 7 master's awarded. *Degree requirements:* For master's, comprehensive exam, oral defense of project or thesis. *Entrance requirements:* For master's, GRE General Test, bachelor's degree from accredited institution with minimum cumulative undergraduate and major GPA of 3.0, academic writing sample. Additional exam requirements/recommendations for international students: Required—TOEFL (minimum score 550 paper-based; 79 iBT), IELTS (minimum score 6.5). *Application deadline:* For fall admission, 6/1 for domestic students, 3/1 for international students; for spring admission, 10/15 for domestic students, 9/1 for international students. Applications are processed on a rolling basis. Application fee: $60. Electronic applications accepted. *Expenses:* Tuition, state resident: full-time $7614; part-time $423 per credit. Tuition, nonresident: full-time $15,552; part-time $864 per credit. Tuition and fees vary according to course level, course load and reciprocity agreements. *Financial support:* In 2014–15, 27 teaching assistantships with full tuition reimbursements (averaging $11,241 per year) were awarded; fellowships with full tuition reimbursements, research assistantships with full tuition reimbursements, Federal Work-Study, scholarships/grants, health care benefits, and unspecified assistantships also available. Support available to part-time students. Financial award application deadline: 7/1; financial award applicants required to submit FAFSA. *Unit head:* Richard Carr, Department Chair, 907-474-7193, Fax: 907-474-5247, E-mail: uaf-english-dept@alaska.edu. *Application contact:* Mary Kreta, Director of Admissions, 907-474-7500, Fax: 907-474-7097, E-mail: admissions@uaf.edu.
Website: http://www.uaf.edu/english

The University of Arizona, College of Humanities, Department of English, Program in Creative Writing, Tucson, AZ 85721. Offers MFA. *Entrance requirements:* Additional exam requirements/recommendations for international students: Required—TOEFL (minimum score 550 paper-based; 79 iBT). Electronic applications accepted.

University of Arkansas, Graduate School, J. William Fulbright College of Arts and Sciences, Department of English, Program in Creative Writing, Fayetteville, AR 72701-1201. Offers MFA. *Degree requirements:* For master's, thesis. Electronic applications accepted.

University of Arkansas at Little Rock, Graduate School, College of Social Sciences and Communication, Department of Rhetoric and Writing, Little Rock, AR 72204-1099. Offers professional and technical writing (MA). Part-time and evening/weekend programs available. *Degree requirements:* For master's, thesis or alternative, oral defense of final project. *Entrance requirements:* For master's, GRE, minimum GPA of 3.0, writing portfolio. *Application deadline:* Applications are processed on a rolling basis. *Expenses:* Tuition, state resident: full-time $6000; part-time $300 per credit hour. Tuition, nonresident: full-time $13,800; part-time $690 per credit hour. *Required fees:* $1126; $603 per term. One-time fee: $40 full-time. *Financial support:* Research assistantships with tuition reimbursements, teaching assistantships with tuition reimbursements, career-related internships or fieldwork, Federal Work-Study, institutionally sponsored loans, and unspecified assistantships available. Support available to part-time students. *Faculty research:* Writing for industry, science, business, and government; composition and rhetorical theory; writing nonfiction; teaching of writing. *Unit head:* Dr. George H. Jensen, Chairperson, 501-569-3160, E-mail: ghjensen@ualr.edu. *Application contact:* Dr. Cynthia A. Nahrwold, Coordinator, 501-569-3316, Fax: 501-569-8279, E-mail: canahrwold@ualr.edu.
Website: http://ualr.edu/rhetoric/

University of Baltimore, Graduate School, Yale Gordon College of Arts and Sciences, Program in Creative Writing and Publishing Arts, Baltimore, MD 21201-5779. Offers MFA. Part-time and evening/weekend programs available. *Entrance requirements:* Additional exam requirements/recommendations for international students: Required—TOEFL.

University of Baltimore, Graduate School, Yale Gordon College of Arts and Sciences, Program in Publications Design, Baltimore, MD 21201-5779. Offers MA. Part-time and evening/weekend programs available. *Degree requirements:* For master's, seminar project. *Entrance requirements:* For master's, minimum GPA of 3.0, portfolio, interview. Additional exam requirements/recommendations for international students: Required—TOEFL (minimum score 550 paper-based). Electronic applications accepted. *Faculty research:* Communication theory, graphic design, media technology.

The University of British Columbia, Faculty of Arts, Creative Writing Program, Vancouver, BC V6T 1Z1, Canada. Offers creative writing (MFA); creative writing and film production (MFA); creative writing and theatre (MFA). Part-time programs available. Postbaccalaureate distance learning degree programs offered (minimal on-campus study). *Degree requirements:* For master's, thesis. *Entrance requirements:* For master's, sample of written work. Additional exam requirements/recommendations for international students: Required—TOEFL (minimum score 550 paper-based). Electronic applications accepted. *Expenses:* Contact institution. *Faculty research:* Writing of fiction; poetry, creative nonfiction, plays for stage, screen, television, radio, writing for children and translation, song lyrics and libretto, new media and graphic novel.

The University of British Columbia, Faculty of Arts and Faculty of Graduate Studies, Department of Theatre and Film, Film Program, Vancouver, BC V6T 1Z2, Canada. Offers creative writing and film production (MFA); film production (MFA, Diploma); film studies (MA). *Degree requirements:* For master's, variable foreign language requirement, comprehensive exam, thesis (MA); thesis or project (MFA). *Entrance requirements:* For master's, portfolio (MFA). Additional exam requirements/recommendations for international students: Required—TOEFL (minimum score 600 paper-based). *Faculty research:* Film theory and violence; American and European cinema; cult cinema; Irish cinema.

University of California, Berkeley, UC Berkeley Extension, Certificate Programs in Writing, Editing and Technical Communication, Berkeley, CA 94720-1500. Offers writing (Postbaccalaureate Certificate). Postbaccalaureate distance learning degree programs offered.

University of California, Davis, Graduate Studies, Program in English, Davis, CA 95616. Offers creative writing (MA); English (MA, PhD). Terminal master's awarded for partial completion of doctoral program. *Degree requirements:* For master's, one foreign language, thesis optional; for doctorate, 2 foreign languages, thesis/dissertation. *Entrance requirements:* For master's and doctorate, GRE General Test, GRE Subject Test, minimum GPA of 3.0, writing sample. Additional exam requirements/recommendations for international students: Required—TOEFL (minimum score 550 paper-based). Electronic applications accepted. *Faculty research:* Feminist theory, ethnic literature, literary theory, history of literature, literature of nature.

University of California, Irvine, School of Humanities, Department of English, Program in Writing, Irvine, CA 92697. Offers creative writing (MFA), including fiction, poetry. *Students:* 32 full-time (16 women); includes 7 minority (1 Black or African American, non-Hispanic/Latino; 2 Asian, non-Hispanic/Latino; 4 Two or more races, non-Hispanic/Latino). Average age 28. 553 applicants, 3% accepted, 12 enrolled. In 2014, 7 master's awarded. *Degree requirements:* For master's, thesis. *Entrance requirements:* For master's, minimum GPA of 3.0, sample of written work. *Application deadline:* For fall admission, 1/15 for domestic and international students. Application fee: $80 ($100 for international students). Electronic applications accepted. *Financial support:* Fellowships with full and partial tuition reimbursements, research assistantships, teaching assistantships with partial tuition reimbursements, institutionally sponsored loans, and tuition waivers (full and partial) available. Financial award application deadline: 3/1; financial award applicants required to submit FAFSA. *Unit head:* Michael Ryan, Director, 949-824-8773, Fax: 949-824-2916, E-mail: mryan@uci.edu. *Application contact:* Diana L. Smith, Graduate Administrator, 949-824-6718, Fax: 949-824-2916, E-mail: smithdl@uci.edu.

University of California, Riverside, Graduate Division, Program in Creative Writing and Writing for the Performing Arts, Riverside, CA 92521. Offers MFA. Program also offered at Palm Desert Graduate Center. *Degree requirements:* For master's, thesis. *Entrance requirements:* For master's, writing sample. Additional exam requirements/recommendations for international students: Required—TOEFL (minimum score 550 paper-based; 80 iBT). Electronic applications accepted. *Expenses:* Tuition, state resident: full-time $5399. Tuition, nonresident: full-time $10,433. *Faculty research:* Nonfiction, playwriting, screenwriting, poetry, fiction.

University of California, San Diego, Graduate Division, Department of Literature, La Jolla, CA 92093. Offers literature (PhD); writing (MFA). *Students:* 75 full-time (47 women); includes 36 minority (1 Black or African American, non-Hispanic/Latino; 2 American Indian or Alaska Native, non-Hispanic/Latino; 8 Asian, non-Hispanic/Latino; 25 Hispanic/Latino), 5 international. 285 applicants, 10% accepted, 16 enrolled. In 2014, 5 master's, 14 doctorates awarded. *Degree requirements:* For master's, thesis; for doctorate, comprehensive exam, thesis/dissertation, 3 quarters of teaching assistantship. *Entrance requirements:* For master's, writing sample; for doctorate, GRE General Test, writing sample. Additional exam requirements/recommendations for international students: Required—TOEFL (minimum score 550 paper-based; 80 iBT), IELTS. *Application deadline:* For fall admission, 12/1 for domestic students. Application fee: $90 ($110 for international students). Electronic applications accepted. *Expenses:* Tuition, state resident: full-time $11,220; part-time $5610 per quarter. Tuition, nonresident: full-time $26,322; part-time $13,161 per quarter. *Required fees:* $570 per quarter. Tuition and fees vary according to program. *Financial support:* Fellowships, research assistantships, teaching assistantships, scholarships/grants, and readerships available. Financial award applicants required to submit FAFSA. *Faculty research:* Chicano/a-Latino/a studies, European studies, film studies and visual culture, Latin American literary and cultural studies, medieval/early modern studies, transnational Africa/African diaspora studies, transnational Asia/Asian diaspora studies. *Unit head:* Stephanie Jed, Chair, 858-534-4618, E-mail: litchair@ucsd.edu. *Application contact:* Kristin Carnohan, PhD Coordinator, 858-534-3217, E-mail: litgrad@ucsd.edu.
Website: http://literature.ucsd.edu

University of California, Santa Barbara, Graduate Division, College of Letters and Sciences, Division of Humanities and Fine Arts, Department of English, Santa Barbara, CA 93106-3170. Offers English (PhD); European medieval studies (PhD); feminist studies (PhD); global studies (PhD); technology and society (PhD); translation studies (PhD); writing studies (PhD); MA/PhD. Terminal master's awarded for partial completion of doctoral program. *Degree requirements:* For doctorate, one foreign language, comprehensive exam, thesis/dissertation. *Entrance requirements:* For doctorate, GRE General Test, GRE Subject Test (English). Additional exam requirements/recommendations for international students: Required—TOEFL (minimum score 550 paper-based; 80 iBT), IELTS (minimum score 7). Electronic applications accepted. *Faculty research:* Medieval, Romantic and Victorian studies; gender studies and feminist theory; literature and the mind; American literature; literature and new media/information culture.

University of California, Santa Cruz, Division of Graduate Studies, Division of Social Sciences, Program in Social Documentation, Santa Cruz, CA 95064. Offers MA. *Entrance requirements:* For master's, resume or curriculum vitae, sample of

documentary production work. Additional exam requirements/recommendations for international students: Required—TOEFL (minimum score 550 paper-based; 83 iBT); Recommended—IELTS (minimum score 8). Electronic applications accepted. *Faculty research:* Documentation of underrepresented areas of community life.

University of Central Arkansas, Graduate School, College of Fine Arts and Communication, Program in Creative Writing, Conway, AR 72035-0001. Offers MFA. *Degree requirements:* For master's, thesis project. *Entrance requirements:* For master's, GRE. Electronic applications accepted.

University of Central Oklahoma, The Jackson College of Graduate Studies, College of Liberal Arts, Department of English, Edmond, OK 73034-5209. Offers creative writing (MA, MFA); traditional studies (MA). Part-time programs available. *Degree requirements:* For master's, variable foreign language requirement, comprehensive exam (for some programs), thesis (for some programs), portfolio. *Entrance requirements:* For master's, GRE, 18-24 hours of course work in English language and literature; writing sample; essay. Additional exam requirements/recommendations for international students: Required—TOEFL (minimum score 550 paper-based; 79 iBT), IELTS (minimum score 6.5). Electronic applications accepted. *Faculty research:* John Milton, Harriet Beecher Stowe.

University of Chicago, Division of the Humanities, Master of Arts Program in the Humanities, Chicago, IL 60637. Offers art history (MA); classics (MA); comparative literature (MA); creative writing (MA); digital humanities (MA); English language and literature (MA); Germanic studies (MA); linguistics (MA); music (MA); philosophy (MA); Romance languages and literatures (MA); South Asian languages and civilizations (MA). *Students:* 83 full-time (41 women), 8 part-time (6 women); includes 14 minority (1 Black or African American, non-Hispanic/Latino; 6 Asian, non-Hispanic/Latino; 6 Hispanic/Latino; 1 Two or more races, non-Hispanic/Latino), 17 international. Average age 26. 153 applicants, 67% accepted, 80 enrolled. *Degree requirements:* For master's, thesis. *Entrance requirements:* For master's, GRE General Test. Additional exam requirements/recommendations for international students: Required—TOEFL (minimum score 600 paper-based; 104 iBT), IELTS (minimum score 7). *Application deadline:* For fall admission, 3/15 for domestic and international students. Application fee: $90. Electronic applications accepted. *Expenses: Tuition:* Full-time $46,899. *Required fees:* $347. *Financial support:* In 2014–15, 100 students received support, including 8 fellowships with partial tuition reimbursements available (averaging $12,000 per year); Federal Work-Study, institutionally sponsored loans, and tuition waivers (partial) also available. Financial award application deadline: 3/15; financial award applicants required to submit FAFSA. *Unit head:* Prof. David Wray, Director, 773-834-1201, E-mail: ma-humanities@uchicago.edu. *Application contact:* Program Coordinator, 773-834-1201, Fax: 773-834-7526, E-mail: ma-humanities@uchicago.edu.
Website: http://maph.uchicago.edu/

University of Colorado Boulder, Graduate School, College of Arts and Sciences, Department of English, Boulder, CO 80309. Offers literature (MA, PhD), including creative writing (MA). *Faculty:* 42 full-time (26 women). *Students:* 114 full-time (65 women), 7 part-time (5 women); includes 19 minority (2 Black or African American, non-Hispanic/Latino; 1 American Indian or Alaska Native, non-Hispanic/Latino; 2 Asian, non-Hispanic/Latino; 11 Hispanic/Latino; 3 Two or more races, non-Hispanic/Latino), 2 international. Average age 30. 508 applicants, 26% accepted, 35 enrolled. In 2014, 35 master's, 3 doctorates awarded. Terminal master's awarded for partial completion of doctoral program. *Degree requirements:* For master's, one foreign language, comprehensive exam, thesis or alternative; for doctorate, 2 foreign languages, comprehensive exam, thesis/dissertation. *Entrance requirements:* For master's, GRE General Test, GRE Subject Test, minimum undergraduate GPA of 3.0; for doctorate, GRE General Test, GRE Subject Test. *Application deadline:* For fall admission, 2/1 for domestic students, 12/1 for international students. Application fee: $50 ($70 for international students). Electronic applications accepted. *Financial support:* In 2014–15, 236 students received support, including 26 fellowships (averaging $3,391 per year), 7 research assistantships with full and partial tuition reimbursements available (averaging $30,902 per year), 74 teaching assistantships with full and partial tuition reimbursements available (averaging $28,450 per year); institutionally sponsored loans, scholarships/grants, health care benefits, and unspecified assistantships also available. Financial award application deadline: 1/1; financial award applicants required to submit FAFSA. *Faculty research:* Literary criticism, English language/literature, modern language/literature, American literature, poetry. *Total annual research expenditures:* $3.9 million.
Website: http://www.colorado.edu/English/

University of Colorado Denver, School of Education and Human Development, Teacher Education Programs, Denver, CO 80217. Offers elementary linguistically diverse education (MA); elementary math and science education (MA); elementary math education (MA); elementary reading and writing (MA); elementary science education (MA); secondary English education (MA); secondary linguistically diverse education (MA); secondary math education (MA); secondary reading and writing (MA); secondary science education (MA); special education (MA). *Accreditation:* NCATE. Part-time and evening/weekend programs available. *Students:* 228 full-time (172 women), 134 part-time (104 women); includes 54 minority (2 Black or African American, non-Hispanic/Latino; 6 Asian, non-Hispanic/Latino; 44 Hispanic/Latino; 2 Two or more races, non-Hispanic/Latino), 8 international. Average age 30. 79 applicants, 76% accepted, 54 enrolled. In 2014, 128 master's awarded. *Degree requirements:* For master's, comprehensive exam. *Entrance requirements:* For master's, GRE or MAT (for those with GPA below 2.75), transcripts, resume, letters of recommendation. Additional exam requirements/recommendations for international students: Required—TOEFL (minimum score 537 paper-based; 75 iBT); Recommended—IELTS (minimum score 6.5). *Application deadline:* For fall admission, 4/15 for domestic students, 4/1 for international students; for spring admission, 9/15 for domestic students, 9/1 for international students; for summer admission, 2/15 for domestic students, 2/1 for international students. Applications are processed on a rolling basis. Application fee: $50 ($75 for international students). Electronic applications accepted. *Expenses:* Expenses: Contact institution. *Financial support:* In 2014–15, 27 students received support. Fellowships, research assistantships, teaching assistantships, Federal Work-Study, institutionally sponsored loans, scholarships/grants, and traineeships available. Financial award application deadline: 4/1; financial award applicants required to submit FAFSA. *Faculty research:* Linguistically diverse education/ESL, elementary reading and writing, elementary teacher education, secondary teacher education, special education. *Unit head:* Cindy Gutierrez, Director, 303-315-4982, E-mail: cindy.gutierrez@ucdenver.edu. *Application contact:* Jason Clark, Director of Recruitment and Retention, 303-315-0183, E-mail: jason.clark@ucdenver.edu.
Website: http://www.ucdenver.edu/academics/colleges/SchoolOfEducation/Academics/MASTERS/Pages/default.aspx

University of Denver, Division of Arts, Humanities and Social Sciences, Department of English, Denver, CO 80208. Offers creative writing (PhD). Part-time programs available. *Faculty:* 19 full-time (8 women), 1 (woman) part-time/adjunct. *Students:* 28 full-time (21 women), 9 part-time (5 women); includes 9 minority (2 Asian, non-Hispanic/Latino; 3 Hispanic/Latino; 4 Two or more races, non-Hispanic/Latino), 3 international. Average age 32. 158 applicants, 20% accepted, 12 enrolled. In 2014, 4 master's, 9 doctorates awarded. *Degree requirements:* For master's, one foreign language, comprehensive exam, thesis; for doctorate, 2 foreign languages, comprehensive exam, thesis/dissertation. *Entrance requirements:* For master's, GRE General Test, GRE Subject Test (advanced literature), bachelor's degree, transcripts, academic essay, statement of intent, three letters of recommendation; for doctorate, GRE General Test, GRE Subject Test (advanced literature), master's degree, transcripts, academic essay, statement of intent, three letters of recommendation, and a writing sample (creative writing program only). Additional exam requirements/recommendations for international students: Required—TOEFL (minimum score 570 paper-based; 88 iBT). *Application deadline:* For fall admission, 1/1 priority date for domestic and international students. Applications are processed on a rolling basis. Application fee: $65. Electronic applications accepted. *Expenses:* Expenses: $1,199 per credit hour. *Financial support:* In 2014–15, 36 students received support, including 29 teaching assistantships with full and partial tuition reimbursements available (averaging $17,366 per year); Federal Work-Study, institutionally sponsored loans, scholarships/grants, and unspecified assistantships also available. Support available to part-time students. Financial award application deadline: 2/15; financial award applicants required to submit FAFSA. *Faculty research:* African diaspora semiotics, Susan Howe's poetics, Renaissance drama and emblematic culture, New England Colonial literature, postmodern literature. *Unit head:* Dr. Linda Bensel-Meyers, Chair, 303-871-2859, Fax: 303-871-2853, E-mail: lbenselm@du.edu. *Application contact:* Dr. Adam Rovner, Director of Graduate Studies, 303-871-2861, Fax: 303-871-2853, E-mail: adam.rovner@du.edu.
Website: http://www.du.edu/ahss/schools/english/

The University of Findlay, Office of Graduate Admissions, Findlay, OH 45840-3653. Offers athletic training (MAT); business (MBA), including health care management, hospitality management, organizational leadership, public management; education (MA Ed), including administration, children's literature, early childhood, human resource development, reading, science, special education, technology; environmental, safety and health management (MSEM); health informatics (MS); occupational therapy (MOT); pharmacy (Pharm D); physical therapy (DPT); physician assistant (MPA); rhetoric and writing (MA); teaching English to speakers of other languages (TESOL) and bilingual education (MA). Part-time and evening/weekend programs available. Postbaccalaureate distance learning degree programs offered (no on-campus study). *Faculty:* 213 full-time (102 women), 62 part-time/adjunct (37 women). *Students:* 690 full-time (385 women), 515 part-time (316 women); includes 101 minority (43 Black or African American, non-Hispanic/Latino; 1 American Indian or Alaska Native, non-Hispanic/Latino; 19 Asian, non-Hispanic/Latino; 27 Hispanic/Latino; 11 Two or more races, non-Hispanic/Latino), 214 international. Average age 28. 765 applicants, 66% accepted, 289 enrolled. In 2014, 225 master's, 104 doctorates awarded. *Degree requirements:* For master's, thesis, cumulative project, capstone project. *Entrance requirements:* For master's, GRE/GMAT, bachelor's degree from accredited institution, minimum undergraduate GPA of 2.5 in last 64 hours of course work; for doctorate, GRE, minimum cumulative GPA of 3.0. Additional exam requirements/recommendations for international students: Required—TOEFL (minimum score 80 iBT). *Application deadline:* Applications are processed on a rolling basis. Application fee: $25. Electronic applications accepted. Tuition and fees vary according to degree level and program. *Financial support:* In 2014–15, 11 research assistantships with full and partial tuition reimbursements (averaging $4,000 per year), 10 teaching assistantships with full and partial tuition reimbursements (averaging $3,600 per year) were awarded; career-related internships or fieldwork, Federal Work-Study, health care benefits, and unspecified assistantships also available. Financial award application deadline: 4/1; financial award applicants required to submit FAFSA. *Unit head:* Christopher M. Harris, Director of Admissions, 419-434-4347, E-mail: harrisc1@findlay.edu. *Application contact:* Austyn Erickson, Graduate Admissions Counselor, 419-434-4693, Fax: 419-434-4898, E-mail: ericksona@findlay.edu.
Website: http://www.findlay.edu/admissions/graduate/Pages/default.aspx

University of Florida, Graduate School, College of Liberal Arts and Sciences, Department of English, Gainesville, FL 32611. Offers creative writing (MFA); English (MA, PhD). *Faculty:* 39 full-time (14 women), 4 part-time/adjunct (all women). *Students:* 93 full-time (58 women), 12 part-time (8 women); includes 20 minority (7 Black or African American, non-Hispanic/Latino; 1 American Indian or Alaska Native, non-Hispanic/Latino; 1 Asian, non-Hispanic/Latino; 11 Hispanic/Latino), 15 international. 192 applicants, 8% accepted, 9 enrolled. In 2014, 7 master's, 11 doctorates awarded. *Degree requirements:* For master's, one foreign language, comprehensive exam, thesis or alternative; for doctorate, one foreign language, comprehensive exam, thesis/dissertation. *Entrance requirements:* For master's and doctorate, GRE General Test, minimum GPA of 3.0. Additional exam requirements/recommendations for international students: Required—TOEFL (minimum score 550 paper-based; 80 iBT), IELTS (minimum score 6). *Application deadline:* For fall admission, 1/15 for domestic and international students; for spring admission, 1/1 for domestic and international students. Application fee: $30. Electronic applications accepted. *Financial support:* In 2014–15, 66 fellowships, 22 research assistantships, 113 teaching assistantships were awarded; unspecified assistantships also available. Financial award application deadline: 1/15; financial award applicants required to submit FAFSA. *Faculty research:* Modern global literatures in English, film and media studies, cultural studies and critical theory, American literature, English literature. *Unit head:* Kenneth Kidd, PhD, Professor and Department Chair, 352-294-2807, Fax: 352-392-0860, E-mail: kbkidd@ufl.edu. *Application contact:* Sid Dobrin, PhD, Professor and Graduate Coordinator, 352-294-2868, Fax: 352-392-0860, E-mail: sdobrin@ufl.edu.
Website: http://web.english.ufl.edu/

University of Georgia, Franklin College of Arts and Sciences, Department of English, Athens, GA 30602. Offers creative writing (MFA, PhD); English (MA, MAT, PhD). *Degree requirements:* For master's, one foreign language, thesis (MA); for doctorate, 2 foreign languages, thesis/dissertation. *Entrance requirements:* For master's and doctorate, GRE General Test. Additional exam requirements/recommendations for international students: Required—TWE. Electronic applications accepted.

University of Houston, College of Liberal Arts and Social Sciences, Department of English, Houston, TX 77204. Offers applied English linguistics (MA); creative writing (MFA); creative writing and literature (MA, PhD); English (MA, PhD). *Degree requirements:* For master's, one foreign language, comprehensive exam (for some programs), thesis (MFA); for doctorate, 2 foreign languages, comprehensive exam, thesis/dissertation. *Entrance requirements:* For master's, GRE General Test, minimum GPA of 3.0 in last 60 hours of course work; for doctorate, GRE General Test, GRE Subject Test (literature), writing sample. Additional exam requirements/recommendations for international students: Required—TOEFL (minimum score 550 paper-based; 79 iBT). Electronic applications accepted.

University of Houston–Victoria, School of Arts and Sciences, Program in Creative Writing, Victoria, TX 77901-4450. Offers MFA. *Degree requirements:* For master's, thesis. *Entrance requirements:* For master's, GRE, two letters of recommendation, twenty- to thirty-page creative writing sample.

University of Idaho, College of Graduate Studies, College of Letters, Arts and Social Sciences, Department of English, Moscow, ID 83844-1102. Offers creative writing (MFA); English (MA, MAT); teaching English as a second language (MA). *Faculty:* 17 full-time. *Students:* 64 full-time, 8 part-time. Average age 31. In 2014, 27 master's awarded. *Entrance requirements:* For master's, minimum GPA of 2.8. Additional exam

Writing

requirements/recommendations for international students: Required—TOEFL (minimum score 550 paper-based). *Application deadline:* For fall admission, 8/1 for domestic students; for spring admission, 12/15 for domestic students. Applications are processed on a rolling basis. Application fee: $60. Electronic applications accepted. *Expenses:* Tuition, state resident: full-time $4784; part-time $280.50 per credit hour. Tuition, nonresident: full-time $18,314; part-time $957.50 per credit hour. *Required fees:* $2000; $58.50 per credit hour. Tuition and fees vary according to program. *Financial support:* Research assistantships and teaching assistantships available. Financial award applicants required to submit FAFSA. *Unit head:* Dr. Scott Slovic, Chair, 208-883-6156, E-mail: englishdept@uidaho.edu. *Application contact:* Sean Scoggin, Graduate Recruitment Coordinator, 208-885-4001, Fax: 208-885-4406, E-mail: graduateadmissions@uidaho.edu.
Website: http://www.uidaho.edu/class/english

University of Illinois at Urbana–Champaign, Graduate College, College of Liberal Arts and Sciences, Department of English, Champaign, IL 61820. Offers creative writing (MFA); English (MA, PhD). *Students:* 116 (76 women). Application fee: $70 ($90 for international students). *Unit head:* Michael Rothberg, Head, 217-333-2391, Fax: 217-333-4321, E-mail: mpr@illinois.edu. *Application contact:* Stephanie Shockey, Office Support Specialist, 217-244-1464, Fax: 217-333-4321, E-mail: shockey@illinois.edu.
Website: http://www.english.illinois.edu/

The University of Iowa, Graduate College, College of Liberal Arts and Sciences, Department of English, Iowa City, IA 52242-1316. Offers English (PhD); literary studies (MA); nonfiction writing (MFA). *Degree requirements:* For master's, thesis (for some programs), exam; for doctorate, comprehensive exam, thesis/dissertation. *Entrance requirements:* For master's and doctorate, GRE General Test, minimum GPA of 3.0. Additional exam requirements/recommendations for international students: Required—TOEFL (minimum score 640 paper-based; 111 iBT). Electronic applications accepted.

The University of Iowa, Graduate College, College of Liberal Arts and Sciences, Department of Spanish and Portuguese, Iowa City, IA 52242-1316. Offers Spanish (MA, PhD); Spanish creative writing (MFA). *Degree requirements:* For master's, thesis optional, exam; for doctorate, comprehensive exam, thesis/dissertation. *Entrance requirements:* For master's and doctorate, GRE General Test, minimum GPA of 3.0. Additional exam requirements/recommendations for international students: Required—TOEFL (minimum score 600 paper-based; 100 iBT). Electronic applications accepted.

The University of Kansas, Graduate Studies, College of Liberal Arts and Sciences, Department of English, Lawrence, KS 66045. Offers creative writing (MFA); English (MA, PhD). Part-time programs available. *Faculty:* 31 full-time, 36 part-time/adjunct. *Students:* 80 full-time (51 women), 5 part-time (2 women); includes 17 minority (6 Black or African American, non-Hispanic/Latino; 1 Asian, non-Hispanic/Latino; 4 Hispanic/Latino; 6 Two or more races, non-Hispanic/Latino), 2 international. Average age 30. 202 applicants, 24% accepted, 25 enrolled. In 2014, 12 master's, 15 doctorates awarded. *Degree requirements:* For master's, one foreign language, comprehensive exam (for some programs), thesis or alternative; for doctorate, 2 foreign languages, comprehensive exam, thesis/dissertation. *Entrance requirements:* For master's and doctorate, GRE General Test, minimum GPA of 3.3. Additional exam requirements/recommendations for international students: Required—TOEFL. *Application deadline:* For fall admission, 12/31 for domestic and international students. Application fee: $55 ($65 for international students). Electronic applications accepted. *Financial support:* Fellowships with full tuition reimbursements, research assistantships with full and partial tuition reimbursements, teaching assistantships with full and partial tuition reimbursements, and unspecified assistantships available. Financial award application deadline: 12/31. *Faculty research:* Ecocriticism and science/science fiction writing; gender and sexuality studies; U.S. ethnic literatures, race, and diaspora studies; composition, rhetoric, and language studies; creative writing. *Unit head:* Anna Neill, Chair, 785-864-2521, E-mail: aneill@ku.edu. *Application contact:* Lydia Ash, Graduate Secretary, 785-864-2518, E-mail: lash@ku.edu.
Website: http://www.english.ku.edu

University of King's College, Graduate and Advanced Programs, Halifax, NS B3H 2A1, Canada. Offers creative nonfiction (MFA); journalism (MJ). *Students:* 46 full-time (34 women), 3 part-time (all women). *Application deadline:* For fall admission, 2/15 for domestic students. Applications are processed on a rolling basis. Application fee: $100. *Expenses:* Tuition, nonresident: full-time $7700. *International tuition:* $8700 full-time. *Required fees:* $1100. *Application contact:* Tara Wigglesworth Hines, Assistant Registrar, 902-422-1271 Ext. 259, Fax: 902-425-8183, E-mail: tara.wigglesworthhines@ukings.ca.
Website: http://www.ukings.ca/graduate-advanced-programs

University of Louisiana at Lafayette, College of Liberal Arts, Department of English, Lafayette, LA 70504. Offers British and American literature (MA), including creative writing, folklore, rhetoric; creative writing (PhD); literature (PhD); rhetoric (PhD). Part-time programs available. Terminal master's awarded for partial completion of doctoral program. *Degree requirements:* For master's, one foreign language, thesis or alternative; for doctorate, 2 foreign languages, comprehensive exam, thesis/dissertation. *Entrance requirements:* For master's, GRE General Test, minimum GPA of 2.75; for doctorate, GRE General Test, minimum GPA of 3.0. Additional exam requirements/recommendations for international students: Required—TOEFL (minimum score 550 paper-based). Electronic applications accepted. *Faculty research:* Composition theory, Southern literature, medieval literature.

University of Louisville, Graduate School, College of Arts and Sciences, Department of English, Louisville, KY 40292. Offers English (MA), including creative writing, literature, rhetoric and composition (MA, PhD); English rhetoric and composition (PhD), including rhetoric and composition (MA, PhD). Part-time programs available. *Students:* 62 full-time (39 women), 20 part-time (10 women); includes 6 minority (2 Black or African American, non-Hispanic/Latino; 2 Hispanic/Latino; 2 Two or more races, non-Hispanic/Latino), 2 international. Average age 29. 94 applicants, 53% accepted, 25 enrolled. In 2014, 18 master's, 4 doctorates awarded. *Degree requirements:* For master's, one foreign language, thesis or culminating project; for doctorate, 2 foreign languages, comprehensive exam, thesis/dissertation. *Entrance requirements:* For master's, GRE General Test, 2 academic letters of recommendation; for doctorate, GRE General Test, 15-20 page critical writing sample, 1000-word statement of professional goals, 3 academic letters of recommendation, transcripts of all college work. Additional exam requirements/recommendations for international students: Required—TOEFL (minimum score 600 paper-based; 100 iBT). *Application deadline:* For fall admission, 8/1 for domestic students, 5/1 priority date for international students; for spring admission, 12/1 for domestic students, 11/1 priority date for international students; for summer admission, 4/1 priority date for international students. Applications are processed on a rolling basis. Application fee: $60. Electronic applications accepted. *Expenses:* Tuition, state resident: full-time $11,326; part-time $630 per credit hour. Tuition, nonresident: full-time $23,568; part-time $1311 per credit hour. *Required fees:* $196. Tuition and fees vary according to program and reciprocity agreements. *Financial support:* Fellowships with full tuition reimbursements, teaching assistantships with full tuition reimbursements, health care benefits, and unspecified assistantships available. Financial award application deadline: 1/5. *Faculty research:* American and English literatures and cultures, rhetoric and composition, critical theory and cultural studies, creative writing. *Unit head:* Dr. Glynis Ridley, Chair, 502-852-6803, E-mail: glynis.ridley@louisville.edu. *Application contact:* Libby Leggett, Director, Graduate Admissions, 502-852-3101, Fax: 502-852-6536, E-mail: gradadm@louisville.edu.
Website: http://www.louisville.edu/english/graduate

The University of Manchester, School of Arts, Histories and Cultures, Manchester, United Kingdom. Offers anthropology, media and performance (PhD); applied theatre professional (PhD); archaeology (PhD); art history and visual studies (PhD); arts management and cultural policy (PhD); classics and ancient history (PhD); composition (PhD); creative writing (PhD); drama (PhD); economic and social history (PhD); electroacoustic composition (PhD); English and American studies (PhD); history (PhD); humanitarianism and conflict response (PhD); museology (PhD); music (PhD); musicology (PhD); religions and theology (PhD).

University of Maryland, College Park, Academic Affairs, College of Arts and Humanities, Department of English, Creative Writing Program, College Park, MD 20742. Offers MA, MFA, PhD. *Degree requirements:* For master's, thesis optional, written exam; for doctorate, one foreign language, oral and written exams. *Entrance requirements:* For master's, GRE General Test, writing sample, 3 letters of recommendation. Additional exam requirements/recommendations for international students: Required—TOEFL. Electronic applications accepted. *Faculty research:* Early British literature, American literature.

University of Massachusetts Amherst, Graduate School, College of Humanities and Fine Arts, Department of English, Amherst, MA 01003. Offers American studies (PhD); composition and rhetoric (PhD); creative writing (MFA); English and American literature (MA, PhD). Part-time programs available. *Faculty:* 49 full-time (24 women). *Students:* 100 full-time (60 women), 76 part-time (50 women); includes 29 minority (2 Black or African American, non-Hispanic/Latino; 6 Asian, non-Hispanic/Latino; 10 Hispanic/Latino; 1 Native Hawaiian or other Pacific Islander, non-Hispanic/Latino; 10 Two or more races, non-Hispanic/Latino), 17 international. Average age 30. 600 applicants, 12% accepted, 29 enrolled. In 2014, 26 master's, 10 doctorates awarded. Terminal master's awarded for partial completion of doctoral program. *Degree requirements:* For master's, one foreign language, thesis optional; for doctorate, one foreign language, comprehensive exam, thesis/dissertation. *Entrance requirements:* For master's, manuscript; for doctorate, GRE General Test, manuscript. Additional exam requirements/recommendations for international students: Required—TOEFL (minimum score 550 paper-based; 80 iBT), IELTS (minimum score 6.5). *Application deadline:* For fall admission, 12/15 for domestic and international students. Applications are processed on a rolling basis. Application fee: $75. Electronic applications accepted. *Expenses:* Tuition, state resident: full-time $1980; part-time $110 per credit. Tuition, nonresident: full-time $14,644; part-time $414 per credit. *Required fees:* $11,417. One-time fee: $357. *Financial support:* Fellowships with full and partial tuition reimbursements, research assistantships with full and partial tuition reimbursements, teaching assistantships with full and partial tuition reimbursements, career-related internships or fieldwork, Federal Work-Study, scholarships/grants, traineeships, health care benefits, tuition waivers (full and partial), and unspecified assistantships available. Support available to part-time students. Financial award application deadline: 12/15. *Unit head:* Dr. Jenny Spencer, Department Head, 413-545-2332, Fax: 413-545-3880. *Application contact:* Lindsay DeSantis, Supervisor of Admissions, 413-545-0722, Fax: 413-577-0010, E-mail: gradadm@grad.umass.edu.
Website: http://www.umass.edu/english/

University of Massachusetts Boston, College of Liberal Arts, Program in Creative Writing, Boston, MA 02125-3393. Offers MFA. *Degree requirements:* For master's, thesis. *Application deadline:* For fall admission, 1/15 for domestic students. *Expenses:* Tuition, state resident: full-time $2590; part-time $108 per credit. Tuition, nonresident: full-time $9758; part-time $406.50 per credit. Tuition and fees vary according to course load and program. *Unit head:* Jill McDonough, Director, 617-287-6700, E-mail: jill.mcdonough@umb.edu. *Application contact:* Peggy Roldan Patel, Graduate Admissions Coordinator, 617-287-6400, Fax: 617-287-6236, E-mail: bos.gadm@dpc.umassp.edu.
Website: http://www.umb.edu/academics/cla/english/grad/mfa

University of Massachusetts Dartmouth, Graduate School, College of Arts and Sciences, Program in Professional Writing, North Dartmouth, MA 02747-2300. Offers MA, Postbaccalaureate Certificate. Part-time programs available. *Faculty:* 22 full-time (13 women), 31 part-time/adjunct (19 women). *Students:* 11 full-time (7 women), 11 part-time (7 women); includes 1 minority (American Indian or Alaska Native, non-Hispanic/Latino), 1 international. Average age 34. 10 applicants, 80% accepted, 7 enrolled. In 2014, 5 master's awarded. *Degree requirements:* For master's, thesis (for some programs), thesis or project. *Entrance requirements:* For master's, MAT (preferred) or GRE, statement of purpose (minimum of 300 words), resume, 3 letters of recommendation, official transcripts, writing sample (minimum of 10 pages); for Postbaccalaureate Certificate, statement of purpose (3 pages), resume, official transcripts. Additional exam requirements/recommendations for international students: Required—TOEFL (minimum score 533 paper-based; 72 iBT), IELTS (minimum score 6). *Application deadline:* For fall admission, 3/1 priority date for domestic students, 2/1 priority date for international students; for spring admission, 12/15 priority date for domestic students, 11/15 priority date for international students. Applications are processed on a rolling basis. Application fee: $60. Electronic applications accepted. *Expenses:* Tuition, state resident: full-time $2071; part-time $86.29 per credit. Tuition, nonresident: full-time $8099; part-time $337.46 per credit. *Required fees:* $16,520; $712.33 per credit. Tuition and fees vary according to course load and reciprocity agreements. *Financial support:* In 2014–15, 7 fellowships with full tuition reimbursements (averaging $14,000 per year) were awarded; career-related internships or fieldwork, Federal Work-Study, and unspecified assistantships also available. Support available to part-time students. Financial award application deadline: 3/1; financial award applicants required to submit FAFSA. *Faculty research:* Rhetoric/communication studies, ethnic literatures, women writers, pedagogy, journalism and related nonfiction, public relations, creative writing, emerging media, technical and professional writing. *Total annual research expenditures:* $32,000. *Unit head:* Christopher Eisenhart, Graduate Program Director, 508-910-6468, Fax: 508-999-9235, E-mail: ceisenhart@umassd.edu. *Application contact:* Steven Briggs, Director of Marketing and Recruitment for Graduate Studies, 508-999-8604, Fax: 508-999-8183, E-mail: graduate@umassd.edu.
Website: http://www.umassd.edu/cas/english/graduateprograms/mainprofessionalwriting/

University of Memphis, Graduate School, College of Arts and Sciences, Department of English, Memphis, TN 38152. Offers African-American literature (Graduate Certificate); applied linguistics (PhD); composition studies (PhD); creative writing (MFA); English as a second language (MA); linguistics (MA); literary and cultural studies (PhD), including African-American literature; literature (MA); professional writing (MA); teaching English as a second language (Graduate Certificate). Part-time and evening/weekend programs available. Postbaccalaureate distance learning degree programs offered (no on-campus study). *Faculty:* 30 full-time (15 women), 1 part-time/adjunct (0 women). *Students:* 89 full-time (45 women), 85 part-time (57 women); includes 35 minority (23 Black or African American, non-Hispanic/Latino; 6 Asian, non-Hispanic/Latino; 5

Hispanic/Latino; 1 Two or more races, non-Hispanic/Latino), 17 international. Average age 35. 83 applicants, 88% accepted, 19 enrolled. In 2014, 29 master's, 6 doctorates awarded. Terminal master's awarded for partial completion of doctoral program. *Degree requirements:* For master's, one foreign language, comprehensive exam, thesis optional; for doctorate, 2 foreign languages, comprehensive exam, thesis/dissertation. *Entrance requirements:* For master's and doctorate, GRE. Additional exam requirements/recommendations for international students: Required—TOEFL. *Application deadline:* For fall admission, 7/1 for domestic students; for spring admission, 10/15 for domestic students. Applications are processed on a rolling basis. Application fee: $35 ($60 for international students). Electronic applications accepted. *Financial support:* In 2014–15, 123 students received support. Research assistantships with full tuition reimbursements available, teaching assistantships with full tuition reimbursements available, Federal Work-Study, scholarships/grants, and unspecified assistantships available. Financial award application deadline: 2/15; financial award applicants required to submit FAFSA. *Faculty research:* Applied linguistics, British and American literature, professional writing, composition studies. *Unit head:* Dr. Joshua Phillips, Chair, 901-678-3067, Fax: 901-678-2226, E-mail: jsphllps@memphis.edu. *Application contact:* Dr. Jeffrey Scraba, Director, Graduate Studies, 901-678-3099, Fax: 901-678-2226, E-mail: jscraba@memphis.edu.
Website: http://www.memphis.edu/english

University of Miami, Graduate School, College of Arts and Sciences, Department of English, Coral Gables, FL 33124. Offers creative writing (MFA); English (MA, PhD). Part-time programs available. Terminal master's awarded for partial completion of doctoral program. *Degree requirements:* For master's, one foreign language, thesis optional; for doctorate, one foreign language, thesis/dissertation. *Entrance requirements:* For master's and doctorate, GRE General Test. Electronic applications accepted. *Faculty research:* Anglo-Irish literature, feminist criticism and theory, Caribbean literature, early modern literature and culture, postcolonial and ethnic studies.

University of Michigan, Horace H. Rackham School of Graduate Studies, College of Literature, Science, and the Arts, Department of English Language and Literature, Helen Zell Writer's Program, Ann Arbor, MI 48109. Offers MFA. *Faculty:* 10 full-time (5 women). *Students:* 44 full-time (29 women); includes 10 minority (2 Black or African American, non-Hispanic/Latino; 5 Asian, non-Hispanic/Latino; 1 Hispanic/Latino; 2 Two or more races, non-Hispanic/Latino), 6 international. 1,060 applicants, 3% accepted, 22 enrolled. In 2014, 22 master's awarded. *Degree requirements:* For master's, comprehensive exam, thesis. *Entrance requirements:* For master's, writing sample. Additional exam requirements/recommendations for international students: Required—TOEFL (minimum score 620 paper-based; 106 iBT). *Application deadline:* For fall admission, 1/1 for domestic and international students. Application fee: $75 ($90 for international students). Electronic applications accepted. *Financial support:* Fellowships with tuition reimbursements, teaching assistantships with tuition reimbursements, and health care benefits available. *Faculty research:* Prose, poetry. *Application contact:* Graduate Admissions Office, 734-763-4139, Fax: 734-763-3128, E-mail: grad.eng.admis@um.cc.umich.edu.
Website: http://www.lsa.umich.edu/writers

University of Michigan–Flint, College of Arts and Sciences, Program in English Language and Literature, Flint, MI 48502-1950. Offers literature (MA); writing and rhetoric (MA). Part-time programs available. *Faculty:* 28 full-time (18 women), 4 part-time/adjunct (2 women). *Students:* 3 full-time (2 women), 21 part-time (15 women); includes 3 minority (1 Black or African American, non-Hispanic/Latino; 1 Hispanic/Latino; 1 Two or more races, non-Hispanic/Latino), 2 international. Average age 36. 10 applicants, 70% accepted, 5 enrolled. In 2014, 20 master's awarded. *Entrance requirements:* For master's, minimum GPA of 3.0, bachelor's degree with major or significant coursework in English or related fields. Additional exam requirements/recommendations for international students: Required—TOEFL (minimum score 84 iBT), IELTS (minimum score 6.5). *Application deadline:* For fall admission, 8/1 for domestic students, 5/1 for international students; for winter admission, 11/15 for domestic students, 9/1 for international students; for spring admission, 3/15 for domestic students, 1/1 for international students; for summer admission, 5/15 for domestic students. Applications are processed on a rolling basis. Application fee: $55. Electronic applications accepted. *Expenses:* Expenses: Contact institution. *Financial support:* Federal Work-Study, scholarships/grants, and unspecified assistantships available. Support available to part-time students. Financial award application deadline: 3/1; financial award applicants required to submit FAFSA. *Unit head:* Dr. Kazuko Hiramatsu, Director, 810-762-3285, E-mail: kazukoh@umflint.edu. *Application contact:* Bradley T. Maki, Director of Graduate Admissions, 810-762-3171, Fax: 810-766-6789, E-mail: bmaki@umflint.edu.
Website: http://www.umflint.edu/graduateprograms/english-language-and-literature-ma

University of Missouri–Kansas City, College of Arts and Sciences, Department of English Language and Literature, Kansas City, MO 64110-2499. Offers creative writing and media arts (MFA); English (MA, PhD). PhD (interdisciplinary) offered through the School of Graduate Studies. Part-time and evening/weekend programs available. *Faculty:* 24 full-time (15 women), 8 part-time/adjunct (6 women). *Students:* 17 full-time (10 women), 34 part-time (21 women); includes 5 minority (2 Black or African American, non-Hispanic/Latino; 1 Asian, non-Hispanic/Latino; 1 Hispanic/Latino; 1 Two or more races, non-Hispanic/Latino). Average age 33. 58 applicants, 43% accepted, 14 enrolled. In 2014, 16 master's awarded. *Degree requirements:* For master's, one foreign language; for doctorate, 2 foreign languages, comprehensive exam, thesis/dissertation. *Entrance requirements:* For master's, GRE General Test, 3 letters of recommendation. Additional exam requirements/recommendations for international students: Required—TOEFL (minimum score 550 paper-based; 80 iBT). *Application deadline:* For fall admission, 1/15 for domestic students, 1/15 priority date for international students. Applications are processed on a rolling basis. Application fee: $45 ($50 for international students). Electronic applications accepted. *Financial support:* In 2014–15, 16 teaching assistantships (averaging $12,150 per year) were awarded; career-related internships or fieldwork, Federal Work-Study, and institutionally sponsored loans also available. Support available to part-time students. Financial award application deadline: 3/1; financial award applicants required to submit FAFSA. *Faculty research:* Creative writing: poetry and prose, computational linguistics, rhetoric and composition, African-American and British literature, print culture. *Unit head:* Dr. Virginia Blanton, Co-Chair, 816-235-2560, Fax: 816-235-1308, E-mail: blantonv@umkc.edu. *Application contact:* Dr. John Cyril Barton, Director of Graduate Studies, 816-235-5206, E-mail: bartonjc@umkc.edu.
Website: http://cas.umkc.edu/english/

The University of Montana, Graduate School, College of Humanities and Sciences, Department of English, Program in Creative Writing, Missoula, MT 59812-0002. Offers fiction (MFA); non-fiction (MFA); poetry (MFA). *Degree requirements:* For master's, final creative paper. *Entrance requirements:* For master's, GRE General Test, sample of written work. Additional exam requirements/recommendations for international students: Required—TOEFL. *Faculty research:* Fiction, poetry, nonfiction.

University of Nebraska at Kearney, Graduate Studies and Research, College of Fine Arts and Humanities, Department of English, Kearney, NE 68849-0001. Offers creative writing (MA); literature (MA). Part-time and evening/weekend programs available. *Faculty:* 13 full-time (8 women). *Students:* 4 part-time (1 woman); includes 1 minority

(Hispanic/Latino). 5 applicants, 80% accepted, 2 enrolled. *Degree requirements:* For master's, comprehensive exam (for some programs), thesis optional, thesis or exam (for literature option). *Entrance requirements:* For master's, GRE General Test, writing sample, three letters of recommendation, letter of interest. Additional exam requirements/recommendations for international students: Recommended—TOEFL (minimum score 550 paper-based; 79 iBT), IELTS (minimum score 6.5). *Application deadline:* For fall admission, 6/15 for domestic students, 5/15 for international students; for spring admission, 10/15 for domestic and international students; for summer admission, 3/15 for domestic and international students. Application fee: $45. Electronic applications accepted. *Expenses:* Tuition, state resident: full-time $3897; part-time $216.50 per credit hour. Tuition, nonresident: full-time $8550; part-time $475 per credit hour. *Required fees:* $414; $23 per credit. $96.50 per semester. One-time fee: $45. Tuition and fees vary according to course load and program. *Financial support:* In 2014–15, 2 teaching assistantships with full tuition reimbursements (averaging $9,900 per year) were awarded; research assistantships, career-related internships or fieldwork, scholarships/grants, and unspecified assistantships also available. Support available to part-time students. Financial award application deadline: 2/28; financial award applicants required to submit FAFSA. *Faculty research:* Narrative theory, popular culture, western and plains literature, women's studies, media studies. *Unit head:* Dr. Samuel J. Umland, Chair, 308-865-8299, E-mail: umlands@unk.edu. *Application contact:* Dr. Martha Kruse, Graduate Program Committee Chair, 308-865-8415, E-mail: krusem@unk.edu.
Website: http://www.unk.edu/academics/english/graduate_program.php

University of Nebraska at Omaha, Graduate Studies, College of Arts and Sciences, Department of English, Omaha, NE 68182. Offers advanced writing (Certificate); English (MA); teaching English to speakers of other languages (Certificate). Part-time and evening/weekend programs available. *Faculty:* 22 full-time (13 women). *Students:* 6 full-time (4 women), 51 part-time (31 women); includes 2 minority (1 Black or African American, non-Hispanic/Latino; 1 Two or more races, non-Hispanic/Latino). Average age 35. 26 applicants, 73% accepted, 12 enrolled. In 2014, 18 master's, 20 other advanced degrees awarded. *Degree requirements:* For master's, comprehensive exam, thesis (for some programs). *Entrance requirements:* For master's, GRE or MAT, minimum GPA of 3.0, transcripts, 3 letters of recommendation, statement of purpose, writing sample; for Certificate, minimum GPA of 3.0, transcripts, statement of purpose. Additional exam requirements/recommendations for international students: Required—TOEFL, IELTS, PTE. *Application deadline:* For fall admission, 8/1 for domestic students; for spring admission, 12/1 for domestic students. Applications are processed on a rolling basis. Application fee: $45. Electronic applications accepted. *Financial support:* In 2014–15, 16 students received support, including 2 research assistantships, 14 teaching assistantships with tuition reimbursements available; fellowships, Federal Work-Study, institutionally sponsored loans, scholarships/grants, tuition waivers (partial), and unspecified assistantships also available. Support available to part-time students. Financial award application deadline: 3/1; financial award applicants required to submit FAFSA. *Unit head:* Dr. Robert Darcy, Chairperson, 402-554-2341, E-mail: graduate@unomaha.edu. *Application contact:* Dr. Tracy Bridgeford, Graduate Program Chair, 402-554-2341, E-mail: graduate@unomaha.edu.

University of Nebraska at Omaha, Graduate Studies, College of Communication, Fine Arts and Media, Writer's Workshop, Omaha, NE 68182. Offers MFA. Postbaccalaureate distance learning degree programs offered (no on-campus study). *Faculty:* 5 full-time (2 women). *Students:* 29 full-time (15 women); includes 5 minority (3 Black or African American, non-Hispanic/Latino; 2 Two or more races, non-Hispanic/Latino). Average age 41. 16 applicants, 69% accepted, 6 enrolled. In 2014, 6 master's awarded. *Entrance requirements:* For master's, 3 letters of recommendation, statement of purpose, writing sample, minimum GPA of 3.0, official transcripts. Additional exam requirements/recommendations for international students: Required—TOEFL, IELTS, PTE. *Application deadline:* For fall admission, 5/1 priority date for domestic and international students; for spring admission, 10/1 priority date for domestic students, 9/1 for international students. Applications are processed on a rolling basis. Application fee: $45. Electronic applications accepted. *Financial support:* Scholarships/grants and tuition waivers (partial) available. Financial award application deadline: 3/1; financial award applicants required to submit FAFSA. *Unit head:* Prof. Lisa Sandlin, Chairperson, 402-554-2341, E-mail: graduate@unomaha.edu. *Application contact:* Prof. Art Homer, Graduate Program Chair, 402-554-2341, E-mail: graduate@unomaha.edu.

University of Nebraska–Lincoln, Graduate College, College of Arts and Sciences, Department of English, Lincoln, NE 68588-0333. Offers composition and rhetoric (MA, PhD); creative writing (MA, PhD); literature studies (MA, PhD). *Degree requirements:* For master's, thesis optional; for doctorate, one foreign language, comprehensive exam, thesis/dissertation. *Entrance requirements:* For master's, writing sample; for doctorate, GRE General Test, writing sample. Additional exam requirements/recommendations for international students: Required—TOEFL (minimum score 600 paper-based). Electronic applications accepted. *Faculty research:* Creative writing, composition and rhetoric, women's studies, North American literature, medieval/Renaissance studies.

University of Nevada, Las Vegas, Graduate College, College of Fine Arts, Department of Film, Las Vegas, NV 89154-5015. Offers writing for dramatic media (MFA). Part-time programs available. *Faculty:* 1 full-time (0 women). *Students:* 9 full-time (5 women), 1 (woman) part-time; includes 3 minority (1 Black or African American, non-Hispanic/Latino; 1 Asian, non-Hispanic/Latino; 1 Two or more races, non-Hispanic/Latino), 1 international. Average age 34. 19 applicants, 26% accepted, 4 enrolled. In 2014, 3 master's awarded. *Degree requirements:* For master's, comprehensive exam, creative project. *Entrance requirements:* Additional exam requirements/recommendations for international students: Required—TOEFL (minimum score 550 paper-based), IELTS (minimum score 7). *Application deadline:* For fall admission, 1/15 for domestic students, 5/1 for international students; for spring admission, 10/1 for international students. Application fee: $60 ($95 for international students). Electronic applications accepted. *Financial support:* In 2014–15, 7 students received support, including 7 teaching assistantships with partial tuition reimbursements available (averaging $13,000 per year); institutionally sponsored loans, scholarships/grants, health care benefits, and unspecified assistantships also available. Financial award application deadline: 3/1. *Faculty research:* Screenplay, stage play, television series, Web entertainment content, production. *Unit head:* Francisco Menendez, Chair/Professor, 702-895-4223, Fax: 702-895-4395, E-mail: francisco.menendez@unlv.edu. *Application contact:* Graduate College Admissions Evaluator, 702-895-3320, Fax: 702-895-4180, E-mail: gradcollege@unlv.edu.
Website: http://film.unlv.edu/

University of Nevada, Las Vegas, Graduate College, College of Liberal Arts, Department of English, Las Vegas, NV 89154-5011. Offers creative writing (MFA); English (MA, PhD). Part-time programs available. *Faculty:* 25 full-time (12 women), 1 part-time/adjunct (0 women). *Students:* 61 full-time (31 women), 15 part-time (7 women); includes 17 minority (1 Black or African American, non-Hispanic/Latino; 3 Asian, non-Hispanic/Latino; 5 Hispanic/Latino; 2 Native Hawaiian or other Pacific Islander, non-Hispanic/Latino; 6 Two or more races, non-Hispanic/Latino), 3 international. Average age 34. 192 applicants, 15% accepted, 18 enrolled. In 2014, 12 master's, 5 doctorates awarded. *Degree requirements:* For master's, one foreign language, comprehensive

exam, thesis (for some programs); for doctorate, 2 foreign languages, comprehensive exam, thesis/dissertation. *Entrance requirements:* For master's, GRE General Test; for doctorate, GRE General Test, GRE Subject Test. Additional exam requirements/recommendations for international students: Required—TOEFL (minimum score 550 paper-based; 80 iBT), IELTS (minimum score 7). *Application deadline:* For fall admission, 1/15 for domestic students, 5/1 for international students; for spring admission, 11/1 for domestic students, 10/1 for international students. Application fee: $60 ($95 for international students). Electronic applications accepted. *Financial support:* In 2014–15, 57 students received support, including 57 teaching assistantships with partial tuition reimbursements available (averaging $13,088 per year); institutionally sponsored loans, scholarships/grants, health care benefits, and unspecified assistantships also available. Financial award application deadline: 3/1. *Faculty research:* Creative writing, poetry, fiction. *Unit head:* Dr. Richard Harp, Chair/Professor, 702-895-1258, Fax: 702-895-4801, E-mail: richard.harp@unlv.edu. *Application contact:* Graduate College Admissions Evaluator, 702-895-3320, Fax: 702-895-4180, E-mail: gradcollege@unlv.edu.
Website: http://english.unlv.edu/

University of New Mexico, Graduate School, College of Arts and Sciences, Program in Creative Writing, Albuquerque, NM 87131. Offers MFA. *Faculty:* 7 full-time (5 women). *Students:* 19 full-time (12 women), 4 part-time (2 women); includes 9 minority (2 Asian, non-Hispanic/Latino; 6 Hispanic/Latino; 1 Two or more races, non-Hispanic/Latino). Average age 32. 65 applicants, 23% accepted, 7 enrolled. In 2014, 3 master's awarded. *Degree requirements:* For master's, comprehensive exam, thesis. *Entrance requirements:* For master's, writing sample. *Application deadline:* For fall admission, 1/15 for domestic and international students. Application fee: $50. Electronic applications accepted. *Financial support:* In 2014–15, 17 students received support, including 17 teaching assistantships with full and partial tuition reimbursements available; health care benefits and unspecified assistantships also available. Financial award application deadline: 1/15. *Faculty research:* Creative writing, fiction, creative non-fiction, poetry. *Unit head:* Dr. Gail Turley Houston, Chair, 505-277-6347, Fax: 505-277-0021, E-mail: ghouston@unm.edu. *Application contact:* N. Ezra Meier, Graduate Advisor, 505-277-4437, Fax: 505-277-0021, E-mail: nezra@unm.edu.
Website: http://english.unm.edu/graduate/master-of-fine-arts/index.html

University of New Mexico, Graduate School, College of Fine Arts, Department of Theatre and Dance, Albuquerque, NM 87131-2039. Offers dance (MFA); dance history (MA); dramatic writing (MFA); theatre education and outreach (MA). *Accreditation:* NASD; NAST. *Faculty:* 8 full-time (4 women), 1 (woman) part-time/adjunct. *Students:* 9 full-time (6 women); includes 3 minority (all Hispanic/Latino). Average age 31. 9 applicants, 44% accepted, 1 enrolled. In 2014, 4 master's awarded. *Degree requirements:* For master's, comprehensive exam (for some programs), thesis (for some programs). *Entrance requirements:* For master's, minimum GPA of 3.0; undergraduate major in theatre, dance or closely-related field; 3 letters of recommendation; letter of intent; BA, BFA, BS, or MA in dance movement science or related field, or equivalent experience (for MFA in dance). *Application deadline:* For fall admission, 4/15 for domestic students; for spring admission, 11/10 for domestic students. Application fee: $50. Electronic applications accepted. *Financial support:* In 2014–15, 1 fellowship (averaging $7,200 per year), 1 research assistantship with partial tuition reimbursement (averaging $3,750 per year), 3 teaching assistantships with partial tuition reimbursements (averaging $4,482 per year) were awarded; Federal Work-Study, health care benefits, tuition waivers (partial), and unspecified assistantships also available. Financial award application deadline: 3/1; financial award applicants required to submit FAFSA. *Faculty research:* Theater education and outreach, choreography, dramatic writing, dance history/criticism. *Unit head:* Bill Liotta, Chair, 505-277-4332, Fax: 505-277-8921, E-mail: wliotta@unm.edu. *Application contact:* Christina Squire, Administrator II, 505-277-7362, Fax: 505-277-8921, E-mail: csquire@unm.edu.
Website: http://theatredance.unm.edu

The University of North Carolina at Greensboro, Graduate School, College of Arts and Sciences, Department of English, Program in Creative Writing, Greensboro, NC 27412-5001. Offers MFA. *Degree requirements:* For master's, comprehensive exam, thesis. *Entrance requirements:* For master's, GRE General Test, minimum GPA of 3.0, writing sample. Additional exam requirements/recommendations for international students: Required—TOEFL. Electronic applications accepted. *Faculty research:* Fiction, poetry, science fiction, film studies.

The University of North Carolina Wilmington, College of Arts and Sciences, Department of Creative Writing, Wilmington, NC 28403-3297. Offers MFA. Part-time programs available. *Faculty:* 17 full-time (10 women). *Students:* 51 full-time (34 women), 24 part-time (14 women); includes 5 minority (1 Black or African American, non-Hispanic/Latino; 3 Hispanic/Latino; 1 Two or more races, non-Hispanic/Latino), 1 international. 280 applicants, 25% accepted, 26 enrolled. In 2014, 23 master's awarded. *Degree requirements:* For master's, comprehensive exam, thesis. *Entrance requirements:* For master's, writing sample. Additional exam requirements/recommendations for international students: Required—TOEFL (minimum score 79 iBT), IELTS. *Application deadline:* For fall admission, 1/5 for domestic students. Application fee: $60. *Expenses:* Tuition, state resident: full-time $3240. Tuition, nonresident: full-time $9208. *Required fees:* $1967. *Financial support:* Career-related internships or fieldwork and Federal Work-Study available. Support available to part-time students. Financial award application deadline: 3/15; financial award applicants required to submit FAFSA. *Unit head:* Dr. Michael White, Chair, 910-962-3519, Fax: 910-962-7461, E-mail: whitem@uncw.edu. *Application contact:* Mark Cox, Graduate Coordinator, 910-962-3331, Fax: 910-962-7461, E-mail: coxm@uncw.edu.
Website: http://uncw.edu/writers/mfa/index.html

University of Northern Iowa, Graduate College, College of Humanities, Arts and Sciences, Department of Languages and Literatures, MA Program in English, Cedar Falls, IA 50614. Offers creative writing (MA); English (MA); literature (MA). Part-time and evening/weekend programs available. *Students:* 14 full-time (9 women), 8 part-time (7 women); includes 2 minority (1 American Indian or Alaska Native, non-Hispanic/Latino; 1 Asian, non-Hispanic/Latino), 1 international. 17 applicants, 41% accepted, 6 enrolled. In 2014, 10 master's awarded. *Degree requirements:* For master's, one foreign language, comprehensive exam, thesis or alternative, portfolio. *Entrance requirements:* Additional exam requirements/recommendations for international students: Required—TOEFL (minimum score 600 paper-based; 100 iBT). *Application deadline:* For fall admission, 8/1 priority date for domestic students. Applications are processed on a rolling basis. Application fee: $50 ($70 for international students). Electronic applications accepted. *Expenses:* Tuition, state resident: full-time $7912; part-time $880 per credit. Tuition, nonresident: full-time $17,906; part-time $880 per credit. *Required fees:* $1101; $325.50 per credit. $465.63 per semester. Tuition and fees vary according to course load and program. *Financial support:* Career-related internships or fieldwork, Federal Work-Study, scholarships/grants, and tuition waivers (full and partial) available. Support available to part-time students. Financial award application deadline: 2/1. *Unit head:* Dr. Anne Myles, Coordinator, 319-273-6911, Fax: 319-273-5807, E-mail: anne.myles@uni.edu. *Application contact:* Laurie S. Russell, Record Analyst, 319-273-2623, Fax: 319-273-2885, E-mail: laurie.russell@uni.edu.
Website: http://www.uni.edu/langlit/

University of North Florida, College of Arts and Sciences, Department of English, Jacksonville, FL 32224. Offers MA. Part-time and evening/weekend programs available. *Faculty:* 9 full-time (4 women). *Students:* 13 full-time (5 women), 32 part-time (22 women); includes 3 minority (2 Hispanic/Latino; 1 Two or more races, non-Hispanic/Latino). Average age 31. 20 applicants, 70% accepted, 10 enrolled. In 2014, 22 master's awarded. *Degree requirements:* For master's, comprehensive exam, thesis optional. *Entrance requirements:* For master's, GRE General Test, minimum GPA of 3.0 in last 60 hours, writing sample. Additional exam requirements/recommendations for international students: Required—TOEFL (minimum score 500 paper-based; 61 iBT). *Application deadline:* For fall admission, 8/1 priority date for domestic students, 5/1 for international students; for spring admission, 12/1 priority date for domestic students, 10/1 for international students; for summer admission, 3/15 for domestic students. Applications are processed on a rolling basis. Application fee: $30. Electronic applications accepted. *Expenses:* Tuition, state resident: full-time $9794; part-time $408.10 per credit hour. Tuition, nonresident: full-time $22,383; part-time $932.61 per credit hour. *Required fees:* $2047; $85.29 per credit hour. Tuition and fees vary according to course load and program. *Financial support:* In 2014–15, 6 students received support. Research assistantships, teaching assistantships, Federal Work-Study, and scholarships/grants available. Financial award application deadline: 4/1; financial award applicants required to submit FAFSA. *Faculty research:* Genre, period, and individual author studies in British, American, and world literature; literary criticism and theory: psychological, new historical and cultural, deconstructive, feminist, narrative, mythic; film and popular culture; online poetry publishing. *Total annual research expenditures:* $45,461. *Unit head:* Dr. Brian A. Striar, Chair, 904-620-1245, Fax: 904-620-3940, E-mail: bstriar@unf.edu. *Application contact:* Dr. Amanda Pascale, Director, The Graduate School, 904-620-1360, Fax: 904-620-1362, E-mail: graduateschool@unf.edu.
Website: http://www.unf.edu/coas/english/

University of North Texas, Robert B. Toulouse School of Graduate Studies, Denton, TX 76203-5459. Offers accounting (MS); applied anthropology (MA, MS); applied behavior analysis (Certificate); applied geography (MA); applied technology and performance improvement (M Ed, MS); art education (MA); art history (MA); art museum education (Certificate); arts leadership (Certificate); audiology (Au D); behavior analysis (MS); behavioral science (PhD); biochemistry and molecular biology (MS); biology (MA, MS); biomedical engineering (MS); business analysis (MS); chemistry (MS); clinical health psychology (PhD); communication studies (MA, MS); computer engineering (MS); computer science (MS); counseling (M Ed, MS), including clinical mental health counseling (MS), college and university counseling, elementary school counseling, secondary school counseling; creative writing (MA); criminal justice (MS); curriculum and instruction (M Ed); decision sciences (MBA); design (MA, MFA), including fashion design (MFA), innovation studies, interior design (MFA); early childhood studies (MS); economics (MS); educational leadership (M Ed, Ed D); educational psychology (MS, PhD), including family studies (MS), gifted and talented (MS), human development (MS), learning and cognition (MS), research, measurement and evaluation (MS); electrical engineering (MS); emergency management (MPA); engineering technology (MS); English (MA); English as a second language (MA); environmental science (MS); finance (MBA, MS); financial management (MPA); French (MA); health services management (MBA); higher education (M Ed, Ed D); history (MA, MS); hospitality management (MS); human resources management (MPA); information science (MS); information systems (PhD); information technologies (MBA); interdisciplinary studies (MA, MS); international studies (MA); international sustainable tourism (MS); jazz studies (MM); journalism (MA, MJ, Graduate Certificate), including interactive and virtual digital communication (Graduate Certificate), narrative journalism (Graduate Certificate), public relations (Graduate Certificate); kinesiology (MS); linguistics (MA); local government management (MPA); logistics (PhD); logistics and supply chain management (MBA); long-term care, senior housing, and aging services (MA); management (PhD); marketing (MBA); mathematics (MA, MS); mechanical and energy engineering (MS, PhD); music (MA), including ethnomusicology, music theory, musicology, performance; music composition (PhD); music education (MM Ed, PhD); nonprofit management (MPA); operations and supply chain management (MBA); performance (MM, DMA); philosophy (MA); political science (MA); professional and technical communication (MA); radio, television and film (MA, MFA); rehabilitation counseling (Certificate); sociology (MA); Spanish (MA); special education (M Ed); speech-language pathology (MA); strategic management (MBA); studio art (MFA); teaching (M Ed); MBA/MS. Part-time and evening/weekend programs available. Postbaccalaureate distance learning degree programs offered. *Faculty:* 651 full-time (215 women), 233 part-time/adjunct (139 women). *Students:* 3,040 full-time (1,598 women), 3,401 part-time (2,097 women); includes 1,740 minority (533 Black or African American, non-Hispanic/Latino; 15 American Indian or Alaska Native, non-Hispanic/Latino; 286 Asian, non-Hispanic/Latino; 746 Hispanic/Latino; 3 Native Hawaiian or other Pacific Islander, non-Hispanic/Latino; 157 Two or more races, non-Hispanic/Latino), 1,145 international. Terminal master's awarded for partial completion of doctoral program. *Degree requirements:* For master's, variable foreign language requirement, comprehensive exam (for some programs), thesis (for some programs); for doctorate, variable foreign language requirement, comprehensive exam (for some programs), thesis/dissertation; for other advanced degree, variable foreign language requirement, comprehensive exam (for some programs). *Entrance requirements:* For master's and doctorate, GRE, GMAT. Additional exam requirements/recommendations for international students: Required—TOEFL (minimum score 550 paper-based; 79 iBT). *Application deadline:* For fall admission, 7/15 for domestic students, 3/15 for international students; for spring admission, 11/15 for domestic students, 9/15 for international students; for summer admission, 5/1 for domestic students. Applications are processed on a rolling basis. Application fee: $60. Electronic applications accepted. *Expenses:* Tuition, state resident: full-time $5450; part-time $3633 per year. Tuition, nonresident: full-time $11,966; part-time $7977 per year. *Required fees:* $1301; $398 per credit hour. $685 per semester. Tuition and fees vary according to program and reciprocity agreements. *Financial support:* Fellowships with partial tuition reimbursements, research assistantships with partial tuition reimbursements, teaching assistantships, career-related internships or fieldwork, Federal Work-Study, institutionally sponsored loans, scholarships/grants, health care benefits, and library assistantships available. Support available to part-time students. Financial award applicants required to submit FAFSA. *Unit head:* Mark Wardell, Dean, 940-565-2383, E-mail: mark.wardell@unt.edu. *Application contact:* Toulouse School of Graduate Studies, 940-565-2383, Fax: 940-565-2141, E-mail: gradsch@unt.edu.
Website: http://tsgs.unt.edu/

University of Notre Dame, Graduate School, College of Arts and Letters, Division of Humanities, Department of English, Creative Writing Program, Notre Dame, IN 46556. Offers MFA. *Degree requirements:* For master's, thesis. *Entrance requirements:* For master's, GRE General Test, minimum GPA of 3.0. Additional exam requirements/recommendations for international students: Required—TOEFL (minimum score 600 paper-based; 80 iBT). Electronic applications accepted. *Faculty research:* Novels, stories, poetry.

University of Oklahoma, Gaylord College of Journalism and Mass Communication, Program in Professional Writing, Norman, OK 73019. Offers MPW. Part-time programs available. *Students:* 10 full-time (5 women), 7 part-time (5 women); includes 5 minority (1 American Indian or Alaska Native, non-Hispanic/Latino; 1 Asian, non-Hispanic/Latino;

1 Hispanic/Latino; 2 Two or more races, non-Hispanic/Latino). Average age 31. 5 applicants, 100% accepted, 3 enrolled. In 2014, 4 master's awarded. *Degree requirements:* For master's, project. *Entrance requirements:* For master's, GRE, 50-page writing sample, 2 letters of recommendation, resume, personal statement, minimum GPA of 3.2. Additional exam requirements/recommendations for international students: Required—TOEFL (minimum score 79 iBT). *Application deadline:* For fall admission, 7/1 for domestic students, 3/1 for international students; for spring admission, 11/1 for domestic students, 9/1 for international students. Application fee: $50 ($100 for international students). Electronic applications accepted. *Expenses:* Tuition, state resident: full-time $4394; part-time $183.10 per credit hour. Tuition, nonresident: full-time $16,970; part-time $707.10 per credit hour. *Required fees:* $2892; $109.95 per credit hour. $126.50 per semester. *Financial support:* In 2014–15, 11 students received support. Career-related internships or fieldwork, institutionally sponsored loans, scholarships/grants, health care benefits, and unspecified assistantships available. Support available to part-time students. Financial award application deadline: 6/1; financial award applicants required to submit FAFSA. *Faculty research:* General fiction, novel writing, non-fiction, screenwriting. *Unit head:* Dr. Katerina Tsetsura, Director of Graduate Studies, 405-325-6195, Fax: 405-325-7565, E-mail: tsetsura@ou.edu. *Application contact:* Larry Laneer, Graduate Advisor, 405-325-2722, Fax: 405-325-7565, E-mail: llaneer@ou.edu.
Website: http://www.ou.edu/content/gaylord/graduate.html

University of Oregon, Graduate School, College of Arts and Sciences, Department of Creative Writing, Eugene, OR 97403. Offers MFA. *Degree requirements:* For master's, thesis, exam. *Entrance requirements:* For master's, minimum GPA of 3.0. Additional exam requirements/recommendations for international students: Required—TOEFL. *Faculty research:* Poetry, fiction, literary nonfiction.

University of Pennsylvania, Graduate School of Education, Division of Reading, Writing, and Literacy, Philadelphia, PA 19104. Offers MS Ed, Ed D, PhD. Part-time programs available. *Students:* 61 full-time (49 women), 31 part-time (22 women); includes 25 minority (11 Black or African American, non-Hispanic/Latino; 6 Asian, non-Hispanic/Latino; 5 Hispanic/Latino; 3 Two or more races, non-Hispanic/Latino), 8 international. 108 applicants, 48% accepted, 33 enrolled. In 2014, 40 master's, 11 doctorates awarded. *Degree requirements:* For master's, comprehensive exam; for doctorate, one foreign language, thesis/dissertation, preliminary exam. *Entrance requirements:* For master's and doctorate, GRE General Test or MAT. Additional exam requirements/recommendations for international students: Required—TOEFL. *Application deadline:* For fall admission, 12/15 priority date for domestic students. Applications are processed on a rolling basis. Application fee: $70. Electronic applications accepted. *Expenses:* Expenses: Contact institution. *Financial support:* Fellowships, institutionally sponsored loans, scholarships/grants, traineeships, health care benefits, and unspecified assistantships available. *Faculty research:* Reading and writing relationships, classroom teachers as researchers, comprehension processes. *Unit head:* Dr. Andrew Porter, Dean, 215-898-7014. *Application contact:* 215-898-6415, Fax: 215-746-6884, E-mail: admissions@gse.upenn.edu.
Website: http://www.gse.upenn.edu

University of Pittsburgh, Dietrich School of Arts and Sciences, Department of English, Pittsburgh, PA 15260. Offers writing (MFA). *Faculty:* 53 full-time (25 women). *Students:* 141 full-time (94 women); includes 32 minority (8 Black or African American, non-Hispanic/Latino; 16 Asian, non-Hispanic/Latino; 8 Hispanic/Latino), 1 international. Average age 30. 309 applicants, 22% accepted, 20 enrolled. In 2014, 19 master's, 11 doctorates awarded. Terminal master's awarded for partial completion of doctoral program. *Degree requirements:* For master's, variable foreign language requirement, thesis; for doctorate, one foreign language, comprehensive exam, thesis/dissertation. *Entrance requirements:* For master's and doctorate, GRE General Test, writing sample. Additional exam requirements/recommendations for international students: Required—TOEFL (minimum score 550 paper-based; 90 iBT). *Application deadline:* For fall admission, 12/10 for domestic and international students. Application fee: $50. Electronic applications accepted. *Expenses:* Tuition, state resident: full-time $20,742; part-time $838 per credit. Tuition, nonresident: full-time $33,960; part-time $1389 per credit. *Required fees:* $800; $205 per term. Tuition and fees vary according to program. *Financial support:* In 2014–15, 106 students received support, including 32 fellowships with full tuition reimbursements available (averaging $21,262 per year), 14 research assistantships with full and partial tuition reimbursements available (averaging $13,980 per year), 60 teaching assistantships with full tuition reimbursements available (averaging $17,310 per year); Federal Work-Study, scholarships/grants, health care benefits, tuition waivers (full and partial), and unspecified assistantships also available. Financial award application deadline: 12/12. *Faculty research:* Cultural studies, literary history and theory, film, composition. *Unit head:* Dr. Don Bialostosky, Chair, 412-624-6509, Fax: 412-624-6639, E-mail: dhb2@pitt.edu. *Application contact:* Jesse Daugherty, Graduate Administrator, 412-624-6549, Fax: 412-624-6639, E-mail: engrad@pitt.edu.
Website: http://www.english.pitt.edu

University of Regina, Faculty of Graduate Studies and Research, Faculty of Arts, Department of English, Regina, SK S4S 0A2, Canada. Offers creative writing and English (MA); English (MA). Part-time programs available. *Faculty:* 18 full-time (8 women), 1 (woman) part-time/adjunct. *Students:* 14 full-time (9 women), 8 part-time (5 women). 19 applicants, 47% accepted. In 2014, 2 master's awarded. *Degree requirements:* For master's, thesis (for some programs). *Entrance requirements:* For master's, writing sample and portfolio of creative material (creative writing and English). Additional exam requirements/recommendations for international students: Required—TOEFL (minimum score 600 paper-based; 100 iBT), IELTS (minimum score 7.5), PTE (minimum score 59). *Application deadline:* For fall admission, 4/15 for domestic and international students; for winter admission, 10/15 for domestic and international students; for spring admission, 2/15 for domestic and international students. Application fee: $100. Electronic applications accepted. *Expenses: Tuition, area resident:* Full-time $4900 Canadian dollars; part-time $837.65 Canadian dollars per semester. *International tuition:* $7900 Canadian dollars full-time. *Required fees:* $396 Canadian dollars; $86.90 Canadian dollars per semester. *Financial support:* In 2014–15, 1 fellowship (averaging $6,000 per year), 1 research assistantship (averaging $5,500 per year), 5 teaching assistantships (averaging $2,427 per year) were awarded; scholarships/grants also available. Financial award application deadline: 6/15. *Faculty research:* British, American, and Canadian literature; sixteenth-, eighteenth-, nineteenth-, and twentieth-century literature; literary theory. *Unit head:* Dr. Troni Grande, Department Head, 306-585-4570, Fax: 306-585-5429, E-mail: troni.grande@uregina.ca. *Application contact:* Dr. Susan Johnston, Graduate Chair, 306-585-4672, Fax: 306-585-5429, E-mail: susan.johnston@uregina.ca.
Website: http://www.uregina.ca/arts/english

University of San Francisco, College of Arts and Sciences, Program in Writing, San Francisco, CA 94117-1080. Offers MFA. Part-time and evening/weekend programs available. *Faculty:* 5 full-time (3 women), 6 part-time/adjunct (1 woman). *Students:* 60 full-time (32 women), 9 part-time (8 women); includes 17 minority (5 Black or African American, non-Hispanic/Latino; 3 Asian, non-Hispanic/Latino; 8 Hispanic/Latino; 1 Two or more races, non-Hispanic/Latino), 2 international. Average age 32. 180 applicants, 62% accepted, 29 enrolled. In 2014, 27 master's awarded. *Degree requirements:* For master's, thesis. *Entrance requirements:* For master's, minimum overall GPA of 2.7, writing sample, 2 letters of recommendation, resume, interview. Additional exam requirements/recommendations for international students: Required—TOEFL (minimum score 550 paper-based; 79 iBT). *Application deadline:* For fall admission, 1/15 for domestic students. Applications are processed on a rolling basis. Application fee: $55 ($65 for international students). *Expenses: Tuition:* Full-time $21,762; part-time $1209 per credit hour. Tuition and fees vary according to degree level, campus/location and program. *Financial support:* In 2014–15, 26 students received support. Fellowships and institutionally sponsored loans available. Support available to part-time students. Financial award application deadline: 3/2; financial award applicants required to submit FAFSA. *Faculty research:* Techniques of teaching the novel to writers, oral history. *Unit head:* Dr. Micah Ballard, Director of Administration, 415-422-6066, Fax: 415-422-6996, E-mail: mfaw@usfca.edu. *Application contact:* Mark Landerghini, Information Contact, 415-422-5101, Fax: 415-422-2217, E-mail: asgraduate@usfca.edu.
Website: http://www.usfca.edu/artsci/writ/

University of South Carolina, The Graduate School, College of Arts and Sciences, Department of English Language and Literature, Columbia, SC 29208. Offers creative writing (MFA); English (MA, PhD); English education (MAT); MLIS/MA. MAT offered in cooperation with the College of Education. Part-time programs available. *Degree requirements:* For master's, one foreign language, comprehensive exam, thesis; for doctorate, 2 foreign languages, comprehensive exam, thesis/dissertation. *Entrance requirements:* For master's, GRE General Test (MFA), GRE Subject Test (MA, MAT), sample of written work; for doctorate, GRE General Test, GRE Subject Test, sample of written work. Additional exam requirements/recommendations for international students: Required—TOEFL. Electronic applications accepted. *Faculty research:* American literature, British literature, composition and rhetoric, linguistics, speech communication.

University of Southern California, Graduate School, Dana and David Dornsife College of Letters, Arts and Sciences, Department of English, Los Angeles, CA 90089. Offers English (MA, PhD); literature and creative writing (PhD). Terminal master's awarded for partial completion of doctoral program. *Degree requirements:* For doctorate, one foreign language, comprehensive exam, thesis/dissertation. *Entrance requirements:* For doctorate, GRE General Test, GRE Subject Test (English literature). Additional exam requirements/recommendations for international students: Required—TOEFL. Electronic applications accepted. *Faculty research:* Creative writing and literature; early modern studies; gender and sexuality; narrative studies; poetry and poetics; media, film, and popular culture; studies in race and minority literature.

University of Southern California, Graduate School, Dana and David Dornsife College of Letters, Arts and Sciences, Master of Professional Writing Program, Los Angeles, CA 90089. Offers MPW. Part-time and evening/weekend programs available. *Degree requirements:* For master's, thesis. *Entrance requirements:* For master's, GRE. Additional exam requirements/recommendations for international students: Required—TOEFL. Electronic applications accepted. *Faculty research:* Creative writing including fiction, creative nonfiction, screenwriting, television writing, playwriting, poetry, Internet writing; publishing in electronic media; book and film reviewing; teaching.

University of Southern Maine, College of Arts and Sciences, Program in Creative Writing, Portland, ME 04104. Offers MFA. *Faculty:* 21 part-time/adjunct (12 women). *Students:* 81 full-time (60 women); includes 10 minority (6 Black or African American, non-Hispanic/Latino; 1 Asian, non-Hispanic/Latino; 2 Hispanic/Latino; 1 Two or more races, non-Hispanic/Latino), 1 international. Average age 38. 61 applicants, 72% accepted, 18 enrolled. In 2014, 50 master's awarded. Application fee: $65. *Expenses: Tuition, area resident:* Full-time $6840; part-time $380 per credit hour. Tuition, state resident: full-time $10,260; part-time $570 per credit hour. Tuition, nonresident: full-time $18,468; part-time $1026 per credit hour. *Required fees:* $830; $83 per credit hour. Tuition and fees vary according to course load and program. *Unit head:* 207-780-4423, E-mail: stonecoastmfa@usm.maine.edu. *Application contact:* Robin Talbot, Associate MFA Director, 207-780-4428, E-mail: rtalbot@usm.maine.edu.
Website: http://usm.maine.edu/stonecoastmfa

University of Southern Mississippi, Graduate School, College of Arts and Letters, Department of English, Hattiesburg, MS 39406-0001. Offers creative writing (MA, PhD); English literature (MA, PhD). *Degree requirements:* For master's, one foreign language, comprehensive exam, thesis; for doctorate, 2 foreign languages, comprehensive exam, thesis/dissertation. *Entrance requirements:* For master's, GRE General Test, minimum GPA of 3.0 in field of study, 2.75 in last 2 years; for doctorate, GRE General Test, minimum GPA of 3.5. Additional exam requirements/recommendations for international students: Required—TOEFL, IELTS. Electronic applications accepted. *Faculty research:* English and American literature, critical theory and cultural studies, creative writing.

University of South Florida, College of Arts and Sciences, Department of English, Tampa, FL 33620-9951. Offers creative writing (MFA), including fiction, poetry; literature (MA, PhD); rhetoric and composition (MA, PhD). Part-time and evening/weekend programs available. *Faculty:* 24 full-time (12 women). *Students:* 73 full-time (52 women), 27 part-time (19 women); includes 16 minority (3 Black or African American, non-Hispanic/Latino; 4 Asian, non-Hispanic/Latino; 7 Hispanic/Latino; 2 Two or more races, non-Hispanic/Latino). Average age 32. 122 applicants, 44% accepted, 25 enrolled. In 2014, 26 master's, 5 doctorates awarded. *Degree requirements:* For master's, thesis (for MFA); thesis or comprehensive examination (for MA); for doctorate, one foreign language, comprehensive exam, thesis/dissertation. *Entrance requirements:* For master's, GRE General Test, minimum undergraduate GPA of 3.5 (for MA), 3.2 (for MFA); three letters of recommendation; personal statement; writing sample from 10 to 20 pages, depending on genre; for doctorate, GRE General Test, minimum graduate GPA of 3.7; three letters of recommendation; 2-3 page personal statement; 2500-word writing sample from English coursework. Additional exam requirements/recommendations for international students: Required—TOEFL (minimum score 550 paper-based; 79 iBT) or IELTS (minimum score 6.5) for MA and PhD; TOEFL (minimum score 600 paper-based) for MFA. *Application deadline:* For fall admission, 2/1 for domestic students, 1/2 for international students. Applications are processed on a rolling basis. Application fee: $30. Electronic applications accepted. *Financial support:* In 2014–15, 81 students received support, including 2 research assistantships (averaging $17,221 per year), 79 teaching assistantships with tuition reimbursements available (averaging $11,576 per year); unspecified assistantships also available. Financial award application deadline: 6/30; financial award applicants required to submit FAFSA. *Faculty research:* British and American literature, rhetoric and composition, world and comparative literatures, creative writing, gender and sexuality studies, women's literature, film and genre studies, literary theory, popular and visual culture, textual and translation studies. *Total annual research expenditures:* $63,565. *Unit head:* Dr. Hunt Hawkins, Professor and Chairperson, 813-974-9492, Fax: 813-974-2270, E-mail: hhawkins@usf.edu. *Application contact:* Dr. Marty Gould, Associate Professor and Graduate Director, 813-974-9474, Fax: 813-974-2270, E-mail: mgould@usf.edu.
Website: http://english.usf.edu/

University of South Florida, Innovative Education, Tampa, FL 33620-9951. *Unit head:* Kathy Barnes, Interdisciplinary Programs Coordinator, 813-974-8031, Fax: 813-974-7061, E-mail: barnesk@usf.edu. *Application contact:* Karen Tylinski, Metro Initiatives, 813-974-9943, Fax: 813-974-7061, E-mail: ktylinsk@usf.edu.
Website: http://www.usf.edu/innovative-education/

Writing

The University of Tampa, Program in Creative Writing, Tampa, FL 33606-1490. Offers MFA. Part-time programs available. *Faculty:* 9 full-time (5 women), 9 part-time/adjunct (3 women). *Students:* 63 full-time (38 women); includes 9 minority (3 Black or African American, non-Hispanic/Latino; 6 Hispanic/Latino), 1 international. Average age 41. 58 applicants, 69% accepted, 24 enrolled. In 2014, 19 master's awarded. *Entrance requirements:* Additional exam requirements/recommendations for international students: Required—TOEFL (minimum score 577 paper-based; 90 iBT); Recommended—IELTS (minimum score 7.5). *Application deadline:* For winter admission, 11/1 for domestic students. Applications are processed on a rolling basis. Application fee: $40. Electronic applications accepted. *Expenses: Tuition:* Full-time $9168; part-time $573 per credit hour. *Required fees:* $80; $40 per term. Tuition and fees vary according to program. *Financial support:* In 2014–15, 25 students received support. Applicants required to submit FAFSA. *Unit head:* Jeff Parker, Director, 813-257-5028, E-mail: jparker@ut.edu. *Application contact:* Brent Benner, Director of Enrollment Management and Admission, 813-257-3002, E-mail: bbenner@ut.edu.
Website: http://www.ut.edu/mfacw/

The University of Tennessee at Chattanooga, Program in English, Chattanooga, TN 37403. Offers creative writing (MA); literary study (MA); rhetoric and writing (MA, Graduate Certificate). Part-time and evening/weekend programs available. *Faculty:* 13 full-time (7 women). *Students:* 18 full-time (13 women), 20 part-time (13 women); includes 4 minority (1 Asian, non-Hispanic/Latino; 1 Hispanic/Latino; 2 Two or more races, non-Hispanic/Latino). Average age 28. 13 applicants, 85% accepted, 8 enrolled. In 2014, 17 master's awarded. *Degree requirements:* For master's, one foreign language, comprehensive exam, thesis. *Entrance requirements:* For master's, GRE General Test or GRE Subject Test (literature), minimum GPA of 3.0 in English. Additional exam requirements/recommendations for international students: Required—TOEFL (minimum score 550 paper-based; 79 iBT), IELTS (minimum score 6). *Application deadline:* For fall admission, 6/13 priority date for domestic students, 6/1 for international students; for spring admission, 10/15 priority date for domestic students, 10/1 for international students. Applications are processed on a rolling basis. Application fee: $30 ($35 for international students). Electronic applications accepted. *Expenses:* Tuition, state resident: full-time $7708; part-time $428 per credit hour. Tuition, nonresident: full-time $23,826; part-time $1323 per credit hour. *Required fees:* $1708; $252 per credit hour. *Financial support:* In 2014–15, 5 research assistantships with tuition reimbursements (averaging $6,445 per year), 6 teaching assistantships with tuition reimbursements (averaging $5,969 per year) were awarded; career-related internships or fieldwork, scholarships/grants, and unspecified assistantships also available. Support available to part-time students. Financial award applicants required to submit FAFSA. *Faculty research:* Technical writing, African-American literature, Milton, creative writing and poetry, American modernism and gender theory. *Total annual research expenditures:* $76,158. *Unit head:* Dr. Christopher Stuart, Department Head, 423-425-2140, Fax: 423-425-2282, E-mail: joe-wilferth@utc.edu. *Application contact:* Dr. J. Randy Walker, Interim Dean of Graduate Studies, 423-425-4478, Fax: 423-425-5223, E-mail: randy-walker@utc.edu.
Website: http://www.utc.edu/Academic/English/

The University of Texas at Austin, Graduate School, College of Liberal Arts, Department of English, Austin, TX 78712-1111. Offers creative writing (MFA); English (MA, PhD). Part-time programs available. Terminal master's awarded for partial completion of doctoral program. *Degree requirements:* For master's, 2 foreign languages; for doctorate, variable foreign language requirement. *Entrance requirements:* For master's and doctorate, GRE General Test. Electronic applications accepted.

The University of Texas at Austin, Graduate School, Michener Center for Writers, Austin, TX 78712-1111. Offers fiction (MFA); playwriting (MFA); poetry (MFA); screenwriting (MFA). Electronic applications accepted.

The University of Texas at El Paso, Graduate School, College of Liberal Arts, Department of Creative Writing, El Paso, TX 79968-0001. Offers creative writing (MFA); creative writing of the Americas (MFA). Part-time and evening/weekend programs available. Postbaccalaureate distance learning degree programs offered (no on-campus study). *Degree requirements:* For master's, thesis. *Entrance requirements:* For master's, minimum GPA of 3.0, letters of recommendation, writing sample. Additional exam requirements/recommendations for international students: Recommended—TOEFL, IELTS. Electronic applications accepted.

The University of Texas at El Paso, Graduate School, College of Liberal Arts, Department of English, El Paso, TX 79968-0001. Offers bilingual professional writing (Certificate); English and American literature (MA); rhetoric and composition (PhD); rhetoric and writing studies (MA); teaching English (MAT). Part-time and evening/weekend programs available. *Degree requirements:* For master's, thesis optional. *Entrance requirements:* For master's, GRE General Test, minimum GPA of 3.0. Additional exam requirements/recommendations for international students: Required—TOEFL. Electronic applications accepted. *Faculty research:* Literature, creative writing, literary theory.

The University of Texas–Pan American, College of Arts and Humanities, Department of English, Edinburg, TX 78539. Offers creative writing (MFA); English (MA, MAIS); English as a second language (MA). Part-time and evening/weekend programs available. *Degree requirements:* For master's, comprehensive exam, thesis optional. *Entrance requirements:* For master's, GRE General Test, minimum GPA of 3.0. *Expenses:* Tuition, state resident: full-time $4187; part-time $232.60 per credit hour. Tuition, nonresident: full-time $10,857; part-time $603.16 per credit hour. *Required fees:* $782; $27.50 per credit hour. $143.35 per semester. *Faculty research:* Oral vs. literary culture, Borderland literature, Mexican-American literature, topics in British and American literature, discourse analysis.

University of the Sacred Heart, Graduate Programs, Department of Communication, San Juan, PR 00914-0383. Offers contemporary culture and media (MA); digital journalism (MA, Certificate); editing for media (MA, Certificate); public relations (MA, Certificate); publicity (MA, Certificate); scriptwriting (MA, Certificate). Part-time and evening/weekend programs available. *Degree requirements:* For master's, thesis.

University of the Sacred Heart, Graduate Programs, Program in Creative Writing, San Juan, PR 00914-0383. Offers MFA, Certificate.

The University of Toledo, College of Graduate Studies, College of Languages, Literature and Social Sciences, Department of English Language and Literature, Toledo, OH 43606-3390. Offers English as a second language (MA); teaching of writing (Certificate). Part-time programs available. *Degree requirements:* For master's, thesis. *Entrance requirements:* For master's, GRE if GPA is less than 3.0, minimum cumulative point-hour ratio of 2.7 for all previous academic work, three letters of recommendation, transcripts from all prior institutions attended, critical essay; for Certificate, statement of purpose, transcripts from all prior institutions attended, 2 letters of recommendation. Additional exam requirements/recommendations for international students: Required—TOEFL (minimum score 550 paper-based; 80 iBT). Electronic applications accepted. *Faculty research:* Literary criticism, linguistics, creative writing, folklore and cultural studies.

University of Toronto, School of Graduate Studies, Faculty of Arts and Science, Department of English, Toronto, ON M5S 2J7, Canada. Offers creative writing (MA); English (MA, PhD); JD/MA. Part-time programs available. *Degree requirements:* For master's, thesis optional; for doctorate, 2 foreign languages, thesis/dissertation. *Entrance requirements:* For master's, minimum B+ average, 2 letters of reference, portfolio (creative writing program); for doctorate, minimum A- average, 2 letters of reference, writing sample. Additional exam requirements/recommendations for international students: Required—TOEFL (minimum score 580 paper-based; 93 iBT), TWE (minimum score 5). Electronic applications accepted.

University of Utah, Graduate School, College of Humanities, Department of English, Salt Lake City, UT 84112. Offers American studies (MA, PhD); British and American literature (MA, PhD); creative writing (MFA, PhD), including fiction, non-fiction, poetry; rhetoric and composition (MA, PhD). *Faculty:* 27 full-time (10 women), 7 part-time/adjunct (2 women). *Students:* 47 full-time (27 women), 25 part-time (16 women); includes 5 minority (1 Black or African American, non-Hispanic/Latino; 2 Asian, non-Hispanic/Latino; 2 Two or more races, non-Hispanic/Latino), 3 international. Average age 35. 285 applicants, 12% accepted, 11 enrolled. In 2014, 7 master's, 7 doctorates awarded. Terminal master's awarded for partial completion of doctoral program. *Degree requirements:* For master's, one foreign language, comprehensive exam (for some programs), thesis (for some programs), 1 standard-level language; exam (for MA); thesis (for MFA); for doctorate, variable foreign language requirement, comprehensive exam, thesis/dissertation, 2 standard-level languages/1 advanced-level language. *Entrance requirements:* For master's and doctorate, GRE General Test, minimum GPA of 3.2. Additional exam requirements/recommendations for international students: Required—TOEFL (minimum score 650 paper-based; 115 iBT); Recommended—IELTS (minimum score 9). *Application deadline:* For fall admission, 12/15 for domestic and international students. Application fee: $55 ($65 for international students). Electronic applications accepted. *Financial support:* In 2014–15, 54 students received support, including 17 fellowships with full tuition reimbursements available (averaging $15,000 per year), 34 teaching assistantships with full tuition reimbursements available (averaging $14,000 per year); health care benefits also available. Financial award application deadline: 12/15; financial award applicants required to submit FAFSA. *Faculty research:* Creative writing including poetics and modern poetry, fiction, and experimental forms; nineteenth and twentieth century British and American literature; American Studies, the American west, and environmental studies; critical theory and practice; race and gender studies. *Total annual research expenditures:* $126,500. *Unit head:* Prof. Barry L. Weller, Department Chair, 801-581-6168, E-mail: barry.weller@utah.edu. *Application contact:* Prof. Howard Horwitz, Director of Graduate Studies, 801-581-7353, E-mail: h.horwitz@english.utah.edu.
Website: http://www.hum.utah.edu/english/

University of Victoria, Faculty of Graduate Studies, Faculty of Fine Arts, Department of Writing, Victoria, BC V8W 2Y2, Canada. Offers MFA. *Entrance requirements:* For master's, portfolio, 2 letters of reference.

University of Virginia, College and Graduate School of Arts and Sciences, Department of English Language and Literature, Program in Creative Writing, Charlottesville, VA 22903. Offers MFA. *Faculty:* 7 full-time (2 women), 1 (woman) part-time/adjunct. *Students:* 26 full-time (16 women); includes 5 minority (3 Asian, non-Hispanic/Latino; 2 Hispanic/Latino), 2 international. Average age 26. 470 applicants, 3% accepted, 10 enrolled. In 2014, 8 master's awarded. *Degree requirements:* For master's, comprehensive exam, thesis. *Entrance requirements:* For master's, GRE General Test, writing sample. Additional exam requirements/recommendations for international students: Required—TOEFL (minimum score 600 paper-based; 90 iBT), IELTS (minimum score 7). *Application deadline:* For fall admission, 1/1 for domestic students, 1/4 for international students. Application fee: $60. Electronic applications accepted. *Expenses:* Tuition, state resident: full-time $14,164; part-time $349 per credit hour. Tuition, nonresident: full-time $23,722; part-time $1300 per credit hour. *Required fees:* $2514. *Financial support:* Fellowships and teaching assistantships available. Financial award application deadline: 1/4; financial award applicants required to submit FAFSA. *Unit head:* Christopher Tilghman, Director, 434-924-8607, Fax: 434-924-1478, E-mail: ct2a@virginia.edu. *Application contact:* Clare Kinney, Director of Graduate Admissions, 434-924-6638, Fax: 434-924-1478, E-mail: crk4h@virginia.edu.
Website: http://www.engl.virginia.edu/creativewriting/

University of Washington, Graduate School, College of Arts and Sciences, Department of English, Program in Creative Writing, Seattle, WA 98195. Offers MFA. *Entrance requirements:* For master's, GRE, GMAT. Additional exam requirements/recommendations for international students: Required—TOEFL (minimum score 550 paper-based). Electronic applications accepted.

University of Washington, Bothell, Program in Creative Writing and Poetics, Bothell, WA 98011-8246. Offers MFA.

University of West Florida, College of Arts and Sciences: Arts, Department of English and Foreign Languages, Pensacola, FL 32514-5750. Offers creative writing (MA); literature (MA). Part-time and evening/weekend programs available. *Degree requirements:* For master's, thesis. *Entrance requirements:* For master's, GRE (minimum score: verbal 500, writing 4.5) or MAT (minimum score 413), official transcripts; two-page statement of purpose; writing sample (2,500 words of literary analysis for literature track or 2,500 words of fiction/non-fiction prose or 10 poems for creative writing track); three letters of recommendation from instructors; 20 hours upper-division undergraduate coursework in English. Additional exam requirements/recommendations for international students: Required—TOEFL (minimum score 550 paper-based). *Faculty research:* Faulkner, Shakespeare, American humor, women's studies, poetry.

University of Windsor, Faculty of Graduate Studies, Faculty of Arts and Social Sciences, Department of English Language, Literature and Creative Writing, Windsor, ON N9B 3P4, Canada. Offers English: creative writing and language and literature (MA); English: language and literature (MA). Part-time programs available. *Degree requirements:* For master's, thesis. *Entrance requirements:* For master's, minimum B average, portfolio. Additional exam requirements/recommendations for international students: Required—TOEFL (minimum score 600 paper-based). Electronic applications accepted. *Faculty research:* Use of gender-related terms in popular culture; international and Aboriginal literatures: expression of cultural identity; critical analysis of authors: Pope, Munroe, Lady Morgan, Orwell, Thomas; the "feminine" voice in literature and contemporary culture.

University of Wisconsin–Eau Claire, College of Arts and Sciences, Program in English, Eau Claire, WI 54702-4004. Offers literature and textual interpretation (MA); writing (MA). Part-time programs available. *Degree requirements:* For master's, oral defense with thesis. *Entrance requirements:* For master's, minimum GPA of 3.25 in English, 3.0 overall; bachelor's degree with minimum of 24 credits in English. Additional exam requirements/recommendations for international students: Required—TOEFL (minimum score 79 iBT).

University of Wisconsin–Madison, Graduate School, College of Letters and Science, Department of English, Madison, WI 53706-1380. Offers applied English linguistics (MA); composition and rhetoric (PhD); creative writing (MFA); English language and

linguistics (PhD); literary studies (MA, PhD). *Degree requirements:* For doctorate, thesis/ dissertation. *Expenses:* Tuition, state resident: full-time $10,723; part-time $745 per credit. Tuition, nonresident: full-time $24,054; part-time $1578 per credit. *Required fees:* $374 per semester. Tuition and fees vary according to course load, program and reciprocity agreements.

University of Wisconsin–Milwaukee, Graduate School, College of Letters and Sciences, Department of English, Milwaukee, WI 53201-0413. Offers creative writing (PhD); English (MA); international technical communication (Certificate); linguistics (PhD); professional writing (PhD); professional writing and communication (Certificate); rhetoric and composition (PhD); MLIS/MA. *Degree requirements:* For master's, thesis or alternative; for doctorate, one foreign language, thesis/dissertation. *Entrance requirements:* For master's, GRE General Test, GRE Subject Test; for doctorate, GRE. Additional exam requirements/recommendations for international students: Required— TOEFL (minimum score 550 paper-based; 79 iBT), IELTS (minimum score 6.5). Electronic applications accepted.

University of Wyoming, College of Arts and Sciences, Department of English, Laramie, WY 82071. Offers creative writing (MFA); English (MA). Part-time programs available. *Degree requirements:* For master's, thesis or alternative, internship. *Entrance requirements:* For master's, GRE General Test, minimum GPA of 3.0. Electronic applications accepted. *Faculty research:* Literature and theory, creative writing, English as a second language, ethnic and women's studies, composition.

Utah State University, School of Graduate Studies, College of Humanities, Arts and Social Sciences, Department of English, Logan, UT 84322. Offers American studies (MA, MS), including folklore, western American literature and culture; English (MA, MS), including literature and writing, technical writing. Part-time and evening/weekend programs available. *Degree requirements:* For master's, thesis or alternative. *Entrance requirements:* For master's, GRE General Test or MAT, minimum GPA of 3.0, recommendation letters, writing samples. Additional exam requirements/ recommendations for international students: Required—TOEFL. *Faculty research:* Scottish enlightenment, material culture, composition theory, creative nonfiction, literary criticism.

Vanderbilt University, Graduate School, Program in Creative Writing, Nashville, TN 37240-1001. Offers MFA. *Students:* 15 full-time (9 women); includes 1 minority (Asian, non-Hispanic/Latino). Average age 26. 613 applicants, 1% accepted, 6 enrolled. In 2014, 1 master's awarded. *Degree requirements:* For master's, comprehensive exam, thesis. *Entrance requirements:* For master's, GRE General Test, sample of written work. Additional exam requirements/recommendations for international students: Required— TOEFL (minimum score 570 paper-based; 88 iBT). *Application deadline:* For fall admission, 1/15 for domestic and international students. Electronic applications accepted. *Expenses: Tuition:* Full-time $42,768; part-time $1782 per credit hour. *Required fees:* $422. One-time fee: $30 full-time. *Financial support:* Fellowships with full and partial tuition reimbursements, teaching assistantships with full and partial tuition reimbursements, Federal Work-Study, institutionally sponsored loans, and health care benefits available. Financial award application deadline: 1/15; financial award applicants required to submit CSS PROFILE or FAFSA. *Unit head:* Dr. Mark Jarman, Director, 615-322-2618, E-mail: mark.jarman@vanderbilt.edu. *Application contact:* Walter B. Bieschke, Program Coordinator for Graduate Admissions, 615-342-0236, E-mail: vandygrad@vanderbilt.edu.
Website: http://www.vanderbilt.edu/creativewriting/

Vermont College of Fine Arts, MFA in Writing for Children and Young Adults Program, Montpelier, VT 05602. Offers MFA. Postbaccalaureate distance learning degree programs offered (minimal on-campus study). *Faculty:* 31 part-time/adjunct (25 women). *Students:* 96 full-time (84 women); includes 8 minority (2 Black or African American, non-Hispanic/Latino; 1 Asian, non-Hispanic/Latino; 4 Hispanic/Latino; 1 Two or more races, non-Hispanic/Latino), 1 international. Average age 40. 47 applicants, 68% accepted, 28 enrolled. In 2014, 42 master's awarded. *Entrance requirements:* For master's, original work, bachelor's degree. *Application deadline:* For fall admission, 3/1 for domestic and international students; for spring admission, 9/1 for domestic and international students. Applications are processed on a rolling basis. Application fee: $75. Electronic applications accepted. Full-time tuition and fees vary according to program. *Financial support:* Scholarships/grants available. Financial award applicants required to submit FAFSA. *Unit head:* Melissa Fisher, Program Director, 802-828-8696, E-mail: melissa.fisher@vcfa.edu. *Application contact:* Ann Cardinal, Director of Student and Alumni Recruitment, 802-828-8589, E-mail: ann.cardinal@vcfa.edu.
Website: http://vcfa.edu/wcya

Vermont College of Fine Arts, MFA in Writing Program, Montpelier, VT 05602. Offers MFA. Postbaccalaureate distance learning degree programs offered (minimal on-campus study). *Faculty:* 39 part-time/adjunct (20 women). *Students:* 129 full-time (93 women); includes 12 minority (2 Black or African American, non-Hispanic/Latino; 3 Asian, non-Hispanic/Latino; 5 Hispanic/Latino; 2 Two or more races, non-Hispanic/Latino), 1 international. Average age 40. 123 applicants, 63% accepted, 36 enrolled. In 2014, 48 master's awarded. *Entrance requirements:* For master's, original work; bachelor's degree; evidence of exceptional academic, literary and/or publishing background. *Application deadline:* For fall admission, 3/20 for domestic and international students; for spring admission, 8/15 for domestic and international students. Application fee: $75. Full-time tuition and fees vary according to program. *Financial support:* Scholarships/grants available. Financial award applicants required to submit FAFSA. *Unit head:* Louise Crowley, Program Director, 802-828-8840, E-mail: louise.crowley@vcfa.edu. *Application contact:* Jason Lamb, Assistant Director of Admissions, 802-828-8829, E-mail: jason.lamb@vcfa.edu.
Website: http://www.vcfa.edu/writing

Virginia Commonwealth University, Graduate School, College of Humanities and Sciences, Department of English, Program in Creative Writing, Richmond, VA 23284-9005. Offers fiction (MFA); fictional poetry (MFA); poetry (MFA). Part-time programs available. *Entrance requirements:* For master's, GRE General Test, portfolio. Additional exam requirements/recommendations for international students: Required—TOEFL (minimum score 600 paper-based; 100 iBT) or IELTS (minimum score 6.5). Electronic applications accepted. *Faculty research:* Poetry, fiction.

Virginia Commonwealth University, Graduate School, College of Humanities and Sciences, Department of English, Program in English, Richmond, VA 23284-9005. Offers literature (MA); writing and rhetoric (MA). Part-time programs available. *Entrance requirements:* For master's, GRE General Test. Additional exam requirements/ recommendations for international students: Required—TWE, TOEFL (minimum score 600 paper-based; 100 iBT) or IELTS (minimum score 6.5). Electronic applications accepted. *Faculty research:* Literature, writing, rhetoric.

Virginia Polytechnic Institute and State University, Graduate School, College of Liberal Arts and Human Sciences, Blacksburg, VA 24061. Offers career and technical education (MS Ed, Ed D, PhD, Ed S); communication (MA); counselor education (MA Ed, Ed D, PhD, Ed S); creative writing (MFA); curriculum and instruction (MA Ed, Ed D, PhD, Ed S); educational leadership and policy studies (MA Ed, Ed D, PhD, Ed S); educational research and evaluation (PhD); English (MA); foreign languages, cultures, and literatures (MA); higher education and student affairs (MA Ed); history (MA); human

development (MS, PhD); material culture and public humanities (MA); philosophy (MA); political science (MA); rhetoric and writing (PhD); science and technology studies (MS, PhD); social, political, ethical, and cultural thought (PhD); sociology (MS, PhD); theater arts (MFA). *Faculty:* 421 full-time (216 women), 2 part-time/adjunct (both women). *Students:* 642 full-time (437 women), 537 part-time (344 women); includes 235 minority (132 Black or African American, non-Hispanic/Latino; 2 American Indian or Alaska Native, non-Hispanic/Latino; 27 Asian, non-Hispanic/Latino; 52 Hispanic/Latino; 1 Native Hawaiian or other Pacific Islander, non-Hispanic/Latino; 21 Two or more races, non-Hispanic/Latino), 81 international. Average age 34. 890 applicants, 46% accepted, 303 enrolled. In 2014, 342 master's, 96 doctorates, 33 other advanced degrees awarded. *Degree requirements:* For master's, comprehensive exam (for some programs), thesis (for some programs); for doctorate, comprehensive exam (for some programs), thesis/dissertation (for some programs). *Entrance requirements:* For master's and doctorate, GRE/GMAT (may vary by department). Additional exam requirements/recommendations for international students: Required—TOEFL (minimum score 550 paper-based). *Application deadline:* For fall admission, 8/1 for domestic students, 4/1 for international students; for spring admission, 1/1 for domestic students, 9/1 for international students. Applications are processed on a rolling basis. Application fee: $75. Electronic applications accepted. *Expenses:* Tuition, state resident: full-time $11,656; part-time $647.50 per credit hour. Tuition, nonresident: full-time $23,351; part-time $1297.25 per credit hour. *Required fees:* $2533; $465.75 per semester. Tuition and fees vary according to course load, campus/location and program. *Financial support:* In 2014–15, 19 research assistantships with full tuition reimbursements (averaging $22,141 per year), 231 teaching assistantships with full tuition reimbursements (averaging $19,470 per year) were awarded. Financial award application deadline: 3/1; financial award applicants required to submit FAFSA. *Total annual research expenditures:* $6.5 million. *Unit head:* Elizabeth Spiller, Dean, 540-231-6779, Fax: 540-231-7157, E-mail: espiller@vt.edu. *Application contact:* Melissa Elliott, Executive Assistant, 540-231-6779, Fax: 540-231-7157, E-mail: elliott1@vt.edu.
Website: http://www.clahs.vt.edu/

Warren Wilson College, MFA Program for Writers, Asheville, NC 28815-9000. Offers MFA. Postbaccalaureate distance learning degree programs offered (minimal on-campus study). *Faculty:* 25 full-time (10 women). *Students:* 83 full-time (68 women); includes 8 minority (2 Black or African American, non-Hispanic/Latino; 4 Asian, non-Hispanic/Latino; 2 Hispanic/Latino). Average age 38. 176 applicants, 11% accepted, 18 enrolled. In 2014, 21 master's awarded. *Degree requirements:* For master's, thesis, public reading, critical essay in 3rd semester. *Entrance requirements:* For master's, manuscript of creative work; personal essay; critical essay. *Application deadline:* For fall admission, 9/1 for domestic and international students; for spring admission, 3/1 for domestic and international students. Application fee: $75. Electronic applications accepted. *Expenses:* Expenses: Contact institution. *Financial support:* In 2014–15, 25 students received support, including 2 fellowships (averaging $18,300 per year); scholarships/grants also available. Financial award application deadline: 3/1; financial award applicants required to submit FAFSA. *Faculty research:* Poetry and fiction writing, analytic writing, creative and analytic study of literature, literary craft instruction. *Unit head:* Prof. Debra Allbery, Director, 828-771-3716, Fax: 828-771-7005, E-mail: dallbery@warren-wilson.edu. *Application contact:* Amber Duntley, MFA Project Manager, 828-771-3717, Fax: 828-771-7005, E-mail: aduntley@warren-wilson.edu.
Website: http://www.wwcmfa.org/

Washington University in St. Louis, Graduate School of Arts and Sciences, Department of English, Writing Program, St. Louis, MO 63130-4899. Offers MFAW. *Degree requirements:* For master's, thesis or written exam. *Entrance requirements:* For master's, GRE General Test, sample of written work. Additional exam requirements/ recommendations for international students: Required—TOEFL. Electronic applications accepted. *Faculty research:* Fiction or poetry-writing workshops and academic courses.

Wayne State University, College of Liberal Arts and Sciences, Department of English, Detroit, MI 48202. Offers comparative literature (MA); English (MA, PhD). Doctoral programs admit for fall only. *Students:* 61 full-time (37 women), 35 part-time (18 women); includes 16 minority (7 Black or African American, non-Hispanic/Latino; 5 Asian, non-Hispanic/Latino; 3 Hispanic/Latino; 1 Two or more races, non-Hispanic/ Latino), 5 international. Average age 34. 136 applicants, 23% accepted, 15 enrolled. In 2014, 12 master's, 8 doctorates awarded. *Degree requirements:* For master's, variable foreign language requirement, essay or thesis; for doctorate, one foreign language, thesis/dissertation. *Entrance requirements:* For master's, statement of purpose; two academic letters of reference; sample essay from previous English course; for doctorate, GRE General Test, statement of purpose; two academic letters of reference; sample essay from previous English course. Additional exam requirements/ recommendations for international students: Required—TOEFL (minimum score 550 paper-based; 79 iBT), TWE (minimum score 5.5), Michigan English Language Assessment Battery (minimum score 85); Recommended—IELTS (minimum score 6.5). *Application deadline:* For fall admission, 3/1 for domestic and international students; for winter admission, 11/1 for domestic and international students; for spring admission, 11/ 1 for domestic students. Application fee: $0. Electronic applications accepted. *Expenses:* Tuition, state resident: full-time $10,294; part-time $571.90 per credit hour. Tuition, nonresident: full-time $29,730; part-time $1238.75 per credit hour. *Required fees:* $1365; $43.50 per credit hour. $291.10 per semester. Tuition and fees vary according to course load and program. *Financial support:* In 2014–15, 56 students received support, including 4 fellowships with full and partial tuition reimbursements available (averaging $17,000 per year), 2 research assistantships with full and partial tuition reimbursements available (averaging $17,994 per year), 31 teaching assistantships with full and partial tuition reimbursements available (averaging $16,540 per year); scholarships/grants, health care benefits, and unspecified assistantships also available. Financial award application deadline: 3/31; financial award applicants required to submit FAFSA. *Faculty research:* English and American literature, cultural studies, composition, linguistics, film. *Unit head:* Dr. Ellen Barton, Professor and Department Chair, 313-577-7692, E-mail: ellen.barton@wayne.edu. *Application contact:* Dr. Carolin Maun, Interim Director of Graduate Studies, 313-577-7694, E-mail: caroline.maun@wayne.edu.
Website: http://clas.wayne.edu/english/

Western Connecticut State University, Division of Graduate Studies, School of Arts and Sciences, Department of English, Danbury, CT 06810-6885. Offers English (MA); literature (MA); TESOL (MA); writing (MA). Part-time programs available. *Degree requirements:* For master's, thesis (for writing option), completion of program in 6 years. *Entrance requirements:* For master's, minimum GPA of 2.5, writing sample. Additional exam requirements/recommendations for international students: Recommended— TOEFL (minimum score 550 paper-based; 79 iBT), IELTS (minimum score 6). *Faculty research:* Developing inquiry in teachers and students, encouraging talent development, analyzing program development and assessment techniques, developing student learning outcomes, encouraging teachers as researchers, assessing the impact of computer technologies.

Western Connecticut State University, Division of Graduate Studies, School of Arts and Sciences, Department of Writing, Linguistics, and Creative Process, Danbury, CT 06810-6885. Offers professional writing (MFA). Part-time programs available. *Degree*

Writing

requirements: For master's, thesis, completion of program within 4 years, enrichment project that compliments course of study. *Entrance requirements:* For master's, 2 writing samples: a 20-50 page portfolio of previous writing and a brief essay. Additional exam requirements/recommendations for international students: Recommended—TOEFL (minimum score 550 paper-based; 79 iBT), IELTS (minimum score 6). *Expenses:* Contact institution. *Faculty research:* Creativity, chaos.

Western Illinois University, School of Graduate Studies, College of Arts and Sciences, Department of English and Journalism, Macomb, IL 61455-1390. Offers English (MA); literary studies (Certificate); professional writing (Certificate); teaching writing (Certificate). Part-time programs available. *Students:* 4 full-time (3 women), 36 part-time (24 women); includes 7 minority (1 Black or African American, non-Hispanic/Latino; 4 Hispanic/Latino; 2 Two or more races, non-Hispanic/Latino). Average age 30. 21 applicants, 95% accepted, 10 enrolled. In 2014, 16 master's, 6 other advanced degrees awarded. *Degree requirements:* For master's, thesis or alternative. *Entrance requirements:* Additional exam requirements/recommendations for international students: Required—TOEFL (minimum score 575 paper-based; 88 iBT). *Application deadline:* Applications are processed on a rolling basis. Application fee: $30. Electronic applications accepted. *Financial support:* In 2014–15, 14 students received support, including 14 teaching assistantships with full tuition reimbursements available (averaging $8,688 per year); research assistantships with full tuition reimbursements available also available. Financial award applicants required to submit FAFSA. *Unit head:* Dr. Mark Mossman, Chairperson, 309-298-1103. *Application contact:* Dr. Nancy Parsons, Associate Provost and Director of Graduate Studies, 309-298-1806, Fax: 309-298-2345, E-mail: grad-office@wiu.edu.
Website: http://wiu.edu/English

Western Kentucky University, Graduate Studies, Potter College of Arts and Letters, Department of English, Bowling Green, KY 42101. Offers education (MA); English (MA Ed); literature (MA), including American literature, British literature, literary theory, women writers, world literature; teaching English as a second language (MA); writing (MA). Part-time and evening/weekend programs available. *Degree requirements:* For master's, comprehensive exam, thesis optional, final exam. *Entrance requirements:* For master's, GRE General Test, minimum GPA of 2.75. Additional exam requirements/recommendations for international students: Required—TOEFL (minimum score 555 paper-based; 79 iBT). *Faculty research:* Improving writing, linking teacher knowledge and performance, Victorian women writers, Kentucky women writers, Kentucky poets.

Western Michigan University, Graduate College, College of Arts and Sciences, Department of English, Kalamazoo, MI 49008. Offers creative writing (MFA, PhD); English (MA, PhD); English teaching (MA). *Degree requirements:* For doctorate, one foreign language, thesis/dissertation. *Application deadline:* For fall admission, 2/1 for domestic students. *Financial support:* Application deadline: 2/15. *Application contact:* Admissions and Orientation, 269-387-2000, Fax: 269-387-2096.

Western New England University, College of Arts and Sciences, Program in Creative Writing, Springfield, MA 01119. Offers MFA. Part-time and evening/weekend programs available. *Students:* 4 part-time (1 woman). Average age 32. *Entrance requirements:* For master's, official transcripts, two letters of recommendation, writing sample. Additional exam requirements/recommendations for international students: Required—TOEFL (minimum score 79 iBT). *Application deadline:* Applications are processed on a rolling basis. Application fee: $30. Electronic applications accepted. *Financial support:* Application deadline: 4/15; applicants required to submit FAFSA. *Unit head:* Pearl Abraham, Director, 413-782-1338, E-mail: pearl.abraham@wne.edu. *Application contact:* Matthew Fox, Director of Admissions for Graduate Students and Adult Learners, 413-782-1517, Fax: 413-782-1777, E-mail: study@wne.edu.

Western State Colorado University, Program in Creative Writing, Gunnison, CO 81231. Offers mainstream genre fiction (MFA); poetry (MFA); screenwriting (MFA). Postbaccalaureate distance learning degree programs offered (minimal on-campus study). *Degree requirements:* For master's, thesis.

Westminster College, Program in Professional Communication, Salt Lake City, UT 84105-3697. Offers MPC, MSC. Part-time and evening/weekend programs available. *Faculty:* 10 full-time (5 women), 3 part-time/adjunct (all women). *Students:* 14 full-time (7 women), 40 part-time (26 women); includes 13 minority (3 Asian, non-Hispanic/Latino; 8 Hispanic/Latino; 2 Two or more races, non-Hispanic/Latino), 3 international. Average age 32. 23 applicants, 70% accepted, 9 enrolled. In 2014, 9 master's awarded. *Degree requirements:* For master's, field project. *Entrance requirements:* For master's, GRE, resume, personal statement of intent, official transcripts, two letters of recommendation. Additional exam requirements/recommendations for international students: Required—TOEFL (minimum score 600 paper-based; 100 iBT), IELTS (minimum score 7.5). *Application deadline:* For fall admission, 8/9 for domestic students, 7/9 for international students; for spring admission, 1/1 for domestic students; for summer admission, 5/1 for domestic students. Applications are processed on a rolling basis. Application fee: $50. Electronic applications accepted. *Expenses:* Expenses: Contact institution. *Financial support:* In 2014–15, 8 students received support. Career-related internships or fieldwork, scholarships/grants, unspecified assistantships, and tuition reimbursements, tuition remission available. Support available to part-time students. Financial award applicants required to submit FAFSA. *Faculty research:* Diversity in higher education, communication pedagogy, mass media law and ethics, impact of new technologies on society, rhetorical theory, feminism and popular culture, critical communication pedagogy. *Unit head:* Dr. Helen Hodgson, Director, 801-832-2821, Fax: 801-832-3102, E-mail: hhodgson@westminstercollege.edu. *Application contact:* Dr. John Baworowsky, Vice President of Enrollment Management, 801-832-2200, Fax: 801-832-3101, E-mail: admission@westminstercollege.edu.
Website: http://www.westminstercollege.edu/mpc

West Virginia University, Eberly College of Arts and Sciences, Department of English, Program in Creative Writing, Morgantown, WV 26506. Offers MFA. Part-time and evening/weekend programs available.

West Virginia Wesleyan College, Program in Creative Writing, Buckhannon, WV 26201. Offers MFA.

Wichita State University, Graduate School, Fairmount College of Liberal Arts and Sciences, Department of English, Wichita, KS 67260. Offers creative writing (MFA); English (MA). Part-time and evening/weekend programs available. *Entrance requirements:* For master's, writing sample (MFA). *Unit head:* Dr. Mary Waters, Chair, 316-978-3130, Fax: 316-978-3548, E-mail: mary.waters@wichita.edu. *Application contact:* Jordan Oleson, Admissions Coordinator, 316-978-3095, Fax: 316-978-3253, E-mail: jordan.oleson@wichita.edu.
Website: http://www.wichita.edu/english

Wilkes University, College of Graduate and Professional Studies, Program in Creative Writing, Wilkes-Barre, PA 18766-0002. Offers MA, MFA. Part-time programs available. Postbaccalaureate distance learning degree programs offered (minimal on-campus study). *Students:* 58 full-time (32 women), 25 part-time (15 women); includes 15 minority (9 Black or African American, non-Hispanic/Latino; 1 Asian, non-Hispanic/Latino; 1 Hispanic/Latino; 1 Native Hawaiian or other Pacific Islander, non-Hispanic/Latino; 3 Two or more races, non-Hispanic/Latino). Average age 39. In 2014, 43 master's awarded. *Entrance requirements:* Additional exam requirements/recommendations for international students: Required—TOEFL (minimum score 550 paper-based; 79 iBT). *Application deadline:* Applications are processed on a rolling basis. Application fee: $35. Electronic applications accepted. *Expenses:* Expenses: Contact institution. *Financial support:* Application deadline: 3/1; applicants required to submit FAFSA. *Unit head:* Dr. Bonnie Culver, Director, 570-408-4527, Fax: 570-408-7846, E-mail: bonnie.culver@wilkes.edu. *Application contact:* Joanne Thomas, Director of Graduate Education, 570-408-4234, Fax: 570-408-7846, E-mail: joanne.thomas1@wilkes.edu.
Website: http://www.wilkes.edu/academics/graduate-programs/masters-programs/creative-writing-ma-mfa/index.aspx

William Paterson University of New Jersey, College of Humanities and Social Sciences, Wayne, NJ 07470-8420. Offers applied sociology (MA); clinical and counseling psychology (MA); creative and professional writing (MFA); English (MA); history (MA); public policy and international affairs (MA). Part-time and evening/weekend programs available. *Faculty:* 32 full-time (16 women), 3 part-time/adjunct (1 woman). *Students:* 50 full-time (30 women), 114 part-time (88 women); includes 64 minority (7 Black or African American, non-Hispanic/Latino; 1 American Indian or Alaska Native, non-Hispanic/Latino; 4 Asian, non-Hispanic/Latino; 50 Hispanic/Latino; 2 Two or more races, non-Hispanic/Latino), 2 international. Average age 34. 115 applicants, 81% accepted, 65 enrolled. In 2014, 42 master's awarded. Terminal master's awarded for partial completion of doctoral program. *Degree requirements:* For master's, thesis (for some programs), internship (for some programs). *Entrance requirements:* For master's, GRE/MAT, minimum GPA of 3.0; 2 letters of recommendation; writing sample/personal statement. Additional exam requirements/recommendations for international students: Required—TOEFL (minimum score 550 paper-based; 79 iBT), IELTS (minimum score 6). *Application deadline:* For fall admission, 6/1 for domestic students, 3/1 for international students; for spring admission, 11/1 for domestic students, 10/1 for international students. Applications are processed on a rolling basis. Application fee: $50. Electronic applications accepted. *Expenses:* Tuition, state resident: full-time $12,413; part-time $564.21 per credit. Tuition, nonresident: full-time $20,487; part-time $931.21 per credit. *Required fees:* $2107; $95.79 per credit. $478.95 per semester. Tuition and fees vary according to course load and degree level. *Financial support:* Research assistantships with full tuition reimbursements, Federal Work-Study, scholarships/grants, and unspecified assistantships available. Support available to part-time students. Financial award application deadline: 4/1; financial award applicants required to submit FAFSA. *Faculty research:* Sexual violence, history of science in Muslim societies, bioethics, teaching writing for transfer, psychological impact of microagressions on minority communities. *Unit head:* Dr. Kara Rabbitt, Dean, 973-720-2731, Fax: 973-720-2955, E-mail: rabbittk@wpunj.edu. *Application contact:* Tinu Adeniran, Associate Director, Graduate Admissions, 973-720-2764, Fax: 973-720-2035, E-mail: adenirant@wpunj.edu.
Website: http://www.wpunj.edu/cohss

Wright State University, School of Graduate Studies, College of Liberal Arts, Department of English Language and Literatures, Dayton, OH 45435. Offers composition and rhetoric (MA); English (MA); literature (MA); teaching English to speakers of other languages (MA). *Degree requirements:* For master's, thesis optional, portfolio. *Entrance requirements:* For master's, 20 hours in upper-level English. Additional exam requirements/recommendations for international students: Required—TOEFL. *Faculty research:* American literature, world literature in English, applied linguistics, writing theory and pedagogy.

Yale University, School of Drama, New Haven, CT 06520. Offers acting (MFA, Certificate); design (MFA, Certificate), including costume design, lighting design, projection design, set design; directing (MFA, Certificate); dramaturgy and dramatic criticism (MFA, DFA); playwriting (MFA, Certificate); sound design (MFA, Certificate); stage management (MFA, Certificate); technical design and production (MFA, Certificate); theater management (MFA); MFA/MBA. *Faculty:* 41 full-time (16 women), 80 part-time/adjunct (30 women). *Students:* 211 full-time (113 women); includes 51 minority (19 Black or African American, non-Hispanic/Latino; 8 Asian, non-Hispanic/Latino; 14 Hispanic/Latino; 10 Two or more races, non-Hispanic/Latino), 32 international. Average age 28. 1,391 applicants, 5% accepted, 66 enrolled. In 2014, 62 master's, 3 doctorates awarded. *Degree requirements:* For master's, comprehensive exam (for some programs), thesis (for some programs); for doctorate, thesis/dissertation, oral and written comprehensive exams. *Entrance requirements:* For master's, GRE (verbal, quantitative, and analytical), in-person audition (for acting); portfolio review (for design). Additional exam requirements/recommendations for international students: Required—TOEFL. *Application deadline:* For fall admission, 1/2 for domestic and international students. Application fee: $110. Electronic applications accepted. *Financial support:* In 2014–15, 203 students received support. Career-related internships or fieldwork, Federal Work-Study, institutionally sponsored loans, scholarships/grants, and health care benefits available. Financial award application deadline: 2/15; financial award applicants required to submit FAFSA. *Unit head:* James Bundy, Dean/Artistic Director of Yale Repertory Theatre, 203-432-1505. *Application contact:* Maria R. Leveton, Registrar/Admissions Administrator, 203-432-1507, Fax: 203-432-9668, E-mail: maria.leveton@yale.edu.
Website: http://www.yale.edu/drama/

ADELPHI UNIVERSITY
College of the Arts and Sciences
Program in Creative Writing

Program of Study

The M.F.A. in Creative Writing offers an intimate learning experience, with opportunities to work full time or part time in multiple genres, including poetry, fiction, creative nonfiction, and dramatic writing. Students hone their craft through workshops, literature classes, a year-long thesis colloquium, and an independent study sequence culminating in the production of a master's degree thesis.

The unique professional development practicum colloquium allows for a hands-on approach and includes meetings with writers, agents, editors, grantors, and arts administrators.

The program enables students to forge connections within the larger New York City–based writing and publishing communities and prepares its graduates for careers in writing, teaching, and arts organizations.

In addition to competitive merit scholarships, all students who have completed Teaching Writing: Theory and Practice (English 638) are eligible to serve as instructors for the undergraduate Introduction to Creative Writing class (English 109). Students work on the University's blog, literary magazine, and social media campaigns as well as serve internships in various arts organizations. The program also has formal relationships with three prestigious national organizations: PEN America, Cave Canem, and the Association of Writers and Writing Programs (AWP).

Research Facilities

The University's primary research holdings are at Swirbul Library and comprise 618,779 volumes (including bound periodicals and government publications); 791,000 items in microformats; 35,000 audiovisual items; and online access to more than 135,000 e-book titles, 87,000 electronic journal titles, and 251 research databases.

Financial Aid

All applications are eligible to be considered for financial aid and are automatically considered for one of six partial (one-half) tuition remissions. Second-year students and students entering with a previous M.A. are eligible for graduate teaching fellowships in the Department of English. There are also opportunities for work-study positions, community service teaching grants, or positions in the Writing Center and Learning Center.

Cost of Study

For the 2015–16 academic year, the tuition rate is $1,110 per credit. University fees range from $370 to $635 per semester.

Living and Housing Costs

Housing may be available on a limited, first-come, first-served basis.

Value

Earning an Adelphi degree means joining a growing network of more than 90,000 alumni. For the tenth straight year, Adelphi was designated a Best Buy by the *Fiske Guide to Colleges*, one of only 20 private universities nationwide to earn that distinction.

Location

Located in historic Garden City, New York, just 23 miles from Manhattan, Adelphi's 75-acre suburban campus is known for the beauty of its landscape and architecture. The campus is a short walk from the Long Island Rail Road and is convenient to New York's major airports and several major highways. Off-campus centers are located in Manhattan, Poughkeepsie, and Suffolk County.

The University and the College

Founded in 1896, Adelphi is a fully accredited, private university with nearly 8,000 undergraduate, graduate, and returning-adult students in the arts and sciences, business, clinical psychology, education, nursing, and social work. Students come from 38 and from 46 countries.

The faculty members of the College of Arts and Sciences place a high priority on students' intellectual development in and out of the classroom and they structure programs to foster that growth. Students analyze original research and other creative work, develop firsthand facility with creative and research methodologies, undertake collaborative work with peers and mentors, engage in serious internships, and hone communication skills.

Applying

A baccalaureate degree is required for admission (the degree does not have to be in English or literature). A student must submit a completed application, a $50 application fee, official college transcripts, two letters of reference from people familiar with the student's writing, a personal statement (1,000-word

maximum and on the subject of the student's writing life and goals), and a manuscript in one genre only (poetry, fiction, dramatic writing, or creative nonfiction). The application deadlines are January 15 for fall enrollment and September 15 for spring enrollment. After those dates, rolling admission is on a space-available basis.

For More Information

Phone: 800. ADELPHI (800-233-5744)
Website: http://english.adelphi.edu/mfa-in-creative-writing/

THE FACULTY AND THEIR RESEARCH

Creative Writing

Judith Baumel, M.A., Johns Hopkins. Contemporary poetry, poetics, translation studies.

Craig Carson, Ph.D., University of California. Restoration/eighteenth-century literature, literary theory, history of the novel, political philosophy, aesthetics.

Catherine Chung, M.F.A., Cornell University. Fiction, creative nonfiction.

Martha Cooley, B.A., Trinity. Creative writing (particularly fiction), modern and contemporary American and European literature, translation studies.

Anton Dudley, M.F.A., New York University. Playwriting, directing, solo performance, cabaret theatre, contemporary drama, development of new works.

Jennifer Fleischner, Ph.D., Columbia University. British and American literature, race and slavery, women's literature, American slavery, biography, historical fiction.

Kermit Frazier, M.F.A., New York University. Playwriting, television writing, contemporary drama, African American drama, the literature of AIDS.

Louise Geddes, Ph.D., CUNY Graduate Center. Renaissance literature, Shakespeare, early modern drama in performance, performance theory, twentieth-century British drama, digital theatre.

Jacqueline Jones LaMon, M.F.A., Indiana. Poetry, introductory creative writing, writing theory and practice.

Lahney Preston-Matto, Ph.D., New York University. Irish and English medieval literature, medieval law, twentieth-century Irish literature, European medieval literature, gender, translation theory.

Michael Matto, Ph.D., New York University. Rhetoric and composition theory, history of the English language, Old English language and literature, cognitive linguistics.

Igor Webb, Ph.D., Stanford. Creative nonfiction, English literature, character development in fiction, translation studies.

Susan Weisser, Ph.D., Columbia University. Nineteenth-century British literature, Woman's studies and feminism, early twentieth-century literature, autobiography and memoir.

Peter West, Ph.D., Emory University. Nineteenth-century American literature and culture, urban literature, the literature of slavery.

Students in the M.F.A. in Creative Writing program hone their craft through workshops, literature classes, and independent study.

The M.F.A. in Creative Writing helps students forge connections within the larger New York City–based writing and publishing community.

ACADEMIC AND PROFESSIONAL PROGRAMS IN INTERDISCIPLINARY STUDIES

Section 14
Interdisciplinary Studies

This section contains a directory of institutions offering graduate work in interdisciplinary studies. Additional information about programs listed in the directory may be obtained by writing directly to the dean of a graduate school or chair of a department at the address given in the directory.

For programs offering related work, see also in this book *Comparative and Interdisciplinary Arts, Humanities,* and *Social Sciences.*

CONTENTS

Interdisciplinary Studies

Alaska Pacific University, Graduate Programs, Liberal Studies Department, Self-Designed Programs, Anchorage, AK 99508-4672. Offers MA. Part-time and evening/weekend programs available. *Degree requirements:* For master's, thesis or project. *Entrance requirements:* For master's, MAT (preferred), GRE General Test or GMAT. *Expenses:* Contact institution.

Amberton University, Graduate School, Program in Professional Development, Garland, TX 75041-5595. Offers MA. Part-time and evening/weekend programs available. Postbaccalaureate distance learning degree programs offered (no on-campus study). *Entrance requirements:* For master's, minimum GPA of 3.0. *Application deadline:* Applications are processed on a rolling basis. *Unit head:* Dr. Don Hebbard, Academic Dean, 972-279-6511 Ext. 153, Fax: 972-279-9773, E-mail: dhebbard@amberton.edu. *Application contact:* Adviser, 972-279-6511 Ext. 180, Fax: 972-279-9773, E-mail: advisor@amberton.edu.
Website: http://www.amberton.edu/programs-and-courses/masters-degree-programs/professional-development/index.html

Antioch University New England, Graduate School, Department of Environmental Studies, Self-Designed Studies Program, Keene, NH 03431-3552. Offers MS. *Degree requirements:* For master's, practicum, seminar, thesis or project. *Entrance requirements:* For master's, detailed proposal. Additional exam requirements/recommendations for international students: Required—TOEFL (minimum score 550 paper-based).

Arizona State University at the Tempe campus, New College of Interdisciplinary Arts and Sciences, Program in Interdisciplinary Studies, Phoenix, AZ 85069-7100. Offers MA. Part-time and evening/weekend programs available. *Degree requirements:* For master's, thesis or alternative, research paper or applied project; interactive Program of Study (iPOS) submitted before completing 50 percent of required credit hours. *Entrance requirements:* For master's, GRE (if GPA less than 3.0 in last 60 hours of undergraduate study), minimum GPA of 3.0 or equivalent in last 2 years of work leading to bachelor's degree, 3 letters of recommendation, official transcripts, personal statement, writing sample of scholarly work or example of professional activities. Additional exam requirements/recommendations for international students: Required—TOEFL, IELTS, or PTE. Electronic applications accepted. *Faculty research:* Comparative politics, foreign policy, world religions, African and African-American folklore, British modernism, English Renaissance drama, physiological psychology, sociology of health and illness, gender/race/class/sexuality, applied ethics, borderland theories.

Athabasca University, Centre for Integrated Studies, Athabasca, AB T9S 3A3, Canada. Offers adult education (MA); community studies (MA); cultural studies (MA); educational studies (MA); global change (MA); work, organization, and leadership (MA). Part-time and evening/weekend programs available. Postbaccalaureate distance learning degree programs offered (no on-campus study). *Degree requirements:* For master's, project. *Entrance requirements:* Additional exam requirements/recommendations for international students: Required—TOEFL (minimum score 560 paper-based). Electronic applications accepted. *Faculty research:* Women's history, literature and culture studies, sustainable development, labor and education.

Baylor University, Graduate School, College of Arts and Sciences, The Institute of Ecological, Earth and Environmental Sciences, Waco, TX 76798. Offers PhD. *Degree requirements:* For doctorate, variable foreign language requirement, comprehensive exam, thesis/dissertation or alternative. *Entrance requirements:* For doctorate, GRE. Additional exam requirements/recommendations for international students: Required—TOEFL (minimum score 550 paper-based; 80 iBT); Recommended—IELTS (minimum score 6.5). Electronic applications accepted. *Faculty research:* Ecosystem processes, environmental toxicology and risk assessment, biogeochemical cycling, chemical fate and transport, conservation management.

Boise State University, College of Arts and Sciences, Program in Interdisciplinary Studies, Boise, ID 83725-0399. Offers MA, MS. Part-time programs available. *Faculty:* 1 full-time. *Students:* 2 full-time (1 woman), 4 part-time (3 women); includes 1 minority (Hispanic/Latino). Average age 40. 7 applicants, 71% accepted, 3 enrolled. In 2014, 2 master's awarded. *Degree requirements:* For master's, thesis. *Entrance requirements:* For master's, minimum GPA of 3.0. *Application deadline:* For fall admission, 10/1 priority date for domestic students; for spring admission, 3/1 priority date for domestic students. Applications are processed on a rolling basis. Application fee: $55. Electronic applications accepted. *Expenses:* Tuition: state resident: part-time $331 per credit hour. Tuition, nonresident: part-time $531 per credit hour. *Financial support:* Career-related internships or fieldwork, Federal Work-Study, and institutionally sponsored loans available. Support available to part-time students. Financial award application deadline: 3/1. *Unit head:* Dr. Daryl Jones, Director, 208-426-1414, Fax: 208-426-3006, E-mail: aprjones@boisestate.edu. *Application contact:* Linda Platt, Office Services Supervisor, Graduate Admission and Degree Services, 208-426-1074, Fax: 208-426-2789, E-mail: lplatt@boisestate.edu.
Website: http://coas.boisestate.edu/interdisciplinary-studies-program/

Bowling Green State University, Graduate College, Interdisciplinary Studies, Bowling Green, OH 43403. Offers M Ed, MA, MS, PhD. Part-time programs available. *Degree requirements:* For master's, thesis or alternative; for doctorate, comprehensive exam, thesis/dissertation. *Entrance requirements:* For master's and doctorate, GRE General Test. Additional exam requirements/recommendations for international students: Required—TOEFL. Electronic applications accepted.

Buffalo State College, State University of New York, The Graduate School, Program in Multidisciplinary Studies, Buffalo, NY 14222-1095. Offers MA, MS. Part-time and evening/weekend programs available. *Degree requirements:* For master's, thesis or project. *Entrance requirements:* For master's, minimum GPA of 2.5. Additional exam requirements/recommendations for international students: Required—TOEFL (minimum score 550 paper-based).

Burlington College, Individualized Master's Program, Burlington, VT 05401-2998. Offers MA. Part-time programs available. Postbaccalaureate distance learning degree programs offered (no on-campus study). *Degree requirements:* For master's, capstone project. *Entrance requirements:* For master's, minimum GPA of 2.5, 2 letters of recommendation, undergraduate transcripts.

California College of the Arts, Graduate Programs, Fine Arts Programs, San Francisco, CA 94107. Offers ceramics (MFA); comics (MFA); film/video/performance (MFA); glass (MFA); interdisciplinary studies (MFA); jewelry/metal arts (MFA); media studies (MFA); painting/drawing (MFA); photography (MFA); printmaking (MFA); sculpture (MFA); social practice (MFA); textiles (MFA); wood/furniture (MFA). *Accreditation:* NASAD. *Degree requirements:* For master's, thesis, exhibit. *Entrance requirements:* For master's, appropriate bachelor's degree, portfolio, resume, 2 letters of recommendation, transcript. Additional exam requirements/recommendations for international students: Required—TOEFL (minimum score 600 paper-based; 100 iBT). Electronic applications accepted.

California Institute of Integral Studies, School of Consciousness and Transformation, San Francisco, CA 94103. Offers anthropology and social change (MA, PhD); creative inquiry/interdisciplinary arts (MFA); East-West psychology (MA, PhD); philosophy and religion (MA, PhD), including Asian and comparative studies, ecology, spirituality, and religion, philosophy, cosmology, and consciousness, women's spirituality; transformative leadership (MA); transformative studies (PhD); writing and consciousness (MFA). Part-time and evening/weekend programs available. Postbaccalaureate distance learning degree programs offered (no on-campus study). *Students:* 385 full-time (256 women), 102 part-time (71 women); includes 124 minority (31 Black or African American, non-Hispanic/Latino; 3 American Indian or Alaska Native, non-Hispanic/Latino; 19 Asian, non-Hispanic/Latino; 39 Hispanic/Latino; 1 Native Hawaiian or other Pacific Islander, non-Hispanic/Latino; 31 Two or more races, non-Hispanic/Latino), 53 international. Average age 43. 196 applicants, 92% accepted, 125 enrolled. In 2014, 75 master's, 41 doctorates awarded. Terminal master's awarded for partial completion of doctoral program. *Degree requirements:* For master's, thesis optional; for doctorate, comprehensive exam, thesis/dissertation, 1 foreign language (for Asian comparative studies). *Entrance requirements:* For master's, minimum GPA of 3.0, letters of recommendation, writing sample; for doctorate, master's degree, minimum GPA of 3.0, letters of recommendation, writing sample. Additional exam requirements/recommendations for international students: Required—TOEFL. *Application deadline:* For fall admission, 2/1 priority date for domestic and international students; for spring admission, 10/15 priority date for domestic and international students. Applications are processed on a rolling basis. Application fee: $65. Electronic applications accepted. *Expenses: Tuition:* Full-time $18,270; part-time $1015 per credit. *Required fees:* $85 per semester hour. *Financial support:* In 2014–15, 445 students received support, including 5 research assistantships (averaging $800 per year), 28 teaching assistantships (averaging $825 per year); career-related internships or fieldwork, Federal Work-Study, and scholarships/grants also available. Support available to part-time students. Financial award application deadline: 4/15; financial award applicants required to submit FAFSA. *Faculty research:* Ecology and sustainability, philosophy and religion, East-West psychology, integrative health, social and cultural anthropology, transformative leadership. *Application contact:* David Townes, Senior Admissions Counselor, 415-575-6152, Fax: 415-575-1268, E-mail: admissions@ciis.edu.
Website: http://www.ciis.edu/

California State University, Bakersfield, Division of Graduate Studies, Program in Interdisciplinary Studies, Bakersfield, CA 93311. Offers MA. *Degree requirements:* For master's, thesis or project. *Entrance requirements:* For master's, minimum GPA of 3.0 in last 90 quarter units, baccalaureate degree. Additional exam requirements/recommendations for international students: Required—TOEFL (minimum score 550 paper-based). Electronic applications accepted. *Faculty research:* Ethics, physical education and health.

California State University, East Bay, Office of Academic Programs and Graduate Studies, Interdisciplinary Programs, Hayward, CA 94542-3000. Offers MA, MS. Part-time programs available. *Degree requirements:* For master's, comprehensive exam, project or thesis. *Entrance requirements:* Additional exam requirements/recommendations for international students: Required—TOEFL (minimum score 550 paper-based). *Application deadline:* For fall admission, 6/30 for domestic and international students. Applications are processed on a rolling basis. Application fee: $55. Electronic applications accepted. *Expenses:* Tuition, state resident: full-time $7830; part-time $1302 per credit hour. Tuition, nonresident: full-time $16,368. *Required fees:* $327 per quarter. Tuition and fees vary according to course load and program. *Financial support:* Fellowships, teaching assistantships, Federal Work-Study, institutionally sponsored loans, and scholarships/grants available. Support available to part-time students. Financial award application deadline: 3/2; financial award applicants required to submit FAFSA. *Unit head:* Jennifer Eagan, Coordinator, 510-885-3716, Fax: 510-885-4777, E-mail: jennifer.eagan@csueastbay.edu. *Application contact:* Dr. Donna Wiley, Interim Associate Vice President for Academic Programs and Graduate Studies, 510-885-3716, Fax: 510-885-4777, E-mail: donna.wiley@csueastbay.edu.
Website: http://www.csueastbay.edu/gradprograms/

California State University, Long Beach, Graduate Studies, Interdisciplinary Studies Program, Long Beach, CA 90840. Offers MA, MS. Part-time programs available. *Degree requirements:* For master's, thesis. *Entrance requirements:* For master's, minimum undergraduate GPA of 3.0. Electronic applications accepted.

California State University, San Bernardino, Graduate Studies, Interdisciplinary Programs, San Bernardino, CA 92407-2397. Offers integrative studies (MA). Part-time and evening/weekend programs available. *Students:* 3 full-time (1 woman), 1 (woman) part-time; includes 2 minority (1 Black or African American, non-Hispanic/Latino; 1 Two or more races, non-Hispanic/Latino). Average age 40. 4 applicants, 50% accepted, 2 enrolled. *Degree requirements:* For master's, thesis or alternative. *Entrance requirements:* Additional exam requirements/recommendations for international students: Required—TOEFL. *Application deadline:* For fall admission, 7/17 for domestic students. Application fee: $55. *Expenses:* Tuition, state resident: full-time $6738; part-time $1302 per term. Tuition, nonresident: full-time $17,898; part-time $248 per unit. *Required fees:* $365 per quarter. Tuition and fees vary according to degree level and program. *Financial support:* Application deadline: 3/1. *Unit head:* Dr. Jeffrey Thompson, Dean of Graduate Studies, 909-537-5058, Fax: 909-537-7034, E-mail: jthompso@csusb.edu. *Application contact:* Olivia Rosas, Associate Vice President for Enrollment Services, 909-537-7577, Fax: 909-537-7034, E-mail: orosas@csusb.edu.

California State University, Stanislaus, College of Humanities and Social Sciences, Programs in Interdisciplinary Studies (MA/MS), Turlock, CA 95382. Offers MA, MS. Part-time and evening/weekend programs available. *Degree requirements:* For master's, thesis. *Entrance requirements:* For master's, GRE, minimum GPA of 3.0, personal statement. Additional exam requirements/recommendations for international students: Required—TOEFL (minimum score 550 paper-based). Electronic applications accepted.

Cambridge College, School of Education, Cambridge, MA 02138-5304. Offers autism specialist (M Ed); autism/behavior analyst (M Ed); behavior analyst (Post-Master's Certificate); behavioral management (M Ed); early childhood teacher (M Ed); education specialist in curriculum and instruction (CAGS); educational leadership (Ed D); elementary teacher (M Ed); English as a second language (M Ed, Certificate); general science (M Ed); health education (Post-Master's Certificate); health/family and consumer sciences (M Ed); history (M Ed); individualized (M Ed); information technology literacy (M Ed); instructional technology (M Ed); interdisciplinary studies (M Ed); library teacher (M Ed); literacy education (M Ed); mathematics (M Ed); mathematics specialist (Certificate); middle school mathematics and science (M Ed);

school administration (M Ed, CAGS); school guidance counselor (M Ed); school nurse education (M Ed); school social worker/school adjustment counselor (M Ed); special education administrator (CAGS); special education/moderate disabilities (M Ed); teaching skills and methodologies (M Ed). Part-time and evening/weekend programs available. Postbaccalaureate distance learning degree programs offered (minimal on-campus study). *Degree requirements:* For master's, thesis, internship/practicum (licensure program only); for doctorate, thesis/dissertation; for other advanced degree, thesis. *Entrance requirements:* For master's, interview, resume, documentation of licensure, 2 professional references; for doctorate, official transcripts, interview, resume, documentation of licensure (if any), written personal statement/essay, portfolio of scholarly and professional work, qualifying assessment, 2 professional references, health insurance, immunizations form; for other advanced degree, official transcripts, interview, resume, documentation of licensure (if any), written personal statement/ essay, 2 professional references, health insurance, immunizations form. Additional exam requirements/recommendations for international students: Required—TOEFL (minimum score 550 paper-based; 79 iBT), Michigan English Language Assessment Battery (minimum score 85); Recommended—IELTS (minimum score 6). Electronic applications accepted. *Expenses:* Contact institution. *Faculty research:* Adult education, accelerated learning, mathematics education, brain compatible learning, special education and law.

Campbell University, Graduate and Professional Programs, School of Education, Buies Creek, NC 27506. Offers elementary education (M Ed); interdisciplinary studies (M Ed); middle grades education (M Ed); physical education (M Ed); school administration (MSA); school counseling (M Ed); secondary education (M Ed). *Accreditation:* NCATE. Part-time and evening/weekend programs available. *Faculty:* 8 full-time, 8 part-time/adjunct. *Students:* 35 full-time (all women), 62 part-time (48 women). *Degree requirements:* For master's, comprehensive exam. *Entrance requirements:* For master's, GRE General Test, minimum GPA of 2.7. *Application deadline:* For fall admission, 8/1 priority date for domestic students; for spring admission, 1/2 priority date for domestic students. Applications are processed on a rolling basis. Application fee: $65. *Financial support:* Career-related internships or fieldwork and Federal Work-Study available. Financial award application deadline: 4/15; financial award applicants required to submit FAFSA. *Faculty research:* Spiritual values and wellness issues in counseling, stress and professional burnout among counselors, thinking strategies, leadership, adaptive technology. *Unit head:* Dr. Karen P. Nery, Dean, 910-893-1631, Fax: 910-893-1999, E-mail: nery@campbell.edu. *Application contact:* Ranae Strickland, Coordinator of Graduate Admissions, 910-814-5515, Fax: 910-814-4718, E-mail: dstrickland@campbell.edu.
Website: http://www.campbell.edu/education/

Central Washington University, Graduate Studies and Research, Individual Studies Program, Ellensburg, WA 98926. Offers M Ed, MA, MS. Part-time programs available. *Degree requirements:* For master's, thesis. *Entrance requirements:* For master's, GRE General Test, minimum GPA of 3.0. Additional exam requirements/recommendations for international students: Required—TOEFL (minimum score 550 paper-based; 79 iBT). Electronic applications accepted.

Clarkson University, Graduate School, Wallace H. Coulter School of Engineering, Program in Interdisciplinary Engineering Science, Potsdam, NY 13699. Offers MS, PhD. Part-time programs available. *Students:* 6 full-time (0 women), 1 (woman) part-time, 2 international. Average age 45. 8 applicants, 63% accepted, 2 enrolled. In 2014, 3 doctorates awarded. Terminal master's awarded for partial completion of doctoral program. *Degree requirements:* For master's, thesis; for doctorate, comprehensive exam, thesis/dissertation, departmental qualifying exam. *Entrance requirements:* For master's and doctorate, GRE, transcripts of all college coursework, resume, personal statement, three letters of recommendation. Additional exam requirements/ recommendations for international students: Required—TOEFL (minimum score 550 paper-based; 80 iBT), IELTS (minimum score 6.5). *Application deadline:* For fall admission, 1/30 priority date for domestic and international students; for spring admission, 9/1 priority date for domestic and international students. Applications are processed on a rolling basis. Application fee: $25 ($35 for international students). Electronic applications accepted. *Expenses: Tuition:* Full-time $16,680; part-time $1390 per credit. *Required fees:* $295 per semester. *Financial support:* In 2014–15, 2 students received support, including fellowships with full tuition reimbursements available (averaging $24,029 per year), 1 research assistantship with full tuition reimbursement available (averaging $24,029 per year), teaching assistantships with full tuition reimbursements available (averaging $24,029 per year); scholarships/grants, tuition waivers (partial), and unspecified assistantships also available. *Unit head:* Dr. William Jemison, Dean, 315-268-6446, Fax: 315-268-4494, E-mail: wjemison@clarkson.edu. *Application contact:* Kelly Sharlow, Assistant to the Dean, 315-268-7929, Fax: 315-268-4494, E-mail: ksharlow@clarkson.edu.
Website: http://www.clarkson.edu/engineering/graduate/interdisciplinary.html

The College of William and Mary, Faculty of Arts and Sciences, Department of Applied Science, Williamsburg, VA 23187-8795. Offers accelerator science (PhD); applied mathematics (PhD); applied mechanics (PhD); applied robotics (PhD); applied science (MS); interface, thin film and surface science (PhD); lasers and optics (PhD); magnetic resonance (PhD); nanotechnology (PhD); non-destructive evaluation (PhD); polymer chemistry (PhD); remote sensing (PhD). Part-time programs available. *Faculty:* 8 full-time (2 women), 2 part-time/adjunct (0 women). *Students:* 28 full-time (11 women), 5 part-time (2 women); includes 5 minority (2 Black or African American, non-Hispanic/ Latino; 2 Asian, non-Hispanic/Latino; 1 Hispanic/Latino), 13 international. Average age 28. 32 applicants, 38% accepted, 7 enrolled. In 2014, 6 master's, 4 doctorates awarded. Terminal master's awarded for partial completion of doctoral program. *Degree requirements:* For master's, comprehensive exam, thesis; for doctorate, comprehensive exam, thesis/dissertation, 4 core courses. *Entrance requirements:* For master's and doctorate, GRE General Test, GRE Subject Test. Additional exam requirements/ recommendations for international students: Required—TOEFL, TWE. *Application deadline:* For fall admission, 2/3 priority date for domestic students, 2/3 for international students; for spring admission, 10/15 priority date for domestic students, 10/14 for international students. Applications are processed on a rolling basis. Application fee: $45. Electronic applications accepted. *Financial support:* Fellowships, research assistantships, teaching assistantships, Federal Work-Study, health care benefits, tuition waivers (full), and unspecified assistantships available. Financial award application deadline: 4/15; financial award applicants required to submit FAFSA. *Faculty research:* Computational biology, non-destructive evaluation, neurophysiology, lasers and optics. *Total annual research expenditures:* $1.7 million. *Unit head:* Dr. Christopher Del Negro, Chair, 757-221-7808, Fax: 757-221-2050, E-mail: cadeln@wm.edu. *Application contact:* Lianne Rios Ashburne, Graduate Program Coordinator, 757-221-2563, Fax: 757-221-2050, E-mail: lrashburne@wm.edu.
Website: http://www.wm.edu/as/appliedscience

Concordia University, School of Graduate Studies, Special Individualized Programs, Montréal, QC H3G 1M8, Canada. Offers M Sc, MA, PhD. *Degree requirements:* For master's, comprehensive exam, thesis; for doctorate, one foreign language, comprehensive exam, thesis/dissertation.

Dalhousie University, Faculty of Graduate Studies, Interdisciplinary PhD Program, Halifax, NS B3H 4H6, Canada. Offers PhD. *Degree requirements:* For doctorate, thesis/ dissertation. *Entrance requirements:* Additional exam requirements/recommendations for international students: Required—TOEFL, IELTS, CANTEST, CAEL, or Michigan English Language Assessment Battery. Electronic applications accepted. *Expenses:* Contact institution.

Dallas Baptist University, Professional Development Program, Dallas, TX 75211-9299. Offers business (MA); counseling (MA); criminal justice (MA); English as a second language (MA); higher education (MA); interdisciplinary (MA); leadership studies (MA); missions (MA); professional life coaching (MA); training and development (MA). Part-time and evening/weekend programs available. *Entrance requirements:* For master's, minimum GPA of 3.0. Additional exam requirements/recommendations for international students: Required—TOEFL, IELTS. *Expenses: Tuition:* Full-time $14,130; part-time $785 per credit hour. *Required fees:* $200 per semester. Tuition and fees vary according to course level and course load.

DePaul University, College of Liberal Arts and Social Sciences, Chicago, IL 60614. Offers Arabic (MA); Chinese (MA); English (MA); French (MA); German (MA); history (MA); interdisciplinary studies (MA, MS); international public service (MS); international studies (MA); Italian (MA); Japanese (MA); leadership and policy studies (MS); liberal studies (MA); new media studies (MA); nonprofit management (MNM); public administration (MPA); public health (MPH); public service management (MS); social work (MSW); sociology (MA); Spanish (MA); sustainable urban development (MA); women and gender studies (MA); writing and publishing (MA); writing, rhetoric, and discourse (MA); MA/PhD. Part-time and evening/weekend programs available. Postbaccalaureate distance learning degree programs offered (no on-campus study). Terminal master's awarded for partial completion of doctoral program. *Degree requirements:* For master's, variable foreign language requirement, comprehensive exam (for some programs), thesis (for some programs). Electronic applications accepted.

DeSales University, Graduate Division, Division of Liberal Arts and Social Sciences, Program in Education, Center Valley, PA 18034-9568. Offers early childhood education Pre K-4 (M Ed); interdisciplinary (M Ed). Part-time and evening/weekend programs available. Postbaccalaureate distance learning degree programs offered (no on-campus study). *Students:* 98 part-time. *Degree requirements:* For master's, thesis project. *Entrance requirements:* Additional exam requirements/recommendations for international students: Required—TOEFL. *Application deadline:* Applications are processed on a rolling basis. Electronic applications accepted. *Financial support:* Application deadline: 5/1. *Unit head:* Dr. Judith Rance-Roney, Chair, 610-282-1100 Ext. 1323, E-mail: judith.rance-roney@desales.edu. *Application contact:* Abigail Wernicki, Director of Graduate Admissions, 610-282-1100 Ext. 1768, E-mail: gradadmissions@desales.edu.

Drew University, Caspersen School of Graduate Studies, Program in Arts and Letters, Madison, NJ 07940-1493. Offers Holocaust and genocide studies (Certificate); interdisciplinary studies (M Litt, D Litt). Part-time and evening/weekend programs available. Terminal master's awarded for partial completion of doctoral program. *Degree requirements:* For master's, thesis optional; for doctorate, thesis/dissertation. *Entrance requirements:* For master's and doctorate, transcripts, writing sample, personal statement, recommendations. Additional exam requirements/recommendations for international students: Required—TOEFL (minimum score 585 paper-based; 95 iBT), TWE. *Expenses:* Contact institution. *Faculty research:* Interdisciplinary studies across art, literature, music, philosophy, religion, and history.

Eastern Washington University, Graduate Studies, Interdisciplinary Studies, Cheney, WA 99004-2431. Offers MA, MS. *Degree requirements:* For master's, comprehensive exam, thesis or alternative. *Entrance requirements:* For master's, minimum GPA of 3.0.

Emory University, Laney Graduate School, Graduate Institute of the Liberal Arts, Atlanta, GA 30322-1100. Offers PhD. *Degree requirements:* For doctorate, one foreign language, comprehensive exam, thesis/dissertation. *Entrance requirements:* For doctorate, GRE General Test. Additional exam requirements/recommendations for international students: Recommended—TOEFL. Electronic applications accepted. *Faculty research:* American cultural criticism, intellectual history, psychoanalysis, history of science, popular culture.

Fitchburg State University, Division of Graduate and Continuing Education, Program in Interdisciplinary Studies, Fitchburg, MA 01420-2697. Offers CAGS. Part-time and evening/weekend programs available. *Entrance requirements:* Additional exam requirements/recommendations for international students: Required—TOEFL (minimum score 550 paper-based; 79 iBT). Electronic applications accepted.

Florida Gulf Coast University, College of Health Professions and Social Work, Department of Health Sciences, Fort Myers, FL 33965-6565. Offers MS. Part-time and evening/weekend programs available. Postbaccalaureate distance learning degree programs offered (no on-campus study). *Faculty:* 58 full-time (42 women), 43 part-time/ adjunct (28 women). *Students:* 3 full-time (2 women), 47 part-time (31 women); includes 13 minority (8 Black or African American, non-Hispanic/Latino; 1 Asian, non-Hispanic/ Latino; 4 Hispanic/Latino). Average age 36. 31 applicants, 77% accepted, 18 enrolled. In 2014, 10 master's awarded. *Degree requirements:* For master's, final project or thesis. *Entrance requirements:* For master's, GRE General Test or MAT, minimum GPA of 3.0. Additional exam requirements/recommendations for international students: Required— TOEFL (minimum score 550 paper-based). *Application deadline:* For fall admission, 7/1 priority date for domestic students; for spring admission, 11/15 for domestic students. Applications are processed on a rolling basis. Application fee: $30. Electronic applications accepted. *Expenses:* Tuition, state resident: full-time $6974. Tuition, nonresident: full-time $28,170. *Required fees:* $1987. Tuition and fees vary according to course load. *Financial support:* In 2014–15, 10 students received support. Career-related internships or fieldwork available. Financial award application deadline: 6/30; financial award applicants required to submit FAFSA. *Faculty research:* Health services administration, gerontology, therapeutic recreation, health professions education, exercise physiology. *Unit head:* Dr. Joan Glacken, Chair, 239-590-7498, Fax: 239-590-7474, E-mail: jglacken@fgcu.edu. *Application contact:* Lynn O'Hare, Administrative Assistant, 239-590-7451, Fax: 239-590-7474, E-mail: lohare@fgcu.edu.
Website: http://www.fgcu.edu/chp/hs/

Florida Institute of Technology, Graduate Programs, College of Science, Program in Interdisciplinary Science, Melbourne, FL 32901-6975. Offers MS. *Students:* 2 full-time (0 women); includes 1 minority (Black or African American, non-Hispanic/Latino). Average age 23. 1 applicant, 100% accepted. In 2014, 9 master's awarded. *Degree requirements:* For master's, comprehensive exam (for some programs), thesis optional. *Entrance requirements:* For master's, STEM undergraduate degree, 2 letters of recommendations, resume, statement of objectives. Additional exam requirements/ recommendations for international students: Required—TOEFL (minimum score 550 paper-based; 79 iBT). *Application deadline:* Applications are processed on a rolling basis. Electronic applications accepted. *Expenses: Tuition:* Part-time $1179 per credit hour. Tuition and fees vary according to campus/location. *Financial support:* Applicants required to submit FAFSA. *Unit head:* Dr. Kastro Hamed, Department Head, 321-674-7206, Fax: 321-674-7598, E-mail: khamed@fit.edu. *Application contact:* Cheryl A.

Brown, Associate Director of Graduate Admissions, 321-674-7581, Fax: 321-723-9468, E-mail: cbrown@fit.edu. Website: http://cos.fit.edu/education/

Fresno Pacific University, Graduate Programs, Individualized Study Program, Fresno, CA 93702-4709. Offers MA. Part-time and evening/weekend programs available. *Degree requirements:* For master's, thesis. *Entrance requirements:* For master's, GMAT, GRE General Test, or MAT, interview. Additional exam requirements/recommendations for international students: Required—TOEFL (minimum score 550 paper-based). *Application deadline:* For fall admission, 7/15 for domestic and international students; for spring admission, 11/15 for domestic and international students. Applications are processed on a rolling basis. Application fee: $90. Electronic applications accepted. *Expenses:* Expenses: $545 per unit. *Financial support:* Scholarships/grants and tuition waivers (full and partial) available. Support available to part-time students. Financial award applicants required to submit FAFSA. *Unit head:* Dr. Rod Janzen, Program Director, 559-453-2210, Fax: 559-453-5558, E-mail: rajanzen@fresno.edu. *Application contact:* Amanda Krum-Stovall, Director of Graduate Admissions, 559-453-2016, E-mail: amanda.krum-stovall@fresno.edu.
Website: http://grad.fresno.edu/programs/individualized-master-arts-program-imap

Frostburg State University, Graduate School, College of Education, Department of Educational Professions, Program in Interdisciplinary Education, Frostburg, MD 21532-1099. Offers M Ed. Part-time and evening/weekend programs available. *Degree requirements:* For master's, thesis or alternative. *Entrance requirements:* Additional exam requirements/recommendations for international students: Required—TOEFL. Electronic applications accepted.

George Mason University, College of Humanities and Social Sciences, Interdisciplinary Studies Program, Fairfax, VA 22030. Offers community college teaching (MAIS); computational social science (MAIS); energy and sustainability (MAIS); film and video studies (MAIS); folklore studies (MAIS); higher education administration (MAIS); neuroethics (MAIS); religion, culture and values (MAIS); social entrepreneurship (MAIS); war and military in society (MAIS); women and gender studies (MAIS). *Faculty:* 11 full-time (3 women), 4 part-time/adjunct (all women). *Students:* 22 full-time (13 women), 87 part-time (51 women); includes 31 minority (21 Black or African American, non-Hispanic/Latino; 2 Asian, non-Hispanic/Latino; 6 Hispanic/Latino; 2 Two or more races, non-Hispanic/Latino), 6 international. Average age 32. 75 applicants, 75% accepted, 28 enrolled. In 2014, 31 master's awarded. *Degree requirements:* For master's, project or thesis. *Entrance requirements:* For master's, 3 letters of recommendation; writing sample; official transcript; resume. Additional exam requirements/recommendations for international students: Required—TOEFL (minimum score 570 paper-based; 80 iBT), IELTS (minimum score 6.5), PTE. *Application deadline:* For fall admission, 3/1 priority date for domestic students; for spring admission, 10/15 for domestic students. Application fee: $65 ($80 for international students). Electronic applications accepted. *Expenses:* Tuition, state resident: full-time $9794; part-time $408 per credit hour. Tuition, nonresident: full-time $26,978; part-time $1124 per credit hour. *Required fees:* $2820; $118 per credit hour. Tuition and fees vary according to course load and program. *Financial support:* In 2014–15, 10 students received support, including 1 fellowship (averaging $6,935 per year), 2 research assistantships with full and partial tuition reimbursements available (averaging $6,499 per year), 8 teaching assistantships with full and partial tuition reimbursements available (averaging $8,271 per year); career-related internships or fieldwork, Federal Work-Study, scholarships/grants, unspecified assistantships, and health care benefits (for full-time research or teaching assistantship recipients) also available. Support available to part-time students. Financial award application deadline: 3/1; financial award applicants required to submit FAFSA. *Faculty research:* Combined English and folklore, religious and cultural studies (Christianity and Muslim society). *Unit head:* Meredith H. Lair, Director, 703-993-2159, Fax: 703-993-1251, E-mail: mlair@gmu.edu. *Application contact:* Lisa Struckmeyer, Administrative Coordinator, 703-993-8762, Fax: 703-993-5585, E-mail: lstruckm@gmu.edu.
Website: http://mais.gmu.edu

George Mason University, College of Humanities and Social Sciences, Program in Global Affairs, Fairfax, VA 22030. Offers MA. *Faculty:* 19 full-time (8 women), 4 part-time/adjunct (3 women). *Students:* 25 full-time (10 women), 31 part-time (24 women); includes 23 minority (6 Black or African American, non-Hispanic/Latino; 6 Asian, non-Hispanic/Latino; 9 Hispanic/Latino; 2 Two or more races, non-Hispanic/Latino), 3 international. Average age 28. 78 applicants, 72% accepted, 23 enrolled. In 2014, 33 master's awarded. *Degree requirements:* For master's, capstone seminar. *Entrance requirements:* For master's, GRE, expanded goals statement, 2 letters of recommendation, evidence of professional competency in a second language tested through Language Testing International or other means approved by the department. Additional exam requirements/recommendations for international students: Required—TOEFL (minimum score 570 paper-based; 80 iBT), IELTS (minimum score 6.5), PTE. *Application deadline:* For fall admission, 3/15 for domestic students, 2/15 for international students; for spring admission, 10/15 for domestic students, 9/15 for international students. Application fee: $65 ($80 for international students). *Expenses:* Tuition, state resident: full-time $9794; part-time $408 per credit hour. Tuition, nonresident: full-time $26,978; part-time $1124 per credit hour. *Required fees:* $2820; $118 per credit hour. Tuition and fees vary according to course load and program. *Financial support:* Career-related internships or fieldwork, Federal Work-Study, and health care benefits (for full-time research or teaching assistantship recipients) available. Financial award application deadline: 3/1; financial award applicants required to submit FAFSA. *Faculty research:* Social movements, globalization, law and economics, comparative politics, global environmentalism and governance, international business and economic development. *Unit head:* Lisa Breglia, Director, 703-993-9184, Fax: 703-993-1244, E-mail: lbreglia@gmu.edu. *Application contact:* Erin McSherry, Graduate Coordinator, 703-993-5056, Fax: 703-993-1244, E-mail: emcsherr@gmu.edu.
Website: http://globalaffairs.gmu.edu

Georgetown University, Graduate School of Arts and Sciences, School of Continuing Studies, Washington, DC 20057. Offers American studies (MALS); Catholic studies (MALS); classical civilizations (MALS); emergency and disaster management (MPS); ethics and the professions (MALS); hospitality management (MPS); human resources management (MPS); humanities (MALS); individualized study (MALS); international affairs (MALS); Islam and Muslim-Christian relations (MALS); journalism (MPS); liberal studies (DLS); literature and society (MALS); medieval and early modern European studies (MALS); public relations and corporate communications (MPS); real estate (MPS); religious studies (MALS); social and public policy (MALS); sports industry management (MPS); systems engineering management (MPS); technology management (MPS); the theory and practice of American democracy (MALS); urban and regional planning (MPS); visual culture (MALS). MPS in systems engineering management offered jointly with Stevens Institute of Technology. *Entrance requirements:* Additional exam requirements/recommendations for international students: Required—TOEFL.

Goddard College, Graduate Division, Master of Arts in Individualized Studies Program, Plainfield, VT 05667-9432. Offers consciousness studies (MA); transformative language arts (MA). Part-time programs available. *Faculty:* 3 full-time (all women), 7 part-time/adjunct (6 women). *Students:* 15 full-time, 10 part-time. Average age 35. 11 applicants, 91% accepted, 10 enrolled. In 2014, 22 master's awarded. *Degree requirements:* For master's, thesis. *Entrance requirements:* For master's, 3 letters of recommendation, interview. *Application deadline:* Applications are processed on a rolling basis. Application fee: $40. Electronic applications accepted. *Expenses:* Expenses: Contact institution. *Financial support:* Scholarships/grants and tuition waivers (full and partial) available. Financial award applicants required to submit FAFSA. *Unit head:* Ruth Farmer, Director, 802-454-8311, Fax: 802-454-7835, E-mail: ruth.farmer@goddard.edu. *Application contact:* Chip Cummings, Admissions Counselor, 800-468-4888 Ext. 221, Fax: 802-454-1029, E-mail: chip.cummings@goddard.edu.
Website: http://www.goddard.edu/academics/ma/individualized-master-arts/

The Graduate Center, City University of New York, Graduate Studies, Interdisciplinary Studies, New York, NY 10016-4039. Offers language in social context (PhD); medieval studies (PhD); public policy (MA, PhD); urban studies (MA, PhD); women's studies (MA, PhD). Terminal master's awarded for partial completion of doctoral program. *Degree requirements:* For master's, thesis; for doctorate, comprehensive exam, thesis/dissertation. *Entrance requirements:* For master's and doctorate, GRE General Test.

Harrison Middleton University, Graduate Program, Tempe, AZ 85282. Offers education (MA, Ed D); humanities (MA); imaginative literature (MA); interdisciplinary studies (DA); jurisprudence (MA); natural science (MA); philosophy and religion (MA); social science (MA). Part-time and evening/weekend programs available. Postbaccalaureate distance learning degree programs offered (no on-campus study). *Degree requirements:* For master's and doctorate, capstone project. *Entrance requirements:* For master's, interview; for doctorate, 2 academic letters of reference, interview, essay. Additional exam requirements/recommendations for international students: Required—TOEFL (minimum score 550 paper-based; 80 iBT). Electronic applications accepted. *Faculty research:* Japanese animation, educational leadership, war art, John Muir's wilderness.

Hiram College, Graduate Studies, Hiram, OH 44234-0067. Offers MAIS. Part-time and evening/weekend programs available. *Degree requirements:* For master's, two seminars, capstone research project. *Entrance requirements:* For master's, bachelor's degree from an accredited institution, 2 letters of recommendation, writing sample, interview.

Hollins University, Graduate Programs, Program in Liberal Studies, Roanoke, VA 24020. Offers humanities (MALS); interdisciplinary studies (MALS); leadership (MALS); liberal studies (CAS); social science (MALS); visual and performing arts (MALS). Part-time and evening/weekend programs available. *Students:* 3 full-time (all women), 37 part-time (32 women); includes 6 minority (4 Black or African American, non-Hispanic/Latino; 1 Hispanic/Latino; 1 Two or more races, non-Hispanic/Latino). Average age 44. 13 applicants, 100% accepted, 9 enrolled. In 2014, 15 master's awarded. *Degree requirements:* For master's, thesis. *Entrance requirements:* For master's, letters of recommendation, interview. Additional exam requirements/recommendations for international students: Required—TOEFL (minimum score 550 paper-based; 79 iBT). *Application deadline:* For fall admission, 7/1 priority date for domestic and international students; for spring admission, 12/10 priority date for domestic and international students. Applications are processed on a rolling basis. Application fee: $40. Electronic applications accepted. *Financial support:* In 2014–15, 7 students received support, including 7 fellowships (averaging $1,000 per year); scholarships/grants also available. Support available to part-time students. Financial award application deadline: 7/15; financial award applicants required to submit FAFSA. *Faculty research:* Diversity, gender and women's studies, political science, leadership. *Unit head:* Dr. Joe Leedom, Director, 540-362-6326, Fax: 540-362-6288, E-mail: jleedom@hollins.edu. *Application contact:* Cathy S. Koon, Manager of Graduate Services, 540-362-6326, Fax: 540-362-6288, E-mail: ckoon@hollins.edu.
Website: http://www.hollins.edu/

Idaho State University, Office of Graduate Studies, Department of Interdisciplinary Studies, Pocatello, ID 83209. Offers general interdisciplinary (M Ed, MA, MNS); waste management and environmental science (MS). Part-time programs available. *Degree requirements:* For master's, comprehensive exam, thesis optional. *Entrance requirements:* For master's, GRE General Test or MAT, minimum GPA of 3.0. Additional exam requirements/recommendations for international students: Required—TOEFL (minimum score 550 paper-based; 80 iBT).

Indiana University Southeast, Master of Interdisciplinary Studies Program, New Albany, IN 47150-6405. Offers MIS, MIS, Graduate Certificate. *Students:* 1 (woman) full-time, 17 part-time (13 women); includes 3 minority (2 Black or African American, non-Hispanic/Latino; 1 American Indian or Alaska Native, non-Hispanic/Latino). Average age 42. 12 applicants, 75% accepted, 9 enrolled. In 2014, 7 master's, 5 other advanced degrees awarded. *Degree requirements:* For master's, thesis or alternative. *Entrance requirements:* For master's, 3 letters of recommendation. *Unit head:* Dr. Deborah Finkel, MLS Director, 812-941-2668, E-mail: sfrench@ius.edu.
Website: http://www.ius.edu/mls/

Iowa State University of Science and Technology, Program in Interdisciplinary Graduate Studies, Ames, IA 50011. Offers MA, MS. *Entrance requirements:* For master's, GRE. Additional exam requirements/recommendations for international students: Recommended—TOEFL (minimum score 550 paper-based; 79 iBT), IELTS (minimum score 6.5). Electronic applications accepted.

Lehigh University, P.C. Rossin College of Engineering and Applied Science and College of Arts and Sciences, Center for Polymer Science and Engineering, Bethlehem, PA 18015. Offers M Eng, MS, PhD. Part-time and evening/weekend programs available. Postbaccalaureate distance learning degree programs offered (no on-campus study). *Faculty:* 19 full-time (1 woman), 1 part-time/adjunct (0 women). *Students:* 2 full-time (1 woman), 17 part-time (2 women); includes 1 minority (Asian, non-Hispanic/Latino). Average age 31. 29 applicants, 21% accepted, 4 enrolled. In 2014, 4 master's, 3 doctorates awarded. Terminal master's awarded for partial completion of doctoral program. *Degree requirements:* For master's, thesis (for some programs); for doctorate, thesis/dissertation. *Entrance requirements:* For master's and doctorate, GRE General Test. Additional exam requirements/recommendations for international students: Required—TOEFL (minimum score 487 paper-based; 85 iBT). *Application deadline:* For fall admission, 7/15 for domestic students, 1/15 for international students; for spring admission, 12/1 for domestic and international students. Applications are processed on a rolling basis. Application fee: $75. Electronic applications accepted. *Financial support:* In 2014–15, 1 student received support, including 1 fellowship (averaging $26,500 per year), 1 research assistantship (averaging $1,000 per year). Financial award application deadline: 1/15. *Faculty research:* Polymer colloids, polymer coatings, blends and composites, polymer interfaces, emulsion polymer. *Unit head:* Dr. Raymond A. Pearson, Director, 610-758-3857, Fax: 610-758-3526, E-mail: rp02@lehigh.edu. *Application contact:* James E. Roberts, Chair, Polymer Education Committee, 610-758-4841, Fax: 610-758-6536, E-mail: jer1@lehigh.edu.
Website: http://www.lehigh.edu/~inpcreng/academics/graduate/polymerscieng.html

Lesley University, Graduate School of Arts and Social Sciences, Cambridge, MA 02138-2790. Offers clinical mental health counseling (MA), including holistic counseling, school and community counseling, trauma studies; counseling psychology (MA, CAGS),

including professional counseling (MA), school counseling (MA); creative writing (MFA); expressive therapies (MA, PhD, CAGS), including art (MA), clinical mental health counseling (MA), dance (MA), expressive therapies (MA), music (MA); independent studies (CAGS); independent study (MA); intercultural relations (MA, CAGS); interdisciplinary studies (MA), including individualized studies, integrative holistic health, mindfulness studies, peace and conflict transformation, trauma sensitive assessment, intervention, and consultation, women's studies; urban environmental leadership (MA). Part-time programs available. Postbaccalaureate distance learning degree programs offered (no on-campus study). *Faculty:* 35 full-time (25 women), 115 part-time/adjunct (90 women). *Students:* 420 full-time (379 women), 514 part-time (414 women); includes 142 minority (50 Black or African American, non-Hispanic/Latino; 5 American Indian or Alaska Native, non-Hispanic/Latino; 16 Asian, non-Hispanic/Latino; 48 Hispanic/Latino; 23 Two or more races, non-Hispanic/Latino), 46 international. Average age 33. In 2014, 475 master's, 11 doctorates, 4 other advanced degrees awarded. *Degree requirements:* For master's, internship, practicum, thesis (for expressive therapies); for doctorate, thesis/dissertation, arts apprenticeship, field placement; for CAGS, thesis, internship (for counseling psychology, expressive therapies). *Entrance requirements:* For master's, MAT (counseling psychology), interview, writing samples, art portfolio; for doctorate, GRE or MAT, interview, master's degree; for CAGS, interview, master's degree. Additional exam requirements/recommendations for international students: Required—TOEFL (minimum score 550 paper-based; 80 iBT). *Application deadline:* Applications are processed on a rolling basis. Application fee: $50. Electronic applications accepted. *Financial support:* Fellowships, career-related internships or fieldwork, Federal Work-Study, scholarships/grants, tuition waivers, and unspecified assistantships available. Financial award applicants required to submit FAFSA. *Faculty research:* Psychotherapy and culture; psychotherapy and psychological trauma; women's issues in art, teaching and psychotherapy; community-based art, psycho-spiritual inquiry. *Unit head:* Dr. Catherine Koverola, Dean, 617-349-8317, Fax: 617-349-8366, E-mail: koverola@lesley.edu. *Application contact:* Martha Sheehan, Director, Graduate Admissions, 888-LESLEYU, Fax: 617-349-8313, E-mail: info@lesley.edu. Website: http://www.lesley.edu/graduate-school-of-arts-and-social-sciences/

Marquette University, Graduate School, Interdisciplinary PhD Program, Milwaukee, WI 53201-1881. Offers PhD. Part-time programs available. *Degree requirements:* For doctorate, thesis/dissertation. *Entrance requirements:* For doctorate, GRE General Test. Additional exam requirements/recommendations for international students: Required—TOEFL (minimum score 630 paper-based). Electronic applications accepted.

Marylhurst University, Department of Interdisciplinary Studies, Marylhurst, OR 97036-0261. Offers MA, MA, MA. Part-time and evening/weekend programs available. *Students:* 29 part-time (24 women); includes 4 minority (2 Native Hawaiian or other Pacific Islander, non-Hispanic/Latino; 2 Two or more races, non-Hispanic/Latino). In 2014, 8 master's awarded. *Degree requirements:* For master's, thesis. *Entrance requirements:* For master's, official transcripts from all previous institutions, personal statement, 2 letters of recommendation, writing sample, interview. Additional exam requirements/recommendations for international students: Required—IELTS (minimum score 6.5), PTE (minimum score 53); Recommended—TOEFL (minimum score 550 paper-based; 79 iBT). *Application deadline:* Applications are processed on a rolling basis. Application fee: $50. Electronic applications accepted. *Expenses: Tuition:* Full-time $21,096; part-time $586 per credit. Tuition and fees vary according to course load, campus/location and program. *Financial support:* Scholarships/grants available. Support available to part-time students. Financial award applicants required to submit FAFSA. *Faculty research:* World religions, spirituality and literature, philosophy, humanities. *Unit head:* Dr. Susan G. Carter, Chair, 503-636-8141, Fax: 503-697-5597, E-mail: scarter@marylhurst.edu. *Application contact:* Maruska Lynch, Graduate Admissions Counselor, 800-634-9982 Ext. 6322, Fax: 503-699-6320, E-mail: admissions@marylhurst.edu. Website: http://www.marylhurst.edu

Marywood University, Academic Affairs, Center for Interdisciplinary Studies, Scranton, PA 18509-1598. Offers human development (PhD), including educational administration, health promotion, higher education administration, instructional leadership, social work. Part-time programs available. *Students:* 31 full-time (21 women), 36 part-time (23 women); includes 3 minority (1 Black or African American, non-Hispanic/Latino; 2 Hispanic/Latino), 2 international. Average age 39. 30 applicants, 63% accepted, 15 enrolled. In 2014, 11 doctorates awarded. *Application deadline:* For fall admission, 1/30 for domestic and international students. Applications are processed on a rolling basis. Application fee: $35. Electronic applications accepted. *Expenses:* Expenses: $885 per credit. *Financial support:* Application deadline: 6/30; applicants required to submit FAFSA. *Unit head:* Dr. Deborah Hokien, Director, 570-348-6279, E-mail: hokien@marywood.edu. *Application contact:* Tammy Manka, Assistant Director of Graduate Admissions, 570-348-6211 Ext. 2322, E-mail: tmanka@marywood.edu. Website: http://www.marywood.edu/academics/gradcatalog/

Massachusetts College of Art and Design, Graduate Programs, MFA Program, Boston, MA 02115-5882. Offers 2D fine arts (MFA), including painting; 3D fine arts (MFA), including ceramics, fibers, glass, jewelry and metalsmithing, sculpture; design (MFA, Postbaccalaureate Certificate), including dynamic media; fine arts (MFA), including interdisciplinary; media arts (MFA, Postbaccalaureate Certificate), including film/video (MFA), photography. *Accreditation:* NASAD. *Faculty:* 31 full-time (15 women), 42 part-time/adjunct (19 women). *Students:* 59 full-time (36 women), 32 part-time (23 women); includes 12 minority (2 Black or African American, non-Hispanic/Latino; 5 Asian, non-Hispanic/Latino; 5 Hispanic/Latino), 18 international. 278 applicants, 38% accepted, 40 enrolled. In 2014, 33 master's, 7 other advanced degrees awarded. *Degree requirements:* For master's, thesis, Exhibition for MFA non design. Thesis document MFA in design and low-residency. *Entrance requirements:* For master's, portfolio, college transcripts, resume, statement of purpose, letters of reference, interview; 6 credits of art history taken prior to or during MFA program; for Postbaccalaureate Certificate, portfolio, college transcripts, resume, statement of purpose, letters of reference, interview. Additional exam requirements/recommendations for international students: Required—TOEFL (minimum score 550 paper-based; 85 iBT); Recommended—IELTS (minimum score 6.5). *Application deadline:* For fall admission, 1/6 priority date for domestic and international students. Application fee: $75. Electronic applications accepted. *Expenses:* Tuition, state resident: full-time $23,400; part-time $780 per credit. Tuition, nonresident: full-time $23,400; part-time $780 per credit. Tuition and fees vary according to course load and program. *Financial support:* In 2014–15, 37 students received support, including 40 teaching assistantships (averaging $2,160 per year); career-related internships or fieldwork, scholarships/grants, tuition waivers (partial), and unspecified assistantships also available. Support available to part-time students. Financial award application deadline: 1/6. *Unit head:* Paul Paturzo, Interim Dean of Graduate Studies, 617-879-7166, E-mail: pjpaturzo@massart.edu. *Application contact:* Isaac Goldstein, Graduate Admissions Counselor, 617-879-7203, Fax: 617-879-7250, E-mail: igoldstein@massart.edu. Website: http://www.massart.edu/Admissions/Graduate_Programs.html

Michigan Technological University, Graduate School, Interdisciplinary Programs, Houghton, MI 49931. Offers atmospheric sciences (PhD); biochemistry and molecular biology (PhD); computational science and engineering (PhD); environmental engineering (PhD); interdisciplinary studies (M Ed, MS, Graduate Certificate). Part-time programs available. *Faculty:* 6 full-time, 3 part-time/adjunct. *Students:* 46 full-time (20 women), 6 part-time (3 women); includes 2 minority (1 Asian, non-Hispanic/Latino; 1 Two or more races, non-Hispanic/Latino), 35 international. Average age 30. 239 applicants, 16% accepted, 9 enrolled. In 2014, 4 doctorates awarded. Terminal master's awarded for partial completion of doctoral program. *Degree requirements:* For master's, comprehensive exam (for some programs), thesis (for some programs); for doctorate, comprehensive exam, thesis/dissertation. *Entrance requirements:* For master's, doctorate, and Graduate Certificate, GRE, statement of purpose, official transcripts, 2-3 letters of recommendation. Additional exam requirements/recommendations for international students: Required—TOEFL or IELTS. *Application deadline:* Applications are processed on a rolling basis. Electronic applications accepted. *Expenses:* Tuition, state resident: full-time $14,769; part-time $820.50 per credit. Tuition, nonresident: full-time $14,769; part-time $820.50 per credit. *Required fees:* $248; $248 per year. Tuition and fees vary according to course load and program. *Financial support:* In 2014–15, 42 students received support, including 6 fellowships with full and partial tuition reimbursements available (averaging $13,824 per year), 25 research assistantships with full and partial tuition reimbursements available (averaging $13,824 per year), 4 teaching assistantships with full and partial tuition reimbursements available (averaging $13,824 per year); career-related internships or fieldwork, Federal Work-Study, scholarships/grants, health care benefits, unspecified assistantships, and cooperative program also available. Financial award applicants required to submit FAFSA. *Faculty research:* Big data, atmospheric sciences, bioinformatics and systems biology, molecular dynamics. *Unit head:* Dr. Jacqueline E. Huntoon, Dean, 906-487-2327, Fax: 906-487-2284, E-mail: jeh@mtu.edu. *Application contact:* Carol T. Wingerson, Administrative Aide, 906-487-2328, Fax: 906-487-2284, E-mail: gradadms@mtu.edu.

Mills College, Graduate Studies, Program in Computer Science, Oakland, CA 94613-1000. Offers computer science (Certificate); interdisciplinary computer science (MA). Part-time programs available. *Faculty:* 4 full-time (3 women), 2 part-time/adjunct (1 woman). *Students:* 16 full-time (all women); includes 9 minority (4 Asian, non-Hispanic/Latino; 4 Hispanic/Latino; 1 Two or more races, non-Hispanic/Latino). Average age 28. 26 applicants, 85% accepted, 9 enrolled. In 2014, 2 master's awarded. *Degree requirements:* For master's, thesis. *Entrance requirements:* For master's, three letters of recommendation. Additional exam requirements/recommendations for international students: Required—TOEFL (minimum score 600 paper-based; 100 iBT) or IELTS (minimum score 7). *Application deadline:* For fall admission, 2/1 priority date for domestic students, 12/15 for international students; for spring admission, 11/1 priority date for domestic students, 10/1 for international students. Applications are processed on a rolling basis. Application fee: $50. Electronic applications accepted. *Expenses: Tuition:* Full-time $31,620; part-time $7905 per course. *Required fees:* $1118. *Financial support:* In 2014–15, 4 students received support, including 13 fellowships with full and partial tuition reimbursements available (averaging $4,173 per year), 4 teaching assistantships with full and partial tuition reimbursements available (averaging $1,866 per year); career-related internships or fieldwork, institutionally sponsored loans, and scholarships/grants also available. Support available to part-time students. Financial award application deadline: 2/1; financial award applicants required to submit FAFSA. *Faculty research:* Dynamical systems, linear programming, theory of computer viruses, interface design, intelligent tutoring systems. *Total annual research expenditures:* $7,483. *Unit head:* Susan S. Wang, Department Head, 510-430-2138, E-mail: wang@mills.edu. *Application contact:* Shrim Bathey, Director of Graduate Admission, 510-430-3309, Fax: 510-430-2159, E-mail: grad-admission@mills.edu. Website: http://www.mills.edu/ics

Minnesota State University Mankato, College of Graduate Studies, Program in Cross-disciplinary Studies, Mankato, MN 56001. Offers MS. Part-time and evening/weekend programs available. *Degree requirements:* For master's, comprehensive exam, thesis or alternative. *Entrance requirements:* For master's, GRE General Test, minimum GPA of 3.0 during previous 2 years. Additional exam requirements/recommendations for international students: Required—TOEFL. *Application deadline:* For fall admission, 7/1 priority date for domestic students; for spring admission, 11/1 for domestic students. Applications are processed on a rolling basis. Application fee: $40. Electronic applications accepted. *Financial support:* Research assistantships with full tuition reimbursements, teaching assistantships with full tuition reimbursements, career-related internships or fieldwork, Federal Work-Study, and unspecified assistantships available. Support available to part-time students. Financial award application deadline: 3/15; financial award applicants required to submit FAFSA. *Unit head:* Chris Mickle, Graduate Coordinator, 507-389-2321. *Application contact:* 507-389-2321, E-mail: grad@mnsu.edu.

Montana State University Billings, College of Education, Department of Educational Theory and Practice, Option in Interdisciplinary Studies, Billings, MT 59101. Offers M Ed. *Degree requirements:* For master's, thesis or alternative. *Entrance requirements:* For master's, GRE General Test or MAT, minimum GPA of 3.0 (undergraduate), 3.25 (graduate). *Application deadline:* For fall admission, 7/15 for domestic students; for spring admission, 12/1 for domestic students. Applications are processed on a rolling basis. Application fee: $40. *Financial support:* Teaching assistantships, career-related internships or fieldwork, Federal Work-Study, institutionally sponsored loans, scholarships/grants, tuition waivers (partial), and unspecified assistantships available. Support available to part-time students. Financial award application deadline: 5/1; financial award applicants required to submit FAFSA. *Unit head:* Dr. Tony Hecimovic, Professor, 406-657-2210, Fax: 406-657-2807, E-mail: thecimovic@msubillings.edu. *Application contact:* David M. Sullivan, Graduate Studies Counselor, 406-657-2053, Fax: 406-657-2299, E-mail: dsullivan@msubillings.edu.

Montana Tech of The University of Montana, Graduate School, Interdisciplinary Program, Butte, MT 59701-8997. Offers MS. Part-time programs available. *Degree requirements:* For master's, comprehensive exam (for some programs), thesis optional. *Entrance requirements:* For master's, GRE General Test, minimum GPA of 3.0. Additional exam requirements/recommendations for international students: Required—TOEFL (minimum score 525 paper-based; 71 iBT). *Expenses:* Tuition, state resident: full-time $5802; part-time $241 per credit. Tuition, nonresident: full-time $15,895; part-time $662 per credit. *Required fees:* $1516; $414 per credit. $207 per semester. One-time fee: $30.

New Mexico State University, Graduate School, Interdisciplinary Program, Las Cruces, NM 88003-8001. Offers MA, MS, PhD. Part-time programs available. Postbaccalaureate distance learning degree programs offered (minimal on-campus study). *Students:* 7 full-time (4 women), 26 part-time (13 women); includes 9 minority (2 Black or African American, non-Hispanic/Latino; 1 Asian, non-Hispanic/Latino; 6 Hispanic/Latino), 3 international. Average age 45. 15 applicants, 73% accepted, 1 enrolled. In 2014, 5 master's, 1 doctorate awarded. *Degree requirements:* For master's, comprehensive exam, thesis; for doctorate, comprehensive exam, thesis/dissertation. *Entrance requirements:* For master's, GRE General Test, minimum GPA of 2.5; for doctorate, GRE General Test, minimum GPA of 3.0. Additional exam requirements/recommendations for international students: Required—TOEFL (minimum score 550 paper-based; 79 iBT), IELTS (minimum score 6.5). *Application deadline:* Applications are processed on a rolling basis. Application fee: $40 ($50 for international students).

Electronic applications accepted. *Expenses:* Tuition, state resident: full-time $3969; part-time $220.50 per credit hour. Tuition, nonresident: full-time $13,838; part-time $768.80 per credit hour. *Required fees:* $853; $47.40 per credit hour. *Financial support:* In 2014–15, 6 students received support, including 4 teaching assistantships (averaging $12,069 per year); career-related internships or fieldwork, Federal Work-Study, scholarships/grants, traineeships, health care benefits, and unspecified assistantships also available. Support available to part-time students. Financial award application deadline: 3/1. *Unit head:* James Maupin, Academic Department Head, 575-646-3195, E-mail: jmaupin@nmsu.edu.
Website: http://idsas.nmsu.edu

New York University, Gallatin School of Individualized Study, New York, NY 10003. Offers MA. Part-time and evening/weekend programs available. *Faculty:* 60 full-time (35 women), 116 part-time/adjunct (64 women). *Students:* 74 full-time (54 women), 69 part-time (47 women); includes 40 minority (18 Black or African American, non-Hispanic/Latino; 8 Asian, non-Hispanic/Latino; 8 Hispanic/Latino; 6 Two or more races, non-Hispanic/Latino), 22 international. Average age 34. 190 applicants, 51% accepted, 39 enrolled. In 2014, 50 master's awarded. *Degree requirements:* For master's, thesis, Gallatin Proseminar, Gallatin Elective, Masters Thesis Seminars. *Entrance requirements:* Additional exam requirements/recommendations for international students: Required—TOEFL. *Application deadline:* For fall admission, 1/15 priority date for domestic and international students; for spring admission, 10/1 for domestic and international students. Applications are processed on a rolling basis. Application fee: $50. Electronic applications accepted. *Expenses:* Expenses: Contact institution. *Financial support:* In 2014–15, 53 students received support, including 1 fellowship with partial tuition reimbursement available (averaging $5,000 per year), 3 research assistantships with full tuition reimbursements available (averaging $20,077 per year); Federal Work-Study, scholarships/grants, and unspecified assistantships also available. Support available to part-time students. Financial award application deadline: 2/1; financial award applicants required to submit FAFSA. *Faculty research:* Arts and performance studies, media studies, political and social thought, literary and cultural studies, environmental and global studies, gender studies. *Application contact:* Frances R. Levin, Director of Enrollment, 212-998-7349, E-mail: gallatin.gradadmissions@nyu.edu.
Website: http://www.gallatin.nyu.edu

Niagara University, Graduate Division of Arts and Sciences, Program in Interdisciplinary Studies, Niagara University, NY 14109. Offers MA. Part-time programs available. *Faculty:* 7 full-time (3 women), 1 part-time/adjunct (0 women). *Students:* 1 full-time (0 women), 10 part-time (6 women); includes 1 minority (Hispanic/Latino). Average age 42. In 2014, 8 master's awarded. *Entrance requirements:* Additional exam requirements/recommendations for international students: Required—TOEFL (minimum score 550 paper-based, 79 iBT), IELTS (minimum score 6), or GMAT/GRE (minimum score 600). *Application deadline:* For fall admission, 8/1 for domestic students. Applications are processed on a rolling basis. Application fee: $30. Tuition and fees vary according to program. *Financial support:* Research assistantships with full and partial tuition reimbursements, teaching assistantships with full and partial tuition reimbursements, career-related internships or fieldwork, Federal Work-Study, scholarships/grants, and unspecified assistantships available. Financial award application deadline: 4/15; financial award applicants required to submit FAFSA. *Unit head:* Dr. Mustafa Gokcek, Director, 716-286-8195, E-mail: gokcek@niagara.edu. *Application contact:* Evan Pierce, Associate Director of Graduate Recruitment, 716-286-8769, Fax: 716-286-8710, E-mail: epierce@niagara.edu.
Website: http://www.niagara.edu/mais

Northeastern University, College of Engineering, Boston, MA 02115-5096. Offers bioengineering (PhD); chemical engineering (MS, PhD); civil engineering (MS, PhD); computer engineering (PhD); computer systems engineering (MS); electrical and computer engineering (MS); electrical and engineering leadership (MS); electrical engineering (PhD); energy systems (MS); engineering leadership (Certificate); engineering management (MRTP); industrial engineering (MS, PhD); information assurance (PhD); information systems (MS); interdisciplinary (PhD); mechanical engineering (MS, PhD); operations research (MS); telecommunication systems management (MS). Part-time programs available. *Expenses:* Contact institution.

Nova Southeastern University, Graduate School of Humanities and Social Sciences, Fort Lauderdale, FL 33314-7796. Offers advanced conflict resolution practice (Graduate Certificate); college student affairs (MS); conflict analysis and resolution (MS, PhD); cross-disciplinary studies (MA); family studies (Graduate Certificate); family systems health care (Graduate Certificate); family therapy (MS, PhD); marriage and family therapy (DMFT); peace studies (Graduate Certificate); qualitative research (Graduate Certificate); solution focused coaching (Graduate Certificate). *Accreditation:* AAMFT/COAMFTE (one or more programs are accredited). Part-time and evening/weekend programs available. Postbaccalaureate distance learning degree programs offered (minimal on-campus study). *Faculty:* 29 full-time (18 women), 27 part-time/adjunct (21 women). *Students:* 502 full-time (363 women), 269 part-time (189 women); includes 415 minority (241 Black or African American, non-Hispanic/Latino; 1 American Indian or Alaska Native, non-Hispanic/Latino; 16 Asian, non-Hispanic/Latino; 136 Hispanic/Latino; 21 Two or more races, non-Hispanic/Latino), 56 international. Average age 37. 424 applicants, 58% accepted, 161 enrolled. In 2014, 140 master's, 50 doctorates, 11 other advanced degrees awarded. *Degree requirements:* For master's, thesis optional, comprehensive exams, portfolios (for some programs), table-top exams (for some programs); for doctorate, comprehensive exam, thesis/dissertation, qualifying exams, portfolios (for some programs). *Entrance requirements:* For master's, interview, minimum GPA of 3.0, writing sample; for doctorate, interview, minimum GPA of 3.5, master's degree in related field, writing sample; for Graduate Certificate, minimum GPA of 3.0. Additional exam requirements/recommendations for international students: Required—TOEFL. *Application deadline:* For fall admission, 5/17 priority date for domestic and international students; for winter admission, 12/1 priority date for domestic and international students; for spring admission, 4/1 priority date for domestic and international students. Applications are processed on a rolling basis. Application fee: $50. Electronic applications accepted. *Financial support:* In 2014–15, 7 students received support, including 26 research assistantships (averaging $15,000 per year); career-related internships or fieldwork, Federal Work-Study, scholarships/grants, and unspecified assistantships also available. Financial award application deadline: 4/1; financial award applicants required to submit CSS PROFILE. *Faculty research:* Conflict resolution, family therapy, peace research, international conflict, multi-disciplinary studies, college student affairs, national security affairs, health care conflict resolution, family systems health care, advanced family systems, qualitative research, solution-focused coaching. *Unit head:* Dr. Honggang Yang, Dean, 954-262-3016, Fax: 954-262-3968, E-mail: yangh@nova.edu. *Application contact:* Marcia Arango, Student Recruitment Coordinator, 954-262-3006, Fax: 954-262-3968, E-mail: marango@nsu.nova.edu.
Website: http://shss.nova.edu/

The Ohio State University, Graduate School, College of Arts and Sciences, Division of Arts and Humanities, Department of Comparative Studies, Columbus, OH 43210. Offers MA, PhD. *Faculty:* 19. *Students:* 24 full-time (12 women); includes 5 minority (2 Black or African American, non-Hispanic/Latino; 2 Asian, non-Hispanic/Latino; 1 Hispanic/Latino), 7 international. Average age 31. In 2014, 5 master's, 7 doctorates awarded. Terminal master's awarded for partial completion of doctoral program. *Degree requirements:* For doctorate, thesis/dissertation. *Entrance requirements:* For master's and doctorate, GRE General Test. Additional exam requirements/recommendations for international students: Required—TOEFL (minimum score 550 paper-based; 79 iBT), Michigan English Language Assessment Battery (minimum score 82); Recommended—IELTS (minimum score 7). *Application deadline:* For fall admission, 11/30 priority date for domestic and international students; for winter admission, 12/1 for domestic students, 11/1 for international students; for spring admission, 3/1 for domestic students, 2/1 for international students. Applications are processed on a rolling basis. Application fee: $60 ($70 for international students). Electronic applications accepted. *Financial support:* Fellowships with tuition reimbursements, research assistantships with tuition reimbursements, teaching assistantships with tuition reimbursements, Federal Work-Study, institutionally sponsored loans, and unspecified assistantships available. Support available to part-time students. *Unit head:* Barry Shank, Chair, 614-688-2559, E-mail: shank.46@osu.edu. *Application contact:* Graduate and Professional Admissions, 614-292-9444, Fax: 614-292-3895, E-mail: gpadmissions@osu.edu.
Website: http://comparativestudies.osu.edu/

Oregon State University, Interdisciplinary/Institutional Programs, Program in Interdisciplinary Studies, Corvallis, OR 97331. Offers MAIS. Program focuses on three areas of study and must include at least one area of study in liberal arts. Part-time programs available. *Students:* 35 full-time (20 women), 5 part-time (0 women); includes 9 minority (7 Hispanic/Latino; 1 Native Hawaiian or other Pacific Islander, non-Hispanic/Latino; 1 Two or more races, non-Hispanic/Latino), 3 international. Average age 32. 29 applicants, 66% accepted, 14 enrolled. In 2014, 19 master's awarded. *Degree requirements:* For master's, thesis optional. *Entrance requirements:* Additional exam requirements/recommendations for international students: Required—TOEFL (minimum score 80 iBT), IELTS (minimum score 6.5). *Application deadline:* For fall admission, 3/1 for domestic students, 4/1 for international students; for winter admission, 9/1 for domestic students, 7/1 for international students; for spring admission, 12/1 for domestic students, 10/1 for international students; for summer admission, 3/1 for domestic students, 1/1 for international students. Application fee: $60. *Expenses:* Tuition, state resident: full-time $11,907; part-time $189 per credit hour. Tuition, nonresident: full-time $19,953; part-time $441 per credit hour. *Required fees:* $1472; $449 per term. One-time fee: $350. Tuition and fees vary according to course load and program. *Financial support:* Fellowships, research assistantships, and teaching assistantships available. Financial award application deadline: 2/1. *Unit head:* Dr. David Bernell, MAIS Program Director, 541-737-6281, E-mail: david.bernell@oregonstate.edu.
Website: http://oregonstate.edu/dept/grad_school/mais.html

Regent University, Graduate School, School of Divinity, Virginia Beach, VA 23464-9800. Offers leadership and renewal (D Min), including Christian leadership and renewal, clinical pastoral education, community transformation, military ministry, ministry leadership coaching; practical theology (M Div, MA), including Biblical studies (M Div, MTS, PhD), chaplain ministry (M Div), Christian theology (M Div, MTS, PhD), church and ministry, history of Christianity (M Div, MTS), inter-cultural studies, interdisciplinary studies (M Div, MA, MTS), worship and renewal; renewal studies (PhD), including Biblical studies (M Div, MTS, PhD), Christian theology (M Div, MTS, PhD), history of global Christianity; theological studies (MTS), including Biblical studies (M Div, MTS, PhD), Christian theology (M Div, MTS, PhD), history of Christianity (M Div, MTS), interdisciplinary studies (M Div, MA, MTS). *Accreditation:* ACIPE; ATS. Part-time programs available. Postbaccalaureate distance learning degree programs offered (minimal on-campus study). *Faculty:* 20 full-time (3 women), 29 part-time/adjunct (3 women). *Students:* 64 full-time (28 women), 616 part-time (258 women); includes 318 minority (269 Black or African American, non-Hispanic/Latino; 7 American Indian or Alaska Native, non-Hispanic/Latino; 16 Asian, non-Hispanic/Latino; 26 Hispanic/Latino), 37 international. Average age 43. 511 applicants, 52% accepted, 187 enrolled. In 2014, 121 master's, 24 doctorates awarded. *Degree requirements:* For master's, comprehensive exam, thesis or alternative, internship; for doctorate, thesis/dissertation or alternative. *Entrance requirements:* For master's, GRE General Test or MAT, minimum undergraduate GPA of 2.75, writing sample, clergy recommendation; for doctorate, M Div or theological master's degree; minimum graduate GPA of 3.5 (PhD), 3.0 (D Min); recommendations; writing sample; transcripts. Additional exam requirements/recommendations for international students: Required—TOEFL (minimum score 577 paper-based). *Application deadline:* For fall admission, 5/1 priority date for domestic students. Applications are processed on a rolling basis. Application fee: $50. Electronic applications accepted. *Expenses:* Expenses: Contact institution. *Financial support:* Fellowships with full and partial tuition reimbursements, career-related internships or fieldwork, scholarships/grants, tuition waivers (full and partial), and unspecified assistantships available. Support available to part-time students. Financial award application deadline: 9/1; financial award applicants required to submit FAFSA. *Faculty research:* Greek and Hebrew, theology, spiritual formation, global missions and world Christianity, women's studies. *Unit head:* Dr. Joseph Umidi, Interim Dean, 757-352-4401, Fax: 757-352-4597, E-mail: joseumi@regent.edu. *Application contact:* Matthew Chadwick, Director of Enrollment Support Services, 800-373-5504, Fax: 757-352-4381, E-mail: admissions@regent.edu.
Website: http://www.regent.edu/acad/schdiv/

Rensselaer Polytechnic Institute, Graduate School, School of Science, Program in Multi-Disciplinary Science, Troy, NY 12180-3590. Offers MS, PhD. *Faculty:* 33 full-time (10 women), 4 part-time/adjunct (0 women). *Students:* 8 full-time (1 woman), 5 international. Average age 32. 4 applicants, 75% accepted, 3 enrolled. In 2014, 2 doctorates awarded. Terminal master's awarded for partial completion of doctoral program. *Degree requirements:* For master's, comprehensive exam (for some programs), thesis optional; for doctorate, comprehensive exam, thesis/dissertation. *Entrance requirements:* For master's, GRE; for doctorate, GRE. Additional exam requirements/recommendations for international students: Required—TOEFL (minimum score 600 paper-based; 100 iBT), IELTS (minimum score 7), PTE (minimum score 68). *Application deadline:* For fall admission, 1/1 priority date for domestic and international students; for spring admission, 8/15 priority date for domestic and international students. Applications are processed on a rolling basis. Application fee: $75. Electronic applications accepted. *Expenses: Tuition:* Full-time $46,700; part-time $1945 per credit. Tuition and fees vary according to course load. *Financial support:* In 2014–15, 7 students received support, including research assistantships (averaging $18,500 per year), teaching assistantships (averaging $18,500 per year); fellowships also available. Financial award application deadline: 1/1. *Total annual research expenditures:* $1.5 million. *Unit head:* Dr. Wilfredo Colon, Graduate Program Director, 518-276-2515, E-mail: colonw@rpi.edu. *Application contact:* Office of Graduate Admissions, 518-276-6216, Fax: 518-276-4072, E-mail: gradadmissions@rpi.edu.
Website: http://rpi.edu/academics/interdisciplinary/multidisciplinaryscience.html

Rochester Institute of Technology, Graduate Enrollment Services, Center for Multidisciplinary Studies, Graduate Programs Department, MS Program in Professional Studies, Rochester, NY 14623-5603. Offers MS. Part-time and evening/weekend programs available. Postbaccalaureate distance learning degree programs offered (no on-campus study). *Students:* 25 full-time (15 women), 42 part-time (21 women); includes

12 minority (4 Black or African American, non-Hispanic/Latino; 1 American Indian or Alaska Native, non-Hispanic/Latino; 2 Asian, non-Hispanic/Latino; 4 Hispanic/Latino; 1 Two or more races, non-Hispanic/Latino), 26 international. Average age 33. 38 applicants, 66% accepted, 16 enrolled. In 2014, 21 master's awarded. *Degree requirements:* For master's, thesis or alternative. *Entrance requirements:* For master's, TOEFL, IELTS, or PTE for non-native English speakers, minimum GPA of 3.0. Additional exam requirements/recommendations for international students: Required—PTE (minimum score 58), TOEFL (minimum score 550 paper-based; 79 iBT) or IELTS (minimum score 6.5). *Application deadline:* For fall admission, 2/15 priority date for domestic and international students; for winter admission, 11/1 for domestic and international students; for spring admission, 12/15 priority date for domestic and international students. Applications are processed on a rolling basis. Application fee: $60. Electronic applications accepted. *Expenses:* Expenses: $1,673 per credit hour. *Financial support:* In 2014–15, 16 students received support. Research assistantships with partial tuition reimbursements available, teaching assistantships with partial tuition reimbursements available, career-related internships or fieldwork, Federal Work-Study, institutionally sponsored loans, scholarships/grants, and unspecified assistantships available. Support available to part-time students. Financial award application deadline: 2/15; financial award applicants required to submit FAFSA. *Unit head:* Dr. James Hall, Graduate Program Director, 585-475-2295, Fax: 585-475-6292, E-mail: cmsi@rit.edu. *Application contact:* Diane Ellison, Associate Vice President, Graduate Enrollment Services, 585-475-2229, Fax: 585-475-7164, E-mail: gradinfo@rit.edu.
Website: http://www.rit.edu/academicaffairs/cms/getting-started/graduate/graduate-degrees-programs

Rosalind Franklin University of Medicine and Science, College of Health Professions, Department of Interprofessional Healthcare Studies, Interprofessional Healthcare Studies Program, North Chicago, IL 60064-3095. Offers interprofessional studies (D Sc). Part-time programs available. Postbaccalaureate distance learning degree programs offered (minimal on-campus study). *Degree requirements:* For doctorate, comprehensive exam, thesis/dissertation. *Entrance requirements:* For doctorate, GRE. Additional exam requirements/recommendations for international students: Required—TOEFL. *Faculty research:* Interprofessional education.

Rutgers, The State University of New Jersey, New Brunswick, Graduate School-New Brunswick, BioMaPS Institute for Quantitative Biology, Piscataway, NJ 08854-8097. Offers computational biology and molecular biophysics (PhD). *Degree requirements:* For doctorate, comprehensive exam, thesis/dissertation. *Entrance requirements:* For doctorate, GRE. Additional exam requirements/recommendations for international students: Required—TOEFL. Electronic applications accepted. *Faculty research:* Structural biology, systems biology, bioinformatics, translational medicine, genomics.

San Diego State University, Graduate and Research Affairs, Interdisciplinary Studies, San Diego, CA 92182. Offers MA, MS. Part-time programs available. *Degree requirements:* For master's, thesis. *Entrance requirements:* For master's, GRE General Test. Additional exam requirements/recommendations for international students: Required—TOEFL. Electronic applications accepted.

San Jose State University, Graduate Studies and Research, Program in Interdisciplinary Studies, San Jose, CA 95192-0001. Offers MA, MS. Electronic applications accepted.

Santa Clara University, School of Education and Counseling Psychology, Santa Clara, CA 95053. Offers alternative and correctional education (Certificate); counseling (MA); counseling psychology (MA); educational administration (MA); interdisciplinary education (MA); teaching (MA). Part-time and evening/weekend programs available. *Faculty:* 27 full-time (16 women), 51 part-time/adjunct (29 women). *Students:* 335 full-time (262 women), 393 part-time (312 women); includes 266 minority (21 Black or African American, non-Hispanic/Latino; 86 Asian, non-Hispanic/Latino; 135 Hispanic/Latino; 24 Two or more races, non-Hispanic/Latino), 35 international. Average age 31. 507 applicants, 67% accepted, 241 enrolled. In 2014 185 master's, 8 other advanced degrees awarded. *Degree requirements:* For master's, comprehensive exam (for some programs), thesis (for some programs); for Certificate, comprehensive exam. *Entrance requirements:* For master's, GRE or MAT, transcript, letters of recommendation, essay. Additional exam requirements/recommendations for international students: Required—TOEFL. *Application deadline:* For fall admission, 6/15 for domestic and international students; for winter admission, 10/15 for domestic and international students; for spring admission, 1/31 for domestic and international students. Applications are processed on a rolling basis. Application fee: $50. Electronic applications accepted. *Expenses:* Expenses: Contact institution. *Financial support:* In 2014–15, 329 students received support. Federal Work-Study, institutionally sponsored loans, and scholarships/grants available. Support available to part-time students. Financial award application deadline: 5/15; financial award applicants required to submit FAFSA. *Faculty research:* Education: meeting the needs of Latino/Latina students, historical and theoretical analysis of language coexistence, early childhood education, teaching of evolution in K-12 science classrooms, transactional learning communities; counseling psychology: grief counseling; maintenance of hope in the face of negative life events; educational and health disparities, with particular focus on Latinos; mindfulness, meditation, and compassion; life transitions. *Total annual research expenditures:* $206,541. *Unit head:* Nicholas Ladany, Dean, 408-554-4455, Fax: 408-554-5038, E-mail: nladany@scu.edu. *Application contact:* Kelly Pjesky, Admissions Director, 408-554-7884, Fax: 408-554-4367, E-mail: kpjesky@scu.edu.
Website: http://www.scu.edu/ecppm/

Sonoma State University, Institute of Interdisciplinary Studies/Special Major, Rohnert Park, CA 94928-3609. Offers MA, MS. Part-time programs available. *Degree requirements:* For master's, thesis or alternative. *Entrance requirements:* For master's, written English proficiency test, minimum GPA of 3.0 in last 60 hours. Additional exam requirements/recommendations for international students: Required—TOEFL (minimum score 500 paper-based).

Sonoma State University, School of Science and Technology, Department of Kinesiology, Rohnert Park, CA 94928. Offers adapted physical education (MA); interdisciplinary (MA); interdisciplinary pre-occupational therapy (MA); lifetime physical activity (MA), including coach education, fitness and wellness; physical education (MA); pre-physical therapy (MA). Part-time programs available. *Degree requirements:* For master's, thesis, oral exam. *Entrance requirements:* For master's, minimum GPA of 2.8. Additional exam requirements/recommendations for international students: Required—TOEFL (minimum score 500 paper-based).

Southern Oregon University, Graduate Studies, Program in Interdisciplinary Studies, Ashland, OR 97520. Offers MIS. Part-time programs available. Postbaccalaureate distance learning degree programs offered (minimal on-campus study). *Faculty:* 212 full-time (92 women), 104 part-time/adjunct (67 women). *Students:* 7 full-time (5 women), 16 part-time (7 women); includes 1 minority (American Indian or Alaska Native, non-Hispanic/Latino). Average age 36. 13 applicants, 77% accepted, 6 enrolled. In 2014, 3 master's awarded. *Degree requirements:* For master's, thesis (for some programs). *Entrance requirements:* For master's, GRE General Test, minimum cumulative GPA of 3.0 in the last 90 quarter credits (60 semester credits) of undergraduate coursework.

Additional exam requirements/recommendations for international students: Required—TOEFL (minimum score 540 paper-based; 76 iBT), IELTS (minimum score 6), ELPT (minimum score 964) or ELS (minimum score 112). *Application deadline:* For fall admission, 7/31 priority date for domestic and international students; for winter admission, 11/15 priority date for domestic students, 11/14 priority date for international students; for spring admission, 1/7 priority date for domestic and international students. Applications are processed on a rolling basis. Application fee: $50. Electronic applications accepted. *Expenses:* Tuition, state resident: full-time $10,225; part-time $1515 per quarter. Tuition, nonresident: full-time $12,782; part-time $1894 per quarter. *Required fees:* $1395; $261 per quarter. *Financial support:* Career-related internships or fieldwork, institutionally sponsored loans, scholarships/grants, and unspecified assistantships available. *Unit head:* Dr. Garth Pittman, Graduate Program Coordinator, 541-552-6671, E-mail: pittman@sou.edu. *Application contact:* Kelly Moutsatson, Director of Admissions, 541-552-6411, Fax: 541-552-8403, E-mail: admissions@sou.edu.
Website: http://www.sou.edu/miis/index.html

State University of New York at Fredonia, College of Liberal Arts and Sciences, Fredonia, NY 14063. Offers biology (MS); interdisciplinary studies (MS); speech pathology (MS); MA/MS. Part-time and evening/weekend programs available. *Students:* 74 full-time (67 women), 9 part-time (5 women); includes 6 minority (3 Asian, non-Hispanic/Latino; 1 Native Hawaiian or other Pacific Islander, non-Hispanic/Latino; 2 Two or more races, non-Hispanic/Latino). Average age 25. In 2014, 49 master's awarded. *Degree requirements:* For master's, comprehensive exam (for some programs), thesis (for some programs). *Entrance requirements:* For master's, GRE. Additional exam requirements/recommendations for international students: Required—TOEFL (minimum score 79 iBT), IELTS (minimum score 6.5), Cambridge English Advanced (minimum score: 52) recommended. *Application deadline:* For fall admission, 4/1 priority date for domestic and international students; for spring admission, 11/1 priority date for domestic students, 11/1 for international students. Applications are processed on a rolling basis. Application fee: $75. Electronic applications accepted. *Financial support:* In 2014–15, 5 students received support. Teaching assistantships with full and partial tuition reimbursements available, tuition waivers (full and partial), and unspecified assistantships available. *Faculty research:* Immunology/microbiology, applied human physiology, ecology and evolution, invertebrate biology, molecular biology, biochemistry, physiology, animal behavior, science education, vertebrate physiology, cell biology, plant biology, developmental biology, aquatic ecology, bilingual language acquisition, bilingual language acquisition and disorders, augmentative and alternate communication with ALS, World War I, Zweig, environmental literature, editing, adolescent literature, pedagogy. *Unit head:* Dr. John L. Kijinski, Dean, 716-673-3173, E-mail: kijinski@fredonia.edu. *Application contact:* Wendy S. Dunst, Interim Graduate Recruitment and Admissions Associate, 716-673-3808, Fax: 716-673-3712, E-mail: wendy.dunst@fredonia.edu.
Website: http://www.fredonia.edu/clas/

Stephen F. Austin State University, Graduate School, College of Applied Arts and Science, Program in Interdisciplinary Studies, Nacogdoches, TX 75962. Offers MIS. Part-time programs available. *Degree requirements:* For master's, comprehensive exam, thesis optional. *Entrance requirements:* For master's, GRE General Test. Additional exam requirements/recommendations for international students: Required—TOEFL (minimum score 550 paper-based).

Teachers College, Columbia University, Graduate Faculty of Education, Interdisciplinary Programs, New York, NY 10027-6696. Offers Ed M, MA, Ed D. Part-time programs available. *Students:* 7 full-time (4 women), 28 part-time (17 women); includes 15 minority (4 Black or African American, non-Hispanic/Latino; 2 American Indian or Alaska Native, non-Hispanic/Latino; 4 Asian, non-Hispanic/Latino; 4 Hispanic/Latino; 1 Two or more races, non-Hispanic/Latino), 5 international. Average age 41. 5 applicants, 20% accepted, 1 enrolled. In 2014, 5 master's, 6 doctorates awarded. Terminal master's awarded for partial completion of doctoral program. *Degree requirements:* For doctorate, thesis/dissertation. Application fee: $65. *Expenses:* Tuition: Full-time $33,552; part-time $1398 per credit. *Required fees:* $418 per semester. *Financial support:* Fellowships, career-related internships or fieldwork, Federal Work-Study, institutionally sponsored loans, and tuition waivers (full and partial) available. Support available to part-time students. Financial award application deadline: 2/1. *Unit head:* William J. Baldwin, Vice Provost, 212-678-3043, E-mail: wjb12@tc.columbia.edu. *Application contact:* Thomas P. Rock, Executive Director of Enrollment Services, 212-678-3710, Fax: 212-678-4171.

Texas A&M University–Texarkana, Graduate Studies and Research, College of Education and Liberal Arts, Texarkana, TX 75505-5518. Offers adult education (MS); curriculum and instruction (M Ed); education (MS); educational administration (M Ed); English (MA); instructional technology (MS); interdisciplinary studies (MA, MS); special education (MS). Part-time and evening/weekend programs available. *Degree requirements:* For master's, comprehensive exam (for some programs), thesis optional. *Entrance requirements:* For master's, minimum GPA of 2.5 on last 60 hours of bachelor's degree. Additional exam requirements/recommendations for international students: Required—TOEFL. Electronic applications accepted.

Texas State University, The Graduate College, College of Applied Arts, Interdisciplinary Studies Program in Occupational Education, San Marcos, TX 78666. Offers MAIS, MSIS. *Faculty:* 2 full-time (0 women), 2 part-time/adjunct (0 women). *Students:* 21 full-time (13 women), 30 part-time (18 women); includes 26 minority (7 Black or African American, non-Hispanic/Latino; 1 Asian, non-Hispanic/Latino; 18 Hispanic/Latino), 2 international. Average age 39. 27 applicants, 85% accepted, 9 enrolled. In 2014, 17 master's awarded. *Degree requirements:* For master's, comprehensive exam, thesis optional. *Entrance requirements:* For master's, minimum GPA of 2.75 for last 60 hours of undergraduate work, statement of personal goals. Additional exam requirements/recommendations for international students: Required—TOEFL (minimum score 550 paper-based; 78 iBT). *Application deadline:* For fall admission, 6/15 priority date for domestic students, 6/1 priority date for international students; for spring admission, 10/15 priority date for domestic students, 10/1 priority date for international students. Applications are processed on a rolling basis. Application fee: $40 ($90 for international students). Electronic applications accepted. *Expenses:* Expenses: $8,834 (tuition and fees combined). *Financial support:* In 2014–15, 39 students received support, including 2 research assistantships (averaging $12,500 per year); teaching assistantships, Federal Work-Study, institutionally sponsored loans, scholarships/grants, health care benefits, and unspecified assistantships also available. Support available to part-time students. Financial award application deadline: 4/1; financial award applicants required to submit FAFSA. *Unit head:* Dr. Matthew Eichler, Director, 512-245-2115, E-mail: me21@txstate.edu. *Application contact:* Dr. Andrea Golato, Dean of Graduate School, 512-245-2581, Fax: 512-245-8365, E-mail: gradcollege@txstate.edu.
Website: http://www.OCED.txstate.edu/

Texas State University, The Graduate College, College of Applied Arts, Interdisciplinary Studies Program in Sustainability, San Marcos, TX 78666. Offers MAIS, MSIS. Part-time programs available. *Students:* 3 full-time (1 woman), 4 part-time (3 women); includes 1 minority (Two or more races, non-Hispanic/Latino). Average age 37.

12 applicants, 83% accepted, 2 enrolled. In 2014, 6 master's awarded. *Degree requirements:* For master's, comprehensive exam, thesis optional. *Entrance requirements:* For master's, GRE (preferred), bachelor's degree from accredited institution, minimum GPA of 2.75 on the last 60 hours of undergraduate work, statement of personal goals, letter of intent to mentor from faculty member who will serve as research advisor and chair the master's committee. Additional exam requirements/recommendations for international students: Required—TOEFL (minimum score 550 paper-based; 78 iBT). *Application deadline:* For fall admission, 6/15 priority date for domestic students, 6/1 for international students; for spring admission, 10/15 priority date for domestic students, 10/1 for international students. Applications are processed on a rolling basis. Application fee: $40 ($90 for international students). *Expenses:* Expenses: $8,834 (tuition and fees combined). *Financial support:* In 2014–15, 5 students received support, including 1 research assistantship (averaging $10,152 per year); teaching assistantships, Federal Work-Study, and scholarships/grants also available. Support available to part-time students. Financial award application deadline: 4/1; financial award applicants required to submit FAFSA. *Faculty research:* Climate change, sustainable clothing. *Total annual research expenditures:* $42,800. *Unit head:* Dr. Gwendolyn Hustvedt, Graduate Advisor, 512-245-4689, E-mail: sustainablemasters@txstate.edu. *Application contact:* Dr. Andrea Golato, Dean of Graduate School, 512-245-2581, Fax: 512-245-8365, E-mail: gradcollege@txstate.edu.
Website: http://psych.txstate.edu

Texas State University, The Graduate College, College of Science and Engineering, Interdisciplinary Studies Program in Elementary Mathematics, Science, and Technology, San Marcos, TX 78666. Offers MSIS. *Students:* 1 full-time (0 women), all international. Average age 25. 1 applicant. In 2014, 1 master's awarded. *Degree requirements:* For master's, comprehensive exam, thesis optional. *Entrance requirements:* For master's, GRE if GPA lower than 2.75 on the last 60 hours of undergraduate course work, baccalaureate degree from regionally-accredited university with minimum GPA of 2.75 on last 60 undergraduate semester hours. Additional exam requirements/recommendations for international students: Required—TOEFL (minimum score 550 paper-based; 78 iBT). *Application deadline:* For fall admission, 6/15 for domestic students, 6/1 for international students; for spring admission, 10/15 for domestic students, 10/1 for international students; for summer admission, 4/15 for domestic students, 3/15 for international students. Applications are processed on a rolling basis. Application fee: $40 ($90 for international students). Electronic applications accepted. *Expenses:* Expenses: $8,834 (tuition and fees combined). *Financial support:* Research assistantships, teaching assistantships, Federal Work-Study, institutionally sponsored loans, scholarships/grants, health care benefits, and unspecified assistantships available. Support available to part-time students. Financial award application deadline: 4/1; financial award applicants required to submit FAFSA. *Unit head:* Dr. Sandra West Moody, Acting Dean, 512-245-3360, Fax: 512-245-8095, E-mail: sw04@txstate.edu. *Application contact:* Dr. Andrea Golato, Dean of Graduate School, 512-245-2581, Fax: 512-245-8365, E-mail: gradcollege@txstate.edu.

Texas Tech University, Graduate School, Interdisciplinary Programs, Lubbock, TX 79409-1030. Offers arid land studies (MS); biotechnology (MS); heritage management (MS); interdisciplinary studies (MA, MS); museum science (MA); wind science and engineering (PhD); JD/MS. Part-time programs available. *Faculty:* 4 full-time (3 women). *Students:* 112 full-time (70 women), 122 part-time (70 women); includes 71 minority (20 Black or African American, non-Hispanic/Latino; 1 American Indian or Alaska Native, non-Hispanic/Latino; 4 Asian, non-Hispanic/Latino; 40 Hispanic/Latino; 6 Two or more races, non-Hispanic/Latino), 43 international. Average age 30. 172 applicants, 65% accepted, 70 enrolled. In 2014, 56 master's, 4 doctorates awarded. Terminal master's awarded for partial completion of doctoral program. *Degree requirements:* For master's, comprehensive exam (for some programs), thesis (for some programs); for doctorate, comprehensive exam, thesis/dissertation (for some programs). *Entrance requirements:* Additional exam requirements/recommendations for international students: Required—TOEFL (minimum score 550 paper-based; 79 iBT). *Application deadline:* For fall admission, 6/1 priority date for domestic students, 1/15 priority date for international students; for spring admission, 9/1 priority date for domestic students, 6/15 priority date for international students. Applications are processed on a rolling basis. Application fee: $60. Electronic applications accepted. *Expenses:* Tuition, state resident: full-time $6310; part-time $262.92 per credit hour. Tuition, nonresident: full-time $14,998; part-time $624.92 per credit hour. *Required fees:* $2701; $36.50 per credit. $912.50 per semester. Tuition and fees vary according to course load. *Financial support:* In 2014–15, 201 students received support, including 196 fellowships (averaging $2,655 per year), 5 research assistantships (averaging $12,144 per year), 2 teaching assistantships (averaging $7,785 per year); scholarships/grants and unspecified assistantships also available. Financial award application deadline: 4/15; financial award applicants required to submit FAFSA. *Total annual research expenditures:* $241,842. *Unit head:* Dr. Mark Sheridan, Vice Provost for Graduate and Postdoctoral Affairs/Dean of the Graduate School, 806-742-2787, Fax: 806-742-1746, E-mail: mark.sheridan@ttu.edu. *Application contact:* Shannon Samson, Coordinator of Graduate School Recruitment, 806-834-5201, Fax: 806-742-1746, E-mail: gradschool@ttu.edu.
Website: http://www.depts.ttu.edu/gradschool/about/INDS/index.php

Trinity Western University, School of Graduate Studies, Program in Interdisciplinary Humanities, Langley, BC V2Y 1Y1, Canada. Offers general humanities (MAIH); specialized (MAIH), including English, history, philosophy. Part-time programs available. *Degree requirements:* For master's, thesis or alternative, 36 semester hours. *Entrance requirements:* For master's, strong undergraduate degree in humanities or English, history or philosophy. Additional exam requirements/recommendations for international students: Recommended—TOEFL. Electronic applications accepted. *Faculty research:* Literary theory, gender, medieval and early modern literature, philosophy of religion, Thomas Merton's poetics.

Tufts University, Graduate School of Arts and Sciences, Interdisciplinary Doctoral Program, Medford, MA 02155. Offers PhD. *Expenses: Tuition:* Full-time $45,590; part-time $1161 per credit hour. *Required fees:* $782. Full-time tuition and fees vary according to degree level, program and student level. Part-time tuition and fees vary according to course load.

Tulane University, School of Science and Engineering, Interdisciplinary PhD Program, New Orleans, LA 70118-5669. Offers PhD. *Expenses: Tuition:* Full-time $46,326; part-time $2574 per credit hour. *Required fees:* $1980; $44.50 per credit hour. $550 per term. Tuition and fees vary according to course load and program.

Union Institute & University, Individualized Master of Arts Program, Cincinnati, OH 45206-1925. Offers creativity studies (MA); health and wellness (MA); history and culture (MA); leadership, public policy, and social issues (MA); literature and writing (MA). Part-time programs available. *Faculty:* 4 full-time (2 women), 3 part-time/adjunct (2 women). *Students:* 14 full-time (11 women), 107 part-time (75 women); includes 36 minority (29 Black or African American, non-Hispanic/Latino; 3 American Indian or Alaska Native, non-Hispanic/Latino; 3 Hispanic/Latino; 1 Two or more races, non-Hispanic/Latino). Average age 40. *Degree requirements:* For master's, thesis. *Entrance requirements:* For master's, transcript, essay, 3 letters of recommendation, resume. *Application deadline:* For spring admission, 3/13 for domestic students. Applications are processed on a rolling basis. Application fee: $50. Electronic applications accepted. *Expenses: Tuition:* Full-time $26,640; part-time $719 per credit hour. *Required fees:* $216; $54 per semester. Part-time tuition and fees vary according to course load, degree level and program. *Financial support:* Career-related internships or fieldwork and tuition waivers available. Financial award applicants required to submit FAFSA. *Unit head:* Andrea Scarpino, Program Director, 802-828-8777. *Application contact:* Director of Admissions, 800-861-6400.
Website: https://www.myunion.edu/academics/masters-programs/master-of-arts/

Union Institute & University, PhD Program in Interdisciplinary Studies, Cincinnati, OH 45206-1925. Offers ethical and creative leadership (PhD), including Martin Luther King studies; humanities and culture (PhD), including Martin Luther King studies; public policy and social change (PhD), including Martin Luther King studies. Program requires participation in brief on-campus residencies twice each year (January and July). Postbaccalaureate distance learning degree programs offered (minimal on-campus study). *Faculty:* 6 full-time (4 women), 9 part-time/adjunct (7 women). *Students:* 92 full-time (51 women), 15 part-time (10 women); includes 37 minority (25 Black or African American, non-Hispanic/Latino; 4 American Indian or Alaska Native, non-Hispanic/Latino; 2 Asian, non-Hispanic/Latino; 3 Hispanic/Latino; 3 Native Hawaiian or other Pacific Islander, non-Hispanic/Latino), 1 international. Average age 46. *Degree requirements:* For doctorate, comprehensive exam, thesis/dissertation. *Entrance requirements:* For doctorate, master's degree, three letters of recommendation, statement of purpose. *Application deadline:* Applications are processed on a rolling basis. Application fee: $50. *Expenses: Tuition:* Full-time $26,640; part-time $719 per credit hour. *Required fees:* $216; $54 per semester. Part-time tuition and fees vary according to course load, degree level and program. *Financial support:* Federal Work-Study, scholarships/grants, and tuition waivers (partial) available. Financial award application deadline: 5/1; financial award applicants required to submit FAFSA. *Faculty research:* Social responsibility, ethical leadership, Martin Luther King studies. *Unit head:* Dr. Arlene Sacks, Dean, 513-861-6400, E-mail: arlene.sacks@myunion.edu. *Application contact:* Admissions Counselor, 800-486-3116.
Website: https://www.myunion.edu/academics/doctoral-programs/phd/

The University of Alabama, Interdisciplinary Programs, Tuscaloosa, AL 35487. Offers PhD. Part-time and evening/weekend programs available. *Students:* 6 full-time (3 women), 8 part-time (6 women); includes 5 minority (all Black or African American, non-Hispanic/Latino). Average age 42. 1 applicant, 100% accepted, 1 enrolled. In 2014, 4 doctorates awarded. *Degree requirements:* For doctorate, comprehensive exam, thesis/dissertation. *Entrance requirements:* For doctorate, GRE (minimum score of 300), MAT (above 50th percentile), GMAT (minimum score 500). Additional exam requirements/recommendations for international students: Required—TOEFL (minimum score 79 iBT), IELTS (minimum score 6.5). *Application deadline:* For fall admission, 5/1 for international students; for winter admission, 9/15 for international students. Applications are processed on a rolling basis. Electronic applications accepted. *Expenses:* Tuition, state resident: full-time $9826. Tuition, nonresident: full-time $24,950. *Unit head:* Dr. Andrew Mark Goodliffe, Assistant Dean of the Graduate School, 205-348-8283, Fax: 205-348-0400, E-mail: amg@ua.edu. *Application contact:* Patrick D. Fuller, Senior Graduate Admissions Counselor, 205-348-5923, Fax: 205-348-0400, E-mail: patrick.d.fuller@ua.edu.
Website: http://graduate.ua.edu

The University of Alabama at Birmingham, School of Engineering, Program in Interdisciplinary Engineering, Birmingham, AL 35294. Offers computational engineering (PhD); environmental health and safety engineering (PhD). *Students:* 12 full-time (1 woman), 26 part-time (7 women); includes 9 minority (6 Black or African American, non-Hispanic/Latino; 2 Asian, non-Hispanic/Latino; 1 Hispanic/Latino), 7 international. Average age 38. In 2014, 4 doctorates awarded. *Degree requirements:* For doctorate, comprehensive exam, thesis/dissertation. *Entrance requirements:* For doctorate, GRE (minimum rank 50% in both Quantitative Reasoning and Verbal Reasoning sections), undergraduate degree in a supporting field, official transcripts, minimum undergraduate GPA of 3.0. Additional exam requirements/recommendations for international students: Required—TOEFL (minimum score 100 iBT). *Application deadline:* For fall admission, 7/1 for domestic students; for spring admission, 11/1 for domestic students; for summer admission, 4/1 for domestic students. *Expenses:* Tuition, state resident: full-time $7090; part-time $370 per credit hour. Tuition, nonresident: full-time $16,072; part-time $869 per credit hour. Full-time tuition and fees vary according to course load and program. *Unit head:* Dr. David Littlefield, Graduate Program Director, 205-934-8460, E-mail: littlefield@uab.edu. *Application contact:* Susan Noblitt Banks, Director of Graduate School Operations, 205-934-8227, Fax: 205-934-8413, E-mail: gradschool@uab.edu.
Website: http://www.uab.edu/engineering/home/degrees-cert/phd?id=189:phd-in-interdisciplinary-engineering&catid=3

The University of Alabama in Huntsville, School of Graduate Studies, Interdisciplinary Studies, Huntsville, AL 35899. Offers MS, PhD, Certificate. Part-time and evening/weekend programs available. Postbaccalaureate distance learning degree programs offered (minimal on-campus study). *Degree requirements:* For master's, comprehensive exam, thesis or alternative, oral and written exams; for doctorate, comprehensive exam, thesis/dissertation, oral and written exams. *Entrance requirements:* For master's and doctorate, GRE General Test, minimum GPA of 3.0; for Certificate, GMAT (minimum score 500), minimum AACSB index of 1080. Additional exam requirements/recommendations for international students: Required—TOEFL (minimum score 500 paper-based; 80 iBT), IELTS (minimum score 6.5). Electronic applications accepted. *Faculty research:* Service discovery, laser technology, macromolecular materials, simulation interoperability, protein structure and function.

University of Alaska Anchorage, College of Arts and Sciences, Program in Interdisciplinary Studies, Anchorage, AK 99508. Offers MA, MS. Part-time programs available. *Entrance requirements:* For master's, GRE General Test, GRE Subject Test, minimum GPA of 3.0. Additional exam requirements/recommendations for international students: Required—TOEFL (minimum score 550 paper-based).

University of Alaska Fairbanks, Graduate School for Interdisciplinary Studies, Fairbanks, AK 99775-7560. Offers indigenous studies (PhD); interdisciplinary studies (MA, MS, PhD). Part-time programs available. *Faculty:* 3 full-time (all women), 1 (woman) part-time/adjunct. *Students:* 10 full-time (all women), 22 part-time (17 women); includes 16 minority (13 American Indian or Alaska Native, non-Hispanic/Latino; 2 Hispanic/Latino; 1 Two or more races, non-Hispanic/Latino). Average age 49. 23 applicants, 13% accepted, 3 enrolled. In 2014, 1 master's, 1 doctorate awarded. *Degree requirements:* For master's, comprehensive exam (for some programs), oral defense of project or thesis; for doctorate, one foreign language, comprehensive exam, thesis/dissertation, oral defense of dissertation. *Entrance requirements:* For master's, GRE General Test, bachelor's degree from accredited institution with minimum cumulative undergraduate and major GPA of 3.0; for doctorate, GRE General Test, minimum cumulative GPA of 3.0. Additional exam requirements/recommendations for international students: Required—TOEFL (minimum score 550 paper-based; 80 iBT). *Application deadline:* For fall admission, 3/1 for domestic and international students; for spring admission, 10/1 for domestic students, 9/1 for international students. Applications are processed on a rolling basis. Application fee: $60. Electronic applications accepted. *Expenses:* Tuition, state resident: full-time $7614; part-time $423 per credit. Tuition, nonresident: full-time $15,552; part-time $864 per credit. Tuition and fees vary according

to course level, course load and reciprocity agreements. *Financial support:* Fellowships with full tuition reimbursements, research assistantships with full tuition reimbursements, teaching assistantships with full tuition reimbursements, career-related internships or fieldwork, Federal Work-Study, scholarships/grants, health care benefits, and unspecified assistantships available. Support available to part-time students. Financial award application deadline: 2/15; financial award applicants required to submit FAFSA. *Unit head:* John Eichelberger, Dean, 907-474-7716, Fax: 907-474-1984, E-mail: fyinds@uaf.edu. *Application contact:* Mary Kreta, Director of Admissions, 907-474-7500, Fax: 907-474-7097, E-mail: admissions@uaf.edu.
Website: http://www.uaf.edu/gradsch/

The University of Arizona, Graduate Interdisciplinary Programs, Tucson, AZ 85721. Offers American Indian studies (MA, PhD); applied mathematics (MS, PMS, PhD), including applied mathematics (MS, PhD), mathematical sciences (PMS); biomedical engineering (MS, PhD); cancer biology (PhD); entomology (MA); entomology and insect science (MS, PhD); genetics (MS, PhD); neuroscience (PhD); physiological sciences (MS, PhD); second language acquisition and teaching (PhD); statistics (MS, PhD); JD/MA. Part-time programs available. *Entrance requirements:* Additional exam requirements/recommendations for international students: Required—TOEFL (minimum score 550 paper-based; 79 iBT).

University of Arkansas, Graduate School, Interdisciplinary Program in Comparative Literature and Cultural Studies, Fayetteville, AR 72701-1201. Offers MA, PhD. *Degree requirements:* For doctorate, 2 foreign languages, comprehensive exam, thesis/dissertation optional. *Entrance requirements:* For doctorate, GRE General Test, official transcripts of all undergraduate and graduate work, three letters of recommendation, writing sample, statement of purpose. Additional exam requirements/recommendations for international students: Required—TOEFL (minimum score 550 paper-based; 80 iBT) or IELTS (minimum score 6.5). *Faculty research:* Literary and cultural theory, cultural studies, postcolonial theory, gender studies, world literature.

University of Arkansas, Graduate School, Interdisciplinary Program in Environmental Dynamics, Fayetteville, AR 72701-1201. Offers PhD. *Degree requirements:* For doctorate, thesis/dissertation. Electronic applications accepted.

University of Arkansas at Little Rock, Graduate School, College of Arts, Humanities, and Social Science, Department of Philosophy and Liberal Studies, Little Rock, AR 72204-1099. Offers MA. *Entrance requirements:* For master's, GRE. *Application deadline:* Applications are processed on a rolling basis. *Expenses:* Tuition, state resident: full-time $6000; part-time $300 per credit hour. Tuition, nonresident: full-time $13,800; part-time $690 per credit hour. *Required fees:* $1126; $603 per term. One-time fee: $40 full-time. *Financial support:* Research assistantships with tuition reimbursements and teaching assistantships with tuition reimbursements available. *Unit head:* Angela Hunter, Interim Chair, 501-683-7066, E-mail: anhunter@ualr.edu.
Website: http://ualr.edu/philosophy/

University of California, Santa Barbara, Graduate Division, College of Letters and Sciences, Division of Social Sciences, Department of Sociology, Santa Barbara, CA 93106-9430. Offers interdisciplinary emphasis: Black studies (PhD); interdisciplinary emphasis: environment and society (PhD); interdisciplinary emphasis: feminist studies (PhD); interdisciplinary emphasis: global studies (PhD); interdisciplinary emphasis: language, interaction and social organization (PhD); interdisciplinary emphasis: quantitative methods in social science (PhD); interdisciplinary emphasis: technology and society (PhD); sociology (PhD); MA/PhD. Terminal master's awarded for partial completion of doctoral program. *Degree requirements:* For doctorate, comprehensive exam, thesis/dissertation. *Entrance requirements:* For doctorate, GRE General Test. Additional exam requirements/recommendations for international students: Required—TOEFL (minimum score 550 paper-based; 80 iBT), IELTS (minimum score 7). Electronic applications accepted. *Faculty research:* Gender and sexualities, race/ethnicity, social movements, conversation analysis, global sociology.

University of California, Santa Cruz, Division of Graduate Studies, Division of the Arts, Department of Music, Santa Cruz, CA 95064. Offers ethnomusicology (MA); music (PhD), including cross-cultural and interdisciplinary studies; music composition (MA, DMA), including world music composition (DMA); music composition (DMA), including computer-assisted (algorithmic) composition ; performance practice (MA). *Degree requirements:* For master's, one foreign language, thesis, recital; for doctorate, one foreign language, thesis/dissertation, qualifying and final examinations. *Entrance requirements:* For master's, GRE General Test, 3 letters of recommendation, writing or composition sample, 10-20 minute unedited recording; for doctorate, GRE General Test, 3 letters of recommendation, writing sample. Additional exam requirements/recommendations for international students: Required—TOEFL (minimum score 550 paper-based; 83 iBT); Recommended—IELTS (minimum score 8). Electronic applications accepted. *Faculty research:* Western music history, new music, composition, ethnomusicology, musicology.

University of Central Florida, College of Graduate Studies, Program in Interdisciplinary Studies, Orlando, FL 32816. Offers gender studies (Certificate); interdisciplinary studies (MS). *Students:* 10 full-time (3 women), 17 part-time (12 women); includes 9 minority (3 Black or African American, non-Hispanic/Latino; 4 Hispanic/Latino; 2 Two or more races, non-Hispanic/Latino), 1 international. Average age 31. 31 applicants, 61% accepted, 10 enrolled. In 2014, 2 master's, 9 other advanced degrees awarded. *Degree requirements:* For master's, thesis or alternative. *Entrance requirements:* For master's, GRE General Test, minimum GPA of 3.0 in last 60 hours. Additional exam requirements/recommendations for international students: Required—TOEFL. Application fee: $30. Electronic applications accepted. *Expenses:* Tuition, state resident: part-time $288.16 per credit hour. Tuition, nonresident: part-time $1073.31 per credit hour. *Financial support:* In 2014–15, 1 student received support, including 1 teaching assistantship (averaging $7,500 per year). *Unit head:* Dr. Michael Hampton, Director, 407-823-0144, E-mail: michael.hampton@ucf.edu. *Application contact:* Barbara Rodriguez Lamas, Director, Admissions and Student Services, 407-823-2766, Fax: 407-823-6442, E-mail: gradadmissions@ucf.edu.
Website: http://www.is.ucf.edu/

University of Central Oklahoma, The Jackson College of Graduate Studies, College of Education and Professional Studies, Department of Adult Education and Safety Science, Edmond, OK 73034-5209. Offers adult and higher education (M Ed), including adult and higher education, interdisciplinary studies, student personnel, training. Part-time programs available. *Degree requirements:* For master's, comprehensive exam (for some programs), thesis (for some programs). *Entrance requirements:* For master's, GRE General Test. Additional exam requirements/recommendations for international students: Required—TOEFL (minimum score 550 paper-based; 79 iBT), IELTS (minimum score 6.5). Electronic applications accepted. *Faculty research:* Violence in the workplace/schools, aging issues, trade and industrial education.

University of Chicago, Division of the Biological Sciences, The Interdisciplinary Scientist Training Program, Chicago, IL 60637-1513. Offers PhD. *Students:* 40 full-time (17 women); includes 14 minority (3 Black or African American, non-Hispanic/Latino; 8 Asian, non-Hispanic/Latino; 2 Hispanic/Latino; 1 Two or more races, non-Hispanic/Latino). Average age 27. *Degree requirements:* For doctorate, thesis/dissertation, ethics class, 2 teaching assistantships. *Entrance requirements:* For doctorate, GRE General Test. Additional exam requirements/recommendations for international students: Required—TOEFL (minimum score 600 paper-based; 104 iBT), IELTS (minimum score 7). *Application deadline:* For fall admission, 12/1 for domestic and international students. Application fee: $90. Electronic applications accepted. *Expenses: Tuition:* Full-time $46,899. *Required fees:* $347. *Financial support:* In 2014–15, 2 students received support, including fellowships (averaging $29,781 per year), research assistantships (averaging $29,781 per year); institutionally sponsored loans, scholarships/grants, traineeships, and health care benefits also available. Financial award applicants required to submit FAFSA. *Unit head:* Dr. Daniel Margoliash, Program Director, 773-702-3224, Fax: 773-702-0037. *Application contact:* Diane Hall, Student Contact, E-mail: djh8@uchicago.edu.

University of Cincinnati, Graduate School, McMicken College of Arts and Sciences, Interdisciplinary Studies Program, Cincinnati, OH 45221. Offers PhD. *Entrance requirements:* For doctorate, GRE General Test. Electronic applications accepted.

University of Colorado Colorado Springs, College of Letters, Arts and Sciences, Master of Sciences Program, Colorado Springs, CO 80933-7150. Offers interdisciplinary sciences (M Sc). Part-time programs available. *Students:* 47 full-time (32 women), 46 part-time (32 women); includes 11 minority (3 Black or African American, non-Hispanic/Latino; 4 Asian, non-Hispanic/Latino; 4 Hispanic/Latino), 6 international. Average age 28. 145 applicants, 40% accepted, 42 enrolled. In 2014, 34 master's awarded. *Degree requirements:* For master's, thesis or alternative. *Entrance requirements:* For master's, minimum GPA of 2.75. Additional exam requirements/recommendations for international students: Required—TOEFL (minimum score 525 paper-based; 80 iBT). *Application deadline:* For fall admission, 3/1 priority date for domestic students, 3/1 for international students; for spring admission, 12/1 for domestic and international students. Applications are processed on a rolling basis. Application fee: $60 ($100 for international students). Electronic applications accepted. *Expenses:* Expenses: Contact institution. *Financial support:* In 2014–15, 21 students received support, including 21 fellowships (averaging $2,600 per year); research assistantships, teaching assistantships, career-related internships or fieldwork, Federal Work-Study, and scholarships/grants also available. Support available to part-time students. Financial award application deadline: 3/1; financial award applicants required to submit FAFSA. *Faculty research:* Molecular and cellular biology, exercise science, ecology and evolution, analytical chemistry, biochemistry, inorganic chemistry, organic chemistry, physical chemistry, health promotion, athletic training and strength and conditioning, athlete development, sport nutrition. *Unit head:* Dr. Kelli Klebe, Dean, 719-255-3779, E-mail: kklebe@uccs.edu. *Application contact:* KrisAnn McBroom, Academic Services Specialist, 719-255-3567, E-mail: kmcbroom@uccs.edu.

University of Florida, Graduate School, College of Public Health and Health Professions, Department of Environmental and Global Health, Gainesville, FL 32610. Offers environmental health (PhD); one health (MHS, PhD). *Faculty:* 13 full-time (5 women), 5 part-time/adjunct (1 woman). *Students:* 5 full-time (4 women), 2 part-time (1 woman); includes 1 minority (Black or African American, non-Hispanic/Latino), 1 international. 12 applicants, 75% accepted, 3 enrolled. In 2014, 3 master's awarded. *Entrance requirements:* For master's and doctorate, GRE, minimum GPA of 3.0. Additional exam requirements/recommendations for international students: Required—TOEFL (minimum score 550 paper-based; 80 iBT), IELTS (minimum score 6). *Application deadline:* For fall admission, 1/1 for domestic students. Application fee: $30. *Financial support:* In 2014–15, 2 fellowships, 12 research assistantships, 7 teaching assistantships were awarded. Financial award applicants required to submit FAFSA. *Unit head:* Dr. Gregory C. Gray, MD, Chair, 352-273-9449, E-mail: gcgray@phhp.ufl.edu. *Application contact:* Office of Admissions, 352-392-1365, E-mail: webrequests@admissions.ufl.edu.
Website: http://egh.phhp.ufl.edu/

University of Houston–Victoria, School of Arts and Sciences, Program in Interdisciplinary Studies, Victoria, TX 77901-4450. Offers MAIS. Part-time and evening/weekend programs available. Postbaccalaureate distance learning degree programs offered (minimal on-campus study). *Degree requirements:* For master's, comprehensive exam or thesis. *Entrance requirements:* For master's, GRE General Test, official transcript, essay. Additional exam requirements/recommendations for international students: Required—TOEFL (minimum score 550 paper-based). Electronic applications accepted.

University of Idaho, College of Graduate Studies, College of Art and Architecture, Program in Bioregional Planning and Community Design, Moscow, ID 83844-2481. Offers MS. *Faculty:* 5 full-time, 1 part-time/adjunct. *Students:* 10 full-time, 5 part-time. Average age 33. In 2014, 6 master's awarded. *Entrance requirements:* Additional exam requirements/recommendations for international students: Required—TOEFL. *Application deadline:* Applications are processed on a rolling basis. Application fee: $60. Electronic applications accepted. *Expenses:* Tuition, state resident: full-time $4784; part-time $280.50 per credit hour. Tuition, nonresident: full-time $18,314; part-time $957.50 per credit hour. *Required fees:* $2000; $58.50 per credit hour. Tuition and fees vary according to program. *Financial support:* Applicants required to submit FAFSA. *Faculty research:* Environment and behavior interaction, geographic trade, design development, economic development, natural resource policy. *Unit head:* Dr. Mark Hoversten, Dean, 208-885-7448, E-mail: bioregionalplanning@uidaho.edu. *Application contact:* Sean Scoggin, Graduate Recruitment Coordinator, 208-885-4001, Fax: 208-805-4406, E-mail: graduateadmissions@uidaho.edu.
Website: http://www.uidaho.edu/caa/biop

University of Idaho, College of Graduate Studies, Program in Interdisciplinary Studies, Moscow, ID 83844-3017. Offers MA, MS. *Students:* 4 part-time. Average age 48. In 2014, 1 master's awarded. *Entrance requirements:* For master's, minimum GPA of 2.8. Additional exam requirements/recommendations for international students: Required—TOEFL. *Application deadline:* For fall admission, 8/1 for domestic students; for spring admission, 12/15 for domestic students. Applications are processed on a rolling basis. Application fee: $60. Electronic applications accepted. *Expenses:* Tuition, state resident: full-time $4784; part-time $280.50 per credit hour. Tuition, nonresident: full-time $18,314; part-time $957.50 per credit hour. *Required fees:* $2000; $58.50 per credit hour. Tuition and fees vary according to program. *Financial support:* Applicants required to submit FAFSA. *Unit head:* Dr. Jie Chen, Dean of Graduate Studies, 208-885-6243, E-mail: uigrad@uidaho.edu. *Application contact:* Stephanie Thomas, Graduate Recruitment Coordinator, 208-885-4001, Fax: 208-885-4406, E-mail: gadms@uidaho.edu.
Website: http://www.uidaho.edu/cogs/academics/interdisciplinarystudies

University of Illinois at Chicago, Graduate College, Program in Learning Sciences, Chicago, IL 60607-7128. Offers PhD. *Students:* 23 full-time (12 women), 3 part-time (2 women); includes 4 minority (1 Black or African American, non-Hispanic/Latino; 1 Asian, non-Hispanic/Latino; 1 Hispanic/Latino; 1 Two or more races, non-Hispanic/Latino), 2 international. Average age 34. 9 applicants, 67% accepted, 2 enrolled. In 2014, 1 doctorate awarded. Application fee: $60. *Expenses:* Tuition, state resident: full-time $11,254; part-time $468 per credit hour. Tuition, nonresident: full-time $23,252; part-time $968 per credit hour. *Required fees:* $1217 per term. Part-time tuition and fees vary according to course load, degree level and program. *Unit head:* Dr. Susan Goldman, Graduate Program Chair, 312-413-3901, E-mail: deana@uic.edu. *Application contact:*

Interdisciplinary Studies

Donald Wink, Director of Graduate Studies, 312-413-3901, E-mail: deana@uic.edu.
Website: http://catalog.uic.edu/gcat/graduate-college/lrsc/

University of Illinois at Springfield, Graduate Programs, College of Liberal Arts and Sciences, Department of Liberal and Integrative Studies, Springfield, IL 62703-5407. Offers MA. Part-time and evening/weekend programs available. *Faculty:* 6 full-time (2 women), 1 (woman) part-time/adjunct. *Students:* 9 full-time (5 women), 39 part-time (19 women); includes 10 minority (7 Black or African American, non-Hispanic/Latino; 1 Asian, non-Hispanic/Latino; 2 Two or more races, non-Hispanic/Latino), 1 international. Average age 38. 38 applicants, 34% accepted, 12 enrolled. In 2014, 8 master's awarded. *Degree requirements:* For master's, project or thesis. *Entrance requirements:* For master's, 2 letters of reference; interview; two- to three-page statement of educational goals, background, and reasons for requesting admission to the program; minimum GPA of 2.5 (for campus-based students), 3.0 (for online students). Additional exam requirements/recommendations for international students: Required—TOEFL (minimum score 500 paper-based; 61 iBT). *Application deadline:* Applications are processed on a rolling basis. Application fee: $60 ($75 for international students). *Expenses:* Tuition, state resident: full-time $7662; part-time $319.25 per credit hour. Tuition, nonresident: full-time $15,966; part-time $665.25 per credit hour. *Financial support:* In 2014–15, fellowships with full tuition reimbursements (averaging $9,900 per year), research assistantships with full tuition reimbursements (averaging $9,600 per year), teaching assistantships with full tuition reimbursements (averaging $9,600 per year) were awarded; career-related internships or fieldwork, Federal Work-Study, scholarships/grants, health care benefits, and unspecified assistantships also available. Support available to part-time students. Financial award application deadline: 11/15; financial award applicants required to submit FAFSA. *Unit head:* Dr. Eric Hadley-Ives, Program Administrator, 217-206-6962, Fax: 217-206-6217, E-mail: hadleyiv@uis.edu. *Application contact:* Dr. Lynn Pardie, Office of Graduate Studies, 800-252-8533, Fax: 217-206-7623, E-mail: lpard1@uis.edu.
Website: http://www.uis.edu/ino/

University of Illinois at Urbana–Champaign, Graduate College, College of Liberal Arts and Sciences, School of Literatures, Cultures and Linguistics, Program in Romance Linguistics, Champaign, IL 61820. Offers PhD. Application fee: $70 ($90 for international students). *Unit head:* Jean-Philippe Mathy, Director, 217-244-2718, Fax: 217-244-8430, E-mail: jmathy@illinois.edu. *Application contact:* Lynn Stanke, Office Support Specialist, 217-333-6269, Fax: 217-244-3050, E-mail: stanke@illinois.edu.

The University of Kansas, University of Kansas Medical Center, School of Medicine, Interdisciplinary Graduate Program in Biomedical Sciences (IGPBS), Kansas City, KS 66160. Offers MA, MPH, MS, PhD, MD/MPH, MD/MS, MD/PhD. *Students:* 15 full-time (10 women); includes 1 minority (Hispanic/Latino), 7 international. Average age 26. 142 applicants, 18% accepted, 15 enrolled. Terminal master's awarded for partial completion of doctoral program. *Degree requirements:* For master's, thesis; for doctorate, comprehensive exam, thesis/dissertation. *Entrance requirements:* For master's and doctorate, GRE. Additional exam requirements/recommendations for international students: Required—TOEFL. *Application deadline:* For fall admission, 1/5 priority date for domestic and international students. Applications are processed on a rolling basis. Application fee: $60. Electronic applications accepted. *Financial support:* In 2014–15, 3 research assistantships with full tuition reimbursements (averaging $24,000 per year), 18 teaching assistantships with full tuition reimbursements (averaging $24,000 per year) were awarded; scholarships/grants and unspecified assistantships also available. Financial award application deadline: 3/1; financial award applicants required to submit FAFSA. *Faculty research:* Cardiovascular biology, neurosciences, signal transduction and cancer biology, molecular biology and genetics, developmental biology. *Unit head:* Dr. Michael J. Werle, Director, 913-588-7491, Fax: 913-588-2710, E-mail: mwerle@kumc.edu. *Application contact:* Miranda Olenhouse, Coordinator, 913-588-2719, Fax: 913-588-2711, E-mail: molenhouse@kumc.edu.
Website: http://www.kumc.edu/igpbs.html

University of Louisville, School of Interdisciplinary and Graduate Studies, Louisville, KY 40292. Offers MA, MS, PhD. Part-time and evening/weekend programs available. *Students:* 13 full-time (6 women), 7 part-time (3 women); includes 4 minority (2 Black or African American, non-Hispanic/Latino; 1 Hispanic/Latino; 1 Two or more races, non-Hispanic/Latino), 2 international. Average age 39. 14 applicants, 79% accepted, 6 enrolled. In 2014, 9 master's, 1 doctorate awarded. Terminal master's awarded for partial completion of doctoral program. *Degree requirements:* For master's, thesis (for some programs); for doctorate, thesis/dissertation. *Entrance requirements:* For master's, GRE General Test, baccalaureate degree, minimum GPA of 3.0; for doctorate, GRE General Test, minimum GPA of 3.0. Additional exam requirements/recommendations for international students: Required—TOEFL (minimum score 550 paper-based; 79 iBT), IELTS (minimum score 6.5). *Application deadline:* For fall admission, 5/1 priority date for international students; for spring admission, 11/1 priority date for international students; for summer admission, 4/1 priority date for international students. Applications are processed on a rolling basis. Application fee: $60. *Expenses:* Tuition, state resident: full-time $11,326; part-time $630 per credit hour. Tuition, nonresident: full-time $23,568; part-time $1311 per credit hour. *Required fees:* $196. Tuition and fees vary according to program and reciprocity agreements. *Financial support:* Fellowships with full tuition reimbursements, career-related internships or fieldwork, Federal Work-Study, institutionally sponsored loans, scholarships/grants, health care benefits, and tuition waivers (full and partial) available. Financial award application deadline: 2/1; financial award applicants required to submit FAFSA. *Unit head:* Dr. Beth A. Boehm, Dean/Vice Provost, 502-852-6590, Fax: 502-852-6616, E-mail: beth.boehm@louisville.edu. *Application contact:* Libby Leggett, Executive Director of Graduate Admissions and Recruitment, 502-852-3108, Fax: 502-852-3111, E-mail: melegg02@louisville.edu.
Website: http://www.graduate.louisville.edu

University of Maine, Graduate School, Interdisciplinary Doctoral Program, Orono, ME 04469. Offers PhD. Part-time and evening/weekend programs available. *Students:* 22 full-time (16 women), 12 part-time (8 women); includes 3 minority (1 Black or African American, non-Hispanic/Latino; 2 American Indian or Alaska Native, non-Hispanic/Latino), 4 international. Average age 42. 9 applicants, 78% accepted, 5 enrolled. In 2014, 7 doctorates awarded. *Degree requirements:* For doctorate, comprehensive exam, thesis/dissertation. *Entrance requirements:* For doctorate, GRE General Test, master's degree. Additional exam requirements/recommendations for international students: Required—TOEFL. *Application deadline:* For fall admission, 4/1 for domestic students; for spring admission, 11/1 for domestic students. Applications are processed on a rolling basis. Application fee: $65. Electronic applications accepted. *Expenses:* Tuition, state resident: part-time $658 per credit hour. Tuition, nonresident: part-time $1550 per credit hour. *Financial support:* In 2014–15, 13 students received support, including 1 fellowship (averaging $20,000 per year), 6 research assistantships (averaging $14,600 per year), 2 teaching assistantships (averaging $14,600 per year). Financial award application deadline: 3/1. *Unit head:* Scott G. Delcourt, Assistant Vice President for Graduate Studies and Senior Associate Dean, 207-581-3291, Fax: 207-581-3232, E-mail: graduate@maine.edu. *Application contact:* Scott G. Delcourt, Assistant Vice President for Graduate Studies and Senior Associate Dean, 207-581-3291, Fax: 207-581-3232, E-mail: graduate@maine.edu.
Website: http://umaine.edu/graduate/

University of Maine, Graduate School, Master of Arts in Interdisciplinary Studies Program, Orono, ME 04469. Offers MA. Part-time and evening/weekend programs available. *Students:* 6 full-time (5 women), 13 part-time (11 women); includes 2 minority (both American Indian or Alaska Native, non-Hispanic/Latino). Average age 44. 8 applicants, 38% accepted, 1 enrolled. In 2014, 5 master's awarded. *Degree requirements:* For master's, thesis or alternative, project. *Entrance requirements:* Additional exam requirements/recommendations for international students: Required—TOEFL. *Application deadline:* For fall admission, 4/1 for domestic students; for spring admission, 11/1 for domestic students. Applications are processed on a rolling basis. Application fee: $65. Electronic applications accepted. *Expenses:* Tuition, state resident: part-time $658 per credit hour. Tuition, nonresident: part-time $1550 per credit hour. *Financial support:* In 2014–15, 1 student received support. Federal Work-Study and institutionally sponsored loans available. Financial award application deadline: 3/1. *Unit head:* Scott G. Delcourt, Assistant Vice President for Graduate Studies and Senior Associate Dean, 207-581-3291, Fax: 207-581-3232, E-mail: graduate@maine.edu. *Application contact:* Scott G. Delcourt, Assistant Vice President for Graduate Studies and Senior Associate Dean, 207-581-3291, Fax: 207-581-3232, E-mail: graduate@maine.edu.
Website: http://umaine.edu/graduate/

University of Manitoba, Faculty of Graduate Studies, Interdisciplinary Programs, Individual Interdisciplinary Programs, Winnipeg, MB R3T 2N2, Canada. Offers M Sc, MA, PhD.

University of Massachusetts Worcester, Graduate School of Biomedical Sciences, Worcester, MA 01655-0115. Offers biochemistry and molecular pharmacology (PhD); bioinformatics and computational biology (PhD); biomedical sciences (millennium program) (PhD); cancer biology (PhD); cell biology (PhD); clinical and population health research (PhD); clinical investigation (MS); immunology and microbiology (PhD); interdisciplinary graduate research (PhD); neuroscience (PhD); translational science (PhD). *Faculty:* 1,367 full-time (516 women), 294 part-time/adjunct (186 women). *Students:* 372 full-time (191 women), 11 part-time (7 women); includes 60 minority (12 Black or African American, non-Hispanic/Latino; 33 Asian, non-Hispanic/Latino; 15 Hispanic/Latino), 139 international. Average age 29. 481 applicants, 22% accepted, 41 enrolled. In 2014, 4 master's, 54 doctorates awarded. Terminal master's awarded for partial completion of doctoral program. *Degree requirements:* For master's, comprehensive exam, thesis; for doctorate, comprehensive exam, thesis/dissertation. *Entrance requirements:* For master's, MD, PhD, DVM, or PharmD; for doctorate, GRE General Test, bachelor's degree. Additional exam requirements/recommendations for international students: Required—TOEFL (minimum score 100 iBT) or IELTS (minimum score 7.5). *Application deadline:* For fall admission, 12/15 for domestic and international students; for spring admission, 5/15 for domestic students. Application fee: $80. Electronic applications accepted. *Expenses:* Expenses: $6,942 state resident; $14,158 nonresident. *Financial support:* In 2014–15, 383 students received support, including research assistantships with full tuition reimbursements available (averaging $30,000 per year); scholarships/grants, health care benefits, tuition waivers (full), and unspecified assistantships also available. Financial award application deadline: 5/16. *Faculty research:* RNA interference, cell/molecular/developmental biology, bioinformatics, clinical/translational research, infectious disease. *Total annual research expenditures:* $241.9 million. *Unit head:* Dr. Anthony Carruthers, Dean, 508-856-4135, E-mail: anthony.carruthers@umassmed.edu. *Application contact:* Dr. Kendall Knight, Assistant Vice Provost for Admissions, 508-856-5628, Fax: 508-856-3659, E-mail: kendall.knight@umassmed.edu.
Website: http://www.umassmed.edu/gsbs/

University of Memphis, Graduate School, College of Arts and Sciences, Department of Earth Sciences, Memphis, TN 38152. Offers archaeology (MS); earth sciences (PhD); geographic information systems (Graduate Certificate), including geographic information systems, GIS educator, GIS planning, GIS professional; geography (MA, MS); geology (MS); geophysics (MS); interdisciplinary (MS). Part-time and evening/weekend programs available. *Faculty:* 13 full-time (3 women), 2 part-time/adjunct (0 women). *Students:* 27 full-time (8 women), 26 part-time (7 women); includes 2 minority (1 Black or African American, non-Hispanic/Latino; 1 Asian, non-Hispanic/Latino), 19 international. Average age 32. 36 applicants, 69% accepted, 7 enrolled. In 2014, 7 master's, 5 doctorates awarded. Terminal master's awarded for partial completion of doctoral program. *Degree requirements:* For master's, comprehensive exam, thesis, seminar presentation; for doctorate, thesis/dissertation. *Entrance requirements:* For master's, GRE General Test, 3 letters of recommendation, statement of research interests; for doctorate, GRE General Test, 2 letters of recommendation, resume, personal statement. Additional exam requirements/recommendations for international students: Required—TOEFL (minimum score 550 paper-based). *Application deadline:* For fall admission, 1/31 for domestic students; for spring admission, 11/1 for domestic students. Applications are processed on a rolling basis. Application fee: $35 ($60 for international students). Electronic applications accepted. *Financial support:* In 2014–15, 18 students received support. Fellowships with full tuition reimbursements available, research assistantships with full tuition reimbursements available, teaching assistantships with full tuition reimbursements available, Federal Work-Study, scholarships/grants, and unspecified assistantships available. Financial award application deadline: 2/15; financial award applicants required to submit FAFSA. *Faculty research:* Hazards, active tectonics, geophysics, hydrology and water resources, spatial analysis. *Unit head:* Dr. M. Jerry Bartholomew, Chair, 901-678-4536, Fax: 901-678-4467, E-mail: jbrthlm1@memphis.edu. *Application contact:* Dr. Arlene Hill, Associate Professor and Graduate Program Coordinator, 901-678-4358, Fax: 901-678-2178, E-mail: dlarsen@memphis.edu.
Website: http://www.memphis.edu/des/

University of Michigan, College of Engineering, Interpro Programs in Engineering, Ann Arbor, MI 48109. Offers automotive engineering (M Eng); design science (PhD); energy systems engineering (MS); financial engineering (MS); global automotive and manufacturing engineering (M Eng); manufacturing engineering (M Eng, D Eng); pharmaceutical engineering (M Eng); robotics and autonomous vehicles (M Eng); MBA/M Eng; MSE/MS. Part-time programs available. Postbaccalaureate distance learning degree programs offered (no on-campus study). *Students:* 187 full-time (46 women), 250 part-time (40 women). 364 applicants, 2% accepted, 3 enrolled. In 2014, 171 master's, 1 doctorate awarded. Terminal master's awarded for partial completion of doctoral program. *Degree requirements:* For master's, capstone project; for doctorate, thesis/dissertation. *Entrance requirements:* For master's, GRE; for doctorate, GRE, 2 years of work experience. Additional exam requirements/recommendations for international students: Required—TOEFL (minimum score 560 paper-based). *Application deadline:* Applications are processed on a rolling basis. Electronic applications accepted. *Financial support:* Fellowships, research assistantships with full tuition reimbursements, teaching assistantships with full tuition reimbursements, career-related internships or fieldwork, scholarships/grants, and unspecified assistantships available. Financial award application deadline: 2/15; financial award applicants required to submit FAFSA. *Faculty research:* Automotive engineering, design science, energy

systems engineering, engineering sustainable systems, financial engineering, global automotive and manufacturing engineering, integrated microsystems, manufacturing engineering, pharmaceutical engineering, robotics and autonomous vehicles. *Total annual research expenditures:* $263,643. *Unit head:* Prof. Panos Papalambros, Director, 734-647-8401, Fax: 734-647-0079, E-mail: pyp@umich.edu. *Application contact:* Patti Mackmiller, Program Manager, 734-764-3071, Fax: 734-647-2243, E-mail: pmackmil@umich.edu.
Website: http://www.isd.engin.umich.edu

University of Minnesota, Twin Cities Campus, Graduate School, College of Liberal Arts, Department of Cultural Studies and Comparative Literature, Program in Comparative Studies in Discourse and Society, Minneapolis, MN 55455-0213. Offers PhD. *Degree requirements:* For doctorate, 2 foreign languages, thesis/dissertation. *Entrance requirements:* For doctorate, GRE General Test, sample of written work. Additional exam requirements/recommendations for international students: Required— TOEFL. *Faculty research:* Cultural theory; music; architecture, space, and urbanism; body and gender; film and popular culture.

University of Missouri, Office of Research and Graduate Studies, School of Natural Resources, Interdisciplinary Certificate Programs, Columbia, MO 65211. Offers Certificate. *Unit head:* Dr. Mark Ryan, Director, 573-882-0314, E-mail: ryanmr@missouri.edu. *Application contact:* Laura Hertel, Coordinator of Student Services, 573-882-1730, E-mail: snr@missouri.edu.

University of Missouri–Kansas City, School of Graduate Studies, Kansas City, MO 64110-2499. Offers interdisciplinary studies (PhD), including art history, cell biology and biophysics, chemistry, computer and electrical engineering, computer science and informatics, economics, education, engineering, English, entrepreneurship and innovation, geosciences, history, mathematics and statistics, molecular biology and biochemistry, music education, oral and craniofacial sciences, pharmaceutical sciences, pharmacology, physics, political science, public affairs and administration, religious studies, social science, telecommunications and computer networking; PMBA/MHA. *Students:* 95 full-time (36 women), 264 part-time (101 women); includes 32 minority (16 Black or African American, non-Hispanic/Latino; 6 Asian, non-Hispanic/Latino; 7 Hispanic/Latino; 1 Native Hawaiian or other Pacific Islander, non-Hispanic/Latino; 2 Two or more races, non-Hispanic/Latino), 152 international. Average age 35. 328 applicants, 24% accepted, 64 enrolled. In 2014, 55 doctorates awarded. *Degree requirements:* For doctorate, comprehensive exam, thesis/dissertation, residency. *Entrance requirements:* For doctorate, GRE General Test, minimum GPA of 2.75 (undergraduate), 3.0 (graduate). Additional exam requirements/recommendations for international students: Required—TOEFL (minimum score 550 paper-based; 80 iBT), TWE (minimum score 4). *Application deadline:* For fall admission, 1/15 priority date for domestic and international students. Applications are processed on a rolling basis. Application fee: $45 ($50 for international students). Electronic applications accepted. *Financial support:* Career-related internships or fieldwork, Federal Work-Study, tuition waivers (partial), and unspecified assistantships available. Support available to part-time students. Financial award application deadline: 3/1; financial award applicants required to submit FAFSA. *Unit head:* Dr. Denis M. Medeiros, Dean, 816-235-1301, Fax: 816-235-1310, E-mail: medeirosd@umkc.edu. *Application contact:* Quincy Bennett Johnson, Coordinator of Admissions and Recruitment, Interdisciplinary PhD Program, 816-235-1559, Fax: 816-235-1310, E-mail: bennettq@umkc.edu.
Website: http://sgs.umkc.edu/

University of Missouri–St. Louis, College of Arts and Sciences, Interdisciplinary Programs, St. Louis, MO 63121. Offers gender studies (Certificate); international studies (Certificate). *Faculty:* 1 full-time (0 women), 17 part-time/adjunct (12 women). *Students:* 1 (woman) full-time, 6 part-time (5 women); includes 3 minority (2 Black or African American, non-Hispanic/Latino; 1 Asian, non-Hispanic/Latino). Average age 35. 23 applicants, 48% accepted, 3 enrolled. In 2014, 5 Certificates awarded. *Entrance requirements:* Additional exam requirements/recommendations for international students: Required—TOEFL (minimum score 550 paper-based; 79 iBT), IELTS (minimum score 6.5). *Application deadline:* For fall admission, 7/1 for domestic and international students; for spring admission, 12/1 for domestic and international students. Applications are processed on a rolling basis. Application fee: $50 ($40 for international students). *Expenses:* Tuition, state resident: full-time $7364; part-time $409.10 per hour. Tuition, nonresident: full-time $18,153; part-time $1008.50 per hour. *Unit head:* Dr. Ronald Yasbin, Dean, 314-516-5501. *Application contact:* Graduate Admissions, 314-516-5458, Fax: 314-516-6996, E-mail: gradadm@umsl.edu.

The University of Montana, Graduate School, College of Humanities and Sciences, Division of Biological Sciences, Interdisciplinary Program in Systems Ecology, Missoula, MT 59812-0002. Offers MS, PhD.

The University of Montana, Graduate School, Program in Interdisciplinary Studies, Missoula, MT 59812-0002. Offers individualized interdisciplinary studies (PhD); interdisciplinary studies (MIS). *Degree requirements:* For doctorate, thesis/dissertation. *Entrance requirements:* For master's, GRE General Test. Additional exam requirements/ recommendations for international students: Required—TOEFL.

University of New Brunswick Fredericton, School of Graduate Studies, Interdisciplinary Studies Program, Fredericton, NB E3B 5A3, Canada. Offers M IDST, PhD. *Faculty:* 76 full-time (40 women), 1 part-time/adjunct (0 women). *Students:* 47 full-time (33 women), 32 part-time (22 women). In 2014, 3 master's, 6 doctorates awarded. *Degree requirements:* For master's, thesis; for doctorate, comprehensive exam, thesis/ dissertation. *Entrance requirements:* For master's, BA honors degree with minimum A-average, minimum GPA of 3.3; for doctorate, master's degree with thesis; minimum A-average. Additional exam requirements/recommendations for international students: Required—TOEFL (minimum score 600 paper-based; 100 iBT), IELTS (minimum score 7), TWE (minimum score 5.5). *Application deadline:* Applications are processed on a rolling basis. Application fee: $50 Canadian dollars. Electronic applications accepted. *Financial support:* In 2014–15, 8 fellowships, 10 research assistantships, 5 teaching assistantships were awarded. *Unit head:* Dr. Linda Eyre, Assistant Dean of Graduate Studies, 506-447-3044, Fax: 506-453-4817, E-mail: gradidst@unb.ca. *Application contact:* Janet Amirault, Graduate Secretary, 506-458-7558, Fax: 506-453-4817, E-mail: jamiraul@unb.ca.
Website: http://go.unb.ca/gradprograms

The University of North Carolina at Charlotte, College of Liberal Arts and Sciences, Interdisciplinary Liberal Arts and Sciences Programs, Charlotte, NC 28223-0001. Offers gerontology (MA, Graduate Certificate); Latin American studies (MA); liberal studies (MA); organizational psychology (PhD); public policy (PhD); women's studies (Graduate Certificate). *Faculty:* 6 full-time (3 women), 5 part-time/adjunct (all women). *Students:* 58 full-time (31 women), 55 part-time (45 women); includes 24 minority (15 Black or African American, non-Hispanic/Latino; 1 Asian, non-Hispanic/Latino; 6 Hispanic/Latino; 1 Native Hawaiian or other Pacific Islander, non-Hispanic/Latino; 1 Two or more races, non-Hispanic/Latino), 12 international. Average age 33. 96 applicants, 46% accepted, 29 enrolled. In 2014, 11 master's, 8 doctorates, 15 other advanced degrees awarded. Terminal master's awarded for partial completion of doctoral program. *Degree requirements:* For master's, thesis or alternative, comprehensive exam or project; for doctorate, thesis/dissertation. *Entrance requirements:* For master's, GRE General Test

or MAT, minimum GPA of 3.0 during previous 2 years, 2.75 overall; for doctorate, GRE, letters of recommendation. Additional exam requirements/recommendations for international students: Required—TOEFL (minimum score 557 paper-based; 83 iBT). *Application deadline:* For fall admission, 5/1 priority date for domestic students, 5/1 for international students; for spring admission, 10/1 priority date for domestic students, 10/ 1 for international students. Applications are processed on a rolling basis. Application fee: $75. Electronic applications accepted. *Expenses:* Tuition, state resident: full-time $4008. Tuition, nonresident: full-time $16,295. *Required fees:* $2755. Tuition and fees vary according to course load and program. *Financial support:* In 2014–15, 24 students received support, including 20 research assistantships (averaging $10,400 per year), 4 teaching assistantships (averaging $8,250 per year); career-related internships or fieldwork, institutionally sponsored loans, scholarships/grants, and unspecified assistantships also available. Support available to part-time students. Financial award application deadline: 4/1; financial award applicants required to submit FAFSA. *Total annual research expenditures:* $15,045. *Unit head:* Dr. Nancy A. Gutierrez, Dean, 704-687-0081, Fax: 704-687-4347, E-mail: ngutierr@uncc.edu. *Application contact:* Kathy B. Giddings, Director of Graduate Admissions, 704-687-5503, Fax: 704-687-3279, E-mail: gradadm@uncc.edu.
Website: http://www.lbst.uncc.edu/

University of Northern British Columbia, Office of Graduate Studies, Prince George, BC V2N 4Z9, Canada. Offers business administration (Diploma); community health science (M Sc); disability management (MA); education (M Ed); first nations studies (MA); gender studies (MA); history (MA); interdisciplinary studies (MA); international studies (MA); mathematical, computer and physical sciences (M Sc); natural resources and environmental studies (M Sc, MA, MNRES, PhD); political science (MA); psychology (M Sc, PhD); social work (MSW). Part-time and evening/weekend programs available. Postbaccalaureate distance learning degree programs offered (no on-campus study). *Degree requirements:* For master's, thesis; for doctorate, thesis/dissertation. *Entrance requirements:* For master's, GRE, minimum B average in undergraduate course work; for doctorate, candidacy exam, minimum A average in graduate course work.

University of North Texas, Robert B. Toulouse School of Graduate Studies, Denton, TX 76203-5459. Offers accounting (MS); applied anthropology (MA, MS); applied behavior analysis (Certificate); applied geography (MA); applied technology and performance improvement (M Ed, MS); art education (MA); art history (MA); art museum education (Certificate); arts leadership (Certificate); audiology (Au D); behavior analysis (MS); behavioral science (PhD); biochemistry and molecular biology (MS); biology (MA, MS); biomedical engineering (MS); business analysis (MS); chemistry (MS); clinical health psychology (PhD); communication studies (MA, MS); computer engineering (MS); computer science (MS); counseling (M Ed, MS), including clinical mental health counseling (MS), college and university counseling, elementary school counseling, secondary school counseling; creative writing (MA); criminal justice (MS); curriculum and instruction (M Ed); decision sciences (MBA); design (MA, MFA), including fashion design (MFA), innovation studies, interior design (MFA); early childhood studies (MS); economics (MS); educational leadership (M Ed, Ed D); educational psychology (MS, PhD), including family studies (MS), gifted and talented (MS), human development (MS), learning and cognition (MS), research, measurement and evaluation (MS); electrical engineering (MS); emergency management (MPA); engineering technology (MS); English (MA); English as a second language (MA); environmental science (MS); finance (MBA, MS); financial management (MPA); French (MA); health services management (MBA); higher education (M Ed, Ed D); history (MA, MS); hospitality management (MS); human resources management (MPA); information science (MS); information systems (PhD); information technologies (MBA); interdisciplinary studies (MA, MS); international studies (MA); international sustainable tourism (MS); jazz studies (MM); journalism (MA, MJ, Graduate Certificate), including interactive and virtual digital communication (Graduate Certificate), narrative journalism (Graduate Certificate), public relations (Graduate Certificate); kinesiology (MS); linguistics (MA); local government management (MPA); logistics (PhD); logistics and supply chain management (MBA); long-term care, senior housing, and aging services (MA); management (PhD); marketing (MBA); mathematics (MA, MS); mechanical and energy engineering (MS, PhD); music (MA), including ethnomusicology, music theory, musicology, performance; music composition (PhD); music education (MM Ed, PhD); nonprofit management (MPA); operations and supply chain management (MBA); performance (MM, DMA); philosophy (MA); political science (MA); professional and technical communication (MA); radio, television and film (MA, MFA); rehabilitation counseling (Certificate); sociology (MA); Spanish (MA); special education (M Ed); speech-language pathology (MA); strategic management (MBA); studio art (MFA); teaching (M Ed); MBA/MS. Part-time and evening/weekend programs available. Postbaccalaureate distance learning degree programs offered. *Faculty:* 651 full-time (215 women), 233 part-time/adjunct (139 women). *Students:* 3,040 full-time (1,598 women), 3,401 part-time (2,097 women); includes 1,740 minority (533 Black or African American, non-Hispanic/Latino; 15 American Indian or Alaska Native, non-Hispanic/Latino; 286 Asian, non-Hispanic/Latino; 746 Hispanic/Latino; 3 Native Hawaiian or other Pacific Islander, non-Hispanic/Latino; 157 Two or more races, non-Hispanic/Latino), 1,145 international. Terminal master's awarded for partial completion of doctoral program. *Degree requirements:* For master's, variable foreign language requirement, comprehensive exam (for some programs), thesis (for some programs); for doctorate, variable foreign language requirement, comprehensive exam (for some programs), thesis/dissertation; for other advanced degree, variable foreign language requirement, comprehensive exam (for some programs). *Entrance requirements:* For master's and doctorate, GRE, GMAT. Additional exam requirements/recommendations for international students: Required—TOEFL (minimum score 550 paper-based; 79 iBT). *Application deadline:* For fall admission, 7/15 for domestic students, 3/15 for international students; for spring admission, 11/15 for domestic students, 9/15 for international students; for summer admission, 5/1 for domestic students. Applications are processed on a rolling basis. Application fee: $60. Electronic applications accepted. *Expenses:* Tuition, state resident: full-time $5450; part-time $3633 per year. Tuition, nonresident: full-time $11,966; part-time $7977 per year. *Required fees:* $1301; $398 per credit hour. $685 per semester. Tuition and fees vary according to program and reciprocity agreements. *Financial support:* Fellowships with partial tuition reimbursements, research assistantships with partial tuition reimbursements, teaching assistantships, career-related internships or fieldwork, Federal Work-Study, institutionally sponsored loans, scholarships/grants, health care benefits, and library assistantships available. Support available to part-time students. Financial award applicants required to submit FAFSA. *Unit head:* Mark Wardell, Dean, 940-565-2383, E-mail: mark.wardell@unt.edu. *Application contact:* Toulouse School of Graduate Studies, 940-565-2383, Fax: 940-565-2141, E-mail: gradsch@unt.edu.
Website: http://tsgs.unt.edu/

University of Oklahoma, Graduate College, Program in Interdisciplinary Studies, Norman, OK 73019-0390. Offers MA, MS, PhD. Part-time and evening/weekend programs available. *Students:* 77 full-time (22 women), 391 part-time (112 women); includes 115 minority (35 Black or African American, non-Hispanic/Latino; 6 American Indian or Alaska Native, non-Hispanic/Latino; 18 Asian, non-Hispanic/Latino; 38 Hispanic/Latino; 3 Native Hawaiian or other Pacific Islander, non-Hispanic/Latino; 15 Two or more races, non-Hispanic/Latino), 19 international. Average age 34. 117

applicants, 83% accepted, 47 enrolled. In 2014, 217 master's, 6 doctorates awarded. *Entrance requirements:* Additional exam requirements/recommendations for international students: Recommended—TOEFL (minimum score 550 paper-based; 79 iBT). *Application deadline:* For fall admission, 6/1 for domestic students, 4/1 for international students; for spring admission, 11/1 for domestic students, 9/1 for international students. Applications are processed on a rolling basis. Application fee: $50 ($100 for international students). Electronic applications accepted. *Expenses:* Tuition, state resident: full-time $4394; part-time $183.10 per credit hour. Tuition, nonresident: full-time $16,970; part-time $707.10 per credit hour. *Required fees:* $2892; $109.95 per credit hour. $126.50 per semester. *Financial support:* In 2014–15, 22 students received support, including 5 research assistantships (averaging $10,523 per year), 1 teaching assistantship (averaging $10,373 per year); unspecified assistantships also available. Financial award applicants required to submit FAFSA. *Unit head:* Lee Williams, Dean, 405-325-3811, Fax: 405-325-5346, E-mail: lwilliams@ou.edu. *Application contact:* Angela Castillo, Academic Counselor II, 405-325-3841, Fax: 405-325-5346, E-mail: acastillo@ou.edu.

University of Oregon, Graduate School, Interdisciplinary Program in Applied Information Management, Eugene, OR 97403. Offers MS. Part-time programs available. Postbaccalaureate distance learning degree programs offered (no on-campus study). *Degree requirements:* For master's, project. *Entrance requirements:* Additional exam requirements/recommendations for international students: Required—TOEFL. Electronic applications accepted. *Expenses:* Contact institution. *Faculty research:* Business management, information design.

University of Ottawa, Faculty of Graduate and Postdoctoral Studies, Interdisciplinary Programs, Ottawa, ON K1N 6N5, Canada. Offers e-business (Certificate); e-commerce (Certificate); finance (Certificate); health services and policies research (Diploma); population health (PhD); population health risk assessment and management (Certificate); public management and governance (Certificate); systems science (Certificate).

University of Pittsburgh, School of Medicine, Graduate Programs in Medicine, Interdisciplinary Biomedical Graduate Program, Pittsburgh, PA 15260. Offers PhD. *Faculty:* 277 full-time (74 women). *Students:* 26 full-time (15 women); includes 6 minority (1 Black or African American, non-Hispanic/Latino; 4 Asian, non-Hispanic/Latino; 1 Hispanic/Latino), 5 international. Average age 23. 426 applicants, 17% accepted, 26 enrolled. *Degree requirements:* For doctorate, comprehensive exam, thesis/dissertation. *Entrance requirements:* For doctorate, GRE General Test, GRE Subject Test, minimum QPA of 3.0. Additional exam requirements/recommendations for international students: Required—TOEFL (minimum score 600 paper-based; 100 iBT), IELTS (minimum score 7). *Application deadline:* For fall admission, 12/1 priority date for domestic and international students. Application fee: $50. Electronic applications accepted. *Expenses:* Tuition, state resident: full-time $20,742; part-time $838 per credit. Tuition, nonresident: full-time $33,960; part-time $1389 per credit. *Required fees:* $800; $205 per term. Tuition and fees vary according to program. *Financial support:* In 2014–15, 26 research assistantships with full tuition reimbursements (averaging $27,000 per year) were awarded; institutionally sponsored loans, scholarships/grants, traineeships, health care benefits, and unspecified assistantships also available. *Faculty research:* Cell biology and molecular physiology, cellular and molecular pathology, immunology, molecular genetics and developmental biology, molecular pharmacology and molecular virology and microbiology. *Unit head:* Dr. John P. Horn, Associate Dean for Graduate Studies, 412-648-8957, Fax: 412-648-1077, E-mail: gradstudies@medschool.pitt.edu. *Application contact:* Graduate Studies Administrator, 412-648-8957, Fax: 412-648-1077, E-mail: gradstudies@medschool.pitt.edu.
Website: http://www.gradbiomed.pitt.edu/

University of Regina, Faculty of Graduate Studies and Research, Faculty of Fine Arts, Department of Visual Arts, Regina, SK S4S 0A2, Canada. Offers ceramics (MFA); drawing (MFA); interdisciplinary studies (MA, MFA); intermedia (MFA); painting (MFA); sculpture (MFA). *Faculty:* 11 full-time (6 women), 3 part-time/adjunct (1 woman). *Students:* 7 full-time (all women), 2 part-time (both women). 11 applicants, 55% accepted. In 2014, 5 master's awarded. *Degree requirements:* For master's, exhibition, support paper, oral defense. *Entrance requirements:* For master's, documentation of recent work. Additional exam requirements/recommendations for international students: Required—TOEFL (minimum score 580 paper-based; 80 iBT), IELTS (minimum score 6.5), PTE (minimum score 59). *Application deadline:* For fall admission, 1/15 for domestic and international students. Application fee: $100. Electronic applications accepted. *Expenses: Tuition, area resident:* Full-time $4900 Canadian dollars; part-time $837.65 Canadian dollars per semester. *International tuition:* $7900 Canadian dollars full-time. *Required fees:* $396 Canadian dollars; $86.90 Canadian dollars per semester. *Financial support:* In 2014–15, 1 fellowship (averaging $6,000 per year), 6 teaching assistantships (averaging $2,427 per year) were awarded; research assistantships and scholarships/grants also available. Financial award application deadline: 6/15. *Faculty research:* Contemporary visual art theory and practice; art history; curatorial practice; print media; drawing/painting, sculpture, and ceramics. *Unit head:* Dr. David Garneau, Department Head, 306-585-5615, Fax: 306-585-5526, E-mail: david.garneau@uregina.ca. *Application contact:* Dr. Robert Truszkowski, Graduate Coordinator, Visual Arts, 306-585-5574, Fax: 306-585-5526, E-mail: robert.truszkowski@uregina.ca.

University of South Alabama, Graduate School, Mobile, AL 36688. Offers MS, PhD. Part-time and evening/weekend programs available. *Faculty:* 15 full-time (4 women), 1 (woman) part-time/adjunct. *Students:* 37 full-time (27 women), 9 part-time (6 women); includes 8 minority (5 Black or African American, non-Hispanic/Latino; 1 American Indian or Alaska Native, non-Hispanic/Latino; 1 Asian, non-Hispanic/Latino; 1 Hispanic/Latino), 1 international. Average age 28. 62 applicants, 34% accepted, 15 enrolled. In 2014, 1 master's, 6 doctorates awarded. *Degree requirements:* For master's, comprehensive exam, research project or thesis; for doctorate, thesis/dissertation. *Entrance requirements:* For master's, GRE, BA/BS in related discipline, minimum undergraduate GPA of 3.0. Additional exam requirements/recommendations for international students: Required—TOEFL (minimum score 525 paper-based; 71 iBT). *Application deadline:* For fall admission, 7/15 priority date for domestic students, 6/15 priority date for international students; for spring admission, 12/1 priority date for domestic students, 11/1 priority date for international students. Applications are processed on a rolling basis. Application fee: $35. Electronic applications accepted. *Expenses:* Tuition, state resident: full-time $9288; part-time $387 per credit hour. Tuition, nonresident: full-time $18,576; part-time $774 per credit hour. Part-time tuition and fees vary according to course load and program. *Financial support:* Fellowships, research assistantships, teaching assistantships, career-related internships or fieldwork, Federal Work-Study, institutionally sponsored loans, scholarships/grants, and unspecified assistantships available. Support available to part-time students. Financial award application deadline: 5/31; financial award applicants required to submit FAFSA. *Unit head:* Dr. B. Keith Harrison, Dean and Associate Vice President for Academic Affairs, 251-460-6310, E-mail: gradschool@southalabama.edu.
Website: http://www.southalabama.edu/graduatemajors/graduateschool/

The University of South Dakota, Graduate School, Interdisciplinary Studies Program, Vermillion, SD 57069-2390. Offers MA. Part-time programs available. Postbaccalaureate distance learning degree programs offered. *Degree requirements:* For master's, thesis or alternative. *Entrance requirements:* For master's, minimum GPA of 2.7; supplemental packet. Additional exam requirements/recommendations for international students: Required—TOEFL (minimum score 550 paper-based; 79 iBT). Electronic applications accepted.

University of South Florida, Morsani College of Medicine and Graduate School, Graduate Programs in Medical Sciences, Tampa, FL 33620-9951. Offers aging and neuroscience (MSMS); allergy, immunology and infectious disease (PhD); anatomy (MSMS, PhD); athletic training (MSMS); bioinformatics and computational biology (MSBCB); biotechnology (MSB); clinical and translational research (MSMS, PhD); health informatics (MSHI, MSMS); health science (MSMS); interdisciplinary medical sciences (MSMS); medical microbiology and immunology (MSMS); metabolic and nutritional medicine (MSMS); molecular medicine (MSMS, PhD); molecular pharmacology and physiology (PhD); neurology (PhD); pathology and laboratory medicine (PhD); pharmacology and therapeutics (PhD); physiology and biophysics (PhD); women's health (MSMS). *Students:* 338 full-time (162 women), 36 part-time (25 women); includes 173 minority (43 Black or African American, non-Hispanic/Latino; 65 Asian, non-Hispanic/Latino; 58 Hispanic/Latino; 7 Two or more races, non-Hispanic/Latino), 24 international. Average age 26. 1,188 applicants, 41% accepted, 271 enrolled. In 2014, 216 master's awarded. Terminal master's awarded for partial completion of doctoral program. *Degree requirements:* For master's, comprehensive exam, thesis; for doctorate, comprehensive exam, thesis/dissertation. *Entrance requirements:* For master's, GRE General Test or GMAT, bachelor's degree or equivalent from regionally-accredited university with minimum GPA of 3.0 in upper-division sciences coursework; prerequisites in general biology, general chemistry, general physics, organic chemistry, quantitative analysis, and integral and differential calculus; for doctorate, GRE General Test (minimum score of 32nd percentile quantitative), bachelor's degree from regionally-accredited university with minimum GPA of 3.0 in upper-division sciences coursework; 3 letters of recommendation; personal interview; 1-2 page personal statement; prerequisites in biology, chemistry, physics, organic chemistry, quantitative analysis, and integral/differential calculus. Additional exam requirements/recommendations for international students: Required—TOEFL (minimum score 550 paper-based; 79 iBT) or IELTS (minimum score 6.5). *Application deadline:* For fall admission, 2/15 for domestic students, 1/2 for international students. Application fee: $30. *Expenses:* Expenses: Contact institution. *Faculty research:* Anatomy, biochemistry, cancer biology, cardiovascular disease, cell biology, immunology, microbiology, molecular biology, neuroscience, pharmacology, physiology. *Unit head:* Dr. Michael Barber, Professor and Associate Dean for Graduate and Postdoctoral Affairs, 813-974-9908, Fax: 813-974-4317, E-mail: mbarber@health.usf.edu. *Application contact:* Dr. Eric Bennett, Graduate Director, PhD Program in Medical Sciences, 813-974-1545, Fax: 813-974-4317, E-mail: esbennet@health.usf.edu.
Website: http://health.usf.edu/nocms/medicine/graduatestudies/

The University of Tennessee at Martin, Graduate Programs, College of Education, Health and Behavioral Sciences, Program in Teaching, Martin, TN 38238-1000. Offers curriculum and instruction (MS Ed), including 7-12, K-6; initial licensure (MS Ed), including elementary, secondary; initial licensure K-12 (MS Ed), including physical education, special education; interdisciplinary (MS Ed). Part-time programs available. *Students:* 7 full-time (4 women), 92 part-time (66 women); includes 9 minority (8 Black or African American, non-Hispanic/Latino; 1 Two or more races, non-Hispanic/Latino). 82 applicants, 68% accepted, 36 enrolled. In 2014, 24 master's awarded. *Degree requirements:* For master's, comprehensive exam. *Entrance requirements:* For master's, GRE General Test, minimum GPA of 2.5. Additional exam requirements/recommendations for international students: Required—TOEFL (minimum score 525 paper-based; 71 iBT). *Application deadline:* For fall admission, 7/27 priority date for domestic students, 7/27 for international students; for spring admission, 12/17 priority date for domestic students, 12/17 for international students. Applications are processed on a rolling basis. Application fee: $30 ($130 for international students). Electronic applications accepted. *Financial support:* Research assistantships with full tuition reimbursements, teaching assistantships with full tuition reimbursements, career-related internships or fieldwork, scholarships/grants, and unspecified assistantships available. Financial award application deadline: 3/1. *Faculty research:* Special education, science/math/technology, school reform, reading. *Unit head:* Dr. Gail Stephens, Interim Dean, 731-881-7127, Fax: 731-881-7975, E-mail: gstephe6@utm.edu. *Application contact:* Jolene L. Cunningham, Student Services Specialist, 731-881-7012, Fax: 731-881-7499, E-mail: jcunningham@utm.edu.

The University of Texas at Arlington, Graduate School, School of Urban and Public Affairs, Program in Interdisciplinary Studies, Arlington, TX 76019. Offers sustainability (MA). Part-time and evening/weekend programs available. *Entrance requirements:* For master's, GRE or GMAT, resume, essay, two letters of recommendation. Additional exam requirements/recommendations for international students: Required—TOEFL (minimum score 550 paper-based). Electronic applications accepted.

The University of Texas at Dallas, School of Interdisciplinary Studies, Richardson, TX 75080. Offers MA. Part-time and evening/weekend programs available. *Faculty:* 3 full-time (2 women). *Students:* 8 full-time (5 women), 11 part-time (6 women); includes 12 minority (6 Black or African American, non-Hispanic/Latino; 3 Asian, non-Hispanic/Latino; 2 Hispanic/Latino; 1 Two or more races, non-Hispanic/Latino). Average age 37. 14 applicants, 71% accepted, 8 enrolled. In 2014, 10 master's awarded. *Degree requirements:* For master's, research project, seminar. *Entrance requirements:* For master's, GRE General Test, minimum GPA of 3.0. Additional exam requirements/recommendations for international students: Required—TOEFL (minimum score 550 paper-based). *Application deadline:* For fall admission, 7/15 for domestic students, 5/1 priority date for international students; for spring admission, 11/15 for domestic students, 9/1 priority date for international students. Applications are processed on a rolling basis. Application fee: $50 ($100 for international students). Electronic applications accepted. *Expenses:* Tuition, state resident: full-time $11,940; part-time $663 per credit. Tuition, nonresident: full-time $22,282; part-time $1238 per credit. *Financial support:* In 2014–15, 9 students received support. Research assistantships with partial tuition reimbursements available, teaching assistantships with partial tuition reimbursements available, career-related internships or fieldwork, Federal Work-Study, institutionally sponsored loans, and scholarships/grants available. Support available to part-time students. Financial award application deadline: 4/30; financial award applicants required to submit FAFSA. *Faculty research:* Education of homeless children and youths. *Total annual research expenditures:* $19,581. *Unit head:* Dr. George Fair, Dean, 972-883-2350, Fax: 972-883-2440, E-mail: gwfair@utdallas.edu. *Application contact:* Rebecca Wiser, Academic Support Coordinator, 972-883-2354, Fax: 972-883-2440, E-mail: rwiser@utdallas.edu.
Website: http://www.utdallas.edu/is

The University of Texas at El Paso, Graduate School, College of Liberal Arts, Master of Arts in Interdisciplinary Studies Program, El Paso, TX 79968-0001. Offers MAIS. Part-time and evening/weekend programs available. *Entrance requirements:* For master's, GRE, minimum GPA of 3.0, letters of recommendation. Additional exam requirements/recommendations for international students: Required—TOEFL; Recommended—IELTS. Electronic applications accepted.

The University of Texas at San Antonio, College of Education and Human Development, Department of Interdisciplinary Learning and Teaching, San Antonio, TX 78249-0617. Offers education (MA), including curriculum and instruction, early childhood and elementary education, instructional technology, reading and literacy, special education; interdisciplinary learning and teaching (PhD). Part-time and evening/weekend programs available. *Faculty:* 26 full-time (19 women), 1 (woman) part-time/adjunct. *Students:* 89 full-time (73 women), 219 part-time (177 women); includes 176 minority (21 Black or African American, non-Hispanic/Latino; 2 American Indian or Alaska Native, non-Hispanic/Latino; 7 Asian, non-Hispanic/Latino; 140 Hispanic/Latino; 6 Two or more races, non-Hispanic/Latino), 11 international. Average age 34. 141 applicants, 91% accepted, 84 enrolled. In 2014, 146 master's, 5 doctorates awarded. *Degree requirements:* For master's, comprehensive exam, thesis optional, 36 hours of course work without thesis (33 with thesis); for doctorate, comprehensive exam, thesis/dissertation, minimum of 60 semester credit hours. *Entrance requirements:* For master's, bachelor's degree with minimum GPA of 3.0 in last 60 hours of coursework; 18 hours of undergraduate coursework in education or related field; for doctorate, GRE, transcripts from all colleges and universities attended, professional vitae demonstrating experience in work environment where education was primary professional emphasis, 3 letters of recommendation, statement of purpose, minimum GPA of 3.5. Additional exam requirements/recommendations for international students: Required—TOEFL (minimum score 550 paper-based; 79 iBT), IELTS (minimum score 6.5). *Application deadline:* For fall admission, 7/1 for domestic students, 4/1 for international students; for spring admission, 11/1 for domestic students, 9/1 for international students. Applications are processed on a rolling basis. Application fee: $45 ($80 for international students). Electronic applications accepted. *Expenses:* Tuition, state resident: full-time $4671; part-time $260 per credit hour. Tuition, nonresident: full-time $18,022; part-time $1001 per credit hour. *Financial support:* Career-related internships or fieldwork, Federal Work-Study, and scholarships/grants available. Support available to part-time students. *Faculty research:* Explorations of science, learning and teaching, family involvement in early childhood, culturally-responsive literacy instruction in diverse settings, STEM education, autism spectrum disorder. *Unit head:* Dr. Maria R. Cortez, Department Chair, 210-458-5969, Fax: 210-458-7281, E-mail: mari.cortez@utsa.edu. *Application contact:* Erin Doran, Student Development Specialist, 210-458-7443, Fax: 210-458-7281, E-mail: erin.doran@utsa.edu.
Website: http://education.utsa.edu/interdisciplinary_learning_and_teaching/

The University of Texas at Tyler, College of Arts and Sciences, Department of Art and Art History, Tyler, TX 75799-0001. Offers art history (MA); interdisciplinary (MAIS); studio art (MFA). *Degree requirements:* For master's, thesis, graduate committee review. *Entrance requirements:* For master's, minimum GPA of 3.0. Additional exam requirements/recommendations for international students: Required—TOEFL. *Faculty research:* Classical myths in contemporary art, social issues in contemporary art, casting methods, Renaissance art.

The University of Texas at Tyler, College of Arts and Sciences, Department of Biology, Tyler, TX 75799-0001. Offers biology (MS); interdisciplinary studies (MSIS). *Degree requirements:* For master's, comprehensive exam, thesis, oral qualifying exam, thesis defense. *Entrance requirements:* For master's, GRE General Test, GRE Subject Test, bachelor's degree in biology or equivalent. Additional exam requirements/recommendations for international students: Required—TOEFL. Electronic applications accepted. *Faculty research:* Phenotypic plasticity and heritability of life history traits, invertebrate ecology and genetics, systematics and phylogenetics of reptiles, hibernation physiology in turtles, landscape ecology, host-microbe interaction, outer membrane proteins in bacteria.

The University of Texas at Tyler, College of Arts and Sciences, Department of Literature and Languages, Tyler, TX 75799-0001. Offers English (MA); interdisciplinary studies (MAIS). Part-time and evening/weekend programs available. *Degree requirements:* For master's, one foreign language, comprehensive exam, thesis optional. *Entrance requirements:* For master's, GRE General Test, minimum GPA of 3.0; four semesters or the equivalent of one foreign language. Additional exam requirements/recommendations for international students: Required—TOEFL. Electronic applications accepted. *Faculty research:* Medieval and Tudor drama, Shakespeare, British Romanticism, British and Irish modernism, American realism, Greek drama, nineteenth-century American literature.

The University of Texas at Tyler, College of Education and Psychology, Department of Psychology and Counseling, Tyler, TX 75799-0001. Offers clinical psychology (MS), including neuropsychology, school psychology; counseling psychology (MA), including general, marriage and family; interdisciplinary studies (MSIS); school counseling (MA). Part-time and evening/weekend programs available. *Degree requirements:* For master's, comprehensive exam, thesis optional. *Entrance requirements:* For master's, GRE General Test, minimum GPA of 3.0. Additional exam requirements/recommendations for international students: Required—TOEFL. Electronic applications accepted. *Faculty research:* Neuropsychology, child abuse, psychometric properties of psychological instruments, maternal behavior, clinical practice issues, victimization of women, post-traumatic stress disorder.

The University of Texas at Tyler, College of Engineering and Computer Science, Department of Computer Science, Tyler, TX 75799-0001. Offers computer science (MS); interdisciplinary studies (MSIS). *Degree requirements:* For master's, comprehensive exam, thesis optional. *Entrance requirements:* For master's, GRE General Test, previous course work in data structures and computer organization, 6 hours of course work in calculus and statistics. Additional exam requirements/recommendations for international students: Required—TOEFL. Electronic applications accepted. *Faculty research:* Database design, software engineering, client-server architecture, visual programming, data mining, computer security, digital image processing, simulation and modeling, computer science education.

The University of Texas Health Science Center at San Antonio, Graduate School of Biomedical Sciences, Integrated Biomedical Sciences Program, San Antonio, TX 78229-3900. Offers PhD. *Degree requirements:* For doctorate, comprehensive exam, thesis/dissertation. *Application deadline:* For fall admission, 1/15 for domestic and international students. *Financial support:* Application deadline: 6/30.
Website: http://gsbs.uthscsa.edu/graduate_programs/integrated-biomedical-sciences

The University of Texas–Pan American, College of Arts and Humanities, Program in Interdisciplinary Studies, Edinburg, TX 78539. Offers MAIS, MSIS. Part-time and evening/weekend programs available. *Degree requirements:* For master's, comprehensive exam, thesis or alternative. *Entrance requirements:* For master's, GRE General Test, minimum GPA of 3.0. *Expenses:* Tuition, state resident: full-time $4187; part-time $232.60 per credit hour. Tuition, nonresident: full-time $10,857; part-time $603.16 per credit hour. *Required fees:* $782; $27.50 per credit hour. $143.35 per semester.

University of the Incarnate Word, School of Graduate Studies and Research, College of Humanities, Arts, and Social Sciences, Program in Multidisciplinary Studies, San Antonio, TX 78209-6397. Offers MA. Part-time and evening/weekend programs available. *Faculty:* 3 full-time (2 women). *Students:* 3 full-time (1 woman), 3 part-time (2 women); includes 4 minority (all Hispanic/Latino). Average age 40. 7 applicants, 100% accepted, 1 enrolled. In 2014, 1 master's awarded. *Degree requirements:* For master's, thesis or capstone experience in one area of focus which incorporates the integration of all disciplines from which work is taken. *Entrance requirements:* For master's, GRE (minimum score 800 verbal and quantitative, 3.5 analytical), MAT (minimum score 40), GMAT (minimum score 450). Additional exam requirements/recommendations for international students: Required—TOEFL (minimum score 560 paper-based; 83 iBT). *Application deadline:* Applications are processed on a rolling basis. Application fee: $20. Electronic applications accepted. *Expenses: Tuition:* Part-time $815 per credit hour. *Required fees:* $86 per credit hour. *Financial support:* Federal Work-Study and scholarships/grants available. Financial award applicants required to submit FAFSA. *Unit head:* Dr. Kevin Vichcales, Dean, School of Graduate Studies and Research, 210-829-3157. *Application contact:* Andrea Cyterski-Acosta, Dean of Enrollment, 210-829-6005, Fax: 210-829-3921, E-mail: admis@uiwtx.edu.
Website: http://www.uiw.edu/gradstudies/documents/mamultidisciplinarystudies.pdf

University of the Incarnate Word, School of Graduate Studies and Research, School of Mathematics, Science, and Engineering, Program in Multidisciplinary Sciences, San Antonio, TX 78209-6397. Offers MA. Part-time and evening/weekend programs available. *Faculty:* 8 full-time (4 women), 1 (woman) part-time/adjunct. *Students:* 17 part-time (16 women); includes 12 minority (1 Asian, non-Hispanic/Latino; 11 Hispanic/Latino). Average age 35. 13 applicants, 100% accepted, 13 enrolled. In 2014, 1 master's awarded. *Degree requirements:* For master's, capstone. *Entrance requirements:* For master's, GRE (minimum score 800 verbal and quantitative, 3.5 analytical), elementary certification with science endorsement (18 hours of science) or secondary certification, or equivalent professional experience teaching service. Additional exam requirements/recommendations for international students: Required—TOEFL (minimum score 560 paper-based; 83 iBT). *Application deadline:* Applications are processed on a rolling basis. Application fee: $20. Electronic applications accepted. *Expenses: Tuition:* Part-time $815 per credit hour. *Required fees:* $86 per credit hour. *Financial support:* Federal Work-Study and scholarships/grants available. Financial award applicants required to submit FAFSA. *Faculty research:* Professional development of in-service high school science teachers. *Unit head:* Dr. Alakananda Chaudhuri, Director, Multidisciplinary Sciences, 210-829-3145, Fax: 210-829-3153, E-mail: alakanan@uiwtx.edu. *Application contact:* Andrea Cyterski-Acosta, Dean of Enrollment, 210-829-6005, Fax: 210-829-3921, E-mail: admis@uiwtx.edu.
Website: http://www.uiw.edu/gradstudies/documents/mamultidisciplinarysciences.pdf

University of Vermont, Graduate College, College of Education and Social Services, Department of Leadership and Developmental Sciences, Interdisciplinary Major, Burlington, VT 05405. Offers M Ed. *Degree requirements:* For master's, thesis or alternative. *Entrance requirements:* Additional exam requirements/recommendations for international students: Required—TOEFL (minimum score 550 paper-based; 80 iBT). Electronic applications accepted.

University of Virginia, College and Graduate School of Arts and Sciences, Program in Art and Architectural History, Charlottesville, VA 22903. Offers MA, PhD. *Faculty:* 21 full-time (10 women), 2 part-time/adjunct (both women). *Students:* 32 full-time (22 women); includes 4 minority (2 Asian, non-Hispanic/Latino; 1 Hispanic/Latino; 1 Two or more races, non-Hispanic/Latino), 1 international. Average age 32. 52 applicants, 15% accepted, 4 enrolled. In 2014, 4 master's, 10 doctorates awarded. *Degree requirements:* For master's, one foreign language, comprehensive exam, thesis; for doctorate, 2 foreign languages, thesis/dissertation, oral exam. *Entrance requirements:* For master's and doctorate, GRE, 2 letters of recommendation. *Application deadline:* For fall admission, 12/7 for domestic and international students. Applications are processed on a rolling basis. Application fee: $60. Electronic applications accepted. *Expenses:* Tuition, state resident: full-time $14,164; part-time $349 per credit hour. Tuition, nonresident: full-time $23,722; part-time $1300 per credit hour. *Required fees:* $2514. *Financial support:* Application deadline: 12/7. *Unit head:* Larry Goedde, Chair, 434-924-3541, Fax: 434-924-3647, E-mail: artdept@virginia.edu.
Website: http://www.virginia.edu/art/phd-program/

University of Washington, Tacoma, Graduate Programs, Interdisciplinary Studies Program, Tacoma, WA 98402-3100. Offers MA. Part-time and evening/weekend programs available. *Degree requirements:* For master's, thesis or project. *Entrance requirements:* For master's, GRE, statement of intended area of focus, two official transcripts from every college attended, copy of current resume, three recommendations. Additional exam requirements/recommendations for international students: Required—TOEFL. Electronic applications accepted. *Faculty research:* American history, political and social theory, political economy of labor, human rights; African-American, labor, and ethnic studies; South Asian art, aesthetics, semiotics, and modes of creative practice; social movements.

The University of Western Ontario, Faculty of Graduate Studies, Center for the Study of Theory and Criticism, London, ON N6A 5B8, Canada. Offers MA, PhD. *Degree requirements:* For master's, one foreign language, thesis; for doctorate, one foreign language, comprehensive exam, thesis/dissertation. *Entrance requirements:* For master's, honors degree or equivalent, minimum B+ average, 2 samples of written work; for doctorate, MA in humanitites or social sciences.

University of Wisconsin–Milwaukee, Graduate School, Program in Multidisciplinary Studies, Milwaukee, WI 53201-0413. Offers PhD. *Degree requirements:* For doctorate, thesis/dissertation. Electronic applications accepted.

Virginia Commonwealth University, Graduate School, Program in Interdisciplinary Studies, Richmond, VA 23284-9005. Offers MIS. Part-time programs available. *Degree requirements:* For master's, thesis optional. *Entrance requirements:* For master's, GRE General Test, minimum GPA of 3.0. Additional exam requirements/recommendations for international students: Required—TOEFL (minimum score 600 paper-based; 100 iBT); Recommended—IELTS (minimum score 6.5). Electronic applications accepted.

Virginia Polytechnic Institute and State University, Graduate School, Intercollege, Blacksburg, VA 24061. Offers genetics, bioinformatics and computational biology (PhD); information technology (MIT); macromolecular science and engineering (MS, PhD). *Students:* 173 full-time (89 women), 657 part-time (229 women); includes 186 minority (65 Black or African American, non-Hispanic/Latino; 64 Asian, non-Hispanic/Latino; 33 Hispanic/Latino; 2 Native Hawaiian or other Pacific Islander, non-Hispanic/Latino; 22 Two or more races, non-Hispanic/Latino), 89 international. Average age 32. 599 applicants, 75% accepted, 343 enrolled. In 2014, 102 master's, 19 doctorates awarded. *Degree requirements:* For master's, comprehensive exam (for some programs), thesis (for some programs); for doctorate, comprehensive exam (for some programs), thesis/dissertation (for some programs). *Entrance requirements:* For master's and doctorate, GRE/GMAT (may vary by department). Additional exam requirements/recommendations for international students: Required—TOEFL (minimum score 550 paper-based). *Application deadline:* For fall admission, 8/1 for domestic students, 4/1 for international students; for spring admission, 1/1 for domestic students, 9/1 for international students. Applications are processed on a rolling basis. Application fee: $75. Electronic applications accepted. *Expenses:* Tuition, state resident: full-time $11,656; part-time $647.50 per credit hour. Tuition, nonresident: full-time $23,351; part-time $1297.25 per credit hour. *Required fees:* $2533; $465.75 per semester. Tuition and fees vary according to course load, campus/location and program. *Financial support:* In 2014–15,

102 research assistantships with full tuition reimbursements (averaging $25,419 per year), 13 teaching assistantships with full tuition reimbursements (averaging $21,101 per year) were awarded. Financial award application deadline: 3/1; financial award applicants required to submit FAFSA. *Unit head:* Dr. Karen P. DePauw, Vice President and Dean for Graduate Education, 540-231-7581, Fax: 540-231-1670, E-mail: kpdepauw@vt.edu. *Application contact:* Graduate Admissions and Academic Progress, 540-231-8636, Fax: 540-231-2039, E-mail: grads@vt.edu.
Website: http://www.graduateschool.vt.edu/graduate_catalog/colleges.htm

Virginia State University, College of Graduate Studies, Program in Interdisciplinary Studies, Petersburg, VA 23806-0001. Offers MIS. Program offered jointly with Virginia Commonwealth University. *Degree requirements:* For master's, thesis optional.

Walden University, Graduate Programs, School of Nursing, Minneapolis, MN 55401. Offers adult-gerontology acute care nurse practitioner (MSN); adult-gerontology nurse practitioner (MSN); education (MSN); family nurse practitioner (MSN); informatics (MSN); leadership and management (MSN); nursing (PhD, Post-Master's Certificate), including education (PhD), healthcare administration (PhD), interdisciplinary health (PhD), leadership (PhD), nursing education (Post-Master's Certificate), nursing informatics (Post-Master's Certificate), nursing leadership and management (Post-Master's Certificate), public health policy (PhD); nursing practice (DNP). *Accreditation:* AACN. Part-time and evening/weekend programs available. Postbaccalaureate distance learning degree programs offered (no on-campus study). *Faculty:* 32 full-time (28 women), 549 part-time/adjunct (500 women). *Students:* 4,555 full-time (4,056 women), 4,442 part-time (4,011 women); includes 3,213 minority (2,044 Black or African American, non-Hispanic/Latino; 44 American Indian or Alaska Native, non-Hispanic/Latino; 528 Asian, non-Hispanic/Latino; 413 Hispanic/Latino; 30 Native Hawaiian or other Pacific Islander, non-Hispanic/Latino; 154 Two or more races, non-Hispanic/Latino), 166 international. Average age 40. 1,978 applicants, 99% accepted, 1884 enrolled. In 2014, 2,118 master's, 46 doctorates, 37 other advanced degrees awarded. *Degree requirements:* For doctorate, thesis/dissertation (for some programs), residency (for some programs), field experience (for some programs). *Entrance requirements:* For master's, bachelor's degree or equivalent in related field or RN; minimum GPA of 2.5; official transcripts; goal statement (for some programs); access to computer and Internet; for doctorate, master's degree or higher; RN; three years of related professional or academic experience; goal statement; access to computer and Internet; for Post-Master's Certificate, relevant work experience; access to computer and Internet. Additional exam requirements/recommendations for international students: Required—TOEFL (minimum score 550 paper-based, 79 iBT), IELTS (minimum score 6.5), Michigan English Language Assessment Battery (minimum score 82), or PTE (minimum score 53). *Application deadline:* Applications are processed on a rolling basis. Application fee: $0. Electronic applications accepted. *Expenses: Tuition:* Full-time $11,925; part-time $500 per credit hour. *Required fees:* $647. *Financial support:* Fellowships, Federal Work-Study, scholarships/grants, unspecified assistantships, and family tuition reduction, active duty/veteran tuition reduction, group tuition reduction, interest-free payment plans, employee tuition reduction available. Support available to part-time students. Financial award applicants required to submit FAFSA. *Unit head:* Dr. Andrea Lindell, Associate Dean, 866-492-5336. *Application contact:* Meghan Thomas, Vice President of Enrollment Management, 866-492-5336, E-mail: info@waldenu.edu.
Website: http://www.waldenu.edu/programs/colleges-schools/nursing

Washington State University, College of Agricultural, Human, and Natural Resource Sciences, Department of Human Development, Pullman, WA 99164-4852. Offers prevention science (PhD). Program also offered at the Spokane campus. Part-time programs available. *Students:* 19 full-time (17 women), 6 part-time (all women); includes 5 minority (1 Black or African American, non-Hispanic/Latino; 1 Asian, non-Hispanic/Latino; 2 Hispanic/Latino; 1 Two or more races, non-Hispanic/Latino), 5 international. Average age 31. 20 applicants, 35% accepted, 6 enrolled. *Degree requirements:* For doctorate, comprehensive exam, thesis/dissertation. *Entrance requirements:* For doctorate, GRE General Test, bachelor's or master's degree in prevention science related field (e.g., communication, educational psychology, human development, nursing, psychology, sociology); written statement specifying qualifications, educational goals, and career objectives; official copies of all college transcripts; three letters of reference. Additional exam requirements/recommendations for international students: Required—TOEFL, IELTS. *Application deadline:* For fall admission, 1/10 priority date for domestic students, 1/1 for international students. Application fee: $75. Electronic applications accepted. *Expenses:* Tuition, state resident: full-time $11,768. Tuition, nonresident: full-time $25,200. *Required fees:* $960. Tuition and fees vary according to program. *Financial support:* In 2014–15, 23 students received support, including 7 research assistantships with full tuition reimbursements available (averaging $14,498 per year), 10 teaching assistantships with full tuition reimbursements available (averaging $13,460 per year); fellowships with full tuition reimbursements available, institutionally sponsored loans, scholarships/grants, health care benefits, and unspecified assistantships also available. Financial award application deadline: 2/15; financial award applicants required to submit FAFSA. *Faculty research:* Prevention science, program implementation and dissemination, drug and alcohol prevention, health communication, equine assisted interventions, obesity prevention, health promotion in emerging adulthood, family processes, disenfranchised youth, rural poverty, adolescent sexuality, cultural competency, community collaborations, parent-child relationships, healthy aging. *Total annual research expenditures:* $551,000. *Unit head:* Dr. Thomas G. Power, Chair/Director of Prevention Science Program, 509-355-8439, Fax: 509-335-2456, E-mail: tompower@wsu.edu. *Application contact:* Graduate School Admissions, 800-GRADWSU, Fax: 509-335-1949, E-mail: gradsch@wsu.edu.
Website: http://hd.wsu.edu/

Wayland Baptist University, Graduate Programs, Program in Multidisciplinary Science, Plainview, TX 79072-6998. Offers multidisciplinary science (MS); nursing (MS). Part-time and evening/weekend programs available. *Faculty:* 29 full-time (16 women), 1 (woman) part-time/adjunct. *Students:* 6 part-time (4 women); includes 4 minority (1 Black or African American, non-Hispanic/Latino; 3 Hispanic/Latino). Average age 42. 4 applicants, 50% accepted, 1 enrolled. In 2014, 6 master's awarded. *Degree requirements:* For master's, comprehensive exam. *Entrance requirements:* For master's, GRE or MAT. Additional exam requirements/recommendations for international students: Required—TOEFL (minimum score 500 paper-based; 61 iBT). *Application deadline:* Applications are processed on a rolling basis. Application fee: $50. Electronic applications accepted. *Expenses: Tuition:* Full-time $8910; part-time $495 per credit hour. *Required fees:* $970; $495 per credit hour. $485 per semester. *Financial support:* Federal Work-Study, institutionally sponsored loans, and scholarships/grants available. Support available to part-time students. Financial award application deadline: 5/1; financial award applicants required to submit FAFSA. *Unit head:* Dr. Scott Franklin, Chairman, Division of Mathematics and Science, 806-291-1115, Fax: 806-291-1968, E-mail: franklins@wbu.edu. *Application contact:* Amanda Stanton, Coordinator of Graduate Studies, 806-291-3423, Fax: 806-291-1950, E-mail: stanton@wbu.edu.

Western Kentucky University, Graduate Studies, College of Education and Behavioral Sciences, School of Teacher Education, Bowling Green, KY 42101. Offers elementary education (MAE, Ed S); exceptional education: learning and behavioral disorders (MAE); exceptional education: moderate and severe disabilities (MAE); instructional design (MS); interdisciplinary early childhood education (MAE); library media education (MS); literacy education (MAE); middle grades education (MAE); secondary education (MAE, Ed S). Part-time and evening/weekend programs available. Postbaccalaureate distance learning degree programs offered (minimal on-campus study). *Degree requirements:* For master's, comprehensive exam. *Entrance requirements:* For master's, GRE General Test. Additional exam requirements/recommendations for international students: Required—TOEFL (minimum score 555 paper-based; 79 iBT). *Faculty research:* Teacher preparation in moderate/severe disabilities.

Western New Mexico University, Graduate Division, Interdisciplinary Studies, Silver City, NM 88062-0680. Offers MA. Part-time programs available. Postbaccalaureate distance learning degree programs offered (no on-campus study). *Students:* 25 full-time (18 women), 195 part-time (115 women); includes 58 minority (13 Black or African American, non-Hispanic/Latino; 3 American Indian or Alaska Native, non-Hispanic/Latino; 4 Asian, non-Hispanic/Latino; 35 Hispanic/Latino; 1 Native Hawaiian or other Pacific Islander, non-Hispanic/Latino; 2 Two or more races, non-Hispanic/Latino), 3 international. Average age 41. 80 applicants, 100% accepted, 42 enrolled. In 2014, 64 master's awarded. *Degree requirements:* For master's, comprehensive exam (for some programs), thesis optional. *Entrance requirements:* For master's, GRE General Test, GRE Subject Test, minimum GPA of 3.2 in last 64 hours of undergraduate study. Additional exam requirements/recommendations for international students: Required—TOEFL (minimum score 550 paper-based). *Application deadline:* For fall admission, 6/1 priority date for domestic and international students; for spring admission, 10/1 priority date for domestic and international students. Application fee: $40. *Expenses:* Tuition, state resident: full-time $1441; part-time $160.10 per credit hour. Tuition, nonresident: full-time $4365; part-time $200.13 per credit hour. *Required fees:* $540 per semester. *Financial support:* In 2014–15, 3 students received support, including 3 fellowships (averaging $4,454 per year); scholarships/grants, tuition waivers (partial), and unspecified assistantships also available. Financial award application deadline: 4/1; financial award applicants required to submit FAFSA. *Unit head:* Dr. Jennifer Coleman, Director of the Graduate Division, 575-538-6106, Fax: 575-538-6650, E-mail: jennifer.coleman@wnmu.edu. *Application contact:* Matthew Lara, Director of Admissions, 575-538-6000, Fax: 575-538-6127, E-mail: laram@wnmu.edu.

West Texas A&M University, Program in Interdisciplinary Studies, Canyon, TX 79016-0001. Offers MA, MS. Part-time and evening/weekend programs available. *Degree requirements:* For master's, comprehensive exam, thesis or alternative. *Entrance requirements:* Additional exam requirements/recommendations for international students: Required—TOEFL. Electronic applications accepted.

Worcester Polytechnic Institute, Graduate Studies and Research, Department of Social Science and Policy Studies, Worcester, MA 01609-2280. Offers interdisciplinary social science (PhD); system dynamics (MS, Graduate Certificate). Part-time and evening/weekend programs available. Postbaccalaureate distance learning degree programs offered (no on-campus study). *Faculty:* 5 full-time (2 women), 2 part-time/adjunct (0 women). *Students:* 2 full-time (1 woman), 13 part-time (2 women); includes 2 minority (1 Black or African American, non-Hispanic/Latino; 1 Hispanic/Latino), 3 international. 8 applicants, 75% accepted, 6 enrolled. In 2014, 2 master's awarded. *Entrance requirements:* For master's and doctorate, GRE General Test, 3 letters of recommendation, statement of purpose. Additional exam requirements/recommendations for international students: Required—TOEFL (minimum score 563 paper-based; 84 iBT), IELTS (minimum score 7). *Application deadline:* For fall admission, 1/1 priority date for domestic students, 1/1 for international students; for spring admission, 10/1 priority date for domestic students, 10/1 for international students. Applications are processed on a rolling basis. Application fee: $70. Electronic applications accepted. *Financial support:* Research assistantships, teaching assistantships, career-related internships or fieldwork, institutionally sponsored loans, scholarships/grants, and unspecified assistantships available. Financial award application deadline: 1/1; financial award applicants required to submit FAFSA. *Unit head:* Dr. James K. Doyle, Head, 508-831-5296, Fax: 508-831-5896, E-mail: doyle@wpi.edu. *Application contact:* Dr. Oleg Pavlov, Graduate Coordinator, 508-831-5296, Fax: 508-831-5896, E-mail: opavlov@wpi.edu.
Website: http://www.wpi.edu/academics/ssps

Worcester Polytechnic Institute, Graduate Studies and Research, Programs in Interdisciplinary Studies, Worcester, MA 01609-2280. Offers bioscience administration (MS); impact engineering (MS); manufacturing engineering management (MS); power systems management (MS); social science (PhD); systems modeling (MS). Part-time and evening/weekend programs available. *Faculty:* 1 part-time/adjunct (0 women). *Students:* 2 full-time (0 women), 74 part-time (15 women); includes 18 minority (3 Black or African American, non-Hispanic/Latino; 7 Asian, non-Hispanic/Latino; 3 Hispanic/Latino; 5 Two or more races, non-Hispanic/Latino), 5 international. 37 applicants, 97% accepted, 29 enrolled. In 2014, 10 master's, 1 doctorate awarded. *Degree requirements:* For master's, thesis; for doctorate, comprehensive exam, thesis/dissertation. *Entrance requirements:* For master's and doctorate, 3 letters of recommendation. Additional exam requirements/recommendations for international students: Required—TOEFL (minimum score 563 paper-based; 84 iBT), IELTS (minimum score 7). *Application deadline:* For fall admission, 1/1 priority date for domestic students, 1/1 for international students; for spring admission, 10/1 priority date for domestic students, 10/1 for international students. Application fee: $70. *Financial support:* Institutionally sponsored loans, scholarships/grants, and unspecified assistantships available. Financial award application deadline: 1/1; financial award applicants required to submit FAFSA. *Unit head:* Dr. Fred J. Looft, Head, 508-831-5231, Fax: 508-831-5491, E-mail: fjlooft@wpi.edu. *Application contact:* Lynne Dougherty, Administrative Assistant, 508-831-5301, Fax: 508-831-5717, E-mail: grad@wpi.edu.

Wright State University, School of Graduate Studies, Interdisciplinary Programs, Program in Interdisciplinary Studies, Dayton, OH 45435. Offers MA, MS. *Degree requirements:* For master's, thesis optional. *Entrance requirements:* Additional exam requirements/recommendations for international students: Required—TOEFL.

York University, Faculty of Graduate Studies, Program in Interdisciplinary Studies, Toronto, ON M3J 1P3, Canada. Offers MA. Part-time programs available. *Degree requirements:* For master's, thesis or alternative. Electronic applications accepted.

ACADEMIC AND PROFESSIONAL PROGRAMS IN THE SOCIAL SCIENCES

Section 15
Area and Cultural Studies

This section contains a directory of institutions offering graduate work in area and cultural studies. Additional information about programs listed in the directory may be obtained by writing directly to the dean of a graduate school or chair of a department at the address given in the directory.

For programs offering related work, see also in this book *Geography, History, Language and Literature, Political Science and International Affairs,* and *Sociology, Anthropology, and Archaeology.*

CONTENTS

Program Directories

African-American Studies

Boston University, Graduate School of Arts and Sciences, Program in African American Studies, Boston, MA 02215. Offers MA. *Students:* 2 full-time (both women); both minorities (1 Black or African American, non-Hispanic/Latino; 1 Two or more races, non-Hispanic/Latino). Average age 23. 8 applicants, 38% accepted, 2 enrolled. In 2014, 3 master's awarded. *Degree requirements:* For master's, one foreign language, comprehensive exam. *Entrance requirements:* For master's, GRE General Test, 2 letters of recommendation, writing sample. Additional exam requirements/ recommendations for international students: Required—TOEFL (minimum score 550 paper-based; 84 iBT). *Application deadline:* For fall admission, 3/1 for domestic and international students. Application fee: $80. Electronic applications accepted. *Expenses: Tuition:* Full-time $45,686; part-time $1428 per credit hour. *Required fees:* $660; $60 per semester. Tuition and fees vary according to program. *Financial support:* In 2014–15, 2 students received support. Federal Work-Study, scholarships/grants, and unspecified assistantships available. Support available to part-time students. Financial award application deadline: 3/1. *Unit head:* John Thornton, Director, 617-358-1423, Fax: 617-353-0455, E-mail: jkthorn@bu.edu. *Application contact:* Deirdre James, Program Administrator, 617-358-1421, Fax: 617-353-0455, E-mail: dejames@bu.edu.
Website: http://www.bu.edu/afam/

Carnegie Mellon University, Dietrich College of Humanities and Social Sciences, Department of History, Pittsburgh, PA 15213-3891. Offers African and African-American diaspora (PhD); culture and power (PhD); labor, politics and social movements (PhD); technology, environment, science and health (PhD); women, gender and the family (PhD). Part-time programs available. *Degree requirements:* For doctorate, oral and written comprehensive exams, dissertation defense. *Entrance requirements:* For doctorate, GRE General Test. Additional exam requirements/recommendations for international students: Required—TOEFL. Electronic applications accepted. *Faculty research:* Anthropology and history, African-American history, technology/environment, cultural history analysis.

Clark Atlanta University, School of Arts and Sciences, Department of African-American Studies, Atlanta, GA 30314. Offers MA, DAH. Part-time programs available. *Faculty:* 1 (woman) part-time/adjunct. *Students:* 14 full-time (6 women), 23 part-time (12 women); includes 33 minority (all Black or African American, non-Hispanic/Latino), 2 international. Average age 36. 11 applicants, 91% accepted, 7 enrolled. In 2014, 1 master's, 2 doctorates awarded. *Degree requirements:* For master's, one foreign language, comprehensive exam, thesis optional; for doctorate, one foreign language, comprehensive exam, thesis/dissertation. *Entrance requirements:* For master's, GRE General Test, minimum GPA of 2.5. Additional exam requirements/recommendations for international students: Required—TOEFL (minimum score 500 paper-based; 61 iBT). *Application deadline:* For fall admission, 4/1 for domestic and international students; for spring admission, 11/1 for domestic and international students. Applications are processed on a rolling basis. Application fee: $40 ($55 for international students). Electronic applications accepted. *Expenses: Tuition:* Full-time $14,904; part-time $828 per credit hour. *Required fees:* $746; $373 per semester. *Financial support:* Scholarships/grants available. Financial award application deadline: 4/30; financial award applicants required to submit FAFSA. *Unit head:* Dr. Stephanie Evans, Chairperson, 404-880-6352, E-mail: sevans@cau.edu. *Application contact:* Michelle Clark-Davis, Graduate Program Admissions, 404-880-6605, E-mail: cauadmissions@cau.edu.

Clark Atlanta University, School of Arts and Sciences, Department of Africana Women's Studies, Atlanta, GA 30314. Offers MA, DAH. Part-time programs available. *Faculty:* 1 full-time (0 women). *Students:* 5 full-time (4 women), 14 part-time (12 women); includes 17 minority (all Black or African American, non-Hispanic/Latino). Average age 33. 6 applicants, 100% accepted, 5 enrolled. In 2014, 1 master's, 1 doctorate awarded. *Degree requirements:* For master's, one foreign language, comprehensive exam, thesis optional; for doctorate, one foreign language, comprehensive exam, thesis/dissertation. *Entrance requirements:* For master's, GRE General Test, minimum GPA of 2.5; for doctorate, GRE General Test, minimum graduate GPA of 3.0. Additional exam requirements/recommendations for international students: Required—TOEFL (minimum score 500 paper-based; 61 iBT). *Application deadline:* For fall admission, 4/1 for domestic and international students; for spring admission, 11/1 for domestic and international students. Applications are processed on a rolling basis. Application fee: $40 ($55 for international students). Electronic applications accepted. *Expenses: Tuition:* Full-time $14,904; part-time $828 per credit hour. *Required fees:* $746; $373 per semester. *Financial support:* Scholarships/grants available. Financial award application deadline: 4/30; financial award applicants required to submit FAFSA. *Faculty research:* Concerns of women of African descent globally. *Unit head:* Dr. Stephanie Evans, Chairperson, 404-880-6352, E-mail: sevans@cau.edu. *Application contact:* Michelle Clark-Davis, Graduate Program Admissions, 404-880-6605, E-mail: cauadmissions@cau.edu.

Columbia University, Graduate School of Arts and Sciences, New York, NY 10027. Offers African-American studies (MA); American studies (MA); anthropology (MA, PhD); art history and archaeology (MA, PhD); astronomy (PhD); biological sciences (PhD); biotechnology (MA); chemical physics (PhD); chemistry (PhD); classical studies (MA, PhD); classics (MA, PhD); climate and society (MA); earth and environmental sciences (PhD); East Asia: regional studies (MA); East Asian languages and cultures (MA, PhD); ecology, evolution and environmental biology (MA), including conservation biology; ecology, evolution, and environmental biology (PhD), including ecology and evolutionary biology, evolutionary primatology; economics (PhD); English and comparative literature (MA, PhD); French and Romance philology (MA, PhD); Germanic languages (MA, PhD); global French studies (MA); Hispanic cultural studies (MA); history (PhD); history and literature (MA); human rights studies (MA); Islamic studies (MA); Italian (MA, PhD); Japanese pedagogy (MA); Jewish studies (MA); Latin America and the Caribbean: regional studies (MA); Latin American and Iberian cultures (PhD); mathematics (MA, PhD), including finance (MA); medieval and Renaissance studies (MA); Middle Eastern, South Asian, and African studies (MA, PhD); modern art: critical and curatorial studies (MA); modern European studies (MA); museum anthropology (MA); music (DMA, PhD); oral history (MA); philosophical foundations of physics (MA); philosophy (MA, PhD); physics (PhD); political science (MA, PhD); psychology (PhD); quantitative methods in the social sciences (MA); religion (MA, PhD); Russia, Eurasia and East Europe: regional studies (MA); Russian translation (MA); Slavic cultures (MA); Slavic languages (MA, PhD); sociology (MA, PhD); South Asian studies (MA); statistics (MA, PhD); theatre (PhD); JD/PhD; MA/MS; MD/PhD; MPA/MA. Dual-degree programs require admission to both Graduate School of Arts and Sciences and another Columbia school. Part-time and evening/weekend programs available. Terminal master's awarded for partial completion of doctoral program. *Degree requirements:* For master's, thesis (for some programs); for doctorate, comprehensive exam, thesis/dissertation. *Entrance requirements:* For master's and doctorate, GRE General Test, GRE Subject Test (for some programs). Electronic applications accepted. *Faculty research:* Humanities, natural sciences, social sciences.

Cornell University, Graduate School, Graduate Fields of Arts and Sciences, Field of African and African-American Studies, Ithaca, NY 14853-0001. Offers African studies (MPS); African-American studies (MPS); Africana studies (PhD). *Degree requirements:* For master's, thesis. *Entrance requirements:* For master's, GRE General Test (recommended), 3 letters of recommendation; for doctorate, GRE General Test (recommended), 3 letters of recommendation, personal statement, writing sample. Additional exam requirements/recommendations for international students: Required—TOEFL (minimum score 550 paper-based; 77 iBT). Electronic applications accepted. *Faculty research:* African-American literature, art, cinema and theater; African-American politics and public policy; African history, politics and art; Caribbean politics and Africana diaspora.

Cornell University, Graduate School, Graduate Fields of Arts and Sciences, Field of English Language and Literature, Ithaca, NY 14853-0001. Offers African-American literature (PhD); American literature after 1865 (PhD); American literature to 1865 (PhD); American studies (PhD); colonial and postcolonial literatures (PhD); creative writing (MFA); cultural studies (PhD); dramatic literature (PhD); English poetry (PhD); English Renaissance to 1660 (PhD); lesbian, bisexual, and gay literary studies (PhD); literary criticism and theory (PhD); Old and Middle English (PhD); prose fiction (PhD); Restoration and the eighteenth-century (PhD); the nineteenth century (PhD); the twentieth century (PhD); women's literature (PhD); MFA/PhD. Terminal master's awarded for partial completion of doctoral program. *Degree requirements:* For master's, one foreign language, thesis; for doctorate, one foreign language, comprehensive exam, thesis/dissertation, teaching experience. *Entrance requirements:* For master's, GRE General Test, 3 letters of recommendation, creative writing sample; for doctorate, GRE General Test, GRE Subject Test (English), 3 letters of recommendation, writing sample. Additional exam requirements/recommendations for international students: Required—TOEFL (minimum score 600 paper-based; 77 iBT). Electronic applications accepted. *Faculty research:* English and American literature, women's writing, ethnic and post-colonial literature, critical theory, medievalism.

Eastern Michigan University, Graduate School, College of Arts and Sciences, Department of Africology and African-American Studies, Ypsilanti, MI 48197. Offers Graduate Certificate. *Faculty:* 3 full-time (1 woman). *Students:* 4 part-time (1 woman); all minorities (all Black or African American, non-Hispanic/Latino). Average age 23. 1 applicant, 100% accepted, 1 enrolled. In 2014, 1 Graduate Certificate awarded. *Entrance requirements:* For degree, bachelor's degree with minimum GPA of 2.7, two letters of reference. *Application deadline:* Applications are processed on a rolling basis. Application fee: $45. *Unit head:* Dr. Victor Okafor, Department Head, 734-487-3460, Fax: 734-487-6891, E-mail: victor.okafor@emich.edu.
Website: http://www.emich.edu/aas/

Georgia State University, College of Arts and Sciences, Department of African-American Studies, Atlanta, GA 30302-3083. Offers MA. Part-time programs available. *Faculty:* 9 full-time (5 women). *Students:* 19 full-time (11 women), 3 part-time (all women); includes 20 minority (19 Black or African American, non-Hispanic/Latino; 1 Hispanic/Latino). Average age 29. 24 applicants, 92% accepted, 13 enrolled. In 2014, 2 master's awarded. *Degree requirements:* For master's, thesis. *Entrance requirements:* For master's, GRE. Additional exam requirements/recommendations for international students: Required—TOEFL (minimum score 550 paper-based; 80 iBT). *Application deadline:* For fall admission, 4/15 for domestic and international students. Application fee: $50. Electronic applications accepted. *Expenses:* Tuition, state resident: full-time $6516; part-time $362 per credit hour. Tuition, nonresident: full-time $22,014; part-time $1223 per credit hour. *Required fees:* $2128 per semester. Tuition and fees vary according to course load and program. *Financial support:* In 2014–15, research assistantships with full and partial tuition reimbursements (averaging $4,200 per year), teaching assistantships with full and partial tuition reimbursements (averaging $4,000 per year) were awarded; health care benefits and unspecified assistantships also available. Financial award applicants required to submit FAFSA. *Faculty research:* HIV prevention education and culturally relevant praxis; African-American women's activism and social movements; narrative therapy and family counseling; African women's history; African-American social movements, civil rights, and Black power movements. *Unit head:* Dr. Akinyele Umoja, Chair, Department of African-American Studies, 404-413-5137, Fax: 404-413-5140, E-mail: aadaku@gsu.edu. *Application contact:* Dr. Sarita Kaya Davis, Graduate Program Director, 404-413-5134, Fax: 404-413-5140, E-mail: saritadavis@gsu.edu.
Website: http://www2.gsu.edu/~wwwaad/

Harvard University, Graduate School of Arts and Sciences, Department of African and African American Studies, Cambridge, MA 02138. Offers PhD.

Indiana University Bloomington, University Graduate School, College of Arts and Sciences, Department of African American and African Diaspora Studies, Bloomington, IN 47405-7000. Offers MA. Part-time programs available. *Faculty:* 3 full-time (1 woman). *Students:* 9 full-time (6 women); includes 6 minority (5 Black or African American, non-Hispanic/Latino; 1 Hispanic/Latino), 2 international. Average age 30. 17 applicants, 41% accepted, 3 enrolled. In 2014, 4 master's awarded. *Entrance requirements:* For master's, GRE, minimum GPA of 3.0. Additional exam requirements/recommendations for international students: Required—TOEFL. *Application deadline:* For fall admission, 1/15 priority date for domestic students, 12/15 for international students; for spring admission, 9/1 for domestic and international students. Applications are processed on a rolling basis. Application fee: $55 ($65 for international students). Electronic applications accepted. *Financial support:* Fellowships with tuition reimbursements, research assistantships with tuition reimbursements, and teaching assistantships with tuition reimbursements available. *Unit head:* Dr. Valerie Grim, Chair, 812-855-3875. *Application contact:* Dr. Carolyn Calloway-Thomas, Director of Graduate Studies, 812-855-3974, E-mail: calloway@indiana.edu.
Website: http://www.indiana.edu/~afroamer/

Michigan State University, The Graduate School, College of Arts and Letters, Program in African American and African Studies, East Lansing, MI 48824. Offers MA, PhD. *Entrance requirements:* Additional exam requirements/recommendations for international students: Required—TOEFL. Electronic applications accepted. *Faculty research:* Black American and diasporic studies, comparative communities of color.

Morgan State University, School of Graduate Studies, College of Liberal Arts, Department of History and Geography, Baltimore, MD 21251. Offers African-American studies (MA); history (MA, PhD); museum studies and historic preservation (MA). Part-time and evening/weekend programs available. *Degree requirements:* For master's, comprehensive exam, thesis; for doctorate, comprehensive exam, thesis/dissertation. *Entrance requirements:* For master's, minimum GPA of 2.5; for doctorate, GRE or MAT.

Additional exam requirements/recommendations for international students: Required—TOEFL (minimum score 550 paper-based). *Faculty research:* Women's history, African diaspora history, urban history.

North Carolina Agricultural and Technical State University, School of Graduate Studies, College of Arts and Sciences, Department of English, Program in English and African-American Literature, Greensboro, NC 27411. Offers MA. Part-time and evening/weekend programs available. *Degree requirements:* For master's, comprehensive exam, qualifying exam. *Entrance requirements:* For master's, GRE General Test, minimum GPA of 3.0.

Northwestern University, The Graduate School, Judd A. and Marjorie Weinberg College of Arts and Sciences, Department of African American Studies, Evanston, IL 60208. Offers PhD.

Oblate School of Theology, Graduate and Professional Programs, San Antonio, TX 78216-6693. Offers African-American pastoral leadership (D Min); divinity (M Div); pastoral leadership (D Min); pastoral ministry (MAP Min); pastoral studies (Certificate); spiritual formation in the local community (D Min); spirituality (MA Sp, PhD); spirituality and ministry (D Min); theology (MA Th); U.S. Hispanic/Latino ministry (D Min); M Div/MA Th. *Accreditation:* ACIPE; ATS (one or more programs are accredited). Part-time programs available. Postbaccalaureate distance learning degree programs offered (no on-campus study). *Faculty:* 23 full-time (8 women), 3 part-time/adjunct (0 women). *Students:* 59 full-time (6 women), 73 part-time (36 women); includes 56 minority (8 Black or African American, non-Hispanic/Latino; 9 Asian, non-Hispanic/Latino; 39 Hispanic/Latino), 41 international. Average age 40. 41 applicants, 88% accepted, 34 enrolled. In 2014, 31 master's, 3 doctorates awarded. *Degree requirements:* For master's, comprehensive exam (for some programs), thesis (for some programs), practicum; for doctorate, one foreign language, comprehensive exam, thesis/dissertation, paper, practicum. *Entrance requirements:* For master's, MAT, interview, course work in theology or religious studies, minimum GPA of 2.5; for doctorate, M Div, MA Th, or MA Sp. Additional exam requirements/recommendations for international students: Required—TOEFL (minimum score 71 iBT). *Application deadline:* For fall admission, 6/15 priority date for domestic and international students; for winter admission, 11/30 for domestic and international students; for spring admission, 11/30 for domestic and international students; for summer admission, 4/1 for domestic and international students. Applications are processed on a rolling basis. Application fee: $65. *Expenses:* Expenses: Contact institution. *Financial support:* In 2014–15, 25 students received support. Scholarships/grants available. Support available to part-time students. Financial award application deadline: 8/1; financial award applicants required to submit FAFSA. *Unit head:* Dr. R. Scott Woodward, Academic Dean, 210-341-1366, Fax: 210-341-4519, E-mail: rsw@ost.edu. *Application contact:* Mario A. Porter, Director of Admissions, 210-341-1366 Ext. 226, Fax: 210-341-4519, E-mail: registrar@ost.edu.

The Ohio State University, Graduate School, College of Arts and Sciences, Division of Arts and Humanities, Department of African-American and African Studies, Columbus, OH 43210. Offers MA, PhD. *Faculty:* 23. *Students:* 13 full-time (9 women); includes 9 minority (7 Black or African American, non-Hispanic/Latino; 2 Two or more races, non-Hispanic/Latino), 2 international. Average age 26. In 2014, 2 master's awarded. *Degree requirements:* For master's, comprehensive exam (for some programs), thesis (for some programs), thesis or comprehensive written examination; for doctorate, thesis/dissertation. *Entrance requirements:* For master's and doctorate, GRE General Test. Additional exam requirements/recommendations for international students: Required—TOEFL (minimum score 550 paper-based; 79 iBT), Michigan English Language Assessment Battery (minimum score 82); Recommended—IELTS (minimum score 7). *Application deadline:* For fall admission, 12/1 priority date for domestic students, 11/30 priority date for international students; for winter admission, 12/1 for domestic students, 11/1 for international students; for spring admission, 3/1 for domestic students, 2/1 for international students. Applications are processed on a rolling basis. Application fee: $60 ($70 for international students). Electronic applications accepted. *Financial support:* Fellowships with tuition reimbursements, research assistantships with tuition reimbursements, teaching assistantships with tuition reimbursements, Federal Work-Study, institutionally sponsored loans, and unspecified assistantships available. Support available to part-time students. *Unit head:* H. Ike Okafor-Newsum, Chair, 614-292-0116, E-mail: newsum.2@osu.edu. *Application contact:* Graduate and Professional Admissions, 614-292-9444, Fax: 614-292-3895, E-mail: gpadmissions@osu.edu.
Website: http://aaas.osu.edu/

Rutgers, The State University of New Jersey, New Brunswick, Graduate School-New Brunswick, Program in History, Piscataway, NJ 08854-8097. Offers African-American history (PhD); early American history (PhD); early modern European history (PhD); east Asian history (PhD); global and comparative history (PhD); history (PhD); history of diplomacy and foreign relations (PhD); history of technology, environment and health (PhD); history of the Atlantic cultures and African diaspora (PhD); Latin American history (PhD); medieval history (PhD); modern European history (PhD); nineteenth and twentieth century American history (PhD); women's and gender history (PhD). *Degree requirements:* For doctorate, thesis/dissertation. *Entrance requirements:* For doctorate, GRE General Test, sample of written work. Electronic applications accepted. *Faculty research:* American history, European history, Afro-American history, women's history, Latin American history.

Syracuse University, College of Arts and Sciences, Program in Pan-African Studies, Syracuse, NY 13244. Offers MA. *Students:* 13 full-time (10 women), 2 part-time (both women); includes 8 minority (6 Black or African American, non-Hispanic/Latino; 2 Two or more races, non-Hispanic/Latino), 6 international. Average age 30. 14 applicants, 43% accepted, 6 enrolled. In 2014, 2 master's awarded. *Degree requirements:* For master's, thesis. *Entrance requirements:* For master's, GRE General Test, research writing sample. Additional exam requirements/recommendations for international students: Required—TOEFL (minimum score 100 iBT). *Application deadline:* For fall admission, 1/10 priority date for domestic and international students. Application fee: $75. Electronic applications accepted. *Expenses: Tuition:* Part-time $1341 per credit. *Financial support:* Fellowships with tuition reimbursements and teaching assistantships with full and partial tuition reimbursements available. Financial award application deadline: 1/1; financial award applicants required to submit FAFSA. *Unit head:* Dr. Kishi Animashaun Ducre, Chair, 315-443-4302, E-mail: kanimash@syr.edu. *Application contact:* Aja Brown, Information Contact, 315-443-5599, E-mail: aabrow02@syr.edu.
Website: http://aas.syr.edu/graduate/index.html

Temple University, College of Liberal Arts, Department of African American Studies, Philadelphia, PA 19122-6096. Offers MA, PhD. *Faculty:* 6 full-time (4 women), 3 part-time/adjunct (2 women). *Students:* 30 full-time (15 women), 3 part-time (1 woman); includes 28 minority (26 Black or African American, non-Hispanic/Latino; 1 American Indian or Alaska Native, non-Hispanic/Latino; 1 Hispanic/Latino), 2 international. 27 applicants, 74% accepted, 9 enrolled. In 2014, 7 master's, 3 doctorates awarded. Terminal master's awarded for partial completion of doctoral program. *Degree requirements:* For master's, comprehensive exam; for doctorate, one foreign language, thesis/dissertation, oral and written qualifying exams. *Entrance requirements:* For master's, GRE, 3 letters of recommendation; minimum GPA of 3.0; for doctorate, GRE, MA in African American studies; 3 letters of recommendation; minimum GPA of 3.0. Additional exam requirements/recommendations for international students: Required—TOEFL (minimum score 550 paper-based; 79 iBT). *Application deadline:* For fall admission, 1/15 for domestic students, 12/15 for international students. Applications are processed on a rolling basis. Application fee: $60. Electronic applications accepted. *Expenses:* Tuition, state resident: full-time $14,490; part-time $805 per credit hour. Tuition, nonresident: full-time $19,850; part-time $1103 per credit hour. *Required fees:* $690. Full-time tuition and fees vary according to class time, course load, degree level, campus/location and program. *Financial support:* Teaching assistantships and Federal Work-Study available. Financial award application deadline: 1/15; financial award applicants required to submit FAFSA. *Faculty research:* African history and civilization, contemporary political and cultural developments, identity, African diaspora history and culture. *Unit head:* Dr. Ama Mazama, Graduate Director, 215-204-1992, Fax: 215-204-5953, E-mail: afam@temple.edu. *Application contact:* Tammey Abner, Graduate Coordinator, 215-204-8491, Fax: 215-204-5953, E-mail: tammy.abner@temple@temple.edu.
Website: http://www.cla.temple.edu/africanamericanstudies

Trinity Lutheran Seminary, Graduate and Professional Programs, Columbus, OH 43209-2334. Offers African American studies (MTS); Biblical studies (MTS, STM); Christian education (MA); Christian spirituality (STM); church in the world (MTS); church music (MA); divinity (M Div); general theological studies (MTS); mission and evangelism (STM); pastoral leadership and practice (STM); youth and family ministry (MA); MSN/MTS; MTS/JD. *Accreditation:* ACIPE; ATS. Part-time programs available. *Faculty:* 11 full-time (5 women), 2 part-time/adjunct (both women). *Students:* 68 full-time (24 women), 43 part-time (18 women); includes 12 minority (10 Black or African American, non-Hispanic/Latino; 1 Asian, non-Hispanic/Latino; 1 Two or more races, non-Hispanic/Latino), 1 international. Average age 35. 45 applicants, 96% accepted, 34 enrolled. In 2014, 34 master's awarded. *Degree requirements:* For master's, variable foreign language requirement, comprehensive exam (for some programs), thesis (for some programs), field experience (for some programs). *Entrance requirements:* For master's, BA or equivalent (for MA, M Div, MTS); M Div, MTS, or equivalent (for STM); audition (for MACM). Additional exam requirements/recommendations for international students: Required—TOEFL. *Application deadline:* For fall admission, 7/15 priority date for domestic and international students. Applications are processed on a rolling basis. Application fee: $25. Electronic applications accepted. *Expenses:* Expenses: $13,760 tuition and fees for degree completion (for D Min). *Financial support:* In 2014–15, 72 students received support. Career-related internships or fieldwork, Federal Work-Study, and scholarships/grants available. Support available to part-time students. Financial award application deadline: 5/1; financial award applicants required to submit FAFSA. *Unit head:* Dr. Brad A. Binau, Academic Dean, 614-235-4136 Ext. 4674, Fax: 614-384-4635, E-mail: bbinau@tlsohio.edu. *Application contact:* Rev. Seth Bridger, Director of Admissions, 614-235-4136 Ext. 4650, Fax: 866-610-8572, E-mail: sbridger@tlsohio.edu.
Website: http://www.tlsohio.edu

University at Albany, State University of New York, College of Arts and Sciences, Department of Africana Studies, Albany, NY 12222-0001. Offers African studies (MA); Afro-American studies (MA). Part-time and evening/weekend programs available. *Entrance requirements:* Additional exam requirements/recommendations for international students: Required—TOEFL (minimum score 550 paper-based). Electronic applications accepted. *Faculty research:* The black family, Afro-centricity in poetry, black women in U.S. literature, African economic development, African American history.

University of California, Berkeley, Graduate Division, College of Letters and Science, Department of African American Studies, Berkeley, CA 94720-1500. Offers PhD. *Degree requirements:* For doctorate, one foreign language, thesis/dissertation. *Entrance requirements:* For doctorate, minimum GPA of 3.0, 3 letters of recommendation. Additional exam requirements/recommendations for international students: Required—TOEFL (minimum score 570 paper-based) or IELTS (minimum score 7). *Faculty research:* Black influence on U. S. foreign policy, black intellectuals, ethnic space in urban society, representation in museums of African-Americans and British Americans during slavery.

University of California, Los Angeles, Graduate Division, College of Letters and Science, Interdepartmental Program in Afro-American Studies, Los Angeles, CA 90095. Offers MA, MA/JD. *Degree requirements:* For master's, one foreign language, comprehensive exam or thesis. *Entrance requirements:* For master's, GRE General Test, bachelor's degree; minimum undergraduate GPA of 3.0 (or its equivalent if letter grade system not used); writing sample. Additional exam requirements/recommendations for international students: Required—TOEFL. Electronic applications accepted.

University of California, Santa Barbara, Graduate Division, College of Letters and Sciences, Division of Social Sciences, Department of Sociology, Santa Barbara, CA 93106-9430. Offers interdisciplinary emphasis: Black studies (PhD); interdisciplinary emphasis: environment and society (PhD); interdisciplinary emphasis: feminist studies (PhD); interdisciplinary emphasis: global studies (PhD); interdisciplinary emphasis: language, interaction and social organization (PhD); interdisciplinary emphasis: quantitative methods in social science (PhD); interdisciplinary emphasis: technology and society (PhD); sociology (PhD); MA/PhD. Terminal master's awarded for partial completion of doctoral program. *Degree requirements:* For doctorate, comprehensive exam, thesis/dissertation. *Entrance requirements:* For doctorate, GRE General Test. Additional exam requirements/recommendations for international students: Required—TOEFL (minimum score 550 paper-based; 80 iBT), IELTS (minimum score 7). Electronic applications accepted. *Faculty research:* Gender and sexualities, race/ethnicity, social movements, conversation analysis, global sociology.

The University of Kansas, Graduate Studies, College of Liberal Arts and Sciences, Department of African and African-American Studies, Lawrence, KS 66045. Offers African and African-American studies (MA); African Studies (Graduate Certificate). Part-time programs available. *Faculty:* 13 full-time, 4 part-time/adjunct. *Students:* 6 full-time (4 women), 3 part-time (2 women); includes 5 minority (4 Black or African American, non-Hispanic/Latino; 1 Hispanic/Latino). Average age 29. 10 applicants, 70% accepted, 4 enrolled. In 2014, 1 master's awarded. *Degree requirements:* For master's, variable foreign language requirement, comprehensive exam, thesis or alternative. *Entrance requirements:* For master's, GRE, all academic transcripts, 3 letters of recommendation, personal statement of purpose, writing sample. Additional exam requirements/recommendations for international students: Required—TOEFL. *Application deadline:* For fall admission, 5/1 for domestic and international students. Application fee: $55 ($65 for international students). Electronic applications accepted. *Faculty research:* African theatre, YaKuur culture, interracial communication, African development and urban planning, African literature, Muslim women in West Africa, identity formation in African and Diasporan settings, African-American history, North African and Arab societies, civil rights, black urban communities. *Unit head:* Dr. Peter Ukpokodu, Chairperson, 785-864-3054, E-mail: ukpokodu@ku.edu. *Application contact:* Lisa Brown, Graduate Admissions Coordinator, 785-864-3038, E-mail: lisah@ku.edu.
Website: http://www.afs.ku.edu

University of Louisville, Graduate School, College of Arts and Sciences, Department of Pan-African Studies, Louisville, KY 40292. Offers African and Diaspora studies (MA); African-American studies (MA); MSSW/MA. Part-time programs available. *Students:* 14

full-time (8 women), 12 part-time (9 women); includes 25 minority (20 Black or African American, non-Hispanic/Latino; 2 Hispanic/Latino; 3 Two or more races, non-Hispanic/Latino). Average age 35. 23 applicants, 87% accepted, 13 enrolled. In 2014, 3 master's awarded. *Degree requirements:* For master's, comprehensive exam, thesis optional. *Entrance requirements:* For master's, GRE General Test. Additional exam requirements/recommendations for international students: Required—TOEFL (minimum score 550 paper-based; 79 iBT). *Application deadline:* For fall admission, 3/15 for domestic students, 5/1 priority date for international students; for spring admission, 10/15 for domestic students, 11/1 priority date for international students; for summer admission, 4/1 priority date for international students. Applications are processed on a rolling basis. Application fee: $60. Electronic applications accepted. *Expenses:* Tuition, state resident: full-time $11,326; part-time $630 per credit hour. Tuition, nonresident: full-time $23,568; part-time $1311 per credit hour. *Required fees:* $196. Tuition and fees vary according to program and reciprocity agreements. *Financial support:* Teaching assistantships available. Financial award application deadline: 3/3; financial award applicants required to submit FAFSA. *Faculty research:* African popular culture, black male identity development, education and retention, contemporary politics in Nigeria, poverty in the Caribbean. *Unit head:* Dr. Ricky L. Jones, Chair, 502-852-0027, E-mail: ricky.jones@louisville.edu. *Application contact:* Libby Leggett, Director, Graduate Admissions, 502-852-3101, E-mail: gradadm@louisville.edu.
Website: http://www.louisville.edu/panafricanstudies

University of Massachusetts Amherst, Graduate School, College of Humanities and Fine Arts, Department of Afro-American Studies, Amherst, MA 01003. Offers MA, PhD. Part-time programs available. *Faculty:* 15 full-time (7 women). *Students:* 35 full-time (24 women), 1 part-time (0 women); includes 23 minority (19 Black or African American, non-Hispanic/Latino; 3 Hispanic/Latino; 1 Two or more races, non-Hispanic/Latino), 7 international. Average age 31. 50 applicants, 20% accepted, 5 enrolled. In 2014, 6 master's, 2 doctorates awarded. Terminal master's awarded for partial completion of doctoral program. *Degree requirements:* For master's, thesis or alternative; for doctorate, comprehensive exam, thesis/dissertation. *Entrance requirements:* For master's and doctorate, writing sample, 3 letters of recommendation. Additional exam requirements/recommendations for international students: Required—TOEFL (minimum score 550 paper-based; 80 iBT), IELTS (minimum score 6.5). *Application deadline:* For fall admission, 1/15 for domestic and international students. Applications are processed on a rolling basis. Application fee: $75. Electronic applications accepted. *Expenses:* Tuition, state resident: full-time $1980; part-time $110 per credit. Tuition, nonresident: full-time $14,644; part-time $414 per credit. *Required fees:* $11,417. One-time fee: $357. *Financial support:* Fellowships with full and partial tuition reimbursements, research assistantships with full and partial tuition reimbursements, teaching assistantships with full and partial tuition reimbursements, career-related internships or fieldwork, Federal Work-Study, scholarships/grants, traineeships, health care benefits, tuition waivers (full and partial), and unspecified assistantships available. Support available to part-time students. Financial award application deadline: 1/15. *Unit head:* Dr. Manish Sinha, Graduate Program Director, 413-545-2751, Fax: 413-545-0628. *Application contact:* Lindsay DeSantis, Supervisor of Admissions, 413-545-0722, Fax: 413-577-0100, E-mail: gradadm@grad.umass.edu.
Website: http://www.umass.edu/afroam/

University of Memphis, Graduate School, College of Arts and Sciences, Department of English, Memphis, TN 38152. Offers African-American literature (Graduate Certificate); applied linguistics (PhD); composition studies (PhD); creative writing (MFA); English as a second language (MA); linguistics (MA); literary and cultural studies (PhD), including African-American literature; literature (MA); professional writing (MA, PhD); teaching English as a second language (Graduate Certificate). Part-time and evening/weekend programs available. Postbaccalaureate distance learning degree programs offered (no on-campus study). *Faculty:* 30 full-time (15 women), 1 part-time/adjunct (0 women). *Students:* 89 full-time (45 women), 85 part-time (57 women); includes 35 minority (23 Black or African American, non-Hispanic/Latino; 6 Asian, non-Hispanic/Latino; 5 Hispanic/Latino; 1 Two or more races, non-Hispanic/Latino), 17 international. Average age 35. 83 applicants, 88% accepted, 19 enrolled. In 2014, 29 master's, 6 doctorates awarded. Terminal master's awarded for partial completion of doctoral program. *Degree requirements:* For master's, one foreign language, comprehensive exam, thesis optional; for doctorate, 2 foreign languages, comprehensive exam, thesis/dissertation. *Entrance requirements:* For master's and doctorate, GRE. Additional exam requirements/recommendations for international students: Required—TOEFL. *Application deadline:* For fall admission, 7/1 for domestic students; for spring admission, 10/15 for domestic students. Applications are processed on a rolling basis. Application fee: $35 ($60 for international students). Electronic applications accepted. *Financial support:* In 2014–15, 123 students received support. Research assistantships with full tuition reimbursements available, teaching assistantships with full tuition reimbursements available, Federal Work-Study, scholarships/grants, and unspecified assistantships available. Financial award application deadline: 2/15; financial award applicants required to submit FAFSA. *Faculty research:* Applied linguistics, British and American literature, professional writing, composition studies. *Unit head:* Dr. Joshua Phillips, Chair, 901-678-3067, Fax: 901-678-2226, E-mail: jsphllps@memphis.edu. *Application contact:* Dr. Jeffrey Scraba, Director, Graduate Studies, 901-678-3099, Fax: 901-678-2226, E-mail: jscraba@memphis.edu.
Website: http://www.memphis.edu/english

University of Wisconsin–Madison, Graduate School, College of Letters and Science, Department of Afro-American Studies, Madison, WI 53706-1380. Offers MA. *Degree requirements:* For master's, thesis or alternative. *Entrance requirements:* For master's, bachelor's degree in related field, minimum GPA of 3.0. Additional exam requirements/recommendations for international students: Required—TOEFL. Electronic applications accepted. *Expenses:* Tuition, state resident: full-time $10,723; part-time $745 per credit. Tuition, nonresident: full-time $24,054; part-time $1578 per credit. *Required fees:* $374 per semester. Tuition and fees vary according to course load, program and reciprocity agreements. *Faculty research:* Afro American art, history, music, literature, and culture.

West Virginia University, Eberly College of Arts and Sciences, Department of History, Morgantown, WV 26506. Offers African history (MA, PhD); African-American history (MA, PhD); American history (MA, PhD); Appalachian/regional history (MA, PhD); East Asian history (MA, PhD); European history (MA, PhD); history of science and technology (MA, PhD); Latin American history (MA). Part-time programs available. *Degree requirements:* For master's, one foreign language, thesis (for some programs), oral exam, thesis defense; for doctorate, one foreign language, comprehensive exam, thesis/dissertation, dissertation defense. *Entrance requirements:* For master's, GRE General Test, minimum GPA of 3.0; for doctorate, GRE General Test. Additional exam requirements/recommendations for international students: Required—TOEFL (minimum score 550 paper-based), IELTS (minimum score 6.5). Electronic applications accepted. *Faculty research:* United States, Appalachia, modern Europe, Africa, colonial and post-colonial societies.

Yale University, Graduate School of Arts and Sciences, Interdisciplinary Program in African-American Studies, New Haven, CT 06520. Offers PhD. *Entrance requirements:* For doctorate, GRE General Test.

African Studies

Arizona State University at the Tempe campus, College of Liberal Arts and Sciences, School of Social Transformation, Tempe, AZ 85287-4902. Offers African studies (Graduate Certificate); gender studies (PhD, Graduate Certificate); justice studies (MS, PhD); social and cultural pedagogy (MA); socio-economic justice (Graduate Certificate); PhD/JD. Part-time programs available. Terminal master's awarded for partial completion of doctoral program. *Degree requirements:* For master's, thesis or alternative, interactive Program of Study (iPOS) submitted before completing 50 percent of required credit hours; for doctorate, comprehensive exam, thesis/dissertation, interactive Program of Study (iPOS) submitted before completing 50 percent of required credit hours. *Entrance requirements:* For master's, GRE or LSAT, minimum GPA of 3.0 or equivalent in last 2 years of work leading to bachelor's degree; for doctorate, GRE or LSAT (for justice studies program), minimum GPA of 3.0 or equivalent in last 2 years of work leading to bachelor's degree. Additional exam requirements/recommendations for international students: Required—TOEFL, IELTS, or PTE. Electronic applications accepted.

California State University, Long Beach, Graduate Studies, College of Liberal Arts, Department of History, Long Beach, CA 90840. Offers Africa and the Middle East (MA); ancient/medieval Europe (MA); Asia (MA); Latin America (MA); modern Europe (MA); United States (MA); world history (MA). Part-time and evening/weekend programs available. *Degree requirements:* For master's, one foreign language, comprehensive exam or thesis. Electronic applications accepted. *Faculty research:* All periods of European and American history, recent Asian and African history.

Carnegie Mellon University, Dietrich College of Humanities and Social Sciences, Department of History, Pittsburgh, PA 15213-3891. Offers African and African-American diaspora (PhD); culture and power (PhD); labor, politics and social movements (PhD); technology, environment, science and health (PhD); women, gender and the family (PhD). Part-time programs available. *Degree requirements:* For doctorate, oral and written comprehensive exams, dissertation defense. *Entrance requirements:* For doctorate, GRE General Test. Additional exam requirements/recommendations for international students: Required—TOEFL. Electronic applications accepted. *Faculty research:* Anthropology and history, African-American history, technology/environment, cultural history analysis.

Claremont Graduate University, Graduate Programs, School of Arts and Humanities, Department of History, Claremont, CA 91711-6160. Offers Africana history (Certificate); American studies and U.S. history (MA, PhD); archival studies (MA); early modern studies (MA, PhD); European studies (MA, PhD); oral history (MA, PhD); MBA/MA; MBA/PhD. *Faculty:* 4 full-time (2 women), 1 part-time/adjunct (0 women). *Students:* 41 full-time (19 women), 25 part-time (10 women); includes 18 minority (2 Black or African American, non-Hispanic/Latino; 1 American Indian or Alaska Native, non-Hispanic/Latino; 6 Asian, non-Hispanic/Latino; 6 Hispanic/Latino; 1 Native Hawaiian or other Pacific Islander, non-Hispanic/Latino; 2 Two or more races, non-Hispanic/Latino). Average age 37. In 2014, 7 master's, 6 doctorates, 1 other advanced degree awarded. Terminal master's awarded for partial completion of doctoral program. *Entrance requirements:* For master's and doctorate, GRE General Test. Additional exam requirements/recommendations for international students: Required—TOEFL (minimum score 550 paper-based; 80 iBT). *Application deadline:* For fall admission, 2/1 priority date for domestic and international students. Applications are processed on a rolling basis. Application fee: $80. Electronic applications accepted. *Expenses: Tuition:* Full-time $41,784; part-time $1741 per credit. *Required fees:* $600; $300 per semester. *Financial support:* Fellowships, research assistantships, Federal Work-Study, institutionally sponsored loans, and scholarships/grants available. Support available to part-time students. Financial award application deadline: 2/15; financial award applicants required to submit FAFSA. *Faculty research:* Intellectual and social history, cultural studies, gender studies, Western history, Chicano history. *Unit head:* Joshua Goode, Chair, 909-607-7430, E-mail: joshua.goode@cgu.edu. *Application contact:* Erma Cross, Admissions and Alumni Coordinator, 909-607-9843, E-mail: erminia.cross@cgu.edu.
Website: http://www.cgu.edu/pages/369.asp

Claremont Graduate University, Graduate Programs, School of Educational Studies, Claremont, CA 91711-6160. Offers Africana education (Certificate); education and policy (MA, PhD); higher education/student affairs (MA, PhD); human development (MA, PhD); public school administration (MA, PhD); quantitative evaluation (MA, PhD); special education (MA, PhD); teacher education (MA); teaching and learning (MA, PhD); urban leadership (PhD); MBA/PhD. PhD program offered jointly with San Diego State University. Part-time programs available. *Faculty:* 16 full-time (9 women), 1 part-time/adjunct (0 women). *Students:* 221 full-time (157 women), 195 part-time (147 women); includes 201 minority (51 Black or African American, non-Hispanic/Latino; 2 American Indian or Alaska Native, non-Hispanic/Latino; 41 Asian, non-Hispanic/Latino; 94 Hispanic/Latino; 2 Native Hawaiian or other Pacific Islander, non-Hispanic/Latino; 11 Two or more races, non-Hispanic/Latino), 14 international. Average age 39. In 2014, 44 master's, 35 doctorates, 13 other advanced degrees awarded. Terminal master's awarded for partial completion of doctoral program. *Entrance requirements:* For master's and doctorate, GRE General Test. Additional exam requirements/recommendations for international students: Required—TOEFL (minimum score 550 paper-based; 80 iBT). *Application deadline:* For fall admission, 4/1 priority date for domestic and international students. Applications are processed on a rolling basis. Application fee: $80. Electronic applications accepted. *Expenses: Tuition:* Full-time $41,784; part-time $1741 per credit. *Required fees:* $600; $300 per semester. *Financial support:* Fellowships, research assistantships, Federal Work-Study, institutionally sponsored loans, and scholarships/grants available. Support available to part-time students. Financial award application deadline: 2/15; financial award applicants required to submit FAFSA. *Faculty research:* Education administration, K-12 and higher education, multicultural education, education policy, diversity in higher education, faculty issues. *Unit head:* Scott Thomas, Dean, 909-621-8075, Fax: 909-621-8734, E-mail:

scott.thomas@cgu.edu. *Application contact:* Rachel Camacho, Assistant Director of Admission, 909-607-9418.
Website: http://www.cgu.edu/pages/267.asp

Columbia University, Graduate School of Arts and Sciences, New York, NY 10027. Offers African-American studies (MA); American studies (MA); anthropology (MA, PhD); art history and archaeology (MA, PhD); astronomy (PhD); biological sciences (PhD); biotechnology (MA); chemical physics (PhD); chemistry (PhD); classical studies (MA, PhD); classics (MA, PhD); climate and society (MA); earth and environmental sciences (PhD); East Asia: regional studies (MA); East Asian languages and cultures (MA, PhD); ecology, evolution and environmental biology (MA), including conservation biology; ecology, evolution, and environmental biology (PhD), including ecology and evolutionary biology, evolutionary primatology; economics (PhD); English and comparative literature (MA, PhD); French and Romance philology (MA, PhD); Germanic languages (MA, PhD); global French studies (MA); Hispanic cultural studies (MA); history (PhD); history and literature (MA); human rights studies (MA); Islamic studies (MA); Italian (MA, PhD); Japanese pedagogy (MA); Jewish studies (MA); Latin America and the Caribbean: regional studies (MA); Latin American and Iberian cultures (PhD); mathematics (MA, PhD), including finance (MA); medieval and Renaissance studies (MA); Middle Eastern, South Asian, and African studies (MA, PhD); modern art: critical and curatorial studies (MA); modern European studies (MA); museum anthropology (MA); music (DMA, PhD); oral history (MA); philosophical foundations of physics (MA); philosophy (MA, PhD); physics (PhD); political science (MA, PhD); psychology (PhD); quantitative methods in the social sciences (MA); religion (MA, PhD); Russia, Eurasia and East Europe: regional studies (MA); Russian translation (MA); Slavic cultures (MA); Slavic languages (MA, PhD); sociology (MA, PhD); South Asian studies (MA); statistics (MA, PhD); theatre (PhD); JD/PhD; MA/MS; MD/PhD; MPA/MA. Dual-degree programs require admission to both Graduate School of Arts and Sciences and another Columbia school. Part-time and evening/weekend programs available. Terminal master's awarded for partial completion of doctoral program. *Degree requirements:* For master's, thesis (for some programs); for doctorate, comprehensive exam, thesis/dissertation. *Entrance requirements:* For master's and doctorate, GRE General Test, GRE Subject Test (for some programs). Electronic applications accepted. *Faculty research:* Humanities, natural sciences, social sciences.

Columbia University, School of International and Public Affairs, Institute of African Studies, New York, NY 10027. Offers Certificate. Students must be enrolled in a separate graduate degree program at Columbia University. Electronic applications accepted.

Cornell University, Graduate School, Graduate Fields of Arts and Sciences, Field of African and African-American Studies, Ithaca, NY 14853-0001. Offers African studies (MPS); African-American studies (MPS); Africana studies (PhD). *Degree requirements:* For master's, thesis. *Entrance requirements:* For master's, GRE General Test (recommended), 3 letters of recommendation; for doctorate, GRE General Test (recommended), 3 letters of recommendation, personal statement, writing sample. Additional exam requirements/recommendations for international students: Required—TOEFL (minimum score 550 paper-based; 77 iBT). Electronic applications accepted. *Faculty research:* African-American literature, art, cinema and theater; African-American politics and public policy; African history, politics and art; Caribbean politics and Africana diaspora.

Cornell University, Graduate School, Graduate Fields of Arts and Sciences, Field of History, Ithaca, NY 14853-0001. Offers African history (MA, PhD); American history (MA, PhD); ancient Greek history (PhD); ancient history (MA, PhD); ancient Roman history (PhD); early modern European history (MA, PhD); English history (MA, PhD); French history (MA, PhD); German history (MA, PhD); history of science (MA, PhD); Korean history (PhD); Latin American history (MA, PhD); medieval Chinese history (MA, PhD); medieval history (MA, PhD); modern Chinese history (MA, PhD); modern European history (MA, PhD); modern Japanese history (MA, PhD); modern Middle Eastern history (PhD); premodern Islamic history (MA, PhD); premodern Japanese history (MA, PhD); Renaissance history (MA, PhD); Russian history (MA, PhD); South Asian history (PhD); Southeast Asian history (MA, PhD). Terminal master's awarded for partial completion of doctoral program. *Degree requirements:* For master's, thesis; for doctorate, 2 foreign languages, comprehensive exam, thesis/dissertation, 1 year of teaching experience. *Entrance requirements:* For master's and doctorate, GRE General Test, writing sample, 3 letters of recommendation. Additional exam requirements/recommendations for international students: Required—TOEFL (minimum score 550 paper-based; 77 iBT). Electronic applications accepted.

Florida International University, College of Arts and Sciences, Program in African and African Diaspora Studies, Miami, FL 33199. Offers MA, MA/PhD. Part-time and evening/weekend programs available. Terminal master's awarded for partial completion of doctoral program. *Degree requirements:* For master's, one foreign language, thesis optional, minimum GPA of 3.0. *Entrance requirements:* For master's, GRE General Test, BA with minimum GPA of 3.0, 2 letters of recommendation, examples of written work. Additional exam requirements/recommendations for international students: Required—TOEFL (minimum score 80 iBT). Electronic applications accepted. *Faculty research:* African diaspora in Latin America, Haitian Creole phonology and culture, racial/ethnic minority sexual health, African-American labor and southern history, gendered perspective of the development of racial science.

Harvard University, Graduate School of Arts and Sciences, Department of African and African American Studies, Cambridge, MA 02138. Offers PhD.

Howard University, Graduate School, Department of African Studies, Washington, DC 20059-0002. Offers MA, PhD. Part-time programs available. *Degree requirements:* For master's, one foreign language, comprehensive exam, thesis, internship; for doctorate, 2 foreign languages, comprehensive exam, thesis/dissertation, field research for some. *Entrance requirements:* For master's, GRE General Test, minimum GPA of 3.0; for doctorate, GRE General Test, minimum GPA of 3.5. Electronic applications accepted. *Faculty research:* African literature and film, economics of Africa, international relations, public policy analysis, gender.

Indiana University Bloomington, University Graduate School, College of Arts and Sciences, School of Global and International Studies, African Studies Program, Bloomington, IN 47405-7000. Offers MA. *Students:* 6 full-time (3 women), 1 (woman) part-time; includes 2 minority (both Black or African American, non-Hispanic/Latino), 4 international. Average age 31. 6 applicants, 67% accepted, 2 enrolled. *Application deadline:* For fall admission, 1/15 for domestic students, 12/1 for international students. Application fee: $55 ($65 for international students). Electronic applications accepted. *Financial support:* Fellowships with tuition reimbursements and teaching assistantships with tuition reimbursements available. *Unit head:* Dr. Samuel Obeng, Director, 812-855-8284, E-mail: sobeng@indiana.edu. *Application contact:* Helen Harrell, Administrative Manager, 812-855-8284, E-mail: hharrell@indiana.edu.
Website: http://www.indiana.edu/~afrist/

Michigan State University, The Graduate School, College of Arts and Letters, Program in African American and African Studies, East Lansing, MI 48824. Offers MA, PhD. *Entrance requirements:* Additional exam requirements/recommendations for international students: Required—TOEFL. Electronic applications accepted. *Faculty research:* Black American and diasporic studies, comparative communities of color.

New York University, Graduate School of Arts and Science, Department of History, New York, NY 10012-1019. Offers African diaspora (PhD); African history (PhD); archival management (Advanced Certificate); Atlantic history (PhD); French studies/history (PhD); Hebrew and Judaic studies/history (PhD); history (MA, PhD), including Europe (PhD), Latin America and the Caribbean (PhD), United States (PhD), women's history (MA); Middle Eastern history (MA); Middle Eastern studies/history (PhD); public history (Advanced Certificate); world history (MA); JD/MA; MA/Advanced Certificate. Part-time programs available. *Faculty:* 43 full-time (19 women). *Students:* 120 full-time (72 women), 43 part-time (29 women); includes 33 minority (15 Black or African American, non-Hispanic/Latino; 1 American Indian or Alaska Native, non-Hispanic/Latino; 4 Asian, non-Hispanic/Latino; 9 Hispanic/Latino; 4 Two or more races, non-Hispanic/Latino), 41 international. Average age 29. 401 applicants, 31% accepted, 38 enrolled. In 2014, 24 master's, 16 doctorates awarded. Terminal master's awarded for partial completion of doctoral program. *Degree requirements:* For master's, seminar paper; for doctorate, one foreign language, thesis/dissertation, oral and written exams; for Advanced Certificate, internship. *Entrance requirements:* For master's, GRE General Test, minimum GPA of 3.0, writing sample; for doctorate, GRE. Additional exam requirements/recommendations for international students: Required—TOEFL. *Application deadline:* For fall admission, 12/18 for domestic and international students. Application fee: $100. *Financial support:* Fellowships with tuition reimbursements, research assistantships, teaching assistantships with tuition reimbursements, career-related internships or fieldwork, Federal Work-Study, institutionally sponsored loans, scholarships/grants, health care benefits, and unspecified assistantships available. Financial award application deadline: 12/18; financial award applicants required to submit FAFSA. *Faculty research:* African, East Asian, medieval, early modern, and modern European history; U.S. history; African and African diaspora; Latin American history; Atlantic world. *Unit head:* Barbara Weinstein, Chair, 212-998-8600, Fax: 212-995-4017, E-mail: history.admissions@nyu.edu. *Application contact:* Stepfanos Geroulanos, Director of Graduate Studies, 212-998-8600, Fax: 212-995-4017, E-mail: history.admissions@nyu.edu.
Website: http://history.as.nyu.edu/

New York University, Graduate School of Arts and Science, Program in Africana Studies, New York, NY 10012-1019. Offers MA. *Students:* 7 full-time (5 women), 2 part-time (both women); includes 7 minority (6 Black or African American, non-Hispanic/Latino; 1 Two or more races, non-Hispanic/Latino). Average age 27. 20 applicants, 70% accepted, 3 enrolled. In 2014, 5 master's awarded. *Degree requirements:* For master's, thesis or alternative. *Entrance requirements:* For master's, GRE, sample of written work. Additional exam requirements/recommendations for international students: Required—TOEFL. *Application deadline:* For fall admission, 1/4 for domestic and international students. Application fee: $95. *Financial support:* Fellowships with tuition reimbursements, Federal Work-Study, and institutionally sponsored loans available. Financial award application deadline: 1/4; financial award applicants required to submit FAFSA. *Faculty research:* Pan-Africanism, black urban studies, film and literature of black Diaspora, cultural politics and theory, politics of identity. *Unit head:* Renee Blake, Director, 212-992-9650, Fax: 212-995-4665, E-mail: africana@nyu.edu. *Application contact:* Raechel Bosch, Graduate Administrator, 212-998-9650, Fax: 212-995-4665, E-mail: africana@nyu.edu.
Website: http://www.nyu.edu/gsas/dept/africana/

New York University, Graduate School of Arts and Science, Program in Museum Studies, New York, NY 10012-1019. Offers museum studies (MA, Advanced Certificate), including Africana studies (MA), Hebrew and Judaic studies (MA), Latin American and Caribbean studies (MA), Near Eastern studies (MA). Part-time and evening/weekend programs available. *Students:* 45 full-time (39 women), 23 part-time (19 women); includes 15 minority (2 American Indian or Alaska Native, non-Hispanic/Latino; 3 Asian, non-Hispanic/Latino; 6 Hispanic/Latino; 4 Two or more races, non-Hispanic/Latino), 19 international. Average age 26. 123 applicants, 81% accepted, 29 enrolled. In 2014, 35 master's, 1 other advanced degree awarded. *Entrance requirements:* For master's, GRE General Test; for Advanced Certificate, master's degree or PhD. Additional exam requirements/recommendations for international students: Required—TOEFL. *Application deadline:* For fall admission, 2/15 for domestic and international students; for spring admission, 11/1 for domestic and international students. Application fee: $100. *Financial support:* Application deadline: 2/15. *Faculty research:* Modern and contemporary art, history of museums and exhibitions, conservation of cultural materials, museum anthropology, ethnography. *Unit head:* Bruce Altshuler, Director, 212-998-8080, Fax: 212-995-4185, E-mail: museum.studies@nyu.edu. *Application contact:* Tatiana Kamorina, Department Administrator, 212-998-8080, Fax: 212-995-4185, E-mail: museum.studies@nyu.edu.
Website: http://www.nyu.edu/fas/program/museumstudies/

Northwestern University, The Graduate School, Judd A. and Marjorie Weinberg College of Arts and Sciences, Program of African Studies, Evanston, IL 60208. Offers Graduate Certificate. *Degree requirements:* For Graduate Certificate, one foreign language. *Faculty research:* Collapsing states in Africa, HIV/AIDS in Africa, Islam in Africa, African philosophy.

The Ohio State University, Graduate School, College of Arts and Sciences, Division of Arts and Humanities, Department of African-American and African Studies, Columbus, OH 43210. Offers MA, PhD. *Faculty:* 23. *Students:* 13 full-time (9 women); includes 9 minority (7 Black or African American, non-Hispanic/Latino; 2 Two or more races, non-Hispanic/Latino), 2 international. Average age 26. In 2014, 2 master's awarded. *Degree requirements:* For master's, comprehensive exam (for some programs), thesis (for some programs), thesis or comprehensive written examination; for doctorate, thesis/dissertation. *Entrance requirements:* For master's and doctorate, GRE General Test. Additional exam requirements/recommendations for international students: Required—TOEFL (minimum score 550 paper-based; 79 iBT), Michigan English Language Assessment Battery (minimum score 82); Recommended—IELTS (minimum score 7). *Application deadline:* For fall admission, 12/1 priority date for domestic students, 11/30 priority date for international students; for winter admission, 12/1 for domestic students, 11/1 for international students; for spring admission, 3/1 for domestic students, 2/1 for international students. Applications are processed on a rolling basis. Application fee: $60 ($70 for international students). Electronic applications accepted. *Financial support:* Fellowships with tuition reimbursements, research assistantships with tuition reimbursements, teaching assistantships with tuition reimbursements, Federal Work-Study, institutionally sponsored loans, and unspecified assistantships available. Support available to part-time students. *Unit head:* H. Ike Okafor-Newsum, Chair, 614-292-0116, E-mail: newsum.2@osu.edu. *Application contact:* Graduate and Professional Admissions, 614-292-9444, Fax: 614-292-3895, E-mail: gpadmissions@osu.edu.
Website: http://aaas.osu.edu/

Ohio University, Graduate College, Center for International Studies, Program in African Studies, Athens, OH 45701. Offers MA. Part-time programs available. *Degree requirements:* For master's, one foreign language, thesis optional. *Entrance requirements:* For master's, minimum GPA of 3.0. Additional exam requirements/recommendations for international students: Required—TOEFL (minimum score 550

paper-based; 80 iBT), IELTS (minimum score 6.5). *Faculty research:* African social sciences and the humanities.

Rice University, Graduate Programs, School of Humanities, Department of Religious Studies, Houston, TX 77251-1892. Offers African religions (PhD); African-American religions (PhD); contemplative studies (PhD); ghosticism, esotericism, mysticism (PhD); Islam (PhD); Jewish thought and philosophy (PhD); modern Christianity in thought and popular culture (PhD); psychology of religion (PhD); the Bible and beyond (PhD). *Degree requirements:* For doctorate, 2 foreign languages, comprehensive exam, thesis/dissertation. *Entrance requirements:* For doctorate, GRE, letters of recommendation, writing sample. Additional exam requirements/recommendations for international students: Required—TOEFL (minimum score 600 paper-based; 90 iBT). Electronic applications accepted. *Faculty research:* Origins and historical development of Islam, history of Christianity, the study of comparative religion, African-American religion, religion and culture.

Rutgers, The State University of New Jersey, New Brunswick, Graduate School-New Brunswick, Program in History, Piscataway, NJ 08854-8097. Offers African-American history (PhD); early American history (PhD); early modern European history (PhD); east Asian history (PhD); global and comparative history (PhD); history (PhD); history of diplomacy and foreign relations (PhD); history of technology, environment and health (PhD); history of the Atlantic cultures and African diaspora (PhD); Latin American history (PhD); medieval history (PhD); modern European history (PhD); nineteenth and twentieth century American history (PhD); women's and gender history (PhD). *Degree requirements:* For doctorate, thesis/dissertation. *Entrance requirements:* For doctorate, GRE General Test, sample of written work. Electronic applications accepted. *Faculty research:* American history, European history, Afro-American history, women's history, Latin American history.

Stony Brook University, State University of New York, Graduate School, College of Arts and Sciences, Department of Africana Studies, Stony Brook, NY 11794. Offers MA, Certificate. *Faculty:* 8 full-time (3 women). *Students:* 2 full-time (both women), 1 (woman) part-time; includes 1 minority (Black or African American, non-Hispanic/Latino), 1 international. Average age 35. 2 applicants. *Degree requirements:* For master's, research thesis project, research seminar. *Entrance requirements:* For master's, GRE General Test, minimum GPA of 3.0, 3 letters of recommendation. *Application deadline:* For fall admission, 1/15 for domestic students; for spring admission, 10/1 for domestic students. Application fee: $100. *Expenses:* Tuition, state resident: full-time $10,370; part-time $432 per credit. Tuition, nonresident: full-time $20,190; part-time $841 per credit. *Required fees:* $1431. *Financial support:* Teaching assistantships available. *Unit head:* Dr. Tracey L. Walters, Chair, 631-632-7475, E-mail: tracey.walters@stonybrook.edu. *Application contact:* Dr. Leslie Owens, Program Director, 631-632-7471, Fax: 631-632-5703, E-mail: leslie.owens@stonybrook.edu.
Website: http://www.stonybrook.edu/commcms/africana-studies//

Syracuse University, College of Arts and Sciences, Program in Pan-African Studies, Syracuse, NY 13244. Offers MA. *Students:* 13 full-time (10 women), 2 part-time (both women); includes 8 minority (6 Black or African American, non-Hispanic/Latino; 2 Two or more races, non-Hispanic/Latino), 6 international. Average age 30. 14 applicants, 43% accepted, 6 enrolled. In 2014, 2 master's awarded. *Degree requirements:* For master's, thesis. *Entrance requirements:* For master's, GRE General Test, research writing sample. Additional exam requirements/recommendations for international students: Required—TOEFL (minimum score 100 iBT). *Application deadline:* For fall admission, 1/10 priority date for domestic and international students. Application fee: $75. Electronic applications accepted. *Expenses: Tuition:* Part-time $1341 per credit. *Financial support:* Fellowships with tuition reimbursements and teaching assistantships with full and partial tuition reimbursements available. Financial award application deadline: 1/1; financial award applicants required to submit FAFSA. *Unit head:* Dr. Kishi Animashaun Ducre, Chair, 315-443-4302, E-mail: kanimash@syr.edu. *Application contact:* Aja Brown, Information Contact, 315-443-5599, E-mail: aabrow02@syr.edu.
Website: http://aas.syr.edu/graduate/index.html

University at Albany, State University of New York, College of Arts and Sciences, Department of Africana Studies, Albany, NY 12222-0001. Offers African studies (MA); Afro-American studies (MA). Part-time and evening/weekend programs available. *Entrance requirements:* Additional exam requirements/recommendations for international students: Required—TOEFL (minimum score 550 paper-based). Electronic applications accepted. *Faculty research:* The black family, Afro-centricity in poetry, black women in U.S. literature, African economic development, African American history.

University of California, Los Angeles, Graduate Division, International Institute, Interdepartmental Program in African Studies, Los Angeles, CA 90095. Offers MA, MPH/MA. *Degree requirements:* For master's, one foreign language, comprehensive exam or thesis. *Entrance requirements:* For master's, GRE General Test, bachelor's degree; minimum undergraduate GPA of 3.0 (or its equivalent if letter grade system not used); writing sample. Additional exam requirements/recommendations for international students: Required—TOEFL. Electronic applications accepted.

University of Connecticut, Graduate School, College of Liberal Arts and Sciences, Field of International Studies, Program in African Studies, Storrs, CT 06269. Offers MA. *Degree requirements:* For master's, comprehensive exam. *Entrance requirements:* For master's, GRE General Test. Additional exam requirements/recommendations for international students: Required—TOEFL (minimum score 550 paper-based). Electronic applications accepted.

University of Florida, Graduate School, College of Liberal Arts and Sciences, Center for African Studies, Gainesville, FL 32611. Offers Certificate. Part-time programs available. *Faculty research:* Governance, human rights, African archaeology, southern African history, wildlife conservation and natural resources.

University of Illinois at Urbana–Champaign, Graduate College, College of Liberal Arts and Sciences, Center for African Studies, Champaign, IL 61820. Offers MA, MA/MS. *Students:* 3 (all women). Application fee: $70 ($90 for international students). *Unit head:* Merle L. Bowen, Director, 217-333-6335, Fax: 217-244-2429, E-mail: bowen@illinois.edu. *Application contact:* Maimouna Barro, Associate Director, 217-333-6335, Fax: 217-244-2429, E-mail: barro@illinois.edu.
Website: http://www.afrst.illinois.edu/

The University of Kansas, Graduate Studies, College of Liberal Arts and Sciences, Department of African and African-American Studies, Lawrence, KS 66045. Offers African and African-American studies (MA); African Studies (Graduate Certificate). Part-time programs available. *Faculty:* 13 full-time, 4 part-time/adjunct. *Students:* 6 full-time (4 women), 3 part-time (2 women); includes 5 minority (4 Black or African American, non-Hispanic/Latino; 1 Hispanic/Latino). Average age 29. 10 applicants, 70% accepted, 4 enrolled. In 2014, 1 master's awarded. *Degree requirements:* For master's, variable foreign language requirement, comprehensive exam, thesis or alternative. *Entrance requirements:* For master's, GRE, all academic transcripts, 3 letters of recommendation, personal statement of purpose, writing sample. Additional exam requirements/recommendations for international students: Required—TOEFL. *Application deadline:* For fall admission, 5/1 for domestic and international students. Application fee: $55 ($65 for international students). Electronic applications accepted. *Faculty research:* African theatre, YaKuur culture, interracial communication, African development and urban planning, African literature, Muslim women in West Africa, identity formation in African and Diasporan settings, African-American history, North African and Arab societies, civil rights, black urban communities. *Unit head:* Dr. Peter Ukpokodu, Chairperson, 785-864-3054, E-mail: ukpokodu@ku.edu. *Application contact:* Lisa Brown, Graduate Admissions Coordinator, 785-864-3038, E-mail: lisah@ku.edu.
Website: http://www.afs.ku.edu

University of Louisville, Graduate School, College of Arts and Sciences, Department of Pan-African Studies, Louisville, KY 40292. Offers African and Diaspora studies (MA); African-American studies (MA); MSSW/MA. Part-time programs available. *Students:* 14 full-time (8 women), 12 part-time (9 women); includes 25 minority (20 Black or African American, non-Hispanic/Latino; 2 Hispanic/Latino; 3 Two or more races, non-Hispanic/Latino). Average age 35. 23 applicants, 87% accepted, 13 enrolled. In 2014, 3 master's awarded. *Degree requirements:* For master's, comprehensive exam, thesis optional. *Entrance requirements:* For master's, GRE General Test. Additional exam requirements/recommendations for international students: Required—TOEFL (minimum score 550 paper-based; 79 iBT). *Application deadline:* For fall admission, 3/15 for domestic students, 5/1 priority date for international students; for spring admission, 10/15 for domestic students, 11/1 priority date for international students; for summer admission, 4/1 priority date for international students. Applications are processed on a rolling basis. Application fee: $60. Electronic applications accepted. *Expenses:* Tuition, state resident: full-time $11,326; part-time $630 per credit hour. Tuition, nonresident: full-time $23,568; part-time $1311 per credit hour. *Required fees:* $196. Tuition and fees vary according to program and reciprocity agreements. *Financial support:* Teaching assistantships available. Financial award application deadline: 3/3; financial award applicants required to submit FAFSA. *Faculty research:* African popular culture, black male identity development, education and retention, contemporary politics in Nigeria, poverty in the Caribbean. *Unit head:* Dr. Ricky L. Jones, Chair, 502-852-0027, E-mail: ricky.jones@louisville.edu. *Application contact:* Libby Leggett, Director, Graduate Admissions, 502-852-3101, E-mail: gradadm@louisville.edu.
Website: http://www.louisville.edu/panafricanstudies

The University of North Carolina at Charlotte, College of Liberal Arts and Sciences, Department of Africana Studies, Charlotte, NC 28223-0001. Offers Graduate Certificate. Part-time programs available. *Faculty:* 5 full-time (1 woman), 1 part-time/adjunct (0 women). *Students:* 4 part-time (all women); all minorities (all Black or African American, non-Hispanic/Latino). Average age 32. 5 applicants, 80% accepted, 4 enrolled. In 2014, 2 Graduate Certificates awarded. *Entrance requirements:* Additional exam requirements/recommendations for international students: Required—TOEFL (minimum score 557 paper-based; 83 iBT). *Application deadline:* For fall admission, 5/1 priority date for domestic students, 5/1 for international students; for spring admission, 10/1 priority date for domestic students, 10/1 for international students. Applications are processed on a rolling basis. Application fee: $75. Electronic applications accepted. *Expenses:* Tuition, state resident: full-time $4008. Tuition, nonresident: full-time $16,295. *Required fees:* $2755. Tuition and fees vary according to course load and program. *Unit head:* Dr. Nancy A. Gutierrez, Dean, 704-687-0081, Fax: 704-687-3228, E-mail: ngutierr@uncc.edu. *Application contact:* Kathy B. Giddings, Director of Graduate Admissions, 704-687-5503, Fax: 704-687-1668, E-mail: gradadm@uncc.edu.
Website: http://africana.uncc.edu/

University of Pennsylvania, School of Arts and Sciences, Program in Africana Studies, Philadelphia, PA 19104. Offers MA, PhD. *Faculty:* 17 full-time (11 women). *Students:* 13 full-time (11 women); includes 8 minority (6 Black or African American, non-Hispanic/Latino; 1 Hispanic/Latino; 1 Two or more races, non-Hispanic/Latino), 3 international. 45 applicants, 9% accepted, 2 enrolled. Application fee: $70. *Unit head:* Dr. Ralph M. Rosen, Associate Dean for Graduate Studies, 215-898-7156, Fax: 215-573-8068, E-mail: grad-dean@sas.upenn.edu. *Application contact:* Arts and Sciences Graduate Admissions, 215-573-5816, Fax: 215-573-8068, E-mail: gdasadmis@sas.upenn.edu.
Website: https://africana.sas.upenn.edu/

University of Pittsburgh, University Center for International Studies, Pittsburgh, PA 15260. Offers African studies (Certificate); Asian studies (Certificate); European Union studies (Certificate); global studies (Certificate); Latin American studies (Certificate); Russian and East European studies (Certificate); West European studies (Certificate). *Students:* 223 full-time (98 women), 11 part-time (1 woman); includes 97 minority (2 Black or African American, non-Hispanic/Latino; 41 Asian, non-Hispanic/Latino; 52 Hispanic/Latino; 2 Two or more races, non-Hispanic/Latino). Average age 31. In 2014, 72 Certificates awarded. *Degree requirements:* For Certificate, one foreign language, study abroad. *Application deadline:* Applications are processed on a rolling basis. *Expenses:* Tuition, state resident: full-time $20,742; part-time $838 per credit. Tuition, nonresident: full-time $33,960; part-time $1389 per credit. *Required fees:* $800; $205 per term. Tuition and fees vary according to program. *Unit head:* Dr. Ariel Armony, Director, 412-648-7374, Fax: 412-624-4672, E-mail: armony@pitt.edu. *Application contact:* Information Contact, 412-624-4141, E-mail: graduate@pitt.edu.
Website: http://www.ucis.pitt.edu

University of South Florida, College of Arts and Sciences, Department of Humanities and Cultural Studies, Tampa, FL 33620-9951. Offers American studies (MA); liberal arts (MA), including Africana studies, film studies, humanities, social and political thought. Part-time and evening/weekend programs available. *Faculty:* 7 full-time (3 women). *Students:* 11 full-time (2 women), 8 part-time (2 women); includes 8 minority (4 Black or African American, non-Hispanic/Latino; 3 Hispanic/Latino; 1 Two or more races, non-Hispanic/Latino), 1 international. Average age 34. 9 applicants, 78% accepted, 5 enrolled. In 2014, 5 master's awarded. *Degree requirements:* For master's, comprehensive exam, thesis, language requirement (for humanities subconcentration). *Entrance requirements:* For master's, GRE General Test (minimum preferred score 59th percentile (153) verbal and 4.5 in analytical writing), minimum GPA of 3.0 in upper-division courses, personal statement, writing sample. Additional exam requirements/recommendations for international students: Required—TOEFL (minimum score 550 paper-based; 79 iBT) or IELTS (minimum score 6.5). *Application deadline:* For fall admission, 2/15 priority date for domestic students, 1/2 for international students; for spring admission, 10/15 priority date for domestic students, 6/1 for international students. Application fee: $30. *Financial support:* In 2014–15, 15 students received support, including 15 teaching assistantships with tuition reimbursements available (averaging $12,437 per year); scholarships/grants also available. Financial award application deadline: 4/1. *Faculty research:* American South, American autobiography, material culture, critical theory, cultural studies, film studies. *Unit head:* Dr. William Cummings, Professor and Chair, 813-974-9380, Fax: 813-974-9409, E-mail: wcummings@usf.edu. *Application contact:* Dr. Brook Sadler, Associate Professor and Graduate Program Director, 813-974-8841, Fax: 813-974-9409, E-mail: brooksadler@usf.edu.
Website: http://humanities.usf.edu/

University of South Florida, Innovative Education, Tampa, FL 33620-9951. *Unit head:* Kathy Barnes, Interdisciplinary Programs Coordinator, 813-974-8031, Fax: 813-974-7061, E-mail: barnesk@usf.edu. *Application contact:* Karen Tylinski, Metro Initiatives, 813-974-9943, Fax: 813-974-7061, E-mail: ktylinsk@usf.edu.
Website: http://www.usf.edu/innovative-education/

The University of Texas at Austin, Graduate School, College of Liberal Arts, John L. Warfield Center for African and African American Studies, Austin, TX 78712-1111. Offers African Diaspora studies (MA, PhD). Part-time programs available. *Degree requirements:* For master's, one foreign language, thesis. *Entrance requirements:* For master's, GRE General Test. Electronic applications accepted.

University of Wisconsin–Madison, Graduate School, College of Letters and Science, Department of African Languages and Literature, Madison, WI 53706-1380. Offers MA, PhD. Part-time programs available. *Degree requirements:* For master's, one foreign language, thesis; for doctorate, 2 foreign languages, comprehensive exam, thesis/dissertation. *Entrance requirements:* For master's, BA in African language and literature; for doctorate, MA in African language and literature. Electronic applications accepted. *Expenses:* Tuition, state resident: full-time $10,723; part-time $745 per credit. Tuition, nonresident: full-time $24,054; part-time $1578 per credit. *Required fees:* $374 per semester. Tuition and fees vary according to course load, program and reciprocity agreements. *Faculty research:* Oral traditions, language pedagogy, stylistics, sociolinguistics, literary criticism.

University of Wisconsin–Madison, Graduate School, College of Letters and Science, Department of History, Madison, WI 53706-1380. Offers African history (MA, PhD); Central Asian history (MA, PhD); comparative world history (MA, PhD); East Asian history (MA, PhD); European history (MA, PhD); gender and women's history (MA, PhD); Latin American and Caribbean history (MA, PhD); Middle Eastern history (MA, PhD); South Asian history (MA, PhD); Southeast Asian history (MA, PhD); United States history (MA, PhD). Terminal master's awarded for partial completion of doctoral program. *Degree requirements:* For master's, thesis (for some programs); for doctorate, variable foreign language requirement, thesis/dissertation. *Entrance requirements:* For master's and doctorate, GRE General Test. Additional exam requirements/recommendations for international students: Required—Michigan English Language Assessment Battery or TOEFL. Electronic applications accepted. *Expenses:* Tuition, state resident: full-time $10,723; part-time $745 per credit. Tuition, nonresident: full-time $24,054; part-time $1578 per credit. *Required fees:* $374 per semester. Tuition and fees vary according to course load, program and reciprocity agreements. *Faculty research:* American, African, European, Asian, Latin American, and Middle Eastern history.

University of Wisconsin–Milwaukee, Graduate School, College of Letters and Sciences, Department of Africology, Milwaukee, WI 53201-0413. Offers PhD. *Degree requirements:* For doctorate, comprehensive exam. *Entrance requirements:* For doctorate, GRE General Test. Additional exam requirements/recommendations for international students: Required—TOEFL (minimum score 550 paper-based; 79 iBT), IELTS (minimum score 6.5). Electronic applications accepted.

Wayne State University, College of Liberal Arts and Sciences, Department of History, Detroit, MI 48202. Offers Africa (PhD); America (PhD); archival administration (Graduate Certificate); Europe (PhD); gender (PhD); history (MA); labor (PhD); science and technology (PhD); world history (PhD, Graduate Certificate); JD/MA; M Ed/MA; MLIS/MA. Doctoral programs admit for fall only. Evening/weekend programs available. *Faculty:* 22 full-time (9 women). *Students:* 32 full-time (14 women), 16 part-time (6 women); includes 4 minority (2 Black or African American, non-Hispanic/Latino; 2 Two or more races, non-Hispanic/Latino). Average age 39. 52 applicants, 37% accepted, 9 enrolled. In 2014, 5 master's awarded. *Degree requirements:* For master's, one foreign language, thesis (for some programs), final oral exam on thesis or essay and seminar; for doctorate, variable foreign language requirement, thesis/dissertation, qualifying exam in 4 fields of history. *Entrance requirements:* For master's, GRE General Test, minimum undergraduate GPA of 3.25 in history, 3.0 overall; at least 18 credits in history and related subjects at the advanced undergraduate level; foreign language; letter of intent; research paper; at least two letters of recommendation from former instructors; for doctorate, GRE General Test, minimum GPA of 3.0; letter of intent; research paper; at least three letters of recommendation from former professors; for Graduate Certificate, baccalaureate degree from accredited college or university; minimum GPA of 3.0, 3.25 in a minimum of eighteen semester credits in history and related subjects at the advanced undergraduate level. Additional exam requirements/recommendations for international students: Required—TOEFL (minimum score 550 paper-based; 79 iBT), TWE (minimum score 5.5), Michigan English Language Assessment Battery (minimum score 85); Recommended—IELTS (minimum score 6.5). *Application deadline:* For fall admission, 2/1 for domestic and international students; for winter admission, 11/1 for domestic students, 10/1 priority date for international students; for spring admission, 3/15 for domestic students, 1/1 priority date for international students. Applications are processed on a rolling basis. Application fee: $0. Electronic applications accepted. *Expenses:* Tuition, state resident: full-time $10,294; part-time $571.90 per credit hour. Tuition, nonresident: full-time $29,730; part-time $1238.75 per credit hour. *Required fees:* $1365; $43.50 per credit hour. $291.10 per semester. Tuition and fees vary according to course load and program. *Financial support:* In 2014–15, 19 students received support, including 1 fellowship with tuition reimbursement available (averaging $16,000 per year), 1 research assistantship with tuition reimbursement available (averaging $17,994 per year), 6 teaching assistantships with tuition reimbursements available (averaging $16,838 per year); scholarships/grants, health care benefits, and unspecified assistantships also available. Financial award application deadline: 3/31; financial award applicants required to submit FAFSA. *Faculty research:* Labor and working class history, urban history, citizenship and politics, gender and women's history. *Unit head:* Dr. Marc W. Kruman, Chair, 313-577-2525, Fax: 313-577-6987, E-mail: mkruman@wayne.edu. *Application contact:* Dr. Gayle McCreedy, Academic Service Officer, 313-577-2592, Fax: 313-577-6987, E-mail: g.mccreedy@wayne.edu. Website: http://clas.wayne.edu/history/

West Virginia University, Eberly College of Arts and Sciences, Department of History, Morgantown, WV 26506. Offers African history (MA, PhD); African-American history (MA, PhD); American history (MA, PhD); Appalachian/regional history (MA, PhD); East Asian history (MA, PhD); European history (MA, PhD); history of science and technology (MA, PhD); Latin American history (MA). Part-time programs available. *Degree requirements:* For master's, one foreign language, thesis (for some programs), oral exam, thesis defense; for doctorate, one foreign language, comprehensive exam, thesis/dissertation, dissertation defense. *Entrance requirements:* For master's, GRE General Test, minimum GPA of 3.0; for doctorate, GRE General Test. Additional exam requirements/recommendations for international students: Required—TOEFL (minimum score 550 paper-based), IELTS (minimum score 6.5). Electronic applications accepted. *Faculty research:* United States, Appalachia, modern Europe, Africa, colonial and post-colonial societies.

Yale University, Graduate School of Arts and Sciences, Interdisciplinary Program in African Studies, New Haven, CT 06520. Offers MA. *Degree requirements:* For master's, one foreign language, thesis. *Entrance requirements:* For master's, GRE General Test.

American Indian/Native American Studies

Central Michigan University, College of Graduate Studies, College of Humanities and Social and Behavioral Sciences, Program in Humanities, Mount Pleasant, MI 48859. Offers humanities (MA), including contemporary issues in the humanities: race, class, and gender, images and ideas of self, Native American issues in modern culture, popular culture studies, the rise of industrial society. Part-time and evening/weekend programs available. *Degree requirements:* For master's, thesis or alternative. Electronic applications accepted. *Faculty research:* Rise of industrial society; images and ideas of self; contemporary issues of race, class, and gender; popular culture; Native American issues in modern culture.

Montana State University, The Graduate School, College of Letters and Science, Department of Native American Studies, Bozeman, MT 59717. Offers MA. Part-time programs available. Postbaccalaureate distance learning degree programs offered (no on-campus study). *Degree requirements:* For master's, comprehensive exam. *Entrance requirements:* For master's, minimum GPA of 3.0; 3 letters of recommendation; 2 academic writing samples; statement of purpose. Additional exam requirements/recommendations for international students: Required—TOEFL (minimum score 550 paper-based). Electronic applications accepted. *Faculty research:* Federal Indian law and policy, contemporary Native film and literature, tribal colleges and Native Americans in higher education, Native veterans, native land rights.

Navajo Technical University, Program in Dine Studies, Crownpoint, NM 87313. Offers MA. *Entrance requirements:* For master's, bachelor's degree, Certificate of Indian Blood (CIB) for tribal eligibility, three letters of recommendation, 500-word essay.

Trent University, Graduate Studies, The Frost Centre for Canadian Studies and Indigenous Studies, Peterborough, ON K9J 7B8, Canada. Offers Canadian studies (PhD); Canadian studies and indigenous studies (MA). Part-time programs available. *Degree requirements:* For master's, thesis. *Entrance requirements:* For master's, honors degree. *Faculty research:* Native community-based socioeconomic development, environmental and social impact inventory, regional studies.

Trent University, Graduate Studies, Program in Indigenous Studies, Peterborough, ON K9J 7B8, Canada. Offers PhD. Part-time programs available. *Degree requirements:* For doctorate, thesis/dissertation. *Entrance requirements:* For doctorate, master's degree.

The University of Arizona, Graduate Interdisciplinary Programs, Graduate Interdisciplinary Program in American Indian Studies, Tucson, AZ 85721. Offers MA, PhD, JD/MA. Part-time programs available. *Degree requirements:* For master's, thesis; for doctorate, one foreign language, comprehensive exam, thesis/dissertation. *Entrance requirements:* For master's, 3 letters of recommendation, 2 writing samples, resume; for doctorate, statement of purpose, 3 letters of recommendation, 2 writing samples, resume. Additional exam requirements/recommendations for international students: Required—TOEFL (minimum score 550 paper-based; 79 iBT). Electronic applications accepted. *Faculty research:* Indian law and policy, Indian societies, Indian language and literature, Indian education.

University of California, Davis, Graduate Studies, Program in Native American Studies, Davis, CA 95616. Offers MA, PhD. Terminal master's awarded for partial completion of doctoral program. *Degree requirements:* For master's, comprehensive exam (for some programs), thesis (for some programs); for doctorate, thesis/dissertation. *Entrance requirements:* For doctorate, GRE. Additional exam requirements/recommendations for international students: Required—TOEFL (minimum score 550 paper-based).

University of California, Los Angeles, Graduate Division, College of Letters and Science, Interdepartmental Program in American Indian Studies, Los Angeles, CA 90095. Offers MA, JD/MA. *Degree requirements:* For master's, comprehensive exam or thesis. *Entrance requirements:* For master's, GRE General Test (recommended), bachelor's degree; minimum undergraduate GPA of 3.0 (or its equivalent if letter grade system not used). Additional exam requirements/recommendations for international students: Required—TOEFL. Electronic applications accepted.

University of Idaho, College of Law, Moscow, ID 83844-2321. Offers business law and entrepreneurship (JD); law (JD); litigation and alternative dispute resolution (JD); Native American law (JD); natural resources and environmental law (JD). *Accreditation:* ABA. *Faculty:* 30 full-time, 7 part-time/adjunct. *Students:* 345 full-time, 7 part-time. Average age 29. *Entrance requirements:* For doctorate, LSAT, Law School Admission Council Credential Assembly Service (CAS) Report. Additional exam requirements/recommendations for international students: Required—TOEFL. *Application deadline:* For fall admission, 2/15 for domestic students. Applications are processed on a rolling basis. Application fee: $50 ($60 for international students). Electronic applications accepted. *Expenses:* Tuition, state resident: full-time $4784; part-time $280.50 per credit hour. Tuition, nonresident: full-time $18,314; part-time $957.50 per credit hour. *Required fees:* $2000; $58.50 per credit hour. Tuition and fees vary according to program. *Financial support:* Career-related internships or fieldwork, Federal Work-Study, and institutionally sponsored loans available. Financial award applicants required to submit FAFSA. *Faculty research:* Transboundary river governance, tribal protection and stewardship, regional water issues, environmental law. *Unit head:* Mark Adams, Dean, 208-885-4977, E-mail: uilaw@uidaho.edu. *Application contact:* Carole Wells, Interim Director of Admissions, 208-885-2300, Fax: 208-885-2252, E-mail: lawadmit@uidaho.edu.
Website: http://www.uidaho.edu/law/

The University of Kansas, Graduate Studies, College of Liberal Arts and Sciences, Indigenous Studies Program, Lawrence, KS 66045-7515. Offers MA, Graduate Certificate, JD/MA. Part-time programs available. *Faculty:* 1 full-time. *Students:* 4 full-time (3 women), 2 part-time (both women); includes 2 minority (both American Indian or Alaska Native, non-Hispanic/Latino). Average age 31. 3 applicants, 67% accepted, 2 enrolled. In 2014, 1 master's awarded. *Degree requirements:* For master's, thesis or alternative. *Entrance requirements:* For master's, GRE, resume, writing sample, minimum GPA of 3.0 (preferred), 3 recommendations, original transcript. Additional exam requirements/recommendations for international students: Required—TOEFL. *Application deadline:* For fall admission, 4/1 priority date for domestic and international students; for spring admission, 10/1 for domestic and international students. Applications are processed on a rolling basis. Application fee: $55 ($65 for international

students). Electronic applications accepted. *Financial support:* Fellowships, research assistantships, teaching assistantships, Federal Work-Study, institutionally sponsored loans, and scholarships/grants available. Support available to part-time students. Financial award application deadline: 3/15; financial award applicants required to submit FAFSA. *Unit head:* Dr. Michael Zogry, Director, 785-864-5271, E-mail: mzogry@ku.edu. *Application contact:* Kay Isbell, Graduate Academic Advisor, 785-864-2306, E-mail: kisbell@ku.edu.
Website: http://www.indigenous.ku.edu

University of Lethbridge, School of Graduate Studies, Lethbridge, AB T1K 3M4, Canada. Offers addictions counseling (M Sc); agricultural biotechnology (M Sc); agricultural studies (M Sc, MA); anthropology (MA); archaeology (M Sc, MA); art (MA, MFA); biochemistry (M Sc); biological sciences (M Sc); biomolecular science (PhD); biosystems and biodiversity (PhD); Canadian studies (MA); chemistry (M Sc); computer science (M Sc); computer science and geographical information science (M Sc); counseling (MC); counseling psychology (M Ed); dramatic arts (MA); earth, space, and physical science (PhD); economics (MA); education (MA); educational leadership (M Ed); English (MA); environmental science (M Sc); evolution and behavior (PhD); exercise science (M Sc); French (MA); French/German (MA); French/Spanish (MA); general education (M Ed); geography (M Sc, MA); German (MA); health sciences (M Sc); individualized multidisciplinary (M Sc, MA); kinesiology (M Sc, MA); management (M Sc), including accounting, finance, general management, human resource management and labor relations, information systems, international management, marketing, policy and strategy; mathematics (M Sc); modern languages (MA); music (M Mus, MA); Native American studies (MA); neuroscience (M Sc, PhD); new media (MA, MFA); nursing (M Sc, MN); philosophy (MA); physics (M Sc); political science (MA); psychology (M Sc, MA); religious studies (MA); sociology (MA); theatre and dramatic arts (MFA); theoretical and computational science (PhD); urban and regional studies (MA); women and gender studies (MA). Part-time and evening/weekend programs available. *Faculty:* 358. *Students:* 445 full-time (243 women), 116 part-time (72 women). Average age 31. 351 applicants, 26% accepted, 87 enrolled. In 2014, 129 master's, 13 doctorates awarded. *Degree requirements:* For master's, thesis (for some programs); for doctorate, comprehensive exam, thesis/dissertation. *Entrance requirements:* For master's, GMAT (for M Sc in management), bachelor's degree in related field, minimum GPA of 3.0 during previous 20 graded semester courses, 2 years' teaching or related experience (M Ed); for doctorate, master's degree, minimum graduate GPA of 3.5. Additional exam requirements/recommendations for international students: Required—TOEFL. Application fee: $100 Canadian dollars. *Financial support:* Fellowships, research assistantships, teaching assistantships, scholarships/grants, health care benefits, and unspecified assistantships available. *Faculty research:* Movement and brain plasticity, gibberellin physiology, photosynthesis, carbon cycling, molecular properties of main-group ring components. *Application contact:* School of Graduate Studies, 403-329-5194, E-mail: sgsinquiries@uleth.ca.
Website: http://www.uleth.ca/graduatestudies/

University of Manitoba, Faculty of Graduate Studies, Faculty of Arts, Department of Native Studies, Winnipeg, MB R3T 2N2, Canada. Offers MA.

University of New Mexico, Graduate School, College of Education, Program in Language, Literacy and Sociocultural Studies, Albuquerque, NM 87131. Offers American Indian education (MA); bilingual education (MA, PhD); educational linguistics (PhD); educational thought and sociocultural studies (MA, PhD); literacy/language arts (MA, PhD); social studies (MA); TESOL (MA, PhD). *Faculty:* 16 full-time (9 women), 6 part-time/adjunct (4 women). *Students:* 63 full-time (45 women), 96 part-time (86 women); includes 84 minority (6 Black or African American, non-Hispanic/Latino; 17 American Indian or Alaska Native, non-Hispanic/Latino; 5 Asian, non-Hispanic/Latino; 52 Hispanic/Latino; 4 Two or more races, non-Hispanic/Latino), 25 international. Average age 36. 50 applicants, 58% accepted, 20 enrolled. In 2014, 36 master's, 4 doctorates awarded. *Degree requirements:* For master's, comprehensive exam, thesis optional; for doctorate, comprehensive exam, thesis/dissertation, research skills. *Entrance requirements:* For master's, letter of intent, 3 letters of recommendation, resume, BA/BS, department demographic form, transcripts; for doctorate, writing sample, letter of intent, 3 letters of recommendation, resume, BA/BS, MA, department demographic form, transcripts. Additional exam requirements/recommendations for international students: Required—TOEFL. *Application deadline:* For fall admission, 12/1 for domestic and international students; for spring admission, 9/15 for domestic and international students. Application fee: $50. Electronic applications accepted. *Financial support:* In 2014–15, 7 students received support, including 7 fellowships (averaging $3,170 per year), 1,318 teaching assistantships with tuition reimbursements available (averaging $3,789 per year); research assistantships, career-related internships or fieldwork, institutionally sponsored loans, scholarships/grants, and unspecified assistantships also available. Support available to part-time students. Financial award application deadline: 3/1; financial award applicants required to submit FAFSA. *Faculty research:* School reform, professional development, history of education, Native American education, politics of education, feminism and issues of sexual identity, critical race theory, bilingualism, literacy reading, adolescent literature, second language acquisition, critical theory and schooling, indigenous languages. *Unit head:* Dr. Lois M. Meyer, Chair, 505-277-7244, Fax: 505-277-8362, E-mail: lsmeyer@unm.edu. *Application contact:* Debra Schaffer, Administrative Assistant, 505-277-0437, Fax: 505-277-8362, E-mail: schaffer@unm.edu.
Website: http://coe.unm.edu/departments/department-of-language-literacy-and-sociocultural-studies/llss-program.html

University of Oklahoma, College of Arts and Sciences, Department of Native American Studies, Norman, OK 73019. Offers MA, JD/MA. Part-time programs available. *Faculty:* 24 full-time (9 women). *Students:* 5 full-time (4 women), 7 part-time (6 women); all minorities (8 American Indian or Alaska Native, non-Hispanic/Latino; 1 Hispanic/Latino; 3 Two or more races, non-Hispanic/Latino). Average age 28. 4 applicants, 100% accepted, 2 enrolled. In 2014, 4 master's awarded. *Degree requirements:* For master's, one foreign language, thesis. *Entrance requirements:* For master's, GRE, minimum GPA of 3.0. Additional exam requirements/recommendations for international students: Required—TOEFL (minimum score 79 iBT). *Application deadline:* For fall admission, 8/1 for domestic students, 4/1 for international students; for spring admission, 12/1 for domestic students, 8/1 for international students. Application fee: $50 ($100 for international students). Electronic applications accepted. *Expenses:* Tuition, state resident: full-time $4394; part-time $183.10 per credit hour. Tuition, nonresident: full-time $16,970; part-time $707.10 per credit hour. *Required fees:* $2892; $109.95 per credit hour. $126.50 per semester. *Financial support:* In 2014–15, 7 students received support, including 6 teaching assistantships with partial tuition reimbursements available (averaging $14,394 per year); career-related internships or fieldwork, Federal Work-Study, institutionally sponsored loans, health care benefits, and unspecified assistantships also available. Financial award application deadline: 6/1; financial award applicants required to submit FAFSA. *Faculty research:* Tribal governance and policy; indigenous media and arts; cultural knowledge, language, and history. *Unit head:* Dr. Amanda Cobb-Greethan, Professor/Director of Native American Studies, 405-325-2312, Fax: 405-325-0842, E-mail: nas@ou.edu.
Website: http://cas.ou.edu/nas-graduate-program

University of Oklahoma, Weitzenhoffer Family College of Fine Arts, School of Art and Art History, Norman, OK 73019. Offers art (MFA), including ceramics, film, painting, photography, printmaking, sculpture, video, visual communication; art history (MA, PhD), including art history (MA), art of the American West (PhD), Native American art (PhD). Part-time programs available. *Faculty:* 25 full-time (6 women). *Students:* 21 full-time (11 women), 11 part-time (7 women); includes 6 minority (4 American Indian or Alaska Native, non-Hispanic/Latino; 2 Two or more races, non-Hispanic/Latino), 1 international. Average age 32. 23 applicants, 48% accepted, 3 enrolled. In 2014, 7 master's awarded. Terminal master's awarded for partial completion of doctoral program. *Degree requirements:* For master's, comprehensive exam, thesis; for doctorate, comprehensive exam, thesis/dissertation. *Entrance requirements:* Additional exam requirements/recommendations for international students: Required—TOEFL (minimum score 79 iBT). *Application deadline:* For fall admission, 1/15 for domestic and international students; for spring admission, 10/1 for domestic and international students. Application fee: $50 ($100 for international students). Electronic applications accepted. *Expenses:* Tuition, state resident: full-time $4394; part-time $183.10 per credit hour. Tuition, nonresident: full-time $16,970; part-time $707.10 per credit hour. *Required fees:* $2892; $109.95 per credit hour. $126.50 per semester. *Financial support:* In 2014–15, 28 students received support, including 1 fellowship (averaging $5,000 per year), 16 teaching assistantships with partial tuition reimbursements available (averaging $10,377 per year); career-related internships or fieldwork, Federal Work-Study, institutionally sponsored loans, scholarships/grants, health care benefits, tuition waivers (full and partial), and unspecified assistantships also available. Support available to part-time students. Financial award application deadline: 6/1; financial award applicants required to submit FAFSA. *Faculty research:* Sculpture, painting, printmaking, technology, ceramics, Native American art, art of American West, Byzantine, Contemporary, Renaissance, Baroque, nineteenth-twentieth century. *Unit head:* 405-325-2691, Fax: 405-325-1668. *Application contact:* 405-325-2691, Fax: 405-325-1668.
Website: http://www.ou.edu/finearts/art_arthistory.html

The University of Tulsa, College of Law, Tulsa, OK 74104. Offers American Indian and indigenous law (LL M); American law for foreign lawyers (LL M); energy and natural resources law (LL M); energy law (MJ); health law (Certificate); Indian law (MJ); law (JD); Native American law (Certificate); natural resources, energy, and environmental law (Certificate); JD/M Tax; JD/MA; JD/MBA; JD/MS. *Accreditation:* ABA. Part-time programs available. Postbaccalaureate distance learning degree programs offered (no on-campus study). *Faculty:* 29 full-time (16 women), 21 part-time/adjunct (6 women). *Students:* 244 full-time (120 women), 22 part-time (9 women); includes 49 minority (4 Black or African American, non-Hispanic/Latino; 11 American Indian or Alaska Native, non-Hispanic/Latino; 2 Asian, non-Hispanic/Latino; 11 Hispanic/Latino; 1 Native Hawaiian or other Pacific Islander, non-Hispanic/Latino; 20 Two or more races, non-Hispanic/Latino), 4 international. Average age 26. 735 applicants, 33% accepted, 86 enrolled. In 2014, 5 master's, 1 doctorate awarded. *Degree requirements:* For master's, thesis optional. *Entrance requirements:* For master's, JD from an ABA-approved U.S. law school or a JD equivalent from non-U.S. university; for doctorate, LSAT, BS or BA from 4-year regionally-accredited college/university; for Certificate, BS or BA from 4-year regionally-accredited college/university. Additional exam requirements/recommendations for international students: Required—TOEFL (minimum score 570 paper-based; 90 iBT), IELTS (minimum score 6.5). *Application deadline:* For fall admission, 2/1 priority date for domestic and international students; for spring admission, 12/5 priority date for domestic and international students. Applications are processed on a rolling basis. Application fee: $30. Electronic applications accepted. *Expenses:* Expenses: Contact institution. *Financial support:* In 2014–15, 218 students received support. Career-related internships or fieldwork, Federal Work-Study, and scholarships/grants available. Support available to part-time students. Financial award application deadline: 8/1; financial award applicants required to submit FAFSA. *Faculty research:* International law, Native American law, criminal law, commercial speech, copyright law. *Unit head:* Lyn Entzeroth, Dean, 918-631-2400, Fax: 918-631-3126, E-mail: lyn-entzeroth@utulsa.edu. *Application contact:* April M. Fox, Assistant Dean of Admissions and Financial Aid, 918-631-2406, Fax: 918-631-3630, E-mail: april-fox@utulsa.edu.
Website: http://www.utulsa.edu/law/

Washington University in St. Louis, Brown School of Social Work, St. Louis, MO 63130-4899. Offers affordable housing and mixed-income community management (Certificate); American Indian and Alaska native (MSW); children, youth and families (MSW); health (MSW); individualized (MSW), including health; mental health (MSW); older adults and aging societies (MSW); public health (MPH), including epidemiology/biostatistics, global health, health policy analysis, urban design; social and economic development (MSW); social work (MSW, PhD), including management (MSW), policy (MSW), research (MSW), sexual health and education (MSW), social entrepreneurship (MSW), system dynamics (MSW); violence and injury prevention (Certificate); JD/MSW; M Arch/MSW; MPH/MBA; MSW/M Div; MSW/MAPS; MSW/MBA; MSW/MPH. MSW/M Div and MSW/MAPS offered in partnership with Eden Theological Seminary. *Accreditation:* CSWE (one or more programs are accredited). *Faculty:* 42 full-time (24 women), 81 part-time/adjunct (49 women). *Students:* 272 full-time (229 women); includes 138 minority (47 Black or African American, non-Hispanic/Latino; 11 American Indian or Alaska Native, non-Hispanic/Latino; 54 Asian, non-Hispanic/Latino; 19 Hispanic/Latino; 7 Two or more races, non-Hispanic/Latino), 47 international. Average age 26. 817 applicants, 62% accepted, 303 enrolled. In 2014, 239 master's, 5 doctorates awarded. *Degree requirements:* For master's, 60 credit hours (MSW), 52 credit hours (MPH); practicum; for doctorate, comprehensive exam, thesis/dissertation. *Entrance requirements:* For master's, For public health: GRE, GMAT, LSAT, or MCAT, minimum GPA of 3.0; for doctorate, GRE, MA or MSW. Additional exam requirements/recommendations for international students: Required—TOEFL (minimum score 100 iBT) or IELTS. *Application deadline:* For fall admission, 3/1 priority date for domestic and international students. Applications are processed on a rolling basis. Application fee: $40. Electronic applications accepted. *Expenses:* Expenses: The tuition rate for new full-time MSW students for the 2015-2016 academic year is $38,234 per year. The tuition rate for new full-time MPH students for the 2015-2016 academic year is $33,132 per year. *Financial support:* In 2014–15, 301 students received support. Fellowships, research assistantships, Federal Work-Study, institutionally sponsored loans, scholarships/grants, health care benefits, tuition waivers (partial), and unspecified assistantships available. Support available to part-time students. Financial award application deadline: 3/1; financial award applicants required to submit FAFSA. *Faculty research:* Mental health services, social development, child welfare, at-risk teens, autism, environmental health, health policy, health communications, obesity, gender and sexuality, violence and injury prevention, chronic disease prevention, poverty, older adults/aging societies, civic engagement, school social work, program evaluation, health disparities. *Unit head:* Jamie L. Adkisson, Director of Recruitment & Admissions, 314-935-3524, Fax: 314-935-4859, E-mail: jadkisson@wustl.edu. *Application contact:* Cate M. Valentine, Admissions Counselor, 314-935-8879, Fax: 314-935-4859, E-mail: cvalentine@wustl.edu.
Website: http://brownschool.wustl.edu

American Studies

American Public University System, AMU/APU Graduate Programs, Charles Town, WV 25414. Offers accounting (MBA, MS); criminal justice (MA), including business administration, emergency and disaster management, general (MA, MS); educational leadership (M Ed); emergency and disaster management (MA); entrepreneurship (MBA); environmental policy and management (MS), including environmental planning, environmental sustainability, fish and wildlife management, general (MA, MS), global environmental management; finance (MBA); general (MBA); global business management (MBA); history (MA), including American history, ancient and classical history, European history, global history, public history; homeland security (MA), including business administration, counter-terrorism studies, criminal justice, cyber, emergency management and public health, intelligence studies, transportation security; homeland security resource allocation (MBA); humanities (MA); information technology (MS), including digital forensics, enterprise software development, information assurance and security, IT project management; information technology management (MBA); intelligence studies (MA), including criminal intelligence, cyber, general (MA, MS), homeland security, intelligence analysis, intelligence collection, intelligence management, intelligence operations, terrorism studies; international relations and conflict resolution (MA), including comparative and security issues, conflict resolution, international and transnational security issues, peacekeeping; legal studies (MA); management (MA), including defense management, general (MA, MS), human resource management, organizational leadership, public administration; marketing (MBA); military history (MA), including American military history, American Revolution, civil war, war since 1945, World War II; military studies (MA), including joint warfare, strategic leadership; national security studies (MA), including general (MA, MS), homeland security, regional security studies, security and intelligence analysis, terrorism studies; nonprofit management (MBA); political science (MA), including American politics and government, comparative government and development, general (MA, MS), international relations, public policy; psychology (MA); public administration (MPA), including disaster management, environmental policy, health policy, human resources, national security, organizational management, security management; public health (MPH); reverse logistics management (MA); school counseling (M Ed); security management (MA); space studies (MS), including aerospace science, general (MA, MS), planetary science; sports and health sciences (MS); teaching (M Ed), including curriculum and instruction for elementary teachers, elementary reading, English language learners, instructional leadership, online learning, special education; transportation and logistics management (MA), including general (MA, MS), maritime engineering management, reverse logistics management. Programs offered via distance learning only. Part-time and evening/weekend programs available. Postbaccalaureate distance learning degree programs offered (no on-campus study). *Faculty:* 426 full-time (236 women), 1,864 part-time/adjunct (880 women). *Students:* 475 full-time (215 women), 10,067 part-time (4,085 women); includes 3,462 minority (1,863 Black or African American, non-Hispanic/Latino; 74 American Indian or Alaska Native, non-Hispanic/Latino; 273 Asian, non-Hispanic/Latino; 831 Hispanic/Latino; 78 Native Hawaiian or other Pacific Islander, non-Hispanic/Latino; 343 Two or more races, non-Hispanic/Latino), 131 international. Average age 36. In 2014, 3,740 master's awarded. *Degree requirements:* For master's, comprehensive exam or practicum. *Entrance requirements:* For master's, official transcript showing earned bachelor's degree from institution accredited by recognized accrediting body. Additional exam requirements/recommendations for international students: Required—TOEFL (minimum score 550 paper-based), IELTS (minimum score 6.5). *Application deadline:* Applications are processed on a rolling basis. Application fee: $0. Electronic applications accepted. *Financial support:* Applicants required to submit FAFSA. *Faculty research:* Military history, criminal justice, management performance, national security. *Unit head:* Dr. Karan Powell, Executive Vice President and Provost, 877-468-6268, Fax: 304-724-3780. *Application contact:* Terry Grant, Vice President of Enrollment Management, 877-468-6268, Fax: 304-724-3780, E-mail: info@apus.edu.
Website: http://www.apus.edu

American University, School of International Service, Washington, DC 20016-8071. Offers comparative and regional studies (Certificate); cross-cultural communication (Certificate); development management (MS); ethics, peace, and global affairs (MA); European studies (Certificate); global environmental policy (MA, Certificate); global information technology (Certificate); international affairs (MA), including comparative and international disability policy, comparative and regional studies, international economic relations, international politics, natural resources and sustainable development, U.S. foreign policy; international communication (MA, Certificate); international development (MA, Certificate); international economic policy (Certificate); international economic relations (Certificate); international media (MA); international peace and conflict resolution (MA, Certificate); international politics (Certificate); international relations (PhD); international service (MIS); peacebuilding (Certificate); social enterprise (MA); the Americas (Certificate); United States foreign policy (Certificate); JD/MA. Part-time and evening/weekend programs available. Postbaccalaureate distance learning degree programs offered (no on-campus study). *Faculty:* 112 full-time (43 women), 59 part-time/adjunct (27 women). *Students:* 545 full-time (335 women), 443 part-time (271 women); includes 231 minority (82 Black or African American, non-Hispanic/Latino; 8 American Indian or Alaska Native, non-Hispanic/Latino; 51 Asian, non-Hispanic/Latino; 81 Hispanic/Latino; 2 Native Hawaiian or other Pacific Islander, non-Hispanic/Latino; 7 Two or more races, non-Hispanic/Latino), 120 international. Average age 28. 1,991 applicants, 70% accepted, 365 enrolled. In 2014, 426 master's, 9 doctorates, 6 other advanced degrees awarded. Terminal master's awarded for partial completion of doctoral program. *Degree requirements:* For master's, one foreign language, comprehensive exam, thesis or alternative; for doctorate, one foreign language, comprehensive exam, thesis/dissertation. *Entrance requirements:* For master's, GRE, transcripts, resume, 2 letters of recommendation, statement of purpose; for doctorate, GRE, transcripts, resume, 3 letters of recommendation, statement of purpose. Additional exam requirements/recommendations for international students: Required—TOEFL (minimum score 600 paper-based; 100 iBT). *Application deadline:* For fall admission, 1/15 for domestic students; for spring admission, 10/1 for domestic students, 9/15 for international students. Application fee: $50. Electronic applications accepted. *Financial support:* Application deadline: 1/15. *Unit head:* Dr. James Goldgeier, Dean, 202-885-1603, Fax: 202-885-2494, E-mail: goldgeier@american.edu. *Application contact:* Jia Jiang, Associate Director, Graduate Education Enrollment, 202-885-1689, Fax: 202-885-1109, E-mail: jiang@american.edu.
Website: http://www.american.edu/sis/

American University of Beirut, Graduate Programs, Faculty of Arts and Sciences, Beirut, Lebanon. Offers anthropology (MA); Arab and Middle Eastern history (PhD); Arabic language and literature (MA, PhD); archaeology (MA); biology (MS); cell and molecular biology (PhD); chemistry (MS); clinical psychology (MA); computational sciences (MS); computer science (MS); economics (MA); English language (MA); English literature (MA); environmental policy planning (MS); financial economics (MAFE); geology (MS); history (MA); mathematics (MA, MS); media studies (MA); Middle Eastern studies (MA); physics (MS); political studies (MA); psychology (MA); public administration (MA); sociology (MA); statistics (MA, MS); theoretical physics (PhD); transnational American studies (MA). Part-time programs available. *Faculty:* 107 full-time (32 women), 6 part-time/adjunct (2 women). *Students:* 230 full-time (161 women), 209 part-time (146 women). Average age 26. 261 applicants, 70% accepted, 83 enrolled. In 2014, 68 master's, 2 doctorates awarded. *Degree requirements:* For master's, one foreign language, comprehensive exam, thesis (for some programs); for doctorate, one foreign language, comprehensive exam, thesis/dissertation. *Entrance requirements:* For master's, GRE (for some MA/MS programs), letter of recommendation; for doctorate, GRE, letters of recommendation. Additional exam requirements/recommendations for international students: Required—TOEFL (minimum score 600 paper-based; 97 iBT), IELTS (minimum score 7). *Application deadline:* For fall admission, 4/1 for domestic and international students; for spring admission, 11/1 for domestic and international students. Application fee: $50. Electronic applications accepted. *Expenses: Tuition:* Full-time $15,462; part-time $859 per credit. *Required fees:* $692. Tuition and fees vary according to course load and program. *Financial support:* Research assistantships, career-related internships or fieldwork, institutionally sponsored loans, scholarships/grants, health care benefits, and unspecified assistantships available. Financial award application deadline: 2/4; financial award applicants required to submit FAFSA. *Faculty research:* Determinants of language proficiency among Arab learners of English as a foreign language; opinion mining, information retrieval, runtime verification, high performance computing; solar and fuel cells, self-organizing systems, heterocyclic chemistry, air and water chemistry; complex analysis, harmonic analysis, number theory; social and political psychology, clinical psychology; thin films physics and technology; theory of soft matter; religious and ethnic conflict; sports and politics. *Total annual research expenditures:* $966,000. *Unit head:* Dr. Patrick McGreevy, Dean, 961-1374374 Ext. 3800, Fax: 961-1744461, E-mail: pm07@aub.edu.lb. *Application contact:* Dr. Salim Kanaan, Director, Admissions Office, 961-1350000 Ext. 2590, Fax: 961-1750775, E-mail: sk00@aub.edu.lb.
Website: http://www.aub.edu.lb/fas/

Appalachian State University, Cratis D. Williams Graduate School, Center for Appalachian Studies, Boone, NC 28608. Offers culture (MA); roots and music (MA); sustainable development (MA). Part-time programs available. *Degree requirements:* For master's, one foreign language, comprehensive exam, thesis optional. *Entrance requirements:* For master's, GRE General Test, 3 letters of recommendation. Additional exam requirements/recommendations for international students: Required—TOEFL (minimum score 570 paper-based; 79 iBT), IELTS (minimum score 6.5). Electronic applications accepted. *Faculty research:* Appalachian culture, sustainable development, Appalachian music.

Armstrong State University, School of Graduate Studies, Program in History, Savannah, GA 31419-1997. Offers American and European history (MA); public history (MA). Part-time and evening/weekend programs available. *Faculty:* 5 full-time (2 women), 1 (woman) part-time/adjunct. *Students:* 6 full-time (5 women), 7 part-time (4 women); includes 3 minority (1 Black or African American, non-Hispanic/Latino; 1 Asian, non-Hispanic/Latino; 1 Hispanic/Latino). Average age 32. 9 applicants, 67% accepted, 5 enrolled. In 2014, 9 master's awarded. *Degree requirements:* For master's, one foreign language, comprehensive exam (for some programs), thesis (for some programs), thesis, internship, or advanced fieldwork. *Entrance requirements:* For master's, GRE General Test, minimum GPA of 3.0, letters of recommendation, BA in history or equivalent. Additional exam requirements/recommendations for international students: Required—TOEFL (minimum score 523 paper-based). *Application deadline:* For fall admission, 6/30 priority date for domestic students, 5/1 priority date for international students; for spring admission, 11/15 priority date for domestic students, 9/15 priority date for international students; for summer admission, 4/15 priority date for domestic students, 9/15 for international students. Applications are processed on a rolling basis. Application fee: $30. Electronic applications accepted. *Expenses:* Tuition, state resident: part-time $206 per credit hour. Tuition, nonresident: part-time $763 per credit hour. *Required fees:* $612 per semester. Tuition and fees vary according to course load, campus/location and program. *Financial support:* In 2014–15, research assistantships with full tuition reimbursements (averaging $5,000 per year) were awarded; career-related internships or fieldwork, Federal Work-Study, and unspecified assistantships also available. Support available to part-time students. Financial award application deadline: 3/15; financial award applicants required to submit FAFSA. *Faculty research:* Public history; European, Latin American, African, and United States history. *Unit head:* Dr. Christopher Curtis, Department Head, 912-344-3051, Fax: 912-344-3451, E-mail: chris.curtis@armstrong.edu. *Application contact:* Kathy Ingram, Associate Director of Graduate/Adult and Nontraditional Students, 912-344-2503, Fax: 912-344-3417, E-mail: graduate@armstrong.edu.
Website: http://www.armstrong.edu/Liberal_Arts/history/history_graduate_program

Baylor University, Graduate School, College of Arts and Sciences, Department of History, Waco, TX 76798. Offers history (MA); religion and culture (PhD); U.S. and Britain (PhD). Part-time programs available. Terminal master's awarded for partial completion of doctoral program. *Degree requirements:* For master's, one foreign language, comprehensive exam, thesis; for doctorate, one foreign language, comprehensive exam, thesis/dissertation. *Entrance requirements:* For master's and doctorate, GRE General Test, 18 semester hours in history. Additional exam requirements/recommendations for international students: Required—TOEFL. *Faculty research:* American religion and culture, medieval women and religion, U.S. women's history, Chinese missions, late nineteenth-century Germany, twentieth-century urban United States.

Baylor University, Graduate School, College of Arts and Sciences, Program in American Studies, Waco, TX 77845. Offers MA. *Degree requirements:* For master's, thesis, final oral exam. *Entrance requirements:* For master's, GRE General Test, 24 semester hours of course work in subjects with American content.

Boston University, Graduate School of Arts and Sciences, Program in American and New England Studies, Boston, MA 02215. Offers PhD. *Students:* 35 full-time (19 women), 6 part-time (4 women); includes 3 minority (2 Black or African American, non-Hispanic/Latino; 1 Two or more races, non-Hispanic/Latino), 1 international. Average age 32. 59 applicants, 17% accepted, 6 enrolled. In 2014, 4 doctorates awarded. *Degree requirements:* For doctorate, one foreign language, comprehensive exam, thesis/dissertation. *Entrance requirements:* For doctorate, GRE General Test, scholarly writing sample, 3 letters of recommendation. Additional exam requirements/recommendations for international students: Required—TOEFL (minimum score 550 paper-based; 84 iBT). *Application deadline:* For fall admission, 1/5 for domestic and

international students. Application fee: $80. Electronic applications accepted. *Expenses: Tuition:* Full-time $45,686; part-time $1428 per credit hour. *Required fees:* $660; $60 per semester. Tuition and fees vary according to program. *Financial support:* In 2014–15, 40 students received support, including 8 fellowships with full tuition reimbursements available (averaging $20,500 per year), 1 research assistantship with full tuition reimbursement available (averaging $20,500 per year), 5 teaching assistantships with full tuition reimbursements available (averaging $20,500 per year); career-related internships or fieldwork, Federal Work-Study, scholarships/grants, health care benefits, and unspecified assistantships also available. Support available to part-time students. Financial award application deadline: 1/5. *Unit head:* Nina Silber, Director, 617-353-9912, Fax: 617-353-2556, E-mail: nsilber@bu.edu. *Application contact:* Benjamin Tocchi, Senior Program Coordinator, 617-353-2948, Fax: 617-353-2556, E-mail: btocchi@bu.edu.
Website: http://www.bu.edu/AMNESP/

Bowling Green State University, Graduate College, College of Arts and Sciences, American Culture Studies Program, Bowling Green, OH 43403. Offers MA, PhD. Part-time programs available. *Degree requirements:* For master's, thesis or alternative; for doctorate, comprehensive exam, thesis/dissertation. *Entrance requirements:* For master's and doctorate, GRE General Test. Additional exam requirements/recommendations for international students: Required—TOEFL. Electronic applications accepted. *Faculty research:* Race and ethnicity, gender, popular culture.

Bowling Green State University, Graduate College, College of Arts and Sciences, Department of Popular Culture, Bowling Green, OH 43403. Offers MA. Part-time programs available. *Degree requirements:* For master's, thesis or alternative. *Entrance requirements:* For master's, GRE General Test. Additional exam requirements/recommendations for international students: Required—TOEFL. Electronic applications accepted. *Faculty research:* Mass media (popular film, TV, and music); folklore/folklife; ritual, festival, celebration, and holidays; global, international, and popular culture; nineteenth century everyday life.

Brown University, Graduate School, Department of American Studies, Providence, RI 02912. Offers American studies (PhD); American studies for international students (MA); public humanities (MA). *Degree requirements:* For doctorate, thesis/dissertation, preliminary exam.

California State University, Fullerton, Graduate Studies, College of Humanities and Social Sciences, Department of American Studies, Fullerton, CA 92834-9480. Offers MA. Part-time programs available. *Students:* 7 full-time (4 women), 21 part-time (14 women); includes 15 minority (1 Black or African American, non-Hispanic/Latino; 2 Asian, non-Hispanic/Latino; 11 Hispanic/Latino; 1 Two or more races, non-Hispanic/Latino), 1 international. Average age 30. 21 applicants, 62% accepted, 10 enrolled. In 2014, 11 master's awarded. *Degree requirements:* For master's, comprehensive exam or thesis. *Entrance requirements:* For master's, minimum GPA of 3.0 in major, 2.5 in last 60 hours. Application fee: $55. *Financial support:* Federal Work-Study, institutionally sponsored loans, and scholarships/grants available. Support available to part-time students. Financial award application deadline: 3/1; financial award applicants required to submit FAFSA. *Unit head:* Dr. Jesse Battan, Chair, 657-278-2441. *Application contact:* Admissions/Applications, 657-278-2371.

California State University, Long Beach, Graduate Studies, College of Liberal Arts, Department of History, Long Beach, CA 90840. Offers Africa and the Middle East (MA); ancient/medieval Europe (MA); Asia (MA); Latin America (MA); modern Europe (MA); United States (MA); world history (MA). Part-time and evening/weekend programs available. *Degree requirements:* For master's, one foreign language, comprehensive exam or thesis. Electronic applications accepted. *Faculty research:* All periods of European and American history, recent Asian and African history.

Central Michigan University, College of Graduate Studies, College of Humanities and Social and Behavioral Sciences, Department of History, Mount Pleasant, MI 48859. Offers European history (Graduate Certificate); history (MA); modern history (Graduate Certificate); United States history (Graduate Certificate); MA/PhD. Part-time programs available. *Degree requirements:* For master's, thesis or alternative. Electronic applications accepted. *Faculty research:* Colonial and revolutionary United States history, modern European history, Latin American and transatlantic history, transnational and comparative history, United States social history.

Claremont Graduate University, Graduate Programs, School of Arts and Humanities, Department of English, Claremont, CA 91711-6160. Offers American studies (MA, PhD); critical theory (MA, PhD); early modern studies (MA, PhD); English (M Phil, MA, PhD); literary theory (PhD); literature (MA, PhD); literature and creative writing (MA); literature and film (MA); MBA/MA; MBA/PhD. Part-time programs available. *Faculty:* 4 full-time (2 women), 2 part-time/adjunct (0 women). *Students:* 70 full-time (51 women), 27 part-time (17 women); includes 31 minority (4 Black or African American, non-Hispanic/Latino; 1 American Indian or Alaska Native, non-Hispanic/Latino; 12 Asian, non-Hispanic/Latino; 6 Hispanic/Latino; 8 Two or more races, non-Hispanic/Latino), 8 international. Average age 36. In 2014, 9 master's, 7 doctorates awarded. *Entrance requirements:* For master's and doctorate, GRE General Test. Additional exam requirements/recommendations for international students: Required—TOEFL (minimum score 550 paper-based; 80 iBT). *Application deadline:* For fall admission, 2/1 priority date for domestic and international students. Applications are processed on a rolling basis. Application fee: $80. Electronic applications accepted. *Expenses: Tuition:* Full-time $41,784; part-time $1741 per credit. *Required fees:* $600; $300 per semester. *Financial support:* Fellowships, Federal Work-Study, institutionally sponsored loans, and scholarships/grants available. Support available to part-time students. Financial award application deadline: 2/15; financial award applicants required to submit FAFSA. *Faculty research:* American, comparative, and English Renaissance literature; modernism; feminist literature and theory. *Unit head:* David Luis-Brown, Chair, E-mail: david.luis-brown@cgu.edu. *Application contact:* Erma Cross, Admissions and Alumni Coordinator, 909-607-9843, E-mail: erminia.cross@cgu.edu.
Website: http://www.cgu.edu/pages/568.asp

Claremont Graduate University, Graduate Programs, School of Arts and Humanities, Department of History, Claremont, CA 91711-6160. Offers Africana history (Certificate); American studies and U.S. history (MA, PhD); archival studies (MA); early modern studies (MA, PhD); European studies (MA, PhD); oral history (MA, PhD); MBA/MA; MBA/PhD. *Faculty:* 4 full-time (2 women), 1 part-time/adjunct (0 women). *Students:* 41 full-time (19 women), 25 part-time (10 women); includes 18 minority (2 Black or African American, non-Hispanic/Latino; 1 American Indian or Alaska Native, non-Hispanic/Latino; 6 Asian, non-Hispanic/Latino; 6 Hispanic/Latino; 1 Native Hawaiian or other Pacific Islander, non-Hispanic/Latino; 2 Two or more races, non-Hispanic/Latino). Average age 37. In 2014, 7 master's, 6 doctorates, 1 other advanced degree awarded. Terminal master's awarded for partial completion of doctoral program. *Entrance requirements:* For master's and doctorate, GRE General Test. Additional exam requirements/recommendations for international students: Required—TOEFL (minimum score 550 paper-based; 80 iBT). *Application deadline:* For fall admission, 2/1 priority date for domestic and international students. Applications are processed on a rolling basis. Application fee: $80. Electronic applications accepted. *Expenses: Tuition:* Full-time $41,784; part-time $1741 per credit. *Required fees:* $600; $300 per semester. *Financial support:* Fellowships, research assistantships, Federal Work-Study, institutionally sponsored loans, and scholarships/grants available. Support available to part-time students. Financial award application deadline: 2/15; financial award applicants required to submit FAFSA. *Faculty research:* Intellectual and social history, cultural studies, gender studies, Western history, Chicano history. *Unit head:* Joshua Goode, Chair, 909-607-7430, E-mail: joshua.goode@cgu.edu. *Application contact:* Erma Cross, Admissions and Alumni Coordinator, 909-607-9843, E-mail: erminia.cross@cgu.edu.
Website: http://www.cgu.edu/pages/369.asp

Clark University, Graduate School, Department of History, Program in American History, Worcester, MA 01610-1477. Offers MA, PhD. *Students:* 11 full-time (4 women), 6 part-time (2 women). Average age 33. 31 applicants, 26% accepted, 5 enrolled. In 2014, 7 master's, 5 doctorates awarded. *Application deadline:* For fall admission, 1/15 for domestic students. Application fee: $75. *Expenses: Tuition:* Full-time $40,380; part-time $1262 per credit hour. *Required fees:* $30. *Financial support:* In 2014–15, fellowships with full and partial tuition reimbursements (averaging $12,090 per year), research assistantships with full and partial tuition reimbursements (averaging $12,090 per year), teaching assistantships with full and partial tuition reimbursements (averaging $12,090 per year) were awarded. *Faculty research:* American political history, comparative history, American family history. *Unit head:* Dr. Willem Klooster, Chair, 508-421-3768. *Application contact:* Diane Fenner, Department Assistant, 508-793-7288, Fax: 508-793-8816, E-mail: dfenner@clarku.edu.

The College at Brockport, State University of New York, School of the Arts, Humanities and Social Sciences, Department of History, Brockport, NY 14420-2997. Offers history (MA), including American history, American/world history, world history. Part-time and evening/weekend programs available. *Faculty:* 11 full-time (5 women). *Students:* 15 full-time (4 women), 19 part-time (6 women); includes 3 minority (2 Hispanic/Latino; 1 Two or more races, non-Hispanic/Latino). 22 applicants, 91% accepted, 17 enrolled. In 2014, 17 master's awarded. *Degree requirements:* For master's, thesis or alternative. *Entrance requirements:* For master's, minimum GPA of 3.0, writing sample, letters of recommendation, statement of objectives. Additional exam requirements/recommendations for international students: Required—TOEFL (minimum score 550 paper-based; 79 iBT), IELTS (minimum score 6.5). *Application deadline:* For fall admission, 7/1 priority date for domestic and international students; for spring admission, 11/15 priority date for domestic and international students; for summer admission, 4/15 for domestic and international students. Application fee: $50. Electronic applications accepted. *Financial support:* In 2014–15, 1 fellowship with tuition reimbursement (averaging $3,750 per year), 2 teaching assistantships with full tuition reimbursements (averaging $6,000 per year) were awarded; Federal Work-Study, scholarships/grants, and unspecified assistantships also available. Support available to part-time students. Financial award application deadline: 3/15; financial award applicants required to submit FAFSA. *Faculty research:* American history, women's history, European history, world history, cultural history. *Unit head:* Dr. Owen Steve Ireland, Chairperson, 585-395-5627, Fax: 585-395-2620, E-mail: oireland@brockport.edu. *Application contact:* Dr. Morag Martin, Graduate Director, 585-395-5690, Fax: 585-395-2620, E-mail: mmartin@brockport.edu.
Website: http://www.brockport.edu/history/grad/

The College of William and Mary, Faculty of Arts and Sciences, Program in American Studies, Williamsburg, VA 23187-8795. Offers MA, PhD, JD/MA. Part-time programs available. *Faculty:* 15 full-time (9 women), 1 (woman) part-time/adjunct. *Students:* 34 full-time (20 women), 3 part-time (all women); includes 7 minority (2 Black or African American, non-Hispanic/Latino; 2 Asian, non-Hispanic/Latino; 1 Hispanic/Latino; 2 Two or more races, non-Hispanic/Latino), 2 international. Average age 31. 58 applicants, 29% accepted, 7 enrolled. In 2014, 7 master's, 6 doctorates awarded. Terminal master's awarded for partial completion of doctoral program. *Degree requirements:* For master's, thesis; for doctorate, one foreign language, comprehensive exam, thesis/dissertation. *Entrance requirements:* For master's, GRE; for doctorate, GRE, MA. Additional exam requirements/recommendations for international students: Required—TOEFL. *Application deadline:* For fall admission, 1/1 for domestic and international students. Application fee: $45. Electronic applications accepted. *Financial support:* In 2014–15, 24 students received support, including 20 fellowships with full tuition reimbursements available (averaging $20,400 per year); career-related internships or fieldwork and unspecified assistantships also available. Financial award application deadline: 1/1. *Faculty research:* Nineteenth- and twentieth-century U.S. cultural history; nineteenth- and twentieth-century American literature; material culture, visual culture, and art historical studies; African-American studies; Native American studies; mass and popular culture studies. *Unit head:* Dr. Charles McGovern, Director, 757-221-1296, Fax: 757-221-1287, E-mail: cfmcgo@wm.edu. *Application contact:* Jean Brown, Program Administrator, 757-221-1275, Fax: 757-221-1287, E-mail: jxbrow@wm.edu.
Website: http://www.wm.edu/americanstudies/

The Colorado College, Education Department, Experienced Teacher Program, Colorado Springs, CO 80903-3294. Offers arts and humanities (MAT); integrated natural sciences (MAT); liberal arts (MAT); Southwest studies (MAT). Programs offered during summer only. Part-time programs available. *Degree requirements:* For master's, thesis, oral exam, 50-page paper. *Expenses:* Contact institution.

Columbia University, Graduate School of Arts and Sciences, New York, NY 10027. Offers African-American studies (MA); American studies (MA); anthropology (MA, PhD); art history and archaeology (MA, PhD); astronomy (PhD); biological sciences (PhD); biotechnology (MA); chemical physics (PhD); chemistry (PhD); classical studies (MA, PhD); classics (MA, PhD); climate and society (MA); earth and environmental sciences (PhD); East Asia: regional studies (MA); East Asian languages and cultures (MA, PhD); ecology, evolution and environmental biology (MA), including conservation biology; ecology, evolution, and environmental biology (PhD), including ecology and evolutionary biology, evolutionary primatology; economics (PhD); English and comparative literature (MA, PhD); French and Romance philology (MA, PhD); Germanic languages (MA, PhD); global French studies (MA); Hispanic cultural studies (MA); history (PhD); history and literature (MA); human rights studies (MA); Islamic studies (MA); Italian (MA, PhD); Japanese pedagogy (MA); Jewish studies (MA); Latin America and the Caribbean: regional studies (MA); Latin American and Iberian cultures (PhD); mathematics (MA, PhD), including finance (MA); medieval and Renaissance studies (MA); Middle Eastern, South Asian, and African studies (MA, PhD); modern art: critical and curatorial studies (MA); modern European studies (MA); museum anthropology (MA); music (DMA, PhD); oral history (MA); philosophical foundations of physics (MA); philosophy (MA, PhD); physics (PhD); political science (MA, PhD); psychology (PhD); quantitative methods in the social sciences (MA); religion (MA, PhD); Russia, Eurasia and East Europe: regional studies (MA); Russian translation (MA); Slavic cultures (MA); Slavic languages (MA, PhD); sociology (MA, PhD); South Asian studies (MA); statistics (MA, PhD); theatre (PhD); JD/PhD; MA/MS; MD/PhD; MPA/MA. Dual-degree programs require admission to both Graduate School of Arts and Sciences and another Columbia school. Part-time and evening/weekend programs available. Terminal master's awarded for partial completion of doctoral program. *Degree requirements:* For master's, thesis (for some programs); for doctorate, comprehensive exam, thesis/dissertation. *Entrance requirements:* For master's and doctorate, GRE General Test, GRE Subject Test (for

some programs). Electronic applications accepted. *Faculty research:* Humanities, natural sciences, social sciences.

Cornell University, Graduate School, Graduate Fields of Arts and Sciences, Field of English Language and Literature, Ithaca, NY 14853-0001. Offers African-American literature (PhD); American literature after 1865 (PhD); American literature to 1865 (PhD); American studies (PhD); colonial and postcolonial literatures (PhD); creative writing (MFA); cultural studies (PhD); dramatic literature (PhD); English poetry (PhD); English Renaissance to 1660 (PhD); lesbian, bisexual, and gay literary studies (PhD); literary criticism and theory (PhD); Old and Middle English (PhD); prose fiction (PhD); Restoration and the eighteenth-century (PhD); the nineteenth century (PhD); the twentieth century (PhD); women's literature (PhD); MFA/PhD. Terminal master's awarded for partial completion of doctoral program. *Degree requirements:* For master's, one foreign language, thesis; for doctorate, one foreign language, comprehensive exam, thesis/dissertation, teaching experience. *Entrance requirements:* For master's, GRE General Test, 3 letters of recommendation, creative writing sample; for doctorate, GRE General Test, GRE Subject Test (English), 3 letters of recommendation, writing sample. Additional exam requirements/recommendations for international students: Required—TOEFL (minimum score 600 paper-based; 77 iBT). Electronic applications accepted. *Faculty research:* English and American literature, women's writing, ethnic and post-colonial literature, critical theory, medievalism.

Cornell University, Graduate School, Graduate Fields of Arts and Sciences, Field of History, Ithaca, NY 14853-0001. Offers African history (MA, PhD); American history (MA, PhD); ancient Greek history (PhD); ancient history (MA, PhD); ancient Roman history (PhD); early modern European history (MA, PhD); English history (MA, PhD); French history (MA, PhD); German history (MA, PhD); history of science (MA, PhD); Korean history (PhD); Latin American history (MA, PhD); medieval Chinese history (MA, PhD); medieval history (MA, PhD); modern Chinese history (MA, PhD); modern European history (MA, PhD); modern Japanese history (MA, PhD); modern Middle Eastern history (PhD); premodern Islamic history (MA, PhD); premodern Japanese history (MA, PhD); Renaissance history (MA, PhD); Russian history (MA, PhD); South Asian history (PhD); Southeast Asian history (MA, PhD). Terminal master's awarded for partial completion of doctoral program. *Degree requirements:* For master's, thesis; for doctorate, 2 foreign languages, comprehensive exam, thesis/dissertation, 1 year of teaching experience. *Entrance requirements:* For master's and doctorate, GRE General Test, writing sample, 3 letters of recommendation. Additional exam requirements/recommendations for international students: Required—TOEFL (minimum score 550 paper-based; 77 iBT). Electronic applications accepted.

Cornell University, Graduate School, Graduate Fields of Arts and Sciences, Field of History of Art, Archaeology and Visual Studies, Ithaca, NY 14853. Offers 19th century art (PhD); African, African American and African diaspora (PhD); American art (PhD); ancient art and archaeology (PhD); Asian American art (PhD); Baroque art (PhD); comparative modernities (PhD); digital art (PhD); East Asian art (PhD); history of photography (PhD); Islamic art (PhD); Latin American art (PhD); medieval art (PhD); modern art (PhD); Renaissance art (PhD); Southeast Asian art (PhD); theory and criticism (PhD); visual studies (PhD). *Degree requirements:* For doctorate, one foreign language, comprehensive exam, thesis/dissertation, general exams in 3 areas. *Entrance requirements:* For doctorate, GRE General Test, sample of written work, 3 letters of recommendation. Additional exam requirements/recommendations for international students: Required—TOEFL (minimum score 550 paper-based; 77 iBT). Electronic applications accepted.

East Carolina University, Graduate School, Thomas Harriot College of Arts and Sciences, Department of History, Greenville, NC 27858-4353. Offers American history (MA); Atlantic world (MA); European history (MA); history education (MA Ed); maritime studies (MA); military history (MA); public history (MA). Part-time and evening/weekend programs available. *Degree requirements:* For master's, one foreign language, comprehensive exam, thesis. *Entrance requirements:* For master's, GRE General Test, GRE Subject Test. Additional exam requirements/recommendations for international students: Required—TOEFL. *Expenses:* Tuition, state resident: full-time $4223. Tuition, nonresident: full-time $16,540. *Required fees:* $2184.

Eastern Michigan University, Graduate School, College of Arts and Sciences, Department of History and Philosophy, Ypsilanti, MI 48197. Offers history (MA, Graduate Certificate), including history (MA), state and local history (Graduate Certificate); philosophy (MA); social sciences (MA, MLS, Graduate Certificate), including social science (MA, Graduate Certificate), social science and American culture (MLS). Part-time and evening/weekend programs available. Postbaccalaureate distance learning degree programs offered (minimal on-campus study). *Faculty:* 24 full-time (7 women). *Students:* 7 full-time (4 women), 62 part-time (24 women); includes 6 minority (4 Black or African American, non-Hispanic/Latino; 1 Hispanic/Latino; 1 Two or more races, non-Hispanic/Latino). Average age 34. 33 applicants, 88% accepted, 19 enrolled. In 2014, 10 master's awarded. *Entrance requirements:* Additional exam requirements/recommendations for international students: Required—TOEFL. *Application deadline:* Applications are processed on a rolling basis. Application fee: $45. *Financial support:* Fellowships, research assistantships with full tuition reimbursements, teaching assistantships with full tuition reimbursements, career-related internships or fieldwork, Federal Work-Study, institutionally sponsored loans, scholarships/grants, tuition waivers (partial), and unspecified assistantships available. Support available to part-time students. Financial award applicants required to submit FAFSA. *Unit head:* Dr. Richard Nation, Department Head, 734-487-1018, Fax: 734-487-6835, E-mail: rnation@emich.edu.
Website: http://www.emich.edu/historyphilosophy

Emory & Henry College, Graduate Programs, Emory, VA 24327-0947. Offers American history (MA Ed); organizational leadership (MCOL); professional studies (M Ed); reading specialist (MA Ed). Part-time and evening/weekend programs available. *Entrance requirements:* For master's, GRE or PRAXIS I, recommendations, writing sample. Additional exam requirements/recommendations for international students: Recommended—TOEFL.

Fairfield University, College of Arts and Sciences, Fairfield, CT 06824. Offers American studies (MA); communication (MA); creative writing (MFA); mathematics (MS); public administration (MPA). Part-time and evening/weekend programs available. Postbaccalaureate distance learning degree programs offered (minimal on-campus study). *Faculty:* 35 full-time (20 women), 5 part-time/adjunct (1 woman). *Students:* 54 full-time (35 women), 65 part-time (37 women); includes 18 minority (4 Black or African American, non-Hispanic/Latino; 4 Asian, non-Hispanic/Latino; 6 Hispanic/Latino; 1 Native Hawaiian or other Pacific Islander, non-Hispanic/Latino; 3 Two or more races, non-Hispanic/Latino), 6 international. Average age 35. 77 applicants, 69% accepted, 27 enrolled. In 2014, 51 master's awarded. *Degree requirements:* For master's, capstone research course. *Entrance requirements:* For master's, minimum GPA of 3.0, 2 letters of recommendation, resume. Additional exam requirements/recommendations for international students: Required—TOEFL (minimum score 550 paper-based; 80 iBT) or IELTS (minimum score 6.5). *Application deadline:* For fall admission, 5/14 for international students; for spring admission, 10/15 for international students. Applications are processed on a rolling basis. Application fee: $60. Electronic applications accepted. *Expenses: Tuition:* Part-time $695 per credit hour. Full-time tuition and fees vary according to degree level and program. *Financial support:* In 2014–15, 41 students received support. Scholarships/grants and unspecified assistantships available. Financial award applicants required to submit FAFSA. *Faculty research:* Ethical theory, media industries, community-based teaching and learning, non commutative algebra and partial differential equations, cancer research in biology and physics. *Unit head:* Dr. James Simon, Dean, 203-254-4000 Ext. 2221, Fax: 203-254-4119, E-mail: jsimon@fairfield.edu. *Application contact:* Marianne Gumpper, Director of Graduate and Continuing Studies Admission, 203-254-4184, Fax: 203-254-4073, E-mail: gradadmis@fairfield.edu.
Website: http://www.fairfield.edu/academics/schoolscollegescenters/collegeofartssciences/graduateprograms/

Florida State University, The Graduate School, College of Fine Arts, School of Dance, Tallahassee, FL 32306-2120. Offers American dance studies (MFA); studio and related studies (MA). *Accreditation:* NASD. *Faculty:* 17 full-time (11 women), 3 part-time/adjunct (2 women). *Students:* 30 full-time (23 women); includes 14 minority (5 Black or African American, non-Hispanic/Latino; 2 Asian, non-Hispanic/Latino; 7 Hispanic/Latino). Average age 28. 25 applicants, 80% accepted, 18 enrolled. In 2014, 8 master's awarded. *Degree requirements:* For master's, comprehensive exam (for some programs), thesis optional, technical proficiency; 1 foreign language (for MA in American dance studies). *Entrance requirements:* For master's, GRE General Test (MA in American dance studies), audition, writing sample, interview (for MFA, MA in dance). Additional exam requirements/recommendations for international students: Required—TOEFL (minimum score 550 paper-based, 80 iBT), IELTS (minimum score 6.5) or Michigan English Language Assessment Battery (minimum score 77). *Application deadline:* For fall admission, 7/1 priority date for domestic and international students; for spring admission, 11/1 priority date for domestic and international students. Applications are processed on a rolling basis. Application fee: $30. Electronic applications accepted. *Expenses:* Tuition, state resident: part-time $403.51 per credit hour. Tuition, nonresident: part-time $1004.85 per credit hour. *Required fees:* $75.81 per credit hour. One-time fee: $20 part-time. Tuition and fees vary according to campus/location. *Financial support:* In 2014–15, 30 students received support, including 1 fellowship with full tuition reimbursement available (averaging $20,000 per year), 10 research assistantships with full tuition reimbursements available (averaging $5,000 per year), 11 teaching assistantships with full tuition reimbursements available (averaging $5,000 per year); scholarships/grants, health care benefits, and unspecified assistantships also available. Financial award application deadline: 6/30; financial award applicants required to submit FAFSA. *Faculty research:* Choreography, performance, dance and cultural significance, American dance history, dance technology. *Unit head:* Prof. Russell Sandifer, Professor and Co-Chair, 850-644-1024, Fax: 850-644-1277, E-mail: rsandifer@fsu.edu. *Application contact:* Stephanie Mills, Academic Coordinator, 850-644-1023, Fax: 850-644-1277, E-mail: smmills@fsu.edu.
Website: http://dance.fsu.edu/

Georgetown University, Graduate School of Arts and Sciences, School of Continuing Studies, Washington, DC 20057. Offers American studies (MALS); Catholic studies (MALS); classical civilizations (MALS); emergency and disaster management (MPS); ethics and the professions (MALS); hospitality management (MPS); human resources management (MPS); humanities (MALS); individualized study (MALS); international affairs (MALS); Islam and Muslim-Christian relations (MALS); journalism (MPS); liberal studies (DLS); literature and society (MALS); medieval and early modern European studies (MALS); public relations and corporate communications (MPS); real estate (MPS); religious studies (MALS); social and public policy (MALS); sports industry management (MPS); systems engineering management (MPS); technology management (MPS); the theory and practice of American democracy (MALS); urban and regional planning (MPS); visual culture (MALS). MPS in systems engineering management offered jointly with Stevens Institute of Technology. *Entrance requirements:* Additional exam requirements/recommendations for international students: Required—TOEFL.

The George Washington University, Columbian College of Arts and Sciences, Department of American Studies, Washington, DC 20052. Offers American studies (PhD); folklife (MA); historic preservation (MA); material culture (MA). Part-time and evening/weekend programs available. *Faculty:* 14 full-time (7 women). *Students:* 18 full-time (12 women), 28 part-time (22 women); includes 7 minority (5 Black or African American, non-Hispanic/Latino; 1 Asian, non-Hispanic/Latino; 1 Two or more races, non-Hispanic/Latino), 3 international. Average age 30. 97 applicants, 30% accepted, 12 enrolled. In 2014, 13 master's, 4 doctorates awarded. Terminal master's awarded for partial completion of doctoral program. *Degree requirements:* For master's, comprehensive exam; for doctorate, one foreign language, thesis/dissertation, general exam. *Entrance requirements:* For master's and doctorate, GRE General Test, minimum GPA of 3.0. Additional exam requirements/recommendations for international students: Required—TOEFL (minimum score 550 paper-based; 80 iBT). *Application deadline:* For fall admission, 1/15 priority date for domestic and international students; for spring admission, 10/1 for domestic students. Application fee: $75. *Financial support:* In 2014–15, 22 students received support. Fellowships, research assistantships, teaching assistantships, career-related internships or fieldwork, Federal Work-Study, institutionally sponsored loans, and tuition waivers available. Financial award application deadline: 1/15. *Unit head:* Melanie McAlister, Chair, 202-994-7244, E-mail: jam@gwu.edu. *Application contact:* Information Contact, 202-994-6070, Fax: 202-994-8651, E-mail: amst@gwu.edu.
Website: http://departments.columbian.gwu.edu/americanstudies/

Georgia College & State University, Graduate School, College of Arts and Sciences, Department of History, Geography and Philosophy, Milledgeville, GA 31061. Offers public history (MA); U. S., Europe and world (MA). Part-time and evening/weekend programs available. *Students:* 4 full-time (1 woman), 6 part-time (3 women); includes 2 minority (1 American Indian or Alaska Native, non-Hispanic/Latino; 1 Hispanic/Latino). Average age 32. 4 applicants, 100% accepted, 4 enrolled. In 2014, 3 master's awarded. *Degree requirements:* For master's, one foreign language, comprehensive exam (for some programs), thesis or alternative. *Entrance requirements:* For master's, GRE, 2 letters of reference, transcript, minimum GPA of 3.0, undergraduate degree in history or other major with substantial work in history, foreign language. Additional exam requirements/recommendations for international students: Recommended—TOEFL (minimum score 550 paper-based; 79 iBT). *Application deadline:* For fall admission, 4/15 for domestic and international students; for spring admission, 11/15 for domestic students, 9/1 for international students; for summer admission, 4/1 for domestic students. Application fee: $40. Electronic applications accepted. *Expenses: Tuition, area resident:* Part-time $283 per credit hour. Tuition, nonresident: part-time $1027 per credit hour. *Required fees:* $995 per semester. Full-time tuition and fees vary according to course load, degree level, campus/location and program. *Financial support:* In 2014–15, 6 research assistantships were awarded; unspecified assistantships also available. Support available to part-time students. Financial award applicants required to submit FAFSA. *Unit head:* Dr. Stephen Auerbach, Graduate Coordinator for MA in History, 478-445-8276, E-mail: stephen.auerbach@gcsu.edu. *Application contact:* Kate Marshall, Graduate Admissions Coordinator, 478-445-1184, Fax: 478-445-1336, E-mail: grad-admit@gcsu.edu.
Website: http://www.gcsu.edu/history/masters.htm

American Studies

Harvard University, Graduate School of Arts and Sciences, Committee on History of American Civilization, Cambridge, MA 02138. Offers PhD. *Degree requirements:* For doctorate, 2 foreign languages, thesis/dissertation. *Entrance requirements:* For doctorate, GRE General Test, GRE Subject Test (recommended). Additional exam requirements/recommendations for international students: Required—TOEFL. *Faculty research:* American history, literature, and religion in the Colonial era; twentieth-century American history, literature, and law; Southern literature, history, and sociology.

Inter American University of Puerto Rico, Metropolitan Campus, Graduate Programs, Program in History, San Juan, PR 00919-1293. Offers American history (PhD); history (MA, PhD).

Kennesaw State University, College of Humanities and Social Sciences, Master of Arts in American Studies Program, Kennesaw, GA 30144. Offers MA. Part-time and evening/weekend programs available. *Students:* 6 full-time (4 women), 24 part-time (15 women); includes 11 minority (5 Black or African American, non-Hispanic/Latino; 1 Asian, non-Hispanic/Latino; 3 Hispanic/Latino; 2 Two or more races, non-Hispanic/Latino), 1 international. Average age 36. 13 applicants, 69% accepted, 7 enrolled. In 2014, 5 master's awarded. *Degree requirements:* For master's, one foreign language, thesis optional. *Entrance requirements:* For master's, GRE. Additional exam requirements/recommendations for international students: Required—TOEFL (minimum score 550 paper-based; 80 iBT), IELTS (minimum score 6.5). *Application deadline:* For fall admission, 6/1 for domestic and international students; for winter admission, 11/1 for domestic and international students; for spring admission, 11/1 for domestic and international students; for summer admission, 4/1 for domestic and international students. Applications are processed on a rolling basis. Application fee: $60. Electronic applications accepted. *Expenses:* Tuition, state resident: part-time $275 per semester hour. Tuition, nonresident: part-time $990 per semester hour. *Financial support:* In 2014–15, 2 research assistantships with full tuition reimbursements (averaging $8,000 per year) were awarded. Financial award application deadline: 4/1; financial award applicants required to submit FAFSA. *Unit head:* Rebecca Hill, Director, 470-578-2431, E-mail: rhill54@kennesaw.edu. *Application contact:* Cherie Miller, Admissions Counselor, 470-578-2431, Fax: 470-578-9172, E-mail: ksugrad@kennesaw.edu.

Lake Forest College, Graduate Program in Liberal Studies, Lake Forest, IL 60045. Offers American studies (MLS); environmental studies (MLS); history and freedom (MLS); writing (MLS). Part-time and evening/weekend programs available. *Faculty:* 11 full-time (5 women), 1 (woman) part-time/adjunct. *Students:* 42 part-time (22 women); includes 4 minority (2 Asian, non-Hispanic/Latino; 2 Hispanic/Latino). Average age 38. 26 applicants, 50% accepted, 9 enrolled. In 2014, 7 master's awarded. *Degree requirements:* For master's, thesis optional, 8 courses, including at least 3 interdisciplinary seminars. *Entrance requirements:* For master's, transcript, essay, interview. Additional exam requirements/recommendations for international students: Required—TOEFL (minimum score 550 paper-based; 83 iBT); Recommended—IELTS (minimum score 6.5). *Application deadline:* For fall admission, 7/15 priority date for domestic students, 6/1 priority date for international students; for winter admission, 12/15 for domestic students, 10/1 for international students; for spring admission, 12/1 priority date for domestic students, 10/1 priority date for international students. Applications are processed on a rolling basis. Application fee: $30. *Expenses:* Expenses: Contact institution. *Financial support:* In 2014–15, 4 students received support. Scholarships/grants and partial tuition grants (for full-time teachers) available. Financial award application deadline: 7/15. *Faculty research:* History of American political thought; American families; electron collisions with molecules; international relations, American foreign policy, and transparency in world politics; ethics and social justice; pacifism. *Unit head:* Prof. D. L. LeMahieu, Director, 847-735-5133, Fax: 847-735-6291, E-mail: lemahieu@lakeforest.edu. *Application contact:* Prof. Carol Gayle, Associate Director, 847-735-5083, Fax: 847-735-6291, E-mail: gayle@lakeforest.edu.
Website: http://www.lakeforest.edu/academics/programs/mls/

La Salle University, School of Arts and Sciences, Program in Education, Philadelphia, PA 19141-1199. Offers American studies (MA); autism spectrum disorders (MA, Certificate); bilingual/bicultural studies (MA); classroom management (MA); dual early childhood and special education (MA); dual middle-level science and math and special education (MA); education (MA); English (MA); English as a second language (Certificate); history (MA); instructional coach (Certificate); instructional leadership (MA); reading specialist (MA, Certificate); secondary education (MA); special education (MA, Certificate). Part-time and evening/weekend programs available. *Degree requirements:* For master's, comprehensive exam. *Entrance requirements:* For master's and Certificate, MAT or GRE, 2 letters of recommendation. Additional exam requirements/recommendations for international students: Required—TOEFL. Electronic applications accepted. Application fee is waived when completed online. *Expenses:* Contact institution.

La Salle University, School of Arts and Sciences, Program in English, Philadelphia, PA 19141-1199. Offers American studies (Certificate); English for educators (MA); English in literary and cultural studies (MA); global literature (Certificate); media studies and the performing and visual arts (Certificate); Philadelphia and regional studies (Certificate). Part-time and evening/weekend programs available. *Degree requirements:* For master's, critical-pedagogical project (for English for educators), thesis or comprehensive examination (for English in literary and cultural studies). *Entrance requirements:* For master's, GRE General Test or MAT, 18 hours of undergraduate course work in English or a related discipline with minimum GPA of 3.0; three letters of recommendation; brief personal statement; writing sample; for Certificate, undergraduate degree in English or a related discipline with minimum GPA of 3.0; 3 letters of recommendation. Additional exam requirements/recommendations for international students: Required—TOEFL. Electronic applications accepted. Application fee is waived when completed online.

La Salle University, School of Arts and Sciences, Program in History, Philadelphia, PA 19141-1199. Offers American history (Certificate); European history (Certificate); history (MA); history for educators (MA); public history (MA); teaching advanced placement history (Certificate); world history (Certificate). Part-time programs available. *Degree requirements:* For master's, thesis or comprehensive exam. *Entrance requirements:* For master's, GRE or MAT, 18 hours of undergraduate coursework in history or a related discipline with minimum GPA of 3.0; two letters of recommendation; brief personal statement (250 to 500 words); writing sample (preferably from an undergraduate research paper). Additional exam requirements/recommendations for international students: Required—TOEFL. Electronic applications accepted. Application fee is waived when completed online.

Lehigh University, College of Arts and Sciences, Department of History, Bethlehem, PA 18015. Offers Atlantic world (PhD); British history (PhD); history (MA); industrial and modern America (PhD); public history (MA). Part-time programs available. *Faculty:* 12 full-time (5 women). *Students:* 25 full-time (9 women), 23 part-time (7 women), 2 international. Average age 34. 28 applicants, 39% accepted, 7 enrolled. In 2014, 4 master's, 1 doctorate awarded. Terminal master's awarded for partial completion of doctoral program. *Degree requirements:* For master's, comprehensive exam (for some programs), comprehensive exam or thesis; for doctorate, comprehensive exam, thesis/dissertation. *Entrance requirements:* For master's, GRE General Test, recommendations, writing sample; for doctorate, GRE General Test, recommendations, writing samples. Additional exam requirements/recommendations for international students: Required—TOEFL. *Application deadline:* For fall admission, 4/15 for domestic and international students; for winter admission, 11/1 priority date for domestic students, 11/15 priority date for international students. Applications are processed on a rolling basis. Application fee: $75. Electronic applications accepted. *Expenses:* Expenses: $1,380 per credit hour. *Financial support:* In 2014–15, 2 fellowships with full tuition reimbursements (averaging $22,500 per year), 10 teaching assistantships with full and partial tuition reimbursements (averaging $19,700 per year) were awarded; research assistantships with full tuition reimbursements, institutionally sponsored loans, scholarships/grants, tuition waivers (full and partial), and unspecified assistantships also available. Support available to part-time students. Financial award application deadline: 1/15. *Faculty research:* Colonial America, modern America, history of technology, Atlantic world. *Total annual research expenditures:* $66,401. *Unit head:* Dr. John K. Smith, Chairman, 610-758-3360, Fax: 610-758-6554, E-mail: jks0@lehigh.edu. *Application contact:* Dr. Roger D. Simon, Graduate Coordinator, 610-758-3368, Fax: 610-758-6554, E-mail: rds2@lehigh.edu.
Website: http://history.cas2.lehigh.edu/

Lehigh University, College of Arts and Sciences, Program in American Studies, Bethlehem, PA 18015. Offers MA, Graduate Certificate. Part-time programs available. *Faculty:* 2 full-time (0 women), 1 (woman) part-time/adjunct. *Students:* 6 full-time (4 women), 2 part-time (0 women); includes 4 minority (2 Black or African American, non-Hispanic/Latino; 2 Hispanic/Latino), 1 international. Average age 25. 8 applicants, 75% accepted, 4 enrolled. In 2014, 7 master's awarded. *Degree requirements:* For master's, thesis. *Entrance requirements:* For master's, GRE, writing sample, essay, minimum GPA of 2.75, 2 letters of recommendation. Additional exam requirements/recommendations for international students: Required—TOEFL (minimum score 85 iBT). *Application deadline:* For fall admission, 1/15 for domestic students, 7/15 for international students; for spring admission, 12/1 for domestic and international students. Applications are processed on a rolling basis. Application fee: $75. Electronic applications accepted. *Financial support:* In 2014–15, 5 students received support, including 1 fellowship with full tuition reimbursement available; institutionally sponsored loans, scholarships/grants, tuition waivers (full and partial), and unspecified assistantships also available. Support available to part-time students. Financial award application deadline: 1/15. *Faculty research:* War; media and video games; social movements; community identity and narrative; traditional eighteenth, nineteenth, and twentieth century literature and history; gender and popular culture. *Unit head:* Prof. John Pettegrew, Director, 610-758-3355, Fax: 610-758-6554, E-mail: amstdgrad@lehigh.edu. *Application contact:* Cassandra L. Petroski, Graduate Coordinator, 610-758-4281, Fax: 610-758-6554, E-mail: amstdgrad@lehigh.edu.
Website: http://american.cas2.lehigh.edu/

Michigan State University, The Graduate School, College of Arts and Letters, Program in American Studies, East Lansing, MI 48824. Offers MA, PhD. *Entrance requirements:* Additional exam requirements/recommendations for international students: Required—TOEFL. Electronic applications accepted.

Mississippi State University, College of Arts and Sciences, Department of History, Mississippi State, MS 39762. Offers U.S. and European history (MA, PhD). Part-time programs available. *Faculty:* 22 full-time (9 women), 1 part-time/adjunct (0 women). *Students:* 46 full-time (17 women), 7 part-time (2 women); includes 5 minority (1 Black or African American, non-Hispanic/Latino; 1 American Indian or Alaska Native, non-Hispanic/Latino; 1 Asian, non-Hispanic/Latino; 1 Hispanic/Latino; 1 Two or more races, non-Hispanic/Latino), 4 international. Average age 29. 31 applicants, 65% accepted, 13 enrolled. In 2014, 7 master's, 2 doctorates awarded. *Degree requirements:* For master's, one foreign language, comprehensive exam, thesis optional; for doctorate, 2 foreign languages, thesis/dissertation, comprehensive oral and written exam. *Entrance requirements:* For master's, minimum GPA of 3.0 on last two years of undergraduate courses; for doctorate, GRE, writing sample, minimum graduate GPA of 3.0. Additional exam requirements/recommendations for international students: Required—TOEFL (minimum score 550 paper-based). *Application deadline:* For fall admission, 4/1 for domestic students, 5/1 for international students; for spring admission, 11/1 for domestic students, 9/1 for international students. Applications are processed on a rolling basis. Application fee: $60. Electronic applications accepted. *Expenses:* Tuition, state resident: full-time $7140; part-time $783 per credit hour. Tuition, nonresident: full-time $18,478; part-time $2043 per credit hour. *Financial support:* In 2014–15, 39 teaching assistantships with full tuition reimbursements (averaging $12,034 per year) were awarded; Federal Work-Study, institutionally sponsored loans, scholarships/grants, and unspecified assistantships also available. Financial award application deadline: 4/1; financial award applicants required to submit FAFSA. *Faculty research:* U.S. political, diplomatic, military, social, and cultural history; modern Europe; Latin America; Asian history; African history. *Unit head:* Dr. Alan I. Marcus, Head, 662-325-3604, Fax: 662-325-1139, E-mail: aim10@msstate.edu. *Application contact:* Dr. Stephen Brain, Graduate Coordinator, 662-325-3604, Fax: 662-325-1139, E-mail: correspondence@history.msstate.edu.
Website: http://www.history.msstate.edu

Monmouth University, The Graduate School, Department of History, West Long Branch, NJ 07764-1898. Offers European history (MA); history of the United States (MA); world history (MA). Part-time and evening/weekend programs available. *Faculty:* 9 full-time (3 women). *Students:* 5 full-time (3 women), 37 part-time (14 women); includes 1 minority (Hispanic/Latino). Average age 35. 22 applicants, 100% accepted, 13 enrolled. In 2014, 16 master's awarded. *Degree requirements:* For master's, comprehensive exam (for some programs), thesis (for some programs). *Entrance requirements:* For master's, minimum GPA of 3.0 in major, 2.5 overall; two letters of recommendation; statement of interest areas and goals. Additional exam requirements/recommendations for international students: Required—TOEFL (minimum score 550 paper-based; 79 iBT), IELTS (minimum score 6) or Michigan English Language Assessment Battery (minimum score 77). *Application deadline:* For fall admission, 7/15 priority date for domestic students, 6/1 for international students; for spring admission, 11/15 priority date for domestic students, 11/1 for international students. Applications are processed on a rolling basis. Application fee: $50. Electronic applications accepted. *Expenses: Tuition:* Full-time $18,072; part-time $1004 per credit. *Required fees:* $157 per semester. *Financial support:* In 2014–15, 29 students received support, including 23 fellowships (averaging $2,264 per year), 4 research assistantships (averaging $7,796 per year); career-related internships or fieldwork, scholarships/grants, and unspecified assistantships also available. Support available to part-time students. Financial award applicants required to submit FAFSA. *Faculty research:* U.S. business; labor; British, German, and French Revolutions; Soviet Union; Africa. *Unit head:* Dr. Maryann Rhett, Program Director, 732-263-5768, Fax: 732-263-5112, E-mail: mrhett@monmouth.edu. *Application contact:* Andrea Thompson, Graduate Admission Counselor, 732-571-3452, Fax: 732-263-5123, E-mail: gradadm@monmouth.edu.
Website: http://www.monmouth.edu/school-of-humanities-social-sciences/ma-in-history.aspx

New Mexico Highlands University, Graduate Studies, College of Arts and Sciences, Department of Social and Behavioral Sciences, Las Vegas, NM 87701. Offers psychology (MS), including clinical psychology/counseling, general psychology; public

affairs (MA), including applied sociology; Southwest studies (MA), including anthropology. Part-time programs available. *Faculty:* 11 full-time (5 women), 3 part-time/adjunct (all women). *Students:* 24 full-time (16 women), 19 part-time (14 women); includes 27 minority (3 Black or African American, non-Hispanic/Latino; 1 American Indian or Alaska Native, non-Hispanic/Latino; 23 Hispanic/Latino), 2 international. Average age 33. 45 applicants, 33% accepted, 15 enrolled. In 2014, 7 master's awarded. *Degree requirements:* For master's, comprehensive exam, thesis or alternative. *Entrance requirements:* For master's, minimum undergraduate GPA of 3.0. Additional exam requirements/recommendations for international students: Required—TOEFL (minimum score 540 paper-based). *Application deadline:* For fall admission, 8/1 priority date for domestic students. Applications are processed on a rolling basis. Application fee: $15. *Financial support:* In 2014–15, 34 teaching assistantships were awarded; career-related internships or fieldwork, Federal Work-Study, institutionally sponsored loans, scholarships/grants, tuition waivers (full and partial), and unspecified assistantships also available. Support available to part-time students. Financial award application deadline: 3/1; financial award applicants required to submit FAFSA. *Faculty research:* Southwest Native American resettlement development, community-level interventions, neurochemistry of personality, comparative criminal justice, social theory and activism. *Unit head:* Dr. Tom Ward, Program Coordinator, 505-454-3196, E-mail: tsward@nmhu.edu. *Application contact:* Diane Trujillo, Administrative Assistant for Graduate Studies, 505-454-3266, Fax: 505-426-2117, E-mail: dtrujillo@nmhu.edu.

New York University, Graduate School of Arts and Science, Program in American Studies, New York, NY 10012-1019. Offers MA, PhD. Part-time programs available. *Faculty:* 4 full-time (1 woman), 2 part-time/adjunct (0 women). *Students:* 32 full-time (22 women), 7 part-time (4 women); includes 17 minority (7 Black or African American, non-Hispanic/Latino; 1 American Indian or Alaska Native, non-Hispanic/Latino; 1 Asian, non-Hispanic/Latino; 7 Hispanic/Latino; 1 Two or more races, non-Hispanic/Latino), 1 international. Average age 33. 186 applicants, 10% accepted, 7 enrolled. In 2014, 4 master's, 5 doctorates awarded. *Degree requirements:* For master's, one foreign language, thesis; for doctorate, 2 foreign languages, thesis/dissertation. *Entrance requirements:* For master's and doctorate, GRE General Test, writing sample. Additional exam requirements/recommendations for international students: Required—TOEFL. *Application deadline:* For fall admission, 12/18 for domestic and international students. Application fee: $100. *Financial support:* Fellowships with tuition reimbursements, teaching assistantships with tuition reimbursements, Federal Work-Study, institutionally sponsored loans, and unspecified assistantships available. Financial award application deadline: 12/18; financial award applicants required to submit FAFSA. *Faculty research:* Cultural politics; race, gender, and sexuality studies; nationalism and transnationalism; science and technology; urban and suburban studies. *Unit head:* Andrew Ross, Director, 212-998-9650, Fax: 212-995-4665, E-mail: amstudies@nyu.edu. *Application contact:* Raechel Bosch, Graduate Administrator, 212-998-9650, Fax: 212-995-4665, E-mail: amstudies@nyu.edu.
Website: http://www.nyu.edu/gsas/dept/amerstu/

New York University, Graduate School of Arts and Science, Program in Irish and Irish American Studies, New York, NY 10012-1019. Offers MA. Part-time programs available. *Students:* 17 full-time (9 women), 15 part-time (10 women); includes 4 minority (1 Black or African American, non-Hispanic/Latino; 1 American Indian or Alaska Native, non-Hispanic/Latino; 1 Asian, non-Hispanic/Latino; 1 Hispanic/Latino), 2 international. Average age 41. 29 applicants, 100% accepted, 19 enrolled. In 2014, 5 master's awarded. *Degree requirements:* For master's, one foreign language. *Entrance requirements:* For master's, GRE General Test. Additional exam requirements/recommendations for international students: Required—TOEFL. *Application deadline:* For fall admission, 3/1 priority date for domestic students, 3/1 for international students. Application fee: $100. *Financial support:* Federal Work-Study, scholarships/grants, health care benefits, and unspecified assistantships available. Financial award application deadline: 3/1. *Unit head:* John Waters, Director of Graduate Studies, 212-998-3950, Fax: 212-995-4373, E-mail: gsas.irishstudies.ma@nyu.edu. *Application contact:* Miriam Nyhan, Graduate Program Administrator, 212-998-3950, Fax: 212-995-4373, E-mail: gsas.irishstudies.ma@nyu.edu.

Northeastern State University, College of Liberal Arts, Department of Social Sciences, Tahlequah, OK 74464-2399. Offers American studies (MA). Part-time and evening/weekend programs available. *Faculty:* 8 full-time (4 women), 1 part-time/adjunct (0 women). *Students:* 2 full-time (1 woman), 9 part-time (2 women); includes 3 minority (1 Black or African American, non-Hispanic/Latino; 2 Two or more races, non-Hispanic/Latino). Average age 36. In 2014, 3 master's awarded. *Degree requirements:* For master's, thesis, written and oral examinations. *Entrance requirements:* For master's, GRE, minimum GPA of 2.5. Additional exam requirements/recommendations for international students: Required—TOEFL. *Application deadline:* For fall admission, 6/1 priority date for domestic students. Applications are processed on a rolling basis. Application fee: $25. Electronic applications accepted. *Expenses:* Tuition, state resident: part-time $178.75 per credit hour. Tuition, nonresident: part-time $451.75 per credit hour. *Required fees:* $37.40 per credit hour. *Financial support:* Teaching assistantships and Federal Work-Study available. Financial award application deadline: 3/1. *Application contact:* Margie Railey, Administrative Assistant, 918-456-5511 Ext. 2093, Fax: 918-458-2061, E-mail: railey@nsouk.edu.
Website: http://catalog.nsuok.edu/preview_program.php?catoid-12&poid-947&returnto-333

Northwestern Oklahoma State University, Program in American Studies, Alva, OK 73717. Offers MA. Part-time programs available. *Faculty:* 12 full-time (4 women). *Students:* 9 full-time (5 women); includes 1 minority (Black or African American, non-Hispanic/Latino). Average age 29. 12 applicants, 100% accepted, 12 enrolled. In 2014, 1 master's awarded. *Degree requirements:* For master's, comprehensive exam, thesis optional. *Entrance requirements:* For master's, GRE or MAT, at least 12 upper-level undergraduate hours in history and/or literature. Application fee: $12. *Faculty research:* Literary history of Oklahoma, Oklahoma Poets Laureate, American naturalism, Lincoln studies, public service and policy studies. *Unit head:* Dr. Shawn Holliday, Director, 580-327-8589, E-mail: spholliday@nwosu.edu. *Application contact:* Rebekah Wagenbach, Coordinator of Graduate Studies, 580-327-8410, E-mail: rmwagenbach@nwosu.edu.
Website: http://www.nwosu.edu/american-studies

Northwestern University, School of Professional Studies, Program in Liberal Studies, Evanston, IL 60208. Offers American studies (MA); history (MA); religious and ethical studies (MA).

Norwich University, College of Graduate and Continuing Studies, Master of Arts in History Program, Northfield, VT 05663. Offers American history (MA); world history (MA). Evening/weekend programs available. Postbaccalaureate distance learning degree programs offered (minimal on-campus study). *Faculty:* 10 part-time/adjunct (2 women). *Students:* 61 full-time (29 women); includes 6 minority (1 Black or African American, non-Hispanic/Latino; 2 American Indian or Alaska Native, non-Hispanic/Latino; 1 Asian, non-Hispanic/Latino; 1 Native Hawaiian or other Pacific Islander, non-Hispanic/Latino; 1 Two or more races, non-Hispanic/Latino). Average age 38. 39 applicants, 95% accepted, 33 enrolled. In 2014, 3 master's awarded. *Degree requirements:* For master's, thesis optional. *Entrance requirements:* For master's, minimum undergraduate GPA of 2.75. Additional exam requirements/recommendations

for international students: Required—TOEFL (minimum score 550 paper-based; 80 iBT), IELTS (minimum score 6.5). *Application deadline:* For fall admission, 8/8 for domestic and international students; for winter admission, 11/7 for domestic and international students; for spring admission, 2/16 for domestic and international students; for summer admission, 5/18 for domestic and international students. Applications are processed on a rolling basis. Electronic applications accepted. *Expenses:* Expenses: Contact institution. *Financial support:* In 2014–15, 21 students received support. Scholarships/grants available. Financial award applicants required to submit FAFSA. *Unit head:* Dr. James Ehrman, Program Director, 802-485-2885, Fax: 802-485-2533, E-mail: jehrman@norwich.edu. *Application contact:* Lars Nielsen, Associate Program Director, 802-485-2853, Fax: 802-485-2533, E-mail: lnielsen@norwich.edu.
Website: http://online.norwich.edu/degree-programs/masters/master-arts-history/overview

Penn State Harrisburg, Graduate School, School of Humanities, Middletown, PA 17057-4898. Offers American studies (MA, PhD); communications (MA); folklore and ethnography (Certificate); heritage and museum practice (Certificate); humanities (MA); writing instruction specialist (Certificate). Evening/weekend programs available. *Unit head:* Dr. Mukund S. Kulkarni, Chancellor, 717-948-6105, Fax: 717-948-6452, E-mail: msk5@psu.edu. *Application contact:* Robert W. Coffman, Jr., Director of Enrollment Management, Admissions, 717-948-6250, Fax: 717-948-6325, E-mail: ric1@psu.edu.
Website: http://harrisburg.psu.edu/humanities

Pepperdine University, Seaver College, Humanities Division, Malibu, CA 90263. Offers MA. Part-time programs available. *Students:* 9 full-time (7 women), 50 part-time (29 women); includes 9 minority (2 Black or African American, non-Hispanic/Latino; 3 Asian, non-Hispanic/Latino; 4 Hispanic/Latino). In 2014, 15 master's awarded. *Degree requirements:* For master's, oral and written exams. *Entrance requirements:* For master's, GRE General Test, writing sample, letters of recommendation. Additional exam requirements/recommendations for international students: Required—TOEFL. *Application deadline:* For fall admission, 2/1 priority date for domestic students. Applications are processed on a rolling basis. Application fee: $65. *Financial support:* Applicants required to submit FAFSA. *Unit head:* Dr. Maire Mullins, Chair/Professor of English, 310-506-4235, Fax: 310-506-7307, E-mail: maire.mullins@pepperdine.edu. *Application contact:* Michael Truschke, Dean of Admission and Enrollment Management, 310-506-6165, Fax: 310-506-4861, E-mail: admission-seaver@pepperdine.edu.
Website: http://seaver.pepperdine.edu/humanities/default.htm

Providence College, Department of History, Providence, RI 02918. Offers American history (MA); modern European history (MA). Part-time and evening/weekend programs available. *Faculty:* 16 full-time (8 women), 2 part-time/adjunct (1 woman). *Students:* 15 full-time (6 women), 29 part-time (7 women); includes 2 minority (both Black or African American, non-Hispanic/Latino). 19 applicants, 100% accepted, 17 enrolled. In 2014, 18 master's awarded. *Degree requirements:* For master's, comprehensive exam, thesis optional. *Entrance requirements:* Additional exam requirements/recommendations for international students: Required—TOEFL (minimum score 577 paper-based; 90 iBT). *Application deadline:* For fall admission, 8/1 priority date for domestic and international students; for spring admission, 12/31 priority date for domestic students, 12/1 priority date for international students. Applications are processed on a rolling basis. Application fee: $55. *Expenses:* Tuition: Part-time $390 per credit. *Financial support:* Career-related internships or fieldwork, institutionally sponsored loans, and unspecified assistantships available. Support available to part-time students. Financial award application deadline: 8/1; financial award applicants required to submit FAFSA. *Faculty research:* American history, Native American history, religion, slavery, Western civilization, labor movements, Japanese and Asian history, Early Modern Europe. *Unit head:* Dr. Paul O'Malley, Program Director, 401-865-2192, Fax: 401-865-1193, E-mail: pomalley@providence.edu. *Application contact:* Phyllis S. Cardullo, Senior Administrative Coordinator, 401-865-2193, Fax: 401-865-1193, E-mail: pcardull@providence.edu.
Website: http://www.providence.edu/history/

Purdue University, Graduate School, College of Liberal Arts, Program in American Studies, West Lafayette, IN 47907. Offers MA, PhD. *Degree requirements:* For master's, essay; for doctorate, one foreign language, thesis/dissertation. *Entrance requirements:* For master's, GRE General Test, minimum undergraduate GPA of 3.0 or equivalent; writing sample; for doctorate, GRE General Test, minimum undergraduate GPA of 3.0 or equivalent; writing sample; master's degree with minimum GPA of 3.0 or equivalent. Additional exam requirements/recommendations for international students: Required—TOEFL (minimum score 550 paper-based; 77 iBT), TWE. Electronic applications accepted. *Faculty research:* African American studies; critical race theory; women, gender and sexuality studies; popular culture; transnational studies; U.S. social movements; ecocriticism.

Regent University, Graduate School, Robertson School of Government, Virginia Beach, VA 23464. Offers government (MA), including American government, international relations, political theory; public administration (MPA), including emergency management and homeland security, general public administration, nonprofit administration and faith-based organizations, public leadership and management. Part-time and evening/weekend programs available. Postbaccalaureate distance learning degree programs offered (minimal on-campus study). *Faculty:* 10 full-time (1 woman), 9 part-time/adjunct (2 women). *Students:* 34 full-time (15 women), 56 part-time (26 women); includes 21 minority (15 Black or African American, non-Hispanic/Latino; 6 Hispanic/Latino), 4 international. Average age 34. 106 applicants, 45% accepted, 33 enrolled. In 2014, 57 master's awarded. *Degree requirements:* For master's, thesis optional, internship. *Entrance requirements:* For master's, GRE General Test or LSAT, minimum undergraduate GPA of 3.0, writing sample, resume, interview, references. Additional exam requirements/recommendations for international students: Required—TOEFL (minimum score 577 paper-based). *Application deadline:* For fall admission, 5/1 priority date for domestic students; for spring admission, 11/1 priority date for domestic students. Applications are processed on a rolling basis. Application fee: $50. Electronic applications accepted. *Expenses:* Expenses: Contact institution. *Financial support:* Career-related internships or fieldwork, scholarships/grants, tuition waivers (full and partial), and unspecified assistantships available. Support available to part-time students. Financial award application deadline: 9/1; financial award applicants required to submit FAFSA. *Faculty research:* Education reform, political character issues, social capital concerns, administrative ethics, Biblical law and public policy. *Unit head:* Dr. Eric Patterson, Dean, 757-352-4616, Fax: 757-352-4735, E-mail: epatterson@regent.edu. *Application contact:* Matthew Chadwick, Director of Enrollment Support Services, 800-373-5504, Fax: 757-352-4381, E-mail: admissions@regent.edu.
Website: http://www.regent.edu/government/

Rice University, Graduate Programs, School of Humanities, Department of Religious Studies, Houston, TX 77251-1892. Offers African religions (PhD); African-American religions (PhD); contemplative studies (PhD); ghosticism, esotericism, mysticism (PhD); Islam (PhD); Jewish thought and philosophy (PhD); modern Christianity in thought and popular culture (PhD); psychology of religion (PhD); the Bible and beyond (PhD). *Degree requirements:* For doctorate, 2 foreign languages, comprehensive exam, thesis/dissertation. *Entrance requirements:* For doctorate, GRE, letters of recommendation,

writing sample. Additional exam requirements/recommendations for international students: Required—TOEFL (minimum score 600 paper-based; 90 iBT). Electronic applications accepted. *Faculty research:* Origins and historical development of Islam, history of Christianity, the study of comparative religion, African-American religion, religion and culture.

Rutgers, The State University of New Jersey, Newark, Graduate School, Program in American Studies, Newark, NJ 07102. Offers MA, PhD. *Entrance requirements:* For master's and doctorate, GRE, minimum undergraduate B average.

Saint Louis University, Graduate Education, College of Arts and Sciences and Graduate Education, Department of American Studies, St. Louis, MO 63103-2097. Offers MA, MA-R, PhD. Part-time programs available. *Degree requirements:* For master's, thesis optional, comprehensive written and oral exams; for doctorate, one foreign language, comprehensive exam, thesis/dissertation, preliminary exams. *Entrance requirements:* For master's, GRE General Test, letters of recommendation, resume; for doctorate, GRE General Test, letters of recommendation, resumé, goal statement, transcripts. Additional exam requirements/recommendations for international students: Required—TOEFL (minimum score 525 paper-based). Electronic applications accepted. *Faculty research:* Urban studies, American religion, intellectual history, southern culture, African-American literature.

Stockton University, School of Graduate and Continuing Studies, Program in American Studies, Galloway, NJ 08205-9441. Offers MA, Certificate. Part-time programs available. *Faculty:* 5 full-time (2 women), 1 part-time/adjunct (0 women). *Students:* 6 full-time (3 women), 15 part-time (10 women); includes 4 minority (1 Black or African American, non-Hispanic/Latino; 3 Hispanic/Latino). Average age 34. 12 applicants, 75% accepted, 9 enrolled. In 2014, 6 master's awarded. *Application deadline:* For fall admission, 7/1 for domestic and international students; for winter admission, 11/1 for international students; for spring admission, 12/1 for domestic students. Applications are processed on a rolling basis. Electronic applications accepted. *Expenses:* Tuition, state resident: full-time $13,694; part-time $570.59 per credit. Tuition, nonresident: full-time $21,080; part-time $878 per credit. *Required fees:* $4118; $171.59 per credit. $80 per term. Tuition and fees vary according to degree level. *Financial support:* In 2014–15, 2 fellowships, 6 research assistantships were awarded; scholarships/grants and unspecified assistantships also available. *Unit head:* Dr. Deborah Gussman, Program Director, 609-626-3640, E-mail: gradschool@stockton.edu. *Application contact:* Tara Williams, Assistant Director of Enrollment Management, 609-626-3640, Fax: 609-626-6050, E-mail: gradschool@stockton.edu.

Texas Christian University, AddRan College of Liberal Arts, Department of History, Fort Worth, TX 76129. Offers United States (MA, PhD). *Faculty:* 14 full-time (3 women). *Students:* 52 full-time (22 women); includes 4 minority (3 Hispanic/Latino; 1 Two or more races, non-Hispanic/Latino), 1 international. Average age 32. 26 applicants, 54% accepted, 11 enrolled. In 2014, 4 master's, 7 doctorates awarded. Terminal master's awarded for partial completion of doctoral program. *Degree requirements:* For master's, comprehensive exam, thesis or alternative; for doctorate, one foreign language, comprehensive exam, thesis/dissertation. *Entrance requirements:* For master's and doctorate, GRE General Test. Additional exam requirements/recommendations for international students: Recommended—TOEFL. *Application deadline:* 2/1 for domestic and international students; for summer admission, 2/1 for domestic and international students. Applications are processed on a rolling basis. Application fee: $60. Electronic applications accepted. *Expenses: Tuition:* Full-time $22,860; part-time $1270 per credit hour. *Financial support:* In 2014–15, 50 students received support, including 3 fellowships with full tuition reimbursements available (averaging $20,000 per year), 15 research assistantships with full tuition reimbursements available (averaging $17,500 per year), 5 teaching assistantships with full tuition reimbursements available (averaging $17,500 per year); tuition waivers also available. Financial award application deadline: 2/1. *Faculty research:* Gender history, military history, popular culture, imperialism, American West. *Total annual research expenditures:* $48,000. *Unit head:* Dr. Jodi Campbell, Associate Professor, 817-257-5882, Fax: 817-257-5650, E-mail: j.campbell@tcu.edu. *Application contact:* Dana Summers, Administrative Assistant, 817-257-7822, Fax: 817-257-5650, E-mail: d.summers@tcu.edu.
Website: http://www.his.tcu.edu/graduate.asp

Trinity College, Graduate Programs, Program in American Studies, Hartford, CT 06106-3100. Offers American culture studies (MA); museums and communities (MA). Part-time and evening/weekend programs available. *Degree requirements:* For master's, thesis or alternative. *Entrance requirements:* For master's, minimum GPA of 3.0.

Universidad de las Américas Puebla, Division of Graduate Studies, School of Social Sciences, Program in American Studies, Puebla, Mexico. Offers MA. Part-time and evening/weekend programs available. *Degree requirements:* For master's, one foreign language, thesis. *Faculty research:* NAFTA, technology, culture, politics and economics in NAFTA region.

University at Buffalo, the State University of New York, Graduate School, College of Arts and Sciences, Department of Transnational Studies, Buffalo, NY 14260. Offers American studies (MA, PhD); Canadian studies (Advanced Certificate); Canadian-American studies (MA); Caribbean Latina/o American studies (MA); global gender studies (MA, PhD). Part-time programs available. Postbaccalaureate distance learning degree programs offered. *Faculty:* 19 full-time (10 women). *Students:* 73 full-time (43 women); includes 20 minority (3 Black or African American, non-Hispanic/Latino; 6 American Indian or Alaska Native, non-Hispanic/Latino; 9 Asian, non-Hispanic/Latino; 2 Hispanic/Latino). Average age 32. 57 applicants, 84% accepted, 16 enrolled. In 2014, 26 master's, 18 doctorates, 1 other advanced degree awarded. *Degree requirements:* For master's, one foreign language, comprehensive exam (for some programs), thesis optional; for doctorate, one foreign language, comprehensive exam, thesis/dissertation; for Advanced Certificate, one foreign language. *Entrance requirements:* For master's, N/A, minimum GPA of 3.0; for doctorate, GRE, minimum GPA of 3.0. Additional exam requirements/recommendations for international students: Required—TOEFL (minimum score 550 paper-based; 79 iBT). *Application deadline:* For fall admission, 8/15 priority date for domestic students, 6/15 priority date for international students; for winter admission, 2/1 for domestic and international students; for spring admission, 1/15 priority date for domestic students, 11/15 priority date for international students. Applications are processed on a rolling basis. Application fee: $75. Electronic applications accepted. *Financial support:* In 2014–15, 16 students received support, including fellowships with full tuition reimbursements available (averaging $6,000 per year), research assistantships (averaging $5,000 per year), teaching assistantships with full tuition reimbursements available (averaging $13,060 per year); career-related internships or fieldwork, institutionally sponsored loans, scholarships/grants, traineeships, health care benefits, and unspecified assistantships also available. Financial award application deadline: 1/4. *Faculty research:* Native American, intercultural and indigenous people's studies, border theory, cultural studies, American pop culture, feminist theory, construction of gender in society. *Unit head:* Dr. Keith Griffler, Chair, 716-645-0802, Fax: 716-645-5977, E-mail: griffler@buffalo.edu. *Application contact:* Karen M. Reinard, Graduate Secretary, 716-645-0797, Fax: 716-645-5976, E-mail: kreinard@buffalo.edu.
Website: http://www.transnationalstudies.buffalo.edu/graduate.shtml

The University of Alabama, Graduate School, College of Arts and Sciences, Department of American Studies, Tuscaloosa, AL 35487. Offers MA. Part-time programs available. *Faculty:* 10 full-time (4 women), 1 part-time/adjunct (0 women). *Students:* 9 full-time (8 women), 1 (woman) part-time; includes 1 minority (Two or more races, non-Hispanic/Latino). Average age 28. 12 applicants, 92% accepted, 8 enrolled. In 2014, 4 master's awarded. *Degree requirements:* For master's, comprehensive exam, thesis optional. *Entrance requirements:* For master's, GRE or MAT. Additional exam requirements/recommendations for international students: Required—TOEFL. *Application deadline:* For fall admission, 1/15 priority date for domestic and international students; for spring admission, 11/30 priority date for domestic and international students; for summer admission, 1/15 for domestic and international students. Applications are processed on a rolling basis. Application fee: $50 ($60 for international students). Electronic applications accepted. *Expenses:* Tuition, state resident: full-time $9826. Tuition, nonresident: full-time $24,950. *Financial support:* In 2014–15, 12 students received support, including 7 teaching assistantships with full tuition reimbursements available (averaging $16,992 per year); career-related internships or fieldwork, health care benefits, tuition waivers (full), and unspecified assistantships also available. Financial award application deadline: 1/10. *Faculty research:* Social and cultural history, popular music and popular culture, African-American arts and education, the culture and environment of the South, gender and sexuality, Asian-American studies, sports, Latino Studies. *Unit head:* Dr. Lynne M. Adrian, Chair and Associate Professor, 205-348-5940, Fax: 205-348-9766, E-mail: ladrian@ua.edu. *Application contact:* Patrick D. Fuller, Senior Graduate Admissions Counselor, 205-348-5923, Fax: 205-348-0400, E-mail: patrick.d.fuller@ua.edu.
Website: http://ams.ua.edu/

University of Colorado Denver, College of Liberal Arts and Sciences, Department of History, Denver, CO 80217. Offers European history (MA); global history (MA); public history (MA); U.S. history (MA). Part-time and evening/weekend programs available. *Faculty:* 14 full-time (6 women), 1 part-time/adjunct (0 women). *Students:* 33 full-time (20 women), 20 part-time (11 women); includes 12 minority (1 Black or African American, non-Hispanic/Latino; 1 American Indian or Alaska Native, non-Hispanic/Latino; 1 Asian, non-Hispanic/Latino; 8 Hispanic/Latino; 1 Two or more races, non-Hispanic/Latino). Average age 34. 27 applicants, 59% accepted, 9 enrolled. In 2014, 9 master's awarded. *Degree requirements:* For master's, comprehensive exam, thesis optional, 36 semester hours (12 courses). *Entrance requirements:* For master's, GRE General Test, writing sample, minimum undergraduate GPA of 3.25, three letters of recommendation, statement of purpose addressing any weaknesses in academic record. Additional exam requirements/recommendations for international students: Required—TOEFL (minimum score 537 paper-based; 75 iBT); Recommended—IELTS (minimum score 6.5). *Application deadline:* For fall admission, 1/20 for domestic and international students; for spring admission, 10/1 for domestic and international students. Application fee: $50 ($75 for international students). Electronic applications accepted. *Financial support:* In 2014–15, 8 students received support. Fellowships, research assistantships, teaching assistantships, Federal Work-Study, institutionally sponsored loans, scholarships/grants, and traineeships available. Financial award application deadline: 4/1; financial award applicants required to submit FAFSA. *Faculty research:* Uses of pre-modern Islamic heritage in modern India; relationship between liberal understandings of democracy, crime, and police discretion; relationships between gender, class, health, and welfare in nineteenth and early twentieth century England; U.S. business cultures and their influences on marketing and personnel practices; intersection of business and political ideologies; social and environmental history of the Rocky Mountain West. *Unit head:* Dr. Pamela Laird, Associate Professor and Chair, 303-556-4497, E-mail: pamela.laird@ucdenver.edu. *Application contact:* Tabitha Fitzpatrick, Program Assistant, 303-315-1776, E-mail: tabitha.fitzpatrick@ucdenver.edu.
Website: http://www.ucdenver.edu/academics/colleges/CLAS/Departments/history/Programs/Masters/Pages/MasterofArts.aspx

University of Dallas, Braniff Graduate School of Liberal Arts, Program in American Studies, Irving, TX 75062-4736. Offers MAS. Part-time programs available. *Degree requirements:* For master's, comprehensive exam. *Entrance requirements:* For master's, GRE General Test. *Faculty research:* Shakespeare, Milton, Melville, Hawthorne, liberty and American literature.

University of Delaware, College of Arts and Sciences, Winterthur Program in American Material Culture, Newark, DE 19716. Offers MA. *Degree requirements:* For master's, thesis. *Entrance requirements:* For master's, GRE General Test, minimum GPA of 3.0. Electronic applications accepted. *Faculty research:* American material culture, American studies, decorative arts.

University of Hawaii at Manoa, Graduate Division, College of Arts and Humanities, Department of American Studies, Honolulu, HI 96822. Offers American studies (MA, PhD); historic preservation (Graduate Certificate); museum studies (Graduate Certificate). Part-time programs available. *Degree requirements:* For master's, comprehensive exam (for some programs), thesis (for some programs); for doctorate, comprehensive exam, thesis/dissertation. *Entrance requirements:* For master's and doctorate, GRE General Test. Additional exam requirements/recommendations for international students: Required—TOEFL (minimum score 600 paper-based; 100 iBT), IELTS (minimum score 7). *Faculty research:* Ethnicity and race, popular culture, historic preservation, arts and culture, international relations.

The University of Iowa, Graduate College, College of Liberal Arts and Sciences, Department of American Studies, Iowa City, IA 52242-1316. Offers MA, PhD. *Degree requirements:* For master's, thesis optional, exam; for doctorate, comprehensive exam, thesis/dissertation. *Entrance requirements:* For master's and doctorate, GRE General Test, minimum GPA of 3.0. Additional exam requirements/recommendations for international students: Required—TOEFL (minimum score 550 paper-based; 81 iBT). Electronic applications accepted.

The University of Kansas, Graduate Studies, College of Liberal Arts and Sciences, Department of American Studies, Lawrence, KS 66045. Offers MA, PhD, MUP/MA. Part-time programs available. *Faculty:* 11 full-time, 2 part-time/adjunct. *Students:* 22 full-time (14 women), 2 part-time (1 woman); includes 4 minority (2 Black or African American, non-Hispanic/Latino; 1 Hispanic/Latino; 1 Two or more races, non-Hispanic/Latino), 2 international. Average age 36. 18 applicants, 56% accepted, 7 enrolled. In 2014, 7 master's, 6 doctorates awarded. Terminal master's awarded for partial completion of doctoral program. *Degree requirements:* For master's, comprehensive exam, thesis or alternative; for doctorate, comprehensive exam, thesis/dissertation. *Entrance requirements:* For master's, GRE General Test; for doctorate, GRE General Test, official transcripts from each college and post-secondary institution attended, statement of academic objectives, resume or curriculum vitae, three letters of recommendation, sample of written academic work. Additional exam requirements/recommendations for international students: Required—TOEFL. *Application deadline:* For fall admission, 12/1 priority date for domestic students, 12/1 for international students; for spring admission, 5/1 for domestic and international students. Applications are processed on a rolling basis. Application fee: $55 ($65 for international students). Electronic applications accepted. *Financial support:* Fellowships with full tuition reimbursements, research

assistantships with partial tuition reimbursements, teaching assistantships with full and partial tuition reimbursements, Federal Work-Study, scholarships/grants, health care benefits, and unspecified assistantships available. Financial award application deadline: 12/21. *Faculty research:* African-American history, community, and religion; jazz, improvisation, and performance; Mexican-American culture and politics; ethnography, oral and social history; literature and theory. *Unit head:* Henry Bial, Chair, 785-864-4011, Fax: 785-864-5772, E-mail: hbial@ku.edu. *Application contact:* Kay Isbell, Graduate Admissions Contact, 785-864-2957, E-mail: kisbell@ku.edu.
Website: http://americanstudies.ku.edu

University of Louisiana at Lafayette, College of Liberal Arts, Department of Modern Languages, Program in Francophone Studies, Lafayette, LA 70504. Offers PhD. *Degree requirements:* For doctorate, 2 foreign languages, comprehensive exam, thesis/dissertation. *Entrance requirements:* For doctorate, GRE General Test, minimum GPA of 2.75. Additional exam requirements/recommendations for international students: Required—TOEFL (minimum score 550 paper-based). Electronic applications accepted. *Faculty research:* Louisiana folklore, eighteenth-century French literature, contemporary criticism.

University of Maryland, College Park, Academic Affairs, College of Arts and Humanities, Department of American Studies, College Park, MD 20742. Offers MA, PhD. *Degree requirements:* For master's, thesis or scholarly paper and exam; for doctorate, thesis/dissertation, 3 comprehensive exams. *Entrance requirements:* For master's, GRE General Test, minimum GPA of 3.0, writing sample, 3 letters of recommendation; for doctorate, GRE General Test. Additional exam requirements/recommendations for international students: Required—TOEFL. Electronic applications accepted. *Faculty research:* Material culture, modes of culture, cultural movements, popular culture, ethnography.

University of Massachusetts Amherst, Graduate School, College of Humanities and Fine Arts, Department of English, Amherst, MA 01003. Offers American studies (PhD); composition and rhetoric (PhD); creative writing (MFA); English and American literature (MA, PhD). Part-time programs available. *Faculty:* 49 full-time (24 women). *Students:* 100 full-time (60 women), 76 part-time (50 women); includes 29 minority (2 Black or African American, non-Hispanic/Latino; 6 Asian, non-Hispanic/Latino; 10 Hispanic/Latino; 1 Native Hawaiian or other Pacific Islander, non-Hispanic/Latino; 10 Two or more races, non-Hispanic/Latino), 17 international. Average age 30. 600 applicants, 12% accepted, 29 enrolled. In 2014, 26 master's, 10 doctorates awarded. Terminal master's awarded for partial completion of doctoral program. *Degree requirements:* For master's, one foreign language, thesis optional; for doctorate, one foreign language, comprehensive exam, thesis/dissertation. *Entrance requirements:* For master's, manuscript; for doctorate, GRE General Test, manuscript. Additional exam requirements/recommendations for international students: Required—TOEFL (minimum score 550 paper-based; 80 iBT), IELTS (minimum score 6.5). *Application deadline:* For fall admission, 12/15 for domestic and international students. Applications are processed on a rolling basis. Application fee: $75. Electronic applications accepted. *Expenses:* Tuition, state resident: full-time $1980; part-time $110 per credit. Tuition, nonresident: full-time $14,644; part-time $414 per credit. Required fees: $11,417. One-time fee: $357. *Financial support:* Fellowships with full and partial tuition reimbursements, research assistantships with full and partial tuition reimbursements, teaching assistantships with full and partial tuition reimbursements, career-related internships or fieldwork, Federal Work-Study, scholarships/grants, traineeships, health care benefits, tuition waivers (full and partial), and unspecified assistantships available. Support available to part-time students. Financial award application deadline: 12/15. *Unit head:* Dr. Jenny Spencer, Department Head, 413-545-2332, Fax: 413-545-3880. *Application contact:* Lindsay DeSantis, Supervisor of Admissions, 413-545-0722, Fax: 413-577-0010, E-mail: gradadm@grad.umass.edu.
Website: http://www.umass.edu/english/

University of Massachusetts Boston, College of Liberal Arts, Program in American Studies, Boston, MA 02125-3393. Offers MA. Part-time and evening/weekend programs available. *Degree requirements:* For master's, thesis or capstone project. *Entrance requirements:* For master's, minimum GPA of 2.75. *Application deadline:* For fall admission, 3/1 for domestic students; for spring admission, 11/1 for domestic students. *Expenses:* Tuition, state resident: full-time $2590; part-time $108 per credit. Tuition, nonresident: full-time $9758; part-time $406.50 per credit. Tuition and fees vary according to course load and program. *Financial support:* Research assistantships with full tuition reimbursements, teaching assistantships with full tuition reimbursements, career-related internships or fieldwork, Federal Work-Study, and unspecified assistantships available. Support available to part-time students. Financial award application deadline: 3/1; financial award applicants required to submit FAFSA. *Faculty research:* War in American culture, immigration history, Latin Americans, history of race and popular music, education and Asian Americans. *Unit head:* Dr. Judy Smith, Director, 617-287-6770, E-mail: amsty@umbsky.cc.umb.edu. *Application contact:* Peggy Roldan Patel, Graduate Admissions Coordinator, 617-287-6400, Fax: 617-287-6236, E-mail: bos.gadm@dpc.umassp.edu.

University of Michigan, Horace H. Rackham School of Graduate Studies, College of Literature, Science, and the Arts, Department of American Culture, Ann Arbor, MI 48109-1045. Offers AM, PhD. *Faculty:* 42 full-time (25 women). *Students:* 42 full-time (25 women); includes 24 minority (7 Black or African American, non-Hispanic/Latino; 1 American Indian or Alaska Native, non-Hispanic/Latino; 8 Asian, non-Hispanic/Latino; 8 Hispanic/Latino), 2 international. 103 applicants, 8% accepted, 6 enrolled. In 2014, 4 master's, 7 doctorates awarded. Terminal master's awarded for partial completion of doctoral program. *Degree requirements:* For doctorate, preliminary exams, field exams, oral defense of dissertation. *Entrance requirements:* For master's, GRE General Test; for doctorate, GRE General Test, sample of written work. Additional exam requirements/recommendations for international students: Required—TOEFL. *Application deadline:* For fall admission, 12/1 for domestic and international students. Application fee: $75 ($90 for international students). Electronic applications accepted. *Financial support:* In 2014–15, 29 students received support, including 29 fellowships with full tuition reimbursements available (averaging $27,900 per year), 12 teaching assistantships with full tuition reimbursements available (averaging $27,900 per year); research assistantships and health care benefits also available. *Faculty research:* Cultural studies, ethnic studies, American culture methodology, literature, history. *Unit head:* June Howard, Chair, 734-763-1460, Fax: 734-936-1967, E-mail: ac.inq@umich.edu. *Application contact:* Marlene Moore, Graduate Student Coordinator, 734-647-9533, Fax: 734-936-1967, E-mail: ac.inq@umich.edu.
Website: http://www.lsa.umich.edu/ac/

University of Michigan–Flint, College of Arts and Sciences, Program in Social Sciences, Flint, MI 48502-1950. Offers gender studies (MA); global studies (MA); U.S. history and politics (MA). Part-time programs available. *Faculty:* 14 full-time (8 women), 5 part-time/adjunct (3 women). *Students:* 1 (woman) full-time, 20 part-time (13 women); includes 8 minority (6 Black or African American, non-Hispanic/Latino; 1 Hispanic/Latino; 1 Two or more races, non-Hispanic/Latino). Average age 41. 8 applicants, 75% accepted, 3 enrolled. In 2014, 7 master's awarded. *Entrance requirements:* For master's, bachelor's degree from accredited institution, minimum overall GPA of 3.0. Additional exam requirements/recommendations for international students: Required—

TOEFL (minimum score 84 iBT), IELTS (minimum score 6.5). *Application deadline:* For fall admission, 8/1 for domestic students, 5/1 for international students; for winter admission, 11/15 for domestic students, 9/1 for international students; for spring admission, 3/15 for domestic students, 1/1 for international students; for summer admission, 5/15 for domestic students. Applications are processed on a rolling basis. Application fee: $55. Electronic applications accepted. *Expenses:* Expenses: Contact institution. *Financial support:* Federal Work-Study, scholarships/grants, and unspecified assistantships available. Support available to part-time students. Financial award application deadline: 3/1; financial award applicants required to submit FAFSA. *Unit head:* Dr. Adam Lutzker, Interim Director, 810-762-3280, Fax: 810-762-3281, E-mail: alutzker@umflint.edu. *Application contact:* Bradley T. Maki, Director of Graduate Admissions, 810-762-3171, Fax: 810-766-6789, E-mail: bmaki@umflint.edu.
Website: http://www.umflint.edu/graduateprograms/social-sciences-ma

University of Michigan–Flint, Graduate Programs, Program in Liberal Studies, Flint, MI 48502-1950. Offers MLS. Part-time programs available. *Faculty:* 1 part-time/adjunct (0 women). *Students:* 4 full-time (all women), 18 part-time (10 women); includes 6 minority (4 Black or African American, non-Hispanic/Latino; 1 American Indian or Alaska Native, non-Hispanic/Latino; 1 Two or more races, non-Hispanic/Latino), 1 international. Average age 41. 7 applicants, 86% accepted, 5 enrolled. In 2014, 4 master's awarded. *Degree requirements:* For master's, thesis or alternative. *Entrance requirements:* For master's, minimum GPA of 3.0, 24 undergraduate credits in humanities and social sciences. Additional exam requirements/recommendations for international students: Required—TOEFL (minimum score 84 iBT), IELTS (minimum score 6.5). *Application deadline:* For fall admission, 8/1 for domestic students, 5/1 for international students; for winter admission, 11/15 for domestic students, 9/1 for international students; for spring admission, 3/15 for domestic students, 1/1 for international students; for summer admission, 5/15 for domestic students. Applications are processed on a rolling basis. Application fee: $55. Electronic applications accepted. Application fee is waived when completed online. *Financial support:* Federal Work-Study, scholarships/grants, and unspecified assistantships available. Support available to part-time students. Financial award application deadline: 3/1; financial award applicants required to submit FAFSA. *Unit head:* Dr. M. Jan Furman, Director, 810-762-3285, E-mail: jfurman@umflint.edu. *Application contact:* Bradley T. Maki, Director of Graduate Admissions, 810-762-3171, Fax: 810-766-6789, E-mail: bmaki@umflint.edu.
Website: http://www.umflint.edu/graduateprograms/liberal-studies-ma

University of Minnesota, Twin Cities Campus, Graduate School, College of Liberal Arts, Department of American Studies, Minneapolis, MN 55455. Offers PhD. *Degree requirements:* For doctorate, one foreign language, comprehensive exam, thesis/dissertation. *Entrance requirements:* For doctorate, GRE General Test, sample of written work, 3 letters of recommendation. Additional exam requirements/recommendations for international students: Required—TOEFL (minimum score 550 paper-based). *Faculty research:* American Indian history, nationalism/transnationalism, gender and sexuality, race and ethnicity.

University of Mississippi, Graduate School, College of Liberal Arts, Interdisciplinary Program in Southern Studies, University, MS 38677. Offers MA. *Entrance requirements:* For master's, GRE General Test, minimum GPA of 3.0. Additional exam requirements/recommendations for international students: Required—TOEFL. Electronic applications accepted.

University of Missouri–St. Louis, College of Arts and Sciences, Department of Political Science, St. Louis, MO 63121. Offers American politics (MA); comparative politics (MA); international politics (MA); political process and behavior (MA); political science (PhD); public administration and public policy (MA); urban and regional politics (MA). Part-time and evening/weekend programs available. *Faculty:* 17 full-time (4 women), 6 part-time/adjunct (2 women). *Students:* 22 full-time (7 women), 35 part-time (20 women); includes 6 minority (5 Black or African American, non-Hispanic/Latino; 1 American Indian or Alaska Native, non-Hispanic/Latino), 5 international. Average age 35. 27 applicants, 63% accepted, 12 enrolled. In 2014, 6 master's, 3 doctorates awarded. Terminal master's awarded for partial completion of doctoral program. *Degree requirements:* For master's, thesis optional; for doctorate, thesis/dissertation. *Entrance requirements:* For master's, GRE General Test, 2 letters of recommendation; for doctorate, GRE General Test, 3 letters of recommendation. Additional exam requirements/recommendations for international students: Required—TOEFL (minimum score 550 paper-based; 79 iBT), IELTS (minimum score 6.5). *Application deadline:* For fall admission, 2/15 priority date for domestic and international students; for spring admission, 10/15 priority date for domestic and international students. Applications are processed on a rolling basis. Application fee: $50 ($40 for international students). Electronic applications accepted. *Expenses:* Tuition, state resident: full-time $7364; part-time $409.10 per hour. Tuition, nonresident: full-time $18,153; part-time $1008.50 per hour. *Financial support:* In 2014–15, 3 research assistantships with full and partial tuition reimbursements (averaging $10,800 per year), 10 teaching assistantships with full and partial tuition reimbursements (averaging $10,800 per year) were awarded; fellowships and career-related internships or fieldwork also available. Support available to part-time students. Financial award application deadline: 3/15; financial award applicants required to submit FAFSA. *Faculty research:* Public policy, urban politics and administration, American government. *Unit head:* Dr. David Kimball, Director of Graduate Studies, 314-516-5521, Fax: 314-516-5268, E-mail: umslpolisci@umsl.edu. *Application contact:* 314-516-5458, Fax: 314-516-6996, E-mail: gradadm@umsl.edu.
Website: http://www.umsl.edu/~polisci/

University of New Mexico, Graduate School, College of Arts and Sciences, Program in American Studies, Albuquerque, NM 87131. Offers MA, PhD. Part-time programs available. *Faculty:* 12 full-time (6 women), 2 part-time/adjunct (1 woman). *Students:* 41 full-time (29 women), 13 part-time (9 women); includes 24 minority (1 Black or African American, non-Hispanic/Latino; 4 American Indian or Alaska Native, non-Hispanic/Latino; 1 Asian, non-Hispanic/Latino; 16 Hispanic/Latino; 2 Two or more races, non-Hispanic/Latino), 2 international. Average age 36. 24 applicants, 71% accepted, 11 enrolled. In 2014, 5 master's, 2 doctorates awarded. *Degree requirements:* For master's, comprehensive exam (for some programs), thesis (for some programs); for doctorate, one foreign language, comprehensive exam, thesis/dissertation. *Entrance requirements:* For master's, BA in related field; for doctorate, MA in related field, complete dossier. Additional exam requirements/recommendations for international students: Required—TOEFL. *Application deadline:* For fall admission, 1/15 for domestic and international students. Application fee: $50. Electronic applications accepted. *Financial support:* In 2014–15, 31 students received support, including 11 research assistantships with partial tuition reimbursements available (averaging $6,287 per year), 15 teaching assistantships with partial tuition reimbursements available (averaging $7,559 per year); Federal Work-Study, health care benefits, tuition waivers (partial), and unspecified assistantships also available. Support available to part-time students. Financial award application deadline: 2/20; financial award applicants required to submit FAFSA. *Faculty research:* Cultural studies, environment/science/technology, gender, race/class/ethnicity, popular culture, Southwest studies. *Unit head:* Dr. Alex Lubin, Chair, 505-277-3929, Fax: 505-277-1208, E-mail: alubin@unm.edu. *Application contact:* Sandy Rodrigue, Department Administrator, 505-277-3929, Fax: 505-277-1208, E-mail: amstudy@unm.edu. Website: http://www.unm.edu/~amstudy/

American Studies

University of New Mexico, Graduate School, College of Fine Arts, Program in Art History, Albuquerque, NM 87131. Offers art history (MA); arts of the Americas (MA); history of architecture (PhD); history of graphic arts (PhD); history of photography (PhD); modern Latin American art history (PhD); Native American art history (PhD); Pre-Columbian art history (PhD); Spanish colonial art history (PhD). Part-time programs available. *Faculty:* 9 full-time (7 women). *Students:* 14 full-time (10 women), 22 part-time (16 women); includes 8 minority (2 American Indian or Alaska Native, non-Hispanic/Latino; 6 Hispanic/Latino), 5 international. Average age 32. 34 applicants, 26% accepted, 5 enrolled. In 2014, 5 master's, 1 doctorate awarded. *Degree requirements:* For master's, one foreign language, comprehensive exam (for some programs), thesis, symposium; for doctorate, 2 foreign languages, comprehensive exam, thesis/dissertation, symposium. *Entrance requirements:* Additional exam requirements/recommendations for international students: Required—TOEFL (minimum score 550 paper-based), IELTS (minimum score 6). *Application deadline:* For fall admission, 1/15 for domestic students; for spring admission, 1/15 for domestic students. Application fee: $50. Electronic applications accepted. *Financial support:* In 2014–15, fellowships (averaging $7,433 per year), research assistantships with tuition reimbursements (averaging $5,216 per year), teaching assistantships with partial tuition reimbursements (averaging $4,005 per year) were awarded; Federal Work-Study, institutionally sponsored loans, scholarships/grants, health care benefits, and unspecified assistantships also available. Support available to part-time students. Financial award application deadline: 3/1; financial award applicants required to submit FAFSA. *Faculty research:* Native American, modern Latin American, pre-Columbian, architectural, American, medieval, Spanish Colonial, and Latin American art; history of photography. *Unit head:* Prof. Mary Tsiongas, Chair, 505-277-5861, Fax: 505-277-5955, E-mail: tsiongas@unm.edu. *Application contact:* Kat Heatherington, Graduate Advisor, 505-277-6672, Fax: 505-277-5955, E-mail: art255@unm.edu.
Website: http://art.unm.edu/

University of Rochester, School of Arts and Sciences, Department of History, Rochester, NY 14627. Offers American history (MA, PhD); European history (MA, PhD); global history (MA, PhD). *Faculty:* 18 full-time (4 women). *Students:* 30 full-time (8 women); includes 4 minority (1 Asian, non-Hispanic/Latino; 1 Hispanic/Latino; 2 Two or more races, non-Hispanic/Latino), 1 international. 32 applicants, 41% accepted, 7 enrolled. In 2014, 5 master's, 7 doctorates awarded. Terminal master's awarded for partial completion of doctoral program. *Degree requirements:* For master's, one foreign language, thesis or alternative; for doctorate, 2 foreign languages, thesis/dissertation, comprehensive oral exam, qualifying exam. *Entrance requirements:* For master's and doctorate, GRE General Test, sample of written work. Additional exam requirements/recommendations for international students: Required—TOEFL. *Application deadline:* For fall admission, 1/15 priority date for domestic students. Application fee: $60. Electronic applications accepted. *Expenses: Tuition:* Full-time $46,150; part-time $1442 per credit hour. *Required fees:* $504. *Financial support:* Fellowships, research assistantships, teaching assistantships, and tuition waivers (full and partial) available. Financial award application deadline: 1/15. *Unit head:* Matthew Lenoe, Chair, 585-275-9355. *Application contact:* Caleb Rood, Secretary, 585-275-2053.
Website: http://www.rochester.edu/College/HIS/

University of Southern California, Graduate School, Dana and David Dornsife College of Letters, Arts and Sciences, Department of American Studies and Ethnicity, Los Angeles, CA 90089. Offers PhD. *Degree requirements:* For doctorate, one foreign language, thesis/dissertation, qualifying exam. *Entrance requirements:* For doctorate, GRE. Additional exam requirements/recommendations for international students: Recommended—TOEFL. Electronic applications accepted. *Faculty research:* Interdisciplinary study of race and ethnicity, regional focus on Los Angeles and the American West, multidisciplinary exploration of culture, interdisciplinary study of gender and sexuality.

University of Southern Maine, College of Arts and Sciences, Program in American and New England Studies, Portland, ME 04104-9300. Offers MA, CGS. Part-time and evening/weekend programs available. *Faculty:* 5 full-time (3 women). *Students:* 5 full-time (3 women), 17 part-time (12 women); includes 3 minority (2 Hispanic/Latino; 1 Two or more races, non-Hispanic/Latino). Average age 36. 9 applicants, 89% accepted, 4 enrolled. In 2014, 9 master's awarded. *Degree requirements:* For master's, thesis optional. *Entrance requirements:* For master's, GRE General Test or MAT. Additional exam requirements/recommendations for international students: Required—TOEFL. *Application deadline:* For fall admission, 3/15 priority date for domestic and international students; for spring admission, 10/1 priority date for domestic and international students. Application fee: $65. *Expenses: Tuition, area resident:* Full-time $6840; part-time $380 per credit hour. Tuition, state resident: full-time $10,260; part-time $570 per credit hour. Tuition, nonresident: full-time $18,468; part-time $1026 per credit hour. *Required fees:* $830; $83 per credit hour. Tuition and fees vary according to course load and program. *Financial support:* Research assistantships, Federal Work-Study, and unspecified assistantships available. Support available to part-time students. *Faculty research:* Social history, regional culture, landscape of literature, material culture, art and architecture. *Unit head:* Dr. Kent Ryden, Director, 207-780-4941, E-mail: kryden@usm.maine.edu. *Application contact:* Mary Sloan, Assistant Dean of Graduate Studies and Director of Graduate Admissions, 207-780-4812, E-mail: gradstudies@usm.maine.edu.
Website: http://www.usm.maine.edu/anes

University of South Florida, College of Arts and Sciences, Department of Humanities and Cultural Studies, Tampa, FL 33620-9951. Offers American studies (MA); liberal arts (MA), including Africana studies, film studies, humanities, social and political thought. Part-time and evening/weekend programs available. *Faculty:* 7 full-time (3 women). *Students:* 11 full-time (2 women), 8 part-time (2 women); includes 8 minority (4 Black or African American, non-Hispanic/Latino; 3 Hispanic/Latino; 1 Two or more races, non-Hispanic/Latino), 1 international. Average age 34. 9 applicants, 78% accepted, 5 enrolled. In 2014, 5 master's awarded. *Degree requirements:* For master's, comprehensive exam, thesis, language requirement (for humanities subconcentration). *Entrance requirements:* For master's, GRE General Test (minimum preferred score 59th percentile (153) verbal and 4.5 in analytical writing), minimum GPA of 3.0 in upper-division courses, personal statement, writing sample. Additional exam requirements/recommendations for international students: Required—TOEFL (minimum score 550 paper-based; 79 iBT) or IELTS (minimum score 6.5). *Application deadline:* For fall admission, 2/15 priority date for domestic students, 1/2 for international students; for spring admission, 10/15 priority date for domestic students, 6/1 for international students. Application fee: $30. *Financial support:* In 2014–15, 15 students received support, including 15 teaching assistantships with tuition reimbursements available (averaging $12,437 per year); scholarships/grants also available. Financial award application deadline: 4/1. *Faculty research:* American South, American autobiography, material culture, critical theory, cultural studies, film studies. *Unit head:* Dr. William Cummings, Professor and Chair, 813-974-9380, Fax: 813-974-9409, E-mail: wcummings@usf.edu. *Application contact:* Dr. Brook Sadler, Associate Professor and Graduate Program Director, 813-974-8841, Fax: 813-974-9409, E-mail: brooksadler@usf.edu.
Website: http://humanities.usf.edu/

The University of Texas at Austin, Graduate School, College of Liberal Arts, Department of American Studies, Austin, TX 78712-1111. Offers MA, PhD. Part-time programs available. *Degree requirements:* For master's, thesis; for doctorate, one foreign language, thesis/dissertation, qualifying oral exam. *Entrance requirements:* For master's and doctorate, GRE General Test, minimum GPA of 3.5. Electronic applications accepted. *Faculty research:* Race, gender, and ethnicity; history of the American West; American design and archaeology; literary cultural history; religion and psychology in American culture.

University of Utah, Graduate School, College of Humanities, Department of English, Salt Lake City, UT 84112. Offers American studies (MA, PhD); British and American literature (MA, PhD); creative writing (MFA, PhD), including fiction, non-fiction, poetry; rhetoric and composition (MA, PhD). *Faculty:* 27 full-time (10 women), 7 part-time/adjunct (2 women). *Students:* 47 full-time (27 women), 25 part-time (16 women); includes 5 minority (1 Black or African American, non-Hispanic/Latino; 2 Asian, non-Hispanic/Latino; 2 Two or more races, non-Hispanic/Latino), 3 international. Average age 35. 285 applicants, 12% accepted, 11 enrolled. In 2014, 7 master's, 7 doctorates awarded. Terminal master's awarded for partial completion of doctoral program. *Degree requirements:* For master's, one foreign language, comprehensive exam (for some programs), thesis (for some programs), 1 standard-level language; exam (for MA); thesis (for MFA); for doctorate, variable foreign language requirement, comprehensive exam, thesis/dissertation, 2 standard-level languages/1 advanced-level language. *Entrance requirements:* For master's and doctorate, GRE General Test, minimum GPA of 3.2. Additional exam requirements/recommendations for international students: Required—TOEFL (minimum score 650 paper-based; 115 iBT); Recommended—IELTS (minimum score 9). *Application deadline:* For fall admission, 12/15 for domestic and international students. Application fee: $55 ($65 for international students). Electronic applications accepted. *Financial support:* In 2014–15, 54 students received support, including 17 fellowships with full tuition reimbursements available (averaging $15,000 per year), 34 teaching assistantships with full tuition reimbursements available (averaging $14,000 per year); health care benefits also available. Financial award application deadline: 12/15; financial award applicants required to submit FAFSA. *Faculty research:* Creative writing including poetics and modern poetry, fiction, and experimental forms; nineteenth and twentieth century British and American literature; American Studies, the American west, and environmental studies; critical theory and practice; race and gender studies. *Total annual research expenditures:* $126,500. *Unit head:* Prof. Barry L. Weller, Department Chair, 801-581-6168, E-mail: barry.weller@utah.edu. *Application contact:* Prof. Howard Horwitz, Director of Graduate Studies, 801-581-7353, E-mail: h.horwitz@english.utah.edu.
Website: http://www.hum.utah.edu/english/

University of Utah, Graduate School, College of Social and Behavioral Science, Department of Political Science, Program in Political Science, Salt Lake City, UT 84112. Offers American politics (MA, MS, PhD); comparative politics (MA, MS, PhD); international relations (MA, MS, PhD); political theory (MA, MS, PhD); public administration (MA, MS, PhD). *Faculty:* 32 full-time (7 women), 10 part-time/adjunct (3 women). *Students:* 67 full-time (25 women); includes 11 minority (1 Black or African American, non-Hispanic/Latino; 1 American Indian or Alaska Native, non-Hispanic/Latino; 4 Asian, non-Hispanic/Latino; 5 Two or more races, non-Hispanic/Latino), 9 international. Average age 34. 35 applicants, 71% accepted, 12 enrolled. In 2014, 6 master's, 6 doctorates awarded. Terminal master's awarded for partial completion of doctoral program. *Degree requirements:* For master's, variable foreign language requirement, thesis or research paper; for doctorate, comprehensive exam, thesis/dissertation. *Entrance requirements:* For master's and doctorate, GRE General Test, minimum GPA of 3.2. Additional exam requirements/recommendations for international students: Required—TOEFL (minimum score 580 paper-based; 61 iBT), IELTS (minimum score 6). *Application deadline:* For fall admission, 1/15 priority date for domestic and international students; for spring admission, 10/1 for domestic and international students. Application fee: $55 ($65 for international students). Electronic applications accepted. *Financial support:* In 2014–15, 4 students received support, including 2 fellowships with full tuition reimbursements available (averaging $15,250 per year), 14 teaching assistantships with full tuition reimbursements available (averaging $13,750 per year); career-related internships or fieldwork, scholarships/grants, health care benefits, and unspecified assistantships also available. Financial award application deadline: 1/15; financial award applicants required to submit FAFSA. *Faculty research:* International politics, comparative politics, political theory, American politics, public administration. *Total annual research expenditures:* $24,651. *Unit head:* Brent Steele, Chair, 801-587-7754, Fax: 801-585-6492, E-mail: brent.steele@utah.edu. *Application contact:* Mary Ann Underwood, Graduate Coordinator/Advisor, 801-581-8608, Fax: 801-585-6492, E-mail: maryann.underwood@poli-sci.utah.edu.
Website: http://www.poli-sci.utah.edu/

University of Wisconsin–Madison, Graduate School, College of Letters and Science, Department of History, Madison, WI 53706-1380. Offers African history (MA, PhD); Central Asian history (MA, PhD); comparative world history (MA, PhD); East Asian history (MA, PhD); European history (MA, PhD); gender and women's history (MA, PhD); Latin American and Caribbean history (MA, PhD); Middle Eastern history (MA, PhD); South Asian history (MA, PhD); Southeast Asian history (MA, PhD); United States history (MA, PhD). Terminal master's awarded for partial completion of doctoral program. *Degree requirements:* For master's, thesis (for some programs); for doctorate, variable foreign language requirement, thesis/dissertation. *Entrance requirements:* For master's and doctorate, GRE General Test. Additional exam requirements/recommendations for international students: Required—Michigan English Language Assessment Battery or TOEFL. Electronic applications accepted. *Expenses:* Tuition, state resident: full-time $10,723; part-time $745 per credit. Tuition, nonresident: full-time $24,054; part-time $1578 per credit. *Required fees:* $374 per semester. Tuition and fees vary according to course load, program and reciprocity agreements. *Faculty research:* American, African, European, Asian, Latin American, and Middle Eastern history.

University of Wyoming, College of Arts and Sciences, American Studies Program, Laramie, WY 82071. Offers MA. Part-time programs available. *Degree requirements:* For master's, thesis optional. *Entrance requirements:* For master's, GRE General Test, minimum GPA of 3.0. *Faculty research:* Material culture, American culture, ethnicity, cultural environments, public culture.

Utah State University, School of Graduate Studies, College of Humanities, Arts and Social Sciences, Department of English and Department of History, Program in American Studies, Logan, UT 84322. Offers folklore (MA, MS); western American literature and culture (MA, MS). Part-time and evening/weekend programs available. *Degree requirements:* For master's, thesis or alternative. *Entrance requirements:* For master's, GRE General Test or MAT, minimum GPA of 3.0, 3 letters of recommendation, writing sample. Additional exam requirements/recommendations for international students: Required—TOEFL. *Faculty research:* Folklore and folklife, American culture, regional studies, material culture, Jewish folklore, Native American folklore.

Villanova University, Graduate School of Liberal Arts and Sciences, Program in Liberal Studies, Villanova, PA 19085. Offers American studies (Certificate); ancient worlds (Certificate); great books (Certificate); interdisciplinary studies (Post-Master's Certificate); liberal studies (MA); peace and justice studies (Certificate). Part-time and

evening/weekend programs available. *Faculty:* 4. *Students:* 10 full-time (7 women), 7 part-time (3 women); includes 1 minority (Black or African American, non-Hispanic/Latino), 3 international. Average age 36. 3 applicants, 100% accepted, 1 enrolled. In 2014, 6 master's awarded. *Degree requirements:* For master's, comprehensive exam. *Entrance requirements:* For master's, statement of goals, 2 recommendation letters. Additional exam requirements/recommendations for international students: Required—TOEFL. *Application deadline:* For fall admission, 3/1 for domestic students, 5/1 for international students; for spring admission, 11/15 for domestic students, 10/15 for international students; for summer admission, 5/1 for domestic students. Applications are processed on a rolling basis. Application fee: $50. Electronic applications accepted. *Financial support:* Research assistantships, scholarships/grants, and unspecified assistantships available. Financial award applicants required to submit FAFSA. *Unit head:* Dr. Marylu Hill, Director, Villanova Center for Liberal Education, 610-519-6936, E-mail: marylu.hill@villanova.edu. *Application contact:* Dean, Graduate School of Liberal Arts and Sciences.
Website: http://www1.villanova.edu/villanova/artsci/liberalstudies.html

Washington State University, College of Liberal Arts, Program in American Studies, Pullman, WA 99164-4010. Offers MA, PhD. Program applications must be made through the Pullman campus. Part-time programs available. *Students:* 15 full-time (8 women), 4 part-time (2 women); includes 10 minority (1 Black or African American, non-Hispanic/Latino; 2 Asian, non-Hispanic/Latino; 6 Hispanic/Latino; 1 Two or more races, non-Hispanic/Latino), 1 international. Average age 34. 43 applicants, 23% accepted, 6 enrolled. In 2014, 4 doctorates awarded. *Degree requirements:* For master's, one foreign language, comprehensive exam, thesis optional, oral exam; for doctorate, one foreign language, comprehensive exam, thesis/dissertation, oral exam. *Entrance requirements:* For master's and doctorate, official college transcripts sent directly from each institution attended, 3-5 page statement of purpose describing areas of interest, minimum GPA of 3.0, writing sample, 3 letters of recommendation. Additional exam requirements/recommendations for international students: Required—TOEFL. *Application deadline:* For fall admission, 1/10 priority date for domestic and international students; for spring admission, 7/1 for domestic and international students. Application fee: $75. *Expenses:* Tuition, state resident: full-time $11,768. Tuition, nonresident: full-time $25,200. *Required fees:* $960. Tuition and fees vary according to program. *Financial support:* In 2014–15, 2 research assistantships (averaging $14,198 per year), 12 teaching assistantships with full and partial tuition reimbursements (averaging $14,129 per year) were awarded; career-related internships or fieldwork, Federal Work-Study, institutionally sponsored loans, health care benefits, and tuition waivers (partial) also available. Financial award application deadline: 2/15; financial award applicants required to submit FAFSA. *Unit head:* Dr. Lisa Guerrero, Director, 509-335*4182, E-mail: laguerre@wsu.edu. *Application contact:* Rose Smetana, Academic Coordinator, 509-335-0012, E-mail: rsmetana@wsu.edu.
Website: http://libarts.wsu.edu/ccgrs/graduate/index.asp

Wayne State University, College of Liberal Arts and Sciences, Department of History, Detroit, MI 48202. Offers Africa (PhD); America (PhD); archival administration (Graduate Certificate); Europe (PhD); gender (PhD); history (MA); labor (PhD); science and technology (PhD); world history (PhD, Graduate Certificate); JD/MA; M Ed/MA; MLIS/MA. Doctoral programs admit for fall only. Evening/weekend programs available. *Faculty:* 22 full-time (9 women). *Students:* 32 full-time (14 women), 16 part-time (6 women); includes 4 minority (2 Black or African American, non-Hispanic/Latino; 2 Two or more races, non-Hispanic/Latino). Average age 39. 52 applicants, 37% accepted, 9 enrolled. In 2014, 5 master's awarded. *Degree requirements:* For master's, one foreign language, thesis (for some programs), final oral exam on thesis or essay and seminar; for doctorate, variable foreign language requirement, thesis/dissertation, qualifying exam in 4 fields of history. *Entrance requirements:* For master's, GRE General Test, minimum undergraduate GPA of 3.25 in history, 3.0 overall; at least 18 credits in history and related subjects at the advanced undergraduate level; foreign language; letter of intent; research paper; at least two letters of recommendation from former instructors;

for doctorate, GRE General Test, minimum GPA of 3.0; letter of intent; research paper; at least three letters of recommendation from former professors; for Graduate Certificate, baccalaureate degree from accredited college or university; minimum GPA of 3.0, 3.25 in a minimum of eighteen semester credits in history and related subjects at the advanced undergraduate level. Additional exam requirements/recommendations for international students: Required—TOEFL (minimum score 550 paper-based; 79 iBT), TWE (minimum score 5.5), Michigan English Language Assessment Battery (minimum score 85); Recommended—IELTS (minimum score 6.5). *Application deadline:* For fall admission, 2/1 for domestic and international students; for winter admission, 11/1 for domestic students, 10/1 priority date for international students; for spring admission, 3/15 for domestic students, 1/1 priority date for international students. Applications are processed on a rolling basis. Application fee: $0. Electronic applications accepted. *Expenses:* Tuition, state resident: full-time $10,294; part-time $571.90 per credit hour. Tuition, nonresident: full-time $29,730; part-time $1238.75 per credit hour. *Required fees:* $1365; $43.50 per credit hour. $291.10 per semester. Tuition and fees vary according to course load and program. *Financial support:* In 2014–15, 19 students received support, including 1 fellowship with tuition reimbursement available (averaging $16,000 per year), 1 research assistantship with tuition reimbursement available (averaging $17,994 per year), 6 teaching assistantships with tuition reimbursements available (averaging $16,838 per year); scholarships/grants, health care benefits, and unspecified assistantships also available. Financial award application deadline: 3/31; financial award applicants required to submit FAFSA. *Faculty research:* Labor and working class history, urban history, citizenship and politics, gender and women's history. *Unit head:* Dr. Marc W. Kruman, Chair, 313-577-2525, Fax: 313-577-6987, E-mail: mkruman@wayne.edu. *Application contact:* Dr. Gayle McCreedy, Academic Service Officer, 313-577-2592, Fax: 313-577-6987, E-mail: g.mccreedy@wayne.edu.
Website: http://clas.wayne.edu/history/

West Virginia University, Eberly College of Arts and Sciences, Department of History, Morgantown, WV 26506. Offers African history (MA, PhD); African-American history (MA, PhD); American history (MA, PhD); Appalachian/regional history (MA, PhD); East Asian history (MA, PhD); European history (MA, PhD); history of science and technology (MA, PhD); Latin American history (MA). Part-time programs available. *Degree requirements:* For master's, one foreign language, thesis (for some programs), oral exam, thesis defense; for doctorate, one foreign language, comprehensive exam, thesis/dissertation, dissertation defense. *Entrance requirements:* For master's, GRE General Test, minimum GPA of 3.0; for doctorate, GRE General Test. Additional exam requirements/recommendations for international students: Required—TOEFL (minimum score 550 paper-based), IELTS (minimum score 6.5). Electronic applications accepted. *Faculty research:* United States, Appalachia, modern Europe, Africa, colonial and post-colonial societies.

Wilfrid Laurier University, Faculty of Graduate and Postdoctoral Studies, Faculty of Arts, Department of Religion and Culture, Waterloo, ON N2L 3C5, Canada. Offers religion and culture (MA); religious diversity of North America (PhD). Part-time programs available. *Degree requirements:* For master's, thesis optional; for doctorate, thesis/dissertation. *Entrance requirements:* For master's, honors BA or the equivalent in religious studies or other interdisciplinary social science or humanities program, minimum B average in overall undergraduate course work, B+ average in the undergraduate major; for doctorate, MA in religious studies, minimum A- average. Additional exam requirements/recommendations for international students: Required—TOEFL (minimum score 89 iBT). Electronic applications accepted. *Faculty research:* Religious diversity in North America.

Yale University, Graduate School of Arts and Sciences, Interdisciplinary Program in American Studies, New Haven, CT 06520. Offers PhD. *Degree requirements:* For doctorate, one foreign language, thesis/dissertation. *Entrance requirements:* For doctorate, GRE General Test.

Asian-American Studies

Binghamton University, State University of New York, Graduate School, School of Arts and Sciences, Department of Asian and Asian American Studies, Vestal, NY 13850. Offers MA, Certificate. *Faculty:* 19 full-time (10 women), 11 part-time/adjunct (8 women). *Students:* 12 full-time (10 women), 2 part-time (1 woman), 12 international. Average age 25. 23 applicants, 65% accepted, 7 enrolled. In 2014, 1 other advanced degree awarded. *Degree requirements:* For master's, variable foreign language requirement, comprehensive exam (for some programs), thesis (for some programs). *Entrance requirements:* For master's, GRE General Test, writing sample. Additional exam requirements/recommendations for international students: Required—TOEFL (minimum score 80 iBT). *Expenses:* Tuition, state resident: full-time $7776; part-time $432 per credit. Tuition, nonresident: full-time $15,138; part-time $841 per credit. *Required fees:* $1754; $213 per credit. Tuition and fees vary according to degree level and program. *Unit head:* Prof. David Stahl, Chair, 607-777-4938, E-mail: dstahl@binghamton.edu. *Application contact:* Kishan Zuber, Recruiting and Admissions Coordinator, 607-777-2151, Fax: 607-777-2501, E-mail: kzuber@binghamton.edu.
Website: http://www.binghamton.edu/aaas/

California State University, Long Beach, Graduate Studies, College of Liberal Arts, Department of Asian and Asian American Studies, Long Beach, CA 90840. Offers Asian studies (MA). Part-time programs available. *Degree requirements:* For master's, one

foreign language, comprehensive exam or thesis. Electronic applications accepted. *Faculty research:* South Asia, China, Japan, Southeast Asia, Asian-Americans in the U.S.

San Francisco State University, Division of Graduate Studies, College of Ethnic Studies, Program in Asian American Studies, San Francisco, CA 94132-1722. Offers MA. *Expenses:* Tuition, state resident: full-time $6738. Tuition, nonresident: full-time $17,898; part-time $372 per credit hour. *Required fees:* $498 per semester. *Unit head:* Dr. Grace J. Yoo, Chair, 415-338-2699, E-mail: aas@sfsu.edu. *Application contact:* Dr. Allyson Tintiangco-Cubales, Coordinator, 415-338-2698, E-mail: aas@sfsu.edu.
Website: http://aas.sfsu.edu/

University of California, Los Angeles, Graduate Division, College of Letters and Science, Program in Asian-American Studies, Los Angeles, CA 90095. Offers MA, MA/MPH, MA/MSW. *Degree requirements:* For master's, one foreign language, comprehensive exam or thesis. *Entrance requirements:* For master's, bachelor's degree; minimum undergraduate GPA of 3.0 (or its equivalent if letter grade system not used); paper or article preferably on Asian Americans. Additional exam requirements/recommendations for international students: Required—TOEFL. Electronic applications accepted.

Asian Studies

Binghamton University, State University of New York, Graduate School, School of Arts and Sciences, Department of Asian and Asian American Studies, Vestal, NY 13850. Offers MA, Certificate. *Faculty:* 19 full-time (10 women), 11 part-time/adjunct (8 women). *Students:* 12 full-time (10 women), 2 part-time (1 woman), 12 international. Average age 25. 23 applicants, 65% accepted, 7 enrolled. In 2014, 1 other advanced degree awarded. *Degree requirements:* For master's, variable foreign language requirement, comprehensive exam (for some programs), thesis (for some programs).

Entrance requirements: For master's, GRE General Test, writing sample. Additional exam requirements/recommendations for international students: Required—TOEFL (minimum score 80 iBT). *Expenses:* Tuition, state resident: full-time $7776; part-time $432 per credit. Tuition, nonresident: full-time $15,138; part-time $841 per credit. *Required fees:* $1754; $213 per credit. Tuition and fees vary according to degree level and program. *Unit head:* Prof. David Stahl, Chair, 607-777-4938, E-mail: dstahl@binghamton.edu. *Application contact:* Kishan Zuber, Recruiting and Admissions

Asian Studies

Coordinator, 607-777-2151, Fax: 607-777-2501, E-mail: kzuber@binghamton.edu.
Website: http://www.binghamton.edu/aaas/

Brown University, Graduate School, Department of Egyptology and Ancient Western Asian Studies, Providence, RI 02912. Offers ancient western Asian studies (PhD); Egyptology (PhD); history of the exact sciences in antiquity (PhD). *Degree requirements:* For doctorate, 2 foreign languages, comprehensive exam, thesis/dissertation. *Entrance requirements:* For doctorate, GRE General Test.

Brown University, Graduate School, Department of Religious Studies, Providence, RI 02912. Offers Asian religious traditions (PhD); religion and critical thought (PhD); religions of the ancient Mediterranean (PhD). *Degree requirements:* For doctorate, 2 foreign languages, thesis/dissertation. *Entrance requirements:* For doctorate, GRE General Test.

California Institute of Integral Studies, School of Consciousness and Transformation, San Francisco, CA 94103. Offers anthropology and social change (MA, PhD); creative inquiry/interdisciplinary arts (MFA); East-West psychology (MA, PhD); philosophy and religion (MA, PhD), including Asian and comparative studies, ecology, spirituality, and religion, philosophy, cosmology, and consciousness, women's spirituality; transformative leadership (MA); transformative studies (PhD); writing and consciousness (MFA). Part-time and evening/weekend programs available. Postbaccalaureate distance learning degree programs offered (no on-campus study). *Students:* 385 full-time (256 women), 102 part-time (71 women); includes 124 minority (31 Black or African American, non-Hispanic/Latino; 3 American Indian or Alaska Native, non-Hispanic/Latino; 19 Asian, non-Hispanic/Latino; 39 Hispanic/Latino; 1 Native Hawaiian or other Pacific Islander, non-Hispanic/Latino; 31 Two or more races, non-Hispanic/Latino), 53 international. Average age 43. 196 applicants, 92% accepted, 125 enrolled. In 2014, 75 master's, 41 doctorates awarded. Terminal master's awarded for partial completion of doctoral program. *Degree requirements:* For master's, thesis optional; for doctorate, comprehensive exam, thesis/dissertation, 1 foreign language (for Asian comparative studies). *Entrance requirements:* For master's, minimum GPA of 3.0, letters of recommendation, writing sample; for doctorate, master's degree, minimum GPA of 3.0, letters of recommendation, writing sample. Additional exam requirements/recommendations for international students: Required—TOEFL. *Application deadline:* For fall admission, 2/1 priority date for domestic and international students; for spring admission, 10/15 priority date for domestic and international students. Applications are processed on a rolling basis. Application fee: $65. Electronic applications accepted. *Expenses: Tuition:* Full-time $18,270; part-time $1015 per credit. *Required fees:* $85 per semester hour. *Financial support:* In 2014–15, 445 students received support, including 5 research assistantships (averaging $800 per year), 28 teaching assistantships (averaging $825 per year); career-related internships or fieldwork, Federal Work-Study, and scholarships/grants also available. Support available to part-time students. Financial award application deadline: 4/15; financial award applicants required to submit FAFSA. *Faculty research:* Ecology and sustainability, philosophy and religion, East-West psychology, integrative health, social and cultural anthropology, transformative leadership. *Application contact:* David Townes, Senior Admissions Counselor, 415-575-6152, Fax: 415-575-1268, E-mail: admissions@ciis.edu.
Website: http://www.ciis.edu/

California State University, Long Beach, Graduate Studies, College of Liberal Arts, Department of Asian and Asian American Studies, Long Beach, CA 90840. Offers Asian studies (MA). Part-time programs available. *Degree requirements:* For master's, one foreign language, comprehensive exam or thesis. Electronic applications accepted. *Faculty research:* South Asia, China, Japan, Southeast Asia, Asian-Americans in the U.S.

California State University, Long Beach, Graduate Studies, College of Liberal Arts, Department of History, Long Beach, CA 90840. Offers Africa and the Middle East (MA); ancient/medieval Europe (MA); Asia (MA); Latin America (MA); modern Europe (MA); United States (MA); world history (MA). Part-time and evening/weekend programs available. *Degree requirements:* For master's, one foreign language, comprehensive exam or thesis. Electronic applications accepted. *Faculty research:* All periods of European and American history, recent Asian and African history.

Columbia University, Graduate School of Arts and Sciences, New York, NY 10027. Offers African-American studies (MA); American studies (MA); anthropology (MA, PhD); art history and archaeology (MA, PhD); astronomy (PhD); biological sciences (PhD); biotechnology (MA); chemical physics (PhD); chemistry (PhD); classical studies (MA, PhD); classics (MA, PhD); climate and society (MA); earth and environmental sciences (PhD); East Asia: regional studies (MA); East Asian languages and cultures (MA, PhD); ecology, evolution and environmental biology (MA), including conservation biology; ecology, evolution, and environmental biology (PhD), including ecology and evolutionary biology, evolutionary primatology; economics (PhD); English and comparative literature (MA, PhD); French and Romance philology (MA, PhD); Germanic languages (MA, PhD); global French studies (MA); Hispanic cultural studies (MA); history (PhD); history and literature (MA); human rights studies (MA); Islamic studies (MA); Italian (MA, PhD); Japanese pedagogy (MA); Jewish studies (MA); Latin America and the Caribbean: regional studies (MA); Latin American and Iberian cultures (PhD); mathematics (MA, PhD), including finance (MA); medieval and Renaissance studies (MA); Middle Eastern, South Asian, and African studies (MA, PhD); modern art: critical and curatorial studies (MA); modern European studies (MA); museum anthropology (MA); music (DMA, PhD); oral history (MA); philosophical foundations of physics (MA); philosophy (MA, PhD); physics (PhD); political science (MA, PhD); psychology (PhD); quantitative methods in the social sciences (MA); religion (MA, PhD); Russia, Eurasia and East Europe: regional studies (MA); Russian translation (MA); Slavic cultures (MA); Slavic languages (MA, PhD); sociology (MA, PhD); South Asian studies (MA); statistics (MA, PhD); theatre (PhD); JD/PhD; MA/MS; MD/PhD; MPA/MA. Dual-degree programs require admission to both Graduate School of Arts and Sciences and another Columbia school. Part-time and evening/weekend programs available. Terminal master's awarded for partial completion of doctoral program. *Degree requirements:* For master's, thesis (for some programs); for doctorate, comprehensive exam, thesis/dissertation. *Entrance requirements:* For master's and doctorate, GRE General Test, GRE Subject Test (for some programs). Electronic applications accepted. *Faculty research:* Humanities, natural sciences, social sciences.

Columbia University, School of International and Public Affairs, Weatherhead East Asian Institute, New York, NY 10027. Offers Asian studies (Certificate). Students must be enrolled in a separate graduate degree program at Columbia University. *Entrance requirements:* For degree, proficiency in East Asian language. Electronic applications accepted.

Columbia University, South Asia Institute, New York, NY 10027. Offers MA, Certificate. Students must be enrolled in a separate graduate degree program at Columbia University. Electronic applications accepted.

Cornell University, Graduate School, Graduate Fields of Arts and Sciences, Field of Asian Literature, Religion and Culture, Ithaca, NY 14853-0001. Offers Asian religions (MA, PhD); Chinese philosophy (PhD); classical Chinese literature (PhD); classical Japanese literature (PhD); East Asian literature and culture (PhD); Korean literature (PhD); modern Chinese literature (PhD); modern Japanese literature (PhD); South Asian literature and culture (PhD); Southeast Asian literature and culture (PhD). *Degree requirements:* For doctorate, comprehensive exam, thesis/dissertation. *Entrance requirements:* For doctorate, GRE General Test, academic writing sample, 3 letters of recommendation. Additional exam requirements/recommendations for international students: Required—TOEFL (minimum score 600 paper-based; 77 iBT). Electronic applications accepted.

Cornell University, Graduate School, Graduate Fields of Arts and Sciences, Field of Asian Studies, Ithaca, NY 14853-0001. Offers East Asian linguistics (MA); East Asian studies (MA); South Asian linguistics (MA); South Asian studies (MA); Southeast Asian linguistics (MA); Southeast Asian studies (MA). *Degree requirements:* For master's, one foreign language, thesis. *Entrance requirements:* For master's, GRE General Test, 3 letters of recommendation. Additional exam requirements/recommendations for international students: Required—TOEFL (minimum score 550 paper-based; 77 iBT). Electronic applications accepted. *Faculty research:* East Asian studies, South Asian studies, Southeast Asian studies.

Cornell University, Graduate School, Graduate Fields of Arts and Sciences, Field of History, Ithaca, NY 14853-0001. Offers African history (MA, PhD); American history (MA, PhD); ancient Greek history (PhD); ancient history (MA, PhD); ancient Roman history (PhD); early modern European history (MA, PhD); English history (MA, PhD); French history (MA, PhD); German history (MA, PhD); history of science (MA, PhD); Korean history (PhD); Latin American history (MA, PhD); medieval Chinese history (MA, PhD); medieval history (MA, PhD); modern Chinese history (MA, PhD); modern European history (MA, PhD); modern Japanese history (MA, PhD); modern Middle Eastern history (PhD); premodern Islamic history (MA, PhD); premodern Japanese history (MA, PhD); Renaissance history (MA, PhD); Russian history (MA, PhD); South Asian history (PhD); Southeast Asian history (MA, PhD). Terminal master's awarded for partial completion of doctoral program. *Degree requirements:* For master's, thesis; for doctorate, 2 foreign languages, comprehensive exam, thesis/dissertation, 1 year of teaching experience. *Entrance requirements:* For master's and doctorate, GRE General Test, writing sample, 3 letters of recommendation. Additional exam requirements/recommendations for international students: Required—TOEFL (minimum score 550 paper-based; 77 iBT). Electronic applications accepted.

Cornell University, Graduate School, Graduate Fields of Arts and Sciences, Field of History of Art, Archaeology and Visual Studies, Ithaca, NY 14853. Offers 19th century art (PhD); African, African American and African diaspora (PhD); American art (PhD); ancient art and archaeology (PhD); Asian American art (PhD); Baroque art (PhD); comparative modernities (PhD); digital art (PhD); East Asian art (PhD); history of photography (PhD); Islamic art (PhD); Latin American art (PhD); medieval art (PhD); modern art (PhD); Renaissance art (PhD); Southeast Asian art (PhD); theory and criticism (PhD); visual studies (PhD). *Degree requirements:* For doctorate, one foreign language, comprehensive exam, thesis/dissertation, general exams in 3 areas. *Entrance requirements:* For doctorate, GRE General Test, sample of written work, 3 letters of recommendation. Additional exam requirements/recommendations for international students: Required—TOEFL (minimum score 550 paper-based; 77 iBT). Electronic applications accepted.

Cornell University, Graduate School, Graduate Fields of Arts and Sciences, Field of Linguistics, Ithaca, NY 14853-0001. Offers applied linguistics (MA, PhD); East Asian linguistics (MA, PhD); English linguistics (MA, PhD); general linguistics (MA, PhD); Germanic linguistics (MA, PhD); Indo-European linguistics (MA, PhD); phonetics (MA, PhD); phonological theory (MA, PhD); Romance linguistics (MA, PhD); second language acquisition (MA, PhD); semantics (MA, PhD); Slavic linguistics (MA, PhD); sociolinguistics (MA, PhD); South Asian linguistics (MA, PhD); Southeast Asian linguistics (MA, PhD); syntactic theory (MA, PhD). Terminal master's awarded for partial completion of doctoral program. *Degree requirements:* For master's, one foreign language, thesis; for doctorate, one foreign language, comprehensive exam, thesis/dissertation. *Entrance requirements:* For master's and doctorate, GRE General Test, 2 letters of recommendation. Additional exam requirements/recommendations for international students: Required—TOEFL (minimum score 600 paper-based; 77 iBT). Electronic applications accepted. *Faculty research:* Phonology and phonetics, syntax and semantics, historical linguistics, philosophy of language, language acquisition.

Creighton University, Graduate School, College of Arts and Sciences, Program in East-West Studies, Omaha, NE 68178-0001. Offers MA. Part-time programs available. *Faculty:* 2 full-time (1 woman), 1 part-time/adjunct (0 women). *Students:* 5 full-time (2 women), 2 part-time (0 women); includes 1 minority (Black or African American, non-Hispanic/Latino), 2 international. Average age 34. 6 applicants, 83% accepted, 4 enrolled. *Degree requirements:* For master's, one foreign language. *Entrance requirements:* For master's, 3 recommendations; personal essay; interview. Additional exam requirements/recommendations for international students: Required—TOEFL. *Application deadline:* For fall admission, 7/1 for domestic and international students; for summer admission, 5/1 for domestic and international students. Application fee: $50. Electronic applications accepted. *Expenses:* Expenses: $40,000 tuition; $1,564 full-time fees per year, $306 part-time. *Financial support:* Application deadline: 5/1; applicants required to submit FAFSA. *Unit head:* Dr. Jinmei Yuan, Associate Professor, 402-280-3309, E-mail: jinmeiyuan@creighton.edu. *Application contact:* Lindsay Johnson, Director of Graduate and Adult Recruitment, 402-280-2703, Fax: 402-280-2423, E-mail: gradschool@creighton.edu.

Dallas Baptist University, Gary Cook School of Leadership, Program in Global Leadership, Dallas, TX 75211-9299. Offers business communication (MA); East Asian studies (MA); ESL (MA); general studies (MA); global leadership (MA); global studies (MA); international business (MA); leading the nonprofit organization (MA); missions (MA); small group ministry (MA); MA/MA. Part-time and evening/weekend programs available. *Entrance requirements:* For master's, minimum GPA of 3.0. Additional exam requirements/recommendations for international students: Required—TOEFL, IELTS. *Expenses: Tuition:* Full-time $14,130; part-time $785 per credit hour. *Required fees:* $200 per semester. Tuition and fees vary according to course level and course load.

Dallas Baptist University, Liberal Arts Program, Dallas, TX 75211-9299. Offers arts (MLA); Christian ministry (MLA); East Asian studies (MLA); English (MLA); English as a second language (MLA); fine arts (MLA); history (MLA); missions (MLA); political science (MLA). Part-time and evening/weekend programs available. *Entrance requirements:* For master's, minimum GPA of 3.0. Additional exam requirements/recommendations for international students: Required—TOEFL. Electronic applications accepted. *Expenses: Tuition:* Full-time $14,130; part-time $785 per credit hour. *Required fees:* $200 per semester. Tuition and fees vary according to course level and course load. *Faculty research:* Milton and seventeenth-century Puritans, inter-Biblical years, nineteenth-century literature, Latin American and Texas history.

Duke University, Graduate School, Department of East Asian Studies, Durham, NC 27708. Offers AM, Certificate. Part-time programs available. *Entrance requirements:* For master's, GRE General Test. Additional exam requirements/recommendations for international students: Required—TOEFL (minimum score 577 paper-based; 90 iBT) or IELTS (minimum score 7). Electronic applications accepted. *Expenses: Tuition:* Full-time $45,760; part-time $2765 per credit. *Required fees:* $978. Full-time tuition and fees vary according to program.

Florida International University, College of Arts and Sciences, Program in Asian Studies, Miami, FL 33199. Offers MA, MA/PhD. Part-time and evening/weekend programs available. *Degree requirements:* For master's, thesis. *Entrance requirements:* For master's, minimum GPA of 3.0, letter of intent, letter of recommendation. Additional exam requirements/recommendations for international students: Required—TOEFL (minimum score 550 paper-based; 80 iBT). Electronic applications accepted.

Florida State University, The Graduate School, College of Social Sciences and Public Policy, Program in Asian Studies, Tallahassee, FL 32306-2161. Offers MA. Part-time programs available. *Faculty:* 3 full-time (all women), 5 part-time/adjunct (1 woman). *Students:* 6 full-time (2 women), 10 part-time (7 women); includes 11 minority (3 Black or African American, non-Hispanic/Latino; 7 Asian, non-Hispanic/Latino; 1 Hispanic/Latino). Average age 24. 11 applicants, 73% accepted, 3 enrolled. In 2014, 1 master's awarded. *Degree requirements:* For master's, one foreign language, comprehensive exam, thesis optional. *Entrance requirements:* For master's, GRE General Test, minimum GPA of 3.0. Additional exam requirements/recommendations for international students: Required—TOEFL (minimum score 550 paper-based; 80 iBT). *Application deadline:* For fall admission, 7/1 for domestic and international students; for spring admission, 11/1 for domestic and international students. Applications are processed on a rolling basis. Application fee: $30. Electronic applications accepted. *Expenses:* Tuition, state resident: part-time $403.51 per credit hour. Tuition, nonresident: part-time $1004.85 per credit hour. *Required fees:* $75.81 per credit hour. One-time fee: $20 part-time. Tuition and fees vary according to campus/location. *Financial support:* In 2014–15, 1 student received support, including 1 research assistantship with full tuition reimbursement available (averaging $5,000 per year); Federal Work-Study, institutionally sponsored loans, and unspecified assistantships also available. Financial award application deadline: 2/15; financial award applicants required to submit FAFSA. *Faculty research:* Art history of the Orient, Asian history and politics. *Unit head:* Dr. Lee K. Metcalf, Director, 850-644-7327, Fax: 850-645-4981, E-mail: lmetcalf@fsu.edu. *Application contact:* Kaley Boggs, Program Specialist, 850-644-4418, Fax: 850-644-4981, E-mail: kboggs@fsu.edu.
Website: http://www.fsu.edu/~asian/

Georgetown University, Graduate School of Arts and Sciences, Edmund A. Walsh School of Foreign Service, Program in Asian Studies, Washington, DC 20057. Offers MA. *Degree requirements:* For master's, comprehensive exam, research project. *Entrance requirements:* Additional exam requirements/recommendations for international students: Required—TOEFL.

The George Washington University, Elliott School of International Affairs, Program in Asian Studies, Washington, DC 20052. Offers MA. Part-time programs available. *Students:* 34 full-time (19 women), 6 part-time (3 women); includes 9 minority (6 Asian, non-Hispanic/Latino; 1 Hispanic/Latino; 2 Two or more races, non-Hispanic/Latino), 15 international. Average age 26. 85 applicants, 14 enrolled. In 2014, 6 master's awarded. *Degree requirements:* For master's, one foreign language, capstone project. *Entrance requirements:* For master's, GRE General Test, 2 years (or the equivalent) of an approved Asian language. Additional exam requirements/recommendations for international students: Required—TOEFL (minimum score 100 iBT), IELTS (minimum score 7). *Application deadline:* For fall admission, 1/15 priority date for domestic students; for spring admission, 10/1 for domestic students. Application fee: $75. Electronic applications accepted. *Financial support:* In 2014–15, 7 students received support. Fellowships with partial tuition reimbursements available and Federal Work-Study available. Financial award application deadline: 1/15; financial award applicants required to submit FAFSA. *Faculty research:* Sino-Soviet studies, Japanese-U.S. relations, Chinese foreign policy, economic development in China. *Unit head:* Prof. Daqing Yang, Director, 202-994-5886, Fax: 202-994-2484, E-mail: asia@gwu.edu. *Application contact:* Nicole A. Campbell, Director of Graduate Admissions, 202-994-7050, Fax: 202-994-9537, E-mail: esiagrad@gwu.edu.
Website: http://www.gwu.edu/graduate-programs/asian-studies

Harvard University, Graduate School of Arts and Sciences, Committee on Inner Asian and Altaic Studies, Cambridge, MA 02138. Offers PhD. *Degree requirements:* For doctorate, 2 foreign languages, thesis/dissertation, oral general exam. *Entrance requirements:* For doctorate, GRE General Test, proficiency in a related foreign language. Additional exam requirements/recommendations for international students: Required—TOEFL.

Harvard University, Graduate School of Arts and Sciences, Committee on Regional Studies–East Asia, Cambridge, MA 02138. Offers Chinese studies (AM); Japanese studies (AM); Korean studies (AM); Mongolian studies (AM); Vietnamese studies (AM). *Degree requirements:* For master's, one foreign language, seminar paper. *Entrance requirements:* For master's, GRE General Test. Additional exam requirements/recommendations for international students: Required—TOEFL.

Harvard University, Graduate School of Arts and Sciences, Department of Sanskrit and Indian Studies, Cambridge, MA 02138. Offers Indian philosophy (AM, PhD); Pali (AM, PhD); Sanskrit (AM, PhD); Tibetan (AM, PhD); Urdu (AM, PhD). Terminal master's awarded for partial completion of doctoral program. *Degree requirements:* For master's, 3 foreign languages; for doctorate, 3 foreign languages, thesis/dissertation. *Entrance requirements:* For master's, GRE General Test; for doctorate, GRE General Test, proficiency in French and German. Additional exam requirements/recommendations for international students: Required—TOEFL.

Indiana University Bloomington, University Graduate School, College of Arts and Sciences, School of Global and International Studies, Department of Central Eurasian Studies, Bloomington, IN 47405-7000. Offers MA, PhD. *Faculty:* 11 full-time (0 women). *Students:* 48 full-time (18 women), 1 part-time (0 women); includes 6 minority (1 Black or African American, non-Hispanic/Latino; 4 Asian, non-Hispanic/Latino; 1 Native Hawaiian or other Pacific Islander, non-Hispanic/Latino), 14 international. Average age 32. 26 applicants, 58% accepted, 5 enrolled. In 2014, 9 master's, 2 doctorates awarded. Terminal master's awarded for partial completion of doctoral program. *Degree requirements:* For master's, one foreign language, thesis; for doctorate, 2 foreign languages, thesis/dissertation, qualifying exams. *Entrance requirements:* For master's, minimum GPA of 3.0, 2 years of a foreign language; for doctorate, minimum GPA of 3.5, 1 research language. Additional exam requirements/recommendations for international students: Required—TOEFL. *Application deadline:* For fall admission, 1/15 priority date for domestic students, 12/1 for international students; for spring admission, 9/15 priority date for domestic students, 8/1 for international students. Applications are processed on a rolling basis. Application fee: $55 ($65 for international students). Electronic applications accepted. *Financial support:* Fellowships with full tuition reimbursements, research assistantships with full tuition reimbursements, teaching assistantships with full tuition reimbursements, and Federal Work-Study available. Financial award application deadline: 2/15. *Faculty research:* Central Asia, Hungarian civilization, Tibetan civilization, Turkish studies, Mongolian philology. *Unit head:* Dr. Jamsheed Choksy, Chair, 812-855-8643, E-mail: jchoksy@indiana.edu. *Application contact:* April Younger, Graduate Secretary, 812-855-2233, E-mail: ayounger@indiana.edu.
Website: http://www.indiana.edu/~ceus/

Indiana University Bloomington, University Graduate School, College of Arts and Sciences, School of Global and International Studies, Department of East Asian Languages and Cultures, Bloomington, IN 47408. Offers Chinese (MA, PhD); Chinese language pedagogy (MA); East Asian studies (MA); Japanese (MA, PhD); Japanese language pedagogy (MA). Part-time programs available. *Faculty:* 21 full-time (11 women), 14 part-time/adjunct (7 women). *Students:* 10 full-time (7 women), 20 part-time (12 women); includes 3 minority (2 Asian, non-Hispanic/Latino; 1 Hispanic/Latino), 15 international. 87 applicants, 31% accepted, 8 enrolled. In 2014, 5 master's awarded. *Degree requirements:* For master's, one foreign language, thesis; for doctorate, 2 foreign languages, comprehensive exam, thesis/dissertation. *Entrance requirements:* Additional exam requirements/recommendations for international students: Required—TOEFL (minimum score 93 iBT). *Application deadline:* For fall admission, 1/1 for domestic students, 12/1 for international students. Application fee: $55 ($65 for international students). Electronic applications accepted. *Financial support:* In 2014–15, 23 students received support, including fellowships with full tuition reimbursements available (averaging $18,000 per year), teaching assistantships with full tuition reimbursements available (averaging $15,750 per year). Financial award application deadline: 2/15. *Faculty research:* Modern East Asian history; politics and society; traditional Chinese thought and society; medieval and premodern Japanese history, literature and society; modern Chinese and Japanese film and literature; Chinese, Japanese, Korean language and linguistics. *Unit head:* Prof. Natsuko Tsujimura, Chair, 812-855-0856, Fax: 812-855-6402, E-mail: tsujimur@indiana.edu. *Application contact:* Stephen Thomas Johnson, Student Services Assistant, 812-856-4959, E-mail: johnsost@indiana.edu.
Website: http://www.indiana.edu/~ealc/index.shtml

Johns Hopkins University, Paul H. Nitze School of Advanced International Studies, Washington, DC 20036. Offers international development (MA, Certificate), including international economics (MA); international economics and finance (MA); international public policy (MIPP); international relations (PhD); international studies (Certificate); Japan studies (MA), including international economics; Korea studies (MA), including international economics; South Asia studies (MA), including international economics; Southeast Asia studies (MA), including international economics; JD/MA; MBA/MA; MHS/MA. Terminal master's awarded for partial completion of doctoral program. *Degree requirements:* For master's, 4-6 international economics courses, 5-6 functional or regional concentration courses, 2 core examinations, proficiency in language other than native language, capstone project; for doctorate, 2 foreign languages, thesis/dissertation, 3 comprehensive exams, economics, quantitative and qualitative course, dissertation prospectus and defense. *Entrance requirements:* For master's, GMAT or GRE General Test, previous course work in economics, foreign language, undergraduate degree; for doctorate, GRE General Test, master's degree. Additional exam requirements/recommendations for international students: Required—TOEFL (minimum score 600 paper-based; 100 iBT) or IELTS (minimum score 7). Electronic applications accepted. *Expenses:* Contact institution. *Faculty research:* Regional studies, international relations, international economics, energy and environment, international development.

Maharishi University of Management, Graduate Studies, Program in Maharishi Vedic Science, Fairfield, IA 52557. Offers MA, PhD. Evening/weekend programs available. *Degree requirements:* For master's, thesis; for doctorate, thesis/dissertation. *Entrance requirements:* For master's, minimum GPA of 3.0; for doctorate, GRE, minimum GPA of 3.0. Additional exam requirements/recommendations for international students: Required—TOEFL. *Faculty research:* Modern science and Vedic science, unification of knowledge, philosophy of science, Sanskrit.

McGill University, Faculty of Graduate and Postdoctoral Studies, Faculty of Arts, Department of East Asian Studies, Montréal, QC H3A 2T5, Canada. Offers MA, PhD.

New York University, Graduate School of Arts and Science, Department of East Asian Studies, New York, NY 10012-1019. Offers MA, PhD. Part-time programs available. *Students:* 13 full-time (7 women), 8 international. Average age 34. In 2014, 4 master's, 2 doctorates awarded. *Degree requirements:* For master's and doctorate, one foreign language. *Entrance requirements:* Additional exam requirements/recommendations for international students: Required—TOEFL. *Application deadline:* For fall admission, 1/4 for domestic and international students. Application fee: $100. Electronic applications accepted. *Financial support:* Fellowships with tuition reimbursements, teaching assistantships with tuition reimbursements, Federal Work-Study, institutionally sponsored loans, scholarships/grants, health care benefits, and unspecified assistantships available. Financial award application deadline: 1/4. *Unit head:* Eliot Borenstein, Acting Chair, 212-998-7620, Fax: 212-995-4682, E-mail: gsas.eas.graduate@nyu.edu. *Application contact:* Tom Looser, Director of Graduate Studies, 212-998-7620, Fax: 212-995-4682, E-mail: gsas.eas.graduate@nyu.edu.

The Ohio State University, Graduate School, East Asian Studies Center, Columbus, OH 43210. Offers MA. *Students:* 8 full-time (1 woman), 1 (woman) part-time; includes 1 minority (Hispanic/Latino), 2 international. Average age 25. In 2014, 2 master's awarded. *Degree requirements:* For master's, thesis optional. *Entrance requirements:* For master's, GRE General Test. Additional exam requirements/recommendations for international students: Required—TOEFL (minimum score 550 paper-based; 79 iBT), IELTS (minimum score 7). *Application deadline:* For fall admission, 12/13 priority date for domestic students, 11/30 priority date for international students; for spring admission, 12/1 for domestic students, 11/1 for international students; for summer admission, 5/15 for domestic students, 4/14 for international students. Applications are processed on a rolling basis. Application fee: $60 ($70 for international students). Electronic applications accepted. *Unit head:* Dr. Philip Brown, Professor, 614-292-0904, E-mail: brown.113@osu.edu. *Application contact:* Graduate and Professional Admissions, 614-292-9444, Fax: 614-292-3895, E-mail: gpadmissions@osu.edu.
Website: http://www.easc.osu.edu/

Ohio University, Graduate College, Center for International Studies, Program in Asian Studies, Athens, OH 45701-2979. Offers MA. Part-time programs available. *Degree requirements:* For master's, one foreign language, thesis optional. *Entrance requirements:* For master's, minimum GPA of 3.0. Additional exam requirements/recommendations for international students: Required—TOEFL (minimum score 550 paper-based; 80 iBT); Recommended—IELTS (minimum score 6.5). Electronic applications accepted. *Faculty research:* Indonesian and Malaysian political, history, literature, media, Islam, and environmental problems.

Princeton University, Graduate School, Department of East Asian Studies, Princeton, NJ 08544-1019. Offers PhD. *Degree requirements:* For doctorate, 2 foreign languages, thesis/dissertation. *Entrance requirements:* For doctorate, GRE General Test, fluency in Japanese and/or Chinese. Additional exam requirements/recommendations for international students: Required—TOEFL (minimum score 600 paper-based). Electronic applications accepted. *Faculty research:* Modern and classical Japanese literature, premodern Chinese and Japanese history, Chinese narrative and poetry.

Rutgers, The State University of New Jersey, New Brunswick, Graduate School-New Brunswick, Program in East Asian Languages and Cultures, Piscataway, NJ 08854-8097. Offers MA. *Degree requirements:* For master's, one foreign language, final exam. *Entrance requirements:* For master's, GRE, official transcripts, two letters of recommendation, personal statement, writing sample. Additional exam requirements/recommendations for international students: Required—TOEFL or IELTS.

Asian Studies

Rutgers, The State University of New Jersey, New Brunswick, Graduate School-New Brunswick, Program in History, Piscataway, NJ 08854-8097. Offers African-American history (PhD); early American history (PhD); early modern European history (PhD); east Asian history (PhD); global and comparative history (PhD); history (PhD); history of diplomacy and foreign relations (PhD); history of technology, environment and health (PhD); history of the Atlantic cultures and African diaspora (PhD); Latin American history (PhD); medieval history (PhD); modern European history (PhD); nineteenth and twentieth century American history (PhD); women's and gender history (PhD). *Degree requirements:* For doctorate, thesis/dissertation. *Entrance requirements:* For doctorate, GRE General Test, sample of written work. Electronic applications accepted. *Faculty research:* American history, European history, Afro-American history, women's history, Latin American history.

St. John's College, Graduate Institute in Liberal Education, Program in Eastern Classics, Santa Fe, NM 87505. Offers MA. Part-time and evening/weekend programs available. *Entrance requirements:* For master's, 2 letters of recommendation. Additional exam requirements/recommendations for international students: Required—TOEFL, TWE. *Expenses:* Contact institution.

St. John's University, St. John's College of Liberal Arts and Sciences, Institute of Asian Studies, Queens, NY 11439. Offers Asian studies (Adv C); Chinese studies (MA, Adv C); East Asian culture studies (Adv C); East Asian studies (MA). Part-time and evening/weekend programs available. *Students:* 8 full-time (5 women), 9 part-time (7 women); includes 6 minority (all Asian, non-Hispanic/Latino), 9 international. Average age 27. 13 applicants, 92% accepted, 3 enrolled. In 2014, 5 master's awarded. *Degree requirements:* For master's, one foreign language, comprehensive exam, thesis optional. *Entrance requirements:* For master's, 6 semester hours of course work in the field, minimum GPA of 3.0. Additional exam requirements/recommendations for international students: Required—TOEFL (minimum score 600 paper-based; 100 iBT), IELTS (minimum score 7). *Application deadline:* For fall admission, 5/1 priority date for domestic and international students; for spring admission, 11/1 priority date for domestic and international students. Applications are processed on a rolling basis. Application fee: $70. Electronic applications accepted. *Expenses: Tuition:* Full-time $20,610; part-time $1145 per credit. *Required fees:* $170 per semester. *Financial support:* Research assistantships and scholarships/grants available. Support available to part-time students. Financial award application deadline: 3/1; financial award applicants required to submit FAFSA. *Faculty research:* East Asian philosophy and religions; government and politics of East Asia; business and economy of East Asia; legal systems and trade relations of East Asian countries; Chinese, Japanese, and Korean languages and civilization; modern China, Japan, and Korea; Chinese, Japanese, and Korean art and history. *Unit head:* Dr. Bernadette Li, Director, 718-990-1657, E-mail: lib@stjohns.edu. *Application contact:* Robert Medrano, Director of Graduate Admission, 718-990-1601, Fax: 718-990-5686, E-mail: gradhelp@stjohns.edu.

San Diego State University, Graduate and Research Affairs, College of Arts and Letters, Center for Asian Studies, San Diego, CA 92182. Offers MA. *Degree requirements:* For master's, one foreign language, thesis. *Entrance requirements:* For master's, GRE General Test, 3 letters of reference, writing sample. Additional exam requirements/recommendations for international students: Required—TOEFL. Electronic applications accepted. *Faculty research:* Language acquisition process, social organization of Asia, economic development.

Seton Hall University, College of Arts and Sciences, Department of Asian Studies, South Orange, NJ 07079-2697. Offers Asian studies (MA). Part-time and evening/weekend programs available. *Faculty:* 5 full-time (2 women), 3 part-time/adjunct (2 women). *Students:* 14 full-time (9 women), 8 part-time (6 women); includes 1 minority (Black or African American, non-Hispanic/Latino), 13 international. Average age 28. 23 applicants, 78% accepted, 9 enrolled. In 2014, 17 master's awarded. *Degree requirements:* For master's, thesis optional. *Entrance requirements:* For master's, strong background in Asian studies or related discipline. Additional exam requirements/recommendations for international students: Required—TOEFL. *Application deadline:* For fall admission, 7/1 priority date for domestic and international students; for spring admission, 11/1 priority date for domestic and international students. Applications are processed on a rolling basis. Application fee: $75. Electronic applications accepted. *Financial support:* Teaching assistantships with full tuition reimbursements, career-related internships or fieldwork, Federal Work-Study, institutionally sponsored loans, and unspecified assistantships available. Financial award applicants required to submit FAFSA. *Faculty research:* Modern Chinese history, contemporary Chinese politics, ancient Chinese history, Hinduism, Asian business, Japanese history. *Unit head:* Dr. Frederick J. Booth, Chair, 973-761-9458, Fax: 973-761-9596, E-mail: frederick.booth@shu.edu. *Application contact:* Dr. Dongdong Chen, Director of Graduate Studies, 973-761-9465, Fax: 973-761-9596, E-mail: dongdong.chen@shu.edu.
Website: http://www.shu.edu/academics/artsci/languages-literatures-cultures/

Stanford University, School of Humanities and Sciences, Center for East Asian Studies, Stanford, CA 94305-9991. Offers MA. *Degree requirements:* For master's, one foreign language, thesis. *Entrance requirements:* For master's, GRE General Test. Additional exam requirements/recommendations for international students: Required—TOEFL. Electronic applications accepted. *Expenses: Tuition:* Full-time $44,184; part-time $982 per credit hour. *Required fees:* $191.

United Theological Seminary of the Twin Cities, Graduate Programs, New Brighton, MN 55112-2598. Offers advanced theological studies (Diploma); justice and peace studies (M Div, MA); leadership toward racial justice (M Div, MA, Certificate); Methodist studies (M Div, MA, Certificate); ministry (D Min); ministry renewal and professional development (Certificate); pastoral care and counseling (M Div, MA, MARL); religion and theology (MA); theological and religious studies (Certificate); theology and the arts (M Div, MA); urban ministry (M Div, MA, MARL); women's studies: religion, theology and ministry (M Div, MA). *Accreditation:* ACIPE; ATS. Part-time and evening/weekend programs available. *Degree requirements:* For master's, thesis; for doctorate, comprehensive exam, thesis/dissertation. *Entrance requirements:* For master's, minimum GPA of 2.75; strong analytical, reflective thinking and writing skills; vocational and academic goals compatible with those of Seminary; for doctorate, M Div or equivalent, minimum GPA of 3.0, 3 years experience in professional ministry; for other advanced degree, BA or equivalent life experience; strong analytical, reflective thinking and writing skills (Certificate); proficiency in English language, previous study of theology at a theological school, recommendation of student's denomination (Diploma). Additional exam requirements/recommendations for international students: Required—TOEFL (minimum score 550 paper-based).

University of Alberta, Faculty of Graduate Studies and Research, Department of East Asian Studies, Edmonton, AB T6G 2E1, Canada. Offers Chinese literature (MA); East Asian interdisciplinary studies (MA); Japanese literature (MA). Part-time programs available. *Degree requirements:* For master's, one foreign language, thesis. *Entrance requirements:* Additional exam requirements/recommendations for international students: Required—TOEFL. Electronic applications accepted. *Faculty research:* Classical Chinese poetry and poetics, Chinese philosophy, modern/contemporary Chinese literature, modern Japanese literature and culture, Japanese women's writing.

The University of Arizona, College of Humanities, Department of East Asian Studies, Tucson, AZ 85721. Offers MA, PhD. Part-time programs available. Terminal master's awarded for partial completion of doctoral program. *Degree requirements:* For master's, one foreign language; for doctorate, 2 foreign languages. *Entrance requirements:* For master's, GRE General Test, 2 letters of recommendation; for doctorate, GRE General Test, 2 letters of recommendation, statement of purpose, writing sample. Additional exam requirements/recommendations for international students: Required—TOEFL (minimum score 550 paper-based; 79 iBT). Electronic applications accepted. *Faculty research:* Chinese history; Chinese/Japanese linguistics, literature, and religion.

University of Bridgeport, College of Public and International Affairs, Bridgeport, CT 06604. Offers East Asian and Pacific Rim studies (MA); global development and peace (MA); global media and communication studies (MA). Part-time and evening/weekend programs available. *Degree requirements:* For master's, thesis. *Entrance requirements:* Additional exam requirements/recommendations for international students: Recommended—TOEFL (minimum score 550 paper-based; 80 iBT), IELTS (minimum score 6.5).

The University of British Columbia, Faculty of Arts, Department of Asian Studies, Vancouver, BC V6T 1Z2, Canada. Offers MA, PhD. *Degree requirements:* For master's, one foreign language, thesis; for doctorate, 2 foreign languages, thesis/dissertation. *Entrance requirements:* For master's, BA; for doctorate, master's degree in Asian studies or equivalent. Additional exam requirements/recommendations for international students: Required—TOEFL (minimum score 570 paper-based; 85 iBT). Electronic applications accepted. *Faculty research:* Language; linguistics; literature; religion and philosophy; premodern history of China, Japan, Korea, South and South East Asia.

The University of British Columbia, Institute of Asian Research, Vancouver, BC V6T 1Z2, Canada. Offers MAAPPS. *Degree requirements:* For master's, thesis optional. *Entrance requirements:* Additional exam requirements/recommendations for international students: Required—TOEFL (minimum score 600 paper-based; 100 iBT). Electronic applications accepted. *Faculty research:* Social cohesion, globalization, social safety nets, policy research, research and development alliances, knowledge-based workshops on Asia-Pacific studies.

University of California, Berkeley, Graduate Division, College of Letters and Science, Department of South and Southeast Asian Studies, Berkeley, CA 94720-1500. Offers Hindi (MA, PhD); Indonesian (MA, PhD); Sanskrit (MA, PhD); Tamil (MA, PhD). Terminal master's awarded for partial completion of doctoral program. *Degree requirements:* For master's, 2 foreign languages, thesis; for doctorate, 2 foreign languages, thesis/dissertation, oral qualifying exam. *Entrance requirements:* For master's and doctorate, GRE General Test, minimum GPA of 3.0, 3 letters of recommendation. Electronic applications accepted.

University of California, Berkeley, Graduate Division, College of Letters and Science, Group in Buddhist Studies, Berkeley, CA 94720-1500. Offers PhD. *Degree requirements:* For doctorate, 4 foreign languages, thesis/dissertation, dissertation defense, qualifying exam. *Entrance requirements:* For doctorate, GRE General Test, MA in Japanese, Chinese, or Sanskrit; minimum GPA of 3.0, 3 letters of recommendation. Electronic applications accepted.

University of California, Berkeley, Graduate Division, Program in International and Area Studies, Group in Asian Studies, Berkeley, CA 94720-1500. Offers Asian studies (PhD); East Asian studies (MA); Northeast Asian studies (MA); South Asian studies (MA); Southeast Asian studies (MA); JD/MA; MBA/MA; MJ/MA. *Degree requirements:* For master's, one foreign language, comprehensive exam or thesis; for doctorate, 2 foreign languages, thesis/dissertation, qualifying exam. *Entrance requirements:* For master's and doctorate, GRE General Test, minimum GPA of 3.0, 3 letters of recommendation.

University of California, Los Angeles, Graduate Division, College of Letters and Science, Department of Asian Languages and Cultures, Los Angeles, CA 90095. Offers MA, PhD. Terminal master's awarded for partial completion of doctoral program. *Degree requirements:* For master's, one foreign language, comprehensive exam or thesis; for doctorate, 2 foreign languages, thesis/dissertation, oral and written qualifying exams. *Entrance requirements:* For master's, GRE General Test, bachelor's degree; minimum undergraduate GPA of 3.0 (or its equivalent if letter grade system not used); writing sample; for doctorate, GRE General Test, master's degree; minimum undergraduate GPA of 3.0 (or its equivalent if letter grade system not used); writing sample. Additional exam requirements/recommendations for international students: Required—TOEFL. Electronic applications accepted.

University of California, Los Angeles, Graduate Division, International Institute, Interdepartmental Program in East Asian Studies, Los Angeles, CA 90095. Offers MA. *Degree requirements:* For master's, one foreign language, comprehensive exam. *Entrance requirements:* For master's, GRE General Test, bachelor's degree; minimum undergraduate GPA of 3.0 (or its equivalent if letter grade system not used). Additional exam requirements/recommendations for international students: Required—TOEFL. Electronic applications accepted.

University of California, Riverside, Graduate Division, Program in Southeast Asian Studies, Riverside, CA 92521. Offers MA. *Faculty:* 6 full-time (5 women). *Students:* 6 full-time (5 women); includes 2 minority (both Asian, non-Hispanic/Latino). Average age 28. 4 applicants, 75% accepted, 2 enrolled. In 2014, 1 master's awarded. *Degree requirements:* For master's, one foreign language, comprehensive exam, thesis, students choose either thesis or comprehensive exam option. *Entrance requirements:* For master's, GRE, statement of purpose to indicate serious interest in Southeast Asian Studies (or specific country or area in this region), writing sample. Additional exam requirements/recommendations for international students: Required—TOEFL, IELTS: no individual section score less than 6; Recommended—IELTS (minimum score 7). *Application deadline:* For fall admission, 1/5 priority date for domestic and international students; for winter admission, 11/15 for domestic students, 7/1 for international students; for spring admission, 3/1 for domestic students, 10/1 for international students. Applications are processed on a rolling basis. Application fee: $80 ($100 for international students). Electronic applications accepted. *Expenses:* Tuition, state resident: full-time $5399. Tuition, nonresident: full-time $10,433. *Financial support:* In 2014–15, 2 students received support, including 2 fellowships with full tuition reimbursements available (averaging $12,900 per year), teaching assistantships with full tuition reimbursements available (averaging $18,000 per year); unspecified assistantships also available. Financial award application deadline: 1/5; financial award applicants required to submit FAFSA. *Faculty research:* Southeast Asian texts, rituals and performance, music and technoculture, dance ethnography, ethnomusicology. *Unit head:* Dr. Mariam Beevi Lam, Director, 951-827-1391, Fax: 951-827-2237, E-mail: mariam.lam@ucr.edu. *Application contact:* Trina B. Elerts, Graduate Program Coordinator, 951-827-1584, Fax: 951-827-2237, E-mail: trina.elerts@ucr.edu.
Website: http://seatrip.ucr.edu/programs/grad.html

University of California, Santa Barbara, Graduate Division, College of Letters and Sciences, Division of Humanities and Fine Arts, Department of East Asian Languages and Cultural Studies, Santa Barbara, CA 93106-7075. Offers applied linguistics (PhD); East Asian languages and cultural studies (MA, PhD); translation studies (PhD). *Degree requirements:* For master's, one foreign language, comprehensive exam (for some

programs), thesis (for some programs); for doctorate, 2 foreign languages, thesis/dissertation, methodology. *Entrance requirements:* For master's and doctorate, GRE General Test. Additional exam requirements/recommendations for international students: Required—TOEFL (minimum score 550 paper-based; 80 iBT), IELTS (minimum score 7). Electronic applications accepted. *Faculty research:* Chinese literature, Chinese film, Japanese society, Japanese literature, East Asian cultural studies.

University of Chicago, Division of the Humanities, Department of East Asian Languages and Civilizations, Chicago, IL 60637. Offers PhD. *Students:* 36 full-time (20 women); includes 3 minority (all Asian, non-Hispanic/Latino), 19 international. 91 applicants, 18% accepted, 4 enrolled. Terminal master's awarded for partial completion of doctoral program. *Degree requirements:* For doctorate, 2 foreign languages, thesis/dissertation. *Entrance requirements:* For doctorate, GRE General Test. Additional exam requirements/recommendations for international students: Required—TOEFL (minimum score 104 iBT), IELTS (minimum score 7). *Application deadline:* For fall admission, 12/15 for domestic and international students. Application fee: $90. Electronic applications accepted. *Expenses:* Tuition: Full-time $46,899. *Required fees:* $347. *Financial support:* Fellowships with full tuition reimbursements, teaching assistantships with tuition reimbursements, Federal Work-Study, institutionally sponsored loans, scholarships/grants, traineeships, and health care benefits available. Financial award application deadline: 12/15; financial award applicants required to submit FAFSA. *Unit head:* Dr. Michael Bourdaghs, Chair, 773-702-1255. *Application contact:* Braden Grams, Assistant Dean of Students, Admissions and Fellowships, 773-702-1552, Fax: 773-834-9148, E-mail: humanitiesadmissions@uchicago.edu.
Website: http://ealc.uchicago.edu/

University of Chicago, Division of the Humanities, Department of South Asian Languages and Civilizations, Chicago, IL 60637. Offers South Asian languages and civilizations (PhD), including Bengali, Hindi, Sanskrit, Tamil, Urdu. *Students:* 27 full-time (17 women); includes 5 minority (1 Black or African American, non-Hispanic/Latino; 2 Asian, non-Hispanic/Latino; 2 Two or more races, non-Hispanic/Latino), 12 international. 39 applicants, 31% accepted, 3 enrolled. Terminal master's awarded for partial completion of doctoral program. *Degree requirements:* For doctorate, 2 foreign languages, thesis/dissertation. *Entrance requirements:* For doctorate, GRE General Test. Additional exam requirements/recommendations for international students: Required—TOEFL (minimum score 104 iBT), IELTS (minimum score 7). *Application deadline:* For fall admission, 12/15 for domestic and international students. Application fee: $90. Electronic applications accepted. *Expenses:* Tuition: Full-time $46,899. *Required fees:* $347. *Financial support:* Fellowships with full tuition reimbursements, teaching assistantships with full tuition reimbursements, Federal Work-Study, institutionally sponsored loans, scholarships/grants, and health care benefits available. Financial award application deadline: 12/15; financial award applicants required to submit FAFSA. *Unit head:* Dr. Ulrike Stark, Chair. *Application contact:* Braden Grams, Assistant Dean of Students, Admissions and Fellowships, 773-702-1552, Fax: 773-834-9148, E-mail: humanitiesadmissions@uchicago.edu.
Website: http://salc.uchicago.edu

University of Chicago, Division of the Humanities, Master of Arts Program in the Humanities, Chicago, IL 60637. Offers art history (MA); classics (MA); comparative literature (MA); creative writing (MA); digital humanities (MA); English language and literature (MA); Germanic studies (MA); linguistics (MA); music (MA); philosophy (MA); Romance languages and literatures (MA); South Asian languages and civilizations (MA). *Students:* 83 full-time (41 women), 8 part-time (6 women); includes 14 minority (1 Black or African American, non-Hispanic/Latino; 6 Asian, non-Hispanic/Latino; 6 Hispanic/Latino; 1 Two or more races, non-Hispanic/Latino), 17 international. Average age 26. 153 applicants, 67% accepted, 80 enrolled. *Degree requirements:* For master's, thesis. *Entrance requirements:* For master's, GRE General Test. Additional exam requirements/recommendations for international students: Required—TOEFL (minimum score 600 paper-based; 104 iBT), IELTS (minimum score 7). *Application deadline:* For fall admission, 3/15 for domestic and international students. Application fee: $90. Electronic applications accepted. *Expenses:* Tuition: Full-time $46,899. *Required fees:* $347. *Financial support:* In 2014–15, 100 students received support, including 8 fellowships with partial tuition reimbursements available (averaging $12,000 per year); Federal Work-Study, institutionally sponsored loans, and tuition waivers (partial) also available. Financial award application deadline: 3/15; financial award applicants required to submit FAFSA. *Unit head:* Prof. David Wray, Director, 773-834-1201, E-mail: ma-humanities@uchicago.edu. *Application contact:* Program Coordinator, 773-834-1201, Fax: 773-834-7526, E-mail: ma-humanities@uchicago.edu.
Website: http://maph.uchicago.edu/

University of Colorado Boulder, Graduate School, College of Arts and Sciences, Department of Asian Languages and Civilizations, Boulder, CO 80309. Offers Chinese (MA, PhD); Japanese (MA, PhD). *Faculty:* 11 full-time (4 women). *Students:* 24 full-time (12 women), 3 part-time (all women); includes 4 minority (2 Asian, non-Hispanic/Latino; 1 Hispanic/Latino; 1 Two or more races, non-Hispanic/Latino), 9 international. Average age 30. 55 applicants, 58% accepted, 12 enrolled. In 2014, 11 master's awarded. Terminal master's awarded for partial completion of doctoral program. *Degree requirements:* For master's, comprehensive exam. *Entrance requirements:* For master's, BA in Chinese or Japanese, minimum undergraduate GPA of 3.0. Additional exam requirements/recommendations for international students: Required—TOEFL. *Application deadline:* For fall admission, 1/1 for domestic students, 12/1 for international students; for spring admission, 10/1 for domestic students, 9/1 for international students. Applications are processed on a rolling basis. Application fee: $50 ($70 for international students). Electronic applications accepted. *Financial support:* In 2014–15, 63 students received support, including 11 fellowships (averaging $3,624 per year), 20 teaching assistantships with full and partial tuition reimbursements available (averaging $26,470 per year); institutionally sponsored loans, scholarships/grants, health care benefits, and unspecified assistantships also available. Financial award application deadline: 2/1; financial award applicants required to submit FAFSA. *Faculty research:* Asian languages/literature, Chinese language/literature, literary criticism, Japanese language/literature. *Total annual research expenditures:* $401,438.
Website: http://alc.colorado.edu/

University of Hawaii at Manoa, Graduate Division, School of Pacific and Asian Studies, Program in Asian Studies, Concentration in Korean Studies, Honolulu, HI 96822. Offers Graduate Certificate. Part-time programs available. *Degree requirements:* For Graduate Certificate, one foreign language. *Entrance requirements:* For degree, GRE. Additional exam requirements/recommendations for international students: Required—TOEFL (minimum score 560 paper-based; 83 iBT), IELTS (minimum score 5).

University of Hawaii at Manoa, Graduate Division, School of Pacific and Asian Studies, Program in Asian Studies, Concentration in Southeast Asian Studies, Honolulu, HI 96822. Offers Graduate Certificate. Part-time programs available. *Degree requirements:* For Graduate Certificate, one foreign language. *Entrance requirements:* For degree, GRE. Additional exam requirements/recommendations for international students: Required—TOEFL (minimum score 560 paper-based; 83 iBT), IELTS (minimum score 5).

University of Illinois at Urbana–Champaign, Graduate College, College of Liberal Arts and Sciences, Center for South Asian and Middle Eastern Studies, Champaign, IL 61820. Offers MA. *Students:* 5 (1 woman). *Degree requirements:* For master's, one foreign language, comprehensive exam, thesis or alternative. Application fee: $70 ($90 for international students). *Unit head:* Valerie Hoffman, Director, 217-333-2681, E-mail: vhoffman@illinois.edu. *Application contact:* Terri L. Gitler, Office Support Associate, 217-244-7331, E-mail: csames@illinois.edu.
Website: http://www.csames.illinois.edu/

University of Illinois at Urbana–Champaign, Graduate College, College of Liberal Arts and Sciences, School of Literatures, Cultures and Linguistics, Department of East Asian Languages and Cultures, Champaign, IL 61820. Offers East Asian languages and cultures (PhD); East Asian studies (MA). *Students:* 16 (8 women). Application fee: $70 ($90 for international students). *Unit head:* Gary Gang Xu, Head, 217-244-4012, Fax: 217-244-2223, E-mail: garyxu@illinois.edu. *Application contact:* Lynn Stanke, Office Support Specialist, 217-333-6269, Fax: 217-244-3050, E-mail: stanke@illinois.edu.
Website: http://www.ealc.illinois.edu/

The University of Iowa, Graduate College, College of Liberal Arts and Sciences, Program in Asian Civilizations, Iowa City, IA 52242-1316. Offers Chinese (MA); Hindi (MA); Sanskrit (MA); South Asian studies (MA). *Degree requirements:* For master's, thesis optional, exam. *Entrance requirements:* For master's, GRE General Test, minimum GPA of 3.0. Additional exam requirements/recommendations for international students: Required—TOEFL (minimum score 590 paper-based; 96 iBT). Electronic applications accepted.

The University of Kansas, Graduate Studies, College of Liberal Arts and Sciences, Department of East Asian Languages and Cultures, Lawrence, KS 66045. Offers MA, MBA/MA. Part-time programs available. *Faculty:* 9 full-time, 14 part-time/adjunct. *Students:* 9 full-time (7 women), 5 part-time (4 women), 5 international. Average age 28. 10 applicants, 50% accepted, 3 enrolled. In 2014, 6 master's awarded. *Degree requirements:* For master's, one foreign language, thesis. *Entrance requirements:* For master's, GRE, 3 letters of recommendation, writing sample, curriculum vitae, statement of purpose. Additional exam requirements/recommendations for international students: Required—TOEFL. *Application deadline:* For fall admission, 4/1 priority date for domestic students, 5/1 for international students; for spring admission, 12/1 priority date for domestic students, 12/1 for international students. Applications are processed on a rolling basis. Application fee: $55 ($65 for international students). Electronic applications accepted. *Financial support:* Fellowships, teaching assistantships with full and partial tuition reimbursements, and unspecified assistantships available. Financial award application deadline: 4/1. *Faculty research:* Gender relations in literature, ancient Chinese law, visual culture of modern Japan, Japanese language pedagogy, Chinese paleography, Korean shamanism, folklore, traditional Chinese and Japanese literature, Chinese linguistics and language pedagogy. *Unit head:* Dr. Margaret Childs, Chair, 785-864-9128, E-mail: mgchilds@ku.edu. *Application contact:* Cari Ann Kreienhop, Graduate Programs and Graduate Admissions Contact, 785-864-3665, E-mail: ckreienhop@ku.edu.
Website: http://ealc.ku.edu/

University of Louisville, Graduate School, College of Arts and Sciences, Program in Asian Studies, Louisville, KY 40292-0001. Offers Graduate Certificate. *Students:* 1 (woman) full-time. Average age 30. In 2014, 1 Graduate Certificate awarded. *Degree requirements:* For Graduate Certificate, one foreign language. *Expenses:* Tuition, state resident: full-time $11,326; part-time $630 per credit hour. Tuition, nonresident: full-time $23,568; part-time $1311 per credit hour. *Required fees:* $196. Tuition and fees vary according to program and reciprocity agreements. *Unit head:* Dr. Shiping Hua, Director, 502-852-3305, E-mail: shiping.hua@louisville.edu. *Application contact:* Libby Leggett, Director, Graduate Admissions, 502-852-3101, Fax: 502-852-6536, E-mail: gradadm@louisville.edu.
Website: http://louisville.edu/asianstudies

University of Maine, Graduate School, College of Liberal Arts and Sciences, Department of History, Orono, ME 04469. Offers Asian studies (MA); Canadian studies (MA); European studies (MA). *Faculty:* 17 full-time (4 women). *Students:* 33 full-time (19 women), 12 part-time (4 women); includes 1 minority (Hispanic/Latino), 3 international. Average age 38. 31 applicants, 65% accepted, 6 enrolled. In 2014, 6 master's, 1 doctorate awarded. *Degree requirements:* For master's, variable foreign language requirement, thesis optional; for doctorate, one foreign language, comprehensive exam, thesis/dissertation. *Entrance requirements:* For master's and doctorate, GRE General Test. Additional exam requirements/recommendations for international students: Required—TOEFL. *Application deadline:* For fall admission, 1/15 priority date for domestic students; for spring admission, 10/15 for domestic students. Applications are processed on a rolling basis. Application fee: $65. Electronic applications accepted. *Expenses:* Tuition, state resident: part-time $658 per credit hour. Tuition, nonresident: part-time $1550 per credit hour. *Financial support:* In 2014–15, 26 students received support, including 4 fellowships (averaging $15,000 per year), 9 teaching assistantships with tuition reimbursements available (averaging $14,600 per year); career-related internships or fieldwork, Federal Work-Study, and tuition waivers (full and partial) also available. Support available to part-time students. Financial award application deadline: 3/1. *Faculty research:* Environmental history, gender history, nationalism, classical, popular culture, Napoleonic, globalization, peasant studies, diplomatic history, military, Native America, Colonial U.S. *Unit head:* Dr. Stephen Miller, Chair, 207-581-1905, Fax: 207-581-1817, E-mail: stephen.miller@maine.edu. *Application contact:* Scott G. Delcourt, Assistant Vice President for Graduate Studies and Senior Associate Dean, 207-581-3291, Fax: 207-581-3232, E-mail: graduate@maine.edu.
Website: http://www.umaine.edu/history/

The University of Manchester, School of Languages, Linguistics and Cultures, Manchester, United Kingdom. Offers Arab world studies (PhD); Chinese studies (M Phil, PhD); East Asian studies (M Phil, PhD); English language (PhD); French studies (M Phil, PhD); German studies (M Phil, PhD); interpreting studies (PhD); Italian studies (M Phil, PhD); Japanese studies (M Phil, PhD); Latin American cultural studies (M Phil, PhD); linguistics (M Phil, PhD); Middle Eastern studies (M Phil, PhD); Polish studies (M Phil, PhD); Portuguese studies (M Phil, PhD); Russian studies (M Phil, PhD); Spanish studies (M Phil, PhD); translation and intercultural studies (M Phil, PhD).

University of Michigan, Horace H. Rackham School of Graduate Studies, College of Literature, Science, and the Arts, Center for Japanese Studies, Ann Arbor, MI 48109-1106. Offers AM, JD/AM, MBA/AM. Part-time programs available. *Faculty:* 45 full-time (19 women), 14 part-time/adjunct (4 women). *Students:* 15 full-time (5 women); includes 4 minority (1 Hispanic/Latino; 3 Two or more races, non-Hispanic/Latino), 1 international. 28 applicants, 68% accepted, 8 enrolled. In 2014, 6 master's awarded. *Degree requirements:* For master's, one foreign language, thesis optional, 6th-term proficiency (3 years) in Japanese language. *Entrance requirements:* For master's, GRE General Test, previous study of Japanese language (highly recommended). Additional exam requirements/recommendations for international students: Required—TOEFL (minimum score 560 paper-based; 84 iBT); Recommended—IELTS (minimum score 6.5). *Application deadline:* For fall admission, 1/10 for domestic and international students. Application fee: $75 ($90 for international students). Electronic applications accepted. *Financial support:* In 2014–15, 9 students received support, including 5

fellowships with full tuition reimbursements available (averaging $15,000 per year); research assistantships with full and partial tuition reimbursements available, teaching assistantships with full and partial tuition reimbursements available, career-related internships or fieldwork, Federal Work-Study, scholarships/grants, health care benefits, unspecified assistantships, and full and partial tuition only scholarships also available. Support available to part-time students. Financial award application deadline: 1/10; financial award applicants required to submit FAFSA. *Faculty research:* Japanese literature; Japanese history (premodern and modern); Japanese linguistics and language pedagogy; modern Japanese society and culture; Japanese elections and politics; gender and sexuality in Japan; Japanese art, art history and visual culture; Japanese film; Buddhism and religion in Japan; Japanese law; Japanese health care (medicine, nursing, psychiatry and social work). *Unit head:* Prof. Jonathan E. Zwicker, PhD, Director, 734-764-6307, Fax: 734-936-2948, E-mail: umcjs@umich.edu. *Application contact:* Carol Stepanchuk, Academic Services Coordinator, 734-764-6307, Fax: 734-936-2948, E-mail: cjsadmissions@umich.edu.
Website: http://www.ii.umich.edu/cjs/

University of Michigan, Horace H. Rackham School of Graduate Studies, College of Literature, Science, and the Arts, Center for South Asian Studies, Ann Arbor, MI 48109. Offers MA, Certificate, MBA/MA. Part-time programs available. *Degree requirements:* For master's, one foreign language, thesis, 24 credits; for Certificate, one foreign language. *Entrance requirements:* For master's, GRE General Test, 3 letters of recommendation; for Certificate, GRE General Test, 2 letters of recommendation, transcripts. Additional exam requirements/recommendations for international students: Required—TOEFL (minimum score 560 paper-based; 84 iBT). Electronic applications accepted. *Faculty research:* History of Islam and South Asia; ethnicity and nationalism; global and transnational feminism; South Asian architecture and urbanism; mysticism and politics in Indian religions.

University of Michigan, Horace H. Rackham School of Graduate Studies, College of Literature, Science, and the Arts, Center for Southeast Asian Studies, Ann Arbor, MI 48109-1106. Offers MA, Graduate Certificate, MBA/MA, MPP/MA. Part-time programs available. *Degree requirements:* For master's, one foreign language, thesis, 25 credits; for Graduate Certificate, one foreign language. *Entrance requirements:* For master's, GRE General Test, 3 recommendations, curriculum vitae; for Graduate Certificate, GRE General Test, 2 recommendations, transcripts, statement of purpose. Additional exam requirements/recommendations for international students: Required—TOEFL (minimum score 560 paper-based; 84 iBT). Electronic applications accepted. *Faculty research:* Politics, political parties, civil society, the law and human rights in Southeast Asia; nationalism and modernity in late colonial Southeast Asia; Islam, religion, language and media; urbanization, globalization and business; pre-modern Southeast Asia in a global/ Eurasian context.

University of Michigan, Horace H. Rackham School of Graduate Studies, College of Literature, Science, and the Arts, Department of Asian Languages and Cultures, Ann Arbor, MI 48104. Offers PhD. *Faculty:* 18 full-time (5 women). *Students:* 21 full-time; includes 8 minority (7 Asian, non-Hispanic/Latino; 1 Hispanic/Latino). Average age 32. 56 applicants, 9% accepted, 3 enrolled. In 2014, 3 doctorates awarded. Terminal master's awarded for partial completion of doctoral program. *Degree requirements:* For doctorate, 2 foreign languages, thesis/dissertation, preliminary exams, oral defense of dissertation. *Entrance requirements:* Additional exam requirements/recommendations for international students: Required—TOEFL (minimum score 600 paper-based; 106 iBT). *Application deadline:* For fall admission, 12/15 for domestic and international students. Application fee: $65 ($75 for international students). Electronic applications accepted. *Financial support:* In 2014–15, 24 students received support. Fellowships with full tuition reimbursements available, teaching assistantships with full tuition reimbursements available, scholarships/grants, and health care benefits available. Financial award application deadline: 12/15. *Faculty research:* Literature, religion, visual culture, history, modern culture. *Unit head:* Prof. Donald S. Lopez, Jr., Chair, 734-764-8286, Fax: 734-647-0157, E-mail: um-alc@umich.edu. *Application contact:* Student Services, 734-734-8286, Fax: 734-647-0157, E-mail: alc-gradservices@umich.edu.
Website: http://www.lsa.umich.edu/asian/

University of Michigan, Horace H. Rackham School of Graduate Studies, College of Literature, Science, and the Arts, The Kenneth G. Lieberthal and Richard H. Rogel Center for Chinese Studies, Ann Arbor, MI 48109. Offers MA, JD/AM, MBA/AM, MPP/ AM. Part-time programs available. *Faculty:* 41 full-time. *Students:* 15 full-time; includes 6 minority (5 Asian, non-Hispanic/Latino; 1 Two or more races, non-Hispanic/Latino). Average age 25. 59 applicants, 31% accepted, 4 enrolled. In 2014, 9 master's awarded. *Degree requirements:* For master's, one foreign language, thesis. *Entrance requirements:* For master's, GRE General Test. Additional exam requirements/ recommendations for international students: Required—TOEFL. *Application deadline:* For winter admission, 1/10 for domestic and international students. Application fee: $75 ($90 for international students). Electronic applications accepted. *Financial support:* Fellowships, Federal Work-Study, institutionally sponsored loans, scholarships/grants, and unspecified assistantships available. Financial award application deadline: 2/1. *Faculty research:* Political and economic reform in China, Chinese religion, history of late Imperial China, Chinese foreign policy, Chinese music and music history. *Unit head:* Mary Gallagher, Director, 734-764-6308, Fax: 734-764-5540. *Application contact:* Carol Stepanchuk, Student Services Coordinator, 734-936-3961, Fax: 734-764-5540, E-mail: cstep@umich.edu.
Website: http://www.ii.umich.edu/lrccs

University of Minnesota, Twin Cities Campus, Graduate School, College of Liberal Arts, Department of Asian Languages and Literatures, Minneapolis, MN 55455-0213. Offers Asian literatures, cultures, and media (PhD). *Degree requirements:* For doctorate, comprehensive exam, thesis/dissertation. *Entrance requirements:* For doctorate, GRE, 3 letters of recommendation. Additional exam requirements/recommendations for international students: Required—TOEFL (minimum score 550 paper-based), IELTS (minimum score 6.5). Electronic applications accepted. *Faculty research:* Gender studies, post-colonial theory, poetics and poetic theory, film studies, post modernist thought.

University of Oregon, Graduate School, College of Arts and Sciences, Program in Asian Studies, Eugene, OR 97403. Offers MA. Part-time programs available. *Degree requirements:* For master's, one foreign language, thesis or alternative. *Entrance requirements:* For master's, GRE General Test. Additional exam requirements/ recommendations for international students: Required—TOEFL. *Faculty research:* East and Southeast Asia, Pacific Islands.

University of Pennsylvania, School of Arts and Sciences, Graduate Group in East Asian Languages and Civilization, Philadelphia, PA 19104. Offers AM, PhD. *Faculty:* 19 full-time (7 women), 3 part-time/adjunct (0 women). *Students:* 50 full-time (34 women), 4 part-time (2 women); includes 4 minority (1 Black or African American, non-Hispanic/ Latino; 3 Asian, non-Hispanic/Latino), 34 international. 162 applicants, 25% accepted, 17 enrolled. In 2014, 9 master's, 6 doctorates awarded. Application fee: $70. *Financial support:* Institutionally sponsored loans, scholarships/grants, traineeships, health care benefits, and unspecified assistantships available. *Unit head:* Dr. Ralph M. Rosen, Associate Dean for Graduate Studies, 215-898-7156, Fax: 215-573-8068, E-mail: grad-dean@sas.upenn.edu. *Application contact:* Arts and Sciences Graduate Admissions, 215-573-5816, Fax: 215-573-8068, E-mail: gdasadmis@sas.upenn.edu.
Website: http://www.sas.upenn.edu/graduate-division

University of Pennsylvania, School of Arts and Sciences, Graduate Group in South Asian Regional Studies, Philadelphia, PA 19104. Offers AM, PhD. *Faculty:* 15 full-time (5 women), 9 part-time/adjunct (2 women). *Students:* 20 full-time (11 women), 3 part-time (0 women); includes 7 minority (4 Asian, non-Hispanic/Latino; 1 Hispanic/Latino; 2 Two or more races, non-Hispanic/Latino), 10 international. 40 applicants, 38% accepted, 8 enrolled. In 2014, 8 master's, 1 doctorate awarded. Terminal master's awarded for partial completion of doctoral program. *Degree requirements:* For master's, one foreign language, thesis, written exam; for doctorate, 3 foreign languages, thesis/dissertation, written exam. *Entrance requirements:* For master's, GRE General Test. Additional exam requirements/recommendations for international students: Required—TOEFL. *Application deadline:* For fall admission, 12/1 priority date for domestic students. Application fee: $70. Electronic applications accepted. *Financial support:* Fellowships, research assistantships, teaching assistantships, institutionally sponsored loans, scholarships/grants, traineeships, health care benefits, and unspecified assistantships available. Financial award application deadline: 12/15. *Faculty research:* South Asian linguistics, literature, and history; economic history. *Unit head:* Dr. Ralph M. Rosen, Associate Dean for Graduate Studies, 215-898-7156, Fax: 215-573-8068, E-mail: grad-dean@sas.upenn.edu. *Application contact:* Arts and Sciences Graduate Admissions, 215-573-5816, Fax: 215-573-8068, E-mail: gdasadmis@sas.upenn.edu.
Website: http://www.southasia.upenn.edu/graduate-programs

University of Pittsburgh, Dietrich School of Arts and Sciences, Department of East Asian Languages and Literatures, Pittsburgh, PA 15260. Offers MA. Part-time programs available. *Faculty:* 25 full-time (15 women), 5 part-time/adjunct (3 women). *Students:* 7 full-time (4 women), 3 international. Average age 25. 43 applicants, 40% accepted, 5 enrolled. In 2014, 3 master's awarded. *Degree requirements:* For master's, one foreign language, thesis, oral comprehensive exam. *Entrance requirements:* For master's, GRE General Test, 2 years of college-level Chinese or Japanese, minimum QPA of 3.0. Additional exam requirements/recommendations for international students: Required—TOEFL (minimum score 90 iBT). *Application deadline:* For fall admission, 1/15 for domestic and international students. Application fee: $50. Electronic applications accepted. *Expenses:* Tuition, state resident: full-time $20,742; part-time $838 per credit. Tuition, nonresident: full-time $33,960; part-time $1389 per credit. *Required fees:* $800; $205 per term. Tuition and fees vary according to program. *Financial support:* In 2014–15, 7 students received support. Scholarships/grants and tuition waivers (full and partial) available. Financial award application deadline: 1/15. *Faculty research:* Chinese literature, film, and poetry; Japanese literature, film, and theater; Chinese society and culture; east Asian foreign policy, security studies, and economic history; Japanese performing arts and fine arts. *Unit head:* Dr. Hiroshi Nara, Chairman and Director of Graduate Studies, 412-624-5579, Fax: 412-624-3458, E-mail: hnara@pitt.edu. *Application contact:* Patrick Fogarty, Graduate Administrator, 412-624-5227, Fax: 412-624-6263, E-mail: pmf23@pitt.edu.
Website: http://www.deall.pitt.edu/

University of Pittsburgh, University Center for International Studies, Pittsburgh, PA 15260. Offers African studies (Certificate); Asian studies (Certificate); European Union studies (Certificate); global studies (Certificate); Latin American studies (Certificate); Russian and East European studies (Certificate); West European studies (Certificate). *Students:* 223 full-time (98 women), 11 part-time (1 woman); includes 97 minority (2 Black or African American, non-Hispanic/Latino; 41 Asian, non-Hispanic/Latino; 52 Hispanic/Latino; 2 Two or more races, non-Hispanic/Latino). Average age 31. In 2014, 72 Certificates awarded. *Degree requirements:* For Certificate, one foreign language, study abroad. *Application deadline:* Applications are processed on a rolling basis. *Expenses:* Tuition, state resident: full-time $20,742; part-time $838 per credit. Tuition, nonresident: full-time $33,960; part-time $1389 per credit. *Required fees:* $800; $205 per term. Tuition and fees vary according to program. *Unit head:* Dr. Ariel Armony, Director, 412-648-7374, Fax: 412-624-4672, E-mail: armony@pitt.edu. *Application contact:* Information Contact, 412-624-4141, E-mail: graduate@pitt.edu.
Website: http://www.ucis.pitt.edu

University of San Francisco, College of Arts and Sciences, Program in Asia Pacific Studies, San Francisco, CA 94117-1080. Offers MA, MA/MBA. Part-time and evening/ weekend programs available. *Faculty:* 5 full-time (2 women), 5 part-time/adjunct (all women). *Students:* 42 full-time (20 women), 1 part-time (0 women); includes 12 minority (5 Asian, non-Hispanic/Latino; 3 Hispanic/Latino; 1 Native Hawaiian or other Pacific Islander, non-Hispanic/Latino; 3 Two or more races, non-Hispanic/Latino), 21 international. Average age 28. 34 applicants, 94% accepted, 19 enrolled. In 2014, 16 master's awarded. *Degree requirements:* For master's, one foreign language, thesis. *Entrance requirements:* For master's, minimum GPA of 3.0. *Application deadline:* For fall admission, 3/1 for domestic students. Applications are processed on a rolling basis. Application fee: $55 ($65 for international students). *Expenses: Tuition:* Full-time $21,762; part-time $1209 per credit hour. Tuition and fees vary according to degree level, campus/location and program. *Financial support:* In 2014–15, 15 students received support. Career-related internships or fieldwork, Federal Work-Study, and institutionally sponsored loans available. Financial award application deadline: 3/2; financial award applicants required to submit FAFSA. *Faculty research:* History of Christianity in China, U.S.-China policy, East Asian economies and political systems, sociolinguistic aspects of Japanese. *Unit head:* Dr. Brian Komei Dempster, Director, 415-422-6357, Fax: 415-422-5933. *Application contact:* Mark Landerghini, Information Contact, 415-422-5101, Fax: 415-422-2217, E-mail: asgraduate@usfca.edu.
Website: http://www.usfca.edu/artsci/apsg/

University of Southern California, Graduate School, Dana and David Dornsife College of Letters, Arts and Sciences, Department of East Asian Languages and Cultures, Los Angeles, CA 90089. Offers classical Chinese literature (MA, PhD); classical Japanese literature (MA, PhD); linguistics (MA, PhD); modern Chinese literature (MA, PhD); modern Japanese literature (MA, PhD); modern Korean literature (MA, PhD). *Degree requirements:* For master's, thesis; for doctorate, 2 foreign languages, comprehensive exam, thesis/dissertation. *Entrance requirements:* For master's and doctorate, GRE, BA in relevant field. Additional exam requirements/recommendations for international students: Required—TOEFL. Electronic applications accepted. *Faculty research:* Gender, visual studies, multimedia, ecocriticism, second language acquisition.

University of Southern California, Graduate School, Dana and David Dornsife College of Letters, Arts and Sciences, East Asian Studies Center, Los Angeles, CA 90089. Offers MA, MA/MBA. Part-time programs available. *Degree requirements:* For master's, one foreign language, thesis, language proficiency in an East Asian language (equivalent to 3 years of study). *Entrance requirements:* For master's, GRE (minimum score 1000). Additional exam requirements/recommendations for international students: Required—TOEFL (minimum score 600 paper-based; 100 iBT). Electronic applications accepted. *Faculty research:* East Asian visual cultures (Chinese, Japanese, and Korean film, culture and art); East Asian politics, society and history; East Asian literature and culture.

The University of Texas at Austin, Graduate School, College of Liberal Arts, Department of Asian Studies, Austin, TX 78712-1111. Offers Asian cultures and languages (MA, PhD); Asian studies (MA). Part-time programs available. *Degree*

requirements: For master's, thesis; for doctorate, 3 foreign languages, thesis/dissertation. *Entrance requirements:* For master's and doctorate, GRE General Test. Electronic applications accepted. *Faculty research:* Modern Taiwanese fiction, modern Japanese literature, religious studies in South Asia during classical period.

University of Toronto, School of Graduate Studies, Faculty of Arts and Science, Department of East Asian Studies, Toronto, ON M5S 2J7, Canada. Offers MA, PhD. Part-time programs available. *Degree requirements:* For master's, thesis optional; for doctorate, 2 foreign languages, comprehensive exam, thesis/dissertation. *Entrance requirements:* For master's, writing sample, 2 letters of recommendation, BA in a specialist or East Asian studies program, minimum B+ average in final year; for doctorate, writing sample, 3 letters of recommendation, MA in East Asian studies. Additional exam requirements/recommendations for international students: Required— TOEFL (minimum score 600 paper-based), TWE (minimum score 5). Electronic applications accepted.

University of Utah, Graduate School, College of Humanities, Asian Studies Program, Salt Lake City, UT 84112. Offers MA. Part-time and evening/weekend programs available. *Students:* 5 full-time (3 women), 1 part-time (0 women). Average age 27. 12 applicants, 33% accepted, 1 enrolled. In 2014, 5 master's awarded. *Degree requirements:* For master's, one foreign language, thesis, 3rd-year proficiency in one Asian language. *Entrance requirements:* For master's, GRE. Additional exam requirements/recommendations for international students: Required—TOEFL (minimum score 580 paper-based). *Application deadline:* For fall admission, 2/1 for domestic and international students; for spring admission, 9/15 for domestic students. Application fee: $55 ($65 for international students). Electronic applications accepted. *Financial support:* In 2014–15, 6 students received support, including 6 fellowships with full tuition reimbursements available (averaging $15,000 per year). Financial award application deadline: 2/1; financial award applicants required to submit FAFSA. *Faculty research:* Asian health studies, history, literature, culture, politics, economics. *Unit head:* Dr. Janet Theiss, Director, 801-585-6477, Fax: 801-581-6105, E-mail: janet.theiss@utah.edu. *Application contact:* Kevin D. Barrett, Academic Advisor, 801-581-6150, Fax: 801-581-6105, E-mail: kevin.barrett@utah.edu.
Website: http://asia-center.utah.edu/

University of Victoria, Faculty of Graduate Studies, Faculty of Humanities, Department of Pacific and Asian Studies, Victoria, BC V8W 2Y2, Canada. Offers MA. *Degree requirements:* For master's, thesis. *Entrance requirements:* For master's, minimum B+ average, writing sample. Additional exam requirements/recommendations for international students: Required—TOEFL (minimum score 575 paper-based), IELTS (minimum score 7). Electronic applications accepted. *Faculty research:* Culture, ethnicity and identity; economy and society; gender studies; languages and linguistics; literature.

University of Virginia, College and Graduate School of Arts and Sciences, Department of East Asian Languages, Literatures, and Cultures, Charlottesville, VA 22903. Offers East Asian studies (MA); MBA/MA. *Faculty:* 16 full-time (13 women), 1 (woman) part-time/adjunct. *Students:* 4 full-time (all women), 2 international. Average age 23. 19 applicants, 26% accepted, 4 enrolled. In 2014, 1 master's awarded. *Degree requirements:* For master's, one foreign language, comprehensive exam, thesis. *Entrance requirements:* For master's, GRE General Test, 2 letters of recommendation. Additional exam requirements/recommendations for international students: Required— TOEFL, IELTS. *Application deadline:* For fall admission, 1/15 for domestic and international students; for winter admission, 9/15 for domestic and international students. Applications are processed on a rolling basis. Application fee: $60. Electronic applications accepted. *Expenses:* Tuition, state resident: full-time $14,164; part-time $349 per credit hour. Tuition, nonresident: full-time $23,722; part-time $1300 per credit hour. *Required fees:* $2514. *Financial support:* Applicants required to submit FAFSA. *Unit head:* Anne Kinney, Chair, 434-982-2304, Fax: 434-243-1528, E-mail: aeb29@virginia.edu.
Website: http://eastasian.virginia.edu/

University of Virginia, College and Graduate School of Arts and Sciences, Department of Middle Eastern and South Asian Languages and Cultures, Charlottesville, VA 22903. Offers Middle Eastern and South Asian studies (MA). *Faculty:* 15 full-time (6 women). *Students:* 6 full-time (4 women), 1 part-time (0 women); includes 2 minority (1 Black or African American, non-Hispanic/Latino; 1 Asian, non-Hispanic/Latino), 2 international. Average age 28. 10 applicants, 100% accepted, 5 enrolled. In 2014, 3 master's awarded. Application fee: $60. *Expenses:* Tuition, state resident: full-time $14,164; part-time $349 per credit hour. Tuition, nonresident: full-time $23,722; part-time $1300 per credit hour. *Required fees:* $2514. *Unit head:* Farzaneh Milani, Chair, 434-243-4930, Fax: 434-243-1528, E-mail: fmm2z@virginia.edu. *Application contact:* Robert Hueckstedt, Director of Graduate Studies, 434-243-8228, Fax: 434-243-1528, E-mail: rah2k@virginia.edu.
Website: http://mesalc.virginia.edu/

University of Washington, Graduate School, College of Arts and Sciences, Department of Asian Languages and Literature, Seattle, WA 98195. Offers Buddhist studies (MA, PhD); Chinese language and literature (MA, PhD); Japanese language and literature (MA, PhD); Korean language and literature (MA, PhD); South Asian language and literature (MA, PhD). *Degree requirements:* For master's, 2 foreign languages, general exam, thesis or 2 research papers; for doctorate, 3 foreign languages, thesis/dissertation, general exam. *Entrance requirements:* For master's, GRE, minimum GPA of 3.0; for doctorate, GRE, master's degree in related field, minimum GPA of 3.0. Additional exam requirements/recommendations for international students: Required— TOEFL. Electronic applications accepted. *Faculty research:* Textual, linguistic, philological, and literary study of languages and literatures of Asia.

University of Washington, Graduate School, College of Arts and Sciences, Henry M. Jackson School of International Studies, China Studies Program, Seattle, WA 98195. Offers MAIS. *Degree requirements:* For master's, one foreign language, thesis optional. *Entrance requirements:* For master's, GRE General Test, minimum GPA of 3.0 in last 2 years. Additional exam requirements/recommendations for international students: Required—TOEFL (minimum score 500 paper-based; 92 iBT), IELTS (minimum score 7). Electronic applications accepted.

University of Washington, Graduate School, College of Arts and Sciences, Henry M. Jackson School of International Studies, Japan Studies Program, Seattle, WA 98195. Offers MAIS. *Degree requirements:* For master's, one foreign language. *Entrance requirements:* For master's, GRE General Test, minimum GPA of 3.0 in last two years. Additional exam requirements/recommendations for international students: Required— TOEFL (minimum score 500 paper-based; 92 iBT), IELTS (minimum score 7). Electronic applications accepted.

University of Washington, Graduate School, College of Arts and Sciences, Henry M. Jackson School of International Studies, Korea Studies Program, Seattle, WA 98195. Offers MAIS. *Degree requirements:* For master's, one foreign language. *Entrance requirements:* For master's, GRE General Test, minimum GPA of 3.0 in last two years. Additional exam requirements/recommendations for international students: Required— TOEFL (minimum score 500 paper-based; 92 iBT), IELTS (minimum score 7). Electronic applications accepted.

University of Washington, Graduate School, College of Arts and Sciences, Henry M. Jackson School of International Studies, Russian, East European and Central Asian Studies Program, Seattle, WA 98195. Offers Central Asian studies (MAIS); East European studies (MAIS); Russian studies (MAIS). *Degree requirements:* For master's, one foreign language, thesis. *Entrance requirements:* For master's, GRE General Test, 2 years of relevant language, minimum GPA of 3.0 in last two years. Additional exam requirements/recommendations for international students: Required—TOEFL (minimum score 500 paper-based; 92 iBT), IELTS (minimum score 7). Electronic applications accepted.

University of Washington, Graduate School, College of Arts and Sciences, Henry M. Jackson School of International Studies, South Asian Studies Program, Seattle, WA 98195. Offers MAIS. *Degree requirements:* For master's, one foreign language, thesis optional. *Entrance requirements:* For master's, GRE General Test, minimum GPA of 3.0 in last two years. Additional exam requirements/recommendations for international students: Required—TOEFL (minimum score 500 paper-based; 92 iBT), IELTS (minimum score 7). Electronic applications accepted.

University of Washington, Graduate School, College of Arts and Sciences, Henry M. Jackson School of International Studies, Southeast Asian Studies Program, Seattle, WA 98195. Offers MAIS. *Degree requirements:* For master's, one foreign language, thesis optional. *Entrance requirements:* For master's, GRE General Test, minimum GPA of 3.0 in last two years. Additional exam requirements/recommendations for international students: Required—TOEFL (minimum score 500 paper-based; 92 iBT), IELTS (minimum score 7). Electronic applications accepted.

University of Wisconsin–Madison, Graduate School, College of Letters and Science, Center for Southeast Asian Studies, Madison, WI 53706. Offers MA. Part-time programs available. *Degree requirements:* For master's, one foreign language, oral defense of seminar paper. Electronic applications accepted. *Expenses:* Tuition, state resident: full-time $10,723; part-time $745 per credit. Tuition, nonresident: full-time $24,054; part-time $1578 per credit. *Required fees:* $374 per semester. Tuition and fees vary according to course load, program and reciprocity agreements. *Faculty research:* Economic development, censorship, political change, pedagogical developments in Indonesia, Philippine historical demography, environment photography.

University of Wisconsin–Madison, Graduate School, College of Letters and Science, Department of East Asian Languages and Literature, Madison, WI 53706-1380. Offers Chinese literature (MA, PhD); Chinese thought (MA, PhD); Japanese linguistics (MA, PhD); Japanese literature (MA, PhD). Part-time programs available. Terminal master's awarded for partial completion of doctoral program. *Degree requirements:* For master's, one foreign language, seminars, written exam; for doctorate, 3 foreign languages, thesis/dissertation, seminars, preliminary exams, oral exams. *Entrance requirements:* For master's, GRE General Test, BA or equivalent in major field; for doctorate, GRE General Test, MA or equivalent in major field. Electronic applications accepted. *Expenses:* Tuition, state resident: full-time $10,723; part-time $745 per credit. Tuition, nonresident: full-time $24,054; part-time $1578 per credit. *Required fees:* $374 per semester. Tuition and fees vary according to course load, program and reciprocity agreements. *Faculty research:* Modern and historical linguistics, literature, literary and cultural history.

University of Wisconsin–Madison, Graduate School, College of Letters and Science, Department of History, Madison, WI 53706-1380. Offers African history (MA, PhD); Central Asian history (MA, PhD); comparative world history (MA, PhD); East Asian history (MA, PhD); European history (MA, PhD); gender and women's history (MA, PhD); Latin American and Caribbean history (MA, PhD); Middle Eastern history (MA, PhD); South Asian history (MA, PhD); Southeast Asian history (MA, PhD); United States history (MA, PhD). Terminal master's awarded for partial completion of doctoral program. *Degree requirements:* For master's, thesis (for some programs); for doctorate, variable foreign language requirement, thesis/dissertation. *Entrance requirements:* For master's and doctorate, GRE General Test. Additional exam requirements/ recommendations for international students: Required—Michigan English Language Assessment Battery or TOEFL. Electronic applications accepted. *Expenses:* Tuition, state resident: full-time $10,723; part-time $745 per credit. Tuition, nonresident: full-time $24,054; part-time $1578 per credit. *Required fees:* $374 per semester. Tuition and fees vary according to course load, program and reciprocity agreements. *Faculty research:* American, African, European, Asian, Latin American, and Middle Eastern history.

University of Wisconsin–Madison, Graduate School, College of Letters and Science, Department of Languages and Cultures of Asia, Madison, WI 53706-1380. Offers civilizations and cultures (PhD); languages and cultures of Asia (MA); languages and literatures (PhD); religions of Asia (PhD). Part-time programs available. Terminal master's awarded for partial completion of doctoral program. *Degree requirements:* For master's, one foreign language, thesis or alternative; for doctorate, 2 foreign languages, thesis/dissertation. *Entrance requirements:* For master's, minimum GPA of 3.0; for doctorate, minimum GPA of 3.25, master's degree. Electronic applications accepted. *Expenses:* Tuition, state resident: full-time $10,723; part-time $745 per credit. Tuition, nonresident: full-time $24,054; part-time $1578 per credit. *Required fees:* $374 per semester. Tuition and fees vary according to course load, program and reciprocity agreements. *Faculty research:* Literature, folklore, religion.

Valparaiso University, Graduate School, Program in Chinese Studies, Valparaiso, IN 46383. Offers MA, JD/MA. Part-time and evening/weekend programs available. *Faculty:* 5 part-time/adjunct (1 woman). *Students:* 1 full-time (0 women), 15 part-time (12 women); includes 7 minority (6 Asian, non-Hispanic/Latino; 1 Hispanic/Latino). Average age 39. In 2014, 9 master's awarded. *Entrance requirements:* For master's, minimum GPA of 3.0, Chinese language proficiency. Additional exam requirements/ recommendations for international students: Required—TOEFL (minimum score 550 paper-based; 80 iBT), IELTS (minimum score 6). *Application deadline:* For fall admission, 4/15 priority date for domestic students. Applications are processed on a rolling basis. Application fee: $30 ($50 for international students). Electronic applications accepted. *Expenses:* Tuition: Full-time $10,710; part-time $595 per credit hour. *Required fees:* $378; $101 per term. Tuition and fees vary according to course load and program. *Financial support:* Scholarships/grants and unspecified assistantships available. Support available to part-time students. Financial award applicants required to submit FAFSA. *Unit head:* Dr. Jennifer A. Ziegler, Dean, Graduate School and Continuing Education, 219-464-5313, Fax: 219-464-5381, E-mail: jennifer.ziegler@valpo.edu. *Application contact:* Jessica Choquette, Graduate Admissions Specialist, 219-464-5313, Fax: 219-464-5381, E-mail: jessica.choquette@valpo.edu.
Website: http://www.valpo.edu/grad/macs/

Washington University in St. Louis, Graduate School of Arts and Sciences, Department of East Asian Languages and Cultures, St. Louis, MO 63130-4899. Offers Chinese (MA); Chinese and comparative literature (PhD); Chinese language and literature (PhD); East Asian studies (MA); Japanese (MA); Japanese and comparative literature (PhD); Japanese language and literature (PhD). Terminal master's awarded for partial completion of doctoral program. *Degree requirements:* For master's, thesis optional; for doctorate, thesis/dissertation. *Entrance requirements:* For master's and doctorate, GRE General Test. Additional exam requirements/recommendations for

international students: Required—TOEFL. Electronic applications accepted. *Faculty research:* Chinese; Japanese; Chinese fiction, theater, poetry, modern literature; Japanese modern and classical fiction, translation theory; East Asian Studies.

West Virginia University, Eberly College of Arts and Sciences, Department of History, Morgantown, WV 26506. Offers African history (MA, PhD); African-American history (MA, PhD); American history (MA, PhD); Appalachian/regional history (MA, PhD); East Asian history (MA, PhD); European history (MA, PhD); history of science and technology (MA, PhD); Latin American history (MA). Part-time programs available. *Degree requirements:* For master's, one foreign language, thesis (for some programs), oral exam, thesis defense; for doctorate, one foreign language, comprehensive exam, thesis/

dissertation, dissertation defense. *Entrance requirements:* For master's, GRE General Test, minimum GPA of 3.0; for doctorate, GRE General Test. Additional exam requirements/recommendations for international students: Required—TOEFL (minimum score 550 paper-based), IELTS (minimum score 6.5). Electronic applications accepted. *Faculty research:* United States, Appalachia, modern Europe, Africa, colonial and post-colonial societies.

Yale University, Graduate School of Arts and Sciences, Program in East Asian Studies, New Haven, CT 06520. Offers MA. *Degree requirements:* For master's, one foreign language. *Entrance requirements:* For master's, GRE General Test.

Canadian Studies

Carleton University, Faculty of Graduate Studies, Faculty of Arts and Social Sciences, School of Canadian Studies, Ottawa, ON K1S 5B6, Canada. Offers MA, PhD. PhD program offered jointly with Trent University. *Degree requirements:* For master's, one foreign language, thesis optional; for doctorate, one foreign language, thesis/dissertation. *Entrance requirements:* For master's, honors degree. Additional exam requirements/recommendations for international students: Required—TOEFL. Electronic applications accepted. *Faculty research:* Modern Canada, cultural studies, women's studies, aboriginal studies and the north, heritage conservation.

Queen's University at Kingston, School of Graduate Studies, Faculty of Arts and Sciences, Department of Political Studies, Kingston, ON K7L 3N6, Canada. Offers Canadian politics (PhD); comparative politics (PhD); gender and politics (PhD); international relations (PhD); political theory (PhD). *Degree requirements:* For master's, thesis or alternative; for doctorate, one foreign language, thesis/dissertation, qualifying exams. *Entrance requirements:* Additional exam requirements/recommendations for international students: Required—TOEFL (minimum score 600 paper-based). *Faculty research:* Canadian politics, comparative politics, political thought, international politics, women and politics.

Saint Mary's University, Faculty of Arts, Program in Atlantic Canada Studies, Halifax, NS B3H 3C3, Canada. Offers MA, Certificate. Part-time and evening/weekend programs available. *Degree requirements:* For master's, thesis. *Entrance requirements:* For master's, honors degree. Electronic applications accepted. *Expenses:* Contact institution.

Trent University, Graduate Studies, The Frost Centre for Canadian Studies and Indigenous Studies, Peterborough, ON K9J 7B8, Canada. Offers Canadian studies (PhD); Canadian studies and indigenous studies (MA). Part-time programs available. *Degree requirements:* For master's, thesis. *Entrance requirements:* For master's, honors degree. *Faculty research:* Native community-based socioeconomic development, environmental and social impact inventory, regional studies.

Université de Saint-Boniface, Program in Canadian Studies, Saint-Boniface, MB R2H 0H7, Canada. Offers MA.

Université de Sherbrooke, Faculty of Letters and Human Sciences, Department of Letters and Communications, Sherbrooke, QC J1K 2R1, Canada. Offers comparative Canadian literature (MA, PhD); French literature (MA, PhD); linguistics (MA); theatre (MA). *Degree requirements:* For master's, thesis or alternative; for doctorate, thesis/dissertation. *Entrance requirements:* For master's, minimum GPA of 2.8; for doctorate, minimum GPA of 3.0.

Université du Québec à Chicoutimi, Graduate Programs, Program in Regional Studies, Chicoutimi, QC G7H 2B1, Canada. Offers MA. Part-time programs available. *Degree requirements:* For master's, thesis. *Entrance requirements:* For master's, appropriate bachelor's degree, proficiency in French.

University at Buffalo, the State University of New York, Graduate School, College of Arts and Sciences, Department of Geography, Buffalo, NY 14260. Offers Canadian studies (Certificate); earth systems science (MA, MS); economic geography and business geographics (MS); environmental modeling and analysis (MA); geographic information science (MA, MS); geography (MA, PhD); GIS and environmental analysis (Certificate); health geography (MS); international trade (MA); transportation and business geographics (MA); urban and regional analysis (MA). Part-time programs available. *Faculty:* 18 full-time (9 women), 1 part-time/adjunct (0 women). *Students:* 87 full-time (37 women), 26 part-time (8 women); includes 78 minority (1 Black or African American, non-Hispanic/Latino; 74 Asian, non-Hispanic/Latino; 3 Hispanic/Latino). Average age 29. 167 applicants, 44% accepted, 32 enrolled. In 2014, 24 master's, 6 doctorates awarded. Terminal master's awarded for partial completion of doctoral program. *Degree requirements:* For master's, thesis (for some programs), project or portfolio; for doctorate, thesis/dissertation. *Entrance requirements:* For master's, GRE General Test, minimum GPA of 2.9; for doctorate, GRE General Test, minimum GPA of 3.0. Additional exam requirements/recommendations for international students: Required—TOEFL (minimum score 550 paper-based; 79 iBT). *Application deadline:* For fall admission, 5/1 priority date for domestic students, 3/10 priority date for international students; for spring admission, 11/1 priority date for domestic students, 9/1 priority date for international students. Applications are processed on a rolling basis. Application fee: $75. Electronic applications accepted. *Financial support:* In 2014–15, 13 students received support, including 8 fellowships with full tuition reimbursements available (averaging $5,500 per year), 13 teaching assistantships with full tuition reimbursements available (averaging $13,800 per year); research assistantships with full tuition reimbursements available, career-related internships or fieldwork, Federal Work-Study, institutionally sponsored loans, traineeships, health care benefits, and unspecified assistantships also available. Financial award application deadline: 1/10. *Faculty research:* International business and world trade, geographic information systems and cartography, transportation, urban and regional analysis, physical and environmental geography. *Total annual research expenditures:* $2.6 million. *Unit head:* Dr. Sharmistha Bagchi-Sen, Chairman, 716-645-0473, Fax: 716-645-2329, E-mail: geosbs@buffalo.edu. *Application contact:* Betsy Crooks, Graduate Secretary, 716-645-0471, Fax: 716-645-2329, E-mail: babraham@buffalo.edu. Website: http://www.geog.buffalo.edu/

University at Buffalo, the State University of New York, Graduate School, College of Arts and Sciences, Department of Transnational Studies, Buffalo, NY 14260. Offers American studies (MA, PhD); Canadian studies (Advanced Certificate); Canadian-American studies (MA); Caribbean Latina/o American studies (MA); global gender studies (MA, PhD). Part-time programs available. Postbaccalaureate distance learning degree programs offered. *Faculty:* 19 full-time (10 women). *Students:* 73 full-time (43 women); includes 20 minority (3 Black or African American, non-Hispanic/Latino; 6 American Indian or Alaska Native, non-Hispanic/Latino; 9 Asian, non-Hispanic/Latino; 2

Hispanic/Latino). Average age 32. 57 applicants, 84% accepted, 16 enrolled. In 2014, 26 master's, 18 doctorates, 1 other advanced degree awarded. *Degree requirements:* For master's, one foreign language, comprehensive exam (for some programs), thesis optional; for doctorate, one foreign language, comprehensive exam, thesis/dissertation; for Advanced Certificate, one foreign language. *Entrance requirements:* For master's, N/A, minimum GPA of 3.0; for doctorate, GRE, minimum GPA of 3.0. Additional exam requirements/recommendations for international students: Required—TOEFL (minimum score 550 paper-based; 79 iBT). *Application deadline:* For fall admission, 8/15 priority date for domestic students, 6/15 priority date for international students; for winter admission, 2/1 for domestic and international students; for spring admission, 1/15 priority date for domestic students, 11/15 priority date for international students. Applications are processed on a rolling basis. Application fee: $75. Electronic applications accepted. *Financial support:* In 2014–15, 16 students received support, including fellowships with full tuition reimbursements available (averaging $6,000 per year), research assistantships (averaging $5,000 per year), teaching assistantships with full tuition reimbursements available (averaging $13,060 per year); career-related internships or fieldwork, institutionally sponsored loans, scholarships/grants, traineeships, health care benefits, and unspecified assistantships also available. Financial award application deadline: 1/4. *Faculty research:* Native American, intercultural and indigenous people's studies, border theory, cultural studies, American pop culture, feminist theory, construction of gender in society. *Unit head:* Dr. Keith Griffler, Chair, 716-645-0802, Fax: 716-645-5977, E-mail: griffler@buffalo.edu. *Application contact:* Karen M. Reinard, Graduate Secretary, 716-645-0797, Fax: 716-645-5976, E-mail: kreinard@buffalo.edu. Website: http://www.transnationalstudies.buffalo.edu/graduate.shtml

University at Buffalo, the State University of New York, Graduate School, College of Arts and Sciences, Program in Canadian Studies, Buffalo, NY 14260. Offers Advanced Certificate. *Unit head:* Munroe Eagles, Director, 716-645-2082, Fax: 716-645-5976, E-mail: eagles@buffalo.edu. *Application contact:* Joseph C. Syracuse, Graduate Enrollment Manager, 716-645-2711, Fax: 716-645-3888, E-mail: jcs32@buffalo.edu. Website: http://www.canadianstudies.buffalo.edu/

University of Lethbridge, School of Graduate Studies, Lethbridge, AB T1K 3M4, Canada. Offers addictions counseling (M Sc); agricultural biotechnology (M Sc); agricultural studies (M Sc, MA); anthropology (MA); archaeology (M Sc, MA); art (MA, MFA); biochemistry (M Sc); biological sciences (M Sc); biomolecular science (PhD); biosystems and biodiversity (PhD); Canadian studies (MA); chemistry (M Sc); computer science (M Sc); computer science and geographical information science (M Sc); counseling (MC); counseling psychology (M Ed); dramatic arts (MA); earth, space, and physical science (PhD); economics (MA); education (MA); educational leadership (M Ed); English (MA); environmental science (M Sc); evolution and behavior (PhD); exercise science (M Sc); French (MA); French/German (MA); French/Spanish (MA); general education (M Ed); geography (M Sc, MA); German (MA); health sciences (M Sc); individualized multidisciplinary (M Sc, MA); kinesiology (M Sc, MA); management (M Sc), including accounting, finance, general management, human resource management and labor relations, information systems, international management, marketing, policy and strategy; mathematics (M Sc); modern languages (MA); music (M Mus, MA); Native American studies (MA); neuroscience (M Sc, PhD); new media (MA, MFA); nursing (M Sc, MN); philosophy (MA); physics (M Sc); political science (MA); psychology (M Sc, MA); religious studies (MA); sociology (MA); theatre and dramatic arts (MFA); theoretical and computational science (PhD); urban and regional studies (MA); women and gender studies (MA). Part-time and evening/weekend programs available. *Faculty:* 358. *Students:* 445 full-time (243 women), 116 part-time (72 women). Average age 31. 351 applicants, 26% accepted, 87 enrolled. In 2014, 129 master's, 13 doctorates awarded. *Degree requirements:* For master's, thesis (for some programs); for doctorate, comprehensive exam, thesis/dissertation. *Entrance requirements:* For master's, GMAT (for M Sc in management), bachelor's degree in related field, minimum GPA of 3.0 during previous 20 graded semester courses, 2 years' teaching or related experience (M Ed); for doctorate, master's degree, minimum graduate GPA of 3.5. Additional exam requirements/recommendations for international students: Required—TOEFL. Application fee: $100 Canadian dollars. *Financial support:* Fellowships, research assistantships, teaching assistantships, scholarships/grants, health care benefits, and unspecified assistantships available. *Faculty research:* Movement and brain plasticity, gibberellin physiology, photosynthesis, carbon cycling, molecular properties of main-group ring components. *Application contact:* School of Graduate Studies, 403-329-5194, E-mail: sgsinquiries@uleth.ca. Website: http://www.uleth.ca/graduatestudies/

University of Maine, Graduate School, College of Liberal Arts and Sciences, Department of History, Orono, ME 04469. Offers Asian studies (MA); Canadian studies (MA); European studies (MA). *Faculty:* 17 full-time (4 women). *Students:* 33 full-time (19 women), 12 part-time (4 women); includes 1 minority (Hispanic/Latino), 3 international. Average age 38. 31 applicants, 65% accepted, 6 enrolled. In 2014, 6 master's, 1 doctorate awarded. *Degree requirements:* For master's, variable foreign language requirement, thesis optional; for doctorate, one foreign language, comprehensive exam, thesis/dissertation. *Entrance requirements:* For master's and doctorate, GRE General Test. Additional exam requirements/recommendations for international students: Required—TOEFL. *Application deadline:* For fall admission, 1/15 priority date for domestic students; for spring admission, 10/15 for domestic students. Applications are processed on a rolling basis. Application fee: $65. Electronic applications accepted. *Expenses:* Tuition, state resident: part-time $658 per credit hour. Tuition, nonresident: part-time $1550 per credit hour. *Financial support:* In 2014–15, 26 students received support, including 4 fellowships (averaging $15,000 per year), 9 teaching assistantships with tuition reimbursements available (averaging $14,600 per year); career-related internships or fieldwork, Federal Work-Study, and tuition waivers (full and partial) also

available. Support available to part-time students. Financial award application deadline: 3/1. *Faculty research:* Environmental history, gender history, nationalism, classical, popular culture, Napoleonic, globalization, peasant studies, diplomatic history, military, Native America, Colonial U.S. *Unit head:* Dr. Stephen Miller, Chair, 207-581-1905, Fax: 207-581-1817, E-mail: stephen.miller@maine.edu. *Application contact:* Scott G. Delcourt, Assistant Vice President for Graduate Studies and Senior Associate Dean, 207-581-3291, Fax: 207-581-3232, E-mail: graduate@maine.edu. Website: http://www.umaine.edu/history/

University of Manitoba, Faculty of Graduate Studies, College Universitaire de Saint Boniface, Program in Canadian Studies, Winnipeg, MB R3T 2N2, Canada. Offers MA.

University of Ottawa, Faculty of Graduate and Postdoctoral Studies, Faculty of Arts, Institute of Canadian Studies, Ottawa, ON K1N 6N5, Canada. Offers economics (PhD); English (PhD); geography (PhD); history (PhD); lettres Franlfcaises (PhD); linguistics (PhD); philosophy (PhD); political science (PhD); psychology (PhD); religious studies (PhD); translation studies (PhD). *Degree requirements:* For doctorate, comprehensive exam, thesis/dissertation.

University of Regina, Faculty of Graduate Studies and Research, Faculty of Arts, Canadian Plains Studies Program, Regina, SK S4S 0A2, Canada. Offers MA, PhD. Offered as a special case program. Part-time programs available. *Faculty:* 1 (woman) part-time/adjunct. *Students:* 2 full-time (1 woman). In 2014, 1 master's, 2 doctorates awarded. *Degree requirements:* For master's, thesis; for doctorate, thesis/dissertation. *Entrance requirements:* Additional exam requirements/recommendations for international students: Required—TOEFL (minimum score 580 paper-based; 80 iBT), IELTS (minimum score 6.5), PTE (minimum score 59). *Application deadline:* Applications are processed on a rolling basis. Application fee: $100. Electronic applications accepted. *Expenses:* Tuition, area resident: Full-time $4900 Canadian dollars; part-time $837.65 Canadian dollars per semester. *International tuition:* $7900 Canadian dollars full-time. *Required fees:* $396 Canadian dollars; $86.90 Canadian dollars per semester. *Financial support:* Fellowships, research assistantships, teaching assistantships, and scholarships/grants available. Financial award application deadline:

6/15. *Unit head:* Dr. Thomas Bredohl, Associate Dean of Arts (Research and Graduate Studies), 306-585-5324, Fax: 306-585-5368, E-mail: thomas.bredohl@uregina.ca.

University of Saskatchewan, College of Graduate Studies and Research, College of Arts and Science, Department of Native Studies, Saskatoon, SK S7N 5A2, Canada. Offers MA, PhD. *Degree requirements:* For master's, thesis; for doctorate, comprehensive exam (for some programs), thesis/dissertation. *Entrance requirements:* Additional exam requirements/recommendations for international students: Required—TOEFL (minimum score 80 iBT); Recommended—IELTS (minimum score 6.5). Electronic applications accepted.

Wilfrid Laurier University, Faculty of Graduate and Postdoctoral Studies, Faculty of Arts, Department of Political Science, Waterloo, ON N2L 3C5, Canada. Offers Canadian political studies (MA); comparative politics/international relations (MA). Part-time programs available. *Degree requirements:* For master's, thesis optional. *Entrance requirements:* For master's, honors bachelor's degree or the equivalent in political science, minimum B average in undergraduate course work. Additional exam requirements/recommendations for international students: Required—TOEFL (minimum score 89 iBT). Electronic applications accepted. *Faculty research:* Political behavior/ political psychology, Canadian political studies, comparative, politics/relations, public opinion and electoral studies, international.

Wilfrid Laurier University, Faculty of Graduate and Postdoctoral Studies, Lyle S. Hallman Faculty of Social Work, Waterloo, ON N2L 3C5, Canada. Offers Aboriginal studies (MSW); community, policy, planning and organizations (MSW); critical social policy and organizational studies (PhD); individuals, families and groups (MSW); social work practice (individuals, families, groups and communities) (PhD); social work practice: individuals, families, groups and communities (PhD). Part-time programs available. *Degree requirements:* For master's, thesis optional; for doctorate, thesis/ dissertation. *Entrance requirements:* For master's, course work in social science, research methodology, and statistics; honors BA with a minimum B average; for doctorate, master's degree in social work, minimum A- average. Additional exam requirements/recommendations for international students: Required—TOEFL (minimum score 89 iBT). Electronic applications accepted. *Expenses:* Contact institution.

Cultural Studies

Ambrose University, Ambrose Seminary, Calgary, AB T3H 0L5, Canada. Offers Chinese ministries (Certificate); Christian studies (Certificate); intercultural ministries (M Div, Certificate); leadership and ministry (Diploma); pastoral ministries (M Div). *Accreditation:* ATS (one or more programs are accredited). Part-time programs available. Postbaccalaureate distance learning degree programs offered (minimal on-campus study). *Faculty:* 7 full-time (0 women), 24 part-time/adjunct (2 women). *Students:* 55 full-time (18 women), 128 part-time (64 women); includes 86 minority (3 Black or African American, non-Hispanic/Latino; 1 American Indian or Alaska Native, non-Hispanic/Latino; 82 Asian, non-Hispanic/Latino). Average age 41. *Degree requirements:* For master's, variable foreign language requirement, internship. *Entrance requirements:* For master's, undergraduate degree from other accredited university or bible college, minimum GPA of 2.0. Additional exam requirements/recommendations for international students: Required—TOEFL (minimum score 560 paper-based, 83 iBT) or IELTS (minimum score 6.5). *Application deadline:* For fall admission, 7/15 for domestic students, 3/1 for international students; for winter admission, 11/15 for domestic students, 7/1 for international students. Applications are processed on a rolling basis. Application fee: $70 ($100 for international students). Electronic applications accepted. *Financial support:* Career-related internships or fieldwork and scholarships/grants available. Support available to part-time students. Financial award application deadline: 3/30. *Faculty research:* Evangelicalism and sociology, missiological trends, chaplaincy, intertestamental studies, postmodernism. *Unit head:* Dr. Paul Spilsbury, Vice-President of Academic Affairs, 403-410-2917, Fax: 403-571-2556, E-mail: pspilsbury@ambrose.edu. *Application contact:* Kalie Eeles, Enrollment Advisor, 403-410-2954, Fax: 403-571-2556, E-mail: enrolment@ambrose.edu. Website: https://ambrose.edu/seminary

American University, School of International Service, Washington, DC 20016-8071. Offers comparative and regional studies (Certificate); cross-cultural communication (Certificate); development management (MS); ethics, peace, and global affairs (MA); European studies (Certificate); global environmental policy (MA, Certificate); global information technology (Certificate); international affairs (MA), including comparative and international disability policy, comparative and regional studies, international economic relations, international politics, natural resources and sustainable development, U.S. foreign policy; international communication (MA, Certificate); international development (MA, Certificate); international economic policy (Certificate); international economic relations (Certificate); international media (MA); international peace and conflict resolution (MA, Certificate); international politics (Certificate); international relations (PhD); international service (MIS); peacebuilding (Certificate); social enterprise (MA); the Americas (Certificate); United States foreign policy (Certificate); JD/MA. Part-time and evening/weekend programs available. Postbaccalaureate distance learning degree programs offered (no on-campus study). *Faculty:* 112 full-time (43 women), 59 part-time/adjunct (27 women). *Students:* 545 full-time (335 women), 443 part-time (271 women); includes 231 minority (82 Black or African American, non-Hispanic/Latino; 8 American Indian or Alaska Native, non-Hispanic/Latino; 51 Asian, non-Hispanic/Latino; 81 Hispanic/Latino; 2 Native Hawaiian or other Pacific Islander, non-Hispanic/Latino; 7 Two or more races, non-Hispanic/ Latino), 120 international. Average age 28. 1,991 applicants, 70% accepted, 365 enrolled. In 2014, 426 master's, 9 doctorates, 6 other advanced degrees awarded. Terminal master's awarded for partial completion of doctoral program. *Degree requirements:* For master's, one foreign language, comprehensive exam, thesis or alternative; for doctorate, one foreign language, comprehensive exam, thesis/ dissertation. *Entrance requirements:* For master's, GRE, transcripts, resume, 2 letters of recommendation, statement of purpose; for doctorate, GRE, transcripts, resume, 3 letters of recommendation, statement of purpose. Additional exam requirements/ recommendations for international students: Required—TOEFL (minimum score 600 paper-based; 100 iBT). *Application deadline:* For fall admission, 1/15 for domestic students; for spring admission, 10/1 for domestic students, 9/15 for international students. Application fee: $50. Electronic applications accepted. *Financial support:* Application deadline: 1/15. *Unit head:* Dr. James Goldgeier, Dean, 202-885-1603, Fax: 202-885-2494, E-mail: goldgeier@american.edu. *Application contact:* Jia Jiang, Associate Director, Graduate Education Enrollment, 202-885-1689, Fax: 202-885-1109, E-mail: jiang@american.edu. Website: http://www.american.edu/sis/

The American University of Paris, Graduate Programs, Paris, France. Offers cross-cultural and sustainable business management (MA); cultural translation (MA); global communications (MA); global communications and civil society (MA); international affairs (MA); international affairs, conflict resolution and civil society development (MA); Middle East and Islamic studies (MA); Middle East and Islamic studies and international affairs (MA); public policy and international affairs (MA); public policy and international law (MA). *Degree requirements:* For master's, thesis (for some programs). *Entrance requirements:* For master's, minimum undergraduate GPA of 3.0. Additional exam requirements/recommendations for international students: Recommended—TOEFL, IELTS. Electronic applications accepted.

Appalachian State University, Cratis D. Williams Graduate School, Center for Appalachian Studies, Boone, NC 28608. Offers culture (MA); roots and music (MA); sustainable development (MA). Part-time programs available. *Degree requirements:* For master's, one foreign language, comprehensive exam, thesis optional. *Entrance requirements:* For master's, GRE General Test, 3 letters of recommendation. Additional exam requirements/recommendations for international students: Required—TOEFL (minimum score 570 paper-based; 79 iBT), IELTS (minimum score 6.5). Electronic applications accepted. *Faculty research:* Appalachian culture, sustainable development, Appalachian music.

Arizona State University at the Tempe campus, College of Liberal Arts and Sciences, Department of English, Program in Film and Media Studies, Tempe, AZ 85287-0402. Offers American media and popular culture (MAS). Part-time and evening/weekend programs available. Postbaccalaureate distance learning degree programs offered (no on-campus study). *Degree requirements:* For master's, integrated project. *Entrance requirements:* For master's, minimum GPA of 3.0 or equivalent in last 2 years of work leading to bachelor's degree. Additional exam requirements/recommendations for international students: Required—TOEFL, IELTS, or PTE. Electronic applications accepted. *Expenses:* Contact institution.

Arizona State University at the Tempe campus, College of Liberal Arts and Sciences, School of International Letters and Cultures, Program in Spanish, Tempe, AZ 85287-0202. Offers cultural studies (PhD); linguistics (MA), including second language acquisition/applied linguistics, sociolinguistics; literature (PhD); literature and culture (MA). Part-time programs available. Terminal master's awarded for partial completion of doctoral program. *Degree requirements:* For master's, thesis, oral defense; written comprehensive exam (literature and culture); portfolio review (linguistics); interactive Program of Study (iPOS) submitted before completing 50 percent of required credit hours; for doctorate, comprehensive exam, thesis/dissertation, interactive Program of Study (iPOS) submitted before completing 50 percent of required credit hours. *Entrance requirements:* For master's, GRE (recommended), BA in Spanish or close equivalent from accredited institution with minimum GPA of 3.5, 3 letters of recommendation, personal statement, academic writing sample; for doctorate, GRE (recommended), MA in Spanish or equivalent from accredited institution with minimum GPA of 3.75, 3 letters of recommendation, personal statement, academic writing sample. Additional exam requirements/recommendations for international students: Required—TOEFL (minimum score 550 paper-based; 83 iBT), IELTS (minimum score 6.5). Electronic applications accepted.

Assemblies of God Theological Seminary, Graduate and Professional Programs, Springfield, MO 65802. Offers Bible theology (PhD); Christian ministries (MA); counseling (MA); divinity (M Div); intercultural ministry (MA); intercultural studies (PhD); ministry (D Min); missiology (D Miss); theological studies (MA). *Accreditation:* ATS. Part-time and evening/weekend programs available. Postbaccalaureate distance learning degree programs offered (minimal on-campus study). *Degree requirements:* For master's, variable foreign language requirement; for doctorate, thesis/dissertation. *Entrance requirements:* For master's, minimum GPA of 2.5; for doctorate, GRE (for PhD in Bible theology), minimum GPA of 3.0. Additional exam requirements/ recommendations for international students: Required—TOEFL (minimum score 550 paper-based; 80 iBT). Electronic applications accepted.

Athabasca University, Centre for Integrated Studies, Athabasca, AB T9S 3A3, Canada. Offers adult education (MA); community studies (MA); cultural studies (MA); educational studies (MA); global change (MA); work, organization, and leadership (MA). Part-time and evening/weekend programs available. Postbaccalaureate distance

learning degree programs offered (no on-campus study). *Degree requirements:* For master's, project. *Entrance requirements:* Additional exam requirements/recommendations for international students: Required—TOEFL (minimum score 560 paper-based). Electronic applications accepted. *Faculty research:* Women's history, literature and culture studies, sustainable development, labor and education.

Baptist Bible College, Graduate School of Theology, Springfield, MO 65803-3498. Offers biblical counseling (MA); biblical studies (MA); church ministry (MA); intercultural studies (MA); theology (M Div). Part-time programs available. *Degree requirements:* For master's, 2 foreign languages, thesis (for some programs). Electronic applications accepted.

Baylor University, Graduate School, College of Arts and Sciences, Department of History, Waco, TX 76798. Offers history (MA); religion and culture (PhD); U.S. and Britain (PhD). Part-time programs available. Terminal master's awarded for partial completion of doctoral program. *Degree requirements:* For master's, one foreign language, comprehensive exam, thesis; for doctorate, one foreign language, comprehensive exam, thesis/dissertation. *Entrance requirements:* For master's and doctorate, GRE General Test, 18 semester hours in history. Additional exam requirements/recommendations for international students: Required—TOEFL. *Faculty research:* American religion and culture, medieval women and religion, U.S. women's history, Chinese missions, late nineteenth-century Germany, twentieth-century urban United States.

Binghamton University, State University of New York, Graduate School, School of Arts and Sciences, Philosophy, Interpretation and Culture Program, Vestal, NY 13850. Offers MA, PhD. *Faculty:* 1 part-time/adjunct (0 women). *Students:* 15 part-time (9 women); includes 3 minority (1 Black or African American, non-Hispanic/Latino; 1 Hispanic/Latino; 1 Native Hawaiian or other Pacific Islander, non-Hispanic/Latino), 8 international. Average age 41. In 2014, 6 doctorates awarded. *Degree requirements:* For doctorate, thesis/dissertation. *Entrance requirements:* Additional exam requirements/recommendations for international students: Required—TOEFL (minimum score 550 paper-based; 80 iBT). Application fee: $75. *Expenses:* Tuition, state resident: full-time $7776; part-time $432 per credit. Tuition, nonresident: full-time $15,138; part-time $841 per credit. *Required fees:* $1754; $213 per credit. Tuition and fees vary according to degree level and program. *Financial support:* In 2014–15, 1 student received support. Career-related internships or fieldwork, Federal Work-Study, institutionally sponsored loans, scholarships/grants, health care benefits, and unspecified assistantships available. Financial award application deadline: 2/15; financial award applicants required to submit FAFSA. *Unit head:* Dr. Nkiru Nzegwu, Coordinator, 607-777-3082, E-mail: panap@binghamton.edu. *Application contact:* Kishan Zuber, Recruiting and Admissions Coordinator, 607-777-2151, Fax: 607-777-2501, E-mail: kzuber@binghamton.edu.

Biola University, Cook School of Intercultural Studies, La Mirada, CA 90639-0001. Offers anthropology (MA); applied linguistics (MA); intercultural education (PhD); intercultural studies (MA, PhD); linguistics (Certificate); linguistics and Biblical languages (MA); missions (MA); teaching English to speakers of other languages (MA, Certificate). Part-time programs available. *Faculty:* 19. *Students:* 86 full-time (41 women), 119 part-time (58 women); includes 68 minority (7 Black or African American, non-Hispanic/Latino; 1 American Indian or Alaska Native, non-Hispanic/Latino; 42 Asian, non-Hispanic/Latino; 14 Hispanic/Latino; 4 Two or more races, non-Hispanic/Latino), 29 international. In 2014, 29 master's, 16 doctorates awarded. *Entrance requirements:* For master's, minimum undergraduate GPA of 3.0; for doctorate, master's degree or equivalent, 3 years of cross-cultural experience, minimum graduate GPA of 3.3. Additional exam requirements/recommendations for international students: Required—TOEFL. *Application deadline:* For fall admission, 7/1 for domestic students, 6/1 for international students; for spring admission, 12/1 for domestic students; for summer admission, 5/1 for domestic students. Applications are processed on a rolling basis. Application fee: $65. Electronic applications accepted. *Financial support:* Scholarships/grants available. Support available to part-time students. Financial award applicants required to submit FAFSA. *Faculty research:* Linguistics, anthropology, intercultural studies, teaching English to speakers of other languages, missions, missiology. *Unit head:* Dr. Bulus Y. Galadima, Dean, 562-903-4844. *Application contact:* Graduate Admissions Office, 562-903-4752, E-mail: graduate.admissions@biola.edu.
Website: http://cook.biola.edu

Biola University, Talbot School of Theology, La Mirada, CA 90639-0001. Offers adult/family ministry (MACE); Bible exposition (MA, Th M); Biblical and theological studies (MA); children's ministry (MACE); Christian education (M Div); cross-cultural education ministry (MACE); educational studies (Ed D, PhD); evangelism and discipleship (M Div); general Christian education (MACE); Messianic Jewish studies (M Div, Certificate); missions and intercultural studies (M Div); New Testament (MA, Th M); Old Testament (MA); Old Testament and Semitics (Th M); pastoral and general ministry (M Div); pastoral care and counseling (M Div); philosophy (MA); spiritual formation (M Div, Certificate); spiritual formation and soul care (MA); theology (Th M, D Min, Certificate); youth ministry (MACE). *Accreditation:* ATS. Part-time and evening/weekend programs available. *Faculty:* 77. *Students:* 581 full-time (140 women), 554 part-time (155 women); includes 522 minority (42 Black or African American, non-Hispanic/Latino; 3 American Indian or Alaska Native, non-Hispanic/Latino; 370 Asian, non-Hispanic/Latino; 78 Hispanic/Latino; 2 Native Hawaiian or other Pacific Islander, non-Hispanic/Latino; 27 Two or more races, non-Hispanic/Latino), 121 international. 437 applicants, 78% accepted, 241 enrolled. In 2014, 182 master's, 33 doctorates awarded. *Entrance requirements:* For master's, bachelor's degree from accredited college or university; minimum GPA of 2.6 (for M Div), 3.0 (for MA); for doctorate, M Div or MA. Additional exam requirements/recommendations for international students: Required—TOEFL (minimum score 600 paper-based; 88 iBT). *Application deadline:* For fall admission, 7/1 for domestic students, 6/1 for international students; for spring admission, 12/1 priority date for domestic students. Applications are processed on a rolling basis. Application fee: $65. Electronic applications accepted. *Financial support:* Scholarships/grants and unspecified assistantships available. Support available to part-time students. Financial award applicants required to submit FAFSA. *Faculty research:* New Testament, Old Testament, spiritual formation, Christian education, theological studies, Christian ministry, preaching and pastoral ministry, language and literature, bible exposition, Christian leadership. *Unit head:* Dr. Clint Arnold, Dean, 562-903-4816, Fax: 562-903-4748. *Application contact:* Graduate Admissions Office, 562-903-4752, E-mail: graduate.admissions@biola.edu.
Website: http://www.talbot.edu/

Boston University, Metropolitan College, Program in Gastronomy, Boston, MA 02215. Offers business (MLA); communications (MLA); food policy (MLA); history and culture (MLA). Part-time and evening/weekend programs available. *Faculty:* 3 full-time (2 women), 14 part-time/adjunct (8 women). *Students:* 4 full-time (all women), 82 part-time (72 women); includes 8 minority (1 Black or African American, non-Hispanic/Latino; 4 Asian, non-Hispanic/Latino; 1 Hispanic/Latino; 2 Two or more races, non-Hispanic/Latino), 7 international. Average age 30. 58 applicants, 76% accepted, 27 enrolled. In 2014, 44 master's awarded. *Degree requirements:* For master's, thesis optional. *Entrance requirements:* Additional exam requirements/recommendations for international students: Required—TOEFL. *Application deadline:* Applications are processed on a rolling basis. Application fee: $80. Electronic applications accepted. *Expenses:* Expenses: $800 per credit part-time; student services fees: $60 per semester; technology fee of $60 per credit (for online courses). *Financial support:* In 2014–15, 4 research assistantships (averaging $4,200 per year) were awarded; career-related internships or fieldwork, scholarships/grants, and unspecified assistantships also available. Support available to part-time students. Financial award applicants required to submit FAFSA. *Faculty research:* Food studies. *Unit head:* Dr. Mary Beaudry, Interim Faculty Coordinator, 617-353-6916, Fax: 617-353-4130, E-mail: gastrmla@bu.edu. *Application contact:* Barbara Rotger, Program Manager, 617-353-6916, Fax: 617-353-4130, E-mail: brotger@bu.edu.
Website: http://www.bu.edu/met/gastronomy

Brock University, Faculty of Graduate Studies, Faculty of Social Sciences, Program in Popular Culture, St. Catharines, ON L2S 3A1, Canada. Offers MA. Part-time programs available. *Degree requirements:* For master's, thesis optional. *Entrance requirements:* For master's, honors BA. Additional exam requirements/recommendations for international students: Required—TOEFL (minimum score 550 paper-based; 80 iBT), IELTS (minimum score 6.5), TWE (minimum score 4). Electronic applications accepted. *Faculty research:* Film and television studies, popular music, historical aspects of popular culture, popular literature.

Carnegie Mellon University, Dietrich College of Humanities and Social Sciences, Department of History, Pittsburgh, PA 15213-3891. Offers African and African-American diaspora (PhD); culture and power (PhD); labor, politics and social movements (PhD); technology, environment, science and health (PhD); women, gender and the family (PhD). Part-time programs available. *Degree requirements:* For doctorate, oral and written comprehensive exams, dissertation defense. *Entrance requirements:* For doctorate, GRE General Test. Additional exam requirements/recommendations for international students: Required—TOEFL. Electronic applications accepted. *Faculty research:* Anthropology and history, African-American history, technology/environment, cultural history analysis.

Central Michigan University, College of Graduate Studies, College of Humanities and Social and Behavioral Sciences, Program in Humanities, Mount Pleasant, MI 48859. Offers humanities (MA), including contemporary issues in the humanities: race, class, and gender, images and ideas of self, Native American issues in modern culture, popular culture studies, the rise of industrial society. Part-time and evening/weekend programs available. *Degree requirements:* For master's, thesis or alternative. Electronic applications accepted. *Faculty research:* Rise of industrial society; images and ideas of self; contemporary issues of race, class, and gender; popular culture; Native American issues in modern culture.

Chapman University, College of Educational Studies, Orange, CA 92866. Offers communication sciences and disorders (MS); counseling (MA), including school counseling (MA, Credential); education (PhD), including cultural and curricular studies, disability studies, leadership studies, school psychology (PhD, Credential); educational psychology (MA); leadership development (MA); pupil personnel services (Credential), including school counseling (MA, Credential), school psychology (PhD, Credential); school psychology (Ed S); single subject (Credential); special education (MA, Credential), including mild/moderate (Credential), moderate/severe (Credential); speech language pathology (Credential); teaching (MA), including elementary education, secondary education. *Accreditation:* Teacher Education Accreditation Council. Part-time and evening/weekend programs available. *Faculty:* 31 full-time (18 women), 78 part-time/adjunct (61 women). *Students:* 257 full-time (206 women), 187 part-time (141 women); includes 186 minority (9 Black or African American, non-Hispanic/Latino; 54 Asian, non-Hispanic/Latino; 104 Hispanic/Latino; 1 Native Hawaiian or other Pacific Islander, non-Hispanic/Latino; 18 Two or more races, non-Hispanic/Latino), 10 international. Average age 29. 614 applicants, 35% accepted, 131 enrolled. In 2014, 128 master's, 10 doctorates awarded. *Entrance requirements:* Additional exam requirements/recommendations for international students: Required—TOEFL (minimum score 550 paper-based; 80 iBT). *Application deadline:* Applications are processed on a rolling basis. Application fee: $60. Electronic applications accepted. *Financial support:* Fellowships and scholarships/grants available. Financial award application deadline: 6/30; financial award applicants required to submit FAFSA. *Unit head:* Dr. Don Cardinal, Dean, 714-997-6781, E-mail: cardinal@chapman.edu. *Application contact:* Admissions Coordinator, 714-997-6714.
Website: http://www.chapman.edu/CES/

Charlotte Christian College and Theological Seminary, Graduate Program, Charlotte, NC 28205. Offers urban Christian ministry (MA), including church planting, multi-cultural studies, sacred music, youth ministry. Part-time and evening/weekend programs available. *Faculty:* 5 full-time (1 woman), 9 part-time/adjunct (2 women). *Students:* 2 full-time (1 woman), 25 part-time (15 women); includes 18 minority (17 Black or African American, non-Hispanic/Latino; 1 Hispanic/Latino), 2 international. Average age 47. 2 applicants, 100% accepted, 2 enrolled. In 2014, 2 master's awarded. *Degree requirements:* For master's, thesis. *Entrance requirements:* For master's, MAT, writing sample/essay. Additional exam requirements/recommendations for international students: Required—TOEFL, IELTS. *Application deadline:* For fall admission, 7/24 for domestic students, 7/18 for international students; for spring admission, 12/11 for domestic students, 12/5 for international students; for summer admission, 4/18 for domestic and international students. Application fee: $50 ($140 for international students). Electronic applications accepted. *Expenses:* Expenses: 1 course: $1,200; 2 courses: $2,300; 3 courses: $3,300; 4 courses $3,900. *Financial support:* In 2014–15, 5 students received support. Federal Work-Study and scholarships/grants available. Financial award application deadline: 4/1; financial award applicants required to submit FAFSA. *Unit head:* Anne Witt, Registrar/Director of International Students, 704-344-6882 Ext. 103, Fax: 704-334-6885, E-mail: abwitt@charlottechristian.edu. *Application contact:* Constance Hemphill, Director of Admissions, 704-334-6882 Ext. 115, Fax: 704-334-6885, E-mail: chemphill@charlottechristian.edu.
Website: http://www.charlottechristian.edu

Claremont Graduate University, Graduate Programs, School of Arts and Humanities, Department of Cultural Studies, Claremont, CA 91711-6160. Offers Africana studies (Certificate); cultural studies (MA, PhD); media studies (MA, PhD); museum studies (MA). Part-time programs available. *Faculty:* 6 full-time (2 women). *Students:* 35 full-time (22 women), 15 part-time (11 women); includes 20 minority (6 Black or African American, non-Hispanic/Latino; 1 American Indian or Alaska Native, non-Hispanic/Latino; 5 Asian, non-Hispanic/Latino; 8 Hispanic/Latino), 7 international. Average age 35. In 2014, 6 master's, 3 doctorates, 1 other advanced degree awarded. *Entrance requirements:* For master's and doctorate, GRE General Test. Additional exam requirements/recommendations for international students: Required—TOEFL (minimum score 550 paper-based; 80 iBT). *Application deadline:* For fall admission, 2/1 priority date for domestic and international students. Applications are processed on a rolling basis. Application fee: $80. Electronic applications accepted. *Expenses: Tuition:* Full-time $41,784; part-time $1741 per credit. *Required fees:* $600; $300 per semester. *Financial support:* Fellowships, research assistantships, Federal Work-Study, institutionally sponsored loans, and scholarships/grants available. Support available to part-time students. Financial award application deadline: 2/15; financial award applicants required to submit FAFSA. *Unit head:* Eve Oishi, Chair, 909-607-7587, E-mail: eve.oishi@cgu.edu. *Application contact:* Amy Sandefur, Assistant Director of

Admissions, 909-607-9101, E-mail: amy.sandefur@cgu.edu. Website: http://www.cgu.edu/pages/441.asp

Columbia International University, Columbia Biblical Seminary and School of Ministry, Columbia, SC 29230-3122. Offers academic ministries (M Div); Bible and theology (Certificate); bible exposition (M Div, MABE); Biblical ministry (Certificate); chaplaincy (M Div); intercultural studies (MAIS); leadership (D Min); member care (D Min); missions (D Min); preaching (D Min); theological studies (MA). *Accreditation:* ATS (one or more programs are accredited). Part-time and evening/weekend programs available. *Faculty:* 14 full-time (1 woman), 9 part-time/adjunct (1 woman). *Students:* 180 full-time (59 women), 218 part-time (61 women); includes 81 minority (58 Black or African American, non-Hispanic/Latino; 1 American Indian or Alaska Native, non-Hispanic/Latino; 18 Asian, non-Hispanic/Latino; 4 Hispanic/Latino), 22 international. Average age 36. 277 applicants, 81% accepted, 117 enrolled. In 2014, 74 master's, 3 doctorates, 15 other advanced degrees awarded. *Degree requirements:* For doctorate, comprehensive exam, thesis/dissertation. *Entrance requirements:* For doctorate, 3 years of ministerial experience, M Div. Additional exam requirements/recommendations for international students: Required—TOEFL. *Application deadline:* For fall admission, 8/1 priority date for domestic and international students; for winter admission, 12/15 priority date for domestic and international students; for spring admission, 1/15 priority date for domestic and international students. Applications are processed on a rolling basis. Application fee: $45. Electronic applications accepted. *Expenses: Tuition:* Full-time $9540; part-time $530 per credit hour. *Required fees:* $480; $240 per semester. *Financial support:* In 2014–15, 120 students received support. Career-related internships or fieldwork, Federal Work-Study, institutionally sponsored loans, and scholarships/grants available. Financial award application deadline: 3/15; financial award applicants required to submit FAFSA. *Unit head:* Dr. Junias Venugopal, Dean, 803-754-4100 Ext. 5330, Fax: 803-786-4209, E-mail: jvenugopal@ciu.edu. *Application contact:* Michelle MacGregor, Director of Admissions, 800-777-2227 Ext. 5335, Fax: 803-786-4209, E-mail: yescbs@ciu.edu.
Website: http://www.ciu.edu/discover-ciu/who-we-are/academics/seminary-school-ministry

Concordia University, School of Theology, Irvine, CA 92612-3299. Offers Christian leadership (MA); research in theology (MA); theology and culture (MA). Part-time and evening/weekend programs available. *Degree requirements:* For master's, project/thesis or vicarage. *Entrance requirements:* For master's, official college transcript(s), statement of intent, 2 references, interview. Additional exam requirements/recommendations for international students: Required—TOEFL. Electronic applications accepted. *Expenses:* Contact institution.

Cornell University, Graduate School, Graduate Fields of Arts and Sciences, Field of English Language and Literature, Ithaca, NY 14853-0001. Offers African-American literature (PhD); American literature after 1865 (PhD); American literature to 1865 (PhD); American studies (PhD); colonial and postcolonial literatures (PhD); creative writing (MFA); cultural studies (PhD); dramatic literature (PhD); English poetry (PhD); English Renaissance to 1660 (PhD); lesbian, bisexual, and gay literary studies (PhD); literary criticism and theory (PhD); Old and Middle English (PhD); prose fiction (PhD); Restoration and the eighteenth-century (PhD); the nineteenth century (PhD); the twentieth century (PhD); women's literature (PhD); MFA/PhD. Terminal master's awarded for partial completion of doctoral program. *Degree requirements:* For master's, one foreign language, thesis; for doctorate, one foreign language, comprehensive exam, thesis/dissertation, teaching experience. *Entrance requirements:* For master's, GRE General Test, 3 letters of recommendation, creative writing sample; for doctorate, GRE General Test, GRE Subject Test (English), 3 letters of recommendation, writing sample. Additional exam requirements/recommendations for international students: Required—TOEFL (minimum score 600 paper-based; 77 iBT). Electronic applications accepted. *Faculty research:* English and American literature, women's writing, ethnic and post-colonial literature, critical theory, medievalism.

Eastern Michigan University, Graduate School, College of Arts and Sciences, Department of Sociology, Anthropology and Criminology, Program in Cultural Museum Studies, Ypsilanti, MI 48197. Offers Graduate Certificate. Part-time and evening/weekend programs available. Postbaccalaureate distance learning degree programs offered (minimal on-campus study). *Students:* 2 full-time (both women), 2 part-time (1 woman); includes 1 minority (Asian, non-Hispanic/Latino). Average age 34. 2 applicants, 100% accepted, 2 enrolled. In 2014, 1 Graduate Certificate awarded. *Entrance requirements:* Additional exam requirements/recommendations for international students: Required—TOEFL. *Application deadline:* Applications are processed on a rolling basis. Application fee: $45. *Financial support:* Fellowships, research assistantships with full tuition reimbursements, teaching assistantships with full tuition reimbursements, career-related internships or fieldwork, Federal Work-Study, institutionally sponsored loans, scholarships/grants, tuition waivers (partial), and unspecified assistantships available. Support available to part-time students. Financial award applicants required to submit FAFSA. *Application contact:* Dr. Liza Cerroni-Long, Advisor, 734-487-0012, Fax: 734-487-9666, E-mail: liza.cerroni-long@emich.edu.

Eastern Michigan University, Graduate School, College of Education, Department of Teacher Education, Program in Urban/Diversity Education, Ypsilanti, MI 48197. Offers MA. *Students:* 6 part-time (all women); includes 3 minority (1 Black or African American, non-Hispanic/Latino; 2 Asian, non-Hispanic/Latino). Average age 27. 2 applicants, 100% accepted, 1 enrolled. In 2014, 4 master's awarded. Application fee: $45. *Application contact:* Dr. Patricia Williams-Boyd, Advisor, 734-487-3260, Fax: 734-487-2101, E-mail: pwilliams1@emich.edu.

Florida State University, The Graduate School, College of Fine Arts, Department of Art History, Tallahassee, FL 32306. Offers art history (MA, PhD); museum and cultural heritage studies (MA); museum studies (Certificate). *Accreditation:* NASAD. Part-time programs available. *Faculty:* 10 full-time (4 women), 10 part-time/adjunct (5 women). *Students:* 52 full-time (46 women), 4 part-time (3 women); includes 8 minority (1 Asian, non-Hispanic/Latino; 4 Hispanic/Latino; 3 Two or more races, non-Hispanic/Latino). Average age 25. 43 applicants, 77% accepted, 17 enrolled. In 2014, 8 master's, 2 doctorates awarded. Terminal master's awarded for partial completion of doctoral program. *Degree requirements:* For master's, one foreign language, thesis (for some programs), capstone project (for some programs); for doctorate, 2 foreign languages, comprehensive exam, thesis/dissertation. *Entrance requirements:* For master's, GRE General Test, minimum GPA of 3.0; for doctorate, GRE General Test, minimum GPA of 3.5. Additional exam requirements/recommendations for international students: Required—TOEFL (minimum score 80 iBT). *Application deadline:* For fall admission, 12/10 for domestic and international students. Applications are processed on a rolling basis. Application fee: $35. Electronic applications accepted. *Expenses:* Expenses: $17,745 in-state, $40,932 out-of-state (for MA and PhD in art history and Certificate in museum studies); $23,660 in-state, $54,576 out-of-state (for MA in museum and cultural heritage studies). *Financial support:* In 2014–15, 33 students received support, including 8 fellowships with full tuition reimbursements available (averaging $10,827 per year), 15 research assistantships with full tuition reimbursements available (averaging $5,175 per year), 8 teaching assistantships with full tuition reimbursements available (averaging $6,109 per year); career-related internships or fieldwork, Federal Work-Study, institutionally sponsored loans, scholarships/grants, and unspecified

assistantships also available. Financial award application deadline: 12/10; financial award applicants required to submit FAFSA. *Faculty research:* Modern art and critical theory, medieval, Renaissance and Baroque, Pre-Columbian and Spanish Colonial, visual arts of the Americas. *Unit head:* Dr. Adam Jolles, Associate Professor of Art History/Department Chair, 850-644-7066, E-mail: ajolles@fsu.edu. *Application contact:* Leah Sherman, Academic Program Specialist/Graduate Student Advisor, 850-644-8207, E-mail: lrsherman@fsu.edu.
Website: http://arthistory.fsu.edu/

Gardner-Webb University, School of Divinity, Boiling Springs, NC 28017. Offers biblical studies (M Div); Christian education and formation (M Div); intercultural studies (M Div); ministry (D Min); missiology (M Div); pastoral care and counseling (M Div); pastoral care and counseling/member care for missionaries (D Min); pastoral studies (M Div); M Div/MA; M Div/MBA. *Accreditation:* ACIPE; ATS. Part-time programs available. *Faculty:* 10 full-time (2 women), 5 part-time/adjunct (1 woman). *Students:* 151 full-time (82 women), 76 part-time (22 women); includes 106 minority (92 Black or African American, non-Hispanic/Latino; 7 Asian, non-Hispanic/Latino; 7 Hispanic/Latino). Average age 41. 110 applicants, 53% accepted, 58 enrolled. *Entrance requirements:* For master's, minimum GPA of 2.6; for doctorate, minimum GPA of 2.75. Additional exam requirements/recommendations for international students: Required—TOEFL (minimum score 500 paper-based; 61 iBT). *Application deadline:* Applications are processed on a rolling basis. Application fee: $40. Electronic applications accepted. *Expenses:* Expenses: Contact institution. *Financial support:* Fellowships, institutionally sponsored loans, and unspecified assistantships available. Support available to part-time students. Financial award application deadline: 5/15. *Faculty research:* Jewish-Christian dialogue, Islam. *Unit head:* Dr. Robert W. Canoy, Sr., Dean, 704-406-4400, Fax: 704-406-3935, E-mail: rcanoy@gardner-webb.edu. *Application contact:* Kheresa Harmon, Director of Admissions, 704-406-3205, Fax: 704-406-3895, E-mail: kharmon@gardner-webb.edu.
Website: http://gardner-webb.edu/academic-programs-and-resources/colleges-and-schools/divinity/index

George Mason University, College of Humanities and Social Sciences, Interdisciplinary Studies Program, Fairfax, VA 22030. Offers community college teaching (MAIS); computational social science (MAIS); energy and sustainability (MAIS); film and video studies (MAIS); folklore studies (MAIS); higher education administration (MAIS); neuroethics (MAIS); religion, culture and values (MAIS); social entrepreneurship (MAIS); war and military in society (MAIS); women and gender studies (MAIS). *Faculty:* 11 full-time (3 women), 4 part-time/adjunct (all women). *Students:* 22 full-time (13 women), 87 part-time (51 women); includes 31 minority (21 Black or African American, non-Hispanic/Latino; 2 Asian, non-Hispanic/Latino; 6 Hispanic/Latino; 2 Two or more races, non-Hispanic/Latino), 6 international. Average age 32. 75 applicants, 75% accepted, 28 enrolled. In 2014, 31 master's awarded. *Degree requirements:* For master's, project or thesis. *Entrance requirements:* For master's, 3 letters of recommendation; writing sample; official transcript; resume. Additional exam requirements/recommendations for international students: Required—TOEFL (minimum score 570 paper-based; 80 iBT), IELTS (minimum score 6.5), PTE. *Application deadline:* For fall admission, 3/1 priority date for domestic students; for spring admission, 10/15 for domestic students. Application fee: $65 ($80 for international students). Electronic applications accepted. *Expenses:* Tuition, state resident: full-time $9794; part-time $408 per credit hour. Tuition, nonresident: full-time $26,978; part-time $1124 per credit hour. *Required fees:* $2820; $118 per credit hour. Tuition and fees vary according to course load and program. *Financial support:* In 2014–15, 10 students received support, including 1 fellowship (averaging $6,935 per year), 2 research assistantships with full and partial tuition reimbursements available (averaging $6,499 per year), 8 teaching assistantships with full and partial tuition reimbursements available (averaging $8,271 per year); career-related internships or fieldwork, Federal Work-Study, scholarships/grants, unspecified assistantships, and health care benefits (for full-time research or teaching assistantship recipients) also available. Support available to part-time students. Financial award application deadline: 3/1; financial award applicants required to submit FAFSA. *Faculty research:* Combined English and folklore, religious and cultural studies (Christianity and Muslim society). *Unit head:* Meredith H. Lair, Director, 703-993-2159, Fax: 703-993-1251, E-mail: mlair@gmu.edu. *Application contact:* Lisa Struckmeyer, Administrative Coordinator, 703-993-8762, Fax: 703-993-5585, E-mail: lstruckm@gmu.edu.
Website: http://mais.gmu.edu

George Mason University, College of Humanities and Social Sciences, Program in Cultural Studies, Fairfax, VA 22030. Offers PhD. *Faculty:* 13 full-time (5 women). *Students:* 32 full-time (21 women), 32 part-time (19 women); includes 10 minority (4 Black or African American, non-Hispanic/Latino; 1 American Indian or Alaska Native, non-Hispanic/Latino; 1 Asian, non-Hispanic/Latino; 2 Hispanic/Latino; 2 Two or more races, non-Hispanic/Latino), 8 international. Average age 34. 42 applicants, 60% accepted, 11 enrolled. In 2014, 5 doctorates awarded. *Degree requirements:* For doctorate, one foreign language, comprehensive exam, thesis/dissertation, foreign language exams. *Entrance requirements:* For doctorate, GRE, expanded goals statement; 3 letters of recommendation from academic sources; writing sample; master's degree in relevant field; official transcripts. Additional exam requirements/recommendations for international students: Required—TOEFL (minimum score 570 paper-based; 80 iBT), IELTS (minimum score 6.5), PTE. *Application deadline:* For fall admission, 1/15 for domestic students. Application fee: $65 ($80 for international students). Electronic applications accepted. *Expenses:* Tuition, state resident: full-time $9794; part-time $408 per credit hour. Tuition, nonresident: full-time $26,978; part-time $1124 per credit hour. *Required fees:* $2820; $118 per credit hour. Tuition and fees vary according to course load and program. *Financial support:* In 2014–15, 27 students received support, including 2 fellowships (averaging $8,651 per year), 4 research assistantships with full and partial tuition reimbursements available (averaging $14,750 per year), 23 teaching assistantships with full and partial tuition reimbursements available (averaging $14,665 per year); career-related internships or fieldwork, Federal Work-Study, scholarships/grants, unspecified assistantships, and health care benefits (for full-time research or teaching assistantship recipients) also available. Support available to part-time students. Financial award application deadline: 3/15; financial award applicants required to submit FAFSA. *Faculty research:* Early Modern cultural studies, Shakespeare and film, feminism, Michel Foucault, science and technology studies. *Unit head:* Denise Albanese, Director, 703-993-2869, Fax: 703-993-2852, E-mail: dalbanes@gmu.edu. *Application contact:* Jonathan Aponte, Information Contact, 703-993-2851, Fax: 703-993-2852, E-mail: japonte@gmu.edu.
Website: http://culturalstudies.gmu.edu

Goucher College, MA and MFA Programs, Baltimore, MD 21204-2794. Offers arts administration (MA); creative nonfiction (MFA); cultural sustainability (MA); digital arts (MFA); environmental studies (MA); historic preservation (MA); management (MA). Part-time and evening/weekend programs available. Postbaccalaureate distance learning degree programs offered (minimal on-campus study). *Faculty:* 83 part-time/adjunct (42 women). *Students:* 72 full-time (58 women), 65 part-time (54 women); includes 39 minority (15 Black or African American, non-Hispanic/Latino; 16 American Indian or Alaska Native, non-Hispanic/Latino; 2 Asian, non-Hispanic/Latino; 4 Hispanic/Latino; 2 Two or more races, non-Hispanic/Latino), 4 international. 120 applicants, 95% accepted,

50 enrolled. In 2014, 63 master's awarded. *Degree requirements:* For master's, thesis, e-portfolio completion. *Entrance requirements:* Additional exam requirements/ recommendations for international students: Required—TOEFL (minimum score 550 paper-based; 80 iBT), IELTS (minimum score 7). *Application deadline:* Applications are processed on a rolling basis. Application fee: $75. *Expenses:* Expenses: $825 per credit; fees vary according to program. *Financial support:* Unspecified assistantships available. Financial award application deadline: 4/15; financial award applicants required to submit FAFSA. *Unit head:* Lynne Lochte, Vice President for New Ventures and Business Strategies, 410-337-6572, E-mail: lynne.lochte@goucher.edu. *Application contact:* Hanora Barron, Admissions Coordinator, 410-337-6200, Fax: 410-337-6085, E-mail: hanora.barron@goucher.edu.
Website: http://www.goucher.edu/grad

Grace Theological Seminary, Graduate and Professional Programs, Winona Lake, IN 46590-9907. Offers biblical studies (Certificate); camp administration (MA); counseling (M Div); exegetical studies (MA); intercultural studies (M Div, MA); local church studies (MA); pastoral studies (M Div); theological studies (MA); theology (D Min, Diploma). *Accreditation:* ATS. Part-time programs available. Postbaccalaureate distance learning degree programs offered (no on-campus study). *Degree requirements:* For master's, thesis optional; for doctorate, 2 foreign languages, thesis/dissertation. *Entrance requirements:* For master's, MAT, minimum GPA of 2.5. Electronic applications accepted. *Faculty research:* Biblical theology, language, and church ministries.

Graduate Theological Union, Graduate Programs, Berkeley, CA 94709-1212. Offers art and religion (MA, PhD, Th D); biblical languages (MA); biblical studies (MA); Biblical studies (PhD, Th D); Buddhist studies (MA); Christian spirituality (MA, PhD, Th D); cultural and historical studies of religions (MA, PhD, Th D); ethics and social theory (PhD, Th D); history (MA, PhD, Th D); homiletics (MA, PhD, Th D); interdisciplinary studies (PhD, Th D, Certificate); Jewish studies (MA, PhD, Th D, Certificate); liturgical studies (MA, PhD, Th D); Near Eastern religions (PhD, Th D); Orthodox Christian studies (MA); religion and psychology (MA, PhD, Th D); religion and society/ethics and social theory (MA); systematic and philosophical theology (MA, PhD, Th D). PhD programs in Jewish studies and Near Eastern religions offered jointly with University of California, Berkeley. *Accreditation:* ATS. Terminal master's awarded for partial completion of doctoral program. *Degree requirements:* For master's, one foreign language, thesis; for doctorate, one foreign language, comprehensive exam, thesis/dissertation. *Entrance requirements:* For master's, GRE General Test; for doctorate, GRE General Test, MA or M Div. Additional exam requirements/recommendations for international students: Required—TOEFL. Electronic applications accepted.

Johnson University, Graduate and Professional Programs, Knoxville, TN 37998-1001. Offers educational technology (MA); intercultural studies (MA); leadership studies (PhD); marriage and family therapy/professional counseling (MA); New Testament (MA); school counseling (MA); teacher education (MA). Part-time and evening/weekend programs available. Postbaccalaureate distance learning degree programs offered (no on-campus study). *Faculty:* 18 full-time (3 women), 39 part-time/adjunct (12 women). *Students:* 112 full-time (46 women), 117 part-time (45 women); includes 22 minority (10 Black or African American, non-Hispanic/Latino; 1 American Indian or Alaska Native, non-Hispanic/Latino; 2 Asian, non-Hispanic/Latino; 5 Hispanic/Latino; 4 Two or more races, non-Hispanic/Latino), 20 international. Average age 30. In 2014, 39 master's awarded. *Degree requirements:* For master's, variable foreign language requirement, comprehensive exam, thesis (for some programs), internships; for doctorate, variable foreign language requirement, comprehensive exam, thesis/dissertation, internships. *Entrance requirements:* For master's, doctorate, and Graduate Certificate, interview, 3 references, transcripts, essay, minimum GPA of 3.0. Additional exam requirements/ recommendations for international students: Required—TOEFL. *Application deadline:* For fall admission, 7/1 for domestic students; for spring admission, 11/1 for domestic students. Application fee: $50. Electronic applications accepted. *Expenses:* Expenses: $16,800; $11,625 (online master's degree); $32,310 (online doctoral degree). *Financial support:* Scholarships/grants available. Financial award application deadline: 4/15; financial award applicants required to submit FAFSA. *Unit head:* Tim Wingfield, VP for Enrollment Services, 865-573-4517. *Application contact:* Stacy Abernathy, Director of Graduate and Non-traditional Admissions, 865-573-4517.

La Salle University, School of Arts and Sciences, Program in English, Philadelphia, PA 19141-1199. Offers American studies (Certificate); English for educators (MA); English in literary and cultural studies (MA); global literature (Certificate); media studies and the performing and visual arts (Certificate); Philadelphia and regional studies (Certificate). Part-time and evening/weekend programs available. *Degree requirements:* For master's, critical-pedagogical project (for English for educators), thesis or comprehensive examination (for English in literary and cultural studies). *Entrance requirements:* For master's, GRE General Test or MAT, 18 hours of undergraduate course work in English or a related discipline with minimum GPA of 3.0; three letters of recommendation; brief personal statement; writing sample; for Certificate, undergraduate degree in English or a related discipline with minimum GPA of 3.0; 3 letters of recommendation. Additional exam requirements/recommendations for international students: Required—TOEFL. Electronic applications accepted. Application fee is waived when completed online.

Lewis & Clark College, Graduate School of Education and Counseling, Department of Counseling Psychology, Portland, OR 97219-7899. Offers marriage, couple and family therapy (MA, MS); professional mental health counseling (MA, MS); professional mental health counseling–addictions (MA, MS); psychological and cultural studies (MA, MS); school psychology (Ed S). *Accreditation:* AAMFT/COAMFTE; ACA. Part-time and evening/weekend programs available. *Degree requirements:* For master's, thesis proposal (MS). *Entrance requirements:* For master's, GRE General Test, minimum undergraduate GPA of 2.75. Additional exam requirements/recommendations for international students: Required—TOEFL (minimum score 575 paper-based). Electronic applications accepted.

Lincoln Christian University, Hargrove School of Adult and Graduate Studies, Lincoln, IL 62656-2167. Offers bible and theology (MA); intercultural studies (MA); marriage and family therapy (MA); organizational leadership (MA); spiritual formation (MA); TESOL (MA). MA in marriage and family therapy offered in Las Vegas, NV; MA in spiritual formation program offered in Bloomington-Normal, IL. Postbaccalaureate distance learning degree programs offered (no on-campus study). *Faculty:* 6 full-time (3 women), 20 part-time/adjunct (3 women). *Students:* 5 full-time (4 women), 137 part-time (53 women); includes 33 minority (19 Black or African American, non-Hispanic/Latino; 3 American Indian or Alaska Native, non-Hispanic/Latino; 1 Asian, non-Hispanic/Latino; 7 Hispanic/Latino; 3 Two or more races, non-Hispanic/Latino), 7 international. Average age 39. 114 applicants, 68% accepted, 62 enrolled. In 2014, 53 master's awarded. *Degree requirements:* For master's, 2.5 cumulative GPA in Undergraduate Degree studies. *Entrance requirements:* For master's, If undergrad cum GPA is lower than 2.5 (on a 4.0 scale) applicant may be required to complete the Miller Analogies Test at an authorized center. Additional exam requirements/recommendations for international students: Required—TOEFL (minimum score 550 paper-based); Recommended—IELTS (minimum score 6). *Application deadline:* For fall admission, 8/1 for domestic students, 3/1 for international students; for spring admission, 11/15 for domestic students, 11/1 for international students. Application fee: $25 ($50 for international students). Application fee is waived when completed online. *Expenses: Tuition:* Full-time $7524; part-time $418 per credit hour. One-time fee: $144. Tuition and fees vary according to campus/location and program. *Financial support:* Applicants required to submit FAFSA.

Maranatha Baptist University, Master of Arts in Intercultural Studies Program, Watertown, WI 53094. Offers MA. Part-time programs available. *Faculty:* 4 full-time (0 women), 5 part-time/adjunct (0 women). *Students:* 1 full-time (0 women), 5 part-time (3 women); includes 1 minority (Two or more races, non-Hispanic/Latino). Average age 24. 1 applicant, 100% accepted, 1 enrolled. *Entrance requirements:* Additional exam requirements/recommendations for international students: Required—TOEFL. *Application deadline:* Applications are processed on a rolling basis. Application fee: $50. *Expenses: Tuition:* Full-time $2655; part-time $295 per credit hour. *Required fees:* $25 per credit hour. Tuition and fees vary according to program. *Financial support:* Scholarships/grants and tuition waivers (full and partial) available. Support available to part-time students. *Unit head:* Dr. Larry Oats, Dean of Maranatha Baptist Seminary, 920-206-2324, Fax: 920-261-9109, E-mail: larry.oats@mbu.edu. *Application contact:* Dr. Jim Harrison, Director of Admissions, 920-206-2327, Fax: 920-261-9109, E-mail: admissions@mbu.edu.
Website: http://www.mbu.edu/seminary/academics/programs/inter-cultural-studies/

McMaster University, School of Graduate Studies, Faculty of Humanities, Department of English and Cultural Studies, Hamilton, ON L8S 4M2, Canada. Offers cultural studies and critical theory (MA); English (MA, PhD). Part-time programs available. *Degree requirements:* For master's, one foreign language, thesis; for doctorate, one foreign language, comprehensive exam, thesis/dissertation. *Entrance requirements:* For master's, honors degree, minimum B+ average in at least 6 full courses of English beyond year 1; for doctorate, MA; minimum A- average in two of three courses. Additional exam requirements/recommendations for international students: Required—TOEFL (minimum score 580 paper-based). *Faculty research:* Literary theory, feminist theory, literature of migration, Bakhting globalization.

New York University, Steinhardt School of Culture, Education, and Human Development, New York, NY 10003. Offers MA, MFA, MM, MPH, MS, DPS, DPT, Ed D, PhD, Advanced Certificate, Post Master's Certificate, Postbaccalaureate Certificate, Advanced Certificate/MPH, MA/Advanced Certificate, MA/MA, MA/MS, MLIS/MA. *Accreditation:* Teacher Education Accreditation Council. Part-time programs available. *Faculty:* 291 full-time (173 women), 740 part-time/adjunct (392 women). *Students:* 2,129 full-time (1,587 women), 1,136 part-time (869 women); includes 854 minority (212 Black or African American, non-Hispanic/Latino; 5 American Indian or Alaska Native, non-Hispanic/Latino; 271 Asian, non-Hispanic/Latino; 288 Hispanic/Latino; 3 Native Hawaiian or other Pacific Islander, non-Hispanic/Latino; 75 Two or more races, non-Hispanic/Latino), 726 international. Average age 31. 6,757 applicants, 42% accepted, 1245 enrolled. In 2014, 1,316 master's, 109 doctorates, 36 other advanced degrees awarded. *Degree requirements:* For master's, thesis (for some programs); for doctorate, comprehensive exam (for some programs), thesis/dissertation. *Entrance requirements:* For doctorate, GRE General Test, interview. Additional exam requirements/ recommendations for international students: Required—TOEFL (minimum score 100 iBT). *Application deadline:* For fall admission, 12/1 priority date for domestic students, 12/1 for international students; for spring admission, 1/1 for domestic and international students. Applications are processed on a rolling basis. Application fee: $75. Electronic applications accepted. *Expenses:* Expenses: Contact institution. *Financial support:* Fellowships with full and partial tuition reimbursements, research assistantships with full and partial tuition reimbursements, teaching assistantships with full and partial tuition reimbursements, career-related internships or fieldwork, Federal Work-Study, institutionally sponsored loans, scholarships/grants, traineeships, tuition waivers (partial), and unspecified assistantships available. Support available to part-time students. Financial award application deadline: 2/1; financial award applicants required to submit FAFSA. *Faculty research:* Equity, urban adolescents, arts in education, globalization, multivariate analysis, psychometrics. *Total annual research expenditures:* $30.4 million. *Unit head:* Dr. Dominic Brewer, Dean, 212-998-5000. *Application contact:* John Myers, Director of Enrollment Management, 212-998-5030, Fax: 212-995-4328, E-mail: steinhardt.gradadmissions@nyu.edu.
Website: http://steinhardt.nyu.edu/

North Central College, Graduate and Continuing Studies Programs, Program in Liberal Studies, Naperville, IL 60566-7063. Offers culture and society (MALS); ethics and public service (MALS); writing, editing, and publishing (MALS). Part-time and evening/weekend programs available. *Faculty:* 8 full-time (2 women), 4 part-time/adjunct (1 woman). *Students:* 2 full-time (1 woman), 24 part-time (14 women); includes 1 minority (Asian, non-Hispanic/Latino). Average age 36. 15 applicants, 73% accepted, 7 enrolled. In 2014, 6 master's awarded. *Degree requirements:* For master's, thesis optional, project. *Entrance requirements:* For master's, interview. Additional exam requirements/ recommendations for international students: Required—TOEFL (minimum score 550 paper-based; 80 iBT). *Application deadline:* For fall admission, 8/15 for domestic students, 7/15 for international students; for winter admission, 12/1 for domestic students, 11/1 for international students; for spring admission, 2/1 for domestic students, 12/1 for international students. Applications are processed on a rolling basis. Application fee: $25. Electronic applications accepted. Application fee is waived when completed online. *Expenses:* Expenses: Contact institution. *Financial support:* In 2014–15, 1 student received support. Scholarships/grants available. Support available to part-time students. Financial award applicants required to submit FAFSA. *Unit head:* Dr. Richard Guzman, Program Coordinator, Liberal Studies, 630-637-5285. *Application contact:* Wendy Kulpinski, Director of Graduate and Continuing Education Admission, 630-637-5808, Fax: 630-637-5844, E-mail: wekulpinski@noctrl.edu.
Website: http://northcentralcollege.edu/admission/liberal-studies

Northern Kentucky University, Office of Graduate Programs, College of Arts and Sciences, Program in English, Highland Heights, KY 41099. Offers composition and rhetoric (Certificate); creative writing (Certificate); cultural studies and discourses (Certificate); English (MA); professional writing (Certificate). Part-time and evening/ weekend programs available. *Faculty:* 13 full-time (6 women), 6 part-time/adjunct (0 women). *Students:* 2 full-time (1 woman), 51 part-time (39 women); includes 3 minority (2 Black or African American, non-Hispanic/Latino; 1 Two or more races, non-Hispanic/ Latino). Average age 36. In 2014, 10 master's, 9 other advanced degrees awarded. *Degree requirements:* For master's, comprehensive exam (for some programs), capstone (thesis, portfolio, project, or exams); 30 hours of credit; for Certificate, 18 hours of credit. *Entrance requirements:* For master's, bachelor's degree in English or related field from regionally-accredited institution with minimum GPA of 3.0 in major or cognate area coursework; official transcripts for all undergraduate and graduate work; two letters of reference; for Certificate, official transcripts for all undergraduate and graduate work; bachelor's degree from regionally-accredited institution; minimum undergraduate GPA of 2.5. Additional exam requirements/recommendations for international students: Required—TOEFL (minimum score 79 iBT); Recommended—IELTS (minimum score 6.5). *Application deadline:* For fall admission, 7/1 priority date for domestic students, 6/1 priority date for international students; for spring admission, 11/1 priority date for domestic students, 10/1 for international students. Application fee: $40. Electronic applications accepted. *Expenses: Tuition, area resident:* Part-time $518 per credit hour.

Tuition, state resident: part-time $630 per credit hour. Tuition, nonresident: part-time $797 per credit hour. *Required fees:* $192 per semester. Tuition and fees vary according to course load, degree level, campus/location, program and reciprocity agreements. *Financial support:* In 2014–15, 8 students received support. Unspecified assistantships available. Financial award applicants required to submit FAFSA. *Unit head:* Dr. John Alberti, Director of English Graduate Studies, 859-572-5619, Fax: 859-572-6093, E-mail: alberti@nku.edu. *Application contact:* Alison Swanson, Graduate Admissions Coordinator, 859-572-6971, E-mail: swansona1@nku.edu.
Website: http://english.nku.edu/gradprogram/

Northwest University, College of Ministry, Kirkland, WA 98033. Offers ministry (MIM); missional leadership (MA); theology and culture (MA). Part-time and evening/weekend programs available. Postbaccalaureate distance learning degree programs offered (no on-campus study). *Faculty:* 6 full-time (1 woman), 8 part-time/adjunct (1 woman). *Students:* 7 full-time (3 women), 81 part-time (19 women); includes 21 minority (2 Black or African American, non-Hispanic/Latino; 6 Asian, non-Hispanic/Latino; 3 Hispanic/Latino; 4 Native Hawaiian or other Pacific Islander, non-Hispanic/Latino; 6 Two or more races, non-Hispanic/Latino). Average age 43. 33 applicants, 97% accepted, 20 enrolled. In 2014, 33 master's awarded. *Degree requirements:* For master's, comprehensive exam (for some programs), thesis (for some programs). *Entrance requirements:* Additional exam requirements/recommendations for international students: Required—TOEFL (minimum score 550 paper-based; 75 iBT). *Application deadline:* For fall admission, 8/1 for domestic students, 4/1 for international students; for spring admission, 12/1 for domestic students, 8/1 for international students. Applications are processed on a rolling basis. Application fee: $50. Electronic applications accepted. *Expenses: Tuition:* Full-time $6894; part-time $684 per credit. *Required fees:* $12.50 per term. One-time fee: $98 full-time; $83 part-time. Tuition and fees vary according to course load, campus/location, program and reciprocity agreements. *Financial support:* In 2014–15, 10 students received support. Federal Work-Study available. *Unit head:* Dr. Wayde Goodall, Dean, 425-889-5211, E-mail: wayde.goodall@northwestu.edu. *Application contact:* Steven Curry, Graduate Enrollment Counselor, College of Ministry, 425-889-7795, E-mail: steven.curry@northwestu.edu.
Website: http://www.northwestu.edu/ministrygrad/

Old Dominion University, College of Arts and Letters, Graduate Program in International Studies, Norfolk, VA 23529. Offers conflict and cooperation (MA, PhD); interdependence and transnationalism (MA, PhD); international cultural studies (MA, PhD); international political economy and development (MA, PhD); modeling and simulation (MA, PhD); U.S. foreign policy and international relations (MA, PhD). Part-time programs available. *Faculty:* 18 full-time (4 women). *Students:* 41 full-time (14 women), 46 part-time (23 women); includes 11 minority (5 Black or African American, non-Hispanic/Latino; 1 Asian, non-Hispanic/Latino; 2 Hispanic/Latino; 3 Two or more races, non-Hispanic/Latino), 24 international. Average age 35. 99 applicants, 54% accepted, 34 enrolled. In 2014, 10 master's, 9 doctorates awarded. Terminal master's awarded for partial completion of doctoral program. *Degree requirements:* For master's, one foreign language, comprehensive exam, thesis optional; for doctorate, one foreign language, comprehensive exam, thesis/dissertation. *Entrance requirements:* For master's, GRE General Test, sample of written work, 2 letters of recommendation; for doctorate, GRE General Test, sample of written work, 3 letters of recommendation. Additional exam requirements/recommendations for international students: Required—TOEFL (minimum score 570 paper-based). *Application deadline:* For fall admission, 1/15 for domestic and international students; for spring admission, 10/15 for domestic and international students. Application fee: $50. Electronic applications accepted. *Expenses:* Tuition, state resident: full-time $10,488; part-time $437 per credit. Tuition, nonresident: full-time $26,136; part-time $1089 per credit. *Required fees:* $64 per semester. One-time fee: $50. *Financial support:* In 2014–15, 20 students received support, including 2 fellowships (averaging $13,000 per year), 5 research assistantships with tuition reimbursements available (averaging $15,000 per year), 7 teaching assistantships with tuition reimbursements available (averaging $15,000 per year); career-related internships or fieldwork, institutionally sponsored loans, scholarships/grants, and unspecified assistantships also available. Support available to part-time students. Financial award application deadline: 2/15; financial award applicants required to submit FAFSA. *Faculty research:* U.S. foreign policy, international security, Transatlantic and Transpacific relations, transnational issues, international political economy and development. *Total annual research expenditures:* $330,391. *Unit head:* Dr. Regina Karp, Graduate Program Director, 757-683-5700, Fax: 757-683-5701, E-mail: rkarp@odu.edu. *Application contact:* Dr. David C. Earnest, Associate Dean, 757-683-6077, Fax: 757-683-5746, E-mail: dearnest@odu.edu.
Website: http://www.al.odu.edu/gpis/

Pacific Northwest College of Art, Program in Critical Theory and Creative Research, Portland, OR 97209. Offers MA, MA/MFA.

Plymouth State University, College of Graduate Studies, Graduate Studies in Education, Program in Integrated Arts, Plymouth, NH 03264-1595. Offers M Ed. *Degree requirements:* For master's, practicum.

Regent University, Graduate School, School of Divinity, Virginia Beach, VA 23464-9800. Offers leadership and renewal (D Min), including Christian leadership and renewal, clinical pastoral education, community transformation, military ministry, ministry leadership coaching; practical theology (M Div, MA), including Biblical studies (M Div, MTS, PhD), chaplain ministry (M Div), Christian theology (M Div, MTS, PhD), church and ministry, history of Christianity (M Div, MTS), inter-cultural studies, interdisciplinary studies (M Div, MA, MTS), worship and renewal; renewal studies (PhD), including Biblical studies (M Div, MTS, PhD), Christian theology (M Div, MTS, PhD), history of global Christianity; theological studies (MTS), including Biblical studies (M Div, MTS, PhD), Christian theology (M Div, MTS, PhD), history of Christianity (M Div, MTS), interdisciplinary studies (M Div, MA, MTS). *Accreditation:* ACIPE; ATS. Part-time programs available. Postbaccalaureate distance learning degree programs offered (minimal on-campus study). *Faculty:* 20 full-time (3 women), 29 part-time/adjunct (3 women). *Students:* 64 full-time (28 women), 616 part-time (258 women); includes 318 minority (269 Black or African American, non-Hispanic/Latino; 7 American Indian or Alaska Native, non-Hispanic/Latino; 16 Asian, non-Hispanic/Latino; 26 Hispanic/Latino), 37 international. Average age 43. 511 applicants, 52% accepted, 187 enrolled. In 2014, 121 master's, 24 doctorates awarded. *Degree requirements:* For master's, comprehensive exam, thesis or alternative, internship; for doctorate, thesis/dissertation or alternative. *Entrance requirements:* For master's, GRE General Test or MAT, minimum undergraduate GPA of 2.75, writing sample, clergy recommendation; for doctorate, M Div or theological master's degree; minimum graduate GPA of 3.5 (PhD), 3.0 (D Min); recommendations; writing sample; transcripts. Additional exam requirements/recommendations for international students: Required—TOEFL (minimum score 577 paper-based). *Application deadline:* For fall admission, 5/1 priority date for domestic students. Applications are processed on a rolling basis. Application fee: $50. Electronic applications accepted. *Expenses:* Expenses: Contact institution. *Financial support:* Fellowships with full and partial tuition reimbursements, career-related internships or fieldwork, scholarships/grants, tuition waivers (full and partial), and unspecified assistantships available. Support available to part-time students. Financial award application deadline: 9/1; financial award applicants required to submit FAFSA.

Faculty research: Greek and Hebrew, theology, spiritual formation, global missions and world Christianity, women's studies. *Unit head:* Dr. Joseph Umidi, Interim Dean, 757-352-4401, Fax: 757-352-4597, E-mail: joseumi@regent.edu. *Application contact:* Matthew Chadwick, Director of Enrollment Support Services, 800-373-5504, Fax: 757-352-4381, E-mail: admissions@regent.edu.
Website: http://www.regent.edu/acad/schdiv/

Regis College, Program in Heritage Studies for a Global Society, Weston, MA 02493. Offers biocultural diversity (MA); cultural heritage in literature (MA); cultural heritage in teaching (MA); cultural heritage in the workplace (MA); public heritage (MA). Part-time programs available. *Degree requirements:* For master's, capstone.

St. Francis Xavier University, Graduate Studies, Department of Celtic Studies, Antigonish, NS B2G 2W5, Canada. Offers MA. *Degree requirements:* For master's, thesis. *Entrance requirements:* Additional exam requirements/recommendations for international students: Required—TOEFL (minimum score 580 paper-based). *Faculty research:* Scottish Gaelic in Nova Scotia.

San Francisco State University, Division of Graduate Studies, College of Health and Social Sciences, Human Sexuality Studies Program, San Francisco, CA 94132-1722. Offers MA. *Expenses:* Tuition, state resident: full-time $6738. Tuition, nonresident: full-time $17,898; part-time $372 per credit hour. *Required fees:* $498 per semester. *Unit head:* Dr. Ed McCaughan, Chair, 415-405-3570, E-mail: sxsdept@sfsu.edu. *Application contact:* Dr. Jessica Fields, Graduate Coordinator, 415-405-0589, E-mail: jfields@sfsu.edu.
Website: http://sxs.sfsu.edu/

School of Visual Arts, Graduate Programs, Critical Theory and the Arts Department, New York, NY 10010-3994. Offers MA. *Degree requirements:* For master's, thesis, 36 credits with minimum cumulative GPA of 3.0. *Entrance requirements:* For master's, writing statement of approximately 1,000 words explaining the development of interest in pursuing an MA; transcripts for previous colleges /universities attended; three letters of recommendation; current resume/curriculum vitae. Additional exam requirements/recommendations for international students: Required—TOEFL (minimum score 600 paper-based; 100 iBT). Electronic applications accepted. *Expenses:* Contact institution.

Simon Fraser University, Office of Graduate Studies, Faculty of Education, Program in Languages, Cultures, and Literacies, Burnaby, BC V5A 1S6, Canada. Offers PhD.

Southern Illinois University Carbondale, Graduate School, College of Liberal Arts, Department of Foreign Languages and Literatures, Carbondale, IL 62901-4701. Offers MA. Part-time programs available. *Faculty:* 18 full-time (5 women), 1 (woman) part-time/adjunct. *Students:* 8 full-time (5 women), 2 part-time (both women), 7 international. Average age 24. 7 applicants, 43% accepted, 3 enrolled. In 2014, 3 master's awarded. *Degree requirements:* For master's, one foreign language, thesis. *Entrance requirements:* For master's, minimum GPA of 2.7. Additional exam requirements/recommendations for international students: Required—TOEFL. *Application deadline:* Applications are processed on a rolling basis. Application fee: $50. *Expenses:* Tuition, state resident: full-time $10,176; part-time $1153 per credit. Tuition, nonresident: full-time $20,814; part-time $1744 per credit. *Required fees:* $7092; $394 per credit. $2364 per semester. *Financial support:* In 2014–15, 9 students received support. Fellowships with full tuition reimbursements available, research assistantships with full tuition reimbursements available, teaching assistantships with full tuition reimbursements available, career-related internships or fieldwork, Federal Work-Study, institutionally sponsored loans, scholarships/grants, and tuition waivers (full) available. Support available to part-time students. Financial award application deadline: 5/15. *Faculty research:* Bibliography, historical linguistics, language pedagogy, philology, commercial facets. *Unit head:* Dr. David Johnson, Chairperson, 618-453-5435, E-mail: mjohnson@siu.edu. *Application contact:* Karen Sweiger-Veil, Administrative Clerk, 618-453-5430, E-mail: kveil@siu.edu.

Stanford University, School of Humanities and Sciences, Department of Anthropology, Stanford, CA 94305-9991. Offers archaeology (MA, PhD); culture and society (MS, PhD); ecology and environment (MA, PhD). Terminal master's awarded for partial completion of doctoral program. *Degree requirements:* For master's, thesis; for doctorate, one foreign language, thesis/dissertation. *Entrance requirements:* For master's and doctorate, GRE General Test. Additional exam requirements/recommendations for international students: Required—TOEFL. Electronic applications accepted. *Expenses: Tuition:* Full-time $44,184; part-time $982 per credit hour. *Required fees:* $191.

Stony Brook University, State University of New York, Graduate School, College of Arts and Sciences, Department of Cultural Analysis and Theory, Stony Brook, NY 11794. Offers comparative literature (MA, PhD); cultural studies (PhD, Certificate). Evening/weekend programs available. *Faculty:* 19 full-time (9 women). *Students:* 43 full-time (30 women), 2 part-time (both women); includes 5 minority (2 Black or African American, non-Hispanic/Latino; 2 Asian, non-Hispanic/Latino; 1 Hispanic/Latino), 16 international. Average age 34. 79 applicants, 35% accepted, 10 enrolled. In 2014, 2 master's, 5 doctorates, 12 other advanced degrees awarded. Terminal master's awarded for partial completion of doctoral program. *Degree requirements:* For master's, 2 foreign languages, exam; for doctorate, 3 foreign languages, comprehensive exam, thesis/dissertation. *Entrance requirements:* For master's and doctorate, GRE General Test, minimum GPA of 3.5 in major, 3.0 overall. Additional exam requirements/recommendations for international students: Required—TOEFL. *Application deadline:* For fall admission, 1/15 for domestic students; for spring admission, 10/1 for domestic students. Application fee: $100. *Expenses:* Tuition, state resident: full-time $10,370; part-time $432 per credit. Tuition, nonresident: full-time $20,190; part-time $841 per credit. *Required fees:* $1431. *Financial support:* In 2014–15, 26 teaching assistantships were awarded; fellowships and research assistantships also available. *Faculty research:* Literary theory, interdisciplinary studies, literary history. *Unit head:* Prof. Robert Harvey, Chair, 631-632-7456, Fax: 631-632-5707, E-mail: robert.harvey@stonybrook.edu. *Application contact:* Mary Moran-Luba, Coordinator, 631-632-7460, Fax: 631-632-5707, E-mail: mary.moran-luba@stonybrook.edu.
Website: http://www.stonybrook.edu/commcms/cat/index.html

Summit University, Graduate Studies, Clarks Summit, PA 18411-1297. Offers Bible (MA); counseling (MA, MS); curriculum and instruction (M Ed); educational administration (M Ed); intercultural studies (MA); literature (MA); missions (MA); organizational leadership (MA); reading specialist (M Ed); secondary English/communications (M Ed); social entrepreneurship (MA); worldview studies (MA). MA in missions program available only for Association of Baptists for World Evangelism missionary personnel. Part-time and evening/weekend programs available. Postbaccalaureate distance learning degree programs offered (no on-campus study). *Entrance requirements:* Additional exam requirements/recommendations for international students: Required—TOEFL (minimum score 500 paper-based).

Taylor College and Seminary, Graduate and Professional Programs, Edmonton, AB T6J 4T3, Canada. Offers Christian studies (Diploma); intercultural studies (MA, Diploma), including intercultural studies (Diploma), TESOL; theology (M Div, MTS). *Accreditation:* ATS. Part-time programs available. Postbaccalaureate distance learning degree programs offered (minimal on-campus study). *Degree requirements:* For master's, thesis optional. *Entrance requirements:* Additional exam requirements/

recommendations for international students: Required—TOEFL (minimum score 550 paper-based; 80 iBT), IELTS (minimum score 6.5). *Faculty research:* Biblical studies, administration and organization, world religions, ethics, missiology.

Texas A&M University, College of Liberal Arts, Department of Performance Studies, College Station, TX 77843. Offers MA. *Faculty:* 4. *Students:* 14 full-time (12 women); includes 4 minority (2 Black or African American, non-Hispanic/Latino; 1 Hispanic/Latino; 1 Two or more races, non-Hispanic/Latino), 2 international. Average age 25. 12 applicants, 58% accepted, 6 enrolled. In 2014, 2 master's awarded. *Degree requirements:* For master's, comprehensive exam (for some programs), thesis or alternative. *Entrance requirements:* For master's, GRE General Test. Additional exam requirements/recommendations for international students: Required—TOEFL. *Application deadline:* For fall admission, 2/15 for domestic students; for spring admission, 10/15 for domestic students. Applications are processed on a rolling basis. Application fee: $50 ($90 for international students). Electronic applications accepted. *Expenses:* Tuition, state resident: full-time $4078; part-time $226.55 per credit hour. Tuition, nonresident: full-time $10,594; part-time $577.55 per credit hour. *Required fees:* $2813; $237.70 per credit hour. $278.50 per semester. Tuition and fees vary according to degree level and student level. *Financial support:* In 2014–15, 14 students received support. Unspecified assistantships available. Financial award applicants required to submit FAFSA. *Unit head:* Dr. Donnlee Dox, Interim Head, 979-458-1870, E-mail: dox@tamu.edu. *Application contact:* Dr. Kirsten Pullen, Director of Graduate Studies, 979-845-2899, Fax: 979-845-5164, E-mail: kpullen@tamu.edu.
Website: http://perf.tamu.edu/

Texas A&M University–Kingsville, College of Graduate Studies, College of Arts and Sciences, Department of Language and Literature, Program in Cultural Studies, Kingsville, TX 78363. Offers MA. *Students:* 2 full-time (1 woman), 2 part-time (both women); all minorities (all Hispanic/Latino). Average age 29. 7 applicants, 86% accepted, 4 enrolled. *Degree requirements:* For master's, variable foreign language requirement, comprehensive exam, thesis (for some programs). *Entrance requirements:* For master's, GRE, MAT, GMAT. Additional exam requirements/recommendations for international students: Required—TOEFL (minimum score 550 paper-based; 79 iBT). *Application deadline:* For fall admission, 8/15 for domestic students, 6/1 for international students; for spring admission, 12/15 for domestic students, 10/1 for international students; for summer admission, 5/15 for domestic students, 4/1 for international students. Applications are processed on a rolling basis. Application fee: $35 ($50 for international students). Electronic applications accepted. *Financial support:* In 2014–15, 2 students received support. Career-related internships or fieldwork, Federal Work-Study, institutionally sponsored loans, scholarships/grants, health care benefits, tuition waivers (full and partial), and unspecified assistantships available. Support available to part-time students. Financial award application deadline: 5/1; financial award applicants required to submit FAFSA. *Unit head:* Dr. Roberto Vela-Cordova, Graduate Coordinator, 361-593-4062, E-mail: roberto.vela@tamuk.edu. *Application contact:* Dr. Mohamed Abdelrahman, Dean of Graduate Students, 361-593-2809, E-mail: mohamed.abdelrahman@tamuk.edu.

Texas Tech University, Graduate School, College of Arts and Sciences, Department of Classical and Modern Languages and Literatures, Lubbock, TX 79409-2071. Offers applied linguistics (MA); classics (MA); German (MA); languages and cultures (MA); Romance languages (MA); Spanish (PhD); MBA/MA. Part-time programs available. *Faculty:* 61 full-time (31 women), 7 part-time/adjunct (4 women). *Students:* 93 full-time (48 women), 15 part-time (10 women); includes 27 minority (1 Black or African American, non-Hispanic/Latino; 22 Hispanic/Latino; 4 Two or more races, non-Hispanic/Latino), 41 international. Average age 32. 60 applicants, 70% accepted, 26 enrolled. In 2014, 26 master's, 7 doctorates awarded. *Degree requirements:* For master's, comprehensive exam, thesis or alternative; for doctorate, comprehensive exam, thesis/dissertation. *Entrance requirements:* For master's and doctorate, GRE General Test. Additional exam requirements/recommendations for international students: Required—TOEFL (minimum score 550 paper-based; 79 iBT). *Application deadline:* For fall admission, 6/1 priority date for domestic students, 1/15 priority date for international students; for spring admission, 9/1 priority date for domestic students, 6/15 priority date for international students. Applications are processed on a rolling basis. Application fee: $60. Electronic applications accepted. *Expenses:* Tuition, state resident: full-time $6310; part-time $262.92 per credit hour. Tuition, nonresident: full-time $14,998; part-time $624.92 per credit hour. *Required fees:* $2701; $36.50 per credit. $912.50 per semester. Tuition and fees vary according to course load. *Financial support:* In 2014–15, 91 students received support, including 78 fellowships (averaging $2,724 per year), 4 research assistantships (averaging $17,800 per year), 82 teaching assistantships (averaging $11,423 per year); Federal Work-Study, scholarships/grants, and unspecified assistantships also available. Financial award application deadline: 4/15; financial award applicants required to submit FAFSA. *Faculty research:* Literature, comparative literature, linguistics, culture, applied linguistics. *Total annual research expenditures:* $1,380. *Unit head:* Dr. Erin Collopy, Chair and Associate Professor, 806-834-8497, Fax: 806-742-3306, E-mail: erin.collopy@ttu.edu. *Application contact:* Liz Hildebrand, Senior Advisor, 806-834-2463, Fax: 806-742-3306, E-mail: liz.hildebrand@ttu.edu.
Website: http://www.depts.ttu.edu/classic_modern/

Trent University, Graduate Studies, Program in Cultural Studies, Peterborough, ON K9J 7B8, Canada. Offers PhD.

Trinity College, Graduate Programs, Program in American Studies, Hartford, CT 06106-3100. Offers American culture studies (MA); museums and communities (MA). Part-time and evening/weekend programs available. *Degree requirements:* For master's, thesis or alternative. *Entrance requirements:* For master's, minimum GPA of 3.0.

Union Institute & University, Individualized Master of Arts Program, Cincinnati, OH 45206-1925. Offers creativity studies (MA); health and wellness (MA); history and culture (MA); leadership, public policy, and social issues (MA); literature and writing (MA). Part-time programs available. *Faculty:* 4 full-time (2 women), 3 part-time/adjunct (2 women). *Students:* 14 full-time (11 women), 107 part-time (75 women); includes 36 minority (29 Black or African American, non-Hispanic/Latino; 3 American Indian or Alaska Native, non-Hispanic/Latino; 3 Hispanic/Latino; 1 Two or more races, non-Hispanic/Latino). Average age 40. *Degree requirements:* For master's, thesis. *Entrance requirements:* For master's, transcript, essay, 3 letters of recommendation, resume. *Application deadline:* For spring admission, 3/13 for domestic students. Applications are processed on a rolling basis. Application fee: $50. Electronic applications accepted. *Expenses: Tuition:* Full-time $26,640; part-time $719 per credit hour. *Required fees:* $216; $54 per semester. Part-time tuition and fees vary according to course load, degree level and program. *Financial support:* Career-related internships or fieldwork and tuition waivers available. Financial award applicants required to submit FAFSA. *Unit head:* Andrea Scarpino, Program Director, 802-828-8777. *Application contact:* Director of Admissions, 800-861-6400.
Website: https://www.myunion.edu/academics/masters-programs/master-of-arts/

Union University, Institute for International and Intercultural Studies, Jackson, TN 38305-3697. Offers MAIS. Part-time and evening/weekend programs available. *Degree requirements:* For master's, capstone course. *Entrance requirements:* For master's, GRE, minimum undergraduate GPA of 3.0, 3 letters of reference. Additional exam requirements/recommendations for international students: Required—TOEFL (minimum score 560 paper-based). *Application deadline:* For fall admission, 8/15 priority date for domestic and international students. Applications are processed on a rolling basis. Application fee: $25 ($50 for international students). Electronic applications accepted. *Expenses: Tuition:* Full-time $6566; part-time $469 per credit hour. *Faculty research:* International education, ethnographic field research, intercultural training for professionals and students, language and culture. *Unit head:* Dr. Cynthia Jayne, Associate Provost, 731-661-5358, Fax: 731-661-5175, E-mail: cjayne@uu.edu. *Application contact:* Susan Bolyard, Program Coordinator, 731-661-5059, Fax: 731-661-5175, E-mail: sbolyard@uu.edu.
Website: http://www.uu.edu/academics/iiis/

University at Buffalo, the State University of New York, Graduate School, College of Arts and Sciences, Department of Transnational Studies, Buffalo, NY 14260. Offers American studies (MA, PhD); Canadian studies (Advanced Certificate); Canadian-American studies (MA); Caribbean Latina/o American studies (MA); global gender studies (MA, PhD). Part-time programs available. Postbaccalaureate distance learning degree programs offered. *Faculty:* 19 full-time (10 women). *Students:* 73 full-time (43 women); includes 20 minority (3 Black or African American, non-Hispanic/Latino; 6 American Indian or Alaska Native, non-Hispanic/Latino; 9 Asian, non-Hispanic/Latino; 2 Hispanic/Latino). Average age 32. 57 applicants, 84% accepted, 16 enrolled. In 2014, 26 master's, 18 doctorates, 1 other advanced degree awarded. *Degree requirements:* For master's, one foreign language, comprehensive exam (for some programs), thesis optional; for doctorate, one foreign language, comprehensive exam, thesis/dissertation; for Advanced Certificate, one foreign language. *Entrance requirements:* For master's, N/A, minimum GPA of 3.0; for doctorate, GRE, minimum GPA of 3.0. Additional exam requirements/recommendations for international students: Required—TOEFL (minimum score 550 paper-based; 79 iBT). *Application deadline:* For fall admission, 8/15 priority date for domestic students, 6/15 priority date for international students; for winter admission, 2/1 for domestic and international students; for spring admission, 1/15 priority date for domestic students, 11/15 priority date for international students. Applications are processed on a rolling basis. Application fee: $75. Electronic applications accepted. *Financial support:* In 2014–15, 16 students received support, including fellowships with full tuition reimbursements available (averaging $6,000 per year), research assistantships (averaging $5,000 per year), teaching assistantships with full tuition reimbursements available (averaging $13,060 per year); career-related internships or fieldwork, institutionally sponsored loans, scholarships/grants, traineeships, health care benefits, and unspecified assistantships also available. Financial award application deadline: 1/4. *Faculty research:* Native American, intercultural and indigenous people's studies, border theory, cultural studies, American pop culture, feminist theory, construction of gender in society. *Unit head:* Dr. Keith Griffler, Chair, 716-645-0802, Fax: 716-645-5977, E-mail: griffler@buffalo.edu. *Application contact:* Karen M. Reinard, Graduate Secretary, 716-645-0797, Fax: 716-645-5976, E-mail: kreinard@buffalo.edu.
Website: http://www.transnationalstudies.buffalo.edu/graduate.shtml

University at Buffalo, the State University of New York, Graduate School, College of Arts and Sciences, Program in Caribbean and Latina/o American Studies, Buffalo, NY 14260. Offers MA. *Unit head:* Dr. Bruce D. McCombe, Dean, 716-645-2711, Fax: 716-645-3888, E-mail: cas-dean@buffalo.edu. *Application contact:* Joseph C. Syracuse, Graduate Enrollment Manager, 716-645-2711, Fax: 716-645-3888, E-mail: jcs32@buffalo.edu.
Website: http://www.caribbeanstudies.buffalo.edu/program/

University of Alaska Fairbanks, College of Liberal Arts, Department of Cross-Cultural Studies, Fairbanks, AK 99775-6300. Offers MA. Part-time programs available. *Faculty:* 3 full-time (2 women). *Students:* 5 part-time (3 women); includes 3 minority (1 American Indian or Alaska Native, non-Hispanic/Latino; 1 Native Hawaiian or other Pacific Islander, non-Hispanic/Latino; 1 Two or more races, non-Hispanic/Latino). Average age 42. 2 applicants. In 2014, 1 master's awarded. *Degree requirements:* For master's, comprehensive exam, project, oral defense of project. *Entrance requirements:* For master's, bachelor's degree from accredited institution with minimum cumulative undergraduate and major GPA of 3.0. Additional exam requirements/recommendations for international students: Required—TOEFL (minimum score 550 paper-based; 79 iBT), IELTS (minimum score 8.5). *Application deadline:* For fall admission, 6/1 for domestic students, 3/1 for international students; for spring admission, 10/15 for domestic students, 9/1 for international students. Applications are processed on a rolling basis. Application fee: $60. Electronic applications accepted. *Expenses:* Tuition, state resident: full-time $7614; part-time $423 per credit. Tuition, nonresident: full-time $15,552; part-time $864 per credit. Tuition and fees vary according to course level, course load and reciprocity agreements. *Financial support:* Fellowships with full tuition reimbursements, research assistantships with full tuition reimbursements, teaching assistantships with full tuition reimbursements, Federal Work-Study, scholarships/grants, health care benefits, and unspecified assistantships available. Support available to part-time students. Financial award application deadline: 7/1; financial award applicants required to submit FAFSA. *Faculty research:* Alaska native literature, oral traditions, history, law and policy, cultures, art; Native American religion and philosophy. *Unit head:* Lawrence Kaplan, Acting Director of the Center for Cross-Cultural Studies, 907-474-1902, Fax: 907-474-1957, E-mail: fycxcs@uaf.edu. *Application contact:* Mary Kreta, Director of Admissions, 907-474-7500, Fax: 907-474-7097, E-mail: admissions@uaf.edu.
Website: http://www.uaf.edu/cxcs

University of California, Davis, Graduate Studies, Graduate Group in Cultural Studies, Davis, CA 95616. Offers MA, PhD. *Degree requirements:* For master's, thesis; for doctorate, thesis/dissertation. *Entrance requirements:* For doctorate, GRE. Additional exam requirements/recommendations for international students: Required—TOEFL (minimum score 550 paper-based). Electronic applications accepted.

University of California, Irvine, School of Humanities, Program in Culture and Theory, Irvine, CA 92697. Offers PhD. *Students:* 17 full-time (13 women); includes 10 minority (1 Black or African American, non-Hispanic/Latino; 6 Asian, non-Hispanic/Latino; 3 Hispanic/Latino). Average age 30. 75 applicants, 9% accepted, 4 enrolled. In 2014, 1 doctorate awarded. Application fee: $90 ($110 for international students). *Unit head:* Nahum Chandler, Director, 949-824-1610, E-mail: n.d.chandler@uci.edu. *Application contact:* James Lee, Faculty Advisor, 949-824-8716, Fax: 949-824-7006, E-mail: jim.lee@uci.edu.
Website: http://www.humanities.uci.edu/cultureandtheory/

University of California, Merced, Graduate Division, School of Social Sciences, Humanities and Arts, Merced, CA 95343. Offers cognitive and information sciences (MA, PhD); psychology (MA, PhD); social sciences (MA, PhD); world cultures (MA, PhD). *Faculty:* 89 full-time (40 women). *Students:* 114 full-time (79 women), 2 part-time (1 woman); includes 43 minority (3 Black or African American, non-Hispanic/Latino; 1 American Indian or Alaska Native, non-Hispanic/Latino; 10 Asian, non-Hispanic/Latino; 24 Hispanic/Latino; 1 Native Hawaiian or other Pacific Islander, non-Hispanic/Latino; 4 Two or more races, non-Hispanic/Latino), 13 international. Average age 32. 127 applicants, 34% accepted, 22 enrolled. In 2014, 3 master's, 11 doctorates awarded.

Degree requirements: For master's, variable foreign language requirement, comprehensive exam, thesis; for doctorate, variable foreign language requirement, comprehensive exam, thesis/dissertation. *Entrance requirements:* For master's and doctorate, GRE. Additional exam requirements/recommendations for international students: Required—TOEFL (minimum score 550 paper-based; 68 iBT); Recommended—IELTS. *Application deadline:* For fall admission, 1/15 for domestic and international students. Application fee: $80 ($100 for international students). Electronic applications accepted. *Expenses:* Tuition, state resident: full-time $11,220; part-time $2805 per semester. *Required fees:* $1940; $970 per semester hour. *Financial support:* In 2014–15, 29 fellowships with full and partial tuition reimbursements (averaging $7,056 per year) were awarded; scholarships/grants also available. *Faculty research:* Psychology, political science, social inequality, interdisciplinary, humanities, cognitive sciences. *Unit head:* Dr. Mark Aldenderfer, Dean, 209-228-7843, Fax: 209-228-4007, E-mail: maldenderfer@ucmerced.edu. *Application contact:* Tsu Ya, Graduate Admissions and Academic Services Manager, 209-228-4521, Fax: 209-228-6906, E-mail: tya@ucmerced.edu.

University of California, Riverside, Graduate Division, Department of Ethnic Studies, Riverside, CA 92521. Offers cultural politics and production (PhD); the state, law, and social transformation (PhD). *Faculty:* 15 full-time (9 women). *Students:* 18 full-time (13 women); includes 16 minority (5 Black or African American, non-Hispanic/Latino; 1 American Indian or Alaska Native, non-Hispanic/Latino; 2 Asian, non-Hispanic/Latino; 7 Hispanic/Latino; 1 Native Hawaiian or other Pacific Islander, non-Hispanic/Latino). Average age 30. 42 applicants, 19% accepted, 4 enrolled. Terminal master's awarded for partial completion of doctoral program. *Degree requirements:* For doctorate, variable foreign language requirement, comprehensive exam, thesis/dissertation. *Entrance requirements:* For doctorate, GRE, Writing Sample, Statement of Purpose, Personal History Statement, Letters of Recommendation (3). Additional exam requirements/recommendations for international students: Required—TOEFL (minimum score 550 paper-based; 80 iBT), Individual section score on IELTS must not be less than 6 in any section. Recommended—IELTS (minimum score 7). *Application deadline:* For fall admission, 1/5 priority date for domestic and international students. Applications are processed on a rolling basis. Application fee: $80 ($100 for international students). Electronic applications accepted. *Expenses:* Tuition, state resident: full-time $5399. Tuition, nonresident: full-time $10,433. *Financial support:* In 2014–15, 10 students received support, including 4 fellowships with full tuition reimbursements available (averaging $10,000 per year), 7 teaching assistantships with full tuition reimbursements available (averaging $18,000 per year); unspecified assistantships also available. Financial award application deadline: 1/5; financial award applicants required to submit FAFSA. *Faculty research:* The political economy of race, class, gender, sexuality, cultural production, the state, law, criminal justice and grass roots responses. *Unit head:* Dr. Dylan Rodriguez, Chair, 951-827-4707, E-mail: dylan.rodriguez@ucr.edu. *Application contact:* Trina B. Elerts, Graduate Program Coordinator, 951-827-1584, E-mail: trina.elerts@ucr.edu.
Website: http://www.ethnicstudies.ucr.edu

University of California, Santa Barbara, Graduate Division, College of Letters and Sciences, Division of Social Sciences, Department of Global and International Studies, Santa Barbara, CA 93106-7065. Offers global culture, ideology, and religion (MA); global government, civil society, and human rights (MA); global studies (PhD); political economy, sustainable development, and the environment (MA). *Degree requirements:* For master's, one foreign language, thesis, 2 years of a second language. *Entrance requirements:* For master's, GRE, 2 years of a second language with minimum B grade in the final term, 3 letters of recommendation, resume/curriculum vitae, personal statement, writing sample. Additional exam requirements/recommendations for international students: Required—TOEFL (minimum score 600 paper-based; 94 iBT), IELTS (minimum score 7). Electronic applications accepted. *Faculty research:* Global culture, ideology, and religion; global governance, civil society, and human rights; political economy, sustainable development and the environment.

University of Denver, Division of Arts, Humanities and Social Sciences, Department of Media, Film and Journalism Studies, Denver, CO 80208. Offers emergent digital practices (MA); international and intercultural communication (MA); strategic communication (MS); student designed emphasis (MA); video production (MA). Part-time programs available. *Faculty:* 14 full-time (8 women), 6 part-time/adjunct (2 women). *Students:* 24 full-time (17 women), 25 part-time (17 women); includes 10 minority (1 Asian, non-Hispanic/Latino; 4 Hispanic/Latino; 5 Two or more races, non-Hispanic/Latino), 4 international. Average age 27. 73 applicants, 89% accepted, 21 enrolled. In 2014, 17 master's awarded. *Degree requirements:* For master's, thesis (for some programs). *Entrance requirements:* For master's, GRE General Test, bachelor's degree, transcripts, personal statement, three letters of recommendation. Additional exam requirements/recommendations for international students: Required—TOEFL (minimum score 620 paper-based; 105 iBT). *Application deadline:* For fall admission, 2/15 priority date for domestic students, 1/1 priority date for international students. Applications are processed on a rolling basis. Application fee: $65. Electronic applications accepted. *Expenses:* Expenses: $1,199 per credit hour. *Financial support:* In 2014–15, 41 students received support, including 7 teaching assistantships with full and partial tuition reimbursements available (averaging $9,515 per year); career-related internships or fieldwork, Federal Work-Study, institutionally sponsored loans, scholarships/grants, and unspecified assistantships also available. Support available to part-time students. Financial award application deadline: 2/15; financial award applicants required to submit FAFSA. *Faculty research:* International and intercultural communication; media law; film history; youth, families, and social media; activist media. *Total annual research expenditures:* $50,000. *Unit head:* Dr. Lynn Schofield Clark, Chair, 303-871-3984, Fax: 303-871-4949, E-mail: lynn.clark@du.edu. *Application contact:* Information Contact, 303-871-2166, E-mail: mfjs@du.edu.
Website: http://www.du.edu/ahss/mfjs/index.html

University of Denver, University College, Denver, CO 80208. Offers geographic information systems (Certificate); global affairs (Certificate), including translation studies, world history and culture; information and communications technology (MCIS), including geographic information systems, information systems security, project management (MCIS, Certificate), software design and programming, technology management, telecommunications technology, Web design and development; leadership and organizations (Certificate), including human capital in organizations, philanthropic leadership, project management (MCIS, Certificate), strategic innovation and change; organizational and professional communication (MPS), including alternative dispute resolution, organizational communication, organizational development and training, public relations and marketing; security management (MAS, Certificate), including emergency planning and response, information security (MAS), organizational security. Part-time and evening/weekend programs available. Postbaccalaureate distance learning degree programs offered (no on-campus study). *Faculty:* 8 full-time (4 women), 133 part-time/adjunct (46 women). *Students:* 54 full-time (21 women), 1,327 part-time (775 women); includes 272 minority (106 Black or African American, non-Hispanic/Latino; 6 American Indian or Alaska Native, non-Hispanic/Latino; 26 Asian, non-Hispanic/Latino; 108 Hispanic/Latino; 1 Native Hawaiian or other Pacific Islander, non-Hispanic/Latino; 25 Two or more races, non-Hispanic/Latino), 116 international. Average age 35. 768 applicants, 95% accepted, 620 enrolled. In 2014, 391 master's, 196 other advanced degrees awarded. *Degree requirements:* For master's, capstone project. *Entrance requirements:* For master's, transcripts, two letters of recommendation, personal statement, resume. Additional exam requirements/recommendations for international students: Required—TOEFL (minimum score 550 paper-based; 80 iBT). *Application deadline:* For fall admission, 6/21 priority date for domestic students, 5/1 priority date for international students; for winter admission, 9/14 priority date for domestic students, 9/19 priority date for international students; for spring admission, 1/11 for domestic students, 12/12 for international students; for summer admission, 3/29 priority date for domestic students, 3/6 priority date for international students. Applications are processed on a rolling basis. Application fee: $75. Electronic applications accepted. *Expenses:* Expenses: $959 per credit hour. *Financial support:* In 2014–15, 19 students received support. Applicants required to submit FAFSA. *Unit head:* Dr. Michael McGuire, Interim Dean, 303-871-3518, E-mail: mmcguire@du.edu. *Application contact:* Information Contact, 303-871-2291, E-mail: ucoladm@du.edu.
Website: http://www.universitycollege.du.edu/

University of Hawaii at Hilo, Program in Hawaiian and Indigenous Language and Culture Revitalization, Hilo, HI 96720-4091. Offers PhD. *Entrance requirements:* Additional exam requirements/recommendations for international students: Required—TOEFL, IELTS. Electronic applications accepted. *Expenses:* Tuition, state resident: full-time $5004; part-time $417 per credit hour. Tuition, nonresident: full-time $11,472; part-time $956 per credit hour. *Required fees:* $388; $139.50 per credit hour. Tuition and fees vary according to course load and program.

University of Hawaii at Hilo, Program in Indigenous Language and Culture Education, Hilo, HI 96720-4091. Offers MA. *Entrance requirements:* Additional exam requirements/recommendations for international students: Required—TOEFL, IELTS. Electronic applications accepted. *Expenses:* Tuition, state resident: full-time $5004; part-time $417 per credit hour. Tuition, nonresident: full-time $11,472; part-time $956 per credit hour. *Required fees:* $388; $139.50 per credit hour. Tuition and fees vary according to course load and program.

University of Hawaii at Manoa, Graduate Division, International Cultural Studies Graduate Certificate Program, Honolulu, HI 96822. Offers Graduate Certificate. Part-time programs available. *Entrance requirements:* For degree, GRE General Test. Additional exam requirements/recommendations for international students: Required—TOEFL (minimum score 540 paper-based; 76 iBT), IELTS (minimum score 5).

University of Houston, College of Liberal Arts and Social Sciences, Department of Modern and Classical Languages, Houston, TX 77204. Offers world cultures and literatures (MA). *Degree requirements:* For master's, one foreign language, thesis optional. *Entrance requirements:* For master's, GRE General Test, minimum GPA of 3.0 in last 60 hours of course work. Additional exam requirements/recommendations for international students: Required—TOEFL (minimum score 500 paper-based). Electronic applications accepted.

University of Houston–Clear Lake, School of Human Sciences and Humanities, Programs in Human Sciences, Houston, TX 77058-1002. Offers behavioral sciences (MA), including criminology, cross cultural studies, general psychology, sociology; clinical psychology (MA); criminology (MA); cross cultural studies (MA); family therapy (MA); fitness and human performance (MA); school psychology (MA). *Accreditation:* AAMFT/COAMFTE. Part-time and evening/weekend programs available. Postbaccalaureate distance learning degree programs offered (minimal on-campus study). *Degree requirements:* For master's, thesis or alternative. *Entrance requirements:* For master's, GRE General Test. Additional exam requirements/recommendations for international students: Required—TOEFL (minimum score 550 paper-based). Electronic applications accepted. *Faculty research:* Smoking cessation, adolescent sexuality, white collar crime, serial murder, human factors/human computer interaction.

The University of Manchester, School of Arts, Histories and Cultures, Manchester, United Kingdom. Offers anthropology, media and performance (PhD); applied theatre professional (PhD); archaeology (PhD); art history and visual studies (PhD); arts management and cultural policy (PhD); classics and ancient history (PhD); composition (PhD); creative writing (PhD); drama (PhD); economic and social history (PhD); electroacoustic composition (PhD); English and American studies (PhD); history (PhD); humanitarianism and conflict response (PhD); museology (PhD); music (PhD); musicology (PhD); religions and theology (PhD).

The University of Manchester, School of Languages, Linguistics and Cultures, Manchester, United Kingdom. Offers Arab world studies (PhD); Chinese studies (M Phil, PhD); East Asian studies (M Phil, PhD); English language (PhD); French studies (M Phil, PhD); German studies (M Phil, PhD); interpreting studies (PhD); Italian studies (M Phil, PhD); Japanese studies (M Phil, PhD); Latin American cultural studies (M Phil, PhD); linguistics (M Phil, PhD); Middle Eastern studies (M Phil, PhD); Polish studies (M Phil, PhD); Portuguese studies (M Phil, PhD); Russian studies (M Phil, PhD); Spanish studies (M Phil, PhD); translation and intercultural studies (M Phil, PhD).

The University of Manchester, School of Social Sciences, Manchester, United Kingdom. Offers ethnographic documentary (M Phil); interdisciplinary study of culture (PhD); philosophy (PhD); politics (PhD); social anthropology (PhD); social anthropology with visual media (PhD); social change (PhD); social statistics (PhD); sociology (PhD); visual anthropology (M Phil).

University of Minnesota, Twin Cities Campus, Graduate School, College of Liberal Arts, Department of Cultural Studies and Comparative Literature, Program in Comparative Studies in Discourse and Society, Minneapolis, MN 55455-0213. Offers PhD. *Degree requirements:* For doctorate, 2 foreign languages, thesis/dissertation. *Entrance requirements:* For doctorate, GRE General Test, sample of written work. Additional exam requirements/recommendations for international students: Required—TOEFL. *Faculty research:* Cultural theory; music; architecture, space, and urbanism; body and gender; film and popular culture.

University of Missouri–St. Louis, College of Arts and Sciences, Interdisciplinary Programs, St. Louis, MO 63121. Offers gender studies (Certificate); international studies (Certificate). *Faculty:* 1 full-time (0 women), 17 part-time/adjunct (12 women). *Students:* 1 (woman) full-time, 6 part-time (5 women); includes 3 minority (2 Black or African American, non-Hispanic/Latino; 1 Asian, non-Hispanic/Latino). Average age 35. 23 applicants, 48% accepted, 3 enrolled. In 2014, 5 Certificates awarded. *Entrance requirements:* Additional exam requirements/recommendations for international students: Required—TOEFL (minimum score 550 paper-based; 79 iBT), IELTS (minimum score 6.5). *Application deadline:* For fall admission, 7/1 for domestic and international students; for spring admission, 12/1 for domestic and international students. Applications are processed on a rolling basis. Application fee: $50 ($40 for international students). *Expenses:* Tuition, state resident: full-time $7364; part-time $409.10 per hour. Tuition, nonresident: full-time $18,153; part-time $1008.50 per hour. *Unit head:* Dr. Ronald Yasbin, Dean, 314-516-5501. *Application contact:* Graduate Admissions, 314-516-5458, Fax: 314-516-6996, E-mail: gradadm@umsl.edu.

The University of Montana, Graduate School, Phyllis J. Washington College of Education and Human Sciences, Department of Counselor Education, Missoula, MT 59812-0002. Offers clinical mental health counseling (MA); counseling and supervision (Ed D); counselor education (Ed S); intercultural youth and family development (MA);

school counseling (MA). *Accreditation:* ACA. *Degree requirements:* For doctorate, thesis/dissertation. *Entrance requirements:* For master's, doctorate, and Ed S, GRE General Test. Additional exam requirements/recommendations for international students: Required—TOEFL.

University of New Mexico, Graduate School, College of Education, Program in Language, Literacy and Sociocultural Studies, Albuquerque, NM 87131. Offers American Indian education (MA); bilingual education (MA, PhD); educational linguistics (PhD); educational thought and sociocultural studies (MA, PhD); literacy/language arts (MA, PhD); social studies (MA); TESOL (MA, PhD). *Faculty:* 16 full-time (9 women), 6 part-time/adjunct (4 women). *Students:* 63 full-time (45 women), 96 part-time (86 women); includes 84 minority (6 Black or African American, non-Hispanic/Latino; 17 American Indian or Alaska Native, non-Hispanic/Latino; 5 Asian, non-Hispanic/Latino; 52 Hispanic/Latino; 4 Two or more races, non-Hispanic/Latino), 25 international. Average age 36. 50 applicants, 58% accepted, 20 enrolled. In 2014, 36 master's, 4 doctorates awarded. *Degree requirements:* For master's, comprehensive exam, thesis optional; for doctorate, comprehensive exam, thesis/dissertation, research skills. *Entrance requirements:* For master's, letter of intent, 3 letters of recommendation, resume, BA/BS, department demographic form, transcripts; for doctorate, writing sample, letter of intent, 3 letters of recommendation, resume, BA/BS, MA, department demographic form, transcripts. Additional exam requirements/recommendations for international students: Required—TOEFL. *Application deadline:* For fall admission, 12/1 for domestic and international students; for spring admission, 9/15 for domestic and international students. Application fee: $50. Electronic applications accepted. *Financial support:* In 2014–15, 7 students received support, including 7 fellowships (averaging $3,170 per year), 1,318 teaching assistantships with tuition reimbursements available (averaging $3,789 per year); research assistantships, career-related internships or fieldwork, institutionally sponsored loans, scholarships/grants, and unspecified assistantships also available. Support available to part-time students. Financial award application deadline: 3/1; financial award applicants required to submit FAFSA. *Faculty research:* School reform, professional development, history of education, Native American education, politics of education, feminism and issues of sexual identity, critical race theory, bilingualism, literacy reading, adolescent literature, second language acquisition, critical theory and schooling, indigenous languages. *Unit head:* Dr. Lois M. Meyer, Chair, 505-277-7244, Fax: 505-277-8362, E-mail: lsmeyer@unm.edu. *Application contact:* Debra Schaffer, Administrative Assistant, 505-277-0437, Fax: 505-277-8362, E-mail: schaffer@unm.edu.
Website: http://coe.unm.edu/departments/department-of-language-literacy-and-sociocultural-studies/llss-program.html

University of Pittsburgh, Graduate Program for Cultural Studies, Pittsburgh, PA 15260. Offers Certificate. Part-time programs available. *Faculty:* 127 full-time (59 women). *Students:* 101 full-time (61 women); includes 25 minority (8 Black or African American, non-Hispanic/Latino; 6 Asian, non-Hispanic/Latino; 11 Hispanic/Latino). 10 applicants, 100% accepted, 10 enrolled. In 2014, 2 Certificates awarded. *Degree requirements:* For Certificate, one foreign language. *Entrance requirements:* For degree, good academic standing in a University of Pittsburgh graduate degree-granting department. *Application deadline:* Applications are processed on a rolling basis. *Expenses:* Tuition, state resident: full-time $20,742; part-time $838 per credit. Tuition, nonresident: full-time $33,960; part-time $1389 per credit. *Required fees:* $800; $205 per term. Tuition and fees vary according to program. *Financial support:* In 2014–15, 2 students received support, including 2 fellowships with full tuition reimbursements available (averaging $18,000 per year). Financial award application deadline: 1/15. *Faculty research:* Diachronic and synchronic cultural critique; cultural politics and critical theory; interdisciplinary approaches to arts, literatures, media, and ethnographies in international cultural contexts. *Unit head:* Dr. Ronald J. Zboray, Director, 412-624-6969, Fax: 412-624-6492, E-mail: zboray@pitt.edu. *Application contact:* Karen E. Lillis, Administrator, 412-624-7232, Fax: 412-624-6492, E-mail: cultural@pitt.edu.
Website: http://www.culturalstudies.pitt.edu

University of Southern California, Graduate School, Dana and David Dornsife College of Letters, Arts and Sciences, Comparative Studies in Literature and Culture Doctoral Program, Los Angeles, CA 90089. Offers comparative literature (PhD); comparative media and culture (PhD); Spanish and Latin American studies (PhD). *Degree requirements:* For doctorate, 2 foreign languages, comprehensive exam, thesis/dissertation. *Entrance requirements:* For doctorate, GRE, competence in language other than English (highly recommended). Additional exam requirements/recommendations for international students: Required—TOEFL. Electronic applications accepted. *Faculty research:* Literary theory, Japanese film and contemporary fiction, Francophone literature and cinema, Latin American and Caribbean literature, Spanish literature and film, nineteenth and twentieth century British and American literature.

University of Southern Maine, College of Management and Human Service, School of Education and Human Development, Program in Counselor Education, Portland, ME 04104-9300. Offers clinical mental health counseling (MS); counseling (CAS); culturally responsive practices in education and human development (CGS); mental health rehabilitation technician/community (CGS); rehabilitation counseling (MS); school counseling (MS); substance abuse counseling (CGS). *Accreditation:* ACA (one or more programs are accredited); CORE; Teacher Education Accreditation Council. Part-time and evening/weekend programs available. *Faculty:* 6 full-time (4 women), 3 part-time/adjunct (2 women). *Students:* 60 full-time (44 women), 82 part-time (67 women); includes 8 minority (2 Black or African American, non-Hispanic/Latino; 1 American Indian or Alaska Native, non-Hispanic/Latino; 1 Asian, non-Hispanic/Latino; 2 Hispanic/Latino; 2 Two or more races, non-Hispanic/Latino). Average age 36. 76 applicants, 75% accepted, 44 enrolled. In 2014, 35 master's, 8 other advanced degrees awarded. *Degree requirements:* For master's, comprehensive exam, thesis or alternative; for other advanced degree, thesis or alternative. *Entrance requirements:* For master's, GRE General Test or MAT, interview; for other advanced degree, master's degree. Additional exam requirements/recommendations for international students: Required—TOEFL (minimum score 550 paper-based; 79 iBT). *Application deadline:* For fall admission, 11/15 for domestic students. Application fee: $65. Electronic applications accepted. *Expenses: Tuition, area resident:* Full-time $6840; part-time $380 per credit hour. Tuition, state resident: full-time $10,260; part-time $570 per credit hour. Tuition, nonresident: full-time $18,468; part-time $1026 per credit hour. *Required fees:* $830; $83 per credit hour. Tuition and fees vary according to course load and program. *Financial support:* Research assistantships, career-related internships or fieldwork, Federal Work-Study, institutionally sponsored loans, scholarships/grants, and unspecified assistantships available. Support available to part-time students. Financial award application deadline: 3/1; financial award applicants required to submit FAFSA. *Faculty research:* Counselor licensure, group dynamics, counseling theories, healthy adaptation, counselor educator well-being. *Unit head:* Adele Baruch, Program Coordinator, 207-780-5317, E-mail: abaruch@usm.maine.edu. *Application contact:* Mary Sloan, Assistant Dean of Graduate Studies and Director of Graduate Admissions, 207-780-4386, E-mail: gradstudies@usm.maine.edu.
Website: http://usm.maine.edu/counselor-education

The University of Texas at Austin, Graduate School, College of Education, Department of Curriculum and Instruction, Austin, TX 78712-1111. Offers bilingual/bicultural education (M Ed, MA, PhD); cultural studies in education (M Ed, MA, PhD); early childhood education (M Ed, MA, PhD); language and literacy studies (M Ed, PhD); learning technologies (M Ed, MA, PhD); physical education (M Ed, MA, PhD). Terminal master's awarded for partial completion of doctoral program. *Degree requirements:* For doctorate, thesis/dissertation. *Entrance requirements:* For master's and doctorate, GRE General Test. Electronic applications accepted.

The University of Texas at Austin, Graduate School, College of Liberal Arts, Department of Anthropology, Program in Cultural Forms, Austin, TX 78712-1111. Offers MA, PhD. Part-time programs available. Terminal master's awarded for partial completion of doctoral program. *Degree requirements:* For master's, one foreign language, thesis, report; for doctorate, one foreign language, thesis/dissertation. *Entrance requirements:* For master's and doctorate, GRE General Test. Electronic applications accepted. *Faculty research:* Expressive culture, gender, genre, folklore and culture of British Isles, ethnography of speaking.

The University of Texas at Austin, Graduate School, College of Liberal Arts, Department of Slavic and Eurasian Studies, Austin, TX 78712-1111. Offers applied linguistics/pedagogy (PhD); literature and culture (PhD); Slavic languages (MA); Slavic linguistics (PhD). *Degree requirements:* For master's, 2 foreign languages, thesis; for doctorate, 3 foreign languages, thesis/dissertation. *Entrance requirements:* For master's and doctorate, GRE General Test. Electronic applications accepted. *Faculty research:* Slavic linguistics; applied linguistics; Russian, Czech, and Slavic literature and culture.

The University of Texas at Austin, Graduate School, College of Liberal Arts, Teresa Lozano Long Institute of Latin American Studies, Austin, TX 78712-1111. Offers cultural politics of Afro-Latin and indigenous peoples (MA); development studies (MA); environmental studies (MA); human rights (MA); Latin American and international law (LL M); JD/MA; MA/MA; MBA/MA; MP Aff/MA; MSCRP/MA. LL M offered jointly with The University of Texas School of Law. *Entrance requirements:* For master's, GRE General Test.

The University of Texas at San Antonio, College of Education and Human Development, Department of Bicultural and Bilingual Studies, San Antonio, TX 78249-0617. Offers bicultural/bilingual studies (MA), including bicultural studies, bicultural/bilingual education; culture, literacy, and language (PhD); teaching English as a second language (MA). Part-time and evening/weekend programs available. *Faculty:* 17 full-time (12 women), 1 part-time/adjunct (0 women). *Students:* 33 full-time (27 women), 106 part-time (80 women); includes 90 minority (3 Black or African American, non-Hispanic/Latino; 5 Asian, non-Hispanic/Latino; 80 Hispanic/Latino; 2 Two or more races, non-Hispanic/Latino), 13 international. Average age 38. 71 applicants, 86% accepted, 33 enrolled. In 2014, 56 master's, 4 doctorates awarded. *Degree requirements:* For master's, one foreign language, comprehensive exam, thesis optional; for doctorate, one foreign language, comprehensive exam, thesis/dissertation. *Entrance requirements:* For master's, bachelor's degree with 18 credit hours in field of study or in another appropriate field of study; for doctorate, GRE General Test, resume or curriculum vitae, 3 letters of recommendation, statement of purpose, master's degree. Additional exam requirements/recommendations for international students: Required—TOEFL (minimum score 550 paper-based; 79 iBT), IELTS (minimum score 6.5). *Application deadline:* For fall admission, 7/1 for domestic students, 4/1 for international students; for spring admission, 11/1 for domestic students, 9/1 for international students. Applications are processed on a rolling basis. Application fee: $45 ($80 for international students). Electronic applications accepted. *Expenses:* Expenses: $8,565 state resident tuition and fees. *Financial support:* In 2014–15, 18 students received support, including 18 fellowships (averaging $28,000 per year), 2 research assistantships (averaging $12,468 per year), 16 teaching assistantships (averaging $11,000 per year); scholarships/grants and unspecified assistantships also available. Financial award application deadline: 4/15. *Faculty research:* Bilingual and ESL teacher preparation; transnational communities; applied linguistics; cultural studies; bilingualism, biliteracy and second language acquisition. *Total annual research expenditures:* $8 million. *Unit head:* Dr. Belinda Bustos Flores, Chair, 210-458-4426, Fax: 210-458-5962, E-mail: belinda.flores@utsa.edu. *Application contact:* Rahnuma Islam, Student Development Specialist, 210-458-6619, Fax: 210-458-5576, E-mail: rahnuma.islam@utsa.edu.
Website: http://education.utsa.edu/bicultural-bilingual_studies

University of the Sacred Heart, Graduate Programs, Department of Communication, Program in Contemporary Culture and Media, San Juan, PR 00914-0383. Offers MA. *Degree requirements:* For master's, thesis.

University of Washington, Bothell, Master of Arts in Cultural Studies Program, Bothell, WA 98011-8246. Offers MA. Evening/weekend programs available. *Degree requirements:* For master's, thesis. *Entrance requirements:* Additional exam requirements/recommendations for international students: Required—TOEFL. Electronic applications accepted.

Washington State University, College of Education, Department of Teaching and Learning, Pullman, WA 99164-2132. Offers cultural studies and social thought in education (PhD); curriculum and instruction (Ed M, MA); English language learners (Ed M, MA); language, literacy and technology (PhD); literacy education (Ed M, MA); mathematics education (PhD); special education (Ed M, MA, PhD); teacher leadership (Ed D); teaching (MIT), including elementary education, secondary education. Programs offered at the Pullman, Spokane, Tri-cities, Vancouver and Global (online) campuses. Part-time programs available. Postbaccalaureate distance learning degree programs offered (no on-campus study). *Faculty:* 54 full-time (37 women), 9 part-time/adjunct (5 women). *Students:* 131 full-time (87 women), 123 part-time (102 women); includes 36 minority (5 Black or African American, non-Hispanic/Latino; 3 American Indian or Alaska Native, non-Hispanic/Latino; 5 Asian, non-Hispanic/Latino; 16 Hispanic/Latino; 7 Two or more races, non-Hispanic/Latino), 35 international. Average age 33. 224 applicants, 42% accepted, 80 enrolled. In 2014, 93 master's, 11 doctorates awarded. *Degree requirements:* For master's, comprehensive exam, thesis, oral or written exam; for doctorate, comprehensive exam, thesis/dissertation, oral and written exam. *Entrance requirements:* For master's, GRE General Test, minimum GPA of 3.0, 3 letters of recommendation, letter of intent, transcripts, resume/curriculum vitae; for doctorate, GRE General Test, minimum GPA of 3.0, 3 letters of recommendation, letter of intent, transcripts, writing sample, resume/curriculum vitae. Additional exam requirements/recommendations for international students: Required—TOEFL (minimum score 550 paper-based; 80 iBT). *Application deadline:* For fall admission, 1/10 priority date for domestic and international students; for spring admission, 9/1 priority date for domestic and international students. Application fee: $75. Electronic applications accepted. *Expenses:* Tuition, state resident: full-time $11,768. Tuition, nonresident: full-time $25,200. *Required fees:* $960. Tuition and fees vary according to program. *Financial support:* In 2014–15, 13 research assistantships (averaging $14,156 per year), 18 teaching assistantships (averaging $13,486 per year) were awarded. Financial award application deadline: 4/1; financial award applicants required to submit FAFSA. *Faculty research:* Intersection of gender, youth cultures and schooling; examination of ideology of power in children's literature; early childhood special education; analyzing pre-service and in-service teacher development; second language acquisition. *Total annual research expenditures:* $361,291. *Unit head:* Dr. Darcy Miller, Professor and Chair, 509-335-4570, E-mail: darcymiller@wsu.edu. *Application contact:* Dr. Jason Sievers,

Director of Graduate Programs, 509-335-9195, Fax: 509-335-5907, E-mail: jasievers@wsu.edu. Website: http://education.wsu.edu/tl/index.html

Wheaton College, Graduate School, Department of Intercultural Studies, Wheaton, IL 60187-5593. Offers evangelism and leadership (MA); intercultural studies (MA); intercultural studies/teaching English as a second language (MA); missions (MA); teaching English as a second language (Certificate). Part-time programs available. *Students:* 33 full-time (19 women), 16 part-time (9 women); includes 10 minority (3 Black or African American, non-Hispanic/Latino; 6 Asian, non-Hispanic/Latino; 1 Hispanic/Latino), 13 international. Average age 33. 31 applicants, 90% accepted, 16 enrolled. In 2014, 53 master's, 1 other advanced degree awarded. *Degree requirements:* For master's, thesis or alternative. *Entrance requirements:* For master's, GRE General Test, MAT. Additional exam requirements/recommendations for international students: Required—TOEFL (minimum score 550 paper-based; 80 iBT), IELTS (minimum score 6.5), TOEFL (minimum score 600 paper-based; 90 iBT) or IELTS (minimum score 7.5) for MA in TESOL. *Application deadline:* For fall admission, 5/1 for domestic students, 1/1 for international students; for spring admission, 11/1 for domestic students. Applications are processed on a rolling basis. Application fee: $30. Electronic applications accepted. *Financial support:* Career-related internships or fieldwork, scholarships/grants, and unspecified assistantships available. Financial award application deadline: 3/1; financial award applicants required to submit FAFSA. *Unit head:* Dr. Robert Gallagher, Chair, 630-752-5948. *Application contact:* Dusty Di Santo, Director of Graduate Admissions, 630-752-5195, Fax: 630-752-5047, E-mail: graduate.admissions@wheaton.edu.
Website: http://www.wheaton.edu/academics/departments/intr

Wilfrid Laurier University, Faculty of Graduate and Postdoctoral Studies, Faculty of Arts, Cultural Analysis and Social Theory Program, Waterloo, ON N2L 3C5, Canada. Offers body politics (MA); cultural representation and social theory (MA); gender, sexuality and embodiment (MA); globalization, identity and social movements (MA). Part-time programs available. *Entrance requirements:* For master's, honours BA in humanities, social science or interdisciplinary program with social theory, minimum B+ in final year of full-time study. Additional exam requirements/recommendations for international students: Required—TOEFL (minimum score 89 iBT). Electronic applications accepted. *Faculty research:* Globalization; identity and social movements; body politics: gender, sexuality and embodiment; cultural representation and social theory.

Wilfrid Laurier University, Faculty of Graduate and Postdoctoral Studies, Faculty of Arts, Department of Communication Studies, Waterloo, ON N2L 3C5, Canada. Offers media, technology and culture (MA); visual communication and culture (MA). *Degree requirements:* For master's, thesis optional. *Entrance requirements:* For master's, honours BA in communication studies or a cognate discipline from an approved university with a minimum B+ overall in last two years of study and in undergraduate major. Additional exam requirements/recommendations for international students: Required—TOEFL (minimum score 89 iBT). Electronic applications accepted. *Faculty research:* Visual communication and culture, media, technology and culture.

East European and Russian Studies

Boston College, Graduate School of Arts and Sciences, Department of Slavic and Eastern Languages, Program in Slavic Studies, Chestnut Hill, MA 02467-3800. Offers MA, MA/JD, MBA/MA. *Degree requirements:* For master's, 3 foreign languages, comprehensive exam, thesis or alternative. *Entrance requirements:* Additional exam requirements/recommendations for international students: Required—TOEFL (minimum score 600 paper-based; 100 iBT). *Application deadline:* For fall admission, 1/15 for domestic students. Application fee: $75. Electronic applications accepted. *Financial support:* Application deadline: 3/1. *Unit head:* Dr. Maxin Shrayer, Director of Graduate Studies, 617-552-3911.
Website: http://www.bc.edu/sl

Brown University, Graduate School, Department of Slavic Languages, Providence, RI 02912. Offers Russian language and literature (AM); Slavic linguistics (AM); Slavic studies (PhD). *Degree requirements:* For master's, one foreign language; for doctorate, 2 foreign languages, thesis/dissertation, preliminary exam.

Carleton University, Faculty of Graduate Studies, Faculty of Public Affairs and Management, Institute of European and Russian Studies, Ottawa, ON K1S 5B6, Canada. Offers European and European Union studies (MA); European integration studies (Diploma); Russian, Eurasian and transition studies (MA). *Degree requirements:* For master's, one foreign language, thesis optional. *Entrance requirements:* For master's, honors degree or equivalent; 2 years of Russian, German or other central east European language. Additional exam requirements/recommendations for international students: Required—TOEFL. *Faculty research:* East-West relations, minority rights in Russia and Eastern Europe.

Columbia University, Graduate School of Arts and Sciences, New York, NY 10027. Offers African-American studies (MA); American studies (MA); anthropology (MA, PhD); art history and archaeology (MA, PhD); astronomy (PhD); biological sciences (PhD); biotechnology (MA); chemical physics (PhD); chemistry (PhD); classical studies (MA, PhD); classics (MA, PhD); climate and society (MA); earth and environmental sciences (PhD); East Asia: regional studies (MA); East Asian languages and cultures (MA, PhD); ecology, evolution and environmental biology (MA), including conservation biology; ecology, evolution, and environmental biology (PhD), including ecology and evolutionary biology, evolutionary primatology; economics (PhD); English and comparative literature (MA, PhD); French and Romance philology (MA, PhD); Germanic languages (MA, PhD); global French studies (MA); Hispanic cultural studies (MA); history (PhD); history and literature (MA); human rights studies (MA); Islamic studies (MA); Italian (MA, PhD); Japanese pedagogy (MA); Jewish studies (MA); Latin America and the Caribbean: regional studies (MA); Latin American and Iberian cultures (PhD); mathematics (MA, PhD), including finance (MA); medieval and Renaissance studies (MA); Middle Eastern, South Asian, and African studies (MA, PhD); modern art: critical and curatorial studies (MA); modern European studies (MA); museum anthropology (MA); music (DMA, PhD); oral history (MA); philosophical foundations of physics (MA); philosophy (MA, PhD); physics (PhD); political science (MA, PhD); psychology (PhD); quantitative methods in the social sciences (MA); religion (MA, PhD); Russia, Eurasia and East Europe: regional studies (MA); Russian translation (MA); Slavic cultures (MA); Slavic languages (MA, PhD); sociology (MA, PhD); South Asian studies (MA); statistics (MA, PhD); theatre (PhD); JD/PhD; MA/MS; MD/PhD; MPA/MA. Dual-degree programs require admission to both Graduate School of Arts and Sciences and another Columbia school. Part-time and evening/weekend programs available. Terminal master's awarded for partial completion of doctoral program. *Degree requirements:* For master's, thesis (for some programs); for doctorate, comprehensive exam, thesis/dissertation. *Entrance requirements:* For master's and doctorate, GRE General Test, GRE Subject Test (for some programs). Electronic applications accepted. *Faculty research:* Humanities, natural sciences, social sciences.

Columbia University, School of International and Public Affairs, The East Central Europe Center, New York, NY 10027. Offers Certificate. Students must be enrolled in a separate graduate degree program at Columbia University. Electronic applications accepted. *Faculty research:* Ethnic politics, modern East Central European history, post-Communist economic and political transitions, East Central European language and literature.

Columbia University, School of International and Public Affairs, The Harriman Institute, New York, NY 10027. Offers Certificate. Students must be enrolled in a separate graduate degree program at Columbia University. Part-time programs available. *Degree requirements:* For Certificate, one foreign language, thesis. *Entrance requirements:* For degree, minimum 2 years of Russian. Electronic applications accepted.

Cornell University, Graduate School, Graduate Fields of Arts and Sciences, Field of History, Ithaca, NY 14853-0001. Offers African history (MA, PhD); American history (MA, PhD); ancient Greek history (PhD); ancient history (MA, PhD); ancient Roman history (PhD); early modern European history (MA, PhD); English history (MA, PhD); French history (MA, PhD); German history (MA, PhD); history of science (MA, PhD); Korean history (PhD); Latin American history (MA, PhD); medieval Chinese history (MA, PhD); medieval history (MA, PhD); modern Chinese history (MA, PhD); modern European history (MA, PhD); modern Japanese history (MA, PhD); modern Middle Eastern history (PhD); premodern Islamic history (MA, PhD); premodern Japanese history (MA, PhD); Renaissance history (MA, PhD); Russian history (MA, PhD); South Asian history (PhD); Southeast Asian history (MA, PhD). Terminal master's awarded for partial completion of doctoral program. *Degree requirements:* For master's, thesis; for doctorate, 2 foreign languages, comprehensive exam, thesis/dissertation, 1 year of teaching experience. *Entrance requirements:* For master's and doctorate, GRE General Test, writing sample, 3 letters of recommendation. Additional exam requirements/recommendations for international students: Required—TOEFL (minimum score 550 paper-based; 77 iBT). Electronic applications accepted.

Florida State University, The Graduate School, College of Social Sciences and Public Policy, Program in Russian and East European Studies, Tallahassee, FL 32306. Offers MA. Part-time programs available. *Faculty:* 2 full-time (1 woman), 4 part-time/adjunct (1 woman). *Students:* 7 full-time (5 women), 2 part-time (0 women); includes 1 minority (Two or more races, non-Hispanic/Latino). Average age 29. 3 applicants, 67% accepted, 1 enrolled. In 2014, 2 master's awarded. *Degree requirements:* For master's, one foreign language, comprehensive exam, thesis optional. *Entrance requirements:* For master's, GRE General Test, minimum GPA of 3.0. Additional exam requirements/recommendations for international students: Required—TOEFL (minimum score 550 paper-based; 80 iBT). *Application deadline:* For fall admission, 7/1 for domestic and international students; for spring admission, 11/1 for domestic and international students. Applications are processed on a rolling basis. Application fee: $30. Electronic applications accepted. *Expenses:* Tuition, state resident: part-time $403.51 per credit hour. Tuition, nonresident: part-time $1004.85 per credit hour. *Required fees:* $75.81 per credit hour. One-time fee: $20 part-time. Tuition and fees vary according to campus/location. *Financial support:* In 2014–15, research assistantships with full tuition reimbursements (averaging $5,000 per year) were awarded; fellowships, career-related internships or fieldwork, Federal Work-Study, institutionally sponsored loans, and unspecified assistantships also available. Financial award application deadline: 2/15; financial award applicants required to submit FAFSA. *Unit head:* Dr. Lee K. Metcalf, Director, 850-644-7327, Fax: 850-645-4981, E-mail: lmetcalf@fsu.edu. *Application contact:* Kaley Boggs, Academic Program Specialist, 850-644-4418, Fax: 850-645-4981, E-mail: kboggs@fsu.edu.
Website: http://www.fsu.edu/~russia/

Georgetown University, Graduate School of Arts and Sciences, Edmund A. Walsh School of Foreign Service, Center for Eurasian, Russian and East European Studies, Washington, DC 20057. Offers MA, MA/JD, MA/PhD. *Degree requirements:* For master's, one foreign language, comprehensive exam, thesis optional. *Entrance requirements:* For master's, GRE General Test. Additional exam requirements/recommendations for international students: Required—TOEFL. *Faculty research:* East-West trade.

The George Washington University, Elliott School of International Affairs, Program in European and Eurasian Studies, Washington, DC 20052. Offers MA. Part-time programs available. *Students:* 18 full-time (6 women), 9 part-time (6 women); includes 1 minority (Black or African American, non-Hispanic/Latino). Average age 27. 47 applicants, 9 enrolled. In 2014, 9 master's awarded. *Degree requirements:* For master's, one foreign language, capstone project. *Entrance requirements:* For master's, GRE General Test, 2 years (or the equivalent) of a modern European language or Russian, 2 semesters of introductory economics (macro or micro). Additional exam requirements/recommendations for international students: Required—TOEFL (minimum score 100 iBT), IELTS (minimum score 7). *Application deadline:* For fall admission, 1/15 priority date for domestic and international students; for spring admission, 10/1 for domestic students. Application fee: $75. Electronic applications accepted. *Financial support:* In 2014–15, 3 students received support. Fellowships with partial tuition reimbursements available and Federal Work-Study available. Financial award application deadline: 1/15; financial award applicants required to submit FAFSA. *Faculty research:* NATO, European economics, European history, European Union. *Unit head:* Peter Rollberg, Director, 202-994-6340, E-mail: rgpeter@gwu.edu. *Application contact:* Nicole A. Campbell, Director of Graduate Admissions, 202-994-7050, Fax: 202-994-9537, E-mail: esiagrad@gwu.edu.
Website: http://elliott.gwu.edu/academics/grad/ees/index.cfm

Harvard University, Graduate School of Arts and Sciences, Committee on Regional Studies-Russia, Eastern Europe, and Central Asia, Cambridge, MA 02138. Offers AM. *Degree requirements:* For master's, one foreign language. *Entrance requirements:* For master's, GRE General Test. Additional exam requirements/recommendations for international students: Required—TOEFL. *Faculty research:* Strategic policy, ethnography and demography of U.S.S.R., non-Russian nationality language training.

Indiana University Bloomington, University Graduate School, College of Arts and Sciences, School of Global and International Studies, Russian and East European

East European and Russian Studies

Institute, Bloomington, IN 47405-7000. Offers MA, Certificate, JD/MA, MA/MA, MBA/MA, MIS/MA, MLS/MA, MPA/MA, MPH/MA, MSSI/MA. Part-time programs available. *Students:* 12 full-time (5 women), 1 (woman) part-time, 1 international. Average age 28. 33 applicants, 48% accepted, 4 enrolled. In 2014, 5 master's awarded. *Degree requirements:* For master's, one foreign language, essay, language proficiency, and written exams; for Certificate, one foreign language, oral and proficiency exams. *Entrance requirements:* For master's, GRE General Test, minimum 2 years of college Russian (for Russian area studies); for Certificate, GRE General Test. Additional exam requirements/recommendations for international students: Required—TOEFL. *Application deadline:* For fall admission, 1/15 for domestic students, 12/1 for international students; for spring admission, 9/15 for domestic students, 8/15 for international students. Applications are processed on a rolling basis. Application fee: $55 ($65 for international students). Electronic applications accepted. *Expenses:* Expenses: $341.51 per credit hour in-state, $1,053.94 out-of-state. *Financial support:* In 2014–15, 1 student received support, including fellowships with tuition reimbursements available (averaging $15,000 per year), research assistantships with tuition reimbursements available (averaging $15,750 per year), teaching assistantships with tuition reimbursements available (averaging $15,750 per year); career-related internships or fieldwork, Federal Work-Study, and institutionally sponsored loans also available. Financial award application deadline: 2/15; financial award applicants required to submit FAFSA. *Faculty research:* Political and economic transition of former Soviet Union and eastern Europe, Russian and Soviet history, Slavic literature and linguistics, education and mass media of former Soviet Union and Eastern Europe. *Unit head:* Prof. Sarah Phillips, Director, 812-855-7309. *Application contact:* Mary Belding, Administrative Secretary, 812-855-3869, Fax: 812-855-6411, E-mail: mebeldin@indiana.edu.
Website: http://www.indiana.edu/~reeiweb/

La Salle University, School of Arts and Sciences, Central and Eastern European Studies Program, Philadelphia, PA 19141-1199. Offers Central and Eastern European studies (MA); intelligence and security studies (Certificate). Part-time and evening/weekend programs available. *Degree requirements:* For master's, one foreign language, proficiency in one Central or Eastern European language; capstone seminar or thesis; for Certificate, one foreign language, evidence of reading knowledge of at least one of the languages of Central or Eastern Europe upon graduation. *Entrance requirements:* For master's and Certificate, bachelor's degree; 2 letters of recommendation. Additional exam requirements/recommendations for international students: Required—TOEFL. Electronic applications accepted. Application fee is waived when completed online. *Expenses:* Contact institution.

The Ohio State University, Graduate School, Center for Slavic and East European Studies, Columbus, OH 43210. Offers MA. *Faculty:* 70. *Students:* 15 full-time (7 women); includes 1 minority (Two or more races, non-Hispanic/Latino). Average age 25. In 2014, 3 master's awarded. *Degree requirements:* For master's, exam or thesis. *Entrance requirements:* For master's, GRE General Test. Additional exam requirements/recommendations for international students: Required—TOEFL (minimum score 550 paper-based; 79 iBT), Michigan English Language Assessment Battery (minimum score 82); Recommended—IELTS (minimum score 7). *Application deadline:* For fall admission, 12/13 priority date for domestic students, 11/30 priority date for international students; for winter admission, 12/1 for domestic students, 11/1 for international students; for spring admission, 12/14 for domestic students, 11/12 for international students; for summer admission, 5/15 for domestic students, 4/14 for international students. Applications are processed on a rolling basis. Application fee: $60 ($70 for international students). Electronic applications accepted. *Financial support:* Fellowships, Federal Work-Study, and institutionally sponsored loans available. Support available to part-time students. *Unit head:* Dr. Yana Hashamova, Director, E-mail: hashamova.1@osu.edu. *Application contact:* Graduate and Professional Admissions, 614-292-9444, Fax: 614-292-3895, E-mail: gpadmissions@osu.edu.
Website: http://slaviccenter.osu.edu

The Ohio State University, Graduate School, College of Arts and Sciences, Division of Arts and Humanities, Department of Slavic and East European Languages and Cultures, Columbus, OH 43210. Offers Slavic linguistics (MA, PhD); Slavic literature, film, and cultural studies (MA, PhD). *Faculty:* 10. *Students:* 15 full-time (9 women), 1 (woman) part-time; includes 1 minority (Hispanic/Latino), 2 international. Average age 30. In 2014, 2 master's, 5 doctorates awarded. Terminal master's awarded for partial completion of doctoral program. *Degree requirements:* For master's, variable foreign language requirement, thesis optional; for doctorate, variable foreign language requirement, thesis/dissertation. *Entrance requirements:* For master's and doctorate, GRE General Test, at least 3 years of Russian language study or equivalent. Additional exam requirements/recommendations for international students: Required—TOEFL (minimum score 550 paper-based; 79 iBT), Michigan English Language Assessment Battery (minimum score 82); Recommended—IELTS (minimum score 7). *Application deadline:* For fall admission, 12/12 priority date for domestic students, 11/30 priority date for international students; for winter admission, 12/1 for domestic students, 11/1 for international students; for spring admission, 3/1 for domestic students, 2/1 for international students. Applications are processed on a rolling basis. Application fee: $60 ($70 for international students). Electronic applications accepted. *Financial support:* Fellowships with tuition reimbursements, teaching assistantships with tuition reimbursements, Federal Work-Study, and institutionally sponsored loans available. Support available to part-time students. *Faculty research:* Polish literature. *Unit head:* Dr. Yana Hashamova, Chair and Professor, 614-292-6733, E-mail: hashamova.1@osu.edu. *Application contact:* Graduate and Professional Admissions, 614-292-9444, Fax: 614-292-3895, E-mail: gpadmissions@osu.edu.
Website: http://slavic.osu.edu/

Stanford University, School of Humanities and Sciences, Center for Russian, East European and Eurasian Studies, Stanford, CA 94305-9991. Offers MA. *Degree requirements:* For master's, one foreign language. *Entrance requirements:* For master's, GRE General Test. Additional exam requirements/recommendations for international students: Required—TOEFL. Electronic applications accepted. *Expenses: Tuition:* Full-time $44,184; part-time $982 per credit hour. *Required fees:* $191.

University of Alberta, Faculty of Graduate Studies and Research, Department of Modern Languages and Cultural Studies, Edmonton, AB T6G 2E1, Canada. Offers applied linguistics (Germanic, Romance, Slavic) (MA); French language, literatures and linguistics (PhD); French language, literatures, and linguistics (MA); Germanic languages, literatures and linguistics (PhD); Germanic languages, literatures, and linguistics (MA); Italian studies (MA); Slavic languages and literatures (Russian, Ukrainian) (MA, PhD); Slavic linguistics (Russian, Ukrainian) (MA, PhD); Spanish and Latin American studies (MA, PhD); Ukrainian folklore (MA, PhD). Part-time programs available. *Degree requirements:* For master's, one foreign language, thesis; for doctorate, 2 foreign languages, comprehensive exam, thesis/dissertation. *Entrance requirements:* For master's and doctorate, 1 language other than English. Additional exam requirements/recommendations for international students: Required—Michigan English Language Assessment Battery or TOEFL (minimum score 550 paper-based). Electronic applications accepted. *Faculty research:* Russian/Ukrainian studies; German studies; contemporary Latin American, French and Francophone studies; Italian studies.

The University of British Columbia, Faculty of Arts and Faculty of Graduate Studies, Department of Central, Eastern and Northern European Studies, Vancouver, BC V6T2Z1, Canada. Offers Germanic studies (MA, PhD). Part-time programs available. *Degree requirements:* For master's, one foreign language, thesis optional, exam; for doctorate, one foreign language, comprehensive exam, thesis/dissertation. *Entrance requirements:* For master's, BA in German; for doctorate, MA in German. Additional exam requirements/recommendations for international students: Required—TOEFL (minimum score 550 paper-based; 80 iBT). Electronic applications accepted. *Faculty research:* Second language acquisition, media theory, performance theory, gender studies, cultural studies.

University of Illinois at Chicago, Graduate College, College of Liberal Arts and Sciences, School of Literatures, Cultural Studies and Linguistics, Department of Slavic and Baltic Languages and Literatures, Chicago, IL 60607-7128. Offers Slavic studies (MA, PhD). Evening/weekend programs available. *Faculty:* 7 full-time (4 women), 1 (woman) part-time/adjunct. *Students:* 8 full-time (4 women), 1 part-time (0 women), 6 international. Average age 31. 6 applicants, 33% accepted, 2 enrolled. In 2014, 1 doctorate awarded. Terminal master's awarded for partial completion of doctoral program. *Degree requirements:* For doctorate, one foreign language, thesis/dissertation. *Entrance requirements:* For master's and doctorate, GRE General Test, minimum GPA of 3.0. Additional exam requirements/recommendations for international students: Required—TOEFL. *Application deadline:* For fall admission, 1/1 priority date for domestic and international students; for spring admission, 11/1 for domestic students, 7/15 for international students. Application fee: $60. Electronic applications accepted. *Expenses:* Tuition, state resident: full-time $11,254; part-time $468 per credit hour. Tuition, nonresident: full-time $23,252; part-time $968 per credit hour. *Required fees:* $1217 per term. Part-time tuition and fees vary according to course load, degree level and program. *Financial support:* In 2014–15, 9 students received support. Fellowships with full tuition reimbursements available, research assistantships with full tuition reimbursements available, teaching assistantships with full tuition reimbursements available, institutionally sponsored loans, and tuition waivers (full) available. Financial award application deadline: 3/1; financial award applicants required to submit FAFSA. *Faculty research:* Twentieth-century Polish literature and culture, Russian and Polish modernisms, nineteenth- and twentieth-century Russian literature, Lithuanian language, Polish-Jewish culture and history, Yiddish literature and language. *Unit head:* Michal Pawel Markowski, Head, 312-996-5218, Fax: 312-413-1044, E-mail: markowsk@uic.edu.
Website: http://lcsl.las.uic.edu/slavic-baltic

University of Illinois at Urbana–Champaign, Graduate College, College of Liberal Arts and Sciences, Russian, East European, and Eurasian Center, Champaign, IL 61820. Offers MA. *Students:* 8 (6 women). Application fee: $70 ($90 for international students). *Unit head:* David Cooper, Director, 217-244-4666, Fax: 217-333-7310, E-mail: dlcoop@illinois.edu. *Application contact:* Alisha Kirchoff, Associate Director, 217-244-4721, Fax: 217-333-1582, E-mail: kirchoff@illinois.edu.
Website: http://www.reeec.illinois.edu/

The University of Kansas, Graduate Studies, College of Liberal Arts and Sciences, Center for Russian, East European and Eurasian Studies, Lawrence, KS 66045. Offers foreign area officer (MA); Russian, East European and Eurasian studies (MA, Graduate Certificate); JD/MA. Part-time programs available. *Faculty:* 2 full-time, 4 part-time/adjunct. *Students:* 6 full-time (0 women); includes 1 minority (Two or more races, non-Hispanic/Latino), 1 international. Average age 27. 8 applicants, 88% accepted, 1 enrolled. In 2014, 6 master's awarded. *Degree requirements:* For master's, one foreign language, comprehensive exam, interdisciplinary capstone research seminar. *Entrance requirements:* For master's, GRE General Test, two-page statement of educational and professional objectives, three letters of recommendation. Additional exam requirements/recommendations for international students: Required—TOEFL. *Application deadline:* For fall admission, 1/1 priority date for domestic and international students. Application fee: $55 ($65 for international students). Electronic applications accepted. *Financial support:* Fellowships with full tuition reimbursements, research assistantships with partial tuition reimbursements, and scholarships/grants available. Financial award application deadline: 1/31; financial award applicants required to submit FAFSA. *Faculty research:* Russian and East Central European history and culture; Ukrainian, Russian, and Central Asian domestic politics and international security; Slavic languages, linguistics, and literatures. *Unit head:* Dr. Mariya Y. Omelicheva, Chair, 785-864-4236, E-mail: omeliche@ku.edu. *Application contact:* Adrienne Landry, Graduate Admissions Contact, 785-864-4237, E-mail: crees@ku.edu.
Website: http://www.crees.ku.edu/

University of Michigan, Horace H. Rackham School of Graduate Studies, College of Literature, Science, and the Arts, Center for Russian, East European, and European Studies, Ann Arbor, MI 48109-1106. Offers AM, Certificate, JD/AM, MBA/AM, MPP/AM. Part-time programs available. *Faculty:* 71 full-time (48 women), 4 part-time/adjunct (2 women). *Students:* 12 full-time (3 women); includes 1 minority (Asian, non-Hispanic/Latino), 1 international. Average age 25. 26 applicants, 69% accepted, 6 enrolled. In 2014, 3 master's, 1 other advanced degree awarded. *Degree requirements:* For master's and Certificate, one foreign language, thesis. *Entrance requirements:* For master's, GRE General Test. Additional exam requirements/recommendations for international students: Required—TOEFL. *Application deadline:* For fall admission, 1/15 for domestic and international students. Application fee: $75 ($90 for international students). Electronic applications accepted. *Financial support:* In 2014–15, 7 students received support, including 4 fellowships with full and partial tuition reimbursements available (averaging $15,000 per year), 2 teaching assistantships with full tuition reimbursements available (averaging $8,000 per year); scholarships/grants also available. Financial award application deadline: 1/20. *Faculty research:* Russia, East Europe, Eurasia, Central Asia, Caucasus. *Unit head:* Dr. Genevieve Zubrzycki, Director, 734-764-0351, Fax: 734-763-4765, E-mail: crees@umich.edu. *Application contact:* Julie E. Burnett, Academic Services Coordinator, 734-764-0351, Fax: 734-763-4765, E-mail: crees.admissions@umich.edu.
Website: http://www.ii.umich.edu/crees

The University of North Carolina at Chapel Hill, Graduate School, College of Arts and Sciences, Department of Slavic Languages and Literatures, Curriculum in Russian and East European Studies, Chapel Hill, NC 27599. Offers MA. Part-time programs available. *Degree requirements:* For master's, one foreign language, thesis. *Entrance requirements:* For master's, GRE General Test. Additional exam requirements/recommendations for international students: Required—TOEFL. Electronic applications accepted. *Faculty research:* Language, area studies, social sciences, sciences, professional schools.

University of Pittsburgh, University Center for International Studies, Pittsburgh, PA 15260. Offers African studies (Certificate); Asian studies (Certificate); European Union studies (Certificate); global studies (Certificate); Latin American studies (Certificate); Russian and East European studies (Certificate); West European studies (Certificate). *Students:* 223 full-time (98 women), 11 part-time (1 woman); includes 97 minority (2 Black or African American, non-Hispanic/Latino; 41 Asian, non-Hispanic/Latino; 52 Hispanic/Latino; 2 Two or more races, non-Hispanic/Latino). Average age 31. In 2014, 72 Certificates awarded. *Degree requirements:* For Certificate, one foreign language,

study abroad. *Application deadline:* Applications are processed on a rolling basis. *Expenses:* Tuition, state resident: full-time $20,742; part-time $838 per credit. Tuition, nonresident: full-time $33,960; part-time $1389 per credit. *Required fees:* $800; $205 per term. Tuition and fees vary according to program. *Unit head:* Dr. Ariel Armony, Director, 412-648-7374, Fax: 412-624-4672, E-mail: armony@pitt.edu. *Application contact:* Information Contact, 412-624-4141, E-mail: graduate@pitt.edu. Website: http://www.ucis.pitt.edu

University of Saskatchewan, College of Graduate Studies and Research, College of Arts and Science, Department of Languages and Linguistics, Saskatoon, SK S7N 5A2, Canada. Offers MA. *Degree requirements:* For master's, 2 foreign languages, thesis. *Entrance requirements:* Additional exam requirements/recommendations for international students: Required—TOEFL (minimum score 80 iBT); Recommended—IELTS (minimum score 6.5). Electronic applications accepted.

The University of Texas at Austin, Graduate School, College of Liberal Arts, Center for Russian, East European, and Eurasian Studies, Austin, TX 78712-1111. Offers MA, JD/MA, MA/MA, MBA/MA, MGPS/MA, MP Aff/MA. Part-time programs available. *Degree requirements:* For master's, one foreign language, report or thesis. *Entrance requirements:* For master's, GRE General Test, 3 years of formal language training or equivalent, minimum GPA of 3.0. Electronic applications accepted. *Faculty research:* East European gypsies, elite transformation and democracy in Eastern Europe, elite partisanship as an intervening variable in Russian politics, post-Soviet youth in Russia.

University of Toronto, School of Graduate Studies, Munk School of Global Affairs, Centre for European, Russian and Eurasian Studies, Toronto, ON M5S 2J7, Canada. Offers MA, JD/MA. *Degree requirements:* For master's, one foreign language, language

proficiency test. *Entrance requirements:* For master's, minimum B+ average in final year, coursework in Russian/East European subjects, 2 years of study in a relevant language. Additional exam requirements/recommendations for international students: Required—TOEFL (minimum score 580 paper-based; 93 iBT), TWE (minimum score 5). Electronic applications accepted.

University of Washington, Graduate School, College of Arts and Sciences, Henry M. Jackson School of International Studies, Russian, East European and Central Asian Studies Program, Seattle, WA 98195. Offers Central Asian studies (MAIS); East European studies (MAIS); Russian studies (MAIS). *Degree requirements:* For master's, one foreign language, thesis. *Entrance requirements:* For master's, GRE General Test, 2 years of relevant language, minimum GPA of 3.0 in last two years. Additional exam requirements/recommendations for international students: Required—TOEFL (minimum score 500 paper-based; 92 iBT), IELTS (minimum score 7). Electronic applications accepted.

Yale University, Graduate School of Arts and Sciences, Department of Slavic Languages and Literatures, New Haven, CT 06520. Offers medieval Slavic literature and philology (PhD); Polish literature (PhD); Russian literature (PhD); Slavic languages and literatures and film studies (PhD). *Degree requirements:* For doctorate, 3 foreign languages, thesis/dissertation. *Entrance requirements:* For doctorate, GRE General Test.

Yale University, Graduate School of Arts and Sciences, Program in Russian and East European Studies, New Haven, CT 06520. Offers MA. *Degree requirements:* For master's, 2 foreign languages. *Entrance requirements:* For master's, GRE General Test.

Ethnic Studies

Cornell University, Graduate School, Graduate Fields of Arts and Sciences, Field of Sociology, Ithaca, NY 14853-0001. Offers economy and society (MA, PhD); gender and life course (MA, PhD); methodology (MA, PhD); organizations (MA, PhD); policy analysis (MA, PhD); political sociology/social movements (MA, PhD); racial and ethnic relations (MA, PhD); social networks (MA, PhD); social psychology (MA, PhD); social stratification (MA, PhD). Terminal master's awarded for partial completion of doctoral program. *Degree requirements:* For master's, thesis; for doctorate, thesis/dissertation, 1 year of teaching experience. *Entrance requirements:* For master's and doctorate, GRE General Test, 2 letters of recommendation, writing sample. Additional exam requirements/recommendations for international students: Required—TOEFL (minimum score 550 paper-based; 77 iBT). Electronic applications accepted. *Faculty research:* Comparative societal analysis, work and family, simulations, social class and mobility, racial segregation and inequality.

Minnesota State University Mankato, College of Graduate Studies, College of Social and Behavioral Sciences, Department of Ethnic Studies, Mankato, MN 56001. Offers MS, Certificate. *Students:* 4 full-time (3 women), 11 part-time (5 women). *Application deadline:* For fall admission, 7/1 for domestic students, 5/1 for international students; for winter admission, 11/1 for domestic students; for spring admission, 10/1 for international students. Applications are processed on a rolling basis. Electronic applications accepted. *Unit head:* Dr. Hanh Huy Phan, Graduate Coordinator, 507-389-1185. *Application contact:* 507-389-2321, E-mail: grad@mnsu.edu. Website: http://sbs.mnsu.edu/ethnic/

Northern Arizona University, Graduate College, College of Social and Behavioral Sciences, Ethnic Studies Program, Flagstaff, AZ 86011. Offers Graduate Certificate. Part-time programs available. *Entrance requirements:* For degree, bachelor's degree with minimum GPA of 2.5. Additional exam requirements/recommendations for international students: Required—TOEFL (minimum score 550 paper-based; 80 iBT), IELTS (minimum score 7). Electronic applications accepted.

San Francisco State University, Division of Graduate Studies, College of Ethnic Studies, Program in Ethnic Studies, San Francisco, CA 94132-1722. Offers MA. *Expenses:* Tuition, state resident: full-time $6738. Tuition, nonresident: full-time $17,898; part-time $372 per credit hour. *Required fees:* $498 per semester. *Unit head:* Dr. Kenneth Monteiro, Dean, 415-338-1694, E-mail: ethnicst@sfsu.edu. *Application contact:* Dr. Laureen Chew, Graduate Coordinator, 415-338-1693, E-mail: ethnicst@sfsu.edu. Website: http://ethnicstudies.sfsu.edu/

United Theological Seminary of the Twin Cities, Graduate Programs, New Brighton, MN 55112-2598. Offers advanced theological studies (Diploma); justice and peace studies (M Div, MA); leadership toward racial justice (M Div, MA, Certificate); Methodist studies (M Div, MA, Certificate); ministry (D Min); ministry renewal and professional development (Certificate); pastoral care and counseling (M Div, MA, MARL); religion and theology (MA); theological and religious studies (Certificate); theology and the arts (M Div, MA); urban ministry (M Div, MA, MARL); women's studies: religion, theology and ministry (M Div, MA). *Accreditation:* ACIPE; ATS. Part-time and evening/weekend programs available. *Degree requirements:* For master's, thesis; for doctorate, comprehensive exam, thesis/dissertation. *Entrance requirements:* For master's, minimum GPA of 2.75; strong analytical, reflective thinking and writing skills; vocational and academic goals compatible with those of Seminary; for doctorate, M Div or equivalent, minimum GPA of 3.0, 3 years experience in professional ministry; for other advanced degree, BA or equivalent life experience; strong analytical, reflective thinking and writing skills (Certificate); proficiency in English language, previous study of theology at a theological school, recommendation of student's denomination (Diploma). Additional exam requirements/recommendations for international students: Required—TOEFL (minimum score 550 paper-based).

Université Laval, Faculty of Letters, Department of History, Programs in Ethnology of French-Speaking People in North America, Québec, QC G1K 7P4, Canada. Offers MA, PhD. Terminal master's awarded for partial completion of doctoral program. *Degree requirements:* For master's, thesis; for doctorate, comprehensive exam, thesis/dissertation. *Entrance requirements:* For master's and doctorate, English exam (comprehension of written English), knowledge of French. Electronic applications accepted.

University of California, Berkeley, Graduate Division, College of Letters and Science, Group in Ethnic Studies, Berkeley, CA 94720-1500. Offers PhD. *Degree requirements:* For doctorate, one foreign language, thesis/dissertation, qualifying exam. *Entrance requirements:* For doctorate, minimum GPA of 3.0, 3 letters of recommendation. *Faculty research:* Gender and race, Asian American visual art, racial theory and politics, Chicana/o literature and visual arts, history of Native North Americans.

University of California, Riverside, Graduate Division, Department of Ethnic Studies, Riverside, CA 92521. Offers cultural politics and production (PhD); the state, law, and social transformation (PhD). *Faculty:* 15 full-time (9 women). *Students:* 18 full-time (13 women); includes 16 minority (5 Black or African American, non-Hispanic/Latino; 1 American Indian or Alaska Native, non-Hispanic/Latino; 2 Asian, non-Hispanic/Latino; 7 Hispanic/Latino; 1 Native Hawaiian or other Pacific Islander, non-Hispanic/Latino). Average age 30. 42 applicants, 19% accepted, 4 enrolled. Terminal master's awarded for partial completion of doctoral program. *Degree requirements:* For doctorate, variable foreign language requirement, comprehensive exam, thesis/dissertation. *Entrance requirements:* For doctorate, GRE, Writing Sample, Statement of Purpose, Personal History Statement, Letters of Recommendation (3). Additional exam requirements/recommendations for international students: Required—TOEFL (minimum score 550 paper-based; 80 iBT), Individual section score on IELTS must not be less than 6 in any section. Recommended—IELTS (minimum score 7). *Application deadline:* For fall admission, 1/5 priority date for domestic and international students. Applications are processed on a rolling basis. Application fee: $80 ($100 for international students). Electronic applications accepted. *Expenses:* Tuition, state resident: full-time $5399. Tuition, nonresident: full-time $10,433. *Financial support:* In 2014–15, 10 students received support, including 4 fellowships with full tuition reimbursements available (averaging $10,000 per year), 7 teaching assistantships with full tuition reimbursements available (averaging $18,000 per year); unspecified assistantships also available. Financial award application deadline: 1/5; financial award applicants required to submit FAFSA. *Faculty research:* The political economy of race, class, gender, sexuality, cultural production, the state, law, criminal justice and grass roots responses. *Unit head:* Dr. Dylan Rodriguez, Chair, 951-827-4707, E-mail: dylan.rodriguez@ucr.edu. *Application contact:* Trina B. Elerts, Graduate Program Coordinator, 951-827-1584, E-mail: trina.elerts@ucr.edu. Website: http://www.ethnicstudies.ucr.edu

University of California, San Diego, Graduate Division, Department of Ethnic Studies, La Jolla, CA 92093. Offers PhD. *Students:* 32 full-time (23 women); includes 25 minority (7 Black or African American, non-Hispanic/Latino; 6 Asian, non-Hispanic/Latino; 11 Hispanic/Latino; 1 Native Hawaiian or other Pacific Islander, non-Hispanic/Latino), 3 international. 74 applicants, 15% accepted, 8 enrolled. In 2014, 2 doctorates awarded. *Degree requirements:* For doctorate, one foreign language, comprehensive exam, thesis/dissertation. *Entrance requirements:* For doctorate, GRE General Test, writing sample. Additional exam requirements/recommendations for international students: Required—TOEFL (minimum score 550 paper-based; 80 iBT), IELTS. *Application deadline:* For fall admission, 1/6 for domestic students. Application fee: $90 ($110 for international students). Electronic applications accepted. *Expenses:* Tuition, state resident: full-time $11,220; part-time $5610 per quarter. Tuition, nonresident: full-time $26,322; part-time $13,161 per quarter. *Required fees:* $570 per quarter. Tuition and fees vary according to program. *Financial support:* Fellowships and scholarships/grants available. Financial award applicants required to submit FAFSA. *Faculty research:* Cultural studies, gender studies, refugee studies, Native American history and culture, theories of performance. *Unit head:* Curtis Marez, Chair, 858-822-4452, E-mail: cmarez@ucsd.edu. *Application contact:* Christa Ludeking, Graduate Coordinator, 858-534-6040, E-mail: ethnicstudiesphd@ucsd.edu. Website: http://ethnicstudies.ucsd.edu

University of Nevada, Las Vegas, Graduate College, College of Liberal Arts, Department of Anthropology and Ethnic Studies, Las Vegas, NV 89154-5003. Offers MA, PhD. Part-time programs available. *Faculty:* 11 full-time (3 women). *Students:* 33 full-time (19 women), 15 part-time (13 women); includes 10 minority (1 Black or African American, non-Hispanic/Latino; 1 Asian, non-Hispanic/Latino; 7 Hispanic/Latino; 1 Two or more races, non-Hispanic/Latino), 1 international. Average age 30. 71 applicants, 20% accepted, 9 enrolled. In 2014, 5 master's awarded. *Degree requirements:* For master's, thesis, oral defense of thesis; for doctorate, comprehensive exam, thesis/dissertation, oral defense of dissertation. *Entrance requirements:* For master's and doctorate, GRE General Test. Additional exam requirements/recommendations for international students: Required—TOEFL (minimum score 550 paper-based; 80 iBT), IELTS (minimum score 7). *Application deadline:* For fall admission, 2/1 for domestic students, 5/1 for international students; for spring admission, 10/1 for international students. Application fee: $60 ($95 for international students). Electronic applications accepted. *Financial support:* In 2014–15, 24 students received support, including 1 fellowship with full tuition reimbursement available (averaging $20,000 per year), 13 research assistantships with partial tuition reimbursements available (averaging $12,538 per year), 10 teaching assistantships with partial tuition reimbursements available (averaging $14,300 per year); institutionally sponsored loans, scholarships/grants, health care benefits, and unspecified assistantships also available. Financial award application deadline: 3/1. *Faculty research:* Food and nutrition, adaptive strategies,

childhood and parenting, sexuality, gender and identity. *Unit head:* Dr. Barbara Roth, Chair/Professor, 702-895-3646, Fax: 702-895-4823, E-mail: barbara.roth@unlv.edu. *Application contact:* Graduate College Admissions Evaluator, 702-895-3320, Fax: 702-895-4180, E-mail: gradcollege@unlv.edu.
Website: http://anthro.unlv.edu/

University of New Mexico, Graduate School, College of Arts and Sciences, Program in Anthropology, Albuquerque, NM 87131-2039. Offers archaeology (MA, MS, PhD); ethnology (MA, MS, PhD); evolutionary anthropology (PhD); public archaeology (MA, MS, PhD). *Faculty:* 24 full-time (10 women). *Students:* 90 full-time (53 women), 32 part-time (25 women); includes 30 minority (4 American Indian or Alaska Native, non-Hispanic/Latino; 2 Asian, non-Hispanic/Latino; 19 Hispanic/Latino; 5 Two or more races, non-Hispanic/Latino), 8 international. Average age 32. 101 applicants, 31% accepted, 20 enrolled. In 2014, 18 master's, 14 doctorates awarded. Terminal master's awarded for partial completion of doctoral program. *Degree requirements:* For master's, comprehensive exam (for some programs), thesis or alternative, 1-2 exams; for doctorate, one foreign language, comprehensive exam, thesis/dissertation, exam, proposal, oral defense, skill and/or second language. *Entrance requirements:* For master's and doctorate, GRE General Test, 3 letters of recommendation, letter of interest, transcripts. Additional exam requirements/recommendations for international students: Required—TOEFL (minimum score 550 paper-based), IELTS (minimum score 7). *Application deadline:* For fall admission, 1/4 for domestic and international students. Application fee: $50. Electronic applications accepted. *Financial support:* In 2014–15, 104 students received support, including 17 fellowships (averaging $9,268 per year), 16 research assistantships with partial tuition reimbursements available (averaging $10,567 per year), 47 teaching assistantships with partial tuition reimbursements available (averaging $8,608 per year); career-related internships or fieldwork, Federal Work-Study, institutionally sponsored loans, scholarships/grants, traineeships, health care benefits, tuition waivers (partial), and unspecified assistantships also available. Support available to part-time students. Financial award application deadline: 3/1; financial award applicants required to submit FAFSA. *Faculty research:* Ethnology, archaeology, evolutionary anthropology, environment, water and land use, gender and social frameworks, Greater Southwest, Latin America, political economy, public anthropology. *Total annual research expenditures:* $1.2 million. *Unit head:* Michael W. Graves, Chair, 505-277-4524, Fax: 505-277-0874, E-mail: mwgraves@unm.edu. *Application contact:* Erika E. Gerety, Program Advisement Coordinator, 505-277-2732, Fax: 505-277-0874, E-mail: erika@unm.edu. Website: http://www.unm.edu/~anthro/

The University of North Carolina at Charlotte, College of Liberal Arts and Sciences, Department of Sociology, Charlotte, NC 28223-0001. Offers health research (MA); mathematical sociology and quantitative methods (MA); organizations, occupations, and work (MA); political sociology (MA); race and gender (MA); social psychology (MA); social theory (MA); sociology of education (MA); stratification (MA). Part-time and evening/weekend programs available. *Faculty:* 16 full-time (10 women). *Students:* 11 full-time (5 women), 2 part-time (0 women); includes 5 minority (4 Black or African American, non-Hispanic/Latino; 1 Hispanic/Latino), 1 international. Average age 29. 14 applicants, 71% accepted, 5 enrolled. In 2014, 6 master's awarded. *Degree requirements:* For master's, thesis or comprehensive exam. *Entrance requirements:* For master's, GRE or MAT, minimum GPA of 3.0 in last 2 years, 2.75 overall. Additional exam requirements/recommendations for international students: Required—TOEFL (minimum score 557 paper-based; 83 iBT). *Application deadline:* For fall admission, 4/15 for domestic and international students; for spring admission, 10/1 for domestic and international students. Application fee: $75. Electronic applications accepted. *Expenses:* Tuition, state resident: full-time $4008. Tuition, nonresident: full-time $16,295. *Required fees:* $2755. Tuition and fees vary according to course load and program. *Financial support:* In 2014–15, 10 students received support, including 5 research assistantships (averaging $10,400 per year), 5 teaching assistantships (averaging $9,200 per year); career-related internships or fieldwork, institutionally sponsored loans, scholarships/grants, and unspecified assistantships also available. Support available to part-time students. Financial award application deadline: 4/1; financial award applicants required to submit FAFSA. *Faculty research:* Impact of race on high school course selection; income inequality within the United States and cross-nationally; small group interaction, nonverbal behaviors, identity, emotions, gender, and expectations; mathematical models of social processes. *Total annual research expenditures:* $413,099. *Unit head:* Dr. Lisa Walker, Chair, 704-687-7825, Fax: 704-687-3091, E-mail: lisa.walker@uncc.edu. *Application contact:* Kathy B. Giddings, Director of Graduate Admissions, 704-687-5503, Fax: 704-687-1668, E-mail: gradadm@uncc.edu.
Website: http://sociology.uncc.edu/

Folklore

George Mason University, College of Humanities and Social Sciences, Interdisciplinary Studies Program, Fairfax, VA 22030. Offers community college teaching (MAIS); computational social science (MAIS); energy and sustainability (MAIS); film and video studies (MAIS); folklore studies (MAIS); higher education administration (MAIS); neuroethics (MAIS); religion, culture and values (MAIS); social entrepreneurship (MAIS); war and military in society (MAIS); women and gender studies (MAIS). *Faculty:* 11 full-time (3 women), 4 part-time/adjunct (all women). *Students:* 22 full-time (13 women), 87 part-time (51 women); includes 31 minority (21 Black or African American, non-Hispanic/Latino; 2 Asian, non-Hispanic/Latino; 6 Hispanic/Latino; 2 Two or more races, non-Hispanic/Latino), 6 international. Average age 32. 75 applicants, 75% accepted, 28 enrolled. In 2014, 31 master's awarded. *Degree requirements:* For master's, project or thesis. *Entrance requirements:* For master's, 3 letters of recommendation; writing sample; official transcript; resume. Additional exam requirements/recommendations for international students: Required—TOEFL (minimum score 570 paper-based; 80 iBT), IELTS (minimum score 6.5), PTE. *Application deadline:* For fall admission, 3/1 priority date for domestic students; for spring admission, 10/15 for domestic students. Application fee: $65 ($80 for international students). Electronic applications accepted. *Expenses:* Tuition, state resident: full-time $9794; part-time $408 per credit hour. Tuition, nonresident: full-time $26,978; part-time $1124 per credit hour. *Required fees:* $2820; $118 per credit hour. Tuition and fees vary according to course load and program. *Financial support:* In 2014–15, 10 students received support, including 1 fellowship (averaging $6,935 per year), 2 research assistantships with full and partial tuition reimbursements available (averaging $6,499 per year), 8 teaching assistantships with full and partial tuition reimbursements available (averaging $8,271 per year); career-related internships or fieldwork, Federal Work-Study, scholarships/grants, unspecified assistantships, and health care benefits (for full-time research or teaching assistantship recipients) also available. Support available to part-time students. Financial award application deadline: 3/1; financial award applicants required to submit FAFSA. *Faculty research:* Combined English and folklore, religious and cultural studies (Christianity and Muslim society). *Unit head:* Meredith H. Lair, Director, 703-993-2159, Fax: 703-993-1251, E-mail: mlair@gmu.edu. *Application contact:* Lisa Struckmeyer, Administrative Coordinator, 703-993-8762, Fax: 703-993-5585, E-mail: lstruckm@gmu.edu.
Website: http://mais.gmu.edu

The George Washington University, Columbian College of Arts and Sciences, Department of American Studies, Washington, DC 20052. Offers American studies (PhD); folklife (MA); historic preservation (MA); material culture (MA). Part-time and evening/weekend programs available. *Faculty:* 14 full-time (7 women). *Students:* 18 full-time (12 women), 28 part-time (22 women); includes 7 minority (5 Black or African American, non-Hispanic/Latino; 1 Asian, non-Hispanic/Latino; 1 Two or more races, non-Hispanic/Latino), 3 international. Average age 30. 97 applicants, 30% accepted, 12 enrolled. In 2014, 13 master's, 4 doctorates awarded. Terminal master's awarded for partial completion of doctoral program. *Degree requirements:* For master's, comprehensive exam; for doctorate, one foreign language, thesis/dissertation, general exam. *Entrance requirements:* For master's and doctorate, GRE General Test, minimum GPA of 3.0. Additional exam requirements/recommendations for international students: Required—TOEFL (minimum score 550 paper-based; 80 iBT). *Application deadline:* For fall admission, 1/15 priority date for domestic and international students; for spring admission, 10/1 for domestic students. Application fee: $75. *Financial support:* In 2014–15, 22 students received support. Fellowships, research assistantships, teaching assistantships, career-related internships or fieldwork, Federal Work-Study, institutionally sponsored loans, and tuition waivers available. Financial award application deadline: 1/15. *Unit head:* Melanie McAlister, Chair, 202-994-7244, E-mail: jam@gwu.edu. *Application contact:* Information Contact, 202-994-6070, Fax: 202-994-8651, E-mail: amst@gwu.edu.
Website: http://departments.columbian.gwu.edu/americanstudies/

Indiana University Bloomington, University Graduate School, College of Arts and Sciences, Department of Folklore and Ethnomusicology, Bloomington, IN 47408-3890. Offers folklore (MA, PhD), including ethnomusicology. Part-time programs available. *Faculty:* 15 full-time (6 women), 4 part-time/adjunct (0 women). *Students:* 81 full-time (48 women), 2 part-time (1 woman); includes 20 minority (9 Black or African American, non-Hispanic/Latino; 4 Asian, non-Hispanic/Latino; 5 Hispanic/Latino; 2 Two or more races, non-Hispanic/Latino), 19 international. Average age 33. 73 applicants, 16% accepted, 10 enrolled. In 2014, 12 master's, 13 doctorates awarded. *Degree requirements:* For master's, one foreign language, comprehensive exam, project, thesis, or exam; for doctorate, 2 foreign languages, comprehensive exam, thesis/dissertation. *Entrance requirements:* For master's, GRE General Test (minimum scores: 151 for Verbal, 150 for Quantitative, 4.5 for Analytical), minimum GPA of 3.0, writing sample; for doctorate, GRE General Test (minimum scores: 151 for Verbal, 150 for Quantitative, 4.5 for Analytical), minimum GPA of 3.0, writing sample. Additional exam requirements/recommendations for international students: Required—TOEFL (minimum score 550 paper-based; 79 iBT). *Application deadline:* For fall admission, 1/2 for domestic students, 12/1 for international students. Application fee: $55 ($65 for international students). Electronic applications accepted. *Financial support:* In 2014–15, 40 students received support, including 4 fellowships with full tuition reimbursements available (averaging $18,000 per year), 15 research assistantships with full tuition reimbursements available (averaging $15,750 per year), 21 teaching assistantships with full tuition reimbursements available (averaging $15,750 per year); Federal Work-Study, scholarships/grants, health care benefits, and unspecified assistantships also available. Financial award application deadline: 3/1; financial award applicants required to submit FAFSA. *Faculty research:* Narrative, performance studies, material culture, popular culture, music. *Unit head:* Dr. John McDowell, Chair, 812-855-0390, Fax: 812-855-4008, E-mail: mcdowell@indiana.edu. *Application contact:* Michelle Melhouse, Graduate Recorder, 812-855-0389, Fax: 812-855-4008, E-mail: mmelhous@indiana.edu.
Website: http://www.indiana.edu/~folklore/

Memorial University of Newfoundland, School of Graduate Studies, Department of Folklore, St. John's, NL A1C 5S7, Canada. Offers MA, PhD. Part-time programs available. *Degree requirements:* For master's, thesis optional; for doctorate, one foreign language, comprehensive exam, thesis/dissertation, oral thesis defense. *Entrance requirements:* For master's, 36 credit hours of course work in folklore, humanities, or social studies; honors degree; for doctorate, MA in folklore or related field. Electronic applications accepted. *Faculty research:* Narrative, folklife, belief theory, methodology, popular culture.

Penn State Harrisburg, Graduate School, School of Humanities, Middletown, PA 17057-4898. Offers American studies (MA, PhD); communications (MA); folklore and ethnography (Certificate); heritage and museum practice (Certificate); humanities (MA); writing instruction specialist (Certificate). Evening/weekend programs available. *Unit head:* Dr. Mukund S. Kulkarni, Chancellor, 717-948-6105, Fax: 717-948-6452, E-mail: msk5@psu.edu. *Application contact:* Robert W. Coffman, Jr., Director of Enrollment Management, Admissions, 717-948-6250, Fax: 717-948-6325, E-mail: ric1@psu.edu.
Website: http://harrisburg.psu.edu/humanities

University of Alberta, Faculty of Graduate Studies and Research, Department of Modern Languages and Cultural Studies, Edmonton, AB T6G 2E1, Canada. Offers applied linguistics (Germanic, Romance, Slavic) (MA); French language, literatures and linguistics (PhD); French language, literatures, and linguistics (MA); Germanic languages, literatures and linguistics (PhD); Germanic languages, literatures, and linguistics (MA); Italian studies (MA); Slavic languages and literatures (Russian, Ukrainian) (MA, PhD); Slavic linguistics (Russian, Ukrainian) (MA, PhD); Spanish and Latin American studies (MA, PhD); Ukrainian folklore (MA, PhD). Part-time programs available. *Degree requirements:* For master's, one foreign language, thesis; for doctorate, 2 foreign languages, comprehensive exam, thesis/dissertation. *Entrance requirements:* For master's and doctorate, 1 language other than English. Additional exam requirements/recommendations for international students: Required—Michigan English Language Assessment Battery or TOEFL (minimum score 550 paper-based). Electronic applications accepted. *Faculty research:* Russian/Ukrainian studies; German studies; contemporary Latin American, French and Francophone studies; Italian studies.

University of California, Berkeley, Graduate Division, College of Letters and Science, Department of Anthropology, Group in Folklore, Berkeley, CA 94720-1500. Offers MA. *Entrance requirements:* For master's, GRE General Test, minimum GPA of 3.0, 3 letters of recommendation.

University of Louisiana at Lafayette, College of Liberal Arts, Department of English, Lafayette, LA 70504. Offers British and American literature (MA), including creative writing, folklore, rhetoric; creative writing (PhD); literature (PhD); rhetoric (PhD). Part-time programs available. Terminal master's awarded for partial completion of doctoral program. *Degree requirements:* For master's, one foreign language, thesis or alternative; for doctorate, 2 foreign languages, comprehensive exam, thesis/dissertation. *Entrance requirements:* For master's, GRE General Test, minimum GPA of 2.75; for doctorate, GRE General Test, minimum GPA of 3.0. Additional exam requirements/recommendations for international students: Required—TOEFL (minimum score 550 paper-based). Electronic applications accepted. *Faculty research:* Composition theory, Southern literature, medieval literature.

The University of North Carolina at Chapel Hill, Graduate School, College of Arts and Sciences, Curriculum in Folklore, Chapel Hill, NC 27599. Offers MA. *Degree requirements:* For master's, one foreign language, comprehensive exam, thesis. *Entrance requirements:* For master's, GRE General Test, minimum GPA of 3.0, writing sample. Electronic applications accepted. *Faculty research:* Public folklore, politics of culture, folklore and feminist theory, belief and health systems, Southern culture.

University of Oregon, Graduate School, College of Arts and Sciences, Folklore Program, Eugene, OR 97403. Offers independent study: folklore (MA, MS). Part-time programs available. *Degree requirements:* For master's, one foreign language, project or thesis. *Entrance requirements:* For master's, GRE General Test, minimum GPA of 3.0. Additional exam requirements/recommendations for international students: Required—TOEFL. *Faculty research:* American folklore, East European folklore, film and folklore, folk religion and belief, ballad.

The University of Texas at Austin, Graduate School, College of Liberal Arts, Department of Anthropology, Program in Cultural Forms, Austin, TX 78712-1111. Offers MA, PhD. Part-time programs available. Terminal master's awarded for partial completion of doctoral program. *Degree requirements:* For master's, one foreign language, thesis, report; for doctorate, one foreign language, thesis/dissertation. *Entrance requirements:* For master's and doctorate, GRE General Test. Electronic applications accepted. *Faculty research:* Expressive culture, gender, genre, folklore and culture of British Isles, ethnography of speaking.

University of Wisconsin–Madison, Graduate School, College of Letters and Science, Department of Scandinavian Studies, Madison, WI 53706-1380. Offers area studies (MA); folklore (PhD); literature (MA, PhD); philology (PhD). Part-time programs available. *Degree requirements:* For master's, 2 foreign languages, exam; for doctorate, thesis/dissertation, exam. *Entrance requirements:* For master's, minimum GPA of 3.25; for doctorate, minimum GPA of 3.5. Electronic applications accepted. *Expenses:* Tuition, state resident: full-time $10,723; part-time $745 per credit. Tuition, nonresident: full-time $24,054; part-time $1578 per credit. *Required fees:* $374 per semester. Tuition and fees vary according to course load, program and reciprocity agreements. *Faculty research:* Historical fiction, Icelandic poetry, nineteenth-century literature, theater, gender studies, folklore.

Utah State University, School of Graduate Studies, College of Humanities, Arts and Social Sciences, Department of English and Department of History, Program in American Studies, Logan, UT 84322. Offers folklore (MA, MS); western American literature and culture (MA, MS). Part-time and evening/weekend programs available. *Degree requirements:* For master's, thesis or alternative. *Entrance requirements:* For master's, GRE General Test or MAT, minimum GPA of 3.0, 3 letters of recommendation, writing sample. Additional exam requirements/recommendations for international students: Required—TOEFL. *Faculty research:* Folklore and folklife, American culture, regional studies, material culture, Jewish folklore, Native American folklore.

Gender Studies

American University, College of Arts and Sciences, Department of Women's, Gender, and Sexuality Studies, Washington, DC 20016. Offers Graduate Certificate. *Faculty:* 2 part-time/adjunct (both women). *Students:* 1 part-time (0 women). Average age 24. In 2014, 1 Graduate Certificate awarded. *Entrance requirements:* For degree, statement of purpose, transcripts, resume. *Unit head:* Dr. Lauren Weis, Director, 202-885-2926, Fax: 202-885-1094, E-mail: weis@american.edu. *Application contact:* Kathleen Clowery, Associate Director, Graduate Enrollment Management, 202-885-3621, Fax: 202-885-2429, E-mail: clowery@american.edu.
Website: http://www.american.edu/cas/wgs/

The American University in Cairo, School of Global Affairs and Public Policy, Cynthia Nelson Institute for Gender and Women's Studies, Cairo, Egypt. Offers gender and justice (MA); gender and women's studies in the Middle East and North Africa (MA); gendered political economies (MA). Tuition and fees vary according to course load and program.

Arizona State University at the Tempe campus, College of Liberal Arts and Sciences, School of Social Transformation, Tempe, AZ 85287-4902. Offers African studies (Graduate Certificate); gender studies (PhD, Graduate Certificate); justice studies (MS, PhD); social and cultural pedagogy (MA); socio-economic justice (Graduate Certificate); PhD/JD. Part-time programs available. Terminal master's awarded for partial completion of doctoral program. *Degree requirements:* For master's, thesis or alternative, interactive Program of Study (iPOS) submitted before completing 50 percent of required credit hours; for doctorate, comprehensive exam, thesis/dissertation, interactive Program of Study (iPOS) submitted before completing 50 percent of required credit hours. *Entrance requirements:* For master's, GRE or LSAT, minimum GPA of 3.0 or equivalent in last 2 years of work leading to bachelor's degree; for doctorate, GRE or LSAT (for justice studies program), minimum GPA of 3.0 or equivalent in last 2 years of work leading to bachelor's degree. Additional exam requirements/recommendations for international students: Required—TOEFL, IELTS, or PTE. Electronic applications accepted.

Brandeis University, Graduate School of Arts and Sciences, Department of Anthropology, Waltham, MA 02454. Offers anthropology (MA, PhD); anthropology and women's and gender studies (MA). Part-time programs available. *Faculty:* 9 full-time (5 women), 1 part-time/adjunct (0 women). *Students:* 32 full-time (20 women), 2 part-time (1 woman); includes 6 minority (2 Black or African American, non-Hispanic/Latino; 2 Asian, non-Hispanic/Latino; 1 Hispanic/Latino; 1 Two or more races, non-Hispanic/Latino), 4 international. 38 applicants, 61% accepted, 14 enrolled. In 2014, 6 master's, 8 doctorates awarded. *Degree requirements:* For master's, thesis or alternative; for doctorate, one foreign language, comprehensive exam, thesis/dissertation. *Entrance requirements:* For master's and doctorate, GRE General Test, sample of written work, resume, letters of recommendation. Additional exam requirements/recommendations for international students: Required—TOEFL (minimum score 600 paper-based; 100 iBT), PTE (minimum score 68); Recommended—IELTS (minimum score 7). *Application deadline:* For fall admission, 1/15 for domestic students. Application fee: $75. Electronic applications accepted. *Financial support:* In 2014–15, 32 students received support, including 8 fellowships with full tuition reimbursements available (averaging $20,800 per year), 24 teaching assistantships with partial tuition reimbursements available (averaging $3,200 per year); Federal Work-Study, scholarships/grants, health care benefits, and tuition waivers (partial) also available. Financial award application deadline: 4/15; financial award applicants required to submit FAFSA. *Faculty research:* Sociocultural anthropology, linguistic anthropology, archaeology, physical anthropology. *Unit head:* Dr. Sarah Lamb, Director of Graduate Studies, 781-736-2210, Fax: 781-736-2232, E-mail: lamb@brandeis.edu. *Application contact:* Laurel Carpenter, Academic Administrator, 781-736-2210, Fax: 781-736-2232, E-mail: lcarpenter@brandeis.edu.
Website: http://www.brandeis.edu/gsas

Brandeis University, Graduate School of Arts and Sciences, Department of English, Waltham, MA 02454-9110. Offers English (MA, PhD); English and women's and gender studies (MA). Part-time programs available. *Degree requirements:* For master's, one foreign language, thesis or alternative; for doctorate, 2 foreign languages, thesis/dissertation, field exam, symposium presentation, prospectus defense. *Entrance requirements:* For master's and doctorate, resume, sample of work, 2 letters of recommendation, statement of purpose, transcript(s). Additional exam requirements/recommendations for international students: Required—TOEFL (minimum score 600 paper-based; 100 iBT); Recommended—IELTS (minimum score 7). Electronic applications accepted. *Faculty research:* Feminist and gender theory, American literature and post-Colonial theory, early modern (Renaissance) English literature, modernism, literature and science, literary theory and philosophy, contemporary poetry.

Brandeis University, Graduate School of Arts and Sciences, Department of Near Eastern and Judaic Studies, Waltham, MA 02454-9110. Offers Near Eastern and Judaic studies (MA, PhD); Near Eastern and Judaic studies and sociology (PhD); Near Eastern and Judaic studies and women's and gender studies (MA); teaching of Hebrew (MAT). Part-time programs available. Terminal master's awarded for partial completion of doctoral program. *Degree requirements:* For master's, one foreign language, thesis or alternative, proseminar, capstone; for doctorate, variable foreign language requirement, comprehensive exam, thesis/dissertation. *Entrance requirements:* For master's and doctorate, 3 letters of recommendation, transcript(s), statement of purpose, writing sample, resume. Additional exam requirements/recommendations for international students: Required—TOEFL (minimum score 600 paper-based; 100 iBT), PTE (minimum score 68); Recommended—IELTS (minimum score 7). Electronic applications accepted. *Faculty research:* Ancient Near East and Bible, Judaic studies, Israel Studies, modern Middle East, Arabic and Islamic civilizations.

Brandeis University, Graduate School of Arts and Sciences, Joint Master's Programs in Women's and Gender Studies, Waltham, MA 02454-9110. Offers anthropology and women's and gender studies (MA); English and women's and gender studies (MA); history and women's and gender studies (MA); Near Eastern and Judaic studies and women's and gender studies (MA); psychology and women's and gender studies (MA); public policy and women's and gender studies (MA); social policy and women's and gender studies (MA); sociology and women's and gender studies (MA); sustainable international development and women's/gender studies (MA). *Degree requirements:* For master's, thesis. *Entrance requirements:* For master's, GRE, sample of written work, resume, statement of purpose, transcript(s), letters of recommendation. Additional exam requirements/recommendations for international students: Required—TOEFL (minimum score 600 paper-based; 100 iBT), PTE (minimum score 68); Recommended—IELTS (minimum score 7). Electronic applications accepted. *Faculty research:* Anthropology, English, history, music, Near Eastern and Judaic studies, public policy, psychology, sociology, and sustainable international development.

Brandeis University, Graduate School of Arts and Sciences, MA Program in Women's and Gender Studies, Waltham, MA 02454-9110. Offers MA. *Degree requirements:* For master's, thesis, proseminar. *Entrance requirements:* For master's, GRE, three letters of recommendation, curriculum vitae or resume, statement of purpose, critical writing sample, transcript(s). Additional exam requirements/recommendations for international students: Required—TOEFL (minimum score 600 paper-based; 100 iBT), PTE (minimum score 68); Recommended—IELTS (minimum score 7). Electronic applications accepted. *Faculty research:* Gender and legal studies, sexuality studies, social and public policy, comparative literature and culture, anthropology, English, music, Near Eastern and Judaic Studies, public policy, sociology, sustainable international development, history, psychology.

California State University, Sacramento, Office of Graduate Studies, College of Education, Department of Teacher Education, Sacramento, CA 95819. Offers behavioral sciences (MA), including gender equity studies; curriculum and instruction (MA); educational technology (MA); language and literacy (MA). Part-time programs available. *Entrance requirements:* Additional exam requirements/recommendations for international students: Required—TOEFL. Electronic applications accepted. *Faculty research:* Technology integration and psychological implications for teaching and learning; inquiry-based research and learning in science and technology; uncovering the process of everyday creativity in teachers and other leaders; universal design as a foundation for inclusion; bullying, cyber-bullying and impact on school success; diversity, social justice in adult/vocational education.

Carnegie Mellon University, Dietrich College of Humanities and Social Sciences, Department of History, Pittsburgh, PA 15213-3891. Offers African and African-American diaspora (PhD); culture and power (PhD); labor, politics and social movements (PhD); technology, environment, science and health (PhD); women, gender and the family (PhD). Part-time programs available. *Degree requirements:* For doctorate, oral and written comprehensive exams, dissertation defense. *Entrance requirements:* For doctorate, GRE General Test. Additional exam requirements/recommendations for international students: Required—TOEFL. Electronic applications accepted. *Faculty research:* Anthropology and history, African-American history, technology/environment, cultural history analysis.

Central European University, Graduate Studies, Department of Gender Studies, Budapest, Hungary. Offers MA, PhD. *Faculty:* 10 full-time (9 women), 6 part-time/adjunct (3 women). *Students:* 95 full-time (77 women). Average age 29. 227 applicants, 23% accepted, 39 enrolled. In 2014, 39 master's, 4 doctorates awarded. *Degree requirements:* For master's, one foreign language, thesis; for doctorate, one foreign

language, comprehensive exam, thesis/dissertation. *Entrance requirements:* For master's and doctorate, interview. Additional exam requirements/recommendations for international students: Required—TOEFL (minimum score 570 paper-based); Recommended—IELTS (minimum score 6.5). *Application deadline:* For fall admission, 1/24 for domestic and international students. Application fee: $40. Electronic applications accepted. *Expenses: Tuition:* Full-time 12,000 euros. *Required fees:* 200 euros. One-time fee: 500 euros full-time. *Financial support:* In 2014–15, 72 students received support, including 72 fellowships (averaging $6,100 per year); career-related internships or fieldwork, scholarships/grants, health care benefits, and tuition waivers (full and partial) also available. *Faculty research:* Theories of gender, gendering theory; science and gender; activism, social movements and policy; gender dimensions of post-state socialism; gendered borders, nationalism, and transnational flows; political violence, war and gender; raced and sexed identities; cultural studies; feminist knowledge production. *Unit head:* Elissa Helms, Head of Department, 36 1 327-3034, Fax: 36-1-327-3296, E-mail: gender@ceu.hu. *Application contact:* Zsuzsanna Jaszberenyi, Admissions Officer, 361-324-3009, Fax: 367-327-3211, E-mail: admissions@ceu.hu.
Website: http://gender.ceu.hu/

Central Michigan University, College of Graduate Studies, College of Humanities and Social and Behavioral Sciences, Program in Humanities, Mount Pleasant, MI 48859. Offers humanities (MA), including contemporary issues in the humanities: race, class, and gender, images and ideas of self, Native American issues in modern culture, popular culture studies, the rise of industrial society. Part-time and evening/weekend programs available. *Degree requirements:* For master's, thesis or alternative. Electronic applications accepted. *Faculty research:* Rise of industrial society; images and ideas of self; contemporary issues of race, class, and gender; popular culture; Native American issues in modern culture.

The College of New Jersey, Graduate Studies, School of Humanities and Social Sciences, Department of Women's and Gender Studies, Ewing, NJ 08628. Offers gender studies (Certificate). Part-time programs available. *Students:* 1 (woman) part-time. In 2014, 1 Certificate awarded. *Entrance requirements:* For degree, two letters of recommendation, official transcripts, essay. Additional exam requirements/recommendations for international students: Required—TOEFL. *Application deadline:* For fall admission, 2/1 priority date for domestic students; for spring admission, 10/1 priority date for domestic students. Application fee: $75. Electronic applications accepted. *Financial support:* Tuition waivers (partial) and unspecified assistantships available. Financial award application deadline: 5/1; financial award applicants required to submit FAFSA. *Unit head:* Anne Marie Nicolosi, Coordinator, 609-771-2276, Fax: 609-637-5164, E-mail: nicolosi@tcnj.edu. *Application contact:* Susan L. Hydro, Director of Graduate and Intersession Programs, 609-771-2300, Fax: 609-637-5105, E-mail: graduate@tcnj.edu.

Cornell University, Graduate School, Graduate Fields of Arts and Sciences, Field of Sociology, Ithaca, NY 14853-0001. Offers economy and society (MA, PhD); gender and life course (MA, PhD); methodology (MA, PhD); organizations (MA, PhD); policy analysis (MA, PhD); political sociology/social movements (MA, PhD); racial and ethnic relations (MA, PhD); social networks (MA, PhD); social psychology (MA, PhD); social stratification (MA, PhD). Terminal master's awarded for partial completion of doctoral program. *Degree requirements:* For master's, thesis; for doctorate, thesis/dissertation, 1 year of teaching experience. *Entrance requirements:* For master's and doctorate, GRE General Test, 2 letters of recommendation, writing sample. Additional exam requirements/recommendations for international students: Required—TOEFL (minimum score 550 paper-based; 77 iBT). Electronic applications accepted. *Faculty research:* Comparative societal analysis, work and family, simulations, social class and mobility, racial segregation and inequality.

Delta State University, Graduate Programs, College of Arts and Sciences, Program in Liberal Studies, Cleveland, MS 38733-0001. Offers evolving human voices (MALS); gender and diversity studies (MALS); globalization studies (MALS); Mississippi Delta studies (MALS); philosophy (MALS); religious studies (MALS). *Students:* 12 full-time (9 women), 7 part-time (5 women); includes 4 minority (all Black or African American, non-Hispanic/Latino). Average age 29. 6 applicants, 83% accepted, 4 enrolled. In 2014, 4 master's awarded. *Degree requirements:* For master's, oral and/or written comprehensive exam. *Application deadline:* For fall admission, 8/1 priority date for domestic students; for spring admission, 12/1 priority date for domestic students. Application fee: $30. *Expenses:* Tuition, state resident: full-time $6012; part-time $334 per credit hour. Tuition, nonresident: full-time $6012; part-time $334 per credit hour. Part-time tuition and fees vary according to course load. *Unit head:* Dr. Paul Hankins, Dean, 662-846-4100, Fax: 662-846-4016, E-mail: phankins@deltastate.edu. *Application contact:* Dr. Beverly Moon, Dean of Graduate Studies, 662-846-4875, Fax: 662-846-4313, E-mail: grad-info@deltastate.edu.
Website: http://www.deltastate.edu/pages/4994.asp

Dominican University of California, School of Arts, Humanities and Social Sciences, Humanities Program, San Rafael, CA 94901-2298. Offers applied music (MA); art history (MA); creative writing (MA); history (MA); literature (MA); philosophy (MA); political theory (MA); religion (MA); women and gender studies (MA). Part-time programs available. *Faculty:* 11 full-time (5 women), 5 part-time/adjunct (2 women). *Students:* 2 full-time (1 woman), 25 part-time (16 women); includes 7 minority (1 Black or African American, non-Hispanic/Latino; 1 American Indian or Alaska Native, non-Hispanic/Latino; 3 Hispanic/Latino; 2 Two or more races, non-Hispanic/Latino). Average age 46. 12 applicants, 83% accepted, 7 enrolled. *Degree requirements:* For master's, thesis or alternative. *Entrance requirements:* For master's, minimum GPA of 3.0, interview. Additional exam requirements/recommendations for international students: Required—TOEFL (minimum score 550 paper-based; 80 iBT), IELTS (minimum score 6.5). *Application deadline:* For fall admission, 5/15 priority date for domestic and international students; for spring admission, 11/15 priority date for domestic and international students. Applications are processed on a rolling basis. Electronic applications accepted. Application fee is waived when completed online. *Expenses:* Expenses: $935 per unit. *Financial support:* Scholarships/grants available. Support available to part-time students. Financial award application deadline: 3/2; financial award applicants required to submit FAFSA. *Unit head:* Dr. Laura Stivers, Acting Dean, 415-458-3734, E-mail: laura.stivers@dominican.edu. *Application contact:* Ryan Purtill, Director, 415-458-3748, Fax: 415-485-3214, E-mail: ryan.purtill@dominican.edu.
Website: http://www.dominican.edu/academics/ahss/graduate-program/index_html

Eastern Michigan University, Graduate School, College of Arts and Sciences, Department of Women's and Gender Studies, Ypsilanti, MI 48197. Offers MA, Graduate Certificate. Part-time and evening/weekend programs available. *Faculty:* 2 full-time (both women). *Students:* 5 full-time (all women), 16 part-time (14 women); includes 4 minority (2 Black or African American, non-Hispanic/Latino; 2 Hispanic/Latino), 2 international. Average age 34. 19 applicants, 63% accepted, 7 enrolled. In 2014, 4 master's, 1 other advanced degree awarded. *Degree requirements:* For master's, thesis, research project, or practicum. *Entrance requirements:* Additional exam requirements/recommendations for international students: Required—TOEFL. *Application deadline:* For fall admission, 6/15 for domestic and international students; for winter admission, 9/15 for domestic and international students; for spring admission, 3/1 for domestic and international students. Applications are processed on a rolling basis. Application fee: $45. *Financial support:* Fellowships, research assistantships with full tuition reimbursements, teaching assistantships with full tuition reimbursements, career-related internships or fieldwork, Federal Work-Study, institutionally sponsored loans, scholarships/grants, tuition waivers (partial), and unspecified assistantships available. Support available to part-time students. Financial award applicants required to submit FAFSA. *Unit head:* Dr. Jacqueline Goodman, Department Head, 734-487-1177, Fax: 734-487-5029, E-mail: jgoodma9@emich.edu. *Application contact:* Dr. Suzanne Gray, Program Advisor, 734-487-1177, Fax: 734-487-5029, E-mail: sgray17@emich.edu.
Website: http://www.emich.edu/wgstudies/

George Mason University, College of Humanities and Social Sciences, Interdisciplinary Studies Program, Fairfax, VA 22030. Offers community college teaching (MAIS); computational social science (MAIS); energy and sustainability (MAIS); film and video studies (MAIS); folklore studies (MAIS); higher education administration (MAIS); neuroethics (MAIS); religion, culture and values (MAIS); social entrepreneurship (MAIS); war and military in society (MAIS); women and gender studies (MAIS). *Faculty:* 11 full-time (3 women), 4 part-time/adjunct (all women). *Students:* 22 full-time (13 women), 87 part-time (51 women); includes 31 minority (21 Black or African American, non-Hispanic/Latino; 2 Asian, non-Hispanic/Latino; 6 Hispanic/Latino; 2 Two or more races, non-Hispanic/Latino), 6 international. Average age 32. 75 applicants, 75% accepted, 28 enrolled. In 2014, 31 master's awarded. *Degree requirements:* For master's, project or thesis. *Entrance requirements:* For master's, 3 letters of recommendation; writing sample; official transcript; resume. Additional exam requirements/recommendations for international students: Required—TOEFL (minimum score 570 paper-based; 80 iBT), IELTS (minimum score 6.5), PTE. *Application deadline:* For fall admission, 3/1 priority date for domestic students; for spring admission, 10/15 for domestic students. Application fee: $65 ($80 for international students). Electronic applications accepted. *Expenses:* Tuition, state resident: full-time $9794; part-time $408 per credit hour. Tuition, nonresident: full-time $26,978; part-time $1124 per credit hour. *Required fees:* $2820; $118 per credit hour. Tuition and fees vary according to course load and program. *Financial support:* In 2014–15, 10 students received support, including 1 fellowship (averaging $6,935 per year), 2 research assistantships with full and partial tuition reimbursements available (averaging $6,499 per year), 8 teaching assistantships with full and partial tuition reimbursements available (averaging $8,271 per year); career-related internships or fieldwork, Federal Work-Study, scholarships/grants, unspecified assistantships, and health care benefits (for full-time research or teaching assistantship recipients) also available. Support available to part-time students. Financial award application deadline: 3/1; financial award applicants required to submit FAFSA. *Faculty research:* Combined English and folklore, religious and cultural studies (Christianity and Muslim society). *Unit head:* Meredith H. Lair, Director, 703-993-2159, Fax: 703-993-1251, E-mail: mlair@gmu.edu. *Application contact:* Lisa Struckmeyer, Administrative Coordinator, 703-993-8762, Fax: 703-993-5585, E-mail: lstruckm@gmu.edu.
Website: http://mais.gmu.edu

The George Washington University, Elliott School of International Affairs, Program in Global Gender Policy, Washington, DC 20052. Offers Graduate Certificate. *Unit head:* Michael Brown, Dean, 202-994-6240, Fax: 202-994-0335, E-mail: elliott@gwu.edu. *Application contact:* Nicole A. Campbell, Director of Graduate Admissions, 202-994-7050, Fax: 202-994-9537, E-mail: esiagrad@gwu.edu.

Indiana University Bloomington, University Graduate School, College of Arts and Sciences, Department of Gender Studies, Bloomington, IN 47405-7000. Offers PhD. *Faculty:* 12 full-time (9 women). *Students:* 27 full-time (23 women); includes 9 minority (4 Black or African American, non-Hispanic/Latino; 1 Asian, non-Hispanic/Latino; 2 Hispanic/Latino; 2 Two or more races, non-Hispanic/Latino), 2 international. Average age 26. 60 applicants, 20% accepted, 5 enrolled. In 2014, 2 doctorates awarded. *Entrance requirements:* Additional exam requirements/recommendations for international students: Required—TOEFL. *Application deadline:* For fall admission, 1/5 priority date for domestic students, 12/1 priority date for international students. Application fee: $55 ($65 for international students). Electronic applications accepted. *Financial support:* In 2014–15, 4 fellowships with tuition reimbursements (averaging $18,000 per year), 2 research assistantships with tuition reimbursements (averaging $15,900 per year), 15 teaching assistantships with tuition reimbursements (averaging $15,750 per year) were awarded. *Unit head:* Brenda R. Weber, Director of Graduate Studies, 812-856-6033, E-mail: brweber@indiana.edu. *Application contact:* Nina Taylor, Graduate Secretary, 812-855-0101, E-mail: nitaylor@indiana.edu.
Website: http://www.indiana.edu/~gender/

Indiana University–Purdue University Indianapolis, School of Liberal Arts, Department of Sociology, Indianapolis, IN 46202. Offers family/gender studies (MA); medical sociology (MA); work/occupations (MA). *Faculty:* 17 full-time (8 women). *Students:* 9 full-time (7 women), 15 part-time (13 women); includes 3 minority (all Black or African American, non-Hispanic/Latino), 2 international. Average age 30. 16 applicants, 69% accepted, 6 enrolled. In 2014, 10 master's awarded. Application fee: $55 ($65 for international students). *Financial support:* Fellowships and teaching assistantships available. *Unit head:* Dr. Robert W. White, Chair, 317-278-5226, E-mail: rwwhite@iupui.edu. *Application contact:* Dr. Carrie E. Foote, Director of Graduate Studies, 317-274-8454, E-mail: foote@iupui.edu.
Website: http://liberalarts.iupui.edu/sociology/

Instituto Tecnologico de Santo Domingo, Graduate School, Area of Humanities and Social Sciences, Santo Domingo, Dominican Republic. Offers accounting (Certificate); adult education (Certificate); applied linguistics (MA); economics (MA); education (M Ed); educational psychology (MA, Certificate); gender and development (MA, Certificate); humanistic studies (MA); international marketing management (Certificate); international relations in the Caribbean basin (Certificate); intervention systems in family therapy (MA); linguistic and literary communication (Certificate); pedagogical support (MA); social science education (M Ed); sustainable human development (MA); terminal illness and death psychology (Certificate); youth and adult education (M Ed).

Memorial University of Newfoundland, School of Graduate Studies, Department of Sociology, St. John's, NL A1C 5S7, Canada. Offers gender (PhD); maritime sociology (PhD); sociology (M Phil, MA); work and development (PhD). Part-time programs available. *Degree requirements:* For master's, comprehensive exam, thesis optional, program journal (M Phil); for doctorate, one foreign language, comprehensive exam, thesis/dissertation, oral defense of thesis. *Entrance requirements:* For master's, 2nd class degree from university of recognized standing in area of study; for doctorate, MA, M Phil, or equivalent. Electronic applications accepted. *Faculty research:* Work and development, gender, maritime sociology.

Middle Tennessee State University, College of Graduate Studies, College of Liberal Arts, Program in Women's and Gender Studies, Murfreesboro, TN 37132. Offers Graduate Certificate. Part-time and evening/weekend programs available. Postbaccalaureate distance learning degree programs offered. *Students:* 2 applicants, 50% accepted. In 2014, 5 Graduate Certificates awarded. *Application deadline:* For fall admission, 6/1 for domestic and international students. Applications are processed on a rolling basis. Application fee: $30. Electronic applications accepted. *Financial support:* Application deadline: 4/1; applicants required to submit FAFSA. *Unit head:* Dr. Mark E.

Byrnes, Dean, 615-898-2534, Fax: 615-904-8279, E-mail: mark.byrnes@mtsu.edu. *Application contact:* Dr. Michael D. Allen, Vice Provost for Research/Dean, 615-898-2840, Fax: 615-904-8020, E-mail: michael.allen@mtsu.edu.

Minnesota State University Mankato, College of Graduate Studies, College of Social and Behavioral Sciences, Department of Gender and Women's Studies, Mankato, MN 56001. Offers MS, Certificate. Part-time programs available. *Students:* 9 full-time (6 women), 4 part-time (3 women). *Degree requirements:* For master's, comprehensive exam, thesis or alternative. *Entrance requirements:* For master's, minimum GPA of 3.0 during previous 2 years of course work. Additional exam requirements/recommendations for international students: Required—TOEFL. *Application deadline:* For fall admission, 7/1 priority date for domestic students; for spring admission, 11/1 for domestic students. Applications are processed on a rolling basis. Application fee: $40. *Financial support:* Research assistantships, teaching assistantships with full tuition reimbursements, career-related internships or fieldwork, Federal Work-Study, institutionally sponsored loans, and unspecified assistantships available. Support available to part-time students. Financial award application deadline: 3/15; financial award applicants required to submit FAFSA. *Unit head:* Dr. Shannon Miller, Graduate Coordinator, 507-389-2077. *Application contact:* 507-389-2321, E-mail: grad@mnsu.edu.
Website: http://sbs.mnsu.edu/women/

Northern Arizona University, Graduate College, College of Social and Behavioral Sciences, Women's and Gender Studies Program, Flagstaff, AZ 86011. Offers Graduate Certificate. Part-time programs available. *Entrance requirements:* Additional exam requirements/recommendations for international students: Required—TOEFL (minimum score 550 paper-based; 80 iBT). Electronic applications accepted.

Northwestern University, The Graduate School, Program in Gender and Sexuality Studies, Evanston, IL 60208. Offers Graduate Certificate. *Faculty research:* Anthropology, gender in Victorian period, autobiography, performance ethnographies, Slavic literature, women in the law.

The Ohio State University, Graduate School, College of Arts and Sciences, Division of Arts and Humanities, Department of Women's, Gender and Sexuality Studies, Columbus, OH 43210. Offers MA, PhD. *Faculty:* 17. *Students:* 24 full-time (21 women), 1 (woman) part-time; includes 9 minority (2 Black or African American, non-Hispanic/Latino; 1 Asian, non-Hispanic/Latino; 3 Hispanic/Latino; 3 Two or more races, non-Hispanic/Latino), 4 international. Average age 28. 39 applicants, 15% accepted, 5 enrolled. In 2014, 2 master's, 3 doctorates awarded. Terminal master's awarded for partial completion of doctoral program. *Degree requirements:* For master's, thesis optional; for doctorate, thesis/dissertation. *Entrance requirements:* For master's and doctorate, GRE (if GPA is less than 3.0 for all work), scholarly writing sample. Additional exam requirements/recommendations for international students: Required—TOEFL (minimum score 550 paper-based; 79 iBT), Michigan English Language Assessment Battery (minimum score 82); Recommended—IELTS (minimum score 7). *Application deadline:* For fall admission, 12/1 priority date for domestic students, 11/15 priority date for international students; for winter admission, 12/1 for domestic students, 11/1 for international students; for spring admission, 3/1 for domestic students, 2/1 for international students. Applications are processed on a rolling basis. Application fee: $60 ($70 for international students). Electronic applications accepted. *Financial support:* Fellowships with tuition reimbursements, research assistantships with tuition reimbursements, teaching assistantships with tuition reimbursements, career-related internships or fieldwork, Federal Work-Study, institutionally sponsored loans, and unspecified assistantships available. Support available to part-time students. *Unit head:* Dr. Jill Bystydzienski, Chair and Professor, 614-292-1021, E-mail: bystydzienski.1@osu.edu. *Application contact:* Graduate and Professional Admissions, 614-292-9444, Fax: 614-292-3895, E-mail: gpadmissions@osu.edu.
Website: http://wgss.osu.edu/

Oregon State University, College of Liberal Arts, Program in Women, Gender, and Sexuality Studies, Corvallis, OR 97331. Offers MA. Part-time programs available. *Faculty:* 7 full-time (6 women), 1 (woman) part-time/adjunct. *Students:* 18 full-time (16 women), 4 part-time (all women); includes 9 minority (1 Black or African American, non-Hispanic/Latino; 1 American Indian or Alaska Native, non-Hispanic/Latino; 5 Hispanic/Latino; 2 Two or more races, non-Hispanic/Latino), 3 international. Average age 32. 26 applicants, 77% accepted, 10 enrolled. In 2014, 3 master's awarded. *Entrance requirements:* Additional exam requirements/recommendations for international students: Required—TOEFL (minimum score 80 iBT), IELTS (minimum score 6.5). *Application deadline:* For fall admission, 1/15 for domestic and international students. Application fee: $60. *Expenses:* Tuition, state resident: full-time $11,907; part-time $189 per credit hour. Tuition, nonresident: full-time $19,953; part-time $441 per credit hour. *Required fees:* $1472; $449 per term. One-time fee: $350. Tuition and fees vary according to course load and program. *Financial support:* Application deadline: 4/1. *Unit head:* Dr. Susan M. Shaw, Professor, 541-737-3082. *Application contact:* Dr. Liddy Detar, Instructor/Advisor, 541-737-4299, E-mail: liddy.detar@oregonstate.edu.
Website: http://liberalarts.oregonstate.edu/slcs/wgss/

Queen's University at Kingston, School of Graduate Studies, Faculty of Arts and Sciences, Department of Political Studies, Kingston, ON K7L 3N6, Canada. Offers Canadian politics (PhD); comparative politics (PhD); gender and politics (PhD); international relations (PhD); political theory (PhD). *Degree requirements:* For master's, thesis or alternative; for doctorate, one foreign language, thesis/dissertation, qualifying exams. *Entrance requirements:* Additional exam requirements/recommendations for international students: Required—TOEFL (minimum score 600 paper-based). *Faculty research:* Canadian politics, comparative politics, political thought, international politics, women and politics.

Roosevelt University, Graduate Division, College of Arts and Sciences, Department of Literature and Languages, Program in Women's and Gender Studies, Chicago, IL 60605. Offers MA, Certificate. Part-time and evening/weekend programs available. *Degree requirements:* For master's, thesis. *Entrance requirements:* For master's, minimum GPA of 2.7. *Faculty research:* Feminist economics; philosophy of feminism; race, class, and gender; women and art; women's history.

Rutgers, The State University of New Jersey, New Brunswick, Graduate School-New Brunswick, Program in Women's and Gender Studies, Piscataway, NJ 08854-8097. Offers MA, PhD. Part-time programs available. *Degree requirements:* For master's, thesis or alternative; for doctorate, comprehensive exam, thesis/dissertation. *Entrance requirements:* For master's and doctorate, GRE General Test, writing sample, 3 letters of recommendation. Additional exam requirements/recommendations for international students: Required—TOEFL. *Faculty research:* Feminist theory, gender and sexuality, global and cultural studies, women in history, literature, and politics, feminist politics.

Saint Mary's University, Faculty of Arts, Program in Women and Gender Studies, Halifax, NS B3H 3C3, Canada. Offers MA. Program offered jointly with Mount Saint Vincent University. Part-time programs available. *Degree requirements:* For master's, thesis. *Entrance requirements:* For master's, honors degree.

San Diego State University, Graduate and Research Affairs, College of Arts and Letters, Program in Lesbian, Gay, Bisexual and Transgender Studies, San Diego, CA 92182. Offers Graduate Certificate.

Simon Fraser University, Office of Graduate Studies, Faculty of Arts and Social Sciences, Department of Gender, Sexuality and Women's Studies, Burnaby, BC V5A 1S6, Canada. Offers MA, PhD. *Degree requirements:* For master's, thesis or alternative; for doctorate, comprehensive exam, thesis/dissertation. *Entrance requirements:* For master's, minimum GPA of 3.0 (on scale of 4.33), or 3.33 based on last 60 credits of undergraduate courses; for doctorate, minimum GPA of 3.5 (on scale of 4.33). Additional exam requirements/recommendations for international students: Recommended—TOEFL (minimum score 580 paper-based; 93 iBT), IELTS (minimum score 7), TWE (minimum score 5). Electronic applications accepted. *Faculty research:* Gender history, feminist labor studies/economics, queer theory, women and media, feminist research methods.

University at Buffalo, the State University of New York, Graduate School, College of Arts and Sciences, Department of Transnational Studies, Buffalo, NY 14260. Offers American studies (MA, PhD); Canadian studies (Advanced Certificate); Canadian-American studies (MA); Caribbean Latina/o American studies (MA); global gender studies (MA, PhD). Part-time programs available. Postbaccalaureate distance learning degree programs offered. *Faculty:* 19 full-time (10 women). *Students:* 73 full-time (43 women); includes 20 minority (3 Black or African American, non-Hispanic/Latino; 6 American Indian or Alaska Native, non-Hispanic/Latino; 9 Asian, non-Hispanic/Latino; 2 Hispanic/Latino). Average age 32. 57 applicants, 84% accepted, 16 enrolled. In 2014, 26 master's, 18 doctorates, 1 other advanced degree awarded. *Degree requirements:* For master's, one foreign language, comprehensive exam (for some programs), thesis optional; for doctorate, one foreign language, comprehensive exam, thesis/dissertation; for Advanced Certificate, one foreign language. *Entrance requirements:* For master's, N/A, minimum GPA of 3.0; for doctorate, GRE, minimum GPA of 3.0. Additional exam requirements/recommendations for international students: Required—TOEFL (minimum score 550 paper-based; 79 iBT). *Application deadline:* For fall admission, 8/15 priority date for domestic students, 6/15 priority date for international students; for winter admission, 2/1 for domestic and international students; for spring admission, 1/15 priority date for domestic students, 11/15 priority date for international students. Applications are processed on a rolling basis. Application fee: $75. Electronic applications accepted. *Financial support:* In 2014–15, 16 students received support, including fellowships with full tuition reimbursements available (averaging $6,000 per year), research assistantships (averaging $5,000 per year), teaching assistantships with full tuition reimbursements available (averaging $13,060 per year); career-related internships or fieldwork, institutionally sponsored loans, scholarships/grants, traineeships, health care benefits, and unspecified assistantships also available. Financial award application deadline: 1/4. *Faculty research:* Native American, intercultural and indigenous people's studies, border theory, cultural studies, American pop culture, feminist theory, construction of gender in society. *Unit head:* Dr. Keith Griffler, Chair, 716-645-0802, Fax: 716-645-5977, E-mail: griffler@buffalo.edu. *Application contact:* Karen M. Reinard, Graduate Secretary, 716-645-0797, Fax: 716-645-5976, E-mail: kreinard@buffalo.edu.
Website: http://www.transnationalstudies.buffalo.edu/graduate.shtml

University at Buffalo, the State University of New York, Graduate School, College of Arts and Sciences, Program in Global Gender Studies, Buffalo, NY 14260. Offers MA, PhD. *Unit head:* Dr. Keith Griffler, Interim Chair, 716-645-0802, Fax: 716-645-5976, E-mail: griffler@buffalo.edu. *Application contact:* Dr. Gwynn Thomas, Director of Graduate Studies, 716-645-2082, E-mail: gmthomas@buffalo.edu.
Website: http://globalgenderstudies.buffalo.edu/

The University of Arizona, College of Social and Behavioral Sciences, Department of Gender and Women's Studies, Tucson, AZ 85721. Offers MA, PhD, Certificate. Part-time programs available. *Degree requirements:* For master's, thesis/project. *Entrance requirements:* For master's and doctorate, GRE (minimum score: 500 verbal, 500 quantitative, 4.5 analytical), 3 letters of recommendation. Additional exam requirements/recommendations for international students: Required—TOEFL (minimum score 600 paper-based; 100 iBT). Electronic applications accepted. *Faculty research:* Gender, race and border studies; sexuality and the body; gender health and science; cultural representation and theory; public policy and social movements.

The University of British Columbia, Faculty of Arts, Institute for Gender, Race, Sexuality, and Social Justice, Vancouver, BC V6T 1Z2, Canada. Offers MA, PhD.

University of California, Los Angeles, Graduate Division, College of Letters and Science, Program in Gender Studies, Los Angeles, CA 90095. Offers MA, PhD. Terminal master's awarded for partial completion of doctoral program. *Degree requirements:* For master's, comprehensive exam, thesis; for doctorate, one foreign language, thesis/dissertation, written and oral qualifying exams. *Entrance requirements:* For doctorate, GRE General Test, bachelor's degree; minimum undergraduate GPA of 3.0 (or its equivalent if letter grade system not used); writing sample. Additional exam requirements/recommendations for international students: Required—TOEFL. Electronic applications accepted.

University of Central Florida, College of Graduate Studies, Program in Interdisciplinary Studies, Orlando, FL 32816. Offers gender studies (Certificate); interdisciplinary studies (MS). *Students:* 10 full-time (3 women), 17 part-time (12 women); includes 9 minority (3 Black or African American, non-Hispanic/Latino; 4 Hispanic/Latino; 2 Two or more races, non-Hispanic/Latino), 1 international. Average age 31. 31 applicants, 61% accepted, 10 enrolled. In 2014, 2 master's, 9 other advanced degrees awarded. *Degree requirements:* For master's, thesis or alternative. *Entrance requirements:* For master's, GRE General Test, minimum GPA of 3.0 in last 60 hours. Additional exam requirements/recommendations for international students: Required—TOEFL. Application fee: $30. Electronic applications accepted. *Expenses:* Tuition, state resident: part-time $288.16 per credit hour. Tuition, nonresident: part-time $1073.31 per credit hour. *Financial support:* In 2014–15, 1 student received support, including 1 teaching assistantship (averaging $7,500 per year). *Unit head:* Dr. Michael Hampton, Director, 407-823-0144, E-mail: michael.hampton@ucf.edu. *Application contact:* Barbara Rodriguez Lamas, Director, Admissions and Student Services, 407-823-2766, Fax: 407-823-6442, E-mail: gradadmissions@ucf.edu.
Website: http://www.is.ucf.edu/

University of Colorado Denver, College of Liberal Arts and Sciences, Program in Humanities, Denver, CO 80217. Offers community health science (MSS); humanities (MH); international studies (MSS); philosophy and theory (MH); social justice (MSS); society and the environment (MSS); visual studies (MH); women's and gender studies (MSS). Part-time and evening/weekend programs available. *Faculty:* 1 full-time (0 women), 1 (woman) part-time/adjunct. *Students:* 49 full-time (37 women), 26 part-time (19 women); includes 14 minority (3 Black or African American, non-Hispanic/Latino; 1 American Indian or Alaska Native, non-Hispanic/Latino; 1 Asian, non-Hispanic/Latino; 6 Hispanic/Latino; 3 Two or more races, non-Hispanic/Latino), 1 international. Average age 35. 27 applicants, 63% accepted, 11 enrolled. In 2014, 16 master's awarded. *Degree requirements:* For master's, 36 credit hours, project or thesis. *Entrance requirements:* For master's, writing sample, statement of purpose/letter of intent, three

letters of recommendation. Additional exam requirements/recommendations for international students: Required—TOEFL (minimum score 537 paper-based; 75 iBT); Recommended—IELTS (minimum score 6.5). *Application deadline:* For fall admission, 5/15 for domestic students, 5/15 priority date for international students; for spring admission, 10/15 for domestic students, 10/15 priority date for international students; for summer admission, 3/15 for domestic and international students. Application fee: $50 ($75 for international students). Electronic applications accepted. *Financial support:* In 2014–15, 4 students received support. Fellowships, research assistantships, teaching assistantships, Federal Work-Study, institutionally sponsored loans, scholarships/grants, and traineeships available. Financial award application deadline: 4/1; financial award applicants required to submit FAFSA. *Faculty research:* Women and gender in the classical Mediterranean, communication theory and democracy, relationship between psychology and philosophy. *Unit head:* Margaret Woodhull, Director of Humanities, 303-315-3568, E-mail: margaret.woodhull@ucdenver.edu. *Application contact:* Angela Beale, Program Assistant, 303-315-3565, E-mail: angela.beale@ucdenver.edu.
Website: http://www.ucdenver.edu/academics/colleges/CLAS/Programs/HumanitiesSocialSciences/Programs/Pages/MasterofHumanities.aspx

University of Florida, Graduate School, College of Liberal Arts and Sciences, Center for Women's Studies and Gender Research, Gainesville, FL 32611. Offers gender and development (Graduate Certificate); women's studies (MA, Graduate Certificate); MA/JD; MA/MA. *Faculty:* 28 full-time (25 women), 34 part-time/adjunct (27 women). *Students:* 9 full-time (6 women), 4 part-time (1 woman); includes 2 minority (1 Asian, non-Hispanic/Latino; 1 Hispanic/Latino), 2 international. 13 applicants, 62% accepted, 6 enrolled. In 2014, 5 master's awarded. Terminal master's awarded for partial completion of doctoral program. *Degree requirements:* For master's, thesis or project. *Entrance requirements:* For master's, GRE General Test (minimum score 1000), minimum GPA of 3.2. Additional exam requirements/recommendations for international students: Required—TOEFL (minimum score 550 paper-based; 80 iBT), IELTS (minimum score 6). *Application deadline:* For fall admission, 1/15 for domestic and international students; for spring admission, 10/1 for domestic and international students. Application fee: $30. Electronic applications accepted. *Financial support:* In 2014–15, 1 fellowship, 1 research assistantship, 7 teaching assistantships were awarded. Financial award application deadline: 1/15; financial award applicants required to submit FAFSA. *Faculty research:* Prejudice, discrimination, intersections, resistance, history. *Total annual research expenditures:* $764. *Unit head:* Dr. Judith W. Page, Director, 352-273-0387, Fax: 352-392-0860, E-mail: page7@ufl.edu. *Application contact:* Anita Anantharam, PhD, Graduate Coordinator, 352-273-0383, Fax: 352-392-4873, E-mail: aanita@ufl.edu.
Website: http://web.wst.ufl.edu/

University of Lethbridge, School of Graduate Studies, Lethbridge, AB T1K 3M4, Canada. Offers addictions counseling (M Sc); agricultural biotechnology (M Sc); agricultural studies (M Sc, MA); anthropology (MA); archaeology (M Sc, MA); art (MA, MFA); biochemistry (M Sc); biological sciences (M Sc); biomolecular science (PhD); biosystems and biodiversity (PhD); Canadian studies (MA); chemistry (M Sc); computer science (M Sc); computer science and geographical information science (M Sc); counseling (MC); counseling psychology (M Ed); dramatic arts (MA); earth, space, and physical science (PhD); economics (MA); education (MA); educational leadership (M Ed); English (MA); environmental science (M Sc); evolution and behavior (PhD); exercise science (M Sc); French (MA); French/German (MA); French/Spanish (MA); general education (M Ed); geography (M Sc, MA); German (MA); health sciences (M Sc); individualized multidisciplinary (M Sc, MA); kinesiology (M Sc, MA); management (M Sc), including accounting, finance, general management, human resource management and labor relations, information systems, international management, marketing, policy and strategy; mathematics (M Sc); modern languages (MA); music (M Mus, MA); Native American studies (MA); neuroscience (M Sc, PhD); new media (MA, MFA); nursing (M Sc, MN); philosophy (MA); physics (M Sc); political science (MA); psychology (M Sc, MA); religious studies (MA); sociology (MA); theatre and dramatic arts (MFA); theoretical and computational science (PhD); urban and regional studies (MA); women and gender studies (MA). Part-time and evening/weekend programs available. *Faculty:* 358. *Students:* 445 full-time (243 women), 116 part-time (72 women). Average age 31. 351 applicants, 26% accepted, 87 enrolled. In 2014, 129 master's, 13 doctorates awarded. *Degree requirements:* For master's, thesis (for some programs); for doctorate, comprehensive exam, thesis/dissertation. *Entrance requirements:* For master's, GMAT (for M Sc in management), bachelor's degree in related field, minimum GPA of 3.0 during previous 20 graded semester courses, 2 years' teaching or related experience (M Ed); for doctorate, master's degree, minimum graduate GPA of 3.5. Additional exam requirements/recommendations for international students: Required—TOEFL. Application fee: $100 Canadian dollars. *Financial support:* Fellowships, research assistantships, teaching assistantships, scholarships/grants, health care benefits, and unspecified assistantships available. *Faculty research:* Movement and brain plasticity, gibberellin physiology, photosynthesis, carbon cycling, molecular properties of main-group ring components. *Application contact:* School of Graduate Studies, 403-329-5194, E-mail: sgsinquiries@uleth.ca.
Website: http://www.uleth.ca/graduatestudies/

University of Maine, Graduate School, College of Liberal Arts and Sciences, Department of English, Orono, ME 04469. Offers composition and pedagogy (MA); gender and literature (MA). Part-time and evening/weekend programs available. *Faculty:* 19 full-time (10 women). *Students:* 25 full-time (18 women), 3 part-time (2 women), 2 international. Average age 29. 41 applicants, 73% accepted, 14 enrolled. In 2014, 3 master's awarded. *Degree requirements:* For master's, one foreign language, thesis optional. *Entrance requirements:* For master's, GRE General Test, minimum GPA of 3.0. Additional exam requirements/recommendations for international students: Required—TOEFL. *Application deadline:* For fall admission, 1/15 priority date for domestic students. Applications are processed on a rolling basis. Application fee: $65. Electronic applications accepted. *Expenses:* Tuition, state resident: part-time $658 per credit hour. Tuition, nonresident: part-time $1550 per credit hour. *Financial support:* In 2014–15, 24 students received support, including 21 teaching assistantships with full tuition reimbursements available (averaging $14,600 per year); Federal Work-Study and tuition waivers (full and partial) also available. Financial award application deadline: 3/1. *Faculty research:* Poetry and poetics, critical studies, medieval studies, gender theory, nineteenth- and twentieth-century literature, Native American literature. *Unit head:* Dr. Richard Brucher, Chair, 207-581-3823, Fax: 207-581-1604. *Application contact:* Scott G. Delcourt, Assistant Vice President for Graduate Studies and Senior Associate Dean, 207-581-3291, Fax: 207-581-3232, E-mail: graduate@maine.edu.
Website: http://english.umaine.edu/

University of Michigan–Flint, College of Arts and Sciences, Program in Social Sciences, Flint, MI 48502-1950. Offers gender studies (MA); global studies (MA); U.S. history and politics (MA). Part-time programs available. *Faculty:* 14 full-time (8 women), 5 part-time/adjunct (3 women). *Students:* 1 (woman) full-time, 20 part-time (13 women); includes 8 minority (6 Black or African American, non-Hispanic/Latino; 1 Hispanic/Latino; 1 Two or more races, non-Hispanic/Latino). Average age 41. 8 applicants, 75% accepted, 3 enrolled. In 2014, 7 master's awarded. *Entrance requirements:* For master's, bachelor's degree from accredited institution, minimum overall GPA of 3.0. Additional exam requirements/recommendations for international students: Required—TOEFL (minimum score 84 iBT), IELTS (minimum score 6.5). *Application deadline:* For fall admission, 8/1 for domestic students, 5/1 for international students; for winter admission, 11/15 for domestic students, 9/1 for international students; for spring admission, 3/15 for domestic students, 1/1 for international students; for summer admission, 5/15 for domestic students. Applications are processed on a rolling basis. Application fee: $55. Electronic applications accepted. *Expenses:* Expenses: Contact institution. *Financial support:* Federal Work-Study, scholarships/grants, and unspecified assistantships available. Support available to part-time students. Financial award application deadline: 3/1; financial award applicants required to submit FAFSA. *Unit head:* Dr. Adam Lutzker, Interim Director, 810-762-3280, Fax: 810-762-3281, E-mail: alutzker@umflint.edu. *Application contact:* Bradley T. Maki, Director of Graduate Admissions, 810-762-3171, Fax: 810-766-6789, E-mail: bmaki@umflint.edu.
Website: http://www.umflint.edu/graduateprograms/social-sciences-ma

University of Missouri–St. Louis, College of Arts and Sciences, Interdisciplinary Programs, St. Louis, MO 63121. Offers gender studies (Certificate); international studies (Certificate). *Faculty:* 1 full-time (0 women), 17 part-time/adjunct (12 women). *Students:* 1 (woman) full-time, 6 part-time (5 women); includes 3 minority (2 Black or African American, non-Hispanic/Latino; 1 Asian, non-Hispanic/Latino). Average age 35. 23 applicants, 48% accepted, 3 enrolled. In 2014, 5 Certificates awarded. *Entrance requirements:* Additional exam requirements/recommendations for international students: Required—TOEFL (minimum score 550 paper-based; 79 iBT), IELTS (minimum score 6.5). *Application deadline:* For fall admission, 7/1 for domestic and international students; for spring admission, 12/1 for domestic and international students. Applications are processed on a rolling basis. Application fee: $50 ($40 for international students). *Expenses:* Tuition, state resident: full-time $7364; part-time $409.10 per hour. Tuition, nonresident: full-time $18,153; part-time $1008.50 per hour. *Unit head:* Dr. Ronald Yasbin, Dean, 314-516-5501. *Application contact:* Graduate Admissions, 314-516-5458, Fax: 314-516-6996, E-mail: gradadm@umsl.edu.

The University of North Carolina at Charlotte, College of Liberal Arts and Sciences, Department of Sociology, Charlotte, NC 28223-0001. Offers health research (MA); mathematical sociology and quantitative methods (MA); organizations, occupations, and work (MA); political sociology (MA); race and gender (MA); social psychology (MA); social theory (MA); sociology of education (MA); stratification (MA). Part-time and evening/weekend programs available. *Faculty:* 16 full-time (10 women). *Students:* 11 full-time (5 women), 2 part-time (0 women); includes 5 minority (4 Black or African American, non-Hispanic/Latino; 1 Hispanic/Latino), 1 international. Average age 29. 14 applicants, 71% accepted, 5 enrolled. In 2014, 6 master's awarded. *Degree requirements:* For master's, thesis or comprehensive exam. *Entrance requirements:* For master's, GRE or MAT, minimum GPA of 3.0 in last 2 years, 2.75 overall. Additional exam requirements/recommendations for international students: Required—TOEFL (minimum score 557 paper-based; 83 iBT). *Application deadline:* For fall admission, 4/15 for domestic and international students; for spring admission, 10/1 for domestic and international students. Application fee: $75. Electronic applications accepted. *Expenses:* Tuition, state resident: full-time $4008. Tuition, nonresident: full-time $16,295. *Required fees:* $2755. Tuition and fees vary according to course load and program. *Financial support:* In 2014–15, 10 students received support, including 5 research assistantships (averaging $10,400 per year), 5 teaching assistantships (averaging $9,200 per year); career-related internships or fieldwork, institutionally sponsored loans, scholarships/grants, and unspecified assistantships also available. Support available to part-time students. Financial award application deadline: 4/1; financial award applicants required to submit FAFSA. *Faculty research:* Impact of race on high school course selection; income inequality within the United States and cross-nationally; small group interaction, nonverbal behaviors, identity, emotions, gender, and expectations; mathematical models of social processes. *Total annual research expenditures:* $413,099. *Unit head:* Dr. Lisa Walker, Chair, 704-687-7825, Fax: 704-687-3091, E-mail: lisa.walker@uncc.edu. *Application contact:* Kathy B. Giddings, Director of Graduate Admissions, 704-687-5503, Fax: 704-687-1668, E-mail: gradadm@uncc.edu.
Website: http://sociology.uncc.edu/

The University of North Carolina at Greensboro, Graduate School, College of Arts and Sciences, Program in Women's and Gender Studies, Greensboro, NC 27412-5001. Offers MA, Certificate. Electronic applications accepted.

University of Northern British Columbia, Office of Graduate Studies, Prince George, BC V2N 4Z9, Canada. Offers business administration (Diploma); community health science (M Sc); disability management (MA); education (M Ed); first nations studies (MA); gender studies (MA); history (MA); interdisciplinary studies (MA); international studies (MA); mathematical, computer and physical sciences (M Sc); natural resources and environmental studies (M Sc, MA, MNRES, PhD); political science (MA); psychology (M Sc, PhD); social work (MSW). Part-time and evening/weekend programs available. Postbaccalaureate distance learning degree programs offered (no on-campus study). *Degree requirements:* For master's, thesis; for doctorate, thesis/dissertation. *Entrance requirements:* For master's, GRE, minimum B average in undergraduate course work; for doctorate, candidacy exam, minimum A average in graduate course work.

University of Northern Iowa, Graduate College, MA Program in Women's and Gender Studies, Cedar Falls, IA 50614. Offers MA. *Students:* 4 full-time (3 women), 3 part-time (all women); includes 1 minority (Asian, non-Hispanic/Latino). 8 applicants, 63% accepted, 1 enrolled. In 2014, 1 master's awarded. *Degree requirements:* For master's, comprehensive exam (for some programs), thesis or alternative. *Entrance requirements:* For master's, minimum GPA of 3.0. Additional exam requirements/recommendations for international students: Required—TOEFL (minimum score 500 paper-based; 61 iBT). *Application deadline:* Applications are processed on a rolling basis. Application fee: $50 ($70 for international students). Electronic applications accepted. *Expenses:* Tuition, state resident: full-time $7912; part-time $880 per credit. Tuition, nonresident: full-time $17,906; part-time $880 per credit. *Required fees:* $1101; $325.50 per credit. $465.63 per semester. Tuition and fees vary according to course load and program. *Financial support:* Application deadline: 2/1. *Unit head:* Dr. Catherine MacGillivray, Interim Director, 319-273-7195, Fax: 319-273-3053, E-mail: catherine.macgillivray@uni.edu. *Application contact:* Laurie S. Russell, Record Analyst, 319-273-2623, Fax: 319-273-2885, E-mail: laurie.russell@uni.edu.
Website: http://www.uni.edu/womenstudies/

University of Oklahoma, College of Arts and Sciences, Women's and Gender Studies Program, Norman, OK 73019. Offers Graduate Certificate. Part-time and evening/weekend programs available. *Students:* 3 full-time (all women), 16 part-time (15 women); includes 2 minority (1 American Indian or Alaska Native, non-Hispanic/Latino; 1 Hispanic/Latino), 1 international. Average age 40. In 2014, 10 Graduate Certificates awarded. *Entrance requirements:* For degree, minimum GPA of 3.0. Additional exam requirements/recommendations for international students: Required—TOEFL (minimum score 79 iBT). *Application deadline:* For fall admission, 3/15 for domestic and international students; for spring admission, 11/15 for domestic and international students. Applications are processed on a rolling basis. Application fee: $50 ($100 for international students). Electronic applications accepted. *Expenses:* Tuition, state resident: full-time $4394; part-time $183.10 per credit hour. Tuition, nonresident: full-time $16,970; part-time $707.10 per credit hour. *Required fees:* $2892; $109.95 per

credit hour. $126.50 per semester. *Financial support:* In 2014–15, 1 research assistantship with partial tuition reimbursement (averaging $11,709 per year), 1 teaching assistantship with partial tuition reimbursement (averaging $10,373 per year) were awarded; unspecified assistantships also available. Financial award application deadline: 6/1; financial award applicants required to submit FAFSA. *Faculty research:* LGBTQ issues, gender and politics, social justice, gender and media, gender and STEM. *Unit head:* Jill Irvine, Director, 405-325-2205, Fax: 405-325-3573, E-mail: jill.irvine@ou.edu. *Application contact:* Katy Hall, Managerial Associate, 405-325-3481, Fax: 405-325-3573, E-mail: katyhall@ou.edu.
Website: http://wgs.ou.edu/

University of Saskatchewan, College of Graduate Studies and Research, College of Arts and Science, Department of Women's and Gender Studies, Saskatoon, SK S7N 5A2, Canada. Offers MA, PhD. *Degree requirements:* For master's, thesis; for doctorate, comprehensive exam (for some programs), thesis/dissertation. *Entrance requirements:* Additional exam requirements/recommendations for international students: Required—TOEFL (minimum score 80 iBT); Recommended—IELTS (minimum score 6.5). Electronic applications accepted.

University of South Florida, College of Arts and Sciences, Department of Women's Studies, Tampa, FL 33620-9951. Offers women's and gender studies (MA). Part-time programs available. *Faculty:* 4 full-time (3 women). *Students:* 9 full-time (8 women); includes 2 minority (both Hispanic/Latino), 2 international. Average age 27. 10 applicants, 70% accepted, 3 enrolled. In 2014, 3 master's awarded. *Degree requirements:* For master's, comprehensive exam, thesis or internship. *Entrance requirements:* For master's, GRE General Test, minimum GPA of 3.0, three letters of recommendation, personal narrative statement of purpose, scholarly writing sample (examples include term paper or research paper); undergraduate major or minor in women's studies (recommended). Additional exam requirements/recommendations for international students: Required—TOEFL (minimum score 550 paper-based; 79 iBT) or IELTS (minimum score 6.5). *Application deadline:* For fall admission, 2/15 for domestic students, 1/2 for international students; for spring admission, 10/15 for domestic students, 6/1 for international students. Applications are processed on a rolling basis. Application fee: $30. *Financial support:* In 2014–15, 9 students received support, including 9 teaching assistantships with tuition reimbursements available (averaging $9,093 per year). Financial award application deadline: 3/1. *Faculty research:* Performance studies, feminist theory and pedagogy; constructions of gender in public discourse, including education, mass media, and popular culture; women's health, reproductive justice, and sexuality; bodies and cultural representations; feminist theory as it relates to learning disabilities, critical race theory, postmodernist and queer theory; hiring practices in higher education, mothering; women of color feminisms. *Unit head:* Dr. Diane Price Herndl, Professor and Chairperson, 813-974-0987, Fax: 813-974-0336, E-mail: priceherndl@usf.edu. *Application contact:* Dr. Kim Golombisky, Associate Professor and Graduate Director, 813-974-0986, Fax: 813-974-0336, E-mail: kgolombi@usf.edu.
Website: http://wgs.usf.edu/

University of South Florida, Innovative Education, Tampa, FL 33620-9951. *Unit head:* Kathy Barnes, Interdisciplinary Programs Coordinator, 813-974-8031, Fax: 813-974-7061, E-mail: barnesk@usf.edu. *Application contact:* Karen Tylinski, Metro Initiatives, 813-974-9943, Fax: 813-974-7061, E-mail: ktylinsk@usf.edu.
Website: http://www.usf.edu/innovative-education/

The University of Toledo, College of Graduate Studies, College of Languages, Literature and Social Sciences, Department of Women's and Gender Studies, Toledo, OH 43606-3390. Offers Certificate. Part-time programs available.

University of Toronto, School of Graduate Studies, Faculty of Arts and Science, Women and Gender Studies Institute, Toronto, ON M5S 2J7, Canada. Offers MA, PhD. *Entrance requirements:* For master's, minimum B+ in final year of undergraduate study. Additional exam requirements/recommendations for international students: Required—TOEFL (minimum score 580 paper-based; 93 iBT), TWE (minimum score 5). Electronic applications accepted.

Wayne State University, College of Liberal Arts and Sciences, Department of History, Detroit, MI 48202. Offers Africa (PhD); America (PhD); archival administration (Graduate Certificate); Europe (PhD); gender (PhD); history (MA); labor (PhD); science and technology (PhD); world history (PhD, Graduate Certificate); JD/MA; M Ed/MA; MLIS/MA. Doctoral programs admit for fall only. Evening/weekend programs available. *Faculty:* 22 full-time (9 women). *Students:* 32 full-time (14 women), 16 part-time (6 women); includes 4 minority (2 Black or African American, non-Hispanic/Latino; 2 Two or more races, non-Hispanic/Latino). Average age 39. 52 applicants, 37% accepted, 9 enrolled. In 2014, 5 master's awarded. *Degree requirements:* For master's, one foreign language, thesis (for some programs), final oral exam on thesis or essay and seminar; for doctorate, variable foreign language requirement, thesis/dissertation, qualifying exam in 4 fields of history. *Entrance requirements:* For master's, GRE General Test, minimum undergraduate GPA of 3.25 in history, 3.0 overall; at least 18 credits in history and related subjects at the advanced undergraduate level; foreign language; letter of intent; research paper; at least two letters of recommendation from former instructors; for doctorate, GRE General Test, minimum GPA of 3.0; letter of intent; research paper; at least three letters of recommendation from former professors; for Graduate Certificate, baccalaureate degree from accredited college or university; minimum GPA of 3.0, 3.25 in a minimum of eighteen semester credits in history and related subjects at the advanced undergraduate level. Additional exam requirements/recommendations for international students: Required—TOEFL (minimum score 550 paper-based; 79 iBT), TWE (minimum score 5.5), Michigan English Language Assessment Battery (minimum score 85); Recommended—IELTS (minimum score 6.5). *Application deadline:* For fall admission, 2/1 for domestic and international students; for winter admission, 11/1 for domestic students, 10/1 priority date for international students; for spring admission, 3/15 for domestic students, 1/1 priority date for international students. Applications are processed on a rolling basis. Application fee: $0. Electronic applications accepted. *Expenses:* Tuition, state resident: full-time $10,294; part-time $571.90 per credit hour. Tuition, nonresident: full-time $29,730; part-time $1238.75 per credit hour. *Required fees:* $1365; $43.50 per credit hour. $291.10 per semester. Tuition and fees vary according to course load and program. *Financial support:* In 2014–15, 19 students received support, including 1 fellowship with tuition reimbursement available (averaging $16,000 per year), 1 research assistantship with tuition reimbursement available (averaging $17,994 per year), 6 teaching assistantships with tuition reimbursements available (averaging $16,838 per year); scholarships/grants, health care benefits, and unspecified assistantships also available. Financial award application deadline: 3/31; financial award applicants required to submit FAFSA. *Faculty research:* Labor and working class history, urban history, citizenship and politics, gender and women's history. *Unit head:* Dr. Marc W. Kruman, Chair, 313-577-2525, Fax: 313-577-6987, E-mail: mkruman@wayne.edu. *Application contact:* Dr. Gayle McCreedy, Academic Service Officer, 313-577-2592, Fax: 313-577-6987, E-mail: g.mccreedy@wayne.edu.
Website: http://clas.wayne.edu/history/

Wilfrid Laurier University, Faculty of Graduate and Postdoctoral Studies, Faculty of Arts, Cultural Analysis and Social Theory Program, Waterloo, ON N2L 3C5, Canada. Offers body politics (MA); cultural representation and social theory (MA); gender, sexuality and embodiment (MA); globalization, identity and social movements (MA). Part-time programs available. *Entrance requirements:* For master's, honours BA in humanities, social science or interdisciplinary program with social theory, minimum B+ in final year of full-time study. Additional exam requirements/recommendations for international students: Required—TOEFL (minimum score 89 iBT). Electronic applications accepted. *Faculty research:* Globalization; identity and social movements; body politics: gender, sexuality and embodiment; cultural representation and social theory.

York University, Faculty of Graduate Studies, Faculty of Liberal Arts and Professional Studies, Program in Gender, Feminist and Women's Studies, Toronto, ON M3J 1P3, Canada. Offers MA, PhD. *Degree requirements:* For master's, thesis or alternative; for doctorate, comprehensive exam, thesis/dissertation. Electronic applications accepted.

Hispanic Studies

Brown University, Graduate School, Department of Hispanic Studies, Providence, RI 02912. Offers PhD. *Degree requirements:* For doctorate, 2 foreign languages, thesis/dissertation, preliminary exam.

California State University, Los Angeles, Graduate Studies, College of Natural and Social Sciences, Department of Chicano Studies, Los Angeles, CA 90032-8530. Offers Mexican-American studies (MA). Part-time and evening/weekend programs available. *Degree requirements:* For master's, one foreign language, comprehensive exam or thesis. *Entrance requirements:* For master's, undergraduate major in Mexican-American studies or related area, 20 upper-division units in Chicano studies, minimum GPA of 2.75 in last 90 quarter units. Additional exam requirements/recommendations for international students: Required—TOEFL (minimum score 500 paper-based). Electronic applications accepted. *Expenses:* Tuition, state resident: full-time $6738; part-time $3609 per year. Tuition, nonresident: full-time $15,666; part-time $8073 per year. Tuition and fees vary according to course load, degree level and program. *Faculty research:* U.S.-Mexican relations, Chicano literature, community organization among Chicanos and Hispanics, Spanish language in the American Southwest.

California State University, Northridge, Graduate Studies, College of Humanities, Department of Chicana and Chicano Studies, Northridge, CA 91330. Offers MA. *Students:* 15 full-time (11 women), 14 part-time (11 women); includes 26 minority (1 Black or African American, non-Hispanic/Latino; 25 Hispanic/Latino), 3 international. Average age 28. *Degree requirements:* For master's, thesis, project. *Entrance requirements:* Additional exam requirements/recommendations for international students: Required—TOEFL. *Application deadline:* For fall admission, 11/30 for domestic students. Application fee: $55. *Expenses: Required fees:* $12,402. *Financial support:* Application deadline: 3/1. *Unit head:* Dr. Christina Ayala-Alcantar, Chair, 818-677-2734.
Website: http://www.csun.edu/chicanostudies/

California State University, San Marcos, College of Humanities, Arts, Behavioral and Social Sciences, Program in Spanish, San Marcos, CA 92096-0001. Offers Hispanic cultures and society (MA); Hispanic language and linguistics (MA); Hispanic literatures and literary theory (MA). Part-time and evening/weekend programs available. *Students:* 1 (woman) full-time, 14 part-time (all women); includes 12 minority (all Hispanic/Latino). Average age 35. *Degree requirements:* For master's, 2 foreign languages, exam. *Entrance requirements:* For master's, GRE General Test, minimum GPA of 3.0 overall and in upper-division Spanish courses, official transcripts, three letters of recommendation, 750-word statement of purpose (in English), academic writing sample (in Spanish). Additional exam requirements/recommendations for international students: Required—TOEFL (minimum score 500 paper-based), TWE (minimum score 4.5). *Application deadline:* For fall admission, 3/15 priority date for domestic students. Applications are processed on a rolling basis. Application fee: $55. Electronic applications accepted. *Expenses:* Tuition, state resident: full-time $6738. *Required fees:* $1692. Tuition and fees vary according to program. *Financial support:* Teaching assistantships available. *Faculty research:* Applied linguistics, Golden Age Spanish literature, Latin American literature, poetry, Chicano studies. *Unit head:* Dr. Michael Hughes, Department Chair, 760-750-8076, E-mail: mhughes@csusm.edu. *Application contact:* Admissions, 760-750-4848, Fax: 760-750-3248, E-mail: apply@csusm.edu.
Website: http://www.csusm.edu/modernlanguages/masters_degree/

Columbia University, Graduate School of Arts and Sciences, New York, NY 10027. Offers African-American studies (MA); American studies (MA); anthropology (MA, PhD); art history and archaeology (MA, PhD); astronomy (PhD); biological sciences (PhD); biotechnology (MA); chemical physics (PhD); chemistry (PhD); classical studies (MA, PhD); classics (MA, PhD); climate and society (MA); earth and environmental sciences (PhD); East Asia: regional studies (MA); East Asian languages and cultures (MA, PhD); ecology, evolution and environmental biology (MA), including conservation biology; ecology, evolution, and environmental biology (PhD), including ecology and evolutionary biology, evolutionary primatology; economics (PhD); English and comparative literature (MA, PhD); French and Romance philology (MA, PhD); Germanic languages (MA, PhD); global French studies (MA); Hispanic cultural studies (MA); history (PhD); history and literature (MA); human rights studies (MA); Islamic studies (MA); Italian (MA, PhD); Japanese pedagogy (MA); Jewish studies (MA); Latin America and the Caribbean: regional studies (MA); Latin American and Iberian cultures (PhD); mathematics (MA, PhD), including finance (MA); medieval and Renaissance studies (MA); Middle Eastern, South Asian, and African studies (MA, PhD); modern art: critical and curatorial studies (MA); modern European studies (MA); museum anthropology (MA); music (DMA, PhD); oral history (MA); philosophical foundations of physics (MA); philosophy (MA, PhD); physics (PhD); political science (MA, PhD); psychology (PhD); quantitative methods in the social sciences (MA); religion (MA, PhD); Russia, Eurasia and East Europe: regional studies (MA); Russian translation (MA); Slavic cultures (MA); Slavic languages (MA, PhD); sociology (MA, PhD); South Asian studies (MA); statistics (MA, PhD); theatre

(PhD); JD/PhD; MA/MS; MD/PhD; MPA/MA. Dual-degree programs require admission to both Graduate School of Arts and Sciences and another Columbia school. Part-time and evening/weekend programs available. Terminal master's awarded for partial completion of doctoral program. *Degree requirements:* For master's, thesis (for some programs); for doctorate, comprehensive exam, thesis/dissertation. *Entrance requirements:* For master's and doctorate, GRE General Test, GRE Subject Test (for some programs). Electronic applications accepted. *Faculty research:* Humanities, natural sciences, social sciences.

Eastern Michigan University, Graduate School, College of Arts and Sciences, Department of World Languages, Ypsilanti, MI 48197. Offers foreign languages (MA, Graduate Certificate), including French (MA), German (MA), German for business (Graduate Certificate), Hispanic language and cultures (Graduate Certificate), Japanese business practices (Graduate Certificate), Spanish (MA). Part-time and evening/weekend programs available. Postbaccalaureate distance learning degree programs offered (minimal on-campus study). *Faculty:* 20 full-time (14 women). *Students:* 5 full-time (4 women), 46 part-time (35 women); includes 10 minority (2 Black or African American, non-Hispanic/Latino; 2 Asian, non-Hispanic/Latino; 6 Hispanic/Latino), 4 international. Average age 33. 46 applicants, 74% accepted, 21 enrolled. In 2014, 23 master's, 1 other advanced degree awarded. *Degree requirements:* For master's, one foreign language. *Entrance requirements:* Additional exam requirements/recommendations for international students: Required—TOEFL. *Application deadline:* Applications are processed on a rolling basis. Application fee: $45. *Financial support:* Fellowships, research assistantships with full tuition reimbursements, teaching assistantships with full tuition reimbursements, career-related internships or fieldwork, Federal Work-Study, institutionally sponsored loans, scholarships/grants, tuition waivers (partial), and unspecified assistantships available. Support available to part-time students. Financial award applicants required to submit FAFSA. *Unit head:* Dr. Rosemary Weston-Gil, Department Head, 734-487-0130, Fax: 734-487-3411, E-mail: rweston3@emich.edu.

La Salle University, School of Arts and Sciences, Hispanic Institute, Philadelphia, PA 19141-1199. Offers bilingual/bicultural studies (MA); ESL specialist (Certificate); interpretation in English-Spanish/Spanish-English (Certificate); teaching English to speakers of other languages (MA); translation and interpretation (MA); translation English/Spanish-Spanish/English (Certificate). Part-time and evening/weekend programs available. *Degree requirements:* For master's, one foreign language, project or thesis. *Entrance requirements:* For master's, GRE, MAT, or GMAT, professional resume; two letters of recommendation; for Certificate, GRE, MAT, or GMAT, professional resume; two letters of recommendation; evidence of an advanced level in Spanish. Additional exam requirements/recommendations for international students: Required—TOEFL. Electronic applications accepted. Application fee is waived when completed online. *Expenses:* Contact institution. *Faculty research:* Puerto Rican literature, cross-cultural communication, English as a second language methodology, Spanish language.

Louisiana State University and Agricultural & Mechanical College, Graduate School, College of Humanities and Social Sciences, Department of Foreign Languages and Literatures, Baton Rouge, LA 70803. Offers Hispanic studies (MA). Part-time programs available. *Faculty:* 20 full-time (9 women). *Students:* 14 full-time (11 women), 2 part-time (1 woman); includes 3 minority (all Hispanic/Latino), 4 international. Average age 29. 10 applicants, 80% accepted, 7 enrolled. In 2014, 5 master's awarded. *Degree requirements:* For master's, 2 foreign languages, thesis optional. *Entrance requirements:* For master's, GRE General Test, minimum GPA of 3.0. Additional exam requirements/recommendations for international students: Required—TOEFL (minimum score 550 paper-based; 79 IBT), IELTS (minimum score 6.5), or PTE (minimum score 59). *Application deadline:* For fall admission, 1/1 priority date for domestic students, 5/15 for international students; for spring admission, 10/15 for domestic and international students; for summer admission, 5/15 for domestic and international students. Applications are processed on a rolling basis. Application fee: $50 ($70 for international students). Electronic applications accepted. *Financial support:* In 2014–15, 14 students received support, including 8 research assistantships with partial tuition reimbursements available (averaging $10,500 per year), 6 teaching assistantships with partial tuition reimbursements available (averaging $10,500 per year); fellowships with full tuition reimbursements available, Federal Work-Study, scholarships/grants, health care benefits, and tuition waivers (full and partial) also available. Financial award application deadline: 4/1; financial award applicants required to submit FAFSA. *Faculty research:* Hispanic cultural studies, linguistics, literary and cultural theory, peninsular and Latin American literature. *Total annual research expenditures:* $548. *Unit head:* Dr. John Pizer, Chair, 225-578-6616, Fax: 225-578-5074, E-mail: pizerj@lsu.edu. *Application contact:* Dr. Andrea Morris, Graduate Adviser, 225-578-6616, Fax: 225-578-5074, E-mail: aemorris@lsu.edu.
Website: http://uiswcmsweb.prod.lsu.edu/hss/fll/

McGill University, Faculty of Graduate and Postdoctoral Studies, Faculty of Arts, Department of Hispanic Studies, Montréal, QC H3A 2T5, Canada. Offers MA, PhD.

Michigan State University, The Graduate School, College of Arts and Letters, Department of Spanish and Portuguese, East Lansing, MI 48824. Offers applied Spanish linguistics (MA); Hispanic cultural studies (PhD); Hispanic literatures (MA). *Entrance requirements:* Additional exam requirements/recommendations for international students: Required—TOEFL. Electronic applications accepted.

Oregon State University, College of Liberal Arts, Program in Contemporary Hispanic Studies, Corvallis, OR 97331. Offers MA. *Faculty:* 7 full-time (5 women). *Students:* 2 full-time (1 woman), 1 (woman) part-time. In 2014, 3 master's awarded. *Entrance requirements:* For master's, ACTFL OPI (Oral Proficiency Interview). *Application deadline:* For fall admission, 4/30 for domestic students. *Expenses:* Tuition, state resident: full-time $11,907; part-time $189 per credit hour. Tuition, nonresident: full-time $19,953; part-time $441 per credit hour. *Required fees:* $1472; $449 per term. One-time fee: $350. Tuition and fees vary according to course load and program. *Unit head:* Dr. Juan Trujillo, Assistant Professor, 541-737-3956, E-mail: jtrujillo@oregonstate.edu. *Application contact:* Graduate School, 541-737-4881, Fax: 541-737-3313, E-mail: graduate.admissions@oregonstate.edu.
Website: http://liberalarts.oregonstate.edu/slcs

Pontifical Catholic University of Puerto Rico, College of Arts and Humanities, Department of Hispanic Studies, Ponce, PR 00717-0777. Offers grammar and writing (Professional Certificate); Hispanic studies (MA). Part-time and evening/weekend programs available. *Degree requirements:* For master's, variable foreign language requirement, comprehensive exam, thesis or alternative. *Entrance requirements:* For master's, GRE General Test, 2 letters of recommendation, interview, minimum GPA of 2.75. Electronic applications accepted.

Queen's University at Kingston, School of Graduate Studies, Faculty of Arts and Sciences, Department of Spanish and Italian, Kingston, ON K7L 3N6, Canada. Offers Spanish language and literature (MA). Part-time programs available. *Degree requirements:* For master's, one foreign language, thesis. *Entrance requirements:* Additional exam requirements/recommendations for international students: Required—TOEFL. Electronic applications accepted. *Faculty research:* Golden Age, nineteenth- and twentieth-century Peninsular novel, literary theory, colonial Latin America, nineteenth-and-twentieth century Latin America.

St. Thomas University, School of Leadership Studies, Program in Hispanic Media, Miami Gardens, FL 33054-6459. Offers MA, Certificate. Part-time and evening/weekend programs available. *Degree requirements:* For master's, comprehensive exam. *Entrance requirements:* Additional exam requirements/recommendations for international students: Required—TOEFL (minimum score 550 paper-based; 79 iBT). Electronic applications accepted.

San Jose State University, Graduate Studies and Research, College of Social Sciences, Department of Mexican American Studies, San Jose, CA 95192-0001. Offers MA. Electronic applications accepted.

Texas A&M International University, Office of Graduate Studies and Research, College of Arts and Sciences, Department of Humanities, Laredo, TX 78041-1900. Offers English (MA); Hispanic studies (PhD); history and political thought (MA); language, literature and translation (MA). *Degree requirements:* For master's, comprehensive exam (for some programs), thesis (for some programs). *Entrance requirements:* For master's, GRE General Test. Additional exam requirements/recommendations for international students: Required—TOEFL (minimum score 550 paper-based; 79 iBT).

Texas A&M University–Kingsville, College of Graduate Studies, College of Arts and Sciences, Department of Language and Literature, Interdisciplinary Program in Hispanic Culture, Kingsville, TX 78363. Offers PhD. *Students:* 1 (woman) full-time; minority (Hispanic/Latino). Average age 49. *Degree requirements:* For doctorate, variable foreign language requirement, comprehensive exam, thesis/dissertation. *Entrance requirements:* For doctorate, GRE, MAT, GMAT, minimum GPA of 3.2, at least three letters of recommendation, demonstrated oral and written proficiency in Spanish. Additional exam requirements/recommendations for international students: Required—TOEFL (minimum score 550 paper-based; 79 iBT). *Application deadline:* For fall admission, 8/15 for domestic students, 6/1 for international students; for spring admission, 12/15 for domestic students, 10/1 for international students; for summer admission, 5/15 for domestic students, 4/1 for international students. Applications are processed on a rolling basis. Application fee: $35 ($50 for international students). Electronic applications accepted. *Financial support:* In 2014–15, 1 student received support, including 1 teaching assistantship (averaging $3,221 per year); career-related internships or fieldwork, Federal Work-Study, institutionally sponsored loans, scholarships/grants, health care benefits, tuition waivers (full and partial), and unspecified assistantships also available. Support available to part-time students. Financial award application deadline: 5/1; financial award applicants required to submit FAFSA. *Unit head:* Dr. Michelle Johnson-Vela, Department Chair, 361-593-2597, E-mail: kfmrj00@tamuk.edu. *Application contact:* Dr. Mohamed Abdelrahman, Dean of Graduate Studies, 361-593-2809, E-mail: mohamed.abdelrahman@tamuk.edu.

University of Alberta, Faculty of Graduate Studies and Research, Department of Modern Languages and Cultural Studies, Edmonton, AB T6G 2E1, Canada. Offers applied linguistics (Germanic, Romance, Slavic) (MA); French language, literatures and linguistics (PhD); French language, literatures, and linguistics (MA); Germanic languages, literatures and linguistics (PhD); Germanic languages, literatures, and linguistics (MA); Italian studies (MA); Slavic languages and literatures (Russian, Ukrainian) (MA, PhD); Slavic linguistics (Russian, Ukrainian) (MA, PhD); Spanish and Latin American studies (MA, PhD); Ukrainian folklore (MA, PhD). Part-time programs available. *Degree requirements:* For master's, one foreign language, thesis; for doctorate, 2 foreign languages, comprehensive exam, thesis/dissertation. *Entrance requirements:* For master's and doctorate, 1 language other than English. Additional exam requirements/recommendations for international students: Required—Michigan English Language Assessment Battery or TOEFL (minimum score 550 paper-based). Electronic applications accepted. *Faculty research:* Russian/Ukrainian studies; German studies; contemporary Latin American, French and Francophone studies; Italian studies.

The University of British Columbia, Faculty of Arts and Faculty of Graduate Studies, Department of French, Hispanic and Italian Studies, Vancouver, BC V6T 1Z1, Canada. Offers French (MA, PhD); Hispanic studies (MA, PhD). Part-time programs available. *Degree requirements:* For master's, thesis optional; for doctorate, 2 foreign languages, comprehensive exam, thesis/dissertation. *Entrance requirements:* For doctorate, MA. Additional exam requirements/recommendations for international students: Required—TOEFL (minimum score 550 paper-based; 80 iBT). Electronic applications accepted. *Faculty research:* Medieval and Renaissance literature, modern literature, romance philology and linguistics, cultural studies, women's literature.

University of California, Riverside, Graduate Division, Department of Hispanic Studies, Riverside, CA 92521-0102. Offers Spanish (MA, PhD). Terminal master's awarded for partial completion of doctoral program. *Degree requirements:* For master's, one foreign language, comprehensive exam; for doctorate, one foreign language, thesis/dissertation, qualifying exams, 1 quarter of teaching experience. *Entrance requirements:* For master's and doctorate, GRE General Test, minimum GPA of 3.0. Additional exam requirements/recommendations for international students: Required—TOEFL (minimum score 550 paper-based; 80 iBT). Electronic applications accepted. *Expenses:* Tuition, state resident: full-time $5399. Tuition, nonresident: full-time $10,433. *Faculty research:* Spanish literature of the sixteenth-, seventeenth- and twentieth-century; pre-Columbian and colonial Latin American literature; nineteenth- and twentieth-century Latin American literature.

University of California, Santa Barbara, Graduate Division, College of Letters and Sciences, Division of Humanities and Fine Arts, Department of Spanish and Portuguese, Santa Barbara, CA 93106-4150. Offers Hispanic languages and literatures (PhD), including European medieval studies, feminist studies, Hispanic linguistics, Hispanic literature, Luso-Brazilian literature; Hispanic linguistics (MA); Luso-Brazilian literature (MA); Spanish or Spanish-American literature (MA); MA/PhD. Spanish Language Institute available during Summer session. Terminal master's awarded for partial completion of doctoral program. *Degree requirements:* For master's, 2 foreign languages, comprehensive exam (for some programs), thesis optional; for doctorate, 3 foreign languages, comprehensive exam, thesis/dissertation. *Entrance requirements:* For master's and doctorate, GRE. Additional exam requirements/recommendations for international students: Required—TOEFL (minimum score 550 paper-based; 80 iBT), IELTS (minimum score 7). Electronic applications accepted. *Faculty research:* Nineteenth-century Spanish and Portuguese literature, Spanish and Spanish-American literature, nineteenth- and twentieth-century Portuguese and Brazilian literatures, Hispanic linguistics, Catalan language and culture.

University of California, Santa Barbara, Graduate Division, College of Letters and Sciences, Division of Social Sciences, Department of Chicana and Chicano Studies, Santa Barbara, CA 93106-4120. Offers MA/PhD. *Entrance requirements:* Additional exam requirements/recommendations for international students: Required—TOEFL (minimum score 550 paper-based; 80 iBT), IELTS (minimum score 7). Electronic applications accepted. *Faculty research:* History and narrative, cultural production, social processes, gender and sexuality studies.

University of Houston, College of Liberal Arts and Social Sciences, Department of Hispanic Studies, Houston, TX 77204. Offers Spanish (MA, PhD). Part-time programs

available. *Degree requirements:* For master's, comprehensive exam, thesis optional; for doctorate, 2 foreign languages, comprehensive exam, thesis/dissertation. *Entrance requirements:* For master's and doctorate, GRE. Additional exam requirements/recommendations for international students: Required—TOEFL (minimum score 550 paper-based; 79 iBT); Recommended—IELTS (minimum score 6.5). Electronic applications accepted.

University of Illinois at Chicago, Graduate College, College of Liberal Arts and Sciences, School of Literatures, Cultural Studies and Linguistics, Department of Hispanic and Italian Studies, Chicago, IL 60607-7128. Offers Hispanic linguistics (PhD). Part-time programs available. *Faculty:* 23 full-time (19 women), 10 part-time/adjunct (7 women). *Students:* 45 full-time (32 women), 15 part-time (9 women); includes 19 minority (18 Hispanic/Latino; 1 Two or more races, non-Hispanic/Latino), 24 international. Average age 29. 50 applicants, 50% accepted, 13 enrolled. In 2014, 10 master's, 2 doctorates awarded. Terminal master's awarded for partial completion of doctoral program. *Degree requirements:* For master's, one foreign language, departmental qualifying exam. *Entrance requirements:* For master's, GRE General Test, minimum GPA of 2.75, undergraduate major in Spanish. Additional exam requirements/recommendations for international students: Required—TOEFL. *Application deadline:* For fall admission, 2/1 for domestic and international students. Applications are processed on a rolling basis. Application fee: $60. Electronic applications accepted. *Expenses:* Tuition, state resident: full-time $11,254; part-time $468 per credit hour. Tuition, nonresident: full-time $23,252; part-time $968 per credit hour. *Required fees:* $1217 per term. Part-time tuition and fees vary according to course load, degree level and program. *Financial support:* In 2014–15, 2 fellowships with full tuition reimbursements were awarded; research assistantships with full tuition reimbursements, teaching assistantships with full tuition reimbursements, Federal Work-Study, scholarships/grants, traineeships, tuition waivers (full), and unspecified assistantships also available. Financial award application deadline: 3/1; financial award applicants required to submit FAFSA. *Faculty research:* Linguistic competence of bilingual speakers as a window to understanding the human faculty of language, neurocognitive processing of language among different speakers and learners, how languages are used within their social contexts. *Unit head:* Prof. Luis Lopez, Professor/Head of the Department of Hispanic and Italian Studies, 312-413-2646, E-mail: luislope@uic.edu. *Application contact:* Prof. Margarita Saona, Associate Professor and Director of Graduate Studies, 312-996-5222, E-mail: saona@uic.edu.
Website: http://lcsl.uic.edu/hispanic-italian

University of Kentucky, Graduate School, College of Arts and Sciences, Program in Hispanic Studies, Lexington, KY 40506-0032. Offers MA, PhD. *Degree requirements:* For master's, one foreign language, comprehensive exam, thesis optional; for doctorate, 2 foreign languages, comprehensive exam, thesis/dissertation. *Entrance requirements:* For master's, GRE General Test, minimum undergraduate GPA of 2.75; for doctorate, GRE General Test, minimum graduate GPA of 3.0. Additional exam requirements/recommendations for international students: Required—TOEFL (minimum score 550 paper-based). Electronic applications accepted. *Faculty research:* Hispanic linguistics, medieval Spanish literature and civilization, Renaissance and Golden Age literature and civilization, Spanish American literature and civilization.

The University of Manchester, School of Languages, Linguistics and Cultures, Manchester, United Kingdom. Offers Arab world studies (PhD); Chinese studies (M Phil, PhD); East Asian studies (M Phil, PhD); English language (PhD); French studies (M Phil, PhD); German studies (M Phil, PhD); interpreting studies (PhD); Italian studies (M Phil, PhD); Japanese studies (M Phil, PhD); Latin American cultural studies (M Phil, PhD); linguistics (M Phil, PhD); Middle Eastern studies (M Phil, PhD); Polish studies (M Phil, PhD); Portuguese studies (M Phil, PhD); Russian studies (M Phil, PhD); Spanish studies (M Phil, PhD); translation and intercultural studies (M Phil, PhD).

University of Nevada, Las Vegas, Graduate College, College of Liberal Arts, Department of World Languages and Cultures, Las Vegas, NV 89154-5047. Offers Hispanic studies (MA). Part-time programs available. *Faculty:* 2 full-time (1 woman). *Students:* 1 full-time (0 women), 12 part-time (11 women); includes 5 minority (all Hispanic/Latino). Average age 34. 8 applicants, 88% accepted, 5 enrolled. In 2014, 2 master's awarded. *Degree requirements:* For master's, one foreign language, comprehensive exam. *Entrance requirements:* Additional exam requirements/recommendations for international students: Required—TOEFL (minimum score 550 paper-based; 80 iBT), IELTS (minimum score 7). *Application deadline:* For fall admission, 8/1 for domestic students, 5/1 for international students; for spring admission, 12/1 for domestic students, 10/1 for international students. Application fee: $60 ($95 for international students). Electronic applications accepted. *Financial support:* In 2014–15, 2 students received support, including 2 teaching assistantships with partial tuition reimbursements available (averaging $12,228 per year); institutionally sponsored loans, scholarships/grants, health care benefits, and unspecified assistantships also available. Financial award application deadline: 3/1. *Faculty research:* Twentieth century Spanish Literature, poetry of the twenties and thirties, and post-Civil War Spanish literature by women; linguistics: social linguistics and dialectology; women narrators of Mexico and Spain; fantastic literature; Judaism in literature in Spanish; Mexican film and Mexican culture. *Unit head:* Dr. Ralph Buechler, Chair/Associate Professor, 702-895-3546, Fax: 702-895-3431, E-mail: ralph.buechler@unlv.edu. *Application contact:* Graduate College Admissions Evaluator, 702-895-3320, Fax: 702-895-4180, E-mail: gradcollege@unlv.edu.
Website: http://liberalarts.unlv.edu/Foreign_Languages/graduates.html

The University of North Carolina at Greensboro, Graduate School, College of Arts and Sciences, Department of Languages, Literatures, and Cultures, Program in Spanish, Greensboro, NC 27412-5001. Offers advanced Spanish language and Hispanic cultural studies (Certificate); Spanish (MA). *Degree requirements:* For master's, one foreign language, comprehensive exam, thesis or alternative. *Entrance requirements:* For master's, GRE General Test, 3-5 minute tape demonstrating foreign language proficiency, composition in Spanish, sample paper in English. Additional exam requirements/recommendations for international students: Required—TOEFL. Electronic applications accepted.

The University of North Carolina Wilmington, College of Arts and Sciences, Department of Foreign Languages and Literatures, Wilmington, NC 28403-3297. Offers Hispanic studies (Graduate Certificate); Spanish (MA). Part-time programs available. Postbaccalaureate distance learning degree programs offered. *Faculty:* 14 full-time (7 women). *Students:* 3 full-time (all women), 11 part-time (8 women); includes 2 minority (both Hispanic/Latino). 8 applicants, 88% accepted, 7 enrolled. In 2014, 13 master's awarded. *Degree requirements:* For master's, one foreign language, comprehensive exam, thesis or alternative. *Entrance requirements:* For master's, GRE. Additional exam requirements/recommendations for international students: Required—TOEFL (minimum score 79 iBT), IELTS. *Application deadline:* For fall admission, 3/1 for domestic students; for spring admission, 11/1 for domestic students. Application fee: $60. *Expenses:* Tuition, state resident: full-time $3240. Tuition, nonresident: full-time $9208. *Required fees:* $1967. *Financial support:* Applicants required to submit FAFSA. *Unit head:* Dr. Michelle Scatton-Tessier, Chair, 910-962-4095, Fax: 910-962-7712, E-mail: scattonm@uncw.edu. *Application contact:* Dr. Brian Chandler, Graduate Coordinator, 910-962-2299, Fax: 910-962-7712, E-mail: chandlerb@uncw.edu.
Website: http://www.uncw.edu/fll/spanish/spngraduate.html

University of Puerto Rico, Mayagüez Campus, Graduate Studies, College of Arts and Sciences, Department of Hispanic Studies, Mayagüez, PR 00681-9000. Offers MA. Part-time programs available. *Faculty:* 26 full-time (18 women). *Students:* 15 full-time (10 women), 6 part-time (all women). 7 applicants, 43% accepted, 3 enrolled. In 2014, 4 master's awarded. *Degree requirements:* For master's, comprehensive exam, thesis. *Entrance requirements:* For master's, minimum GPA of 2.75, BA in Hispanic studies or its equivalent. *Application deadline:* For fall admission, 2/15 for domestic and international students; for spring admission, 9/15 for domestic and international students. Applications are processed on a rolling basis. Application fee: $25. *Expenses: Tuition, area resident:* Full-time $2466; part-time $822 per credit. *International tuition:* $6371 full-time. *Required fees:* $1095; $1095 per year. Tuition and fees vary according to course level, course load and reciprocity agreements. *Financial support:* In 2014–15, 8 students received support, including 3 research assistantships (averaging $1,500 per year), 8 teaching assistantships (averaging $6,342 per year); fellowships with full tuition reimbursements available, Federal Work-Study, institutionally sponsored loans, and unspecified assistantships also available. *Faculty research:* Spanish literature, Hispanic-American literature, Puerto Rican literature, stylistics, linguistics. *Unit head:* Dr. Maribel Acosta, Director, 787-265-3843, Fax: 787-265-3843, E-mail: macostalugo@gmail.com.
Website: http://www.uprm.edu/hispanicos/

University of Puerto Rico, Río Piedras Campus, College of Humanities, Department of Hispanic Studies, San Juan, PR 00931-3300. Offers Hispanic linguistics (PhD); Hispanic studies (MA); Latin American literature (PhD); Puerto Rican literature (PhD); Spanish literature (PhD). Part-time programs available. *Degree requirements:* For master's, one foreign language, comprehensive exam, thesis; for doctorate, one foreign language, comprehensive exam, thesis/dissertation. *Entrance requirements:* For master's, PAEG or GRE, interview, minimum GPA of 3.0, letter of recommendation (2); for doctorate, PAEG or GRE, interview, master's degree, minimum GPA of 3.0, letter of recommendation (2). *Faculty research:* Poetry of Luis Palés Matos, short stories in Puerto Rico, language in the social process, "Decima Popular", Anglicism.

The University of Texas at Austin, Graduate School, College of Liberal Arts, Center for Mexican American Studies, Austin, TX 78712-1111. Offers MA.

University of Victoria, Faculty of Graduate Studies, Faculty of Humanities, Department of Hispanic and Italian Studies, Victoria, BC V8W 2Y2, Canada. Offers Hispanic and Italian studies (MA); Hispanic studies (MA). *Degree requirements:* For master's, one foreign language, comprehensive exam, thesis (for some programs). *Entrance requirements:* For master's, undergraduate major in Hispanic studies, minimum B+ average. Additional exam requirements/recommendations for international students: Required—TOEFL (minimum score 575 paper-based), IELTS (minimum score 7). Electronic applications accepted. *Faculty research:* Medieval/Renaissance Spanish and Italian literature, Golden Age literature, Latin American literature.

Villanova University, Graduate School of Liberal Arts and Sciences, Department of Romance Languages and Literatures, Villanova, PA 19085-1699. Offers Hispanic studies (MA). Part-time and evening/weekend programs available. *Faculty:* 3. *Students:* 13 full-time (7 women), 2 part-time (both women); includes 4 minority (all Hispanic/Latino), 6 international. Average age 29. 9 applicants, 100% accepted, 4 enrolled. In 2014, 6 master's awarded. *Degree requirements:* For master's, one foreign language, comprehensive exam. *Entrance requirements:* For master's, minimum GPA of 3.0, writing sample in Spanish. Additional exam requirements/recommendations for international students: Required—TOEFL. *Application deadline:* For fall admission, 3/1 for domestic students, 5/1 for international students; for spring admission, 11/15 for domestic students, 10/15 for international students; for summer admission, 5/1 for domestic students. Applications are processed on a rolling basis. Application fee: $50. Electronic applications accepted. *Financial support:* Teaching assistantships with tuition reimbursements, scholarships/grants, and unspecified assistantships available. Financial award applicants required to submit FAFSA. *Unit head:* Dr. Adriano Duque, Director, 610-519-7478.
Website: http://www1.villanova.edu/villanova/artsci/romancelanglit/academics/graduateprograminhispanicstudies.html

Holocaust and Genocide Studies

Chapman University, Wilkinson College of Humanities and Social Sciences, Program in War and Society, Orange, CA 92866. Offers MA. *Entrance requirements:* For master's, GRE or minimum cumulative GPA of 3.0, official transcripts, 500-word essay, writing sample, two letters of recommendation, resume. *Application deadline:* Applications are processed on a rolling basis. *Unit head:* Dr. Patrick Fuery, Dean, 714-516-4580, E-mail: fuery@chapman.edu. *Application contact:* Eva Yen, Director of Graduate Admissions, 714-997-6786, Fax: 714-997-6713, E-mail: eyen@chapman.edu.
Website: http://www.chapman.edu/wilkinson/graduate-studies/ma-warsociety.aspx

Clark University, Graduate School, Department of History, Program in Holocaust History, Worcester, MA 01610-1477. Offers PhD. *Students:* 22 full-time (14 women), 1 part-time (0 women), 10 international. Average age 33. 23 applicants, 17% accepted, 4 enrolled. In 2014, 2 doctorates awarded. *Degree requirements:* For doctorate, thesis/dissertation. *Entrance requirements:* Additional exam requirements/recommendations for international students: Required—TOEFL. *Application deadline:* For fall admission, 1/15 for domestic students. Application fee: $75. *Expenses: Tuition:* Full-time $40,380; part-time $1262 per credit hour. *Required fees:* $30. *Financial support:* In 2014–15, fellowships with full and partial tuition reimbursements (averaging $12,090 per year), research assistantships with full and partial tuition reimbursements (averaging $12,090 per year), teaching assistantships with full and partial tuition reimbursements (averaging $12,090 per year) were awarded; tuition waivers (partial) also available. *Faculty research:* Jewish persecution, children and survivors, Germany's role in the Holocaust.

Holocaust and Genocide Studies

Unit head: Deborah Dwork, Professor, 508-793-8897. *Application contact:* Mary Jane Rein, Executive Director, 508-793-8897, Fax: 508-793-8827, E-mail: mrein@clarku.edu.

Drew University, Caspersen School of Graduate Studies, Program in Arts and Letters, Madison, NJ 07940-1493. Offers Holocaust and genocide studies (Certificate); interdisciplinary studies (M Litt, D Litt). Part-time and evening/weekend programs available. Terminal master's awarded for partial completion of doctoral program. *Degree requirements:* For master's, thesis optional; for doctorate, thesis/dissertation. *Entrance requirements:* For master's and doctorate, transcripts, writing sample, personal statement, recommendations. Additional exam requirements/recommendations for international students: Required—TOEFL (minimum score 585 paper-based; 95 iBT), TWE. *Expenses:* Contact institution. *Faculty research:* Interdisciplinary studies across art, literature, music, philosophy, religion, and history.

Gratz College, Graduate Programs, Programs in Holocaust and Genocide Studies, Melrose Park, PA 19027. Offers MA, Graduate Certificate. Postbaccalaureate distance learning degree programs offered (no on-campus study).

Kean University, College of Humanities and Social Sciences, Program in Holocaust and Genocide Studies, Union, NJ 07083. Offers MA. Part-time programs available. *Faculty:* 14 full-time (5 women). *Students:* 10 full-time (7 women), 30 part-time (22 women); includes 7 minority (5 Black or African American, non-Hispanic/Latino; 2 Hispanic/Latino). Average age 34. 28 applicants, 100% accepted, 22 enrolled. In 2014, 2 master's awarded. *Degree requirements:* For master's, thesis. *Entrance requirements:* For master's, minimum cumulative GPA of 3.0, official transcripts from all institutions attended, two letters of recommendation from professional associates, personal statement, professional resume/curriculum vitae. Additional exam requirements/recommendations for international students: Required—TOEFL (minimum score 550 paper-based; 79 iBT). *Application deadline:* For fall admission, 6/1 for domestic and international students; for spring admission, 12/1 for domestic and international students. Applications are processed on a rolling basis. Application fee: $75 ($150 for international students). Electronic applications accepted. *Expenses:* Tuition, state resident: full-time $12,461; part-time $607 per credit. Tuition, nonresident: full-time $16,889; part-time $744 per credit. *Required fees:* $3141; $143 per credit. Tuition and fees vary according to course load, degree level and program. *Financial support:* In 2014–15, 2 research assistantships with full tuition reimbursements (averaging $3,742 per year) were awarded; scholarships/grants and unspecified assistantships also available. Financial award applicants required to submit FAFSA. *Unit head:* Dr. Catherine Nicholson, Program Coordinator, 908-737-0259, E-mail: dklein@kean.edu. *Application contact:* Reenat Hasan, Assistant Director of Graduate Admissions, 908-737-7134, Fax: 908-737-7135, E-mail: hasanr@kean.edu.
Website: http://grad.kean.edu/mahgs

Seton Hill University, Program in Genocide and Holocaust Studies, Greensburg, PA 15601. Offers Certificate. Part-time and evening/weekend programs available. Postbaccalaureate distance learning degree programs offered (no on-campus study). *Faculty:* 1 full-time (0 women), 2 part-time/adjunct (0 women). *Students:* 1 (woman) full-time, 5 part-time (all women); includes 1 minority (American Indian or Alaska Native, non-Hispanic/Latino), 1 international. Average age 37. 22 applicants, 36% accepted, 6 enrolled. In 2014, 2 Certificates awarded. *Entrance requirements:* For degree, letter of recommendation, resume, personal statements. Additional exam requirements/recommendations for international students: Required—TOEFL (minimum score 600 paper-based; 100 iBT), IELTS (minimum score 6.5). *Application deadline:* Applications are processed on a rolling basis. Application fee: $0. Electronic applications accepted. *Expenses: Tuition:* Full-time $7362; part-time $818 per credit. *Required fees:* $34 per credit. *Financial support:* In 2014–15, 2 students received support. Scholarships/grants available. Financial award application deadline: 8/15; financial award applicants required to submit FAFSA. *Faculty research:* Comparative genocide, the Holocaust, conflict in Israel/Palestine, international human rights. *Unit head:* Dr. James Paharik, Program Advisor, 724-838-1073, E-mail: jpaharik@setonhill.edu. *Application contact:* Debbie Fredo, Program Counselor, 724-838-4367, E-mail: fredo@setonhill.edu.
Website: http://www.setonhill.edu/academics/certificateprograms/genocide_and_holocaust_studies

Stockton University, School of Graduate and Continuing Studies, Program in Holocaust and Genocide Studies, Galloway, NJ 08205-9441. Offers MA. Part-time and evening/weekend programs available. *Faculty:* 4 full-time (3 women). *Students:* 3 full-time (2 women), 13 part-time (9 women); includes 2 minority (both Hispanic/Latino). Average age 34. 7 applicants, 86% accepted, 6 enrolled. In 2014, 8 master's awarded. *Degree requirements:* For master's, thesis optional. *Entrance requirements:* Additional exam requirements/recommendations for international students: Required—TOEFL. *Application deadline:* For fall admission, 7/1 for domestic and international students; for spring admission, 12/1 for domestic students, 11/1 for international students. Applications are processed on a rolling basis. Application fee: $50. Electronic applications accepted. *Expenses:* Tuition, state resident: full-time $13,694; part-time $570.59 per credit. Tuition, nonresident: full-time $21,080; part-time $878 per credit. *Required fees:* $4118; $171.59 per credit. $80 per term. Tuition and fees vary according to degree level. *Financial support:* In 2014–15, 12 students received support, including 2 fellowships, 7 research assistantships with partial tuition reimbursements available; career-related internships or fieldwork, Federal Work-Study, scholarships/grants, and unspecified assistantships also available. Financial award application deadline: 3/1; financial award applicants required to submit FAFSA. *Faculty research:* Women and the Holocaust, survivor perspectives, liberty and persecution. *Unit head:* Dr. Marion Hussong, Program Director, 609-626-3640, Fax: 609-626-6050, E-mail: mahg@stockton.edu. *Application contact:* Tara Williams, Assistant Director of Graduate Enrollment Management, 609-626-3640, Fax: 609-626-6050, E-mail: gradschool@stockton.edu.

West Chester University of Pennsylvania, College of Arts and Sciences, Department of History, West Chester, PA 19383. Offers history (M Ed, MA); Holocaust and genocide studies (MA, Certificate). Part-time and evening/weekend programs available. *Faculty:* 7 full-time (3 women). *Students:* 8 full-time (6 women), 30 part-time (13 women); includes 3 minority (1 Black or African American, non-Hispanic/Latino; 1 American Indian or Alaska Native, non-Hispanic/Latino; 1 Two or more races, non-Hispanic/Latino). Average age 29. 21 applicants, 95% accepted, 13 enrolled. In 2014, 17 master's awarded. *Degree requirements:* For master's, comprehensive exam (for MA in history and M Ed); thesis or comprehensive exam (for MA in Holocaust and genocide studies); for Certificate, 18 hours of coursework. *Entrance requirements:* For master's, statement of professional goals; writing sample, minimum GPA of 3.0 in history, and three letters of recommendation (for history); minimum GPA of 2.8 and two letters of recommendation (for Holocaust and genocide studies); for Certificate, statement of professional goals, two letters of recommendation, minimum GPA of 2.8. Additional exam requirements/recommendations for international students: Required—TOEFL (minimum score 550 paper-based; 80 iBT). *Application deadline:* For fall admission, 4/15 priority date for domestic students, 3/15 for international students; for spring admission, 10/15 priority date for domestic students, 9/1 for international students. Applications are processed on a rolling basis. Application fee: $45. Electronic applications accepted. *Expenses:* Tuition, state resident: full-time $8172; part-time $454 per credit. Tuition, nonresident: full-time $12,258; part-time $681 per credit. *Required fees:* $2231; $110.78 per credit. Tuition and fees vary according to campus/location and program. *Financial support:* Unspecified assistantships available. Support available to part-time students. Financial award application deadline: 2/15; financial award applicants required to submit FAFSA. *Unit head:* Dr. Wayne Hanley, Chair, 610-436-2201, E-mail: whanley@wcupa.edu. *Application contact:* Dr. Jonathan Friedman, Graduate Coordinator of Holocaust and Genocide Studies, 610-436-2972, E-mail: jfriedman@wcupa.edu.
Website: http://www.wcupa.edu/_academics/sch_cas.his/

Jewish Studies

American Jewish University, Graduate School of Nonprofit Management, Program in Jewish Communal Studies, Bel Air, CA 90077-1599. Offers MAJCS. *Degree requirements:* For master's, thesis. *Entrance requirements:* For master's, GMAT or GRE General Test, interview.

Biola University, Talbot School of Theology, La Mirada, CA 90639-0001. Offers adult/family ministry (MACE); Bible exposition (MA, Th M); Biblical and theological studies (MA); children's ministry (MACE); Christian education (M Div); cross-cultural education ministry (MACE); educational studies (Ed D, PhD); evangelism and discipleship (M Div); general Christian education (MACE); Messianic Jewish studies (M Div, Certificate); missions and intercultural studies (M Div); New Testament (MA, Th M); Old Testament (MA); Old Testament and Semitics (Th M); pastoral and general ministry (M Div); pastoral care and counseling (M Div); philosophy (MA); spiritual formation (M Div, Certificate); spiritual formation and soul care (MA); theology (Th M, D Min, Certificate); youth ministry (MACE). *Accreditation:* ATS. Part-time and evening/weekend programs available. *Faculty:* 77. *Students:* 581 full-time (140 women), 554 part-time (155 women); includes 522 minority (42 Black or African American, non-Hispanic/Latino; 3 American Indian or Alaska Native, non-Hispanic/Latino; 370 Asian, non-Hispanic/Latino; 78 Hispanic/Latino; 2 Native Hawaiian or other Pacific Islander, non-Hispanic/Latino; 27 Two or more races, non-Hispanic/Latino), 121 international. 437 applicants, 78% accepted, 241 enrolled. In 2014, 182 master's, 33 doctorates awarded. *Entrance requirements:* For master's, bachelor's degree from accredited college or university; minimum GPA of 2.6 (for M Div), 3.0 (for MA); for doctorate, M Div or MA. Additional exam requirements/recommendations for international students: Required—TOEFL (minimum score 600 paper-based; 88 iBT). *Application deadline:* For fall admission, 7/1 for domestic students, 6/1 for international students; for spring admission, 12/1 priority date for domestic students. Applications are processed on a rolling basis. Application fee: $65. Electronic applications accepted. *Financial support:* Scholarships/grants and unspecified assistantships available. Support available to part-time students. Financial award applicants required to submit FAFSA. *Faculty research:* New Testament, Old Testament, spiritual formation, Christian education, theological studies, Christian ministry, preaching and pastoral ministry, language and literature, bible exposition, Christian leadership. *Unit head:* Dr. Clint Arnold, Dean, 562-903-4816, Fax: 562-903-4748. *Application contact:* Graduate Admissions Office, 562-903-4752, E-mail: graduate.admissions@biola.edu.
Website: http://www.talbot.edu/

Brandeis University, Graduate School of Arts and Sciences, Department of Near Eastern and Judaic Studies, Waltham, MA 02454-9110. Offers Near Eastern and Judaic studies (MA, PhD); Near Eastern and Judaic studies and sociology (PhD); Near Eastern and Judaic studies and women's and gender studies (MA); teaching of Hebrew (MAT). Part-time programs available. Terminal master's awarded for partial completion of doctoral program. *Degree requirements:* For master's, one foreign language, thesis or alternative, proseminar, capstone; for doctorate, variable foreign language requirement, comprehensive exam, thesis/dissertation. *Entrance requirements:* For master's and doctorate, 3 letters of recommendation, transcript(s), statement of purpose, writing sample, resume. Additional exam requirements/recommendations for international students: Required—TOEFL (minimum score 600 paper-based; 100 iBT), PTE (minimum score 68); Recommended—IELTS (minimum score 7). Electronic applications accepted. *Faculty research:* Ancient Near East and Bible, Judaic studies, Israel Studies, modern Middle East, Arabic and Islamic civilizations.

Brandeis University, Graduate School of Arts and Sciences, Hornstein Jewish Professional Leadership Program, Waltham, MA 02454-9110. Offers MA/MA, MBA/MA, MPP/MA. Part-time programs available. *Entrance requirements:* Additional exam requirements/recommendations for international students: Required—TOEFL (minimum score 600 paper-based; 100 iBT), PTE (minimum score 68); Recommended—IELTS (minimum score 7). Electronic applications accepted. *Faculty research:* Leadership, business, non-profit, public policy, Near Eastern and Judaic Studies, Jewish identity, Israel-Diaspora relations.

Brooklyn College of the City University of New York, School of Humanities and Social Sciences, Department of Judaic Studies, Brooklyn, NY 11210-2889. Offers MA. Part-time and evening/weekend programs available. *Degree requirements:* For master's, 2 foreign languages, comprehensive exam or thesis. *Entrance requirements:* For master's, 18 upper-level credits in Judaic studies, interview, 2 letters of recommendation. Additional exam requirements/recommendations for international students: Required—TOEFL (minimum score 525 paper-based; 70 iBT). Electronic applications accepted. *Faculty research:* Biblical studies, Talmud and Midrash, modern Jewish history and thought.

Central Yeshiva Tomchei Tmimim-Lubavitch, Graduate Programs, Brooklyn, NY 11230. Offers Jewish/Judaic studies (MA); Talmudic studies (MA). *Accreditation:* AARTS.

Columbia University, Graduate School of Arts and Sciences, New York, NY 10027. Offers African-American studies (MA); American studies (MA); anthropology (MA, PhD); art history and archaeology (MA, PhD); astronomy (PhD); biological sciences (PhD); biotechnology (MA); chemical physics (PhD); chemistry (PhD); classical studies (MA, PhD); classics (MA, PhD); climate and society (MA); earth and environmental sciences (PhD); East Asia: regional studies (MA); East Asian languages and cultures (MA, PhD);

ecology, evolution and environmental biology (MA), including conservation biology; ecology, evolution, and environmental biology (PhD), including ecology and evolutionary biology, evolutionary primatology; economics (PhD); English and comparative literature (MA, PhD); French and Romance philology (MA, PhD); Germanic languages (MA, PhD); global French studies (MA); Hispanic cultural studies (MA); history (PhD); history and literature (MA); human rights studies (MA); Islamic studies (MA); Italian (MA, PhD); Japanese pedagogy (MA); Jewish studies (MA); Latin America and the Caribbean: regional studies (MA); Latin American and Iberian cultures (PhD); mathematics (MA, PhD), including finance (MA); medieval and Renaissance studies (MA); Middle Eastern, South Asian, and African studies (MA, PhD); modern art: critical and curatorial studies (MA); modern European studies (MA); museum anthropology (MA); music (DMA, PhD); oral history (MA); philosophical foundations of physics (MA); philosophy (MA, PhD); physics (PhD); political science (MA, PhD); psychology (PhD); quantitative methods in the social sciences (MA); religion (MA, PhD); Russia, Eurasia and East Europe: regional studies (MA); Russian translation (MA); Slavic cultures (MA); Slavic languages (MA, PhD); sociology (MA, PhD); South Asian studies (MA); statistics (MA, PhD); theatre (PhD); JD/PhD; MA/MS; MD/PhD; MPA/MA. Dual-degree programs require admission to both Graduate School of Arts and Sciences and another Columbia school. Part-time and evening/weekend programs available. Terminal master's awarded for partial completion of doctoral program. *Degree requirements:* For master's, thesis (for some programs); for doctorate, comprehensive exam, thesis/dissertation. *Entrance requirements:* For master's and doctorate, GRE General Test, GRE Subject Test (for some programs). Electronic applications accepted. *Faculty research:* Humanities, natural sciences, social sciences.

Concordia University, School of Graduate Studies, Faculty of Arts and Science, Department of Religion, Program in Judaic Studies, Montréal, QC H3G 1M8, Canada. Offers MA. *Degree requirements:* For master's, one foreign language, comprehensive exam, thesis optional. *Entrance requirements:* For master's, Hebrew exam, honors degree in Judaic studies or equivalent. Additional exam requirements/recommendations for international students: Required—TOEFL. *Faculty research:* Jewish religious reflections and modern philosophy of religion, Judaism and modernity, Judaism in late antiquity.

Cornell University, Graduate School, Graduate Fields of Arts and Sciences, Field of Near Eastern Studies, Ithaca, NY 14853-0001. Offers ancient Near Eastern studies (MA, PhD); Arabic and Islamic studies (MA, PhD); biblical studies (MA, PhD); Hebrew and Judaic studies (MA, PhD). Terminal master's awarded for partial completion of doctoral program. *Degree requirements:* For master's, one foreign language, thesis; for doctorate, 2 foreign languages, comprehensive exam, thesis/dissertation. *Entrance requirements:* For master's and doctorate, GRE General Test, 2 years of 1 Near Eastern language, 3 letters of recommendation, writing sample. Additional exam requirements/recommendations for international students: Required—TOEFL (minimum score 550 paper-based; 77 iBT). Electronic applications accepted. *Faculty research:* Ancient Near East (including archeology), Hebrew and Judaic studies (including Bible), early Christianity, Arabic and Islamic studies, modern Middle East.

The Criswell College, Graduate School of the Bible, Dallas, TX 75246-1537. Offers biblical studies (M Div); Christian leadership (MA); counseling (MA); Jewish studies (MA); ministry (MA); theological and biblical studies (MA). Part-time programs available. *Degree requirements:* For master's, 2 foreign languages, thesis optional. *Entrance requirements:* For master's, GRE General Test, minimum GPA of 2.5. Electronic applications accepted. *Faculty research:* Emphasis on biblical languages (Hebrew and Greek), expository preaching and evangelism in the local church.

Dallas Theological Seminary, Graduate Programs, Dallas, TX 75204-6499. Offers adult education (Th M); apologetics (Th M); Bible backgrounds (Th M); Bible translation (Th M); Biblical and theological studies (Certificate); biblical counseling (MA); biblical exegesis and linguistics (MA); biblical exposition (PhD); biblical studies (MA); Biblical theology (Th M); children's education (Th M); Christian education (MA, D Min); Christian leadership (MA); cross-cultural ministries (MA); educational administration (Th M); educational leadership (Th M); evangelism and discipleship (Th M); exposition of Biblical books (Th M); family life education (Th M); general studies (Th M); Hebrew and cognate studies (Th M); hermeneutics (Th M); historical theology (Th M); homiletics (Th M); intercultural ministries (Th M); Jesus studies (Th M); leadership studies (Th M); media and communication (MA); media arts (Th M); ministry (D Min); ministry with women (Th M); New Testament studies (Th M, PhD); Old Testament studies (Th M, PhD); parachurch ministries (Th M); pastoral care and counseling (Th M); pastoral theology and practice (Th M); philosophy (Th M); sacred theology (STM); spiritual formation (Th M); systematic theology (Th M); teaching in Christian institutions (Th M); theological studies (PhD); urban ministries (Th M); worship studies (Th M); youth education (Th M). *Accreditation:* ATS (one or more programs are accredited). Part-time programs available. Postbaccalaureate distance learning degree programs offered (no on-campus study). *Degree requirements:* For master's, variable foreign language requirement, thesis (for some programs); for doctorate, 2 foreign languages, thesis/dissertation. *Entrance requirements:* For master's, GRE or MAT (if minimum undergraduate cumulative GPA is below 2.5 or undergraduate degree is unaccredited). Additional exam requirements/recommendations for international students: Required—TOEFL (minimum score 575 paper-based; 85 iBT), TWE. Electronic applications accepted.

Graduate Theological Union, Graduate Programs, Berkeley, CA 94709-1212. Offers art and religion (MA, PhD, Th D); biblical languages (MA); biblical studies (MA); Biblical studies (PhD, Th D); Buddhist studies (MA); Christian spirituality (MA, PhD, Th D); cultural and historical studies of religions (MA, PhD, Th D); ethics and social theory (PhD, Th D); history (MA, PhD, Th D); homiletics (MA, PhD, Th D); interdisciplinary studies (PhD, Th D); Jewish studies (MA, PhD, Th D, Certificate); liturgical studies (MA, PhD, Th D); Near Eastern religions (PhD, Th D); Orthodox Christian studies (MA); religion and psychology (MA, PhD, Th D); religion and society/ethics and social theory (MA); systematic and philosophical theology (MA, PhD, Th D). PhD programs in Jewish studies and Near Eastern religions offered jointly with University of California, Berkeley. *Accreditation:* ATS. Terminal master's awarded for partial completion of doctoral program. *Degree requirements:* For master's, one foreign language, thesis; for doctorate, one foreign language, comprehensive exam, thesis/dissertation. *Entrance requirements:* For master's, GRE General Test; for doctorate, GRE General Test, MA or M Div. Additional exam requirements/recommendations for international students: Required—TOEFL. Electronic applications accepted.

Gratz College, Graduate Programs, Program in Jewish-Christian Studies, Melrose Park, PA 19027. Offers Graduate Certificate. Postbaccalaureate distance learning degree programs offered (no on-campus study).

Gratz College, Graduate Programs, Program in Jewish Studies, Melrose Park, PA 19027. Offers MA, Certificate. Part-time programs available. Postbaccalaureate distance learning degree programs offered. *Degree requirements:* For master's, one foreign language, comprehensive exam, thesis optional.

Harvard University, Graduate School of Arts and Sciences, Department of Near Eastern Languages and Civilizations, Cambridge, MA 02138. Offers Akkadian and Sumerian (AM, PhD); Arabic (AM, PhD); Armenian (AM, PhD); biblical history (AM, PhD); Hebrew (AM, PhD); Indo-Muslim culture (AM, PhD); Iranian (AM, PhD); Jewish history and literature (AM, PhD); Persian (AM, PhD); Semitic philology (AM, PhD); Syro-Palestinian archaeology (AM, PhD); Turkish (AM, PhD). *Degree requirements:* For doctorate, variable foreign language requirement, thesis/dissertation, general exams. *Entrance requirements:* For master's, GRE General Test; for doctorate, GRE General Test, proficiency in a Near Eastern language. Additional exam requirements/recommendations for international students: Required—TOEFL.

Hebrew College, Cantor Educator Program, Newton Centre, MA 02459. Offers MJ Ed. *Entrance requirements:* For master's, GRE, interview. Additional exam requirements/recommendations for international students: Required—TOEFL.

Hebrew College, Program in Jewish Studies, Newton Centre, MA 02459. Offers Jewish liturgical music (Certificate); Jewish music education (Certificate); Jewish studies (MA). Part-time and evening/weekend programs available. Postbaccalaureate distance learning degree programs offered (minimal on-campus study). *Degree requirements:* For master's, one foreign language. *Entrance requirements:* For master's, GRE, interview. Additional exam requirements/recommendations for international students: Required—TOEFL.

Hebrew Union College–Jewish Institute of Religion, School of Graduate Studies, Program in Judaic Studies, New York, NY 10012-1186. Offers MAJS. Part-time programs available. *Degree requirements:* For master's, one foreign language, thesis. *Entrance requirements:* For master's, GRE, minimum 2 years of college-level Hebrew. *Faculty research:* Philosophy and theology, Bible, Hebrew, history and Rabbinics.

Indiana University Bloomington, University Graduate School, College of Arts and Sciences, Borns Jewish Studies Program, Bloomington, IN 47405. Offers MA. *Faculty:* 23 full-time (8 women). *Students:* 2 full-time (1 woman); includes 1 minority (Hispanic/Latino). Average age 24. 11 applicants, 18% accepted, 2 enrolled. In 2014, 2 master's awarded. *Application deadline:* For fall admission, 1/15 for domestic students, 12/1 for international students; for winter admission, 1/15 for domestic students. Application fee: $55 ($65 for international students). Electronic applications accepted. *Financial support:* Fellowships with full and partial tuition reimbursements available. *Faculty research:* Jewish studies, religious studies, history, Holocaust study. *Unit head:* Mark Roseman, Director, 812-855-0453, Fax: 812-855-4314, E-mail: marrosem@indiana.edu. *Application contact:* Tracy Richardson, Administrative Secretary, 812-855-0453, Fax: 812-855-4314, E-mail: tracrich@indiana.edu.
Website: http://www.indiana.edu/~jsp/index.shtml

The Jewish Theological Seminary, The Graduate School, New York, NY 10027-4649. Offers ancient Judaism (MA, DHL, PhD); Bible and ancient Semitic languages (MA, DHL, PhD); interdepartmental studies (MA); Jewish art and visual culture (MA); Jewish gender and women's studies (MA); Jewish history (MA, DHL, PhD); Jewish literature (MA, DHL, PhD); Jewish philosophy (DHL); Jewish thought (MA, PhD); liturgy (MA, DHL, PhD); medieval Jewish studies (MA, DHL, PhD); Midrash (DHL); Midrash and scriptural interpretation (MA, PhD); modern Jewish studies (MA, DHL, PhD); Talmud and rabbinics (MA, DHL, PhD); MA/MSW. MA/MSW offered jointly with Columbia University. *Accreditation:* ACIPE. Part-time programs available. Terminal master's awarded for partial completion of doctoral program. *Degree requirements:* For master's, one foreign language, comprehensive exam (for some programs), thesis (for some programs); for doctorate, 3 foreign languages, comprehensive exam (for some programs), thesis/dissertation. *Entrance requirements:* For master's, GRE or MAT, 3 letters of recommendation, writing sample; for doctorate, GRE or MAT, 3 letters of recommendation, writing research sample. Additional exam requirements/recommendations for international students: Required—TOEFL.

The Jewish Theological Seminary, William Davidson Graduate School of Jewish Education, New York, NY 10027-4649. Offers MA, Ed D. Offered in conjunction with Rabbinical School; H. L. Miller Cantorial School and College of Jewish Music; Teacher's College, Columbia University; and Union Theological Seminary. Part-time programs available. Postbaccalaureate distance learning degree programs offered (minimal on-campus study). *Degree requirements:* For master's, one foreign language, thesis optional; for doctorate, one foreign language, comprehensive exam, thesis/dissertation. *Entrance requirements:* For master's, GRE or MAT, 3 letters of recommendation; for doctorate, GRE or MAT, writing sample, 3 letters of recommendation. Additional exam requirements/recommendations for international students: Recommended—TOEFL.

McGill University, Faculty of Graduate and Postdoctoral Studies, Faculty of Arts, Department of Jewish Studies, Montréal, QC H3A 2T5, Canada. Offers MA.

New York University, Graduate School of Arts and Science, Program in Museum Studies, New York, NY 10012-1019. Offers museum studies (MA, Advanced Certificate), including Africana studies (MA), Hebrew and Judaic studies (MA), Latin American and Caribbean studies (MA), Near Eastern studies (MA). Part-time and evening/weekend programs available. *Students:* 45 full-time (39 women), 23 part-time (19 women); includes 15 minority (2 American Indian or Alaska Native, non-Hispanic/Latino; 3 Asian, non-Hispanic/Latino; 6 Hispanic/Latino; 4 Two or more races, non-Hispanic/Latino), 19 international. Average age 26. 123 applicants, 81% accepted, 29 enrolled. In 2014, 35 master's, 1 other advanced degree awarded. *Entrance requirements:* For master's, GRE General Test; for Advanced Certificate, master's degree or PhD. Additional exam requirements/recommendations for international students: Required—TOEFL. *Application deadline:* For fall admission, 2/15 for domestic and international students; for spring admission, 11/1 for domestic and international students. Application fee: $100. *Financial support:* Application deadline: 2/15. *Faculty research:* Modern and contemporary art, history of museums and exhibitions, conservation of cultural materials, museum anthropology, ethnography. *Unit head:* Bruce Altshuler, Director, 212-998-8080, Fax: 212-995-4185, E-mail: museum.studies@nyu.edu. *Application contact:* Tatiana Kamorina, Department Administrator, 212-998-8080, Fax: 212-995-4185, E-mail: museum.studies@nyu.edu.
Website: http://www.nyu.edu/fas/program/museumstudies/

New York University, Graduate School of Arts and Science, Skirball Department of Hebrew and Judaic Studies, New York, NY 10012-1019. Offers Hebrew and Judaic studies (MA, PhD); Hebrew and Judaic studies/museum studies (MA). Part-time programs available. *Students:* 59 full-time (32 women), 12 part-time (8 women); includes 2 minority (1 Hispanic/Latino; 1 Two or more races, non-Hispanic/Latino), 18 international. Average age 30. 75 applicants, 51% accepted, 16 enrolled. In 2014, 18 master's, 13 doctorates awarded. Terminal master's awarded for partial completion of doctoral program. *Degree requirements:* For master's, 2 foreign languages, comprehensive exam, thesis optional; for doctorate, 4 foreign languages, comprehensive exam, thesis/dissertation. *Entrance requirements:* For master's and doctorate, GRE General Test. Additional exam requirements/recommendations for international students: Required—TOEFL. *Application deadline:* For fall admission, 1/4 priority date for domestic students, 1/4 for international students. Application fee: $100. *Financial support:* Fellowships with tuition reimbursements, teaching assistantships with tuition reimbursements, Federal Work-Study, and institutionally sponsored loans available. Financial award application deadline: 1/4; financial award applicants required to submit FAFSA. *Faculty research:* Post-Biblical and Talmudic literature and history, mysticism, Bible and ancient Near East, medieval and modern Jewish history, medieval and modern Jewish philosophy. *Unit head:* David Engel, Chair, 212-998-8980, Fax: 212-995-4178, E-mail: gsas.hebrewjudaic@nyu.edu. *Application contact:* Jeffrey

Rubenstein, Director of Graduate Studies, 212-998-8980, Fax: 212-995-4178, E-mail: gsas.hebrewjudaic@nyu.edu.
Website: http://www.nyu.edu/gsas/dept/hebrew/

New York University, Steinhardt School of Culture, Education, and Human Development, Department of Humanities and Social Sciences in the Professions, Program in Education and Jewish Studies, New York, NY 10012-1019. Offers MA, PhD, MA/MA. Part-time programs available. *Faculty:* 1 full-time (0 women). *Students:* 16 full-time (8 women), 12 part-time (8 women); includes 3 minority (all Hispanic/Latino), 1 international. Average age 29. 14 applicants, 79% accepted, 7 enrolled. In 2014, 5 master's, 2 doctorates awarded. *Degree requirements:* For doctorate, thesis/dissertation. *Entrance requirements:* For doctorate, GRE General Test, interview. Additional exam requirements/recommendations for international students: Required—TOEFL (minimum score 100 iBT). *Application deadline:* For fall admission, 12/1 priority date for domestic and international students. Applications are processed on a rolling basis. Application fee: $75. Electronic applications accepted. *Financial support:* Fellowships with full and partial tuition reimbursements, teaching assistantships with partial tuition reimbursements, career-related internships or fieldwork, Federal Work-Study, institutionally sponsored loans, scholarships/grants, tuition waivers (partial), and unspecified assistantships available. Support available to part-time students. Financial award application deadline: 2/1; financial award applicants required to submit FAFSA. *Faculty research:* Jewish education, educational history, Judaic studies. *Unit head:* Prof. Harold Wechsler, Director, 212-992-9423, Fax: 212-995-4178, E-mail: hw29@nyu.edu. *Application contact:* 212-998-5030, Fax: 212-995-4328, E-mail: steinhardt.gradadmissions@nyu.edu.
Website: http://steinhardt.nyu.edu/humsocsci/jewish

Reconstructionist Rabbinical College, Graduate Programs, Wyncote, PA 19095-1898. Offers Jewish studies (MAJS); rabbinics (MAHL, DHL); women's studies (Certificate). Certificate offered jointly with Temple University. Part-time programs available. *Degree requirements:* For master's, one foreign language, thesis (MAJS), completion of rabbinical program (MAHL); for doctorate, one foreign language. *Entrance requirements:* For master's, GRE General Test; placement examinations in Hebrew and Judaism (MAHL); for doctorate, GRE General Test, placement examinations in Hebrew and Judaism. *Faculty research:* Bible, Hebrew Semitic texts, contemporary Judaism.

Rice University, Graduate Programs, School of Humanities, Department of Religious Studies, Houston, TX 77251-1892. Offers African religions (PhD); African-American religions (PhD); contemplative studies (PhD); ghosticism, esotericism, mysticism (PhD); Islam (PhD); Jewish thought and philosophy (PhD); modern Christianity in thought and popular culture (PhD); psychology of religion (PhD); the Bible and beyond (PhD). *Degree requirements:* For doctorate, 2 foreign languages, comprehensive exam, thesis/dissertation. *Entrance requirements:* For doctorate, GRE, letters of recommendation, writing sample. Additional exam requirements/recommendations for international students: Required—TOEFL (minimum score 600 paper-based; 90 iBT). Electronic applications accepted. *Faculty research:* Origins and historical development of Islam, history of Christianity, the study of comparative religion, African-American religion, religion and culture.

Rutgers, The State University of New Jersey, New Brunswick, Graduate School-New Brunswick, Department of Jewish Studies, New Brunswick, NJ 08901. Offers MA, Certificate. Part-time programs available.

Seton Hall University, College of Arts and Sciences, Department of Religion, South Orange, NJ 07079-2697. Offers Jewish-Christian Studies (MA). Part-time and evening/weekend programs available. *Faculty:* 4 full-time (0 women). *Students:* 9 full-time (5 women), 8 part-time (5 women); includes 6 minority (1 Asian, non-Hispanic/Latino; 2 Hispanic/Latino; 3 Native Hawaiian or other Pacific Islander, non-Hispanic/Latino), 1 international. Average age 45. 6 applicants, 100% accepted, 5 enrolled. In 2014, 1 master's awarded. *Degree requirements:* For master's, thesis optional. *Entrance requirements:* For master's, interview or suitable correspondence with department chair. Additional exam requirements/recommendations for international students: Required—TOEFL. *Application deadline:* For fall admission, 7/1 priority date for domestic and international students; for spring admission, 11/1 priority date for domestic and international students. Applications are processed on a rolling basis. Application fee: $75. Electronic applications accepted. *Financial support:* Fellowships, research assistantships, career-related internships or fieldwork, Federal Work-Study, scholarships/grants, tuition waivers (full and partial), and unspecified assistantships available. Support available to part-time students. Financial award application deadline: 8/31; financial award applicants required to submit FAFSA. *Faculty research:* Jewish-Christian issues, Biblical studies, Holocaust studies. *Unit head:* Prof. KC Choi, Chair, 973-761-9462, E-mail: kijoo.choi@shu.edu. *Application contact:* Fr. Lawrence Frizzell, Program Chair, 973-761-9751, Fax: 973-761-9596, E-mail: lawrence.frizzell@shu.edu.
Website: http://www.shu.edu/academics/artsci/religion/

Southern Evangelical Seminary, Graduate Programs, Matthews, NC 28105. Offers apologetics (MA, D Min, Certificate); Christian education (MA); church ministry (MA, Certificate); divinity (Certificate), including apologetics (M Div, Certificate); Islamic studies (MA, Certificate); Jewish studies (MA); philosophy (MA); philosophy of religion (PhD); religion (MA); theology (M Div), including apologetics (M Div, Certificate), Biblical studies; youth ministry (MA). Part-time and evening/weekend programs available. Postbaccalaureate distance learning degree programs offered. *Degree requirements:* For master's, thesis (for some programs); for doctorate, 2 foreign languages, comprehensive exam (for some programs), thesis/dissertation. *Entrance requirements:* Additional exam requirements/recommendations for international students: Required—TOEFL (minimum score 600 paper-based).

Spertus Institute for Jewish Learning and Leadership, Graduate Programs, Program in Jewish Studies, Chicago, IL 60605-1901. Offers MAJPS, MAJS, MSJE, MSJS, DJS, DSJS. Part-time and evening/weekend programs available. Postbaccalaureate distance learning degree programs offered (minimal on-campus study). *Degree requirements:* For master's, one foreign language, thesis (for some programs); for doctorate, one foreign language, thesis/dissertation. *Entrance requirements:* For master's, interview, BAJS (MAJS); for doctorate, MAJS.

Telshe Yeshiva–Chicago, Graduate Program, Chicago, IL 60625-5598. Offers Second Talmudic Degree. *Accreditation:* AARTS.

Touro College, Graduate School of Jewish Studies, New York, NY 10010. Offers MA. Part-time programs available. *Faculty:* 4 full-time, 20 part-time/adjunct. *Students:* 10 full-time (3 women), 24 part-time (13 women), 1 international. *Degree requirements:* For master's, one foreign language, thesis. *Entrance requirements:* For master's, previous course work in Jewish studies, proficiency in Hebrew. Application fee: $40. *Financial support:* Tuition waivers (full and partial) available. Support available to part-time students. *Faculty research:* Medieval and modern Jewish history, Jewish philosophy, Holocaust studies, Jewish education. *Unit head:* Dr. Michael Shmidman, Dean, 212-213-2230.

Towson University, Baltimore Hebrew Institute, Towson, MD 21252-0001. Offers Jewish communal service (MAJCS, Postbaccalaureate Certificate); Jewish education (MAJE, Postbaccalaureate Certificate); Jewish studies (MAJS). *Students:* 6 full-time (3 women), 22 part-time (13 women); includes 3 minority (2 Black or African American, non-Hispanic/Latino; 1 Hispanic/Latino). *Entrance requirements:* For master's, bachelor's degree, minimum GPA of 3.0, letters of recommendation, statement of intent, sample of work, interview, resume; for Postbaccalaureate Certificate, bachelor's degree, minimum GPA of 3.0, statement of intent, sample of work, interview, 2 letters of recommendation, resume. Additional exam requirements/recommendations for international students: Required—TOEFL. *Application deadline:* Applications are processed on a rolling basis. Application fee: $45. Electronic applications accepted. *Unit head:* Dr. Hana Bor, Director, 410-704-4719, E-mail: hbor@towson.edu. *Application contact:* Alicia Arkell-Kleis, Information Contact, 410-704-6004, E-mail: grads@towson.edu.
Website: http://www.towson.edu/bhi/

University of California, Berkeley, Graduate Division, College of Letters and Science, Program in Jewish Studies, Berkeley, CA 94720-1500. Offers PhD. Program held jointly with Graduate Theological Union. *Entrance requirements:* For doctorate, GRE General Test, 3 letters of recommendation.

University of California, San Diego, Graduate Division, Department of History, La Jolla, CA 92093. Offers history (MA, PhD); Judaic studies (MA). *Students:* 91 full-time (36 women), 4 part-time (all women); includes 26 minority (3 Black or African American, non-Hispanic/Latino; 2 American Indian or Alaska Native, non-Hispanic/Latino; 2 Asian, non-Hispanic/Latino; 19 Hispanic/Latino), 18 international. 178 applicants, 17% accepted, 19 enrolled. In 2014, 5 master's, 9 doctorates awarded. *Degree requirements:* For master's, one foreign language, comprehensive exam; for doctorate, one foreign language, thesis/dissertation. *Entrance requirements:* For master's and doctorate, GRE General Test, minimum GPA of 3.0. Additional exam requirements/recommendations for international students: Required—TOEFL (minimum score 550 paper-based), IELTS. *Application deadline:* For fall admission, 1/5 for domestic students. Application fee: $90 ($110 for international students). Electronic applications accepted. *Expenses:* Tuition, state resident: full-time $11,220; part-time $5610 per quarter. Tuition, nonresident: full-time $26,322; part-time $13,161 per quarter. *Required fees:* $570 per quarter. Tuition and fees vary according to program. *Financial support:* Fellowships, research assistantships, teaching assistantships, career-related internships or fieldwork, scholarships/grants, and readerships available. Financial award applicants required to submit FAFSA. *Faculty research:* Ancient history, east Asian history, history of science, Judaic studies, Chinese studies. *Unit head:* David Gutierrez, Chair, 858-534-1996, E-mail: dggutierrez@ucsd.edu. *Application contact:* Amber Rieder, Graduate Coordinator, 858-822-0664, E-mail: arieder@ucsd.edu.
Website: http://history.ucsd.edu

University of Connecticut, Graduate School, College of Liberal Arts and Sciences, Field of International Studies, Program in Judaic Studies, Storrs, CT 06269. Offers MA. *Entrance requirements:* Additional exam requirements/recommendations for international students: Required—TOEFL (minimum score 550 paper-based). Electronic applications accepted.

University of Florida, Graduate School, College of Liberal Arts and Sciences, Department of History, Gainesville, FL 32611. Offers historic preservation (MA, PhD); history (MA, PhD); Jewish studies (MA); women's and gender studies (PhD); JD/MA; JD/PhD. Part-time programs available. *Faculty:* 26 full-time (9 women), 9 part-time/adjunct (5 women). *Students:* 59 full-time (21 women), 14 part-time (6 women); includes 7 minority (4 Black or African American, non-Hispanic/Latino; 3 Hispanic/Latino), 6 international. 112 applicants, 21% accepted, 11 enrolled. In 2014, 6 master's, 14 doctorates awarded. Terminal master's awarded for partial completion of doctoral program. *Degree requirements:* For master's, variable foreign language requirement, thesis optional, 30 credit hours; for doctorate, variable foreign language requirement, comprehensive exam, thesis/dissertation, 90 credit hours. *Entrance requirements:* For master's and doctorate, GRE General Test, minimum GPA of 3.0. Additional exam requirements/recommendations for international students: Required—TOEFL (minimum score 550 paper-based; 80 iBT), IELTS (minimum score 6). *Application deadline:* For fall admission, 1/1 priority date for domestic students, 1/1 for international students. Applications are processed on a rolling basis. Application fee: $30. Electronic applications accepted. *Financial support:* In 2014–15, 15 fellowships, 9 research assistantships, 44 teaching assistantships were awarded; career-related internships or fieldwork and unspecified assistantships also available. Financial award application deadline: 1/15; financial award applicants required to submit FAFSA. *Faculty research:* Latin American and Caribbean history, nineteenth century U.S. history, medieval European history, African history and Atlantic world history. *Unit head:* Ida L. Altman, PhD, Professor and Chair, 352-392-6927, Fax: 352-392-6927, E-mail: ialtman@ufl.edu. *Application contact:* Elizabeth Dale, PhD, Graduate Coordinator, 352-273-3387, Fax: 352-392-6927, E-mail: edale@ufl.edu.
Website: http://www.history.ufl.edu/

University of Florida, Graduate School, College of Liberal Arts and Sciences, Department of Religion, Gainesville, FL 32611-7410. Offers Jewish studies (MA); religion (MA, PhD); tropical conservation and development (MA, PhD); women's and gender studies (MA, PhD). Part-time programs available. *Faculty:* 10 full-time (3 women), 15 part-time/adjunct (7 women). *Students:* 21 full-time (13 women), 2 part-time (1 woman); includes 4 minority (3 Asian, non-Hispanic/Latino; 1 Hispanic/Latino), 3 international. Average age 33. 29 applicants, 48% accepted, 3 enrolled. In 2014, 3 master's, 2 doctorates awarded. *Degree requirements:* For master's, one foreign language, thesis optional; for doctorate, one foreign language, comprehensive exam, thesis/dissertation. *Entrance requirements:* For master's, GRE General Test, minimum GPA of 3.0. Additional exam requirements/recommendations for international students: Required—TOEFL (minimum score 550 paper-based; 80 iBT), IELTS (minimum score 6). *Application deadline:* For fall admission, 6/1 priority date for domestic students. Applications are processed on a rolling basis. Electronic applications accepted. *Financial support:* In 2014–15, 6 fellowships, 3 research assistantships, 18 teaching assistantships were awarded; Federal Work-Study and unspecified assistantships also available. Financial award applicants required to submit FAFSA. *Faculty research:* Religion in America, Christian thought, Islam, religions of India, comparative religion. *Unit head:* Manuel A. Vasquez, PhD, Professor and Chair, 352-392-1625, Fax: 352-392-7395, E-mail: manuelv@ufl.edu. *Application contact:* Terje Ostebo, PhD, Director of Graduate Studies, 352-392-2175, Fax: 352-392-7395, E-mail: manuelv@ufl.edu.
Website: http://religion.ufl.edu/

University of Maryland, College Park, Academic Affairs, College of Arts and Humanities, Meyerhoff Center for Jewish Studies, College Park, MD 20742. Offers MA. *Degree requirements:* For master's, thesis or 2 major research papers. *Entrance requirements:* For master's, GRE General Test, 3 letters of recommendation, writing sample. Additional exam requirements/recommendations for international students: Required—TOEFL.

University of Michigan, Horace H. Rackham School of Graduate Studies, College of Literature, Science, and the Arts, Department of Near Eastern Studies, Ann Arbor, MI 49286. Offers ancient Near Eastern studies (AM, PhD); Arabic for professional purposes (AM); Arabic language and literature (AM, PhD); Armenian studies (AM, PhD); Christianity in late antiquity (AM, PhD); Egyptology (AM, PhD); Hebrew Bible and ancient Israel (AM, PhD); Hebrew literature (AM, PhD); Islamic studies (AM, PhD); Jewish cultural studies (AM, PhD); Jewish mysticism (AM, PhD); Persian and Iranian

studies (AM, PhD); Rabbinic literature (AM, PhD); Second Temple Judaism (AM, PhD); teaching of Arabic as a foreign language (AM); Turkish studies (AM, PhD). *Faculty:* 22 full-time (5 women), 1 (woman) part-time/adjunct. *Students:* 37 full-time (16 women); includes 2 minority (both Asian, non-Hispanic/Lâtino), 11 international. Average age 32. 72 applicants, 19% accepted, 6 enrolled. In 2014, 7 master's, 3 doctorates awarded. Terminal master's awarded for partial completion of doctoral program. *Degree requirements:* For master's, 2 foreign languages; for doctorate, 4 foreign languages, comprehensive exam, thesis/dissertation, preliminary exams, oral defense of dissertation. *Entrance requirements:* Additional exam requirements/recommendations for international students: Required—TOEFL (minimum score 560 paper-based; 84 iBT). *Application deadline:* For fall admission, 12/15 for domestic and international students. Application fee: $65 ($75 for international students). Electronic applications accepted. *Financial support:* In 2014–15, 22 students received support. Fellowships with full tuition reimbursements available, teaching assistantships with full tuition reimbursements available, scholarships/grants, health care benefits, unspecified assistantships, and spring/summer stipends available. Financial award application deadline: 12/15. *Faculty research:* Middle and Near Eastern literatures, languages, cultures from ancient times to the present. *Unit head:* Prof. Gottfried Hagen, Chair, 734-764-0314, E-mail: ghagen@umich.edu. *Application contact:* Student Services, 734-764-0315, E-mail: nes-gradservices@umich.edu.
Website: http://www.umich.edu/~neareast/

University of Michigan, Horace H. Rackham School of Graduate Studies, College of Literature, Science, and the Arts, Jean and Samuel Frankel Center for Judaic Studies, Ann Arbor, MI 48178. Offers MA, Graduate Certificate. Part-time programs available. *Faculty:* 30 full-time (12 women). *Students:* 12 full-time (5 women). Average age 28. 9 applicants, 100% accepted, 5 enrolled. In 2014, 2 master's, 1 other advanced degree awarded. *Degree requirements:* For master's, thesis, fourth-term proficiency in either Hebrew or Yiddish; for Graduate Certificate, capstone course (including public lecture), reading knowledge of 1 Jewish language. *Entrance requirements:* For master's, GRE General Test; for Graduate Certificate, admission to a U-M doctoral program. Additional exam requirements/recommendations for international students: Required—TOEFL (minimum score 560 paper-based). *Application deadline:* For fall admission, 1/10 for domestic and international students; for winter admission, 9/1 for domestic and international students. Application fee: $75 ($90 for international students). Electronic applications accepted. *Financial support:* In 2014–15, 12 fellowships (averaging $2,700 per year) were awarded; summer research fellowships also available. *Faculty research:* American Jewish experience; classical Judaism/religious studies; global and transnational studies; Jewish literature, language and translation; social science; visual studies. *Unit head:* Prof. Deborah Dash Moore, Director, 734-763-9047, Fax: 734-936-2186, E-mail: ddmoore@umich.edu. *Application contact:* Brittin Alissa Jones, Student/Fellow Coordinator, 734-615-6097, Fax: 734-936-2186, E-mail: brittinp@umich.edu.
Website: http://www.lsa.umich.edu/judaic

University of St. Michael's College, Faculty of Theology, Toronto, ON M5S 1J4, Canada. Offers Catholic leadership (MA); eastern Christian studies (Diploma); religious education (Diploma); theological studies (Diploma); theology (M Div, MA, MRE, MTS, D Min, PhD, Th D); theology and Jewish studies (MA). Th D offered jointly with University of Toronto. *Accreditation:* ATS (one or more programs are accredited). Part-time programs available. *Degree requirements:* For master's, thesis (for some programs), 1 foreign language (MA), 2 foreign languages (Th M); for doctorate, 3 foreign languages, comprehensive exam, thesis/dissertation; for other advanced degree, thesis optional. *Entrance requirements:* For master's, M Div or BA, course work in an ancient or modern language, minimum GPA of 3.3; for doctorate, MA in theology, Th M, or M Div with thesis, minimum GPA of 3.7; for other advanced degree, minimum GPA of 2.7. Additional exam requirements/recommendations for international students: Required—TOEFL (minimum score 600 paper-based). Electronic applications accepted. *Expenses:* Contact institution. *Faculty research:* Patristics, eastern Christianity, ecology and theology, ecumenism, Jewish Christian studies.

University of Wisconsin–Madison, Graduate School, College of Letters and Science, Department of Hebrew and Semitic Studies, Madison, WI 53706-1380. Offers MA, PhD. Terminal master's awarded for partial completion of doctoral program. *Degree requirements:* For master's, 2 foreign languages; for doctorate, thesis/dissertation. *Entrance requirements:* For master's and doctorate, GRE. Electronic applications accepted. *Expenses:* Tuition, state resident: full-time $10,723; part-time $745 per credit. Tuition, nonresident: full-time $24,054; part-time $1578 per credit. *Required fees:* $374 per semester. Tuition and fees vary according to course load, program and reciprocity agreements. *Faculty research:* Biblical language and literature, Northwest Semitic languages.

University of Wisconsin–Milwaukee, Graduate School, College of Letters and Sciences, Interdepartmental Program in Foreign Language and Literature, Milwaukee, WI 53201-0413. Offers classics and Hebrew studies (MAFLL); comparative literature (MAFLL); French and Italian (MAFLL); German (MAFLL); Slavic studies (MAFLL); translation (Certificate). Part-time programs available. *Degree requirements:* For master's, 2 foreign languages, thesis or alternative. *Entrance requirements:* Additional exam requirements/recommendations for international students: Required—TOEFL (minimum score 550 paper-based; 79 iBT), IELTS (minimum score 6.5). Electronic applications accepted.

Washington University in St. Louis, Graduate School of Arts and Sciences, Department of Jewish, Islamic, and Near Eastern Languages and Cultures, St. Louis, MO 63130-4899. Offers Islamic and Near Eastern studies (MA); Jewish studies (MA). *Degree requirements:* For master's, one foreign language, thesis (for some programs). *Entrance requirements:* For master's, GRE General Test. Additional exam requirements/recommendations for international students: Required—TOEFL. Electronic applications accepted. *Faculty research:* Islamic and Near Eastern studies (Islamic history, Arabic language and literature, modern Middle East history), Jewish studies (Hebrew Bible, Rabbinic literature, Jewish history, modern Hebrew literature).

Yeshiva University, Bernard Revel Graduate School of Jewish Studies, New York, NY 10033-3201. Offers MA, PhD. Part-time programs available. Terminal master's awarded for partial completion of doctoral program. *Degree requirements:* For master's, comprehensive exam; for doctorate, 2 foreign languages, comprehensive exam, thesis/dissertation. *Entrance requirements:* For master's and doctorate, GRE General Test (recommended), reading knowledge of Hebrew, minimum GPA of 3.0. *Faculty research:* Bible, Jewish history, Jewish philosophy and mysticism, Talmud, Semitic languages.

Latin American Studies

Boricua College, Program in Latin American and Caribbean Studies, New York, NY 10032-1560. Offers MA. Program offered in Brooklyn and Manhattan. Evening/weekend programs available. *Degree requirements:* For master's, thesis. *Entrance requirements:* For master's, interview by the faculty.

Boston University, Graduate School of Arts and Sciences, Frederick S. Pardee School of Global Studies, Boston, MA 02215. Offers international affairs (MA); international relations and environmental policy (MA); international relations and international communication (MA); international relations and religion (MA); international relations, mid-career (MA); Latin American studies (MA); MA/JD; MBA/MA. *Faculty:* 33 full-time (8 women), 10 part-time/adjunct (4 women). *Students:* 78 full-time (50 women), 15 part-time (11 women); includes 12 minority (3 Black or African American, non-Hispanic/Latino; 5 Asian, non-Hispanic/Latino; 3 Hispanic/Latino; 1 Two or more races, non-Hispanic/Latino), 26 international. Average age 25. 338 applicants, 68% accepted, 36 enrolled. In 2014, 51 master's awarded. *Degree requirements:* For master's, one foreign language, capstone. *Entrance requirements:* For master's, GRE General Test, 3 letters of recommendation, transcript of all prior college coursework, statement of purpose. Additional exam requirements/recommendations for international students: Required—TOEFL (minimum score 600 paper-based; 94 iBT). *Application deadline:* For fall admission, 4/15 for domestic and international students; for spring admission, 10/15 for domestic and international students. Applications are processed on a rolling basis. Application fee: $80. Electronic applications accepted. *Expenses: Tuition:* Full-time $45,686; part-time $1428 per credit hour. *Required fees:* $660; $60 per semester. Tuition and fees vary according to program. *Financial support:* In 2014–15, 21 students received support. Federal Work-Study, scholarships/grants, and unspecified assistantships available. Financial award application deadline: 1/3; financial award applicants required to submit FAFSA. *Faculty research:* International relations, area studies, political economy, global development policy, global climate. *Unit head:* Adil Najam, Dean, 617-353-9279, Fax: 617-353-9290, E-mail: psgs@bu.edu. *Application contact:* Michael Williams, Graduate Program Administrator, 617-353-9349, Fax: 617-353-9290, E-mail: psgsgrad@bu.edu.
Website: http://www.bu.edu/PardeeSchool

Boston University, Graduate School of Arts and Sciences, Program in Latin American Studies, Boston, MA 02215. Offers MA. *Students:* 14 applicants, 71% accepted, 1 enrolled. In 2014, 2 master's awarded. *Degree requirements:* For master's, one foreign language, paper and oral defense. *Entrance requirements:* For master's, GRE General Test, 3 letters of recommendation, official transcripts of all prior college coursework, statement of purpose. Additional exam requirements/recommendations for international students: Required—TOEFL (minimum score 600 paper-based; 94 iBT). *Application deadline:* For fall admission, 4/15 for domestic students. Application fee: $80. Electronic applications accepted. *Expenses: Tuition:* Full-time $45,686; part-time $1428 per credit hour. *Required fees:* $660; $60 per semester. Tuition and fees vary according to program. *Financial support:* Federal Work-Study and scholarships/grants available. Financial award application deadline: 1/5. *Unit head:* James Iffland, Director, 617-353-6216, Fax: 617-353-9290, E-mail: iffland@bu.edu. *Application contact:* Michael Williams, Graduate Program Administrator, 617-353-9349, Fax: 617-353-9290, E-mail: mawillia@bu.edu. Website: http://www.bu.edu/ir/graduate/programs/latin-american-studies/

Brown University, Graduate School, Department of Portuguese and Brazilian Studies, Providence, RI 02912. Offers Brazilian studies (AM); English as a second language and cross-cultural studies (AM); Portuguese and Brazilian studies (AM, PhD); Portuguese bilingual education and cross-cultural studies (AM). *Degree requirements:* For doctorate, thesis/dissertation.

California State University, Long Beach, Graduate Studies, College of Liberal Arts, Department of History, Long Beach, CA 90840. Offers Africa and the Middle East (MA); ancient/medieval Europe (MA); Asia (MA); Latin America (MA); modern Europe (MA); United States (MA); world history (MA). Part-time and evening/weekend programs available. *Degree requirements:* For master's, one foreign language, comprehensive exam or thesis. Electronic applications accepted. *Faculty research:* All periods of European and American history, recent Asian and African history.

California State University, Los Angeles, Graduate Studies, College of Natural and Social Sciences, Department of Latin American Studies, Los Angeles, CA 90032-8530. Offers MA. Part-time and evening/weekend programs available. *Degree requirements:* For master's, one foreign language, comprehensive exam, thesis. *Entrance requirements:* For master's, minimum GPA of 2.5. Additional exam requirements/recommendations for international students: Required—TOEFL (minimum score 500 paper-based). Electronic applications accepted. *Expenses:* Tuition, state resident: full-time $6738; part-time $3609 per year. Tuition, nonresident: full-time $15,666; part-time $8073 per year. Tuition and fees vary according to course load, degree level and program. *Faculty research:* Central America, Cuba, Third World development, labor history, redemocratization.

Centro de Estudios Avanzados de Puerto Rico y el Caribe, Graduate Program in Puerto Rican and Caribbean Studies, Old San Juan, PR 00902-3970. Offers Puerto Rican and Caribbean history (MA, PhD); Puerto Rican and Caribbean literature (MA, PhD); Puerto Rican studies (MA). Part-time and evening/weekend programs available. *Degree requirements:* For master's, comprehensive exam, thesis; for doctorate, 2 foreign languages, comprehensive exam, thesis/dissertation. *Entrance requirements:* For master's and doctorate, interview. *Faculty research:* Literature, history, art, folklore, and culture of Puerto Rico and Caribbean countries.

Cleveland State University, College of Graduate Studies, College of Liberal Arts and Social Sciences, Department of Modern Languages, Cleveland, OH 44115. Offers French (M Ed); Spanish (M Ed, MA), including language and linguistics (MA), Latin American studies (MA), peninsular studies (MA), Spanish (MA). Part-time and evening/weekend programs available. *Faculty:* 6 full-time (3 women), 1 (woman) part-time/adjunct. *Students:* 5 full-time (1 woman), 11 part-time (9 women); includes 7 minority (all Hispanic/Latino), 2 international. Average age 35. 7 applicants, 57% accepted, 2 enrolled. In 2014, 5 master's awarded. *Degree requirements:* For master's, one foreign language, comprehensive exam, thesis optional. *Entrance requirements:* For master's, undergraduate major in Spanish or equivalent, essay in Spanish, writing sample, 2 letters of reference, ACTFL "advanced low" oral proficiency rating. Additional exam requirements/recommendations for international students: Required—TOEFL

(minimum score 525 paper-based; 65 iBT). *Application deadline:* For fall admission, 7/25 priority date for domestic students; for spring admission, 12/15 priority date for domestic students. Applications are processed on a rolling basis. Application fee: $30. Electronic applications accepted. *Expenses:* Tuition, state resident: full-time $9566; part-time $531 per credit hour. Tuition, nonresident: full-time $17,980; part-time $999 per credit hour. *Required fees:* $25 per semester. Tuition and fees vary according to degree level and program. *Financial support:* In 2014–15, 5 students received support, including 5 teaching assistantships with full tuition reimbursements available (averaging $8,000 per year); Federal Work-Study and unspecified assistantships also available. Financial award application deadline: 4/1. *Faculty research:* Peninsular poetry and prose, sociolinguistics, Latin American and Caribbean literature, Arabic diaspora in Latin America, border literature. *Unit head:* Dr. Antonio Medina-Rivera, Chairperson, 216-523-7175, Fax: 216-687-4650, E-mail: a.medinarivera@csuohio.edu. *Application contact:* Dr. Stephen Gingerich, Graduate Director, 216-687-4677, Fax: 216-687-4650, E-mail: s.gingerich@csuohio.edu.
Website: http://www.csuohio.edu/class/world-languages/world-languages

Columbia University, Graduate School of Arts and Sciences, New York, NY 10027. Offers African-American studies (MA); American studies (MA); anthropology (MA, PhD); art history and archaeology (MA, PhD); astronomy (PhD); biological sciences (PhD); biotechnology (MA); chemical physics (PhD); chemistry (PhD); classical studies (MA, PhD); classics (MA, PhD); climate and society (MA); earth and environmental sciences (PhD); East Asia: regional studies (MA); East Asian languages and cultures (MA, PhD); ecology, evolution and environmental biology (MA), including conservation biology; ecology, evolution, and environmental biology (PhD), including ecology and evolutionary biology, evolutionary primatology; economics (PhD); English and comparative literature (MA, PhD); French and Romance philology (MA, PhD); Germanic languages (MA, PhD); global French studies (MA); Hispanic cultural studies (MA); history (PhD); history and literature (MA); human rights studies (MA); Islamic studies (MA); Italian (MA, PhD); Japanese pedagogy (MA); Jewish studies (MA); Latin America and the Caribbean: regional studies (MA); Latin American and Iberian cultures (PhD); mathematics (MA, PhD), including finance (MA); medieval and Renaissance studies (MA); Middle Eastern, South Asian, and African studies (MA, PhD); modern art: critical and curatorial studies (MA); modern European studies (MA); museum anthropology (MA); music (DMA, PhD); oral history (MA); philosophical foundations of physics (MA); philosophy (MA, PhD); physics (PhD); political science (MA, PhD); psychology (PhD); quantitative methods in the social sciences (MA); religion (MA, PhD); Russia, Eurasia and East Europe: regional studies (MA); Russian translation (MA); Slavic cultures (MA); Slavic languages (MA, PhD); sociology (MA, PhD); South Asian studies (MA); statistics (MA, PhD); theatre (PhD); JD/PhD; MA/MS; MD/PhD; MPA/MA. Dual-degree programs require admission to both Graduate School of Arts and Sciences and another Columbia school. Part-time and evening/weekend programs available. Terminal master's awarded for partial completion of doctoral program. *Degree requirements:* For master's, thesis (for some programs); for doctorate, comprehensive exam, thesis/dissertation. *Entrance requirements:* For master's and doctorate, GRE General Test, GRE Subject Test (for some programs). Electronic applications accepted. *Faculty research:* Humanities, natural sciences, social sciences.

Columbia University, School of International and Public Affairs, Institute of Latin American Studies, New York, NY 10027. Offers Latin American and Caribbean studies (MA); Latin American studies (Certificate). Students must also be enrolled in a separate graduate degree program at Columbia University. *Degree requirements:* For master's, 2 foreign languages, thesis. Electronic applications accepted. *Faculty research:* Rights vs. efficiency in a globalized era, citizenship and governance in Latin America and Western Europe.

Cornell University, Graduate School, Graduate Fields of Arts and Sciences, Field of Archaeology, Ithaca, NY 14853-0001. Offers environmental archaeology (MA); historical archaeology (MA); Latin American archaeology (MA); medieval archaeology (MA); Mediterranean and Near Eastern archaeology (MA); Stone Age archaeology (MA). *Degree requirements:* For master's, one foreign language, thesis. *Entrance requirements:* For master's, GRE General Test, 3 letters of recommendation, sample of written work. Additional exam requirements/recommendations for international students: Required—TOEFL (minimum score 550 paper-based; 77 iBT). Electronic applications accepted. *Faculty research:* Anatolia, Lydia, Sardis, classical and Hellenistic Greece, science in archaeology, North American Indians, Stone Age Africa, Mayan trade.

Cornell University, Graduate School, Graduate Fields of Arts and Sciences, Field of History, Ithaca, NY 14853-0001. Offers African history (MA, PhD); American history (MA, PhD); ancient Greek history (PhD); ancient history (MA, PhD); ancient Roman history (PhD); early modern European history (MA, PhD); English history (MA, PhD); French history (MA, PhD); German history (MA, PhD); history of science (MA, PhD); Korean history (PhD); Latin American history (MA, PhD); medieval Chinese history (MA, PhD); medieval history (MA, PhD); modern Chinese history (MA, PhD); modern European history (MA, PhD); modern Japanese history (MA, PhD); modern Middle Eastern history (PhD); premodern Islamic history (MA, PhD); premodern Japanese history (MA, PhD); Renaissance history (MA, PhD); Russian history (MA, PhD); South Asian history (PhD); Southeast Asian history (MA, PhD). Terminal master's awarded for partial completion of doctoral program. *Degree requirements:* For master's, thesis; for doctorate, 2 foreign languages, comprehensive exam, thesis/dissertation, 1 year of teaching experience. *Entrance requirements:* For master's and doctorate, GRE General Test, writing sample, 3 letters of recommendation. Additional exam requirements/recommendations for international students: Required—TOEFL (minimum score 550 paper-based; 77 iBT). Electronic applications accepted.

Cornell University, Graduate School, Graduate Fields of Arts and Sciences, Field of History of Art, Archaeology and Visual Studies, Ithaca, NY 14853. Offers 19th century art (PhD); African, African American and African diaspora (PhD); American art (PhD); ancient art and archaeology (PhD); Asian American art (PhD); Baroque art (PhD); comparative modernities (PhD); digital art (PhD); East Asian art (PhD); history of photography (PhD); Islamic art (PhD); Latin American art (PhD); medieval art (PhD); modern art (PhD); Renaissance art (PhD); Southeast Asian art (PhD); theory and criticism (PhD); visual studies (PhD). *Degree requirements:* For doctorate, one foreign language, comprehensive exam, thesis/dissertation, general exams in 3 areas. *Entrance requirements:* For doctorate, GRE General Test, sample of written work, 3 letters of recommendation. Additional exam requirements/recommendations for international students: Required—TOEFL (minimum score 550 paper-based; 77 iBT). Electronic applications accepted.

Duke University, Graduate School, Department of History, Durham, NC 27708. Offers history (AM, PhD); Latin American studies (PhD); JD/AM. *Degree requirements:* For doctorate, 2 foreign languages, thesis/dissertation. *Entrance requirements:* For doctorate, GRE General Test. Additional exam requirements/recommendations for international students: Required—TOEFL (minimum score 577 paper-based; 90 iBT) or IELTS (minimum score 7). Electronic applications accepted. *Expenses: Tuition:* Full-time $45,760; part-time $2765 per credit. *Required fees:* $978. Full-time tuition and fees vary according to program.

Florida International University, College of Arts and Sciences, Program in Latin American and Caribbean Studies, Miami, FL 33199. Offers MA. Part-time and evening/weekend programs available. *Degree requirements:* For master's, one foreign language, thesis or alternative. *Entrance requirements:* For master's, GRE General Test (minimum score 1000); GMAT, LSAT, or EXADEP (minimum 62nd percentile), minimum GPA of 3.0, 3 letters of recommendation, letter of intent. Additional exam requirements/recommendations for international students: Required—TOEFL (minimum score 550 paper-based; 80 iBT). Electronic applications accepted.

Georgetown University, Graduate School of Arts and Sciences, Edmund A. Walsh School of Foreign Service, Center for Latin American Studies, Washington, DC 20057-1026. Offers MA, MA/JD, MA/PhD. Part-time and evening/weekend programs available. *Degree requirements:* For master's, one foreign language, comprehensive exam, thesis optional. *Entrance requirements:* For master's, GRE General Test, minimum B average. Additional exam requirements/recommendations for international students: Required—TOEFL. Electronic applications accepted.

The George Washington University, Elliott School of International Affairs, Program in Latin American and Hemispheric Studies, Washington, DC 20052. Offers MA. Part-time programs available. *Students:* 12 full-time (7 women), 5 part-time (2 women); includes 8 minority (1 Black or African American, non-Hispanic/Latino; 1 Asian, non-Hispanic/Latino; 6 Hispanic/Latino). Average age 26. 28 applicants, 6 enrolled. In 2014, 9 master's awarded. *Degree requirements:* For master's, one foreign language, capstone project. *Entrance requirements:* For master's, GRE General Test, 2 years (or the equivalent) of Spanish or Portuguese. Additional exam requirements/recommendations for international students: Required—TOEFL (minimum score 100 iBT), IELTS (minimum score 7). *Application deadline:* For fall admission, 1/15 priority date for domestic and international students; for spring admission, 10/1 for domestic students. Application fee: $75. Electronic applications accepted. *Financial support:* In 2014–15, 4 students received support. Fellowships with partial tuition reimbursements available, Federal Work-Study, and scholarships/grants available. Financial award application deadline: 1/15; financial award applicants required to submit FAFSA. *Faculty research:* Democracy and change in Andean nations, rural economic development, peasant cooperatives and political change. *Unit head:* Robert Maguire, Director, 202-994-4060, E-mail: lasp@gwu.edu. *Application contact:* Nicole A. Campbell, Director of Graduate Admissions, 202-994-7050, Fax: 202-994-9537, E-mail: esiagrad@gwu.edu.
Website: http://elliott.gwu.edu/latin-american-studies

Georgia State University, College of Arts and Sciences, Department of Modern and Classical Languages, Atlanta, GA 30302-3083. Offers French (MA), including applied linguistics and pedagogy, French studies, literature and culture; Latin American studies (Certificate); Spanish (MA); translation and interpretation (Certificate), including interpretation, translation. Part-time programs available. *Faculty:* 19 full-time (10 women). *Students:* 32 full-time (21 women), 19 part-time (12 women); includes 18 minority (7 Black or African American, non-Hispanic/Latino; 3 Asian, non-Hispanic/Latino; 6 Hispanic/Latino; 2 Two or more races, non-Hispanic/Latino), 3 international. Average age 35. 22 applicants, 100% accepted, 12 enrolled. In 2014, 10 master's, 14 other advanced degrees awarded. *Degree requirements:* For master's, 2 foreign languages, comprehensive exam, thesis or alternative, Graduate Foreign Language Reading Exam. *Entrance requirements:* For master's, GRE, statement of purpose, writing sample in the target language, 2 letters of recommendation, official transcripts; for Certificate, entrance examination involving translating one passage from English to the target language and one passage from the target language to English, 3 letters of recommendation, resume/curriculum vitae, official transcripts. Additional exam requirements/recommendations for international students: Required—TOEFL (minimum score 79 iBT). *Application deadline:* For fall admission, 3/15 priority date for domestic and international students; for spring admission, 11/15 priority date for domestic and international students. Application fee: $50. Electronic applications accepted. *Expenses:* Tuition, state resident: full-time $6516; part-time $362 per credit hour. Tuition, nonresident: full-time $22,014; part-time $1223 per credit hour. *Required fees:* $2128 per semester. Tuition and fees vary according to course load and program. *Financial support:* Applicants required to submit FAFSA. *Faculty research:* French literature and culture, Francophone literature and culture, Latin American literature and culture, Spanish literature and culture, Hispanic linguistics. *Unit head:* Dr. Fernando Reati, Department Chair, 404-413-5984, Fax: 404-413-5982, E-mail: freati@gsu.edu. *Application contact:* Amber Amari, Director, Graduate and Scheduling Services, 404-413-5037, E-mail: aamari@gsu.edu.
Website: http://www.gsu.edu/~wwwmcl/

Indiana University Bloomington, University Graduate School, College of Arts and Sciences, School of Global and International Studies, Center for Latin American and Caribbean Studies, Bloomington, IN 47405. Offers MA, MBA/MA, MIS/MA, MLS/MA, MPA/MA, MPH/MA. Part-time programs available. *Students:* 7 full-time (5 women); includes 2 minority (both Hispanic/Latino). Average age 27. 26 applicants, 73% accepted, 7 enrolled. In 2014, 3 master's awarded. *Degree requirements:* For master's, one foreign language, oral and written exam. *Entrance requirements:* For master's, GRE General Test. Additional exam requirements/recommendations for international students: Required—TOEFL. *Application deadline:* For fall admission, 1/15 priority date for domestic students, 12/1 for international students; for spring admission, 9/1 for domestic and international students. Applications are processed on a rolling basis. Application fee: $55 ($65 for international students). Electronic applications accepted. *Financial support:* Fellowships with tuition reimbursements, research assistantships with tuition reimbursements, teaching assistantships with tuition reimbursements, career-related internships or fieldwork, Federal Work-Study, institutionally sponsored loans, scholarships/grants, and unspecified assistantships available. Financial award application deadline: 7/15; financial award applicants required to submit FAFSA. *Unit head:* Dr. Shane Greene, Director, 812-855-9097, Fax: 812-855-5345, E-mail: lsgreene@indiana.edu. *Application contact:* Katie Novak, Academic Secretary, 812-855-1836, Fax: 812-855-5345, E-mail: clacs@indiana.edu.
Website: http://www.indiana.edu/~clacs/

La Salle University, School of Arts and Sciences, Hispanic Institute, Philadelphia, PA 19141-1199. Offers bilingual/bicultural studies (MA); ESL specialist (Certificate); interpretation in English-Spanish/Spanish-English (Certificate); teaching English to speakers of other languages (MA); translation and interpretation (MA); translation English/Spanish-Spanish/English (Certificate). Part-time and evening/weekend programs available. *Degree requirements:* For master's, one foreign language, project or thesis. *Entrance requirements:* For master's, GRE, MAT, or GMAT, professional resume; two letters of recommendation; for Certificate, GRE, MAT, or GMAT, professional resume; two letters of recommendation; evidence of an advanced level in Spanish. Additional exam requirements/recommendations for international students: Required—TOEFL. Electronic applications accepted. Application fee is waived when completed online. *Expenses:* Contact institution. *Faculty research:* Puerto Rican literature, cross-cultural communication, English as a second language methodology, Spanish language.

Michigan State University, The Graduate School, College of Social Science, Program in Chicano/Latino Studies, East Lansing, MI 48824. Offers PhD. *Entrance requirements:* Additional exam requirements/recommendations for international students: Required—TOEFL. Electronic applications accepted.

New York University, Graduate School of Arts and Science, Center for Latin American and Caribbean Studies, New York, NY 10012-1019. Offers MA, JD/MA. Part-time programs available. *Students:* 20 full-time (13 women), 5 part-time (4 women); includes 15 minority (1 Black or African American, non-Hispanic/Latino; 13 Hispanic/Latino; 1 Two or more races, non-Hispanic/Latino), 5 international. Average age 27. 41 applicants, 93% accepted, 14 enrolled. In 2014, 12 master's awarded. *Degree requirements:* For master's, one foreign language, thesis or alternative, major project. *Entrance requirements:* For master's, GRE General Test, knowledge of Portuguese or Spanish. Additional exam requirements/recommendations for international students: Required—TOEFL. *Application deadline:* For fall admission, 2/1 priority date for domestic students, 2/1 for international students. Application fee: $100. *Financial support:* Fellowships with tuition reimbursements, teaching assistantships with tuition reimbursements, Federal Work-Study, institutionally sponsored loans, scholarships/grants, health care benefits, and unspecified assistantships available. Financial award application deadline: 2/1; financial award applicants required to submit FAFSA. *Faculty research:* Latin American politics, Caribbean societies, Andean history, political economy of cultural policies. *Unit head:* Jill Lane, Director, 212-998-8686, Fax: 212-995-4163, E-mail: clacs.info@nyu.edu. *Application contact:* Amalia Cordova, Program Administrator, 212-998-8686, Fax: 212-995-4163, E-mail: clacs.info@nyu.edu. Website: http://clacs.as.nyu.edu/

New York University, Graduate School of Arts and Science, Program in Museum Studies, New York, NY 10012-1019. Offers museum studies (MA, Advanced Certificate), including Africana studies (MA), Hebrew and Judaic studies (MA), Latin American and Caribbean studies (MA), Near Eastern studies (MA). Part-time and evening/weekend programs available. *Students:* 45 full-time (39 women), 23 part-time (19 women); includes 15 minority (2 American Indian or Alaska Native, non-Hispanic/Latino; 3 Asian, non-Hispanic/Latino; 6 Hispanic/Latino; 4 Two or more races, non-Hispanic/Latino), 19 international. Average age 26. 123 applicants, 81% accepted, 29 enrolled. In 2014, 35 master's, 1 other advanced degree awarded. *Entrance requirements:* For master's, GRE General Test; for Advanced Certificate, master's degree or PhD. Additional exam requirements/recommendations for international students: Required—TOEFL. *Application deadline:* For fall admission, 2/15 for domestic and international students; for spring admission, 11/1 for domestic and international students. Application fee: $100. *Financial support:* Application deadline: 2/15. *Faculty research:* Modern and contemporary art, history of museums and exhibitions, conservation of cultural materials, museum anthropology, ethnography. *Unit head:* Bruce Altshuler, Director, 212-998-8080, Fax: 212-995-4185, E-mail: museum.studies@nyu.edu. *Application contact:* Tatiana Kamorina, Department Administrator, 212-998-8080, Fax: 212-995-4185, E-mail: museum.studies@nyu.edu. Website: http://www.nyu.edu/fas/program/museumstudies/

Northeastern Illinois University, College of Graduate Studies and Research, College of Arts and Sciences, Program in Latin American Literatures and Cultures, Chicago, IL 60625-4699. Offers MA.

The Ohio State University, Graduate School, Center for Latin American Studies, Columbus, OH 43210. Offers MA. In 2014, 1 master's awarded. *Entrance requirements:* For master's, GRE General Test. Additional exam requirements/recommendations for international students: Required—TOEFL (minimum score 550 paper-based; 79 iBT), IELTS (minimum score 7). *Application deadline:* For fall admission, 12/13 priority date for domestic students, 11/30 priority date for international students; for spring admission, 12/14 for domestic students, 11/12 for international students; for summer admission, 5/15 for domestic students, 4/14 for international students. Applications are processed on a rolling basis. Application fee: $60 ($70 for international students). Electronic applications accepted. *Financial support:* Fellowships with tuition reimbursements available. *Unit head:* Dr. Abril Trigo, Director, 614-292-8695, E-mail: trigo.1@osu.edu. *Application contact:* Graduate and Professional Admissions, 614-292-9444, Fax: 614-292-3895, E-mail: gpadmissions@osu.edu. Website: http://clas.osu.edu

Ohio University, Graduate College, Center for International Studies, Program in Latin American Studies, Athens, OH 45701-2979. Offers MA. Part-time programs available. *Degree requirements:* For master's, one foreign language, thesis optional. *Entrance requirements:* For master's, minimum GPA of 3.0. Additional exam requirements/recommendations for international students: Required—TOEFL (minimum score 550 paper-based; 80 iBT), IELTS (minimum score 6.5). Electronic applications accepted. *Faculty research:* Central America, Ecuador, Brazil, transnational migration, microfinance.

San Diego State University, Graduate and Research Affairs, College of Arts and Letters, Center for Latin American Studies, San Diego, CA 92182. Offers MA, MBA/MA. *Degree requirements:* For master's, 2 foreign languages, thesis or alternative. *Entrance requirements:* For master's, GRE General Test, 3 letters of reference. Additional exam requirements/recommendations for international students: Required—TOEFL. Electronic applications accepted. *Faculty research:* Latin American politics and economics.

Simon Fraser University, Office of Graduate Studies, Faculty of Arts and Social Sciences, Latin American Studies Program, Vancouver, BC V6B 5K3, Canada. Offers MA, Graduate Certificate. *Degree requirements:* For master's, one foreign language, thesis; for Graduate Certificate, one foreign language, Spanish or Portuguese language exam. *Entrance requirements:* For master's, minimum GPA of 3.0 (on scale of 4.33), or 3.33 based on last 60 credits of undergraduate courses; for Graduate Certificate, current enrollment in a master's or doctoral program. Additional exam requirements/recommendations for international students: Recommended—TOEFL (minimum score 580 paper-based; 93 iBT), IELTS (minimum score 7), TWE (minimum score 5). Electronic applications accepted. *Faculty research:* Theories and strategies of development, political economy, globalization, political sociology, health communications and promotion.

Tulane University, School of Liberal Arts, Roger Thayer Stone Center for Latin American Studies, New Orleans, LA 70118-5669. Offers MA, PhD, MBA/MA, MCL/MA. Terminal master's awarded for partial completion of doctoral program. *Degree requirements:* For master's, one foreign language, thesis optional; for doctorate, 2 foreign languages, thesis/dissertation. *Entrance requirements:* For master's, GRE General Test, minimum B average in undergraduate course work; for doctorate, GRE General Test. Additional exam requirements/recommendations for international students: Required—TOEFL. Electronic applications accepted. *Expenses: Tuition:* Full-time $46,326; part-time $2574 per credit hour. *Required fees:* $1980; $44.50 per credit hour. $550 per term. Tuition and fees vary according to course load and program.

University at Albany, State University of New York, College of Arts and Sciences, Department of Latin American, Caribbean, and U.S. Latino Studies, Albany, NY 12222-0001. Offers MA, PhD, Certificate. Part-time programs available. *Degree requirements:* For master's, thesis. *Entrance requirements:* For master's, ability to read and write Spanish. Additional exam requirements/recommendations for international students: Required—TOEFL (minimum score 550 paper-based). Electronic applications accepted. *Faculty research:* Meso-American anthropology, Latin American women's studies, Latinos in the U.S.

University at Buffalo, the State University of New York, Graduate School, College of Arts and Sciences, Department of Transnational Studies, Buffalo, NY 14260. Offers American studies (MA, PhD); Canadian studies (Advanced Certificate); Canadian-American studies (MA); Caribbean Latina/o American studies (MA); global gender studies (MA, PhD). Part-time programs available. Postbaccalaureate distance learning degree programs offered. *Faculty:* 19 full-time (10 women). *Students:* 73 full-time (43 women); includes 20 minority (3 Black or African American, non-Hispanic/Latino; 6 American Indian or Alaska Native, non-Hispanic/Latino; 9 Asian, non-Hispanic/Latino; 2 Hispanic/Latino). Average age 32. 57 applicants, 84% accepted, 16 enrolled. In 2014, 26 master's, 18 doctorates, 1 other advanced degree awarded. *Degree requirements:* For master's, one foreign language, comprehensive exam (for some programs), thesis optional; for doctorate, one foreign language, comprehensive exam, thesis/dissertation; for Advanced Certificate, one foreign language. *Entrance requirements:* For master's, N/A, minimum GPA of 3.0; for doctorate, GRE, minimum GPA of 3.0. Additional exam requirements/recommendations for international students: Required—TOEFL (minimum score 550 paper-based; 79 iBT). *Application deadline:* For fall admission, 8/15 priority date for domestic students, 6/15 priority date for international students; for winter admission, 2/1 for domestic and international students; for spring admission, 1/15 priority date for domestic students, 11/15 priority date for international students. Applications are processed on a rolling basis. Application fee: $75. Electronic applications accepted. *Financial support:* In 2014–15, 16 students received support, including fellowships with full tuition reimbursements available (averaging $6,000 per year), research assistantships (averaging $5,000 per year), teaching assistantships with full tuition reimbursements available (averaging $13,060 per year); career-related internships or fieldwork, institutionally sponsored loans, scholarships/grants, traineeships, health care benefits, and unspecified assistantships also available. Financial award application deadline: 1/4. *Faculty research:* Native American, intercultural and indigenous people's studies, border theory, cultural studies, American pop culture, feminist theory, construction of gender in society. *Unit head:* Dr. Keith Griffler, Chair, 716-645-0802, Fax: 716-645-5977, E-mail: griffler@buffalo.edu. *Application contact:* Karen M. Reinard, Graduate Secretary, 716-645-0797, Fax: 716-645-5976, E-mail: kreinard@buffalo.edu. Website: http://www.transnationalstudies.buffalo.edu/graduate.shtml

University at Buffalo, the State University of New York, Graduate School, College of Arts and Sciences, Program in Caribbean and Latina/o American Studies, Buffalo, NY 14260. Offers MA. *Unit head:* Dr. Bruce D. McCombe, Dean, 716-645-2711, Fax: 716-645-3888, E-mail: cas-dean@buffalo.edu. *Application contact:* Joseph C. Syracuse, Graduate Enrollment Manager, 716-645-2711, Fax: 716-645-3888, E-mail: jcs32@buffalo.edu. Website: http://www.caribbeanstudies.buffalo.edu/program/

The University of Arizona, College of Social and Behavioral Sciences, Center for Latin American Studies, Tucson, AZ 85721. Offers MA. Part-time programs available. *Degree requirements:* For master's, 2 foreign languages, comprehensive exam, thesis optional. *Entrance requirements:* For master's, GRE, 2 letters of recommendation, resume. Additional exam requirements/recommendations for international students: Required—TOEFL (minimum score 550 paper-based; 79 iBT). Electronic applications accepted. *Faculty research:* Comparative analyses of national identities and of democratization across Latin America, environmental problems and management along the U.S.-Mexican border, integration efforts along the Peru/Ecuador border, social justice issues in Guatemala.

University of California, Berkeley, Graduate Division, Program in International and Area Studies, Group in Latin American Studies, Berkeley, CA 94720-1500. Offers MA, MJ/MA. *Degree requirements:* For master's, 2 foreign languages. *Entrance requirements:* For master's, GRE General Test, minimum GPA of 3.0, reading knowledge of Spanish or Portuguese, 3 letters of recommendation. Additional exam requirements/recommendations for international students: Required—TOEFL. Electronic applications accepted. *Faculty research:* Rural development, border communities, political economy, geography, history.

University of California, Los Angeles, Graduate Division, International Institute, Interdepartmental Program in Latin American Studies, Los Angeles, CA 90095. Offers MA, M Ed/MA, MA/MA, MBA/MA, MLIS/MA, MPH/MA. *Degree requirements:* For master's, 2 foreign languages, comprehensive exam or thesis. *Entrance requirements:* For master's, GRE General Test, bachelor's degree; minimum undergraduate GPA of 3.0 (or its equivalent if letter grade system not used); language requirement. Additional exam requirements/recommendations for international students: Required—TOEFL. Electronic applications accepted.

University of California, San Diego, Graduate Division, Latin American Studies Program, La Jolla, CA 92093. Offers MA. *Students:* 16 full-time (14 women); includes 7 minority (all Hispanic/Latino), 4 international. 27 applicants, 67% accepted, 8 enrolled. In 2014, 7 master's awarded. *Degree requirements:* For master's, one foreign language, thesis. *Entrance requirements:* For master's, GRE General Test, minimum GPA of 3.0; writing sample. Additional exam requirements/recommendations for international students: Required—TOEFL (minimum score 550 paper-based; 80 iBT), IELTS (minimum score 7). *Application deadline:* For fall admission, 1/15 for domestic students. Application fee: $90 ($110 for international students). Electronic applications accepted. *Expenses:* Tuition, state resident: full-time $11,220; part-time $5610 per quarter. Tuition, nonresident: full-time $26,322; part-time $13,161 per quarter. *Required fees:* $570 per quarter. Tuition and fees vary according to program. *Financial support:* Fellowships, research assistantships, teaching assistantships, scholarships/grants, unspecified assistantships, and readerships available. Financial award applicants required to submit FAFSA. *Faculty research:* Early civilizations; archaeology; psychological and medical anthropology; politics; race, gender and transnational cultural studies. *Unit head:* Leon Zamosc, Director, 858-822-5033, E-mail: lzamosc@ucsd.edu. *Application contact:* Brittany Wright, Graduate Coordinator, 858-534-7967, E-mail: bloy@ucsd.edu.

University of California, Santa Barbara, Graduate Division, College of Letters and Sciences, Division of Humanities and Fine Arts, Program in Latin American and Iberian Studies, Santa Barbara, CA 93106-4150. Offers MA. *Degree requirements:* For master's, one foreign language, comprehensive exam (for some programs), thesis. *Entrance requirements:* For master's, GRE. Additional exam requirements/recommendations for international students: Required—TOEFL (minimum score 550 paper-based; 80 iBT), IELTS (minimum score 7). Electronic applications accepted. *Faculty research:* Political science, anthropology, history, sociology, Portuguese.

University of Chicago, Division of the Social Sciences and Division of the Humanities, Center for Latin American Studies, Chicago, IL 60637. Offers MA. *Students:* 2 full-time (0 women); both minorities (both Hispanic/Latino). 10 applicants, 70% accepted, 2 enrolled. In 2014, 5 master's awarded. *Degree requirements:* For master's, one foreign language, thesis. *Entrance requirements:* For master's, GRE General Test. Additional exam requirements/recommendations for international students: Required—TOEFL (minimum score 104 iBT), IELTS (minimum score 7). *Application deadline:* For fall admission, 1/5 priority date for domestic and international students. Application fee: $90. Electronic applications accepted. *Expenses:* Tuition: Full-time $46,899. *Required fees:* $347. *Financial support:* In 2014–15, 2 students received support. Federal Work-Study,

institutionally sponsored loans, and scholarships/grants available. Financial award application deadline: 1/5. *Unit head:* Prof. Mauricio Tenorio, Director. *Application contact:* Office of the Dean of Students, 773-702-8415, E-mail: admissions@ssd.uchicago.edu.
Website: http://clas.uchicago.edu

University of Connecticut, Graduate School, College of Liberal Arts and Sciences, Field of International Studies, Program in Latin American Studies, Storrs, CT 06269. Offers MA. *Degree requirements:* For master's, comprehensive exam. *Entrance requirements:* For master's, GRE General Test. Additional exam requirements/recommendations for international students: Required—TOEFL (minimum score 550 paper-based). Electronic applications accepted.

University of Florida, Graduate School, College of Liberal Arts and Sciences, Center for Latin American Studies, Gainesville, FL 32611. Offers Latin American studies (MA, Certificate); sustainable development practice (MDP); tropical conservation and development (MA); JD/MA. Part-time programs available. *Faculty:* 3 part-time/adjunct (all women). *Students:* 16 full-time (13 women), 4 part-time (3 women); includes 8 minority (1 Black or African American, non-Hispanic/Latino; 7 Hispanic/Latino). 57 applicants, 63% accepted, 18 enrolled. In 2014, 4 master's awarded. *Degree requirements:* For master's, thesis. *Entrance requirements:* For master's, GRE General Test, minimum GPA of 3.0. Additional exam requirements/recommendations for international students: Required—TOEFL (minimum score 550 paper-based; 80 iBT), IELTS (minimum score 6). *Application deadline:* For fall admission, 6/1 priority date for domestic students. Applications are processed on a rolling basis. Application fee: $30. Electronic applications accepted. *Financial support:* In 2014–15, 15 fellowships, 19 research assistantships, 3 teaching assistantships were awarded; career-related internships or fieldwork, Federal Work-Study, institutionally sponsored loans, and unspecified assistantships also available. Financial award application deadline: 3/1; financial award applicants required to submit FAFSA. *Faculty research:* Tropical conservation and development; ethnicity in the Americas, Brazil, and Cuba; North American Free Trade Agreement (NAFTA). *Unit head:* Philip Williams, PhD, Director, 352-273-4702, Fax: 352-392-7682, E-mail: pjw@latam.ufl.edu. *Application contact:* Richmond F. Brown, PhD, Associate Director, 352-273-4708, Fax: 352-392-7682, E-mail: rfbrown@ufl.edu.
Website: http://www.latam.ufl.edu/

University of Illinois at Chicago, Graduate College, College of Liberal Arts and Sciences, Latin American and Latino Studies Program, Chicago, IL 60607-7128. Offers MA. *Faculty:* 12 full-time (8 women), 10 part-time/adjunct (6 women). *Students:* 9 full-time (7 women), 1 (woman) part-time; includes 8 minority (1 American Indian or Alaska Native, non-Hispanic/Latino; 7 Hispanic/Latino), 1 international. Average age 31. 14 applicants, 64% accepted, 4 enrolled. In 2014, 5 master's awarded. Application fee: $60. *Expenses:* Tuition, state resident: full-time $11,254; part-time $468 per credit hour. Tuition, nonresident: full-time $23,252; part-time $968 per credit hour. *Required fees:* $1217 per term. Part-time tuition and fees vary according to course load, degree level and program. *Faculty research:* Representation of nation, race, gender and labor in film; Colonial political discourse and social resistance; social structures and religious rituals among the Maya; rural development and ecology in Mexico; Latina reproductive rights; youth activism; transnational Cuban migration; globalization and labor strategies of women in Brazil; Mexican hometown associations; local, national and global immigrant rights struggles. *Unit head:* Prof. Amalia Pallares, Director, 312-413-3773, Fax: 312-996-1796, E-mail: amalia@uic.edu. *Application contact:* Receptionist, 312-413-2550, E-mail: gradcoll@uic.edu.
Website: http://www.uic.edu/las/latamst/programs/masters.shtml

University of Illinois at Urbana–Champaign, Graduate College, College of Liberal Arts and Sciences, Center for Latin American and Caribbean Studies, Champaign, IL 61820. Offers Latin American studies (MA). *Students:* 6 (4 women). Application fee: $70 ($90 for international students). *Unit head:* Dara Ellen Goldman, Director, 217-333-3182, Fax: 217-244-7333, E-mail: degoldma@illinois.edu. *Application contact:* Angelina Cotler, Associate Director, 217-333-8419, Fax: 217-244-7333, E-mail: cotler@illinois.edu.
Website: http://www.clacs.illinois.edu/

The University of Kansas, Graduate Studies, College of Liberal Arts and Sciences, Latin American and Caribbean Studies Program, Lawrence, KS 66045. Offers Brazilian studies (Graduate Certificate); Central American and Mexican studies (Graduate Certificate); Latin American studies (MA). Part-time programs available. *Faculty:* 1 full-time, 2 part-time/adjunct. *Students:* 2 full-time (both women), 6 part-time (2 women); includes 4 minority (3 Hispanic/Latino; 1 Two or more races, non-Hispanic/Latino), 1 international. Average age 35. 2 applicants, 100% accepted, 1 enrolled. *Degree requirements:* For master's, 2 foreign languages, comprehensive exam, thesis optional. *Entrance requirements:* For master's, GRE, minimum GPA of 3.0, references, writing sample. Additional exam requirements/recommendations for international students: Required—TOEFL. *Application deadline:* For fall admission, 4/2 priority date for domestic students, 1/15 priority date for international students; for spring admission, 11/15 for domestic and international students. Applications are processed on a rolling basis. Application fee: $55 ($65 for international students). Electronic applications accepted. *Financial support:* Fellowships with full tuition reimbursements, research assistantships with full and partial tuition reimbursements, teaching assistantships with full and partial tuition reimbursements, scholarships/grants, and unspecified assistantships available. Financial award application deadline: 2/1. *Faculty research:* Economic development and its environmental repercussions; national and popular cultures; indigenous peoples and their languages; social, cultural and environmental history; medical practice and anthropology. *Unit head:* Santa Arias, Director, 785-864-4213, E-mail: sarias@ku.edu. *Application contact:* Alyssa McDonald, Graduate Admissions Contact, 785-864-9814, E-mail: mcdonalda@ku.edu.
Website: https://latamst.ku.edu/

The University of Manchester, School of Languages, Linguistics and Cultures, Manchester, United Kingdom. Offers Arab world studies (PhD); Chinese studies (M Phil, PhD); East Asian studies (M Phil, PhD); English language (PhD); French studies (M Phil, PhD); German studies (M Phil, PhD); interpreting studies (PhD); Italian studies (M Phil, PhD); Japanese studies (M Phil, PhD); Latin American cultural studies (M Phil, PhD); linguistics (M Phil, PhD); Middle Eastern studies (M Phil, PhD); Polish studies (M Phil, PhD); Portuguese studies (M Phil, PhD); Russian studies (M Phil, PhD); Spanish studies (M Phil, PhD); translation and intercultural studies (M Phil, PhD).

University of Massachusetts Dartmouth, Graduate School, College of Arts and Sciences, Department of Portuguese, North Dartmouth, MA 02747-2300. Offers Luso-Afro Brazilian studies (PhD); Portuguese (MA). Part-time programs available. *Faculty:* 5 full-time (2 women), 2 part-time/adjunct (1 woman). *Students:* 9 full-time (7 women), 5 part-time (4 women); includes 7 minority (2 Black or African American, non-Hispanic/Latino; 5 Hispanic/Latino), 4 international. Average age 40. 9 applicants, 78% accepted, 4 enrolled. In 2014, 2 master's, 1 doctorate awarded. Terminal master's awarded for partial completion of doctoral program. *Degree requirements:* For master's, comprehensive exam (for some programs), written exam or research project; for doctorate, comprehensive exam, thesis/dissertation. *Entrance requirements:* For master's, GRE (recommended), statement of purpose (minimum of 300 words), resume,

3 letters of recommendation, official transcripts, writing samples in Portuguese (minimum of 10 pages); for doctorate, GRE (recommended), statement of purpose (minimum of 300 words), resume, 3 letters of recommendation, official transcripts, scholarly writing sample (minimum of 10 pages). Additional exam requirements/recommendations for international students: Required—TOEFL (minimum score 500 paper-based). *Application deadline:* For fall admission, 2/1 priority date for domestic students, 1/1 priority date for international students; for spring admission, 11/15 priority date for domestic students, 10/15 priority date for international students. Applications are processed on a rolling basis. Application fee: $60. Electronic applications accepted. *Expenses:* Tuition, state resident: full-time $2071; part-time $86.29 per credit. Tuition, nonresident: full-time $8099; part-time $337.46 per credit. *Required fees:* $16,520; $712.33 per credit. Tuition and fees vary according to course load and reciprocity agreements. *Financial support:* In 2014–15, 9 fellowships with full tuition reimbursements (averaging $18,295 per year) were awarded; Federal Work-Study and unspecified assistantships also available. Support available to part-time students. Financial award application deadline: 3/1; financial award applicants required to submit FAFSA. *Faculty research:* Translation studies, literature in Luso-Afro-Brazilian studies, literary and cultural theory, gender studies, studies in ethnicity and migration, bi-and multilingualism. *Total annual research expenditures:* $32,000. *Unit head:* Victor J. Mendes, Graduate Program Director, 508-999-8338, Fax: 508-910-9272, E-mail: vmendes@umassd.edu. *Application contact:* Steven Briggs, Director of Marketing and Recruitment for Graduate Studies, 508-999-8604, Fax: 508-999-8183, E-mail: graduate@umassd.edu.
Website: http://www.umassd.edu/cas/departmentsanddegreeprograms/portuguese/

University of Miami, Graduate School, College of Arts and Sciences, Department of Latin American and Caribbean Studies, Coral Gables, FL 33124. Offers Latin American studies (MA). Part-time programs available. *Degree requirements:* For master's, comprehensive exam (for some programs), thesis, linguistic competency in Spanish or Portuguese, reading competency in a second Latin American language. *Entrance requirements:* For master's, GRE, 3 letters of recommendation. Additional exam requirements/recommendations for international students: Required—TOEFL. Electronic applications accepted. *Faculty research:* Literary, media, religious, visual and cultural studies; environment and tourism studies; US-Latin American Relations and drug trafficking; migration, globalization, and social movements; democratization, regime transitions, and citizenship.

University of New Mexico, Graduate School, College of Arts and Sciences, Program in Latin American Studies, Albuquerque, NM 87131. Offers MA, PhD, JD/MA, MA/MA, MA/MPH, MBA/MA, MCRP/MA. Part-time programs available. *Faculty:* 9 full-time (4 women). *Students:* 16 full-time (10 women), 4 part-time (2 women); includes 8 minority (all Hispanic/Latino), 1 international. Average age 28. 17 applicants, 71% accepted, 9 enrolled. In 2014, 9 master's awarded. *Degree requirements:* For master's, one foreign language, comprehensive exam (for some programs), thesis (for some programs); for doctorate, 2 foreign languages, comprehensive exam, thesis/dissertation. *Entrance requirements:* For master's, GRE General Test, intermediate competence in Spanish, Portuguese or indigenous Latin American language; for doctorate, GRE General Test, master's degree in related field, one Latin American language. Additional exam requirements/recommendations for international students: Required—TOEFL. *Application deadline:* For fall admission, 2/1 priority date for domestic and international students; for spring admission, 11/1 for domestic and international students. Application fee: $50. Electronic applications accepted. *Financial support:* In 2014–15, 15 students received support, including 2 fellowships with full tuition reimbursements available (averaging $15,000 per year), 11 research assistantships with full tuition reimbursements available (averaging $13,000 per year), 2 teaching assistantships with full tuition reimbursements available (averaging $14,410 per year); Federal Work-Study, scholarships/grants, health care benefits, tuition waivers (full), and unspecified assistantships also available. Financial award application deadline: 2/1; financial award applicants required to submit FAFSA. *Unit head:* Dr. Susan Tiano, Director, 505-277-2961, Fax: 505-277-5989, E-mail: stiano@unm.edu. *Application contact:* Matias Fontenla, Associate Director for Academic Programs, 505-277-2961, Fax: 505-277-5989, E-mail: fontenla@unm.edu.
Website: http://laii.unm.edu

University of New Mexico, Graduate School, College of Fine Arts, Program in Art History, Albuquerque, NM 87131. Offers art history (MA); arts of the Americas (MA); history of architecture (PhD); history of graphic arts (PhD); history of photography (PhD); modern Latin American art history (PhD); Native American art history (PhD); Pre-Columbian art history (PhD); Spanish colonial art history (PhD). Part-time programs available. *Faculty:* 9 full-time (7 women). *Students:* 14 full-time (10 women), 22 part-time (16 women); includes 8 minority (2 American Indian or Alaska Native, non-Hispanic/Latino; 6 Hispanic/Latino), 5 international. Average age 32. 34 applicants, 26% accepted, 5 enrolled. In 2014, 5 master's, 1 doctorate awarded. *Degree requirements:* For master's, one foreign language, comprehensive exam (for some programs), thesis, symposium; for doctorate, 2 foreign languages, comprehensive exam, thesis/dissertation, symposium. *Entrance requirements:* Additional exam requirements/recommendations for international students: Required—TOEFL (minimum score 550 paper-based), IELTS (minimum score 6). *Application deadline:* For fall admission, 1/15 for domestic students; for spring admission, 1/15 for domestic students. Application fee: $50. Electronic applications accepted. *Financial support:* In 2014–15, fellowships (averaging $7,433 per year), research assistantships with tuition reimbursements (averaging $5,216 per year), teaching assistantships with partial tuition reimbursements (averaging $4,005 per year) were awarded; Federal Work-Study, institutionally sponsored loans, scholarships/grants, health care benefits, and unspecified assistantships also available. Support available to part-time students. Financial award application deadline: 3/1; financial award applicants required to submit FAFSA. *Faculty research:* Native American, modern Latin American, pre-Columbian, architectural, American, medieval, Spanish Colonial, and Latin American art; history of photography. *Unit head:* Prof. Mary Tsiongas, Chair, 505-277-5861, Fax: 505-277-5955, E-mail: tsiongas@unm.edu. *Application contact:* Kat Heatherington, Graduate Advisor, 505-277-6672, Fax: 505-277-5955, E-mail: art255@unm.edu.
Website: http://art.unm.edu/

The University of North Carolina at Chapel Hill, Graduate School, College of Arts and Sciences, Department of Political Science, Chapel Hill, NC 27599. Offers Latin American studies (Certificate); political science (MA, PhD); trans-Atlantic studies (MA). *Degree requirements:* For master's, comprehensive exam; for doctorate, one foreign language, comprehensive exam, thesis/dissertation. *Entrance requirements:* For master's and doctorate, GRE General Test, minimum GPA of 3.0 recommended. Electronic applications accepted.

The University of North Carolina at Charlotte, College of Liberal Arts and Sciences, Interdisciplinary Liberal Arts and Sciences Programs, Charlotte, NC 28223-0001. Offers gerontology (MA, Graduate Certificate); Latin American studies (MA); liberal studies (MA); organizational psychology (PhD); public policy (PhD); women's studies (Graduate Certificate). *Faculty:* 6 full-time (3 women), 5 part-time/adjunct (all women). *Students:* 58 full-time (31 women), 55 part-time (45 women); includes 24 minority (15 Black or African American, non-Hispanic/Latino; 1 Asian, non-Hispanic/Latino; 6 Hispanic/Latino; 1

Native Hawaiian or other Pacific Islander, non-Hispanic/Latino; 1 Two or more races, non-Hispanic/Latino, 12 international. Average age 33. 96 applicants, 46% accepted, 29 enrolled. In 2014, 11 master's, 8 doctorates, 15 other advanced degrees awarded. Terminal master's awarded for partial completion of doctoral program. *Degree requirements:* For master's, thesis or alternative, comprehensive exam or project; for doctorate, thesis/dissertation. *Entrance requirements:* For master's, GRE General Test or MAT, minimum GPA of 3.0 during previous 2 years, 2.75 overall; for doctorate, GRE, letters of recommendation. Additional exam requirements/recommendations for international students: Required—TOEFL (minimum score 557 paper-based; 83 iBT). *Application deadline:* For fall admission, 5/1 priority date for domestic students, 5/1 for international students; for spring admission, 10/1 priority date for domestic students, 10/1 for international students. Applications are processed on a rolling basis. Application fee: $75. Electronic applications accepted. *Expenses:* Tuition, state resident: full-time $4008. Tuition, nonresident: full-time $16,295. *Required fees:* $2755. Tuition and fees vary according to course load and program. *Financial support:* In 2014–15, 24 students received support, including 20 research assistantships (averaging $10,400 per year), 4 teaching assistantships (averaging $8,250 per year); career-related internships or fieldwork, institutionally sponsored loans, scholarships/grants, and unspecified assistantships also available. Support available to part-time students. Financial award application deadline: 4/1; financial award applicants required to submit FAFSA. *Total annual research expenditures:* $15,045. *Unit head:* Dr. Nancy A. Gutierrez, Dean, 704-687-0081, Fax: 704-687-4347, E-mail: ngutierr@uncc.edu. *Application contact:* Kathy B. Giddings, Director of Graduate Admissions, 704-687-5503, Fax: 704-687-3279, E-mail: gradadm@uncc.edu.
Website: http://www.lbst.uncc.edu/

University of Notre Dame, Graduate School, College of Arts and Letters, Division of Humanities, Department of Romance Languages and Literatures, Notre Dame, IN 46556. Offers French and Francophone studies (MA); Iberian and Latin American studies (MA); Italian studies (MA); Romance literatures (MA). *Degree requirements:* For master's, 2 foreign languages, comprehensive exam, thesis optional. *Entrance requirements:* For master's, GRE General Test, BA in target language. Additional exam requirements/recommendations for international students: Required—TOEFL (minimum score 600 paper-based; 80 iBT). Electronic applications accepted. *Faculty research:* Literature of discovery and exploration, modern literature, literary criticism, medieval literature, feminist critical theory.

University of Pittsburgh, University Center for International Studies, Pittsburgh, PA 15260. Offers African studies (Certificate); Asian studies (Certificate); European Union studies (Certificate); global studies (Certificate); Latin American studies (Certificate); Russian and East European studies (Certificate); West European studies (Certificate). *Students:* 223 full-time (98 women), 11 part-time (1 woman); includes 97 minority (2 Black or African American, non-Hispanic/Latino; 41 Asian, non-Hispanic/Latino; 52 Hispanic/Latino; 2 Two or more races, non-Hispanic/Latino). Average age 31. In 2014, 72 Certificates awarded. *Degree requirements:* For Certificate, one foreign language, study abroad. *Application deadline:* Applications are processed on a rolling basis. *Expenses:* Tuition, state resident: full-time $20,742; part-time $838 per credit. Tuition, nonresident: full-time $33,960; part-time $1389 per credit. *Required fees:* $800; $205 per term. Tuition and fees vary according to program. *Unit head:* Dr. Ariel Armony, Director, 412-648-7374, Fax: 412-624-4672, E-mail: armony@pitt.edu. *Application contact:* Information Contact, 412-624-4141, E-mail: graduate@pitt.edu.
Website: http://www.ucis.pitt.edu

University of Southern California, Graduate School, Dana and David Dornsife College of Letters, Arts and Sciences, Comparative Studies in Literature and Culture Doctoral Program, Los Angeles, CA 90089. Offers comparative literature (PhD); comparative media and culture (PhD); Spanish and Latin American studies (PhD). *Degree requirements:* For doctorate, 2 foreign languages, comprehensive exam, thesis/dissertation. *Entrance requirements:* For doctorate, GRE, competence in language other than English (highly recommended). Additional exam requirements/recommendations for international students: Required—TOEFL. Electronic applications accepted. *Faculty research:* Literary theory, Japanese film and contemporary fiction, Francophone literature and cinema, Latin American and Caribbean literature, Spanish literature and film, nineteenth and twentieth century British and American literature.

University of South Florida, College of Arts and Sciences, Department of Government and International Affairs, Tampa, FL 33620-9951. Offers government (PhD); Latin American, Caribbean and Latino studies (MA); political science (MA), including comparative government and politics, international relations, public policy. Part-time and evening/weekend programs available. *Faculty:* 10 full-time (1 woman). *Students:* 56 full-time (29 women), 47 part-time (23 women); includes 18 minority (6 Black or African American, non-Hispanic/Latino; 1 Asian, non-Hispanic/Latino; 9 Hispanic/Latino; 2 Two or more races, non-Hispanic/Latino), 9 international. Average age 33. 73 applicants, 51% accepted, 25 enrolled. In 2014, 45 master's, 2 doctorates awarded. *Degree requirements:* For master's, comprehensive exam, thesis; for doctorate, comprehensive exam, thesis/dissertation. *Entrance requirements:* For master's, GRE General Test, minimum GPA of 3.0 in upper-division undergraduate course work; letters of recommendation (2 for MPA, 3 for MPS); 500-word personal statement and undergraduate background in political science or related fields (for MPS); one-page career statement (for MPA); for doctorate, GRE General Test, 500-word personal statement, three letters of recommendation, transcripts of MA/BA coursework, writing sample. Additional exam requirements/recommendations for international students: Required—TOEFL (minimum score 550 paper-based; 79 iBT) or IELTS (minimum score 6.5). *Application deadline:* For fall admission, 2/15 for domestic students, 1/2 for international students; for spring admission, 10/15 for domestic students, 6/1 for international students. Applications are processed on a rolling basis. Application fee: $30. Electronic applications accepted. *Financial support:* In 2014–15, 18 students received support, including 18 teaching assistantships with tuition reimbursements available (averaging $12,390 per year); unspecified assistantships also available. Financial award application deadline: 4/1. *Faculty research:* Citizenship and identity, social movements, global governance, American politics, public policy. *Unit head:* Dr. Steven Tauber, Associate Professor and Interim Chair, 813-974-2278, Fax: 813-974-0832, E-mail: stauber@usf.edu. *Application contact:* Dr. Bernd Reiter, Associate Professor and Director of Graduate Studies, 813-974-3583, Fax: 813-974-0832, E-mail: breiter@usf.edu.
Website: http://gia.usf.edu/

University of South Florida, Innovative Education, Tampa, FL 33620-9951. *Unit head:* Kathy Barnes, Interdisciplinary Programs Coordinator, 813-974-8031, Fax: 813-974-7061, E-mail: barnesk@usf.edu. *Application contact:* Karen Tylinski, Metro Initiatives, 813-974-9943, Fax: 813-974-7061, E-mail: ktylinsk@usf.edu.
Website: http://www.usf.edu/innovative-education/

The University of Texas at Austin, Graduate School, College of Liberal Arts, Teresa Lozano Long Institute of Latin American Studies, Austin, TX 78712-1111. Offers cultural politics of Afro-Latin and indigenous peoples (MA); development studies (MA); environmental studies (MA); human rights (MA); Latin American and international law (LL M); JD/MA; MA/MA; MBA/MA; MP Aff/MA; MSCRP/MA. LL M offered jointly with

The University of Texas School of Law. *Entrance requirements:* For master's, GRE General Test.

The University of Texas at Dallas, School of Arts and Humanities, Program in Humanities, Richardson, TX 75080. Offers aesthetic studies (MA, PhD); history (MA); history of ideas (MA, PhD); humanities (MA, PhD); Latin American studies (MA); studies in literature (MA, PhD). *Faculty:* 35 full-time (11 women), 1 part-time/adjunct (0 women). *Students:* 148 full-time (94 women), 151 part-time (97 women); includes 78 minority (21 Black or African American, non-Hispanic/Latino; 4 American Indian or Alaska Native, non-Hispanic/Latino; 14 Asian, non-Hispanic/Latino; 28 Hispanic/Latino; 11 Two or more races, non-Hispanic/Latino), 16 international. Average age 39. 127 applicants, 46% accepted, 40 enrolled. In 2014, 40 master's, 15 doctorates awarded. *Degree requirements:* For master's, one foreign language, portfolio, thesis, or capstone project; for doctorate, one foreign language, thesis/dissertation. *Entrance requirements:* For master's, minimum GPA of 3.3 in upper-level coursework in field; for doctorate, field examinations, minimum GPA of 3.3 in upper-level coursework in field. Additional exam requirements/recommendations for international students: Required—TOEFL (minimum score 550 paper-based). *Application deadline:* For fall admission, 7/15 for domestic students, 5/1 priority date for international students; for spring admission, 11/15 for domestic students, 9/1 priority date for international students. Applications are processed on a rolling basis. Application fee: $50 ($100 for international students). Electronic applications accepted. *Expenses:* Tuition, state resident: full-time $11,940; part-time $663 per credit. Tuition, nonresident: full-time $22,282; part-time $1238 per credit. *Financial support:* In 2014–15, 161 students received support. Research assistantships with partial tuition reimbursements available, teaching assistantships with partial tuition reimbursements available, career-related internships or fieldwork, Federal Work-Study, institutionally sponsored loans, scholarships/grants, and unspecified assistantships available. Support available to part-time students. Financial award application deadline: 4/30; financial award applicants required to submit FAFSA. *Faculty research:* Holocaust studies, U.S./Mexico studies, translation studies, art history research, Chinese studies. *Unit head:* Dr. Michael Wilson, III, Associate Dean for Graduate Education, 972-883-2756, Fax: 972-883-2989, E-mail: mwilson@utdallas.edu. *Application contact:* Alice Salazar, Coordinator, 972-883-2756, Fax: 972-883-2989, E-mail: alice.salazar1@utdallas.edu.
Website: http://www.utdallas.edu/ah/programs/graduate

University of Utah, Graduate School, College of Humanities, Latin American Studies Program, Salt Lake City, UT 84112. Offers MA. Part-time and evening/weekend programs available. *Students:* 3 full-time (0 women). 1 applicant, 100% accepted, 3 enrolled. *Degree requirements:* For master's, 2 foreign languages, thesis, third-year proficiency in one of the two major Latin American languages, first-year proficiency in the other (Spanish or Portuguese). *Entrance requirements:* For master's, GRE, minimum undergraduate GPA of 3.0, graduate 3.4. Additional exam requirements/recommendations for international students: Required—TOEFL (minimum score 580 paper-based). *Application deadline:* For fall admission, 2/1 priority date for domestic and international students. Application fee: $55 ($65 for international students). Electronic applications accepted. *Financial support:* Application deadline: 4/15. *Faculty research:* Latin American health studies, history, literature, culture, politics, economics. *Unit head:* Dr. Rebecca Horn, Director, 801-581-5294, E-mail: rebecca.horn@history.utah.edu. *Application contact:* Kevin D. Barrett, Academic Coordinator, 801-584-6150, Fax: 801-581-6105, E-mail: kevin.barrett@utah.edu.
Website: http://latin-american-studies.utah.edu/

University of Wisconsin–Madison, Graduate School, College of Letters and Science, Department of History, Madison, WI 53706-1380. Offers African history (MA, PhD); Central Asian history (MA, PhD); comparative world history (MA, PhD); East Asian history (MA, PhD); European history (MA, PhD); gender and women's history (MA, PhD); Latin American and Caribbean history (MA, PhD); Middle Eastern history (MA, PhD); South Asian history (MA, PhD); Southeast Asian history (MA, PhD); United States history (MA, PhD). Terminal master's awarded for partial completion of doctoral program. *Degree requirements:* For master's, thesis (for some programs); for doctorate, variable foreign language requirement, thesis/dissertation. *Entrance requirements:* For master's and doctorate, GRE General Test. Additional exam requirements/recommendations for international students: Required—Michigan English Language Assessment Battery or TOEFL. Electronic applications accepted. *Expenses:* Tuition, state resident: full-time $10,723; part-time $745 per credit. Tuition, nonresident: full-time $24,054; part-time $1578 per credit. *Required fees:* $374 per semester. Tuition and fees vary according to course load, program and reciprocity agreements. *Faculty research:* American, African, European, Asian, Latin American, and Middle Eastern history.

University of Wisconsin–Madison, Graduate School, College of Letters and Science, Latin American, Caribbean and Iberian Studies Program, Madison, WI 53706-1380. Offers MA, MA/JD. *Degree requirements:* For master's, 2 foreign languages, thesis. *Entrance requirements:* For master's, minimum GPA of 3.0. Electronic applications accepted. *Expenses:* Tuition, state resident: full-time $10,723; part-time $745 per credit. Tuition, nonresident: full-time $24,054; part-time $1578 per credit. *Required fees:* $374 per semester. Tuition and fees vary according to course load, program and reciprocity agreements. *Faculty research:* Development, gender, social movements, cultural studies, history.

Vanderbilt University, Graduate School, Program in Latin American Studies, Nashville, TN 37240-1001. Offers MA, LL M/MA, MBA/MA. *Faculty:* 1 (woman) full-time. *Students:* 6 full-time (5 women); includes 3 minority (1 Black or African American, non-Hispanic/Latino; 2 Hispanic/Latino). Average age 24. 17 applicants, 59% accepted, 6 enrolled. In 2014, 7 master's awarded. *Degree requirements:* For master's, 2 foreign languages, thesis or alternative. *Entrance requirements:* For master's, GRE General Test. Additional exam requirements/recommendations for international students: Required—TOEFL (minimum score 570 paper-based; 88 iBT). *Application deadline:* For fall admission, 1/15 for domestic and international students. Application fee: $0. Electronic applications accepted. *Expenses:* Tuition: Full-time $42,768; part-time $1782 per credit hour. *Required fees:* $422. One-time fee: $30 full-time. *Financial support:* Teaching assistantships with full tuition reimbursements, Federal Work-Study, institutionally sponsored loans, and health care benefits available. Financial award application deadline: 1/15; financial award applicants required to submit CSS PROFILE or FAFSA. *Faculty research:* Latin American and Iberian studies, anthropology, history, Spanish and Portuguese, social and political science. *Unit head:* Dr. William F. Robinson, Associate Director of Center for Latin American Studies, 615-343-1935, Fax: 615-343-6002, E-mail: william.f.robinson@vanderbilt.edu. *Application contact:* Norma Antillon, Administrative Assistant, 615-322-2527, Fax: 615-343-6002, E-mail: norma.g.antillon@vanderbilt.edu.
Website: http://www.vanderbilt.edu/clas/graduate-programs/

West Virginia University, Eberly College of Arts and Sciences, Department of History, Morgantown, WV 26506. Offers African history (MA, PhD); African-American history (MA, PhD); American history (MA, PhD); Appalachian/regional history (MA, PhD); East Asian history (MA, PhD); European history (MA, PhD); history of science and technology (MA, PhD); Latin American history (MA). Part-time programs available. *Degree requirements:* For master's, one foreign language, thesis (for some programs), oral exam, thesis defense; for doctorate, one foreign language, comprehensive exam, thesis/

dissertation, dissertation defense. *Entrance requirements:* For master's, GRE General Test, minimum GPA of 3.0; for doctorate, GRE General Test. Additional exam requirements/recommendations for international students: Required—TOEFL (minimum score 550 paper-based), IELTS (minimum score 6.5). Electronic applications accepted. *Faculty research:* United States, Appalachia, modern Europe, Africa, colonial and post-colonial societies.

Yale University, Graduate School of Arts and Sciences, Department of Spanish and Portuguese, New Haven, CT 06520. Offers Latin American literature (PhD); Luso-Brazilian and Spanish/Spanish American literatures (PhD); Spanish peninsular literature (PhD). Terminal master's awarded for partial completion of doctoral program. *Degree requirements:* For doctorate, 3 foreign languages, thesis/dissertation. *Entrance requirements:* For doctorate, GRE General Test.

Near and Middle Eastern Studies

The American University in Cairo, School of Global Affairs and Public Policy, Middle East Studies Program, Cairo, Egypt. Offers MA, Diploma. *Degree requirements:* For master's, proficiency in French or German, proficiency in Arabic (for international students). *Entrance requirements:* Additional exam requirements/recommendations for international students: Required—English entrance exam and/or TOEFL. Tuition and fees vary according to course load and program.

The American University in Cairo, School of Humanities and Social Sciences, Department of Arab and Islamic Civilizations, Cairo, Egypt. Offers Arabic language and literature (MA); Islamic art and architecture (MA); Islamic studies (MA, Diploma); Middle Eastern history (MA). Part-time programs available. *Degree requirements:* For master's, thesis optional, proficiency in French or German. *Entrance requirements:* Additional exam requirements/recommendations for international students: Required—English entrance exam and/or TOEFL. Electronic applications accepted. Tuition and fees vary according to course load and program. *Faculty research:* History of early Islam, Ayyubid, and Mamluk periods; nineteenth- and twentieth-century Middle East Islamic jurisprudence; contemporary Arabic literary criticism.

The American University in Cairo, School of Humanities and Social Sciences, Department of Sociology, Anthropology, Psychology, and Egyptology, Cairo, Egypt. Offers Egyptology and Coptology (MA); psychology (MA); sociology and anthropology (MA). *Degree requirements:* For master's, one foreign language, thesis. *Entrance requirements:* Additional exam requirements/recommendations for international students: Required—English entrance exam and/or TOEFL. Electronic applications accepted. Tuition and fees vary according to course load and program. *Faculty research:* Development, gender, sociopolitical economic formulations, social science indigenization, Arab world.

American University of Beirut, Graduate Programs, Faculty of Arts and Sciences, Beirut, Lebanon. Offers anthropology (MA); Arab and Middle Eastern history (PhD); Arabic language and literature (MA, PhD); archaeology (MA); biology (MS); cell and molecular biology (PhD); chemistry (MS); clinical psychology (MA); computational sciences (MS); computer science (MS); economics (MA); English language (MA); English literature (MA); environmental policy planning (MS); financial economics (MAFE); geology (MS); history (MA); mathematics (MA, MS); media studies (MA); Middle Eastern studies (MA); physics (MS); political studies (MA); psychology (MA); public administration (MA); sociology (MA); statistics (MA, MS); theoretical physics (PhD); transnational American studies (MA). Part-time programs available. *Faculty:* 107 full-time (32 women), 6 part-time/adjunct (2 women). *Students:* 230 full-time (161 women), 209 part-time (146 women). Average age 26. 261 applicants, 70% accepted, 83 enrolled. In 2014, 68 master's, 2 doctorates awarded. *Degree requirements:* For master's, one foreign language, comprehensive exam, thesis (for some programs); for doctorate, one foreign language, comprehensive exam, thesis/dissertation. *Entrance requirements:* For master's, GRE (for some MA/MS programs), letter of recommendation; for doctorate, GRE, letters of recommendation. Additional exam requirements/recommendations for international students: Required—TOEFL (minimum score 600 paper-based; 97 iBT), IELTS (minimum score 7). *Application deadline:* For fall admission, 4/1 for domestic and international students; for spring admission, 11/1 for domestic and international students. Application fee: $50. Electronic applications accepted. *Expenses: Tuition:* Full-time $15,462; part-time $859 per credit. *Required fees:* $692. Tuition and fees vary according to course load and program. *Financial support:* Research assistantships, career-related internships or fieldwork, institutionally sponsored loans, scholarships/grants, health care benefits, and unspecified assistantships available. Financial award application deadline: 2/4; financial award applicants required to submit FAFSA. *Faculty research:* Determinants of language proficiency among Arab learners of English as a foreign language; opinion mining, information retrieval, runtime verification, high performance computing; solar and fuel cells, self-organizing systems, heterocyclic chemistry, air and water chemistry; complex analysis, harmonic analysis, number theory; social and political psychology, clinical psychology; thin films physics and technology; theory of soft matter; religious and ethnic conflict; sports and politics. *Total annual research expenditures:* $966,000. *Unit head:* Dr. Patrick McGreevy, Dean, 961-1374374 Ext. 3800, Fax: 961-1744461, E-mail: pm07@aub.edu.lb. *Application contact:* Dr. Salim Kanaan, Director, Admissions Office, 961-1350000 Ext. 2590, Fax: 961-1750775, E-mail: sk00@aub.edu.lb.
Website: http://www.aub.edu.lb/fas/

The American University of Paris, Graduate Programs, Paris, France. Offers cross-cultural and sustainable business management (MA); cultural translation (MA); global communications (MA); global communications and civil society (MA); international affairs (MA); international affairs, conflict resolution and civil society development (MA); Middle East and Islamic studies (MA); Middle East and Islamic studies and international affairs (MA); public policy and international affairs (MA); public policy and international law (MA). *Degree requirements:* For master's, thesis (for some programs). *Entrance requirements:* For master's, minimum undergraduate GPA of 3.0. Additional exam requirements/recommendations for international students: Recommended—TOEFL, IELTS. Electronic applications accepted.

Brandeis University, Graduate School of Arts and Sciences, Department of Near Eastern and Judaic Studies, Waltham, MA 02454-9110. Offers Near Eastern and Judaic studies (MA, PhD); Near Eastern and Judaic studies and sociology (PhD); Near Eastern and Judaic studies and women's and gender studies (MA); teaching of Hebrew (MAT). Part-time programs available. Terminal master's awarded for partial completion of doctoral program. *Degree requirements:* For master's, one foreign language, thesis or alternative, proseminar, capstone; for doctorate, variable foreign language requirement, comprehensive exam, thesis/dissertation. *Entrance requirements:* For master's and doctorate, 3 letters of recommendation, transcript(s), statement of purpose, writing sample, resume. Additional exam requirements/recommendations for international students: Required—TOEFL (minimum score 600 paper-based; 100 iBT), PTE (minimum score 68); Recommended—IELTS (minimum score 7). Electronic applications accepted. *Faculty research:* Ancient Near East and Bible, Judaic studies, Israel Studies, modern Middle East, Arabic and Islamic civilizations.

Brown University, Graduate School, Department of Egyptology and Ancient Western Asian Studies, Providence, RI 02912. Offers ancient western Asian studies (PhD); Egyptology (PhD); history of the exact sciences in antiquity (PhD). *Degree requirements:* For doctorate, 2 foreign languages, comprehensive exam, thesis/dissertation. *Entrance requirements:* For doctorate, GRE General Test.

California State University, Long Beach, Graduate Studies, College of Liberal Arts, Department of History, Long Beach, CA 90840. Offers Africa and the Middle East (MA); ancient/medieval Europe (MA); Asia (MA); Latin America (MA); modern Europe (MA); United States (MA); world history (MA). Part-time and evening/weekend programs available. *Degree requirements:* For master's, one foreign language, comprehensive exam or thesis. Electronic applications accepted. *Faculty research:* All periods of European and American history, recent Asian and African history.

The Catholic University of America, School of Arts and Sciences, Department of Semitic and Egyptian Languages and Literatures, Washington, DC 20064. Offers Ancient Near East (Biblical Hebrew/Aramaic) (MA, PhD); Arabic (PhD); Christian Near East (Biblical Hebrew/Aramaic) (MA); Coptic (MA, PhD); Syriac (MA). Part-time programs available. *Faculty:* 3 full-time (0 women), 1 part-time/adjunct (0 women). *Students:* 10 full-time (2 women), 16 part-time (3 women); includes 3 minority (1 Hispanic/Latino; 2 Two or more races, non-Hispanic/Latino), 1 international. Average age 34. 11 applicants, 73% accepted, 4 enrolled. In 2014, 7 master's, 2 doctorates awarded. *Degree requirements:* For master's, one foreign language, comprehensive exam; for doctorate, 2 foreign languages, comprehensive exam, thesis/dissertation. *Entrance requirements:* For master's and doctorate, GRE General Test, statement of purpose, official copies of academic transcripts, three letters of recommendation. Additional exam requirements/recommendations for international students: Required—TOEFL (minimum score 580 paper-based). *Application deadline:* For fall admission, 7/15 priority date for domestic students, 7/1 for international students; for spring admission, 11/15 priority date for domestic students, 11/1 for international students. Applications are processed on a rolling basis. Application fee: $55. Electronic applications accepted. *Expenses: Tuition:* Full-time $40,200; part-time $1600 per credit hour. *Required fees:* $400; $195 per semester. One-time fee: $425. *Financial support:* Fellowships, research assistantships, teaching assistantships, Federal Work-Study, scholarships/grants, tuition waivers (full and partial), and unspecified assistantships available. Financial award application deadline: 2/1; financial award applicants required to submit FAFSA. *Faculty research:* Christian history and literature of the Near East, Biblical Hebrew, Arabic Christianity, Coptic, Syriac. *Unit head:* Dr. Edward M. Cook, Chair, 202-319-5083, Fax: 202-319-4735, E-mail: cooke@cua.edu. *Application contact:* Director of Graduate Admissions, 202-319-5057, Fax: 202-319-6533, E-mail: cua-admissions@cua.edu.
Website: http://semitics.cua.edu/

Columbia University, Graduate School of Arts and Sciences, New York, NY 10027. Offers African-American studies (MA); American studies (MA); anthropology (MA, PhD); art history and archaeology (MA, PhD); astronomy (PhD); biological sciences (PhD); biotechnology (MA); chemical physics (PhD); chemistry (PhD); classical studies (MA, PhD); classics (MA, PhD); climate and society (MA); earth and environmental sciences (PhD); East Asia: regional studies (MA); East Asian languages and cultures (MA, PhD); ecology, evolution and environmental biology (MA), including conservation biology; ecology, evolution, and environmental biology (PhD), including ecology and evolutionary biology, evolutionary primatology; economics (PhD); English and comparative literature (MA, PhD); French and Romance philology (MA, PhD); Germanic languages (MA, PhD); global French studies (MA); Hispanic cultural studies (MA); history (PhD); history and literature (MA); human rights studies (MA); Islamic studies (MA); Italian (MA, PhD); Japanese pedagogy (MA); Jewish studies (MA); Latin America and the Caribbean: regional studies (MA); Latin American and Iberian cultures (PhD); mathematics (MA, PhD), including finance (MA); medieval and Renaissance studies (MA); Middle Eastern, South Asian, and African studies (MA, PhD); modern art: critical and curatorial studies (MA); modern European studies (MA); museum anthropology (MA); music (DMA, PhD); oral history (MA); philosophical foundations of physics (MA); philosophy (MA, PhD); physics (PhD); political science (MA, PhD); psychology (PhD); quantitative methods in the social sciences (MA); religion (MA, PhD); Russia, Eurasia and East Europe: regional studies (MA); Russian translation (MA); Slavic cultures (MA); Slavic languages (MA, PhD); sociology (MA, PhD); South Asian studies (MA); statistics (MA, PhD); theatre (PhD); JD/PhD; MA/MS; MD/PhD; MPA/MA. Dual-degree programs require admission to both Graduate School of Arts and Sciences and another Columbia school. Part-time and evening/weekend programs available. Terminal master's awarded for partial completion of doctoral program. *Degree requirements:* For master's, thesis (for some programs); for doctorate, comprehensive exam, thesis/dissertation. *Entrance requirements:* For master's and doctorate, GRE General Test, GRE Subject Test (for some programs). Electronic applications accepted. *Faculty research:* Humanities, natural sciences, social sciences.

Columbia University, School of International and Public Affairs, Middle East Institute, New York, NY 10027. Offers Certificate. Students must also be enrolled in a separate graduate degree program at Columbia University. Electronic applications accepted.

Cornell University, Graduate School, Graduate Fields of Arts and Sciences, Field of Archaeology, Ithaca, NY 14853-0001. Offers environmental archaeology (MA); historical archaeology (MA); Latin American archaeology (MA); medieval archaeology (MA); Mediterranean and Near Eastern archaeology (MA); Stone Age archaeology (MA). *Degree requirements:* For master's, one foreign language, thesis. *Entrance requirements:* For master's, GRE General Test, 3 letters of recommendation, sample of written work. Additional exam requirements/recommendations for international students: Required—TOEFL (minimum score 550 paper-based; 77 iBT). Electronic applications accepted. *Faculty research:* Anatolia, Lydia, Sardis, classical and Hellenistic Greece, science in archaeology, North American Indians, Stone Age Africa, Mayan trade.

Cornell University, Graduate School, Graduate Fields of Arts and Sciences, Field of History, Ithaca, NY 14853-0001. Offers African history (MA, PhD); American history (MA, PhD); ancient Greek history (PhD); ancient history (MA, PhD); ancient Roman history (PhD); early modern European history (MA, PhD); English history (MA, PhD);

French history (MA, PhD); German history (MA, PhD); history of science (MA, PhD); Korean history (PhD); Latin American history (MA, PhD); medieval Chinese history (MA, PhD); medieval history (MA, PhD); modern Chinese history (MA, PhD); modern European history (MA, PhD); modern Japanese history (MA, PhD); modern Middle Eastern history (PhD); premodern Islamic history (MA, PhD); premodern Japanese history (MA, PhD); Renaissance history (MA, PhD); Russian history (MA, PhD); South Asian history (PhD); Southeast Asian history (MA, PhD). Terminal master's awarded for partial completion of doctoral program. *Degree requirements:* For master's, thesis; for doctorate, 2 foreign languages, comprehensive exam, thesis/dissertation, 1 year of teaching experience. *Entrance requirements:* For master's and doctorate, GRE General Test, writing sample, 3 letters of recommendation. Additional exam requirements/recommendations for international students: Required—TOEFL (minimum score 550 paper-based; 77 iBT). Electronic applications accepted.

Cornell University, Graduate School, Graduate Fields of Arts and Sciences, Field of History of Art, Archaeology and Visual Studies, Ithaca, NY 14853. Offers 19th century art (PhD); African, African American and African diaspora (PhD); American art (PhD); ancient art and archaeology (PhD); Asian American art (PhD); Baroque art (PhD); comparative modernities (PhD); digital art (PhD); East Asian art (PhD); history of photography (PhD); Islamic art (PhD); Latin American art (PhD); medieval art (PhD); modern art (PhD); Renaissance art (PhD); Southeast Asian art (PhD); theory and criticism (PhD); visual studies (PhD). *Degree requirements:* For doctorate, one foreign language, comprehensive exam, thesis/dissertation, general exams in 3 areas. *Entrance requirements:* For doctorate, GRE General Test, sample of written work, 3 letters of recommendation. Additional exam requirements/recommendations for international students: Required—TOEFL (minimum score 550 paper-based; 77 iBT). Electronic applications accepted.

Cornell University, Graduate School, Graduate Fields of Arts and Sciences, Field of Near Eastern Studies, Ithaca, NY 14853-0001. Offers ancient Near Eastern studies (MA, PhD); Arabic and Islamic studies (MA, PhD); biblical studies (MA, PhD); Hebrew and Judaic studies (MA, PhD). Terminal master's awarded for partial completion of doctoral program. *Degree requirements:* For master's, one foreign language, thesis; for doctorate, 2 foreign languages, comprehensive exam, thesis/dissertation. *Entrance requirements:* For master's and doctorate, GRE General Test, 2 years of 1 Near Eastern language, 3 letters of recommendation, writing sample. Additional exam requirements/recommendations for international students: Required—TOEFL (minimum score 550 paper-based; 77 iBT). Electronic applications accepted. *Faculty research:* Ancient Near East (including archeology), Hebrew and Judaic studies (including Bible), early Christianity, Arabic and Islamic studies, modern Middle East.

George Mason University, College of Humanities and Social Sciences, Center for Global Islamic Studies, Fairfax, VA 22030. Offers Middle East and Islamic studies (MA). *Faculty:* 16 full-time (6 women). *Students:* 8 full-time (4 women), 12 part-time (9 women); includes 4 minority (2 Black or African American, non-Hispanic/Latino; 1 Asian, non-Hispanic/Latino; 1 Hispanic/Latino), 2 international. Average age 28. 29 applicants, 76% accepted, 8 enrolled. In 2014, 2 master's awarded. *Entrance requirements:* For master's, GRE, resume, 3 letters of recommendation, goals statement, writing sample, official transcripts. Additional exam requirements/recommendations for international students: Required—TOEFL (minimum score 570 paper-based; 80 iBT), IELTS (minimum score 6.5), PTE. Application fee: $65 ($80 for international students). *Expenses:* Tuition, state resident: full-time $9794; part-time $408 per credit hour. Tuition, nonresident: full-time $26,978; part-time $1124 per credit hour. *Required fees:* $2820; $118 per credit hour. Tuition and fees vary according to course load and program. *Financial support:* In 2014–15, 4 students received support, including 3 research assistantships with full and partial tuition reimbursements available (averaging $6,265 per year), 2 teaching assistantships with full and partial tuition reimbursements available (averaging $8,785 per year). *Total annual research expenditures:* $235,388. *Unit head:* Bassam S. Haddad, Middle East Studies Program Director, 703-993-2962, Fax: 703-993-1399, E-mail: bhaddad@gmu.edu. *Application contact:* Melissa Bejjani, Program Contact, E-mail: meis@gmu.edu.
Website: http://meis.gmu.edu

Georgetown University, Graduate School of Arts and Sciences, Edmund A. Walsh School of Foreign Service, The Center for Contemporary Arab Studies, Washington, DC 20057. Offers MA, Certificate, MA/JD, MA/PhD. *Degree requirements:* For master's, one foreign language, comprehensive exam, thesis or alternative, proficiency in Arabic. *Entrance requirements:* For master's, GRE, minimum GPA of 3.0. Additional exam requirements/recommendations for international students: Required—TOEFL (minimum score 600 paper-based; 100 iBT). Electronic applications accepted. *Faculty research:* Contemporary Arab world.

The George Washington University, Columbian College of Arts and Sciences, Department of Religion, Washington, DC 20052. Offers Islam (MA), including Hinduism and Islam. Part-time and evening/weekend programs available. *Faculty:* 8 full-time (3 women). *Students:* 8 full-time (4 women); includes 4 minority (3 Asian, non-Hispanic/Latino; 1 Hispanic/Latino), 3 international. Average age 27. 12 applicants, 83% accepted, 4 enrolled. In 2014, 2 master's awarded. *Degree requirements:* For master's, one foreign language, comprehensive exam, thesis. *Entrance requirements:* For master's, GRE General Test, interview, minimum GPA of 3.0. Additional exam requirements/recommendations for international students: Required—TOEFL (minimum score 550 paper-based; 80 iBT). *Application deadline:* For fall admission, 4/1 priority date for domestic students, 1/15 priority date for international students; for spring admission, 10/1 priority date for domestic students, 9/1 priority date for international students. Applications are processed on a rolling basis. Application fee: $75. Electronic applications accepted. *Financial support:* In 2014–15, 1 student received support. Federal Work-Study and tuition waivers available. *Unit head:* Dr. Robert Eisen, Chair, 202-994-4780, Fax: 202-994-9379, E-mail: eisen@gwu.edu. *Application contact:* Information Contact, 202-994-6325, Fax: 202-994-9379, E-mail: religion@gwu.edu.
Website: http://www.gwu.edu/~religion/

The George Washington University, Elliott School of International Affairs, Program in Middle East Studies, Washington, DC 20052. Offers MA. Part-time programs available. *Students:* 36 full-time (21 women), 23 part-time (11 women); includes 7 minority (1 Black or African American, non-Hispanic/Latino; 1 American Indian or Alaska Native, non-Hispanic/Latino; 2 Asian, non-Hispanic/Latino; 1 Hispanic/Latino; 2 Two or more races, non-Hispanic/Latino), 5 international. Average age 26. 96 applicants, 21 enrolled. In 2014, 25 master's awarded. *Degree requirements:* For master's, one foreign language, capstone project. *Entrance requirements:* For master's, GRE General Test, 2 years (or equivalent) of an approved regional language. Additional exam requirements/recommendations for international students: Required—TOEFL (minimum score 100 iBT), IELTS (minimum score 7). *Application deadline:* For fall admission, 1/15 priority date for domestic and international students; for spring admission, 10/1 for domestic students. Application fee: $75. Electronic applications accepted. *Financial support:* In 2014–15, 7 students received support. Fellowships with partial tuition reimbursements available, Federal Work-Study, and scholarships/grants available. Financial award application deadline: 1/15; financial award applicants required to submit FAFSA. *Unit head:* Prof. Marc Lynch, Director, 202-994-9249, E-mail: mesp@gwu.edu. *Application contact:* Nicole A. Campbell, Director of Graduate Admissions, 202-994-7050, Fax: 202-994-9537, E-mail: esiagrad@gwu.edu. Website: http://elliott.gwu.edu/middle-east-studies

Harvard University, Graduate School of Arts and Sciences, Committee on Middle Eastern Studies, Cambridge, MA 02138. Offers anthropology and Middle Eastern studies (PhD); economics and Middle Eastern studies (PhD); fine arts and Middle Eastern studies (PhD); history and Middle Eastern studies (PhD); regional studies–Middle East (AM). Terminal master's awarded for partial completion of doctoral program. *Degree requirements:* For master's, one foreign language; for doctorate, 2 foreign languages, thesis/dissertation. *Entrance requirements:* For master's, GRE General Test; for doctorate, GRE General Test, 1 year of course work in Middle Eastern regional studies, proficiency in a related language. Additional exam requirements/recommendations for international students: Required—TOEFL.

Harvard University, Graduate School of Arts and Sciences, Department of Near Eastern Languages and Civilizations, Cambridge, MA 02138. Offers Akkadian and Sumerian (AM, PhD); Arabic (AM, PhD); Armenian (AM, PhD); biblical history (AM, PhD); Hebrew (AM, PhD); Indo-Muslim culture (AM, PhD); Iranian (AM, PhD); Jewish history and literature (AM, PhD); Persian (AM, PhD); Semitic philology (AM, PhD); Syro-Palestinian archaeology (AM, PhD); Turkish (AM, PhD). *Degree requirements:* For doctorate, variable foreign language requirement, thesis/dissertation, general exams. *Entrance requirements:* For master's, GRE General Test; for doctorate, GRE General Test, proficiency in a Near Eastern language. Additional exam requirements/recommendations for international students: Required—TOEFL.

Johns Hopkins University, Zanvyl Krieger School of Arts and Sciences, Department of Near Eastern Studies, Baltimore, MD 21218-2699. Offers archaeology (PhD); Assyriology (PhD); Egyptology (PhD); Hebrew Bible/Northwest Semitics (PhD). *Degree requirements:* For doctorate, 2 foreign languages, comprehensive exam, thesis/dissertation. *Entrance requirements:* For doctorate, GRE. Additional exam requirements/recommendations for international students: Required—TOEFL (minimum score 600 paper-based; 100 iBT); Recommended—IELTS. Electronic applications accepted. *Faculty research:* Egyptology, Assyriology, Hebrew Bible/Northwest Semitic languages, Demotic Egyptian, archaeology.

Liberty University, Helms School of Government, Lynchburg, VA 24515. Offers criminal justice (MS); public policy (MA), including campaigns and elections, international affairs, Middle East affairs, public administration, public policy. Part-time programs available. Postbaccalaureate distance learning degree programs offered (no on-campus study). *Students:* 248 full-time (119 women), 522 part-time (209 women); includes 194 minority (157 Black or African American, non-Hispanic/Latino; 8 American Indian or Alaska Native, non-Hispanic/Latino; 7 Asian, non-Hispanic/Latino; 5 Hispanic/Latino; 1 Native Hawaiian or other Pacific Islander, non-Hispanic/Latino; 16 Two or more races, non-Hispanic/Latino), 14 international. Average age 34. 837 applicants, 55% accepted, 226 enrolled. In 2014, 65 degrees awarded. *Entrance requirements:* For master's, minimum undergraduate GPA of 3.0. Additional exam requirements/recommendations for international students: Required—TOEFL (minimum score 600 paper-based; 100 iBT). *Application deadline:* Applications are processed on a rolling basis. Application fee: $50. Electronic applications accepted. *Unit head:* Shawn D. Akers, Dean, 434-592-4986. *Application contact:* Jay Bridge, Director of Admissions, 800-424-9595, Fax: 800-628-7977, E-mail: gradadmissions@liberty.edu.

McGill University, Faculty of Graduate and Postdoctoral Studies, Faculty of Arts, Institute of Islamic Studies, Montréal, QC H3A 2T5, Canada. Offers MA, PhD, Diploma.

New York University, Graduate School of Arts and Science, Hagop Kevorkian Center for Near Eastern Studies, Department of Middle Eastern and Islamic Studies, New York, NY 10012-1019. Offers Middle Eastern and Islamic studies (MA, PhD); Middle Eastern and Islamic studies/history (PhD). Part-time programs available. *Faculty:* 17 full-time (6 women). *Students:* 37 full-time (17 women), 1 part-time (0 women); includes 2 minority (both Asian, non-Hispanic/Latino), 14 international. Average age 32. 101 applicants, 7% accepted, 4 enrolled. In 2014, 9 doctorates awarded. Terminal master's awarded for partial completion of doctoral program. *Degree requirements:* For master's, 2 foreign languages, thesis; for doctorate, 4 foreign languages, comprehensive exam, thesis/dissertation. *Entrance requirements:* For doctorate, GRE General Test. Additional exam requirements/recommendations for international students: Required—TOEFL. *Application deadline:* For fall admission, 12/18 for domestic and international students. Application fee: $100. *Financial support:* Fellowships with tuition reimbursements, teaching assistantships with tuition reimbursements, Federal Work-Study, and institutionally sponsored loans available. Financial award application deadline: 12/18; financial award applicants required to submit FAFSA. *Faculty research:* Middle Eastern history, Arabic/Persian/Turkish language and literature, cultures and societies of Middle East, Islamic studies. *Unit head:* Zvi Ben-Dor Benite, Chair, 212-998-8880, Fax: 212-995-4689, E-mail: mideast.studies@nyu.edu. *Application contact:* Everett Rowson, Atcing Director of Graduate Studies, 212-998-8880, Fax: 212-995-4689, E-mail: mideast.studies@nyu.edu.
Website: http://www.nyu.edu/gsas/dept/mideast/

New York University, Graduate School of Arts and Science, Hagop Kevorkian Center for Near Eastern Studies, Program in Near Eastern Studies, New York, NY 10012-1019. Offers Near Eastern studies (MA); Near Eastern studies/journalism (MA); Near Eastern studies/museum studies (MA). Part-time programs available. *Faculty:* 2 full-time (0 women). *Students:* 28 full-time (15 women), 12 part-time (9 women); includes 3 minority (1 Black or African American, non-Hispanic/Latino; 1 Asian, non-Hispanic/Latino; 1 Hispanic/Latino), 10 international. Average age 26. 73 applicants, 79% accepted, 22 enrolled. In 2014, 22 master's awarded. *Degree requirements:* For master's, one foreign language, thesis. *Entrance requirements:* For master's, GRE General Test. Additional exam requirements/recommendations for international students: Required—TOEFL. *Application deadline:* For fall admission, 1/4 for domestic and international students. Application fee: $100. *Financial support:* Fellowships with tuition reimbursements, teaching assistantships with tuition reimbursements, Federal Work-Study, and institutionally sponsored loans available. Financial award application deadline: 1/4; financial award applicants required to submit FAFSA. *Faculty research:* Politics, political economy, anthropology, history and culture of the Middle East. *Unit head:* Helga Tawil-Souri, Acting Director, 212-998-8877, Fax: 212-995-4144, E-mail: kevorkian.center@nyu.edu. *Application contact:* Greta Scharnweber, Associate Director, 212-998-8877, Fax: 212-995-4144, E-mail: kevorkian.center@nyu.edu.
Website: http://neareaststudies.as.nyu.edu/

New York University, Graduate School of Arts and Science, Program in Museum Studies, New York, NY 10012-1019. Offers museum studies (MA, Advanced Certificate), including Africana studies (MA), Hebrew and Judaic studies (MA), Latin American and Caribbean studies (MA), Near Eastern studies (MA). Part-time and evening/weekend programs available. *Students:* 45 full-time (39 women), 23 part-time (19 women); includes 15 minority (2 American Indian or Alaska Native, non-Hispanic/Latino; 3 Asian, non-Hispanic/Latino; 6 Hispanic/Latino; 4 Two or more races, non-Hispanic/Latino), 19 international. Average age 26. 123 applicants, 81% accepted, 29 enrolled. In 2014, 35 master's, 1 other advanced degree awarded. *Entrance requirements:* For master's, GRE General Test; for Advanced Certificate, master's degree or PhD. Additional exam requirements/recommendations for international

students: Required—TOEFL. *Application deadline:* For fall admission, 2/15 for domestic and international students; for spring admission, 11/1 for domestic and international students. Application fee: $100. *Financial support:* Application deadline: 2/15. *Faculty research:* Modern and contemporary art, history of museums and exhibitions, conservation of cultural materials, museum anthropology, ethnography. *Unit head:* Bruce Altshuler, Director, 212-998-8080, Fax: 212-995-4185, E-mail: museum.studies@nyu.edu. *Application contact:* Tatiana Kamorina, Department Administrator, 212-998-8080, Fax: 212-995-4185, E-mail: museum.studies@nyu.edu.
Website: http://www.nyu.edu/fas/program/museumstudies/

Princeton University, Graduate School, Department of Near Eastern Studies, Princeton, NJ 08544-1019. Offers MA, PhD. *Degree requirements:* For master's, one foreign language, thesis; for doctorate, 2 foreign languages, thesis/dissertation. *Entrance requirements:* For master's and doctorate, GRE General Test. Additional exam requirements/recommendations for international students: Required—TOEFL. Electronic applications accepted.

Rice University, Graduate Programs, School of Humanities, Department of Religious Studies, Houston, TX 77251-1892. Offers African religions (PhD); African-American religions (PhD); contemplative studies (PhD); gnosticism, esotericism, mysticism (PhD); Islam (PhD); Jewish thought and philosophy (PhD); modern Christianity in thought and popular culture (PhD); psychology of religion (PhD); the Bible and beyond (PhD). *Degree requirements:* For doctorate, 2 foreign languages, comprehensive exam, thesis/dissertation. *Entrance requirements:* For doctorate, GRE, letters of recommendation, writing sample. Additional exam requirements/recommendations for international students: Required—TOEFL (minimum score 600 paper-based; 90 iBT). Electronic applications accepted. *Faculty research:* Origins and historical development of Islam, history of Christianity, the study of comparative religion, African-American religion, religion and culture.

Southern Evangelical Seminary, Graduate Programs, Matthews, NC 28105. Offers apologetics (MA, D Min, Certificate); Christian education (MA); church ministry (MA, Certificate); divinity (Certificate), including apologetics (M Div, Certificate); Islamic studies (MA, Certificate); Jewish studies (MA); philosophy (MA); philosophy of religion (PhD); religion (MA); theology (M Div), including apologetics (M Div, Certificate), Biblical studies; youth ministry (MA). Part-time and evening/weekend programs available. Postbaccalaureate distance learning degree programs offered. *Degree requirements:* For master's, thesis (for some programs); for doctorate, 2 foreign languages, comprehensive exam (for some programs), thesis/dissertation. *Entrance requirements:* Additional exam requirements/recommendations for international students: Required—TOEFL (minimum score 600 paper-based).

The University of Arizona, College of Social and Behavioral Sciences, Department of Near Eastern Studies, Tucson, AZ 85721. Offers MA, PhD. Part-time and evening/weekend programs available. Terminal master's awarded for partial completion of doctoral program. *Degree requirements:* For master's, one foreign language; for doctorate, 3 foreign languages, thesis/dissertation. *Entrance requirements:* For master's, GRE General Test, 3 letters of recommendation, statement of purpose, curriculum vitae, writing sample; for doctorate, GRE General Test, 3 letters of recommendation, curriculum vitae, writing sample. Additional exam requirements/recommendations for international students: Required—TOEFL (minimum score 550 paper-based; 79 iBT). Electronic applications accepted.

University of California, Berkeley, Graduate Division, College of Letters and Science, Department of Near Eastern Studies, Group in Near Eastern Religions, Berkeley, CA 94720-1500. Offers PhD. Program offered jointly with Graduate Theological Union. *Degree requirements:* For doctorate, 2 foreign languages, thesis/dissertation, qualifying exam. *Entrance requirements:* For doctorate, GRE General Test, MA or equivalent in Near Eastern studies or related field; minimum GPA of 3.0, 3 letters of recommendation.

University of California, Berkeley, Graduate Division, College of Letters and Science, Department of Near Eastern Studies, Program in Near Eastern Studies, Berkeley, CA 94720-1500. Offers MA, PhD. *Degree requirements:* For doctorate, 2 foreign languages, thesis/dissertation, qualifying exam. *Entrance requirements:* For master's and doctorate, GRE General Test, minimum GPA of 3.0, 3 letters of recommendation.

University of California, Los Angeles, Graduate Division, College of Letters and Science, Department of Near Eastern Languages and Cultures, Los Angeles, CA 90034. Offers MA, PhD. *Degree requirements:* For master's, one foreign language, comprehensive exam; for doctorate, 2 foreign languages, thesis/dissertation, oral and written qualifying exams. *Entrance requirements:* For master's, GRE General Test, bachelor's degree; minimum undergraduate GPA of 3.25 (or its equivalent if letter grade system not used); for doctorate, GRE General Test, master's degree; minimum undergraduate GPA of 3.25 (or its equivalent if letter grade system not used). Additional exam requirements/recommendations for international students: Required—TOEFL. Electronic applications accepted.

University of California, Los Angeles, Graduate Division, College of Letters and Science, Interdepartmental Program in Indo-European Studies, Los Angeles, CA 90095. Offers PhD. *Degree requirements:* For doctorate, 2 foreign languages, thesis/dissertation, oral and written qualifying exams. *Entrance requirements:* For doctorate, bachelor's degree; minimum undergraduate GPA of 3.0 (or its equivalent if letter grade system not used); writing sample; competence in Latin. Additional exam requirements/recommendations for international students: Required—TOEFL. Electronic applications accepted.

University of California, Los Angeles, Graduate Division, International Institute, Interdepartmental Program in Islamic Studies, Los Angeles, CA 90095. Offers MA, PhD, MPH/MA. *Degree requirements:* For master's, one foreign language, comprehensive exam; for doctorate, one foreign language, thesis/dissertation, oral and written qualifying exams. *Entrance requirements:* For master's, GRE General Test, bachelor's degree; minimum undergraduate GPA of 3.0 (or its equivalent if letter grade system not used); language requirement; for doctorate, GRE General Test, master's degree; minimum undergraduate GPA of 3.0 (or its equivalent if letter grade system not used); proficiency in Arabic. Additional exam requirements/recommendations for international students: Required—TOEFL. Electronic applications accepted.

University of Chicago, Divinity School, PhD Program, Chicago, IL 60637. Offers anthropology and sociology of religions (PhD); bible (PhD); history of Christianity (PhD); history of Judaism (PhD); history of religions (PhD); Islamic studies (PhD); philosophy of religions (PhD); religion and literature (PhD); religions in America (PhD); religious ethics (PhD); theology (PhD). *Students:* 164 full-time (50 women); includes 18 minority (5 Black or African American, non-Hispanic/Latino; 8 Asian, non-Hispanic/Latino; 1 Hispanic/Latino; 4 Two or more races, non-Hispanic/Latino), 28 international. 185 applicants, 12% accepted, 18 enrolled. *Degree requirements:* For doctorate, 2 foreign languages, comprehensive exam, thesis/dissertation. *Entrance requirements:* For doctorate, GRE General Test. Additional exam requirements/recommendations for international students: Required—TOEFL (minimum score 600 paper-based; 104 iBT), IELTS (minimum score 7). *Application deadline:* For fall admission, 12/15 for domestic and international students. Application fee: $75. Electronic applications accepted. *Expenses: Tuition:* Full-time $46,899. *Required fees:* $347. *Financial support:* Fellowships, Federal Work-Study, institutionally sponsored loans, and scholarships/grants available. Financial award application deadline: 12/15; financial award applicants required to submit FAFSA. *Faculty research:* Anthropology and sociology of religions, history of religions, theology, religious ethics, philosophy of religions, Bible, history of Christianity/Judaism, Islamic studies, religions in America. *Unit head:* Dr. Margaret M. Mitchell, Dean/Professor of New Testament and Early Christian Literature, 773-702-8200. *Application contact:* John W. Howell, Coordinator for Recruiting and Admissions, 773-702-8249, Fax: 773-834-4581, E-mail: divinityadmissions@uchicago.edu.
Website: http://divinity.uchicago.edu/doctoral-program-phd

University of Chicago, Division of the Humanities, Department of Near Eastern Languages and Civilizations, Chicago, IL 60637. Offers PhD. *Students:* 126 full-time (47 women); includes 14 minority (4 Asian, non-Hispanic/Latino; 7 Hispanic/Latino; 3 Two or more races, non-Hispanic/Latino), 30 international. 143 applicants, 32% accepted, 14 enrolled. Terminal master's awarded for partial completion of doctoral program. *Degree requirements:* For doctorate, 2 foreign languages, comprehensive exam, thesis/dissertation. *Entrance requirements:* For doctorate, GRE General Test. Additional exam requirements/recommendations for international students: Required—TOEFL (minimum score 104 iBT), IELTS (minimum score 7). *Application deadline:* For fall admission, 12/15 for domestic and international students. Application fee: $90. Electronic applications accepted. *Expenses: Tuition:* Full-time $46,899. *Required fees:* $347. *Financial support:* Fellowships with full tuition reimbursements, teaching assistantships with full tuition reimbursements, Federal Work-Study, institutionally sponsored loans, scholarships/grants, and health care benefits available. Financial award application deadline: 12/15; financial award applicants required to submit FAFSA. *Unit head:* Dr. Theo van den Hout, Chair, 773-702-9512. *Application contact:* Braden Grams, Assistant Dean of Students, Admissions and Fellowships, 773-702-1552, Fax: 773-834-9148, E-mail: humanitiesadmissions@uchicago.edu.
Website: http://nelc.uchicago.edu/

University of Chicago, Division of the Social Sciences and Division of the Humanities, Center for Middle Eastern Studies, Chicago, IL 60637. Offers MA. *Students:* 23 full-time (15 women); includes 2 minority (1 Asian, non-Hispanic/Latino; 1 Hispanic/Latino), 7 international. 35 applicants, 86% accepted. In 2014, 11 master's awarded. *Degree requirements:* For master's, one foreign language, thesis. *Entrance requirements:* For master's, GRE General Test. Additional exam requirements/recommendations for international students: Required—TOEFL (minimum score 104 iBT), IELTS (minimum score 7). *Application deadline:* For fall admission, 1/5 for domestic and international students. Application fee: $90. Electronic applications accepted. *Expenses: Tuition:* Full-time $46,899. *Required fees:* $347. *Financial support:* In 2014–15, 8 students received support. Federal Work-Study, institutionally sponsored loans, and scholarships/grants available. Financial award application deadline: 1/5. *Unit head:* Prof. Hakan Karateke, Director. *Application contact:* Office of the Dean of Students, 773-702-8415, E-mail: admissions@ssd.uchicago.edu.
Website: http://cmes.uchicago.edu

University of Illinois at Urbana–Champaign, Graduate College, College of Liberal Arts and Sciences, Center for South Asian and Middle Eastern Studies, Champaign, IL 61820. Offers MA. *Students:* 5 (1 woman). *Degree requirements:* For master's, one foreign language, comprehensive exam, thesis or alternative. Application fee: $70 ($90 for international students). *Unit head:* Valerie Hoffman, Director, 217-333-2681, E-mail: vhoffman@illinois.edu. *Application contact:* Terri L. Gitler, Office Support Associate, 217-244-7331, E-mail: csames@illinois.edu.
Website: http://www.csames.illinois.edu/

The University of Kansas, Graduate Studies, College of Liberal Arts and Sciences, Center for Russian, East European and Eurasian Studies, Lawrence, KS 66045. Offers foreign area officer (MA); Russian, East European and Eurasian studies (MA, Graduate Certificate); JD/MA. Part-time programs available. *Faculty:* 2 full-time, 4 part-time/adjunct. *Students:* 6 full-time (0 women); includes 1 minority (Two or more races, non-Hispanic/Latino), 1 international. Average age 27. 8 applicants, 88% accepted, 1 enrolled. In 2014, 6 master's awarded. *Degree requirements:* For master's, one foreign language, comprehensive exam, interdisciplinary capstone research seminar. *Entrance requirements:* For master's, GRE General Test, two-page statement of educational and professional objectives, three letters of recommendation. Additional exam requirements/recommendations for international students: Required—TOEFL. *Application deadline:* For fall admission, 1/1 priority date for domestic and international students. Application fee: $55 ($65 for international students). Electronic applications accepted. *Financial support:* Fellowships with full tuition reimbursements, research assistantships with partial tuition reimbursements, and scholarships/grants available. Financial award application deadline: 1/31; financial award applicants required to submit FAFSA. *Faculty research:* Russian and East Central European history and culture; Ukrainian, Russian, and Central Asian domestic politics and international security; Slavic languages, linguistics, and literatures. *Unit head:* Dr. Mariya Y. Omelicheva, Chair, 785-864-4236, E-mail: omeliche@ku.edu. *Application contact:* Adrienne Landry, Graduate Admissions Contact, 785-864-4237, E-mail: crees@ku.edu.
Website: http://www.crees.ku.edu/

The University of Manchester, Faculty of Life Sciences, Manchester, United Kingdom. Offers adaptive organismal biology (M Phil, PhD); animal biology (M Phil, PhD); biochemistry (M Phil, PhD); bioinformatics (M Phil, PhD); biomolecular sciences (M Phil, PhD); biotechnology (M Phil, PhD); cell biology (M Phil, PhD); cell matrix research (M Phil, PhD); channels and transporters (M Phil, PhD); developmental biology (M Phil, PhD); Egyptology (M Phil, PhD); environmental biology (M Phil, PhD); evolutionary biology (M Phil, PhD); gene expression (M Phil, PhD); genetics (M Phil, PhD); history of science, technology and medicine (M Phil, PhD); immunology (M Phil, PhD); integrative neurobiology and behavior (M Phil, PhD); membrane trafficking (M Phil, PhD); microbiology (M Phil, PhD); molecular and cellular neuroscience (M Phil, PhD); molecular biology (M Phil, PhD); molecular cancer studies (M Phil, PhD); neuroscience (M Phil, PhD); ophthalmology (M Phil, PhD); optometry (M Phil, PhD); organelle function (M Phil, PhD); pharmacology (M Phil, PhD); physiology (M Phil, PhD); plant sciences (M Phil, PhD); stem cell research (M Phil, PhD); structural biology (M Phil, PhD); systems neuroscience (M Phil, PhD); toxicology (M Phil, PhD).

The University of Manchester, School of Languages, Linguistics and Cultures, Manchester, United Kingdom. Offers Arab world studies (PhD); Chinese studies (M Phil, PhD); East Asian studies (M Phil, PhD); English language (PhD); French studies (M Phil, PhD); German studies (M Phil, PhD); interpreting studies (PhD); Italian studies (M Phil, PhD); Japanese studies (M Phil, PhD); Latin American cultural studies (M Phil, PhD); linguistics (M Phil, PhD); Middle Eastern studies (M Phil, PhD); Polish studies (M Phil, PhD); Portuguese studies (M Phil, PhD); Russian studies (M Phil, PhD); Spanish studies (M Phil, PhD); translation and intercultural studies (M Phil, PhD).

University of Memphis, Graduate School, College of Arts and Sciences, Department of History, Memphis, TN 38152. Offers ancient Egyptian history (MA, PhD). Postbaccalaureate distance learning degree programs offered (no on-campus study). *Faculty:* 20 full-time (10 women), 1 (woman) part-time/adjunct. *Students:* 38 full-time (25 women), 47 part-time (23 women); includes 13 minority (12 Black or African American, non-Hispanic/Latino; 1 Hispanic/Latino), 3 international. Average age 36. 38 applicants, 32% accepted, 10 enrolled. In 2014, 13 master's, 5 doctorates awarded. *Degree requirements:* For master's, comprehensive exam, thesis optional; for doctorate, one

foreign language, comprehensive exam, thesis/dissertation, 60 credits plus 12 dissertation credits, 2 research seminars. *Entrance requirements:* For master's, GRE General Test or MAT, 18 undergraduate hours of course work in history with minimum GPA of 3.0, 2 letters of recommendation, writing sample; for doctorate, GRE General Test, GRE Subject Test, MA in history or related field, three letters of recommendation, writing sample, statement of purpose. Additional exam requirements/recommendations for international students: Required—TOEFL. *Application deadline:* For fall admission, 1/15 for domestic students; for spring admission, 9/15 for domestic students. Applications are processed on a rolling basis. Application fee: $35 ($60 for international students). Electronic applications accepted. *Financial support:* In 2014–15, 54 students received support. Research assistantships with full tuition reimbursements available, teaching assistantships with full tuition reimbursements available, career-related internships or fieldwork, Federal Work-Study, scholarships/grants, and unspecified assistantships available. Financial award application deadline: 2/15; financial award applicants required to submit FAFSA. *Faculty research:* African/African-American history; U.S. history; ancient Egyptian history; modern European history; women, gender, and family studies. *Unit head:* Dr. Aram Goudsouzian, Chairman, 901-678-2515, Fax: 901-678-2720, E-mail: agoudszn@memphis.edu. *Application contact:* Dr. Daniel Unowsky, Coordinator of Graduate Studies, 901-678-3385, Fax: 901-678-2720, E-mail: dunowsky@memphis.edu.
Website: http://history.memphis.edu/

University of Michigan, Horace H. Rackham School of Graduate Studies, College of Literature, Science, and the Arts, Department of Near Eastern Studies, Ann Arbor, MI 49286. Offers ancient Near Eastern studies (AM, PhD); Arabic for professional purposes (AM); Arabic language and literature (AM, PhD); Armenian studies (AM, PhD); Christianity in late antiquity (AM, PhD); Egyptology (AM, PhD); Hebrew Bible and ancient Israel (AM, PhD); Hebrew literature (AM, PhD); Islamic studies (AM, PhD); Jewish cultural studies (AM, PhD); Jewish mysticism (AM, PhD); Persian and Iranian studies (AM, PhD); Rabbinic literature (AM, PhD); Second Temple Judaism (AM, PhD); teaching of Arabic as a foreign language (AM); Turkish studies (AM, PhD). *Faculty:* 22 full-time (5 women), 1 (woman) part-time/adjunct. *Students:* 37 full-time (16 women); includes 2 minority (both Asian, non-Hispanic/Latino), 11 international. Average age 32. 72 applicants, 19% accepted, 6 enrolled. In 2014, 7 master's, 3 doctorates awarded. Terminal master's awarded for partial completion of doctoral program. *Degree requirements:* For master's, 2 foreign languages; for doctorate, 4 foreign languages, comprehensive exam, thesis/dissertation, preliminary exams, oral defense of dissertation. *Entrance requirements:* Additional exam requirements/recommendations for international students: Required—TOEFL (minimum score 560 paper-based; 84 iBT). *Application deadline:* For fall admission, 12/15 for domestic and international students. Application fee: $65 ($75 for international students). Electronic applications accepted. *Financial support:* In 2014–15, 22 students received support. Fellowships with full tuition reimbursements available, teaching assistantships with full tuition reimbursements available, scholarships/grants, health care benefits, unspecified assistantships, and spring/summer stipends available. Financial award application deadline: 12/15. *Faculty research:* Middle and Near Eastern literatures, languages, cultures from ancient times to the present. *Unit head:* Prof. Gottfried Hagen, Chair, 734-764-0314, E-mail: ghagen@umich.edu. *Application contact:* Student Services, 734-764-0315, E-mail: nes-gradservices@umich.edu.
Website: http://www.umich.edu/~neareast/

University of Michigan, Horace H. Rackham School of Graduate Studies, Interdepartmental Program in Modern Middle Eastern and North African Studies, Ann Arbor, MI 48109. Offers AM, JD/AM, MBA/AM. *Degree requirements:* For master's, one foreign language, thesis or alternative. *Entrance requirements:* For master's, GRE General Test. Additional exam requirements/recommendations for international students: Required—TOEFL (minimum score 560 paper-based; 84 iBT). Electronic applications accepted. *Faculty research:* The Middle East and North Africa.

University of Pennsylvania, School of Arts and Sciences, Graduate Group in Near Eastern Languages and Civilization, Philadelphia, PA 19104. Offers AM, PhD. *Faculty:* 23 full-time (10 women), 4 part-time/adjunct (0 women). *Students:* 26 full-time (11 women), 4 part-time (0 women); includes 2 minority (1 Hispanic/Latino; 1 Two or more races, non-Hispanic/Latino), 5 international. 52 applicants, 13% accepted, 3 enrolled. In 2014, 7 master's, 1 doctorate awarded. Application fee: $70. *Financial support:* Institutionally sponsored loans, scholarships/grants, traineeships, health care benefits, and unspecified assistantships available. *Unit head:* Dr. Ralph M. Rosen, Associate Dean for Graduate Studies, 215-898-7156, Fax: 215-573-8068, E-mail: grad-dean@sas.upenn.edu. *Application contact:* Arts and Sciences Graduate Admissions, 215-573-5816, Fax: 215-573-8068, E-mail: gdasadmis@sas.upenn.edu.
Website: http://www.sas.upenn.edu/graduate-division

University of South Africa, College of Human Sciences, Pretoria, South Africa. Offers adult education (M Ed); African languages (MA, PhD); African politics (MA, PhD); Afrikaans (MA, PhD); ancient history (MA, PhD); ancient Near Eastern studies (MA, PhD); anthropology (MA, PhD); applied linguistics (MA); Arabic (MA, PhD); archaeology (MA); art history (MA); Biblical archaeology (MA); Biblical studies (M Th, D Th, PhD); Christian spirituality (M Th, D Th); church history (M Th, D Th); classical studies (MA, PhD); clinical psychology (MA); communication (MA, PhD); comparative education (M Ed, Ed D); consulting psychology (D Admin, D Com, PhD); curriculum studies (M Ed, Ed D); development studies (M Admin, MA, D Admin, PhD); didactics (M Ed, Ed D); education (M Tech); education management (M Ed, Ed D); educational psychology (M Ed); English (MA); environmental education (M Ed); French (MA, PhD); German (MA, PhD); Greek (MA); guidance and counseling (M Ed); health studies (MA, PhD), including health sciences education (MA), health services management (MA), medical and surgical nursing science (critical care general) (MA), midwifery and neonatal nursing science (MA), trauma and emergency care (MA); history (MA, PhD); history of education (Ed D); inclusive education (M Ed, Ed D); information and communications technology policy and regulation (MA); information science (MA, MIS, PhD); international politics (MA, PhD); Islamic studies (MA, PhD); Italian (MA, PhD); Judaica (MA, PhD); linguistics (MA, PhD); mathematical education (M Ed); mathematics education (MA); missiology (M Th, D Th); modern Hebrew (MA, PhD); musicology (MA, MMus, D Mus, PhD); natural science education (M Ed); New Testament (M Th, D Th); Old Testament (D Th); pastoral therapy (M Th, D Th); philosophy (MA); philosophy of education (M Ed, Ed D); politics (MA, PhD); Portuguese (MA, PhD); practical theology (M Th, D Th); psychology (MA, MS, PhD); psychology of education (M Ed, Ed D); public health (MA); religious studies (MA, D Th, PhD); Romance languages (MA); Russian (MA, PhD); Semitic languages (MA, PhD); social behavior studies in HIV/AIDS (MA); social science (mental health) (MA); social science in development studies (MA); social science in psychology (MA); social science in social work (MA); social science in sociology (MA); social work (MSW, DSW, PhD); socio-education (M Ed, Ed D); sociolinguistics (MA); sociology (MA, PhD); Spanish (MA, PhD); systematic theology (M Th, D Th); TESOL (teaching English to speakers of other languages) (MA); theological ethics (M Th, D Th); theory of literature (MA, PhD); urban ministries (D Th); urban ministry (M Th).

The University of Texas at Austin, Graduate School, College of Liberal Arts, Department of Middle Eastern Studies, Austin, TX 78712-1111. Offers Middle Eastern languages and cultures (MA, PhD); Middle Eastern studies (MA); JD/MA; MA/M Sc; MA/MA; MBA/MA; MPA/MA. *Degree requirements:* For master's, one foreign language, comprehensive exam, thesis; for doctorate, 2 foreign languages, comprehensive exam, thesis/dissertation. *Entrance requirements:* For master's and doctorate, GRE General Test. Additional exam requirements/recommendations for international students: Required—TOEFL. Electronic applications accepted. *Faculty research:* Islamic studies, Persian language and literature, Hebrew language, Jewish studies, Arabic literature and language.

University of Toronto, School of Graduate Studies, Faculty of Arts and Science, Department of Near and Middle Eastern Civilizations, Toronto, ON M5S 2J7, Canada. Offers MA, PhD. Part-time programs available. *Degree requirements:* For master's, thesis optional; for doctorate, 2 foreign languages, thesis/dissertation, language proficiency exams. *Entrance requirements:* For master's, BA in relevant area, minimum B+ average in final year, prior coursework in ancient Near Eastern or Islamic civilizations, 2 letters of reference; for doctorate, MA in relevant area with a minimum A-average, 2 letters of reference. Additional exam requirements/recommendations for international students: Required—TOEFL (minimum score 580 paper-based; 93 iBT), TWE (minimum score 5). Electronic applications accepted.

University of Utah, Graduate School, College of Humanities, Program in Middle East Studies, Salt Lake City, UT 84112. Offers Arabic (MA, PhD); Hebrew (MA); history (MA, PhD); Persian (MA, PhD); political science (MA, PhD). *Students:* 1 full-time (0 women), 8 part-time (3 women); includes 1 minority (Asian, non-Hispanic/Latino), 3 international. Average age 40. In 2014, 5 master's, 1 doctorate awarded. Terminal master's awarded for partial completion of doctoral program. *Degree requirements:* For master's, 2 foreign languages, comprehensive exam, thesis optional; for doctorate, 3 foreign languages, comprehensive exam, thesis/dissertation. *Entrance requirements:* For master's, GRE General Test, minimum GPA of 3.2; for doctorate, GRE General Test, MA in Middle East studies or equivalent, minimum GPA of 3.2. Additional exam requirements/recommendations for international students: Required—TOEFL (minimum score 580 paper-based; 92 iBT); Recommended—IELTS (minimum score 7). *Application deadline:* For fall admission, 1/15 priority date for domestic and international students. Application fee: $55 ($65 for international students). Electronic applications accepted. *Financial support:* In 2014–15, 5 students received support, including 2 teaching assistantships with full tuition reimbursements available (averaging $13,500 per year); fellowships and unspecified assistantships also available. Financial award application deadline: 1/15. *Faculty research:* Islamic studies; Middle Eastern history; political science; Judaic studies; anthropology; Arabic, Persian, Hebrew, and Turkish language and literature. *Unit head:* Johanna Watzinger-Tharp, Director, 801-581-7148, Fax: 801-581-6105, E-mail: j.tharp@utah.edu. *Application contact:* Kellie Hubbard, Academic Advisor, 801-581-5362, Fax: 801-581-6105, E-mail: kellie.hubbard@utah.edu.
Website: http://www.mec.utah.edu

University of Virginia, College and Graduate School of Arts and Sciences, Department of Middle Eastern and South Asian Languages and Cultures, Charlottesville, VA 22903. Offers Middle Eastern and South Asian studies (MA). *Faculty:* 15 full-time (6 women). *Students:* 6 full-time (4 women), 1 part-time (0 women); includes 2 minority (1 Black or African American, non-Hispanic/Latino; 1 Asian, non-Hispanic/Latino), 2 international. Average age 28. 10 applicants, 100% accepted, 5 enrolled. In 2014, 3 master's awarded. Application fee: $60. *Expenses:* Tuition, state resident: full-time $14,164; part-time $349 per credit hour. Tuition, nonresident: full-time $23,722; part-time $1300 per credit hour. *Required fees:* $2514. *Unit head:* Farzaneh Milani, Chair, 434-243-4930, Fax: 434-243-1528, E-mail: fmm2z@virginia.edu. *Application contact:* Robert Hueckstedt, Director of Graduate Studies, 434-243-8228, Fax: 434-243-1528, E-mail: rah2k@virginia.edu.
Website: http://mesalc.virginia.edu/

University of Washington, Graduate School, College of Arts and Sciences, Department of Near Eastern Languages and Civilization, Seattle, WA 98195. Offers MA. *Degree requirements:* For master's, 2 foreign languages, exams. *Entrance requirements:* For master's, GRE, minimum GPA of 3.0. Additional exam requirements/recommendations for international students: Required—TOEFL. Electronic applications accepted. *Faculty research:* Arabic, Hebrew, Persian, and Turkish literature; Islamic civilization and religion; Central Asian Turkic language and literature; Hebrew Bible and ancient Near East; ancient Christianity.

University of Washington, Graduate School, College of Arts and Sciences, Henry M. Jackson School of International Studies, Middle East Studies Program, Seattle, WA 98195. Offers MAIS. *Degree requirements:* For master's, one foreign language, thesis optional. *Entrance requirements:* For master's, GRE General Test, minimum GPA of 3.0 in last two years. Additional exam requirements/recommendations for international students: Required—TOEFL (minimum score 500 paper-based; 92 iBT), IELTS (minimum score 7). Electronic applications accepted.

University of Washington, Graduate School, Interdisciplinary Program in Near and Middle Eastern Studies, Seattle, WA 98195. Offers PhD. *Degree requirements:* For doctorate, 3 foreign languages, thesis/dissertation. *Entrance requirements:* For doctorate, GRE General Test, minimum GPA of 3.0. Additional exam requirements/recommendations for international students: Required—TOEFL. Electronic applications accepted.

University of Waterloo, Graduate Studies, Faculty of Arts, Department of Classical Studies, Waterloo, ON N2L 3G1, Canada. Offers ancient Mediterranean cultures (MA). *Degree requirements:* For master's, one foreign language. *Faculty research:* Ancient history, philosophy, anthropology, religion, culture.

University of Wisconsin–Madison, Graduate School, College of Letters and Science, Department of History, Madison, WI 53706-1380. Offers African history (MA, PhD); Central Asian history (MA, PhD); comparative world history (MA, PhD); East Asian history (MA, PhD); European history (MA, PhD); gender and women's history (MA, PhD); Latin American and Caribbean history (MA, PhD); Middle Eastern history (MA, PhD); South Asian history (MA, PhD); Southeast Asian history (MA, PhD); United States history (MA, PhD). Terminal master's awarded for partial completion of doctoral program. *Degree requirements:* For master's, thesis (for some programs); for doctorate, variable foreign language requirement, thesis/dissertation. *Entrance requirements:* For master's and doctorate, GRE General Test. Additional exam requirements/recommendations for international students: Required—Michigan English Language Assessment Battery or TOEFL. Electronic applications accepted. *Expenses:* Tuition, state resident: full-time $10,723; part-time $745 per credit. Tuition, nonresident: full-time $24,054; part-time $1578 per credit. *Required fees:* $374 per semester. Tuition and fees vary according to course load, program and reciprocity agreements. *Faculty research:* American, African, European, Asian, Latin American, and Middle Eastern history.

Washington University in St. Louis, Graduate School of Arts and Sciences, Department of Jewish, Islamic, and Near Eastern Languages and Cultures, St. Louis, MO 63130-4899. Offers Islamic and Near Eastern studies (MA); Jewish studies (MA). *Degree requirements:* For master's, one foreign language, thesis (for some programs). *Entrance requirements:* For master's, GRE General Test. Additional exam requirements/recommendations for international students: Required—TOEFL. Electronic applications accepted. *Faculty research:* Islamic and Near Eastern studies (Islamic history, Arabic

language and literature, modern Middle East history), Jewish studies (Hebrew Bible, Rabbinic literature, Jewish history, modern Hebrew literature).

Wayne State University, College of Liberal Arts and Sciences, Department of Classical and Modern Languages, Literatures, and Cultures, Program in Near Eastern Languages, Detroit, MI 48202. Offers Arabic (MA); Hebrew (MA). *Students:* 5 full-time (2 women), 2 part-time (1 woman); includes 3 minority (1 Asian, non-Hispanic/Latino; 2 Two or more races, non-Hispanic/Latino). Average age 26. 10 applicants, 40% accepted, 1 enrolled. In 2014, 4 master's awarded. *Degree requirements:* For master's, one foreign language, thesis or essay. *Entrance requirements:* For master's, GRE (recommended), letter of intent, 5-7 page sample of writing in English, three confidential letters of recommendation, minimum undergraduate GPA of 3.0, two years of Arabic language with minimum GPA of 3.5 in Arabic courses, prior coursework in Islamic/Near Eastern studies (preferred), adequate knowledge of at least one Semitic language and Near Eastern culture. Additional exam requirements/recommendations for international students: Required—TOEFL (minimum score 550 paper-based; 79 iBT), TWE (minimum score 5.5), Michigan English Language Assessment Battery (minimum score 85); Recommended—IELTS (minimum score 6.5). *Application deadline:* For fall admission, 6/1 priority date for domestic students, 5/1 priority date for international students; for winter admission, 10/1 priority date for domestic students, 9/1 priority date for international students; for spring admission, 2/1 priority date for domestic students, 1/1 priority date for international students. Applications are processed on a rolling basis.

Application fee: $0. Electronic applications accepted. *Expenses:* Tuition, state resident: full-time $10,294; part-time $571.90 per credit hour. Tuition, nonresident: full-time $29,730; part-time $1238.75 per credit hour. *Required fees:* $1365; $43.50 per credit hour. $291.10 per semester. Tuition and fees vary according to course load and program. *Financial support:* Fellowships, teaching assistantships with tuition reimbursements, scholarships/grants, health care benefits, and unspecified assistantships available. Support available to part-time students. Financial award application deadline: 3/31; financial award applicants required to submit FAFSA. *Faculty research:* Modern Middle East history, Arabic language and culture studies, Chinese linguistics, Islamic studies, Judaic studies. *Unit head:* Dr. Anne Duggan, Chair, E-mail: a.duggan@wayne.edu. *Application contact:* Vanessa DeGifis, Assistant Professor/Student Advisor, 313-577-0481, E-mail: vdegifis@wayne.edu. Website: http://clas.wayne.edu/languages/manel

Yale University, Graduate School of Arts and Sciences, Department of Near Eastern Languages and Civilizations, New Haven, CT 06520. Offers Arabic and Islamic studies (MA, PhD); archaeology of the ancient Near East (MA, PhD); Assyriology (MA, PhD); Egyptology (MA, PhD); Graeco-Arabic studies (MA, PhD); Northwest Semitic, Bible, comparative Semitics (MA, PhD). *Degree requirements:* For doctorate, 2 foreign languages, thesis/dissertation. *Entrance requirements:* For doctorate, GRE General Test.

Northern Studies

University of Alaska Fairbanks, College of Liberal Arts, Department of Northern Studies, Fairbanks, AK 99775-6460. Offers environmental politics and policy (MA); Northern history (MA). Part-time programs available. *Faculty:* 1 (woman) full-time. *Students:* 16 full-time (8 women), 17 part-time (13 women); includes 1 minority (Two or more races, non-Hispanic/Latino), 2 international. Average age 37. 15 applicants, 47% accepted, 7 enrolled. In 2014, 7 master's awarded. *Degree requirements:* For master's, comprehensive exam, oral defense of project or thesis. *Entrance requirements:* For master's, bachelor's degree from accredited institution with minimum cumulative undergraduate and major GPA of 3.0. Additional exam requirements/recommendations for international students: Required—TOEFL (minimum score 550 paper-based; 79 iBT), IELTS (minimum score 6.5). *Application deadline:* For fall admission, 6/1 for domestic students, 3/1 for international students; for spring admission, 10/15 for domestic students, 9/1 for international students. Applications are processed on a rolling basis. Application fee: $60. Electronic applications accepted. *Expenses:* Tuition, state resident: full-time $7614; part-time $423 per credit. Tuition, nonresident: full-time $15,552; part-time $864 per credit. Tuition and fees vary according to course level, course load and reciprocity agreements. *Financial support:* In 2014–15, 4 research assistantships with full tuition reimbursements (averaging $6,012 per year), 10 teaching assistantships with full tuition reimbursements (averaging $8,530 per year) were awarded; fellowships with full tuition reimbursements, career-related internships or fieldwork, Federal Work-Study, scholarships/grants, health care benefits, and unspecified assistantships also available. Support available to part-time students. Financial award application deadline: 1/1; financial award applicants required to submit FAFSA. *Unit head:* Mary Ehrlander, Director, 907-474-7126, Fax: 907-474-5817, E-mail: fynors@uaf.edu. *Application contact:* Mary Kreta, Director of Admissions, 907-474-7500, Fax: 907-474-7097, E-mail: admissions@uaf.edu. Website: http://www.uaf.edu/northern/

University of Manitoba, Faculty of Graduate Studies, Faculty of Arts, Department of Icelandic Language and Literature, Winnipeg, MB R3T 2N2, Canada. Offers MA.

Pacific Area/Pacific Rim Studies

University of Guam, Office of Graduate Studies, College of Liberal Arts and Social Sciences, Micronesian Studies Program, Mangilao, GU 96923. Offers MA. *Degree requirements:* For master's, thesis. *Entrance requirements:* For master's, GRE General Test. Additional exam requirements/recommendations for international students: Required—TOEFL. *Faculty research:* Adolescent suicide in Micronesia, history of Micronesia, traditional agriculture in the Pacific, Micronesian languages, health and cultural practices.

University of Hawaii at Manoa, Graduate Division, School of Pacific and Asian Studies, Program in Pacific Island Studies, Honolulu, HI 96822. Offers MA, Graduate Certificate. Part-time programs available. *Degree requirements:* For master's, thesis optional. *Entrance requirements:* Additional exam requirements/recommendations for international students: Required—TOEFL (minimum score 580 paper-based; 92 iBT), IELTS (minimum score 5).

University of San Francisco, College of Arts and Sciences, Program in Asia Pacific Studies, San Francisco, CA 94117-1080. Offers MA, MA/MBA. Part-time and evening/weekend programs available. *Faculty:* 5 full-time (2 women), 5 part-time/adjunct (all women). *Students:* 42 full-time (20 women), 1 part-time (0 women); includes 12 minority (5 Asian, non-Hispanic/Latino; 3 Hispanic/Latino; 1 Native Hawaiian or other Pacific Islander, non-Hispanic/Latino; 3 Two or more races, non-Hispanic/Latino), 21 international. Average age 28. 34 applicants, 94% accepted, 19 enrolled. In 2014, 16 master's awarded. *Degree requirements:* For master's, one foreign language, thesis.

Entrance requirements: For master's, minimum GPA of 3.0. *Application deadline:* For fall admission, 3/1 for domestic students. Applications are processed on a rolling basis. Application fee: $55 ($65 for international students). *Expenses:* Tuition: Full-time $21,762; part-time $1209 per credit hour. Tuition and fees vary according to degree level, campus/location and program. *Financial support:* In 2014–15, 15 students received support. Career-related internships or fieldwork, Federal Work-Study, and institutionally sponsored loans available. Financial award application deadline: 3/2; financial award applicants required to submit FAFSA. *Faculty research:* History of Christianity in China, U.S.-China policy, East Asian economies and political systems, sociolinguistic aspects of Japanese. *Unit head:* Dr. Brian Komei Dempster, Director, 415-422-6357, Fax: 415-422-5933. *Application contact:* Mark Landerghini, Information Contact, 415-422-5101, Fax: 415-422-2217, E-mail: asgraduate@usfca.edu. Website: http://www.usfca.edu/artsci/apsg/

University of Victoria, Faculty of Graduate Studies, Faculty of Humanities, Department of Pacific and Asian Studies, Victoria, BC V8W 2Y2, Canada. Offers MA. *Degree requirements:* For master's, thesis. *Entrance requirements:* For master's, minimum B+ average, writing sample. Additional exam requirements/recommendations for international students: Required—TOEFL (minimum score 575 paper-based), IELTS (minimum score 7). Electronic applications accepted. *Faculty research:* Culture, ethnicity and identity; economy and society; gender studies; languages and linguistics; literature.

Western European Studies

American Public University System, AMU/APU Graduate Programs, Charles Town, WV 25414. Offers accounting (MBA, MS); criminal justice (MA), including business administration, emergency and disaster management, general (MA, MS); educational leadership (M Ed); emergency and disaster management (MA); entrepreneurship (MBA); environmental policy and management (MS), including environmental planning, environmental sustainability, fish and wildlife management, general (MA, MS), global environmental management; finance (MBA); general (MBA); global business management (MBA); history (MA), including American history, ancient and classical history, European history, global history, public history; homeland security (MA), including business administration, counter-terrorism studies, criminal justice, cyber, emergency management and public health, intelligence studies, transportation security; homeland security resource allocation (MBA); humanities (MA); information technology (MS), including digital forensics, enterprise software development, information assurance and security, IT project management; information technology management (MBA); intelligence studies (MA), including criminal intelligence, cyber, general (MA, MS), homeland security, intelligence analysis, intelligence collection, intelligence

management, intelligence operations, terrorism studies; international relations and conflict resolution (MA), including comparative and security issues, conflict resolution, international and transnational security issues, peacekeeping; legal studies (MA); management (MA), including defense management, general (MA, MS), human resource management, organizational leadership, public administration; marketing (MBA); military history (MA), including American military history, American Revolution, civil war, war since 1945, World War II; military studies (MA), including joint warfare, strategic leadership; national security studies (MA), including general (MA, MS), homeland security, regional security studies, security and intelligence analysis, terrorism studies; nonprofit management (MBA); political science (MA), including American politics and government, comparative government and development, general (MA, MS), international relations, public policy; psychology (MA); public administration (MPA), including disaster management, environmental policy, health policy, human resources, national security, organizational management, security management; public health (MPH); reverse logistics management (MA); school counseling (M Ed); security management (MA); space studies (MS), including aerospace science, general (MA,

MS), planetary science; sports and health sciences (MS); teaching (M Ed), including curriculum and instruction for elementary teachers, elementary reading, English language learners, instructional leadership, online learning, special education; transportation and logistics management (MA), including general (MA, MS), maritime engineering management, reverse logistics management. Programs offered via distance learning only. Part-time and evening/weekend programs available. Postbaccalaureate distance learning degree programs offered (no on-campus study). *Faculty:* 426 full-time (236 women), 1,864 part-time/adjunct (880 women). *Students:* 475 full-time (215 women), 10,067 part-time (4,085 women); includes 3,462 minority (1,863 Black or African American, non-Hispanic/Latino; 74 American Indian or Alaska Native, non-Hispanic/Latino; 273 Asian, non-Hispanic/Latino; 831 Hispanic/Latino; 78 Native Hawaiian or other Pacific Islander, non-Hispanic/Latino; 343 Two or more races, non-Hispanic/Latino), 131 international. Average age 36. In 2014, 3,740 master's awarded. *Degree requirements:* For master's, comprehensive exam or practicum. *Entrance requirements:* For master's, official transcript showing earned bachelor's degree from institution accredited by recognized accrediting body. Additional exam requirements/recommendations for international students: Required—TOEFL (minimum score 550 paper-based), IELTS (minimum score 6.5). *Application deadline:* Applications are processed on a rolling basis. Application fee: $0. Electronic applications accepted. *Financial support:* Applicants required to submit FAFSA. *Faculty research:* Military history, criminal justice, management performance, national security. *Unit head:* Dr. Karan Powell, Executive Vice President and Provost, 877-468-6268, Fax: 304-724-3780. *Application contact:* Terry Grant, Vice President of Enrollment Management, 877-468-6268, Fax: 304-724-3780, E-mail: info@apus.edu.
Website: http://www.apus.edu

American University, School of International Service, Washington, DC 20016-8071. Offers comparative and regional studies (Certificate); cross-cultural communication (Certificate); development management (MS); ethics, peace, and global affairs (MA); European studies (Certificate); global environmental policy (MA, Certificate); global information technology (Certificate); international affairs (MA), including comparative and international disability policy, comparative and regional studies, international economic relations, international politics, natural resources and sustainable development, U.S. foreign policy; international communication (MA, Certificate); international development (MA, Certificate); international economic policy (Certificate); international economic relations (Certificate); international media (MA); international peace and conflict resolution (MA, Certificate); international politics (Certificate); international relations (PhD); international service (MIS); peacebuilding (Certificate); social enterprise (MA); the Americas (Certificate); United States foreign policy (Certificate); JD/MA. Part-time and evening/weekend programs available. Postbaccalaureate distance learning degree programs offered (no on-campus study). *Faculty:* 112 full-time (43 women), 59 part-time/adjunct (27 women). *Students:* 545 full-time (335 women), 443 part-time (271 women); includes 231 minority (82 Black or African American, non-Hispanic/Latino; 8 American Indian or Alaska Native, non-Hispanic/Latino; 51 Asian, non-Hispanic/Latino; 81 Hispanic/Latino; 2 Native Hawaiian or other Pacific Islander, non-Hispanic/Latino; 7 Two or more races, non-Hispanic/Latino), 120 international. Average age 28. 1,991 applicants, 70% accepted, 365 enrolled. In 2014, 426 master's, 9 doctorates, 6 other advanced degrees awarded. Terminal master's awarded for partial completion of doctoral program. *Degree requirements:* For master's, one foreign language, comprehensive exam, thesis or alternative; for doctorate, one foreign language, comprehensive exam, thesis/dissertation. *Entrance requirements:* For master's, GRE, transcripts, resume, 2 letters of recommendation, statement of purpose; for doctorate, GRE, transcripts, resume, 3 letters of recommendation, statement of purpose. Additional exam requirements/recommendations for international students: Required—TOEFL (minimum score 600 paper-based; 100 iBT). *Application deadline:* For fall admission, 1/15 for domestic students; for spring admission, 10/1 for domestic students, 9/15 for international students. Application fee: $50. Electronic applications accepted. *Financial support:* Application deadline: 1/15. *Unit head:* Dr. James Goldgeier, Dean, 202-885-1603, Fax: 202-885-2494, E-mail: goldgeier@american.edu. *Application contact:* Jia Jiang, Associate Director, Graduate Education Enrollment, 202-885-1689, Fax: 202-885-1109, E-mail: jiang@american.edu.
Website: http://www.american.edu/sis/

Armstrong State University, School of Graduate Studies, Program in History, Savannah, GA 31419-1997. Offers American and European history (MA); public history (MA). Part-time and evening/weekend programs available. *Faculty:* 5 full-time (2 women), 1 (woman) part-time/adjunct. *Students:* 6 full-time (5 women), 7 part-time (4 women); includes 3 minority (1 Black or African American, non-Hispanic/Latino; 1 Asian, non-Hispanic/Latino; 1 Hispanic/Latino). Average age 32. 9 applicants, 67% accepted, 5 enrolled. In 2014, 9 master's awarded. *Degree requirements:* For master's, one foreign language, comprehensive exam (for some programs), thesis (for some programs), thesis, internship, or advanced fieldwork. *Entrance requirements:* For master's, GRE General Test, minimum GPA of 3.0, letters of recommendation, BA in history or equivalent. Additional exam requirements/recommendations for international students: Required—TOEFL (minimum score 523 paper-based). *Application deadline:* For fall admission, 6/30 priority date for domestic students, 5/1 priority date for international students; for spring admission, 11/15 priority date for domestic students, 9/15 priority date for international students; for summer admission, 4/15 priority date for domestic students, 9/15 for international students. Applications are processed on a rolling basis. Application fee: $30. Electronic applications accepted. *Expenses:* Tuition, state resident: part-time $206 per credit hour. Tuition, nonresident: part-time $763 per credit hour. *Required fees:* $612 per semester. Tuition and fees vary according to course load, campus/location and program. *Financial support:* In 2014–15, research assistantships with full tuition reimbursements (averaging $5,000 per year) were awarded; career-related internships or fieldwork, Federal Work-Study, and unspecified assistantships also available. Support available to part-time students. Financial award application deadline: 3/15; financial award applicants required to submit FAFSA. *Faculty research:* Public history; European, Latin American, African, and United States history. *Unit head:* Dr. Christopher Curtis, Department Head, 912-344-3051, Fax: 912-344-3451, E-mail: chris.curtis@armstrong.edu. *Application contact:* Kathy Ingram, Associate Director of Graduate/Adult and Nontraditional Students, 912-344-2503, Fax: 912-344-3417, E-mail: graduate@armstrong.edu.
Website: http://www.armstrong.edu/Liberal_Arts/history/history_graduate_program

Baylor University, Graduate School, College of Arts and Sciences, Department of History, Waco, TX 76798. Offers history (MA); religion and culture (PhD); U.S. and Britain (PhD). Part-time programs available. Terminal master's awarded for partial completion of doctoral program. *Degree requirements:* For master's, one foreign language, comprehensive exam, thesis; for doctorate, one foreign language, comprehensive exam, thesis/dissertation. *Entrance requirements:* For master's and doctorate, GRE General Test, 18 semester hours in history. Additional exam requirements/recommendations for international students: Required—TOEFL. *Faculty research:* American religion and culture, medieval women and religion, U.S. women's history, Chinese missions, late nineteenth-century Germany, twentieth-century urban United States.

Boston College, Graduate School of Arts and Sciences, Department of History, Chestnut Hill, MA 02467-3800. Offers European national studies (MA); history (MA, PhD); medieval studies (MA). *Faculty:* 43 full-time. *Students:* 61 full-time (30 women); includes 4 minority (1 Black or African American, non-Hispanic/Latino; 1 Asian, non-Hispanic/Latino; 1 Hispanic/Latino; 1 Two or more races, non-Hispanic/Latino), 5 international. 194 applicants, 29% accepted, 20 enrolled. In 2014, 13 master's, 7 doctorates awarded. Terminal master's awarded for partial completion of doctoral program. *Degree requirements:* For master's, one foreign language, comprehensive exam, thesis optional; for doctorate, 2 foreign languages, comprehensive exam, thesis/dissertation. *Entrance requirements:* For master's and doctorate, GRE General Test, writing sample. Additional exam requirements/recommendations for international students: Required—TOEFL (minimum score 600 paper-based; 100 iBT), IELTS (minimum score 7). *Application deadline:* For fall admission, 1/2 for domestic and international students. Application fee: $75. Electronic applications accepted. *Financial support:* In 2014–15, fellowships with full tuition reimbursements (averaging $21,000 per year), teaching assistantships with full tuition reimbursements (averaging $21,000 per year) were awarded; Federal Work-Study, scholarships/grants, health care benefits, and unspecified assistantships also available. Support available to part-time students. Financial award application deadline: 3/1; financial award applicants required to submit FAFSA. *Faculty research:* U.S. history, medieval history, early modern European history, Latin American history, Asian history, transnational history. *Unit head:* Dr. Kevin Kenny, Chairperson, 617-552-1196, E-mail: kevin.kenny@bc.edu. *Application contact:* Dr. Prasannan Pathasarathi, Director of Graduate Studies, 617-552-3781, E-mail: pathasa@bc.edu.
Website: http://www.bc.edu/history

Brown University, Graduate School, Department of Portuguese and Brazilian Studies, Providence, RI 02912. Offers Brazilian studies (AM); English as a second language and cross-cultural studies (AM); Portuguese and Brazilian studies (AM, PhD); Portuguese bilingual education and cross-cultural studies (AM). *Degree requirements:* For doctorate, thesis/dissertation.

California State University, Long Beach, Graduate Studies, College of Liberal Arts, Department of History, Long Beach, CA 90840. Offers Africa and the Middle East (MA); ancient/medieval Europe (MA); Asia (MA); Latin America (MA); modern Europe (MA); United States (MA); world history (MA). Part-time and evening/weekend programs available. *Degree requirements:* For master's, one foreign language, comprehensive exam or thesis. Electronic applications accepted. *Faculty research:* All periods of European and American history, recent Asian and African history.

Carleton University, Faculty of Graduate Studies, Faculty of Public Affairs and Management, Institute of European and Russian Studies, Ottawa, ON K1S 5B6, Canada. Offers European and European Union studies (MA); European integration studies (Diploma); Russian, Eurasian and transition studies (MA). *Degree requirements:* For master's, one foreign language, thesis optional. *Entrance requirements:* For master's, honors degree or equivalent; 2 years of Russian, German or other central east European language. Additional exam requirements/recommendations for international students: Required—TOEFL. *Faculty research:* East-West relations, minority rights in Russia and Eastern Europe.

The Catholic University of America, School of Arts and Sciences, Department of History, Washington, DC 20064. Offers history (MA, PhD); religion and society in the late medieval and early modern world (MA); MA/JD; MSLS/MA. Part-time programs available. *Faculty:* 15 full-time (6 women). *Students:* 11 full-time (4 women), 23 part-time (11 women); includes 2 minority (both Two or more races, non-Hispanic/Latino), 2 international. Average age 31. 24 applicants, 58% accepted, 1 enrolled. In 2014, 3 master's, 4 doctorates awarded. *Degree requirements:* For master's, one foreign language, comprehensive exam, thesis optional; for doctorate, 2 foreign languages, comprehensive exam, thesis/dissertation. *Entrance requirements:* For master's and doctorate, GRE General Test, statement of purpose, official copies of academic transcripts, three letters of recommendation, writing sample. Additional exam requirements/recommendations for international students: Required—TOEFL (minimum score 580 paper-based). *Application deadline:* For fall admission, 7/15 priority date for domestic students, 7/1 for international students; for spring admission, 11/15 priority date for domestic students, 11/1 for international students. Applications are processed on a rolling basis. Application fee: $55. Electronic applications accepted. *Expenses: Tuition:* Full-time $40,200; part-time $1600 per credit hour. *Required fees:* $400; $195 per semester. One-time fee: $425. *Financial support:* Fellowships, research assistantships, teaching assistantships, Federal Work-Study, scholarships/grants, tuition waivers (full and partial), and unspecified assistantships available. Financial award application deadline: 2/1; financial award applicants required to submit FAFSA. *Faculty research:* Modern European intellectual history, history of mathematics and sciences, Renaissance, Catholic reformation, medieval women and gender. *Unit head:* Dr. Jerry Muller, Chair, 202-319-5484, Fax: 202-319-5569, E-mail: mullerj@cua.edu. *Application contact:* Director of Graduate Admissions, 202-319-5057, Fax: 202-319-6533, E-mail: cua-admissions@cua.edu.
Website: http://history.cua.edu/

Central Michigan University, College of Graduate Studies, College of Humanities and Social and Behavioral Sciences, Department of History, Mount Pleasant, MI 48859. Offers European history (Graduate Certificate); history (MA); modern history (Graduate Certificate); United States history (Graduate Certificate); MA/PhD. Part-time programs available. *Degree requirements:* For master's, thesis or alternative. Electronic applications accepted. *Faculty research:* Colonial and revolutionary United States history, modern European history, Latin American and transatlantic history, transnational and comparative history, United States social history.

Claremont Graduate University, Graduate Programs, School of Arts and Humanities, Department of History, Claremont, CA 91711-6160. Offers Africana history (Certificate); American studies and U.S. history (MA, PhD); archival studies (MA); early modern studies (MA, PhD); European studies (MA, PhD); oral history (MA, PhD); MBA/MA; MBA/PhD. *Faculty:* 4 full-time (2 women), 1 part-time/adjunct (0 women). *Students:* 41 full-time (19 women), 25 part-time (10 women); includes 18 minority (2 Black or African American, non-Hispanic/Latino; 1 American Indian or Alaska Native, non-Hispanic/Latino; 6 Asian, non-Hispanic/Latino; 6 Hispanic/Latino; 1 Native Hawaiian or other Pacific Islander, non-Hispanic/Latino; 2 Two or more races, non-Hispanic/Latino). Average age 37. In 2014, 7 master's, 6 doctorates, 1 other advanced degree awarded. Terminal master's awarded for partial completion of doctoral program. *Entrance requirements:* For master's and doctorate, GRE General Test. Additional exam requirements/recommendations for international students: Required—TOEFL (minimum score 550 paper-based; 80 iBT). *Application deadline:* For fall admission, 2/1 priority date for domestic and international students. Applications are processed on a rolling basis. Application fee: $80. Electronic applications accepted. *Expenses: Tuition:* Full-time $41,784; part-time $1741 per credit. *Required fees:* $600; $300 per semester. *Financial support:* Fellowships, research assistantships, Federal Work-Study, institutionally sponsored loans, and scholarships/grants available. Support available to part-time students. Financial award application deadline: 2/15; financial award applicants required to submit FAFSA. *Faculty research:* Intellectual and social history, cultural studies, gender studies, Western history, Chicano history. *Unit head:* Joshua

Goode, Chair, 909-607-7430, E-mail: joshua.goode@cgu.edu. *Application contact:* Erma Cross, Admissions and Alumni Coordinator, 909-607-9843, E-mail: erminia.cross@cgu.edu.
Website: http://www.cgu.edu/pages/369.asp

Columbia University, Graduate School of Arts and Sciences, New York, NY 10027. Offers African-American studies (MA); American studies (MA); anthropology (MA, PhD); art history and archaeology (MA, PhD); astronomy (PhD); biological sciences (PhD); biotechnology (MA); chemical physics (PhD); chemistry (PhD); classical studies (MA, PhD); classics (MA, PhD); climate and society (MA); earth and environmental sciences (PhD); East Asia: regional studies (MA); East Asian languages and cultures (MA, PhD); ecology, evolution and environmental biology (MA), including conservation biology; ecology, evolution, and environmental biology (PhD), including ecology and evolutionary biology, evolutionary primatology; economics (PhD); English and comparative literature (MA, PhD); French and Romance philology (MA, PhD); Germanic languages (MA, PhD); global French studies (MA); Hispanic cultural studies (MA); history (PhD); history and literature (MA); human rights studies (MA); Islamic studies (MA); Italian (MA, PhD); Japanese pedagogy (MA); Jewish studies (MA); Latin America and the Caribbean: regional studies (MA); Latin American and Iberian cultures (PhD); mathematics (MA, PhD), including finance (MA); medieval and Renaissance studies (MA); Middle Eastern, South Asian, and African studies (MA, PhD); modern art: critical and curatorial studies (MA); modern European studies (MA); museum anthropology (MA); music (DMA, PhD); oral history (MA); philosophical foundations of physics (MA); philosophy (MA, PhD); physics (PhD); political science (MA, PhD); psychology (PhD); quantitative methods in the social sciences (MA); religion (MA, PhD); Russia, Eurasia and East Europe: regional studies (MA); Russian translation (MA); Slavic cultures (MA); Slavic languages (MA, PhD); sociology (MA, PhD); South Asian studies (MA); statistics (MA, PhD); theatre (PhD); JD/PhD; MA/MS; MD/PhD; MPA/MA. Dual-degree programs require admission to both Graduate School of Arts and Sciences and another Columbia school. Part-time and evening/weekend programs available. Terminal master's awarded for partial completion of doctoral program. *Degree requirements:* For master's, thesis (for some programs); for doctorate, comprehensive exam, thesis/dissertation. *Entrance requirements:* For master's and doctorate, GRE General Test, GRE Subject Test (for some programs). Electronic applications accepted. *Faculty research:* Humanities, natural sciences, social sciences.

Columbia University, School of International and Public Affairs, Blinken European Institute, New York, NY 10027. Offers Certificate. Students must be enrolled in a separate graduate degree program at Columbia University. Electronic applications accepted.

Cornell University, Graduate School, Graduate Fields of Arts and Sciences, Field of History, Ithaca, NY 14853-0001. Offers African history (MA, PhD); American history (MA, PhD); ancient Greek history (PhD); ancient history (MA, PhD); ancient Roman history (PhD); early modern European history (MA, PhD); English history (MA, PhD); French history (MA, PhD); German history (MA, PhD); history of science (MA, PhD); Korean history (PhD); Latin American history (MA, PhD); medieval Chinese history (MA, PhD); medieval history (MA, PhD); modern Chinese history (MA, PhD); modern European history (MA, PhD); modern Japanese history (MA, PhD); modern Middle Eastern history (PhD); premodern Islamic history (MA, PhD); premodern Japanese history (MA, PhD); Renaissance history (MA, PhD); Russian history (MA, PhD); South Asian history (PhD); Southeast Asian history (MA, PhD). Terminal master's awarded for partial completion of doctoral program. *Degree requirements:* For master's, thesis; for doctorate, 2 foreign languages, comprehensive exam, thesis/dissertation, 1 year of teaching experience. *Entrance requirements:* For master's and doctorate, GRE General Test, writing sample, 3 letters of recommendation. Additional exam requirements/recommendations for international students: Required—TOEFL (minimum score 550 paper-based; 77 iBT). Electronic applications accepted.

Creighton University, Graduate School, College of Arts and Sciences, Program in East-West Studies, Omaha, NE 68178-0001. Offers MA. Part-time programs available. *Faculty:* 2 full-time (1 woman), 1 part-time/adjunct (0 women). *Students:* 5 full-time (2 women), 2 part-time (0 women); includes 1 minority (Black or African American, non-Hispanic/Latino), 2 international. Average age 34. 6 applicants, 83% accepted, 4 enrolled. *Degree requirements:* For master's, one foreign language. *Entrance requirements:* For master's, 3 recommendations; personal essay; interview. Additional exam requirements/recommendations for international students: Required—TOEFL. *Application deadline:* For fall admission, 7/1 for domestic and international students; for summer admission, 5/1 for domestic and international students. Application fee: $50. Electronic applications accepted. *Expenses:* Expenses: $40,000 tuition; $1,564 full-time fees per year, $306 part-time. *Financial support:* Application deadline: 5/1; applicants required to submit FAFSA. *Unit head:* Dr. Jinmei Yuan, Associate Professor, 402-280-3309, E-mail: jinmeiyuan@creighton.edu. *Application contact:* Lindsay Johnson, Director of Graduate and Adult Recruitment, 402-280-2703, Fax: 402-280-2423, E-mail: gradschool@creighton.edu.

East Carolina University, Graduate School, Thomas Harriot College of Arts and Sciences, Department of History, Greenville, NC 27858-4353. Offers American history (MA); Atlantic world (MA); European history (MA); history education (MA Ed); maritime studies (MA); military history (MA); public history (MA). Part-time and evening/weekend programs available. *Degree requirements:* For master's, one foreign language, comprehensive exam, thesis. *Entrance requirements:* For master's, GRE General Test, GRE Subject Test. Additional exam requirements/recommendations for international students: Required—TOEFL. *Expenses:* Tuition, state resident: full-time $4223. Tuition, nonresident: full-time $16,540. *Required fees:* $2184.

Georgetown University, Graduate School of Arts and Sciences, Edmund A. Walsh School of Foreign Service, BMW Center for German and European Studies, Washington, DC 20057. Offers MA, MA/JD, MA/PhD. *Degree requirements:* For master's, 2 foreign languages, comprehensive exam. *Entrance requirements:* For master's, GRE General Test. Additional exam requirements/recommendations for international students: Required—TOEFL. Electronic applications accepted. *Faculty research:* Transatlantic relations, European Union, German and European Studies.

The George Washington University, Elliott School of International Affairs, Program in European and Eurasian Studies, Washington, DC 20052. Offers MA. Part-time programs available. *Students:* 18 full-time (6 women), 9 part-time (6 women); includes 1 minority (Black or African American, non-Hispanic/Latino). Average age 27. 47 applicants, 9 enrolled. In 2014, 9 master's awarded. *Degree requirements:* For master's, one foreign language, capstone project. *Entrance requirements:* For master's, GRE General Test, 2 years (or the equivalent) of a modern European language or Russian, 2 semesters of introductory economics (macro or micro). Additional exam requirements/recommendations for international students: Required—TOEFL (minimum score 100 iBT), IELTS (minimum score 7). *Application deadline:* For fall admission, 1/15 priority date for domestic and international students; for spring admission, 10/1 for domestic students. Application fee: $75. Electronic applications accepted. *Financial support:* In 2014–15, 3 students received support. Fellowships with partial tuition reimbursements available and Federal Work-Study available. Financial award application deadline: 1/15; financial award applicants required to submit FAFSA. *Faculty research:* NATO, European economics, European history, European Union. *Unit head:* Peter Rollberg, Director, 202-994-6340, E-mail: rgpeter@gwu.edu. *Application contact:* Nicole A. Campbell, Director of Graduate Admissions, 202-994-7050, Fax: 202-994-9537, E-mail: esiagrad@gwu.edu.
Website: http://elliott.gwu.edu/academics/grad/ees/index.cfm

Georgia College & State University, Graduate School, College of Arts and Sciences, Department of History, Geography and Philosophy, Milledgeville, GA 31061. Offers public history (MA); U. S., Europe and world (MA). Part-time and evening/weekend programs available. *Students:* 4 full-time (1 woman), 6 part-time (3 women); includes 2 minority (1 American Indian or Alaska Native, non-Hispanic/Latino; 1 Hispanic/Latino). Average age 32. 4 applicants, 100% accepted, 4 enrolled. In 2014, 3 master's awarded. *Degree requirements:* For master's, one foreign language, comprehensive exam (for some programs), thesis or alternative. *Entrance requirements:* For master's, GRE, 2 letters of reference, transcript, minimum GPA of 3.0, undergraduate degree in history or other major with substantial work in history, foreign language. Additional exam requirements/recommendations for international students: Recommended—TOEFL (minimum score 550 paper-based; 79 iBT). *Application deadline:* For fall admission, 4/15 for domestic and international students; for spring admission, 11/15 for domestic students, 9/1 for international students; for summer admission, 4/1 for domestic students. Application fee: $40. Electronic applications accepted. *Expenses: Tuition, area resident:* Part-time $283 per credit hour. Tuition, nonresident: part-time $1027 per credit hour. *Required fees:* $995 per semester. Full-time tuition and fees vary according to course load, degree level, campus/location and program. *Financial support:* In 2014–15, 6 research assistantships were awarded; unspecified assistantships also available. Support available to part-time students. Financial award applicants required to submit FAFSA. *Unit head:* Dr. Stephen Auerbach, Graduate Coordinator for MA in History, 478-445-8276, E-mail: stephen.auerbach@gcsu.edu. *Application contact:* Kate Marshall, Graduate Admissions Coordinator, 478-445-1184, Fax: 478-445-1336, E-mail: grad-admit@gcsu.edu.
Website: http://www.gcsu.edu/history/masters.htm

Indiana University Bloomington, University Graduate School, College of Arts and Sciences, School of Global and International Studies, Institute for European Studies, Bloomington, IN 47405. Offers MA, MA/MBA, MPA/MA. Part-time programs available. *Faculty:* 16 full-time (5 women), 1 (woman) part-time/adjunct. *Students:* 3 full-time (1 woman). Average age 30. *Degree requirements:* For master's, one foreign language, thesis. *Entrance requirements:* For master's, GRE General Test. Additional exam requirements/recommendations for international students: Required—TOEFL. *Application deadline:* For fall admission, 1/15 priority date for domestic students, 12/15 for international students; for spring admission, 9/1 priority date for domestic students, 9/1 for international students. Applications are processed on a rolling basis. Application fee: $55 ($65 for international students). Electronic applications accepted. *Financial support:* In 2014–15, 5 students received support, including 2 research assistantships with full tuition reimbursements available (averaging $15,750 per year); fellowships, teaching assistantships, Federal Work-Study, scholarships/grants, health care benefits, and unspecified assistantships also available. Financial award applicants required to submit FAFSA. *Faculty research:* European integration, economics of Europe, European Union, European culture and identity, expansion of European Union. *Unit head:* Dr. Timothy Hellwig, Director, 812-855-1456, Fax: 812-855-7695, E-mail: thellwig@indiana.edu. *Application contact:* Megan Immerzeel, Administrative Secretary, 812-855-3280, Fax: 812-855-7695, E-mail: euroinst@indiana.edu.
Website: http://www.iub.edu/~euroinst/

La Salle University, School of Arts and Sciences, Program in History, Philadelphia, PA 19141-1199. Offers American history (Certificate); European history (Certificate); history (MA); history for educators (MA); public history (MA); teaching advanced placement history (Certificate); world history (Certificate). Part-time programs available. *Degree requirements:* For master's, thesis or comprehensive exam. *Entrance requirements:* For master's, GRE or MAT, 18 hours of undergraduate coursework in history or a related discipline with minimum GPA of 3.0; two letters of recommendation; brief personal statement (250 to 500 words); writing sample (preferably from an undergraduate research paper). Additional exam requirements/recommendations for international students: Required—TOEFL. Electronic applications accepted. Application fee is waived when completed online.

Mississippi State University, College of Arts and Sciences, Department of History, Mississippi State, MS 39762. Offers U.S. and European history (MA, PhD). Part-time programs available. *Faculty:* 22 full-time (9 women), 1 part-time/adjunct (0 women). *Students:* 46 full-time (17 women), 7 part-time (2 women); includes 5 minority (1 Black or African American, non-Hispanic/Latino; 1 American Indian or Alaska Native, non-Hispanic/Latino; 1 Asian, non-Hispanic/Latino; 1 Hispanic/Latino; 1 Two or more races, non-Hispanic/Latino), 4 international. Average age 29. 31 applicants, 65% accepted, 13 enrolled. In 2014, 7 master's, 2 doctorates awarded. *Degree requirements:* For master's, one foreign language, comprehensive exam, thesis optional; for doctorate, 2 foreign languages, thesis/dissertation, comprehensive oral and written exam. *Entrance requirements:* For master's, minimum GPA of 3.0 on last two years of undergraduate courses; for doctorate, GRE, writing sample, minimum graduate GPA of 3.0. Additional exam requirements/recommendations for international students: Required—TOEFL (minimum score 550 paper-based). *Application deadline:* For fall admission, 4/1 for domestic students, 5/1 for international students; for spring admission, 11/1 for domestic students, 9/1 for international students. Applications are processed on a rolling basis. Application fee: $60. Electronic applications accepted. *Expenses:* Tuition, state resident: full-time $7140; part-time $783 per credit hour. Tuition, nonresident: full-time $18,478; part-time $2043 per credit hour. *Financial support:* In 2014–15, 39 teaching assistantships with full tuition reimbursements (averaging $12,034 per year) were awarded; Federal Work-Study, institutionally sponsored loans, scholarships/grants, and unspecified assistantships also available. Financial award application deadline: 4/1; financial award applicants required to submit FAFSA. *Faculty research:* U.S. political, diplomatic, military, social, and cultural history; modern Europe; Latin America; Asian history; African history. *Unit head:* Dr. Alan I. Marcus, Head, 662-325-3604, Fax: 662-325-1139, E-mail: aim10@msstate.edu. *Application contact:* Dr. Stephen Brain, Graduate Coordinator, 662-325-3604, Fax: 662-325-1139, E-mail: correspondence@history.msstate.edu.
Website: http://www.history.msstate.edu

Monmouth University, The Graduate School, Department of History, West Long Branch, NJ 07764-1898. Offers European history (MA); history of the United States (MA); world history (MA). Part-time and evening/weekend programs available. *Faculty:* 9 full-time (3 women). *Students:* 5 full-time (3 women), 37 part-time (14 women); includes 1 minority (Hispanic/Latino). Average age 35. 22 applicants, 100% accepted, 13 enrolled. In 2014, 16 master's awarded. *Degree requirements:* For master's, comprehensive exam (for some programs), thesis (for some programs). *Entrance requirements:* For master's, minimum GPA of 3.0 in major, 2.5 overall; two letters of recommendation; statement of interest areas and goals. Additional exam requirements/recommendations for international students: Required—TOEFL (minimum score 550 paper-based; 79 iBT), IELTS (minimum score 6) or Michigan English Language Assessment Battery (minimum score 77). *Application deadline:* For fall admission, 7/15 priority date for domestic students, 6/1 for international students; for spring admission,

11/15 priority date for domestic students, 11/1 for international students. Applications are processed on a rolling basis. Application fee: $50. Electronic applications accepted. *Expenses: Tuition:* Full-time $18,072; part-time $1004 per credit. *Required fees:* $157 per semester. *Financial support:* In 2014–15, 29 students received support, including 23 fellowships (averaging $2,264 per year), 4 research assistantships (averaging $7,796 per year); career-related internships or fieldwork, scholarships/grants, and unspecified assistantships also available. Support available to part-time students. Financial award applicants required to submit FAFSA. *Faculty research:* U.S. business; labor; British, German, and French Revolutions; Soviet Union; Africa. *Unit head:* Dr. Maryann Rhett, Program Director, 732-263-5768, Fax: 732-263-5112, E-mail: mrhett@monmouth.edu. *Application contact:* Andrea Thompson, Graduate Admission Counselor, 732-571-3452, Fax: 732-263-5123, E-mail: gradadm@monmouth.edu.
Website: http://www.monmouth.edu/school-of-humanities-social-sciences/ma-in-history.aspx

New York University, Graduate School of Arts and Science, Center for European Studies, New York, NY 10012-1019. Offers MA. *Faculty:* 4 full-time (0 women). *Students:* 10 full-time (7 women), 1 (woman) part-time; includes 2 minority (both Two or more races, non-Hispanic/Latino), 3 international. Average age 27. 14 applicants, 93% accepted, 8 enrolled. In 2014, 4 master's awarded. *Entrance requirements:* For master's, GRE General Test. Additional exam requirements/recommendations for international students: Required—TOEFL. *Application deadline:* For fall admission, 2/1 priority date for domestic students, 2/1 for international students. Application fee: $100. Electronic applications accepted. *Financial support:* Fellowships with tuition reimbursements, teaching assistantships, career-related internships or fieldwork, Federal Work-Study, institutionally sponsored loans, and scholarships/grants available. Financial award application deadline: 2/1; financial award applicants required to submit FAFSA. *Faculty research:* Xenophobia, migration, and identity politics in Europe; European Union and political economy; Central Eastern Europe. *Unit head:* Larry Wolff, Director, 212-998-3838, Fax: 212-995-4188, E-mail: european.studies@nyu.edu. *Application contact:* Mikhala Stein, Administrator, 212-998-3838, Fax: 212-995-4188, E-mail: european.studies@nyu.edu.
Website: http://www.nyu.edu/gsas/dept/europe/

San Diego State University, Graduate and Research Affairs, College of Arts and Letters, Department of European Studies, San Diego, CA 92182. Offers MA. *Degree requirements:* For master's, one foreign language. *Entrance requirements:* For master's, GRE General Test. Additional exam requirements/recommendations for international students: Required—TOEFL. Electronic applications accepted.

University of Colorado Denver, College of Liberal Arts and Sciences, Department of History, Denver, CO 80217. Offers European history (MA); global history (MA); public history (MA); U.S. history (MA). Part-time and evening/weekend programs available. *Faculty:* 14 full-time (6 women), 1 part-time/adjunct (0 women). *Students:* 33 full-time (20 women), 20 part-time (11 women); includes 12 minority (1 Black or African American, non-Hispanic/Latino; 1 American Indian or Alaska Native, non-Hispanic/Latino; 1 Asian, non-Hispanic/Latino; 8 Hispanic/Latino; 1 Two or more races, non-Hispanic/Latino). Average age 34. 27 applicants, 59% accepted, 9 enrolled. In 2014, 9 master's awarded. *Degree requirements:* For master's, comprehensive exam, thesis optional, 36 semester hours (12 courses). *Entrance requirements:* For master's, GRE General Test, writing sample, minimum undergraduate GPA of 3.25, three letters of recommendation, statement of purpose addressing any weaknesses in academic record. Additional exam requirements/recommendations for international students: Required—TOEFL (minimum score 537 paper-based; 75 iBT); Recommended—IELTS (minimum score 6.5). *Application deadline:* For fall admission, 1/20 for domestic and international students; for spring admission, 10/1 for domestic and international students. Application fee: $50 ($75 for international students). Electronic applications accepted. *Financial support:* In 2014–15, 8 students received support. Fellowships, research assistantships, teaching assistantships, Federal Work-Study, institutionally sponsored loans, scholarships/grants, and traineeships available. Financial award application deadline: 4/1; financial award applicants required to submit FAFSA. *Faculty research:* Uses of pre-modern Islamic heritage in modern India; relationship between liberal understandings of democracy, crime, and police discretion; relationships between gender, class, health, and welfare in nineteenth and early twentieth century England; U.S. business cultures and their influences on marketing and personnel practices; intersection of business and political ideologies; social and environmental history of the Rocky Mountain West. *Unit head:* Dr. Pamela Laird, Associate Professor and Chair, 303-556-4497, E-mail: pamela.laird@ucdenver.edu. *Application contact:* Tabitha Fitzpatrick, Program Assistant, 303-315-1776, E-mail: tabitha.fitzpatrick@ucdenver.edu. Website: http://www.ucdenver.edu/academics/colleges/CLAS/Departments/history/Programs/Masters/Pages/MasterofArts.aspx

University of Connecticut, Graduate School, College of Liberal Arts and Sciences, Field of International Studies, Program in European Studies, Storrs, CT 06269. Offers MA. *Degree requirements:* For master's, comprehensive exam. *Entrance requirements:* For master's, GRE General Test. Additional exam requirements/recommendations for international students: Required—TOEFL (minimum score 550 paper-based). Electronic applications accepted.

University of Connecticut, Graduate School, College of Liberal Arts and Sciences, Field of International Studies, Program in Italian History and Culture, Storrs, CT 06269. Offers MA. *Entrance requirements:* Additional exam requirements/recommendations for international students: Required—TOEFL (minimum score 550 paper-based). Electronic applications accepted.

University of Guelph, Graduate Studies, College of Arts, School of Languages and Literatures, Program in European Studies, Guelph, ON N1G 2W1, Canada. Offers MA. *Degree requirements:* For master's, research paper. *Entrance requirements:* For master's, curriculum vitae, writing sample, 2 letters of recommendation.

University of Illinois at Urbana–Champaign, Graduate College, College of Liberal Arts and Sciences, European Union Center, Champaign, IL 61820. Offers MA. *Students:* 8 (6 women). *Degree requirements:* For master's, one foreign language. Application fee: $70 ($90 for international students). *Unit head:* Anna Stenport, Director, 217-265-7515, Fax: 217-333-6270, E-mail: aws@illinois.edu. *Application contact:* Kim Rice, Office Manager, 217-265-4194, Fax: 217-333-6270, E-mail: kimrice@illinois.edu.
Website: http://www.euc.illinois.edu/

University of Maine, Graduate School, College of Liberal Arts and Sciences, Department of History, Orono, ME 04469. Offers Asian studies (MA); Canadian studies (MA); European studies (MA). *Faculty:* 17 full-time (4 women). *Students:* 33 full-time (19 women), 12 part-time (4 women); includes 1 minority (Hispanic/Latino), 3 international. Average age 38. 31 applicants, 65% accepted, 6 enrolled. In 2014, 6 master's, 1 doctorate awarded. *Degree requirements:* For master's, variable foreign language requirement, thesis optional; for doctorate, one foreign language, comprehensive exam, thesis/dissertation. *Entrance requirements:* For master's and doctorate, GRE General

Test. Additional exam requirements/recommendations for international students: Required—TOEFL. *Application deadline:* For fall admission, 1/15 priority date for domestic students; for spring admission, 10/15 for domestic students. Applications are processed on a rolling basis. Application fee: $65. Electronic applications accepted. *Expenses:* Tuition, state resident: part-time $658 per credit hour. Tuition, nonresident: part-time $1550 per credit hour. *Financial support:* In 2014–15, 26 students received support, including 4 fellowships (averaging $15,000 per year), 9 teaching assistantships with tuition reimbursements available (averaging $14,600 per year); career-related internships or fieldwork, Federal Work-Study, and tuition waivers (full and partial) also available. Support available to part-time students. Financial award application deadline: 3/1. *Faculty research:* Environmental history, gender history, nationalism, classical, popular culture, Napoleonic, globalization, peasant studies, diplomatic history, military, Native America, Colonial U.S. *Unit head:* Dr. Stephen Miller, Chair, 207-581-1905, Fax: 207-581-1817, E-mail: stephen.miller@maine.edu. *Application contact:* Scott G. Delcourt, Assistant Vice President for Graduate Studies and Senior Associate Dean, 207-581-3291, Fax: 207-581-3232, E-mail: graduate@maine.edu.
Website: http://www.umaine.edu/history/

University of Nevada, Reno, Graduate School, Interdisciplinary Program in Basque Studies, Reno, NV 89557. Offers PhD. *Degree requirements:* For doctorate, thesis/dissertation. *Entrance requirements:* For doctorate, GRE General Test, master's degree in related field, minimum GPA of 3.0. Additional exam requirements/recommendations for international students: Required—TOEFL (minimum score 500 paper-based; 61 iBT), IELTS (minimum score 6). Electronic applications accepted. *Faculty research:* Ethnic groups, Basque society, migration studies, symbolic anthropology, terrorism.

University of Pittsburgh, University Center for International Studies, Pittsburgh, PA 15260. Offers African studies (Certificate); Asian studies (Certificate); European Union studies (Certificate); global studies (Certificate); Latin American studies (Certificate); Russian and East European studies (Certificate); West European studies (Certificate). *Students:* 223 full-time (98 women), 11 part-time (1 woman); includes 97 minority (2 Black or African American, non-Hispanic/Latino; 41 Asian, non-Hispanic/Latino; 52 Hispanic/Latino; 2 Two or more races, non-Hispanic/Latino). Average age 31. In 2014, 72 Certificates awarded. *Degree requirements:* For Certificate, one foreign language, study abroad. *Application deadline:* Applications are processed on a rolling basis. *Expenses:* Tuition, state resident: full-time $20,742; part-time $838 per credit. Tuition, nonresident: full-time $33,960; part-time $1389 per credit. *Required fees:* $800; $205 per term. Tuition and fees vary according to program. *Unit head:* Dr. Ariel Armony, Director, 412-648-7374, Fax: 412-624-4672, E-mail: armony@pitt.edu. *Application contact:* Information Contact, 412-624-4141, E-mail: graduate@pitt.edu.
Website: http://www.ucis.pitt.edu

University of Rochester, School of Arts and Sciences, Department of History, Rochester, NY 14627. Offers American history (MA, PhD); European history (MA, PhD); global history (MA, PhD). *Faculty:* 18 full-time (4 women). *Students:* 30 full-time (8 women); includes 4 minority (1 Asian, non-Hispanic/Latino; 1 Hispanic/Latino; 2 Two or more races, non-Hispanic/Latino), 1 international. 32 applicants, 41% accepted, 7 enrolled. In 2014, 5 master's, 7 doctorates awarded. Terminal master's awarded for partial completion of doctoral program. *Degree requirements:* For master's, one foreign language, thesis or alternative; for doctorate, 2 foreign languages, thesis/dissertation, comprehensive oral exam, qualifying exam. *Entrance requirements:* For master's and doctorate, GRE General Test, sample of written work. Additional exam requirements/recommendations for international students: Required—TOEFL. *Application deadline:* For fall admission, 1/15 priority date for domestic students. Application fee: $60. Electronic applications accepted. *Expenses: Tuition:* Full-time $46,150; part-time $1442 per credit hour. *Required fees:* $504. *Financial support:* Fellowships, research assistantships, teaching assistantships, and tuition waivers (full and partial) available. Financial award application deadline: 1/15. *Unit head:* Matthew Lenoe, Chair, 585-275-9355. *Application contact:* Caleb Rood, Secretary, 585-275-2053.
Website: http://www.rochester.edu/College/HIS/

Wayne State University, College of Liberal Arts and Sciences, Department of History, Detroit, MI 48202. Offers Africa (PhD); America (PhD); archival administration (Graduate Certificate); Europe (PhD); gender (PhD); history (MA); labor (PhD); science and technology (PhD); world history (PhD, Graduate Certificate); JD/MA; M Ed/MA; MLIS/MA. Doctoral programs admit for fall only. Evening/weekend programs available. *Faculty:* 22 full-time (9 women). *Students:* 32 full-time (14 women), 16 part-time (6 women); includes 4 minority (2 Black or African American, non-Hispanic/Latino; 2 Two or more races, non-Hispanic/Latino). Average age 39. 52 applicants, 37% accepted, 9 enrolled. In 2014, 5 master's awarded. *Degree requirements:* For master's, one foreign language, thesis (for some programs), final oral exam on thesis or essay and seminar; for doctorate, variable foreign language requirement, thesis/dissertation, qualifying exam in 4 fields of history. *Entrance requirements:* For master's, GRE General Test, minimum undergraduate GPA of 3.25 in history, 3.0 overall; at least 18 credits in history and related subjects at the advanced undergraduate level; foreign language; letter of intent; research paper; at least two letters of recommendation from former instructors; for doctorate, GRE General Test, minimum GPA of 3.0; letter of intent; research paper; at least three letters of recommendation from former professors; for Graduate Certificate, baccalaureate degree from accredited college or university; minimum GPA of 3.0, 3.25 in a minimum of eighteen semester credits in history and related subjects at the advanced undergraduate level. Additional exam requirements/recommendations for international students: Required—TOEFL (minimum score 550 paper-based; 79 iBT), TWE (minimum score 5.5), Michigan English Language Assessment Battery (minimum score 85); Recommended—IELTS (minimum score 6.5). *Application deadline:* For fall admission, 2/1 for domestic and international students; for winter admission, 11/1 for domestic students, 10/1 priority date for international students; for spring admission, 3/15 for domestic students, 1/1 priority date for international students. Applications are processed on a rolling basis. Application fee: $0. Electronic applications accepted. *Expenses:* Tuition, state resident: full-time $10,294; part-time $571.90 per credit hour. Tuition, nonresident: full-time $29,730; part-time $1238.75 per credit hour. *Required fees:* $1365; $43.50 per credit hour. $291.10 per semester. Tuition and fees vary according to course load and program. *Financial support:* In 2014–15, 19 students received support, including 1 fellowship with tuition reimbursement available (averaging $16,000 per year), 1 research assistantship with tuition reimbursement available (averaging $17,994 per year), 6 teaching assistantships with tuition reimbursements available (averaging $16,838 per year); scholarships/grants, health care benefits, and unspecified assistantships also available. Financial award application deadline: 3/31; financial award applicants required to submit FAFSA. *Faculty research:* Labor and working class history, urban history, citizenship and politics, gender and women's history. *Unit head:* Dr. Marc W. Kruman, Chair, 313-577-2525, Fax: 313-577-6987, E-mail: mkruman@wayne.edu. *Application contact:* Dr. Gayle McCreedy, Academic Service Officer, 313-577-2592, Fax: 313-577-6987, E-mail: g.mccreedy@wayne.edu.
Website: http://clas.wayne.edu/history/

Women's Studies

American University, College of Arts and Sciences, Department of Women's, Gender, and Sexuality Studies, Washington, DC 20016. Offers Graduate Certificate. *Faculty:* 2 part-time/adjunct (both women). *Students:* 1 part-time (0 women). Average age 24. In 2014, 1 Graduate Certificate awarded. *Entrance requirements:* For degree, statement of purpose, transcripts, resume. *Unit head:* Dr. Lauren Weis, Director, 202-885-2926, Fax: 202-885-1094, E-mail: weis@american.edu. *Application contact:* Kathleen Clowery, Associate Director, Graduate Enrollment Management, 202-885-3621, Fax: 202-885-2429, E-mail: clowery@american.edu.
Website: http://www.american.edu/cas/wgs/

The American University in Cairo, School of Global Affairs and Public Policy, Cynthia Nelson Institute for Gender and Women's Studies, Cairo, Egypt. Offers gender and justice (MA); gender and women's studies in the Middle East and North Africa (MA); gendered political economies (MA). Tuition and fees vary according to course load and program.

Benedictine University, Graduate Programs, Program in Leadership, Lisle, IL 60532-0900. Offers MS. *Degree requirements:* For master's, capstone.

Brandeis University, Graduate School of Arts and Sciences, Department of Anthropology, Waltham, MA 02454. Offers anthropology (MA, PhD); anthropology and women's and gender studies (MA). Part-time programs available. *Faculty:* 9 full-time (5 women), 1 part-time/adjunct (0 women). *Students:* 32 full-time (20 women), 2 part-time (1 woman); includes 6 minority (2 Black or African American, non-Hispanic/Latino; 2 Asian, non-Hispanic/Latino; 1 Hispanic/Latino; 1 Two or more races, non-Hispanic/Latino), 4 international. 38 applicants, 61% accepted, 14 enrolled. In 2014, 6 master's, 8 doctorates awarded. *Degree requirements:* For master's, thesis or alternative; for doctorate, one foreign language, comprehensive exam, thesis/dissertation. *Entrance requirements:* For master's and doctorate, GRE General Test, sample of written work, resume, letters of recommendation. Additional exam requirements/recommendations for international students: Required—TOEFL (minimum score 600 paper-based; 100 iBT), PTE (minimum score 68); Recommended—IELTS (minimum score 7). *Application deadline:* For fall admission, 1/15 for domestic students. Application fee: $75. Electronic applications accepted. *Financial support:* In 2014–15, 32 students received support, including 8 fellowships with full tuition reimbursements available (averaging $20,800 per year), 24 teaching assistantships with partial tuition reimbursements available (averaging $3,200 per year); Federal Work-Study, scholarships/grants, health care benefits, and tuition waivers (partial) also available. Financial award application deadline: 4/15; financial award applicants required to submit FAFSA. *Faculty research:* Sociocultural anthropology, linguistic anthropology, archaeology, physical anthropology. *Unit head:* Dr. Sarah Lamb, Director of Graduate Studies, 781-736-2210, Fax: 781-736-2232, E-mail: lamb@brandeis.edu. *Application contact:* Laurel Carpenter, Academic Administrator, 781-736-2210, Fax: 781-736-2232, E-mail: lcarpenter@brandeis.edu.
Website: http://www.brandeis.edu/gsas

Brandeis University, Graduate School of Arts and Sciences, Department of English, Waltham, MA 02454-9110. Offers English (MA, PhD); English and women's and gender studies (MA). Part-time programs available. *Degree requirements:* For master's, one foreign language, thesis or alternative; for doctorate, 2 foreign languages, thesis/dissertation, field exam, symposium presentation, prospectus defense. *Entrance requirements:* For master's and doctorate, resume, sample of work, 2 letters of recommendation, statement of purpose, transcript(s). Additional exam requirements/recommendations for international students: Required—TOEFL (minimum score 600 paper-based; 100 iBT); Recommended—IELTS (minimum score 7). Electronic applications accepted. *Faculty research:* Feminist and gender theory, American literature and post-Colonial theory, early modern (Renaissance) English literature, modernism, literature and science, literary theory and philosophy, contemporary poetry.

Brandeis University, Graduate School of Arts and Sciences, Department of Near Eastern and Judaic Studies, Waltham, MA 02454-9110. Offers Near Eastern and Judaic studies (MA, PhD); Near Eastern and Judaic studies and sociology (PhD); Near Eastern and Judaic studies and women's and gender studies (MA); teaching of Hebrew (MAT). Part-time programs available. Terminal master's awarded for partial completion of doctoral program. *Degree requirements:* For master's, one foreign language, thesis or alternative, proseminar, capstone; for doctorate, variable foreign language requirement, comprehensive exam, thesis/dissertation. *Entrance requirements:* For master's and doctorate, 3 letters of recommendation, transcript(s), statement of purpose, writing sample, resume. Additional exam requirements/recommendations for international students: Required—TOEFL (minimum score 600 paper-based; 100 iBT), PTE (minimum score 68); Recommended—IELTS (minimum score 7). Electronic applications accepted. *Faculty research:* Ancient Near East and Bible, Judaic studies, Israel Studies, modern Middle East, Arabic and Islamic civilizations.

Brandeis University, Graduate School of Arts and Sciences, Joint Master's Programs in Women's and Gender Studies, Waltham, MA 02454-9110. Offers anthropology and women's and gender studies (MA); English and women's and gender studies (MA); history and women's and gender studies (MA); Near Eastern and Judaic studies and women's and gender studies (MA); psychology and women's and gender studies (MA); public policy and women's and gender studies (MA); social policy and women's and gender studies (MA); sociology and women's and gender studies (MA); sustainable international development and women's/gender studies (MA). *Degree requirements:* For master's, thesis. *Entrance requirements:* For master's, GRE, sample of written work, resume, statement of purpose, transcript(s), letters of recommendation. Additional exam requirements/recommendations for international students: Required—TOEFL (minimum score 600 paper-based; 100 iBT), PTE (minimum score 68); Recommended—IELTS (minimum score 7). Electronic applications accepted. *Faculty research:* Anthropology, English, history, music, Near Eastern and Judaic studies, public policy, psychology, sociology, and sustainable international development.

Brandeis University, Graduate School of Arts and Sciences, MA Program in Women's and Gender Studies, Waltham, MA 02454-9110. Offers MA. *Degree requirements:* For master's, thesis, proseminar. *Entrance requirements:* For master's, GRE, three letters of recommendation, curriculum vitae or resume, statement of purpose, critical writing sample, transcript(s). Additional exam requirements/recommendations for international students: Required—TOEFL (minimum score 600 paper-based; 100 iBT), PTE (minimum score 68); Recommended—IELTS (minimum score 7). Electronic applications accepted. *Faculty research:* Gender and legal studies, sexuality studies, social and public policy, comparative literature and culture, anthropology, English, music, Near Eastern and Judaic Studies, public policy, sociology, sustainable international development, history, psychology.

California Institute of Integral Studies, School of Consciousness and Transformation, San Francisco, CA 94103. Offers anthropology and social change (MA, PhD); creative inquiry/interdisciplinary arts (MFA); East-West psychology (MA, PhD); philosophy and religion (MA, PhD), including Asian and comparative studies, ecology, spirituality, and religion, philosophy, cosmology, and consciousness, women's spirituality; transformative leadership (MA); transformative studies (PhD); writing and consciousness (MFA). Part-time and evening/weekend programs available. Postbaccalaureate distance learning degree programs offered (no on-campus study). *Students:* 385 full-time (256 women), 102 part-time (71 women); includes 124 minority (31 Black or African American, non-Hispanic/Latino; 3 American Indian or Alaska Native, non-Hispanic/Latino; 19 Asian, non-Hispanic/Latino; 39 Hispanic/Latino; 1 Native Hawaiian or other Pacific Islander, non-Hispanic/Latino; 31 Two or more races, non-Hispanic/Latino), 53 international. Average age 43. 196 applicants, 92% accepted, 125 enrolled. In 2014, 75 master's, 41 doctorates awarded. Terminal master's awarded for partial completion of doctoral program. *Degree requirements:* For master's, thesis optional; for doctorate, comprehensive exam, thesis/dissertation, 1 foreign language (for Asian comparative studies). *Entrance requirements:* For master's, minimum GPA of 3.0, letters of recommendation, writing sample; for doctorate, master's degree, minimum GPA of 3.0, letters of recommendation, writing sample. Additional exam requirements/recommendations for international students: Required—TOEFL. *Application deadline:* For fall admission, 2/1 priority date for domestic and international students; for spring admission, 10/15 priority date for domestic and international students. Applications are processed on a rolling basis. Application fee: $65. Electronic applications accepted. *Expenses: Tuition:* Full-time $18,270; part-time $1015 per credit. *Required fees:* $85 per semester hour. *Financial support:* In 2014–15, 445 students received support, including 5 research assistantships (averaging $800 per year), 28 teaching assistantships (averaging $825 per year); career-related internships or fieldwork, Federal Work-Study, and scholarships/grants also available. Support available to part-time students. Financial award application deadline: 4/15; financial award applicants required to submit FAFSA. *Faculty research:* Ecology and sustainability, philosophy and religion, East-West psychology, integrative health, social and cultural anthropology, transformative leadership. *Application contact:* David Townes, Senior Admissions Counselor, 415-575-6152, Fax: 415-575-1268, E-mail: admissions@ciis.edu.
Website: http://www.ciis.edu/

Carnegie Mellon University, Dietrich College of Humanities and Social Sciences, Department of History, Pittsburgh, PA 15213-3891. Offers African and African-American diaspora (PhD); culture and power (PhD); labor, politics and social movements (PhD); technology, environment, science and health (PhD); women, gender and the family (PhD). Part-time programs available. *Degree requirements:* For doctorate, oral and written comprehensive exams, dissertation defense. *Entrance requirements:* For doctorate, GRE General Test. Additional exam requirements/recommendations for international students: Required—TOEFL. Electronic applications accepted. *Faculty research:* Anthropology and history, African-American history, technology/environment, cultural history analysis.

Chatham University, Program in Business Administration, Pittsburgh, PA 15232-2826. Offers business administration (MBA); healthcare management (MBA); sustainability (MBA); women's leadership (MBA). Part-time and evening/weekend programs available. *Faculty:* 1 full-time (0 women), 8 part-time/adjunct (5 women). *Students:* 17 full-time (10 women), 39 part-time (31 women); includes 9 minority (5 Black or African American, non-Hispanic/Latino; 2 Asian, non-Hispanic/Latino; 1 Hispanic/Latino; 1 Two or more races, non-Hispanic/Latino), 11 international. Average age 30. 51 applicants, 55% accepted, 18 enrolled. In 2014, 4 master's awarded. *Entrance requirements:* For master's, minimum GPA of 3.0, letters of recommendation. Additional exam requirements/recommendations for international students: Required—TOEFL (minimum score 600 paper-based; 100 iBT), IELTS (minimum score 7), TWE. *Application deadline:* For fall admission, 4/1 for domestic and international students; for spring admission, 11/1 for domestic students, 10/1 for international students. Applications are processed on a rolling basis. Application fee: $45. Electronic applications accepted. Application fee is waived when completed online. *Expenses: Tuition:* Full-time $15,318; part-time $851 per credit hour. *Required fees:* $440; $24 per credit hour. Tuition and fees vary according to course load, program and reciprocity agreements. *Financial support:* Applicants required to submit FAFSA. *Unit head:* Dr. Rachel Chung, Director of Business and Entrepreneurship Program, 412-365-2433. *Application contact:* Katie Noel, Assistant Director of Graduate Admission, 412-365-2758, Fax: 412-365-1609, E-mail: gradadmissions@chatham.edu.
Website: http://www.chatham.edu/mba

Claremont Graduate University, Graduate Programs, School of Arts and Humanities, Department of Religion, Claremont, CA 91711-6160. Offers Hebrew Bible (MA, PhD); history of Christianity and religions of North America (MA, PhD); New Testament (MA, PhD); philosophy of religion and theology (MA, PhD); theology, ethics and culture (MA, PhD); women's studies in religion (MA, PhD); MA/PhD; MBA/PhD. Part-time programs available. *Faculty:* 7 full-time (3 women), 2 part-time/adjunct (0 women). *Students:* 153 full-time (58 women), 31 part-time (16 women); includes 33 minority (12 Black or African American, non-Hispanic/Latino; 1 American Indian or Alaska Native, non-Hispanic/Latino; 7 Asian, non-Hispanic/Latino; 10 Hispanic/Latino; 1 Native Hawaiian or other Pacific Islander, non-Hispanic/Latino; 2 Two or more races, non-Hispanic/Latino), 14 international. Average age 37. In 2014, 15 master's, 13 doctorates awarded. Terminal master's awarded for partial completion of doctoral program. *Entrance requirements:* For master's and doctorate, GRE General Test. Additional exam requirements/recommendations for international students: Required—TOEFL (minimum score 550 paper-based; 80 iBT). *Application deadline:* For fall admission, 2/1 priority date for domestic and international students. Applications are processed on a rolling basis. Application fee: $80. Electronic applications accepted. *Expenses: Tuition:* Full-time $41,784; part-time $1741 per credit. *Required fees:* $600; $300 per semester. *Financial support:* Fellowships, research assistantships, teaching assistantships, Federal Work-Study, institutionally sponsored loans, and scholarships/grants available. Support available to part-time students. Financial award application deadline: 2/15; financial award applicants required to submit FAFSA. *Unit head:* Tammi Schneider, Chair, E-mail: tammi.schneider@cgu.edu. *Application contact:* Erma Cross, Admissions and Alumni Coordinator, 909-607-9843, E-mail: erminia.cross@cgu.edu.
Website: http://www.cgu.edu/pages/674.asp

Claremont Graduate University, Graduate Programs, School of Arts and Humanities, Program in Applied Women's Studies, Claremont, CA 91711-6160. Offers MA. *Faculty:* 2 full-time (both women). *Students:* 10 full-time (all women), 2 part-time (both women); includes 5 minority (3 Black or African American, non-Hispanic/Latino; 1 Hispanic/Latino; 1 Two or more races, non-Hispanic/Latino). Average age 29. In 2014, 8 master's awarded. *Entrance requirements:* For master's, GRE General Test. Additional exam requirements/recommendations for international students: Required—TOEFL (minimum score 550 paper-based; 80 iBT). *Application deadline:* For fall admission, 2/1 priority date for domestic and international students. Applications are processed on a rolling

basis. Application fee: $80. Electronic applications accepted. *Expenses: Tuition:* Full-time $41,784; part-time $1741 per credit. *Required fees:* $600; $300 per semester. *Financial support:* Fellowships, research assistantships, teaching assistantships, Federal Work-Study, institutionally sponsored loans, and scholarships/grants available. Support available to part-time students. Financial award application deadline: 2/15; financial award applicants required to submit FAFSA. *Unit head:* Linda Perkins, Director, 909-621-8696, E-mail: linda.perkins@cgu.edu. *Application contact:* Amy Sandefur, Assistant Director of Admissions, 909-607-9101, E-mail: amy.sandefur@cgu.edu. Website: http://www.cgu.edu/pages/1477.asp

Clark Atlanta University, School of Arts and Sciences, Department of Africana Women's Studies, Atlanta, GA 30314. Offers MA, DAH. Part-time programs available. *Faculty:* 1 full-time (0 women). *Students:* 5 full-time (4 women), 14 part-time (12 women); includes 17 minority (all Black or African American, non-Hispanic/Latino). Average age 33. 6 applicants, 100% accepted, 5 enrolled. In 2014, 1 master's, 1 doctorate awarded. *Degree requirements:* For master's, one foreign language, comprehensive exam, thesis optional; for doctorate, one foreign language, comprehensive exam, thesis/dissertation. *Entrance requirements:* For master's, GRE General Test, minimum GPA of 2.5; for doctorate, GRE General Test, minimum graduate GPA of 3.0. Additional exam requirements/recommendations for international students: Required—TOEFL (minimum score 500 paper-based; 61 iBT). *Application deadline:* For fall admission, 4/1 for domestic and international students; for spring admission, 11/1 for domestic and international students. Applications are processed on a rolling basis. Application fee: $40 ($55 for international students). Electronic applications accepted. *Expenses: Tuition:* Full-time $14,904; part-time $828 per credit hour. *Required fees:* $746; $373 per semester. *Financial support:* Scholarships/grants available. Financial award application deadline: 4/30; financial award applicants required to submit FAFSA. *Faculty research:* Concerns of women of African descent globally. *Unit head:* Dr. Stephanie Evans, Chairperson, 404-880-6352, E-mail: sevans@cau.edu. *Application contact:* Michelle Clark-Davis, Graduate Program Admissions, 404-880-6605, E-mail: cauadmissions@cau.edu.

Cornell University, Graduate School, Graduate Fields of Arts and Sciences, Field of English Language and Literature, Ithaca, NY 14853-0001. Offers African-American literature (PhD); American literature after 1865 (PhD); American literature to 1865 (PhD); American studies (PhD); colonial and postcolonial literatures (PhD); creative writing (MFA); cultural studies (PhD); dramatic literature (PhD); English poetry (PhD); English Renaissance to 1660 (PhD); lesbian, bisexual, and gay literary studies (PhD); literary criticism and theory (PhD); Old and Middle English (PhD); prose fiction (PhD); Restoration and the eighteenth-century (PhD); the nineteenth century (PhD); the twentieth century (PhD); women's literature (PhD); MFA/PhD. Terminal master's awarded for partial completion of doctoral program. *Degree requirements:* For master's, one foreign language, thesis; for doctorate, one foreign language, comprehensive exam, thesis/dissertation, teaching experience. *Entrance requirements:* For master's, GRE General Test, 3 letters of recommendation, creative writing sample; for doctorate, GRE General Test, GRE Subject Test (English), 3 letters of recommendation, writing sample. Additional exam requirements/recommendations for international students: Required—TOEFL (minimum score 600 paper-based; 77 iBT). Electronic applications accepted. *Faculty research:* English and American literature, women's writing, ethnic and post-colonial literature, critical theory, medievalism.

DePaul University, College of Liberal Arts and Social Sciences, Chicago, IL 60614. Offers Arabic (MA); Chinese (MA); English (MA); French (MA); German (MA); history (MA); interdisciplinary studies (MA, MS); international public service (MS); international studies (MA); Italian (MA); Japanese (MA); leadership and policy studies (MS); liberal studies (MA); new media studies (MA); nonprofit management (MNM); public administration (MPA); public health (MPH); public service management (MS); social work (MSW); sociology (MA); Spanish (MA); sustainable urban development (MA); women and gender studies (MA); writing and publishing (MA); writing, rhetoric, and discourse (MA); MA/PhD. Part-time and evening/weekend programs available. Postbaccalaureate distance learning degree programs offered (no on-campus study). Terminal master's awarded for partial completion of doctoral program. *Degree requirements:* For master's, variable foreign language requirement, comprehensive exam (for some programs), thesis (for some programs). Electronic applications accepted.

Dominican University of California, School of Arts, Humanities and Social Sciences, Humanities Program, San Rafael, CA 94901-2298. Offers applied music (MA); art history (MA); creative writing (MA); history (MA); literature (MA); philosophy (MA); political theory (MA); religion (MA); women and gender studies (MA). Part-time programs available. *Faculty:* 11 full-time (5 women), 5 part-time/adjunct (2 women). *Students:* 2 full-time (1 woman), 25 part-time (16 women); includes 7 minority (1 Black or African American, non-Hispanic/Latino; 1 American Indian or Alaska Native, non-Hispanic/Latino; 3 Hispanic/Latino; 2 Two or more races, non-Hispanic/Latino). Average age 46. 12 applicants, 83% accepted, 7 enrolled. *Degree requirements:* For master's, thesis or alternative. *Entrance requirements:* For master's, minimum GPA of 3.0, interview. Additional exam requirements/recommendations for international students: Required—TOEFL (minimum score 550 paper-based; 80 iBT), IELTS (minimum score 6.5). *Application deadline:* For fall admission, 5/15 priority date for domestic and international students; for spring admission, 11/15 priority date for domestic and international students. Applications are processed on a rolling basis. Electronic applications accepted. Application fee is waived when completed online. *Expenses:* Expenses: $935 per unit. *Financial support:* Scholarships/grants available. Support available to part-time students. Financial award application deadline: 3/2; financial award applicants required to submit FAFSA. *Unit head:* Dr. Laura Stivers, Acting Dean, 415-458-3734, E-mail: laura.stivers@dominican.edu. *Application contact:* Ryan Purtill, Director, 415-458-3748, Fax: 415-485-3214, E-mail: ryan.purtill@dominican.edu. Website: http://www.dominican.edu/academics/ahss/graduate-program/index_html

Eastern Michigan University, Graduate School, College of Arts and Sciences, Department of Women's and Gender Studies, Ypsilanti, MI 48197. Offers MA, Graduate Certificate. Part-time and evening/weekend programs available. *Faculty:* 2 full-time (both women). *Students:* 5 full-time (all women), 16 part-time (14 women); includes 4 minority (2 Black or African American, non-Hispanic/Latino; 2 Hispanic/Latino), 2 international. Average age 34. 19 applicants, 63% accepted, 7 enrolled. In 2014, 4 master's, 1 other advanced degree awarded. *Degree requirements:* For master's, thesis, research project, or practicum. *Entrance requirements:* Additional exam requirements/recommendations for international students: Required—TOEFL. *Application deadline:* For fall admission, 6/15 for domestic and international students; for winter admission, 9/15 for domestic and international students; for spring admission, 3/1 for domestic and international students. Applications are processed on a rolling basis. Application fee: $45. *Financial support:* Fellowships, research assistantships with full tuition reimbursements, teaching assistantships with full tuition reimbursements, career-related internships or fieldwork, Federal Work-Study, institutionally sponsored loans, scholarships/grants, tuition waivers (partial), and unspecified assistantships available. Support available to part-time students. Financial award applicants required to submit FAFSA. *Unit head:* Dr. Jacqueline Goodman, Department Head, 734-487-1177, Fax: 734-487-5029, E-mail: jgoodma9@emich.edu. *Application contact:* Dr. Suzanne Gray, Program Advisor, 734-

487-1177, Fax: 734-487-5029, E-mail: sgray17@emich.edu. Website: http://www.emich.edu/wgstudies/

Emory University, Laney Graduate School, Department of Comparative Literature, Atlanta, GA 30322-1100. Offers comparative literature (PhD); philosophy (Certificate); psychoanalytic studies (PhD); women's studies (Certificate). *Degree requirements:* For doctorate, 2 foreign languages, comprehensive exam, thesis/dissertation. *Entrance requirements:* For doctorate, GRE General Test, minimum GPA of 3.0. Additional exam requirements/recommendations for international students: Required—TOEFL. Electronic applications accepted. *Faculty research:* Literary theory, psychoanalysis trauma and testimony, literature and religion, literature and technology, literature and philosophy, politics and global culture, literature and aesthetics.

Emory University, Laney Graduate School, Department of Spanish and Portuguese, Atlanta, GA 30322-1100. Offers comparative literature (Certificate); film studies (Certificate); Spanish (PhD); women's studies (Certificate). *Degree requirements:* For doctorate, 2 foreign languages, comprehensive exam, thesis/dissertation. *Entrance requirements:* For doctorate, GRE General Test. Additional exam requirements/recommendations for international students: Required—TOEFL. Electronic applications accepted. *Faculty research:* Spanish literature, Spanish American literature, literary theory, criticism, cultural studies.

Emory University, Laney Graduate School, Department of Women's, Gender, and Sexuality Studies, Atlanta, GA 30322-1100. Offers PhD. *Degree requirements:* For doctorate, comprehensive exam, thesis/dissertation. *Entrance requirements:* For doctorate, GRE General Test, writing sample. Additional exam requirements/recommendations for international students: Required—TOEFL. Electronic applications accepted. *Faculty research:* Feminist theory, women's literature, African-American literature, gender in cross-cultural perspective, public policy and globalization.

Florida Atlantic University, Dorothy F. Schmidt College of Arts and Letters, Center for Women, Gender and Sexuality Studies, Boca Raton, FL 33431-0991. Offers MA, Certificate. Part-time programs available. *Degree requirements:* For master's, comprehensive exam, thesis or alternative. *Entrance requirements:* For master's, GRE General Test, minimum GPA of 3.0. Additional exam requirements/recommendations for international students: Required—TOEFL (minimum score 500 paper-based; 61 iBT), IELTS (minimum score 6). Electronic applications accepted. *Expenses:* Tuition, state resident: full-time $7396; part-time $369.82 per credit hour. Tuition, nonresident: full-time $19,392; part-time $1024.81 per credit hour. Tuition and fees vary according to course load. *Faculty research:* Women and science/technology, feminist theory, violence against women, women and international development, feminist medical anthropology.

George Mason University, College of Humanities and Social Sciences, Interdisciplinary Studies Program, Fairfax, VA 22030. Offers community college teaching (MAIS); computational social science (MAIS); energy and sustainability (MAIS); film and video studies (MAIS); folklore studies (MAIS); higher education administration (MAIS); neuroethics (MAIS); religion, culture and values (MAIS); social entrepreneurship (MAIS); war and military in society (MAIS); women and gender studies (MAIS). *Faculty:* 11 full-time (3 women), 4 part-time/adjunct (all women). *Students:* 22 full-time (13 women), 87 part-time (51 women); includes 31 minority (21 Black or African American, non-Hispanic/Latino; 2 Asian, non-Hispanic/Latino; 6 Hispanic/Latino; 2 Two or more races, non-Hispanic/Latino), 6 international. Average age 32. 75 applicants, 75% accepted, 28 enrolled. In 2014, 31 master's awarded. *Degree requirements:* For master's, project or thesis. *Entrance requirements:* For master's, 3 letters of recommendation; writing sample; official transcript; resume. Additional exam requirements/recommendations for international students: Required—TOEFL (minimum score 570 paper-based; 80 iBT), IELTS (minimum score 6.5), PTE. *Application deadline:* For fall admission, 3/1 priority date for domestic students; for spring admission, 10/15 for domestic students. Application fee: $65 ($80 for international students). Electronic applications accepted. *Expenses:* Tuition, state resident: full-time $9794; part-time $408 per credit hour. Tuition, nonresident: full-time $26,978; part-time $1124 per credit hour. *Required fees:* $2820; $118 per credit hour. Tuition and fees vary according to course load and program. *Financial support:* In 2014–15, 10 students received support, including 1 fellowship (averaging $6,935 per year), 2 research assistantships with full and partial tuition reimbursements available (averaging $6,499 per year), 8 teaching assistantships with full and partial tuition reimbursements available (averaging $8,271 per year); career-related internships or fieldwork, Federal Work-Study, scholarships/grants, unspecified assistantships, and health care benefits (for full-time research or teaching assistantship recipients) also available. Support available to part-time students. Financial award application deadline: 3/1; financial award applicants required to submit FAFSA. *Faculty research:* Combined English and folklore, religious and cultural studies (Christianity and Muslim society). *Unit head:* Meredith H. Lair, Director, 703-993-2159, Fax: 703-993-1251, E-mail: mlair@gmu.edu. *Application contact:* Lisa Struckmeyer, Administrative Coordinator, 703-993-8762, Fax: 703-993-5585, E-mail: lstruckm@gmu.edu. Website: http://mais.gmu.edu

The George Washington University, Columbian College of Arts and Sciences, Department of Women's Studies, Washington, DC 20052. Offers MA, Certificate. Part-time and evening/weekend programs available. *Faculty:* 1 (woman) full-time. *Students:* 12 full-time (all women), 7 part-time (all women); includes 4 minority (1 Black or African American, non-Hispanic/Latino; 3 Hispanic/Latino), 2 international. Average age 29. 35 applicants, 71% accepted, 9 enrolled. In 2014, 4 master's, 3 other advanced degrees awarded. *Degree requirements:* For master's, comprehensive exam, thesis or alternative. *Entrance requirements:* For master's, GRE General Test, minimum GPA of 3.0. Additional exam requirements/recommendations for international students: Required—TOEFL (minimum score 550 paper-based; 80 iBT). *Application deadline:* For fall admission, 4/1 priority date for domestic students, 1/15 priority date for international students; for spring admission, 10/1 priority date for domestic students, 9/1 priority date for international students. Applications are processed on a rolling basis. Application fee: $75. Electronic applications accepted. *Financial support:* In 2014–15, 2 students received support. Fellowships with tuition reimbursements available, teaching assistantships with tuition reimbursements available, Federal Work-Study, institutionally sponsored loans, and tuition waivers available. Financial award application deadline: 1/15. *Unit head:* Dr. Daniel Moshenberg, Director, 202-994-9086, Fax: 202-994-7249. *Application contact:* Information Contact, 202-994-6942, Fax: 202-994-2249, E-mail: wstu@gwu.edu. Website: http://www.gwu.edu/~wstu/

Georgia State University, College of Arts and Sciences, Institute for Women's, Gender, and Sexuality Studies, Atlanta, GA 30302-3083. Offers MA, Graduate Certificate. Part-time programs available. *Faculty:* 4 full-time (all women). *Students:* 9 full-time (7 women), 3 part-time (all women); includes 6 minority (2 Black or African American, non-Hispanic/Latino; 3 Asian, non-Hispanic/Latino; 1 Two or more races, non-Hispanic/Latino). Average age 34. 20 applicants, 80% accepted, 11 enrolled. *Degree requirements:* For master's, comprehensive exam, thesis or alternative. *Entrance requirements:* For master's, GRE, two official transcripts from each college or university attended, three letters of recommendation addressing student's ability to undertake graduate study, 750-1000 word statement of purpose, academic writing sample; for

Graduate Certificate, GRE, two official transcripts from each college or university attended, three letters of recommendation addressing student's ability to undertake graduate study, 750-1000 word statement of purpose, academic writing sample. Additional exam requirements/recommendations for international students: Required—TOEFL (minimum score 550 paper-based; 80 iBT). *Application deadline:* For fall admission, 2/15 for domestic and international students. Application fee: $50. Electronic applications accepted. *Expenses:* Tuition, state resident: full-time $6516; part-time $362 per credit hour. Tuition, nonresident: full-time $22,014; part-time $1223 per credit hour. *Required fees:* $2128 per semester. Tuition and fees vary according to course load and program. *Financial support:* In 2014–15, research assistantships with full tuition reimbursements (averaging $7,000 per year), teaching assistantships with full tuition reimbursements (averaging $7,500 per year) were awarded; career-related internships or fieldwork, health care benefits, and unspecified assistantships also available. Financial award application deadline: 2/15. *Faculty research:* Gender, sexuality, and youth studies; gender and neoliberalism; transnational feminisms; cultural studies; queer theories. *Unit head:* Dr. Susan Talburt, Director, 404-413-6581, Fax: 404-413-6585, E-mail: stalburt@gsu.edu. *Application contact:* Dr. Amira Jarmakani, Director of Graduate Studies, 404-413-6583, Fax: 404-413-6585, E-mail: amira@gsu.edu.
Website: http://www2.gsu.edu/~wwwwsi/

The Graduate Center, City University of New York, Graduate Studies, Interdisciplinary Studies, New York, NY 10016-4039. Offers language in social context (PhD); medieval studies (PhD); public policy (MA, PhD); urban studies (MA, PhD); women's studies (MA, PhD). Terminal master's awarded for partial completion of doctoral program. *Degree requirements:* For master's, thesis; for doctorate, comprehensive exam, thesis/dissertation. *Entrance requirements:* For master's and doctorate, GRE General Test.

Inter American University of Puerto Rico, Metropolitan Campus, Graduate Programs, Program in Women's and Gender Studies, San Juan, PR 00919-1293. Offers MA.

The Jewish Theological Seminary, The Graduate School, New York, NY 10027-4649. Offers ancient Judaism (MA, DHL, PhD); Bible and ancient Semitic languages (MA, DHL, PhD); interdepartmental studies (MA); Jewish art and visual culture (MA); Jewish gender and women's studies (MA); Jewish history (MA, DHL, PhD); Jewish literature (MA, DHL, PhD); Jewish philosophy (DHL); Jewish thought (MA, PhD); liturgy (MA, DHL, PhD); medieval Jewish studies (MA, DHL, PhD); Midrash (DHL); Midrash and scriptural interpretation (MA, PhD); modern Jewish studies (MA, DHL, PhD); Talmud and rabbinics (MA, DHL, PhD); MA/MSW. MA/MSW offered jointly with Columbia University. *Accreditation:* ACIPE. Part-time programs available. Terminal master's awarded for partial completion of doctoral program. *Degree requirements:* For master's, one foreign language, comprehensive exam (for some programs), thesis (for some programs); for doctorate, 3 foreign languages, comprehensive exam (for some programs), thesis/dissertation. *Entrance requirements:* For master's, GRE or MAT, 3 letters of recommendation, writing sample; for doctorate, GRE or MAT, 3 letters of recommendation, writing research sample. Additional exam requirements/recommendations for international students: Required—TOEFL.

Kansas State University, Graduate School, College of Arts and Sciences, Department of Women's Studies, Manhattan, KS 66506. Offers Graduate Certificate. *Students:* 4 full-time (all women), 4 part-time (all women); includes 2 minority (both Hispanic/Latino). 3 applicants, 33% accepted. In 2014, 7 Graduate Certificates awarded. *Financial support:* In 2014–15, 1 teaching assistantship (averaging $6,600 per year) was awarded. *Unit head:* Michele Janette, Head, 785-532-5738, Fax: 785-532-3299, E-mail: mjanette@ksu.edu. *Application contact:* Shannon Fox, Administrative Assistant, 785-532-6191, Fax: 785-532-2983, E-mail: grad@ksu.edu.
Website: http://www.k-state.edu/womst/

Lakehead University, Graduate Studies, Department of History, Thunder Bay, ON P7B 5E1, Canada. Offers gerontology (MA); history (MA); women's studies (MA). Part-time programs available. *Degree requirements:* For master's, one foreign language, thesis. *Entrance requirements:* For master's, minimum B average. Additional exam requirements/recommendations for international students: Required—TOEFL. *Faculty research:* Canadian history, British history, Russian/German history, women's studies.

Lakehead University, Graduate Studies, Faculty of Education, Thunder Bay, ON P7B 5E1, Canada. Offers educational studies (PhD); gerontology (M Ed); women's studies (M Ed). Part-time and evening/weekend programs available. *Degree requirements:* For master's, project or thesis. *Entrance requirements:* For master's, minimum B average. Additional exam requirements/recommendations for international students: Required—TOEFL. *Faculty research:* Art education, AIDS education, language arts education, gerontology, women's studies.

Lakehead University, Graduate Studies, Faculty of Social Sciences and Humanities, Department of English, Thunder Bay, ON P7B 5E1, Canada. Offers English (MA); women's studies (MA). Part-time and evening/weekend programs available. *Degree requirements:* For master's, one foreign language, thesis optional. *Entrance requirements:* For master's, minimum B average. Additional exam requirements/recommendations for international students: Required—TOEFL. *Faculty research:* Rhetoric and literary studies, children's literature, nineteenth- and twentieth-century American literature, modern literature, women's studies.

Lakehead University, Graduate Studies, Faculty of Social Sciences and Humanities, Department of Sociology, Thunder Bay, ON P7B 5E1, Canada. Offers gerontology (MA); health services and policy research (MA); sociology (MA); women's studies (MA). Part-time and evening/weekend programs available. *Degree requirements:* For master's, research project or thesis. *Entrance requirements:* For master's, minimum B average. Additional exam requirements/recommendations for international students: Required—TOEFL. *Faculty research:* Sociology of medicine, cultural and social change, health human resources, gerontology, women's studies.

Lakehead University, Graduate Studies, School of Social Work, Thunder Bay, ON P7B 5E1, Canada. Offers gerontology (MSW); social work (MSW); women's studies (MSW). Part-time programs available. *Degree requirements:* For master's, thesis or project. *Entrance requirements:* For master's, minimum B average. Additional exam requirements/recommendations for international students: Required—TOEFL. *Faculty research:* Clinical psychology, social work and practice theory, long-term care, health care for frail elderly, women's studies.

Lakehead University, Graduate Studies, Women's Studies Collaborative Program, Thunder Bay, ON P7B 5E1, Canada. Offers M Ed, MA, MSW. Part-time programs available. *Degree requirements:* For master's, thesis (for some programs). *Entrance requirements:* Additional exam requirements/recommendations for international students: Required—TOEFL. *Faculty research:* Feminist thought, feminist pedagogy, women of literature, Canadian women's history, well-being of women.

Lesley University, Graduate School of Arts and Social Sciences, Cambridge, MA 02138-2790. Offers clinical mental health counseling (MA), including holistic counseling, school and community counseling, trauma studies; counseling psychology (MA, CAGS), including professional counseling (MA), school counseling (MA); creative writing (MFA); expressive therapies (MA, PhD, CAGS), including art (MA), clinical mental health counseling (MA), dance (MA), expressive therapies (MA), music (MA); independent studies (CAGS); independent study (MA); intercultural relations (MA, CAGS); interdisciplinary studies (MA), including individualized studies, integrative holistic health, mindfulness studies, peace and conflict transformation, trauma sensitive assessment, intervention, and consultation, women's studies; urban environmental leadership (MA). Part-time programs available. Postbaccalaureate distance learning degree programs offered (no on-campus study). *Faculty:* 35 full-time (25 women), 115 part-time/adjunct (90 women). *Students:* 420 full-time (379 women), 514 part-time (414 women); includes 142 minority (50 Black or African American, non-Hispanic/Latino; 5 American Indian or Alaska Native, non-Hispanic/Latino; 16 Asian, non-Hispanic/Latino; 48 Hispanic/Latino; 23 Two or more races, non-Hispanic/Latino), 46 international. Average age 33. In 2014, 475 master's, 11 doctorates, 4 other advanced degrees awarded. *Degree requirements:* For master's, internship, practicum, thesis (for expressive therapies); for doctorate, thesis/dissertation, arts apprenticeship, field placement; for CAGS, thesis, internship (for counseling psychology, expressive therapies). *Entrance requirements:* For master's, MAT (counseling psychology), interview, writing samples, art portfolio; for doctorate, GRE or MAT, interview, master's degree; for CAGS, interview, master's degree. Additional exam requirements/recommendations for international students: Required—TOEFL (minimum score 550 paper-based; 80 iBT). *Application deadline:* Applications are processed on a rolling basis. Application fee: $50. Electronic applications accepted. *Financial support:* Fellowships, career-related internships or fieldwork, Federal Work-Study, scholarships/grants, tuition waivers, and unspecified assistantships available. Financial award applicants required to submit FAFSA. *Faculty research:* Psychotherapy and culture; psychotherapy and psychological trauma; women's issues in art, teaching and psychotherapy; community-based art, psycho-spiritual inquiry. *Unit head:* Dr. Catherine Koverola, Dean, 617-349-8317, Fax: 617-349-8366, E-mail: koverola@lesley.edu. *Application contact:* Martha Sheehan, Director, Graduate Admissions, 888-LESLEYU, Fax: 617-349-8313, E-mail: info@lesley.edu.
Website: http://www.lesley.edu/graduate-school-of-arts-and-social-sciences/

Memorial University of Newfoundland, School of Graduate Studies, Interdisciplinary Program in Women's Studies, St. John's, NL A1C 5S7, Canada. Offers MWS.

Middle Tennessee State University, College of Graduate Studies, College of Liberal Arts, Program in Women's and Gender Studies, Murfreesboro, TN 37132. Offers Graduate Certificate. Part-time and evening/weekend programs available. Postbaccalaureate distance learning degree programs offered. *Students:* 2 applicants, 50% accepted. In 2014, 5 Graduate Certificates awarded. *Application deadline:* For fall admission, 6/1 for domestic and international students. Applications are processed on a rolling basis. Application fee: $30. Electronic applications accepted. *Financial support:* Application deadline: 4/1; applicants required to submit FAFSA. *Unit head:* Dr. Mark E. Byrnes, Dean, 615-898-2534, Fax: 615-904-8279, E-mail: mark.byrnes@mtsu.edu. *Application contact:* Dr. Michael D. Allen, Vice Provost for Research/Dean, 615-898-2840, Fax: 615-904-8020, E-mail: michael.allen@mtsu.edu.

Minnesota State University Mankato, College of Graduate Studies, College of Social and Behavioral Sciences, Department of Gender and Women's Studies, Mankato, MN 56001. Offers MS, Certificate. Part-time programs available. *Students:* 9 full-time (6 women), 4 part-time (3 women). *Degree requirements:* For master's, comprehensive exam, thesis or alternative. *Entrance requirements:* For master's, minimum GPA of 3.0 during previous 2 years of course work. Additional exam requirements/recommendations for international students: Required—TOEFL. *Application deadline:* For fall admission, 7/1 priority date for domestic students; for spring admission, 11/1 for domestic students. Applications are processed on a rolling basis. Application fee: $40. *Financial support:* Research assistantships, teaching assistantships with full tuition reimbursements, career-related internships or fieldwork, Federal Work-Study, institutionally sponsored loans, and unspecified assistantships available. Support available to part-time students. Financial award application deadline: 3/15; financial award applicants required to submit FAFSA. *Unit head:* Dr. Shannon Miller, Graduate Coordinator, 507-389-2077. *Application contact:* 507-389-2321, E-mail: grad@mnsu.edu.
Website: http://sbs.mnsu.edu/women/

Mount Saint Vincent University, Graduate Programs, Department of Women's Studies, Halifax, NS B3M 2J6, Canada. Offers MA. Program offered jointly with Dalhousie University, Saint Mary's University. Part-time programs available. *Degree requirements:* For master's, thesis. Electronic applications accepted.

Northern Arizona University, Graduate College, College of Social and Behavioral Sciences, Women's and Gender Studies Program, Flagstaff, AZ 86011. Offers Graduate Certificate. Part-time programs available. *Entrance requirements:* Additional exam requirements/recommendations for international students: Required—TOEFL (minimum score 550 paper-based; 80 iBT). Electronic applications accepted.

The Ohio State University, Graduate School, College of Arts and Sciences, Division of Arts and Humanities, Department of Women's, Gender and Sexuality Studies, Columbus, OH 43210. Offers MA, PhD. *Faculty:* 17. *Students:* 24 full-time (21 women), 1 (woman) part-time; includes 9 minority (2 Black or African American, non-Hispanic/Latino; 1 Asian, non-Hispanic/Latino; 3 Hispanic/Latino; 3 Two or more races, non-Hispanic/Latino), 4 international. Average age 28. 39 applicants, 15% accepted, 5 enrolled. In 2014, 2 master's, 3 doctorates awarded. Terminal master's awarded for partial completion of doctoral program. *Degree requirements:* For master's, thesis optional; for doctorate, thesis/dissertation. *Entrance requirements:* For master's and doctorate, GRE (if GPA is less than 3.0 for all work), scholarly writing sample. Additional exam requirements/recommendations for international students: Required—TOEFL (minimum score 550 paper-based; 79 iBT), Michigan English Language Assessment Battery (minimum score 82); Recommended—IELTS (minimum score 7). *Application deadline:* For fall admission, 12/1 priority date for domestic students, 11/15 priority date for international students; for winter admission, 12/1 for domestic students, 11/1 for international students; for spring admission, 3/1 for domestic students, 2/1 for international students. Applications are processed on a rolling basis. Application fee: $60 ($70 for international students). Electronic applications accepted. *Financial support:* Fellowships with tuition reimbursements, research assistantships with tuition reimbursements, teaching assistantships with tuition reimbursements, career-related internships or fieldwork, Federal Work-Study, institutionally sponsored loans, and unspecified assistantships available. Support available to part-time students. *Unit head:* Dr. Jill Bystydzienski, Chair and Professor, 614-292-1021, E-mail: bystydzienski.1@osu.edu. *Application contact:* Graduate and Professional Admissions, 614-292-9444, Fax: 614-292-3895, E-mail: gpadmissions@osu.edu.
Website: http://wgss.osu.edu/

Oregon State University, College of Liberal Arts, Program in Women, Gender, and Sexuality Studies, Corvallis, OR 97331. Offers MA. Part-time programs available. *Faculty:* 7 full-time (6 women), 1 (woman) part-time/adjunct. *Students:* 18 full-time (16 women), 4 part-time (all women); includes 9 minority (1 Black or African American, non-Hispanic/Latino; 1 American Indian or Alaska Native, non-Hispanic/Latino; 5 Hispanic/Latino; 2 Two or more races, non-Hispanic/Latino), 3 international. Average age 32. 26 applicants, 77% accepted, 10 enrolled. In 2014, 3 master's awarded. *Entrance requirements:* Additional exam requirements/recommendations for international students: Required—TOEFL (minimum score 80 iBT), IELTS (minimum score 6.5).

Application deadline: For fall admission, 1/15 for domestic and international students. Application fee: $60. *Expenses:* Tuition, state resident: full-time $11,907; part-time $189 per credit hour. Tuition, nonresident: full-time $19,953; part-time $441 per credit hour. *Required fees:* $1472; $449 per term. One-time fee: $350. Tuition and fees vary according to course load and program. *Financial support:* Application deadline: 4/1. *Unit head:* Dr. Susan M. Shaw, Professor, 541-737-3082. *Application contact:* Dr. Liddy Detar, Instructor/Advisor, 541-737-4299, E-mail: liddy.detar@oregonstate.edu. Website: http://liberalarts.oregonstate.edu/slcs/wgss/

Queen's University at Kingston, School of Graduate Studies, Faculty of Arts and Sciences, Department of Sociology, Kingston, ON K7L 3N6, Canada. Offers communication and Information technology (MA, PhD); feminist sociology (MA, PhD); socio-legal studies (MA, PhD); sociological theory (MA, PhD). Part-time programs available. *Degree requirements:* For master's, thesis; for doctorate, comprehensive exam, thesis/dissertation. *Entrance requirements:* For master's, honors bachelors degree in sociology; for doctorate, honors bachelors degree, masters degree in sociology. Additional exam requirements/recommendations for international students: Required—TOEFL. *Faculty research:* Social change and modernization, social control, deviance and criminology, surveillance.

Reconstructionist Rabbinical College, Graduate Programs, Wyncote, PA 19095-1898. Offers Jewish studies (MAJS); rabbinics (MAHL, DHL); women's studies (Certificate). Certificate offered jointly with Temple University. Part-time programs available. *Degree requirements:* For master's, one foreign language, thesis (MAJS), completion of rabbinical program (MAHL); for doctorate, one foreign language. *Entrance requirements:* For master's, GRE General Test; placement examinations in Hebrew and Judaism (MAHL); for doctorate, GRE General Test, placement examinations in Hebrew and Judaism. *Faculty research:* Bible, Hebrew Semitic texts, contemporary Judaism.

Roosevelt University, Graduate Division, College of Arts and Sciences, Department of Literature and Languages, Program in Women's and Gender Studies, Chicago, IL 60605. Offers MA, Certificate. Part-time and evening/weekend programs available. *Degree requirements:* For master's, thesis. *Entrance requirements:* For master's, minimum GPA of 2.7. *Faculty research:* Feminist economics; philosophy of feminism; race, class, and gender; women and art; women's history.

Rutgers, The State University of New Jersey, New Brunswick, Graduate School-New Brunswick, Department of Political Science, Piscataway, NJ 08854-8097. Offers American politics (PhD); comparative politics (PhD); international relations (PhD); political theory (PhD); public law (PhD); United Nations and global policy studies (MA); women and politics (PhD). *Degree requirements:* For doctorate, one foreign language, comprehensive exam, thesis/dissertation. *Entrance requirements:* For master's, bachelor's degree from accredited U.S. college or university or a comparable institution in another country; for doctorate, GRE General Test. Additional exam requirements/recommendations for international students: Required—TOEFL.

Rutgers, The State University of New Jersey, New Brunswick, Graduate School-New Brunswick, Program in Women's and Gender Studies, Piscataway, NJ 08854-8097. Offers MA, PhD. Part-time programs available. *Degree requirements:* For master's, thesis or alternative; for doctorate, comprehensive exam, thesis/dissertation. *Entrance requirements:* For master's and doctorate, GRE General Test, writing sample, 3 letters of recommendation. Additional exam requirements/recommendations for international students: Required—TOEFL. *Faculty research:* Feminist theory, gender and sexuality, global and cultural studies, women in history, literature, and politics, feminist politics.

Saint Mary's University, Faculty of Arts, Program in Women and Gender Studies, Halifax, NS B3H 3C3, Canada. Offers MA. Program offered jointly with Mount Saint Vincent University. Part-time programs available. *Degree requirements:* For master's, thesis. *Entrance requirements:* For master's, honors degree.

San Diego State University, Graduate and Research Affairs, College of Arts and Letters, Department of Women's Studies, San Diego, CA 92182. Offers MA. *Entrance requirements:* For master's, GRE General Test, 2 letters of reference. Additional exam requirements/recommendations for international students: Required—TOEFL. Electronic applications accepted.

San Francisco State University, Division of Graduate Studies, College of Liberal and Creative Arts, Department of Women and Gender Studies, San Francisco, CA 94132-1722. Offers MA. Part-time and evening/weekend programs available. *Expenses:* Tuition, state resident: full-time $6738. Tuition, nonresident: full-time $17,898; part-time $372 per credit hour. *Required fees:* $498 per semester. *Unit head:* Dr. Deborah Cohler, Chair, 415-338-3065, E-mail: dcohler@sfsu.edu. *Application contact:* Dr. Nan Alamilla Boyd, Graduate Advisor, 415-338-1516, E-mail: alamilla@sfsu.edu. Website: http://wgsdept.sfsu.edu/

Sarah Lawrence College, Graduate Studies, Program in Women's History, Bronxville, NY 10708-5999. Offers MA. Part-time programs available. *Degree requirements:* For master's, thesis. *Entrance requirements:* For master's, previous course work in history, minimum B average in undergraduate course work. Additional exam requirements/recommendations for international students: Required—TOEFL (minimum score 600 paper-based). Electronic applications accepted.

Simon Fraser University, Office of Graduate Studies, Faculty of Arts and Social Sciences, Department of Gender, Sexuality and Women's Studies, Burnaby, BC V5A 1S6, Canada. Offers MA, PhD. *Degree requirements:* For master's, thesis or alternative; for doctorate, comprehensive exam, thesis/dissertation. *Entrance requirements:* For master's, minimum GPA of 3.0 (on scale of 4.33), or 3.33 based on last 60 credits of undergraduate courses; for doctorate, minimum GPA of 3.5 (on scale of 4.33). Additional exam requirements/recommendations for international students: Recommended—TOEFL (minimum score 580 paper-based; 93 iBT), IELTS (minimum score 7), TWE (minimum score 5). Electronic applications accepted. *Faculty research:* Gender history, feminist labor studies/economics, queer theory, women and media, feminist research methods.

Smith College, Graduate and Special Programs, Center for Women in Mathematics Post-Baccalaureate Program, Northampton, MA 01063. Offers Postbaccalaureate Certificate. Part-time programs available. *Faculty:* 12 full-time (5 women). *Students:* 9 full-time (all women); includes 3 minority (all Black or African American, non-Hispanic/Latino). Average age 24. 37 applicants, 38% accepted, 9 enrolled. In 2014, 12 Postbaccalaureate Certificates awarded. *Application deadline:* For fall admission, 3/15 for domestic students; for spring admission, 10/15 for domestic students. Application fee: $60. *Expenses: Tuition:* Full-time $33,360; part-time $1390 per credit. *Financial support:* In 2014–15, 9 students received support. Scholarships/grants and tuition waivers (full) available. Support available to part-time students. *Unit head:* Ruth Haas, Director, 413-585-3872, E-mail: rhaas@smith.edu. *Application contact:* Ruth Morgan, Program Assistant, 413-585-3050, Fax: 413-585-3054, E-mail: rmorgan@smith.edu. Website: http://www.smith.edu/gradstudy/nondegree_math.php

Sofia University, Hybrid: Face-to-Face/Online Programs, Palo Alto, CA 94303. Offers counseling psychology (MA); psychology (PhD), including transpersonal psychology; spiritual guidance (MA); transpersonal psychology (MA, Certificate); women's spirituality (MA, Certificate). Postbaccalaureate distance learning degree programs offered

(minimal on-campus study). *Entrance requirements:* For master's, bachelor's degree; for doctorate, bachelor's degree; master's degree. Electronic applications accepted.

Southeastern Baptist Theological Seminary, Graduate and Professional Programs, Wake Forest, NC 27588-1889. Offers advanced biblical studies (M Div); Christian education (M Div, MACE); Christian ethics (PhD); Christian ministry (M Div); Christian planting (M Div); church music (MACM); counseling (MACO); evangelism (PhD); language (M Div); ministry (D Min); New Testament (PhD); Old Testament (PhD); philosophy (PhD); theology (Th M, PhD); women's studies (M Div). *Accreditation:* ACIPE; ATS (one or more programs are accredited). *Degree requirements:* For master's, thesis (for some programs), oral exam; for doctorate, thesis/dissertation, fieldwork. *Entrance requirements:* For master's, Cooperative English Test, minimum GPA of 2.0, M Div or equivalent (Th M); for doctorate, GRE General Test or MAT, Cooperative English Test, M Div or equivalent, 3 years of professional experience.

Southern Connecticut State University, School of Graduate Studies, School of Arts and Sciences, Program in Women's Studies, New Haven, CT 06515-1355. Offers MA. Part-time and evening/weekend programs available. *Degree requirements:* For master's, thesis or alternative. *Entrance requirements:* For master's, interview. Electronic applications accepted.

Stony Brook University, State University of New York, Graduate School, College of Arts and Sciences, Program in Women's Studies, Stony Brook, NY 11794. Offers Certificate. In 2014, 3 Certificates awarded. *Degree requirements:* For Certificate, interdisciplinary research colloquium. *Entrance requirements:* For degree, GRE, minimum GPA of 2.75, 3 letters of recommendation. *Expenses:* Tuition, state resident: full-time $10,370; part-time $432 per credit. Tuition, nonresident: full-time $20,190; part-time $841 per credit. *Required fees:* $1431. *Unit head:* Dr. Robert Harvey, Chair, 631-632-7460, Fax: 631-632-5707, E-mail: robert.harvey@stonybrook.edu. *Application contact:* Prof. Lisa Diedrich, Director of Graduate Studies, 631-632-1765, Fax: 632-5707, E-mail: lisa.diedrich@stonybrook.edu. Website: http://www.stonybrook.edu/commcms/cat/graduate/WomenGenderStudies.html

Texas Woman's University, Graduate School, College of Arts and Sciences, Department of Women's Studies, Denton, TX 76201. Offers MA, PhD. Part-time programs available. Terminal master's awarded for partial completion of doctoral program. *Degree requirements:* For master's, comprehensive exam, thesis (for some programs); for doctorate, comprehensive exam, thesis/dissertation. *Entrance requirements:* For master's, 2 letters of reference, personal essay; for doctorate, personal essay, writing sample, curriculum vitae, 2 reference letters. Additional exam requirements/recommendations for international students: Required—TOEFL (minimum score 550 paper-based; 79 iBT). Electronic applications accepted. *Faculty research:* Feminist/womanist theories and epistemologies, history of U.S. feminism, U.S. women of color, feminism and religion/spirituality, critical race theories.

Towson University, Program in Women's Studies, Towson, MD 21252-0001. Offers MS, Postbaccalaureate Certificate. *Students:* 9 full-time (7 women), 2 part-time (both women); includes 6 minority (4 Black or African American, non-Hispanic/Latino; 2 Hispanic/Latino). *Degree requirements:* For master's, thesis optional. *Entrance requirements:* For master's, bachelor's degree with minimum GPA of 3.0, 9 credits of course work in women's studies and/or the social sciences, essay, 2 letters of recommendation; for Postbaccalaureate Certificate, bachelor's degree, 9 units in women's studies and/or the social sciences, 2 letters of recommendation, essay. *Application deadline:* Applications are processed on a rolling basis. Application fee: $45. Electronic applications accepted. *Financial support:* Application deadline: 4/1. *Unit head:* Dr. Kate Wilkinson, Graduate Program Director, 410-704-5744, E-mail: kwilkinson@towson.edu. *Application contact:* Alicia Arkell-Kleis, Information Contact, 410-704-6004, E-mail: grads@towson.edu. Website: http://gtad.towson.edu/program/master/wmst-ms/

United Theological Seminary of the Twin Cities, Graduate Programs, New Brighton, MN 55112-2598. Offers advanced theological studies (Diploma); justice and peace studies (M Div, MA); leadership toward racial justice (M Div, MA, Certificate); Methodist studies (M Div, MA, Certificate); ministry (D Min); ministry renewal and professional development (Certificate); pastoral care and counseling (M Div, MA, MARL); religion and theology (MA); theological and religious studies (Certificate); theology and the arts (M Div, MA); urban ministry (M Div, MA, MARL); women's studies: religion, theology and ministry (M Div, MA). *Accreditation:* ACIPE; ATS. Part-time and evening/weekend programs available. *Degree requirements:* For master's, thesis; for doctorate, comprehensive exam, thesis/dissertation. *Entrance requirements:* For master's, minimum GPA of 2.75; strong analytical, reflective thinking and writing skills; vocational and academic goals compatible with those of Seminary; for doctorate, M Div or equivalent, minimum GPA of 3.0, 3 years experience in professional ministry; for other advanced degree, BA or equivalent life experience; strong analytical, reflective thinking and writing skills (Certificate); proficiency in English language, previous study of theology at a theological school, recommendation of student's denomination (Diploma). Additional exam requirements/recommendations for international students: Required—TOEFL (minimum score 550 paper-based).

Université Laval, Faculty of Social Sciences, Program in Feminist Studies, Québec, QC G1K 7P4, Canada. Offers Diploma. Part-time programs available. *Entrance requirements:* For degree, knowledge of French, comprehension of written English. Electronic applications accepted.

University at Albany, State University of New York, College of Arts and Sciences, Department of Women's, Gender and Sexuality Studies, Albany, NY 12222-0001. Offers MA. *Entrance requirements:* Additional exam requirements/recommendations for international students: Required—TOEFL (minimum score 550 paper-based). Electronic applications accepted. *Faculty research:* Feminist pedagogy, lesbian and gay studies, women in the African diaspora, women's health policy, literature of feminism.

The University of Alabama, Graduate School, College of Arts and Sciences, Department of Gender and Race Studies, Tuscaloosa, AL 35487. Offers women's studies (MA). Part-time programs available. *Faculty:* 8 full-time (6 women), 1 (woman) part-time/adjunct. *Students:* 23 full-time (19 women), 6 part-time (all women); includes 16 minority (15 Black or African American, non-Hispanic/Latino; 1 Two or more races, non-Hispanic/Latino). Average age 26. 16 applicants, 81% accepted, 9 enrolled. In 2014, 9 master's awarded. *Degree requirements:* For master's, comprehensive exam, thesis optional. *Entrance requirements:* For master's, MAT or GRE. Additional exam requirements/recommendations for international students: Required—TOEFL. *Application deadline:* For fall admission, 3/7 priority date for domestic students, 3/7 for international students. Applications are processed on a rolling basis. Application fee: $50 ($60 for international students). Electronic applications accepted. *Expenses:* Tuition, state resident: full-time $9826. Tuition, nonresident: full-time $24,950. *Financial support:* In 2014–15, 6 students received support, including 3 research assistantships with tuition reimbursements available (averaging $10,908 per year), 3 teaching assistantships with tuition reimbursements available (averaging $10,908 per year); health care benefits and unspecified assistantships also available. Financial award application deadline: 4/1. *Faculty research:* Black feminist theory, African-American women's discursive practices, black women's leadership, feminist theory, queer theory.

Women's Studies

Unit head: Dr. DoVeanna S. Minor, Chair, 205-348-8462, Fax: 205-348-3584, E-mail: dfulton@as.ua.edu. *Application contact:* Patrick D. Fuller, Senior Graduate Admissions Counselor, 205-348-5923, Fax: 205-348-0400, E-mail: patrick.d.fuller@ua.edu. Website: http://www.as.ua.edu/grs/

The University of Arizona, College of Social and Behavioral Sciences, Department of Gender and Women's Studies, Tucson, AZ 85721. Offers MA, PhD, Certificate. Part-time programs available. *Degree requirements:* For master's, thesis/project. *Entrance requirements:* For master's and doctorate, GRE (minimum score: 500 verbal, 500 quantitative, 4.5 analytical), 3 letters of recommendation. Additional exam requirements/recommendations for international students: Required—TOEFL (minimum score 600 paper-based; 100 iBT). Electronic applications accepted. *Faculty research:* Gender, race and border studies; sexuality and the body; gender health and science; cultural representation and theory; public policy and social movements.

University of California, Santa Barbara, Graduate Division, College of Letters and Sciences, Division of Humanities and Fine Arts, Department of English, Santa Barbara, CA 93106-3170. Offers English (PhD); European medieval studies (PhD); feminist studies (PhD); global studies (PhD); technology and society (PhD); translation studies (PhD); writing studies (PhD); MA/PhD. Terminal master's awarded for partial completion of doctoral program. *Degree requirements:* For doctorate, one foreign language, comprehensive exam, thesis/dissertation. *Entrance requirements:* For doctorate, GRE General Test, GRE Subject Test (English). Additional exam requirements/recommendations for international students: Required—TOEFL (minimum score 550 paper-based; 80 iBT), IELTS (minimum score 7). Electronic applications accepted. *Faculty research:* Medieval, Romantic and Victorian studies; gender studies and feminist theory; literature and the mind; American literature; literature and new media/information culture.

University of California, Santa Barbara, Graduate Division, College of Letters and Sciences, Division of Humanities and Fine Arts, Department of History, Santa Barbara, CA 93106-9410. Offers European medieval studies (PhD); global studies (PhD); public historical studies (PhD); technology and society (PhD); women's studies (PhD); MA/PhD. *Degree requirements:* For doctorate, variable foreign language requirement, comprehensive exam, thesis/dissertation. *Entrance requirements:* For doctorate, GRE. Additional exam requirements/recommendations for international students: Required—TOEFL (minimum score 550 paper-based; 80 iBT), IELTS (minimum score 7). Electronic applications accepted. *Faculty research:* Europe, United States, Latin America, Africa, Middle East, East Asia.

University of California, Santa Barbara, Graduate Division, College of Letters and Sciences, Division of Humanities and Fine Arts, Department of History of Art and Architecture, Santa Barbara, CA 93106-2014. Offers art history (PhD), including art history, European medieval studies, feminist studies; MA/PhD. Terminal master's awarded for partial completion of doctoral program. *Degree requirements:* For doctorate, 2 foreign languages, comprehensive exam, thesis/dissertation. *Entrance requirements:* For doctorate, GRE. Additional exam requirements/recommendations for international students: Required—TOEFL (minimum score 550 paper-based; 80 iBT), IELTS (minimum score 7). Electronic applications accepted. *Faculty research:* History of architecture, Renaissance-Italian, Baroque, American, Chinese, Japanese, contemporary, Northern Renaissance.

University of California, Santa Barbara, Graduate Division, College of Letters and Sciences, Division of Humanities and Fine Arts, Department of Religious Studies, Santa Barbara, CA 93106-3130. Offers ancient Mediterranean studies (PhD); cognitive science (PhD); European medieval studies (PhD); feminist studies (PhD); global studies (PhD); religious studies (MA, PhD); translation studies (PhD); MA/PhD. Terminal master's awarded for partial completion of doctoral program. *Degree requirements:* For master's, one foreign language, comprehensive exam (for some programs), thesis (for some programs), colloquium; for doctorate, 2 foreign languages, thesis/dissertation, methodology, colloquium. *Entrance requirements:* For master's and doctorate, GRE General Test. Additional exam requirements/recommendations for international students: Required—TOEFL (minimum score 550 paper-based; 80 iBT), IELTS (minimum score 7). Electronic applications accepted. *Faculty research:* Area studies; religious traditions; theory and method in the study of religion; religion, culture, and politics; spirituality and religious experience.

University of California, Santa Barbara, Graduate Division, College of Letters and Sciences, Division of Humanities and Fine Arts, Department of Spanish and Portuguese, Santa Barbara, CA 93106-4150. Offers Hispanic languages and literatures (PhD), including European medieval studies, feminist studies, Hispanic linguistics, Hispanic literature, Luso-Brazilian literature; Hispanic linguistics (MA); Luso-Brazilian literature (MA); Spanish or Spanish-American literature (MA); MA/PhD. Spanish Language Institute available during Summer session. Terminal master's awarded for partial completion of doctoral program. *Degree requirements:* For master's, 2 foreign languages, comprehensive exam (for some programs), thesis optional; for doctorate, 3 foreign languages, comprehensive exam, thesis/dissertation. *Entrance requirements:* For master's and doctorate, GRE. Additional exam requirements/recommendations for international students: Required—TOEFL (minimum score 550 paper-based; 80 iBT), IELTS (minimum score 7). Electronic applications accepted. *Faculty research:* Nineteenth-century Spanish and Portuguese literature, Spanish and Spanish-American literature, nineteenth- and twentieth-century Portuguese and Brazilian literatures, Hispanic linguistics, Catalan language and culture.

University of California, Santa Barbara, Graduate Division, College of Letters and Sciences, Division of Humanities and Fine Arts, Department of Theater and Dance, Santa Barbara, CA 93106-7060. Offers theater studies (MA, PhD), including European medieval studies (PhD), feminist studies (PhD), theatre studies (PhD); MA/PhD. Terminal master's awarded for partial completion of doctoral program. *Degree requirements:* For master's, comprehensive exam, thesis; for doctorate, one foreign language, comprehensive exam, thesis/dissertation. *Entrance requirements:* For master's and doctorate, GRE. Additional exam requirements/recommendations for international students: Required—TOEFL (minimum score 550 paper-based; 80 iBT), IELTS (minimum score 7). Electronic applications accepted. *Faculty research:* English and American theater and Ancient Greek; Spanish, Latin American and Caribbean performance; Renaissance and Baroque drama and intercultural theory; East Asian performance, gender and nationalism; Korean cultural studies, Russian literature, and Slavic folklore; history of German theater, Shakespeare, and European opera; postcolonialism, performance-based ethnography, globalism and national identity formation in Africa.

University of California, Santa Barbara, Graduate Division, College of Letters and Sciences, Division of Humanities and Fine Arts, Program in Comparative Literature, Santa Barbara, CA 93106-4130. Offers comparative literature (PhD); East Asian literatures (PhD); feminist studies (PhD); French (PhD); global studies (PhD); translation studies (PhD); MA/PhD. *Degree requirements:* For doctorate, 2 foreign languages, comprehensive exam, thesis/dissertation. *Entrance requirements:* For doctorate, GRE. Additional exam requirements/recommendations for international students: Required—TOEFL (minimum score 550 paper-based; 80 iBT), IELTS (minimum score 7). Electronic

applications accepted. *Faculty research:* Comparative literary studies in global context, critical theory, translation studies, media technological studies, trauma studies.

University of California, Santa Barbara, Graduate Division, College of Letters and Sciences, Division of Social Sciences, Department of Communication, Santa Barbara, CA 93106-4020. Offers cognitive science (PhD); communication (PhD); feminist studies (PhD); language, interaction and social organization (PhD); quantitative methods in the social sciences (PhD); society and technology (PhD); MA/PhD. Terminal master's awarded for partial completion of doctoral program. *Degree requirements:* For doctorate, comprehensive exam, thesis/dissertation. *Entrance requirements:* For doctorate, GRE. Additional exam requirements/recommendations for international students: Required—TOEFL (minimum score 80 iBT), IELTS (minimum score 7). Electronic applications accepted. *Faculty research:* Interpersonal, intercultural, organizational, health, media.

University of California, Santa Barbara, Graduate Division, College of Letters and Sciences, Division of Social Sciences, Department of Feminist Studies, Santa Barbara, CA 93106-7110. Offers MA, PhD, MA/PhD. Terminal master's awarded for partial completion of doctoral program. *Degree requirements:* For master's, thesis (for some programs); for doctorate, one foreign language, comprehensive exam, thesis/dissertation. *Entrance requirements:* For master's and doctorate, GRE. Additional exam requirements/recommendations for international students: Required—TOEFL (minimum score 550 paper-based; 80 iBT), IELTS (minimum score 7). Electronic applications accepted. *Faculty research:* Genders and sexualities, productive and reproductive labors, race and nation, discourse and theory, media and new technologies.

University of California, Santa Barbara, Graduate Division, College of Letters and Sciences, Division of Social Sciences, Department of Sociology, Santa Barbara, CA 93106-9430. Offers interdisciplinary emphasis: Black studies (PhD); interdisciplinary emphasis: environment and society (PhD); interdisciplinary emphasis: feminist studies (PhD); interdisciplinary emphasis: global studies (PhD); interdisciplinary emphasis: language, interaction and social organization (PhD); interdisciplinary emphasis: quantitative methods in social science (PhD); interdisciplinary emphasis: technology and society (PhD); sociology (PhD); MA/PhD. Terminal master's awarded for partial completion of doctoral program. *Degree requirements:* For doctorate, comprehensive exam, thesis/dissertation. *Entrance requirements:* For doctorate, GRE General Test. Additional exam requirements/recommendations for international students: Required—TOEFL (minimum score 550 paper-based; 80 iBT), IELTS (minimum score 7). Electronic applications accepted. *Faculty research:* Gender and sexualities, race/ethnicity, social movements, conversation analysis, global sociology.

University of Cincinnati, Graduate School, McMicken College of Arts and Sciences, Department of Women's, Gender, and Sexuality Studies, Cincinnati, OH 45221-0164. Offers MA, Certificate, MA/JD. Part-time programs available. Terminal master's awarded for partial completion of doctoral program. *Degree requirements:* For master's, comprehensive exam, final paper/project. *Entrance requirements:* For master's, GRE General Test, 3 letters of recommendation. Additional exam requirements/recommendations for international students: Required—TOEFL (minimum score 600 paper-based), IELTS (minimum score 6.5). Electronic applications accepted. *Faculty research:* Feminist legal issues, sexuality, international political economy, Latin America, cultural/literary and environmental studies.

University of Colorado Denver, College of Liberal Arts and Sciences, Program in Humanities, Denver, CO 80217. Offers community health science (MSS); humanities (MH); international studies (MSS); philosophy and theory (MH); social justice (MSS); society and the environment (MSS); visual studies (MH); women's and gender studies (MSS). Part-time and evening/weekend programs available. *Faculty:* 1 full-time (0 women), 1 (woman) part-time/adjunct. *Students:* 49 full-time (37 women), 26 part-time (19 women); includes 14 minority (3 Black or African American, non-Hispanic/Latino; 1 American Indian or Alaska Native, non-Hispanic/Latino; 1 Asian, non-Hispanic/Latino; 6 Hispanic/Latino; 3 Two or more races, non-Hispanic/Latino), 1 international. Average age 35. 27 applicants, 63% accepted, 11 enrolled. In 2014, 16 master's awarded. *Degree requirements:* For master's, 36 credit hours, project or thesis. *Entrance requirements:* For master's, writing sample, statement of purpose/letter of intent, three letters of recommendation. Additional exam requirements/recommendations for international students: Required—TOEFL (minimum score 537 paper-based; 75 iBT); Recommended—IELTS (minimum score 6.5). *Application deadline:* For fall admission, 5/15 for domestic students, 5/15 priority date for international students; for spring admission, 10/15 for domestic students, 10/15 priority date for international students; for summer admission, 3/15 for domestic and international students. Application fee: $50 ($75 for international students). Electronic applications accepted. *Financial support:* In 2014–15, 4 students received support. Fellowships, research assistantships, teaching assistantships, Federal Work-Study, institutionally sponsored loans, scholarships/grants, and traineeships available. Financial award application deadline: 4/1; financial award applicants required to submit FAFSA. *Faculty research:* Women and gender in the classical Mediterranean, communication theory and democracy, relationship between psychology and philosophy. *Unit head:* Margaret Woodhull, Director of Humanities, 303-315-3568, E-mail: margaret.woodhull@ucdenver.edu. *Application contact:* Angela Beale, Program Assistant, 303-315-3565, E-mail: angela.beale@ucdenver.edu.
Website: http://www.ucdenver.edu/academics/colleges/CLAS/Programs/HumanitiesSocialSciences/Programs/Pages/MasterofHumanities.aspx

University of Florida, Graduate School, College of Liberal Arts and Sciences, Center for Women's Studies and Gender Research, Gainesville, FL 32611. Offers gender and development (Graduate Certificate); women's studies (MA, Graduate Certificate); MA/JD; MA/MA. *Faculty:* 28 full-time (25 women), 34 part-time/adjunct (27 women). *Students:* 9 full-time (6 women), 4 part-time (1 woman); includes 2 minority (1 Asian, non-Hispanic/Latino; 1 Hispanic/Latino), 2 international. 13 applicants, 62% accepted, 6 enrolled. In 2014, 5 master's awarded. Terminal master's awarded for partial completion of doctoral program. *Degree requirements:* For master's, thesis or project. *Entrance requirements:* For master's, GRE General Test (minimum score 1000), minimum GPA of 3.2. Additional exam requirements/recommendations for international students: Required—TOEFL (minimum score 550 paper-based; 80 iBT), IELTS (minimum score 6). *Application deadline:* For fall admission, 1/15 for domestic and international students; for spring admission, 10/1 for domestic and international students. Application fee: $30. Electronic applications accepted. *Financial support:* In 2014–15, 1 fellowship, 1 research assistantship, 7 teaching assistantships were awarded. Financial award application deadline: 1/15; financial award applicants required to submit FAFSA. *Faculty research:* Prejudice, discrimination, intersections, resistance, history. *Total annual research expenditures:* $764. *Unit head:* Dr. Judith W. Page, Director, 352-273-0387, Fax: 352-392-0860, E-mail: page7@ufl.edu. *Application contact:* Anita Anantharam, PhD, Graduate Coordinator, 352-273-0383, Fax: 352-392-4873, E-mail: aanita@ufl.edu. Website: http://web.wst.ufl.edu/

University of Georgia, Franklin College of Arts and Sciences, Institute for Women's Studies, Athens, GA 30602. Offers Certificate.

University of Hawaii at Manoa, Graduate Division, College of Social Sciences, Advanced Women's Studies Program, Honolulu, HI 96822. Offers Graduate Certificate. Part-time programs available. *Entrance requirements:* Additional exam requirements/

recommendations for international students: Required—TOEFL (minimum score 500 paper-based; 61 iBT), IELTS (minimum score 5).

The University of Iowa, Graduate College, College of Liberal Arts and Sciences, Department of Gender, Women's and Sexuality Studies, Iowa City, IA 52242-1316. Offers Certificate. *Entrance requirements:* Additional exam requirements/ recommendations for international students: Required—TOEFL (minimum score 550 paper-based; 81 iBT).

University of Lethbridge, School of Graduate Studies, Lethbridge, AB T1K 3M4, Canada. Offers addictions counseling (M Sc); agricultural biotechnology (M Sc); agricultural studies (M Sc, MA); anthropology (MA); archaeology (M Sc, MA); art (MA, MFA); biochemistry (M Sc); biological sciences (M Sc); biomolecular science (PhD); biosystems and biodiversity (PhD); Canadian studies (MA); chemistry (M Sc); computer science (M Sc); computer science and geographical information science (M Sc); counseling (MC); counseling psychology (M Ed); dramatic arts (MA); earth, space, and physical science (PhD); economics (MA); education (MA); educational leadership (M Ed); English (MA); environmental science (M Sc); evolution and behavior (PhD); exercise science (M Sc); French (MA); French/German (MA); French/Spanish (MA); general education (M Ed); geography (M Sc, MA); German (MA); health sciences (M Sc); individualized multidisciplinary (M Sc, MA); kinesiology (M Sc, MA); management (M Sc), including accounting, finance, general management, human resource management and labor relations, information systems, international management, marketing, policy and strategy; mathematics (M Sc); modern languages (MA); music (M Mus, MA); Native American studies (MA); neuroscience (M Sc, PhD); new media (MA, MFA); nursing (M Sc, MN); philosophy (MA); physics (M Sc); political science (MA); psychology (M Sc, MA); religious studies (MA); sociology (MA); theatre and dramatic arts (MFA); theoretical and computational science (PhD); urban and regional studies (MA); women and gender studies (MA). Part-time and evening/weekend programs available. *Faculty:* 358. *Students:* 445 full-time (243 women), 116 part-time (72 women). Average age 31. 351 applicants, 26% accepted, 87 enrolled. In 2014, 129 master's, 13 doctorates awarded. *Degree requirements:* For master's, thesis (for some programs); for doctorate, comprehensive exam, thesis/dissertation. *Entrance requirements:* For master's, GMAT (for M Sc in management), bachelor's degree in related field, minimum GPA of 3.0 during previous 20 graded semester courses, 2 years' teaching or related experience (M Ed); for doctorate, master's degree, minimum graduate GPA of 3.5. Additional exam requirements/recommendations for international students: Required—TOEFL. Application fee: $100 Canadian dollars. *Financial support:* Fellowships, research assistantships, teaching assistantships, scholarships/grants, health care benefits, and unspecified assistantships available. *Faculty research:* Movement and brain plasticity, gibberellin physiology, photosynthesis, carbon cycling, molecular properties of main-group ring components. *Application contact:* School of Graduate Studies, 403-329-5194, E-mail: sgsinquiries@uleth.ca.
Website: http://www.uleth.ca/graduatestudies/

University of Louisville, Graduate School, College of Arts and Sciences, Department of Women's and Gender Studies, Louisville, KY 40292. Offers MA, Certificate, MSSW/MA. Part-time programs available. *Students:* 20 full-time (18 women), 5 part-time (all women); includes 3 minority (all Black or African American, non-Hispanic/Latino). Average age 27. 21 applicants, 90% accepted, 9 enrolled. In 2014, 4 master's, 2 other advanced degrees awarded. *Degree requirements:* For master's, thesis or alternative. *Entrance requirements:* For master's, GRE. Additional exam requirements/recommendations for international students: Required—TOEFL. *Application deadline:* For fall admission, 8/1 for domestic students, 5/1 priority date for international students; for spring admission, 12/20 for domestic students, 11/1 priority date for international students; for summer admission, 4/1 priority date for international students. Applications are processed on a rolling basis. Application fee: $60. Electronic applications accepted. *Expenses:* Tuition, state resident: full-time $11,326; part-time $630 per credit hour. Tuition, nonresident: full-time $23,568; part-time $1311 per credit hour. *Required fees:* $196. Tuition and fees vary according to program and reciprocity agreements. *Financial support:* Teaching assistantships with full tuition reimbursements and scholarships/grants available. Financial award application deadline: 5/1; financial award applicants required to submit FAFSA. *Faculty research:* Gender representation in popular media; intersections of race, class, gender and sexuality in U.S. popular culture and popular music; interconnectedness between the performance of identity and racialized body politics for African diaspora women and men; nineteenth century women/gender in the U.S.; medicine as a gendered practice; gender, race, and class dynamics in parenting and the workplace. *Unit head:* Dr. Nancy M. Theriot, Chairperson, 502-852-8160, Fax: 502-852-4421, E-mail: nancyt@louisville.edu. *Application contact:* Libby Leggett, Director, Graduate Admissions, 502-852-3101, Fax: 502-852-6536, E-mail: gradadm@louisville.edu.
Website: http://louisville.edu/wgs/

University of Maryland, Baltimore County, The Graduate School, College of Arts, Humanities and Social Sciences, Program in Gender and Women's Studies, Baltimore, MD 21250. Offers Postbaccalaureate Certificate. Part-time and evening/weekend programs available. *Students:* 1 applicant, 100% accepted. *Application deadline:* Applications are processed on a rolling basis. Application fee: $0. Electronic applications accepted. *Expenses:* Tuition, state resident: part-time $557. Tuition, nonresident: part-time $922. *Required fees:* $122 per semester. One-time fee: $200 part-time. *Financial support:* In 2014–15, 1 teaching assistantship with partial tuition reimbursement (averaging $7,500 per year) was awarded; health care benefits and unspecified assistantships also available. *Faculty research:* Feminist theory, reproductive and sexual politics, U.S. women's history. *Unit head:* Dr. Carole McCann, Director/Associate Professor, 410-455-2161, E-mail: mccann@umbc.edu. *Application contact:* Kathryn Nee, Coordinator of Domestic Admissions, 410-455-2944, E-mail: nee@umbc.edu.
Website: http://www.umbc.edu/gwstudies/

University of Maryland, College Park, Academic Affairs, College of Arts and Humanities, Department of Women's Studies, College Park, MD 20742. Offers MA, PhD. *Degree requirements:* For master's, thesis or alternative; for doctorate, one foreign language, thesis/dissertation or alternative. *Entrance requirements:* For master's, GRE General Test, writing sample, 3 letters of recommendation. Additional exam requirements/recommendations for international students: Required—TOEFL. *Faculty research:* Gender roles, national and global diversity, sexuality.

University of Michigan, Horace H. Rackham School of Graduate Studies, College of Literature, Science, and the Arts, Department of Women's Studies, Ann Arbor, MI 48109. Offers English and women's studies (PhD); history and women's studies (PhD); LGBTQ studies (Certificate); psychology and women's studies (PhD); women's studies (Certificate). *Faculty:* 36 full-time. *Students:* 58 full-time (48 women). 119 applicants, 8% accepted, 6 enrolled. In 2014, 7 doctorates, 4 other advanced degrees awarded. *Degree requirements:* For doctorate, variable foreign language requirement, comprehensive exam (for some programs), thesis/dissertation. *Entrance requirements:* For doctorate, GRE General Test, previous undergraduate coursework in women's studies. *Application deadline:* For fall admission, 12/1 for domestic and international students. Application fee: $75 ($90 for international students). Electronic applications accepted. *Financial support:* In 2014–15, fellowships with full tuition reimbursements (averaging $18,000 per year), research assistantships with full tuition reimbursements (averaging $18,000

per year), teaching assistantships with full tuition reimbursements (averaging $18,000 per year) were awarded; scholarships/grants, health care benefits, tuition waivers (full), and unspecified assistantships also available. *Faculty research:* LGBTQ studies, sexuality studies, feminist science studies, global feminism, health studies, international studies, cultural studies. *Unit head:* Lilia Cortina, Director of Graduate Studies, 734-763-2047, Fax: 734-647-4943, E-mail: lilia@umich.edu. *Application contact:* Aimee Germain, Graduate Program Coordinator, 734-763-2047, Fax: 734-647-4943, E-mail: wsdgradinquiry@umich.edu.
Website: http://www.lsa.umich.edu/women/

University of Minnesota, Twin Cities Campus, Graduate School, College of Liberal Arts, Department of Gender, Women, and Sexuality Studies, Minneapolis, MN 55455-0213. Offers feminist studies (PhD). *Degree requirements:* For doctorate, comprehensive exam, thesis/dissertation. *Entrance requirements:* For doctorate, GRE. Additional exam requirements/recommendations for international students: Required—TOEFL (minimum score 550 paper-based). Electronic applications accepted. *Faculty research:* Transnational feminist theories, critical development theory, feminist postcolonialisms, feminist science studies and studying of health, literature, Asian diasporas, sexuality and queer theory.

University of New Mexico, Graduate School, College of Arts and Sciences, Program in Women Studies, Albuquerque, NM 87131. Offers Graduate Certificate. Part-time programs available. *Students:* 2 applicants, 100% accepted, 1 enrolled. In 2014, 5 Graduate Certificates awarded. *Entrance requirements:* For degree, enrollment in degree-granting program. Additional exam requirements/recommendations for international students: Required—TOEFL. *Application deadline:* Applications are processed on a rolling basis. Application fee: $50. *Financial support:* In 2014–15, 1 research assistantship with partial tuition reimbursement (averaging $3,428 per year), 3 teaching assistantships with partial tuition reimbursements (averaging $7,395 per year) were awarded; health care benefits and unspecified assistantships also available. Support available to part-time students. Financial award application deadline: 2/15; financial award applicants required to submit FAFSA. *Faculty research:* Global feminism; queer and sexuality studies; race, gender, and feminisms. *Unit head:* Dr. Barbara O. Reyes, Director, 505-277-3854, Fax: 505-277-1208, E-mail: breyes3@unm.edu. *Application contact:* Vicki Hall, Academic Administrator III, 505-277-6131, Fax: 505-277-0351, E-mail: vhall@unm.edu.
Website: http://www.unm.edu/~womenst/

The University of North Carolina at Charlotte, College of Liberal Arts and Sciences, Interdisciplinary Liberal Arts and Sciences Programs, Charlotte, NC 28223-0001. Offers gerontology (MA, Graduate Certificate); Latin American studies (MA); liberal studies (MA); organizational psychology (PhD); public policy (PhD); women's studies (Graduate Certificate). *Faculty:* 6 full-time (3 women), 5 part-time/adjunct (all women). *Students:* 58 full-time (31 women), 55 part-time (45 women); includes 24 minority (15 Black or African American, non-Hispanic/Latino; 1 Asian, non-Hispanic/Latino; 6 Hispanic/Latino; 1 Native Hawaiian or other Pacific Islander, non-Hispanic/Latino; 1 Two or more races, non-Hispanic/Latino), 12 international. Average age 33. 96 applicants, 46% accepted, 29 enrolled. In 2014, 11 master's, 8 doctorates, 15 other advanced degrees awarded. Terminal master's awarded for partial completion of doctoral program. *Degree requirements:* For master's, thesis or alternative, comprehensive exam or project; for doctorate, thesis/dissertation. *Entrance requirements:* For master's, GRE General Test or MAT, minimum GPA of 3.0 during previous 2 years, 2.75 overall; for doctorate, GRE, letters of recommendation. Additional exam requirements/recommendations for international students: Required—TOEFL (minimum score 557 paper-based; 83 iBT). *Application deadline:* For fall admission, 5/1 priority date for domestic students, 5/1 for international students; for spring admission, 10/1 priority date for domestic students, 10/1 for international students. Applications are processed on a rolling basis. Application fee: $75. Electronic applications accepted. *Expenses:* Tuition, state resident: full-time $4008. Tuition, nonresident: full-time $16,295. *Required fees:* $2755. Tuition and fees vary according to course load and program. *Financial support:* In 2014–15, 24 students received support, including 20 research assistantships (averaging $10,400 per year), 4 teaching assistantships (averaging $8,250 per year); career-related internships or fieldwork, institutionally sponsored loans, scholarships/grants, and unspecified assistantships also available. Support available to part-time students. Financial award application deadline: 4/1; financial award applicants required to submit FAFSA. *Total annual research expenditures:* $15,045. *Unit head:* Dr. Nancy A. Gutierrez, Dean, 704-687-0081, Fax: 704-687-4347, E-mail: ngutierr@uncc.edu. *Application contact:* Kathy B. Giddings, Director of Graduate Admissions, 704-687-5503, Fax: 704-687-3279, E-mail: gradadm@uncc.edu.
Website: http://www.lbst.uncc.edu/

The University of North Carolina at Greensboro, Graduate School, College of Arts and Sciences, Department of English, Greensboro, NC 27412-5001. Offers creative writing (MFA); English (M Ed, MA, PhD, Certificate), including American literature (PhD), English (M Ed, MA), English literature (PhD), rhetoric and composition (PhD), technical writing (Certificate), women's studies (Certificate). *Degree requirements:* For master's, comprehensive exam; for doctorate, variable foreign language requirement, thesis/dissertation, preliminary exam. *Entrance requirements:* For master's, GRE General Test, minimum GPA of 3.0; for doctorate, GRE General Test, GRE Subject Test, critical writing sample, minimum GPA of 3.0. Additional exam requirements/recommendations for international students: Required—TOEFL. Electronic applications accepted.

The University of North Carolina at Greensboro, Graduate School, College of Arts and Sciences, Program in Women's and Gender Studies, Greensboro, NC 27412-5001. Offers MA, Certificate. Electronic applications accepted.

University of Northern Iowa, Graduate College, MA Program in Women's and Gender Studies, Cedar Falls, IA 50614. Offers MA. *Students:* 4 full-time (3 women), 3 part-time (all women); includes 1 minority (Asian, non-Hispanic/Latino). 8 applicants, 63% accepted, 1 enrolled. In 2014, 1 master's awarded. *Degree requirements:* For master's, comprehensive exam (for some programs), thesis or alternative. *Entrance requirements:* For master's, minimum GPA of 3.0. Additional exam requirements/recommendations for international students: Required—TOEFL (minimum score 500 paper-based; 61 iBT). *Application deadline:* Applications are processed on a rolling basis. Application fee: $50 ($70 for international students). Electronic applications accepted. *Expenses:* Tuition, state resident: full-time $7912; part-time $880 per credit. Tuition, nonresident: full-time $17,906; part-time $880 per credit. *Required fees:* $1101; $325.50 per credit. $465.63 per semester. Tuition and fees vary according to course load and program. *Financial support:* Application deadline: 2/1. *Unit head:* Dr. Catherine MacGillivray, Interim Director, 319-273-7195, Fax: 319-273-3053, E-mail: catherine.macgillivray@uni.edu. *Application contact:* Laurie S. Russell, Record Analyst, 319-273-2623, Fax: 319-273-2885, E-mail: laurie.russell@uni.edu.
Website: http://www.uni.edu/womenstudies/

University of Oklahoma, College of Arts and Sciences, Women's and Gender Studies Program, Norman, OK 73019. Offers Graduate Certificate. Part-time and evening/weekend programs available. *Students:* 3 full-time (all women), 16 part-time (15 women); includes 2 minority (1 American Indian or Alaska Native, non-Hispanic/Latino; 1 Hispanic/Latino), 1 international. Average age 40. In 2014, 10 Graduate Certificates awarded. *Entrance requirements:* For degree, minimum GPA of 3.0. Additional exam

requirements/recommendations for international students: Required—TOEFL (minimum score 79 iBT). *Application deadline:* For fall admission, 3/15 for domestic and international students; for spring admission, 11/15 for domestic and international students. Applications are processed on a rolling basis. Application fee: $50 ($100 for international students). Electronic applications accepted. *Expenses:* Tuition, state resident: full-time $4394; part-time $183.10 per credit hour. Tuition, nonresident: full-time $16,970; part-time $707.10 per credit hour. *Required fees:* $2892; $109.95 per credit hour. $126.50 per semester. *Financial support:* In 2014–15, 1 research assistantship with partial tuition reimbursement (averaging $11,709 per year), 1 teaching assistantship with partial tuition reimbursement (averaging $10,373 per year) were awarded; unspecified assistantships also available. Financial award application deadline: 6/1; financial award applicants required to submit FAFSA. *Faculty research:* LGBTQ issues, gender and politics, social justice, gender and media, gender and STEM. *Unit head:* Jill Irvine, Director, 405-325-2205, Fax: 405-325-3573, E-mail: jill.irvine@ou.edu. *Application contact:* Katy Hall, Managerial Associate, 405-325-3481, Fax: 405-325-3573, E-mail: katyhall@ou.edu.
Website: http://wgs.ou.edu/

University of Ottawa, Faculty of Graduate and Postdoctoral Studies, Faculty of Social Sciences, Institute of Women's Studies, Ottawa, ON K1N 6N5, Canada. Offers criminology (MA, MCA); education (MA); English (MA); history (MA); human kinetics (MA); law (LL M); lettres Franlfcaises (MA); nursing (M Sc); pastoral studies (MA); political science (MA); religious studies (MA); sociology (MA). *Degree requirements:* For master's, thesis or alternative.

University of Pittsburgh, Dietrich School of Arts and Sciences, Gender, Sexuality, and Women's Studies Program, Pittsburgh, PA 15260. Offers Doctoral Certificate, Master's Certificate. Part-time programs available. *Faculty:* 119 full-time (91 women), 2 part-time/adjunct (both women). *Students:* 57 full-time (47 women); includes 16 minority (5 Black or African American, non-Hispanic/Latino; 7 Asian, non-Hispanic/Latino; 4 Hispanic/Latino). Average age 27. 17 applicants, 100% accepted, 17 enrolled. In 2014, 2 Master's Certificates awarded. *Degree requirements:* For other advanced degree, scholarly essay. *Entrance requirements:* For degree, good academic standing in a University of Pittsburgh graduate degree-granting department. *Application deadline:* Applications are processed on a rolling basis. Application fee: $0. Electronic applications accepted. *Expenses:* Tuition, state resident: full-time $20,742; part-time $838 per credit. Tuition, nonresident: full-time $33,960; part-time $1389 per credit. *Required fees:* $800; $205 per term. Tuition and fees vary according to program. *Financial support:* Application deadline: 2/9. *Faculty research:* Global feminisms; gender and interpersonal violence; race and gender studies; gender and sustainability; representation and gender in media, arts, and literature; masculinities; concepts of the body. *Unit head:* Dr. Todd Reeser, Director, 412-624-6486, Fax: 412-624-6492, E-mail: gsws@pitt.edu. *Application contact:* Karen E. Lillis, Administrator, 412-624-7232, Fax: 412-624-6492, E-mail: lillis@pitt.edu.
Website: http://www.gsws.pitt.edu/students/

University of Regina, Faculty of Graduate Studies and Research, Faculty of Arts, Department of Women's and Gender Studies, Regina, SK S4S 0A2, Canada. Offers MA. Offered as a special case program. Part-time programs available. *Faculty:* 4 full-time (all women), 1 (woman) part-time/adjunct. *Students:* 1 applicant. In 2014, 1 master's awarded. *Degree requirements:* For master's, thesis. *Entrance requirements:* Additional exam requirements/recommendations for international students: Required—TOEFL (minimum score 580 paper-based; 80 iBT), IELTS (minimum score 6.5), PTE (minimum score 59). *Application deadline:* Applications are processed on a rolling basis. Application fee: $100. Electronic applications accepted. *Expenses: Tuition, area resident:* Full-time $4900 Canadian dollars; part-time $837.65 Canadian dollars per semester. *International tuition:* $7900 Canadian dollars full-time. *Required fees:* $396 Canadian dollars; $86.90 Canadian dollars per semester. *Financial support:* Fellowships, research assistantships, teaching assistantships, and scholarships/grants available. Financial award application deadline: 6/15. *Faculty research:* Feminist theory; mapping sexualities; mapping gender; women, feminism, and globalization. *Unit head:* Dr. Darlene Juschka, Graduate Program Coordinator, 306-585-5280, E-mail: darlene.juschka@uregina.ca. *Application contact:* Cordelia McDonald, Administrative Assistant, 306-585-4189, E-mail: cordelia.mcdonald@uregina.ca.
Website: http://www.uregina.ca/arts/womens-gender-studies

University of Saskatchewan, College of Graduate Studies and Research, College of Arts and Science, Department of Women's and Gender Studies, Saskatoon, SK S7N 5A2, Canada. Offers MA, PhD. *Degree requirements:* For master's, thesis; for doctorate, comprehensive exam (for some programs), thesis/dissertation. *Entrance requirements:* Additional exam requirements/recommendations for international students: Required—TOEFL (minimum score 80 iBT); Recommended—IELTS (minimum score 6.5). Electronic applications accepted.

University of South Carolina, The Graduate School, College of Arts and Sciences, Program in Women's Studies, Columbia, SC 29208. Offers Certificate. Part-time programs available. *Entrance requirements:* For degree, GRE General Test or MAT. Additional exam requirements/recommendations for international students: Required—TOEFL. Electronic applications accepted. *Faculty research:* Health; pedagogy; intersection of race, class, gender; public policy; politics of culture and representations, feminist political economics.

University of South Florida, College of Arts and Sciences, Department of Women's Studies, Tampa, FL 33620-9951. Offers women's and gender studies (MA). Part-time programs available. *Faculty:* 4 full-time (3 women). *Students:* 9 full-time (8 women); includes 2 minority (both Hispanic/Latino), 2 international. Average age 27. 10 applicants, 70% accepted, 3 enrolled. In 2014, 3 master's awarded. *Degree requirements:* For master's, comprehensive exam, thesis or internship. *Entrance requirements:* For master's, GRE General Test, minimum GPA of 3.0, three letters of recommendation, personal narrative statement of purpose, scholarly writing sample (examples include term paper or research paper); undergraduate major or minor in women's studies (recommended). Additional exam requirements/recommendations for international students: Required—TOEFL (minimum score 550 paper-based; 79 iBT) or IELTS (minimum score 6.5). *Application deadline:* For fall admission, 2/15 for domestic students, 1/2 for international students; for spring admission, 10/15 for domestic students, 6/1 for international students. Applications are processed on a rolling basis. Application fee: $30. *Financial support:* In 2014–15, 9 students received support, including 9 teaching assistantships with tuition reimbursements available (averaging $9,093 per year). Financial award application deadline: 3/1. *Faculty research:* Performance studies, feminist theory and pedagogy; constructions of gender in public discourse, including education, mass media, and popular culture; women's health, reproductive justice, and sexuality; bodies and cultural representations; feminist theory as it relates to learning disabilities, critical race theory, postmodernist and queer theory; hiring practices in higher education, mothering; women of color feminisms. *Unit head:* Dr. Diane Price Herndl, Professor and Chairperson, 813-974-0987, Fax: 813-974-0336, E-mail: priceherndl@usf.edu. *Application contact:* Dr. Kim Golombisky, Associate Professor and Graduate Director, 813-974-0986, Fax: 813-974-0336, E-mail: kgolombi@usf.edu.
Website: http://wgs.usf.edu/

The University of Toledo, College of Graduate Studies, College of Languages, Literature and Social Sciences, Department of Women's and Gender Studies, Toledo, OH 43606-3390. Offers Certificate. Part-time programs available.

University of Toronto, School of Graduate Studies, Faculty of Arts and Science, Women and Gender Studies Institute, Toronto, ON M5S 2J7, Canada. Offers MA, PhD. *Entrance requirements:* For master's, minimum B+ in final year of undergraduate study. Additional exam requirements/recommendations for international students: Required—TOEFL (minimum score 580 paper-based; 93 iBT), TWE (minimum score 5). Electronic applications accepted.

University of Washington, Graduate School, College of Arts and Sciences, Department of Gender, Women and Sexuality Studies, Seattle, WA 98195. Offers PhD. Terminal master's awarded for partial completion of doctoral program. *Degree requirements:* For doctorate, one foreign language, thesis/dissertation, exam. *Entrance requirements:* For doctorate, GRE General Test. Additional exam requirements/recommendations for international students: Required—TOEFL. Electronic applications accepted. *Faculty research:* Women's history in U.S. and China; Native American ethnography and identity; women, science, and technology; political economy of development, feminism and nationalism.

University of Wisconsin–Madison, Graduate School, College of Letters and Science, Department of History, Madison, WI 53706-1380. Offers African history (MA, PhD); Central Asian history (MA, PhD); comparative world history (MA, PhD); East Asian history (MA, PhD); European history (MA, PhD); gender and women's history (MA, PhD); Latin American and Caribbean history (MA, PhD); Middle Eastern history (MA, PhD); South Asian history (MA, PhD); Southeast Asian history (MA, PhD); United States history (MA, PhD). Terminal master's awarded for partial completion of doctoral program. *Degree requirements:* For master's, thesis (for some programs); for doctorate, variable foreign language requirement, thesis/dissertation. *Entrance requirements:* For master's and doctorate, GRE General Test. Additional exam requirements/recommendations for international students: Required—Michigan English Language Assessment Battery or TOEFL. Electronic applications accepted. *Expenses:* Tuition, state resident: full-time $10,723; part-time $745 per credit. Tuition, nonresident: full-time $24,054; part-time $1578 per credit. *Required fees:* $374 per semester. Tuition and fees vary according to course load, program and reciprocity agreements. *Faculty research:* American, African, European, Asian, Latin American, and Middle Eastern history.

University of Wisconsin–Milwaukee, Graduate School, College of Letters and Sciences, Program in Women's Studies, Milwaukee, WI 53201-0413. Offers MA. Part-time programs available. *Entrance requirements:* For master's, three letters of recommendation, sample of written work, letter of intent. Electronic applications accepted.

Western Seminary, Graduate Programs, Program in Ministry and Leadership, Portland, OR 97215-3367. Offers chaplaincy (MA); coaching (MA); Jewish ministry (MA); pastoral care to women (MA); youth ministry (MA). *Degree requirements:* For master's, practicum. *Entrance requirements:* Additional exam requirements/recommendations for international students: Required—TOEFL.

Western Seminary–Sacramento Campus, Graduate Certificate Programs, Sacramento, CA 95821. Offers Bible (Graduate Certificate); coaching (Graduate Certificate); pastoral care to women (Graduate Certificate); theology (Graduate Certificate); youth and family (Graduate Certificate). Postbaccalaureate distance learning degree programs offered. *Entrance requirements:* For degree, essays, undergraduate transcripts, 4 recommendations. Additional exam requirements/recommendations for international students: Required—TOEFL.

Western Seminary–Sacramento Campus, Graduate Diploma Programs, Sacramento, CA 95821. Offers Bible and theology (Graduate Diploma); ministry (Graduate Diploma); pastoral care to women (Graduate Diploma). *Entrance requirements:* For degree, essays, undergraduate transcripts, 4 recommendations. Additional exam requirements/recommendations for international students: Required—TOEFL.

Western Seminary–San Jose Campus, Graduate Programs, Los Gatos, CA 95032-4520. Offers Bible and theology (Graduate Diploma); Bible, camp and conference ministry (CGS); Biblical and theological studies (MA), including exegetical track, theological track; coaching (CGS); expositional ministry (M Div); marital and family therapy (MA); ministry (Graduate Diploma); ministry and leadership (MA), including camp and conference ministry, coaching, pastoral care to women, youth ministry; pastoral care to women (CGS, Graduate Diploma); pastoral ministry (M Div); theology (CGS); youth and family (CGS). Part-time and evening/weekend programs available. Postbaccalaureate distance learning degree programs offered (minimal on-campus study). *Entrance requirements:* For master's, minimum GPA of 3.0. Electronic applications accepted.

York University, Faculty of Graduate Studies, Faculty of Liberal Arts and Professional Studies, Program in Gender, Feminist and Women's Studies, Toronto, ON M3J 1P3, Canada. Offers MA, PhD. *Degree requirements:* For master's, thesis or alternative; for doctorate, comprehensive exam, thesis/dissertation. Electronic applications accepted.

Section 16
Communication and Media

This section contains a directory of institutions offering graduate work in communication and media, followed by an in-depth entries submitted by institutions that chose to prepare detailed program descriptions. Additional information about programs listed in the directory but not augmented by an in-depth entry may be obtained by writing directly to the dean of a graduate school or chair of a department at the address given in the directory.

For programs offering related work, see also in this book *Film, Television, and Video; Language and Literature;* and *Psychology and Counseling.* In the other guides in this series:

Graduate Programs in Engineering & Applied Sciences

See *Computer Science and Information Technology* and *Telecommunications*

Graduate Programs in Business, Education, Information Studies, Law & Social Work

See *Advertising and Public Relations*

CONTENTS

Program Directories

Displays and Close-Ups

See also:

Communication—General

Abilene Christian University, Graduate School, College of Arts and Sciences, Department of Communication, Program in Communication, Abilene, TX 79699-9100. Offers MA. Part-time programs available. *Faculty:* 9 part-time/adjunct (4 women). *Students:* 10 full-time (6 women), 4 part-time (2 women); includes 2 minority (1 Black or African American, non-Hispanic/Latino; 1 Hispanic/Latino). 31 applicants, 42% accepted, 6 enrolled. In 2014, 5 master's awarded. *Degree requirements:* For master's, comprehensive exam, thesis optional. *Entrance requirements:* For master's, GRE General Test. Additional exam requirements/recommendations for international students: Required—TOEFL (minimum score 550 paper-based; 90 iBT), IELTS (minimum score 6.5), PTE. *Application deadline:* For fall admission, 4/1 priority date for domestic students; for spring admission, 11/1 for domestic students. Applications are processed on a rolling basis. Application fee: $50. Electronic applications accepted. *Expenses: Tuition:* Full-time $18,228; part-time $1016 per credit hour. *Financial support:* In 2014–15, 11 students received support. Teaching assistantships and Federal Work-Study available. Support available to part-time students. Financial award application deadline: 4/1; financial award applicants required to submit FAFSA. *Faculty research:* Intercultural communication, family communication, forensics, organizational communication. *Unit head:* Dr. Lauren Lemley, Graduate Director, 325-674-2136, Fax: 325-674-6966, E-mail: lauren.lemly@acu.edu. *Application contact:* Corey Patterson, Director of Graduate Admission and Recruiting, 325-674-6566, Fax: 325-674-6717, E-mail: gradinfo@acu.edu.
Website: http://www.acu.edu/graduate/degree-programs/communication/index.html

American University, School of Communication, Washington, DC 20016-8001. Offers MA, MFA, PhD. *Accreditation:* ACEJMC (one or more programs are accredited). Part-time and evening/weekend programs available. *Faculty:* 39 full-time (20 women). *Students:* 159 full-time (106 women), 232 part-time (153 women); includes 119 minority (82 Black or African American, non-Hispanic/Latino; 3 American Indian or Alaska Native, non-Hispanic/Latino; 13 Asian, non-Hispanic/Latino; 17 Hispanic/Latino; 4 Two or more races, non-Hispanic/Latino), 44 international. 604 applicants, 61% accepted, 196 enrolled. In 2014, 185 master's, 3 doctorates awarded. *Degree requirements:* For master's, comprehensive exam, thesis or alternative; for doctorate, comprehensive exam, thesis/dissertation. *Entrance requirements:* For doctorate, GRE General Test. Additional exam requirements/recommendations for international students: Required—TOEFL (minimum score 600 paper-based; 100 iBT), IELTS (minimum score 7). *Application deadline:* For fall admission, 2/1 priority date for domestic and international students; for spring admission, 11/1 for domestic and international students. Applications are processed on a rolling basis. Application fee: $55. Electronic applications accepted. *Financial support:* In 2014–15, 108 students received support, including 6 fellowships with partial tuition reimbursements available (averaging $23,000 per year), 30 research assistantships with partial tuition reimbursements available (averaging $15,000 per year), 30 teaching assistantships with partial tuition reimbursements available (averaging $15,000 per year); career-related internships or fieldwork, Federal Work-Study, institutionally sponsored loans, scholarships/grants, and tuition waivers (partial) also available. Support available to part-time students. Financial award application deadline: 2/1; financial award applicants required to submit FAFSA. *Faculty research:* New communication technology, documentaries and public broadcasting, litigation and public relations, dissident media, race and gender and the media, international journalism and human rights, social media. *Unit head:* Jeffrey Rutenbeck, Dean, 202-885-2058, Fax: 202-885-2099, E-mail: jeff@american.edu. *Application contact:* Sharmeen Ahsan-Bracciale, Director of Graduate Services, 202-885-2040, Fax: 202-885-2019, E-mail: sharmeen@american.edu.
Website: http://www.soc.american.edu/

The American University in Cairo, School of Global Affairs and Public Policy, Department of Journalism and Mass Communication, Cairo, Egypt. Offers journalism and mass communication (MA); television and digital journalism (MA). Part-time programs available. *Degree requirements:* For master's, thesis (for some programs). *Entrance requirements:* For master's, English entrance exam, GMAT. Electronic applications accepted. Tuition and fees vary according to course load and program. *Faculty research:* Mass media and national development/censorship, intercultural photo communication, comparative journalism/television.

The American University of Paris, Graduate Programs, Paris, France. Offers cross-cultural and sustainable business management (MA); cultural translation (MA); global communications (MA); global communications and civil society (MA); international affairs (MA); international affairs, conflict resolution and civil society development (MA); Middle East and Islamic studies (MA); Middle East and Islamic studies and international affairs (MA); public policy and international affairs (MA); public policy and international law (MA). *Degree requirements:* For master's, thesis (for some programs). *Entrance requirements:* For master's, minimum undergraduate GPA of 3.0. Additional exam requirements/recommendations for international students: Recommended—TOEFL, IELTS. Electronic applications accepted.

Andrews University, School of Graduate Studies, College of Arts and Sciences, Interdisciplinary Studies in Communication Program, Berrien Springs, MI 49104. Offers MA. *Faculty:* 5 full-time (4 women). *Students:* 5 full-time (3 women), 2 part-time (0 women); includes 4 minority (all Black or African American, non-Hispanic/Latino), 2 international. Average age 29. 9 applicants, 22% accepted, 1 enrolled. In 2014, 10 master's awarded. *Application deadline:* Applications are processed on a rolling basis. Application fee: $40. Tuition and fees vary according to course level. *Unit head:* Dr. Delyse E. Steyn, Area Coordinator, 269-471-3126. *Application contact:* Monica Wringer, Supervisor of Graduate Admission, 800-253-2874, Fax: 269-471-3228, E-mail: graduate@andrews.edu.

Angelo State University, College of Graduate Studies, College of Arts and Sciences, Department of Communication, Mass Media and Theatre, San Angelo, TX 76909. Offers communication systems management (MA). Part-time and evening/weekend programs available. *Degree requirements:* For master's, comprehensive exam, thesis optional. *Entrance requirements:* Additional exam requirements/recommendations for international students: Required—TOEFL or IELTS. Electronic applications accepted.

Arizona State University at the Tempe campus, College of Liberal Arts and Sciences, Hugh Downs School of Human Communication, Tempe, AZ 85287. Offers communication (PhD). Evening/weekend programs available. *Degree requirements:* For doctorate, comprehensive exam, thesis/dissertation, interactive Program of Study (iPOS) submitted before completing 50 percent of required credit hours. *Entrance requirements:* For doctorate, GRE, minimum GPA of 3.0 or equivalent in last 2 years of work leading to bachelor's degree. Additional exam requirements/recommendations for international students: Required—TOEFL, IELTS, or PTE. Electronic applications accepted.

Arizona State University at the Tempe campus, New College of Interdisciplinary Arts and Sciences, Program in Communication Studies, Phoenix, AZ 85069-7100. Offers MA. Part-time and evening/weekend programs available. *Degree requirements:* For master's, thesis, applied project or written comprehensive exam; interactive Program of Study (iPOS) submitted before completing 50 percent of required credit hours. *Entrance requirements:* For master's, GRE (if GPA less than 3.0 in last 60 hours of undergraduate study), minimum GPA of 3.0 or equivalent in last 2 years of work leading to bachelor's degree, 3 letters of recommendation, official transcripts, writing sample of scholarly work or example of professional activities. Additional exam requirements/recommendations for international students: Required—TOEFL, IELTS, or PTE. Electronic applications accepted. *Faculty research:* Organizational, applied, and environmental communication; intergenerational family communication and its connectedness to wellness; communication in personal and work relationships; popular culture; technology and culture; cultural dimensions of new mobile communication and computing technologies.

Arkansas State University, Graduate School, College of Media and Communication, State University, AR 72467. Offers MA, MSMC, Graduate Certificate, SCCT. Part-time programs available. *Faculty:* 13 full-time (6 women). *Students:* 21 full-time (12 women), 36 part-time (17 women); includes 22 minority (18 Black or African American, non-Hispanic/Latino; 1 American Indian or Alaska Native, non-Hispanic/Latino; 1 Asian, non-Hispanic/Latino; 2 Hispanic/Latino), 18 international. Average age 27. 51 applicants, 63% accepted, 22 enrolled. In 2014, 27 master's awarded. *Degree requirements:* For master's and other advanced degree, one foreign language, comprehensive exam, thesis or alternative. *Entrance requirements:* For master's, GRE General Test, appropriate bachelor's degree, letters of reference; official transcripts, immunization records; for other advanced degree, GRE, interview, master's degree, official transcript, immunization records. Additional exam requirements/recommendations for international students: Required—TOEFL (minimum score 550 paper-based; 79 iBT), IELTS (minimum score 6), PTE (minimum score 56). *Application deadline:* For fall admission, 7/1 for domestic and international students; for spring admission, 11/15 for domestic students, 11/14 for international students. Applications are processed on a rolling basis. Application fee: $30 ($40 for international students). Electronic applications accepted. *Expenses:* Tuition, state resident: full-time $4392; part-time $244 per credit hour. Tuition, nonresident: full-time $8784; part-time $488 per credit hour. *International tuition:* $9484 full-time. *Required fees:* $1134; $63 per credit hour. $25 per term. Tuition and fees vary according to course load and program. *Financial support:* In 2014–15, 13 students received support. Career-related internships or fieldwork, scholarships/grants, and unspecified assistantships available. Financial award application deadline: 7/1; financial award applicants required to submit FAFSA. *Unit head:* Dr. Brad Rawlins, Dean, 870-972-2468, Fax: 870-972-3856, E-mail: brawlins@astate.edu. *Application contact:* Vickey Ring, Graduate Admissions Coordinator, 870-972-3029, Fax: 870-972-3857, E-mail: vickeyring@astate.edu.
Website: http://www.astate.edu/college/communications/index.dot

Auburn University, Graduate School, College of Liberal Arts, Department of Communication and Journalism, Auburn University, AL 36849. Offers communication (MA); communication studies (Graduate Certificate); mass communications (MA). Part-time programs available. *Faculty:* 28 full-time (16 women), 6 part-time/adjunct (3 women). *Students:* 21 full-time (16 women), 4 part-time (1 woman); includes 3 minority (2 Black or African American, non-Hispanic/Latino; 1 Hispanic/Latino), 4 international. Average age 25. 55 applicants, 38% accepted, 7 enrolled. In 2014, 17 master's awarded. *Degree requirements:* For master's, thesis (for some programs). *Entrance requirements:* For master's, GRE General Test. *Application deadline:* For fall admission, 7/7 for domestic students; for spring admission, 11/24 for domestic students. Applications are processed on a rolling basis. Application fee: $50 ($60 for international students). Electronic applications accepted. *Expenses:* Tuition, state resident: full-time $8586; part-time $477 per credit hour. Tuition, nonresident: full-time $25,758; part-time $1431 per credit hour. *Required fees:* $804 per semester. Tuition and fees vary according to degree level and program. *Financial support:* Teaching assistantships and Federal Work-Study available. Support available to part-time students. Financial award application deadline: 3/15; financial award applicants required to submit FAFSA. *Unit head:* Dr. Jennifer Adams, Chair, 334-844-2727. *Application contact:* Dr. George Flowers, Dean of the Graduate School, 334-844-2125.
Website: http://www.cla.auburn.edu/cmjn/

Austin Peay State University, College of Graduate Studies, College of Arts and Letters, Department of Communication, Clarksville, TN 37044. Offers communication arts (MA). Part-time and evening/weekend programs available. Postbaccalaureate distance learning degree programs offered (no on-campus study). *Degree requirements:* For master's, comprehensive exam, thesis (for some programs). *Entrance requirements:* For master's, GRE General Test, 3 letters of recommendation. Additional exam requirements/recommendations for international students: Required—TOEFL (minimum score 500 paper-based). Electronic applications accepted.

Ball State University, Graduate School, College of Communication, Information, and Media, Muncie, IN 47306-1099. Offers MA, MS. Part-time programs available. Postbaccalaureate distance learning degree programs offered (no on-campus study). *Faculty:* 24 full-time (7 women), 2 part-time/adjunct (0 women). *Students:* 113 full-time (42 women), 78 part-time (43 women); includes 18 minority (12 Black or African American, non-Hispanic/Latino; 5 Hispanic/Latino; 1 Two or more races, non-Hispanic/Latino), 24 international. Average age 28. 179 applicants, 79% accepted, 98 enrolled. In 2014, 80 master's awarded. *Degree requirements:* For master's, comprehensive exam (for some programs), thesis (for some programs). *Entrance requirements:* For master's, GRE (for some programs). Additional exam requirements/recommendations for international students: Required—TOEFL (minimum score 550 paper-based), IELTS (minimum score 6.5). *Application deadline:* For fall admission, 1/1 priority date for international students; for spring admission, 7/1 priority date for international students. Applications are processed on a rolling basis. Application fee: $50. Electronic applications accepted. *Financial support:* In 2014–15, 90 students received support, including 41 research assistantships with partial tuition reimbursements available (averaging $7,995 per year), 31 teaching assistantships with partial tuition reimbursements available (averaging $10,620 per year); unspecified assistantships also available. Financial award application deadline: 3/1. *Unit head:* Roger Lavery, Dean, 765-285-6000, Fax: 765-285-6002, E-mail: rlavery@bsu.edu. *Application contact:* Dr. Robert Morris, Associate Provost for Research and Dean of the Graduate School, 765-285-4723, Fax: 765-285-1328, E-mail: rmorris@bsu.edu.
Website: http://cms.bsu.edu/academics/collegesanddepartments/ccim

Barry University, College of Arts and Sciences, Department of Communication, Miami Shores, FL 33161-6695. Offers broadcasting (Certificate); communication (MA), including broadcast communication, public relations and corporate communications; organizational communication (MS). Part-time and evening/weekend programs

available. *Degree requirements:* For master's, thesis (for some programs). *Entrance requirements:* For master's, GRE General Test, MAT, minimum GPA of 3.0. Electronic applications accepted. *Faculty research:* Organizational communication, broadcast communication, intercultural communication, advertising, leadership.

Baylor University, Graduate School, College of Arts and Sciences, Department of Communication, Waco, TX 76798. Offers MA. Part-time programs available. *Degree requirements:* For master's, thesis optional. *Entrance requirements:* For master's, GRE General Test, transcripts; 3 letters of recommendation; personal statement of intent; scholarly writing sample. Additional exam requirements/recommendations for international students: Required—TOEFL, IELTS, PTE. Electronic applications accepted. *Faculty research:* Rhetoric, interpersonal and family communication, organizational communication, film and digital media, new technology.

Bellarmine University, School of Communication, Louisville, KY 40205-0671. Offers MA. Part-time and evening/weekend programs available. *Faculty:* 4 full-time (3 women). *Students:* 1 full-time (0 women), 31 part-time (29 women); includes 7 minority (5 Black or African American, non-Hispanic/Latino; 2 Hispanic/Latino). Average age 30. In 2014, 18 master's awarded. *Entrance requirements:* For master's, GRE, GMAT or LSAT. Additional exam requirements/recommendations for international students: Required—TOEFL (minimum score 550 paper-based; 80 iBT). *Application deadline:* Applications are processed on a rolling basis. Application fee: $40. Tuition and fees vary according to program. *Unit head:* Dr. Lara Needham, Dean, 502-272-7965, E-mail: lneedham@bellarmine.edu. *Application contact:* Dr. Sara Pettingill, Dean of Graduate Admission, 502-272-8401, Fax: 502-272-8002, E-mail: spettingill@bellarmine.edu.
Website: http://www.bellarmine.edu/admissions/graduate/majorsandprograms/mactop.aspx

Bethel University, Graduate School, St. Paul, MN 55112-6999. Offers autism spectrum disorders (Certificate); business administration (MBA); communication (MA); counseling psychology (MA); educational leadership (Ed D); gerontology (MA); international baccalaureate education (Certificate); K-12 education (MA); literacy education (MA, Certificate); nurse educator (Certificate); nurse leader (Certificate); nurse-midwifery (MS); nursing (MS); physician assistant (MS); postsecondary teaching (Certificate); special education (MA); strategic leadership (MA); teaching (MA). Part-time and evening/weekend programs available. Postbaccalaureate distance learning degree programs offered (no on-campus study). *Faculty:* 13 full-time (7 women), 89 part-time/adjunct (43 women). *Students:* 739 full-time (484 women), 337 part-time (219 women); includes 175 minority (96 Black or African American, non-Hispanic/Latino; 2 American Indian or Alaska Native, non-Hispanic/Latino; 40 Asian, non-Hispanic/Latino; 20 Hispanic/Latino; 1 Native Hawaiian or other Pacific Islander, non-Hispanic/Latino; 16 Two or more races, non-Hispanic/Latino), 26 international. Average age 35. 1,354 applicants, 42% accepted, 421 enrolled. In 2014, 166 master's, 9 doctorates, 11 other advanced degrees awarded. *Degree requirements:* For master's, comprehensive exam (for some programs), thesis (for some programs); for doctorate, comprehensive exam, thesis/dissertation. *Entrance requirements:* Additional exam requirements/recommendations for international students: Required—TOEFL (minimum score 550 paper-based, 80 iBT) or IELTS. *Application deadline:* Applications are processed on a rolling basis. Application fee: $0. Electronic applications accepted. *Financial support:* Teaching assistantships, career-related internships or fieldwork, and scholarships/grants available. Support available to part-time students. Financial award applicants required to submit FAFSA. *Unit head:* Dick Crombie, Vice-President/Dean, 651-635-8000, Fax: 651-635-8004, E-mail: gs@bethel.edu. *Application contact:* Director of Admissions, 651-635-8000, Fax: 651-635-8004, E-mail: gs@bethel.edu.
Website: https://www.bethel.edu/graduate/

Boise State University, College of Social Sciences and Public Affairs, Department of Communication, Boise, ID 83725-0399. Offers MA. Part-time programs available. *Faculty:* 15 full-time (all women), 3 part-time/adjunct (all women). *Students:* 7 full-time (4 women), 13 part-time (7 women); includes 3 minority (1 Asian, non-Hispanic/Latino; 2 Hispanic/Latino), 4 international. Average age 37. 14 applicants, 64% accepted, 2 enrolled. In 2014, 2 master's awarded. *Degree requirements:* For master's, thesis. *Entrance requirements:* For master's, minimum GPA of 3.0, writing sample. *Application deadline:* For fall admission, 3/1 priority date for domestic students; for spring admission, 10/1 priority date for domestic students. Applications are processed on a rolling basis. Application fee: $55. Electronic applications accepted. *Expenses:* Tuition, state resident: part-time $331 per credit hour. Tuition, nonresident: part-time $531 per credit hour. *Financial support:* In 2014–15, 6 students received support, including 1 research assistantship with full tuition reimbursement available (averaging $8,096 per year), 5 teaching assistantships with full tuition reimbursements available (averaging $8,096 per year); career-related internships or fieldwork, Federal Work-Study, and unspecified assistantships also available. Financial award application deadline: 3/1. *Unit head:* Dr. Teresa Boucher, Interim Department Head, 208-426-1922, E-mail: tbouche@boisestate.edu. *Application contact:* Linda Platt, Supervisor, Graduate Admission and Degree Services, 208-426-1074, Fax: 208-426-2789, E-mail: lplatt@boisestate.edu.
Website: http://sspa.boisestate.edu/communication/graduate/

Boston University, College of Communication, Boston, MA 02215. Offers MA, MFA, MS, PhD, JD/MS, MBA/MS. Part-time programs available. *Faculty:* 67 full-time, 73 part-time/adjunct. *Students:* 285 full-time (232 women), 24 part-time (16 women); includes 31 minority (12 Black or African American, non-Hispanic/Latino; 7 Asian, non-Hispanic/Latino; 5 Hispanic/Latino; 7 Two or more races, non-Hispanic/Latino), 120 international. Average age 24. 910 applicants, 55% accepted, 186 enrolled. In 2014, 128 master's awarded. *Degree requirements:* For master's, comprehensive exam (for some programs), thesis (for some programs); for doctorate, comprehensive exam, thesis/dissertation. *Entrance requirements:* For master's, GRE General Test, transcripts, essays, 3 letters of recommendation, resume; for doctorate, GRE General Test, transcripts, essays, 3 letters of recommendation, resume, writing sample. Additional exam requirements/recommendations for international students: Required—TOEFL (minimum score 600 paper-based; 100 iBT), IELTS. *Application deadline:* For fall admission, 5/1 for domestic and international students. Applications are processed on a rolling basis. Application fee: $80. Electronic applications accepted. *Expenses: Tuition:* Full-time $45,686; part-time $1428 per credit hour. *Required fees:* $660; $60 per semester. Tuition and fees vary according to program. *Financial support:* Teaching assistantships with partial tuition reimbursements, career-related internships or fieldwork, Federal Work-Study, institutionally sponsored loans, scholarships/grants, and unspecified assistantships available. Support available to part-time students. Financial award application deadline: 5/1; financial award applicants required to submit FAFSA. *Unit head:* Thomas Fiedler, Dean, 617-353-3450, Fax: 617-358-0399, E-mail: comdean@bu.edu. *Application contact:* Manny Dotel, Assistant Director, Graduate Affairs, 617-353-3481, E-mail: comgrad@bu.edu.
Website: http://www.bu.edu/com/grad/

Boston University, Graduate School of Arts and Sciences, Frederick S. Pardee School of Global Studies, Boston, MA 02215. Offers international affairs (MA); international relations and environmental policy (MA); international relations and international communication (MA); international relations and religion (MA); international relations, mid-career (MA); Latin American studies (MA); MA/JD; MBA/MA. *Faculty:* 33 full-time (8 women), 10 part-time/adjunct (4 women). *Students:* 78 full-time (50 women), 15 part-time (11 women); includes 12 minority (3 Black or African American, non-Hispanic/Latino; 5 Asian, non-Hispanic/Latino; 3 Hispanic/Latino; 1 Two or more races, non-Hispanic/Latino), 26 international. Average age 25. 338 applicants, 68% accepted, 36 enrolled. In 2014, 51 master's awarded. *Degree requirements:* For master's, one foreign language, capstone. *Entrance requirements:* For master's, GRE General Test, 3 letters of recommendation, transcript of all prior college coursework, statement of purpose. Additional exam requirements/recommendations for international students: Required—TOEFL (minimum score 600 paper-based; 94 iBT). *Application deadline:* For fall admission, 4/15 for domestic and international students; for spring admission, 10/15 for domestic and international students. Applications are processed on a rolling basis. Application fee: $80. Electronic applications accepted. *Expenses: Tuition:* Full-time $45,686; part-time $1428 per credit hour. *Required fees:* $660; $60 per semester. Tuition and fees vary according to program. *Financial support:* In 2014–15, 21 students received support. Federal Work-Study, scholarships/grants, and unspecified assistantships available. Financial award application deadline: 1/3; financial award applicants required to submit FAFSA. *Faculty research:* International relations, area studies, political economy, global development policy, global climate. *Unit head:* Adil Najam, Dean, 617-353-9279, Fax: 617-353-9290, E-mail: psgs@bu.edu. *Application contact:* Michael Williams, Graduate Program Administrator, 617-353-9349, Fax: 617-353-9290, E-mail: psgsgrad@bu.edu.
Website: http://www.bu.edu/PardeeSchool

Bowling Green State University, Graduate College, College of Arts and Sciences, School of Communication Studies, Bowling Green, OH 43403. Offers MA, PhD. Part-time programs available. Terminal master's awarded for partial completion of doctoral program. *Degree requirements:* For master's, thesis or alternative; for doctorate, comprehensive exam, thesis/dissertation. *Entrance requirements:* For master's and doctorate, GRE General Test. Additional exam requirements/recommendations for international students: Required—TOEFL. Electronic applications accepted.

Brandeis University, Rabb School of Continuing Studies, Division of Graduate Professional Studies, Master of Science in Virtual Management Program, Waltham, MA 02454-9110. Offers MS. Part-time programs available. Postbaccalaureate distance learning degree programs offered (no on-campus study). *Faculty:* 2 full-time (1 woman), 33 part-time/adjunct (10 women). *Students:* 5 part-time (all women); includes 3 minority (1 Black or African American, non-Hispanic/Latino; 1 Asian, non-Hispanic/Latino; 1 Hispanic/Latino). Average age 35. In 2014, 4 master's awarded. *Entrance requirements:* For master's, resume, official transcripts, recommendations, goal statements. Additional exam requirements/recommendations for international students: Required—TOEFL (minimum score 600 paper-based; 100 iBT), IELTS (minimum score 7), PTE (minimum score 68). *Application deadline:* For fall admission, 8/11 priority date for domestic students, 8/15 priority date for international students; for winter admission, 11/15 for domestic students; for spring admission, 12/15 priority date for domestic and international students; for summer admission, 4/14 priority date for domestic and international students. Applications are processed on a rolling basis. Application fee: $50. Electronic applications accepted.
Website: http://www.brandeis.edu/gps

Brigham Young University, Graduate Studies, College of Fine Arts and Communications, School of Communications, Provo, UT 84602. Offers mass communications (MA). Part-time programs available. *Faculty:* 16 full-time (2 women). *Students:* 17 full-time (10 women), 26 part-time (15 women); includes 5 minority (3 Asian, non-Hispanic/Latino; 2 Hispanic/Latino), 7 international. Average age 30. 20 applicants, 60% accepted, 11 enrolled. In 2014, 8 master's awarded. *Degree requirements:* For master's, comprehensive exam, thesis. *Entrance requirements:* For master's, GRE, minimum GPA of 3.0 in last 60 hours of course work. Additional exam requirements/recommendations for international students: Required—TOEFL (minimum score 580 paper-based; 85 iBT). *Application deadline:* For fall admission, 3/31 priority date for domestic and international students. Applications are processed on a rolling basis. Application fee: $50. Electronic applications accepted. *Expenses: Tuition:* Full-time $6310; part-time $371 per credit hour. Tuition and fees vary according to program and student's religious affiliation. *Financial support:* In 2014–15, 17 students received support, including 20 research assistantships with full and partial tuition reimbursements available (averaging $4,229 per year), 7 teaching assistantships with full and partial tuition reimbursements available (averaging $3,815 per year); career-related internships or fieldwork, institutionally sponsored loans, scholarships/grants, unspecified assistantships, and supplementary awards also available. Financial award application deadline: 4/30; financial award applicants required to submit FAFSA. *Faculty research:* Ethics, international, magazine, newspaper, media effects. *Unit head:* Dr. Edward E. Adams, Director, 801-422-2997, Fax: 801-422-0160, E-mail: comms_secretary@byu.edu. *Application contact:* Dr. Mark A. Callister, Graduate Coordinator, 801-422-6143, Fax: 801-422-0160, E-mail: mark_callister@byu.edu.
Website: http://cfac.byu.edu/departments/communications

California Baptist University, Program in Communication, Riverside, CA 92503. Offers MA. Part-time and evening/weekend programs available. Postbaccalaureate distance learning degree programs offered (minimal on-campus study). *Degree requirements:* For master's, thesis or alternative, comprehensive project and defended paper. *Entrance requirements:* For master's, bachelor's degree, official transcripts, 2 recommendations, current resume, 500-word essay, minimum GPA of 2.5. Additional exam requirements/recommendations for international students: Required—TOEFL (minimum score 80 iBT). *Application deadline:* For fall admission, 8/1 priority date for domestic students, 7/1 priority date for international students; for spring admission, 12/1 priority date for domestic students, 11/1 priority date for international students. Applications are processed on a rolling basis. Application fee: $45. Electronic applications accepted. *Financial support:* Applicants required to submit CSS PROFILE or FAFSA. *Unit head:* Dr. David Poole, Vice President of Online and Professional Studies, 951-343-3901, E-mail: dpoole@calbaptist.edu. *Application contact:* Dr. Patricia Hernandez, Program Director of MA in Communication, 951-343-3979, E-mail: phernandez@calbaptist.edu.
Website: http://www.cbuonline.edu/programs/program/master-of-arts-in-communication-

California State University, Chico, Office of Graduate Studies, College of Communication and Education, Department of Communication Arts and Sciences, Program in Communication Studies, Chico, CA 95929-0722. Offers MA. *Faculty:* 4 full-time (2 women). *Students:* 4 full-time (3 women), 9 part-time (5 women); includes 2 minority (both Hispanic/Latino), 1 international. Average age 26. 20 applicants, 65% accepted, 9 enrolled. In 2014, 11 master's awarded. *Degree requirements:* For master's, thesis or project. *Entrance requirements:* For master's, GRE, three letters of recommendation, example of writing, one-page statement of purpose, minimum GPA of 3.0. Additional exam requirements/recommendations for international students: Required—TOEFL (minimum score 550 paper-based; 80 iBT), IELTS (minimum score 6.5), PTE (minimum score 59). *Application deadline:* For fall admission, 3/1 priority date for domestic students, 3/1 for international students; for spring admission, 9/15 priority date for domestic students, 9/15 for international students. Application fee: $55. Electronic applications accepted. *Expenses:* Tuition, state resident: full-time $7002.

Tuition, nonresident: full-time $18,162. *Required fees:* $1530. Tuition and fees vary according to program. *Financial support:* Teaching assistantships, career-related internships or fieldwork, scholarships/grants, traineeships, and unspecified assistantships available. Financial award application deadline: 3/1; financial award applicants required to submit FAFSA. *Unit head:* Dr. Suzanne B. Miller, Department Chair, 530-898-5751, Fax: 530-898-4096, E-mail: cmst@csuchico.edu. *Application contact:* Judy L. Rice, Graduate Coordinator, 530-898-5751, Fax: 530-898-3342, E-mail: jlrice@csuchico.edu.
Website: http://catalog.csuchico.edu/viewer/15/COMM/CMSTNONEMA.html

California State University, East Bay, Office of Academic Programs and Graduate Studies, College of Letters, Arts, and Social Sciences, Department of Communication, Hayward, CA 94542-3000. Offers MA. Part-time programs available. *Degree requirements:* For master's, comprehensive exam, project, thesis, or exam. *Entrance requirements:* For master's, GRE, minimum GPA of 3.0 in field; 3 letters of recommendation; sample of scholarly writing. Additional exam requirements/recommendations for international students: Required—TOEFL (minimum score 550 paper-based). *Application deadline:* For fall admission, 6/30 for domestic and international students. Applications are processed on a rolling basis. Application fee: $55. Electronic applications accepted. *Expenses:* Tuition, state resident: full-time $7830; part-time $1302 per credit hour. Tuition, nonresident: full-time $16,368. *Required fees:* $327 per quarter. Tuition and fees vary according to course load and program. *Financial support:* Fellowships, teaching assistantships, career-related internships or fieldwork, Federal Work-Study, institutionally sponsored loans, scholarships/grants, and unspecified assistantships available. Support available to part-time students. Financial award application deadline: 3/2; financial award applicants required to submit FAFSA. *Unit head:* Dr. Gale Young, Chair, 510-885-3292, Fax: 510-885-4099, E-mail: gale.young@csueastbay.edu. *Application contact:* Dr. Donna Wiley, Interim Associate Vice President for Academic Programs and Graduate Studies, 510-885-3716, Fax: 510-885-4777, E-mail: donna.wiley@csueastbay.edu.
Website: http://www20.csueastbay.edu/class/departments/communication/

California State University, Fresno, Division of Graduate Studies, College of Arts and Humanities, Department of Communication, Fresno, CA 93740-8027. Offers MA. Part-time and evening/weekend programs available. *Degree requirements:* For master's, thesis or alternative. *Entrance requirements:* For master's, GRE General Test, minimum GPA of 3.1. Additional exam requirements/recommendations for international students: Required—TOEFL. Electronic applications accepted. *Faculty research:* Learning styles, education, critical thinking.

California State University, Fullerton, Graduate Studies, College of Communications, Department of Communications, Fullerton, CA 92834-9480. Offers advertising (MA); mass communications research and theory (MA); professional communications (MA); tourism and entertainment (MA). Part-time programs available. *Students:* 18 full-time (17 women), 18 part-time (12 women); includes 17 minority (2 Black or African American, non-Hispanic/Latino; 5 Asian, non-Hispanic/Latino; 10 Hispanic/Latino), 2 international. Average age 27. 48 applicants, 42% accepted, 10 enrolled. In 2014, 25 master's awarded. *Degree requirements:* For master's, project or thesis. *Entrance requirements:* For master's, GRE General Test. Application fee: $55. *Financial support:* Teaching assistantships, career-related internships or fieldwork, Federal Work-Study, institutionally sponsored loans, and scholarships/grants available. Support available to part-time students. Financial award application deadline: 3/1; financial award applicants required to submit FAFSA. *Unit head:* Dr. Diane F. Witmer, Chair, 657-278-7008. *Application contact:* Coordinator, 657-278-3832.

California State University, Fullerton, Graduate Studies, College of Communications, Department of Human Communications, Fullerton, CA 92834-9480. Offers communication studies (MA); communicative disorders (MA). *Accreditation:* ASHA. Part-time programs available. *Students:* 74 full-time (62 women), 37 part-time (27 women); includes 55 minority (1 Black or African American, non-Hispanic/Latino; 24 Asian, non-Hispanic/Latino; 24 Hispanic/Latino; 1 Native Hawaiian or other Pacific Islander, non-Hispanic/Latino; 5 Two or more races, non-Hispanic/Latino), 3 international. Average age 29. 414 applicants, 12% accepted, 43 enrolled. In 2014, 37 master's awarded. *Degree requirements:* For master's, comprehensive exam, thesis or alternative. *Entrance requirements:* For master's, minimum GPA of 3.0 in major. Application fee: $55. *Financial support:* Teaching assistantships, career-related internships or fieldwork, Federal Work-Study, institutionally sponsored loans, and scholarships/grants available. Support available to part-time students. Financial award application deadline: 3/1; financial award applicants required to submit FAFSA. *Faculty research:* Speech therapy. *Unit head:* Dr. John Reinard, Chair, 657-278-3617. *Application contact:* Admissions/Applications, 657-278-2371.

California State University, Long Beach, Graduate Studies, College of Liberal Arts, Department of Communication Studies, Long Beach, CA 90840. Offers MA. Part-time programs available. *Degree requirements:* For master's, comprehensive exam or thesis. *Entrance requirements:* For master's, GRE. Electronic applications accepted. *Faculty research:* Rhetoric, public address, communication theory, interpersonal communication, intercultural communication.

California State University, Los Angeles, Graduate Studies, College of Arts and Letters, Department of Communication Studies, Los Angeles, CA 90032-8530. Offers MA, MFA. Part-time and evening/weekend programs available. *Degree requirements:* For master's, comprehensive exam or thesis. *Entrance requirements:* For master's, minimum GPA of 2.75 in last 90 units of course work. Additional exam requirements/recommendations for international students: Required—TOEFL (minimum score 500 paper-based). Electronic applications accepted. *Expenses:* Tuition, state resident: full-time $6738; part-time $3609 per year. Tuition, nonresident: full-time $15,666; part-time $8073 per year. Tuition and fees vary according to course load, degree level and program. *Faculty research:* Organizational, interpersonal, intercultural, and instructional communication; rhetorical theories.

California State University, Northridge, Graduate Studies, College of Arts, Media, and Communication, Northridge, CA 91330. Offers MA, MFA, MM. Part-time and evening/weekend programs available. *Students:* 126 full-time (82 women), 103 part-time (59 women); includes 68 minority (14 Black or African American, non-Hispanic/Latino; 13 Asian, non-Hispanic/Latino; 32 Hispanic/Latino; 9 Two or more races, non-Hispanic/Latino), 38 international. Average age 33. *Entrance requirements:* Additional exam requirements/recommendations for international students: Required—TOEFL. *Application deadline:* For fall admission, 11/30 for domestic students. Application fee: $55. *Expenses: Required fees:* $12,402. *Financial support:* Teaching assistantships, career-related internships or fieldwork, Federal Work-Study, and unspecified assistantships available. Support available to part-time students. Financial award application deadline: 3/1. *Unit head:* Jay Jay Kvapil, Dean, 818-677-2246, E-mail: kvapil@csun.edu.

California State University, Sacramento, Office of Graduate Studies, College of Arts and Letters, Department of Communication Studies, Sacramento, CA 95819. Offers MA. Part-time programs available. *Degree requirements:* For master's, thesis or project; writing proficiency exam. *Entrance requirements:* For master's, GRE, minimum GPA of 3.25 during previous 2 years. Additional exam requirements/recommendations for international students: Required—TOEFL. Electronic applications accepted.

California State University, San Bernardino, Graduate Studies, College of Arts and Letters, Department of Communication Studies, San Bernardino, CA 92407-2397. Offers communication studies (MA); integrated marketing communication (MA). *Students:* 4 full-time (all women), 16 part-time (11 women); includes 7 minority (2 Black or African American, non-Hispanic/Latino; 2 Asian, non-Hispanic/Latino; 3 Hispanic/Latino), 4 international. Average age 29. 37 applicants, 32% accepted, 5 enrolled. In 2014, 4 master's awarded. *Degree requirements:* For master's, comprehensive exam. *Entrance requirements:* Additional exam requirements/recommendations for international students: Required—TOEFL. *Application deadline:* For fall admission, 7/17 for domestic students. Application fee: $55. *Expenses:* Tuition, state resident: full-time $6738; part-time $1302 per term. Tuition, nonresident: full-time $17,898; part-time $248 per unit. *Required fees:* $365 per quarter. Tuition and fees vary according to degree level and program. *Unit head:* Dr. Michael Salvador, Chair, 909-537-5820, Fax: 909-537-7009, E-mail: salvador@csusb.edu. *Application contact:* Dr. Jeffrey Thompson, Dean of Graduate Studies, 909-537-5058, Fax: 909-537-7034, E-mail: jthompso@csusb.edu.

Carleton University, Faculty of Graduate Studies, Faculty of Public Affairs and Management, School of Journalism and Communication, Program in Communication, Ottawa, ON K1S 5B6, Canada. Offers MA, PhD. *Degree requirements:* For master's, thesis optional; for doctorate, comprehensive exam, thesis/dissertation. *Entrance requirements:* For master's, honors degree. Additional exam requirements/recommendations for international students: Required—TOEFL. *Faculty research:* History of communication and media systems, communication/information technologies and society, communication and social relations, communication policy and political economy.

Carnegie Mellon University, Dietrich College of Humanities and Social Sciences, Department of English, Pittsburgh, PA 15213-3891. Offers communication planning and design (M Des); literary and cultural studies (MA, PhD); professional writing (MAPW), including editing and publishing, policy and non-profit communication, public and media relations / corporate communications, science or healthcare communication, technical writing, writing for new media, writing for print media; rhetoric (MA, PhD). Part-time programs available. Terminal master's awarded for partial completion of doctoral program. *Degree requirements:* For doctorate, 2 foreign languages, comprehensive exam, thesis/dissertation. *Entrance requirements:* For master's and doctorate, GRE General Test. Additional exam requirements/recommendations for international students: Required—TOEFL, TWE. *Faculty research:* Cognitive processes in discourse with emphasis on writing, testing, and evaluation.

Central Connecticut State University, School of Graduate Studies, College of Liberal Arts and Social Sciences, Department of Communication, New Britain, CT 06050-4010. Offers organizational communication (MS); public relations/promotions (Certificate). Part-time and evening/weekend programs available. *Faculty:* 6 full-time (1 woman). *Students:* 4 full-time (3 women), 28 part-time (23 women); includes 6 minority (3 Black or African American, non-Hispanic/Latino; 2 Hispanic/Latino; 1 Two or more races, non-Hispanic/Latino). Average age 28. 26 applicants, 27% accepted, 4 enrolled. In 2014, 8 master's, 1 other advanced degree awarded. *Degree requirements:* For master's, comprehensive exam, thesis or alternative; for Certificate, qualifying exam. *Entrance requirements:* For master's, minimum undergraduate GPA of 3.0, resume, references, essay. Additional exam requirements/recommendations for international students: Required—TOEFL (minimum score 550 paper-based; 79 iBT). *Application deadline:* For fall admission, 6/1 for domestic students, 5/1 for international students; for spring admission, 11/1 for domestic and international students. Applications are processed on a rolling basis. Application fee: $50. Electronic applications accepted. *Expenses: Tuition, area resident:* Full-time $5730; part-time $534 per credit. Tuition, state resident: full-time $8596; part-time $534 per credit. Tuition, nonresident: full-time $15,964; part-time $548 per credit. *Required fees:* $4211; $215 per credit. *Financial support:* In 2014–15, 3 students received support, including 1 research assistantship; career-related internships or fieldwork, Federal Work-Study, scholarships/grants, and unspecified assistantships also available. Support available to part-time students. Financial award application deadline: 3/1; financial award applicants required to submit FAFSA. *Faculty research:* Organizational communication, mass communication, intercultural communication, political communication, information management. *Unit head:* Dr. Christopher Pudlinski, Chair, 860-832-2690, E-mail: pudlinskic@ccsu.edu. *Application contact:* Patricia Gardner, Associate Director of Graduate Studies, 860-832-2350, Fax: 860-832-2362, E-mail: graduateadmissions@ccsu.edu.
Website: http://web.ccsu.edu/communication/

Central Michigan University, College of Graduate Studies, College of Communication and Fine Arts, Department of Communication and Dramatic Arts, Mount Pleasant, MI 48859. Offers communication (MA), including communication and dramatic arts. Part-time programs available. *Degree requirements:* For master's, thesis. *Entrance requirements:* Additional exam requirements/recommendations for international students: Recommended—TOEFL (minimum score 100 iBT), IELTS. Electronic applications accepted. *Faculty research:* Communication theory, interpersonal/nonverbal communication, organizational communication, family and interpersonal communication, political communication.

Clarion University of Pennsylvania, Office of Transfer, Adult and Graduate Admissions, Online Master of Science Programs, Clarion, PA 16214. Offers library science (MSLS); mass media arts and journalism (MS). Part-time programs available. Postbaccalaureate distance learning degree programs offered (no on-campus study). *Faculty:* 23 full-time (14 women). *Students:* 93 full-time (72 women), 561 part-time (444 women); includes 40 minority (16 Black or African American, non-Hispanic/Latino; 2 American Indian or Alaska Native, non-Hispanic/Latino; 7 Asian, non-Hispanic/Latino; 9 Hispanic/Latino; 1 Native Hawaiian or other Pacific Islander, non-Hispanic/Latino; 5 Two or more races, non-Hispanic/Latino). Average age 32. 165 applicants, 84% accepted, 120 enrolled. In 2014, 184 master's awarded. *Degree requirements:* For master's, comprehensive exam, thesis or alternative. *Entrance requirements:* For master's, minimum QPA of 3.0. Additional exam requirements/recommendations for international students: Required—TOEFL (minimum score 600 paper-based; 100 iBT), IELTS (minimum score 7.5). *Application deadline:* For fall admission, 8/1 priority date for domestic students, 4/15 priority date for international students; for spring admission, 12/1 priority date for domestic students, 9/15 priority date for international students. Applications are processed on a rolling basis. Application fee: $40. Electronic applications accepted. Tuition and fees vary according to degree level, campus/location and program. *Financial support:* In 2014–15, 12 research assistantships with full and partial tuition reimbursements (averaging $9,240 per year) were awarded. Support available to part-time students. Financial award application deadline: 3/1. *Unit head:* Dr. Myrna Kuehn, Chair, 814-393-2245, Fax: 814-393-2186. *Application contact:* Michelle Ritzler, Assistant Director, Graduate Programs, 814-393-2337, Fax: 814-393-2030, E-mail: gradstudies@clarion.edu.
Website: http://www.clarion.edu/991/

Clark University, Graduate School, College of Professional and Continuing Education, Program in Professional Communication, Worcester, MA 01610-1477. Offers MSPC.

Students: 24 full-time (19 women), 16 part-time (14 women); includes 4 minority (1 Black or African American, non-Hispanic/Latino; 2 Asian, non-Hispanic/Latino; 1 Hispanic/Latino), 16 international. Average age 28. 70 applicants, 81% accepted, 22 enrolled. In 2014, 44 master's awarded. *Degree requirements:* For master's, thesis optional. *Entrance requirements:* Additional exam requirements/recommendations for international students: Required—TOEFL. *Application deadline:* Applications are processed on a rolling basis. Application fee: $75. Electronic applications accepted. *Expenses: Tuition:* Full-time $40,380; part-time $1262 per credit hour. *Required fees:* $30. *Unit head:* William Fisher, Dean, 508-793-7676. *Application contact:* Ethan Bernstein, Director of Graduate Admissions, 508-793-7373, E-mail: gradadmissions@clarku.edu.
Website: http://copace.clarku.edu/graduate-programs/masters-professional-communication/

Clemson University, Graduate School, College of Architecture, Arts, and Humanities, Department of Communication Studies, Clemson, SC 29634. Offers communication, technology and society (MA). Part-time programs available. *Faculty:* 26 full-time (14 women), 1 part-time/adjunct (0 women). *Students:* 21 full-time (14 women), 1 international. Average age 24. 53 applicants, 34% accepted, 13 enrolled. In 2014, 5 master's awarded. *Degree requirements:* For master's, comprehensive exam (for some programs), thesis (for some programs). *Entrance requirements:* Additional exam requirements/recommendations for international students: Required—TOEFL. *Application deadline:* For fall admission, 2/1 priority date for domestic and international students. Applications are processed on a rolling basis. Electronic applications accepted. *Financial support:* In 2014–15, 18 students received support, including 3 research assistantships (averaging $16,000 per year), 15 teaching assistantships (averaging $16,000 per year); tuition waivers (full) also available. *Unit head:* Dr. Karyn O. Jones, Interim Chair, 864-656-3855, E-mail: karynj@clemson.edu. *Application contact:* Dr. James B. London, Associate Dean for Research and Graduate Studies, 864-656-3927, E-mail: london1@clemson.edu.
Website: http://www.clemson.edu/caah/communication/

Clemson University, Graduate School, College of Architecture, Arts, and Humanities, Department of English, Program in Professional Communication, Clemson, SC 29634. Offers MA. Part-time programs available. *Students:* 24 full-time (16 women), 5 part-time (all women); includes 8 minority (3 Black or African American, non-Hispanic/Latino; 3 Hispanic/Latino; 2 Two or more races, non-Hispanic/Latino). Average age 27. 24 applicants, 71% accepted, 12 enrolled. In 2014, 8 master's awarded. *Degree requirements:* For master's, one foreign language, thesis or alternative, oral exam. *Entrance requirements:* For master's, GRE General Test, minimum GPA of 3.0. Additional exam requirements/recommendations for international students: Required—TOEFL, IELTS. *Application deadline:* For fall admission, 2/1 priority date for domestic students, 2/1 for international students; for spring admission, 11/1 priority date for domestic students, 11/1 for international students. Applications are processed on a rolling basis. Application fee: $70 ($80 for international students). Electronic applications accepted. *Financial support:* In 2014–15, 10 students received support, including 10 teaching assistantships with partial tuition reimbursements available (averaging $18,839 per year); fellowships with full and partial tuition reimbursements available, research assistantships with partial tuition reimbursements available, career-related internships or fieldwork, institutionally sponsored loans, scholarships/grants, health care benefits, and unspecified assistantships also available. Support available to part-time students. Financial award application deadline: 4/1; financial award applicants required to submit FAFSA. *Faculty research:* Usability and user experience design, rhetoric, intercultural communication, digital publishing, social media authoring, technical writing. *Unit head:* Dr. Sean Williams, Chair, 864-656-3151, Fax: 864-656-1345, E-mail: sean@clemson.edu. *Application contact:* Dr. Tharon Howard, Graduate Coordinator, 864-656-6689, Fax: 864-656-1345, E-mail: tharon@clemson.edu.
Website: http://www.clemson.edu/caah/english/graduate/mapc/index.html

Clemson University, Graduate School, College of Architecture, Arts, and Humanities, Program in Rhetorics, Communication and Information Design, Clemson, SC 29634. Offers PhD. *Students:* 23 full-time (12 women), 6 part-time (3 women); includes 4 minority (2 Black or African American, non-Hispanic/Latino; 2 Hispanic/Latino), 4 international. Average age 33. 22 applicants, 32% accepted, 7 enrolled. In 2014, 3 doctorates awarded. *Degree requirements:* For doctorate, thesis/dissertation (for some programs). *Entrance requirements:* For doctorate, GRE, master's degree in English, communications studies, art, professional communication or related field; portfolio; 3 letters of reference; minimum graduate GPA of 3.5. Additional exam requirements/recommendations for international students: Required—TOEFL (minimum score 550 paper-based). *Application deadline:* For fall admission, 2/1 priority date for domestic students, 4/15 for international students. Applications are processed on a rolling basis. Application fee: $70 ($80 for international students). Electronic applications accepted. *Financial support:* In 2014–15, 16 students received support, including 4 fellowships (averaging $5,000 per year), 16 teaching assistantships with partial tuition reimbursements available (averaging $24,834 per year); research assistantships, career-related internships or fieldwork, institutionally sponsored loans, scholarships/grants, health care benefits, and unspecified assistantships also available. Support available to part-time students. *Faculty research:* Historiography and philology, multimodal writing, health communication, future of the book, readability studies, politics and rhetoric. *Unit head:* Dr. Victor Vitanza, Director, 864-656-6411, Fax: 864-656-0599, E-mail: sophist@clemson.edu. *Application contact:* Dr. James B. London, Associate Dean for Research and Graduate Studies, 864-656-3927, E-mail: london1@clemson.edu.
Website: http://www.clemson.edu/caah/rcid/

Clemson University, Graduate School, College of Business and Behavioral Science, Department of Graphic Communications, Clemson, SC 29634. Offers MS. *Faculty:* 10 full-time (3 women), 2 part-time/adjunct (1 woman). *Students:* 9 full-time (8 women), 2 part-time (both women), 1 international. Average age 27. 8 applicants, 25% accepted, 2 enrolled. In 2014, 7 master's awarded. *Entrance requirements:* For master's, GRE General Test. Additional exam requirements/recommendations for international students: Required—TOEFL. *Application deadline:* For fall admission, 4/15 for international students; for spring admission, 9/15 for international students. Application fee: $70 ($80 for international students). Electronic applications accepted. *Financial support:* In 2014–15, 11 students received support, including 2 fellowships (averaging $12,500 per year); research assistantships with partial tuition reimbursements available, teaching assistantships with partial tuition reimbursements available, career-related internships or fieldwork, institutionally sponsored loans, scholarships/grants, health care benefits, and unspecified assistantships also available. Support available to part-time students. Financial award applicants required to submit FAFSA. *Total annual research expenditures:* $55,749. *Unit head:* Dr. Samuel T. Ingram, Chair, 864-656-3447, E-mail: sting@clemson.edu. *Application contact:* Nancy Leininger, Coordinator, 864-656-3447, Fax: 864-656-5344, E-mail: lnancy@clemson.edu.
Website: http://graphics.clemson.edu/

Cleveland State University, College of Graduate Studies, College of Liberal Arts and Social Sciences, School of Communication, Cleveland, OH 44115. Offers applied communication theory and methodology (MA); culture, communication and health care (Certificate). Part-time and evening/weekend programs available. *Faculty:* 10 full-time (3 women). *Students:* 20 part-time (11 women); includes 4 minority (3 Black or African American, non-Hispanic/Latino; 1 Asian, non-Hispanic/Latino), 4 international. Average age 34. 14 applicants, 93% accepted, 5 enrolled. In 2014, 5 master's awarded. *Degree requirements:* For master's, variable foreign language requirement, comprehensive exam (for some programs), thesis, project, comprehensive exam, or collaborative project. *Entrance requirements:* For master's, GRE or MAT, minimum undergraduate GPA of 2.75, 2 letters of recommendation, statement of interest. Additional exam requirements/recommendations for international students: Required—TOEFL (minimum score 525 paper-based; 65 iBT). *Application deadline:* For fall admission, 8/25 priority date for domestic students, 5/15 priority date for international students; for spring admission, 1/15 priority date for domestic students, 11/1 priority date for international students. Applications are processed on a rolling basis. Application fee: $30. Electronic applications accepted. *Expenses:* Expenses: $9,615 full-time, in-state tuition and fees. *Financial support:* In 2014–15, 14 students received support, including 5 research assistantships with full and partial tuition reimbursements available (averaging $11,000 per year), 9 teaching assistantships with full and partial tuition reimbursements available (averaging $11,000 per year); tuition waivers (full and partial) and unspecified assistantships also available. Financial award application deadline: 8/1. *Faculty research:* Interpersonal, organizational, and mass communication; health communication. *Unit head:* Dr. George B. Ray, Director, 216-687-4631, Fax: 216-687-5435, E-mail: g.ray@csuohio.edu. *Application contact:* Dr. Gary Pettey, Communication Graduate Program Director, 216-687-4641, Fax: 216-687-5435, E-mail: g.pettey@csuohio.edu.
Website: http://www.csuohio.edu/class/communication/communication

Cleveland State University, College of Graduate Studies, Maxine Goodman Levin College of Urban Affairs, Program in Urban Studies and Public Affairs, Cleveland, OH 44115. Offers communication (PhD); public administration (PhD); urban policy and development (PhD). Part-time and evening/weekend programs available. *Faculty:* 23 full-time (11 women), 23 part-time/adjunct (6 women). *Students:* 10 full-time (6 women), 26 part-time (13 women); includes 5 minority (4 Black or African American, non-Hispanic/Latino; 1 Asian, non-Hispanic/Latino), 10 international. Average age 40. 32 applicants, 34% accepted, 2 enrolled. In 2014, 3 doctorates awarded. *Degree requirements:* For doctorate, comprehensive exam, thesis/dissertation. *Entrance requirements:* For doctorate, GRE General Test (minimum score: verbal and quantitative 50th percentile, analytical writing 4.0), minimum GPA of 3.5. Additional exam requirements/recommendations for international students: Required—TOEFL (minimum score 525 paper-based; 65 iBT), IELTS, or ITEP. *Application deadline:* For fall admission, 1/31 for domestic and international students. Application fee: $30. Electronic applications accepted. *Expenses:* Expenses: $9,615 full-time, in-state tuition and fees. *Financial support:* In 2014–15, 15 students received support, including 7 research assistantships with full and partial tuition reimbursements available (averaging $9,200 per year), 3 teaching assistantships with full and partial tuition reimbursements available (averaging $8,600 per year); scholarships/grants and unspecified assistantships also available. Support available to part-time students. Financial award application deadline: 3/1; financial award applicants required to submit FAFSA. *Faculty research:* Urban and public policy, public affairs. *Unit head:* Dr. Wendy Kellogg, Director, 216-687-5265, E-mail: w.kellogg@csuohio.edu. *Application contact:* David Arrighi, Graduate Academic Advisor, 216-523-7522, Fax: 216-687-5398, E-mail: urbanprograms@csuohio.edu.
Website: http://urban.csuohio.edu/academics/graduate/phd/

The College at Brockport, State University of New York, School of the Arts, Humanities and Social Sciences, Department of Communication, Brockport, NY 14420-2997. Offers MA. Part-time and evening/weekend programs available. *Faculty:* 6 full-time (2 women). *Students:* 5 full-time (3 women), 6 part-time (2 women); includes 2 minority (1 Black or African American, non-Hispanic/Latino; 1 Asian, non-Hispanic/Latino), 2 international. 12 applicants, 92% accepted, 7 enrolled. In 2014, 9 master's awarded. *Degree requirements:* For master's, thesis or alternative, research project. *Entrance requirements:* For master's, minimum GPA of 3.0, letters of recommendation. Additional exam requirements/recommendations for international students: Required—TOEFL (minimum score 550 paper-based; 79 iBT), IELTS (minimum score 6.5). *Application deadline:* For fall admission, 7/15 priority date for domestic and international students; for spring admission, 11/15 priority date for domestic students; for summer admission, 4/1 priority date for domestic and international students. Application fee: $50. Electronic applications accepted. *Financial support:* In 2014–15, 1 fellowship with full tuition reimbursement (averaging $7,500 per year), 2 teaching assistantships with full tuition reimbursements (averaging $6,000 per year) were awarded; Federal Work-Study, scholarships/grants, and unspecified assistantships also available. Support available to part-time students. Financial award application deadline: 3/15; financial award applicants required to submit FAFSA. *Faculty research:* Organizational communication, rhetorical theory and criticism, media theory and criticism, interpersonal communication, communication theory. *Unit head:* Dr. Monica Brasted, Chairperson, 585-395-2511, Fax: 585-395-5771, E-mail: mbrasted@brockport.edu. *Application contact:* Dr. Alex Lyon, Graduate Director, 585-395-5772, Fax: 585-395-5771, E-mail: alyon@brockport.edu.
Website: http://www.brockport.edu/cmc/grad/

College of Charleston, Graduate School, School of Humanities and Social Sciences, Program in Communication, Charleston, SC 29424-0001. Offers MA. Part-time and evening/weekend programs available. *Degree requirements:* For master's, comprehensive exam or thesis. *Entrance requirements:* For master's, GRE, writing sample; 2 letters of recommendation; minimum GPA of 2.75 overall, 3.0 in major. Additional exam requirements/recommendations for international students: Required—TOEFL (minimum score 81 iBT). Electronic applications accepted.

The College of New Rochelle, Graduate School, Division of Art and Communication Studies, Program in Communication Studies, New Rochelle, NY 10805-2308. Offers MS, Certificate. Part-time and evening/weekend programs available. *Degree requirements:* For master's, thesis or alternative, thesis or comprehensive exam. *Entrance requirements:* For master's, GRE General Test, interview, minimum GPA of 3.0. Additional exam requirements/recommendations for international students: Required—TOEFL. *Expenses: Tuition:* Part-time $894 per credit. *Required fees:* $325 per semester.

Columbia University, Graduate School of Business, Doctoral Program in Business, New York, NY 10027. Offers business (PhD), including accounting, decision, risk, and operations, finance and economics, management, marketing. *Accreditation:* AACSB. *Degree requirements:* For doctorate, comprehensive exam, thesis/dissertation, major field exam, research paper, thesis proposal. *Entrance requirements:* For doctorate, GMAT or GRE (finance), 2 letters of reference, resume. Additional exam requirements/recommendations for international students: Required—TOEFL. Electronic applications accepted. *Expenses:* Contact institution. *Faculty research:* Human decision making and behavioral research; real estate market and mortgage defaults; financial crisis and corporate governance; international business; security analysis and accounting.

Columbia University, Graduate School of Business, MBA Program, New York, NY 10027. Offers accounting (MBA); decision, risk, and operations (MBA); entrepreneurship (MBA); finance and economics (MBA); healthcare and pharmaceutical management

(MBA); human resource management (MBA); international business (MBA); leadership and ethics (MBA); management (MBA); marketing (MBA); media (MBA); private equity (MBA); real estate (MBA); social enterprise (MBA); value investing (MBA); DDS/MBA; JD/MBA; MBA/MIA; MBA/MPH; MBA/MS; MD/MBA. *Entrance requirements:* For master's, GMAT, 2 letters of recommendation. Additional exam requirements/recommendations for international students: Required—TOEFL. Electronic applications accepted. *Expenses:* Contact institution. *Faculty research:* Human decision making and behavioral research; real estate market and mortgage defaults; financial crisis and corporate governance; international business; security analysis and accounting.

Columbia University, School of Continuing Education, Program in Communications Practice, New York, NY 10027. Offers MS. Electronic applications accepted.

Concordia University, School of Graduate Studies, Faculty of Arts and Science, Department of Communication Studies, Montréal, QC H3G 1M8, Canada. Offers communication (PhD); communication studies (Diploma); media studies (MA). PhD program offered jointly with Université de Montréal and Université du Québec à Montréal. *Degree requirements:* For master's, thesis optional; for doctorate, one foreign language, comprehensive exam, thesis/dissertation, research practicum, seminar. *Entrance requirements:* For master's, bachelor's degree in communications, 2 years of media-related experience; for doctorate, MA in communications. *Faculty research:* Communication and development, organizational communication, cultural studies, rhetoric, future studies.

Cornell University, Graduate School, Graduate Fields of Agriculture and Life Sciences, Field of Communication, Ithaca, NY 14853-0001. Offers communication (MS, PhD); human-computer interaction (MS, PhD); language and communication (MS, PhD); media communication and society (MS, PhD); organizational communication (MS, PhD); science, environment and health communication (MS, PhD); social psychology of communication (MS, PhD). *Degree requirements:* For master's, thesis (MS); for doctorate, comprehensive exam, thesis/dissertation. *Entrance requirements:* For master's and doctorate, GRE General Test, 3 letters of recommendation. Additional exam requirements/recommendations for international students: Required—TOEFL (minimum score 600 paper-based; 100 iBT). Electronic applications accepted. *Faculty research:* Mass communication, communication technologies, science and environmental communication.

DePaul University, College of Communication, Chicago, IL 60614. Offers digital communication and media arts (MA); health communication (MA); journalism (MA); media and cinema studies (MA); organizational and multicultural communication (MA); public relations and advertising (MA); relational communication (MA). Part-time and evening/weekend programs available. *Entrance requirements:* Additional exam requirements/recommendations for international students: Required—TOEFL (minimum score 590 paper-based; 96 iBT), IELTS (minimum score 7.5) or PTE. Electronic applications accepted.

DEREE - The American College of Greece, Graduate Programs, Athens, Greece. Offers applied psychology (MS); communication (MA); leadership (MS); marketing (MS).

DeVry University, Graduate Programs, Downers Grove, IL 60515. Offers accounting and financial management (MAFM); business administration (MBA); education (MS); educational technology (MS); electrical engineering (MS); human resources management (MHRM); information systems management (MISM); network and communications management (MNCM); project management (MPM); public administration (MPA).

Drake University, School of Journalism and Mass Communication, Des Moines, IA 50311-4516. Offers MCL. *Faculty:* 6 full-time (5 women), 1 part-time/adjunct (0 women). *Students:* 1 full-time (0 women), 21 part-time (19 women); includes 2 minority (1 Black or African American, non-Hispanic/Latino; 1 Asian, non-Hispanic/Latino). Average age 30. 7 applicants, 100% accepted, 7 enrolled. *Unit head:* Dr. Kathleen Richardson, Dean, 515-271-2295, Fax: 515-271-4518, E-mail: kathleen.richardson@drake.edu.

Drexel University, College of Arts and Sciences, Department of Culture and Communication, Philadelphia, PA 19104-2875. Offers communication (MS), including public communication, science communication, technical communication; publication management (MS). Part-time and evening/weekend programs available. *Degree requirements:* For master's, internship, professional portfolio. *Entrance requirements:* Additional exam requirements/recommendations for international students: Required—TOEFL. Electronic applications accepted. *Faculty research:* Science information and attitudes, science influence on literature, process of technical writing, document design, software documentation.

Drury University, Program in Communication, Springfield, MO 65802. Offers MA. Part-time and evening/weekend programs available. *Entrance requirements:* For master's, GMAT or MAT. Additional exam requirements/recommendations for international students: Required—TOEFL. Electronic applications accepted. *Expenses:* Contact institution.

Duquesne University, Graduate School of Liberal Arts, Department of Communication and Rhetorical Studies, Pittsburgh, PA 15282-0001. Offers communication (MA); rhetoric (PhD). Part-time and evening/weekend programs available. *Faculty:* 10 full-time (4 women), 5 part-time/adjunct (3 women). *Students:* 99 full-time (58 women), 9 part-time (6 women); includes 12 minority (8 Black or African American, non-Hispanic/Latino; 1 Asian, non-Hispanic/Latino; 2 Hispanic/Latino; 1 Two or more races, non-Hispanic/Latino), 21 international. Average age 34. 86 applicants, 55% accepted, 20 enrolled. In 2014, 13 master's, 6 doctorates awarded. *Degree requirements:* For master's, thesis optional, practicum; for doctorate, 2 foreign languages, comprehensive exam, thesis/dissertation. *Entrance requirements:* For master's and doctorate, GRE General Test. Additional exam requirements/recommendations for international students: Required—TOEFL. *Application deadline:* For fall admission, 2/1 priority date for domestic and international students; for spring admission, 11/1 priority date for domestic and international students. Applications are processed on a rolling basis. Electronic applications accepted. Application fee is waived when completed online. *Expenses: Tuition:* Full-time $18,882; part-time $1049 per credit. *Required fees:* $1800; $100 per credit. Tuition and fees vary according to program. *Financial support:* In 2014–15, 9 research assistantships with full tuition reimbursements (averaging $10,000 per year), 10 teaching assistantships with full tuition reimbursements (averaging $17,000 per year) were awarded; career-related internships or fieldwork, Federal Work-Study, institutionally sponsored loans, scholarships/grants, tuition waivers (full and partial), and unspecified assistantships also available. Financial award application deadline: 5/1. *Unit head:* Dr. Ronald Arnett, Chair, 412-396-5076, E-mail: arnett@duq.edu. *Application contact:* Linda Rendulic, Assistant to the Dean, 412-396-6460, E-mail: rendulic@duq.edu.
Website: http://www.duq.edu/academics/schools/liberal-arts/graduate-school/programs/communication-

Eastern Michigan University, Graduate School, College of Arts and Sciences, Department of Communication, Media and Theatre Arts, Program in Communication, Ypsilanti, MI 48197. Offers MA. Part-time and evening/weekend programs available. Postbaccalaureate distance learning degree programs offered (minimal on-campus study). *Students:* 11 full-time (5 women), 33 part-time (20 women); includes 20 minority (14 Black or African American, non-Hispanic/Latino; 3 Hispanic/Latino; 3 Two or more races, non-Hispanic/Latino), 2 international. Average age 29. 36 applicants, 81% accepted, 18 enrolled. In 2014, 8 master's awarded. *Degree requirements:* For master's, thesis or alternative. *Entrance requirements:* Additional exam requirements/recommendations for international students: Required—TOEFL. *Application deadline:* Applications are processed on a rolling basis. Application fee: $45. *Financial support:* Fellowships, research assistantships with full tuition reimbursements, teaching assistantships with full tuition reimbursements, career-related internships or fieldwork, Federal Work-Study, institutionally sponsored loans, scholarships/grants, tuition waivers (partial), and unspecified assistantships available. Support available to part-time students. Financial award applicants required to submit FAFSA. *Unit head:* Dr. Donald Ritzenhein, Coordinator, 734-487-3131, Fax: 734-487-3443, E-mail: dritzenh@emich.edu.

Eastern New Mexico University, Graduate School, College of Fine Arts, Portales, NM 88130. Offers communicative arts and sciences (MA). Part-time programs available. Postbaccalaureate distance learning degree programs offered (minimal on-campus study). *Degree requirements:* For master's, comprehensive exam, thesis optional. *Entrance requirements:* For master's, minimum GPA of 3.0, submission of writing sample. Additional exam requirements/recommendations for international students: Required—TOEFL (minimum score 550 paper-based; 79 iBT), IELTS (minimum score 6). Electronic applications accepted.

Eastern University, Graduate Education Programs, St. Davids, PA 19087-3696. Offers ESL program specialist (K-12) (Certificate); general supervisor (PreK-12) (Certificate); health and physical education (K-12) (Certificate); middle level (4-8) (Certificate); multicultural education (M Ed); pre K-4 (Certificate); pre K-4 with special education (Certificate); reading (M Ed); reading specialist (K-12) (Certificate); reading supervisor (K-12) (Certificate); school health services (M Ed); school health supervisor (Certificate); school nurse (Certificate); school principalship (K-12) (Certificate); secondary biology education (7-12) (Certificate); secondary chemistry education (7-12) (Certificate); secondary communication education (7-12) (Certificate); secondary education (7-12) (Certificate); secondary English education (7-12) (Certificate); secondary math education (7-12) (Certificate); secondary social studies education (7-12) (Certificate); special education (M Ed); special education (7-12) (Certificate); special education (Pre K-8) (Certificate); special education supervisor (N-12) (Certificate); TESOL (M Ed); world language (Certificate), including French, Spanish. Part-time and evening/weekend programs available. Postbaccalaureate distance learning degree programs offered (no on-campus study). *Faculty:* 22 full-time (11 women), 26 part-time/adjunct (18 women). *Students:* 57 full-time (42 women), 241 part-time (174 women); includes 106 minority (80 Black or African American, non-Hispanic/Latino; 1 American Indian or Alaska Native, non-Hispanic/Latino; 6 Asian, non-Hispanic/Latino; 15 Hispanic/Latino; 1 Native Hawaiian or other Pacific Islander, non-Hispanic/Latino; 3 Two or more races, non-Hispanic/Latino), 4 international. Average age 34. 109 applicants, 95% accepted, 85 enrolled. In 2014, 74 master's awarded. *Entrance requirements:* For master's, minimum GPA of 2.5; for Certificate, minimum GPA of 3.0. Additional exam requirements/recommendations for international students: Required—TOEFL. *Application deadline:* For fall admission, 8/14 for domestic students; for spring admission, 12/20 for domestic students. Applications are processed on a rolling basis. Application fee: $35. Application fee is waived when completed online. *Expenses: Tuition:* Full-time $15,600; part-time $650 per credit. *Required fees:* $30; $27.50 per semester. One-time fee: $50. Tuition and fees vary according to course load, degree level and program. *Financial support:* In 2014–15, 84 students received support, including 6 research assistantships with partial tuition reimbursements available (averaging $7,710 per year); scholarships/grants and unspecified assistantships also available. Financial award application deadline: 3/15; financial award applicants required to submit FAFSA. *Unit head:* Harry Gutelius, Associate Dean, 610-341-1729. *Application contact:* Michael Perpiglia, Associate Director of Enrollment, 610-341-5947, Fax: 484-581-1276, E-mail: mperpigl@eastern.edu.
Website: http://www.eastern.edu/academics/programs/loeb-school-education-0/graduateprograms

Eastern Washington University, Graduate Studies, College of Social and Behavioral Sciences and Social Work, Department of Communication Studies, Cheney, WA 99004-2431. Offers MSC. Part-time and evening/weekend programs available. *Degree requirements:* For master's, comprehensive exam, thesis or alternative. *Entrance requirements:* For master's, GRE General Test, minimum GPA of 3.0.

East Tennessee State University, School of Graduate Studies, College of Arts and Sciences, Department of Communication and Performance, Johnson City, TN 37614. Offers professional communication (MA), including communication studies, storytelling and theatre, strategic communication. Program offered with Department of Mass Communications. Part-time programs available. *Faculty:* 17 full-time (7 women). *Students:* 11 full-time (8 women); includes 1 minority (Two or more races, non-Hispanic/Latino), 4 international. Average age 26. 18 applicants, 72% accepted, 7 enrolled. In 2014, 7 master's awarded. *Degree requirements:* For master's, comprehensive exam, thesis optional. *Entrance requirements:* For master's, GRE General Test, minimum GPA of 3.0; three letters of recommendation. Additional exam requirements/recommendations for international students: Required—TOEFL (minimum score 550 paper-based; 79 iBT). *Application deadline:* For fall admission, 6/1 for domestic students, 4/30 for international students; for spring admission, 11/1 for domestic students, 9/30 for international students. Application fee: $35 ($45 for international students). Electronic applications accepted. *Financial support:* In 2014–15, 17 students received support, including 6 research assistantships with full tuition reimbursements available (averaging $6,000 per year), 4 teaching assistantships with full tuition reimbursements available (averaging $6,000 per year); career-related internships or fieldwork, institutionally sponsored loans, scholarships/grants, and unspecified assistantships also available. Financial award application deadline: 7/1; financial award applicants required to submit FAFSA. *Faculty research:* Political communications, visual communication, depictions of gender and ethnicity in print and online media and online corporate media, presidential rhetoric and newspaper coverage of presidential speeches. *Application contact:* Angela Edwards, Graduate Specialist, 423-439-4703, Fax: 423-439-5624, E-mail: edwardag@etsu.edu.
Website: http://www.etsu.edu/cas/comm_perform/

Edinboro University of Pennsylvania, Department of Communication Studies, Edinboro, PA 16444. Offers MA. Part-time and evening/weekend programs available. *Degree requirements:* For master's, thesis or alternative, competency exam. *Entrance requirements:* For master's, GRE or MAT, minimum QPA of 2.5. Electronic applications accepted.

Emerson College, Graduate Studies, School of Communication, Department of Communication Studies, Boston, MA 02116-4624. Offers communication management (MA). Part-time and evening/weekend programs available. *Faculty:* 16 full-time (7 women), 3 part-time/adjunct (all women). *Students:* 36 full-time (30 women), 4 part-time (3 women); includes 2 minority (1 Black or African American, non-Hispanic/Latino; 1 Hispanic/Latino), 19 international. Average age 26. 118 applicants, 36% accepted, 12 enrolled. In 2014, 21 master's awarded. *Entrance requirements:* For master's, GMAT or GRE General Test. Additional exam requirements/recommendations for international

students: Required—TOEFL (minimum score 550 paper-based; 80 iBT), IELTS (minimum score 6.5). *Application deadline:* For fall admission, 3/1 priority date for domestic and international students; for spring admission, 11/1 for domestic and international students. Applications are processed on a rolling basis. Application fee: $60 ($75 for international students). Electronic applications accepted. *Expenses: Tuition:* Part-time $1145 per credit. *Financial support:* In 2014–15, 8 students received support, including 8 fellowships (averaging $8,625 per year); research assistantships, Federal Work-Study, scholarships/grants, and unspecified assistantships also available. Financial award application deadline: 3/1; financial award applicants required to submit FAFSA. *Unit head:* Dr. Gregory Payne, Interim Chair, 617-824-8491, E-mail: gregory_payne@emerson.edu. *Application contact:* Leanda Ferland, Office of Graduate Admission, 617-824-8610, Fax: 617-824-8614, E-mail: gradapp@emerson.edu.
Website: http://www.emerson.edu/graduate_admission

Fairfield University, College of Arts and Sciences, Fairfield, CT 06824. Offers American studies (MA); communication (MA); creative writing (MFA); mathematics (MS); public administration (MPA). Part-time and evening/weekend programs available. Postbaccalaureate distance learning degree programs offered (minimal on-campus study). *Faculty:* 35 full-time (20 women), 5 part-time/adjunct (1 woman). *Students:* 54 full-time (35 women), 65 part-time (37 women); includes 18 minority (4 Black or African American, non-Hispanic/Latino; 4 Asian, non-Hispanic/Latino; 6 Hispanic/Latino; 1 Native Hawaiian or other Pacific Islander, non-Hispanic/Latino; 3 Two or more races, non-Hispanic/Latino), 6 international. Average age 35. 77 applicants, 69% accepted, 27 enrolled. In 2014, 51 master's awarded. *Degree requirements:* For master's, capstone research course. *Entrance requirements:* For master's, minimum GPA of 3.0, 2 letters of recommendation, resume. Additional exam requirements/recommendations for international students: Required—TOEFL (minimum score 550 paper-based; 80 iBT) or IELTS (minimum score 6.5). *Application deadline:* For fall admission, 5/14 for international students; for spring admission, 10/15 for international students. Applications are processed on a rolling basis. Application fee: $60. Electronic applications accepted. *Expenses: Tuition:* Part-time $695 per credit hour. Full-time tuition and fees vary according to degree level and program. *Financial support:* In 2014–15, 41 students received support. Scholarships/grants and unspecified assistantships available. Financial award applicants required to submit FAFSA. *Faculty research:* Ethical theory, media industries, community-based teaching and learning, non commutative algebra and partial differential equations, cancer research in biology and physics. *Unit head:* Dr. James Simon, Dean, 203-254-4000 Ext. 2221, Fax: 203-254-4119, E-mail: jsimon@fairfield.edu. *Application contact:* Marianne Gumpper, Director of Graduate and Continuing Studies Admission, 203-254-4184, Fax: 203-254-4073, E-mail: gradadmis@fairfield.edu.
Website: http://www.fairfield.edu/academics/schoolscollegescenters/collegeofartssciences/graduateprograms/

Fairleigh Dickinson University, Metropolitan Campus, University College: Arts, Sciences, and Professional Studies, School of Art and Media Studies, Program in Media and Communications, Teaneck, NJ 07666-1914. Offers MA.

Fitchburg State University, Division of Graduate and Continuing Education, Program in Applied Communications, Fitchburg, MA 01420-2697. Offers applied communications (MS, Certificate); health communication (MS); library media (MS); technical and professional writing (MS). Part-time and evening/weekend programs available. *Entrance requirements:* Additional exam requirements/recommendations for international students: Required—TOEFL (minimum score 550 paper-based; 79 iBT). Electronic applications accepted.

Florida Atlantic University, Dorothy F. Schmidt College of Arts and Letters, School of Communication and Multimedia Studies, Boca Raton, FL 33431-0991. Offers communication studies (MA); film and video (Certificate); media, technology and entertainment (MFA). Part-time programs available. *Degree requirements:* For master's, one foreign language, comprehensive exam (for some programs), thesis (for some programs). *Entrance requirements:* For master's, GRE General Test, minimum GPA of 3.0, essay, letters of recommendation. Electronic applications accepted. *Expenses:* Tuition, state resident: full-time $7396; part-time $369.82 per credit hour. Tuition, nonresident: full-time $19,392; part-time $1024.81 per credit hour. Tuition and fees vary according to course load. *Faculty research:* Cultural studies, gender studies, film, communication theory, journalism, new media.

Florida Institute of Technology, Graduate Programs, College of Psychology and Liberal Arts, Program in Global Strategic Communication, Melbourne, FL 32901-6975. Offers MS. *Students:* 11 full-time (10 women), 11 part-time (10 women); includes 4 minority (1 Black or African American, non-Hispanic/Latino; 3 Hispanic/Latino), 6 international. Average age 34. 26 applicants, 62% accepted, 7 enrolled. In 2014, 2 master's awarded. *Degree requirements:* For master's, comprehensive exam, 36 credit hours, thesis or final exam. *Entrance requirements:* For master's, GRE General Test (recommended), minimum GPA of 3.0, 2 letters of recommendation, discursive writing sample, display of work experience in the field. Additional exam requirements/recommendations for international students: Required—TOEFL (minimum score 550 paper-based; 79 iBT). *Application deadline:* Applications are processed on a rolling basis. Electronic applications accepted. *Expenses: Tuition:* Part-time $1179 per credit hour. Tuition and fees vary according to campus/location. *Financial support:* Applicants required to submit FAFSA. *Unit head:* Dr. Robert A. Taylor, Associate Dean, 321-674-7384, Fax: 321-674-8109, E-mail: rotaylor@fit.edu. *Application contact:* Cheryl A. Brown, Associate Director of Graduate Admissions, 321-674-7581, Fax: 321-723-9468, E-mail: cbrown@fit.edu.
Website: http://cpla.fit.edu/sac/global-strategic-communication/

Florida International University, School of Journalism and Mass Communication, Miami, FL 33199. Offers mass communication (MS), including global strategic communications, Spanish language journalism. *Accreditation:* ACEJMC. Part-time and evening/weekend programs available. *Degree requirements:* For master's, thesis optional. *Entrance requirements:* For master's, 2 letters of recommendation; minimum GPA of 3.0 during last 60 hours of upper-level work; resume. Additional exam requirements/recommendations for international students: Required—TOEFL (minimum score 550 paper-based; 80 iBT). Electronic applications accepted. *Faculty research:* Post-Hurricane Andrew population studies, Central American journalism, employment discrimination.

Florida State University, The Graduate School, College of Communication and Information, School of Communication, Tallahassee, FL 32306. Offers communication theory and research (PhD); integrated marketing communication (MA, MS); media and communication studies (MA, MS). Part-time programs available. *Faculty:* 26 full-time (11 women), 4 part-time/adjunct (1 woman). *Students:* 68 full-time (48 women), 105 part-time (71 women); includes 83 minority (15 Black or African American, non-Hispanic/Latino; 46 Asian, non-Hispanic/Latino; 19 Hispanic/Latino; 3 Two or more races, non-Hispanic/Latino). Average age 24. 206 applicants, 30% accepted, 41 enrolled. In 2014, 98 master's, 10 doctorates awarded. *Degree requirements:* For master's, thesis (for some programs); for doctorate, comprehensive exam, thesis/dissertation. *Entrance requirements:* For master's, GRE General Test, minimum GPA of 3.0; for doctorate, GRE General Test, minimum GPA of 3.3 in graduate course work. Additional exam requirements/recommendations for international students: Required—TOEFL (minimum score 600 paper-based; 100 iBT), IELTS (minimum score 7). *Application deadline:* For fall admission, 7/1 priority date for domestic students, 5/1 priority date for international students; for spring admission, 11/1 priority date for domestic and international students; for summer admission, 3/1 priority date for domestic and international students. Applications are processed on a rolling basis. Application fee: $30. Electronic applications accepted. *Expenses:* Tuition, state resident: part-time $403.51 per credit hour. Tuition, nonresident: part-time $1004.85 per credit hour. *Required fees:* $75.81 per credit hour. One-time fee: $20 part-time. Tuition and fees vary according to campus/location. *Financial support:* In 2014–15, 89 students received support, including 6 research assistantships with full tuition reimbursements available (averaging $7,816 per year), 83 teaching assistantships with full tuition reimbursements available (averaging $7,816 per year); fellowships, career-related internships or fieldwork, Federal Work-Study, institutionally sponsored loans, scholarships/grants, tuition waivers (partial), and unspecified assistantships also available. Support available to part-time students. Financial award application deadline: 2/1; financial award applicants required to submit FAFSA. *Faculty research:* Communication in the public interest; strategic communication; media and technology; multicultural, intercultural, and international communication. *Total annual research expenditures:* $67,063. *Unit head:* Dr. Gary Heald, Director, 850-644-5034, Fax: 850-644-8642, E-mail: gheald@fsu.edu. *Application contact:* Natashia Hinson-Turner, Graduate Coordinator, 850-644-5034, Fax: 850-644-8642, E-mail: natashia.turner@cci.fsu.edu.
Website: http://www.cci.fsu.edu

Fort Hays State University, Graduate School, College of Arts and Sciences, Department of Communication, Hays, KS 67601-4099. Offers MS. Part-time programs available. *Degree requirements:* For master's, comprehensive exam, thesis optional. *Entrance requirements:* Additional exam requirements/recommendations for international students: Required—TOEFL (minimum score 550 paper-based). Electronic applications accepted. *Faculty research:* Listening skills development, oral sensory motor skills, speech, reading, articulation in preschool children.

George Mason University, College of Humanities and Social Sciences, Department of Communication, Fairfax, VA 22030. Offers MA, PhD, Certificate. *Faculty:* 41 full-time (14 women), 38 part-time/adjunct (20 women). *Students:* 44 full-time (23 women), 33 part-time (27 women); includes 14 minority (6 Black or African American, non-Hispanic/Latino; 2 Asian, non-Hispanic/Latino; 4 Hispanic/Latino; 2 Two or more races, non-Hispanic/Latino), 6 international. Average age 30. 119 applicants, 45% accepted, 31 enrolled. In 2014, 13 master's, 3 doctorates awarded. *Degree requirements:* For master's, comprehensive exam, thesis or project; for doctorate, comprehensive exam, thesis/dissertation. *Entrance requirements:* For master's, GRE, expanded goals statement; 3 letters of recommendation; resume; official transcripts; for doctorate, GRE, 3 letters of recommendation; expanded goals statement; resume; official transcript; writing sample; for Certificate, GRE, expanded goals statement, resume, 2 letters of recommendation, official transcripts. Additional exam requirements/recommendations for international students: Required—TOEFL (minimum score 570 paper-based; 80 iBT), IELTS (minimum score 6.5), PTE. *Application deadline:* For fall admission, 3/1 priority date for domestic students. Application fee: $65 ($80 for international students). Electronic applications accepted. *Expenses:* Tuition, state resident: full-time $9794; part-time $408 per credit hour. Tuition, nonresident: full-time $26,978; part-time $1124 per credit hour. *Required fees:* $2820; $118 per credit hour. Tuition and fees vary according to course load and program. *Financial support:* In 2014–15, 28 students received support, including 1 fellowship (averaging $8,000 per year), 10 research assistantships with full and partial tuition reimbursements available (averaging $14,980 per year), 23 teaching assistantships with full and partial tuition reimbursements available (averaging $11,363 per year); career-related internships or fieldwork, Federal Work-Study, scholarships/grants, unspecified assistantships, and health care benefits (for full-time research or teaching assistantship recipients) also available. Financial award application deadline: 3/1; financial award applicants required to submit FAFSA. *Faculty research:* Theoretical and multi-methodological promotion, disease prevention, quality of care, risk assessment, crisis management, consumer/provider relationships, health campaigns, communication policy. *Total annual research expenditures:* $1.4 million. *Unit head:* Dr. Anne M. Nicotera, Chair, 703-993-8296, Fax: 703-993-1096, E-mail: anicoter@gmu.edu. *Application contact:* Brittany Sanders, Graduate Programs Coordinator, 703-993-1090, Fax: 703-993-1096, E-mail: bsander7@gmu.edu.
Website: http://communication.gmu.edu

Georgetown University, Graduate School of Arts and Sciences, Program in Communication, Culture, and Technology, Washington, DC 20057. Offers MA. Part-time and evening/weekend programs available. *Degree requirements:* For master's, thesis (for some programs). *Entrance requirements:* For master's, GRE General Test, 3 letters of recommendation, writing sample. Additional exam requirements/recommendations for international students: Required—TOEFL (minimum score 600 paper-based). Electronic applications accepted.

The George Washington University, Elliott School of International Affairs, Program in Global Communication, Washington, DC 20052. Offers MA. Part-time programs available. *Students:* 43 full-time (28 women), 21 part-time (17 women); includes 11 minority (4 Black or African American, non-Hispanic/Latino; 3 Asian, non-Hispanic/Latino; 3 Hispanic/Latino; 1 Two or more races, non-Hispanic/Latino), 25 international. Average age 27. 139 applicants, 26 enrolled. In 2014, 16 master's awarded. *Degree requirements:* For master's, one foreign language, capstone project. *Entrance requirements:* For master's, GRE general test, 2 years (or equivalent) of a modern, spoken, foreign language; introductory microeconomics/macroeconomics. Additional exam requirements/recommendations for international students: Required—TOEFL (minimum score 100 iBT), IELTS (minimum score 7). *Application deadline:* For fall admission, 1/15 priority date for domestic and international students; for spring admission, 10/1 for domestic students. Electronic applications accepted. *Financial support:* Fellowships, Federal Work-Study, and scholarships/grants available. Financial award application deadline: 1/15; financial award applicants required to submit FAFSA. *Unit head:* Prof. Sean Aday, 202-994-8137, E-mail: ipdgc@gwu.edu. *Application contact:* Nicole A. Campbell, Director of Graduate Admissions, 202-994-7050, Fax: 202-994-9537, E-mail: esiagrad@gwu.edu.
Website: http://www.gwu.edu/~elliott/academics/grad/gc/

Georgia State University, College of Arts and Sciences, Department of Communication, Atlanta, GA 30302-3083. Offers film, video, and digital imaging (MA), including critical studies, production, screenwriting; human communication and social influence (MA); mass communication (MA); media and society (PhD); moving image studies (PhD); public communication (PhD); rhetoric and politics (PhD). Part-time programs available. *Faculty:* 35 full-time (18 women). *Students:* 102 full-time (51 women), 40 part-time (15 women); includes 37 minority (20 Black or African American, non-Hispanic/Latino; 4 Asian, non-Hispanic/Latino; 6 Hispanic/Latino; 7 Two or more races, non-Hispanic/Latino), 14 international. Average age 33. 154 applicants, 39% accepted, 30 enrolled. In 2014, 25 master's, 5 doctorates awarded. *Degree requirements:* For master's, variable foreign language requirement, thesis (for some programs); for doctorate, comprehensive exam, thesis/dissertation. *Entrance requirements:* For master's, GRE; for doctorate, GRE. Additional exam requirements/recommendations for international students: Required—TOEFL (minimum score 550

paper-based; 80 iBT), IELTS (minimum score 6.5). *Application deadline:* For fall admission, 2/10 for domestic and international students; for spring admission, 10/15 for domestic and international students. Application fee: $50. Electronic applications accepted. *Expenses:* Tuition, state resident: full-time $6516; part-time $362 per credit hour. Tuition, nonresident: full-time $22,014; part-time $1223 per credit hour. *Required fees:* $2128 per semester. Tuition and fees vary according to course load and program. *Financial support:* In 2014–15, fellowships with tuition reimbursements (averaging $15,000 per year), teaching assistantships with tuition reimbursements (averaging $15,000 per year) were awarded; career-related internships or fieldwork and unspecified assistantships also available. Financial award applicants required to submit FAFSA. *Faculty research:* New media, mass media and journalism, rhetoric, film and media studies, film production. *Unit head:* Dr. David Cheshier, Chair, 404-413-5649, Fax: 404-413-5634, E-mail: dcheshier@gsu.edu. *Application contact:* Dr. Jennifer Barker, Associate Professor, 404-413-5793, Fax: 404-413-5634, E-mail: jmbarker@gsu.edu. Website: http://communication.gsu.edu

Gonzaga University, School of Professional Studies, Program in Communication and Leadership Studies, Spokane, WA 99258. Offers MA. Part-time and evening/weekend programs available. Postbaccalaureate distance learning degree programs offered (no on-campus study). *Faculty:* 6 full-time (3 women), 11 part-time/adjunct (2 women). *Students:* 18 full-time (13 women), 271 part-time (189 women); includes 53 minority (16 Black or African American, non-Hispanic/Latino; 4 American Indian or Alaska Native, non-Hispanic/Latino; 8 Asian, non-Hispanic/Latino; 17 Hispanic/Latino; 2 Native Hawaiian or other Pacific Islander, non-Hispanic/Latino; 6 Two or more races, non-Hispanic/Latino), 5 international. Average age 36. 33 applicants, 76% accepted, 19 enrolled. In 2014, 129 master's awarded. *Degree requirements:* For master's, thesis optional. *Entrance requirements:* For master's, MAT or GRE. Additional exam requirements/recommendations for international students: Recommended—TOEFL (minimum score 580 paper-based; 88 iBT), IELTS (minimum score 6.5). *Application deadline:* Applications are processed on a rolling basis. Application fee: $50. Electronic applications accepted. *Expenses:* Expenses: Contact institution. *Financial support:* In 2014–15, 6 students received support. Application deadline: 2/1; applicants required to submit FAFSA. *Unit head:* Dr. Michael Hazel, Department Chair, 509-313-3679, E-mail: hazelm@gonzag.edu. *Application contact:* Megan Taylor, Department Coordinator, 866-380-5323.

Governors State University, College of Arts and Sciences, Program in Communication and Training, University Park, IL 60484. Offers communication studies (MA); instructional and training technology (MA); media communication (MA). Part-time and evening/weekend programs available. *Degree requirements:* For master's, thesis or alternative.

Grand Valley State University, College of Liberal Arts and Sciences, School of Communications, Allendale, MI 49401-9403. Offers MS. Part-time and evening/weekend programs available. *Faculty:* 3 full-time (1 woman), 1 part-time/adjunct (0 women). *Students:* 10 full-time (6 women), 45 part-time (31 women); includes 9 minority (1 Black or African American, non-Hispanic/Latino; 1 Asian, non-Hispanic/Latino; 7 Hispanic/Latino), 4 international. Average age 31. 30 applicants, 93% accepted, 14 enrolled. In 2014, 17 master's awarded. *Degree requirements:* For master's, thesis or alternative. *Entrance requirements:* For master's, minimum GPA of 3.0 in last 60 hours, 2 letters of recommendation. Additional exam requirements/recommendations for international students: Required—TOEFL (minimum score 550 paper-based). *Application deadline:* For fall admission, 8/15 priority date for domestic students; for winter admission, 12/15 priority date for domestic students; for spring admission, 4/15 priority date for domestic students. Applications are processed on a rolling basis. Application fee: $30. Electronic applications accepted. *Expenses:* Tuition, state resident: full-time $10,602; part-time $589 per credit hour. Tuition, nonresident: full-time $14,022; part-time $779 per credit hour. Tuition and fees vary according to degree level and program. *Financial support:* In 2014–15, 7 students received support, including 4 fellowships (averaging $7,383 per year); 3 research assistantships with tuition reimbursements available (averaging $7,587 per year); career-related internships or fieldwork, Federal Work-Study, and institutionally sponsored loans also available. Support available to part-time students. Financial award application deadline: 4/15. *Faculty research:* Communication technology, databases, organizational communication, systems theory, public relations and advertising. *Unit head:* Dr. Anthony Thompson, Director, 616-331-3606, Fax: 616-895-2700, E-mail: thompsoa@gvsu.edu. *Application contact:* Dr. Alex Nesterenko, Coordinator, 616-331-3668, Fax: 616-331-2700, E-mail: nesterea@gvsu.edu.

Harvard University, Extension School, Cambridge, MA 02138-3722. Offers applied sciences (CAS); biotechnology (ALM); educational technologies (ALM); educational technology (CET); English for graduate and professional studies (DGP); environmental management (ALM, CEM); information technology (ALM); journalism (ALM); liberal arts (ALM); management (ALM, CM); mathematics for teaching (ALM); museum studies (ALM); premedical studies (Diploma); publication and communication (CPC). Part-time and evening/weekend programs available. *Degree requirements:* For master's, thesis. *Entrance requirements:* For master's, 3 completed graduate courses with grade of B or higher. Additional exam requirements/recommendations for international students: Required—TOEFL (minimum score 600 paper-based), TWE (minimum score 5). *Expenses:* Contact institution.

Hawai`i Pacific University, College of Humanities and Social Sciences, Program in Communication, Honolulu, HI 96813. Offers MA. Part-time and evening/weekend programs available. *Faculty:* 6 full-time (2 women), 1 (woman) part-time/adjunct. *Students:* 44 full-time (27 women), 22 part-time (13 women); includes 30 minority (2 Black or African American, non-Hispanic/Latino; 10 Asian, non-Hispanic/Latino; 5 Hispanic/Latino; 13 Two or more races, non-Hispanic/Latino). Average age 30. 60 applicants, 88% accepted, 30 enrolled. In 2014, 31 master's awarded. *Degree requirements:* For master's, thesis. *Entrance requirements:* Additional exam requirements/recommendations for international students: Recommended—TOEFL (minimum score 550 paper-based; 80 iBT), TWE (minimum score 5). *Application deadline:* For fall admission, 2/15 priority date for domestic students; for spring admission, 10/15 priority date for domestic students. Applications are processed on a rolling basis. Application fee: $50. Electronic applications accepted. *Expenses: Tuition:* Full-time $15,570; part-time $865 per credit. *Required fees:* $13. One-time fee: $50. Tuition and fees vary according to course load and program. *Financial support:* In 2014–15, 26 students received support. Career-related internships or fieldwork, Federal Work-Study, scholarships/grants, tuition waivers, and unspecified assistantships available. Financial award application deadline: 3/1; financial award applicants required to submit FAFSA. *Unit head:* Dr. John Hart, Department Chair, 808-544-0805, Fax: 808-544-1424, E-mail: jhart@hpu.edu. *Application contact:* Danny Lam, Assistant Director of Graduate Admissions, 808-543-8034, Fax: 808-544-0280, E-mail: grad@hpu.edu. Website: http://www.hpu.edu/CHSS/Communication/MA_COM/index.html

Hofstra University, Lawrence Herbert School of Communication, Hempstead, NY 11549. Offers documentary studies and production (MFA); journalism and public relations (MA), including journalism, public relations; rhetorical studies (MA). Part-time and evening/weekend programs available. *Faculty:* 21 full-time (8 women), 10 part-time/adjunct (5 women). *Students:* 66 full-time (48 women), 38 part-time (23 women); includes 47 minority (23 Black or African American, non-Hispanic/Latino; 2 American Indian or Alaska Native, non-Hispanic/Latino; 2 Asian, non-Hispanic/Latino; 18 Hispanic/Latino; 2 Two or more races, non-Hispanic/Latino), 17 international. Average age 28. 129 applicants, 67% accepted, 34 enrolled. In 2014, 17 master's awarded. *Degree requirements:* For master's, thesis, thesis project, minimum GPA of 3.0. *Entrance requirements:* For master's, letters of recommendation, interview. Additional exam requirements/recommendations for international students: Required—TOEFL (minimum score 550 paper-based; 80 iBT). *Application deadline:* Applications are processed on a rolling basis. Application fee: $70 ($75 for international students). Electronic applications accepted. *Expenses: Tuition:* Full-time $20,610; part-time $1145 per credit hour. *Required fees:* $970; $165 per term. Tuition and fees vary according to program. *Financial support:* In 2014–15, 46 students received support, including 20 fellowships with full and partial tuition reimbursements available (averaging $3,725 per year), 9 research assistantships with full and partial tuition reimbursements available (averaging $4,757 per year); Federal Work-Study, institutionally sponsored loans, scholarships/grants, tuition waivers (full and partial), and unspecified assistantships also available. Support available to part-time students. Financial award applicants required to submit FAFSA. *Faculty research:* Public relations for non-profit organizations, multimedia and the future of news, performance of race and gender, global public relations, political communication. *Unit head:* Dr. Evan W. Cornog, Dean, 516-463-5215, Fax: 516-463-4866, E-mail: comewc@hofstra.edu. *Application contact:* Sunil Samuel, Assistant Vice President of Admissions, 516-463-4723, Fax: 516-463-4664, E-mail: graduateadmission@hofstra.edu. Website: http://www.hofstra.edu/academics/colleges/soc/

Howard University, School of Communications, Washington, DC 20059-0002. Offers MA, MFA, MS, PhD. Part-time and evening/weekend programs available. Terminal master's awarded for partial completion of doctoral program. *Degree requirements:* For master's, comprehensive exam (for some programs), thesis optional; for doctorate, one foreign language, comprehensive exam, thesis/dissertation. *Entrance requirements:* For master's, GRE General Test, minimum GPA of 3.0; for doctorate, GRE General Test, minimum GPA of 3.2. Additional exam requirements/recommendations for international students: Required—TOEFL. Electronic applications accepted. *Expenses:* Contact institution. *Faculty research:* Communication disorders, intercultural communication, communication skills, race and media.

Illinois Institute of Technology, Graduate College, Lewis College of Human Sciences, Department of Humanities, Chicago, IL 60616. Offers information architecture (MS); technical communication (PhD); technical communication and information design (MS). Part-time programs available. *Faculty:* 17 full-time (10 women), 22 part-time/adjunct (14 women). *Students:* 11 full-time (6 women), 5 part-time (0 women); includes 5 minority (2 Black or African American, non-Hispanic/Latino; 1 Hispanic/Latino; 1 Native Hawaiian or other Pacific Islander, non-Hispanic/Latino; 1 Two or more races, non-Hispanic/Latino), 2 international. Average age 36. 29 applicants, 24% accepted, 5 enrolled. In 2014, 4 master's, 1 doctorate awarded. *Degree requirements:* For master's, comprehensive exam, thesis or alternative; for doctorate, comprehensive exam, thesis/dissertation. *Entrance requirements:* For master's, GRE General Test (minimum score 144 Quantitative, 153 Verbal, and 4.0 Analytical Writing), minimum undergraduate GPA of 3.0; 2 letters of recommendation from faculty or supervisors, professional statement discussing academic goals; for doctorate, GRE General Test (minimum score 144 Quantitative, 153 Verbal, and 4.0 Analytical Writing), Applicants must have completed a bachelor's or master's degree in a field that, in combination with the 27-credit hour technical core, would provide a solid basis for advanced academic work leading to original research in the field. 3 letters of recommendation from faculty or supervisors, professional statement discussing academic goals. Additional exam requirements/recommendations for international students: Required—TOEFL (minimum score 95 iBT); Recommended—IELTS (minimum score 7). *Application deadline:* For fall admission, 5/1 for domestic and international students; for spring admission, 10/15 for domestic and international students. Applications are processed on a rolling basis. Application fee: $50. Electronic applications accepted. *Expenses: Tuition:* Full-time $22,500; part-time $1250 per credit hour. *Required fees:* $30 per course. $260 per semester. One-time fee: $235. Tuition and fees vary according to course load and program. *Financial support:* Fellowships with partial tuition reimbursements, research assistantships with partial tuition reimbursements, teaching assistantships with partial tuition reimbursements, career-related internships or fieldwork, Federal Work-Study, institutionally sponsored loans, scholarships/grants, health care benefits, tuition waivers (partial), and unspecified assistantships available. Support available to part-time students. Financial award applicants required to submit FAFSA. *Faculty research:* Linguistics, punishment theory, political communication, gender and technology, philosophical and ethical issues in neuroscience. *Unit head:* Maureen Flanagan, Professor and Chair, 312-567-3563, Fax: 312-567-5187, E-mail: maureen.flanagan@iit.edu. *Application contact:* Rishab Malhotra, Director, Graduate Admission, 866-472-3448, Fax: 312-567-3138, E-mail: inquiry.grad@iit.edu. Website: http://www.iit.edu/csl/hum/

Illinois State University, Graduate School, College of Arts and Sciences, School of Communication, Normal, IL 61790-2200. Offers MA, MS. *Degree requirements:* For master's, thesis or alternative. *Entrance requirements:* For master's, GRE General Test, minimum GPA of 2.8 in last 60 hours of course work. Additional exam requirements/recommendations for international students: Required—TOEFL.

Indiana State University, College of Graduate and Professional Studies, College of Arts and Sciences, Department of Communication, Terre Haute, IN 47809. Offers communication studies (MA, MS); radio, television and film (MA, MS). Part-time programs available. *Degree requirements:* For master's, thesis (for some programs), oral and written exam. *Entrance requirements:* For master's, GRE General Test. Additional exam requirements/recommendations for international students: Required—TOEFL. *Faculty research:* Women in media, communication apprehension, media history.

Indiana University Bloomington, University Graduate School, College of Arts and Sciences, The Media School, Department of Telecommunications, Bloomington, IN 47405-7000. Offers mass communications (PhD); telecommunications (MA, MS). *Faculty:* 11 full-time (4 women). *Students:* 51 full-time (29 women), 1 part-time (0 women); includes 5 minority (1 American Indian or Alaska Native, non-Hispanic/Latino; 2 Asian, non-Hispanic/Latino; 1 Hispanic/Latino; 1 Two or more races, non-Hispanic/Latino), 14 international. Average age 30. 62 applicants, 32% accepted, 14 enrolled. In 2014, 13 master's, 6 doctorates awarded. Terminal master's awarded for partial completion of doctoral program. *Degree requirements:* For master's, thesis (for some programs); for doctorate, thesis/dissertation. *Entrance requirements:* For master's, GRE General Test, minimum undergraduate GPA of 3.0, 3 letters of recommendation; for doctorate, GRE General Test, minimum graduate GPA of 3.5, 3 letters of recommendation. Additional exam requirements/recommendations for international students: Required—TOEFL. *Application deadline:* For fall admission, 1/15 priority date for domestic students, 12/1 for international students. Applications are processed on a rolling basis. Application fee: $55 ($65 for international students). Electronic applications accepted. *Financial support:* In 2014–15, fellowships with full tuition reimbursements (averaging $18,000 per year), research assistantships (averaging $15,750 per year),

teaching assistantships (averaging $15,750 per year) were awarded; tuition waivers (full) also available. *Faculty research:* Media processes and effects, media law and policy, media management, media design and production. *Unit head:* Dr. Walter Gantz, Chair, 812-855-1621, E-mail: gantz@indiana.edu. *Application contact:* Tamera Theodore, Graduate Program Administrator, 812-855-2017, E-mail: ttheodor@indiana.edu.
Website: http://www.indiana.edu/~telecom/index.shtml

Indiana University of Pennsylvania, School of Graduate Studies and Research, College of Education and Educational Technology, Department of Communications Media, Indiana, PA 15705-1087. Offers adult education and communications technology (MA); communications media and instructional technology (PhD). Part-time and evening/weekend programs available. *Faculty:* 11 full-time (4 women). *Students:* 15 full-time (6 women), 41 part-time (20 women); includes 6 minority (4 Black or African American, non-Hispanic/Latino; 2 Two or more races, non-Hispanic/Latino), 3 international. Average age 38. 48 applicants, 25% accepted, 9 enrolled. In 2014, 12 doctorates awarded. Terminal master's awarded for partial completion of doctoral program. *Degree requirements:* For doctorate, comprehensive exam, thesis/dissertation. *Entrance requirements:* For doctorate, GRE, goal statement, resume, writing sample, two letters of recommendation. Additional exam requirements/recommendations for international students: Required—TOEFL (minimum score 540 paper-based). *Application deadline:* Applications are processed on a rolling basis. Application fee: $50. Electronic applications accepted. *Financial support:* In 2014–15, 1 fellowship with full tuition reimbursement (averaging $4,890 per year), 9 research assistantships with full and partial tuition reimbursements (averaging $6,249 per year), 3 teaching assistantships with partial tuition reimbursements (averaging $23,305 per year) were awarded; career-related internships or fieldwork, Federal Work-Study, scholarships/grants, tuition waivers (full), and unspecified assistantships also available. Support available to part-time students. Financial award application deadline: 4/15; financial award applicants required to submit FAFSA. *Unit head:* Dr. Mark Piwinsky, Chairperson, 724-357-2492, Fax: 724-357-5503, E-mail: mark.piwinsky@iup.edu. *Application contact:* Dr. Zachary Stiegler, Graduate Coordinator, 724-357-3219, E-mail: zachary.stiegler@iup.edu.
Website: http://www.iup.edu/commmedia/

Indiana University–Purdue University Fort Wayne, College of Arts and Sciences, Department of Communication, Fort Wayne, IN 46805-1499. Offers professional communication (MA, MS). Part-time programs available. *Faculty:* 9 full-time (4 women). *Students:* 5 full-time (3 women), 19 part-time (12 women); includes 5 minority (3 Black or African American, non-Hispanic/Latino; 1 Asian, non-Hispanic/Latino; 1 Hispanic/Latino), 2 international. Average age 31. 21 applicants, 90% accepted, 14 enrolled. In 2014, 12 master's awarded. *Entrance requirements:* For master's, minimum GPA of 3.0. Additional exam requirements/recommendations for international students: Required—TOEFL (minimum score 550 paper-based; 79 iBT); Recommended—TWE. *Application deadline:* For fall admission, 4/15 priority date for domestic students, 2/15 priority date for international students; for spring admission, 11/30 priority date for domestic students, 9/15 priority date for international students. Applications are processed on a rolling basis. Application fee: $55 ($60 for international students). Electronic applications accepted. *Financial support:* In 2014–15, 6 teaching assistantships with partial tuition reimbursements (averaging $13,522 per year) were awarded; scholarships/grants also available. Support available to part-time students. Financial award application deadline: 3/1; financial award applicants required to submit FAFSA. *Faculty research:* Cosmetic surgery and Chinese women, First Amendment and online information. *Total annual research expenditures:* $30,752. *Unit head:* Dr. Marcia Dixson, Chair/Associate Professor, 260-481-6558, Fax: 260-481-6183, E-mail: dixson@ipfw.edu. *Application contact:* Dr. Steven Carr, Graduate Program Director, 260-481-6545, Fax: 260-481-6183, E-mail: carr@ipfw.edu.
Website: http://www.ipfw.edu/comm/

Indiana University–Purdue University Indianapolis, School of Liberal Arts, Department of Communication Studies, Indianapolis, IN 46225. Offers applied communication (MA); health communication (PhD). Part-time programs available. *Students:* 13 full-time (10 women), 23 part-time (17 women); includes 7 minority (4 Black or African American, non-Hispanic/Latino; 1 Asian, non-Hispanic/Latino; 2 Hispanic/Latino), 7 international. 28 applicants, 50% accepted, 9 enrolled. In 2014, 12 master's awarded. *Degree requirements:* For master's, comprehensive exam, thesis; for doctorate, thesis/dissertation. *Entrance requirements:* For doctorate, master's degree. Additional exam requirements/recommendations for international students: Required—TOEFL; Recommended—IELTS. *Application deadline:* For fall admission, 1/15 priority date for domestic and international students; for spring admission, 5/14 for domestic students, 5/15 for international students. Application fee: $60. Electronic applications accepted. *Financial support:* In 2014–15, 7 students received support, including 1 fellowship with full tuition reimbursement available (averaging $25,000 per year), 3 research assistantships with partial tuition reimbursements available (averaging $15,000 per year), 5 teaching assistantships (averaging $2,500 per year); career-related internships or fieldwork, Federal Work-Study, institutionally sponsored loans, scholarships/grants, health care benefits, tuition waivers, and unspecified assistantships also available. Support available to part-time students. Financial award application deadline: 2/1. *Unit head:* Prof. Jennifer Bute, Director of Graduate Studies, 317-274-2090, E-mail: jjbute@iupui.edu. *Application contact:* Candice L. Smith, Coordinator of Academic and Graduate Programs, 317-274-8305, E-mail: canlsmit@iupui.edu.
Website: http://liberalarts.iupui.edu/comm/

Instituto Tecnologico de Santo Domingo, Graduate School, Area of Humanities and Social Sciences, Santo Domingo, Dominican Republic. Offers accounting (Certificate); adult education (Certificate); applied linguistics (MA); economics (MA); education (M Ed); educational psychology (MA, Certificate); gender and development (MA, Certificate); humanistic studies (MA); international marketing management (Certificate); international relations in the Caribbean basin (Certificate); intervention systems in family therapy (MA); linguistic and literary communication (Certificate); pedagogical support (MA); social science education (M Ed); sustainable human development (MA); terminal illness and death psychology (Certificate); youth and adult education (M Ed).

Instituto Tecnológico y de Estudios Superiores de Monterrey, Campus Ciudad Obregón, Programs in Education, Program in Communications, Ciudad Obregón, Mexico. Offers ME.

Instituto Tecnológico y de Estudios Superiores de Monterrey, Campus Monterrey, Graduate and Research Division, Program in Natural and Social Sciences, Monterrey, Mexico. Offers biotechnology (MS); chemistry (MS, PhD); communications (MS); education (MA). Part-time programs available. *Degree requirements:* For master's, one foreign language, thesis; for doctorate, one foreign language, thesis/dissertation. *Entrance requirements:* For master's, EXADEP; for doctorate, EXADEP, master's degree in related field. Additional exam requirements/recommendations for international students: Required—TOEFL. *Faculty research:* Cultural industries, mineral substances, bioremediation, food processing, CQ in industrial chemical processing.

Ithaca College, Roy H. Park School of Communications, Program in Communications, Ithaca, NY 14850. Offers MS. Part-time programs available. *Faculty:* 4 full-time (1 woman). *Students:* 11 full-time (8 women), 15 part-time (9 women); includes 3 minority (1 Black or African American, non-Hispanic/Latino; 1 Hispanic/Latino; 1 Two or more races, non-Hispanic/Latino), 7 international. Average age 27. 22 applicants, 64% accepted, 7 enrolled. In 2014, 17 master's awarded. *Degree requirements:* For master's, thesis optional. *Entrance requirements:* For master's, minimum GPA of 3.0. Additional exam requirements/recommendations for international students: Required—TOEFL (minimum score 550 paper-based; 80 iBT). *Application deadline:* For fall admission, 2/15 priority date for domestic and international students; for spring admission, 12/1 priority date for domestic and international students. Applications are processed on a rolling basis. Application fee: $40. Electronic applications accepted. *Expenses:* Expenses: Contact institution. *Financial support:* In 2014–15, 20 students received support, including 13 teaching assistantships (averaging $10,406 per year); career-related internships or fieldwork, Federal Work-Study, scholarships/grants, and unspecified assistantships also available. Support available to part-time students. Financial award application deadline: 3/1; financial award applicants required to submit CSS PROFILE or FAFSA. *Faculty research:* Managing corporate communication and learning, social systems design, crisis communication and diversity, social marketing, instructional design and interactive technologies. *Unit head:* Dr. Cory Young, Chair, 607-274-3143, Fax: 607-274-1263, E-mail: gps@ithaca.edu. *Application contact:* Gerard Turbide, Director, Office of Admission, 607-274-3143, Fax: 607-274-1263, E-mail: gps@ithaca.edu.
Website: http://www.ithaca.edu/rhp/gradcomm/

James Madison University, The Graduate School, College of Arts and Letters, School of Communication Studies, Harrisonburg, VA 22807. Offers communication and advocacy (MA), including environmental communication. *Faculty:* 22 full-time (13 women), 1 (woman) part-time/adjunct. *Students:* 16 full-time (11 women), 1 part-time (0 women); includes 3 minority (2 Black or African American, non-Hispanic/Latino; 1 Two or more races, non-Hispanic/Latino). Average age 28. 18 applicants, 100% accepted, 9 enrolled. Electronic applications accepted. *Expenses:* Tuition, state resident: full-time $7812; part-time $434 per credit hour. Tuition, nonresident: full-time $20,430; part-time $1135 per credit hour. *Financial support:* In 2014–15, 19 students received support, including 1 fellowship, 7 teaching assistantships with full tuition reimbursements available (averaging $8,837 per year); 11 assistantships (averaging $7112) also available. Financial award application deadline: 3/1; financial award applicants required to submit FAFSA. *Unit head:* Dr. Eric Fife, Director of the School of Communication Studies, 540-568-6449, E-mail: fifeem@jmu.edu. *Application contact:* Lynette D. Michael, Director of Graduate Admissions and Student Records, 540-568-6131 Ext. 6395, Fax: 540-568-7860, E-mail: michaeld@jmu.edu.
Website: http://www.jmu.edu/commstudies/

Johns Hopkins University, Zanvyl Krieger School of Arts and Sciences, Advanced Academic Programs, Program in Communication, Washington, DC 20036. Offers MA, MA/MBA. Part-time and evening/weekend programs available. Postbaccalaureate distance learning degree programs offered (no on-campus study). *Degree requirements:* For master's, thesis. *Entrance requirements:* For master's, minimum GPA of 3.0, strong writing skills. Additional exam requirements/recommendations for international students: Required—TOEFL (minimum score 100 iBT). Electronic applications accepted.

Kansas State University, Graduate School, College of Arts and Sciences, A. Q. Miller School of Journalism and Mass Communications, Manhattan, KS 66506. Offers advertising (MS); community journalism (MS); global communication (MS); health communication (MS); media management (MS); public relations (MS). Part-time and evening/weekend programs available. *Faculty:* 15 full-time (7 women), 1 (woman) part-time/adjunct. *Students:* 15 full-time (9 women), 5 part-time (3 women); includes 2 minority (both Hispanic/Latino), 9 international. Average age 26. 10 applicants, 80% accepted, 6 enrolled. In 2014, 10 master's awarded. *Degree requirements:* For master's, comprehensive exam, thesis. *Entrance requirements:* For master's, GRE General Test, minimum GPA of 3.0. Additional exam requirements/recommendations for international students: Required—TOEFL (minimum score 79 iBT). *Application deadline:* For fall admission, 2/1 priority date for domestic and international students; for spring admission, 8/1 priority date for domestic and international students. Applications are processed on a rolling basis. Application fee: $50 ($75 for international students). Electronic applications accepted. *Financial support:* In 2014–15, 2 research assistantships with full tuition reimbursements (averaging $11,180 per year), 7 teaching assistantships with full tuition reimbursements (averaging $7,729 per year) were awarded; scholarships/grants, health care benefits, and unspecified assistantships also available. Financial award application deadline: 2/1; financial award applicants required to submit FAFSA. *Faculty research:* Health communication, risk communication, strategic communications, community journalism, global communication. *Total annual research expenditures:* $219,641. *Unit head:* Dr. Birgit Wassmuth, Director, 785-532-6890, Fax: 785-532-5484, E-mail: wassmuth@ksu.edu. *Application contact:* Dr. Nancy Muturi, Associate Director of Graduate Studies, 785-532-3890, Fax: 785-532-5484, E-mail: nmuturi@ksu.edu.
Website: http://jmc.ksu.edu/

Kansas State University, Graduate School, College of Arts and Sciences, Department of Communication Studies, Manhattan, KS 66505. Offers MA. *Faculty:* 8 full-time (3 women). *Students:* 18 full-time (9 women), 3 part-time (all women), 2 international. Average age 20. 14 applicants, 64% accepted, 9 enrolled. In 2014, 7 master's awarded. *Degree requirements:* For master's, thesis or alternative. *Entrance requirements:* For master's, GRE General Test (recommended), minimum GPA of 3.0. Additional exam requirements/recommendations for international students: Required—TOEFL. *Application deadline:* For fall admission, 2/15 priority date for domestic students, 2/1 priority date for international students; for spring admission, 8/1 for domestic and international students. Applications are processed on a rolling basis. Application fee: $50 ($75 for international students). Electronic applications accepted. *Financial support:* Career-related internships or fieldwork, institutionally sponsored loans, and scholarships/grants available. Support available to part-time students. Financial award application deadline: 3/1; financial award applicants required to submit FAFSA. *Faculty research:* Debate, message preparation, speech criticism, engagement in the democratic process. *Unit head:* Dr. Colene Lind, Graduate Director, 785-532-6818, Fax: 785-532-3714, E-mail: colenejlind@ksu.edu.
Website: http://commstudies.k-state.edu

Kansas State University, Graduate School, College of Engineering, Department of Electrical and Computer Engineering, Manhattan, KS 66506. Offers electrical engineering (MS), including bioengineering, communication systems, design of computer systems, electrical engineering, energy and power systems, integrated circuits and devices, real time embedded systems, renewable energy, signal processing. Part-time and evening/weekend programs available. Postbaccalaureate distance learning degree programs offered (no on-campus study). *Faculty:* 21 full-time (4 women), 1 (woman) part-time/adjunct. *Students:* 38 full-time (8 women), 45 part-time (6 women); includes 13 minority (4 Black or African American, non-Hispanic/Latino; 8 Asian, non-Hispanic/Latino; 1 Hispanic/Latino), 37 international. Average age 28. 126 applicants, 29% accepted, 14 enrolled. In 2014, 22 master's, 5 doctorates awarded. *Degree requirements:* For master's, thesis or alternative, final exam; for doctorate, thesis/dissertation, final exam, preliminary exams. *Entrance requirements:* For master's, GRE General Test, bachelor's degree in electrical engineering or computer science, minimum

GPA of 3.0; for doctorate, GRE General Test. Additional exam requirements/recommendations for international students: Required—TOEFL (minimum score 600 paper-based; 85 iBT). *Application deadline:* For fall admission, 1/1 priority date for domestic and international students; for spring admission, 8/1 priority date for domestic and international students. Applications are processed on a rolling basis. Application fee: $50 ($75 for international students). Electronic applications accepted. *Financial support:* In 2014–15, 40 students received support, including 22 research assistantships with tuition reimbursements available (averaging $12,100 per year), 18 teaching assistantships with full tuition reimbursements available (averaging $12,220 per year); career-related internships or fieldwork, institutionally sponsored loans, and scholarships/grants also available. Support available to part-time students. Financial award application deadline: 3/1; financial award applicants required to submit FAFSA. *Faculty research:* Energy systems and renewable energy, computer systems and real time embedded systems, communication systems and signal processing, integrated circuits and devices, bioengineering. *Total annual research expenditures:* $1.3 million. *Unit head:* Dr. Don Gruenbacher, Head, 785-532-5600, Fax: 785-532-1188, E-mail: grue@k-state.edu. *Application contact:* Dr. Andrew Rys, Graduate Program Director, 785-532-4665, Fax: 785-532-1188, E-mail: andrys@k-state.edu.
Website: http://www.ece.k-state.edu/

Kean University, College of Humanities and Social Sciences, Program in Communication Studies, Union, NJ 07083. Offers MA. Part-time programs available. *Faculty:* 14 full-time (7 women). *Students:* 14 full-time (11 women), 26 part-time (22 women); includes 18 minority (11 Black or African American, non-Hispanic/Latino; 6 Hispanic/Latino; 1 Two or more races, non-Hispanic/Latino), 2 international. Average age 36. 20 applicants, 70% accepted, 9 enrolled. In 2014, 6 master's awarded. *Degree requirements:* For master's, comprehensive exam, thesis optional. *Entrance requirements:* For master's, GRE General Test, minimum cumulative GPA of 3.0, official transcripts from all institutions attended, three letters of recommendation, professional resume/curriculum vitae, personal statement. Additional exam requirements/recommendations for international students: Required—TOEFL (minimum score 550 paper-based; 79 iBT). *Application deadline:* For fall admission, 6/1 for domestic and international students; for spring admission, 12/1 for domestic and international students. Applications are processed on a rolling basis. Application fee: $75 ($150 for international students). Electronic applications accepted. *Expenses:* Tuition, state resident: full-time $12,461; part-time $607 per credit. Tuition, nonresident: full-time $16,889; part-time $744 per credit. *Required fees:* $3141; $143 per credit. Tuition and fees vary according to course load, degree level and program. *Financial support:* In 2014–15, 3 research assistantships with full tuition reimbursements (averaging $3,742 per year) were awarded; scholarships/grants and unspecified assistantships also available. Financial award applicants required to submit FAFSA. *Unit head:* Dr. Wenli Yuan, Program Coordinator, 908-737-0471, E-mail: wyuan@kean.edu. *Application contact:* Steven Koch, Admissions Counselor, 908-737-7136, Fax: 908-737-7135, E-mail: skoch@kean.edu.
Website: http://grad.kean.edu/masters-programs/communication-studies

Kennesaw State University, College of Humanities and Social Sciences, Program in Integrated Global Communication, Kennesaw, GA 30144. Offers MA. *Students:* 24 full-time (21 women); includes 8 minority (5 Black or African American, non-Hispanic/Latino; 2 Hispanic/Latino; 1 Two or more races, non-Hispanic/Latino), 4 international. Average age 29. 19 applicants, 68% accepted, 13 enrolled. In 2014, 14 master's awarded. *Entrance requirements:* For master's, GRE, BA or BS in communication or related field from accredited college or university; official transcripts; two-page resume; 500-word personal statement; three letters of recommendation. Additional exam requirements/recommendations for international students: Required—TOEFL (minimum score 550 paper-based; 80 iBT), IELTS (minimum score 6.5). *Application deadline:* For fall admission, 6/1 for domestic and international students. Application fee: $60. Electronic applications accepted. *Expenses:* Tuition, state resident: part-time $275 per semester hour. Tuition, nonresident: part-time $990 per semester hour. *Financial support:* In 2014–15, 2 research assistantships with full tuition reimbursements (averaging $8,000 per year) were awarded; unspecified assistantships also available. Financial award application deadline: 4/1; financial award applicants required to submit FAFSA. *Unit head:* Dr. Buddy Mayo, Director, 470-578-3638, E-mail: cmayo5@kennesaw.edu. *Application contact:* Jeannine Jones, Admissions Counselor, 470-578-6298, Fax: 470-578-9172, E-mail: ksugrad@kennesaw.edu.
Website: http://communication.hss.kennesaw.edu/programs/maigc/

Kent State University, College of Communication and Information, School of Communication Studies, Kent, OH 44242-0001. Offers communication and information (PhD); communication studies (MA). Part-time programs available. *Faculty:* 16 full-time (12 women). *Students:* 33 full-time (28 women), 10 part-time (7 women); includes 3 minority (2 Asian, non-Hispanic/Latino; 1 Hispanic/Latino), 15 international. Average age 29. 92 applicants, 52% accepted, 36 enrolled. In 2014, 7 master's awarded. *Degree requirements:* For master's, thesis, project, internship, or coursework; for doctorate, variable foreign language requirement, thesis/dissertation. *Entrance requirements:* For master's, GRE General Test, minimum GPA of 3.0, goal statement, writing sample, 3 letters of recommendation. Additional exam requirements/recommendations for international students: Required—TOEFL (minimum score: paper-based 525, iBT 71), Michigan English Language Assessment Battery (minimum score of 75), IELTS (minimum score of 6.0), PTE Academic (minimum score of 48), or completion of ELS level 112 Intensive Program. *Application deadline:* For fall admission, 1/15 for domestic students; for spring admission, 11/15 for domestic students. Application fee: $45 ($70 for international students). Electronic applications accepted. *Expenses:* Tuition, state resident: full-time $8730; part-time $485 per credit hour. Tuition, nonresident: full-time $14,886; part-time $827 per credit hour. Tuition and fees vary according to campus/location and program. *Financial support:* Research assistantships with full tuition reimbursements, teaching assistantships with full tuition reimbursements, career-related internships or fieldwork, Federal Work-Study, scholarships/grants, and unspecified assistantships available. Financial award application deadline: 2/1. *Unit head:* Paul Haridakis, Professor and Director, 330-672-0180, E-mail: pharidak@kent.edu. *Application contact:* Dr. Mei-Chen Lin, Associate Professor and Graduate Coordinator, 330-672-2659, Fax: 330-672-3510, E-mail: comm@kent.edu.
Website: http://www.kent.edu/comm/

La Salle University, School of Arts and Sciences, Program in Professional and Business Communication, Philadelphia, PA 19141-1199. Offers communication consulting and development (MA); communication management (MA); general professional communication (MA); professional and business communication (Certificate); public relations (MA); social and new media (Certificate). Part-time and evening/weekend programs available. Postbaccalaureate distance learning degree programs offered (minimal on-campus study). *Degree requirements:* For master's, practicum. *Entrance requirements:* For master's, writing assessment, professional resume; minimum overall B average; two letters of recommendation (if GPA below 3.25); brief personal statement (about 500 words); interview; for Certificate, writing assessment, minimum GPA of 2.75 in undergraduate studies; brief personal statement (about 500 words); interview. Additional exam requirements/recommendations for international students: Required—TOEFL. Electronic applications accepted. Application fee is waived when completed online. *Expenses:* Contact institution.

Lasell College, Graduate and Professional Studies in Communication, Newton, MA 02466-2709. Offers health communication (MSC, Graduate Certificate); integrated marketing communication (MSC, Graduate Certificate); public relations (MSC, Graduate Certificate). Part-time and evening/weekend programs available. Postbaccalaureate distance learning degree programs offered (minimal on-campus study). *Faculty:* 5 full-time (3 women), 10 part-time/adjunct (5 women). *Students:* 50 full-time (37 women), 94 part-time (74 women); includes 40 minority (25 Black or African American, non-Hispanic/Latino; 2 American Indian or Alaska Native, non-Hispanic/Latino; 4 Asian, non-Hispanic/Latino; 8 Hispanic/Latino; 1 Two or more races, non-Hispanic/Latino), 19 international. Average age 30. *Entrance requirements:* For master's and Graduate Certificate, bachelor's degree from an accredited institution. Additional exam requirements/recommendations for international students: Required—TOEFL (minimum score 550 paper-based; 79 iBT), IELTS. *Application deadline:* For fall admission, 8/31 priority date for domestic students, 6/30 priority date for international students; for spring admission, 12/31 priority date for domestic students, 10/31 priority date for international students. Applications are processed on a rolling basis. Electronic applications accepted. *Expenses: Tuition:* Full-time $10,700; part-time $595 per credit. *Required fees:* $160; $80 per semester. *Financial support:* Available to part-time students. Application deadline: 8/31; applicants required to submit FAFSA. *Unit head:* Dr. Joan Dolamore, Dean of Graduate and Professional Studies, 617-243-2485, Fax: 617-243-2450, E-mail: gradinfo@lasell.edu. *Application contact:* Adrienne Franciosi, Director of Graduate Admission, 617-243-2214, Fax: 617-243-2450, E-mail: gradinfo@lasell.edu.
Website: http://www.lasell.edu/academics/graduate-and-professional-studies/programs-of-study/master-of-science-in-communication.html

La Sierra University, College of Arts and Sciences, Department of English and Communication, Riverside, CA 92515. Offers communication (MA), including public relations/advertising, theory emphasis; English (MA), including literary emphasis, writing emphasis. Part-time programs available. *Degree requirements:* For master's, one foreign language. *Entrance requirements:* For master's, GRE General Test.

Liberty University, School of Communication and Creative Arts, Lynchburg, VA 24515. Offers strategic communication (MA); studio and digital arts (MFA). Part-time programs available. *Students:* 68 full-time (49 women), 97 part-time (62 women); includes 36 minority (28 Black or African American, non-Hispanic/Latino; 2 Asian, non-Hispanic/Latino; 2 Hispanic/Latino; 4 Two or more races, non-Hispanic/Latino), 16 international. Average age 32. 278 applicants, 40% accepted, 67 enrolled. In 2014, 15 degrees awarded. *Degree requirements:* For master's, thesis (for some programs). *Entrance requirements:* For master's, minimum undergraduate GPA of 3.0, faculty recommendation, written statement of purpose, writing sample. Additional exam requirements/recommendations for international students: Required—TOEFL (minimum score 600 paper-based; 100 iBT). *Application deadline:* For fall admission, 6/1 for domestic students; for spring admission, 11/1 for domestic students. Applications are processed on a rolling basis. Application fee: $50. Electronic applications accepted. *Financial support:* Federal Work-Study and unspecified assistantships available. Financial award applicants required to submit FAFSA. *Unit head:* Dr. Norman Mintle, Dean, 434-582-2077, E-mail: cvkramer@liberty.edu. *Application contact:* Dr. Terry Elam, Director of Graduate Admissions, 434-582-2111, Fax: 434-582-7836, E-mail: gradadmissions@liberty.edu.

Lindenwood University, Graduate Programs, School of Accelerated Degree Programs, St. Charles, MO 63301-1695. Offers administration (MSA); business administration (MBA); communications (MA); criminal justice and administration (MS); gerontology (MA); healthcare administration (MS); human resource management (MS); information technology (Certificate); managing information technology (MS); writing (MFA). Part-time and evening/weekend programs available. Postbaccalaureate distance learning degree programs offered (no on-campus study). *Faculty:* 22 full-time (9 women), 96 part-time/adjunct (34 women). *Students:* 811 full-time (488 women), 169 part-time (113 women); includes 374 minority (312 Black or African American, non-Hispanic/Latino; 6 American Indian or Alaska Native, non-Hispanic/Latino; 8 Asian, non-Hispanic/Latino; 26 Hispanic/Latino; 22 Two or more races, non-Hispanic/Latino), 25 international. Average age 35. 891 applicants, 65% accepted, 513 enrolled. In 2014, 498 master's awarded. *Degree requirements:* For master's, thesis (for some programs), minimum cumulative GPA of 3.0. *Entrance requirements:* For master's, interview, minimum GPA of 3.0. Additional exam requirements/recommendations for international students: Required—TOEFL (minimum score 550 paper-based; 80 iBT). *Application deadline:* For fall admission, 10/3 priority date for domestic and international students; for winter admission, 1/4 priority date for domestic and international students; for spring admission, 4/5 priority date for domestic and international students. Applications are processed on a rolling basis. Application fee: $30 ($100 for international students). Electronic applications accepted. *Expenses: Tuition:* Full-time $15,230; part-time $440 per credit hour. *Required fees:* $205 per semester. Tuition and fees vary according to course level, course load and degree level. *Financial support:* In 2014–15, 479 students received support. Career-related internships or fieldwork, institutionally sponsored loans, scholarships/grants, tuition waivers (partial), and unspecified assistantships available. Financial award application deadline: 6/30; financial award applicants required to submit FAFSA. *Unit head:* Dr. Gina Ganahl, Dean, 636-949-4501, Fax: 636-949-4505, E-mail: gganahl@lindenwood.edu. *Application contact:* Tyler Kostich, Director of Evening and Graduate Admissions, 636-949-4138, Fax: 636-949-4109, E-mail: adultadmissions@lindenwood.edu.
Website: http://www.lindenwood.edu/lead/

Lindenwood University, Graduate Programs, School of Communications, St. Charles, MO 63301-1695. Offers broadcast (MA); communications studies (MA); interactive media and Web design (MA); journalism (MA). Part-time and evening/weekend programs available. *Faculty:* 8 full-time (1 woman), 4 part-time/adjunct (1 woman). *Students:* 16 full-time (13 women), 2 part-time (0 women); includes 3 minority (2 Black or African American, non-Hispanic/Latino; 1 Asian, non-Hispanic/Latino), 4 international. Average age 27. 11 applicants, 55% accepted, 5 enrolled. In 2014, 4 master's awarded. *Degree requirements:* For master's, thesis (for some programs), minimum cumulative GPA of 3.0. *Entrance requirements:* For master's, GRE, minimum GPA of 3.0, resume. Additional exam requirements/recommendations for international students: Required—TOEFL (minimum score 550 paper-based; 80 iBT). *Application deadline:* For fall admission, 8/24 priority date for domestic and international students; for spring admission, 1/25 priority date for domestic and international students. Applications are processed on a rolling basis. Application fee: $30 ($100 for international students). Electronic applications accepted. *Expenses: Tuition:* Full-time $15,230; part-time $440 per credit hour. *Required fees:* $205 per semester. Tuition and fees vary according to course level, course load and degree level. *Financial support:* In 2014–15, 3 students received support. Career-related internships or fieldwork, Federal Work-Study, institutionally sponsored loans, scholarships/grants, tuition waivers (partial), and unspecified assistantships available. Financial award application deadline: 6/30; financial award applicants required to submit FAFSA. *Unit head:* Mike Wall, Dean, 636-949-4880, E-mail: mwall@lindenwood.edu. *Application contact:* Tyler Kostich, Director of Evening and Graduate Admissions, 636-949-4138, Fax: 636-949-4109, E-mail: adultadmissions@lindenwood.edu.
Website: http://www.lindenwood.edu/communications/

Lindenwood University–Belleville, Graduate Programs, Belleville, IL 62226. Offers business administration (MBA); communications (MA), including digital and multimedia, media management, promotions, training and development; counseling (MA); criminal justice administration (MS); education (MA); healthcare administration (MS); human resource management (MS); school administration (MA); teaching (MAT).

Louisiana State University and Agricultural & Mechanical College, Graduate School, College of Humanities and Social Sciences, Department of Communication Studies, Baton Rouge, LA 70803. Offers MA, PhD. *Faculty:* 12 full-time (6 women). *Students:* 31 full-time (14 women), 5 part-time (1 woman); includes 6 minority (4 Black or African American, non-Hispanic/Latino; 2 Hispanic/Latino), 2 international. Average age 33. 46 applicants, 46% accepted, 7 enrolled. In 2014, 4 master's, 8 doctorates awarded. *Degree requirements:* For master's, thesis; for doctorate, one foreign language, thesis/dissertation. *Entrance requirements:* For master's and doctorate, GRE General Test, minimum GPA of 3.0. Additional exam requirements/recommendations for international students: Required—TOEFL (minimum score 550 paper-based; 79 iBT), IELTS (minimum score 6.5), or PTE (minimum score 59). *Application deadline:* For fall admission, 1/1 priority date for domestic students, 5/15 for international students; for spring admission, 10/15 for domestic and international students; for summer admission, 5/15 for domestic and international students. Applications are processed on a rolling basis. Application fee: $50 ($70 for international students). Electronic applications accepted. *Financial support:* In 2014–15, 31 students received support, including 1 fellowship with full and partial tuition reimbursement available (averaging $16,479 per year), 26 teaching assistantships with full and partial tuition reimbursements available (averaging $11,173 per year); research assistantships with full and partial tuition reimbursements available, career-related internships or fieldwork, Federal Work-Study, institutionally sponsored loans, scholarships/grants, health care benefits, tuition waivers (full and partial), and unspecified assistantships also available. Support available to part-time students. Financial award applicants required to submit FAFSA. *Faculty research:* Rhetorical theory and criticism, performance studies, interpersonal communication. *Total annual research expenditures:* $44,244. *Unit head:* Dr. Renee Edwards, Chair, 225-578-4172, Fax: 225-578-4828, E-mail: edwards@lsu.edu. *Application contact:* Dr. Loretta Pecchioni, Graduate Adviser, 225-578-6812, Fax: 225-578-4828, E-mail: lpecch1@lsu.edu.
Website: http://www.lsu.edu/CMST

Marist College, Graduate Programs, School of Communication and the Arts, Poughkeepsie, NY 12601-1387. Offers communication (MA); integrated marketing communication (MA); museum studies (MA). Part-time programs available. Postbaccalaureate distance learning degree programs offered (no on-campus study). *Degree requirements:* For master's, thesis or comprehensive exam. *Entrance requirements:* For master's, GRE, minimum undergraduate GPA of 3.0, resume, 3 letters of recommendation. Additional exam requirements/recommendations for international students: Required—TOEFL (minimum score 550 paper-based; 80 iBT); Recommended—IELTS (minimum score 6.5). Electronic applications accepted.

Marquette University, Graduate School, Diederich College of Communication, Milwaukee, WI 53201-1881. Offers advertising and public relations (MA); communication studies (MA); digital storytelling (Certificate); journalism (MA); mass communication (MA); science, health and environmental communication (MA). *Accreditation:* ACEJMC (one or more programs are accredited). Part-time and evening/weekend programs available. *Degree requirements:* For master's, comprehensive exam, thesis or alternative. *Entrance requirements:* For master's, GRE, official transcripts from all current and previous colleges/universities except Marquette, three letters of recommendation, statement of academic and professional goals. Additional exam requirements/recommendations for international students: Required—TOEFL (minimum score 530 paper-based). Electronic applications accepted. *Faculty research:* Urban journalism, gender and communication, intercultural communication, religious communication.

Marshall University, Academic Affairs Division, College of Liberal Arts, Department of Communication Studies, Huntington, WV 25755. Offers MA. *Students:* 11 full-time (7 women), 1 (woman) part-time; includes 1 minority (Black or African American, non-Hispanic/Latino). Average age 29. In 2014, 11 master's awarded. *Degree requirements:* For master's, thesis optional. *Entrance requirements:* For master's, GRE General Test. Application fee: $40. *Financial support:* Fellowships available. *Unit head:* Dr. Camilla Brammer, Chair, 304-696-2810, E-mail: brammer@marshall.edu. *Application contact:* Fax: 304-746-1902, E-mail: services@marshall.edu.

Marywood University, Academic Affairs, Insalaco College of Creative and Performing Arts, Department of Communication Arts, Scranton, PA 18509-1598. Offers MA. Part-time programs available. *Students:* 19 full-time (10 women), 7 part-time (5 women); includes 1 minority (Hispanic/Latino), 8 international. Average age 29. In 2014, 17 master's awarded. *Application deadline:* For fall admission, 4/1 for domestic students, 3/31 for international students; for spring admission, 11/15 for domestic students, 8/31 for international students. Applications are processed on a rolling basis. Application fee: $35. Electronic applications accepted. *Expenses: Tuition:* Part-time $775 per credit. *Required fees:* $688 per semester. Tuition and fees vary according to degree level and campus/location. *Financial support:* Application deadline: 6/30; applicants required to submit FAFSA. *Unit head:* Dr. Michael Mirabito, Chair, 570-348-6211 Ext. 2630, E-mail: mirabito@.marywood.edu. *Application contact:* Tammy Manka, Assistant Director of Graduate Admissions, 570-348-6211 Ext. 2322, E-mail: tmanka@marywood.edu.
Website: http://www.marywood.edu/commarts/

McGill University, Faculty of Graduate and Postdoctoral Studies, Faculty of Arts, Department of Art History and Communication Studies, Montréal, QC H3A 2T5, Canada. Offers MA, PhD.

Michigan State University, The Graduate School, College of Communication Arts and Sciences, Department of Communication, East Lansing, MI 48824. Offers MA, PhD. *Entrance requirements:* Additional exam requirements/recommendations for international students: Required—TOEFL (minimum score 580 paper-based). Electronic applications accepted.

Minnesota State University Mankato, College of Graduate Studies, College of Arts and Humanities, Department of Communication Studies, Mankato, MN 56001. Offers communication education (Certificate); communication studies (MA, MS); forensics (MFA); professional communication (Certificate). *Students:* 21 full-time (9 women), 31 part-time (22 women). *Degree requirements:* For master's, one foreign language, comprehensive exam, thesis. *Entrance requirements:* For master's, minimum GPA of 3.0 during previous 2 years, writing sample. *Application deadline:* For fall admission, 7/1 priority date for domestic students, 5/1 for international students; for spring admission, 11/1 for domestic students, 10/1 for international students. Applications are processed on a rolling basis. Application fee: $40. Electronic applications accepted. *Financial support:* Research assistantships, teaching assistantships with full tuition reimbursements, career-related internships or fieldwork, Federal Work-Study, and institutionally sponsored loans available. Support available to part-time students. Financial award application deadline: 3/15; financial award applicants required to submit FAFSA. *Unit head:* Dr. Christopher Brown, Chairperson, 507-389-2510. *Application contact:* 507-389-2321, E-mail: grad@mnsu.edu. Website: http://www.mnsu.edu/cmst/

Mississippi College, Graduate School, College of Arts and Sciences, School of Christian Studies and the Arts, Department of Communication, Clinton, MS 39058. Offers applied communication (MSC); public relations and corporate communication (MSC). Part-time programs available. *Degree requirements:* For master's, comprehensive exam, thesis optional. *Entrance requirements:* For master's, GRE or NTE, minimum GPA of 2.5. Additional exam requirements/recommendations for international students: Recommended—TOEFL, IELTS. Electronic applications accepted.

Missouri State University, Graduate College, College of Arts and Letters, Department of Communication and Mass Media, Springfield, MO 65897. Offers MA. Part-time programs available. *Faculty:* 13 full-time (8 women). *Students:* 23 full-time (12 women), 12 part-time (8 women); includes 4 minority (3 Black or African American, non-Hispanic/Latino; 1 Hispanic/Latino), 4 international. Average age 30. 25 applicants, 88% accepted, 17 enrolled. In 2014, 19 master's awarded. *Degree requirements:* For master's, comprehensive exam, thesis or alternative. *Entrance requirements:* For master's, GRE General Test, minimum GPA of 3.0. Additional exam requirements/recommendations for international students: Required—TOEFL (minimum score 550 paper-based; 79 iBT). *Application deadline:* For fall admission, 7/20 for domestic students, 5/1 for international students; for spring admission, 12/20 for domestic students, 9/1 for international students. Applications are processed on a rolling basis. Application fee: $35 ($50 for international students). Electronic applications accepted. *Expenses:* Tuition, state resident: full-time $2250; part-time $250 per credit hour. Tuition, nonresident: full-time $4509; part-time $501 per credit hour. Tuition and fees vary according to course level, course load and program. *Financial support:* In 2014–15, 12 teaching assistantships with full tuition reimbursements (averaging $8,450 per year) were awarded; career-related internships or fieldwork, Federal Work-Study, institutionally sponsored loans, scholarships/grants, and unspecified assistantships also available. Support available to part-time students. Financial award application deadline: 3/31; financial award applicants required to submit FAFSA. *Faculty research:* Conflict resolution, media analysis, intercultural communication, political communication, communication theory and organizational praxis. *Unit head:* Dr. Shawn Wahl, Interim Head, 417-836-4423, Fax: 417-836-4774, E-mail: communication@missouristate.edu. *Application contact:* Misty Stewart, Coordinator of Graduate Admissions and Recruitment, 417-836-6079, Fax: 417-836-6200, E-mail: mistystewart@missouristate.edu.
Website: http://communication.missouristate.edu/

Missouri State University, Graduate College, Interdisciplinary Program in Administrative Studies, Springfield, MO 65897. Offers applied communication (MS); criminal justice (MS); environmental management (MS); homeland security (MS); sports management (MS). Part-time and evening/weekend programs available. Postbaccalaureate distance learning degree programs offered (no on-campus study). *Students:* 17 full-time (9 women), 64 part-time (29 women); includes 10 minority (4 Black or African American, non-Hispanic/Latino; 1 Asian, non-Hispanic/Latino; 2 Hispanic/Latino; 3 Two or more races, non-Hispanic/Latino), 3 international. Average age 33. 48 applicants, 73% accepted, 21 enrolled. In 2014, 16 master's awarded. *Degree requirements:* For master's, comprehensive exam, thesis or alternative. *Entrance requirements:* For master's, GRE, GMAT if GPA less than 3.0. Additional exam requirements/recommendations for international students: Required—TOEFL (minimum score 550 paper-based; 79 iBT). *Application deadline:* For fall admission, 7/20 priority date for domestic students; for spring admission, 12/20 priority date for domestic students. Applications are processed on a rolling basis. Application fee: $35 ($50 for international students). Electronic applications accepted. *Expenses:* Tuition, state resident: full-time $2250; part-time $250 per credit hour. Tuition, nonresident: full-time $4509; part-time $501 per credit hour. Tuition and fees vary according to course level, course load and program. *Financial support:* Career-related internships or fieldwork, Federal Work-Study, institutionally sponsored loans, scholarships/grants, and unspecified assistantships available. Support available to part-time students. Financial award application deadline: 3/31; financial award applicants required to submit FAFSA. *Unit head:* Dr. Gerald Masterson, Program Coordinator, 417-836-5251, Fax: 417-836-6888, E-mail: msas@missouristate.edu. *Application contact:* Misty Stewart, Coordinator of Graduate Recruitment, 417-836-6079, Fax: 417-836-6200, E-mail: mistystewart@missouristate.edu.
Website: http://msas.missouristate.edu

Monmouth University, The Graduate School, Department of Corporate and Public Communication, West Long Branch, NJ 07764-1898. Offers corporate and public communication (MA); human resources management and communication (Certificate); public service communication (Certificate); strategic public relations and new media (Certificate). Part-time and evening/weekend programs available. *Faculty:* 9 full-time (7 women). *Students:* 7 full-time (4 women), 24 part-time (19 women); includes 6 minority (1 Black or African American, non-Hispanic/Latino; 3 Hispanic/Latino; 2 Two or more races, non-Hispanic/Latino), 1 international. Average age 31. 23 applicants, 91% accepted, 13 enrolled. In 2014, 12 master's awarded. *Degree requirements:* For master's, comprehensive exam (for some programs), thesis (for some programs), project. *Entrance requirements:* For master's, GRE, baccalaureate degree with minimum GPA of 3.0 in major, 2.75 overall; two letters of recommendation, personal essay (750 words or less describing preparation for study and personal objectives), digital or hard copy portfolio of select samples of work including a writing sample, resume. Additional exam requirements/recommendations for international students: Required—TOEFL (minimum score 550 paper-based; 79 iBT), IELTS (minimum score 6), Michigan English Language Assessment Battery (minimum score 77). *Application deadline:* For fall admission, 7/15 priority date for domestic students, 6/1 for international students; for spring admission, 11/15 priority date for domestic students, 11/1 for international students. Applications are processed on a rolling basis. Application fee: $50. Electronic applications accepted. *Expenses: Tuition:* Full-time $18,072; part-time $1004 per credit. *Required fees:* $157 per semester. *Financial support:* In 2014–15, 28 students received support, including 19 fellowships (averaging $2,898 per year), 3 research assistantships (averaging $9,030 per year); scholarships/grants and unspecified assistantships also available. Support available to part-time students. Financial award applicants required to submit FAFSA. *Faculty research:* Service-learning, history of television, feminism and the media, executive communication, public relations pedagogy. *Unit head:* Dr. Deanna Shoemaker, Program Director, 732-263-5449, Fax: 732-571-3609, E-mail: dshoemak@monmouth.edu. *Application contact:* Andrea Thompson, Graduate Admission Counselor, 732-571-3452, Fax: 732-263-5123, E-mail: gradadm@monmouth.edu.
Website: http://www.monmouth.edu/cpc

Montana State University Billings, College of Arts and Sciences, Department of Communication and Theater, Billings, MT 59101. Offers public relations (MS). Part-time programs available. Postbaccalaureate distance learning degree programs offered. *Degree requirements:* For master's, thesis optional. *Entrance requirements:* For master's, GRE General Test, minimum undergraduate GPA of 3.0, 3 letters of recommendation. *Application deadline:* For fall admission, 3/15 for domestic students, 7/15 for international students; for spring admission, 10/15 for domestic students, 12/1 for international students. Applications are processed on a rolling basis. Application fee: $40. *Financial support:* Teaching assistantships, career-related internships or fieldwork,

Federal Work-Study, institutionally sponsored loans, and scholarships/grants available. Support available to part-time students. Financial award application deadline: 5/1; financial award applicants required to submit FAFSA. *Unit head:* Dr. Sarah Keller, Chair, 406-896-5824, E-mail: skeller@msubillings.edu. *Application contact:* David M. Sullivan, Graduate Studies Counselor, 406-657-2053, Fax: 406-657-2299, E-mail: dsullivan@msubillings.edu.

Moore College of Art & Design, Program in Social Engagement, Philadelphia, PA 19103. Offers MA. Part-time programs available. *Degree requirements:* For master's, thesis. Application fee: $60. *Expenses: Tuition:* Full-time $31,584; part-time $1504 per credit. *Unit head:* Daniel Tucker, Program Manager, E-mail: dtucker@moore.edu. *Application contact:* Stefan Schechs, Associate Director of Admissions, 215-965-4016, Fax: 215-568-3547, E-mail: sschechs@moore.edu. Website: http://moore.edu/academics/graduate-studies/ma-in-social-engagement

Morehead State University, Graduate Programs, Caudill College of Arts, Humanities and Social Sciences, Department of Communication, Media and Leadership Studies, Morehead, KY 40351. Offers communication (MA). Part-time and evening/weekend programs available. *Degree requirements:* For master's, comprehensive exam, exit assessment, written examination, oral interview. *Entrance requirements:* For master's, GRE General Test, bachelor's degree in communications or closely related field. Additional exam requirements/recommendations for international students: Required—TOEFL (minimum score 500 paper-based). Electronic applications accepted. *Faculty research:* Mass media effects, organizational communications, advertising/public relations.

New Mexico State University, College of Arts and Sciences, Department of Communication Studies, Las Cruces, NM 88003-8001. Offers MA. Part-time programs available. *Faculty:* 6 full-time (2 women). *Students:* 13 full-time (7 women), 7 part-time (3 women); includes 6 minority (1 Black or African American, non-Hispanic/Latino; 5 Hispanic/Latino), 2 international. Average age 35. 19 applicants, 74% accepted, 6 enrolled. In 2014, 13 master's awarded. *Degree requirements:* For master's, comprehensive exam (for some programs), thesis (for some programs). *Entrance requirements:* For master's, minimum GPA of 3.0. Additional exam requirements/recommendations for international students: Required—TOEFL (minimum score 550 paper-based; 79 iBT), IELTS (minimum score 6.5). *Application deadline:* For fall admission, 7/1 priority date for domestic students; for spring admission, 4/1 priority date for domestic students. Applications are processed on a rolling basis. Application fee: $40 ($50 for international students). Electronic applications accepted. *Expenses: Tuition,* state resident: full-time $3969; part-time $220.50 per credit hour. Tuition, nonresident: full-time $13,838; part-time $768.80 per credit hour. *Required fees:* $853; $47.40 per credit hour. *Financial support:* In 2014–15, 16 students received support, including 1 fellowship (averaging $800 per year), 1 research assistantship (averaging $2,000 per year), 10 teaching assistantships (averaging $16,261 per year); career-related internships or fieldwork, Federal Work-Study, scholarships/grants, traineeships, health care benefits, and unspecified assistantships also available. Support available to part-time students. Financial award application deadline: 3/1. *Faculty research:* Interpersonal, organizational, intercultural, political, and health communication. *Total annual research expenditures:* $23,906. *Unit head:* Dr. Kenneth Hacker, Academic Department Head, 575-646-2801, Fax: 575-646-1603, E-mail: comstudy@nmsu.edu. Website: http://commstudies.nmsu.edu

New York Institute of Technology, College of Arts and Sciences, Department of Communication Arts, Old Westbury, NY 11568-8000. Offers MA. Part-time and evening/weekend programs available. *Degree requirements:* For master's, thesis or alternative. *Entrance requirements:* For master's, minimum QPA of 2.85. Additional exam requirements/recommendations for international students: Required—TOEFL (minimum score 550 paper-based; 79 iBT), IELTS (minimum score 6). Electronic applications accepted. *Faculty research:* Journalism, digital and social media, communication arts, TV and society, film and culture.

New York University, Steinhardt School of Culture, Education, and Human Development, Department of Media, Culture and Communication, New York, NY 10010. Offers media, culture and communication (MA, PhD); MLIS/MA. Part-time programs available. *Faculty:* 35 full-time (17 women), 43 part-time/adjunct (19 women). *Students:* 98 full-time (68 women), 38 part-time (30 women); includes 27 minority (5 Black or African American, non-Hispanic/Latino; 12 Asian, non-Hispanic/Latino; 5 Hispanic/Latino; 1 Native Hawaiian or other Pacific Islander, non-Hispanic/Latino; 4 Two or more races, non-Hispanic/Latino), 55 international. Average age 33. 550 applicants, 24% accepted, 46 enrolled. In 2014, 57 master's, 6 doctorates awarded. Terminal master's awarded for partial completion of doctoral program. *Degree requirements:* For master's, thesis (for some programs); for doctorate, thesis/dissertation. *Entrance requirements:* For master's, GRE General Test; for doctorate, GRE General Test, interview. Additional exam requirements/recommendations for international students: Required—TOEFL (minimum score 100 iBT). *Application deadline:* For fall admission, 12/1 priority date for domestic and international students; for spring admission, 10/1 for domestic and international students. Applications are processed on a rolling basis. Application fee: $75. Electronic applications accepted. *Financial support:* Fellowships with full and partial tuition reimbursements, teaching assistantships with full and partial tuition reimbursements, career-related internships or fieldwork, Federal Work-Study, institutionally sponsored loans, scholarships/grants, tuition waivers (partial), and unspecified assistantships available. Support available to part-time students. Financial award application deadline: 2/1; financial award applicants required to submit FAFSA. *Faculty research:* Digital media and new technologies, media criticism, flow of media and culture transnationally and transculturally. *Unit head:* Prof. Lisa Gitelman, Chairperson, 212-998-5191, Fax: 212-995-4046, E-mail: lg91@nyu.edu. *Application contact:* 212-998-5030, Fax: 212-995-4328, E-mail: steinhardt.gradadmissions@nyu.edu. Website: http://steinhardt.nyu.edu/mcc

Norfolk State University, School of Graduate Studies, School of Liberal Arts, Department of Media and Communication, Norfolk, VA 23504. Offers MA. Part-time programs available. *Degree requirements:* For master's, thesis. *Entrance requirements:* For master's, GRE, minimum GPA of 2.5, letters of recommendation. Additional exam requirements/recommendations for international students: Required—TOEFL.

North Carolina State University, Graduate School, College of Humanities and Social Sciences, Department of Communication, Raleigh, NC 27695. Offers MS. Part-time programs available. *Degree requirements:* For master's, thesis optional. *Entrance requirements:* For master's, GRE, minimum undergraduate GPA of 3.0 during last 60 hours. Electronic applications accepted. *Faculty research:* Instructional communication, political communication, organizational conflict management, intercultural communication, communication technology.

North Dakota State University, College of Graduate and Interdisciplinary Studies, College of Arts, Humanities and Social Sciences, Department of Communication, Fargo, ND 58108. Offers communication (PhD); mass communication (MA, MS); speech communication (MA, MS). Part-time programs available. Postbaccalaureate distance learning degree programs offered (no on-campus study). Terminal master's awarded for partial completion of doctoral program. *Degree requirements:* For master's, thesis (for

some programs); for doctorate, comprehensive exam, thesis/dissertation, 2-3 publications. *Entrance requirements:* For master's, GRE, minimum undergraduate GPA of 3.25; for doctorate, GRE, minimum undergraduate GPA of 3.5. Additional exam requirements/recommendations for international students: Required—TOEFL (minimum score 600 paper-based; 100 iBT), IELTS (minimum score 7). Electronic applications accepted. *Faculty research:* Communication and rhetorical theory, organizational communication, broadcast and print journalism, international communication, public relations and advertising.

Northeastern State University, College of Liberal Arts, Department of Communication, Art and Theatre, Tahlequah, OK 74464-2399. Offers communication (MA). Part-time and evening/weekend programs available. *Faculty:* 3 full-time (1 woman). *Students:* 10 full-time (7 women), 7 part-time (5 women); includes 5 minority (1 Black or African American, non-Hispanic/Latino; 3 American Indian or Alaska Native, non-Hispanic/Latino; 1 Two or more races, non-Hispanic/Latino). Average age 30. In 2014, 9 master's awarded. *Degree requirements:* For master's, comprehensive exam. *Entrance requirements:* For master's, GRE, MAT, minimum GPA of 2.5. Additional exam requirements/recommendations for international students: ·Required—TOEFL. *Application deadline:* For fall admission, 6/1 priority date for domestic students. Applications are processed on a rolling basis. Application fee: $25. Electronic applications accepted. *Expenses:* Tuition, state resident: part-time $178.75 per credit hour. Tuition, nonresident: part-time $451.75 per credit hour. *Required fees:* $37.40 per credit hour. *Financial support:* Teaching assistantships and Federal Work-Study available. Financial award application deadline: 3/1. *Unit head:* Dr. Hsin-I (Sydney) Yueh, Graduate Program Director, 918-444-4725, E-mail: yueh@nsuok.edu. *Application contact:* Margie Railey, Administrative Assistant, 918-456-5511 Ext. 2093, Fax: 918-458-2061, E-mail: railey@nsouk.edu. Website: http://academics.nsuok.edu/communicationstudies/MasterofArts.aspx

Northern Arizona University, Graduate College, College of Social and Behavioral Sciences, School of Communication, Flagstaff, AZ 86011. Offers MA. Part-time programs available. *Degree requirements:* For master's, thesis or project. *Entrance requirements:* For master's, GRE General Test. Additional exam requirements/recommendations for international students: Required—TOEFL (minimum score 550 paper-based; 80 iBT), IELTS (minimum score 7). Electronic applications accepted.

Northern Illinois University, Graduate School, College of Liberal Arts and Sciences, Department of Communication, De Kalb, IL 60115-2854. Offers communication studies (MA). Part-time programs available. *Faculty:* 24 full-time (11 women), 1 part-time/adjunct (0 women). *Students:* 29 full-time (12 women), 7 part-time (4 women); includes 9 minority (1 Black or African American, non-Hispanic/Latino; 1 Asian, non-Hispanic/Latino; 5 Hispanic/Latino; 2 Two or more races, non-Hispanic/Latino), 2 international. Average age 27. 29 applicants, 69% accepted, 9 enrolled. In 2014, 19 master's awarded. *Degree requirements:* For master's, comprehensive exam, thesis optional. *Entrance requirements:* For master's, GRE General Test, minimum GPA of 2.75. Additional exam requirements/recommendations for international students: Required—TOEFL (minimum score 550 paper-based). *Application deadline:* For fall admission, 6/1 for domestic students, 5/1 for international students; for spring admission, 11/1 for domestic students, 10/1 for international students. Applications are processed on a rolling basis. Application fee: $40. Electronic applications accepted. *Financial support:* In 2014–15, 30 teaching assistantships with full tuition reimbursements were awarded; fellowships with full tuition reimbursements, research assistantships with full tuition reimbursements, career-related internships or fieldwork, Federal Work-Study, scholarships/grants, tuition waivers (full), and unspecified assistantships also available. Support available to part-time students. Financial award applicants required to submit FAFSA. *Faculty research:* Journalism, history film studies, rhetoric or criticism, globalization, mass media law. *Unit head:* Dr. Gary Burns, Chair, 815-753-7028, Fax: 815-753-7109, E-mail: gburns@niu.edu. *Application contact:* Dr. Kathleen Valde, Director, Graduate Studies, 815-753-7005, E-mail: kvalde@niu.edu. Website: http://www.comm.niu.edu/

Northern Kentucky University, Office of Graduate Programs, College of Informatics, Program in Communication, Highland Heights, KY 41099. Offers communication (MA); communication teaching (Certificate); documentary studies (Certificate); public relations (Certificate); relationships (Certificate). Part-time and evening/weekend programs available. *Faculty:* 7 full-time (4 women), 1 part-time/adjunct (0 women). *Students:* 9 full-time (1 woman), 17 part-time (11 women); includes 3 minority (all Black or African American, non-Hispanic/Latino), 2 international. Average age 30. In 2014, 13 master's, 2 other advanced degrees awarded. Terminal master's awarded for partial completion of doctoral program. *Degree requirements:* For master's, comprehensive exams, thesis or applied capstone project. *Entrance requirements:* For master's, GRE, minimum GPA of 3.0, 3 letters of recommendation, letter of intent. Additional exam requirements/recommendations for international students: Required—TOEFL (minimum score 79 iBT); Recommended—IELTS (minimum score 6.5). *Application deadline:* For fall admission, 8/1 for domestic students, 6/1 for international students; for spring admission, 12/1 for domestic students, 10/1 for international students. Applications are processed on a rolling basis. Application fee: $40. Electronic applications accepted. *Expenses: Tuition,* area resident: Part-time $518 per credit hour. Tuition, state resident: part-time $630 per credit hour. Tuition, nonresident: part-time $797 per credit hour. *Required fees:* $192 per semester. Tuition and fees vary according to course load, degree level, campus/location, program and reciprocity agreements. *Financial support:* In 2014–15, 7 students received support. Unspecified assistantships available. Financial award applicants required to submit FAFSA. *Faculty research:* Mediating effect of health communication, organizational communication, quantitative and qualitative research methods, family and interpersonal communication. *Unit head:* Dr. Andrea Lambert-South, Graduate Program Director, 859-572-6615, E-mail: lamberta3@nku.edu. *Application contact:* Alison Swanson, Graduate Admissions Coordinator, 859-572-6971, E-mail: swansona1@nku.edu. Website: http://informatics.nku.edu/content/informatics/departments/communication/programs/communication—m-a—.html

Northwestern University, The Graduate School, School of Communication, Department of Communication Studies, Evanston, IL 60208. Offers communication studies (PhD), including interaction and social influence, rhetoric and public culture; managerial communication (MSC); media, technology and society (PhD); technology and social behavior (PhD). PhD admissions and degree offered through The Graduate School. Terminal master's awarded for partial completion of doctoral program. *Degree requirements:* For doctorate, thesis/dissertation. *Entrance requirements:* For master's and doctorate, GRE General Test. Additional exam requirements/recommendations for international students: Required—TOEFL. Electronic applications accepted.

Notre Dame of Maryland University, Graduate Studies, Program in Contemporary Communication, Baltimore, MD 21210-2476. Offers MA. Part-time and evening/weekend programs available. *Degree requirements:* For master's, thesis optional. *Entrance requirements:* For master's, minimum GPA of 3.0. Additional exam requirements/recommendations for international students: Required—TOEFL (minimum score 500 paper-based; 61 iBT). Electronic applications accepted.

The Ohio State University, Graduate School, College of Arts and Sciences, School of Communication, Columbus, OH 43210. Offers MA, PhD. *Faculty:* 27. *Students:* 68 full-

time (43 women); includes 9 minority (3 Black or African American, non-Hispanic/Latino; 1 Asian, non-Hispanic/Latino; 3 Hispanic/Latino; 2 Two or more races, non-Hispanic/Latino), 11 international. Average age 29. In 2014, 12 master's, 12 doctorates awarded. *Degree requirements:* For doctorate, thesis/dissertation. *Entrance requirements:* For master's and doctorate, GRE. Additional exam requirements/recommendations for international students: Required—TOEFL (minimum score 640 paper-based; 111 iBT); Recommended—IELTS (minimum score 8.5). *Application deadline:* For fall admission, 12/1 priority date for domestic and international students; for winter admission, 12/1 for domestic students, 11/1 for international students; for spring admission, 3/1 for domestic students, 2/1 for international students. Applications are processed on a rolling basis. Application fee: $60 ($70 for international students). Electronic applications accepted. *Financial support:* Fellowships with tuition reimbursements, research assistantships with tuition reimbursements, and teaching assistantships with tuition reimbursements available. *Unit head:* Dr. Daniel McDonald, Professor and Director, 614-292-0451, E-mail: mcdonald.221@osu.edu. *Application contact:* Graduate and Professional Admissions, 614-292-9444, Fax: 614-292-3895, E-mail: gpadmissions@osu.edu.
Website: http://www.comm.ohio-state.edu/

Ohio University, Graduate College, Scripps College of Communication, Athens, OH 45701-2979. Offers MA, MCTP, MS, PhD. Part-time programs available. *Degree requirements:* For master's, comprehensive exam (for some programs), thesis or alternative; for doctorate, comprehensive exam, thesis/dissertation. *Entrance requirements:* For master's and doctorate, GRE General Test. Additional exam requirements/recommendations for international students: Required—TOEFL or IELTS. Electronic applications accepted. *Expenses:* Contact institution.

Our Lady of the Lake University of San Antonio, College of Arts and Sciences, Program in English, San Antonio, TX 78207-4689. Offers English and communication arts (MA); English education (MA); English language and literature (MA); writing (MA); MA/MFA. Program offered jointly with University of the Incarnate Word and St. Mary's University. Part-time and evening/weekend programs available. *Degree requirements:* For master's, comprehensive exam, thesis optional. *Entrance requirements:* For master's, GRE General Test or MAT, minimum GPA of 3.0 in last 60 hours, 2.5 overall. Additional exam requirements/recommendations for international students: Required—TOEFL. Electronic applications accepted. *Faculty research:* Writing theory and research, contemporary Southern literature, popular culture, poetry, literature of the Southwest.

Penn State Harrisburg, Graduate School, School of Humanities, Middletown, PA 17057-4898. Offers American studies (MA, PhD); communications (MA); folklore and ethnography (Certificate); heritage and museum practice (Certificate); humanities (MA); writing instruction specialist (Certificate). Evening/weekend programs available. *Unit head:* Dr. Mukund S. Kulkarni, Chancellor, 717-948-6105, Fax: 717-948-6452, E-mail: msk5@psu.edu. *Application contact:* Robert W. Coffman, Jr., Director of Enrollment Management, Admissions, 717-948-6250, Fax: 717-948-6325, E-mail: ric1@psu.edu.
Website: http://harrisburg.psu.edu/humanities

Penn State University Park, Graduate School, College of the Liberal Arts, Department of Communication Arts and Sciences, University Park, PA 16802. Offers MA, PhD. *Unit head:* Dr. Susan Welch, Dean, 814-865-7691, Fax: 814-863-2085, E-mail: swelch@psu.edu. *Application contact:* Lori A. Stania, Director, Graduate Student Services, 814-867-5278, Fax: 814-863-4627, E-mail: gswww@psu.edu.
Website: http://cas.la.psu.edu/

Pepperdine University, Seaver College, Division of Communication, Malibu, CA 90263. Offers communication (MA, MS); media production (MA). Part-time programs available. *Students:* 3 full-time (2 women), 27 part-time (20 women); includes 6 minority (2 Asian, non-Hispanic/Latino; 2 Hispanic/Latino; 1 Native Hawaiian or other Pacific Islander, non-Hispanic/Latino; 1 Two or more races, non-Hispanic/Latino), 2 international. In 2014, 5 master's awarded. *Entrance requirements:* For master's, GRE General Test, letters of recommendation, writing sample. Additional exam requirements/recommendations for international students: Required—TOEFL. *Application deadline:* For fall admission, 2/1 priority date for domestic students, 2/1 for international students. Applications are processed on a rolling basis. Application fee: $65. Electronic applications accepted. *Financial support:* Research assistantships, teaching assistantships, career-related internships or fieldwork, and scholarships/grants available. Support available to part-time students. Financial award applicants required to submit FAFSA. *Unit head:* Dr. Kenneth E. Waters, Chair/Professor of Journalism, 310-506-4245, E-mail: ken.waters@pepperdine.edu. *Application contact:* Michael Truschke, Dean of Admission and Enrollment Management, 310-506-6165, Fax: 310-506-4861, E-mail: admission-seaver@pepperdine.edu.

Pittsburg State University, Graduate School, College of Arts and Sciences, Department of Communication, Pittsburg, KS 66762. Offers applied communication (MA); communication education (MA); theatre (MA). *Degree requirements:* For master's, thesis or alternative.

Point Park University, School of Communication, Pittsburgh, PA 15222-1984. Offers MA. Part-time and evening/weekend programs available. *Degree requirements:* For master's, comprehensive exam (for some programs), thesis or alternative. *Entrance requirements:* For master's, GRE (if GPA less than 2.75), minimum GPA of 2.75, 2 letters of recommendation, statement of intent. Additional exam requirements/recommendations for international students: Required—TOEFL (minimum score 570 paper-based; 88 iBT), IELTS (minimum score 6.5); Recommended—TWE (minimum score 5). Electronic applications accepted.

Purdue University, Graduate School, College of Liberal Arts, Department of Communication, West Lafayette, IN 47907. Offers MA, MS, PhD. *Degree requirements:* For master's, comprehensive exams or thesis; for doctorate, thesis/dissertation. *Entrance requirements:* For master's and doctorate, GRE General Test, minimum undergraduate GPA of 3.0 or equivalent. Additional exam requirements/recommendations for international students: Required—TOEFL (minimum score 600 paper-based; 77 iBT). Electronic applications accepted. *Faculty research:* Interpersonal communication, mass communication, organizational communication, public affairs and issue management, rhetorical studies.

Purdue University Calumet, Graduate Studies Office, School of Liberal Arts and Social Sciences, Department of Communication and Creative Arts, Hammond, IN 46323-2094. Offers communication (MA). Part-time and evening/weekend programs available. *Degree requirements:* For master's, comprehensive exam, thesis or extended course work. *Entrance requirements:* For master's, minimum GPA of 3.0. Additional exam requirements/recommendations for international students: Required—TOEFL. Electronic applications accepted. *Faculty research:* International communication, gender studies, political rhetoric, media effects, media accountability.

Queen's University at Kingston, School of Graduate Studies, Faculty of Arts and Sciences, Department of Sociology, Kingston, ON K7L 3N6, Canada. Offers communication and Information technology (MA, PhD); feminist sociology (MA, PhD); socio-legal studies (MA, PhD); sociological theory (MA, PhD). Part-time programs available. *Degree requirements:* For master's, thesis; for doctorate, comprehensive exam, thesis/dissertation. *Entrance requirements:* For master's, honors bachelors degree in sociology; for doctorate, honors bachelors degree, masters degree in sociology. Additional exam requirements/recommendations for international students: Required—TOEFL. *Faculty research:* Social change and modernization, social control, deviance and criminology, surveillance.

Quincy University, Master of Arts in Communication Program, Quincy, IL 62301-2699. Offers MA. Part-time and evening/weekend programs available. Postbaccalaureate distance learning degree programs offered (no on-campus study). *Students:* 5 full-time (3 women), 8 part-time (4 women). *Degree requirements:* For master's, capstone project: thesis, internship, or creative project. *Entrance requirements:* For master's, official transcripts, two recommendations, minimum cumulative undergraduate GPA of 3.0, resume. Additional exam requirements/recommendations for international students: Required—TOEFL (minimum score 550 paper-based; 79 iBT). *Application deadline:* Applications are processed on a rolling basis. Application fee: $25. Electronic applications accepted. *Expenses: Tuition:* Full-time $9600; part-time $400 per semester hour. Tuition and fees vary according to course load, campus/location and program. *Financial support:* Applicants required to submit FAFSA. *Unit head:* Christine Tracy, Assistant Professor, Communication, 217-228-5432 Ext. 3105, E-mail: tracych@quincy.edu. *Application contact:* Office of Admissions, 217-228-5210, Fax: 217-228-5479, E-mail: admissions@quincy.edu.
Website: http://www.quincy.edu/academics/graduate-programs/communication

Quinnipiac University, School of Communications, Hamden, CT 06518-1940. Offers MS. Part-time and evening/weekend programs available. Postbaccalaureate distance learning degree programs offered (no on-campus study). *Faculty:* 14 full-time (8 women), 24 part-time/adjunct (7 women). *Students:* 32 full-time (21 women), 108 part-time (76 women); includes 29 minority (17 Black or African American, non-Hispanic/Latino; 4 Asian, non-Hispanic/Latino; 7 Hispanic/Latino; 1 Two or more races, non-Hispanic/Latino), 1 international. 61 applicants, 85% accepted, 37 enrolled. In 2014, 96 master's awarded. *Entrance requirements:* Additional exam requirements/recommendations for international students: Required—TOEFL (minimum score 575 paper-based; 90 iBT), IELTS (minimum score 6.5). *Application deadline:* For fall admission, 7/30 priority date for domestic students, 4/30 priority date for international students; for spring admission, 12/15 priority date for domestic students, 9/15 priority date for international students. Applications are processed on a rolling basis. Application fee: $45. Electronic applications accepted. *Expenses: Tuition:* Part-time $920 per credit. *Required fees:* $222 per semester. Tuition and fees vary according to course load and program. *Financial support:* In 2014–15, 6 students received support, including 1 fellowship with full tuition reimbursement available; career-related internships or fieldwork, Federal Work-Study, scholarships/grants, and unspecified assistantships also available. Support available to part-time students. Financial award application deadline: 6/1; financial award applicants required to submit FAFSA. *Application contact:* Office of Graduate Admissions, 203-582-8672, Fax: 203-582-3443, E-mail: graduate@quinnipiac.edu.
Website: http://www.quinnipiac.edu/gradprograms

Regent University, Graduate School, School of Communication and the Arts, Virginia Beach, VA 23464-9800. Offers acting (MFA); communication (MA, PhD), including political communication (MA), strategic communication (MA); directing for cinema/television (MFA); film and TV (MA), including producing, production, script writing; journalism (MA); producing for cinema/television (MFA); script and screenwriting (MFA); theatre (MA). Part-time programs available. Postbaccalaureate distance learning degree programs offered (minimal on-campus study). *Faculty:* 20 full-time (3 women), 26 part-time/adjunct (7 women). *Students:* 89 full-time (49 women), 211 part-time (125 women); includes 92 minority (69 Black or African American, non-Hispanic/Latino; 2 American Indian or Alaska Native, non-Hispanic/Latino; 2 Asian, non-Hispanic/Latino; 19 Hispanic/Latino), 10 international. Average age 35. 199 applicants, 53% accepted, 77 enrolled. In 2014, 48 master's, 8 doctorates awarded. *Degree requirements:* For master's, thesis or alternative; for doctorate, thesis/dissertation. *Entrance requirements:* For master's, GRE General Test or MAT, minimum undergraduate GPA of 3.0, writing sample, computer literacy survey, recommendation, resume, interview, audition (for MFA programs); for doctorate, GRE General Test, minimum graduate GPA of 3.0, writing sample, computer literacy survey, recommendation, interview, transcripts. Additional exam requirements/recommendations for international students: Required—TOEFL (minimum score 577 paper-based). *Application deadline:* For fall admission, 3/1 priority date for domestic students; for spring admission, 10/1 priority date for domestic students. Applications are processed on a rolling basis. Application fee: $50. Electronic applications accepted. *Expenses:* Expenses: Contact institution. *Financial support:* Fellowships with full and partial tuition reimbursements, career-related internships or fieldwork, scholarships/grants, tuition waivers (full and partial), and unspecified assistantships available. Support available to part-time students. Financial award application deadline: 9/1; financial award applicants required to submit FAFSA. *Faculty research:* Southern gospel music, education and entertainment, celebrities and the media, journalism and ethics, C.S. Lewis. *Unit head:* Dr. Mitch Land, Dean, 757-352-4916, Fax: 757-352-4291, E-mail: mland@regent.edu. *Application contact:* Matthew Chadwick, Director of Enrollment Support Services, 800-373-5504, Fax: 757-352-4381, E-mail: admissions@regent.edu.
Website: http://www.regent.edu/acad/schcom/

Rochester Institute of Technology, Graduate Enrollment Services, College of Imaging Arts and Sciences, School of Media Sciences, Rochester, NY 14623-5603. Offers print media (MS). Part-time programs available. *Students:* 11 full-time (5 women), 1 part-time, 11 international. Average age 24. 16 applicants, 56% accepted, 4 enrolled. In 2014, 6 master's awarded. *Degree requirements:* For master's, thesis. *Entrance requirements:* For master's, GRE and TOEFL, IELTS, or PTE for non-native English speakers, recommended minimum GPA of 3.0. Additional exam requirements/recommendations for international students: Required—PTE (minimum score 58), TOEFL (minimum score 550 paper-based; 79 iBT) or IELTS (minimum score 6.5). *Application deadline:* For fall admission, 2/15 priority date for domestic and international students; for spring admission, 12/15 priority date for domestic and international students. Applications are processed on a rolling basis. Application fee: $60. Electronic applications accepted. *Expenses:* Expenses: $1,673 per credit hour. *Financial support:* In 2014–15, 8 students received support. Research assistantships with partial tuition reimbursements available, teaching assistantships with partial tuition reimbursements available, career-related internships or fieldwork, Federal Work-Study, institutionally sponsored loans, scholarships/grants, and unspecified assistantships available. Support available to part-time students. Financial award application deadline: 8/30; financial award applicants required to submit FAFSA. *Faculty research:* Content management, publishing workflows, typography and layout, business trends, color management, electronic publishing, multi-media, digital printing/publishing and applications of printing. *Unit head:* Dr. Gregory D'Amico, Graduate Program Director, 585-475-5992, E-mail: mxcppr@rit.edu. *Application contact:* Diane Ellison, Associate Vice President, Graduate Enrollment Services, 585-475-2229, Fax: 585-475-7164, E-mail: gradinfo@rit.edu.
Website: http://cias.rit.edu/schools/media-sciences

Rochester Institute of Technology, Graduate Enrollment Services, College of Liberal Arts, School of Communication, Rochester, NY 14623-5604. Offers communication and digital media (Advanced Certificate); communication and media technologies (MS). Part-time programs available. Postbaccalaureate distance learning degree programs offered (no on-campus study). *Students:* 12 full-time (8 women), 17 part-time (all women);

includes 1 minority (Hispanic/Latino), 23 international. Average age 26. 32 applicants, 59% accepted, 12 enrolled. In 2014, 16 master's awarded. *Degree requirements:* For master's, thesis or alternative, thesis or project. *Entrance requirements:* For master's, TOEFL, IELTS, or PTE for non-native English speakers, recommended minimum GPA of 3.0, writing sample. Additional exam requirements/recommendations for international students: Required—PTE (minimum score 58), TOEFL (minimum score 550 paper-based; 79 iBT) or IELTS (minimum score 6.5). *Application deadline:* For fall admission, 2/15 priority date for domestic and international students; for winter admission, 11/1 for domestic and international students; for spring admission, 12/15 priority date for domestic and international students. Applications are processed on a rolling basis. Application fee: $60. Electronic applications accepted. *Expenses:* Expenses: $1,673 per credit hour. *Financial support:* In 2014–15, 14 students received support. Research assistantships with partial tuition reimbursements available, teaching assistantships with partial tuition reimbursements available, career-related internships or fieldwork, Federal Work-Study, institutionally sponsored loans, scholarships/grants, and unspecified assistantships available. Support available to part-time students. Financial award applicants required to submit FAFSA. *Faculty research:* The analysis of communication problems, the development of solutions, and the creation of messages as a result of their combined training in the social sciences, humanities, and applied technologies. *Unit head:* Dr. Patrick Scanlon, Director, 585-475-2449, Fax: 585-475-7732, E-mail: pmsgsl@rit.edu. *Application contact:* Diane Ellison, Associate Vice President, Graduate Enrollment Services, 585-475-2229, Fax: 585-475-7164, E-mail: gradinfo@rit.edu. Website: http://www.rit.edu/cla/communication/

Roosevelt University, Graduate Division, College of Arts and Sciences, Department of Communication, Chicago, IL 60605. Offers integrated marketing communications (MSIMC); journalism (MSJ). Part-time and evening/weekend programs available.

Rutgers, The State University of New Jersey, New Brunswick, School of Communication, Information and Library Studies, Program in Communication, Library and Information Science and Media Studies, Piscataway, NJ 08854-8097. Offers PhD. Part-time programs available. *Degree requirements:* For doctorate, comprehensive exam, thesis/dissertation, qualifying exams. *Entrance requirements:* For doctorate, GRE General Test, proficiency in statistics. Additional exam requirements/recommendations for international students: Required—TOEFL (minimum score 600 paper-based). Electronic applications accepted. *Faculty research:* Information science, media studies.

Sacred Heart University, Graduate Programs, College of Arts and Sciences, Department of Communications, Fairfield, CT 06825-1000. Offers corporate communication and public relations (MA Comm); digital/multimedia journalism (MA Comm); digital/multimedia production (MA Comm). Part-time and evening/weekend programs available. *Faculty:* 10 full-time (2 women). *Students:* 62 full-time (31 women), 27 part-time (14 women); includes 25 minority (16 Black or African American, non-Hispanic/Latino; 8 Hispanic/Latino; 1 Native Hawaiian or other Pacific Islander, non-Hispanic/Latino), 4 international. Average age 26. 117 applicants, 90% accepted, 69 enrolled. In 2014, 40 master's awarded. *Degree requirements:* For master's, thesis or alternative. *Entrance requirements:* For master's, bachelor's degree. Additional exam requirements/recommendations for international students: Required—PTE; Recommended—TOEFL (minimum score 570 paper-based; 80 iBT), IELTS (minimum score 6.5). *Application deadline:* Applications are processed on a rolling basis. Application fee: $60. Electronic applications accepted. *Expenses: Tuition:* Full-time $24,559; part-time $649 per credit. *Financial support:* Unspecified assistantships available. Financial award applicants required to submit FAFSA. *Unit head:* Dr. Andrew Miller, Chair, 203-396-8087, E-mail: millera@sacredheart.edu. *Application contact:* Kathy Dilks, Executive Director of Graduate Admissions, 203-365-7619, Fax: 203-365-4732, E-mail: gradustudies@sacredheart.edu.
Website: http://www.sacredheart.edu/academics/collegeofartssciences/academicdepartments/communicationmediastudies/

Saginaw Valley State University, College of Arts and Behavioral Sciences, Program in Communication and Digital Media Design, University Center, MI 48710. Offers MA. Part-time and evening/weekend programs available. *Students:* 13 full-time (9 women), 11 part-time (5 women); includes 3 minority (all Black or African American, non-Hispanic/Latino), 9 international. Average age 31. 15 applicants, 80% accepted, 6 enrolled. In 2014, 6 master's awarded. *Degree requirements:* For master's, thesis. *Entrance requirements:* For master's, minimum GPA of 3.0. Additional exam requirements/recommendations for international students: Required—TOEFL (minimum score 540 paper-based). *Application deadline:* For fall admission, 7/15 for international students; for winter admission, 11/15 for international students; for spring admission, 4/15 for international students. Applications are processed on a rolling basis. Application fee: $30 ($90 for international students). Electronic applications accepted. *Expenses:* Tuition, state resident: full-time $8957; part-time $497.60 per credit hour. Tuition, nonresident: full-time $17,081; part-time $948.95 per credit hour. *Required fees:* $263; $14.60 per credit hour. Tuition and fees vary according to degree level. *Financial support:* Federal Work-Study and scholarships/grants available. Support available to part-time students. Financial award application deadline: 4/1; financial award applicants required to submit FAFSA. *Unit head:* Dr. Robert Drew, Professor of Communication, 989-964-7495, E-mail: rdrew@svsu.edu. *Application contact:* Jenna Briggs, Director, Graduate and International Admissions, 989-964-6096, Fax: 989-964-2788, E-mail: gradadm@svsu.edu.
Website: http://www.svsu.edu/communicationdigitalmedia/

Saint Louis University, Graduate Education, College of Arts and Sciences and Graduate Education, Department of Communication, St. Louis, MO 63103-2097. Offers MA, MA-R. Part-time programs available. *Degree requirements:* For master's, thesis (for some programs), comprehensive oral and written exams. *Entrance requirements:* For master's, GRE General Test, letters of recommendation, resume, interview. Additional exam requirements/recommendations for international students: Required—TOEFL (minimum score 525 paper-based). Electronic applications accepted. *Faculty research:* Media studies, organizational communication, dialogue, intercultural communication, qualitative research methods.

St. Mary's University, Graduate School, Department of English and Communication Studies, Program in Communication Studies, San Antonio, TX 78228-8507. Offers communication studies (MA); public communication, public policy and public leadership (Certificate); JD/MA. Part-time programs available. Postbaccalaureate distance learning degree programs offered (minimal on-campus study). *Faculty:* 7 full-time (3 women), 3 part-time/adjunct (2 women). *Students:* 4 full-time (all women), 13 part-time (9 women); includes 12 minority (2 Black or African American, non-Hispanic/Latino; 9 Hispanic/Latino; 1 Native Hawaiian or other Pacific Islander, non-Hispanic/Latino), 2 international. Average age 27. 17 applicants, 29% accepted, 4 enrolled. In 2014, 1 master's awarded. *Degree requirements:* For master's, comprehensive exam. *Entrance requirements:* For master's, GRE General Test, MAT, GPA X Average GRE Score [(Verbal + Quantitative) / Analytical writing minimum of 4.0 = 1350; Up to 10 percent of students in the program may be accepted with less than the minimum index if they demonstrate to the Graduate Communication Committee that they can perform at the graduate level. Additional exam requirements/recommendations for international students: Required—TOEFL (minimum score 550 paper-based; 80 iBT). *Application deadline:* For fall admission, 8/1 priority date for domestic students. Applications are processed on a rolling basis. Application

fee: $0. Electronic applications accepted. *Expenses: Tuition:* Full-time $15,070; part-time $800 per credit hour. *Required fees:* $156 per semester. *Financial support:* In 2014–15, 1 research assistantship (averaging $7,000 per year) was awarded; career-related internships or fieldwork, Federal Work-Study, institutionally sponsored loans, scholarships/grants, and health care benefits also available. Financial award application deadline: 3/31; financial award applicants required to submit FAFSA. *Faculty research:* Media and power; rise of the political right; income inequality and social justice; development communication; interpersonal and rhetorical communication; social movements; gender, critical theory; cultural and postcolonial theory. *Unit head:* Dr. Kathleen Maloney, Associate Professor of English and Communication Studies, 210-431-2005, E-mail: kmaloney@stmarytx.edu.
Website: https://www.stmarytx.edu/academics/graduate/masters/communication/

St. Thomas University, School of Leadership Studies, Miami Gardens, FL 33054-6459. Offers MA, MPS, MS, Ed D, Certificate. Part-time and evening/weekend programs available. *Entrance requirements:* Additional exam requirements/recommendations for international students: Required—TOEFL (minimum score 550 paper-based; 79 iBT).

Sam Houston State University, College of Humanities and Social Sciences, Department of Communication Studies, Huntsville, TX 77341. Offers MA. Part-time and evening/weekend programs available. Postbaccalaureate distance learning degree programs offered (no on-campus study). *Faculty:* 6 full-time (2 women). *Students:* 7 full-time (5 women), 3 part-time (1 woman); includes 2 minority (1 Black or African American, non-Hispanic/Latino; 1 Hispanic/Latino). Average age 34. 13 applicants, 77% accepted, 7 enrolled. In 2014, 1 master's awarded. *Degree requirements:* For master's, comprehensive exam, thesis optional. *Entrance requirements:* For master's, GRE General Test, three letters of recommendation. Additional exam requirements/recommendations for international students: Required—TOEFL (minimum score 550 paper-based; 79 iBT), IELTS (minimum score 6.5). *Application deadline:* For fall admission, 8/1 for domestic students, 6/25 for international students; for spring admission, 12/1 for domestic students, 11/12 for international students; for summer admission, 5/15 for domestic students, 4/9 for international students. Applications are processed on a rolling basis. Application fee: $45 ($75 for international students). Electronic applications accepted. *Expenses:* Tuition, state resident: full-time $2286; part-time $254 per credit hour. Tuition, nonresident: full-time $5544; part-time $616 per credit hour. *Required fees:* $440 per semester. Tuition and fees vary according to course load and campus/location. *Financial support:* In 2014–15, 3 research assistantships (averaging $7,685 per year) were awarded; career-related internships or fieldwork, Federal Work-Study, scholarships/grants, tuition waivers, and unspecified assistantships also available. Support available to part-time students. Financial award application deadline: 3/15; financial award applicants required to submit FAFSA. *Unit head:* Dr. Terry Thibodeaux, Chair, 936-294-1356, Fax: 936-294-1336, E-mail: scm_tmt@shsu.edu. *Application contact:* Dr. Frances Brandau, Graduate Advisor/Associate Professor, 936-294-4668, Fax: 936-294-1336, E-mail: scm_feb@shsu.edu.
Website: http://www.shsu.edu/academics/communication-studies/

San Diego State University, Graduate and Research Affairs, College of Professional Studies and Fine Arts, School of Communication, San Diego, CA 92182. Offers advertising and public relations (MA); critical-cultural studies (MA); interaction studies (MA); intercultural and international studies (MA); new media studies (MA); news and information studies (MA); telecommunications and media management (MA). *Degree requirements:* For master's, thesis. *Entrance requirements:* For master's, GRE General Test, 3 letters of recommendation. Additional exam requirements/recommendations for international students: Required—TOEFL. Electronic applications accepted.

San Jose State University, Graduate Studies and Research, College of Social Sciences, Department of Communication Studies, San Jose, CA 95192-0001. Offers MA. *Degree requirements:* For master's, comprehensive exam, thesis or alternative, project. *Entrance requirements:* For master's, minimum GPA of 3.0. Electronic applications accepted.

Seton Hall University, College of Arts and Sciences, Department of Communication, South Orange, NJ 07079-2697. Offers corporate and professional communication (MA); museum professions (MA), including exhibition development, museum education, museum management, museum registration; strategic communication (MA); strategic communication and leadership (MA). Part-time and evening/weekend programs available. Postbaccalaureate distance learning degree programs offered (minimal on-campus study). *Faculty:* 3 full-time (1 woman), 15 part-time/adjunct (6 women). *Students:* 31 full-time (21 women), 105 part-time (69 women); includes 47 minority (34 Black or African American, non-Hispanic/Latino; 3 Asian, non-Hispanic/Latino; 10 Hispanic/Latino), 6 international. Average age 32. 114 applicants, 74% accepted, 40 enrolled. In 2014, 65 master's awarded. *Degree requirements:* For master's, thesis. *Entrance requirements:* Additional exam requirements/recommendations for international students: Required—TOEFL. *Application deadline:* For fall admission, 7/1 priority date for domestic and international students; for spring admission, 11/1 priority date for domestic and international students. Applications are processed on a rolling basis. Application fee: $75. Electronic applications accepted. *Financial support:* Research assistantships, career-related internships or fieldwork, Federal Work-Study, and unspecified assistantships available. Financial award applicants required to submit FAFSA. *Faculty research:* Managerial communication, communication consulting, communication and development. *Unit head:* Prof. Deirdre Yates, Chair, 973-761-9474, Fax: 973-761-9234, E-mail: deirdre.yates@shu.edu. *Application contact:* Dr. Richard Dool, Director of Graduate Studies, 973-761-9490, Fax: 973-761-9234, E-mail: rrichard.dool@shu.edu.
Website: http://www.shu.edu/academics/artsci/communication-arts/

Shippensburg University of Pennsylvania, School of Graduate Studies, College of Arts and Sciences, Department of Communication/Journalism, Shippensburg, PA 17257-2299. Offers communication studies (MS). Part-time and evening/weekend programs available. *Faculty:* 5 full-time (2 women), 2 part-time/adjunct (1 woman). *Students:* 10 full-time (4 women), 11 part-time (9 women), 2 international. Average age 28. 23 applicants, 65% accepted, 10 enrolled. In 2014, 9 master's awarded. *Degree requirements:* For master's, 6-credit thesis or 3-credit professional project, candidacy. *Entrance requirements:* For master's, GRE or MAT (if GPA less than 2.75), 3 professional references, resume, essay, 500-word statement of purpose. Additional exam requirements/recommendations for international students: Required—TOEFL (minimum score 580 paper-based); Recommended—IELTS (minimum score 6). *Application deadline:* For fall admission, 4/30 for international students; for spring admission, 9/30 for international students. Applications are processed on a rolling basis. Application fee: $45. Electronic applications accepted. *Expenses:* Expenses: Contact institution. *Financial support:* In 2014–15, 7 research assistantships with full tuition reimbursements (averaging $5,000 per year) were awarded; career-related internships or fieldwork, scholarships/grants, unspecified assistantships, and resident hall director and student payroll positions also available. Support available to part-time students. Financial award application deadline: 3/1; financial award applicants required to submit FAFSA. *Unit head:* Dr. Kimberly D. Garris, Program Coordinator, 717-477-1521, Fax: 717-477-4013, E-mail: kdgarr@ship.edu. *Application contact:* Jeremy R. Goshorn, Assistant Dean of Graduate Admissions, 717-477-1231, Fax: 717-477-4016, E-mail: jrgoshorn@ship.edu. Website: http://www.ship.edu/communication-journalism/

Shippensburg University of Pennsylvania, School of Graduate Studies, College of Arts and Sciences, Department of Sociology and Anthropology, Shippensburg, PA 17257-2299. Offers organizational development and leadership (MS), including business, communications, environmental management, higher education structure and policy, historical administration, individual and organizational development, management information systems, public organizations, social structures and organizations. Part-time and evening/weekend programs available. *Faculty:* 4 full-time (all women). *Students:* 11 full-time (4 women), 42 part-time (26 women); includes 11 minority (7 Black or African American, non-Hispanic/Latino; 1 Asian, non-Hispanic/Latino; 2 Hispanic/Latino; 1 Two or more races, non-Hispanic/Latino), 2 international. Average age 30. 53 applicants, 60% accepted, 17 enrolled. In 2014, 21 master's awarded. *Degree requirements:* For master's, capstone experience including internship. *Entrance requirements:* For master's, interview (if GPA less than 2.75), resume, personal goals statement. Additional exam requirements/recommendations for international students: Required—TOEFL (minimum score 580 paper-based); Recommended—IELTS (minimum score 6). *Application deadline:* For fall admission, 4/30 for international students; for spring admission, 9/30 for international students. Applications are processed on a rolling basis. Application fee: $45. Electronic applications accepted. *Expenses: Tuition, area resident:* Part-time $454 per credit. Tuition, state resident: part-time $454 per credit. Tuition, nonresident: part-time $681 per credit. *Required fees:* $133 per credit. *Financial support:* In 2014–15, 15 research assistantships with full tuition reimbursements (averaging $5,000 per year) were awarded; career-related internships or fieldwork, scholarships/grants, unspecified assistantships, and resident hall director and student payroll positions also available. Support available to part-time students. Financial award applicants required to submit FAFSA. *Unit head:* Dr. Barbara Denison, Program Coordinator, 717-477-1735, Fax: 717-477-4011, E-mail: bjdeni@ship.edu. *Application contact:* Jeremy R. Goshorn, Assistant Dean of Graduate Admissions, 717-477-1231, Fax: 717-477-4016, E-mail: jrgoshorn@ship.edu.
Website: http://www.ship.edu/odl/

Simmons College, School of Management, Boston, MA 02115. Offers business administration (MBA); management (MS), including communications management, non-profit management; marketing (MBA); MBA/MSW; MS/MA. *Accreditation:* AACSB. Part-time and evening/weekend programs available. *Faculty:* 23 full-time (17 women), 13 part-time/adjunct (11 women). *Students:* 35 full-time (all women), 209 part-time (190 women); includes 62 minority (32 Black or African American, non-Hispanic/Latino; 1 American Indian or Alaska Native, non-Hispanic/Latino; 13 Asian, non-Hispanic/Latino; 11 Hispanic/Latino; 1 Native Hawaiian or other Pacific Islander, non-Hispanic/Latino; 4 Two or more races, non-Hispanic/Latino), 12 international. Average age 32. 223 applicants, 88% accepted, 80 enrolled. In 2014, 133 master's awarded. *Entrance requirements:* For master's, GMAT or GRE. Additional exam requirements/recommendations for international students: Required—TOEFL. *Application deadline:* Applications are processed on a rolling basis. Application fee: $75. Electronic applications accepted. *Expenses: Tuition:* Full-time $19,500; part-time $975 per credit. *Financial support:* Scholarships/grants and unspecified assistantships available. Financial award applicants required to submit FAFSA. *Faculty research:* Gender and organizations, leadership, health care management. *Unit head:* Cathy Minehan, Dean, 617-521-2846. *Application contact:* Melissa Terrio, Director of Graduate Admissions, 617-521-3840, Fax: 617-521-3880, E-mail: somadm@simmons.edu.
Website: http://www.simmons.edu/som

Simon Fraser University, Office of Graduate Studies, School of Communication, Burnaby, BC V5A 1S6, Canada. Offers MA, PhD, MA/MA. MA/MA program in global communication offered jointly with the Communication University of China. *Degree requirements:* For master's, thesis or alternative, annual formal review; for doctorate, comprehensive exam, thesis/dissertation, annual formal review. *Entrance requirements:* For master's, minimum GPA of 3.0 (on scale of 4.33), or 3.33 based on last 60 credits of undergraduate courses; for doctorate, minimum GPA of 3.5 (on scale of 4.33). Additional exam requirements/recommendations for international students: Recommended—TOEFL (minimum score 580 paper-based; 93 iBT), IELTS (minimum score 7), TWE (minimum score 5). Electronic applications accepted. *Faculty research:* Cultural policy and politics; globalization, social change, and social justice; history and theory of communication; media and cultural studies; technology and society.

South Dakota State University, Graduate School, College of Arts and Science, Department of Journalism and Mass Communication, Brookings, SD 57007. Offers communication studies and journalism (MS). Part-time and evening/weekend programs available. *Degree requirements:* For master's, thesis, oral exam. *Entrance requirements:* Additional exam requirements/recommendations for international students: Required—TOEFL (minimum score 550 paper-based; 79 iBT). *Faculty research:* Mass communication applications.

Southeastern Louisiana University, College of Arts, Humanities and Social Sciences, Department of Languages and Communication, Hammond, LA 70402. Offers organizational communication (MA). Part-time and evening/weekend programs available. *Faculty:* 6 full-time (4 women). *Students:* 12 full-time (8 women), 20 part-time (15 women); includes 12 minority (7 Black or African American, non-Hispanic/Latino; 4 Hispanic/Latino; 1 Two or more races, non-Hispanic/Latino), 1 international. Average age 27. In 2014, 5 master's awarded. *Degree requirements:* For master's, comprehensive exam, thesis optional. *Entrance requirements:* For master's, GRE General Test (minimum score of 800), bachelor's degree in communication or related field, minimum GPA of 3.0. Additional exam requirements/recommendations for international students: Required—TOEFL (minimum score 500 paper-based; 61 iBT). *Application deadline:* For fall admission, 7/15 priority date for domestic students, 6/1 priority date for international students; for spring admission, 12/1 priority date for domestic students, 10/1 priority date for international students. Applications are processed on a rolling basis. Application fee: $20 ($30 for international students). Electronic applications accepted. *Financial support:* In 2014–15, 14 research assistantships (averaging $8,292 per year) were awarded; Federal Work-Study, institutionally sponsored loans, scholarships/grants, traineeships, and unspecified assistantships also available. Support available to part-time students. Financial award application deadline: 5/1; financial award applicants required to submit FAFSA. *Faculty research:* Intercultural studies, communication apprehension, small group relationships, minority health studies, romantic relations. *Total annual research expenditures:* $4,180. *Unit head:* Dr. Lucia Guzzi Harrison, Department Head, 985-549-2105, Fax: 985-549-5014, E-mail: lharrison@selu.edu. *Application contact:* Sandra Meyers, Graduate Admissions Analyst, 985-549-5620, Fax: 985-549-5632, E-mail: admissions@selu.edu.
Website: http://www.selu.edu/acad_research/depts/lang_comm/

Southern Illinois University Carbondale, Graduate School, College of Mass Communication and Media Arts, Carbondale, IL 62901-4701. Offers MA, MFA, PhD, MBA/MA. Part-time programs available. *Faculty:* 35 full-time (9 women), 2 part-time/adjunct (0 women). *Students:* 66 full-time (29 women), 33 part-time (18 women); includes 11 minority (8 Black or African American, non-Hispanic/Latino; 2 Asian, non-Hispanic/Latino; 1 Hispanic/Latino), 32 international. Average age 28. 69 applicants, 48% accepted, 19 enrolled. In 2014, 22 master's, 10 doctorates awarded. *Degree requirements:* For doctorate, thesis/dissertation. *Entrance requirements:* For doctorate,

GRE General Test, minimum GPA of 3.25. Additional exam requirements/recommendations for international students: Required—TOEFL. *Application deadline:* Applications are processed on a rolling basis. Application fee: $50. *Expenses:* Tuition, state resident: full-time $10,176; part-time $1153 per credit. Tuition, nonresident: full-time $20,814; part-time $1744 per credit. *Required fees:* $7092; $394 per credit. $2364 per semester. *Financial support:* In 2014–15, 75 students received support. Fellowships, research assistantships, teaching assistantships, career-related internships or fieldwork, Federal Work-Study, institutionally sponsored loans, and tuition waivers (full) available. Support available to part-time students. *Unit head:* Dr. Dafna Lemish, Interim Dean, 618-453-7708, E-mail: dafnalemish@siu.edu. *Application contact:* Georgia Norman, Administrative Aide, 618-453-3785, E-mail: mcmagrad@siu.edu.

Southern Polytechnic State University, School of Arts and Sciences, Department of English, Technical Communication, and Media Arts, Marietta, GA 30060-2896. Offers communications management (Postbaccalaureate Certificate); content development (Postbaccalaureate Certificate); information and instructional design (MSIID); information design and communication (MS); instructional design (Postbaccalaureate Certificate); technical communication (Graduate Certificate); visual communication and graphics (Postbaccalaureate Certificate). Part-time and evening/weekend programs available. Postbaccalaureate distance learning degree programs offered (no on-campus study). *Degree requirements:* For master's, thesis optional; for other advanced degree, thesis optional, 18 hours completed through thesis option (6 hours), internship option (6 hours) or advanced coursework option (6 hours). *Entrance requirements:* For master's, GRE, statement of purpose, writing sample, timed essay; for other advanced degree, writing sample, professional recommendations. Additional exam requirements/recommendations for international students: Required—TOEFL (minimum score 550 paper-based; 79 iBT), IELTS (minimum score 6.5). Electronic applications accepted. *Faculty research:* Usability, user-centered design, instructional design, information architecture, information design, content strategy.

Southern Utah University, Program in Communication, Cedar City, UT 84720-2498. Offers MA. Part-time and evening/weekend programs available. Postbaccalaureate distance learning degree programs offered. *Students:* 17 full-time (9 women), 36 part-time (23 women); includes 6 minority (2 Black or African American, non-Hispanic/Latino; 1 American Indian or Alaska Native, non-Hispanic/Latino; 2 Hispanic/Latino; 1 Native Hawaiian or other Pacific Islander, non-Hispanic/Latino). Average age 31. 22 applicants, 77% accepted, 14 enrolled. In 2014, 19 master's awarded. *Entrance requirements:* For master's, GRE. Additional exam requirements/recommendations for international students: Required—TOEFL (minimum score 550 paper-based, 79 iBT) or IELTS (minimum score 6). *Application deadline:* For fall admission, 6/15 for domestic and international students; for spring admission, 10/15 for domestic and international students. Applications are processed on a rolling basis. Application fee: $60 ($65 for international students). Electronic applications accepted. *Expenses:* Expenses: Contact institution. *Financial support:* Teaching assistantships with tuition reimbursements and unspecified assistantships available. Financial award application deadline: 3/15. *Unit head:* Dr. Arthur Challis, Department Chair, 435-586-7994, Fax: 435-865-8352, E-mail: challis@suu.edu. *Application contact:* Dr. Matthew Barton, Graduate Coordinator, 435-586-7970, Fax: 435-865-8352, E-mail: bartonm@suu.edu.
Website: http://www.suu.edu/hss/comm/masters/

Spring Arbor University, School of Arts and Sciences, Spring Arbor, MI 49283-9799. Offers communication (MA); spiritual formation and leadership (MA). Part-time programs available. Postbaccalaureate distance learning degree programs offered (no on-campus study). *Degree requirements:* For master's, thesis (for some programs). *Entrance requirements:* For master's, GRE (minimum score of 40th percentile and taken within last 5 years), bachelor's degree from regionally-accredited college or university, minimum GPA of 3.0 for at least the last two years of the bachelor's degree, at least two recommendations from professional/academic individuals. Additional exam requirements/recommendations for international students: Required—TOEFL (minimum score 600 paper-based). *Expenses:* Contact institution.

Stanford University, School of Humanities and Sciences, Department of Communication, Stanford, CA 94305-9991. Offers communication theory and research (PhD); journalism (MA); media studies (MA). *Faculty:* 13 full-time (4 women), 1 part-time/adjunct (0 women). *Students:* 66 full-time (39 women). Average age 29. 152 applicants, 25% accepted, 31 enrolled. In 2014, 25 master's, 3 doctorates awarded. Terminal master's awarded for partial completion of doctoral program. *Degree requirements:* For master's, thesis, project; for doctorate, thesis/dissertation, qualifying examination, area examination, 2 projects. *Entrance requirements:* For master's and doctorate, GRE General Test. Additional exam requirements/recommendations for international students: Required—TOEFL (minimum score 650 paper-based; 115 iBT). *Application deadline:* For fall admission, 12/2 for domestic students, 12/3 for international students. Application fee: $125. Electronic applications accepted. *Expenses: Tuition:* Full-time $44,184; part-time $982 per credit hour. *Required fees:* $191. *Financial support:* Fellowships, research assistantships, and teaching assistantships available. *Unit head:* James T. Hamilton, Chair, 650-723-5448, E-mail: jayth@stanford.edu. *Application contact:* Katrin Wheeler, Student Services Manager, 650-724-8920, Fax: 650-725-2472, E-mail: comm-studentservices@stanford.edu.
Website: http://communication.stanford.edu/

State University of New York College at Potsdam, School of Arts and Sciences, Department of English and Communication, Potsdam, NY 13676. Offers MA. Part-time and evening/weekend programs available. *Degree requirements:* For master's, one foreign language, thesis or alternative. *Entrance requirements:* For master's, minimum GPA of 3.0 in last 60 hours of undergraduate course work. Additional exam requirements/recommendations for international students: Required—TOEFL (minimum score 550 paper-based; 80 iBT), IELTS (minimum score 6). Electronic applications accepted.

Stephen F. Austin State University, Graduate School, College of Applied Arts and Science, Department of Communication, Nacogdoches, TX 75962. Offers communication (MA); mass communication (MA). Part-time programs available. *Degree requirements:* For master's, comprehensive exam, thesis optional. *Entrance requirements:* For master's, GRE General Test. Additional exam requirements/recommendations for international students: Required—TOEFL (minimum score 550 paper-based).

Stevens Institute of Technology, Graduate School, Charles V. Schaefer Jr. School of Engineering, Department of Electrical and Computer Engineering, Program in Electrical Engineering, Hoboken, NJ 07030. Offers computer architecture and digital systems (M Eng); electrical engineering (PhD); microelectronics and photonics science and technology (M Eng); signal processing for communications (M Eng); telecommunications systems engineering (M Eng); wireless communications (M Eng, Certificate). *Degree requirements:* For master's, thesis optional; for doctorate, variable foreign language requirement, thesis/dissertation. *Entrance requirements:* For master's, doctorate, and Certificate, GRE. Additional exam requirements/recommendations for international students: Required—TOEFL. Electronic applications accepted.

Communication—General

Stevenson University, Program in Communication Studies, Stevenson, MD 21153. Offers MS. *Degree requirements:* For master's, project or thesis. *Entrance requirements:* For master's, baccalaureate degree, official transcripts, minimum cumulative GPA of 3.0, writing sample. *Expenses:* Expenses: $670 per credit. *Application contact:* Angela Reynolds, Director, Recruitment and Admissions, 443-352-4414, Fax: 443-352-4440, E-mail: amreynolds@stevenson.edu.
Website: http://www.stevenson.edu/graduate-professional-studies/graduate-programs/communication-studies/index.html

Suffolk University, College of Arts and Sciences, Department of Communication and Journalism, Boston, MA 02108-2770. Offers communication studies (MAC); integrated marketing communication (MAC); public relations and advertising (MAC). Part-time and evening/weekend programs available. *Faculty:* 7 full-time (5 women). *Students:* 27 full-time (22 women), 16 part-time (12 women); includes 5 minority (2 Black or African American, non-Hispanic/Latino; 1 Asian, non-Hispanic/Latino; 2 Hispanic/Latino), 19 international. Average age 25. 88 applicants, 56% accepted, 6 enrolled. In 2014, 46 master's awarded. *Degree requirements:* For master's, thesis optional. *Entrance requirements:* For master's, GRE General Test, MAT, or GMAT, 2 letters of recommendation, resume. Additional exam requirements/recommendations for international students: Required—TOEFL (minimum score 550 paper-based; 80 iBT). *Application deadline:* For fall admission, 6/15 priority date for domestic students, 6/15 for international students; for spring admission, 11/1 priority date for domestic students, 11/1 for international students. Applications are processed on a rolling basis. Application fee: $50. Electronic applications accepted. *Expenses:* Expenses: Contact institution. *Financial support:* In 2014–15, 36 students received support, including 36 fellowships (averaging $8,788 per year); career-related internships or fieldwork, Federal Work-Study, and institutionally sponsored loans also available. Support available to part-time students. Financial award application deadline: 4/1; financial award applicants required to submit FAFSA. *Faculty research:* Branding law and management, health care communication, gender roles and violence in video games, new media, political communication. *Unit head:* Gloria Boone, Chair, 617-573-8501, Fax: 617-742-6982, E-mail: gboone@suffolk.edu. *Application contact:* Cory Meyers, Director of Graduate Admissions, 617-573-8302, Fax: 617-305-1733, E-mail: grad.admission@suffolk.edu.
Website: http://www.suffolk.edu/college/departments/10483.php

Summit University, Baptist Bible Seminary, Clarks Summit, PA 18411-1297. Offers Biblical apologetics (MA); church education (M Div, M Min); church planting (M Div, M Min); global ministry (M Div, M Min); leadership in communication (D Min); leadership in counseling and spiritual development (D Min); leadership in global ministry (D Min); leadership in pastoral ministry (D Min); leadership in theological studies (D Min); military chaplaincy (M Div); ministry (PhD); organizational leadership (M Min); outreach pastor (M Div, M Min); pastoral counseling (M Div, M Min); pastoral leadership (M Div, M Min); theology (Th M); worship ministries leadership (M Div, M Min); youth pastor (M Div, M Min). Part-time and evening/weekend programs available. Postbaccalaureate distance learning degree programs offered (minimal on-campus study). Terminal master's awarded for partial completion of doctoral program. *Degree requirements:* For master's, 2 foreign languages, thesis, oral exam (for M Div); for doctorate, 2 foreign languages, comprehensive exam (for some programs), thesis/dissertation, oral exam. *Entrance requirements:* For doctorate, Greek and Hebrew entrance exams (for PhD). Electronic applications accepted.

Summit University, Graduate Studies, Clarks Summit, PA 18411-1297. Offers Bible (MA); counseling (MA, MS); curriculum and instruction (M Ed); educational administration (M Ed); intercultural studies (MA); literature (MA); missions (MA); organizational leadership (MA); reading specialist (M Ed); secondary English/communications (M Ed); social entrepreneurship (MA); worldview studies (MA). MA in missions program available only for Association of Baptists for World Evangelism missionary personnel. Part-time and evening/weekend programs available. Postbaccalaureate distance learning degree programs offered (no on-campus study). *Entrance requirements:* Additional exam requirements/recommendations for international students: Required—TOEFL (minimum score 500 paper-based).

Syracuse University, College of Visual and Performing Arts, Program in Communication and Rhetorical Studies, Syracuse, NY 13244. Offers MA. Part-time programs available. *Students:* 13 full-time (8 women), 7 part-time (4 women); includes 5 minority (2 Black or African American, non-Hispanic/Latino; 3 Hispanic/Latino), 1 international. Average age 26. 44 applicants, 50% accepted, 8 enrolled. In 2014, 8 master's awarded. *Degree requirements:* For master's, comprehensive exam (for some programs), thesis (for some programs). *Entrance requirements:* For master's, GRE General Test, writing sample. Additional exam requirements/recommendations for international students: Required—TOEFL (minimum score 100 iBT). *Application deadline:* For fall admission, 2/1 priority date for domestic and international students. Application fee: $75. Electronic applications accepted. *Expenses: Tuition:* Part-time $1341 per credit. *Financial support:* In 2014–15, 9 students received support. Fellowships with full tuition reimbursements available, teaching assistantships with full and partial tuition reimbursements available, and tuition waivers available. Financial award application deadline: 1/1; financial award applicants required to submit FAFSA. *Unit head:* Dr. Charles Morris, Chair, 315-443-2308, E-mail: admissg@syr.edu. *Application contact:* Joseph Morley, Information Contact, 315-443-7175, E-mail: admissg@syr.edu.
Website: http://vpa.syr.edu/

Syracuse University, S. I. Newhouse School of Public Communications, Syracuse, NY 13244. Offers MA, MS, PhD, JD/MA, JD/MS, MS/MA. *Accreditation:* ACEJMC (one or more programs are accredited). Postbaccalaureate distance learning degree programs offered (minimal on-campus study). *Faculty:* 70 full-time (26 women), 42 part-time/adjunct (20 women). *Students:* 261 full-time (180 women), 73 part-time (48 women); includes 79 minority (44 Black or African American, non-Hispanic/Latino; 8 Asian, non-Hispanic/Latino; 22 Hispanic/Latino; 5 Two or more races, non-Hispanic/Latino), 102 international. Average age 28. 723 applicants, 68% accepted, 226 enrolled. In 2014, 275 master's, 4 doctorates awarded. *Degree requirements:* For master's, comprehensive exam (for some programs); for doctorate, thesis/dissertation, qualifying exams. *Entrance requirements:* For master's and doctorate, GRE General Test. Additional exam requirements/recommendations for international students: Required—TOEFL (minimum score 100 iBT), IELTS (minimum score 7). *Application deadline:* For fall admission, 1/15 priority date for domestic and international students; for summer admission, 1/15 priority date for domestic and international students. Application fee: $45. Electronic applications accepted. *Expenses: Tuition:* Part-time $1341 per credit. *Financial support:* Fellowships with full tuition reimbursements, research assistantships with partial tuition reimbursements, scholarships/grants, and instructional associate positions with partial tuition reimbursements available. Financial award application deadline: 2/1. *Faculty research:* Media convergence, political reporting, interactive multimedia, popular television, advertising effectiveness. *Unit head:* Lorraine Branham,, Dean, 315-443-3372. *Application contact:* Graduate Records Office, 315-443-4039, Fax: 315-443-1834, E-mail: pcgrad@syr.edu.
Website: http://newhouse.syr.edu/

Teachers College, Columbia University, Graduate Faculty of Education, Department of Math, Science and Technology, Program in Communications, New York, NY 10027. Offers Ed M, MA, Ed D. Part-time and evening/weekend programs available. *Faculty:* 8 full-time, 6 part-time/adjunct. *Students:* 14 full-time (10 women), 34 part-time (24 women); includes 13 minority (1 Black or African American, non-Hispanic/Latino; 5 Asian, non-Hispanic/Latino; 5 Hispanic/Latino; 2 Two or more races, non-Hispanic/Latino), 22 international. Average age 29. 55 applicants, 31% accepted, 9 enrolled. In 2014, 14 master's, 1 doctorate awarded. Terminal master's awarded for partial completion of doctoral program. *Degree requirements:* For master's, integrative project; for doctorate, comprehensive exam, thesis/dissertation. *Entrance requirements:* For doctorate, GRE General Test or MAT, writing sample; interview (recommended). *Application deadline:* For fall admission, 1/15 for domestic students; for spring admission, 11/1 for domestic students. Applications are processed on a rolling basis. Application fee: $65. Electronic applications accepted. *Expenses: Tuition:* Full-time $33,552; part-time $1398 per credit. *Required fees:* $418 per semester. *Financial support:* Career-related internships or fieldwork, Federal Work-Study, institutionally sponsored loans, and tuition waivers (full and partial) available. Support available to part-time students. Financial award applicants required to submit FAFSA. *Faculty research:* Television and youth, application of digital technology to education reform. *Unit head:* Prof. Lalitha Vasudevan, Program Coordinator, 212-678-6660, E-mail: lmv2102@tc.columbia.edu. *Application contact:* Deanna Ghozati, Assistant Director of Admission, 212-678-4018, Fax: 212-678-4171, E-mail: ghozati@tc.edu.
Website: http://www.tc.edu/mst/ccte/

Temple University, College of Health Professions and Social Work, Department of Communication Sciences and Disorders, Philadelphia, PA 19122. Offers communication sciences (PhD); speech-language-hearing (MA). *Accreditation:* ASHA. *Faculty:* 15 full-time (12 women), 9 part-time/adjunct (all women). *Students:* 59 full-time (55 women), 8 part-time (all women); includes 13 minority (2 Black or African American, non-Hispanic/Latino; 2 Asian, non-Hispanic/Latino; 7 Hispanic/Latino; 2 Two or more races, non-Hispanic/Latino). 375 applicants, 26% accepted, 32 enrolled. In 2014, 23 master's awarded. *Degree requirements:* For master's, comprehensive exam; for doctorate, comprehensive exam, thesis/dissertation. *Entrance requirements:* For master's, GRE General Test, minimum GPA of 3.0, 2 letters of reference, statement of goals; for doctorate, GRE General Test, minimum GPA of 3.0, 3 letters of reference, statement of goals, writing sample, resume. Additional exam requirements/recommendations for international students: Required—TOEFL (minimum score 550 paper-based; 79 iBT). *Application deadline:* For fall admission, 1/1 for domestic and international students; for spring admission, 11/1 for domestic students, 10/1 for international students. Application fee: $60. Electronic applications accepted. *Expenses:* Tuition, state resident: full-time $14,490; part-time $805 per credit hour. Tuition, nonresident: full-time $19,850; part-time $1103 per credit hour. *Required fees:* $690. Full-time tuition and fees vary according to class time, course load, degree level, campus/location and program. *Financial support:* Federal Work-Study, institutionally sponsored loans, and unspecified assistantships available. Financial award application deadline: 1/15. *Faculty research:* Bilingualism; biliteracy; adult neurogenic language disorders, including aphasia; dementia; school readiness. *Unit head:* Dr. Carol Scheffner Hammer, Department Chair, 215-204-7543, E-mail: cjhammer@temple.edu. *Application contact:* Dawn Dandridge, Coordinator of Outreach, 215-204-9005, E-mail: ddandrid@temple.edu.
Website: http://chpsw.temple.edu/commsci/home

Temple University, School of Media and Communication, Philadelphia, PA 19122-6096. Offers MA, MJ, MS, PhD. Part-time and evening/weekend programs available. *Faculty:* 58 full-time (27 women), 79 part-time/adjunct (35 women). *Students:* 83 full-time (56 women), 40 part-time (25 women); includes 13 minority (6 Black or African American, non-Hispanic/Latino; 2 Asian, non-Hispanic/Latino; 3 Hispanic/Latino; 2 Two or more races, non-Hispanic/Latino), 37 international. 163 applicants, 48% accepted, 37 enrolled. In 2014, 33 master's, 9 doctorates awarded. *Degree requirements:* For master's, comprehensive exam (for some programs); for doctorate, one foreign language, comprehensive exam, thesis/dissertation. *Entrance requirements:* For master's and doctorate, GRE General Test, minimum GPA of 3.0. Additional exam requirements/recommendations for international students: Required—TOEFL. *Application deadline:* For fall admission, 12/15 for international students. Application fee: $60. Electronic applications accepted. *Expenses:* Tuition, state resident: full-time $14,490; part-time $805 per credit hour. Tuition, nonresident: full-time $19,850; part-time $1103 per credit hour. *Required fees:* $690. Full-time tuition and fees vary according to class time, course load, degree level, campus/location and program. *Financial support:* Fellowships, teaching assistantships with partial tuition reimbursements, career-related internships or fieldwork, Federal Work-Study, institutionally sponsored loans, tuition waivers (full and partial), and unspecified assistantships available. Financial award application deadline: 1/15; financial award applicants required to submit FAFSA. *Unit head:* David Boardman, Dean, 215-204-8422, Fax: 215-204-4811, E-mail: dboardman@temple.edu. *Application contact:* Nicole McKenna, Director, Office of Research and Graduate Studies, 215-204-1497, Fax: 215-204-0310, E-mail: nmckenna@temple.edu.
Website: http://smc.temple.edu/

Texas A&M University, College of Liberal Arts, Department of Communication, College Station, TX 77843. Offers MA, PhD. *Faculty:* 16. *Students:* 39 full-time (21 women), 15 part-time (9 women); includes 9 minority (3 Black or African American, non-Hispanic/Latino; 2 Asian, non-Hispanic/Latino; 4 Hispanic/Latino), 8 international. Average age 31. 62 applicants, 32% accepted, 13 enrolled. In 2014, 6 master's, 6 doctorates awarded. *Degree requirements:* For master's, thesis or alternative; for doctorate, thesis/dissertation. *Entrance requirements:* For master's, GRE General Test. Additional exam requirements/recommendations for international students: Required—TOEFL. *Application deadline:* For fall admission, 2/15 priority date for domestic students; for spring admission, 10/15 for domestic students. Applications are processed on a rolling basis. Application fee: $50 ($90 for international students). Electronic applications accepted. *Expenses:* Tuition, state resident: full-time $4078; part-time $226.55 per credit hour. Tuition, nonresident: full-time $10,594; part-time $577.55 per credit hour. *Required fees:* $2813; $237.70 per credit hour. $278.50 per semester. Tuition and fees vary according to degree level and student level. *Financial support:* In 2014–15, 40 students received support, including 9 fellowships with full and partial tuition reimbursements available (averaging $12,256 per year), 3 research assistantships with full and partial tuition reimbursements available (averaging $4,880 per year), 37 teaching assistantships with full and partial tuition reimbursements available (averaging $7,785 per year); career-related internships or fieldwork, institutionally sponsored loans, scholarships/grants, traineeships, health care benefits, tuition waivers (full and partial), and unspecified assistantships also available. Support available to part-time students. Financial award application deadline: 2/1; financial award applicants required to submit FAFSA. *Faculty research:* Rhetoric and public affairs, communication and health, communication and organizations. *Unit head:* Dr. J. Kevin Barge, Head, 979-845-5514, E-mail: kbarge@tamu.edu. *Application contact:* Dr. Charles Conrad, Graduate Program Director, 979-845-5530, E-mail: c-conrad@tamu.edu.
Website: http://communication.tamu.edu/html/home.html

Texas A&M University–Corpus Christi, College of Graduate Studies, College of Liberal Arts, Corpus Christi, TX 78412-5503. Offers communication (MA); English (MA); history (MA); psychology (MA); public administration (MPA); studio art (MA, MFA). Part-time and evening/weekend programs available. *Students:* 85 full-time (56 women), 100

part-time (68 women); includes 85 minority (3 Black or African American, non-Hispanic/Latino; 2 American Indian or Alaska Native, non-Hispanic/Latino; 4 Asian, non-Hispanic/Latino; 74 Hispanic/Latino; 2 Two or more races, non-Hispanic/Latino), 12 international. Average age 31. 206 applicants, 60% accepted, 83 enrolled. In 2014, 64 master's awarded. *Degree requirements:* For master's, comprehensive exam, thesis (for some programs). *Entrance requirements:* For master's, GRE General Test. Additional exam requirements/recommendations for international students: Required—TOEFL. *Application deadline:* For fall admission, 7/15 priority date for domestic students, 5/1 priority date for international students; for spring admission, 11/15 priority date for domestic students, 9/1 priority date for international students. Applications are processed on a rolling basis. Application fee: $50 ($70 for international students). Electronic applications accepted. *Financial support:* Research assistantships, teaching assistantships, career-related internships or fieldwork, Federal Work-Study, institutionally sponsored loans, scholarships/grants, health care benefits, and unspecified assistantships available. Support available to part-time students. Financial award application deadline: 3/15; financial award applicants required to submit FAFSA. *Unit head:* Dr. Mark Hartlaub, Interim Dean, 361-825-2659, Fax: 361-825-5844, E-mail: mark.hartlaub@tamucc.edu. *Application contact:* Graduate Admissions Coordinator, 361-825-2177, Fax: 361-825-2755, E-mail: gradweb@tamucc.edu.
Website: http://cla.tamucc.edu/

Texas Southern University, Tavis Smiley School of Communication, Houston, TX 77004-4584. Offers MA. Part-time programs available. *Degree requirements:* For master's, comprehensive exam, thesis. *Entrance requirements:* For master's, GRE General Test, minimum GPA of 2.5. Additional exam requirements/recommendations for international students: Required—TOEFL. Electronic applications accepted.

Texas State University, The Graduate College, College of Fine Arts and Communication, San Marcos, TX 78666. Offers MA, MFA, MM. Part-time and evening/weekend programs available. *Faculty:* 72 full-time (31 women), 12 part-time/adjunct (3 women). *Students:* 144 full-time (65 women), 65 part-time (37 women); includes 64 minority (7 Black or African American, non-Hispanic/Latino; 3 Asian, non-Hispanic/Latino; 51 Hispanic/Latino; 3 Two or more races, non-Hispanic/Latino), 20 international. Average age 30. 180 applicants, 64% accepted, 64 enrolled. In 2014, 85 master's awarded. *Degree requirements:* For master's, comprehensive exam, thesis (for some programs). *Entrance requirements:* For master's, GRE General Test (for some programs), baccalaureate degree from regionally-accredited institution, minimum GPA of 2.75 in last 60 hours of course work. Additional exam requirements/recommendations for international students: Required—TOEFL (minimum score 550 paper-based; 78 iBT). *Application deadline:* For fall admission, 6/15 priority date for domestic students, 6/1 for international students; for spring admission, 10/15 priority date for domestic students, 10/1 for international students. Applications are processed on a rolling basis. Application fee: $40 ($90 for international students). Electronic applications accepted. *Expenses:* Expenses: $8,834 (tuition and fees combined). *Financial support:* In 2014–15, 140 students received support, including 7 research assistantships (averaging $12,467 per year), 87 teaching assistantships (averaging $11,116 per year); career-related internships or fieldwork, Federal Work-Study, institutionally sponsored loans, scholarships/grants, and unspecified assistantships also available. Support available to part-time students. Financial award application deadline: 4/1; financial award applicants required to submit FAFSA. *Faculty research:* Emergency communication, landscape of Hispanic advancement, assessing portrayals. *Unit head:* Dr. John Fleming, Interim Dean, 512-245-2308, Fax: 512-245-8386, E-mail: jf18@txstate.edu. *Application contact:* Dr. Andrea Golato, Dean of Graduate School, 512-245-2581, Fax: 512-245-8365, E-mail: gradcollege@txstate.edu.
Website: http://www.finearts.txstate.edu.edu/

Texas State University, The Graduate College, College of Fine Arts and Communication, Department of Communication Studies, Program in Communication Studies, San Marcos, TX 78666. Offers MA. Part-time and evening/weekend programs available. *Faculty:* 8 full-time (6 women), 1 part-time/adjunct (0 women). *Students:* 35 full-time (23 women), 10 part-time (5 women); includes 12 minority (3 Black or African American, non-Hispanic/Latino; 8 Hispanic/Latino; 1 Two or more races, non-Hispanic/Latino), 2 international. Average age 27. 43 applicants, 70% accepted, 19 enrolled. In 2014, 19 master's awarded. *Degree requirements:* For master's, comprehensive exam, thesis optional. *Entrance requirements:* For master's, GRE (preferred), baccalaureate degree from regionally-accredited institution with minimum GPA of 3.2 in last 60 hours of undergraduate course work. Additional exam requirements/recommendations for international students: Required—TOEFL (minimum score 550 paper-based; 78 iBT). *Application deadline:* For fall admission, 3/7 priority date for domestic students, 3/7 for international students; for spring admission, 11/15 priority date for domestic students, 10/1 for international students; for summer admission, 3/1 for domestic and international students. Applications are processed on a rolling basis. Application fee: $40 ($90 for international students). Electronic applications accepted. *Expenses:* Expenses: $8,834 (tuition and fees combined). *Financial support:* In 2014–15, 26 students received support, including 2 research assistantships (averaging $14,700 per year), 25 teaching assistantships (averaging $14,544 per year); career-related internships or fieldwork, Federal Work-Study, institutionally sponsored loans, scholarships/grants, and unspecified assistantships also available. Support available to part-time students. Financial award application deadline: 4/1; financial award applicants required to submit FAFSA. *Faculty research:* Emergency communications, firefighting action, assessing portrayals. *Total annual research expenditures:* $117,415. *Unit head:* Dr. Maureen Keeley, Graduate Adviser, 512-245-3133, Fax: 512-245-3138, E-mail: mk09@txstate.edu. *Application contact:* Dr. Andrea Golato, Dean of Graduate School, 512-245-2581, Fax: 512-245-8365, E-mail: gradcollege@txstate.edu.
Website: http://www.finearts.txstate.edu/commstudies/

Texas Tech University, Graduate School, College of Arts and Sciences, Department of Communication Studies, Lubbock, TX 79409-3083. Offers MA. Part-time programs available. *Faculty:* 13 full-time (5 women), 4 part-time/adjunct (2 women). *Students:* 14 full-time (9 women), 1 (woman) part-time; includes 6 minority (1 Black or African American, non-Hispanic/Latino; 5 Hispanic/Latino), 2 international. Average age 24. 19 applicants, 37% accepted, 7 enrolled. In 2014, 10 master's awarded. *Degree requirements:* For master's, thesis. *Entrance requirements:* For master's, GRE. Additional exam requirements/recommendations for international students: Required—TOEFL (minimum score 550 paper-based; 79 iBT). *Application deadline:* For fall admission, 6/1 priority date for domestic students, 1/15 priority date for international students; for spring admission, 9/1 priority date for domestic students, 6/15 priority date for international students. Applications are processed on a rolling basis. Application fee: $60. Electronic applications accepted. *Expenses:* Tuition, state resident: full-time $6310; part-time $262.92 per credit hour. Tuition, nonresident: full-time $14,998; part-time $624.92 per credit hour. *Required fees:* $2701; $36.50 per credit. $912.50 per semester. Tuition and fees vary according to course load. *Financial support:* In 2014–15, 15 students received support, including 4 fellowships (averaging $1,725 per year), 14 teaching assistantships (averaging $10,571 per year); unspecified assistantships also available. Financial award application deadline: 4/15; financial award applicants required to submit FAFSA. *Faculty research:* Health communication, crisis communication, organizational communication, rhetoric, instructional communication, interpersonal communication, religious communication. *Unit head:* Dr. Narissra Punyanunt-Carter, Interim Chair, 806-742-3911, E-mail: n.punyanunt@ttu.edu. *Application contact:* Dr. Amy Heuman, Graduate Advisor, 806-742-3911, E-mail: a.heuman@ttu.edu.
Website: http://www.depts.ttu.edu/communicationstudies/

Tiffin University, Program in Humanities, Tiffin, OH 44883-2161. Offers art and visual media (MH); communication (MH); creative writing (MH); English (MH); film studies (MH); humanities (MH); individualized studies (MH). Part-time and evening/weekend programs available. Postbaccalaureate distance learning degree programs offered (no on-campus study). *Entrance requirements:* For master's, work experience. Additional exam requirements/recommendations for international students: Required—TOEFL (minimum score 550 paper-based; 79 iBT).

Towson University, Program in Communications Management, Towson, MD 21252-0001. Offers MS. *Students:* 15 part-time (12 women); includes 2 minority (both Black or African American, non-Hispanic/Latino). *Degree requirements:* For master's, thesis. *Entrance requirements:* For master's, bacehlor's degree with 24 credits in mass communications, public relations, advertising or communication studies; advanced writing and basic statistics courses; professional experience; minimum GPA of 3.0; letter of recommendation; resume. Additional exam requirements/recommendations for international students: Required—TOEFL. *Application deadline:* For fall admission, 1/15 for domestic students. Application fee: $45. Electronic applications accepted. *Financial support:* Application deadline: 4/1. *Unit head:* Dr. Beth Haller, Graduate Program Director, 410-704-2442, E-mail: bhaller@towson.edu. *Application contact:* Alicia Arkell-Kleis, Information Contact, 410-704-6004, Fax: 410-704-4675, E-mail: grads@towson.edu.
Website: http://grad.towson.edu/program/master/comg-ms/

Trinity International University, Trinity Graduate School, Deerfield, IL 60015-1284. Offers bioethics (MA); communication and culture (MA); counseling psychology (MA); instructional leadership (M Ed); teaching (MA). Part-time and evening/weekend programs available. Postbaccalaureate distance learning degree programs offered (minimal on-campus study). *Degree requirements:* For master's, comprehensive exam. *Entrance requirements:* For master's, GRE General Test or MAT, minimum undergraduate GPA of 3.0. Additional exam requirements/recommendations for international students: Required—TOEFL (minimum score 580 paper-based), TWE (minimum score 4). Electronic applications accepted.

Trinity Washington University, School of Business and Graduate Studies, Washington, DC 20017-1094. Offers business administration (MBA); communication (MA); international security studies (MA); organizational management (MSA), including federal program management, human resource management, nonprofit management, organizational development, public and community health. Part-time and evening/weekend programs available. *Degree requirements:* For master's, thesis (for some programs), capstone project (MSA). *Entrance requirements:* For master's, minimum GPA of 2.5. Additional exam requirements/recommendations for international students: Required—TOEFL (minimum score 550 paper-based).

Troy University, Graduate School, College of Communication and Fine Arts, Troy, AL 36082. Offers strategic communication (MS). Part-time and evening/weekend programs available. *Faculty:* 4 full-time (3 women), 2 part-time/adjunct (0 women). *Students:* 43 full-time (33 women), 74 part-time (53 women); includes 67 minority (58 Black or African American, non-Hispanic/Latino; 1 American Indian or Alaska Native, non-Hispanic/Latino; 2 Hispanic/Latino; 6 Two or more races, non-Hispanic/Latino). Average age 29. 43 applicants, 100% accepted, 35 enrolled. In 2014, 19 master's awarded. *Degree requirements:* For master's, comprehensive exam, thesis optional, minimum GPA of 3.0, admission to candidacy. *Entrance requirements:* For master's, GRE (minimum score of 850 on old exam or 290 on new exam), MAT (minimum score of 385) or GMAT (minimum score of 380), bachelor's degree; minimum undergraduate GPA of 2.5 or 3.0 on last 30 semester hours. Additional exam requirements/recommendations for international students: Required—TOEFL (minimum score 523 paper-based; 70 iBT), IELTS (minimum score 6). *Application deadline:* For fall admission, 6/1 for international students; for spring admission, 10/15 for international students. Application fee: $50. *Expenses:* Tuition, state resident: full-time $6570; part-time $365 per credit hour. Tuition, nonresident: full-time $13,140; part-time $730 per credit hour. *Required fees:* $365 per credit hour. *Unit head:* Dr. Larry Blocher, Dean, 334-670-3869, Fax: 334-670-3547, E-mail: lblocher@troy.edu. *Application contact:* Jessica A. Kimbro, Director of Graduate Admissions, 334-670-3178, E-mail: jacord@troy.edu.

Université de Montréal, Faculty of Arts and Sciences, Department of Communication, Montréal, QC H3C 3J7, Canada. Offers communication (PhD); communication sciences (M Sc). *Degree requirements:* For master's, thesis; for doctorate, one foreign language, thesis/dissertation, general exam. *Entrance requirements:* For doctorate, proficiency in French. Electronic applications accepted. *Faculty research:* Mass media/new communication technologies, organizational communication.

Université du Québec à Montréal, Graduate Programs, Program in Communications, Montréal, QC H3C 3P8, Canada. Offers MA, PhD. PhD offered jointly with Concordia University and Université de Montréal. Part-time programs available. *Degree requirements:* For master's, thesis; for doctorate, thesis/dissertation. *Entrance requirements:* For master's, appropriate bachelor's degree or equivalent, proficiency in French; for doctorate, appropriate master's degree or equivalent, proficiency in French.

Université du Québec à Trois-Rivières, Graduate Programs, Program in Social Communication, Trois-Rivières, QC G9A 5H7, Canada. Offers MA, DESS.

University at Albany, State University of New York, College of Arts and Sciences, Department of Communication, Albany, NY 12222-0001. Offers communication (MA); sociology and communication (PhD). Part-time programs available. *Degree requirements:* For master's, comprehensive exam, thesis or alternative; for doctorate, comprehensive exam, thesis/dissertation. *Entrance requirements:* For master's, minimum GPA of 3.0; for doctorate, GRE, minimum GPA of 3.0. Additional exam requirements/recommendations for international students: Required—TOEFL (minimum score 550 paper-based). Electronic applications accepted. *Faculty research:* Language and social interaction, campaign communication, media agenda-setting, high-speed management, organizational boundary-spanning.

University at Buffalo, the State University of New York, Graduate School, College of Arts and Sciences, Department of Communication, Buffalo, NY 14260. Offers MA, PhD. *Faculty:* 14 full-time (4 women), 16 part-time/adjunct (9 women). *Students:* 19 full-time (12 women), 15 part-time (6 women); includes 13 minority (1 Black or African American, non-Hispanic/Latino; 11 Asian, non-Hispanic/Latino; 1 Hispanic/Latino), 1 international. Average age 30. 92 applicants, 35% accepted, 7 enrolled. In 2014, 5 master's, 3 doctorates awarded. Terminal master's awarded for partial completion of doctoral program. *Degree requirements:* For master's, thesis; for doctorate, comprehensive exam, thesis/dissertation. *Entrance requirements:* For master's and doctorate, GRE General Test, minimum GPA of 3.0. Additional exam requirements/recommendations for international students: Required—TOEFL (minimum score 600 paper-based; 100 iBT); Recommended—TWE. *Application deadline:* For fall admission, 1/15 priority date for domestic students, 4/1 priority date for international students. Applications are processed on a rolling basis. Application fee: $75. Electronic applications accepted. *Financial support:* In 2014–15, 1 fellowship with full tuition reimbursement (averaging

$13,560 per year), 2 research assistantships with full tuition reimbursements (averaging $18,173 per year), 13 teaching assistantships with full tuition reimbursements (averaging $13,650 per year) were awarded; career-related internships or fieldwork, institutionally sponsored loans, health care benefits, and unspecified assistantships also available. Financial award application deadline: 1/15; financial award applicants required to submit FAFSA. *Faculty research:* Technology, health, international, interpersonal. *Total annual research expenditures:* $692,963. *Unit head:* Dr. Thomas H. Feeley, Chairman, 716-645-1160, Fax: 716-645-2086, E-mail: thfeeley@buffalo.edu. *Application contact:* Rose Gryckiewicz, Graduate Program Coordinator, 716-645-1505, Fax: 716-645-2086, E-mail: rfg@buffalo.edu.
Website: http://www.cas.buffalo.edu/communication

The University of Akron, Graduate School, Buchtel College of Arts and Sciences, School of Communication, Akron, OH 44325. Offers MA. Part-time and evening/weekend programs available. *Faculty:* 13 full-time (10 women), 1 part-time/adjunct (0 women). *Students:* 19 full-time (16 women), 7 part-time (all women); includes 6 minority (5 Black or African American, non-Hispanic/Latino; 1 Hispanic/Latino), 1 international. Average age 34. 10 applicants, 90% accepted, 6 enrolled. In 2014, 16 master's awarded. *Degree requirements:* For master's, thesis, project or written comprehensive exam. *Entrance requirements:* For master's, GRE, essay of no more than 500 words outlining reasons for wanting to attend the program. Additional exam requirements/recommendations for international students: Required—TOEFL (minimum score 550 paper-based; 79 iBT), IELTS (minimum score 6.5). *Application deadline:* For fall admission, 5/1 for domestic and international students. Application fee: $45 ($70 for international students). Electronic applications accepted. *Expenses:* Tuition, state resident: full-time $7578; part-time $421 per credit hour. Tuition, nonresident: full-time $12,977; part-time $721 per credit hour. *Required fees:* $1388; $35 per credit hour. Tuition and fees vary according to course load. *Financial support:* In 2014–15, 12 teaching assistantships with full tuition reimbursements were awarded; unspecified assistantships also available. *Faculty research:* Communications theory, business and organization communications, criticism of communications, film and video studies, interpersonal and intercultural communications. *Total annual research expenditures:* $30,775. *Unit head:* Dr. Therese Lueck, Interim Director, 330-972-6093, E-mail: tlueck@uakron.edu. *Application contact:* Dr. Tang Tang, Graduate Director, 330-972-7606, E-mail: tang@uakron.edu.
Website: http://www.uakron.edu/schlcomm/

The University of Alabama, Graduate School, College of Communication and Information Sciences, Tuscaloosa, AL 35487-0172. Offers MA, MFA, MLIS, PhD. *Accreditation:* ACEJMC (one or more programs are accredited at the [master's] level). *Faculty:* 59 full-time (25 women), 3 part-time/adjunct (1 woman). *Students:* 170 full-time (112 women), 184 part-time (140 women); includes 42 minority (25 Black or African American, non-Hispanic/Latino; 1 American Indian or Alaska Native, non-Hispanic/Latino; 4 Asian, non-Hispanic/Latino; 7 Hispanic/Latino; 5 Two or more races, non-Hispanic/Latino), 30 international. Average age 32. 335 applicants, 57% accepted, 136 enrolled. In 2014, 153 master's, 12 doctorates awarded. *Degree requirements:* For master's, comprehensive exam, thesis or alternative; for doctorate, comprehensive exam, thesis/dissertation. *Entrance requirements:* For master's, GRE; for doctorate, GRE, minimum graduate GPA of 3.0, master's degree. Additional exam requirements/recommendations for international students: Required—TOEFL (minimum score 600 paper-based; 100 iBT). *Application deadline:* For fall admission, 2/15 priority date for domestic and international students; for winter admission, 11/1 priority date for international students; for spring admission, 11/1 priority date for domestic students. Applications are processed on a rolling basis. Application fee: $50 ($60 for international students). Electronic applications accepted. *Expenses:* Tuition, state resident: full-time $9826. Tuition, nonresident: full-time $24,950. *Financial support:* In 2014–15, 78 students received support, including 3 fellowships with tuition reimbursements available (averaging $15,000 per year), 34 research assistantships with tuition reimbursements available (averaging $13,045 per year), 38 teaching assistantships with tuition reimbursements available (averaging $13,045 per year); institutionally sponsored loans, health care benefits, and unspecified assistantships also available. Financial award application deadline: 2/15. *Faculty research:* Mass media research; media effects; information studies; cultural, critical, and rhetorical studies; electronic media; law and policy. *Unit head:* Dr. Jennings Bryant, Associate Dean for Graduate Studies, 205-348-8593, Fax: 205-348-6774. *Application contact:* Diane Shaddix, Information Contact, 205-348-8593, Fax: 205-348-6774, E-mail: dshaddix@bama.ua.edu.
Website: http://www.cis.ua.edu

The University of Alabama at Birmingham, College of Arts and Sciences, Program in Communication Management, Birmingham, AL 35294. Offers MA. Part-time and evening/weekend programs available. *Students:* 12 full-time (9 women), 13 part-time (12 women); includes 11 minority (all Black or African American, non-Hispanic/Latino), 4 international. Average age 29. In 2014, 25 master's awarded. *Degree requirements:* For master's, comprehensive exam (for some programs), thesis (for some programs). *Entrance requirements:* For master's, GRE (recommended) or MAT, minimum undergraduate GPA of 3.0, letters of reference. Application fee: $45 ($60 for international students). Electronic applications accepted. *Expenses:* Tuition, state resident: full-time $7090; part-time $370 per credit hour. Tuition, nonresident: full-time $16,072; part-time $869 per credit hour. Full-time tuition and fees vary according to course load and program. *Unit head:* Dr. Jonathan H. Amsbary, Graduate Program Director, 205-934-3877, Fax: 205-934-8916, E-mail: amsbary@uab.edu. *Application contact:* Susan Noblitt Banks, Director of Graduate School Operations, 205-934-8227, Fax: 205-934-8413, E-mail: gradschool@uab.edu.
Website: http://www.uab.edu/cas/communication/graduate-program

University of Alaska Fairbanks, College of Liberal Arts, Department of Communications, Fairbanks, AK 99775-5680. Offers professional communication (MA). Part-time programs available. *Faculty:* 4 full-time (2 women). *Students:* 6 full-time (3 women), 4 part-time (all women); includes 2 minority (1 Black or African American, non-Hispanic/Latino; 1 American Indian or Alaska Native, non-Hispanic/Latino), 1 international. Average age 34. 11 applicants, 82% accepted, 5 enrolled. In 2014, 6 master's awarded. *Degree requirements:* For master's, comprehensive exam, thesis, oral defense of thesis. *Entrance requirements:* For master's, bachelor's degree from accredited institution with minimum cumulative undergraduate and major GPA of 3.0, academic writing sample. Additional exam requirements/recommendations for international students: Required—TOEFL (minimum score 550 paper-based; 79 iBT), IELTS (minimum score 6.5). *Application deadline:* For fall admission, 6/1 for domestic students, 3/1 for international students; for spring admission, 10/15 for domestic students, 9/1 for international students. Applications are processed on a rolling basis. Application fee: $60. Electronic applications accepted. *Expenses:* Tuition, state resident: full-time $7614; part-time $423 per credit. Tuition, nonresident: full-time $15,552; part-time $864 per credit. Tuition and fees vary according to course level, course load and reciprocity agreements. *Financial support:* In 2014–15, 6 teaching assistantships with full tuition reimbursements (averaging $11,078 per year) were awarded; fellowships with full tuition reimbursements, Federal Work-Study, scholarships/grants, tuition waivers, and unspecified assistantships also available. Support available to part-time students. Financial award application deadline: 7/1; financial award applicants required to submit FAFSA. *Faculty research:* Interpersonal

communications, health communications, intercultural communications, politeness and face management in conversation, gender communication. *Unit head:* Dr. Peter DeCaro, Department Chair, 907-474-6591, Fax: 907-474-5858, E-mail: fycomm@uaf.edu. *Application contact:* Mary Kreta, Director of Admissions, 907-474-7500, Fax: 907-474-7097, E-mail: admissions@uaf.edu.
Website: http://www.uaf.edu/comm/

University of Alberta, Faculty of Extension, Edmonton, AB T6G 2E1, Canada. Offers communications and technology (MA).

University of Alberta, Faculty of Graduate Studies and Research, Program in Communications and Technology, Edmonton, AB T6G 2E1, Canada. Offers MACT.

The University of Arizona, College of Social and Behavioral Sciences, Department of Communication, Tucson, AZ 85721. Offers MA, PhD. Part-time programs available. Terminal master's awarded for partial completion of doctoral program. *Degree requirements:* For master's, thesis optional; for doctorate, comprehensive exam, thesis/dissertation. *Entrance requirements:* For master's, GRE General Test, minimum GPA of 3.25, writing sample, 3 letters of recommendation; for doctorate, GRE General Test, minimum GPA of 3.5, writing sample, 3 letters of recommendation, statement of purpose. Additional exam requirements/recommendations for international students: Required—TOEFL (minimum score 600 paper-based; 90 iBT). Electronic applications accepted. *Faculty research:* Health communication, new communication technologies.

University of Arkansas, Graduate School, J. William Fulbright College of Arts and Sciences, Department of Communication, Fayetteville, AR 72701-1201. Offers MA. Part-time programs available. *Degree requirements:* For master's, thesis. *Entrance requirements:* For master's, GRE General Test. Electronic applications accepted.

University of Bridgeport, College of Public and International Affairs, Bridgeport, CT 06604. Offers East Asian and Pacific Rim studies (MA); global development and peace (MA); global media and communication studies (MA). Part-time and evening/weekend programs available. *Degree requirements:* For master's, thesis. *Entrance requirements:* Additional exam requirements/recommendations for international students: Recommended—TOEFL (minimum score 550 paper-based; 80 iBT), IELTS (minimum score 6.5).

University of Calgary, Faculty of Graduate Studies, Faculty of Arts, Department of Communication and Culture, Calgary, AB T2N 1N4, Canada. Offers MA, MCS, PhD. Part-time and evening/weekend programs available. *Degree requirements:* For master's, project (MCS), thesis (MA); for doctorate, thesis/dissertation. *Entrance requirements:* For master's, minimum GPA of 3.0; for doctorate, master's degree, minimum GPA of 3.0, BA degree, min GPA of 3.0. Additional exam requirements/recommendations for international students: Required—TOEFL (minimum score 600 paper-based); Recommended—IELTS (minimum score 8). Electronic applications accepted. *Faculty research:* Science communications, structuration theory, organizational communication, communication theory, media law.

University of California, Davis, Graduate Studies, Program in Communication, Davis, CA 95616. Offers MA. *Degree requirements:* For master's, comprehensive exam (for some programs), thesis (for some programs). *Entrance requirements:* For master's, GRE. Additional exam requirements/recommendations for international students: Required—TOEFL (minimum score 550 paper-based).

University of California, San Diego, Graduate Division, Department of Communication, La Jolla, CA 92093. Offers PhD. *Students:* 49 full-time (33 women), 3 part-time (2 women); includes 15 minority (5 Black or African American, non-Hispanic/Latino; 4 Asian, non-Hispanic/Latino; 5 Hispanic/Latino; 1 Native Hawaiian or other Pacific Islander, non-Hispanic/Latino), 10 international. 112 applicants, 16% accepted, 10 enrolled. In 2014, 6 doctorates awarded. *Degree requirements:* For doctorate, one foreign language, comprehensive exam, thesis/dissertation, 3 quarters of teaching assistantship. *Entrance requirements:* For doctorate, GRE General Test, demonstrated competence in a natural language other than English. Additional exam requirements/recommendations for international students: Required—TOEFL (minimum score 550 paper-based; 80 iBT), IELTS. *Application deadline:* For fall admission, 12/14 for domestic students. Application fee: $90 ($110 for international students). Electronic applications accepted. *Expenses:* Tuition, state resident: full-time $11,220; part-time $5610 per quarter. Tuition, nonresident: full-time $26,322; part-time $13,161 per quarter. *Required fees:* $570 per quarter. Tuition and fees vary according to program. *Financial support:* Fellowships, research assistantships, teaching assistantships, and scholarships/grants available. Financial award applicants required to submit FAFSA. *Faculty research:* Communication and culture, communication as a social force, communication and the person, communications and science studies. *Unit head:* Valerie Hartouni, Chair, 858-534-2366, E-mail: vhartouni@ucsd.edu. *Application contact:* Zachary Dake, Graduate Coordinator, 858-534-2379, E-mail: zdake@ucsd.edu.
Website: http://communication.ucsd.edu

University of California, Santa Barbara, Graduate Division, College of Letters and Sciences, Division of Social Sciences, Department of Communication, Santa Barbara, CA 93106-4020. Offers cognitive science (PhD); communication (PhD); feminist studies (PhD); language, interaction and social organization (PhD); quantitative methods in the social sciences (PhD); society and technology (PhD); MA/PhD. Terminal master's awarded for partial completion of doctoral program. *Degree requirements:* For doctorate, comprehensive exam, thesis/dissertation. *Entrance requirements:* For doctorate, GRE. Additional exam requirements/recommendations for international students: Required—TOEFL (minimum score 80 iBT), IELTS (minimum score 7). Electronic applications accepted. *Faculty research:* Interpersonal, intercultural, organizational, health, media.

University of California, Santa Cruz, Division of Graduate Studies, Division of Physical and Biological Sciences, Program in Science Communication, Santa Cruz, CA 95064. Offers Certificate. *Entrance requirements:* For degree, GRE General Test, GRE Subject Test, bachelor's degree in science. Additional exam requirements/recommendations for international students: Required—TOEFL (minimum score 550 paper-based; 83 iBT); Recommended—IELTS (minimum score 8). Electronic applications accepted. *Faculty research:* Science writing.

University of Central Florida, College of Sciences, Nicholson School of Communication, Orlando, FL 32816. Offers communication (MA). Part-time and evening/weekend programs available. *Faculty:* 41 full-time (18 women), 20 part-time/adjunct (11 women). *Students:* 34 full-time (24 women), 33 part-time (26 women); includes 17 minority (6 Black or African American, non-Hispanic/Latino; 3 Asian, non-Hispanic/Latino; 7 Hispanic/Latino; 1 Two or more races, non-Hispanic/Latino), 8 international. Average age 27. 69 applicants, 71% accepted, 35 enrolled. In 2014, 27 master's, 9 other advanced degrees awarded. *Degree requirements:* For master's, thesis or comprehensive exam. *Entrance requirements:* For master's, GRE General Test, minimum GPA of 3.0 in last 60 hours of course work. Additional exam requirements/recommendations for international students: Required—TOEFL. *Application deadline:* For fall admission, 7/15 for domestic students; for spring admission, 12/7 for domestic students. Application fee: $30. Electronic applications accepted. *Expenses:* Tuition, state resident: part-time $288.16 per credit hour. Tuition, nonresident: part-time $1073.31 per credit hour. *Financial support:* In 2014–15, 19 students received support, including 4 fellowships with partial tuition reimbursements

available (averaging $4,800 per year), 4 research assistantships with partial tuition reimbursements available (averaging $7,100 per year), 14 teaching assistantships with partial tuition reimbursements available (averaging $7,100 per year); career-related internships or fieldwork, Federal Work-Study, institutionally sponsored loans, tuition waivers (partial), and unspecified assistantships also available. Financial award application deadline: 3/1; financial award applicants required to submit FAFSA. *Faculty research:* Persuasion, communication apprehension, nonverbal communication, conflict resolution. *Unit head:* Dr. Robert Chandler, Director, 407-823-1411, E-mail: robert.chandler@ucf.edu. *Application contact:* Barbara Rodriguez Lamas, Director, Admissions and Student Services, 407-823-2766, Fax: 407-823-6442, E-mail: gradadmissions@ucf.edu.
Website: http://communication.cos.ucf.edu/

University of Central Missouri, The Graduate School, Warrensburg, MO 64093. Offers accountancy (MA); accounting (MBA); applied mathematics (MS); aviation safety (MA); biology (MS); business administration (MBA); career and technical education leadership (MS); college student personnel administration (MS); communication (MA); computer science (MS); counseling (MS); criminal justice (MS); educational leadership (Ed D); educational technology (MS); elementary and early childhood education (MSE); English (MA); environmental studies (MA); finance (MBA); history (MA); human services/educational technology (Ed S); human services/learning resources (Ed S); human services/professional counseling (Ed S); industrial hygiene (MS); industrial management (MS); information systems (MBA); information technology (MS); kinesiology (MS); library science and information services (MS); literacy education (MSE); marketing (MBA); mathematics (MS); music (MA); occupational safety management (MS); psychology (MS); rural family nursing (MS); school administration (MSE); social gerontology (MS); sociology (MA); special education (MSE); speech language pathology (MS); superintendency (Ed S); teaching (MAT); teaching English as a second language (MA); technology (MS); technology management (PhD); theatre (MA). Part-time programs available. *Faculty:* 314 full-time (137 women), 24 part-time/adjunct (14 women). *Students:* 1,624 full-time (542 women), 1,773 part-time (1,055 women); includes 194 minority (104 Black or African American, non-Hispanic/Latino; 6 American Indian or Alaska Native, non-Hispanic/Latino; 23 Asian, non-Hispanic/Latino; 41 Hispanic/Latino; 3 Native Hawaiian or other Pacific Islander, non-Hispanic/Latino; 17 Two or more races, non-Hispanic/Latino), 1,592 international. Average age 31. 2,800 applicants, 63% accepted, 1223 enrolled. In 2014, 796 master's, 81 other advanced degrees awarded. *Degree requirements:* For master's and Ed S, comprehensive exam (for some programs), thesis (for some programs). *Entrance requirements:* Additional exam requirements/recommendations for international students: Required—TOEFL (minimum score 550 paper-based; 79 iBT). *Application deadline:* For fall admission, 6/1 for domestic students; for spring admission, 10/1 for domestic and international students. Applications are processed on a rolling basis. Application fee: $30 ($75 for international students). Electronic applications accepted. *Expenses:* Tuition, state resident: full-time $6630; part-time $276.25 per credit hour. Tuition, nonresident: full-time $13,260; part-time $552.50 per credit hour. *Required fees:* $29 per credit hour. Tuition and fees vary according to campus/location. *Financial support:* In 2014–15, 118 students received support, including 271 research assistantships with full and partial tuition reimbursements available (averaging $7,500 per year), 109 teaching assistantships with full and partial tuition reimbursements available (averaging $7,500 per year); career-related internships or fieldwork, Federal Work-Study, scholarships/grants, and administrative and laboratory assistantships also available. Support available to part-time students. Financial award application deadline: 3/1; financial award applicants required to submit FAFSA. *Unit head:* Tina Church-Hockett, Director of Graduate School and International Admissions, 660-543-4621, Fax: 660-543-4778, E-mail: church@ucmo.edu. *Application contact:* Brittany Lawrence, Graduate Student Services Coordinator, 660-543-4621, Fax: 660-543-4778, E-mail: gradinfo@ucmo.edu.
Website: http://www.ucmo.edu/graduate/

University of Cincinnati, Graduate School, McMicken College of Arts and Sciences, Department of Communication, Cincinnati, OH 45221. Offers MA. Part-time programs available. *Degree requirements:* For master's, comprehensive exam, thesis or alternative. *Entrance requirements:* For master's, GRE General Test, undergraduate course work in communication. Additional exam requirements/recommendations for international students: Required—TOEFL. Electronic applications accepted. *Faculty research:* Political communication, health communication, organizational communication, interpersonal communication.

University of Colorado Boulder, Graduate School, College of Arts and Sciences, Department of Communication, Boulder, CO 80309. Offers MA, PhD. *Faculty:* 17 full-time (8 women). *Students:* 40 full-time (25 women), 2 part-time (both women); includes 6 minority (1 Asian, non-Hispanic/Latino; 5 Hispanic/Latino), 4 international. Average age 29. 71 applicants, 13% accepted, 9 enrolled. In 2014, 11 master's, 6 doctorates awarded. Terminal master's awarded for partial completion of doctoral program. *Degree requirements:* For master's, comprehensive exam, thesis optional; for doctorate, comprehensive exam, thesis/dissertation. *Entrance requirements:* For master's and doctorate, GRE General Test, minimum undergraduate GPA of 3.2. *Application deadline:* For fall admission, 12/15 for domestic and international students; for spring admission, 9/15 for domestic students, 8/15 for international students. Applications are processed on a rolling basis. Application fee: $50 ($70 for international students). Electronic applications accepted. *Financial support:* In 2014–15, 89 students received support, including 2 fellowships (averaging $1,000 per year), 2 research assistantships with full and partial tuition reimbursements available (averaging $32,125 per year), 36 teaching assistantships with full and partial tuition reimbursements available (averaging $36,802 per year); institutionally sponsored loans, scholarships/grants, health care benefits, and unspecified assistantships also available. Financial award application deadline: 12/15; financial award applicants required to submit FAFSA. *Faculty research:* Communications, organizational theory and behavior, social sciences: humanistic emphasis, democracy. *Total annual research expenditures:* $18,632.
Website: http://www.colorado.edu/cs

University of Colorado Boulder, Graduate School, School of Journalism and Mass Communication, Boulder, CO 80309. Offers communication (PhD), including media studies; mass communication research (MA); newsgathering (MA). *Accreditation:* ACEJMC (one or more programs are accredited). *Faculty:* 18 full-time (7 women). *Students:* 50 full-time (29 women), 10 part-time (8 women); includes 6 minority (1 Black or African American, non-Hispanic/Latino; 5 Hispanic/Latino), 10 international. Average age 29. 82 applicants, 65% accepted, 19 enrolled. In 2014, 13 master's, 3 doctorates awarded. Terminal master's awarded for partial completion of doctoral program. *Degree requirements:* For master's, comprehensive exam, thesis or alternative; for doctorate, comprehensive exam, thesis/dissertation. *Entrance requirements:* For master's, GRE General Test, minimum undergraduate GPA of 2.75; for doctorate, GRE General Test, minimum undergraduate GPA of 3.2, 3.5 graduate. *Application deadline:* For fall admission, 2/1 for domestic students, 12/1 for international students. Applications are processed on a rolling basis. Application fee: $50 ($70 for international students). Electronic applications accepted. *Financial support:* In 2014–15, 106 students received support, including 9 fellowships (averaging $4,749 per year), 17 research assistantships with full and partial tuition reimbursements available (averaging $27,900 per year), 21 teaching assistantships with full and partial tuition reimbursements available (averaging $28,721 per year); institutionally sponsored loans, scholarships/grants, health care benefits, and unspecified assistantships also available. Financial award application deadline: 3/1; financial award applicants required to submit FAFSA. *Faculty research:* Mass communication/media, journalism, electronic media, print media, television.
Website: http://www.colorado.edu/cmci/

University of Colorado Colorado Springs, College of Letters, Arts and Sciences, Department of Communication, Colorado Springs, CO 80933-7150. Offers MA. Part-time programs available. *Faculty:* 17 full-time (12 women), 16 part-time/adjunct (10 women). *Students:* 10 full-time (6 women), 34 part-time (18 women); includes 6 minority (1 Black or African American, non-Hispanic/Latino; 1 American Indian or Alaska Native, non-Hispanic/Latino; 4 Hispanic/Latino), 6 international. Average age 32. 15 applicants, 73% accepted, 8 enrolled. In 2014, 19 master's awarded. *Degree requirements:* For master's, thesis optional. *Entrance requirements:* For master's, GRE. Additional exam requirements/recommendations for international students: Recommended—TOEFL (minimum score 550 paper-based; 80 iBT). *Application deadline:* Applications are processed on a rolling basis. Application fee: $60 ($100 for international students). Electronic applications accepted. *Expenses:* Tuition, state resident: full-time $9900; part-time $1892 per course. Tuition, nonresident: full-time $18,792; part-time $3375 per course. One-time fee: $100. Tuition and fees vary according to course load, program and reciprocity agreements. *Financial support:* In 2014–15, 11 students received support, including 1 teaching assistantship (averaging $5,625 per year); fellowships, career-related internships or fieldwork, Federal Work-Study, and scholarships/grants also available. Support available to part-time students. Financial award application deadline: 3/1; financial award applicants required to submit FAFSA. *Faculty research:* Instructional communication, popular culture, strategic communication efforts in public relations, the impact of gender and culture on leadership behavior, leadership succession, organizational trust, intercultural communication, psychological and social effects of media, organizational communication. *Unit head:* Dr. Sherwyn Morreale, Director of Graduate Studies, 719-255-4115, Fax: 719-255-4030, E-mail: smorreal@uccs.edu. *Application contact:* Debbie MacDonald, Program Assistant, 719-255-4114, Fax: 719-255-4030, E-mail: debbie.macdonald@uccs.edu.
Website: http://www.uccs.edu/comm/

University of Colorado Denver, College of Liberal Arts and Sciences, Department of Communication, Denver, CO 80217. Offers MA. Part-time and evening/weekend programs available. *Faculty:* 12 full-time (6 women), 1 (woman) part-time/adjunct. *Students:* 10 full-time (6 women), 8 part-time (6 women); includes 2 minority (1 Black or African American, non-Hispanic/Latino; 1 Hispanic/Latino), 1 international. Average age 31. 17 applicants, 65% accepted, 4 enrolled. In 2014, 6 master's awarded. *Degree requirements:* For master's, comprehensive exam, 33 credits; thesis or substantial writing project. *Entrance requirements:* For master's, GRE General Test (minimum score of 153) or LSAT (minimum score of 150), minimum undergraduate GPA of 3.25, three letters of recommendation, two official transcripts, resume, academic writing sample. Additional exam requirements/recommendations for international students: Required—TOEFL (minimum score 80 iBT); Recommended—IELTS (minimum score 6.5). *Application deadline:* For fall admission, 2/1 for domestic students, 1/1 priority date for international students; for spring admission, 10/1 for domestic students, 9/1 priority date for international students. Application fee: $50 ($75 for international students). Electronic applications accepted. *Financial support:* In 2014–15, 2 students received support. Fellowships, research assistantships, teaching assistantships, Federal Work-Study, institutionally sponsored loans, scholarships/grants, and traineeships available. Financial award application deadline: 4/1; financial award applicants required to submit FAFSA. *Faculty research:* Diversity, difference, and intercultural communication; health communication/medical rhetoric; organizational communication; rhetoric and public affairs; social justice and civic engagement. *Unit head:* Dr. Stephen Hartnett, Professor and Department Chair, 303-315-1914, E-mail: stephen.hartnett@ucdenver.edu. *Application contact:* Michelle Medal, Program Assistant, 303-315-1919, E-mail: michelle.medal@ucdenver.edu.
Website: http://www.ucdenver.edu/academics/colleges/CLAS/Departments/communication/Programs/Masters/Pages/Overview.aspx

University of Connecticut, Graduate School, College of Liberal Arts and Sciences, Department of Communication Sciences, Program in Communication Processes, Storrs, CT 06269. Offers MA. *Degree requirements:* For master's, comprehensive exam. *Entrance requirements:* For master's, GRE General Test. Additional exam requirements/recommendations for international students: Required—TOEFL (minimum score 550 paper-based). Electronic applications accepted.

University of Dayton, Department of Communication, Dayton, OH 45469. Offers MA. Part-time and evening/weekend programs available. *Faculty:* 10 full-time (5 women), 1 part-time/adjunct (0 women). *Students:* 26 full-time (20 women), 4 part-time (all women); includes 1 minority (Two or more races, non-Hispanic/Latino), 17 international. Average age 26. 81 applicants, 32% accepted, 10 enrolled. In 2014, 14 master's awarded. *Degree requirements:* For master's, comprehensive exam, thesis optional. *Entrance requirements:* For master's, GRE General Test, minimum undergraduate GPA of 3.0, 3 letters of recommendation, statement of purpose. Additional exam requirements/recommendations for international students: Required—TOEFL (minimum score 550 paper-based; 80 iBT). *Application deadline:* For fall admission, 3/1 for domestic students, 3/1 priority date for international students; for spring admission, 11/1 for international students. Applications are processed on a rolling basis. Application fee: $0 ($50 for international students). Electronic applications accepted. *Expenses: Tuition:* Full-time $10,176; part-time $848 per credit. *Required fees:* $25; $25 per course. Part-time tuition and fees vary according to course level, course load, degree level and program. *Financial support:* In 2014–15, 1 research assistantship with full tuition reimbursement (averaging $10,700 per year), 8 teaching assistantships with full tuition reimbursements (averaging $10,700 per year) were awarded; institutionally sponsored loans, health care benefits, and unspecified assistantships also available. Financial award application deadline: 3/1; financial award applicants required to submit FAFSA. *Faculty research:* Public relations, law and policy, digital communication, organizational communication, political communication, rhetoric, interpersonal communication, health communication, communication theory. *Unit head:* Dr. Jon A. Hess, Chair, 937-229-2028, E-mail: jhess1@udayton.edu. *Application contact:* Dr. JeeHee Han, Graduate Program Director, 937-229-2486, E-mail: jhan01@udayton.edu.
Website: https://www.udayton.edu/artssciences/academics/communication/welcome/index.php

University of Delaware, College of Arts and Sciences, Department of Communication, Newark, DE 19716. Offers MA. Part-time and evening/weekend programs available. *Degree requirements:* For master's, comprehensive exam (for some programs), thesis (for some programs). *Entrance requirements:* For master's, GRE General Test, minimum GPA of 3.0. Additional exam requirements/recommendations for international students: Required—TOEFL (minimum score 600 paper-based). Electronic applications accepted. *Faculty research:* Politics and the media, online social interaction technologies, mass communication law, media and the perceptions of reality, the role of communication in public opinion processes, small group research, communication during resource dilemmas.

Communication—General

University of Dubuque, Program in Communication, Dubuque, IA 52001-5099. Offers information technologies communication (MAC); leadership and management (MAC); strategic and corporate communication (MAC). Part-time and evening/weekend programs available. *Degree requirements:* For master's, thesis optional. *Entrance requirements:* For master's, GRE, minimum GPA of 2.5, 3 recommendations. Additional exam requirements/recommendations for international students: Required—TOEFL (minimum score 550 paper-based). Electronic applications accepted. *Faculty research:* Intercultural communication, management communication.

University of Florida, Graduate School, College of Journalism and Communications, Gainesville, FL 32611. Offers advertising (M Adv); journalism (MAMC); mass communication (MAMC, PhD); public relations (MAMC); telecommunication (MAMC); JD/MAMC; JD/PhD. *Accreditation:* ACEJMC (one or more programs are accredited). Part-time programs available. Postbaccalaureate distance learning degree programs offered. *Faculty:* 33 full-time (17 women), 3 part-time/adjunct (2 women). *Students:* 148 full-time (103 women), 201 part-time (144 women); includes 77 minority (29 Black or African American, non-Hispanic/Latino; 8 Asian, non-Hispanic/Latino; 40 Hispanic/Latino), 72 international. 410 applicants, 39% accepted, 86 enrolled. In 2014, 107 master's, 12 doctorates awarded. *Degree requirements:* For master's, comprehensive exam (for some programs), thesis; for doctorate, comprehensive exam (for some programs), thesis/dissertation. *Entrance requirements:* For master's and doctorate, GRE General Test 156 Verbal, 146 Quantitative, minimum GPA of 3.0. resume, statement of goals, 3 letters of recommendation. Additional exam requirements/recommendations for international students: Required—TOEFL (minimum score 550 paper-based; 80 iBT), IELTS (minimum score 6). *Application deadline:* For fall admission, 4/1 for domestic students, 1/30 for international students; for spring admission, 4/15 for domestic students, 7/15 for international students. Applications are processed on a rolling basis. Application fee: $30. Electronic applications accepted. *Financial support:* Career-related internships or fieldwork, Federal Work-Study, institutionally sponsored loans, and unspecified assistantships available. Support available to part-time students. Financial award application deadline: 3/15; financial award applicants required to submit FAFSA. *Faculty research:* Translational communication in science, technology, engineering, medicine, and health; international and intercultural communication; audience analysis and media effects; social interest communication, grassroots activism, and civic engagement; corporate social responsibility. *Total annual research expenditures:* $1.1 million. *Unit head:* Diane McFarlin, Dean, 352-392-0466, Fax: 352-392-1794, E-mail: dmcfarlin@ufl.edu. *Application contact:* Debbie M. Treise, PhD, Senior Associate Dean, Division of Graduate Studies and Research, 352-392-6557, E-mail: dtreise@jou.ufl.edu. Website: http://www.jou.ufl.edu/

University of Georgia, Grady School of Journalism and Mass Communication, Athens, GA 30602. Offers journalism and mass communication (MA); mass communication (PhD). *Degree requirements:* For master's, comprehensive exam, thesis (MA); for doctorate, comprehensive exam, thesis/dissertation. *Entrance requirements:* For master's and doctorate, GRE General Test. Additional exam requirements/recommendations for international students: Required—TOEFL, TWE for Ph D. Electronic applications accepted.

University of Hartford, College of Arts and Sciences, Program in Communication, West Hartford, CT 06117-1599. Offers MA. Part-time and evening/weekend programs available. *Degree requirements:* For master's, comprehensive exam, thesis optional. *Entrance requirements:* For master's, GRE, 3 letters of recommendation. Additional exam requirements/recommendations for international students: Required—TOEFL (minimum score 550 paper-based). Electronic applications accepted. *Expenses:* Contact institution. *Faculty research:* Communication reticence, relational communication, media literacy, journalism history, media audience attitude and behavior.

University of Hawaii at Manoa, Graduate Division, College of Social Sciences, School of Communications, Honolulu, HI 96822. Offers communication (MA); telecommunication and information resource management (Graduate Certificate). Part-time programs available. *Degree requirements:* For master's, thesis optional. *Entrance requirements:* Additional exam requirements/recommendations for international students: Required—TOEFL (minimum score 600 paper-based; 100 iBT), IELTS (minimum score 7). *Faculty research:* Communication technology policy and development, intercultural communication, organizational communication.

University of Houston, College of Liberal Arts and Social Sciences, School of Communication, Houston, TX 77204. Offers health communication (MA); mass communication studies (MA); public relations studies (MA); speech communication (MA). Part-time programs available. *Degree requirements:* For master's, comprehensive exam (for some programs), thesis (for some programs), 30-33 hours. *Entrance requirements:* For master's, GRE. Additional exam requirements/recommendations for international students: Required—TOEFL. Electronic applications accepted.

University of Illinois at Chicago, Graduate College, College of Liberal Arts and Sciences, Department of Communication, Chicago, IL 60607-7128. Offers MA, PhD. Evening/weekend programs available. *Faculty:* 16 full-time (11 women), 2 part-time/adjunct (1 woman). *Students:* 15 full-time (11 women), 19 part-time (16 women); includes 6 minority (3 Black or African American, non-Hispanic/Latino; 1 Asian, non-Hispanic/Latino; 1 Hispanic/Latino; 1 Two or more races, non-Hispanic/Latino), 6 international. Average age 32. 51 applicants, 25% accepted, 3 enrolled. In 2014, 4 master's awarded. *Degree requirements:* For master's, thesis. *Entrance requirements:* For master's, GRE General Test, minimum GPA of 3.0 in last 90 hours. Additional exam requirements/recommendations for international students: Required—TOEFL. *Application deadline:* For fall admission, 2/1 for domestic and international students. Applications are processed on a rolling basis. Application fee: $40. Electronic applications accepted. *Expenses:* Tuition, state resident: full-time $11,254; part-time $468 per credit hour. Tuition, nonresident: full-time $23,252; part-time $968 per credit hour. *Required fees:* $1217 per term. Part-time tuition and fees vary according to course load, degree level and program. *Financial support:* In 2014–15, 3 students received support, including 1 fellowship with full tuition reimbursement available; research assistantships with full tuition reimbursements available, teaching assistantships with full tuition reimbursements available, career-related internships or fieldwork, Federal Work-Study, scholarships/grants, traineeships, tuition waivers (full), and unspecified assistantships also available. Support available to part-time students. Financial award application deadline: 3/1; financial award applicants required to submit FAFSA. *Faculty research:* Organizational, political, and interpersonal communication; public relations. *Unit head:* Prof. Zizi Papacharissi, Head, 312-996-3188, E-mail: zizi@uic.edu. *Application contact:* Andrew Rojecki, Director of Graduate Studies, 312-996-4460, E-mail: arojecki@uic.edu. Website: http://comm.uic.edu

University of Illinois at Springfield, Graduate Programs, College of Liberal Arts and Sciences, Program in Communication, Springfield, IL 62703-5407. Offers MA. Part-time and evening/weekend programs available. *Faculty:* 2 full-time (both women). *Students:* 11 full-time (8 women), 9 part-time (8 women); includes 3 minority (2 Black or African American, non-Hispanic/Latino; 1 Two or more races, non-Hispanic/Latino), 1 international. Average age 29. 27 applicants, 48% accepted, 8 enrolled. In 2014, 14 master's awarded. *Degree requirements:* For master's, comprehensive exam, thesis, or

project. *Entrance requirements:* For master's, in-house writing exam, departmental writing proficiency exam, minimum undergraduate GPA of 3.0. Additional exam requirements/recommendations for international students: Required—TOEFL (minimum score 580 paper-based). *Application deadline:* Applications are processed on a rolling basis. Application fee: $60 ($75 for international students). Electronic applications accepted. *Expenses:* Tuition, state resident: full-time $7662; part-time $319.25 per credit hour. Tuition, nonresident: full-time $15,966; part-time $665.25 per credit hour. *Financial support:* In 2014–15, fellowships with full tuition reimbursements (averaging $9,900 per year), research assistantships with full tuition reimbursements (averaging $9,600 per year), teaching assistantships with full tuition reimbursements (averaging $9,600 per year) were awarded; career-related internships or fieldwork, Federal Work-Study, scholarships/grants, health care benefits, and unspecified assistantships also available. Support available to part-time students. Financial award application deadline: 11/15; financial award applicants required to submit FAFSA. *Unit head:* Dr. Amie Kincaid, Program Administrator, 217-206-8415, Fax: 217-206-6217, E-mail: akinc2@uis.edu. *Application contact:* Dr. Lynn Pardie, Office of Graduate Studies, 800-252-8533, Fax: 217-206-7623, E-mail: lpard1@uis.edu.

University of Illinois at Urbana–Champaign, Graduate College, College of Liberal Arts and Sciences, Department of Communication, Champaign, IL 61820. Offers MA, PhD. Part-time and evening/weekend programs available. Postbaccalaureate distance learning degree programs offered (no on-campus study). *Students:* 92 (71 women). Terminal master's awarded for partial completion of doctoral program. Application fee: $70 ($90 for international students). *Unit head:* John Caughlin, Head, 217-333-2683, Fax: 217-244-1598, E-mail: caughlin@illinois.edu. *Application contact:* Mary Strum, Office Support Specialist, 217-244-1595, Fax: 217-244-1598, E-mail: strum@illinois.edu. Website: http://www.communication.illinois.edu/

University of Illinois at Urbana–Champaign, Graduate College, College of Media, Institute of Communications Research, Champaign, IL 61820. Offers communications and media (PhD). *Students:* 41 (28 women). Application fee: $70 ($90 for international students). *Faculty research:* Feminist cultural studies, media technology, international communications, Latino studies, economics of media. *Unit head:* William Berry, Head, 217-333-1602, Fax: 217-244-7695, E-mail: weberry@illinois.edu. *Application contact:* Theresa L. Harris, Office Manager, 217-333-1549, Fax: 217-333-1549, E-mail: tharris@illinois.edu. Website: http://www.media.illinois.edu/icr/

The University of Iowa, Graduate College, College of Liberal Arts and Sciences, Department of Communication Studies, Iowa City, IA 52242-1316. Offers interpersonal communication and relationships (MA, PhD); media studies (MA, PhD); rhetoric and public advocacy (MA, PhD). *Degree requirements:* For master's, thesis optional, exam; for doctorate, comprehensive exam, thesis/dissertation. *Entrance requirements:* For master's and doctorate, GRE General Test, minimum GPA of 3.0. Additional exam requirements/recommendations for international students: Required—TOEFL (minimum score 550 paper-based; 81 iBT). Electronic applications accepted.

The University of Kansas, Graduate Studies, College of Liberal Arts and Sciences, Department of Communication Studies, Lawrence, KS 66045-7574. Offers MA, PhD. Evening/weekend programs available. *Faculty:* 14 full-time, 7 part-time/adjunct. *Students:* 60 full-time (31 women), 7 part-time (4 women); includes 5 minority (1 Black or African American, non-Hispanic/Latino; 1 Asian, non-Hispanic/Latino; 1 Hispanic/Latino; 1 Native Hawaiian or other Pacific Islander, non-Hispanic/Latino; 1 Two or more races, non-Hispanic/Latino), 5 international. Average age 29. 48 applicants, 52% accepted, 15 enrolled. In 2014, 13 master's, 8 doctorates awarded. *Degree requirements:* For master's, comprehensive exam (for some programs), thesis or alternative; for doctorate, comprehensive exam, thesis/dissertation. *Entrance requirements:* For master's, GRE General Test, minimum GPA of 3.1; for doctorate, GRE General Test, minimum GPA of 3.2 (undergraduate), 3.6 (graduate). Additional exam requirements/recommendations for international students: Required—TOEFL. *Application deadline:* For fall admission, 5/5 priority date for domestic and international students; for spring admission, 11/15 priority date for domestic and international students.. Applications are processed on a rolling basis. Application fee: $55 ($65 for international students). Electronic applications accepted. *Financial support:* Fellowships with tuition reimbursements, research assistantships, teaching assistantships with full and partial tuition reimbursements, and unspecified assistantships available. Financial award application deadline: 1/15; financial award applicants required to submit FAFSA. *Faculty research:* Rhetoric, interpersonal communication, organizational communication, intercultural communication, legal communication. *Unit head:* Tom D. Beisecker, Chair, 785-864-9882, E-mail: south40@ku.edu. *Application contact:* Suzanne Grachek, Administrative Associate, Office Manager, 785-864-9867, E-mail: sgrachek@ku.edu. Website: http://www.coms.ku.edu

University of Kentucky, Graduate School, College of Communication and Information, Program in Communication, Lexington, KY 40506-0032. Offers MA, PhD. *Degree requirements:* For master's, comprehensive exam, thesis optional; for doctorate, comprehensive exam, thesis/dissertation. *Entrance requirements:* For master's, GRE General Test, minimum undergraduate GPA of 2.75; for doctorate, GRE General Test, minimum graduate GPA of 3.0, undergraduate 2.75. Additional exam requirements/recommendations for international students: Required—TOEFL (minimum score 550 paper-based). Electronic applications accepted. *Faculty research:* Public service campaigns, health communication, mass media law and public policy, political communication, international and intercultural communication.

University of Louisiana at Lafayette, College of Liberal Arts, Department of Communication, Lafayette, LA 70504. Offers mass communications (MS). Part-time programs available. *Degree requirements:* For master's, thesis optional. *Entrance requirements:* For master's, GRE General Test, minimum GPA of 2.75. Additional exam requirements/recommendations for international students: Required—TOEFL (minimum score 550 paper-based). Electronic applications accepted. *Faculty research:* Mass media problems, issues and ethics, mass communication, historical studies, conflict of interest and law and ethics in journalism, contemporary issues and trends in publications.

University of Louisiana at Monroe, Graduate School, College of Arts, Education, and Sciences, Department of Communication, Monroe, LA 71209-0001. Offers MA. *Degree requirements:* For master's, thesis. *Entrance requirements:* For master's, GRE (minimum verbal and quantitative score: 900). Additional exam requirements/recommendations for international students: Required—TOEFL (minimum score 500 paper-based; 61 iBT). Electronic applications accepted. *Faculty research:* Interactive media, rhetoric progress, interpersonal, journalism history, gender/multicultural issues, forensics.

University of Louisville, Graduate School, College of Arts and Sciences, Department of Communication, Louisville, KY 40292-0001. Offers MA. Part-time and evening/weekend programs available. Postbaccalaureate distance learning degree programs offered (no on-campus study). *Students:* 17 full-time (12 women), 9 part-time (7 women); includes 5 minority (3 Black or African American, non-Hispanic/Latino; 1 Hispanic/Latino; 1 Two or more races, non-Hispanic/Latino), 2 international. Average

age 28. 22 applicants, 59% accepted, 10 enrolled. In 2014, 2 master's awarded. *Degree requirements:* For master's, comprehensive exam (for some programs), thesis or alternative. *Entrance requirements:* For master's, GRE General Test. Additional exam requirements/recommendations for international students: Required—TOEFL (minimum score 550 paper-based; 79 iBT). *Application deadline:* For fall admission, 7/1 for domestic students, 5/1 priority date for international students; for spring admission, 11/1 for domestic students, 11/1 priority date for international students; for summer admission, 4/1 priority date for international students. Applications are processed on a rolling basis. Application fee: $60. Electronic applications accepted. *Expenses:* Tuition, state resident: full-time $11,326; part-time $630 per credit hour. Tuition, nonresident: full-time $23,568; part-time $1311 per credit hour. *Required fees:* $196. Tuition and fees vary according to program and reciprocity agreements. *Financial support:* Research assistantships with full tuition reimbursements, teaching assistantships with full and partial tuition reimbursements, scholarships/grants, tuition waivers (partial), and unspecified assistantships available. Support available to part-time students. Financial award applicants required to submit FAFSA. *Faculty research:* Health communication, interpersonal communication, computer-mediated communication, strategic communication, mass communication. *Unit head:* Dr. Al Futrell, Chair, E-mail: al@louisville.edu. *Application contact:* Libby Leggett, Director, Graduate Admissions, 502-852-3101, Fax: 502-852-6536, E-mail: gradadm@louisville.edu.
Website: http://louisville.edu/communication

University of Maine, Graduate School, College of Liberal Arts and Sciences, Department of Communication and Journalism, Orono, ME 04469. Offers communication (MA, PhD); mass communication (MA). Part-time programs available. *Faculty:* 8 full-time (3 women), 7 part-time/adjunct (3 women). *Students:* 16 full-time (8 women), 1 (woman) part-time, 3 international. Average age 27. 21 applicants, 52% accepted, 7 enrolled. In 2014, 4 master's, 3 doctorates awarded. *Degree requirements:* For master's, thesis (for some programs); for doctorate, comprehensive exam, thesis/dissertation. *Entrance requirements:* For master's, GRE General Test. Additional exam requirements/recommendations for international students: Required—TOEFL. *Application deadline:* For fall admission, 2/1 priority date for domestic students. Applications are processed on a rolling basis. Application fee: $65. Electronic applications accepted. *Expenses:* Tuition, state resident: part-time $658 per credit hour. Tuition, nonresident: part-time $1550 per credit hour. *Financial support:* In 2014–15, 14 students received support, including 14 teaching assistantships with full tuition reimbursements available (averaging $14,600 per year); career-related internships or fieldwork, Federal Work-Study, institutionally sponsored loans, and tuition waivers (full and partial) also available. Support available to part-time students. Financial award application deadline: 3/1. *Faculty research:* Rhetorical theory, semiotics, discourse analysis, gender and communication, children's talk/communication disorders. *Total annual research expenditures:* $104,293. *Unit head:* Dr. Nathan Stormer, Chair, 207-581-1938, Fax: 207-581-1286, E-mail: nathan@maine.edu. *Application contact:* Scott G. Delcourt, Assistant Vice President for Graduate Studies and Senior Associate Dean, 207-581-3291, Fax: 207-581-3232, E-mail: graduate@maine.edu.
Website: http://cmj.umaine.edu/graduate-program/

University of Maryland, Baltimore County, The Graduate School, College of Arts, Humanities and Social Sciences, Department of Modern Languages and Linguistics, Program in Intercultural Communication, Baltimore, MD 21250. Offers MA. Part-time and evening/weekend programs available. *Faculty:* 17 full-time (9 women), 2 part-time/adjunct (1 woman). *Students:* 25 full-time (20 women), 7 part-time (5 women); includes 9 minority (8 Black or African American, non-Hispanic/Latino; 1 Hispanic/Latino), 13 international. 15 applicants, 87% accepted, 7 enrolled. In 2014, 10 master's awarded. *Degree requirements:* For master's, one foreign language, comprehensive exam (for some programs), thesis (for some programs). *Entrance requirements:* For master's, GRE General Test, minimum GPA of 3.0, 3 letters of recommendation, self-evaluation and statement of support, resume. Additional exam requirements/recommendations for international students: Required—TOEFL (minimum score 550 paper-based; 80 iBT). *Application deadline:* For fall admission, 1/31 for domestic and international students. Application fee: $50. Electronic applications accepted. *Expenses:* Tuition, state resident: part-time $557. Tuition, nonresident: part-time $922. *Required fees:* $122 per semester. One-time fee: $200 part-time. *Financial support:* In 2014–15, 8 students received support, including 6 teaching assistantships with full tuition reimbursements available (averaging $12,190 per year); Federal Work-Study, scholarships/grants, and tuition waivers (partial) also available. Financial award application deadline: 1/31; financial award applicants required to submit FAFSA. *Faculty research:* Comparative television research-cross-cultural; cultural studies; social developments in Latin America; intercultural communication; French civilization and cultural studies; language, gender and sexuality; sociolinguistics; African linguistics; immigrants in U.S. and Latin American societies. *Unit head:* Dr. Denis Provencher, Director, 410-455-2109 Ext. 52636, Fax: 410-455-2636, E-mail: provench@umbc.edu.
Website: http://www.umbc.edu/mll/incc/

University of Maryland, College Park, Academic Affairs, College of Arts and Humanities, Department of Communication, College Park, MD 20742. Offers MA, PhD. *Degree requirements:* For master's, thesis optional; for doctorate, comprehensive exam, thesis/dissertation. *Entrance requirements:* For master's, GRE General Test, minimum GPA of 3.0, sample of scholarly writing, 3 letters of recommendation, statement of goals and experiences; for doctorate, GRE General Test. Additional exam requirements/recommendations for international students: Required—TOEFL. Electronic applications accepted. *Faculty research:* Health communication, interpersonal communication, persuasion, intercultural communication, contemporary rhetoric theory.

University of Massachusetts Amherst, Graduate School, College of Social and Behavioral Sciences, Department of Communication, Amherst, MA 01003. Offers MA, PhD. Part-time programs available. *Faculty:* 28 full-time (14 women). *Students:* 64 full-time (41 women), 7 part-time (3 women); includes 11 minority (4 Asian, non-Hispanic/Latino; 5 Hispanic/Latino; 2 Two or more races, non-Hispanic/Latino), 32 international. Average age 35. 131 applicants, 18% accepted, 7 enrolled. In 2014, 1 master's, 9 doctorates awarded. Terminal master's awarded for partial completion of doctoral program. *Degree requirements:* For master's, thesis or alternative; for doctorate, comprehensive exam, thesis/dissertation. *Entrance requirements:* For master's and doctorate, GRE General Test, 3 letters of recommendation. Additional exam requirements/recommendations for international students: Required—TOEFL (minimum score 550 paper-based; 80 iBT), IELTS (minimum score 6.5). *Application deadline:* For fall admission, 1/2 for domestic and international students. Applications are processed on a rolling basis. Application fee: $75. Electronic applications accepted. *Expenses:* Tuition, state resident: full-time $1980; part-time $110 per credit. Tuition, nonresident: full-time $14,644; part-time $414 per credit. *Required fees:* $11,417. One-time fee: $357. *Financial support:* Fellowships with full and partial tuition reimbursements, research assistantships with full and partial tuition reimbursements, teaching assistantships with full and partial tuition reimbursements, career-related internships or fieldwork, Federal Work-Study, scholarships/grants, traineeships, health care benefits, tuition waivers (full and partial), and unspecified assistantships available. Support available to part-time students. Financial award application deadline: 1/2; financial award applicants required to submit FAFSA. *Unit head:* Dr. Leda Cooks, Graduate Program Director, 413-545-2795, Fax: 413-545-6399, E-mail: jariceh@comm.umass.edu. *Application contact:* Lindsay DeSantis, Supervisor of Admissions, 413-545-0722, Fax: 413-577-0010, E-mail: gradadm@grad.umass.edu.
Website: http://www.umass.edu/communication/

University of Memphis, Graduate School, College of Communication and Fine Arts, Department of Communication, Memphis, TN 38152. Offers communication (MA); communication arts (PhD); film and video production (MA). Part-time programs available. *Faculty:* 12 full-time (5 women). *Students:* 20 full-time (10 women), 18 part-time (6 women); includes 8 minority (4 Black or African American, non-Hispanic/Latino; 1 Asian, non-Hispanic/Latino; 2 Hispanic/Latino; 1 Two or more races, non-Hispanic/Latino). Average age 35. 47 applicants, 55% accepted, 6 enrolled. In 2014, 3 master's, 6 doctorates awarded. *Degree requirements:* For master's, comprehensive exam, thesis or alternative; for doctorate, comprehensive exam, thesis/dissertation. *Entrance requirements:* For master's and doctorate, GRE General Test. Additional exam requirements/recommendations for international students: Required—TOEFL (minimum score 600 paper-based). *Application deadline:* For fall admission, 2/1 for domestic and international students. Application fee: $35 ($60 for international students). *Financial support:* In 2014–15, 27 students received support. Research assistantships with full tuition reimbursements available, teaching assistantships with full tuition reimbursements available, Federal Work-Study, scholarships/grants, and unspecified assistantships available. Financial award application deadline: 2/15; financial award applicants required to submit FAFSA. *Faculty research:* Rhetoric, media studies, applied communication (health communication). *Unit head:* Dr. Sandra Sarkela, Chair, 901-678-3173, Fax: 901-678-4331, E-mail: ssarkela@memphis.edu. *Application contact:* Dr. Amanda Young, Coordinator of Graduate Studies, 901-678-3612, Fax: 901-678-4331, E-mail: ajyoung@memphis.edu.
Website: http://www.memphis.edu/ccfa/index.php

University of Miami, Graduate School, School of Communication, Coral Gables, FL 33124. Offers communication (PhD); communication studies (MA); film studies (MA, PhD); motion pictures (MFA), including production, producing, and screenwriting; print journalism (MA); public relations (MA); Spanish language journalism (MA); television broadcast journalism (MA). Part-time programs available. *Degree requirements:* For master's, comprehensive exam (for some programs), thesis (for some programs); for doctorate, comprehensive exam, thesis/dissertation. *Entrance requirements:* For master's, GRE General Test; for doctorate, GRE General Test, master's thesis or scholarly research. Additional exam requirements/recommendations for international students: Required—TOEFL (minimum score 600 paper-based; 100 iBT). Electronic applications accepted. *Faculty research:* Communication studies, mass communication, international/interpersonal communication, film studies, journalism.

University of Michigan, Horace H. Rackham School of Graduate Studies, College of Literature, Science, and the Arts, Department of Communication Studies, Ann Arbor, MI 48109-1285. Offers PhD. *Faculty:* 21 full-time (9 women). *Students:* 29 full-time (22 women); includes 8 minority (5 Black or African American, non-Hispanic/Latino; 2 Hispanic/Latino; 1 Two or more races, non-Hispanic/Latino), 6 international. Average age 29. 94 applicants, 14% accepted, 6 enrolled. In 2014, 5 doctorates awarded. *Degree requirements:* For doctorate, comprehensive exam, thesis/dissertation, first-year research project, 2 terms in student instructor position, publications, presentations. *Entrance requirements:* For doctorate, GRE, U.S. bachelor's degree or its equivalent from accredited institution. Additional exam requirements/recommendations for international students: Required—TOEFL (minimum score 600 paper-based; 102 iBT). *Application deadline:* For fall admission, 12/1 for domestic and international students. Application fee: $75 ($90 for international students). Electronic applications accepted. *Expenses:* Expenses: $10,203.19/term for MI resident pre-candidates; $20,446.19/term for non-MI resident pre-candidates; $5,501.19/term for candidates. *Financial support:* In 2014–15, 29 students received support, including 28 fellowships with full tuition reimbursements available (averaging $18,757 per year), 2 research assistantships with full tuition reimbursements available (averaging $18,971 per year), 21 teaching assistantships with full tuition reimbursements available (averaging $19,827 per year); scholarships/grants, health care benefits, tuition waivers (full), and unspecified assistantships also available. Financial award application deadline: 4/30; financial award applicants required to submit FAFSA. *Faculty research:* Political communication; media, culture and society; media effects; race, gender, and the media; new media, media law and policy. *Unit head:* Prof. Susan J. Douglas, Professor and Chair, 734-764-0420, Fax: 734-764-3288, E-mail: sdoug@umich.edu. *Application contact:* Amy B. Eaton, Graduate Program Coordinator, 734-615-8974, Fax: 734-764-3288, E-mail: lsa-commphd@umich.edu.
Website: http://www.lsa.umich.edu/comm/

University of Minnesota, Twin Cities Campus, Graduate School, College of Design, Department of Design, Housing, and Apparel, Minneapolis, MN 55455-0213. Offers apparel (MA, MS, PhD); design communication (MA, MS, PhD); housing studies (MA, MS, PhD, Postbaccalaureate Certificate); interactive design (MFA); interior design (MA, MS, PhD). Part-time programs available. *Degree requirements:* For master's and Postbaccalaureate Certificate, comprehensive exam, thesis (for some programs); for doctorate, comprehensive exam, thesis/dissertation. *Entrance requirements:* For master's, GRE General Test, minimum GPA of 3.0 (preferred), portfolio, 3 letters of recommendation; for doctorate, GRE General Test, minimum GPA of 3.0 (preferred), portfolio, 3 letters of recommendation, writing sample; for Postbaccalaureate Certificate, GRE General Test, minimum GPA of 3.0 (preferred). Additional exam requirements/recommendations for international students: Required—TOEFL (minimum score 550 paper-based; 79 iBT). Electronic applications accepted. *Faculty research:* Housing policy and community development; consumer behavior; interactive design; design history; social, cultural, and behavioral issues related to designed environments.

University of Minnesota, Twin Cities Campus, Graduate School, College of Liberal Arts, Department of Communication Studies, Minneapolis, MN 55455-0213. Offers MA, PhD. *Degree requirements:* For master's, thesis or alternative; for doctorate, thesis/dissertation. *Entrance requirements:* For master's, GRE General Test, minimum GPA of 3.0; for doctorate, GRE General Test, minimum graduate GPA of 3.5. Additional exam requirements/recommendations for international students: Required—TOEFL. Electronic applications accepted. *Faculty research:* Rhetorical studies, communication theory, media studies, gender and communication, public address.

University of Missouri, Office of Research and Graduate Studies, College of Arts and Science, Department of Communication, Columbia, MO 65211. Offers MA, PhD. *Faculty:* 14 full-time (8 women). *Students:* 31 full-time (22 women), 8 part-time (4 women); includes 3 minority (1 Asian, non-Hispanic/Latino; 1 Hispanic/Latino; 1 Two or more races, non-Hispanic/Latino), 3 international. Average age 30. 124 applicants, 9% accepted, 10 enrolled. In 2014, 2 master's, 6 doctorates awarded. Terminal master's awarded for partial completion of doctoral program. *Degree requirements:* For doctorate, comprehensive exam, thesis/dissertation. *Entrance requirements:* For master's and doctorate, GRE General Test (minimum score 500 verbal, 500 quantitative, 4.0 analytical preferred), minimum GPA of 3.0. Additional exam requirements/recommendations for international students: Required—TOEFL (minimum score 600 paper-based; 100 iBT). *Application deadline:* For fall admission, 1/15 priority date for domestic students, 1/15 for international students. Applications are processed on a rolling basis. Application fee: $55 ($75 for international students). Electronic applications

accepted. *Financial support:* Fellowships with full tuition reimbursements, research assistantships with full tuition reimbursements, teaching assistantships with full tuition reimbursements, institutionally sponsored loans, health care benefits, and unspecified assistantships available. *Faculty research:* Interpersonal, mass media, organizational, and political communication. *Unit head:* Department Chair, 573-882-0525, E-mail: portermj@missouri.edu. *Application contact:* Martha Crump, Administrative Assistant, 573-882-4432, E-mail: crumpm@missouri.edu. Website: https://communication.missouri.edu/?q=grad/about

University of Missouri, Office of Research and Graduate Studies, School of Journalism, Columbia, MO 65211. Offers center for the digital globe (Certificate); European Union studies (Certificate); health communications (MA); interactive media (MA); journalism (PhD); media management (MA); strategic communication (MA). *Accreditation:* ACEJMC (one or more programs are accredited). Part-time programs available. *Faculty:* 75 full-time (38 women), 3 part-time/adjunct (1 woman). *Students:* 159 full-time (104 women), 88 part-time (54 women); includes 33 minority (8 Black or African American, non-Hispanic/Latino; 11 Asian, non-Hispanic/Latino; 11 Hispanic/Latino; 3 Two or more races, non-Hispanic/Latino, 57 international. Average age 29. 239 applicants, 55% accepted, 78 enrolled. In 2014, 73 master's, 8 doctorates awarded. Terminal master's awarded for partial completion of doctoral program. *Degree requirements:* For master's, thesis (for some programs); for doctorate, 2 foreign languages, thesis/dissertation. *Entrance requirements:* For master's and doctorate, GRE General Test, minimum GPA of 3.0. Additional exam requirements/recommendations for international students: Required—TOEFL (minimum score 600 paper-based; 100 iBT). *Application deadline:* For fall admission, 12/15 priority date for domestic and international students; for winter admission, 9/1 priority date for domestic and international students. Applications are processed on a rolling basis. Application fee: $55 ($75 for international students). Electronic applications accepted. *Financial support:* Fellowships with tuition reimbursements, research assistantships with tuition reimbursements, teaching assistantships with tuition reimbursements, career-related internships or fieldwork, institutionally sponsored loans, scholarships/grants, health care benefits, and unspecified assistantships available. Support available to part-time students. *Faculty research:* Strategic communication, convergence journalism, journalism studies, international programs, photojournalism, magazine journalism, radio-television journalism. *Unit head:* Dr. Esther Thorson, Associate Dean, 573-882-9590, E-mail: thorsone@missouri.edu. *Application contact:* Ginny Cowell, Administrative Assistant, 573-882-4852, E-mail: cowellvj@missouri.edu. Website: http://www.journalism.missouri.edu/graduate/

University of Missouri–St. Louis, College of Fine Arts and Communication, Department of Communication, St. Louis, MO 63121. Offers MA. Part-time and evening/weekend programs available. *Faculty:* 7 full-time (6 women), 1 (woman) part-time/adjunct. *Students:* 4 full-time (2 women), 10 part-time (6 women); includes 5 minority (all Black or African American, non-Hispanic/Latino), 2 international. Average age 29. 16 applicants, 44% accepted, 4 enrolled. In 2014, 8 master's awarded. *Degree requirements:* For master's, thesis optional. *Entrance requirements:* For master's, 3 letters of recommendation, minimum GPA of 3.25; BA in communication or related discipline. Additional exam requirements/recommendations for international students: Recommended—TOEFL (minimum score 600 paper-based; 79 iBT), IELTS (minimum score 6.5). *Application deadline:* For fall admission, 7/1 for domestic and international students; for spring admission, 12/1 for domestic and international students. Application fee: $50 ($40 for international students). Electronic applications accepted. *Expenses:* Tuition, state resident: full-time $7364; part-time $409.10 per hour. Tuition, nonresident: full-time $18,153; part-time $1008.50 per hour. *Financial support:* In 2014–15, 5 teaching assistantships (averaging $11,520 per year) were awarded. Financial award application deadline: 4/1; financial award applicants required to submit FAFSA. *Faculty research:* Theory and methodology: intercultural, interpersonal, and mass organizational. *Unit head:* Dr. Alice Hall, Director of Graduate Studies, 314-516-5485, Fax: 314-516-5816, E-mail: halla@umsl.edu. *Application contact:* 314-516-5458, Fax: 314-516-6996, E-mail: gradadm@umsl.edu. Website: http://www.umsl.edu/~comm/

The University of Montana, Graduate School, College of Humanities and Sciences, Department of Communication Studies, Missoula, MT 59812-0002. Offers MA. *Degree requirements:* For master's, thesis (for some programs). *Entrance requirements:* For master's, GRE General Test. Additional exam requirements/recommendations for international students: Required—TOEFL (minimum score 525 paper-based). *Faculty research:* Conflict management, organizational communication, language, personal relationships, rhetoric.

University of Nebraska at Omaha, Graduate Studies, College of Communication, Fine Arts and Media, School of Communication, Omaha, NE 68182. Offers communication (MA); human resources and training (Certificate); technical communication (Certificate). Part-time and evening/weekend programs available. *Faculty:* 23 full-time (12 women). *Students:* 8 full-time (5 women), 28 part-time (23 women); includes 4 minority (1 Black or African American, non-Hispanic/Latino; 2 Hispanic/Latino; 1 Two or more races, non-Hispanic/Latino), 3 international. Average age 31. 33 applicants, 67% accepted, 15 enrolled. In 2014, 18 master's, 6 other advanced degrees awarded. *Degree requirements:* For master's, comprehensive exam, thesis (for some programs). *Entrance requirements:* For master's, minimum GPA of 3.0, 15 undergraduate communication courses, resume, statement of purpose, 3 letters of recommendation. Additional exam requirements/recommendations for international students: Required—TOEFL, IELTS, PTE. *Application deadline:* For fall admission, 3/1 priority date for domestic and international students; for spring admission, 10/1 priority date for domestic and international students. Applications are processed on a rolling basis. Application fee: $45. Electronic applications accepted. *Financial support:* In 2014–15, 13 students received support, including 6 research assistantships with tuition reimbursements available, 7 teaching assistantships with tuition reimbursements available; fellowships, Federal Work-Study, institutionally sponsored loans, scholarships/grants, tuition waivers (partial), and unspecified assistantships also available. Support available to part-time students. Financial award application deadline: 3/1; financial award applicants required to submit FAFSA. *Unit head:* Dr. Hugh Reilly, Director, 402-554-2341, E-mail: graduate@unomaha.edu. *Application contact:* Dr. Adam Tyma, Graduate Program Chair, 402-554-2341, E-mail: graduate@unomaha.edu.

University of Nebraska–Lincoln, Graduate College, College of Arts and Sciences, Department of Communication Studies, Lincoln, NE 68588. Offers instructional communication (MA, PhD); interpersonal communication (MA, PhD); marketing, communication studies, and advertising (MA, PhD); organizational communication (MA, PhD); rhetoric and culture (MA, PhD). *Degree requirements:* For master's, thesis optional; for doctorate, comprehensive exam, thesis/dissertation. *Entrance requirements:* For master's and doctorate, GRE General Test, writing sample. Additional exam requirements/recommendations for international students: Required—TOEFL (minimum score 600 paper-based). Electronic applications accepted. *Faculty research:* Message strategies, gender communication, political communication, organizational communication, instructional communication.

University of Nevada, Las Vegas, Graduate College, Greenspun College of Urban Affairs, Department of Communication Studies, Las Vegas, NV 89154-4052. Offers MA. Part-time programs available. *Faculty:* 4 full-time (3 women), 1 part-time/adjunct (0 women). *Students:* 12 full-time (8 women); includes 5 minority (1 Asian, non-Hispanic/Latino; 1 Hispanic/Latino; 3 Two or more races, non-Hispanic/Latino). Average age 29. 20 applicants, 75% accepted, 7 enrolled. In 2014, 11 master's awarded. *Degree requirements:* For master's, comprehensive exam (for some programs), thesis (for some programs). *Entrance requirements:* For master's, GRE General Test. Additional exam requirements/recommendations for international students: Required—TOEFL (minimum score 550 paper-based; 80 iBT), IELTS (minimum score 7). *Application deadline:* For fall admission, 1/15 for domestic students, 5/1 for international students; for spring admission, 10/1 for international students. Application fee: $60 ($95 for international students). Electronic applications accepted. *Financial support:* In 2014–15, 12 students received support, including 12 teaching assistantships with partial tuition reimbursements available (averaging $10,263 per year); institutionally sponsored loans, scholarships/grants, health care benefits, and unspecified assistantships also available. Financial award application deadline: 3/1. *Faculty research:* Rhetoric/public address and persuasion, argumentation, debate; interpersonal, family and health communication, conflict resolution; media and political communication; sex and gender, inter-cultural communication; cultural studies, memory studies, food studies. *Unit head:* Dr. David Henry, Chair/Professor, 702-895-3030, Fax: 702-895-4805, E-mail: david.henry@unlv.edu. *Application contact:* Graduate College Admissions Evaluator, 702-895-3320, Fax: 702-895-4180, E-mail: gradcollege@unlv.edu. Website: http://communicationstudies.unlv.edu/

University of New Mexico, Graduate School, College of Arts and Sciences, Program in Communication and Journalism, Albuquerque, NM 87131-2039. Offers communication (MA, PhD). Part-time programs available. *Faculty:* 16 full-time (10 women), 2 part-time/adjunct (0 women). *Students:* 35 full-time (23 women), 15 part-time (10 women); includes 22 minority (2 Black or African American, non-Hispanic/Latino; 10 American Indian or Alaska Native, non-Hispanic/Latino; 1 Asian, non-Hispanic/Latino; 4 Hispanic/Latino; 1 Native Hawaiian or other Pacific Islander, non-Hispanic/Latino; 4 Two or more races, non-Hispanic/Latino), 13 international. Average age 32. 41 applicants, 46% accepted, 17 enrolled. In 2014, 9 master's, 7 doctorates awarded. *Degree requirements:* For master's, 30 hours of class work and 6-hour thesis or project, or 36 hours of class work and comprehensive exam; for doctorate, 2 foreign languages, comprehensive exam, thesis/dissertation. *Entrance requirements:* For master's, GRE General Test, letters of recommendation, letter of intent, curriculum vitae, transcripts; for doctorate, GRE General Test, letters of recommendation, writing sample, letter of intent, curriculum vitae, transcripts. Additional exam requirements/recommendations for international students: Required—TOEFL (minimum score 550 paper-based). *Application deadline:* For fall admission, 1/15 for domestic and international students. Application fee: $50. Electronic applications accepted. *Financial support:* In 2014–15, 46 students received support, including 2 fellowships with tuition reimbursements available (averaging $13,800 per year), 2 research assistantships (averaging $9,439 per year), 47 teaching assistantships with tuition reimbursements available (averaging $10,639 per year); career-related internships or fieldwork, scholarships/grants, health care benefits, and unspecified assistantships also available. Financial award application deadline: 3/1; financial award applicants required to submit FAFSA. *Faculty research:* Health communication, intercultural communication, interpersonal/organizational communication, mass communication. *Unit head:* Dr. Karen Foss, Chair, 505-277-5305, Fax: 505-277-2068, E-mail: kfoss@unm.edu. *Application contact:* Gregoria Arienda Cavazos, Student Advisement Coordinator, 505-277-5305, Fax: 505-277-2068, E-mail: cjadvise@unm.edu. Website: http://www.unm.edu/~cjdept/

The University of North Carolina at Chapel Hill, Graduate School, College of Arts and Sciences, Department of Communication Studies, Chapel Hill, NC 27599. Offers PhD. *Degree requirements:* For doctorate, comprehensive exam, thesis/dissertation. *Entrance requirements:* For doctorate, GRE General Test, minimum GPA of 3.0. Additional exam requirements/recommendations for international students: Required—TOEFL (minimum score 550 paper-based; 79 iBT). Electronic applications accepted.

The University of North Carolina at Charlotte, College of Liberal Arts and Sciences, Department of Communication Studies, Charlotte, NC 28223-0001. Offers communication studies (Graduate Certificate); health communication (MA); organizational communication (MA); public relations and international public relations (MA); rhetoric, media studies, and popular culture (MA). Part-time and evening/weekend programs available. *Faculty:* 15 full-time (8 women). *Students:* 11 full-time (8 women), 12 part-time (9 women); includes 3 minority (2 Black or African American, non-Hispanic/Latino; 1 Two or more races, non-Hispanic/Latino), 2 international. Average age 27. 49 applicants, 49% accepted, 11 enrolled. In 2014, 11 master's awarded. Terminal master's awarded for partial completion of doctoral program. *Degree requirements:* For master's, project, thesis, or comprehensive exam. *Entrance requirements:* For master's, GRE General Test, minimum GPA of 2.75 overall. Additional exam requirements/recommendations for international students: Required—TOEFL (minimum score 557 paper-based; 83 iBT). *Application deadline:* For fall admission, 3/1 for domestic and international students; for spring admission, 11/15 for domestic students, 10/1 for international students. Application fee: $75. Electronic applications accepted. *Expenses:* Tuition, state resident: full-time $4008. Tuition, nonresident: full-time $16,295. *Required fees:* $2755. Tuition and fees vary according to course load and program. *Financial support:* In 2014–15, 10 students received support, including 10 teaching assistantships (averaging $14,981 per year); career-related internships or fieldwork, institutionally sponsored loans, scholarships/grants, and unspecified assistantships also available. Support available to part-time students. Financial award application deadline: 4/1; financial award applicants required to submit FAFSA. *Faculty research:* Rhetorical approaches to analyzing public relations controversies, participant empowerment and engagement in community-based participatory action research, human factors constraining the management of knowledge in a large financial services organization, models of Internet governance, race and class politics of mediated sports. *Unit head:* Dr. Shawn Long, Chair, 704-687-0783, Fax: 704-687-6900, E-mail: shawn.long@uncc.edu. *Application contact:* Kathy B. Giddings, Director of Graduate Admissions, 704-687-5503, Fax: 704-687-1668, E-mail: gradadm@uncc.edu. Website: http://gradcomm.uncc.edu/

The University of North Carolina at Greensboro, Graduate School, College of Arts and Sciences, Department of Communication Studies, Greensboro, NC 27412-5001. Offers MA. Part-time programs available. *Degree requirements:* For master's, thesis or alternative. *Entrance requirements:* For master's, GRE General Test, MAT, or PRAXIS. Additional exam requirements/recommendations for international students: Required—TOEFL. Electronic applications accepted.

University of North Dakota, Graduate School, College of Arts and Sciences, School of Communication, Grand Forks, ND 58202. Offers communication (MA); communication and public discourse (PhD). Part-time programs available. *Degree requirements:* For master's, comprehensive exam, thesis or alternative; for doctorate, thesis/dissertation. *Entrance requirements:* For master's and doctorate, GRE General Test, minimum GPA of 3.0. Additional exam requirements/recommendations for international students: Required—TOEFL (minimum score 550 paper-based; 79 iBT), IELTS (minimum score

6.5). Electronic applications accepted. *Faculty research:* Communication technologies, mass communication in diverse society, acculturation and socialization functions.

University of Northern Colorado, Graduate School, College of Humanities and Social Sciences, School of Communication, Program in Communication Studies, Greeley, CO 80639. Offers MA. Part-time programs available. *Degree requirements:* For master's, comprehensive exam, thesis or alternative. *Entrance requirements:* For master's, GRE General Test, 3 letters of recommendation. Electronic applications accepted.

University of Northern Iowa, Graduate College, College of Humanities, Arts and Sciences, Department of Communication Studies, Cedar Falls, IA 50614. Offers MA. Part-time and evening/weekend programs available. *Students:* 20 full-time (6 women), 15 part-time (11 women); includes 7 minority (5 Black or African American, non-Hispanic/Latino; 2 Asian, non-Hispanic/Latino), 2 international. 48 applicants, 35% accepted, 12 enrolled. In 2014, 13 master's awarded. *Degree requirements:* For master's, comprehensive exam, thesis or alternative. *Entrance requirements:* For master's, minimum GPA of 3.0. Additional exam requirements/recommendations for international students: Required—TOEFL (minimum score 500 paper-based; 61 iBT). *Application deadline:* For fall admission, 8/1 priority date for domestic students. Applications are processed on a rolling basis. Application fee: $50 ($70 for international students). Electronic applications accepted. *Expenses:* Tuition, state resident: full-time $7912; part-time $880 per credit. Tuition, nonresident: full-time $17,906; part-time $880 per credit. *Required fees:* $1101; $325.50 per credit. $465.63 per semester. Tuition and fees vary according to course load and program. *Financial support:* Career-related internships or fieldwork, Federal Work-Study, scholarships/grants, and tuition waivers (full and partial) available. Support available to part-time students. Financial award application deadline: 2/1. *Unit head:* Dr. Tom Hall, Coordinator, 319-273-7159, Fax: 319-273-7356, E-mail: tom.hall@uni.edu. *Application contact:* Laurie S. Russell, Record Analyst, 319-273-2623, Fax: 319-273-2885, E-mail: laurie.russell@uni.edu. Website: http://www.uni.edu/commstudies/graduate-program

University of North Texas, Robert B. Toulouse School of Graduate Studies, Denton, TX 76203-5459. Offers accounting (MS); applied anthropology (MA, MS); applied behavior analysis (Certificate); applied geography (MA); applied technology and performance improvement (M Ed, MS); art education (MA); art history (MA); art museum education (Certificate); arts leadership (Certificate); audiology (Au D); behavior analysis (MS); behavioral science (PhD); biochemistry and molecular biology (MS); biology (MA, MS); biomedical engineering (MS); business analysis (MS); chemistry (MS); clinical health psychology (PhD); communication studies (MA, MS); computer engineering (MS); computer science (MS); counseling (M Ed, MS), including clinical mental health counseling (MS), college and university counseling, elementary school counseling, secondary school counseling; creative writing (MA); criminal justice (MS); curriculum and instruction (M Ed); decision sciences (MBA); design (MA, MFA), including fashion design (MFA), innovation studies, interior design (MFA); early childhood studies (MS); economics (MS); educational leadership (M Ed, Ed D); educational psychology (MS, PhD), including family studies (MS), gifted and talented (MS), human development (MS), learning and cognition (MS), research, measurement and evaluation (MS); electrical engineering (MS); emergency management (MPA); engineering technology (MS); English (MA); English as a second language (MA); environmental science (MS); finance (MBA, MS); financial management (MPA); French (MA); health services management (MBA); higher education (M Ed, Ed D); history (MA, MS); hospitality management (MS); human resources management (MPA); information science (MS); information systems (PhD); information technologies (MBA); interdisciplinary studies (MA, MS); international studies (MA); international sustainable tourism (MS); jazz studies (MM); journalism (MA, MJ, Graduate Certificate), including interactive and virtual digital communication (Graduate Certificate), narrative journalism (Graduate Certificate), public relations (Graduate Certificate); kinesiology (MS); linguistics (MA); local government management (MPA); logistics (PhD); logistics and supply chain management (MBA); long-term care, senior housing, and aging services (MA); management (PhD); marketing (MBA); mathematics (MA, MS); mechanical and energy engineering (MS, PhD); music (MA), including ethnomusicology, music theory, musicology, performance; music composition (PhD); music education (MM Ed, PhD); nonprofit management (MPA); operations and supply chain management (MBA); performance (MM, DMA); philosophy (MA); political science (MA); professional and technical communication (MA); radio, television and film (MA, MFA); rehabilitation counseling (Certificate); sociology (MA); Spanish (MA); special education (M Ed); speech-language pathology (MA); strategic management (MBA); studio art (MFA); teaching (M Ed); MBA/MS. Part-time and evening/weekend programs available. Postbaccalaureate distance learning degree programs offered. *Faculty:* 651 full-time (215 women), 233 part-time/adjunct (139 women). *Students:* 3,040 full-time (1,598 women), 3,401 part-time (2,097 women); includes 1,740 minority (533 Black or African American, non-Hispanic/Latino; 15 American Indian or Alaska Native, non-Hispanic/Latino; 286 Asian, non-Hispanic/Latino; 746 Hispanic/Latino; 3 Native Hawaiian or other Pacific Islander, non-Hispanic/Latino; 157 Two or more races, non-Hispanic/Latino), 1,145 international. Terminal master's awarded for partial completion of doctoral program. *Degree requirements:* For master's, variable foreign language requirement, comprehensive exam (for some programs), thesis (for some programs); for doctorate, variable foreign language requirement, comprehensive exam (for some programs), thesis/dissertation; for other advanced degree, variable foreign language requirement, comprehensive exam (for some programs). *Entrance requirements:* For master's and doctorate, GRE, GMAT. Additional exam requirements/recommendations for international students: Required—TOEFL (minimum score 550 paper-based; 79 iBT). *Application deadline:* For fall admission, 7/15 for domestic students, 3/15 for international students; for spring admission, 11/15 for domestic students, 9/15 for international students; for summer admission, 5/1 for domestic students. Applications are processed on a rolling basis. Application fee: $60. Electronic applications accepted. *Expenses:* Tuition, state resident: full-time $5450; part-time $3633 per year. Tuition, nonresident: full-time $11,966; part-time $7977 per year. *Required fees:* $1301; $398 per credit hour. $685 per semester. Tuition and fees vary according to program and reciprocity agreements. *Financial support:* Fellowships with partial tuition reimbursements, research assistantships with partial tuition reimbursements, teaching assistantships, career-related internships or fieldwork, Federal Work-Study, institutionally sponsored loans, scholarships/grants, health care benefits, and library assistantships available. Support available to part-time students. Financial award applicants required to submit FAFSA. *Unit head:* Mark Wardell, Dean, 940-565-2383, E-mail: mark.wardell@unt.edu. *Application contact:* Toulouse School of Graduate Studies, 940-565-2383, Fax: 940-565-2141, E-mail: gradsch@unt.edu. Website: http://tsgs.unt.edu/

University of Oklahoma, College of Arts and Sciences, Department of Communication, Norman, OK 73019. Offers communication (MA, PhD); organizational communication (MA). Part-time and evening/weekend programs available. Postbaccalaureate distance learning degree programs offered (no on-campus study). *Faculty:* 19 full-time (9 women). *Students:* 30 full-time (19 women), 54 part-time (27 women); includes 27 minority (8 Black or African American, non-Hispanic/Latino; 3 American Indian or Alaska Native, non-Hispanic/Latino; 1 Asian, non-Hispanic/Latino; 10 Hispanic/Latino; 5 Two or more races, non-Hispanic/Latino), 8 international. Average age 35. 45 applicants, 53% accepted, 11 enrolled. In 2014, 13 master's, 4 doctorates awarded. Terminal master's awarded for partial completion of doctoral program. *Degree requirements:* For master's, variable foreign language requirement, comprehensive exam (for some programs), thesis optional; for doctorate, variable foreign language requirement, comprehensive exam, thesis/dissertation. *Entrance requirements:* For doctorate, GRE. Additional exam requirements/recommendations for international students: Required—TOEFL (minimum score 79 iBT). *Application deadline:* For fall admission, 2/1 for domestic and international students; for spring admission, 11/1 for domestic students, 9/1 for international students. Application fee: $50 ($100 for international students). Electronic applications accepted. *Expenses:* Tuition, state resident: full-time $4394; part-time $183.10 per credit hour. Tuition, nonresident: full-time $16,970; part-time $707.10 per credit hour. *Required fees:* $2892; $109.95 per credit hour. $126.50 per semester. *Financial support:* In 2014–15, 36 students received support, including 1 research assistantship with partial tuition reimbursement available (averaging $10,372 per year), 29 teaching assistantships with partial tuition reimbursements available (averaging $16,189 per year); scholarships/grants and unspecified assistantships also available. Financial award application deadline: 6/1; financial award applicants required to submit FAFSA. *Faculty research:* Intercultural/international communication, interpersonal communication/social influence, political/mass communication, health communication, organizational communication, communication technology. *Total annual research expenditures:* $744,456. *Unit head:* Dr. Michael W. Kramer, Chair and Professor, 405-325-9503, Fax: 405-325-7625, E-mail: mkramer@ou.edu. *Application contact:* Dr. Elaine Hsieh, Graduate Liaison and Associate Professor, 405-325-3154, Fax: 405-325-7625, E-mail: ehsieh@ou.edu.
Website: http://cas.ou.edu/comm

University of Oregon, Graduate School, School of Journalism and Communication, Eugene, OR 97403. Offers journalism (MA, MS); media studies (MA, MS, PhD); multimedia journalism (MA, MS); strategic communication (MA, MS). *Accreditation:* ASHA. Part-time programs available. *Degree requirements:* For master's, thesis or alternative. *Entrance requirements:* For master's, GRE General Test; for doctorate, master's degree. *Faculty research:* Impact of mass communication, media technology, media accountability, craft attitudes, media economics.

University of Ottawa, Faculty of Graduate and Postdoctoral Studies, Faculty of Arts, Department of Communication, Ottawa, ON K1N 6N5, Canada. Offers MA. Electronic applications accepted. *Faculty research:* Media studies, organizational communications.

University of Pennsylvania, Annenberg School for Communication, Philadelphia, PA 19104. Offers PhD. *Faculty:* 19 full-time (8 women), 5 part-time/adjunct (1 woman). *Students:* 78 full-time (48 women), 3 part-time (1 woman); includes 11 minority (3 Black or African American, non-Hispanic/Latino; 2 Asian, non-Hispanic/Latino; 4 Hispanic/Latino; 2 Two or more races, non-Hispanic/Latino), 30 international. 326 applicants, 6% accepted, 14 enrolled. In 2014, 13 doctorates awarded. *Degree requirements:* For doctorate, thesis/dissertation. *Entrance requirements:* For doctorate, GRE General Test. *Application deadline:* For fall admission, 1/2 for domestic students. Application fee: $70. Electronic applications accepted. *Financial support:* In 2014–15, 80 students received support. Fellowships, research assistantships, teaching assistantships, institutionally sponsored loans, scholarships/grants, traineeships, health care benefits, and unspecified assistantships available. Financial award application deadline: 12/15. *Unit head:* Dr. Michael X. Delli Carpini, Dean, 215-898-7041, E-mail: dean@asc.upenn.edu. *Application contact:* Joanne Murray, Graduate Studies Coordinator, 215-898-7041, Fax: 215-898-2024.
Website: http://www.asc.upenn.edu/

University of Pittsburgh, Dietrich School of Arts and Sciences, Department of Communication, Pittsburgh, PA 15260. Offers MA, PhD. *Faculty:* 11 full-time (4 women). *Students:* 43 full-time (23 women); includes 14 minority (5 Black or African American, non-Hispanic/Latino; 2 Asian, non-Hispanic/Latino; 7 Hispanic/Latino), 2 international. Average age 29. 88 applicants, 9% accepted, 8 enrolled. In 2014, 1 master's, 10 doctorates awarded. *Degree requirements:* For master's, comprehensive exam, thesis optional; for doctorate, comprehensive exam, thesis/dissertation. *Entrance requirements:* For master's and doctorate, GRE General Test, sample of written work, curriculum vitae. Additional exam requirements/recommendations for international students: Required—TOEFL (minimum score 577 paper-based; 90 iBT), IELTS (minimum score 7). *Application deadline:* For fall admission, 1/2 priority date for domestic and international students. Application fee: $50. Electronic applications accepted. *Expenses:* Tuition, state resident: full-time $20,742; part-time $838 per credit. Tuition, nonresident: full-time $33,960; part-time $1389 per credit. *Required fees:* $800; $205 per term. Tuition and fees vary according to program. *Financial support:* In 2014–15, 28 students received support, including 22 fellowships with full tuition reimbursements available (averaging $17,370 per year), 2 teaching assistantships with full tuition reimbursements available (averaging $16,710 per year); Federal Work-Study, scholarships/grants, health care benefits, tuition waivers (full), and unspecified assistantships also available. Financial award application deadline: 1/2; financial award applicants required to submit FAFSA. *Faculty research:* Media and cultural studies, public argument and discourse, rhetoric of science, history, criticism and theory of rhetoric. *Unit head:* Dr. Lester Olson, Department Chair, 412-624-1564, Fax: 412-624-1878, E-mail: olson@pitt.edu. *Application contact:* Dr. John Lyne, Director of Graduate Studies, 412-648-7664, Fax: 412-624-1878, E-mail: jlyne@pitt.edu.
Website: http://www.comm.pitt.edu/

University of Portland, Department of Communication Studies, Portland, OR 97203-5798. Offers communication (MA); management communication (MS). Part-time and evening/weekend programs available. *Faculty:* 5 full-time (3 women), 1 part-time/adjunct (0 women). *Students:* 7 full-time (4 women), 10 part-time (7 women); includes 2 minority (1 Hispanic/Latino; 1 Two or more races, non-Hispanic/Latino), 2 international. Average age 28. In 2014, 7 master's awarded. *Degree requirements:* For master's, thesis optional. *Entrance requirements:* For master's, GRE General Test, minimum GPA of 3.25, 3 letters of recommendation, resume, statement of goals, official transcripts. Additional exam requirements/recommendations for international students: Required—TOEFL (minimum score 600 paper-based; 100 iBT), IELTS (minimum score 7.5). *Application deadline:* For fall admission, 7/15 priority date for domestic and international students; for spring admission, 12/15 priority date for domestic and international students. Applications are processed on a rolling basis. Application fee: $50. *Expenses:* Tuition: Full-time $19,260; part-time $1070 per credit hour. Tuition and fees vary according to program. *Financial support:* Career-related internships or fieldwork, Federal Work-Study, scholarships/grants, and tuition waivers (partial) available. Financial award application deadline: 3/1; financial award applicants required to submit FAFSA. *Unit head:* Dr. Jeff Kerssen-Griep, Director, 503-943-7229, E-mail: kerssen@up.edu. *Application contact:* Allison Able, Graduate Program Coordinator, 503-943-7107, Fax: 503-943-7315, E-mail: able@up.edu.
Website: http://college.up.edu/commstudies/default.aspx?cid-1377&PID-286

University of Puerto Rico, Río Piedras Campus, School of Communication, Program in Communication Theory and Research, San Juan, PR 00931-3300. Offers MA.

University of Rhode Island, Graduate School, College of Arts and Sciences, Department of Communication Studies, Kingston, RI 02881. Offers MA. Part-time programs available. *Faculty:* 33 full-time (17 women), 2 part-time/adjunct (both women). *Students:* 10 full-time (8 women), 18 part-time (11 women); includes 5 minority (4 Black or African American, non-Hispanic/Latino; 1 American Indian or Alaska Native, non-

Hispanic/Latino), 5 international. In 2014, 10 master's awarded. *Degree requirements:* For master's, comprehensive exam (for some programs), thesis optional. *Entrance requirements:* For master's, GRE, 2 letters of recommendation. Additional exam requirements/recommendations for international students: Required—TOEFL (minimum score 550 paper-based; 88 iBT). *Application deadline:* For fall admission, 7/15 for domestic students, 2/1 for international students. Application fee: $65. Electronic applications accepted. *Expenses:* Tuition, state resident: full-time $11,532; part-time $641 per credit. Tuition, nonresident: full-time $23,606; part-time $1311 per credit. *Required fees:* $1442; $39 per credit. $35 per semester. One-time fee: $155. *Financial support:* In 2014–15, 2 research assistantships with full tuition reimbursements (averaging $16,072 per year), 5 teaching assistantships with full tuition reimbursements (averaging $15,844 per year) were awarded. Financial award application deadline: 2/1; financial award applicants required to submit FAFSA. *Total annual research expenditures:* $41,820. *Unit head:* Dr. Kevin McClure, Chair, 401-874-4726, Fax: 401-874-4722, E-mail: kmcclure@uri.edu. *Application contact:* Dr. Abran Salazar, Director of Graduate Studies, 401-874-9015, E-mail: abran_salazar@uri.edu.
Website: http://www.uri.edu/artsci/com/

University of South Africa, College of Human Sciences, Pretoria, South Africa. Offers adult education (M Ed); African languages (MA, PhD); African politics (MA, PhD); Afrikaans (MA, PhD); ancient history (MA, PhD); ancient Near Eastern studies (MA, PhD); anthropology (MA, PhD); applied linguistics (MA); Arabic (MA, PhD); archaeology (MA); art history (MA); Biblical archaeology (MA); Biblical studies (M Th, D Th, PhD); Christian spirituality (M Th, D Th); church history (M Th, D Th); classical studies (MA, PhD); clinical psychology (MA); communication (MA, PhD); comparative education (M Ed, Ed D); consulting psychology (D Admin, D Com, PhD); curriculum studies (M Ed, Ed D); development studies (M Admin, MA, D Admin, PhD); didactics (M Ed, Ed D); education (M Tech); education management (M Ed, Ed D); educational psychology (M Ed); English (MA); environmental education (M Ed); French (MA, PhD); German (MA, PhD); Greek (MA); guidance and counseling (M Ed); health studies (MA, PhD), including health sciences education (MA), health services management (MA), medical and surgical nursing science (critical care general) (MA), midwifery and neonatal nursing science (MA), trauma and emergency care (MA); history (MA, PhD); history of education (Ed D); inclusive education (M Ed, Ed D); information and communications technology policy and regulation (MA); information science (MA, MIS, PhD); international politics (MA, PhD); Islamic studies (MA, PhD); Italian (MA, PhD); Judaica (MA, PhD); linguistics (MA, PhD); mathematical education (M Ed); mathematics education (MA); missiology (M Th, D Th); modern Hebrew (MA, PhD); musicology (MA, MMus, D Mus, PhD); natural science education (M Ed); New Testament (M Th, D Th); Old Testament (D Th); pastoral therapy (M Th, D Th); philosophy (MA); philosophy of education (M Ed, Ed D); politics (MA, PhD); Portuguese (MA, PhD); practical theology (M Th, D Th); psychology (MA, MS, PhD); psychology of education (M Ed, Ed D); public health (MA); religious studies (MA, D Th, PhD); Romance languages (MA); Russian (MA, PhD); Semitic languages (MA, PhD); social behavior studies in HIV/AIDS (MA); social science (mental health) (MA); social science in development studies (MA); social science in psychology (MA); social science in social work (MA); social science in sociology (MA); social work (MSW, DSW, PhD); socio-education (M Ed, Ed D); sociolinguistics (MA); sociology (MA, PhD); Spanish (MA, PhD); systematic theology (M Th, D Th); TESOL (teaching English to speakers of other languages) (MA); theological ethics (M Th, D Th); theory of literature (MA, PhD); urban ministries (D Th); urban ministry (M Th).

University of South Alabama, College of Arts and Sciences, Department of Communication, Mobile, AL 36688. Offers MA. *Faculty:* 6 full-time (2 women). *Students:* 25 full-time (19 women), 5 part-time (2 women); includes 6 minority (5 Black or African American, non-Hispanic/Latino; 1 American Indian or Alaska Native, non-Hispanic/Latino), 2 international. Average age 28. 18 applicants, 44% accepted, 6 enrolled. In 2014, 12 master's awarded. *Degree requirements:* For master's, comprehensive exam, thesis optional, minimum of 34 semesters hours, including 3 hours of thesis or project work; minimum of 25 semester hours in communication. *Entrance requirements:* For master's, GRE, GMAT, minimum GPA of 3.0, BA in communication or 36 semester hours. Additional exam requirements/recommendations for international students: Required—TOEFL (minimum score 525 paper-based). *Application deadline:* For fall admission, 7/15 priority date for domestic students, 6/15 priority date for international students; for spring admission, 12/1 priority date for domestic students, 11/1 priority date for international students. Applications are processed on a rolling basis. Application fee: $35. Electronic applications accepted. *Expenses:* Tuition, state resident: full-time $9288; part-time $387 per credit hour. Tuition, nonresident: full-time $18,576; part-time $774 per credit hour. Part-time tuition and fees vary according to course load and program. *Financial support:* Fellowships, research assistantships, teaching assistantships, career-related internships or fieldwork, Federal Work-Study, institutionally sponsored loans, scholarships/grants, and unspecified assistantships available. Support available to part-time students. Financial award application deadline: 5/31; financial award applicants required to submit FAFSA. *Unit head:* Dr. James Aucoin, Chair, 251-380-2800, Fax: 251-380-2850, E-mail: jaucoin@southalabama.edu. *Application contact:* Dr. Richard Ward, Graduate Coordinator, Communication, 251-380-2800, Fax: 251-380-2850, E-mail: rward@southalabama.edu.
Website: http://comm.southalabama.edu/index.php/programs/graduate-studies.html

The University of South Dakota, Graduate School, College of Arts and Sciences, Department of Communication Studies, Vermillion, SD 57069-2390. Offers MA. Part-time programs available. *Degree requirements:* For master's, comprehensive exam (for some programs), thesis (for some programs). *Entrance requirements:* For master's, minimum GPA of 2.7. Additional exam requirements/recommendations for international students: Required—TOEFL (minimum score 575 paper-based; 79 iBT). Electronic applications accepted. *Faculty research:* Male/female communication, interpersonal communication, relational communication, rhetoric and public address, organizational communication.

University of Southern California, Graduate School, Annenberg School for Communication and Journalism, School of Communication, Program in Communication, Los Angeles, CA 90089. Offers culture and community (PhD); global and transnational communication (PhD); groups, organizations and networks (PhD); health communication and social dynamics (PhD); information, political economy and entertainment (PhD); new media and technology (PhD); rhetoric, politics and public media (PhD). *Students:* 105 full-time (76 women); includes 829 minority (8 Black or African American, non-Hispanic/Latino; 810 Asian, non-Hispanic/Latino; 7 Hispanic/Latino; 4 Two or more races, non-Hispanic/Latino), 41 international. Average age 27. 229 applicants, 14% accepted, 19 enrolled. In 2014, 16 doctorates awarded. *Degree requirements:* For doctorate, thesis/dissertation. *Entrance requirements:* For doctorate, GRE General Test, resume or curriculum vitae, scholarly writing, 3 letters of recommendation, statement of purpose. Additional exam requirements/recommendations for international students: Required—TOEFL (minimum score 114 iBT) or IELTS; Recommended—TWE. *Application deadline:* For fall admission, 11/1 for domestic and international students. Application fee: $85. Electronic applications accepted. *Financial support:* In 2014–15, 18 students received support, including 18 fellowships with full tuition reimbursements available (averaging $74,000 per year); health care benefits and unspecified assistantships also available. Financial award application deadline: 11/1; financial award applicants required to submit FAFSA. *Faculty research:* Computer-mediated communication, public health campaigns, communication democracy and the public sphere, new communication technologies in organizations, communication and community. *Unit head:* Dr. Peter Monge, Director of the PhD Program, 213-740-0921, E-mail: monge@usc.edu. *Application contact:* Allyson Hill, Associate Dean for Admissions, 213-821-0770, Fax: 213-740-1933, E-mail: ascadm@usc.edu.
Website: http://www.annenberg.usc.edu

University of Southern California, Graduate School, Annenberg School for Communication and Journalism, School of Communication, Program in Global Communication, Los Angeles, CA 90089. Offers MA/M Sc. Program offered jointly with London School of Economics. *Students:* 45 full-time (35 women); includes 3 minority (1 Asian, non-Hispanic/Latino; 2 Hispanic/Latino), 39 international. Average age 24. 278 applicants, 22% accepted, 45 enrolled. *Entrance requirements:* Additional exam requirements/recommendations for international students: Required—TOEFL (minimum score 114 iBT) or IELTS. *Application deadline:* For fall admission, 2/1 priority date for domestic and international students. Applications are processed on a rolling basis. Application fee: $0. Electronic applications accepted. *Financial support:* In 2014–15, 16 research assistantships with partial tuition reimbursements (averaging $10,000 per year) were awarded; Federal Work-Study, institutionally sponsored loans, scholarships/grants, health care benefits, tuition waivers (partial), and unspecified assistantships also available. Support available to part-time students. Financial award application deadline: 1/15; financial award applicants required to submit FAFSA. *Faculty research:* New technology, audience analysis, globalization, entertainment industry, integrated communication. *Unit head:* Dr. Patricia Riley, Director, 213-740-3949, Fax: 213-740-0013, E-mail: priley@usc.edu. *Application contact:* Allyson Hill, Associate Dean for Admissions, 213-821-0770, Fax: 213-740-1933, E-mail: ascadm@usc.edu.
Website: http://www.annenberg.usc.edu

University of Southern California, Graduate School, Annenberg School for Communication and Journalism, School of Communication, Program in Public Diplomacy, Los Angeles, CA 90089. Offers MPD. Part-time programs available. *Students:* 41 full-time (0 women), 3 part-time (0 women); includes 12 minority (3 Black or African American, non-Hispanic/Latino; 4 Asian, non-Hispanic/Latino; 5 Hispanic/Latino), 12 international. Average age 26. 60 applicants, 75% accepted, 18 enrolled. In 2014, 26 master's awarded. *Degree requirements:* For master's, thesis. *Entrance requirements:* For master's, GRE, resume, writing samples, statement of purpose, recommendation letters. Additional exam requirements/recommendations for international students: Required—TOEFL (minimum score 114 iBT) or IELTS (minimum score 8). *Application deadline:* For fall admission, 1/15 priority date for domestic and international students. Application fee: $85. Electronic applications accepted. *Financial support:* In 2014–15, 4 fellowships with partial tuition reimbursements (averaging $39,000 per year) were awarded; career-related internships or fieldwork, Federal Work-Study, and scholarships/grants also available. Support available to part-time students. Financial award application deadline: 1/15; financial award applicants required to submit FAFSA. *Unit head:* Dr. Nicholas Cull, Director, 213-821-4080, E-mail: cull@usc.edu. *Application contact:* Allyson Hill, Associate Dean for Admissions, 213-821-0770, Fax: 213-740-1933, E-mail: ascadm@usc.edu.
Website: http://www.annenberg.usc.edu

University of Southern Indiana, Graduate Studies, College of Liberal Arts, Program in Communication, Evansville, IN 47712-3590. Offers MA. Part-time and evening/weekend programs available. *Faculty:* 11 full-time (4 women). *Students:* 5 full-time (3 women), 13 part-time (10 women); includes 2 minority (1 Hispanic/Latino; 1 Two or more races, non-Hispanic/Latino), 1 international. Average age 32. In 2014, 6 master's awarded. *Entrance requirements:* For master's, GRE, written letter of intent, three professional letters of recommendation. Additional exam requirements/recommendations for international students: Required—TOEFL (minimum score 550 paper-based; 79 iBT), IELTS (minimum score 6). *Application deadline:* For fall admission, 8/1 for domestic students, 3/1 for international students. Applications are processed on a rolling basis. Application fee: $40. Electronic applications accepted. *Financial support:* Federal Work-Study, scholarships/grants, and unspecified assistantships available. Financial award application deadline: 3/1; financial award applicants required to submit FAFSA. *Unit head:* Dr. Karen Bonnell, Interim Director, 812-464-1968, E-mail: kbonnell@usi.edu. *Application contact:* Dr. Mayola Rowser, Director, Graduate Studies, 812-465-7016, E-mail: mrowser@usi.edu.
Website: http://www.usi.edu/liberalarts/master-of-arts-in-communication

University of South Florida, College of Arts and Sciences, Department of Communication, Tampa, FL 33620-9951. Offers MA, PhD. Part-time programs available. *Faculty:* 13 full-time (6 women). *Students:* 39 full-time (22 women), 17 part-time (10 women); includes 17 minority (5 Black or African American, non-Hispanic/Latino; 2 Asian, non-Hispanic/Latino; 8 Hispanic/Latino; 2 Two or more races, non-Hispanic/Latino), 1 international. Average age 36. 69 applicants, 38% accepted, 11 enrolled. In 2014, 5 master's, 8 doctorates awarded. *Degree requirements:* For master's, comprehensive exam, thesis (for some programs); for doctorate, comprehensive exam, thesis/dissertation. *Entrance requirements:* For master's, GRE General Test (minimum preferred score of 59th percentile (153) verbal), minimum GPA of 3.0, two letters of recommendation, writing sample, statement of purpose, resume; for doctorate, GRE General Test (minimum preferred score of 59th percentile (153) verbal), three letters of recommendation, writing sample, statement of purpose, resume. Additional exam requirements/recommendations for international students: Required—TOEFL (minimum score 550 paper-based; 79 iBT). *Application deadline:* For fall admission, 1/15 for domestic students, 1/2 for international students; for spring admission, 11/1 for domestic students, 6/1 for international students. Applications are processed on a rolling basis. Application fee: $30. Electronic applications accepted. *Financial support:* In 2014–15, 32 students received support, including 32 teaching assistantships with full tuition reimbursements available (averaging $9,875 per year); unspecified assistantships also available. Financial award application deadline: 1/15; financial award applicants required to submit FAFSA. *Faculty research:* Organizational, interpersonal, and health communication; media and cultural studies; rhetoric; performance studies; qualitative research methods. *Unit head:* Dr. David Payne, Associate Professor and Interim Chair, 813-974-2145, Fax: 813-974-6817, E-mail: dpayne@usf.edu. *Application contact:* Dr. Ambar Basu, Associate Professor and Graduate Program Director, 813-974-2145, Fax: 813-974-6817, E-mail: abasu@usf.edu.
Website: http://communication.usf.edu/

The University of Tennessee, Graduate School, College of Communication and Information, Knoxville, TN 37996. Offers advertising (MS, PhD); broadcasting (MS, PhD); communications (MS, PhD); information sciences (MS, PhD); journalism (MS, PhD); public relations (MS, PhD); speech communication (MS, PhD). Part-time and evening/weekend programs available. Postbaccalaureate distance learning degree programs offered (no on-campus study). *Degree requirements:* For master's, thesis or alternative; for doctorate, thesis/dissertation. *Entrance requirements:* For master's and doctorate, GRE General Test, minimum GPA of 2.7. Additional exam requirements/recommendations for international students: Required—TOEFL. Electronic applications accepted.

The University of Texas at Arlington, Graduate School, College of Liberal Arts, Department of Communication, Arlington, TX 76019. Offers MA. Part-time and evening/weekend programs available. *Degree requirements:* For master's, comprehensive exam (for some programs), thesis or alternative. *Entrance requirements:* For master's, GRE General Test. Additional exam requirements/recommendations for international students: Required—TOEFL (minimum score 550 paper-based). Electronic applications accepted.

The University of Texas at Austin, Graduate School, College of Communication, Department of Communication Studies, Austin, TX 78712-1111. Offers MA, PhD. *Entrance requirements:* For master's and doctorate, GRE General Test. Electronic applications accepted.

The University of Texas at Dallas, School of Behavioral and Brain Sciences, Program in Communication Sciences and Disorders, Richardson, TX 75080. Offers communication disorders (MS); communication science and disorders (PhD). Part-time and evening/weekend programs available. *Faculty:* 14 full-time (9 women), 13 part-time/adjunct (all women). *Students:* 236 full-time (230 women), 11 part-time (all women); includes 51 minority (2 Black or African American, non-Hispanic/Latino; 13 Asian, non-Hispanic/Latino; 21 Hispanic/Latino; 15 Two or more races, non-Hispanic/Latino), 9 international. Average age 25. 575 applicants, 13% accepted, 62 enrolled. In 2014, 120 master's, 1 doctorate awarded. *Degree requirements:* For doctorate, thesis/dissertation. *Entrance requirements:* For master's and doctorate, GRE General Test, minimum GPA of 3.0 in upper-level course work in field. Additional exam requirements/recommendations for international students: Required—TOEFL (minimum score 550 paper-based). *Application deadline:* For fall admission, 7/15 for domestic students, 5/1 priority date for international students; for spring admission, 11/15 for domestic students, 9/1 priority date for international students. Applications are processed on a rolling basis. Application fee: $50 ($100 for international students). Electronic applications accepted. *Expenses:* Tuition, state resident: full-time $11,940; part-time $663 per credit. Tuition, nonresident: full-time $22,282; part-time $1238 per credit. *Financial support:* In 2014–15, 174 students received support, including 6 research assistantships with partial tuition reimbursements available (averaging $17,708 per year), 16 teaching assistantships with partial tuition reimbursements available (averaging $16,857 per year); fellowships, Federal Work-Study, institutionally sponsored loans, scholarships/grants, and unspecified assistantships also available. Support available to part-time students. Financial award application deadline: 4/30; financial award applicants required to submit FAFSA. *Faculty research:* Developmental neurolinguistics, brain plasticity and biofeedback treatment, autism spectrum disorders, speech production, neurogenic speech and language disorders. *Unit head:* Dr. Robert D. Stillman, Program Head, 214-905-3106, Fax: 972-883-3022, E-mail: stillman@utdallas.edu. *Application contact:* 972-883-3106, Fax: 972-883-3022, E-mail: commsciphd@utdallas.edu.
Website: http://bbs.utdallas.edu/csd/

The University of Texas at El Paso, Graduate School, College of Liberal Arts, Department of Communication, El Paso, TX 79968. Offers MA. Part-time and evening/weekend programs available. Terminal master's awarded for partial completion of doctoral program. *Degree requirements:* For master's, thesis optional. *Entrance requirements:* For master's, GRE General Test, minimum GPA of 3.0. Additional exam requirements/recommendations for international students: Required—TOEFL. Electronic applications accepted. *Faculty research:* Intercultural communication, international communication, rhetorical theories, cultural and media studies, health communication.

The University of Texas at San Antonio, College of Liberal and Fine Arts, Department of Communication, San Antonio, TX 78249. Offers MA. Part-time and evening/weekend programs available. Postbaccalaureate distance learning degree programs offered (minimal on-campus study). *Faculty:* 15 full-time (6 women). *Students:* 4 full-time (all women), 18 part-time (10 women); includes 17 minority (2 Black or African American, non-Hispanic/Latino; 15 Hispanic/Latino). Average age 27. 26 applicants, 58% accepted, 9 enrolled. In 2014, 12 master's awarded. *Degree requirements:* For master's, comprehensive exam, thesis optional, 36 course hours. *Entrance requirements:* For master's, GRE, minimum GPA of 3.0 (last 60 hours), statement of purpose, two academic letters of recommendation. Additional exam requirements/recommendations for international students: Required—TOEFL (minimum score 550 paper-based; 79 iBT), IELTS (minimum score 6.5). *Application deadline:* For fall admission, 7/1 for domestic students, 4/1 priority date for international students; for spring admission, 11/1 for domestic students, 9/1 for international students. Applications are processed on a rolling basis. Application fee: $45 ($80 for international students). Electronic applications accepted. *Expenses:* Expenses: $1,100 tuition and fees per 3 hour course for in-state residents; $3495 for out-of-state/international residents. *Financial support:* In 2014–15, 11 students received support, including 4 fellowships, 2 research assistantships (averaging $2,000 per year), 6 teaching assistantships (averaging $2,000 per year); career-related internships or fieldwork, Federal Work-Study, institutionally sponsored loans, scholarships/grants, traineeships, health care benefits, and unspecified assistantships also available. Support available to part-time students. Financial award application deadline: 2/15; financial award applicants required to submit FAFSA. *Faculty research:* Organizational communication, health communication, interpersonal communication, intercultural communication, new media and digital media. *Total annual research expenditures:* $2,300. *Unit head:* Dr. Paul LeBlanc, Department Chair, 210-458-7724, Fax: 210-458-5991, E-mail: paul.leblanc@utsa.edu. *Application contact:* Mary Tutor, Program Coordinator, 210-458-7750, E-mail: mary.tutor@utsa.edu.
Website: http://communication.utsa.edu/

The University of Texas at Tyler, College of Arts and Sciences, Department of Communication, Tyler, TX 75799-0001. Offers communication (MA); interdisciplinary studies (MAIS, MSIS). Part-time programs available. *Degree requirements:* For master's, comprehensive exam. *Entrance requirements:* For master's, GRE General Test, minimum GPA of 2.5. Additional exam requirements/recommendations for international students: Required—TOEFL. Electronic applications accepted. *Faculty research:* Organizational communication, feminist criticism, religions communication, mass media.

The University of Texas–Pan American, College of Arts and Humanities, Department of Communication, Edinburg, TX 78539. Offers communication (MA); communication training and consulting (Graduate Certificate); strategic communication and media relations (Graduate Certificate); theatre (MA). *Accreditation:* NAST. Part-time and evening/weekend programs available. *Degree requirements:* For master's, comprehensive exam, thesis or alternative. *Entrance requirements:* For master's, minimum GPA of 3.0. Additional exam requirements/recommendations for international students: Required—TOEFL. *Expenses:* Tuition, state resident: full-time $4187; part-time $232.60 per credit hour. Tuition, nonresident: full-time $10,857; part-time $603.16 per credit hour. *Required fees:* $782; $27.50 per credit hour. $143.35 per semester. *Faculty research:* Rhetorical theory, intercultural and mass communication, American theatre, multicultural theatre and drama, television and film.

University of the Incarnate Word, School of Graduate Studies and Research, H-E-B School of Business and Administration, Programs in Administration, San Antonio, TX 78209-6397. Offers adult education (MAA); communication arts (MAA); healthcare administration (MAA); instructional technology (MAA); nutrition (MAA); organizational development (MAA); sports management (MAA). Part-time and evening/weekend programs available. Postbaccalaureate distance learning degree programs offered (no on-campus study). *Faculty:* 13 full-time (5 women), 14 part-time/adjunct (5 women). *Students:* 33 full-time (18 women), 33 part-time (21 women); includes 37 minority (7 Black or African American, non-Hispanic/Latino; 1 Asian, non-Hispanic/Latino; 28 Hispanic/Latino; 1 Two or more races, non-Hispanic/Latino), 11 international. Average age 31. 61 applicants, 75% accepted, 12 enrolled. In 2014, 35 master's awarded. *Degree requirements:* For master's, capstone. *Entrance requirements:* For master's, GRE, GMAT, undergraduate degree, minimum GPA of 2.5. Additional exam requirements/recommendations for international students: Required—TOEFL (minimum score 560 paper-based; 83 iBT). *Application deadline:* Applications are processed on a rolling basis. Application fee: $20. Electronic applications accepted. *Expenses: Tuition:* Part-time $815 per credit hour. *Required fees:* $86 per credit hour. *Financial support:* Federal Work-Study and scholarships/grants available. Financial award applicants required to submit FAFSA. *Unit head:* Dr. Mark Teachout, Programs Director, 210-829-3177, Fax: 210-805-3564, E-mail: teachout@uiwtx.edu. *Application contact:* Andrea Cyterski-Acosta, Dean of Enrollment, 210-829-6005, Fax: 210-829-3921, E-mail: admis@uiwtx.edu.
Website: http://www.uiw.edu/maa/

University of the Incarnate Word, School of Graduate Studies and Research, School of Media and Design, Program in Communication Arts, San Antonio, TX 78209-6397. Offers MA. Part-time and evening/weekend programs available. *Faculty:* 3 full-time (2 women). *Students:* 8 full-time (7 women), 23 part-time (13 women); includes 24 minority (3 Black or African American, non-Hispanic/Latino; 21 Hispanic/Latino), 2 international. Average age 29. 8 applicants, 88% accepted, 4 enrolled. In 2014, 16 master's awarded. *Degree requirements:* For master's, thesis or alternative. *Entrance requirements:* For master's, GMAT, GRE General Test, interview, writing sample. Additional exam requirements/recommendations for international students: Required—TOEFL (minimum score 560 paper-based; 83 iBT). *Application deadline:* Applications are processed on a rolling basis. Application fee: $20. Electronic applications accepted. *Expenses: Tuition:* Part-time $815 per credit hour. *Required fees:* $86 per credit hour. *Financial support:* Federal Work-Study and scholarships/grants available. Financial award applicants required to submit FAFSA. *Faculty research:* Impact of media on society, the new media of the Internet, convergent media vs. traditional media, social media and effect on society, technological transformation of media production, mobile technologies, Arab Spring, theories of communication. *Unit head:* Dr. Valerie Greenberg, Director of Communication Arts Graduate Program, 210-829-3891, Fax: 210-829-3196, E-mail: greenber@uiwtx.edu. *Application contact:* Andrea Cyterski-Acosta, Dean of Enrollment, 210-829-6005, Fax: 210-829-3921, E-mail: admis@uiwtx.edu.
Website: http://uiw.edu/commarts/grad_prog.html

University of the Pacific, College of the Pacific, Department of Communication, Stockton, CA 95211-0197. Offers MA. *Students:* 12 part-time (4 women); includes 5 minority (1 Black or African American, non-Hispanic/Latino; 1 Asian, non-Hispanic/Latino; 1 Hispanic/Latino; 2 Two or more races, non-Hispanic/Latino). Average age 26. 18 applicants, 56% accepted, 4 enrolled. In 2014, 8 master's awarded. *Degree requirements:* For master's, thesis. *Entrance requirements:* For master's, GRE General Test. Additional exam requirements/recommendations for international students: Required—TOEFL (minimum score 475 paper-based). *Application deadline:* For fall admission, 3/1 priority date for domestic students; for spring admission, 10/1 for domestic students. Applications are processed on a rolling basis. Application fee: $75. *Financial support:* In 2014–15, 10 teaching assistantships were awarded. Support available to part-time students. Financial award application deadline: 3/1; financial award applicants required to submit FAFSA. *Unit head:* Dr. Qingwen Dong, Chairman, 209-946-2505, E-mail: qdong@pacific.edu. *Application contact:* Information Contact, 209-946-2261.

University of the Sacred Heart, Graduate Programs, Department of Communication, San Juan, PR 00914-0383. Offers contemporary culture and media (MA); digital journalism (MA, Certificate); editing for media (MA, Certificate); public relations (MA, Certificate); publicity (MA, Certificate); scriptwriting (MA, Certificate). Part-time and evening/weekend programs available. *Degree requirements:* For master's, thesis.

The University of Toledo, College of Graduate Studies, College of Communication and the Arts, Department of Communication, Toledo, OH 43606-3390. Offers Certificate. Part-time programs available. *Entrance requirements:* For degree, minimum GPA of 2.7 for all prior academic work, transcripts from all prior institutions attended; statement of purpose. Electronic applications accepted.

University of Utah, Graduate School, College of Humanities, Department of Communication, Salt Lake City, UT 84112. Offers MA, MS, PhD. *Faculty:* 26 full-time (12 women), 13 part-time/adjunct (5 women). *Students:* 53 full-time (33 women), 25 part-time (16 women); includes 16 minority (1 American Indian or Alaska Native, non-Hispanic/Latino; 4 Asian, non-Hispanic/Latino; 8 Hispanic/Latino; 3 Two or more races, non-Hispanic/Latino), 9 international. Average age 35. 99 applicants, 31% accepted, 15 enrolled. In 2014, 10 master's, 6 doctorates awarded. Terminal master's awarded for partial completion of doctoral program. *Degree requirements:* For master's, thesis or alternative; for doctorate, comprehensive exam, thesis/dissertation. *Entrance requirements:* For master's and doctorate, GRE General Test, minimum GPA of 3.0. Additional exam requirements/recommendations for international students: Required—TOEFL (minimum score 500 paper-based; 90 iBT); Recommended—IELTS. *Application deadline:* For fall admission, 12/15 for domestic students, 11/15 for international students. Application fee: $55 ($65 for international students). Electronic applications accepted. *Financial support:* In 2014–15, 13 students received support, including 9 fellowships with full tuition reimbursements available (averaging $14,000 per year), 1 research assistantship with full tuition reimbursement available (averaging $14,000 per year), 3 teaching assistantships with full tuition reimbursements available (averaging $14,000 per year); health care benefits and unspecified assistantships also available. Financial award application deadline: 1/15. *Faculty research:* CommSHER (Communicating Science, Health, Environment, Risk), critical/cultural studies, interpersonal/organizational communication, new media technologies, rhetoric. *Unit head:* Dr. Kent A. Ono, Chair, 801-585-9128, Fax: 801-585-6255, E-mail: kent.ono@utah.edu. *Application contact:* Dr. Helene Shugart, Director of Graduate Studies, 801-581-5686, Fax: 801-585-6255, E-mail: h.shugart@utah.edu.
Website: http://www.communication.utah.edu

University of Vermont, Graduate College, College of Nursing and Health Sciences, Department of Communication Sciences and Disorders, Burlington, VT 05405. Offers MS. *Accreditation:* ASHA. *Entrance requirements:* For master's, GRE General Test. Additional exam requirements/recommendations for international students: Required—TOEFL (minimum score 550 paper-based; 80 iBT). Electronic applications accepted.

University of Washington, Graduate School, College of Arts and Sciences, Department of Communication, Seattle, WA 98195. Offers MA, MC, PhD. Part-time programs available. Terminal master's awarded for partial completion of doctoral program. *Degree requirements:* For master's, thesis, project (MC); for doctorate, thesis/dissertation. *Entrance requirements:* For master's and doctorate, GRE, minimum GPA of 3.0, writing sample. Additional exam requirements/recommendations for international students: Required—TOEFL. Electronic applications accepted. *Faculty research:*

Communication—General

Communication and culture, communication technology and society, international communication, political communication, rhetoric and critical studies.

University of Washington, Graduate School, College of Arts and Sciences, School of Art, Division of Design, Seattle, WA 98195. Offers industrial design (MFA); visual communication design (MFA).

University of West Florida, College of Arts and Sciences: Arts, Department of Communication Arts, Pensacola, FL 32514-5750. Offers MA. Part-time and evening/weekend programs available. *Degree requirements:* For master's, thesis or alternative. *Entrance requirements:* For master's, GRE (minimum score: verbal 470, writing 4.0), MAT (minimum score 413), or GMAT (minimum score of 400), minimum GPA of 3.2; official transcripts; undergraduate degree in related field; three letters of reference; current curriculum vitae/resume. Additional exam requirements/recommendations for international students: Required—TOEFL (minimum score 550 paper-based). *Faculty research:* Equity studies.

University of Windsor, Faculty of Graduate Studies, Faculty of Arts and Social Sciences, Department of Communication Studies, Windsor, ON N9B 3P4, Canada. Offers communication and social justice (MA). *Degree requirements:* For master's, thesis. *Entrance requirements:* For master's, writing sample/media production or multimedia portfolio. Additional exam requirements/recommendations for international students: Required—TOEFL (minimum score 600 paper-based). Electronic applications accepted. *Faculty research:* Sociology of news, media ownership and control, communication networks and social movements, issues of media representation.

University of Wisconsin–Madison, Graduate School, College of Letters and Science, Department of Communication Arts, Madison, WI 53706-1380. Offers communication science (MA, PhD); film (MA, PhD); media and cultural studies (MA, PhD); rhetoric (MA, PhD). Terminal master's awarded for partial completion of doctoral program. *Degree requirements:* For master's, one foreign language, thesis (for some programs); for doctorate, one foreign language, thesis/dissertation. *Entrance requirements:* For master's and doctorate, GRE General Test, minimum GPA of 3.5. Electronic applications accepted. *Expenses:* Tuition, state resident: full-time $10,723; part-time $745 per credit. Tuition, nonresident: full-time $24,054; part-time $1578 per credit. *Required fees:* $374 per semester. Tuition and fees vary according to course load, program and reciprocity agreements.

University of Wisconsin–Madison, Graduate School, College of Letters and Science, School of Journalism and Mass Communication, Madison, WI 53706-1380. Offers family and consumer journalism (PhD); journalism and mass communication (MA); mass communication (PhD). Part-time programs available. *Degree requirements:* For master's, thesis (for some programs); for doctorate, thesis/dissertation. *Entrance requirements:* For master's, GRE General Test, minimum GPA of 3.0; for doctorate, GRE General Test, minimum GPA of 3.5. Additional exam requirements/recommendations for international students: Required—TOEFL. Electronic applications accepted. *Expenses:* Tuition, state resident: full-time $10,723; part-time $745 per credit. Tuition, nonresident: full-time $24,054; part-time $1578 per credit. *Required fees:* $374 per semester. Tuition and fees vary according to course load, program and reciprocity agreements. *Faculty research:* International/development communication; strategic mass communication; mass communication and the individual; science, technology, and environment communication; mass communication and societal institutions.

University of Wisconsin–Milwaukee, Graduate School, College of Letters and Sciences, Department of Communication, Milwaukee, WI 53201-0413. Offers communication (MA, PhD); mediation and negotiation (Certificate); rhetorical leadership (Certificate). Part-time programs available. *Degree requirements:* For master's, thesis or alternative; for doctorate, comprehensive exam. *Entrance requirements:* For master's, GRE General Test, minimum GPA of 3.0. Additional exam requirements/recommendations for international students: Required—TOEFL (minimum score 550 paper-based; 79 iBT), IELTS (minimum score 6). Electronic applications accepted.

University of Wisconsin–Stevens Point, College of Fine Arts and Communication, Division of Communication, Stevens Point, WI 54481-3897. Offers interpersonal communication (MA); media studies (MA); organizational communication (MA); public relations (MA). Part-time programs available. *Degree requirements:* For master's, thesis or alternative. *Entrance requirements:* For master's, GRE. Additional exam requirements/recommendations for international students: Required—TOEFL (minimum score 575 paper-based). *Faculty research:* Communication theory and research, film history.

University of Wisconsin–Superior, Graduate Division, Department of Communicating Arts, Superior, WI 54880-4500. Offers mass communication (MA); speech communication (MA); theater (MA). Part-time programs available. *Degree requirements:* For master's, comprehensive exam, thesis or alternative, position paper or project. *Entrance requirements:* For master's, minimum GPA of 2.75. Electronic applications accepted. *Faculty research:* Multimedia technology, ethics in journalism, diversity, electronic portfolio assessment.

University of Wisconsin–Whitewater, School of Graduate Studies, College of Arts and Communications, Department of Communication, Whitewater, WI 53190-1790. Offers corporate communication (MS); mass communication (MS). Part-time and evening/weekend programs available. Postbaccalaureate distance learning degree programs offered (no on-campus study). *Degree requirements:* For master's, thesis or alternative. *Entrance requirements:* For master's, 2 letters of recommendation, goal statement. Additional exam requirements/recommendations for international students: Required—TOEFL (minimum score 550 paper-based; 80 iBT), IELTS (minimum score 6). Electronic applications accepted.

University of Wyoming, College of Arts and Sciences, Department of Communication and Journalism, Laramie, WY 82071. Offers communication (MA). Part-time programs available. *Degree requirements:* For master's, thesis. *Entrance requirements:* For master's, GRE General Test, minimum GPA of 3.0. *Faculty research:* Personal relations, nonverbal behavior, media management, communication technology, conversation analysis.

Utah State University, School of Graduate Studies, College of Humanities, Arts and Social Sciences, Department of Journalism and Communication, Logan, UT 84322. Offers MA, MS. Part-time programs available. *Degree requirements:* For master's, comprehensive exam, thesis. *Entrance requirements:* For master's, GRE General Test or MAT, minimum GPA of 3.0. Additional exam requirements/recommendations for international students: Required—TOEFL. Electronic applications accepted. *Faculty research:* Race and gender and media, history of censorship, internet design and advertising, technology gap.

Valparaiso University, Graduate School, Program in Media and Communication, Valparaiso, IN 46383. Offers digital media (MS); sports media (MS, Certificate). Part-time and evening/weekend programs available. *Students:* 17 full-time (6 women), 11 part-time (8 women); includes 4 minority (2 Black or African American, non-Hispanic/Latino; 1 Hispanic/Latino; 1 Two or more races, non-Hispanic/Latino), 11 international. Average age 27. In 2014, 24 master's, 2 other advanced degrees awarded. *Entrance requirements:* For master's, minimum GPA of 3.0, undergraduate minor in communication. Additional exam requirements/recommendations for international students: Required—TOEFL (minimum score 550 paper-based; 80 iBT), IELTS (minimum score 6). *Application deadline:* Applications are processed on a rolling basis. Application fee: $30 ($50 for international students). Electronic applications accepted. *Expenses: Tuition:* Full-time $10,710; part-time $595 per credit hour. *Required fees:* $378; $101 per term. Tuition and fees vary according to course load and program. *Financial support:* Available to part-time students. Applicants required to submit FAFSA. *Unit head:* Dr. Jennifer A. Ziegler, Dean, Graduate School and Continuing Education, 219-464-5313, Fax: 219-464-5381, E-mail: jennifer.ziegler@valpo.edu. *Application contact:* Jessica Choquette, Graduate Admissions Specialist, 219-464-5313, Fax: 219-464-5381, E-mail: jessica.choquette@valpo.edu.
Website: http://www.valpo.edu/grad/programs/masters.php

Villanova University, Graduate School of Liberal Arts and Sciences, Department of Communication, Villanova, PA 19085-1699. Offers MA. Part-time and evening/weekend programs available. *Students:* 15 full-time (13 women), 17 part-time (12 women); includes 8 minority (4 Black or African American, non-Hispanic/Latino; 1 Asian, non-Hispanic/Latino; 1 Hispanic/Latino; 2 Two or more races, non-Hispanic/Latino), 3 international. Average age 27. 22 applicants, 68% accepted, 10 enrolled. In 2014, 14 master's awarded. *Degree requirements:* For master's, comprehensive exam (for some programs), thesis optional. *Entrance requirements:* For master's, GRE or GMAT, minimum GPA of 3.0, writing sample, statement of goals, 3 letters of recommendation. Additional exam requirements/recommendations for international students: Required—TOEFL. *Application deadline:* For fall admission, 5/1 priority date for international students; for spring admission, 10/15 priority date for international students. Applications are processed on a rolling basis. Application fee: $50. Electronic applications accepted. *Financial support:* Research assistantships, teaching assistantships, scholarships/grants, and unspecified assistantships available. Financial award applicants required to submit FAFSA. *Unit head:* Dr. Heidi Rose, Director of Graduate Studies, 610-519-6939.
Website: http://www1.villanova.edu/villanova/artsci/communication/academic/graduate.html

Virginia Commonwealth University, Graduate School, College of Humanities and Sciences, School of Mass Communications, Program in Media, Art, and Text, Richmond, VA 23284-9005. Offers PhD. *Entrance requirements:* For doctorate, GRE. Additional exam requirements/recommendations for international students: Required—TOEFL (minimum score 600 paper-based; 100 iBT); Recommended—IELTS (minimum score 6.5). Electronic applications accepted.

Virginia Polytechnic Institute and State University, Graduate School, College of Liberal Arts and Human Sciences, Blacksburg, VA 24061. Offers career and technical education (MS Ed, Ed D, PhD, Ed S); communication (MA); counselor education (MA Ed, Ed D, PhD, Ed S); creative writing (MFA); curriculum and instruction (MA Ed, Ed D, PhD, Ed S); educational leadership and policy studies (MA Ed, Ed D, PhD, Ed S); educational research and evaluation (PhD); English (MA); foreign languages, cultures, and literatures (MA); higher education and student affairs (MA Ed); history (MA); human development (MS, PhD); material culture and public humanities (MA); philosophy (MA); political science (MA); rhetoric and writing (PhD); science and technology studies (MS, PhD); social, political, ethical, and cultural thought (PhD); sociology (MS, PhD); theater arts (MFA). *Faculty:* 421 full-time (216 women), 2 part-time/adjunct (both women). *Students:* 642 full-time (437 women), 537 part-time (344 women); includes 235 minority (132 Black or African American, non-Hispanic/Latino; 2 American Indian or Alaska Native, non-Hispanic/Latino; 27 Asian, non-Hispanic/Latino; 52 Hispanic/Latino; 1 Native Hawaiian or other Pacific Islander, non-Hispanic/Latino; 21 Two or more races, non-Hispanic/Latino), 81 international. Average age 34. 890 applicants, 46% accepted, 303 enrolled. In 2014, 342 master's, 96 doctorates, 33 other advanced degrees awarded. *Degree requirements:* For master's, comprehensive exam (for some programs), thesis (for some programs); for doctorate, comprehensive exam (for some programs), thesis/dissertation (for some programs). *Entrance requirements:* For master's and doctorate, GRE/GMAT (may vary by department). Additional exam requirements/recommendations for international students: Required—TOEFL (minimum score 550 paper-based). *Application deadline:* For fall admission, 8/1 for domestic students, 4/1 for international students; for spring admission, 1/1 for domestic students, 9/1 for international students. Applications are processed on a rolling basis. Application fee: $75. Electronic applications accepted. *Expenses:* Tuition, state resident: full-time $11,656; part-time $647.50 per credit hour. Tuition, nonresident: full-time $23,351; part-time $1297.25 per credit hour. *Required fees:* $2533; $465.75 per semester. Tuition and fees vary according to course load, campus/location and program. *Financial support:* In 2014–15, 19 research assistantships with full tuition reimbursements (averaging $22,141 per year), 231 teaching assistantships with full tuition reimbursements (averaging $19,470 per year) were awarded. Financial award application deadline: 3/1; financial award applicants required to submit FAFSA. *Total annual research expenditures:* $6.5 million. *Unit head:* Elizabeth Spiller, Dean, 540-231-6779, Fax: 540-231-7157, E-mail: espiller@vt.edu. *Application contact:* Melissa Elliott, Executive Assistant, 540-231-6779, Fax: 540-231-7157, E-mail: elliott1@vt.edu.
Website: http://www.clahs.vt.edu/

Wake Forest University, Graduate School of Arts and Sciences, Department of Communication, Winston-Salem, NC 27109. Offers speech communication (MA). Part-time programs available. *Degree requirements:* For master's, one foreign language, thesis. *Entrance requirements:* For master's, GRE General Test, writing sample. Additional exam requirements/recommendations for international students: Required—TOEFL (minimum score 79 iBT). Electronic applications accepted.

Walden University, Graduate Programs, School of Management, Minneapolis, MN 55401. Offers accounting (MBA, MS, DBA), including accounting for the professional (MS), accounting with CPA emphasis (MS), self-designed (MS); advanced project management (Graduate Certificate); applied project management (Graduate Certificate); auditing (Graduate Certificate); bridge to business administration (Post-Doctoral Certificate); bridge to management (Post-Doctoral Certificate); business administration (EMBA); business management (Graduate Certificate); communication (MS, Graduate Certificate); corporate finance (MBA); entrepreneurship (DBA); entrepreneurship and small business (MBA); finance (DBA); global supply chain management (DBA); healthcare management (MBA, DBA); human resource management (MBA, MS, Graduate Certificate), including functional human resource management (MS), general program (MS), integrating functional and strategic human resource management (MS), organizational strategy (MS); human resources management (DBA); information systems management (DBA); international business (MBA, DBA); leadership (MBA, MS, DBA), including general program (MS), human resource leadership (MS), leader development (MS), self-designed (MS); management (MS, PhD), including finance (PhD), general program (MS), healthcare management (MS), human resource management (MS), human resources management (PhD), information systems management (PhD), leadership (MS), leadership and organizational change (PhD), marketing (MS), project management (MS), strategy and operations (MS); marketing (MBA, DBA); project management (MBA, MS, DBA); self-designed (MBA, DBA); social impact management (DBA); technology entrepreneurship (DBA). Part-time and evening/weekend programs available. Postbaccalaureate distance learning degree programs offered (no on-campus study). *Faculty:* 35 full-time (13 women), 379 part-time/adjunct (152 women). *Students:* 4,349 full-time (2,435 women),

2,495 part-time (1,472 women); includes 3,873 minority (3,177 Black or African American, non-Hispanic/Latino; 21 American Indian or Alaska Native, non-Hispanic/Latino; 164 Asian, non-Hispanic/Latino; 353 Hispanic/Latino; 15 Native Hawaiian or other Pacific Islander, non-Hispanic/Latino; 143 Two or more races, non-Hispanic/Latino), 59 international. Average age 41. 2,198 applicants, 98% accepted, 2000 enrolled. In 2014, 788 master's, 139 doctorates, 53 other advanced degrees awarded. *Degree requirements:* For master's, thesis (for some programs), residency (for EMBA); for doctorate, thesis/dissertation (for some programs), residency. *Entrance requirements:* For master's, bachelor's degree or higher; minimum GPA of 2.5; official transcripts; goal statement (for some programs); access to computer and Internet; for doctorate, master's degree or higher; three years of related professional or academic experience (preferred); minimum GPA of 3.0; goal statement and current resume (for select programs); official transcripts; access to computer and Internet; for other advanced degree, relevant work experience; access to computer and Internet. Additional exam requirements/recommendations for international students: Required—TOEFL (minimum score 550 paper-based, 79 iBT), IELTS (minimum score 6.5), Michigan English Language Assessment Battery (minimum score 82), or PTE (minimum score 53). *Application deadline:* Applications are processed on a rolling basis. Application fee: $0. Electronic applications accepted. *Expenses: Tuition:* Full-time $11,925; part-time $500 per credit hour. *Required fees:* $647. *Financial support:* Fellowships, Federal Work-Study, scholarships/grants, unspecified assistantships, and family tuition reduction, active duty/veteran tuition reduction, group tuition reduction, interest-free payment plans, employee tuition reduction available. Support available to part-time students. Financial award applicants required to submit FAFSA. *Unit head:* Dr. Freda Turner, Associate Dean, 866-492-5336. *Application contact:* Meghan Thomas, Vice President of Enrollment Management, 866-492-5336, E-mail: info@waldenu.edu. Website: http://www.waldenu.edu/programs/colleges-schools/management

Washington State University, The Edward R. Murrow College of Communication, Pullman, WA 99164-2520. Offers communication (MA, PhD); strategic communication (MA). MA in strategic communication offered at the Global (online) campus. *Students:* 45 full-time (34 women), 48 part-time (37 women); includes 16 minority (4 Black or African American, non-Hispanic/Latino; 1 American Indian or Alaska Native, non-Hispanic/Latino; 2 Asian, non-Hispanic/Latino; 7 Hispanic/Latino; 2 Two or more races, non-Hispanic/Latino), 15 international. Average age 31. 150 applicants, 49% accepted, 58 enrolled. In 2014, 7 master's, 1 doctorate awarded. *Degree requirements:* For master's, comprehensive exam (for some programs), thesis optional, oral exam; for doctorate, comprehensive exam, thesis/dissertation. *Entrance requirements:* For master's, GRE General Test, minimum GPA of 3.25, 3 letters of recommendation; for doctorate, GRE General Test, minimum undergraduate GPA of 3.25, graduate 3.5; MA in communication; 3 letters of recommendation. Additional exam requirements/recommendations for international students: Required—TOEFL (minimum score 580 paper-based). *Application deadline:* For fall admission, 1/10 priority date for domestic and international students. Applications are processed on a rolling basis. Application fee: $75. Electronic applications accepted. *Expenses:* Tuition, state resident: full-time $11,768. Tuition, nonresident: full-time $25,200. *Required fees:* $960. Tuition and fees vary according to program. *Financial support:* In 2014–15, 36 students received support, including 4 research assistantships with full and partial tuition reimbursements available (averaging $10,648 per year), 21 teaching assistantships with full and partial tuition reimbursements available (averaging $13,625 per year); career-related internships or fieldwork, Federal Work-Study, institutionally sponsored loans, tuition waivers (partial), and teaching associateships also available. Financial award application deadline: 2/15; financial award applicants required to submit FAFSA. *Faculty research:* Communication technology, health communication, science communication, political communication, intercultural communication. *Unit head:* Dr. Prabu David, Associate Dean for Academic Affairs, 509-335-0041, E-mail: prabu.david@wsu.edu. *Application contact:* Graduate School Admissions, 800-GRADWSU, Fax: 509-335-1949, E-mail: gradsch@wsu.edu. Website: http://communication.wsu.edu/

Wayne State College, School of Education and Counseling, Department of Educational Foundations and Leadership, Program in Curriculum and Instruction, Wayne, NE 68787. Offers alternative education (MSE); business and information technology education (MSE); communication arts education (MSE); early childhood education (MSE); elementary education (MSE); English as a second language (MSE); English education (MSE); family and consumer sciences education (MSE); industrial technology and vocational education (MSE); learning communities (MSE); mathematics education (MSE); music education (MSE); science education (MSE); social science education (MSE). *Accreditation:* NCATE. Part-time and evening/weekend programs available. *Degree requirements:* For master's, comprehensive exam, thesis optional. *Entrance requirements:* For master's, GRE General Test. Additional exam requirements/recommendations for international students: Required—TOEFL (minimum score 550 paper-based).

Wayne State University, College of Fine, Performing and Communication Arts, Department of Communication, Detroit, MI 48202. Offers communication (PhD), including democratic participation and culture, identity and representation, media, society and culture, risk, crisis and conflict, wellness, worklife and relationships; communication and new media (Graduate Certificate); communication studies (MA); dispute resolution (MADR, Graduate Certificate); health communication (Graduate Certificate); journalism (MA); media arts (MA); media studies (MA); public relations and organizational communication (MA); JD/MADR. Doctoral programs admit for fall only. *Students:* 63 full-time (34 women), 82 part-time (63 women); includes 48 minority (40 Black or African American, non-Hispanic/Latino; 3 Asian, non-Hispanic/Latino; 3 Hispanic/Latino; 2 Two or more races, non-Hispanic/Latino), 13 international. Average age 35. 177 applicants, 40% accepted, 38 enrolled. In 2014, 33 master's, 4 doctorates, 9 other advanced degrees awarded. *Degree requirements:* For master's, thesis (for some programs), thesis or essay; for doctorate, thesis/dissertation. *Entrance requirements:* For master's, GRE (if undergraduate GPA less than 3.2), personal statement; BA or BS in communication or related field with minimum upper-division GPA of 3.2 and sample of academic writing (for MA); minimum upper-division undergraduate GPA of 3.0 and 3 letters of recommendation (for MADR); for doctorate, GRE, MA in communication or related field with minimum GPA of 3.5, three letters of recommendation; personal statement; sample of written scholarship; for Graduate Certificate, minimum upper-division GPA of 3.0, personal statement. Additional exam requirements/recommendations for international students: Required—TOEFL (minimum score 600 paper-based; 100 iBT), IELTS (minimum score 6.5), TWE (minimum score 6). *Application deadline:* For fall admission, 8/1 for domestic and international students; for winter admission, 11/1 for domestic and international students; for spring admission, 4/1 for domestic and international students. Application fee: $0. Electronic applications accepted. *Expenses:* Expenses: Contact institution. *Financial support:* In 2014–15, 48 students received support, including 3 fellowships with tuition reimbursements available (averaging $16,000 per year), 20 teaching assistantships with tuition reimbursements available (averaging $16,540 per year); research assistantships with tuition reimbursements available, scholarships/grants, and unspecified assistantships also available. Financial award application deadline: 3/31; financial award applicants required to submit FAFSA. *Faculty research:* Rhetorical theory and criticism; mass media theory

and research; argumentation; organizational communication; risk and crisis communication; interpersonal, family, and health communication. *Unit head:* Dr. Lee Wilikins, Chair, 313-577-2943, E-mail: eh8899@wayne.edu. *Application contact:* Dr. Pradeep Sopory, Director of Graduate Studies, 313-577-2945, E-mail: psopory@wayne.edu.
Website: http://comm.wayne.edu/

Weber State University, Telitha E. Lindquist College of Arts and Humanities, Department of Communication, Ogden, UT 84408-1001. Offers MPC. Part-time and evening/weekend programs available. *Faculty:* 10 full-time (7 women), 2 part-time/adjunct (both women). *Students:* 8 full-time (4 women), 35 part-time (16 women); includes 1 minority (Hispanic/Latino), 1 international. Average age 33. In 2014, 23 master's awarded. *Entrance requirements:* For master's, GRE. Additional exam requirements/recommendations for international students: Required—TOEFL (minimum score 550 paper-based; 85 iBT). *Application deadline:* For fall admission, 4/1 for domestic students. Application fee: $60 ($90 for international students). Electronic applications accepted. *Expenses:* Tuition, state resident: part-time $1638 per year. Tuition, nonresident: part-time $4912 per year. Tuition and fees vary according to course load and program. *Financial support:* In 2014–15, 8 students received support. Scholarships/grants available. Financial award application deadline: 4/1; financial award applicants required to submit FAFSA. *Unit head:* Dr. Kathryn Edwards, Program Director, 801-626-6571, Fax: 801-626-7760, E-mail: kedwards@weber.edu. *Application contact:* Shari Love, Office Specialist, 801-626-7499, Fax: 801-626-7975, E-mail: slove@weber.edu.
Website: http://www.weber.edu/mpc

Webster University, School of Communications, St. Louis, MO 63119-3194. Offers MA. Part-time and evening/weekend programs available. Postbaccalaureate distance learning degree programs offered. *Degree requirements:* For master's, thesis (for some programs). *Entrance requirements:* For master's, 36 hours of graduate course work. Additional exam requirements/recommendations for international students: Required—TOEFL.

West Chester University of Pennsylvania, College of Arts and Sciences, Department of Communication Studies, West Chester, PA 19383. Offers MA. Part-time and evening/weekend programs available. *Faculty:* 7 full-time (4 women), 1 part-time/adjunct (0 women). *Students:* 8 full-time (3 women), 6 part-time (5 women); includes 3 minority (all Black or African American, non-Hispanic/Latino). Average age 25. 8 applicants, 100% accepted, 5 enrolled. In 2014, 9 master's awarded. *Degree requirements:* For master's, comprehensive exam, thesis optional. *Entrance requirements:* For master's, GRE in at least 50th percentile in two of the three tested areas (not required for applicants with a GPA of 3.5 or better), minimum GPA of 2.8 overall, 3.0 in major; writing sample; two letters of reference; courses or experience that indicate skill in public speaking, communication theory, and communication (or related) research. Additional exam requirements/recommendations for international students: Required—TOEFL (minimum score 550 paper-based; 80 iBT). *Application deadline:* For fall admission, 4/15 priority date for domestic students, 3/15 for international students; for spring admission, 10/15 priority date for domestic students, 9/1 for international students. Applications are processed on a rolling basis. Application fee: $45. Electronic applications accepted. *Expenses:* Tuition, state resident: full-time $8172; part-time $454 per credit. Tuition, nonresident: full-time $12,258; part-time $681 per credit. *Required fees:* $2231; $110.78 per credit. Tuition and fees vary according to campus/location and program. *Financial support:* Unspecified assistantships available. Support available to part-time students. Financial award application deadline: 2/15; financial award applicants required to submit FAFSA. *Faculty research:* Rhetorical communication, media/social media, intercultural communication, interpersonal and group communication, conflict management. *Unit head:* Dr. Timothy Brown, Chair, 610-436-2500, Fax: 610-436-2500, E-mail: tbrown@wcupa.edu. *Application contact:* Dr. Mary Braz, Graduate Coordinator, 610-436-3328, E-mail: mbraz@wcupa.edu.
Website: http://communication.wcupa.edu/

Western Illinois University, School of Graduate Studies, College of Fine Arts and Communication, Department of Communication, Macomb, IL 61455-1390. Offers MA. Part-time programs available. *Students:* 15 full-time (9 women), 7 part-time (5 women); includes 6 minority (5 Black or African American, non-Hispanic/Latino; 1 Hispanic/Latino), 3 international. Average age 25. 14 applicants, 64% accepted, 7 enrolled. In 2014, 5 master's awarded. *Degree requirements:* For master's, comprehensive exam (for some programs), thesis or alternative. *Entrance requirements:* Additional exam requirements/recommendations for international students: Required—TOEFL (minimum score 580 paper-based; 92 iBT). *Application deadline:* Applications are processed on a rolling basis. Application fee: $30. Electronic applications accepted. *Financial support:* In 2014–15, 12 students received support, including 6 research assistantships with full tuition reimbursements available (averaging $7,544 per year), 6 teaching assistantships with full tuition reimbursements available (averaging $8,688 per year). Financial award applicants required to submit FAFSA. *Unit head:* Dr. Peter Jorgensen, Chairperson, 309-298-1507. *Application contact:* Dr. Nancy Parsons, Associate Provost and Director of Graduate Studies, 309-298-1806, Fax: 309-298-2345, E-mail: grad-office@wiu.edu.
Website: http://wiu.edu/comm

Western Kentucky University, Graduate Studies, Potter College of Arts and Letters, Department of Communication, Bowling Green, KY 42101. Offers communication (MA); organizational communication (Graduate Certificate). Part-time and evening/weekend programs available. *Degree requirements:* For master's, comprehensive exam, thesis optional, final exam. *Entrance requirements:* For master's, GRE General Test, minimum GPA of 2.75. Additional exam requirements/recommendations for international students: Required—TOEFL (minimum score 555 paper-based; 79 iBT). *Faculty research:* Public rhetoric and public address organization communication, teamwork in communication, intercultural crisis communication.

Western Michigan University, Graduate College, College of Arts and Sciences, School of Communication, Kalamazoo, MI 49008. Offers MA. *Application deadline:* For fall admission, 2/15 for domestic students. *Financial support:* Application deadline: 2/15. *Application contact:* Admissions and Orientation, 269-387-2000, Fax: 269-387-2096.

Western New England University, College of Arts and Sciences, Program in Communication, Springfield, MA 01119. Offers public relations (MA). Part-time and evening/weekend programs available. *Students:* 17 part-time (13 women); includes 3 minority (2 Black or African American, non-Hispanic/Latino; 1 Hispanic/Latino). Average age 36. *Degree requirements:* For master's, independent study or thesis. *Entrance requirements:* For master's, official transcript, personal statement, resume, three letters of recommendation. Additional exam requirements/recommendations for international students: Required—TOEFL (minimum score 79 iBT). *Application deadline:* Applications are processed on a rolling basis. Application fee: $30. Electronic applications accepted. *Financial support:* Application deadline: 4/15; applicants required to submit FAFSA. *Unit head:* Dr. Saeed Ghahramani, Dean, 413-782-1218, Fax: 413-796-2118, E-mail: sghahram@wne.edu. *Application contact:* Matthew Fox, Director of Recruiting and Marketing for Adult Learners, 413-782-1517, Fax: 413-782-1777, E-mail: study@wne.edu.

Westminster College, Program in Professional Communication, Salt Lake City, UT 84105-3697. Offers MPC, MSC. Part-time and evening/weekend programs available. *Faculty:* 10 full-time (5 women), 3 part-time/adjunct (all women). *Students:* 14 full-time (7 women), 40 part-time (26 women); includes 13 minority (3 Asian, non-Hispanic/Latino; 8 Hispanic/Latino; 2 Two or more races, non-Hispanic/Latino), 3 international. Average age 32. 23 applicants, 70% accepted, 9 enrolled. In 2014, 9 master's awarded. *Degree requirements:* For master's, field project. *Entrance requirements:* For master's, GRE, resume, personal statement of intent, official transcripts, two letters of recommendation. Additional exam requirements/recommendations for international students: Required—TOEFL (minimum score 600 paper-based; 100 iBT), IELTS (minimum score 7.5). *Application deadline:* For fall admission, 8/9 for domestic students, 7/9 for international students; for spring admission, 1/1 for domestic students; for summer admission, 5/1 for domestic students. Applications are processed on a rolling basis. Application fee: $50. Electronic applications accepted. *Expenses:* Expenses: Contact institution. *Financial support:* In 2014–15, 8 students received support. Career-related internships or fieldwork, scholarships/grants, unspecified assistantships, and tuition reimbursements, tuition remission available. Support available to part-time students. Financial award applicants required to submit FAFSA. *Faculty research:* Diversity in higher education, communication pedagogy, mass media law and ethics, impact of new technologies on society, rhetorical theory, feminism and popular culture, critical communication pedagogy. *Unit head:* Dr. Helen Hodgson, Director, 801-832-2821, Fax: 801-832-3102, E-mail: hhodgson@westminstercollege.edu. *Application contact:* Dr. John Baworowsky, Vice President of Enrollment Management, 801-832-2200, Fax: 801-832-3101, E-mail: admission@westminstercollege.edu.
Website: http://www.westminstercollege.edu/mpc

West Texas A&M University, College of Fine Arts and Humanities, Department of Communication, Canyon, TX 79016-0001. Offers MA. Part-time programs available. *Degree requirements:* For master's, comprehensive exam, thesis optional. *Entrance requirements:* For master's, GRE General Test, 24 hours of undergraduate communications courses, 1 letter of recommendation, interview with communication advisor. Additional exam requirements/recommendations for international students: Required—TOEFL (minimum score 550 paper-based). Electronic applications accepted. *Faculty research:* Comparison student learning in basic public speaking in traditional versus online format, impact of supervisor immediacy and power on organizational outcomes, storytelling, gender, nonverbal.

West Virginia University, Eberly College of Arts and Sciences, Department of Communication Studies, Morgantown, WV 26506. Offers communication in instruction (MA); communication studies (PhD); communication theory and research (MA); corporate and organizational communication (MA). Part-time programs available. *Degree requirements:* For master's, comprehensive exam (for some programs), thesis (for some programs); for doctorate, comprehensive exam, thesis/dissertation. *Entrance requirements:* For master's and doctorate, minimum GPA of 3.0. Additional exam requirements/recommendations for international students: Required—TOEFL. Electronic applications accepted. *Faculty research:* Instructional communication, interpersonal communication, health communication, influence, instructional communication, social influence.

Wichita State University, Graduate School, Fairmount College of Liberal Arts and Sciences, Elliott School of Communication, Wichita, KS 67260. Offers MA. Part-time programs available. *Unit head:* Dr. Matthew Cecil, Director, 316-978-3185, Fax: 316-978-3006, E-mail: matthew.cecil@wichita.edu. *Application contact:* Jordan Oleson, Admissions Coordinator, 316-978-3095, E-mail: jordan.oleson@wichita.edu.
Website: http://www.wichita.edu/esc

Wilfrid Laurier University, Faculty of Graduate and Postdoctoral Studies, Faculty of Arts, Department of Communication Studies, Waterloo, ON N2L 3C5, Canada. Offers media, technology and culture (MA); visual communication and culture (MA). *Degree requirements:* For master's, thesis optional. *Entrance requirements:* For master's, honours BA in communication studies or a cognate discipline from an approved university with a minimum B+ overall in last two years of study and in undergraduate major. Additional exam requirements/recommendations for international students: Required—TOEFL (minimum score 89 iBT). Electronic applications accepted. *Faculty research:* Visual communication and culture, media, technology and culture.

William Paterson University of New Jersey, College of the Arts and Communication, Wayne, NJ 07470-8420. Offers art (MFA); music (MM); professional communication (MA). *Accreditation:* NASAD. Part-time and evening/weekend programs available. *Faculty:* 23 full-time (15 women), 11 part-time/adjunct (6 women). *Students:* 32 full-time (13 women), 18 part-time (11 women); includes 9 minority (2 Black or African American, non-Hispanic/Latino; 3 Asian, non-Hispanic/Latino; 4 Hispanic/Latino), 5 international. Average age 32. 79 applicants, 59% accepted, 24 enrolled. In 2014, 26 master's awarded. *Degree requirements:* For master's, comprehensive exam (for some programs), thesis (for some programs). *Entrance requirements:* For master's, GRE, minimum GPA of 2.75; audition; 2 letters of recommendation; portfolio with letter of intent. Additional exam requirements/recommendations for international students: Required—TOEFL (minimum score 550 paper-based; 79 iBT), IELTS (minimum score 6). *Application deadline:* For fall admission, 6/1 for domestic students, 3/1 for international students; for spring admission, 11/5 for domestic students, 10/15 for international students. Applications are processed on a rolling basis. Application fee: $50. Electronic applications accepted. *Expenses:* Tuition, state resident: full-time $12,413; part-time $564.21 per credit. Tuition, nonresident: full-time $20,487; part-time $931.21 per credit. *Required fees:* $2107; $95.79 per credit. $478.95 per semester. Tuition and fees vary according to course load and degree level. *Financial support:* Research assistantships with full tuition reimbursements, career-related internships or fieldwork, Federal Work-Study, scholarships/grants, and unspecified assistantships available. Support available to part-time students. Financial award application deadline: 4/1; financial award applicants required to submit FAFSA. *Unit head:* Daryl Moore, Dean, 973-720-2232, E-mail: moored@wpunj.edu. *Application contact:* Christina Aiello, Assistant Director, Graduate Admissions, 973-720-2506, Fax: 973-720-2035, E-mail: aielloc@wpunj.edu.
Website: http://www.wpunj.edu/coac

York University, Faculty of Graduate Studies, Program in Communication and Culture, Toronto, ON M3J 1P3, Canada. Offers MA, PhD. Program offered jointly with Ryerson University. *Degree requirements:* For master's, thesis or alternative; for doctorate, comprehensive exam, thesis/dissertation. Electronic applications accepted.

Arts Journalism

Academy of Art University, Graduate Program, Program in Fashion Journalism, San Francisco, CA 94105-3410. Offers MA. Part-time programs available. Postbaccalaureate distance learning degree programs offered (no on-campus study). *Students:* 18 full-time (all women), 16 part-time (13 women); includes 16 minority (11 Black or African American, non-Hispanic/Latino; 1 American Indian or Alaska Native, non-Hispanic/Latino; 2 Hispanic/Latino; 2 Two or more races, non-Hispanic/Latino), 10 international. Average age 27. 28 applicants, 100% accepted, 18 enrolled. In 2014, 11 master's awarded. *Degree requirements:* For master's, final review. *Entrance requirements:* For master's, statement of intent; resume; portfolio/reel; official college transcripts. *Application deadline:* Applications are processed on a rolling basis. Application fee: $100. Electronic applications accepted. *Expenses: Tuition:* Part-time $910 per unit. *Financial support:* Career-related internships or fieldwork and Federal Work-Study available. Support available to part-time students. Financial award application deadline: 8/10; financial award applicants required to submit FAFSA. *Unit head:* 800-544-ARTS, E-mail: info@academyart.edu. *Application contact:* 800-544-ARTS, E-mail: info@academyart.edu.
Website: http://www.academyart.edu/academics/fashion/graduate-degrees

School of the Art Institute of Chicago, Graduate Division, Program in New Arts Journalism, Chicago, IL 60603-3103. Offers MA. *Entrance requirements:* Additional exam requirements/recommendations for international students: Required—TOEFL, IELTS.

Syracuse University, S. I. Newhouse School of Public Communications, Program in Arts Journalism, Syracuse, NY 13244. Offers MA. *Students:* 16 full-time (11 women), 1 (woman) part-time; includes 2 minority (1 Black or African American, non-Hispanic/Latino; 1 Hispanic/Latino), 3 international. Average age 24. 33 applicants, 70% accepted, 16 enrolled. In 2014, 15 master's awarded. *Degree requirements:* For master's, capstone project. *Entrance requirements:* For master's, GRE General Test. Additional exam requirements/recommendations for international students: Required—TOEFL (minimum score 600 paper-based; 100 iBT). *Application deadline:* For fall admission, 2/1 for domestic students, 2/1 priority date for international students; for summer admission, 1/15 for domestic students, 1/15 priority date for international students. Application fee: $45. Electronic applications accepted. *Expenses: Tuition:* Part-time $1341 per credit. *Financial support:* Fellowships with full tuition reimbursements, research assistantships with partial tuition reimbursements, and teaching assistantships with partial tuition reimbursements available. Financial award application deadline: 2/1. *Unit head:* Johanna Keller, Director, 315-443-9251, Fax: 315-443-3946, E-mail: pcgrad@syr.edu. *Application contact:* Graduate Records Office, 315-443-4039, Fax: 315-443-1834, E-mail: pcgrad@syr.edu.
Website: http://newhouse.syr.edu/

Broadcast Journalism

Emerson College, Graduate Studies, School of Communication, Department of Journalism, Boston, MA 02116-4624. Offers journalism (MA), including broadcast journalism, print/multimedia journalism. *Faculty:* 16 full-time (8 women), 8 part-time/adjunct (5 women). *Students:* 40 full-time (33 women), 1 part-time (0 women); includes 9 minority (5 Black or African American, non-Hispanic/Latino; 3 Hispanic/Latino; 1 Two or more races, non-Hispanic/Latino), 11 international. Average age 24. 112 applicants, 46% accepted, 16 enrolled. In 2014, 22 master's awarded. *Entrance requirements:* For master's, GRE General Test. Additional exam requirements/recommendations for international students: Required—TOEFL (minimum score 550 paper-based; 80 iBT), IELTS (minimum score 6.5). *Application deadline:* For fall admission, 3/1 priority date for domestic and international students. Applications are processed on a rolling basis. Application fee: $60 ($75 for international students). Electronic applications accepted. *Expenses: Tuition:* Part-time $1145 per credit. *Financial support:* In 2014–15, 12 students received support, including 12 fellowships with partial tuition reimbursements available (averaging $11,000 per year); research assistantships with partial tuition reimbursements available, Federal Work-Study, scholarships/grants, and unspecified assistantships also available. Financial award application deadline: 3/1; financial award applicants required to submit FAFSA. *Faculty research:* Journalism. *Unit head:* Prof. Paul Niwa, Interim Chair, 617-824-8805, E-mail: ted_gup@emerson.edu. *Application contact:* Leanda Ferland, Office of Graduate Admission, 617-824-8610, Fax: 617-824-8614, E-mail: gradapp@emerson.edu.
Website: http://www.emerson.edu/graduate_admission

Northwestern University, Medill School of Journalism, Media, and Integrated Marketing Communications, Evanston, IL 60208. Offers integrated marketing communications (MSIMC), including brand strategy, content marketing, direct and interactive marketing, marketing analytics, strategic communications; interactive publishing (MSJ); magazine writing/editing (MSJ); reporting (MSJ); video/broadcast (MSJ). *Accreditation:* ACEJMC (one or more programs are accredited). *Entrance requirements:* For master's, GRE General Test, GMAT or LSAT (for MSJ). Additional exam requirements/recommendations for international students: Required—TOEFL. Electronic applications accepted. *Expenses:* Contact institution. *Faculty research:* Web business journalism, cultural stereotypes, voter apathy, digital television.

Quinnipiac University, School of Communications, Program in Journalism, Hamden, CT 06518-1940. Offers journalism (MS), including broadcast/multimedia, writing; sports journalism (MS), including broadcast/multimedia, writing. Part-time and evening/weekend programs available. Postbaccalaureate distance learning degree programs offered (no on-campus study). *Faculty:* 5 full-time (2 women), 12 part-time/adjunct (2 women). *Students:* 10 full-time (7 women), 3 part-time (2 women); includes 3 minority (all Black or African American, non-Hispanic/Latino). 16 applicants, 81% accepted, 5 enrolled. In 2014, 20 master's awarded. *Degree requirements:* For master's, project. *Entrance requirements:* For master's, minimum GPA of 2.8, portfolio or writing sample. Additional exam requirements/recommendations for international students: Required—TOEFL (minimum score 575 paper-based; 90 iBT), IELTS (minimum score 6.5). *Application deadline:* For fall admission, 7/30 priority date for domestic students, 4/30 priority date for international students; for spring admission, 12/15 priority date for domestic students, 9/15 priority date for international students. Applications are processed on a rolling basis. Application fee: $45. Electronic applications accepted. *Expenses: Tuition:* Part-time $920 per credit. *Required fees:* $222 per semester. Tuition and fees vary according to course load and program. *Financial support:* In 2014–15, 3 students received support. Fellowships with tuition reimbursements available, career-related internships or fieldwork, Federal Work-Study, scholarships/grants, and unspecified assistantships available. Support available to part-time students. Financial award application deadline: 6/1; financial award applicants required to submit FAFSA. *Faculty research:* Journalism history, federal law enforcement and journalism, social media and journalism, online journalism, sports journalism, American football history and media, journalism and film, McCarthyism and journalism. *Application contact:* Office of Graduate Admissions, 800-462-1944, Fax: 203-582-3443, E-mail: graduate@quinnipiac.edu.
Website: http://www.quinnipiac.edu/gradjournalism

Quinnipiac University, School of Communications, Program in Sports Journalism, Hamden, CT 06518-1940. Offers MS. Part-time and evening/weekend programs available. Postbaccalaureate distance learning degree programs offered (no on-campus study). *Faculty:* 5 full-time (2 women), 12 part-time/adjunct (2 women). *Students:* 6 full-time (1 woman), 1 (woman) part-time. 5 applicants, 100% accepted, 5 enrolled. *Entrance requirements:* For master's, minimum GPA of 2.8, portfolio or writing sample. Additional exam requirements/recommendations for international students: Required—TOEFL (minimum score 575 paper-based; 90 iBT), IELTS (minimum score 6.5). *Application deadline:* For fall admission, 7/30 priority date for domestic students, 4/30 priority date for international students; for spring admission, 12/15 priority date for domestic students, 9/30 priority date for international students. Applications are processed on a rolling basis. Application fee: $45. Electronic applications accepted. *Expenses: Tuition:* Part-time $920 per credit. *Required fees:* $222 per semester. Tuition and fees vary according to course load and program. *Financial support:* In 2014–15, 1 student received support. Fellowships with tuition reimbursements available, career-related internships or fieldwork, Federal Work-Study, scholarships/grants, and unspecified assistantships available. Support available to part-time students. Financial award application deadline: 6/1; financial award applicants required to submit FAFSA. *Application contact:* Office of Graduate Admissions, 203-582-8672, Fax: 203-582-3443, E-mail: graduate@quinnipiac.edu.
Website: http://www.quinnipiac.edu/school-of-communications/graduate-programs/master-of-science-in-sports-journalism/

Syracuse University, S. I. Newhouse School of Public Communications, Program in Broadcast and Digital Journalism, Syracuse, NY 13244. Offers MS. *Students:* 35 full-time (26 women), 1 part-time (0 women); includes 11 minority (9 Black or African American, non-Hispanic/Latino; 2 Hispanic/Latino), 1 international. Average age 25. 90 applicants, 82% accepted, 34 enrolled. In 2014, 39 master's awarded. *Degree requirements:* For master's, capstone course. *Entrance requirements:* For master's,

GRE General Test. Additional exam requirements/recommendations for international students: Required—TOEFL (minimum score 100 iBT). *Application deadline:* For fall admission, 2/1 for domestic and international students; for summer admission, 1/15 priority date for domestic and international students. Application fee: $45. Electronic applications accepted. *Expenses: Tuition:* Part-time $1341 per credit. *Financial support:* Fellowships with full tuition reimbursements, research assistantships with partial tuition reimbursements, and teaching assistantships with partial tuition reimbursements available. Financial award application deadline: 2/1. *Unit head:* Prof. Chris Tuohey, Chair, 315-443-4118, E-mail: pcgrad@syr.edu. *Application contact:* Graduate Records Office, 315-443-5749, Fax: 315-443-1834, E-mail: pcgrad@syr.edu.
Website: http://newhouse.syr.edu/

University of Maryland, College Park, Academic Affairs, Phillip Merrill College of Journalism, College Park, MD 20742. Offers broadcast journalism (MA); journalism (MA); journalism and media studies (PhD); online news (MA); public affairs reporting (MA). *Accreditation:* ACEJMC (one or more programs are accredited). Part-time and evening/weekend programs available. *Faculty:* 22 full-time (13 women), 53 part-time/adjunct (23 women). *Students:* 63 full-time (35 women), 6 part-time (2 women); includes 16 minority (9 Black or African American, non-Hispanic/Latino; 4 Asian, non-Hispanic/Latino; 3 Hispanic/Latino), 14 international. 117 applicants, 38% accepted, 15 enrolled. In 2014, 22 master's, 6 doctorates awarded. *Degree requirements:* For doctorate, thesis/dissertation, preliminary written and oral comprehensive exams. *Entrance requirements:* For master's and doctorate, GRE General Test, minimum GPA of 3.0, 3 letters of recommendation. Additional exam requirements/recommendations for international students: Required—TOEFL. *Application deadline:* For fall admission, 2/1 for domestic and international students; for summer admission, 2/1 for domestic and international students. Application fee: $75. Electronic applications accepted. *Financial support:* In 2014–15, 9 fellowships with full and partial tuition reimbursements (averaging $24,407 per year), 25 teaching assistantships (averaging $17,009 per year) were awarded; career-related internships or fieldwork, Federal Work-Study, and scholarships/grants also available. Support available to part-time students. Financial award applicants required to submit FAFSA. *Faculty research:* Mass communication theory, specialized journalism, new telecommunication technologies, press integration. *Total annual research expenditures:* $230,123. *Unit head:* Lucy A. Dalglish, Dean, 301-405-8806, Fax: 301-314-1978, E-mail: dalglish@umd.edu. *Application contact:* Dr. Charles A. Caramello, Dean of Graduate School, 301-405-0358, Fax: 301-314-9305, E-mail: ccaramel@umd.edu.
Website: http://www.journalism.umd.edu/

University of Miami, Graduate School, School of Communication, Coral Gables, FL 33124. Offers communication (PhD); communication studies (MA); film studies (MA, PhD); motion pictures (MFA), including production, producing, and screenwriting; print journalism (MA); public relations (MA); Spanish language journalism (MA); television broadcast journalism (MA). Part-time programs available. *Degree requirements:* For master's, comprehensive exam (for some programs), thesis (for some programs); for doctorate, comprehensive exam, thesis/dissertation. *Entrance requirements:* For master's, GRE General Test; for doctorate, GRE General Test, master's thesis or scholarly research. Additional exam requirements/recommendations for international students: Required—TOEFL (minimum score 600 paper-based; 100 iBT). Electronic applications accepted. *Faculty research:* Communication studies, mass communication, international/interpersonal communication, film studies, journalism.

University of the Sacred Heart, Graduate Programs, Department of Communication, San Juan, PR 00914-0383. Offers contemporary culture and media (MA); digital journalism (MA, Certificate); editing for media (MA, Certificate); public relations (MA, Certificate); publicity (MA, Certificate); scriptwriting (MA, Certificate). Part-time and evening/weekend programs available. *Degree requirements:* For master's, thesis.

Corporate and Organizational Communication

Argosy University, Schaumburg, Graduate School of Business and Management, Schaumburg, IL 60173-5403. Offers accounting (DBA, Adv C); customized professional concentration (MBA, DBA); finance (MBA, Certificate); fraud examination (MBA); healthcare administration (MBA, Certificate); human resource management (MS); information systems (Adv C, Certificate); information systems management (MBA); international business (MBA, DBA, Adv C, Certificate); management (MBA, MSM, DBA, Adv C, Certificate); marketing (MBA, DBA, Adv C, Certificate); organizational leadership (MS, Ed D); public administration (MBA); sustainable management (MBA).

Armstrong State University, School of Graduate Studies, Program in Professional Communication and Leadership, Savannah, GA 31419-1997. Offers MA, Certificate. Part-time and evening/weekend programs available. *Faculty:* 13 full-time (6 women), 4 part-time/adjunct (3 women). *Students:* 22 full-time (16 women), 46 part-time (29 women); includes 28 minority (24 Black or African American, non-Hispanic/Latino; 1 Asian, non-Hispanic/Latino; 3 Hispanic/Latino). Average age 34. 32 applicants, 81% accepted, 23 enrolled. In 2014, 10 master's awarded. *Degree requirements:* For master's, comprehensive exam, project. *Entrance requirements:* For master's, minimum GPA of 2.5, letters of recommendation, letter of intent, resume. Additional exam requirements/recommendations for international students: Required—TOEFL (minimum score 523 paper-based). *Application deadline:* For fall admission, 6/1 priority date for domestic students, 5/1 priority date for international students; for spring admission, 11/15 priority date for domestic students, 9/15 priority date for international students; for summer admission, 4/15 for domestic students, 9/15 priority date for international students. Application fee: $30. *Expenses: Tuition:* state resident: part-time $206 per credit hour. Tuition, nonresident: part-time $763 per credit hour. *Required fees:* $612 per semester. Tuition and fees vary according to course load, campus/location and program. *Financial support:* In 2014–15, research assistantships with full tuition reimbursements (averaging $5,000 per year) were awarded; scholarships/grants and unspecified assistantships also available. Financial award application deadline: 3/15; financial award applicants required to submit FAFSA. *Faculty research:* Organizational communication, conflict resolution and mediation, rhetoric and language identity, brand identity and marketing, communication theory. *Unit head:* Dr. Chris Hendricks, Program Coordinator, 912-344-2725, E-mail: chris.hendricks@armstrong.edu. *Application contact:* Kathy Ingram, Associate Director of Graduate/Adult and Nontraditional Students, 912-344-2503, Fax: 912-344-3417, E-mail: graduate@armstrong.edu.
Website: http://www.armstrong.edu/Majors/degree/master_professional_communication_leadership

Assumption College, Department of Business Studies, Worcester, MA 01609-1296. Offers accounting (MBA); business administration (CAGS); finance/economics (MBA);

frontline management (CGS); general business (MBA); human resources (MBA); international business (MBA); management (MBA); marketing (MBA); nonprofit leadership (MBA, CGS); organizational communication (CGS). Part-time and evening/weekend programs available. *Faculty:* 6 full-time (2 women), 16 part-time/adjunct (6 women). *Students:* 39 full-time (20 women), 135 part-time (76 women); includes 28 minority (11 Black or African American, non-Hispanic/Latino; 1 American Indian or Alaska Native, non-Hispanic/Latino; 4 Asian, non-Hispanic/Latino; 10 Hispanic/Latino; 1 Native Hawaiian or other Pacific Islander, non-Hispanic/Latino; 1 Two or more races, non-Hispanic/Latino), 3 international. Average age 30. 53 applicants, 57% accepted, 18 enrolled. In 2014, 57 master's awarded. *Degree requirements:* For master's, thesis, capstone. *Entrance requirements:* For master's and other advanced degree, 3 letters of recommendation, resume, essay. Additional exam requirements/recommendations for international students: Required—TOEFL (minimum score 540 paper-based; 76 iBT), IELTS (minimum score 6). *Application deadline:* For fall admission, 10/1 for domestic and international students; for winter admission, 2/1 for domestic and international students; for spring admission, 4/1 for domestic and international students. Applications are processed on a rolling basis. Application fee: $30. Electronic applications accepted. *Expenses: Tuition:* Full-time $10,620; part-time $590 per credit. *Required fees:* $20 per term. Full-time tuition and fees vary according to course load and program. *Financial support:* In 2014–15, 23 students received support. Tuition waivers (full and partial), unspecified assistantships, and institutional discounts available. Financial award application deadline: 5/1; financial award applicants required to submit FAFSA. *Faculty research:* Workplace diversity, dynamics of team interaction, utilization of leased employees, experiential learning project on due diligence market for prostheses. *Unit head:* Eric Drouart, Director, 508-767-7457, E-mail: edrouart@assumption.edu. *Application contact:* Dr. Landy Johnson, Director of Operations for Graduate and Professional Studies, 508-767-7666, Fax: 508-767-7030, E-mail: graduate@assumption.edu.
Website: http://graduate.assumption.edu/mba/assumption-mba

Barry University, College of Arts and Sciences, Department of Communication, Miami Shores, FL 33161-6695. Offers broadcasting (Certificate); communication (MA), including broadcast communication, public relations and corporate communications; organizational communication (MS). Part-time and evening/weekend programs available. *Degree requirements:* For master's, thesis (for some programs). *Entrance requirements:* For master's, GRE General Test, MAT, minimum GPA of 3.0. Electronic applications accepted. *Faculty research:* Organizational communication, broadcast communication, intercultural communication, advertising, leadership.

Corporate and Organizational Communication

Baruch College of the City University of New York, Weissman School of Arts and Sciences, Program in Corporate Communication, New York, NY 10010-5585. Offers MA. Part-time and evening/weekend programs available. *Faculty:* 7 full-time (3 women), 5 part-time/adjunct (0 women). *Students:* 17 full-time (14 women), 27 part-time (21 women); includes 10 minority (6 Black or African American, non-Hispanic/Latino; 4 Hispanic/Latino), 13 international. Average age 30. 31 applicants, 74% accepted, 13 enrolled. In 2014, 39 master's awarded. *Degree requirements:* For master's, thesis or alternative. *Entrance requirements:* For master's, GRE/GMAT (may be waived for some applicants), 3 letters of recommendation; personal essay; resume; official transcripts. Additional exam requirements/recommendations for international students: Required—TOEFL. *Application deadline:* For fall admission, 5/1 for domestic and international students; for spring admission, 12/1 for domestic and international students. Applications are processed on a rolling basis. Application fee: $135. Electronic applications accepted. *Financial support:* Applicants required to submit FAFSA. *Faculty research:* Media history; cultural studies; film studies; social implications of contemporary digital media; improving public argument; intercultural and international aspects of communication; intercultural friendship formation; use of technology in communication education; strategic corporate communication; immersive spectatorship; global corporate communication; communications strategy development; public and media relations; crisis management; work and life balance. *Unit head:* Prof. Michael Goodman, Director, 646-312-3723, Fax: 646-312-3721, E-mail: michael.goodman@baruch.cuny.edu. *Application contact:* Michael J. Lovaglio, Director of Graduate Programs, 646-312-3897, Fax: 646-312-3871, E-mail: wsas.graduate.studies@baruch.cuny.edu.
Website: http://www.baruch.cuny.edu/wsas/academics/corporate_communication/index.htm

Bellevue University, Graduate School, College of Arts and Sciences, Bellevue, NE 68005-3098. Offers clinical counseling (MS); healthcare administration (MHA); human services (MA); international security and intelligence studies (MS); managerial communication (MA). Postbaccalaureate distance learning degree programs offered.

Boston University, Metropolitan College, Program in Gastronomy, Boston, MA 02215. Offers business (MLA); communications (MLA); food policy (MLA); history and culture (MLA). Part-time and evening/weekend programs available. *Faculty:* 3 full-time (2 women), 14 part-time/adjunct (8 women). *Students:* 4 full-time (all women), 82 part-time (72 women); includes 8 minority (1 Black or African American, non-Hispanic/Latino; 4 Asian, non-Hispanic/Latino; 1 Hispanic/Latino; 2 Two or more races, non-Hispanic/Latino), 7 international. Average age 30. 58 applicants, 76% accepted, 27 enrolled. In 2014, 44 master's awarded. *Degree requirements:* For master's, thesis optional. *Entrance requirements:* Additional exam requirements/recommendations for international students: Required—TOEFL. *Application deadline:* Applications are processed on a rolling basis. Application fee: $80. Electronic applications accepted. *Expenses:* Expenses: $800 per credit part-time; student services fees: $60 per semester; technology fee of $60 per credit (for online courses). *Financial support:* In 2014–15, 4 research assistantships (averaging $4,200 per year) were awarded; career-related internships or fieldwork, scholarships/grants, and unspecified assistantships also available. Support available to part-time students. Financial award applicants required to submit FAFSA. *Faculty research:* Food studies. *Unit head:* Dr. Mary Beaudry, Interim Faculty Coordinator, 617-353-6916, Fax: 617-353-4130, E-mail: gastrmla@bu.edu. *Application contact:* Barbara Rotger, Program Manager, 617-353-6916, Fax: 617-353-4130, E-mail: brotger@bu.edu.
Website: http://www.bu.edu/met/gastronomy

Bowie State University, Graduate Programs, Program in Organizational Communication, Bowie, MD 20715-9465. Offers MA, Certificate. Part-time and evening/weekend programs available. *Students:* 70 full-time (40 women), 35 part-time (15 women); includes 91 minority (75 Black or African American, non-Hispanic/Latino; 1 Hispanic/Latino; 15 Two or more races, non-Hispanic/Latino), 4 international. Average age 31. 25 applicants, 80% accepted, 18 enrolled. In 2014, 16 master's awarded. *Degree requirements:* For master's, comprehensive exam, thesis optional, research paper. *Entrance requirements:* For master's, minimum GPA of 2.5. *Application deadline:* For fall admission, 4/1 priority date for domestic and international students; for spring admission, 11/1 priority date for domestic and international students. Applications are processed on a rolling basis. Application fee: $40. Electronic applications accepted. *Expenses:* Tuition, state resident: full-time $8928; part-time $372 per credit. Tuition, nonresident: full-time $16,176; part-time $674 per credit. *Required fees:* $2141. *Financial support:* Application deadline: 4/1. *Faculty research:* International telecommunications, developmental communications. *Unit head:* Dr. Chukwuka Onwumechili, Coordinator, 301-860-3709, Fax: 301-860-3728, E-mail: conwumechili@bowiestate.edu. *Application contact:* Angela Issac, Information Contact, 301-860-4000.

California State University, San Bernardino, Graduate Studies, College of Arts and Letters, Department of Communication Studies, San Bernardino, CA 92407-2397. Offers communication studies (MA); integrated marketing communication (MA). *Students:* 4 full-time (all women), 16 part-time (11 women); includes 7 minority (2 Black or African American, non-Hispanic/Latino; 2 Asian, non-Hispanic/Latino; 3 Hispanic/Latino), 4 international. Average age 29. 37 applicants, 32% accepted, 5 enrolled. In 2014, 4 master's awarded. *Degree requirements:* For master's, comprehensive exam. *Entrance requirements:* Additional exam requirements/recommendations for international students: Required—TOEFL. *Application deadline:* For fall admission, 7/17 for domestic students. Application fee: $55. *Expenses:* Tuition, state resident: full-time $6738; part-time $1302 per term. Tuition, nonresident: full-time $17,898; part-time $248 per unit. *Required fees:* $365 per quarter. Tuition and fees vary according to degree level and program. *Unit head:* Dr. Michael Salvador, Chair, 909-537-5820, Fax: 909-537-7009, E-mail: salvador@csusb.edu. *Application contact:* Dr. Jeffrey Thompson, Dean of Graduate Studies, 909-537-5058, Fax: 909-537-7034, E-mail: jthompso@csusb.edu.

Canisius College, Graduate Division, College of Arts and Sciences, Department of Communication Studies, Buffalo, NY 14208-1098. Offers communication and leadership (MS). Part-time and evening/weekend programs available. *Faculty:* 10 full-time (4 women), 1 (woman) part-time/adjunct. *Students:* 6 full-time (4 women), 18 part-time (10 women); includes 1 minority (Black or African American, non-Hispanic/Latino), 2 international. Average age 29. 23 applicants, 65% accepted, 6 enrolled. In 2014, 24 master's awarded. *Degree requirements:* For master's, thesis. *Entrance requirements:* For master's, GRE, official transcript of all college work. Additional exam requirements/recommendations for international students: Required—TOEFL (minimum score 550 paper-based, 80 iBT), IELTS (minimum score 6.5), or CAEL (minimum score 70). *Application deadline:* For fall admission, 7/15 priority date for domestic students; for spring admission, 4/15 priority date for domestic students. Applications are processed on a rolling basis. Application fee: $25. Electronic applications accepted. Application fee is waived when completed online. *Financial support:* Career-related internships or fieldwork, Federal Work-Study, scholarships/grants, and unspecified assistantships available. Support available to part-time students. Financial award application deadline: 4/30; financial award applicants required to submit FAFSA. *Faculty research:* Conflict and communication, health and communication, leadership. *Unit head:* Dr. Rosanne L.

Hartman, Graduate Program Director/Professor, Communication and Leadership, 716-888-2589, Fax: 716-888-3118, E-mail: hartmanr@canisius.edu. *Application contact:* Kathleen B. Davis, Vice President of Enrollment Management, 716-888-2500, Fax: 716-888-3195, E-mail: daviskb@canisius.edu.
Website: http://www.canisius.edu/graduate/

Carnegie Mellon University, Dietrich College of Humanities and Social Sciences, Department of English, Program in Professional Writing, Pittsburgh, PA 15213-3891. Offers editing and publishing (MAPW); policy and non-profit communication (MAPW); public and media relations/corporate communications (MAPW); science or healthcare communication (MAPW); technical writing (MAPW); writing for new media (MAPW); writing for print media (MAPW). Part-time programs available. *Entrance requirements:* For master's, GRE General Test. Additional exam requirements/recommendations for international students: Required—TOEFL, TWE.

Central Connecticut State University, School of Graduate Studies, College of Liberal Arts and Social Sciences, Department of Communication, New Britain, CT 06050-4010. Offers organizational communication (MS); public relations/promotions (Certificate). Part-time and evening/weekend programs available. *Faculty:* 6 full-time (1 woman). *Students:* 4 full-time (3 women), 28 part-time (23 women); includes 6 minority (3 Black or African American, non-Hispanic/Latino; 2 Hispanic/Latino; 1 Two or more races, non-Hispanic/Latino). Average age 28. 26 applicants, 27% accepted, 4 enrolled. In 2014, 8 master's, 1 other advanced degree awarded. *Degree requirements:* For master's, comprehensive exam, thesis or alternative; for Certificate, qualifying exam. *Entrance requirements:* For master's, minimum undergraduate GPA of 3.0, resume, references, essay. Additional exam requirements/recommendations for international students: Required—TOEFL (minimum score 550 paper-based; 79 iBT). *Application deadline:* For fall admission, 6/1 for domestic students, 5/1 for international students; for spring admission, 11/1 for domestic and international students. Applications are processed on a rolling basis. Application fee: $50. Electronic applications accepted. *Expenses:* Tuition, area resident: Full-time $5730; part-time $534 per credit. Tuition, state resident: full-time $8596; part-time $534 per credit. Tuition, nonresident: full-time $15,964; part-time $548 per credit. *Required fees:* $4211; $215 per credit. *Financial support:* In 2014–15, 3 students received support, including 1 research assistantship; career-related internships or fieldwork, Federal Work-Study, scholarships/grants, and unspecified assistantships also available. Support available to part-time students. Financial award application deadline: 3/1; financial award applicants required to submit FAFSA. *Faculty research:* Organizational communication, mass communication, intercultural communication, political communication, information management. *Unit head:* Dr. Christopher Pudlinski, Chair, 860-832-2690, E-mail: pudlinskic@ccsu.edu. *Application contact:* Patricia Gardner, Associate Director of Graduate Studies, 860-832-2350, Fax: 860-832-2362, E-mail: graduateadmissions@ccsu.edu.
Website: http://web.ccsu.edu/communication/

City College of the City University of New York, Graduate School, College of Liberal Arts and Science, Division of the Humanities and Arts, Department of Media and Communication Arts, Program in Branding and Integrated Communications, New York, NY 10031. Offers MPS.

Columbia University, Graduate School of Business, MBA Program, New York, NY 10027. Offers accounting (MBA); decision, risk, and operations (MBA); entrepreneurship (MBA); finance and economics (MBA); healthcare and pharmaceutical management (MBA); human resource management (MBA); international business (MBA); leadership and ethics (MBA); management (MBA); marketing (MBA); media (MBA); private equity (MBA); real estate (MBA); social enterprise (MBA); value investing (MBA); DDS/MBA; JD/MBA; MBA/MIA; MBA/MPH; MBA/MS; MD/MBA. *Entrance requirements:* For master's, GMAT, 2 letters of recommendation. Additional exam requirements/recommendations for international students: Required—TOEFL. Electronic applications accepted. *Expenses:* Contact institution. *Faculty research:* Human decision making and behavioral research; real estate market and mortgage defaults; financial crisis and corporate governance; international business; security analysis and accounting.

Columbia University, School of Continuing Education, Program in Strategic Communications, New York, NY 10027. Offers MS. Part-time and evening/weekend programs available. *Entrance requirements:* For master's, minimum undergraduate GPA of 3.0. Additional exam requirements/recommendations for international students: Required—American Language Program placement test. Electronic applications accepted. *Faculty research:* Marketing communications, public relations, crisis management.

Concordia University, St. Paul, College of Arts and Letters, St. Paul, MN 55104-5494. Offers strategic communication management (MA). Evening/weekend programs available. *Faculty:* 4 part-time/adjunct (1 woman). *Students:* 31 full-time (20 women), 3 part-time (all women); includes 5 minority (1 Black or African American, non-Hispanic/Latino; 1 American Indian or Alaska Native, non-Hispanic/Latino; 1 Asian, non-Hispanic/Latino; 1 Hispanic/Latino; 1 Native Hawaiian or other Pacific Islander, non-Hispanic/Latino). Average age 33. 23 applicants, 52% accepted, 9 enrolled. In 2014, 14 master's awarded. *Degree requirements:* For master's, thesis optional. *Entrance requirements:* For master's, official transcripts from regionally-accredited institution stating the conferral of bachelor's degree with minimum cumulative GPA of 3.0; personal statement; current professional resume. Additional exam requirements/recommendations for international students: Recommended—TOEFL (minimum score 547 paper-based; 78 iBT), IELTS (minimum score 6). *Application deadline:* For fall admission, 8/1 for domestic and international students; for spring admission, 12/1 for domestic and international students; for summer admission, 5/1 for domestic and international students. Applications are processed on a rolling basis. Application fee: $50. Electronic applications accepted. *Expenses:* Tuition: Full-time $4416; part-time $368 per credit. Tuition and fees vary according to degree level and program. *Financial support:* Applicants required to submit FAFSA. *Unit head:* Dr. David Lumpp, Dean, 651-641-8217, E-mail: lumpp@csp.edu. *Application contact:* Kimberly Craig, Associate Vice President, Cohort Enrollment Management, 651-603-6223, Fax: 651-603-6320, E-mail: craig@csp.edu.

Concordia University Wisconsin, Graduate Programs, School of Business and Legal Studies, MBA Program, Mequon, WI 53097-2402. Offers finance (MBA); health care administration (MBA); human resource management (MBA); international business (MBA); international business-bilingual English/Chinese (MBA); management (MBA); management information systems (MBA); managerial communications (MBA); marketing (MBA); public administration (MBA); risk management (MBA). Postbaccalaureate distance learning degree programs offered (minimal on-campus study). *Degree requirements:* For master's, comprehensive exam, thesis or alternative. *Entrance requirements:* Additional exam requirements/recommendations for international students: Required—TOEFL. *Expenses:* Contact institution.

Cornell University, Graduate School, Graduate Fields of Agriculture and Life Sciences, Field of Communication, Ithaca, NY 14853-0001. Offers communication (MS, PhD); human-computer interaction (MS, PhD); language and communication (MS, PhD); media communication and society (MS, PhD); organizational communication (MS, PhD); science, environment and health communication (MS, PhD); social psychology of communication (MS, PhD). *Degree requirements:* For master's, thesis (MS); for

doctorate, comprehensive exam, thesis/dissertation. *Entrance requirements:* For master's and doctorate, GRE General Test, 3 letters of recommendation. Additional exam requirements/recommendations for international students: Required—TOEFL (minimum score 600 paper-based; 100 iBT). Electronic applications accepted. *Faculty research:* Mass communication, communication technologies, science and environmental communication.

Dallas Baptist University, College of Business, Business Administration Program, Dallas, TX 75211-9299. Offers accounting (MBA); business communication (MBA); conflict resolution management (MBA); entrepreneurship (MBA); finance (MBA); health care management (MBA); international business (MBA); leading the non-profit organization (MBA); management (MBA); management information systems (MBA); marketing (MBA); project management (MBA); technology and engineering (MBA). *Accreditation:* ACBSP. Part-time and evening/weekend programs available. *Entrance requirements:* For master's, GMAT, minimum GPA of 3.0. Additional exam requirements/recommendations for international students: Required—TOEFL, IELTS. Electronic applications accepted. *Expenses: Tuition:* Full-time $14,130; part-time $785 per credit hour. *Required fees:* $200 per semester. Tuition and fees vary according to course level and course load. *Faculty research:* Sports management, services marketing, retailing, strategic management, financial planning/investments.

Dallas Baptist University, Gary Cook School of Leadership, Program in Global Leadership, Dallas, TX 75211-9299. Offers business communication (MA); East Asian studies (MA); ESL (MA); general studies (MA); global leadership (MA); global studies (MA); international business (MA); leading the nonprofit organization (MA); missions (MA); small group ministry (MA); MA/MA. Part-time and evening/weekend programs available. *Entrance requirements:* For master's, minimum GPA of 3.0. Additional exam requirements/recommendations for international students: Required—TOEFL, IELTS. *Expenses: Tuition:* Full-time $14,130; part-time $785 per credit hour. *Required fees:* $200 per semester. Tuition and fees vary according to course level and course load.

DePaul University, College of Communication, Chicago, IL 60614. Offers digital communication and media arts (MA); health communication (MA); journalism (MA); media and cinema studies (MA); organizational and multicultural communication (MA); public relations and advertising (MA); relational communication (MA). Part-time and evening/weekend programs available. *Entrance requirements:* Additional exam requirements/recommendations for international students: Required—TOEFL (minimum score 590 paper-based; 96 iBT), IELTS (minimum score 7.5) or PTE. Electronic applications accepted.

Drexel University, College of Arts and Sciences, Department of Culture and Communication, Program in Communication, Philadelphia, PA 19104-2875. Offers public communication (MS); science communication (MS); technical communication (MS). Part-time and evening/weekend programs available. *Degree requirements:* For master's, internship, professional portfolio. *Entrance requirements:* For master's, GRE or minimum GPA of 3.0. Additional exam requirements/recommendations for international students: Required—TOEFL. Electronic applications accepted.

Eastern Michigan University, Graduate School, Academic Affairs Division, Ypsilanti, MI 48197. Offers individualized studies (MA, MS); integrated marketing communications (MS). *Students:* 2 part-time (both women); includes 1 minority (Black or African American, non-Hispanic/Latino), 1 international. Average age 43. 191 applicants, 86% accepted, 61 enrolled. In 2014, 4 master's awarded. *Entrance requirements:* Additional exam requirements/recommendations for international students: Required—TOEFL. Application fee: $45. *Unit head:* Dr. Jeffrey Kentor, Dean, 734-487-0042, Fax: 734-487-0050, E-mail: jkentor@emich.edu. *Application contact:* Graduate Admissions, 734-487-2400, Fax: 734-487-6559, E-mail: graduate.admissions@emich.edu.

Eastern Michigan University, Graduate School, College of Business, Department of Marketing, Program in Integrated Marketing Communications, Ypsilanti, MI 48197. Offers MS. *Students:* 25 full-time (18 women), 33 part-time (28 women); includes 17 minority (12 Black or African American, non-Hispanic/Latino; 1 Asian, non-Hispanic/Latino; 4 Two or more races, non-Hispanic/Latino), 1 international. Average age 36. 37 applicants, 70% accepted, 16 enrolled. In 2014, 33 master's awarded. Application fee: $45. *Application contact:* K. Michelle Henry, Director, Academic Services, 734-487-4444, Fax: 734-478-1316, E-mail: cob.graduate@emich.edu.

East Tennessee State University, School of Graduate Studies, College of Arts and Sciences, Department of Communication and Performance, Johnson City, TN 37614. Offers professional communication (MA), including communication studies, storytelling and theatre, strategic communication. Program offered with Department of Mass Communications. Part-time programs available. *Faculty:* 17 full-time (7 women). *Students:* 11 full-time (8 women); includes 1 minority (Two or more races, non-Hispanic/Latino), 4 international. Average age 26. 18 applicants, 72% accepted, 7 enrolled. In 2014, 7 master's awarded. *Degree requirements:* For master's, comprehensive exam, thesis optional. *Entrance requirements:* For master's, GRE General Test, minimum GPA of 3.0; three letters of recommendation. Additional exam requirements/recommendations for international students: Required—TOEFL (minimum score 550 paper-based; 79 iBT). *Application deadline:* For fall admission, 6/1 for domestic students, 4/30 for international students; for spring admission, 11/1 for domestic students, 9/30 for international students. Application fee: $35 ($45 for international students). Electronic applications accepted. *Financial support:* In 2014–15, 17 students received support, including 6 research assistantships with full tuition reimbursements available (averaging $6,000 per year), 4 teaching assistantships with full tuition reimbursements available (averaging $6,000 per year); career-related internships or fieldwork, institutionally sponsored loans, scholarships/grants, and unspecified assistantships also available. Financial award application deadline: 7/1; financial award applicants required to submit FAFSA. *Faculty research:* Political communications, visual communication, depictions of gender and ethnicity in print and online media and online corporate media, presidential rhetoric and newspaper coverage of presidential speeches. *Application contact:* Angela Edwards, Graduate Specialist, 423-439-4703, Fax: 423-439-5624, E-mail: edwardag@etsu.edu.
Website: http://www.etsu.edu/cas/comm_perform/

Emerson College, Graduate Studies, School of Communication, Department of Communication Studies, Program in Communication Management, Boston, MA 02116-4624. Offers MA. Part-time and evening/weekend programs available. *Students:* 36 full-time (30 women), 4 part-time (3 women); includes 2 minority (1 Black or African American, non-Hispanic/Latino; 1 Hispanic/Latino), 19 international. Average age 26. 118 applicants, 36% accepted, 12 enrolled. In 2014, 21 master's awarded. *Entrance requirements:* For master's, GMAT or GRE General Test. Additional exam requirements/recommendations for international students: Required—TOEFL (minimum score 550 paper-based; 80 iBT), IELTS (minimum score 6.5). *Application deadline:* For fall admission, 3/1 priority date for domestic and international students; for spring admission, 11/1 for domestic and international students. Applications are processed on a rolling basis. Application fee: $60 ($75 for international students). Electronic applications accepted. *Expenses: Tuition:* Part-time $1145 per credit. *Financial support:* In 2014–15, 8 students received support, including 8 fellowships with partial tuition reimbursements available (averaging $8,625 per year); research assistantships with partial tuition reimbursements available, Federal Work-Study, scholarships/grants, and unspecified assistantships also available. Financial award application deadline: 3/1; financial award applicants required to submit FAFSA. *Faculty research:* Organizational management, corporate and organizational communication. *Unit head:* Prof. Linda Gallant, Graduate Program Director, 617-824-8491, E-mail: linda_gallant@emerson.edu. *Application contact:* Leanda Ferland, Office of Graduate Admission, 617-824-8610, Fax: 617-824-8614, E-mail: gradapp@emerson.edu. Website: http://www.emerson.edu/graduate_admission

Emerson College, Graduate Studies, School of Communication, Department of Marketing Communication, Program in Integrated Marketing Communication, Boston, MA 02116-4624. Offers MA. Part-time and evening/weekend programs available. *Faculty:* 16 full-time (7 women), 7 part-time/adjunct (2 women). *Students:* 131 full-time (99 women), 22 part-time (18 women); includes 9 minority (4 Black or African American, non-Hispanic/Latino; 1 Asian, non-Hispanic/Latino; 4 Hispanic/Latino), 90 international. Average age 24. 263 applicants, 72% accepted, 53 enrolled. In 2014, 68 master's awarded. *Entrance requirements:* For master's, GMAT or GRE General Test. Additional exam requirements/recommendations for international students: Required—TOEFL (minimum score 550 paper-based; 80 iBT), IELTS (minimum score 6.5). *Application deadline:* For fall admission, 6/1 priority date for domestic students, 5/1 priority date for international students; for spring admission, 11/1 priority date for domestic students. Applications are processed on a rolling basis. Application fee: $60 ($75 for international students). Electronic applications accepted. *Expenses: Tuition:* Part-time $1145 per credit. *Financial support:* In 2014–15, 17 students received support, including 17 fellowships with partial tuition reimbursements available (averaging $9,300 per year), 16 research assistantships with partial tuition reimbursements available (averaging $10,000 per year); Federal Work-Study, scholarships/grants, and unspecified assistantships also available. Financial award application deadline: 3/1; financial award applicants required to submit FAFSA. *Faculty research:* Marketing, international business. *Unit head:* Prof. Lu An Reeb, Graduate Program Director, 617-824-8492, E-mail: cathy_waters@emerson.edu. *Application contact:* Sean Ganas, Office of Graduate Admission, 617-824-8610, Fax: 617-824-8614, E-mail: gradapp@emerson.edu. Website: http://www.emerson.edu/graduate_admission

Fairleigh Dickinson University, College at Florham, Maxwell Becton College of Arts and Sciences, Department of English, Communication and Philosophy, Program in Corporate and Organizational Communication, Madison, NJ 07940-1099. Offers MA, MA/MBA. *Entrance requirements:* For master's, GRE General Test.

Florida State University, The Graduate School, College of Communication and Information, School of Communication, Tallahassee, FL 32306. Offers communication theory and research (PhD); integrated marketing communication (MA, MS); media and communication studies (MA, MS). Part-time programs available. *Faculty:* 26 full-time (11 women), 4 part-time/adjunct (1 woman). *Students:* 68 full-time (48 women), 105 part-time (71 women); includes 83 minority (15 Black or African American, non-Hispanic/Latino; 46 Asian, non-Hispanic/Latino; 19 Hispanic/Latino; 3 Two or more races, non-Hispanic/Latino). Average age 24. 206 applicants, 30% accepted, 41 enrolled. In 2014, 98 master's, 10 doctorates awarded. *Degree requirements:* For master's, thesis (for some programs); for doctorate, comprehensive exam, thesis/dissertation. *Entrance requirements:* For master's, GRE General Test, minimum GPA of 3.0; for doctorate, GRE General Test, minimum GPA of 3.3 in graduate course work. Additional exam requirements/recommendations for international students: Required—TOEFL (minimum score 600 paper-based; 100 iBT), IELTS (minimum score 7). *Application deadline:* For fall admission, 7/1 priority date for domestic students, 5/1 priority date for international students; for spring admission, 11/1 priority date for domestic and international students; for summer admission, 3/1 priority date for domestic and international students. Applications are processed on a rolling basis. Application fee: $30. Electronic applications accepted. *Expenses:* Tuition, state resident: part-time $403.51 per credit hour. Tuition, nonresident: part-time $1004.85 per credit hour. *Required fees:* $75.81 per credit hour. One-time fee: $20 part-time. Tuition and fees vary according to campus/location. *Financial support:* In 2014–15, 89 students received support, including 6 research assistantships with full tuition reimbursements available (averaging $7,816 per year), 83 teaching assistantships with full tuition reimbursements available (averaging $7,816 per year); fellowships, career-related internships or fieldwork, Federal Work-Study, institutionally sponsored loans, scholarships/grants, tuition waivers (partial), and unspecified assistantships also available. Support available to part-time students. Financial award application deadline: 2/1; financial award applicants required to submit FAFSA. *Faculty research:* Communication in the public interest; strategic communication; media and technology; multicultural, intercultural, and international communication. *Total annual research expenditures:* $67,063. *Unit head:* Dr. Gary Heald, Director, 850-644-5034, Fax: 850-644-8642, E-mail: gheald@fsu.edu. *Application contact:* Natashia Hinson-Turner, Graduate Coordinator, 850-644-5034, Fax: 850-644-8642, E-mail: natashia.turner@cci.fsu.edu. Website: http://www.cci.fsu.edu

Fordham University, Gabelli School of Business, New York, NY 10023. Offers accounting (MBA); communications and media management (MBA); executive business administration (EMBA), including management; finance (MBA); global finance (MS); information systems (MBA, MS); management systems (MBA); marketing (MBA); media management (MS); taxation (MS); taxation and public accountancy (MTA); JD/MBA; MBA/MIM; MS/MBA. MBA/MIM offered jointly with Thunderbird School of Global Management. *Accreditation:* AACSB. Part-time and evening/weekend programs available. *Faculty:* 131 full-time (61 women), 61 part-time/adjunct (13 women). *Students:* 1,233 full-time (708 women), 588 part-time (274 women); includes 1,032 minority (73 Black or African American, non-Hispanic/Latino; 7 American Indian or Alaska Native, non-Hispanic/Latino; 846 Asian, non-Hispanic/Latino; 103 Hispanic/Latino; 3 Native Hawaiian or other Pacific Islander, non-Hispanic/Latino), 53 international. Average age 28. 3,701 applicants, 51% accepted, 718 enrolled. In 2014, 916 master's awarded. *Degree requirements:* For master's, Internships - required for MSQF, recommended for MBA, optional for most other programs. *Entrance requirements:* For master's, GMAT/GRE, 2 letters of recommendation, resume, 2 essays, transcripts. Additional exam requirements/recommendations for international students: Required—TOEFL (minimum score 600 paper-based; 100 iBT). *Application deadline:* For fall admission, 6/1 priority date for domestic students, 5/1 priority date for international students; for winter admission, 11/1 for domestic students, 10/1 priority date for international students; for spring admission, 11/1 priority date for domestic students, 2/1 priority date for international students; for summer admission, 3/1 priority date for domestic students. Applications are processed on a rolling basis. Application fee: $130. Electronic applications accepted. *Expenses:* Expenses: $1,306 per credit. *Financial support:* In 2014–15, 53 students received support, including fellowships (averaging $25,838 per year); research assistantships, career-related internships or fieldwork, institutionally sponsored loans, scholarships/grants, and unspecified assistantships also available. Support available to part-time students. Financial award application deadline: 6/15; financial award applicants required to submit FAFSA. *Unit head:* Dr. Donna Rapaccioli, Dean, 212-636-6165, Fax: 212-307-1779, E-mail: rapaccioli@fordham.edu. *Application contact:* Patricia Caffrey, Director of Admissions and Financial Aid, 212-636-6200, Fax: 212-636-7076, E-mail: admissionsgb@fordham.edu. Website: http://www.fordham.edu/info/20451/graduate_business

Corporate and Organizational Communication

Franklin University, Marketing and Communication Program, Columbus, OH 43215-5399. Offers MS. Part-time and evening/weekend programs available. *Entrance requirements:* For master's, minimum undergraduate GPA of 2.75. Additional exam requirements/recommendations for international students: Required—TOEFL (minimum score 550 paper-based). Electronic applications accepted.

Golden Gate University, Ageno School of Business, San Francisco, CA 94105-2968. Offers accounting (MBA); business administration (EMBA, MBA, PMBA, DBA); finance (MBA, MS, Certificate); financial planning (MS, Certificate); healthcare information systems (Certificate); human resource management (MBA, MS); human resources management (Certificate); information systems (MS); information technology (MBA); information technology management (Certificate); integrated marketing and communications (MS, Certificate); international business (MBA); management (MBA); marketing (MBA, MS, Certificate); operations supply chain management (Certificate); psychology (MA, Certificate); public administration (EMPA); public relations (MS, Certificate); technical market analysis (Certificate); JD/MBA. Part-time and evening/weekend programs available. *Degree requirements:* For doctorate, thesis/dissertation, qualifying examination. *Entrance requirements:* For master's, GMAT (MBA), minimum GPA of 2.5 (MS). Additional exam requirements/recommendations for international students: Required—TOEFL (minimum score 550 paper-based; 79 iBT). Electronic applications accepted. *Expenses:* Contact institution.

HEC Montreal, School of Business Administration, Graduate Diploma Programs in Administration, Program in Marketing Communication, Montréal, QC H3T 2A7, Canada. Offers Graduate Diploma. All courses are given in French. *Students:* 85 part-time (74 women). 88 applicants, 45% accepted, 37 enrolled. In 2014, 80 Graduate Diplomas awarded. *Degree requirements:* For Graduate Diploma, one foreign language. *Entrance requirements:* For degree, bachelor's degree in administration (for marketing option), two years of work experience. *Application deadline:* For fall admission, 4/15 for domestic and international students. Application fee: $83 Canadian dollars. Electronic applications accepted. *Financial support:* Research assistantships, teaching assistantships, and scholarships/grants available. Financial award application deadline: 9/2. *Unit head:* Silvia Ponce, Director, 514-340-6393, Fax: 514-340-6915, E-mail: silvia.ponce@hec.ca. *Application contact:* Jo Anne Audet, Administrative Director, 514-340-1315, Fax: 514-340-6411, E-mail: joanne.audet@hec.ca.
Website: http://www.hec.ca/programmes_formations/des/dess/dess_communication_marketing/index.html

High Point University, Norcross Graduate School, High Point, NC 27268. Offers business administration (MBA); educational leadership (M Ed); elementary education (M Ed); history (MA); nonprofit management (MA); secondary math (M Ed); special education (M Ed); strategic communication (MA); teaching elementary education k-6 (MAT); teaching secondary mathematics 9-12 (MAT). *Accreditation:* NCATE. Part-time and evening/weekend programs available. *Degree requirements:* For master's, comprehensive exam (for some programs), thesis (for some programs). *Entrance requirements:* For master's, GMAT (MBA), GRE, MAT, minimum GPA of 3.0. Additional exam requirements/recommendations for international students: Required—TOEFL (minimum score 550 paper-based). Electronic applications accepted.

Howard University, School of Communications, Department of Communication and Culture, Washington, DC 20059-0002. Offers intercultural communication (MA, PhD); organizational communication (MA, PhD). Offered through the Graduate School of Arts and Sciences. Part-time programs available. Terminal master's awarded for partial completion of doctoral program. *Degree requirements:* For master's, comprehensive exam or thesis; for doctorate, one foreign language, comprehensive exam, thesis/dissertation. *Entrance requirements:* For master's, English proficiency exam, GRE General Test, minimum GPA of 3.0; for doctorate, English proficiency exam, GRE General Test, master's degree in related field, minimum GPA of 3.5. Additional exam requirements/recommendations for international students: Required—TOEFL. *Faculty research:* Media effects, black discourse, development communication, African-American organizations.

Illinois Institute of Technology, Stuart School of Business, Program in Marketing Analytics and Communication, Chicago, IL 60661. Offers MS, MBA/MS. Part-time and evening/weekend programs available. *Faculty:* 36 full-time (10 women), 12 part-time/adjunct (2 women). *Students:* 98 full-time (65 women), 11 part-time (6 women); includes 3 minority (1 Black or African American, non-Hispanic/Latino; 2 Asian, non-Hispanic/Latino), 101 international. Average age 25. 389 applicants, 61% accepted, 36 enrolled. In 2014, 65 master's awarded. *Entrance requirements:* For master's, GRE (minimum score 1000) or GMAT (500). Additional exam requirements/recommendations for international students: Required—TOEFL (minimum score 600 paper-based; 85 iBT); Recommended—IELTS (minimum score 7). *Application deadline:* For fall admission, 8/1 for domestic students, 5/1 for international students; for spring admission, 12/15 for domestic students, 10/15 for international students. Applications are processed on a rolling basis. Application fee: $75. Electronic applications accepted. *Expenses:* Expenses: Contact institution. *Financial support:* Career-related internships or fieldwork, Federal Work-Study, institutionally sponsored loans, scholarships/grants, traineeships, health care benefits, and tuition waivers (partial) available. Support available to part-time students. Financial award applicants required to submit FAFSA. *Unit head:* M. Krishna Erramilli, Professor, 312-906-6573, Fax: 312-906-6549, E-mail: krish@stuart.iit.edu. *Application contact:* Rishab Malhotra, Director, Graduate Admission, 866-472-3448, Fax: 312-567-3138, E-mail: inquiry.grad@iit.edu.
Website: http://www.stuart.iit.edu/graduateprograms/ms/marketing_comm/index.shtml

Iowa State University of Science and Technology, Department of English, Ames, IA 50011. Offers creative writing (MFA); English (MA); rhetoric and professional communication (PhD). *Degree requirements:* For master's, thesis or alternative; for doctorate, thesis/dissertation. *Entrance requirements:* For master's, GRE General Test, sample of written work, resume, portfolio in creative writing; for doctorate, GRE General Test, sample of written work, resume. Additional exam requirements/recommendations for international students: Required—TOEFL (minimum score 600 paper-based; 100 iBT), IELTS (minimum score 7). Electronic applications accepted. *Faculty research:* Creative writing, literature, rhetoric, composition and professional communication, teaching English as a second language, applied linguistics.

Iowa State University of Science and Technology, Program in Rhetoric and Professional Communication, Ames, IA 50011. Offers PhD. *Entrance requirements:* For doctorate, GRE, official academic transcripts, resume, three letters of recommendation, writing sample. Additional exam requirements/recommendations for international students: Required—TOEFL (minimum score 640 paper-based; 111 iBT), IELTS (minimum score 7.5). Electronic applications accepted.

Iowa State University of Science and Technology, Program in Rhetoric, Composition, and Professional Communication, Ames, IA 50011. Offers MA. *Entrance requirements:* For master's, GRE, official academic transcripts, resume, three letters of recommendation, writing sample. Additional exam requirements/recommendations for international students: Required—TOEFL (minimum score 600 paper-based; 100 iBT), IELTS (minimum score 7). Electronic applications accepted.

John Carroll University, Graduate School, Department of Communications Management, University Heights, OH 44118-4581. Offers MA. Part-time and evening/weekend programs available. *Degree requirements:* For master's, comprehensive exam, thesis or project. *Entrance requirements:* For master's, GRE General Test, minimum GPA of 3.0. Additional exam requirements/recommendations for international students: Required—TOEFL. Electronic applications accepted. *Faculty research:* Communication law, media ethics, international studies, international broadcasting, media history.

La Salle University, School of Arts and Sciences, Program in Professional and Business Communication, Philadelphia, PA 19141-1199. Offers communication consulting and development (MA); communication management (MA); general professional communication (MA); professional and business communication (Certificate); public relations (MA); social and new media (Certificate). Part-time and evening/weekend programs available. Postbaccalaureate distance learning degree programs offered (minimal on-campus study). *Degree requirements:* For master's, practicum. *Entrance requirements:* For master's, writing assessment, professional resume; minimum overall B average; two letters of recommendation (if GPA below 3.25); brief personal statement (about 500 words); interview; for Certificate, writing assessment, minimum GPA of 2.75 in undergraduate studies; brief personal statement (about 500 words); interview. Additional exam requirements/recommendations for international students: Required—TOEFL. Electronic applications accepted. Application fee is waived when completed online. *Expenses:* Contact institution.

Lasell College, Graduate and Professional Studies in Communication, Newton, MA 02466-2709. Offers health communication (MSC, Graduate Certificate); integrated marketing communication (MSC, Graduate Certificate); public relations (MSC, Graduate Certificate). Part-time and evening/weekend programs available. Postbaccalaureate distance learning degree programs offered (minimal on-campus study). *Faculty:* 5 full-time (3 women), 10 part-time/adjunct (5 women). *Students:* 50 full-time (37 women), 94 part-time (74 women); includes 40 minority (25 Black or African American, non-Hispanic/Latino; 2 American Indian or Alaska Native, non-Hispanic/Latino; 4 Asian, non-Hispanic/Latino; 8 Hispanic/Latino; 1 Two or more races, non-Hispanic/Latino), 19 international. Average age 30. *Entrance requirements:* For master's and Graduate Certificate, bachelor's degree from an accredited institution. Additional exam requirements/recommendations for international students: Required—TOEFL (minimum score 550 paper-based; 79 iBT), IELTS. *Application deadline:* For fall admission, 8/31 priority date for domestic students, 6/30 priority date for international students; for spring admission, 12/31 priority date for domestic students, 10/31 priority date for international students. Applications are processed on a rolling basis. Electronic applications accepted. *Expenses: Tuition:* Full-time $10,700; part-time $595 per credit. *Required fees:* $160; $80 per semester. *Financial support:* Available to part-time students. Application deadline: 8/31; applicants required to submit FAFSA. *Unit head:* Dr. Joan Dolamore, Dean of Graduate and Professional Studies, 617-243-2485, Fax: 617-243-2450, E-mail: gradinfo@lasell.edu. *Application contact:* Adrienne Franciosi, Director of Graduate Admission, 617-243-2214, Fax: 617-243-2450, E-mail: gradinfo@lasell.edu.
Website: http://www.lasell.edu/academics/graduate-and-professional-studies/programs-of-study/master-of-science-in-communication.html

Loyola University Chicago, Graduate School of Business, Marketing Department, Chicago, IL 60611. Offers integrated marketing communications (MSIMC); MSIMC/MBA. Part-time and evening/weekend programs available. *Faculty:* 13 full-time (9 women), 3 part-time/adjunct (0 women). *Students:* 24 full-time (17 women), 24 part-time (16 women); includes 4 minority (1 Asian, non-Hispanic/Latino; 2 Hispanic/Latino; 1 Native Hawaiian or other Pacific Islander, non-Hispanic/Latino), 38 international. Average age 25. 116 applicants, 50% accepted, 20 enrolled. In 2014, 21 master's awarded. *Entrance requirements:* For master's, GMAT or GRE, a completed application form, official transcripts, two letters of recommendation, statement of purpose, resume. Additional exam requirements/recommendations for international students: Required—TOEFL (minimum score 90 iBT) or IELTS (minimum score 6.5). *Application deadline:* For fall admission, 7/15 for domestic and international students; for winter admission, 10/1 for domestic and international students; for spring admission, 1/15 for domestic and international students; for summer admission, 4/1 for domestic and international students. Applications are processed on a rolling basis. Application fee: $50. Electronic applications accepted. Application fee is waived when completed online. *Expenses:* Expenses: $4275 per course. *Financial support:* Scholarships/grants and unspecified assistantships available. Financial award application deadline: 3/15. *Faculty research:* Brand strategy, consumer behavior, digital/interactive marketing, international marketing. *Unit head:* Dr. Joan Phillips, Chair, Marketing Department, 312-915-7815, E-mail: jphillips@luc.edu. *Application contact:* Lauren Griffin, Enrollment Advisor, Quinlan School of Business Graduate Programs, 312-915-6124, Fax: 312-915-7207, E-mail: lgriffin3@luc.edu.
Website: http://www.luc.edu/quinlan/mba/masters-in-marketing/index.shtml

Manhattanville College, School of Graduate and Professional Studies, Program in Marketing Communication Management, Purchase, NY 10577-2132. Offers MS. Part-time and evening/weekend programs available. *Degree requirements:* For master's, final project. *Entrance requirements:* Additional exam requirements/recommendations for international students: Required—TOEFL. *Expenses: Tuition:* Full-time $16,110; part-time $895 per credit. *Required fees:* $60 per semester. Part-time tuition and fees vary according to course load and program.

Marist College, Graduate Programs, School of Communication and the Arts, Program in Integrated Marketing Communication, Poughkeepsie, NY 12601-1387. Offers MA. *Entrance requirements:* For master's, GRE or GMAT, official undergraduate/graduate transcripts from all institutions attended; current resume; completed recommendation forms for three references; personal statement.

Metropolitan College of New York, Program in Media Management, New York, NY 10013. Offers MBA. Evening/weekend programs available. *Degree requirements:* For master's, thesis, 10 day study abroad. *Entrance requirements:* For master's, GMAT or GRE General Test, appropriate work experience, interview, minimum GPA of 2.7. Additional exam requirements/recommendations for international students: Required—TOEFL (minimum score 600 paper-based). Electronic applications accepted. *Expenses:* Contact institution.

Minnesota State University Mankato, College of Graduate Studies, College of Arts and Humanities, Department of Communication Studies, Mankato, MN 56001. Offers communication education (Certificate); communication studies (MA, MS); forensics (MFA); professional communication (Certificate). *Students:* 21 full-time (9 women), 31 part-time (22 women). *Degree requirements:* For master's, one foreign language, comprehensive exam, thesis. *Entrance requirements:* For master's, minimum GPA of 3.0 during previous 2 years, writing sample. *Application deadline:* For fall admission, 7/1 priority date for domestic students, 5/1 for international students; for spring admission, 11/1 for domestic students, 10/1 for international students. Applications are processed on a rolling basis. Application fee: $40. Electronic applications accepted. *Financial support:* Research assistantships, teaching assistantships with full tuition reimbursements, career-related internships or fieldwork, Federal Work-Study, and institutionally sponsored loans available. Support available to part-time students. Financial award application deadline: 3/15; financial award applicants required to submit FAFSA. *Unit head:* Dr. Christopher Brown, Chairperson, 507-389-2510. *Application contact:* 507-389-2321, E-mail: grad@mnsu.edu. Website: http://www.mnsu.edu/cmst/

Mississippi College, Graduate School, College of Arts and Sciences, School of Christian Studies and the Arts, Department of Communication, Clinton, MS 39058. Offers applied communication (MSC); public relations and corporate communication (MSC). Part-time programs available. *Degree requirements:* For master's, comprehensive exam, thesis optional. *Entrance requirements:* For master's, GRE or NTE, minimum GPA of 2.5. Additional exam requirements/recommendations for international students: Recommended—TOEFL, IELTS. Electronic applications accepted.

Monmouth University, The Graduate School, Department of Corporate and Public Communication, West Long Branch, NJ 07764-1898. Offers corporate and public communication (MA); human resources management and communication (Certificate); public service communication (Certificate); strategic public relations and new media (Certificate). Part-time and evening/weekend programs available. *Faculty:* 9 full-time (7 women). *Students:* 7 full-time (4 women), 24 part-time (19 women); includes 6 minority (1 Black or African American, non-Hispanic/Latino; 3 Hispanic/Latino; 2 Two or more races, non-Hispanic/Latino), 1 international. Average age 31. 23 applicants, 91% accepted, 13 enrolled. In 2014, 12 master's awarded. *Degree requirements:* For master's, comprehensive exam (for some programs), thesis (for some programs), project. *Entrance requirements:* For master's, GRE, baccalaureate degree with minimum GPA of 3.0 in major, 2.75 overall; two letters of recommendation, personal essay (750 words or less describing preparation for study and personal objectives), digital or hard copy portfolio of select samples of work including a writing sample, resume. Additional exam requirements/recommendations for international students: Required—TOEFL (minimum score 550 paper-based; 79 iBT), IELTS (minimum score 6), Michigan English Language Assessment Battery (minimum score 77). *Application deadline:* For fall admission, 7/15 priority date for domestic students, 6/1 for international students; for spring admission, 11/15 priority date for domestic students, 11/1 for international students. Applications are processed on a rolling basis. Application fee: $50. Electronic applications accepted. *Expenses: Tuition:* Full-time $18,072; part-time $1004 per credit. *Required fees:* $157 per semester. *Financial support:* In 2014–15, 28 students received support, including 19 fellowships (averaging $2,898 per year), 3 research assistantships (averaging $9,030 per year); scholarships/grants and unspecified assistantships also available. Support available to part-time students. Financial award applicants required to submit FAFSA. *Faculty research:* Service-learning, history of television, feminism and the media, executive communication, public relations pedagogy. *Unit head:* Dr. Deanna Shoemaker, Program Director, 732-263-5449, Fax: 732-571-3609, E-mail: dshoemak@monmouth.edu. *Application contact:* Andrea Thompson, Graduate Admission Counselor, 732-571-3452, Fax: 732-263-5123, E-mail: gradadm@monmouth.edu.
Website: http://www.monmouth.edu/cpc

Murray State University, College of Business and Public Affairs, Program in Organizational Communication, Murray, KY 42071. Offers MA, MS. Part-time programs available. *Degree requirements:* For master's, thesis (for some programs). *Entrance requirements:* For master's, minimum GPA of 2.5 for conditional admittance, 3.0 for unconditional admittance. Additional exam requirements/recommendations for international students: Required—TOEFL (minimum score 550 paper-based). *Faculty research:* Organizational learning, organizational culture, leadership, health communication, personality.

National University, Academic Affairs, College of Letters and Sciences, La Jolla, CA 92037-1011. Offers applied linguistics (MA); biology (MS); counseling psychology (MA), including licensed professional clinical counseling, marriage and family therapy; creative writing (MFA); English (MA), including Gothic studies, rhetoric; film studies (MA); forensic and crime science (Certificate); forensic studies (MFS), including criminalistics, investigation; history (MA); human behavior (MA); mathematics for educators (MS); performance psychology (MA); strategic communications (MA). Part-time and evening/weekend programs available. Postbaccalaureate distance learning degree programs offered (no on-campus study). *Faculty:* 69 full-time (34 women), 100 part-time/adjunct (55 women). *Students:* 727 full-time (532 women), 349 part-time (240 women); includes 505 minority (128 Black or African American, non-Hispanic/Latino; 5 American Indian or Alaska Native, non-Hispanic/Latino; 52 Asian, non-Hispanic/Latino; 260 Hispanic/Latino; 9 Native Hawaiian or other Pacific Islander, non-Hispanic/Latino; 51 Two or more races, non-Hispanic/Latino), 4 international. Average age 34. In 2014, 569 master's awarded. *Degree requirements:* For master's, thesis (for some programs). *Entrance requirements:* For master's, interview, minimum GPA of 2.5. Additional exam requirements/recommendations for international students: Required—TOEFL (minimum score 550 paper-based; 79 iBT), IELTS (minimum score 6). *Application deadline:* Applications are processed on a rolling basis. Application fee: $60 ($65 for international students). Electronic applications accepted. *Expenses: Tuition:* Full-time $14,184; part-time $1773 per course. *Financial support:* Career-related internships or fieldwork, institutionally sponsored loans, scholarships/grants, and tuition waivers (partial) available. Support available to part-time students. Financial award application deadline: 6/30; financial award applicants required to submit FAFSA. *Unit head:* College of Letters and Sciences, 800-628-8648, E-mail: cols@nu.edu. *Application contact:* Frank Rojas, Interim Vice President for Enrollment Services, 800-628-8648, E-mail: advisor@nu.edu.
Website: http://www.nu.edu/OurPrograms/CollegeOfLettersAndSciences.html

National University, Academic Affairs, School of Business and Management, La Jolla, CA 92037-1011. Offers business administration (MBA), including financial management, human resource management, integrated marketing communications, international business, management accounting, marketing, mobile marketing and social media, organizational leadership, professional golf management; global management (MGM). Part-time and evening/weekend programs available. Postbaccalaureate distance learning degree programs offered (no on-campus study). *Faculty:* 32 full-time (9 women), 74 part-time/adjunct (23 women). *Students:* 727 full-time (347 women), 280 part-time (145 women); includes 478 minority (136 Black or African American, non-Hispanic/Latino; 8 American Indian or Alaska Native, non-Hispanic/Latino; 119 Asian, non-Hispanic/Latino; 159 Hispanic/Latino; 14 Native Hawaiian or other Pacific Islander, non-Hispanic/Latino; 42 Two or more races, non-Hispanic/Latino), 164 international. Average age 33. In 2014, 784 master's awarded. *Degree requirements:* For master's, thesis (for some programs). *Entrance requirements:* For master's, interview, minimum GPA of 2.5. Additional exam requirements/recommendations for international students: Required—TOEFL (minimum score 550 paper-based; 79 iBT), IELTS (minimum score 6). *Application deadline:* Applications are processed on a rolling basis. Application fee: $60 ($65 for international students). Electronic applications accepted. *Expenses: Tuition:* Full-time $14,184; part-time $1773 per course. *Financial support:* Career-related internships or fieldwork, scholarships/grants, and tuition waivers (partial) available. Support available to part-time students. Financial award application deadline: 6/30; financial award applicants required to submit FAFSA. *Unit head:* School of Business and Management, 800-628-8648, Fax: 858-642-8719, E-mail: sobm@nu.edu. *Application contact:* Frank Rojas, Vice President for Enrollment Services, 800-628-8648, E-mail: advisor@nu.edu.
Website: http://www.nu.edu/OurPrograms/SchoolOfBusinessAndManagement.html

New Mexico State University, College of Arts and Sciences, Department of English, Las Cruces, NM 88003-8001. Offers creative writing (MA, MFA); English studies for teachers (MA); literature (MA); rhetoric and professional communication (MA, PhD). Part-time programs available. *Faculty:* 20 full-time (11 women), 3 part-time/adjunct (1 woman). *Students:* 65 full-time (41 women), 29 part-time (20 women); includes 30 minority (2 Black or African American, non-Hispanic/Latino; 2 American Indian or Alaska Native, non-Hispanic/Latino; 2 Asian, non-Hispanic/Latino; 22 Hispanic/Latino; 2 Two or more races, non-Hispanic/Latino), 4 international. Average age 33. 104 applicants, 19% accepted, 15 enrolled. In 2014, 18 master's, 2 doctorates awarded. *Degree requirements:* For master's, one foreign language, thesis (for some programs); for doctorate, comprehensive exam, thesis/dissertation, internship. *Entrance requirements:* For master's and doctorate, sample of written work. Additional exam requirements/recommendations for international students: Required—TOEFL (minimum score 550 paper-based; 79 iBT), IELTS (minimum score 6.5). *Application deadline:* For fall admission, 2/1 for domestic and international students. Application fee: $40 ($50 for international students). Electronic applications accepted. *Expenses:* Tuition, state resident: full-time $3969; part-time $220.50 per credit hour. Tuition, nonresident: full-time $13,838; part-time $768.80 per credit hour. *Required fees:* $853; $47.40 per credit hour. *Financial support:* In 2014–15, 61 students received support, including 17 fellowships (averaging $3,970 per year), 49 teaching assistantships (averaging $16,313 per year); career-related internships or fieldwork, Federal Work-Study, institutionally sponsored loans, scholarships/grants, traineeships, health care benefits, and unspecified assistantships also available. Support available to part-time students. Financial award application deadline: 3/1. *Faculty research:* Composition research, history and theory of rhetoric, technical/professional communication, creative writing, English and American literature. *Total annual research expenditures:* $5,069. *Unit head:* Dr. Barry L. Thatcher, Head, 575-646-2319, Fax: 575-646-7725, E-mail: bathatch@nmsu.edu. *Application contact:* Dr. Tracey Eileen Miller-Tomlinson, Director of Graduate Studies, 575-646-2213, Fax: 575-646-7725, E-mail: tomlin@nmsu.edu.
Website: http://english.nmsu.edu

New York University, School of Continuing and Professional Studies, Division of Programs in Business, Program in Integrated Marketing, New York, NY 10012-1019. Offers brand management (MS); digital marketing (MS); marketing analytics (MS). Part-time and evening/weekend programs available. *Faculty:* 3 full-time (2 women), 91 part-time/adjunct (29 women). *Students:* 435 full-time (339 women), 154 part-time (124 women); includes 71 minority (19 Black or African American, non-Hispanic/Latino; 31 Asian, non-Hispanic/Latino; 19 Hispanic/Latino; 2 Two or more races, non-Hispanic/Latino), 444 international. Average age 25. 922 applicants, 67% accepted, 263 enrolled. In 2014, 192 master's awarded. *Degree requirements:* For master's, comprehensive exam, thesis, capstone; writing of complete business plan. *Entrance requirements:* For master's, GRE or GMAT (only upon request), bachelor's degree, resume with relevant professional work, internship or volunteer experience, two letters of recommendation, statement of purpose. Additional exam requirements/recommendations for international students: Required—TOEFL (minimum score 600 paper-based; 100 iBT), IELTS (minimum score 7). *Application deadline:* For fall admission, 2/1 priority date for domestic and international students; for spring admission, 10/15 priority date for domestic students, 8/15 priority date for international students. Applications are processed on a rolling basis. Application fee: $150. Electronic applications accepted. *Financial support:* In 2014–15, 51 students received support, including 51 fellowships (averaging $3,012 per year); Federal Work-Study and scholarships/grants also available. Support available to part-time students. Financial award application deadline: 4/1; financial award applicants required to submit FAFSA. *Faculty research:* Branding, digital marketing, Web analytics, consumer behavior, customer loyalty, campaign planning and management. *Unit head:* Paula Payton, Academic Director, 212-992-3228, E-mail: pp64@nyu.edu. *Application contact:* Admissions Office, 212-998-7100, E-mail: scps.gradadmissions@nyu.edu.
Website: http://www.sps.nyu.edu/areas-of-study/marketing/graduate-programs/ms-integrated-marketing/

New York University, School of Continuing and Professional Studies, Division of Programs in Business, Programs in Marketing and Public Relations, New York, NY 10012-1019. Offers corporate and organizational communication (MS); public relations management (MS). Part-time and evening/weekend programs available. *Faculty:* 2 full-time (0 women), 48 part-time/adjunct (18 women). *Students:* 260 full-time (226 women), 121 part-time (95 women); includes 63 minority (26 Black or African American, non-Hispanic/Latino; 10 Asian, non-Hispanic/Latino; 25 Hispanic/Latino; 2 Two or more races, non-Hispanic/Latino), 227 international. Average age 25. 375 applicants, 78% accepted, 128 enrolled. In 2014, 171 master's awarded. *Degree requirements:* For master's, thesis. *Entrance requirements:* For master's, GRE or GMAT (only upon request), bachelor's degree, resume with relevant professional work, internship or volunteer experience, two letters of recommendation, statement of purpose. Additional exam requirements/recommendations for international students: Required—TOEFL (minimum score 600 paper-based; 100 iBT), IELTS (minimum score 7). *Application deadline:* For fall admission, 2/1 priority date for domestic and international students; for spring admission, 10/15 priority date for domestic students, 8/15 priority date for international students. Applications are processed on a rolling basis. Application fee: $150. Electronic applications accepted. *Financial support:* In 2014–15, 68 students received support, including 68 fellowships (averaging $2,269 per year). Financial award application deadline: 4/1; financial award applicants required to submit FAFSA. *Unit head:* Angela Ambrosini, Academic Director, 212-992-3288, E-mail: aa152@nyu.edu. *Application contact:* Admissions Office, 212-998-7100, E-mail: sps.gradadmissions@nyu.edu.
Website: http://www.sps.nyu.edu/academics/departments/marketing-and-pr.html

Northeastern University, College of Professional Studies, Boston, MA 02115-5096. Offers applied nutrition (MS); commerce and economic development (MS); corporate and organizational communication (MS); digital media (MPS); geographic information technology (MPS); global studies and international affairs (MS); homeland security (MA); human services (MS); informatics (MPS); leadership (MS); nonprofit management (MS); project management (MS); regulatory affairs for drugs, biologics, and medical devices (MS); regulatory affairs of food and food industries (MS); respiratory care leadership (MS); technical communication (MS). Postbaccalaureate distance learning degree programs offered (no on-campus study).

Northwestern University, The Graduate School, School of Communication, Department of Communication Studies, Evanston, IL 60208. Offers communication studies (PhD), including interaction and social influence, rhetoric and public culture; managerial communication (MSC); media, technology and society (PhD); technology and social behavior (PhD). PhD admissions and degree offered through The Graduate School. Terminal master's awarded for partial completion of doctoral program. *Degree requirements:* For doctorate, thesis/dissertation. *Entrance requirements:* For master's and doctorate, GRE General Test. Additional exam requirements/recommendations for international students: Required—TOEFL. Electronic applications accepted.

Northwestern University, Medill School of Journalism, Media, and Integrated Marketing Communications, Integrated Marketing Communications Program, Evanston, IL 60208. Offers brand strategy (MSIMC); content marketing (MSIMC); direct and interactive marketing (MSIMC); marketing analytics (MSIMC); strategic communications (MSIMC). Part-time programs available. *Entrance requirements:* For master's, GRE

General Test or GMAT, full-time work experience (preferred). Additional exam requirements/recommendations for international students: Required—TOEFL. Electronic applications accepted. *Faculty research:* Data mining, business to business marketing, values in advertising, political advertising.

Ohio University, Graduate College, Scripps College of Communication, School of Communication Studies, Athens, OH 45701-2979. Offers health communication (PhD); organizational communication (MA); relating and organizing (PhD); rhetoric and public culture (PhD). Part-time programs available. Postbaccalaureate distance learning degree programs offered (minimal on-campus study). Terminal master's awarded for partial completion of doctoral program. *Degree requirements:* For master's, capstone; for doctorate, comprehensive exam, thesis/dissertation. *Entrance requirements:* For master's, GRE; for doctorate, GRE General Test, minimum GPA of 3.0. Additional exam requirements/recommendations for international students: Required—TOEFL (minimum score 550 paper-based; 80 iBT) or IELTS (minimum score 6.5). Electronic applications accepted. *Faculty research:* Rhetoric and public culture, relating and organizing, health communication.

Queens University of Charlotte, School of Communication, Charlotte, NC 28274-0002. Offers organizational and strategic communication (MA). Part-time and evening/weekend programs available. *Degree requirements:* For master's, capstone course. *Entrance requirements:* Additional exam requirements/recommendations for international students: Required—TOEFL. *Expenses:* Contact institution.

Radford University, College of Graduate and Professional Studies, College of Humanities and Behavioral Sciences, Program in Corporate and Professional Communication, Radford, VA 24142. Offers corporate and professional communication (MS). Part-time and evening/weekend programs available. *Faculty:* 6 full-time (4 women). *Students:* 11 full-time (7 women), 4 part-time (1 woman); includes 4 minority (2 Hispanic/Latino; 2 Two or more races, non-Hispanic/Latino). Average age 26. 8 applicants, 100% accepted, 6 enrolled. In 2014, 10 master's awarded. *Degree requirements:* For master's, comprehensive exam, thesis optional. *Entrance requirements:* For master's, GRE, minimum GPA of 2.75; short essay; 3 letters of reference, resume, official transcripts. Additional exam requirements/recommendations for international students: Required—TOEFL (minimum score 550 paper-based; 79 iBT), IELTS (minimum score 6.5). *Application deadline:* For fall admission, 2/15 priority date for domestic students, 12/1 for international students; for spring admission, 7/1 for international students. Applications are processed on a rolling basis. Application fee: $50. Electronic applications accepted. *Expenses:* Tuition, state resident: full-time $7187; part-time $299 per credit hour. Tuition, nonresident: full-time $16,394; part-time $683 per credit hour. *Required fees:* $2974; $125 per credit hour. Tuition and fees vary according to course load and program. *Financial support:* In 2014–15, 11 students received support, including 3 research assistantships (averaging $9,000 per year), 8 teaching assistantships with partial tuition reimbursements available (averaging $10,500 per year); career-related internships or fieldwork, Federal Work-Study, institutionally sponsored loans, and scholarships/grants also available. Financial award application deadline: 3/1; financial award applicants required to submit FAFSA. *Faculty research:* Rhetoric and persuasion in organizations, media relations, organizational legitimacy, issues management, social capital. *Unit head:* Dr. Lynn Zoch, Director, School of Communication, 540-831-6553, Fax: 540-831-5883, E-mail: comm@radford.edu. *Application contact:* Rebecca Conner, Director, Graduate Enrollment, 540-831-6296, Fax: 540-831-6061, E-mail: gradcollege@radford.edu.
Website: http://www.radford.edu/content/chbs/home/comm.html

Regent University, Graduate School, School of Communication and the Arts, Virginia Beach, VA 23464-9800. Offers acting (MFA); communication (MA, PhD), including political communication (MA), strategic communication (MA); directing for cinema/television (MFA); film and TV (MA), including producing, production, script writing; journalism (MA); producing for cinema/television (MFA); script and screenwriting (MFA); theatre (MA). Part-time programs available. Postbaccalaureate distance learning degree programs offered (minimal on-campus study). *Faculty:* 20 full-time (3 women), 26 part-time/adjunct (7 women). *Students:* 89 full-time (49 women), 211 part-time (125 women); includes 92 minority (69 Black or African American, non-Hispanic/Latino; 2 American Indian or Alaska Native, non-Hispanic/Latino; 2 Asian, non-Hispanic/Latino; 19 Hispanic/Latino), 10 international. Average age 35. 199 applicants, 53% accepted, 77 enrolled. In 2014, 48 master's, 8 doctorates awarded. *Degree requirements:* For master's, thesis or alternative; for doctorate, thesis/dissertation. *Entrance requirements:* For master's, GRE General Test or MAT, minimum undergraduate GPA of 3.0, writing sample, computer literacy survey, recommendation, resume, interview, audition (for MFA programs); for doctorate, GRE General Test, minimum graduate GPA of 3.0, writing sample, computer literacy survey, recommendation, interview, transcripts. Additional exam requirements/recommendations for international students: Required—TOEFL (minimum score 577 paper-based). *Application deadline:* For fall admission, 3/1 priority date for domestic students; for spring admission, 10/1 priority date for domestic students. Applications are processed on a rolling basis. Application fee: $50. Electronic applications accepted. *Expenses:* Expenses: Contact institution. *Financial support:* Fellowships with full and partial tuition reimbursements, career-related internships or fieldwork, scholarships/grants, tuition waivers (full and partial), and unspecified assistantships available. Support available to part-time students. Financial award application deadline: 9/1; financial award applicants required to submit FAFSA. *Faculty research:* Southern gospel music, education and entertainment, celebrities and the media, journalism and ethics, C.S. Lewis. *Unit head:* Dr. Mitch Land, Dean, 757-352-4916, Fax: 757-352-4291, E-mail: mland@regent.edu. *Application contact:* Matthew Chadwick, Director of Enrollment Support Services, 800-373-5504, Fax: 757-352-4381, E-mail: admissions@regent.edu.
Website: http://www.regent.edu/acad/schcom/

Regis College, Program in Organizational and Professional Communication, Weston, MA 02493. Offers MS. Part-time and evening/weekend programs available. *Degree requirements:* For master's, thesis. *Entrance requirements:* For master's, GRE or MAT. Additional exam requirements/recommendations for international students: Required—TOEFL (minimum score 550 paper-based).

Rider University, College of Liberal Arts, Education, and Sciences, Lawrenceville, NJ 08648-3001. Offers applied psychology (MA); business communication (MA). Part-time and evening/weekend programs available. *Entrance requirements:* For master's, official transcripts, current resume, two professional letters of recommendation, statement of aims and objectives, personal interview by invitation of faculty. Additional exam requirements/recommendations for international students: Required—TOEFL (minimum score 550 paper-based). Electronic applications accepted.

Roosevelt University, Graduate Division, College of Arts and Sciences, Department of Communication, Program in Integrated Marketing Communications, Chicago, IL 60605. Offers MSIMC. Part-time and evening/weekend programs available. *Faculty research:* Print journalism, urban high school journalism.

Rowan University, Graduate School, College of Communication and Creative Arts, Integrated Marketing Communication and New Media Certificate of Graduate Study Program, Glassboro, NJ 08028-1701. Offers CGS. *Students:* 5 full-time (4 women), 11 part-time (10 women); includes 5 minority (3 Black or African American, non-Hispanic/Latino; 1 Asian, non-Hispanic/Latino; 1 Hispanic/Latino). Average age 28. 2 applicants, 100% accepted, 2 enrolled. *Application deadline:* For fall admission, 8/1 for domestic students; for spring admission, 2/1 for domestic students, 2/15 for international students; for summer admission, 4/1 for domestic and international students. Applications are processed on a rolling basis. Application fee: $65. Electronic applications accepted. *Expenses: Tuition, area resident:* Part-time $648 per credit. Tuition, state resident: part-time $648 per credit. Tuition, nonresident: part-time $648 per credit. *Required fees:* $145 per credit. Tuition and fees vary according to degree level, campus/location, program and student level. *Unit head:* Dr. Horacio Sosa, Vice President, Global Learning and Partnerships, 856-256-4747, Fax: 856-256-5638, E-mail: sosa@rowan.edu. *Application contact:* Admissions and Enrollment Services, 856-256-4747, Fax: 856-256-5637, E-mail: globaladmissions@rowan.edu.

Sacred Heart University, Graduate Programs, College of Arts and Sciences, Department of Communications, Fairfield, CT 06825-1000. Offers corporate communication and public relations (MA Comm); digital/multimedia journalism (MA Comm); digital/multimedia production (MA Comm). Part-time and evening/weekend programs available. *Faculty:* 10 full-time (2 women). *Students:* 62 full-time (31 women), 27 part-time (14 women); includes 25 minority (16 Black or African American, non-Hispanic/Latino; 8 Hispanic/Latino; 1 Native Hawaiian or other Pacific Islander, non-Hispanic/Latino), 4 international. Average age 26. 117 applicants, 90% accepted, 69 enrolled. In 2014, 40 master's awarded. *Degree requirements:* For master's, thesis or alternative. *Entrance requirements:* For master's, bachelor's degree. Additional exam requirements/recommendations for international students: Required—PTE; Recommended—TOEFL (minimum score 570 paper-based; 80 iBT), IELTS (minimum score 6.5). *Application deadline:* Applications are processed on a rolling basis. Application fee: $60. Electronic applications accepted. *Expenses: Tuition:* Full-time $24,559; part-time $649 per credit. *Financial support:* Unspecified assistantships available. Financial award applicants required to submit FAFSA. *Unit head:* Dr. Andrew Miller, Chair, 203-396-8087, E-mail: millera@sacredheart.edu. *Application contact:* Kathy Dilks, Executive Director of Graduate Admissions, 203-365-7619, Fax: 203-365-4732, E-mail: gradstudies@sacredheart.edu.
Website: http://www.sacredheart.edu/academics/collegeofartssciences/academicdepartments/communicationmediastudies/

St. Bonaventure University, School of Graduate Studies, Russell J. Jandoli School of Journalism and Mass Communication, Program in Integrated Marketing Communications, St. Bonaventure, NY 14778-2284. Offers MA. Weekend format option offered at Buffalo Center (Hamburg, NY). Evening/weekend programs available. *Faculty:* 5 full-time (3 women), 9 part-time/adjunct (5 women). *Students:* 58 full-time (41 women), 16 part-time (10 women); includes 10 minority (6 Black or African American, non-Hispanic/Latino; 3 Hispanic/Latino; 1 Two or more races, non-Hispanic/Latino), 2 international. Average age 26. 46 applicants, 83% accepted, 25 enrolled. In 2014, 32 master's awarded. *Entrance requirements:* For master's, transcripts, two letters of recommendation, personal statement. Additional exam requirements/recommendations for international students: Required—TOEFL (minimum score 550 paper-based; 79 iBT). *Application deadline:* For fall admission, 6/5 for domestic students, 2/1 for international students; for spring admission, 10/15 for domestic students, 7/1 for international students. Applications are processed on a rolling basis. Application fee: $0. Electronic applications accepted. *Expenses:* Expenses: Contact institution. *Financial support:* In 2014–15, 2 research assistantships were awarded; Federal Work-Study, scholarships/grants, health care benefits, and unspecified assistantships also available. Support available to part-time students. *Unit head:* Dr. Richard Lee, Director, 716-375-2563, Fax: 716-375-2588, E-mail: rlee@sbu.edu. *Application contact:* Bruce Campbell, Director of Graduate Admissions, 716-375-2429, Fax: 716-375-4015, E-mail: gradsch@sbu.edu.
Website: http://www.sbu.edu/academics/schools/journalism-and-mass-communications/graduate-degrees/ma-integrated-marketing-communications

St. Bonaventure University, School of Graduate Studies, Russell J. Jandoli School of Journalism and Mass Communication, Program in Strategic Leadership, St. Bonaventure, NY 14778-2284. Offers MA. Part-time programs available. Postbaccalaureate distance learning degree programs offered (no on-campus study). *Faculty:* 2 full-time (both women), 1 (woman) part-time/adjunct. *Students:* 9 full-time (8 women), 16 part-time (8 women); includes 3 minority (2 Black or African American, non-Hispanic/Latino; 1 American Indian or Alaska Native, non-Hispanic/Latino). Average age 37. 12 applicants, 83% accepted, 9 enrolled. *Degree requirements:* For master's, portfolio, project. *Entrance requirements:* For master's, personal statement, bachelor's degree, transcripts, three years of work experience, current resume. Additional exam requirements/recommendations for international students: Required—TOEFL (minimum score 550 paper-based; 79 iBT). *Application deadline:* For fall admission, 6/15 for domestic students, 2/1 for international students; for spring admission, 10/15 for domestic students, 7/1 for international students. Application fee: $0. *Expenses:* Expenses: Contact institution. *Financial support:* Federal Work-Study, scholarships/grants, and health care benefits available. Support available to part-time students. *Unit head:* Dr. Kimberly Young, Director, 716-375-2076, Fax: 716-375-2588, E-mail: kyoung@sbu.edu. *Application contact:* Bruce Campbell, Director of Graduate Admissions, 716-375-2429, Fax: 716-375-4015, E-mail: gradsch@sbu.edu.
Website: http://www.sbu.edu/academics/schools/journalism-and-mass-communications/graduate-degrees/ms-strategic-leadership-(online)

Seton Hall University, College of Arts and Sciences, Department of Communication, South Orange, NJ 07079-2697. Offers corporate and professional communication (MA); museum professions (MA), including exhibition development, museum education, museum management, museum registration; strategic communication (MA); strategic communication and leadership (MA). Part-time and evening/weekend programs available. Postbaccalaureate distance learning degree programs offered (minimal on-campus study). *Faculty:* 3 full-time (1 woman), 15 part-time/adjunct (6 women). *Students:* 31 full-time (21 women), 105 part-time (69 women); includes 47 minority (34 Black or African American, non-Hispanic/Latino; 3 Asian, non-Hispanic/Latino; 10 Hispanic/Latino), 6 international. Average age 32. 114 applicants, 74% accepted, 40 enrolled. In 2014, 65 master's awarded. *Degree requirements:* For master's, thesis. *Entrance requirements:* Additional exam requirements/recommendations for international students: Required—TOEFL. *Application deadline:* For fall admission, 7/1 priority date for domestic and international students; for spring admission, 11/1 priority date for domestic and international students. Applications are processed on a rolling basis. Application fee: $75. Electronic applications accepted. *Financial support:* Research assistantships, career-related internships or fieldwork, Federal Work-Study, and unspecified assistantships available. Financial award applicants required to submit FAFSA. *Faculty research:* Managerial communication, communication consulting, communication and development. *Unit head:* Prof. Deirdre Yates, Chair, 973-761-9474, Fax: 973-761-9234, E-mail: deirdre.yates@shu.edu. *Application contact:* Dr. Richard Dool, Director of Graduate Studies, 973-761-9490, Fax: 973-761-9234, E-mail: rrichard.dool@shu.edu.
Website: http://www.shu.edu/academics/artsci/communication-arts/

Southern Illinois University Edwardsville, Graduate School, College of Arts and Sciences, Department of Applied Communication Studies, Program in Corporate and Organizational Communication, Edwardsville, IL 62026. Offers MA. Part-time and

evening/weekend programs available. *Students:* 6 full-time (3 women), 2 part-time (both women); includes 3 minority (all Black or African American, non-Hispanic/Latino). 9 applicants, 78% accepted. In 2014, 2 master's awarded. *Degree requirements:* For master's, comprehensive exam (for some programs), thesis (for some programs). *Entrance requirements:* Additional exam requirements/recommendations for international students: Required—TOEFL (minimum score 550 paper-based, 79 iBT), IELTS (minimum score 6.5), Michigan Test of English Language Proficiency or PTE. *Application deadline:* For fall admission, 7/18 for domestic students, 6/1 for international students; for spring admission, 12/12 for domestic students, 10/1 for international students; for summer admission, 4/24 for domestic students, 3/1 for international students. Applications are processed on a rolling basis. Application fee: $30. Electronic applications accepted. *Expenses:* Tuition, state resident: full-time $5026. Tuition, nonresident: full-time $12,566. *International tuition:* $25,136 full-time. *Required fees:* $1682. Tuition and fees vary according to course load, campus/location and program. *Financial support:* Institutionally sponsored loans, scholarships/grants, and unspecified assistantships available. Financial award application deadline: 3/1; financial award applicants required to submit FAFSA. *Unit head:* Dr. Jocelyn DeGroot Brown, Program Director, 618-650-5828, E-mail: jocbrow@siue.edu. *Application contact:* Melissa K. Mace, Assistant Director of Graduate and International Recruitment, 618-650-2756, Fax: 618-650-3618, E-mail: mmace@siue.edu.
Website: http://www.siue.edu/artsandsciences/spc/

Spalding University, Graduate Studies, College of Social Sciences and Humanities, Program in Business and Communication, Louisville, KY 40203-2188. Offers MSBC. Part-time and evening/weekend programs available. *Faculty:* 5 full-time (3 women), 5 part-time/adjunct (2 women). *Students:* 37 full-time (22 women), 33 part-time (22 women); includes 25 minority (23 Black or African American, non-Hispanic/Latino; 2 Two or more races, non-Hispanic/Latino). Average age 38. 44 applicants, 86% accepted, 38 enrolled. In 2014, 48 master's awarded. *Entrance requirements:* For master's, GRE or GMAT, personal essay, interview, letters of recommendation, transcripts, resume. Additional exam requirements/recommendations for international students: Required—TOEFL (minimum score 535 paper-based). *Application deadline:* Applications are processed on a rolling basis. Application fee: $30. *Financial support:* In 2014–15, 1 research assistantship (averaging $3,540 per year) was awarded; scholarships/grants and unspecified assistantships also available. Financial award application deadline: 3/30; financial award applicants required to submit FAFSA. *Faculty research:* Curriculum development, consumer behavior, interdisciplinary pedagogy. *Unit head:* Dr. Robin Hinkle, Director, 502-873-4244, E-mail: rhinkle@spalding.edu. *Application contact:* Claire Elder, Administrative Assistant, 502-873-7120, E-mail: celder@spalding.edu.

Stevens Institute of Technology, Graduate School, Wesley J. Howe School of Technology Management, Program in Professional Communications, Hoboken, NJ 07030. Offers Certificate.

Suffolk University, College of Arts and Sciences, Department of Communication and Journalism, Boston, MA 02108-2770. Offers communication studies (MAC); integrated marketing communication (MAC); public relations and advertising (MAC). Part-time and evening/weekend programs available. *Faculty:* 7 full-time (5 women). *Students:* 27 full-time (22 women), 16 part-time (12 women); includes 5 minority (2 Black or African American, non-Hispanic/Latino; 1 Asian, non-Hispanic/Latino; 2 Hispanic/Latino), 19 international. Average age 25. 88 applicants, 56% accepted, 6 enrolled. In 2014, 46 master's awarded. *Degree requirements:* For master's, thesis optional. *Entrance requirements:* For master's, GRE General Test, MAT, or GMAT, 2 letters of recommendation, resume. Additional exam requirements/recommendations for international students: Required—TOEFL (minimum score 550 paper-based; 80 iBT). *Application deadline:* For fall admission, 6/15 priority date for domestic students, 6/15 for international students; for spring admission, 11/1 priority date for domestic students, 11/1 for international students. Applications are processed on a rolling basis. Application fee: $50. Electronic applications accepted. *Expenses:* Expenses: Contact institution. *Financial support:* In 2014–15, 36 students received support, including 36 fellowships (averaging $8,788 per year); career-related internships or fieldwork, Federal Work-Study, and institutionally sponsored loans also available. Support available to part-time students. Financial award application deadline: 4/1; financial award applicants required to submit FAFSA. *Faculty research:* Branding law and management, health care communication, gender roles and violence in video games, new media, political communication. *Unit head:* Gloria Boone, Chair, 617-573-8501, Fax: 617-742-6982, E-mail: gboone@suffolk.edu. *Application contact:* Cory Meyers, Director of Graduate Admissions, 617-573-8302, Fax: 617-305-1733, E-mail: grad.admission@suffolk.edu.
Website: http://www.suffolk.edu/college/departments/10483.php

Temple University, School of Media and Communication, Department of Strategic Communication, Philadelphia, PA 19122-6096. Offers communication management (MS). Part-time and evening/weekend programs available. *Faculty:* 10 full-time (3 women), 12 part-time/adjunct (8 women). *Students:* 7 full-time (all women), 18 part-time (12 women); includes 1 minority (Hispanic/Latino), 5 international. 37 applicants, 46% accepted, 8 enrolled. In 2014, 20 master's awarded. *Degree requirements:* For master's, capstone. *Entrance requirements:* For master's, GRE General Test. Additional exam requirements/recommendations for international students: Required—TOEFL (minimum score 620 paper-based; 105 iBT). *Application deadline:* For fall admission, 2/15 for domestic and international students; for spring admission, 11/1 for domestic and international students. Application fee: $60. Electronic applications accepted. *Expenses:* Expenses: Contact institution. *Financial support:* Career-related internships or fieldwork and Federal Work-Study available. Financial award application deadline: 1/15; financial award applicants required to submit FAFSA. *Unit head:* Dr. Guillermo Caliendo, Assistant Professor and Graduate Director, 215-204-0656, E-mail: gcaliendo@temple.edu. *Application contact:* Nicole McKenna, Director, Office of Research and Graduate Studies, 215-204-1497, Fax: 215-204-0310, E-mail: nmckenna@temple.edu.
Website: http://smc.temple.edu/strc/

Towson University, Program in Communications Management, Towson, MD 21252-0001. Offers MS. *Students:* 15 part-time (12 women); includes 2 minority (both Black or African American, non-Hispanic/Latino). *Degree requirements:* For master's, thesis. *Entrance requirements:* For master's, bacehlor's degree with 24 credits in mass communications, public relations, advertising or communication studies; advanced writing and basic statistics courses; professional experience; minimum GPA of 3.0; letter of recommendation; resume. Additional exam requirements/recommendations for international students: Required—TOEFL. *Application deadline:* For fall admission, 1/15 for domestic students. Application fee: $45. Electronic applications accepted. *Financial support:* Application deadline: 4/1. *Unit head:* Dr. Beth Haller, Graduate Program Director, 410-704-2442, E-mail: bhaller@towson.edu. *Application contact:* Alicia Arkell-Kleis, Information Contact, 410-704-6004, Fax: 410-704-4675, E-mail: grads@towson.edu.
Website: http://grad.towson.edu/program/master/comg-ms/

Troy University, Graduate School, College of Communication and Fine Arts, Troy, AL 36082. Offers strategic communication (MS). Part-time and evening/weekend programs available. *Faculty:* 4 full-time (3 women), 2 part-time/adjunct (0 women). *Students:* 43 full-time (33 women), 74 part-time (53 women); includes 67 minority (58 Black or African American, non-Hispanic/Latino; 1 American Indian or Alaska Native, non-Hispanic/Latino; 2 Hispanic/Latino; 6 Two or more races, non-Hispanic/Latino). Average age 29. 43 applicants, 100% accepted, 35 enrolled. In 2014, 19 master's awarded. *Degree requirements:* For master's, comprehensive exam, thesis optional, minimum GPA of 3.0, admission to candidacy. *Entrance requirements:* For master's, GRE (minimum score of 850 on old exam or 290 on new exam), MAT (minimum score of 385) or GMAT (minimum score of 380), bachelor's degree; minimum undergraduate GPA of 2.5 or 3.0 on last 30 semester hours. Additional exam requirements/recommendations for international students: Required—TOEFL (minimum score 523 paper-based; 70 iBT), IELTS (minimum score 6). *Application deadline:* For fall admission, 6/1 for international students; for spring admission, 10/15 for international students. Application fee: $50. *Expenses:* Tuition, state resident: full-time $6570; part-time $365 per credit hour. Tuition, nonresident: full-time $13,140; part-time $730 per credit hour. *Required fees:* $365 per credit hour. *Unit head:* Dr. Larry Blocher, Dean, 334-670-3869, Fax: 334-670-3547, E-mail: lblocher@troy.edu. *Application contact:* Jessica A. Kimbro, Director of Graduate Admissions, 334-670-3178, E-mail: jacord@troy.edu.

Universidad Autonoma de Guadalajara, Graduate Programs, Guadalajara, Mexico. Offers administrative law and justice (LL M); advertising and corporate communications (MA); architecture (M Arch); business (MBA); computational science (MCC); education (Ed M, Ed D); English-Spanish translation (MA); entrepreneurship and management (MBA); integrated management of digital animation (MA); international business (MIB); international corporate law (LL M); internet technologies (MS); manufacturing systems (MMS); occupational health (MS); philosophy (MA, PhD); power electronics (MS); quality systems (MQS); renewable energy (MS); social evaluation of projects (MBA); strategic market research (MBA); tax law (MA); teaching mathematics (MA).

Universidad Iberoamericana, Graduate School, Santo Domingo D.N., Dominican Republic. Offers business administration (MBA, PMBA); constitutional law (LL M); dentistry (DMD); educational management (MA); integrated marketing communication (MA); psychopedagogical intervention (M Ed); real estate law (LL M); strategic management of human talent (MM).

Université de Sherbrooke, Faculty of Administration, Program in Marketing Communications, Sherbrooke, QC J1K 2R1, Canada. Offers M Adm. *Degree requirements:* For master's, one foreign language, thesis. *Entrance requirements:* For master's, bachelor's degree in related field, minimum GPA of 3.0 (on 4.3 scale). Electronic applications accepted.

University of Alaska Fairbanks, College of Liberal Arts, Department of Communications, Fairbanks, AK 99775-5680. Offers professional communication (MA). Part-time programs available. *Faculty:* 4 full-time (2 women). *Students:* 6 full-time (3 women), 4 part-time (all women); includes 2 minority (1 Black or African American, non-Hispanic/Latino; 1 American Indian or Alaska Native, non-Hispanic/Latino), 1 international. Average age 34. 11 applicants, 82% accepted, 5 enrolled. In 2014, 6 master's awarded. *Degree requirements:* For master's, comprehensive exam, thesis, oral defense of thesis. *Entrance requirements:* For master's, bachelor's degree from accredited institution with minimum cumulative undergraduate and major GPA of 3.0, academic writing sample. Additional exam requirements/recommendations for international students: Required—TOEFL (minimum score 550 paper-based; 79 iBT), IELTS (minimum score 6.5). *Application deadline:* For fall admission, 6/1 for domestic students, 3/1 for international students; for spring admission, 10/15 for domestic students, 9/1 for international students. Applications are processed on a rolling basis. Application fee: $60. Electronic applications accepted. *Expenses:* Tuition, state resident: full-time $7614; part-time $423 per credit. Tuition, nonresident: full-time $15,552; part-time $864 per credit. Tuition and fees vary according to course level, course load and reciprocity agreements. *Financial support:* In 2014–15, 6 teaching assistantships with full tuition reimbursements (averaging $11,078 per year) were awarded; fellowships with full tuition reimbursements, Federal Work-Study, scholarships/grants, tuition waivers, and unspecified assistantships also available. Support available to part-time students. Financial award application deadline: 7/1; financial award applicants required to submit FAFSA. *Faculty research:* Interpersonal communications, health communications, intercultural communications, politeness and face management in conversation, gender communication. *Unit head:* Dr. Peter DeCaro, Department Chair, 907-474-6591, Fax: 907-474-5858, E-mail: fycomm@uaf.edu. *Application contact:* Mary Kreta, Director of Admissions, 907-474-7500, Fax: 907-474-7097, E-mail: admissions@uaf.edu.
Website: http://www.uaf.edu/comm/

University of Colorado Denver, Business School, Program in Marketing, Denver, CO 80217. Offers brand management and marketing communication (MS); global marketing (MS); high-tech and entrepreneurial marketing (MS); marketing for sustainability (MS); marketing research (MS); sports and entertainment marketing (MS). Part-time and evening/weekend programs available. *Students:* 37 full-time (17 women), 13 part-time (6 women); includes 6 minority (1 Black or African American, non-Hispanic/Latino; 1 Asian, non-Hispanic/Latino; 2 Hispanic/Latino; 2 Two or more races, non-Hispanic/Latino), 16 international. Average age 29. 63 applicants, 57% accepted, 12 enrolled. In 2014, 20 master's awarded. *Degree requirements:* For master's, 30 semester hours (21 of marketing core courses, 9 of marketing electives). *Entrance requirements:* For master's, GMAT, resume, essay, two letters of recommendation, financial statements (for international applicants). Additional exam requirements/recommendations for international students: Required—TOEFL (minimum score 525 paper-based; 71 iBT); Recommended—IELTS (minimum score 6.5). *Application deadline:* For fall admission, 4/15 priority date for domestic students, 3/15 priority date for international students; for spring admission, 10/15 priority date for domestic students, 9/15 priority date for international students; for summer admission, 2/15 priority date for domestic students, 1/15 priority date for international students. Applications are processed on a rolling basis. Application fee: $50 ($75 for international students). Electronic applications accepted. *Expenses:* Expenses: Contact institution. *Financial support:* In 2014–15, 14 students received support. Fellowships, research assistantships, teaching assistantships, Federal Work-Study, institutionally sponsored loans, scholarships/grants, and traineeships available. Financial award application deadline: 4/1; financial award applicants required to submit FAFSA. *Faculty research:* Marketing issues in the Chinese environment, impact of individual difference and contextual factors on the risk-taking behaviors of managers making new-business creation decisions, attribution theory perspective of conflict between marketers and engineers, organizational identity and identification, international market entry strategies. *Unit head:* Vicki Lane, Director of Marketing Program, 303-315-8468, E-mail: vicki.lane@ucdenver.edu. *Application contact:* Shelly Townley, Admissions Director, Graduate Programs, 303-315-8202, E-mail: shelly.townley@ucdenver.edu.
Website: http://www.ucdenver.edu/academics/colleges/business/degrees/ms/marketing/Pages/Marketing.aspx

University of Connecticut, Graduate School, College of Liberal Arts and Sciences, Department of Communication Sciences, Program in Communication Processes and Marketing Communication, Storrs, CT 06269. Offers PhD. *Degree requirements:* For doctorate, thesis/dissertation. *Entrance requirements:* For doctorate, GMAT or GRE General Test. Additional exam requirements/recommendations for international

students: Required—TOEFL (minimum score 550 paper-based). Electronic applications accepted.

University of Denver, Division of Arts, Humanities and Social Sciences, Department of Media, Film and Journalism Studies, Denver, CO 80208. Offers emergent digital practices (MA); international and intercultural communication (MA); strategic communication (MS); student designed emphasis (MA); video production (MA). Part-time programs available. *Faculty:* 14 full-time (8 women), 6 part-time/adjunct (2 women). *Students:* 24 full-time (17 women), 25 part-time (17 women); includes 10 minority (1 Asian, non-Hispanic/Latino; 4 Hispanic/Latino; 5 Two or more races, non-Hispanic/ Latino), 4 international. Average age 27. 73 applicants, 89% accepted, 21 enrolled. In 2014, 17 master's awarded. *Degree requirements:* For master's, thesis (for some programs). *Entrance requirements:* For master's, GRE General Test, bachelor's degree, transcripts, personal statement, three letters of recommendation. Additional exam requirements/recommendations for international students: Required—TOEFL (minimum score 620 paper-based; 105 iBT). *Application deadline:* For fall admission, 2/15 priority date for domestic students, 1/1 priority date for international students. Applications are processed on a rolling basis. Application fee: $65. Electronic applications accepted. *Expenses:* Expenses: $1,199 per credit hour. *Financial support:* In 2014–15, 41 students received support, including 7 teaching assistantships with full and partial tuition reimbursements available (averaging $9,515 per year); career-related internships or fieldwork, Federal Work-Study, institutionally sponsored loans, scholarships/grants, and unspecified assistantships also available. Support available to part-time students. Financial award application deadline: 2/15; financial award applicants required to submit FAFSA. *Faculty research:* International and intercultural communication; media law; film history; youth, families, and social media; activist media. *Total annual research expenditures:* $50,000. *Unit head:* Dr. Lynn Schofield Clark, Chair, 303-871-3984, Fax: 303-871-4949, E-mail: lynn.clark@du.edu. *Application contact:* Information Contact, 303-871-2166, E-mail: mfjs@du.edu.
Website: http://www.du.edu/ahss/mfjs/index.html

University of Denver, University College, Denver, CO 80208. Offers geographic information systems (Certificate); global affairs (Certificate), including translation studies, world history and culture; information and communications technology (MCIS), including geographic information systems, information systems security, project management (MCIS, Certificate), software design and programming, technology management, telecommunications technology, Web design and development; leadership and organizations (Certificate), including human capital in organizations, philanthropic leadership, project management (MCIS, Certificate), strategic innovation and change; organizational and professional communication (MPS), including alternative dispute resolution, organizational communication, organizational development and training, public relations and marketing; security management (MAS, Certificate), including emergency planning and response, information security (MAS), organizational security. Part-time and evening/weekend programs available. Postbaccalaureate distance learning degree programs offered (no on-campus study). *Faculty:* 8 full-time (4 women), 133 part-time/adjunct (46 women). *Students:* 54 full-time (21 women), 1,327 part-time (775 women); includes 272 minority (106 Black or African American, non-Hispanic/Latino; 6 American Indian or Alaska Native, non-Hispanic/ Latino; 26 Asian, non-Hispanic/Latino; 108 Hispanic/Latino; 1 Native Hawaiian or other Pacific Islander, non-Hispanic/Latino; 25 Two or more races, non-Hispanic/Latino), 116 international. Average age 35. 768 applicants, 95% accepted, 620 enrolled. In 2014, 391 master's, 196 other advanced degrees awarded. *Degree requirements:* For master's, capstone project. *Entrance requirements:* For master's, transcripts, two letters of recommendation, personal statement, resume. Additional exam requirements/ recommendations for international students: Required—TOEFL (minimum score 550 paper-based; 80 iBT). *Application deadline:* For fall admission, 6/21 priority date for domestic students, 5/1 priority date for international students; for winter admission, 9/14 priority date for domestic students, 9/19 priority date for international students; for spring admission, 1/11 for domestic students, 12/12 for international students; for summer admission, 3/29 priority date for domestic students, 3/6 priority date for international students. Applications are processed on a rolling basis. Application fee: $75. Electronic applications accepted. *Expenses:* Expenses: $959 per credit hour. *Financial support:* In 2014–15, 19 students received support. Applicants required to submit FAFSA. *Unit head:* Dr. Michael McGuire, Interim Dean, 303-871-3518, E-mail: mmcguire@du.edu. *Application contact:* Information Contact, 303-871-2291, E-mail: ucoladm@du.edu.
Website: http://www.universitycollege.du.edu/

University of Missouri, Office of Research and Graduate Studies, School of Journalism, Columbia, MO 65211. Offers center for the digital globe (Certificate); European Union studies (Certificate); health communications (MA); interactive media (MA); journalism (PhD); media management (MA); strategic communication (MA). *Accreditation:* ACEJMC (one or more programs are accredited). Part-time programs available. *Faculty:* 75 full-time (38 women), 3 part-time/adjunct (1 woman). *Students:* 159 full-time (104 women), 88 part-time (54 women); includes 33 minority (8 Black or African American, non-Hispanic/Latino; 11 Asian, non-Hispanic/Latino; 11 Hispanic/ Latino; 3 Two or more races, non-Hispanic/Latino), 57 international. Average age 29. 239 applicants, 55% accepted, 78 enrolled. In 2014, 73 master's, 8 doctorates awarded. Terminal master's awarded for partial completion of doctoral program. *Degree requirements:* For master's, thesis (for some programs); for doctorate, 2 foreign languages, thesis/dissertation. *Entrance requirements:* For master's and doctorate, GRE General Test, minimum GPA of 3.0. Additional exam requirements/ recommendations for international students: Required—TOEFL (minimum score 600 paper-based; 100 iBT). *Application deadline:* For fall admission, 12/15 priority date for domestic and international students; for winter admission, 9/1 priority date for domestic and international students. Applications are processed on a rolling basis. Application fee: $55 ($75 for international students). Electronic applications accepted. *Financial support:* Fellowships with tuition reimbursements, research assistantships with tuition reimbursements, teaching assistantships with tuition reimbursements, career-related internships or fieldwork, institutionally sponsored loans, scholarships/grants, health care benefits, and unspecified assistantships available. Support available to part-time students. *Faculty research:* Strategic communication, convergence journalism, journalism studies, international programs, photojournalism, magazine journalism, radio-television journalism. *Unit head:* Dr. Esther Thorson, Associate Dean, 573-882-9590, E-mail: thorsone@missouri.edu. *Application contact:* Ginny Cowell, Administrative Assistant, 573-882-4852, E-mail: cowellvj@missouri.edu.
Website: http://www.journalism.missouri.edu/graduate/

University of Nebraska–Lincoln, Graduate College, College of Arts and Sciences, Department of Communication Studies, Lincoln, NE 68588. Offers instructional communication (MA, PhD); interpersonal communication (MA, PhD); marketing, communication studies, and advertising (MA, PhD); organizational communication (MA, PhD); rhetoric and culture (MA, PhD). *Degree requirements:* For master's, thesis optional; for doctorate, comprehensive exam, thesis/dissertation. *Entrance requirements:* For master's and doctorate, GRE General Test, writing sample. Additional exam requirements/recommendations for international students: Required—TOEFL (minimum score 600 paper-based). Electronic applications accepted. *Faculty research:* Message strategies, gender communication, political communication, organizational communication, instructional communication.

The University of North Carolina at Charlotte, College of Liberal Arts and Sciences, Department of Communication Studies, Charlotte, NC 28223-0001. Offers communication studies (Graduate Certificate); health communication (MA); organizational communication (MA); public relations and international public relations (MA); rhetoric, media studies, and popular culture (MA). Part-time and evening/weekend programs available. *Faculty:* 15 full-time (8 women). *Students:* 11 full-time (8 women), 12 part-time (9 women); includes 3 minority (2 Black or African American, non-Hispanic/ Latino; 1 Two or more races, non-Hispanic/Latino), 2 international. Average age 27. 49 applicants, 49% accepted, 11 enrolled. In 2014, 11 master's awarded. Terminal master's awarded for partial completion of doctoral program. *Degree requirements:* For master's, project, thesis, or comprehensive exam. *Entrance requirements:* For master's, GRE General Test, minimum GPA of 2.75 overall. Additional exam requirements/ recommendations for international students: Required—TOEFL (minimum score 557 paper-based; 83 iBT). *Application deadline:* For fall admission, 3/1 for domestic and international students; for spring admission, 11/15 for domestic students, 10/1 for international students. Application fee: $75. Electronic applications accepted. *Expenses:* Tuition, state resident: full-time $4008. Tuition, nonresident: full-time $16,295. *Required fees:* $2755. Tuition and fees vary according to course load and program. *Financial support:* In 2014–15, 10 students received support, including 10 teaching assistantships (averaging $14,981 per year); career-related internships or fieldwork, institutionally sponsored loans, scholarships/grants, and unspecified assistantships also available. Support available to part-time students. Financial award application deadline: 4/1; financial award applicants required to submit FAFSA. *Faculty research:* Rhetorical approaches to analyzing public relations controversies, participant empowerment and engagement in community-based participatory action research, human factors constraining the management of knowledge in a large financial services organization, models of Internet governance, race and class politics of mediated sports. *Unit head:* Dr. Shawn Long, Chair, 704-687-0783, Fax: 704-687-6900, E-mail: shawn.long@uncc.edu. *Application contact:* Kathy B. Giddings, Director of Graduate Admissions, 704-687-5503, Fax: 704-687-1668, E-mail: gradadm@uncc.edu.
Website: http://gradcomm.uncc.edu/

University of Oklahoma, College of Arts and Sciences, Department of Communication, Norman, OK 73019. Offers communication (MA, PhD); organizational communication (MA). Part-time and evening/weekend programs available. Postbaccalaureate distance learning degree programs offered (no on-campus study). *Faculty:* 19 full-time (9 women). *Students:* 30 full-time (19 women), 54 part-time (27 women); includes 27 minority (8 Black or African American, non-Hispanic/Latino; 3 American Indian or Alaska Native, non-Hispanic/Latino; 1 Asian, non-Hispanic/Latino; 10 Hispanic/Latino; 5 Two or more races, non-Hispanic/Latino), 8 international. Average age 35. 45 applicants, 53% accepted, 11 enrolled. In 2014, 13 master's, 4 doctorates awarded. Terminal master's awarded for partial completion of doctoral program. *Degree requirements:* For master's, variable foreign language requirement, comprehensive exam (for some programs), thesis optional; for doctorate, variable foreign language requirement, comprehensive exam, thesis/dissertation. *Entrance requirements:* For doctorate, GRE. Additional exam requirements/recommendations for international students: Required—TOEFL (minimum score 79 iBT). *Application deadline:* For fall admission, 2/1 for domestic and international students; for spring admission, 11/1 for domestic students, 9/1 for international students. Application fee: $50 ($100 for international students). Electronic applications accepted. *Expenses:* Tuition, state resident: full-time $4394; part-time $183.10 per credit hour. Tuition, nonresident: full-time $16,970; part-time $707.10 per credit hour. *Required fees:* $2892; $109.95 per credit hour. $126.50 per semester. *Financial support:* In 2014–15, 36 students received support, including 1 research assistantship with partial tuition reimbursement available (averaging $10,372 per year), 29 teaching assistantships with partial tuition reimbursements available (averaging $16,189 per year); scholarships/grants and unspecified assistantships also available. Financial award application deadline: 6/1; financial award applicants required to submit FAFSA. *Faculty research:* Intercultural/international communication, interpersonal communication/social influence, political/mass communication, health communication, organizational communication, communication technology. *Total annual research expenditures:* $744,456. *Unit head:* Dr. Michael W. Kramer, Chair and Professor, 405-325-9503, Fax: 405-325-7625, E-mail: mkramer@ou.edu. *Application contact:* Dr. Elaine Hsieh, Graduate Liaison and Associate Professor, 405-325-3154, Fax: 405-325-7625, E-mail: ehsieh@ou.edu.
Website: http://cas.ou.edu/comm

University of Portland, Department of Communication Studies, Portland, OR 97203-5798. Offers communication (MA); management communication (MS). Part-time and evening/weekend programs available. *Faculty:* 5 full-time (3 women), 1 part-time/adjunct (0 women). *Students:* 7 full-time (4 women), 10 part-time (7 women); includes 2 minority (1 Hispanic/Latino; 1 Two or more races, non-Hispanic/Latino), 2 international. Average age 28. In 2014, 7 master's awarded. *Degree requirements:* For master's, thesis optional. *Entrance requirements:* For master's, GRE General Test, minimum GPA of 3.25, 3 letters of recommendation, resume, statement of goals, official transcripts. Additional exam requirements/recommendations for international students: Required—TOEFL (minimum score 600 paper-based; 100 iBT), IELTS (minimum score 7.5). *Application deadline:* For fall admission, 7/15 priority date for domestic and international students; for spring admission, 12/15 priority date for domestic and international students. Applications are processed on a rolling basis. Application fee: $50. *Expenses: Tuition:* Full-time $19,260; part-time $1070 per credit hour. Tuition and fees vary according to program. *Financial support:* Career-related internships or fieldwork, Federal Work-Study, scholarships/grants, and tuition waivers (partial) available. Financial award application deadline: 3/1; financial award applicants required to submit FAFSA. *Unit head:* Dr. Jeff Kerssen-Griep, Director, 503-943-7229, E-mail: kerssen@up.edu. *Application contact:* Allison Able, Graduate Program Coordinator, 503-943-7107, Fax: 503-943-7315, E-mail: able@up.edu.
Website: http://college.up.edu/commstudies/default.aspx?cid-1377&PID-286

University of St. Thomas, Graduate Studies, Opus College of Business, Master of Business Communication Program, Minneapolis, MN 55403. Offers MBC. Part-time and evening/weekend programs available. *Entrance requirements:* For master's, GMAT or GRE. Additional exam requirements/recommendations for international students: Required—TOEFL (minimum score 80 iBT), IELTS (minimum score 6.5), or Michigan English Language Assessment Battery. Electronic applications accepted.

University of Southern California, Graduate School, Annenberg School for Communication and Journalism, School of Communication, Program in Communication Management, Los Angeles, CA 90089. Offers MCM, JD/MCM, MCM/MAJCS. Part-time and evening/weekend programs available. Postbaccalaureate distance learning degree programs offered (no on-campus study). *Students:* 239 full-time, 82 part-time; includes 98 minority (25 Black or African American, non-Hispanic/Latino; 29 Asian, non-Hispanic/ Latino; 39 Hispanic/Latino; 1 Native Hawaiian or other Pacific Islander, non-Hispanic/ Latino; 4 Two or more races, non-Hispanic/Latino), 138 international. Average age 25. 506 applicants, 48% accepted, 141 enrolled. In 2014, 141 master's awarded. *Degree requirements:* For master's, professional project. *Entrance requirements:* For master's, GRE General Test or GMAT, resume, writing samples, recommendation letters, statement of purpose. Additional exam requirements/recommendations for international students: Required—TOEFL (minimum score 114 iBT) or IELTS. *Application deadline:*

For fall admission, 5/1 priority date for domestic students, 1/15 priority date for international students; for spring admission, 10/1 for domestic students, 9/1 for international students. Applications are processed on a rolling basis. Application fee: $85. Electronic applications accepted. *Financial support:* Career-related internships or fieldwork, Federal Work-Study, institutionally sponsored loans, and scholarships/grants available. Support available to part-time students. Financial award application deadline: 1/2; financial award applicants required to submit FAFSA. *Faculty research:* Global communication, communication law and policy, entertainment management, marketing communication, strategic and corporate communication management. *Unit head:* Dr. Rebecca Weintraub, Director, 213-821-0764, Fax: 213-740-8036, E-mail: weintrau@usc.edu. *Application contact:* Allyson Hill, Associate Dean for Admissions, 213-821-0770, Fax: 213-740-1933, E-mail: ascadm@usc.edu.
Website: http://www.annenberg.usc.edu

University of South Florida, College of Arts and Sciences, School of Mass Communications, Tampa, FL 33620-9951. Offers media studies (MA), including media studies; multimedia journalism studies (MA); strategic communication management (MA). Part-time and evening/weekend programs available. *Faculty:* 10 full-time (3 women). *Students:* 17 full-time (13 women), 17 part-time (6 women); includes 5 minority (2 Black or African American, non-Hispanic/Latino; 1 Asian, non-Hispanic/Latino; 2 Hispanic/Latino), 7 international. Average age 29. 40 applicants, 65% accepted, 14 enrolled. In 2014, 15 master's awarded. *Degree requirements:* For master's, comprehensive exam, thesis optional. *Entrance requirements:* For master's, GRE General Test (minimum score of 153 verbal and 144 quantitative preferred), minimum GPA of 3.0 in last 60 hours of course work, three letters of recommendation, letter of intent, resume. Additional exam requirements/recommendations for international students: Required—TOEFL (minimum score 550 paper-based; 79 iBT) or IELTS (minimum score 6.5). *Application deadline:* For fall admission, 2/15 for domestic students, 1/2 for international students; for spring admission, 10/15 for domestic students, 6/1 for international students. Application fee: $30. Electronic applications accepted. *Financial support:* In 2014–15, 9 students received support, including 9 teaching assistantships with tuition reimbursements available (averaging $10,513 per year); unspecified assistantships also available. Financial award application deadline: 2/28. *Faculty research:* First Amendment analysis, civic journalism, public opinion, media ethics, media effects research in sports public relations, public relations management, advertisement, telecommunications. *Total annual research expenditures:* $52,955. *Unit head:* Dr. Jim Andrews, Interim Director and Associate Professor, 813-974-2108, Fax: 813-974-2592, E-mail: jimandrews@usf.edu. *Application contact:* Dr. Michael Mitrook, Assistant Professor, 813-974-8890, Fax: 813-974-2592, E-mail: mmitrook@.usf.edu.
Website: http://masscom.usf.edu/grad/

University of South Florida, Innovative Education, Tampa, FL 33620-9951. *Unit head:* Kathy Barnes, Interdisciplinary Programs Coordinator, 813-974-8031, Fax: 813-974-7061, E-mail: barnesk@usf.edu. *Application contact:* Karen Tylinski, Metro Initiatives, 813-974-9943, Fax: 813-974-7061, E-mail: ktylinsk@usf.edu.
Website: http://www.usf.edu/innovative-education/

University of Wisconsin–Stevens Point, College of Fine Arts and Communication, Division of Communication, Stevens Point, WI 54481-3897. Offers interpersonal communication (MA); media studies (MA); organizational communication (MA); public relations (MA). Part-time programs available. *Degree requirements:* For master's, thesis or alternative. *Entrance requirements:* For master's, GRE. Additional exam requirements/recommendations for international students: Required—TOEFL (minimum score 575 paper-based). *Faculty research:* Communication theory and research, film history.

University of Wisconsin–Whitewater, School of Graduate Studies, College of Arts and Communications, Department of Communication, Whitewater, WI 53190-1790. Offers corporate communication (MS); mass communication (MS). Part-time and evening/weekend programs available. Postbaccalaureate distance learning degree programs offered (no on-campus study). *Degree requirements:* For master's, thesis or alternative. *Entrance requirements:* For master's, 2 letters of recommendation, goal statement. Additional exam requirements/recommendations for international students: Required—TOEFL (minimum score 550 paper-based; 80 iBT), IELTS (minimum score 6). Electronic applications accepted.

Washington State University, The Edward R. Murrow College of Communication, Pullman, WA 99164-2520. Offers communication (MA, PhD); strategic communication (MA). MA in strategic communication offered at the Global (online) campus. *Students:* 45 full-time (34 women), 48 part-time (37 women); includes 16 minority (4 Black or African American, non-Hispanic/Latino; 1 American Indian or Alaska Native, non-Hispanic/Latino; 2 Asian, non-Hispanic/Latino; 7 Hispanic/Latino; 2 Two or more races, non-Hispanic/Latino), 15 international. Average age 31. 150 applicants, 49% accepted, 58 enrolled. In 2014, 7 master's, 1 doctorate awarded. *Degree requirements:* For master's, comprehensive exam (for some programs), thesis optional, oral exam; for doctorate, comprehensive exam, thesis/dissertation. *Entrance requirements:* For master's, GRE General Test, minimum GPA of 3.25, 3 letters of recommendation; for doctorate, GRE General Test, minimum undergraduate GPA of 3.25, graduate 3.5; MA in communication; 3 letters of recommendation. Additional exam requirements/recommendations for international students: Required—TOEFL (minimum score 580 paper-based). *Application deadline:* For fall admission, 1/10 priority date for domestic and international students. Applications are processed on a rolling basis. Application fee: $75. Electronic applications accepted. *Expenses:* Tuition, state resident: full-time $11,768. Tuition, nonresident: full-time $25,200. *Required fees:* $960. Tuition and fees vary according to program. *Financial support:* In 2014–15, 36 students received support, including 4 research assistantships with full and partial tuition reimbursements available (averaging $10,648 per year), 21 teaching assistantships with full and partial tuition reimbursements available (averaging $13,625 per year); career-related internships or fieldwork, Federal Work-Study, institutionally sponsored loans, tuition waivers (partial), and teaching associateships also available. Financial award application deadline: 2/15; financial award applicants required to submit FAFSA. *Faculty research:* Communication technology, health communication, science communication, political communication, intercultural communication. *Unit head:* Dr. Prabu David, Associate Dean for Academic Affairs, 509-335-0041, E-mail: prabu.david@wsu.edu. *Application contact:* Graduate School Admissions, 800-GRADWSU, Fax: 509-335-1949, E-mail: gradsch@wsu.edu.
Website: http://communication.wsu.edu/

Webster University, School of Communications, Program in Communications Management, St. Louis, MO 63119-3194. Offers MA.

Western Kentucky University, Graduate Studies, Potter College of Arts and Letters, Department of Communication, Bowling Green, KY 42101. Offers communication (MA); organizational communication (Graduate Certificate). Part-time and evening/weekend programs available. *Degree requirements:* For master's, comprehensive exam, thesis optional, final exam. *Entrance requirements:* For master's, GRE General Test, minimum GPA of 2.75. Additional exam requirements/recommendations for international students: Required—TOEFL (minimum score 555 paper-based; 79 iBT). *Faculty research:* Public rhetoric and public address organization communication, teamwork in communication, intercultural crisis communication.

West Virginia University, Eberly College of Arts and Sciences, Department of Communication Studies, Morgantown, WV 26506. Offers communication in instruction (MA); communication studies (PhD); communication theory and research (MA); corporate and organizational communication (MA). Part-time programs available. *Degree requirements:* For master's, comprehensive exam (for some programs), thesis (for some programs); for doctorate, comprehensive exam, thesis/dissertation. *Entrance requirements:* For master's and doctorate, minimum GPA of 3.0. Additional exam requirements/recommendations for international students: Required—TOEFL. Electronic applications accepted. *Faculty research:* Instructional communication, interpersonal communication, health communication, influence, instructional communication, social influence.

West Virginia University, Reed College of Media, Program in Digital Marketing Communications, Morgantown, WV 26506. Offers Graduate Certificate. Postbaccalaureate distance learning degree programs offered (no on-campus study). *Entrance requirements:* For degree, resume. Electronic applications accepted.

West Virginia University, Reed College of Media, Program in Integrated Marketing Communications, Morgantown, WV 26501. Offers MS, Graduate Certificate. Part-time programs available. Postbaccalaureate distance learning degree programs offered (no on-campus study). *Entrance requirements:* For master's, GRE or GMAT (waived with minimum undergraduate GPA of 3.3 or at least 6 years of related professional experience), undergraduate transcript, resume; letters of recommendation (strongly recommended). Additional exam requirements/recommendations for international students: Required—TOEFL.

Health Communication

Boston University, Metropolitan College, Program in Health Communication, Boston, MA 02215. Offers MS. Part-time programs available. Postbaccalaureate distance learning degree programs offered (no on-campus study). *Faculty:* 1 full-time (0 women), 9 part-time/adjunct (5 women). *Students:* 76 part-time (68 women); includes 15 minority (7 Black or African American, non-Hispanic/Latino; 2 Asian, non-Hispanic/Latino; 3 Hispanic/Latino; 3 Two or more races, non-Hispanic/Latino), 1 international. Average age 37. 30 applicants, 93% accepted, 28 enrolled. In 2014, 44 master's awarded. *Entrance requirements:* For master's, bachelor's degree, minimum GPA of 3.0, some professional experience. Additional exam requirements/recommendations for international students: Required—TOEFL (minimum score 100 iBT). *Application deadline:* For fall admission, 7/13 for domestic students; for spring admission, 11/21 for domestic students; for summer admission, 3/28 for domestic students. Applications are processed on a rolling basis. Application fee: $80. Electronic applications accepted. *Expenses:* Expenses: $800 per credit part-time; student services fees: $60 per semester; technology fee of $60 per credit (for online courses). *Financial support:* Available to part-time students. Applicants required to submit FAFSA. *Faculty research:* Public relations and health communication. *Unit head:* Dr. Tanya Zlateva, Interim Dean, 617-353-3010, Fax: 617-353-6066, E-mail: metdean@bu.edu. *Application contact:* Sonia M. Parker, Assistant Dean, 617-353-2975, E-mail: soparker@bu.edu.
Website: http://www.bu.edu/online/online_programs/graduate_degree/master_health_communication/

Brandman University, School of Nursing and Health Professions, Irvine, CA 92618. Offers health administration (MHA); health risk and crisis communication (MS).

Chapman University, Wilkinson College of Humanities and Social Sciences, Health and Strategic Communication Program, Orange, CA 92866. Offers MS. Part-time and evening/weekend programs available. *Faculty:* 13 full-time (9 women), 18 part-time/adjunct (10 women). *Students:* 7 full-time (6 women); includes 1 minority (Asian, non-Hispanic/Latino). Average age 27. 21 applicants, 67% accepted, 6 enrolled. In 2014, 8 master's awarded. *Entrance requirements:* For master's, GRE, minimum undergraduate GPA of 3.0. Additional exam requirements/recommendations for international students: Required—TOEFL (minimum score 550 paper-based; 80 iBT). *Application deadline:* Applications are processed on a rolling basis. Application fee: $60. Electronic applications accepted. *Financial support:* Fellowships, Federal Work-Study, and scholarships/grants available. Financial award applicants required to submit FAFSA. *Unit head:* Dr. Lisa Sparks, Chair, 714-997-6703, E-mail: sparks@chapman.edu. *Application contact:* Shannon McCance, Admission Counselor, 714-997-6711, E-mail: smccance@chapman.edu.
Website: http://www.chapman.edu/wilkinson/graduate-studies/ms-health-communication/index.aspx

Cleveland State University, College of Graduate Studies, College of Liberal Arts and Social Sciences, School of Communication, Cleveland, OH 44115. Offers applied communication theory and methodology (MA); culture, communication and health care (Certificate). Part-time and evening/weekend programs available. *Faculty:* 10 full-time (3 women). *Students:* 20 part-time (11 women); includes 4 minority (3 Black or African American, non-Hispanic/Latino; 1 Asian, non-Hispanic/Latino), 4 international. Average age 34. 14 applicants, 93% accepted, 5 enrolled. In 2014, 5 master's awarded. *Degree requirements:* For master's, variable foreign language requirement, comprehensive exam (for some programs), thesis, project, comprehensive exam, or collaborative project. *Entrance requirements:* For master's, GRE or MAT, minimum undergraduate GPA of 2.75, 2 letters of recommendation, statement of interest. Additional exam requirements/recommendations for international students: Required—TOEFL (minimum score 525 paper-based; 65 iBT). *Application deadline:* For fall admission, 8/25 priority date for domestic students, 5/15 priority date for international students; for spring admission, 1/15 priority date for domestic students, 11/1 priority date for international students. Applications are processed on a rolling basis. Application fee: $30. Electronic applications accepted. *Expenses:* Expenses: $9,615 full-time, in-state tuition and fees. *Financial support:* In 2014–15, 14 students received support, including 5 research assistantships with full and partial tuition reimbursements available (averaging $11,000 per year), 9 teaching assistantships with full and partial tuition reimbursements available

(averaging $11,000 per year); tuition waivers (full and partial) and unspecified assistantships also available. Financial award application deadline: 8/1. *Faculty research:* Interpersonal, organizational, and mass communication; health communication. *Unit head:* Dr. George B. Ray, Director, 216-687-4631, Fax: 216-687-5435, E-mail: g.ray@csuohio.edu. *Application contact:* Dr. Gary Pettey, Communication Graduate Program Director, 216-687-4641, Fax: 216-687-5435, E-mail: g.pettey@csuohio.edu.
Website: http://www.csuohio.edu/class/communication/communication

Cornell University, Graduate School, Graduate Fields of Agriculture and Life Sciences, Field of Communication, Ithaca, NY 14853-0001. Offers communication (MS, PhD); human-computer interaction (MS, PhD); language and communication (MS, PhD); media communication and society (MS, PhD); organizational communication (MS, PhD); science, environment and health communication (MS, PhD); social psychology of communication (MS, PhD). *Degree requirements:* For master's, thesis (MS); for doctorate, comprehensive exam, thesis/dissertation. *Entrance requirements:* For master's and doctorate, GRE General Test, 3 letters of recommendation. Additional exam requirements/recommendations for international students: Required—TOEFL (minimum score 600 paper-based; 100 iBT). Electronic applications accepted. *Faculty research:* Mass communication, communication technologies, science and environmental communication.

DePaul University, College of Communication, Chicago, IL 60614. Offers digital communication and media arts (MA); health communication (MA); journalism (MA); media and cinema studies (MA); organizational and multicultural communication (MA); public relations and advertising (MA); relational communication (MA). Part-time and evening/weekend programs available. *Entrance requirements:* Additional exam requirements/recommendations for international students: Required—TOEFL (minimum score 590 paper-based; 96 iBT), IELTS (minimum score 7.5) or PTE. Electronic applications accepted.

East Carolina University, Graduate School, College of Fine Arts and Communication, School of Communication, Greenville, NC 27858-4353. Offers health communication (MA). *Entrance requirements:* For master's, GRE. *Expenses:* Tuition, state resident: full-time $4223. Tuition, nonresident: full-time $16,540. *Required fees:* $2184.

Emerson College, Graduate Studies, School of Communication, Department of Communication Sciences and Disorders, Program in Health Communication, Boston, MA 02116-4624. Offers MA. Program offered jointly with Tufts University. Part-time programs available. *Students:* 21 full-time (16 women), 2 part-time (both women); includes 7 minority (1 Black or African American, non-Hispanic/Latino; 2 Asian, non-Hispanic/Latino; 2 Hispanic/Latino; 2 Two or more races, non-Hispanic/Latino), 4 international. Average age 26. 135 applicants, 22% accepted, 10 enrolled. In 2014, 20 master's awarded. *Entrance requirements:* For master's, GMAT or GRE General Test. Additional exam requirements/recommendations for international students: Required—TOEFL (minimum score 550 paper-based; 80 iBT), IELTS (minimum score 6.5). *Application deadline:* For fall admission, 3/1 priority date for domestic students, 3/1 for international students. Applications are processed on a rolling basis. Application fee: $60 ($75 for international students). Electronic applications accepted. *Expenses: Tuition:* Part-time $1145 per credit. *Financial support:* In 2014–15, 8 students received support, including 8 fellowships with partial tuition reimbursements available (averaging $8,000 per year); research assistantships with partial tuition reimbursements available, Federal Work-Study, scholarships/grants, and unspecified assistantships also available. Financial award application deadline: 3/1; financial award applicants required to submit FAFSA. *Faculty research:* Health promotion, health communications. *Unit head:* Dr. Timothy Edgar, Graduate Program Director, 617-824-8492, E-mail: timothy_edgar@emerson.edu. *Application contact:* Leanda Ferland, Office of Graduate Admission, 617-824-8610, Fax: 617-824-8614, E-mail: gradapp@emerson.edu.
Website: http://www.emerson.edu/graduate_admission

Fitchburg State University, Division of Graduate and Continuing Education, Program in Applied Communications, Fitchburg, MA 01420-2697. Offers applied communications (MS, Certificate); health communication (MS); library media (MS); technical and professional writing (MS). Part-time and evening/weekend programs available. *Entrance requirements:* Additional exam requirements/recommendations for international students: Required—TOEFL (minimum score 550 paper-based; 79 iBT). Electronic applications accepted.

The George Washington University, Milken Institute School of Public Health, Department of Global Health, Washington, DC 20052. Offers global health (Dr PH); global health communication (MPH). *Accreditation:* CEPH. *Faculty:* 14 full-time (8 women). *Students:* 48 full-time (38 women), 68 part-time (55 women); includes 43 minority (18 Black or African American, non-Hispanic/Latino; 1 American Indian or Alaska Native, non-Hispanic/Latino; 8 Asian, non-Hispanic/Latino; 12 Hispanic/Latino; 4 Two or more races, non-Hispanic/Latino), 5 international. Average age 29. 292 applicants, 64% accepted, 34 enrolled. In 2014, 47 master's, 1 doctorate awarded. *Degree requirements:* For master's, case study or special project. *Entrance requirements:* For master's, GMAT, GRE General Test, or MCAT. Additional exam requirements/recommendations for international students: Required—TOEFL. *Application deadline:* For fall admission, 4/15 priority date for domestic students, 4/15 for international students; for spring admission, 11/1 for domestic and international students. Applications are processed on a rolling basis. Application fee: $75. *Financial support:* In 2014–15, 24 students received support. Tuition waivers available. Financial award application deadline: 2/15. *Unit head:* Dr. James Tielsch, Chair, 202-994-0270, Fax: 202-994-1955, E-mail: jtielsch@gwu.edu. *Application contact:* Jane Smith, Director of Admissions, 202-994-0248, Fax: 202-994-1860, E-mail: sphhsinfo@gwumc.edu.

Indiana University–Purdue University Indianapolis, School of Liberal Arts, Department of Communication Studies, Indianapolis, IN 46225. Offers applied communication (MA); health communication (PhD). Part-time programs available. *Students:* 13 full-time (10 women), 23 part-time (17 women); includes 7 minority (4 Black or African American, non-Hispanic/Latino; 1 Asian, non-Hispanic/Latino; 2 Hispanic/Latino), 7 international. 28 applicants, 50% accepted, 9 enrolled. In 2014, 12 master's awarded. *Degree requirements:* For master's, comprehensive exam, thesis; for doctorate, thesis/dissertation. *Entrance requirements:* For doctorate, master's degree. Additional exam requirements/recommendations for international students: Required—TOEFL; Recommended—IELTS. *Application deadline:* For fall admission, 1/15 priority date for domestic and international students; for spring admission, 5/14 for domestic students, 5/15 for international students. Application fee: $60. Electronic applications accepted. *Financial support:* In 2014–15, 7 students received support, including 1 fellowship with full tuition reimbursement available (averaging $25,000 per year), 3 research assistantships with partial tuition reimbursements available (averaging $15,000 per year), 5 teaching assistantships (averaging $2,500 per year); career-related internships or fieldwork, Federal Work-Study, institutionally sponsored loans, scholarships/grants, health care benefits, tuition waivers, and unspecified assistantships also available. Support available to part-time students. Financial award application deadline: 2/1. *Unit head:* Prof. Jennifer Bute, Director of Graduate Studies, 317-274-2090, E-mail: jjbute@iupui.edu. *Application contact:* Candice L. Smith, Coordinator of Academic and Graduate Programs, 317-274-8305, E-mail: canlsmit@iupui.edu.
Website: http://liberalarts.iupui.edu/comm/

Johns Hopkins University, Bloomberg School of Public Health, Department of Health, Behavior and Society, Baltimore, MD 21218-2699. Offers genetic counseling (Sc M); health education and health communication (MSPH); social and behavioral sciences (Dr PH, PhD); social factors in health (MHS). *Degree requirements:* For master's, comprehensive exam (for some programs), thesis (for some programs); for doctorate, comprehensive exam, thesis/dissertation. *Entrance requirements:* For master's, GRE, curriculum vitae, 3 letters of recommendation; for doctorate, GRE, transcripts, curriculum vitae, 3 recommendation letters. Additional exam requirements/recommendations for international students: Required—TOEFL (minimum score 600 paper-based; 100 iBT). Electronic applications accepted. *Faculty research:* Social determinants of health and structural and community-level inventions to improve health, communication and health education, behavioral and social aspects of genetic counseling.

Kansas State University, Graduate School, College of Arts and Sciences, A. Q. Miller School of Journalism and Mass Communications, Manhattan, KS 66506. Offers advertising (MS); community journalism (MS); global communication (MS); health communication (MS); media management (MS); public relations (MS). Part-time and evening/weekend programs available. *Faculty:* 15 full-time (7 women), 1 (woman) part-time/adjunct. *Students:* 15 full-time (9 women), 5 part-time (3 women); includes 2 minority (both Hispanic/Latino), 9 international. Average age 26. 10 applicants, 80% accepted, 6 enrolled. In 2014, 10 master's awarded. *Degree requirements:* For master's, comprehensive exam, thesis. *Entrance requirements:* For master's, GRE General Test, minimum GPA of 3.0. Additional exam requirements/recommendations for international students: Required—TOEFL (minimum score 79 iBT). *Application deadline:* For fall admission, 2/1 priority date for domestic and international students; for spring admission, 8/1 priority date for domestic and international students. Applications are processed on a rolling basis. Application fee: $50 ($75 for international students). Electronic applications accepted. *Financial support:* In 2014–15, 2 research assistantships with full tuition reimbursements (averaging $11,180 per year), 7 teaching assistantships with full tuition reimbursements (averaging $7,729 per year) were awarded; scholarships/grants, health care benefits, and unspecified assistantships also available. Financial award application deadline: 2/1; financial award applicants required to submit FAFSA. *Faculty research:* Health communication, risk communication, strategic communications, community journalism, global communication. *Total annual research expenditures:* $219,641. *Unit head:* Dr. Birgit Wassmuth, Director, 785-532-6890, Fax: 785-532-5484, E-mail: wassmuth@ksu.edu. *Application contact:* Dr. Nancy Muturi, Associate Director of Graduate Studies, 785-532-3890, Fax: 785-532-5484, E-mail: nmuturi@ksu.edu.
Website: http://jmc.ksu.edu/

Lasell College, Graduate and Professional Studies in Communication, Newton, MA 02466-2709. Offers health communication (MSC, Graduate Certificate); integrated marketing communication (MSC, Graduate Certificate); public relations (MSC, Graduate Certificate). Part-time and evening/weekend programs available. Postbaccalaureate distance learning degree programs offered (minimal on-campus study). *Faculty:* 5 full-time (3 women), 10 part-time/adjunct (5 women). *Students:* 50 full-time (37 women), 94 part-time (74 women); includes 40 minority (25 Black or African American, non-Hispanic/Latino; 2 American Indian or Alaska Native, non-Hispanic/Latino; 4 Asian, non-Hispanic/Latino; 8 Hispanic/Latino; 1 Two or more races, non-Hispanic/Latino), 19 international. Average age 30. *Entrance requirements:* For master's and Graduate Certificate, bachelor's degree from an accredited institution. Additional exam requirements/recommendations for international students: Required—TOEFL (minimum score 550 paper-based; 79 iBT), IELTS. *Application deadline:* For fall admission, 8/31 priority date for domestic students, 6/30 priority date for international students; for spring admission, 12/31 priority date for domestic students, 10/31 priority date for international students. Applications are processed on a rolling basis. Electronic applications accepted. *Expenses: Tuition:* Full-time $10,700; part-time $595 per credit. *Required fees:* $160; $80 per semester. *Financial support:* Available to part-time students. Application deadline: 8/31; applicants required to submit FAFSA. *Unit head:* Dr. Joan Dolamore, Dean of Graduate and Professional Studies, 617-243-2485, Fax: 617-243-2450, E-mail: gradinfo@lasell.edu. *Application contact:* Adrienne Franciosi, Director of Graduate Admission, 617-243-2214, Fax: 617-243-2450, E-mail: gradinfo@lasell.edu.
Website: http://www.lasell.edu/academics/graduate-and-professional-studies/programs-of-study/master-of-science-in-communication.html

Marquette University, Graduate School, Diederich College of Communication, Milwaukee, WI 53201-1881. Offers advertising and public relations (MA); communication studies (MA); digital storytelling (Certificate); journalism (MA); mass communication (MA); science, health and environmental communication (MA). *Accreditation:* ACEJMC (one or more programs are accredited). Part-time and evening/weekend programs available. *Degree requirements:* For master's, comprehensive exam, thesis or alternative. *Entrance requirements:* For master's, GRE, official transcripts from all current and previous colleges/universities except Marquette, three letters of recommendation, statement of academic and professional goals. Additional exam requirements/recommendations for international students: Required—TOEFL (minimum score 530 paper-based). Electronic applications accepted. *Faculty research:* Urban journalism, gender and communication, intercultural communication, religious communication.

Michigan State University, The Graduate School, College of Communication Arts and Sciences, Program in Health Communication, East Lansing, MI 48824. Offers MA. *Entrance requirements:* Additional exam requirements/recommendations for international students: Required—TOEFL. Electronic applications accepted. *Faculty research:* Mass communication and public health, health communication for diverse populations, descriptive and analytical epidemiology.

Ohio University, Graduate College, Scripps College of Communication, School of Communication Studies, Athens, OH 45701-2979. Offers health communication (PhD); organizational communication (MA); relating and organizing (PhD); rhetoric and public culture (PhD). Part-time programs available. Postbaccalaureate distance learning degree programs offered (minimal on-campus study). Terminal master's awarded for partial completion of doctoral program. *Degree requirements:* For master's, capstone; for doctorate, comprehensive exam, thesis/dissertation. *Entrance requirements:* For master's, GRE; for doctorate, GRE General Test, minimum GPA of 3.0. Additional exam requirements/recommendations for international students: Required—TOEFL (minimum score 550 paper-based; 80 iBT) or IELTS (minimum score 6.5). Electronic applications accepted. *Faculty research:* Rhetoric and public culture, relating and organizing, health communication.

Southern Illinois University Edwardsville, Graduate School, College of Arts and Sciences, Department of Applied Communication Studies, Program in Health Communication, Edwardsville, IL 62026. Offers MA. Part-time and evening/weekend programs available. *Students:* 4 full-time (all women), 8 part-time (7 women); includes 2 minority (1 Black or African American, non-Hispanic/Latino; 1 Hispanic/Latino). 5 applicants, 100% accepted. In 2014, 3 master's awarded. *Degree requirements:* For master's, comprehensive exam (for some programs), thesis (for some programs). *Entrance requirements:* Additional exam requirements/recommendations for international students: Required—TOEFL (minimum score 550 paper-based, 79 iBT),

IELTS (minimum score 6.5), Michigan Test of English Language Proficiency or PTE. *Application deadline:* For fall admission, 7/18 for domestic students, 6/1 for international students; for spring admission, 12/12 for domestic students, 10/1 for international students; for summer admission, 4/24 for domestic students, 3/1 for international students. Applications are processed on a rolling basis. Application fee: $30. Electronic applications accepted. *Expenses:* Tuition, state resident: full-time $5026. Tuition, nonresident: full-time $12,566. *International tuition:* $25,136 full-time. *Required fees:* $1682. Tuition and fees vary according to course load, campus/location and program. *Financial support:* Institutionally sponsored loans, scholarships/grants, and unspecified assistantships available. Financial award application deadline: 3/1; financial award applicants required to submit FAFSA. *Unit head:* Dr. Jocelyn DeGroot Brown, Program Director, 618-650-5828, E-mail: jocbrow@siue.edu. *Application contact:* Melissa K. Mace, Assistant Director of Graduate and International Recruitment, 618-650-2756, Fax: 618-650-3618, E-mail: mmace@siue.edu.

Stony Brook University, State University of New York, School of Journalism, Stony Brook, NY 11794. Offers health communication (Certificate); journalism (MS). *Faculty:* 12 full-time (4 women), 25 part-time/adjunct (10 women). *Students:* 8 full-time (5 women), 2 part-time (1 woman); includes 2 minority (1 Black or African American, non-Hispanic/Latino; 1 Hispanic/Latino). In 2014, 3 master's awarded. *Entrance requirements:* For master's, GRE. Additional exam requirements/recommendations for international students: Required—TOEFL (minimum score 600 paper-based; 100 iBT). *Application deadline:* For fall admission, 4/30 for domestic students; for spring admission, 10/1 for domestic students. *Expenses:* Tuition, state resident: full-time $10,370; part-time $432 per credit. Tuition, nonresident: full-time $20,190; part-time $841 per credit. *Required fees:* $1431. *Faculty research:* Journalism, newspaper journalism, literacy, media management, civic education, radio journalism. *Total annual research expenditures:* $395,717. *Unit head:* Prof. Howard Schneider, Dean, 631-632-7403, E-mail: howard.schneider@stonybrook.edu. *Application contact:* Maureen Robinson, Coordinator, 631-632-1073, E-mail: maureen.robinson@stonybrook.edu.
Website: https://journalism.cc.stonybrook.edu/

Stony Brook University, State University of New York, Stony Brook University Medical Center, Health Sciences Center, School of Medicine, Program in Public Health, Stony Brook, NY 11794. Offers community health (MPH); evaluation sciences (MPH); family violence (MPH); health communication (Certificate); health economics (MPH); population health (MPH); substance abuse (MPH). *Accreditation:* CEPH. *Students:* 46 full-time (35 women), 18 part-time (16 women); includes 29 minority (5 Black or African American, non-Hispanic/Latino; 14 Asian, non-Hispanic/Latino; 10 Hispanic/Latino), 4 international. Average age 29. 168 applicants, 46% accepted, 31 enrolled. In 2014, 23 master's awarded. *Entrance requirements:* For master's, GRE, 3 references, bachelor's degree from accredited college or university with minimum GPA of 3.0, essays, interview. Additional exam requirements/recommendations for international students: Required—TOEFL (minimum score 85 iBT). *Application deadline:* For fall admission, 6/1 for domestic students, 3/15 for international students. Application fee: $100. Electronic applications accepted. *Expenses:* Tuition, state resident: full-time $10,370; part-time $432 per credit. Tuition, nonresident: full-time $20,190; part-time $841 per credit. *Required fees:* $1431. *Financial support:* Fellowships available. *Faculty research:* Population health, health service research, health economics. *Unit head:* Dr. Lisa A. Benz Scott, Director, 631-444-9396, Fax: 631-444-3480, E-mail: lisa.benzscott@stonybrook.edu. *Application contact:* Senior Academic Coordinator, 631-444-9396, Fax: 631-444-3480, E-mail: joanmarie.maniaci@stonybrook.edu.
Website: http://publichealth.stonybrookmedicine.edu/

Tufts University, School of Medicine, Public Health and Professional Degree Programs, Boston, MA 02111. Offers biomedical sciences (MS); development and regulation of medicines and devices (MS, Certificate); health communication (MS); pain research, education and policy (MS, Certificate); physician assistant (MS); public health (MPH, Dr PH). MS programs offered jointly with Emerson College. *Accreditation:* CEPH (one or more programs are accredited). Part-time and evening/weekend programs available. *Faculty:* 83 full-time (34 women), 44 part-time/adjunct (18 women). *Students:* 387 full-time (221 women), 94 part-time (66 women); includes 162 minority (21 Black or African American, non-Hispanic/Latino; 1 American Indian or Alaska Native, non-Hispanic/Latino; 97 Asian, non-Hispanic/Latino; 24 Hispanic/Latino; 19 Two or more races, non-Hispanic/Latino), 28 international. Average age 27. 1,239 applicants, 57% accepted, 302 enrolled. In 2014, 181 degrees awarded. *Degree requirements:* For master's, thesis (for some programs); for doctorate, thesis/dissertation. *Entrance requirements:* For master's, GRE General Test, MCAT, GMAT. Additional exam requirements/recommendations for international students: Required—TOEFL (minimum score 100 iBT). *Application deadline:* For fall admission, 1/15 priority date for domestic students, 1/15 for international students; for spring admission, 10/25 priority date for domestic students, 10/25 for international students. Applications are processed on a rolling basis. Application fee: $70. Electronic applications accepted. *Expenses:* Expenses: $4,804 per credit, $494 in fees (for MPH, MS in health communication, MS/Certificate in pain research, education and policy, part-time Dr PH, and Certificate in development and regulation of medicines and devices); $41,456, $494 in fees (for MS in biomedical sciences); $37,222, $494 in fees (for full-time Dr PH); $24,753, $360 in fees (for MS in physician assistant). *Financial support:* In 2014–15, 14 students received support, including 1 fellowship (averaging $3,000 per year), 21 research assistantships (averaging $500 per year), 35 teaching assistantships (averaging $2,000 per year); Federal Work-Study and scholarships/grants also available. Support available to part-time students. Financial award application deadline: 2/4; financial award applicants required to submit FAFSA. *Faculty research:* Environmental and occupational health, nutrition, epidemiology, health communication, health services management and policy, biostatics, protein interaction, mRNA processing, vascular pathology. *Unit head:* Dr. Aviva Must, Dean, 617-636-0935, Fax: 617-636-0898, E-mail: aviva.must@tufts.edu. *Application contact:* Emily Keily, Director of Admissions, 617-636-0935, Fax: 617-636-0898, E-mail: med-phpd@tufts.edu.
Website: http://publichealth.tufts.edu

Tulane University, School of Public Health and Tropical Medicine, Department of Global community Health and Behavioral Sciences, New Orleans, LA 70118-5669. Offers community health sciences (MPH); global community health and behavioral sciences (Dr PH, PhD); health education and communication (MPH); maternal and child health (MPH); nutrition (MPH); JD/MPH; MD/MPH; MSW/MPH. Part-time programs available. *Degree requirements:* For doctorate, comprehensive exam, thesis/dissertation. *Entrance requirements:* For master's and doctorate, GRE General Test. Additional exam requirements/recommendations for international students: Required—TOEFL. Electronic applications accepted. *Expenses: Tuition:* Full-time $46,326; part-time $2574 per credit hour. *Required fees:* $1980; $44.50 per credit hour. $550 per term. Tuition and fees vary according to course load and program.

University of Florida, Graduate School, College of Health and Human Performance, Department of Health Education and Behavior, Gainesville, FL 32611. Offers health and human performance (PhD), including health behavior; health communication (Graduate Certificate); health education and behavior (MS). *Accreditation:* NCATE (one or more programs are accredited). Part-time programs available. *Faculty:* 10 full-time (3 women), 3 part-time/adjunct (2 women). *Students:* 38 full-time (33 women), 5 part-time (all women); includes 18 minority (6 Black or African American, non-Hispanic/Latino; 7 Asian, non-Hispanic/Latino; 5 Hispanic/Latino), 1 international. 20 applicants, 85% accepted, 16 enrolled. In 2014, 20 master's, 6 doctorates awarded. Terminal master's awarded for partial completion of doctoral program. *Degree requirements:* For master's, comprehensive exam, thesis (for some programs); for doctorate, comprehensive exam, thesis/dissertation. *Entrance requirements:* For master's and doctorate, GRE General Test score 293, minimum GPA of 3.0. Additional exam requirements/recommendations for international students: Required—TOEFL (minimum score 550 paper-based; 80 iBT), IELTS (minimum score 6). *Application deadline:* For fall admission, 1/1 priority date for domestic students, 1/1 for international students; for spring admission, 11/3 for domestic students, 10/1 for international students; for summer admission, 3/2 for domestic and international students. Applications are processed on a rolling basis. Application fee: $30. Electronic applications accepted. *Financial support:* In 2014–15, 1 fellowship, 4 research assistantships, 16 teaching assistantships were awarded; career-related internships or fieldwork and institutionally sponsored loans also available. Financial award application deadline: 2/1; financial award applicants required to submit FAFSA. *Faculty research:* Community-based participatory research; health disparities issues; health; cancer prevention and control; obesity-related issues; community capacity building; training community health workers; use of community based research principles to design, implement, an evaluate community health worker interventions; obesity; weight management; health literacy; health disparities (ethnic, gender, age, urban/rural); tailored health messages; entertainment education; COPD. *Total annual research expenditures:* $281,171. *Unit head:* Thomas Clanton, PhD, Professor and Interim Department Chair, 352-294-1712 Ext. 1281, Fax: 352-392-1909, E-mail: tclanton@hhp.ufl.edu. *Application contact:* Robert M Weiler, PhD, Professor and Graduate Coordinator, 352-294-1808, Fax: 352-392-1909, E-mail: rweiler@hhp.ufl.edu.
Website: http://heb.hhp.ufl.edu/

University of Florida, Graduate School, College of Journalism and Communications, Program in Mass Communication, Gainesville, FL 32611. Offers international/intercultural communication (MAMC); journalism (MAMC); mass communication (MAMC, PhD), including clinical translational science (MAMC); public relations (MAMC); science/health communication (MAMC); telecommunication (MAMC). *Entrance requirements:* For master's and doctorate, GRE General Test, minimum GPA of 3.0.

University of Houston, College of Liberal Arts and Social Sciences, School of Communication, Houston, TX 77204. Offers health communication (MA); mass communication studies (MA); public relations studies (MA); speech communication (MA). Part-time programs available. *Degree requirements:* For master's, comprehensive exam (for some programs), thesis (for some programs), 30-33 hours. *Entrance requirements:* For master's, GRE. Additional exam requirements/recommendations for international students: Required—TOEFL. Electronic applications accepted.

University of Missouri, Office of Research and Graduate Studies, School of Journalism, Columbia, MO 65211. Offers center for the digital globe (Certificate); European Union studies (Certificate); health communications (MA); interactive media (MA); journalism (PhD); media management (MA); strategic communication (MA). *Accreditation:* ACEJMC (one or more programs are accredited). Part-time programs available. *Faculty:* 75 full-time (38 women), 3 part-time/adjunct (1 woman). *Students:* 159 full-time (104 women), 88 part-time (54 women); includes 33 minority (8 Black or African American, non-Hispanic/Latino; 11 Asian, non-Hispanic/Latino; 11 Hispanic/Latino; 3 Two or more races, non-Hispanic/Latino), 57 international. Average age 29. 239 applicants, 55% accepted, 78 enrolled. In 2014, 73 master's, 8 doctorates awarded. Terminal master's awarded for partial completion of doctoral program. *Degree requirements:* For master's, thesis (for some programs); for doctorate, 2 foreign languages, thesis/dissertation. *Entrance requirements:* For master's and doctorate, GRE General Test, minimum GPA of 3.0. Additional exam requirements/recommendations for international students: Required—TOEFL (minimum score 600 paper-based; 100 iBT). *Application deadline:* For fall admission, 12/15 priority date for domestic and international students; for winter admission, 9/1 priority date for domestic and international students. Applications are processed on a rolling basis. Application fee: $55 ($75 for international students). Electronic applications accepted. *Financial support:* Fellowships with tuition reimbursements, research assistantships with tuition reimbursements, teaching assistantships with tuition reimbursements, career-related internships or fieldwork, institutionally sponsored loans, scholarships/grants, health care benefits, and unspecified assistantships available. Support available to part-time students. *Faculty research:* Strategic communication, convergence journalism, journalism studies, international programs, photojournalism, magazine journalism, radio-television journalism. *Unit head:* Dr. Esther Thorson, Associate Dean, 573-882-9590, E-mail: thorsone@missouri.edu. *Application contact:* Ginny Cowell, Administrative Assistant, 573-882-4852, E-mail: cowellvj@missouri.edu.
Website: http://www.journalism.missouri.edu/graduate/

The University of North Carolina at Charlotte, College of Liberal Arts and Sciences, Department of Communication Studies, Charlotte, NC 28223-0001. Offers communication studies (Graduate Certificate); health communication (MA); organizational communication (MA); public relations and international public relations (MA); rhetoric, media studies, and popular culture (MA). Part-time and evening/weekend programs available. *Faculty:* 15 full-time (8 women). *Students:* 11 full-time (8 women), 12 part-time (9 women); includes 3 minority (2 Black or African American, non-Hispanic/Latino; 1 Two or more races, non-Hispanic/Latino), 2 international. Average age 27. 49 applicants, 49% accepted, 11 enrolled. In 2014, 11 master's awarded. Terminal master's awarded for partial completion of doctoral program. *Degree requirements:* For master's, project, thesis, or comprehensive exam. *Entrance requirements:* For master's, GRE General Test, minimum GPA of 2.75 overall. Additional exam requirements/recommendations for international students: Required—TOEFL (minimum score 557 paper-based; 83 iBT). *Application deadline:* For fall admission, 3/1 for domestic and international students; for spring admission, 11/15 for domestic students, 10/1 for international students. Application fee: $75. Electronic applications accepted. *Expenses:* Tuition, state resident: full-time $4008. Tuition, nonresident: full-time $16,295. *Required fees:* $2755. Tuition and fees vary according to course load and program. *Financial support:* In 2014–15, 10 students received support, including 10 teaching assistantships (averaging $14,981 per year); career-related internships or fieldwork, institutionally sponsored loans, scholarships/grants, and unspecified assistantships also available. Support available to part-time students. Financial award application deadline: 4/1; financial award applicants required to submit FAFSA. *Faculty research:* Rhetorical approaches to analyzing public relations controversies, participant empowerment and engagement in community-based participatory action research, human factors constraining the management of knowledge in a large financial services organization, models of Internet governance, race and class politics of mediated sports. *Unit head:* Dr. Shawn Long, Chair, 704-687-0783, Fax: 704-687-6900, E-mail: shawn.long@uncc.edu. *Application contact:* Kathy B. Giddings, Director of Graduate Admissions, 704-687-5503, Fax: 704-687-1668, E-mail: gradadm@uncc.edu.
Website: http://gradcomm.uncc.edu/

University of Southern California, Graduate School, Annenberg School for Communication and Journalism, School of Communication, Program in Communication, Los Angeles, CA 90089. Offers culture and community (PhD); global and transnational

Health Communication

communication (PhD); groups, organizations and networks (PhD); health communication and social dynamics (PhD); information, political economy and entertainment (PhD); new media and technology (PhD); rhetoric, politics and public media (PhD). *Students:* 105 full-time (76 women); includes 829 minority (8 Black or African American, non-Hispanic/Latino; 810 Asian, non-Hispanic/Latino; 7 Hispanic/Latino; 4 Two or more races, non-Hispanic/Latino), 41 international. Average age 27. 229 applicants, 14% accepted, 19 enrolled. In 2014, 16 doctorates awarded. *Degree requirements:* For doctorate, thesis/dissertation. *Entrance requirements:* For doctorate, GRE General Test, resume or curriculum vitae, scholarly writing, 3 letters of recommendation, statement of purpose. Additional exam requirements/recommendations for international students: Required—TOEFL (minimum score 114 iBT) or IELTS; Recommended—TWE. *Application deadline:* For fall admission, 11/1 for domestic and international students. Application fee: $85. Electronic applications accepted. *Financial support:* In 2014–15, 18 students received support, including 18 fellowships with full tuition reimbursements available (averaging $74,000 per year); health care benefits and unspecified assistantships also available. Financial award application deadline: 11/1; financial award applicants required to submit FAFSA. *Faculty research:* Computer-mediated communication, public health campaigns, communication democracy and the public sphere, new communication technologies in organizations, communication and community. *Unit head:* Dr. Peter Monge, Director of the PhD Program, 213-740-0921, E-mail: monge@usc.edu. *Application contact:* Allyson Hill, Associate Dean for Admissions, 213-821-0770, Fax: 213-740-1933, E-mail: ascadm@usc.edu.
Website: http://www.annenberg.usc.edu

University of Southern California, Keck School of Medicine and Graduate School, Graduate Programs in Medicine, Department of Preventive Medicine, Master of Public Health Program, Los Angeles, CA 90032. Offers biostatistics-epidemiology (MPH); child and family health (MPH); environmental health (MPH); global health leadership (MPH); health communication (MPH); health education and promotion (MPH); public health policy (MPH). *Accreditation:* CEPH. Part-time and evening/weekend programs available. *Faculty:* 22 full-time (12 women), 3 part-time/adjunct (0 women). *Students:* 182 full-time (142 women), 35 part-time (25 women); includes 120 minority (19 Black or African American, non-Hispanic/Latino; 64 Asian, non-Hispanic/Latino; 37 Hispanic/Latino), 33 international. Average age 24. 236 applicants, 70% accepted, 71 enrolled. In 2014, 99 master's awarded. *Degree requirements:* For master's, practicum, final report, oral presentation. *Entrance requirements:* For master's, GRE General Test, MCAT, GMAT, minimum GPA of 3.0. Additional exam requirements/recommendations for international students: Required—TOEFL (minimum score 600 paper-based; 90 iBT). *Application deadline:* For fall admission, 6/1 priority date for domestic and international students; for spring admission, 10/1 priority date for domestic and international students; for summer admission, 3/1 for domestic and international students. Applications are processed on a rolling basis. Application fee: $85. Electronic applications accepted. *Expenses:* Expenses: $1,602 per unit. *Financial support:* Career-related internships or fieldwork, Federal Work-Study, institutionally sponsored loans, and scholarships/grants available. Support available to part-time students. Financial award application deadline: 5/4; financial award applicants required to submit CSS PROFILE or FAFSA. *Faculty*

research: Substance abuse prevention, cancer and heart disease prevention, mass media and health communication research, health promotion, treatment compliance. *Unit head:* Dr. Louise A. Rohrbach, Director, 323-442-8237, Fax: 323-442-8297, E-mail: rohrbac@usc.edu. *Application contact:* Valerie Burris, Admissions Counselor, 323-442-7257, Fax: 323-442-8297, E-mail: valeriem@usc.edu.
Website: http://mph.usc.edu/

Wayne State University, College of Fine, Performing and Communication Arts, Department of Communication, Detroit, MI 48202. Offers communication (PhD), including democratic participation and culture, identity and representation, media, society and culture, risk, crisis and conflict, wellness, worklife and relationships; communication and new media (Graduate Certificate); communication studies (MA); dispute resolution (MADR, Graduate Certificate); health communication (Graduate Certificate); journalism (MA); media arts (MA); media studies (MA); public relations and organizational communication (MA); JD/MADR. Doctoral programs admit for fall only. *Students:* 63 full-time (34 women), 82 part-time (63 women); includes 48 minority (40 Black or African American, non-Hispanic/Latino; 3 Asian, non-Hispanic/Latino; 3 Hispanic/Latino; 2 Two or more races, non-Hispanic/Latino), 13 international. Average age 35. 177 applicants, 40% accepted, 38 enrolled. In 2014, 33 master's, 4 doctorates, 9 other advanced degrees awarded. *Degree requirements:* For master's, thesis (for some programs), thesis or essay; for doctorate, thesis/dissertation. *Entrance requirements:* For master's, GRE (if undergraduate GPA less than 3.2), personal statement; BA or BS in communication or related field with minimum upper-division GPA of 3.2 and sample of academic writing (for MA); minimum upper-division undergraduate GPA of 3.0 and 3 letters of recommendation (for MADR); for doctorate, GRE, MA in communication or related field with minimum GPA of 3.5, three letters of recommendation; personal statement; sample of written scholarship; for Graduate Certificate, minimum upper-division GPA of 3.0, personal statement. Additional exam requirements/recommendations for international students: Required—TOEFL (minimum score 600 paper-based; 100 iBT), IELTS (minimum score 6.5), TWE (minimum score 6). *Application deadline:* For fall admission, 8/1 for domestic and international students; for winter admission, 11/1 for domestic and international students; for spring admission, 4/1 for domestic and international students. Application fee: $0. Electronic applications accepted. *Expenses:* Expenses: Contact institution. *Financial support:* In 2014–15, 48 students received support, including 3 fellowships with tuition reimbursements available (averaging $16,000 per year), 20 teaching assistantships with tuition reimbursements available (averaging $16,540 per year); research assistantships with tuition reimbursements available, scholarships/grants, and unspecified assistantships also available. Financial award application deadline: 3/31; financial award applicants required to submit FAFSA. *Faculty research:* Rhetorical theory and criticism; mass media theory and research; argumentation; organizational communication; risk and crisis communication; interpersonal, family, and health communication. *Unit head:* Dr. Lee Wilikins, Chair, 313-577-2943, E-mail: eh8899@wayne.edu. *Application contact:* Dr. Pradeep Sopory, Director of Graduate Studies, 313-577-2945, E-mail: psopory@wayne.edu.
Website: http://comm.wayne.edu/

Internet and Interactive Multimedia

Academy of Art University, Graduate Program, School of Multimedia Communications, San Francisco, CA 94105-3410. Offers MA. Part-time programs available. Postbaccalaureate distance learning degree programs offered. *Faculty:* 4 full-time (0 women), 14 part-time/adjunct (4 women). *Students:* 94 full-time (56 women), 40 part-time (24 women); includes 20 minority (10 Black or African American, non-Hispanic/Latino; 1 American Indian or Alaska Native, non-Hispanic/Latino; 2 Asian, non-Hispanic/Latino; 5 Hispanic/Latino; 1 Native Hawaiian or other Pacific Islander, non-Hispanic/Latino; 1 Two or more races, non-Hispanic/Latino), 94 international. Average age 28. 43 applicants, 100% accepted, 18 enrolled. In 2014, 81 master's awarded. *Degree requirements:* For master's, final review. *Entrance requirements:* For master's, statement of intent; resume; portfolio/reel; official college transcripts. *Application deadline:* Applications are processed on a rolling basis. Application fee: $100. Electronic applications accepted. *Expenses:* Tuition: Part-time $910 per unit. *Financial support:* Career-related internships or fieldwork and Federal Work-Study available. Support available to part-time students. Financial award application deadline: 8/10; financial award applicants required to submit FAFSA. *Unit head:* 800-544-ARTS, E-mail: info@academyart.edu. *Application contact:* 800-544-ARTS, E-mail: info@academyart.edu.
Website: http://www.academyart.edu/multimedia-communications-school/

Alfred University, Graduate School, New York State College of Ceramics, School of Art and Design, Alfred, NY 14802. Offers ceramic art (MFA); electronic integrated art (MFA); glass art (MFA); sculpture (MFA). *Accreditation:* NASAD. *Degree requirements:* For master's, thesis, exhibit. *Entrance requirements:* For master's, portfolio. Additional exam requirements/recommendations for international students: Required—TOEFL (minimum score 550 paper-based; 80 iBT), IELTS (minimum score 6). Electronic applications accepted. *Faculty research:* Ceramic art, sculpture, glass art, new media, time-based media.

Boston University, Metropolitan College, Department of Computer Science, Boston, MA 02215. Offers computer information systems (MS), including computer networks, database management and business intelligence, health informatics, IT project management, security, Web application development; computer networks (Certificate); digital forensics (Certificate); health informatics (Certificate); information technology project management (Certificate); software engineering in health care systems (Certificate); telecommunications (MS), including security. Part-time and evening/weekend programs available. Postbaccalaureate distance learning degree programs offered (no on-campus study). *Faculty:* 13 full-time (3 women), 43 part-time/adjunct (3 women). *Students:* 76 full-time (22 women), 768 part-time (188 women); includes 251 minority (68 Black or African American, non-Hispanic/Latino; 1 American Indian or Alaska Native, non-Hispanic/Latino; 117 Asian, non-Hispanic/Latino; 57 Hispanic/Latino; 2 Native Hawaiian or other Pacific Islander, non-Hispanic/Latino; 6 Two or more races, non-Hispanic/Latino), 130 international. Average age 34. 463 applicants, 79% accepted, 248 enrolled. In 2014, 222 master's, 25 other advanced degrees awarded. *Degree requirements:* For master's, thesis optional. *Entrance requirements:* For master's and Certificate, official transcripts from regionally-accredited bachelor's degree program, 3 letters of recommendation, professional resume, personal statement. Additional exam requirements/recommendations for international students: Required—TOEFL (minimum score 84 iBT), IELTS. *Application deadline:* For fall admission, 6/1 priority date for international students; for spring admission, 10/1 priority date for international students.

Applications are processed on a rolling basis. Application fee: $80. Electronic applications accepted. *Expenses:* Expenses: $800 per credit part-time; student services fees: $60 per semester; technology fee of $60 per credit (for online courses). *Financial support:* In 2014–15, 11 research assistantships (averaging $8,400 per year) were awarded; unspecified assistantships also available. Support available to part-time students. Financial award applicants required to submit FAFSA. *Faculty research:* Medical informatics, Web technologies, telecom and networks, security and forensics, software engineering, programming languages, multimedia and artificial intelligence (AI), information systems and IT project management. *Unit head:* Dr. Anatoly Temkin, Chairman, 617-353-2566, Fax: 617-353-2367, E-mail: csinfo@bu.edu. *Application contact:* Lesley Moreau, Academic Program Coordinator, 617-353-2566, Fax: 617-353-2367, E-mail: metcs@bu.edu.
Website: http://www.bu.edu/csmet/

Brooklyn College of the City University of New York, School of Visual, Media and Performing Arts, Program in Performance and Interactive Media Arts, Brooklyn, NY 11210-2889. Offers MFA. *Entrance requirements:* For master's, 2 letters of recommendation, resume, portfolio, interview. Additional exam requirements/recommendations for international students: Required—TOEFL (minimum score 550 paper-based; 61 iBT). Electronic applications accepted.

California State University, East Bay, Office of Academic Programs and Graduate Studies, College of Letters, Arts, and Social Sciences, Multimedia Program, Hayward, CA 94542-3000. Offers MA. Part-time programs available. *Degree requirements:* For master's, multimedia project or thesis. *Entrance requirements:* For master's, minimum GPA of 2.5; resume; 2 letters of recommendation; multimedia portfolio; statement of purpose. Additional exam requirements/recommendations for international students: Required—TOEFL (minimum score 550 paper-based). *Application deadline:* For fall admission, 6/30 for domestic and international students. Application fee: $55. Electronic applications accepted. *Expenses:* Tuition, state resident: full-time $7830; part-time $1302 per credit hour. Tuition, nonresident: full-time $16,368. *Required fees:* $327 per quarter. Tuition and fees vary according to course load and program. *Financial support:* Fellowships, teaching assistantships, Federal Work-Study, institutionally sponsored loans, and scholarships/grants available. Support available to part-time students. Financial award application deadline: 3/1; financial award applicants required to submit FAFSA. *Unit head:* Gwyan Rhabyt, Director, 510-885-3161. *Application contact:* Dr. Donna Wiley, Interim Associate Vice President for Academic Programs and Graduate Studies, 510-885-3716, Fax: 510-885-4777, E-mail: donna.wiley@csueastbay.edu.
Website: http://multimedia.csueastbay.edu.

Concordia University, School of Graduate Studies, Faculty of Engineering and Computer Science, Concordia Institute for Information Systems Engineering (CIISE), Montréal, QC H3G 1M8, Canada. Offers 3D graphics and game development (Certificate); information systems security (M Eng, MA Sc); quality systems engineering (M Eng, MA Sc); service engineering and network management (Certificate).

DePaul University, College of Computing and Digital Media, Chicago, IL 60604. Offers animation (MA, MFA); business information technology (MS); cinema (MFA); cinema production (MS); computational finance (MS); computer and information sciences (PhD); computer game development (MS); computer information and network security (MS); computer science (MS); e-commerce technology (MS); health informatics (MS); human-

computer interaction (MS); information systems (MS); information technology project management (MS); network engineering and management (MS); predictive analytics (MS); screenwriting (MFA); software engineering (MS); JD/MS. Part-time and evening/weekend programs available. Postbaccalaureate distance learning degree programs offered (no on-campus study). *Degree requirements:* For master's, thesis (for some programs); for doctorate, comprehensive exam, thesis/dissertation. *Entrance requirements:* For master's, GRE or GMAT (for MS in computational finance only), bachelor's degree, resume (MS in predictive analytics only), IT experience (MS in information technology project management only), portfolio review (all MFA programs and MA in animation); for doctorate, GRE, master's degree in computer science. Additional exam requirements/recommendations for international students: Required—TOEFL (minimum score 590 paper-based; 80 iBT), IELTS (minimum score 6.5), PTE (minimum score 53). Electronic applications accepted. *Expenses:* Contact institution. *Faculty research:* Data mining, computer science, human-computer interaction, security, animation and film.

Duquesne University, Graduate School of Liberal Arts, Department of Journalism and Media Arts, Pittsburgh, PA 15282-0001. Offers MS, Certificate. Part-time and evening/weekend programs available. *Faculty:* 10 full-time (2 women), 3 part-time/adjunct (0 women). *Students:* 36 full-time (19 women), 3 part-time (2 women); includes 7 minority (5 Black or African American, non-Hispanic/Latino; 1 American Indian or Alaska Native, non-Hispanic/Latino; 1 Hispanic/Latino), 4 international. Average age 25. 33 applicants, 67% accepted, 18 enrolled. In 2014, 16 master's awarded. *Entrance requirements:* For master's, GRE General Test, portfolio, writing sample. Additional exam requirements/recommendations for international students: Required—TOEFL. *Application deadline:* For fall admission, 8/1 for domestic students, 5/1 for international students; for spring admission, 11/1 for domestic students. Applications are processed on a rolling basis. Electronic applications accepted. *Expenses: Tuition:* Full-time $18,882; part-time $1049 per credit. *Required fees:* $1800; $100 per credit. Tuition and fees vary according to program. *Financial support:* In 2014–15, 5 teaching assistantships (averaging $8,600 per year) were awarded; Federal Work-Study also available. Support available to part-time students. Financial award application deadline: 5/1. *Unit head:* Dr. Michael Dillon, Director, 412-396-1311, E-mail: dillonm@duq.edu. *Application contact:* Linda Rendulic, Assistant to the Dean, 412-396-6400, E-mail: rendulic@duq.edu.
Website: http://www.duq.edu/academics/schools/liberal-arts/graduate-school/programs/media-arts-and-technology

Elon University, Program in Interactive Media, Elon, NC 27244-2010. Offers MA. *Faculty:* 16 full-time (5 women). *Students:* 32 full-time (20 women); includes 12 minority (9 Black or African American, non-Hispanic/Latino; 1 American Indian or Alaska Native, non-Hispanic/Latino; 2 Asian, non-Hispanic/Latino). Average age 25. 55 applicants, 82% accepted, 32 enrolled. In 2014, 40 master's awarded. *Degree requirements:* For master's, 6-hour capstone. *Entrance requirements:* For master's, GRE. Additional exam requirements/recommendations for international students: Required—TOEFL (minimum score 550 paper-based; 79 iBT). *Application deadline:* For fall admission, 5/1 priority date for domestic students. Applications are processed on a rolling basis. Application fee: $50. Electronic applications accepted. *Expenses:* Expenses: Contact institution. *Financial support:* Federal Work-Study and scholarships/grants available. Financial award application deadline: 3/15; financial award applicants required to submit FAFSA. *Faculty research:* Effects of service-learning (local and international) on the quality of learning for interactive media students, pedagogy for visual communication, impact of reviewer comments on consumer product and news perceptions, visual communication, social media in pedagogy. *Unit head:* Dr. Paul Parsons, Dean of the School of Communications, 336-278-5724, E-mail: pparsons@elon.edu. *Application contact:* Art Fadde, Director of Graduate Admissions, 800-334-8448 Ext. 3, Fax: 336-278-7699, E-mail: afadde@elon.edu.
Website: http://www.elon.edu/imedia

Excelsior College, School of Business and Technology, Albany, NY 12203-5159. Offers business administration (MBA); cybersecurity (MS); cybersecurity management (MBA, Graduate Certificate); health care management (MBA); human performance technology (MBA); leadership (MBA); social media management (MBA); technology management (MBA). Part-time and evening/weekend programs available. Postbaccalaureate distance learning degree programs offered (no on-campus study). *Faculty:* 34 part-time/adjunct (14 women). *Students:* 1,469 part-time (447 women); includes 605 minority (318 Black or African American, non-Hispanic/Latino; 7 American Indian or Alaska Native, non-Hispanic/Latino; 50 Asian, non-Hispanic/Latino; 165 Hispanic/Latino; 8 Native Hawaiian or other Pacific Islander, non-Hispanic/Latino; 57 Two or more races, non-Hispanic/Latino), 12 international. Average age 38. In 2014, 108 master's awarded. *Application deadline:* Applications are processed on a rolling basis. Application fee: $110. *Expenses: Tuition:* Part-time $620 per credit hour. *Financial support:* Scholarships/grants available. *Unit head:* Dr. Karl Lawrence, Dean, 888-647-2388. *Application contact:* Admissions, 888-647-2388 Ext. 133, Fax: 518-464-8777, E-mail: admissions@excelsior.edu.

Fairfield University, School of Engineering, Fairfield, CT 06824. Offers automated manufacturing (CAS); database management (CAS); electrical and computer engineering (MS); information security (CAS); management of technology (MS); mechanical engineering (MS); network technology (CAS); software engineering (MS); Web application development (CAS). Part-time and evening/weekend programs available. *Faculty:* 4 full-time (1 woman), 18 part-time/adjunct (5 women). *Students:* 193 full-time (50 women), 69 part-time (11 women); includes 20 minority (4 Black or African American, non-Hispanic/Latino; 6 Asian, non-Hispanic/Latino; 10 Hispanic/Latino), 199 international. Average age 27. 516 applicants, 64% accepted, 124 enrolled. In 2014, 38 master's awarded. *Degree requirements:* For master's, thesis, capstone course. *Entrance requirements:* For master's, interview, minimum GPA of 2.8, resume, 2 recommendations. Additional exam requirements/recommendations for international students: Required—TOEFL (minimum score 550 paper-based; 80 iBT) or IELTS (minimum score 6.5). *Application deadline:* For fall admission, 5/15 for international students; for spring admission, 10/15 for international students. Applications are processed on a rolling basis. Application fee: $60. Electronic applications accepted. *Expenses:* Expenses: $750 per credit hour. *Financial support:* In 2014–15, 30 students received support. Scholarships/grants and unspecified assistantships available. Financial award applicants required to submit FAFSA. *Faculty research:* Ocean dynamics modeling, thermo fluids, Web/mobile software applications, microwaves/electromagnetics, micro/nano manufacturing. *Unit head:* Dr. Bruce Berdanier, Dean, 203-254-4147, Fax: 203-254-4013, E-mail: bberdanier@fairfield.edu. *Application contact:* Marianne Gumpper, Director of Graduate and Continuing Studies Admission, 203-254-4184, Fax: 203-254-4073, E-mail: gradadmis@fairfield.edu.
Website: http://www.fairfield.edu/academics/schoolscollegescenters/schoolofengineering/graduateprograms/

Full Sail University, Education Media Design and Technology Master of Science Program - Online, Winter Park, FL 32792-7437. Offers MS. Postbaccalaureate distance learning degree programs offered (no on-campus study). *Entrance requirements:* Additional exam requirements/recommendations for international students: Required—TOEFL (minimum score 550 paper-based; 79 iBT).

Full Sail University, Game Design Master of Science Program - Campus, Winter Park, FL 32792-7437. Offers MS.

Full Sail University, Internet Marketing Master of Science Program - Online, Winter Park, FL 32792-7437. Offers MS. Postbaccalaureate distance learning degree programs offered.

Gannon University, School of Graduate Studies, College of Engineering and Business, School of Engineering and Computer Science, Program in Computer and Information Science, Erie, PA 16541-0001. Offers applied computer science (MSCIS); information systems (MSCIS); Web development (MSCIS). Part-time and evening/weekend programs available. *Degree requirements:* For master's, thesis (for some programs), directed research. *Entrance requirements:* For master's, GRE or GMAT, letters of recommendation, resume, transcripts, baccalaureate degree in computer and information science or related field, minimum GPA of 2.5. Additional exam requirements/recommendations for international students: Required—TOEFL (minimum score 79 iBT). Electronic applications accepted.

Georgetown University, Graduate School of Arts and Sciences, Program in Communication, Culture, and Technology, Washington, DC 20057. Offers MA. Part-time and evening/weekend programs available. *Degree requirements:* For master's, thesis (for some programs). *Entrance requirements:* For master's, GRE General Test, 3 letters of recommendation, writing sample. Additional exam requirements/recommendations for international students: Required—TOEFL (minimum score 600 paper-based). Electronic applications accepted.

Georgia Institute of Technology, Graduate Studies, Ivan Allen College of Liberal Arts, School of Literature, Media, and Communication, Atlanta, GA 30332-0001. Offers digital media (MS, PhD). Part-time programs available. *Students:* 33 full-time (11 women), 3 part-time (1 woman); includes 10 minority (4 Black or African American, non-Hispanic/Latino; 4 Asian, non-Hispanic/Latino; 2 Hispanic/Latino), 3 international. Average age 28. 68 applicants, 51% accepted, 8 enrolled. In 2014, 14 master's, 1 doctorate awarded. Terminal master's awarded for partial completion of doctoral program. *Degree requirements:* For master's, thesis optional, project studio, paid internship, responsible conduct of research training; for doctorate, comprehensive exam, thesis/dissertation, portfolio review, responsible conduct of research training. *Entrance requirements:* For master's, GRE, cumulative GPA of 3.0 or better (MS HCI), three letters of recommendation, transcripts from each college/university attended, design portfolio, statement of purpose; for doctorate, GRE, three letters of recommendation, transcripts from each college/university attended, design portfolio, statement of purpose. Additional exam requirements/recommendations for international students: Required—TOEFL (minimum score 650 paper-based; 114 iBT). *Application deadline:* For fall admission, 1/8 priority date for domestic and international students. Applications are processed on a rolling basis. Application fee: $75. Electronic applications accepted. *Expenses:* Tuition, state resident: full-time $12,344; part-time $515 per credit hour. Tuition, nonresident: full-time $27,600; part-time $1150 per credit hour. *Required fees:* $1196 per term. Part-time tuition and fees vary according to course load. *Financial support:* Fellowships, research assistantships, teaching assistantships, career-related internships or fieldwork, Federal Work-Study, institutionally sponsored loans, tuition waivers (partial), and unspecified assistantships available. Support available to part-time students. Financial award application deadline: 5/1. *Faculty research:* New media studies. *Total annual research expenditures:* $1.2 million. *Unit head:* Michael Nitsche, Director, 404-894-7000, E-mail: michael.nitsche@lmc.gatech.edu. *Application contact:* Michael Terrell, Graduate Coordinator, 404-385-7551, E-mail: michael.terrell@lmc.gatech.edu.
Website: http://lmc.gatech.edu

Indiana University–Purdue University Indianapolis, School of Informatics and Computing, Indianapolis, IN 46202. Offers bioinformatics (MS, PhD); health informatics (MS, PhD); human-computer interaction (MS, PhD); information and library science (MLS); media arts and science (MS). Part-time and evening/weekend programs available. *Faculty:* 3 full-time (0 women). *Students:* 199 full-time (101 women), 229 part-time (159 women); includes 49 minority (18 Black or African American, non-Hispanic/Latino; 15 Asian, non-Hispanic/Latino; 10 Hispanic/Latino; 6 Two or more races, non-Hispanic/Latino), 102 international. Average age 34. 268 applicants, 63% accepted, 133 enrolled. In 2014, 144 master's awarded. *Degree requirements:* For master's, thesis optional; for doctorate, thesis/dissertation. *Entrance requirements:* For master's, minimum undergraduate GPA of 3.0, graduate 3.2. Additional exam requirements/recommendations for international students: Required—TOEFL. *Application deadline:* For fall admission, 3/15 for domestic students; for spring admission, 10/15 for domestic students. Application fee: $60 ($65 for international students). Electronic applications accepted. *Financial support:* Fellowships, research assistantships, teaching assistantships, career-related internships or fieldwork, Federal Work-Study, institutionally sponsored loans, and scholarships/grants available. Support available to part-time students. *Unit head:* Dr. Robert B. Schnabel, Dean. *Application contact:* Elizabeth Bunge, Graduate Admissions Coordinator, 317-278-9200, E-mail: ebunge@iupui.edu.
Website: http://soic.iupui.edu/

Ithaca College, Roy H. Park School of Communications, Executive Master's in Communications Innovation Program, Ithaca, NY 14850. Offers MS. Part-time and evening/weekend programs available. Postbaccalaureate distance learning degree programs offered (minimal on-campus study). *Faculty:* 4 full-time (1 woman). *Students:* 11 part-time (7 women); includes 1 minority (Black or African American, non-Hispanic/Latino), 1 international. Average age 33. 11 applicants, 100% accepted, 5 enrolled. *Degree requirements:* For master's, project. *Entrance requirements:* For master's, minimum GPA of 3.0. Additional exam requirements/recommendations for international students: Required—TOEFL (minimum score 550 paper-based; 80 iBT). *Application deadline:* For fall admission, 2/15 priority date for domestic and international students; for spring admission, 12/1 priority date for domestic and international students. Applications are processed on a rolling basis. Application fee: $40. Electronic applications accepted. *Expenses:* Expenses: Contact institution. *Financial support:* In 2014–15, 6 students received support. Career-related internships or fieldwork, Federal Work-Study, scholarships/grants, and unspecified assistantships available. Support available to part-time students. Financial award application deadline: 3/1; financial award applicants required to submit CSS PROFILE or FAFSA. *Unit head:* Bob Regan, Director, E-mail: rregan@ithaca.edu. *Application contact:* Gerard Turbide, Director, Office of Admission, 607-274-3143, Fax: 607-274-1263, E-mail: gps@ithaca.edu.
Website: http://www.ithaca.edu/gradprograms/innovation/

Kutztown University of Pennsylvania, College of Visual and Performing Arts, Program in Communication Design, Kutztown, PA 19530-0730. Offers MFA. Part-time programs available. *Faculty:* 4 full-time (1 woman). *Students:* 4 full-time (3 women), 1 international. Average age 28. 5 applicants, 80% accepted, 3 enrolled. *Degree requirements:* For master's, thesis optional. *Entrance requirements:* Additional exam requirements/recommendations for international students: Required—TOEFL (minimum score 550 paper-based; 79 iBT). *Application deadline:* For fall admission, 3/1 priority date for domestic and international students. Applications are processed on a rolling basis. Application fee: $35. Electronic applications accepted. *Expenses: Tuition, area resident:* Part-time $454 per credit. Tuition, state resident: part-time $454 per credit. Tuition, nonresident: part-time $681 per credit. *Required fees:* $85 per credit. *Financial*

support: Career-related internships or fieldwork, Federal Work-Study, scholarships/grants, and unspecified assistantships available. Financial award application deadline: 3/1; financial award applicants required to submit FAFSA. *Unit head:* Todd McFeely, Chairperson, 610-683-4531, Fax: 610-683-4619, E-mail: mcfeely@kutztown.edu. *Application contact:* Kelly Hish, Admissions Clerk, 610-683-4200, Fax: 610-683-1393, E-mail: graduate@kutztown.edu.
Website: http://kucd.kutztown.edu/mfa.php

Lindenwood University, Graduate Programs, School of Communications, St. Charles, MO 63301-1695. Offers broadcast (MA); communications studies (MA); interactive media and Web design (MA); journalism (MA). Part-time and evening/weekend programs available. *Faculty:* 8 full-time (1 woman), 4 part-time/adjunct (1 woman). *Students:* 16 full-time (13 women), 2 part-time (0 women); includes 3 minority (2 Black or African American, non-Hispanic/Latino; 1 Asian, non-Hispanic/Latino), 4 international. Average age 27. 11 applicants, 55% accepted, 5 enrolled. In 2014, 4 master's awarded. *Degree requirements:* For master's, thesis (for some programs), minimum cumulative GPA of 3.0. *Entrance requirements:* For master's, GRE, minimum GPA of 3.0, resume. Additional exam requirements/recommendations for international students: Required—TOEFL (minimum score 550 paper-based; 80 iBT). *Application deadline:* For fall admission, 8/24 priority date for domestic and international students; for spring admission, 1/25 priority date for domestic and international students. Applications are processed on a rolling basis. Application fee: $30 ($100 for international students). Electronic applications accepted. *Expenses: Tuition:* Full-time $15,230; part-time $440 per credit hour. *Required fees:* $205 per semester. Tuition and fees vary according to course level, course load and degree level. *Financial support:* In 2014–15, 3 students received support. Career-related internships or fieldwork, Federal Work-Study, institutionally sponsored loans, scholarships/grants, tuition waivers (partial), and unspecified assistantships available. Financial award application deadline: 6/30; financial award applicants required to submit FAFSA. *Unit head:* Mike Wall, Dean, 636-949-4880, E-mail: mwall@lindenwood.edu. *Application contact:* Tyler Kostich, Director of Evening and Graduate Admissions, 636-949-4138, Fax: 636-949-4109, E-mail: adultadmissions@lindenwood.edu.
Website: http://www.lindenwood.edu/communications/

Lindenwood University–Belleville, Graduate Programs, Belleville, IL 62226. Offers business administration (MBA); communications (MA), including digital and multimedia, media management, promotions, training and development; counseling (MA); criminal justice administration (MS); education (MA); healthcare administration (MS); human resource management (MS); school administration (MA); teaching (MAT).

Lindsey Wilson College, Louisville Center for Design, Columbia, KY 42728. Offers interactive design (MA). Postbaccalaureate distance learning degree programs offered (no on-campus study).

Lynn University, Eugene M. and Christine E. Lynn College of International Communication, Boca Raton, FL 33431-5598. Offers communication and media - digital media (MS); communication and media - media studies and practice (MS); digital media (Certificate). Part-time and evening/weekend programs available. *Faculty:* 5 full-time (4 women). *Students:* 24 full-time (17 women), 9 part-time (7 women); includes 8 minority (4 Black or African American, non-Hispanic/Latino; 3 Hispanic/Latino; 1 Two or more races, non-Hispanic/Latino), 11 international. Average age 28. 19 applicants, 95% accepted, 12 enrolled. In 2014, 13 master's awarded. *Degree requirements:* For master's, project or thesis. *Entrance requirements:* For master's, resume, letter of recommendation, official transcripts, bachelor's degree from accredited institution, personal statement. Additional exam requirements/recommendations for international students: Required—TOEFL (minimum score 550 paper-based; 80 iBT), IELTS (minimum score 6.5). *Application deadline:* Applications are processed on a rolling basis. Application fee: $45. Electronic applications accepted. *Expenses: Tuition:* Full-time $16,200; part-time $675 per credit hour. Tuition and fees vary according to class time, course load, degree level and program. *Financial support:* In 2014–15, 12 students received support. Career-related internships or fieldwork, Federal Work-Study, institutionally sponsored loans, scholarships/grants, tuition waivers (partial), and unspecified assistantships available. Support available to part-time students. Financial award application deadline: 8/1; financial award applicants required to submit FAFSA. *Unit head:* Dr. David L. Jaffe, Dean, 561-237-7099, Fax: 561-237-7097, E-mail: djaffe@lynn.edu. *Application contact:* Steven Pruitt, Director of Graduate Admission, 561-237-7834, Fax: 561-237-7100, E-mail: admission@lynn.edu.
Website: http://www.lynn.edu/academics/colleges/international-communication

Marlboro College, Graduate and Professional Studies, Program in Teaching with Technology, Brattleboro, VT 05301. Offers MAT, Certificate. Part-time and evening/weekend programs available. Postbaccalaureate distance learning degree programs offered (minimal on-campus study). *Degree requirements:* For master's, 30 credits including capstone project. *Entrance requirements:* For master's, letter of intent, 2 letters of recommendation, transcripts. Electronic applications accepted. *Expenses: Tuition:* Full-time $45,900; part-time $765 per credit.

Mount Mary University, Graduate Division, Program in English, Milwaukee, WI 53222-4597. Offers creative writing (MA); writing for social media (MA). Part-time and evening/weekend programs available. *Faculty:* 2 full-time (both women), 3 part-time/adjunct (1 woman). *Students:* 16 full-time (14 women), 15 part-time (14 women); includes 7 minority (4 Black or African American, non-Hispanic/Latino; 3 Two or more races, non-Hispanic/Latino), 1 international. Average age 39. 10 applicants, 60% accepted, 5 enrolled. In 2014, 17 master's awarded. *Degree requirements:* For master's, comprehensive exam, thesis or alternative. *Entrance requirements:* For master's, minimum GPA of 2.75. Additional exam requirements/recommendations for international students: Required—TOEFL (minimum score 550 paper-based, 80 iBT) or IELTS (minimum score 6.5). *Application deadline:* For fall admission, 8/1 for domestic and international students; for spring admission, 12/1 for domestic and international students; for summer admission, 5/1 for domestic and international students. Applications are processed on a rolling basis. Application fee: $50 ($0 for international students). Electronic applications accepted. *Expenses:* Expenses: Contact institution. *Financial support:* In 2014–15, 1 student received support. Career-related internships or fieldwork and Federal Work-Study available. Support available to part-time students. Financial award application deadline: 5/1; financial award applicants required to submit FAFSA. *Unit head:* Ann Angel, Graduate Program Chair, 414-258-4810, E-mail: angela@mtmary.edu. *Application contact:* Dr. Douglas J. Mickelson, Dean for Graduate Education, 414-256-1252, Fax: 414-256-0167, E-mail: mickelsd@mtmary.edu.
Website: http://www.mtmary.edu/majors-programs/graduate/english/index.html

National University, Academic Affairs, School of Business and Management, La Jolla, CA 92037-1011. Offers business administration (MBA), including financial management, human resource management, integrated marketing communications, international business, management accounting, marketing, mobile marketing and social media, organizational leadership, professional golf management; global management (MGM). Part-time and evening/weekend programs available. Postbaccalaureate distance learning degree programs offered (no on-campus study). *Faculty:* 32 full-time (9 women), 74 part-time/adjunct (23 women). *Students:* 727 full-time (347 women), 280 part-time (145 women); includes 478 minority (136 Black or African American, non-Hispanic/Latino; 8 American Indian or Alaska Native, non-Hispanic/Latino; 119 Asian, non-Hispanic/Latino; 159 Hispanic/Latino; 14 Native Hawaiian or other Pacific Islander, non-Hispanic/Latino; 42 Two or more races, non-Hispanic/Latino), 164 international. Average age 33. In 2014, 784 master's awarded. *Degree requirements:* For master's, thesis (for some programs). *Entrance requirements:* For master's, interview, minimum GPA of 2.5. Additional exam requirements/recommendations for international students: Required—TOEFL (minimum score 550 paper-based; 79 iBT), IELTS (minimum score 6). *Application deadline:* Applications are processed on a rolling basis. Application fee: $60 ($65 for international students). Electronic applications accepted. *Expenses: Tuition:* Full-time $14,184; part-time $1773 per course. *Financial support:* Career-related internships or fieldwork, scholarships/grants, and tuition waivers (partial) available. Support available to part-time students. Financial award application deadline: 6/30; financial award applicants required to submit FAFSA. *Unit head:* School of Business and Management, 800-628-8648, Fax: 858-642-8719, E-mail: sobm@nu.edu. *Application contact:* Frank Rojas, Vice President for Enrollment Services, 800-628-8648, E-mail: advisor@nu.edu.
Website: http://www.nu.edu/OurPrograms/SchoolOfBusinessAndManagement.html

National University, Academic Affairs, School of Professional Studies, La Jolla, CA 92037-1011. Offers criminal justice (MCJ); digital cinema (MFA); digital journalism (MA); juvenile justice (MS); professional screen writing (MFA); public administration (MPA), including human resource management, organizational leadership, public finance. Part-time and evening/weekend programs available. Postbaccalaureate distance learning degree programs offered (no on-campus study). *Faculty:* 19 full-time (8 women), 28 part-time/adjunct (7 women). *Students:* 277 full-time (141 women), 140 part-time (80 women); includes 248 minority (102 Black or African American, non-Hispanic/Latino; 23 Asian, non-Hispanic/Latino; 102 Hispanic/Latino; 5 Native Hawaiian or other Pacific Islander, non-Hispanic/Latino; 16 Two or more races, non-Hispanic/Latino), 8 international. Average age 37. *Degree requirements:* For master's, thesis (for some programs). *Entrance requirements:* For master's, interview, minimum GPA of 2.5. Additional exam requirements/recommendations for international students: Required—TOEFL (minimum score 550 paper-based; 79 iBT), IELTS (minimum score 6). *Application deadline:* Applications are processed on a rolling basis. Application fee: $60 ($65 for international students). Electronic applications accepted. *Expenses: Tuition:* Full-time $14,184; part-time $1773 per course. *Financial support:* Career-related internships or fieldwork, institutionally sponsored loans, scholarships/grants, and tuition waivers (partial) available. Support available to part-time students. Financial award application deadline: 6/30; financial award applicants required to submit FAFSA. *Unit head:* School of Professional Studies, 800-628-8648, E-mail: sops@nu.edu. *Application contact:* Frank Rojas, Vice President for Enrollment Services, 800-628-8648, E-mail: advisor@nu.edu.
Website: http://www.nu.edu/OurPrograms/School-of-Professional-Studies.html

New Mexico Highlands University, Graduate Studies, College of Arts and Sciences, Department of Computer Sciences, Las Vegas, NM 87701. Offers media arts and computer science (MS), including computer science. *Faculty:* 4 full-time (0 women). *Students:* 6 full-time (2 women), 9 part-time (3 women); includes 3 minority (all Hispanic/Latino), 12 international. Average age 28. 3 applicants, 100% accepted, 3 enrolled. In 2014, 9 master's awarded. *Degree requirements:* For master's, comprehensive exam, thesis. *Entrance requirements:* For master's, minimum undergraduate GPA of 3.0. Additional exam requirements/recommendations for international students: Required—TOEFL (minimum score 540 paper-based). Application fee: $15. *Financial support:* In 2014–15, 7 students received support, including 8 research assistantships, 12 teaching assistantships; career-related internships or fieldwork, Federal Work-Study, institutionally sponsored loans, scholarships/grants, tuition waivers (full and partial), and unspecified assistantships also available. Support available to part-time students. Financial award application deadline: 3/1; financial award applicants required to submit FAFSA. *Faculty research:* Advanced digital compositing, photographic installations and exhibition design, pattern recognition, parallel and distributed computing, computer security education. *Unit head:* Dr. John Jeffries, Department Chair, 505-454-3480, E-mail: jjeffries@nmhu.edu. *Application contact:* Diane Trujillo, Administrative Assistant for Graduate Studies, 505-454-3266, Fax: 505-426-2117, E-mail: dtrujillo@nmhu.edu.
Website: http://www.nmhu.edu/current-students/graduate/arts-and-sciences/masters-in-computer-and-mathematical-sciences/

New York University, Polytechnic School of Engineering, Department of Technology, Culture and Society, New York, NY 10012-1019. Offers integrated digital media (MS, Graduate Certificate). Part-time and evening/weekend programs available. *Faculty:* 17 full-time (5 women), 33 part-time/adjunct (14 women). *Students:* 45 full-time (25 women), 7 part-time (4 women); includes 16 minority (5 Black or African American, non-Hispanic/Latino; 6 Asian, non-Hispanic/Latino; 5 Hispanic/Latino), 24 international. Average age 26. 78 applicants, 42% accepted, 27 enrolled. In 2014, 16 master's awarded. *Degree requirements:* For master's, comprehensive exam (for some programs), thesis (for some programs). *Entrance requirements:* Additional exam requirements/recommendations for international students: Required—TOEFL (minimum score 550 paper-based; 80 iBT); Recommended—IELTS (minimum score 6.5). *Application deadline:* For fall admission, 2/15 priority date for domestic and international students; for spring admission, 11/1 priority date for domestic and international students. Applications are processed on a rolling basis. Application fee: $75. Electronic applications accepted. *Financial support:* Fellowships, research assistantships, teaching assistantships, career-related internships or fieldwork, institutionally sponsored loans, scholarships/grants, and unspecified assistantships available. Support available to part-time students. Financial award applicants required to submit FAFSA. *Faculty research:* Trade magazine journalism, technical writing, financial reporting, medical and science reporting, industrial advertising and public relations. *Total annual research expenditures:* $106,957. *Unit head:* Prof. Kristen Day, Head, 718-260-3999, E-mail: kday@poly.edu. *Application contact:* Raymond Lutzky, Director, Graduate Enrollment Management, 718-637-5984, Fax: 718-260-3624, E-mail: rlutzky@poly.edu.

New York University, Polytechnic School of Engineering, Major in Integrated Digital Media, New York, NY 10012-1019. Offers MS, Graduate Certificate. Part-time programs available. *Students:* 45 full-time (25 women), 7 part-time (4 women); includes 16 minority (5 Black or African American, non-Hispanic/Latino; 6 Asian, non-Hispanic/Latino; 5 Hispanic/Latino), 24 international. Average age 26. 78 applicants, 42% accepted, 27 enrolled. In 2014, 16 master's awarded. *Entrance requirements:* Additional exam requirements/recommendations for international students: Required—TOEFL (minimum score 550 paper-based; 80 iBT); Recommended—IELTS (minimum score 6.5). *Application deadline:* For fall admission, 2/15 priority date for domestic and international students; for spring admission, 11/1 priority date for domestic and international students. Applications are processed on a rolling basis. Application fee: $75. Electronic applications accepted. *Financial support:* Institutionally sponsored loans, scholarships/grants, and unspecified assistantships available. Support available to part-time students. *Unit head:* Dr. R. Luke DuBois, Program Director, 646-997-0719, E-mail: dubois@nyu.edu. *Application contact:* Raymond Lutzky, Director, Graduate Enrollment Management, 718-637-5984, Fax: 718-260-3624, E-mail: rlutzky@poly.edu.
Website: http://engineering.nyu.edu/academics/programs/integrated-digital-media-ms

New York University, Tisch School of the Arts, Interactive Telecommunications Program, New York, NY 10012-1019. Offers MPS. *Faculty:* 9 full-time, 40 part-time/

adjunct. *Students:* 214 full-time (105 women), 9 part-time (6 women); includes 41 minority (5 Black or African American, non-Hispanic/Latino; 1 American Indian or Alaska Native, non-Hispanic/Latino; 22 Asian, non-Hispanic/Latino; 9 Hispanic/Latino; 4 Two or more races, non-Hispanic/Latino), 108 international. 361 applicants, 63% accepted, 117 enrolled. In 2014, 102 master's awarded. *Degree requirements:* For master's, thesis. *Entrance requirements:* Additional exam requirements/recommendations for international students: Required—TOEFL (minimum score 600 paper-based; 100 iBT) or IELTS (minimum score 6). *Application deadline:* For fall admission, 12/1 priority date for domestic and international students. Application fee: $60. Electronic applications accepted. *Financial support:* In 2014–15, 90 students received support, including 24 fellowships with full and partial tuition reimbursements available; career-related internships or fieldwork, Federal Work-Study, institutionally sponsored loans, scholarships/grants, and tuition waivers (partial) also available. Financial award application deadline: 2/15; financial award applicants required to submit FAFSA. *Faculty research:* Interactive narrative/storytelling, interactive media, Web technology, physical computing, ubiquitous computing. *Unit head:* Dan O'Sullivan, Chair, 212-998-1880, Fax: 212-998-1898, E-mail: itp.inquiries@nyu.edu. *Application contact:* Dan Sandford, Director of Graduate Admissions, 212-998-1918, Fax: 212-995-4060, E-mail: tisch.gradadmissions@nyu.edu.
Website: http://www.itp.tisch.nyu.edu/

North Central College, Graduate and Continuing Studies Programs, Department of Computer Science, Naperville, IL 60566-7063. Offers Web and Internet applications (MS). Part-time and evening/weekend programs available. *Faculty:* 4 full-time (2 women). *Students:* 3 full-time (0 women), 6 part-time (1 woman); includes 1 minority (Asian, non-Hispanic/Latino), 1 international. Average age 27. 15 applicants, 47% accepted, 2 enrolled. In 2014, 5 master's awarded. *Degree requirements:* For master's, thesis optional, project. *Entrance requirements:* For master's, interview. Additional exam requirements/recommendations for international students: Required—TOEFL (minimum score 550 paper-based; 80 iBT). *Application deadline:* For fall admission, 8/15 for domestic students, 7/15 for international students; for winter admission, 12/1 for domestic students, 11/1 for international students; for spring admission, 2/1 for domestic students, 12/1 for international students. Applications are processed on a rolling basis. Application fee: $25. Electronic applications accepted. Application fee is waived when completed online. *Expenses:* Expenses: Contact institution. *Financial support:* Scholarships/grants available. Support available to part-time students. Financial award applicants required to submit FAFSA. *Unit head:* Dr. Caroline St. Clair, Program Coordinator, Web and Internet Applications, 630-637-5171, Fax: 630-637-5172, E-mail: cstclair@noctrl.edu. *Application contact:* Wendy Kulpinski, Director of Graduate and Continuing Education Admission, 630-637-5808, Fax: 630-637-5819, E-mail: wekulpinski@noctrl.edu.

Northeastern University, College of Professional Studies, Boston, MA 02115-5096. Offers applied nutrition (MS); commerce and economic development (MS); corporate and organizational communication (MS); digital media (MPS); geographic information technology (MPS); global studies and international affairs (MS); homeland security (MA); human services (MS); informatics (MPS); leadership (MS); nonprofit management (MS); project management (MS); regulatory affairs for drugs, biologics, and medical devices (MS); regulatory affairs of food and food industries (MS); respiratory care leadership (MS); technical communication (MS). Postbaccalaureate distance learning degree programs offered (no on-campus study).

Northwestern University, School of Professional Studies, Program in Information Systems, Evanston, IL 60208. Offers analytics and business intelligence (MS); database and Internet technologies (MS); information systems (MS); information systems management (MS); information systems security (MS); medical informatics (MS); software project management and development (MS).

The Ohio State University, Graduate School, College of Arts and Sciences, Division of Arts and Humanities, Department of Design, Columbus, OH 43210. Offers design (MA); design research and development (MFA); digital animation and interactive media (MFA). *Accreditation:* NASAD. Part-time programs available. *Faculty:* 16. *Students:* 20 full-time (11 women), 3 part-time (2 women); includes 6 minority (2 Black or African American, non-Hispanic/Latino; 3 Asian, non-Hispanic/Latino; 1 Hispanic/Latino), 8 international. Average age 29. In 2014, 6 master's awarded. *Degree requirements:* For master's, project or thesis. *Entrance requirements:* For master's, GRE General Test (for all applicants with cumulative GPA below 3.0), portfolio. Additional exam requirements/recommendations for international students: Recommended—TOEFL (minimum score 550 paper-based; 79 iBT). *Application deadline:* For fall admission, 12/13 priority date for domestic students, 11/30 priority date for international students; for winter admission, 12/1 for domestic students, 11/1 for international students; for spring admission, 3/1 for domestic students, 2/1 for international students. Applications are processed on a rolling basis. Application fee: $60 ($70 for international students). Electronic applications accepted. *Financial support:* Fellowships with tuition reimbursements, research assistantships with tuition reimbursements, teaching assistantships with tuition reimbursements, career-related internships or fieldwork, Federal Work-Study, institutionally sponsored loans, and unspecified assistantships available. Support available to part-time students. Financial award application deadline: 5/1. *Unit head:* Mary Anne Beecher, PhD, Chair, 614-688-6746, E-mail: beecher.17@osu.edu. *Application contact:* Graduate and Professional Admissions, 614-292-9444, Fax: 614-292-3895, E-mail: gpadmissions@osu.edu.
Website: http://design.osu.edu/

Pace University, Seidenberg School of Computer Science and Information Systems, New York, NY 10038. Offers computer science (MS); computing science (DPS); information systems (MS); Internet technology (MS); large computing systems (Certificate); network administration (Certificate); security and information assurance (Certificate); software development and engineering (MS, Certificate); telecommunications (Certificate); telecommunications systems and networks (MS). Part-time and evening/weekend programs available. *Faculty:* 26 full-time (7 women), 7 part-time/adjunct (2 women). *Students:* 167 full-time (57 women), 324 part-time (90 women); includes 182 minority (83 Black or African American, non-Hispanic/Latino; 1 American Indian or Alaska Native, non-Hispanic/Latino; 46 Asian, non-Hispanic/Latino; 47 Hispanic/Latino; 5 Two or more races, non-Hispanic/Latino), 132 international. Average age 35. 441 applicants, 84% accepted, 157 enrolled. In 2014, 115 master's, 7 doctorates, 9 other advanced degrees awarded. *Degree requirements:* For master's, thesis or alternative, capstone course; for doctorate, comprehensive exam (for some programs), thesis/dissertation. *Entrance requirements:* For master's, GRE General Test. Additional exam requirements/recommendations for international students: Required—TOEFL. *Application deadline:* For fall admission, 8/1 priority date for domestic students, 6/1 for international students; for spring admission, 12/1 for domestic students, 10/1 for international students. Applications are processed on a rolling basis. Application fee: $70. Electronic applications accepted. *Expenses:* Expenses: Contact institution. *Financial support:* Research assistantships and career-related internships or fieldwork available. Support available to part-time students. Financial award applicants required to submit FAFSA. *Faculty research:* Computer security and forensics, cybersecurity, telehealth, mobile computing, distributed teams, robotics. *Total annual research expenditures:* $685,824. *Unit head:* Dr. Amar Gupta, Dean, Seidenberg School of

Computer Science and Information Systems, 914-773-3750, Fax: 914-773-3533, E-mail: agupta@pace.edu. *Application contact:* Susan Ford-Goldschein, Director of Graduate Admissions, 914-422-4283, Fax: 914-422-4287, E-mail: gradwp@pace.edu.
Website: http://www.pace.edu/seidenberg

Philadelphia University, School of Engineering and Textiles, Program in Interactive Design and Media, Philadelphia, PA 19144. Offers MS. *Entrance requirements:* For master's, portfolio. Additional exam requirements/recommendations for international students: Required—TOEFL (minimum score 550 paper-based; 79 iBT). Electronic applications accepted.

Pratt Institute, School of Art and Design, Program in Digital Arts, Brooklyn, NY 11205-3899. Offers MFA, MS/MFA. *Accreditation:* NASAD. *Faculty:* 5 full-time (1 woman), 27 part-time/adjunct (8 women). *Students:* 65 full-time (40 women), 6 part-time (4 women); includes 5 minority (3 Asian, non-Hispanic/Latino; 2 Hispanic/Latino), 59 international. Average age 25. 218 applicants, 20% accepted, 20 enrolled. In 2014, 27 master's awarded. *Degree requirements:* For master's, thesis, exhibit. *Entrance requirements:* For master's, portfolio or video tape, letters of recommendation. Additional exam requirements/recommendations for international students: Required—TOEFL (minimum score 550 paper-based; 79 iBT). *Application deadline:* For fall admission, 1/5 for domestic and international students; for spring admission, 10/1 for domestic and international students. Applications are processed on a rolling basis. Application fee: $50 ($90 for international students). Electronic applications accepted. *Financial support:* Career-related internships or fieldwork, Federal Work-Study, institutionally sponsored loans, scholarships/grants, health care benefits, and unspecified assistantships available. Support available to part-time students. Financial award application deadline: 2/1; financial award applicants required to submit FAFSA. *Unit head:* Peter Patchen, Chair, 718-636-3693, E-mail: ppatchen@pratt.edu. *Application contact:* Young Hah, Director of Graduate Admissions, 718-636-3683, Fax: 718-399-4242, E-mail: yhah@pratt.edu.
Website: https://www.pratt.edu/academics/school-of-art/graduate-school-of-art/digital-arts-grad/

See Display on page 153 and Close-Up on page 203.

Quinnipiac University, School of Communications, Program in Interactive Media, Hamden, CT 06518-1940. Offers interactive media (MS); production (MS); social media (MS). Part-time and evening/weekend programs available. Postbaccalaureate distance learning degree programs offered (no on-campus study). *Faculty:* 5 full-time (2 women), 12 part-time/adjunct (2 women). *Students:* 9 full-time (7 women), 96 part-time (67 women); includes 26 minority (14 Black or African American, non-Hispanic/Latino; 4 Asian, non-Hispanic/Latino; 7 Hispanic/Latino; 1 Two or more races, non-Hispanic/Latino). 24 applicants, 92% accepted, 18 enrolled. In 2014, 69 master's awarded. *Entrance requirements:* For master's, minimum GPA of 2.8, portfolio or writing sample. Additional exam requirements/recommendations for international students: Required—TOEFL (minimum score 575 paper-based; 90 iBT), IELTS (minimum score 6.5). *Application deadline:* For fall admission, 7/30 priority date for domestic students, 4/30 priority date for international students; for spring admission, 12/30 priority date for domestic students, 9/15 priority date for international students. Applications are processed on a rolling basis. Application fee: $45. Electronic applications accepted. *Expenses:* Tuition: Part-time $920 per credit. *Required fees:* $222 per semester. Tuition and fees vary according to course load and program. *Financial support:* Career-related internships or fieldwork and unspecified assistantships available. Support available to part-time students. Financial award application deadline: 6/1; financial award applicants required to submit FAFSA. *Faculty research:* User experience, social media, semiotics and communication, online distribution of news, Web-based interventions for research. *Unit head:* Phillip Simon, Director, 203-582-8274, E-mail: phillip.simon@quinnipiac.edu. *Application contact:* Quinnipiac University Online Admissions Office, 800-462-1944, E-mail: quonlineadmissions@quinnipiac.edu.
Website: https://quonline.quinnipiac.edu/online-programs/online-graduate-programs/ms-in-interactive-media/

Robert Morris University, Graduate Studies, School of Communications and Information Systems, Moon Township, PA 15108-1189. Offers communication and information systems (MS); competitive intelligence systems (MS); information security and assurance (MS); information systems and communications (D Sc); information systems management (MS); information technology project management (MS); Internet information systems (MS); organizational leadership (MS). Part-time and evening/weekend programs available. Postbaccalaureate distance learning degree programs offered (no on-campus study). *Faculty:* 25 full-time (10 women), 4 part-time/adjunct (0 women). *Students:* 320 part-time (117 women); includes 71 minority (38 Black or African American, non-Hispanic/Latino; 1 American Indian or Alaska Native, non-Hispanic/Latino; 6 Asian, non-Hispanic/Latino; 4 Hispanic/Latino; 22 Two or more races, non-Hispanic/Latino), 46 international. Average age 34. 267 applicants, 42% accepted, 85 enrolled. In 2014, 84 master's, 14 doctorates awarded. *Degree requirements:* For doctorate, thesis/dissertation. *Entrance requirements:* For doctorate, employer letter of endorsement, interview. Additional exam requirements/recommendations for international students: Required—TOEFL (minimum score 550 paper-based; 79 iBT). *Application deadline:* For fall admission, 7/1 priority date for domestic and international students; for spring admission, 11/1 priority date for domestic and international students. Applications are processed on a rolling basis. Application fee: $35. Electronic applications accepted. *Expenses:* Expenses: Contact institution. *Financial support:* Research assistantships with partial tuition reimbursements, institutionally sponsored loans, and unspecified assistantships available. Support available to part-time students. Financial award application deadline: 5/1. *Unit head:* Dr. Barbara J. Levine, Dean, 412-397-6460, Fax: 412-397-6469, E-mail: levine@rmu.edu. *Application contact:* 412-397-5200, Fax: 412-397-5915, E-mail: graduateadmissions@rmu.edu.
Website: http://www.rmu.edu/web/cms/schools/scis/Pages/default.aspx

Rochester Institute of Technology, Graduate Enrollment Services, College of Liberal Arts, School of Communication, Rochester, NY 14623-5604. Offers communication and digital media (Advanced Certificate); communication and media technologies (MS). Part-time programs available. Postbaccalaureate distance learning degree programs offered (no on-campus study). *Students:* 12 full-time (8 women), 17 part-time (all women); includes 1 minority (Hispanic/Latino), 23 international. Average age 26. 32 applicants, 59% accepted, 12 enrolled. In 2014, 16 master's awarded. *Degree requirements:* For master's, thesis or alternative, thesis or project. *Entrance requirements:* For master's, TOEFL, IELTS, or PTE for non-native English speakers, recommended minimum GPA of 3.0, writing sample. Additional exam requirements/recommendations for international students: Required—PTE (minimum score 58), TOEFL (minimum score 550 paper-based; 79 iBT) or IELTS (minimum score 6.5). *Application deadline:* For fall admission, 2/15 priority date for domestic and international students; for winter admission, 11/1 for domestic and international students; for spring admission, 12/15 priority date for domestic and international students. Applications are processed on a rolling basis. Application fee: $60. Electronic applications accepted. *Expenses:* Expenses: $1,673 per credit hour. *Financial support:* In 2014–15, 14 students received support. Research assistantships with partial tuition reimbursements available, teaching assistantships with partial tuition reimbursements available, career-related internships or fieldwork, Federal Work-Study, institutionally sponsored loans, scholarships/grants, and unspecified

assistantships available. Support available to part-time students. Financial award applicants required to submit FAFSA. *Faculty research:* The analysis of communication problems, the development of solutions, and the creation of messages as a result of their combined training in the social sciences, humanities, and applied technologies. *Unit head:* Dr. Patrick Scanlon, Director, 585-475-2449, Fax: 585-475-7732, E-mail: pmsgsl@rit.edu. *Application contact:* Diane Ellison, Associate Vice President, Graduate Enrollment Services, 585-475-2229, Fax: 585-475-7164, E-mail: gradinfo@rit.edu. Website: http://www.rit.edu/cla/communication/.

Rochester Institute of Technology, Graduate Enrollment Services, Golisano College of Computing and Information Sciences, Information Science and Technologies Department, Advanced Certificate Program in Web Development, Rochester, NY 14623-5608. Offers Advanced Certificate. Part-time and evening/weekend programs available. *Students:* 2 applicants. In 2014, 2 Advanced Certificates awarded. *Entrance requirements:* For degree, TOEFL, IELTS, or PTE for non-native English speakers, minimum GPA of 3.0. Additional exam requirements/recommendations for international students: Required—TOEFL (minimum score 570 paper-based; 88 iBT) or IELTS (minimum score 6.5). *Application deadline:* Applications are processed on a rolling basis. Application fee: $60. Electronic applications accepted. *Expenses:* Expenses: $1,673 per credit hour. *Financial support:* Federal Work-Study, institutionally sponsored loans, and scholarships/grants available. Support available to part-time students. Financial award applicants required to submit FAFSA. *Faculty research:* Interactive computing, fundamentals of interactive design, Web and multimedia programming, the impact of networked technologies in Web communications. *Unit head:* Dr. Peter Lutz, Graduate Program Director, 585-475-2700, Fax: 585-475-6584, E-mail: informaticsgrad@rit.edu. *Application contact:* Diane Ellison, Associate Vice President, Graduate Enrollment Services, 585-475-2229, Fax: 585-475-7164, E-mail: gradinfo@rit.edu. Website: http://www.ist.rit.edu/degrees/graduate/advanced-cert.php

Rocky Mountain College of Art + Design, Program in Education, Leadership + Emerging Technologies, Lakewood, CO 80214. Offers MA. Postbaccalaureate distance learning degree programs offered (no on-campus study).

Sacred Heart University, Graduate Programs, College of Arts and Sciences, Department of Computer Science, Fairfield, CT 06825-1000. Offers computer game design and development (Graduate Certificate); computer science and information technology (MS); computer science gaming (MS); cybersecurity (MS); database design (Graduate Certificate); information technology (Graduate Certificate); information technology and network security (Graduate Certificate); interactive multimedia (Graduate Certificate); Web development (Graduate Certificate). Part-time and evening/weekend programs available. *Faculty:* 6 full-time (2 women), 18 part-time/adjunct (5 women). *Students:* 266 full-time (100 women), 69 part-time (15 women); includes 30 minority (11 Black or African American, non-Hispanic/Latino; 7 Asian, non-Hispanic/Latino; 12 Hispanic/Latino; 265 international. Average age 26. 1,010 applicants, 56% accepted, 166 enrolled. In 2014, 50 master's awarded. *Degree requirements:* For master's, thesis or alternative. *Entrance requirements:* For master's, bachelor's degree, minimum GPA of 3.0. Additional exam requirements/recommendations for international students: Required—PTE; Recommended—TOEFL (minimum score 570 paper-based; 80 iBT), IELTS (minimum score 6.5). *Application deadline:* For fall admission, 5/15 for international students; for spring admission, 10/30 for international students. Applications are processed on a rolling basis. Application fee: $60. Electronic applications accepted. *Expenses:* Tuition: Full-time $24,559; part-time $649 per credit. *Financial support:* Unspecified assistantships available. Financial award applicants required to submit FAFSA. *Unit head:* Domenick Pinto, Academic Director and Chairperson, 203-371-7789, Fax: 203-371-0506, E-mail: pintod@sacredheart.edu. *Application contact:* Kathy Dilks, Executive Director of Graduate Admissions, 203-365-7619, Fax: 203-365-4732, E-mail: gradstudies@sacredheart.edu. Website: http://www.sacredheart.edu/academics/collegeofartssciences/academicdepartments/computerscienceinformationtechnology/graduatedegreesandcertificates/

Sam Houston State University, College of Fine Arts and Mass Communication, Department of Mass Communication, Huntsville, TX 77341. Offers digital media (MA). Part-time programs available. *Faculty:* 13 full-time (5 women), 1 (woman) part-time/adjunct. *Students:* 5 full-time (0 women), 3 part-time (2 women); includes 2 minority (1 Asian, non-Hispanic/Latino; 1 Two or more races, non-Hispanic/Latino), 1 international. Average age 36. 8 applicants, 100% accepted, 8 enrolled. *Degree requirements:* For master's, comprehensive exam (for some programs), thesis optional. *Entrance requirements:* For master's, GRE General Test, personal statement, digital media portfolio. *Application deadline:* For fall admission, 8/1 for domestic students, 6/25 for international students; for spring admission, 12/1 for domestic students, 11/12 for international students; for summer admission, 5/15 for domestic students, 4/9 for international students. Applications are processed on a rolling basis. Application fee: $45 ($75 for international students). Electronic applications accepted. *Expenses:* Tuition, state resident: full-time $2286; part-time $254 per credit hour. Tuition, nonresident: full-time $5544; part-time $616 per credit hour. *Required fees:* $440 per semester. Tuition and fees vary according to course load and campus/location. *Financial support:* In 2014–15, 5 research assistantships (averaging $4,739 per year) were awarded; career-related internships or fieldwork, Federal Work-Study, scholarships/grants, tuition waivers (partial), and unspecified assistantships also available. Support available to part-time students. Financial award application deadline: 3/15; financial award applicants required to submit FAFSA. *Unit head:* Dr. Jean Bodon, Chair, 936-294-4419, Fax: 936-294-1888, E-mail: bodon@shsu.edu. *Application contact:* Dr. Robin Johnson, Graduate Program Director, 936-294-1499, Fax: 936-294-1888, E-mail: robin.johnson@shsu.edu. Website: http://www.shsu.edu/academics/mass-communication/

San Diego State University, Graduate and Research Affairs, College of Professional Studies and Fine Arts, School of Communication, San Diego, CA 92182. Offers advertising and public relations (MA); critical-cultural studies (MA); interaction studies (MA); intercultural and international studies (MA); new media studies (MA); news and information studies (MA); telecommunications and media management (MA). *Degree requirements:* For master's, thesis. *Entrance requirements:* For master's, GRE General Test, 3 letters of recommendation. Additional exam requirements/recommendations for international students: Required—TOEFL. Electronic applications accepted.

Savannah College of Art and Design, Graduate School, Program in Interactive Design and Game Development, Savannah, GA 31402-3146. Offers MA, MFA, Graduate Certificate. Part-time programs available. Postbaccalaureate distance learning degree programs offered (no on-campus study). *Faculty:* 16 full-time (4 women), 5 part-time/adjunct (1 woman). *Students:* 53 full-time (17 women), 44 part-time (14 women); includes 14 minority (6 Black or African American, non-Hispanic/Latino; 6 Asian, non-Hispanic/Latino; 2 Hispanic/Latino), 37 international. Average age 28. 113 applicants, 42% accepted, 24 enrolled. In 2014, 22 master's awarded. *Degree requirements:* For master's, thesis (for some programs), final project (for MA); internship (for MFA). *Entrance requirements:* For master's, portfolio (in digital or multimedia format). Additional exam requirements/recommendations for international students: Required—TOEFL (minimum score 550 paper-based, 85 iBT), IELTS (minimum score 6.5), or

ACTFL. *Application deadline:* For fall admission, 4/1 for domestic and international students. Applications are processed on a rolling basis. Application fee: $40. Electronic applications accepted. *Expenses:* Tuition: Full-time $34,605; part-time $3845 per course. One-time fee: $500. Tuition and fees vary according to course load. *Financial support:* Fellowships, career-related internships or fieldwork, Federal Work-Study, and scholarships/grants available. Financial award application deadline: 4/1; financial award applicants required to submit FAFSA. *Unit head:* SuAnne Fu, Interim Chair. *Application contact:* Jenny Jaquillard, Executive Director of Admissions, Recruitment and Events, 912-525-5100, Fax: 912-525-5985, E-mail: admission@scad.edu. Website: http://www.scad.edu/academics/programs/interactive-design-and-game-development

School of Visual Arts, Graduate Programs, Interaction Design Department, New York, NY 10010-3994. Offers MFA. *Degree requirements:* For master's, thesis, 60 credits, residency of two academic years, thesis project. *Entrance requirements:* For master's, portfolio, statement of purpose, resume. Additional exam requirements/recommendations for international students: Required—TOEFL (minimum score 550 paper-based; 79 iBT). Electronic applications accepted. *Faculty research:* Data analysis and visualization, service design, interaction design.

School of Visual Arts, Graduate Programs, Program in Photography, Video and Related Media, New York, NY 10010-3994. Offers MFA. *Accreditation:* NASAD. *Degree requirements:* For master's, thesis, 60 credits and all course requirements; minimum GPA of 3.3; thesis project. *Entrance requirements:* For master's, portfolio (still images and/or videos) through SlideRoom. Additional exam requirements/recommendations for international students: Required—TOEFL (minimum score 550 paper-based; 79 iBT). Electronic applications accepted. *Faculty research:* Contemporary and responsible creative initiatives, including experimental, narrative or documentary video, installation and conceptual art, tableau and real-world-witness photography.

Southern New Hampshire University, School of Business, Manchester, NH 03106-1045. Offers accounting (MBA, MS, Graduate Certificate); accounting finance (MS); accounting/auditing (MS); accounting/forensic accounting (MS); accounting/taxation (MS); athletic administration (MBA, Graduate Certificate); business administration (IMBA, MBA, Certificate, Graduate Certificate), including accounting (Certificate), business administration (MBA), business information systems (Graduate Certificate), human resource management (Certificate); corporate social responsibility (MBA); entrepreneurship (MBA); finance (MBA, MS, Graduate Certificate); finance/corporate finance (MS); finance/investments and securities (MS); forensic accounting (MBA); healthcare informatics (MBA); healthcare management (MBA); human resource management (Graduate Certificate); information technology (MS, Graduate Certificate); information technology management (MBA); international business (Graduate Certificate); international business and information technology (Graduate Certificate); international finance (Graduate Certificate); international sport management (Graduate Certificate); justice studies (MBA); leadership of nonprofit organizations (Graduate Certificate); marketing (MBA, MS, Graduate Certificate); operations and project management (MS); operations and supply chain management (MBA, Graduate Certificate); organizational leadership (MS); project management (MBA, Graduate Certificate); Six Sigma (MBA); Six Sigma quality (Graduate Certificate); social media marketing (MBA); sport management (MBA, MS, Graduate Certificate); sustainability and environmental compliance (MBA); workplace conflict management (MBA); MBA/Certificate. *Accreditation:* ACBSP. Part-time and evening/weekend programs available. Postbaccalaureate distance learning degree programs offered (no on-campus study). Terminal master's awarded for partial completion of doctoral program. *Degree requirements:* For master's, one foreign language, comprehensive exam (for some programs), thesis or alternative. *Entrance requirements:* For master's, minimum GPA of 2.5. Additional exam requirements/recommendations for international students: Required—TOEFL (minimum score 500 paper-based). Electronic applications accepted.

Southern Polytechnic State University, School of Arts and Sciences, Department of English, Technical Communication, and Media Arts, Marietta, GA 30060-2896. Offers communications management (Postbaccalaureate Certificate); content development (Postbaccalaureate Certificate); information and instructional design (MSIID); information design and communication (MS); instructional design (Postbaccalaureate Certificate); technical communication (Graduate Certificate); visual communication and graphics (Postbaccalaureate Certificate). Part-time and evening/weekend programs available. Postbaccalaureate distance learning degree programs offered (no on-campus study). *Degree requirements:* For master's, thesis optional; for other advanced degree, thesis optional, 18 hours completed through thesis option (6 hours), internship option (6 hours) or advanced coursework option (6 hours). *Entrance requirements:* For master's, GRE, statement of purpose, writing sample, timed essay; for other advanced degree, writing sample, professional recommendations. Additional exam requirements/recommendations for international students: Required—TOEFL (minimum score 550 paper-based; 79 iBT), IELTS (minimum score 6.5). Electronic applications accepted. *Faculty research:* Usability, user-centered design, instructional design, information architecture, information design, content strategy.

Stevens Institute of Technology, Graduate School, Charles V. Schaefer Jr. School of Engineering, Department of Computer Science, Hoboken, NJ 07030. Offers computer graphics (Certificate); computer science (MS, PhD); computer systems (Certificate); database management systems (Certificate); distributed systems (Certificate); elements of computer science (Certificate); enterprise computing (Certificate); enterprise security and information assurance (Certificate); health informatics (Certificate); multimedia experience and management (Certificate); networks and systems administration (Certificate); security and privacy (Certificate); service oriented computing (Certificate); software design (Certificate); theoretical computer science (Certificate). Part-time and evening/weekend programs available. Terminal master's awarded for partial completion of doctoral program. *Degree requirements:* For master's, thesis optional; for doctorate, variable foreign language requirement, comprehensive exam, thesis/dissertation. *Entrance requirements:* For master's and doctorate, GRE, minimum GPA of 3.0. Additional exam requirements/recommendations for international students: Required—TOEFL. Electronic applications accepted. *Faculty research:* Semantics, reliability theory, programming language, cyber security.

Tennessee Technological University, College of Graduate Studies, College of Engineering, Department of Computer Science, Cookeville, TN 38505. Offers computer software and scientific applications (MS); Internet-based computing (MS). Part-time programs available. *Students:* 8 full-time (0 women), 6 part-time (1 woman), 6 international. 125 applicants, 10% accepted, 7 enrolled. In 2014, 8 master's awarded. *Degree requirements:* For master's, thesis or alternative. *Entrance requirements:* For master's, GRE. Additional exam requirements/recommendations for international students: Required—TOEFL (minimum score 550 paper-based; 79 iBT), IELTS (minimum score 5.5), PTE (minimum score 53), or TOEIC (Test of English as an International Communication). *Application deadline:* For fall admission, 8/1 for domestic students, 5/1 for international students; for spring admission, 12/1 for domestic students, 10/1 for international students. Applications are processed on a rolling basis. Application fee: $35 ($40 for international students). Electronic applications accepted. *Expenses:* Tuition, state resident: full-time $9783; part-time $492 per credit hour. Tuition, nonresident: full-time $24,071; part-time $1179 per credit hour. *Financial support:* In

2014–15, 4 research assistantships (averaging $7,500 per year), 3 teaching assistantships (averaging $7,500 per year) were awarded. Financial award application deadline: 4/1. *Unit head:* Dr. Doug Talbert, Interim Chairperson, 931-372-3691, Fax: 931-372-3686, E-mail: dtalbert@tntech.edu. *Application contact:* Shelia K. Kendrick, Coordinator of Graduate Studies, 931-372-3808, Fax: 931-372-3497, E-mail: skendrick@tntech.edu.

Touro College, Graduate School of Technology, New York, NY 10010. Offers information systems (MS); instructional technology (MS); Web and multimedia design (MA). *Students:* 73 full-time (32 women), 74 part-time (23 women); includes 83 minority (22 Black or African American, non-Hispanic/Latino; 1 American Indian or Alaska Native, non-Hispanic/Latino; 48 Asian, non-Hispanic/Latino; 10 Hispanic/Latino; 1 Native Hawaiian or other Pacific Islander, non-Hispanic/Latino; 1 Two or more races, non-Hispanic/Latino), 3 international. *Unit head:* Dr. Isaac Herskowitz, Dean of the Graduate School of Technology, 202-463-0400 Ext. 5231, E-mail: issac.herskowitz@touro.edu. Website: http://www.touro.edu/gst/

Towson University, Program in Applied Information Technology, Towson, MD 21252-0001. Offers applied information technology (MS, D Sc); database management systems (Postbaccalaureate Certificate); information security and assurance (Postbaccalaureate Certificate); information systems management (Postbaccalaureate Certificate); Internet applications development (Postbaccalaureate Certificate); networking technologies (Postbaccalaureate Certificate); software engineering (Postbaccalaureate Certificate). *Students:* 132 full-time (44 women), 219 part-time (73 women); includes 118 minority (71 Black or African American, non-Hispanic/Latino; 1 American Indian or Alaska Native, non-Hispanic/Latino; 23 Asian, non-Hispanic/Latino; 12 Hispanic/Latino; 2 Native Hawaiian or other Pacific Islander, non-Hispanic/Latino; 9 Two or more races, non-Hispanic/Latino), 85 international. *Entrance requirements:* For master's and Postbaccalaureate Certificate, bachelor's degree, minimum GPA of 3.0; for doctorate, master's degree in computer science, information systems, information technology, or closely-related areas; minimum GPA of 3.0; 2 letters of recommendation; resume. Additional exam requirements/recommendations for international students: Required—TOEFL. *Application deadline:* Applications are processed on a rolling basis. Application fee: $45. Electronic applications accepted. *Unit head:* Dr. Suranjan Chakraborty, Graduate Program Director, 410-704-4769, E-mail: schakraborty@towson.edu. *Application contact:* Alicia Arkell-Kleis, Information Contact, 410-704-6004, E-mail: grads@towson.edu. Website: http://grad.towson.edu/program/master/ait-ms/

Towson University, Program in Interactive Media Design, Towson, MD 21252-0001. Offers Postbaccalaureate Certificate. Postbaccalaureate distance learning degree programs offered (no on-campus study). *Students:* 1 (woman) full-time, 17 part-time (12 women); includes 7 minority (6 Black or African American, non-Hispanic/Latino; 1 Two or more races, non-Hispanic/Latino). *Entrance requirements:* For degree, minimum GPA of 3.0, resume, letter of intent; bachelor's degree in art or art education, or a bachelor's degree in another discipline with a minimum of 9 credits of course work in studio art and/or professional experience working in the field of art education or graphic design. *Application deadline:* Applications are processed on a rolling basis. Application fee: $45. Electronic applications accepted. *Unit head:* Prof. Bridget Sullivan, Graduate Program Director, 410-704-2802, E-mail: bsullivan@towson.edu. *Application contact:* Alicia Arkell-Kleis, Information Contact, 410-704-6004, E-mail: grads@towson.edu. Website: http://grad.towson.edu/program/certificate/iamd-pbc/index.asp

Universidad Autonoma de Guadalajara, Graduate Programs, Guadalajara, Mexico. Offers administrative law and justice (LL M); advertising and corporate communications (MA); architecture (M Arch); business (MBA); computational science (MCC); education (Ed M, Ed D); English-Spanish translation (MA); entrepreneurship and management (MBA); integrated management of digital animation (MA); international business (MIB); international corporate law (LL M); internet technologies (MS); manufacturing systems (MMS); occupational health (MS); philosophy (MA, PhD); power electronics (MS); quality systems (MQS); renewable energy (MS); social evaluation of projects (MBA); strategic market research (MBA); tax law (MA); teaching mathematics (MA).

University of Advancing Technology, Master of Science Program in Technology, Tempe, AZ 85283-1042. Offers advancing computer science (MS); emerging technologies (MS); game production and management (MS); information assurance (MS); technology leadership (MS). *Degree requirements:* For master's, project or thesis. *Entrance requirements:* Additional exam requirements/recommendations for international students: Required—TOEFL (minimum score 550 paper-based). Electronic applications accepted. *Faculty research:* Artificial intelligence, fractals, organizational management.

University of Denver, University College, Denver, CO 80208. Offers geographic information systems (Certificate); global affairs (Certificate), including translation studies, world history and culture; information and communications technology (MCIS), including geographic information systems, information systems security, project management (MCIS, Certificate), software design and programming, technology management, telecommunications technology, Web design and development; leadership and organizations (Certificate), including human capital in organizations, philanthropic leadership, project management (MCIS, Certificate), strategic innovation and change; organizational and professional communication (MPS), including alternative dispute resolution, organizational communication, organizational development and training, public relations and marketing; security management (MAS, Certificate), including emergency planning and response, information security (MAS), organizational security. Part-time and evening/weekend programs available. Postbaccalaureate distance learning degree programs offered (no on-campus study). *Faculty:* 8 full-time (4 women), 133 part-time/adjunct (46 women). *Students:* 54 full-time (21 women), 1,327 part-time (775 women); includes 272 minority (106 Black or African American, non-Hispanic/Latino; 6 American Indian or Alaska Native, non-Hispanic/Latino; 26 Asian, non-Hispanic/Latino; 108 Hispanic/Latino; 1 Native Hawaiian or other Pacific Islander, non-Hispanic/Latino; 25 Two or more races, non-Hispanic/Latino), 116 international. Average age 35. 768 applicants, 95% accepted, 620 enrolled. In 2014, 391 master's, 196 other advanced degrees awarded. *Degree requirements:* For master's, capstone project. *Entrance requirements:* For master's, transcripts, two letters of recommendation, personal statement, resume. Additional exam requirements/recommendations for international students: Required—TOEFL (minimum score 550 paper-based; 80 iBT). *Application deadline:* For fall admission, 6/21 priority date for domestic students, 5/1 priority date for international students; for winter admission, 9/14 priority date for domestic students, 9/19 priority date for international students; for spring admission, 1/11 for domestic students, 12/12 for international students; for summer admission, 3/29 priority date for domestic students, 3/6 priority date for international students. Applications are processed on a rolling basis. Application fee: $75. Electronic applications accepted. *Expenses:* Expenses: $959 per credit hour. *Financial support:* In 2014–15, 19 students received support. Applicants required to submit FAFSA. *Unit head:* Dr. Michael McGuire, Interim Dean, 303-871-3518, E-mail: mmcguire@du.edu. *Application contact:* Information Contact, 303-871-2291, E-mail: ucoladm@du.edu. Website: http://www.universitycollege.du.edu/

University of Georgia, Terry College of Business, Program in Internet Technology, Athens, GA 30602. Offers MIT. Postbaccalaureate distance learning degree programs offered (no on-campus study). *Degree requirements:* For master's, capstone project.

University of Miami, Graduate School, College of Arts and Sciences, Department of Art and Art History, Coral Gables, FL 33124. Offers art history (MA); ceramics/glass (MFA); graphic design/multimedia (MFA); painting (MFA); photography/digital imaging (MFA); printmaking (MFA); sculpture (MFA). Part-time programs available. *Degree requirements:* For master's, variable foreign language requirement, thesis, exhibit (MFA), comprehensive exam (MA). *Entrance requirements:* For master's, GRE General Test (MA), research paper (MA), slide portfolio (MFA). Additional exam requirements/recommendations for international students: Required—TOEFL. Electronic applications accepted. *Faculty research:* Installation art, public art.

University of Missouri, Office of Research and Graduate Studies, School of Journalism, Columbia, MO 65211. Offers center for the digital globe (Certificate); European Union studies (Certificate); health communications (MA); interactive media (MA); journalism (PhD); media management (MA); strategic communication (MA). *Accreditation:* ACEJMC (one or more programs are accredited). Part-time programs available. *Faculty:* 75 full-time (38 women), 3 part-time/adjunct (1 woman). *Students:* 159 full-time (104 women), 88 part-time (54 women); includes 33 minority (8 Black or African American, non-Hispanic/Latino; 11 Asian, non-Hispanic/Latino; 11 Hispanic/Latino; 3 Two or more races, non-Hispanic/Latino), 57 international. Average age 29. 239 applicants, 55% accepted, 78 enrolled. In 2014, 73 master's, 8 doctorates awarded. Terminal master's awarded for partial completion of doctoral program. *Degree requirements:* For master's, thesis (for some programs); for doctorate, 2 foreign languages, thesis/dissertation. *Entrance requirements:* For master's and doctorate, GRE General Test, minimum GPA of 3.0. Additional exam requirements/recommendations for international students: Required—TOEFL (minimum score 600 paper-based; 100 iBT). *Application deadline:* For fall admission, 12/15 priority date for domestic and international students; for winter admission, 9/1 priority date for domestic and international students. Applications are processed on a rolling basis. Application fee: $55 ($75 for international students). Electronic applications accepted. *Financial support:* Fellowships with tuition reimbursements, research assistantships with tuition reimbursements, teaching assistantships with tuition reimbursements, career-related internships or fieldwork, institutionally sponsored loans, scholarships/grants, health care benefits, and unspecified assistantships available. Support available to part-time students. *Faculty research:* Strategic communication, convergence journalism, journalism studies, international programs, photojournalism, magazine journalism, radio-television journalism. *Unit head:* Dr. Esther Thorson, Associate Dean, 573-882-9590, E-mail: thorsone@missouri.edu. *Application contact:* Ginny Cowell, Administrative Assistant, 573-882-4852, E-mail: cowellvj@missouri.edu. Website: http://www.journalism.missouri.edu/graduate/

The University of Montana, Graduate School, College of Visual and Performing Arts, School of Media Arts, Missoula, MT 59812-0002. Offers digital filmmaking (MFA); integrated digital media (MFA).

University of North Texas, Robert B. Toulouse School of Graduate Studies, Denton, TX 76203-5459. Offers accounting (MS); applied anthropology (MA, MS); applied behavior analysis (Certificate); applied geography (MA); applied technology and performance improvement (M Ed, MS); art education (MA); art history (MA); art museum education (Certificate); arts leadership (Certificate); audiology (Au D); behavior analysis (MS); behavioral science (PhD); biochemistry and molecular biology (MS); biology (MA, MS); biomedical engineering (MS); business analysis (MS); chemistry (MS); clinical health psychology (PhD); communication studies (MA, MS); computer engineering (MS); computer science (MS); counseling (M Ed, MS), including clinical mental health counseling (MS), college and university counseling, elementary school counseling, secondary school counseling; creative writing (MA); criminal justice (MS); curriculum and instruction (M Ed); decision sciences (MBA); design (MA, MFA), including fashion design (MFA), innovation studies, interior design (MFA); early childhood studies (MS); economics (MS); educational leadership (M Ed, Ed D); educational psychology (MS, PhD), including family studies (MS), gifted and talented (MS), human development (MS), learning and cognition (MS), research, measurement and evaluation (MS); electrical engineering (MS); emergency management (MPA); engineering technology (MS); English (MA); English as a second language (MA); environmental science (MS); finance (MBA, MS); financial management (MPA); French (MA); health services management (MBA); higher education (M Ed, Ed D); history (MA, MS); hospitality management (MS); human resources management (MPA); information science (MS); information systems (PhD); information technologies (MBA); interdisciplinary studies (MA, MS); international studies (MA); international sustainable tourism (MS); jazz studies (MM); journalism (MA, MJ, Graduate Certificate), including interactive and virtual digital communication (Graduate Certificate), narrative journalism (Graduate Certificate), public relations (Graduate Certificate); kinesiology (MS); linguistics (MA); local government management (MPA); logistics (PhD); logistics and supply chain management (MBA); long-term care, senior housing, and aging services (MA); management (PhD); marketing (MBA); mathematics (MA, MS); mechanical and energy engineering (MS, PhD); music (MA), including ethnomusicology, music theory, musicology, performance; music composition (PhD); music education (MM Ed, PhD); nonprofit management (MPA); operations and supply chain management (MBA); performance (MM, DMA); philosophy (MA); political science (MA); professional and technical communication (MA); radio, television and film (MA, MFA); rehabilitation counseling (Certificate); sociology (MA); Spanish (MA); special education (M Ed); speech-language pathology (MA); strategic management (MBA); studio art (MFA); teaching (M Ed); MBA/MS. Part-time and evening/weekend programs available. Postbaccalaureate distance learning degree programs offered. *Faculty:* 651 full-time (215 women), 233 part-time/adjunct (139 women). *Students:* 3,040 full-time (1,598 women), 3,401 part-time (2,097 women); includes 1,740 minority (533 Black or African American, non-Hispanic/Latino; 15 American Indian or Alaska Native, non-Hispanic/Latino; 286 Asian, non-Hispanic/Latino; 746 Hispanic/Latino; 3 Native Hawaiian or other Pacific Islander, non-Hispanic/Latino; 157 Two or more races, non-Hispanic/Latino), 1,145 international. Terminal master's awarded for partial completion of doctoral program. *Degree requirements:* For master's, variable foreign language requirement, comprehensive exam (for some programs), thesis (for some programs); for doctorate, variable foreign language requirement, comprehensive exam (for some programs), thesis/dissertation; for other advanced degree, variable foreign language requirement, comprehensive exam (for some programs). *Entrance requirements:* For master's and doctorate, GRE, GMAT. Additional exam requirements/recommendations for international students: Required—TOEFL (minimum score 550 paper-based; 79 iBT). *Application deadline:* For fall admission, 7/15 for domestic students, 3/15 for international students; for spring admission, 11/15 for domestic students, 9/15 for international students; for summer admission, 5/1 for domestic students. Applications are processed on a rolling basis. Application fee: $60. Electronic applications accepted. *Expenses:* Tuition, state resident: full-time $5450; part-time $3633 per year. Tuition, nonresident: full-time $11,966; part-time $7977 per year. *Required fees:* $1301; $398 per credit hour. $685 per semester. Tuition and fees vary according to program and reciprocity agreements. *Financial support:* Fellowships with partial tuition reimbursements, research assistantships with partial tuition reimbursements, teaching assistantships, career-related internships or fieldwork,

Federal Work-Study, institutionally sponsored loans, scholarships/grants, health care benefits, and library assistantships available. Support available to part-time students. Financial award applicants required to submit FAFSA. *Unit head:* Mark Wardell, Dean, 940-565-2383, E-mail: mark.wardell@unt.edu. *Application contact:* Toulouse School of Graduate Studies, 940-565-2383, Fax: 940-565-2141, E-mail: gradsch@unt.edu.
Website: http://tsgs.unt.edu/

University of Pennsylvania, School of Design, Department of Fine Arts, Philadelphia, PA 19104. Offers emerging design and research (Certificate); fine arts (MFA); time-based and interactive media (Certificate). *Faculty:* 5 full-time (2 women). *Students:* 36 full-time (22 women), 1 part-time (0 women); includes 14 minority (4 Black or African American, non-Hispanic/Latino; 1 American Indian or Alaska Native, non-Hispanic/Latino; 1 Asian, non-Hispanic/Latino; 4 Hispanic/Latino; 4 Two or more races, non-Hispanic/Latino), 4 international. 119 applicants, 41% accepted, 18 enrolled. In 2014, 19 master's, 13 other advanced degrees awarded. *Entrance requirements:* For master's, portfolio. Additional exam requirements/recommendations for international students: Required—TOEFL, IELTS. *Application deadline:* For fall admission, 1/14 priority date for domestic and international students. Application fee: $80. Electronic applications accepted. *Financial support:* Teaching assistantships and scholarships/grants available. Financial award application deadline: 2/15; financial award applicants required to submit FAFSA. *Faculty research:* Painting, sculpture, printmaking, animation, video, installation, sound, emerging design practices, photography. *Unit head:* Marilyn Jordan Taylor, Dean, 215-898-6520, E-mail: mjtaylor@design.upenn.edu. *Application contact:* Office of Admissions and Financial Aid, 215-898-6520, E-mail: admissions@design.upenn.edu.
Website: http://www.design.upenn.edu/fine-arts

University of San Francisco, College of Arts and Sciences, Web Science Program, San Francisco, CA 94117-1080. Offers MS. *Faculty:* 8 full-time (4 women). *Students:* 4 full-time (1 woman), 1 international. Average age 28. 1 applicant. In 2014, 4 master's awarded. *Application deadline:* For fall admission, 3/1 for domestic students; for spring admission, 10/15 for domestic students. *Expenses: Tuition:* Full-time $21,762; part-time $1209 per credit hour. Tuition and fees vary according to degree level, campus/location and program. *Financial support:* In 2014–15, 1 student received support. *Unit head:* Dr. Sophie Engle, Graduate Director, 415-422-6530, Fax: 415-422-5800. *Application contact:* Mark Landerghini, Graduate Adviser, 415-422-5101, E-mail: asgraduate@usfca.edu.
Website: http://www1.cs.usfca.edu/grad/msws/

University of Southern California, Graduate School, School of Cinematic Arts, Interactive Media Division, Los Angeles, CA 90089. Offers interactive media (MFA); media arts and practice (PhD). *Degree requirements:* For master's, thesis, thesis project. *Entrance requirements:* Additional exam requirements/recommendations for international students: Required—TOEFL (minimum score 600 paper-based; 100 iBT). Electronic applications accepted. *Expenses:* Contact institution. *Faculty research:* Immersive media, mobile media, stereoscopic, game design and development, serious games and games for health and learning, experiments in game play.

University of Southern California, Graduate School, Viterbi School of Engineering, Department of Computer Science, Los Angeles, CA 90089. Offers computer networks (MS); computer science (MS, PhD); computer security (MS); game development (MS); high performance computing and simulations (MS); human language technology (MS); intelligent robotics (MS); multimedia and creative technologies (MS); software engineering (MS). Part-time and evening/weekend programs available. Postbaccalaureate distance learning degree programs offered (no on-campus study). *Entrance requirements:* For master's and doctorate, GRE General Test. Additional exam requirements/recommendations for international students: Required—TOEFL. Electronic applications accepted. *Faculty research:* Databases, computer graphics and computer vision, software engineering, networks and security, robotics, multimedia and virtual reality.

University of Southern California, Graduate School, Viterbi School of Engineering, Ming Hsieh Department of Electrical Engineering, Los Angeles, CA 90089. Offers computer engineering (MS, PhD); electric power (MS); electrical engineering (MS, PhD, Engr); engineering technology commercialization (Graduate Certificate); multimedia and creative technologies (MS); telecommunications (MS); VLSI design (MS); wireless health technology (MS). Part-time programs available. Postbaccalaureate distance learning degree programs offered (no on-campus study). Terminal master's awarded for partial completion of doctoral program. *Degree requirements:* For master's, thesis optional; for doctorate, thesis/dissertation. *Entrance requirements:* For master's and doctorate, GRE General Test. Additional exam requirements/recommendations for international students: Recommended—TOEFL. Electronic applications accepted. *Faculty research:* Communications, computer engineering and networks, control systems, integrated circuits and systems, electromagnetics and energy conversion, micro electro-mechanical systems and nanotechnology, photonics and quantum electronics, plasma research, signal and image processing.

University of South Florida, College of Arts and Sciences, School of Mass Communications, Tampa, FL 33620-9951. Offers media studies (MA), including media studies; multimedia journalism studies (MA); strategic communication management (MA). Part-time and evening/weekend programs available. *Faculty:* 10 full-time (3 women). *Students:* 17 full-time (13 women), 17 part-time (6 women); includes 5 minority (2 Black or African American, non-Hispanic/Latino; 1 Asian, non-Hispanic/Latino; 2 Hispanic/Latino), 7 international. Average age 29. 40 applicants, 65% accepted, 14 enrolled. In 2014, 15 master's awarded. *Degree requirements:* For master's, comprehensive exam, thesis optional. *Entrance requirements:* For master's, GRE General Test (minimum score of 153 verbal and 144 quantitative preferred), minimum GPA of 3.0 in last 60 hours of course work, three letters of recommendation, letter of intent, resume. Additional exam requirements/recommendations for international students: Required—TOEFL (minimum score 550 paper-based; 79 iBT) or IELTS (minimum score 6.5). *Application deadline:* For fall admission, 2/15 for domestic students, 1/2 for international students; for spring admission, 10/15 for domestic students, 6/1 for international students. Application fee: $30. Electronic applications accepted. *Financial support:* In 2014–15, 9 students received support, including 9 teaching assistantships with tuition reimbursements available (averaging $10,513 per year); unspecified assistantships also available. Financial award application deadline: 2/28. *Faculty research:* First Amendment analysis, civic journalism, public opinion, media ethics, media effects research in sports public relations, public relations management, advertisement, telecommunications. *Total annual research expenditures:* $52,955. *Unit head:* Dr. Jim Andrews, Interim Director and Associate Professor, 813-974-2108, Fax: 813-974-2592, E-mail: jimandrews@usf.edu. *Application contact:* Dr. Michael Mitrook, Assistant Professor, 813-974-8890, Fax: 813-974-2592, E-mail: mmitrook@.usf.edu.
Website: http://masscom.usf.edu/grad/

University of South Florida, Innovative Education, Tampa, FL 33620-9951. *Unit head:* Kathy Barnes, Interdisciplinary Programs Coordinator, 813-974-8031, Fax: 813-974-7061, E-mail: barnesk@usf.edu. *Application contact:* Karen Tylinski, Metro Initiatives, 813-974-9943, Fax: 813-974-7061, E-mail: ktylinsk@usf.edu.
Website: http://www.usf.edu/innovative-education/

The University of Texas at Dallas, School of Arts, Technology, and Emerging Communication, Richardson, TX 75080. Offers arts and technology (MA, MFA, PhD); emerging media and communication (MA). *Faculty:* 20 full-time (7 women), 1 part-time/adjunct (0 women). *Students:* 124 full-time (53 women), 70 part-time (30 women); includes 60 minority (16 Black or African American, non-Hispanic/Latino; 1 American Indian or Alaska Native, non-Hispanic/Latino; 11 Asian, non-Hispanic/Latino; 21 Hispanic/Latino; 11 Two or more races, non-Hispanic/Latino), 20 international. Average age 33. 127 applicants, 43% accepted, 37 enrolled. In 2014, 45 master's awarded. *Degree requirements:* For master's and doctorate, portfolio, thesis, or capstone project. *Entrance requirements:* For master's and doctorate, minimum GPA of 3.3 in upper-level coursework in field. Additional exam requirements/recommendations for international students: Required—TOEFL (minimum score 550 paper-based). *Application deadline:* For fall admission, 7/15 for domestic students, 5/1 priority date for international students; for spring admission, 11/15 for domestic students, 9/1 priority date for international students. Applications are processed on a rolling basis. Application fee: $50 ($100 for international students). Electronic applications accepted. *Expenses:* Tuition, state resident: full-time $11,940; part-time $663 per credit. Tuition, nonresident: full-time $22,282; part-time $1238 per credit. *Financial support:* In 2014–15, 103 students received support, including 8 research assistantships with partial tuition reimbursements available (averaging $12,192 per year), 20 teaching assistantships with partial tuition reimbursements available (averaging $10,350 per year); career-related internships or fieldwork, Federal Work-Study, institutionally sponsored loans, scholarships/grants, and unspecified assistantships also available. Support available to part-time students. Financial award application deadline: 4/30; financial award applicants required to submit FAFSA. *Faculty research:* Motion capture, conversational/interactive robotics, simulations as modern teaching tools. *Total annual research expenditures:* $910,856. *Unit head:* Dr. Frank Dufour, Director, PhD Arts and Technology Program, 972-883-4129, E-mail: frank.dufour@utdallas.edu. *Application contact:* Roger Malina, Associate Director, Arts and Technology, 972-883-2023, E-mail: roger.malina@utdallas.edu.
Website: http://www.utdallas.edu/atec/

University of the Sacred Heart, Graduate Programs, Department of Communication, San Juan, PR 00914-0383. Offers contemporary culture and media (MA); digital journalism (MA, Certificate); editing for media (MA, Certificate); public relations (MA, Certificate); publicity (MA, Certificate); scriptwriting (MA, Certificate). Part-time and evening/weekend programs available. *Degree requirements:* For master's, thesis.

University of the Sacred Heart, Graduate Programs, Department of Education, San Juan, PR 00914-0383. Offers early childhood education (M Ed); information technology and multimedia (Certificate); instruction systems and education technology (M Ed), including English, information technology and multimedia, instructional design, mathematics, Spanish. Part-time and evening/weekend programs available. *Degree requirements:* For master's, thesis. *Entrance requirements:* For master's, EXADEP, minimum undergraduate GPA of 2.75, interview.

University of Utah, Graduate School, College of Engineering, Program in Entertainment Arts and Engineering, Salt Lake City, UT 84112. Offers game art (MEAE); game engineering (MEAE); game production (MEAE); technical art (MEAE). Part-time programs available. *Faculty:* 6 full-time, 8 part-time/adjunct (2 women). *Students:* 94 full-time (12 women), 1 (woman) part-time; includes 7 minority (2 Asian, non-Hispanic/Latino; 2 Hispanic/Latino; 1 Native Hawaiian or other Pacific Islander, non-Hispanic/Latino; 2 Two or more races, non-Hispanic/Latino), 38 international. Average age 27. 160 applicants, 50% accepted, 60 enrolled. In 2014, 23 master's awarded. *Entrance requirements:* For master's, GRE (recommended for game engineering and game production track applicants). Additional exam requirements/recommendations for international students: Required—TOEFL (minimum score 550 paper-based; 80 iBT), IELTS (minimum score 6.5). *Application deadline:* For fall admission, 2/28 for domestic and international students. Application fee: $65. Electronic applications accepted. *Expenses:* Expenses: Contact institution. *Financial support:* In 2014–15, 50 research assistantships with partial tuition reimbursements (averaging $6,750 per year), 53 teaching assistantships with partial tuition reimbursements (averaging $6,750 per year) were awarded; career-related internships or fieldwork, health care benefits, tuition waivers (partial), and unspecified assistantships also available. *Faculty research:* Games for health, simulation. *Unit head:* Corrinne Lewis, Academic Program Manager, 801-585-6491, E-mail: corrinne.lewis@utah.edu. *Application contact:* Hallie Huber, Program Coordinator/Academic Advisor, 801-581-5460, E-mail: hallie.huber@utah.edu.
Website: http://eae.utah.edu/

Virginia Commonwealth University, Graduate School, School of the Arts, Department of Graphic Design, Richmond, VA 23284-9005. Offers design/visual communications (MFA); interior environment (MFA). *Accreditation:* NASAD. *Degree requirements:* For master's, thesis, exhibition. *Entrance requirements:* For master's, portfolio. Additional exam requirements/recommendations for international students: Required—TOEFL (minimum score 600 paper-based; 100 iBT). Electronic applications accepted. *Faculty research:* Conducting visual or theoretical research, and in investigating the intersection of function and expression in design problem solving.

Virginia Polytechnic Institute and State University, Graduate School, College of Architecture and Urban Studies, Blacksburg, VA 24061. Offers architecture (MS Arch); architecture and design research (PhD); building/construction science and management (MS); creative technologies (MFA); environmental design and planning (PhD); landscape architecture (MLA); planning, governance, and globalization (PhD); public administration (MPA); public administration/public affairs (PhD, Certificate); public and international affairs (MPIA); urban and regional planning (MURP); MS/MA. *Accreditation:* ASLA (one or more programs are accredited). *Faculty:* 133 full-time (54 women), 2 part-time/adjunct (1 woman). *Students:* 316 full-time (166 women), 237 part-time (108 women); includes 104 minority (46 Black or African American, non-Hispanic/Latino; 1 American Indian or Alaska Native, non-Hispanic/Latino; 20 Asian, non-Hispanic/Latino; 21 Hispanic/Latino; 16 Two or more races, non-Hispanic/Latino), 108 international. Average age 32. 609 applicants, 50% accepted, 108 enrolled. In 2014, 155 master's, 29 doctorates awarded. *Degree requirements:* For master's, comprehensive exam (for some programs), thesis (for some programs); for doctorate, comprehensive exam (for some programs), thesis/dissertation (for some programs). *Entrance requirements:* For master's and doctorate, GRE/GMAT (may vary by department). Additional exam requirements/recommendations for international students: Required—TOEFL (minimum score 550 paper-based). *Application deadline:* For fall admission, 8/1 for domestic students, 4/1 for international students; for spring admission, 1/1 for domestic students, 9/1 for international students. Applications are processed on a rolling basis. Application fee: $75. Electronic applications accepted. *Expenses:* Tuition, state resident: full-time $11,656; part-time $647.50 per credit hour. Tuition, nonresident: full-time $23,351; part-time $1297.25 per credit hour. *Required fees:* $2533; $465.75 per semester. Tuition and fees vary according to course load, campus/location and program. *Financial support:* In 2014–15, 13 research assistantships with full tuition reimbursements (averaging $20,302 per year), 44 teaching assistantships with full tuition reimbursements (averaging $19,484 per year) were awarded. Financial award application deadline: 3/1; financial award applicants required to submit FAFSA. *Total annual research expenditures:* $3.2 million. *Unit head:* Dr. A. J. Davis, Dean, 540-231-6416, Fax: 540-231-6332, E-mail: davisa@vt.edu. *Application contact:* Christine

Mattsson-Coon, Executive Assistant, 540-231-6416, Fax: 540-231-6332, E-mail: cmattsso@vt.edu. Website: http://www.caus.vt.edu/

Western Illinois University, School of Graduate Studies, College of Education and Human Services, Department of Instructional Design and Technology, Macomb, IL 61455-1390. Offers distance learning (Certificate); educational technology specialist (Certificate); graphic applications (Certificate); instructional design and technology (MS); multimedia (Certificate); technology integration in education (Certificate); training development (Certificate). Part-time programs available. Postbaccalaureate distance learning degree programs offered (no on-campus study). *Students:* 18 full-time (12 women), 59 part-time (32 women); includes 16 minority (11 Black or African American, non-Hispanic/Latino; 1 American Indian or Alaska Native, non-Hispanic/Latino; 3 Asian, non-Hispanic/Latino; 1 Hispanic/Latino), 5 international. Average age 35. 20 applicants, 85% accepted, 12 enrolled. In 2014, 25 master's, 11 other advanced degrees awarded. *Degree requirements:* For master's, thesis or alternative. *Entrance requirements:* Additional exam requirements/recommendations for international students: Required—TOEFL (minimum score 550 paper-based; 80 iBT). *Application deadline:* Applications are processed on a rolling basis. Application fee: $30. Electronic applications accepted. *Financial support:* In 2014–15, 11 students received support, including 5 research assistantships with full tuition reimbursements available (averaging $7,544 per year), 7 teaching assistantships with full tuition reimbursements available (averaging $8,688 per year). Financial award applicants required to submit FAFSA. *Unit head:* Dr. Hoyet Hemphill, Chairperson, 309-298-1952. *Application contact:* Dr. Nancy Parsons, Associate Provost and Director of Graduate Studies, 309-298-1806, Fax: 309-298-2345, E-mail: grad-office@wiu.edu.
Website: http://wiu.edu/idt

Wilmington University, College of Technology, New Castle, DE 19720-6491. Offers geographic information systems (MS); information assurance (MS); information systems technologies (MS); Internet/Web design (MS); management and management information systems (MS). Part-time and evening/weekend programs available. *Faculty:* 5 full-time (2 women), 53 part-time/adjunct (14 women). *Students:* 674 full-time (197 women), 131 part-time (55 women); includes 48 minority (35 Black or African American, non-Hispanic/Latino; 3 American Indian or Alaska Native, non-Hispanic/Latino; 6 Asian, non-Hispanic/Latino; 4 Hispanic/Latino), 708 international. Average age 27. 679 applicants, 100% accepted, 423 enrolled. In 2014, 102 master's awarded. *Entrance requirements:* Additional exam requirements/recommendations for international students: Required—TOEFL (minimum score 500 paper-based). *Application deadline:* Applications are processed on a rolling basis. Application fee: $35. Electronic applications accepted. *Unit head:* Dr. Edward L. Guthrie, Dean, 302-356-6870. *Application contact:* Laura Morris, Director of Admissions, 877-967-5464, E-mail: infocenter@wilmu.edu.
Website: http://www.wilmu.edu/technology/

Worcester Polytechnic Institute, Graduate Studies and Research, Program in Interactive Media and Game Development, Worcester, MA 01609-2280. Offers MS. Part-time and evening/weekend programs available. *Students:* 21 full-time (6 women), 1 part-time (0 women); includes 2 minority (1 Black or African American, non-Hispanic/Latino; 1 Asian, non-Hispanic/Latino), 14 international. 55 applicants, 73% accepted, 10 enrolled. In 2014, 2 master's awarded. *Entrance requirements:* For master's, GRE (recommended), 3 letters of recommendation, statement of purpose, portfolio (recommended). Additional exam requirements/recommendations for international students: Required—TOEFL (minimum score 563 paper-based; 84 iBT), IELTS (minimum score 7). *Application deadline:* For fall admission, 1/1 for domestic and international students; for spring admission, 10/1 for domestic and international students. Applications are processed on a rolling basis. Electronic applications accepted. *Financial support:* Research assistantships and teaching assistantships available. *Unit head:* Charles Rich, Graduate Coordinator, 508-831-4977, Fax: 508-831-5776, E-mail: rich@wpi.edu. *Application contact:* Tricia Desmarais, Administrative Assistant, 508-831-6470, Fax: 508-831-5776, E-mail: td@wpi.edu.
Website: http://www.wpi.edu/academics/imgd

Journalism

American University, School of Communication, Program in Journalism and Public Affairs, Washington, DC 20016-8001. Offers interactive journalism (MA). *Accreditation:* ACEJMC; NASPAA. *Faculty:* 13 full-time (5 women), 4 part-time/adjunct (all women). *Students:* 28 full-time (22 women). 137 applicants, 55% accepted, 30 enrolled. In 2014, 28 master's awarded. *Degree requirements:* For master's, comprehensive exam, thesis or alternative. *Entrance requirements:* Additional exam requirements/recommendations for international students: Required—TOEFL (minimum score 600 paper-based; 100 iBT), IELTS (minimum score 7). *Application deadline:* For fall admission, 2/1 priority date for domestic students, 4/1 priority date for international students. Applications are processed on a rolling basis. Application fee: $55. Electronic applications accepted. *Financial support:* In 2014–15, 3 fellowships with full and partial tuition reimbursements (averaging $27,000 per year), 14 research assistantships with partial tuition reimbursements (averaging $7,000 per year), 3 teaching assistantships with partial tuition reimbursements (averaging $7,000 per year) were awarded; career-related internships or fieldwork, Federal Work-Study, institutionally sponsored loans, scholarships/grants, tuition waivers (partial), and unspecified assistantships also available. Financial award application deadline: 2/1; financial award applicants required to submit FAFSA. *Faculty research:* Government and media effects of journalistic practices and policies, race and gender and the media, investigative reporting, computer-assisted reporting. *Unit head:* Prof. John Watson, Division Director, 202-885-2083, Fax: 202-885-2099, E-mail: jwatson@american.edu. *Application contact:* Sharmeen Ahsan-Bracciale, Graduate Admissions Office, 202-885-2040, Fax: 202-885-2019, E-mail: sharmeen@american.edu.
Website: http://www.american.edu/soc/journalism/index.cfm

American University, School of Communication, Weekend Programs in Communication, Washington, DC 20016-8001. Offers interactive journalism (MA); media entrepreneurship (MA); producing for film and video (MA); strategic communication (MA). *Accreditation:* ACEJMC. Part-time and evening/weekend programs available. *Degree requirements:* For master's, comprehensive exam, thesis or alternative. *Entrance requirements:* Additional exam requirements/recommendations for international students: Required—TOEFL (minimum score 600 paper-based; 100 iBT). *Application deadline:* For fall admission, 8/1 for domestic students. Applications are processed on a rolling basis. Application fee: $50. Electronic applications accepted. *Financial support:* Fellowships and institutionally sponsored loans available. Financial award applicants required to submit FAFSA. *Unit head:* Prof. Rose Ann Robertson, Associate Dean for Academic Administration, 202-885-2002, E-mail: rrobert@american.edu. *Application contact:* Sharmeen Ahsan-Bracciale, Director of Graduate Services, 202-885-3940, Fax: 202-885-2019, E-mail: sharmeen@american.edu.
Website: http://american.edu/soc/admissions/weekend.cfm

The American University in Cairo, School of Global Affairs and Public Policy, Department of Journalism and Mass Communication, Cairo, Egypt. Offers journalism and mass communication (MA); television and digital journalism (MA). Part-time programs available. *Degree requirements:* For master's, thesis (for some programs). *Entrance requirements:* For master's, English entrance exam, GMAT. Electronic applications accepted. Tuition and fees vary according to course load and program. *Faculty research:* Mass media and national development/censorship, intercultural photo communication, comparative journalism/television.

Angelo State University, College of Graduate Studies, College of Arts and Sciences, Department of Communication, Mass Media and Theatre, San Angelo, TX 76909. Offers communication systems management (MA). Part-time and evening/weekend programs available. *Degree requirements:* For master's, comprehensive exam, thesis optional. *Entrance requirements:* Additional exam requirements/recommendations for international students: Required—TOEFL or IELTS. Electronic applications accepted.

Arizona State University at the Tempe campus, Walter Cronkite School of Journalism and Mass Communication, Phoenix, AZ 85004. Offers journalism and mass communication (PhD); mass communication (MMC). *Accreditation:* ACEJMC. Terminal master's awarded for partial completion of doctoral program. *Degree requirements:* For master's, 9-hour professional capstone experience; interactive Program of Study (iPOS) submitted before completing 50 percent of required credit hours; for doctorate, comprehensive exam, thesis/dissertation, interactive Program of Study (iPOS) submitted before completing 50 percent of required credit hours. *Entrance requirements:* For master's and doctorate, GRE, minimum GPA of 3.0 or equivalent in last 2 years of work leading to bachelor's degree. Additional exam requirements/recommendations for international students: Required—TOEFL, IELTS, or PTE. Electronic applications accepted. *Expenses:* Contact institution.

Arkansas State University, Graduate School, College of Media and Communication, Department of Media, State University, AR 72467. Offers MSMC. Part-time programs available. *Faculty:* 10 full-time (5 women). *Students:* 14 full-time (8 women), 22 part-time (6 women); includes 11 minority (9 Black or African American, non-Hispanic/Latino; 1 Asian, non-Hispanic/Latino; 1 Hispanic/Latino), 15 international. Average age 27. 27 applicants, 67% accepted, 13 enrolled. In 2014, 14 master's awarded. *Degree requirements:* For master's, comprehensive exam, thesis or alternative. *Entrance requirements:* For master's, GRE General Test or MAT, appropriate bachelor's degree, letters of reference, educational experience, professional experience, official transcripts, immunization records. Additional exam requirements/recommendations for international students: Required—TOEFL (minimum score 550 paper-based; 79 iBT), IELTS (minimum score 6), PTE (minimum score 56). *Application deadline:* For fall admission, 7/1 for domestic and international students; for spring admission, 11/15 for domestic students, 11/14 for international students. Applications are processed on a rolling basis. Application fee: $30 ($40 for international students). Electronic applications accepted. *Expenses:* Tuition, state resident: full-time $4392; part-time $244 per credit hour. Tuition, nonresident: full-time $8784; part-time $488 per credit hour. *International tuition:* $9484 full-time. *Required fees:* $1134; $63 per credit hour. $25 per term. Tuition and fees vary according to course load and program. *Financial support:* In 2014–15, 2 students received support. Career-related internships or fieldwork, scholarships/grants, and unspecified assistantships available. Financial award application deadline: 7/1; financial award applicants required to submit FAFSA. *Unit head:* Dr. Osabuohien Amienyi, Chair, 870-972-3070, Fax: 870-972-2997, E-mail: osami@astate.edu. *Application contact:* Vickey Ring, Graduate Admissions Coordinator, 870-972-3029, Fax: 870-972-3857, E-mail: vickeyring@astate.edu.
Website: http://www.astate.edu/college/communications/about

Arkansas Tech University, College of Arts and Humanities, Russellville, AR 72801. Offers English (M Ed, MA); history (MA); liberal arts (MLA); multi-media journalism (MA); psychology (MS); teaching English as a second language (MA). Part-time programs available. *Students:* 70 full-time (39 women), 105 part-time (72 women); includes 20 minority (3 Black or African American, non-Hispanic/Latino; 2 American Indian or Alaska Native, non-Hispanic/Latino; 1 Asian, non-Hispanic/Latino; 10 Hispanic/Latino; 4 Two or more races, non-Hispanic/Latino), 51 international. Average age 30. In 2014, 63 master's awarded. *Degree requirements:* For master's, comprehensive exam (for some programs), thesis (for some programs), project. *Entrance requirements:* For master's, GRE General Test or GMAT. Additional exam requirements/recommendations for international students: Required—TOEFL (minimum score 550 paper-based; 79 iBT), IELTS (minimum score 6). *Application deadline:* For fall admission, 3/1 priority date for domestic students, 5/1 priority date for international students; for spring admission, 10/1 priority date for domestic and international students. Applications are processed on a rolling basis. Application fee: $25 ($75 for international students). Electronic applications accepted. *Expenses:* Tuition, state resident: full-time $6264; part-time $261 per credit hour. Tuition, nonresident: full-time $12,528; part-time $522 per credit hour. *Required fees:* $423 per semester. Tuition and fees vary according to course load. *Financial support:* In 2014–15, research assistantships with full tuition reimbursements (averaging $4,800 per year), teaching assistantships with full tuition reimbursements (averaging $4,800 per year) were awarded; career-related internships or fieldwork, Federal Work-Study, scholarships/grants, health care benefits, and unspecified assistantships also available. Support available to part-time students. Financial award application deadline: 4/15; financial award applicants required to submit FAFSA. *Unit head:* Dr. Jeffrey Woods, Dean, 479-968-0274, Fax: 479-964-0812, E-mail: jwoods@atu.edu. *Application contact:* Dr. Mary B. Gunter, Dean of Graduate College, 479-968-0398, Fax: 479-964-0542, E-mail: gradcollege@atu.edu.
Website: http://www.atu.edu/humanities/

Ball State University, Graduate School, College of Communication, Information, and Media, Department of Journalism, Muncie, IN 47306-1099. Offers journalism (MA); public relations (MA). *Faculty:* 8 full-time (0 women), 2 part-time/adjunct (0 women). *Students:* 25 full-time (13 women), 36 part-time (26 women); includes 9 minority (6 Black or African American, non-Hispanic/Latino; 2 Hispanic/Latino; 1 Two or more races, non-Hispanic/Latino), 11 international. Average age 31. 49 applicants, 65% accepted, 20 enrolled. In 2014, 17 master's awarded. *Entrance requirements:* For master's, resume. Application fee: $50. *Financial support:* In 2014–15, 16 students received support,

including 9 research assistantships with partial tuition reimbursements available (averaging $8,704 per year), 1 teaching assistantship with partial tuition reimbursement available (averaging $9,946 per year); unspecified assistantships also available. Financial award application deadline: 3/1. *Faculty research:* Image studies, readership surveys, audience perception studies. *Unit head:* Dr. William J. Willis, Chairperson, 765-285-8201, Fax: 765-285-7997, E-mail: jwillis@bsu.edu. *Application contact:* Dan Waechter, Information Contact, 765-285-8221, Fax: 765-285-7997, E-mail: dwaechter@bsu.edu.
Website: http://www.bsu.edu/jounalism/

Baylor University, Graduate School, College of Arts and Sciences, Department of Journalism, Public Relations and New Media, Waco, TX 76798. Offers international journalism (MIJ); journalism (MA). *Degree requirements:* For master's, proficiency in 1 foreign language (for MIJ). *Entrance requirements:* For master's, GRE General Test. *Faculty research:* International politics, mass media and society, journalism history, editing practices.

Bob Jones University, Graduate Programs, Greenville, SC 29614. Offers accountancy (MS); Bible (MA); Bible translation (MA); Biblical studies (Certificate); broadcast management (MS); business administration (MBA); church history (MA, PhD); church ministries (MA); church music (MM); cinema and video production (MA); counseling (MS); curriculum and instruction (Ed D); divinity (M Div); dramatic production (MA); educational leadership (MS, Ed D, Ed S); elementary education (M Ed, MAT); English (M Ed, MA, MAT); fine arts (MA); graphic design (MA); history (M Ed, MA); illustration (MA); interpretative speech (MA); mathematics (M Ed, MAT); medical missions (Certificate); ministry (MM, D Min); multi-categorical special education (M Ed, MAT); music (M Ed); New Testament interpretation (PhD); Old Testament interpretation (PhD); orchestral instrument performance (MM); organ performance (MM); pastoral studies (MA); personnel services (MS, Ed S); piano pedagogy (MM); piano performance (MM); platform arts (MA); radio and television broadcasting (MS); rhetoric and public address (MA); secondary education (M Ed); studio art (MA); teaching Bible (MA); theology (MA, PhD); voice performance (MM); youth ministries (MA); M Div/MM.

Boston University, College of Communication, Department of Journalism, Boston, MA 02215. Offers MS. Part-time programs available. *Faculty:* 24 full-time, 15 part-time/adjunct. *Students:* 72 full-time (57 women), 6 part-time (3 women); includes 6 minority (3 Asian, non-Hispanic/Latino; 3 Two or more races, non-Hispanic/Latino), 20 international. Average age 24. 210 applicants, 72% accepted, 42 enrolled. In 2014, 55 master's awarded. *Degree requirements:* For master's, thesis. *Entrance requirements:* For master's, GRE General Test, resume, writing samples, letters of recommendation. Additional exam requirements/recommendations for international students: Required—TOEFL (minimum score 600 paper-based; 100 iBT), IELTS. *Application deadline:* For fall admission, 5/1 for domestic and international students. Applications are processed on a rolling basis. Application fee: $80. Electronic applications accepted. *Expenses: Tuition:* Full-time $45,686; part-time $1428 per credit hour. *Required fees:* $660; $60 per semester. Tuition and fees vary according to program. *Financial support:* Teaching assistantships with partial tuition reimbursements, career-related internships or fieldwork, Federal Work-Study, institutionally sponsored loans, scholarships/grants, and unspecified assistantships available. Support available to part-time students. Financial award application deadline: 5/1; financial award applicants required to submit FAFSA. *Unit head:* William McKeen, Chairman, 617-353-3484, Fax: 617-353-1086, E-mail: wmckeen@bu.edu. *Application contact:* Manny Dotel, Assistant Director, Graduate Affairs, 617-353-3481, E-mail: comgrad@bu.edu.
Website: http://www.bu.edu/com/academics/journalism/

California State University, Fresno, Division of Graduate Studies, College of Arts and Humanities, Department of Mass Communication and Journalism, Fresno, CA 93740-8027. Offers MA. Part-time and evening/weekend programs available. *Degree requirements:* For master's, thesis. *Entrance requirements:* For master's, GRE General Test, minimum GPA of 3.0. Additional exam requirements/recommendations for international students: Required—TOEFL. Electronic applications accepted.

California State University, Northridge, Graduate Studies, College of Arts, Media, and Communication, Department of Journalism, Northridge, CA 91330. Offers mass communication (MA). Part-time and evening/weekend programs available. *Students:* 18 full-time (10 women), 8 part-time (4 women); includes 12 minority (4 Black or African American, non-Hispanic/Latino; 2 Asian, non-Hispanic/Latino; 4 Hispanic/Latino; 2 Two or more races, non-Hispanic/Latino), 6 international. Average age 29. *Degree requirements:* For master's, thesis. *Entrance requirements:* For master's, GRE General Test. Additional exam requirements/recommendations for international students: Required—TOEFL. *Application deadline:* For fall admission, 11/30 for domestic students. Application fee: $55. *Expenses: Required fees:* $12,402. *Financial support:* Career-related internships or fieldwork and Federal Work-Study available. Financial award application deadline: 3/1. *Unit head:* Linda Bowen, Chair, 818-677-3135.
Website: http://www.csun.edu/journalism/

Carleton University, Faculty of Graduate Studies, Faculty of Public Affairs and Management, School of Journalism and Communication, Ottawa, ON K1S 5B6, Canada. Offers communication (MA, PhD); journalism (MJ). *Degree requirements:* For master's, thesis optional; for doctorate, comprehensive exam, thesis/dissertation. *Entrance requirements:* For master's, honors degree. Additional exam requirements/recommendations for international students: Required—TOEFL. *Faculty research:* Specialized print reporting, broadcast journalism, journalism studies.

Columbia College Chicago, Graduate School, Department of Journalism, Chicago, IL 60605-1996. Offers MA. *Faculty:* 16 full-time (10 women), 25 part-time/adjunct (14 women). *Students:* 10 full-time (6 women); includes 4 minority (3 Black or African American, non-Hispanic/Latino; 1 Hispanic/Latino), 1 international. Average age 27. *Degree requirements:* For master's, thesis. *Entrance requirements:* For master's, self-assessment essay, work sample, interview, letters of recommendation. Additional exam requirements/recommendations for international students: Required—TOEFL (minimum score 600 paper-based; 100 iBT). *Application deadline:* For fall admission, 1/15 for domestic and international students. Applications are processed on a rolling basis. Application fee: $55 ($100 for international students). Electronic applications accepted. *Expenses:* Expenses: $1,033 per credit hour; fees: $352 per semester. *Financial support:* In 2014–15, 16 students received support, including 8 fellowships, 8 research assistantships; career-related internships or fieldwork, Federal Work-Study, scholarships/grants, and unspecified assistantships also available. Support available to part-time students. Financial award application deadline: 8/13; financial award applicants required to submit FAFSA. *Unit head:* Curtis Lawrence, Program Director, 312-369-8905, E-mail: clawrence@colum.edu. *Application contact:* Kara Leffler, Associate Director of Graduate Admissions, 312-369-7262, Fax: 312-369-8024, E-mail: kleffler@colum.edu.
Website: http://www.colum.edu/Admissions/Graduate/programs/graduate-journalism-program/index.php

Columbia University, Fu Foundation School of Engineering and Applied Science, Department of Computer Science, New York, NY 10027. Offers computer science (MS, Eng Sc D, PhD); computer science and journalism (MS). PhD offered through the Graduate School of Arts and Sciences. Part-time programs available. Postbaccalaureate distance learning degree programs offered (no on-campus study). *Faculty:* 46 full-time (8 women), 32 part-time/adjunct (4 women). *Students:* 333 full-time (95 women), 229 part-time (58 women); includes 61 minority (2 Black or African American, non-Hispanic/Latino; 45 Asian, non-Hispanic/Latino; 6 Hispanic/Latino; 8 Two or more races, non-Hispanic/Latino), 418 international. 1,818 applicants, 25% accepted, 227 enrolled. In 2014, 182 master's, 12 doctorates awarded. Terminal master's awarded for partial completion of doctoral program. *Degree requirements:* For master's, thesis optional; for doctorate, comprehensive exam, thesis/dissertation, candidacy exam. *Entrance requirements:* For master's and doctorate, GRE General Test. Additional exam requirements/recommendations for international students: Required—TOEFL, IELTS, PTE. *Application deadline:* For fall admission, 12/15 priority date for domestic and international students; for spring admission, 10/1 priority date for domestic and international students. Application fee: $85. Electronic applications accepted. *Financial support:* In 2014–15, 135 students received support, including 9 fellowships with full tuition reimbursements available (averaging $32,059 per year), 108 research assistantships with full tuition reimbursements available (averaging $28,809 per year), 18 teaching assistantships with full tuition reimbursements available (averaging $6,000 per year); health care benefits also available. Financial award application deadline: 12/15; financial award applicants required to submit FAFSA. *Faculty research:* Natural language processing, machine learning, software systems, network systems, computer security, computational biology, foundations of computer science, vision and graphics. *Unit head:* Dr. Julia B. Hirschberg, Professor and Chair, Computer Science, 212-939-7114, E-mail: julia@cs.columbia.edu. *Application contact:* Remiko O. Moss, Assistant Director, 212-939-7002, Fax: 212-666-0140, E-mail: remimoss@cs.columbia.edu.
Website: http://www.cs.columbia.edu/

Columbia University, Graduate School of Journalism, New York, NY 10027. Offers MA, MS, PhD, JD/MS, MIA/MS, MS/MBA. *Accreditation:* ACEJMC. Part-time programs available. *Degree requirements:* For master's, thesis; for doctorate, thesis/dissertation. *Entrance requirements:* For master's, writing test, 2-3 samples of journalistic work, minimum typing speed of 50 words per minute; for doctorate, GRE. Additional exam requirements/recommendations for international students: Required—TOEFL. *Expenses:* Contact institution. *Faculty research:* International communication, communication technologies, ethics in journalism, journalism history.

Concordia University, School of Graduate Studies, Faculty of Arts and Science, Department of Journalism, Montréal, QC H3G 1M8, Canada. Offers Diploma. *Degree requirements:* For Diploma, one foreign language. *Entrance requirements:* Additional exam requirements/recommendations for international students: Required—departmental English test or TOEFL.

CUNY Graduate School of Journalism, Graduate Program, New York, NY 10018. Offers entrepreneurial journalism (MA, Advanced Certificate); journalism (MA). *Accreditation:* ACEJMC. *Degree requirements:* For master's, internship, final or capstone project. *Entrance requirements:* For master's, GRE, admissions exam, 3 letters of recommendation, resume, interview, 3 writing samples. Additional exam requirements/recommendations for international students: Required—TOEFL (minimum score 105 iBT). Electronic applications accepted.

DePaul University, College of Communication, Chicago, IL 60614. Offers digital communication and media arts (MA); health communication (MA); journalism (MA); media and cinema studies (MA); organizational and multicultural communication (MA); public relations and advertising (MA); relational communication (MA). Part-time and evening/weekend programs available. *Entrance requirements:* Additional exam requirements/recommendations for international students: Required—TOEFL (minimum score 590 paper-based; 96 iBT), IELTS (minimum score 7.5) or PTE. Electronic applications accepted.

Drexel University, School of Journalism, Philadelphia, PA 19104-2875. Offers MA. *Entrance requirements:* Additional exam requirements/recommendations for international students: Required—TOEFL.

Emerson College, Graduate Studies, School of Communication, Department of Journalism, Boston, MA 02116-4624. Offers journalism (MA), including broadcast journalism, print/multimedia journalism. *Faculty:* 16 full-time (8 women), 8 part-time/adjunct (5 women). *Students:* 40 full-time (33 women), 1 part-time (0 women); includes 9 minority (5 Black or African American, non-Hispanic/Latino; 3 Hispanic/Latino; 1 Two or more races, non-Hispanic/Latino), 11 international. Average age 24. 112 applicants, 46% accepted, 16 enrolled. In 2014, 22 master's awarded. *Entrance requirements:* For master's, GRE General Test. Additional exam requirements/recommendations for international students: Required—TOEFL (minimum score 550 paper-based; 80 iBT), IELTS (minimum score 6.5). *Application deadline:* For fall admission, 3/1 priority date for domestic and international students. Applications are processed on a rolling basis. Application fee: $60 ($75 for international students). Electronic applications accepted. *Expenses: Tuition:* Part-time $1145 per credit. *Financial support:* In 2014–15, 12 students received support, including 12 fellowships with partial tuition reimbursements available (averaging $11,000 per year); research assistantships with partial tuition reimbursements available, Federal Work-Study, scholarships/grants, and unspecified assistantships also available. Financial award application deadline: 3/1; financial award applicants required to submit FAFSA. *Faculty research:* Journalism. *Unit head:* Prof. Paul Niwa, Interim Chair, 617-824-8805, E-mail: ted_gup@emerson.edu. *Application contact:* Leanda Ferland, Office of Graduate Admission, 617-824-8610, Fax: 617-824-8614, E-mail: gradapp@emerson.edu.
Website: http://www.emerson.edu/graduate_admission

Florida Agricultural and Mechanical University, Division of Graduate Studies, Research, and Continuing Education, School of Journalism and Graphic Communication, Tallahassee, FL 32307-3200. Offers journalism (MS). *Degree requirements:* For master's, comprehensive exam, thesis (for some programs). *Entrance requirements:* For master's, GRE General Test, minimum GPA of 3.0. Additional exam requirements/recommendations for international students: Required—TOEFL.

Florida International University, School of Journalism and Mass Communication, Miami, FL 33199. Offers mass communication (MS), including global strategic communications, Spanish language journalism. *Accreditation:* ACEJMC. Part-time and evening/weekend programs available. *Degree requirements:* For master's, thesis optional. *Entrance requirements:* For master's, 2 letters of recommendation; minimum GPA of 3.0 during last 60 hours of upper-level work; resume. Additional exam requirements/recommendations for international students: Required—TOEFL (minimum score 550 paper-based; 80 iBT). Electronic applications accepted. *Faculty research:* Post-Hurricane Andrew population studies, Central American journalism, employment discrimination.

Full Sail University, New Media Journalism Master of Arts Program - Online, Winter Park, FL 32792-7437. Offers MA.

Georgetown University, Graduate School of Arts and Sciences, School of Continuing Studies, Washington, DC 20057. Offers American studies (MALS); Catholic studies (MALS); classical civilizations (MALS); emergency and disaster management (MPS); ethics and the professions (MALS); hospitality management (MPS); human resources management (MPS); humanities (MALS); individualized study (MALS); international affairs (MALS); Islam and Muslim-Christian relations (MALS); journalism (MPS); liberal

studies (DLS); literature and society (MALS); medieval and early modern European studies (MALS); public relations and corporate communications (MPS); real estate (MPS); religious studies (MALS); social and public policy (MALS); sports industry management (MPS); systems engineering management (MPS); technology management (MPS); the theory and practice of American democracy (MALS); urban and regional planning (MPS); visual culture (MALS). MPS in systems engineering management offered jointly with Stevens Institute of Technology. *Entrance requirements:* Additional exam requirements/recommendations for international students: Required—TOEFL.

Harvard University, Extension School, Cambridge, MA 02138-3722. Offers applied sciences (CAS); biotechnology (ALM); educational technologies (ALM); educational technology (CET); English for graduate and professional studies (DGP); environmental management (ALM, CEM); information technology (ALM); journalism (ALM); liberal arts (ALM); management (ALM, CM); mathematics for teaching (ALM); museum studies (ALM); premedical studies (Diploma); publication and communication (CPC). Part-time and evening/weekend programs available. *Degree requirements:* For master's, thesis. *Entrance requirements:* For master's, 3 completed graduate courses with grade of B or higher. Additional exam requirements/recommendations for international students: Required—TOEFL (minimum score 600 paper-based), TWE (minimum score 5). *Expenses:* Contact institution.

Hofstra University, Lawrence Herbert School of Communication, Programs in Journalism and Public Relations, Hempstead, NY 11549. Offers journalism (MA); public relations (MA). Part-time and evening/weekend programs available. *Students:* 43 full-time (31 women), 25 part-time (15 women); includes 34 minority (17 Black or African American, non-Hispanic/Latino; 2 American Indian or Alaska Native, non-Hispanic/Latino; 2 Asian, non-Hispanic/Latino; 12 Hispanic/Latino; 1 Two or more races, non-Hispanic/Latino), 8 international. Average age 28. 107 applicants, 65% accepted, 26 enrolled. In 2014, 6 master's awarded. *Degree requirements:* For master's, thesis. *Entrance requirements:* For master's, minimum GPA of 2.75; bachelor's degree. Additional exam requirements/recommendations for international students: Required—TOEFL (minimum score 550 paper-based; 95 iBT). *Application deadline:* Applications are processed on a rolling basis. Application fee: $70 ($75 for international students). Electronic applications accepted. *Expenses: Tuition:* Full-time $20,610; part-time $1145 per credit hour. *Required fees:* $970; $165 per term. Tuition and fees vary according to program. *Financial support:* In 2014–15, 28 students received support, including 10 fellowships with full and partial tuition reimbursements available (averaging $2,950 per year), 4 research assistantships with full and partial tuition reimbursements available (averaging $4,650 per year); Federal Work-Study, institutionally sponsored loans, scholarships/grants, and tuition waivers (full and partial) also available. Support available to part-time students. Financial award applicants required to submit FAFSA. *Faculty research:* Media ethics/law; environmental, science and health journalism; multimedia/future of news, new media; race, gender, cultural issues; social justice. *Unit head:* Dr. Carol T. Fletcher, Chairperson, 516-463-6464, Fax: 516-463-4866, E-mail: jrnctf@hofstra.edu. *Application contact:* Sunil Samuel, Assistant Vice President of Admissions, 516-463-4723, Fax: 516-463-4664, E-mail: graduateadmission@hofstra.edu.
Website: http://www.hofstra.edu/academics/colleges/soc/

Indiana University Bloomington, University Graduate School, College of Arts and Sciences, The Media School, School of Journalism, Bloomington, IN 47405-7000. Offers journalism (MA, MAT); mass communication (PhD); MA/JD; MA/MA. *Faculty:* 11 full-time (5 women). *Students:* 52 full-time (33 women), 6 part-time (5 women); includes 6 minority (5 Black or African American, non-Hispanic/Latino; 1 Two or more races, non-Hispanic/Latino), 28 international. Average age 30. 83 applicants, 61% accepted, 11 enrolled. In 2014, 22 master's, 2 doctorates awarded. Terminal master's awarded for partial completion of doctoral program. *Degree requirements:* For master's, thesis (for some programs); for doctorate, thesis/dissertation. *Entrance requirements:* For master's and doctorate, GRE General Test. Additional exam requirements/recommendations for international students: Required—TOEFL. *Application deadline:* For fall admission, 1/15 priority date for domestic students; for spring admission, 9/1 priority date for domestic students. Applications are processed on a rolling basis. Application fee: $55 ($65 for international students). *Financial support:* Fellowships, research assistantships with full tuition reimbursements, teaching assistantships with partial tuition reimbursements, career-related internships or fieldwork, Federal Work-Study, institutionally sponsored loans, and tuition waivers (full) available. Financial award application deadline: 1/15. *Faculty research:* Political communication, international communication, communication history, communication law, visual communication. *Unit head:* Bonnie Brownlee, Chair, 812-855-0570, E-mail: brownlee@indiana.edu. *Application contact:* Lesa Major, Associate Dean, Research and Graduate Studies, 812-855-8111, E-mail: lhmajor@indiana.edu.
Website: http://journalism.indiana.edu/

Iowa State University of Science and Technology, Greenlee School of Journalism and Mass Communication, Ames, IA 50011. Offers MS. *Entrance requirements:* For master's, GRE General Test. Additional exam requirements/recommendations for international students: Required—TOEFL (minimum score 570 paper-based; 88 iBT), IELTS (minimum score 6.5). Electronic applications accepted.

Kansas State University, Graduate School, College of Arts and Sciences, A. Q. Miller School of Journalism and Mass Communications, Manhattan, KS 66506. Offers advertising (MS); community journalism (MS); global communication (MS); health communication (MS); media management (MS); public relations (MS). Part-time and evening/weekend programs available. *Faculty:* 15 full-time (7 women), 1 (woman) part-time/adjunct. *Students:* 15 full-time (9 women), 5 part-time (3 women); includes 2 minority (both Hispanic/Latino), 9 international. Average age 26. 10 applicants, 80% accepted, 6 enrolled. In 2014, 10 master's awarded. *Degree requirements:* For master's, comprehensive exam, thesis. *Entrance requirements:* For master's, GRE General Test, minimum GPA of 3.0. Additional exam requirements/recommendations for international students: Required—TOEFL (minimum score 79 iBT). *Application deadline:* For fall admission, 2/1 priority date for domestic and international students; for spring admission, 8/1 priority date for domestic and international students. Applications are processed on a rolling basis. Application fee: $50 ($75 for international students). Electronic applications accepted. *Financial support:* In 2014–15, 2 research assistantships with full tuition reimbursements (averaging $11,180 per year), 7 teaching assistantships with full tuition reimbursements (averaging $7,729 per year) were awarded; scholarships/grants, health care benefits, and unspecified assistantships also available. Financial award application deadline: 2/1; financial award applicants required to submit FAFSA. *Faculty research:* Health communication, risk communication, strategic communications, community journalism, global communication. *Total annual research expenditures:* $219,641. *Unit head:* Dr. Birgit Wassmuth, Director, 785-532-6890, Fax: 785-532-5484, E-mail: wassmuth@ksu.edu. *Application contact:* Dr. Nancy Muturi, Associate Director of Graduate Studies, 785-532-3890, Fax: 785-532-5484, E-mail: nmuturi@ksu.edu.
Website: http://jmc.ksu.edu/

Kent State University, College of Communication and Information, School of Journalism and Mass Communication, Kent, OH 44242-0001. Offers media

management (MA); public relations (MA); reporting and editing (MA), including broadcast, convergence, journalism educators, magazine, newspaper. Part-time programs available. *Faculty:* 28 full-time (13 women). *Students:* 21 full-time (15 women), 173 part-time (127 women); includes 24 minority (14 Black or African American, non-Hispanic/Latino; 1 American Indian or Alaska Native, non-Hispanic/Latino; 2 Asian, non-Hispanic/Latino; 1 Hispanic/Latino; 6 Two or more races, non-Hispanic/Latino), 7 international. Average age 37. 112 applicants, 68% accepted, 50 enrolled. In 2014, 117 master's awarded. *Degree requirements:* For master's, thesis or project. *Entrance requirements:* For master's, GRE General Test, minimum GPA of 3.0, transcripts, goal statement, statement of desired concentration, resume, 3 letters of recommendation. Additional exam requirements/recommendations for international students: Required—TOEFL (minimum score: paper-based 525, iBT 71), Michigan English Language Assessment Battery (minimum score of 75), IELTS (minimum score of 6.0), PTE Academic (minimum score of 48), or completion of ELS level 112 Intensive Program. *Application deadline:* For fall admission, 7/1 for domestic students, 3/1 for international students; for spring admission, 12/1 for domestic students, 10/30 for international students; for summer admission, 5/1 for domestic students. Application fee: $45 ($70 for international students). Electronic applications accepted. *Expenses:* Tuition, state resident: full-time $8730; part-time $485 per credit hour. Tuition, nonresident: full-time $14,886; part-time $827 per credit hour. Tuition and fees vary according to campus/location and program. *Financial support:* Research assistantships with full tuition reimbursements, teaching assistantships with full tuition reimbursements, career-related internships or fieldwork, Federal Work-Study, scholarships/grants, and unspecified assistantships available. Financial award application deadline: 2/1. *Unit head:* Thor Wasbotten, Director and Professor, 330-672-4066, E-mail: thor@kent.edu. *Application contact:* Joe Murray, Graduate Coordinator and Associate Professor, 330-672-2572, E-mail: jmc@kent.edu.
Website: http://www.kent.edu/jmc

Lindenwood University, Graduate Programs, School of Communications, St. Charles, MO 63301-1695. Offers broadcast (MA); communications studies (MA); interactive media and Web design (MA); journalism (MA). Part-time and evening/weekend programs available. *Faculty:* 8 full-time (1 woman), 4 part-time/adjunct (1 woman). *Students:* 16 full-time (13 women), 2 part-time (0 women); includes 3 minority (2 Black or African American, non-Hispanic/Latino; 1 Asian, non-Hispanic/Latino), 4 international. Average age 27. 11 applicants, 55% accepted, 5 enrolled. In 2014, 4 master's awarded. *Degree requirements:* For master's, thesis (for some programs), minimum cumulative GPA of 3.0. *Entrance requirements:* For master's, GRE, minimum GPA of 3.0, resume. Additional exam requirements/recommendations for international students: Required—TOEFL (minimum score 550 paper-based; 80 iBT). *Application deadline:* For fall admission, 8/24 priority date for domestic and international students; for spring admission, 1/25 priority date for domestic and international students. Applications are processed on a rolling basis. Application fee: $30 ($100 for international students). Electronic applications accepted. *Expenses: Tuition:* Full-time $15,230; part-time $440 per credit hour. *Required fees:* $205 per semester. Tuition and fees vary according to course level, course load and degree level. *Financial support:* In 2014–15, 3 students received support. Career-related internships or fieldwork, Federal Work-Study, institutionally sponsored loans, scholarships/grants, tuition waivers (partial), and unspecified assistantships available. Financial award application deadline: 6/30; financial award applicants required to submit FAFSA. *Unit head:* Mike Wall, Dean, 636-949-4880, E-mail: mwall@lindenwood.edu. *Application contact:* Tyler Kostich, Director of Evening and Graduate Admissions, 636-949-4138, Fax: 636-949-4109, E-mail: adultadmissions@lindenwood.edu.
Website: http://www.lindenwood.edu/communications/

Marquette University, Graduate School, Diederich College of Communication, Milwaukee, WI 53201-1881. Offers advertising and public relations (MA); communication studies (MA); digital storytelling (Certificate); journalism (MA); mass communication (MA); science, health and environmental communication (MA). *Accreditation:* ACEJMC (one or more programs are accredited). Part-time and evening/weekend programs available. *Degree requirements:* For master's, comprehensive exam, thesis or alternative. *Entrance requirements:* For master's, GRE, official transcripts from all current and previous colleges/universities except Marquette, three letters of recommendation, statement of academic and professional goals. Additional exam requirements/recommendations for international students: Required—TOEFL (minimum score 530 paper-based). Electronic applications accepted. *Faculty research:* Urban journalism, gender and communication, intercultural communication, religious communication.

Marshall University, Academic Affairs Division, College of Arts and Media, School of Journalism and Mass Communications, Huntington, WV 25755. Offers MAJ. *Faculty:* 6 full-time (2 women). *Students:* 6 full-time (4 women), 6 part-time (5 women). Average age 26. In 2014, 7 master's awarded. *Degree requirements:* For master's, thesis optional. *Entrance requirements:* For master's, GRE General Test. Application fee: $40. *Unit head:* Dr. Janet Dooley, Chair, 304-696-2734, E-mail: dooley@marshall.edu. *Application contact:* Dr. Robert Rabe, Graduate Coordinator, 304-696-4636, E-mail: rabe@marshall.edu.

Michigan State University, The Graduate School, College of Communication Arts and Sciences, School of Journalism, East Lansing, MI 48824. Offers MA. *Entrance requirements:* Additional exam requirements/recommendations for international students: Required—TOEFL. Electronic applications accepted.

National University, Academic Affairs, School of Professional Studies, La Jolla, CA 92037-1011. Offers criminal justice (MCJ); digital cinema (MFA); digital journalism (MA); juvenile justice (MS); professional screen writing (MFA); public administration (MPA), including human resource management, organizational leadership, public finance. Part-time and evening/weekend programs available. Postbaccalaureate distance learning degree programs offered (no on-campus study). *Faculty:* 19 full-time (8 women), 28 part-time/adjunct (7 women). *Students:* 277 full-time (141 women), 140 part-time (80 women); includes 248 minority (102 Black or African American, non-Hispanic/Latino; 23 Asian, non-Hispanic/Latino; 102 Hispanic/Latino; 5 Native Hawaiian or other Pacific Islander, non-Hispanic/Latino; 16 Two or more races, non-Hispanic/Latino), 8 international. Average age 37. *Degree requirements:* For master's, thesis (for some programs). *Entrance requirements:* For master's, interview, minimum GPA of 2.5. Additional exam requirements/recommendations for international students: Required—TOEFL (minimum score 550 paper-based; 79 iBT), IELTS (minimum score 6). *Application deadline:* Applications are processed on a rolling basis. Application fee: $60 ($65 for international students). Electronic applications accepted. *Expenses: Tuition:* Full-time $14,184; part-time $1773 per course. *Financial support:* Career-related internships or fieldwork, institutionally sponsored loans, scholarships/grants, and tuition waivers (partial) available. Support available to part-time students. Financial award application deadline: 6/30; financial award applicants required to submit FAFSA. *Unit head:* School of Professional Studies, 800-628-8648, E-mail: sops@nu.edu. *Application contact:* Frank Rojas, Vice President for Enrollment Services, 800-628-8648, E-mail: advisor@nu.edu.
Website: http://www.nu.edu/OurPrograms/School-of-Professional-Studies.html

Journalism

New York University, Graduate School of Arts and Science, Department of Biology, New York, NY 10012-1019. Offers biology (PhD); biomedical journalism (MS); cancer and molecular biology (PhD); computational biology (PhD); computers in biological research (MS); developmental genetics (PhD); general biology (MS); immunology and microbiology (PhD); molecular genetics (PhD); neurobiology (PhD); oral biology (MS); plant biology (PhD); recombinant DNA technology (MS); MS/MBA. Part-time programs available. *Faculty:* 24 full-time (5 women). *Students:* 153 full-time (88 women), 27 part-time (16 women); includes 40 minority (6 Black or African American, non-Hispanic/Latino; 22 Asian, non-Hispanic/Latino; 8 Hispanic/Latino; 4 Two or more races, non-Hispanic/Latino; 71 international. Average age 27. 394 applicants, 56% accepted, 77 enrolled. In 2014, 68 master's, 9 doctorates awarded. Terminal master's awarded for partial completion of doctoral program. *Degree requirements:* For master's, thesis or alternative, qualifying paper; for doctorate, comprehensive exam, thesis/dissertation. *Entrance requirements:* For master's and doctorate, GRE General Test. Additional exam requirements/recommendations for international students: Required—TOEFL. *Application deadline:* For fall admission, 12/1 priority date for domestic students, 12/1 for international students. Application fee: $100. *Financial support:* Fellowships with tuition reimbursements, research assistantships with tuition reimbursements, teaching assistantships with tuition reimbursements, career-related internships or fieldwork, Federal Work-Study, institutionally sponsored loans, scholarships/grants, health care benefits, and unspecified assistantships available. Financial award application deadline: 12/1; financial award applicants required to submit FAFSA. *Faculty research:* Genomics, molecular and cell biology, development and molecular genetics, molecular evolution of plants and animals. *Unit head:* Stephen Small, Chair, 212-998-8200, Fax: 212-995-4015, E-mail: biology.admissions@nyu.edu. *Application contact:* Ken Birnbaum, Director of Graduate Studies, PhD Programs, 212-998-8200, Fax: 212-995-4015, E-mail: biology.admissions@nyu.edu.
Website: http://biology.as.nyu.edu/

New York University, Graduate School of Arts and Science, Department of Journalism, New York, NY 10012-1019. Offers biomedical journalism (MS); cultural reporting and criticism (MA); French studies/journalism (MA); journalism (MA); Latin American and Caribbean studies/journalism (MA); Near Eastern studies/journalism (MA); science and environmental reporting (Advanced Certificate); MA/Advanced Certificate. *Accreditation:* ACEJMC. Part-time programs available. *Students:* 197 full-time (155 women), 13 part-time (11 women); includes 38 minority (7 Black or African American, non-Hispanic/Latino; 14 Asian, non-Hispanic/Latino; 10 Hispanic/Latino; 7 Two or more races, non-Hispanic/Latino), 64 international. Average age 26. 314 applicants, 70% accepted, 90 enrolled. In 2014, 111 master's, 25 other advanced degrees awarded. *Degree requirements:* For master's, written projects. *Entrance requirements:* For master's, GRE General Test, sample of written work. Additional exam requirements/recommendations for international students: Required—TOEFL. *Application deadline:* For fall admission, 1/4 priority date for domestic students, 1/4 for international students. Application fee: $100. *Financial support:* Fellowships with tuition reimbursements, teaching assistantships with tuition reimbursements, Federal Work-Study, institutionally sponsored loans, scholarships/grants, and tuition waivers (partial) available. Financial award application deadline: 1/4; financial award applicants required to submit FAFSA. *Faculty research:* Newspaper, magazine, and broadcast journalism; business and financial reporting; media studies. *Unit head:* Perri Klass, Chair, 212-998-7980, Fax: 212-995-4148, E-mail: graduate.journalism@nyu.edu. *Application contact:* Charles Seife, Director of Graduate Studies, 212-998-7980, Fax: 212-995-4148, E-mail: graduate.journalism@nyu.edu.
Website: http://journalism.nyu.edu/graduate/

Northeastern University, College of Arts, Media and Design, Boston, MA 02115-5096. Offers architecture (M Arch); information design and visualization (MFA); journalism (MA); studio art (MFA). *Entrance requirements:* Additional exam requirements/recommendations for international students: Required—TOEFL (minimum score 100 iBT), IELTS. Electronic applications accepted.

Northwestern University, Medill School of Journalism, Media, and Integrated Marketing Communications, Evanston, IL 60208. Offers integrated marketing communications (MSIMC), including brand strategy, content marketing, direct and interactive marketing, marketing analytics, strategic communications; interactive publishing (MSJ); magazine writing/editing (MSJ); reporting (MSJ); video/broadcast (MSJ). *Accreditation:* ACEJMC (one or more programs are accredited). *Entrance requirements:* For master's, GRE General Test, GMAT or LSAT (for MSJ). Additional exam requirements/recommendations for international students: Required—TOEFL. Electronic applications accepted. *Expenses:* Contact institution. *Faculty research:* Web business journalism, cultural stereotypes, voter apathy, digital television.

Ohio University, Graduate College, Scripps College of Communication, E.W. Scripps School of Journalism, Athens, OH 45701-2979. Offers MS, PhD. Part-time programs available. *Degree requirements:* For master's, thesis or alternative; for doctorate, comprehensive exam, thesis/dissertation. *Entrance requirements:* For master's and doctorate, GRE General Test, minimum GPA of 3.0. Additional exam requirements/recommendations for international students: Required—TOEFL (minimum score 550 paper-based; 80 iBT) or IELTS (minimum score 6.5). Electronic applications accepted. *Faculty research:* Newspaper, magazine, broadcasting, public relations, advertising.

Point Park University, School of Communication, Pittsburgh, PA 15222-1984. Offers MA. Part-time and evening/weekend programs available. *Degree requirements:* For master's, comprehensive exam (for some programs), thesis or alternative. *Entrance requirements:* For master's, GRE (if GPA less than 2.75), minimum GPA of 2.75, 2 letters of recommendation, statement of intent. Additional exam requirements/recommendations for international students: Required—TOEFL (minimum score 570 paper-based; 88 iBT), IELTS (minimum score 6.5); Recommended—TWE (minimum score 5). Electronic applications accepted.

Quinnipiac University, School of Communications, Program in Journalism, Hamden, CT 06518-1940. Offers journalism (MS), including broadcast/multimedia, writing; sports journalism (MS), including broadcast/multimedia, writing. Part-time and evening/weekend programs available. Postbaccalaureate distance learning degree programs offered (no on-campus study). *Faculty:* 5 full-time (2 women), 12 part-time/adjunct (2 women). *Students:* 10 full-time (7 women), 3 part-time (2 women); includes 3 minority (all Black or African American, non-Hispanic/Latino). 16 applicants, 81% accepted, 5 enrolled. In 2014, 20 master's awarded. *Degree requirements:* For master's, project. *Entrance requirements:* For master's, minimum GPA of 2.8, portfolio or writing sample. Additional exam requirements/recommendations for international students: Required—TOEFL (minimum score 575 paper-based; 90 iBT), IELTS (minimum score 6.5). *Application deadline:* For fall admission, 7/30 priority date for domestic students, 4/30 priority date for international students; for spring admission, 12/15 priority date for domestic students, 9/15 priority date for international students. Applications are processed on a rolling basis. Application fee: $45. Electronic applications accepted. *Expenses:* Tuition: Part-time $920 per credit. *Required fees:* $222 per semester. Tuition and fees vary according to course load and program. *Financial support:* In 2014–15, 3 students received support. Fellowships with tuition reimbursements available, career-related internships or fieldwork, Federal Work-Study, scholarships/grants, and unspecified assistantships available. Support available to part-time students. Financial

award application deadline: 6/1; financial award applicants required to submit FAFSA. *Faculty research:* Journalism history, federal law enforcement and journalism, social media and journalism, online journalism, sports journalism, American football history and media, journalism and film, McCarthyism and journalism. *Application contact:* Office of Graduate Admissions, 800-462-1944, Fax: 203-582-3443, E-mail: graduate@quinnipiac.edu.
Website: http://www.quinnipiac.edu/gradjournalism

Regent University, Graduate School, School of Communication and the Arts, Virginia Beach, VA 23464-9800. Offers acting (MFA); communication (MA, PhD), including political communication (MA), strategic communication (MA); directing for cinema/television (MFA); film and TV (MA), including producing, production, script writing; journalism (MA); producing for cinema/television (MFA); script and screenwriting (MFA); theatre (MA). Part-time programs available. Postbaccalaureate distance learning degree programs offered (minimal on-campus study). *Faculty:* 20 full-time (3 women), 26 part-time/adjunct (7 women). *Students:* 89 full-time (49 women), 211 part-time (125 women); includes 92 minority (69 Black or African American, non-Hispanic/Latino; 2 American Indian or Alaska Native, non-Hispanic/Latino; 2 Asian, non-Hispanic/Latino; 19 Hispanic/Latino), 10 international. Average age 35. 199 applicants, 53% accepted, 77 enrolled. In 2014, 48 master's, 8 doctorates awarded. *Degree requirements:* For master's, thesis or alternative; for doctorate, thesis/dissertation. *Entrance requirements:* For master's, GRE General Test or MAT, minimum undergraduate GPA of 3.0, writing sample, computer literacy survey, recommendation, resume, interview, audition (for MFA programs); for doctorate, GRE General Test, minimum graduate GPA of 3.0, writing sample, computer literacy survey, recommendation, interview, transcripts. Additional exam requirements/recommendations for international students: Required—TOEFL (minimum score 577 paper-based). *Application deadline:* For fall admission, 3/1 priority date for domestic students; for spring admission, 10/1 priority date for domestic students. Applications are processed on a rolling basis. Application fee: $50. Electronic applications accepted. *Expenses:* Expenses: Contact institution. *Financial support:* Fellowships with full and partial tuition reimbursements, career-related internships or fieldwork, scholarships/grants, tuition waivers (full and partial), and unspecified assistantships available. Support available to part-time students. Financial award application deadline: 9/1; financial award applicants required to submit FAFSA. *Faculty research:* Southern gospel music, education and entertainment, celebrities and the media, journalism and ethics, C.S. Lewis. *Unit head:* Dr. Mitch Land, Dean, 757-352-4916, Fax: 757-352-4291, E-mail: mland@regent.edu. *Application contact:* Matthew Chadwick, Director of Enrollment Support Services, 800-373-5504, Fax: 757-352-4381, E-mail: admissions@regent.edu.
Website: http://www.regent.edu/acad/schcom/

Roosevelt University, Graduate Division, College of Arts and Sciences, Department of Communication, Program in Journalism, Chicago, IL 60605. Offers MSJ. Part-time and evening/weekend programs available.

Sacred Heart University, Graduate Programs, College of Arts and Sciences, Department of Communications, Fairfield, CT 06825-1000. Offers corporate communication and public relations (MA Comm); digital/multimedia journalism (MA Comm); digital/multimedia production (MA Comm). Part-time and evening/weekend programs available. *Faculty:* 10 full-time (2 women). *Students:* 62 full-time (31 women), 27 part-time (14 women); includes 25 minority (16 Black or African American, non-Hispanic/Latino; 8 Hispanic/Latino; 1 Native Hawaiian or other Pacific Islander, non-Hispanic/Latino), 4 international. Average age 26. 117 applicants, 90% accepted, 69 enrolled. In 2014, 40 master's awarded. *Degree requirements:* For master's, thesis or alternative. *Entrance requirements:* For master's, bachelor's degree. Additional exam requirements/recommendations for international students: Required—PTE; Recommended—TOEFL (minimum score 570 paper-based; 80 iBT), IELTS (minimum score 6.5). *Application deadline:* Applications are processed on a rolling basis. Application fee: $60. Electronic applications accepted. *Expenses:* Tuition: Full-time $24,559; part-time $649 per credit. *Financial support:* Unspecified assistantships available. Financial award applicants required to submit FAFSA. *Unit head:* Dr. Andrew Miller, Chair, 203-396-8087, E-mail: millera@sacredheart.edu. *Application contact:* Kathy Dilks, Executive Director of Graduate Admissions, 203-365-7619, Fax: 203-365-4732, E-mail: gradstudies@sacredheart.edu.
Website: http://www.sacredheart.edu/academics/collegeofartssciences/academicdepartments/communicationmediastudies/

School of the Art Institute of Chicago, Graduate Division, Program in New Arts Journalism, Chicago, IL 60603-3103. Offers MA. *Entrance requirements:* Additional exam requirements/recommendations for international students: Required—TOEFL, IELTS.

South Dakota State University, Graduate School, College of Arts and Science, Department of Journalism and Mass Communication, Brookings, SD 57007. Offers communication studies and journalism (MS). Part-time and evening/weekend programs available. *Degree requirements:* For master's, thesis, oral exam. *Entrance requirements:* Additional exam requirements/recommendations for international students: Required—TOEFL (minimum score 550 paper-based; 79 iBT). *Faculty research:* Mass communication applications.

Southern Illinois University Carbondale, Graduate School, College of Mass Communication and Media Arts, Department of Journalism, Carbondale, IL 62901-4701. Offers PhD. *Expenses:* Tuition, state resident: full-time $10,176; part-time $1153 per credit. Tuition, nonresident: full-time $20,814; part-time $1744 per credit. *Required fees:* $7092; $394 per credit. $2364 per semester. *Unit head:* William Frievogel, Director, 618-453-2121. *Application contact:* Lu Lyons, Supervisor, Admissions, 618-453-4512, E-mail: llyons@siu.edu.

Stanford University, School of Humanities and Sciences, Department of Communication, Stanford, CA 94305-9991. Offers communication theory and research (PhD); journalism (MA); media studies (MA). *Faculty:* 13 full-time (4 women), 1 part-time/adjunct (0 women). *Students:* 66 full-time (39 women). Average age 29. 152 applicants, 25% accepted, 31 enrolled. In 2014, 25 master's, 3 doctorates awarded. Terminal master's awarded for partial completion of doctoral program. *Degree requirements:* For master's, thesis, project; for doctorate, thesis/dissertation, qualifying examination, area examination, 2 projects. *Entrance requirements:* For master's and doctorate, GRE General Test. Additional exam requirements/recommendations for international students: Required—TOEFL (minimum score 650 paper-based; 115 iBT). *Application deadline:* For fall admission, 12/2 for domestic students, 12/3 for international students. Application fee: $125. Electronic applications accepted. *Expenses:* Tuition: Full-time $44,184; part-time $982 per credit hour. *Required fees:* $191. *Financial support:* Fellowships, research assistantships, and teaching assistantships available. *Unit head:* James T. Hamilton, Chair, 650-723-5448, E-mail: jayth@stanford.edu. *Application contact:* Katrin Wheeler, Student Services Manager, 650-724-8920, Fax: 650-725-2472, E-mail: comm-studentservices@stanford.edu.
Website: http://communication.stanford.edu/

Stony Brook University, State University of New York, School of Journalism, Stony Brook, NY 11794. Offers health communication (Certificate); journalism (MS). *Faculty:* 12 full-time (4 women), 25 part-time/adjunct (10 women). *Students:* 8 full-time (5 women), 2 part-time (1 woman); includes 2 minority (1 Black or African American, non-

Hispanic/Latino; 1 Hispanic/Latino). In 2014, 3 master's awarded. *Entrance requirements:* For master's, GRE. Additional exam requirements/recommendations for international students: Required—TOEFL (minimum score 600 paper-based; 100 iBT). *Application deadline:* For fall admission, 4/30 for domestic students; for spring admission, 10/1 for domestic students. *Expenses:* Tuition, state resident: full-time $10,370; part-time $432 per credit. Tuition, nonresident: full-time $20,190; part-time $841 per credit. *Required fees:* $1431. *Faculty research:* Journalism, newspaper journalism, literacy, media management, civic education, radio journalism. *Total annual research expenditures:* $395,717. *Unit head:* Prof. Howard Schneider, Dean, 631-632-7403, E-mail: howard.schneider@stonybrook.edu. *Application contact:* Maureen Robinson, Coordinator, 631-632-1073, E-mail: maureen.robinson@stonybrook.edu.
Website: https://journalism.cc.stonybrook.edu/

Syracuse University, S. I. Newhouse School of Public Communications, Program in Arts Journalism, Syracuse, NY 13244. Offers MA. *Students:* 16 full-time (11 women), 1 (woman) part-time; includes 2 minority (1 Black or African American, non-Hispanic/Latino; 1 Hispanic/Latino), 3 international. Average age 24. 33 applicants, 70% accepted, 16 enrolled. In 2014, 15 master's awarded. *Degree requirements:* For master's, capstone project. *Entrance requirements:* For master's, GRE General Test. Additional exam requirements/recommendations for international students: Required—TOEFL (minimum score 600 paper-based; 100 iBT). *Application deadline:* For fall admission, 2/1 for domestic students, 2/1 priority date for international students; for summer admission, 1/15 for domestic students, 1/15 priority date for international students. Application fee: $45. Electronic applications accepted. *Expenses: Tuition:* Part-time $1341 per credit. *Financial support:* Fellowships with full tuition reimbursements, research assistantships with partial tuition reimbursements, and teaching assistantships with partial tuition reimbursements available. Financial award application deadline: 2/1. *Unit head:* Johanna Keller, Director, 315-443-9251, Fax: 315-443-3946, E-mail: pcgrad@syr.edu. *Application contact:* Graduate Records Office, 315-443-4039, Fax: 315-443-1834, E-mail: pcgrad@syr.edu.
Website: http://newhouse.syr.edu/

Syracuse University, S. I. Newhouse School of Public Communications, Program in Broadcast and Digital Journalism, Syracuse, NY 13244. Offers MS. *Students:* 35 full-time (26 women), 1 part-time (0 women); includes 11 minority (9 Black or African American, non-Hispanic/Latino; 2 Hispanic/Latino), 1 international. Average age 25. 90 applicants, 82% accepted, 34 enrolled. In 2014, 39 master's awarded. *Degree requirements:* For master's, capstone course. *Entrance requirements:* For master's, GRE General Test. Additional exam requirements/recommendations for international students: Required—TOEFL (minimum score 100 iBT). *Application deadline:* For fall admission, 2/1 for domestic and international students; for summer admission, 1/15 priority date for domestic and international students. Application fee: $45. Electronic applications accepted. *Expenses: Tuition:* Part-time $1341 per credit. *Financial support:* Fellowships with full tuition reimbursements, research assistantships with partial tuition reimbursements, and teaching assistantships with partial tuition reimbursements available. Financial award application deadline: 2/1. *Unit head:* Prof. Chris Tuohey, Chair, 315-443-4118, E-mail: pcgrad@syr.edu. *Application contact:* Graduate Records Office, 315-443-5749, Fax: 315-443-1834, E-mail: pcgrad@syr.edu.
Website: http://newhouse.syr.edu/

Syracuse University, S. I. Newhouse School of Public Communications, Program in Computational Journalism, Syracuse, NY 13244. Offers MS. *Entrance requirements:* For master's, GRE. Additional exam requirements/recommendations for international students: Required—TOEFL (minimum score 100 iBT). *Application deadline:* For summer admission, 1/15 priority date for domestic and international students. Application fee: $45. Electronic applications accepted. Application fee is waived when completed online. *Expenses: Tuition:* Part-time $1341 per credit. *Financial support:* Application deadline: 1/15. *Unit head:* Stephen Masiclat, Co-Director, 315-443-3372. *Application contact:* Graduate Programs Office, 315-443-4039, Fax: 315-443-1834, E-mail: pcgrad@syr.edu.
Website: http://newhouse.syr.edu/

Syracuse University, S. I. Newhouse School of Public Communications, Program in Magazine, Newspaper and Online Journalism, Syracuse, NY 13244. Offers MA. *Students:* 22 full-time (12 women), 3 part-time (2 women); includes 11 minority (7 Black or African American, non-Hispanic/Latino; 1 Asian, non-Hispanic/Latino; 3 Hispanic/Latino), 5 international. Average age 24. 81 applicants, 78% accepted, 20 enrolled. In 2014, 34 master's awarded. *Degree requirements:* For master's, capstone course. *Entrance requirements:* For master's, GRE General Test. Additional exam requirements/recommendations for international students: Required—TOEFL (minimum score 600 paper-based; 100 iBT). *Application deadline:* For fall admission, 2/1 for domestic students, 2/1 priority date for international students; for summer admission, 1/15 priority date for domestic and international students. Application fee: $45. Electronic applications accepted. *Expenses: Tuition:* Part-time $1341 per credit. *Financial support:* Fellowships with full tuition reimbursements, research assistantships with partial tuition reimbursements, and teaching assistantships with partial tuition reimbursements available. Financial award application deadline: 2/1; financial award applicants required to submit FAFSA. *Unit head:* Melissa Chessher, Director, 315-443-4004, Fax: 315-443-3946, E-mail: pcgrad@syr.edu. *Application contact:* Graduate Records Office, 315-443-4039, Fax: 315-443-1834, E-mail: pcgrad@syr.edu.
Website: http://newhouse.syr.edu/

Temple University, School of Media and Communication, Department of Journalism, Philadelphia, PA 19122-6096. Offers MJ. Part-time and evening/weekend programs available. *Faculty:* 14 full-time (6 women), 21 part-time/adjunct (8 women). *Students:* 6 full-time (5 women), 11 part-time (7 women); includes 5 minority (1 Black or African American, non-Hispanic/Latino; 2 Hispanic/Latino; 2 Two or more races, non-Hispanic/Latino), 2 international. 28 applicants, 54% accepted, 7 enrolled. In 2014, 8 master's awarded. *Degree requirements:* For master's, comprehensive exam, written exam. *Entrance requirements:* For master's, GRE General Test, minimum GPA of 3.0. Additional exam requirements/recommendations for international students: Required—TOEFL (minimum score 620 paper-based; 105 iBT). *Application deadline:* For fall admission, 3/1 for domestic and international students; for spring admission, 11/1 for domestic and international students. Applications are processed on a rolling basis. Application fee: $60. Electronic applications accepted. *Expenses:* Expenses: Contact institution. *Financial support:* Career-related internships or fieldwork and Federal Work-Study available. Financial award application deadline: 1/15; financial award applicants required to submit FAFSA. *Faculty research:* Journalism history, advertising research, media law, media institutions. *Unit head:* Dr. Patrick L. Murphy, Associate Dean for Research and Graduate Studies, Associate Professor, 215-204-3876, Fax: 215-204-1974, E-mail: murphy.p@temple.edu. *Application contact:* Nicole McKenna, Director, Office of Research and Graduate Studies, 215-204-1497, Fax: 215-204-0310, E-mail: nmckenna@temple.edu.
Website: http://www.temple.edu/journalism/

Texas Christian University, Bob Schieffer College of Communication, School of Journalism, Fort Worth, TX 76129-0002. Offers MS. *Faculty:* 5 full-time (2 women). *Students:* 2 full-time (both women). 7 applicants, 29% accepted. In 2014, 3 master's awarded. *Expenses: Tuition:* Full-time $22,860; part-time $1270 per credit hour. *Unit head:* Dr. John Tisdale, Interim Director, 817-257-6554, E-mail: j.tisdale@tcu.edu. *Application contact:* Dr. Daxton Stewart, Director of Graduate Studies/Associate Dean, 817-257-5918, Fax: 817-257-5921, E-mail: d.stewart@tcu.edu.
Website: http://journalism.tcu.edu/

Université Laval, Faculty of Letters, Department of Information and Communication, Program in International Journalism, Québec, QC G1K 7P4, Canada. Offers Diploma. Offered jointly with École Supérieure De Journalisme De Lille (France). *Entrance requirements:* For degree, English exam, French exam, test on international current events, interview, knowledge of French, knowledge of English. Electronic applications accepted.

The University of Alabama, Graduate School, College of Communication and Information Sciences, Department of Journalism, Tuscaloosa, AL 35487-0172. Offers MA. *Faculty:* 6 full-time (1 woman). *Students:* 13 full-time (7 women), 4 part-time (1 woman); includes 2 minority (both Black or African American, non-Hispanic/Latino), 1 international. Average age 28. 22 applicants, 64% accepted, 11 enrolled. In 2014, 10 master's awarded. Terminal master's awarded for partial completion of doctoral program. *Degree requirements:* For master's, comprehensive exam (for some programs), thesis or alternative. *Entrance requirements:* For master's, GRE, minimum GPA of 3.0. Additional exam requirements/recommendations for international students: Required—TOEFL (minimum score 550 paper-based; 79 iBT). *Application deadline:* For fall admission, 3/31 priority date for domestic students, 1/15 priority date for international students; for spring admission, 11/1 priority date for domestic students, 9/15 priority date for international students. Applications are processed on a rolling basis. Application fee: $50 ($60 for international students). Electronic applications accepted. *Expenses:* Tuition, state resident: full-time $9826. Tuition, nonresident: full-time $24,950. *Financial support:* In 2014–15, 11 students received support, including 7 research assistantships with full and partial tuition reimbursements available (averaging $12,000 per year), 4 teaching assistantships with full and partial tuition reimbursements available (averaging $12,000 per year); career-related internships or fieldwork, Federal Work-Study, institutionally sponsored loans, scholarships/grants, health care benefits, and unspecified assistantships also available. Financial award application deadline: 2/15; financial award applicants required to submit FAFSA. *Faculty research:* Journalistic processes, practices and ethics, media effects, media sociology, history, law. *Unit head:* Dr. Jennifer Greer, Department Chair, 205-348-6304, Fax: 205-348-2780, E-mail: jdgreer@ua.edu. *Application contact:* Dr. Wilson Lowrey, Graduate Coordinator, 205-348-8608, Fax: 205-348-2780, E-mail: wlowrey@ua.edu.
Website: http://www.jn.ua.edu/

The University of Arizona, College of Social and Behavioral Sciences, School of Journalism, Tucson, AZ 85721. Offers international journalism studies (MA); professional journalism (MA). Part-time programs available. *Degree requirements:* For master's, project. *Entrance requirements:* For master's, GRE, minimum GPA of 3.0. Additional exam requirements/recommendations for international students: Required—TOEFL. Electronic applications accepted. *Faculty research:* Press law, military censorship, Latin American press, media and minorities, reporting public affairs.

University of Arkansas, Graduate School, J. William Fulbright College of Arts and Sciences, Department of Journalism, Fayetteville, AR 72701-1201. Offers MA.

The University of British Columbia, Faculty of Arts and Faculty of Graduate Studies, School of Journalism, Vancouver, BC V6T 1Z2, Canada. Offers MJ. *Degree requirements:* For master's, thesis, 3 month internship. *Entrance requirements:* For master's, portfolio, resume with cover letter, letters of reference. Additional exam requirements/recommendations for international students: Required—TOEFL (minimum score 615 paper-based), IELTS (minimum score 7.5). Electronic applications accepted. *Expenses:* Contact institution. *Faculty research:* New media, media coverage, journalistic ethics, international journalism, multimedia.

University of California, Berkeley, Graduate Division, Graduate School of Journalism, Berkeley, CA 94720-1500. Offers MJ, JD/MJ, MJ/MA. *Accreditation:* ACEJMC. *Degree requirements:* For master's, project. *Entrance requirements:* For master's, GRE General Test, 3 work samples, minimum GPA of 3.0, 3 letters of recommendation. Additional exam requirements/recommendations for international students: Required—TOEFL (minimum score 600 paper-based). *Faculty research:* Documentary, new media, print (newspaper and magazine), broadcast (television and radio), photography.

University of Colorado Boulder, Graduate School, School of Journalism and Mass Communication, Boulder, CO 80309. Offers communication (PhD), including media studies; mass communication research (MA); newsgathering (MA). *Accreditation:* ACEJMC (one or more programs are accredited). *Faculty:* 18 full-time (7 women). *Students:* 50 full-time (29 women), 10 part-time (8 women); includes 6 minority (1 Black or African American, non-Hispanic/Latino; 5 Hispanic/Latino), 10 international. Average age 29. 82 applicants, 65% accepted, 19 enrolled. In 2014, 13 master's, 3 doctorates awarded. Terminal master's awarded for partial completion of doctoral program. *Degree requirements:* For master's, comprehensive exam, thesis or alternative; for doctorate, comprehensive exam, thesis/dissertation. *Entrance requirements:* For master's, GRE General Test, minimum undergraduate GPA of 2.75; for doctorate, GRE General Test, minimum undergraduate GPA of 3.2, 3.5 graduate. *Application deadline:* For fall admission, 2/1 for domestic students, 12/1 for international students. Applications are processed on a rolling basis. Application fee: $50 ($70 for international students). Electronic applications accepted. *Financial support:* In 2014–15, 106 students received support, including 9 fellowships (averaging $4,749 per year), 17 research assistantships with full and partial tuition reimbursements available (averaging $27,900 per year), 21 teaching assistantships with full and partial tuition reimbursements available (averaging $28,721 per year); institutionally sponsored loans, scholarships/grants, health care benefits, and unspecified assistantships also available. Financial award application deadline: 3/1; financial award applicants required to submit FAFSA. *Faculty research:* Mass communication/media, journalism, electronic media, print media, television.
Website: http://www.colorado.edu/cmci/

University of Florida, Graduate School, College of Journalism and Communications, Program in Mass Communication, Gainesville, FL 32611. Offers international/intercultural communication (MAMC); journalism (MAMC); mass communication (MAMC, PhD), including clinical translational science (MAMC); public relations (MAMC); science/health communication (MAMC); telecommunication (MAMC). *Entrance requirements:* For master's and doctorate, GRE General Test, minimum GPA of 3.0.

University of Georgia, Grady School of Journalism and Mass Communication, Athens, GA 30602. Offers journalism and mass communication (MA); mass communication (PhD). *Degree requirements:* For master's, comprehensive exam, thesis (MA); for doctorate, comprehensive exam, thesis/dissertation. *Entrance requirements:* For master's and doctorate, GRE General Test. Additional exam requirements/recommendations for international students: Required—TOEFL, TWE for Ph D. Electronic applications accepted.

University of Illinois at Springfield, Graduate Programs, College of Public Affairs and Administration, Public Affairs Reporting Program, Springfield, IL 62703-5407. Offers MA. Part-time and evening/weekend programs available. *Faculty:* 1 full-time (0 women). *Students:* 16 full-time (12 women); includes 6 minority (all Black or African American, non-Hispanic/Latino). Average age 27. 22 applicants, 77% accepted, 16 enrolled. In

2014, 14 master's awarded. *Degree requirements:* For master's, internship, professional portfolio. *Entrance requirements:* For master's, literacy/competency writing test, interview, written work sample, 3 letters of reference. Additional exam requirements/recommendations for international students: Required—TOEFL (minimum score 500 paper-based; 61 iBT). Application fee: $60 ($75 for international students). Electronic applications accepted. *Expenses:* Tuition, state resident: full-time $7662; part-time $319.25 per credit hour. Tuition, nonresident: full-time $15,966; part-time $665.25 per credit hour. *Financial support:* In 2014–15, fellowships with full tuition reimbursements (averaging $9,900 per year), research assistantships with full tuition reimbursements (averaging $9,600 per year), teaching assistantships with full tuition reimbursements (averaging $9,600 per year) were awarded; career-related internships or fieldwork, Federal Work-Study, scholarships/grants, health care benefits, and unspecified assistantships also available. Support available to part-time students. Financial award application deadline: 11/15; financial award applicants required to submit FAFSA. *Unit head:* Dr. Charles Wheeler, Director, 217-206-6535, Fax: 217-206-7807, E-mail: cwhee1@uis.edu. *Application contact:* Dr. Lynn Pardie, Office of Graduate Studies, 800-252-8533, Fax: 217-206-7623, E-mail: lpard1@uis.edu.
Website: http://www.uis.edu/publicaffairsreporting/

University of Illinois at Urbana–Champaign, Graduate College, College of Media, Department of Journalism, Champaign, IL 61820. Offers MS, MS/JD, MS/MBA. *Accreditation:* ACEJMC. *Students:* 10 (7 women). Application fee: $70 ($90 for international students). *Unit head:* Rich Martin, Interim Head, 217-265-9461, Fax: 217-333-7931, E-mail: richmart@illinois.edu. *Application contact:* Nancy Benson, Advisor, 217-244-9327, Fax: 217-333-7931, E-mail: nbenson@illinois.edu.
Website: http://www.media.illinois.edu/journalism/

The University of Iowa, Graduate College, College of Liberal Arts and Sciences, School of Journalism and Mass Communication, Iowa City, IA 52242-1316. Offers journalism and media communication (MA); mass communication (PhD); strategic communication (MA); JD/MA; JD/PhD. *Degree requirements:* For master's, thesis optional, exam; for doctorate, comprehensive exam, thesis/dissertation. *Entrance requirements:* For master's and doctorate, GRE General Test, minimum GPA of 3.0. Additional exam requirements/recommendations for international students: Required—TOEFL (minimum score 637 paper-based; 110 iBT). Electronic applications accepted. *Faculty research:* Verbal and visual aspects of historical, legal, social, and cross-cultural communication.

The University of Kansas, Graduate Studies, School of Journalism and Mass Communications, Lawrence, KS 66045. Offers journalism (MS). *Accreditation:* ACEJMC. Part-time programs available. *Faculty:* 24 full-time, 13 part-time/adjunct. *Students:* 23 full-time (13 women), 35 part-time (24 women); includes 6 minority (1 Black or African American, non-Hispanic/Latino; 1 American Indian or Alaska Native, non-Hispanic/Latino; 1 Asian, non-Hispanic/Latino; 2 Hispanic/Latino; 1 Two or more races, non-Hispanic/Latino), 5 international. Average age 30. 46 applicants, 48% accepted, 15 enrolled. In 2014, 17 master's awarded. *Degree requirements:* For master's, comprehensive exam, thesis. *Entrance requirements:* For master's, GRE General Test, minimum GPA of 3.0. Additional exam requirements/recommendations for international students: Required—TOEFL or IELTS. *Application deadline:* For fall admission, 2/1 for domestic and international students; for spring admission, 11/1 for domestic and international students. Application fee: $55 ($65 for international students). Electronic applications accepted. *Financial support:* Fellowships, research assistantships, teaching assistantships with full and partial tuition reimbursements, career-related internships or fieldwork, scholarships/grants, and unspecified assistantships available. Support available to part-time students. Financial award application deadline: 2/1; financial award applicants required to submit FAFSA. *Faculty research:* Advertising, creativity, public relations, integrated marketing communication; media economics, online journalism; new media, visual communication; health communication, sports communication; political journalism, press law. *Unit head:* Scott Reinardy, Associate Dean for Graduate Studies, 785-864-7691, E-mail: reinardy@ku.edu. *Application contact:* Jammie A. Johnson, Graduate Advisor Administrative Assistant, 785-864-7649, E-mail: jamjohn@ku.edu.
Website: http://www.journalism.ku.edu/

University of King's College, Graduate and Advanced Programs, Halifax, NS B3H 2A1, Canada. Offers creative nonfiction (MFA); journalism (MJ). *Students:* 46 full-time (34 women), 3 part-time (all women). *Application deadline:* For fall admission, 2/15 for domestic students. Applications are processed on a rolling basis. Application fee: $100. *Expenses:* Tuition, nonresident: full-time $7700. International tuition: $8700 full-time. *Required fees:* $1100. *Application contact:* Tara Wigglesworth Hines, Assistant Registrar, 902-422-1271 Ext. 259, Fax: 902-425-8183, E-mail: tara.wigglesworthhines@ukings.ca.
Website: http://www.ukings.ca/graduate-advanced-programs

University of Maryland, College Park, Academic Affairs, Phillip Merrill College of Journalism, College Park, MD 20742. Offers broadcast journalism (MA); journalism (MA); journalism and media studies (PhD); online news (MA); public affairs reporting (MA). *Accreditation:* ACEJMC (one or more programs are accredited). Part-time and evening/weekend programs available. *Faculty:* 22 full-time (13 women), 53 part-time/adjunct (23 women). *Students:* 63 full-time (35 women), 6 part-time (2 women); includes 16 minority (9 Black or African American, non-Hispanic/Latino; 4 Asian, non-Hispanic/Latino; 3 Hispanic/Latino), 14 international. 117 applicants, 38% accepted, 15 enrolled. In 2014, 22 master's, 6 doctorates awarded. *Degree requirements:* For doctorate, thesis/dissertation, preliminary written and oral comprehensive exams. *Entrance requirements:* For master's and doctorate, GRE General Test, minimum GPA of 3.0, 3 letters of recommendation. Additional exam requirements/recommendations for international students: Required—TOEFL. *Application deadline:* For fall admission, 2/1 for domestic and international students; for summer admission, 2/1 for domestic and international students. Application fee: $75. Electronic applications accepted. *Financial support:* In 2014–15, 9 fellowships with full and partial tuition reimbursements (averaging $24,407 per year), 25 teaching assistantships (averaging $17,009 per year) were awarded; career-related internships or fieldwork, Federal Work-Study, and scholarships/grants also available. Support available to part-time students. Financial award applicants required to submit FAFSA. *Faculty research:* Mass communication theory, specialized journalism, new telecommunication technologies, press integration. *Total annual research expenditures:* $230,123. *Unit head:* Lucy A. Dalglish, Dean, 301-405-8806, Fax: 301-314-1978, E-mail: dalglish@umd.edu. *Application contact:* Dr. Charles A. Caramello, Dean of Graduate School, 301-405-0358, Fax: 301-314-9305, E-mail: ccaramel@umd.edu.
Website: http://www.journalism.umd.edu/

University of Memphis, Graduate School, College of Communication and Fine Arts, Department of Journalism, Memphis, TN 38152. Offers MA. Part-time and evening/weekend programs available. Postbaccalaureate distance learning degree programs offered (no on-campus study). *Faculty:* 7 full-time (3 women), 2 part-time/adjunct (1 woman). *Students:* 19 full-time (10 women), 44 part-time (26 women); includes 16 minority (12 Black or African American, non-Hispanic/Latino; 1 American Indian or Alaska Native, non-Hispanic/Latino; 1 Asian, non-Hispanic/Latino; 1 Hispanic/Latino; 1 Two or more races, non-Hispanic/Latino), 2 international. Average age 33. 17

applicants, 82% accepted, 10 enrolled. In 2014, 14 master's awarded. *Degree requirements:* For master's, comprehensive exam, thesis (for some programs), culminating experience: project, thesis, or referred paper. *Entrance requirements:* For master's, GRE General Test, MAT, transcripts, resume, goal statement. Additional exam requirements/recommendations for international students: Required—TOEFL (minimum score 600 paper-based). *Application deadline:* For fall admission, 6/1 for domestic and international students; for spring admission, 10/1 for domestic and international students. Applications are processed on a rolling basis. Application fee: $35 ($60 for international students). *Financial support:* In 2014–15, 25 students received support. Research assistantships with full tuition reimbursements available, teaching assistantships with full tuition reimbursements available, Federal Work-Study, scholarships/grants, and unspecified assistantships available. Support available to part-time students. Financial award application deadline: 2/15; financial award applicants required to submit FAFSA. *Faculty research:* Spirit of libel law, statistical software packages, college yearbooks, computer-assisted grammar project, newspaper in education. *Unit head:* Dr. David Arant, Chair, 901-678-2401, Fax: 901-678-4287, E-mail: darant@memphis.edu. *Application contact:* Dr. Rick Fischer, Coordinator of Graduate Studies, 901-678-2853, Fax: 901-678-4287, E-mail: rfischer@memphis.edu.
Website: http://memphis.edu/journalism/

University of Miami, Graduate School, School of Communication, Coral Gables, FL 33124. Offers communication (PhD); communication studies (MA); film studies (MA, PhD); motion pictures (MFA), including production, producing, and screenwriting; print journalism (MA); public relations (MA); Spanish language journalism (MA); television broadcast journalism (MA). Part-time programs available. *Degree requirements:* For master's, comprehensive exam (for some programs), thesis (for some programs); for doctorate, comprehensive exam, thesis/dissertation. *Entrance requirements:* For master's, GRE General Test; for doctorate, GRE General Test, master's thesis or scholarly research. Additional exam requirements/recommendations for international students: Required—TOEFL (minimum score 600 paper-based; 100 iBT). Electronic applications accepted. *Faculty research:* Communication studies, mass communication, international/interpersonal communication, film studies, journalism.

University of Mississippi, Graduate School, School of Journalism and New Media, University, MS 38677. Offers journalism (MA). *Degree requirements:* For master's, thesis.

University of Missouri, Office of Research and Graduate Studies, School of Journalism, Columbia, MO 65211. Offers center for the digital globe (Certificate); European Union studies (Certificate); health communications (MA); interactive media (MA); journalism (PhD); media management (MA); strategic communication (MA). *Accreditation:* ACEJMC (one or more programs are accredited). Part-time programs available. *Faculty:* 75 full-time (38 women), 3 part-time/adjunct (1 woman). *Students:* 159 full-time (104 women), 88 part-time (54 women); includes 33 minority (8 Black or African American, non-Hispanic/Latino; 11 Asian, non-Hispanic/Latino; 11 Hispanic/Latino; 3 Two or more races, non-Hispanic/Latino), 57 international. Average age 29. 239 applicants, 55% accepted, 78 enrolled. In 2014, 73 master's, 8 doctorates awarded. Terminal master's awarded for partial completion of doctoral program. *Degree requirements:* For master's, thesis (for some programs); for doctorate, 2 foreign languages, thesis/dissertation. *Entrance requirements:* For master's and doctorate, GRE General Test, minimum GPA of 3.0. Additional exam requirements/recommendations for international students: Required—TOEFL (minimum score 600 paper-based; 100 iBT). *Application deadline:* For fall admission, 12/15 priority date for domestic and international students; for winter admission, 9/1 priority date for domestic and international students. Applications are processed on a rolling basis. Application fee: $55 ($75 for international students). Electronic applications accepted. *Financial support:* Fellowships with tuition reimbursements, research assistantships with tuition reimbursements, teaching assistantships with tuition reimbursements, career-related internships or fieldwork, institutionally sponsored loans, scholarships/grants, health care benefits, and unspecified assistantships available. Support available to part-time students. *Faculty research:* Strategic communication, convergence journalism, journalism studies, international programs, photojournalism, magazine journalism, radio-television journalism. *Unit head:* Dr. Esther Thorson, Associate Dean, 573-882-9590, E-mail: thorsone@missouri.edu. *Application contact:* Ginny Cowell, Administrative Assistant, 573-882-4852, E-mail: cowellvj@missouri.edu.
Website: http://www.journalism.missouri.edu/graduate/

The University of Montana, Graduate School, School of Journalism, Missoula, MT 59812-0002. Offers MA. *Degree requirements:* For master's, thesis or alternative, professional project. *Entrance requirements:* For master's, GRE. Additional exam requirements/recommendations for international students: Required—TOEFL (minimum score 580 paper-based). Electronic applications accepted. *Faculty research:* Native American issues, natural resources, public affairs, economy, photojournalism, multimedia, media law.

University of Nebraska–Lincoln, Graduate College, College of Journalism and Mass Communications, Lincoln, NE 68588. Offers marketing, communication and advertising (MA); professional journalism (MA). Postbaccalaureate distance learning degree programs offered (no on-campus study). *Degree requirements:* For master's, thesis. *Entrance requirements:* For master's, samples of work. Additional exam requirements/recommendations for international students: Required—TOEFL (minimum score 600 paper-based). Electronic applications accepted. *Faculty research:* Interactive media and the Internet, community newspapers, children's radio, advertising involvement, telecommunications policy.

University of Nevada, Las Vegas, Graduate College, Greenspun College of Urban Affairs, School of Journalism and Media Studies, Las Vegas, NV 89154-5007. Offers MA. *Faculty:* 5 full-time (0 women), 1 part-time/adjunct (0 women). *Students:* 12 full-time (9 women), 7 part-time (4 women); includes 7 minority (1 Black or African American, non-Hispanic/Latino; 3 Asian, non-Hispanic/Latino; 3 Hispanic/Latino), 2 international. Average age 29. 14 applicants, 79% accepted, 6 enrolled. In 2014, 11 master's awarded. *Entrance requirements:* For master's, GRE General Test. Additional exam requirements/recommendations for international students: Required—TOEFL (minimum score 550 paper-based; 80 iBT), IELTS (minimum score 7). *Application deadline:* For fall admission, 3/15 for domestic students, 5/1 for international students; for spring admission, 10/1 for international students. Application fee: $60 ($95 for international students). Electronic applications accepted. *Financial support:* In 2014–15, 8 students received support, including 1 research assistantship with partial tuition reimbursement available (averaging $10,000 per year), 7 teaching assistantships with partial tuition reimbursements available (averaging $10,000 per year); institutionally sponsored loans, scholarships/grants, health care benefits, and unspecified assistantships also available. Financial award application deadline: 3/1. *Faculty research:* Journalism, mass communication and media history; media law, First Amendment theory, First Amendment law, privacy, obscenity, libel; visual literacy, aesthetics and rhetoric, social psychology of visually-mediated world; global media, audience reception theory and research, video criticism, and advertising; intersection of society and media technologies, emerging technology. *Unit head:* Dr. Lawrence Mullen, Director/Professor, 702-895-4491, E-mail: lawrence.mullen@unlv.edu. *Application contact:* Graduate

College Admissions Evaluator, 702-895-3320, Fax: 702-895-4180, E-mail: gradcollege@unlv.edu. Website: http://journalism.unlv.edu/

University of Nevada, Reno, Graduate School, Donald W. Reynolds School of Journalism, Reno, NV 89557. Offers MA. *Degree requirements:* For master's, thesis. *Entrance requirements:* For master's, GRE General Test, minimum GPA of 2.75. Additional exam requirements/recommendations for international students: Required—TOEFL (minimum score 500 paper-based; 61 iBT), IELTS (minimum score 6). Electronic applications accepted. *Faculty research:* Interactive environmental journalism.

University of North Texas, Robert B. Toulouse School of Graduate Studies, Denton, TX 76203-5459. Offers accounting (MS); applied anthropology (MA, MS); applied behavior analysis (Certificate); applied geography (MA); applied technology and performance improvement (M Ed, MS); art education (MA); art history (MA); art museum education (Certificate); arts leadership (Certificate); audiology (Au D); behavior analysis (MS); behavioral science (PhD); biochemistry and molecular biology (MS); biology (MA, MS); biomedical engineering (MS); business analysis (MS); chemistry (MS); clinical health psychology (PhD); communication studies (MA, MS); computer engineering (MS); computer science (MS); counseling (M Ed, MS), including clinical mental health counseling (MS), college and university counseling, elementary school counseling, secondary school counseling; creative writing (MA); criminal justice (MS); curriculum and instruction (M Ed); decision sciences (MBA); design (MA, MFA), including fashion design (MFA), innovation studies, interior design (MFA); early childhood studies (MS); economics (MS); educational leadership (M Ed, Ed D); educational psychology (MS, PhD), including family studies (MS), gifted and talented (MS), human development (MS), learning and cognition (MS), research, measurement and evaluation (MS); electrical engineering (MS); emergency management (MPA); engineering technology (MS); English (MA); English as a second language (MA); environmental science (MS); finance (MBA, MS); financial management (MPA); French (MA); health services management (MBA); higher education (M Ed, Ed D); history (MA, MS); hospitality management (MS); human resources management (MPA); information science (MS); information systems (PhD); information technologies (MBA); interdisciplinary studies (MA, MS); international studies (MA); international sustainable tourism (MS); jazz studies (MM); journalism (MA, MJ, Graduate Certificate), including interactive and virtual digital communication (Graduate Certificate), narrative journalism (Graduate Certificate), public relations (Graduate Certificate); kinesiology (MS); linguistics (MA); local government management (MPA); logistics (PhD); logistics and supply chain management (MBA); long-term care, senior housing, and aging services (MA); management (PhD); marketing (MBA); mathematics (MA, MS); mechanical and energy engineering (MS, PhD); music (MA), including ethnomusicology, music theory, musicology, performance; music composition (PhD); music education (MM Ed, PhD); nonprofit management (MPA); operations and supply chain management (MBA); performance (MM, DMA); philosophy (MA); political science (MA); professional and technical communication (MA); radio, television and film (MA, MFA); rehabilitation counseling (Certificate); sociology (MA); Spanish (MA); special education (M Ed); speech-language pathology (MA); strategic management (MBA); studio art (MFA); teaching (M Ed); MBA/MS. Part-time and evening/weekend programs available. Postbaccalaureate distance learning degree programs offered. *Faculty:* 651 full-time (215 women), 233 part-time/adjunct (139 women). *Students:* 3,040 full-time (1,598 women), 3,401 part-time (2,097 women); includes 1,740 minority (533 Black or African American, non-Hispanic/Latino; 15 American Indian or Alaska Native, non-Hispanic/Latino; 286 Asian, non-Hispanic/Latino; 746 Hispanic/Latino; 3 Native Hawaiian or other Pacific Islander, non-Hispanic/Latino; 157 Two or more races, non-Hispanic/Latino), 1,145 international. Terminal master's awarded for partial completion of doctoral program. *Degree requirements:* For master's, variable foreign language requirement, comprehensive exam (for some programs), thesis (for some programs); for doctorate, variable foreign language requirement, comprehensive exam (for some programs), thesis/dissertation; for other advanced degree, variable foreign language requirement, comprehensive exam (for some programs). *Entrance requirements:* For master's and doctorate, GRE, GMAT. Additional exam requirements/recommendations for international students: Required—TOEFL (minimum score 550 paper-based; 79 iBT). *Application deadline:* For fall admission, 7/15 for domestic students, 3/15 for international students; for spring admission, 11/15 for domestic students, 9/15 for international students; for summer admission, 5/1 for domestic students. Applications are processed on a rolling basis. Application fee: $60. Electronic applications accepted. *Expenses:* Tuition, state resident: full-time $5450; part-time $3633 per year. Tuition, nonresident: full-time $11,966; part-time $7977 per year. *Required fees:* $1301; $398 per credit hour. $685 per semester. Tuition and fees vary according to program and reciprocity agreements. *Financial support:* Fellowships with partial tuition reimbursements, research assistantships with partial tuition reimbursements, teaching assistantships, career-related internships or fieldwork, Federal Work-Study, institutionally sponsored loans, scholarships/grants, health care benefits, and library assistantships available. Support available to part-time students. Financial award applicants required to submit FAFSA. *Unit head:* Mark Wardell, Dean, 940-565-2383, E-mail: mark.wardell@unt.edu. *Application contact:* Toulouse School of Graduate Studies, 940-565-2383, Fax: 940-565-2141, E-mail: gradsch@unt.edu. Website: http://tsgs.unt.edu/

University of Oklahoma, Gaylord College of Journalism and Mass Communication, Program in Journalism and Mass Communication, Norman, OK 73019. Offers MA, PhD. Part-time programs available. *Students:* 30 full-time (18 women), 23 part-time (8 women); includes 5 minority (2 Black or African American, non-Hispanic/Latino; 1 American Indian or Alaska Native, non-Hispanic/Latino; 1 Hispanic/Latino; 1 Two or more races, non-Hispanic/Latino), 15 international. Average age 31. 38 applicants, 47% accepted, 12 enrolled. In 2014, 14 master's, 4 doctorates awarded. *Degree requirements:* For master's, comprehensive exam (for some programs), thesis (for some programs); for doctorate, comprehensive exam, thesis/dissertation. *Entrance requirements:* For master's, GRE, 2 letters of recommendation, resume, personal statement, writing sample, minimum GPA of 3.2; for doctorate, GRE, 3 letters of recommendation, resume, personal statement, writing sample, minimum GPA of 3.5. Additional exam requirements/recommendations for international students: Required—TOEFL (minimum score 79 iBT). *Application deadline:* For fall admission, 7/1 for domestic students, 3/1 for international students; for spring admission, 11/1 for domestic students, 9/1 for international students. Application fee: $50 ($100 for international students). Electronic applications accepted. *Expenses:* Tuition, state resident: full-time $4394; part-time $183.10 per credit hour. Tuition, nonresident: full-time $16,970; part-time $707.10 per credit hour. *Required fees:* $2892; $109.95 per credit hour. $126.50 per semester. *Financial support:* In 2014–15, 37 students received support. Career-related internships or fieldwork, institutionally sponsored loans, scholarships/grants, health care benefits, and unspecified assistantships available. Support available to part-time students. Financial award application deadline: 6/1; financial award applicants required to submit FAFSA. *Faculty research:* Global and international public relations, crisis communication, strategic communication, advertising planning, digital advertising, media management, media studies, mass communication, women and leadership, digital media, health communication, ethics in journalism and media, broadcasting and production, critical and cultural theories. *Unit head:* Dr. Katerina Tsetsura, Director of Graduate Studies, 405-325-6195, Fax: 405-325-7565, E-mail: tsetsura@ou.edu. *Application contact:* Larry Laneer, Graduate Advisor, 405-325-2722, Fax: 405-325-7565, E-mail: llaneer@ou.edu. Website: http://www.ou.edu/content/gaylord/graduate.html

University of Oregon, Graduate School, School of Journalism and Communication, Eugene, OR 97403. Offers journalism (MA, MS); media studies (MA, MS, PhD); multimedia journalism (MA, MS); strategic communication (MA, MS). *Accreditation:* ASHA. Part-time programs available. *Degree requirements:* For master's, thesis or alternative. *Entrance requirements:* For master's, GRE General Test; for doctorate, master's degree. *Faculty research:* Impact of mass communication, media technology, media accountability, craft attitudes, media economics.

University of Puerto Rico, Río Piedras Campus, School of Communication, Program in Journalism, San Juan, PR 00931-3300. Offers MA.

University of Regina, Faculty of Graduate Studies and Research, Faculty of Arts, School of Journalism, Regina, SK S4S 0A2, Canada. Offers MJ. Part-time programs available. *Faculty:* 4 full-time (2 women). *Degree requirements:* For master's, project. *Entrance requirements:* For master's, written project concept; statement of interest; statement of ability. Additional exam requirements/recommendations for international students: Required—TOEFL (minimum score 580 paper-based; 80 iBT), IELTS (minimum score 6.5), PTE (minimum score 59). *Application deadline:* For fall admission, 1/15 for domestic and international students. Application fee: $100. Electronic applications accepted. *Expenses: Tuition, area resident:* Full-time $4900 Canadian dollars; part-time $837.65 Canadian dollars per semester. *International tuition:* $7900 Canadian dollars full-time. *Required fees:* $396 Canadian dollars; $86.90 Canadian dollars per semester. *Financial support:* Fellowships, research assistantships, teaching assistantships, and scholarships/grants available. Financial award application deadline: 6/15. *Unit head:* Mitch Diamantopolous, Head, 306-585-4090, Fax: 306-585-4867, E-mail: mitch.diamantopolous@uregina.ca. *Application contact:* Patricia Elliott, Graduate Program Coordinator, 306-585-4449, Fax: 306-585-4867, E-mail: patricia.elliott@uregina.ca.
Website: http://www.uregina.ca/arts/journalism/

University of South Carolina, The Graduate School, College of Mass Communications and Information Studies, School of Journalism and Mass Communications, Columbia, SC 29208. Offers MA, MMC, PhD. *Accreditation:* ACEJMC. Part-time programs available. *Degree requirements:* For master's, comprehensive exam, thesis (for some programs); for doctorate, one foreign language, comprehensive exam, thesis/dissertation. *Entrance requirements:* For master's and doctorate, GRE General Test, minimum GPA of 3.0. Additional exam requirements/recommendations for international students: Required—TOEFL (minimum score 600 paper-based; 75 iBT). Electronic applications accepted. *Faculty research:* Ethics, communications law, international communications, science/health/environmental/risk communications, convergent media.

University of Southern California, Graduate School, Annenberg School for Communication and Journalism, School of Journalism, Program in Journalism, Los Angeles, CA 90089. Offers MS. Program enrolls new students to Summer term only. *Students:* 36 full-time (26 women); includes 18 minority (6 Black or African American, non-Hispanic/Latino; 1 American Indian or Alaska Native, non-Hispanic/Latino; 5 Asian, non-Hispanic/Latino; 6 Hispanic/Latino), 7 international. Average age 25. In 2014, 40 master's awarded. *Degree requirements:* For master's, comprehensive exam, thesis optional. *Entrance requirements:* For master's, GRE General Test, resume, writing samples, letters of recommendation, statement of purpose. Additional exam requirements/recommendations for international students: Required—TOEFL (minimum score 114 iBT) or IELTS (minimum score 8). *Application deadline:* For summer admission, 1/4 priority date for domestic students, 12/1 priority date for international students. Application fee: $85. Electronic applications accepted. *Financial support:* In 2014–15, 4 fellowships with full tuition reimbursements (averaging $72,408 per year), 4 teaching assistantships with full tuition reimbursements (averaging $72,408 per year) were awarded; career-related internships or fieldwork, Federal Work-Study, institutionally sponsored loans, scholarships/grants, health care benefits, and unspecified assistantships also available. Support available to part-time students. Financial award application deadline: 1/2; financial award applicants required to submit FAFSA. *Unit head:* Willow Bay, Director, 213-740-3914, Fax: 213-740-8624, E-mail: jourbks@usc.edu. *Application contact:* Allyson Hill, Associate Dean for Admissions, 213-821-0770, Fax: 213-740-1933, E-mail: ascadm@usc.edu.
Website: http://www.annenberg.usc.edu

University of Southern California, Graduate School, Annenberg School for Communication and Journalism, School of Journalism, Program in Specialized Journalism, Los Angeles, CA 90089. Offers specialized journalism (MA); specialized journalism (the arts) (MA). Program enrolls new students to Summer term only. Part-time programs available. *Students:* 28 full-time, 4 part-time; includes 11 minority (5 Black or African American, non-Hispanic/Latino; 1 Asian, non-Hispanic/Latino; 4 Hispanic/Latino; 1 Two or more races, non-Hispanic/Latino), 4 international. Average age 35. 73 applicants, 70% accepted, 22 enrolled. In 2014, 24 master's awarded. *Degree requirements:* For master's, thesis, professional project. *Entrance requirements:* For master's, GRE General Test, resume, portfolio of professional work, letters of recommendation, statement of purpose. Additional exam requirements/recommendations for international students: Required—TOEFL (minimum score 114 iBT) or IELTS (minimum score 8). *Application deadline:* For summer admission, 1/31 priority date for domestic and international students. Applications are processed on a rolling basis. Application fee: $85. Electronic applications accepted. *Financial support:* In 2014–15, 4 fellowships with full tuition reimbursements (averaging $74,208 per year), 2 research assistantships with full tuition reimbursements (averaging $74,208 per year) were awarded; Federal Work-Study, scholarships/grants, and health care benefits also available. Support available to part-time students. Financial award application deadline: 1/2; financial award applicants required to submit FAFSA. *Unit head:* Willow Bay, Director, 213-743-5324. *Application contact:* Allyson Hill, Associate Dean for Admissions, 213-821-0770, Fax: 213-740-1933, E-mail: ascadm@usc.edu.

University of South Florida, College of Arts and Sciences, School of Mass Communications, Tampa, FL 33620-9951. Offers media studies (MA), including media studies; multimedia journalism studies (MA); strategic communication management (MA). Part-time and evening/weekend programs available. *Faculty:* 10 full-time (3 women). *Students:* 17 full-time (13 women), 17 part-time (6 women); includes 5 minority (2 Black or African American, non-Hispanic/Latino; 1 Asian, non-Hispanic/Latino; 2 Hispanic/Latino), 7 international. Average age 29. 40 applicants, 65% accepted, 14 enrolled. In 2014, 15 master's awarded. *Degree requirements:* For master's, comprehensive exam, thesis optional. *Entrance requirements:* For master's, GRE General Test (minimum score of 153 verbal and 144 quantitative preferred), minimum GPA of 3.0 in last 60 hours of course work, three letters of recommendation, letter of intent, resume. Additional exam requirements/recommendations for international students: Required—TOEFL (minimum score 550 paper-based; 79 iBT) or IELTS (minimum score 6.5). *Application deadline:* For fall admission, 2/15 for domestic students, 1/2 for international students; for spring admission, 10/15 for domestic students, 6/1 for international students. Application fee: $30. Electronic applications accepted. *Financial support:* In 2014–15, 9 students received support, including 9 teaching assistantships with tuition reimbursements available (averaging $10,513 per year); unspecified assistantships also available. Financial award application deadline: 2/

Journalism

28. *Faculty research:* First Amendment analysis, civic journalism, public opinion, media ethics, media effects research in sports public relations, public relations management, advertisement, telecommunications. *Total annual research expenditures:* $52,955. *Unit head:* Dr. Jim Andrews, Interim Director and Associate Professor, 813-974-2108, Fax: 813-974-2592, E-mail: jimandrews@usf.edu. *Application contact:* Dr. Michael Mitrook, Assistant Professor, 813-974-8890, Fax: 813-974-2592, E-mail: mmitrook@.usf.edu. Website: http://masscom.usf.edu/grad/

University of South Florida, Innovative Education, Tampa, FL 33620-9951. *Unit head:* Kathy Barnes, Interdisciplinary Programs Coordinator, 813-974-8031, Fax: 813-974-7061, E-mail: barnesk@usf.edu. *Application contact:* Karen Tylinski, Metro Initiatives, 813-974-9943, Fax: 813-974-7061, E-mail: ktylinsk@usf.edu. Website: http://www.usf.edu/innovative-education/

University of South Florida, St. Petersburg, College of Arts and Sciences, St. Petersburg, FL 33701. Offers digital journalism and design (MA); environmental science and policy (MA, MS); Florida studies (MLA); journalism and media studies (MA); liberal studies (MLA); psychology (MA). Part-time programs available. Postbaccalaureate distance learning degree programs offered (no on-campus study). *Degree requirements:* For master's, comprehensive exam, thesis or project. *Entrance requirements:* For master's, GRE, LSAT, MCAT (varies by program), letter of intent, 3 letters of recommendation, writing samples, bachelor's degree from regionally-accredited institution with minimum GPA of 3.0 overall or in upper two years. Additional exam requirements/recommendations for international students: Required—TOEFL (minimum score 550 paper-based; 79 iBT); Recommended—IELTS. Electronic applications accepted.

The University of Tennessee, Graduate School, College of Communication and Information, Knoxville, TN 37996. Offers advertising (MS, PhD); broadcasting (MS, PhD); communications (MS, PhD); information sciences (MS, PhD); journalism (MS, PhD); public relations (MS, PhD); speech communication (MS, PhD). Part-time and evening/weekend programs available. Postbaccalaureate distance learning degree programs offered (no on-campus study). *Degree requirements:* For master's, thesis or alternative; for doctorate, thesis/dissertation. *Entrance requirements:* For master's and doctorate, GRE General Test, minimum GPA of 2.7. Additional exam requirements/recommendations for international students: Required—TOEFL. Electronic applications accepted.

The University of Texas at Austin, Graduate School, College of Communication, School of Journalism, Austin, TX 78712-1111. Offers MA, PhD, MA/MA, MBA/MA, MP Aff/MA. Part-time programs available. *Degree requirements:* For master's, thesis; for doctorate, one foreign language, thesis/dissertation. *Entrance requirements:* For master's and doctorate, GRE General Test. Electronic applications accepted. *Faculty research:* Politics of race, gender, and sexuality; visual ethics; media law and ethics; national television violence study; agenda setting and public opinion.

The University of Western Ontario, Faculty of Graduate Studies, Faculty of Information and Media Studies, Program in Journalism, London, ON N6A 5B8, Canada. Offers MA. *Degree requirements:* For master's, internship. *Entrance requirements:* For master's, honors degree, minimum B average during previous 2 years of course work. Additional exam requirements/recommendations for international students: Required—TOEFL (minimum score 640 paper-based), TWE (minimum score 5). Electronic applications accepted.

University of Wisconsin–Madison, Graduate School, College of Agricultural and Life Sciences, Department of Life Sciences Communication, Madison, WI 53706-1380. Offers life sciences communication (MPS, MS); mass communications (PhD). Part-time programs available. Terminal master's awarded for partial completion of doctoral program. *Degree requirements:* For master's, thesis (for some programs); for doctorate, thesis/dissertation. *Entrance requirements:* For master's, GRE; for doctorate, GRE, master's degree in a communication field or related area of study. Additional exam requirements/recommendations for international students: Required—TOEFL. Electronic applications accepted. *Expenses:* Tuition, state resident: full-time $10,723; part-time $745 per credit. Tuition, nonresident: full-time $24,054; part-time $1578 per credit. *Required fees:* $374 per semester. Tuition and fees vary according to course load, program and reciprocity agreements. *Faculty research:* Science and risk communication, new communication technologies, health communication, mass communication, political communication, history of communication, indigenous communication.

University of Wisconsin–Madison, Graduate School, College of Letters and Science, School of Journalism and Mass Communication, Program in Journalism and Mass Communication, Madison, WI 53706-1380. Offers MA. *Expenses:* Tuition, state resident: full-time $10,723; part-time $745 per credit. Tuition, nonresident: full-time $24,054; part-time $1578 per credit. *Required fees:* $374 per semester. Tuition and fees vary according to course load, program and reciprocity agreements.

Virginia Commonwealth University, Graduate School, College of Humanities and Sciences, School of Mass Communications, Program in Mass Communications, Richmond, VA 23284-9005. Offers multimedia journalism (MS); strategic public relations (MS). *Degree requirements:* For master's, comprehensive exam, thesis optional. *Entrance requirements:* For master's, GRE General Test. Additional exam requirements/recommendations for international students: Required—TOEFL (minimum score 600 paper-based; 100 iBT); Recommended—IELTS (minimum score 6.5). Electronic applications accepted. *Faculty research:* Multimedia journalism, strategic public relations.

Wayne State University, College of Fine, Performing and Communication Arts, Department of Communication, Detroit, MI 48202. Offers communication (PhD), including democratic participation and culture, identity and representation, media, society and culture, risk, crisis and conflict, wellness, worklife and relationships; communication and new media (Graduate Certificate); communication studies (MA); dispute resolution (MADR, Graduate Certificate); health communication (Graduate Certificate); journalism (MA); media arts (MA); media studies (MA); public relations and organizational communication (MA); JD/MADR. Doctoral programs admit for fall only. *Students:* 63 full-time (34 women), 82 part-time (63 women); includes 48 minority (40 Black or African American, non-Hispanic/Latino; 3 Asian, non-Hispanic/Latino; 3 Hispanic/Latino; 2 Two or more races, non-Hispanic/Latino), 13 international. Average age 35. 177 applicants, 40% accepted, 38 enrolled. In 2014, 33 master's, 4 doctorates, 9 other advanced degrees awarded. *Degree requirements:* For master's, thesis (for some programs), thesis or essay; for doctorate, thesis/dissertation. *Entrance requirements:* For master's, GRE (if undergraduate GPA less than 3.2), personal statement; BA or BS in communication or related field with minimum upper-division GPA of 3.2 and sample of academic writing (for MA); minimum upper-division undergraduate GPA of 3.0 and 3 letters of recommendation (for MADR); for doctorate, GRE, MA in communication or related field with minimum GPA of 3.5, three letters of recommendation; personal statement; sample of written scholarship; for Graduate Certificate, minimum upper-division GPA of 3.0, personal statement. Additional exam requirements/recommendations for international students: Required—TOEFL (minimum score 600 paper-based; 100 iBT), IELTS (minimum score 6.5), TWE (minimum score 6). *Application deadline:* For fall admission, 8/1 for domestic and international students; for winter admission, 11/1 for domestic and international students; for spring admission, 4/1 for domestic and international students. Application fee: $0. Electronic applications accepted. *Expenses:* Expenses: Contact institution. *Financial support:* In 2014–15, 48 students received support, including 3 fellowships with tuition reimbursements available (averaging $16,000 per year), 20 teaching assistantships with tuition reimbursements available (averaging $16,540 per year); research assistantships with tuition reimbursements available, scholarships/grants, and unspecified assistantships also available. Financial award application deadline: 3/31; financial award applicants required to submit FAFSA. *Faculty research:* Rhetorical theory and criticism; mass media theory and research; argumentation; organizational communication; risk and crisis communication; interpersonal, family, and health communication. *Unit head:* Dr. Lee Wilikins, Chair, 313-577-2943, E-mail: eh8899@wayne.edu. *Application contact:* Dr. Pradeep Sopory, Director of Graduate Studies, 313-577-2945, E-mail: psopory@wayne.edu. Website: http://comm.wayne.edu/

West Virginia University, Reed College of Media, Morgantown, WV 26506. Offers digital marketing communications (Graduate Certificate); integrated marketing communications (MS); journalism (MSJ). MS program taught exclusively online. Part-time programs available. Postbaccalaureate distance learning degree programs offered (no on-campus study). *Degree requirements:* For master's, thesis or alternative. *Entrance requirements:* For master's, GRE General Test, minimum GPA of 3.0, writing samples. Additional exam requirements/recommendations for international students: Required—TOEFL. Electronic applications accepted. *Faculty research:* History, law, and women in media; press management; public opinion; advertising effectiveness; international advertising.

Mass Communication

American University, School of Communication, Program in International Media, Washington, DC 20016-8001. Offers MA. Part-time and evening/weekend programs available. *Faculty:* 1 (woman) full-time, 7 part-time/adjunct (4 women). *Students:* 17 full-time (12 women), 1 (woman) part-time; includes 2 minority (both Hispanic/Latino), 7 international. 38 applicants, 39% accepted, 4 enrolled. In 2014, 3 master's awarded. *Degree requirements:* For master's, one foreign language, comprehensive exam, thesis or alternative. *Entrance requirements:* For master's, GRE General Test, bachelor's degree with minimum cumulative GPA of 3.3, 2 letters of reference. Additional exam requirements/recommendations for international students: Required—TOEFL (minimum score 600 paper-based; 100 iBT), IELTS (minimum score 7). *Application deadline:* For fall admission, 2/1 priority date for domestic students, 2/1 for international students; for spring admission, 11/1 for domestic and international students. Applications are processed on a rolling basis. Application fee: $55. Electronic applications accepted. *Financial support:* In 2014–15, 6 research assistantships with partial tuition reimbursements (averaging $8,000 per year) were awarded; career-related internships or fieldwork, Federal Work-Study, scholarships/grants, and unspecified assistantships also available. Financial award application deadline: 2/1; financial award applicants required to submit FAFSA. *Unit head:* Christine Lawrence, Interim Director, 202-885-2062, Fax: 202-885-2099, E-mail: claw@american.edu. *Application contact:* Sharmeen Ahsan-Bracciale, Graduate Admissions Office, 202-885-2040, Fax: 202-885-2019, E-mail: sharmeen@american.edu.

American University, School of Communication, Program in Public Communication, Washington, DC 20016-8001. Offers MA. *Accreditation:* ACEJMC. Part-time and evening/weekend programs available. *Degree requirements:* For master's, comprehensive exam, thesis or alternative. *Entrance requirements:* For master's, GRE General Test. Additional exam requirements/recommendations for international students: Required—TOEFL (minimum score 600 paper-based; 100 iBT), IELTS (minimum score 7). *Application deadline:* For fall admission, 2/1 priority date for domestic students, 4/1 priority date for international students. Applications are

processed on a rolling basis. Application fee: $50. Electronic applications accepted. *Financial support:* Research assistantships with partial tuition reimbursements, teaching assistantships with partial tuition reimbursements, career-related internships or fieldwork, Federal Work-Study, institutionally sponsored loans, scholarships/grants, tuition waivers (partial), and unspecified assistantships available. Financial award application deadline: 2/1; financial award applicants required to submit FAFSA. *Faculty research:* Litigation and public relations, cross-cultural and intercultural communication, statistical public relations, African-Americans and women in public communication, international public relations. *Application contact:* Sharmeen Ahsan-Bracciale, Director of Graduate Services, 202-885-3940, Fax: 202-885-2019, E-mail: sharmeen@american.edu. Website: http://www.american.edu/soc/communication/degrees/MA-SCOM.cfm

American University, School of Communication, Weekend Programs in Communication, Washington, DC 20016-8001. Offers interactive journalism (MA); media entrepreneurship (MA); producing for film and video (MA); strategic communication (MA). *Accreditation:* ACEJMC. Part-time and evening/weekend programs available. *Degree requirements:* For master's, comprehensive exam, thesis or alternative. *Entrance requirements:* Additional exam requirements/recommendations for international students: Required—TOEFL (minimum score 600 paper-based; 100 iBT). *Application deadline:* For fall admission, 8/1 for domestic students. Applications are processed on a rolling basis. Application fee: $50. Electronic applications accepted. *Financial support:* Fellowships and institutionally sponsored loans available. Financial award applicants required to submit FAFSA. *Unit head:* Prof. Rose Ann Robertson, Associate Dean for Academic Administration, 202-885-2002, E-mail: rrobert@american.edu. *Application contact:* Sharmeen Ahsan-Bracciale, Director of Graduate Services, 202-885-3940, Fax: 202-885-2019, E-mail: sharmeen@american.edu. Website: http://american.edu/soc/admissions/weekend.cfm

American University, School of International Service, Washington, DC 20016-8071. Offers comparative and regional studies (Certificate); cross-cultural communication (Certificate); development management (MS); ethics, peace, and global affairs (MA); European studies (Certificate); global environmental policy (MA, Certificate); global information technology (Certificate); international affairs (MA), including comparative and international disability policy, comparative and regional studies, international economic relations, international politics, natural resources and sustainable development, U.S. foreign policy; international communication (MA, Certificate); international development (MA, Certificate); international economic policy (Certificate); international economic relations (Certificate); international media (MA); international peace and conflict resolution (MA, Certificate); international politics (Certificate); international relations (PhD); international service (MIS); peacebuilding (Certificate); social enterprise (MA); the Americas (Certificate); United States foreign policy (Certificate); JD/MA. Part-time and evening/weekend programs available. Postbaccalaureate distance learning degree programs offered (no on-campus study). *Faculty:* 112 full-time (43 women), 59 part-time/adjunct (27 women). *Students:* 545 full-time (335 women), 443 part-time (271 women); includes 231 minority (82 Black or African American, non-Hispanic/Latino; 8 American Indian or Alaska Native, non-Hispanic/Latino; 51 Asian, non-Hispanic/Latino; 81 Hispanic/Latino; 2 Native Hawaiian or other Pacific Islander, non-Hispanic/Latino; 7 Two or more races, non-Hispanic/Latino), 120 international. Average age 28. 1,991 applicants, 70% accepted, 365 enrolled. In 2014, 426 master's, 9 doctorates, 6 other advanced degrees awarded. Terminal master's awarded for partial completion of doctoral program. *Degree requirements:* For master's, one foreign language, comprehensive exam, thesis or alternative; for doctorate, one foreign language, comprehensive exam, thesis/dissertation. *Entrance requirements:* For master's, GRE, transcripts, resume, 2 letters of recommendation, statement of purpose; for doctorate, GRE, transcripts, resume, 3 letters of recommendation, statement of purpose. Additional exam requirements/recommendations for international students: Required—TOEFL (minimum score 600 paper-based; 100 iBT). *Application deadline:* For fall admission, 1/15 for domestic students; for spring admission, 10/1 for domestic students, 9/15 for international students. Application fee: $50. Electronic applications accepted. *Financial support:* Application deadline: 1/15. *Unit head:* Dr. James Goldgeier, Dean, 202-885-1603, Fax: 202-885-2494, E-mail: goldgeier@american.edu. *Application contact:* Jia Jiang, Associate Director, Graduate Education Enrollment, 202-885-1689, Fax: 202-885-1109, E-mail: jiang@american.edu.
Website: http://www.american.edu/sis/

Arizona State University at the Tempe campus, Walter Cronkite School of Journalism and Mass Communication, Phoenix, AZ 85004. Offers journalism and mass communication (PhD); mass communication (MMC). *Accreditation:* ACEJMC. Terminal master's awarded for partial completion of doctoral program. *Degree requirements:* For master's, 9-hour professional capstone experience; interactive Program of Study (iPOS) submitted before completing 50 percent of required credit hours; for doctorate, comprehensive exam, thesis/dissertation, interactive Program of Study (iPOS) submitted before completing 50 percent of required credit hours. *Entrance requirements:* For master's and doctorate, GRE, minimum GPA of 3.0 or equivalent in last 2 years of work leading to bachelor's degree. Additional exam requirements/recommendations for international students: Required—TOEFL, IELTS, or PTE. Electronic applications accepted. *Expenses:* Contact institution.

Auburn University, Graduate School, College of Liberal Arts, Department of Communication and Journalism, Auburn University, AL 36849. Offers communication (MA); communication studies (Graduate Certificate); mass communications (MA). Part-time programs available. *Faculty:* 28 full-time (16 women), 6 part-time/adjunct (3 women). *Students:* 21 full-time (16 women), 4 part-time (1 woman); includes 3 minority (2 Black or African American, non-Hispanic/Latino; 1 Hispanic/Latino), 4 international. Average age 25. 55 applicants, 38% accepted, 7 enrolled. In 2014, 17 master's awarded. *Degree requirements:* For master's, thesis (for some programs). *Entrance requirements:* For master's, GRE General Test. *Application deadline:* For fall admission, 7/7 for domestic students; for spring admission, 11/24 for domestic students. Applications are processed on a rolling basis. Application fee: $50 ($60 for international students). Electronic applications accepted. *Expenses:* Tuition, state resident: full-time $8586; part-time $477 per credit hour. Tuition, nonresident: full-time $25,758; part-time $1431 per credit hour. *Required fees:* $804 per semester. Tuition and fees vary according to degree level and program. *Financial support:* Teaching assistantships and Federal Work-Study available. Support available to part-time students. Financial award application deadline: 3/15; financial award applicants required to submit FAFSA. *Unit head:* Dr. Jennifer Adams, Chair, 334-844-2727. *Application contact:* Dr. George Flowers, Dean of the Graduate School, 334-844-2125.
Website: http://www.cla.auburn.edu/cmjn/

Boston University, College of Communication, Department of Mass Communication, Advertising, and Public Relations, Boston, MA 02215. Offers advertising (MS); JD/MS. Part-time programs available. *Faculty:* 26 full-time, 33 part-time/adjunct. *Students:* 138 full-time (117 women), 9 part-time (6 women); includes 12 minority (5 Black or African American, non-Hispanic/Latino; 3 Asian, non-Hispanic/Latino; 1 Hispanic/Latino; 3 Two or more races, non-Hispanic/Latino), 83 international. Average age 25. 429 applicants, 48% accepted, 81 enrolled. In 2014, 18 master's awarded. *Degree requirements:* For master's, comprehensive exam (for some programs), thesis (for some programs). *Entrance requirements:* For master's, GRE General Test, resume, letters of recommendation. Additional exam requirements/recommendations for international students: Required—TOEFL (minimum score 600 paper-based; 100 iBT), IELTS. *Application deadline:* For fall admission, 5/1 for domestic and international students. Applications are processed on a rolling basis. Application fee: $80. Electronic applications accepted. *Expenses: Tuition:* Full-time $45,686; part-time $1428 per credit hour. *Required fees:* $660; $60 per semester. Tuition and fees vary according to program. *Financial support:* Research assistantships, teaching assistantships with partial tuition reimbursements, career-related internships or fieldwork, Federal Work-Study, institutionally sponsored loans, scholarships/grants, and unspecified assistantships available. Support available to part-time students. Financial award application deadline: 5/1; financial award applicants required to submit FAFSA. *Unit head:* T. Barton Carter, Chairman, 617-353-3482, E-mail: comlaw@bu.edu. *Application contact:* Manny Dotel, Assistant Director, Graduate Affairs, 617-353-3481, E-mail: comgrad@bu.edu.
Website: http://www.bu.edu/com/academics/masscomm-ad-pr/

Brigham Young University, Graduate Studies, College of Fine Arts and Communications, School of Communications, Provo, UT 84602. Offers mass communications (MA). Part-time programs available. *Faculty:* 16 full-time (2 women). *Students:* 17 full-time (10 women), 26 part-time (15 women); includes 5 minority (3 Asian, non-Hispanic/Latino; 2 Hispanic/Latino), 7 international. Average age 30. 20 applicants, 60% accepted, 11 enrolled. In 2014, 8 master's awarded. *Degree requirements:* For master's, comprehensive exam, thesis. *Entrance requirements:* For master's, GRE, minimum GPA of 3.0 in last 60 hours of course work. Additional exam requirements/recommendations for international students: Required—TOEFL (minimum score 580 paper-based; 85 iBT). *Application deadline:* For fall admission, 3/31 priority date for domestic and international students. Applications are processed on a rolling

basis. Application fee: $50. Electronic applications accepted. *Expenses: Tuition:* Full-time $6310; part-time $371 per credit hour. Tuition and fees vary according to program and student's religious affiliation. *Financial support:* In 2014–15, 17 students received support, including 20 research assistantships with full and partial tuition reimbursements available (averaging $4,229 per year), 7 teaching assistantships with full and partial tuition reimbursements available (averaging $3,815 per year); career-related internships or fieldwork, institutionally sponsored loans, scholarships/grants, unspecified assistantships, and supplementary awards also available. Financial award application deadline: 4/30; financial award applicants required to submit FAFSA. *Faculty research:* Ethics, international, magazine, newspaper, media effects. *Unit head:* Dr. Edward E. Adams, Director, 801-422-2997, Fax: 801-422-0160, E-mail: comms_secretary@byu.edu. *Application contact:* Dr. Mark A. Callister, Graduate Coordinator, 801-422-6143, Fax: 801-422-0160, E-mail: mark_callister@byu.edu.
Website: http://cfac.byu.edu/departments/communications

California State University, Fresno, Division of Graduate Studies, College of Arts and Humanities, Department of Mass Communication and Journalism, Fresno, CA 93740-8027. Offers MA. Part-time and evening/weekend programs available. *Degree requirements:* For master's, thesis. *Entrance requirements:* For master's, GRE General Test, minimum GPA of 3.0. Additional exam requirements/recommendations for international students: Required—TOEFL. Electronic applications accepted.

California State University, Fullerton, Graduate Studies, College of Communications, Department of Communications, Fullerton, CA 92834-9480. Offers advertising (MA); mass communications research and theory (MA); professional communications (MA); tourism and entertainment (MA). Part-time programs available. *Students:* 18 full-time (17 women), 18 part-time (12 women); includes 17 minority (2 Black or African American, non-Hispanic/Latino; 5 Asian, non-Hispanic/Latino; 10 Hispanic/Latino), 2 international. Average age 27. 48 applicants, 42% accepted, 10 enrolled. In 2014, 25 master's awarded. *Degree requirements:* For master's, project or thesis. *Entrance requirements:* For master's, GRE General Test. Application fee: $55. *Financial support:* Teaching assistantships, career-related internships or fieldwork, Federal Work-Study, institutionally sponsored loans, and scholarships/grants available. Support available to part-time students. Financial award application deadline: 3/1; financial award applicants required to submit FAFSA. *Unit head:* Dr. Diane F. Witmer, Chair, 657-278-7008. *Application contact:* Coordinator, 657-278-3832.

California State University, Northridge, Graduate Studies, College of Arts, Media, and Communication, Department of Journalism, Northridge, CA 91330. Offers mass communication (MA). Part-time and evening/weekend programs available. *Students:* 18 full-time (10 women), 8 part-time (4 women); includes 12 minority (4 Black or African American, non-Hispanic/Latino; 2 Asian, non-Hispanic/Latino; 4 Hispanic/Latino; 2 Two or more races, non-Hispanic/Latino), 6 international. Average age 29. *Degree requirements:* For master's, thesis. *Entrance requirements:* For master's, GRE General Test. Additional exam requirements/recommendations for international students: Required—TOEFL. *Application deadline:* For fall admission, 11/30 for domestic students. Application fee: $55. *Expenses: Required fees:* $12,402. *Financial support:* Career-related internships or fieldwork and Federal Work-Study available. Financial award application deadline: 3/1. *Unit head:* Linda Bowen, Chair, 818-677-3135.
Website: http://www.csun.edu/journalism/

The College of Saint Rose, Graduate Studies, School of Arts and Humanities, Department of Public Communications, Albany, NY 12203-1419. Offers MA. Part-time and evening/weekend programs available. *Degree requirements:* For master's, final project or thesis. *Entrance requirements:* For master's, minimum undergraduate GPA of 3.0, 2 writing samples. Additional exam requirements/recommendations for international students: Required—TOEFL (minimum score 550 paper-based). Electronic applications accepted.

Colorado State University, Graduate School, College of Liberal Arts, Department of Journalism and Technical Communication, Fort Collins, CO 80523-1785. Offers public communication and technology (MS, PhD); technical communication (MS). Part-time programs available. *Faculty:* 16 full-time (8 women). *Students:* 31 full-time (23 women), 37 part-time (26 women); includes 9 minority (2 Black or African American, non-Hispanic/Latino; 1 American Indian or Alaska Native, non-Hispanic/Latino; 4 Hispanic/Latino; 2 Two or more races, non-Hispanic/Latino), 6 international. Average age 33. 36 applicants, 67% accepted, 20 enrolled. In 2014, 6 master's, 2 doctorates awarded. *Degree requirements:* For master's, variable foreign language requirement, comprehensive exam (for some programs), thesis (for some programs); for doctorate, variable foreign language requirement, comprehensive exam (for some programs), thesis/dissertation (for some programs). *Entrance requirements:* For master's, GRE General Test, samples of written work, letters of recommendation, resume or curriculum vitae, 3 writing/communication projects, statement of purpose, transcripts; for doctorate, GRE General Test, master's degree, minimum GPA of 3.0, scholarly/professional work, letters of recommendation, statement of career plans, resume, transcripts. Additional exam requirements/recommendations for international students: Required—TOEFL (minimum score 550 paper-based; 80 iBT). *Application deadline:* For fall admission, 2/15 priority date for domestic students, 12/15 priority date for international students; for spring admission, 6/15 priority date for domestic students. Applications are processed on a rolling basis. Application fee: $50. Electronic applications accepted. *Expenses:* Tuition, state resident: full-time $9348; part-time $519 per credit. Tuition, nonresident: full-time $22,916; part-time $1273 per credit. *Required fees:* $1584. *Financial support:* In 2014–15, 36 students received support, including 4 research assistantships with full and partial tuition reimbursements available (averaging $14,586 per year), 32 teaching assistantships with partial tuition reimbursements available (averaging $14,327 per year); career-related internships or fieldwork, Federal Work-Study, institutionally sponsored loans, scholarships/grants, traineeships, and unspecified assistantships also available. Support available to part-time students. Financial award application deadline: 3/1; financial award applicants required to submit FAFSA. *Faculty research:* Technical/science communication, public relations, health/risk communication, Web/new media technologies, environmental communication. *Total annual research expenditures:* $1.1 million. *Unit head:* Dr. Greg Luft, Chair, 970-491-1979, Fax: 970-491-2908, E-mail: greg.luft@colostate.edu. *Application contact:* Dr. Linda Kidder, Graduate Program Coordinator, 970-491-5132, Fax: 970-491-2908, E-mail: linda.kidder@colostate.edu.
Website: http://journalism.colostate.edu/

Drexel University, College of Arts and Sciences, Department of Culture and Communication, Program in Communication, Philadelphia, PA 19104-2875. Offers public communication (MS); science communication (MS); technical communication (MS). Part-time and evening/weekend programs available. *Degree requirements:* For master's, internship, professional portfolio. *Entrance requirements:* For master's, GRE or minimum GPA of 3.0. Additional exam requirements/recommendations for international students: Required—TOEFL. Electronic applications accepted.

Florida International University, School of Journalism and Mass Communication, Miami, FL 33199. Offers mass communication (MS), including global strategic communications, Spanish language journalism. *Accreditation:* ACEJMC. Part-time and evening/weekend programs available. *Degree requirements:* For master's, thesis optional. *Entrance requirements:* For master's, 2 letters of recommendation; minimum GPA of 3.0 during last 60 hours of upper-level work; resume. Additional exam

requirements/recommendations for international students: Required—TOEFL (minimum score 550 paper-based; 80 iBT). Electronic applications accepted. *Faculty research:* Post-Hurricane Andrew population studies, Central American journalism, employment discrimination.

The George Washington University, Columbian College of Arts and Sciences, School of Media and Public Affairs, Washington, DC 20052. Offers MA, Graduate Certificate. *Accreditation:* NASPAA. *Faculty:* 25 full-time (10 women). *Students:* 26 full-time (16 women), 11 part-time (8 women); includes 8 minority (1 Asian, non-Hispanic/Latino; 7 Hispanic/Latino), 7 international. Average age 26. 85 applicants, 56% accepted, 21 enrolled. In 2014, 22 master's, 16 other advanced degrees awarded. *Degree requirements:* For master's, thesis optional. *Entrance requirements:* For master's, GRE General Test. Additional exam requirements/recommendations for international students: Required—TOEFL (minimum score 550 paper-based; 80 iBT). *Application deadline:* For fall admission, 4/1 priority date for domestic students, 1/15 priority date for international students; for spring admission, 10/1 priority date for domestic students, 9/1 priority date for international students. Applications are processed on a rolling basis. Application fee: $75. Electronic applications accepted. *Financial support:* In 2014–15, fellowships with tuition reimbursements (averaging $10,000 per year), teaching assistantships with tuition reimbursements (averaging $5,000 per year) were awarded. Financial award application deadline: 1/15. *Unit head:* Frank Sesno, Director, 202-994-9553, E-mail: sesno@gwu.edu. *Application contact:* Information Contact, 202-994-6227, Fax: 202-994-5806, E-mail: smpa@gwu.edu.
Website: http://www.gwu.edu/~smpa/

Georgia State University, College of Arts and Sciences, Department of Communication, Atlanta, GA 30302-3083. Offers film, video, and digital imaging (MA), including critical studies, production, screenwriting; human communication and social influence (MA); mass communication (MA); media and society (PhD); moving image studies (PhD); public communication (PhD); rhetoric and politics (PhD). Part-time programs available. *Faculty:* 35 full-time (18 women). *Students:* 102 full-time (51 women), 40 part-time (15 women); includes 37 minority (20 Black or African American, non-Hispanic/Latino; 4 Asian, non-Hispanic/Latino; 6 Hispanic/Latino; 7 Two or more races, non-Hispanic/Latino), 14 international. Average age 33. 154 applicants, 39% accepted, 30 enrolled. In 2014, 25 master's, 5 doctorates awarded. *Degree requirements:* For master's, variable foreign language requirement, thesis (for some programs); for doctorate, comprehensive exam, thesis/dissertation. *Entrance requirements:* For master's, GRE; for doctorate, GRE. Additional exam requirements/recommendations for international students: Required—TOEFL (minimum score 550 paper-based; 80 iBT), IELTS (minimum score 6.5). *Application deadline:* For fall admission, 2/10 for domestic and international students; for spring admission, 10/15 for domestic and international students. Application fee: $50. Electronic applications accepted. *Expenses:* Tuition, state resident: full-time $6516; part-time $362 per credit hour. Tuition, nonresident: full-time $22,014; part-time $1223 per credit hour. *Required fees:* $2128 per semester. Tuition and fees vary according to course load and program. *Financial support:* In 2014–15, fellowships with tuition reimbursements (averaging $15,000 per year), teaching assistantships with tuition reimbursements (averaging $15,000 per year) were awarded; career-related internships or fieldwork and unspecified assistantships also available. Financial award applicants required to submit FAFSA. *Faculty research:* New media, mass media and journalism, rhetoric, film and media studies, film production. *Unit head:* Dr. David Cheshier, Chair, 404-413-5649, Fax: 404-413-5634, E-mail: dcheshier@gsu.edu. *Application contact:* Dr. Jennifer Barker, Associate Professor, 404-413-5793, Fax: 404-413-5634, E-mail: jmbarker@gsu.edu.
Website: http://communication.gsu.edu

Grambling State University, School of Graduate Studies and Research, College of Professional Studies, Department of Mass Communication, Grambling, LA 71245. Offers MA. Part-time programs available. *Degree requirements:* For master's, comprehensive exam, thesis optional. *Entrance requirements:* For master's, GRE, minimum GPA of 2.5 on last degree. Additional exam requirements/recommendations for international students: Required—TOEFL (minimum score 500 paper-based; 62 iBT). Electronic applications accepted.

Howard University, School of Communications, Division of Mass Communication and Media Studies, Washington, DC 20059-0002. Offers mass communication (MA, PhD); media studies (MA, PhD). Part-time and evening/weekend programs available. *Degree requirements:* For master's, comprehensive exam (for some programs), thesis optional; for doctorate, one foreign language, comprehensive exam, thesis/dissertation. *Entrance requirements:* For master's, GRE, minimum GPA of 3.0; for doctorate, GRE, minimum graduate GPA of 3.5. Additional exam requirements/recommendations for international students: Required—TOEFL. Electronic applications accepted. *Faculty research:* Advertising, public relations, journalism new media.

Indiana University Bloomington, University Graduate School, College of Arts and Sciences, The Media School, Department of Telecommunications, Program in Mass Communications, Bloomington, IN 47405-7000. Offers PhD. *Faculty:* 17 full-time (6 women). *Students:* 31 full-time (17 women); includes 4 minority (1 American Indian or Alaska Native, non-Hispanic/Latino; 2 Asian, non-Hispanic/Latino; 1 Two or more races, non-Hispanic/Latino), 7 international. Average age 32. 14 applicants, 36% accepted, 4 enrolled. In 2014, 3 doctorates awarded. *Degree requirements:* For doctorate, comprehensive exam, thesis/dissertation. *Entrance requirements:* For doctorate, GRE General Test, minimum graduate GPA of 3.5, 3 letters of recommendation. Additional exam requirements/recommendations for international students: Required—TOEFL (minimum score 600 paper-based; 100 iBT). *Application deadline:* For fall admission, 1/15 priority date for domestic students, 12/1 priority date for international students. Applications are processed on a rolling basis. Application fee: $55 ($65 for international students). Electronic applications accepted. *Financial support:* Application deadline: 1/15. *Faculty research:* Media processes and effects, media law and policy, economics of media and virtual worlds. *Application contact:* Tamera Theodore, Graduate Program Administrator, 812-855-2017, E-mail: ttheodor@indiana.edu.
Website: http://www.indiana.edu/~telecom/index.shtml

Indiana University Bloomington, University Graduate School, College of Arts and Sciences, The Media School, School of Journalism, Bloomington, IN 47405-7000. Offers journalism (MA, MAT); mass communication (PhD); MA/JD; MA/MA. *Faculty:* 11 full-time (5 women). *Students:* 52 full-time (33 women), 6 part-time (5 women); includes 6 minority (5 Black or African American, non-Hispanic/Latino; 1 Two or more races, non-Hispanic/Latino), 28 international. Average age 30. 83 applicants, 61% accepted, 11 enrolled. In 2014, 22 master's, 2 doctorates awarded. Terminal master's awarded for partial completion of doctoral program. *Degree requirements:* For master's, thesis (for some programs); for doctorate, thesis/dissertation. *Entrance requirements:* For master's and doctorate, GRE General Test. Additional exam requirements/recommendations for international students: Required—TOEFL. *Application deadline:* For fall admission, 1/15 priority date for domestic students; for spring admission, 9/1 priority date for domestic students. Applications are processed on a rolling basis. Application fee: $55 ($65 for international students). *Financial support:* Fellowships, research assistantships with full tuition reimbursements, teaching assistantships with partial tuition reimbursements, career-related internships or fieldwork, Federal Work-Study, institutionally sponsored loans, and tuition waivers (full) available. Financial award application deadline: 1/15. *Faculty research:* Political communication, international communication, communication history, communication law, visual communication. *Unit head:* Bonnie Brownlee, Chair, 812-855-0570, E-mail: brownlee@indiana.edu. *Application contact:* Lesa Major, Associate Dean, Research and Graduate Studies, 812-855-8111, E-mail: lhmajor@indiana.edu.
Website: http://journalism.indiana.edu/

Iona College, School of Arts and Science, Department of Mass Communication, New Rochelle, NY 10801-1890. Offers non-profit public relations (Certificate). *Accreditation:* ACEJMC (one or more programs are accredited). Part-time and evening/weekend programs available. *Faculty:* 4 full-time (1 woman), 1 (woman) part-time/adjunct. *Students:* 12 full-time (10 women), 22 part-time (16 women); includes 7 minority (4 Black or African American, non-Hispanic/Latino; 3 Hispanic/Latino), 8 international. Average age 27. 27 applicants, 41% accepted, 5 enrolled. In 2014, 15 master's, 6 other advanced degrees awarded. *Degree requirements:* For master's, comprehensive exam (for some programs), thesis or alternative. *Entrance requirements:* For master's, GRE General Test if undergraduate GPA is below 3.0. Additional exam requirements/recommendations for international students: Required—TOEFL (minimum score 550 paper-based; 80 iBT), IELTS (minimum score 6). *Application deadline:* For fall admission, 8/1 for domestic students, 5/1 for international students; for spring admission, 1/1 for domestic students, 9/1 for international students. Applications are processed on a rolling basis. Application fee: $50. Electronic applications accepted. *Expenses:* Expenses: Contact institution. *Financial support:* In 2014–15, 2 students received support. Scholarships/grants, tuition waivers (partial), and unspecified assistantships available. Support available to part-time students. Financial award application deadline: 4/15; financial award applicants required to submit FAFSA. *Faculty research:* Media ecology, new media, corporate communication, media images, organizational learning in public relations, media law, medicine ethics. *Unit head:* Robert Petrausch, PhD, Chair, 914-633-2354, E-mail: rpetausch@iona.edu. *Application contact:* Amanda St. Bernard, Assistant Director, Graduate Admissions, 914-633-2440, Fax: 914-633-2277, E-mail: astbernard@iona.edu.
Website: http://www.iona.edu/Academics/School-of-Arts-Science/Departments/Mass-Communication/Graduate-Programs.aspx

Iowa State University of Science and Technology, Greenlee School of Journalism and Mass Communication, Ames, IA 50011. Offers MS. *Entrance requirements:* For master's, GRE General Test. Additional exam requirements/recommendations for international students: Required—TOEFL (minimum score 570 paper-based; 88 iBT), IELTS (minimum score 6.5). Electronic applications accepted.

Jackson State University, Graduate School, College of Liberal Arts, Department of Mass Communications, Jackson, MS 39217. Offers MS. Part-time and evening/weekend programs available. *Degree requirements:* For master's, comprehensive exam, thesis optional. *Entrance requirements:* For master's, GRE General Test. Additional exam requirements/recommendations for international students: Required—TOEFL (minimum score 520 paper-based; 67 iBT).

Kansas State University, Graduate School, College of Arts and Sciences, A. Q. Miller School of Journalism and Mass Communications, Manhattan, KS 66506. Offers advertising (MS); community journalism (MS); global communication (MS); health communication (MS); media management (MS); public relations (MS). Part-time and evening/weekend programs available. *Faculty:* 15 full-time (7 women), 1 (woman) part-time/adjunct. *Students:* 15 full-time (9 women), 5 part-time (3 women); includes 2 minority (both Hispanic/Latino), 9 international. Average age 26. 10 applicants, 80% accepted, 6 enrolled. In 2014, 10 master's awarded. *Degree requirements:* For master's, comprehensive exam, thesis. *Entrance requirements:* For master's, GRE General Test, minimum GPA of 3.0. Additional exam requirements/recommendations for international students: Required—TOEFL (minimum score 79 iBT). *Application deadline:* For fall admission, 2/1 priority date for domestic and international students; for spring admission, 8/1 priority date for domestic and international students. Applications are processed on a rolling basis. Application fee: $50 ($75 for international students). Electronic applications accepted. *Financial support:* In 2014–15, 2 research assistantships with full tuition reimbursements (averaging $11,180 per year), 7 teaching assistantships with full tuition reimbursements (averaging $7,729 per year) were awarded; scholarships/grants, health care benefits, and unspecified assistantships also available. Financial award application deadline: 2/1; financial award applicants required to submit FAFSA. *Faculty research:* Health communication, risk communication, strategic communications, community journalism, global communication. *Total annual research expenditures:* $219,641. *Unit head:* Dr. Birgit Wassmuth, Director, 785-532-6890, Fax: 785-532-5484, E-mail: wassmuth@ksu.edu. *Application contact:* Dr. Nancy Muturi, Associate Director of Graduate Studies, 785-532-3890, Fax: 785-532-5484, E-mail: nmuturi@ksu.edu.
Website: http://jmc.ksu.edu/

Kent State University, College of Communication and Information, School of Journalism and Mass Communication, Kent, OH 44242-0001. Offers media management (MA); public relations (MA); reporting and editing (MA), including broadcast, convergence, journalism educators, magazine, newspaper. Part-time programs available. *Faculty:* 28 full-time (13 women). *Students:* 21 full-time (15 women), 173 part-time (127 women); includes 24 minority (14 Black or African American, non-Hispanic/Latino; 1 American Indian or Alaska Native, non-Hispanic/Latino; 2 Asian, non-Hispanic/Latino; 1 Hispanic/Latino; 6 Two or more races, non-Hispanic/Latino), 7 international. Average age 37. 112 applicants, 68% accepted, 50 enrolled. In 2014, 117 master's awarded. *Degree requirements:* For master's, thesis or project. *Entrance requirements:* For master's, GRE General Test, minimum GPA of 3.0, transcripts, goal statement, statement of desired concentration, resume, 3 letters of recommendation. Additional exam requirements/recommendations for international students: Required—TOEFL (minimum score: paper-based 525, iBT 71), Michigan English Language Assessment Battery (minimum score of 75), IELTS (minimum score of 6.0), PTE Academic (minimum score of 48), or completion of ELS level 112 Intensive Program. *Application deadline:* For fall admission, 7/1 for domestic students, 3/1 for international students; for spring admission, 12/1 for domestic students, 10/30 for international students; for summer admission, 5/1 for domestic students. Application fee: $45 ($70 for international students). Electronic applications accepted. *Expenses:* Tuition, state resident: full-time $8730; part-time $485 per credit hour. Tuition, nonresident: full-time $14,886; part-time $827 per credit hour. Tuition and fees vary according to campus/location and program. *Financial support:* Research assistantships with full tuition reimbursements, teaching assistantships with full tuition reimbursements, career-related internships or fieldwork, Federal Work-Study, scholarships/grants, and unspecified assistantships available. Financial award application deadline: 2/1. *Unit head:* Thor Wasbotten, Director and Professor, 330-672-4066, E-mail: thor@kent.edu. *Application contact:* Joe Murray, Graduate Coordinator and Associate Professor, 330-672-2572, E-mail: jmc@kent.edu.
Website: http://www.kent.edu/jmc

Louisiana State University and Agricultural & Mechanical College, Graduate School, Manship School of Mass Communication, Baton Rouge, LA 70803. Offers MMC, PhD, JD/MMC. *Accreditation:* ACEJMC. Part-time programs available. Postbaccalaureate distance learning degree programs offered (minimal on-campus

study). *Faculty:* 24 full-time (12 women). *Students:* 62 full-time (42 women), 14 part-time (11 women); includes 20 minority (15 Black or African American, non-Hispanic/Latino; 1 Asian, non-Hispanic/Latino; 3 Hispanic/Latino; 1 Two or more races, non-Hispanic/Latino), 16 international. Average age 27. 62 applicants, 48% accepted, 22 enrolled. In 2014, 20 master's, 3 doctorates awarded. *Degree requirements:* For master's, thesis; for doctorate, thesis/dissertation. *Entrance requirements:* For master's, GRE General Test, minimum GPA of 3.0. Additional exam requirements/recommendations for international students: Required—TOEFL (minimum score 550 paper-based; 79 IBT), IELTS (minimum score 6.5), or PTE (minimum score 59). *Application deadline:* For fall admission, 1/1 priority date for domestic students, 5/15 for international students; for spring admission, 10/15 for domestic and international students; for summer admission, 5/15 for domestic and international students. Applications are processed on a rolling basis. Application fee: $50 ($70 for international students). Electronic applications accepted. *Financial support:* In 2014–15, 61 students received support, including 1 fellowship (averaging $33,839 per year), 31 research assistantships with full and partial tuition reimbursements available (averaging $15,839 per year), 14 teaching assistantships with full and partial tuition reimbursements available (averaging $15,557 per year); career-related internships or fieldwork, Federal Work-Study, institutionally sponsored loans, scholarships/grants, health care benefits, tuition waivers (full and partial), and unspecified assistantships also available. Support available to part-time students. Financial award application deadline: 3/1; financial award applicants required to submit FAFSA. *Faculty research:* Media effects, political communication, new media technologies, persuasive communication, journalism processes and practice. *Total annual research expenditures:* $82,923. *Unit head:* Dr. Jerry Ceppos, Dean, 225-578-3488, Fax: 225-578-2125, E-mail: jceppos@lsu.edu. *Application contact:* Dr. Amy L. Reynolds, Associate Dean of Graduate Studies and Research, 225-578-9294, Fax: 225-578-2125, E-mail: areynolds@lsu.edu.
Website: http://www.manship.lsu.edu/

Lynn University, Eugene M. and Christine E. Lynn College of International Communication, Boca Raton, FL 33431-5598. Offers communication and media - digital media (MS); communication and media - media studies and practice (MS); digital media (Certificate). Part-time and evening/weekend programs available. *Faculty:* 5 full-time (4 women). *Students:* 24 full-time (17 women), 9 part-time (7 women); includes 8 minority (4 Black or African American, non-Hispanic/Latino; 3 Hispanic/Latino; 1 Two or more races, non-Hispanic/Latino), 11 international. Average age 28. 19 applicants, 95% accepted, 12 enrolled. In 2014, 13 master's awarded. *Degree requirements:* For master's, project or thesis. *Entrance requirements:* For master's, resume, letter of recommendation, official transcripts, bachelor's degree from accredited institution, personal statement. Additional exam requirements/recommendations for international students: Required—TOEFL (minimum score 550 paper-based; 80 iBT), IELTS (minimum score 6.5). *Application deadline:* Applications are processed on a rolling basis. Application fee: $45. Electronic applications accepted. *Expenses: Tuition:* Full-time $16,200; part-time $675 per credit hour. Tuition and fees vary according to class time, course load, degree level and program. *Financial support:* In 2014–15, 12 students received support. Career-related internships or fieldwork, Federal Work-Study, institutionally sponsored loans, scholarships/grants, tuition waivers (partial), and unspecified assistantships available. Support available to part-time students. Financial award application deadline: 8/1; financial award applicants required to submit FAFSA. *Unit head:* Dr. David L. Jaffe, Dean, 561-237-7099, Fax: 561-237-7097, E-mail: djaffe@lynn.edu. *Application contact:* Steven Pruitt, Director of Graduate Admission, 561-237-7834, Fax: 561-237-7100, E-mail: admission@lynn.edu.
Website: http://www.lynn.edu/academics/colleges/international-communication

Marquette University, Graduate School, Diederich College of Communication, Milwaukee, WI 53201-1881. Offers advertising and public relations (MA); communication studies (MA); digital storytelling (Certificate); journalism (MA); mass communication (MA); science, health and environmental communication (MA). *Accreditation:* ACEJMC (one or more programs are accredited). Part-time and evening/weekend programs available. *Degree requirements:* For master's, comprehensive exam, thesis or alternative. *Entrance requirements:* For master's, GRE, official transcripts from all current and previous colleges/universities except Marquette, three letters of recommendation, statement of academic and professional goals. Additional exam requirements/recommendations for international students: Required—TOEFL (minimum score 530 paper-based). Electronic applications accepted. *Faculty research:* Urban journalism, gender and communication, intercultural communication, religious communication.

Middle Tennessee State University, College of Graduate Studies, College of Mass Communication, Program in Mass Communication, Murfreesboro, TN 37132. Offers MS. Part-time and evening/weekend programs available. Postbaccalaureate distance learning degree programs offered. *Faculty:* 9 full-time (4 women). *Students:* 9 full-time (5 women), 21 part-time (15 women); includes 7 minority (5 Black or African American, non-Hispanic/Latino; 1 Asian, non-Hispanic/Latino; 1 Two or more races, non-Hispanic/Latino), 1 international. 69 applicants, 39% accepted. In 2014, 7 master's awarded. *Degree requirements:* For master's, comprehensive exam, thesis optional. *Entrance requirements:* For master's, GRE. Additional exam requirements/recommendations for international students: Required—TOEFL (minimum score 525 paper-based; 71 iBT) or IELTS (minimum score 6). *Application deadline:* For fall admission, 6/1 for domestic and international students. Applications are processed on a rolling basis. Application fee: $30. *Financial support:* In 2014–15, 10 students received support. Tuition waivers available. Support available to part-time students. Financial award application deadline: 4/1. *Unit head:* Ken Paulson, Dean, 615-898-2195, Fax: 615-898-5682, E-mail: ken.paulson@mtsu.edu. *Application contact:* Dr. Michael D. Allen, Vice Provost for Research/Dean, 615-898-2840, Fax: 615-904-8020, E-mail: michael.allen@mtsu.edu.
Website: http://www.mtsu.edu/mcgrad/

Murray State University, College of Business and Public Affairs, Program in Mass Communications, Murray, KY 42071. Offers MA, MS. Part-time programs available. *Entrance requirements:* Additional exam requirements/recommendations for international students: Required—TOEFL (minimum score 550 paper-based). *Faculty research:* AH media on the Internet, visual communication and learning, persuasion, media framing, history of radio and wireless technology.

North Dakota State University, College of Graduate and Interdisciplinary Studies, College of Arts, Humanities and Social Sciences, Department of Communication, Fargo, ND 58108. Offers communication (PhD); mass communication (MA, MS); speech communication (MA, MS). Part-time programs available. Postbaccalaureate distance learning degree programs offered (no on-campus study). Terminal master's awarded for partial completion of doctoral program. *Degree requirements:* For master's, thesis (for some programs); for doctorate, comprehensive exam, thesis/dissertation, 2-3 publications. *Entrance requirements:* For master's, GRE, minimum undergraduate GPA of 3.25; for doctorate, GRE, minimum undergraduate GPA of 3.5. Additional exam requirements/recommendations for international students: Required—TOEFL (minimum score 600 paper-based; 100 iBT), IELTS (minimum score 7). Electronic applications accepted. *Faculty research:* Communication and rhetorical theory, organizational communication, broadcast and print journalism, international communication, public relations and advertising.

Oklahoma State University, College of Arts and Sciences, School of Media and Strategic Communications, Stillwater, OK 74078. Offers mass communication (MS). *Faculty:* 21 full-time (9 women), 5 part-time/adjunct (2 women). *Students:* 9 full-time (5 women), 12 part-time (6 women); includes 3 minority (1 Black or African American, non-Hispanic/Latino; 2 Two or more races, non-Hispanic/Latino). Average age 29. 13 applicants, 69% accepted, 8 enrolled. In 2014, 8 master's awarded. *Degree requirements:* For master's, thesis, project/creative component. *Entrance requirements:* For master's, GRE, minimum GPA of 3.0. Additional exam requirements/recommendations for international students: Required—TOEFL (minimum score 550 paper-based; 79 iBT). *Application deadline:* For fall admission, 3/1 priority date for international students; for spring admission, 8/1 priority date for international students. Applications are processed on a rolling basis. Application fee: $40 ($75 for international students). Electronic applications accepted. *Expenses:* Tuition, state resident: full-time $4488; part-time $187 per credit hour. Tuition, nonresident: full-time $18,360; part-time $765 per credit hour. *Required fees:* $2413; $100.55 per credit hour. Tuition and fees vary according to campus/location. *Financial support:* In 2014–15, 5 teaching assistantships (averaging $19,200 per year) were awarded; research assistantships, career-related internships or fieldwork, Federal Work-Study, scholarships/grants, health care benefits, tuition waivers (partial), and unspecified assistantships also available. Support available to part-time students. Financial award application deadline: 3/1; financial award applicants required to submit FAFSA. *Unit head:* Dr. Derina Holtzhausen, Director, 405-744-7676, Fax: 405-744-7104, E-mail: derina.holtzhausen@okstate.edu.
Website: http://media.okstate.edu

Penn State University Park, Graduate School, College of Communications, Department of Communications, University Park, PA 16802. Offers mass communications (PhD); media studies (MA). *Unit head:* Dr. Marie C. Hardin, Dean, 814-863-1484, Fax: 814-863-8044, E-mail: mch208@psu.edu. *Application contact:* Lori A. Stania, Director, Graduate Student Services, 814-867-5278, Fax: 814-863-4627, E-mail: gswww@psu.edu.
Website: http://comm.psu.edu/

Point Park University, School of Communication, Pittsburgh, PA 15222-1984. Offers MA. Part-time and evening/weekend programs available. *Degree requirements:* For master's, comprehensive exam (for some programs), thesis or alternative. *Entrance requirements:* For master's, GRE (if GPA less than 2.75), minimum GPA of 2.75, 2 letters of recommendation, statement of intent. Additional exam requirements/recommendations for international students: Required—TOEFL (minimum score 570 paper-based; 88 iBT), IELTS (minimum score 6.5); Recommended—TWE (minimum score 5). Electronic applications accepted.

St. Cloud State University, School of Graduate Studies, College of Liberal Arts, Department of Mass Communications, St. Cloud, MN 56301-4498. Offers MS. *Degree requirements:* For master's, thesis or alternative. *Entrance requirements:* For master's, minimum GPA of 2.75. Additional exam requirements/recommendations for international students: Required—Michigan English Language Assessment Battery; Recommended—TOEFL (minimum score 600 paper-based), IELTS (minimum score 6.5). Electronic applications accepted.

San Jose State University, Graduate Studies and Research, College of Applied Sciences and Arts, School of Journalism and Mass Communications, San Jose, CA 95192-0001. Offers mass communications (MS). *Accreditation:* ACEJMC. Part-time programs available. *Degree requirements:* For master's, thesis or alternative. *Entrance requirements:* For master's, GRE, minimum GPA of 3.0. Electronic applications accepted. *Faculty research:* Communications theory, mass media effects, public relations, international communications.

Southern Illinois University Carbondale, Graduate School, College of Mass Communication and Media Arts, Department of Mass Communication and Media Arts, Carbondale, IL 62901-4701. Offers MA, MFA. *Students:* 36 full-time (14 women), 17 part-time (8 women); includes 2 minority (1 Black or African American, non-Hispanic/Latino; 1 Asian, non-Hispanic/Latino), 20 international. 38 applicants, 34% accepted, 9 enrolled. In 2014, 11 master's awarded. Application fee: $50. *Expenses:* Tuition, state resident: full-time $10,176; part-time $1153 per credit. Tuition, nonresident: full-time $20,814; part-time $1744 per credit. *Required fees:* $7092; $394 per credit. $2364 per semester. *Unit head:* Prof. Deborah Tudor, Director of Graduate Studies, 618-453-3267, E-mail: dtudor@siu.edu. *Application contact:* Georgia Norman, Administrative Aide, 618-453-3785, E-mail: mcmagrad@siu.edu.

Southern Illinois University Edwardsville, Graduate School, College of Arts and Sciences, Department of Mass Communications, Program in Mass Communications, Edwardsville, IL 62026. Offers MS. Part-time and evening/weekend programs available. *Faculty:* 10 full-time (2 women). *Students:* 7 full-time (4 women), 12 part-time (7 women); includes 4 minority (2 Black or African American, non-Hispanic/Latino; 1 American Indian or Alaska Native, non-Hispanic/Latino; 1 Asian, non-Hispanic/Latino), 4 international. 13 applicants, 54% accepted. In 2014, 6 master's awarded. *Degree requirements:* For master's, comprehensive exam (for some programs), thesis (for some programs). *Entrance requirements:* Additional exam requirements/recommendations for international students: Required—TOEFL (minimum score 550 paper-based; 79 iBT), IELTS (minimum score 6.5). *Application deadline:* For fall admission, 7/24 for domestic students, 7/15 for international students; for spring admission, 12/11 for domestic students, 11/15 for international students; for summer admission, 4/29 for domestic students, 4/15 for international students. Applications are processed on a rolling basis. Application fee: $30. Electronic applications accepted. *Expenses:* Tuition, state resident: full-time $5026. Tuition, nonresident: full-time $12,566. *International tuition:* $25,136 full-time. *Required fees:* $1682. Tuition and fees vary according to course load, campus/location and program. *Financial support:* In 2014–15, 9 students received support, including 4 research assistantships with full tuition reimbursements available, 5 teaching assistantships with full tuition reimbursements available; fellowships with full tuition reimbursements available, career-related internships or fieldwork, institutionally sponsored loans, scholarships/grants, and unspecified assistantships also available. Financial award application deadline: 3/1; financial award applicants required to submit FAFSA. *Unit head:* Dr. Elza Ibroscheva, Director, 618-650-2242, E-mail: eibrosc@siue.edu. *Application contact:* Melissa K. Mace, Assistant Director of Admissions for Graduate and International Recruitment, 618-650-2756, Fax: 618-650-3618, E-mail: mmace@siue.edu.
Website: http://www.siue.edu/MASSCOMM/

Southern University and Agricultural and Mechanical College, Graduate School, College of Arts and Humanities, Department of Mass Communication, Baton Rouge, LA 70813. Offers MA. *Degree requirements:* For master's, comprehensive exam, thesis. *Entrance requirements:* For master's, GRE General Test. Additional exam requirements/recommendations for international students: Required—TOEFL (minimum score 525 paper-based). *Faculty research:* Photojournalism, textbook on broadcast.

Stephen F. Austin State University, Graduate School, College of Applied Arts and Science, Department of Communication, Nacogdoches, TX 75962. Offers communication (MA); mass communication (MA). Part-time programs available. *Degree requirements:* For master's, comprehensive exam, thesis optional. *Entrance*

requirements: For master's, GRE General Test. Additional exam requirements/recommendations for international students: Required—TOEFL (minimum score 550 paper-based).

Syracuse University, S. I. Newhouse School of Public Communications, Program in Communications Management, Syracuse, NY 13244. Offers MS. Part-time and evening/weekend programs available. Postbaccalaureate distance learning degree programs offered (minimal on-campus study). *Students:* 1 (woman) full-time, 43 part-time (31 women); includes 5 minority (4 Black or African American, non-Hispanic/Latino; 1 Hispanic/Latino), 6 international. Average age 43. 15 applicants, 67% accepted, 9 enrolled. In 2014, 22 master's awarded. *Degree requirements:* For master's, comprehensive exam, internship. *Entrance requirements:* For master's, GRE General Test, minimum 5 years of experience in public relations or related field; portfolio; 3 letters of recommendation including 1 from current employer, client, or business partner. Additional exam requirements/recommendations for international students: Required—TOEFL (minimum score 100 iBT). *Application deadline:* For fall admission, 5/15 priority date for domestic and international students. Application fee: $45. Electronic applications accepted. *Expenses: Tuition:* Part-time $1341 per credit. *Financial support:* Application deadline: 1/1; applicants required to submit FAFSA. *Unit head:* Maria Russell, Academic Director, 315-443-3368, E-mail: commgt@syr.edu. *Application contact:* Graduate Records Office, 315-443-5749, E-mail: pcgrad@syr.edu.
Website: http://newhouse.syr.edu/

Syracuse University, S. I. Newhouse School of Public Communications, Program in Mass Communications, Syracuse, NY 13244. Offers PhD. *Students:* 16 full-time (12 women), 4 part-time (1 woman); includes 3 minority (1 Black or African American, non-Hispanic/Latino; 2 Asian, non-Hispanic/Latino), 8 international. Average age 33. 55 applicants, 11% accepted, 5 enrolled. In 2014, 4 doctorates awarded. *Degree requirements:* For doctorate, comprehensive exam, thesis/dissertation, qualifying exams. *Entrance requirements:* For doctorate, GRE General Test. Additional exam requirements/recommendations for international students: Required—TOEFL (minimum score 100 iBT). *Application deadline:* For fall admission, 12/1 priority date for domestic and international students. Application fee: $45. Electronic applications accepted. *Expenses: Tuition:* Part-time $1341 per credit. *Financial support:* Fellowships with full tuition reimbursements, research assistantships with partial tuition reimbursements, teaching assistantships with partial tuition reimbursements, career-related internships or fieldwork, and tuition waivers (partial) available. Financial award application deadline: 12/10. *Unit head:* Dr. Dennis Kinsey, Director of Doctoral Studies, 315-443-3372, Fax: 315-443-3946, E-mail: masscomm@syr.edu. *Application contact:* Amy Arends, Doctoral Office, 315-443-3372, E-mail: masscomm@syr.edu.
Website: http://newhouse.syr.edu/

Texas Christian University, Bob Schieffer College of Communication, School of Strategic Communication, Fort Worth, TX 76129. Offers MS. Part-time programs available. *Faculty:* 7 full-time (6 women). *Students:* 13 full-time (7 women), 2 part-time (1 woman); includes 1 minority (Black or African American, non-Hispanic/Latino), 4 international. Average age 26. 11 applicants, 45% accepted, 5 enrolled. In 2014, 5 master's awarded. *Entrance requirements:* For master's, GRE General Test, 15 semester hours (five courses) in undergraduate journalism, advertising or public relations, or substantial professional experience in a communication discipline as determined by the graduate faculty. Additional exam requirements/recommendations for international students: Recommended—TOEFL (minimum score 100 iBT). *Application deadline:* For fall admission, 6/1 for domestic and international students; for spring admission, 10/15 for domestic and international students. Applications are processed on a rolling basis. Application fee: $60. Electronic applications accepted. *Expenses: Tuition:* Full-time $22,860; part-time $1270 per credit hour. *Financial support:* In 2014–15, 7 students received support, including 6 teaching assistantships (averaging $9,000 per year); tuition waivers also available. Financial award application deadline: 2/15; financial award applicants required to submit FAFSA. *Faculty research:* Social and digital media, advertising and public relations, health communication, crisis communication, ethics. *Unit head:* Dr. Jacque Lambiase, Director, 817-257-6552, Fax: 817-257-7322, E-mail: j.lambiase@tcu.edu. *Application contact:* Dr. Julie O'Neil, Graduate Director, 817-257-6966, Fax: 817-257-7322, E-mail: j.oneil@tcu.edu.
Website: http://stco.tcu.edu/

Texas State University, The Graduate College, College of Fine Arts and Communication, School of Journalism and Mass Communication, San Marcos, TX 78666. Offers MA. *Faculty:* 8 full-time (5 women), 3 part-time/adjunct (0 women). *Students:* 28 full-time (14 women), 4 part-time (all women); includes 13 minority (1 Asian, non-Hispanic/Latino; 10 Hispanic/Latino; 2 Two or more races, non-Hispanic/Latino), 15 international. Average age 29. In 2014, 22 master's awarded. *Degree requirements:* For master's, comprehensive exam, thesis optional. *Entrance requirements:* For master's, GRE General Test, departmental grammar test, minimum GPA of 3.0 in last 60 hours of course work. Additional exam requirements/recommendations for international students: Required—TOEFL (minimum score 550 paper-based; 78 iBT). *Application deadline:* For fall admission, 2/1 priority date for domestic students, 2/1 for international students; for spring admission, 10/15 priority date for domestic students, 10/1 for international students. Applications are processed on a rolling basis. Application fee: $40 ($90 for international students). Electronic applications accepted. *Financial support:* In 2014–15, 7 students received support, including 11 teaching assistantships; research assistantships, career-related internships or fieldwork, Federal Work-Study, and institutionally sponsored loans also available. Support available to part-time students. Financial award application deadline: 4/1; financial award applicants required to submit FAFSA. *Unit head:* Dr. Sandhya Rao, Graduate Advisor, 512-245-2656, Fax: 512-245-7649, E-mail: sr02@txstate.edu. *Application contact:* Dr. Andrea Golato, Dean of the Graduate College, 512-245-2581, Fax: 512-245-8365, E-mail: gradcollege@txstate.edu.
Website: http://www.masscomm.txstate.edu/

Texas Tech University, Graduate School, College of Media and Communication, Lubbock, TX 79409. Offers mass communications (MA, PhD). Part-time and evening/weekend programs available. Postbaccalaureate distance learning degree programs offered. *Faculty:* 40 full-time (13 women), 3 part-time/adjunct (all women). *Students:* 73 full-time (49 women), 49 part-time (27 women); includes 19 minority (4 Black or African American, non-Hispanic/Latino; 1 Asian, non-Hispanic/Latino; 12 Hispanic/Latino; 2 Two or more races, non-Hispanic/Latino), 21 international. Average age 28. 119 applicants, 67% accepted, 56 enrolled. In 2014, 47 master's, 7 doctorates awarded. *Degree requirements:* For master's, thesis optional; for doctorate, comprehensive exam, thesis/dissertation. *Entrance requirements:* For doctorate, GRE. Additional exam requirements/recommendations for international students: Required—TOEFL (minimum score 550 paper-based; 79 iBT). *Application deadline:* For fall admission, 6/1 priority date for domestic students, 1/15 priority date for international students; for spring admission, 9/1 priority date for domestic students, 6/15 priority date for international students. Applications are processed on a rolling basis. Application fee: $60. Electronic applications accepted. *Expenses:* Tuition, state resident: full-time $6310; part-time $262.92 per credit hour. Tuition, nonresident: full-time $14,998; part-time $624.92 per credit hour. *Required fees:* $2701; $36.50 per credit. $912.50 per semester. Tuition and fees vary according to course load. *Financial support:* In 2014–15, 80 students received support, including 72 fellowships (averaging $4,013 per year), 23 research assistantships (averaging $14,321 per year), 29 teaching assistantships (averaging $9,172 per year); career-related internships or fieldwork, scholarships/grants, and unspecified assistantships also available. Support available to part-time students. Financial award application deadline: 4/15; financial award applicants required to submit FAFSA. *Faculty research:* Media effects, political communication, health communication, critical/cultural, Hispanic and international communication. *Total annual research expenditures:* $123,809. *Unit head:* Dr. Coy Callison, Graduate Director, 806-834-5344, E-mail: coy.callison@ttu.edu. *Application contact:* Shannon Samson, Coordinator of Graduate School Recruitment, 806-834-5201, Fax: 806-742-1746, E-mail: gradschool@ttu.edu.
Website: http://www.depts.ttu.edu/comc/

Université Laval, Faculty of Letters, Department of Information and Communication, Program in Public Communication, Québec, QC G1K 7P4, Canada. Offers MA, PhD. Part-time programs available. *Degree requirements:* For master's, thesis (for some programs). *Entrance requirements:* For master's, knowledge of French, knowledge of English. Electronic applications accepted.

The University of Alabama, Graduate School, College of Communication and Information Sciences, Communication and Information Sciences Program, Tuscaloosa, AL 35487-0172. Offers PhD. *Faculty:* 9 full-time (2 women). *Students:* 42 full-time (24 women), 9 part-time (5 women); includes 5 minority (3 Black or African American, non-Hispanic/Latino; 1 American Indian or Alaska Native, non-Hispanic/Latino; 1 Asian, non-Hispanic/Latino), 19 international. Average age 33. 37 applicants, 43% accepted, 11 enrolled. In 2014, 12 doctorates awarded. *Degree requirements:* For doctorate, comprehensive exam, thesis/dissertation. *Entrance requirements:* For doctorate, GRE, master's degree, minimum undergraduate and graduate GPA of 3.0. Additional exam requirements/recommendations for international students: Required—TOEFL. *Application deadline:* For fall admission, 2/15 for domestic and international students; for winter admission, 11/1 for domestic and international students. Application fee: $50 ($60 for international students). *Expenses:* Tuition, state resident: full-time $9826. Tuition, nonresident: full-time $24,950. *Financial support:* In 2014–15, 4 fellowships with full tuition reimbursements (averaging $15,000 per year), 14 research assistantships with full tuition reimbursements (averaging $13,045 per year), 10 teaching assistantships with full tuition reimbursements (averaging $13,045 per year) were awarded; institutionally sponsored loans, health care benefits, and unspecified assistantships also available. Financial award application deadline: 2/15. *Faculty research:* Mass media; mass media effects; information studies; cultural, critical and rhetorical studies; policy and law; electronic media. *Unit head:* Dr. Jennings Bryant, Associate Dean for Graduate Studies, 205-348-8593, Fax: 205-348-6774. *Application contact:* Diane Shaddix, Information Contact, 205-348-8593, Fax: 205-348-6774, E-mail: dshaddix@bama.ua.edu.
Website: http://www.cis.ua.edu/graduate

University of Arkansas at Little Rock, Graduate School, College of Social Sciences and Communication, School of Mass Communication, Little Rock, AR 72204-1099. Offers MA. Part-time and evening/weekend programs available. *Degree requirements:* For master's, comprehensive exam, thesis optional. *Entrance requirements:* For master's, GRE General Test, minimum GPA of 2.7. *Application deadline:* Applications are processed on a rolling basis. *Expenses:* Tuition, state resident: full-time $6000; part-time $300 per credit hour. Tuition, nonresident: full-time $13,800; part-time $690 per credit hour. *Required fees:* $1126; $603 per term. One-time fee: $40 full-time. *Financial support:* Research assistantships with tuition reimbursements, career-related internships or fieldwork, Federal Work-Study, institutionally sponsored loans, and unspecified assistantships available. Support available to part-time students. *Faculty research:* Theory and practice of mass communication, social role of the mass media. *Unit head:* Dr. OLaf Hoerschelmann, Director, 501-569-3250. *Application contact:* Dr. Kwasi Boateng, Coordinator, 501-569-3250, E-mail: kxboateng@ualr.edu.
Website: http://ualr.edu/masscomm/

University of Colorado Boulder, Graduate School, School of Journalism and Mass Communication, Boulder, CO 80309. Offers communication (PhD), including media studies; mass communication research (MA); newsgathering (MA). *Accreditation:* ACEJMC (one or more programs are accredited). *Faculty:* 18 full-time (7 women). *Students:* 50 full-time (29 women), 10 part-time (8 women); includes 6 minority (1 Black or African American, non-Hispanic/Latino; 5 Hispanic/Latino), 10 international. Average age 29. 82 applicants, 65% accepted, 19 enrolled. In 2014, 13 master's, 3 doctorates awarded. Terminal master's awarded for partial completion of doctoral program. *Degree requirements:* For master's, comprehensive exam, thesis or alternative; for doctorate, comprehensive exam, thesis/dissertation. *Entrance requirements:* For master's, GRE General Test, minimum undergraduate GPA of 2.75; for doctorate, GRE General Test, minimum undergraduate GPA of 3.2, 3.5 graduate. *Application deadline:* For fall admission, 2/1 for domestic students, 12/1 for international students. Applications are processed on a rolling basis. Application fee: $50 ($70 for international students). Electronic applications accepted. *Financial support:* In 2014–15, 106 students received support, including 9 fellowships (averaging $4,749 per year), 17 research assistantships with full and partial tuition reimbursements available (averaging $27,900 per year), 21 teaching assistantships with full and partial tuition reimbursements available (averaging $28,721 per year); institutionally sponsored loans, scholarships/grants, health care benefits, and unspecified assistantships also available. Financial award application deadline: 3/1; financial award applicants required to submit FAFSA. *Faculty research:* Mass communication/media, journalism, electronic media, print media, television.
Website: http://www.colorado.edu/cmci/

University of Denver, Division of Arts, Humanities and Social Sciences, Department of Media, Film and Journalism Studies, Denver, CO 80208. Offers emergent digital practices (MA); international and intercultural communication (MA); strategic communication (MS); student designed emphasis (MA); video production (MA). Part-time programs available. *Faculty:* 14 full-time (8 women), 6 part-time/adjunct (2 women). *Students:* 24 full-time (17 women), 25 part-time (17 women); includes 10 minority (1 Asian, non-Hispanic/Latino; 4 Hispanic/Latino; 5 Two or more races, non-Hispanic/Latino), 4 international. Average age 27. 73 applicants, 89% accepted, 21 enrolled. In 2014, 17 master's awarded. *Degree requirements:* For master's, thesis (for some programs). *Entrance requirements:* For master's, GRE General Test, bachelor's degree, transcripts, personal statement, three letters of recommendation. Additional exam requirements/recommendations for international students: Required—TOEFL (minimum score 620 paper-based; 105 iBT). *Application deadline:* For fall admission, 2/15 priority date for domestic students, 1/1 priority date for international students. Applications are processed on a rolling basis. Application fee: $65. Electronic applications accepted. *Expenses:* Expenses: $1,199 per credit hour. *Financial support:* In 2014–15, 41 students received support, including 7 teaching assistantships with full and partial tuition reimbursements available (averaging $9,515 per year); career-related internships or fieldwork, Federal Work-Study, institutionally sponsored loans, scholarships/grants, and unspecified assistantships also available. Support available to part-time students. Financial award application deadline: 2/15; financial award applicants required to submit FAFSA. *Faculty research:* International and intercultural communication; media law; film history; youth, families, and social media; activist media. *Total annual research*

expenditures: $50,000. *Unit head:* Dr. Lynn Schofield Clark, Chair, 303-871-3984, Fax: 303-871-4949, E-mail: lynn.clark@du.edu. *Application contact:* Information Contact, 303-871-2166, E-mail: mfjs@du.edu.
Website: http://www.du.edu/ahss/mfjs/index.html

University of Florida, Graduate School, College of Journalism and Communications, Program in Mass Communication, Gainesville, FL 32611. Offers international/intercultural communication (MAMC); journalism (MAMC); mass communication (MAMC, PhD), including clinical translational science (MAMC); public relations (MAMC); science/health communication (MAMC); telecommunication (MAMC). *Entrance requirements:* For master's and doctorate, GRE General Test, minimum GPA of 3.0.

University of Georgia, Grady School of Journalism and Mass Communication, Athens, GA 30602. Offers journalism and mass communication (MA); mass communication (PhD). *Degree requirements:* For master's, comprehensive exam, thesis (MA); for doctorate, comprehensive exam, thesis/dissertation. *Entrance requirements:* For master's and doctorate, GRE General Test. Additional exam requirements/recommendations for international students: Required—TOEFL, TWE for Ph D. Electronic applications accepted.

University of Houston, College of Liberal Arts and Social Sciences, School of Communication, Houston, TX 77204. Offers health communication (MA); mass communication studies (MA); public relations studies (MA); speech communication (MA). Part-time programs available. *Degree requirements:* For master's, comprehensive exam (for some programs), thesis (for some programs), 30-33 hours. *Entrance requirements:* For master's, GRE. Additional exam requirements/recommendations for international students: Required—TOEFL. Electronic applications accepted.

The University of Iowa, Graduate College, College of Liberal Arts and Sciences, School of Journalism and Mass Communication, Iowa City, IA 52242-1316. Offers journalism and media communication (MA); mass communication (PhD); strategic communication (MA); JD/MA; JD/PhD. *Degree requirements:* For master's, thesis optional, exam; for doctorate, comprehensive exam, thesis/dissertation. *Entrance requirements:* For master's and doctorate, GRE General Test, minimum GPA of 3.0. Additional exam requirements/recommendations for international students: Required—TOEFL (minimum score 637 paper-based; 110 iBT). Electronic applications accepted. *Faculty research:* Verbal and visual aspects of historical, legal, social, and cross-cultural communication.

University of Louisiana at Lafayette, College of Liberal Arts, Department of Communication, Lafayette, LA 70504. Offers mass communications (MS). Part-time programs available. *Degree requirements:* For master's, thesis optional. *Entrance requirements:* For master's, GRE General Test, minimum GPA of 2.75. Additional exam requirements/recommendations for international students: Required—TOEFL (minimum score 550 paper-based). Electronic applications accepted. *Faculty research:* Mass media problems, issues and ethics, mass communication, historical studies, conflict of interest and law and ethics in journalism, contemporary issues and trends in publications.

University of Maine, Graduate School, College of Liberal Arts and Sciences, Department of Communication and Journalism, Orono, ME 04469. Offers communication (MA, PhD); mass communication (MA). Part-time programs available. *Faculty:* 8 full-time (3 women), 7 part-time/adjunct (3 women). *Students:* 16 full-time (8 women), 1 (woman) part-time, 3 international. Average age 27. 21 applicants, 52% accepted, 7 enrolled. In 2014, 4 master's, 3 doctorates awarded. *Degree requirements:* For master's, thesis (for some programs); for doctorate, comprehensive exam, thesis/dissertation. *Entrance requirements:* For master's, GRE General Test. Additional exam requirements/recommendations for international students: Required—TOEFL. *Application deadline:* For fall admission, 2/1 priority date for domestic students. Applications are processed on a rolling basis. Application fee: $65. Electronic applications accepted. *Expenses:* Tuition, state resident: part-time $658 per credit hour. Tuition, nonresident: part-time $1550 per credit hour. *Financial support:* In 2014–15, 14 students received support, including 14 teaching assistantships with full tuition reimbursements available (averaging $14,600 per year); career-related internships or fieldwork, Federal Work-Study, institutionally sponsored loans, and tuition waivers (full and partial) also available. Support available to part-time students. Financial award application deadline: 3/1. *Faculty research:* Rhetorical theory, semiotics, discourse analysis, gender and communication, children's talk/communication disorders. *Total annual research expenditures:* $104,293. *Unit head:* Dr. Nathan Stormer, Chair, 207-581-1938, Fax: 207-581-1286, E-mail: nathan@maine.edu. *Application contact:* Scott G. Delcourt, Assistant Vice President for Graduate Studies and Senior Associate Dean, 207-581-3291, Fax: 207-581-3232, E-mail: graduate@maine.edu.
Website: http://cmj.umaine.edu/graduate-program/

University of Michigan, Horace H. Rackham School of Graduate Studies, College of Literature, Science, and the Arts, Department of Communication Studies, Ann Arbor, MI 48109-1285. Offers PhD. *Faculty:* 21 full-time (9 women). *Students:* 29 full-time (22 women); includes 8 minority (5 Black or African American, non-Hispanic/Latino; 2 Hispanic/Latino; 1 Two or more races, non-Hispanic/Latino), 6 international. Average age 29. 94 applicants, 14% accepted, 6 enrolled. In 2014, 5 doctorates awarded. *Degree requirements:* For doctorate, comprehensive exam, thesis/dissertation, first-year research project, 2 terms in student instructor position, publications, presentations. *Entrance requirements:* For doctorate, GRE, U.S. bachelor's degree or its equivalent from accredited institution. Additional exam requirements/recommendations for international students: Required—TOEFL (minimum score 600 paper-based; 102 iBT). *Application deadline:* For fall admission, 12/1 for domestic and international students. Application fee: $75 ($90 for international students). Electronic applications accepted. *Expenses:* Expenses: $10,203.19/term for MI resident pre-candidates; $20,446.19/term for non-MI resident pre-candidates; $5,501.19/term for candidates. *Financial support:* In 2014–15, 29 students received support, including 28 fellowships with full tuition reimbursements available (averaging $18,757 per year), 2 research assistantships with full tuition reimbursements available (averaging $18,971 per year), 21 teaching assistantships with full tuition reimbursements available (averaging $19,827 per year); scholarships/grants, health care benefits, tuition waivers (full), and unspecified assistantships also available. Financial award application deadline: 4/30; financial award applicants required to submit FAFSA. *Faculty research:* Political communication; media, culture and society; media effects; race, gender, and the media; new media, media law and policy. *Unit head:* Prof. Susan J. Douglas, Professor and Chair, 734-764-0420, Fax: 734-764-3288, E-mail: sdoug@umich.edu. *Application contact:* Amy B. Eaton, Graduate Program Coordinator, 734-615-8974, Fax: 734-764-3288, E-mail: lsa-commphd@umich.edu.
Website: http://www.lsa.umich.edu/comm/

University of Minnesota, Twin Cities Campus, Graduate School, College of Liberal Arts, School of Journalism and Mass Communication, Minneapolis, MN 55455-0213. Offers mass communication (MA, PhD); strategic communication (professional program) (MA). *Degree requirements:* For master's, thesis; for doctorate, comprehensive exam, thesis/dissertation. *Entrance requirements:* For master's, GRE; GMAT (for strategic communications program), letters of recommendation, minimum undergraduate GPA of 3.0, writing sample; two years professional experience (for strategic communications program); for doctorate, GRE, letters of recommendation, minimum undergraduate GPA of 3.0, writing sample. Additional exam requirements/recommendations for international students: Required—TOEFL (minimum score 79 iBT). Electronic applications accepted. *Faculty research:* Communication law, regulation, and ethics; history; mass media effects; new media, health communication.

University of Nebraska–Lincoln, Graduate College, College of Journalism and Mass Communications, Lincoln, NE 68588. Offers marketing, communication and advertising (MA); professional journalism (MA). Postbaccalaureate distance learning degree programs offered (no on-campus study). *Degree requirements:* For master's, thesis. *Entrance requirements:* For master's, samples of work. Additional exam requirements/recommendations for international students: Required—TOEFL (minimum score 600 paper-based). Electronic applications accepted. *Faculty research:* Interactive media and the Internet, community newspapers, children's radio, advertising involvement, telecommunications policy.

The University of North Carolina at Chapel Hill, Graduate School, School of Journalism and Mass Communication, Chapel Hill, NC 27599. Offers mass communication (MA, PhD); technology and communication (MA). *Accreditation:* ACEJMC (one or more programs are accredited). Part-time programs available. Postbaccalaureate distance learning degree programs offered (minimal on-campus study). *Degree requirements:* For master's, comprehensive exam, thesis; for doctorate, comprehensive exam, thesis/dissertation. *Entrance requirements:* For master's and doctorate, GRE General Test, minimum GPA of 3.0. Additional exam requirements/recommendations for international students: Required—TOEFL (minimum score 620 paper-based; 105 iBT); Recommended—IELTS (minimum score 7.5). Electronic applications accepted. *Expenses:* Contact institution. *Faculty research:* Media processes and production, legal and regulatory issues, media effects, media history.

University of Oklahoma, Gaylord College of Journalism and Mass Communication, Program in Journalism and Mass Communication, Norman, OK 73019. Offers MA, PhD. Part-time programs available. *Students:* 30 full-time (18 women), 23 part-time (8 women); includes 5 minority (2 Black or African American, non-Hispanic/Latino; 1 American Indian or Alaska Native, non-Hispanic/Latino; 1 Hispanic/Latino; 1 Two or more races, non-Hispanic/Latino), 15 international. Average age 31. 38 applicants, 47% accepted, 12 enrolled. In 2014, 14 master's, 4 doctorates awarded. *Degree requirements:* For master's, comprehensive exam (for some programs), thesis (for some programs); for doctorate, comprehensive exam, thesis/dissertation. *Entrance requirements:* For master's, GRE, 2 letters of recommendation, resume, personal statement, writing sample, minimum GPA of 3.2; for doctorate, GRE, 3 letters of recommendation, resume, personal statement, writing sample, minimum GPA of 3.5. Additional exam requirements/recommendations for international students: Required—TOEFL (minimum score 79 iBT). *Application deadline:* For fall admission, 7/1 for domestic students, 3/1 for international students; for spring admission, 11/1 for domestic students, 9/1 for international students. Application fee: $50 ($100 for international students). Electronic applications accepted. *Expenses:* Tuition, state resident: full-time $4394; part-time $183.10 per credit hour. Tuition, nonresident: full-time $16,970; part-time $707.10 per credit hour. *Required fees:* $2892; $109.95 per credit hour. $126.50 per semester. *Financial support:* In 2014–15, 37 students received support. Career-related internships or fieldwork, institutionally sponsored loans, scholarships/grants, health care benefits, and unspecified assistantships available. Support available to part-time students. Financial award application deadline: 6/1; financial award applicants required to submit FAFSA. *Faculty research:* Global and international public relations, crisis communication, strategic communication, advertising planning, digital advertising, media management, media studies, mass communication, women and leadership, digital media, health communication, ethics in journalism and media, broadcasting and production, critical and cultural theories. *Unit head:* Dr. Katerina Tsetsura, Director of Graduate Studies, 405-325-6195, Fax: 405-325-7565, E-mail: tsetsura@ou.edu. *Application contact:* Larry Laneer, Graduate Advisor, 405-325-2722, Fax: 405-325-7565, E-mail: llaneer@ou.edu.
Website: http://www.ou.edu/content/gaylord/graduate.html

University of Puerto Rico, Río Piedras Campus, School of Communication, San Juan, PR 00931-3300. Offers MA. Part-time programs available. *Degree requirements:* For master's, comprehensive exam, thesis. *Entrance requirements:* For master's, GRE, PAEG, minimum GPA of 3.0, 2 letters of recommendation, interview.

University of Southern Mississippi, Graduate School, College of Arts and Letters, School of Mass Communication and Journalism, Hattiesburg, MS 39406-0001. Offers mass communication (MA, MS, PhD); public relations (MS). Part-time programs available. *Degree requirements:* For master's, comprehensive exam, thesis optional; for doctorate, comprehensive exam, thesis/dissertation. *Entrance requirements:* For master's, GRE General Test, minimum GPA of 3.0 in field of study, 2.75 in last 2 years; for doctorate, GRE General Test, minimum GPA of 3.5. Additional exam requirements/recommendations for international students: Required—TOEFL, IELTS.

University of South Florida, College of Arts and Sciences, School of Mass Communications, Tampa, FL 33620-9951. Offers media studies (MA), including media studies; multimedia journalism studies (MA); strategic communication management (MA). Part-time and evening/weekend programs available. *Faculty:* 10 full-time (3 women). *Students:* 17 full-time (13 women), 17 part-time (6 women); includes 5 minority (2 Black or African American, non-Hispanic/Latino; 1 Asian, non-Hispanic/Latino; 2 Hispanic/Latino), 7 international. Average age 29. 40 applicants, 65% accepted, 14 enrolled. In 2014, 15 master's awarded. *Degree requirements:* For master's, comprehensive exam, thesis optional. *Entrance requirements:* For master's, GRE General Test (minimum score of 153 verbal and 144 quantitative preferred), minimum GPA of 3.0 in last 60 hours of course work, three letters of recommendation, letter of intent, resume. Additional exam requirements/recommendations for international students: Required—TOEFL (minimum score 550 paper-based; 79 iBT) or IELTS (minimum score 6.5). *Application deadline:* For fall admission, 2/15 for domestic students, 1/2 for international students; for spring admission, 10/15 for domestic students, 6/1 for international students. Application fee: $30. Electronic applications accepted. *Financial support:* In 2014–15, 9 students received support, including 9 teaching assistantships with tuition reimbursements available (averaging $10,513 per year); unspecified assistantships also available. Financial award application deadline: 2/28. *Faculty research:* First Amendment analysis, civic journalism, public opinion, media ethics, media effects research in sports public relations, public relations management, advertisement, telecommunications. *Total annual research expenditures:* $52,955. *Unit head:* Dr. Jim Andrews, Interim Director and Associate Professor, 813-974-2108, Fax: 813-974-2592, E-mail: jimandrews@usf.edu. *Application contact:* Dr. Michael Mitrook, Assistant Professor, 813-974-8890, Fax: 813-974-2592, E-mail: mmitrook@.usf.edu.
Website: http://masscom.usf.edu/grad/

University of South Florida, Innovative Education, Tampa, FL 33620-9951. *Unit head:* Kathy Barnes, Interdisciplinary Programs Coordinator, 813-974-8031, Fax: 813-974-7061, E-mail: barnesk@usf.edu. *Application contact:* Karen Tylinski, Metro Initiatives, 813-974-9943, Fax: 813-974-7061, E-mail: ktylinsk@usf.edu.
Website: http://www.usf.edu/innovative-education/

Mass Communication

University of Wisconsin–Madison, Graduate School, College of Letters and Science, School of Journalism and Mass Communication, Program in Journalism and Mass Communication, Madison, WI 53706-1380. Offers MA. *Expenses:* Tuition, state resident: full-time $10,723; part-time $745 per credit. Tuition, nonresident: full-time $24,054; part-time $1578 per credit. *Required fees:* $374 per semester. Tuition and fees vary according to course load, program and reciprocity agreements.

University of Wisconsin–Madison, Graduate School, College of Letters and Science, School of Journalism and Mass Communication, Program in Mass Communication, Madison, WI 53706-1380. Offers PhD. *Degree requirements:* For doctorate, thesis/ dissertation. *Expenses:* Tuition, state resident: full-time $10,723; part-time $745 per credit. Tuition, nonresident: full-time $24,054; part-time $1578 per credit. *Required fees:* $374 per semester. Tuition and fees vary according to course load, program and reciprocity agreements.

University of Wisconsin–Superior, Graduate Division, Department of Communicating Arts, Superior, WI 54880-4500. Offers mass communication (MA); speech communication (MA); theater (MA). Part-time programs available. *Degree requirements:* For master's, comprehensive exam, thesis or alternative, position paper or project. *Entrance requirements:* For master's, minimum GPA of 2.75. Electronic applications accepted. *Faculty research:* Multimedia technology, ethics in journalism, diversity, electronic portfolio assessment.

University of Wisconsin–Whitewater, School of Graduate Studies, College of Arts and Communications, Department of Communication, Whitewater, WI 53190-1790. Offers corporate communication (MS); mass communication (MS). Part-time and evening/ weekend programs available. Postbaccalaureate distance learning degree programs offered (no on-campus study). *Degree requirements:* For master's, thesis or alternative. *Entrance requirements:* For master's, 2 letters of recommendation, goal statement. Additional exam requirements/recommendations for international students: Required— TOEFL (minimum score 550 paper-based; 80 iBT), IELTS (minimum score 6). Electronic applications accepted.

Virginia Commonwealth University, Graduate School, College of Humanities and Sciences, School of Mass Communications, Program in Mass Communications, Richmond, VA 23284-9005. Offers multimedia journalism (MS); strategic public relations (MS). *Degree requirements:* For master's, comprehensive exam, thesis optional. *Entrance requirements:* For master's, GRE General Test. Additional exam requirements/ recommendations for international students: Required—TOEFL (minimum score 600 paper-based; 100 iBT); Recommended—IELTS (minimum score 6.5). Electronic applications accepted. *Faculty research:* Multimedia journalism, strategic public relations.

Media Studies

American University, School of Communication, Film and Electronic Media Program, Washington, DC 20016-8001. Offers MFA. Part-time and evening/weekend programs available. *Degree requirements:* For master's, comprehensive exam, thesis or alternative. *Entrance requirements:* For master's, GRE General Test. Additional exam requirements/recommendations for international students: Required—TOEFL (minimum score 600 paper-based; 100 iBT), IELTS. *Application deadline:* For fall admission, 2/1 priority date for domestic and international students; for spring admission, 11/15 for domestic and international students. Applications are processed on a rolling basis. Application fee: $50. Electronic applications accepted. *Financial support:* Fellowships with partial tuition reimbursements, research assistantships with partial tuition reimbursements, teaching assistantships with partial tuition reimbursements, career-related internships or fieldwork, Federal Work-Study, institutionally sponsored loans, scholarships/grants, tuition waivers (partial), and unspecified assistantships available. Financial award application deadline: 2/1; financial award applicants required to submit FAFSA. *Faculty research:* Documentary film production, social media, media and public policy, visual literacy, new technology. *Unit head:* Prof. John Douglass, Director, Film and Media Arts Division, 202-885-2045, Fax: 202-885-2019, E-mail: jdougla@american.edu. *Application contact:* Sharmeen Ahsan-Bracciale, Director of Graduate Student Services, 202-885-3940, Fax: 202-885-2019, E-mail: sharmeen@american.edu.
Website: http://www.american.edu/soc/film/degrees/MFA-FLEM.cfm

American University, School of Communication, PhD Program in Communication, Washington, DC 20016-8001. Offers media industries and institutions (PhD); media, public issues, and engagement (PhD); media, technology, and culture (PhD). *Faculty:* 10 full-time (4 women). *Students:* 15 full-time (12 women), 1 (woman) part-time; includes 3 minority (1 Asian, non-Hispanic/Latino; 2 Hispanic/Latino), 5 international. 64 applicants, 17% accepted, 5 enrolled. In 2014, 3 doctorates awarded. *Degree requirements:* For doctorate, comprehensive exam, thesis/dissertation. *Entrance requirements:* For doctorate, GRE General Test. Additional exam requirements/ recommendations for international students: Required—TOEFL (minimum score 600 paper-based; 100 iBT), IELTS (minimum score 7). *Application deadline:* For fall admission, 12/15 priority date for domestic students, 12/15 for international students. Applications are processed on a rolling basis. Application fee: $55. Electronic. applications accepted. *Financial support:* In 2014–15, 16 research assistantships with full and partial tuition reimbursements (averaging $42,000 per year) were awarded; Federal Work-Study, scholarships/grants, and unspecified assistantships also available. Financial award application deadline: 2/1; financial award applicants required to submit FAFSA. *Faculty research:* Public policy advocacy; social impact of mass media and communication policies; science, health, and environmental communication; intercultural and international strategic communication. *Unit head:* Prof. Kathryn Montgomery, Director, 202-885-2680, Fax: 202-885-2099, E-mail: kcm@american.edu. *Application contact:* Sharmeen Ahsan-Bracciale, Director of Graduate Services, 202-885-2040, Fax: 202-885-2019, E-mail: sharmeen@american.edu.
Website: http://www.american.edu/soc/communication-studies/degrees/phd-in-communication.cfm

American University of Beirut, Graduate Programs, Faculty of Arts and Sciences, Beirut, Lebanon. Offers anthropology (MA); Arab and Middle Eastern history (PhD); Arabic language and literature (MA, PhD); archaeology (MA); biology (MS); cell and molecular biology (PhD); chemistry (MS); clinical psychology (MA); computational sciences (MS); computer science (MS); economics (MA); English language (MA); English literature (MA); environmental policy planning (MS); financial economics (MAFE); geology (MS); history (MA); mathematics (MA, MS); media studies (MA); Middle Eastern studies (MA); physics (MS); political studies (MA); psychology (MA); public administration (MA); sociology (MA); statistics (MA, MS); theoretical physics (PhD); transnational American studies (MA). Part-time programs available. *Faculty:* 107 full-time (32 women), 6 part-time/adjunct (2 women). *Students:* 230 full-time (161 women), 209 part-time (146 women). Average age 26. 261 applicants, 70% accepted, 83 enrolled. In 2014, 68 master's, 2 doctorates awarded. *Degree requirements:* For master's, one foreign language, comprehensive exam, thesis (for some programs); for doctorate, one foreign language, comprehensive exam, thesis/dissertation. *Entrance requirements:* For master's, GRE (for some MA/MS programs), letter of recommendation; for doctorate, GRE, letters of recommendation. Additional exam requirements/recommendations for international students: Required—TOEFL (minimum score 600 paper-based; 97 iBT), IELTS (minimum score 7). *Application deadline:* For fall admission, 4/1 for domestic and international students; for spring admission, 11/1 for domestic and international students. Application fee: $50. Electronic applications accepted. *Expenses: Tuition:* Full-time $15,462; part-time $859 per credit. *Required fees:* $692. Tuition and fees vary according to course load and program. *Financial support:* Research assistantships, career-related internships or fieldwork, institutionally sponsored loans, scholarships/grants, health care benefits, and unspecified assistantships available. Financial award application deadline: 2/4; financial award applicants required to submit FAFSA. *Faculty research:* Determinants of language proficiency among Arab learners of English as a foreign language; opinion mining,

information retrieval, runtime verification, high performance computing; solar and fuel cells, self-organizing systems, heterocyclic chemistry, air and water chemistry; complex analysis, harmonic analysis, number theory; social and political psychology, clinical psychology; thin films physics and technology; theory of soft matter; religious and ethnic conflict; sports and politics. *Total annual research expenditures:* $966,000. *Unit head:* Dr. Patrick McGreevy, Dean, 961-1374374 Ext. 3800, Fax: 961-1744461, E-mail: pm07@aub.edu.lb. *Application contact:* Dr. Salim Kanaan, Director, Admissions Office, 961-1350000 Ext. 2590, Fax: 961-1750775, E-mail: sk00@aub.edu.lb.
Website: http://www.aub.edu.lb/fas/

Arizona State University at the Tempe campus, College of Liberal Arts and Sciences, Department of English, Program in Film and Media Studies, Tempe, AZ 85287-0402. Offers American media and popular culture (MAS). Part-time and evening/weekend programs available. Postbaccalaureate distance learning degree programs offered (no on-campus study). *Degree requirements:* For master's, integrated project. *Entrance requirements:* For master's, minimum GPA of 3.0 or equivalent in last 2 years of work leading to bachelor's degree. Additional exam requirements/recommendations for international students: Required—TOEFL, IELTS, or PTE. Electronic applications accepted. *Expenses:* Contact institution.

Arizona State University at the Tempe campus, Herberger Institute for Design and the Arts, School of Arts, Media and Engineering, Tempe, AZ 85287-8709. Offers media arts and sciences (PhD). *Degree requirements:* For doctorate, comprehensive exam, thesis/dissertation, interactive Program of Study (iPOS) submitted before completing 50 percent of required credit hours. *Entrance requirements:* For doctorate, GRE, minimum GPA of 3.25 in last 2 years of work leading to bachelor's degree, portfolio of supporting material, statement of educational/career goals, 3 letters of recommendation, resume/ curriculum vitae. Additional exam requirements/recommendations for international students: Required—TOEFL, IELTS, or PTE. Electronic applications accepted.

Arkansas State University, Graduate School, College of Media and Communication, Department of Media, State University, AR 72467. Offers MSMC. Part-time programs available. *Faculty:* 10 full-time (5 women). *Students:* 14 full-time (8 women), 22 part-time (6 women); includes 11 minority (9 Black or African American, non-Hispanic/Latino; 1 Asian, non-Hispanic/Latino; 1 Hispanic/Latino), 15 international. Average age 27. 27 applicants, 67% accepted, 13 enrolled. In 2014, 14 master's awarded. *Degree requirements:* For master's, comprehensive exam, thesis or alternative. *Entrance requirements:* For master's, GRE General Test or MAT, appropriate bachelor's degree, letters of reference, educational experience, professional experience, official transcripts, immunization records. Additional exam requirements/recommendations for international students: Required—TOEFL (minimum score 550 paper-based; 79 iBT), IELTS (minimum score 6), PTE (minimum score 56). *Application deadline:* For fall admission, 7/1 for domestic and international students; for spring admission, 11/15 for domestic students, 11/14 for international students. Applications are processed on a rolling basis. Application fee: $30 ($40 for international students). Electronic applications accepted. *Expenses:* Tuition, state resident: full-time $4392; part-time $244 per credit hour. Tuition, nonresident: full-time $8784; part-time $488 per credit hour. *International tuition:* $9484 full-time. *Required fees:* $1134; $63 per credit hour. $25 per term. Tuition and fees vary according to course load and program. *Financial support:* In 2014–15, 2 students received support. Career-related internships or fieldwork, scholarships/grants, and unspecified assistantships available. Financial award application deadline: 7/1; financial award applicants required to submit FAFSA. *Unit head:* Dr. Osabuohien Amienyi, Chair, 870-972-3070, Fax: 870-972-2997, E-mail: osami@astate.edu. *Application contact:* Vickey Ring, Graduate Admissions Coordinator, 870-972-3029, Fax: 870-972-3857, E-mail: vickeyring@astate.edu.
Website: http://www.astate.edu/college/communications/about

Bob Jones University, Graduate Programs, Greenville, SC 29614. Offers accountancy (MS); Bible (MA); Bible translation (MA); Biblical studies (Certificate); broadcast management (MS); business administration (MBA); church history (MA, PhD); church ministries (MA); church music (MM); cinema and video production (MA); counseling (MS); curriculum and instruction (Ed D); divinity (M Div); dramatic production (MA); educational leadership (MS, Ed D, Ed S); elementary education (M Ed, MAT); English (M Ed, MA, MAT); fine arts (MA); graphic design (MA); history (M Ed, MA); illustration (MA); interpretative speech (MA); mathematics (M Ed, MAT); medical missions (Certificate); ministry (MM, D Min); multi-categorical special education (M Ed, MAT); music (M Ed); New Testament interpretation (PhD); Old Testament interpretation (PhD); orchestral instrument performance (MM); organ performance (MM); pastoral studies (MA); personnel services (MS, Ed S); piano pedagogy (MM); piano performance (MM); platform arts (MA); radio and television broadcasting (MS); rhetoric and public address (MA); secondary education (M Ed); studio art (MA); teaching Bible (MA); theology (MA, PhD); voice performance (MM); youth ministries (MA); M Div/MM.

Boston University, College of Communication, Department of Film and Television, Boston, MA 02215. Offers MFA, MS, MBA/MS. Part-time programs available. *Faculty:* 17 full-time, 25 part-time/adjunct. *Students:* 68 full-time (52 women), 7 part-time (5 women); includes 11 minority (7 Black or African American, non-Hispanic/Latino; 3

Hispanic/Latino; 1 Two or more races, non-Hispanic/Latino), 16 international. Average age 25. 223 applicants, 51% accepted, 53 enrolled. In 2014, 14 master's awarded. *Degree requirements:* For master's, thesis. *Entrance requirements:* For master's, GRE General Test, resume, writing and creative samples, letters of recommendation. Additional exam requirements/recommendations for international students: Required—TOEFL (minimum score 600 paper-based; 100 iBT), IELTS. *Application deadline:* For fall admission, 5/1 for domestic and international students. Applications are processed on a rolling basis. Application fee: $80. Electronic applications accepted. *Expenses: Tuition:* Full-time $45,686; part-time $1428 per credit hour. *Required fees:* $660; $60 per semester. Tuition and fees vary according to program. *Financial support:* Teaching assistantships with partial tuition reimbursements, career-related internships or fieldwork, Federal Work-Study, institutionally sponsored loans, scholarships/grants, and unspecified assistantships available. Support available to part-time students. Financial award application deadline: 5/1; financial award applicants required to submit FAFSA. *Unit head:* Paul Schneider, Chairman, 617-353-3483, Fax: 617-353-1084, E-mail: ftvchair@bu.edu. *Application contact:* Manny Dotel, Assistant Director, Graduate Affairs, 617-353-3481, E-mail: comgrad@bu.edu.
Website: http://www.bu.edu/com/academics/film-tv/

Boston University, College of Communication, Division of Emerging Media Studies, Boston, MA 02215. Offers MA, PhD. Part-time programs available. *Students:* 7 full-time (6 women), 2 part-time (both women); includes 2 minority (1 Asian, non-Hispanic/Latino; 1 Hispanic/Latino), 1 international. 48 applicants, 60% accepted, 10 enrolled. In 2014, 7 master's awarded. *Degree requirements:* For master's, thesis; for doctorate, comprehensive exam, thesis/dissertation. *Entrance requirements:* For master's and doctorate, GRE, resume, writing samples, letters of recommendation. Additional exam requirements/recommendations for international students: Required—TOEFL (minimum score 600 paper-based; 100 iBT), IELTS. *Application deadline:* For fall admission, 5/1 for domestic and international students. Applications are processed on a rolling basis. Application fee: $80. Electronic applications accepted. *Expenses: Tuition:* Full-time $45,686; part-time $1428 per credit hour. *Required fees:* $660; $60 per semester. Tuition and fees vary according to program. *Financial support:* Fellowships, research assistantships, teaching assistantships, career-related internships or fieldwork, Federal Work-Study, institutionally sponsored loans, scholarships/grants, health care benefits, and unspecified assistantships available. Financial award application deadline: 5/1; financial award applicants required to submit FAFSA. *Unit head:* Dr. James Katz, Professor of Emerging Media/Chair of the Division of Emerging Media Studies, 617-353-7733, E-mail: katz2020@bu.edu. *Application contact:* Manny Dotel, Assistant Director, Graduate Affairs, 617-353-3481, E-mail: comgrad@bu.edu.
Website: http://www.bu.edu/com/academics/emerging-media/

Brooklyn College of the City University of New York, School of Visual, Media and Performing Arts, Department of Television and Radio, Brooklyn, NY 11210-2889. Offers media studies (MS); television production (MFA). Part-time and evening/weekend programs available. *Degree requirements:* For master's, comprehensive exam. *Entrance requirements:* For master's, GRE General Test or MAT, 12 credits in television/radio with a minimum B average, 2 letters of recommendation. Additional exam requirements/recommendations for international students: Required—TOEFL (minimum score 580 paper-based; 92 iBT). Electronic applications accepted. *Faculty research:* Criticism, research methods, audience behavior, policy and regulation, program history, international television and radio.

California College of the Arts, Graduate Programs, Fine Arts Programs, San Francisco, CA 94107. Offers ceramics (MFA); comics (MFA); film/video/performance (MFA); glass (MFA); interdisciplinary studies (MFA); jewelry/metal arts (MFA); media studies (MFA); painting/drawing (MFA); photography (MFA); printmaking (MFA); sculpture (MFA); social practice (MFA); textiles (MFA); wood/furniture (MFA). *Accreditation:* NASAD. *Degree requirements:* For master's, thesis, exhibit. *Entrance requirements:* For master's, appropriate bachelor's degree, portfolio, resume, 2 letters of recommendation, transcript. Additional exam requirements/recommendations for international students: Required—TOEFL (minimum score 600 paper-based; 100 iBT). Electronic applications accepted.

Carnegie Mellon University, School of Computer Science and College of Fine Arts, Program in Entertainment Technology, Pittsburgh, PA 15213-3891. Offers MET.

Central Michigan University, College of Graduate Studies, College of Communication and Fine Arts, School of Broadcasting and Cinematic Arts, Mount Pleasant, MI 48859. Offers electronic media management (MA); electronic media production (MA); electronic media studies (MA); film theory and criticism (MA). Part-time programs available. *Degree requirements:* For master's, thesis or alternative. *Entrance requirements:* For master's, undergraduate degree in broadcasting, film studies, or an associated discipline with minimum GPA of 2.7. Electronic applications accepted. *Faculty research:* Multimedia production, film history and criticism, writing and promotions, international broadcasting and media systems, history of American broadcasting.

Champlain College, Graduate Studies, Burlington, VT 05402-0670. Offers business (MBA); digital forensic management (MS); digital forensic science (MS); early childhood education (M Ed); emergent media (MFA, MS); health care administration (MS); law (MS); managing innovation and information technology (MS); mediation and applied conflict studies (MS). MS in emergent media program held in Shanghai. Part-time programs available. Postbaccalaureate distance learning degree programs offered (no on-campus study). *Degree requirements:* For master's, capstone project. *Entrance requirements:* Additional exam requirements/recommendations for international students: Required—TOEFL (minimum score 550 paper-based; 80 iBT). Electronic applications accepted.

City College of the City University of New York, Graduate School, College of Liberal Arts and Science, Division of the Humanities and Arts, Department of Media and Communication Arts, Program in Media Arts Production, New York, NY 10031-9198. Offers MFA.

Claremont Graduate University, Graduate Programs, School of Arts and Humanities, Department of Cultural Studies, Claremont, CA 91711-6160. Offers Africana studies (Certificate); cultural studies (MA, PhD); media studies (MA, PhD); museum studies (MA). Part-time programs available. *Faculty:* 6 full-time (2 women). *Students:* 35 full-time (22 women), 15 part-time (11 women); includes 20 minority (6 Black or African American, non-Hispanic/Latino; 1 American Indian or Alaska Native, non-Hispanic/Latino; 5 Asian, non-Hispanic/Latino; 8 Hispanic/Latino), 7 international. Average age 35. In 2014, 6 master's, 3 doctorates, 1 other advanced degree awarded. *Entrance requirements:* For master's and doctorate, GRE General Test. Additional exam requirements/recommendations for international students: Required—TOEFL (minimum score 550 paper-based; 80 iBT). *Application deadline:* For fall admission, 2/1 priority date for domestic and international students. Applications are processed on a rolling basis. Application fee: $80. Electronic applications accepted. *Expenses: Tuition:* Full-time $41,784; part-time $1741 per credit. *Required fees:* $600; $300 per semester. *Financial support:* Fellowships, research assistantships, Federal Work-Study, institutionally sponsored loans, and scholarships/grants available. Support available to part-time students. Financial award application deadline: 2/15; financial award applicants required to submit FAFSA. *Unit head:* Eve Oishi, Chair, 909-607-7587, E-mail: eve.oishi@cgu.edu. *Application contact:* Amy Sandefur, Assistant Director of Admissions, 909-607-9101, E-mail: amy.sandefur@cgu.edu.
Website: http://www.cgu.edu/pages/441.asp

College of Staten Island of the City University of New York, Graduate Programs, Division of Humanities and Social Sciences, Program in Cinema and Media Studies, Staten Island, NY 10314-6600. Offers MA. Part-time and evening/weekend programs available. *Faculty:* 5 full-time (3 women). *Students:* 15 part-time (9 women). Average age 28. 16 applicants, 44% accepted, 5 enrolled. In 2014, 3 master's awarded. *Degree requirements:* For master's, comprehensive exam (for some programs), thesis optional, 36 credits in cinema and media studies courses. *Entrance requirements:* For master's, bachelor's degree with minimum B average in undergraduate cinema studies or communications courses; 10-12 page writing sample; three letters of recommendation; one- to two-page statement of intent detailing interest in field, background in film and media studies, and/or research interests. Additional exam requirements/recommendations for international students: Required—TOEFL (minimum score 550 paper-based; 79 iBT), IELTS (minimum score 6.5). *Application deadline:* For fall admission, 4/15 priority date for domestic and international students; for spring admission, 11/25 priority date for domestic and international students. Applications are processed on a rolling basis. Application fee: $125. Electronic applications accepted. *Expenses:* Tuition, state resident: full-time $9650; part-time $405 per credit. Tuition, nonresident: full-time $17,880; part-time $745 per credit. *Required fees:* $141.10 per semester. Tuition and fees vary according to program. *Financial support:* In 2014–15, 2 students received support, including 2 fellowships (averaging $1,000 per year), 1 research assistantship (averaging $11,654 per year), 3 teaching assistantships (averaging $3,000 per year); career-related internships or fieldwork, Federal Work-Study, and scholarships/grants also available. Support available to part-time students. Financial award applicants required to submit FAFSA. *Unit head:* Dr. Cindy Wong, Graduate Program Coordinator, 718-982-2541, Fax: 718-982-2710, E-mail: cinemamasters@csi.cuny.edu. *Application contact:* Sasha Spence, Assistant Director for Graduate Admissions, 718-982-2019, Fax: 718-982-2500, E-mail: sasha.spence@csi.cuny.edu.
Website: http://csivc.csi.cuny.edu/mediaculture/files

Concordia University, School of Graduate Studies, Faculty of Arts and Science, Department of Communication Studies, Montréal, QC H3G 1M8, Canada. Offers communication (PhD); communication studies (Diploma); media studies (MA). PhD program offered jointly with Université de Montréal and Université du Québec à Montréal. *Degree requirements:* For master's, thesis optional; for doctorate, one foreign language, comprehensive exam, thesis/dissertation, research practicum, seminar. *Entrance requirements:* For master's, bachelor's degree in communications, 2 years of media-related experience; for doctorate, MA in communications. *Faculty research:* Communication and development, organizational communication, cultural studies, rhetoric, future studies.

Concordia University, School of Graduate Studies, Faculty of Fine Arts, Department of Studio Arts, Montréal, QC H3G 1M8, Canada. Offers studio arts (MFA), including film production, open media, painting, photography, print media, sculpture, ceramics and fibers. *Degree requirements:* For master's, thesis or alternative. *Entrance requirements:* For master's, portfolio.

Cornell University, Graduate School, Graduate Fields of Agriculture and Life Sciences, Field of Communication, Ithaca, NY 14853-0001. Offers communication (MS, PhD); human-computer interaction (MS, PhD); language and communication (MS, PhD); media communication and society (MS, PhD); organizational communication (MS, PhD); science, environment and health communication (MS, PhD); social psychology of communication (MS, PhD). *Degree requirements:* For master's, thesis (MS); for doctorate, comprehensive exam, thesis/dissertation. *Entrance requirements:* For master's and doctorate, GRE General Test, 3 letters of recommendation. Additional exam requirements/recommendations for international students: Required—TOEFL (minimum score 600 paper-based; 100 iBT). Electronic applications accepted. *Faculty research:* Mass communication, communication technologies, science and environmental communication.

Dallas Theological Seminary, Graduate Programs, Dallas, TX 75204-6499. Offers adult education (Th M); apologetics (Th M); Bible backgrounds (Th M); Bible translation (Th M); Biblical and theological studies (Certificate); biblical counseling (MA); biblical exegesis and linguistics (MA); biblical exposition (PhD); biblical studies (MA); Biblical theology (Th M); children's education (Th M); Christian education (MA, D Min); Christian leadership (MA); cross-cultural ministries (MA); educational administration (Th M); educational leadership (Th M); evangelism and discipleship (Th M); exposition of Biblical books (Th M); family life education (Th M); general studies (Th M); Hebrew and cognate studies (Th M); hermeneutics (Th M); historical theology (Th M); homiletics (Th M); intercultural ministries (Th M); Jesus studies (Th M); leadership studies (Th M); media and communication (MA); media arts (Th M); ministry (D Min); ministry with women (Th M); New Testament studies (Th M, PhD); Old Testament studies (Th M, PhD); parachurch ministries (Th M); pastoral care and counseling (Th M); pastoral theology and practice (Th M); philosophy (Th M); sacred theology (STM); spiritual formation (Th M); systematic theology (Th M); teaching in Christian institutions (Th M); theological studies (PhD); urban ministries (Th M); worship studies (Th M); youth education (Th M). *Accreditation:* ATS (one or more programs are accredited). Part-time programs available. Postbaccalaureate distance learning degree programs offered (no on-campus study). *Degree requirements:* For master's, variable foreign language requirement, thesis (for some programs); for doctorate, 2 foreign languages, thesis/dissertation. *Entrance requirements:* For master's, GRE or MAT (if minimum undergraduate cumulative GPA is below 2.5 or undergraduate degree is unaccredited). Additional exam requirements/recommendations for international students: Required—TOEFL (minimum score 575 paper-based; 85 iBT), TWE. Electronic applications accepted.

DePaul University, College of Communication, Chicago, IL 60614. Offers digital communication and media arts (MA); health communication (MA); journalism (MA); media and cinema studies (MA); organizational and multicultural communication (MA); public relations and advertising (MA); relational communication (MA). Part-time and evening/weekend programs available. *Entrance requirements:* Additional exam requirements/recommendations for international students: Required—TOEFL (minimum score 590 paper-based; 96 iBT), IELTS (minimum score 7.5) or PTE. Electronic applications accepted.

DePaul University, College of Liberal Arts and Social Sciences, Chicago, IL 60614. Offers Arabic (MA); Chinese (MA); English (MA); French (MA); German (MA); history (MA); interdisciplinary studies (MA, MS); international public service (MS); international studies (MA); Italian (MA); Japanese (MA); leadership and policy studies (MS); liberal studies (MA); new media studies (MA); nonprofit management (MNM); public administration (MPA); public health (MPH); public service management (MS); social work (MSW); sociology (MA); Spanish (MA); sustainable urban development (MA); women and gender studies (MA); writing and publishing (MA); writing, rhetoric, and discourse (MA); MA/PhD. Part-time and evening/weekend programs available. Postbaccalaureate distance learning degree programs offered (no on-campus study). Terminal master's awarded for partial completion of doctoral program. *Degree requirements:* For master's, variable foreign language requirement, comprehensive

exam (for some programs), thesis (for some programs). Electronic applications accepted.

Digital Media Arts College, Graduate Programs, Boca Raton, FL 33487. Offers graphic design (MFA); special FX animation (MFA).

Duke University, Graduate School, Master of Fine Arts in Experimental and Documentary Arts Program, Durham, NC 27708. Offers MFA. *Degree requirements:* For master's, thesis, final project. *Entrance requirements:* For master's, portfolio. Additional exam requirements/recommendations for international students: Required—TOEFL (minimum score 577 paper-based; 90 iBT) or IELTS (minimum score 7). Electronic applications accepted. *Expenses: Tuition:* Full-time $45,760; part-time $2765 per credit. *Required fees:* $978. Full-time tuition and fees vary according to program.

Emerson College, Graduate Studies, School of the Arts, Department of Visual and Media Arts, Program in Media Art, Boston, MA 02116-4624. Offers MFA. *Faculty:* 48 full-time (17 women), 7 part-time/adjunct (1 woman). *Students:* 72 full-time (38 women), 10 part-time (3 women); includes 12 minority (6 Black or African American, non-Hispanic/Latino; 1 Asian, non-Hispanic/Latino; 5 Hispanic/Latino), 26 international. Average age 28. 190 applicants, 34% accepted, 20 enrolled. In 2014, 19 master's awarded. *Entrance requirements:* For master's, creative portfolio. Additional exam requirements/recommendations for international students: Required—TOEFL (minimum score 550 paper-based; 80 iBT), IELTS (minimum score 6.5). *Application deadline:* For fall admission, 2/15 for domestic and international students. Applications are processed on a rolling basis. Application fee: $60 ($75 for international students). Electronic applications accepted. *Expenses: Tuition:* Part-time $1145 per credit. *Financial support:* In 2014–15, 21 students received support, including 21 fellowships with full and partial tuition reimbursements available (averaging $15,186 per year); research assistantships with partial tuition reimbursements available, Federal Work-Study, scholarships/grants, and unspecified assistantships also available. Financial award application deadline: 1/15; financial award applicants required to submit FAFSA. *Faculty research:* Media studies. *Unit head:* Prof. L. Marc Fields, Graduate Program Director, 617-824-8800, E-mail: l_marc_fields@emerson.edu. *Application contact:* Leanda Ferland, Office of Graduate Admission, 617-824-8610, Fax: 617-824-8614, E-mail: gradapp@emerson.edu.
Website: http://www.emerson.edu/graduate_admission

Fairleigh Dickinson University, Metropolitan Campus, University College: Arts, Sciences, and Professional Studies, School of Art and Media Studies, Program in Media and Communications, Teaneck, NJ 07666-1914. Offers MA.

Fielding Graduate University, Graduate Programs, School of Psychology, Santa Barbara, CA 93105-3814. Offers clinical psychology (PhD, Graduate Certificate), including forensic psychology (PhD), health psychology (PhD), neuropsychology (PhD), parent-infant mental health (PhD), violence prevention and control (PhD); clinical psychology respecialization (Post-Doctoral Certificate); media psychology (MA, PhD), including forensic psychology (PhD); neuropsychology (Post-Doctoral Certificate). *Accreditation:* APA. Postbaccalaureate distance learning degree programs offered (minimal on-campus study). *Faculty:* 33 full-time (21 women), 40 part-time/adjunct (20 women). *Students:* 502 full-time (366 women), 79 part-time (62 women); includes 186 minority (69 Black or African American, non-Hispanic/Latino; 8 American Indian or Alaska Native, non-Hispanic/Latino; 23 Asian, non-Hispanic/Latino; 62 Hispanic/Latino; 1 Native Hawaiian or other Pacific Islander, non-Hispanic/Latino; 23 Two or more races, non-Hispanic/Latino), 4 international. Average age 45. 215 applicants, 56% accepted, 78 enrolled. In 2014, 15 master's, 54 doctorates, 9 other advanced degrees awarded. Terminal master's awarded for partial completion of doctoral program. *Degree requirements:* For master's, thesis or alternative, capstone project; for doctorate, comprehensive exam, thesis/dissertation. *Entrance requirements:* For master's, BA from regionally-accredited institution or equivalent, minimum GPA of 2.5; for doctorate, BA or MA from regionally-accredited institution or equivalent, writing sample, minimum GPA of 3.0. *Application deadline:* For fall admission, 3/6 for domestic students, 2/6 for international students; for spring admission, 11/1 for domestic and international students; for summer admission, 3/1 for domestic students, 2/1 for international students. Application fee: $75. Electronic applications accepted. *Expenses: Tuition:* Full-time $25,650; part-time $2880 per course. Tuition and fees vary according to degree level and program. *Financial support:* In 2014–15, 88 students received support, including 14 teaching assistantships (averaging $1,200 per year); scholarships/grants, health care benefits, tuition waivers (partial), and unspecified assistantships also available. Support available to part-time students. *Unit head:* Dr. Gerald Porter, Provost and Senior Vice President, 805-898-2940, E-mail: gporter@fielding.edu. *Application contact:* Enrollment Coordinator, 800-340-1099 Ext. 4098, Fax: 805-687-9793, E-mail: psyadmissions@fielding.edu.
Website: http://www.fielding.edu/programs/psy/default.aspx

Florida Atlantic University, Dorothy F. Schmidt College of Arts and Letters, School of Communication and Multimedia Studies, Boca Raton, FL 33431-0991. Offers communication studies (MA); film and video (Certificate); media, technology and entertainment (MFA). Part-time programs available. *Degree requirements:* For master's, one foreign language, comprehensive exam (for some programs), thesis (for some programs). *Entrance requirements:* For master's, GRE General Test, minimum GPA of 3.0, essay, letters of recommendation. Electronic applications accepted. *Expenses:* Tuition, state resident: full-time $7396; part-time $369.82 per credit hour. Tuition, nonresident: full-time $19,392; part-time $1024.81 per credit hour. Tuition and fees vary according to course load. *Faculty research:* Cultural studies, gender studies, film, communication theory, journalism, new media.

Florida State University, The Graduate School, College of Communication and Information, School of Communication, Tallahassee, FL 32306. Offers communication theory and research (PhD); integrated marketing communication (MA, MS); media and communication studies (MA, MS). Part-time programs available. *Faculty:* 26 full-time (11 women), 4 part-time/adjunct (1 woman). *Students:* 68 full-time (48 women), 105 part-time (71 women); includes 83 minority (15 Black or African American, non-Hispanic/Latino; 46 Asian, non-Hispanic/Latino; 19 Hispanic/Latino; 3 Two or more races, non-Hispanic/Latino). Average age 24. 206 applicants, 30% accepted, 41 enrolled. In 2014, 98 master's, 10 doctorates awarded. *Degree requirements:* For master's, thesis (for some programs); for doctorate, comprehensive exam, thesis/dissertation. *Entrance requirements:* For master's, GRE General Test, minimum GPA of 3.0; for doctorate, GRE General Test, minimum GPA of 3.3 in graduate course work. Additional exam requirements/recommendations for international students: Required—TOEFL (minimum score 600 paper-based; 100 iBT), IELTS (minimum score 7). *Application deadline:* For fall admission, 7/1 priority date for domestic students, 5/1 priority date for international students; for spring admission, 11/1 priority date for domestic and international students; for summer admission, 3/1 priority date for domestic and international students. Applications are processed on a rolling basis. Application fee: $30. Electronic applications accepted. *Expenses:* Tuition, state resident: part-time $403.51 per credit hour. Tuition, nonresident: part-time $1004.85 per credit hour. *Required fees:* $75.81 per credit hour. One-time fee: $20 part-time. Tuition and fees vary according to campus/location. *Financial support:* In 2014–15, 89 students received support, including 6 research assistantships with full tuition reimbursements available (averaging $7,816 per year), 83 teaching assistantships with full tuition reimbursements available (averaging $7,816 per year); fellowships, career-related internships or fieldwork, Federal Work-Study, institutionally sponsored loans, scholarships/grants, tuition waivers (partial), and unspecified assistantships also available. Support available to part-time students. Financial award application deadline: 2/1; financial award applicants required to submit FAFSA. *Faculty research:* Communication in the public interest; strategic communication; media and technology; multicultural, intercultural, and international communication. *Total annual research expenditures:* $67,063. *Unit head:* Dr. Gary Heald, Director, 850-644-5034, Fax: 850-644-8642, E-mail: gheald@fsu.edu. *Application contact:* Natashia Hinson-Turner, Graduate Coordinator, 850-644-5034, Fax: 850-644-8642, E-mail: natashia.turner@cci.fsu.edu.
Website: http://www.cci.fsu.edu

Fordham University, Gabelli School of Business, New York, NY 10023. Offers accounting (MBA); communications and media management (MBA); executive business administration (EMBA), including management; finance (MBA); global finance (MS); information systems (MBA, MS); management systems (MBA); marketing (MBA); media management (MS); taxation (MS); taxation and public accountancy (MTA); JD/MBA; MBA/MIM; MS/MBA. MBA/MIM offered jointly with Thunderbird School of Global Management. *Accreditation:* AACSB. Part-time and evening/weekend programs available. *Faculty:* 131 full-time (61 women), 61 part-time/adjunct (13 women). *Students:* 1,233 full-time (708 women), 588 part-time (274 women); includes 1,032 minority (73 Black or African American, non-Hispanic/Latino; 7 American Indian or Alaska Native, non-Hispanic/Latino; 846 Asian, non-Hispanic/Latino; 103 Hispanic/Latino; 3 Native Hawaiian or other Pacific Islander, non-Hispanic/Latino), 53 international. Average age 28. 3,701 applicants, 51% accepted, 718 enrolled. In 2014, 916 master's awarded. *Degree requirements:* For master's, Internships - required for MSQF, recommended for MBA, optional for most other programs. *Entrance requirements:* For master's, GMAT/GRE, 2 letters of recommendation, resume, 2 essays, transcripts. Additional exam requirements/recommendations for international students: Required—TOEFL (minimum score 600 paper-based; 100 iBT). *Application deadline:* For fall admission, 6/1 priority date for domestic students, 5/1 priority date for international students; for winter admission, 11/1 for domestic students, 10/1 priority date for international students; for spring admission, 11/1 priority date for domestic students, 2/1 priority date for international students; for summer admission, 3/1 priority date for domestic students. Applications are processed on a rolling basis. Application fee: $130. Electronic applications accepted. *Expenses:* Expenses: $1,306 per credit. *Financial support:* In 2014–15, 53 students received support, including fellowships (averaging $25,838 per year); research assistantships, career-related internships or fieldwork, institutionally sponsored loans, scholarships/grants, and unspecified assistantships also available. Support available to part-time students. Financial award application deadline: 6/15; financial award applicants required to submit FAFSA. *Unit head:* Dr. Donna Rapaccioli, Dean, 212-636-6165, Fax: 212-307-1779, E-mail: rapaccioli@fordham.edu. *Application contact:* Patricia Caffrey, Director of Admissions and Financial Aid, 212-636-6200, Fax: 212-636-7076, E-mail: admissionsgb@fordham.edu.
Website: http://www.fordham.edu/info/20451/graduate_business

Full Sail University, Media Design Master of Fine Arts Program - Online, Winter Park, FL 32792-7437. Offers MFA. Postbaccalaureate distance learning degree programs offered.

George Mason University, College of Humanities and Social Sciences, Department of History and Art History, Program in History, Fairfax, VA 22030. Offers history (MA); new media and information technology (PhD); public and applied history (PhD). *Faculty:* 45 full-time (18 women), 8 part-time/adjunct (4 women). *Students:* 66 full-time (32 women), 136 part-time (58 women); includes 19 minority (4 Black or African American, non-Hispanic/Latino; 3 Asian, non-Hispanic/Latino; 9 Hispanic/Latino; 3 Two or more races, non-Hispanic/Latino), 4 international. Average age 36. 145 applicants, 54% accepted, 42 enrolled. In 2014, 42 master's, 4 doctorates awarded. *Degree requirements:* For master's, comprehensive exam, translation language exam; for doctorate, comprehensive exam, thesis/dissertation. *Entrance requirements:* For master's, GRE (waived for students who received their undergraduate degree 10 or more years ago or hold another graduate degree), expanded goals statement; 2 letters of recommendation; resume; official transcript; for doctorate, GRE, expanded goals statement; 3 letters of recommendation; writing sample; official transcripts. Additional exam requirements/recommendations for international students: Required—TOEFL (minimum score 570 paper-based; 80 iBT), IELTS (minimum score 6.5), PTE. *Application deadline:* For fall admission, 3/15 priority date for domestic students; for spring admission, 11/1 priority date for domestic students. Application fee: $65 ($80 for international students). Electronic applications accepted. *Expenses:* Tuition, state resident: full-time $9794; part-time $408 per credit hour. Tuition, nonresident: full-time $26,978; part-time $1124 per credit hour. *Required fees:* $2820; $118 per credit hour. Tuition and fees vary according to course load and program. *Financial support:* In 2014–15, 31 students received support, including 2 fellowships with full tuition reimbursements available (averaging $7,151 per year), 16 research assistantships with full and partial tuition reimbursements available (averaging $17,210 per year), 14 teaching assistantships with full and partial tuition reimbursements available (averaging $14,330 per year); career-related internships or fieldwork, Federal Work-Study, scholarships/grants, unspecified assistantships, and health care benefits (for full-time research or teaching assistantship recipients) also available. Support available to part-time students. Financial award application deadline: 3/1; financial award applicants required to submit FAFSA. *Faculty research:* History and new media, American history (digital), building digital archives in the 1930's. *Unit head:* Randolph Scully, History Program Director, 703-993-1259, Fax: 703-993-1251, E-mail: rscully@gmu.edu. *Application contact:* Nicole Anne Roth, Graduate Program Coordinator, 703-993-1248, Fax: 703-993-1251, E-mail: nroth@gmu.edu.
Website: http://historyarthistory.gmu.edu/programs/la-ma-hist

George Mason University, College of Visual and Performing Arts, Art and Visual Technology Program, Fairfax, VA 22030. Offers drawing (MFA); graphic design (MFA); new media art (MFA); painting (MFA); photography (MFA); printmaking (MFA); sculpture (MFA). *Accreditation:* NASAD. *Faculty:* 21 full-time (11 women), 36 part-time/adjunct (22 women). *Students:* 5 full-time (4 women), 12 part-time (2 women); includes 3 minority (1 Black or African American, non-Hispanic/Latino; 2 Two or more races, non-Hispanic/Latino). Average age 40. 25 applicants, 20% accepted, 3 enrolled. In 2014, 4 master's awarded. *Degree requirements:* For master's, comprehensive experience, studio project or thesis. *Entrance requirements:* For master's, official transcripts; 3 letters of recommendation; letter of intent; resume; professional goals statement. Additional exam requirements/recommendations for international students: Required—TOEFL (minimum score 570 paper-based; 80 iBT), IELTS (minimum score 6.5), PTE. *Application deadline:* For fall admission, 1/15 for domestic and international students. Application fee: $65 ($80 for international students). Electronic applications accepted. *Expenses:* Tuition, state resident: full-time $9794; part-time $408 per credit hour. Tuition, nonresident: full-time $26,978; part-time $1124 per credit hour. *Required fees:* $2820; $118 per credit hour. Tuition and fees vary according to course load and program. *Financial support:* In 2014–15, 2 students received support, including 2 teaching assistantships with full and partial tuition reimbursements available (averaging $6,696 per year); career-related internships or fieldwork, Federal Work-Study, scholarships/grants, unspecified assistantships, and health care benefits (for full-time research or teaching assistantship

recipients) also available. Support available to part-time students. Financial award application deadline: 3/1; financial award applicants required to submit FAFSA. *Faculty research:* Digital arts, painting, photography, print-making, sculpture; combined art forms in in-disciplinary projects including installation, performance, publishing, time or writing-based; combined creative and critical approaches. *Unit head:* Peter Winant, Director, 703-993-8385, Fax: 703-993-8798, E-mail: pwinant@gmu.edu. *Application contact:* Asma Ormazad, Graduate Studies Administrative Assistant, 703-993-9773, Fax: 703-993-8255, E-mail: aomarzad@gmu.edu.
Website: http://soa.gmu.edu

Georgetown University, Graduate School of Arts and Sciences, School of Continuing Studies, Washington, DC 20057. Offers American studies (MALS); Catholic studies (MALS); classical civilizations (MALS); emergency and disaster management (MPS); ethics and the professions (MALS); hospitality management (MPS); human resources management (MPS); humanities (MALS); individualized study (MALS); international affairs (MALS); Islam and Muslim-Christian relations (MALS); journalism (MPS); liberal studies (DLS); literature and society (MALS); medieval and early modern European studies (MALS); public relations and corporate communications (MPS); real estate (MPS); religious studies (MALS); social and public policy (MALS); sports industry management (MPS); systems engineering management (MPS); technology management (MPS); the theory and practice of American democracy (MALS); urban and regional planning (MPS); visual culture (MALS). MPS in systems engineering management offered jointly with Stevens Institute of Technology. *Entrance requirements:* Additional exam requirements/recommendations for international students: Required—TOEFL.

Georgia State University, College of Arts and Sciences, Department of Communication, Atlanta, GA 30302-3083. Offers film, video, and digital imaging (MA), including critical studies, production, screenwriting; human communication and social influence (MA); mass communication (MA); media and society (PhD); moving image studies (PhD); public communication (PhD); rhetoric and politics (PhD). Part-time programs available. *Faculty:* 35 full-time (18 women). *Students:* 102 full-time (51 women), 40 part-time (15 women); includes 37 minority (20 Black or African American, non-Hispanic/Latino; 4 Asian, non-Hispanic/Latino; 6 Hispanic/Latino; 7 Two or more races, non-Hispanic/Latino), 14 international. Average age 33. 154 applicants, 39% accepted, 30 enrolled. In 2014, 25 master's, 5 doctorates awarded. *Degree requirements:* For master's, variable foreign language requirement, thesis (for some programs); for doctorate, comprehensive exam, thesis/dissertation. *Entrance requirements:* For master's, GRE; for doctorate, GRE. Additional exam requirements/recommendations for international students: Required—TOEFL (minimum score 550 paper-based; 80 iBT), IELTS (minimum score 6.5). *Application deadline:* For fall admission, 2/10 for domestic and international students; for spring admission, 10/15 for domestic and international students. Application fee: $50. Electronic applications accepted. *Expenses:* Tuition, state resident: full-time $6516; part-time $362 per credit hour. Tuition, nonresident: full-time $22,014; part-time $1223 per credit hour. *Required fees:* $2128 per semester. Tuition and fees vary according to course load and program. *Financial support:* In 2014–15, fellowships with tuition reimbursements (averaging $15,000 per year), teaching assistantships with tuition reimbursements (averaging $15,000 per year) were awarded; career-related internships or fieldwork and unspecified assistantships also available. Financial award applicants required to submit FAFSA. *Faculty research:* New media, mass media and journalism, rhetoric, film and media studies, film production. *Unit head:* Dr. David Cheshier, Chair, 404-413-5649, Fax: 404-413-5634, E-mail: dcheshier@gsu.edu. *Application contact:* Dr. Jennifer Barker, Associate Professor, 404-413-5793, Fax: 404-413-5634, E-mail: jmbarker@gsu.edu.
Website: http://communication.gsu.edu

Governors State University, College of Arts and Sciences, Program in Communication and Training, University Park, IL 60484. Offers communication studies (MA); instructional and training technology (MA); media communication (MA). Part-time and evening/weekend programs available. *Degree requirements:* For master's, thesis or alternative.

Howard University, School of Communications, Division of Mass Communication and Media Studies, Washington, DC 20059-0002. Offers mass communication (MA, PhD); media studies (MA, PhD). Part-time and evening/weekend programs available. *Degree requirements:* For master's, comprehensive exam (for some programs), thesis optional; for doctorate, one foreign language, comprehensive exam, thesis/dissertation. *Entrance requirements:* For master's, GRE, minimum GPA of 3.0; for doctorate, GRE, minimum graduate GPA of 3.5. Additional exam requirements/recommendations for international students: Required—TOEFL. Electronic applications accepted. *Faculty research:* Advertising, public relations, journalism new media.

Hunter College of the City University of New York, Graduate School, School of Arts and Sciences, Department of Film and Media Studies, Program in Integrated Media Arts, New York, NY 10065-5085. Offers MFA. Part-time and evening/weekend programs available. *Faculty:* 2 full-time (1 woman). *Students:* 5 full-time (4 women), 46 part-time (35 women); includes 17 minority (6 Black or African American, non-Hispanic/Latino; 1 American Indian or Alaska Native, non-Hispanic/Latino; 5 Asian, non-Hispanic/Latino; 5 Hispanic/Latino), 15 international. Average age 33. 60 applicants, 42% accepted, 13 enrolled. In 2014, 11 master's awarded. *Entrance requirements:* For master's, GRE General Test, 3 letters of recommendation, portfolio of media works, minimum GPA of 3.0. Additional exam requirements/recommendations for international students: Required—TOEFL, TWE. *Application deadline:* For fall admission, 2/1 for domestic students. *Financial support:* Federal Work-Study and tuition waivers (partial) available. Support available to part-time students. *Faculty research:* Nonfiction production, Internet as medium, public interest journalism, social and historical roots of media arts. *Unit head:* Kelly Anderson, Deputy Chair, 212-772-6008. *Application contact:* Mary Flanagan, New Media Advisor, 212-650-3219, E-mail: maryflanagan@hunter.cuny.edu.
Website: http://filmmedia.hunter.cuny.edu/

Indiana State University, College of Graduate and Professional Studies, College of Arts and Sciences, Department of Communication, Terre Haute, IN 47809. Offers communication studies (MA, MS); radio, television and film (MA, MS). Part-time programs available. *Degree requirements:* For master's, thesis (for some programs), oral and written exam. *Entrance requirements:* For master's, GRE General Test. Additional exam requirements/recommendations for international students: Required—TOEFL. *Faculty research:* Women in media, communication apprehension, media history.

Indiana University Bloomington, University Graduate School, College of Arts and Sciences, The Media School, Department of Communication and Culture, Bloomington, IN 47405-7000. Offers communication and culture (MA); film and media studies (PhD); performance and ethnography (PhD); rhetoric and public culture (PhD). *Faculty:* 22 full-time (13 women), 1 (woman) part-time/adjunct. *Students:* 75 full-time (41 women); includes 7 minority (1 Black or African American, non-Hispanic/Latino; 5 Hispanic/Latino; 1 Two or more races, non-Hispanic/Latino), 7 international. 116 applicants, 15% accepted, 8 enrolled. In 2014, 7 master's, 7 doctorates awarded. *Degree requirements:* For master's, comprehensive exam; for doctorate, one foreign language, comprehensive exam, thesis/dissertation, student teaching. *Entrance requirements:* For master's and doctorate, GRE General Test, minimum GPA of 3.0, 3 letters of recommendation, writing sample, personal statement. Additional exam requirements/recommendations for international students: Required—TOEFL (minimum score 550 paper-based) or IELTS. *Application deadline:* For fall admission, 1/2 for domestic students, 12/1 for international students; for winter admission, 1/2 for domestic students, 12/1 for international students. Application fee: $55 ($65 for international students). Electronic applications accepted. *Financial support:* Fellowships with full tuition reimbursements, research assistantships with full tuition reimbursements, and teaching assistantships with full tuition reimbursements available. Financial award application deadline: 1/2. *Faculty research:* Rhetoric and public culture, film and media studies, performance ethnography. *Unit head:* Prof. Jane Goodman, Chair, 812-855-3232, Fax: 812-855-6014, E-mail: cmcl@indiana.edu. *Application contact:* Kathy P. Teige, Graduate Secretary, 812-855-6389, Fax: 812-855-6014, E-mail: kteige@indiana.edu.
Website: http://www.indiana.edu/~cmcl/

Indiana University of Pennsylvania, School of Graduate Studies and Research, College of Education and Educational Technology, Department of Communications Media, Program in Communications Media and Instructional Technology, Indiana, PA 15705-1087. Offers PhD. *Faculty:* 11 full-time (4 women). *Students:* 15 full-time (6 women), 41 part-time (20 women); includes 6 minority (4 Black or African American, non-Hispanic/Latino; 2 Two or more races, non-Hispanic/Latino), 3 international. Average age 38. 48 applicants, 25% accepted, 9 enrolled. In 2014, 12 doctorates awarded. Application fee: $50. *Financial support:* In 2014–15, 1 fellowship with full tuition reimbursement (averaging $4,890 per year), 9 research assistantships with full and partial tuition reimbursements (averaging $6,249 per year), 3 teaching assistantships with partial tuition reimbursements (averaging $23,305 per year) were awarded. *Unit head:* Dr. Zachary Stiegler, Coordinator, 724-357-3219, E-mail: zachary.stiegler@iup.edu.
Website: http://www.iup.edu/commmedia/programs/phdcmit/

Kutztown University of Pennsylvania, College of Visual and Performing Arts, Program in Electronic Media, Kutztown, PA 19530-0730. Offers MS. Part-time and evening/weekend programs available. *Students:* 1 full-time (0 women). Average age 27. In 2014, 9 master's awarded. *Degree requirements:* For master's, thesis. *Entrance requirements:* For master's, GRE General Test. Additional exam requirements/recommendations for international students: Required—TOEFL (minimum score 550 paper-based; 79 iBT). *Application deadline:* For fall admission, 8/1 priority date for domestic and international students; for spring admission, 12/1 priority date for domestic and international students. Applications are processed on a rolling basis. Application fee: $35. Electronic applications accepted. *Expenses: Tuition, area resident:* Part-time $454 per credit. Tuition, state resident: part-time $454 per credit. Tuition, nonresident: part-time $681 per credit. *Required fees:* $85 per credit. *Financial support:* Career-related internships or fieldwork, Federal Work-Study, scholarships/grants, and unspecified assistantships available. Financial award application deadline: 3/1; financial award applicants required to submit FAFSA. *Unit head:* Dr. Helen Bieber, Chairperson, 610-683-4496, Fax: 610-683-4659, E-mail: bieber@kutztown.edu. *Application contact:* Kelly Hish, Admissions Clerk, 610-683-4200, Fax: 610-683-1393, E-mail: graduate@kutztown.edu.

La Salle University, School of Arts and Sciences, Program in English, Philadelphia, PA 19141-1199. Offers American studies (Certificate); English for educators (MA); English in literary and cultural studies (MA); global literature (Certificate); media studies and the performing and visual arts (Certificate); Philadelphia and regional studies (Certificate). Part-time and evening/weekend programs available. *Degree requirements:* For master's, critical-pedagogical project (for English for educators), thesis or comprehensive examination (for English in literary and cultural studies). *Entrance requirements:* For master's, GRE General Test or MAT, 18 hours of undergraduate course work in English or a related discipline with minimum GPA of 3.0; three letters of recommendation; brief personal statement; writing sample; for Certificate, undergraduate degree in English or a related discipline with minimum GPA of 3.0; 3 letters of recommendation. Additional exam requirements/recommendations for international students: Required—TOEFL. Electronic applications accepted. Application fee is waived when completed online.

La Salle University, School of Arts and Sciences, Program in Professional and Business Communication, Philadelphia, PA 19141-1199. Offers communication consulting and development (MA); communication management (MA); general professional communication (MA); professional and business communication (Certificate); public relations (MA); social and new media (Certificate). Part-time and evening/weekend programs available. Postbaccalaureate distance learning degree programs offered (minimal on-campus study). *Degree requirements:* For master's, practicum. *Entrance requirements:* For master's, writing assessment, professional resume; minimum overall B average; two letters of recommendation (if GPA below 3.25); brief personal statement (about 500 words); interview; for Certificate, writing assessment, minimum GPA of 2.75 in undergraduate studies; brief personal statement (about 500 words); interview. Additional exam requirements/recommendations for international students: Required—TOEFL. Electronic applications accepted. Application fee is waived when completed online. *Expenses:* Contact institution.

Lindenwood University–Belleville, Graduate Programs, Belleville, IL 62226. Offers business administration (MBA); communications (MA), including digital and multimedia, media management, promotions, training and development; counseling (MA); criminal justice administration (MS); education (MA); healthcare administration (MS); human resource management (MS); school administration (MA); teaching (MAT).

Louisiana State University and Agricultural & Mechanical College, Graduate School, Manship School of Mass Communication, Baton Rouge, LA 70803. Offers MMC, PhD, JD/MMC. *Accreditation:* ACEJMC. Part-time programs available. Postbaccalaureate distance learning degree programs offered (minimal on-campus study). *Faculty:* 24 full-time (12 women). *Students:* 62 full-time (42 women), 14 part-time (11 women); includes 20 minority (15 Black or African American, non-Hispanic/Latino; 1 Asian, non-Hispanic/Latino; 3 Hispanic/Latino; 1 Two or more races, non-Hispanic/Latino), 16 international. Average age 27. 62 applicants, 48% accepted, 22 enrolled. In 2014, 20 master's, 3 doctorates awarded. *Degree requirements:* For master's, thesis; for doctorate, thesis/dissertation. *Entrance requirements:* For master's, GRE General Test, minimum GPA of 3.0. Additional exam requirements/recommendations for international students: Required—TOEFL (minimum score 550 paper-based; 79 IBT), IELTS (minimum score 6.5), or PTE (minimum score 59). *Application deadline:* For fall admission, 1/1 priority date for domestic students, 5/15 for international students; for spring admission, 10/15 for domestic and international students; for summer admission, 5/15 for domestic and international students. Applications are processed on a rolling basis. Application fee: $50 ($70 for international students). Electronic applications accepted. *Financial support:* In 2014–15, 61 students received support, including 1 fellowship (averaging $33,839 per year), 31 research assistantships with full and partial tuition reimbursements available (averaging $15,839 per year), 14 teaching assistantships with full and partial tuition reimbursements available (averaging $15,557 per year); career-related internships or fieldwork, Federal Work-Study, institutionally sponsored loans, scholarships/grants, health care benefits, tuition waivers (full and partial), and unspecified assistantships also available. Support available to part-time students. Financial award application deadline: 3/1; financial award applicants required

to submit FAFSA. *Faculty research:* Media effects, political communication, new media technologies, persuasive communication, journalism processes and practice. *Total annual research expenditures:* $82,923. *Unit head:* Dr. Jerry Ceppos, Dean, 225-578-3488, Fax: 225-578-2125, E-mail: jceppos@lsu.edu. *Application contact:* Dr. Amy L. Reynolds, Associate Dean of Graduate Studies and Research, 225-578-9294, Fax: 225-578-2125, E-mail: areynolds@lsu.edu.
Website: http://www.manship.lsu.edu/

Loyola University Maryland, Graduate Programs, Loyola College of Arts and Sciences, Department of Communication, Baltimore, MD 21210-2699. Offers emerging media (MA). Part-time programs available. Postbaccalaureate distance learning degree programs offered (minimal on-campus study). *Degree requirements:* For master's, capstone project.

Lynn University, College of Business and Management, Boca Raton, FL 33431-5598. Offers financial valuation and investment management (MBA); hospitality management (MBA); international business management (MBA); marketing (MBA); media management (MBA); sports management (MBA). Part-time and evening/weekend programs available. Postbaccalaureate distance learning degree programs offered. *Faculty:* 13 full-time (3 women), 12 part-time/adjunct (6 women). *Students:* 228 full-time (96 women), 111 part-time (58 women); includes 71 minority (43 Black or African American, non-Hispanic/Latino; 1 Asian, non-Hispanic/Latino; 25 Hispanic/Latino; 2 Two or more races, non-Hispanic/Latino), 81 international. Average age 29. 205 applicants, 95% accepted, 149 enrolled. In 2014, 152 degrees awarded. *Degree requirements:* For master's, strategic management seminar. *Entrance requirements:* For master's, bachelor's degree from accredited institution, resume, letter of recommendation, official transcripts, essay/personal statement. Additional exam requirements/recommendations for international students: Required—TOEFL (minimum score 550 paper-based; 80 iBT), IELTS (minimum score 6.5). *Application deadline:* For fall admission, 8/17 for domestic students, 8/3 for international students; for spring admission, 12/15 for domestic students, 11/24 for international students; for summer admission, 4/17 for domestic students, 4/3 for international students. Applications are processed on a rolling basis. Application fee: $45. Electronic applications accepted. *Expenses: Tuition:* Full-time $16,200; part-time $675 per credit hour. Tuition and fees vary according to class time, course load, degree level and program. *Financial support:* In 2014–15, 80 students received support. Career-related internships or fieldwork, Federal Work-Study, scholarships/grants, tuition waivers (full and partial), and unspecified assistantships available. Support available to part-time students. Financial award application deadline: 3/1; financial award applicants required to submit FAFSA. *Faculty research:* Labor relations, dynamic balance in leisure-time skills, ethics in athletics, hotel development. *Unit head:* Dr. Ralph Norcio, Senior Associate Dean, 561-237-7010, Fax: 561-237-7014, E-mail: rnorcio@lynn.edu. *Application contact:* Steven Pruitt, Director of Graduate and Undergraduate Evening Admission, 561-237-7834, Fax: 561-237-7100, E-mail: spruitt@lynn.edu.
Website: http://www.lynn.edu/academics/colleges/business-and-management

Lynn University, Eugene M. and Christine E. Lynn College of International Communication, Boca Raton, FL 33431-5598. Offers communication and media - digital media (MS); communication and media - media studies and practice (MS); digital media (Certificate). Part-time and evening/weekend programs available. *Faculty:* 5 full-time (4 women). *Students:* 24 full-time (17 women), 9 part-time (7 women); includes 8 minority (4 Black or African American, non-Hispanic/Latino; 3 Hispanic/Latino; 1 Two or more races, non-Hispanic/Latino), 11 international. Average age 28. 19 applicants, 95% accepted, 12 enrolled. In 2014, 13 master's awarded. *Degree requirements:* For master's, project or thesis. *Entrance requirements:* For master's, resume, letter of recommendation, official transcripts, bachelor's degree from accredited institution, personal statement. Additional exam requirements/recommendations for international students: Required—TOEFL (minimum score 550 paper-based; 80 iBT), IELTS (minimum score 6.5). *Application deadline:* Applications are processed on a rolling basis. Application fee: $45. Electronic applications accepted. *Expenses: Tuition:* Full-time $16,200; part-time $675 per credit hour. Tuition and fees vary according to class time, course load, degree level and program. *Financial support:* In 2014–15, 12 students received support. Career-related internships or fieldwork, Federal Work-Study, institutionally sponsored loans, scholarships/grants, tuition waivers (partial), and unspecified assistantships available. Support available to part-time students. Financial award application deadline: 8/1; financial award applicants required to submit FAFSA. *Unit head:* Dr. David L. Jaffe, Dean, 561-237-7099, Fax: 561-237-7097, E-mail: djaffe@lynn.edu. *Application contact:* Steven Pruitt, Director of Graduate Admission, 561-237-7834, Fax: 561-237-7100, E-mail: admission@lynn.edu.
Website: http://www.lynn.edu/academics/colleges/international-communication

Maryland Institute College of Art, Graduate Studies, Program in Critical Studies, Baltimore, MD 21201. Offers MA. *Faculty:* 1 (woman) full-time, 4 part-time/adjunct (2 women). *Students:* 5 full-time (1 woman). Average age 27. 25 applicants, 32% accepted, 5 enrolled. In 2014, 5 master's awarded. *Degree requirements:* For master's, thesis. *Entrance requirements:* For master's, essay, bachelor's degree in any field. Additional exam requirements/recommendations for international students: Required—TOEFL (minimum score 550 paper-based; 80 iBT), IELTS (minimum score 6.5). *Application deadline:* For fall admission, 1/15 for domestic and international students. Application fee: $75. *Expenses:* Expenses: Contact institution. *Financial support:* In 2014–15, 5 fellowships (averaging $13,000 per year), 5 teaching assistantships (averaging $3,200 per year) were awarded; career-related internships or fieldwork and scholarships/grants also available. Financial award application deadline: 1/15. *Unit head:* Dr. Jennie Hirsh, Director, 410-225-5274, Fax: 410-225-5275, E-mail: graduate@mica.edu. *Application contact:* Chris D. Harring, Director, Graduate Admission, 410-225-2256, Fax: 410-225-5275, E-mail: graduate@mica.edu.
Website: http://www.mica.edu/Programs_of_Study/Graduate_Programs/Critical_Studies_(MA).html

Massachusetts College of Art and Design, Graduate Programs, MFA Program, Boston, MA 02115-5882. Offers 2D fine arts (MFA), including painting; 3D fine arts (MFA), including ceramics, fibers, glass, jewelry and metalsmithing, sculpture; design (MFA, Postbaccalaureate Certificate), including dynamic media; fine arts (MFA), including interdisciplinary; media arts (MFA, Postbaccalaureate Certificate), including film/video (MFA), photography. *Accreditation:* NASAD. *Faculty:* 31 full-time (15 women), 42 part-time/adjunct (19 women). *Students:* 59 full-time (36 women), 32 part-time (23 women); includes 12 minority (2 Black or African American, non-Hispanic/Latino; 5 Asian, non-Hispanic/Latino; 5 Hispanic/Latino), 18 international. 278 applicants, 38% accepted, 40 enrolled. In 2014, 33 master's, 7 other advanced degrees awarded. *Degree requirements:* For master's, thesis, Exhibition for MFA non design. Thesis document MFA in design and low-residency. *Entrance requirements:* For master's, portfolio, college transcripts, resume, statement of purpose, letters of reference, interview; 6 credits of art history taken prior to or during MFA program; for Postbaccalaureate Certificate, portfolio, college transcripts, resume, statement of purpose, letters of reference, interview. Additional exam requirements/recommendations for international students: Required—TOEFL (minimum score 550 paper-based; 85 iBT); Recommended—IELTS (minimum score 6.5). *Application deadline:* For fall admission, 1/6 priority date for domestic and international students. Application fee: $75. Electronic applications accepted. *Expenses:* Tuition, state resident: full-time $23,400; part-time $780 per credit. Tuition, nonresident: full-time $23,400; part-time $780 per credit. Tuition and fees vary according to course load and program. *Financial support:* In 2014–15, 37 students received support, including 40 teaching assistantships (averaging $2,160 per year); career-related internships or fieldwork, scholarships/grants, tuition waivers (partial), and unspecified assistantships also available. Support available to part-time students. Financial award application deadline: 1/6. *Unit head:* Paul Paturzo, Interim Dean of Graduate Studies, 617-879-7166, E-mail: pjpaturzo@massart.edu. *Application contact:* Isaac Goldstein, Graduate Admissions Counselor, 617-879-7203, Fax: 617-879-7250, E-mail: igoldstein@massart.edu.
Website: http://www.massart.edu/Admissions/Graduate_Programs.html

Massachusetts Institute of Technology, School of Architecture and Planning, Program in Media Arts and Sciences, Cambridge, MA 02139. Offers media arts and sciences (SM, PhD); media technology (SM). *Faculty:* 20 full-time (5 women). *Students:* 156 full-time (48 women), 1 part-time (0 women); includes 27 minority (1 Black or African American, non-Hispanic/Latino; 19 Asian, non-Hispanic/Latino; 4 Hispanic/Latino; 3 Two or more races, non-Hispanic/Latino), 71 international. Average age 29. 690 applicants, 11% accepted, 66 enrolled. In 2014, 26 master's, 20 doctorates awarded. Terminal master's awarded for partial completion of doctoral program. *Degree requirements:* For master's, thesis; for doctorate, comprehensive exam, thesis/dissertation. *Entrance requirements:* Additional exam requirements/recommendations for international students: Required—IELTS (minimum score 7). *Application deadline:* For fall admission, 12/15 for domestic and international students. Application fee: $75. Electronic applications accepted. *Expenses: Tuition:* Full-time $44,720; part-time $699 per unit. *Required fees:* $296. *Financial support:* In 2014–15, 150 students received support, including 19 fellowships (averaging $35,900 per year), 131 research assistantships (averaging $34,300 per year); teaching assistantships, Federal Work-Study, institutionally sponsored loans, scholarships/grants, health care benefits, and unspecified assistantships also available. Financial award application deadline: 4/15; financial award applicants required to submit FAFSA. *Faculty research:* Human machine interaction, communications technologies, new media technologies, physical computing, learning and creativity. *Total annual research expenditures:* $20.2 million. *Unit head:* Prof. Patricia Maes, Acting Academic Head, 617-253-5960, Fax: 617-253-8542. *Application contact:* Graduate Admissions, 617-253-5114, Fax: 617-253-8542, E-mail: mas@media.mit.edu.
Website: http://www.media.mit.edu/admissions/

Massachusetts Institute of Technology, School of Humanities, Arts, and Social Sciences, Programs in Comparative Media/Science writing, Program in Comparative Media Studies, Cambridge, MA 02139. Offers SM. *Faculty:* 8 full-time (2 women). *Students:* 19 full-time (11 women); includes 4 minority (2 Asian, non-Hispanic/Latino; 1 Hispanic/Latino; 1 Two or more races, non-Hispanic/Latino), 4 international. Average age 27. 103 applicants, 10% accepted, 8 enrolled. In 2014, 7 master's awarded. *Degree requirements:* For master's, thesis. *Entrance requirements:* For master's, GRE General Test. Additional exam requirements/recommendations for international students: Required—IELTS (minimum score 7). *Application deadline:* For fall admission, 1/15 for domestic and international students. Application fee: $75. Electronic applications accepted. *Expenses: Tuition:* Full-time $44,720; part-time $699 per unit. *Required fees:* $296. *Financial support:* In 2014–15, 19 students received support, including 2 fellowships (averaging $34,100 per year), 17 research assistantships (averaging $32,800 per year); teaching assistantships, Federal Work-Study, institutionally sponsored loans, scholarships/grants, health care benefits, and unspecified assistantships also available. Financial award application deadline: 4/15; financial award applicants required to submit FAFSA. *Faculty research:* Media history and theory; game design, learning games, and creative computing; civic media; digital humanities. *Total annual research expenditures:* $691,000. *Unit head:* T.L. Taylor, Interim Director, 617-253-3599, Fax: 617-258-5133, E-mail: cmsw@mit.edu. *Application contact:* Graduate Contact, 617-253-3599, Fax: 617-258-5133, E-mail: cms-admissions@mit.edu.
Website: http://cms.mit.edu/education/comparative-media-studies/masters/

Metropolitan College of New York, Program in Media Management, New York, NY 10013. Offers MBA. Evening/weekend programs available. *Degree requirements:* For master's, thesis, 10 day study abroad. *Entrance requirements:* For master's, GMAT or GRE General Test, appropriate work experience, interview, minimum GPA of 2.7. Additional exam requirements/recommendations for international students: Required—TOEFL (minimum score 600 paper-based). Electronic applications accepted. *Expenses:* Contact institution.

Michigan State University, The Graduate School, College of Communication Arts and Sciences, Department of Telecommunication, Information Studies, and Media, East Lansing, MI 48824. Offers digital media arts and technology (MA); information and telecommunication management (MA); information, policy and society (MA); serious game design (MA). *Entrance requirements:* Additional exam requirements/recommendations for international students: Required—TOEFL. Electronic applications accepted.

Michigan State University, The Graduate School, College of Communication Arts and Sciences, Program in Communication Arts and Sciences–Media and Information Studies, East Lansing, MI 48824. Offers PhD. *Entrance requirements:* Additional exam requirements/recommendations for international students: Required—TOEFL. Electronic applications accepted. *Faculty research:* Mass media, comparative media.

Missouri Western State University, Program in Digital Media, St. Joseph, MO 64507-2294. Offers MAA. Part-time programs available. *Students:* 7 full-time (1 woman), 6 part-time (2 women); includes 1 minority (Black or African American, non-Hispanic/Latino), 3 international. Average age 31. 2 applicants, 100% accepted, 2 enrolled. In 2014, 2 master's awarded. *Entrance requirements:* For master's, minimum GPA of 2.75, curriculum vitae, interview, 3 letters of reference, letter of intent, portfolio. Additional exam requirements/recommendations for international students: Recommended—TOEFL (minimum score 70 iBT), IELTS (minimum score 6). *Application deadline:* For fall admission, 7/15 for domestic and international students; for spring admission, 11/1 for domestic students, 10/15 for international students; for summer admission, 4/29 for domestic students. Applications are processed on a rolling basis. Application fee: $45 ($50 for international students). Electronic applications accepted. *Expenses:* Tuition, state resident: full-time $5506; part-time $305.91 per credit hour. Tuition, nonresident: full-time $10,075; part-time $559.71 per credit hour. *Required fees:* $504; $99 per credit hour. $176 per semester. Tuition and fees vary according to course load and program. *Financial support:* Scholarships/grants and unspecified assistantships available. Support available to part-time students. *Unit head:* Dr. Bob Bergland, Professor, 816-271-4446, E-mail: bergland@missouriwestern.edu. *Application contact:* Dr. Benjamin D. Caldwell, Dean of the Graduate School, 816-271-4394, Fax: 816-271-4525, E-mail: graduate@missouriwestern.edu.
Website: http://www.missouriwestern.edu/digitalmedia/

Monmouth University, The Graduate School, Department of Corporate and Public Communication, West Long Branch, NJ 07764-1898. Offers corporate and public communication (MA); human resources management and communication (Certificate); public service communication (Certificate); strategic public relations and new media (Certificate). Part-time and evening/weekend programs available. *Faculty:* 9 full-time (7

women). *Students:* 7 full-time (4 women), 24 part-time (19 women); includes 6 minority (1 Black or African American, non-Hispanic/Latino; 3 Hispanic/Latino; 2 Two or more races, non-Hispanic/Latino), 1 international. Average age 31. 23 applicants, 91% accepted, 13 enrolled. In 2014, 12 master's awarded. *Degree requirements:* For master's, comprehensive exam (for some programs), thesis (for some programs), project. *Entrance requirements:* For master's, GRE, baccalaureate degree with minimum GPA of 3.0 in major, 2.75 overall; two letters of recommendation, personal essay (750 words or less describing preparation for study and personal objectives), digital or hard copy portfolio of select samples of work including a writing sample, resume. Additional exam requirements/recommendations for international students: Required—TOEFL (minimum score 550 paper-based; 79 iBT), IELTS (minimum score 6), Michigan English Language Assessment Battery (minimum score 77). *Application deadline:* For fall admission, 7/15 priority date for domestic students, 6/1 for international students; for spring admission, 11/15 priority date for domestic students, 11/1 for international students. Applications are processed on a rolling basis. Application fee: $50. Electronic applications accepted. *Expenses: Tuition:* Full-time $18,072; part-time $1004 per credit. *Required fees:* $157 per semester. *Financial support:* In 2014–15, 28 students received support, including 19 fellowships (averaging $2,898 per year), 3 research assistantships (averaging $9,030 per year); scholarships/grants and unspecified assistantships also available. Support available to part-time students. Financial award applicants required to submit FAFSA. *Faculty research:* Service-learning, history of television, feminism and the media, executive communication, public relations pedagogy. *Unit head:* Dr. Deanna Shoemaker, Program Director, 732-263-5449, Fax: 732-571-3609, E-mail: dshoemak@monmouth.edu. *Application contact:* Andrea Thompson, Graduate Admission Counselor, 732-571-3452, Fax: 732-263-5123, E-mail: gradadm@monmouth.edu.
Website: http://www.monmouth.edu/cpc

New Mexico Highlands University, Graduate Studies, College of Arts and Sciences, Department of Computer Sciences, Las Vegas, NM 87701. Offers media arts and computer science (MS), including computer science. *Faculty:* 4 full-time (0 women). *Students:* 6 full-time (2 women), 9 part-time (3 women); includes 3 minority (all Hispanic/Latino), 12 international. Average age 28. 3 applicants, 100% accepted, 3 enrolled. In 2014, 9 master's awarded. *Degree requirements:* For master's, comprehensive exam, thesis. *Entrance requirements:* For master's, minimum undergraduate GPA of 3.0. Additional exam requirements/recommendations for international students: Required—TOEFL (minimum score 540 paper-based). Application fee: $15. *Financial support:* In 2014–15, 7 students received support, including 8 research assistantships, 12 teaching assistantships; career-related internships or fieldwork, Federal Work-Study, institutionally sponsored loans, scholarships/grants, tuition waivers (full and partial), and unspecified assistantships also available. Support available to part-time students. Financial award application deadline: 3/1; financial award applicants required to submit FAFSA. *Faculty research:* Advanced digital compositing, photographic installations and exhibition design, pattern recognition, parallel and distributed computing, computer security education. *Unit head:* Dr. John Jeffries, Department Chair, 505-454-3480, E-mail: jjeffries@nmhu.edu. *Application contact:* Diane Trujillo, Administrative Assistant for Graduate Studies, 505-454-3266, Fax: 505-426-2117, E-mail: dtrujillo@nmhu.edu.
Website: http://www.nmhu.edu/current-students/graduate/arts-and-sciences/masters-in-computer-and-mathematical-sciences/

The New School, The New School for Public Engagement, Program in Media Studies, New York, NY 10011. Offers documentary media studies (Graduate Certificate); media management (Graduate Certificate); media studies (MA). Part-time and evening/weekend programs available. Postbaccalaureate distance learning degree programs offered (no on-campus study). *Degree requirements:* For master's, thesis optional. *Entrance requirements:* For master's, interview. Additional exam requirements/recommendations for international students: Required—TOEFL (minimum score 600 paper-based; 100 iBT). Electronic applications accepted. *Faculty research:* Effect of technology on society, effect of U. S. media on international affairs, effect of media on corporate affairs.

New York University, Graduate School of Arts and Science, Department of Anthropology, Program in Culture and Media, New York, NY 10012-1019. Offers MA/Advanced Certificate, PhD/Advanced Certificate. *Faculty:* 1 (woman) full-time. *Students:* 6 full-time (all women); includes 2 minority (1 American Indian or Alaska Native, non-Hispanic/Latino; 1 Hispanic/Latino), 1 international. Average age 30. 25 applicants, 8% accepted, 1 enrolled. *Entrance requirements:* Additional exam requirements/recommendations for international students: Required—TOEFL. *Application deadline:* For fall admission, 12/18 priority date for domestic students, 12/18 for international students. Application fee: $100. *Financial support:* Fellowships, research assistantships, teaching assistantships, career-related internships or fieldwork, institutionally sponsored loans, scholarships/grants, health care benefits, and unspecified assistantships available. Financial award application deadline: 12/18. *Faculty research:* Critical history of ethnographic film, ethnography of media, indigenous media, politics of reproduction and disability, social movements. *Unit head:* Faye Ginsburg, Director, 212-998-3759, Fax: 212-995-4730, E-mail: anthropology@nyu.edu. *Application contact:* Pegi Vail, Associate Director, 212-998-3759, Fax: 212-995-4730, E-mail: anthropology@nyu.edu.
Website: http://www.nyu.edu/gsas/dept/anthro/

New York University, School of Continuing and Professional Studies, The Preston Robert Tisch Center for Hospitality, Tourism, and Sports Management, Program in Sports Business, New York, NY 10012-1019. Offers global sports media (MS); professional and collegiate sports operations (MS); sports business (Advanced Certificate); sports law (MS); sports marketing and sales (MS). Part-time and evening/weekend programs available. *Faculty:* 6 full-time (2 women), 26 part-time/adjunct (3 women). *Students:* 69 full-time (20 women), 57 part-time (19 women); includes 29 minority (7 Black or African American, non-Hispanic/Latino; 1 American Indian or Alaska Native, non-Hispanic/Latino; 7 Asian, non-Hispanic/Latino; 12 Hispanic/Latino; 2 Two or more races, non-Hispanic/Latino), 42 international. Average age 25. 122 applicants, 67% accepted, 37 enrolled. In 2014, 56 master's, 5 other advanced degrees awarded. *Degree requirements:* For master's, thesis. *Entrance requirements:* For master's, GRE or GMAT (only upon request), bachelor's degree, resume with relevant professional work, internship or volunteer experience, two letters of recommendation, statement of purpose. Additional exam requirements/recommendations for international students: Required—TOEFL (minimum score 600 paper-based; 100 iBT), IELTS (minimum score 7). *Application deadline:* For fall admission, 2/1 priority date for domestic and international students; for spring admission, 10/15 priority date for domestic students, 8/15 priority date for international students. Applications are processed on a rolling basis. Application fee: $150. Electronic applications accepted. *Financial support:* In 2014–15, 47 students received support, including 41 fellowships (averaging $2,260 per year); Federal Work-Study and scholarships/grants also available. Support available to part-time students. Financial award application deadline: 4/1; financial award applicants required to submit FAFSA. *Faculty research:* Implications of college football's bowl coalition series from a legal, economic, and academic perspective; social history of sports. *Unit head:* Arthur Miller, Associate Dean and Director, and University Professor, 212-998-9100. *Application contact:* Admissions Office, 212-998-7100, E-mail: sps.gradadmissions@nyu.edu.
Website: http://www.sps.nyu.edu/areas-of-study/tisch/graduate-programs/ms-sports-business/

New York University, Steinhardt School of Culture, Education, and Human Development, Department of Media, Culture and Communication, New York, NY 10010. Offers media, culture and communication (MA, PhD); MLIS/MA. Part-time programs available. *Faculty:* 35 full-time (17 women), 43 part-time/adjunct (19 women). *Students:* 98 full-time (68 women), 38 part-time (30 women); includes 27 minority (5 Black or African American, non-Hispanic/Latino; 12 Asian, non-Hispanic/Latino; 5 Hispanic/Latino; 1 Native Hawaiian or other Pacific Islander, non-Hispanic/Latino; 4 Two or more races, non-Hispanic/Latino), 55 international. Average age 33. 550 applicants, 24% accepted, 46 enrolled. In 2014, 57 master's, 6 doctorates awarded. Terminal master's awarded for partial completion of doctoral program. *Degree requirements:* For master's, thesis (for some programs); for doctorate, thesis/dissertation. *Entrance requirements:* For master's, GRE General Test; for doctorate, GRE General Test, interview. Additional exam requirements/recommendations for international students: Required—TOEFL (minimum score 100 iBT). *Application deadline:* For fall admission, 12/1 priority date for domestic and international students; for spring admission, 10/1 for domestic and international students. Applications are processed on a rolling basis. Application fee: $75. Electronic applications accepted. *Financial support:* Fellowships with full and partial tuition reimbursements, teaching assistantships with full and partial tuition reimbursements, career-related internships or fieldwork, Federal Work-Study, institutionally sponsored loans, scholarships/grants, tuition waivers (partial), and unspecified assistantships available. Support available to part-time students. Financial award application deadline: 2/1; financial award applicants required to submit FAFSA. *Faculty research:* Digital media and new technologies, media criticism, flow of media and culture transnationally and transculturally. *Unit head:* Prof. Lisa Gitelman, Chairperson, 212-998-5191, Fax: 212-995-4046, E-mail: lg91@nyu.edu. *Application contact:* 212-998-5030, Fax: 212-995-4328, E-mail: steinhardt.gradadmissions@nyu.edu.
Website: http://steinhardt.nyu.edu/mcc

Norfolk State University, School of Graduate Studies, School of Liberal Arts, Department of Media and Communication, Norfolk, VA 23504. Offers MA. Part-time programs available. *Degree requirements:* For master's, thesis. *Entrance requirements:* For master's, GRE, minimum GPA of 2.5, letters of recommendation. Additional exam requirements/recommendations for international students: Required—TOEFL.

Northern Kentucky University, Office of Graduate Programs, College of Informatics, Program in Communication, Highland Heights, KY 41099. Offers communication (MA); communication teaching (Certificate); documentary studies (Certificate); public relations (Certificate); relationships (Certificate). Part-time and evening/weekend programs available. *Faculty:* 7 full-time (4 women), 1 part-time/adjunct (0 women). *Students:* 9 full-time (1 woman), 17 part-time (11 women); includes 3 minority (all Black or African American, non-Hispanic/Latino), 2 international. Average age 30. In 2014, 13 master's, 2 other advanced degrees awarded. Terminal master's awarded for partial completion of doctoral program. *Degree requirements:* For master's, comprehensive exams, thesis or applied capstone project. *Entrance requirements:* For master's, GRE, minimum GPA of 3.0, 3 letters of recommendation, letter of intent. Additional exam requirements/recommendations for international students: Required—TOEFL (minimum score 79 iBT); Recommended—IELTS (minimum score 6.5). *Application deadline:* For fall admission, 8/1 for domestic students, 6/1 for international students; for spring admission, 12/1 for domestic students, 10/1 for international students. Applications are processed on a rolling basis. Application fee: $40. Electronic applications accepted. *Expenses: Tuition, area resident:* Part-time $518 per credit hour. Tuition, state resident: part-time $630 per credit hour. Tuition, nonresident: part-time $797 per credit hour. *Required fees:* $192 per semester. Tuition and fees vary according to course load, degree level, campus/location, program and reciprocity agreements. *Financial support:* In 2014–15, 7 students received support. Unspecified assistantships available. Financial award applicants required to submit FAFSA. *Faculty research:* Mediating effect of health communication, organizational communication, quantitative and qualitative research methods, family and interpersonal communication. *Unit head:* Dr. Andrea Lambert-South, Graduate Program Director, 859-572-6615, E-mail: lamberta3@nku.edu. *Application contact:* Alison Swanson, Graduate Admissions Coordinator, 859-572-6971, E-mail: swansona1@nku.edu.
Website: http://informatics.nku.edu/content/informatics/departments/communication/programs/communication—m-a—.html

Northwestern University, The Graduate School, Kellogg School of Management, Management Programs, Evanston, IL 60208. Offers accounting information and management (MBA, PhD); analytical finance (MBA); business administration (MBA); decision sciences (MBA); entrepreneurship and innovation (MBA); finance (MBA, PhD); health enterprise management (MBA); human resources management (MBA); international business (MBA); management and organizations (MBA, PhD); management and organizations and sociology (PhD); management and strategy (MBA); management studies (MS); managerial analytics (MBA); managerial economics (MBA); managerial economics and strategy (PhD); marketing (MBA, PhD); marketing management (MBA); media management (MBA); operations management (MBA, PhD); real estate (MBA); social enterprise at Kellogg (MBA); JD/MBA. Part-time and evening/weekend programs available. Terminal master's awarded for partial completion of doctoral program. *Degree requirements:* For doctorate, thesis/dissertation, 2 years of coursework, qualifying (field) exam and candidacy, summer research papers and presentations to faculty, proposal defense, final exam/defense. *Entrance requirements:* For master's, GMAT, GRE, interview, 2 letters of recommendation, college transcripts, resume, essays, Kellogg honor code; for doctorate, GMAT, GRE, statement of purpose, transcripts, 2 letters of recommendation, resume, interview. Additional exam requirements/recommendations for international students: Required—TOEFL, IELTS. Electronic applications accepted. *Expenses:* Contact institution. *Faculty research:* Business cycles and international finance, health policy, networks, non-market strategy, consumer psychology.

Northwestern University, The Graduate School, School of Communication, Department of Communication Studies, Evanston, IL 60208. Offers communication studies (PhD), including interaction and social influence, rhetoric and public culture; managerial communication (MSC); media, technology and society (PhD); technology and social behavior (PhD). PhD admissions and degree offered through The Graduate School. Terminal master's awarded for partial completion of doctoral program. *Degree requirements:* For doctorate, thesis/dissertation. *Entrance requirements:* For master's and doctorate, GRE General Test. Additional exam requirements/recommendations for international students: Required—TOEFL. Electronic applications accepted.

Northwestern University, The Graduate School, School of Communication, Department of Radio, Television and Film, Evanston, IL 60208. Offers documentary media (MFA); screen cultures (MA, PhD); writing for the screen and stage (MFA). Admissions and degrees offered through The Graduate School. Part-time programs available. Terminal master's awarded for partial completion of doctoral program. *Degree requirements:* For master's, comprehensive exam or thesis; for doctorate, thesis/dissertation, qualifying exam. *Entrance requirements:* For master's and doctorate, GRE General Test. Additional exam requirements/recommendations for international

students: Required—TOEFL. Electronic applications accepted. *Faculty research:* Art and new media, media theory and criticism, gender, media history, documentary.

Ohio University, Graduate College, Scripps College of Communication, School of Media Arts and Studies, Athens, OH 45701-2979. Offers mass communication (PhD); media arts and studies (MA). *Degree requirements:* For master's, comprehensive exam (for some programs), thesis or alternative; for doctorate, comprehensive exam, thesis/dissertation. *Entrance requirements:* For master's, GRE General Test or MAT, minimum GPA of 3.0; for doctorate, GRE General Test or MAT. Additional exam requirements/recommendations for international students: Required—TOEFL (minimum score 600 paper-based; 100 iBT) or IELTS (minimum score 7). Electronic applications accepted. *Faculty research:* Media and development communication, new media and society, industry studies.

Ohio University, Graduate College, Scripps College of Communication, School of Visual Communication, Athens, OH 45701-2979. Offers MA. *Accreditation:* NASAD. *Entrance requirements:* For master's, minimum GPA of 2.5, portfolio. Additional exam requirements/recommendations for international students: Required—TOEFL (minimum score 600 paper-based; 100 iBT) or IELTS (minimum score 7). Electronic applications accepted. *Faculty research:* Photojournalism (including documentary photography), commercial photography (including illustrative photography), picture editing, informational graphics/publication design, interactive multimedia, visual media management.

Pace University, Dyson College of Arts and Sciences, Program in Media and Communication Arts, New York, NY 10038. Offers MA. Part-time and evening/weekend programs available. *Students:* 11 full-time (9 women), 29 part-time (23 women); includes 15 minority (8 Black or African American, non-Hispanic/Latino; 1 Asian, non-Hispanic/Latino; 4 Hispanic/Latino; 2 Two or more races, non-Hispanic/Latino), 8 international. Average age 28. 32 applicants, 78% accepted, 15 enrolled. In 2014, 15 master's awarded. *Degree requirements:* For master's, comprehensive exam. *Entrance requirements:* For master's, portfolio containing examples of prior work (press releases, advertisements, presentations, writing samples, etc.). Additional exam requirements/recommendations for international students: Required—TOEFL. *Application deadline:* For fall admission, 8/1 priority date for domestic students, 6/1 for international students; for spring admission, 12/1 for domestic students, 10/1 for international students. Applications are processed on a rolling basis. Application fee: $70. Electronic applications accepted. *Expenses: Tuition:* Part-time $1120 per credit. *Required fees:* $266 per semester. Tuition and fees vary according to course load, degree level and program. *Financial support:* Applicants required to submit FAFSA. *Unit head:* Dr. Maria T. Luskay, Director, 914-773-3353, E-mail: mluskay@pace.edu. *Application contact:* Susan Ford-Goldschein, Director of Admissions, 212-346-1531, Fax: 212-346-1585, E-mail: gradnyc@pace.edu.
Website: http://www.pace.edu/dyson/academic-departments-and-programs/mediacomm/graduate-programs/

Penn State University Park, Graduate School, College of Communications, Department of Communications, University Park, PA 16802. Offers mass communications (PhD); media studies (MA). *Unit head:* Dr. Marie C. Hardin, Dean, 814-863-1484, Fax: 814-863-8044, E-mail: mch208@psu.edu. *Application contact:* Lori A. Stania, Director, Graduate Student Services, 814-867-5278, Fax: 814-863-4627, E-mail: gswww@psu.edu.
Website: http://comm.psu.edu/

Pepperdine University, Seaver College, Division of Communication, Malibu, CA 90263. Offers communication (MA, MS); media production (MA). Part-time programs available. *Students:* 3 full-time (2 women), 27 part-time (20 women); includes 6 minority (2 Asian, non-Hispanic/Latino; 2 Hispanic/Latino; 1 Native Hawaiian or other Pacific Islander, non-Hispanic/Latino; 1 Two or more races, non-Hispanic/Latino), 2 international. In 2014, 5 master's awarded. *Entrance requirements:* For master's, GRE General Test, letters of recommendation, writing sample. Additional exam requirements/recommendations for international students: Required—TOEFL. *Application deadline:* For fall admission, 2/1 priority date for domestic students, 2/1 for international students. Applications are processed on a rolling basis. Application fee: $65. Electronic applications accepted. *Financial support:* Research assistantships, teaching assistantships, career-related internships or fieldwork, and scholarships/grants available. Support available to part-time students. Financial award applicants required to submit FAFSA. *Unit head:* Dr. Kenneth E. Waters, Chair/Professor of Journalism, 310-506-4245, E-mail: ken.waters@pepperdine.edu. *Application contact:* Michael Truschke, Dean of Admission and Enrollment Management, 310-506-6165, Fax: 310-506-4861, E-mail: admission-seaver@pepperdine.edu.

 Pratt Institute, School of Liberal Arts and Sciences, Program in Media Studies, Brooklyn, NY 11205-3899. Offers MA. *Faculty:* 9 full-time (5 women), 3 part-time/adjunct (1 woman). *Students:* 16 full-time (12 women), 2 part-time (1 woman); includes 4 minority (1 Black or African American, non-Hispanic/Latino; 1 Asian, non-Hispanic/Latino; 2 Hispanic/Latino), 6 international. Average age 25. 30 applicants, 97% accepted, 8 enrolled. *Entrance requirements:* For master's, BA, BS, or BFA from accredited institution; statement of purpose; 10-20 pages of relevant writing samples; transcripts of undergraduate coursework; three letters of recommendation. *Application deadline:* For fall admission, 1/5 for domestic and international students; for spring admission, 10/1 for domestic and international students. Application fee: $50 ($90 for international students). Electronic applications accepted. *Financial support:* Application deadline: 2/1; applicants required to submit FAFSA. *Unit head:* Maria Damon, Chair, 718-636-3790, E-mail: mdamon@pratt.edu. *Application contact:* Young Hah, Director of Graduate Admissions, 718-636-3683, Fax: 718-399-4242, E-mail: yhah@pratt.edu.
Website: https://www.pratt.edu/academics/liberal-arts-and-sciences/graduate-media-studies/

See Display on this page and Close-Up on page 767.

Robert Morris University Illinois, Morris Graduate School of Management, Chicago, IL 60605. Offers accounting (MBA); accounting/finance (MBA); business analytics (MIS); design and media (MM); educational technology (MM); health care administration (MM); higher education administration (MM); human resource management (MBA); information security (MIS); information systems (MIS); law enforcement administration (MM); management (MBA); management/finance (MBA); management/human resource management (MBA); mobile computing (MIS); sports administration (MM). Part-time and evening/weekend programs available. *Faculty:* 5 full-time (2 women), 27 part-time/adjunct (8 women). *Students:* 237 full-time (122 women), 180 part-time (109 women); includes 222 minority (128 Black or African American, non-Hispanic/Latino; 2 American Indian or Alaska Native, non-Hispanic/Latino; 18 Asian, non-Hispanic/Latino; 68 Hispanic/Latino; 1 Native Hawaiian or other Pacific Islander, non-Hispanic/Latino; 5 Two or more races, non-Hispanic/Latino), 26 international. Average age 33. 191 applicants, 63% accepted, 104 enrolled. In 2014, 234 master's awarded. *Entrance requirements:* For master's, official transcripts, two letters of recommendation. Additional exam requirements/recommendations for international students: Required—TOEFL (minimum score 550 paper-based). *Application deadline:* Applications are processed on a rolling basis. Application fee: $20 ($100 for international students). Electronic applications

accepted. *Expenses: Tuition:* Full-time $14,400; part-time $2400 per course. *Financial support:* In 2014–15, 339 students received support. Federal Work-Study and scholarships/grants available. Support available to part-time students. Financial award applicants required to submit FAFSA. *Unit head:* Kayed Akkawi, Dean, 312-935-6050, Fax: 312-935-6020, E-mail: kakkawi@robertmorris.edu. *Application contact:* Catherine Lockwood, Vice President of Adult Undergraduate and Graduate Education, 312-935-6050, Fax: 312-935-6020, E-mail: clockwood@robertmorris.edu.

Rochester Institute of Technology, Graduate Enrollment Services, College of Liberal Arts, School of Communication, Rochester, NY 14623-5604. Offers communication and digital media (Advanced Certificate); communication and media technologies (MS). Part-time programs available. Postbaccalaureate distance learning degree programs offered (no on-campus study). *Students:* 12 full-time (8 women), 17 part-time (all women); includes 1 minority (Hispanic/Latino), 23 international. Average age 26. 32 applicants, 59% accepted, 12 enrolled. In 2014, 16 master's awarded. *Degree requirements:* For master's, thesis or alternative, thesis or project. *Entrance requirements:* For master's, TOEFL, IELTS, or PTE for non-native English speakers, recommended minimum GPA of 3.0, writing sample. Additional exam requirements/recommendations for international students: Required—PTE (minimum score 58), TOEFL (minimum score 550 paper-based; 79 iBT) or IELTS (minimum score 6.5). *Application deadline:* For fall admission, 2/15 priority date for domestic and international students; for winter admission, 11/1 for domestic and international students; for spring admission, 12/15 priority date for domestic and international students. Applications are processed on a rolling basis. Application fee: $60. Electronic applications accepted. *Expenses:* Expenses: $1,673 per credit hour. *Financial support:* In 2014–15, 14 students received support. Research assistantships with partial tuition reimbursements available, teaching assistantships with partial tuition reimbursements available, career-related internships or fieldwork, Federal Work-Study, institutionally sponsored loans, scholarships/grants, and unspecified assistantships available. Support available to part-time students. Financial award applicants required to submit FAFSA. *Faculty research:* The analysis of communication problems, the development of solutions, and the creation of messages as a result of their combined training in the social sciences, humanities, and applied technologies. *Unit head:* Dr. Patrick Scanlon, Director, 585-475-2449, Fax: 585-475-7732, E-mail: pmsgsl@rit.edu. *Application contact:* Diane Ellison, Associate Vice President, Graduate Enrollment Services, 585-475-2229, Fax: 585-475-7164, E-mail: gradinfo@rit.edu.
Website: http://www.rit.edu/cla/communication/

Rowan University, Graduate School, College of Communication and Creative Arts, Integrated Marketing Communication and New Media Certificate of Graduate Study Program, Glassboro, NJ 08028-1701. Offers CGS. *Students:* 5 full-time (4 women), 11 part-time (10 women); includes 5 minority (3 Black or African American, non-Hispanic/Latino; 1 Asian, non-Hispanic/Latino; 1 Hispanic/Latino). Average age 28. 2 applicants, 100% accepted, 2 enrolled. *Application deadline:* For fall admission, 8/1 for domestic students; for spring admission, 2/1 for domestic students, 2/15 for international students; for summer admission, 4/1 for domestic and international students. Applications are processed on a rolling basis. Application fee: $65. Electronic applications accepted. *Expenses: Tuition, area resident:* Part-time $648 per credit. Tuition, state resident: part-time $648 per credit. Tuition, nonresident: part-time $648 per credit. *Required fees:* $145 per credit. Tuition and fees vary according to degree level, campus/location, program and student level. *Unit head:* Dr. Horacio Sosa, Vice President, Global Learning and Partnerships, 856-256-4747, Fax: 856-256-5638, E-mail: sosa@rowan.edu. *Application contact:* Admissions and Enrollment Services, 856-256-4747, Fax: 856-256-5637, E-mail: globaladmissions@rowan.edu.

Rutgers, The State University of New Jersey, New Brunswick, School of Communication, Information and Library Studies, Program in Communication, Library and Information Science and Media Studies, Piscataway, NJ 08854-8097. Offers PhD. Part-time programs available. *Degree requirements:* For doctorate, comprehensive exam, thesis/dissertation, qualifying exams. *Entrance requirements:* For doctorate, GRE General Test, proficiency in statistics. Additional exam requirements/recommendations for international students: Required—TOEFL (minimum score 600 paper-based). Electronic applications accepted. *Faculty research:* Information science, media studies.

Saginaw Valley State University, College of Arts and Behavioral Sciences, Program in Communication and Digital Media Design, University Center, MI 48710. Offers MA. Part-time and evening/weekend programs available. *Students:* 13 full-time (9 women), 11 part-time (5 women); includes 3 minority (all Black or African American, non-Hispanic/Latino), 9 international. Average age 31. 15 applicants, 80% accepted, 6 enrolled. In 2014, 6 master's awarded. *Degree requirements:* For master's, thesis. *Entrance requirements:* For master's, minimum GPA of 3.0. Additional exam requirements/recommendations for international students: Required—TOEFL (minimum score 540 paper-based). *Application deadline:* For fall admission, 7/15 for international students; for winter admission, 11/15 for international students; for spring admission, 4/15 for international students. Applications are processed on a rolling basis. Application fee: $30 ($90 for international students). Electronic applications accepted. *Expenses:* Tuition, state resident: full-time $8957; part-time $497.60 per credit hour. Tuition, nonresident: full-time $17,081; part-time $948.95 per credit hour. *Required fees:* $263; $14.60 per credit hour. Tuition and fees vary according to degree level. *Financial support:* Federal Work-Study and scholarships/grants available. Support available to part-time students. Financial award application deadline: 4/1; financial award applicants required to submit FAFSA. *Unit head:* Dr. Robert Drew, Professor of Communication, 989-964-7495, E-mail: rdrew@svsu.edu. *Application contact:* Jenna Briggs, Director, Graduate and International Admissions, 989-964-6096, Fax: 989-964-2788, E-mail: gradadm@svsu.edu.
Website: http://www.svsu.edu/communicationdigitalmedia/

St. Edward's University, Bill Munday School of Business, Area of Digital Media Management, Austin, TX 78704. Offers MBA. *Students:* 37 full-time (16 women), 1 part-time (0 women); includes 17 minority (3 Black or African American, non-Hispanic/Latino; 1 American Indian or Alaska Native, non-Hispanic/Latino; 4 Asian, non-Hispanic/Latino; 8 Hispanic/Latino; 1 Two or more races, non-Hispanic/Latino), 3 international. Average age 27. 69 applicants, 46% accepted, 23 enrolled. In 2014, 18 master's awarded. *Entrance requirements:* For master's, GRE or GMAT, interview, 2 letters of recommendation, minimum GPA of 3.0 in last 60 hours of course work. Additional exam requirements/recommendations for international students: Required—TOEFL (minimum score 79 iBT) or IELTS (minimum score 6). *Application deadline:* For fall admission, 2/15 priority date for domestic and international students. Applications are processed on a rolling basis. Application fee: $50. Electronic applications accepted. *Expenses:* Expenses: Contact institution. *Unit head:* Russell Rains, Director, 512-428-1220, Fax: 512-448-8492, E-mail: russellr@stedwards.edu. *Application contact:* Office of Admission, 512-448-8500, Fax: 512-464-8877, E-mail: seu.admit@stedwards.edu.
Website: http://www.stedwards.edu

San Diego State University, Graduate and Research Affairs, College of Professional Studies and Fine Arts, School of Communication, San Diego, CA 92182. Offers advertising and public relations (MA); critical-cultural studies (MA); interaction studies (MA); intercultural and international studies (MA); new media studies (MA); news and information studies (MA); telecommunications and media management (MA). *Degree requirements:* For master's, thesis. *Entrance requirements:* For master's, GRE General Test, 3 letters of recommendation. Additional exam requirements/recommendations for international students: Required—TOEFL. Electronic applications accepted.

San Diego State University, Graduate and Research Affairs, College of Professional Studies and Fine Arts, School of Theater, Television and Film, Program in Television, Film, and New Media Production, San Diego, CA 92182. Offers MA. *Entrance requirements:* For master's, GRE General Test, 3 letters of recommendation, resume, sample reel, influential book list, influential films list, hobby list. Additional exam requirements/recommendations for international students: Required—TOEFL. Electronic applications accepted. *Faculty research:* Experimental film and television programs, documentary film, television research and production.

San Francisco State University, Division of Graduate Studies, College of Liberal and Creative Arts, Department of Broadcast and Electronic Communication Arts, San Francisco, CA 94132-1722. Offers MA. *Expenses:* Tuition, state resident: full-time $6738. Tuition, nonresident: full-time $17,898; part-time $372 per credit hour. *Required fees:* $498 per semester. *Unit head:* Dr. Scott Patterson, Chair, 415-338-1787, Fax: 415-338-1168, E-mail: spatters@sfsu.edu. *Application contact:* Dr. Nancy Reist, Graduate Coordinator, 415-338-1787, Fax: 415-338-1168, E-mail: sami@sfsu.edu.
Website: http://beca.sfsu.edu/

Savannah College of Art and Design, Graduate School, Program in Motion Media Design, Savannah, GA 31402-3146. Offers MA, MFA. Part-time programs available. Postbaccalaureate distance learning degree programs offered (no on-campus study). *Faculty:* 10 full-time (2 women), 5 part-time/adjunct (2 women). *Students:* 38 full-time (21 women), 37 part-time (18 women); includes 21 minority (15 Black or African American, non-Hispanic/Latino; 3 Asian, non-Hispanic/Latino; 3 Hispanic/Latino), 28 international. Average age 30. 47 applicants, 47% accepted, 15 enrolled. In 2014, 23 master's awarded. *Degree requirements:* For master's, thesis (for some programs), final project (for MA); internship (for MFA). *Entrance requirements:* For master's, portfolio. Additional exam requirements/recommendations for international students: Required—TOEFL (minimum score 550 paper-based, 85 iBT), IELTS (minimum score 6.5), or ACTFL. *Application deadline:* For fall admission, 4/1 for domestic and international students. Applications are processed on a rolling basis. Application fee: $40. Electronic applications accepted. *Expenses: Tuition:* Full-time $34,605; part-time $3845 per course. One-time fee: $500. Tuition and fees vary according to course load. *Financial support:* Fellowships, career-related internships or fieldwork, Federal Work-Study, and scholarships/grants available. Financial award application deadline: 4/1; financial award applicants required to submit FAFSA. *Unit head:* John Colette, Chair. *Application contact:* Jenny Jaquillard, Executive Director of Admissions, Recruitment and Events, 912-525-5100, Fax: 912-525-5985, E-mail: admission@scad.edu.
Website: http://www.scad.edu/academics/programs/motion-media-design

Savannah College of Art and Design, Graduate School, Program in Performing Arts, Savannah, GA 31402-3146. Offers MFA. *Faculty:* 11 full-time (5 women), 5 part-time/adjunct (4 women). *Students:* 50 full-time (32 women), 2 part-time (1 woman); includes 22 minority (14 Black or African American, non-Hispanic/Latino; 1 American Indian or Alaska Native, non-Hispanic/Latino; 4 Asian, non-Hispanic/Latino; 2 Hispanic/Latino; 1 Two or more races, non-Hispanic/Latino), 3 international. Average age 27. 88 applicants, 49% accepted, 24 enrolled. In 2014, 12 master's awarded. *Degree requirements:* For master's, thesis. *Entrance requirements:* For master's, audition, interview. Additional exam requirements/recommendations for international students: Required—TOEFL (minimum score 550 paper-based, 85 iBT), IELTS (minimum score 6.5), or ACTFL. *Application deadline:* For fall admission, 4/1 for domestic and international students. Applications are processed on a rolling basis. Application fee: $40. Electronic applications accepted. *Expenses: Tuition:* Full-time $34,605; part-time $3845 per course. One-time fee: $500. Tuition and fees vary according to course load. *Financial support:* Fellowships, career-related internships or fieldwork, Federal Work-Study, and scholarships/grants available. Financial award application deadline: 4/1; financial award applicants required to submit FAFSA. *Unit head:* Michael Wainstein, Chair. *Application contact:* Jenny Jaquillard, Executive Director of Admissions, Recruitment and Events, 912-525-5100, Fax: 912-525-5985, E-mail: admission@scad.edu.
Website: http://www.scad.edu/academics/programs/performing-arts

Southern Illinois University Carbondale, Graduate School, College of Mass Communication and Media Arts, Department of Mass Communication and Media Arts, Carbondale, IL 62901-4701. Offers MA, MFA. *Students:* 36 full-time (14 women), 17 part-time (8 women); includes 2 minority (1 Black or African American, non-Hispanic/Latino; 1 Asian, non-Hispanic/Latino), 20 international. 38 applicants, 34% accepted, 9 enrolled. In 2014, 11 master's awarded. Application fee: $50. *Expenses:* Tuition, state resident: full-time $10,176; part-time $1153 per credit. Tuition, nonresident: full-time $20,814; part-time $1744 per credit. *Required fees:* $7092; $394 per credit. $2364 per semester. *Unit head:* Prof. Deborah Tudor, Director of Graduate Studies, 618-453-3267, E-mail: dtudor@siu.edu. *Application contact:* Georgia Norman, Administrative Aide, 618-453-3785, E-mail: mcmagrad@siu.edu.

Southern Illinois University Carbondale, Graduate School, College of Mass Communication and Media Arts, Department of Professional Media and Media Management Studies, Carbondale, IL 62901-4701. Offers MA. *Students:* 25 full-time (12 women), 16 part-time (10 women); includes 9 minority (7 Black or African American, non-Hispanic/Latino; 1 Asian, non-Hispanic/Latino; 1 Hispanic/Latino), 8 international. 21 applicants, 71% accepted, 8 enrolled. In 2014, 10 master's awarded. Application fee: $50. *Expenses:* Tuition, state resident: full-time $10,176; part-time $1153 per credit. Tuition, nonresident: full-time $20,814; part-time $1744 per credit. *Required fees:* $7092; $394 per credit. $2364 per semester. *Unit head:* Prof. Deborah Tudor, Director, 618-453-3267, E-mail: dtudor@siu.edu. *Application contact:* Georgia Norman, Supervisor, Admissions, 618-453-3785, E-mail: mcmagrad@siu.edu.

Southern Illinois University Carbondale, Graduate School, College of Mass Communication and Media Arts, Program in Media Theory and Research, Carbondale, IL 62901-4701. Offers MA. *Students:* 5 full-time (3 women), 4 international. 10 applicants, 50% accepted, 2 enrolled. In 2014, 1 master's awarded. Application fee: $50. *Expenses:* Tuition, state resident: full-time $10,176; part-time $1153 per credit. Tuition, nonresident: full-time $20,814; part-time $1744 per credit. *Required fees:* $7092; $394 per credit. $2364 per semester. *Unit head:* Prof. Deborah Tudor, Director of Graduate Studies, 618-453-3267, E-mail: dtudor@siu.edu. *Application contact:* Georgia Norman, Supervisor, Admissions, 618-453-3785, E-mail: mcmagrad@siu.edu.

Southern Illinois University Edwardsville, Graduate School, College of Arts and Sciences, Department of Mass Communications, Program in Media Literacy, Edwardsville, IL 62026. Offers Postbaccalaureate Certificate. Part-time and evening/weekend programs available. *Entrance requirements:* Additional exam requirements/recommendations for international students: Required—TOEFL (minimum score 550 paper-based; 79 iBT), IELTS (minimum score 6.5). *Application deadline:* For fall admission, 7/24 for domestic students, 7/15 for international students; for spring admission, 12/11 for domestic students, 11/15 for international students; for summer admission, 4/29 for domestic students, 4/15 for international students. Applications are processed on a rolling basis. Application fee: $30. Electronic applications accepted. *Expenses:* Tuition, state resident: full-time $5026. Tuition, nonresident: full-time

$12,566. *International tuition:* $25,136 full-time. *Required fees:* $1682. Tuition and fees vary according to course load, campus/location and program. *Financial support:* Fellowships with full tuition reimbursements, research assistantships with full tuition reimbursements, teaching assistantships with full tuition reimbursements, institutionally sponsored loans, scholarships/grants, and unspecified assistantships available. Financial award application deadline: 3/1; financial award applicants required to submit FAFSA. *Unit head:* Dr. Elza Ibroscheva, Program Director, 618-650-2242, E-mail: eibrosc@siue.edu. *Application contact:* Melissa K. Mace, Assistant Director of Admissions for Graduate and International Recruitment, 618-650-2756, Fax: 618-650-3618, E-mail: mmace@siue.edu.
Website: http://www.siue.edu/MASSCOMM/

Stanford University, School of Humanities and Sciences, Department of Communication, Stanford, CA 94305-9991. Offers communication theory and research (PhD); journalism (MA); media studies (MA). *Faculty:* 13 full-time (4 women), 1 part-time/adjunct (0 women). *Students:* 66 full-time (39 women). Average age 29. 152 applicants, 25% accepted, 31 enrolled. In 2014, 25 master's, 3 doctorates awarded. Terminal master's awarded for partial completion of doctoral program. *Degree requirements:* For master's, thesis, project; for doctorate, thesis/dissertation, qualifying examination, area examination, 2 projects. *Entrance requirements:* For master's and doctorate, GRE General Test. Additional exam requirements/recommendations for international students: Required—TOEFL (minimum score 650 paper-based; 115 iBT). *Application deadline:* For fall admission, 12/2 for domestic students, 12/3 for international students. Application fee: $125. Electronic applications accepted. *Expenses: Tuition:* Full-time $44,184; part-time $982 per credit hour. *Required fees:* $191. *Financial support:* Fellowships, research assistantships, and teaching assistantships available. *Unit head:* James T. Hamilton, Chair, 650-723-5448, E-mail: jayth@stanford.edu. *Application contact:* Katrin Wheeler, Student Services Manager, 650-724-8920, Fax: 650-725-2472, E-mail: comm-studentservices@stanford.edu.
Website: http://communication.stanford.edu/

Syracuse University, S. I. Newhouse School of Public Communications, Program in Media Studies, Syracuse, NY 13244. Offers MA. *Students:* 19 full-time (13 women), 4 part-time (2 women); includes 4 minority (2 Black or African American, non-Hispanic/Latino; 1 Asian, non-Hispanic/Latino; 1 Hispanic/Latino), 13 international. Average age 25. 63 applicants, 57% accepted, 11 enrolled. In 2014, 10 master's awarded. *Degree requirements:* For master's, thesis. *Entrance requirements:* For master's, GRE General Test. Additional exam requirements/recommendations for international students: Required—TOEFL (minimum score 600 paper-based; 100 iBT). *Application deadline:* For fall admission, 1/15 priority date for domestic and international students. Application fee: $45. Electronic applications accepted. *Expenses: Tuition:* Part-time $1341 per credit. *Financial support:* Fellowships with full tuition reimbursements, research assistantships with partial tuition reimbursements, and teaching assistantships with partial tuition reimbursements available. Financial award application deadline: 1/1. *Unit head:* Bradley Gorham, Director of Media Studies Program, 315-443-3372, Fax: 315-443-3946, E-mail: pcgrad@syr.edu. *Application contact:* Graduate Records Office, 315-443-4039, E-mail: pcgrad@syr.edu.
Website: http://newhouse.syr.edu/

Syracuse University, S. I. Newhouse School of Public Communications, Program in New Media Management, Syracuse, NY 13244. Offers MS. *Students:* 21 full-time (18 women), 1 (woman) part-time; includes 3 minority (1 Asian, non-Hispanic/Latino; 2 Hispanic/Latino), 16 international. Average age 24. 63 applicants, 78% accepted, 19 enrolled. In 2014, 30 master's awarded. *Degree requirements:* For master's, thesis optional, capstone course. *Entrance requirements:* For master's, GRE General Test or GMAT. Additional exam requirements/recommendations for international students: Required—TOEFL (minimum score 600 paper-based; 100 iBT). *Application deadline:* For fall admission, 2/1 for domestic and international students; for summer admission, 1/15 priority date for domestic and international students. Application fee: $45. Electronic applications accepted. *Expenses: Tuition:* Part-time $1341 per credit. *Financial support:* Fellowships with full tuition reimbursements, research assistantships with partial tuition reimbursements, and teaching assistantships with partial tuition reimbursements available. Financial award application deadline: 2/1. *Unit head:* Prof. Stephen Masiclat, Director, 315-443-9243, Fax: 315-443-3946, E-mail: pcgrad@syr.edu. *Application contact:* Graduate Records Office, 315-443-4039, Fax: 315-334-1834, E-mail: pcgrad@syr.edu.
Website: http://newhouse.syr.edu/

Syracuse University, S. I. Newhouse School of Public Communications, Program in Television, Radio, and Film, Syracuse, NY 13244. Offers MA. *Students:* 48 full-time (33 women), 4 part-time (2 women); includes 15 minority (8 Black or African American, non-Hispanic/Latino; 1 Asian, non-Hispanic/Latino; 4 Hispanic/Latino; 2 Two or more races, non-Hispanic/Latino), 19 international. Average age 25. 74 applicants, 84% accepted, 44 enrolled. In 2014, 36 master's awarded. *Degree requirements:* For master's, comprehensive exam. *Entrance requirements:* For master's, GRE General Test. Additional exam requirements/recommendations for international students: Required—TOEFL (minimum score 600 paper-based; 100 iBT). *Application deadline:* For fall admission, 2/1 for domestic and international students; for summer admission, 1/15 priority date for domestic and international students. Application fee: $45. Electronic applications accepted. *Expenses: Tuition:* Part-time $1341 per credit. *Financial support:* Fellowships with full tuition reimbursements, research assistantships with partial tuition reimbursements, and teaching assistantships with partial tuition reimbursements available. Financial award application deadline: 1/15. *Unit head:* Michael Schoonmaker, Chair, 315-443-4004, Fax: 315-443-3946, E-mail: pcgrad@syr.edu. *Application contact:* Graduate Records Office, 315-443-4039, Fax: 315-443-1834, E-mail: pcgrad@syr.edu.
Website: http://newhouse.syr.edu/

Temple University, School of Media and Communication, Department of Media Studies and Production, Philadelphia, PA 19122-6096. Offers MA. Part-time programs available. *Faculty:* 15 full-time (7 women), 15 part-time/adjunct (5 women). *Students:* 70 full-time (44 women), 11 part-time (6 women); includes 7 minority (5 Black or African American, non-Hispanic/Latino; 2 Asian, non-Hispanic/Latino), 30 international. 98 applicants, 48% accepted, 22 enrolled. In 2014, 5 master's awarded. *Degree requirements:* For master's, thesis optional. *Entrance requirements:* For master's, GRE General Test, minimum GPA of 3.0. Additional exam requirements/recommendations for international students: Required—TOEFL (minimum score 600 paper-based; 100 iBT). *Application deadline:* For fall admission, 2/15 for domestic and international students. Application fee: $60. Electronic applications accepted. *Expenses:* Expenses: Contact institution. *Financial support:* Career-related internships or fieldwork and Federal Work-Study available. Financial award application deadline: 1/15; financial award applicants required to submit FAFSA. *Faculty research:* Media institutions, international communications, communication policy, media theory. *Unit head:* Dr. Nancy Morris, Chair, 215-204-8394, E-mail: amorri@temple.edu. *Application contact:* Nicole McKenna, Director, Office of Research and Graduate Studies, 215-204-1497, Fax: 215-204-0310, E-mail: nmckenna@temple.edu.
Website: http://smc.temple.edu/msp/

Trinity College, Graduate Programs, Program in English, Hartford, CT 06106-3100. Offers literary studies (MA); writing, rhetoric, and media arts (MA). Part-time and evening/weekend programs available. *Degree requirements:* For master's, thesis (for some programs). *Entrance requirements:* For master's, minimum GPA of 3.0.

University at Buffalo, the State University of New York, Graduate School, College of Arts and Sciences, Department of Media Study, Buffalo, NY 14260. Offers film studies (MAH); media arts production (MFA); media study (PhD); new media design (Certificate); M Arch/MFA. *Faculty:* 11 full-time (4 women), 3 part-time/adjunct (1 woman). *Students:* 59 (33 women); includes 20 minority (1 Black or African American, non-Hispanic/Latino; 17 Asian, non-Hispanic/Latino; 1 Hispanic/Latino; 1 Two or more races, non-Hispanic/Latino). Average age 26. 66 applicants, 20% accepted, 10 enrolled. In 2014, 15 master's awarded. Terminal master's awarded for partial completion of doctoral program. *Degree requirements:* For master's, thesis, Thesis and media project; for doctorate, thesis/dissertation, qualifying exam, dissertation includes media project. *Entrance requirements:* For master's, portfolio; for doctorate, GRE, portfolio. Additional exam requirements/recommendations for international students: Required—TOEFL (minimum score 550 paper-based; 79 iBT). *Application deadline:* For fall admission, 1/7 priority date for domestic and international students. Applications are processed on a rolling basis. Application fee: $75. Electronic applications accepted. *Financial support:* In 2014–15, 11 students received support, including 2 fellowships (averaging $4,000 per year), 11 teaching assistantships with full tuition reimbursements available (averaging $13,480 per year); career-related internships or fieldwork, Federal Work-Study, scholarships/grants, health care benefits, and unspecified assistantships also available. Support available to part-time students. Financial award application deadline: 1/5; financial award applicants required to submit FAFSA. *Faculty research:* Digital arts, video, documentary, film, game design, digital poetics, locative media. *Total annual research expenditures:* $44,875. *Unit head:* Prof. Josephine Anstey, Chair, 716-645-6902, Fax: 716-645-6979, E-mail: jranstey@buffalo.edu. *Application contact:* Ann Mangan, Academic Advisor & Graduate Coordinator, 716-645-0945, Fax: 716-645-6979, E-mail: annmanga@buffalo.edu.
Website: http://mediastudy.buffalo.edu/

The University of Alabama, Graduate School, College of Communication and Information Sciences, Department of Telecommunication and Film, Tuscaloosa, AL 35487-0152. Offers MA. *Faculty:* 14 full-time (4 women). *Students:* 8 full-time (4 women), 1 part-time (0 women); includes 2 minority (1 Black or African American, non-Hispanic/Latino; 1 Two or more races, non-Hispanic/Latino), 3 international. Average age 25. 17 applicants, 53% accepted, 7 enrolled. In 2014, 4 master's awarded. Terminal master's awarded for partial completion of doctoral program. *Degree requirements:* For master's, comprehensive exam, thesis or alternative. *Entrance requirements:* For master's, GRE, minimum GPA of 3.0. Additional exam requirements/recommendations for international students: Required—TOEFL (minimum score 600 paper-based; 79 iBT). *Application deadline:* For fall admission, 4/15 priority date for domestic students, 1/15 priority date for international students; for spring admission, 11/1 for domestic students, 10/1 priority date for international students. Applications are processed on a rolling basis. Application fee: $50 ($60 for international students). Electronic applications accepted. *Expenses:* Tuition, state resident: full-time $9826. Tuition, nonresident: full-time $24,950. *Financial support:* In 2014–15, 6 students received support, including 2 research assistantships with tuition reimbursements available (averaging $9,825 per year), 2 teaching assistantships with tuition reimbursements available (averaging $9,825 per year); institutionally sponsored loans also available. Financial award application deadline: 2/15. *Faculty research:* Entertainment theory, news and public affairs, effects of telecommunications, management, media law and policy. *Unit head:* Dr. Gary A. Copeland, Chair, 205-348-6350, Fax: 205-348-5162, E-mail: copeland@ua.edu. *Application contact:* Dr. Shuhua Zhou, Graduate Coordinator, 205-348-8653, Fax: 205-348-5162, E-mail: szhou@bama.ua.edu.
Website: http://www.tcf.ua.edu

University of Bridgeport, College of Public and International Affairs, Bridgeport, CT 06604. Offers East Asian and Pacific Rim studies (MA); global development and peace (MA); global media and communication studies (MA). Part-time and evening/weekend programs available. *Degree requirements:* For master's, thesis. *Entrance requirements:* Additional exam requirements/recommendations for international students: Recommended—TOEFL (minimum score 550 paper-based; 80 iBT), IELTS (minimum score 6.5).

University of California, Los Angeles, Graduate Division, School of Theater, Film and Television, Department of Film, Television, and Digital Media, Los Angeles, CA 90034. Offers animation (MFA); cinema and media studies (MA, PhD); cinematography (MFA); production (MFA); screenwriting (MFA). *Degree requirements:* For master's, comprehensive exam; for doctorate, one foreign language, thesis/dissertation, oral and written qualifying exams. *Entrance requirements:* For master's, GRE General Test (for MA applicants), bachelor's degree; minimum undergraduate GPA of 3.0 (or its equivalent if letter grade system not used); writing sample (for MA); for doctorate, GRE General Test, master's degree; minimum undergraduate GPA of 3.0 (or its equivalent if letter grade system not used); writing sample. Additional exam requirements/recommendations for international students: Required—TOEFL. Electronic applications accepted. *Expenses:* Contact institution.

University of California, Santa Barbara, Graduate Division, College of Letters and Sciences, Division of Humanities and Fine Arts, Department of Media Arts and Technology, Santa Barbara, CA 93106-6065. Offers MS, PhD. Terminal master's awarded for partial completion of doctoral program. *Degree requirements:* For master's, thesis; for doctorate, comprehensive exam, thesis/dissertation. *Entrance requirements:* For master's and doctorate, GRE. Additional exam requirements/recommendations for international students: Required—TOEFL (minimum score 550 paper-based; 80 iBT), IELTS (minimum score 7). Electronic applications accepted. *Faculty research:* Transarchitectures and worldmaking, virtual and mixed reality, visualization, intelligent space and interactive installation, human-computer interaction.

University of Chicago, Division of the Humanities, Department of Cinema and Media Studies, Chicago, IL 60637. Offers PhD. *Students:* 37 full-time (21 women); includes 5 minority (3 Black or African American, non-Hispanic/Latino; 2 Two or more races, non-Hispanic/Latino), 13 international. 124 applicants, 31% accepted, 6 enrolled. Terminal master's awarded for partial completion of doctoral program. *Degree requirements:* For doctorate, 2 foreign languages, thesis/dissertation. *Entrance requirements:* For doctorate, GRE General Test. Additional exam requirements/recommendations for international students: Required—TOEFL (minimum score 104 iBT), IELTS (minimum score 7). *Application deadline:* For fall admission, 12/15 for domestic and international students. Application fee: $90. Electronic applications accepted. *Expenses: Tuition:* Full-time $46,899. *Required fees:* $347. *Financial support:* Fellowships with full tuition reimbursements, teaching assistantships with tuition reimbursements, institutionally sponsored loans, scholarships/grants, and health care benefits available. Financial award application deadline: 12/15; financial award applicants required to submit FAFSA. *Unit head:* Dr. James Chandler, Chair, 773-702-8274. *Application contact:* Braden Grams, Assistant Dean of Students, Admissions and Fellowships, 773-702-1552, Fax: 773-834-9148, E-mail: humanitiesadmissions@uchicago.edu.
Website: http://humanities.uchicago.edu/cmtes/cms/

University of Colorado Boulder, Graduate School, College of Engineering and Applied Science, Alliance for Technology, Learning, and Society Program, Boulder, CO 80309.

Offers information and communication technology for development (MS); technology, media, and society (PhD). *Students:* 37 full-time (23 women), 6 part-time (3 women); includes 8 minority (3 Black or African American, non-Hispanic/Latino; 2 American Indian or Alaska Native, non-Hispanic/Latino; 2 Hispanic/Latino; 1 Two or more races, non-Hispanic/Latino), 5 international. Average age 36. 42 applicants, 57% accepted, 16 enrolled. In 2014, 10 master's, 3 doctorates awarded. *Entrance requirements:* For master's, minimum undergraduate GPA of 3.0. *Application deadline:* For fall admission, 1/9 for domestic students, 12/1 for international students; for spring admission, 11/15 for domestic and international students. Application fee: $50 ($70 for international students). Electronic applications accepted. *Financial support:* In 2014–15, 53 students received support, including 20 fellowships (averaging $13,335 per year), 10 research assistantships with full and partial tuition reimbursements available (averaging $38,254 per year), 2 teaching assistantships with full and partial tuition reimbursements available (averaging $41,842 per year); institutionally sponsored loans, scholarships/grants, health care benefits, and unspecified assistantships also available. Financial award application deadline: 1/15; financial award applicants required to submit FAFSA. *Faculty research:* Evaluation of the Dissector Tool based on the Visible Human Data Project, assessing student outcomes for SENCER (an NSF-sponsored program using civic engagement to increase the interest and learning in undergraduate science at over 300 U.S. universities). Website: http://www.colorado.edu/ATLAS/

University of Colorado Boulder, Graduate School, School of Journalism and Mass Communication, Program in Communication, Boulder, CO 80309. Offers media studies (PhD). *Students:* 22 full-time (12 women), 4 part-time (all women), 6 international. Average age 33. 26 applicants, 42% accepted, 5 enrolled. In 2014, 3 doctorates awarded. *Entrance requirements:* For doctorate, GRE General Test, minimum undergraduate GPA of 3.25. Additional exam requirements/recommendations for international students: Required—TOEFL. *Application deadline:* For fall admission, 2/15 for domestic and international students. Application fee: $50 ($70 for international students). Electronic applications accepted. *Financial support:* In 2014–15, 56 students received support, including 3 fellowships (averaging $11,681 per year), 10 research assistantships with full and partial tuition reimbursements available (averaging $33,458 per year), 11 teaching assistantships with full and partial tuition reimbursements available (averaging $38,986 per year); institutionally sponsored loans, scholarships/grants, health care benefits, and unspecified assistantships also available. Financial award application deadline: 3/1; financial award applicants required to submit FAFSA. Website: http://journalism.colorado.edu/academics/graduate/doctoral-degree/

University of Florida, Graduate School, College of Journalism and Communications, Gainesville, FL 32611. Offers advertising (M Adv); journalism (MAMC); mass communication (MAMC, PhD); public relations (MAMC); telecommunication (MAMC); JD/MAMC; JD/PhD. *Accreditation:* ACEJMC (one or more programs are accredited). Part-time programs available. Postbaccalaureate distance learning degree programs offered. *Faculty:* 33 full-time (17 women), 3 part-time/adjunct (2 women). *Students:* 148 full-time (103 women), 201 part-time (144 women); includes 77 minority (29 Black or African American, non-Hispanic/Latino; 8 Asian, non-Hispanic/Latino; 40 Hispanic/Latino), 72 international. 410 applicants, 39% accepted, 86 enrolled. In 2014, 107 master's, 12 doctorates awarded. *Degree requirements:* For master's, comprehensive exam (for some programs), thesis; for doctorate, comprehensive exam (for some programs), thesis/dissertation. *Entrance requirements:* For master's and doctorate, GRE General Test 156 Verbal, 146 Quantitative, minimum GPA of 3.0. resume, statement of goals, 3 letters of recommendation. Additional exam requirements/recommendations for international students: Required—TOEFL (minimum score 550 paper-based; 80 iBT), IELTS (minimum score 6). *Application deadline:* For fall admission, 4/1 for domestic students, 1/30 for international students; for spring admission, 4/15 for domestic students, 7/15 for international students. Applications are processed on a rolling basis. Application fee: $30. Electronic applications accepted. *Financial support:* Career-related internships or fieldwork, Federal Work-Study, institutionally sponsored loans, and unspecified assistantships available. Support available to part-time students. Financial award application deadline: 3/15; financial award applicants required to submit FAFSA. *Faculty research:* Translational communication in science, technology, engineering, medicine, and health; international and intercultural communication; audience analysis and media effects; social interest communication, grassroots activism, and civic engagement; corporate social responsibility. *Total annual research expenditures:* $1.1 million. *Unit head:* Diane McFarlin, Dean, 352-392-0466, Fax: 352-392-1794, E-mail: dmcfarlin@ufl.edu. *Application contact:* Debbie M. Treise, PhD, Senior Associate Dean, Division of Graduate Studies and Research, 352-392-6557, E-mail: dtreise@jou.ufl.edu. Website: http://www.jou.ufl.edu/

University of Illinois at Urbana–Champaign, Graduate College, College of Fine and Applied Arts, School of Art and Design, Program in Design and Media, Champaign, IL 61820. Offers art and design (MFA), including new media; graphic design (MFA); industrial design (MFA). *Accreditation:* NASAD. *Students:* 11 (8 women). Application fee: $70 ($90 for international students). *Unit head:* Ernest Scott, Chair, 217-333-1579, E-mail: ernscott@illinois.edu. *Application contact:* Ellen de Waard, Coordinator of Graduate Academic Affairs, 217-333-0642, Fax: 217-244-7688, E-mail: edewaard@illinois.edu. Website: http://www.art.illinois.edu

University of Illinois at Urbana–Champaign, Graduate College, College of Media, Institute of Communications Research, Champaign, IL 61820. Offers communications and media (PhD). *Students:* 41 (28 women). Application fee: $70 ($90 for international students). *Faculty research:* Feminist cultural studies, media technology, international communications, Latino studies, economics of media. *Unit head:* William Berry, Head, 217-333-1602, Fax: 217-244-7695, E-mail: weberry@illinois.edu. *Application contact:* Theresa L. Harris, Office Manager, 217-333-1549, Fax: 217-333-1549, E-mail: tharris@illinois.edu. Website: http://www.media.illinois.edu/icr/

The University of Iowa, Graduate College, College of Liberal Arts and Sciences, Department of Communication Studies, Iowa City, IA 52242-1316. Offers interpersonal communication and relationships (MA, PhD); media studies (MA, PhD); rhetoric and public advocacy (MA, PhD). *Degree requirements:* For master's, thesis optional, exam; for doctorate, comprehensive exam, thesis/dissertation. *Entrance requirements:* For master's and doctorate, GRE General Test, minimum GPA of 3.0. Additional exam requirements/recommendations for international students: Required—TOEFL (minimum score 550 paper-based; 81 iBT). Electronic applications accepted.

The University of Iowa, Graduate College, College of Liberal Arts and Sciences, School of Journalism and Mass Communication, Iowa City, IA 52242-1316. Offers journalism and media communication (MA); mass communication (PhD); strategic communication (MA); JD/MA; JD/PhD. *Degree requirements:* For master's, thesis optional, exam; for doctorate, comprehensive exam, thesis/dissertation. *Entrance requirements:* For master's and doctorate, GRE General Test, minimum GPA of 3.0. Additional exam requirements/recommendations for international students: Required—TOEFL (minimum score 637 paper-based; 110 iBT). Electronic applications accepted. *Faculty research:* Verbal and visual aspects of historical, legal, social, and cross-cultural communication.

The University of Kansas, Graduate Studies, College of Liberal Arts and Sciences, Department of Film and Media Studies, Lawrence, KS 66045. Offers MA, PhD. *Faculty:* 11 full-time, 4 part-time/adjunct. *Students:* 18 full-time (6 women), 1 (woman) part-time; includes 3 minority (1 American Indian or Alaska Native, non-Hispanic/Latino; 1 Asian, non-Hispanic/Latino; 1 Two or more races, non-Hispanic/Latino), 2 international. Average age 33. 13 applicants, 54% accepted, 1 enrolled. In 2014, 3 doctorates awarded. *Degree requirements:* For master's, thesis; for doctorate, one foreign language, comprehensive exam, thesis/dissertation. *Entrance requirements:* For master's, GRE General Test, minimum GPA of 3.0; for doctorate, GRE General Test, minimum GPA of 3.5; MA in film or related field. Additional exam requirements/recommendations for international students: Required—TOEFL or IELTS. *Application deadline:* For fall admission, 1/1 for domestic and international students. Application fee: $55 ($65 for international students). Electronic applications accepted. *Financial support:* Teaching assistantships with full and partial tuition reimbursements available. Financial award application deadline: 1/1; financial award applicants required to submit FAFSA. *Faculty research:* Latin American cinema, Japanese and East Asian cinema, new media/cultural geography of media, film history, film theory and visual culture. *Unit head:* Dr. Tamara L. Falicov, Chair, 785-864-1353, E-mail: tfalicov@ku.edu. *Application contact:* Karla Conrad, Graduate Secretary, 785-864-1340, E-mail: kmconrad@ku.edu. Website: http://film.ku.edu/

University of Lethbridge, School of Graduate Studies, Lethbridge, AB T1K 3M4, Canada. Offers addictions counseling (M Sc); agricultural biotechnology (M Sc); agricultural studies (M Sc, MA); anthropology (MA); archaeology (M Sc, MA); art (MA, MFA); biochemistry (M Sc); biological sciences (M Sc); biomolecular science (PhD); biosystems and biodiversity (PhD); Canadian studies (MA); chemistry (M Sc); computer science (M Sc); computer science and geographical information science (M Sc); counseling (MC); counseling psychology (M Ed); dramatic arts (MA); earth, space, and physical science (PhD); economics (MA); education (MA); educational leadership (M Ed); English (MA); environmental science (M Sc); evolution and behavior (PhD); exercise science (M Sc); French (MA); French/German (MA); French/Spanish (MA); general education (M Ed); geography (M Sc, MA); German (MA); health sciences (M Sc); individualized multidisciplinary (M Sc, MA); kinesiology (M Sc, MA); management (M Sc), including accounting, finance, general management, human resource management and labor relations, information systems, international management, marketing, policy and strategy; mathematics (M Sc); modern languages (MA); music (M Mus, MA); Native American studies (MA); neuroscience (M Sc, PhD); new media (MA, MFA); nursing (M Sc, MN); philosophy (MA); physics (M Sc); political science (MA); psychology (M Sc, MA); religious studies (MA); sociology (MA); theatre and dramatic arts (MFA); theoretical and computational science (PhD); urban and regional studies (MA); women and gender studies (MA). Part-time and evening/weekend programs available. *Faculty:* 358. *Students:* 445 full-time (243 women), 116 part-time (72 women). Average age 31. 351 applicants, 26% accepted, 87 enrolled. In 2014, 129 master's, 13 doctorates awarded. *Degree requirements:* For master's, thesis (for some programs); for doctorate, comprehensive exam, thesis/dissertation. *Entrance requirements:* For master's, GMAT (for M Sc in management), bachelor's degree in related field, minimum GPA of 3.0 during previous 20 graded semester courses, 2 years' teaching or related experience (M Ed); for doctorate, master's degree, minimum graduate GPA of 3.5. Additional exam requirements/recommendations for international students: Required—TOEFL. Application fee: $100 Canadian dollars. *Financial support:* Fellowships, research assistantships, teaching assistantships, scholarships/grants, health care benefits, and unspecified assistantships available. *Faculty research:* Movement and brain plasticity, gibberellin physiology, photosynthesis, carbon cycling, molecular properties of main-group ring compounds. *Application contact:* School of Graduate Studies, 403-329-5194, E-mail: sgsinquiries@uleth.ca. Website: http://www.uleth.ca/graduatestudies/

University of Maryland, College Park, Academic Affairs, Phillip Merrill College of Journalism, College Park, MD 20742. Offers broadcast journalism (MA); journalism (MA); journalism and media studies (PhD); online news (MA); public affairs reporting (MA). *Accreditation:* ACEJMC (one or more programs are accredited). Part-time and evening/weekend programs available. *Faculty:* 22 full-time (13 women), 53 part-time/adjunct (23 women). *Students:* 63 full-time (35 women), 6 part-time (2 women); includes 16 minority (9 Black or African American, non-Hispanic/Latino; 4 Asian, non-Hispanic/Latino; 3 Hispanic/Latino), 14 international. 117 applicants, 38% accepted, 15 enrolled. In 2014, 22 master's, 6 doctorates awarded. *Degree requirements:* For doctorate, thesis/dissertation, preliminary written and oral comprehensive exams. *Entrance requirements:* For master's and doctorate, GRE General Test, minimum GPA of 3.0, 3 letters of recommendation. Additional exam requirements/recommendations for international students: Required—TOEFL. *Application deadline:* For fall admission, 2/1 for domestic and international students; for summer admission, 2/1 for domestic and international students. Application fee: $75. Electronic applications accepted. *Financial support:* In 2014–15, 9 fellowships with full and partial tuition reimbursements (averaging $24,407 per year), 25 teaching assistantships (averaging $17,009 per year) were awarded; career-related internships or fieldwork, Federal Work-Study, and scholarships/grants also available. Support available to part-time students. Financial award applicants required to submit FAFSA. *Faculty research:* Mass communication theory, specialized journalism, new telecommunication technologies, press integration. *Total annual research expenditures:* $230,123. *Unit head:* Lucy A. Dalglish, Dean, 301-405-8806, Fax: 301-314-1978, E-mail: dalglish@umd.edu. *Application contact:* Dr. Charles A. Caramello, Dean of Graduate School, 301-405-0358, Fax: 301-314-9305, E-mail: ccaramel@umd.edu. Website: http://www.journalism.umd.edu/

University of Michigan, Horace H. Rackham School of Graduate Studies, School of Music, Theatre, and Dance, Program in Media Arts, Ann Arbor, MI 48109-2085. Offers MA. *Entrance requirements:* For master's, GRE, portfolio. Additional exam requirements/recommendations for international students: Required—TOEFL.

University of Missouri, Office of Research and Graduate Studies, School of Journalism, Columbia, MO 65211. Offers center for the digital globe (Certificate); European Union studies (Certificate); health communications (MA); interactive media (MA); journalism (PhD); media management (MA); strategic communication (MA). *Accreditation:* ACEJMC (one or more programs are accredited). Part-time programs available. *Faculty:* 75 full-time (38 women), 3 part-time/adjunct (1 woman). *Students:* 159 full-time (104 women), 88 part-time (54 women); includes 33 minority (8 Black or African American, non-Hispanic/Latino; 11 Asian, non-Hispanic/Latino; 11 Hispanic/Latino; 3 Two or more races, non-Hispanic/Latino), 57 international. Average age 29. 239 applicants, 55% accepted, 78 enrolled. In 2014, 73 master's, 8 doctorates awarded. Terminal master's awarded for partial completion of doctoral program. *Degree requirements:* For master's, thesis (for some programs); for doctorate, 2 foreign languages, thesis/dissertation. *Entrance requirements:* For master's and doctorate, GRE General Test, minimum GPA of 3.0. Additional exam requirements/recommendations for international students: Required—TOEFL (minimum score 600 paper-based; 100 iBT). *Application deadline:* For fall admission, 12/15 priority date for domestic and international students; for winter admission, 9/1 priority date for domestic and international students. Applications are processed on a rolling basis. Application fee: $55 ($75 for international students). Electronic applications accepted. *Financial*

support: Fellowships with tuition reimbursements, research assistantships with tuition reimbursements, teaching assistantships with tuition reimbursements, career-related internships or fieldwork, institutionally sponsored loans, scholarships/grants, health care benefits, and unspecified assistantships available. Support available to part-time students. *Faculty research:* Strategic communication, convergence journalism, journalism studies, international programs, photojournalism, magazine journalism, radio-television journalism. *Unit head:* Dr. Esther Thorson, Associate Dean, 573-882-9590, E-mail: thorsone@missouri.edu. *Application contact:* Ginny Cowell, Administrative Assistant, 573-882-4852, E-mail: cowellvj@missouri.edu.
Website: http://www.journalism.missouri.edu/graduate/

University of Missouri–Kansas City, College of Arts and Sciences, Department of English Language and Literature, Kansas City, MO 64110-2499. Offers creative writing and media arts (MFA); English (MA, PhD). PhD (interdisciplinary) offered through the School of Graduate Studies. Part-time and evening/weekend programs available. *Faculty:* 24 full-time (15 women), 8 part-time/adjunct (6 women). *Students:* 17 full-time (10 women), 34 part-time (21 women); includes 5 minority (2 Black or African American, non-Hispanic/Latino; 1 Asian, non-Hispanic/Latino; 1 Hispanic/Latino; 1 Two or more races, non-Hispanic/Latino). Average age 33. 58 applicants, 43% accepted, 14 enrolled. In 2014, 16 master's awarded. *Degree requirements:* For master's, one foreign language; for doctorate, 2 foreign languages, comprehensive exam, thesis/dissertation. *Entrance requirements:* For master's, GRE General Test, 3 letters of recommendation. Additional exam requirements/recommendations for international students: Required—TOEFL (minimum score 550 paper-based; 80 iBT). *Application deadline:* For fall admission, 1/15 for domestic students, 1/15 priority date for international students. Applications are processed on a rolling basis. Application fee: $45 ($50 for international students). Electronic applications accepted. *Financial support:* In 2014–15, 16 teaching assistantships (averaging $12,150 per year) were awarded; career-related internships or fieldwork, Federal Work-Study, and institutionally sponsored loans also available. Support available to part-time students. Financial award application deadline: 3/1; financial award applicants required to submit FAFSA. *Faculty research:* Creative writing: poetry and prose, computational linguistics, rhetoric and composition, African-American and British literature, print culture. *Unit head:* Dr. Virginia Blanton, Co-Chair, 816-235-2560, Fax: 816-235-1308, E-mail: blantonv@umkc.edu. *Application contact:* Dr. John Cyril Barton, Director of Graduate Studies, 816-235-5206, E-mail: bartonjc@umkc.edu.
Website: http://cas.umkc.edu/english/

University of Nevada, Las Vegas, Graduate College, Greenspun College of Urban Affairs, School of Journalism and Media Studies, Las Vegas, NV 89154-5007. Offers MA. *Faculty:* 5 full-time (0 women), 1 part-time/adjunct (0 women). *Students:* 12 full-time (9 women), 7 part-time (4 women); includes 7 minority (1 Black or African American, non-Hispanic/Latino; 3 Asian, non-Hispanic/Latino; 3 Hispanic/Latino), 2 international. Average age 29. 14 applicants, 79% accepted, 6 enrolled. In 2014, 11 master's awarded. *Entrance requirements:* For master's, GRE General Test. Additional exam requirements/recommendations for international students: Required—TOEFL (minimum score 550 paper-based; 80 iBT), IELTS (minimum score 7). *Application deadline:* For fall admission, 3/15 for domestic students, 5/1 for international students; for spring admission, 10/1 for international students. Application fee: $60 ($95 for international students). Electronic applications accepted. *Financial support:* In 2014–15, 8 students received support, including 1 research assistantship with partial tuition reimbursement available (averaging $10,000 per year), 7 teaching assistantships with partial tuition reimbursements available (averaging $10,000 per year); institutionally sponsored loans, scholarships/grants, health care benefits, and unspecified assistantships also available. Financial award application deadline: 3/1. *Faculty research:* Journalism, mass communication and media history; media law, First Amendment theory, First Amendment law, privacy, obscenity, libel; visual literacy, aesthetics and rhetoric, social psychology of visually-mediated world; global media, audience reception theory and research, video criticism, and advertising; intersection of society and media technologies, emerging technology. *Unit head:* Dr. Lawrence Mullen, Director/Professor, 702-895-4491, E-mail: lawrence.mullen@unlv.edu. *Application contact:* Graduate College Admissions Evaluator, 702-895-3320, Fax: 702-895-4180, E-mail: gradcollege@unlv.edu.
Website: http://journalism.unlv.edu/

The University of North Carolina at Charlotte, College of Liberal Arts and Sciences, Department of Communication Studies, Charlotte, NC 28223-0001. Offers communication studies (Graduate Certificate); health communication (MA); organizational communication (MA); public relations and international public relations (MA); rhetoric, media studies, and popular culture (MA). Part-time and evening/weekend programs available. *Faculty:* 15 full-time (8 women). *Students:* 11 full-time (8 women), 12 part-time (9 women); includes 3 minority (2 Black or African American, non-Hispanic/Latino; 1 Two or more races, non-Hispanic/Latino), 2 international. Average age 27. 49 applicants, 49% accepted, 11 enrolled. In 2014, 11 master's awarded. Terminal master's awarded for partial completion of doctoral program. *Degree requirements:* For master's, project, thesis, or comprehensive exam. *Entrance requirements:* For master's, GRE General Test, minimum GPA of 2.75 overall. Additional exam requirements/recommendations for international students: Required—TOEFL (minimum score 557 paper-based; 83 iBT). *Application deadline:* For fall admission, 3/1 for domestic and international students; for spring admission, 11/15 for domestic students, 10/1 for international students. Application fee: $75. Electronic applications accepted. *Expenses:* Tuition, state resident: full-time $4008. Tuition, nonresident: full-time $16,295. *Required fees:* $2755. Tuition and fees vary according to course load and program. *Financial support:* In 2014–15, 10 students received support, including 10 teaching assistantships (averaging $14,981 per year); career-related internships or fieldwork, institutionally sponsored loans, scholarships/grants, and unspecified assistantships also available. Support available to part-time students. Financial award application deadline: 4/1; financial award applicants required to submit FAFSA. *Faculty research:* Rhetorical approaches to analyzing public relations controversies, participant empowerment and engagement in community-based participatory action research, human factors constraining the management of knowledge in a large financial services organization, models of Internet governance, race and class politics of mediated sports. *Unit head:* Dr. Shawn Long, Chair, 704-687-0783, Fax: 704-687-6900, E-mail: shawn.long@uncc.edu. *Application contact:* Kathy B. Giddings, Director of Graduate Admissions, 704-687-5503, Fax: 704-687-1668, E-mail: gradadm@uncc.edu.
Website: http://gradcomm.uncc.edu/

The University of North Carolina at Greensboro, Graduate School, College of Arts and Sciences, Department of Media Studies, Greensboro, NC 27412-5001. Offers film and video production (MFA).

University of Oregon, Graduate School, School of Architecture and Allied Arts, Program in Arts and Administration, Eugene, OR 97403. Offers arts management (MA, MS); media management (MA, MS). *Degree requirements:* For master's, summer internship, thesis/project. *Entrance requirements:* For master's, minimum GPA of 3.0; bachelor's degree in history, practice of visual, performing arts or other related degree. Additional exam requirements/recommendations for international students: Required—TOEFL. *Faculty research:* Museum education, arts program evaluation, community arts, information management, arts marketing.

University of Oregon, Graduate School, School of Journalism and Communication, Eugene, OR 97403. Offers journalism (MA, MS); media studies (MA, MS, PhD); multimedia journalism (MA, MS); strategic communication (MA, MS). *Accreditation:* ASHA. Part-time programs available. *Degree requirements:* For master's, thesis or alternative. *Entrance requirements:* For master's, GRE General Test; for doctorate, master's degree. *Faculty research:* Impact of mass communication, media technology, media accountability, craft attitudes, media economics.

University of South Carolina, The Graduate School, College of Arts and Sciences, Department of Art, Division of Media Arts, Columbia, SC 29208. Offers MMA. *Degree requirements:* For master's, thesis. *Entrance requirements:* For master's, GRE General Test, interview, portfolio. Additional exam requirements/recommendations for international students: Required—TOEFL. Electronic applications accepted. *Faculty research:* Three dimensional imaging, script writing.

University of Southern California, Graduate School, Annenberg School for Communication and Journalism, School of Communication, Program in Communication, Los Angeles, CA 90089. Offers culture and community (PhD); global and transnational communication (PhD); groups, organizations and networks (PhD); health communication and social dynamics (PhD); information, political economy and entertainment (PhD); new media and technology (PhD); rhetoric, politics and public media (PhD). *Students:* 105 full-time (76 women); includes 829 minority (8 Black or African American, non-Hispanic/Latino; 810 Asian, non-Hispanic/Latino; 7 Hispanic/Latino; 4 Two or more races, non-Hispanic/Latino), 41 international. Average age 27. 229 applicants, 14% accepted, 19 enrolled. In 2014, 16 doctorates awarded. *Degree requirements:* For doctorate, thesis/dissertation. *Entrance requirements:* For doctorate, GRE General Test, resume or curriculum vitae, scholarly writing, 3 letters of recommendation, statement of purpose. Additional exam requirements/recommendations for international students: Required—TOEFL (minimum score 114 iBT) or IELTS; Recommended—TWE. *Application deadline:* For fall admission, 11/1 for domestic and international students. Application fee: $85. Electronic applications accepted. *Financial support:* In 2014–15, 18 students received support, including 18 fellowships with full tuition reimbursements available (averaging $74,000 per year); health care benefits and unspecified assistantships also available. Financial award application deadline: 11/1; financial award applicants required to submit FAFSA. *Faculty research:* Computer-mediated communication, public health campaigns, communication democracy and the public sphere, new communication technologies in organizations, communication and community. *Unit head:* Dr. Peter Monge, Director of the PhD Program, 213-740-0921, E-mail: monge@usc.edu. *Application contact:* Allyson Hill, Associate Dean for Admissions, 213-821-0770, Fax: 213-740-1933, E-mail: ascadm@usc.edu.
Website: http://www.annenberg.usc.edu

University of Southern California, Graduate School, Annenberg School for Communication and Journalism, School of Communication, Program in Communication Management, Los Angeles, CA 90089. Offers MCM, JD/MCM, MCM/MAJCS. Part-time and evening/weekend programs available. Postbaccalaureate distance learning degree programs offered (no on-campus study). *Students:* 239 full-time, 82 part-time; includes 98 minority (25 Black or African American, non-Hispanic/Latino; 29 Asian, non-Hispanic/Latino; 39 Hispanic/Latino; 1 Native Hawaiian or other Pacific Islander, non-Hispanic/Latino; 4 Two or more races, non-Hispanic/Latino), 138 international. Average age 25. 506 applicants, 48% accepted, 141 enrolled. In 2014, 141 master's awarded. *Degree requirements:* For master's, professional project. *Entrance requirements:* For master's, GRE General Test or GMAT, resume, writing samples, recommendation letters, statement of purpose. Additional exam requirements/recommendations for international students: Required—TOEFL (minimum score 114 iBT) or IELTS. *Application deadline:* For fall admission, 5/1 priority date for domestic students, 1/15 priority date for international students; for spring admission, 10/1 for domestic students, 9/1 for international students. Applications are processed on a rolling basis. Application fee: $85. Electronic applications accepted. *Financial support:* Career-related internships or fieldwork, Federal Work-Study, institutionally sponsored loans, and scholarships/grants available. Support available to part-time students. Financial award application deadline: 1/2; financial award applicants required to submit FAFSA. *Faculty research:* Global communication, communication law and policy, entertainment management, marketing communication, strategic and corporate communication management. *Unit head:* Dr. Rebecca Weintraub, Director, 213-821-0764, Fax: 213-740-8036, E-mail: weintrau@usc.edu. *Application contact:* Allyson Hill, Associate Dean for Admissions, 213-821-0770, Fax: 213-740-1933, E-mail: ascadm@usc.edu.
Website: http://www.annenberg.usc.edu

University of Southern California, Graduate School, Annenberg School for Communication and Journalism, School of Communication, Program in Digital Social Media, Los Angeles, CA 90089. Offers MS. Part-time and evening/weekend programs available. *Students:* 14 full-time (9 women), 2 part-time (both women); includes 4 minority (2 Black or African American, non-Hispanic/Latino; 1 Asian, non-Hispanic/Latino; 1 Hispanic/Latino), 6 international. Average age 29. 33 applicants, 39% accepted, 12 enrolled. *Degree requirements:* For master's, dynamic digital media site or app launch. *Entrance requirements:* For master's, GRE General Test, resume, statement of purpose, writing sample, two letters of recommendation. Additional exam requirements/recommendations for international students: Required—TOEFL (minimum score 115 iBT) or IELTS (minimum recommended score 8). *Application deadline:* For spring admission, 10/15 for domestic and international students. Applications are processed on a rolling basis. Application fee: $85. Electronic applications accepted. *Financial support:* Career-related internships or fieldwork and Federal Work-Study available. Financial award applicants required to submit FAFSA. *Unit head:* Dr. Karen North, Clinical Professor of Communication and Director, Digital Social Media, 310-235-4444, E-mail: knorth@usc.edu. *Application contact:* Allyson Hill, Associate Dean of Admissions, 213-821-0770, E-mail: ascadm@usc.edu.
Website: http://www.annenberg.usc.edu

University of Southern California, Graduate School, Dana and David Dornsife College of Letters, Arts and Sciences, Comparative Studies in Literature and Culture Doctoral Program, Los Angeles, CA 90089. Offers comparative literature (PhD); comparative media and culture (PhD); Spanish and Latin American studies (PhD). *Degree requirements:* For doctorate, 2 foreign languages, comprehensive exam, thesis/dissertation. *Entrance requirements:* For doctorate, GRE, competence in language other than English (highly recommended). Additional exam requirements/recommendations for international students: Required—TOEFL. Electronic applications accepted. *Faculty research:* Literary theory, Japanese film and contemporary fiction, Francophone literature and cinema, Latin American and Caribbean literature, Spanish literature and film, nineteenth and twentieth century British and American literature.

University of Southern California, Graduate School, School of Cinematic Arts, Interactive Media Division, Los Angeles, CA 90089. Offers interactive media (MFA); media arts and practice (PhD). *Degree requirements:* For master's, thesis, thesis project. *Entrance requirements:* Additional exam requirements/recommendations for international students: Required—TOEFL (minimum score 600 paper-based; 100 iBT). Electronic applications accepted. *Expenses:* Contact institution. *Faculty research:*

Immersive media, mobile media, stereoscopic, game design and development, serious games and games for health and learning, experiments in game play.

University of Southern California, Graduate School, School of Cinematic Arts, Interdivisional Program in Media Arts and Practice, Los Angeles, CA 90089. Offers PhD. *Degree requirements:* For doctorate, 2 foreign languages, thesis/dissertation. *Entrance requirements:* For doctorate, GRE, portfolio. Additional exam requirements/ recommendations for international students: Required—TOEFL. Electronic applications accepted. *Faculty research:* Transmedia, theory and history of emerging technologies; documentary and experimental film and video; interactive media design; telepresence research and mobile media.

University of South Florida, College of Arts and Sciences, School of Mass Communications, Tampa, FL 33620-9951. Offers media studies (MA), including media studies; multimedia journalism studies (MA); strategic communication management (MA). Part-time and evening/weekend programs available. *Faculty:* 10 full-time (3 women). *Students:* 17 full-time (13 women), 17 part-time (6 women); includes 5 minority (2 Black or African American, non-Hispanic/Latino; 1 Asian, non-Hispanic/Latino; 2 Hispanic/Latino), 7 international. Average age 29. 40 applicants, 65% accepted, 14 enrolled. In 2014, 15 master's awarded. *Degree requirements:* For master's, comprehensive exam, thesis optional. *Entrance requirements:* For master's, GRE General Test (minimum score of 153 verbal and 144 quantitative preferred), minimum GPA of 3.0 in last 60 hours of course work, three letters of recommendation, letter of intent, resume. Additional exam requirements/recommendations for international students: Required—TOEFL (minimum score 550 paper-based; 79 iBT) or IELTS (minimum score 6.5). *Application deadline:* For fall admission, 2/15 for domestic students, 1/2 for international students; for spring admission, 10/15 for domestic students, 6/1 for international students. Application fee: $30. Electronic applications accepted. *Financial support:* In 2014–15, 9 students received support, including 9 teaching assistantships with tuition reimbursements available (averaging $10,513 per year); unspecified assistantships also available. Financial award application deadline: 2/28. *Faculty research:* First Amendment analysis, civic journalism, public opinion, media ethics, media effects research in sports public relations, public relations management, advertisement, telecommunications. *Total annual research expenditures:* $52,955. *Unit head:* Dr. Jim Andrews, Interim Director and Associate Professor, 813-974-2108, Fax: 813-974-2592, E-mail: jimandrews@usf.edu. *Application contact:* Dr. Michael Mitrook, Assistant Professor, 813-974-8890, Fax: 813-974-2592, E-mail: mmitrook@.usf.edu. Website: http://masscom.usf.edu/grad/

University of South Florida, St. Petersburg, College of Arts and Sciences, St. Petersburg, FL 33701. Offers digital journalism and design (MA); environmental science and policy (MA, MS); Florida studies (MLA); journalism and media studies (MA); liberal studies (MLA); psychology (MA). Part-time programs available. Postbaccalaureate distance learning degree programs offered (no on-campus study). *Degree requirements:* For master's, comprehensive exam, thesis or project. *Entrance requirements:* For master's, GRE, LSAT, MCAT (varies by program), letter of intent, 3 letters of recommendation, writing samples, bachelor's degree from regionally-accredited institution with minimum GPA of 3.0 overall or in upper two years. Additional exam requirements/recommendations for international students: Required—TOEFL (minimum score 550 paper-based; 79 iBT); Recommended—IELTS. Electronic applications accepted.

The University of Tennessee, Graduate School, College of Communication and Information, Knoxville, TN 37996. Offers advertising (MS, PhD); broadcasting (MS, PhD); communications (MS, PhD); information sciences (MS, PhD); journalism (MS, PhD); public relations (MS, PhD); speech communication (MS, PhD). Part-time and evening/weekend programs available. Postbaccalaureate distance learning degree programs offered (no on-campus study). *Degree requirements:* For master's, thesis or alternative; for doctorate, thesis/dissertation. *Entrance requirements:* For master's and doctorate, GRE General Test, minimum GPA of 2.7. Additional exam requirements/ recommendations for international students: Required—TOEFL. Electronic applications accepted.

The University of Texas at Austin, Graduate School, College of Communication, Department of Radio-Television-Film, Austin, TX 78712-1111. Offers film and media production (MFA); media studies (MA, PhD); screenwriting (MFA). *Degree requirements:* For master's, thesis (for some programs); for doctorate, thesis/ dissertation. *Entrance requirements:* For master's and doctorate, GRE General Test. Electronic applications accepted. *Faculty research:* International communication, film studies, media and culture, telecommunication and new media, gender and sexuality.

The University of Western Ontario, Faculty of Graduate Studies, Faculty of Information and Media Studies, Programs in Media Studies, London, ON N6A 5B8, Canada. Offers MA, PhD. Part-time programs available. *Degree requirements:* For master's, thesis; for doctorate, comprehensive exam, thesis/dissertation. *Entrance requirements:* For master's, 2 letters of reference; for doctorate, MA in media studies, communications or related field. Additional exam requirements/recommendations for international students: Required—TOEFL (minimum score 625 paper-based), TWE (minimum score 5). Electronic applications accepted. *Faculty research:* Media cultures, media industries, media technologies.

University of Wisconsin–Madison, Graduate School, College of Letters and Science, Department of Communication Arts, Madison, WI 53706-1380. Offers communication science (MA, PhD); film (MA, PhD); media and cultural studies (MA, PhD); rhetoric (MA, PhD). Terminal master's awarded for partial completion of doctoral program. *Degree requirements:* For master's, one foreign language, thesis (for some programs); for doctorate, one foreign language, thesis/dissertation. *Entrance requirements:* For master's and doctorate, GRE General Test, minimum GPA of 3.5. Electronic applications accepted. *Expenses:* Tuition, state resident: full-time $10,723; part-time $745 per credit. Tuition, nonresident: full-time $24,054; part-time $1578 per credit. *Required fees:* $374 per semester. Tuition and fees vary according to course load, program and reciprocity agreements.

University of Wisconsin–Milwaukee, Graduate School, College of Letters and Sciences, Department of Media Studies, Milwaukee, WI 53201-0413. Offers media studies (MA); rhetorical leadership (Certificate). Part-time programs available. *Degree requirements:* For master's, thesis or alternative. *Entrance requirements:* For master's, GRE General Test, minimum GPA of 3.0. Additional exam requirements/ recommendations for international students: Required—TOEFL (minimum score 550 paper-based; 79 iBT), IELTS (minimum score 6.5). Electronic applications accepted.

University of Wisconsin–Stevens Point, College of Fine Arts and Communication, Division of Communication, Stevens Point, WI 54481-3897. Offers interpersonal communication (MA); media studies (MA); organizational communication (MA); public relations (MA). Part-time programs available. *Degree requirements:* For master's, thesis or alternative. *Entrance requirements:* For master's, GRE. Additional exam requirements/recommendations for international students: Required—TOEFL (minimum score 575 paper-based). *Faculty research:* Communication theory and research, film history.

Valparaiso University, Graduate School, Program in Media and Communication, Valparaiso, IN 46383. Offers digital media (MS); sports media (MS, Certificate). Part-time and evening/weekend programs available. *Students:* 17 full-time (6 women), 11 part-time (8 women); includes 4 minority (2 Black or African American, non-Hispanic/ Latino; 1 Hispanic/Latino; 1 Two or more races, non-Hispanic/Latino), 11 international. Average age 27. In 2014, 24 master's, 2 other advanced degrees awarded. *Entrance requirements:* For master's, minimum GPA of 3.0, undergraduate minor in communication. Additional exam requirements/recommendations for international students: Required—TOEFL (minimum score 550 paper-based; 80 iBT), IELTS (minimum score 6). *Application deadline:* Applications are processed on a rolling basis. Application fee: $30 ($50 for international students). Electronic applications accepted. *Expenses: Tuition:* Full-time $10,710; part-time $595 per credit hour. *Required fees:* $378; $101 per term. Tuition and fees vary according to course load and program. *Financial support:* Available to part-time students. Applicants required to submit FAFSA. *Unit head:* Dr. Jennifer A. Ziegler, Dean, Graduate School and Continuing Education, 219-464-5313, Fax: 219-464-5381, E-mail: jennifer.ziegler@valpo.edu. *Application contact:* Jessica Choquette, Graduate Admissions Specialist, 219-464-5313, Fax: 219-464-5381, E-mail: jessica.choquette@valpo.edu. Website: http://www.valpo.edu/grad/programs/masters.php

Virginia Commonwealth University, Graduate School, College of Humanities and Sciences, Department of English, Richmond, VA 23284-9005. Offers creative writing (MFA), including fiction, fictional poetry, poetry; English (MA), including literature, writing and rhetoric; media, art, and text (PhD). Part-time programs available. *Degree requirements:* For master's, thesis optional. *Entrance requirements:* For master's, GRE General Test, portfolio (MFA); for doctorate, GRE General Test. Additional exam requirements/recommendations for international students: Required—TOEFL (minimum score 600 paper-based; 100 iBT) or IELTS (minimum score 6.5). Electronic applications accepted.

Virginia Commonwealth University, Graduate School, College of Humanities and Sciences, School of Mass Communications, Program in Media, Art, and Text, Richmond, VA 23284-9005. Offers PhD. *Entrance requirements:* For doctorate, GRE. Additional exam requirements/recommendations for international students: Required—TOEFL (minimum score 600 paper-based; 100 iBT); Recommended—IELTS (minimum score 6.5). Electronic applications accepted.

Virginia State University, College of Graduate Studies, College of Humanities and Social Sciences, Department of Mass Communications, Petersburg, VA 23806-0001. Offers media management (MA).

Wayne State University, College of Fine, Performing and Communication Arts, Department of Communication, Detroit, MI 48202. Offers communication (PhD), including democratic participation and culture, identity and representation, media, society and culture, risk, crisis and conflict, wellness, worklife and relationships; communication and new media (Graduate Certificate); communication studies (MA); dispute resolution (MADR, Graduate Certificate); health communication (Graduate Certificate); journalism (MA); media arts (MA); media studies (MA); public relations and organizational communication (MA); JD/MADR. Doctoral programs admit for fall only. *Students:* 63 full-time (34 women), 82 part-time (63 women); includes 48 minority (40 Black or African American, non-Hispanic/Latino; 3 Asian, non-Hispanic/Latino; 3 Hispanic/Latino; 2 Two or more races, non-Hispanic/Latino), 13 international. Average age 35. 177 applicants, 40% accepted, 38 enrolled. In 2014, 33 master's, 4 doctorates, 9 other advanced degrees awarded. *Degree requirements:* For master's, thesis (for some programs), thesis or essay; for doctorate, thesis/dissertation. *Entrance requirements:* For master's, GRE (if undergraduate GPA less than 3.2), personal statement; BA or BS in communication or related field with minimum upper-division GPA of 3.2 and sample of academic writing (for MA); minimum upper-division undergraduate GPA of 3.0 and 3 letters of recommendation (for MADR); for doctorate, GRE, MA in communication or related field with minimum GPA of 3.5, three letters of recommendation; personal statement; sample of written scholarship; for Graduate Certificate, minimum upper-division GPA of 3.0, personal statement. Additional exam requirements/recommendations for international students: Required—TOEFL (minimum score 600 paper-based; 100 iBT), IELTS (minimum score 6.5), TWE (minimum score 6). *Application deadline:* For fall admission, 8/1 for domestic and international students; for winter admission, 11/1 for domestic and international students; for spring admission, 4/1 for domestic and international students. Application fee: $0. Electronic applications accepted. *Expenses:* Expenses: Contact institution. *Financial support:* In 2014–15, 48 students received support, including 3 fellowships with tuition reimbursements available (averaging $16,000 per year), 20 teaching assistantships with tuition reimbursements available (averaging $16,540 per year); research assistantships with tuition reimbursements available, scholarships/grants, and unspecified assistantships also available. Financial award application deadline: 3/31; financial award applicants required to submit FAFSA. *Faculty research:* Rhetorical theory and criticism; mass media theory and research; argumentation; organizational communication; risk and crisis communication; interpersonal, family, and health communication. *Unit head:* Dr. Lee Wilkins, Chair, 313-577-2943, E-mail: eh8899@wayne.edu. *Application contact:* Dr. Pradeep Sopory, Director of Graduate Studies, 313-577-2945, E-mail: psopory@wayne.edu. Website: http://comm.wayne.edu/

Webster University, George Herbert Walker School of Business and Technology, Department of Business, St. Louis, MO 63119-3194. Offers business and organizational security management (MBA); decision support systems (MBA); environmental management (MBA); finance (MBA, MS); forensic accounting (MS); gerontology (MBA); human resources development (MBA); human resources management (MBA); information technology management (MBA); international business (MA, MBA); international relations (MBA); management and leadership (MBA); marketing (MBA); media communications (MBA); procurement and acquisitions management (MBA); Web services (MBA). *Accreditation:* ACBSP. Part-time and evening/weekend programs available. Postbaccalaureate distance learning degree programs offered (no on-campus study). *Degree requirements:* For master's, comprehensive exam (for some programs), thesis (for some programs). *Entrance requirements:* Additional exam requirements/ recommendations for international students: Required—TOEFL.

Webster University, School of Communications, Program in Media Communications, St. Louis, MO 63119-3194. Offers MA.

Webster University, School of Communications, Program in Media Literacy, St. Louis, MO 63119-3194. Offers MA.

West Virginia State University, Media Studies Graduate Program, Institute, WV 25112-1000. Offers MA. *Degree requirements:* For master's, thesis, Comprehensive exam may be taken in lieu of a thesis. *Entrance requirements:* For master's, GRE (950), Undergraduate GPA of 3.0, Letters of Recommendation. Additional exam requirements/ recommendations for international students: Required—TOEFL (minimum score 550 paper-based). Electronic applications accepted.

Media Studies

Wilfrid Laurier University, Faculty of Graduate and Postdoctoral Studies, Faculty of Arts, Department of Communication Studies, Waterloo, ON N2L 3C5, Canada. Offers media, technology and culture (MA); visual communication and culture (MA). *Degree requirements:* For master's, thesis optional. *Entrance requirements:* For master's, honours BA in communication studies or a cognate discipline from an approved university with a minimum B+ overall in last two years of study and in undergraduate major. Additional exam requirements/recommendations for international students: Required—TOEFL (minimum score 89 iBT). Electronic applications accepted. *Faculty research:* Visual communication and culture, media, technology and culture.

Publishing

Arizona State University at the Tempe campus, College of Liberal Arts and Sciences, School of Historical, Philosophical and Religious Studies, Tempe, AZ 85287-4301. Offers European history (MA, PhD); medieval studies (Graduate Certificate); North American history (MA, PhD); philosophy (MA, PhD); public history (MA); religious studies (MA, PhD); Renaissance studies (Graduate Certificate); scholarly publishing (Graduate Certificate). Part-time programs available. Terminal master's awarded for partial completion of doctoral program. *Degree requirements:* For master's, thesis or alternative, interactive Program of Study (iPOS) submitted before completing 50 percent of required credit hours; for doctorate, variable foreign language requirement, comprehensive exam, thesis/dissertation, interactive Program of Study (iPOS) submitted before completing 50 percent of required credit hours. *Entrance requirements:* For master's and doctorate, GRE, minimum GPA of 3.0 or equivalent in last 2 years of work leading to bachelor's degree. Additional exam requirements/recommendations for international students: Required—TOEFL, IELTS, or PTE. Electronic applications accepted.

Brown University, Graduate School, School of Engineering, Providence, RI 02912. Offers biomedical engineering (Sc M, PhD); chemical and biochemical engineering (Sc M, PhD); electrical sciences and computer engineering (Sc M, PhD); fluid and thermal sciences (Sc M, PhD); materials science and engineering (Sc M, PhD); mechanics of solids and structures (Sc M, PhD). *Degree requirements:* For doctorate, thesis/dissertation, preliminary exam.

Carnegie Mellon University, Dietrich College of Humanities and Social Sciences, Department of English, Program in Professional Writing, Pittsburgh, PA 15213-3891. Offers editing and publishing (MAPW); policy and non-profit communication (MAPW); public and media relations/corporate communications (MAPW); science or healthcare communication (MAPW); technical writing (MAPW); writing for new media (MAPW); writing for print media (MAPW). Part-time programs available. *Entrance requirements:* For master's, GRE General Test. Additional exam requirements/recommendations for international students: Required—TOEFL, TWE.

DePaul University, College of Liberal Arts and Social Sciences, Chicago, IL 60614. Offers Arabic (MA); Chinese (MA); English (MA); French (MA); German (MA); history (MA); interdisciplinary studies (MA, MS); international public service (MS); international studies (MA); Italian (MA); Japanese (MA); leadership and policy studies (MS); liberal studies (MA); new media studies (MA); nonprofit management (MNM); public administration (MPA); public health (MPH); public service management (MS); social work (MSW); sociology (MA); Spanish (MA); sustainable urban development (MA); women and gender studies (MA); writing and publishing (MA); writing, rhetoric, and discourse (MA); MA/PhD. Part-time and evening/weekend programs available. Postbaccalaureate distance learning degree programs offered (no on-campus study). Terminal master's awarded for partial completion of doctoral program. *Degree requirements:* For master's, variable foreign language requirement, comprehensive exam (for some programs), thesis (for some programs). Electronic applications accepted.

Drexel University, College of Arts and Sciences, Department of Culture and Communication, Program in Publication Management, Philadelphia, PA 19104-2875. Offers MS. Part-time and evening/weekend programs available. *Degree requirements:* For master's, research project. *Entrance requirements:* Additional exam requirements/recommendations for international students: Required—TOEFL. Electronic applications accepted.

Emerson College, Graduate Studies, School of the Arts, Department of Writing, Literature and Publishing, Program in Publishing and Writing, Boston, MA 02116-4624. Offers MA. Part-time and evening/weekend programs available. *Students:* 105 full-time (92 women), 13 part-time (11 women); includes 24 minority (5 Black or African American, non-Hispanic/Latino; 2 Asian, non-Hispanic/Latino; 16 Hispanic/Latino; 1 Two or more races, non-Hispanic/Latino), 7 international. Average age 25. 180 applicants, 59% accepted, 48 enrolled. In 2014, 43 master's awarded. *Degree requirements:* For master's, thesis or alternative. *Entrance requirements:* For master's, GRE General Test, 15-page writing sample. Additional exam requirements/recommendations for international students: Required—TOEFL (minimum score 550 paper-based; 80 iBT), IELTS (minimum score 6.5). *Application deadline:* For fall admission, 3/1 priority date for domestic and international students. Applications are processed on a rolling basis. Application fee: $60 ($75 for international students). Electronic applications accepted. *Expenses: Tuition:* Part-time $1145 per credit. *Financial support:* In 2014–15, 23 students received support, including 23 fellowships with partial tuition reimbursements available (averaging $8,696 per year); research assistantships with partial tuition reimbursements available, Federal Work-Study, scholarships/grants, and unspecified assistantships also available. Financial award application deadline: 3/1; financial award applicants required to submit FAFSA. *Faculty research:* Publishing. *Unit head:* Prof. Lisa Diercks, Graduate Program Director, 617-824-8750, E-mail: lisa_diercks@emerson.edu. *Application contact:* Leanda Ferland, Office of Graduate Admission, 617-824-8610, Fax: 617-824-8614, E-mail: gradapp@emerson.edu.
Website: http://www.emerson.edu/graduate_admission

The George Washington University, College of Professional Studies, Program in Publishing, Washington, DC 20052. Offers MPS. Program offered in Alexandria, VA. *Students:* 73 part-time (67 women); includes 14 minority (7 Black or African American, non-Hispanic/Latino; 2 Asian, non-Hispanic/Latino; 4 Hispanic/Latino; 1 Two or more races, non-Hispanic/Latino), 1 international. Average age 31. 93 applicants, 92% accepted, 40 enrolled. In 2014, 38 master's awarded. *Entrance requirements:* For master's, minimum cumulative GPA of 3.0. *Application deadline:* For fall admission, 4/1 for domestic and international students. Electronic applications accepted. *Unit head:* Dr. Arnold Grossblatt, Director, 202-994-7220, E-mail: arnieg@gwu.edu. *Application contact:* Kristin Williams, Associate Provost, Grad Enroll, 202-994-0467, Fax: 202-994-0371, E-mail: ksw@gwu.edu.
Website: http://nearyou.gwu.edu/pubs/

New York University, School of Continuing and Professional Studies, Center for Publishing, New York, NY 10012-1019. Offers digital and print media (MS). Part-time and evening/weekend programs available. *Faculty:* 1 (woman) full-time, 34 part-time/adjunct (17 women). *Students:* 45 full-time (42 women), 62 part-time (54 women); includes 24 minority (8 Black or African American, non-Hispanic/Latino; 6 Asian, non-Hispanic/Latino; 6 Hispanic/Latino; 4 Two or more races, non-Hispanic/Latino), 24 international. Average age 25. 114 applicants, 63% accepted, 36 enrolled. In 2014, 58 master's awarded. *Degree requirements:* For master's, thesis. *Entrance requirements:* For master's, GRE or GMAT (only upon request), bachelor's degree, resume with relevant professional work, internship or volunteer experience, two letters of recommendation, statement of purpose. Additional exam requirements/recommendations for international students: Required—TOEFL (minimum score 600 paper-based; 100 iBT), IELTS (minimum score 7). *Application deadline:* For fall admission, 2/1 priority date for domestic and international students; for spring admission, 10/15 priority date for domestic students, 8/15 priority date for international students. Applications are processed on a rolling basis. Application fee: $150. Electronic applications accepted. *Financial support:* In 2014–15, 40 students received support, including 37 fellowships (averaging $2,405 per year); Federal Work-Study and scholarships/grants also available. Support available to part-time students. Financial award application deadline: 4/1; financial award applicants required to submit FAFSA. *Unit head:* Andrea Chambers, Academic Director and Clinical Assistant Professor, 212-992-3232. *Application contact:* Admissions Office, 212-998-7100, E-mail: sps.gradadmissions@nyu.edu.
Website: http://www.sps.nyu.edu/publishing

North Central College, Graduate and Continuing Studies Programs, Program in Liberal Studies, Naperville, IL 60566-7063. Offers culture and society (MALS); ethics and public service (MALS); writing, editing, and publishing (MALS). Part-time and evening/weekend programs available. *Faculty:* 8 full-time (2 women), 4 part-time/adjunct (1 woman). *Students:* 2 full-time (1 woman), 24 part-time (14 women); includes 1 minority (Asian, non-Hispanic/Latino). Average age 36. 15 applicants, 73% accepted, 7 enrolled. In 2014, 6 master's awarded. *Degree requirements:* For master's, thesis optional, project. *Entrance requirements:* For master's, interview. Additional exam requirements/recommendations for international students: Required—TOEFL (minimum score 550 paper-based; 80 iBT). *Application deadline:* For fall admission, 8/15 for domestic students, 7/15 for international students; for winter admission, 12/1 for domestic students, 11/1 for international students; for spring admission, 2/1 for domestic students, 12/1 for international students. Applications are processed on a rolling basis. Application fee: $25. Electronic applications accepted. Application fee is waived when completed online. *Expenses:* Expenses: Contact institution. *Financial support:* In 2014–15, 1 student received support. Scholarships/grants available. Support available to part-time students. Financial award applicants required to submit FAFSA. *Unit head:* Dr. Richard Guzman, Program Coordinator, Liberal Studies, 630-637-5285. *Application contact:* Wendy Kulpinski, Director of Graduate and Continuing Education Admission, 630-637-5808, Fax: 630-637-5844, E-mail: wekulpinski@noctrl.edu.
Website: http://northcentralcollege.edu/admission/liberal-studies

Northwestern University, Medill School of Journalism, Media, and Integrated Marketing Communications, Evanston, IL 60208. Offers integrated marketing communications (MSIMC), including brand strategy, content marketing, direct and interactive marketing, marketing analytics, strategic communications; interactive publishing (MSJ); magazine writing/editing (MSJ); reporting (MSJ); video/broadcast (MSJ). *Accreditation:* ACEJMC (one or more programs are accredited). *Entrance requirements:* For master's, GRE General Test, GMAT or LSAT (for MSJ). Additional exam requirements/recommendations for international students: Required—TOEFL. Electronic applications accepted. *Expenses:* Contact institution. *Faculty research:* Web business journalism, cultural stereotypes, voter apathy, digital television.

Pace University, Dyson College of Arts and Sciences, Program in Publishing, New York, NY 10038. Offers book publishing (Certificate); business side of publishing (Certificate); digital publishing (Certificate); magazine publishing (Certificate); publishing (MS). Part-time and evening/weekend programs available. Postbaccalaureate distance learning degree programs offered. *Faculty:* 2 full-time (1 woman), 14 part-time/adjunct (9 women). *Students:* 83 full-time (66 women), 21 part-time (17 women); includes 34 minority (13 Black or African American, non-Hispanic/Latino; 5 Asian, non-Hispanic/Latino; 12 Hispanic/Latino; 4 Two or more races, non-Hispanic/Latino), 13 international. Average age 26. 84 applicants, 93% accepted, 40 enrolled. In 2014, 35 master's, 1 other advanced degree awarded. *Degree requirements:* For master's, internship or thesis. *Entrance requirements:* For master's, GRE General Test, two letters of recommendation, personal statement, resume, all official transcripts. Additional exam requirements/recommendations for international students: Required—TOEFL. *Application deadline:* For fall admission, 8/1 priority date for domestic students, 6/1 for international students; for spring admission, 12/1 priority date for domestic students, 10/1 for international students. Applications are processed on a rolling basis. Application fee: $70. Electronic applications accepted. *Expenses: Tuition:* Part-time $1120 per credit. *Required fees:* $266 per semester. Tuition and fees vary according to course load, degree level and program. *Financial support:* Research assistantships and career-related internships or fieldwork available. Support available to part-time students. Financial award applicants required to submit FAFSA. *Unit head:* Prof. Sherman Raskin, MS in Publishing Program Director, 212-346-1431, E-mail: puboffice@pace.edu. *Application contact:* Susan Ford-Goldschein, Director of Graduate Admissions, 212-346-1531, Fax: 212-346-1585, E-mail: gradnyc@pace.edu.
Website: http://www.pace.edu/dyson/academic-departments-and-programs/publishing

Rosemont College, Schools of Graduate and Professional Studies, Publishing Program, Rosemont, PA 19010-1699. Offers MA. Part-time programs available. Postbaccalaureate distance learning degree programs offered. *Faculty:* 9 part-time/adjunct (5 women). *Students:* 16 full-time (all women), 25 part-time (23 women); includes 8 minority (5 Black or African American, non-Hispanic/Latino; 1 Asian, non-Hispanic/Latino; 1 Hispanic/Latino; 1 Two or more races, non-Hispanic/Latino), 3 international. Average age 31. 46 applicants, 52% accepted, 11 enrolled. In 2014, 23 master's awarded. *Degree requirements:* For master's, comprehensive exam (for some programs), thesis. *Entrance requirements:* For master's, 3 letters of recommendation. Additional exam requirements/recommendations for international students: Required—TOEFL. *Application deadline:* Applications are processed on a rolling basis. Application

fee: $50. Electronic applications accepted. Application fee is waived when completed online. *Financial support:* Institutionally sponsored loans and unspecified assistantships available. Financial award applicants required to submit FAFSA. *Unit head:* Anne Willkomm, Program Director, 610-527-0200 Ext. 2336, Fax: 610-526-2964, E-mail: awillkimm@rosemont.edu. *Application contact:* Graduate Admissions Counselor, 610-527-0200 Ext. 2596, Fax: 610-520-4399, E-mail: gpsadmissions@rosemont.edu. Website: http://www.rosemont.edu

Rowan University, Graduate School, College of Communication and Creative Arts, Program in Editing and Publishing, Glassboro, NJ 08028-1701. Offers CGS. *Faculty:* 1 full-time (0 women). *Students:* 1 part-time (0 women). Average age 26. 1 applicant, 100% accepted, 1 enrolled. *Application deadline:* For fall admission, 8/1 for domestic students; for spring admission, 11/1 for domestic students. Applications are processed on a rolling basis. Application fee: $65. Electronic applications accepted. *Expenses: Tuition, area resident:* Part-time $648 per credit. Tuition, state resident: part-time $648 per credit. Tuition, nonresident: part-time $648 per credit. *Required fees:* $145 per credit. Tuition and fees vary according to degree level, campus/location, program and student level. *Unit head:* Dr. Horacio Sosa, Vice President, Global Learning and Partnerships, 856-256-4747, Fax: 856-256-5638, E-mail: sosa@rowan.edu. *Application contact:* Admissions and Enrollment Services, 856-256-4747, Fax: 856-256-5637, E-mail: globaladmissions@rowan.edu.

Sam Houston State University, College of Humanities and Social Sciences, Department of English, Huntsville, TX 77341. Offers creative writing, editing, and publishing (MFA); English (MA). Part-time programs available. *Faculty:* 25 full-time (13 women), 2 part-time/adjunct (0 women). *Students:* 12 full-time (6 women), 26 part-time (15 women); includes 7 minority (2 Black or African American, non-Hispanic/Latino; 2 American Indian or Alaska Native, non-Hispanic/Latino; 1 Hispanic/Latino; 2 Two or more races, non-Hispanic/Latino), 1 international. Average age 33. 17 applicants, 82% accepted, 12 enrolled. In 2014, 16 master's awarded. *Degree requirements:* For master's, comprehensive exam, thesis optional. *Entrance requirements:* For master's, GRE General Test, creative writing sample, letters of recommendation. Additional exam requirements/recommendations for international students: Required—TOEFL (minimum score 550 paper-based; 79 iBT), IELTS (minimum score 6.5). *Application deadline:* For fall admission, 3/15 priority date for domestic students, 6/25 for international students; for spring admission, 10/15 priority date for domestic students, 11/12 for international students. Applications are processed on a rolling basis. Application fee: $45 ($75 for international students). Electronic applications accepted. *Expenses:* Tuition, state resident: full-time $2286; part-time $254 per credit hour. Tuition, nonresident: full-time $5544; part-time $616 per credit hour. *Required fees:* $440 per semester. Tuition and

fees vary according to course load and campus/location. *Financial support:* In 2014–15, 14 research assistantships (averaging $7,240 per year), 11 teaching assistantships (averaging $7,206 per year) were awarded; career-related internships or fieldwork, Federal Work-Study, scholarships/grants, tuition waivers (partial), and unspecified assistantships also available. Support available to part-time students. Financial award application deadline: 3/15; financial award applicants required to submit FAFSA. *Unit head:* Dr. Helena Halmari, Chair, 936-294-1404, Fax: 936-294-1408, E-mail: eng_shh@shsu.edu. *Application contact:* Dr. Paul Child, Advisor, 936-294-1412, Fax: 936-294-1408, E-mail: eng_pwc@shsu.edu. Website: http://www.shsu.edu/~eng_www/

Simon Fraser University, Office of Graduate Studies, Faculty of Arts and Social Sciences, Canadian Institute for Studies in Publishing, Vancouver, BC V6B 5K3, Canada. Offers M Pub. *Degree requirements:* For master's, internship, internship project report. *Entrance requirements:* For master's, minimum GPA of 3.0 (on scale of 4.33), or 3.33 based on last 60 credits of undergraduate courses. Additional exam requirements/recommendations for international students: Recommended—TOEFL (minimum score 580 paper-based; 93 iBT), IELTS (minimum score 7), TWE (minimum score 5). Electronic applications accepted. *Expenses:* Contact institution. *Faculty research:* History of publishing, electronic publishing, editing, multimedia, publication design, communications technology, copyright and intellectual property.

University of Baltimore, Graduate School, Yale Gordon College of Arts and Sciences, Program in Creative Writing and Publishing Arts, Baltimore, MD 21201-5779. Offers MFA. Part-time and evening/weekend programs available. *Entrance requirements:* Additional exam requirements/recommendations for international students: Required—TOEFL.

University of Baltimore, Graduate School, Yale Gordon College of Arts and Sciences, Program in Publications Design, Baltimore, MD 21201-5779. Offers MA. Part-time and evening/weekend programs available. *Degree requirements:* For master's, seminar project. *Entrance requirements:* For master's, minimum GPA of 3.0, portfolio, interview. Additional exam requirements/recommendations for international students: Required—TOEFL (minimum score 550 paper-based). Electronic applications accepted. *Faculty research:* Communication theory, graphic design, media technology.

University of Houston–Victoria, School of Arts and Sciences, Program in Publishing, Victoria, TX 77901-4450. Offers MS. *Entrance requirements:* For master's, GMAT or GRE, 2 letters of recommendation, writing sample. Additional exam requirements/recommendations for international students: Required—TOEFL. Electronic applications accepted.

Rhetoric

Abilene Christian University, Graduate School, College of Arts and Sciences, Department of English, Abilene, TX 79699-9100. Offers composition/rhetoric (MA); literature (MA); writing (MA). Part-time programs available. *Faculty:* 17 part-time/adjunct (7 women). *Students:* 12 full-time (6 women), 7 part-time (6 women); includes 2 minority (both Hispanic/Latino), 1 international. 20 applicants, 45% accepted, 7 enrolled. In 2014, 4 master's awarded. *Degree requirements:* For master's, one foreign language, comprehensive exam (for some programs), thesis (for some programs). *Entrance requirements:* For master's, GRE General Test. Additional exam requirements/recommendations for international students: Required—TOEFL (minimum score 550 paper-based; 90 iBT), IELTS (minimum score 6.5), PTE. *Application deadline:* For fall admission, 4/1 priority date for domestic students; for spring admission, 11/1 for domestic students. Applications are processed on a rolling basis. Application fee: $50. Electronic applications accepted. *Expenses:* Tuition: Full-time $18,228; part-time $1016 per credit hour. *Financial support:* In 2014–15, 14 students received support, including 6 teaching assistantships with partial tuition reimbursements available (averaging $5,800 per year); Federal Work-Study also available. Support available to part-time students. Financial award application deadline: 4/1; financial award applicants required to submit FAFSA. *Faculty research:* Feminism, Shakespearean dimensions of new literature, poetic consciousness, deconstruction myths. *Unit head:* Dr. Dana McMichael, Graduate Director, 325-674-2083, Fax: 325-674-2408, E-mail: dana.mcmichael@acu.edu. *Application contact:* Corey Patterson, Director of Graduate Admission and Recruiting, 325-674-6566, Fax: 325-674-6717, E-mail: gradinfo@acu.edu.

Arizona State University at the Tempe campus, College of Liberal Arts and Sciences, Department of English, Tempe, AZ 85287-0302. Offers applied linguistics (PhD); creative writing (MFA); English (MA, PhD), including comparative literature (MA), linguistics (MA), literature, rhetoric and composition (MA), rhetoric, composition, and linguistics (PhD); film and media studies (MAS), including American media and popular culture; linguistics (Graduate Certificate); teaching English to speakers of other languages (MTESOL); translation studies (Graduate Certificate). Terminal master's awarded for partial completion of doctoral program. *Degree requirements:* For master's, variable foreign language requirement, comprehensive exam (for some programs), thesis (for some programs), interactive Program of Study (iPOS) submitted before completing 50 percent of required credit hours; for doctorate, variable foreign language requirement, comprehensive exam, thesis/dissertation, interactive Program of Study (iPOS) submitted before completing 50 percent of required credit hours. *Entrance requirements:* For master's and doctorate, GRE, minimum GPA of 3.0 or equivalent in last 2 years of work leading to bachelor's degree. Additional exam requirements/recommendations for international students: Required—TOEFL, IELTS, or PTE. Electronic applications accepted.

Ball State University, Graduate School, College of Communication, Information, and Media, Department of Communication Studies, Muncie, IN 47306-1099. Offers speech, public address, forensics, and rhetoric (MA). *Faculty:* 7 full-time (6 women). *Students:* 17 full-time (14 women), 13 part-time (11 women); includes 3 minority (1 Black or African American, non-Hispanic/Latino; 2 Hispanic/Latino), 6 international. Average age 27. 23 applicants, 91% accepted, 16 enrolled. In 2014, 12 master's awarded. *Entrance requirements:* For master's, GRE General Test. Application fee: $50. *Financial support:* In 2014–15, 22 students received support, including 25 teaching assistantships with partial tuition reimbursements available (averaging $11,056 per year); unspecified assistantships also available. Financial award application deadline: 3/1. *Unit head:* Glen Stamp, Chairperson, 765-285-1882, Fax: 765-285-2736, E-mail: gstamp@bsu.edu. *Application contact:* Dr. Robert Morris, Associate Provost for Research and Dean of the Graduate School, 765-285-4723, Fax: 765-285-1328, E-mail: rmorris@bsu.edu. Website: http://cms.bsu.edu/academics/collegesanddepartments/communicationstudies

Bob Jones University, Graduate Programs, Greenville, SC 29614. Offers accountancy (MS); Bible (MA); Bible translation (MA); Biblical studies (Certificate); broadcast

management (MS); business administration (MBA); church history (MA, PhD); church ministries (MA); church music (MM); cinema and video production (MA); counseling (MS); curriculum and instruction (Ed D); divinity (M Div); dramatic production (MA); educational leadership (MS, Ed D, Ed S); elementary education (M Ed, MAT); English (M Ed, MA, MAT); fine arts (MA); graphic design (MA); history (M Ed, MA); illustration (MA); interpretative speech (MA); mathematics (M Ed, MAT); medical missions (Certificate); ministry (MM, D Min); multi-categorical special education (M Ed, MAT); music (M Ed); New Testament interpretation (PhD); Old Testament interpretation (PhD); orchestral instrument performance (MM); organ performance (MM); pastoral studies (MA); personnel services (MS, Ed S); piano pedagogy (MM); piano performance (MM); platform arts (MA); radio and television broadcasting (MS); rhetoric and public address (MA); secondary education (M Ed); studio art (MA); teaching Bible (MA); theology (MA, PhD); voice performance (MM); youth ministries (MA); M Div/MM.

Bowling Green State University, Graduate College, College of Arts and Sciences, Department of English, Program in English, Bowling Green, OH 43403. Offers English (MA, PhD); literature (MA); rhetoric and writing (PhD); scientific and technical communication (MA). Part-time programs available. *Degree requirements:* For master's, thesis or alternative; for doctorate, comprehensive exam, thesis/dissertation, foreign language or proficiency in Old English. *Entrance requirements:* For master's and doctorate, GRE General Test. Additional exam requirements/recommendations for international students: Required—TOEFL. Electronic applications accepted. *Faculty research:* Postmodern literary theory, rhetorical theory, ethnic American literature, literature and culture, composition pedagogy.

Brigham Young University, Graduate Studies, College of Humanities, Department of English, Provo, UT 84602-1001. Offers creative writing (MFA); literature (MA); rhetoric/composition (MA). *Faculty:* 61 full-time (22 women). *Students:* 71 full-time (52 women), 5 part-time (all women). Average age 24. 71 applicants, 51% accepted, 31 enrolled. In 2014, 22 master's awarded. *Degree requirements:* For master's, thesis. *Entrance requirements:* For master's, GRE General Test, creative portfolio (for MFA). Additional exam requirements/recommendations for international students: Required—TOEFL (minimum score 213 paper-based). *Application deadline:* For fall admission, 1/15 for domestic and international students. Application fee: $50. Electronic applications accepted. *Expenses: Tuition:* Full-time $6310; part-time $371 per credit hour. Tuition and fees vary according to program and student's religious affiliation. *Financial support:* In 2014–15, 10 research assistantships (averaging $4,000 per year), 62 teaching assistantships (averaging $6,000 per year) were awarded; career-related internships or fieldwork, institutionally sponsored loans, scholarships/grants, and tuition waivers (partial) also available. Support available to part-time students. Financial award application deadline: 3/15. *Faculty research:* English literature, American literature, rhetoric, creative writing. *Unit head:* Prof. Phillip Snyder, Head, 801-422-2487, Fax: 801-422-0221, E-mail: phillip_snyder@byu.edu. *Application contact:* Lou Ann C. Crisler, Graduate Secretary, 801-422-8673, Fax: 801-422-0221, E-mail: louann_crisler@byu.edu. Website: http://english.byu.edu/

California State University, Dominguez Hills, College of Arts and Humanities, Department of English, Carson, CA 90747-0001. Offers English (MA); rhetoric and composition (Certificate); teaching English as a second language (Certificate). Part-time and evening/weekend programs available. *Faculty:* 8 full-time (4 women). *Students:* 35 full-time (23 women), 42 part-time (24 women); includes 40 minority (10 Black or African American, non-Hispanic/Latino; 9 Asian, non-Hispanic/Latino; 20 Hispanic/Latino; 1 Two or more races, non-Hispanic/Latino), 11 international. Average age 35. 35 applicants, 77% accepted, 21 enrolled. In 2014, 29 master's awarded. *Degree requirements:* For master's, comprehensive exam (for some programs), thesis or alternative. *Entrance requirements:* For master's, minimum GPA of 3.0 in last 60 units. Additional exam requirements/recommendations for international students: Required—TOEFL (minimum

score 550 paper-based). *Application deadline:* Applications are processed on a rolling basis. Application fee: $55. Electronic applications accepted. *Expenses:* Tuition, state resident: full-time $6738; part-time $3960 per year. Tuition, nonresident: full-time $13,434; part-time $8370 per year. *Required fees:* $623; $623 per year. *Faculty research:* Gender studies, transnationalism, discourse analysis, visual culture, Shakespeare. *Unit head:* Dr. Timothy Chin, Chair, 310-243-3322, E-mail: english@csudh.edu. *Application contact:* Brandy McLelland, Director of Student Information Services/Registrar, 310-243-3645, E-mail: bmclelland@csudh.edu.
Website: http://www4.csudh.edu/english/index

California State University, Northridge, Graduate Studies, College of Humanities, Department of English, Northridge, CA 91330. Offers creative writing (MA); literature (MA); rhetoric and composition theory (MA). Part-time and evening/weekend programs available. *Students:* 36 full-time (22 women), 84 part-time (53 women); includes 39 minority (3 Black or African American, non-Hispanic/Latino; 10 Asian, non-Hispanic/Latino; 22 Hispanic/Latino; 4 Two or more races, non-Hispanic/Latino), 1 international. Average age 32. *Degree requirements:* For master's, thesis or alternative. *Entrance requirements:* For master's, writing proficiency test, GRE General Test or minimum GPA of 3.0. Additional exam requirements/recommendations for international students: Required—TOEFL. *Application deadline:* For fall admission, 11/30 for domestic students. Application fee: $55. *Expenses: Required fees:* $12,402. *Financial support:* Teaching assistantships available. Financial award application deadline: 3/1. *Faculty research:* Reading improvement, professional writing, Dickens, Shaw, English as a second language. *Unit head:* Jackie Stallcup, Chair, 818-677-3434. *Application contact:* Dr. Marjie Seagoe, Graduate Studies Secretary, 818-677-3433.
Website: http://www.csun.edu/english/index.php

California State University, Stanislaus, College of Humanities and Social Sciences, Program in English (MA), Turlock, CA 95382. Offers literature (Certificate); rhetoric and teaching writing (MA); teaching English to speakers of other languages (MA). Part-time programs available. *Degree requirements:* For master's, comprehensive exam, thesis or alternative. *Entrance requirements:* For master's, GRE, minimum GPA of 3.0, 2 letters of reference, personal statement. Additional exam requirements/recommendations for international students: Required—TOEFL (minimum score 575 paper-based), TWE (minimum score 4). Electronic applications accepted. *Faculty research:* Transnational literacies, Renaissance and medieval literature, abolition writings and slave narratives, qualitative writing.

Carnegie Mellon University, Dietrich College of Humanities and Social Sciences, Department of English, Pittsburgh, PA 15213-3891. Offers communication planning and design (M Des); literary and cultural studies (MA, PhD); professional writing (MAPW), including editing and publishing, policy and non-profit communication, public and media relations / corporate communications, science or healthcare communication, technical writing, writing for new media, writing for print media; rhetoric (MA, PhD). Part-time programs available. Terminal master's awarded for partial completion of doctoral program. *Degree requirements:* For doctorate, 2 foreign languages, comprehensive exam, thesis/dissertation. *Entrance requirements:* For master's and doctorate, GRE General Test. Additional exam requirements/recommendations for international students: Required—TOEFL, TWE. *Faculty research:* Cognitive processes in discourse with emphasis on writing, testing, and evaluation.

The Catholic University of America, School of Arts and Sciences, Department of English Language and Literature, Washington, DC 20064. Offers English language and literature (MA, PhD); rhetoric (Certificate); MSLS/MA. Part-time programs available. *Faculty:* 15 full-time (5 women), 1 (woman) part-time/adjunct. *Students:* 19 full-time (11 women), 35 part-time (23 women); includes 5 minority (1 Black or African American, non-Hispanic/Latino; 3 Hispanic/Latino; 1 Two or more races, non-Hispanic/Latino), 3 international. Average age 29. 52 applicants, 48% accepted, 8 enrolled. In 2014, 7 master's, 5 doctorates awarded. *Degree requirements:* For master's, one foreign language, comprehensive exam; for doctorate, 2 foreign languages, comprehensive exam, thesis/dissertation. *Entrance requirements:* For master's and doctorate, GRE General Test, statement of purpose, official copies of academic transcripts, three letters of recommendation, writing sample. Additional exam requirements/recommendations for international students: Required—TOEFL (minimum score 580 paper-based). *Application deadline:* For fall admission, 7/15 priority date for domestic students, 7/1 for international students; for spring admission, 11/15 priority date for domestic students, 11/1 for international students. Applications are processed on a rolling basis. Application fee: $55. Electronic applications accepted. *Expenses: Tuition:* Full-time $40,200; part-time $1600 per credit hour. *Required fees:* $400; $195 per semester. One-time fee: $425. *Financial support:* Fellowships, research assistantships, teaching assistantships, Federal Work-Study, scholarships/grants, tuition waivers (full and partial), and unspecified assistantships available. Financial award application deadline: 2/1; financial award applicants required to submit FAFSA. *Faculty research:* Medieval literature, theory and history of rhetoric, Renaissance literature, religion and literature, English and American drama. *Unit head:* Dr. Ernest Suarez, Chair, 202-319-5488, Fax: 202-319-4188, E-mail: suarez@cua.edu. *Application contact:* Director of Graduate Admissions, 202-319-5057, Fax: 202-319-6533, E-mail: cua-admissions@cua.edu.
Website: http://english.cua.edu/

Clemson University, Graduate School, College of Architecture, Arts, and Humanities, Program in Rhetorics, Communication and Information Design, Clemson, SC 29634. Offers PhD. *Students:* 23 full-time (12 women), 6 part-time (3 women); includes 4 minority (2 Black or African American, non-Hispanic/Latino; 2 Hispanic/Latino), 4 international. Average age 33. 22 applicants, 32% accepted, 7 enrolled. In 2014, 3 doctorates awarded. *Degree requirements:* For doctorate, thesis/dissertation (for some programs). *Entrance requirements:* For doctorate, GRE, master's degree in English, communications studies, art, professional communication or related field; portfolio; 3 letters of reference; minimum graduate GPA of 3.5. Additional exam requirements/recommendations for international students: Required—TOEFL (minimum score 550 paper-based). *Application deadline:* For fall admission, 2/1 priority date for domestic students, 4/15 for international students. Applications are processed on a rolling basis. Application fee: $70 ($80 for international students). Electronic applications accepted. *Financial support:* In 2014–15, 16 students received support, including 4 fellowships (averaging $5,000 per year), 16 teaching assistantships with partial tuition reimbursements available (averaging $24,834 per year); research assistantships, career-related internships or fieldwork, institutionally sponsored loans, scholarships/grants, health care benefits, and unspecified assistantships also available. Support available to part-time students. *Faculty research:* Historiography and philology, multimodal writing, health communication, future of the book, readability studies, politics and rhetoric. *Unit head:* Dr. Victor Vitanza, Director, 864-656-6411, Fax: 864-656-0599, E-mail: sophist@clemson.edu. *Application contact:* Dr. James B. London, Associate Dean for Research and Graduate Studies, 864-656-3927, E-mail: london1@clemson.edu.
Website: http://www.clemson.edu/caah/rcid/

DePaul University, College of Liberal Arts and Social Sciences, Chicago, IL 60614. Offers Arabic (MA); Chinese (MA); English (MA); French (MA); German (MA); history (MA); interdisciplinary studies (MA, MS); international public service (MS); international studies (MA); Italian (MA); Japanese (MA); leadership and policy studies (MS); liberal studies (MA); new media studies (MA); nonprofit management (MNM); public administration (MPA); public health (MPH); public service management (MS); social work (MSW); sociology (MA); Spanish (MA); sustainable urban development (MA); women and gender studies (MA); writing and publishing (MA); writing, rhetoric, and discourse (MA); MA/PhD. Part-time and evening/weekend programs available. Postbaccalaureate distance learning degree programs offered (no on-campus study). Terminal master's awarded for partial completion of doctoral program. *Degree requirements:* For master's, variable foreign language requirement, comprehensive exam (for some programs), thesis (for some programs). Electronic applications accepted.

Duquesne University, Graduate School of Liberal Arts, Department of Communication and Rhetorical Studies, Pittsburgh, PA 15282-0001. Offers communication (MA); rhetoric (PhD). Part-time and evening/weekend programs available. *Faculty:* 10 full-time (4 women), 5 part-time/adjunct (3 women). *Students:* 99 full-time (58 women), 9 part-time (6 women); includes 12 minority (8 Black or African American, non-Hispanic/Latino; 1 Asian, non-Hispanic/Latino; 2 Hispanic/Latino; 1 Two or more races, non-Hispanic/Latino), 21 international. Average age 34. 86 applicants, 55% accepted, 20 enrolled. In 2014, 13 master's, 6 doctorates awarded. *Degree requirements:* For master's, thesis optional, practicum; for doctorate, 2 foreign languages, comprehensive exam, thesis/dissertation. *Entrance requirements:* For master's and doctorate, GRE General Test. Additional exam requirements/recommendations for international students: Required—TOEFL. *Application deadline:* For fall admission, 2/1 priority date for domestic and international students; for spring admission, 11/1 priority date for domestic and international students. Applications are processed on a rolling basis. Electronic applications accepted. Application fee is waived when completed online. *Expenses: Tuition:* Full-time $18,882; part-time $1049 per credit. *Required fees:* $1800; $100 per credit. Tuition and fees vary according to program. *Financial support:* In 2014–15, 9 research assistantships with full tuition reimbursements (averaging $10,000 per year), 10 teaching assistantships with full tuition reimbursements (averaging $17,000 per year) were awarded; career-related internships or fieldwork, Federal Work-Study, institutionally sponsored loans, scholarships/grants, tuition waivers (full and partial), and unspecified assistantships also available. Financial award application deadline: 5/1. *Unit head:* Dr. Ronald Arnett, Chair, 412-396-5076, E-mail: arnett@duq.edu. *Application contact:* Linda Rendulic, Assistant to the Dean, 412-396-6460, E-mail: rendulic@duq.edu.
Website: http://www.duq.edu/academics/schools/liberal-arts/graduate-school/programs/communication-

East Carolina University, Graduate School, Thomas Harriot College of Arts and Sciences, Department of English, Greenville, NC 27858-4353. Offers creative writing (MA); English studies (MA); linguistics (MA); literature (MA); multicultural and transnational literatures (MA, Certificate); rhetoric and composition (MA); rhetoric, writing, and professional communication (PhD); teaching English in the two-year college (Certificate); teaching English to speakers of other languages (MA, Certificate); technical and professional communication (MA). Part-time and evening/weekend programs available. *Degree requirements:* For master's, one foreign language, comprehensive exam, thesis optional. *Entrance requirements:* For master's, GRE General Test, MAT (for MA Ed). Additional exam requirements/recommendations for international students: Required—TOEFL. *Expenses:* Tuition, state resident: full-time $4223. Tuition, nonresident: full-time $16,540. *Required fees:* $2184.

Eastern Washington University, Graduate Studies, College of Arts, Letters and Education, Department of English, Cheney, WA 99004-2431. Offers literature (MA); rhetoric, composition, and technical communication (MA); teaching English as a second language (MA). *Degree requirements:* For master's, comprehensive exam, thesis or alternative. *Entrance requirements:* For master's, GRE General Test, minimum GPA of 3.0.

Florida Atlantic University, Dorothy F. Schmidt College of Arts and Letters, Department of English, Boca Raton, FL 33431-0991. Offers American literature (MA); British literature (MA); creative nonfiction (MFA); creative writing (MA); English (MAT); fiction (MFA); multicultural and world literacies (MA); poetry (MFA); rhetoric and composition (MA); science fiction and fantasy (MA). Part-time programs available. *Degree requirements:* For master's, one foreign language, thesis. *Entrance requirements:* For master's, GRE General Test, minimum GPA of 3.0, writing samples, 2 letters of recommendation. Additional exam requirements/recommendations for international students: Required—TOEFL (minimum score 500 paper-based; 61 iBT), IELTS (minimum score 6). Electronic applications accepted. *Expenses:* Tuition, state resident: full-time $7396; part-time $369.82 per credit hour. Tuition, nonresident: full-time $19,392; part-time $1024.81 per credit hour. Tuition and fees vary according to course load. *Faculty research:* African-American writers, critical theory, British-American, Asian-American.

Florida State University, The Graduate School, College of Arts and Sciences, Department of English, Tallahassee, FL 32312. Offers creative writing (MFA); English (PhD), including creative writing, literature, rhetoric and composition; literature (MA); rhetoric and composition (MA). Part-time programs available. *Faculty:* 47 full-time (24 women), 2 part-time/adjunct (1 woman). *Students:* 142 full-time (80 women), 31 part-time (23 women); includes 44 minority (17 Black or African American, non-Hispanic/Latino; 1 American Indian or Alaska Native, non-Hispanic/Latino; 12 Asian, non-Hispanic/Latino; 5 Hispanic/Latino; 9 Two or more races, non-Hispanic/Latino), 9 international. Average age 30. 307 applicants, 20% accepted, 38 enrolled. In 2014, 21 master's, 24 doctorates awarded. *Degree requirements:* For master's, one foreign language, thesis (for some programs), 33 hours of coursework including capstone essay, thesis or portfolio (MA); 45 hours of coursework including 9-12 thesis hours (MFA); for doctorate, comprehensive exam, thesis/dissertation, 27 hours of coursework, 24 hours of dissertation work. *Entrance requirements:* For master's and doctorate, GRE General Test, sample of written work, 3 letters of recommendation, resume. Additional exam requirements/recommendations for international students: Required—TOEFL. *Application deadline:* For fall admission, 1/1 priority date for domestic and international students. Application fee: $30. Electronic applications accepted. *Expenses:* Tuition, state resident: part-time $403.51 per credit hour. Tuition, nonresident: part-time $1004.85 per credit hour. *Required fees:* $75.81 per credit hour. One-time fee: $20 part-time. Tuition and fees vary according to campus/location. *Financial support:* In 2014–15, 132 students received support, including 5 fellowships with full and partial tuition reimbursements available, teaching assistantships with full and partial tuition reimbursements available (averaging $13,250 per year); career-related internships or fieldwork, Federal Work-Study, and institutionally sponsored loans also available. Financial award application deadline: 8/1; financial award applicants required to submit FAFSA. *Faculty research:* British and Irish literature, American literature, creative writing, rhetoric and composition, multiethnic transnational literature, history of text technology. *Unit head:* Dr. Eric Walker, Chairman, 850-644-4230, Fax: 850-644-0811, E-mail: ewalker@fsu.edu. *Application contact:* Ginger Martin, Senior Graduate Academic Coordinator, 850-644-1081, Fax: 850-644-9656, E-mail: vmartin@fsu.edu.
Website: http://english.fsu.edu/

George Mason University, College of Humanities and Social Sciences, Department of English, Fairfax, VA 22030. Offers creative writing (MFA), including fiction; English (MA,

Certificate); linguistics (PhD); writing and rhetoric (PhD). *Faculty:* 78 full-time (45 women), 35 part-time/adjunct (21 women). *Students:* 103 full-time (71 women), 140 part-time (105 women); includes 36 minority (10 Black or African American, non-Hispanic/Latino; 8 Asian, non-Hispanic/Latino; 12 Hispanic/Latino; 6 Two or more races, non-Hispanic/Latino), 14 international. Average age 32. 267 applicants, 52% accepted, 67 enrolled. In 2014, 68 master's, 11 other advanced degrees awarded. *Degree requirements:* For master's, thesis (for some programs), proficiency in a foreign language by course work or translation test; for doctorate, thesis/dissertation, 2 graduating papers. *Entrance requirements:* For master's, official transcripts; expanded goals statement; writing sample; portfolio; 2 letters of recommendation; for doctorate, GRE, expanded goals statement; 3 letters of recommendation; writing sample; introductory course in linguistics; official transcripts; for Certificate, official transcripts; expanded goals statement; 3 letters of recommendation; portfolio and writing sample (for professional writing and rhetoric); resume and writing sample (for folklore). Additional exam requirements/recommendations for international students: Required—TOEFL (minimum score 570 paper-based; 80 iBT), IELTS (minimum score 6.5), PTE. *Application deadline:* For fall admission, 3/15 priority date for domestic students; for spring admission, 10/15 priority date for domestic students. Application fee: $65 ($80 for international students). Electronic applications accepted. *Expenses:* Tuition, state resident: full-time $9794; part-time $408 per credit hour. Tuition, nonresident: full-time $26,978; part-time $1124 per credit hour. *Required fees:* $2820; $118 per credit hour. Tuition and fees vary according to course load and program. *Financial support:* In 2014–15, 72 students received support, including 3 fellowships (averaging $1,823 per year), 6 research assistantships with full and partial tuition reimbursements available (averaging $14,605 per year), 65 teaching assistantships with full and partial tuition reimbursements available (averaging $11,909 per year); career-related internships or fieldwork, Federal Work-Study, scholarships/grants, unspecified assistantships, and health care benefits (for full-time research or teaching assistantship recipients) also available. Support available to part-time students. Financial award application deadline: 3/1; financial award applicants required to submit FAFSA. *Faculty research:* Literature, professional writing and editing, writing of fiction or poetry. *Total annual research expenditures:* $84,493. *Unit head:* Debra Lattanzi-Shutika, Chair, 703-993-1170, Fax: 703-993-1161, E-mail: dshutika@gmu.edu. *Application contact:* Alex Walsh, Graduate Admissions Coordinator, 703-993-1185, Fax: 703-993-1161, E-mail: awalsh7@gmu.edu.
Website: http://english.gmu.edu

Georgia State University, College of Arts and Sciences, Department of Communication, Atlanta, GA 30302-3083. Offers film, video, and digital imaging (MA), including critical studies, production, screenwriting; human communication and social influence (MA); mass communication (MA); media and society (PhD); moving image studies (PhD); public communication (PhD); rhetoric and politics (PhD). Part-time programs available. *Faculty:* 35 full-time (18 women). *Students:* 102 full-time (51 women), 40 part-time (15 women); includes 37 minority (20 Black or African American, non-Hispanic/Latino; 4 Asian, non-Hispanic/Latino; 6 Hispanic/Latino; 7 Two or more races, non-Hispanic/Latino), 14 international. Average age 33. 154 applicants, 39% accepted, 30 enrolled. In 2014, 25 master's, 5 doctorates awarded. *Degree requirements:* For master's, variable foreign language requirement, thesis (for some programs); for doctorate, comprehensive exam, thesis/dissertation. *Entrance requirements:* For master's, GRE; for doctorate, GRE. Additional exam requirements/recommendations for international students: Required—TOEFL (minimum score 550 paper-based; 80 iBT), IELTS (minimum score 6.5). *Application deadline:* For fall admission, 2/10 for domestic and international students; for spring admission, 10/15 for domestic and international students. Application fee: $50. Electronic applications accepted. *Expenses:* Tuition, state resident: full-time $6516; part-time $362 per credit hour. Tuition, nonresident: full-time $22,014; part-time $1223 per credit hour. *Required fees:* $2128 per semester. Tuition and fees vary according to course load and program. *Financial support:* In 2014–15, fellowships with tuition reimbursements (averaging $15,000 per year), teaching assistantships with tuition reimbursements (averaging $15,000 per year) were awarded; career-related internships or fieldwork and unspecified assistantships also available. Financial award applicants required to submit FAFSA. *Faculty research:* New media, mass media and journalism, rhetoric, film and media studies, film production. *Unit head:* Dr. David Cheshier, Chair, 404-413-5649, Fax: 404-413-5634, E-mail: dcheshier@gsu.edu. *Application contact:* Dr. Jennifer Barker, Associate Professor, 404-413-5793, Fax: 404-413-5634, E-mail: jmbarker@gsu.edu.
Website: http://communication.gsu.edu

Georgia State University, College of Arts and Sciences, Department of English, Atlanta, GA 30302-3083. Offers creative writing (MA, MFA, PhD), including creative writing (PhD), fiction (MA, MFA), poetry (MA, MFA); English (MA, PhD); literary studies (MA, PhD); rhetoric and composition (MA, PhD). Part-time programs available. *Faculty:* 46 full-time (21 women). *Students:* 119 full-time (79 women), 79 part-time (56 women); includes 22 minority (10 Black or African American, non-Hispanic/Latino; 8 Asian, non-Hispanic/Latino; 2 Hispanic/Latino; 2 Two or more races, non-Hispanic/Latino), 9 international. Average age 37. 203 applicants, 44% accepted, 32 enrolled. In 2014, 14 master's, 13 doctorates awarded. *Degree requirements:* For master's, one foreign language, thesis, 30 hours of coursework plus 6 hours of thesis credit; for doctorate, one foreign language, comprehensive exam, thesis/dissertation, second exam. *Entrance requirements:* For master's and doctorate, GRE. Additional exam requirements/recommendations for international students: Required—TOEFL (minimum score 550 paper-based; 80 iBT). *Application deadline:* For fall admission, 1/15 for domestic and international students. Application fee: $50. Electronic applications accepted. *Expenses:* Tuition, state resident: full-time $6516; part-time $362 per credit hour. Tuition, nonresident: full-time $22,014; part-time $1223 per credit hour. *Required fees:* $2128 per semester. Tuition and fees vary according to course load and program. *Financial support:* In 2014–15, research assistantships with full tuition reimbursements (averaging $6,000 per year), teaching assistantships with full tuition reimbursements (averaging $15,000 per year) were awarded; career-related internships or fieldwork, traineeships, and health care benefits also available. Financial award application deadline: 2/15. *Faculty research:* British and American literature and transnational literatures in English, literary theory and cultural studies, creative writing (fiction and poetry), rhetoric and composition, new media and digital humanities. *Unit head:* Dr. Calvin Thomas, Director of Graduate Studies in English, 404-413-5808, Fax: 404-413-5830, E-mail: cthomas@gsu.edu. *Application contact:* Amber Amari, Director, Graduate and Scheduling Services, 404-413-5037, E-mail: aamari@gsu.edu.
Website: http://www.english.gsu.edu

Hofstra University, Lawrence Herbert School of Communication, Program in Rhetorical Studies, Hempstead, NY 11549. Offers MA. Part-time and evening/weekend programs available. *Students:* 13 full-time (8 women), 8 part-time (7 women); includes 11 minority (6 Black or African American, non-Hispanic/Latino; 4 Hispanic/Latino; 1 Two or more races, non-Hispanic/Latino), 2 international. Average age 28. 15 applicants, 80% accepted, 8 enrolled. In 2014, 7 master's awarded. *Degree requirements:* For master's, thesis. *Entrance requirements:* For master's, 2 letters of recommendation, interview. Additional exam requirements/recommendations for international students: Required—TOEFL (minimum score 550 paper-based; 80 iBT). *Application deadline:* Applications are processed on a rolling basis. Application fee: $70 ($75 for international students). Electronic applications accepted. *Expenses: Tuition:* Full-time $20,610; part-time $1145 per credit hour. *Required fees:* $970; $165 per term. Tuition and fees vary according to program. *Financial support:* In 2014–15, 12 students received support, including 7 fellowships with full and partial tuition reimbursements available (averaging $3,214 per year), 3 research assistantships with full and partial tuition reimbursements available (averaging $3,018 per year); Federal Work-Study, institutionally sponsored loans, scholarships/grants, tuition waivers (full and partial), and unspecified assistantships also available. Support available to part-time students. Financial award applicants required to submit FAFSA. *Faculty research:* Performance of race and gender, public deliberation, civic engagement, political communication, popular culture, health communication. *Unit head:* Dr. Andrew Spieldenner, Program Director, 516-463-5955, Fax: 516-463-7012, E-mail: sphazs@hofstra.edu. *Application contact:* Sunil Samuel, Assistant Vice President of Admissions, 516-463-4723, Fax: 516-463-4664, E-mail: graduateadmission@hofstra.edu.
Website: http://www.hofstra.edu/academics/colleges/soc/

Idaho State University, Office of Graduate Studies, College of Arts and Letters, Department of Communication and Rhetorical Studies, Pocatello, ID 83209-8115. Offers communication and rhetorical studies (MA). Part-time programs available. *Degree requirements:* For master's, comprehensive exam, paper or thesis. *Entrance requirements:* For master's, GRE General Test, minimum GPA of 3.0 in all upper-level courses. Additional exam requirements/recommendations for international students: Required—TOEFL (minimum score 550 paper-based; 80 iBT). Electronic applications accepted. *Faculty research:* Metaphor and cognition in organizational groups and teams; rhetorical criticism of contemporary culture, including music, film, television, and advertising; communication pedagogy; the effect of language on organizational identification and commitment; risk communication and crisis communication.

Indiana University Bloomington, University Graduate School, College of Arts and Sciences, The Media School, Department of Communication and Culture, Bloomington, IN 47405-7000. Offers communication and culture (MA); film and media studies (PhD); performance and ethnography (PhD); rhetoric and public culture (PhD). *Faculty:* 22 full-time (13 women), 1 (woman) part-time/adjunct. *Students:* 75 full-time (41 women); includes 7 minority (1 Black or African American, non-Hispanic/Latino; 5 Hispanic/Latino; 1 Two or more races, non-Hispanic/Latino), 7 international. 116 applicants, 15% accepted, 8 enrolled. In 2014, 7 master's, 7 doctorates awarded. *Degree requirements:* For master's, comprehensive exam; for doctorate, one foreign language, comprehensive exam, thesis/dissertation, student teaching. *Entrance requirements:* For master's and doctorate, GRE General Test, minimum GPA of 3.0, 3 letters of recommendation, writing sample, personal statement. Additional exam requirements/recommendations for international students: Required—TOEFL (minimum score 550 paper-based) or IELTS. *Application deadline:* For fall admission, 1/2 for domestic students, 12/1 for international students; for winter admission, 1/2 for domestic students, 12/1 for international students. Application fee: $55 ($65 for international students). Electronic applications accepted. *Financial support:* Fellowships with full tuition reimbursements, research assistantships with full tuition reimbursements, and teaching assistantships with full tuition reimbursements available. Financial award application deadline: 1/2. *Faculty research:* Rhetoric and public culture, film and media studies, performance ethnography. *Unit head:* Prof. Jane Goodman, Chair, 812-855-3232, Fax: 812-855-6014, E-mail: cmcl@indiana.edu. *Application contact:* Kathy P. Teige, Graduate Secretary, 812-855-6389, Fax: 812-855-6014, E-mail: kteige@indiana.edu.
Website: http://www.indiana.edu/~cmcl/

Iowa State University of Science and Technology, Department of English, Ames, IA 50011. Offers creative writing (MFA); English (MA); rhetoric and professional communication (PhD). *Degree requirements:* For master's, thesis or alternative; for doctorate, thesis/dissertation. *Entrance requirements:* For master's, GRE General Test, sample of written work, resume, portfolio in creative writing; for doctorate, GRE General Test, sample of written work, resume. Additional exam requirements/recommendations for international students: Required—TOEFL (minimum score 600 paper-based; 100 iBT), IELTS (minimum score 7). Electronic applications accepted. *Faculty research:* Creative writing, literature, rhetoric, composition and professional communication, teaching English as a second language, applied linguistics.

Iowa State University of Science and Technology, Program in Rhetoric and Professional Communication, Ames, IA 50011. Offers PhD. *Entrance requirements:* For doctorate, GRE, official academic transcripts, resume, three letters of recommendation, writing sample. Additional exam requirements/recommendations for international students: Required—TOEFL (minimum score 640 paper-based; 111 iBT), IELTS (minimum score 7.5). Electronic applications accepted.

Iowa State University of Science and Technology, Program in Rhetoric, Composition, and Professional Communication, Ames, IA 50011. Offers MA. *Entrance requirements:* For master's, GRE, official academic transcripts, resume, three letters of recommendation, writing sample. Additional exam requirements/recommendations for international students: Required—TOEFL (minimum score 600 paper-based; 100 iBT), IELTS (minimum score 7). Electronic applications accepted.

James Madison University, The Graduate School, College of Arts and Letters, School of Writing, Rhetoric, and Technical Communication, Harrisonburg, VA 22807. Offers MA, MS. Part-time programs available. *Faculty:* 20 full-time (11 women), 1 (woman) part-time/adjunct. *Students:* 13 full-time (10 women), 3 part-time (2 women); includes 3 minority (1 Black or African American, non-Hispanic/Latino; 1 Asian, non-Hispanic/Latino; 1 Hispanic/Latino). Average age 28. 12 applicants, 83% accepted, 8 enrolled. In 2014, 8 master's awarded. *Degree requirements:* For master's, one foreign language, thesis. *Application deadline:* For fall admission, 5/31 for domestic students; for spring admission, 8/31 for domestic students. Application fee: $55. Electronic applications accepted. *Expenses:* Tuition, state resident: full-time $7812; part-time $434 per credit hour. Tuition, nonresident: full-time $20,430; part-time $1135 per credit hour. *Financial support:* In 2014–15, 12 students received support, including 1 fellowship, 2 teaching assistantships with full tuition reimbursements available (averaging $8,837 per year); career-related internships or fieldwork, Federal Work-Study, and 9 assistantships (averaging $7112) also available. Financial award application deadline: 3/1; financial award applicants required to submit FAFSA. *Unit head:* Dr. Traci A. Zimmerman, Director of the School of Writing, Rhetoric and Technical Communication, 540-568-2334, E-mail: zimmerta@jmu.edu. *Application contact:* Lynette D. Michael, Director of Graduate Admissions and Student Records, 540-568-6131 Ext. 6395, Fax: 540-568-7860, E-mail: michaeld@jmu.edu.
Website: http://www.jmu.edu/wrtc/

Kent State University, College of Arts and Sciences, Department of English, Kent, OH 44242-0001. Offers creative writing (MFA); English (PhD); English for teachers (MA); literature and writing (MA); rhetoric and composition (PhD); teaching English as a second language (MA); TESL/TEFL (Certificate). MFA program offered jointly with Cleveland State University, The University of Akron, and Youngstown State University. Part-time programs available. *Faculty:* 49 full-time (33 women). *Students:* 124 full-time (94 women), 25 part-time (17 women); includes 10 minority (1 Black or African American, non-Hispanic/Latino; 4 Asian, non-Hispanic/Latino; 2 Hispanic/Latino; 3 Two or more races, non-Hispanic/Latino), 30 international. Average age 32. 284 applicants, 61% accepted, 65 enrolled. In 2014, 42 master's, 9 doctorates, 1 other advanced degree

awarded. Terminal master's awarded for partial completion of doctoral program. *Degree requirements:* For master's, one foreign language, thesis; for doctorate, one foreign language, comprehensive exam, thesis/dissertation. *Entrance requirements:* For master's and doctorate, GRE General Test, minimum GPA of 3.0, transcript, 8-15 page writing sample, resume, letter of intent, 3 letters of recommendation; for Certificate, minimum GPA of 3.0, transcripts. Additional exam requirements/recommendations for international students: Required—TOEFL (minimum score: paper-based 525, iBT 71), Michigan English Language Assessment Battery (minimum score of 75), IELTS (minimum score of 6.0), PTE Academic (minimum score of 48), or completion of ELS level 112 Intensive Program. *Application deadline:* For fall admission, 1/15 for domestic students, 2/1 for international students. Application fee: $45 ($70 for international students). Electronic applications accepted. *Expenses:* Tuition, state resident: full-time $8730; part-time $485 per credit hour. Tuition, nonresident: full-time $14,886; part-time $827 per credit hour. Tuition and fees vary according to campus/location and program. *Financial support:* Fellowships with full tuition reimbursements, research assistantships with full tuition reimbursements, teaching assistantships with full tuition reimbursements, career-related internships or fieldwork, Federal Work-Study, and unspecified assistantships available. Financial award application deadline: 2/1. *Unit head:* Dr. Robery Trogdon, Chair, 330-672-2676, E-mail: rcorthel@kent.edu. *Application contact:* Kevin Floyd, Graduate Student Coordinator, 330-672-2676, E-mail: english@kent.edu. Website: http://www.kent.edu/english/

Michigan State University, The Graduate School, College of Arts and Letters, Program in Rhetoric and Writing, East Lansing, MI 48824. Offers critical studies in literacy and pedagogy (MA); digital rhetoric and professional writing (MA); rhetoric and writing (PhD). *Entrance requirements:* Additional exam requirements/recommendations for international students: Required—TOEFL. Electronic applications accepted. *Faculty research:* Rhetoric, writing and communication studies; media studies; technical communication, writing for digital environments.

Michigan Technological University, Graduate School, College of Sciences and Arts, Department of Humanities, Houghton, MI 49931. Offers rhetoric and technical communication (MS, PhD). Part-time programs available. *Faculty:* 33 full-time (21 women), 6 part-time/adjunct (4 women). *Students:* 35 full-time (23 women), 10 part-time (7 women), 17 international. Average age 35. 62 applicants, 29% accepted, 12 enrolled. In 2014, 2 master's, 7 doctorates awarded. Terminal master's awarded for partial completion of doctoral program. *Degree requirements:* For master's, comprehensive exam (for some programs), thesis (for some programs); for doctorate, one foreign language, comprehensive exam, thesis/dissertation. *Entrance requirements:* For master's and doctorate, GRE, statement of purpose, official transcripts, 3 letters of recommendation, resume/curriculum vitae, writing sample (10-15 pages). Additional exam requirements/recommendations for international students: Required—TOEFL (recommended score 100 iBT) or IELTS. *Application deadline:* For fall admission, 1/15 priority date for domestic and international students; for spring admission, 10/15 for domestic and international students. Applications are processed on a rolling basis. Electronic applications accepted. *Expenses:* Tuition, state resident: full-time $14,769; part-time $820.50 per credit. Tuition, nonresident: full-time $14,769; part-time $820.50 per credit. *Required fees:* $248; $248 per year. Tuition and fees vary according to course load and program. *Financial support:* In 2014–15, 33 students received support, including 1 fellowship with full and partial tuition reimbursement available (averaging $13,824 per year), 2 research assistantships with full and partial tuition reimbursements available (averaging $13,824 per year), 29 teaching assistantships with full and partial tuition reimbursements available (averaging $13,824 per year); career-related internships or fieldwork, Federal Work-Study, scholarships/grants, health care benefits, unspecified assistantships, and cooperative program also available. Financial award applicants required to submit FAFSA. *Faculty research:* Rhetoric and composition; communication and cultural studies; studies of science, technology, and society; technical communication and digital media. *Total annual research expenditures:* $27,970. *Unit head:* Dr. Ronald L. Strickland, Chair, 906-487-2376, Fax: 906-487-3559, E-mail: rlstrick@mtu.edu. *Application contact:* Katy Ellenich, Administrative Aide, 906-487-2540, Fax: 906-487-3559, E-mail: kmelleni@mtu.edu. Website: http://www.hu.mtu.edu/index.php

Missouri Western State University, Program in Assessment, St. Joseph, MO 64507-2294. Offers autism spectrum disorders (MAS, Graduate Certificate); TESOL (MAS, Graduate Certificate); writing (MAS). Part-time programs available. *Students:* 1 (woman) full-time, 46 part-time (39 women); includes 6 minority (3 Black or African American, non-Hispanic/Latino; 1 American Indian or Alaska Native, non-Hispanic/Latino; 1 Asian, non-Hispanic/Latino; 1 Hispanic/Latino), 1 international. Average age 36. 6 applicants, 100% accepted, 4 enrolled. In 2014, 15 master's, 3 other advanced degrees awarded. *Entrance requirements:* For master's, minimum GPA of 2.75. Additional exam requirements/recommendations for international students: Recommended—TOEFL (minimum score 70 iBT), IELTS (minimum score 6). *Application deadline:* For fall admission, 7/15 for domestic and international students; for spring admission, 11/1 for domestic students, 10/15 for international students; for summer admission, 4/29 for domestic students. Applications are processed on a rolling basis. Application fee: $45 ($50 for international students). Electronic applications accepted. *Expenses:* Tuition, state resident: full-time $5506; part-time $305.91 per credit hour. Tuition, nonresident: full-time $10,075; part-time $559.71 per credit hour. *Required fees:* $504; $99 per credit hour. $176 per semester. Tuition and fees vary according to course load and program. *Financial support:* Scholarships/grants and unspecified assistantships available. Support available to part-time students. *Unit head:* Dr. Susan Bashinski, Director of Graduate Programs in Education, 816-271-5629, E-mail: sbashinski@missouriwestern.edu. *Application contact:* Dr. Benjamin D. Caldwell, Dean of the Graduate School, 816-271-4394, Fax: 816-271-4525, E-mail: graduate@missouriwestern.edu. Website: https://www.missouriwestern.edu/masa/

Monmouth University, The Graduate School, Department of English, West Long Branch, NJ 07764-1898. Offers creative writing (MA); literature (MA); rhetoric and writing (MA). Part-time and evening/weekend programs available. *Faculty:* 11 full-time (7 women). *Students:* 9 full-time (6 women), 33 part-time (25 women); includes 2 minority (1 Black or African American, non-Hispanic/Latino; 1 Asian, non-Hispanic/Latino). Average age 30. 25 applicants, 88% accepted, 15 enrolled. In 2014, 18 master's awarded. *Degree requirements:* For master's, comprehensive exam (for some programs), thesis. *Entrance requirements:* For master's, minimum overall GPA of 2.75, fifteen or more credits in literature or related field, essay of 1,000 words describing interest and goals, two letters of recommendation, creative writing sample. Additional exam requirements/recommendations for international students: Required—TOEFL (minimum score 550 paper-based; 79 iBT), IELTS (minimum score 6), Michigan English Language Assessment Battery (minimum score 77). *Application deadline:* For fall admission, 7/15 for domestic students, 6/1 for international students; for spring admission, 11/15 for domestic students, 11/1 for international students. Application fee: $50. *Expenses: Tuition:* Full-time $18,072; part-time $1004 per credit. *Required fees:* $157 per semester. *Financial support:* In 2014–15, 30 students received support, including 26 fellowships (averaging $2,521 per year), 2 research assistantships (averaging $5,198 per year); career-related internships or fieldwork, scholarships/grants, and unspecified assistantships also available. Support available to part-time students. Financial award applicants required to submit FAFSA. *Faculty research:* Renaissance and medieval literature, nineteenth century American literature, eighteenth century British literature and women's studies, Old and Middle English, African diaspora and African post-colonial literature. *Unit head:* Dr. Jeffrey Jackson, Program Director, 732-571-3439, Fax: 732-263-5242, E-mail: jejackso@monmouth.edu. *Application contact:* Andrea Thompson, Graduate Admission Counselor, 732-571-3452, Fax: 732-263-5123, E-mail: gradadm@monmouth.edu.
Website: http://www.monmouth.edu/school-of-humanities-social-sciences/ma-english.aspx

National University, Academic Affairs, College of Letters and Sciences, La Jolla, CA 92037-1011. Offers applied linguistics (MA); biology (MS); counseling psychology (MA), including licensed professional clinical counseling, marriage and family therapy; creative writing (MFA); English (MA), including Gothic studies, rhetoric; film studies (MA); forensic and crime science (Certificate); forensic studies (MFS), including criminalistics, investigation; history (MA); human behavior (MA); mathematics for educators (MS); performance psychology (MA); strategic communications (MA). Part-time and evening/weekend programs available. Postbaccalaureate distance learning degree programs offered (no on-campus study). *Faculty:* 69 full-time (34 women), 100 part-time/adjunct (55 women). *Students:* 727 full-time (532 women), 349 part-time (240 women); includes 505 minority (128 Black or African American, non-Hispanic/Latino; 5 American Indian or Alaska Native, non-Hispanic/Latino; 52 Asian, non-Hispanic/Latino; 260 Hispanic/Latino; 9 Native Hawaiian or other Pacific Islander, non-Hispanic/Latino; 51 Two or more races, non-Hispanic/Latino), 4 international. Average age 34. In 2014, 569 master's awarded. *Degree requirements:* For master's, thesis (for some programs). *Entrance requirements:* For master's, interview, minimum GPA of 2.5. Additional exam requirements/recommendations for international students: Required—TOEFL (minimum score 550 paper-based; 79 iBT), IELTS (minimum score 6). *Application deadline:* Applications are processed on a rolling basis. Application fee: $60 ($65 for international students). Electronic applications accepted. *Expenses: Tuition:* Full-time $14,184; part-time $1773 per course. *Financial support:* Career-related internships or fieldwork, institutionally sponsored loans, scholarships/grants, and tuition waivers (partial) available. Support available to part-time students. Financial award application deadline: 6/30; financial award applicants required to submit FAFSA. *Unit head:* College of Letters and Sciences, 800-628-8648, E-mail: cols@nu.edu. *Application contact:* Frank Rojas, Interim Vice President for Enrollment Services, 800-628-8648, E-mail: advisor@nu.edu.
Website: http://www.nu.edu/OurPrograms/CollegeOfLettersAndSciences.html

New Mexico Highlands University, Graduate Studies, College of Arts and Sciences, Department of English, Las Vegas, NM 87701. Offers English (MA), including creative writing, language, rhetoric and composition, literature. *Faculty:* 3 full-time (2 women). *Students:* 11 full-time (5 women), 7 part-time (6 women); includes 7 minority (1 Black or African American, non-Hispanic/Latino; 1 American Indian or Alaska Native, non-Hispanic/Latino; 3 Hispanic/Latino; 2 Two or more races, non-Hispanic/Latino), 1 international. Average age 37. 6 applicants, 100% accepted, 4 enrolled. In 2014, 4 master's awarded. *Degree requirements:* For master's, comprehensive exam, thesis. *Entrance requirements:* For master's, minimum undergraduate GPA of 3.0. Additional exam requirements/recommendations for international students: Required—TOEFL (minimum score 540 paper-based). *Application deadline:* For fall admission, 8/1 priority date for domestic students. Applications are processed on a rolling basis. Application fee: $15. *Financial support:* In 2014–15, 22 teaching assistantships were awarded; career-related internships or fieldwork, Federal Work-Study, institutionally sponsored loans, scholarships/grants, tuition waivers (full and partial), and unspecified assistantships also available. Support available to part-time students. Financial award application deadline: 3/1; financial award applicants required to submit FAFSA. *Faculty research:* Twentieth-century literature, life path writing in homeless shelters, native American philosophy, medieval intellectual and cultural history, creating pedagogical tools for teaching law. *Unit head:* Dr. Helen Blythe, Chair, 505-454-3329, E-mail: helenblythe@nmhu.edu. *Application contact:* Diane Trujillo, Administrative Assistant, Graduate Studies, 505-454-3266, Fax: 505-426-2117, E-mail: dtrujillo@nmhu.edu.

New Mexico State University, College of Arts and Sciences, Department of English, Las Cruces, NM 88003-8001. Offers creative writing (MA, MFA); English studies for teachers (MA); literature (MA); rhetoric and professional communication (MA, PhD). Part-time programs available. *Faculty:* 20 full-time (11 women), 3 part-time/adjunct (1 woman). *Students:* 65 full-time (41 women), 29 part-time (20 women); includes 30 minority (2 Black or African American, non-Hispanic/Latino; 2 American Indian or Alaska Native, non-Hispanic/Latino; 2 Asian, non-Hispanic/Latino; 22 Hispanic/Latino; 2 Two or more races, non-Hispanic/Latino), 4 international. Average age 33. 104 applicants, 19% accepted, 15 enrolled. In 2014, 18 master's, 2 doctorates awarded. *Degree requirements:* For master's, one foreign language, thesis (for some programs); for doctorate, comprehensive exam, thesis/dissertation, internship. *Entrance requirements:* For master's and doctorate, sample of written work. Additional exam requirements/recommendations for international students: Required—TOEFL (minimum score 550 paper-based; 79 iBT), IELTS (minimum score 6.5). *Application deadline:* For fall admission, 2/1 for domestic and international students. Application fee: $40 ($50 for international students). Electronic applications accepted. *Expenses:* Tuition, state resident: full-time $3969; part-time $220.50 per credit hour. Tuition, nonresident: full-time $13,838; part-time $768.80 per credit hour. *Required fees:* $853; $47.40 per credit hour. *Financial support:* In 2014–15, 61 students received support, including 17 fellowships (averaging $3,970 per year), 49 teaching assistantships (averaging $16,313 per year); career-related internships or fieldwork, Federal Work-Study, institutionally sponsored loans, scholarships/grants, traineeships, health care benefits, and unspecified assistantships also available. Support available to part-time students. Financial award application deadline: 3/1. *Faculty research:* Composition research, history and theory of rhetoric, technical/professional communication, creative writing, English and American literature. *Total annual research expenditures:* $5,069. *Unit head:* Dr. Barry L. Thatcher, Head, 575-646-2319, Fax: 575-646-7725, E-mail: bathatch@nmsu.edu. *Application contact:* Dr. Tracey Eileen Miller-Tomlinson, Director of Graduate Studies, 575-646-2213, Fax: 575-646-7725, E-mail: tomlin@nmsu.edu.
Website: http://english.nmsu.edu

North Carolina State University, Graduate School, College of Humanities and Social Sciences, Program in Communication, Rhetoric, and Digital Media, Raleigh, NC 27695. Offers PhD.

North Dakota State University, College of Graduate and Interdisciplinary Studies, College of Arts, Humanities and Social Sciences, Department of English, Fargo, ND 58108. Offers English (MA, MS); rhetoric, writing and culture (PhD). Part-time programs available. *Degree requirements:* For master's, one foreign language, thesis. *Entrance requirements:* Additional exam requirements/recommendations for international students: Required—TOEFL (minimum score 600 paper-based; 100 iBT), IELTS (minimum score 7). Electronic applications accepted. *Faculty research:* American and English literature, women's studies, language attitudes, composition practices, computers and composition.

See Display on next page and Close-Up on page 765.

Northern Arizona University, Graduate College, College of Arts and Letters, Department of English, Flagstaff, AZ 86011. Offers applied linguistics (PhD); English (MA, MFA), including creative writing (MFA), general English studies (MA), literature (MA), rhetoric and the teaching of writing (MA), secondary English education (MA); professional writing (Certificate); teaching English as a second language (MA, Certificate). Part-time programs available. *Degree requirements:* For master's, comprehensive exam (for some programs), thesis (for some programs), departmental qualifying exam; for doctorate, comprehensive exam, thesis/dissertation, departmental qualifying exam. *Entrance requirements:* For master's, minimum GPA of 3.0 or GRE; for doctorate, GRE General Test. Additional exam requirements/recommendations for international students: Required—TOEFL (minimum score 550 paper-based; 80 iBT), IELTS (minimum score 7), TOEFL (minimum score 600 paper-based; 100 iBT) for PhD; TOEFL (minimum score 570 paper-based; 89 iBT) for MA. Electronic applications accepted.

Northern Kentucky University, Office of Graduate Programs, College of Arts and Sciences, Program in English, Highland Heights, KY 41099. Offers composition and rhetoric (Certificate); creative writing (Certificate); cultural studies and discourses (Certificate); English (MA); professional writing (Certificate). Part-time and evening/weekend programs available. *Faculty:* 13 full-time (6 women), 6 part-time/adjunct (0 women). *Students:* 2 full-time (1 woman), 51 part-time (39 women); includes 3 minority (2 Black or African American, non-Hispanic/Latino; 1 Two or more races, non-Hispanic/Latino). Average age 36. In 2014, 10 master's, 9 other advanced degrees awarded. *Degree requirements:* For master's, comprehensive exam (for some programs), capstone (thesis, portfolio, project, or exams); 30 hours of credit; for Certificate, 18 hours of credit. *Entrance requirements:* For master's, bachelor's degree in English or related field from regionally-accredited institution with minimum GPA of 3.0 in major or cognate area coursework; official transcripts for all undergraduate and graduate work; two letters of reference; for Certificate, official transcripts for all undergraduate and graduate work; bachelor's degree from regionally-accredited institution; minimum undergraduate GPA of 2.5. Additional exam requirements/recommendations for international students: Required—TOEFL (minimum score 79 iBT); Recommended—IELTS (minimum score 6.5). *Application deadline:* For fall admission, 7/1 priority date for domestic students, 6/1 priority date for international students; for spring admission, 11/1 priority date for domestic students, 10/1 for international students. Application fee: $40. Electronic applications accepted. *Expenses: Tuition, area resident:* Part-time $518 per credit hour. Tuition, state resident: part-time $630 per credit hour. Tuition, nonresident: part-time $797 per credit hour. *Required fees:* $192 per semester. Tuition and fees vary according to course load, degree level, campus/location, program and reciprocity agreements. *Financial support:* In 2014–15, 8 students received support. Unspecified assistantships available. Financial award applicants required to submit FAFSA. *Unit head:* Dr. John Alberti, Director of English Graduate Studies, 859-572-5619, Fax: 859-572-6093, E-mail: alberti@nku.edu. *Application contact:* Alison Swanson, Graduate Admissions Coordinator, 859-572-6971, E-mail: swansona1@nku.edu. Website: http://english.nku.edu/gradprogram/

Northwestern University, The Graduate School, School of Communication, Department of Communication Studies, Evanston, IL 60208. Offers communication studies (PhD), including interaction and social influence, rhetoric and public culture; managerial communication (MSC); media, technology and society (PhD); technology and social behavior (PhD). PhD admissions and degree offered through The Graduate School. Terminal master's awarded for partial completion of doctoral program. *Degree requirements:* For doctorate, thesis/dissertation. *Entrance requirements:* For master's and doctorate, GRE General Test. Additional exam requirements/recommendations for international students: Required—TOEFL. Electronic applications accepted.

Ohio University, Graduate College, Scripps College of Communication, School of Communication Studies, Athens, OH 45701-2979. Offers health communication (PhD); organizational communication (MA); relating and organizing (PhD); rhetoric and public culture (PhD). Part-time programs available. Postbaccalaureate distance learning degree programs offered (minimal on-campus study). Terminal master's awarded for partial completion of doctoral program. *Degree requirements:* For master's, capstone; for doctorate, comprehensive exam, thesis/dissertation. *Entrance requirements:* For master's, GRE; for doctorate, GRE General Test, minimum GPA of 3.0. Additional exam requirements/recommendations for international students: Required—TOEFL (minimum score 550 paper-based; 80 iBT) or IELTS (minimum score 6.5). Electronic applications accepted. *Faculty research:* Rhetoric and public culture, relating and organizing, health communication.

Rensselaer Polytechnic Institute, Graduate School, School of Humanities, Arts, and Social Sciences, Programs in Communication and Rhetoric, Troy, NY 12180-3590. Offers MS, PhD. *Faculty:* 16 full-time (8 women). *Students:* 13 full-time (7 women), 2 part-time (0 women); includes 2 minority (1 Black or African American, non-Hispanic/Latino; 1 Hispanic/Latino). Average age 30. 25 applicants, 40% accepted, 3 enrolled. In 2014, 1 master's awarded. Terminal master's awarded for partial completion of doctoral program. *Degree requirements:* For master's, thesis optional; for doctorate, comprehensive exam, thesis/dissertation. *Entrance requirements:* For master's and doctorate, GRE. Additional exam requirements/recommendations for international students: Required—TOEFL (minimum score 570 paper-based; 88 iBT), IELTS (minimum score 6.5), PTE (minimum score 60). *Application deadline:* For fall admission, 1/1 priority date for domestic and international students; for spring admission, 8/15 priority date for domestic and international students. Applications are processed on a rolling basis. Application fee: $75. Electronic applications accepted. *Expenses: Tuition:* Full-time $46,700; part-time $1945 per credit. Tuition and fees vary according to course load. *Financial support:* In 2014–15, 12 students received support, including research assistantships with full tuition reimbursements available (averaging $18,500 per year), teaching assistantships with full tuition reimbursements available (averaging $18,500 per year); fellowships also available. Financial award application deadline: 1/1. *Faculty research:* Communication, game studies, human computer interaction, literary theory, media studies, rhetoric, visual design, writing studies. *Unit head:* Dr. Katya Haskins, Graduate Program Director, 518-276-4047, E-mail: haskie@rpi.edu. *Application contact:* Office of Graduate Admissions, 518-276-6216, E-mail: gradadmissions@rpi.edu. Website: http://www.cm.rpi.edu/pl/graduate

Rowan University, Graduate School, College of Communication and Creative Arts, Writing, Composition, and Rhetoric Certificate of Graduate Study Program, Glassboro, NJ 08028-1701. Offers CGS. *Expenses: Tuition, area resident:* Part-time $648 per credit. Tuition, state resident: part-time $648 per credit. Tuition, nonresident: part-time $648 per credit. *Required fees:* $145 per credit. Tuition and fees vary according to degree level, campus/location, program and student level. *Unit head:* Dr. Horacio Sosa, Vice President, Global Learning and Partnerships, 856-256-4747, Fax: 856-256-5638, E-mail: sosa@rowan.edu. *Application contact:* Admissions and Enrollment Services, 856-256-4747, Fax: 856-256-5637, E-mail: globaladmissions@rowan.edu.

Salisbury University, Program in English, Salisbury, MD 21801-6837. Offers composition and rhetoric (MA); English (MA); literature (MA); TESOL (MA). Part-time and evening/weekend programs available. *Faculty:* 11 full-time (5 women). *Students:* 9 full-time (6 women), 24 part-time (19 women); includes 6 minority (3 Black or African American, non-Hispanic/Latino; 2 Hispanic/Latino; 1 Two or more races, non-Hispanic/Latino), 3 international. Average age 32. 11 applicants, 100% accepted, 11 enrolled. In 2014, 20 master's awarded. *Degree requirements:* For master's, comprehensive exam (for some programs), thesis optional. *Entrance requirements:* For master's, GRE, MAT, PRAXIS I, 2 letters of recommendation; personal statement. Additional exam

requirements/recommendations for international students: Required—TOEFL (minimum score 550 paper-based; 79 iBT), IELTS (minimum score 6.5). *Application deadline:* For fall admission, 3/15 for domestic and international students; for spring admission, 10/1 for domestic and international students. Applications are processed on a rolling basis. Application fee: $65. Electronic applications accepted. *Expenses:* Expenses: $358 per credit hour for residents; $647 for non-residents; $78 fees. *Financial support:* In 2014–15, 12 teaching assistantships with full tuition reimbursements (averaging $9,498 per year) were awarded; career-related internships or fieldwork, institutionally sponsored loans, and unspecified assistantships also available. Support available to part-time students. Financial award application deadline: 3/1; financial award applicants required to submit FAFSA. *Faculty research:* American literature; British literature; linguistics, film, rhetoric and composition. *Unit head:* Dr. Christopher Vilmar, Graduate Program Director, English, 410-677-6511, Fax: -, E-mail: csvilmar@salisbury.edu.
Website: http://www.salisbury.edu/gsr/gradstudies/ENGpage.html

San Diego State University, Graduate and Research Affairs, College of Arts and Letters, Department of Rhetoric and Writing Studies, San Diego, CA 92182. Offers MA. Part-time programs available. *Degree requirements:* For master's, thesis. *Entrance requirements:* For master's, GRE General Test, writing sample, 3 letters of reference. Additional exam requirements/recommendations for international students: Required—TOEFL. Electronic applications accepted.

Southern Illinois University Carbondale, Graduate School, College of Liberal Arts, Department of English, Carbondale, IL 62901-4701. Offers composition (MA, PhD), including composition, literature, rhetoric; creative writing (MFA). *Faculty:* 33 full-time (14 women), 1 (woman) part-time/adjunct. *Students:* 66 full-time (40 women), 34 part-time (20 women); includes 2 minority (both Hispanic/Latino), 7 international. 158 applicants, 22% accepted, 24 enrolled. In 2014, 18 master's, 9 doctorates awarded. *Degree requirements:* For master's, one foreign language, thesis; for doctorate, 2 foreign languages, thesis/dissertation. *Entrance requirements:* For master's, GRE General Test, GRE Subject Test, minimum GPA of 2.7; for doctorate, GRE General Test, GRE Subject Test, minimum GPA of 3.25. Additional exam requirements/recommendations for international students: Required—TOEFL. *Application deadline:* For fall admission, 2/15 for domestic students; for spring admission, 11/15 for domestic students. Applications are processed on a rolling basis. Application fee: $50. *Expenses:* Tuition, state resident: full-time $10,176; part-time $1153 per credit. Tuition, nonresident: full-time $20,814; part-time $1744 per credit. *Required fees:* $7092; $394 per credit. $2364 per semester. *Financial support:* In 2014–15, 2 fellowships with full tuition reimbursements, 5 research assistantships with full tuition reimbursements, 72 teaching assistantships with full tuition reimbursements were awarded; career-related internships or fieldwork, Federal Work-Study, institutionally sponsored loans, and tuition waivers (full) also available. Support available to part-time students. *Faculty research:* British literature, English literature, modern Continental literature, literary criticism and theory, film studies, Irish studies. *Unit head:* Dr. Ryan Netzley, Chair, 618-453-6894, E-mail: rnetzley@siu.edu. *Application contact:* Patty Norris, Administrative Clerk, 618-453-6894, Fax: 618-453-3253, E-mail: gradengl@siu.edu.
Website: http://english.siuc.edu/

Syracuse University, College of Arts and Sciences, Program in Composition and Cultural Rhetoric, Syracuse, NY 13244. Offers PhD. *Students:* 29 full-time (19 women), 2 part-time (1 woman); includes 9 minority (3 Black or African American, non-Hispanic/Latino; 5 Hispanic/Latino; 1 Two or more races, non-Hispanic/Latino). Average age 33. 47 applicants, 11% accepted, 4 enrolled. In 2014, 5 doctorates awarded. *Degree requirements:* For doctorate, comprehensive exam, thesis/dissertation. *Entrance requirements:* For doctorate, GRE. Additional exam requirements/recommendations for international students: Required—TOEFL (minimum score 100 iBT). *Application deadline:* For fall admission, 1/15 priority date for domestic and international students. Application fee: $75. Electronic applications accepted. *Expenses: Tuition:* Part-time $1341 per credit. *Financial support:* Fellowships with full and partial tuition reimbursements and teaching assistantships with full and partial tuition reimbursements available. Financial award application deadline: 1/1; financial award applicants required to submit FAFSA. *Unit head:* Prof. Eileen Schell, Graduate Chair, 315-443-5146, E-mail: eeschell@syr.edu. *Application contact:* Kristen Krause, Office Coordinator III, 315-443-5146, E-mail: kkrause@syr.edu.
Website: http://ccr.syr.edu/

Syracuse University, College of Visual and Performing Arts, Program in Communication and Rhetorical Studies, Syracuse, NY 13244. Offers MA. Part-time programs available. *Students:* 13 full-time (8 women), 7 part-time (4 women); includes 5 minority (2 Black or African American, non-Hispanic/Latino; 3 Hispanic/Latino), 1 international. Average age 26. 44 applicants, 50% accepted, 8 enrolled. In 2014, 8 master's awarded. *Degree requirements:* For master's, comprehensive exam (for some programs), thesis (for some programs). *Entrance requirements:* For master's, GRE General Test, writing sample. Additional exam requirements/recommendations for international students: Required—TOEFL (minimum score 100 iBT). *Application deadline:* For fall admission, 2/1 priority date for domestic and international students. Application fee: $75. Electronic applications accepted. *Expenses: Tuition:* Part-time $1341 per credit. *Financial support:* In 2014–15, 9 students received support. Fellowships with full tuition reimbursements available, teaching assistantships with full and partial tuition reimbursements available, and tuition waivers available. Financial award application deadline: 1/1; financial award applicants required to submit FAFSA. *Unit head:* Dr. Charles Morris, Chair, 315-443-2308, E-mail: admissg@syr.edu. *Application contact:* Joseph Morley, Information Contact, 315-443-7175, E-mail: admissg@syr.edu.
Website: http://vpa.syr.edu/

Texas Christian University, AddRan College of Liberal Arts, Department of English, Fort Worth, TX 76129. Offers English (MA, PhD); rhetoric and composition (PhD). *Faculty:* 12 full-time (7 women), 1 (woman) part-time/adjunct. *Students:* 53 full-time (39 women); includes 8 minority (1 Black or African American, non-Hispanic/Latino; 4 Hispanic/Latino; 3 Two or more races, non-Hispanic/Latino), 1 international. Average age 30. 33 applicants, 48% accepted, 11 enrolled. In 2014, 4 master's, 2 doctorates awarded. *Degree requirements:* For master's, one foreign language, thesis; for doctorate, one foreign language, comprehensive exam, thesis/dissertation. *Entrance requirements:* For master's and doctorate, GRE General Test. Additional exam requirements/recommendations for international students: Recommended—TOEFL. *Application deadline:* For fall admission, 1/10 for domestic and international students; for winter admission, 1/10 for domestic and international students; for spring admission, 10/15 for domestic and international students. Application fee: $60. Electronic applications accepted. *Expenses: Tuition:* Full-time $22,860; part-time $1270 per credit hour. *Financial support:* In 2014–15, 51 students received support, including 4 fellowships with full tuition reimbursements available (averaging $21,000 per year), 4 research assistantships with full tuition reimbursements available, 24 teaching assistantships with full tuition reimbursements available (averaging $17,000 per year); Federal Work-Study, tuition waivers, and unspecified assistantships also available. Financial award application deadline: 1/10; financial award applicants required to submit FAFSA. *Faculty research:* Rhetoric, print culture and periodicals, new media writing, literary theory, women's studies. *Total annual research expenditures:* $6,500. *Unit head:* Dr. Mona Narain, Director of Graduate Studies, 817-257-7240, Fax: 817-257-6238, E-mail: m.narain@tcu.edu.
Website: http://www.eng.tcu.edu/

Texas State University, The Graduate College, College of Liberal Arts, Department of English, Program in Rhetoric and Composition, San Marcos, TX 78666. Offers MA. Part-time programs available. *Faculty:* 6 full-time (4 women). *Students:* 8 full-time (4 women), 6 part-time (3 women); includes 6 minority (1 Black or African American, non-Hispanic/Latino; 3 Hispanic/Latino; 2 Two or more races, non-Hispanic/Latino). Average age 33. 9 applicants, 67% accepted, 4 enrolled. In 2014, 10 master's awarded. *Degree requirements:* For master's, comprehensive exam, thesis optional. *Entrance requirements:* For master's, GRE (preferred), baccalaureate degree from regionally-accredited university with minimum GPA of 2.75 on last 60 undergraduate semester hours, 3.0 in minimum of 12 hours of undergraduate English courses. Additional exam requirements/recommendations for international students: Required—TOEFL (minimum score 550 paper-based; 78 iBT). *Application deadline:* For fall admission, 6/15 for domestic students, 6/1 for international students; for spring admission, 11/1 for domestic students, 10/1 for international students; for summer admission, 4/15 for domestic students, 3/15 for international students. Applications are processed on a rolling basis. Application fee: $40 ($90 for international students). Electronic applications accepted. *Expenses:* Expenses: $8,834 (tuition and fees combined). *Financial support:* In 2014–15, 8 students received support, including 1 research assistantship (averaging $14,579 per year), 6 teaching assistantships (averaging $13,485 per year); Federal Work-Study, institutionally sponsored loans, scholarships/grants, and unspecified assistantships also available. Support available to part-time students. Financial award application deadline: 4/1; financial award applicants required to submit FAFSA. *Unit head:* Dr. Rebecca Jackson, Graduate Advisor, 512-245-2163, E-mail: rj10@txstate.edu. *Application contact:* Dr. Andrea Golato, Dean of Graduate School, 512-245-2581, Fax: 512-245-8365, E-mail: gradcollege@txstate.edu.
Website: http://www.english.txstate.edu

Texas Tech University, Graduate School, College of Arts and Sciences, Department of English, Lubbock, TX 79409-3091. Offers English (MA, PhD); technical communication (MA); technical communication and rhetoric (PhD). Part-time programs available. Postbaccalaureate distance learning degree programs offered (minimal on-campus study). *Faculty:* 62 full-time (35 women), 8 part-time/adjunct (4 women). *Students:* 92 full-time (55 women), 91 part-time (63 women); includes 24 minority (5 Black or African American, non-Hispanic/Latino; 2 American Indian or Alaska Native, non-Hispanic/Latino; 6 Asian, non-Hispanic/Latino; 6 Hispanic/Latino; 5 Two or more races, non-Hispanic/Latino), 9 international. Average age 34. 197 applicants, 36% accepted, 48 enrolled. In 2014, 12 master's, 14 doctorates awarded. Terminal master's awarded for partial completion of doctoral program. *Degree requirements:* For master's, variable foreign language requirement, comprehensive exam, thesis optional; for doctorate, variable foreign language requirement, comprehensive exam, thesis/dissertation. *Entrance requirements:* For master's and doctorate, GRE General Test. Additional exam requirements/recommendations for international students: Required—TOEFL (minimum score 550 paper-based; 79 iBT), IELTS (minimum score 6.5). *Application deadline:* For fall admission, 6/1 priority date for domestic students, 1/15 priority date for international students; for spring admission, 9/1 priority date for domestic students, 6/15 priority date for international students. Applications are processed on a rolling basis. Application fee: $60. Electronic applications accepted. *Expenses:* Tuition, state resident: full-time $6310; part-time $262.92 per credit hour. Tuition, nonresident: full-time $14,998; part-time $624.92 per credit hour. *Required fees:* $2701; $36.50 per credit. $912.50 per semester. Tuition and fees vary according to course load. *Financial support:* In 2014–15, 112 students received support, including 94 fellowships (averaging $2,592 per year), 8 research assistantships (averaging $19,331 per year), 89 teaching assistantships (averaging $14,644 per year); career-related internships or fieldwork, Federal Work-Study, scholarships/grants, and unspecified assistantships also available. Financial award application deadline: 12/15; financial award applicants required to submit FAFSA. *Faculty research:* American, British, and comparative literature; creative writing; linguistics; film; technical communication and rhetoric. *Total annual research expenditures:* $64,530. *Unit head:* Dr. Bruce Clarke, Professor, 806-742-2501, Fax: 806-742-0989, E-mail: bruce.clarke@ttu.edu. *Application contact:* Dr. Brian J. McFadden, Director of Graduate Studies, 806-742-2501 Ext. 246, Fax: 806-742-0989, E-mail: english.gradadvisor@ttu.edu.
Website: http://www.english.ttu.edu/

Texas Woman's University, Graduate School, College of Arts and Sciences, Department of English, Speech, and Foreign Languages, Denton, TX 76201. Offers English (MA); rhetoric (PhD). Part-time programs available. *Degree requirements:* For master's, comprehensive exam, thesis; for doctorate, comprehensive exam, thesis/dissertation. *Entrance requirements:* For master's, GRE General Test (preferred minimum score 153 [500 old version] verbal, 138 [350 old version] quantitative), 3 letters of reference, minimum GPA of 3.0 on previous upper-division and graduate work; for doctorate, GRE General Test (preferred minimum score 153 [500 old version] verbal, 138 [350 old version] quantitative), writing sample, 3 letters of reference, interview (for graduate assistants), minimum GPA of 3.0 on previous upper-division and graduate work. Additional exam requirements/recommendations for international students: Recommended—TOEFL (minimum score 600 paper-based; 100 iBT). Electronic applications accepted. *Faculty research:* British and American literature, rhetoric: historical and applied, composition studies and technology, literary theory and criticism, women's literature and feminist rhetoric.

The University of Alabama, Graduate School, College of Arts and Sciences, Department of English, Tuscaloosa, AL 35487. Offers applied linguistics (PhD); composition and rhetoric (PhD); creative writing (MFA), including fiction, poetry; literature (MA, PhD); rhetoric and composition (MA); teaching English as a second language (MATESOL). *Faculty:* 34 full-time (19 women). *Students:* 129 full-time (70 women), 9 part-time (8 women); includes 18 minority (9 Black or African American, non-Hispanic/Latino; 1 Asian, non-Hispanic/Latino; 5 Hispanic/Latino; 3 Two or more races, non-Hispanic/Latino), 7 international. Average age 28. 318 applicants, 18% accepted, 42 enrolled. In 2014, 39 master's, 2 doctorates awarded. *Degree requirements:* For master's, one foreign language, comprehensive exam, thesis optional; for doctorate, 2 foreign languages, comprehensive exam, thesis/dissertation. *Entrance requirements:* For master's, GRE (minimum score of 300, except for MFA), minimum GPA of 3.0, critical writing sample; for doctorate, GRE (minimum score of 300), minimum GPA of 3.5 on master's or equivalent graduate work, critical writing sample. Additional exam requirements/recommendations for international students: Required—TOEFL (minimum score 100 iBT). *Application deadline:* For fall admission, 12/31 priority date for domestic and international students. Application fee: $50 ($60 for international students). Electronic applications accepted. *Expenses:* Tuition, state resident: full-time $9826. Tuition, nonresident: full-time $24,950. *Financial support:* In 2014–15, 11 fellowships with full tuition reimbursements (averaging $15,000 per year), 1 research assistantship with full tuition reimbursement (averaging $12,366 per year), 112 teaching assistantships with full tuition reimbursements (averaging $12,366 per year) were awarded; career-related internships or fieldwork, scholarships/grants, health care benefits, and unspecified assistantships also available. Financial award application deadline: 12/31. *Faculty research:* American literature, British literature, composition/

rhetoric, applied linguistics, creative writing. *Unit head:* Prof. Joel Brouwer, Department Chair, 205-348-9524, Fax: 205-348-1388, E-mail: joel.brouwer@ua.edu. *Application contact:* Jennifer Fuqua, Graduate Coordinator, 205-348-0766, Fax: 205-348-1388, E-mail: jfuqua@ua.edu.

The University of Alabama at Birmingham, College of Arts and Sciences, Program in English, Birmingham, AL 35294. Offers creative writing (MA); literature (MA); rhetoric and composition (MA). Part-time programs available. *Students:* 13 full-time (12 women), 12 part-time (4 women); includes 1 minority (Black or African American, non-Hispanic/Latino). Average age 29. In 2014, 11 master's awarded. *Degree requirements:* For master's, one foreign language, comprehensive exam, thesis or alternative. *Entrance requirements:* For master's, GRE General Test or MAT, minimum GPA of 2.75. *Application deadline:* For fall admission, 7/1 for domestic students; for spring admission, 11/1 for domestic students. Applications are processed on a rolling basis. Application fee: $45 ($60 for international students). Electronic applications accepted. *Expenses:* Tuition, state resident: full-time $7090; part-time $370 per credit hour. Tuition, nonresident: full-time $16,072; part-time $869 per credit hour. Full-time tuition and fees vary according to course load and program. *Financial support:* Teaching assistantships and career-related internships or fieldwork available. *Unit head:* Dr. Gale Temple, Program Director, 205-934-8593, Fax: 205-975-6610, E-mail: gtemple@uab.edu. *Application contact:* Susan Noblitt Banks, Director of Graduate School Operations, 205-934-8227, Fax: 205-934-8413, E-mail: gradschool@uab.edu.
Website: http://www.uab.edu/cas/english/academic-programs

The University of Arizona, College of Humanities, Department of English, Rhetoric, Composition and the Teaching of English Program, Tucson, AZ 85721. Offers MA, PhD. *Degree requirements:* For master's, one foreign language, comprehensive exam; for doctorate, one foreign language, comprehensive exam, thesis/dissertation. *Entrance requirements:* For doctorate, GRE General Test, 3 letters of recommendation, writing sample. Additional exam requirements/recommendations for international students: Required—TOEFL (minimum score 550 paper-based; 79 iBT). Electronic applications accepted.

University of Arkansas at Little Rock, Graduate School, College of Social Sciences and Communication, Department of Rhetoric and Writing, Little Rock, AR 72204-1099. Offers professional and technical writing (MA). Part-time and evening/weekend programs available. *Degree requirements:* For master's, thesis or alternative, oral defense of final project. *Entrance requirements:* For master's, GRE, minimum GPA of 3.0, writing portfolio. *Application deadline:* Applications are processed on a rolling basis. *Expenses:* Tuition, state resident: full-time $6000; part-time $300 per credit hour. Tuition, nonresident: full-time $13,800; part-time $690 per credit hour. *Required fees:* $1126; $603 per term. One-time fee: $40 full-time. *Financial support:* Research assistantships with tuition reimbursements, teaching assistantships with tuition reimbursements, career-related internships or fieldwork, Federal Work-Study, institutionally sponsored loans, and unspecified assistantships available. Support available to part-time students. *Faculty research:* Writing for industry, science, business, and government; composition and rhetorical theory; writing nonfiction; teaching of writing. *Unit head:* Dr. George H. Jensen, Chairperson, 501-569-3160, E-mail: ghjensen@ualr.edu. *Application contact:* Dr. Cynthia A. Nahrwold, Coordinator, 501-569-3316, Fax: 501-569-8279, E-mail: canahrwold@ualr.edu.
Website: http://ualr.edu/rhetoric/

University of California, Berkeley, Graduate Division, College of Letters and Science, Department of Rhetoric, Berkeley, CA 94720-1500. Offers PhD. *Degree requirements:* For doctorate, 2 foreign languages, thesis/dissertation, qualifying exam. *Entrance requirements:* For doctorate, GRE General Test, minimum GPA of 3.0, 3 letters of recommendation. *Faculty research:* History and theory of rhetoric, public discourse (law, politics, and science), literature and philosophy, film.

University of Colorado Denver, College of Liberal Arts and Sciences, Department of English, Denver, CO 80217. Offers applied linguistics (MA); literature (MA); rhetoric and teaching of writing (MA). Part-time and evening/weekend programs available. *Faculty:* 23 full-time (13 women), 1 (woman) part-time/adjunct. *Students:* 21 full-time (17 women), 16 part-time (10 women); includes 5 minority (1 Black or African American, non-Hispanic/Latino; 1 Asian, non-Hispanic/Latino; 3 Hispanic/Latino), 2 international. Average age 28. 19 applicants, 58% accepted, 4 enrolled. In 2014, 19 master's awarded. *Degree requirements:* For master's, variable foreign language requirement, comprehensive exam (for some programs), thesis (for some programs), minimum of 33 credit hours (for literature program), 30 (for rhetoric and teaching of writing and applied linguistics programs). *Entrance requirements:* For master's, GRE General Test, minimum GPA of 3.0 in undergraduate courses, critical writing sample, letters of recommendation, completion of 24 semester hours in English courses (at least 16 at the upper-division level), statement of purpose. Additional exam requirements/recommendations for international students: Required—TOEFL (minimum score 537 paper-based; 75 iBT); Recommended—IELTS (minimum score 6.5). *Application deadline:* For fall admission, 4/1 for domestic and international students; for spring admission, 10/1 for domestic and international students; for summer admission, 4/1 for domestic and international students. Application fee: $50 ($75 for international students). Electronic applications accepted. *Financial support:* In 2014–15, 9 students received support. Fellowships, research assistantships, teaching assistantships, Federal Work-Study, institutionally sponsored loans, scholarships/grants, traineeships, and unspecified assistantships available. Financial award application deadline: 4/1; financial award applicants required to submit FAFSA. *Faculty research:* Literature, rhetoric, teaching of writing, applied linguistics. *Unit head:* Prof. Nancy Ciccone, Chair, 303-556-8395, E-mail: nancy.ciccone@ucdenver.edu. *Application contact:* English Department, 303-556-2584, Fax: 303-556-2959.
Website: http://www.ucdenver.edu/academics/colleges/CLAS/Departments/english/Programs/Masters/Pages/Overview.aspx

The University of Findlay, Office of Graduate Admissions, Findlay, OH 45840-3653. Offers athletic training (MAT); business (MBA), including health care management, hospitality management, organizational leadership, public management; education (MA Ed), including administration, children's literature, early childhood, human resource development, reading, science, special education, technology; environmental, safety and health management (MSEM); health informatics (MS); occupational therapy (MOT); pharmacy (Pharm D); physical therapy (DPT); physician assistant (MPA); rhetoric and writing (MA); teaching English to speakers of other languages (TESOL) and bilingual education (MA). Part-time and evening/weekend programs available. Postbaccalaureate distance learning degree programs offered (no on-campus study). *Faculty:* 213 full-time (102 women), 62 part-time/adjunct (37 women). *Students:* 690 full-time (385 women), 515 part-time (316 women); includes 101 minority (43 Black or African American, non-Hispanic/Latino; 1 American Indian or Alaska Native, non-Hispanic/Latino; 19 Asian, non-Hispanic/Latino; 27 Hispanic/Latino; 11 Two or more races, non-Hispanic/Latino), 214 international. Average age 28. 765 applicants, 66% accepted, 289 enrolled. In 2014, 225 master's, 104 doctorates awarded. *Degree requirements:* For master's, thesis, cumulative project, capstone project. *Entrance requirements:* For master's, GRE/GMAT, bachelor's degree from accredited institution, minimum undergraduate GPA of 2.5 in last 64 hours of course work; for doctorate, GRE, minimum cumulative GPA of 3.0. Additional exam requirements/recommendations for international students: Required—

TOEFL (minimum score 80 iBT). *Application deadline:* Applications are processed on a rolling basis. Application fee: $25. Electronic applications accepted. Tuition and fees vary according to degree level and program. *Financial support:* In 2014–15, 11 research assistantships with full and partial tuition reimbursements (averaging $4,000 per year), 10 teaching assistantships with full and partial tuition reimbursements (averaging $3,600 per year) were awarded; career-related internships or fieldwork, Federal Work-Study, health care benefits, and unspecified assistantships also available. Financial award application deadline: 4/1; financial award applicants required to submit FAFSA. *Unit head:* Christopher M. Harris, Director of Admissions, 419-434-4347, E-mail: harrisc1@findlay.edu. *Application contact:* Austyn Erickson, Graduate Admissions Counselor, 419-434-4693, Fax: 419-434-4898, E-mail: ericksona@findlay.edu.
Website: http://www.findlay.edu/admissions/graduate/Pages/default.aspx

University of Houston–Downtown, College of Humanities and Social Sciences, Department of English, Program in Rhetoric and Composition, Houston, TX 77002. Offers MA. Part-time and evening/weekend programs available. *Faculty:* 6 full-time (3 women), 1 (woman) part-time/adjunct. *Students:* 4 full-time (2 women), 7 part-time (5 women); includes 6 minority (5 Black or African American, non-Hispanic/Latino; 1 Hispanic/Latino). Average age 36. 17 applicants, 82% accepted, 11 enrolled. *Entrance requirements:* For master's, essay, resume, 2 letters of recommendation, transcripts, 10-15 page sample of academic writing. Additional exam requirements/recommendations for international students: Required—TOEFL (minimum score 600 paper-based; 86 iBT). *Application deadline:* For fall admission, 5/15 for domestic and international students; for spring admission, 11/15 for domestic and international students. Application fee: $35 ($60 for international students). Electronic applications accepted. *Expenses:* Expenses: $260 per credit state resident; $572 nonresident. *Unit head:* Dr. Michelle Moosally, Chair, 713-221-8254, Fax: 713-226-5205, E-mail: moosallym@uhd.edu. *Application contact:* Ceshia Love, Director of Graduate and International Admissions, 713-221-8093, Fax: 713-223-7408, E-mail: gradadmissions@uhd.edu.
Website: https://www.uhd.edu/academics/humanities/graduate-programs/masters-arts-rhetoric-composition/Pages/marc-index.aspx

The University of Iowa, Graduate College, College of Liberal Arts and Sciences, Department of Communication Studies, Iowa City, IA 52242-1316. Offers interpersonal communication and relationships (MA, PhD); media studies (MA, PhD); rhetoric and public advocacy (MA, PhD). *Degree requirements:* For master's, thesis optional, exam; for doctorate, comprehensive exam, thesis/dissertation. *Entrance requirements:* For master's and doctorate, GRE General Test, minimum GPA of 3.0. Additional exam requirements/recommendations for international students: Required—TOEFL (minimum score 550 paper-based; 81 iBT). Electronic applications accepted.

University of Louisiana at Lafayette, College of Liberal Arts, Department of English, Lafayette, LA 70504. Offers British and American literature (MA), including creative writing, folklore, rhetoric; creative writing (PhD); literature (PhD); rhetoric (PhD). Part-time programs available. Terminal master's awarded for partial completion of doctoral program. *Degree requirements:* For master's, one foreign language, thesis or alternative; for doctorate, 2 foreign languages, comprehensive exam, thesis/dissertation. *Entrance requirements:* For master's, GRE General Test, minimum GPA of 2.75; for doctorate, GRE General Test, minimum GPA of 3.0. Additional exam requirements/recommendations for international students: Required—TOEFL (minimum score 550 paper-based). Electronic applications accepted. *Faculty research:* Composition theory, Southern literature, medieval literature.

University of Louisville, Graduate School, College of Arts and Sciences, Department of English, Louisville, KY 40292. Offers English (MA), including creative writing, literature, rhetoric and composition (MA, PhD); English rhetoric and composition (PhD), including rhetoric and composition (MA, PhD). Part-time programs available. *Students:* 62 full-time (39 women), 20 part-time (10 women); includes 6 minority (2 Black or African American, non-Hispanic/Latino; 2 Hispanic/Latino; 2 Two or more races, non-Hispanic/Latino), 2 international. Average age 29. 94 applicants, 53% accepted, 25 enrolled. In 2014, 18 master's, 4 doctorates awarded. *Degree requirements:* For master's, one foreign language, thesis or culminating project; for doctorate, 2 foreign languages, comprehensive exam, thesis/dissertation. *Entrance requirements:* For master's, GRE General Test, 2 academic letters of recommendation; for doctorate, GRE General Test, 15-20 page critical writing sample, 1000-word statement of professional goals, 3 academic letters of recommendation, transcripts of all college work. Additional exam requirements/recommendations for international students: Required—TOEFL (minimum score 600 paper-based; 100 iBT). *Application deadline:* For fall admission, 8/1 for domestic students, 5/1 priority date for international students; for spring admission, 12/1 for domestic students, 11/1 priority date for international students; for summer admission, 4/1 priority date for international students. Applications are processed on a rolling basis. Application fee: $60. Electronic applications accepted. *Expenses:* Tuition, state resident: full-time $11,326; part-time $630 per credit hour. Tuition, nonresident: full-time $23,568; part-time $1311 per credit hour. *Required fees:* $196. Tuition and fees vary according to program and reciprocity agreements. *Financial support:* Fellowships with full tuition reimbursements, teaching assistantships with full tuition reimbursements, health care benefits, and unspecified assistantships available. Financial award application deadline: 1/5. *Faculty research:* American and English literatures and cultures, rhetoric and composition, critical theory and cultural studies, creative writing. *Unit head:* Dr. Glynis Ridley, Chair, 502-852-6803, E-mail: glynis.ridley@louisville.edu. *Application contact:* Libby Leggett, Director, Graduate Admissions, 502-852-3101, Fax: 502-852-6536, E-mail: gradadm@louisville.edu.
Website: http://www.louisville.edu/english/graduate

University of Massachusetts Amherst, Graduate School, College of Humanities and Fine Arts, Department of English, Amherst, MA 01003. Offers American studies (PhD); composition and rhetoric (PhD); creative writing (MFA); English and American literature (MA, PhD). Part-time programs available. *Faculty:* 49 full-time (24 women). *Students:* 100 full-time (60 women), 76 part-time (50 women); includes 29 minority (2 Black or African American, non-Hispanic/Latino; 6 Asian, non-Hispanic/Latino; 10 Hispanic/Latino; 1 Native Hawaiian or other Pacific Islander, non-Hispanic/Latino; 10 Two or more races, non-Hispanic/Latino), 17 international. Average age 30. 600 applicants, 12% accepted, 29 enrolled. In 2014, 26 master's, 10 doctorates awarded. Terminal master's awarded for partial completion of doctoral program. *Degree requirements:* For master's, one foreign language, thesis optional; for doctorate, one foreign language, comprehensive exam, thesis/dissertation. *Entrance requirements:* For master's, manuscript; for doctorate, GRE General Test, manuscript. Additional exam requirements/recommendations for international students: Required—TOEFL (minimum score 550 paper-based; 80 iBT), IELTS (minimum score 6.5). *Application deadline:* For fall admission, 12/15 for domestic and international students. Applications are processed on a rolling basis. Application fee: $75. Electronic applications accepted. *Expenses:* Tuition, state resident: full-time $1980; part-time $110 per credit. Tuition, nonresident: full-time $14,644; part-time $414 per credit. *Required fees:* $11,417. One-time fee: $357. *Financial support:* Fellowships with full and partial tuition reimbursements, research assistantships with full and partial tuition reimbursements, teaching assistantships with full and partial tuition reimbursements, career-related internships or fieldwork, Federal Work-Study, scholarships/grants, traineeships, health

care benefits, tuition waivers (full and partial), and unspecified assistantships available. Support available to part-time students. Financial award application deadline: 12/15. *Unit head:* Dr. Jenny Spencer, Department Head, 413-545-2332, Fax: 413-545-3880. *Application contact:* Lindsay DeSantis, Supervisor of Admissions, 413-545-0722, Fax: 413-577-0010, E-mail: gradadm@grad.umass.edu.
Website: http://www.umass.edu/english/

University of Michigan–Flint, College of Arts and Sciences, Program in English Language and Literature, Flint, MI 48502-1950. Offers literature (MA); writing and rhetoric (MA). Part-time programs available. *Faculty:* 28 full-time (18 women), 4 part-time/adjunct (2 women). *Students:* 3 full-time (2 women), 21 part-time (15 women); includes 3 minority (1 Black or African American, non-Hispanic/Latino; 1 Hispanic/Latino; 1 Two or more races, non-Hispanic/Latino), 2 international. Average age 36. 10 applicants, 70% accepted, 5 enrolled. In 2014, 20 master's awarded. *Entrance requirements:* For master's, minimum GPA of 3.0, bachelor's degree with major or significant coursework in English or related fields. Additional exam requirements/recommendations for international students: Required—TOEFL (minimum score 84 iBT), IELTS (minimum score 6.5). *Application deadline:* For fall admission, 8/1 for domestic students, 5/1 for international students; for winter admission, 11/15 for domestic students, 9/1 for international students; for spring admission, 3/15 for domestic students, 1/1 for international students; for summer admission, 5/15 for domestic students. Applications are processed on a rolling basis. Application fee: $55. Electronic applications accepted. *Expenses:* Expenses: Contact institution. *Financial support:* Federal Work-Study, scholarships/grants, and unspecified assistantships available. Support available to part-time students. Financial award application deadline: 3/1; financial award applicants required to submit FAFSA. *Unit head:* Dr. Kazuko Hiramatsu, Director, 810-762-3285, E-mail: kazukoh@umflint.edu. *Application contact:* Bradley T. Maki, Director of Graduate Admissions, 810-762-3171, Fax: 810-766-6789, E-mail: bmaki@umflint.edu.
Website: http://www.umflint.edu/graduateprograms/english-language-and-literature-ma

University of Nebraska–Lincoln, Graduate College, College of Arts and Sciences, Department of Communication Studies, Lincoln, NE 68588. Offers instructional communication (MA, PhD); interpersonal communication (MA, PhD); marketing, communication studies, and advertising (MA, PhD); organizational communication (MA, PhD); rhetoric and culture (MA, PhD). *Degree requirements:* For master's, thesis optional; for doctorate, comprehensive exam, thesis/dissertation. *Entrance requirements:* For master's and doctorate, GRE General Test, writing sample. Additional exam requirements/recommendations for international students: Required—TOEFL (minimum score 600 paper-based). Electronic applications accepted. *Faculty research:* Message strategies, gender communication, political communication, organizational communication, instructional communication.

University of Nebraska–Lincoln, Graduate College, College of Arts and Sciences, Department of English, Lincoln, NE 68588-0333. Offers composition and rhetoric (MA, PhD); creative writing (MA, PhD); literature studies (MA, PhD). *Degree requirements:* For master's, thesis optional; for doctorate, one foreign language, comprehensive exam, thesis/dissertation. *Entrance requirements:* For master's, writing sample; for doctorate, GRE General Test, writing sample. Additional exam requirements/recommendations for international students: Required—TOEFL (minimum score 600 paper-based). Electronic applications accepted. *Faculty research:* Creative writing, composition and rhetoric, women's studies, North American literature, medieval/Renaissance studies.

The University of North Carolina at Charlotte, College of Liberal Arts and Sciences, Department of Communication Studies, Charlotte, NC 28223-0001. Offers communication studies (Graduate Certificate); health communication (MA); organizational communication (MA); public relations and international public relations (MA); rhetoric, media studies, and popular culture (MA). Part-time and evening/weekend programs available. *Faculty:* 15 full-time (8 women). *Students:* 11 full-time (8 women), 12 part-time (9 women); includes 3 minority (2 Black or African American, non-Hispanic/Latino; 1 Two or more races, non-Hispanic/Latino), 2 international. Average age 27. 49 applicants, 49% accepted, 11 enrolled. In 2014, 11 master's awarded. Terminal master's awarded for partial completion of doctoral program. *Degree requirements:* For master's, project, thesis, or comprehensive exam. *Entrance requirements:* For master's, GRE General Test, minimum GPA of 2.75 overall. Additional exam requirements/recommendations for international students: Required—TOEFL (minimum score 557 paper-based; 83 iBT). *Application deadline:* For fall admission, 3/1 for domestic and international students; for spring admission, 11/15 for domestic students, 10/1 for international students. Application fee: $75. Electronic applications accepted. *Expenses:* Tuition, state resident: full-time $4008. Tuition, nonresident: full-time $16,295. *Required fees:* $2755. Tuition and fees vary according to course load and program. *Financial support:* In 2014–15, 10 students received support, including 10 teaching assistantships (averaging $14,981 per year); career-related internships or fieldwork, institutionally sponsored loans, scholarships/grants, and unspecified assistantships also available. Support available to part-time students. Financial award application deadline: 4/1; financial award applicants required to submit FAFSA. *Faculty research:* Rhetorical approaches to analyzing public relations controversies, participant empowerment and engagement in community-based participatory action research, human factors constraining the management of knowledge in a large financial services organization, models of Internet governance, race and class politics of mediated sports. *Unit head:* Dr. Shawn Long, Chair, 704-687-0783, Fax: 704-687-6900, E-mail: shawn.long@uncc.edu. *Application contact:* Kathy B. Giddings, Director of Graduate Admissions, 704-687-5503, Fax: 704-687-1668, E-mail: gradadm@uncc.edu.
Website: http://gradcomm.uncc.edu/

The University of North Carolina at Greensboro, Graduate School, College of Arts and Sciences, Department of English, Program in English, Greensboro, NC 27412-5001. Offers American literature (PhD); English (M Ed, MA); English literature (PhD); rhetoric and composition (PhD). *Degree requirements:* For master's, comprehensive exam, thesis or alternative; for doctorate, variable foreign language requirement, thesis/dissertation, preliminary exam. *Entrance requirements:* For master's, GRE General Test, GRE Subject Test, minimum GPA of 3.0; for doctorate, GRE General Test, GRE Subject Test, critical writing sample, minimum GPA of 3.0. Additional exam requirements/recommendations for international students: Required—TOEFL. Electronic applications accepted.

University of Southern California, Graduate School, Annenberg School for Communication and Journalism, School of Communication, Program in Communication, Los Angeles, CA 90089. Offers culture and community (PhD); global and transnational communication (PhD); groups, organizations and networks (PhD); health communication and social dynamics (PhD); information, political economy and entertainment (PhD); new media and technology (PhD); rhetoric, politics and public media (PhD). *Students:* 105 full-time (76 women); includes 829 minority (8 Black or African American, non-Hispanic/Latino; 810 Asian, non-Hispanic/Latino; 7 Hispanic/Latino; 4 Two or more races, non-Hispanic/Latino), 41 international. Average age 27. 229 applicants, 14% accepted, 19 enrolled. In 2014, 16 doctorates awarded. *Degree requirements:* For doctorate, thesis/dissertation. *Entrance requirements:* For doctorate, GRE General Test, resume or curriculum vitae, scholarly writing, 3 letters of recommendation, statement of purpose. Additional exam requirements/

recommendations for international students: Required—TOEFL (minimum score 114 iBT) or IELTS; Recommended—TWE. *Application deadline:* For fall admission, 11/1 for domestic and international students. Application fee: $85. Electronic applications accepted. *Financial support:* In 2014–15, 18 students received support, including 18 fellowships with full tuition reimbursements available (averaging $74,000 per year); health care benefits and unspecified assistantships also available. Financial award application deadline: 11/1; financial award applicants required to submit FAFSA. *Faculty research:* Computer-mediated communication, public health campaigns, communication democracy and the public sphere, new communication technologies in organizations, communication and community. *Unit head:* Dr. Peter Monge, Director of the PhD Program, 213-740-0921, E-mail: monge@usc.edu. *Application contact:* Allyson Hill, Associate Dean for Admissions, 213-821-0770, Fax: 213-740-1933, E-mail: ascadm@usc.edu.
Website: http://www.annenberg.usc.edu

University of South Florida, College of Arts and Sciences, Department of English, Tampa, FL 33620-9951. Offers creative writing (MFA), including fiction, poetry; literature (MA, PhD); rhetoric and composition (MA, PhD). Part-time and evening/weekend programs available. *Faculty:* 24 full-time (12 women). *Students:* 73 full-time (52 women), 27 part-time (19 women); includes 16 minority (3 Black or African American, non-Hispanic/Latino; 4 Asian, non-Hispanic/Latino; 7 Hispanic/Latino; 2 Two or more races, non-Hispanic/Latino). Average age 32. 122 applicants, 44% accepted, 25 enrolled. In 2014, 26 master's, 5 doctorates awarded. *Degree requirements:* For master's, thesis (for MFA); thesis or comprehensive examination (for MA); for doctorate, one foreign language, comprehensive exam, thesis/dissertation. *Entrance requirements:* For master's, GRE General Test, minimum undergraduate GPA of 3.5 (for MA), 3.2 (for MFA); three letters of recommendation; personal statement; writing sample from 10 to 20 pages, depending on genre; for doctorate, GRE General Test, minimum graduate GPA of 3.7; three letters of recommendation; 2-3 page personal statement; 2500-word writing sample from English coursework. Additional exam requirements/recommendations for international students: Required—TOEFL (minimum score 550 paper-based; 79 iBT) or IELTS (minimum score 6.5) for MA and PhD; TOEFL (minimum score 600 paper-based) for MFA. *Application deadline:* For fall admission, 2/1 for domestic students, 1/2 for international students. Applications are processed on a rolling basis. Application fee: $30. Electronic applications accepted. *Financial support:* In 2014–15, 81 students received support, including 2 research assistantships (averaging $17,221 per year), 79 teaching assistantships with tuition reimbursements available (averaging $11,576 per year); unspecified assistantships also available. Financial award application deadline: 6/30; financial award applicants required to submit FAFSA. *Faculty research:* British and American literature, rhetoric and composition, world and comparative literatures, creative writing, gender and sexuality studies, women's literature, film and genre studies, literary theory, popular and visual culture, textual and translation studies. Total annual research expenditures: $63,565. *Unit head:* Dr. Hunt Hawkins, Professor and Chairperson, 813-974-9492, Fax: 813-974-2270, E-mail: hhawkins@usf.edu. *Application contact:* Dr. Marty Gould, Associate Professor and Graduate Director, 813-974-9474, Fax: 813-974-2270, E-mail: mgould@usf.edu.
Website: http://english.usf.edu

The University of Tennessee at Chattanooga, Program in English, Chattanooga, TN 37403. Offers creative writing (MA); literary study (MA); rhetoric and writing (MA, Graduate Certificate). Part-time and evening/weekend programs available. *Faculty:* 13 full-time (7 women). *Students:* 18 full-time (13 women), 20 part-time (13 women); includes 4 minority (1 Asian, non-Hispanic/Latino; 1 Hispanic/Latino; 2 Two or more races, non-Hispanic/Latino). Average age 28. 13 applicants, 85% accepted, 8 enrolled. In 2014, 17 master's awarded. *Degree requirements:* For master's, one foreign language, comprehensive exam, thesis. *Entrance requirements:* For master's, GRE General Test or GRE Subject Test (literature), minimum GPA of 3.0 in English. Additional exam requirements/recommendations for international students: Required—TOEFL (minimum score 550 paper-based; 79 iBT), IELTS (minimum score 6). *Application deadline:* For fall admission, 6/13 priority date for domestic students, 6/1 for international students; for spring admission, 10/15 priority date for domestic students, 10/1 for international students. Applications are processed on a rolling basis. Application fee: $30 ($35 for international students). Electronic applications accepted. *Expenses:* Tuition, state resident: full-time $7708; part-time $428 per credit hour. Tuition, nonresident: full-time $23,826; part-time $1323 per credit hour. *Required fees:* $1708; $252 per credit hour. *Financial support:* In 2014–15, 5 research assistantships with tuition reimbursements (averaging $6,445 per year), 6 teaching assistantships with tuition reimbursements (averaging $5,969 per year) were awarded; career-related internships or fieldwork, scholarships/grants, and unspecified assistantships also available. Support available to part-time students. Financial award applicants required to submit FAFSA. *Faculty research:* Technical writing, African-American literature, Milton, creative writing and poetry, American modernism and gender theory. Total annual research expenditures: $76,158. *Unit head:* Dr. Christopher Stuart, Department Head, 423-425-2140, Fax: 423-425-2282, E-mail: joe.wilferth@utc.edu. *Application contact:* Dr. J. Randy Walker, Interim Dean of Graduate Studies, 423-425-4478, Fax: 423-425-5223, E-mail: randy-walker@utc.edu.
Website: http://www.utc.edu/Academic/English/

The University of Texas at El Paso, Graduate School, College of Liberal Arts, Department of English, El Paso, TX 79968-0001. Offers bilingual professional writing (Certificate); English and American literature (MA); rhetoric and composition (PhD); rhetoric and writing studies (MA); teaching English (MAT). Part-time and evening/weekend programs available. *Degree requirements:* For master's, thesis optional. *Entrance requirements:* For master's, GRE General Test, minimum GPA of 3.0. Additional exam requirements/recommendations for international students: Required—TOEFL. Electronic applications accepted. *Faculty research:* Literature, creative writing, literary theory.

University of Utah, Graduate School, College of Humanities, Department of English, Salt Lake City, UT 84112. Offers American studies (MA, PhD); British and American literature (MA, PhD); creative writing (MFA, PhD), including fiction, non-fiction, poetry; rhetoric and composition (MA, PhD). *Faculty:* 27 full-time (10 women), 7 part-time/adjunct (2 women). *Students:* 47 full-time (27 women), 25 part-time (16 women); includes 5 minority (1 Black or African American, non-Hispanic/Latino; 2 Asian, non-Hispanic/Latino; 2 Two or more races, non-Hispanic/Latino), 3 international. Average age 35. 285 applicants, 12% accepted, 11 enrolled. In 2014, 7 master's, 7 doctorates awarded. Terminal master's awarded for partial completion of doctoral program. *Degree requirements:* For master's, one foreign language, comprehensive exam (for some programs), thesis (for some programs), 1 standard-level language; exam (for MA); thesis (for MFA); for doctorate, variable foreign language requirement, comprehensive exam, thesis/dissertation, 2 standard-level languages/1 advanced-level language. *Entrance requirements:* For master's and doctorate, GRE General Test, minimum GPA of 3.2. Additional exam requirements/recommendations for international students: Required—TOEFL (minimum score 650 paper-based; 115 iBT); Recommended—IELTS (minimum score 9). *Application deadline:* For fall admission, 12/15 for domestic and international students. Application fee: $55 ($65 for international students). Electronic applications accepted. *Financial support:* In 2014–15, 54 students received support, including 17 fellowships with full tuition reimbursements available (averaging $15,000

per year), 34 teaching assistantships with full tuition reimbursements available (averaging $14,000 per year); health care benefits also available. Financial award application deadline: 12/15; financial award applicants required to submit FAFSA. *Faculty research:* Creative writing including poetics and modern poetry, fiction, and experimental forms; nineteenth and twentieth century British and American literature; American Studies, the American west, and environmental studies; critical theory and practice; race and gender studies. *Total annual research expenditures:* $126,500. *Unit head:* Prof. Barry L. Weller, Department Chair, 801-581-6168, E-mail: barry.weller@utah.edu. *Application contact:* Prof. Howard Horwitz, Director of Graduate Studies, 801-581-7353, E-mail: h.horwitz@english.utah.edu.
Website: http://www.hum.utah.edu/english/

University of Wisconsin–Madison, Graduate School, College of Letters and Science, Department of Communication Arts, Madison, WI 53706-1380. Offers communication science (MA, PhD); film (MA, PhD); media and cultural studies (MA, PhD); rhetoric (MA, PhD). Terminal master's awarded for partial completion of doctoral program. *Degree requirements:* For master's, one foreign language, thesis (for some programs); for doctorate, one foreign language, thesis/dissertation. *Entrance requirements:* For master's and doctorate, GRE General Test, minimum GPA of 3.5. Electronic applications accepted. *Expenses:* Tuition, state resident: full-time $10,723; part-time $745 per credit. Tuition, nonresident: full-time $24,054; part-time $1578 per credit. *Required fees:* $374 per semester. Tuition and fees vary according to course load, program and reciprocity agreements.

University of Wisconsin–Milwaukee, Graduate School, College of Letters and Sciences, Department of Communication, Milwaukee, WI 53201-0413. Offers communication (MA, PhD); mediation and negotiation (Certificate); rhetorical leadership (Certificate). Part-time programs available. *Degree requirements:* For master's, thesis or alternative; for doctorate, comprehensive exam. *Entrance requirements:* For master's, GRE General Test, minimum GPA of 3.0. Additional exam requirements/recommendations for international students: Required—TOEFL (minimum score 550 paper-based; 79 iBT), IELTS (minimum score 6). Electronic applications accepted.

University of Wisconsin–Milwaukee, Graduate School, College of Letters and Sciences, Department of English, Milwaukee, WI 53201-0413. Offers creative writing (PhD); English (MA); international technical communication (Certificate); linguistics (PhD); professional writing (PhD); professional writing and communication (Certificate); rhetoric and composition (PhD); MLIS/MA. *Degree requirements:* For master's, thesis or alternative; for doctorate, one foreign language, thesis/dissertation. *Entrance requirements:* For master's, GRE General Test, GRE Subject Test; for doctorate, GRE. Additional exam requirements/recommendations for international students: Required—TOEFL (minimum score 550 paper-based; 79 iBT), IELTS (minimum score 6.5). Electronic applications accepted.

Valdosta State University, Department of English, Valdosta, GA 31698. Offers literature (MA); rhetoric and composition (MA); studies for language arts teachers (MA). Part-time programs available. *Faculty:* 12 full-time (9 women). *Students:* 6 full-time (5 women), 24 part-time (14 women); includes 2 minority (1 Black or African American, non-Hispanic/Latino; 1 Two or more races, non-Hispanic/Latino). Average age 24. 7 applicants, 71% accepted, 4 enrolled. *Degree requirements:* For master's, one foreign language, thesis, comprehensive written and/or oral exams. *Entrance requirements:* For master's, GRE General Test, minimum GPA of 3.0. Additional exam requirements/recommendations for international students: Required—TOEFL (minimum score 523 paper-based). *Application deadline:* For fall admission, 7/1 for domestic and international students; for spring admission, 11/1 for domestic and international students. Applications are processed on a rolling basis. Application fee: $35. Electronic applications accepted. *Expenses:* Tuition, state resident: part-time $236 per credit hour. Tuition, nonresident: part-time $850 per credit hour. *Required fees:* $1032 per semester. *Financial support:* In 2014–15, 11 students received support, including 6 research assistantships with full tuition reimbursements available (averaging $4,000 per year), 7 teaching assistantships with full tuition reimbursements available (averaging $8,000 per year); institutionally sponsored loans, scholarships/grants, and unspecified

assistantships also available. Support available to part-time students. Financial award application deadline: 7/1; financial award applicants required to submit FAFSA. *Faculty research:* American literature, creative writing. *Unit head:* Dr. Mark Smith, Head, 229-333-5946, E-mail: marksmit@valdosta.edu. *Application contact:* Jessica Powers, Admissions Specialist, 229-333-5694, Fax: 229-245-3853, E-mail: jldevane@valdosta.edu.

Virginia Commonwealth University, Graduate School, College of Humanities and Sciences, Department of English, Program in English, Richmond, VA 23284-9005. Offers literature (MA); writing and rhetoric (MA). Part-time programs available. *Entrance requirements:* For master's, GRE General Test. Additional exam requirements/recommendations for international students: Required—TWE, TOEFL (minimum score 600 paper-based; 100 iBT) or IELTS (minimum score 6.5). Electronic applications accepted. *Faculty research:* Literature, writing, rhetoric.

Virginia Polytechnic Institute and State University, Graduate School, College of Liberal Arts and Human Sciences, Blacksburg, VA 24061. Offers career and technical education (MS Ed, Ed D, PhD, Ed S); communication (MA); counselor education (MA Ed, Ed D, PhD, Ed S); creative writing (MFA); curriculum and instruction (MA Ed, Ed D, PhD, Ed S); educational leadership and policy studies (MA Ed, Ed D, PhD, Ed S); educational research and evaluation (PhD); English (MA); foreign languages, cultures, and literatures (MA); higher education and student affairs (MA Ed); history (MA); human development (MS, PhD); material culture and public humanities (MA); philosophy (MA); political science (MA); rhetoric and writing (PhD); science and technology studies (MS, PhD); social, political, ethical, and cultural thought (PhD); sociology (MS, PhD); theater arts (MFA). *Faculty:* 421 full-time (216 women), 2 part-time/adjunct (both women). *Students:* 642 full-time (437 women), 537 part-time (344 women); includes 235 minority (132 Black or African American, non-Hispanic/Latino; 2 American Indian or Alaska Native, non-Hispanic/Latino; 27 Asian, non-Hispanic/Latino; 52 Hispanic/Latino; 1 Native Hawaiian or other Pacific Islander, non-Hispanic/Latino; 21 Two or more races, non-Hispanic/Latino), 81 international. Average age 34. 890 applicants, 46% accepted, 303 enrolled. In 2014, 342 master's, 96 doctorates, 33 other advanced degrees awarded. *Degree requirements:* For master's, comprehensive exam (for some programs), thesis (for some programs); for doctorate, comprehensive exam (for some programs), thesis/dissertation (for some programs). *Entrance requirements:* For master's and doctorate, GRE/GMAT (may vary by department). Additional exam requirements/recommendations for international students: Required—TOEFL (minimum score 550 paper-based). *Application deadline:* For fall admission, 8/1 for domestic students, 4/1 for international students; for spring admission, 1/1 for domestic students, 9/1 for international students. Applications are processed on a rolling basis. Application fee: $75. Electronic applications accepted. *Expenses:* Tuition, state resident: full-time $11,656; part-time $647.50 per credit hour. Tuition, nonresident: full-time $23,351; part-time $1297.25 per credit hour. *Required fees:* $2533; $465.75 per semester. Tuition and fees vary according to course load, campus/location and program. *Financial support:* In 2014–15, 19 research assistantships with full tuition reimbursements (averaging $22,141 per year), 231 teaching assistantships with full tuition reimbursements (averaging $19,470 per year) were awarded. Financial award application deadline: 3/1; financial award applicants required to submit FAFSA. *Total annual research expenditures:* $6.5 million. *Unit head:* Elizabeth Spiller, Dean, 540-231-6779, Fax: 540-231-7157, E-mail: espiller@vt.edu. *Application contact:* Melissa Elliott, Executive Assistant, 540-231-6779, Fax: 540-231-7157, E-mail: elliott1@vt.edu.
Website: http://www.clahs.vt.edu/

Wright State University, School of Graduate Studies, College of Liberal Arts, Department of English Language and Literatures, Dayton, OH 45435. Offers composition and rhetoric (MA); English (MA); literature (MA); teaching English to speakers of other languages (MA). *Degree requirements:* For master's, thesis optional, portfolio. *Entrance requirements:* For master's, 20 hours in upper-level English. Additional exam requirements/recommendations for international students: Required—TOEFL. *Faculty research:* American literature, world literature in English, applied linguistics, writing theory and pedagogy.

Speech and Interpersonal Communication

Arkansas State University, Graduate School, College of Media and Communication, Department of Communication, State University, AR 72467. Offers MA, Graduate Certificate, SCCT. Part-time programs available. *Faculty:* 3 full-time (1 woman). *Students:* 7 full-time (4 women), 14 part-time (11 women); includes 11 minority (9 Black or African American, non-Hispanic/Latino; 1 American Indian or Alaska Native, non-Hispanic/Latino; 1 Hispanic/Latino), 3 international. Average age 27. 24 applicants, 58% accepted, 9 enrolled. In 2014, 13 master's awarded. *Degree requirements:* For master's, one foreign language, comprehensive exam, thesis or alternative; for other advanced degree, comprehensive exam. *Entrance requirements:* For master's, GRE General Test or MAT, appropriate bachelor's degree, writing sample, letter of recommendation, official transcripts, immunization records; for other advanced degree, GRE or MAT, appropriate master's degree, interview, official transcript, immunization records. Additional exam requirements/recommendations for international students: Required—TOEFL (minimum score 550 paper-based; 79 iBT), IELTS (minimum score 6), PTE (minimum score 56). *Application deadline:* For fall admission, 7/1 for domestic and international students; for spring admission, 11/15 for domestic students, 11/14 for international students. Applications are processed on a rolling basis. Application fee: $30 ($40 for international students). Electronic applications accepted. *Expenses:* Tuition, state resident: full-time $4392; part-time $244 per credit hour. Tuition, nonresident: full-time $8784; part-time $488 per credit hour. *International tuition:* $9484 full-time. *Required fees:* $1134; $63 per credit hour. $25 per term. Tuition and fees vary according to course load and program. *Financial support:* In 2014–15, 11 students received support. Teaching assistantships, career-related internships or fieldwork, scholarships/grants, and unspecified assistantships available. Financial award application deadline: 7/1; financial award applicants required to submit FAFSA. *Unit head:* Dr. Marceline Thompson-Hayes, Interim Chair, 870-972-2091, Fax: 870-972-3856, E-mail: mhayes@astate.edu. *Application contact:* Vickey Ring, Graduate Admissions Coordinator, 870-972-3029, Fax: 870-972-3857, E-mail: vickeyring@astate.edu.
Website: http://www.astate.edu/college/communications/about

Ball State University, Graduate School, College of Communication, Information, and Media, Department of Communication Studies, Muncie, IN 47306-1099. Offers speech, public address, forensics, and rhetoric (MA). *Faculty:* 7 full-time (6 women). *Students:* 17 full-time (14 women), 13 part-time (11 women); includes 3 minority (1 Black or African American, non-Hispanic/Latino; 2 Hispanic/Latino), 6 international. Average age 27. 23 applicants, 91% accepted, 16 enrolled. In 2014, 12 master's awarded. *Entrance*

requirements: For master's, GRE General Test. Application fee: $50. *Financial support:* In 2014–15, 22 students received support, including 25 teaching assistantships with partial tuition reimbursements available (averaging $11,056 per year); unspecified assistantships also available. Financial award application deadline: 3/1. *Unit head:* Glen Stamp, Chairperson, 765-285-1882, Fax: 765-285-2736, E-mail: gstamp@bsu.edu. *Application contact:* Dr. Robert Morris, Associate Provost for Research and Dean of the Graduate School, 765-285-4723, Fax: 765-285-1328, E-mail: rmorris@bsu.edu.
Website: http://cms.bsu.edu/academics/collegesanddepartments/communicationstudies

Bob Jones University, Graduate Programs, Greenville, SC 29614. Offers accountancy (MS); Bible (MA); Bible translation (MA); Biblical studies (Certificate); broadcast management (MS); business administration (MBA); church history (MA, PhD); church ministries (MA); church music (MM); cinema and video production (MA); counseling (MS); curriculum and instruction (Ed D); divinity (M Div); dramatic production (MA); educational leadership (MS, Ed D, Ed S); elementary education (M Ed, MAT); English (M Ed, MA, MAT); fine arts (MA); graphic design (MA); history (M Ed, MA); illustration (MA); interpretative speech (MA); mathematics (M Ed, MAT); medical missions (Certificate); ministry (MM, D Min); multi-categorical special education (M Ed, MAT); music (M Ed); New Testament interpretation (PhD); Old Testament interpretation (PhD); orchestral instrument performance (MM); organ performance (MM); pastoral studies (MA); personnel services (MS, Ed S); piano pedagogy (MM); piano performance (MM); platform arts (MA); radio and television broadcasting (MS); rhetoric and public address (MA); secondary education (M Ed); studio art (MA); teaching Bible (MA); theology (MA, PhD); voice performance (MM); youth ministries (MA); M Div/MM.

Bowling Green State University, Graduate College, College of Arts and Sciences, School of Communication Studies, Program of Communication Studies, Bowling Green, OH 43403. Offers MA, PhD. Terminal master's awarded for partial completion of doctoral program. *Degree requirements:* For master's, thesis or alternative; for doctorate, comprehensive exam, thesis/dissertation. *Entrance requirements:* For master's and doctorate, GRE General Test. Additional exam requirements/recommendations for international students: Required—TOEFL. Electronic applications accepted. *Faculty research:* Rhetorical theory and criticism, culture and communication, interpersonal/organizational communication.

Brooklyn College of the City University of New York, School of Humanities and Social Sciences, Department of Speech Communication Arts and Sciences, Brooklyn,

NY 11210-2889. Offers audiology (Au D); speech (MA), including public communication; speech-language pathology (MS). Au D offered jointly with Hunter College of the City University of New York. *Accreditation:* ASHA (one or more programs are accredited). Part-time programs available. Terminal master's awarded for partial completion of doctoral program. *Degree requirements:* For master's, comprehensive exam, NTE. *Entrance requirements:* For master's, GRE, minimum GPA of 3.0, interview, essay. Additional exam requirements/recommendations for international students: Required—TOEFL (minimum score 500 paper-based; 61 iBT). Electronic applications accepted. *Faculty research:* Language and learning disorders, aphasia, auditory disorders, public and business communication, voice and fluency disorders.

California State University, Fullerton, Graduate Studies, College of Communications, Department of Human Communications, Fullerton, CA 92834-9480. Offers communication studies (MA); communicative disorders (MA). *Accreditation:* ASHA. Part-time programs available. *Students:* 74 full-time (62 women), 37 part-time (27 women); includes 55 minority (1 Black or African American, non-Hispanic/Latino; 24 Asian, non-Hispanic/Latino; 24 Hispanic/Latino; 1 Native Hawaiian or other Pacific Islander, non-Hispanic/Latino; 5 Two or more races, non-Hispanic/Latino), 3 international. Average age 29. 414 applicants, 12% accepted, 43 enrolled. In 2014, 37 master's awarded. *Degree requirements:* For master's, comprehensive exam, thesis or alternative. *Entrance requirements:* For master's, minimum GPA of 3.0 in major. Application fee: $55. *Financial support:* Teaching assistantships, career-related internships or fieldwork, Federal Work-Study, institutionally sponsored loans, and scholarships/grants available. Support available to part-time students. Financial award application deadline: 3/1; financial award applicants required to submit FAFSA. *Faculty research:* Speech therapy. *Unit head:* Dr. John Reinard, Chair, 657-278-3617. *Application contact:* Admissions/Applications, 657-278-2371.

California State University, Fullerton, Graduate Studies, College of Humanities and Social Sciences, Program in Linguistics, Fullerton, CA 92834-9480. Offers analysis of specific language structures (MA); anthropological linguistics (MA); applied linguistics (MA); communication and semantics (MA); disorders of communication (MA); experimental phonetics (MA). Part-time programs available. *Students:* 45 full-time (28 women), 14 part-time (10 women); includes 11 minority (6 Asian, non-Hispanic/Latino; 5 Hispanic/Latino), 38 international. Average age 29. 36 applicants, 75% accepted, 21 enrolled. In 2014, 10 master's awarded. *Degree requirements:* For master's, one foreign language, thesis or alternative, project. *Entrance requirements:* For master's, minimum GPA of 3.0, undergraduate major in linguistics or related field. Application fee: $55. *Financial support:* Career-related internships or fieldwork, Federal Work-Study, institutionally sponsored loans, and scholarships/grants available. Support available to part-time students. Financial award application deadline: 3/1; financial award applicants required to submit FAFSA. *Unit head:* Dr. Franz Muller-Gotama, Adviser, 657-278-2441. *Application contact:* Admissions/Applications, 657-278-2371.

California State University, Northridge, Graduate Studies, College of Arts, Media, and Communication, Department of Communication Studies, Northridge, CA 91330. Offers MA. *Students:* 23 full-time (18 women), 19 part-time (14 women); includes 15 minority (5 Black or African American, non-Hispanic/Latino; 3 Asian, non-Hispanic/Latino; 6 Hispanic/Latino; 1 Two or more races, non-Hispanic/Latino), 6 international. Average age 30. *Entrance requirements:* For master's, GRE General Test. Additional exam requirements/recommendations for international students: Required—TOEFL. *Application deadline:* For fall admission, 11/30 for domestic students. Application fee: $55. *Expenses: Required fees:* $12,402. *Financial support:* Teaching assistantships available. Financial award application deadline: 3/1. *Unit head:* Kathryn Sorrells, Chair, 818-677-2853.
Website: http://www.csun.edu/CommunicationStudies/

Colorado State University, Graduate School, College of Liberal Arts, Department of Communication Studies, Fort Collins, CO 80523-1783. Offers MA. *Faculty:* 15 full-time (7 women). *Students:* 19 full-time (14 women), 13 part-time (11 women); includes 3 minority (1 Black or African American, non-Hispanic/Latino; 1 Hispanic/Latino; 1 Two or more races, non-Hispanic/Latino), 1 international. Average age 25. 34 applicants, 56% accepted, 12 enrolled. In 2014, 4 master's awarded. *Entrance requirements:* For master's, GRE General Test, minimum GPA of 3.0, writing sample, letters of recommendation, transcripts. Additional exam requirements/recommendations for international students: Required—TOEFL (minimum score 550 paper-based; 80 iBT). *Application deadline:* For fall admission, 1/31 priority date for domestic and international students. Applications are processed on a rolling basis. Application fee: $50. Electronic applications accepted. *Expenses:* Tuition, state resident: full-time $9348; part-time $519 per credit. Tuition, nonresident: full-time $22,916; part-time $1273 per credit. *Required fees:* $1584. *Financial support:* In 2014–15, 6 students received support, including 2 research assistantships (averaging $9,508 per year), 4 teaching assistantships with full and partial tuition reimbursements available (averaging $13,270 per year); scholarships/grants and unspecified assistantships also available. Financial award application deadline: 3/1; financial award applicants required to submit FAFSA. *Faculty research:* Rhetorical theory and criticism, media and popular culture, intercultural communication, freedom of speech, communication theory. *Total annual research expenditures:* $198,650. *Unit head:* Dr. Sue Pendell, Head, 970-491-6140, Fax: 970-491-2160, E-mail: sue.pendell@colostate.edu. *Application contact:* Dr. Karrin Anderson, Director of Graduate Studies, 970-491-6893, Fax: 970-491-2160, E-mail: karrin.anderson@colostate.edu.
Website: http://communicationstudies.colostate.edu/

Eastern Illinois University, Graduate School, College of Arts and Humanities, Department of Communication Studies, Charleston, IL 61920. Offers community college pedagogy (MA). Part-time and evening/weekend programs available. *Faculty:* 11. *Students:* 20 full-time (15 women), 10 part-time (5 women); includes 5 minority (2 Black or African American, non-Hispanic/Latino; 1 American Indian or Alaska Native, non-Hispanic/Latino; 2 Hispanic/Latino), 3 international. Average age 27. 36 applicants, 53% accepted, 11 enrolled. In 2014, 10 master's awarded. *Degree requirements:* For master's, comprehensive exam (for some programs), thesis (for some programs). *Entrance requirements:* For master's, GMAT or GRE. Additional exam requirements/recommendations for international students: Required—TOEFL (minimum score 500 paper-based; 61 iBT), IELTS (minimum score 6). *Application deadline:* For fall admission, 5/15 for domestic and international students; for spring admission, 10/15 for domestic and international students. Applications are processed on a rolling basis. Application fee: $30. Electronic applications accepted. *Expenses:* Tuition, state resident: full-time $3113; part-time $283 per credit hour. Tuition, nonresident: full-time $7469; part-time $679 per credit hour. *Required fees:* $2287; $96 per credit hour. Tuition and fees vary according to course load. *Financial support:* In 2014–15, 32 students received support, including 12 teaching assistantships with full tuition reimbursements available (averaging $7,830 per year); career-related internships or fieldwork, Federal Work-Study, and unspecified assistantships also available. Support available to part-time students. Financial award application deadline: 3/1; financial award applicants required to submit FAFSA. *Unit head:* Stephen King, Chairperson, 217-581-2016, Fax: 217-581-5718, E-mail: saking@eiu.edu. *Application contact:* Matt Gill, Graduate Coordinator, 217-581-6306, Fax: 217-581-5718, E-mail: mjgill@eiu.edu.
Website: http://www.eiu.edu/commstudiesgrad/index.php

Georgia State University, College of Arts and Sciences, Department of Communication, Atlanta, GA 30302-3083. Offers film, video, and digital imaging (MA), including critical studies, production, screenwriting; human communication and social influence (MA); mass communication (MA); media and society (PhD); moving image studies (PhD); public communication (PhD); rhetoric and politics (PhD). Part-time programs available. *Faculty:* 35 full-time (18 women). *Students:* 102 full-time (51 women), 40 part-time (15 women); includes 37 minority (20 Black or African American, non-Hispanic/Latino; 4 Asian, non-Hispanic/Latino; 6 Hispanic/Latino; 7 Two or more races, non-Hispanic/Latino), 14 international. Average age 33. 154 applicants, 39% accepted, 30 enrolled. In 2014, 25 master's, 5 doctorates awarded. *Degree requirements:* For master's, variable foreign language requirement, thesis (for some programs); for doctorate, comprehensive exam, thesis/dissertation. *Entrance requirements:* For master's, GRE; for doctorate, GRE. Additional exam requirements/recommendations for international students: Required—TOEFL (minimum score 550 paper-based; 80 iBT), IELTS (minimum score 6.5). *Application deadline:* For fall admission, 2/10 for domestic and international students; for spring admission, 10/15 for domestic and international students. Application fee: $50. Electronic applications accepted. *Expenses:* Tuition, state resident: full-time $6516; part-time $362 per credit hour. Tuition, nonresident: full-time $22,014; part-time $1223 per credit hour. *Required fees:* $2128 per semester. Tuition and fees vary according to course load and program. *Financial support:* In 2014–15, fellowships with tuition reimbursements (averaging $15,000 per year), teaching assistantships with tuition reimbursements (averaging $15,000 per year) were awarded; career-related internships or fieldwork and unspecified assistantships also available. Financial award applicants required to submit FAFSA. *Faculty research:* New media, mass media and journalism, rhetoric, film and media studies, film production. *Unit head:* Dr. David Cheshier, Chair, 404-413-5649, Fax: 404-413-5634, E-mail: dcheshier@gsu.edu. *Application contact:* Dr. Jennifer Barker, Associate Professor, 404-413-5793, Fax: 404-413-5634, E-mail: jmbarker@gsu.edu.
Website: http://communication.gsu.edu

Idaho State University, Office of Graduate Studies, College of Arts and Letters, Department of Communication and Rhetorical Studies, Pocatello, ID 83209-8115. Offers communication and rhetorical studies (MA). Part-time programs available. *Degree requirements:* For master's, comprehensive exam, paper or thesis. *Entrance requirements:* For master's, GRE General Test, minimum GPA of 3.0 in all upper-level courses. Additional exam requirements/recommendations for international students: Required—TOEFL (minimum score 550 paper-based; 80 iBT). Electronic applications accepted. *Faculty research:* Metaphor and cognition in organizational groups and teams; rhetorical criticism of contemporary culture, including music, film, television, and advertising; communication pedagogy; the effect of language on organizational identification and commitment; risk communication and crisis communication.

Indiana University Bloomington, University Graduate School, College of Arts and Sciences, The Media School, Department of Communication and Culture, Bloomington, IN 47405-7000. Offers communication and culture (MA); film and media studies (PhD); performance and ethnography (PhD); rhetoric and public culture (PhD). *Faculty:* 22 full-time (13 women), 1 (woman) part-time/adjunct. *Students:* 75 full-time (41 women); includes 7 minority (1 Black or African American, non-Hispanic/Latino; 5 Hispanic/Latino; 1 Two or more races, non-Hispanic/Latino), 7 international. 116 applicants, 15% accepted, 8 enrolled. In 2014, 7 master's, 7 doctorates awarded. *Degree requirements:* For master's, comprehensive exam; for doctorate, one foreign language, comprehensive exam, thesis/dissertation, student teaching. *Entrance requirements:* For master's and doctorate, GRE General Test, minimum GPA of 3.0, 3 letters of recommendation, writing sample, personal statement. Additional exam requirements/recommendations for international students: Required—TOEFL (minimum score 550 paper-based) or IELTS. *Application deadline:* For fall admission, 1/2 for domestic students, 12/1 for international students; for winter admission, 1/2 for domestic students, 12/1 for international students. Application fee: $55 ($65 for international students). Electronic applications accepted. *Financial support:* Fellowships with full tuition reimbursements, research assistantships with full tuition reimbursements, and teaching assistantships with full tuition reimbursements available. Financial award application deadline: 1/2. *Faculty research:* Rhetoric and public culture, film and media studies, performance ethnography. *Unit head:* Prof. Jane Goodman, Chair, 812-855-3232, Fax: 812-855-6014, E-mail: cmcl@indiana.edu. *Application contact:* Kathy P. Teige, Graduate Secretary, 812-855-6389, Fax: 812-855-6014, E-mail: kteige@indiana.edu.
Website: http://www.indiana.edu/~cmcl/

Louisiana Tech University, Graduate School, College of Liberal Arts, Department of Speech, Ruston, LA 71272. Offers audiology (Au D); speech-language pathology (MA). *Accreditation:* ASHA (one or more programs are accredited). *Degree requirements:* For master's, thesis or alternative. *Entrance requirements:* For master's, GRE General Test. *Application deadline:* For fall admission, 1/15 for domestic students; for spring admission, 2/3 for domestic students. Application fee: $40. *Financial support:* Fellowships, career-related internships or fieldwork, Federal Work-Study, institutionally sponsored loans, and unspecified assistantships available. Financial award application deadline: 2/1. *Unit head:* Dr. Brenda L. Heiman, Interim Head, 318-257-4764, Fax: 318-257-4492. *Application contact:* Marilyn J. Robinson, Assistant to the Dean of the Graduate School, 318-257-2924, Fax: 318-257-4487.
Website: http://www.latech.edu/speech/

Marquette University, Graduate School, Diederich College of Communication, Milwaukee, WI 53201-1881. Offers advertising and public relations (MA); communication studies (MA); digital storytelling (Certificate); journalism (MA); mass communication (MA); science, health and environmental communication (MA). *Accreditation:* ACEJMC (one or more programs are accredited). Part-time and evening/weekend programs available. *Degree requirements:* For master's, comprehensive exam, thesis or alternative. *Entrance requirements:* For master's, GRE, official transcripts from all current and previous colleges/universities except Marquette, three letters of recommendation, statement of academic and professional goals. Additional exam requirements/recommendations for international students: Required—TOEFL (minimum score 530 paper-based). Electronic applications accepted. *Faculty research:* Urban journalism, gender and communication, intercultural communication, religious communication.

New York University, Steinhardt School of Culture, Education, and Human Development, Department of Media, Culture and Communication, New York, NY 10010. Offers media, culture and communication (MA, PhD); MLIS/MA. Part-time programs available. *Faculty:* 35 full-time (17 women), 43 part-time/adjunct (19 women). *Students:* 98 full-time (68 women), 38 part-time (30 women); includes 27 minority (5 Black or African American, non-Hispanic/Latino; 12 Asian, non-Hispanic/Latino; 5 Hispanic/Latino; 1 Native Hawaiian or other Pacific Islander, non-Hispanic/Latino; 4 Two or more races, non-Hispanic/Latino), 55 international. Average age 33. 550 applicants, 24% accepted, 46 enrolled. In 2014, 57 master's, 6 doctorates awarded. Terminal master's awarded for partial completion of doctoral program. *Degree requirements:* For master's, thesis (for some programs); for doctorate, thesis/dissertation. *Entrance requirements:* For master's, GRE General Test; for doctorate, GRE General Test, interview. Additional exam requirements/recommendations for international students: Required—TOEFL (minimum score 100 iBT). *Application deadline:* For fall admission, 12/1 priority date for

domestic and international students; for spring admission, 10/1 for domestic and international students. Applications are processed on a rolling basis. Application fee: $75. Electronic applications accepted. *Financial support:* Fellowships with full and partial tuition reimbursements, teaching assistantships with full and partial tuition reimbursements, career-related internships or fieldwork, Federal Work-Study, institutionally sponsored loans, scholarships/grants, tuition waivers (partial), and unspecified assistantships available. Support available to part-time students. Financial award application deadline: 2/1; financial award applicants required to submit FAFSA. *Faculty research:* Digital media and new technologies, media criticism, flow of media and culture transnationally and transculturally. *Unit head:* Prof. Lisa Gitelman, Chairperson, 212-998-5191, Fax: 212-995-4046, E-mail: lg91@nyu.edu. *Application contact:* 212-998-5030, Fax: 212-995-4328, E-mail: steinhardt.gradadmissions@nyu.edu.
Website: http://steinhardt.nyu.edu/mcc

North Dakota State University, College of Graduate and Interdisciplinary Studies, College of Arts, Humanities and Social Sciences, Department of Communication, Fargo, ND 58108. Offers communication (PhD); mass communication (MA, MS); speech communication (MA, MS). Part-time programs available. Postbaccalaureate distance learning degree programs offered (no on-campus study). Terminal master's awarded for partial completion of doctoral program. *Degree requirements:* For master's, thesis (for some programs); for doctorate, comprehensive exam, thesis/dissertation, 2-3 publications. *Entrance requirements:* For master's, GRE, minimum undergraduate GPA of 3.25; for doctorate, GRE, minimum undergraduate GPA of 3.5. Additional exam requirements/recommendations for international students: Required—TOEFL (minimum score 600 paper-based; 100 iBT), IELTS (minimum score 7). Electronic applications accepted. *Faculty research:* Communication and rhetorical theory, organizational communication, broadcast and print journalism, international communication, public relations and advertising.

Northeastern Illinois University, College of Graduate Studies and Research, College of Arts and Sciences, Program in Communication, Media and Theatre, Chicago, IL 60625-4699. Offers MA. Part-time and evening/weekend programs available. *Degree requirements:* For master's, comprehensive exam, oral exams, thesis or 3 term papers. *Entrance requirements:* For master's, 15 undergraduate hours in speech and performing arts, minimum GPA of 2.75. Additional exam requirements/recommendations for international students: Required—TOEFL (minimum score 550 paper-based; 79 iBT). Electronic applications accepted. *Faculty research:* Creative drama, family communication, fine arts and general education, playwriting techniques, interpersonal communications.

Northwestern University, The Graduate School, School of Communication, Department of Performance Studies, Evanston, IL 60208. Offers MA, PhD. Admissions and degrees offered through The Graduate School. Part-time programs available. Terminal master's awarded for partial completion of doctoral program. *Degree requirements:* For master's, recital; for doctorate, one foreign language, thesis/dissertation, recital. *Entrance requirements:* For master's and doctorate, GRE General Test. Additional exam requirements/recommendations for international students: Required—TOEFL. *Faculty research:* Adaptation/performance of literature, ethnography of performance, critical cultural studies, performance theory, intercultural performance, gender studies.

Ohio University, Graduate College, Scripps College of Communication, School of Communication Studies, Athens, OH 45701-2979. Offers health communication (PhD); organizational communication (MA); relating and organizing (PhD); rhetoric and public culture (PhD). Part-time programs available. Postbaccalaureate distance learning degree programs offered (minimal on-campus study). Terminal master's awarded for partial completion of doctoral program. *Degree requirements:* For master's, capstone; for doctorate, comprehensive exam, thesis/dissertation. *Entrance requirements:* For master's, GRE; for doctorate, GRE General Test, minimum GPA of 3.0. Additional exam requirements/recommendations for international students: Required—TOEFL (minimum score 550 paper-based; 80 iBT) or IELTS (minimum score 6.5). Electronic applications accepted. *Faculty research:* Rhetoric and public culture, relating and organizing, health communication.

Old Dominion University, College of Arts and Letters, Program in Lifespan and Digital Communication, Norfolk, VA 23529. Offers MA. *Accreditation:* NASAD. Part-time and evening/weekend programs available. *Faculty:* 15 full-time (5 women). *Students:* 11 full-time (9 women), 14 part-time (10 women); includes 11 minority (8 Black or African American, non-Hispanic/Latino; 1 Hispanic/Latino; 2 Two or more races, non-Hispanic/Latino), 1 international. Average age 30. 14 applicants, 86% accepted, 12 enrolled. In 2014, 4 master's awarded. *Degree requirements:* For master's, thesis optional, comprehensive exam (for non-thesis students of a project). *Entrance requirements:* For master's, GRE. Additional exam requirements/recommendations for international students: Recommended—TOEFL (minimum score 550 paper-based; 79 iBT). *Application deadline:* For fall admission, 6/15 for domestic students, 4/15 for international students. Applications are processed on a rolling basis. Application fee: $50. Electronic applications accepted. *Expenses:* Tuition, state resident: full-time $10,488; part-time $437 per credit. Tuition, nonresident: full-time $26,136; part-time $1089 per credit. *Required fees:* $64 per semester. One-time fee: $50. *Financial support:* In 2014–15, 8 students received support, including 1 research assistantship (averaging $10,000 per year), 4 teaching assistantships (averaging $10,000 per year); 3 graduate assistantships ($5000 per term) also available. Financial award application deadline: 6/15. *Faculty research:* Family communication, digital media studies, lifespan communication, social media, screenwriting. *Unit head:* Dr. Thomas J. Socha, Graduate Program Director, 757-683-3833, E-mail: tsocha@odu.edu. *Application contact:* Dr. David C. Earnest, Associate Dean, 757-683-6077, Fax: 757-683-5746, E-mail: dearnest@odu.edu.
Website: http://www.odu.edu/~tsocha/Masters/ma-index.shtml

Portland State University, Graduate Studies, College of Liberal Arts and Sciences, Department of Communication, Portland, OR 97207-0751. Offers general speech communication (MA, MS, Certificate). Part-time programs available. *Faculty:* 10 full-time (5 women), 8 part-time/adjunct (4 women). *Students:* 17 full-time (13 women), 9 part-time (6 women); includes 6 minority (1 Black or African American, non-Hispanic/Latino; 1 American Indian or Alaska Native, non-Hispanic/Latino; 1 Asian, non-Hispanic/Latino; 1 Hispanic/Latino; 2 Two or more races, non-Hispanic/Latino), 1 international. Average age 32. 19 applicants, 68% accepted, 9 enrolled. In 2014, 11 master's awarded. *Degree requirements:* For master's, variable foreign language requirement, thesis optional. *Entrance requirements:* For master's, GRE (encouraged for all, required only for students who select the thesis option and/or who receive an assistantship), minimum GPA of 3.0 in upper-division course work or 2.75 overall, 3 letters of recommendation, statement of purpose, writing samples. Additional exam requirements/recommendations for international students: Required—TOEFL (minimum score 600 paper-based; 100 iBT). *Application deadline:* For fall admission, 2/1 priority date for domestic and international students. Applications are processed on a rolling basis. Application fee: $65. Electronic applications accepted. *Expenses:* Tuition, state resident: part-time $222 per credit. Tuition, nonresident: part-time $527 per credit. *Required fees:* $22 per contact hour. $100 per quarter. Tuition and fees vary according to program. *Financial support:* In 2014–15, 1 research assistantship with full tuition reimbursement (averaging $10,130 per year), 10 teaching assistantships with full and partial tuition reimbursements (averaging $5,765 per year) were awarded; career-related internships or fieldwork, Federal Work-Study, scholarships/grants, and unspecified assistantships also available. Support available to part-time students. Financial award application deadline: 3/1; financial award applicants required to submit FAFSA. *Total annual research expenditures:* $68,797. *Unit head:* Prof. Jeffrey Robinson, PhD, Chair, 503-725-3599, Fax: 503-725-5385, E-mail: jeffreyr@pdx.edu. *Application contact:* Prof. Cynthia-Lou Coleman, PhD, 503-725-5384, Fax: 503-725-5385, E-mail: hallie2@pdx.edu.
Website: http://www.pdx.edu/communication/

Rensselaer Polytechnic Institute, Graduate School, School of Humanities, Arts, and Social Sciences, Programs in Communication and Rhetoric, Troy, NY 12180-3590. Offers MS, PhD. *Faculty:* 16 full-time (8 women). *Students:* 13 full-time (7 women), 2 part-time (0 women); includes 2 minority (1 Black or African American, non-Hispanic/Latino; 1 Hispanic/Latino). Average age 30. 25 applicants, 40% accepted, 3 enrolled. In 2014, 1 master's awarded. Terminal master's awarded for partial completion of doctoral program. *Degree requirements:* For master's, thesis optional; for doctorate, comprehensive exam, thesis/dissertation. *Entrance requirements:* For master's and doctorate, GRE. Additional exam requirements/recommendations for international students: Required—TOEFL (minimum score 570 paper-based; 88 iBT), IELTS (minimum score 6.5), PTE (minimum score 60). *Application deadline:* For fall admission, 1/1 priority date for domestic and international students; for spring admission, 8/15 priority date for domestic and international students. Applications are processed on a rolling basis. Application fee: $75. Electronic applications accepted. *Expenses:* Tuition: Full-time $46,700; part-time $1945 per credit. Tuition and fees vary according to course load. *Financial support:* In 2014–15, 12 students received support, including research assistantships with full tuition reimbursements available (averaging $18,500 per year), teaching assistantships with full tuition reimbursements available (averaging $18,500 per year); fellowships also available. Financial award application deadline: 1/1. *Faculty research:* Communication, game studies, human computer interaction, literary theory, media studies, rhetoric, visual design, writing studies. *Unit head:* Dr. Katya Haskins, Graduate Program Director, 518-276-4047, E-mail: haskie@rpi.edu. *Application contact:* Office of Graduate Admissions, 518-276-6216, E-mail: gradadmissions@rpi.edu.
Website: http://www.cm.rpi.edu/pl/graduate

San Francisco State University, Division of Graduate Studies, College of Liberal and Creative Arts, Department of Communication Studies, San Francisco, CA 94132-1722. Offers MA. Part-time programs available. *Application deadline:* Applications are processed on a rolling basis. *Expenses:* Tuition, state resident: full-time $6738. Tuition, nonresident: full-time $17,898; part-time $372 per credit hour. *Required fees:* $498 per semester. *Financial support:* Teaching assistantships available. *Unit head:* Dr. Christina Sabee, Chair, 415-338-1597, E-mail: csabee@sfsu.edu. *Application contact:* Dr. Karen E. Lovaas, Graduate Advisor, 415-338-1713, E-mail: klovaas@sfsu.edu.
Website: http://communicationstudies.sfsu.edu/

San Jose State University, Graduate Studies and Research, College of Social Sciences, Department of History, San Jose, CA 95192-0001. Offers history (MA); history education (MA). *Degree requirements:* For master's, comprehensive exam, thesis or alternative. *Entrance requirements:* For master's, bachelor's degree or 15 units of course work in history, minimum GPA of 3.0. Electronic applications accepted.

Seton Hall University, School of Health and Medical Sciences, Program in Speech-Language Pathology, South Orange, NJ 07079-2697. Offers MS. *Accreditation:* ASHA. *Entrance requirements:* For master's, GRE, bachelor's degree, clinical experience; minimum GPA of 3.0, undergraduate preprofessional coursework in communication sciences and disorders. Additional exam requirements/recommendations for international students: Recommended—TOEFL. Electronic applications accepted. *Faculty research:* Child language disorders, motor speech control, voice disorders, dysphagia, early intervention/teaming.

Southern Illinois University Carbondale, Graduate School, College of Liberal Arts, Department of Communication Studies, Carbondale, IL 62901-4701. Offers MA, MS, PhD. *Faculty:* 16 full-time (8 women). *Students:* 43 full-time (21 women), 31 part-time (18 women); includes 10 minority (4 Black or African American, non-Hispanic/Latino; 1 American Indian or Alaska Native, non-Hispanic/Latino; 2 Asian, non-Hispanic/Latino; 3 Hispanic/Latino), 7 international. 55 applicants, 38% accepted, 20 enrolled. In 2014, 5 master's, 10 doctorates awarded. *Degree requirements:* For master's, one foreign language, thesis or alternative; for doctorate, one foreign language, thesis/dissertation. *Entrance requirements:* For master's, GRE General Test or MAT, minimum GPA of 2.7; for doctorate, GRE General Test or MAT, minimum GPA of 3.25. Additional exam requirements/recommendations for international students: Required—TOEFL. *Application deadline:* For fall admission, 2/1 for domestic students. Application fee: $50. *Expenses:* Tuition, state resident: full-time $10,176; part-time $1153 per credit. Tuition, nonresident: full-time $20,814; part-time $1744 per credit. *Required fees:* $7092; $394 per credit. $2364 per semester. *Financial support:* In 2014–15, 61 students received support, including 4 fellowships with full tuition reimbursements available, 4 research assistantships with full tuition reimbursements available, 50 teaching assistantships with full tuition reimbursements available; Federal Work-Study, institutionally sponsored loans, and tuition waivers (full) also available. Support available to part-time students. *Unit head:* Dr. Nathan Stucky, Chair, 618-453-2291, E-mail: nstucky@siu.edu. *Application contact:* Laura Sims, Office Administrator, 618-453-2214, E-mail: lsims@siu.edu.

Southern Illinois University Edwardsville, Graduate School, College of Arts and Sciences, Department of Applied Communication Studies, Program in Interpersonal Communication, Edwardsville, IL 62026. Offers MA. Part-time and evening/weekend programs available. *Students:* 1 (woman) full-time, 9 part-time (8 women); includes 1 minority (Two or more races, non-Hispanic/Latino). 1 applicant, 100% accepted. In 2014, 2 master's awarded. *Degree requirements:* For master's, comprehensive exam (for some programs), thesis (for some programs). *Entrance requirements:* Additional exam requirements/recommendations for international students: Required—TOEFL (minimum score 550 paper-based, 79 iBT), IELTS (minimum score 6.5), Michigan Test of English Language Proficiency or PTE. *Application deadline:* For fall admission, 7/18 for domestic students, 6/1 for international students; for spring admission, 12/12 for domestic students, 10/1 for international students; for summer admission, 4/24 for domestic students, 3/1 for international students. Applications are processed on a rolling basis. Application fee: $30. Electronic applications accepted. *Expenses:* Tuition, state resident: full-time $5026. Tuition, nonresident: full-time $12,566. *International tuition:* $25,136 full-time. *Required fees:* $1682. Tuition and fees vary according to course load, campus/location and program. *Financial support:* Institutionally sponsored loans, scholarships/grants, and unspecified assistantships available. Financial award application deadline: 3/1; financial award applicants required to submit FAFSA. *Unit head:* Dr. Jocelyn DeGroot Brown, Program Director, 618-650-5828, E-mail: jocbrow@siue.edu. *Application contact:* Melissa K. Mace, Assistant Director of Graduate and International Recruitment, 618-650-2756, Fax: 618-650-3618, E-mail: mmace@siue.edu.
Website: http://www.siue.edu/artsandsciences/spc/

Speech and Interpersonal Communication

Texas Christian University, Bob Schieffer College of Communication, Department of Communication Studies, Fort Worth, TX 76129. Offers MS. Part-time programs available. *Faculty:* 12 full-time (5 women). *Students:* 10 full-time (7 women), 1 part-time (0 women), 1 international. Average age 25. 9 applicants, 89% accepted, 7 enrolled. In 2014, 7 master's awarded. *Degree requirements:* For master's, comprehensive exams or thesis. *Entrance requirements:* For master's, GRE General Test. Additional exam requirements/recommendations for international students: Required—TOEFL (minimum score 550 paper-based; 80 iBT). *Application deadline:* For fall and spring admission, 2/15 for domestic and international students. Application fee: $60. Electronic applications accepted. *Expenses: Tuition:* Full-time $22,860; part-time $1270 per credit hour. *Financial support:* In 2014–15, 10 students received support, including 9 teaching assistantships with full tuition reimbursements available (averaging $11,000 per year); tuition waivers also available. Financial award application deadline: 2/15. *Faculty research:* Interpersonal communication, social media, health communication, organizational communication, instructional communication. *Unit head:* Dr. Paul King, Professor/Chair, 817-257-6466, Fax: 817-257-6580, E-mail: p.king@tcu.edu. *Application contact:* Dr. Paul Schrodt, Professor and Graduate Director, 817-257-5674, Fax: 817-257-6580, E-mail: p.schrodt@tcu.edu.
Website: http://www.commstudies.tcu.edu

The University of Alabama, Graduate School, College of Communication and Information Sciences, Department of Communication Studies, Tuscaloosa, AL 35487. Offers MA. *Faculty:* 14 full-time (9 women). *Students:* 25 full-time (14 women), 2 part-time (0 women); includes 7 minority (5 Black or African American, non-Hispanic/Latino; 1 Asian, non-Hispanic/Latino; 1 Two or more races, non-Hispanic/Latino), 3 international. Average age 27. 35 applicants, 63% accepted, 10 enrolled. In 2014, 15 master's awarded. *Degree requirements:* For master's, comprehensive exam (for some programs), thesis (for some programs), colloquium presentation; capstone portfolio (for some programs). *Entrance requirements:* For master's, GRE, MAT, minimum GPA of 3.0. Additional exam requirements/recommendations for international students: Required—TOEFL (minimum score 550 paper-based). *Application deadline:* For fall admission, 5/1 for domestic students, 4/1 for international students; for spring admission, 11/1 for domestic students, 10/1 for international students; for summer admission, 3/1 for domestic and international students. Applications are processed on a rolling basis. Application fee: $50 ($60 for international students). Electronic applications accepted. *Expenses:* Tuition, state resident: full-time $9826. Tuition, nonresident: full-time $24,950. *Financial support:* In 2014–15, 16 students received support, including 1 fellowship with full tuition reimbursement available, 13 teaching assistantships with full tuition reimbursements available (averaging $12,366 per year); health care benefits, unspecified assistantships, and one teaching stipend (one semester $3,000) also available. Financial award application deadline: 3/1. *Faculty research:* Rhetorical studies, organizational communication, interpersonal communication, gender and communication, health communication. *Unit head:* Dr. Beth S. Bennett, Department Chair, 205-348-8073, E-mail: bbennett@ua.edu. *Application contact:* Dr. Jane Stuart Baker, Coordinator of Admissions, 205-348-4175, E-mail: jsbaker@ua.edu.
Website: http://www.comstudies.ua.edu/

University of Arkansas at Little Rock, Graduate School, College of Social Sciences and Communication, Department of Speech Communication, Little Rock, AR 72204-1099. Offers applied communication studies (MA). Part-time and evening/weekend programs available. *Degree requirements:* For master's, comprehensive exam, internship, paper, or thesis. *Entrance requirements:* For master's, GRE General Test, MAT, minimum GPA of 2.7. *Application deadline:* Applications are processed on a rolling basis. *Expenses:* Tuition, state resident: full-time $6000; part-time $300 per credit hour. Tuition, nonresident: full-time $13,800; part-time $690 per credit hour. *Required fees:* $1126; $603 per term. One-time fee: $40 full-time. *Financial support:* Research assistantships, career-related internships or fieldwork, Federal Work-Study, institutionally sponsored loans, and unspecified assistantships available. *Faculty research:* Communication theory and applications, managerial communication, human resource training and development, relational communication. *Unit head:* Dr. Carol Thompson, Interim Chair, 501-569-3159, E-mail: clthompson@ualr.edu. *Application contact:* Dr. Gerald W. Driskill, Graduate Program Coordinator, 501-569-8385, E-mail: gwdriskill@ualr.edu.
Website: http://ualr.edu/speechcomm/

University of California, Santa Barbara, Graduate Division, College of Letters and Sciences, Division of Social Sciences, Department of Sociology, Santa Barbara, CA 93106-9430. Offers interdisciplinary emphasis: Black studies (PhD); interdisciplinary emphasis: environment and society (PhD); interdisciplinary emphasis: feminist studies (PhD); interdisciplinary emphasis: global studies (PhD); interdisciplinary emphasis: language, interaction and social organization (PhD); interdisciplinary emphasis: quantitative methods in social science (PhD); interdisciplinary emphasis: technology and society (PhD); sociology (PhD); MA/PhD. Terminal master's awarded for partial completion of doctoral program. *Degree requirements:* For doctorate, comprehensive exam, thesis/dissertation. *Entrance requirements:* For doctorate, GRE General Test. Additional exam requirements/recommendations for international students: Required—TOEFL (minimum score 550 paper-based; 80 iBT), IELTS (minimum score 7). Electronic applications accepted. *Faculty research:* Gender and sexualities, race/ethnicity, social movements, conversation analysis, global sociology.

University of Denver, Division of Arts, Humanities and Social Sciences, Department of Communication Studies, Denver, CO 80208. Offers MA, PhD. Part-time programs available. *Faculty:* 11 full-time (8 women), 1 part-time/adjunct (0 women). *Students:* 24 full-time (16 women), 8 part-time (6 women); includes 9 minority (1 Black or African American, non-Hispanic/Latino; 1 Asian, non-Hispanic/Latino; 7 Hispanic/Latino), 4 international. Average age 31. 64 applicants, 48% accepted, 12 enrolled. In 2014, 1 master's, 2 doctorates awarded. *Degree requirements:* For master's, comprehensive exam or thesis; for doctorate, one foreign language, thesis/dissertation. *Entrance requirements:* For master's, GRE General Test, bachelor's degree in communication or a related field, transcripts, essay, resume or curriculum vitae, three letters of recommendation; for doctorate, GRE General Test, bachelor's or master's degree in communication or related field, transcripts, essay, resume or curriculum vitae, three letters of recommendation. Additional exam requirements/recommendations for international students: Required—TOEFL (minimum score 570 paper-based; 88 iBT). *Application deadline:* For fall admission, 12/15 priority date for domestic and international students; for winter admission, 3/15 priority date for domestic and international students; for spring admission, 6/15 for domestic students, 6/15 priority date for international students. Applications are processed on a rolling basis. Application fee: $65. Electronic applications accepted. *Expenses:* Expenses: $1,199 per credit hour. *Financial support:* In 2014–15, 27 students received support, including 16 teaching assistantships with full and partial tuition reimbursements available (averaging $17,000 per year); career-related internships or fieldwork, Federal Work-Study, institutionally sponsored loans, scholarships/grants, and unspecified assistantships also available. Support available to part-time students. Financial award application deadline: 2/15; financial award applicants required to submit FAFSA. *Faculty research:* Successful community collaborative efforts, long-term marriages, cross-ethnic friendships, public dialogue about environmental risk, women's international cooperation. *Unit head:* Dr. Christina R. Foust, Chair, 303-871-4330, Fax: 303-871-4316, E-mail: cfoust@du.edu. *Application contact:* Dr. Mary Claire Morr Serweicz, Associate Professor/Director of Graduate Studies, 303-871-4332, Fax: 303-871-4316, E-mail: mserewic@du.edu.
Website: http://www.du.edu/ahss/schools/comn/index.html

University of Georgia, Franklin College of Arts and Sciences, Department of Speech Communication, Athens, GA 30602. Offers interpersonal and health communication (MA, PhD); rhetorical studies (MA, PhD). *Degree requirements:* For master's, thesis; for doctorate, one foreign language, thesis/dissertation. *Entrance requirements:* For master's and doctorate, GRE General Test. Electronic applications accepted.

University of Hawaii at Manoa, Graduate Division, College of Arts and Humanities, Department of Speech, Honolulu, HI 96822. Offers MA. Part-time programs available. *Degree requirements:* For master's, thesis optional. *Entrance requirements:* For master's, GRE General Test. Additional exam requirements/recommendations for international students: Required—TOEFL (minimum score 600 paper-based; 100 iBT), IELTS (minimum score 7). *Faculty research:* Social influence, relational management, message processing, intercultural communication.

University of Houston, College of Liberal Arts and Social Sciences, School of Communication, Houston, TX 77204. Offers health communication (MA); mass communication studies (MA); public relations studies (MA); speech communication (MA). Part-time programs available. *Degree requirements:* For master's, comprehensive exam (for some programs), thesis (for some programs), 30-33 hours. *Entrance requirements:* For master's, GRE. Additional exam requirements/recommendations for international students: Required—TOEFL. Electronic applications accepted.

The University of Iowa, Graduate College, College of Liberal Arts and Sciences, Department of Communication Studies, Iowa City, IA 52242-1316. Offers interpersonal communication and relationships (MA, PhD); media studies (MA, PhD); rhetoric and public advocacy (MA, PhD). *Degree requirements:* For master's, thesis optional, exam; for doctorate, comprehensive exam, thesis/dissertation. *Entrance requirements:* For master's and doctorate, GRE General Test, minimum GPA of 3.0. Additional exam requirements/recommendations for international students: Required—TOEFL (minimum score 550 paper-based; 81 iBT). Electronic applications accepted.

University of Louisiana at Monroe, Graduate School, College of Arts, Education, and Sciences, School of Education, Program in Curriculum and Instruction, Monroe, LA 71209-0001. Offers art education (M Ed); biology education (M Ed); chemistry education (M Ed); curriculum and instruction (Ed D); early childhood education (M Ed); earth science education (M Ed); educational leadership (M Ed); elementary education (1-5) (M Ed); English as a second language (M Ed); English education (M Ed); family and consumer education (M Ed); French education (M Ed); history education (M Ed); math education (M Ed); middle school education (M Ed); music education (M Ed); reading education (K-12) (M Ed); Spanish education (M Ed); special education - academically gifted (M Ed); special education - early intervention (M Ed); special education - educational diagnostician (M Ed); special education - mild/moderate disabilities (M Ed); speech education (M Ed). *Accreditation:* NCATE. *Degree requirements:* For master's, comprehensive exam (for some programs), thesis; for doctorate, thesis/dissertation, internships. *Entrance requirements:* For master's, GRE General Test; for doctorate, GRE General Test, minimum undergraduate GPA of 2.75, graduate 3.25. Additional exam requirements/recommendations for international students: Required—TOEFL (minimum score 500 paper-based; 61 iBT). Electronic applications accepted.

University of Maryland, College Park, Academic Affairs, College of Behavioral and Social Sciences, Department of Hearing and Speech Sciences, College Park, MD 20742. Offers audiology (MA, PhD); hearing and speech sciences (Au D); language pathology (MA, PhD); neuroscience (PhD); speech (MA, PhD). *Accreditation:* ASHA (one or more programs are accredited). *Degree requirements:* For master's, thesis optional; for doctorate, thesis/dissertation, written and oral exams. *Entrance requirements:* For master's, GRE General Test, minimum GPA of 3.5, 3 letters of recommendation; for doctorate, GRE General Test, minimum GPA of 3.5. Additional exam requirements/recommendations for international students: Required—TOEFL. Electronic applications accepted. *Faculty research:* Speech perception, language acquisition, bilingualism, hearing loss.

University of Nebraska–Lincoln, Graduate College, College of Arts and Sciences, Department of Communication Studies, Lincoln, NE 68588. Offers instructional communication (MA, PhD); interpersonal communication (MA, PhD); marketing, communication studies, and advertising (MA, PhD); organizational communication (MA, PhD); rhetoric and culture (MA, PhD). *Degree requirements:* For master's, thesis optional; for doctorate, comprehensive exam, thesis/dissertation. *Entrance requirements:* For master's and doctorate, GRE General Test, writing sample. Additional exam requirements/recommendations for international students: Required—TOEFL (minimum score 600 paper-based). Electronic applications accepted. *Faculty research:* Message strategies, gender communication, political communication, organizational communication, instructional communication.

University of Nevada, Reno, Graduate School, College of Liberal Arts, Department of Speech Communications, Reno, NV 89557. Offers MA. *Degree requirements:* For master's, thesis optional. *Entrance requirements:* For master's, GRE General Test, minimum GPA of 2.75. Additional exam requirements/recommendations for international students: Required—TOEFL (minimum score 500 paper-based; 61 iBT), IELTS (minimum score 6). Electronic applications accepted. *Faculty research:* Rhetorical theory and criticism; communications/sex roles; judicial, legal, contextual, and behavioral approaches to communication theory.

University of South Carolina, The Graduate School, College of Education, Department of Instruction and Teacher Education, Program in Secondary Education, Columbia, SC 29208. Offers art education (IMA, MAT); business education (IMA, MAT); English (MAT); foreign language (MAT); health education (MAT); mathematics (MAT); science (IMA, MAT); secondary (Ed D); secondary education (MT, PhD); social studies (MAT); theatre and speech (MAT). IMA and MT offered jointly with the subject areas. *Accreditation:* NCATE. *Degree requirements:* For master's, comprehensive exam, thesis (for some programs), foreign language (MA); for doctorate, one foreign language, comprehensive exam, thesis/dissertation. *Entrance requirements:* For master's, GRE General Test or MAT, teaching certificate (IMA, M Ed), interview; for doctorate, GRE General Test or MAT, interview. *Faculty research:* Middle school programs, professional development, school collaboration.

University of Southern Mississippi, Graduate School, College of Arts and Letters, Department of Communication Studies, Hattiesburg, MS 39406-0001. Offers MA, MS, PhD. Part-time programs available. *Degree requirements:* For master's, comprehensive exam, thesis optional; for doctorate, comprehensive exam, thesis/dissertation. *Entrance requirements:* For master's, GRE General Test, minimum GPA of 3.0 in last 60 hours and in major; for doctorate, GRE General Test, minimum GPA of 3.5. Additional exam requirements/recommendations for international students: Required—TOEFL, IELTS. *Faculty research:* Persuasion and social influence, interpersonal communication, organizational communication, political communication, crisis communication, public advocacy.

The University of Tennessee, Graduate School, College of Communication and Information, Knoxville, TN 37996. Offers advertising (MS, PhD); broadcasting (MS,

PhD); communications (MS, PhD); information sciences (MS, PhD); journalism (MS, PhD); public relations (MS, PhD); speech communication (MS, PhD). Part-time and evening/weekend programs available. Postbaccalaureate distance learning degree programs offered (no on-campus study). *Degree requirements:* For master's, thesis or alternative; for doctorate, thesis/dissertation. *Entrance requirements:* For master's and doctorate, GRE General Test, minimum GPA of 2.7. Additional exam requirements/recommendations for international students: Required—TOEFL. Electronic applications accepted.

University of Wisconsin–Madison, Graduate School, College of Letters and Science, Department of Communicative Disorders, Madison, WI 53706-1380. Offers normal aspects of speech, language and hearing (MS, PhD); speech-language pathology (MS, PhD); MS/PhD. *Accreditation:* ASHA (one or more programs are accredited). *Degree requirements:* For doctorate, thesis/dissertation. *Entrance requirements:* For master's and doctorate, GRE. Electronic applications accepted. *Expenses:* Tuition, state resident: full-time $10,723; part-time $745 per credit. Tuition, nonresident: full-time $24,054; part-time $1578 per credit. *Required fees:* $374 per semester. Tuition and fees vary according to course load, program and reciprocity agreements. *Faculty research:* Language disorders in children and adults, disorders of speech production, intelligibility, fluency, hearing impairment, deafness.

University of Wisconsin–Stevens Point, College of Fine Arts and Communication, Division of Communication, Stevens Point, WI 54481-3897. Offers interpersonal communication (MA); media studies (MA); organizational communication (MA); public relations (MA). Part-time programs available. *Degree requirements:* For master's, thesis or alternative. *Entrance requirements:* For master's, GRE. Additional exam requirements/recommendations for international students: Required—TOEFL (minimum score 575 paper-based). *Faculty research:* Communication theory and research, film history.

University of Wisconsin–Superior, Graduate Division, Department of Communicating Arts, Superior, WI 54880-4500. Offers mass communication (MA); speech communication (MA); theater (MA). Part-time programs available. *Degree requirements:* For master's, comprehensive exam, thesis or alternative, position paper or project. *Entrance requirements:* For master's, minimum GPA of 2.75. Electronic applications accepted. *Faculty research:* Multimedia technology, ethics in journalism, diversity, electronic portfolio assessment.

Wake Forest University, Graduate School of Arts and Sciences, Department of Communication, Winston-Salem, NC 27109. Offers speech communication (MA). Part-time programs available. *Degree requirements:* For master's, one foreign language, thesis. *Entrance requirements:* For master's, GRE General Test, writing sample. Additional exam requirements/recommendations for international students: Required—TOEFL (minimum score 79 iBT). Electronic applications accepted.

Washington University in St. Louis, School of Medicine, Program in Audiology and Communication Sciences, St. Louis, MO 63110. Offers audiology (Au D); deaf education (MS); speech and hearing sciences (PhD). *Accreditation:* ASHA (one or more programs are accredited). *Faculty:* 22 full-time (12 women), 18 part-time/adjunct (12 women). *Students:* 73 full-time (71 women). Average age 24. 136 applicants, 25% accepted, 24 enrolled. In 2014, 10 master's, 11 doctorates awarded. *Degree requirements:* For master's, comprehensive exam, thesis, independent study project, oral exam; for doctorate, comprehensive exam, thesis/dissertation, capstone project. *Entrance requirements:* For master's and doctorate, GRE General Test, minimum B average in previous college/university coursework (recommended). Additional exam requirements/recommendations for international students: Required—TOEFL (minimum score 100 iBT). *Application deadline:* For fall admission, 2/15 for domestic and international students. Application fee: $60 ($80 for international students). Electronic applications accepted. *Expenses:* Expenses: Contact institution. *Financial support:* In 2014–15, 72 students received support, including 73 fellowships with full and partial tuition reimbursements available (averaging $15,000 per year), 6 teaching assistantships with partial tuition reimbursements available (averaging $1,000 per year); career-related internships or fieldwork, Federal Work-Study, institutionally sponsored loans, scholarships/grants, traineeships, health care benefits, tuition waivers (partial), and unspecified assistantships also available. Financial award application deadline: 2/15; financial award applicants required to submit FAFSA. *Faculty research:* Audiology, deaf education, speech and hearing sciences, sensory neuroscience. *Unit head:* Dr. William W. Clark, Program Director, 314-747-0104, Fax: 314-747-0105. *Application contact:* Elizabeth A. Elliott, Director, Finance and Student Academic Affairs, 314-747-0104, Fax: 314-747-0105, E-mail: elliottb@wustl.edu.
Website: http://pacs.wustl.edu/

Technical Communication

Auburn University, Graduate School, College of Liberal Arts, Department of English, Auburn University, AL 36849. Offers English (MA, PhD); technical communication (MTPC). Part-time programs available. *Faculty:* 40 full-time (20 women), 24 part-time/adjunct (14 women). *Students:* 31 full-time (20 women), 45 part-time (30 women); includes 6 minority (5 Black or African American, non-Hispanic/Latino; 1 Hispanic/Latino). Average age 28. 90 applicants, 43% accepted, 18 enrolled. In 2014, 25 master's, 4 doctorates, 1 other advanced degree awarded. *Degree requirements:* For master's, one foreign language, thesis optional, written exam; for doctorate, 2 foreign languages, thesis/dissertation, oral and written exams. *Entrance requirements:* For master's, GRE General Test, sample of written work; for doctorate, GRE General Test, GRE Subject Test, sample of written work. *Application deadline:* For fall admission, 7/7 for domestic students; for spring admission, 11/24 for domestic students. Applications are processed on a rolling basis. Application fee: $50 ($60 for international students). Electronic applications accepted. *Expenses:* Tuition, state resident: full-time $8586; part-time $477 per credit hour. Tuition, nonresident: full-time $25,758; part-time $1431 per credit hour. *Required fees:* $804 per semester. Tuition and fees vary according to degree level and program. *Financial support:* Fellowships, teaching assistantships, and Federal Work-Study available. Support available to part-time students. Financial award application deadline: 3/15; financial award applicants required to submit FAFSA. *Faculty research:* English literature, American literature, linguistics, rhetoric and composition, literary theory. *Unit head:* Dr. Jeremy M. Downes, Chair, 334-844-9079. *Application contact:* Dr. George Flowers, Dean of the Graduate School, 334-844-2125.

Boise State University, College of Arts and Sciences, Department of English, Boise, ID 83725-0399. Offers creative writing (MFA); English (MA); technical communication (MA). Part-time programs available. *Faculty:* 34 full-time, 14 part-time/adjunct. *Students:* 45 full-time (29 women), 29 part-time (17 women); includes 8 minority (1 Black or African American, non-Hispanic/Latino; 2 Asian, non-Hispanic/Latino; 5 Hispanic/Latino). Average age 37. 200 applicants, 97% accepted, 25 enrolled. In 2014, 30 master's awarded. *Degree requirements:* For master's, thesis. *Entrance requirements:* For master's, GRE, minimum GPA of 3.0. *Application deadline:* For fall admission, 7/17 priority date for domestic students; for spring admission, 12/5 priority date for domestic students. Applications are processed on a rolling basis. Application fee: $55. Electronic applications accepted. *Expenses:* Tuition, state resident: part-time $331 per credit hour. Tuition, nonresident: part-time $531 per credit hour. *Financial support:* In 2014–15, 31 teaching assistantships with full tuition reimbursements (averaging $9,368 per year) were awarded; research assistantships with full tuition reimbursements, career-related internships or fieldwork, Federal Work-Study, institutionally sponsored loans, and unspecified assistantships also available. Support available to part-time students. Financial award application deadline: 3/1. *Unit head:* Dr. Michelle Payne, Chair, 208-426-3426, Fax: 208-426-4373, E-mail: mpayne@boisestate.edu. *Application contact:* Linda Platt, Supervisor, Graduate Admission and Degree Services, 208-426-1074, E-mail: lplatt@boisestate.edu.
Website: http://english.boisestate.edu/graduate-programs/

Bowling Green State University, Graduate College, College of Arts and Sciences, Department of English, Program in English, Bowling Green, OH 43403. Offers English (MA, PhD); literature (MA); rhetoric and writing (PhD); scientific and technical communication (MA). Part-time programs available. *Degree requirements:* For master's, thesis or alternative; for doctorate, comprehensive exam, thesis/dissertation, foreign language or proficiency in Old English. *Entrance requirements:* For master's and doctorate, GRE General Test. Additional exam requirements/recommendations for international students: Required—TOEFL. Electronic applications accepted. *Faculty research:* Postmodern literary theory, rhetorical theory, ethnic American literature, literature and culture, composition pedagogy.

Colorado State University, Graduate School, College of Liberal Arts, Department of Journalism and Technical Communication, Fort Collins, CO 80523-1785. Offers public communication and technology (MS, PhD); technical communication (MS). Part-time programs available. *Faculty:* 16 full-time (8 women). *Students:* 31 full-time (23 women), 37 part-time (26 women); includes 9 minority (2 Black or African American, non-Hispanic/Latino; 1 American Indian or Alaska Native, non-Hispanic/Latino; 4 Hispanic/Latino; 2 Two or more races, non-Hispanic/Latino), 6 international. Average age 33. 36 applicants, 67% accepted, 20 enrolled. In 2014, 6 master's, 2 doctorates awarded. *Degree requirements:* For master's, variable foreign language requirement, comprehensive exam (for some programs), thesis (for some programs); for doctorate, variable foreign language requirement, comprehensive exam (for some programs), thesis/dissertation (for some programs). *Entrance requirements:* For master's, GRE General Test, samples of written work, letters of recommendation, resume or curriculum vitae, 3 writing/communication projects, statement of purpose, transcripts; for doctorate, GRE General Test, master's degree, minimum GPA of 3.0, scholarly/professional work, letters of recommendation, statement of career plans, resume, transcripts. Additional exam requirements/recommendations for international students: Required—TOEFL (minimum score 550 paper-based; 80 iBT). *Application deadline:* For fall admission, 2/15 priority date for domestic students, 12/15 priority date for international students; for spring admission, 6/15 priority date for domestic students. Applications are processed on a rolling basis. Application fee: $50. Electronic applications accepted. *Expenses:* Tuition, state resident: full-time $9348; part-time $519 per credit. Tuition, nonresident: full-time $22,916; part-time $1273 per credit. *Required fees:* $1584. *Financial support:* In 2014–15, 36 students received support, including 4 research assistantships with full and partial tuition reimbursements available (averaging $14,586 per year), 32 teaching assistantships with partial tuition reimbursements available (averaging $14,327 per year); career-related internships or fieldwork, Federal Work-Study, institutionally sponsored loans, scholarships/grants, traineeships, and unspecified assistantships also available. Support available to part-time students. Financial award application deadline: 3/1; financial award applicants required to submit FAFSA. *Faculty research:* Technical/science communication, public relations, health/risk communication, Web/new media technologies, environmental communication. *Total annual research expenditures:* $1.1 million. *Unit head:* Dr. Greg Luft, Chair, 970-491-1979, Fax: 970-491-2908, E-mail: greg.luft@colostate.edu. *Application contact:* Dr. Linda Kidder, Graduate Program Coordinator, 970-491-5132, Fax: 970-491-2908, E-mail: linda.kidder@colostate.edu.
Website: http://journalism.colostate.edu/

Drexel University, College of Arts and Sciences, Department of Culture and Communication, Program in Communication, Philadelphia, PA 19104-2875. Offers public communication (MS); science communication (MS); technical communication (MS). Part-time and evening/weekend programs available. *Degree requirements:* For master's, internship, professional portfolio. *Entrance requirements:* For master's, GRE or minimum GPA of 3.0. Additional exam requirements/recommendations for international students: Required—TOEFL. Electronic applications accepted.

East Carolina University, Graduate School, Thomas Harriot College of Arts and Sciences, Department of English, Greenville, NC 27858-4353. Offers creative writing (MA); English studies (MA); linguistics (MA); literature (MA); multicultural and transnational literatures (MA, Certificate); rhetoric and composition (MA); rhetoric, writing, and professional communication (PhD); teaching English in the two-year college (Certificate); teaching English to speakers of other languages (MA, Certificate); technical and professional communication (MA). Part-time and evening/weekend programs available. *Degree requirements:* For master's, one foreign language, comprehensive exam, thesis optional. *Entrance requirements:* For master's, GRE General Test, MAT (for MA Ed). Additional exam requirements/recommendations for international students: Required—TOEFL. *Expenses:* Tuition, state resident: full-time $4223. Tuition, nonresident: full-time $16,540. *Required fees:* $2184.

Eastern Michigan University, Graduate School, College of Arts and Sciences, Department of English Language and Literature, Programs in Written Communication, Ypsilanti, MI 48197. Offers technical communications (MA, Graduate Certificate); written communications (MA). Part-time and evening/weekend programs available. Postbaccalaureate distance learning degree programs offered (minimal on-campus study). *Students:* 2 full-time (both women), 15 part-time (9 women); includes 1 minority (Two or more races, non-Hispanic/Latino). Average age 34. 12 applicants, 42% accepted, 3 enrolled. In 2014, 11 master's, 1 other advanced degree awarded. *Entrance requirements:* Additional exam requirements/recommendations for international students: Required—TOEFL. *Application deadline:* Applications are processed on a

rolling basis. Application fee: $45. *Financial support:* Fellowships, research assistantships with full tuition reimbursements, teaching assistantships with full tuition reimbursements, career-related internships or fieldwork, Federal Work-Study, institutionally sponsored loans, scholarships/grants, tuition waivers (partial), and unspecified assistantships available. Support available to part-time students. Financial award applicants required to submit FAFSA. *Application contact:* Dr. Steve Benninghoff, Program Coordinator, 734-487-2075, Fax: 734-483-9744, E-mail: steve.benninghoff@emich.edu.

Eastern Washington University, Graduate Studies, College of Arts, Letters and Education, Department of English, Cheney, WA 99004-2431. Offers literature (MA); rhetoric, composition, and technical communication (MA); teaching English as a second language (MA). *Degree requirements:* For master's, comprehensive exam, thesis or alternative. *Entrance requirements:* For master's, GRE General Test, minimum GPA of 3.0.

Harvard University, Harvard Graduate School of Education, Master's Programs in Education, Cambridge, MA 02138. Offers arts in education (Ed M); education policy and management (Ed M); higher education (Ed M); human development and psychology (Ed M); international education policy (Ed M); language and literacy (Ed M); learning and teaching (Ed M); mind, brain, and education (Ed M); prevention science and practice (Ed M); school leadership (Ed M); special studies (Ed M); teacher education (Ed M); technology, innovation, and education (Ed M). Part-time programs available. *Faculty:* 66 full-time (35 women), 82 part-time/adjunct (41 women). *Students:* 595 full-time (441 women), 71 part-time (48 women); includes 170 minority (33 Black or African American, non-Hispanic/Latino; 2 American Indian or Alaska Native, non-Hispanic/Latino; 69 Asian, non-Hispanic/Latino; 46 Hispanic/Latino; 20 Two or more races, non-Hispanic/Latino), 117 international. Average age 28. 1,741 applicants, 51% accepted, 613 enrolled. In 2014, 589 master's awarded. *Entrance requirements:* For master's, GRE General Test, statement of purpose, 3 letters of recommendation, resume, official transcripts. Additional exam requirements/recommendations for international students: Required—TOEFL (minimum score 613 paper-based; 104 iBT), TWE (minimum score 5). *Application deadline:* For fall admission, 1/5 for domestic and international students. Application fee: $85. Electronic applications accepted. *Expenses:* Expenses: Contact institution. *Financial support:* In 2014–15, 365 students received support, including 10 fellowships with full and partial tuition reimbursements available (averaging $15,790 per year), 6 teaching assistantships (averaging $4,281 per year); research assistantships, career-related internships or fieldwork, Federal Work-Study, institutionally sponsored loans, scholarships/grants, health care benefits, tuition waivers (full and partial), and unspecified assistantships also available. Support available to part-time students. Financial award application deadline: 2/1; financial award applicants required to submit FAFSA. *Faculty research:* Learning and development, educational leadership and organizations, education policy analysis. *Total annual research expenditures:* $34.3 million. *Unit head:* Jennifer L. Petrallia, Assistant Dean, 617-495-8445. *Application contact:* Information Contact, 617-495-3414, Fax: 617-496-3577, E-mail: gseadmissions@harvard.edu.
Website: http://www.gse.harvard.edu/

Lawrence Technological University, College of Arts and Sciences, Southfield, MI 48075-1058. Offers computer science (MS); educational technology (MA); science education (MA); technical communication (MS); training and performance (MA). Part-time and evening/weekend programs available. *Faculty:* 8 full-time (4 women), 16 part-time/adjunct (7 women). *Students:* 108 part-time (49 women); includes 46 minority (12 Black or African American, non-Hispanic/Latino; 31 Asian, non-Hispanic/Latino; 1 Hispanic/Latino; 2 Two or more races, non-Hispanic/Latino), 5 international. Average age 31. 765 applicants, 22% accepted, 43 enrolled. In 2014, 28 master's awarded. *Degree requirements:* For master's, thesis (for some programs). *Entrance requirements:* Additional exam requirements/recommendations for international students: Required—TOEFL (minimum score 550 paper-based; 79 iBT). *Application deadline:* For fall admission, 8/1 priority date for domestic students, 5/29 for international students; for spring admission, 12/1 priority date for domestic students, 10/15 for international students. Applications are processed on a rolling basis. Application fee: $50. Electronic applications accepted. *Expenses: Tuition:* Full-time $14,700; part-time $1050 per credit hour. *Required fees:* $150. One-time fee: $150 part-time. *Financial support:* In 2014–15, 8 students received support, including 2 research assistantships (averaging $6,338 per year); Federal Work-Study also available. Financial award application deadline: 4/1; financial award applicants required to submit FAFSA. *Unit head:* Dr. Hsiao-Ping Moore, Dean, 248-204-3500, Fax: 248-204-3518, E-mail: scidean@ltu.edu. *Application contact:* Jane Rohrback, Director of Admissions, 248-204-3160, Fax: 248-204-2228, E-mail: admissions@ltu.edu.
Website: http://www.ltu.edu/arts_sciences/graduate.asp

Michigan Technological University, Graduate School, College of Sciences and Arts, Department of Humanities, Houghton, MI 49931. Offers rhetoric and technical communication (MS, PhD). Part-time programs available. *Faculty:* 33 full-time (21 women), 6 part-time/adjunct (4 women). *Students:* 35 full-time (23 women), 10 part-time (7 women), 17 international. Average age 35. 62 applicants, 29% accepted, 12 enrolled. In 2014, 2 master's, 7 doctorates awarded. Terminal master's awarded for partial completion of doctoral program. *Degree requirements:* For master's, comprehensive exam (for some programs), thesis (for some programs); for doctorate, one foreign language, comprehensive exam, thesis/dissertation. *Entrance requirements:* For master's and doctorate, GRE, statement of purpose, official transcripts, 3 letters of recommendation, resume/curriculum vitae, writing sample (10-15 pages). Additional exam requirements/recommendations for international students: Required—TOEFL (recommended score 100 iBT) or IELTS. *Application deadline:* For fall admission, 1/15 priority date for domestic and international students; for spring admission, 10/15 for domestic and international students. Applications are processed on a rolling basis. Electronic applications accepted. *Expenses:* Tuition, state resident: full-time $14,769; part-time $820.50 per credit. Tuition, nonresident: full-time $14,769; part-time $820.50 per credit. *Required fees:* $248; $248 per year. Tuition and fees vary according to course load and program. *Financial support:* In 2014–15, 33 students received support, including 1 fellowship with full and partial tuition reimbursement available (averaging $13,824 per year), 2 research assistantships with full and partial tuition reimbursements available (averaging $13,824 per year), 29 teaching assistantships with full and partial tuition reimbursements available (averaging $13,824 per year); career-related internships or fieldwork, Federal Work-Study, scholarships/grants, health care benefits, unspecified assistantships, and cooperative program also available. Financial award applicants required to submit FAFSA. *Faculty research:* Rhetoric and composition; communication and cultural studies; studies of science, technology, and society; technical communication and digital media. *Total annual research expenditures:* $27,970. *Unit head:* Dr. Ronald L. Strickland, Chair, 906-487-2376, Fax: 906-487-3559, E-mail: rlstrick@mtu.edu. *Application contact:* Katy Ellenich, Administrative Aide, 906-487-2540, Fax: 906-487-3559, E-mail: kmelleni@mtu.edu.
Website: http://www.hu.mtu.edu/index.php

Minnesota State University Mankato, College of Graduate Studies, College of Arts and Humanities, Department of English, Mankato, MN 56001. Offers creative writing (MFA); English (MAT); English studies (MA); teaching English as a second language (MA, Certificate); technical communication (MA, Certificate). Part-time programs available. *Students:* 50 full-time (29 women), 108 part-time (78 women). *Degree requirements:* For master's, one foreign language, comprehensive exam, thesis or alternative. *Entrance requirements:* For master's, minimum GPA of 3.0 during previous 2 years, writing sample (MFA). Additional exam requirements/recommendations for international students: Required—TOEFL (minimum score 500 paper-based; 61 iBT). *Application deadline:* For fall admission, 7/1 for domestic students, 5/1 for international students. Applications are processed on a rolling basis. Application fee: $40. Electronic applications accepted. *Financial support:* Research assistantships with full tuition reimbursements, teaching assistantships with full tuition reimbursements, career-related internships or fieldwork, Federal Work-Study, and unspecified assistantships available. Financial award application deadline: 3/15; financial award applicants required to submit FAFSA. *Faculty research:* Keats and Christianity. *Unit head:* Dr. Nancy Drescher, Chairperson, 507-389-5504. *Application contact:* 507-389-2321, E-mail: grad@mnsu.edu.
Website: http://english.mnsu.edu/

Missouri Western State University, Program in Written Communication, St. Joseph, MO 64507-2294. Offers technical communication (MAA); writing studies (MAA). Part-time programs available. *Students:* 3 full-time (all women), 12 part-time (9 women); includes 2 minority (1 American Indian or Alaska Native, non-Hispanic/Latino; 1 Two or more races, non-Hispanic/Latino), 3 international. Average age 32. 8 applicants, 100% accepted, 7 enrolled. In 2014, 2 degrees awarded. *Entrance requirements:* For master's, minimum GPA of 3.0, essay, letters of reference, portfolio. Additional exam requirements/recommendations for international students: Recommended—TOEFL (minimum score 70 iBT), IELTS (minimum score 6). *Application deadline:* For fall admission, 7/15 for domestic and international students; for spring admission, 11/1 for domestic students, 10/15 for international students; for summer admission, 4/29 for domestic students. Applications are processed on a rolling basis. Application fee: $45 ($50 for international students). Electronic applications accepted. *Expenses:* Tuition, state resident: full-time $5506; part-time $305.91 per credit hour. Tuition, nonresident: full-time $10,075; part-time $559.71 per credit hour. *Required fees:* $504; $99 per credit hour. $176 per semester. Tuition and fees vary according to course load and program. *Financial support:* Scholarships/grants and unspecified assistantships available. Support available to part-time students. *Unit head:* Dr. Michael Charlton, Associate Professor/Director of Graduate Studies, 816-271-4323, E-mail: mcharlton@missouriwestern.edu. *Application contact:* Dr. Benjamin D. Caldwell, Dean of the Graduate School, 816-271-4394, Fax: 816-271-4525, E-mail: graduate@missouriwestern.edu.
Website: https://www.missouriwestern.edu/eml/maawc/

Montana Tech of The University of Montana, Graduate School, Department of Technical Communication, Butte, MT 59701-8997. Offers MS. Part-time programs available. *Degree requirements:* For master's, project or thesis. *Entrance requirements:* For master's, GRE General Test, minimum GPA of 3.0. Additional exam requirements/recommendations for international students: Required—TOEFL (minimum score 525 paper-based; 71 iBT). Electronic applications accepted. *Expenses:* Tuition, state resident: full-time $5802; part-time $241 per credit. Tuition, nonresident: full-time $15,895; part-time $662 per credit. *Required fees:* $1516; $414 per credit. $207 per semester. One-time fee: $30. *Faculty research:* Environmental concerns and the Big Hole River, history of Butte mining, African studies, multicultural communications.

New Jersey Institute of Technology, College of Science and Liberal Arts, Newark, NJ 07102. Offers applied mathematics (MS); applied physics (M Sc, PhD); applied statistics (MS); biology (MS, PhD); biostatistics (MS); chemistry (MS, PhD); computational biology (MS); environmental science (MS, PhD); history (MA, MAT); materials science and engineering (MS, PhD); mathematical and computational finance (MS); mathematics science (PhD); pharmaceutical chemistry (MS); professional and technical communications (MS). Part-time and evening/weekend programs available. Terminal master's awarded for partial completion of doctoral program. *Degree requirements:* For master's, thesis optional; for doctorate, thesis/dissertation. *Entrance requirements:* For master's, GRE General Test; for doctorate, GRE General Test, minimum graduate GPA of 3.5. Additional exam requirements/recommendations for international students: Required—TOEFL (minimum score 550 paper-based; 79 iBT). Electronic applications accepted.

North Carolina State University, Graduate School, College of Humanities and Social Sciences, Department of English, Program in Technical Communication, Raleigh, NC 27695. Offers MS. *Degree requirements:* For master's, thesis optional. *Entrance requirements:* For master's, GRE General Test. Electronic applications accepted. *Faculty research:* Workplace writing, organizational socialization and power, integrated and multimedia documentation systems, technical communication management, usability testing theories.

North Central College, Graduate and Continuing Studies Programs, Program in Leadership Studies, Naperville, IL 60566-7063. Offers higher education leadership (MLD); professional leadership (MLD); social entrepreneurship (MLD); sports leadership (MLD). Part-time and evening/weekend programs available. *Faculty:* 7 full-time (1 woman), 11 part-time/adjunct (5 women). *Students:* 34 full-time (21 women), 26 part-time (13 women); includes 10 minority (4 Black or African American, non-Hispanic/Latino; 1 Asian, non-Hispanic/Latino; 5 Hispanic/Latino), 3 international. Average age 28. 80 applicants, 55% accepted, 21 enrolled. In 2014, 38 master's awarded. *Degree requirements:* For master's, thesis optional, project. *Entrance requirements:* For master's, interview. Additional exam requirements/recommendations for international students: Required—TOEFL (minimum score 550 paper-based; 80 iBT). *Application deadline:* For fall admission, 8/15 for domestic students, 7/15 for international students; for winter admission, 12/1 for domestic students, 11/1 for international students; for spring admission, 2/1 for domestic students, 12/1 for international students. Applications are processed on a rolling basis. Application fee: $25. Electronic applications accepted. Application fee is waived when completed online. *Expenses:* Expenses: Contact institution. *Financial support:* In 2014–15, 1 student received support. Scholarships/grants available. Support available to part-time students. Financial award applicants required to submit FAFSA. *Unit head:* Dr. Thomas Cavenagh, Program Coordinator, Leadership Studies, 630-637-5285. *Application contact:* Wendy Kulpinski, Director of Graduate and Continuing Education Admission, 630-637-5808, Fax: 630-637-5844, E-mail: wekulpinski@noctrl.edu.

Northeastern University, College of Professional Studies, Boston, MA 02115-5096. Offers applied nutrition (MS); commerce and economic development (MS); corporate and organizational communication (MS); digital media (MPS); geographic information technology (MPS); global studies and international affairs (MS); homeland security (MA); human services (MS); informatics (MPS); leadership (MS); nonprofit management (MS); project management (MS); regulatory affairs for drugs, biologics, and medical devices (MS); regulatory affairs of food and food industries (MS); respiratory care leadership (MS); technical communication (MS). Postbaccalaureate distance learning degree programs offered (no on-campus study).

Rensselaer Polytechnic Institute, Graduate School, School of Humanities, Arts, and Social Sciences, Program in Technical Communication, Troy, NY 12180-3590. Offers MS. Part-time programs available. *Faculty:* 3 full-time (1 woman), 1 part-time/adjunct (0

women). *Students:* 4 applicants. *Degree requirements:* For master's, thesis optional. *Entrance requirements:* For master's, GRE. Additional exam requirements/recommendations for international students: Required—TOEFL (minimum score 570 paper-based; 88 iBT), IELTS (minimum score 6.5), PTE (minimum score 60). *Application deadline:* For fall admission, 1/1 priority date for domestic and international students; for spring admission, 8/15 priority date for domestic and international students. Applications are processed on a rolling basis. Application fee: $75. Electronic applications accepted. *Expenses: Tuition:* Full-time $46,700; part-time $1945 per credit. Tuition and fees vary according to course load. *Financial support:* Application deadline: 1/1. *Faculty research:* Human-computer interaction, usability, technical writing, integrating textual and graphic information for electronic media. *Unit head:* Dr. Katya Haskins, Graduate Program Director, 518-276-4047, E-mail: haskie@rpi.edu. *Application contact:* Office of Graduate Admissions, 518-276-6216, E-mail: gradadmissions@rpi.edu.
Website: http://www.cm.rpi.edu/pl/ms-technical-communication-649

Southern Polytechnic State University, School of Arts and Sciences, Department of English, Technical Communication, and Media Arts, Marietta, GA 30060-2896. Offers communications management (Postbaccalaureate Certificate); content development (Postbaccalaureate Certificate); information and instructional design (MSIID); information design and communication (MS); instructional design (Postbaccalaureate Certificate); technical communication (Graduate Certificate); visual communication and graphics (Postbaccalaureate Certificate). Part-time and evening/weekend programs available. Postbaccalaureate distance learning degree programs offered (no on-campus study). *Degree requirements:* For master's, thesis optional; for other advanced degree, thesis optional, 18 hours completed through thesis option (6 hours), internship option (6 hours) or advanced coursework option (6 hours). *Entrance requirements:* For master's, GRE, statement of purpose, writing sample, timed essay; for other advanced degree, writing sample, professional recommendations. Additional exam requirements/recommendations for international students: Required—TOEFL (minimum score 550 paper-based; 79 iBT), IELTS (minimum score 6.5). Electronic applications accepted. *Faculty research:* Usability, user-centered design, instructional design, information architecture, information design, content strategy.

Texas State University, The Graduate College, College of Liberal Arts, Department of English, Program in Technical Communication, San Marcos, TX 78666. Offers MA. *Faculty:* 7 full-time (4 women). *Students:* 13 full-time (11 women), 28 part-time (18 women); includes 7 minority (2 Black or African American, non-Hispanic/Latino; 4 Hispanic/Latino; 1 Two or more races, non-Hispanic/Latino). Average age 32. 19 applicants, 89% accepted, 11 enrolled. In 2014, 10 master's awarded. *Degree requirements:* For master's, comprehensive exam, thesis optional. *Entrance requirements:* For master's, GRE (preferred), baccalaureate degree from regionally-accredited university with minimum GPA of 2.75 on last 60 undergraduate semester hours, 3.0 in minimum of 12 hours of undergraduate English courses. Additional exam requirements/recommendations for international students: Required—TOEFL (minimum score 550 paper-based; 78 iBT). *Application deadline:* For fall admission, 6/15 priority date for domestic students, 6/1 for international students; for spring admission, 11/1 priority date for domestic students, 10/1 for international students; for summer admission, 4/15 for domestic students, 3/15 for international students. Applications are processed on a rolling basis. Application fee: $40 ($90 for international students). Electronic applications accepted. *Expenses:* Expenses: $8,834 (tuition and fees combined). *Financial support:* In 2014–15, 18 students received support, including 3 research assistantships (averaging $12,180 per year), 1 teaching assistantship (averaging $14,914 per year); Federal Work-Study and institutionally sponsored loans also available. Support available to part-time students. Financial award application deadline: 4/1. *Unit head:* Dr. Miriam Williams, Graduate Advisor, 512-245-3015, Fax: 512-245-8546, E-mail: mw32@txstate.edu. *Application contact:* Dr. Andrea Golato, Dean of Graduate School, 512-245-2581, Fax: 512-245-8365, E-mail: gradcollege@txstate.edu.
Website: http://www.english.txstate.edu/

University of Houston–Downtown, College of Humanities and Social Sciences, Department of English, Program in Technical Communication, Houston, TX 77002. Offers MS. Part-time programs available. *Faculty:* 6 full-time (3 women), 1 (woman) part-time/adjunct. *Students:* 3 full-time (all women), 23 part-time (17 women); includes 10 minority (7 Black or African American, non-Hispanic/Latino; 1 Asian, non-Hispanic/Latino; 1 Hispanic/Latino; 1 Two or more races, non-Hispanic/Latino), 1 international. Average age 39. 11 applicants, 91% accepted, 5 enrolled. In 2014, 3 master's awarded. *Entrance requirements:* For master's, GRE (for students with lower than 3.0 GPA), essay, resume, 2 letters of recommendation, transcripts. Additional exam requirements/recommendations for international students: Required—TOEFL (minimum score 600 paper-based; 86 iBT). *Application deadline:* For fall admission, 7/15 for domestic and international students; for spring admission, 11/15 for domestic and international students. Application fee: $35 ($60 for international students). Electronic applications accepted. *Expenses:* Expenses: $260 per credit state resident, $572 nonresident. *Financial support:* Applicants required to submit FAFSA. *Faculty research:* Environmental rhetoric, instructional design, usability, assessment, presentation slides. *Unit head:* Dr. Michelle Moosally, Chair, 713-221-8254, Fax: 713-226-5205, E-mail: moosallym@uhd.edu. *Application contact:* Ceshia Love, Director of Graduate and International Admissions, 713-221-8093, Fax: 713-223-7408, E-mail: gradadmissions@uhd.edu.
Website: https://www.uhd.edu/academics/humanities/graduate-programs/master-science-technical-communication/Pages/mstc-index.aspx

University of Nebraska at Omaha, Graduate Studies, College of Communication, Fine Arts and Media, School of Communication, Omaha, NE 68182. Offers communication (MA); human resources and training (Certificate); technical communication (Certificate). Part-time and evening/weekend programs available. *Faculty:* 23 full-time (12 women). *Students:* 8 full-time (5 women), 28 part-time (23 women); includes 4 minority (1 Black or African American, non-Hispanic/Latino; 2 Hispanic/Latino; 1 Two or more races, non-Hispanic/Latino), 3 international. Average age 31. 33 applicants, 67% accepted, 15 enrolled. In 2014, 18 master's, 6 other advanced degrees awarded. *Degree requirements:* For master's, comprehensive exam, thesis (for some programs). *Entrance requirements:* For master's, minimum GPA of 3.0, 15 undergraduate communication courses, resume, statement of purpose, 3 letters of recommendation. Additional exam requirements/recommendations for international students: Required—TOEFL, IELTS, PTE. *Application deadline:* For fall admission, 3/1 priority date for domestic and international students; for spring admission, 10/1 priority date for domestic and international students. Applications are processed on a rolling basis. Application fee: $45. Electronic applications accepted. *Financial support:* In 2014–15, 13 students received support, including 6 research assistantships with tuition reimbursements available, 7 teaching assistantships with tuition reimbursements available; fellowships, Federal Work-Study, institutionally sponsored loans, scholarships/grants, tuition waivers (partial), and unspecified assistantships also available. Support available to part-time students. Financial award application deadline: 3/1; financial award applicants required to submit FAFSA. *Unit head:* Dr. Hugh Reilly, Director, 402-554-2341, E-mail: graduate@unomaha.edu. *Application contact:* Dr. Adam Tyma, Graduate Program Chair, 402-554-2341, E-mail: graduate@unomaha.edu.

The University of North Carolina at Charlotte, College of Liberal Arts and Sciences, Department of English, Charlotte, NC 28223-0001. Offers English (MA); English education (MA); technical communication (Graduate Certificate). Part-time and evening/weekend programs available. *Faculty:* 31 full-time (16 women). *Students:* 30 full-time (22 women), 60 part-time (37 women); includes 16 minority (11 Black or African American, non-Hispanic/Latino; 1 American Indian or Alaska Native, non-Hispanic/Latino; 2 Hispanic/Latino; 1 Native Hawaiian or other Pacific Islander, non-Hispanic/Latino; 1 Two or more races, non-Hispanic/Latino), 4 international. Average age 31. 46 applicants, 83% accepted, 28 enrolled. In 2014, 13 master's, 4 other advanced degrees awarded. *Degree requirements:* For master's, comprehensive exam, thesis optional. *Entrance requirements:* For master's, GRE General Test, minimum undergraduate GPA of 3.0 in major, 2.75 overall. Additional exam requirements/recommendations for international students: Required—TOEFL (minimum score 557 paper-based; 83 iBT). *Application deadline:* For fall admission, 5/1 priority date for domestic students, 5/1 for international students; for spring admission, 10/1 priority date for domestic students, 10/1 for international students. Applications are processed on a rolling basis. Application fee: $75. Electronic applications accepted. *Expenses:* Tuition, state resident: full-time $4008. Tuition, nonresident: full-time $16,295. *Required fees:* $2755. Tuition and fees vary according to course load and program. *Financial support:* In 2014–15, 19 students received support, including 19 teaching assistantships (averaging $7,740 per year); career-related internships or fieldwork, institutionally sponsored loans, scholarships/grants, and unspecified assistantships also available. Support available to part-time students. Financial award application deadline: 4/1; financial award applicants required to submit FAFSA. *Faculty research:* Narrative, pragmatics and stance in medical discourse and Alzheimer's speech; online discourse and digital corpora of speech. *Total annual research expenditures:* $102,408. *Unit head:* Dr. Mark West, Interim Chair, 704-687-0618, Fax: 704-687-1401, E-mail: miwest@uncc.edu. *Application contact:* Kathy B. Giddings, Director of Graduate Admissions, 704-687-5503, Fax: 704-687-1668, E-mail: gradadm@uncc.edu.
Website: http://english.uncc.edu/MA-English/graduate-programs.html

University of South Florida, Innovative Education, Tampa, FL 33620-9951. *Unit head:* Kathy Barnes, Interdisciplinary Programs Coordinator, 813-974-8031, Fax: 813-974-7061, E-mail: barnesk@usf.edu. *Application contact:* Karen Tylinski, Metro Initiatives, 813-974-9943, Fax: 813-974-7061, E-mail: ktylinsk@usf.edu.
Website: http://www.usf.edu/innovative-education/

University of Washington, Graduate School, College of Engineering, Department of Human Centered Design and Engineering, Seattle, WA 98195-2315. Offers human centered design and engineering (MS, PhD); user centered design (MS, PhD). Part-time and evening/weekend programs available. *Faculty:* 15 full-time (9 women). *Students:* 104 full-time (65 women), 81 part-time (49 women). Average age 32. 641 applicants, 30% accepted, 134 enrolled. In 2014, 60 master's, 2 doctorates awarded. Terminal master's awarded for partial completion of doctoral program. *Degree requirements:* For master's, thesis or alternative; for doctorate, comprehensive exam, thesis/dissertation, preliminary, general, and final exams. *Entrance requirements:* For master's, minimum GPA of 3.0, transcripts, 3 letters of recommendation, curriculum vitae, personal statement of objectives; for doctorate, GRE General Test, minimum GPA of 3.0, transcripts, 3 letters of recommendation, curriculum vitae, personal statement of objectives. Additional exam requirements/recommendations for international students: Required—TOEFL (minimum score 600 paper-based; 102 iBT). *Application deadline:* For fall admission, 1/15 for domestic and international students. Application fee: $85. Electronic applications accepted. *Expenses:* Expenses: Contact institution. *Financial support:* In 2014–15, 29 students received support, including 3 fellowships with full tuition reimbursements available, 17 research assistantships with full tuition reimbursements available, 9 teaching assistantships with full tuition reimbursements available; career-related internships or fieldwork, institutionally sponsored loans, and tuition waivers (full) also available. Financial award application deadline: 2/28; financial award applicants required to submit FAFSA. *Faculty research:* Usability testing; rhetorical and empirical exploration of basic communication phenomena; computer documentation; technology assessment; educational assessment; Web, multimedia and user interface design. *Total annual research expenditures:* $2.1 million. *Unit head:* Dr. David McDonald, Professor/Chair, 206-685-2945, Fax: 206-543-8858, E-mail: hcdechr@uw.edu. *Application contact:* Pat Reilly, Academic Services Manager, 206-543-1798, Fax: 206-543-8858, E-mail: preilly@uw.edu.
Website: http://www.hcde.washington.edu/

University of Wisconsin–Milwaukee, Graduate School, College of Letters and Sciences, Department of English, Milwaukee, WI 53201-0413. Offers creative writing (PhD); English (MA); international technical communication (Certificate); linguistics (PhD); professional writing (PhD); professional writing and communication (Certificate); rhetoric and composition (PhD); MLIS/MA. *Degree requirements:* For master's, thesis or alternative; for doctorate, one foreign language, thesis/dissertation. *Entrance requirements:* For master's, GRE General Test, GRE Subject Test; for doctorate, GRE. Additional exam requirements/recommendations for international students: Required—TOEFL (minimum score 550 paper-based; 79 iBT), IELTS (minimum score 6.5). Electronic applications accepted.

NORTH DAKOTA STATE UNIVERSITY
College of Arts, Humanities and Social Sciences

NDSU GRADUATE SCHOOL

 For more information, visit http://petersons.to/nndstateartshumanities

Programs of Study

The College of Arts, Humanities and Social Sciences at North Dakota State University equips students with the skills and knowledge to thrive in their professional and personal lives, including the following:

- Ability to think critically
- Ability to effectively communicate in all media
- Understanding the diverse ideas that constitute the intellectual marketplace
- Recognition of the significance of all traditions in creating cultures throughout the world

The college offers several graduate programs through eight of its twelve departments: Architecture and Landscape Architecture; Communication; Criminal Justice and Political Science; Emergency Management; English; History, Philosophy, and Religious Studies; Music; and Sociology and Anthropology.

Department of Architecture and Landscape Architecture: The Department of Architecture and Landscape Architecture focuses on the challenges related to designing landscapes and built environments. It offers a nationally accredited Master of Architecture (M.Arch.) program for individuals interested in pursuing advanced careers in the field.

Department of Communication: The Department of Communication provides students with the expertise to build rewarding careers in a wide variety of professions. Its graduate programs include the Master of Arts (M.A.) in Communication, Master of Science (M.S.) in Communication, Doctor of Philosophy (Ph.D.) in Communication, and an online master's degree.

Department of Criminal Justice and Political Science: The Department of Criminal Justice and Political Science prepares students for positions that protect and serve people and communities, create and strengthen political and social systems, and enhance quality of life. It offers both M.S. and Ph.D. degrees in Criminal Justice.

Department of Emergency Management: The Department of Emergency Management trains students to protect people and communities and facilitates research that strengthens theory and practice in the field. It has two graduate programs: the M.S. in Emergency Management and Ph.D. in Emergency Management.

Department of English: The Department of English cultivates students' appreciation, knowledge, and understanding of the English language. It offers the following graduate programs: the M.A. in English Composition; M.A. in English Literature; and Ph.D. in English: Rhetoric, Writing, and Culture.

Department of History, Philosophy, and Religious Studies: The Department of History, Philosophy, and Religious Studies encourages active learning and provides diverse learning opportunities. It provides the M.A. in History and Ph.D. in History programs.

Challey School of Music: The Challey School of Music prepares students for excellence in musical performance and scholarship. It provides a Master of Music program with options in performance, conducting, and music education, as well as a Doctor of Musical Arts program with options in performance and conducting.

Department of Sociology and Anthropology: The Department of Sociology and Anthropology provides comprehensive study of human behavior in social settings. It has six graduate programs: the M.A. in Anthropology, M.S. in Anthropology, M.S. in Natural Resources Management (social science option), Ph.D. in Natural Resources Management (social science option), M.S. in Sociology, and an online master's in Community Development.

Research

Faculty members and students actively engage in research regarding a wide range of subjects. Faculty members are awarded millions of dollars in research grants and contracts annually, and their work is published in more than 100 peer-reviewed publications each year.

Students assist faculty members with their research and conduct individual research that contributes to the body of knowledge in their fields.

Financial Aid

Graduate students in the College of Arts, Humanities and Social Sciences may receive financial aid from employer tuition reimbursement programs, fellowships, graduate assistantships (teaching or research), loans (through federal programs or private lenders), military and veteran assistance, and scholarships from the university and private funders.

Cost of Study

The most current information on tuition and fees can be found online at https://www.ndsu.edu/bisonconnection/accounts/tuition.

Living and Housing Costs

Information about on-campus housing for graduate students can be found at www.ndsu.edu/reslife/general_apartment_information. While there is no specific residence hall for graduate students, they are able to live in the University apartments. There are also numerous housing options in the Fargo community.

Faculty

Faculty members, like Stephenson J. Beck, Ph.D., are talented teachers and scholars. Dr. Beck is an associate professor and the director of graduate studies in the Department of Communication. His research focuses on relational communication in groups, communication strategy, and macro-cognition. His goal is to understand how people alter messages to achieve individual and group goals and to examine how this process influences group processes and message perception.

Dr. Beck has authored and co-authored many articles and books about his research. He has also presented his work at several conferences, colloquia, and symposia. In addition, he has served on editorial boards of journals, participated in policy and planning and other committees, and operated a consulting practice.

Student Life

North Dakota State University provides students with the resources and opportunities to create vibrant and fulfilling college careers. They receive academic, career, support, and wellness services from the following departments:

- Career Center
- Counseling Center
- Graduate Center for Writers
- Office of International Student and Study Abroad Services
- Office of Multicultural Programs
- Wallman Wellness Center

Social resources include arts and culture, community outreach, intramural sports, recreational programs, and student organizations.

Location

North Dakota State University is located on the eastern edge of North Dakota in Fargo, the state's largest community. With its sister city, Moorhead, Minnesota, directly across the Red River, Fargo is one of the largest metropolitan centers between Minneapolis

North Dakota State University

and Seattle and offers a family-friendly environment with excellent schools, safe neighborhoods, and a low crime rate; an active arts and cultural scene, including a symphony, civic opera company, art museums, and community theater; and many places to shop and eat, including numerous restaurants, coffee shops, and a newly refurbished downtown district.

The University

In 1890, North Dakota State University became North Dakota's first land-grant university. Today, this esteemed research institution offers more than 14,700 students 100 undergraduate majors, 84 master's programs, and 51 doctoral programs.

It is recognized nationally and internationally for providing high quality education, excellent service, and innovative research. In fact, the Carnegie Commission on Higher Education ranked North Dakota State University within the top 108 universities in the country. In addition, the National Science Foundation determined that several of its programs rank within the top 100.

Correspondence and Information

College of Arts, Humanities and Social Sciences
Graduate School
North Dakota State University
Department 2820, P.O. Box 6050
Fargo, North Dakota 58108-6050
Phone: 701-231-7033
       800-608-6378 (toll-free)
E-mail: ndsu.grad.school@ndsu.edu
Website: www.ndsu.edu/gradschool
      facebook.com/ndsugradschool (Facebook)
      @NDSUGradSchool (Twitter)

The College of Arts, Humanities and Social Sciences is at the center of the Liberal and Fine Arts on the campus of NDSU. The departments in this college offer high-quality graduate degree programs in the humanities, social sciences, and the fine arts.

PRATT INSTITUTE
School of Liberal Arts

 For more information, visit http://petersons.to/prattmediastudies

Programs of Study

Pratt has been educating professionals for productive careers since its founding in 1887. Pratt's School of Liberal Arts offers an outstanding professional art and design education taught by a faculty of working professionals who bring high standards and current practices to the classroom. Faculty members have received more than eighteen Tiffany, Fulbright, and Guggenheim awards as well as other prestigious professional honors.

Pratt offers master's degrees in a variety of programs, including Master of Arts in Media Studies; Master of Fine Arts in Performance and Performance Studies; Master of Fine Arts in Writing, and Master of Science in History of Art and Design. Pratt also offers a dual degree in Art History and Library Science and a dual degree in Art History and Fine Art.

Graduates of Pratt's liberal arts programs have the competitive edge needed to obtain top administrative and creative positions in design studios, businesses, various industries, and arts organizations; Students can choose from a wide array of course offerings, including art and design history, comparative literature, philosophy, foreign languages, and social sciences. The graduate programs require the completion of 30 to 68 credits (75 credits for the M.S./M.F.A. dual-degree program) and last from 1-1/2 to 3 years, depending on the curriculum and the number of prerequisites that have been met at the time of admission. For the granting of degrees, all of the graduate programs require the submission of a thesis or a comparable effort.

Media Studies at Pratt is an intensive 30-credit, three-semester theory and practice M.A., shaped in relation to Pratt's art/design/architecture environment and to the lively social space and theoretical scene of Brooklyn and New York City. Classes in media theory and media practice are small, following seminar and workshop formats, and all are taught by professors on Pratt Institute's Brooklyn campus.

The graduate degree offers students the freedom and flexibility to design their own program of study. The M.A. in Media Studies at Pratt is designed to train students to think and make critically, whether their final destination is a Ph.D. program or a professional career in the arts, media, or communication.

The curriculum emphasizes studies of media in their various forms, including film, video, television, radio, writing, smart phones, and other computerized forms of media convergence. Alongside their theoretical investigations, students are also encouraged to become media makers. Guided by a diverse and exceptional faculty, students study the logics and processes of media, and they explore cultural technologies of expression, representation, and manipulation. Students learn to analyze a variety of media forms (cinema, photography, audio-phonic, and social media), along with the aesthetic, social, economic and political contexts in which these media operate. They also work also work on textual analysis, interpretation, and semiotics and gain expertise in media history and theory.

Research Facilities

The Pratt Library contains 186,589 bound volumes, serial backfiles, and other material (including government documents); 251,603 audiovisual materials; and 3,996 microforms. The library also subscribes to 925 periodicals.

Pratt maintains numerous studios, shops, and technical facilities for work in all media as well as state-of-the-art computer facilities. Digital arts labs include state-of-the-art Macintosh, PC/NT, and UNIX operating systems as well as digital video and audio systems. Pratt also has extensive gallery space for exhibitions.

Financial Aid

Financial aid awards are offered through a variety of institutional, state, and federally funded programs. These include Graduate Scholarships awarded by departments to incoming students on the basis of merit, endowed and restricted scholarships for continuing students, and student employment. Assistantships are awarded on a competitive basis to continuing students in all departments. Special alumni-sponsored fellowships are also available.

Cost of Study

Graduate tuition for 2015–16 is $28,638 per year (full-time, 18 credits, $1,591 per credit) and student fees are $1,932 per year. The cost of books and supplies varies widely, depending on the program in which the student is enrolled.

Living and Housing Costs

Campus housing continues to be expanded to meet students' needs and is available for single students on a first-come, first-served basis. Housing costs average $17,646 per academic year. Pratt offers limited graduate student housing two blocks away from the campus. There is a plentiful supply of moderately priced rentals in the immediate area and in adjacent neighborhoods for married students seeking housing and for those students choosing to reside off campus.

Student Group

In educating more than four generations of students to be creative, technically skilled, and adaptable professionals, Pratt has gained an international reputation that attracts about 4,550 undergraduate and graduate students annually from forty-eight states and eighty-one countries.

Location

Pratt Institute's 25-acre, parklike main campus is situated among the turn-of-the-century mansions, Victorian brownstones, and wide, tree-lined boulevards of Clinton Hill, one of Brooklyn's historic neighborhoods. Midtown Manhattan, the heart of New York City, is only 25 minutes away by subway and offers students a vast array of professional, cultural, and recreational opportunities. Pratt also maintains a satellite facility in Manhattan's Chelsea district. Pratt Manhattan houses the Institute's graduate arts and cultural management, communications/packaging design, design management, facilities management, historic preservation, library and information science, and urban design; it also offers Associate of Occupational Studies (A.O.S.) and Associate of Applied Science (A.A.S.) degree programs.

The Institute

A private, nonsectarian institute of higher education, Pratt Institute was founded by industrialist and philanthropist Charles Pratt. Changing with the needs and requirements of the professional world for which it prepares its graduates, Pratt today educates 3,149 undergraduate and 1,478 graduate students for careers in art and design, architecture, and library and information science.

Applying

The deadline for applications and all supporting materials, including portfolio, is January 5. Applicants should complete the application process online. Early submission of applications with all necessary credentials is highly desirable. For applicants who intend to file for financial aid, applications and all supporting documents should be received no later than January 5 for the fall semester and October 1 for the spring semester. Applications received after these dates are considered if openings exist in a particular program.

Correspondence and Information

Graduate Admissions Office
Pratt Institute
200 Willoughby Avenue
Brooklyn, New York 11205
United States
Phone: 718-636-3514
         800-331-0834 (toll-free)
Fax: 718-399-4242
E-mail: admissions@pratt.edu
Websites: www.pratt.edu
          www.pratt.edu/admissions/request-information

THE FACULTY

Andrew Barnes, Dean of the School of Liberal Arts and Sciences

HISTORY OF ART AND DESIGN
Dorothea Dietrich, Chair and Professor; Ph.D., Yale.
Gayle Rodda Kurtz, Assistant Chair; Ph.D., CUNY Graduate Center.
Sonya Abrego, Visiting Instructor; M.Phil., Bard.
Kelly Rae Aldridge, Visiting Instructor; M.A., Stony Brook, SUNY.
Lisa Banner, Visiting Associate Professor; Ph.D., NYU.
Agnes Berecz, Visiting Assistant Professor; Ph.D., Universite Paris I.
Sam Bryan, Adjunct Associate Professor; D.A., Carnegie Mellon.
Corey D'Augustine, Visiting Assistant Professor; M.A., NYU.
Edward DeCarbo, Adjunct Associate Professor; Ph.D., Indiana.
Eva Diaz, Assistant Professor; Ph.D., Princeton.
Mary Douglas Edwards, Adjunct Professor; Ph.D., Columbia.
Charles Eppley, Visiting Instructor; M.A., Stony Brook, SUNY.
Diana Gisolfi, Professor; Ph.D., Chicago.
Dimitri Hazzikostas, Assistant Professor; Ph.D., Columbia.
Frima Fox Hofrichter, Professor; Ph.D., Rutgers.
Heather Horton, Visiting Assistant Professor; Ph.D., NYU.

Pratt Institute

Susan Karnet, Visiting Instructor; M.F.A., Hunter.
Dara Kiese, Visiting Assistant Professor; Ph.D., CUNY Graduate Center.
Vivien Knussi, Adjunct Instructor; Ph.D., Columbia.
Marilyn Kushner, Visiting Professor; Ph.D., Northwestern.
Thomas La Padula, Adjunct Professor; M.F.A., Syracuse.
Anca Lasc, Assistant Professor; Ph.D., USC.
Jacob Lewis, Visiting Instructor; Ph.D., Northwestern.
Rael Lewis, Visiting Assistant Professor; Ph.D., Stanford.
Michele LiCalsi, Visiting Assistant Professor; M.A., NYU.
William Lorenzo, Visiting Assistant Professor; B.F.A., CUNY, Brooklyn.
Elizabeth Meggs, Visiting Instructor; B.F.A., Virginia Commonwealth.
Juan Monroy, Visiting Assistant Professor; M.A., NYU.
Marsha Morton, Professor; Ph.D., NYU.
Evan Neely, Adjunct Assistant Professor; Ph.D., Columbia.
Nicholas Parkinson, Visiting Instructor; M.A., Stony Brook, SUNY.
Joyce Polistena, Adjunct Professor; Ph.D., CUNY Graduate Center.
Katarina V. Posch, Associate Professor; Ph.D., Tokyo University of Fine Arts and Music.
Elena Rossi-Snook, Visiting Assistant Professor; M.A., University of East Anglia.
Ann Schoenfeld, Adjunct Assistant Professor; Ph.D., CUNY Graduate Center.
Dorothy Shepard, Adjunct Professor; Ph.D., Bryn Mawr.
Elizabeth St. George, Visiting Instructor; M.A., Bard.
Jack Toolin, Visiting Assistant Professor; M.F.A., San Jose State.
Alice Walkiewicz, Visiting Instructor; M.Phil., CUNY Graduate Center.
Bor-Hua Wang, Adjunct Assistant Professor; Ph.D., Columbia.
Sarah Wilkins, Visiting Assistant Professor; Ph.D., Rutgers.
Karyn Zieve, Visiting Assistant Professor; Ph.D., NYU.

MEDIA STUDIES
Maria Damon, Chair, Humanities and Media Studies.
Jonathan Beller, Director of Media Studies program, Professor; Ph.D. Duke.
Stephanie Boluk, Assistant Professor; Ph.D., Florida.
Allen Feldman, Visiting Professor; Ph.D., New School.
Ira Livingston, Professor; Ph.D., Stanford.
Mendi Obadike, Assistant Professor; Ph.D., Duke.
Minh-Ha Pham, Assistant Professor; Ph.D., Berkeley.
Ethan Spigland, Professor; M.F.A., NYU.
Christopher Vitale, Associate Professor; Ph.D., NYU.

PERFORMANCE AND PERFORMANCE STUDIES
Maria Damon, Chair, Humanities and Media Studies.
Tracie Morris Director of Performance and Performance Studies program, Professor; Ph.D., NYU.
Donald Andreasen, Adjunct Associate Professor; M.F.A., New School.
Youmna Chlala, Associate Professor; M.F.A., California College of the Arts.
Steven Doloff, Professor; Ph.D., CUNY Graduate Center.
Lisabeth During, Associate Professor; Ph.D., Cambridge (U.K.).
James Hannaham, Associate Professor; M.F.A. Texas at Austin.
Ann Holder, Associate Professor; Ph.D. Boston College.
May Joseph, Professor.
Ira Livingston, Professor; Ph.D., Stanford.
Jennifer Miller, Associate Professor.
Mendi Obadike; Ph.D., Duke.

WRITING
Maria Damon, Chair, Humanities and Media Studies.
Christina Hawkey, Director of Writing program, Professor; M.F.A., Massachusetts Amherst.
Youmna Chlala, Associate Professor; M.F.A., California College of Art.
Laura Elrick, Assistant Professor; M.A., NYU.
James Hannaham, Associate Professor; M.F.A., Texas at Austin.
Samantha Hunt, Professor; M.F.A., Warren Wilson.
Rachel Levitsky, Associate Professor; M.F.A., Naropa.
Tracie Morris, Professor; Ph.D., NYU.
Anna Moschovakis; M.F.A., Bard.
Mendi Obadike, Associate Professor; Ph.D., Duke.

© 2015 Bob Handelman

© 2015 Bob Handelman

Section 17
Conflict Resolution and Mediation/Peace Studies

This section contains a directory of institutions offering graduate work in conflict resolution and mediation/peace studies. Additional information about programs listed in the directory but not augmented by an in-depth entry may be obtained by writing directly to the dean of a graduate school or chair of a department at the address given in the directory.

For programs offering related work, see also in this book *Political Science and International Affairs* and *Public, Regional, and Industrial Affairs*. In another guide in this series:

Graduate Programs in Business, Education, Information Studies, Law & Social Work
See *Business Administration and Management* and *Law*

CONTENTS

Program Directory

Conflict Resolution and Mediation/Peace Studies

Abilene Christian University, Graduate School, College of Arts and Sciences, Department of Conflict Resolution, Abilene, TX 79699-9100. Offers conflict resolution (Certificate); conflict resolution and reconciliation (MA). Part-time and evening/weekend programs available. Postbaccalaureate distance learning degree programs offered (minimal on-campus study). *Faculty:* 3 full-time (0 women), 2 part-time/adjunct (1 woman). *Students:* 45 full-time (29 women), 31 part-time (23 women); includes 30 minority (25 Black or African American, non-Hispanic/Latino; 5 Hispanic/Latino). 32 applicants, 78% accepted, 18 enrolled. In 2014, 30 master's, 50 other advanced degrees awarded. *Degree requirements:* For master's, practicum. *Entrance requirements:* Additional exam requirements/recommendations for international students: Required—TOEFL (minimum score 550 paper-based; 90 iBT), IELTS (minimum score 6.5), PTE. *Application deadline:* For fall admission, 8/15 priority date for domestic students; for winter admission, 10/1 priority date for domestic students; for spring admission, 12/15 priority date for domestic students; for summer admission, 4/15 priority date for domestic students. Applications are processed on a rolling basis. Application fee: $100. Electronic applications accepted. *Expenses:* Expenses: Contact institution. *Financial support:* In 2014–15, 1 student received support. Available to part-time students. Applicants required to submit FAFSA. *Unit head:* Dr. Garry P. Bailey, Graduate Director, 325-674-2015, Fax: 325-674-2427, E-mail: garrybailey@acu.edu. *Application contact:* Corey Patterson, Director of Graduate Admission and Recruiting, 325-674-6566, Fax: 325-674-6717, E-mail: gradinfo@acu.edu.
Website: http://www.mediate.com/ccr/

Abilene Christian University, Graduate School, College of Education and Human Services, Graduate Studies in Education, Leadership of Learning Program, Abilene, TX 79699-9100. Offers leadership of digital learning (M Ed, Certificate), including digital learning (M Ed), leadership of learning (Certificate); leadership of learning (M Ed), including conflict resolution, principalship. Part-time programs available. Postbaccalaureate distance learning degree programs offered (no on-campus study). *Students:* 19 full-time (16 women), 14 part-time (11 women); includes 12 minority (4 Black or African American, non-Hispanic/Latino; 1 Asian, non-Hispanic/Latino; 6 Hispanic/Latino; 1 Two or more races, non-Hispanic/Latino). 19 applicants, 32% accepted, 4 enrolled. In 2014, 14 master's awarded. *Degree requirements:* For master's, comprehensive exam, practicum. *Entrance requirements:* Additional exam requirements/recommendations for international students: Required—TOEFL (minimum score 550 paper-based; 90 iBT), IELTS (minimum score 6.5), PTE. *Application deadline:* For fall admission, 8/15 priority date for domestic students; for winter admission, 10/1 priority date for domestic students; for spring admission, 12/15 priority date for domestic students; for summer admission, 4/15 for domestic students. Applications are processed on a rolling basis. Application fee: $50. Electronic applications accepted. *Expenses:* Expenses: Contact institution. *Financial support:* In 2014–15, 1 student received support. Application deadline: 4/1; applicants required to submit FAFSA. *Unit head:* Dr. Lloyd Goldsmith, Graduate Director, 325-674-2946, Fax: 325-674-2123, E-mail: lloyd.goldsmith@acu.edu. *Application contact:* Corey Patterson, Director of Graduate Admission and Recruiting, 325-674-6566, Fax: 325-674-6717, E-mail: gradinfo@acu.edu.

American Public University System, AMU/APU Graduate Programs, Charles Town, WV 25414. Offers accounting (MBA, MS); criminal justice (MA), including business administration, emergency and disaster management, general (MA, MS); educational leadership (M Ed); emergency and disaster management (MA); entrepreneurship (MBA); environmental policy and management (MS), including environmental planning, environmental sustainability, fish and wildlife management, general (MA, MS), global environmental management; finance (MBA); general (MBA); global business management (MBA); history (MA), including American history, ancient and classical history, European history, global history, public history; homeland security (MA), including business administration, counter-terrorism studies, criminal justice, cyber, emergency management and public health, intelligence studies, transportation security; homeland security resource allocation (MBA); humanities (MA); information technology (MS), including digital forensics, enterprise software development, information assurance and security, IT project management; information technology management (MBA); intelligence studies (MA), including criminal intelligence, cyber, general (MA, MS), homeland security, intelligence analysis, intelligence collection, intelligence management, intelligence operations, terrorism studies; international relations and conflict resolution (MA), including comparative and security issues, conflict resolution, international and transnational security issues, peacekeeping; legal studies (MA); management (MA), including defense management, general (MA, MS), human resource management, organizational leadership, public administration; marketing (MBA); military history (MA), including American military history, American Revolution, civil war, war since 1945, World War II; military studies (MA), including joint warfare, strategic leadership; national security studies (MA), including general (MA, MS), homeland security, regional security studies, security and intelligence analysis, terrorism studies; nonprofit management (MBA); political science (MA), including American politics and government, comparative government and development, general (MA, MS), international relations, public policy; psychology (MA); public administration (MPA), including disaster management, environmental policy, health policy, human resources, national security, organizational management, security management; public health (MPH); reverse logistics management (MA); school counseling (M Ed); security management (MA); space studies (MS), including aerospace science, general (MA, MS), planetary science; sports and health sciences (MS); teaching (M Ed), including curriculum and instruction for elementary teachers, elementary reading, English language learners, instructional leadership, online learning, special education; transportation and logistics management (MA), including general (MA, MS), maritime engineering management, reverse logistics management. Programs offered via distance learning only. Part-time and evening/weekend programs available. Postbaccalaureate distance learning degree programs offered (no on-campus study). *Faculty:* 426 full-time (236 women), 1,864 part-time/adjunct (880 women). *Students:* 475 full-time (215 women), 10,067 part-time (4,085 women); includes 3,462 minority (1,863 Black or African American, non-Hispanic/Latino; 74 American Indian or Alaska Native, non-Hispanic/Latino; 273 Asian, non-Hispanic/Latino; 831 Hispanic/Latino; 78 Native Hawaiian or other Pacific Islander, non-Hispanic/Latino; 343 Two or more races, non-Hispanic/Latino), 131 international. Average age 36. In 2014, 3,740 master's awarded. *Degree requirements:* For master's, comprehensive exam or practicum. *Entrance requirements:* For master's, official transcript showing earned bachelor's degree from institution accredited by recognized accrediting body. Additional exam requirements/recommendations for international students: Required—TOEFL (minimum score 550 paper-based), IELTS (minimum score 6.5). *Application deadline:* Applications are processed on a rolling basis. Application fee: $0. Electronic applications accepted. *Financial support:* Applicants required to submit FAFSA. *Faculty research:* Military history, criminal justice, management performance, national security. *Unit head:* Dr. Karan Powell, Executive Vice President and Provost, 877-468-6268, Fax: 304-724-3780. *Application contact:* Terry Grant, Vice President of Enrollment Management, 877-468-6268, Fax: 304-724-3780, E-mail: info@apus.edu.
Website: http://www.apus.edu

American University, School of International Service, Washington, DC 20016-8071. Offers comparative and regional studies (Certificate); cross-cultural communication (Certificate); development management (MS); ethics, peace, and global affairs (MA); European studies (Certificate); global environmental policy (MA, Certificate); global information technology (Certificate); international affairs (MA), including comparative and international disability policy, comparative and regional studies, international economic relations, international politics, natural resources and sustainable development, U.S. foreign policy; international communication (MA, Certificate); international development (MA, Certificate); international economic policy (Certificate); international economic relations (Certificate); international media (MA); international peace and conflict resolution (MA, Certificate); international politics (Certificate); international relations (PhD); international service (MIS); peacebuilding (Certificate); social enterprise (MA); the Americas (Certificate); United States foreign policy (Certificate); JD/MA. Part-time and evening/weekend programs available. Postbaccalaureate distance learning degree programs offered (no on-campus study). *Faculty:* 112 full-time (43 women), 59 part-time/adjunct (27 women). *Students:* 545 full-time (335 women), 443 part-time (271 women); includes 231 minority (82 Black or African American, non-Hispanic/Latino; 8 American Indian or Alaska Native, non-Hispanic/Latino; 51 Asian, non-Hispanic/Latino; 81 Hispanic/Latino; 2 Native Hawaiian or other Pacific Islander, non-Hispanic/Latino; 7 Two or more races, non-Hispanic/Latino), 120 international. Average age 28. 1,991 applicants, 70% accepted, 365 enrolled. In 2014, 426 master's, 9 doctorates, 6 other advanced degrees awarded. Terminal master's awarded for partial completion of doctoral program. *Degree requirements:* For master's, one foreign language, comprehensive exam, thesis or alternative; for doctorate, one foreign language, comprehensive exam, thesis/dissertation. *Entrance requirements:* For master's, GRE, transcripts, resume, 2 letters of recommendation, statement of purpose; for doctorate, GRE, transcripts, resume, 3 letters of recommendation, statement of purpose. Additional exam requirements/recommendations for international students: Required—TOEFL (minimum score 600 paper-based; 100 iBT). *Application deadline:* For fall admission, 1/15 for domestic students; for spring admission, 10/1 for domestic students, 9/15 for international students. Application fee: $50. Electronic applications accepted. *Financial support:* Application deadline: 1/15. *Unit head:* Dr. James Goldgeier, Dean, 202-885-1603, Fax: 202-885-2494, E-mail: goldgeier@american.edu. *Application contact:* Jia Jiang, Associate Director, Graduate Education Enrollment, 202-885-1689, Fax: 202-885-1109, E-mail: jiang@american.edu.
Website: http://www.american.edu/sis/

The American University of Paris, Graduate Programs, Paris, France. Offers cross-cultural and sustainable business management (MA); cultural translation (MA); global communications (MA); global communications and civil society (MA); international affairs (MA); international affairs, conflict resolution and civil society development (MA); Middle East and Islamic studies (MA); Middle East and Islamic studies and international affairs (MA); public policy and international affairs (MA); public policy and international law (MA). *Degree requirements:* For master's, thesis (for some programs). *Entrance requirements:* For master's, minimum undergraduate GPA of 3.0. Additional exam requirements/recommendations for international students: Recommended—TOEFL, IELTS. Electronic applications accepted.

Anabaptist Mennonite Biblical Seminary, Graduate and Professional Programs, Elkhart, IN 46517-1999. Offers Christian formation (MA); divinity (M Div); mission and evangelism (MA); peace studies (MA); theological studies (MA, Certificate). *Accreditation:* ACIPE; ATS. Part-time programs available. *Degree requirements:* For master's, comprehensive exam, thesis optional. *Entrance requirements:* For master's and Certificate, 3 letters of reference. Additional exam requirements/recommendations for international students: Required—TOEFL (minimum score 550 paper-based). Electronic applications accepted. *Faculty research:* Biblical studies, theology, church history, church leadership.

Antioch University Midwest, Graduate Programs, Program in Conflict Analysis and Management, Yellow Springs, OH 45387-1609. Offers MA. Part-time and evening/weekend programs available. Postbaccalaureate distance learning degree programs offered (minimal on-campus study). *Degree requirements:* For master's, thesis or alternative. *Entrance requirements:* For master's, resume, goal statement, interview. Electronic applications accepted. *Expenses:* Contact institution.

Arcadia University, Graduate Studies, Program in International Peace and Conflict Resolution, Glenside, PA 19038-3295. Offers MAIPCR. Part-time and evening/weekend programs available. *Degree requirements:* For master's, one foreign language. *Entrance requirements:* For master's, GRE. Additional exam requirements/recommendations for international students: Required—TOEFL. *Expenses:* Contact institution.

Baptist Theological Seminary at Richmond, Graduate and Professional Programs, Richmond, VA 23227. Offers Biblical interpretation (M Div); Christian education (M Div); Christian ministry (MCM); justice and peacebuilding (D Min); theological studies (MTS, Graduate Certificate); M Div/MS; M Div/MSW. *Accreditation:* ATS. Part-time programs available. Postbaccalaureate distance learning degree programs offered (minimal on-campus study). *Faculty:* 7 full-time (2 women), 14 part-time/adjunct (6 women). *Students:* 45 full-time (27 women), 40 part-time (24 women); includes 10 minority (9 Black or African American, non-Hispanic/Latino; 1 Hispanic/Latino), 3 international. *Degree requirements:* For doctorate, one foreign language, comprehensive exam, thesis/dissertation, field study, independent study. *Entrance requirements:* For master's, BA/BS, 2 references, resume, official transcripts; for doctorate, MAT, M Div, 3 years of full-time ministry experience, minimum GPA of 2.75, 3 references, resume, official transcripts, writing sample, personal statement. Additional exam requirements/recommendations for international students: Required—TOEFL (minimum score 550 paper-based). *Application deadline:* For fall admission, 7/1 for domestic students, 5/1 for international students; for winter admission, 12/15 for domestic students, 9/1 for international students; for spring admission, 1/15 for domestic students, 10/1 for international students. Applications are processed on a rolling basis. Application fee: $35. *Financial support:* Teaching assistantships, scholarships/grants, and tuition waivers (partial) available. Financial award application deadline: 2/1. *Faculty research:* Biblical studies, pastoral care, church history, theology, ministry. *Unit head:* Dr. Ronald W. Crawford, President, 804-204-1201, Fax: 804-355-8182, E-mail: rcrawford@btsr.edu. *Application contact:* Melissa Fallen, Director of Admissions and Recruitment, 804-204-1208, E-mail: admissions@btsr.edu.
Website: http://www.btsr.edu/programs/degree-programs/

Bethany Theological Seminary, Graduate and Professional Programs, Richmond, IN 47374-4019. Offers biblical studies (MA Th); ministry studies (M Div); peace studies (M Div, MA Th); theological studies (MA Th, CATS); youth ministry (M Div). *Accreditation:* ACIPE; ATS. Part-time programs available. Postbaccalaureate distance learning degree programs offered (minimal on-campus study). *Degree requirements:* For master's, thesis (for some programs). *Entrance requirements:* For master's, letters of reference. Additional exam requirements/recommendations for international students: Required—TOEFL (minimum score 550 paper-based).

Bethel University, Graduate Programs, McKenzie, TN 38201. Offers administration and supervision (MA Ed); business administration (MBA); conflict resolution (MA); physician assistant studies (MS). Part-time and evening/weekend programs available. *Degree requirements:* For master's, thesis (for some programs). *Entrance requirements:* For master's, GRE General Test or MAT, minimum undergraduate GPA of 2.5.

Brandeis University, The Heller School for Social Policy and Management, Program in Coexistence and Conflict, Waltham, MA 02454-9110. Offers MA, MA/MA. MA/MA program offered in conjunction with Program in Sustainable International Development. *Degree requirements:* For master's, thesis, internship. *Entrance requirements:* For master's, 3 letters of recommendation, curriculum vitae or resume, 5 years of field experience. Additional exam requirements/recommendations for international students: Required—TOEFL (minimum score 600 paper-based; 100 iBT). Electronic applications accepted. *Faculty research:* Intercommunal conflicts, strategic intervention, conflict resolution, coexistence and conflict, international and inter-governmental organizations.

California State University, Dominguez Hills, College of Arts and Humanities, Program in Negotiation, Conflict Resolution and Peacebuilding, Carson, CA 90747-0001. Offers MA. Part-time and evening/weekend programs available. Postbaccalaureate distance learning degree programs offered (no on-campus study). *Faculty:* 2 full-time (1 woman), 3 part-time/adjunct (2 women). *Students:* 29 full-time (14 women), 106 part-time (70 women); includes 60 minority (27 Black or African American, non-Hispanic/Latino; 1 American Indian or Alaska Native, non-Hispanic/Latino; 3 Asian, non-Hispanic/Latino; 24 Hispanic/Latino; 1 Native Hawaiian or other Pacific Islander, non-Hispanic/Latino; 4 Two or more races, non-Hispanic/Latino), 2 international. Average age 41. 64 applicants, 83% accepted, 30 enrolled. In 2014, 40 master's awarded. *Degree requirements:* For master's, portfolio. *Entrance requirements:* For master's, minimum GPA of 3.2, 3 letters of recommendation. Additional exam requirements/recommendations for international students: Required—TOEFL (minimum score 550 paper-based). *Application deadline:* For fall admission, 5/1 for domestic and international students; for spring admission, 12/1 for domestic and international students. Application fee: $55. Electronic applications accepted. *Expenses:* Tuition, state resident: full-time $6738; part-time $3960 per year. Tuition, nonresident: full-time $13,434; part-time $8370 per year. *Required fees:* $623; $623 per year. *Faculty research:* Ethnic conflict, mediator ethics, teacher training, global conflict resolution (including role of ombuds), optimal multicultural process. *Unit head:* Dr. Rudy Vanterpool, Interim Director, 310-243-2295, Fax: 310-516-4268, E-mail: rvanterpool@csudh.edu. *Application contact:* Penny A. Roebuck, Administrative Coordinator, 310-243-3237, Fax: 310-516-4268, E-mail: plabaun@csudh.edu.
Website: http://www4.csudh.edu/negotiation/

Cambridge College, School of Management, Cambridge, MA 02138-5304. Offers business negotiation and conflict resolution (M Mgt); general business (M Mgt); health care informatics (M Mgt); health care management (M Mgt); leadership in human and organizational dynamics (M Mgt); non-profit and public organization management (M Mgt); small business development (M Mgt); technology management (M Mgt). Part-time and evening/weekend programs available. *Degree requirements:* For master's, thesis, seminars. *Entrance requirements:* For master's, resume, 2 professional references. Additional exam requirements/recommendations for international students: Required—TOEFL (minimum score 550 paper-based; 79 iBT), Michigan English Language Assessment Battery (minimum score 85); Recommended—IELTS (minimum score 6). Electronic applications accepted. *Expenses:* Contact institution. *Faculty research:* Negotiation, mediation and conflict resolution; leadership; management of diverse organizations; case studies and simulation methodologies for management education, digital as a second language: social networking for digital immigrants, non-profit and public management.

Carleton University, Faculty of Graduate Studies, Faculty of Public Affairs and Management, Department of Law, Ottawa, ON K1S 5B6, Canada. Offers conflict resolution (Certificate); legal studies (MA). *Degree requirements:* For master's, thesis. *Entrance requirements:* For master's, honors degree. Additional exam requirements/recommendations for international students: Required—TOEFL. *Faculty research:* Legal and social theory; women, law, and gender relations; law, crime, and social order; political economy of law; international law.

Champlain College, Graduate Studies, Burlington, VT 05402-0670. Offers business (MBA); digital forensic management (MS); digital forensic science (MS); early childhood education (M Ed); emergent media (MFA, MS); health care administration (MS); law (MS); managing innovation and information technology (MS); mediation and applied conflict studies (MS). MS in emergent media program held in Shanghai. Part-time programs available. Postbaccalaureate distance learning degree programs offered (no on-campus study). *Degree requirements:* For master's, capstone project. *Entrance requirements:* Additional exam requirements/recommendations for international students: Required—TOEFL (minimum score 550 paper-based; 80 iBT). Electronic applications accepted.

Colorado Technical University Colorado Springs, Graduate Studies, Program in Management, Colorado Springs, CO 80907-3896. Offers accounting (MBA, MSA); business administration (MBA); finance (MBA); human resources management (MBA); logistics/supply chain management (MBA); management (DM); marketing (MBA); mediation and dispute resolution (MBA); operations management (MBA); project management (MBA); technology management (MBA). Part-time and evening/weekend programs available. Postbaccalaureate distance learning degree programs offered. *Degree requirements:* For master's, thesis or alternative; for doctorate, thesis/dissertation. *Entrance requirements:* For doctorate, minimum graduate GPA of 3.0, 5 years of related work experience. *Faculty research:* Sexual harassment, performance evaluation, critical thinking.

Colorado Technical University Denver South, Programs in Business Administration and Management, Aurora, CO 80014. Offers accounting (MBA); business administration (MBA); business administration and management (EMBA); finance (MBA); human resource management (MBA); marketing (MBA); mediation and dispute resolution (MBA); operations management (MBA); project management (MBA); technology management (MBA). Part-time and evening/weekend programs available. *Degree requirements:* For master's, thesis or alternative. *Entrance requirements:* For master's, minimum undergraduate GPA of 3.0, resume.

Columbia College, Graduate Programs, Department of Human Relations, Columbia, SC 29203-5998. Offers interpersonal relations/conflict management (Certificate); organizational behavior/conflict management (Certificate); organizational change and leadership (MA). Part-time and evening/weekend programs available. Postbaccalaureate distance learning degree programs offered. *Degree requirements:* For master's, thesis, practicum. *Entrance requirements:* For master's, GRE General Test, MAT, 2 letters of recommendation, minimum GPA of 3.2. Additional exam requirements/recommendations for international students: Required—TOEFL. Electronic applications accepted. *Expenses:* Contact institution. *Faculty research:* Envisioning and the resolution of conflict, environmental conflict resolution, crisis negotiation.

Columbia University, School of Continuing Education, Program in Negotiation and Conflict Resolution, New York, NY 10027. Offers MS. Part-time programs available. *Entrance requirements:* For master's, 2 letters of recommendation, professional resume. Electronic applications accepted.

Cornell University, Graduate School, Graduate Fields of Architecture, Art and Planning, Field of Regional Science, Ithaca, NY 14853-0001. Offers environmental studies (MA, MS, PhD); international spatial problems (MA, MS, PhD); location theory (MA, MS, PhD); multiregional economic analysis (MA, MS, PhD); peace science (MA, MS, PhD); planning methods (MA, MS, PhD); urban and regional economics (MA, MS, PhD). Terminal master's awarded for partial completion of doctoral program. *Degree requirements:* For master's, thesis; for doctorate, comprehensive exam, thesis/dissertation. *Entrance requirements:* For master's and doctorate, GRE General Test, 2 letters of recommendation. Additional exam requirements/recommendations for international students: Required—TOEFL (minimum score 600 paper-based; 77 iBT). Electronic applications accepted. *Faculty research:* Urban and regional growth, spatial economics, formation of spatial patterns by socioeconomic systems, non-linear dynamics and complex systems, environmental-economic systems.

Creighton University, School of Law, Program in Negotiation and Conflict Resolution, Omaha, NE 68178. Offers MS, Certificate. Part-time and evening/weekend programs available. Postbaccalaureate distance learning degree programs offered (minimal on-campus study). *Faculty:* 7 full-time (3 women), 8 part-time/adjunct (6 women). *Students:* 41 full-time (26 women), 61 part-time (34 women); includes 20 minority (15 Black or African American, non-Hispanic/Latino; 3 Asian, non-Hispanic/Latino; 1 Hispanic/Latino; 1 Native Hawaiian or other Pacific Islander, non-Hispanic/Latino). Average age 39. 30 applicants, 93% accepted, 25 enrolled. In 2014, 60 master's awarded. *Degree requirements:* For master's, thesis or alternative, practicum. *Entrance requirements:* Additional exam requirements/recommendations for international students: Required—TOEFL. *Application deadline:* Applications are processed on a rolling basis. Application fee: $50. Electronic applications accepted. *Expenses: Tuition:* Full-time $14,040; part-time $780 per credit hour. *Required fees:* $153 per semester. Tuition and fees vary according to course load, campus/location, program, reciprocity agreements and student's religious affiliation. *Financial support:* Institutionally sponsored loans available. Financial award applicants required to submit FAFSA. *Faculty research:* Nationalism/identity and conflict; complex adaptive items and conflict engagement; history, memory and conflict; culture and conflict. *Unit head:* Prof. Patrick Borchers, Director/Professor of Law, 402-280-3852, Fax: 402-280-3756, E-mail: patrickborchers@creighton.edu. *Application contact:* Bryan Hanson, Assistant Director, 402-280-3852, Fax: 402-280-3756, E-mail: bryanhanson@creighton.edu.
Website: http://law.creighton.edu/werner-institute

Dallas Baptist University, College of Business, Business Administration Program, Dallas, TX 75211-9299. Offers accounting (MBA); business communication (MBA); conflict resolution management (MBA); entrepreneurship (MBA); finance (MBA); health care management (MBA); international business (MBA); leading the non-profit organization (MBA); management (MBA); management information systems (MBA); marketing (MBA); project management (MBA); technology and engineering (MBA). *Accreditation:* ACBSP. Part-time and evening/weekend programs available. *Entrance requirements:* For master's, GMAT, minimum GPA of 3.0. Additional exam requirements/recommendations for international students: Required—TOEFL, IELTS. Electronic applications accepted. *Expenses: Tuition:* Full-time $14,130; part-time $785 per credit hour. *Required fees:* $200 per semester. Tuition and fees vary according to course level and course load. *Faculty research:* Sports management, services marketing, retailing, strategic management, financial planning/investments.

Dallas Baptist University, College of Business, Management Program, Dallas, TX 75211-9299. Offers conflict resolution management (MA); general management (MA); health care management (MA); human resource management (MA); organizational management (MA); performance management (MA); professional sales and management optimization (MA). Part-time and evening/weekend programs available. *Entrance requirements:* For master's, GRE General Test, minimum GPA of 3.0. Additional exam requirements/recommendations for international students: Required—TOEFL, IELTS. Electronic applications accepted. *Expenses: Tuition:* Full-time $14,130; part-time $785 per credit hour. *Required fees:* $200 per semester. Tuition and fees vary according to course level and course load. *Faculty research:* Organizational behavior, conflict personalities.

Dominican University, School of Professional and Continuing Studies, River Forest, IL 60305-1099. Offers conflict resolution (MA). Part-time and evening/weekend programs available. Postbaccalaureate distance learning degree programs offered (minimal on-campus study). *Faculty:* 13 part-time/adjunct (4 women). *Students:* 31 full-time (27 women), 18 part-time (13 women); includes 24 minority (19 Black or African American, non-Hispanic/Latino; 5 Hispanic/Latino). Average age 32. 19 applicants, 63% accepted, 15 enrolled. In 2014, 12 master's awarded. *Entrance requirements:* For master's, bachelor's degree in any subject, two letters of recommendation. Additional exam requirements/recommendations for international students: Required—TOEFL (minimum score 550 paper-based; 79 iBT). *Application deadline:* Applications are processed on a rolling basis. Application fee: $25. *Expenses:* Expenses: $535 per credit hour, $100 per year in fees. *Unit head:* Dr. Matthew Hlinak, Assistant Provost for Continuing Studies and Special Initiatives, 708-714-9056, E-mail: mhlinak@dom.edu. *Application contact:* Monica Halloran, Associate Director of Academic Advising, 708-714-9007, Fax: 708-714-9126, E-mail: mhallora@dom.edu.
Website: http://continuingstudies.dom.edu/

Duquesne University, Graduate School of Liberal Arts, Graduate Center for Social and Public Policy, Pittsburgh, PA 15282-0001. Offers conflict resolution and peace studies (Certificate); social and public policy (MA, Certificate). Part-time and evening/weekend programs available. *Faculty:* 6 full-time (2 women), 1 (woman) part-time/adjunct. *Students:* 25 full-time (16 women), 2 part-time (1 woman); includes 4 minority (1 Black or African American, non-Hispanic/Latino; 1 Asian, non-Hispanic/Latino; 2 Two or more races, non-Hispanic/Latino), 2 international. Average age 29. 32 applicants, 63% accepted, 10 enrolled. In 2014, 16 master's awarded. *Degree requirements:* For master's, thesis. *Entrance requirements:* For master's, GRE General Test. Additional exam requirements/recommendations for international students: Required—TOEFL. *Application deadline:* For fall admission, 4/30 priority date for domestic and international students; for spring admission, 11/1 priority date for domestic and international students. Applications are processed on a rolling basis. Electronic applications accepted. *Expenses: Tuition:* Full-time $18,882; part-time $1049 per credit. *Required fees:* $1800; $100 per credit. Tuition and fees vary according to program. *Financial support:* In 2014–15, 20 students received support, including 13 teaching assistantships with full and partial tuition reimbursements available (averaging $10,000 per year); career-related internships or fieldwork, institutionally sponsored loans, scholarships/grants, tuition

waivers (full and partial), and unspecified assistantships also available. Support available to part-time students. Financial award application deadline: 5/1. *Faculty research:* Program evaluation, environmental policy, criminal justice policy, health care policy. *Total annual research expenditures:* $30,000. *Unit head:* Dr. Michael Irwin, Director, 412-396-6488, E-mail: irwinm@duq.edu. *Application contact:* Linda Rendulic, Assistant to the Dean, 412-396-6400, E-mail: rendulic@duq.edu.
Website: http://www.duq.edu/academics/schools/liberal-arts/graduate-school/programs/social-and-public-policy

Eastern Mennonite University, Program in Conflict Transformation, Harrisonburg, VA 22802-2462. Offers MA, Graduate Certificate. Part-time programs available. *Degree requirements:* For master's, practicum. *Entrance requirements:* For master's, minimum undergraduate GPA of 2.75. Additional exam requirements/recommendations for international students: Required—TOEFL (minimum score 550 paper-based). Electronic applications accepted. *Expenses:* Contact institution. *Faculty research:* Restorative justice, negotiation, security in an age of terror, trauma recovery, development, peacebuilding.

Fresno Pacific University, Graduate Programs, Program in Peacemaking and Conflict Studies, Fresno, CA 93702-4709. Offers church conflict and peacemaking (Certificate); mediation (Certificate); peacemaking and conflict studies (MA); restorative justice (Certificate). Part-time and evening/weekend programs available. *Degree requirements:* For master's, thesis. *Entrance requirements:* For master's, GMAT, MAT, GRE, interview, writing sample, three references. Additional exam requirements/recommendations for international students: Required—TOEFL (minimum score 550 paper-based). *Application deadline:* For fall admission, 7/15 for domestic and international students; for spring admission, 11/15 for domestic and international students. Applications are processed on a rolling basis. Application fee: $90. Electronic applications accepted. *Expenses:* Expenses: $545 per unit. *Financial support:* Career-related internships or fieldwork, scholarships/grants, and tuition waivers (full and partial) available. Support available to part-time students. Financial award applicants required to submit FAFSA. *Unit head:* Dr. Peter Smith, Director, 559-453-3466, Fax: 559-252-4800, E-mail: peter.smith@fresno.edu. *Application contact:* Amanda Krum-Stovall, Director of Graduate Admissions, 559-453-2016, E-mail: amanda.krum-stovall@fresno.edu.
Website: http://grad.fresno.edu/programs/peacemaking-and-conflict-studies-pacs-program

Future Generations Graduate School, Program in Applied Community Change, Conservation, and Peacebuilding, Franklin, WV 26807. Offers conservation (MA); peacebuilding (MA). *Degree requirements:* For master's, one foreign language, applied practicum research. *Entrance requirements:* For master's, bachelor's degree, community involvement. Additional exam requirements/recommendations for international students: Required—TOEFL. Electronic applications accepted. *Faculty research:* Sustainable communities, community engagement, peacebuilding, seed-scale community development.

George Mason University, School for Conflict Analysis and Resolution, Arlington, VA 22201. Offers MS, PhD, Certificate. Part-time and evening/weekend programs available. *Faculty:* 21 full-time (11 women), 21 part-time/adjunct (7 women). *Students:* 130 full-time (72 women), 164 part-time (97 women); includes 75 minority (43 Black or African American, non-Hispanic/Latino; 15 Asian, non-Hispanic/Latino; 14 Hispanic/Latino; 3 Two or more races, non-Hispanic/Latino), 36 international. Average age 34. 343 applicants, 41% accepted, 89 enrolled. In 2014, 70 master's, 15 doctorates, 5 other advanced degrees awarded. *Degree requirements:* For master's, thesis optional; for doctorate, one foreign language, comprehensive exam, thesis/dissertation, oral defense of dissertation. *Entrance requirements:* For master's, 2 official copies of transcripts; 3 letters of recommendation; expanded goals statement; resume; baccalaureate degree from accredited institution with minimum GPA of 3.0; for doctorate, baccalaureate and master's degrees from regionally-accredited institution; minimum GPA of 3.0; 2 official copies of transcripts; expanded goals statement; 3 letters of recommendation; writing sample; resume; for Certificate, baccalaureate degree from accredited institution with minimum GPA of 3.0; 2 official copies of transcripts; letter of intent; 2 letters of recommendation; resume. Additional exam requirements/recommendations for international students: Required—TOEFL (minimum score 570 paper-based; 80 iBT), IELTS (minimum score 6.5), PTE. *Application deadline:* For fall admission, 5/1 priority date for domestic students; for spring admission, 10/1 priority date for domestic students. Application fee: $65 ($80 for international students). Electronic applications accepted. *Expenses:* Tuition, state resident: full-time $9794; part-time $408 per credit hour. Tuition, nonresident: full-time $26,978; part-time $1124 per credit hour. *Required fees:* $2820; $118 per credit hour. Tuition and fees vary according to course load and program. *Financial support:* In 2014–15, 43 students received support, including 6 fellowships (averaging $7,414 per year), 27 research assistantships with full and partial tuition reimbursements available (averaging $15,206 per year), 14 teaching assistantships with full and partial tuition reimbursements available (averaging $8,910 per year); career-related internships or fieldwork, Federal Work-Study, scholarships/grants, unspecified assistantships, and health care benefits (for full-time research or teaching assistantship recipients) also available. Support available to part-time students. Financial award application deadline: 3/1; financial award applicants required to submit FAFSA. *Faculty research:* Preventive diplomacy, conflict/dispute resolution, peace/security, political violence, international terrorism. *Total annual research expenditures:* $1.4 million. *Unit head:* Kevin Avruch, Dean, 703-993-3607, Fax: 703-993-1302, E-mail: kavruch@gmu.edu. *Application contact:* Monique Williams, Director of Graduate Admissions, 703-993-3655, Fax: 703-993-1302, E-mail: mwilli43@gmu.edu.
Website: http://scar.gmu.edu

George Mason University, School of Policy, Government, and International Affairs, Program in Peace Operations, Arlington, VA 22201. Offers MS. *Faculty:* 9 full-time (4 women), 5 part-time/adjunct (2 women). *Students:* 18 full-time (10 women), 43 part-time (21 women); includes 16 minority (5 Black or African American, non-Hispanic/Latino; 3 Asian, non-Hispanic/Latino; 7 Hispanic/Latino; 1 Two or more races, non-Hispanic/Latino), 1 international. Average age 30. 27 applicants, 78% accepted, 14 enrolled. In 2014, 30 master's awarded. *Degree requirements:* For master's, thesis or alternative. *Entrance requirements:* For master's, GRE (for students seeking merit-based scholarships), 750-1000 word goal statement; resume; two copies of official transcript; two letters of recommendation. Additional exam requirements/recommendations for international students: Required—TOEFL (minimum score 575 paper-based; 80 iBT), IELTS (minimum score 6.5), PTE. *Application deadline:* For fall admission, 6/1 priority date for domestic students, 5/1 priority date for international students; for spring admission, 12/1 priority date for domestic students, 11/1 priority date for international students. Applications are processed on a rolling basis. Application fee: $65 ($80 for international students). Electronic applications accepted. *Expenses:* Expenses: Contact institution. *Financial support:* Research assistantships, teaching assistantships, career-related internships or fieldwork, Federal Work-Study, scholarships/grants, unspecified assistantships, and health care benefits (for full-time research or teaching assistantship recipients) available. Financial award application deadline: 3/1; financial award applicants required to submit FAFSA. *Unit head:* Travis Major, Director of Graduate Admissions, 703-993-3183, Fax: 703-993-4876, E-mail: tmajor@gmu.edu.
Website: http://spgia.gmu.edu/programs/graduate-degrees/master-of-science-in-peace-operations/

George Mason University, School of Policy, Government, and International Affairs, Program in Public Administration, Fairfax, VA 22030. Offers administration of justice (Certificate); association management (Certificate); biodefense (MS, PhD); critical analysis and strategic response to terrorism (Certificate); emergency management and homeland security (Certificate); nonprofit management (Certificate); political science (MA, PhD); public administration (MPA); public management (Certificate). *Accreditation:* NASPAA (one or more programs are accredited). *Entrance requirements:* For degree, expanded goals statement; 3 letters of recommendation; official transcripts; resume. Additional exam requirements/recommendations for international students: Required—TOEFL, IELTS, PTE. Application fee: $65 ($80 for international students). Electronic applications accepted. *Expenses:* Expenses: Contact institution. *Financial support:* Fellowships, research assistantships with full and partial tuition reimbursements, teaching assistantships with full and partial tuition reimbursements, career-related internships or fieldwork, Federal Work-Study, scholarships/grants, and unspecified assistantships available. Support available to part-time students. Financial award application deadline: 3/1; financial award applicants required to submit FAFSA. *Application contact:* Peg Koback, Education Support Specialist, 703-993-3707, Fax: 703-993-1399, E-mail: mkoback@gmu.edu.
Website: http://pia.gmu.edu/

Georgetown University, Graduate School of Arts and Sciences, Department of Government, Program in Conflict Resolution, Washington, DC 20057. Offers MA.

Georgetown University, Graduate School of Arts and Sciences, Edmund A. Walsh School of Foreign Service, Center for Security Studies, Washington, DC 20057. Offers MA, MA/JD, MA/PhD.

Henley-Putnam University, Master of Science Program in Strategic Security and Protection Management, San Jose, CA 95131. Offers extremist organizations (MS). Part-time programs available. Postbaccalaureate distance learning degree programs offered (no on-campus study). *Faculty:* 17 part-time/adjunct (2 women). *Students:* 21 full-time (0 women), 41 part-time (8 women); includes 5 minority (3 Black or African American, non-Hispanic/Latino; 1 American Indian or Alaska Native, non-Hispanic/Latino; 1 Hispanic/Latino). Average age 36. 6 applicants, 100% accepted, 6 enrolled. In 2014, 23 master's awarded. *Degree requirements:* For master's, comprehensive exam, thesis. *Entrance requirements:* For master's, bachelor's degree from institution accredited by an agency recognized by the U.S. Department of Education and/or the Council for Higher Education Accreditation, background check. Additional exam requirements/recommendations for international students: Required—TOEFL (minimum score 650 paper-based; 79 iBT); Recommended—IELTS. *Application deadline:* Applications are processed on a rolling basis. *Expenses:* Expenses: Contact institution. *Financial support:* Scholarships/grants and unspecified assistantships available. *Unit head:* Dr. Scott Catino, Associate Dean, 408-453-9900, E-mail: scatino@henley-putnam.edu. *Application contact:* Nancy Reggio, Director of Admissions, 888-852-8746, E-mail: nreggio@henley-putnam.edu.

Henley-Putnam University, Master of Science Program in Terrorism and Counterterrorism Studies, San Jose, CA 95131. Offers intelligence operations (MS); protective intelligence (MS). Part-time programs available. Postbaccalaureate distance learning degree programs offered (no on-campus study). *Faculty:* 22 part-time/adjunct (5 women). *Students:* 55 full-time (12 women), 72 part-time (18 women); includes 11 minority (5 Black or African American, non-Hispanic/Latino; 4 Asian, non-Hispanic/Latino; 2 Hispanic/Latino). Average age 35. 17 applicants, 100% accepted, 17 enrolled. In 2014, 23 master's awarded. *Degree requirements:* For master's, thesis. *Entrance requirements:* For master's, bachelor's degree from institution accredited by an agency recognized by the U.S. Department of Education and/or the Council for Higher Education Accreditation, background check. Additional exam requirements/recommendations for international students: Required—TOEFL (minimum score 650 paper-based; 79 iBT); Recommended—IELTS (minimum score 7). *Application deadline:* Applications are processed on a rolling basis. *Expenses:* Expenses: Contact institution. *Financial support:* Scholarships/grants and unspecified assistantships available. *Unit head:* Diane Maye, Associate Dean, 408-453-9900, E-mail: dmaye@henley-putnam.edu. *Application contact:* Nancy Reggio, Director of Admissions, 888-852-8746 Ext. 9928, E-mail: nreggio@henley-putnam.edu.
Website: http://www.henley-putnam.edu/programs/masters/terrorism-and-counterterrorism-studies.aspx

Hult International Business School, Program in International Relations - Hult London Campus, London WC 1B 4JP, United Kingdom. Offers conflict resolution (MA); diplomacy (MA); international public law (MA); international relations (MA); Middle East international security (MA); politics (MA); security studies (MA); terrorism (MA); U.S. foreign policy (MA). Part-time programs available. *Entrance requirements:* Additional exam requirements/recommendations for international students: Required—TOEFL (minimum score 580 paper-based), TWE (minimum score 5). Electronic applications accepted. *Faculty research:* American foreign politics, Middle East, security studies.

Kansas State University, Graduate School, College of Human Ecology, School of Family Studies and Human Services, Manhattan, KS 66506. Offers communication sciences and disorders (MS); conflict resolution (Graduate Certificate); early childhood education (MS); family and community service (MS); family studies (MS); life span human development (MS); marriage and family therapy (MS); personal financial planning (MS, Graduate Certificate); youth development (MS, Graduate Certificate). *Accreditation:* AAMFT/COAMFTE; ASHA. Part-time programs available. Postbaccalaureate distance learning degree programs offered (no on-campus study). *Faculty:* 39 full-time (26 women), 9 part-time/adjunct (7 women). *Students:* 69 full-time (57 women), 141 part-time (99 women); includes 48 minority (15 Black or African American, non-Hispanic/Latino; 3 American Indian or Alaska Native, non-Hispanic/Latino; 3 Asian, non-Hispanic/Latino; 21 Hispanic/Latino; 2 Native Hawaiian or other Pacific Islander, non-Hispanic/Latino; 4 Two or more races, non-Hispanic/Latino), 3 international. Average age 31. 203 applicants, 38% accepted, 57 enrolled. In 2014, 48 master's, 28 other advanced degrees awarded. *Degree requirements:* For master's, comprehensive exam (for some programs), thesis optional. *Entrance requirements:* For master's, GRE, minimum GPA of 3.0 in last 2 years of undergraduate study. Additional exam requirements/recommendations for international students: Required—TOEFL (minimum score 600 paper-based). *Application deadline:* For fall admission, 2/1 priority date for domestic students, 1/1 priority date for international students; for spring admission, 10/1 priority date for domestic students, 8/1 priority date for international students; for summer admission, 2/1 priority date for domestic students, 12/1 priority date for international students. Applications are processed on a rolling basis. Application fee: $50 ($75 for international students). Electronic applications accepted. *Financial support:* In 2014–15, 25 research assistantships (averaging $10,000 per year), 9 teaching assistantships with full tuition reimbursements (averaging $10,000 per year) were awarded; unspecified assistantships also available. Financial award application deadline: 3/1. *Faculty research:* Health and security of military families, personal and family risk assessment and evaluation, disorders of communication and swallowing, families and health, financial decision-making. *Total annual research expenditures:* $8.4 million. *Unit head:* Dr. Dottie Durband, Director, 785-532-5510, Fax: 785-532-5505,

E-mail: dottie@ksu.edu. *Application contact:* Connie Fechter, Administrative Specialist, 785-532-5510, Fax: 785-532-5505, E-mail: fechter@ksu.edu.
Website: http://www.he.k-state.edu/fshs/

Kennesaw State University, College of Humanities and Social Sciences, PhD Program in International Conflict Management, Kennesaw, GA 30144. Offers PhD. *Students:* 22 full-time (13 women), 24 part-time (15 women); includes 10 minority (8 Black or African American, non-Hispanic/Latino; 2 Hispanic/Latino), 17 international. Average age 38. 37 applicants, 35% accepted, 7 enrolled. *Degree requirements:* For doctorate, one foreign language, thesis/dissertation. *Entrance requirements:* For doctorate, GRE, portfolio of documents, copy of transcripts from all universities previously attended, resume, statement of goals and objectives, academic writing sample, three letters of recommendation. Additional exam requirements/recommendations for international students: Required—TOEFL (minimum score 90 iBT), IELTS (minimum score 7). *Application deadline:* For fall admission, 2/1 for domestic and international students. Application fee: $60. Electronic applications accepted. *Expenses:* Tuition, state resident: part-time $275 per semester hour. Tuition, nonresident: part-time $990 per semester hour. *Financial support:* In 2014–15, 5 research assistantships with full tuition reimbursements (averaging $15,000 per year) were awarded; fellowships, teaching assistantships, and unspecified assistantships also available. Financial award application deadline: 4/1; financial award applicants required to submit FAFSA. *Unit head:* Dr. Brandon Lundy, Director, 470-578-2893, E-mail: phdhss@kennesaw.edu. *Application contact:* Nicole Densmore, Admissions Counselor, 470-578-6127, Fax: 470-578-9172, E-mail: ksugrad@kennesaw.edu.
Website: http://phd.hss.kennesaw.edu/

Kennesaw State University, College of Humanities and Social Sciences, Program in Conflict Management, Kennesaw, GA 30144. Offers MSCM. Evening/weekend programs available. *Students:* 41 full-time (23 women); includes 15 minority (12 Black or African American, non-Hispanic/Latino; 1 Asian, non-Hispanic/Latino; 1 Hispanic/Latino; 1 Two or more races, non-Hispanic/Latino), 3 international. Average age 38. 32 applicants, 88% accepted, 21 enrolled. In 2014, 22 master's awarded. *Entrance requirements:* For master's, GMAT, GRE, LSAT. Additional exam requirements/recommendations for international students: Required—TOEFL (minimum score 550 paper-based; 80 iBT), IELTS (minimum score 6.5). *Application deadline:* For fall admission, 6/1 for domestic and international students. Applications are processed on a rolling basis. Application fee: $60. Electronic applications accepted. *Expenses:* Tuition, state resident: part-time $275 per semester hour. Tuition, nonresident: part-time $990 per semester hour. *Financial support:* In 2014–15, 2 research assistantships with full tuition reimbursements (averaging $8,000 per year) were awarded; Federal Work-Study and unspecified assistantships also available. Support available to part-time students. Financial award application deadline: 4/1; financial award applicants required to submit FAFSA. *Unit head:* Dr. Sherrill Hayes, Director, 470-578-6081, E-mail: shayes32@kennesaw.edu. *Application contact:* Ansley Wood, Admissions Counselor, 470-578-6637, Fax: 470-578-9172, E-mail: ksugrad@kennesaw.edu.
Website: http://www.kennesaw.edu/

Lesley University, Graduate School of Arts and Social Sciences, Cambridge, MA 02138-2790. Offers clinical mental health counseling (MA), including holistic counseling, school and community counseling, trauma studies; counseling psychology (MA, CAGS), including professional counseling (MA), school counseling (MA); creative writing (MFA); expressive therapies (MA, PhD, CAGS), including art (MA), clinical mental health counseling (MA), dance (MA), expressive therapies (MA), music (MA); independent studies (CAGS); independent study (MA); intercultural relations (MA, CAGS); interdisciplinary studies (MA), including individualized studies, integrative holistic health, mindfulness studies, peace and conflict transformation, trauma sensitive assessment, intervention, and consultation, women's studies; urban environmental leadership (MA). Part-time programs available. Postbaccalaureate distance learning degree programs offered (no on-campus study). *Faculty:* 35 full-time (25 women), 115 part-time/adjunct (90 women). *Students:* 420 full-time (379 women), 514 part-time (414 women); includes 142 minority (50 Black or African American, non-Hispanic/Latino; 5 American Indian or Alaska Native, non-Hispanic/Latino; 16 Asian, non-Hispanic/Latino; 48 Hispanic/Latino; 23 Two or more races, non-Hispanic/Latino), 46 international. Average age 33. In 2014, 475 master's, 11 doctorates, 4 other advanced degrees awarded. *Degree requirements:* For master's, internship, practicum, thesis (for expressive therapies); for doctorate, thesis/dissertation, arts apprenticeship, field placement; for CAGS, thesis, internship (for counseling psychology, expressive therapies). *Entrance requirements:* For master's, MAT (counseling psychology), interview, writing samples, art portfolio; for doctorate, GRE or MAT, interview, master's degree; for CAGS, interview, master's degree. Additional exam requirements/recommendations for international students: Required—TOEFL (minimum score 550 paper-based; 80 iBT). *Application deadline:* Applications are processed on a rolling basis. Application fee: $50. Electronic applications accepted. *Financial support:* Fellowships, career-related internships or fieldwork, Federal Work-Study, scholarships/grants, tuition waivers, and unspecified assistantships available. Financial award applicants required to submit FAFSA. *Faculty research:* Psychotherapy and culture; psychotherapy and psychological trauma; women's issues in art, teaching and psychotherapy; community-based art, psycho-spiritual inquiry. *Unit head:* Dr. Catherine Koverola, Dean, 617-349-8317, Fax: 617-349-8366, E-mail: koverola@lesley.edu. *Application contact:* Martha Sheehan, Director, Graduate Admissions, 888-LESLEYU, Fax: 617-349-8313, E-mail: info@lesley.edu.
Website: http://www.lesley.edu/graduate-school-of-arts-and-social-sciences/

Lipscomb University, Graduate School of Business, Nashville, TN 37204-3951. Offers accountancy (M Acc); accounting (MBA); conflict management (MBA); financial services (MBA); health care informatics (MBA); healthcare management (MBA); human resources (MHR); information security (MBA); leadership (MBA); nonprofit management (MBA); professional accountancy (Certificate); sports management (MBA); strategic human resources (MBA); sustainability (MBA); MBA/MS. *Accreditation:* ACBSP. Part-time and evening/weekend programs available. *Faculty:* 14 full-time (1 woman), 15 part-time/adjunct (4 women). *Students:* 121 full-time (71 women), 113 part-time (47 women); includes 36 minority (23 Black or African American, non-Hispanic/Latino; 11 Hispanic/Latino; 2 Two or more races, non-Hispanic/Latino), 7 international. Average age 32. 145 applicants, 79% accepted, 69 enrolled. In 2014, 106 master's awarded. *Entrance requirements:* For master's, GMAT, transcripts, interview, 2 references, resume. Additional exam requirements/recommendations for international students: Required—TOEFL (minimum score 570 paper-based). *Application deadline:* For fall admission, 6/15 for domestic students, 2/1 for international students; for winter admission, 6/1 for international students; for spring admission, 11/15 for domestic students. Applications are processed on a rolling basis. Application fee: $50 ($75 for international students). Electronic applications accepted. *Expenses:* Expenses: $1,230 per credit hour (for MBA and PMBA); $1,150 (for M Acc); $1,125 (for MHR); $1,100 (for MM). *Financial support:* Career-related internships or fieldwork, scholarships/grants, tuition waivers (partial), and unspecified assistantships available. Support available to part-time students. Financial award application deadline: 7/1; financial award applicants required to submit FAFSA. *Faculty research:* Impact of spirituality on organization commitment, women in corporate leadership, psychological empowerment, training. *Unit head:* Joe Ivey, Associate Dean of Graduate Business Programs, 615-966-6229, Fax: 615-966-1818, E-mail: joe.ivey@lipscomb.edu. *Application contact:* Lisa Shacklett, Assistant Dean of Enrollment and Marketing, 615-966-5968, E-mail: lisa.shacklett@lipscomb.edu.
Website: http://www.lipscomb.edu/business/Graduate-Programs

Lipscomb University, Institute for Conflict Management, Nashville, TN 37204-3951. Offers MA, Certificate. Part-time and evening/weekend programs available. *Faculty:* 4 full-time (1 woman), 2 part-time/adjunct (1 woman). *Students:* 11 full-time (7 women), 17 part-time (12 women); includes 3 minority (1 Black or African American, non-Hispanic/Latino; 1 Hispanic/Latino; 1 Two or more races, non-Hispanic/Latino). Average age 41. In 2014, 9 master's, 6 other advanced degrees awarded. *Degree requirements:* For master's, thesis optional, externship. *Entrance requirements:* For master's, GRE, GMAT, LSAT or equivalent, 3 years of work experience. Additional exam requirements/recommendations for international students: Required—TOEFL (minimum score 570 paper-based; 80 iBT). *Application deadline:* For fall admission, 7/15 for domestic students; for spring admission, 12/15 for domestic students. Applications are processed on a rolling basis. Application fee: $50 ($75 for international students). Electronic applications accepted. *Expenses:* Expenses: $1,230 per credit hour. *Financial support:* Tuition waivers (full) available. Financial award applicants required to submit FAFSA. *Faculty research:* Generationally generated conflict, cross-cultural conflict, risk and injury reduction in healthcare, spiritual formation. *Unit head:* Dr. Steve Joiner, Managing Director, 615-966-7141, Fax: 615-966-7143, E-mail: steve.joiner@lipscomb.edu. *Application contact:* Dr. Phyllis Hildreth, Academic Director, 615-966-5695, Fax: 615-966-7143, E-mail: phyllis.hildreth@lipscomb.edu.
Website: http://lipscomb.edu/icm

Marquette University, Graduate School, College of Professional Studies, Milwaukee, WI 53201-1881. Offers criminal justice administration (MLS, Certificate); dispute resolution (MDR, MLS); health care administration (MLS); leadership studies (Certificate); non-profit sector administration (MLS); public service (MAPS, MLS); sports leadership (MLS). Part-time and evening/weekend programs available. Postbaccalaureate distance learning degree programs offered (no on-campus study). *Degree requirements:* For master's, comprehensive exam (for some programs). *Entrance requirements:* For master's, GRE General Test (preferred), GMAT, or LSAT, official transcripts from all current and previous colleges/universities except Marquette, three letters of recommendation, statement of purpose. Additional exam requirements/recommendations for international students: Required—TOEFL. Electronic applications accepted.

Middlebury Institute of International Studies, Graduate School of International Policy and Management, Program in Nonproliferation and Terrorism Studies, Monterey, CA 93940-2691. Offers MA. *Degree requirements:* For master's, one foreign language. *Entrance requirements:* For master's, minimum GPA of 3.0, proficiency in a foreign language. Additional exam requirements/recommendations for international students: Required—TOEFL (minimum score 550 paper-based; 80 iBT). *Application deadline:* For fall admission, 3/5 priority date for domestic and international students; for spring admission, 10/1 priority date for domestic and international students. Application fee: $50. Application fee is waived when completed online. *Expenses: Tuition:* Full-time $36,020; part-time $1715 per credit. *Required fees:* $53 per semester. *Financial support:* Application deadline: 3/15; applicants required to submit FAFSA. *Unit head:* Jeffrey Knopf, Chair, 831-647-7174, Fax: 831-647-4199, E-mail: jknopf@miis.edu. *Application contact:* 831-647-4123, Fax: 831-647-6405, E-mail: admit@miis.edu.
Website: http://www.miis.edu/academics/programs/npts

Montclair State University, The Graduate School, College of Humanities and Social Sciences, Conflict Management in the Workplace Certificate Program, Montclair, NJ 07043-1624. Offers Certificate. *Students:* 1 (woman) full-time, 4 part-time (2 women); all minorities (3 Black or African American, non-Hispanic/Latino; 2 Hispanic/Latino). Average age 33. 1 applicant. *Application deadline:* Applications are processed on a rolling basis. *Expenses:* Tuition, state resident: full-time $9960; part-time $553.35 per credit. Tuition, nonresident: full-time $15,074; part-time $837.43 per credit. *Required fees:* $1595; $88.63 per credit. Tuition and fees vary according to degree level and program. *Unit head:* Dr. Jack Baldwin LeClair, Coordinator. *Application contact:* Amy Aiello, Executive Director of The Graduate School, 973-655-5147, Fax: 973-655-7869, E-mail: graduate.school@montclair.edu.

Montclair State University, The Graduate School, College of Humanities and Social Sciences, MA Program in Law and Governance, Montclair, NJ 07043-1624. Offers conflict management and peace studies (MA); governance, compliance and regulation (MA); intellectual property (MA); law and governance (MA); legal management (MA). Part-time and evening/weekend programs available. *Faculty:* 13 full-time (6 women), 25 part-time/adjunct (8 women). *Students:* 11 full-time (6 women), 23 part-time (13 women); includes 17 minority (8 Black or African American, non-Hispanic/Latino; 2 Asian, non-Hispanic/Latino; 5 Hispanic/Latino; 2 Two or more races, non-Hispanic/Latino), 2 international. Average age 31. 32 applicants, 44% accepted, 10 enrolled. In 2014, 27 master's awarded. *Degree requirements:* For master's, thesis or comprehensive exam. *Entrance requirements:* For master's, GRE General Test, minimum cumulative GPA of 2.75 for undergraduate work, 2 letters of recommendation, essay. Additional exam requirements/recommendations for international students: Required—TOEFL (minimum score 83 iBT) or IELTS (minimum score 6.5). *Application deadline:* Applications are processed on a rolling basis. Application fee: $60. Electronic applications accepted. *Expenses:* Tuition, state resident: full-time $9960; part-time $553.35 per credit. Tuition, nonresident: full-time $15,074; part-time $837.43 per credit. *Required fees:* $1595; $88.63 per credit. Tuition and fees vary according to degree level and program. *Financial support:* In 2014–15, 1 research assistantship with full tuition reimbursement (averaging $7,000 per year) was awarded; Federal Work-Study, scholarships/grants, and unspecified assistantships also available. Support available to part-time students. Financial award application deadline: 3/1; financial award applicants required to submit FAFSA. *Unit head:* Dr. William Berlin, Chair, 973-655-7576, E-mail: berlinw@mail.montclair.edu. *Application contact:* Amy Aiello, Director of Graduate Admissions and Operations, 973-655-5147, Fax: 973-655-7869, E-mail: graduate.school@montclair.edu.
Website: http://www.montclair.edu/graduate/programs-of-study/law-and-governance/

National Defense University, College of International Security Affairs, Washington, DC 20319-5066. Offers strategic security studies (MA), including conflict management, counterterrorism, homeland defense/ security, international security studies. Part-time and evening/weekend programs available. *Degree requirements:* For master's, thesis. *Entrance requirements:* Additional exam requirements/recommendations for international students: Required—TOEFL.

Naval Postgraduate School, Departments and Academic Groups, Department of National Security Affairs, Monterey, CA 93943. Offers national security affairs (MA); security studies (MA), including civil-military relations, combating terrorism: policy and strategy, defense decision-making and planning, Europe and Eurasia, Far East, Southeast Asia, the Pacific, homeland security and defense, Middle East, South Asia, Sub-Saharan Africa, stabilization and reconstruction, western hemisphere. Program only open to commissioned officers of the United States and friendly nations and selected United States federal civilian employees. Part-time programs available. *Degree requirements:* For master's, thesis (for some programs). *Faculty research:* Privatizing welfare in the Middle East; social construction of Russia's resurgence; institutions,

ethnicity and political mobilization in South Africa; Hezbollah; China's strategic interests in Cambodia.

New York University, School of Continuing and Professional Studies, Center for Global Affairs, New York, NY 10012-1019. Offers global affairs (MS), including environment/energy policy, human rights and international law, international development and humanitarian assistance, international relations, peace building, private sector, transnational security; global energy (Advanced Certificate); peacebuilding (Advanced Certificate); transnational security (Advanced Certificate). Part-time and evening/weekend programs available. *Faculty:* 11 full-time (6 women), 32 part-time/adjunct (14 women). *Students:* 156 full-time (105 women), 136 part-time (86 women); includes 79 minority (24 Black or African American, non-Hispanic/Latino; 17 Asian, non-Hispanic/Latino; 37 Hispanic/Latino; 1 Two or more races, non-Hispanic/Latino), 66 international. Average age 28. 357 applicants, 72% accepted, 98 enrolled. In 2014, 144 master's awarded. *Degree requirements:* For master's, thesis. *Entrance requirements:* For master's, GRE or GMAT (only upon request), bachelor's degree, resume with relevant professional work, internship or volunteer experience, two letters of recommendation, statement of purpose. Additional exam requirements/recommendations for international students: Required—TOEFL (minimum score 600 paper-based; 100 iBT), IELTS (minimum score 7). *Application deadline:* For fall admission, 2/1 priority date for domestic and international students; for spring admission, 10/15 priority date for domestic students, 8/15 priority date for international students. Applications are processed on a rolling basis. Application fee: $150. Electronic applications accepted. *Financial support:* In 2014–15, 99 students received support, including 95 fellowships (averaging $2,218 per year); Federal Work-Study and scholarships/grants also available. Support available to part-time students. Financial award application deadline: 4/1; financial award applicants required to submit FAFSA. *Unit head:* Vera Jelinek, Divisional Dean and Clinical Associate Professor, 212-992-8380. *Application contact:* Office of Admissions, 212-998-7100, E-mail: sps.gradadmissions@nyu.edu.
Website: http://www.sps.nyu.edu/academics/departments/global-affairs.html

Norwich University, College of Graduate and Continuing Studies, Master of Arts in Diplomacy Program, Northfield, VT 05663. Offers international commerce (MA); international conflict management (MA); international terrorism (MA). Evening/weekend programs available. Postbaccalaureate distance learning degree programs offered (minimal on-campus study). *Faculty:* 2 full-time (0 women), 21 part-time/adjunct (2 women). *Students:* 174 full-time (50 women); includes 36 minority (27 Black or African American, non-Hispanic/Latino; 6 Hispanic/Latino; 3 Two or more races, non-Hispanic/Latino). Average age 35. 87 applicants, 98% accepted, 65 enrolled. In 2014, 123 master's awarded. *Degree requirements:* For master's, comprehensive exam, thesis optional. *Entrance requirements:* For master's, minimum undergraduate GPA of 2.75. Additional exam requirements/recommendations for international students: Required—TOEFL (minimum score 550 paper-based; 80 iBT), IELTS (minimum score 6.5). *Application deadline:* For fall admission, 8/8 for domestic and international students; for winter admission, 11/7 for domestic and international students; for spring admission, 2/16 for domestic and international students; for summer admission, 5/18 for domestic and international students. Applications are processed on a rolling basis. Electronic applications accepted. *Expenses:* Expenses: Contact institution. *Financial support:* In 2014–15, 111 students received support. Scholarships/grants available. Financial award applicants required to submit FAFSA. *Unit head:* Dr. Lasha Tchantouridze, Program Director, 802-485-2095, Fax: 802-485-2533, E-mail: ltchanto@norwich.edu. *Application contact:* Fianna Verret, Associate Program Director, 802-485-2783, Fax: 802-485-2533, E-mail: fverret@norwich.edu.
Website: http://online.norwich.edu/degree-programs/masters/master-arts-diplomacy/overview

Nova Southeastern University, Graduate School of Humanities and Social Sciences, Fort Lauderdale, FL 33314-7796. Offers advanced conflict resolution practice (Graduate Certificate); college student affairs (MS); conflict analysis and resolution (MS, PhD); cross-disciplinary studies (MA); family studies (Graduate Certificate); family systems health care (Graduate Certificate); family therapy (MS, PhD); marriage and family therapy (DMFT); peace studies (Graduate Certificate); qualitative research (Graduate Certificate); solution focused coaching (Graduate Certificate). *Accreditation:* AAMFT/COAMFTE (one or more programs are accredited). Part-time and evening/weekend programs available. Postbaccalaureate distance learning degree programs offered (minimal on-campus study). *Faculty:* 29 full-time (18 women), 27 part-time/adjunct (21 women). *Students:* 502 full-time (363 women), 269 part-time (189 women); includes 415 minority (241 Black or African American, non-Hispanic/Latino; 1 American Indian or Alaska Native, non-Hispanic/Latino; 16 Asian, non-Hispanic/Latino; 136 Hispanic/Latino; 21 Two or more races, non-Hispanic/Latino), 56 international. Average age 37. 424 applicants, 58% accepted, 161 enrolled. In 2014, 140 master's, 50 doctorates, 11 other advanced degrees awarded. *Degree requirements:* For master's, thesis optional, comprehensive exams, portfolios (for some programs), table-top exams (for some programs); for doctorate, comprehensive exam, thesis/dissertation, qualifying exams, portfolios (for some programs). *Entrance requirements:* For master's, interview, minimum GPA of 3.0, writing sample; for doctorate, interview, minimum GPA of 3.5, master's degree in related field, writing sample; for Graduate Certificate, minimum GPA of 3.0. Additional exam requirements/recommendations for international students: Required—TOEFL. *Application deadline:* For fall admission, 5/17 priority date for domestic and international students; for winter admission, 12/1 priority date for domestic and international students; for spring admission, 4/1 priority date for domestic and international students. Applications are processed on a rolling basis. Application fee: $50. Electronic applications accepted. *Financial support:* In 2014–15, 7 students received support, including 26 research assistantships (averaging $15,000 per year); career-related internships or fieldwork, Federal Work-Study, scholarships/grants, and unspecified assistantships also available. Financial award application deadline: 4/1; financial award applicants required to submit CSS PROFILE. *Faculty research:* Conflict resolution, family therapy, peace research, international conflict, multi-disciplinary studies, college student affairs, national security affairs, health care conflict resolution, family systems health care, advanced family systems, qualitative research, solution-focused coaching. *Unit head:* Dr. Honggang Yang, Dean, 954-262-3016, Fax: 954-262-3968, E-mail: yangh@nova.edu. *Application contact:* Marcia Arango, Student Recruitment Coordinator, 954-262-3006, Fax: 954-262-3968, E-mail: marango@nsu.nova.edu.
Website: http://shss.nova.edu/

Old Dominion University, College of Arts and Letters, Graduate Program in International Studies, Norfolk, VA 23529. Offers conflict and cooperation (MA, PhD); interdependence and transnationalism (MA, PhD); international cultural studies (MA, PhD); international political economy and development (MA, PhD); modeling and simulation (MA, PhD); U.S. foreign policy and international relations (MA, PhD). Part-time programs available. *Faculty:* 18 full-time (4 women). *Students:* 41 full-time (14 women), 46 part-time (23 women); includes 11 minority (5 Black or African American, non-Hispanic/Latino; 1 Asian, non-Hispanic/Latino; 2 Hispanic/Latino; 3 Two or more races, non-Hispanic/Latino), 24 international. Average age 35. 99 applicants, 54% accepted, 34 enrolled. In 2014, 10 master's, 9 doctorates awarded. Terminal master's awarded for partial completion of doctoral program. *Degree requirements:* For master's, one foreign language, comprehensive exam, thesis optional; for doctorate, one foreign language, comprehensive exam, thesis/dissertation. *Entrance requirements:* For master's, GRE General Test, sample of written work, 2 letters of recommendation; for doctorate, GRE General Test, sample of written work, 3 letters of recommendation. Additional exam requirements/recommendations for international students: Required—TOEFL (minimum score 570 paper-based). *Application deadline:* For fall admission, 1/15 for domestic and international students; for spring admission, 10/15 for domestic and international students. Application fee: $50. Electronic applications accepted. *Expenses:* Tuition, state resident: full-time $10,488; part-time $437 per credit. Tuition, nonresident: full-time $26,136; part-time $1089 per credit. *Required fees:* $64 per semester. One-time fee: $50. *Financial support:* In 2014–15, 20 students received support, including 2 fellowships (averaging $13,000 per year), 5 research assistantships with tuition reimbursements available (averaging $15,000 per year), 7 teaching assistantships with tuition reimbursements available (averaging $15,000 per year); career-related internships or fieldwork, institutionally sponsored loans, scholarships/grants, and unspecified assistantships also available. Support available to part-time students. Financial award application deadline: 2/15; financial award applicants required to submit FAFSA. *Faculty research:* U.S. foreign policy, international security, Transatlantic and Transpacific relations, transnational issues, international political economy and development. *Total annual research expenditures:* $330,391. *Unit head:* Dr. Regina Karp, Graduate Program Director, 757-683-5700, Fax: 757-683-5701, E-mail: rkarp@odu.edu. *Application contact:* Dr. David C. Earnest, Associate Dean, 757-683-6077, Fax: 757-683-5746, E-mail: dearnest@odu.edu.
Website: http://www.al.odu.edu/gpis/

Pepperdine University, School of Law, Master of Dispute Resolution Program, Malibu, CA 90263. Offers MDR. *Students:* 13 full-time (9 women), 17 part-time (7 women); includes 8 minority (2 Black or African American, non-Hispanic/Latino; 2 Asian, non-Hispanic/Latino; 3 Hispanic/Latino; 1 Two or more races, non-Hispanic/Latino), 7 international. In 2014, 35 master's awarded. *Entrance requirements:* For master's, GRE/LSAT, letters of recommendation. *Application deadline:* For fall admission, 2/15 for domestic students; for spring admission, 8/15 for domestic students. Application fee: $60. *Unit head:* Dr. Peter Robinson, Managing Director, Straus Institute for Dispute Resolution, 310-506-4655, E-mail: peter.robinson@pepperdine.edu. *Application contact:* Shellee S. Warnes, Associate Director, Straus Institute for Dispute Resolution, 310-506-7455, E-mail: shellee.warnes@pepperdine.edu.
Website: http://law.pepperdine.edu/degrees-programs/master-of-dispute-resolution/

Pepperdine University, School of Law, Master of Laws in Dispute Resolution Program, Malibu, CA 90263. Offers LL M. *Students:* 16 full-time (10 women), 17 part-time (9 women); includes 2 minority (1 Black or African American, non-Hispanic/Latino; 1 Hispanic/Latino), 15 international. In 2014, 18 master's awarded. *Entrance requirements:* For master's, GRE General Test or LSAT, JD from ABA-accredited institution. Additional exam requirements/recommendations for international students: Required—TOEFL. *Application deadline:* For fall admission, 2/15 for domestic and international students; for spring admission, 8/15 for domestic and international students. Applications are processed on a rolling basis. Application fee: $60. Electronic applications accepted. *Expenses:* Expenses: Contact institution. *Financial support:* Career-related internships or fieldwork, Federal Work-Study, institutionally sponsored loans, and scholarships/grants available. Support available to part-time students. Financial award application deadline: 4/1; financial award applicants required to submit FAFSA. *Unit head:* Dr. Peter Robinson, Director, Institute for Dispute Resolution, 310-506-4655, Fax: 310-506-4266, E-mail: peter.robinson@pepperdine.edu. *Application contact:* Shellee S. Warnes, Assistant Director, Academic Programs, 310-506-7455, Fax: 310-506-4266, E-mail: shellee.warnes@pepperdine.edu.
Website: https://law.pepperdine.edu/degrees-programs/master-of-laws-dispute-resolution/

Portland State University, Graduate Studies, College of Liberal Arts and Sciences, Program in Conflict Resolution, Portland, OR 97207-0751. Offers MA, MS. *Faculty:* 8 full-time (4 women), 3 part-time/adjunct (2 women). *Students:* 43 full-time (27 women), 23 part-time (19 women); includes 11 minority (3 Black or African American, non-Hispanic/Latino; 1 American Indian or Alaska Native, non-Hispanic/Latino; 2 Asian, non-Hispanic/Latino; 4 Hispanic/Latino; 1 Two or more races, non-Hispanic/Latino), 8 international. Average age 34. 52 applicants, 71% accepted, 25 enrolled. In 2014, 27 master's awarded. *Degree requirements:* For master's, thesis or alternative, practicum. *Entrance requirements:* For master's, 3 letters of recommendation. Additional exam requirements/recommendations for international students: Required—TOEFL (minimum score 550 paper-based; 80 iBT), IELTS (minimum score 6.5). *Application deadline:* For fall admission, 3/30 for domestic students, 3/1 for international students; for winter admission, 9/1 for domestic students, 8/1 for international students; for spring admission, 11/1 for domestic and international students. Application fee: $50. *Expenses:* Tuition, state resident: part-time $222 per credit. Tuition, nonresident: part-time $527 per credit. *Required fees:* $22 per contact hour. $100 per quarter. Tuition and fees vary according to program. *Financial support:* In 2014–15, 1 teaching assistantship with full tuition reimbursement (averaging $5,958 per year) was awarded; Federal Work-Study also available. *Total annual research expenditures:* $84,699. *Unit head:* Dr. Robert Gould, Director, 503-725-3502, E-mail: gouldr@pdx.edu. *Application contact:* Stephenie Jahnke, Program Administrator, 503-725-9175, E-mail: jahnkes@pdx.edu.
Website: http://www.conflictresolution.pdx.edu/

Royal Roads University, Graduate Studies, Peace and Conflict Studies Program, Victoria, BC V9B 5Y2, Canada. Offers conflict analysis (G Dip); conflict analysis and management (MA); disaster and emergency management (MA); human security and peacebuilding (MA). Postbaccalaureate distance learning degree programs offered (minimal on-campus study). *Degree requirements:* For master's, thesis. *Entrance requirements:* For master's, 5-7 years of related work experience. Additional exam requirements/recommendations for international students: Required—TOEFL (paper-based 570) or IELTS (7) recommended. Electronic applications accepted. *Faculty research:* Conflict analysis, ethno-political conflict reconciliation, international relations, displaced persons.

St. Mary's University, Graduate School, Graduate Department of International Relations, San Antonio, TX 78228-8507. Offers international conflict resolution (MA); security policy (MA); JD/MA. Part-time and evening/weekend programs available. Postbaccalaureate distance learning degree programs offered (no on-campus study). *Faculty:* 4 full-time (2 women), 1 part-time/adjunct (0 women). *Students:* 15 full-time (9 women), 64 part-time (21 women); includes 31 minority (5 Black or African American, non-Hispanic/Latino; 1 American Indian or Alaska Native, non-Hispanic/Latino; 6 Asian, non-Hispanic/Latino; 18 Hispanic/Latino; 1 Native Hawaiian or other Pacific Islander, non-Hispanic/Latino), 7 international. Average age 32. 54 applicants, 65% accepted, 25 enrolled. In 2014, 34 master's, 7 other advanced degrees awarded. *Degree requirements:* For master's, one foreign language, comprehensive exam, thesis optional, Demonstration of a working knowledge of a foreign language. *Entrance requirements:* For master's, GRE General Test, GPA x Verbal GRE Score = 450. Minimum writing score is 4.0. Additional exam requirements/recommendations for international students: Required—TOEFL (minimum score 550 paper-based; 80 iBT), IELTS (minimum score 6). *Application deadline:* Applications are processed on a rolling basis. Application fee: $0. Electronic applications accepted. *Expenses: Tuition:* Full-time

$15,070; part-time $800 per credit hour. *Required fees:* $156 per semester. *Financial support:* In 2014–15, 4 research assistantships (averaging $7,000 per year) were awarded; Federal Work-Study, scholarships/grants, tuition waivers (full), unspecified assistantships, and grant for active-duty and retired military, DOD employees, and their spouses also available. Financial award application deadline: 3/31; financial award applicants required to submit FAFSA. *Faculty research:* World religions and global affairs; human security and conflict transformation; military, security, peacekeeping; development studies, sustainability and the environment; migration and immigration policy. *Unit head:* Dr. Aaron Tyler, Chair Graduate International Relations, 210-436-3111, Fax: 210-431-4336, E-mail: atyler@stmarytx.edu.
Website: https://www.stmarytx.edu/academics/graduate/masters/internationalrelations/

Saint Paul University, Faculty of Human Sciences, Program in Conflict Studies, Ottawa, ON K1S 1C4, Canada. Offers MA. Part-time programs available. *Entrance requirements:* For master's, H=honors BA, B average.

Salisbury University, Program in Conflict Analysis and Dispute Resolution, Salisbury, MD 21801-6837. Offers MA. Part-time programs available. *Faculty:* 6 full-time (0 women). *Students:* 33 full-time (19 women), 6 part-time (5 women); includes 13 minority (11 Black or African American, non-Hispanic/Latino; 1 Asian, non-Hispanic/Latino; 1 Two or more races, non-Hispanic/Latino), 2 international. Average age 31. 25 applicants, 92% accepted, 19 enrolled. In 2014, 13 master's awarded. *Degree requirements:* For master's, thesis optional. *Entrance requirements:* For master's, minimum undergraduate GPA of 3.0; 3 letters of recommendation; personal statement; writing sample. Additional exam requirements/recommendations for international students: Required—TOEFL (minimum score 550 paper-based; 79 iBT), IELTS (minimum score 6.5). *Application deadline:* For fall admission, 4/14 priority date for domestic and international students. Applications are processed on a rolling basis. Application fee: $65. Electronic applications accepted. *Expenses:* Expenses: $358 per credit hour for residents; $647 for non-residents; $78 fees. *Financial support:* In 2014–15, 2 students received support, including 6 teaching assistantships with full tuition reimbursements available (averaging $7,500 per year); institutionally sponsored loans and unspecified assistantships also available. Support available to part-time students. Financial award application deadline: 3/1; financial award applicants required to submit FAFSA. *Faculty research:* International conflict, organizational conflict, indigenous conflict resolution, non-violence movement and tendencies, environmental change and conflicts stemming from ecologic issues and human interactions. *Unit head:* Dr. Ignaciyas Soosaipillai, Chair, Center for Conflict Resolution, 410-543-6435, E-mail: iksoosaipillai@salisbury.edu. *Application contact:* Dr. Jacques Koko, Graduate Program Director, 410-677-0135, E-mail: jlkoko@salisbury.edu.
Website: http://www.salisbury.edu/gsr/gradstudies/CADRpage

Salve Regina University, Program in Humanities, Newport, RI 02840-4192. Offers humanitarian assistance (MA); humanities (PhD); public humanities (MA); religion, peace and justice (MA). Part-time and evening/weekend programs available. Postbaccalaureate distance learning degree programs offered (no on-campus study). *Faculty:* 1 full-time (0 women), 6 part-time/adjunct (2 women). *Students:* 3 full-time (0 women), 88 part-time (52 women); includes 9 minority (3 Black or African American, non-Hispanic/Latino; 2 Asian, non-Hispanic/Latino; 1 Hispanic/Latino; 1 Native Hawaiian or other Pacific Islander, non-Hispanic/Latino; 2 Two or more races, non-Hispanic/Latino), 2 international. Average age 48. 13 applicants, 85% accepted, 11 enrolled. In 2014, 3 master's, 3 doctorates awarded. *Degree requirements:* For master's, thesis optional; for doctorate, one foreign language, comprehensive exam, thesis/dissertation. *Entrance requirements:* For master's, GMAT, GRE General Test, or MAT; for doctorate, GRE General Test. Additional exam requirements/recommendations for international students: Required—TOEFL (minimum score 600 paper-based; 100 iBT) or IELTS. *Application deadline:* For fall admission, 3/15 priority date for domestic and international students; for spring admission, 9/15 priority date for domestic and international students. Applications are processed on a rolling basis. Application fee: $60. Electronic applications accepted. *Expenses: Tuition:* Full-time $8550; part-time $475 per credit. *Required fees:* $50 per term. Tuition and fees vary according to course level, course load and degree level. *Financial support:* Career-related internships or fieldwork and Federal Work-Study available. Support available to part-time students. Financial award application deadline: 3/1; financial award applicants required to submit FAFSA. *Unit head:* Dr. Michael Budd, Director, 401-341-3284, E-mail: michael.budd@salve.edu. *Application contact:* Kelly Alverson, Director of Graduate Admissions, 401-341-2153, Fax: 401-341-2973, E-mail: kelly.alverson@salve.edu.
Website: http://www.salve.edu/graduate-studies/humanities

Southern Methodist University, Annette Caldwell Simmons School of Education and Human Development, Department of Dispute Resolution and Counseling, Dallas, TX 75275. Offers counseling (MS); dispute resolution (MA). Part-time programs available. *Degree requirements:* For master's, practica experience, 2 internships (counseling). *Entrance requirements:* For master's, minimum undergraduate GPA of 2.75 (for dispute resolution), 3.0 (for counseling); 3 letters of recommendation. Additional exam requirements/recommendations for international students: Required—TOEFL. Electronic applications accepted.

Southern New Hampshire University, School of Business, Manchester, NH 03106-1045. Offers accounting (MBA, MS, Graduate Certificate); accounting finance (MS); accounting/auditing (MS); accounting/forensic accounting (MS); accounting/taxation (MS); athletic administration (MBA, Graduate Certificate); business administration (IMBA, MBA, Certificate, Graduate Certificate), including accounting (Certificate), business administration (MBA), business information systems (Graduate Certificate), human resource management (Certificate); corporate social responsibility (MBA); entrepreneurship (MBA); finance (MBA, MS, Graduate Certificate); finance/corporate finance (MS); finance/investments and securities (MS); forensic accounting (MBA); healthcare informatics (MBA); healthcare management (MBA); human resource management (Graduate Certificate); information technology (MS, Graduate Certificate); information technology management (MBA); international business (Graduate Certificate); international business and information technology (Graduate Certificate); international finance (Graduate Certificate); international sport management (Graduate Certificate); justice studies (MBA); leadership of nonprofit organizations (Graduate Certificate); marketing (MBA, MS, Graduate Certificate); operations and project management (MS); operations and supply chain management (MBA, Graduate Certificate); organizational leadership (MS); project management (MBA, Graduate Certificate); Six Sigma (MBA); Six Sigma quality (Graduate Certificate); social media marketing (MBA); sport management (MBA, MS, Graduate Certificate); sustainability and environmental compliance (MBA); workplace conflict management (MBA); MBA/Certificate. *Accreditation:* ACBSP. Part-time and evening/weekend programs available. Postbaccalaureate distance learning degree programs offered (no on-campus study). Terminal master's awarded for partial completion of doctoral program. *Degree requirements:* For master's, one foreign language, comprehensive exam (for some programs), thesis or alternative. *Entrance requirements:* For master's, minimum GPA of 2.5. Additional exam requirements/recommendations for international students: Required—TOEFL (minimum score 500 paper-based). Electronic applications accepted.

Syracuse University, Maxwell School of Citizenship and Public Affairs, Program in Conflict Resolution, Syracuse, NY 13244. Offers CAS. Part-time programs available. *Students:* 5 part-time (all women). Average age 49. 14 applicants, 100% accepted, 2 enrolled. In 2014, 39 CASs awarded. *Entrance requirements:* Additional exam requirements/recommendations for international students: Required—TOEFL (minimum score 100 iBT). *Application deadline:* For fall admission, 2/1 priority date for domestic and international students. Applications are processed on a rolling basis. Application fee: $75. Electronic applications accepted. *Expenses: Tuition:* Part-time $1341 per credit. *Unit head:* Prof. Catherine Gerard, Director, 315-443-2367, E-mail: parc@syr.edu. *Application contact:* Debbie Toole, Fax: 315-443-3423, E-mail: datoole@syr.edu.
Website: http://www.maxwell.syr.edu/

Trident University International, College of Business Administration, Program in Business Administration, Cypress, CA 90630. Offers business administration (PhD); conflict and negotiation management (MBA); criminal justice administration (MBA); entrepreneurship (MBA); finance (MBA); general management (MBA); government accounting (MBA); human resource management (MBA); information security and digital assurance management (MBA); information technology management (MBA); international business (MBA); logistics management (MBA); marketing (MBA); project management (MBA); public management (MBA); quality management (MBA); strategic leadership (MBA). Part-time and evening/weekend programs available. Postbaccalaureate distance learning degree programs offered (no on-campus study). *Degree requirements:* For doctorate, comprehensive exam, thesis/dissertation, defense of dissertation. *Entrance requirements:* For master's, minimum GPA of 2.5 (students with GPA 3.0 or greater may transfer up to 30% of graduate level credits); for doctorate, minimum GPA of 3.4, curriculum vitae, course work in research methods or statistics. Additional exam requirements/recommendations for international students: Required—TOEFL. Electronic applications accepted.

Tufts University, The Fletcher School of Law and Diplomacy, Medford, MA 02155. Offers LL M, MA, MALD, MIB, PhD, DVM/MA, JD/MALD, MALD/MA, MALD/MBA, MALD/MS, MD/MA. Postbaccalaureate distance learning degree programs offered (minimal on-campus study). *Degree requirements:* For master's, one foreign language, thesis; for doctorate, one foreign language, comprehensive exam, thesis/dissertation, dissertation defense. *Entrance requirements:* For master's and doctorate, GMAT or GRE General Test. Additional exam requirements/recommendations for international students: Required—TOEFL (minimum score 600 paper-based; 100 iBT), IELTS (minimum score 7). Electronic applications accepted. *Expenses:* Contact institution. *Faculty research:* Negotiation and conflict resolution, international organizations, international business and economic law, security studies, development economics.

United States International University, School of Arts and Sciences, Nairobi, Kenya. Offers counseling psychology (MA), including chemical dependency, health psychology; international relations (MA), including development studies, diplomacy and foreign policy, peace and conflict studies. Part-time and evening/weekend programs available. *Degree requirements:* For master's, thesis, practicum. *Entrance requirements:* For master's, GRE General Test, 2 letters of recommendation, resume. Additional exam requirements/recommendations for international students: Required—TOEFL. *Faculty research:* Trauma in children, African intellectualism, psychological assessment tools.

United Theological Seminary of the Twin Cities, Graduate Programs, New Brighton, MN 55112-2598. Offers advanced theological studies (Diploma); justice and peace studies (M Div, MA); leadership toward racial justice (M Div, MA, Certificate); Methodist studies (M Div, MA, Certificate); ministry (D Min); ministry renewal and professional development (Certificate); pastoral care and counseling (M Div, MA, MARL); religion and theology (MA); theological and religious studies (Certificate); theology and the arts (M Div, MA); urban ministry (M Div, MA, MARL); women's studies: religion, theology and ministry (M Div, MA). *Accreditation:* ACIPE; ATS. Part-time and evening/weekend programs available. *Degree requirements:* For master's, thesis; for doctorate, comprehensive exam, thesis/dissertation. *Entrance requirements:* For master's, minimum GPA of 2.75; strong analytical, reflective thinking and writing skills; vocational and academic goals compatible with those of Seminary; for doctorate, M Div or equivalent, minimum GPA of 3.0, 3 years experience in professional ministry; for other advanced degree, BA or equivalent life experience; strong analytical, reflective thinking and writing skills (Certificate); proficiency in English language, previous study of theology at a theological school, recommendation of student's denomination (Diploma). Additional exam requirements/recommendations for international students: Required—TOEFL (minimum score 550 paper-based).

Universidad del Turabo, Graduate Programs, School of Social Sciences and Humanities, Programs in Public Affairs, Gurabo, PR 00778-3030. Offers arts administration (MPA); conflict and mediation studies (MPA); criminal justice studies (MPA); forensic science (MPA); human services administration (MPA). *Entrance requirements:* For master's, GRE, EXADEP, interview.

Université de Sherbrooke, Faculty of Law, Sherbrooke, QC J1K 2R1, Canada. Offers alternative dispute resolution (LL M, Diploma); business law (Diploma); common law (JD); criminal and penal law (Diploma); health law (LL M, Diploma); international law (LL M); law (LL D); legal management (Diploma); notarial law (Diploma); transnational law (Diploma). Part-time and evening/weekend programs available. *Degree requirements:* For master's, thesis; for Diploma, one foreign language. *Entrance requirements:* For master's and Diploma, LL B. Electronic applications accepted.

University of Arkansas at Little Rock, Graduate School, College of Social Sciences and Communication, Program in Conflict Mediation, Little Rock, AR 72204-1099. Offers Graduate Certificate. *Application deadline:* For fall admission, 6/1 for domestic students; for spring admission, 10/15 for domestic students; for summer admission, 3/15 for domestic students. Application fee: $40. *Expenses:* Tuition, state resident: full-time $6000; part-time $300 per credit hour. Tuition, nonresident: full-time $13,800; part-time $690 per credit hour. *Required fees:* $1126; $603 per term. One-time fee: $40 full-time. *Unit head:* Dr. Jerry G. Stevenson, Coordinator, 501-569-3211, E-mail: jgstevenson@ualr.edu.
Website: http://ualr.edu/iog/publiccollaboration/cpc-programsservices/graduate-certificate/

University of Baltimore, Graduate School, College of Public Affairs, Program in Negotiations and Conflict Management, Baltimore, MD 21201-5779. Offers MS. Part-time and evening/weekend programs available. *Degree requirements:* For master's, thesis optional, internship. *Entrance requirements:* For master's, minimum GPA of 3.0. Additional exam requirements/recommendations for international students: Required—TOEFL (minimum score 550 paper-based). Electronic applications accepted. *Faculty research:* Communication and conflict, conflict management systems theory.

University of Bridgeport, College of Public and International Affairs, Bridgeport, CT 06604. Offers East Asian and Pacific Rim studies (MA); global development and peace (MA); global media and communication studies (MA). Part-time and evening/weekend programs available. *Degree requirements:* For master's, thesis. *Entrance requirements:* Additional exam requirements/recommendations for international students: Recommended—TOEFL (minimum score 550 paper-based; 80 iBT), IELTS (minimum score 6.5).

University of Denver, Josef Korbel School of International Studies, Program in Conflict Resolution, Denver, CO 80208. Offers MA. Part-time programs available. *Faculty:* 1

(woman) full-time, 2 part-time/adjunct (1 woman). *Students:* 12 full-time (9 women), 2 part-time (1 woman); includes 3 minority (2 Hispanic/Latino; 1 Two or more races, non-Hispanic/Latino), 1 international. Average age 25. 29 applicants, 100% accepted, 9 enrolled. In 2014, 10 master's awarded. *Degree requirements:* For master's, thesis optional, internship. *Entrance requirements:* For master's, GRE General Test or GMAT, bachelor's degree, transcripts, statement of purpose, writing sample, two letters of recommendation. Additional exam requirements/recommendations for international students: Required—TOEFL (minimum score 587 paper-based; 95 iBT). *Application deadline:* For fall admission, 2/1 priority date for domestic and international students; for winter admission, 11/1 priority date for domestic and international students; for spring admission, 1/15 priority date for domestic and international students. Applications are processed on a rolling basis. Application fee: $65. Electronic applications accepted. *Expenses:* Expenses: $1,199 per credit hour. *Financial support:* In 2014–15, 5 students received support, including 1 teaching assistantship; career-related internships or fieldwork, Federal Work-Study, scholarships/grants, tuition waivers (partial), and unspecified assistantships also available. Support available to part-time students. Financial award application deadline: 2/15; financial award applicants required to submit FAFSA. *Unit head:* Dr. Karen Feste, Director, 303-871-2418, Fax: 303-871-2456, E-mail: kfeste@du.edu. *Application contact:* Information Contact, 303-871-6477, E-mail: cri@du.edu.
Website: http://www.du.edu/con-res/

University of Denver, University College, Denver, CO 80208. Offers geographic information systems (Certificate); global affairs (Certificate), including translation studies, world history and culture; information and communications technology (MCIS), including geographic information systems, information systems security, project management (MCIS, Certificate), software design and programming, technology management, telecommunications technology, Web design and development; leadership and organizations (Certificate), including human capital in organizations, philanthropic leadership, project management (MCIS, Certificate), strategic innovation and change; organizational and professional communication (MPS), including alternative dispute resolution, organizational communication, organizational development and training, public relations and marketing; security management (MAS, Certificate), including emergency planning and response, information security (MAS), organizational security. Part-time and evening/weekend programs available. Postbaccalaureate distance learning degree programs offered (no on-campus study). *Faculty:* 8 full-time (4 women), 133 part-time/adjunct (46 women). *Students:* 54 full-time (21 women), 1,327 part-time (775 women); includes 272 minority (106 Black or African American, non-Hispanic/Latino; 6 American Indian or Alaska Native, non-Hispanic/Latino; 26 Asian, non-Hispanic/Latino; 108 Hispanic/Latino; 1 Native Hawaiian or other Pacific Islander, non-Hispanic/Latino; 25 Two or more races, non-Hispanic/Latino), 116 international. Average age 35. 768 applicants, 95% accepted, 620 enrolled. In 2014, 391 master's, 196 other advanced degrees awarded. *Degree requirements:* For master's, capstone project. *Entrance requirements:* For master's, transcripts, two letters of recommendation, personal statement, resume. Additional exam requirements/recommendations for international students: Required—TOEFL (minimum score 550 paper-based; 80 iBT). *Application deadline:* For fall admission, 6/21 priority date for domestic students, 5/1 priority date for international students; for winter admission, 9/14 priority date for domestic students, 9/19 priority date for international students; for spring admission, 1/11 for domestic students, 12/12 for international students; for summer admission, 3/29 priority date for domestic students, 3/6 priority date for international students. Applications are processed on a rolling basis. Application fee: $75. Electronic applications accepted. *Expenses:* Expenses: $959 per credit hour. *Financial support:* In 2014–15, 19 students received support. Applicants required to submit FAFSA. *Unit head:* Dr. Michael McGuire, Interim Dean, 303-871-3518, E-mail: mmcguire@du.edu. *Application contact:* Information Contact, 303-871-2291, E-mail: ucoladm@du.edu.
Website: http://www.universitycollege.du.edu/

University of Hawaii at Manoa, Graduate Division, College of Social Sciences, Spark M. Matsunaga Institute for Peace, Honolulu, HI 96822. Offers conflict resolution (Graduate Certificate). Part-time programs available. *Entrance requirements:* For degree, GRE General Test. Additional exam requirements/recommendations for international students: Required—TOEFL (minimum score 540 paper-based; 76 iBT), IELTS (minimum score 5).

University of Idaho, College of Law, Moscow, ID 83844-2321. Offers business law and entrepreneurship (JD); law (JD); litigation and alternative dispute resolution (JD); Native American law (JD); natural resources and environmental law (JD). *Accreditation:* ABA. *Faculty:* 30 full-time, 7 part-time/adjunct. *Students:* 345 full-time, 7 part-time. Average age 29. *Entrance requirements:* For doctorate, LSAT, Law School Admission Council Credential Assembly Service (CAS) Report. Additional exam requirements/recommendations for international students: Required—TOEFL. *Application deadline:* For fall admission, 2/15 for domestic students. Applications are processed on a rolling basis. Application fee: $50 ($60 for international students). Electronic applications accepted. *Expenses:* Tuition, state resident: full-time $4784; part-time $280.50 per credit hour. Tuition, nonresident: full-time $18,314; part-time $957.50 per credit hour. *Required fees:* $2000; $58.50 per credit hour. Tuition and fees vary according to program. *Financial support:* Career-related internships or fieldwork, Federal Work-Study, and institutionally sponsored loans available. Financial award applicants required to submit FAFSA. *Faculty research:* Transboundary river governance, tribal protection and stewardship, regional water issues, environmental law. *Unit head:* Mark Adams, Dean, 208-885-4977, E-mail: uilaw@uidaho.edu. *Application contact:* Carole Wells, Interim Director of Admissions, 208-885-2300, Fax: 208-885-2252, E-mail: lawadmit@uidaho.edu.
Website: http://www.uidaho.edu/law/

The University of Manchester, School of Arts, Histories and Cultures, Manchester, United Kingdom. Offers anthropology, media and performance (PhD); applied theatre professional (PhD); archaeology (PhD); art history and visual studies (PhD); arts management and cultural policy (PhD); classics and ancient history (PhD); composition (PhD); creative writing (PhD); drama (PhD); economic and social history (PhD); electroacoustic composition (PhD); English and American studies (PhD); history (PhD); humanitarianism and conflict response (PhD); museology (PhD); music (PhD); musicology (PhD); religions and theology (PhD).

University of Massachusetts Amherst, Graduate School, College of Natural Sciences, Department of Psychological and Brain Sciences, Amherst, MA 01003. Offers clinical psychology (MS, PhD); cognitive psychology (MS, PhD); developmental science (MS, PhD); psychology of peace and violence (MS, PhD); social psychology (MS, PhD). *Accreditation:* APA (one or more programs are accredited). *Faculty:* 62 full-time (31 women). *Students:* 47 full-time (32 women), 14 part-time (11 women); includes 12 minority (2 Black or African American, non-Hispanic/Latino; 6 Asian, non-Hispanic/Latino; 3 Hispanic/Latino; 1 Two or more races, non-Hispanic/Latino), 9 international. Average age 27. 317 applicants, 7% accepted, 11 enrolled. In 2014, 12 master's, 10 doctorates awarded. Terminal master's awarded for partial completion of doctoral program. *Degree requirements:* For master's, thesis; for doctorate, comprehensive exam, thesis/dissertation. *Entrance requirements:* For master's and doctorate, GRE General Test, 3 letters of recommendation. Additional exam requirements/recommendations for international students: Required—TOEFL (minimum score 550 paper-based; 80 iBT), IELTS (minimum score 6.5). *Application deadline:* For fall admission, 12/1 for domestic and international students. Applications are processed on a rolling basis. Application fee: $75. Electronic applications accepted. *Expenses:* Tuition, state resident: full-time $1980; part-time $110 per credit. Tuition, nonresident: full-time $14,644; part-time $414 per credit. *Required fees:* $11,417. One-time fee: $357. *Financial support:* Fellowships with full and partial tuition reimbursements, research assistantships with full and partial tuition reimbursements, teaching assistantships with full and partial tuition reimbursements, career-related internships or fieldwork, Federal Work-Study, scholarships/grants, traineeships, health care benefits, tuition waivers (full and partial), and unspecified assistantships available. Support available to part-time students. Financial award application deadline: 12/1. *Unit head:* Dr. Michael Constantino, Graduate Program Director, 413-545-2503, Fax: 413-545-0996. *Application contact:* Lindsay DeSantis, Supervisor of Admissions, 413-545-0722, Fax: 413-577-0010, E-mail: gradadm@grad.umass.edu.
Website: http://www.psych.umass.edu/

University of Massachusetts Boston, John W. McCormack Graduate School of Policy and Global Studies, Program in Conflict Resolution, Boston, MA 02125-3393. Offers MA, Certificate. MA program accepts applications for fall admission only; Certificate program accepts applications for spring admission only. *Degree requirements:* For master's, practicum, final project. *Entrance requirements:* For master's, MAT or GRE, minimum GPA of 2.75; for Certificate, minimum GPA of 2.75. *Application deadline:* For fall admission, 3/1 for domestic students; for spring admission, 11/1 for domestic students. *Expenses:* Tuition, state resident: full-time $2590; part-time $108 per credit. Tuition, nonresident: full-time $9758; part-time $406.50 per credit. Tuition and fees vary according to course load and program. *Financial support:* Research assistantships with full tuition reimbursements, teaching assistantships with full tuition reimbursements, career-related internships or fieldwork, Federal Work-Study, and unspecified assistantships available. Support available to part-time students. Financial award application deadline: 3/1. *Faculty research:* Mediation and negotiation, justice and conflict, cross-cultural mediation, environmental fairness, dispute resolution theory and ethics. *Unit head:* Dr. David Matz, Director, 617-287-7376. *Application contact:* Peggy Roldan Patel, Graduate Admissions Coordinator, 617-287-6400, Fax: 617-287-6236, E-mail: bos.gadm@dpc.umassp.edu.

University of Massachusetts Boston, John W. McCormack Graduate School of Policy and Global Studies, Program in Global Governance and Human Security, Boston, MA 02125-3393. Offers MA. *Expenses:* Tuition, state resident: full-time $2590; part-time $108 per credit. Tuition, nonresident: full-time $9758; part-time $406.50 per credit. Tuition and fees vary according to course load and program. *Unit head:* Dr. Stephen Crosby, Dean, 617-287-5550, E-mail: stephen.crosby@umb.edu. *Application contact:* Peggy Roldan Patel, Graduate Admissions Coordinator, 617-287-6400, Fax: 617-287-6236, E-mail: bos.gadm@dpc.umassp.edu.

University of Massachusetts Lowell, College of Fine Arts, Humanities and Social Sciences, Program in Peace and Conflict Studies, Lowell, MA 01854. Offers MA, Graduate Certificate. *Degree requirements:* For master's, practicum, project, or thesis. *Entrance requirements:* For master's, GRE, GMAT, or LSAT, bachelor's degree from accredited institution college or university, minimum undergraduate GPA of 3.0, 18 credits of peace and conflict studies related coursework, three letters of reference, personal statement, resume or curriculum vitae. Additional exam requirements/recommendations for international students: Required—TOEFL.

University of Missouri, Office of Research and Graduate Studies and School of Law, Program in Dispute Resolution, Columbia, MO 65211. Offers LL M, Certificate. *Students:* 8 full-time (6 women), 5 part-time (0 women), 8 international. Average age 38. 35 applicants, 54% accepted, 11 enrolled. In 2014, 14 master's, 41 Certificates awarded. *Entrance requirements:* Additional exam requirements/recommendations for international students: Required—TOEFL (minimum score 600 paper-based; 100 iBT). *Application deadline:* For fall admission, 1/1 for domestic students. Applications are processed on a rolling basis. Application fee: $55 ($75 for international students). Electronic applications accepted. *Financial support:* Fellowships, research assistantships, teaching assistantships, institutionally sponsored loans, scholarships/grants, health care benefits, and unspecified assistantships available. Support available to part-time students. *Faculty research:* Children and the law, family law, Constitutional law, youth sports, arbitration, environmental law, bankruptcy, taxation, American legal history, ethics and professionalism, civil procedure. *Unit head:* Dr. Paul Ladehoff, Director, 573-884-7813, E-mail: ladehoffp@missouri.edu. *Application contact:* Karen Neylon, Coordinator, 573-882-2020, E-mail: neylonk@missouri.edu.
Website: http://law.missouri.edu/csdr/llm/

University of Missouri, School of Law, Columbia, MO 65211. Offers dispute resolution (LL M); law (JD); JD/MA; JD/MBA; JD/MPA. *Accreditation:* ABA. *Students:* 348 full-time (132 women), 20 part-time (12 women); includes 54 minority (31 Black or African American, non-Hispanic/Latino; 1 American Indian or Alaska Native, non-Hispanic/Latino; 3 Asian, non-Hispanic/Latino; 5 Hispanic/Latino; 14 Two or more races, non-Hispanic/Latino), 2 international. Average age 26. *Entrance requirements:* For doctorate, LSAT. Additional exam requirements/recommendations for international students: Required—TOEFL. *Application deadline:* For fall admission, 3/1 priority date for domestic students. Applications are processed on a rolling basis. *Expenses:* Expenses: Contact institution. *Financial support:* Fellowships, Federal Work-Study, and institutionally sponsored loans available. Financial award application deadline: 3/1; financial award applicants required to submit FAFSA. *Unit head:* Gary Myers, Dean, 573-882-3246, E-mail: myers@missouri.edu. *Application contact:* Lisa E. Key, Assistant Dean for Career Development and Student Services, 573-884-2949, E-mail: keye@missouri.edu.
Website: http://www.law.missouri.edu/

University of New Brunswick Fredericton, School of Graduate Studies, Policy Studies Program, Fredericton, NB E3B 5A3, Canada. Offers citizen engagement/dispute resolution (M Phil); community development (M Phil); international development (M Phil); leadership (M Phil); sustainability/environmental issues (M Phil); worldviews (M Phil). Part-time programs available. *Faculty:* 17 full-time (9 women), 1 part-time/adjunct (0 women). *Students:* 14 full-time (7 women), 4 part-time (3 women). In 2014, 3 master's awarded. *Degree requirements:* For master's, thesis, report. *Entrance requirements:* For master's, minimum GPA of 3.5. Additional exam requirements/recommendations for international students: Required—TWE (minimum score 5.5), TOEFL (minimum score 600 paper-based; 100 iBT) or IELTS (minimum score 7). *Application deadline:* Applications are processed on a rolling basis. Application fee: $50 Canadian dollars. Electronic applications accepted. *Financial support:* In 2014–15, 3 fellowships, research assistantships (averaging $5,600 per year), teaching assistantships (averaging $4,400 per year) were awarded. *Faculty research:* International development, worldviews, citizenship/dispute resolution, sustainability/environmental issues, leadership, community development. *Unit head:* Dr. Linda Eyre, Dean of Graduate Studies, 506-447-3044, Fax: 506-453-4817, E-mail: gradidst@unb.ca. *Application contact:* Janet Amirault, Graduate Secretary, 506-458-7558, Fax: 506-453-4817, E-mail: jamiraul@unb.ca.
Website: http://www.unb.ca/gradstudies/programs/mphil/index.html

University of New Haven, Graduate School, College of Arts and Sciences, Program in Industrial and Organizational Psychology, West Haven, CT 06516-1916. Offers conflict management (MA); human resource management (MA); industrial organizational psychology (MA); organizational development (MA); psychology of conflict management (Certificate). Part-time and evening/weekend programs available. *Degree requirements:* For master's, thesis or alternative, internship or practicum. *Entrance requirements:* Additional exam requirements/recommendations for international students: Required—TOEFL (minimum score 80 iBT), IELTS, PTE (minimum score 53). Electronic applications accepted. Application fee is waived when completed online. *Expenses:* Contact institution.

The University of North Carolina at Greensboro, Graduate School, School of Health and Human Sciences, Department of Peace and Conflict Studies, Greensboro, NC 27412-5001. Offers MA, Certificate. Electronic applications accepted.

The University of North Carolina Wilmington, College of Arts and Sciences, Department of Public and International Affairs, Wilmington, NC 28403-3297. Offers coastal and ocean policy (MS); conflict management (Graduate Certificate); conflict management and resolution (MA); public administration (MPA). *Accreditation:* NASPAA. Part-time programs available. *Faculty:* 14 full-time (4 women). *Students:* 54 full-time (32 women), 67 part-time (44 women); includes 17 minority (11 Black or African American, non-Hispanic/Latino; 1 American Indian or Alaska Native, non-Hispanic/Latino; 1 Asian, non-Hispanic/Latino; 4 Hispanic/Latino), 1 international. 55 applicants, 100% accepted, 39 enrolled. In 2014, 26 master's awarded. *Degree requirements:* For master's, comprehensive exam, thesis or alternative, practicum. *Entrance requirements:* For master's, GRE, GMAT. Additional exam requirements/recommendations for international students: Required—TOEFL (minimum score 79 iBT), IELTS. *Application deadline:* For fall admission, 4/15 for domestic students; for spring admission, 11/5 for domestic students. Application fee: $60. *Expenses:* Tuition, state resident: full-time $3240. Tuition, nonresident: full-time $9208. *Required fees:* $1967. *Financial support:* Application deadline: 3/15; applicants required to submit FAFSA. *Unit head:* Dr. Earl Sheridan, Chair, 910-962-3222, Fax: 910-962-3286, E-mail: sheridan@uncw.edu. *Application contact:* Dr. Mark Imperial, MPA Program Director and Internship Coordinator/Program Director, Master of Coastal and Ocean Policy, 910-962-7928, Fax: 910-962-3286, E-mail: imperialm@uncw.edu.
Website: http://www.uncw.edu/pia/graduate/index.html

University of Notre Dame, Graduate School, College of Arts and Letters, Division of Social Science, Joan B. Kroc Institute for International Peace Studies, Notre Dame, IN 46556. Offers MA, PhD. *Degree requirements:* For master's, one foreign language, comprehensive exam, thesis optional; for doctorate, one foreign language, comprehensive exam, thesis/dissertation. *Entrance requirements:* For master's, GRE General Test. Additional exam requirements/recommendations for international students: Required—TOEFL (minimum score 600 paper-based; 80 iBT). Electronic applications accepted. *Faculty research:* The role of international norms and institutions in peacemaking; the impact of religious, philosophical, and cultural influences on peace; the dynamics of intergroup conflict and conflict transformation; the promotion of social, economic, and environmental justice.

University of Phoenix–Online Campus, College of Social Science, Phoenix, AZ 85034-7209. Offers mediation (Certificate); psychology (MS), including behavioral health, industrial-organizational, psychology. Evening/weekend programs available. Postbaccalaureate distance learning degree programs offered. *Entrance requirements:* Additional exam requirements/recommendations for international students: Required—TOEFL, TOEIC (Test of English as an International Communication), Berlitz Online English Proficiency Exam, PTE, or IELTS. Electronic applications accepted. *Expenses:* Contact institution.

University of San Diego, Joan B. Kroc School of Peace Studies, San Diego, CA 92110-2492. Offers peace and justice studies (MA). *Faculty:* 4 full-time (2 women), 1 part-time/adjunct (0 women). *Students:* 29 full-time (21 women), 4 part-time (3 women); includes 6 minority (1 Black or African American, non-Hispanic/Latino; 2 Asian, non-Hispanic/Latino; 2 Hispanic/Latino; 1 Two or more races, non-Hispanic/Latino), 7 international. Average age 28. 87 applicants, 71% accepted, 18 enrolled. In 2014, 25 master's awarded. *Degree requirements:* For master's, capstone project. *Entrance requirements:* For master's, GRE General Test, minimum GPA of 3.0. Additional exam requirements/recommendations for international students: Required—TOEFL (minimum score 580 paper-based; 83 iBT), TWE. *Application deadline:* For fall admission, 1/15 for domestic and international students. Application fee: $45. Electronic applications accepted. *Financial support:* In 2014–15, 29 students received support. Career-related internships or fieldwork, Federal Work-Study, institutionally sponsored loans, scholarships/grants, and unspecified assistantships available. Support available to part-time students. Financial award application deadline: 4/1; financial award applicants required to submit FAFSA. *Faculty research:* Conflict analysis and resolution, human security and peacebuilding, development and peacebuilding, human rights and transitional justice, religion and peacebuilding. *Unit head:* Dr. Patricia Marquez, Dean, 619-260-7919. *Application contact:* Monica Mahon, Associate Director of Graduate Admissions, 619-260-4524, Fax: 619-260-4158, E-mail: grads@sandiego.edu.
Website: http://www.sandiego.edu/peacestudies/

University of the Sacred Heart, Graduate Programs, Program in Systems of Justice, San Juan, PR 00914-0383. Offers human rights and anti-discriminatory processes (MASJ); mediation and transformation of conflicts (MASJ).

University of Victoria, Faculty of Graduate Studies, Faculty of Human and Social Development, School of Public Administration, Victoria, BC V8W 2Y2, Canada. Offers dispute resolution (MADR); public administration (MPA, PhD); MPA/LL B. Part-time and evening/weekend programs available. Postbaccalaureate distance learning degree programs offered. *Degree requirements:* For master's, thesis (for some programs), report; for doctorate, thesis/dissertation, candidacy exam. *Entrance requirements:* For master's, GMAT or GRE General Test, professional resume; for doctorate, GMAT or GRE General Test. Additional exam requirements/recommendations for international students: Required—TOEFL (minimum score 610 paper-based). Electronic applications accepted. *Faculty research:* Policy analysis, local government, performance management, energy markets, labor markets.

University of Wisconsin–Milwaukee, Graduate School, College of Letters and Sciences, Department of Communication, Milwaukee, WI 53201-0413. Offers communication (MA, PhD); mediation and negotiation (Certificate); rhetorical leadership (Certificate). Part-time programs available. *Degree requirements:* For master's, thesis or alternative; for doctorate, comprehensive exam. *Entrance requirements:* For master's, GRE General Test, minimum GPA of 3.0. Additional exam requirements/recommendations for international students: Required—TOEFL (minimum score 550 paper-based; 79 iBT), IELTS (minimum score 6). Electronic applications accepted.

University of Wisconsin–Milwaukee, Graduate School, College of Letters and Sciences, Interdepartmental Program in Human Resources and Labor Relations, Milwaukee, WI 53201-0413. Offers human resources and labor relations (MHRLR); international human resources and labor relations (Certificate); mediation and negotiation (Certificate). Part-time programs available. *Entrance requirements:* For master's, GMAT or GRE General Test. Additional exam requirements/recommendations for international students: Required—TOEFL (minimum score 550 paper-based; 79 iBT), IELTS (minimum score 6.5). Electronic applications accepted.

Walden University, Graduate Programs, School of Public Policy and Administration, Minneapolis, MN 55401. Offers criminal justice (MPA, MPP, MS, Graduate Certificate), including emergency management (MS, PhD), general program (MS, PhD), homeland security and policy coordination (MS, PhD), law and public policy (MS, PhD), policy analysis (MS, PhD), public management and leadership (MS, PhD), self-designed (MS), terrorism, mediation, and peace (MS, PhD); criminal justice leadership and executive management (MS), including emergency management (MS, PhD), general program (MS, PhD), homeland security and policy coordination (MS, PhD), law and public policy (MS, PhD), policy analysis (MS, PhD), public management and leadership (MS, PhD), self-designed, terrorism, mediation, and peace (MS, PhD); emergency management (MPA, MPP, MS), including criminal justice (MS, PhD), general program (MS, PhD), homeland security (MS), public management and leadership (MS, PhD), terrorism and emergency management (MS); general program (MPA, MPP); government management (Graduate Certificate); health policy (MPA, MPP); homeland security (Graduate Certificate); homeland security and policy coordination (MPA, MPP); international nongovernmental organizations (MPA, MPP); law and public policy (MPA, MPP); local government management for sustainable communities (MPA, MPP); nonprofit management (Graduate Certificate); nonprofit management and leadership (MPA, MPP, MS); online teaching in higher education (Post-Master's Certificate); policy analysis (MPA); public management and leadership (MPA, MPP, Graduate Certificate); public policy (Graduate Certificate); public policy and administration (PhD), including criminal justice (MS, PhD), emergency management (MS, PhD), general program (MS, PhD), health policy, homeland security and policy coordination (MS, PhD), international nongovernmental organizations, law and public policy (MS, PhD), local government management for sustainable communities, nonprofit management and leadership, policy analysis (MS, PhD), public management and leadership (MS, PhD), terrorism, mediation, and peace (MS, PhD); strategic planning and public policy (Graduate Certificate); terrorism, mediation, and peace (MPA, MPP). Part-time and evening/weekend programs available. Postbaccalaureate distance learning degree programs offered (no on-campus study). *Faculty:* 13 full-time (5 women), 151 part-time/adjunct (65 women). *Students:* 1,009 full-time (573 women), 1,632 part-time (954 women); includes 1,553 minority (1,307 Black or African American, non-Hispanic/Latino; 15 American Indian or Alaska Native, non-Hispanic/Latino; 38 Asian, non-Hispanic/Latino; 127 Hispanic/Latino; 66 Two or more races, non-Hispanic/Latino), 15 international. Average age 42. 665 applicants, 97% accepted, 616 enrolled. In 2014, 317 master's, 95 doctorates, 34 other advanced degrees awarded. *Degree requirements:* For doctorate, thesis/dissertation, residency. *Entrance requirements:* For master's, bachelor's degree or higher; minimum GPA of 2.5; official transcripts; goal statement (for some programs); access to computer and Internet; for doctorate, master's degree or higher; three years of related professional or academic experience (preferred); minimum GPA of 3.0; goal statement and current resume (for select programs); official transcripts; access to computer and Internet; for other advanced degree, relevant work experience; access to computer and Internet. Additional exam requirements/recommendations for international students: Required—TOEFL (minimum score 550 paper-based, 79 iBT), IELTS (minimum score 6.5), Michigan English Language Assessment Battery (minimum score 82), or PTE (minimum score 53). *Application deadline:* Applications are processed on a rolling basis. Application fee: $0. Electronic applications accepted. *Expenses: Tuition:* Full-time $11,925; part-time $500 per credit hour. *Required fees:* $647. *Financial support:* Fellowships, Federal Work-Study, scholarships/grants, unspecified assistantships, and family tuition reduction, active duty/veteran tuition reduction, group tuition reduction, interest-free payment plans, employee tuition reduction available. Support available to part-time students. Financial award applicants required to submit FAFSA. *Unit head:* Dr. Shana Garrett, Associate Dean, 866-492-5336. *Application contact:* Meghan Thomas, Vice President of Enrollment Management, 866-492-5336, E-mail: info@waldenu.edu.
Website: http://www.waldenu.edu/programs/colleges-schools/public-policy-and-administration

Wayne State University, College of Fine, Performing and Communication Arts, Department of Communication, Program in Dispute Resolution, Detroit, MI 48202. Offers MADR, Graduate Certificate, JD/MADR. *Faculty:* 23 full-time (13 women). *Students:* 6 full-time (4 women), 19 part-time (14 women); includes 10 minority (all Black or African American, non-Hispanic/Latino), 2 international. Average age 41. 21 applicants, 33% accepted, 5 enrolled. In 2014, 7 master's, 2 other advanced degrees awarded. *Entrance requirements:* For master's, GMAT, GRE General Test, or LSAT, bachelor's degree with minimum undergraduate upper-division GPA of 3.0; personal statement, three letters of recommendation; for Graduate Certificate, graduate or advanced degree from accredited educational institution or active pursuit of such a degree at Wayne State University; minimum undergraduate upper-division GPA of 3.0; personal statement of 200 words outlining interest in program; three letters of recommendation. Additional exam requirements/recommendations for international students: Required—TOEFL (minimum score 550 paper-based; 79 iBT), Michigan English Language Assessment Battery (minimum score 85); Recommended—IELTS (minimum score 6.5), TWE (minimum score 5.5). *Application deadline:* For fall admission, 8/1 for domestic students, 5/1 priority date for international students; for winter admission, 11/1 for domestic students, 9/1 priority date for international students; for spring admission, 4/1 for domestic students, 1/1 for international students. Application fee: $0. Electronic applications accepted. *Expenses:* Expenses: Contact institution. *Financial support:* In 2014–15, 5 students received support. Fellowships, teaching assistantships, scholarships/grants, and unspecified assistantships available. Financial award application deadline: 3/31; financial award applicants required to submit FAFSA. *Faculty research:* Interpersonal communication, rhetoric, crisis communication, mass communication. *Unit head:* Dr. Lee C. Wilkins, Professor and Chair, 313-577-2959, E-mail: lee.wilkins@wayne.edu. *Application contact:* Dr. Bill Warters, Academic Director, 313-993-7482, E-mail: w.warters@wayne.edu.
Website: http://comm.wayne.edu/madr.php

Wayne State University, College of Liberal Arts and Sciences, Center for Peace and Conflict Studies, Detroit, MI 48202. Offers peace and security studies (Graduate Certificate). *Faculty:* 3 full-time, 10 part-time/adjunct. *Students:* 4 part-time (3 women). 3 applicants. In 2014, 2 Graduate Certificates awarded. *Degree requirements:* For Graduate Certificate, internship or practicum. *Entrance requirements:* For degree, admission to masters's degree program at WSU or University of Windsor, or graduate of master's degree program in approved discipline at an accredited institution. Additional exam requirements/recommendations for international students: Required—TOEFL (minimum score 550 paper-based; 79 iBT), Michigan English Language Assessment Battery (minimum score 85); Recommended—IELTS (minimum score 6.5). *Application deadline:* For fall admission, 6/1 priority date for domestic students, 5/1 priority date for international students; for winter admission, 10/1 priority date for domestic students, 9/1 priority date for international students; for spring admission, 2/1 priority date for domestic students, 1/1 priority date for international students; for summer admission, 2/1 priority date for domestic students, 1/1 priority date for international students. Applications are processed on a rolling basis. Application fee: $0. Electronic applications accepted. *Expenses:* Tuition, state resident: full-time $10,294; part-time $571.90 per credit hour.

Conflict Resolution and Mediation/Peace Studies

Tuition, nonresident: full-time $29,730; part-time $1238.75 per credit hour. *Required fees:* $1365; $43.50 per credit hour. $291.10 per semester. Tuition and fees vary according to course load and program. *Financial support:* Scholarships/grants available. Financial award application deadline: 3/31; financial award applicants required to submit FAFSA. *Unit head:* Dr. Frederic Pearson, Professor and Program Director, 313-577-3453, E-mail: fredericpearson@wayne.edu.
Website: http://clas.wayne.edu/cpcs/

Wilfrid Laurier University, Faculty of Graduate and Postdoctoral Studies, School of International Policy and Governance, Global Governance Program, Waterloo, ON N2L 3C5, Canada. Offers conflict and security (PhD); global environment (PhD); global justice and human rights (PhD); global political economy (PhD); global social governance (PhD); multilateral institutions and diplomacy (PhD). Offered jointly with University of Waterloo. *Degree requirements:* For doctorate, thesis/dissertation. *Entrance requirements:* For doctorate, MA in political science, history, economics, international development studies, international peace studies, globalization studies, environmental studies or related field with minimum A-. Additional exam requirements/recommendations for international students: Required—TOEFL (minimum score 89 iBT). Electronic applications accepted. *Faculty research:* Global political economy, global environment, conflict and security, global justice and human rights, multilateral institutions and diplomacy.

Willamette University, College of Law, Salem, OR 97301-3922. Offers dispute resolution (LL M); law (MLS, JD); transnational law (LL M); JD/MBA. *Accreditation:* ABA. Part-time programs available. *Faculty:* 30 full-time (13 women), 7 part-time/adjunct (1 woman). *Students:* 335 full-time (147 women), 6 part-time (4 women); includes 55 minority (4 Black or African American, non-Hispanic/Latino; 6 American Indian or Alaska Native, non-Hispanic/Latino; 20 Asian, non-Hispanic/Latino; 21 Hispanic/Latino; 4 Native Hawaiian or other Pacific Islander, non-Hispanic/Latino), 20 international. Average age 27. 499 applicants, 72% accepted, 100 enrolled. In 2014, 6 master's, 121 doctorates awarded. *Degree requirements:* For master's, thesis, 25 credit hours (for LL M); 26 credit hours (for MLS); for doctorate, thesis/dissertation, 90 credit hours. *Entrance requirements:* For master's, bachelor's degree (for MLS); domestic or foreign JD (for LL M); for doctorate, LSAT. Additional exam requirements/recommendations for international students: Required—TOEFL (minimum score 480 paper-based; 45 iBT); Recommended—IELTS (minimum score 5). *Application deadline:* For fall admission, 3/1 priority date for domestic students, 3/1 for international students. Applications are processed on a rolling basis. Application fee: $50. Electronic applications accepted. Application fee is waived when completed online. *Expenses:* Expenses: $37,625 full-time (10-16 credits), $1,448 per credit part-time (5-9 credits). *Financial support:* In 2014–15, 239 students received support. Federal Work-Study, scholarships/grants, tuition waivers (partial), and unspecified assistantships available. Financial award application deadline: 3/1; financial award applicants required to submit FAFSA. *Faculty research:* Dispute resolution, international law, business law, law and government, sustainability. *Unit head:* Curtis Bridgeman, Dean, 503-370-6024, Fax: 503-370-6828, E-mail: cbridgma@willamette.edu. *Application contact:* Carolyn Dennis, Assistant Dean for Admission, 503-370-6282, Fax: 503-370-6087, E-mail: law-admission@willamette.edu.
Website: http://www.willamette.edu/wucl/

Yeshiva University, Benjamin N. Cardozo School of Law, New York, NY 10003-4301. Offers comparative legal thought (LL M); dispute resolution and advocacy (LL M); general studies (LL M); intellectual property law (LL M); law (JD). *Accreditation:* ABA. *Faculty:* 61 full-time (24 women), 92 part-time/adjunct (38 women). *Students:* 992 full-time (506 women), 85 part-time (48 women); includes 277 minority (65 Black or African American, non-Hispanic/Latino; 88 Asian, non-Hispanic/Latino; 112 Hispanic/Latino; 1 Native Hawaiian or other Pacific Islander, non-Hispanic/Latino; 11 Two or more races, non-Hispanic/Latino), 69 international. Average age 24. 2,913 applicants, 50% accepted, 339 enrolled. In 2014, 70 master's, 391 doctorates awarded. *Entrance requirements:* For doctorate, LSAT, 2 letters of recommendation. *Application deadline:* For fall admission, 4/1 priority date for domestic students; for spring admission, 12/1 for domestic students. Applications are processed on a rolling basis. Application fee: $75. Electronic applications accepted. *Expenses:* Expenses: Contact institution. *Financial support:* In 2014–15, 778 students received support, including 87 research assistantships (averaging $1,599 per year); career-related internships or fieldwork, Federal Work-Study, institutionally sponsored loans, scholarships/grants, health care benefits, and tuition waivers (full and partial) also available. Support available to part-time students. Financial award application deadline: 3/1; financial award applicants required to submit FAFSA. *Faculty research:* Corporate and commercial law, intellectual property law, criminal law and litigation, Constitutional law, legal theory and jurisprudence. *Unit head:* David G. Martinidez, Dean of Admissions, 212-790-0357, Fax: 212-790-0482, E-mail: lawinfo@yu.edu.
Website: http://www.cardozo.yu.edu/

Section 18
Criminology and Forensics

This section contains a directory of institutions offering graduate work in criminology and forensics. Additional information about programs listed in the directory but not augmented by an in-depth entry may be obtained by writing directly to the dean of a graduate school or chair of a department at the address given in the directory.

For programs offering related work, see also in this book *Political Science and International Affairs, Psychology and Counseling,* and *Sociology, Anthropology, and Archaeology.* In another guide in this series:

Graduate Programs in Business, Education, Information Studies, Law & Social Work

See *Law* and *Social Work*

CONTENTS

Program Directories

Displays and Close-Ups

See:

Criminal Justice and Criminology

Adler University, Programs in Psychology, Chicago, IL 60602. Offers advanced Adlerian psychotherapy (Certificate); art therapy (MA); clinical neuropsychology (Certificate); clinical psychology (Psy D); community psychology (MA); counseling and organizational psychology (MA); counseling psychology (MA); criminology (MA); emergency management leadership (MA); forensic psychology (MA); marriage and family counseling (MA); marriage and family therapy (Certificate); military psychology (MA); nonprofit management (MA); organizational psychology (MA); police psychology (MA); public policy and administration (MA); rehabilitation counseling (MA); sport and health psychology (MA); substance abuse counseling (Certificate); Psy D/Certificate; Psy D/MACAT; Psy D/MACP; Psy D/MAMFC; Psy D/MASAC. *Accreditation:* APA. Part-time and evening/weekend programs available. Postbaccalaureate distance learning degree programs offered (minimal on-campus study). Terminal master's awarded for partial completion of doctoral program. *Degree requirements:* For master's, thesis or alternative, oral exam, practicum; for doctorate, thesis/dissertation, clinical exam, internship, oral exam, practicum, written qualifying exam. *Entrance requirements:* For master's, 12 semester hours in psychology, minimum GPA of 3.0; for doctorate, 18 semester hours in psychology, minimum GPA of 3.25; for Certificate, appropriate master's or doctoral degree. Additional exam requirements/recommendations for international students: Required—TOEFL (minimum score 550 paper-based; 79 iBT). Electronic applications accepted.

See Display on page 969 and Close-Up on page 1207.

Adrian College, Graduate Programs, Adrian, MI 49221-2575. Offers accounting (MS); athletic training (MS); criminal justice (MA). *Degree requirements:* For master's, comprehensive exam (for some programs), thesis (for some programs), thesis, internship or practicum with corresponding in-depth paper and/or presentation. *Entrance requirements:* For master's, appropriate undergraduate degree, minimum cumulative and major GPA of 3.0, personal statement.

Albany State University, College of Arts and Humanities, Albany, GA 31705-2717. Offers English education (M Ed); public administration (MPA), including community and economic development administration, criminal justice administration, general administration, health administration and policy, human resources management, public policy, water resources management; social work (MSW). Part-time programs available. *Degree requirements:* For master's, comprehensive exam, professional portfolio (for MPA), internship, capstone report. *Entrance requirements:* For master's, GRE, MAT, minimum GPA of 3.0, official transcript, pre-medical record/certificate of immunization, letters of reference. Electronic applications accepted. *Faculty research:* HIV prevention for minority students.

Albany State University, College of Sciences and Health Professions, Albany, GA 31705-2717. Offers criminal justice (MS), including corrections, forensic science, law enforcement, public administration; mathematics education (M Ed); nursing (MSN), including RN to MSN family nurse practitioner, RN to MSN nurse educator; science education (M Ed). Part-time and evening/weekend programs available. Postbaccalaureate distance learning degree programs offered. *Degree requirements:* For master's, comprehensive exam, thesis. *Entrance requirements:* For master's, GRE or MAT, official transcript, letters of recommendations, pre-medical/certificate of immunizations. Electronic applications accepted.

Albertus Magnus College, Master of Science in Criminal Justice Program, New Haven, CT 06511-1189. Offers corrections administration (MS); juvenile justice (MS). Postbaccalaureate distance learning degree programs offered (no on-campus study). *Degree requirements:* For master's, thesis. *Entrance requirements:* For master's, bachelor's degree from regionally-accredited college or university with minimum GPA of 3.0 in criminal justice, 2.8 overall; undergraduate major in criminal justice or completion of 18 criminal justice credits; interview; two letters of recommendation; one-page personal statement. Application fee: $50. *Financial support:* Career-related internships or fieldwork available. Support available to part-time students. *Unit head:* Michael Geary, Coordinator, 203-773-8088, E-mail: mgeary@albertus.edu. *Application contact:* Dr. Sean O'Connell, Vice President for Academic Affairs, 203-777-8539, Fax: 203-777-3701, E-mail: soconnell@albertus.edu.
Website: http://www.albertus.edu/graduate-degrees/graduate-degree-programs/criminal-justice/

Alliant International University–San Francisco, California School of Forensic Studies, Program in Applied Criminology, San Francisco, CA 94133-1221. Offers victimology (MS). *Entrance requirements:* For master's, 3 essays, resume. Additional exam requirements/recommendations for international students: Required—TOEFL (minimum score 550 paper-based; 80 iBT). Electronic applications accepted.

American Public University System, AMU/APU Graduate Programs, Charles Town, WV 25414. Offers accounting (MBA, MS); criminal justice (MA), including business administration, emergency and disaster management, general (MA, MS); educational leadership (M Ed); emergency and disaster management (MA); entrepreneurship (MBA); environmental policy and management (MS), including environmental planning, environmental sustainability, fish and wildlife management, general (MA, MS), global environmental management; finance (MBA); general (MBA); global business management (MBA); history (MA), including American history, ancient and classical history, European history, global history, public history; homeland security (MA), including business administration, counter-terrorism studies, criminal justice, cyber, emergency management and public health, intelligence studies, transportation security; homeland security resource allocation (MBA); humanities (MA); information technology (MS), including digital forensics, enterprise software development, information assurance and security, IT project management; information technology management (MBA); intelligence studies (MA), including criminal intelligence, cyber, general (MA, MS), homeland security, intelligence analysis, intelligence collection, intelligence management, intelligence operations, terrorism studies; international relations and conflict resolution (MA), including comparative and security issues, conflict resolution, international and transnational security issues, peacekeeping; legal studies (MA); management (MA), including defense management, general (MA, MS), human resource management, organizational leadership, public administration; marketing (MBA); military history (MA), including American military history, American Revolution, civil war, war since 1945, World War II; military studies (MA), including joint warfare, strategic leadership; national security studies (MA), including general (MA, MS), homeland security, regional security studies, security and intelligence analysis, terrorism studies; nonprofit management (MBA); political science (MA), including American politics and government, comparative government and development, general (MA, MS), international relations, public policy; psychology (MA); public administration (MPA), including disaster management, environmental policy, health policy, human resources, national security, organizational management, security management; public health (MPH); reverse logistics management (MA); school counseling (M Ed); security

management (MA); space studies (MS), including aerospace science, general (MA, MS), planetary science; sports and health sciences (MS); teaching (M Ed), including curriculum and instruction for elementary teachers, elementary reading, English language learners, instructional leadership, online learning, special education; transportation and logistics management (MA), including general (MA, MS), maritime engineering management, reverse logistics management. Programs offered via distance learning only. Part-time and evening/weekend programs available. Postbaccalaureate distance learning degree programs offered (no on-campus study). *Faculty:* 426 full-time (236 women), 1,864 part-time/adjunct (880 women). *Students:* 475 full-time (215 women), 10,067 part-time (4,085 women); includes 3,462 minority (1,863 Black or African American, non-Hispanic/Latino; 74 American Indian or Alaska Native, non-Hispanic/Latino; 273 Asian, non-Hispanic/Latino; 831 Hispanic/Latino; 78 Native Hawaiian or other Pacific Islander, non-Hispanic/Latino; 343 Two or more races, non-Hispanic/Latino), 131 international. Average age 36. In 2014, 3,740 master's awarded. *Degree requirements:* For master's, comprehensive exam or practicum. *Entrance requirements:* For master's, official transcript showing earned bachelor's degree from institution accredited by recognized accrediting body. Additional exam requirements/recommendations for international students: Required—TOEFL (minimum score 550 paper-based), IELTS (minimum score 6.5). *Application deadline:* Applications are processed on a rolling basis. Application fee: $0. Electronic applications accepted. *Financial support:* Applicants required to submit FAFSA. *Faculty research:* Military history, criminal justice, management performance, national security. *Unit head:* Dr. Karan Powell, Executive Vice President and Provost, 877-468-6268, Fax: 304-724-3780. *Application contact:* Terry Grant, Vice President of Enrollment Management, 877-468-6268, Fax: 304-724-3780, E-mail: info@apus.edu.
Website: http://www.apus.edu

American University of Puerto Rico, Program in Criminal Justice, Bayamón, PR 00960-2037. Offers MA. Evening/weekend programs available. *Faculty:* 4 part-time/adjunct (1 woman). *Students:* 7 full-time (2 women), 4 part-time (2 women); all minorities (all Hispanic/Latino). Average age 32. 2 applicants, 100% accepted, 2 enrolled. In 2014, 6 master's awarded. *Degree requirements:* For master's, comprehensive exam. *Entrance requirements:* For master's, interviews; recommendations. *Application deadline:* For fall admission, 8/1 for domestic students; for winter admission, 10/15 for domestic students; for spring admission, 3/22 for domestic students. Applications are processed on a rolling basis. Application fee: $25. *Expenses: Tuition:* Full-time $5280; part-time $240 per credit. *Required fees:* $45 per term. *Financial support:* In 2014–15, 8 students received support, including 9 fellowships (averaging $500 per year). Financial award applicants required to submit FAFSA. *Unit head:* Prof. Carmen T. Landron-Rivera, Assistant to the Dean of Faculty, 787-620-2040 Ext. 2182, Fax: 787-620-2958, E-mail: clandron@aupr.edu. *Application contact:* Keren I. Llanos-Figueroa, Information Contact, 787-620-2040 Ext. 2021, Fax: 787-785-7377, E-mail: oficnaadmisiones@aupr.edu.

Anderson University, Command College, Anderson, SC 29621-4035. Offers executive leadership (MA). Postbaccalaureate distance learning degree programs offered. *Entrance requirements:* For master's, minimum undergraduate GPA of 2.75, 5 years of experience working in criminal justice field, resume. *Expenses:* Expenses: $403 per semester hour. *Financial support:* Application deadline: 3/1; applicants required to submit FAFSA. *Application contact:* Mallory Knight, Graduate Admission Counselor, 864-231-2182, Fax: 864-231-2115, E-mail: malloryknight@andersonuniversity.edu.

Anna Maria College, Graduate Division, Program in Criminal Justice, Paxton, MA 01612. Offers criminal justice (MS). Part-time and evening/weekend programs available. *Degree requirements:* For master's, capstone project or thesis. *Entrance requirements:* For master's, bachelor's degree in related field, minimum GPA of 2.7. Additional exam requirements/recommendations for international students: Required—TOEFL (minimum score 500 paper-based). Electronic applications accepted.

Anna Maria College, Graduate Division, Program in Justice Administration, Paxton, MA 01612. Offers MS. Part-time and evening/weekend programs available. *Degree requirements:* For master's, capstone project. *Entrance requirements:* Additional exam requirements/recommendations for international students: Required—TOEFL (minimum score 500 paper-based). Electronic applications accepted.

Anna Maria College, Graduate Division, Program in Security Management, Paxton, MA 01612. Offers MA. *Degree requirements:* For master's, thesis.

Appalachian State University, Cratis D. Williams Graduate School, Department of Government and Justice Studies, Boone, NC 28608. Offers criminal justice (MS); political science (MA), including American government, environmental politics and policy analysis, international relations; public administration (MPA), including public management, town, city and county management. Part-time programs available. Postbaccalaureate distance learning degree programs offered (no on-campus study). *Degree requirements:* For master's, variable foreign language requirement, comprehensive exam, thesis optional. *Entrance requirements:* For master's, GRE General Test, 3 letters of recommendation. Additional exam requirements/recommendations for international students: Required—TOEFL (minimum score 570 paper-based; 79 iBT), IELTS (minimum score 6.5). Electronic applications accepted. *Faculty research:* Campaign finance, emerging democracies, bureaucratic politics, judicial behavior, administration of justice.

Arizona State University at the Tempe campus, College of Public Programs, School of Criminology and Criminal Justice, Phoenix, AZ 85004. Offers corrections management (Graduate Certificate); criminal justice (MA); criminology and criminal justice (MS, PhD); law enforcement administration (Graduate Certificate). Part-time and evening/weekend programs available. Postbaccalaureate distance learning degree programs offered (minimal on-campus study). Terminal master's awarded for partial completion of doctoral program. *Degree requirements:* For master's, thesis or alternative, policy analysis project, interactive Program of Study (iPOS) submitted before completing 50 percent of required credit hours; for doctorate, comprehensive exam, thesis/dissertation, interactive Program of Study (iPOS) submitted before completing 50 percent of required credit hours. *Entrance requirements:* For master's, GRE (MS), minimum GPA of 3.0 or equivalent in last 2 years of work leading to bachelor's degree; for doctorate, GRE, minimum GPA of 3.0 or equivalent in last 2 years of work leading to bachelor's degree, 2 letters of recommendation, resume, personal statement. Additional exam requirements/recommendations for international students: Required—TOEFL, IELTS, or PTE. Electronic applications accepted.

Arkansas State University, Graduate School, College of Humanities and Social Sciences, Department of Criminology, Sociology, and Geography, State University, AR 72467. Offers criminal justice (MA); sociology (MA); sociology education (SCCT). Part-time programs available. *Faculty:* 9 full-time (5 women). *Students:* 5 full-time (1 woman), 20 part-time (12 women); includes 12 minority (all Black or African American, non-

Hispanic/Latino), 2 international. Average age 34. 27 applicants, 52% accepted, 12 enrolled. In 2014, 11 master's, 1 other advanced degree awarded. *Degree requirements:* For master's, one foreign language, comprehensive exam, thesis or alternative; for SCCT, comprehensive exam. *Entrance requirements:* For master's, GRE General Test or MAT, appropriate bachelor's degree, letters of recommendation, official transcripts, immunization records; for SCCT, GRE General Test or MAT, interview, master's degree, official transcript, immunization records. Additional exam requirements/recommendations for international students: Required—TOEFL (minimum score 550 paper-based; 79 iBT), IELTS (minimum score 6), PTE (minimum score 56). *Application deadline:* For fall admission, 5/1 for domestic and international students; for spring admission, 11/1 for domestic and international students. Applications are processed on a rolling basis. Application fee: $30 ($40 for international students). Electronic applications accepted. *Expenses:* Tuition, state resident: full-time $4392; part-time $244 per credit hour. Tuition, nonresident: full-time $8784; part-time $488 per credit hour. *International tuition:* $9484 full-time. *Required fees:* $1134; $63 per credit hour. $25 per term. Tuition and fees vary according to course load and program. *Financial support:* In 2014–15, 4 students received support. Career-related internships or fieldwork, scholarships/grants, and unspecified assistantships available. Financial award application deadline: 7/1; financial award applicants required to submit FAFSA. *Unit head:* Dr. Leslie McCallister, Chair, 870-972-3705, Fax: 870-972-3694, E-mail: lmccallister@astate.edu. *Application contact:* Vickey Ring, Graduate Admissions Coordinator, 870-972-3029, Fax: 870-972-3857, E-mail: vickeyring@astate.edu. Website: http://www.astate.edu/college/humanities-and-social-sciences/departments/criminology-sociology-and-geography/

Armstrong State University, School of Graduate Studies, Program in Criminal Justice, Savannah, GA 31419-1997. Offers criminal justice (MS); cyber crime (Certificate). Part-time and evening/weekend programs available. *Faculty:* 8 full-time (4 women), 2 part-time/adjunct (1 woman). *Students:* 10 full-time (2 women), 12 part-time (7 women); includes 5 minority (2 Black or African American, non-Hispanic/Latino; 3 Hispanic/Latino). Average age 31. 15 applicants, 53% accepted, 6 enrolled. In 2014, 3 master's, 5 other advanced degrees awarded. *Degree requirements:* For master's, comprehensive exam, field practicum or thesis. *Entrance requirements:* For master's, GRE General Test (minimum score 150 on verbal, 141 on quantitative, or 4 on analytical section) or MAT, minimum GPA of 2.5, 2 letters of recommendation, letter of intent (500-1000 words). Additional exam requirements/recommendations for international students: Required—TOEFL (minimum score 523 paper-based). *Application deadline:* For fall admission, 6/1 priority date for domestic students, 5/1 priority date for international students; for spring admission, 11/15 priority date for domestic students, 9/15 priority date for international students; for summer admission, 4/15 priority date for domestic students, 9/15 for international students. Applications are processed on a rolling basis. Application fee: $30. Electronic applications accepted. *Expenses:* Tuition, state resident: part-time $206 per credit hour. Tuition, nonresident: part-time $763 per credit hour. *Required fees:* $612 per semester. Tuition and fees vary according to course load, campus/location and program. *Financial support:* In 2014–15, research assistantships with full tuition reimbursements (averaging $5,000 per year) were awarded; career-related internships or fieldwork, Federal Work-Study, scholarships/grants, and unspecified assistantships also available. Support available to part-time students. Financial award application deadline: 3/15; financial award applicants required to submit FAFSA. *Faculty research:* International crime/globalization, cyber-crime, influence of social science research on judicial decision-making. *Unit head:* Dr. Daniel Skidmore-Hess, Department Head, 912-344-2532, Fax: 912-344-3438, E-mail: daniel.skidmore-hess@armstrong.edu. *Application contact:* Kathy Ingram, Associate Director of Graduate/Adult and Nontraditional Students, 912-344-2503, Fax: 912-344-3417, E-mail: graduate@armstrong.edu. Website: http://www.armstrong.edu/Liberal_Arts/criminal_justice_soc_and_pol_science/cjsocpols_graduate_program

Ashworth College, Graduate Programs, Norcross, GA 30092. Offers business administration (MBA); criminal justice (MS); health care administration (MBA, MS); human resource management (MBA, MS); international business (MBA); management (MS); marketing (MBA, MS).

Auburn University at Montgomery, College of Public Policy and Justice, Department of Justice and Public Safety, Montgomery, AL 36124-4023. Offers criminal studies (MSJPS); homeland security (MSJPS); homeland security and emergency management (MS); legal studies (MSJPS); organizational leadership (MSJPS); paralegal (Certificate). Part-time and evening/weekend programs available. *Faculty:* 6 full-time (3 women), 4 part-time/adjunct (0 women). *Students:* 12 full-time (7 women), 43 part-time (26 women); includes 19 minority (all Black or African American, non-Hispanic/Latino). Average age 32. 34 applicants, 79% accepted, 15 enrolled. In 2014, 20 master's awarded. *Degree requirements:* For master's, comprehensive exam, thesis optional. *Entrance requirements:* For master's, GRE General Test or MAT. *Application deadline:* Applications are processed on a rolling basis. Electronic applications accepted. *Expenses:* Tuition, state resident: full-time $6264; part-time $348 per credit hour. Tuition, nonresident: full-time $14,094; part-time $783 per credit hour. *Financial support:* Career-related internships or fieldwork and scholarships/grants available. Support available to part-time students. Financial award application deadline: 3/1; financial award applicants required to submit FAFSA. *Faculty research:* Law enforcement, corrections, juvenile justice. *Unit head:* Dr. Ralph Ioimo, Head, 334-244-3691, Fax: 334-244-3244, E-mail: rioimo@aum.edu. *Application contact:* Shinae Yoon, Administrative Associate, 334-244-3692, Fax: 334-244-3244, E-mail: syoon1@aum.edu.

Aurora University, College of Professional Studies, Aurora, IL 60506-4892. Offers business (MBA); criminal justice (MS); nursing (MSN); social work (MSW, DSW). Part-time and evening/weekend programs available. *Entrance requirements:* Additional exam requirements/recommendations for international students: Required—TOEFL (minimum score 550 paper-based). Electronic applications accepted.

Ball State University, Graduate School, College of Sciences and Humanities, Department of Political Science, Program in Public Administration, Muncie, IN 47306-1099. Offers criminal justice (MPA); public administration (MPA), including criminal justice. *Students:* 10 full-time (5 women), 2 part-time (1 woman); includes 1 minority (American Indian or Alaska Native, non-Hispanic/Latino), 3 international. Average age 25. 8 applicants, 63% accepted, 2 enrolled. In 2014, 5 master's awarded. *Entrance requirements:* For master's, GRE General Test. Application fee: $50. *Financial support:* In 2014–15, 3 students received support, including 5 research assistantships with partial tuition reimbursements available (averaging $10,117 per year), 1 teaching assistantship with partial tuition reimbursement available (averaging $8,675 per year); unspecified assistantships also available. Financial award application deadline: 3/1. *Faculty research:* Employment training programs, personnel and labor relations, planning. *Unit head:* Dr. Joseph Losco, Director, 765-285-8780, Fax: 765-285-5345, E-mail: jlosco@bsu.edu. *Application contact:* Dr. Gary Crawley, Associate Provost for Research and Dean of the Graduate School, 765-285-8785, E-mail: gcrawley@bsu.edu. Website: http://www.bsu.edu/poli-sci/

Baylor University, School of Law, Waco, TX 76798-7288. Offers administrative practice (JD); business litigation (JD); business transactions (JD); criminal practice (JD); estate planning (JD); general civil litigation (JD); healthcare (JD); intellectual property (JD); law (JD); real estate and natural resources (JD); JD/M Tax; JD/MBA; JD/MPPA. *Accreditation:* ABA. *Entrance requirements:* For doctorate, LSAT. Additional exam requirements/recommendations for international students: Recommended—TOEFL. Electronic applications accepted. Application fee is waived when completed online. *Expenses:* Contact institution.

Bellevue University, Graduate School, College of Information Technology, Bellevue, NE 68005-3098. Offers computer information systems (MS); cybersecurity (MS); management of information systems (MS); project management (MPM).

Bellevue University, Graduate School, College of Professional Studies, Bellevue, NE 68005-3098. Offers instructional design and development (MS); justice administration and criminal management (MS); leadership (MA); organizational performance (MS); public administration (MPA); security management (MS).

Boise State University, College of Social Sciences and Public Affairs, Program in Criminal Justice Administration, Boise, ID 83725-0399. Offers criminal justice (MA); victim services (Graduate Certificate). *Faculty:* 8 full-time, 2 part-time/adjunct. *Students:* 9 full-time (5 women), 25 part-time (19 women); includes 6 minority (1 Asian, non-Hispanic/Latino; 5 Hispanic/Latino), 1 international. 23 applicants, 96% accepted, 10 enrolled. In 2014, 6 master's awarded. *Degree requirements:* For master's, thesis. *Entrance requirements:* For master's, minimum GPA of 3.0. *Application deadline:* For fall admission, 3/1 priority date for domestic students; for spring admission, 10/1 priority date for domestic students. Applications are processed on a rolling basis. Application fee: $55. Electronic applications accepted. *Expenses:* Tuition, state resident: part-time $331 per credit hour. Tuition, nonresident: part-time $531 per credit hour. *Financial support:* In 2014–15, 2 students received support. Federal Work-Study and institutionally sponsored loans available. Financial award application deadline: 3/1; financial award applicants required to submit FAFSA. *Unit head:* Dr. Jeremy Ball, Department Chair, 208-426-3769, E-mail: jeremyball@boisestate.edu. *Application contact:* Linda Platt, Supervisor, Graduate Admission and Degree Services, 208-426-1074, Fax: 208-426-2789, E-mail: lplatt@boisestate.edu. Website: http://sspa.boisetstate.edu/criminaljustice/graduate/

Boston University, Metropolitan College, Program in Criminal Justice, Boston, MA 02215. Offers MCJ. Part-time and evening/weekend programs available. Postbaccalaureate distance learning degree programs offered (no on-campus study). *Faculty:* 5 full-time (2 women), 4 part-time/adjunct (0 women). *Students:* 6 full-time (2 women), 345 part-time (200 women); includes 62 minority (30 Black or African American, non-Hispanic/Latino; 8 Asian, non-Hispanic/Latino; 16 Hispanic/Latino; 1 Native Hawaiian or other Pacific Islander, non-Hispanic/Latino; 7 Two or more races, non-Hispanic/Latino), 12 international. Average age 32. 133 applicants, 83% accepted, 82 enrolled. In 2014, 228 master's awarded. *Degree requirements:* For master's, comprehensive examination (for on-campus program only). *Entrance requirements:* Additional exam requirements/recommendations for international students: Required—TOEFL (minimum score 84 iBT). *Application deadline:* For fall admission, 7/15 for domestic students, 7/15 priority date for international students; for spring admission, 12/15 for domestic students, 11/15 priority date for international students. Applications are processed on a rolling basis. Application fee: $80. Electronic applications accepted. *Expenses:* Expenses: $800 per credit part-time; student services fees: $60 per semester; technology fee of $60 per credit (for online courses). *Financial support:* In 2014–15, 1 student received support, including 8 research assistantships (averaging $4,200 per year); scholarships/grants and unspecified assistantships also available. Support available to part-time students. Financial award application deadline: 6/15; financial award applicants required to submit FAFSA. *Faculty research:* Criminal justice administration and planning, criminology, police, corrections, collective violence, juvenile issues, cybersecurity, forensic psychology. *Unit head:* Dr. Daniel P. LeClair, Chair, 617-353-3025, Fax: 617-358-3595, E-mail: dleclair@bu.edu. *Application contact:* Dr. Mary Ellen Mastrorilli, Assistant Professor and Associate Chair, 617-353-3025, E-mail: memastro@bu.edu. Website: http://www.bu.edu/met/cj/

Bowling Green State University, Graduate College, College of Health and Human Services, Program in Criminal Justice, Bowling Green, OH 43403. Offers MSCJ. Part-time and evening/weekend programs available. Postbaccalaureate distance learning degree programs offered (no on-campus study). *Degree requirements:* For master's, thesis or alternative. *Entrance requirements:* For master's, GRE General Test. Additional exam requirements/recommendations for international students: Required—TOEFL. Electronic applications accepted.

Bridgewater State University, College of Graduate Studies, School of Arts and Sciences, Department of Sociology, Program in Criminal Justice, Bridgewater, MA 02325-0001. Offers MS. *Entrance requirements:* For master's, GRE General Test.

Buffalo State College, State University of New York, The Graduate School, Faculty of Applied Science and Education, Department of Criminal Justice, Buffalo, NY 14222-1095. Offers MS. Part-time and evening/weekend programs available. *Degree requirements:* For master's, comprehensive exam, project. *Entrance requirements:* For master's, minimum GPA of 3.0. Additional exam requirements/recommendations for international students: Required—TOEFL (minimum score 550 paper-based).

California Coast University, School of Criminal Justice, Santa Ana, CA 92701. Offers MS.

California State University, Fresno, Division of Graduate Studies, College of Social Sciences, Department of Criminology, Fresno, CA 93740-8027. Offers MS. Part-time and evening/weekend programs available. *Degree requirements:* For master's, thesis or alternative. *Entrance requirements:* For master's, GRE General Test, minimum GPA of 3.0. Additional exam requirements/recommendations for international students: Required—TOEFL. Electronic applications accepted. *Faculty research:* Substance abuse, gangs vs. law enforcement, needs of female offenders, battered women, crime victims.

California State University, Long Beach, Graduate Studies, College of Health and Human Services, Department of Criminal Justice, Long Beach, CA 90840. Offers criminal justice (MS); emergency services administration (MS). Part-time programs available. *Degree requirements:* For master's, comprehensive course or thesis. *Entrance requirements:* For master's, minimum GPA of 3.0. Electronic applications accepted.

California State University, Los Angeles, Graduate Studies, College of Health and Human Services, Department of Criminal Justice and Criminalistics, Los Angeles, CA 90032-8530. Offers criminal justice (MS); criminalistics (MS). Part-time and evening/weekend programs available. *Degree requirements:* For master's, thesis. *Entrance requirements:* For master's, minimum GPA of 2.75. Additional exam requirements/recommendations for international students: Required—TOEFL (minimum score 500 paper-based). *Expenses:* Tuition, state resident: full-time $6738; part-time $3609 per year. Tuition, nonresident: full-time $15,666; part-time $8073 per year. Tuition and fees vary according to course load, degree level and program.

California State University, Sacramento, Office of Graduate Studies, College of Health and Human Services, Division of Criminal Justice, Sacramento, CA 95819. Offers MS. Part-time programs available. *Degree requirements:* For master's, thesis or

project. *Entrance requirements:* For master's, GRE, BA in criminal justice or equivalent, minimum GPA of 2.5 during previous 2 years of course work. Additional exam requirements/recommendations for international students: Required—TOEFL. Electronic applications accepted.

California State University, San Bernardino, Graduate Studies, College of Social and Behavioral Sciences, Department of Criminal Justice, San Bernardino, CA 92407-2397. Offers MA. Part-time programs available. *Students:* 3 full-time (all women), 14 part-time (8 women); includes 9 minority (2 Black or African American, non-Hispanic/Latino; 6 Hispanic/Latino; 1 Two or more races, non-Hispanic/Latino), 2 international. Average age 24. 21 applicants, 62% accepted, 6 enrolled. In 2014, 4 master's awarded. *Entrance requirements:* Additional exam requirements/recommendations for international students: Required—TOEFL. *Application deadline:* For fall admission, 7/17 for domestic students. Application fee: $55. *Expenses:* Tuition, state resident: full-time $6738; part-time $1302 per term. Tuition, nonresident: full-time $17,898; part-time $248 per unit. *Required fees:* $365 per quarter. Tuition and fees vary according to degree level and program. *Financial support:* Institutionally sponsored loans available. *Faculty research:* Crime seriousness, fear of crime, victimization, corrections management, crime correlates. *Unit head:* Dr. Larry Gaines, Chair, 909-537-5508, Fax: 909-537-7025, E-mail: lgaines@csusb.edu. *Application contact:* Dr. Jeffrey Thompson, Associate Vice Dean of Graduate Studies, 909-537-5058, E-mail: jthompso@csusb.edu.

California State University, Stanislaus, College of Humanities and Social Sciences, Program in Criminal Justice (MA), Turlock, CA 95382. Offers MA. Part-time programs available. *Degree requirements:* For master's, comprehensive exam, thesis or alternative. *Entrance requirements:* For master's, minimum GPA of 3.0, 3 letters of reference, personal statement. Electronic applications accepted. *Faculty research:* Police gerontology services, hate crimes, juvenile justice, masculinities and modern society, nutrition and criminal behavior.

California University of Pennsylvania, School of Graduate Studies and Research, College of Liberal Arts, Department of Justice, Law and Society, California, PA 15419-1394. Offers social science - criminal justice (MA). Part-time and evening/weekend programs available. *Degree requirements:* For master's, comprehensive exam, thesis optional. *Entrance requirements:* For master's, MAT, minimum GPA of 3.0. Additional exam requirements/recommendations for international students: Required—TOEFL (minimum score 550 paper-based; 80 iBT). Electronic applications accepted. *Expenses:* Tuition, state resident: full-time $10,896; part-time $454 per credit. Tuition, nonresident: full-time $16,344; part-time $681 per credit. *Required fees:* $2425. *Faculty research:* Ethics and law, ethics in police practice, law and morality, police policy, St. Thomas Aquinas and crime.

Calumet College of Saint Joseph, Program in Public Safety Administration, Whiting, IN 46394-2195. Offers MS.

Capella University, School of Public Service Leadership, Doctoral Programs in Healthcare, Minneapolis, MN 55402. Offers criminal justice (PhD); emergency management (PhD); epidemiology (Dr PH); general health administration (DHA); general public administration (DPA); health advocacy and leadership (Dr PH); health care administration (PhD); health care leadership (DHA); health policy advocacy (DHA); multidisciplinary human services (PhD); nonprofit management and leadership (PhD); public safety leadership (PhD); social and community services (PhD).

Capella University, School of Public Service Leadership, Master's Programs in Healthcare, Minneapolis, MN 55402. Offers criminal justice (MS); emergency management (MS); general public health (MPH); gerontology (MS); health administration (MHA); health care operations (MHA); health management policy (MPH); health policy (MHA); homeland security (MS); multidisciplinary human services (MS); public administration (MPA); public safety leadership (MS); social and community services (MS); social behavioral sciences (MPH); MS/MPA.

Caribbean University, Graduate School, Bayamón, PR 00960-0493. Offers administration and supervision (MA Ed); criminal justice (MA); curriculum and instruction (MA Ed, PhD), including elementary education (MA Ed), English education (MA Ed), history education (MA Ed), mathematics education (MA Ed), primary education (MA Ed), science education (MA Ed), Spanish education (MA Ed); educational technology in instructional systems (MA Ed); gerontology (MSN); human resources (MBA); museology, archiving and art history (MA Ed); neonatal pediatrics (MSN); physical education (MA Ed); special education (MA Ed). *Entrance requirements:* For master's, interview, minimum GPA of 2.5.

Carnegie Mellon University, H. John Heinz III College, School of Information Systems and Management, Master of Science in Information Security Policy and Management Program, Pittsburgh, PA 15213-3891. Offers MSISPM. *Entrance requirements:* For master's, GRE or GMAT, college-level course in advanced algebra/pre-calculus; college-level courses in economics and statistics (recommended). Additional exam requirements/recommendations for international students: Required—TOEFL or IELTS.

Central Connecticut State University, School of Graduate Studies, College of Liberal Arts and Social Sciences, Department of Criminology and Criminal Justice, New Britain, CT 06050-4010. Offers criminal justice (MS). Part-time and evening/weekend programs available. *Faculty:* 8 full-time (3 women). *Students:* 5 full-time (4 women), 34 part-time (25 women); includes 17 minority (6 Black or African American, non-Hispanic/Latino; 1 Asian, non-Hispanic/Latino; 8 Hispanic/Latino; 1 Native Hawaiian or other Pacific Islander, non-Hispanic/Latino; 1 Two or more races, non-Hispanic/Latino). Average age 29. 25 applicants, 68% accepted, 8 enrolled. In 2014, 6 master's awarded. *Degree requirements:* For master's, comprehensive exam, thesis or alternative. *Entrance requirements:* For master's, minimum undergraduate GPA of 3.0, essay, resume. Additional exam requirements/recommendations for international students: Required—TOEFL (minimum score 550 paper-based; 79 iBT). *Application deadline:* For fall admission, 6/1 for domestic students, 5/1 for international students; for spring admission, 11/1 for domestic and international students. Applications are processed on a rolling basis. Application fee: $50. Electronic applications accepted. *Expenses: Tuition, area resident:* Full-time $5730; part-time $534 per credit. Tuition, state resident: full-time $8596; part-time $534 per credit. Tuition, nonresident: full-time $15,964; part-time $548 per credit. *Required fees:* $4211; $215 per credit. *Financial support:* In 2014–15, 2 students received support. Application deadline: 3/1; applicants required to submit FAFSA. *Unit head:* Dr. Kathleen Bantley, Chair, 860-832-3005, E-mail: bantleyk@ccsu.edu. *Application contact:* Patricia Gardner, Associate Director of Graduate Studies, 860-832-2350, Fax: 860-832-2362, E-mail: graduateadmissions@ccsu.edu.
Website: http://web.ccsu.edu/criminology/

Chaminade University of Honolulu, Graduate Services, Program in Criminal Justice Administration, Honolulu, HI 96816-1578. Offers criminal justice administration (MSCJA); homeland security leadership development (MSCJA, Certificate). Part-time and evening/weekend programs available. Postbaccalaureate distance learning degree programs offered (no on-campus study). *Degree requirements:* For master's, comprehensive exam. *Entrance requirements:* For master's, minimum undergraduate GPA of 3.0, 3 letters of recommendation. Additional exam requirements/recommendations for international students: Required—TOEFL (minimum score 550 paper-based). Electronic applications accepted. *Faculty research:* Penology, juvenile delinquency, multicultural and ethnic diversity in criminology, law enforcement administration and training, homeland security.

Charleston Southern University, Department of Criminal Justice, Charleston, SC 29423-8087. Offers MSCJ. Part-time and evening/weekend programs available. *Degree requirements:* For master's, comprehensive exam, thesis optional. *Entrance requirements:* For master's, GRE or MAT, bachelor's degree in criminal justice. Additional exam requirements/recommendations for international students: Required—TOEFL (minimum score 550 paper-based; 79 iBT).

Chicago State University, School of Graduate and Professional Studies, College of Arts and Sciences, Department of Criminal Justice, Philosophy, and Political Science, Chicago, IL 60628. Offers criminal justice (MS). Part-time and evening/weekend programs available. *Entrance requirements:* For master's, minimum GPA of 2.75. *Faculty research:* Gang crime.

Clark Atlanta University, School of Arts and Sciences, Department of Criminal Justice, Atlanta, GA 30314. Offers MA. Part-time programs available. *Faculty:* 1 full-time (0 women). *Students:* 8 full-time (7 women), 2 part-time (1 woman); includes 6 minority (all Black or African American, non-Hispanic/Latino), 2 international. Average age 24. 7 applicants, 100% accepted, 3 enrolled. In 2014, 5 master's awarded. *Degree requirements:* For master's, one foreign language, comprehensive exam, thesis. *Entrance requirements:* For master's, GRE General Test, minimum GPA of 2.5. Additional exam requirements/recommendations for international students: Required—TOEFL (minimum score 500 paper-based; 61 iBT). *Application deadline:* For fall admission, 4/1 for domestic and international students; for spring admission, 11/1 for domestic and international students. Applications are processed on a rolling basis. Application fee: $40 ($55 for international students). *Expenses: Tuition:* Full-time $14,904; part-time $828 per credit hour. *Required fees:* $746; $373 per semester. *Financial support:* Career-related internships or fieldwork, Federal Work-Study, scholarships/grants, and unspecified assistantships available. Support available to part-time students. Financial award application deadline: 4/30; financial award applicants required to submit FAFSA. *Faculty research:* Race and crime, black ex-offenders in the labor market. *Unit head:* Dr. Obie Clayton, Chairperson, 404-880-8681, E-mail: oclayton@cau.edu. *Application contact:* Michelle Clark-Davis, Graduate Program Admissions, 404-880-6605, E-mail: cauadmissions@cau.edu.

College of Saint Elizabeth, Program in Justice Studies, Morristown, NJ 07960-6989. Offers justice administration and public service (MA). Part-time programs available. *Degree requirements:* For master's, thesis or alternative. *Entrance requirements:* For master's, minimum GPA of 3.0, writing sample, interview. Additional exam requirements/recommendations for international students: Required—TOEFL. Electronic applications accepted.

Colorado State University–Global Campus, Graduate Programs, Greenwood Village, CO 80111. Offers criminal justice and law enforcement administration (MS); education leadership (MS); finance (MS); healthcare administration and management (MS); human resource management (MHRM); information technology management (MITM); international management (MS); management (MS); organizational leadership (MS); professional accounting (MPA); project management (MS); teaching and learning (MS). Postbaccalaureate distance learning degree programs offered (no on-campus study).

Colorado Technical University Colorado Springs, Graduate Studies, Program in Criminal Justice, Colorado Springs, CO 80907-3896. Offers MSM. Postbaccalaureate distance learning degree programs offered.

Colorado Technical University Denver South, Program in Computer Science, Aurora, CO 80014. Offers computer systems security (MSCS); database systems (MSCS); software engineering (MSCS). Part-time and evening/weekend programs available. *Degree requirements:* For master's, thesis or alternative. *Entrance requirements:* For master's, minimum undergraduate GPA of 3.0, resume.

Columbia College, Master of Science in Criminal Justice Program, Columbia, MO 65216-0002. Offers MSCJ. Part-time and evening/weekend programs available. Postbaccalaureate distance learning degree programs offered (no on-campus study). *Faculty:* 4 full-time (0 women), 19 part-time/adjunct (9 women). *Students:* 22 full-time (13 women), 145 part-time (71 women); includes 39 minority (25 Black or African American, non-Hispanic/Latino; 12 Hispanic/Latino; 2 Two or more races, non-Hispanic/Latino), 2 international. Average age 38. 32 applicants, 78% accepted, 17 enrolled. In 2014, 46 master's awarded. *Degree requirements:* For master's, final exams, culminating experience (intensive writing seminar). *Entrance requirements:* Additional exam requirements/recommendations for international students: Required—TOEFL (minimum score 550 paper-based; 79 iBT). *Application deadline:* For fall admission, 8/9 priority date for domestic and international students; for spring admission, 12/27 priority date for domestic and international students. Applications are processed on a rolling basis. Application fee: $55. Electronic applications accepted. *Expenses: Tuition:* Part-time $340 per credit hour. Tuition and fees vary according to campus/location. *Financial support:* Federal Work-Study and scholarships/grants available. Financial award application deadline: 3/1; financial award applicants required to submit FAFSA. *Unit head:* Dr. Mike Lyman, Graduate Program Coordinator, 573-875-7472, E-mail: mlyman@ccis.edu. *Application contact:* Stephanie Johnson, Director of Admissions, 573-875-7352, Fax: 573-875-7506, E-mail: sjohnson@ccis.edu.
Website: http://www.ccis.edu/graduate/academics/degrees.asp?MSCJ

Columbia Southern University, College of Safety and Emergency Services, Orange Beach, AL 36561. Offers criminal justice administration (MS); emergency services management (MS); occupational safety and health (MS), including environmental management. Part-time and evening/weekend programs available. Postbaccalaureate distance learning degree programs offered (no on-campus study). *Entrance requirements:* For master's, bachelor's degree from accredited/approved institution. Additional exam requirements/recommendations for international students: Required—TOEFL. Electronic applications accepted.

Concordia University, St. Paul, College of Education and Science, St. Paul, MN 55104-5494. Offers criminal justice (MA); curriculum and instruction (MA Ed), including K-12 reading; differentiated instruction (MA Ed); early childhood education (MA Ed); educational leadership (MA Ed); educational technology (MA Ed); exercise science (MA); family life education (MA); forensic mental health (MA); K-12 principal licensure (Ed S); K-12 reading (Certificate); physical therapy (DPT); special education (MA Ed, Certificate), including autism spectrum disorder (MA Ed), emotional and behavioral disorders (MA Ed), learning disabilities (MA Ed); sports management (MA); superintendent (Ed S). *Accreditation:* NCATE. Part-time and evening/weekend programs available. Postbaccalaureate distance learning degree programs offered (minimal on-campus study). *Faculty:* 16 full-time (9 women), 122 part-time/adjunct (72 women). *Students:* 1,147 full-time (810 women), 118 part-time (84 women); includes 147 minority (71 Black or African American, non-Hispanic/Latino; 12 American Indian or Alaska Native, non-Hispanic/Latino; 28 Asian, non-Hispanic/Latino; 20 Hispanic/Latino; 1 Native Hawaiian or other Pacific Islander, non-Hispanic/Latino; 15 Two or more races, non-Hispanic/Latino), 47 international. Average age 34. 874 applicants, 64% accepted, 440 enrolled. In 2014, 348 master's, 85 other advanced degrees awarded. *Degree requirements:* For master's, thesis (for some programs); for doctorate, clinical internships; capstone projects; for other advanced degree, e-folio review of

competencies. *Entrance requirements:* For master's, official transcripts from regionally-accredited institution stating the conferral of a bachelor's degree with minimum cumulative GPA of 3.0; personal statement; professional resume; practitioner in field through work or volunteerism; resume; for doctorate, GRE (taken within last five years), bachelor's degree with minimum cumulative GPA of 3.0; 100 physical therapy observation hours; 2 letters of recommendation; for other advanced degree, at least three years of teaching experience, master's degree, valid MN teaching license. Additional exam requirements/recommendations for international students: Recommended—TOEFL (minimum score 547 paper-based; 78 iBT), IELTS (minimum score 6). *Application deadline:* For fall admission, 8/1 for domestic and international students; for spring admission, 12/1 for domestic and international students; for summer admission, 5/1 for domestic and international students. Applications are processed on a rolling basis. Application fee: $50. Electronic applications accepted. *Expenses: Tuition:* Full-time $4416; part-time $368 per credit. Tuition and fees vary according to degree level and program. *Financial support:* Applicants required to submit FAFSA. *Unit head:* Dr. Donald Helmstetter, Dean, 651-641-8227, Fax: 651-641-8807, E-mail: helmstetter@csp.edu. *Application contact:* Kimberly Craig, Associate Vice President, Cohort Enrollment Management, 651-603-6223, Fax: 651-603-6320, E-mail: craig@csp.edu.

Coppin State University, Division of Graduate Studies, Division of Arts and Sciences, Department of Criminal Justice and Law Enforcement, Baltimore, MD 21216-3698. Offers criminal justice (MS). Part-time and evening/weekend programs available. *Degree requirements:* For master's, thesis optional. *Entrance requirements:* For master's, GRE, minimum GPA of 3.0.

Curry College, Graduate Studies, Program in Criminal Justice, Milton, MA 02186-9984. Offers MA. Part-time and evening/weekend programs available. *Degree requirements:* For master's, thesis. *Entrance requirements:* For master's, resume, recommendations, interview. Additional exam requirements/recommendations for international students: Required—TOEFL (minimum score 550 paper-based; 80 iBT). *Expenses:* Contact institution.

Dallas Baptist University, Professional Development Program, Dallas, TX 75211-9299. Offers business (MA); counseling (MA); criminal justice (MA); English as a second language (MA); higher education (MA); interdisciplinary (MA); leadership studies (MA); missions (MA); professional life coaching (MA); training and development (MA). Part-time and evening/weekend programs available. *Entrance requirements:* For master's, minimum GPA of 3.0. Additional exam requirements/recommendations for international students: Required—TOEFL, IELTS. *Expenses: Tuition:* Full-time $14,130; part-time $785 per credit hour. *Required fees:* $200 per semester. Tuition and fees vary according to course level and course load.

Defiance College, Program in Business Administration, Defiance, OH 43512-1610. Offers criminal justice (MBA); health care (MBA); leadership (MBA); sport management (MBA). Part-time and evening/weekend programs available. *Degree requirements:* For master's, thesis. *Entrance requirements:* For master's, minimum GPA of 2.5. Additional exam requirements/recommendations for international students: Recommended—TOEFL.

Delta State University, Graduate Programs, College of Arts and Sciences, Division of Social Sciences and History, Program in Social Justice and Criminology, Cleveland, MS 38733-0001. Offers MSJC. Part-time programs available. Postbaccalaureate distance learning degree programs offered. *Faculty:* 2 full-time (1 woman), 2 part-time/adjunct (1 woman). *Students:* 11 full-time (4 women), 14 part-time (8 women); includes 13 minority (12 Black or African American, non-Hispanic/Latino; 1 Hispanic/Latino). Average age 30. 16 applicants, 75% accepted, 9 enrolled. In 2014, 5 master's awarded. *Degree requirements:* For master's, thesis or alternative. *Application deadline:* For fall admission, 8/1 priority date for domestic students; for spring admission, 12/1 priority date for domestic students. Applications are processed on a rolling basis. Application fee: $30. *Expenses:* Tuition, state resident: full-time $6012; part-time $334 per credit hour. Tuition, nonresident: full-time $6012; part-time $334 per credit hour. Part-time tuition and fees vary according to course load. *Financial support:* Research assistantships, career-related internships or fieldwork, Federal Work-Study, and institutionally sponsored loans available. Support available to part-time students. Financial award application deadline: 6/1. *Unit head:* Dr. Paulette Miekle, Chair, 662-846-4065, Fax: 662-846-4016, E-mail: pmeikleyaw@deltastate.edu. *Application contact:* Dr. Beverly Moon, Dean of Graduate Studies, 662-846-4873, Fax: 662-846-4313, E-mail: grad-info@deltastate.edu.
Website: http://www.deltastate.edu/pages/3189.asp

DeSales University, Graduate Division, Division of Liberal Arts and Social Sciences, Program in Criminal Justice, Center Valley, PA 18034-9568. Offers criminal justice (MACJ); digital forensics (MACJ); investigative forensics (MACJ). Part-time programs available. Postbaccalaureate distance learning degree programs offered (no on-campus study). *Students:* 41 part-time. *Entrance requirements:* Additional exam requirements/recommendations for international students: Required—TOEFL. *Application deadline:* Applications are processed on a rolling basis. Electronic applications accepted. *Unit head:* Dr. Katherine Ramsland, Director, 610-282-1100 Ext. 1445, Fax: 610-282-0787, E-mail: katherine.ramsland@desales.edu. *Application contact:* Abigail Wernicki, Director of Graduate Admissions, 610-282-1100 Ext. 1768, Fax: 610-282-2869, E-mail: gradadmissions@desales.edu.

Drury University, Program in Criminology/Criminal Justice, Springfield, MO 65802. Offers criminal justice (MS); criminology (MA). Part-time and evening/weekend programs available. *Degree requirements:* For master's, thesis (for some programs). *Entrance requirements:* For master's, GMAT or MAT. Additional exam requirements/recommendations for international students: Required—TOEFL. Electronic applications accepted. *Expenses:* Contact institution. *Faculty research:* Gangs, fear of crime, social justice, social change and law, drug laws in Iran.

East Carolina University, Graduate School, College of Human Ecology, Department of Criminal Justice, Greenville, NC 27858-4353. Offers criminal justice (MS); criminal justice education (Certificate); public management and leadership (Certificate); security studies (Certificate). Part-time and evening/weekend programs available. Postbaccalaureate distance learning degree programs offered (no on-campus study). *Degree requirements:* For master's, thesis, internship. *Entrance requirements:* For master's, GRE or MAT, bachelor's degree in criminal justice or related field. Additional exam requirements/recommendations for international students: Required—TOEFL. *Expenses:* Tuition, state resident: full-time $4223. Tuition, nonresident: full-time $16,540. *Required fees:* $2184. *Faculty research:* Corrections, policing, international criminal justice, terrorism.

East Carolina University, Graduate School, Thomas Harriot College of Arts and Sciences, Department of Political Science, Greenville, NC 27858-4353. Offers community health administration (Certificate); public administration (MPA); security studies (Certificate). *Accreditation:* NASPAA. Part-time and evening/weekend programs available. *Degree requirements:* For master's, one foreign language, comprehensive exam. *Entrance requirements:* For master's, GRE General Test. Additional exam requirements/recommendations for international students: Required—TOEFL. *Expenses:* Tuition, state resident: full-time $4223. Tuition, nonresident: full-time $16,540. *Required fees:* $2184.

East Central University, School of Graduate Studies, Department of Human Resources, Ada, OK 74820. Offers administration (MSHR); counseling (MSHR); criminal justice (MSHR); human services (MSHR); rehabilitation counseling (MSHR). *Accreditation:* CORE. Part-time and evening/weekend programs available. *Degree requirements:* For master's, thesis optional. *Entrance requirements:* For master's, GRE General Test, MAT, minimum GPA of 2.5. Electronic applications accepted.

Eastern Kentucky University, The Graduate School, College of Justice and Safety, Program in Correctional and Juvenile Justice Studies, Richmond, KY 40475-3102. Offers MS. *Degree requirements:* For master's, comprehensive exam (for some programs), thesis (for some programs). *Entrance requirements:* For master's, GRE.

Eastern Kentucky University, The Graduate School, College of Justice and Safety, Program in Criminal Justice and Police Studies, Richmond, KY 40475-3102. Offers criminal justice (MS); criminal justice education (MS); police studies (MS). Part-time programs available. *Degree requirements:* For master's, thesis optional. *Entrance requirements:* For master's, GRE General Test, minimum GPA of 3.0.

Eastern Kentucky University, The Graduate School, College of Justice and Safety, Program in Loss Prevention and Safety, Richmond, KY 40475-3102. Offers MS. *Entrance requirements:* For master's, GRE.

Eastern Michigan University, Graduate School, College of Arts and Sciences, Department of Sociology, Anthropology and Criminology, Program in Criminology and Criminal Justice, Ypsilanti, MI 48197. Offers MA. *Students:* 3 full-time (2 women), 25 part-time (22 women); includes 10 minority (8 Black or African American, non-Hispanic/Latino; 1 American Indian or Alaska Native, non-Hispanic/Latino; 1 Two or more races, non-Hispanic/Latino). Average age 38. 17 applicants, 76% accepted, 5 enrolled. In 2014, 5 master's awarded. Application fee: $45. *Application contact:* Dr. Marilyn Corsianos, Graduate Coordinator, 734-487-0012, Fax: 734-487-9666, E-mail: mcorsiano@emich.edu.

East Tennessee State University, School of Graduate Studies, College of Arts and Sciences, Department of Criminal Justice and Criminology, Johnson City, TN 37614. Offers MA, Postbaccalaureate Certificate. Part-time and evening/weekend programs available. *Faculty:* 12 full-time (5 women). *Students:* 17 full-time (10 women), 14 part-time (10 women); includes 1 minority (Black or African American, non-Hispanic/Latino). Average age 32. 33 applicants, 52% accepted, 13 enrolled. In 2014, 11 master's, 6 other advanced degrees awarded. *Degree requirements:* For master's, comprehensive exam, thesis optional; for Postbaccalaureate Certificate, practicum. *Entrance requirements:* For master's, GRE General Test, minimum GPA of 3.0; for Postbaccalaureate Certificate, minimum GPA of 2.5, three letters of recommendation. Additional exam requirements/recommendations for international students: Required—TOEFL (minimum score 550 paper-based; 79 iBT). *Application deadline:* For fall admission, 6/1 for domestic students, 4/30 for international students; for spring admission, 11/1 for domestic students, 9/30 for international students. Application fee: $35 ($45 for international students). Electronic applications accepted. *Financial support:* In 2014–15, 17 students received support, including 4 research assistantships with full and partial tuition reimbursements available (averaging $5,600 per year), 9 teaching assistantships with full tuition reimbursements available (averaging $6,000 per year); career-related internships or fieldwork, institutionally sponsored loans, scholarships/grants, and unspecified assistantships also available. Financial award application deadline: 7/1; financial award applicants required to submit FAFSA. *Faculty research:* Adolescent work experience and delinquency, violence against women, prisons and inmates, death penalty, women and crime, juvenile justice and alternative education. *Unit head:* Dr. Larry Miller, Chair, 423-439-5964, Fax: 423-439-4660, E-mail: millerls@etsu.edu. *Application contact:* Angela Edwards, Graduate Specialist, 423-439-4703, Fax: 423-439-5624, E-mail: edwardag@etsu.edu.
Website: http://www.etsu.edu/cas/cj/

Everest University, Graduate Programs, Jacksonville, FL 32256. Offers business (MBA); criminal justice (MS).

Everest University, Program in Criminal Justice, Tampa, FL 33619. Offers MS. Part-time and evening/weekend programs available. Postbaccalaureate distance learning degree programs offered (minimal on-campus study). *Degree requirements:* For master's, thesis optional, externship, research practicum. *Entrance requirements:* Additional exam requirements/recommendations for international students: Required—TOEFL (minimum score 550 paper-based).

Everest University, Program in Criminal Justice, Pompano Beach, FL 33062. Offers MS.

Excelsior College, School of Business and Technology, Albany, NY 12203-5159. Offers business administration (MBA); cybersecurity (MS); cybersecurity management (MBA, Graduate Certificate); health care management (MBA); human performance technology (MBA); leadership (MBA); social media management (MBA); technology management (MBA). Part-time and evening/weekend programs available. Postbaccalaureate distance learning degree programs offered (no on-campus study). *Faculty:* 34 part-time/adjunct (14 women). *Students:* 1,469 part-time (447 women); includes 605 minority (318 Black or African American, non-Hispanic/Latino; 7 American Indian or Alaska Native, non-Hispanic/Latino; 50 Asian, non-Hispanic/Latino; 165 Hispanic/Latino; 8 Native Hawaiian or other Pacific Islander, non-Hispanic/Latino; 57 Two or more races, non-Hispanic/Latino), 12 international. Average age 38. In 2014, 108 master's awarded. *Application deadline:* Applications are processed on a rolling basis. Application fee: $110. *Expenses: Tuition:* Part-time $620 per credit hour. *Financial support:* Scholarships/grants available. *Unit head:* Dr. Karl Lawrence, Dean, 888-647-2388. *Application contact:* Admissions, 888-647-2388 Ext. 133, Fax: 518-464-8777, E-mail: admissions@excelsior.edu.

Fairleigh Dickinson University, Metropolitan Campus, University College: Arts, Sciences, and Professional Studies, School of Criminal Justice and Legal Studies, Program in Criminal Justice, Teaneck, NJ 07666-1914. Offers MA.

Fairmont State University, Program in Criminal Justice, Fairmont, WV 26554. Offers MS. Part-time and evening/weekend programs available. Postbaccalaureate distance learning degree programs offered. *Faculty:* 4 part-time/adjunct (2 women). *Students:* 17 full-time (6 women), 13 part-time (8 women); includes 3 minority (1 Black or African American, non-Hispanic/Latino; 1 Asian, non-Hispanic/Latino; 1 Two or more races, non-Hispanic/Latino). Average age 27. 18 applicants, 67% accepted, 11 enrolled. In 2014, 6 master's awarded. *Degree requirements:* For master's, thesis or comprehensive exam. *Entrance requirements:* For master's, GRE, minimum GPA of 3.0. Additional exam requirements/recommendations for international students: Required—TOEFL. *Application deadline:* For fall admission, 5/1 for domestic and international students. Applications are processed on a rolling basis. Application fee: $40. Electronic applications accepted. *Expenses:* Tuition, state resident: full-time $3404; part-time $367 per credit hour. Tuition, nonresident: full-time $7291; part-time $799 per credit hour. *Financial support:* In 2014–15, 5 students received support. *Unit head:* Dr. Jennifer Myers, Director, Graduate Program in Criminal Justice, 304-367-4936, Fax: 304-367-4785, E-mail: jennifer.myers@fairmontstate.edu. *Application contact:* Jack Kirby,

Criminal Justice and Criminology

Director of Graduate Studies, 304-367-4101, E-mail: jack.kirby@fairmontstate.edu. Website: http://www.fairmontstate.edu/graduatestudies/CJ_Overview.asp

Faulkner University, Alabama Christian College of Arts and Sciences, Department of Criminal Justice, Montgomery, AL 36109-3398. Offers MJA. Postbaccalaureate distance learning degree programs offered (no on-campus study). *Degree requirements:* For master's, research project. *Entrance requirements:* For master's, MAT, GRE or GMAT, minimum overall GPA of 2.5, major 3.0; 3 letters of recommendation; letter of intent; resume.

Fayetteville State University, Graduate School, Program in Criminal Justice, Fayetteville, NC 28301-4298. Offers MA. *Faculty:* 14 full-time (8 women). *Students:* 14 full-time (9 women), 24 part-time (15 women); includes 21 minority (20 Black or African American, non-Hispanic/Latino; 1 Asian, non-Hispanic/Latino). Average age 34. 13 applicants, 100% accepted, 13 enrolled. In 2014, 13 master's awarded. *Application deadline:* For fall admission, 4/15 for domestic students; for spring admission, 10/15 for domestic students. Application fee: $40. *Unit head:* Dr. Miriam Delone, Interim Chair, 910-672-1478, Fax: 910-672-1908, E-mail: mdelone@uncfsu.edu. *Application contact:* 910-672-1478, Fax: 910-672-1908, E-mail: mdelone@uncfsu.edu.

Ferris State University, College of Education and Human Services, School of Criminal Justice, Big Rapids, MI 49307. Offers criminal justice administration (MSCJ). Part-time and evening/weekend programs available. *Faculty:* 7 full-time (3 women). *Students:* 7 full-time (3 women), 48 part-time (22 women); includes 19 minority (11 Black or African American, non-Hispanic/Latino; 1 Asian, non-Hispanic/Latino; 6 Hispanic/Latino; 1 Two or more races, non-Hispanic/Latino). Average age 34. 35 applicants, 100% accepted, 28 enrolled. In 2014, 25 master's awarded. *Degree requirements:* For master's, comprehensive exam or thesis/dissertation. *Entrance requirements:* For master's, bachelor's degree in criminal justice or related field, minimum GPA of 3.0. Additional exam requirements/recommendations for international students: Required—TOEFL (minimum score 500 paper-based; 61 iBT). *Application deadline:* For fall admission, 8/15 for domestic students; for winter admission, 12/15 for domestic students; for spring admission, 3/15 for domestic students. Applications are processed on a rolling basis. Application fee: $0. Electronic applications accepted. Tuition and fees vary according to degree level and program. *Financial support:* In 2014–15, 1 research assistantship (averaging $4,850 per year) was awarded; Federal Work-Study and unspecified assistantships also available. Support available to part-time students. Financial award applicants required to submit FAFSA. *Faculty research:* Policy enactment, health and safety issues, criminological theory, juvenile justice, policy techniques, problem-based learning. *Unit head:* Dr. Gregory P. Vanderkooi, Professor/Graduate Program Coordinator, 231-591-2458, Fax: 231-591-3792, E-mail: vanderkg@ferris.edu. *Application contact:* Sara P. Rasmussen, Secretary, 231-591-3652, Fax: 231-591-3792, E-mail: sararasmussen@ferris.edu.
Website: http://www.ferris.edu/education/cj/

Florida Agricultural and Mechanical University, Division of Graduate Studies, Research, and Continuing Education, College of Social Sciences, Arts and Humanities, Department of History and Political Science, Program in Applied Social Science, Tallahassee, FL 32307-3200. Offers criminal justice (MASS); history (MASS); political science (MASS); public administration (MASS). Part-time programs available. *Degree requirements:* For master's, thesis optional. *Entrance requirements:* For master's, GRE General Test, minimum GPA of 3.0. *Faculty research:* Southern history, black history, election trends, Presidential history.

Florida Atlantic University, College of Design and Social Inquiry, School of Criminology and Criminal Justice, Boca Raton, FL 33431-0991. Offers MS. Part-time and evening/weekend programs available. Postbaccalaureate distance learning degree programs offered. *Degree requirements:* For master's, thesis optional. *Entrance requirements:* For master's, GRE General Test, minimum GPA of 3.0, undergraduate course work in statistics and criminology. Additional exam requirements/recommendations for international students: Required—TOEFL (minimum score 550 paper-based; 61 iBT), IELTS (minimum score 6). Electronic applications accepted. *Expenses:* Tuition, state resident: full-time $7396; part-time $369.82 per credit hour. Tuition, nonresident: full-time $19,392; part-time $1024.81 per credit hour. Tuition and fees vary according to course load. *Faculty research:* Restorative, justice corrections, logic modeling, criminal justice management, crime causation.

Florida Gulf Coast University, College of Arts and Sciences, Program in Criminal Justice Studies, Fort Myers, FL 33965-6565. Offers MS. *Faculty:* 230 full-time (93 women), 158 part-time/adjunct (72 women). *Students:* 6 full-time (4 women), 6 part-time (2 women); includes 4 minority (2 Black or African American, non-Hispanic/Latino; 2 Hispanic/Latino). Average age 36. 7 applicants, 71% accepted, 5 enrolled. In 2014, 2 master's awarded. *Entrance requirements:* For master's, GRE General Test, minimum GPA of 3.0. Additional exam requirements/recommendations for international students: Required—TOEFL (minimum score 550 paper-based). *Application deadline:* For fall admission, 3/1 for domestic students; for spring admission, 11/1 for domestic students. Applications are processed on a rolling basis. Application fee: $30. Electronic applications accepted. *Expenses:* Tuition, state resident: full-time $6974. Tuition, nonresident: full-time $28,170. *Required fees:* $1987. Tuition and fees vary according to course load. *Financial support:* In 2014–15, 1 student received support. Application deadline: 6/30; applicants required to submit FAFSA. *Unit head:* Shawn Keller, Program Chair, 239-590-4248, E-mail: skeller@fgcu.edu. *Application contact:* Mary Zager, Associate Professor/Chair, Division of Justice Studies, 239-590-7832, Fax: 239-590-7843, E-mail: mzager@fgcu.edu.

Florida International University, College of Arts and Sciences, Department of Criminal Justice, Miami, FL 33199. Offers MS. Part-time and evening/weekend programs available. *Degree requirements:* For master's, thesis optional. *Entrance requirements:* For master's, minimum undergraduate GPA of 3.0. Additional exam requirements/recommendations for international students: Required—TOEFL (minimum score 550 paper-based; 80 iBT). Electronic applications accepted.

Florida State University, The Graduate School, College of Criminology and Criminal Justice, Tallahassee, FL 32306-1127. Offers criminology (MSC); criminology and criminal justice (MA, PhD), including corrections (MA), global security (MA), policing (MA), victimology (MA); MPA/MSC; MS/MSW. Part-time programs available. Postbaccalaureate distance learning degree programs offered (no on-campus study). *Faculty:* 17 full-time (4 women). *Students:* 117 full-time (69 women), 100 part-time (64 women); includes 58 minority (26 Black or African American, non-Hispanic/Latino; 1 American Indian or Alaska Native, non-Hispanic/Latino; 3 Asian, non-Hispanic/Latino; 27 Hispanic/Latino; 1 Two or more races, non-Hispanic/Latino), 15 international. 151 applicants, 83% accepted, 69 enrolled. In 2014, 40 master's, 6 doctorates awarded. Terminal master's awarded for partial completion of doctoral program. *Degree requirements:* For master's, thesis optional; for doctorate, comprehensive exam, thesis/dissertation. *Entrance requirements:* For master's, GRE General Test; for doctorate, GRE General Test, area paper or thesis. Additional exam requirements/recommendations for international students: Required—TOEFL (minimum score 600 paper-based; 100 iBT). *Application deadline:* For fall admission, 7/1 for domestic and international students; for spring admission, 11/1 for domestic and international students. Applications are processed on a rolling basis. Application fee: $30. Electronic

applications accepted. *Expenses:* Tuition, state resident: part-time $403.51 per credit hour. Tuition, nonresident: part-time $1004.85 per credit hour. *Required fees:* $75.81 per credit hour. One-time fee: $20 part-time. Tuition and fees vary according to campus/location. *Financial support:* In 2014–15, 4 fellowships with full tuition reimbursements (averaging $20,000 per year), 29 research assistantships with full tuition reimbursements (averaging $14,500 per year), 15 teaching assistantships with full tuition reimbursements (averaging $14,500 per year) were awarded; Federal Work-Study, institutionally sponsored loans, scholarships/grants, tuition waivers (partial), and unspecified assistantships also available. Financial award application deadline: 1/15; financial award applicants required to submit FAFSA. *Faculty research:* Criminological theory, criminal justice administration and planning, criminal justice policy and evaluation, law and social control, biosocial criminology. *Unit head:* Dr. Thomas G. Blomberg, Dean, 850-644-7365, Fax: 850-644-9614. *Application contact:* Margarita Frankeberger, Graduate Student Coordinator, 850-644-7373, Fax: 850-644-9614, E-mail: mfrankeberger@fsu.edu.
Website: http://www.criminology.fsu.edu/

George Mason University, College of Humanities and Social Sciences, Department of Criminology, Law and Society, Fairfax, VA 22030. Offers MA, PhD. Part-time programs available. *Faculty:* 25 full-time (19 women), 49 part-time/adjunct (13 women). *Students:* 32 full-time (21 women), 33 part-time (27 women); includes 13 minority (6 Black or African American, non-Hispanic/Latino; 1 Asian, non-Hispanic/Latino; 5 Hispanic/Latino; 1 Two or more races, non-Hispanic/Latino), 4 international. Average age 30. 97 applicants, 43% accepted, 17 enrolled. In 2014, 9 master's, 3 doctorates awarded. Terminal master's awarded for partial completion of doctoral program. *Degree requirements:* For master's, thesis; for doctorate, thesis/dissertation, two comprehensive exams. *Entrance requirements:* For master's, GRE, personal goal statement, transcripts, 3 letters of recommendation, writing sample, resume; for doctorate, GRE, personal goal statement, transcripts, 3 letters of recommendation, writing sample, resume. Additional exam requirements/recommendations for international students: Required—TOEFL (minimum score 570 paper-based; 80 iBT), IELTS (minimum score 6.5), PTE. *Application deadline:* For fall admission, 2/1 priority date for domestic students. Application fee: $65 ($80 for international students). Electronic applications accepted. *Expenses:* Tuition, state resident: full-time $9794; part-time $408 per credit hour. Tuition, nonresident: full-time $26,978; part-time $1124 per credit hour. *Required fees:* $2820; $118 per credit hour. Tuition and fees vary according to course load and program. *Financial support:* In 2014–15, 23 students received support, including 1 fellowship (averaging $8,000 per year), 17 research assistantships with full and partial tuition reimbursements available (averaging $23,802 per year), 6 teaching assistantships with full and partial tuition reimbursements available (averaging $21,037 per year); career-related internships or fieldwork, Federal Work-Study, scholarships/grants, unspecified assistantships, and health care benefits (for full-time research or teaching assistantship recipients) also available. Support available to part-time students. Financial award application deadline: 3/1; financial award applicants required to submit FAFSA. *Faculty research:* Health care and justice agencies, public opinion on criminal justice issues and survey methods, police and crime control, police organizations and their reform, crime and place, counterterrorism, social equity and diversity issues, community corrections, prisons and prisoner reentry, evidence-based crime policy, courts and corrections, homeland security, risk and vulnerability assessment, experimental criminology, crime prevention, meta analysis and quantitative research methods. Total annual research expenditures: $3.7 million. *Unit head:* David B. Wilson, Chair, 703-993-4701, Fax: 703-993-8316, E-mail: dwilsonb@gmu.edu. *Application contact:* Mary Schifferli, Graduate Coordinator, 703-993-9417, Fax: 703-993-8316, E-mail: mschiffe@gmu.edu.
Website: http://cls.gmu.edu/

George Mason University, School of Policy, Government, and International Affairs, Program in Public Administration, Fairfax, VA 22030. Offers administration of justice (Certificate); association management (Certificate); biodefense (MS, PhD); critical analysis and strategic response to terrorism (Certificate); emergency management and homeland security (Certificate); nonprofit management (Certificate); political science (MA, PhD); public administration (MPA); public management (Certificate). *Accreditation:* NASPAA (one or more programs are accredited). *Entrance requirements:* For degree, expanded goals statement; 3 letters of recommendation; official transcripts; resume. Additional exam requirements/recommendations for international students: Required—TOEFL, IELTS, PTE. Application fee: $65 ($80 for international students). Electronic applications accepted. *Expenses:* Expenses: Contact institution. *Financial support:* Fellowships, research assistantships with full and partial tuition reimbursements, teaching assistantships with full and partial tuition reimbursements, career-related internships or fieldwork, Federal Work-Study, scholarships/grants, and unspecified assistantships available. Support available to part-time students. Financial award application deadline: 3/1; financial award applicants required to submit FAFSA. *Application contact:* Peg Koback, Education Support Specialist, 703-993-3707, Fax: 703-993-1399, E-mail: mkoback@gmu.edu.
Website: http://pia.gmu.edu/

The George Washington University, Columbian College of Arts and Sciences, Department of Forensic Sciences, Washington, DC 20052. Offers crime scene investigation (MFS); forensic chemistry (MFS); forensic molecular biology (MFS); forensic toxicology (MFS); high-technology crime investigation (MS); security management (MFS). MFS in high-technology crime investigation and MFS in security management offered in Arlington, VA. Part-time and evening/weekend programs available. *Faculty:* 8 full-time (1 woman). *Students:* 57 full-time (53 women), 42 part-time (32 women); includes 29 minority (15 Black or African American, non-Hispanic/Latino; 1 American Indian or Alaska Native, non-Hispanic/Latino; 7 Asian, non-Hispanic/Latino; 6 Hispanic/Latino), 7 international. Average age 27. 163 applicants, 64% accepted, 36 enrolled. In 2014, 50 master's, 3 other advanced degrees awarded. *Degree requirements:* For master's, comprehensive exam. *Entrance requirements:* For master's, GRE General Test, minimum GPA of 3.0. Additional exam requirements/recommendations for international students: Required—TOEFL (minimum score 550 paper-based; 80 iBT). *Application deadline:* For fall admission, 1/16 priority date for international students; for spring admission, 10/1 priority date for domestic students, 9/1 priority date for international students. Applications are processed on a rolling basis. Application fee: $75. Electronic applications accepted. *Financial support:* In 2014–15, 19 students received support. Fellowships with partial tuition reimbursements available, Federal Work-Study, and tuition waivers available. *Unit head:* Dr. Victor Weedn, Chair, 202-994-6977, E-mail: vweedn@gwu.edu. *Application contact:* 202-994-6210, Fax: 202-994-6213, E-mail: askccas@gwu.edu.
Website: http://www.gwu.edu/~forensic/

The George Washington University, Columbian College of Arts and Sciences, Department of Sociology, Program in Criminology, Washington, DC 20052. Offers MA. *Students:* 6 full-time (all women), 3 part-time (all women); includes 3 minority (2 Black or African American, non-Hispanic/Latino; 1 Asian, non-Hispanic/Latino). Average age 25. 23 applicants, 43% accepted, 5 enrolled. In 2014, 4 master's awarded. *Degree requirements:* For master's, comprehensive exam. *Entrance requirements:* For master's, GRE General Test, minimum GPA of 3.0. Additional exam requirements/recommendations for international students: Required—TOEFL (minimum score 550

paper-based). *Application deadline:* For fall admission, 4/1 priority date for domestic and international students; for spring admission, 10/1 priority date for domestic and international students. Applications are processed on a rolling basis. Application fee: $75. Electronic applications accepted. *Financial support:* In 2014–15, fellowships with full tuition reimbursements (averaging $10,000 per year), teaching assistantships (averaging $5,000 per year) were awarded. Financial award application deadline: 2/1. *Unit head:* Ronald Weitzer, Director, 202-994-6895. *Application contact:* Information Contact, 202-994-6345, Fax: 202-994-3239, E-mail: soc@gwu.edu.
Website: http://www.gwu.edu/graduate-programs/criminology

Georgia College & State University, Graduate School, College of Arts and Sciences, Department of Government and Sociology, Program in Criminal Justice, Milledgeville, GA 31061. Offers MSCJ. Part-time and evening/weekend programs available. *Students:* 2 full-time (0 women), 14 part-time (10 women); includes 7 minority (6 Black or African American, non-Hispanic/Latino; 1 Two or more races, non-Hispanic/Latino). Average age 30. 2 applicants, 50% accepted, 1 enrolled. In 2014, 4 master's awarded. *Degree requirements:* For master's, comprehensive exam, thesis optional, capstone project. *Entrance requirements:* For master's, GRE or MAT, 3 letters of recommendation, transcripts. Additional exam requirements/recommendations for international students: Required—TOEFL (minimum score 550 paper-based; 79 iBT). *Application deadline:* For fall admission, 7/1 for domestic students, 4/1 for international students; for spring admission, 11/1 for domestic students; for summer admission, 4/1 for domestic students. Application fee: $40. Electronic applications accepted. *Expenses: Tuition, area resident:* Part-time $283 per credit hour. Tuition, nonresident: part-time $1027 per credit hour. *Required fees:* $995 per semester. Full-time tuition and fees vary according to course load, degree level, campus/location and program. *Financial support:* In 2014–15, 2 research assistantships with full tuition reimbursements were awarded; unspecified assistantships also available. Financial award applicants required to submit FAFSA. *Unit head:* Dr. Sara Doude, Program Coordinator, 478-445-4257, E-mail: sara.doude@gcsu.edu. *Application contact:* Kate Marshall, Graduate Admissions Coordinator, 478-445-1184, Fax: 478-445-1336, E-mail: grad-admit@gcsu.edu.

Georgia State University, Andrew Young School of Policy Studies, Department of Criminal Justice and Criminology, Atlanta, GA 30302-4018. Offers criminal justice (MS, PhD); public administration (MS). Part-time programs available. *Faculty:* 13 full-time (4 women). *Students:* 37 full-time (26 women), 5 part-time (3 women); includes 15 minority (9 Black or African American, non-Hispanic/Latino; 1 American Indian or Alaska Native, non-Hispanic/Latino; 2 Asian, non-Hispanic/Latino; 2 Hispanic/Latino; 1 Two or more races, non-Hispanic/Latino), 3 international. Average age 30. 41 applicants, 49% accepted, 10 enrolled. In 2014, 11 master's, 1 doctorate awarded. Terminal master's awarded for partial completion of doctoral program. *Degree requirements:* For master's, thesis optional; for doctorate, comprehensive exam, thesis/dissertation. *Entrance requirements:* For master's, GRE; for doctorate, GRE. Additional exam requirements/recommendations for international students: Required—TOEFL (minimum score 603 paper-based; 100 iBT) or IELTS (minimum score 7). *Application deadline:* For fall admission, 2/15 for domestic and international students; for spring admission, 10/1 for domestic and international students. Application fee: $50. Electronic applications accepted. *Expenses:* Tuition, state resident: full-time $6516; part-time $362 per credit hour. Tuition, nonresident: full-time $22,014; part-time $1223 per credit hour. *Required fees:* $2128 per semester. Tuition and fees vary according to course load and program. *Financial support:* In 2014–15, fellowships with full tuition reimbursements (averaging $22,000 per year), research assistantships with full tuition reimbursements (averaging $14,000 per year), teaching assistantships with full tuition reimbursements (averaging $14,000 per year) were awarded; career-related internships or fieldwork, Federal Work-Study, scholarships/grants, traineeships, health care benefits, and unspecified assistantships also available. Financial award application deadline: 2/15. *Faculty research:* Urban violence, drugs, victimization, criminal justice, criminology. *Unit head:* Dr. Brian K. Payne, Professor of Criminal Justice and Criminology/Department Chair, 404-413-1020, Fax: 404-413-1030, E-mail: bpayne@gsu.edu. *Application contact:* Charisma Parker, Admissions Coordinator, 404-413-0030, Fax: 404-413-0023, E-mail: cparker28@gsu.edu.
Website: http://aysps.gsu.edu/cj/

Georgia State University, Andrew Young School of Policy Studies, Department of Public Management and Policy, Atlanta, GA 30303. Offers criminal justice (MPA); disaster management (Certificate); disaster policy (MPA); environmental policy (PhD); health policy (PhD); management and finance (MPA); nonprofit management (MPA, Certificate); nonprofit policy (MPA); planning and economic development (MPP, Certificate); policy analysis and evaluation (MPA), including planning and economic development; public and nonprofit management (PhD); public finance and budgeting (PhD), including science and technology policy, urban and regional economic development; public finance policy (MPA), including social policy; public health (MPA). *Accreditation:* NASPAA (one or more programs are accredited). Part-time programs available. *Faculty:* 14 full-time (7 women). *Students:* 136 full-time (80 women), 85 part-time (47 women); includes 81 minority (60 Black or African American, non-Hispanic/Latino; 7 Asian, non-Hispanic/Latino; 11 Hispanic/Latino; 3 Two or more races, non-Hispanic/Latino), 25 international. Average age 30. 269 applicants, 59% accepted, 64 enrolled. In 2014, 80 master's, 7 other advanced degrees awarded. Terminal master's awarded for partial completion of doctoral program. *Degree requirements:* For master's, thesis optional; for doctorate, comprehensive exam, thesis/dissertation. *Entrance requirements:* For master's and doctorate, GRE. Additional exam requirements/recommendations for international students: Required—TOEFL (minimum score 603 paper-based; 100 iBT) or IELTS (minimum score 7). *Application deadline:* For fall admission, 2/15 for domestic and international students; for spring admission, 10/1 for domestic and international students. Application fee: $50. Electronic applications accepted. *Expenses:* Tuition, state resident: full-time $6516; part-time $362 per credit hour. Tuition, nonresident: full-time $22,014; part-time $1223 per credit hour. *Required fees:* $2128 per semester. Tuition and fees vary according to course load and program. *Financial support:* In 2014–15, fellowships (averaging $8,194 per year), research assistantships (averaging $8,068 per year), teaching assistantships (averaging $3,600 per year) were awarded; institutionally sponsored loans, scholarships/grants, health care benefits, and unspecified assistantships also available. Financial award application deadline: 2/1. *Faculty research:* Public budgeting and finance, public management, nonprofit management, performance measurement and management, urban development. *Unit head:* Dr. Gregory Burr Lewis, Chair and Professor, 404-413-0114, Fax: 404-413-0104, E-mail: glewis@gsu.edu. *Application contact:* Charisma Parker, Admissions Coordinator, 404-413-0030, Fax: 404-413-0023, E-mail: cparker28@gsu.edu.
Website: http://aysps.gsu.edu/pmap/

The Graduate Center, City University of New York, Graduate Studies, Program in Criminal Justice, New York, NY 10016-4039. Offers PhD. *Degree requirements:* For doctorate, one foreign language, thesis/dissertation. *Entrance requirements:* For doctorate, GRE General Test, writing sample. Additional exam requirements/recommendations for international students: Required—TOEFL. Electronic applications accepted.

Grambling State University, School of Graduate Studies and Research, College of Professional Studies, Department of Criminal Justice, Grambling, LA 71245. Offers MS. Part-time programs available. *Degree requirements:* For master's, comprehensive exam, thesis optional. *Entrance requirements:* For master's, GRE, minimum GPA of 2.5 on last degree and in four core courses. Additional exam requirements/recommendations for international students: Required—TOEFL (minimum score 500 paper-based; 62 iBT). Electronic applications accepted.

Grand Valley State University, College of Community and Public Service, School of Criminal Justice, Allendale, MI 49401-9403. Offers MS. Part-time and evening/weekend programs available. *Faculty:* 4 full-time (2 women). *Students:* 13 full-time (10 women), 15 part-time (7 women); includes 6 minority (1 Black or African American, non-Hispanic/Latino; 1 Asian, non-Hispanic/Latino; 4 Hispanic/Latino). Average age 32. 16 applicants, 75% accepted, 5 enrolled. In 2014, 4 master's awarded. *Degree requirements:* For master's, thesis or alternative. *Entrance requirements:* For master's, minimum GPA of 3.0. Additional exam requirements/recommendations for international students: Required—TOEFL. *Application deadline:* For fall admission, 7/30 priority date for domestic students; for winter admission, 12/10 priority date for domestic students; for spring admission, 4/10 priority date for domestic students. Application fee: $30. *Expenses:* Tuition, state resident: full-time $10,602; part-time $589 per credit hour. Tuition, nonresident: full-time $14,022; part-time $779 per credit hour. Tuition and fees vary according to degree level and program. *Financial support:* In 2014–15, 9 students received support, including 1 fellowship (averaging $750 per year), 8 research assistantships with full tuition reimbursements available (averaging $5,588 per year); career-related internships or fieldwork, Federal Work-Study, scholarships/grants, and unspecified assistantships also available. Support available to part-time students. Financial award application deadline: 5/1. *Faculty research:* Correctional administration, juvenile justice issues/gangs, women's issues, leadership, program/policy evaluation. *Unit head:* Dr. Kathleen Bailey, Director, 616-331-7148, Fax: 616-331-7155, E-mail: baileyk@gvsu.edu. *Application contact:* Tracey James-Heer, Associate Director for Graduate Recruitment, 616-331-2025, Fax: 616-486-6476, E-mail: james-ht@gvsu.edu.
Website: http://www.gvsu.edu/cj/

Hilbert College, Program in Criminal Justice Administration, Hamburg, NY 14075-1597. Offers MS. Evening/weekend programs available. *Faculty:* 5 full-time (2 women), 7 part-time/adjunct (1 woman). *Students:* 9 full-time (6 women), 6 part-time (4 women); includes 2 minority (1 Black or African American, non-Hispanic/Latino; 1 Two or more races, non-Hispanic/Latino). Average age 33. 22 applicants, 32% accepted, 6 enrolled. In 2014, 6 master's awarded. *Degree requirements:* For master's, final capstone project. *Entrance requirements:* For master's, admissions statement/essay, official transcripts from all prior colleges, two letters of recommendation, current resume, relevant work experience, baccalaureate degree from accredited college or university with minimum cumulative GPA of 3.0, personal interview. Additional exam requirements/recommendations for international students: Recommended—TOEFL. *Application deadline:* Applications are processed on a rolling basis. Application fee: $20. Electronic applications accepted. Application fee is waived when completed online. *Expenses:* Expenses: Contact institution. *Financial support:* In 2014–15, 8 students received support. Scholarships/grants available. Financial award application deadline: 7/1; financial award applicants required to submit FAFSA. *Unit head:* Dr. Martin Floss, Chair, 716-649-7900 Ext. 307, Fax: 716-649-0702, E-mail: mfloss@hilbert.edu. *Application contact:* Kim Chiarmonte, Director, Center for Adult and Graduate Studies, 716-926-8948, Fax: 716-649-0702, E-mail: kchiarmonte@hilbert.edu.
Website: http://www.hilbert.edu/grad/ms-cja

Holy Family University, Graduate School, School of Arts and Sciences, Program in Criminal Justice, Philadelphia, PA 19114. Offers MA. Part-time and evening/weekend programs available. *Entrance requirements:* For master's, 2 letters of recommendation, official transcripts of all college or university work, writing sample. Additional exam requirements/recommendations for international students: Required—TOEFL (minimum score 550 paper-based; 79 iBT), IELTS (minimum score 6), PTE (minimum score 54). Electronic applications accepted.

Husson University, Program in Criminal Justice Administration, Bangor, ME 04401-2999. Offers MS. Part-time programs available. *Faculty:* 5 full-time (3 women), 2 part-time/adjunct (0 women). *Students:* 10 full-time (3 women), 4 part-time (0 women); includes 1 minority (Two or more races, non-Hispanic/Latino). Average age 33. 2 applicants, 100% accepted, 2 enrolled. In 2014, 12 master's awarded. *Degree requirements:* For master's, thesis optional. *Entrance requirements:* For master's, GMAT or GRE, 2 letters of recommendation. Additional exam requirements/recommendations for international students: Required—TOEFL (minimum score 550 paper-based; 80 iBT). *Application deadline:* For fall admission, 8/1 for domestic students. Applications are processed on a rolling basis. Application fee: $50. Electronic applications accepted. *Expenses:* Expenses: Contact institution. *Financial support:* Career-related internships or fieldwork and unspecified assistantships available. Financial award application deadline: 4/15; financial award applicants required to submit FAFSA. *Unit head:* John Michaud, Director, School of Legal Studies, 207-941-7037, E-mail: michaudj@husson.edu. *Application contact:* Kristen Card, Director of Graduate Admissions, 207-404-5660, E-mail: cardk@husson.edu.
Website: http://www.husson.edu/index.php?cat_id-611

Illinois State University, Graduate School, College of Applied Science and Technology, Department of Criminal Justice Sciences, Normal, IL 61790-2200. Offers MA, MS. *Degree requirements:* For master's, thesis or alternative. *Entrance requirements:* For master's, GRE General Test, minimum GPA of 2.6 in last 60 hours of course work. *Faculty research:* Graduate practicum for victim assistance and advocacy, graduate practicum in adult probation cases, graduate practicum in youth intervention program.

Indiana State University, College of Graduate and Professional Studies, College of Arts and Sciences, Department of Criminology and Criminal Justice, Terre Haute, IN 47809. Offers MA, MS. Part-time programs available. Postbaccalaureate distance learning degree programs offered (no on-campus study). *Degree requirements:* For master's, thesis (for some programs). *Entrance requirements:* For master's, minimum GPA of 2.75 in undergraduate work, 3.0 in previous graduate work. Additional exam requirements/recommendations for international students: Required—TOEFL (minimum score 550 paper-based). Electronic applications accepted. *Faculty research:* Violent crime, rape attitudes, classification of offenders, substance abuse, domestic violence.

Indiana University Bloomington, University Graduate School, College of Arts and Sciences, Department of Criminal Justice, Bloomington, IN 47405. Offers crime and youth development (MA, PhD); crime, law and psychology (MA, PhD); criminal justice (MA, PhD); criminal justice institutions and practices (MA, PhD); criminology (MA, PhD); developmental criminology (MA, PhD); interdisciplinary studies in crime and punishment (PhD); interdisciplinary studies of crime and punishment (MA); the relationship between crime and gender, race and ethnicity (MA, PhD); theoretical analyses of criminology (MA, PhD). Part-time programs available. *Faculty:* 11 full-time (3 women). *Students:* 27 full-time (15 women); includes 3 minority (1 Black or African American, non-Hispanic/Latino; 1 American Indian or Alaska Native, non-Hispanic/Latino; 1 Asian, non-Hispanic/Latino), 3 international. Average age 31. 25 applicants, 32% accepted, 7 enrolled. In 2014, 1 master's, 1 doctorate awarded. Terminal master's awarded for partial

completion of doctoral program. *Degree requirements:* For master's, thesis optional; for doctorate, comprehensive exam, thesis/dissertation, foreign language or research practicum. *Entrance requirements:* For master's and doctorate, GRE General Test. Additional exam requirements/recommendations for international students: Required—TOEFL (minimum score 600 paper-based; 100 iBT); Recommended—TWE. *Application deadline:* For fall admission, 1/15 for domestic students, 12/1 for international students. Application fee: $55 ($65 for international students). Electronic applications accepted. *Financial support:* In 2014–15, fellowships with full tuition reimbursements (averaging $18,000 per year), 17 teaching assistantships with full tuition reimbursements (averaging $15,750 per year) were awarded; research assistantships with full tuition reimbursements, Federal Work-Study, health care benefits, tuition waivers (full), and unspecified assistantships also available. Financial award application deadline: 1/15. *Faculty research:* Violence, crime, juveniles, psychology and law, cross-cultural studies. *Unit head:* Prof. Michael Grossberg, Chair, 812-856-1210, E-mail: grossb@indiana.edu. *Application contact:* Ruth Cord, Graduate Secretary, 812-856-4675, Fax: 812-855-5522, E-mail: rkapusti@indiana.edu.
Website: http://www.indiana.edu/~crimjust/

Indiana University Northwest, School of Public and Environmental Affairs, Gary, IN 46408-1197. Offers criminal justice (MPA); environmental affairs (Graduate Certificate); health services (MPA); nonprofit management (Certificate); public management (MPA). *Accreditation:* NASPAA (one or more programs are accredited). Part-time programs available. *Faculty:* 5 full-time (3 women). *Students:* 12 full-time (7 women), 39 part-time (23 women); includes 37 minority (26 Black or African American, non-Hispanic/Latino; 1 Asian, non-Hispanic/Latino; 9 Hispanic/Latino; 1 Two or more races, non-Hispanic/Latino). Average age 38. 30 applicants, 93% accepted, 25 enrolled. In 2014, 29 master's, 15 other advanced degrees awarded. *Entrance requirements:* For master's, GRE General Test or GMAT, letters of recommendation. *Application deadline:* For fall admission, 8/15 priority date for domestic students. Applications are processed on a rolling basis. *Financial support:* Career-related internships or fieldwork, Federal Work-Study, and tuition waivers (partial) available. Support available to part-time students. Financial award application deadline: 3/1. *Faculty research:* Employment in income security policies, evidence in criminal justice, equal employment law, social welfare policy and welfare reform, public finance in developing countries. *Unit head:* Dr. Barbara Peat, Department Chair, 219-981-5645, E-mail: bpeat@iun.edu. *Application contact:* Susan Zinner, 219-980-6836, E-mail: speanw@iun.edu.
Website: http://www.iun.edu/spea/index.htm

Indiana University of Pennsylvania, School of Graduate Studies and Research, College of Health and Human Services, Department of Criminology, Doctoral Program in Criminology, Indiana, PA 15705-1087. Offers PhD. Part-time programs available. *Faculty:* 16 full-time (8 women). *Students:* 14 full-time (11 women), 16 part-time (7 women); includes 1 minority (Asian, non-Hispanic/Latino), 5 international. Average age 30. 32 applicants, 44% accepted, 5 enrolled. In 2014, 2 doctorates awarded. *Degree requirements:* For doctorate, one foreign language, comprehensive exam, thesis/dissertation. *Entrance requirements:* For doctorate, GRE, 3 letters of recommendation, writing sample. Additional exam requirements/recommendations for international students: Required—TOEFL (minimum score 540 paper-based). *Application deadline:* Applications are processed on a rolling basis. Application fee: $50. Electronic applications accepted. *Financial support:* In 2014–15, 3 fellowships with full tuition reimbursements (averaging $1,948 per year), 13 research assistantships with full and partial tuition reimbursements (averaging $11,789 per year), 4 teaching assistantships with partial tuition reimbursements (averaging $23,305 per year) were awarded; Federal Work-Study, scholarships/grants, and unspecified assistantships also available. Support available to part-time students. Financial award application deadline: 4/15; financial award applicants required to submit FAFSA. *Unit head:* Dr. Erika Frenzel, Graduate Coordinator, 724-357-5976, E-mail: e.frenzel@iup.edu.
Website: http://www.iup.edu/grad/criminologyphd/default.aspx

Indiana University of Pennsylvania, School of Graduate Studies and Research, College of Health and Human Services, Department of Criminology, Master's Program in Criminology, Indiana, PA 15705-1087. Offers MA. Part-time programs available. Postbaccalaureate distance learning degree programs offered (no on-campus study). *Faculty:* 16 full-time (8 women). *Students:* 31 full-time (15 women), 17 part-time (10 women); includes 9 minority (8 Black or African American, non-Hispanic/Latino; 1 Two or more races, non-Hispanic/Latino). Average age 26. 86 applicants, 48% accepted, 27 enrolled. In 2014, 27 master's awarded. *Degree requirements:* For master's, thesis optional. *Entrance requirements:* For master's, 2 letters of recommendation. Additional exam requirements/recommendations for international students: Required—TOEFL (minimum score 540 paper-based). *Application deadline:* For fall admission, 4/15 priority date for domestic students. Applications are processed on a rolling basis. Application fee: $50. Electronic applications accepted. *Financial support:* In 2014–15, 13 research assistantships with full and partial tuition reimbursements (averaging $3,458 per year) were awarded; fellowships, career-related internships or fieldwork, Federal Work-Study, scholarships/grants, and unspecified assistantships also available. Support available to part-time students. Financial award application deadline: 4/15; financial award applicants required to submit FAFSA. *Unit head:* Dr. Jennifer Gossett, Graduate Coordinator, 724-357-5608, E-mail: jennifer.gossett@iup.edu.
Website: http://www.iup.edu/grad/criminology/default.aspx

Indiana University–Purdue University Indianapolis, School of Public and Environmental Affairs, Indianapolis, IN 46202. Offers criminal justice and public safety (MS); homeland security and emergency management (Graduate Certificate); library management (Graduate Certificate); nonprofit management (Graduate Certificate); public affairs (MPA); public management (Graduate Certificate); social entrepreneurship: nonprofit and public benefit organizations (Graduate Certificate); JD/MPA; MLS/NMC; MLS/PMC; MPA/MA. *Accreditation:* CAHME (one or more programs are accredited); NASPAA. Part-time and evening/weekend programs available. Postbaccalaureate distance learning degree programs offered (no on-campus study). *Entrance requirements:* For master's, GRE General Test, GMAT or LSAT, minimum GPA of 3.0 (preferred). Additional exam requirements/recommendations for international students: Required—TOEFL (minimum score 93 iBT), IELTS (minimum score 6.5). Electronic applications accepted. *Faculty research:* Nonprofit and public management, public policy, urban policy, sustainability policy, disaster preparedness and recovery, vehicular safety, homicide, offender rehabilitation and re-entry.

Inter American University of Puerto Rico, Aguadilla Campus, Graduate School, Aguadilla, PR 00605. Offers accounting (MBA); counseling psychology specializing in family (MS); criminal justice (MA); educative management and leadership (MA); elementary education (M Ed); finance (MBA); human resources (MBA); industrial management (MBA); management information systems (MBA); marketing (MBA). Part-time and evening/weekend programs available. *Degree requirements:* For master's, comprehensive exam. *Entrance requirements:* For master's, EXADEP, 2 letters of recommendation, minimum GPA of 2.5. Electronic applications accepted.

Inter American University of Puerto Rico, Metropolitan Campus, Graduate Programs, Program in Criminal Justice, San Juan, PR 00919-1293. Offers MA. Part-time and evening/weekend programs available. *Degree requirements:* For master's, comprehensive exam. *Entrance requirements:* For master's, GRE or EXADEP, interview. Electronic applications accepted.

Inter American University of Puerto Rico, Ponce Campus, Graduate School, Mercedita, PR 00715-1602. Offers accounting (MBA); biology (M Ed); chemistry (M Ed); criminal justice (MA); elementary education (M Ed); English as a Second Language (M Ed); finance (MBA); history (M Ed); human resources (MBA); marketing (MBA); mathematics (M Ed); Spanish (M Ed). *Entrance requirements:* For master's, minimum GPA of 2.5.

Iona College, School of Arts and Science, Department of Criminal Justice, New Rochelle, NY 10801-1890. Offers forensic criminology (Certificate). Part-time and evening/weekend programs available. *Faculty:* 2 full-time (0 women), 4 part-time/adjunct (1 woman). *Students:* 17 full-time (12 women), 11 part-time (4 women); includes 12 minority (5 Black or African American, non-Hispanic/Latino; 6 Hispanic/Latino; 1 Two or more races, non-Hispanic/Latino). Average age 29. 10 applicants, 100% accepted, 7 enrolled. In 2014, 6 master's awarded. *Degree requirements:* For master's, thesis (for some programs), thesis or literature review. *Entrance requirements:* For master's, minimum GPA of 3.0. Additional exam requirements/recommendations for international students: Required—TOEFL (minimum score 550 paper-based; 80 iBT), IELTS (minimum score 6.5). *Application deadline:* For fall admission, 8/1 priority date for domestic students, 5/1 priority date for international students; for spring admission, 1/1 priority date for domestic students, 9/1 priority date for international students. Applications are processed on a rolling basis. Application fee: $50. Electronic applications accepted. *Expenses: Tuition:* Part-time $985 per credit. *Required fees:* $245 per term. *Financial support:* In 2014–15, 3 students received support. Unspecified assistantships available. Financial award application deadline: 4/15; financial award applicants required to submit FAFSA. *Faculty research:* Juvenile justice, criminology, victimology, policing, social justice, security threat assessment. *Unit head:* Cathryn Lavery, PhD, Chair, 914-633-2597, E-mail: clavery@iona.edu. *Application contact:* Frank Boughner, Director, Graduate Admissions, 914-633-2420, Fax: 914-633-2277, E-mail: fboughner@iona.edu.
Website: http://www.iona.edu/Academics/School-of-Arts-Science/Departments/Criminal-Justice/Graduate-Programs.aspx

Jackson State University, Graduate School, College of Liberal Arts, Department of Sociology, Jackson, MS 39217. Offers criminology and justice services (MA); sociology (MA). Part-time and evening/weekend programs available. *Degree requirements:* For master's, comprehensive exam, thesis or alternative. *Entrance requirements:* For master's, GRE General Test. Additional exam requirements/recommendations for international students: Required—TOEFL (minimum score 520 paper-based; 67 iBT).

Jacksonville State University, College of Graduate Studies and Continuing Education, College of Arts and Sciences, Department of Criminal Justice, Jacksonville, AL 36265-1602. Offers MS. Part-time and evening/weekend programs available. *Faculty:* 3 full-time (0 women), 1 (woman) part-time/adjunct. *Students:* 9 full-time (3 women), 16 part-time (10 women); includes 15 minority (13 Black or African American, non-Hispanic/Latino; 1 American Indian or Alaska Native, non-Hispanic/Latino; 1 Hispanic/Latino). Average age 30. 20 applicants, 55% accepted, 9 enrolled. In 2014, 13 master's awarded. *Degree requirements:* For master's, comprehensive exam, thesis (for some programs). *Entrance requirements:* For master's, GRE General Test or MAT. Additional exam requirements/recommendations for international students: Required—TOEFL (minimum score 500 paper-based; 61 iBT). *Application deadline:* Applications are processed on a rolling basis. Application fee: $35. Electronic applications accepted. *Financial support:* In 2014–15, 6 students received support. Available to part-time students. Application deadline: 4/1; applicants required to submit FAFSA. *Unit head:* Dr. Richard Davis, Head, 256-782-5347, E-mail: rpdavis@jsu.edu. *Application contact:* Dr. Jean Pugliese, Associate Dean, 256-782-5329, Fax: 256-782-5321, E-mail: pugliese@jsu.edu.

John Jay College of Criminal Justice of the City University of New York, Graduate Studies, Program in Protection Management, New York, NY 10019-1093. Offers MS. Part-time and evening/weekend programs available. *Degree requirements:* For master's, thesis or alternative. *Entrance requirements:* For master's, minimum B average. Additional exam requirements/recommendations for international students: Required—TOEFL (minimum score 500 paper-based).

John Jay College of Criminal Justice of the City University of New York, Graduate Studies, Programs in Criminal Justice, New York, NY 10019-1093. Offers criminal justice (MA, PhD); criminology and deviance (PhD); forensic psychology (PhD); forensic science (PhD); international crime and justice (MA); law and philosophy (PhD); organizational behavior (PhD); public policy (PhD). Part-time and evening/weekend programs available. Terminal master's awarded for partial completion of doctoral program. *Degree requirements:* For master's, thesis or alternative; for doctorate, one foreign language, thesis/dissertation. *Entrance requirements:* For master's, GRE General Test, minimum B average; for doctorate, GRE General Test. Additional exam requirements/recommendations for international students: Required—TOEFL (minimum score 500 paper-based).

Johnson & Wales University, Graduate School, MS Program in Criminal Justice Management, Providence, RI 02903-3703. Offers MS.

Kaplan University, Davenport Campus, School of Criminal Justice, Davenport, IA 52807-2095. Offers corrections (MSCJ); global issues in criminal justice (MSCJ); law (MSCJ); leadership and executive management (MSCJ); policing (MSCJ). Part-time and evening/weekend programs available. Postbaccalaureate distance learning degree programs offered (no on-campus study). *Entrance requirements:* Additional exam requirements/recommendations for international students: Required—TOEFL (minimum score 550 paper-based; 80 iBT). Electronic applications accepted.

Kean University, College of Business and Public Management, Program in Criminal Justice, Union, NJ 07083. Offers MA. Part-time programs available. *Faculty:* 14 full-time (4 women). *Students:* 9 full-time (3 women), 9 part-time (3 women); includes 16 minority (7 Black or African American, non-Hispanic/Latino; 1 Asian, non-Hispanic/Latino; 8 Hispanic/Latino). Average age 33. 9 applicants, 78% accepted, 7 enrolled. In 2014, 3 master's awarded. *Degree requirements:* For master's, comprehensive exam, thesis optional. *Entrance requirements:* For master's, GRE (minimum Analytic Writing score of 3.5), 3 reference letters, minimum GPA of 3.0, writing sample, official transcripts from all institutions attended, personal statement, resume, sample of scholarly work from undergraduate studies. Additional exam requirements/recommendations for international students: Required—TOEFL (minimum score 550 paper-based; 79 iBT). *Application deadline:* For fall admission, 6/1 for domestic and international students; for spring admission, 12/1 for domestic and international students. Applications are processed on a rolling basis. Application fee: $75 ($150 for international students). Electronic applications accepted. *Expenses:* Tuition, state resident: full-time $12,461; part-time $607 per credit. Tuition, nonresident: full-time $16,889; part-time $744 per credit. *Required fees:* $3141; $143 per credit. Tuition and fees vary according to course load, degree level and program. *Financial support:* In 2014–15, 3 research assistantships with full tuition reimbursements (averaging $3,742 per year) were awarded; scholarships/grants and unspecified assistantships also available. Financial award applicants required to submit FAFSA. *Unit head:* Dr. Pat McManimon, Program

Coordinator, 908-737-4309, E-mail: pmcmanim@kean.edu. *Application contact:* Steven Koch, Admissions Coordinator, 908-737-7136, Fax: 908-737-7135, E-mail: skoch@kean.edu.
Website: http://grad.kean.edu/masters-programs/criminal-justice

Keiser University, MA in Criminal Justice-Homeland Security Program, Ft. Lauderdale, FL 33309. Offers MA.

Keiser University, MA in Criminal Justice Program, Ft. Lauderdale, FL 33309. Offers MA. Part-time programs available. Postbaccalaureate distance learning degree programs offered (no on-campus study).

Kennesaw State University, College of Humanities and Social Sciences, Program in Criminal Justice, Kennesaw, GA 30144. Offers MS. Part-time programs available. *Students:* 13 full-time (7 women), 17 part-time (13 women); includes 16 minority (9 Black or African American, non-Hispanic/Latino; 1 Asian, non-Hispanic/Latino; 4 Hispanic/Latino; 2 Two or more races, non-Hispanic/Latino), 1 international. Average age 28. 17 applicants, 71% accepted, 9 enrolled. In 2014, 2 master's awarded. *Degree requirements:* For master's, research project or thesis. *Entrance requirements:* For master's, GRE. Additional exam requirements/recommendations for international students: Required—TOEFL (minimum score 550 paper-based; 80 iBT), IELTS (minimum score 6.5). *Application deadline:* For fall admission, 6/1 for domestic and international students; for spring admission, 11/1 for domestic and international students. Applications are processed on a rolling basis. Application fee: $60. Electronic applications accepted. *Expenses:* Tuition, state resident: part-time $275 per semester hour. Tuition, nonresident: part-time $990 per semester hour. *Financial support:* In 2014–15, 2 research assistantships with full tuition reimbursements (averaging $8,000 per year) were awarded; unspecified assistantships also available. Financial award application deadline: 4/1; financial award applicants required to submit FAFSA. *Unit head:* Dr. Sutham Cobkit, Director, 470-578-4734, Fax: 770-499-3423, E-mail: scobkit@kennesaw.edu. *Application contact:* Admissions Counselor, 470-578-4377, Fax: 470-578-9172, E-mail: ksugrad@kennesaw.edu.
Website: http://scj.hss.kennesaw.edu/programs/mscj/

Keuka College, Program in Criminal Justice Administration, Keuka Park, NY 14478-0098. Offers MS. Part-time and evening/weekend programs available. *Faculty:* 6 part-time/adjunct (2 women). *Students:* 9 full-time (3 women). 89 applicants, 100% accepted. In 2014, 9 master's awarded. *Application deadline:* For fall admission, 8/15 for domestic students; for winter admission, 12/15 for domestic students; for spring admission, 4/15 for domestic students. Application fee: $30. *Expenses:* Expenses: Contact institution. *Unit head:* Dr. Tom Tremer, Program Director, 315-279-5672, E-mail: ttremer@mail.keuka.edu. *Application contact:* Fred Hoyle, Dean of Enrollment, 315-279-5413, Fax: 315-279-5386, E-mail: admissions@mail.keuka.edu.

Lamar University, College of Graduate Studies, College of Arts and Sciences, Department of Sociology, Social Work, and Criminal Justice, Beaumont, TX 77710. Offers criminal justice (MS). Part-time programs available. *Faculty:* 5 full-time (1 woman). *Students:* 10 full-time (8 women), 117 part-time (66 women); includes 92 minority (62 Black or African American, non-Hispanic/Latino; 1 American Indian or Alaska Native, non-Hispanic/Latino; 27 Hispanic/Latino; 2 Two or more races, non-Hispanic/Latino). Average age 35. 116 applicants, 81% accepted, 18 enrolled. In 2014, 8 master's awarded. *Degree requirements:* For master's, thesis or alternative, applied projects. *Entrance requirements:* For master's, GRE General Test. Additional exam requirements/recommendations for international students: Required—TOEFL (minimum score 550 paper-based; 79 iBT), IELTS (minimum score 6.5). *Application deadline:* For fall admission, 8/10 for domestic students, 7/1 for international students; for spring admission, 1/5 for domestic students, 12/1 for international students. Applications are processed on a rolling basis. Application fee: $25 ($50 for international students). *Expenses:* Tuition, state resident: full-time $5724; part-time $1908 per semester. Tuition, nonresident: full-time $12,240; part-time $4080 per semester. *Required fees:* $1940; $318 per credit hour. *Financial support:* In 2014–15, 3 fellowships with partial tuition reimbursements (averaging $1,000 per year) were awarded; career-related internships or fieldwork, Federal Work-Study, and scholarships/grants also available. Support available to part-time students. Financial award application deadline: 4/1; financial award applicants required to submit FAFSA. *Faculty research:* Corrections, planning and evaluations, juveniles, terrorism, Mexican criminal justice. *Unit head:* Dr. Stuart Wright, Chair, 409-880-8542, Fax: 409-880-2324. *Application contact:* Melissa Gallien, Director, Admissions and Academic Services, 409-880-8888, Fax: 409-880-7419, E-mail: gradmissions@lamar.edu.
Website: http://artssciences.lamar.edu/sociology-social-work-criminal-justice

Lewis University, College of Arts and Sciences, Program in Criminal/Social Justice, Romeoville, IL 60446. Offers MS. Part-time and evening/weekend programs available. *Students:* 9 full-time (5 women), 88 part-time (37 women); includes 35 minority (20 Black or African American, non-Hispanic/Latino; 1 American Indian or Alaska Native, non-Hispanic/Latino; 1 Asian, non-Hispanic/Latino; 12 Hispanic/Latino; 1 Two or more races, non-Hispanic/Latino), 1 international. Average age 32. *Entrance requirements:* For master's, bachelor's degree or a minimum of 12 related hours in criminal/social justice, 2 letters of recommendation, minimum GPA of 3.0, interview. Additional exam requirements/recommendations for international students: Required—TOEFL (minimum score 550 paper-based; 80 iBT). *Application deadline:* For fall admission, 5/1 priority date for international students; for spring admission, 11/15 priority date for international students. Applications are processed on a rolling basis. Application fee: $40. Electronic applications accepted. *Financial support:* Federal Work-Study, scholarships/grants, tuition waivers (full and partial), and unspecified assistantships available. Financial award application deadline: 5/1; financial award applicants required to submit FAFSA. *Faculty research:* Community policing, management, terrorism, biological warfare, drugs. *Unit head:* Dr. Calvin Edwards, Chair of Justice, Law and Public Safety Studies, 815-838-0500, Fax: 815-836-5870, E-mail: koloshsa@lewisu.edu. *Application contact:* Michelle Mega, Coordinator, 815-838-0500 Ext. 5342, Fax: 815-836-5342, E-mail: megami@lewisu.edu.
Website: http://www.lewisu.edu/academics/masterscrim/index.htm

Liberty University, Helms School of Government, Lynchburg, VA 24515. Offers criminal justice (MS); public policy (MA), including campaigns and elections, international affairs, Middle East affairs, public administration, public policy. Part-time programs available. Postbaccalaureate distance learning degree programs offered (no on-campus study). *Students:* 248 full-time (119 women), 522 part-time (209 women); includes 194 minority (157 Black or African American, non-Hispanic/Latino; 8 American Indian or Alaska Native, non-Hispanic/Latino; 7 Asian, non-Hispanic/Latino; 5 Hispanic/Latino; 1 Native Hawaiian or other Pacific Islander, non-Hispanic/Latino; 16 Two or more races, non-Hispanic/Latino), 14 international. Average age 34. 837 applicants, 55% accepted, 226 enrolled. In 2014, 65 degrees awarded. *Entrance requirements:* For master's, minimum undergraduate GPA of 3.0. Additional exam requirements/recommendations for international students: Required—TOEFL (minimum score 600 paper-based; 100 iBT). *Application deadline:* Applications are processed on a rolling basis. Application fee: $50. Electronic applications accepted. *Unit head:* Shawn D. Akers, Dean, 434-592-4986. *Application contact:* Jay Bridge, Director of Admissions, 800-424-9595, Fax: 800-628-7977, E-mail: gradadmissions@liberty.edu.

Liberty University, School of Behavioral Sciences, Lynchburg, VA 24515. Offers advanced clinical skills (PhD); clinical mental health counseling (MA); counselor education and supervision (PhD); human services counseling (MA), including addictions and recovery, business, child and family law, Christian ministries, criminal justice, crisis response and trauma, executive leadership, health and wellness, life coaching, marriage and family, military resilience; marriage and family therapy (MA); military resilience (Certificate); professional counseling (MA). Part-time programs available. Postbaccalaureate distance learning degree programs offered (minimal on-campus study). *Students:* 3,009 full-time (2,433 women), 6,251 part-time (4,981 women); includes 2,959 minority (2,520 Black or African American, non-Hispanic/Latino; 49 American Indian or Alaska Native, non-Hispanic/Latino; 51 Asian, non-Hispanic/Latino; 97 Hispanic/Latino; 9 Native Hawaiian or other Pacific Islander, non-Hispanic/Latino; 233 Two or more races, non-Hispanic/Latino), 153 international. Average age 38. 6,645 applicants, 55% accepted, 2039 enrolled. In 2014, 2,410 master's, 11 doctorates, 2 other advanced degrees awarded. *Application deadline:* Applications are processed on a rolling basis. Application fee: $50. Electronic applications accepted. *Financial support:* Applicants required to submit FAFSA. *Unit head:* Dr. Ronald Hawkins, Founding Dean, School of Behavioral Sciences. *Application contact:* Jay Bridge, Director of Admissions, 800-424-9595, Fax: 800-628-7977, E-mail: gradadmissions@liberty.edu.

Liberty University, School of Business, Lynchburg, VA 24515. Offers accounting (MBA, MS, DBA); business administration (MBA); criminal justice (MBA); cyber security (MS); executive leadership (MA); healthcare (MBA); human resources (DBA); information systems (MS), including information assurance, technology management; international business (MBA, DBA); leadership (MBA, DBA); marketing (MBA, MS, DBA), including digital marketing and advertising (MS), project management (MS), public relations (MS), sports marketing and media (MS); project management (MBA, DBA); public administration (MBA); public relations (MBA). Part-time programs available. Postbaccalaureate distance learning degree programs offered (minimal on-campus study). *Students:* 1,520 full-time (813 women), 4,179 part-time (1,982 women); includes 1,402 minority (1,110 Black or African American, non-Hispanic/Latino; 30 American Indian or Alaska Native, non-Hispanic/Latino; 82 Asian, non-Hispanic/Latino; 59 Hispanic/Latino; 7 Native Hawaiian or other Pacific Islander, non-Hispanic/Latino; 114 Two or more races, non-Hispanic/Latino), 119 international. Average age 35. 5,645 applicants, 49% accepted, 1445 enrolled. In 2014, 1,474 master's, 63 other advanced degrees awarded. *Entrance requirements:* For master's, minimum undergraduate GPA of 3.0, 15 hours of upper-level business courses. Additional exam requirements/recommendations for international students: Required—TOEFL (minimum score 600 paper-based; 100 iBT). *Application deadline:* Applications are processed on a rolling basis. Application fee: $50. Electronic applications accepted. *Expenses:* Expenses: Contact institution. *Unit head:* Dr. Scott Hicks, Dean, 434-592-4808, Fax: 434-582-2366, E-mail: smhicks@liberty.edu. *Application contact:* Jay Bridge, Director of Graduate Admissions, 800-424-9595, Fax: 800-628-7977, E-mail: gradadmissions@liberty.edu.
Website: http://www.liberty.edu/academics/business/index.cfm?PID-149

Lincoln University, Graduate Studies, Jefferson City, MO 65101. Offers business administration (MBA), including accounting, entrepreneurship, management, public administration and policy; educational leadership (Ed S), including elementary leadership, secondary leadership, superintendency; guidance and counseling (M Ed), including community/agency counseling, elementary school, secondary school; history (MA); school administration and supervision (M Ed), including elementary school administration, secondary school administration, special education administration; school teaching (M Ed), including elementary school teaching, secondary school teaching; sociology (MA); sociology/criminal justice (MA). Part-time and evening/weekend programs available. Postbaccalaureate distance learning degree programs offered (minimal on-campus study). *Students:* 57 full-time (35 women), 83 part-time (50 women); includes 64 minority (47 Black or African American, non-Hispanic/Latino; 1 American Indian or Alaska Native, non-Hispanic/Latino; 14 Asian, non-Hispanic/Latino; 1 Hispanic/Latino; 1 Two or more races, non-Hispanic/Latino), 9 international. Average age 33. 60 applicants, 68% accepted, 31 enrolled. In 2014, 52 master's, 2 other advanced degrees awarded. *Degree requirements:* For master's and Ed S, comprehensive exam, thesis optional. *Entrance requirements:* For master's and Ed S, GRE, MAT or GMAT, minimum GPA of 2.75 in major, 2.5 overall; 3 letters of recommendation; minimum C average in English composition; personal statement of purpose. Additional exam requirements/recommendations for international students: Required—TOEFL (minimum score 500 paper-based; 61 iBT). *Application deadline:* For fall admission, 8/1 priority date for domestic and international students; for spring admission, 12/1 priority date for domestic and international students; for summer admission, 5/1 priority date for domestic and international students. Applications are processed on a rolling basis. Application fee: $30. *Expenses:* Tuition, state resident: full-time $6840; part-time $285 per credit hour. Tuition, nonresident: full-time $12,720; part-time $530 per credit hour. *Required fees:* $737; $737 per year. *Financial support:* In 2014–15, 1 fellowship with tuition reimbursement, 11 research assistantships with tuition reimbursements were awarded; Federal Work-Study and scholarships/grants also available. Support available to part-time students. Financial award application deadline: 3/1; financial award applicants required to submit FAFSA. *Unit head:* Dr. Linda S. Bickel, Dean, 573-681-5247, Fax: 573-681-5106, E-mail: gradschool@lincolnu.edu. *Application contact:* Irasema Steck, Administrative Assistant, 573-681-5247, Fax: 573-681-5106, E-mail: gradschool@lincolnu.edu.
Website: http://www.lincolnu.edu/web/graduate-studies/graduate-studies

Lindenwood University, Graduate Programs, School of Accelerated Degree Programs, St. Charles, MO 63301-1695. Offers administration (MSA); business administration (MBA); communications (MA); criminal justice and administration (MS); gerontology (MA); healthcare administration (MS); human resource management (MS); information technology (Certificate); managing information technology (MS); writing (MFA). Part-time and evening/weekend programs available. Postbaccalaureate distance learning degree programs offered (no on-campus study). *Faculty:* 22 full-time (9 women), 96 part-time/adjunct (34 women). *Students:* 811 full-time (488 women), 169 part-time (113 women); includes 374 minority (312 Black or African American, non-Hispanic/Latino; 6 American Indian or Alaska Native, non-Hispanic/Latino; 8 Asian, non-Hispanic/Latino; 26 Hispanic/Latino; 22 Two or more races, non-Hispanic/Latino), 25 international. Average age 35. 891 applicants, 65% accepted, 513 enrolled. In 2014, 498 master's awarded. *Degree requirements:* For master's, thesis (for some programs), minimum cumulative GPA of 3.0. *Entrance requirements:* For master's, interview, minimum GPA of 3.0. Additional exam requirements/recommendations for international students: Required—TOEFL (minimum score 550 paper-based; 80 iBT). *Application deadline:* For fall admission, 10/3 priority date for domestic and international students; for winter admission, 1/4 priority date for domestic and international students; for spring admission, 4/5 priority date for domestic and international students. Applications are processed on a rolling basis. Application fee: $30 ($100 for international students). Electronic applications accepted. *Expenses: Tuition:* Full-time $15,230; part-time $440 per credit hour. *Required fees:* $205 per semester. Tuition and fees vary according to course level, course load and degree level. *Financial support:* In 2014–15, 479 students received support. Career-related internships or fieldwork, institutionally sponsored loans, scholarships/grants, tuition waivers (partial), and unspecified assistantships available. Financial award application deadline: 6/30; financial award applicants required

to submit FAFSA. *Unit head:* Dr. Gina Ganahl, Dean, 636-949-4501, Fax: 636-949-4505, E-mail: gganahl@lindenwood.edu. *Application contact:* Tyler Kostich, Director of Evening and Graduate Admissions, 636-949-4138, Fax: 636-949-4109, E-mail: adultadmissions@lindenwood.edu.
Website: http://www.lindenwood.edu/lead/

Lindenwood University–Belleville, Graduate Programs, Belleville, IL 62226. Offers business administration (MBA); communications (MA), including digital and multimedia, media management, promotions, training and development; counseling (MA); criminal justice administration (MS); education (MA); healthcare administration (MS); human resource management (MS); school administration (MA); teaching (MAT).

Long Island University–Brentwood Campus, College of Liberal Arts and Sciences, Brentwood, NY 11717. Offers criminal justice (MS); healthcare administration (MPA). Part-time programs available. *Students:* 1 part-time (0 women). Average age 36. 2 applicants. In 2014, 6 master's awarded. *Entrance requirements:* Additional exam requirements/recommendations for international students: Required—TOEFL (minimum score 79 iBT), IELTS. *Application deadline:* Applications are processed on a rolling basis. Application fee: $50. Electronic applications accepted. *Expenses: Tuition:* Part-time $1132 per credit hour. *Required fees:* $434 per semester. *Financial support:* Federal Work-Study, scholarships/grants, and unspecified assistantships available. Financial award applicants required to submit FAFSA. *Unit head:* Dr. Donna Di Donato, Dean and Chief Operating Officer LIU Brentwoood, 631-287 8010, Fax: 631-287 8575. *Application contact:* Christina Seifert, Director of Admissions LIU Brentwood, 631-287 8505 Ext. 26, Fax: 631-2878575, E-mail: christina.seifert@liu.edu.
Website: http://liu.edu/brentwood

Longwood University, College of Graduate and Professional Studies, Department of Sociology, Anthropology, and Criminal Justice Studies, Farmville, VA 23909. Offers criminal justice and social policy (MS). Part-time and evening/weekend programs available. *Faculty:* 11 full-time (5 women), 2 part-time/adjunct (0 women). *Students:* 5 full-time (3 women), 2 part-time (1 woman); includes 1 minority (Hispanic/Latino). 7 applicants, 71% accepted, 1 enrolled. In 2014, 3 master's awarded. *Degree requirements:* For master's, comprehensive exam (for some programs), thesis (for some programs). *Entrance requirements:* For master's, minimum GPA of 2.75, bachelor's degree from regionally-accredited institution, 2 recommendations, 500-word personal essay, official transcripts. Additional exam requirements/recommendations for international students: Required—TOEFL (minimum score 570 paper-based), IELTS (minimum score 6.5). *Application deadline:* For fall admission, 5/1 priority date for domestic students; for spring admission, 10/1 priority date for domestic students; for summer admission, 2/1 priority date for domestic students. Applications are processed on a rolling basis. Application fee: $50. Electronic applications accepted. *Expenses:* Tuition, state resident: part-time $430 per credit hour. Tuition, nonresident: part-time $1001 per credit hour. Tuition and fees vary according to campus/location and program. *Financial support:* Career-related internships or fieldwork and Federal Work-Study available. Financial award applicants required to submit FAFSA. *Unit head:* Dr. William C. Burger, Graduate Program Coordinator - Sociology/Criminal Justice & Social Policy, 434-395-2247, E-mail: burgerwc@longwood.edu. *Application contact:* College of Graduate and Professional Studies, 434-395-2380, Fax: 434-395-2750, E-mail: graduate@longwood.edu.
Website: http://www.longwood.edu/sacjs/

Loyola University Chicago, Graduate School, Department of Criminal Justice and Criminology, Chicago, IL 60660. Offers MA. Part-time and evening/weekend programs available. *Faculty:* 8 full-time (1 woman), 12 part-time/adjunct (1 woman). *Students:* 14 full-time (9 women), 5 part-time (3 women); includes 7 minority (3 Black or African American, non-Hispanic/Latino; 3 Hispanic/Latino; 1 Two or more races, non-Hispanic/Latino). Average age 26. 36 applicants, 58% accepted, 14 enrolled. In 2014, 16 master's awarded. *Degree requirements:* For master's, thesis or alternative, comprehensive exams. *Entrance requirements:* For master's, GRE, minimum GPA of 3.0. Additional exam requirements/recommendations for international students: Required—TOEFL (minimum score 550 paper-based). *Application deadline:* For fall admission, 2/1 priority date for domestic students. Application fee: $50. Electronic applications accepted. Application fee is waived when completed online. *Expenses: Tuition:* Full-time $17,370; part-time $965 per credit. *Required fees:* $138 per semester. *Financial support:* In 2014–15, 1 student received support, including research assistantships with partial tuition reimbursements available (averaging $7,800 per year); career-related internships or fieldwork and scholarships/grants also available. Financial award application deadline: 2/1; financial award applicants required to submit FAFSA. *Faculty research:* Crime and delinquency causation, effectiveness and efficiency of criminal justice system. *Total annual research expenditures:* $120,000. *Unit head:* Dr. Deborah Baskin, Chair, 312-915-7568, Fax: 312-915-7650, E-mail: dbaskin@luc.edu. *Application contact:* Dr. Loretta Stalans, Graduate Program Director, 312-915-7567, Fax: 312-915-7650, E-mail: lstalan@luc.edu.

Loyola University New Orleans, College of Social Sciences, Program in Criminal Justice, New Orleans, LA 70118-6195. Offers MCJ. Part-time and evening/weekend programs available. *Faculty:* 6 full-time (2 women), 17 part-time/adjunct (7 women). *Students:* 34 full-time (27 women), 38 part-time (22 women); includes 32 minority (20 Black or African American, non-Hispanic/Latino; 1 American Indian or Alaska Native, non-Hispanic/Latino; 1 Asian, non-Hispanic/Latino; 10 Hispanic/Latino). Average age 33. 37 applicants, 73% accepted, 24 enrolled. In 2014, 34 master's awarded. *Degree requirements:* For master's, comprehensive exam, research and practicum. *Entrance requirements:* For master's, GRE, resume, interview, letters of recommendation, work experience, transcript from accredited university. Additional exam requirements/recommendations for international students: Required—TOEFL (minimum score 550 paper-based). *Application deadline:* For fall admission, 8/1 priority date for domestic and international students; for spring admission, 1/5 priority date for domestic and international students. Applications are processed on a rolling basis. Application fee: $20. Electronic applications accepted. Application fee is waived when completed online. *Expenses:* Expenses: Contact institution. *Financial support:* In 2014–15, 3 research assistantships (averaging $4,000 per year) were awarded; scholarships/grants and unspecified assistantships also available. Financial award application deadline: 5/1; financial award applicants required to submit FAFSA. *Faculty research:* Physical and social aspects of disasters, reconciling interpretations of gang behaviors and processes with viewpoints of actual gang members, examining the social network dynamics of deviant populations, investigating the future of criminal innovation, navigating racial/ethnic dynamics in criminology, human trafficking, criminology and forensic science. *Unit head:* Dr. William E. Thornton, Chair, 504-865-3323, Fax: 504-865-3883, E-mail: crimjust@loyno.edu. *Application contact:* Clarissa Koederitz, Executive Assistant to the Chair, 504-865-3323, Fax: 504-865-3883, E-mail: crimjust@loyno.edu.
Website: http://css.loyno.edu/criminaljustice/master-of-criminal-justice

Lynn University, College of Arts and Sciences, Boca Raton, FL 33431-5598. Offers applied psychology (MS); criminal justice administration (MS); emergency planning and administration (MS). Part-time and evening/weekend programs available. Postbaccalaureate distance learning degree programs offered (no on-campus study). *Faculty:* 4 full-time (2 women), 10 part-time/adjunct (8 women). *Students:* 77 full-time (58 women), 36 part-time (21 women); includes 23 minority (12 Black or African American, non-Hispanic/Latino; 2 Asian, non-Hispanic/Latino; 9 Hispanic/Latino), 11 international. Average age 32. 103 applicants, 96% accepted, 71 enrolled. In 2014, 27 master's awarded. *Degree requirements:* For master's, comprehensive exam (for some programs), thesis (for some programs). *Entrance requirements:* For master's, bachelor's degree from accredited institution, resume, letter of recommendation, essay of professional goals, official transcripts. Additional exam requirements/recommendations for international students: Required—TOEFL (minimum score 550 paper-based; 80 iBT), IELTS (minimum score 6.5). *Application deadline:* For fall admission, 8/17 for domestic students, 8/3 for international students; for spring admission, 12/15 for domestic students, 11/24 for international students; for summer admission, 4/17 for domestic students, 4/6 for international students. Applications are processed on a rolling basis. Application fee: $45. Electronic applications accepted. *Expenses: Tuition:* Full-time $16,200; part-time $675 per credit hour. Tuition and fees vary according to class time, course load, degree level and program. *Financial support:* In 2014–15, 33 students received support. Career-related internships or fieldwork, Federal Work-Study, scholarships/grants, tuition waivers (full and partial), and unspecified assistantships available. Support available to part-time students. Financial award application deadline: 3/1; financial award applicants required to submit FAFSA. *Faculty research:* Terrorism, criminological theory, corrections, emergency planning, counseling. *Unit head:* Dr. Katrina Carter-Tellison, Dean, 561-237-7412, E-mail: kcartertellison@lynn.edu. *Application contact:* Steven Pruitt, Director of Graduate Admission, 561-237-7834, Fax: 561-237-7100, E-mail: admissionpm@lynn.edu.
Website: http://www.lynn.edu/academics/colleges/arts-and-sciences/

Madonna University, School of Business, Livonia, MI 48150-1173. Offers business administration (MBA); international business (MSBA); leadership studies (MSBA); leadership studies in criminal justice (MSBA); quality and operations management (MSBA). Part-time and evening/weekend programs available. Postbaccalaureate distance learning degree programs offered (minimal on-campus study). *Degree requirements:* For master's, thesis (for some programs), foreign language proficiency (international business). *Entrance requirements:* For master's, GMAT, GRE General Test, minimum GPA of 3.0. Electronic applications accepted. *Faculty research:* Management, women in management, future studies.

Marian University, School of Business and Public Safety, Fond du Lac, WI 54935-4699. Offers criminal justice leadership (MS); organizational leadership and quality (MS). Part-time and evening/weekend programs available. *Faculty:* 7 part-time/adjunct (2 women). *Students:* 51 part-time (31 women); includes 2 minority (1 Asian, non-Hispanic/Latino; 1 Two or more races, non-Hispanic/Latino). Average age 37. In 2014, 32 master's awarded. *Degree requirements:* For master's, comprehensive group project. *Entrance requirements:* For master's, 3 years of managerial experience, minimum GPA of 2.75, letters of professional reference. Additional exam requirements/recommendations for international students: Required—TOEFL (minimum score 525 paper-based; 70 iBT). *Application deadline:* Applications are processed on a rolling basis. Application fee: $25. Electronic applications accepted. *Expenses:* Expenses: Contact institution. *Financial support:* In 2014–15, 1 student received support. Institutionally sponsored loans available. Financial award application deadline: 3/1; financial award applicants required to submit FAFSA. *Faculty research:* Organizational values, statistical decision-making, learning organization, quality planning, customer research. *Unit head:* Dr. Jeffrey G. Reed, Dean, Marian School of Business, 920-923-8759, Fax: 920-923-7167, E-mail: jreed@marianuniversity.edu. *Application contact:* Jordan Baitinger, Admission Counselor, 920-923-8609, Fax: 920-923-7167, E-mail: jlbaitinger16@marianuniversity.edu.

Marquette University, Graduate School, College of Professional Studies, Milwaukee, WI 53201-1881. Offers criminal justice administration (MLS, Certificate); dispute resolution (MDR, MLS); health care administration (MLS); leadership studies (Certificate); non-profit sector administration (MLS); public service (MAPS, MLS); sports leadership (MLS). Part-time and evening/weekend programs available. Postbaccalaureate distance learning degree programs offered (no on-campus study). *Degree requirements:* For master's, comprehensive exam (for some programs). *Entrance requirements:* For master's, GRE General Test (preferred), GMAT, or LSAT, official transcripts from all current and previous colleges/universities except Marquette, three letters of recommendation, statement of purpose. Additional exam requirements/recommendations for international students: Required—TOEFL. Electronic applications accepted.

Marshall University, Academic Affairs Division, College of Science, Department of Criminal Justice, Huntington, WV 25755. Offers MS. Evening/weekend programs available. *Students:* 10 full-time (8 women), 2 part-time (1 woman); includes 2 minority (1 Black or African American, non-Hispanic/Latino; 1 Asian, non-Hispanic/Latino). Average age 27. In 2014, 4 master's awarded. *Degree requirements:* For master's, thesis optional. *Entrance requirements:* For master's, GRE General Test. Application fee: $40. *Unit head:* Dr. Brian Morgan, Chair, 304-696-6469, E-mail: morgan16@marshall.edu. *Application contact:* Information Contact, Fax: 304-746-1902, E-mail: services@marshall.edu.

Marywood University, Academic Affairs, Munley College of Liberal Arts and Sciences, Department of Social Sciences, Scranton, PA 18509-1598. Offers criminal justice (MS). *Students:* 12 full-time (9 women), 1 (woman) part-time; includes 3 minority (1 Black or African American, non-Hispanic/Latino; 1 Hispanic/Latino; 1 Native Hawaiian or other Pacific Islander, non-Hispanic/Latino). Average age 27. In 2014, 8 master's awarded. *Application deadline:* For fall admission, 4/1 for domestic students, 3/31 for international students; for spring admission, 11/1 for domestic students, 8/31 for international students. Applications are processed on a rolling basis. Application fee: $35. Electronic applications accepted. *Expenses: Tuition:* Part-time $775 per credit. *Required fees:* $688 per semester. Tuition and fees vary according to degree level and campus/location. *Financial support:* Application deadline: 6/30; applicants required to submit FAFSA. *Unit head:* Dr. Patrick Seffrin, Graduate Program Director, 570-348-6211 Ext. 2582, E-mail: seffrin@marywood.edu. *Application contact:* Tammy Manka, Assistant Director of Graduate Admissions, 570-348-6211 Ext. 2322, E-mail: tmanka@marywood.edu.
Website: http://www.marywood.edu/socsci/

McNeese State University, Doré School of Graduate Studies, College of Liberal Arts, Department of Social Sciences, Lake Charles, LA 70609. Offers criminal justice (MS). *Entrance requirements:* For master's, GRE, minimum undergraduate GPA of 3.0, 3 letters of recommendation, autobiography.

Mercyhurst University, Graduate Studies, Program in Administration of Justice, Erie, PA 16546. Offers administration of justice (MS). Part-time and evening/weekend programs available. *Degree requirements:* For master's, thesis optional. *Entrance requirements:* For master's, GRE, resume, essay, three professional references, transcripts. Additional exam requirements/recommendations for international students: Required—TOEFL. Electronic applications accepted. *Faculty research:* Research methods, criminal justice administration, juvenile justice.

Mercyhurst University, Graduate Studies, Program in Applied Intelligence, Erie, PA 16546. Offers MS, Certificate. *Entrance requirements:* For master's, GRE or MAT, resume, essay, three professional references, transcripts. Additional exam

requirements/recommendations for international students: Required—TOEFL. Electronic applications accepted.

Methodist University, School of Graduate Studies, Program in Justice Administration, Fayetteville, NC 28311-1498. Offers MJA. Part-time and evening/weekend programs available. *Entrance requirements:* For master's, bachelor's degree in criminal justice or related discipline with minimum overall GPA of 3.0 from accredited institution. Additional exam requirements/recommendations for international students: Required—TOEFL (minimum score 500 paper-based; 60 iBT).

Metropolitan State University, School of Law Enforcement and Criminal Justice, St. Paul, MN 55106-5000. Offers criminal justice (MS). Part-time and evening/weekend programs available. *Degree requirements:* For master's, thesis. *Entrance requirements:* For master's, resume, letters of reference, minimum GPA of 3.0. Additional exam requirements/recommendations for international students: Required—TOEFL (minimum score 550 paper-based). Electronic applications accepted.

Michigan State University, The Graduate School, College of Social Science, School of Criminal Justice, East Lansing, MI 48824. Offers criminal justice (MS, PhD); forensic science (MS); law enforcement intelligence and analysis (MS). Postbaccalaureate distance learning degree programs offered. *Entrance requirements:* Additional exam requirements/recommendations for international students: Required—TOEFL. Electronic applications accepted.

Middle Tennessee State University, College of Graduate Studies, College of Behavioral and Health Sciences, Department of Criminal Justice Administration, Murfreesboro, TN 37132. Offers MCJ. Program offered jointly with Tennessee State University. Part-time and evening/weekend programs available. Postbaccalaureate distance learning degree programs offered. *Faculty:* 9 full-time (1 woman), 1 (woman) part-time/adjunct. *Students:* 10 full-time (4 women), 27 part-time (13 women); includes 13 minority (9 Black or African American, non-Hispanic/Latino; 1 American Indian or Alaska Native, non-Hispanic/Latino; 1 Asian, non-Hispanic/Latino; 1 Hispanic/Latino; 1 Two or more races, non-Hispanic/Latino), 1 international. 66 applicants, 58% accepted. In 2014, 2 master's awarded. *Degree requirements:* For master's, comprehensive exam, thesis. *Entrance requirements:* For master's, GRE or MAT. Additional exam requirements/recommendations for international students: Required—TOEFL (minimum score 525 paper-based; 71 iBT) or IELTS (minimum score 6). *Application deadline:* For fall admission, 6/1 for domestic and international students. Applications are processed on a rolling basis. Application fee: $25 ($30 for international students). Electronic applications accepted. *Financial support:* Tuition waivers available. Support available to part-time students. Financial award application deadline: 4/1; financial award applicants required to submit FAFSA. *Unit head:* Dr. Lance Selva, Interim Chair, 615-898-2630, Fax: 615-898-5159, E-mail: lance.selva@mtsu.edu. *Application contact:* Dr. Michael D. Allen, Vice Provost for Research/Dean, 615-898-2840, Fax: 615-904-8020, E-mail: michael.allen@mtsu.edu.

Midwestern State University, Billie Doris McAda Graduate School, Robert D. and Carol Gunn College of Health Sciences and Human Services, Department of Criminal Justice and Health Services Administration, Wichita Falls, TX 76308. Offers criminal justice (MA); health information management (MHA); health services administration (Graduate Certificate); medical practice management (MHA); public and community sector health care management (MHA); rural and urban hospital management (MHA). Part-time and evening/weekend programs available. *Degree requirements:* For master's, comprehensive exam, thesis. *Entrance requirements:* For master's, GRE. Additional exam requirements/recommendations for international students: Required—TOEFL (minimum score 550 paper-based). *Application deadline:* For fall admission, 7/1 priority date for domestic students, 4/1 for international students; for spring admission, 11/1 priority date for domestic students, 8/1 for international students. Applications are processed on a rolling basis. Application fee: $35 ($50 for international students). Electronic applications accepted. *Financial support:* Teaching assistantships with partial tuition reimbursements, career-related internships or fieldwork, Federal Work-Study, institutionally sponsored loans, scholarships/grants, tuition waivers (partial), and unspecified assistantships available. Support available to part-time students. Financial award application deadline: 3/1; financial award applicants required to submit FAFSA. *Faculty research:* Universal service policy, telehealth, bullying, healthcare financial management, public health ethics. *Unit head:* Dr. Nathan Moran, Chair, 940-397-4752, Fax: 940-397-6291, E-mail: nathan.moran@mwsu.edu.
Website: http://www.mwsu.edu/academics/hs2/health-admin/

Mississippi College, Graduate School, College of Arts and Sciences, School of Humanities and Social Sciences, Department of History, Political Science, Administration of Justice, and Paralegal Studies, Clinton, MS 39058. Offers administration of justice (MSS); history (M Ed, MA, MSS); paralegal studies (Certificate); political science (MSS); social sciences (M Ed, MSS). Part-time programs available. *Degree requirements:* For master's, one foreign language, comprehensive exam, thesis (for some programs). *Entrance requirements:* For master's, GRE or NTE, minimum GPA of 2.5. Additional exam requirements/recommendations for international students: Recommended—TOEFL, IELTS. Electronic applications accepted.

Mississippi Valley State University, Department of Criminal Justice and Social Work, Itta Bena, MS 38941-1400. Offers criminal justice (MS). Part-time and evening/weekend programs available. *Degree requirements:* For master's, thesis optional. *Entrance requirements:* For master's, minimum GPA of 2.5. Electronic applications accepted. *Faculty research:* Police in the criminal justice system, the United States and international terrorism.

Missouri Southern State University, Program in Criminal Justice Administration, Joplin, MO 64801-1595. Offers MS. Program offered jointly with Southeast Missouri State University. Postbaccalaureate distance learning degree programs offered. *Degree requirements:* For master's, thesis optional. *Entrance requirements:* For master's, minimum undergraduate GPA of 2.5.

Missouri State University, Graduate College, College of Humanities and Public Affairs, Department of Criminology and Criminal Justice, Springfield, MO 65897. Offers criminology (MS); homeland security and defense (Certificate). Part-time programs available. *Faculty:* 7 full-time (2 women). *Students:* 20 full-time (12 women), 33 part-time (20 women); includes 9 minority (3 Black or African American, non-Hispanic/Latino; 1 American Indian or Alaska Native, non-Hispanic/Latino; 2 Hispanic/Latino; 3 Two or more races, non-Hispanic/Latino). Average age 31. 19 applicants, 95% accepted, 16 enrolled. In 2014, 1 master's awarded. *Degree requirements:* For master's, comprehensive exam, thesis or alternative. *Entrance requirements:* For master's, bachelor's degree in criminology, criminal justice, or sociology; minimum undergraduate GPA of 3.0. Additional exam requirements/recommendations for international students: Required—TOEFL (minimum score 550 paper-based; 79 iBT). *Application deadline:* For fall admission, 7/20 for domestic students, 5/1 for international students; for spring admission, 12/20 for domestic students, 9/1 for international students. Applications are processed on a rolling basis. Application fee: $35 ($50 for international students). Electronic applications accepted. *Expenses:* Tuition, state resident: full-time $2250; part-time $250 per credit hour. Tuition, nonresident: full-time $4509; part-time $501 per credit hour. Tuition and fees vary according to course level, course load and program. *Financial support:* Federal Work-Study, institutionally sponsored loans, and unspecified

assistantships available. Financial award application deadline: 3/1; financial award applicants required to submit FAFSA. *Faculty research:* Homeland security initiatives, juvenile policy and programs, law enforcement and drug abuse. *Unit head:* Dr. Brett Garland, Program Director, 417-836-6954, E-mail: brettgarland@missouristate.edu. *Application contact:* Misty Stewart, Coordinator of Graduate Recruitment, 417-836-6079, Fax: 417-836-6200, E-mail: mistystewart@missouristate.edu.
Website: http://criminology.missouristate.edu/

Missouri State University, Graduate College, Interdisciplinary Program in Administrative Studies, Springfield, MO 65897. Offers applied communication (MS); criminal justice (MS); environmental management (MS); homeland security (MS); sports management (MS). Part-time and evening/weekend programs available. Postbaccalaureate distance learning degree programs offered (no on-campus study). *Students:* 17 full-time (9 women), 64 part-time (29 women); includes 10 minority (4 Black or African American, non-Hispanic/Latino; 1 Asian, non-Hispanic/Latino; 2 Hispanic/Latino; 3 Two or more races, non-Hispanic/Latino), 3 international. Average age 33. 48 applicants, 73% accepted, 21 enrolled. In 2014, 16 master's awarded. *Degree requirements:* For master's, comprehensive exam, thesis or alternative. *Entrance requirements:* For master's, GRE, GMAT if GPA less than 3.0. Additional exam requirements/recommendations for international students: Required—TOEFL (minimum score 550 paper-based; 79 iBT). *Application deadline:* For fall admission, 7/20 priority date for domestic students; for spring admission, 12/20 priority date for domestic students. Applications are processed on a rolling basis. Application fee: $35 ($50 for international students). Electronic applications accepted. *Expenses:* Tuition, state resident: full-time $2250; part-time $250 per credit hour. Tuition, nonresident: full-time $4509; part-time $501 per credit hour. Tuition and fees vary according to course level, course load and program. *Financial support:* Career-related internships or fieldwork, Federal Work-Study, institutionally sponsored loans, scholarships/grants, and unspecified assistantships available. Support available to part-time students. Financial award application deadline: 3/31; financial award applicants required to submit FAFSA. *Unit head:* Dr. Gerald Masterson, Program Coordinator, 417-836-5251, Fax: 417-836-6888, E-mail: msas@missouristate.edu. *Application contact:* Misty Stewart, Coordinator of Graduate Recruitment, 417-836-6079, Fax: 417-836-6200, E-mail: mistystewart@missouristate.edu.
Website: http://msas.missouristate.edu

Molloy College, Criminal Justice Program, Rockville Centre, NY 11571-5002. Offers MS. *Faculty:* 5 full-time (2 women), 2 part-time/adjunct (0 women). *Students:* 20 full-time (12 women), 10 part-time (5 women); includes 13 minority (7 Black or African American, non-Hispanic/Latino; 1 Asian, non-Hispanic/Latino; 4 Hispanic/Latino; 1 Two or more races, non-Hispanic/Latino), 1 international. Average age 28. 9 applicants, 56% accepted, 4 enrolled. In 2014, 20 master's awarded. Application fee: $60. *Expenses: Tuition:* Full-time $17,640; part-time $980 per credit. *Required fees:* $900. *Faculty research:* Police performance management, law and policing, mass murder, human trafficking, comparing police methods at international level. *Unit head:* Dr. John Eterno, Associate Dean/Graduate Program Director, 516-323-3806, E-mail: jeterno@molloy.edu. *Application contact:* Alina Haitz, Assistant Director of Graduate Admissions, 516-323-4008, E-mail: ahaitz@molloy.edu.

Monmouth University, The Graduate School, Department of Criminal Justice, West Long Branch, NJ 07764-1898. Offers criminal justice (MA, Certificate); homeland security (MS, Certificate). Part-time and evening/weekend programs available. Postbaccalaureate distance learning degree programs offered (minimal on-campus study). *Faculty:* 4 full-time (0 women), 5 part-time/adjunct (1 woman). *Students:* 22 full-time (12 women), 33 part-time (16 women); includes 11 minority (4 Black or African American, non-Hispanic/Latino; 1 Asian, non-Hispanic/Latino; 5 Hispanic/Latino; 1 Two or more races, non-Hispanic/Latino). Average age 27. 32 applicants, 97% accepted, 21 enrolled. In 2014, 18 master's awarded. *Degree requirements:* For master's, comprehensive exam (for some programs), thesis (for some programs). *Entrance requirements:* For master's, baccalaureate degree with minimum GPA of 3.0 in major, 2.5 overall; two letters of recommendation; personal essay. Additional exam requirements/recommendations for international students: Required—TOEFL (minimum score 550 paper-based; 79 iBT), IELTS (minimum score 6), TOEFL (minimum score 550 paper-based; 79 iBT), IELTS (minimum score 6), Michigan English Language Assessment Battery (minimum score 77) or Certificate of Advanced English (minimum score B2). *Application deadline:* For fall admission, 7/15 priority date for domestic students, 6/1 for international students; for spring admission, 11/15 priority date for domestic students, 11/1 for international students. Applications are processed on a rolling basis. Application fee: $50. Electronic applications accepted. *Expenses: Tuition:* Full-time $18,072; part-time $1004 per credit. *Required fees:* $157 per semester. *Financial support:* In 2014–15, 50 students received support, including 43 fellowships (averaging $2,881 per year), 4 research assistantships (averaging $5,198 per year); career-related internships or fieldwork, scholarships/grants, and unspecified assistantships also available. Support available to part-time students. Financial award applicants required to submit FAFSA. *Faculty research:* Violent crimes, criminal pathology, terrorism, computer crime, comparative criminal justice systems, homeland security. *Unit head:* John Comiskey, Program Director, Homeland Security, 732-571-3448, Fax: 732-263-5148, E-mail: jcomiske@monmouth.edu. *Application contact:* Andrea Thompson, Graduate Admission Counselor, 732-571-3452, Fax: 732-263-5123, E-mail: gradadm@monmouth.edu.
Website: http://www.monmouth.edu/academics/criminal_justice/default.asp

Monroe College, King Graduate School, Bronx, NY 10468-5407. Offers business management (MBA); criminal justice (MS); executive leadership in hospitality management (MS); public health (MPH). Program also offered in New Rochelle, NY. Postbaccalaureate distance learning degree programs offered.

Morehead State University, Graduate Programs, Caudill College of Arts, Humanities and Social Sciences, Department of Sociology, Social Work and Criminology, Morehead, KY 40351. Offers criminology (MA); general sociology (MA); gerontology (MA); sociology regional analysis (MA); sociology/chemical dependency (MA). Part-time and evening/weekend programs available. *Degree requirements:* For master's, comprehensive exam, thesis (for some programs). *Entrance requirements:* For master's, GRE General Test, minimum GPA of 3.0 in sociology, 2.75 overall; 18 hours of course work in sociology, writing sample. Additional exam requirements/recommendations for international students: Required—TOEFL (minimum score 500 paper-based). Electronic applications accepted. *Faculty research:* Death and dying; aging, drinking, and drugs; economic development; adult children of alcoholics.

Mount Mercy University, Program in Criminal Justice, Cedar Rapids, IA 52402-4797. Offers MA. Evening/weekend programs available. Postbaccalaureate distance learning degree programs offered (minimal on-campus study). *Degree requirements:* For master's, capstone.

National University, Academic Affairs, School of Education, La Jolla, CA 92037-1011. Offers applied behavior analysis (Certificate); applied school leadership (MS); autism (Certificate); best practices (Certificate); e-teaching and learning (Certificate); early childhood education (Certificate); education (MA), including best practices (M Ed, MA), e-teaching and learning (M Ed, MA), education technology, teacher leadership (M Ed, MA), teaching and learning in a global society (M Ed, MA), teaching mathematics (M Ed,

MA); education with preliminary multiple or single subject (M Ed), including best practices (M Ed, MA), e-teaching and learning (M Ed, MA), educational technology (M Ed, MA), teacher leadership (M Ed, MA), teaching and learning in a global society (M Ed, MA), teaching mathematics (M Ed, MA); educational administration (MS); educational and instructional technology (MS); educational counseling (MS); educational technology (Certificate); higher education administration (MS); innovative school leadership (MS); instructional leadership (MS); juvenile justice special education (MS); reading (Certificate); school psychology (MS); special education (MS), including deaf and hard-of-hearing, mild/moderate disabilities, moderate/severe disabilities; teacher leadership (Certificate); teaching (MA), including applied behavioral analysis, autism, best practices (M Ed, MA), e-teaching and learning (M Ed, MA), early childhood education, educational technology (M Ed, MA), reading, special education, teacher leadership (M Ed, MA), teaching and learning in a global society (M Ed, MA), teaching mathematics (M Ed, MA); teaching mathematics (Certificate). Part-time and evening/weekend programs available. Postbaccalaureate distance learning degree programs offered (no on-campus study). *Faculty:* 83 full-time (50 women), 309 part-time/adjunct (188 women). *Students:* 2,563 full-time (1,811 women), 1,992 part-time (1,374 women); includes 2,016 minority (363 Black or African American, non-Hispanic/Latino; 22 American Indian or Alaska Native, non-Hispanic/Latino; 273 Asian, non-Hispanic/Latino; 1,188 Hispanic/Latino; 27 Native Hawaiian or other Pacific Islander, non-Hispanic/Latino; 143 Two or more races, non-Hispanic/Latino), 2 international. Average age 34. In 2014, 1,813 master's awarded. *Degree requirements:* For master's, thesis (for some programs). *Entrance requirements:* For master's, interview, minimum GPA of 2.5. Additional exam requirements/recommendations for international students: Required—TOEFL (minimum score 550 paper-based; 79 iBT), IELTS (minimum score 6). *Application deadline:* Applications are processed on a rolling basis. Application fee: $60 ($65 for international students). Electronic applications accepted. *Expenses: Tuition:* Full-time $14,184; part-time $1773 per course. *Financial support:* Career-related internships or fieldwork, institutionally sponsored loans, scholarships/grants, and tuition waivers (partial) available. Support available to part-time students. Financial award application deadline: 6/30. *Faculty research:* Teacher education, special education, educational effectiveness, teaching abroad, school counseling. *Unit head:* School of Education, 800-628-8648, E-mail: soe@nu.edu. *Application contact:* Frank Rojas, Vice President for Enrollment Services, 800-628-8648, E-mail: advisor@nu.edu.
Website: http://www.nu.edu/OurPrograms/SchoolOfEducation.html

National University, Academic Affairs, School of Professional Studies, La Jolla, CA 92037-1011. Offers criminal justice (MCJ); digital cinema (MFA); digital journalism (MA); juvenile justice (MS); professional screen writing (MFA); public administration (MPA), including human resource management, organizational leadership, public finance. Part-time and evening/weekend programs available. Postbaccalaureate distance learning degree programs offered (no on-campus study). *Faculty:* 19 full-time (8 women), 28 part-time/adjunct (7 women). *Students:* 277 full-time (141 women), 140 part-time (80 women); includes 248 minority (102 Black or African American, non-Hispanic/Latino; 23 Asian, non-Hispanic/Latino; 102 Hispanic/Latino; 5 Native Hawaiian or other Pacific Islander, non-Hispanic/Latino; 16 Two or more races, non-Hispanic/Latino), 8 international. Average age 37. *Degree requirements:* For master's, thesis (for some programs). *Entrance requirements:* For master's, interview, minimum GPA of 2.5. Additional exam requirements/recommendations for international students: Required—TOEFL (minimum score 550 paper-based; 79 iBT), IELTS (minimum score 6). *Application deadline:* Applications are processed on a rolling basis. Application fee: $60 ($65 for international students). Electronic applications accepted. *Expenses: Tuition:* Full-time $14,184; part-time $1773 per course. *Financial support:* Career-related internships or fieldwork, institutionally sponsored loans, scholarships/grants, and tuition waivers (partial) available. Support available to part-time students. Financial award application deadline: 6/30; financial award applicants required to submit FAFSA. *Unit head:* School of Professional Studies, 800-628-8648, E-mail: sops@nu.edu. *Application contact:* Frank Rojas, Vice President for Enrollment Services, 800-628-8648, E-mail: advisor@nu.edu.
Website: http://www.nu.edu/OurPrograms/School-of-Professional-Studies.html

New Charter University, College of Public Policy and Administration, Program in Criminal Justice, San Francisco, CA 94105. Offers MS. Part-time and evening/weekend programs available. Postbaccalaureate distance learning degree programs offered (no on-campus study). *Entrance requirements:* For master's, course work in calculus, statistics. Additional exam requirements/recommendations for international students: Required—TOEFL (minimum score 550 paper-based).

New Jersey City University, Graduate Studies and Continuing Education, College of Professional Studies, Department of Criminal Justice, Jersey City, NJ 07305-1597. Offers MS. Part-time and evening/weekend programs available. *Faculty:* 6 full-time (2 women), 1 (woman) part-time/adjunct. *Students:* 21 full-time (10 women), 38 part-time (28 women); includes 46 minority (31 Black or African American, non-Hispanic/Latino; 1 American Indian or Alaska Native, non-Hispanic/Latino; 1 Asian, non-Hispanic/Latino; 12 Hispanic/Latino; 1 Two or more races, non-Hispanic/Latino), 1 international. Average age 32. 26 applicants, 81% accepted, 21 enrolled. In 2014, 12 master's awarded. *Degree requirements:* For master's, thesis or alternative. *Entrance requirements:* Additional exam requirements/recommendations for international students: Required—TOEFL (minimum score 79 iBT). *Application deadline:* For fall admission, 8/1 priority date for domestic students; for spring admission, 12/1 for domestic students. Applications are processed on a rolling basis. Application fee: $0. *Expenses: Tuition, area resident:* Part-time $538 per credit. Tuition, state resident: part-time $538 per credit. Tuition, nonresident: part-time $948 per credit. *Financial support:* Unspecified assistantships available. *Unit head:* Dr. David Chiabi, Chairperson, 201-200-3492, E-mail: swilliams@njcu.edu. *Application contact:* Jose Balda, Director of Admissions, E-mail: jbalda@njcu.edu.

New Jersey City University, Graduate Studies and Continuing Education, College of Professional Studies, Program in National Security Studies, Jersey City, NJ 07305-1597. Offers civil security leadership (D Sc); national security studies (MS). Part-time programs available. *Faculty:* 2 full-time (0 women), 5 part-time/adjunct (0 women). *Students:* 17 full-time (5 women), 79 part-time (15 women); includes 40 minority (22 Black or African American, non-Hispanic/Latino; 6 Asian, non-Hispanic/Latino; 11 Hispanic/Latino; 1 Two or more races, non-Hispanic/Latino), 2 international. Average age 38. 39 applicants, 100% accepted, 34 enrolled. In 2014, 12 master's awarded. *Entrance requirements:* Additional exam requirements/recommendations for international students: Required—TOEFL (minimum score 79 iBT). Application fee: $50. *Expenses: Tuition, area resident:* Part-time $538 per credit. Tuition, state resident: part-time $538 per credit. Tuition, nonresident: part-time $948 per credit. *Unit head:* Dr. Tsung (Bill) Soo Hoo, Chair, 201-200-3492, E-mail: bsoohoo@njcu.edu. *Application contact:* Jose Balda, Director of Admission, E-mail: jbalda@njcu.edu.
Website: http://www.njcu.edu/grad/national-security-studies/

New Mexico State University, College of Arts and Sciences, Department of Criminal Justice, Las Cruces, NM 88003-8001. Offers MCJ. Part-time and evening/weekend programs available. Postbaccalaureate distance learning degree programs offered (no on-campus study). *Faculty:* 7 full-time (2 women), 3 part-time/adjunct (2 women). *Students:* 18 full-time (9 women), 40 part-time (28 women); includes 39 minority (5 Black or African American, non-Hispanic/Latino; 1 American Indian or Alaska Native, non-Hispanic/Latino; 1 Asian, non-Hispanic/Latino; 30 Hispanic/Latino; 2 Two or more races, non-Hispanic/Latino). Average age 31. 22 applicants, 86% accepted, 15 enrolled. In 2014, 22 master's awarded. *Degree requirements:* For master's, comprehensive exam, thesis optional, oral and written exams. *Entrance requirements:* For master's, minimum GPA of 3.0. Additional exam requirements/recommendations for international students: Required—TOEFL (minimum score 550 paper-based; 79 iBT), IELTS (minimum score 6.5). *Application deadline:* For fall admission, 4/1 for domestic and international students; for spring admission, 3/1 priority date for domestic students, 11/1 priority date for international students. Application fee: $40 ($50 for international students). Electronic applications accepted. *Expenses:* Tuition, state resident: full-time $3969; part-time $220.50 per credit hour. Tuition, nonresident: full-time $13,838; part-time $768.80 per credit hour. *Required fees:* $853; $47.40 per credit hour. *Financial support:* In 2014–15, 11 students received support, including 7 teaching assistantships (averaging $16,377 per year); career-related internships or fieldwork, Federal Work-Study, scholarships/grants, traineeships, health care benefits, and unspecified assistantships also available. Support available to part-time students. Financial award application deadline: 3/1. *Faculty research:* Juvenile justice, jails and prison administration, courts and legal decision-making, victim studies, policy and evaluation research. *Total annual research expenditures:* $3,771. *Unit head:* Dr. Carlos Posadas, Academic Department Head, 575-646-3316, Fax: 575-646-2827, E-mail: cposadas@nmsu.edu. *Application contact:* Dr. Dulcinea Lara, Graduate Program Director, 575-646-3316, Fax: 575-646-2827, E-mail: dulcinea@nmsu.edu.
Website: http://crimjust.nmsu.edu

Niagara University, Graduate Division of Arts and Sciences, Department of Criminal Justice, Niagara University, NY 14109. Offers criminal justice administration (MS). Part-time programs available. *Faculty:* 5 full-time (2 women). *Students:* 22 full-time (12 women), 9 part-time (2 women); includes 4 minority (2 Black or African American, non-Hispanic/Latino; 1 Hispanic/Latino; 1 Two or more races, non-Hispanic/Latino), 13 international. Average age 29. In 2014, 17 master's awarded. *Entrance requirements:* For master's, GRE. Additional exam requirements/recommendations for international students: Required—TOEFL (minimum score 550 paper-based, 79 iBT), IELTS (minimum score 6), or GMAT/GRE (minimum score 600). *Application deadline:* For fall admission, 8/1 for domestic students. Applications are processed on a rolling basis. Application fee: $30. Tuition and fees vary according to program. *Financial support:* Research assistantships with full and partial tuition reimbursements, teaching assistantships with full and partial tuition reimbursements, career-related internships or fieldwork, Federal Work-Study, scholarships/grants, and unspecified assistantships available. Support available to part-time students. Financial award application deadline: 4/15; financial award applicants required to submit FAFSA. *Unit head:* Dr. Timothy Ireland, Dean, 716-286-8060, Fax: 716-286-8061, E-mail: toi@niagara.edu. *Application contact:* Ronald Winkley, Director, 716-286-8089, Fax: 716-286-8061, E-mail: rwinkley@niagara.edu.
Website: http://www.niagara.edu/graduate-crj

Norfolk State University, School of Graduate Studies, School of Liberal Arts, Department of Sociology, Program in Criminal Justice, Norfolk, VA 23504. Offers MA.

North Carolina Central University, College of Behavioral and Social Sciences, Department of Criminal Justice, Durham, NC 27707-3129. Offers MS. Part-time and evening/weekend programs available. *Degree requirements:* For master's, one foreign language, comprehensive exam, thesis or alternative. *Entrance requirements:* For master's, GRE, minimum GPA of 3.0 in major, 2.5 overall. Additional exam requirements/recommendations for international students: Required—TOEFL.

North Dakota State University, College of Graduate and Interdisciplinary Studies, College of Arts, Humanities and Social Sciences, Department of Criminal Justice and Political Science, Fargo, ND 58108. Offers criminal justice (PhD); criminal justice administration (MS). Part-time programs available. Terminal master's awarded for partial completion of doctoral program. *Degree requirements:* For master's, thesis; for doctorate, comprehensive exam, thesis/dissertation. *Entrance requirements:* For master's, minimum GPA of 3.0 in last 60 credit hours, approved bachelor's degree, course work in research methods and statistics; for doctorate, GRE General Test, minimum GPA of 3.0 over last 60 credit hours, 3 letters of recommendation. Additional exam requirements/recommendations for international students: Required—TOEFL (minimum score 525 paper-based; 71 iBT). *Faculty research:* Corrections, policing, drugs and crime, gender and crime, criminology.

Northeastern State University, College of Liberal Arts, Department of Criminal Justice and Legal Studies, Tahlequah, OK 74464-2399. Offers criminal justice (MS). Part-time and evening/weekend programs available. *Faculty:* 2 full-time (1 woman). *Students:* 18 full-time (9 women), 28 part-time (13 women); includes 21 minority (4 Black or African American, non-Hispanic/Latino; 8 American Indian or Alaska Native, non-Hispanic/Latino; 1 Hispanic/Latino; 8 Two or more races, non-Hispanic/Latino). Average age 33. In 2014, 14 master's awarded. *Degree requirements:* For master's, thesis optional, oral exam. *Entrance requirements:* For master's, MAT or GRE, minimum GPA of 2.5. Additional exam requirements/recommendations for international students: Required—TOEFL. *Application deadline:* For fall admission, 6/1 priority date for domestic students. Applications are processed on a rolling basis. Application fee: $25. Electronic applications accepted. *Expenses:* Tuition, state resident: part-time $178.75 per credit hour. Tuition, nonresident: part-time $451.75 per credit hour. *Required fees:* $37.40 per credit hour. *Financial support:* Teaching assistantships and Federal Work-Study available. Financial award application deadline: 3/1. *Unit head:* Dr. Rob Wallace, Chair, 918-444-3520, Fax: 918-444-2348, E-mail: wallace@nsuok.edu. *Application contact:* Margie Railey, Administrative Assistant, 918-456-5511 Ext. 2093, Fax: 918-458-2061, E-mail: railey@nsouk.edu.
Website: http://academics.nsuok.edu/criminaljustice/GraduateStudies.aspx

Northeastern University, College of Social Sciences and Humanities, Boston, MA 02115. Offers criminology and criminal justice (MSCJ); criminology and justice policy (PhD); economics (MA, PhD); English (MA, PhD); law and public policy (MS, PhD); political science (MA, PhD); public administration (MPA); public history (MA); security and resilience studies (MS); sociology (MA, PhD); urban and regional policy (MS); world history (MA, PhD). *Degree requirements:* For doctorate, variable foreign language requirement, comprehensive exam, thesis/dissertation. *Entrance requirements:* For master's and doctorate, GRE. Additional exam requirements/recommendations for international students: Required—TOEFL, IELTS. Electronic applications accepted.

Northern Arizona University, Graduate College, College of Social and Behavioral Sciences, Department of Criminology and Criminal Justice, Flagstaff, AZ 86011. Offers applied criminology (MS). Part-time programs available. Postbaccalaureate distance learning degree programs offered. *Degree requirements:* For master's, thesis, internship, comprehensive exam, or practicum. *Entrance requirements:* For master's, minimum GPA of 3.0. Additional exam requirements/recommendations for international students: Required—TOEFL (minimum score 550 paper-based; 80 iBT), IELTS (minimum score 7). Electronic applications accepted.

Northern Michigan University, Office of Graduate Education and Research, College of Health Sciences and Professional Studies, School of Education, Leadership and Public

Service, Marquette, MI 49855-5301. Offers administration and supervision (MAE); elementary education (MAE); higher education in student affairs (MA); instruction (MAE); learning disabilities (MAE); public administration (MPA), including criminal justice administration, human resource administration, public administration, public management, state and local government; reading education (MAE), including reading, reading specialist; science education (MS); secondary education (MAE). *Accreditation:* Teacher Education Accreditation Council. Part-time programs available. Postbaccalaureate distance learning degree programs offered (no on-campus study). *Faculty:* 11 full-time (6 women). *Students:* 38 full-time (23 women), 211 part-time (157 women); includes 11 minority (1 Black or African American, non-Hispanic/Latino; 8 American Indian or Alaska Native, non-Hispanic/Latino; 1 Hispanic/Latino; 1 Two or more races, non-Hispanic/Latino). Average age 32. 121 applicants, 88% accepted, 87 enrolled. In 2014, 48 master's awarded. *Degree requirements:* For master's, thesis (for some programs). *Entrance requirements:* For master's, minimum GPA of 3.0. Additional exam requirements/recommendations for international students: Required—TOEFL (minimum score 550 paper-based; 79 iBT), IELTS (minimum score 6.5). *Application deadline:* For fall admission, 7/1 priority date for domestic students; for winter admission, 11/15 for domestic students; for spring admission, 3/17 for domestic students. Applications are processed on a rolling basis. Application fee: $50. Electronic applications accepted. *Expenses: Tuition,* state resident: full-time $7716; part-time $441 per credit hour. Tuition, nonresident: full-time $10,812; part-time $634.50 per credit hour. *Required fees:* $31.88 per semester. Tuition and fees vary according to course load, degree level and program. *Financial support:* Research assistantships with full tuition reimbursements, career-related internships or fieldwork, Federal Work-Study, institutionally sponsored loans, and unspecified assistantships available. Support available to part-time students. Financial award application deadline: 3/1; financial award applicants required to submit FAFSA. *Unit head:* Dr. Joseph Lubig, Associate Dean, School of Education, Leadership, and Public Service, 906-227-2780, Fax: 906-227-2764, E-mail: jlubig@nmu.edu. *Application contact:* Nancy E. Carter, Certification Counselor and Graduate Programs Coordinator, 906-227-1625, Fax: 906-227-2764, E-mail: ncarter@nmu.edu.
Website: http://www.nmu.edu/education/

Oklahoma City University, Petree College of Arts and Sciences, Division of Sociology and Justice Studies, Oklahoma City, OK 73106-1402. Offers MA, MS. Part-time and evening/weekend programs available. *Faculty:* 1 full-time (0 women). *Students:* 7 full-time (all women), 13 part-time (11 women); includes 5 minority (2 Black or African American, non-Hispanic/Latino; 1 American Indian or Alaska Native, non-Hispanic/Latino; 2 Hispanic/Latino), 1 international. Average age 32. 16 applicants, 88% accepted, 10 enrolled. In 2014, 9 master's awarded. *Degree requirements:* For master's, thesis or alternative. *Entrance requirements:* For master's, minimum GPA of 3.0, two letters of recommendation. Additional exam requirements/recommendations for international students: Required—TOEFL (minimum score 550 paper-based; 80 iBT). *Application deadline:* Applications are processed on a rolling basis. Application fee: $50. Electronic applications accepted. *Expenses: Tuition:* Part-time $936 per credit hour. *Required fees:* $115 per credit hour. One-time fee: $250. Tuition and fees vary according to course load, degree level, program and student's religious affiliation. *Financial support:* In 2014–15, 4 students received support. Career-related internships or fieldwork, Federal Work-Study, institutionally sponsored loans, scholarships/grants, and tuition waivers available. Support available to part-time students. Financial award application deadline: 6/1; financial award applicants required to submit FAFSA. *Faculty research:* Victims, police, corrections, security, women and crime. *Unit head:* Robert Spinks, Director, 405-208-5368, Fax: 405-208-5447, E-mail: bspinks@okcu.edu. *Application contact:* Matthew Harrington, Director, Graduate Admissions, 800-633-7242, Fax: 405-208-5916, E-mail: gadmissions@okcu.edu.
Website: http://www.okcu.edu/petree/soc/

Old Dominion University, College of Arts and Letters, Program in Criminology and Criminal Justice, Norfolk, VA 23529. Offers PhD. *Faculty:* 19 full-time (11 women). *Students:* 12 full-time (6 women), 12 part-time (8 women); includes 4 minority (1 Black or African American, non-Hispanic/Latino; 1 Asian, non-Hispanic/Latino; 1 Hispanic/Latino; 1 Native Hawaiian or other Pacific Islander, non-Hispanic/Latino). Average age 32. 18 applicants, 56% accepted, 6 enrolled. In 2014, 4 doctorates awarded. *Degree requirements:* For doctorate, comprehensive exam, thesis/dissertation. *Entrance requirements:* For doctorate, GRE General Test, MA; minimum graduate GPA of 3.25; theory, methods, and statistics graduate coursework; letters of reference; writing sample. Additional exam requirements/recommendations for international students: Required—TOEFL. *Application deadline:* For fall admission, 1/15 for domestic and international students. Application fee: $50. Electronic applications accepted. *Expenses:* Tuition, state resident: full-time $10,488; part-time $437 per credit. Tuition, nonresident: full-time $26,136; part-time $1089 per credit. *Required fees:* $64 per semester. One-time fee: $50. *Financial support:* In 2014–15, 11 students received support, including 11 teaching assistantships with full tuition reimbursements available (averaging $15,000 per year). Financial award application deadline: 1/15. *Faculty research:* Inequality, crime and justice; domestic violence; community justice; criminological theory; methods; policing; courts and corrections; state crime. *Unit head:* Dr. Dawn L. Rothe, Graduate Program Director, 757-683-3935, Fax: 757-683-5634, E-mail: drothe@odu.edu. *Application contact:* Dr. David C. Earnest, Associate Dean, 757-683-6077, Fax: 757-683-5746, E-mail: dearnest@odu.edu.
Website: http://al.odu.edu/sociology/phdprogram/index.shtml

Penn State Harrisburg, Graduate School, School of Public Affairs, Middletown, PA 17057-4898. Offers criminal justice (MA); health administration (MHA); long term care (Certificate); non-profit administration (Certificate); policy analysis and evaluation (Certificate); public administration (MPA, PhD); public budgeting and financial management (Certificate); public sector human resource management (Certificate). *Accreditation:* NASPAA. *Unit head:* Dr. Mukund S. Kulkarni, Chancellor, 717-948-6105, Fax: 717-948-6452, E-mail: msk5@psu.edu. *Application contact:* Robert W. Coffman, Jr., Director of Enrollment Management, Admissions, 717-948-6250, Fax: 717-948-6325, E-mail: ric1@psu.edu.
Website: http://harrisburg.psu.edu/public-affairs

Penn State University Park, Graduate School, College of the Liberal Arts, Department of Sociology and Criminology, University Park, PA 16802. Offers criminology (MA, PhD); sociology (MA, PhD). *Unit head:* Dr. Susan Welch, Dean, 814-865-7691, Fax: 814-863-2085, E-mail: swelch@psu.edu. *Application contact:* Lori A. Stania, Director, Graduate Student Services, 814-867-5278, Fax: 814-863-4627, E-mail: gswww@psu.edu.
Website: http://sociology.la.psu.edu/

Point Park University, School of Arts and Sciences, Department of Criminal Justice and Intelligence Studies, Pittsburgh, PA 15222-1984. Offers criminal justice administration (MS). Evening/weekend programs available. *Degree requirements:* For master's, comprehensive exam (for some programs), thesis or alternative. *Entrance requirements:* For master's, minimum GPA of 2.75, resume, 2 letters of recommendation. Additional exam requirements/recommendations for international students: Required—TOEFL (minimum score 550 paper-based; 79 iBT). Electronic applications accepted.

Pontifical Catholic University of Puerto Rico, College of Graduate Studies in Behavioral Science and Community Affairs, Program in Criminology, Ponce, PR 00717-0777. Offers MA. Part-time and evening/weekend programs available. *Degree requirements:* For master's, thesis. *Entrance requirements:* For master's, EXADEP, 3 letters of recommendation, interview, minimum GPA of 2.75.

Pontificia Universidad Catolica Madre y Maestra, Graduate School, Faculty of Social and Administrative Sciences, Santiago, Dominican Republic. Offers business administration (MBA), including business development, finance, international business, management skills (M Mgmt, MBA), marketing, operations, strategic cost management, strategy, tourist destination planning and management; law (LL M), including civil law, corporate business law, criminal law, international relations, real estate law; management (M Mgmt), including higher financial management, insurance program administration, management skills (M Mgmt, MBA); psychology (MA), including clinical child and adolescent psychology, forensic psychology; strategic human resources (EMBA).

Portland State University, Graduate Studies, College of Urban and Public Affairs, Hatfield School of Government, Division of Criminology and Criminal Justice, Portland, OR 97207-0751. Offers MS, PhD. Part-time programs available. *Faculty:* 12 full-time (5 women), 8 part-time/adjunct (0 women). *Students:* 18 full-time (12 women), 4 part-time (3 women); includes 4 minority (2 Black or African American, non-Hispanic/Latino; 2 Hispanic/Latino). Average age 28. 26 applicants, 73% accepted, 17 enrolled. In 2014, 13 master's awarded. *Degree requirements:* For master's, thesis or alternative, comprehensive oral exam; for doctorate, comprehensive exam, thesis/dissertation. *Entrance requirements:* For master's, minimum GPA of 3.2 overall or graduate. Additional exam requirements/recommendations for international students: Required—TOEFL (minimum score 550 paper-based; 80 iBT). *Application deadline:* For fall admission, 2/1 priority date for domestic and international students. Application fee: $50. *Expenses:* Tuition, state resident: part-time $222 per credit. Tuition, nonresident: part-time $527 per credit. *Required fees:* $22 per contact hour. $100 per quarter. Tuition and fees vary according to program. *Financial support:* In 2014–15, 1 research assistantship with full tuition reimbursement (averaging $9,855 per year), 11 teaching assistantships with full tuition reimbursements (averaging $7,095 per year) were awarded; career-related internships or fieldwork, Federal Work-Study, scholarships/grants, and unspecified assistantships also available. Support available to part-time students. Financial award application deadline: 3/1; financial award applicants required to submit FAFSA. *Faculty research:* History of criminal justice, mental health issues, international terrorism, offender assessment, domestic violence. *Total annual research expenditures:* $95,462. *Unit head:* Dr. Brian C. Renauer, Chair, 503-725-8090, Fax: 503-725-5162, E-mail: renauer@pdx.edu. *Application contact:* Dr. Kathy Perrin, Office Manager, 503-725-4014, Fax: 503-725-5162, E-mail: perrin@pdx.edu.
Website: http://www.pdx.edu/cupa/criminology-criminal-justice

Radford University, College of Graduate and Professional Studies, College of Humanities and Behavioral Sciences, Program in Criminal Justice, Radford, VA 24142. Offers criminal justice (MA, MS). Part-time programs available. *Faculty:* 6 full-time (3 women). *Students:* 11 full-time (6 women), 4 part-time (2 women); includes 3 minority (2 Black or African American, non-Hispanic/Latino; 1 Hispanic/Latino). Average age 26. 11 applicants, 91% accepted, 4 enrolled. In 2014, 23 master's, 10 other advanced degrees awarded. *Degree requirements:* For master's, comprehensive exam, thesis optional. *Entrance requirements:* For master's, minimum GPA of 2.9; 2 letters of reference; original writing sample, resume, official transcripts. Additional exam requirements/recommendations for international students: Required—TOEFL (minimum score 550 paper-based; 79 iBT), IELTS (minimum score 6.5). *Application deadline:* For fall admission, 2/15 priority date for domestic students, 12/1 for international students; for spring admission, 7/1 for international students. Applications are processed on a rolling basis. Application fee: $50. Electronic applications accepted. *Expenses:* Tuition, state resident: full-time $7187; part-time $299 per credit hour. Tuition, nonresident: full-time $16,394; part-time $683 per credit hour. *Required fees:* $2974; $125 per credit hour. Tuition and fees vary according to course load and program. *Financial support:* In 2014–15, 7 students received support, including 5 research assistantships (averaging $7,729 per year), 2 teaching assistantships with partial tuition reimbursements available (averaging $10,500 per year); career-related internships or fieldwork, Federal Work-Study, institutionally sponsored loans, scholarships/grants, and unspecified assistantships also available. Financial award application deadline: 3/1; financial award applicants required to submit FAFSA. *Faculty research:* Spatial issues and crime, gun violence, rural crime, gender and criminal issues, interpersonal violence. *Unit head:* Dr. Lori Elis, Graduate Coordinator, 540-831-6775, Fax: 540-831-6075, E-mail: lelis@radford.edu. *Application contact:* Rebecca Conner, Director, Graduate Enrollment, 540-831-6296, Fax: 540-831-6061, E-mail: gradcollege@radford.edu.
Website: http://www.radford.edu/content/chbs/home/criminal-justice/programs/graduate.html

Regis University, College for Professional Studies, School of Humanities and Social Sciences, MS in Criminology Program, Denver, CO 80221-1099. Offers MS. Part-time and evening/weekend programs available. Postbaccalaureate distance learning degree programs offered (no on-campus study). *Faculty:* 3 full-time (1 woman), 19 part-time/adjunct (5 women). *Students:* 114 full-time (87 women), 61 part-time (50 women); includes 66 minority (30 Black or African American, non-Hispanic/Latino; 2 American Indian or Alaska Native, non-Hispanic/Latino; 24 Hispanic/Latino; 2 Native Hawaiian or other Pacific Islander, non-Hispanic/Latino; 8 Two or more races, non-Hispanic/Latino), 1 international. Average age 35. 43 applicants, 91% accepted, 36 enrolled. In 2014, 68 master's awarded. *Degree requirements:* For master's, thesis, capstone final research project. *Entrance requirements:* For master's, official transcript reflecting baccalaureate degree awarded from regionally-accredited college or university, two letters of recommendation, resume, essays, interview. Additional exam requirements/recommendations for international students: Required—TOEFL (minimum score 550 paper-based; 82 iBT). *Application deadline:* Applications are processed on a rolling basis. Application fee: $75. Electronic applications accepted. *Expenses:* Expenses: Contact institution. *Financial support:* In 2014–15, 1 student received support. Federal Work-Study and scholarships/grants available. Financial award application deadline: 4/15; financial award applicants required to submit FAFSA. *Unit head:* Don E. Lindley, Chair, 303-458-4928, Fax: 303-964-5539, E-mail: dlindley@regis.edu. *Application contact:* Sarah Engel, Director of Admissions, 303-458-4900, Fax: 303-964-5534, E-mail: regisadm@regis.edu.
Website: http://regis.edu/CPS/Academics/Degrees-and-Programs/Graduate-Programs/MS-Criminology.aspx

Robert Morris University Illinois, Morris Graduate School of Management, Chicago, IL 60605. Offers accounting (MBA); accounting/finance (MBA); business analytics (MIS); design and media (MM); educational technology (MM); health care administration (MM); higher education administration (MM); human resource management (MBA); information security (MIS); information systems (MIS); law enforcement administration (MM); management (MBA); management/finance (MBA); management/human resource management (MBA); mobile computing (MIS); sports administration (MM). Part-time and evening/weekend programs available. *Faculty:* 5 full-time (2 women), 27 part-time/adjunct (8 women). *Students:* 237 full-time (122 women), 180 part-time (109 women);

includes 222 minority (128 Black or African American, non-Hispanic/Latino; 2 American Indian or Alaska Native, non-Hispanic/Latino; 18 Asian, non-Hispanic/Latino; 68 Hispanic/Latino; 1 Native Hawaiian or other Pacific Islander, non-Hispanic/Latino; 5 Two or more races, non-Hispanic/Latino), 26 international. Average age 33. 191 applicants, 63% accepted, 104 enrolled. In 2014, 234 master's awarded. *Entrance requirements:* For master's, official transcripts, two letters of recommendation. Additional exam requirements/recommendations for international students: Required—TOEFL (minimum score 550 paper-based). *Application deadline:* Applications are processed on a rolling basis. Application fee: $20 ($100 for international students). Electronic applications accepted. *Expenses: Tuition:* Full-time $14,400; part-time $2400 per course. *Financial support:* In 2014–15, 339 students received support. Federal Work-Study and scholarships/grants available. Support available to part-time students. Financial award applicants required to submit FAFSA. *Unit head:* Kayed Akkawi, Dean, 312-935-6050, Fax: 312-935-6020, E-mail: kakkawi@robertmorris.edu. *Application contact:* Catherine Lockwood, Vice President of Adult Undergraduate and Graduate Education, 312-935-6050, Fax: 312-935-6020, E-mail: clockwood@robertmorris.edu.

Rochester Institute of Technology, Graduate Enrollment Services, College of Liberal Arts, Criminal Justice Department, MS Program in Criminal Justice, Rochester, NY 14623-5604. Offers MS. Part-time programs available. *Students:* 2 full-time (1 woman), 9 part-time (6 women); includes 6 minority (2 Black or African American, non-Hispanic/Latino; 2 Asian, non-Hispanic/Latino; 2 Hispanic/Latino). Average age 28. 9 applicants, 22% accepted, 1 enrolled. *Degree requirements:* For master's, thesis. *Entrance requirements:* For master's, GRE and TOEFL, IELTS, or PTE for non-native English speakers, recommended minimum GPA of 3.0. Additional exam requirements/recommendations for international students: Required—PTE (minimum score 58), TOEFL (minimum score 550 paper-based; 79 iBT) or IELTS (minimum score 6.5). *Application deadline:* For fall admission, 2/15 priority date for domestic and international students; for spring admission, 12/15 priority date for domestic and international students. Applications are processed on a rolling basis. Electronic applications accepted. *Expenses:* Expenses: $1,673 per credit hour. *Financial support:* In 2014–15, 6 students received support. Research assistantships with partial tuition reimbursements available, teaching assistantships with partial tuition reimbursements available, career-related internships or fieldwork, Federal Work-Study, institutionally sponsored loans, scholarships/grants, and unspecified assistantships available. Support available to part-time students. Financial award applicants required to submit FAFSA. *Unit head:* Dr. John McCluskey, Graduate Program Director, 585-475-2666, E-mail: jdmgcj@rit.edu. *Application contact:* Diane Ellison, Associate Vice President, Graduate Enrollment Services, 585-475-2229, Fax: 585-475-7164, E-mail: gradinfo@rit.edu.
Website: http://www.rit.edu/cla/criminaljustice/ms/overview

Roger Williams University, School of Justice Studies, Bristol, RI 02809. Offers criminal justice (MS); cybersecurity (MS); leadership (MS), including health care administration (MPA, MS), public management (MPA, MS); public administration (MPA), including health care administration (MPA, MS), public management (MPA, MS); MS/JD. Part-time and evening/weekend programs available. Postbaccalaureate distance learning degree programs offered. *Faculty:* 4 full-time (2 women), 5 part-time/adjunct (0 women). *Students:* 13 full-time (7 women), 88 part-time (41 women); includes 10 minority (4 Black or African American, non-Hispanic/Latino; 2 Asian, non-Hispanic/Latino; 4 Hispanic/Latino), 5 international. Average age 36. 69 applicants, 61% accepted, 24 enrolled. In 2014, 30 master's awarded. *Degree requirements:* For master's, comprehensive exam, thesis optional. *Entrance requirements:* For master's, 2 letters of recommendation. Additional exam requirements/recommendations for international students: Recommended—TOEFL (minimum score 85 iBT), IELTS. *Application deadline:* Applications are processed on a rolling basis. Application fee: $50. Electronic applications accepted. *Expenses:* Expenses: $14,724. *Financial support:* Application deadline: 6/15; applicants required to submit FAFSA. *Unit head:* Dr. Stephanie Manzi, Dean, 401-254-3021, Fax: 401-254-3431, E-mail: smanzi@rwu.edu. *Application contact:* Lori Vales, Graduate Admissions Coordinator, 401-254-6200, Fax: 401-254-3557, E-mail: gradadmit@rwu.edu.
Website: http://www.rwu.edu/academics/departments/criminaljustice.htm#graduate

Rowan University, Graduate School, College of Humanities and Social Sciences, Law/Justice Department, Program in Criminal Justice, Glassboro, NJ 08028-1701. Offers MA. Part-time and evening/weekend programs available. *Faculty:* 5 full-time (3 women). *Students:* 5 full-time (4 women), 23 part-time (13 women); includes 7 minority (3 Black or African American, non-Hispanic/Latino; 2 Asian, non-Hispanic/Latino; 2 Hispanic/Latino). Average age 30. 38 applicants, 37% accepted, 12 enrolled. In 2014, 23 master's awarded. *Degree requirements:* For master's, thesis. *Entrance requirements:* For master's, GRE General Test. Additional exam requirements/recommendations for international students: Required—TOEFL. *Application deadline:* For fall admission, 8/1 for domestic students, 5/1 for international students; for spring admission, 11/1 for domestic students, 12/1 for international students. Applications are processed on a rolling basis. Application fee: $65. Electronic applications accepted. *Expenses: Tuition, area resident:* Part-time $648 per credit. Tuition, state resident: part-time $648 per credit. Tuition, nonresident: part-time $648 per credit. *Required fees:* $145 per credit. Tuition and fees vary according to degree level, campus/location, program and student level. *Financial support:* Career-related internships or fieldwork, scholarships/grants, health care benefits, and unspecified assistantships available. *Unit head:* Dr. Horacio Sosa, Vice President, Global Learning and Partnerships, 856-256-4747, Fax: 856-256-5638, E-mail: lalovic-hand@rowan.edu. *Application contact:* Admissions and Enrollment Services, 856-256-4747, Fax: 856-256-5637, E-mail: globaladmissions@rowan.edu.

Rutgers, The State University of New Jersey, Camden, Graduate School of Arts and Sciences, Program in Criminal Justice, Camden, NJ 08102. Offers MA, MPA/MA. Part-time and evening/weekend programs available. *Degree requirements:* For master's, comprehensive exam, thesis optional, 30 credits. *Entrance requirements:* For master's, GRE, 3 letters of recommendation; statement of personal, professional, and academic goals. Additional exam requirements/recommendations for international students: Required—TOEFL, IELTS. Electronic applications accepted. *Faculty research:* Criminal justice policy, public management, children in the criminal justice system, violence, gender and crime.

Rutgers, The State University of New Jersey, Newark, Graduate School, School of Criminal Justice, Doctoral Program in Criminal Justice, Newark, NJ 07102. Offers PhD. *Degree requirements:* For doctorate, thesis/dissertation. *Entrance requirements:* Additional exam requirements/recommendations for international students: Required—TOEFL.

Rutgers, The State University of New Jersey, Newark, Graduate School, School of Criminal Justice, Master's Program in Criminal Justice, Newark, NJ 07102. Offers MA. *Entrance requirements:* For master's, GRE, minimum undergraduate B average. Additional exam requirements/recommendations for international students: Required—TOEFL.

Sacred Heart University, Graduate Programs, College of Arts and Sciences, Department of Criminal Justice, Fairfield, CT 06825-1000. Offers MA. Part-time and evening/weekend programs available. *Faculty:* 5 full-time (2 women). *Students:* 16 full-time (11 women), 30 part-time (13 women); includes 19 minority (16 Black or African American, non-Hispanic/Latino; 2 Hispanic/Latino; 1 Two or more races, non-Hispanic/Latino), 2 international. Average age 29. 19 applicants, 95% accepted, 14 enrolled. In 2014, 21 master's awarded. *Degree requirements:* For master's, comprehensive exam, thesis optional. *Entrance requirements:* For master's, BA/BS with minimum GPA of 3.0. Additional exam requirements/recommendations for international students: Required—PTE; Recommended—TOEFL (minimum score 570 paper-based; 80 iBT), IELTS (minimum score 6.5). *Application deadline:* For fall admission, 3/1 for domestic students; for spring admission, 11/1 for domestic students. Applications are processed on a rolling basis. Application fee: $60. Electronic applications accepted. *Expenses: Tuition:* Full-time $24,559; part-time $649 per credit. *Financial support:* Unspecified assistantships available. Financial award applicants required to submit FAFSA. *Unit head:* Dr. Jim McCabe, Chair, 203-396-8002, E-mail: mccabej@sacredheart.edu. *Application contact:* Kathy Dilks, Executive Director of Graduate Admissions, 203-365-7619, Fax: 203-365-4732, E-mail: gradstudies@sacredheart.edu.
Website: http://www.sacredheart.edu/academics/collegeofartssciences/academicdepartments/criminaljustice/masterofartsincriminaljustice/

St. Ambrose University, College of Arts and Sciences, Program in Criminal Justice, Davenport, IA 52803-2898. Offers criminal justice (MCJ); juvenile justice education (MCJ). Part-time and evening/weekend programs available. *Degree requirements:* For master's, thesis (for some programs), practicum or project. *Entrance requirements:* For master's, 2 years of work experience, 2 letters of recommendation, personal interview. Additional exam requirements/recommendations for international students: Required—TOEFL. Electronic applications accepted. *Faculty research:* Community policing.

St. Cloud State University, School of Graduate Studies, College of Social Sciences, Department of Criminal Justice, Program in Criminal Justice, St. Cloud, MN 56301-4498. Offers criminal justice administration (MS). Part-time and evening/weekend programs available. Postbaccalaureate distance learning degree programs offered (no on-campus study). *Entrance requirements:* For master's, minimum overall GPA in previous undergraduate and graduate records or in last half of undergraduate work. Electronic applications accepted.

St. John's University, St. John's College of Liberal Arts and Sciences, Department of Sociology and Anthropology, Queens, NY 11439. Offers criminology and justice (MA); sociology (MA). Part-time and evening/weekend programs available. *Students:* 37 full-time (27 women), 14 part-time (10 women); includes 28 minority (12 Black or African American, non-Hispanic/Latino; 4 Asian, non-Hispanic/Latino; 12 Hispanic/Latino), 8 international. Average age 27. 62 applicants, 74% accepted, 18 enrolled. In 2014, 34 master's awarded. *Degree requirements:* For master's, comprehensive exam, thesis optional. *Entrance requirements:* For master's, 18 undergraduate credits in social sciences, minimum GPA of 3.0, bachelor's degree. Additional exam requirements/recommendations for international students: Required—TOEFL (minimum score 600 paper-based; 100 iBT), IELTS (minimum score 7). *Application deadline:* For fall admission, 5/1 priority date for domestic and international students; for spring admission, 11/1 priority date for domestic and international students. Applications are processed on a rolling basis. Application fee: $70. Electronic applications accepted. *Expenses: Tuition:* Full-time $20,610; part-time $1145 per credit. *Required fees:* $170 per semester. *Financial support:* Research assistantships, career-related internships or fieldwork, and scholarships/grants available. Support available to part-time students. Financial award application deadline: 3/1; financial award applicants required to submit FAFSA. *Faculty research:* Community studies and gentrification, global financial crisis, insurance fraud, globalization, immigration and human rights. *Unit head:* Dr. Roberta Villalon, Chair, 718-990-5663, E-mail: villalonr@stjohns.edu. *Application contact:* Robert Medrano, Director of Graduate Admission, 718-990-1601, Fax: 718-990-5686, E-mail: gradhelp@stjohns.edu.

Saint Joseph's University, College of Arts and Sciences, Department of Criminal Justice, Philadelphia, PA 19131-1395. Offers administration/police executive (MS); behavior analysis (MS, Post-Master's Certificate); criminal justice (MS); criminology (MS); federal law (MS); intelligence and crime (MS); probation, parole, and corrections (MS). Part-time and evening/weekend programs available. Postbaccalaureate distance learning degree programs offered (no on-campus study). *Faculty:* 6 full-time (4 women), 42 part-time/adjunct (16 women). *Students:* 31 full-time (21 women), 401 part-time (276 women); includes 158 minority (104 Black or African American, non-Hispanic/Latino; 7 Asian, non-Hispanic/Latino; 31 Hispanic/Latino; 16 Two or more races, non-Hispanic/Latino), 3 international. Average age 32. 226 applicants, 68% accepted, 115 enrolled. In 2014, 188 master's awarded. *Degree requirements:* For master's, thesis. *Entrance requirements:* For master's, GRE General Test or minimum GPA of 3.0, 2 letters of recommendation, personal statement, resume, official transcripts. Additional exam requirements/recommendations for international students: Required—TOEFL (minimum score 550 paper-based; 80 iBT). *Application deadline:* For fall admission, 7/15 priority date for domestic students, 4/15 for international students; for winter admission, 1/15 for international students; for spring admission, 11/15 priority date for domestic students, 10/15 for international students. Applications are processed on a rolling basis. Application fee: $35. Electronic applications accepted. *Financial support:* In 2014–15, 8 students received support. Career-related internships or fieldwork and unspecified assistantships available. Financial award applicants required to submit FAFSA. *Faculty research:* Housing mobility and the intergenerational transmission of neighborhood poverty, fair trade. *Total annual research expenditures:* $17,309. *Unit head:* Sylvia DeSantis, Director. *Application contact:* Elisabeth Woodward, Director of Marketing and Admissions, Graduate Arts and Sciences, 610-660-3131, Fax: 610-660-3131, E-mail: gradstudies@sju.edu.
Website: http://www.sju.edu/majors-programs/graduate-arts-sciences/masters/criminal-justice-ms

Saint Leo University, Graduate Studies in Public Safety Administration, Saint Leo, FL 33574-6665. Offers criminal justice (MS), including corrections, critical incident management, forensic science, legal studies. Part-time and evening/weekend programs available. Postbaccalaureate distance learning degree programs offered (minimal on-campus study). *Faculty:* 9 full-time (1 woman), 24 part-time/adjunct (5 women). *Students:* 789 full-time (464 women), 10 part-time (7 women); includes 438 minority (347 Black or African American, non-Hispanic/Latino; 4 American Indian or Alaska Native, non-Hispanic/Latino; 8 Asian, non-Hispanic/Latino; 75 Hispanic/Latino; 4 Two or more races, non-Hispanic/Latino), 3 international. Average age 38. In 2014, 219 master's awarded. *Degree requirements:* For master's, comprehensive project. *Entrance requirements:* For master's, bachelor's degree with minimum GPA of 3.0 from regionally-accredited college or university. Additional exam requirements/recommendations for international students: Required—TOEFL (minimum score 550 paper-based; 80 iBT). *Application deadline:* For fall admission, 7/1 priority date for domestic and international students; for spring admission, 11/1 priority date for domestic and international students. Applications are processed on a rolling basis. Application fee: $80. Electronic applications accepted. *Expenses:* Expenses: Contact institution. *Financial support:* In 2014–15, 16 students received support. Scholarships/grants and health care benefits available. Financial award application deadline: 3/1; financial award applicants required to submit FAFSA. *Unit head:* Dr. Robert Diemer, Director of Department of Public Safety Administration, 352-588-8974, Fax: 352-588-8289, E-mail: robert.diemer@saintleo.edu. *Application contact:* Joshua Stagner, Director of Graduate

Admission, 800-707-8846, Fax: 352-588-7873, E-mail: grad.admissions@saintleo.edu.
Website: http://www.saintleo.edu/academics/graduate/criminal-justice.aspx

Saint Mary's University, Faculty of Arts, Program in Criminology, Halifax, NS B3H 3C3, Canada. Offers MA. Part-time programs available. *Degree requirements:* For master's, thesis. *Entrance requirements:* For master's, honors degree, official transcripts, sample of academic written work, 2 letters of recommendation. Electronic applications accepted. *Expenses:* Contact institution.

Saint Peter's University, Program in Criminal Justice Administration, Jersey City, NJ 07306-5997. Offers federal law enforcement administration (MA); police administration (MA). Part-time and evening/weekend programs available. *Entrance requirements:* Additional exam requirements/recommendations for international students: Required—TOEFL. Electronic applications accepted.

St. Thomas University, School of Business, Department of Management, Miami Gardens, FL 33054-6459. Offers accounting (MBA); general management (MSM, Certificate); health management (MBA, MSM, Certificate); human resource management (MBA, MSM, Certificate); international business (MBA, MIB, MSM, Certificate); justice administration (MSM, Certificate); management accounting (MSM, Certificate); public management (MSM, Certificate); sports administration (MS). Part-time and evening/weekend programs available. *Degree requirements:* For master's, comprehensive exam. *Entrance requirements:* For master's, interview, minimum GPA of 3.0 or GMAT. Additional exam requirements/recommendations for international students: Required—TOEFL (minimum score 550 paper-based; 79 iBT). Electronic applications accepted.

Salem State University, School of Graduate Studies, Program in Criminal Justice, Salem, MA 01970-5353. Offers MS. Part-time and evening/weekend programs available. *Entrance requirements:* For master's, GRE or MAT. Additional exam requirements/recommendations for international students: Required—TOEFL (minimum score 550 paper-based; 80 iBT) or IELTS (minimum score 5.5).

Salve Regina University, Program in Administration of Justice and Homeland Security, Newport, RI 02840-4192. Offers administration of justice and homeland security (MS); cybersecurity and intelligence (CGS); leadership in justice (CGS). Part-time and evening/weekend programs available. Postbaccalaureate distance learning degree programs offered (no on-campus study). *Faculty:* 2 full-time (0 women), 6 part-time/adjunct (1 woman). *Students:* 18 full-time (10 women), 58 part-time (15 women); includes 6 minority (1 Black or African American, non-Hispanic/Latino; 4 Hispanic/Latino; 1 Two or more races, non-Hispanic/Latino). Average age 31. 15 applicants, 100% accepted, 15 enrolled. In 2014, 23 master's awarded. *Entrance requirements:* For master's, GMAT, GRE General Test, or MAT. Additional exam requirements/recommendations for international students: Required—TOEFL (minimum score 600 paper-based; 100 iBT). *Application deadline:* For fall admission, 3/5 priority date for domestic students, 3/15 priority date for international students; for spring admission, 9/15 priority date for domestic students, 9/5 priority date for international students. Applications are processed on a rolling basis. Application fee: $60. Electronic applications accepted. *Expenses: Tuition:* Full-time $8550; part-time $475 per credit. *Required fees:* $50 per term. Tuition and fees vary according to course level, course load and degree level. *Financial support:* Career-related internships or fieldwork and Federal Work-Study available. Support available to part-time students. Financial award application deadline: 3/1; financial award applicants required to submit FAFSA. *Unit head:* David Smith, Director, 401-341-3210, E-mail: david.smith@salve.edu. *Application contact:* Nicole Ferreira, Associate Director of Graduate Admissions, 401-341-2462, Fax: 401-341-2973, E-mail: nicole.ferreira@salve.edu.
Website: http://www.salve.edu/graduate-studies/administration-of-justice-and-homeland-security

Sam Houston State University, College of Criminal Justice, Department of Criminal Justice and Criminology, Huntsville, TX 77341. Offers criminal justice (MS, PhD); criminal justice and criminology (MA); criminal justice leadership and management (MS); victim services management (MS). Part-time and evening/weekend programs available. Postbaccalaureate distance learning degree programs offered (no on-campus study). *Faculty:* 31 full-time (12 women), 3 part-time/adjunct (1 woman). *Students:* 47 full-time (29 women), 217 part-time (94 women); includes 87 minority (41 Black or African American, non-Hispanic/Latino; 3 American Indian or Alaska Native, non-Hispanic/Latino; 6 Asian, non-Hispanic/Latino; 33 Hispanic/Latino; 1 Native Hawaiian or other Pacific Islander, non-Hispanic/Latino; 3 Two or more races, non-Hispanic/Latino), 15 international. Average age 35. 150 applicants, 78% accepted, 100 enrolled. In 2014, 93 master's, 15 doctorates awarded. *Degree requirements:* For master's, comprehensive exam (for some programs), thesis (for some programs); for doctorate, comprehensive exam, thesis/dissertation. *Entrance requirements:* For master's, GRE, personal essay, official transcripts, three recommendation letters, resume; for doctorate, GRE, personal essay, official transcripts, three recommendation letters, resume, master's degree. Additional exam requirements/recommendations for international students: Required—TOEFL (minimum score 550 paper-based; 79 iBT), IELTS (minimum score 6.5). *Application deadline:* For fall admission, 2/1 for domestic and international students; for spring admission, 9/1 for domestic and international students; for summer admission, 4/1 for domestic and international students. Applications are processed on a rolling basis. Application fee: $45 ($75 for international students). Electronic applications accepted. *Expenses:* Tuition, state resident: full-time $2286; part-time $254 per credit hour. Tuition, nonresident: full-time $5544; part-time $616 per credit hour. *Required fees:* $440 per semester. Tuition and fees vary according to course load and campus/location. *Financial support:* In 2014–15, 53 research assistantships (averaging $13,084 per year), 15 teaching assistantships (averaging $13,336 per year) were awarded; career-related internships or fieldwork, Federal Work-Study, scholarships/grants, tuition waivers (partial), and unspecified assistantships also available. Support available to part-time students. Financial award application deadline: 3/15; financial award applicants required to submit FAFSA. *Unit head:* Dr. Gaylene Armstrong, Chair, 936-294-4506, Fax: 936-294-1638, E-mail: garmstrong@shsu.edu. *Application contact:* Doris Powell-Pratt, Graduate Advising Coordinator, 936-294-3637, Fax: 936-294-4055, E-mail: icc_dcp@shsu.edu.
Website: http://www.shsu.edu/academics/criminal-justice/departments/criminal-justice-and-criminology/index.html

San Diego State University, Graduate and Research Affairs, College of Professional Studies and Fine Arts, School of Public Affairs, Program in Criminal Justice Administration, San Diego, CA 92182. Offers MPA. Part-time programs available. *Entrance requirements:* For master's, GRE General Test, 2 letters of reference. Additional exam requirements/recommendations for international students: Required—TOEFL. Electronic applications accepted.

San Diego State University, Graduate and Research Affairs, College of Professional Studies and Fine Arts, School of Public Affairs, Program in Criminal Justice and Criminology, San Diego, CA 92182. Offers MS. *Entrance requirements:* For master's, GRE General Test, 2 letters of reference. Additional exam requirements/recommendations for international students: Required—TOEFL. Electronic applications accepted.

San Francisco State University, Division of Graduate Studies, College of Health and Social Sciences, Public Administration Program, San Francisco, CA 94132-1722. Offers criminal justice administration (MPA); environmental administration and policy (MPA); nonprofit administration (MPA); public management (MPA); public policy (MPA); urban administration (MPA). *Accreditation:* NASPAA. *Expenses:* Tuition, state resident: full-time $6738. Tuition, nonresident: full-time $17,898; part-time $372 per credit hour. *Required fees:* $498 per semester. *Unit head:* Dr. Elizabeth Brown, Director of the School of Public Affairs and Civic Engagement, 415-817-4455, Fax: 415-817-4464, E-mail: mpa@sfsu.edu. *Application contact:* Dr. Sheldon Gen, Graduate Coordinator, 415-817-4458, Fax: 415-817-4464, E-mail: sgen@sfsu.edu.
Website: http://mpa.sfsu.edu/

San Jose State University, Graduate Studies and Research, College of Applied Sciences and Arts, Department of Justice Studies, San Jose, CA 95192-0001. Offers MS. Part-time programs available. *Degree requirements:* For master's, thesis or alternative. *Entrance requirements:* For master's, GRE or LSAT, minimum GPA of 3.0. Additional exam requirements/recommendations for international students: Required—TOEFL. Electronic applications accepted. *Faculty research:* Employee stress, interagency cooperation, prison industries, application of death penalty sentences, sucrose ingestion and delinquency.

Seattle University, College of Arts and Sciences, Department of Criminal Justice, Seattle, WA 98122-1090. Offers crime analysis (Certificate); criminal justice (MACJ). Part-time and evening/weekend programs available. *Faculty:* 7 full-time (3 women), 2 part-time/adjunct (1 woman). *Students:* 16 full-time (13 women), 60 part-time (48 women); includes 22 minority (3 Black or African American, non-Hispanic/Latino; 4 Asian, non-Hispanic/Latino; 10 Hispanic/Latino; 1 Native Hawaiian or other Pacific Islander, non-Hispanic/Latino; 4 Two or more races, non-Hispanic/Latino). Average age 28. 58 applicants, 62% accepted, 23 enrolled. In 2014, 18 master's, 2 Certificates awarded. *Degree requirements:* For master's, comprehensive exam or thesis. *Entrance requirements:* For master's, minimum GPA of 3.0; undergraduate degree in criminal justice or related social, behavioral, or physical science, or related coursework and/or volunteer or supervised experience; letters of recommendation; writing sample. Additional exam requirements/recommendations for international students: Required—TOEFL, IELTS. *Application deadline:* For fall admission, 3/15 for domestic and international students. Application fee: $55. Electronic applications accepted. *Financial support:* In 2014–15, 32 students received support. Applicants required to submit FAFSA. *Faculty research:* Criminal justice program evaluation, ex-offender reentry, policing issues, restorative justice, psychopathy. *Unit head:* Dr. Elaine Gunnison, Graduate Program Director, 206-296-2430, E-mail: gunnisone@seattleu.edu. *Application contact:* Janet Shandley, Associate Dean of Graduate Admissions, 206-296-5900, Fax: 206-298-5656, E-mail: grad_admissions@seattleu.edu.
Website: https://www.seattleu.edu/artsci/criminal-graduate/

Shippensburg University of Pennsylvania, School of Graduate Studies, College of Education and Human Services, Department of Criminal Justice, Shippensburg, PA 17257-2299. Offers MS. Part-time and evening/weekend programs available. *Faculty:* 7 full-time (4 women). *Students:* 14 full-time (8 women), 22 part-time (13 women); includes 10 minority (5 Black or African American, non-Hispanic/Latino; 1 Asian, non-Hispanic/Latino; 1 Hispanic/Latino; 1 Native Hawaiian or other Pacific Islander, non-Hispanic/Latino; 2 Two or more races, non-Hispanic/Latino). Average age 29. 36 applicants, 81% accepted, 22 enrolled. In 2014, 13 master's awarded. *Degree requirements:* For master's, thesis optional, internship, practicum, or thesis. *Entrance requirements:* For master's, GRE or MAT (if GPA less than 2.75), 500-word statement of interest. Additional exam requirements/recommendations for international students: Required—TOEFL (minimum score 580 paper-based); Recommended—IELTS (minimum score 6). *Application deadline:* For fall admission, 4/30 for international students; for spring admission, 9/30 for international students. Applications are processed on a rolling basis. Application fee: $45. Electronic applications accepted. *Expenses: Tuition, area resident:* Part-time $454 per credit. Tuition, state resident: part-time $454 per credit. Tuition, nonresident: part-time $681 per credit. *Required fees:* $133 per credit. *Financial support:* In 2014–15, 7 research assistantships with full tuition reimbursements (averaging $5,000 per year) were awarded; career-related internships or fieldwork, scholarships/grants, unspecified assistantships, and resident hall director and student payroll positions also available. Support available to part-time students. Financial award application deadline: 3/1; financial award applicants required to submit FAFSA. *Unit head:* Dr. Matthew D. Fetzer, Assistant Professor, 717-477-1558, Fax: 717-477-4087, E-mail: mdfetzer@ship.edu. *Application contact:* Jeremy R. Goshorn, Assistant Dean of Graduate Admissions, 717-477-1231, Fax: 717-477-4016, E-mail: jrgoshorn@ship.edu.
Website: http://www.ship.edu/criminal_justice/

Simon Fraser University, Office of Graduate Studies, Faculty of Arts and Social Sciences, School of Criminology, Burnaby, BC V5A 1S6, Canada. Offers applied legal studies (MA); criminology (MA, PhD). *Degree requirements:* For master's, thesis or alternative, practicum; for doctorate, thesis/dissertation. *Entrance requirements:* For master's, minimum GPA of 3.0 (on scale of 4.33), or 3.33 based on last 60 credits of undergraduate courses; for doctorate, minimum GPA of 3.5 (on scale of 4.33). Additional exam requirements/recommendations for international students: Recommended—TOEFL (minimum score 580 paper-based; 93 iBT), IELTS (minimum score 7), TWE (minimum score 5). Electronic applications accepted. *Faculty research:* Media and crime, feminist jurisprudence, policy evaluation, forensic entomology, restorative justice.

Simpson College, Department of Social Sciences, Indianola, IA 50125-1297. Offers criminal justice (MACJ). Evening/weekend programs available.

Slippery Rock University of Pennsylvania, Graduate Studies (Recruitment), College of Liberal Arts, Department of Criminology and Criminal Justice, Slippery Rock, PA 16057-1383. Offers criminal justice (MA). Part-time and evening/weekend programs available. Postbaccalaureate distance learning degree programs offered (no on-campus study). *Faculty:* 5 full-time (3 women). *Students:* 19 full-time (14 women), 26 part-time (10 women); includes 10 minority (8 Black or African American, non-Hispanic/Latino; 2 Hispanic/Latino). Average age 30. 44 applicants, 77% accepted, 23 enrolled. In 2014, 9 master's awarded. *Degree requirements:* For master's, comprehensive exam (for some programs), thesis (for some programs). *Entrance requirements:* For master's, minimum GPA of 2.75, three letters of recommendation, personal statement. Additional exam requirements/recommendations for international students: Required—TOEFL (minimum score 550 paper-based; 80 iBT). *Application deadline:* For fall admission, 3/1 priority date for domestic students, 5/1 priority date for international students; for spring admission, 10/1 priority date for domestic students, 9/1 priority date for international students. Applications are processed on a rolling basis. Application fee: $25 ($30 for international students). Electronic applications accepted. *Expenses:* Expenses: $546.10 per credit in-state resident; $568.45 per credit nonresident. *Financial support:* Career-related internships or fieldwork, Federal Work-Study, institutionally sponsored loans, scholarships/grants, and tuition waivers (partial) available. Support available to part-time students. Financial award application deadline: 5/1; financial award applicants required to submit FAFSA. *Unit head:* Dr. David Champion, Graduate Coordinator, 724-738-4462, Fax: 724-738-4822, E-mail: david.champion@sru.edu. *Application contact:* Brandi Weber-Mortimer, Director of Graduate Admissions, 724-738-2051, Fax: 724-738-2146,

E-mail: graduate.admissions@sru.edu.
Website: http://www.sru.edu/academics/graduate-programs/criminal-justice-master-of-arts

Southeast Missouri State University, School of Graduate Studies, Department of Criminal Justice and Sociology, Cape Girardeau, MO 63701-4799. Offers criminal justice (MS), including community policing administration, criminal justice administration. Part-time programs available. Postbaccalaureate distance learning degree programs offered (minimal on-campus study). *Faculty:* 6 full-time (4 women), 1 part-time/adjunct (0 women). *Students:* 5 full-time (2 women), 39 part-time (23 women); includes 13 minority (10 Black or African American, non-Hispanic/Latino; 2 Hispanic/Latino; 1 Two or more races, non-Hispanic/Latino), 1 international. Average age 35. 16 applicants, 100% accepted, 14 enrolled. In 2014, 24 master's awarded. *Degree requirements:* For master's, comprehensive exam, thesis. *Entrance requirements:* For master's, GRE, minimum undergraduate GPA of 2.75, 3.25 in last 4 semesters of undergraduate work. Additional exam requirements/recommendations for international students: Required—TOEFL (minimum score 550 paper-based; 79 iBT), IELTS (minimum score 6), PTE (minimum score 53). *Application deadline:* For fall admission, 8/1 for domestic students, 6/1 for international students; for spring admission, 11/21 for domestic students, 10/1 for international students; for summer admission, 5/15 for domestic students. Applications are processed on a rolling basis. Application fee: $30 ($40 for international students). Electronic applications accepted. *Expenses:* Tuition, state resident: full-time $5256; part-time $292 per credit hour. Tuition, nonresident: full-time $9288; part-time $516 per credit hour. *Financial support:* In 2014–15, 5 students received support. Career-related internships or fieldwork, Federal Work-Study, scholarships/grants, traineeships, tuition waivers (full), and unspecified assistantships available. Financial award application deadline: 6/30; financial award applicants required to submit FAFSA. *Faculty research:* Death penalty research, perspectives of incorporating technology in the classroom, prison programming, evaluation of state probation and parole systems, international police response to domestic violence. *Unit head:* Dr. Diana Bruns, Department of Criminal Justice and Sociology Chair, 573-651-2541, Fax: 573-986-6417, E-mail: dbruns@semo.edu. *Application contact:* Dr. John Wade, Professor, 573-651-2541, Fax: 573-986-6417, E-mail: jwade@semo.edu.
Website: http://www.semo.edu/criminaljustice/

Southern Illinois University Carbondale, Graduate School, College of Liberal Arts, Department of Criminology and Criminal Justice, Carbondale, IL 62901-4701. Offers MA. *Faculty:* 10 full-time (3 women). *Students:* 20 full-time (9 women), 13 part-time (7 women); includes 5 minority (1 Black or African American, non-Hispanic/Latino; 2 Asian, non-Hispanic/Latino; 2 Hispanic/Latino), 4 international. 41 applicants, 51% accepted, 12 enrolled. In 2014, 2 master's awarded. *Degree requirements:* For master's, thesis optional. *Entrance requirements:* For master's, GRE General Test, minimum GPA of 2.7. Additional exam requirements/recommendations for international students: Required—TOEFL. *Application deadline:* Applications are processed on a rolling basis. Application fee: $50. *Expenses:* Tuition, state resident: full-time $10,176; part-time $1153 per credit. Tuition, nonresident: full-time $20,814; part-time $1744 per credit. *Required fees:* $7092; $394 per credit. $2364 per semester. *Financial support:* In 2014–15, 2 fellowships with full tuition reimbursements, 5 research assistantships with full tuition reimbursements, 13 teaching assistantships with full tuition reimbursements were awarded; career-related internships or fieldwork, Federal Work-Study, and institutionally sponsored loans also available. Support available to part-time students. *Faculty research:* Corrections, criminology, law enforcement, crime prevention, victims of crime. *Total annual research expenditures:* $300,000. *Unit head:* Joseph Schafer, Chair, 618-453-6376. *Application contact:* Melanie Terbrak, Graduate Secretary, 618-453-6372, Fax: 618-453-6377, E-mail: mlterbrak@siu.edu.
Website: http://ccj.siuc.edu/

Southern University and Agricultural and Mechanical College, Graduate School, Nelson Mandela School of Public Policy and Urban Affairs, Department of Criminal Justice, Baton Rouge, LA 70813. Offers MS. *Entrance requirements:* Additional exam requirements/recommendations for international students: Required—TOEFL (minimum score 525 paper-based).

Southern University at New Orleans, School of Graduate Studies, New Orleans, LA 70126-1009. Offers criminal justice (MA); management information systems (MS); museum studies (MA); social work (MSW). *Accreditation:* CSWE. Part-time and evening/weekend programs available. *Degree requirements:* For master's, thesis. *Entrance requirements:* For master's, GRE/GMAT. Additional exam requirements/recommendations for international students: Required—TOEFL.

South University, Graduate Programs, College of Arts and Sciences, Program in Criminal Justice, Savannah, GA 31406. Offers MS.

South University, Graduate Programs, College of Business, Savannah, GA 31406. Offers corrections (MBA); entrepreneurship and small business (MBA); healthcare administration (MBA); hospitality management (MBA); leadership (MS); public administration (MPA); sustainability (MBA).

South University, Program in Criminal Justice, Columbia, SC 29203. Offers MS.

South University, Program in Criminal Justice, Montgomery, AL 36116-1120. Offers MS.

South University, Program in Criminal Justice, Tampa, FL 33614. Offers MS.

South University, Program in Criminal Justice, Royal Palm Beach, FL 33411. Offers MS.

Southwestern College, Professional Studies Programs, Wichita, KS 67207. Offers accountancy (MA); business administration (MBA); leadership (MS); management (MS); security administration (MS); specialized ministries (MA); theological studies (MA). Part-time and evening/weekend programs available. Postbaccalaureate distance learning degree programs offered (minimal on-campus study). *Faculty:* 34 part-time/adjunct (11 women). *Students:* 100 part-time (37 women); includes 24 minority (10 Black or African American, non-Hispanic/Latino; 3 Asian, non-Hispanic/Latino; 6 Hispanic/Latino; 5 Two or more races, non-Hispanic/Latino). Average age 37. 75 applicants, 71% accepted, 22 enrolled. In 2014, 78 master's awarded. *Degree requirements:* For master's, practicum/capstone project. *Entrance requirements:* For master's, baccalaureate degree; minimum GPA of 2.5 (for MA and MS), 3.0 (for MBA). Additional exam requirements/recommendations for international students: Required—TOEFL (minimum score 550 paper-based). *Application deadline:* For fall admission, 8/1 for domestic students; for spring admission, 12/1 for domestic students. Applications are processed on a rolling basis. Application fee: $0. Electronic applications accepted. *Expenses:* Expenses: $10,836. *Financial support:* In 2014–15, 5 students received support. Federal Work-Study, tuition waivers (partial), and unspecified assistantships available. Financial award application deadline: 4/1; financial award applicants required to submit FAFSA. *Unit head:* Susan Backofen, Vice President for Enrollment Management, 888-684-5335 Ext. 214, Fax: 316-688-5218, E-mail: susan.backofen@sckans.edu. *Application contact:* 888-684-5335, Fax: 316-688-5218, E-mail: enrollment@sckans.edu.
Website: http://www.southwesterncollege.org

Southwest University, Program in Criminal Justice, Kenner, LA 70062. Offers MS.

Stockton University, School of Graduate and Continuing Studies, Program in Criminal Justice, Galloway, NJ 08205-9441. Offers MA. Part-time and evening/weekend programs available. *Faculty:* 6 full-time (4 women), 1 part-time/adjunct (0 women). *Students:* 15 full-time (13 women), 12 part-time (9 women); includes 3 minority (1 Black or African American, non-Hispanic/Latino; 2 Hispanic/Latino). Average age 24. 29 applicants, 83% accepted, 16 enrolled. In 2014, 13 master's awarded. *Degree requirements:* For master's, comprehensive exam (for some programs), thesis, student portfolio project. *Entrance requirements:* For master's, GRE General Test, minimum GPA of 3.0. Additional exam requirements/recommendations for international students: Required—TOEFL. *Application deadline:* For fall admission, 7/1 for domestic and international students; for spring admission, 12/1 for domestic students, 11/1 for international students. Applications are processed on a rolling basis. Application fee: $50. Electronic applications accepted. *Expenses:* Tuition, state resident: full-time $13,694; part-time $570.59 per credit. Tuition, nonresident: full-time $21,080; part-time $878 per credit. *Required fees:* $4118; $171.59 per credit. $80 per term. Tuition and fees vary according to degree level. *Financial support:* In 2014–15, 12 students received support, including 1 fellowship, 9 research assistantships with partial tuition reimbursements available; career-related internships or fieldwork, Federal Work-Study, scholarships/grants, and unspecified assistantships also available. Support available to part-time students. Financial award application deadline: 3/1; financial award applicants required to submit FAFSA. *Faculty research:* Homeland security, forensic psychology, corrections, sex crimes, violent crimes. *Unit head:* Dr. Christine Tartaro, Director, 609-626-3640, E-mail: christine.tartaro@stockton.edu. *Application contact:* Tara Williams, Assistant Director of Graduate Enrollment Management, 609-626-3640, Fax: 609-626-6050, E-mail: gradschool@stockton.edu.

Suffolk University, College of Arts and Sciences, Department of Sociology, Boston, MA 02108-2770. Offers MSCJS, MSCJS/JD, MSCJS/MPA, MSCJS/MSMHC. Part-time programs available. *Faculty:* 4 full-time (2 women), 1 part-time/adjunct (0 women). *Students:* 23 full-time (17 women), 17 part-time (12 women); includes 13 minority (10 Black or African American, non-Hispanic/Latino; 1 Asian, non-Hispanic/Latino; 2 Hispanic/Latino), 2 international. Average age 26. 86 applicants, 66% accepted, 28 enrolled. In 2014, 34 master's awarded. *Entrance requirements:* For master's, 2 letters of recommendation, resume. Additional exam requirements/recommendations for international students: Required—TOEFL (minimum score 550 paper-based; 80 iBT). *Application deadline:* For fall admission, 6/15 priority date for domestic students, 6/15 for international students; for spring admission, 11/1 priority date for domestic students, 11/1 for international students. Applications are processed on a rolling basis. Application fee: $50. Electronic applications accepted. *Expenses:* Expenses: Contact institution. *Financial support:* In 2014–15, 26 students received support, including 26 fellowships (averaging $7,545 per year); career-related internships or fieldwork, Federal Work-Study, and institutionally sponsored loans also available. Support available to part-time students. Financial award application deadline: 4/1; financial award applicants required to submit FAFSA. *Faculty research:* Restorative justice, anti-gang initiative, healthcare for female ex-offenders, violence against women, juvenile justice and the courts. *Unit head:* Erika Gebo, Associate Professor/Chair, 617-557-1594, Fax: 671-994-4278, E-mail: egebo@suffolk.edu. *Application contact:* Cory Meyers, Director of Graduate Admissions, 617-573-8302, Fax: 617-305-1733, E-mail: grad.admission@suffolk.edu.
Website: http://www.suffolk.edu/college/departments/12638.php

Sul Ross State University, School of Professional Studies, Department of Criminal Justice, Alpine, TX 79832. Offers MS, MS/MA. *Entrance requirements:* For master's, GRE General Test, minimum GPA of 2.5 in last 60 hours of undergraduate work.

Tarleton State University, College of Graduate Studies, College of Liberal and Fine Arts, Department of Criminal Justice, Stephenville, TX 76402. Offers MCJ. Part-time and evening/weekend programs available. *Degree requirements:* For master's, comprehensive exam (for some programs), thesis optional. *Entrance requirements:* For master's, GRE General Test, minimum GPA of 3.0. Additional exam requirements/recommendations for international students: Required—TOEFL (minimum score 550 paper-based; 80 iBT). Electronic applications accepted.

Temple University, College of Liberal Arts, Department of Criminal Justice, Philadelphia, PA 19122-6096. Offers MA, PhD. Part-time programs available. *Faculty:* 21 full-time (12 women), 17 part-time/adjunct (7 women). *Students:* 32 full-time (23 women), 2 part-time (0 women); includes 5 minority (2 Black or African American, non-Hispanic/Latino; 2 Asian, non-Hispanic/Latino; 1 Hispanic/Latino), 3 international. 48 applicants, 23% accepted, 9 enrolled. In 2014, 4 master's awarded. Terminal master's awarded for partial completion of doctoral program. *Degree requirements:* For master's, thesis optional; for doctorate, thesis/dissertation, qualifying exams. *Entrance requirements:* For master's, GRE General Test, minimum GPA of 3.0, 3 letters of recommendation; for doctorate, GRE General Test, 3 letters of recommendation. Additional exam requirements/recommendations for international students: Required—TOEFL (minimum score 550 paper-based; 79 iBT). *Application deadline:* For fall admission, 12/15 for domestic students, 11/30 for international students. Application fee: $60. Electronic applications accepted. *Expenses:* Tuition, state resident: full-time $14,490; part-time $805 per credit hour. Tuition, nonresident: full-time $19,850; part-time $1103 per credit hour. *Required fees:* $690. Full-time tuition and fees vary according to class time, course load, degree level, campus/location and program. *Financial support:* Research assistantships with tuition reimbursements, teaching assistantships with tuition reimbursements, career-related internships or fieldwork, and Federal Work-Study available. Financial award application deadline: 1/15. *Faculty research:* Policy analysis and program evaluation; geography of crime and justice; criminal behavior; rehabilitation and behavioral change; policing, security, and crime prevention; juvenile delinquency and juvenile justice. *Unit head:* Dr. Kate Auerhahn, Graduate Director, 215-204-1354, Fax: 215-204-3872, E-mail: auehahn@temple.edu. *Application contact:* LaSaundra Scott, Coordinator, 215-204-1376, Fax: 215-204-3872, E-mail: lscott01@temple.edu.
Website: http://www.temple.edu/cj/

Tennessee State University, The School of Graduate Studies and Research, College of Liberal Arts, Department of Criminal Justice, Nashville, TN 37209-1561. Offers MCJ. Program offered jointly with Middle Tennessee State University. *Degree requirements:* For master's, thesis. *Entrance requirements:* For master's, GRE General Test or MAT. Electronic applications accepted.

Texas A&M International University, Office of Graduate Studies and Research, College of Arts and Sciences, Department of Public Affairs and Social Research, Laredo, TX 78041-1900. Offers criminal justice (MS); history and political thought (MA); political science (MA); public administration (MPA). *Degree requirements:* For master's, comprehensive exam (for some programs), thesis (for some programs). *Entrance requirements:* For master's, GRE General Test. Additional exam requirements/recommendations for international students: Required—TOEFL (minimum score 550 paper-based; 79 iBT).

Texas A&M University–Central Texas, Graduate Studies and Research, Killeen, TX 76549. Offers accounting (MS); business administration (MBA); clinical mental health counseling (MS); criminal justice (MCJ); curriculum and instruction (M Ed); educational administration (M Ed); educational psychology - experimental psychology (MS); history (MA); human resource management (MS); information systems (MS); liberal studies

(MS); management and leadership (MS); marriage and family therapy (MS); mathematics (MS); political science (MA); school counseling (M Ed); school psychology (Ed S).

Texas A&M University–Kingsville, College of Graduate Studies, College of Arts and Sciences, Department of Psychology and Sociology, Program in Criminology, Kingsville, TX 78363. Offers MS. *Students:* 8 full-time (3 women), 2 part-time (both women); includes 9 minority (1 Black or African American, non-Hispanic/Latino; 8 Hispanic/Latino), 1 international. Average age 26. 11 applicants, 100% accepted, 8 enrolled. *Degree requirements:* For master's, variable foreign language requirement, comprehensive exam, thesis (for some programs). *Entrance requirements:* For master's, GRE, MAT, GMAT. Additional exam requirements/recommendations for international students: Required—TOEFL (minimum score 550 paper-based; 79 iBT). *Application deadline:* For fall admission, 8/15 for domestic students, 6/1 for international students; for spring admission, 12/15 for domestic students, 10/1 for international students; for summer admission, 5/15 for domestic students, 4/1 for international students. Applications are processed on a rolling basis. Application fee: $35 ($50 for international students). Electronic applications accepted. *Financial support:* In 2014–15, 6 students received support, including 1 teaching assistantship (averaging $8,176 per year); career-related internships or fieldwork, Federal Work-Study, institutionally sponsored loans, scholarships/grants, health care benefits, tuition waivers (full and partial), and unspecified assistantships also available. Support available to part-time students. Financial award application deadline: 5/1; financial award applicants required to submit FAFSA. *Unit head:* Dr. Richard Miller, Department Chair, 361-593-4181, Fax: 361-593-2707, E-mail: richard.miller@tamuk.edu. *Application contact:* Dr. Lloyd Dempster, Graduate Coordinator, 361-593-4181, E-mail: lloyd.dempster@tamuk.edu.
Website: http://www.tamuk.edu/artsci/psycsoci/crim/

Texas Christian University, AddRan College of Liberal Arts, Department of Criminal Justice, Fort Worth, TX 76129. Offers criminal justice and criminology (MS). Postbaccalaureate distance learning degree programs offered (no on-campus study). *Faculty:* 4 full-time (1 woman). *Students:* 17 full-time (8 women); includes 9 minority (4 Black or African American, non-Hispanic/Latino; 1 Asian, non-Hispanic/Latino; 4 Hispanic/Latino). Average age 34. 26 applicants, 88% accepted, 17 enrolled. *Degree requirements:* For master's, thesis optional. *Entrance requirements:* Additional exam requirements/recommendations for international students: Recommended—TOEFL. *Application deadline:* For fall admission, 4/1 for domestic and international students. Application fee: $60. Electronic applications accepted. *Expenses:* Expenses: Contact institution. *Financial support:* Applicants required to submit FAFSA. *Faculty research:* Cybercrime, sex offenders, prisoner reentry, criminological theory, policing. *Unit head:* Johnny Nhan, Director/Associate Professor, 626-391-3871, E-mail: j.nhan@tcu.edu. *Application contact:* Pam Carlisle, Administrative Assistant, 817-257-5846, Fax: 817-257-7737, E-mail: p.carlisle@tcu.edu.
Website: http://www.cjp.tcu.edu/

Texas Southern University, School of Public Affairs, Program in Administration of Justice, Houston, TX 77004-4584. Offers MS, PhD. Electronic applications accepted.

Texas State University, The Graduate College, College of Applied Arts, Program in Criminal Justice, San Marcos, TX 78666. Offers MSCJ, PhD. Part-time and evening/weekend programs available. *Faculty:* 14 full-time (4 women), 1 (woman) part-time/adjunct. *Students:* 51 full-time (34 women), 36 part-time (20 women); includes 27 minority (5 Black or African American, non-Hispanic/Latino; 2 Asian, non-Hispanic/Latino; 18 Hispanic/Latino; 2 Two or more races, non-Hispanic/Latino), 5 international. Average age 31. 58 applicants, 60% accepted, 14 enrolled. In 2014, 34 master's, 6 doctorates awarded. *Degree requirements:* For master's, comprehensive exam, thesis (for some programs); for doctorate, comprehensive exam, thesis/dissertation. *Entrance requirements:* For master's, GRE, bachelor's degree, minimum GPA of 3.0 in last 60 hours of course work; for doctorate, GRE (minimum combined Verbal and Quantitative score of 1000), master's degree in criminal justice or related field; minimum GPA of 3.5 in graduate courses; 3 letters of recommendation; personal/goals statement. Additional exam requirements/recommendations for international students: Required—TOEFL (minimum score 550 paper-based; 78 iBT). *Application deadline:* For fall admission, 6/15 priority date for domestic students, 6/1 for international students; for spring admission, 10/15 priority date for domestic students, 10/1 for international students. Applications are processed on a rolling basis. Application fee: $40 ($90 for international students). Electronic applications accepted. *Expenses:* Expenses: $8,834 (tuition and fees combined). *Financial support:* In 2014–15, 52 students received support, including 9 research assistantships (averaging $19,302 per year), 21 teaching assistantships (averaging $21,384 per year); Federal Work-Study, institutionally sponsored loans, and unspecified assistantships also available. Support available to part-time students. Financial award application deadline: 4/1; financial award applicants required to submit FAFSA. *Faculty research:* Geographic profiling, illegal crossing, criminal hunt pattern, reducing inmate rape, counterterrorism, displaced residents, Texas Youth Commission (TYC) classification systems. *Total annual research expenditures:* $4.4 million. *Unit head:* Dr. Beth Sanders, Graduate Advisor, 512-245-2174, Fax: 512-245-8063, E-mail: bs47@txstate.edu. *Application contact:* Dr. Andrea Golato, Dean of the Graduate College, 512-245-2581, Fax: 512-245-8365, E-mail: gradcollege@txstate.edu.
Website: http://www.cj.txstate.edu/

Tiffin University, Program in Criminal Justice, Tiffin, OH 44883-2161. Offers crime analysis (MSCJ); criminal behavior (MSCJ); forensic psychology (MSCJ); homeland security administration (MSCJ); justice administration (MSCJ). Part-time and evening/weekend programs available. Postbaccalaureate distance learning degree programs offered (no on-campus study). *Degree requirements:* For master's, thesis optional. *Entrance requirements:* For master's, minimum undergraduate GPA of 2.5, work experience. Additional exam requirements/recommendations for international students: Required—TOEFL (minimum score 550 paper-based; 79 iBT). Electronic applications accepted. *Faculty research:* Terrorism, intelligence, homeland security, guns and crime.

Trident University International, College of Business Administration, Program in Business Administration, Cypress, CA 90630. Offers business administration (PhD); conflict and negotiation management (MBA); criminal justice administration (MBA); entrepreneurship (MBA); finance (MBA); general management (MBA); government accounting (MBA); human resource management (MBA); information security and digital assurance management (MBA); information technology management (MBA); international business (MBA); logistics management (MBA); marketing (MBA); project management (MBA); public management (MBA); quality management (MBA); strategic leadership (MBA). Part-time and evening/weekend programs available. Postbaccalaureate distance learning degree programs offered (no on-campus study). *Degree requirements:* For doctorate, comprehensive exam, thesis/dissertation, defense of dissertation. *Entrance requirements:* For master's, minimum GPA of 2.5 (students with GPA 3.0 or greater may transfer up to 30% of graduate level credits); for doctorate, minimum GPA of 3.4, curriculum vitae, course work in research methods or statistics. Additional exam requirements/recommendations for international students: Required—TOEFL. Electronic applications accepted.

Trine University, Program in Criminal Justice, Angola, IN 46703-1764. Offers emergency management (MS); forensic psychology (MS); law (MS); public administration (MS). Part-time and evening/weekend programs available. *Students:* 46 part-time (39 women). In 2014, 20 master's awarded. *Entrance requirements:* Additional exam requirements/recommendations for international students: Required—TOEFL. *Expenses: Tuition:* Full-time $12,000; part-time $670 per credit hour. Tuition and fees vary according to degree level, campus/location, program and student level. *Financial support:* Application deadline: 3/1; applicants required to submit FAFSA. *Unit head:* Barbara E. Molargik-Fitch, JD, Director, 260-203-2693, Fax: 260-203-2965, E-mail: molargik-fitchb@trine.edu. *Application contact:* Cherie Ditto, Director of SPS Enrollment Services, 260-702-3592, E-mail: dittoc@trine.edu.
Website: http://www.trine.edu/academics/majors-and-minors/graduate/criminal-justice/index.aspx

Troy University, Graduate School, College of Arts and Sciences, Program in Criminal Justice, Troy, AL 36082. Offers MS. Part-time and evening/weekend programs available. *Faculty:* 6 full-time (3 women), 5 part-time/adjunct (2 women). *Students:* 49 full-time (23 women), 197 part-time (132 women); includes 164 minority (144 Black or African American, non-Hispanic/Latino; 2 American Indian or Alaska Native, non-Hispanic/Latino; 1 Asian, non-Hispanic/Latino; 7 Hispanic/Latino; 10 Two or more races, non-Hispanic/Latino). Average age 36. 119 applicants, 94% accepted, 68 enrolled. In 2014, 68 master's awarded. *Degree requirements:* For master's, comprehensive exam, research course, minimum GPA of 3.0, admission to candidacy. *Entrance requirements:* For master's, GRE (minimum score of 850 on old exam or 290 on new exam), MAT (minimum score of 385) or GMAT (minimum score of 380), bachelor's degree; minimum undergraduate GPA of 2.5 or 3.0 on last 30 semester hours. Additional exam requirements/recommendations for international students: Required—TOEFL (minimum score 523 paper-based; 70 iBT), IELTS (minimum score 6). *Application deadline:* Applications are processed on a rolling basis. Application fee: $50. Electronic applications accepted. *Expenses:* Tuition, state resident: full-time $6570; part-time $365 per credit hour. Tuition, nonresident: full-time $13,140; part-time $730 per credit hour. *Required fees:* $365 per credit hour. *Financial support:* Available to part-time students. Applicants required to submit FAFSA. *Faculty research:* Crime victims, criminal justice personnel issues, disability issues in criminal justice. *Unit head:* Dr. Jeffrey Lee, Chairman, 334-670-3439, Fax: 334-670-3753, E-mail: jlee22079@troy.edu. *Application contact:* Jessica A. Kimbro, Director of Graduate Admissions, 334-670-3178, E-mail: jacord@troy.edu.

Troy University, Graduate School, College of Arts and Sciences, Program in Public Administration, Troy, AL 36082. Offers government contracting (MPA); health care administration (MPA); justice administration (MPA); national security affairs (MPA); nonprofit management (MPA); public human resources management (MPA); public management (MPA). *Accreditation:* NASPAA. Part-time and evening/weekend programs available. Postbaccalaureate distance learning degree programs offered (no on-campus study). *Faculty:* 14 full-time (9 women), 8 part-time/adjunct (4 women). *Students:* 56 full-time (37 women), 255 part-time (154 women); includes 181 minority (157 Black or African American, non-Hispanic/Latino; 4 Asian, non-Hispanic/Latino; 14 Hispanic/Latino; 6 Two or more races, non-Hispanic/Latino). Average age 32. 182 applicants, 67% accepted, 64 enrolled. In 2014, 108 master's awarded. *Degree requirements:* For master's, capstone course with minimum B grade, minimum GPA of 3.0, admission to candidacy. *Entrance requirements:* For master's, GRE (minimum score of 920 on old exam or 294 on new exam), MAT (minimum score of 400) or GMAT (minimum score of 490), bachelor's degree; minimum undergraduate GPA of 2.5 or 3.0 on last 30 semester hours, letter of recommendation; essay, resume. Additional exam requirements/recommendations for international students: Required—TOEFL (minimum score 523 paper-based; 70 iBT), IELTS (minimum score 6). *Application deadline:* Applications are processed on a rolling basis. Application fee: $50. Electronic applications accepted. *Expenses:* Tuition, state resident: full-time $6570; part-time $365 per credit hour. Tuition, nonresident: full-time $13,140; part-time $730 per credit hour. *Required fees:* $365 per credit hour. *Financial support:* Available to part-time students. Applicants required to submit FAFSA. *Unit head:* Dr. Pamela Trump Dunning, Director, 334-808-6507, Fax: 334-670-5647, E-mail: pdunningl@troy.edu. *Application contact:* Jessica A. Kimbro, Director of Graduate Admissions, 334-670-3178, E-mail: jacord@troy.edu.

Troy University, Graduate School, College of Business, Program in Business Administration, Troy, AL 36082. Offers accounting (EMBA, MBA); criminal justice (EMBA); finance (MBA); general management (EMBA, MBA); healthcare management (EMBA); information systems (EMBA, MBA); international economic development (MBA). *Accreditation:* ACBSP. Part-time and evening/weekend programs available. *Faculty:* 19 full-time (4 women), 2 part-time/adjunct (0 women). *Students:* 105 full-time (55 women), 239 part-time (123 women); includes 175 minority (114 Black or African American, non-Hispanic/Latino; 4 American Indian or Alaska Native, non-Hispanic/Latino; 40 Asian, non-Hispanic/Latino; 8 Hispanic/Latino; 1 Native Hawaiian or other Pacific Islander, non-Hispanic/Latino; 8 Two or more races, non-Hispanic/Latino). Average age 29. 281 applicants, 63% accepted, 35 enrolled. In 2014, 218 master's awarded. *Degree requirements:* For master's, minimum GPA of 3.0, capstone course, research course. *Entrance requirements:* For master's, GMAT (minimum score 500) or GRE (minimum score 900 on old exam or 294 on new exam), bachelor's degree; minimum undergraduate GPA of 2.5 or 3.0 on last 30 semester hours, letter of recommendation. Additional exam requirements/recommendations for international students: Required—TOEFL (minimum score 523 paper-based; 70 iBT), IELTS (minimum score 6). *Application deadline:* Applications are processed on a rolling basis. Application fee: $50. *Expenses:* Tuition, state resident: full-time $6570; part-time $365 per credit hour. Tuition, nonresident: full-time $13,140; part-time $730 per credit hour. *Required fees:* $365 per credit hour. *Unit head:* Dr. Bob Wheatley, Director, Graduate Business Programs, 334-670-3194, Fax: 334-670-3599, E-mail: rwheat@troy.edu. *Application contact:* Jessica A. Kimbro, Director of Graduate Admissions, 334-670-3178, E-mail: jacord@troy.edu.

Troy University, Graduate School, College of Education, Program in Counseling and Psychology, Troy, AL 36082. Offers agency counseling (Ed S); clinical mental health (MS); community counseling (MS, Ed S); corrections counseling (MS); rehabilitation counseling (MS); school psychology (MS, Ed S); school psychometry (MS); social service counseling (MS); student affairs counseling (MS); substance abuse counseling (MS). *Accreditation:* ACA; CORE; NCATE. Part-time and evening/weekend programs available. *Faculty:* 41 full-time (18 women), 32 part-time/adjunct (18 women). *Students:* 358 full-time (286 women), 503 part-time (425 women); includes 572 minority (481 Black or African American, non-Hispanic/Latino; 3 American Indian or Alaska Native, non-Hispanic/Latino; 5 Asian, non-Hispanic/Latino; 62 Hispanic/Latino; 21 Two or more races, non-Hispanic/Latino). Average age 34. 248 applicants, 86% accepted, 139 enrolled. In 2014, 212 master's, 4 other advanced degrees awarded. *Degree requirements:* For master's, comprehensive exam, thesis. *Entrance requirements:* For master's, GRE (minimum score of 850 on old exam or 290 on new exam), GMAT (minimum score of 380), or MAT (minimum score of 385), bachelor's degree; minimum undergraduate GPA of 2.5 or 3.0 on last 30 semester hours, letter of recommendation. Additional exam requirements/recommendations for international students: Required—TOEFL (minimum score 523 paper-based; 70 iBT), IELTS (minimum score 6). *Application deadline:* Applications are processed on a rolling basis. Application fee: $50. Electronic applications accepted. *Expenses:* Tuition, state resident: full-time $6570; part-time $365 per credit hour. Tuition, nonresident: full-time $13,140; part-time $730 per credit hour. *Required fees:* $365 per credit hour. *Unit head:* Dr. Andrew Creamer,

Chair, 334-670-3350, Fax: 334-670-3291, E-mail: acreamer@troy.edu. *Application contact:* Jessica A. Kimbro, Director of Graduate Admissions, 334-670-3178, E-mail: jacord@troy.edu.

Universidad del Este, Graduate School, Carolina, PR 00984. Offers accounting (MBA); adult education (M Ed); agribusiness (MBA); criminal justice and criminology (MA); curriculum and instruction - early education (M Ed); curriculum and instruction - elementary (M Ed); curriculum and instruction - English (M Ed); curriculum and instruction - Spanish (M Ed); human resources (MBA); information security management (MBA); information technology and Web business development (MBA); management (MBA); public policy (MPA); social work (MA), including clinical social work; special education (M Ed); strategic leadership (MBA).

Universidad del Turabo, Graduate Programs, School of Social Sciences and Humanities, Programs in Public Affairs, Program in Criminal Justice Studies, Gurabo, PR 00778-3030. Offers MPA. *Entrance requirements:* For master's, GRE, EXADEP, interview.

Université de Montréal, Faculty of Arts and Sciences, School of Criminology, Montréal, QC H3C 3J7, Canada. Offers M Sc, PhD. Terminal master's awarded for partial completion of doctoral program. *Degree requirements:* For master's, thesis; for doctorate, thesis/dissertation, general exam. *Entrance requirements:* For master's, B Sc in criminology or the equivalent; for doctorate, M Sc in criminology or equivalent. Electronic applications accepted. *Faculty research:* Criminal behavior, criminality, prison population, victims of crime, female offenders.

University at Albany, State University of New York, School of Criminal Justice, Albany, NY 12222-0001. Offers MA, PhD, MSW/MA. Part-time programs available. *Degree requirements:* For doctorate, thesis/dissertation. *Entrance requirements:* For master's and doctorate, GRE General Test. Additional exam requirements/recommendations for international students: Required—TOEFL (minimum score 550 paper-based). Electronic applications accepted. *Faculty research:* Causes of delinquency, comparative policing, world crime data, correctional policy, family violence.

The University of Alabama, Graduate School, College of Arts and Sciences, Department of Criminal Justice, Tuscaloosa, AL 35487. Offers MS. Part-time programs available. *Faculty:* 11 full-time (7 women). *Students:* 24 full-time (12 women), 9 part-time (4 women); includes 3 minority (all Black or African American, non-Hispanic/Latino), 1 international. Average age 27. 21 applicants, 57% accepted, 8 enrolled. In 2014, 6 master's awarded. *Degree requirements:* For master's, comprehensive exam (for some programs), thesis (for some programs), thesis or comprehensive exam. *Entrance requirements:* For master's, GRE. Additional exam requirements/recommendations for international students: Recommended—TOEFL. *Application deadline:* For fall admission, 6/15 for domestic and international students; for winter admission, 11/1 for domestic and international students; for spring admission, 11/15 for domestic and international students. Applications are processed on a rolling basis. Application fee: $50 ($60 for international students). Electronic applications accepted. *Expenses:* Tuition, state resident: full-time $9826. Tuition, nonresident: full-time $24,950. *Financial support:* In 2014–15, 25 teaching assistantships with partial tuition reimbursements (averaging $6,570 per year) were awarded; fellowships, health care benefits, and unspecified assistantships also available. Financial award application deadline: 2/15; financial award applicants required to submit FAFSA. *Faculty research:* Social deviance, sociology of HIV/AIDS, terrorism, cyber crime, juvenile delinquency. *Total annual research expenditures:* $30,000. *Unit head:* Dr. Lesley W. Reid, Department Chair, 205-348-7795, Fax: 205-348-7795, E-mail: lwreid@ua.edu. *Application contact:* Dr. Adam Lankford, Associate Professor and Director of Graduate Studies, 205-348-9901, Fax: 205-348-9901, E-mail: adam.lankford@ua.edu.
Website: http://cj.ua.edu

The University of Alabama at Birmingham, College of Arts and Sciences, Program in Criminal Justice, Birmingham, AL 35294. Offers MSCJ. Evening/weekend programs available. Postbaccalaureate distance learning degree programs offered (no on-campus study). *Students:* 7 full-time (4 women), 5 part-time (2 women); includes 7 minority (all Black or African American, non-Hispanic/Latino). Average age 30. In 2014, 4 master's awarded. *Degree requirements:* For master's, thesis or alternative. *Entrance requirements:* For master's, GRE General Test. Additional exam requirements/recommendations for international students: Required—TOEFL, TWE. *Application deadline:* For fall admission, 7/1 for domestic students. Applications are processed on a rolling basis. Application fee: $45 ($60 for international students). Electronic applications accepted. *Expenses:* Tuition, state resident: full-time $7090; part-time $370 per credit hour. Tuition, nonresident: full-time $16,072; part-time $869 per credit hour. Full-time tuition and fees vary according to course load and program. *Financial support:* Research assistantships, career-related internships or fieldwork, and scholarships/grants available. Financial award applicants required to submit FAFSA. *Unit head:* Dr. Heith Copes, Director of Graduate Studies in Forensic Science, 205-934-2067, Fax: 205-934-2067, E-mail: jhcopes@uab.edu. *Application contact:* Susan Noblitt Banks, Director of Graduate School Operations, 205-934-8227, Fax: 205-934-8413, E-mail: gradschool@uab.edu.
Website: http://www.uab.edu/cas/justice-sciences/graduate-programs/master-of-science-in-criminal-justice-mscj

The University of Alabama in Huntsville, School of Graduate Studies, Interdisciplinary Studies, Interdisciplinary Program in Information Assurance and Security, Huntsville, AL 35899. Offers computer engineering (MS), including computer science; information systems (Certificate). Part-time and evening/weekend programs available. *Degree requirements:* For master's, comprehensive exam, thesis. *Entrance requirements:* For master's, GRE General Test, minimum GPA of 3.0; for Certificate, GMAT, minimum GPA of 3.0. Additional exam requirements/recommendations for international students: Required—TOEFL (minimum score 550 paper-based; 80 iBT), IELTS (minimum score 6.5). Electronic applications accepted. *Faculty research:* Service discovery, enterprise security, security metrics, cryptography, network security.

University of Alaska Fairbanks, College of Liberal Arts, Department of Justice, Fairbanks, AK 99775-6120. Offers MA. Part-time programs available. Postbaccalaureate distance learning degree programs offered (no on-campus study). *Faculty:* 4 full-time (0 women). *Students:* 2 full-time (1 woman), 13 part-time (7 women); includes 3 minority (1 American Indian or Alaska Native, non-Hispanic/Latino; 2 Hispanic/Latino). Average age 36. 19 applicants, 37% accepted, 6 enrolled. In 2014, 4 master's awarded. *Degree requirements:* For master's, comprehensive exam, oral defense of project or thesis. *Entrance requirements:* For master's, bachelor's degree from accredited institution with minimum cumulative undergraduate and major GPA of 3.0. Additional exam requirements/recommendations for international students: Required—TOEFL (minimum score 550 paper-based; 79 iBT), IELTS (minimum score 6.5). *Application deadline:* For fall admission, 6/1 for domestic students, 3/1 for international students; for spring admission, 10/15 for domestic students, 9/1 for international students. Applications are processed on a rolling basis. Application fee: $60. Electronic applications accepted. *Expenses:* Tuition, state resident: full-time $7614; part-time $423 per credit. Tuition, nonresident: full-time $15,552; part-time $864 per credit. Tuition and fees vary according to course level, course load and reciprocity agreements. *Financial support:* Federal Work-Study, scholarships/grants, and health care benefits available. Support available to part-time students. Financial award application deadline: 7/1; financial award applicants required to submit FAFSA. *Total annual research expenditures:* $3,000. *Unit head:* Micheal Daku, Department Chair, 907-474-5500, Fax: 907-474-6510, E-mail: fyjust@uaf.edu. *Application contact:* Mary Kreta, Director of Admissions, 907-474-7500, Fax: 907-474-7097, E-mail: admissions@uaf.edu.
Website: http://www.uaf.edu/justice/

University of Alberta, Faculty of Graduate Studies and Research, Department of Sociology, Edmonton, AB T6G 2E1, Canada. Offers criminal justice (MA); demography (MA, PhD); sociology (MA, PhD). Part-time programs available. *Degree requirements:* For master's, thesis (for some programs); for doctorate, thesis/dissertation. *Faculty research:* Criminology, knowledge and culture, methods and theory, population studies, stratification.

University of Antelope Valley, Program in Criminal Justice, Lancaster, CA 93534. Offers MS. *Degree requirements:* For master's, capstone project. *Entrance requirements:* For master's, official transcripts documenting earned bachelor's degree from nationally- or regionally-accredited institution with minimum cumulative GPA of 2.0.

University of Arkansas at Little Rock, Graduate School, College of Social Sciences and Communication, Department of Criminal Justice, Little Rock, AR 72204-1099. Offers MA, MS, PhD. MS program is offered by distance education. Part-time and evening/weekend programs available. *Degree requirements:* For master's, thesis defense or written comprehensive exam; for doctorate, thesis/dissertation. *Entrance requirements:* For master's, GRE General Test or MAT, interview, minimum GPA of 2.75. Additional exam requirements/recommendations for international students: Required—TOEFL (minimum score 550 paper-based; 79 iBT). *Application deadline:* Applications are processed on a rolling basis. *Expenses:* Tuition, state resident: full-time $6000; part-time $300 per credit hour. Tuition, nonresident: full-time $13,800; part-time $690 per credit hour. *Required fees:* $1126; $603 per term. One-time fee: $40 full-time. *Financial support:* Fellowships, research assistantships with tuition reimbursements, teaching assistantships with tuition reimbursements, career-related internships or fieldwork, Federal Work-Study, institutionally sponsored loans, and unspecified assistantships available. Support available to part-time students. *Faculty research:* Dissemination and analysis of behavioral science knowledge, leadership and managerial skills, philosophy of individual rights and humane treatment. *Unit head:* Dr. Mary L. Parker, Chairperson, 501-569-8589, E-mail: mlparker@ualr.edu. *Application contact:* Dr. Jeff Walker, Coordinator, 501-569-3083, E-mail: jtwalker@ualr.edu.
Website: http://ualr.edu/criminaljustice/

University of Baltimore, Graduate School, College of Public Affairs, Program in Criminal Justice, Baltimore, MD 21201-5779. Offers MS, JD/MS. Part-time and evening/weekend programs available. *Degree requirements:* For master's, thesis or alternative. *Entrance requirements:* For master's, interview, minimum GPA of 2.8. Additional exam requirements/recommendations for international students: Required—TOEFL (minimum score 550 paper-based). Electronic applications accepted. *Faculty research:* Drugs and violence, police and community policing, women and crime, victimization, correction in community.

University of California, Irvine, School of Social Ecology, Department of Criminology, Law and Society, Irvine, CA 92697. Offers MAS, PhD. *Students:* 114 full-time (68 women), 62 part-time (26 women); includes 73 minority (12 Black or African American, non-Hispanic/Latino; 1 American Indian or Alaska Native, non-Hispanic/Latino; 16 Asian, non-Hispanic/Latino; 30 Hispanic/Latino; 14 Two or more races, non-Hispanic/Latino), 12 international. Average age 31. 176 applicants, 53% accepted, 70 enrolled. In 2014, 47 master's, 8 doctorates awarded. *Degree requirements:* For doctorate, thesis/dissertation, research project. *Entrance requirements:* For master's and doctorate, GRE General Test, minimum GPA of 3.0. Additional exam requirements/recommendations for international students: Required—TOEFL (minimum score 550 paper-based). *Application deadline:* For fall admission, 1/15 priority date for domestic and international students. Application fee: $90 ($110 for international students). Electronic applications accepted. *Financial support:* Fellowships, research assistantships with full tuition reimbursements, teaching assistantships, institutionally sponsored loans, traineeships, health care benefits, and unspecified assistantships available. Financial award application deadline: 3/1; financial award applicants required to submit FAFSA. *Faculty research:* White-collar and corporate crime; immigration, the poor, homelessness, and governmental regulation; sentencing, community corrections, and diversion; mathematical and scientific evidence in jury trials; legal and criminological theory development. *Unit head:* Prof. Cheryl Maxon, Department Chair, 949-824-5150, E-mail: cmaxson@uci.edu. *Application contact:* Leslie Noel, Graduate Coordinator, 949-824-1442, Fax: 949-824-3001, E-mail: lknoel@uci.edu.
Website: http://cls.soceco.uci.edu/

University of Central Florida, College of Health and Public Affairs, Department of Criminal Justice and Legal Studies, Orlando, FL 32816. Offers corrections leadership (Certificate); criminal justice (MS, PhD); juvenile justice leadership (Certificate); police leadership (Certificate). Part-time and evening/weekend programs available. *Faculty:* 28 full-time (9 women), 12 part-time/adjunct (3 women). *Students:* 54 full-time (29 women), 148 part-time (85 women); includes 88 minority (35 Black or African American, non-Hispanic/Latino; 5 Asian, non-Hispanic/Latino; 41 Hispanic/Latino; 7 Two or more races, non-Hispanic/Latino), 3 international. Average age 32. 134 applicants, 81% accepted, 67 enrolled. In 2014, 95 master's, 39 other advanced degrees awarded. *Degree requirements:* For master's, thesis or alternative. *Entrance requirements:* For master's, GRE General Test, minimum GPA of 3.0. Additional exam requirements/recommendations for international students: Required—TOEFL. *Application deadline:* For fall admission, 7/15 for domestic students; for spring admission, 4/15 for domestic students. Electronic applications accepted. *Expenses:* Tuition, state resident: part-time $288.16 per credit hour. Tuition, nonresident: part-time $1073.31 per credit hour. *Financial support:* In 2014–15, 8 students received support, including 3 fellowships (averaging $10,000 per year), 5 teaching assistantships with partial tuition reimbursements available (averaging $6,200 per year); career-related internships or fieldwork, Federal Work-Study, institutionally sponsored loans, tuition waivers (partial), and unspecified assistantships also available. Financial award application deadline: 3/1; financial award applicants required to submit FAFSA. *Unit head:* Dr. Roberto Potter, Interim Chair, 407-823-2603, E-mail: roberto.potter@ucf.edu. *Application contact:* Barbara Rodriguez Lamas, Director, Admissions and Student Services, 407-823-2766, Fax: 407-823-6442, E-mail: gradadmissions@ucf.edu.
Website: http://www.cohpa.ucf.edu/crim.jus/

University of Central Missouri, The Graduate School, Warrensburg, MO 64093. Offers accountancy (MA); accounting (MBA); applied mathematics (MS); aviation safety (MA); biology (MS); business administration (MBA); career and technical education leadership (MS); college student personnel administration (MS); communication (MA); computer science (MS); counseling (MS); criminal justice (MS); educational leadership (Ed D); educational technology (MS); elementary and early childhood education (MSE); English (MA); environmental studies (MA); finance (MBA); history (MA); human services/educational technology (Ed S); human services/learning resources (Ed S); human services/professional counseling (Ed S); industrial hygiene (MS); industrial management (MS); information systems (MBA); information technology (MS); kinesiology (MS); library

science and information services (MS); literacy education (MSE); marketing (MBA); mathematics (MS); music (MA); occupational safety management (MS); psychology (MS); rural family nursing (MS); school administration (MSE); social gerontology (MS); sociology (MA); special education (MSE); speech language pathology (MS); superintendency (Ed S); teaching (MAT); teaching English as a second language (MA); technology (MS); technology management (PhD); theatre (MA). Part-time programs available. *Faculty:* 314 full-time (137 women), 24 part-time/adjunct (14 women). *Students:* 1,624 full-time (542 women), 1,773 part-time (1,055 women); includes 194 minority (104 Black or African American, non-Hispanic/Latino; 6 American Indian or Alaska Native, non-Hispanic/Latino; 23 Asian, non-Hispanic/Latino; 41 Hispanic/Latino; 3 Native Hawaiian or other Pacific Islander, non-Hispanic/Latino; 17 Two or more races, non-Hispanic/Latino), 1,592 international. Average age 31. 2,800 applicants, 63% accepted, 1223 enrolled. In 2014, 796 master's, 81 other advanced degrees awarded. *Degree requirements:* For master's and Ed S, comprehensive exam (for some programs), thesis (for some programs). *Entrance requirements:* Additional exam requirements/recommendations for international students: Required—TOEFL (minimum score 550 paper-based; 79 iBT). *Application deadline:* For fall admission, 6/1 for domestic students; for spring admission, 10/1 for domestic and international students. Applications are processed on a rolling basis. Application fee: $30 ($75 for international students). Electronic applications accepted. *Expenses:* Tuition, state resident: full-time $6630; part-time $276.25 per credit hour. Tuition, nonresident: full-time $13,260; part-time $552.50 per credit hour. *Required fees:* $29 per credit hour. Tuition and fees vary according to campus/location. *Financial support:* In 2014–15, 118 students received support, including 271 research assistantships with full and partial tuition reimbursements available (averaging $7,500 per year), 109 teaching assistantships with full and partial tuition reimbursements available (averaging $7,500 per year); career-related internships or fieldwork, Federal Work-Study, scholarships/grants, and administrative and laboratory assistantships also available. Support available to part-time students. Financial award application deadline: 3/1; financial award applicants required to submit FAFSA. *Unit head:* Tina Church-Hockett, Director of Graduate School and International Admissions, 660-543-4621, Fax: 660-543-4778, E-mail: church@ucmo.edu. *Application contact:* Brittany Lawrence, Graduate Student Services Coordinator, 660-543-4621, Fax: 660-543-4778, E-mail: gradinfo@ucmo.edu. Website: http://www.ucmo.edu/graduate/

University of Central Oklahoma, The Jackson College of Graduate Studies, College of Liberal Arts, School of Criminal Justice, Edmond, OK 73034-5209. Offers crime and intelligence analysis (MA); criminal justice management and administration (MA). Part-time programs available. *Entrance requirements:* Additional exam requirements/recommendations for international students: Required—TOEFL (minimum score 550 paper-based; 79 iBT), IELTS (minimum score 6.5). Electronic applications accepted. *Faculty research:* Gender issues, violent offenders.

University of Cincinnati, Graduate School, College of Education, Criminal Justice, and Human Services, Division of Criminal Justice, Cincinnati, OH 45221. Offers MS, PhD. Part-time programs available. Postbaccalaureate distance learning degree programs offered (no on-campus study). *Degree requirements:* For master's, thesis or alternative; for doctorate, thesis/dissertation. *Entrance requirements:* For master's, GRE or MAT, minimum GPA of 3.0; for doctorate, minimum GPA of 3.5. Additional exam requirements/recommendations for international students: Required—TOEFL (minimum score 550 paper-based), OEPT 3. Electronic applications accepted.

University of Colorado Colorado Springs, School of Public Affairs, Colorado Springs, CO 80933-7150. Offers criminal justice (MCJ); public administration (MPA). *Accreditation:* NASPAA. Part-time and evening/weekend programs available. Postbaccalaureate distance learning degree programs offered (minimal on-campus study). *Faculty:* 12 full-time (6 women), 17 part-time/adjunct (8 women). *Students:* 23 full-time (11 women), 104 part-time (49 women); includes 37 minority (13 Black or African American, non-Hispanic/Latino; 1 American Indian or Alaska Native, non-Hispanic/Latino; 6 Asian, non-Hispanic/Latino; 15 Hispanic/Latino; 1 Native Hawaiian or other Pacific Islander, non-Hispanic/Latino; 1 Two or more races, non-Hispanic/Latino), 7 international. Average age 35. 49 applicants, 90% accepted, 32 enrolled. In 2014, 34 master's awarded. *Degree requirements:* For master's, internship, capstone project, or thesis. *Entrance requirements:* For master's, GRE General Test, GMAT, LSAT, minimum GPA of 3.0. Additional exam requirements/recommendations for international students: Recommended—TOEFL (minimum score 550 paper-based; 80 iBT). *Application deadline:* For fall admission, 6/1 for domestic and international students; for spring admission, 11/1 for domestic and international students. Applications are processed on a rolling basis. Application fee: $60 ($100 for international students). *Expenses:* Expenses: Contact institution. *Financial support:* In 2014–15, 28 students received support, including 1 teaching assistantship (averaging $6,000 per year); fellowships, career-related internships or fieldwork, Federal Work-Study, and scholarships/grants also available. Support available to part-time students. Financial award application deadline: 3/1; financial award applicants required to submit FAFSA. *Faculty research:* Intimate partner violence, risk and protective factors for violent victimization, intersections of race, class, gender and crime, effective interventions for adult and juvenile offenders, sex trafficking, sentencing disparities for disadvantaged populations, child maltreatment, biosocial and developmental explanations of crime, public personnel management, organizational behavior and development, strategic leadership, national security, program evaluation, social policy, group dynamics. *Total annual research expenditures:* $120,922. *Unit head:* Dr. Terry Schwartz, Interim Dean, 719-255-4047, E-mail: tschwart@uccs.edu. *Application contact:* Crista Hill, Outreach Student Services Specialist, 719-255-4993, Fax: 719-255-4183, E-mail: chill12@uccs.edu. Website: http://www.uccs.edu/spa/

University of Colorado Denver, School of Public Affairs, Program in Criminology and Criminal Justice, Denver, CO 80217. Offers criminal justice (MCJ), including criminal justice, domestic violence, emergency management and homeland security. Part-time and evening/weekend programs available. *Students:* 40 full-time (27 women), 22 part-time (10 women); includes 12 minority (1 Black or African American, non-Hispanic/Latino; 3 Asian, non-Hispanic/Latino; 8 Hispanic/Latino), 1 international. Average age 33. 28 applicants, 71% accepted, 12 enrolled. In 2014, 22 master's awarded. *Degree requirements:* For master's, thesis or alternative, 36-39 semester credit hours. *Entrance requirements:* For master's, GRE, GMAT, LSAT, recommendations, official transcripts, current resume, essay. Additional exam requirements/recommendations for international students: Required—TOEFL (minimum score 537 paper-based; 75 iBT); Recommended—IELTS (minimum score 6.5). *Application deadline:* For fall admission, 3/15 priority date for domestic students, 3/1 priority date for international students; for spring admission, 10/15 priority date for domestic students, 10/1 priority date for international students. Application fee: $50 ($75 for international students). Electronic applications accepted. *Expenses:* Expenses: Contact institution. *Financial support:* In 2014–15, 10 students received support. Fellowships, research assistantships, teaching assistantships, Federal Work-Study, institutionally sponsored loans, scholarships/grants, traineeships, and unspecified assistantships available. Financial award application deadline: 4/1; financial award applicants required to submit FAFSA. *Faculty research:* White collar crime, women and the criminal justice system, applied family violence issues, intimate partner violence and domestic violence interventions, juvenile

delinquency. *Unit head:* Dr. Callie Rennison, MCJ Program Director, 303-315-2813, Fax: 303-315-2229, E-mail: callie.rennison@ucdenver.edu. *Application contact:* Brendan Hardy, Director of Student Recruitment, 303-315-2227, Fax: 303-315-2229, E-mail: brendan.hardy@ucdenver.edu. Website: http://ucdenver.edu/academics/colleges/SPA/Academics/programs/CriminalJustice/Pages/index.aspx

University of Colorado Denver, School of Public Affairs, Program in Public Affairs and Administration, Denver, CO 80127. Offers public administration (MPA), including domestic violence, emergency management and homeland security, environmental policy, management and law, homeland security and defense, local government, nonprofit management, public administration; public affairs (PhD). *Accreditation:* NASPAA. Part-time and evening/weekend programs available. Postbaccalaureate distance learning degree programs offered (no on-campus study). *Students:* 275 full-time (176 women), 140 part-time (93 women); includes 70 minority (7 Black or African American, non-Hispanic/Latino; 4 American Indian or Alaska Native, non-Hispanic/Latino; 9 Asian, non-Hispanic/Latino; 44 Hispanic/Latino; 2 Native Hawaiian or other Pacific Islander, non-Hispanic/Latino; 4 Two or more races, non-Hispanic/Latino), 19 international. Average age 34. 243 applicants, 71% accepted, 97 enrolled. In 2014, 127 master's, 5 doctorates awarded. *Degree requirements:* For master's, thesis or alternative, 36-39 credit hours; for doctorate, comprehensive exam, thesis/dissertation, minimum of 66 semester hours, including at least 30 hours of dissertation. *Entrance requirements:* For master's, GRE, GMAT or LSAT, resume, essay, transcripts, recommendations; for doctorate, GRE, resume, essay, transcripts, recommendations. Additional exam requirements/recommendations for international students: Required—TOEFL (minimum score 550 paper-based; 80 iBT); Recommended—IELTS (minimum score 6.5). *Application deadline:* For fall admission, 2/1 priority date for domestic students, 1/15 priority date for international students; for spring admission, 10/15 priority date for domestic students, 10/1 priority date for international students. Application fee: $50 ($75 for international students). Electronic applications accepted. *Expenses:* Expenses: Contact institution. *Financial support:* In 2014–15, 60 students received support. Fellowships with partial tuition reimbursements available, research assistantships with partial tuition reimbursements available, teaching assistantships with partial tuition reimbursements available, Federal Work-Study, institutionally sponsored loans, scholarships/grants, traineeships, and unspecified assistantships available. Financial award application deadline: 4/1; financial award applicants required to submit FAFSA. *Faculty research:* Housing, education and the social and economic issues of vulnerable populations; nonprofit governance and management; education finance, effectiveness and reform; P-20 education initiatives; municipal government accountability. *Unit head:* Dr. Christine Martell, Director of MPA Program, 303-315-2716, Fax: 303-315-2229, E-mail: christine.martell@ucdenver.edu. *Application contact:* Dawn Savage, Student Services Coordinator, 303-315-2743, Fax: 303-315-2229, E-mail: dawn.savage@ucdenver.edu. Website: http://www.ucdenver.edu/academics/colleges/SPA/Academics/programs/PublicAffairsAdmin/Pages/index.aspx

University of Delaware, College of Arts and Sciences, Department of Sociology and Criminal Justice, Newark, DE 19716. Offers criminology (MA, PhD); sociology (MA, PhD). *Degree requirements:* For master's, thesis; for doctorate, comprehensive exam, thesis/dissertation. *Entrance requirements:* For master's and doctorate, GRE, 3 letters of recommendation. Additional exam requirements/recommendations for international students: Required—TOEFL. Electronic applications accepted. *Faculty research:* Sex and gender, criminology/deviance, theory, methods, collective behavior.

University of Denver, University College, Denver, CO 80208. Offers geographic information systems (Certificate); global affairs (Certificate), including translation studies, world history and culture; information and communications technology (MCIS), including geographic information systems, information systems security, project management (MCIS, Certificate), software design and programming, technology management, telecommunications technology, Web design and development; leadership and organizations (Certificate), including human capital in organizations, philanthropic leadership, project management (MCIS, Certificate), strategic innovation and change; organizational and professional communication (MPS), including alternative dispute resolution, organizational communication, organizational development and training, public relations and marketing; security management (MAS, Certificate), including emergency planning and response, information security (MAS), organizational security. Part-time and evening/weekend programs available. Postbaccalaureate distance learning degree programs offered (no on-campus study). *Faculty:* 8 full-time (4 women), 133 part-time/adjunct (46 women). *Students:* 54 full-time (21 women), 1,327 part-time (775 women); includes 272 minority (106 Black or African American, non-Hispanic/Latino; 6 American Indian or Alaska Native, non-Hispanic/Latino; 26 Asian, non-Hispanic/Latino; 108 Hispanic/Latino; 1 Native Hawaiian or other Pacific Islander, non-Hispanic/Latino; 25 Two or more races, non-Hispanic/Latino), 116 international. Average age 35. 768 applicants, 95% accepted, 620 enrolled. In 2014, 391 master's, 196 other advanced degrees awarded. *Degree requirements:* For master's, capstone project. *Entrance requirements:* For master's, transcripts, two letters of recommendation, personal statement, resume. Additional exam requirements/recommendations for international students: Required—TOEFL (minimum score 550 paper-based; 80 iBT). *Application deadline:* For fall admission, 6/21 priority date for domestic students, 5/1 priority date for international students; for winter admission, 9/14 priority date for domestic students, 9/19 priority date for international students; for spring admission, 1/11 for domestic students, 12/12 for international students; for summer admission, 3/29 priority date for domestic students, 3/6 priority date for international students. Applications are processed on a rolling basis. Application fee: $75. Electronic applications accepted. *Expenses:* Expenses: $959 per credit hour. *Financial support:* In 2014–15, 19 students received support. Applicants required to submit FAFSA. *Unit head:* Dr. Michael McGuire, Interim Dean, 303-871-3518, E-mail: mmcguire@du.edu. *Application contact:* Information Contact, 303-871-2291, E-mail: ucoladm@du.edu. Website: http://www.universitycollege.du.edu/

University of Detroit Mercy, College of Liberal Arts and Education, Department of Criminal Justice and Human Services, Program in Criminal Justice Studies, Detroit, MI 48221. Offers MA. Part-time and evening/weekend programs available. *Degree requirements:* For master's, thesis or alternative. *Entrance requirements:* For master's, minimum GPA of 2.75. *Faculty research:* Socialization and social control, law and correction practices.

University of Detroit Mercy, College of Liberal Arts and Education, Department of Criminal Justice and Human Services, Program in Security Administration, Detroit, MI 48221. Offers MS. Part-time and evening/weekend programs available. *Degree requirements:* For master's, thesis or alternative. *Entrance requirements:* For master's, minimum GPA of 2.75. *Faculty research:* Physical information and personnel security.

University of Florida, Graduate School, College of Liberal Arts and Sciences, Department of Sociology and Criminology and Law, Gainesville, FL 32611. Offers criminology, law, and society (MA, PhD); sociology (MA, PhD), including sociology, tropical conservation and development, women's and gender studies (PhD); MA/JD. Part-time programs available. *Faculty:* 19 full-time (9 women), 9 part-time/adjunct (6 women). *Students:* 85 full-time (62 women), 9 part-time (5 women); includes 24 minority

(12 Black or African American, non-Hispanic/Latino; 4 Asian, non-Hispanic/Latino; 8 Hispanic/Latino), 22 international. 80 applicants, 34% accepted, 14 enrolled. In 2014, 17 doctorates awarded. Terminal master's awarded for partial completion of doctoral program. *Degree requirements:* For master's, thesis optional; for doctorate, comprehensive exam, thesis/dissertation. *Entrance requirements:* For master's and doctorate, GRE, minimum GPA of 3.0. Additional exam requirements/recommendations for international students: Required—TOEFL (minimum score 550 paper-based; 80 iBT), IELTS (minimum score 6). *Application deadline:* For fall admission, 1/15 for domestic and international students; for spring admission, 6/1 for domestic and international students. Applications are processed on a rolling basis. Application fee: $30. Electronic applications accepted. *Financial support:* In 2014–15, 10 fellowships, 7 research assistantships, 59 teaching assistantships were awarded. Financial award application deadline: 1/15; financial award applicants required to submit FAFSA. *Faculty research:* Law and society, juvenile justice, criminal investigation procedures, deviance, biosocial criminology, environmental sociology, comparative race and ethnic studies, health and aging, families and gender. *Unit head:* Richard Hollinger, PhD, Professor and Chair, 352-392-0265, Fax: 352-392-6568, E-mail: rhollin@ufl.edu. *Application contact:* Barbara Zsembik, PhD, Associate Professor of Sociology/Graduate Coordinator/Associate Chair, 352-294-7190, Fax: 352-392-6568, E-mail: zsembik@soc.ufl.edu.
Website: http://soccrim.clas.ufl.edu/

University of Great Falls, Graduate Studies, Program in Criminal Justice, Great Falls, MT 59405. Offers MSM. Part-time and evening/weekend programs available. *Degree requirements:* For master's, thesis optional. *Entrance requirements:* For master's, GRE General Test or MAT, 3 letters of recommendation. Additional exam requirements/recommendations for international students: Required—TOEFL (minimum score 500 paper-based). Electronic applications accepted. *Faculty research:* Delinquency, domestic violence law.

University of Guelph, Graduate Studies, College of Social and Applied Human Sciences, Department of Criminology and Criminal Justice Policy, Guelph, ON N1G 2W1, Canada. Offers MA. *Degree requirements:* For master's, thesis or major paper. *Entrance requirements:* For master's, minimum B+ average during previous 2 years of coursework. Electronic applications accepted.

University of Guelph, Graduate Studies, College of Social and Applied Human Sciences, Department of Sociology and Anthropology, Guelph, ON N1G 2W1, Canada. Offers anthropology (MA); crime and criminal justice policy (MA); sociology (MA, PhD). *Degree requirements:* For master's, thesis or major paper; for doctorate, comprehensive exam, thesis/dissertation. *Entrance requirements:* For master's, minimum B+ average during previous 2 years of course work, honors BA or equivalent; for doctorate, must have an MA in Sociology, must have 80% or higher in graduate level studies. Additional exam requirements/recommendations for international students: Required—TOEFL (minimum score 550 paper-based; 89 iBT) or IELTS (minimum score 6.5). Electronic applications accepted. *Faculty research:* Rural and development sociology; education, employment, and the workplace; race, ethnicity, and native studies; criminology and deviance; social psychology.

University of Houston–Clear Lake, School of Human Sciences and Humanities, Programs in Human Sciences, Houston, TX 77058-1002. Offers behavioral sciences (MA), including criminology, cross cultural studies, general psychology, sociology; clinical psychology (MA); criminology (MA); cross cultural studies (MA); family therapy (MA); fitness and human performance (MA); school psychology (MA). *Accreditation:* AAMFT/COAMFTE. Part-time and evening/weekend programs available. Postbaccalaureate distance learning degree programs offered (minimal on-campus study). *Degree requirements:* For master's, thesis or alternative. *Entrance requirements:* For master's, GRE General Test. Additional exam requirements/recommendations for international students: Required—TOEFL (minimum score 550 paper-based). Electronic applications accepted. *Faculty research:* Smoking cessation, adolescent sexuality, white collar crime, serial murder, human factors/human computer interaction.

University of Houston–Downtown, College of Business, Master of Security Management for Executives Program, Houston, TX 77002. Offers MSM. Part-time and evening/weekend programs available. *Faculty:* 2 full-time (0 women). *Students:* 16 part-time (5 women); includes 8 minority (3 Black or African American, non-Hispanic/Latino; 2 Asian, non-Hispanic/Latino; 2 Hispanic/Latino; 1 Two or more races, non-Hispanic/Latino). Average age 40. In 2014, 22 master's awarded. *Degree requirements:* For master's, capstone project. *Entrance requirements:* For master's, letter of intent, 3 letters of recommendation from supervisors indicating probability of applicant's success in program, proof of three years of paid work experience with supervisory or managerial responsibilities. Additional exam requirements/recommendations for international students: Required—TOEFL (minimum score 550 paper-based; 80 iBT). *Application deadline:* For fall admission, 8/1 for domestic students, 5/1 for international students; for spring admission, 11/15 for domestic students. Application fee: $35 ($60 for international students). Electronic applications accepted. *Expenses:* Expenses: $260 per credit state resident, $572 nonresident. *Financial support:* Federal Work-Study available. Financial award applicants required to submit FAFSA. *Unit head:* Dr. D. Michael Fields, Dean, College of Business, 713-221-8179, Fax: 713-221-8675, E-mail: fieldsd@uhd.edu. *Application contact:* Ceshia Love, Director of Graduate and International Admissions, 713-221-8093, Fax: 713-223-7408, E-mail: gradadmissions@uhd.edu.
Website: https://www.uhd.edu/academics/business/graduate-programs/Pages/msme-index.aspx

University of Houston–Downtown, College of Public Service, Department of Criminal Justice, Houston, TX 77002. Offers MS. Part-time and evening/weekend programs available. Postbaccalaureate distance learning degree programs offered (no on-campus study). *Faculty:* 11 full-time (6 women). *Students:* 25 full-time (17 women), 60 part-time (35 women); includes 63 minority (34 Black or African American, non-Hispanic/Latino; 3 Asian, non-Hispanic/Latino; 24 Hispanic/Latino; 2 Two or more races, non-Hispanic/Latino), 2 international. Average age 33. 45 applicants, 78% accepted, 26 enrolled. In 2014, 18 master's awarded. *Degree requirements:* For master's, thesis or project. *Entrance requirements:* For master's, personal statement, 3 letters of recommendation, minimum GPA of 3.0 on last 60 hours. Additional exam requirements/recommendations for international students: Required—TOEFL (minimum score 550 paper-based; 80 iBT). *Application deadline:* For fall admission, 8/1 for domestic students, 5/1 for international students; for spring admission, 11/15 for domestic students, 10/1 for international students. Application fee: $35 ($60 for international students). Electronic applications accepted. *Expenses:* Expenses: $260 per credit state resident, $572 nonresident. *Financial support:* Federal Work-Study and scholarships/grants available. Financial award applicants required to submit FAFSA. *Faculty research:* Policing issues, issues in security, community supervision, legal and other issues in prisons, juvenile justice. *Unit head:* Dr. Barbara Belbot, Chair, 713-221-8983, Fax: 713-221-2726, E-mail: belbotb@uhd.edu. *Application contact:* Ceshia Love, Director of Graduate and International Admissions, 713-221-8093, Fax: 713-223-7408, E-mail: gradadmissions@uhd.edu.
Website: http://www.uhd.edu/mscj/

University of Illinois at Chicago, Graduate College, College of Liberal Arts and Sciences, Department of Criminology, Law, and Justice, Chicago, IL 60607-7128. Offers MA, PhD. Evening/weekend programs available. *Faculty:* 13 full-time (6 women), 9 part-time/adjunct (2 women). *Students:* 44 full-time (33 women), 17 part-time (8 women); includes 28 minority (13 Black or African American, non-Hispanic/Latino; 1 Asian, non-Hispanic/Latino; 9 Hispanic/Latino; 2 Native Hawaiian or other Pacific Islander, non-Hispanic/Latino; 3 Two or more races, non-Hispanic/Latino), 5 international. Average age 32. 84 applicants, 33% accepted, 17 enrolled. In 2014, 11 master's, 3 doctorates awarded. *Degree requirements:* For master's, thesis. *Entrance requirements:* For master's, GRE General Test, minimum GPA of 3.0. Additional exam requirements/recommendations for international students: Required—TOEFL. *Application deadline:* For fall admission, 1/1 priority date for domestic and international students. Applications are processed on a rolling basis. Application fee: $60. Electronic applications accepted. *Expenses:* Tuition, state resident: full-time $11,254; part-time $468 per credit hour. Tuition, nonresident: full-time $23,252; part-time $968 per credit hour. *Required fees:* $1217 per term. Part-time tuition and fees vary according to course load, degree level and program. *Financial support:* Fellowships with full tuition reimbursements, research assistantships with full tuition reimbursements, teaching assistantships with full tuition reimbursements, career-related internships or fieldwork, Federal Work-Study, institutionally sponsored loans, scholarships/grants, traineeships, tuition waivers (full), and unspecified assistantships available. Financial award application deadline: 3/1; financial award applicants required to submit FAFSA. *Faculty research:* Sentencing probation, police and court use of scientific evidence, community mediation and conflict resolution. *Total annual research expenditures:* $296,000. *Unit head:* Prof. Lisa Frohmann, Head, 312-996-5290, E-mail: lfrohman@uic.edu. *Application contact:* Prof. Paul Schewe, Director of Graduate Studies, 312-413-2626, E-mail: schewepa@uic.edu.
Website: http://clj.las.uic.edu/

University of Louisiana at Monroe, Graduate School, College of Business and Social Sciences, Department of Criminal Justice, Monroe, LA 71209-0001. Offers MA. Part-time and evening/weekend programs available. *Degree requirements:* For master's, thesis optional. *Entrance requirements:* For master's, GRE General Test, minimum GPA of 2.5. Additional exam requirements/recommendations for international students: Required—TOEFL (minimum score 500 paper-based; 61 iBT). Electronic applications accepted.

University of Louisville, Graduate School, College of Arts and Sciences, Department of Justice Administration, Louisville, KY 40292. Offers MS, PhD. Part-time and evening/weekend programs available. Postbaccalaureate distance learning degree programs offered (no on-campus study). *Students:* 72 full-time (26 women), 75 part-time (27 women); includes 29 minority (16 Black or African American, non-Hispanic/Latino; 1 Asian, non-Hispanic/Latino; 7 Hispanic/Latino; 5 Two or more races, non-Hispanic/Latino), 1 international. Average age 36. 68 applicants, 78% accepted, 36 enrolled. In 2014, 11 master's awarded. *Degree requirements:* For master's, comprehensive exam (for some programs), thesis (for some programs), professional paper. *Entrance requirements:* For master's, GRE General Test, 2 letters of recommendation. Additional exam requirements/recommendations for international students: Required—TOEFL (minimum score 550 paper-based; 79 iBT). *Application deadline:* For fall admission, 7/1 for domestic students, 5/1 priority date for international students; for spring admission, 11/15 for domestic students, 11/1 priority date for international students; for summer admission, 4/1 priority date for international students. Applications are processed on a rolling basis. Application fee: $60. Electronic applications accepted. *Expenses:* Tuition, state resident: full-time $11,326; part-time $630 per credit hour. Tuition, nonresident: full-time $23,568; part-time $1311 per credit hour. *Required fees:* $196. Tuition and fees vary according to program and reciprocity agreements. *Financial support:* Research assistantships with full tuition reimbursements and health care benefits available. Financial award application deadline: 8/1; financial award applicants required to submit FAFSA. *Faculty research:* Applied research, program evaluation and policy analysis in criminal justice; juvenile sex offender research; theoretical criminology; crime analysis; organizational and leadership management. *Unit head:* Dr. Deborah G. Keeling, Chair, 502-852-6567, Fax: 502-852-0065, E-mail: dgwilson@louisville.edu. *Application contact:* Libby Leggett, Director, Graduate Admissions, 502-852-3101, Fax: 502-852-6536, E-mail: gradadm@louisville.edu.
Website: https://louisville.edu/justiceadministration/

University of Management and Technology, Program in Criminal Justice, Arlington, VA 22209. Offers homeland security (MS). Part-time and evening/weekend programs available. Postbaccalaureate distance learning degree programs offered (no on-campus study). *Entrance requirements:* Additional exam requirements/recommendations for international students: Required—TOEFL (minimum score 530 paper-based; 71 iBT).

University of Management and Technology, Program in Management, Arlington, VA 22209. Offers acquisition management (MS, AC); criminal justice administration (MS); general management (MS); project management (MS, AC). Part-time and evening/weekend programs available. Postbaccalaureate distance learning degree programs offered (no on-campus study). *Entrance requirements:* For master's, 3 recommendations, resume. Additional exam requirements/recommendations for international students: Required—TOEFL (minimum score 530 paper-based; 71 iBT). Electronic applications accepted.

The University of Manchester, School of Law, Manchester, United Kingdom. Offers bioethics and medical jurisprudence (PhD); criminology (M Phil, PhD); law (M Phil, PhD).

University of Maryland, College Park, Academic Affairs, College of Behavioral and Social Sciences, Department of Criminology and Criminal Justice, College Park, MD 20742. Offers MA, PhD, JD/MA. Part-time and evening/weekend programs available. Terminal master's awarded for partial completion of doctoral program. *Degree requirements:* For master's, comprehensive exam, thesis optional; for doctorate, comprehensive exam, thesis/dissertation. *Entrance requirements:* For master's, GRE General Test, minimum GPA of 3.0, 3 letters of recommendation; for doctorate, GRE General Test. Additional exam requirements/recommendations for international students: Required—TOEFL. Electronic applications accepted. *Faculty research:* Theory, crime prevention, death penalty, criminal justice technology, policy.

University of Maryland Eastern Shore, Graduate Programs, Department of Criminal Justice, Princess Anne, MD 21853-1299. Offers MS. Part-time and evening/weekend programs available. *Degree requirements:* For master's, comprehensive exam, thesis optional. *Entrance requirements:* For master's, GRE General Test, interview. Additional exam requirements/recommendations for international students: Required—TOEFL (minimum score 80 iBT).

University of Massachusetts Lowell, College of Fine Arts, Humanities and Social Sciences, School of Criminology and Justice Studies, Lowell, MA 01854. Offers criminal justice (MA); criminology and criminal justice (PhD); security studies (MA, MS). Part-time and evening/weekend programs available. *Degree requirements:* For master's, thesis optional. *Entrance requirements:* For master's, GRE General Test or MAT. Electronic applications accepted. *Faculty research:* Family violence, criminal justice management, corrections, policing, delinquency.

University of Memphis, Graduate School, College of Arts and Sciences, Department of Criminology and Criminal Justice, Memphis, TN 38152. Offers MA. Part-time programs available. *Faculty:* 3 full-time (0 women), 1 (woman) part-time/adjunct. *Students:* 11 full-time (7 women), 16 part-time (8 women); includes 13 minority (9 Black or African

American, non-Hispanic/Latino; 3 Hispanic/Latino; 1 Two or more races, non-Hispanic/Latino), 1 international. Average age 33. 15 applicants, 87% accepted, 5 enrolled. In 2014, 16 master's awarded. *Degree requirements:* For master's, comprehensive exam, thesis optional. *Entrance requirements:* For master's, GRE General Test, minimum GPA of 3.0. Additional exam requirements/recommendations for international students: Required—TOEFL. *Application deadline:* For fall admission, 6/1 for domestic students; for spring admission, 11/1 for domestic students. Application fee: $35 ($60 for international students). *Financial support:* In 2014–15, 11 students received support. Research assistantships with full tuition reimbursements available, teaching assistantships with full tuition reimbursements available, career-related internships or fieldwork, Federal Work-Study, institutionally sponsored loans, scholarships/grants, tuition waivers (partial), and unspecified assistantships available. Financial award application deadline: 2/15; financial award applicants required to submit FAFSA. *Faculty research:* Violence, crime prevention, crime analysis, survey research, crisis intervention. *Unit head:* Prof. W. Randolph Dupont, Chair, 901-678-2737, Fax: 901-678-5279, E-mail: rdupont@memphis.edu. *Application contact:* Dr. K. B. Turner, Coordinator of Graduate Studies, 901-678-2737, Fax: 901-678-5279, E-mail: kbturner@memphis.edu.
Website: http://www.memphis.edu/cjustice/

University of Michigan–Flint, Graduate Programs, Program in Public Administration, Flint, MI 48502-1950. Offers administration of non-profit agencies (MPA); criminal justice administration (MPA); educational administration (MPA); healthcare administration (MPA). Part-time programs available. *Faculty:* 1 full-time (0 women), 8 part-time/adjunct (3 women). *Students:* 15 full-time (9 women), 118 part-time (81 women); includes 35 minority (26 Black or African American, non-Hispanic/Latino; 1 American Indian or Alaska Native, non-Hispanic/Latino; 7 Hispanic/Latino; 1 Two or more races, non-Hispanic/Latino), 5 international. Average age 33. 69 applicants, 75% accepted, 38 enrolled. In 2014, 43 master's awarded. *Degree requirements:* For master's, thesis or alternative, internship. *Entrance requirements:* For master's, minimum GPA of 3.0; 1 course each in American government, microeconomics and statistics. Additional exam requirements/recommendations for international students: Required—TOEFL (minimum score 84 iBT), IELTS (minimum score 6.5). *Application deadline:* For fall admission, 8/1 for domestic students, 5/1 for international students; for winter admission, 11/15 for domestic students, 9/1 for international students; for spring admission, 3/15 for domestic students, 1/1 for international students; for summer admission, 5/15 for domestic students. Applications are processed on a rolling basis. Application fee: $55. Electronic applications accepted. Application fee is waived when completed online. *Expenses:* Expenses: Contact institution. *Financial support:* Career-related internships or fieldwork, Federal Work-Study, and scholarships/grants available. Support available to part-time students. Financial award application deadline: 3/1; financial award applicants required to submit FAFSA. *Unit head:* Dr. Kathryn Schellenberg, Director, 810-762-3340, E-mail: kathsch@umflint.edu. *Application contact:* Bradley T. Maki, Director of Graduate Admissions, 810-762-3171, Fax: 810-766-6789, E-mail: bmaki@umflint.edu.
Website: http://www.umflint.edu/graduateprograms/public-administration-mpa

University of Minnesota, Duluth, Graduate School, College of Liberal Arts, Department of Sociology/Anthropology, Program in Criminology, Duluth, MN 55812-2496. Offers MA. Part-time and evening/weekend programs available. *Degree requirements:* For master's, thesis or alternative. *Entrance requirements:* For master's, minimum GPA of 3.0, letter of recommendation, personal statement. Additional exam requirements/recommendations for international students: Required—TOEFL. *Faculty research:* Restorative justice, juvenile delinquency, social justice, program evaluation.

University of Missouri–Kansas City, College of Arts and Sciences, Department of Criminal Justice and Criminology, Kansas City, MO 64110-2499. Offers MS. Part-time and evening/weekend programs available. *Faculty:* 8 full-time (5 women), 5 part-time/adjunct (2 women). *Students:* 3 full-time (1 woman), 21 part-time (14 women); includes 8 minority (6 Black or African American, non-Hispanic/Latino; 1 American Indian or Alaska Native, non-Hispanic/Latino; 1 Hispanic/Latino). Average age 28. 32 applicants, 44% accepted, 8 enrolled. In 2014, 8 master's awarded. *Degree requirements:* For master's, thesis optional. *Entrance requirements:* For master's, GRE, minimum GPA of 3.0 in major, 2.7 overall. Additional exam requirements/recommendations for international students: Required—TOEFL (minimum score 550 paper-based; 80 iBT). *Application deadline:* For fall admission, 3/1 for domestic and international students; for spring admission, 11/1 for domestic and international students. Applications are processed on a rolling basis. Application fee: $45 ($50 for international students). Electronic applications accepted. *Financial support:* In 2014–15, 4 teaching assistantships with full and partial tuition reimbursements (averaging $11,200 per year) were awarded; research assistantships with full tuition reimbursements, career-related internships or fieldwork, Federal Work-Study, institutionally sponsored loans, and tuition waivers (partial) also available. Support available to part-time students. Financial award application deadline: 3/1; financial award applicants required to submit FAFSA. *Faculty research:* Death penalty, community corrections, urban community and neighborhoods. *Unit head:* Dr. Ken Novak, Chair, 816-235-1599, Fax: 816-235-5193, E-mail: novakk@umkc.edu. *Application contact:* Dr. Alexander Holsinger, Director, Graduate Program, 816-235-5288, Fax: 816-235-5193, E-mail: holsingera@umkc.edu.
Website: http://cas.umkc.edu/CJC/

University of Missouri–St. Louis, College of Arts and Sciences, Department of Criminology and Criminal Justice, St. Louis, MO 63121. Offers MA, PhD. *Faculty:* 16 full-time (7 women), 1 part-time/adjunct (0 women). *Students:* 16 full-time (12 women), 39 part-time (23 women); includes 9 minority (5 Black or African American, non-Hispanic/Latino; 3 Hispanic/Latino; 1 Two or more races, non-Hispanic/Latino), 1 international. Average age 29. 115 applicants, 35% accepted, 15 enrolled. In 2014, 14 master's, 3 doctorates awarded. *Degree requirements:* For doctorate, thesis/dissertation. *Entrance requirements:* For master's, essay; 2 letters of recommendation; for doctorate, GRE General Test, writing sample, 3 letters of recommendation. Additional exam requirements/recommendations for international students: Required—TOEFL (minimum score 550 paper-based; 65 iBT), IELTS (minimum score 6.5). *Application deadline:* For fall admission, 2/1 priority date for domestic and international students. Applications are processed on a rolling basis. Application fee: $50 ($40 for international students). Electronic applications accepted. *Expenses:* Tuition, state resident: full-time $7364; part-time $409.10 per hour. Tuition, nonresident: full-time $18,153; part-time $1008.50 per hour. *Financial support:* In 2014–15, 3 research assistantships with full and partial tuition reimbursements (averaging $13,500 per year), 15 teaching assistantships with full and partial tuition reimbursements (averaging $13,500 per year) were awarded; fellowships with full tuition reimbursements and career-related internships or fieldwork also available. Financial award applicants required to submit FAFSA. *Faculty research:* Crime control, criminological theory, juvenile delinquency, violence, drugs. *Unit head:* Dr. Beth Huebner, Director of Graduate Studies, 314-516-5031, Fax: 314-516-5048, E-mail: huebner@umsl.edu. *Application contact:* 314-516-5458, Fax: 314-516-6996, E-mail: gradadm@umsl.edu.

The University of Montana, Graduate School, College of Humanities and Sciences, Department of Sociology, Missoula, MT 59812-0002. Offers criminology (MA); inequality and social justice (MA); rural and environmental change (MA); sociology (MA). *Entrance requirements:* For master's, GRE General Test. Additional exam requirements/recommendations for international students: Required—TOEFL. *Faculty research:* Housing, homelessness, hunger, infant mortality, work safety.

University of Nebraska at Omaha, Graduate Studies, College of Public Affairs and Community Service, School of Criminology and Criminal Justice, Omaha, NE 68182. Offers MA, MS, PhD. Part-time and evening/weekend programs available. *Faculty:* 20 full-time (8 women). *Students:* 32 full-time (25 women), 61 part-time (38 women); includes 23 minority (9 Black or African American, non-Hispanic/Latino; 2 Asian, non-Hispanic/Latino; 5 Hispanic/Latino; 7 Two or more races, non-Hispanic/Latino), 2 international. Average age 30. 74 applicants, 47% accepted, 23 enrolled. In 2014, 13 master's, 4 doctorates awarded. Terminal master's awarded for partial completion of doctoral program. *Degree requirements:* For master's, comprehensive exam, thesis (for some programs); for doctorate, comprehensive exam, thesis/dissertation. *Entrance requirements:* For master's, GRE General Test, previous course work in criminal justice, statistics, and research methods; minimum GPA of 3.0; official transcripts; statement of purpose; 2 letters of recommendation; for doctorate, GRE General Test, master's degree, minimum undergraduate GPA of 3.0, 3 letters of recommendation, statement of purpose, writing sample, resume. Additional exam requirements/recommendations for international students: Required—TOEFL, IELTS, PTE. *Application deadline:* For fall admission, 2/1 for domestic and international students; for spring admission, 12/1 priority date for domestic and international students; for summer admission, 4/30 for domestic and international students. Applications are processed on a rolling basis. Application fee: $45. Electronic applications accepted. *Financial support:* In 2014–15, 21 students received support, including 13 research assistantships with tuition reimbursements available, 8 teaching assistantships with tuition reimbursements available; career-related internships or fieldwork, Federal Work-Study, institutionally sponsored loans, scholarships/grants, tuition waivers (partial), and unspecified assistantships also available. Support available to part-time students. Financial award application deadline: 3/1; financial award applicants required to submit FAFSA. *Unit head:* Dr. Candice Batton, Director, 402-554-2341, E-mail: graduate@unomaha.edu. *Application contact:* Lisa Sample, Graduate Program Chair, 402-554-2341, E-mail: graduate@unomaha.edu.

University of Nevada, Las Vegas, Graduate College, Greenspun College of Urban Affairs, Department of Criminal Justice, Las Vegas, NV 89154-5009. Offers MA, PhD. Part-time programs available. *Faculty:* 6 full-time (3 women). *Students:* 12 full-time (5 women), 6 part-time (3 women); includes 8 minority (1 Black or African American, non-Hispanic/Latino; 1 American Indian or Alaska Native, non-Hispanic/Latino; 1 Asian, non-Hispanic/Latino; 3 Hispanic/Latino; 2 Two or more races, non-Hispanic/Latino), 2 international. Average age 31. 26 applicants, 54% accepted, 5 enrolled. In 2014, 14 master's awarded. *Degree requirements:* For master's, comprehensive exam (for some programs), thesis (for some programs). *Entrance requirements:* Additional exam requirements/recommendations for international students: Required—TOEFL (minimum score 550 paper-based; 80 iBT), IELTS (minimum score 7). *Application deadline:* For fall admission, 2/1 for domestic students, 5/1 for international students; for spring admission, 10/1 for international students. Application fee: $60 ($95 for international students). Electronic applications accepted. *Financial support:* In 2014–15, 10 students received support, including 3 research assistantships with partial tuition reimbursements available (averaging $11,458 per year), 7 teaching assistantships with partial tuition reimbursements available (averaging $10,000 per year); institutionally sponsored loans, scholarships/grants, health care benefits, and unspecified assistantships also available. Financial award application deadline: 3/1. *Faculty research:* Administration of justice, corrections, criminological theory, policing, sociology of law. *Total annual research expenditures:* $58,374. *Unit head:* Dr. Joel Lieberman, Chair/Associate Professor, 702-895-0249, Fax: 702-895-0252, E-mail: joel.lieberman@unlv.edu. *Application contact:* Graduate College Admissions Evaluator, 702-895-3320, Fax: 702-895-4180, E-mail: gradcollege@unlv.edu.
Website: http://criminaljustice.unlv.edu/grad/

University of Nevada, Reno, Graduate School, College of Liberal Arts, School of Social Research and Justice Studies, Department of Criminal Justice, Reno, NV 89557. Offers MA. *Degree requirements:* For master's, comprehensive exam, thesis optional. *Entrance requirements:* For master's, GRE or LSAT, undergraduate degree in criminal justice with minimum GPA of 3.0. Additional exam requirements/recommendations for international students: Required—TOEFL (minimum score 500 paper-based; 61 iBT), IELTS (minimum score 6). Electronic applications accepted. *Faculty research:* Criminal justice system, social policy interaction.

University of Nevada, Reno, Graduate School, College of Liberal Arts, School of Social Research and Justice Studies, Program in Justice Management, Reno, NV 89557. Offers MJM. Part-time programs available. Postbaccalaureate distance learning degree programs offered (no on-campus study). *Degree requirements:* For master's, thesis optional. *Entrance requirements:* For master's, minimum GPA of 2.75. Additional exam requirements/recommendations for international students: Required—TOEFL (minimum score 500 paper-based; 61 iBT), IELTS (minimum score 6). Electronic applications accepted. *Faculty research:* Justice administration, adult justice management, juvenile justice management.

University of New Haven, Graduate School, Henry C. Lee College of Criminal Justice and Forensic Sciences, Program in Criminal Justice, West Haven, CT 06516-1916. Offers crime analysis (MS); criminal justice (MS, PhD); criminal justice management (MS, Certificate); forensic computer investigation (MS, Certificate); forensic psychology (MS); information protection and security (Certificate); victim advocacy and services management (Certificate); victimology (MS). Part-time and evening/weekend programs available. Postbaccalaureate distance learning degree programs offered (no on-campus study). *Degree requirements:* For master's, thesis or alternative. *Entrance requirements:* Additional exam requirements/recommendations for international students: Required—TOEFL (minimum score 80 iBT), IELTS, PTE (minimum score 53). Electronic applications accepted. Application fee is waived when completed online. *Expenses: Tuition:* Full-time $22,248; part-time $824 per credit hour. *Required fees:* $45 per trimester.

University of New Haven, Graduate School, Henry C. Lee College of Criminal Justice and Forensic Sciences, Program in Investigations, West Haven, CT 06516-1916. Offers criminal investigations (MS); financial crimes investigations (MS); forensic computer investigations (MS). *Expenses: Tuition:* Full-time $22,248; part-time $824 per credit hour. *Required fees:* $45 per trimester.

University of North Alabama, College of Arts and Sciences, Department of Criminal Justice, Florence, AL 35632-0001. Offers MSCJ. Part-time and evening/weekend programs available. *Faculty:* 3 full-time (1 woman), 1 part-time/adjunct (0 women). *Students:* 10 full-time (6 women), 9 part-time (7 women); includes 6 minority (4 Black or African American, non-Hispanic/Latino; 2 Hispanic/Latino), 5 international. Average age 28. 15 applicants, 80% accepted, 10 enrolled. In 2014, 20 master's awarded. *Degree requirements:* For master's, comprehensive exam. *Entrance requirements:* For master's, GRE General Test, MAT. Additional exam requirements/recommendations for international students: Required—TOEFL (minimum score 550 paper-based; 79 iBT), IELTS (minimum score 6). *Application deadline:* For fall admission, 7/1 priority date for domestic students, 7/1 for international students; for spring admission, 11/1 for domestic and international students. Applications are processed on a rolling basis. Application

fee: $25 ($50 for international students). Electronic applications accepted. *Expenses:* Tuition, state resident: full-time $5166; part-time $1722 per semester. Tuition, nonresident: full-time $10,332; part-time $3444 per semester. *Required fees:* $393.50 per semester. *Unit head:* Dr. Yaschica Williams, Chair, 256-765-5045, E-mail: ywilliams@una.edu. *Application contact:* Hillary N. Coats, Graduate Admissions Coordinator, 256-765-4447, E-mail: graduate@una.edu.
Website: http://www.una.edu/criminaljustice/

The University of North Carolina at Charlotte, College of Liberal Arts and Sciences, Department of Criminal Justice and Criminology, Charlotte, NC 28223-0001. Offers MS. Part-time and evening/weekend programs available. *Faculty:* 14 full-time (7 women). *Students:* 8 full-time (6 women), 9 part-time (5 women); includes 3 minority (2 Black or African American, non-Hispanic/Latino; 1 Hispanic/Latino). Average age 26. 13 applicants, 54% accepted, 5 enrolled. In 2014, 14 master's awarded. *Degree requirements:* For master's, thesis or comprehensive exam. *Entrance requirements:* For master's, GRE General Test or MAT, minimum GPA of 3.0 in undergraduate major, 2.75 overall. Additional exam requirements/recommendations for international students: Required—TOEFL (minimum score 557 paper-based; 83 iBT). *Application deadline:* For fall admission, 4/1 for domestic and international students; for spring admission, 10/1 for domestic and international students. Application fee: $75. Electronic applications accepted. *Expenses:* Tuition, state resident: full-time $4008. Tuition, nonresident: full-time $16,295. *Required fees:* $2755. Tuition and fees vary according to course load and program. *Financial support:* In 2014–15, 7 students received support, including 2 research assistantships (averaging $12,520 per year), 5 teaching assistantships (averaging $13,000 per year); fellowships, career-related internships or fieldwork, Federal Work-Study, institutionally sponsored loans, scholarships/grants, and unspecified assistantships also available. Support available to part-time students. Financial award application deadline: 4/1; financial award applicants required to submit FAFSA. *Faculty research:* The relationship among psychology, law, and politics; gang membership and its relationship to delinquent behaviors, capital punishment, and family violence; the impact of globalization on crime in India; police use of force, firearms, and non-lethal weapons in various countries around the world. *Total annual research expenditures:* $74,629. *Unit head:* Dr. Beth E. Bjerregaard, Chair, 704-687-0738, Fax: 704-687-3349, E-mail: bebjerre@uncc.edu. *Application contact:* Kathy B. Giddings, Director of Graduate Admissions, 704-687-5503, Fax: 704-687-1668, E-mail: gradadm@uncc.edu.
Website: http://criminaljustice.uncc.edu/graduate-programs

The University of North Carolina at Greensboro, Graduate School, College of Arts and Sciences, Department of Sociology, Greensboro, NC 27412-5001. Offers criminology (MA); sociology (MA). Part-time programs available. *Degree requirements:* For master's, comprehensive exam, thesis. *Entrance requirements:* For master's, GRE General Test. Additional exam requirements/recommendations for international students: Required—TOEFL. Electronic applications accepted.

The University of North Carolina Wilmington, College of Arts and Sciences, Department of Sociology and Criminology, Wilmington, NC 28403-3297. Offers MA. *Faculty:* 18 full-time (11 women). *Students:* 15 full-time (9 women), 8 part-time (6 women); includes 4 minority (3 Black or African American, non-Hispanic/Latino; 1 Hispanic/Latino). 26 applicants, 81% accepted, 11 enrolled. In 2014, 10 master's awarded. *Degree requirements:* For master's, comprehensive exam, thesis or internship. *Entrance requirements:* Additional exam requirements/recommendations for international students: Required—TOEFL (minimum score 79 iBT), IELTS. *Application deadline:* For fall admission, 2/15 for domestic students. Application fee: $60. Electronic applications accepted. *Expenses:* Tuition, state resident: full-time $3240. Tuition, nonresident: full-time $9208. *Required fees:* $1967. *Financial support:* Unspecified assistantships available. Financial award applicants required to submit FAFSA. *Unit head:* Dr. Leslie Hossfeld, Chair, 910-962-7849, Fax: 910-962-7385, E-mail: hossfeldl@uncw.edu. *Application contact:* Dr. Christina Lanier, Graduate Coordinator, 910-962-7691, Fax: 910-962-7385, E-mail: lanierc@uncw.edu.
Website: http://www.uncw.edu/socgrad/index.html

University of North Dakota, Graduate School, College of Arts and Sciences, Program in Criminal Justice, Grand Forks, ND 58202. Offers PhD. Part-time programs available. *Entrance requirements:* For doctorate, GRE General Test. Additional exam requirements/recommendations for international students: Required—TOEFL (minimum score 550 paper-based; 79 iBT), IELTS (minimum score 6.5). Electronic applications accepted.

University of Northern Colorado, Graduate School, College of Humanities and Social Sciences, School of Sociology and Criminal Justice, Greeley, CO 80639. Offers criminal justice (MA); sociology (MA).

University of North Florida, College of Arts and Sciences, Department of Criminology and Criminal Justice, Jacksonville, FL 32224. Offers criminal justice (MS). *Faculty:* 4 full-time (2 women), 2 part-time/adjunct (1 woman). *Students:* 17 full-time (15 women), 26 part-time (20 women); includes 22 minority (16 Black or African American, non-Hispanic/Latino; 1 Asian, non-Hispanic/Latino; 3 Hispanic/Latino; 2 Two or more races, non-Hispanic/Latino). Average age 30. 34 applicants, 50% accepted, 11 enrolled. In 2014, 17 master's awarded. *Degree requirements:* For master's, comprehensive exam, thesis optional. *Entrance requirements:* For master's, GRE General Test, minimum GPA of 3.0 in last 60 hours, letters of recommendation. Additional exam requirements/recommendations for international students: Required—TOEFL (minimum score 500 paper-based; 61 iBT). *Application deadline:* For fall admission, 7/1 priority date for domestic students, 5/1 for international students; for spring admission, 11/1 priority date for domestic students, 10/1 for international students. Application fee: $30. Electronic applications accepted. *Expenses:* Tuition, state resident: full-time $9794; part-time $408.10 per credit hour. Tuition, nonresident: full-time $22,383; part-time $932.61 per credit hour. *Required fees:* $2047; $85.29 per credit hour. Tuition and fees vary according to course load and program. *Financial support:* In 2014–15, 7 students received support. Research assistantships, teaching assistantships, Federal Work-Study, scholarships/grants, and unspecified assistantships available. Financial award application deadline: 4/1; financial award applicants required to submit FAFSA. *Unit head:* Dr. David Forde, Chair, 904-620-2313, E-mail: david.forde@unf.edu. *Application contact:* Dr. Amanda Pascale, Director, The Graduate School, 904-620-1360, Fax: 904-620-1362, E-mail: graduateschool@unf.edu.
Website: http://www.unf.edu/coas/ccj/

University of North Georgia, Department of Political Science and Criminal Justice, Dahlonega, GA 30597. Offers criminal justice (MS); international affairs (MAIA); public administration (MPA). Part-time and evening/weekend programs available. Postbaccalaureate distance learning degree programs offered (no on-campus study). *Degree requirements:* For master's, thesis optional, internship. *Entrance requirements:* For master's, GRE or GMAT, minimum undergraduate GPA of 2.5, 3 letters of recommendation. Additional exam requirements/recommendations for international students: Required—TOEFL (minimum score 550 paper-based; 79 iBT), IELTS (minimum score 6.5). Electronic applications accepted.

University of North Texas, Robert B. Toulouse School of Graduate Studies, Denton, TX 76203-5459. Offers accounting (MS); applied anthropology (MA, MS); applied behavior analysis (Certificate); applied geography (MA); applied technology and performance improvement (M Ed, MS); art education (MA); art history (MA); art museum education (Certificate); arts leadership (Certificate); audiology (Au D); behavior analysis (MS); behavioral science (PhD); biochemistry and molecular biology (MS); biology (MA, MS); biomedical engineering (MS); business analysis (MS); chemistry (MS); clinical health psychology (PhD); communication studies (MA, MS); computer engineering (MS); computer science (MS); counseling (M Ed, MS), including clinical mental health counseling (MS), college and university counseling, elementary school counseling, secondary school counseling; creative writing (MA); criminal justice (MS); curriculum and instruction (M Ed); decision sciences (MBA); design (MA, MFA), including fashion design (MFA), innovation studies, interior design (MFA); early childhood studies (MS); economics (MS); educational leadership (M Ed, Ed D); educational psychology (MS, PhD), including family studies (MS), gifted and talented (MS), human development (MS), learning and cognition (MS), research, measurement and evaluation (MS); electrical engineering (MS); emergency management (MPA); engineering technology (MS); English (MA); English as a second language (MA); environmental science (MS); finance (MBA, MS); financial management (MPA); French (MA); health services management (MBA); higher education (M Ed, Ed D); history (MA, MS); hospitality management (MS); human resources management (MPA); information science (MS); information systems (PhD); information technologies (MBA); interdisciplinary studies (MA, MS); international studies (MA); international sustainable tourism (MS); jazz studies (MM); journalism (MA, MJ, Graduate Certificate), including interactive and virtual digital communication (Graduate Certificate), narrative journalism (Graduate Certificate), public relations (Graduate Certificate); kinesiology (MS); linguistics (MA); local government management (MPA); logistics (PhD); logistics and supply chain management (MBA); long-term care, senior housing, and aging services (MA); management (PhD); marketing (MBA); mathematics (MA, MS); mechanical and energy engineering (MS, PhD); music (MA), including ethnomusicology, music theory, musicology, performance; music composition (PhD); music education (MM Ed, PhD); nonprofit management (MPA); operations and supply chain management (MBA); performance (MM, DMA); philosophy (MA); political science (MA); professional and technical communication (MA); radio, television and film (MA, MFA); rehabilitation counseling (Certificate); sociology (MA); Spanish (MA); special education (M Ed); speech-language pathology (MA); strategic management (MBA); studio art (MFA); teaching (M Ed); MBA/MS. Part-time and evening/weekend programs available. Postbaccalaureate distance learning degree programs offered. *Faculty:* 651 full-time (215 women), 233 part-time/adjunct (139 women). *Students:* 3,040 full-time (1,598 women), 3,401 part-time (2,097 women); includes 1,740 minority (533 Black or African American, non-Hispanic/Latino; 15 American Indian or Alaska Native, non-Hispanic/Latino; 286 Asian, non-Hispanic/Latino; 746 Hispanic/Latino; 3 Native Hawaiian or other Pacific Islander, non-Hispanic/Latino; 157 Two or more races, non-Hispanic/Latino), 1,145 international. Terminal master's awarded for partial completion of doctoral program. *Degree requirements:* For master's, variable foreign language requirement, comprehensive exam (for some programs), thesis (for some programs); for doctorate, variable foreign language requirement, comprehensive exam (for some programs), thesis/dissertation; for other advanced degree, variable foreign language requirement, comprehensive exam (for some programs). *Entrance requirements:* For master's and doctorate, GRE, GMAT. Additional exam requirements/recommendations for international students: Required—TOEFL (minimum score 550 paper-based; 79 iBT). *Application deadline:* For fall admission, 7/15 for domestic students, 3/15 for international students; for spring admission, 11/15 for domestic students, 9/15 for international students; for summer admission, 5/1 for domestic students. Applications are processed on a rolling basis. Application fee: $60. Electronic applications accepted. *Expenses:* Tuition, state resident: full-time $5450; part-time $3633 per year. Tuition, nonresident: full-time $11,966; part-time $7977 per year. *Required fees:* $1301; $398 per credit hour. $685 per semester. Tuition and fees vary according to program and reciprocity agreements. *Financial support:* Fellowships with partial tuition reimbursements, research assistantships with partial tuition reimbursements, teaching assistantships, career-related internships or fieldwork, Federal Work-Study, institutionally sponsored loans, scholarships/grants, health care benefits, and library assistantships available. Support available to part-time students. Financial award applicants required to submit FAFSA. *Unit head:* Mark Wardell, Dean, 940-565-2383, E-mail: mark.wardell@unt.edu. *Application contact:* Toulouse School of Graduate Studies, 940-565-2383, Fax: 940-565-2141, E-mail: gradsch@unt.edu.
Website: http://tsgs.unt.edu/

University of Ottawa, Faculty of Graduate and Postdoctoral Studies, Faculty of Social Sciences, Department of Criminology, Ottawa, ON K1N 6N5, Canada. Offers MA, MCA, PhD. *Degree requirements:* For master's, thesis or alternative. *Entrance requirements:* For master's, honors bachelor's degree or equivalent, minimum B average. Electronic applications accepted. *Faculty research:* Creation and reform of criminal policies in Canada.

University of Pennsylvania, School of Arts and Sciences, Graduate Group in Criminology, Philadelphia, PA 19104. Offers MA, MS, PhD. *Faculty:* 17 full-time (3 women). *Students:* 16 full-time (11 women), 3 part-time (all women); includes 4 minority (1 Black or African American, non-Hispanic/Latino; 1 Asian, non-Hispanic/Latino; 1 Hispanic/Latino; 1 Two or more races, non-Hispanic/Latino), 4 international. 94 applicants, 23% accepted, 13 enrolled. In 2014, 20 master's, 1 doctorate awarded. Application fee: $70. *Financial support:* Institutionally sponsored loans, scholarships/grants, traineeships, health care benefits, and unspecified assistantships available. *Unit head:* Dr. Ralph M. Rosen, Associate Dean for Graduate Studies, 215-898-7156, Fax: 215-573-8068, E-mail: grad-dean@sas.upenn.edu. *Application contact:* Arts and Sciences Graduate Admissions, 215-573-5816, Fax: 215-573-8068, E-mail: gdasadmis@sas.upenn.edu.
Website: http://www.sas.upenn.edu/graduate-division

University of Phoenix–Augusta Campus, College of Criminal Justice and Security, Augusta, GA 30909-4583. Offers administration of justice and security (MS).

University of Phoenix–Austin Campus, College of Criminal Justice and Security, Austin, TX 78759. Offers administration of justice and security (MS). Postbaccalaureate distance learning degree programs offered.

University of Phoenix–Bay Area Campus, College of Criminal Justice and Security, San Jose, CA 95134-1805. Offers administration of justice and security (MS).

University of Phoenix–Birmingham Campus, College of Social and Behavioral Science, Birmingham, AL 35242. Offers administration of justice and security (MS); psychology (MS).

University of Phoenix–Dallas Campus, College of Criminal Justice and Security, Dallas, TX 75251. Offers administration of justice and security (MS). Postbaccalaureate distance learning degree programs offered. *Degree requirements:* For master's, thesis (for some programs). *Entrance requirements:* For master's, minimum undergraduate GPA of 2.5, 3 years of work experience. Additional exam requirements/recommendations for international students: Required—TOEFL (minimum score 550 paper-based; 79 iBT). Electronic applications accepted.

University of Phoenix–Des Moines Campus, College of Criminal Justice and Security, Des Moines, IA 50309. Offers administration of justice and security (MS). Postbaccalaureate distance learning degree programs offered.

University of Phoenix–Jersey City Campus, College of Criminal Justice and Security, Jersey City, NJ 07310. Offers administration of justice and security (MS). Postbaccalaureate distance learning degree programs offered.

University of Phoenix–Kansas City Campus, College of Criminal Justice and Security, Kansas City, MO 64131. Offers administration of justice and security (MS). Evening/weekend programs available. Postbaccalaureate distance learning degree programs offered. *Degree requirements:* For master's, thesis (for some programs). *Entrance requirements:* For master's, 3 years work experience, minimum undergraduate GPA of 2.5. Additional exam requirements/recommendations for international students: Required—TOEFL (minimum score 550 paper-based).

University of Phoenix–Memphis Campus, College of Criminal Justice and Security, Cordova, TN 38018. Offers administration of justice and security (MS).

University of Phoenix–Online Campus, College of Justice and Security, Phoenix, AZ 85034-7209. Offers administration of justice and security (MS), including administration of justice and security, global and homeland security, law enforcement organizations; public administration (MPA). Evening/weekend programs available. Postbaccalaureate distance learning degree programs offered. *Entrance requirements:* Additional exam requirements/recommendations for international students: Required—TOEFL, TOEIC (Test of English as an International Communication), Berlitz Online English Proficiency Exam, PTE, or IELTS. Electronic applications accepted. *Expenses:* Contact institution.

University of Phoenix–Phoenix Campus, College of Criminal Justice and Security, Tempe, AZ 85282-2371. Offers administration of justice and security (MS); global and homeland security (MS); law enforcement organizations (MS); public administration (MPA). Evening/weekend programs available. Postbaccalaureate distance learning degree programs offered. *Entrance requirements:* Additional exam requirements/recommendations for international students: Required—TOEFL, TOEIC (Test of English as an International Communication), Berlitz Online English Proficiency Exam, PTE, or IELTS. Electronic applications accepted. *Expenses:* Contact institution.

University of Phoenix–St. Louis Campus, College of Criminal Justice and Security, St. Louis, MO 63043. Offers administration of justice and security (MS). Evening/weekend programs available. *Degree requirements:* For master's, thesis (for some programs). *Entrance requirements:* For master's, minimum undergraduate GPA of 2.5, 3 years work experience. Additional exam requirements/recommendations for international students: Required—TOEFL (minimum score 550 paper-based; 79 iBT). Electronic applications accepted.

University of Phoenix–San Antonio Campus, College of Criminal Justice and Security, San Antonio, TX 78230. Offers administration of justice and security (MS).

University of Phoenix–Savannah Campus, College of Criminal Justice and Security, Savannah, GA 31405-7400. Offers administration of justice and security (MS).

University of Phoenix–Southern California Campus, College of Criminal Justice and Security, Costa Mesa, CA 92626. Offers administration of justice and security (MS), including administration of justice and security, global and homeland security, law enforcement organizations; public administration (MPA). Evening/weekend programs available. Postbaccalaureate distance learning degree programs offered. *Entrance requirements:* Additional exam requirements/recommendations for international students: Required—TOEFL, TOEIC (Test of English as an International Communication), Berlitz Online English Proficiency Exam, PTE, or IELTS. Electronic applications accepted. *Expenses:* Contact institution.

University of Phoenix–Washington D.C. Campus, College of Criminal Justice and Security, Washington, DC 20001. Offers administration of justice and security (MS).

University of Phoenix–Western Washington Campus, College of Criminal Justice and Security, Tukwila, WA 98188. Offers administration of justice and security (MS). Evening/weekend programs available. *Degree requirements:* For master's, thesis (for some programs). *Entrance requirements:* For master's, minimum undergraduate GPA of 2.5, 3 years of work experience. Additional exam requirements/recommendations for international students: Required—TOEFL (minimum score 550 paper-based; 79 iBT). Electronic applications accepted.

University of Pittsburgh, School of Law, Master of Studies in Law Program, Pittsburgh, PA 15260. Offers business law (MSL), including commercial law, corporate law, general business law, international business, tax law; Constitutional law (MSL); criminal law and justice (MSL); disability law (MSL); education law (MSL); elder and estate planning law (MSL); employment and labor law (MSL); energy law (MSL); environmental and real estate law (MSL); family law (MSL); health law (MSL); intellectual property and technology law (MSL); international and human rights law (MSL); jurisprudence (MSL); personal injury and civil litigation (MSL); regulatory law (MSL); self-designed (MSL); sports and entertainment law (MSL). Part-time programs available. *Faculty:* 36 full-time (13 women), 120 part-time/adjunct (33 women). *Students:* 2 full-time (both women), 7 part-time (3 women); includes 2 minority (1 Black or African American, non-Hispanic/Latino; 1 Asian, non-Hispanic/Latino). Average age 29. 19 applicants, 95% accepted, 9 enrolled. In 2014, 4 master's awarded. *Entrance requirements:* Additional exam requirements/recommendations for international students: Required—TOEFL (minimum score 600 paper-based; 100 iBT). *Application deadline:* For fall admission, 6/30 for domestic students, 5/1 for international students. Applications are processed on a rolling basis. Application fee: $0. *Expenses:* Tuition, state resident: full-time $20,742; part-time $838 per credit. Tuition, nonresident: full-time $33,960; part-time $1389 per credit. *Required fees:* $800; $205 per term. Tuition and fees vary according to program. *Faculty research:* Law, health law, business law, contracts, intellectual property, environmental law. *Unit head:* Prof. Alan Meisel, Director, 412-648-1384, Fax: 412-648-2649, E-mail: meisel@pitt.edu. *Application contact:* Beth Ann Pischke, Administrative Coordinator, 412-648-7120, Fax: 412-648-2649, E-mail: pischke@pitt.edu.
Website: http://www.law.pitt.edu/msl

University of Regina, Faculty of Graduate Studies and Research, Faculty of Arts, Department of Justice Studies, Regina, SK S4S 0A2, Canada. Offers justice studies (MA); police studies (MA). Part-time programs available. *Faculty:* 4 full-time (2 women). *Students:* 4 full-time (2 women), 8 part-time (4 women). 8 applicants, 38% accepted. In 2014, 9 master's awarded. *Degree requirements:* For master's, thesis. *Entrance requirements:* For master's, writing sample. Additional exam requirements/recommendations for international students: Required—TOEFL (minimum score 580 paper-based; 80 iBT), IELTS (minimum score 6.5), PTE (minimum score 59). *Application deadline:* For fall admission, 1/15 for domestic and international students. Application fee: $100. Electronic applications accepted. *Expenses:* Tuition, area resident: Full-time $4900 Canadian dollars; part-time $837.65 Canadian dollars per semester. *International tuition:* $7900 Canadian dollars full-time. *Required fees:* $396 Canadian dollars; $86.90 Canadian dollars per semester. *Financial support:* In 2014–15, 1 fellowship (averaging $6,000 per year), 5 teaching assistantships (averaging $2,427 per year) were awarded; research assistantships also available. Financial award application deadline: 6/15. *Faculty research:* Restorative and social justice, policing, public policy, social policy and planning. *Unit head:* Dr. Hirsch Greenberg, Department Head, 306-585-4038, Fax: 306-585-4815, E-mail: hirsch.greenberg@uregina.ca. *Application contact:* Dr. Nick Jones, Graduate Program Coordinator, 306-585-4862, Fax: 306-585-4815, E-mail: nick.jones@uregina.ca.
Website: http://www.uregina.ca/arts/justice-studies

University of South Africa, College of Law, Pretoria, South Africa. Offers correctional services management (M Tech); criminology (MA, PhD); law (LL M, LL D); penology (MA, PhD); police science (MA, PhD); policing (M Tech); security risk management (M Tech); social science in criminology (MA).

University of South Carolina, The Graduate School, College of Arts and Sciences, Department of Criminology and Criminal Justice, Columbia, SC 29208. Offers MA, PhD, JD/MA. Part-time and evening/weekend programs available. *Degree requirements:* For master's, comprehensive exam, thesis; for doctorate, comprehensive exam, thesis/dissertation. *Entrance requirements:* For master's and doctorate, GRE. Additional exam requirements/recommendations for international students: Required—TOEFL. Electronic applications accepted. *Faculty research:* Juvenile delinquency, substance abuse, policy development, minority issues, law enforcement services.

The University of South Dakota, Graduate School, College of Arts and Sciences, Program in Administrative Studies, Vermillion, SD 57069-2390. Offers alcohol and drug studies (MSA); criminal justice (MSA); health services administration (MSA); human resource management (MSA); interdisciplinary (MSA); long term care administration (MSA); organizational leadership (MSA). Part-time and evening/weekend programs available. Postbaccalaureate distance learning degree programs offered (no on-campus study). *Degree requirements:* For master's, thesis or alternative. *Entrance requirements:* For master's, 3 years of work or experience, minimum GPA of 2.7, resume. Additional exam requirements/recommendations for international students: Required—TOEFL (minimum score 550 paper-based; 79 iBT). Electronic applications accepted.

University of Southern Mississippi, Graduate School, College of Science and Technology, Department of Administration of Justice, Hattiesburg, MS 39406-0001. Offers administration of justice (PhD); corrections (MA, MS); forensics (MS); juvenile justice (MA, MS); law enforcement (MA, MS). Part-time programs available. *Degree requirements:* For master's, comprehensive exam, thesis; for doctorate, comprehensive exam, thesis/dissertation. *Entrance requirements:* For master's, GRE General Test, minimum GPA of 2.75 in last 60 hours, 3.0 in field of study; for doctorate, GRE General Test, minimum GPA of 3.5. Additional exam requirements/recommendations for international students: Required—TOEFL, IELTS. *Faculty research:* Crime in the family, police training models, humanities and criminal justice.

University of South Florida, College of Behavioral and Community Sciences, Department of Criminology, Tampa, FL 33620-9951. Offers criminal justice administration (MA); criminology (MA, PhD). *Faculty:* 13 full-time (4 women). *Students:* 31 full-time (19 women), 63 part-time (34 women); includes 24 minority (9 Black or African American, non-Hispanic/Latino; 2 Asian, non-Hispanic/Latino; 11 Hispanic/Latino; 1 Native Hawaiian or other Pacific Islander, non-Hispanic/Latino; 1 Two or more races, non-Hispanic/Latino), 1 international. Average age 34. 127 applicants, 46% accepted, 37 enrolled. In 2014, 29 master's, 4 doctorates awarded. *Degree requirements:* For master's, comprehensive exam (for some programs), thesis (for some programs); for doctorate, comprehensive exam, thesis/dissertation. *Entrance requirements:* For master's, GRE General Test (for MA in criminology with minimum preferred scores of 153 verbal, 144 quantitative, and 4.0 in analytical writing, statement of purpose; minimum GPA of 3.0 in all upper-division coursework for bachelor's degree, three letters of recommendation, and writing sample (for criminology); minimum undergraduate GPA of 3.0, work experience in the criminal justice field, and two letters of recommendation (for criminal justice administration); for doctorate, GRE General Test (minimum preferred scores of 153 verbal, 144 quantitative, and 4.0 in analytical writing or combined score of 1000 on old scoring), minimum GPA of 3.0 in all upper-division coursework for bachelor's degree or 3.4 in graduate coursework; three letters of recommendation; statement of purpose; sample of academic written work. Additional exam requirements/recommendations for international students: Required—TOEFL (minimum score 550 paper-based; 79 iBT) or IELTS (minimum score 6.5). *Application deadline:* For fall admission, 1/15 for domestic students, 1/2 for international students; for spring admission, 9/30 for domestic students, 6/1 for international students. Application fee: $30. Electronic applications accepted. *Financial support:* In 2014–15, 21 students received support, including 2 research assistantships (averaging $14,172 per year), 15 teaching assistantships with tuition reimbursements available (averaging $11,702 per year). *Faculty research:* Juvenile justice and delinquency, substance use and abuse, macro-level models of criminal behavior, race and social control, violence. *Total annual research expenditures:* $443,559. *Unit head:* Dr. Michael Leiber, Professor and Chair, 813-974-9704, Fax: 813-974-2803, E-mail: mjleiber@usf.edu. *Application contact:* Dr. Ojmarrh Mitchell, Associate Professor and Graduate Director, 813-974-2815, Fax: 813-974-2803, E-mail: omitchell@usf.edu.
Website: http://criminology.cbcs.usf.edu/

University of South Florida, Innovative Education, Tampa, FL 33620-9951. *Unit head:* Kathy Barnes, Interdisciplinary Programs Coordinator, 813-974-8031, Fax: 813-974-7061, E-mail: barnesk@usf.edu. *Application contact:* Karen Tylinski, Metro Initiatives, 813-974-9943, Fax: 813-974-7061, E-mail: ktylinsk@usf.edu.
Website: http://www.usf.edu/innovative-education/

University of South Florida Sarasota-Manatee, College of Arts and Sciences, Sarasota, FL 34243. Offers criminal justice administration (MA). Part-time and evening/weekend programs available. Postbaccalaureate distance learning degree programs offered (minimal on-campus study). *Faculty:* 4 full-time (3 women). *Students:* 16 part-time (11 women); includes 5 minority (1 Black or African American, non-Hispanic/Latino; 2 American Indian or Alaska Native, non-Hispanic/Latino; 2 Hispanic/Latino). Average age 34. 18 applicants, 28% accepted, 3 enrolled. In 2014, 8 master's awarded. *Degree requirements:* For master's, comprehensive exam (for some programs), thesis, research grant proposal (equivalent to a master's thesis). *Entrance requirements:* For master's, GRE if upper-level GPA is below 3.0, two letters of recommendation; 1-2 page statement of purpose. Additional exam requirements/recommendations for international students: Required—TOEFL (minimum score 550 paper-based; 79 iBT), IELTS (minimum score 6.5). *Application deadline:* For fall admission, 3/1 priority date for domestic students, 3/1 for international students; for spring admission, 10/1 priority date for domestic students, 10/1 for international students. Applications are processed on a rolling basis. Application fee: $30. Electronic applications accepted. *Expenses:* Expenses: Contact institution. *Financial support:* Career-related internships or fieldwork, institutionally sponsored loans, scholarships/grants, health care benefits, and unspecified assistantships available. Support available to part-time students. Financial award application deadline: 3/1; financial award applicants required to submit FAFSA. *Faculty research:* Criminological theories; relationships among race, racism, and crime; law enforcement information sharing; directive communication in gerontological practice; age bias and prejudicial views toward older people. *Unit head:* Dr. Jane Rose, Dean, 941-359-4469, Fax: 941-359-4489, E-mail: jane.rose@sar.usf.edu. *Application contact:* Andy Telatovich, Director, Admissions, 941-359-4330, Fax: 941-359-4585, E-mail: atelatovich@sar.usf.edu.
Website: http://usfsm.edu/college-of-arts-sciences/

Criminal Justice and Criminology

The University of Tennessee, Graduate School, College of Arts and Sciences, Department of Sociology, Knoxville, TN 37996. Offers criminology (MA, PhD); energy, environment, and resource policy (MA, PhD); political economy (MA, PhD). Part-time programs available. *Degree requirements:* For master's, thesis or alternative; for doctorate, thesis/dissertation. *Entrance requirements:* For master's, GRE General Test, minimum GPA of 3.0; for doctorate, GRE General Test, minimum GPA of 3.5. Additional exam requirements/recommendations for international students: Required—TOEFL. Electronic applications accepted.

The University of Tennessee at Chattanooga, Program in Criminal Justice, Chattanooga, TN 37403. Offers MSCJ. Part-time and evening/weekend programs available. *Faculty:* 5 full-time (2 women). *Students:* 16 full-time (8 women), 16 part-time (9 women); includes 8 minority (4 Black or African American, non-Hispanic/Latino; 2 Hispanic/Latino; 2 Two or more races, non-Hispanic/Latino). Average age 28. 22 applicants, 82% accepted, 11 enrolled. In 2014, 8 master's awarded. *Degree requirements:* For master's, thesis optional, qualifying exams, internship. *Entrance requirements:* For master's, GRE General Test or MAT. Additional exam requirements/recommendations for international students: Required—TOEFL (minimum score 550 paper-based; 79 iBT), IELTS (minimum score 6). *Application deadline:* For fall admission, 6/13 priority date for domestic students, 6/1 for international students; for spring admission, 10/15 priority date for domestic students, 10/1 for international students. Applications are processed on a rolling basis. Application fee: $30 ($35 for international students). Electronic applications accepted. *Expenses:* Tuition, state resident: full-time $7708; part-time $428 per credit hour. Tuition, nonresident: full-time $23,826; part-time $1323 per credit hour. *Required fees:* $1708; $252 per credit hour. *Financial support:* In 2014–15, 6 research assistantships with tuition reimbursements (averaging $6,861 per year), 2 teaching assistantships with tuition reimbursements (averaging $6,855 per year) were awarded; career-related internships or fieldwork, scholarships/grants, and unspecified assistantships also available. Support available to part-time students. Financial award applicants required to submit FAFSA. *Faculty research:* Violence against women, crime prevention, police accountability, criminal justice privatization, public policy. *Unit head:* Dr. Tammy Garland, Acting Department Head, 423-425-5245, Fax: 423-425-2228, E-mail: tammy-garland@utc.edu. *Application contact:* Dr. J. Randy Walker, Interim Dean of Graduate Studies, 423-425-4478, Fax: 423-425-5223, E-mail: randy-walker@utc.edu.
Website: http://www.utc.edu/Academic/CriminalJustice/degree-master-general.php

The University of Texas at Arlington, Graduate School, College of Liberal Arts, Department of Criminology and Criminal Justice, Arlington, TX 76019. Offers MA. Part-time and evening/weekend programs available. *Degree requirements:* For master's, comprehensive exam, thesis or alternative. *Entrance requirements:* For master's, GRE General Test, minimum GPA of 3.0 in last 60 hours of undergraduate course work, 3 letters of recommendation. Additional exam requirements/recommendations for international students: Required—TOEFL (minimum score 550 paper-based).

The University of Texas at Dallas, School of Economic, Political and Policy Sciences, Program in Criminology, Richardson, TX 75080. Offers criminology (MS, PhD); justice administration and leadership (MS). Part-time and evening/weekend programs available. *Faculty:* 11 full-time (4 women), 1 part-time/adjunct (0 women). *Students:* 51 full-time (29 women), 27 part-time (12 women); includes 32 minority (15 Black or African American, non-Hispanic/Latino; 5 Asian, non-Hispanic/Latino; 12 Hispanic/Latino), 1 international. Average age 33. 92 applicants, 38% accepted, 22 enrolled. In 2014, 29 master's, 1 doctorate awarded. *Degree requirements:* For master's, thesis; for doctorate, thesis/dissertation. *Entrance requirements:* For master's, GRE General Test, minimum GPA of 3.0 in upper-level course work in field; for doctorate, GRE (minimum combined verbal and quantitative score of 1200), minimum GPA of 3.2 in upper-level course work in field. Additional exam requirements/recommendations for international students: Required—TOEFL (minimum score 550 paper-based). *Application deadline:* For fall admission, 7/15 for domestic students, 5/1 priority date for international students; for spring admission, 11/15 for domestic students, 9/1 priority date for international students. Applications are processed on a rolling basis. Application fee: $50 ($100 for international students). Electronic applications accepted. *Expenses:* Tuition, state resident: full-time $11,940; part-time $663 per credit. Tuition, nonresident: full-time $22,282; part-time $1238 per credit. *Financial support:* In 2014–15, 41 students received support, including 4 research assistantships with partial tuition reimbursements available (averaging $12,488 per year), 13 teaching assistantships with partial tuition reimbursements available (averaging $12,115 per year); career-related internships or fieldwork, Federal Work-Study, institutionally sponsored loans, scholarships/grants, and unspecified assistantships also available. Support available to part-time students. Financial award application deadline: 4/30; financial award applicants required to submit FAFSA. *Faculty research:* Developmental criminology, domestic violence, mental health and violence, the death penalty, corrections. *Unit head:* Dr. John L. Worrall, Program Head, 972-883-4893, Fax: 972-883-2735, E-mail: worrall@utdallas.edu. *Application contact:* Laurel Brown, Graduate Program Administrator, 972-883-4982, Fax: 972-883-2735, E-mail: lbrown@utdallas.edu.
Website: http://www.utdallas.edu/epps/criminology/

The University of Texas at San Antonio, College of Public Policy, Department of Criminal Justice, San Antonio, TX 78207. Offers criminology (MS). Part-time and evening/weekend programs available. *Faculty:* 6 full-time (1 woman). *Students:* 12 full-time (6 women), 15 part-time (7 women); includes 20 minority (3 Black or African American, non-Hispanic/Latino; 1 American Indian or Alaska Native, non-Hispanic/Latino; 14 Hispanic/Latino; 2 Two or more races, non-Hispanic/Latino). Average age 28. 18 applicants, 83% accepted, 11 enrolled. In 2014, 15 master's awarded. *Degree requirements:* For master's, variable foreign language requirement, minimum of 36 semester credit hours; thesis or written comprehensive exams. *Entrance requirements:* For master's, minimum GPA of 3.0 in last 60 hours of undergraduate course work; 2 letters of recommendation; resume; 18 credit hours in criminal justice, criminology or closely-related discipline. Additional exam requirements/recommendations for international students: Required—TOEFL (minimum score 550 paper-based; 79 iBT), IELTS (minimum score 6.5). *Application deadline:* For fall admission, 7/1 for domestic students, 4/1 for international students; for spring admission, 11/1 for domestic students, 9/1 for international students. Application fee: $45 ($80 for international students). Electronic applications accepted. *Expenses:* Expenses: Contact institution. *Financial support:* In 2014–15, 7 students received support, including 10 research assistantships (averaging $8,037 per year), 2 teaching assistantships (averaging $8,037 per year). Financial award application deadline: 2/15. *Faculty research:* Criminological theory, crime prevention, administration of justice, correctional interventions, evidence-based practices and program evaluation. *Total annual research expenditures:* $14,395. *Unit head:* Dr. Richard Hartley, Associate Professor and Chair, 210-458-2535, Fax: 210-458-2680, E-mail: richard.hartley@utsa.edu. *Application contact:* Dr. Marie Tillyer, Associate Professor/Graduate Advisor of Record, 210-458-2682, Fax: 210-459-2680, E-mail: marie.tillyer@utsa.edu.
Website: http://copp.utsa.edu/department/about-us/

The University of Texas at Tyler, College of Arts and Sciences, Department of Social Sciences, Tyler, TX 75799-0001. Offers criminal justice (MS); public administration (MPA); sociology (MS). Part-time and evening/weekend programs available. *Degree requirements:* For master's, comprehensive exam, thesis optional. *Entrance requirements:* For master's, GRE General Test, minimum GPA of 3.0. Additional exam requirements/recommendations for international students: Required—TOEFL. *Faculty research:* Urban segregation, minority business, violent crime, gender discrimination.

The University of Texas of the Permian Basin, Office of Graduate Studies, College of Arts and Sciences, Department of Social Sciences, Program in Criminal Justice Administration, Odessa, TX 79762-0001. Offers MS. Part-time and evening/weekend programs available. *Degree requirements:* For master's, comprehensive exam (for some programs), thesis (for some programs). *Entrance requirements:* For master's, GRE General Test, 3 letters of recommendation. Additional exam requirements/recommendations for international students: Required—TOEFL (minimum score 550 paper-based).

The University of Texas–Pan American, College of Social and Behavioral Sciences, Department of Criminal Justice, Edinburg, TX 78539. Offers MS. Part-time and evening/weekend programs available. Postbaccalaureate distance learning degree programs offered (no on-campus study). *Degree requirements:* For master's, comprehensive exam, applied project or thesis. *Entrance requirements:* For master's, minimum GPA of 2.75. *Expenses:* Tuition, state resident: full-time $4187; part-time $232.60 per credit hour. Tuition, nonresident: full-time $10,857; part-time $603.16 per credit hour. *Required fees:* $782; $27.50 per credit hour. $143.35 per semester. *Faculty research:* Comparative criminal justice systems, death penalty, community policing, Hispanic women.

University of the Fraser Valley, Graduate Studies, Abbotsford, BC V2S 7M8, Canada. Offers criminal justice (MA); social work (MSW). Evening/weekend programs available. *Degree requirements:* For master's, thesis optional, major research paper. *Entrance requirements:* For master's, bachelor's degree, work experience in related field. Additional exam requirements/recommendations for international students: Recommended—TOEFL (minimum score 88 iBT), IELTS (minimum score 6.5), TWE. Electronic applications accepted. *Expenses:* Contact institution. *Faculty research:* Criminal justice, criminology, social work, child welfare.

The University of Toledo, College of Graduate Studies, College of Social Justice and Human Service, Department of Criminal Justice and Social Work, Toledo, OH 43606-3390. Offers child advocacy (Certificate); criminal justice (MA); elder law (Certificate); juvenile justice (Certificate); patient advocacy (Certificate); social work (MSW); JD/MA. *Accreditation:* CSWE. Part-time programs available. *Degree requirements:* For master's, comprehensive exam, thesis. *Entrance requirements:* For master's and Certificate, minimum cumulative GPA of 2.7 for all previous academic work, letters of recommendation. Additional exam requirements/recommendations for international students: Required—TOEFL (minimum score 550 paper-based; 80 iBT). Electronic applications accepted.

University of Toronto, School of Graduate Studies, Faculty of Arts and Science, Centre for Criminology and Sociolegal Studies, Toronto, ON M5S 2J7, Canada. Offers MA, PhD, JD/MA. Part-time programs available. *Degree requirements:* For doctorate, comprehensive exam, thesis/dissertation. *Entrance requirements:* For master's, 2 letters of reference, bachelor's degree in social science or humanities, minimum B+ average in last 2 years of undergraduate study; for doctorate, 2 letters of reference, MA in criminology or equivalent, minimum A- average. Additional exam requirements/recommendations for international students: Required—TOEFL (minimum score 580 paper-based; 93 iBT), TWE (minimum score 5). Electronic applications accepted.

University of West Florida, College of Professional Studies, Department of Research and Advanced Studies, Pensacola, FL 32514-5750. Offers administration (MSA), including acquisition and contract administration, biomedical/pharmaceutical, criminal justice administration, database administration, education leadership, healthcare administration, human performance technology, leadership, nursing administration, public administration, software engineering and administration; college student personnel administration (M Ed), including college personnel administration, guidance and counseling; curriculum and instruction (M Ed, Ed S); educational leadership (M Ed); middle and secondary level education and ESOL (M Ed). Part-time and evening/weekend programs available. *Entrance requirements:* For master's, GRE or MAT, official transcripts; minimum undergraduate GPA of 3.0; letter of intent; three letters of recommendation; resume. Additional exam requirements/recommendations for international students: Required—TOEFL (minimum score 550 paper-based).

University of West Florida, College of Professional Studies, School of Justice Studies and Social Work, Department of Justice Studies, Pensacola, FL 32514-5750. Offers criminal justice (MS). Part-time and evening/weekend programs available. *Degree requirements:* For master's, thesis optional. *Entrance requirements:* For master's, GRE or MAT, official transcripts; minimum undergraduate cumulative GPA of 3.0; 3 letters of recommendation; personal statement. Additional exam requirements/recommendations for international students: Required—TOEFL (minimum score 550 paper-based). Electronic applications accepted.

University of West Georgia, College of Social Sciences, Department of Criminology, Carrollton, GA 30118. Offers MA. Part-time and evening/weekend programs available. *Faculty:* 10 full-time (6 women). *Students:* 20 full-time (14 women), 5 part-time (3 women); includes 10 minority (9 Black or African American, non-Hispanic/Latino; 1 Asian, non-Hispanic/Latino). Average age 28. 15 applicants, 100% accepted, 12 enrolled. In 2014, 7 master's awarded. *Degree requirements:* For master's, one foreign language, thesis optional. *Entrance requirements:* For master's, GRE General Test (recommended combined score of 295), minimum GPA of 2.5, references, intellectual biography. Additional exam requirements/recommendations for international students: Required—TOEFL (minimum score 523 paper-based; 69 iBT); Recommended—IELTS (minimum score 6). *Application deadline:* For fall admission, 7/31 for domestic students, 6/1 for international students; for spring admission, 11/30 for domestic students, 10/15 for international students. Applications are processed on a rolling basis. Application fee: $40. Electronic applications accepted. *Financial support:* In 2014–15, 2 students received support, including 13 research assistantships with full tuition reimbursements available (averaging $3,923 per year), 1 teaching assistantship with full tuition reimbursement available (averaging $3,000 per year); unspecified assistantships also available. Financial award application deadline: 4/1; financial award applicants required to submit FAFSA. *Faculty research:* Policing, methods evaluation and policy, public opinion and statistics, life course criminology. *Unit head:* Dr. David Jenks, Chair, 678-839-5199, Fax: 678-839-6506, E-mail: djenks@westga.edu. *Application contact:* Trish Wells, Graduate Studies Associate, 678-839-5170, Fax: 678-839-5171, E-mail: pwells@westga.edu.
Website: http://criminology.westga.edu

University of Windsor, Faculty of Graduate Studies, Faculty of Arts and Social Sciences, Department of Sociology and Anthropology, Windsor, ON N9B 3P4, Canada. Offers criminology (MA); sociology (MA); sociology-social justice (PhD). Part-time programs available. *Degree requirements:* For master's, thesis; for doctorate, comprehensive exam, thesis/dissertation. *Entrance requirements:* For master's, minimum B+ average; for doctorate, writing sample, minimum B+ average. Additional exam requirements/recommendations for international students: Required—TOEFL (minimum score 560 paper-based). Electronic applications accepted. *Faculty research:*

Power and social change; criminology/deviance; social psychology; comparative development; race and ethnic relations; family, sex, and gender, social justice.

University of Wisconsin–Milwaukee, Graduate School, School of Social Welfare, Department of Criminal Justice, Milwaukee, WI 53201-0413. Offers administration (MS); corrections (MS); law enforcement (MS). Part-time programs available. *Degree requirements:* For master's, thesis or alternative. *Entrance requirements:* For master's, GRE General Test, MAT. Additional exam requirements/recommendations for international students: Required—TOEFL (minimum score 550 paper-based; 79 iBT), IELTS (minimum score 6.5). Electronic applications accepted.

University of Wisconsin–Platteville, School of Graduate Studies, Distance Learning Center, Online Master of Science in Criminal Justice Program, Platteville, WI 53818-3099. Offers MS. Part-time and evening/weekend programs available. Postbaccalaureate distance learning degree programs offered (no on-campus study). *Degree requirements:* For master's, thesis or alternative. *Entrance requirements:* Additional exam requirements/recommendations for international students: Required—TOEFL (minimum score 500 paper-based; 61 iBT), IELTS (minimum score 6). Electronic applications accepted. *Expenses:* Contact institution.

Upper Iowa University, Online Master's Programs, Fayette, IA 52142-1857. Offers accounting (MBA); corporate financial management (MBA); global business (MBA); health and human services (MPA); higher education administration (MHEA); homeland security (MPA); human resources management (MBA); justice administration (MPA); organizational development (MBA); public personnel management (MPA); quality management (MBA). MBA also available at Madison, WI campus. Part-time programs available. Postbaccalaureate distance learning degree programs offered (no on-campus study). *Degree requirements:* For master's, research project. *Entrance requirements:* For master's, GMAT, GRE, or minimum GPA of 2.7 during last 60 hours. Additional exam requirements/recommendations for international students: Required—TOEFL (minimum score 570 paper-based). Electronic applications accepted. *Faculty research:* Total quality management, CQI, teams, organization culture and climate, management.

Urbana University, College of Social and Behavioral Sciences, Urbana, OH 43078-2091. Offers criminal justice administration (MA). *Entrance requirements:* For master's, 3 letters of recommendation.

Utica College, Program in Economic Crime and Fraud Management, Utica, NY 13502-4892. Offers MBA. Part-time and evening/weekend programs available. Postbaccalaureate distance learning degree programs offered (minimal on-campus study). *Faculty:* 7 full-time (0 women). *Students:* 6 full-time (4 women), 101 part-time (57 women); includes 38 minority (22 Black or African American, non-Hispanic/Latino; 5 Asian, non-Hispanic/Latino; 11 Hispanic/Latino). Average age 32. 34 applicants, 100% accepted, 33 enrolled. In 2014, 31 master's awarded. *Entrance requirements:* For master's, BS, minimum GPA of 3.0. Additional exam requirements/recommendations for international students: Required—TOEFL (minimum score 525 paper-based). *Application deadline:* Applications are processed on a rolling basis. Application fee: $50. Electronic applications accepted. *Expenses:* Expenses: Contact institution. *Financial support:* Career-related internships or fieldwork, scholarships/grants, tuition waivers (partial), and unspecified assistantships available. Support available to part-time students. Financial award application deadline: 3/15; financial award applicants required to submit FAFSA. *Unit head:* Dr. R. Bruce McBride, Director of Economic Crime Graduate Programs, 315-792-3808, E-mail: rmcbride@utica.edu. *Application contact:* John D. Rowe, Director of Graduate Admissions, 315-792-3824, Fax: 315-792-3003, E-mail: jrowe@utica.edu.
Website: http://onlineuticacollege.com/programs/mba-fraud-management.asp

Utica College, Program in Economic Crime Management, Utica, NY 13502-4892. Offers MS. Part-time and evening/weekend programs available. Postbaccalaureate distance learning degree programs offered (minimal on-campus study). *Faculty:* 4 full-time (0 women). *Students:* 68 part-time (37 women); includes 22 minority (14 Black or African American, non-Hispanic/Latino; 1 Asian, non-Hispanic/Latino; 7 Hispanic/Latino). Average age 39. 21 applicants, 95% accepted, 16 enrolled. In 2014, 21 master's awarded. *Degree requirements:* For master's, thesis. *Entrance requirements:* For master's, BS, minimum GPA of 3.0. Additional exam requirements/recommendations for international students: Required—TOEFL (minimum score 525 paper-based). *Application deadline:* Applications are processed on a rolling basis. Application fee: $50. Electronic applications accepted. *Expenses:* Expenses: Contact institution. *Financial support:* Career-related internships or fieldwork, scholarships/grants, tuition waivers (partial), and unspecified assistantships available. Support available to part-time students. Financial award application deadline: 3/15; financial award applicants required to submit FAFSA. *Unit head:* Dr. R. Bruce McBride, Director of Economic Crime Graduate Programs, 315-792-3808, E-mail: rmcbride@utica.edu. *Application contact:* John D. Rowe, Director of Graduate Admissions, 315-792-3824, Fax: 315-792-3003, E-mail: jrowe@utica.edu.

Valdosta State University, Department of Sociology, Anthropology, and Criminal Justice, Valdosta, GA 31698. Offers criminal justice (MS); sociology (MS). *Accreditation:* AAMFT/COAMFTE. Part-time and evening/weekend programs available. *Faculty:* 15 full-time (6 women). *Students:* 13 full-time (9 women), 16 part-time (11 women); includes 12 minority (10 Black or African American, non-Hispanic/Latino; 2 Two or more races, non-Hispanic/Latino), 1 international. Average age 23. 9 applicants, 89% accepted, 8 enrolled. In 2014, 10 master's awarded. *Degree requirements:* For master's, thesis or alternative, comprehensive written and/or oral exams. *Entrance requirements:* For master's, GRE General Test or MAT (sociology, marriage and family therapy), minimum GPA of 2.5. Additional exam requirements/recommendations for international students: Required—TOEFL (minimum score 523 paper-based). *Application deadline:* For fall admission, 7/1 for domestic and international students; for spring admission, 11/15 for domestic and international students. Applications are processed on a rolling basis. Application fee: $35. Electronic applications accepted. *Expenses:* Tuition, state resident: part-time $236 per credit hour. Tuition, nonresident: part-time $850 per credit hour. *Required fees:* $1032 per semester. *Financial support:* In 2014–15, 4 students received support, including 5 research assistantships with full tuition reimbursements available (averaging $3,652 per year); career-related internships or fieldwork, institutionally sponsored loans, scholarships/grants, and unspecified assistantships also available. Support available to part-time students. Financial award application deadline: 7/1; financial award applicants required to submit FAFSA. *Unit head:* Dr. Darrell Ross, Head, 229-333-5943, Fax: 229-333-5492. *Application contact:* Michelle Jordan, Admissions Specialist, 229-333-5694, Fax: 229-245-3853, E-mail: sojordan@valdosta.edu.

Virginia College in Birmingham, Virginia College Online, Birmingham, AL 35209. Offers business administration (MBA); criminal justice (MCJ); cybersecurity (MC). Part-time and evening/weekend programs available. Postbaccalaureate distance learning degree programs offered (no on-campus study).

Virginia Commonwealth University, Graduate School, College of Humanities and Sciences, Wilder School of Government and Public Affairs, Department of Criminal Justice, Richmond, VA 23284-9005. Offers MS, CCJA. Part-time and evening/weekend programs available. *Degree requirements:* For master's, thesis or comprehensive exam. *Entrance requirements:* For master's, GRE, LSAT or GMAT, minimum cumulative GPA of 3.0. Additional exam requirements/recommendations for international students: Required—TOEFL (minimum score 600 paper-based; 100 iBT); Recommended—IELTS (minimum score 6.5). Electronic applications accepted.

Virginia State University, College of Graduate Studies, College of Humanities and Social Sciences, Department of Sociology and Criminal Justice, Petersburg, VA 23806-0001. Offers criminal justice (MS).

Walden University, Graduate Programs, School of Public Policy and Administration, Minneapolis, MN 55401. Offers criminal justice (MPA, MPP, MS, Graduate Certificate), including emergency management (MS, PhD), general program (MS, PhD), homeland security and policy coordination (MS, PhD), law and public policy (MS, PhD), policy analysis (MS, PhD), public management and leadership (MS, PhD), self-designed (MS), terrorism, mediation, and peace (MS, PhD); criminal justice leadership and executive management (MS), including emergency management (MS, PhD), general program (MS, PhD), homeland security and policy coordination (MS, PhD), law and public policy (MS, PhD), policy analysis (MS, PhD), public management and leadership (MS, PhD), self-designed, terrorism, mediation, and peace (MS, PhD); emergency management (MPA, MPP, MS), including criminal justice (MS, PhD), general program (MS, PhD), homeland security (MS), public management and leadership (MS, PhD), terrorism and emergency management (MS); general program (MPA, MPP); government management (Graduate Certificate); health policy (MPA, MPP); homeland security (Graduate Certificate); homeland security and policy coordination (MPA, MPP); international nongovernmental organizations (MPA, MPP); law and public policy (MPA, MPP); local government management for sustainable communities (MPA, MPP); nonprofit management (Graduate Certificate); nonprofit management and leadership (MPA, MPP, MS); online teaching in higher education (Post-Master's Certificate); policy analysis (MPA); public management and leadership (MPA, MPP, Graduate Certificate); public policy (Graduate Certificate); public policy and administration (PhD), including criminal justice (MS, PhD), emergency management (MS, PhD), general program (MS, PhD), health policy, homeland security and policy coordination (MS, PhD), international nongovernmental organizations, law and public policy (MS, PhD), local government management for sustainable communities, nonprofit management and leadership, policy analysis (MS, PhD), public management and leadership (MS, PhD), terrorism, mediation, and peace (MS, PhD); strategic planning and public policy (Graduate Certificate); terrorism, mediation, and peace (MPA, MPP). Part-time and evening/weekend programs available. Postbaccalaureate distance learning degree programs offered (no on-campus study). *Faculty:* 13 full-time (5 women), 151 part-time/adjunct (65 women). *Students:* 1,009 full-time (573 women), 1,632 part-time (954 women); includes 1,553 minority (1,307 Black or African American, non-Hispanic/Latino; 15 American Indian or Alaska Native, non-Hispanic/Latino; 38 Asian, non-Hispanic/Latino; 127 Hispanic/Latino; 66 Two or more races, non-Hispanic/Latino), 15 international. Average age 42. 665 applicants, 97% accepted, 616 enrolled. In 2014, 317 master's, 95 doctorates, 34 other advanced degrees awarded. *Degree requirements:* For doctorate, thesis/dissertation, residency. *Entrance requirements:* For master's, bachelor's degree or higher; minimum GPA of 2.5; official transcripts; goal statement (for some programs); access to computer and Internet; for doctorate, master's degree or higher; three years of related professional or academic experience (preferred); minimum GPA of 3.0; goal statement and current resume (for select programs); official transcripts; access to computer and Internet; for other advanced degree, relevant work experience; access to computer and Internet. Additional exam requirements/recommendations for international students: Required—TOEFL (minimum score 550 paper-based, 79 iBT), IELTS (minimum score 6.5), Michigan English Language Assessment Battery (minimum score 82), or PTE (minimum score 53). *Application deadline:* Applications are processed on a rolling basis. Application fee: $0. Electronic applications accepted. *Expenses: Tuition:* Full-time $11,925; part-time $500 per credit hour. *Required fees:* $647. *Financial support:* Fellowships, Federal Work-Study, scholarships/grants, unspecified assistantships, and family tuition reduction, active duty/veteran tuition reduction, group tuition reduction, interest-free payment plans, employee tuition reduction available. Support available to part-time students. Financial award applicants required to submit FAFSA. *Unit head:* Dr. Shana Garrett, Associate Dean, 866-492-5336. *Application contact:* Meghan Thomas, Vice President of Enrollment Management, 866-492-5336, E-mail: info@waldenu.edu.
Website: http://www.waldenu.edu/programs/colleges-schools/public-policy-and-administration

Walden University, Graduate Programs, School of Social Work and Human Services, Minneapolis, MN 55401. Offers addictions (MSW); addictions and social work (DSW); children, families, and couples (MSW); clinical expertise (DSW); criminal justice (DSW); crisis and trauma (MSW); disaster, crisis, and intervention (DSW); forensic populations and settings (MSW); general program (MSW); human services (MS, PhD), including clinical social work (PhD), criminal justice, disaster, crisis and intervention, family studies and intervention strategies (PhD), family studies and interventions, general program, human services administration, public health, social policy analysis and planning; medical social work (MSW, DSW); military families and culture (MSW); policy practice (DSW); social work (PhD), including addictions and social work, clinical expertise, disaster, crisis and intervention (MS, PhD), family studies and interventions (MS, PhD), medical social work, policy practice, social work administration; social work administration (DSW). Part-time and evening/weekend programs available. Postbaccalaureate distance learning degree programs offered (no on-campus study). *Faculty:* 18 full-time (11 women), 236 part-time/adjunct (156 women). *Students:* 1,400 full-time (1,205 women), 884 part-time (759 women); includes 1,586 minority (1,373 Black or African American, non-Hispanic/Latino; 20 American Indian or Alaska Native, non-Hispanic/Latino; 16 Asian, non-Hispanic/Latino; 120 Hispanic/Latino; 57 Two or more races, non-Hispanic/Latino), 14 international. Average age 40. 892 applicants, 96% accepted, 826 enrolled. In 2014, 61 master's, 14 doctorates awarded. *Degree requirements:* For master's, residency (for some programs); for doctorate, thesis/dissertation, residency. *Entrance requirements:* For master's, bachelor's degree or higher; minimum GPA of 2.5; official transcripts; goal statement (for some programs); access to computer and Internet; for doctorate, master's degree or higher; three years of related professional or academic experience (preferred); minimum GPA of 3.0; goal statement and current resume (for select programs); official transcripts; access to computer and Internet. Additional exam requirements/recommendations for international students: Required—TOEFL (minimum score 550 paper-based, 79 iBT), IELTS (minimum score 6.5), Michigan English Language Assessment Battery (minimum score 82), or PTE (minimum score 53). *Application deadline:* Applications are processed on a rolling basis. Application fee: $0. Electronic applications accepted. *Expenses: Tuition:* Full-time $11,925; part-time $500 per credit hour. *Required fees:* $647. *Financial support:* Fellowships, Federal Work-Study, scholarships/grants, unspecified assistantships, and family tuition reduction, active duty/veteran tuition reduction, group tuition reduction, interest-free payment plans, employee tuition reduction available. Support available to part-time students. Financial award applicants required to submit FAFSA. *Unit head:* Dr. Savitri Dixon-Saxon, Associate Dean, 866-492-5336. *Application contact:* Meghan Thomas, Vice President of Enrollment Management, 866-492-5336, E-mail: info@waldenu.edu.
Website: http://www.waldenu.edu/colleges-schools/school-of-social-work-and-human-services/academic-programs

Criminal Justice and Criminology

Washburn University, School of Applied Studies, Department of Criminal Justice and Legal Studies, Topeka, KS 66621. Offers MCJ. Part-time and evening/weekend programs available. Postbaccalaureate distance learning degree programs offered (minimal on-campus study). *Students:* 10 full-time (8 women), 16 part-time (9 women). Average age 36. 8 applicants, 88% accepted, 7 enrolled. In 2014, 12 master's awarded. *Degree requirements:* For master's, thesis or alternative, continuous enrollment each fall and spring semester, completion of all program requirements within seven years of entry (MCJ). *Entrance requirements:* For master's, GRE, 3 letters of reference, minimum GPA of 3.0 for undergraduate degree, short biography, official transcripts. Additional exam requirements/recommendations for international students: Required—TOEFL (minimum score 79 iBT). *Application deadline:* For fall admission, 4/1 priority date for domestic and international students; for spring admission, 11/1 priority date for domestic and international students. Applications are processed on a rolling basis. Application fee: $35. Electronic applications accepted. *Expenses:* Tuition, state resident: full-time $6120; part-time $340 per credit hour. Tuition, nonresident: full-time $12,456; part-time $692 per credit hour. *Required fees:* $86; $43 per semester. Tuition and fees vary according to program. *Financial support:* Institutionally sponsored loans and scholarships/grants available. Support available to part-time students. Financial award application deadline: 3/1. *Faculty research:* Practitioner behavior, police management and training, field and institutional correction administration, terrorism, police training, sex slaves. *Unit head:* Dr. Patricia Dahl, Program Director, 785-670-1413, Fax: 785-670-1027, E-mail: patricia.dahl@washburn.edu.
Website: http://www.washburn.edu/academics/college-schools/applied-studies/departments/criminal-justice-legal-studies/index.html

Washington State University, College of Liberal Arts, Program in Criminal Justice and Criminology, Pullman, WA 99164. Offers MA, PhD. MA program also offered at Spokane and Global (online) campuses. Postbaccalaureate distance learning degree programs offered (no on-campus study). *Students:* 46 full-time (20 women), 12 part-time (6 women); includes 13 minority (2 Black or African American, non-Hispanic/Latino; 8 Hispanic/Latino; 2 Native Hawaiian or other Pacific Islander, non-Hispanic/Latino; 1 Two or more races, non-Hispanic/Latino), 8 international. Average age 32. 50 applicants, 62% accepted, 18 enrolled. In 2014, 9 master's, 3 doctorates awarded. *Degree requirements:* For master's, comprehensive exam (for some programs), thesis, oral exam; for doctorate, comprehensive exam, thesis/dissertation, oral or written exam. *Entrance requirements:* For master's, GRE General Test, major in criminal justice, sociology, psychology, liberal arts, or a related field; strong writing and analytical skills; minimum GPA of 3.0; for doctorate, GRE General Test, major in criminal justice, sociology, psychology, liberal arts, or a related field; strong writing and analytical skills. Additional exam requirements/recommendations for international students: Required—TOEFL, IELTS. *Application deadline:* For fall admission, 1/10 priority date for domestic and international students. Application fee: $75. Electronic applications accepted. *Expenses:* Tuition, state resident: full-time $11,768. Tuition, nonresident: full-time $25,200. *Required fees:* $960. Tuition and fees vary according to program. *Financial support:* In 2014–15, 5 research assistantships with full and partial tuition reimbursements (averaging $14,198 per year), 23 teaching assistantships with full and partial tuition reimbursements (averaging $14,162 per year) were awarded; career-related internships or fieldwork, Federal Work-Study, institutionally sponsored loans, health care benefits, tuition waivers (partial), and teaching associateships also available. Financial award application deadline: 2/15; financial award applicants required to submit FAFSA. *Faculty research:* Community policing, community justice, corrections policy, crime prevention policy, criminal justice management. *Unit head:* Dr. David Brody, Chair, 509-335-8611, Fax: 509-335-7990. *Application contact:* Dee Dee Torgeson, Graduate and Student Records Coordinator, 509-335-4249, Fax: 509-335-4513, E-mail: torgeson@wsu.edu.
Website: http://libarts.wsu.edu/crimj/

Wayland Baptist University, Graduate Programs, Programs in Behavioral and Social Sciences, Plainview, TX 79072-6998. Offers counseling (MA); government administration (MPA); history (MA); homeland security (MPA); justice administration (MPA). Part-time and evening/weekend programs available. Postbaccalaureate distance learning degree programs offered. *Faculty:* 19 full-time (5 women), 18 part-time/adjunct (8 women). *Students:* 17 full-time (12 women), 428 part-time (264 women); includes 208 minority (66 Black or African American, non-Hispanic/Latino; 6 American Indian or Alaska Native, non-Hispanic/Latino; 14 Asian, non-Hispanic/Latino; 98 Hispanic/Latino; 4 Native Hawaiian or other Pacific Islander, non-Hispanic/Latino; 20 Two or more races, non-Hispanic/Latino). Average age 38. 152 applicants, 93% accepted, 67 enrolled. In 2014, 158 master's awarded. *Degree requirements:* For master's, comprehensive exam. *Entrance requirements:* For master's, GRE, MAT. Additional exam requirements/recommendations for international students: Required—TOEFL (minimum score 500 paper-based; 61 iBT). *Application deadline:* Applications are processed on a rolling basis. Application fee: $50. Electronic applications accepted. *Expenses: Tuition:* Full-time $8910; part-time $495 per credit hour. *Required fees:* $970; $495 per credit hour. $485 per semester. *Financial support:* Federal Work-Study, institutionally sponsored loans, and scholarships/grants available. Support available to part-time students. Financial award application deadline: 5/1; financial award applicants required to submit FAFSA. *Unit head:* Dr. Estelle Owens, Chairman, 806-291-1171, Fax: 806-291-1972, E-mail: owensest@wbu.edu. *Application contact:* Amanda Stanton, Graduate Studies, 806-291-3423, Fax: 806-291-1950, E-mail: stanton@wbu.edu.

Wayne State University, College of Liberal Arts and Sciences, Department of Criminal Justice, Detroit, MI 48202. Offers MS. Postbaccalaureate distance learning degree programs offered (no on-campus study). *Faculty:* 9 full-time (3 women), 3 part-time/adjunct (1 woman). *Students:* 3 full-time (all women), 41 part-time (26 women); includes 17 minority (15 Black or African American, non-Hispanic/Latino; 2 Hispanic/Latino). Average age 29. 59 applicants, 42% accepted, 16 enrolled. In 2014, 14 master's awarded. *Degree requirements:* For master's, comprehensive exam, three-credit essay, thesis, or capstone seminar. *Entrance requirements:* For master's, GRE (for applicants with a GPA of 2.75-2.99), minimum GPA of 3.0 (written statement and writing sample if less), bachelor's degree from accredited college or university, 2 letters of recommendation, personal statement. Additional exam requirements/recommendations for international students: Required—TOEFL (minimum score 550 paper-based; 79 iBT), TWE (minimum score 5.5), Michigan English Language Assessment Battery (minimum score 85); Recommended—IELTS (minimum score 6.5). *Application deadline:* For fall admission, 6/1 for domestic students, 5/1 priority date for international students; for winter admission, 10/1 priority date for domestic students, 9/1 priority date for international students; for spring admission, 2/1 for domestic students, 1/1 for international students. Application fee: $0. Electronic applications accepted. *Expenses:* Tuition, state resident: full-time $10,294; part-time $571.90 per credit hour. Tuition, nonresident: full-time $29,730; part-time $1238.75 per credit hour. *Required fees:* $1365; $43.50 per credit hour. $291.10 per semester. Tuition and fees vary according to course load and program. *Financial support:* In 2014–15, 15 students received support, including 1 teaching assistantship with tuition reimbursement available (averaging $16,838 per year); scholarships/grants, health care benefits, and unspecified assistantships also available. Financial award application deadline: 3/31; financial award applicants required to submit FAFSA. *Faculty research:* Criminology, juvenile delinquency and justice, law, policing, corrections, social deviance. *Unit head:* Dr.

Bradley Smith, Interim Chair, 313-577-3281, Fax: 313-577-9977, E-mail: bradsmith@wayne.edu. *Application contact:* Dr. Jennifer Wareham, Associate Professor/Graduate Director, 313-577-0772, Fax: 313-577-9977, E-mail: jwareham@wayne.edu.
Website: http://clas.wayne.edu/CRJ/

Webber International University, Graduate School of Business, Babson Park, FL 33827-0096. Offers accounting (MBA); criminal justice management (MBA); management (MBA); sports management (MBA). Part-time and evening/weekend programs available. *Faculty:* 8 full-time (1 woman). *Students:* 42 full-time (20 women), 17 part-time (11 women). Average age 27. 33 applicants, 100% accepted, 33 enrolled. In 2014, 24 master's awarded. *Degree requirements:* For master's, thesis or alternative. *Entrance requirements:* For master's, previous course work in financial and managerial accounting. Additional exam requirements/recommendations for international students: Required—TOEFL. *Application deadline:* For fall admission, 5/15 priority date for domestic students. Applications are processed on a rolling basis. Application fee: $50 ($75 for international students). *Expenses: Required fees:* $1974. Full-time tuition and fees vary according to course load and program. *Financial support:* In 2014–15, 8 students received support. Fellowships with partial tuition reimbursements available available. Support available to part-time students. Financial award application deadline: 8/15; financial award applicants required to submit FAFSA. *Faculty research:* Finance strategy, market research, investments, Intranet. *Unit head:* Dr. Nikos Orphanoudakis, Dean, 863-638-2925, Fax: 863-638-2823, E-mail: drnikos@webber.edu. *Application contact:* Jeanne Sobierajski, MBA Marketing Director, 863-638-2927, Fax: 863-638-2823, E-mail: mba@webber.edu.
Website: http://www.webber.edu

Webster University, George Herbert Walker School of Business and Technology, Department of Business, St. Louis, MO 63119-3194. Offers business and organizational security management (MBA); decision support systems (MBA); environmental management (MBA); finance (MBA, MS); forensic accounting (MS); gerontology (MBA); human resources development (MBA); human resources management (MBA); information technology management (MBA); international business (MA, MBA); international relations (MBA); management and leadership (MBA); marketing (MBA); media communications (MBA); procurement and acquisitions management (MBA); Web services (MBA). *Accreditation:* ACBSP. Part-time and evening/weekend programs available. Postbaccalaureate distance learning degree programs offered (no on-campus study). *Degree requirements:* For master's, comprehensive exam (for some programs), thesis (for some programs). *Entrance requirements:* Additional exam requirements/recommendations for international students: Required—TOEFL.

Webster University, George Herbert Walker School of Business and Technology, Department of Management, St. Louis, MO 63119-3194. Offers business and organizational security management (MA); health administration (MHA); health care management (MA); health services management (MA); human resources development (MA); human resources management (MA); information technology management (MS); management and leadership (MA); marketing (MA); nonprofit leadership (MA); procurement and acquisitions management (MA); public administration (MPA); space systems operations management (MS). Part-time and evening/weekend programs available. Postbaccalaureate distance learning degree programs offered (no on-campus study). *Degree requirements:* For master's, thesis (for some programs). *Entrance requirements:* Additional exam requirements/recommendations for international students: Required—TOEFL.

West Chester University of Pennsylvania, College of Business and Public Affairs, Department of Criminal Justice, West Chester, PA 19383. Offers MS. Part-time and evening/weekend programs available. *Faculty:* 5 full-time (3 women), 2 part-time/adjunct (both women). *Students:* 10 full-time (all women), 35 part-time (24 women); includes 21 minority (16 Black or African American, non-Hispanic/Latino; 1 Asian, non-Hispanic/Latino; 3 Hispanic/Latino; 1 Two or more races, non-Hispanic/Latino). Average age 27. 42 applicants, 98% accepted, 28 enrolled. In 2014, 16 master's awarded. *Degree requirements:* For master's, 15-credit core (law, research, ethics, theories, and capstone independent research project); 15 additional credits of criminal justice electives. *Entrance requirements:* For master's, minimum GPA of 3.0; two letters of recommendation. Additional exam requirements/recommendations for international students: Required—TOEFL (minimum score 550 paper-based; 80 iBT). *Application deadline:* For fall admission, 4/15 priority date for domestic students, 3/15 for international students; for spring admission, 10/15 priority date for domestic students, 9/1 for international students. Applications are processed on a rolling basis. Application fee: $45. Electronic applications accepted. *Expenses:* Expenses: Contact institution. *Financial support:* Unspecified assistantships available. Support available to part-time students. Financial award application deadline: 2/15; financial award applicants required to submit FAFSA. *Faculty research:* Criminal law, criminal procedure, Constitutional interpretation, drug and alcohol prevention, drug courts, mental health courts, legislation related to sex offending, animal cruelty, pharmaceutical battery, terrorism, law enforcement. *Unit head:* Dr. Mary Brewster, Chair, 610-436-2630, Fax: 610-738-0491, E-mail: mbrewster@wcupa.edu. *Application contact:* Dr. Jane Tucker, Graduate Coordinator, 610-436-2648, Fax: 610-738-0491, E-mail: jtucker@wcupa.edu.

Western Connecticut State University, Division of Graduate Studies, Ancell School of Business, Program in Justice Administration, Danbury, CT 06810-6885. Offers MS. Part-time programs available. *Degree requirements:* For master's, comprehensive exam or research project, completion of program within 6 years. *Entrance requirements:* For master's, GMAT, GRE, LSAT, or MAT. Additional exam requirements/recommendations for international students: Recommended—TOEFL (minimum score 550 paper-based; 79 iBT), IELTS (minimum score 6). *Faculty research:* Examination of prison life as portrayed by the film industry.

Western Illinois University, School of Graduate Studies, College of Education and Human Services, School of Law Enforcement and Justice Administration, Macomb, IL 61455-1390. Offers law enforcement and justice administration (MA); police executive administration (Certificate). Part-time programs available. *Students:* 20 full-time (10 women), 25 part-time (6 women); includes 11 minority (5 Black or African American, non-Hispanic/Latino; 6 Hispanic/Latino). Average age 31. 40 applicants, 100% accepted, 17 enrolled. In 2014, 16 master's, 7 other advanced degrees awarded. *Degree requirements:* For master's, thesis or alternative. *Entrance requirements:* For master's, GRE or MAT, minimum GPA of 3.0. Additional exam requirements/recommendations for international students: Required—TOEFL (minimum score 520 paper-based; 68 iBT). *Application deadline:* Applications are processed on a rolling basis. Application fee: $30. Electronic applications accepted. *Financial support:* In 2014–15, 6 students received support, including 1 research assistantship with full tuition reimbursement available (averaging $7,544 per year), 5 teaching assistantships with full tuition reimbursements available (averaging $8,688 per year). Financial award applicants required to submit FAFSA. *Unit head:* Dr. Terry Mors, Director, 309-298-1038. *Application contact:* Dr. Nancy Parsons, Associate Provost and Director of Graduate Studies, 309-298-1806, Fax: 309-298-2345, E-mail: grad-office@wiu.edu.
Website: http://wiu.edu/leja

Western Kentucky University, Graduate Studies, Potter College of Arts and Letters, Department of Sociology, Bowling Green, KY 42101. Offers criminology (MA); sociology

(MA). Postbaccalaureate distance learning degree programs offered. *Degree requirements:* For master's, comprehensive exam, thesis optional, final exam. *Entrance requirements:* For master's, GRE General Test, minimum GPA of 3.0. Additional exam requirements/recommendations for international students: Required—TOEFL (minimum score 555 paper-based; 79 iBT). *Faculty research:* Criminology/delinquency, quantitative and survey research methodology, occupations/professions, sex and gender, demography.

Western Oregon University, Graduate Programs, College of Liberal Arts and Sciences, Division of Social Science, Monmouth, OR 97361-1394. Offers criminal justice (MA, MS). Part-time and evening/weekend programs available. *Degree requirements:* For master's, thesis optional, written exams. *Entrance requirements:* For master's, minimum GPA of 3.0. Additional exam requirements/recommendations for international students: Required—TOEFL (minimum score 550 paper-based; 79 iBT), IELTS (minimum score 6.5). *Faculty research:* Prison to community transition of adult felons, community justice, restorative justice, parole and probation.

Westfield State University, Division of Graduate and Continuing Education, Department of Criminal Justice, Westfield, MA 01086. Offers MS. Part-time and evening/weekend programs available. *Degree requirements:* For master's, comprehensive exam, thesis (for some programs). *Entrance requirements:* For master's, GRE General Test or MAT, minimum undergraduate GPA of 2.7.

West Liberty University, School of Professional Studies, West Liberty, WV 26074. Offers justice leadership (MPS); organizational leadership (MPS).

West Texas A&M University, College of Education and Social Sciences, Department of Political Science and Criminal Justice, Canyon, TX 79016-0001. Offers criminal justice (MA). Part-time and evening/weekend programs available. *Degree requirements:* For master's, comprehensive exam, thesis optional. *Entrance requirements:* For master's, GRE General Test. Additional exam requirements/recommendations for international students: Required—TOEFL (minimum score 550 paper-based). Electronic applications accepted. *Faculty research:* Racial profiling, changing nature of prisons, campus police and parking services.

West Virginia State University, Master of Science Program in Law Enforcement and Administration, Institute, WV 25112-1000. Offers MS. *Degree requirements:* For master's, comprehensive exam, internship, paper. *Entrance requirements:* For master's, GRE (50th Percentile) or MAT (50th Percentile), minimum undergraduate GPA of 2.7, 3 letters of recommendation, completion of course in statistics/research methods, interview. Additional exam requirements/recommendations for international students: Required—TOEFL (minimum score 550 paper-based). Electronic applications accepted.

Wichita State University, Graduate School, Fairmount College of Liberal Arts and Sciences, School of Community Affairs, Wichita, KS 67260. Offers criminal justice (MA). Part-time programs available. Postbaccalaureate distance learning degree programs offered (no on-campus study). *Unit head:* Dr. Michael Birzer, Director, 316-978-7200, Fax: 316-978-3626, E-mail: michael.birzer@wichita.edu. *Application contact:* Jordan Oleson, Admissions Coordinator, 316-978-3095, Fax: 316-978-3253, E-mail: jordan.oleson@wichita.edu.
Website: http://www.sjcny.edu

Widener University, College of Arts and Sciences, Program in Criminal Justice, Chester, PA 19013-5792. Offers MA, Psy D/MA. Part-time and evening/weekend programs available. *Degree requirements:* For master's, project. *Entrance requirements:* For master's, interview, minimum undergraduate GPA of 3.0. *Expenses:* Contact institution. *Faculty research:* Criminal law and procedure, corrections, domestic violence.

Wilfrid Laurier University, Laurier Brantford, Brantford, ON N3T 2Y3, Canada. Offers criminology (MA), including culture, crime and policy, international crime and justice, media criminology. *Degree requirements:* For master's, thesis. *Entrance requirements:* For master's, honours bachelor's degree with major in criminology or equivalent degree;

minimum B+ average in final year and in all criminology courses. Additional exam requirements/recommendations for international students: Required—TOEFL (minimum score 89 iBT). Electronic applications accepted.

Wilmington University, College of Social and Behavioral Sciences, New Castle, DE 19720-6491. Offers administration of human services (MS); administration of justice (MS); clinical mental health counseling (MS); homeland security (MS). *Accreditation:* ACA. Part-time and evening/weekend programs available. *Faculty:* 7 full-time (4 women), 70 part-time/adjunct (28 women). *Students:* 175 full-time (141 women), 468 part-time (350 women); includes 296 minority (266 Black or African American, non-Hispanic/Latino; 5 American Indian or Alaska Native, non-Hispanic/Latino; 3 Asian, non-Hispanic/Latino; 18 Hispanic/Latino; 2 Native Hawaiian or other Pacific Islander, non-Hispanic/Latino; 2 Two or more races, non-Hispanic/Latino), 4 international. Average age 35. 251 applicants, 100% accepted, 157 enrolled. In 2014, 170 master's awarded. *Entrance requirements:* Additional exam requirements/recommendations for international students: Required—TOEFL (minimum score 500 paper-based). *Application deadline:* Applications are processed on a rolling basis. Application fee: $35. Electronic applications accepted. *Financial support:* Applicants required to submit FAFSA. *Unit head:* Dr. Christian A. Trowbridge, Dean, 302-295-1151, Fax: 302-328-5164. *Application contact:* Laura Morris, Director of Admissions, 877-967-5464, E-mail: inquire@wilmcoll.edu.
Website: http://www.wilmu.edu/behavioralscience/

Wright State University, School of Graduate Studies, College of Liberal Arts, Program in Applied Behavioral Science, Dayton, OH 45435. Offers criminal justice and social problems (MA); international and comparative politics (MA). *Degree requirements:* For master's, thesis optional. *Entrance requirements:* Additional exam requirements/recommendations for international students: Required—TOEFL. *Faculty research:* Training and development, criminal justice and social problems, community systems, human factors, industrial/organizational psychology.

Xavier University, College of Social Sciences, Health and Education, Department of Criminal Justice, Cincinnati, OH 45207. Offers MS. Part-time and evening/weekend programs available. *Faculty:* 3 full-time (1 woman), 1 part-time/adjunct (0 women). *Students:* 4 full-time (2 women), 4 part-time (3 women); includes 2 minority (both Black or African American, non-Hispanic/Latino). Average age 26. 10 applicants, 50% accepted, 4 enrolled. In 2014, 7 master's awarded. *Degree requirements:* For master's, comprehensive exam, thesis. *Entrance requirements:* For master's, MAT, GRE, or LSAT, minimum GPA of 2.7; official transcript; 2 letters of recommendation. Additional exam requirements/recommendations for international students: Required—TOEFL (minimum score 550 paper-based; 79 iBT). *Application deadline:* For fall admission, 8/15 for domestic students. Applications are processed on a rolling basis. Application fee: $35. Electronic applications accepted. Application fee is waived when completed online. *Expenses:* Expenses: $585 per credit hour. *Financial support:* In 2014-15, 3 students received support. Career-related internships or fieldwork, scholarships/grants, and unspecified assistantships available. Support available to part-time students. Financial award applicants required to submit FAFSA. *Faculty research:* Women and crime, crime policy, policing. *Unit head:* Dr. Y. Gail Hurst, Chair, 513-745-1070, Fax: 513-745-3220, E-mail: hurst@xavier.edu. *Application contact:* Roger Bosse, Graduate Services Director, 513-745-3357, Fax: 513-745-1048, E-mail: bosse@xavier.edu.
Website: http://www.xavier.edu/criminal-justice-grad/

Youngstown State University, Graduate School, Bitonte College of Health and Human Services, Department of Criminal Justice, Youngstown, OH 44555-0001. Offers MS. Part-time and evening/weekend programs available. *Degree requirements:* For master's, thesis optional. *Entrance requirements:* For master's, minimum GPA of 2.7. Additional exam requirements/recommendations for international students: Required—TOEFL. *Faculty research:* Police human resource allocation, police administration, computerized test development, criminal law.

Forensic Sciences

Alabama State University, College of Science, Mathematics and Technology, Department of Physical Sciences, Montgomery, AL 36101-0271. Offers forensic science (MS). *Faculty:* 2 full-time (1 woman), 1 part-time/adjunct (0 women). *Students:* 9 full-time (6 women), 2 part-time (both women); includes 8 minority (7 Black or African American, non-Hispanic/Latino; 1 American Indian or Alaska Native, non-Hispanic/Latino), 2 international. Average age 27. 26 applicants, 35% accepted, 7 enrolled. Application fee: $25. *Unit head:* Dr. Azriel Gorski, Dean, 334-229-6705, Fax: 334-229-6103, E-mail: agorski@alasu.edu. *Application contact:* Dr. William Person, Dean of Graduate Studies, 334-229-4274, Fax: 334-229-4928, E-mail: wperson@alasu.edu.
Website: http://www.alasu.edu/academics/colleges—departments/science-mathematics-technology/physical-sciences/index.aspx

Albany State University, College of Sciences and Health Professions, Albany, GA 31705-2717. Offers criminal justice (MS), including corrections, forensic science, law enforcement, public administration; mathematics education (M Ed); nursing (MSN), including RN to MSN family nurse practitioner, RN to MSN nurse educator; science education (M Ed). Part-time and evening/weekend programs available. Postbaccalaureate distance learning degree programs offered. *Degree requirements:* For master's, comprehensive exam, thesis. *Entrance requirements:* For master's, GRE or MAT, official transcript, letters of recommendations, pre-medical/certificate of immunizations. Electronic applications accepted.

Alliant International University–Irvine, California School of Forensic Studies, Irvine, CA 92606. Offers Psy D. *Degree requirements:* For doctorate, comprehensive exam, thesis/dissertation, internship. *Entrance requirements:* For doctorate, minimum GPA of 3.0, recommendations, essay. Additional exam requirements/recommendations for international students: Required—TOEFL (minimum score 80 iBT), TWE (minimum score 5). Electronic applications accepted. *Faculty research:* Detecting deception, psychological safety of undercover police officers, domestic violence, risk assessment, competency evaluations.

American Public University System, AMU/APU Graduate Programs, Charles Town, WV 25414. Offers accounting (MBA, MS); criminal justice (MA), including business administration, emergency and disaster management, general (MA, MS); educational leadership (M Ed); emergency and disaster management (MA); entrepreneurship (MBA); environmental policy and management (MS), including environmental planning, environmental sustainability, fish and wildlife management, general (MA, MS), global environmental management; finance (MBA); general (MBA); global business management (MBA); history (MA), including American history, ancient and classical

history, European history, global history, public history; homeland security (MA), including business administration, counter-terrorism studies, criminal justice, cyber, emergency management and public health, intelligence studies, transportation security; homeland security resource allocation (MBA); humanities (MA); information technology (MS), including digital forensics, enterprise software development, information assurance and security, IT project management; information technology management (MBA); intelligence studies (MA), including criminal intelligence, cyber, general (MA, MS), homeland security, intelligence analysis, intelligence collection, intelligence management, intelligence operations, terrorism studies; international relations and conflict resolution (MA), including comparative and security issues, conflict resolution, international and transnational security issues, peacekeeping; legal studies (MA); management (MA), including defense management, general (MA, MS), human resource management, organizational leadership, public administration; marketing (MBA); military history (MA), including American military history, American Revolution, civil war, war since 1945, World War II; military studies (MA), including joint warfare, strategic leadership; national security studies (MA), including general (MA, MS), homeland security, regional security studies, security and intelligence analysis, terrorism studies; nonprofit management (MBA); political science (MA), including American politics and government, comparative government and development, general (MA, MS), international relations, public policy; psychology (MA); public administration (MPA), including disaster management, environmental policy, health policy, human resources, national security, organizational management, security management; public health (MPH); reverse logistics management (MA); school counseling (M Ed); security management (MA); space studies (MS), including aerospace science, general (MA, MS), planetary science; sports and health sciences (MS); teaching (M Ed), including curriculum and instruction for elementary teachers, elementary reading, English language learners, instructional leadership, online learning, special education; transportation and logistics management (MA), including general (MA, MS), maritime engineering management, reverse logistics management. Programs offered via distance learning only. Part-time and evening/weekend programs available. Postbaccalaureate distance learning degree programs offered (no on-campus study). *Faculty:* 426 full-time (236 women), 1,864 part-time/adjunct (880 women). *Students:* 475 full-time (215 women), 10,067 part-time (4,085 women); includes 3,462 minority (1,863 Black or African American, non-Hispanic/Latino; 74 American Indian or Alaska Native, non-Hispanic/Latino; 273 Asian, non-Hispanic/Latino; 831 Hispanic/Latino; 78 Native Hawaiian or other Pacific Islander, non-Hispanic/Latino; 343 Two or more races, non-Hispanic/Latino), 131 international. Average age 36. In 2014, 3,740 master's awarded.

Forensic Sciences

Degree requirements: For master's, comprehensive exam or practicum. *Entrance requirements:* For master's, official transcript showing earned bachelor's degree from institution accredited by recognized accrediting body. Additional exam requirements/recommendations for international students: Required—TOEFL (minimum score 550 paper-based), IELTS (minimum score 6.5). *Application deadline:* Applications are processed on a rolling basis. Application fee: $0. Electronic applications accepted. *Financial support:* Applicants required to submit FAFSA. *Faculty research:* Military history, criminal justice, management performance, national security. *Unit head:* Dr. Karan Powell, Executive Vice President and Provost, 877-468-6268, Fax: 304-724-3780. *Application contact:* Terry Grant, Vice President of Enrollment Management, 877-468-6268, Fax: 304-724-3780, E-mail: info@apus.edu.
Website: http://www.apus.edu

Arcadia University, Graduate Studies, Program in Forensic Science, Glenside, PA 19038-3295. Offers MSFS. *Expenses:* Contact institution.

Bay Path University, Program in Forensics, Longmeadow, MA 01106-2292. Offers MS. Part-time and evening/weekend programs available. Postbaccalaureate distance learning degree programs offered. *Students:* 7 full-time (6 women), 7 part-time (all women); includes 4 minority (1 Black or African American, non-Hispanic/Latino; 1 Asian, non-Hispanic/Latino; 2 Hispanic/Latino). Average age 27. 27 applicants, 59% accepted, 12 enrolled. In 2014, 9 master's awarded. *Degree requirements:* For master's, 39 credits with minimum B- grade in all coursework; final portfolio. *Entrance requirements:* For master's, BS in forensic science or a natural science, minimum cumulative GPA of 3.0. *Application deadline:* Applications are processed on a rolling basis. Application fee: $45. Electronic applications accepted. Application fee is waived when completed online. *Expenses:* Expenses: Contact institution. *Financial support:* In 2014–15, 4 students received support. Scholarships/grants available. Financial award applicants required to submit FAFSA. *Unit head:* Dr. Sandra Haddad, Program Director, 413-565-1355. *Application contact:* Diane Ranaldi, Dean of Graduate Admissions, 413-565-1332, Fax: 413-565-1250, E-mail: dranaldi@baypath.edu.
Website: http://graduate.baypath.edu/Graduate-Programs/Programs-On-Campus/MS-Programs/Forensics

Boston University, School of Medicine, Division of Graduate Medical Sciences, Program in Biomedical Forensic Sciences, Boston, MA 02118. Offers MS. Part-time and evening/weekend programs available. Postbaccalaureate distance learning degree programs offered. *Degree requirements:* For master's, thesis. *Application deadline:* For fall admission, 7/1 for domestic and international students. *Expenses:* Tuition: Full-time $45,686; part-time $1428 per credit hour. *Required fees:* $660; $60 per semester. Tuition and fees vary according to program. *Unit head:* Dr. Robin Cotton, Director, 617-638-1950, E-mail: rwcotton@bu.edu. *Application contact:* Patricia Jones, Executive Financial Coordinator, 617-414-2315, E-mail: psterlin@bu.edu.
Website: http://www.bumc.bu.edu/biomedforensic/

Boston University, School of Medicine, Division of Graduate Medical Sciences, Program in Forensic Anthropology, Boston, MA 02215. Offers MS. *Expenses:* Tuition: Full-time $45,686; part-time $1428 per credit hour. *Required fees:* $660; $60 per semester. Tuition and fees vary according to program. *Financial support:* Applicants required to submit FAFSA. *Unit head:* Dr. Tara L. Moore, Co-Director, 617-638-4054, Fax: 617-638-4922, E-mail: tlmoore@bu.edu. *Application contact:* Patricia Jones, Executive Financial Coordinator, 617-414-2315, E-mail: psterlin@bu.edu.
Website: http://www.bumc.bu.edu/gms/forensicanthro-masters-program/

Carlow University, College of Leadership and Social Change, MBA Program, Pittsburgh, PA 15213-3165. Offers business administration (MBA); fraud and forensics (MBA); healthcare management (MBA); project management (MBA). Part-time and evening/weekend programs available. Postbaccalaureate distance learning degree programs offered (no on-campus study). *Students:* 75 full-time (59 women), 27 part-time (18 women); includes 20 minority (16 Black or African American, non-Hispanic/Latino; 3 Asian, non-Hispanic/Latino; 1 Two or more races, non-Hispanic/Latino), 4 international. Average age 31. 55 applicants, 95% accepted, 35 enrolled. In 2014, 49 master's awarded. *Entrance requirements:* For master's, minimum undergraduate GPA of 3.0; essay; resume; transcripts; two recommendations. Additional exam requirements/recommendations for international students: Required—TOEFL (minimum score 550 paper-based). *Application deadline:* Applications are processed on a rolling basis. Electronic applications accepted. Application fee is waived when completed online. *Expenses:* Tuition: Full-time $9750; part-time $785 per credit. Part-time tuition and fees vary according to degree level and program. *Unit head:* Dr. Enrique Mu, Chair, MBA Program, 412-578-8729, E-mail: emu@carlow.edu. *Application contact:* Kimberly Lipniskis, Director Enrollment Management, Graduate, 412-578-6671, Fax: 412-578-6321, E-mail: klipniskis@carlow.edu.
Website: http://www.carlow.edu/Business_Administration.aspx

Cedar Crest College, Program in Forensic Science, Allentown, PA 18104-6196. Offers MS. *Faculty:* 8 full-time (5 women). *Students:* 15 full-time (13 women), 7 part-time (6 women). In 2014, 6 master's awarded. *Degree requirements:* For master's, thesis. *Entrance requirements:* For master's, GRE. *Application deadline:* For fall admission, 1/2 priority date for domestic students. Applications are processed on a rolling basis. Electronic applications accepted. *Expenses:* Expenses: Contact institution. *Financial support:* In 2014–15, 4 students received support. Unspecified assistantships available. *Faculty research:* Genotyping of low copy number DNA, presumptive and confirmatory testing of gamma hydroxyl butyrate (GHB) and gamma-butyrolactone (GBL). *Unit head:* Dr. Lawrence A. Quarino, Director and Associate Professor, 610-606-4666 Ext. 3507, Fax: 610-740-3787, E-mail: laquarin@cedarcrest.edu. *Application contact:* Mary Ellen Hickes, Director of School of Adult and Graduate Education, 610-606-4666, E-mail: sage@cedarcrest.edu.

Chaminade University of Honolulu, Graduate Services, Program in Forensic Science, Honolulu, HI 96816-1578. Offers MSFS, Certificate. Part-time programs available. *Degree requirements:* For master's, comprehensive exam, thesis or alternative. *Entrance requirements:* For master's, GRE, 2 letters of recommendation. Additional exam requirements/recommendations for international students: Required—TOEFL (minimum score 550 paper-based). Electronic applications accepted.

Champlain College, Graduate Studies, Burlington, VT 05402-0670. Offers business (MBA); digital forensic management (MS); digital forensic science (MS); early childhood education (M Ed); emergent media (MFA, MS); health care administration (MS); law (MS); managing innovation and information technology (MS); mediation and applied conflict studies (MS). MS in emergent media program held in Shanghai. Part-time programs available. Postbaccalaureate distance learning degree programs offered (no on-campus study). *Degree requirements:* For master's, capstone project. *Entrance requirements:* Additional exam requirements/recommendations for international students: Required—TOEFL (minimum score 550 paper-based; 80 iBT). Electronic applications accepted.

The College at Brockport, State University of New York, School of Business Administration and Economics, Brockport, NY 14420-2997. Offers forensic accounting (MS). Part-time programs available. *Faculty:* 5 full-time (1 woman), 1 part-time/adjunct (0 women). *Students:* 13 full-time (5 women), 8 part-time (5 women); includes 4 minority (3 Black or African American, non-Hispanic/Latino; 1 Asian, non-Hispanic/Latino). 29

applicants, 79% accepted, 19 enrolled. In 2014, 16 master's awarded. *Entrance requirements:* For master's, GMAT or GRE General Test. Additional exam requirements/recommendations for international students: Required—TOEFL (minimum score 550 paper-based; 79 iBT), IELTS (minimum score 6.5). *Application deadline:* For fall admission, 7/1 priority date for domestic and international students; for spring admission, 12/1 priority date for domestic and international students. Application fee: $50. Electronic applications accepted. *Financial support:* Career-related internships or fieldwork, Federal Work-Study, scholarships/grants, and unspecified assistantships available. Financial award application deadline: 3/15; financial award applicants required to submit FAFSA. *Unit head:* Dr. James Cordeiro, Department Chair, 585-395-5793, Fax: 585-395-2542. *Application contact:* Dr. Donald A. Kent, Graduate Director, 585-395-5521, Fax: 585-395-2515, E-mail: dkent@brockport.edu.
Website: http://www.brockport.edu/bus-econ/

DeSales University, Graduate Division, Division of Liberal Arts and Social Sciences, Program in Criminal Justice, Center Valley, PA 18034-9568. Offers criminal justice (MACJ); digital forensics (MACJ); investigative forensics (MACJ). Part-time programs available. Postbaccalaureate distance learning degree programs offered (no on-campus study). *Students:* 41 part-time. *Entrance requirements:* Additional exam requirements/recommendations for international students: Required—TOEFL. *Application deadline:* Applications are processed on a rolling basis. Electronic applications accepted. *Unit head:* Dr. Katherine Ramsland, Director, 610-282-1100 Ext. 1445, Fax: 610-282-0787, E-mail: katherine.ramsland@desales.edu. *Application contact:* Abigail Wernicki, Director of Graduate Admissions, 610-282-1100 Ext. 1768, Fax: 610-282-2869, E-mail: gradadmissions@desales.edu.

Duquesne University, Bayer School of Natural and Environmental Sciences, Program in Forensic Science and Law, Pittsburgh, PA 15282-0001. Offers MS. *Faculty:* 5 full-time (3 women), 13 part-time/adjunct (7 women). *Students:* 18 full-time (12 women). Average age 22. In 2014, 10 master's awarded. *Degree requirements:* For master's, comprehensive exam. *Entrance requirements:* For master's, SAT or ACT, 1 recommendation form; minimum total QPA of 3.0, 2.5 in math and science. *Application deadline:* For fall admission, 7/1 for domestic and international students. Applications are processed on a rolling basis. Application fee: $0. Electronic applications accepted. *Expenses:* Expenses: $1,077 per credit; fees: $100 per credit. *Financial support:* In 2014–15, 17 students received support. Career-related internships or fieldwork and scholarships/grants available. Financial award application deadline: 5/1. *Faculty research:* Extraction protocols, mass spectrometry, synthetic fiber analysis, synthetic polymer characterization, trace analysis, amplification of DNA, methods for labeling DNA, construction of a genetic profile, experiential exploration of mitochondrial DNA, the Y-chromosome, amelogenin. *Total annual research expenditures:* $51,667. *Unit head:* Dr. Federick W. Fochtman, Director, 412-396-6373, Fax: 412-396-1402, E-mail: fochtman@duq.edu. *Application contact:* Valerie L. Lijewski, Academic Advisor, 412-396-1084, Fax: 412-396-1402, E-mail: lijewski@duq.edu.
Website: http://www.duq.edu/academics/schools/natural-and-environmental-sciences/academic-programs/forensic-science-and-law

Florida Atlantic University, College of Business, School of Accounting, Boca Raton, FL 33431-0991. Offers accounting (MAC, MBA, PhD); accounting information systems (MAC); business valuation (Exec MAC); forensic accounting (Exec MAC); taxation (MAC). *Accreditation:* AACSB. Part-time and evening/weekend programs available. Postbaccalaureate distance learning degree programs offered (minimal on-campus study). *Degree requirements:* For master's, comprehensive exam, thesis optional. *Entrance requirements:* For master's, GMAT with minimum score 500 (preferred) or GRE (minimum score 1000 old test, 153 Verbal, 144 Quantitative, 4 Writing) taken within last 5 years, BS in accounting or equivalent, minimum GPA of 3.0 in last 60 hours of undergraduate study. Additional exam requirements/recommendations for international students: Required—TOEFL (minimum score 600 paper-based; 61 iBT), IELTS (minimum score 6). *Expenses:* Tuition, state resident: full-time $7396; part-time $369.82 per credit hour. Tuition, nonresident: full-time $19,392; part-time $1024.81 per credit hour. Tuition and fees vary according to course load. *Faculty research:* Systems and computer applications, accounting theory, information systems.

Florida Gulf Coast University, College of Arts and Sciences, Program in Criminal Forensic Studies, Fort Myers, FL 33965-6565. Offers MS. *Faculty:* 230 full-time (93 women), 158 part-time/adjunct (72 women). *Students:* 5 full-time (3 women), 5 part-time (3 women); includes 3 minority (1 Black or African American, non-Hispanic/Latino; 1 Hispanic/Latino; 1 Two or more races, non-Hispanic/Latino). Average age 29. In 2014, 5 master's awarded. *Entrance requirements:* For master's, GRE General Test, minimum GPA of 3.0. Additional exam requirements/recommendations for international students: Required—TOEFL (minimum score 550 paper-based). *Application deadline:* For fall admission, 4/1 for domestic students; for spring admission, 11/15 for domestic students. Applications are processed on a rolling basis. Application fee: $30. Electronic applications accepted. *Expenses:* Tuition, state resident: full-time $6974. Tuition, nonresident: full-time $28,170. *Required fees:* $1987. Tuition and fees vary according to course load. *Financial support:* In 2014–15, 3 students received support. Research assistantships, career-related internships or fieldwork, and tuition waivers (full and partial) available. Support available to part-time students. Financial award application deadline: 6/30; financial award applicants required to submit FAFSA. *Unit head:* Heather Walsh-Haney, Professor, 239-590-7693, Fax: 239-590-7846, E-mail: hwalsh@fgcu.edu. *Application contact:* Debora Haring, Interim Assistant Director, Graduate Studies, 239-590-7908, Fax: 239-590-7843, E-mail: dharing@fgcu.edu.

Florida International University, College of Arts and Sciences, Department of Chemistry and Biochemistry, Program in Forensic Science, Miami, FL 33199. Offers MS, PhD. Part-time programs available. *Degree requirements:* For master's, thesis optional. *Entrance requirements:* For master's, GRE, minimum GPA of 3.0, 3 letters of recommendation. Additional exam requirements/recommendations for international students: Required—TOEFL (minimum score 550 paper-based). Electronic applications accepted.

George Mason University, College of Science, Program in Forensic Science, Fairfax, VA 22030. Offers MS, Advanced Certificate. *Faculty:* 3 full-time (2 women), 3 part-time/adjunct (2 women). *Students:* 31 full-time (25 women), 46 part-time (33 women); includes 37 minority (17 Black or African American, non-Hispanic/Latino; 3 Asian, non-Hispanic/Latino; 9 Hispanic/Latino; 8 Two or more races, non-Hispanic/Latino), 1 international. Average age 29. 59 applicants, 71% accepted, 24 enrolled. In 2014, 36 master's awarded. *Degree requirements:* For master's, research project or thesis; capstone course. *Entrance requirements:* For master's, BA/BS in related field with minimum GPA of 3.0; 3 letters of recommendation; 2 copies of official transcripts; current resume; expanded goals statement; for Advanced Certificate, BA/BS with minimum GPA of 3.0; 2 copies of official transcripts; current resume. Additional exam requirements/recommendations for international students: Required—TOEFL (minimum score 570 paper-based; 80 iBT), IELTS (minimum score 6.5), PTE. *Application deadline:* For fall admission, 4/15 priority date for domestic students; for spring admission, 11/15 priority date for domestic students. Application fee: $65 ($80 for international students). Electronic applications accepted. *Expenses:* Expenses: Contact institution. *Financial support:* In 2014–15, 1 student received support, including 1 teaching assistantship with full and partial tuition reimbursement available (averaging $14,500 per year); career-

related internships or fieldwork, Federal Work-Study, scholarships/grants, and unspecified assistantships also available. Support available to part-time students. Financial award application deadline: 3/1; financial award applicants required to submit FAFSA. *Faculty research:* Forensic laboratory tests, criminal procedures, forensic chemistry and biology. *Unit head:* Mary E. O'Toole, Director, 703-993-5059, Fax: 703-993-3535, E-mail: motoole2@gmu.edu. *Application contact:* Emily Rancourt, Graduate Program Coordinator, 703-993-5234, Fax: 703-993-1993, E-mail: erancour@gmu.edu. Website: http://forensicscience.gmu.edu/

George Mason University, Volgenau School of Engineering, Department of Electrical and Computer Engineering, Fairfax, VA 22030. Offers computer engineering (MS); computer forensics (MS); electrical and computer engineering (PhD, Certificate); electrical engineering (MS); telecommunications (MS). MS programs offered jointly with Old Dominion University, University of Virginia, Virginia Commonwealth University, and Virginia Polytechnic Institute and State University. *Faculty:* 31 full-time (4 women), 41 part-time/adjunct (5 women). *Students:* 258 full-time (77 women), 275 part-time (51 women); includes 113 minority (33 Black or African American, non-Hispanic/Latino; 54 Asian, non-Hispanic/Latino; 17 Hispanic/Latino; 1 Native Hawaiian or other Pacific Islander, non-Hispanic/Latino; 8 Two or more races, non-Hispanic/Latino), 237 international. Average age 30. 554 applicants, 69% accepted, 158 enrolled. In 2014, 153 master's, 4 doctorates, 24 other advanced degrees awarded. *Degree requirements:* For master's, thesis optional; for doctorate, comprehensive exam, thesis or scholarly paper. *Entrance requirements:* For master's, GRE, personal goals statement; 2 official copies of transcripts; self-evaluation form; 3 letters of recommendation; resume; official bank statement; photocopy of passport; proof of financial support; for doctorate, GRE (waived for GMU electrical and computer engineering master's graduates with minimum GPA of 3.0), personal goals statement; 2 official copies of transcripts; self-evaluation form; 3 letters of recommendation; resume; official bank statement; photocopy of passport; proof of financial support. Additional exam requirements/recommendations for international students: Required—TOEFL (minimum score 575 paper-based; 80 iBT), IELTS (minimum score 6.5), PTE. *Application deadline:* For fall admission, 1/15 priority date for domestic students; for spring admission, 8/15 priority date for domestic students. Applications are processed on a rolling basis. Application fee: $65 ($80 for international students). Electronic applications accepted. *Expenses:* Expenses: Contact institution. *Financial support:* In 2014–15, 68 students received support, including 33 research assistantships with full and partial tuition reimbursements available (averaging $18,359 per year), 38 teaching assistantships with full and partial tuition reimbursements available (averaging $11,521 per year); career-related internships or fieldwork, Federal Work-Study, scholarships/grants, unspecified assistantships, and health care benefits (for full-time research or teaching assistantship recipients) also available. Support available to part-time students. Financial award application deadline: 3/1; financial award applicants required to submit FAFSA. *Faculty research:* Communication networks, signal processing, system failure diagnosis, multiprocessors, material processing using microwave energy. *Total annual research expenditures:* $2.3 million. *Unit head:* Andre Manitius, Chair, 703-993-1570, Fax: 703-993-1601, E-mail: amanitiu@gmu.edu. *Application contact:* Jammie Chang, Academic Program Coordinator, 703-993-1570, Fax: 703-993-1601, E-mail: jchangn@gmu.edu. Website: http://ece.gmu.edu/

The George Washington University, Columbian College of Arts and Sciences, Department of Forensic Sciences, Washington, DC 20052. Offers crime scene investigation (MFS); forensic chemistry (MFS); forensic molecular biology (MFS); forensic toxicology (MFS); high-technology crime investigation (MS); security management (MFS). MFS in high-technology crime investigation and MFS in security management offered in Arlington, VA. Part-time and evening/weekend programs available. *Faculty:* 8 full-time (1 woman). *Students:* 57 full-time (53 women), 42 part-time (32 women); includes 29 minority (15 Black or African American, non-Hispanic/Latino; 1 American Indian or Alaska Native, non-Hispanic/Latino; 7 Asian, non-Hispanic/Latino; 6 Hispanic/Latino), 7 international. Average age 27. 163 applicants, 64% accepted, 36 enrolled. In 2014, 50 master's, 3 other advanced degrees awarded. *Degree requirements:* For master's, comprehensive exam. *Entrance requirements:* For master's, GRE General Test, minimum GPA of 3.0. Additional exam requirements/recommendations for international students: Required—TOEFL (minimum score 550 paper-based; 80 iBT). *Application deadline:* For fall admission, 1/16 priority date for international students; for spring admission, 10/1 priority date for domestic students, 9/1 priority date for international students. Applications are processed on a rolling basis. Application fee: $75. Electronic applications accepted. *Financial support:* In 2014–15, 19 students received support. Fellowships with partial tuition reimbursements available, Federal Work-Study, and tuition waivers available. *Unit head:* Dr. Victor Weedn, Chair, 202-994-6977, E-mail: vweedn@gwu.edu. *Application contact:* 202-994-6210, Fax: 202-994-6213, E-mail: askccas@gwu.edu. Website: http://www.gwu.edu/~forensic/

Georgia State University, Andrew Young School of Policy Studies, School of Social Work, Atlanta, GA 30294. Offers child welfare leadership (Certificate); community partnerships (MSW); forensic social work (Certificate). *Accreditation:* CSWE. Part-time programs available. *Faculty:* 13 full-time (8 women). *Students:* 86 full-time (78 women), 7 part-time (6 women); includes 63 minority (50 Black or African American, non-Hispanic/Latino; 1 Asian, non-Hispanic/Latino; 6 Hispanic/Latino; 1 Native Hawaiian or other Pacific Islander, non-Hispanic/Latino; 5 Two or more races, non-Hispanic/Latino). Average age 29. 116 applicants, 71% accepted, 40 enrolled. In 2014, 48 master's, 4 other advanced degrees awarded. *Entrance requirements:* For master's, GRE; for Certificate, GRE. Additional exam requirements/recommendations for international students: Required—TOEFL, TOEFL (minimum score 550 paper-based; 100 iBT) or IELTS (minimum score 7). *Application deadline:* For fall admission, 2/1 priority date for domestic and international students. Application fee: $50. Electronic applications accepted. *Expenses:* Tuition, state resident: full-time $6516; part-time $362 per credit hour. Tuition, nonresident: full-time $22,014; part-time $1223 per credit hour. *Required fees:* $2128 per semester. Tuition and fees vary according to course load and program. *Financial support:* In 2014–15, research assistantships with tuition reimbursements (averaging $4,000 per year), teaching assistantships with tuition reimbursements (averaging $4,000 per year) were awarded; career-related internships or fieldwork, institutionally sponsored loans, scholarships/grants, tuition waivers, and unspecified assistantships also available. Financial award application deadline: 2/1; financial award applicants required to submit FAFSA. *Faculty research:* Community partnership, non-profit organizations, child welfare practice and policy, gerontological practice and policy, restorative justice. *Unit head:* Renanda Dear, Director of Student and Community Services, 404-413-1057, Fax: 404-413-1075, E-mail: rwood@gsu.edu. *Application contact:* Charisma Parker, Admissions Coordinator, 404-413-0030, Fax: 404-413-0023, E-mail: cparker28@gsu.edu. Website: http://aysps.gsu.edu/socialwork

Golden Gate University, School of Accounting, San Francisco, CA 94105-2968. Offers accounting (M Ac, MSA, Graduate Certificate); forensic accounting (M Ac, MSA, Graduate Certificate); taxation (M Ac). Part-time and evening/weekend programs available. *Entrance requirements:* For master's, minimum GPA of 3.0. Additional exam requirements/recommendations for international students: Required—TOEFL.

Electronic applications accepted. *Faculty research:* Forensic accounting, audit, tax, CPA exam.

Indiana University–Purdue University Indianapolis, School of Science, Forensic and Investigative Sciences Program, Indianapolis, IN 46202. Offers MS. *Students:* 1 (woman) full-time, 2 part-time (both women). 8 applicants, 50% accepted, 3 enrolled. In 2014, 1 master's awarded. *Entrance requirements:* For master's, GRE General Test, bachelor's degree in chemistry, biology, forensic science, pharmacology/toxicology, or related science from accredited institution; minimum GPA of 3.0 for all undergraduate work. Application fee: $55 ($65 for international students). *Unit head:* Dr. John Goodpaster, Director of Forensic Sciences Program, 317-274-6881, E-mail: jvgoodpa@iupui.edu. *Application contact:* Administrative Office, 317-274-6882, E-mail: forsci@iupui.edu. Website: http://forensic.iupui.edu/

Iona College, School of Arts and Science, Department of Criminal Justice, New Rochelle, NY 10801-1890. Offers forensic criminology (Certificate). Part-time and evening/weekend programs available. *Faculty:* 2 full-time (0 women), 4 part-time/adjunct (1 woman). *Students:* 17 full-time (12 women), 11 part-time (4 women); includes 12 minority (5 Black or African American, non-Hispanic/Latino; 6 Hispanic/Latino; 1 Two or more races, non-Hispanic/Latino). Average age 29. 10 applicants, 100% accepted, 7 enrolled. In 2014, 6 master's awarded. *Degree requirements:* For master's, thesis (for some programs), thesis or literature review. *Entrance requirements:* For master's, minimum GPA of 3.0. Additional exam requirements/recommendations for international students: Required—TOEFL (minimum score 550 paper-based; 80 iBT), IELTS (minimum score 6.5). *Application deadline:* For fall admission, 8/1 priority date for domestic students, 5/1 priority date for international students; for spring admission, 1/1 priority date for domestic students, 9/1 priority date for international students. Applications are processed on a rolling basis. Application fee: $50. Electronic applications accepted. *Expenses: Tuition:* Part-time $985 per credit. *Required fees:* $245 per term. *Financial support:* In 2014–15, 3 students received support. Unspecified assistantships available. Financial award application deadline: 4/15; financial award applicants required to submit FAFSA. *Faculty research:* Juvenile justice, criminology, victimology, policing, social justice, security threat assessment. *Unit head:* Cathryn Lavery, PhD, Chair, 914-633-2597, E-mail: clavery@iona.edu. *Application contact:* Frank Boughner, Director, Graduate Admissions, 914-633-2420, Fax: 914-633-2277, E-mail: fboughner@iona.edu. Website: http://www.iona.edu/Academics/School-of-Arts-Science/Departments/Criminal-Justice/Graduate-Programs.aspx

John Jay College of Criminal Justice of the City University of New York, Graduate Studies, Program in Forensic Computing, New York, NY 10019-1093. Offers MS. Part-time and evening/weekend programs available. *Degree requirements:* For master's, thesis or alternative. *Entrance requirements:* For master's, GRE General Test, minimum B average. Additional exam requirements/recommendations for international students: Required—TOEFL (minimum score 500 paper-based). .

John Jay College of Criminal Justice of the City University of New York, Graduate Studies, Program in Forensic Science, New York, NY 10019-1093. Offers MS. Part-time and evening/weekend programs available. *Degree requirements:* For master's, thesis. *Entrance requirements:* For master's, GRE, minimum B average. Additional exam requirements/recommendations for international students: Required—TOEFL (minimum score 500 paper-based).

John Jay College of Criminal Justice of the City University of New York, Graduate Studies, Programs in Criminal Justice, New York, NY 10019-1093. Offers criminal justice (MA, PhD); criminology and deviance (PhD); forensic psychology (PhD); forensic science (PhD); international crime and justice (MA); law and philosophy (PhD); organizational behavior (PhD); public policy (PhD). Part-time and evening/weekend programs available. Terminal master's awarded for partial completion of doctoral program. *Degree requirements:* For master's, thesis or alternative; for doctorate, one foreign language, thesis/dissertation. *Entrance requirements:* For master's, GRE General Test, minimum B average; for doctorate, GRE General Test. Additional exam requirements/recommendations for international students: Required—TOEFL (minimum score 500 paper-based).

La Salle University, College of Professional and Continuing Studies, Program in Economic Crime Forensics, Philadelphia, PA 19141-1199. Offers corporate fraud (MS); fraud and forensic accounting (Certificate); network security (MS). Part-time and evening/weekend programs available. Postbaccalaureate distance learning degree programs offered (no on-campus study). *Entrance requirements:* For master's, minimum GPA of 3.0; professional resume; letters of recommendation; personal interview; for Certificate, professional resume, 200-word essay. Additional exam requirements/recommendations for international students: Required—TOEFL. Electronic applications accepted. Application fee is waived when completed online.

Marshall University, Academic Affairs Division, Forensic Science Center, Huntington, WV 25755. Offers MS. *Students:* 35 full-time (27 women); includes 5 minority (1 Asian, non-Hispanic/Latino; 2 Hispanic/Latino; 2 Two or more races, non-Hispanic/Latino), 1 international. Average age 24. In 2014, 20 master's awarded. *Degree requirements:* For master's, comprehensive exam, thesis optional. *Entrance requirements:* For master's, GRE General Test, undergraduate degree in a natural science, forensic science, or equivalent course work in a related field; 1 year of undergraduate coursework in general chemistry, organic chemistry, physics and biology, with 1 year of associated laboratory for each course. Additional exam requirements/recommendations for international students: Required—TOEFL. *Application deadline:* For fall admission, 3/1 for domestic and international students. Application fee: $40. *Expenses:* Expenses: Contact institution. *Financial support:* In 2014–15, 12 research assistantships with full tuition reimbursements (averaging $4,000 per year), teaching assistantships with full tuition reimbursements (averaging $6,000 per year) were awarded; career-related internships or fieldwork, Federal Work-Study, institutionally sponsored loans, tuition waivers (partial), and unspecified assistantships also available. Financial award application deadline: 8/27; financial award applicants required to submit FAFSA. *Faculty research:* STR analysis of DNA for human identification, forensic analytical chemistry, digital forensics/computer forensics examination, microbial source tracking. *Total annual research expenditures:* $6.5 million. *Unit head:* Dr. Terry W. Fenger, Director, 304-690-4373, Fax: 304-690-4360, E-mail: fenger@marshall.edu. *Application contact:* Kelly Preston, Senior Administrative Secretary, 304-690-4363 Ext. 248, Fax: 304-690-4371, E-mail: forensics@marshall.edu. Website: http://forensics.marshall.edu/

McGill University, Faculty of Graduate and Postdoctoral Studies, Faculty of Dentistry, Montréal, QC H3A 2T5, Canada. Offers forensic dentistry (Certificate); oral and maxillofacial surgery (M Sc, PhD).

Mercyhurst University, Graduate Studies, Program in Forensic and Biological Anthropology, Erie, PA 16546. Offers MS. *Entrance requirements:* For master's, GRE or MAT, undergraduate degree in related field, interview, resume, essay, three professional references, transcripts. Additional exam requirements/recommendations for international students: Required—TOEFL.

Forensic Sciences

Michigan State University, The Graduate School, College of Social Science, School of Criminal Justice, East Lansing, MI 48824. Offers criminal justice (MS, PhD); forensic science (MS); law enforcement intelligence and analysis (MS). Postbaccalaureate distance learning degree programs offered. *Entrance requirements:* Additional exam requirements/recommendations for international students: Required—TOEFL. Electronic applications accepted.

Missouri Western State University, Program in Forensic Investigations, St. Joseph, MO 64507-2294. Offers MAS, Graduate Certificate. Part-time programs available. *Students:* 3 full-time (2 women), 6 part-time (5 women); includes 1 minority (Two or more races, non-Hispanic/Latino). Average age 32. 5 applicants, 60% accepted, 2 enrolled. In 2014, 1 master's, 1 other advanced degree awarded. *Entrance requirements:* For master's, minimum GPA of 2.75. Additional exam requirements/recommendations for international students: Recommended—TOEFL (minimum score 70 iBT), IELTS (minimum score 6). *Application deadline:* For fall admission, 7/15 for domestic and international students; for spring admission, 11/1 for domestic students, 10/15 for international students; for summer admission, 4/29 for domestic students. Applications are processed on a rolling basis. Application fee: $45 ($50 for international students). Electronic applications accepted. *Expenses:* Tuition, state resident: full-time $5506; part-time $305.91 per credit hour. Tuition, nonresident: full-time $10,075; part-time $559.71 per credit hour. *Required fees:* $504; $99 per credit hour. $176 per semester. Tuition and fees vary according to course load and program. *Financial support:* Scholarships/grants and unspecified assistantships available. Support available to part-time students. *Unit head:* Dr. Monty Smith, Assistant Professor, 816-271-4434, E-mail: msmith84@missouriwestern.edu. *Application contact:* Dr. Benjamin D. Caldwell, Dean of the Graduate School, 816-271-4394, Fax: 816-271-4525, E-mail: graduate@missouriwestern.edu.
Website: https://www.missouriwestern.edu/cj-ls-swk/forensic-investigation/

National University, Academic Affairs, College of Letters and Sciences, La Jolla, CA 92037-1011. Offers applied linguistics (MA); biology (MS); counseling psychology (MA), including licensed professional clinical counseling, marriage and family therapy; creative writing (MFA); English (MA), including Gothic studies, rhetoric; film studies (MA); forensic and crime science (Certificate); forensic studies (MFS), including criminalistics, investigation; history (MA); human behavior (MA); mathematics for educators (MS); performance psychology (MA); strategic communications (MA). Part-time and evening/weekend programs available. Postbaccalaureate distance learning degree programs offered (no on-campus study). *Faculty:* 69 full-time (34 women), 100 part-time/adjunct (55 women). *Students:* 727 full-time (532 women), 349 part-time (240 women); includes 505 minority (128 Black or African American, non-Hispanic/Latino; 5 American Indian or Alaska Native, non-Hispanic/Latino; 52 Asian, non-Hispanic/Latino; 260 Hispanic/Latino; 9 Native Hawaiian or other Pacific Islander, non-Hispanic/Latino; 51 Two or more races, non-Hispanic/Latino), 4 international. Average age 34. In 2014, 569 master's awarded. *Degree requirements:* For master's, thesis (for some programs). *Entrance requirements:* For master's, interview, minimum GPA of 2.5. Additional exam requirements/recommendations for international students: Required—TOEFL (minimum score 550 paper-based; 79 iBT), IELTS (minimum score 6). *Application deadline:* Applications are processed on a rolling basis. Application fee: $60 ($65 for international students). Electronic applications accepted. *Expenses:* Tuition: Full-time $14,184; part-time $1773 per course. *Financial support:* Career-related internships or fieldwork, institutionally sponsored loans, scholarships/grants, and tuition waivers (partial) available. Support available to part-time students. Financial award application deadline: 6/30; financial award applicants required to submit FAFSA. *Unit head:* College of Letters and Sciences, 800-628-8648, E-mail: cols@nu.edu. *Application contact:* Frank Rojas, Interim Vice President for Enrollment Services, 800-628-8648, E-mail: advisor@nu.edu.
Website: http://www.nu.edu/OurPrograms/CollegeOfLettersAndSciences.html

National University, Academic Affairs, School of Engineering and Computing, La Jolla, CA 92037-1011. Offers computer science (MS), including advanced computing, database engineering, software engineering; cyber security and information assurance (MS), including computer forensics, ethical hacking and penetration testing, health information assurance, information assurance and security; data analytics (MS); engineering management (MS), including enterprise architecture, project management, systems engineering, technology management; environmental engineering (MS); homeland security and emergency management (MS); management information systems (MS); project management (Certificate); sustainability management (MS); wireless communications (MS). Part-time and evening/weekend programs available. Postbaccalaureate distance learning degree programs offered (no on-campus study). *Faculty:* 24 full-time (5 women), 21 part-time/adjunct (5 women). *Students:* 275 full-time (72 women), 86 part-time (24 women); includes 147 minority (41 Black or African American, non-Hispanic/Latino; 48 Asian, non-Hispanic/Latino; 37 Hispanic/Latino; 7 Native Hawaiian or other Pacific Islander, non-Hispanic/Latino; 14 Two or more races, non-Hispanic/Latino), 95 international. Average age 33. In 2014, 281 master's awarded. *Degree requirements:* For master's, thesis (for some programs). *Entrance requirements:* For master's, interview, minimum GPA of 2.5. Additional exam requirements/recommendations for international students: Required—TOEFL (minimum score 550 paper-based; 79 iBT), IELTS (minimum score 6). *Application deadline:* Applications are processed on a rolling basis. Application fee: $60 ($65 for international students). Electronic applications accepted. *Expenses:* Tuition: Full-time $14,184; part-time $1773 per course. *Financial support:* Career-related internships or fieldwork, institutionally sponsored loans, scholarships/grants, and tuition waivers (partial) available. Support available to part-time students. Financial award application deadline: 6/30; financial award applicants required to submit FAFSA. *Faculty research:* Educational technology, scholarships in science. *Unit head:* School of Engineering and Computing, 800-628-8648, E-mail: soec@nu.edu. *Application contact:* Frank Rojas, Vice President for Enrollment Services, 800-628-8648, E-mail: advisor@nu.edu.
Website: http://www.nu.edu/OurPrograms/SchoolOfEngineeringAndTechnology.html

Nebraska Wesleyan University, University College, Program in Forensic Science, Lincoln, NE 68504-2796. Offers MFS. Part-time and evening/weekend programs available.

Oklahoma State University Center for Health Sciences, Graduate Program in Forensic Sciences, Tulsa, OK 74107. Offers forensic biology/DNA (MS); forensic pathology/death scene investigations (MS); forensic psychology (MS). Part-time and evening/weekend programs available. Postbaccalaureate distance learning degree programs offered (no on-campus study). *Faculty:* 3 full-time (0 women), 17 part-time/adjunct (8 women). *Students:* 13 full-time (11 women), 19 part-time (15 women); includes 7 minority (3 American Indian or Alaska Native, non-Hispanic/Latino; 1 Asian, non-Hispanic/Latino; 3 Hispanic/Latino), 1 international. Average age 31. 35 applicants, 43% accepted, 10 enrolled. In 2014, 11 master's awarded. *Degree requirements:* For master's, comprehensive exam, thesis (for some programs), creative component (for non-thesis options). *Entrance requirements:* For master's, MAT (for options in forensic science administration and forensic document examination) or GRE General Test, professional experience (for options in forensic science administration and forensic document examination). Additional exam requirements/recommendations for international students: Required—TOEFL (minimum score 100 iBT) or IELTS (minimum score 7.0). *Application deadline:* For fall admission, 3/1 for domestic and international

students; for spring admission, 10/1 for domestic and international students; for summer admission, 7/1 for domestic and international students. Applications are processed on a rolling basis. Application fee: $50 ($75 for international students). Electronic applications accepted. *Expenses:* Tuition, state resident: full-time $22,835. Tuition, nonresident: full-time $44,966. *Required fees:* $1259. *Financial support:* In 2014–15, 20 students received support, including 8 research assistantships (averaging $12,000 per year); career-related internships or fieldwork, Federal Work-Study, and tuition waivers (partial) also available. Support available to part-time students. Financial award application deadline: 4/1; financial award applicants required to submit FAFSA. *Faculty research:* Studies on the variability in chromosomal DNA; development/enhancement of accessory methods useful for forensic DNA typing; development of universal methods useful for discriminating pathogenic bacteria; forensic dentistry; forensic chemistry in the areas of controlled substances, explosives, and technology; therapeutic jurisprudence, issues involving inmates and their families, institutional stress suicide. *Total annual research expenditures:* $58,000. *Unit head:* Dr. Robert W. Allen, Director, 918-561-1108, Fax: 918-561-8414. *Application contact:* Cathy Newsome, Coordinator, 918-561-1108, Fax: 918-561-8414, E-mail: cathy.newsome@okstate.edu.
Website: http://www.healthsciences.okstate.edu/forensic/index.cfm

Pace University, Dyson College of Arts and Sciences, Program in Forensic Science, New York, NY 10038. Offers MS. Part-time and evening/weekend programs available. *Students:* 26 full-time (16 women), 7 part-time (6 women); includes 14 minority (6 Black or African American, non-Hispanic/Latino; 1 American Indian or Alaska Native, non-Hispanic/Latino; 4 Asian, non-Hispanic/Latino; 2 Hispanic/Latino; 1 Two or more races, non-Hispanic/Latino), 6 international. Average age 25. 32 applicants, 75% accepted, 13 enrolled. In 2014, 20 master's awarded. *Entrance requirements:* For master's, two letters of recommendation, personal statement, resume, official transcripts. Additional exam requirements/recommendations for international students: Required—TOEFL. *Application deadline:* For fall admission, 8/1 priority date for domestic students, 6/1 for international students; for spring admission, 12/1 priority date for domestic students, 10/1 for international students. Application fee: $70. Electronic applications accepted. *Expenses:* Tuition: Part-time $1120 per credit. *Required fees:* $266 per semester. Tuition and fees vary according to course load, degree level and program. *Financial support:* Application deadline: 2/15; applicants required to submit FAFSA. *Unit head:* Dr. Demos Athanasopolous, Director, Forensic Science Program, 212-346-1763, E-mail: dathanasopolous@pace.edu. *Application contact:* Susan Ford-Goldschein, Director of Graduate Admissions, 212-346-1531, Fax: 212-346-1585, E-mail: gradnyc@pace.edu.
Website: http://www.pace.edu/dyson/academic-departments-and-programs/forensic-science

Philadelphia College of Osteopathic Medicine, Graduate and Professional Programs, Graduate Programs in Forensic Medicine, Philadelphia, PA 19131. Offers MS. Evening/weekend programs available. *Faculty:* 2 full-time (0 women), 2 part-time/adjunct (1 woman). *Students:* 63 full-time (49 women); includes 17 minority (6 Black or African American, non-Hispanic/Latino; 2 Asian, non-Hispanic/Latino; 1 Hispanic/Latino; 8 Two or more races, non-Hispanic/Latino). Average age 28. 39 applicants, 67% accepted, 21 enrolled. In 2014, 42 master's awarded. *Degree requirements:* For master's, capstone project. *Entrance requirements:* For master's, minimum GPA of 3.0; coursework in biology, chemistry, anatomy and physiology or completion of PCOM pathway program. Additional exam requirements/recommendations for international students: Required—TOEFL (minimum score 79 iBT). *Application deadline:* Applications are processed on a rolling basis. Application fee: $50. Electronic applications accepted. *Financial support:* In 2014–15, 11 students received support. Federal Work-Study, institutionally sponsored loans, and scholarships/grants available. Financial award application deadline: 3/15; financial award applicants required to submit FAFSA. *Unit head:* Dr. Gregory McDonald, Chair, 215-871-6760, Fax: 215-871-6792. *Application contact:* Johnathan Cox, Assistant Director of Admissions, 215-871-6700, Fax: 215-871-6719, E-mail: johnathancox@pcom.edu.
Website: http://www.pcom.edu

Saint Leo University, Graduate Studies in Public Safety Administration, Saint Leo, FL 33574-6665. Offers criminal justice (MS), including corrections, critical incident management, forensic science, legal studies. Part-time and evening/weekend programs available. Postbaccalaureate distance learning degree programs offered (minimal on-campus study). *Faculty:* 9 full-time (1 woman), 24 part-time/adjunct (5 women). *Students:* 789 full-time (464 women), 10 part-time (7 women); includes 438 minority (347 Black or African American, non-Hispanic/Latino; 4 American Indian or Alaska Native, non-Hispanic/Latino; 8 Asian, non-Hispanic/Latino; 75 Hispanic/Latino; 4 Two or more races, non-Hispanic/Latino), 3 international. Average age 38. In 2014, 219 master's awarded. *Degree requirements:* For master's, comprehensive project. *Entrance requirements:* For master's, bachelor's degree with minimum GPA of 3.0 from regionally-accredited college or university. Additional exam requirements/recommendations for international students: Required—TOEFL (minimum score 550 paper-based; 80 iBT). *Application deadline:* For fall admission, 7/1 priority date for domestic and international students; for spring admission, 11/1 priority date for domestic and international students. Applications are processed on a rolling basis. Application fee: $80. Electronic applications accepted. *Expenses:* Expenses: Contact institution. *Financial support:* In 2014–15, 16 students received support. Scholarships/grants and health care benefits available. Financial award application deadline: 3/1; financial award applicants required to submit FAFSA. *Unit head:* Dr. Robert Diemer, Director of Department of Public Safety Administration, 352-588-8974, Fax: 352-588-8289, E-mail: robert.diemer@saintleo.edu. *Application contact:* Joshua Stagner, Director of Graduate Admission, 800-707-8846, Fax: 352-588-7873, E-mail: grad.admissions@saintleo.edu.
Website: http://www.saintleo.edu/academics/graduate/criminal-justice.aspx

Sam Houston State University, College of Criminal Justice, Department of Forensic Science, Huntsville, TX 77341. Offers MS. Part-time programs available. *Faculty:* 6 full-time (4 women). *Students:* 27 full-time (26 women); includes 7 minority (4 Black or African American, non-Hispanic/Latino; 3 Hispanic/Latino), 1 international. Average age 24. 9 applicants, 100% accepted, 7 enrolled. In 2014, 16 master's awarded. *Degree requirements:* For master's, comprehensive exam. *Entrance requirements:* For master's, GRE, official transcripts, three letters of recommendation, personal essay. Additional exam requirements/recommendations for international students: Required—TOEFL (minimum score 550 paper-based; 79 iBT), IELTS (minimum score 6.5). *Application deadline:* For fall admission, 12/31 for domestic and international students. Applications are processed on a rolling basis. Application fee: $45 ($75 for international students). Electronic applications accepted. *Expenses:* Tuition, state resident: full-time $2286; part-time $254 per credit hour. Tuition, nonresident: full-time $5544; part-time $616 per credit hour. *Required fees:* $440 per semester. Tuition and fees vary according to course load and campus/location. *Financial support:* In 2014–15, 15 research assistantships (averaging $7,510 per year) were awarded; career-related internships or fieldwork, Federal Work-Study, scholarships/grants, tuition waivers, and unspecified assistantships also available. Support available to part-time students. Financial award application deadline: 3/15; financial award applicants required to submit FAFSA. *Unit head:* Dr. Sarah Kerrigan, Chair, 936-294-4370, Fax: 936-294-4905, E-mail: sarah.kerrigan@shsu.edu. *Application contact:* Doris Powell-Pratt, Graduate Advising

Coordinator, 936-294-3637, Fax: 936-294-4055, E-mail: icc_dcp@shsu.edu. Website: http://forensics.shsu.edu/

Sam Houston State University, College of Sciences, Department of Computer Science, Huntsville, TX 77341. Offers computing and information science (MS); digital forensics (MS); information assurance and security (MS). Part-time programs available. *Faculty:* 12 full-time (3 women), 1 (woman) part-time/adjunct. *Students:* 37 full-time (8 women), 49 part-time (10 women); includes 25 minority (12 Black or African American, non-Hispanic/Latino; 3 Asian, non-Hispanic/Latino; 9 Hispanic/Latino; 1 Two or more races, non-Hispanic/Latino), 32 international. Average age 32. 73 applicants, 40% accepted, 21 enrolled. In 2014, 7 master's awarded. *Degree requirements:* For master's, comprehensive exam, thesis optional, internship; for doctorate, comprehensive exam, thesis/dissertation. *Entrance requirements:* For master's, GRE General Test, letters of recommendation. Additional exam requirements/recommendations for international students: Required—TOEFL (minimum score 550 paper-based; 79 iBT), IELTS (minimum score 6.5). *Application deadline:* For fall admission, 8/1 for domestic students, 6/25 for international students; for spring admission, 12/1 for domestic students, 11/12 for international students; for summer admission, 5/15 for domestic students, 4/9 for international students. Applications are processed on a rolling basis. Application fee: $45 ($75 for international students). Electronic applications accepted. *Expenses:* Tuition, state resident: full-time $2286; part-time $254 per credit hour. Tuition, nonresident: full-time $5544; part-time $616 per credit hour. *Required fees:* $440 per semester. Tuition and fees vary according to course load and campus/location. *Financial support:* In 2014–15, 19 research assistantships (averaging $6,013 per year) were awarded; career-related internships or fieldwork, Federal Work-Study, scholarships/grants, tuition waivers (partial), and unspecified assistantships also available. Support available to part-time students. Financial award application deadline: 3/15; financial award applicants required to submit FAFSA. *Unit head:* Dr. Peter Cooper, Chair/Professor, 936-294-1569, Fax: 936-294-4312, E-mail: css_pac@shsu.edu. *Application contact:* Dr. Jihuang Ji, Associate Professor/Graduate Advisor, 936-294-1579, Fax: 936-294-4312, E-mail: csc_jxj@shsu.edu. Website: http://cs.shsu.edu/

Seattle University, College of Arts and Sciences, Department of Criminal Justice, Seattle, WA 98122-1090. Offers crime analysis (Certificate); criminal justice (MACJ). Part-time and evening/weekend programs available. *Faculty:* 7 full-time (3 women), 2 part-time/adjunct (1 woman). *Students:* 16 full-time (13 women), 60 part-time (48 women); includes 22 minority (3 Black or African American, non-Hispanic/Latino; 4 Asian, non-Hispanic/Latino; 10 Hispanic/Latino; 1 Native Hawaiian or other Pacific Islander, non-Hispanic/Latino; 4 Two or more races, non-Hispanic/Latino). Average age 28. 58 applicants, 62% accepted, 23 enrolled. In 2014, 18 master's, 2 Certificates awarded. *Degree requirements:* For master's, comprehensive exam or thesis. *Entrance requirements:* For master's, minimum GPA of 3.0; undergraduate degree in criminal justice or related social, behavioral, or physical science, or related coursework and/or volunteer or supervised experience; letters of recommendation; writing sample. Additional exam requirements/recommendations for international students: Required—TOEFL, IELTS. *Application deadline:* For fall admission, 3/15 for domestic and international students. Application fee: $55. Electronic applications accepted. *Financial support:* In 2014–15, 32 students received support. Applicants required to submit FAFSA. *Faculty research:* Criminal justice program evaluation, ex-offender reentry, policing issues, restorative justice, psychopathy. *Unit head:* Dr. Elaine Gunnison, Graduate Program Director, 206-296-2430, E-mail: gunnisone@seattleu.edu. *Application contact:* Janet Shandley, Associate Dean of Graduate Admissions, 206-296-5900, Fax: 206-298-5656, E-mail: grad_admissions@seattleu.edu. Website: https://www.seattleu.edu/artsci/criminal-graduate/

Stevenson University, Program in Forensic Science, Owings Mills, MD 21117. Offers MS. Program offered in partnership with Maryland State Police Forensic Sciences Division. *Faculty:* 4 full-time (3 women), 5 part-time/adjunct (2 women). *Students:* 28 full-time (25 women), 23 part-time (21 women); includes 23 minority (20 Black or African American, non-Hispanic/Latino; 1 American Indian or Alaska Native, non-Hispanic/Latino; 1 Asian, non-Hispanic/Latino; 1 Hispanic/Latino). Average age 27. 49 applicants, 67% accepted, 25 enrolled. In 2014, 13 master's awarded. *Degree requirements:* For master's, capstone course. *Entrance requirements:* For master's, bachelor's degree in chemistry, biology, physics, or a related science with minimum cumulative and science/math GPA of 3.2; course/lab work in general biology, general chemistry, organic chemistry, physics, cell biology, molecular genetics, analytical chemistry, instrumental analysis, human anatomy and physiology, biotechniques, and biochemistry. Additional exam requirements/recommendations for international students: Required—TOEFL (minimum score 550 paper-based), IELTS (minimum score 6.5). *Application deadline:* Applications are processed on a rolling basis. Application fee: $0. Electronic applications accepted. *Expenses:* Expenses: $645 per credit, $125 fee. *Unit head:* John Tobin, PhD, Coordinator, 443-352-4142, Fax: 443-394-0538, E-mail: jtobin@stevenson.edu. *Application contact:* William Wellein, Enrollment Counselor, 443-352-5843, Fax: 443-394-0538, E-mail: wwellein@stevenson.edu. Website: http://www.stevenson.edu

Stevenson University, Program in Forensic Studies, Owings Mills, MD 21117. Offers computer forensics (MS); criminalistics (MS); forensic accounting (MS); forensic legal professional (MS); interdisciplinary track (MS); investigations (MS). Postbaccalaureate distance learning degree programs offered (minimal on-campus study). *Faculty:* 5 full-time (3 women), 15 part-time/adjunct (2 women). *Students:* 14 full-time (12 women), 130 part-time (110 women); includes 64 minority (61 Black or African American, non-Hispanic/Latino; 2 Asian, non-Hispanic/Latino; 1 Hispanic/Latino). Average age 30. 77 applicants, 79% accepted, 33 enrolled. In 2014, 58 master's awarded. *Degree requirements:* For master's, capstone course. *Entrance requirements:* Additional exam requirements/recommendations for international students: Required—TOEFL (minimum score 550 paper-based), IELTS (minimum score 6.5). *Application deadline:* Applications are processed on a rolling basis. Application fee: $0. Electronic applications accepted. *Expenses:* Expenses: $645 per credit, $125 fee. *Unit head:* Thomas Coogan, JD, Associate Dean, 443-352-4075, Fax: 443-394-0538, E-mail: tcoogan@stevenson.edu. *Application contact:* William Wellein, Enrollment Counselor, 443-352-5843, Fax: 443-394-0538, E-mail: wwellein@stevenson.edu.

Syracuse University, College of Arts and Sciences, Program in Biomedical Forensic Science, Syracuse, NY 13244. Offers MS. Part-time programs available. *Students:* 15 full-time (10 women), 1 part-time (0 women); includes 7 minority (3 Black or African American, non-Hispanic/Latino; 1 Asian, non-Hispanic/Latino; 2 Hispanic/Latino; 1 Two or more races, non-Hispanic/Latino), 1 international. Average age 25. 38 applicants, 61% accepted, 11 enrolled. *Entrance requirements:* For master's, GRE or MCAT, interview. *Application deadline:* For fall admission, 2/15 priority date for domestic and international students; for spring admission, 11/1 priority date for domestic and international students; for summer admission, 2/15 priority date for domestic and international students. Applications are processed on a rolling basis. Application fee: $75. Electronic applications accepted. *Expenses: Tuition:* Part-time $1341 per credit. *Financial support:* Fellowships with full tuition reimbursements, research assistantships with full and partial tuition reimbursements, and teaching assistantships with full and partial tuition reimbursements available. *Unit head:* Dr. Michael M. Sponsler, Director of

Curricular Programs for the Forensic and National Security Sciences Institute, 315-443-0326, E-mail: forensics@syr.edu. *Application contact:* Same as above. Website: http://forensics.syr.edu/index.html

Syracuse University, College of Arts and Sciences, Program in Forensic Science, Syracuse, NY 13244. Offers MS. Part-time programs available. *Students:* 32 full-time (26 women), 5 part-time (4 women); includes 9 minority (4 Black or African American, non-Hispanic/Latino; 4 Hispanic/Latino; 1 Two or more races, non-Hispanic/Latino), 4 international. Average age 25. 45 applicants, 80% accepted, 18 enrolled. In 2014, 15 master's awarded. *Degree requirements:* For master's, internship. *Entrance requirements:* For master's, GRE General Test, telephone interview. Additional exam requirements/recommendations for international students: Required—TOEFL (minimum score 100 iBT). *Application deadline:* For fall admission, 2/15 priority date for domestic and international students; for spring admission, 11/1 priority date for domestic and international students; for summer admission, 2/15 for domestic students, 2/16 priority date for international students. Applications are processed on a rolling basis. Application fee: $75. Electronic applications accepted. *Expenses: Tuition:* Part-time $1341 per credit. *Financial support:* Fellowships with full tuition reimbursements, research assistantships, and teaching assistantships available. Financial award application deadline: 1/1; financial award applicants required to submit FAFSA. *Unit head:* Dr. Michael M. Sponsler, Director of Curricular Programs for the Forensic and National Security Sciences Institute, 315-443-4347, E-mail: sponsler@syr.edu. *Application contact:* same as above. Website: http://forensics.syr.edu/index.html

Texas Tech University, Graduate School, College of Arts and Sciences, Interdisciplinary Program in Forensic Science, Lubbock, TX 79409. Offers MS. *Students:* 18 full-time (15 women), 12 part-time (5 women); includes 8 minority (2 Black or African American, non-Hispanic/Latino; 6 Hispanic/Latino), 2 international. Average age 26. 13 applicants, 77% accepted, 4 enrolled. In 2014, 10 master's awarded. *Degree requirements:* For master's, thesis (for some programs), internship with comprehensive exam. *Entrance requirements:* Additional exam requirements/recommendations for international students: Required—TOEFL (minimum score 550 paper-based; 79 iBT). Application fee: $60. *Expenses:* Tuition, state resident: full-time $6310; part-time $262.92 per credit hour. Tuition, nonresident: full-time $14,998; part-time $624.92 per credit hour. *Required fees:* $2701; $36.50 per credit. $912.50 per semester. Tuition and fees vary according to course load. *Financial support:* In 2014–15, 10 students received support, including 9 fellowships (averaging $2,689 per year), 1 research assistantship (averaging $17,400 per year). Financial award application deadline: 4/15; financial award applicants required to submit FAFSA. *Faculty research:* Forensic anthropology, forensic psychology. *Unit head:* Dr. Robert Paine, Director, 806-834-8375, Fax: 806-743-7932, E-mail: robert.paine@ttu.edu. *Application contact:* Dr. Jorge Iber, Associate Dean, 806-742-3833, Fax: 806-742-3893, E-mail: jorge.iber@ttu.edu.

Towson University, Program in Forensic Science, Towson, MD 21252-0001. Offers MS. *Students:* 43 full-time (34 women), 6 part-time (all women); includes 15 minority (12 Black or African American, non-Hispanic/Latino; 2 Asian, non-Hispanic/Latino; 1 Hispanic/Latino), 2 international. *Entrance requirements:* For master's, minimum GPA of 3.0; bachelor's degree in biological sciences, chemistry, forensic chemistry, or related field. *Application deadline:* Applications are processed on a rolling basis. Application fee: $45. Electronic applications accepted. *Unit head:* Mark Profili, Graduate Program Director, 410-704-2668, E-mail: mprofili@towson.edu. *Application contact:* Alicia Arkell-Kleis, Information Contact, 410-704-6004, Fax: 410-704-4675, E-mail: grads@towson.edu. Website: http://grad.towson.edu/program/master/frsc-ms/

Universidad del Turabo, Graduate Programs, School of Social Sciences and Humanities, Programs in Public Affairs, Program in Forensic Science, Gurabo, PR 00778-3030. Offers MPA.

University at Albany, State University of New York, College of Arts and Sciences, Department of Biological Sciences, Albany, NY 12222-0001. Offers biodiversity, conservation, and policy (MS); ecology and evolutionary biology (PhD); forensic biology (MS); molecular, cellular, developmental, and neural biology (PhD). *Degree requirements:* For master's, one foreign language; for doctorate, one foreign language, thesis/dissertation. *Entrance requirements:* For master's and doctorate, GRE General Test. Additional exam requirements/recommendations for international students: Required—TOEFL (minimum score 550 paper-based). Electronic applications accepted. *Faculty research:* Interferon, neural development, RNA self-splicing, behavioral ecology, DNA repair enzymes.

University at Albany, State University of New York, School of Business, Department of Accounting, Albany, NY 12222-0001. Offers accounting (MS); forensic accounting (MS); professional accounting (MS); tax practice (MS); taxation (MS). *Accreditation:* AACSB. *Degree requirements:* For master's, research project. *Entrance requirements:* For master's, GMAT. Additional exam requirements/recommendations for international students: Required—TOEFL (minimum score 550 paper-based). Electronic applications accepted. *Faculty research:* Professional ethics, statistical analysis, cost management systems, accounting theory.

The University of Alabama at Birmingham, College of Arts and Sciences, Program in Computer Forensics and Security Management, Birmingham, AL 35294. Offers MS. Interdisciplinary program offered jointly with College of Arts and Sciences and School of Business. *Students:* 4 full-time (1 woman), 6 part-time (2 women); includes 2 minority (1 Black or African American, non-Hispanic/Latino; 1 Hispanic/Latino), 3 international. Average age 34. In 2014, 3 master's awarded. *Degree requirements:* For master's, field practicum (internship). *Entrance requirements:* For master's, GRE General Test (minimum combined score of 320) or GMAT (minimum total score of 550), minimum GPA of 3.0. *Application deadline:* For fall admission, 3/1 for domestic students. Application fee: $45 ($60 for international students). Electronic applications accepted. *Expenses:* Tuition, state resident: full-time $7090; part-time $370 per credit hour. Tuition, nonresident: full-time $16,072; part-time $869 per credit hour. Full-time tuition and fees vary according to course load and program. *Unit head:* Dr. Anthony Skjellum, Program Co-Director, Computer and Information Sciences, 205-934-2213, Fax: 205-934-5473, E-mail: tony@cis.uab.edu. *Application contact:* Dr. John J. Sloan, III, Program Co-Director, Justice Sciences, 205-934-2069, E-mail: prof@uab.edu. Website: http://www.uab.edu/cas/justice-sciences/graduate-programs/master-of-science-in-computer-forensics-and-security-management-mscfsm

The University of Alabama at Birmingham, College of Arts and Sciences, Program in Forensic Science, Birmingham, AL 35294. Offers MSFS. *Students:* 11 full-time (8 women), 2 part-time (1 woman); includes 2 minority (1 Black or African American, non-Hispanic/Latino; 1 Two or more races, non-Hispanic/Latino). Average age 23. In 2014, 10 master's awarded. *Entrance requirements:* For master's, GRE, minimum GPA of 3.0. Additional exam requirements/recommendations for international students: Required—TOEFL, TWE. *Application deadline:* For fall admission, 1/31 priority date for domestic students. Application fee: $45 ($60 for international students). Electronic applications accepted. *Expenses:* Tuition, state resident: full-time $7090; part-time $370 per credit hour. Tuition, nonresident: full-time $16,072; part-time $869 per credit hour. Full-time tuition and fees vary according to course load and program. *Financial support:*

Forensic Sciences

Research assistantships and scholarships/grants available. *Unit head:* Dr. Elizabeth Gardner, Graduate Program Director, 205-934-0668, E-mail: eagard@uab.edu. *Application contact:* Susan Noblitt Banks, Director of Graduate School Operations, 205-934-8227, Fax: 205-934-8413, E-mail: gradschool@uab.edu.
Website: http://www.uab.edu/cas/justice-sciences/graduate-programs/master-of-science-in-forensic-science-msfs

University of California, Davis, Graduate Studies, Graduate Group in Forensic Science, Davis, CA 95616. Offers MS. *Degree requirements:* For master's, thesis. *Entrance requirements:* Additional exam requirements/recommendations for international students: Required—TOEFL (minimum score 550 paper-based), IELTS (minimum score 7). Electronic applications accepted.

University of Central Florida, College of Engineering and Computer Science, Department of Electrical Engineering and Computer Science, Program in Computer Science, Orlando, FL 32816. Offers computer science (MS, PhD); digital forensics (MS). Part-time and evening/weekend programs available. *Students:* 192 full-time (53 women), 122 part-time (22 women); includes 49 minority (11 Black or African American, non-Hispanic/Latino; 12 Asian, non-Hispanic/Latino; 23 Hispanic/Latino; 3 Two or more races, non-Hispanic/Latino), 137 international. Average age 30. 371 applicants, 71% accepted, 99 enrolled. In 2014, 75 master's, 6 doctorates awarded. *Degree requirements:* For master's, thesis or alternative; for doctorate, thesis/dissertation, candidacy exam, departmental qualifying exam. *Entrance requirements:* For master's, GRE General Test, GRE Subject Test, minimum GPA of 3.0 in last 60 hours; for doctorate, GRE Subject Test, minimum GPA of 3.0 in last 60 hours. Additional exam requirements/recommendations for international students: Required—TOEFL. *Application deadline:* For fall admission, 7/15 priority date for domestic students; for spring admission, 12/1 priority date for domestic students. Application fee: $30. Electronic applications accepted. *Expenses:* Tuition, state resident: part-time $288.16 per credit hour. Tuition, nonresident: part-time $1073.31 per credit hour. *Financial support:* In 2014–15, 88 students received support, including 23 fellowships with partial tuition reimbursements available (averaging $6,300 per year), 46 research assistantships with partial tuition reimbursements available (averaging $10,600 per year), 46 teaching assistantships with partial tuition reimbursements available (averaging $11,100 per year); career-related internships or fieldwork, Federal Work-Study, institutionally sponsored loans, tuition waivers (partial), and unspecified assistantships also available. Financial award application deadline: 3/1; financial award applicants required to submit FAFSA. *Faculty research:* Parallel processing, databases, algorithms, virtual reality. *Unit head:* Dr. Gary Leavens, Chair, 407-882-0185, E-mail: leavens@ucf.edu. *Application contact:* Barbara Rodriguez Lamas, Director, Admissions and Student Services, 407-823-2766, Fax: 407-823-6442, E-mail: gradadmissions@ucf.edu.
Website: http://web.eecs.ucf.edu/

University of Central Oklahoma, The Jackson College of Graduate Studies, College of Liberal Arts, School of Criminal Justice, Edmond, OK 73034-5209. Offers crime and intelligence analysis (MA); criminal justice management and administration (MA). Part-time programs available. *Entrance requirements:* Additional exam requirements/recommendations for international students: Required—TOEFL (minimum score 550 paper-based; 79 iBT), IELTS (minimum score 6.5). Electronic applications accepted. *Faculty research:* Gender issues, violent offenders.

University of Central Oklahoma, The Jackson College of Graduate Studies, Forensic Science Institute, Edmond, OK 73034-5209. Offers biology/chemistry (MS); forensic science (MS). *Degree requirements:* For master's, thesis. *Entrance requirements:* For master's, GRE, official transcripts. Additional exam requirements/recommendations for international students: Required—TOEFL (minimum score 550 paper-based; 79 iBT), IELTS (minimum score 6.5). Electronic applications accepted.

University of Charleston, Master of Forensic Accounting Program, Charleston, WV 25304-1099. Offers EMFA. Part-time programs available. Postbaccalaureate distance learning degree programs offered (minimal on-campus study). *Degree requirements:* For master's, capstone project with mock trial testimony. *Entrance requirements:* Additional exam requirements/recommendations for international students: Required—TOEFL. *Application deadline:* Applications are processed on a rolling basis. Application fee: $50. Electronic applications accepted. *Financial support:* Applicants required to submit FAFSA. *Unit head:* Robert James Rufus, Coordinator, 304-522-8770, E-mail: mfacc@ucwv.edu. *Application contact:* Bobby Redd, Admissions Representative, 304-860-5621, E-mail: bobbyredd@ucwv.edu.
Website: http://www.ucwv.edu/Forensic-Accounting/

University of Colorado Denver, Business School, Program in Accounting, Denver, CO 80217. Offers auditing and forensic accounting (MS); controllership/financial officer (MS); information systems audit control (MS); taxation (MS). *Accreditation:* AACSB. Part-time and evening/weekend programs available. *Students:* 114 full-time (59 women), 35 part-time (18 women); includes 31 minority (4 Black or African American, non-Hispanic/Latino; 13 Asian, non-Hispanic/Latino; 12 Hispanic/Latino; 2 Two or more races, non-Hispanic/Latino), 24 international. Average age 31. 87 applicants, 63% accepted, 25 enrolled. In 2014, 67 master's awarded. *Degree requirements:* For master's, 30 semester hours. *Entrance requirements:* For master's, GMAT (waived for students who already hold a graduate degree, or an undergraduate degree from CU Denver), essay, resume, two letters of recommendation; financial statements (for international students). Additional exam requirements/recommendations for international students: Required—TOEFL (minimum score 537 paper-based; 75 iBT); Recommended—IELTS (minimum score 6.5). *Application deadline:* For fall admission, 4/15 priority date for domestic students, 3/15 priority date for international students; for spring admission, 10/15 priority date for domestic students, 9/15 priority date for international students; for summer admission, 2/15 priority date for domestic students, 1/15 priority date for international students. Applications are processed on a rolling basis. Application fee: $50 ($75 for international students). Electronic applications accepted. *Expenses:* Expenses: Contact institution. *Financial support:* In 2014–15, 13 students received support. Fellowships, research assistantships, teaching assistantships, Federal Work-Study, institutionally sponsored loans, scholarships/grants, and traineeships available. Financial award application deadline: 4/1; financial award applicants required to submit FAFSA. *Faculty research:* Transfer pricing, behavioral accounting, environmental accounting, health services, international auditing. *Unit head:* Clifford Young, Associate Dean, 303-315-8000, E-mail: clifford.young@ucdenver.edu. *Application contact:* Shelly Townley, Admissions Director, Graduate Programs, 303-315-8202, E-mail: shelly.townley@ucdenver.edu.
Website: http://www.ucdenver.edu/academics/colleges/business/degrees/ms/accounting/Pages/Accounting.aspx

University of Colorado Denver, College of Arts and Media, Denver, CO 80217. Offers recording arts (MS), including media forensics, recording arts. Part-time and evening/weekend programs available. *Faculty:* 32 full-time (11 women), 2 part-time/adjunct (1 woman). *Students:* 23 full-time (5 women), 4 part-time (2 women); includes 6 minority (2 Asian, non-Hispanic/Latino; 3 Hispanic/Latino; 1 Two or more races, non-Hispanic/Latino), 1 international. Average age 34. 19 applicants, 74% accepted, 8 enrolled. In 2014, 8 master's awarded. *Degree requirements:* For master's, thesis, 34 credits, thesis/portfolio. *Entrance requirements:* For master's, GRE General Test (minimum scores higher than 50th percentile for all sections), minimum undergraduate GPA of 3.0, portfolio, resume, interview, 3 letters of recommendation. Additional exam requirements/recommendations for international students: Required—TOEFL (minimum score 70 iBT). *Application deadline:* For fall admission, 4/1 for domestic students, 3/1 for international students. Application fee: $50 ($75 for international students). Electronic applications accepted. *Expenses:* Expenses: Contact institution. *Financial support:* In 2014–15, 2 students received support. Federal Work-Study, institutionally sponsored loans, scholarships/grants, traineeships, and unspecified assistantships available. Financial award application deadline: 4/1; financial award applicants required to submit FAFSA. *Faculty research:* Audio forensics, audio pedagogy, concert recordings, digital audio workstations, music law. *Total annual research expenditures:* $29,822. *Unit head:* Laurence Kaptain, Dean, 303-352-3559, E-mail: laurence.kaptain@ucdenver.edu. *Application contact:* Megan Sforzini, Program Assistant, 303-352-3833, E-mail: megan.sforzini@ucdenver.edu.
Website: http://www.ucdenver.edu/academics/colleges/CAM/programs/meis/masterdegree/Pages/index.aspx

University of Florida, Graduate School, College of Pharmacy, Programs in Forensic Science, Gainesville, FL 32611. Offers clinical toxicology (Certificate); drug chemistry (Certificate); environmental forensics (Certificate); forensic death investigation (Certificate); forensic DNA and serology (MSP, Certificate); forensic drug chemistry (MSP); forensic science (MSP); forensic toxicology (Certificate). Part-time and evening/weekend programs available. Postbaccalaureate distance learning degree programs offered (no on-campus study). *Faculty:* 13 full-time (3 women). *Students:* 33 full-time (28 women), 214 part-time (166 women); includes 47 minority (18 Black or African American, non-Hispanic/Latino; 1 American Indian or Alaska Native, non-Hispanic/Latino; 9 Asian, non-Hispanic/Latino; 19 Hispanic/Latino), 9 international. In 2014, 109 master's awarded. *Degree requirements:* For master's, comprehensive exam. *Entrance requirements:* For master's, GRE General Test, minimum GPA of 3.0. Additional exam requirements/recommendations for international students: Required—TOEFL (minimum score 550 paper-based; 80 iBT), IELTS (minimum score 6). Application fee: $30. *Financial support:* Applicants required to submit FAFSA. *Unit head:* Dr. Ian Tibbett, Director, 352-273-6871, Fax: 352-273-8716, E-mail: itebbett@ufl.edu. *Application contact:* Dr. Ian Tibbett, Director, 352-273-6871, Fax: 352-273-8716, E-mail: itebbett@ufl.edu.
Website: http://www.forensicscience.ufl.edu/

University of Houston–Victoria, School of Arts and Sciences, Program in Biomedical Sciences, Victoria, TX 77901-4450. Offers biological sciences (MS); biomedical sciences (MS); forensic science (MS).

University of Illinois at Chicago, College of Pharmacy and Graduate College, Graduate Programs in Pharmacy, Program in Forensic Science, Chicago, IL 60607-7128. Offers MS. *Faculty:* 15 full-time (4 women), 10 part-time/adjunct (2 women). *Students:* 5 full-time (all women); includes 1 minority (Hispanic/Latino). Average age 30. 43 applicants, 19% accepted, 5 enrolled. In 2014, 19 master's awarded. *Degree requirements:* For master's, thesis. *Entrance requirements:* For master's, GRE General Test. Additional exam requirements/recommendations for international students: Required—TOEFL. *Application deadline:* For fall admission, 1/1 for domestic students, 2/15 for international students. Application fee: $60. *Expenses:* Tuition, state resident: full-time $11,254; part-time $468 per credit hour. Tuition, nonresident: full-time $23,252; part-time $968 per credit hour. *Required fees:* $1217 per term. Part-time tuition and fees vary according to course load, degree level and program. *Financial support:* Fellowships with full tuition reimbursements, research assistantships with full tuition reimbursements, teaching assistantships with full tuition reimbursements, career-related internships or fieldwork, Federal Work-Study, institutionally sponsored loans, and tuition waivers (full) available. Financial award application deadline: 2/1; financial award applicants required to submit FAFSA. *Faculty research:* Interpretation of physical evidence, utilization of physical evidence, analytical toxicology of controlled substances, automated fingerprint systems, dye and ink characterizations. *Unit head:* Prof. Albert Karl Larsen, Director, Forensic Science Graduate Studies, 312-996-2250, E-mail: forensicdgs@uic.edu. *Application contact:* Jackie Perry, Graduate College Receptionist, 312-413-2550, Fax: 312-413-0185, E-mail: gradcoll@uic.edu.
Website: http://www.uic.edu/pharmacy/depts/Forensic_Science/

University of New Haven, Graduate School, Henry C. Lee College of Criminal Justice and Forensic Sciences, Program in Criminal Justice, West Haven, CT 06516-1916. Offers crime analysis (MS); criminal justice (MS, PhD); criminal justice management (MS, Certificate); forensic computer investigation (MS, Certificate); forensic psychology (MS); information protection and security (Certificate); victim advocacy and services management (Certificate); victimology (MS). Part-time and evening/weekend programs available. Postbaccalaureate distance learning degree programs offered (no on-campus study). *Degree requirements:* For master's, thesis or alternative. *Entrance requirements:* Additional exam requirements/recommendations for international students: Required—TOEFL (minimum score 80 iBT), IELTS, PTE (minimum score 53). Electronic applications accepted. Application fee is waived when completed online. *Expenses: Tuition:* Full-time $22,248; part-time $824 per credit hour. *Required fees:* $45 per trimester.

University of New Haven, Graduate School, Henry C. Lee College of Criminal Justice and Forensic Sciences, Program in Fire Science, West Haven, CT 06516-1916. Offers emergency management (MS, Certificate); fire administration (MS); fire science (MS); fire science technology (Certificate); fire/arson investigation (MS, Certificate); forensic science/fire science (Certificate); public safety management (MS, Certificate). Part-time and evening/weekend programs available. *Degree requirements:* For master's, thesis or alternative, research project or internship. *Entrance requirements:* Additional exam requirements/recommendations for international students: Required—TOEFL (minimum score 80 iBT), IELTS, PTE (minimum score 53). Electronic applications accepted. Application fee is waived when completed online. *Expenses: Tuition:* Full-time $22,248; part-time $824 per credit hour. *Required fees:* $45 per trimester.

University of New Haven, Graduate School, Henry C. Lee College of Criminal Justice and Forensic Sciences, Program in Forensic Science, West Haven, CT 06516-1916. Offers criminalistics (MS, Certificate); fire science (MS). Part-time and evening/weekend programs available. *Degree requirements:* For master's, thesis or alternative, research project or internship. *Entrance requirements:* For master's, GRE. Additional exam requirements/recommendations for international students: Required—TOEFL (minimum score 80 iBT), IELTS, PTE (minimum score 53). Electronic applications accepted. Application fee is waived when completed online. *Expenses: Tuition:* Full-time $22,248; part-time $824 per credit hour. *Required fees:* $45 per trimester.

University of New Haven, Graduate School, Henry C. Lee College of Criminal Justice and Forensic Sciences, Program in Forensic Technology, West Haven, CT 06516-1916. Offers MS. *Degree requirements:* For master's, internship or research project. *Expenses: Tuition:* Full-time $22,248; part-time $824 per credit hour. *Required fees:* $45 per trimester.

University of North Texas Health Science Center at Fort Worth, Graduate School of Biomedical Sciences, Fort Worth, TX 76107-2699. Offers anatomy and cell biology (MS, PhD); biochemistry and molecular biology (MS, PhD); biomedical sciences (MS, PhD);

biotechnology (MS); forensic genetics (MS); integrative physiology (MS, PhD); medical science (MS); microbiology and immunology (MS, PhD); pharmacology (MS, PhD); science education (MS); DO/MS; DO/PhD. Terminal master's awarded for partial completion of doctoral program. *Degree requirements:* For master's, thesis; for doctorate, thesis/dissertation. *Entrance requirements:* For master's and doctorate, GRE General Test. Additional exam requirements/recommendations for international students: Required—TOEFL. *Expenses:* Contact institution. *Faculty research:* Alzheimer's disease, aging, eye diseases, cancer, cardiovascular disease.

University of Rhode Island, Graduate School, College of Arts and Sciences, Department of Computer Science and Statistics, Kingston, RI 02881. Offers applied mathematics (PhD), including computer science, statistics; computer science (MS, PhD); digital forensics (Graduate Certificate); statistics (MS). Part-time programs available. *Faculty:* 12 full-time (6 women). *Students:* 30 full-time (10 women), 49 part-time (8 women); includes 15 minority (5 Black or African American, non-Hispanic/Latino; 1 American Indian or Alaska Native, non-Hispanic/Latino; 7 Asian, non-Hispanic/Latino; 2 Hispanic/Latino), 16 international. In 2014, 5 master's, 3 doctorates awarded. *Degree requirements:* For master's, comprehensive exam (for some programs), thesis optional; for doctorate, comprehensive exam, thesis/dissertation. *Entrance requirements:* For master's and doctorate, GRE, 2 letters of recommendation. Additional exam requirements/recommendations for international students: Required—TOEFL (minimum score 550 paper-based). *Application deadline:* For fall admission, 7/15 for domestic students, 2/1 for international students; for spring admission, 11/15 for domestic students, 7/15 for international students. Application fee: $65. Electronic applications accepted. *Expenses:* Tuition, state resident: full-time $11,532; part-time $641 per credit. Tuition, nonresident: full-time $23,606; part-time $1311 per credit. *Required fees:* $1442; $39 per credit. $35 per semester. One-time fee: $155. *Financial support:* In 2014–15, 4 research assistantships with full and partial tuition reimbursements (averaging $14,430 per year), 12 teaching assistantships with full and partial tuition reimbursements (averaging $15,298 per year) were awarded. Financial award application deadline: 2/1; financial award applicants required to submit FAFSA. *Faculty research:* Bioinformatics, computer and digital forensics, behavioral model of pedestrian dynamics, real-time distributed object computing, cryptography. *Total annual research expenditures:* $371,046. *Unit head:* Dr. Joan Peckham, Chair, 401-874-2701, Fax: 401-874-4617, E-mail: joan@cs.uri.edu. *Application contact:* E-mail: grad-inquiries@cs.uri.edu.
Website: http://www.cs.uri.edu/

University of St. Francis, College of Arts and Sciences, Joliet, IL 60435-6169. Offers advanced generalist forensic social work (Post-Master's Certificate); physician assistant practice (MS); social work (MSW). *Faculty:* 7 full-time (6 women), 1 part-time/adjunct (0 women). *Students:* 97 full-time (73 women), 23 part-time (21 women); includes 52 minority (22 Black or African American, non-Hispanic/Latino; 6 Asian, non-Hispanic/Latino; 18 Hispanic/Latino; 6 Two or more races, non-Hispanic/Latino), 1 international. Average age 30. 85 applicants, 51% accepted, 28 enrolled. In 2014, 55 master's awarded. *Entrance requirements:* Additional exam requirements/recommendations for international students: Required—TOEFL (minimum score 550 paper-based; 79 iBT), IELTS (minimum score 6.5). *Application deadline:* Applications are processed on a rolling basis. Application fee: $30. Electronic applications accepted. Application fee is waived when completed online. *Expenses:* Expenses: Contact institution. *Financial support:* In 2014–15, 8 students received support. Career-related internships or fieldwork, scholarships/grants, tuition waivers (partial), and unspecified assistantships available. Support available to part-time students. Financial award applicants required to submit FAFSA. *Unit head:* Dr. Robert Kase, Dean, 815-740-3367, Fax: 815-740-6366. *Application contact:* Sandra Sloka, Director of Admissions for Graduate and Degree Completion Programs, 800-735-7500, Fax: 815-740-3431, E-mail: ssloka@stfrancis.edu.
Website: http://www.stfrancis.edu/academics/cas

University of Southern Mississippi, Graduate School, College of Science and Technology, Department of Administration of Justice, Hattiesburg, MS 39406-0001. Offers administration of justice (PhD); corrections (MA, MS); forensics (MS); juvenile justice (MA, MS); law enforcement (MA, MS). Part-time programs available. *Degree requirements:* For master's, comprehensive exam, thesis; for doctorate, comprehensive exam, thesis/dissertation. *Entrance requirements:* For master's, GRE General Test, minimum GPA of 2.75 in last 60 hours, 3.0 in field of study; for doctorate, GRE General Test, minimum GPA of 3.5. Additional exam requirements/recommendations for international students: Required—TOEFL, IELTS. *Faculty research:* Crime in the family, police training models, humanities and criminal justice.

Utica College, Program in Cybersecurity, Utica, NY 13502-4892. Offers MS. Part-time and evening/weekend programs available. Postbaccalaureate distance learning degree programs offered. *Faculty:* 5 full-time (0 women), 8 part-time/adjunct (0 women). *Students:* 2 full-time (0 women), 285 part-time (85 women); includes 74 minority (29 Black or African American, non-Hispanic/Latino; 6 American Indian or Alaska Native, non-Hispanic/Latino; 14 Asian, non-Hispanic/Latino; 21 Hispanic/Latino; 4 Two or more races, non-Hispanic/Latino). Average age 35. 194 applicants, 97% accepted, 153 enrolled. In 2014, 70 master's awarded. *Entrance requirements:* For master's, BS, minimum GPA of 3.0. Additional exam requirements/recommendations for international students: Recommended—TOEFL (minimum score 525 paper-based). *Application deadline:* Applications are processed on a rolling basis. Electronic applications accepted. *Expenses: Tuition:* Full-time $33,216; part-time $706 per credit hour. *Required fees:* $520; $50 per course. Tuition and fees vary according to course load, degree level, campus/location and program. *Financial support:* Application deadline: 3/15; applicants required to submit FAFSA. *Faculty research:* Steganography and data hiding, cryptography. *Unit head:* Joseph Giordano, Chair, 315-792-2521. *Application contact:* John D. Rowe, Director of Graduate Admissions, 315-792-3824, Fax: 315-792-3003, E-mail: jrowe@utica.edu.
Website: http://www.onlineuticacollege.com/programs/masters-cybersecurity.asp

Virginia Commonwealth University, Graduate School, College of Humanities and Sciences, Department of Forensic Science, Richmond, VA 23284-9005. Offers forensic biology (MS); forensic chemistry/drugs and toxicology (MS); forensic chemistry/trace (MS); forensic physical evidence (MS). Part-time programs available. *Entrance requirements:* For master's, GRE General Test, bachelor's degree in a natural science discipline, including forensic science, or a degree with equivalent work. Additional exam requirements/recommendations for international students: Required—TOEFL (minimum score 600 paper-based; 100 iBT) or IELTS (minimum score 6.5). Electronic applications accepted.

Walden University, Graduate Programs, School of Social Work and Human Services, Minneapolis, MN 55401. Offers addictions (MSW); addictions and social work (DSW); children, families, and couples (MSW); clinical expertise (DSW); criminal justice (DSW); crisis and trauma (MSW); disaster, crisis, and intervention (DSW); forensic populations and settings (MSW); general program (MSW); human services (MS, PhD), including clinical social work (PhD), criminal justice, disaster, crisis and intervention, family studies and intervention strategies (PhD), family studies and interventions, general program, human services administration, public health, social policy analysis and planning; medical social work (MSW, DSW); military families and culture (MSW); policy practice (DSW); social work (PhD), including addictions and social work, clinical expertise, disaster, crisis and intervention (MS, PhD), family studies and interventions (MS, PhD), medical social work, policy practice, social work administration; social work administration (DSW). Part-time and evening/weekend programs available. Postbaccalaureate distance learning degree programs offered (no on-campus study). *Faculty:* 18 full-time (11 women), 236 part-time/adjunct (156 women). *Students:* 1,400 full-time (1,205 women), 884 part-time (759 women); includes 1,586 minority (1,373 Black or African American, non-Hispanic/Latino; 20 American Indian or Alaska Native, non-Hispanic/Latino; 16 Asian, non-Hispanic/Latino; 120 Hispanic/Latino; 57 Two or more races, non-Hispanic/Latino), 14 international. Average age 40. 892 applicants, 96% accepted, 826 enrolled. In 2014, 61 master's, 14 doctorates awarded. *Degree requirements:* For master's, residency (for some programs); for doctorate, thesis/dissertation, residency. *Entrance requirements:* For master's, bachelor's degree or higher; minimum GPA of 2.5; official transcripts; goal statement (for some programs); access to computer and Internet; for doctorate, master's degree or higher; three years of related professional or academic experience (preferred); minimum GPA of 3.0; goal statement and current resume (for select programs); official transcripts; access to computer and Internet. Additional exam requirements/recommendations for international students: Required—TOEFL (minimum score 550 paper-based, 79 iBT), IELTS (minimum score 6.5), Michigan English Language Assessment Battery (minimum score 82), or PTE (minimum score 53). *Application deadline:* Applications are processed on a rolling basis. Application fee: $0. Electronic applications accepted. *Expenses: Tuition:* Full-time $11,925; part-time $500 per credit hour. *Required fees:* $647. *Financial support:* Fellowships, Federal Work-Study, scholarships/grants, unspecified assistantships, and family tuition reduction, active duty/veteran tuition reduction, group tuition reduction, interest-free payment plans, employee tuition reduction available. Support available to part-time students. Financial award applicants required to submit FAFSA. *Unit head:* Dr. Savitri Dixon-Saxon, Associate Dean, 866-492-5336. *Application contact:* Meghan Thomas, Vice President of Enrollment Management, 866-492-5336, E-mail: info@waldenu.edu.
Website: http://www.waldenu.edu/colleges-schools/school-of-social-work-and-human-services/academic-programs

Webster University, George Herbert Walker School of Business and Technology, Department of Business, St. Louis, MO 63119-3194. Offers business and organizational security management (MBA); decision support systems (MBA); environmental management (MBA); finance (MBA, MS); forensic accounting (MS); gerontology (MBA); human resources development (MBA); human resources management (MBA); information technology management (MBA); international business (MA, MBA); international relations (MBA); management and leadership (MBA); marketing (MBA); media communications (MBA); procurement and acquisitions management (MBA); Web services (MBA). *Accreditation:* ACBSP. Part-time and evening/weekend programs available. Postbaccalaureate distance learning degree programs offered (no on-campus study). *Degree requirements:* For master's, comprehensive exam (for some programs), thesis (for some programs). *Entrance requirements:* Additional exam requirements/recommendations for international students: Required—TOEFL.

West Virginia University, Eberly College of Arts and Sciences, Department of Biology, Morgantown, WV 26506. Offers cell and molecular biology (MS, PhD); environmental and evolutionary biology (MS, PhD); forensic biology (MS, PhD); genomic biology (MS, PhD); neurobiology (MS, PhD). Terminal master's awarded for partial completion of doctoral program. *Degree requirements:* For master's, thesis, final exam; for doctorate, thesis/dissertation, preliminary and final exams. *Entrance requirements:* For master's, GRE General Test, GRE Subject Test, minimum GPA of 3.0; for doctorate, GRE General Test, minimum GPA of 3.0. Additional exam requirements/recommendations for international students: Required—TOEFL. *Faculty research:* Environmental biology, genetic engineering, developmental biology, global change, biodiversity.

Section 19
Economics

This section contains a directory of institutions offering graduate work in economics, followed by an in-depth entry submitted by an institution that chose to prepare a detailed program description. Additional information about programs listed in the directory but not augmented by an in-depth entry may be obtained by writing directly to the dean of a graduate school or chair of a department at the address given in the directory.

For programs offering related work, see also in this book *Family and Consumer Sciences, Political Science and International Affairs,* and *Public, Regional, and Industrial Affairs.* In the other guides in this series:

Graduate Programs in the Physical Sciences, Mathematics, Agricultural Sciences, the Environment & Natural Resources
See *Agricultural and Food Sciences* and *Mathematical Sciences*

Graduate Programs in Engineering & Applied Sciences
See *Computer Science and Information Technology; Geological, Mineral/Mining, and Petroleum Engineering;* and *Industrial Engineering*

Graduate Programs in Business, Education, Information Studies, Law & Social Work
See *Business Administration and Management*

CONTENTS

Program Directories

Display and Close-Up

Agricultural Economics and Agribusiness

Alcorn State University, School of Graduate Studies, School of Agriculture and Applied Science, Lorman, MS 39096-7500. Offers agricultural economics (MS Ag); agronomy (MS Ag); animal science (MS Ag). *Degree requirements:* For master's, thesis optional. *Faculty research:* Aquatic systems, dairy herd improvement, fruit production, alternative farming practices.

American University of Beirut, Graduate Programs, Faculty of Agricultural and Food Sciences, Beirut, Lebanon. Offers agricultural economics (MS); animal sciences (MS); ecosystem management (MSES); food technology (MS); irrigation (MS); nutrition (MS); plant protection (MS); plant science (MS); poultry science (MS); rural community development (MS). Part-time programs available. *Faculty:* 17 full-time (4 women), 4 part-time/adjunct (1 woman). *Students:* 15 full-time (13 women), 58 part-time (40 women). Average age 26. 60 applicants, 55% accepted, 12 enrolled. In 2014, 33 master's awarded. *Degree requirements:* For master's, one foreign language, comprehensive exam, thesis (for some programs). *Entrance requirements:* Additional exam requirements/recommendations for international students: Required—TOEFL (minimum score 600 paper-based; 100 iBT), IELTS (minimum score 7.5). *Application deadline:* For fall admission, 2/10 for domestic and international students; for spring admission, 11/3 for domestic and international students. Application fee: $50. Electronic applications accepted. *Expenses: Tuition:* Full-time $15,462; part-time $859 per credit. *Required fees:* $692. Tuition and fees vary according to course load and program. *Financial support:* In 2014–15, 1 research assistantship with partial tuition reimbursement (averaging $1,800 per year), 34 teaching assistantships with full and partial tuition reimbursements (averaging $1,220 per year) were awarded; scholarships/grants, health care benefits, and unspecified assistantships also available. Financial award application deadline: 2/2. *Faculty research:* Nutrition and non-communicable diseases in Lebanon, nutritional assessment in Arab youth, establishing food trails across Lebanon, feasibility of groundwater recharge in improving rural livelihoods, landscape atlas for Lebanon. *Total annual research expenditures:* $618,504. *Unit head:* Prof. Nahla Hwalla, Dean, 961-1343002 Ext. 4400, Fax: 961-1744460, E-mail: nahla@aub.edu.lb. *Application contact:* Dr. Rabih Talhouk, Director, Graduate Council, 961-1350000 Ext. 4386, Fax: 961-1374374, E-mail: graduate.council@aub.edu.lb.
Website: http://www.aub.edu.lb/fafs/fafs_home/Pages/index.aspx

Arizona State University at the Tempe campus, W. P. Carey School of Business, Morrison School of Agribusiness, Mesa, AZ 85212. Offers PhD. Part-time and evening/weekend programs available. *Entrance requirements:* Additional exam requirements/recommendations for international students: Required—TOEFL (minimum score 550 paper-based; 80 iBT), IELTS (minimum score 6.5); Recommended—TWE. Electronic applications accepted. *Faculty research:* Consumer behavior and marketing strategies in food markets, supply-chain management, derivatives and risk management, international agricultural trade and policy.

Auburn University, Graduate School, College of Agriculture, Department of Agricultural Economics and Rural Sociology, Auburn University, AL 36849. Offers agricultural economics (M Ag, MS). Part-time programs available. *Faculty:* 15 full-time (4 women). *Students:* 5 full-time (3 women), 1 part-time (0 women); includes 1 minority (Black or African American, non-Hispanic/Latino), 3 international. Average age 25. 12 applicants, 83% accepted, 2 enrolled. In 2014, 6 master's awarded. *Degree requirements:* For master's, thesis (for some programs). *Entrance requirements:* For master's, GRE General Test. *Application deadline:* For fall admission, 7/7 for domestic students; for spring admission, 11/24 for domestic students. Applications are processed on a rolling basis. Application fee: $50 ($60 for international students). Electronic applications accepted. *Expenses:* Tuition, state resident: full-time $8586; part-time $477 per credit hour. Tuition, nonresident: full-time $25,758; part-time $1431 per credit hour. *Required fees:* $804 per semester. Tuition and fees vary according to degree level and program. *Financial support:* Research assistantships, teaching assistantships, and Federal Work-Study available. Support available to part-time students. Financial award application deadline: 3/15; financial award applicants required to submit FAFSA. *Unit head:* Dr. Deacue Fields, Chair, 334-844-4800. *Application contact:* Dr. George Flowers, Dean of the Graduate School, 334-844-2125.
Website: http://www.ag.auburn.edu/agec/

California Polytechnic State University, San Luis Obispo, College of Agriculture, Food and Environmental Sciences, Department of Agribusiness, San Luis Obispo, CA 93407. Offers MS. Part-time programs available. *Faculty:* 2 full-time (1 woman), 1 part-time/adjunct (0 women). *Students:* 3 part-time (1 woman), 2 international. Average age 39. In 2014, 3 master's awarded. *Degree requirements:* For master's, comprehensive exam, thesis. *Application deadline:* For fall admission, 4/1 for domestic students, 11/30 for international students; for winter admission, 10/1 for domestic students, 6/30 for international students; for spring admission, 10/1 for domestic students. Applications are processed on a rolling basis. Application fee: $55. Electronic applications accepted. *Expenses:* Tuition, state resident: full-time $6738; part-time $3906 per year. Tuition, nonresident: full-time $15,666; part-time $8370 per year. *Required fees:* $3447; $1001 per quarter. One-time fee: $3447 full-time; $3003 part-time. *Financial support:* Fellowships, research assistantships, teaching assistantships, career-related internships or fieldwork, Federal Work-Study, institutionally sponsored loans, scholarships/grants, and unspecified assistantships available. Support available to part-time students. Financial award application deadline: 3/2; financial award applicants required to submit FAFSA. *Faculty research:* Agribusiness management, commodity marketing, international and domestic agribusiness. *Unit head:* Dr. James Ahern, Graduate Coordinator, 805-756-5030, Fax: 805-756-5040, E-mail: jahern@calpoly.edu. *Application contact:* Dr. Mark Shelton, Associate Dean/Graduate Coordinator, 805-756-2161, Fax: 805-756-6577, E-mail: mshelton@calpoly.edu.
Website: http://agb.calpoly.edu/

Colorado State University, Graduate School, College of Agricultural Sciences, Department of Agricultural and Resource Economics, Fort Collins, CO 80523-1172. Offers MS, PhD. Part-time programs available. *Faculty:* 20 full-time (4 women). *Students:* 23 full-time (8 women), 25 part-time (7 women); includes 2 minority (1 Black or African American, non-Hispanic/Latino; 1 Hispanic/Latino), 16 international. Average age 30. 60 applicants, 60% accepted, 9 enrolled. In 2014, 9 master's awarded. Terminal master's awarded for partial completion of doctoral program. *Degree requirements:* For master's, thesis or technical paper; for doctorate, comprehensive exam, thesis/dissertation. *Entrance requirements:* For master's, minimum GPA of 3.0, economics background, transcripts, 3 letters of recommendation, written statement; for doctorate, GRE, minimum GPA of 3.0, MS in economics or agricultural economics, transcripts, 3 letters of recommendation, written statement. Additional exam requirements/recommendations for international students: Required—TOEFL (minimum score 550 paper-based; 80 iBT), IELTS (minimum score 6.5). *Application deadline:* For fall admission, 2/1 priority date for domestic and international students; for spring admission, 7/1 priority date for domestic and international students. Applications are processed on a rolling basis. Application fee: $50. Electronic applications accepted. *Expenses:* Tuition, state resident: full-time $9348; part-time $519 per credit. Tuition, nonresident: full-time $22,916; part-time $1273 per credit. *Required fees:* $1584. *Financial support:* In 2014–15, 22 students received support, including 2 fellowships with full tuition reimbursements available (averaging $58,550 per year), 12 research assistantships with full tuition reimbursements available (averaging $14,776 per year), 8 teaching assistantships with full tuition reimbursements available (averaging $10,119 per year); Federal Work-Study, scholarships/grants, and unspecified assistantships also available. Financial award application deadline: 3/1; financial award applicants required to submit FAFSA. *Faculty research:* Outdoor recreation industry, sustainable agriculture, agricultural water law and policy, food safety issues, economic and rural development, agricultural policy. *Total annual research expenditures:* $2.8 million. *Unit head:* Dr. Gregory Perry, Head, 970-491-6955, Fax: 970-491-2067, E-mail: greg.perry@colostate.edu. *Application contact:* Denise Davis, Program Assistant II, 970-491-6955, Fax: 970-491-2067, E-mail: denise.davis@colostate.edu.
Website: http://dare.colostate.edu/index.aspx

Cornell University, Graduate School, Graduate Fields of Agriculture and Life Sciences, Field of Applied Economics and Management, Ithaca, NY 14853-0001. Offers agricultural finance (MS, PhD); applied econometrics and qualitative analysis (MS, PhD); economics of development (MS, PhD); environmental economics (MS, PhD); environmental management (MPS); farm management and production economics (MS, PhD); marketing and food distribution (MS, PhD); public policy analysis (MS, PhD); resource economics (PhD). *Entrance requirements:* For master's and doctorate, GRE. Additional exam requirements/recommendations for international students: Required—TOEFL.

Cornell University, Graduate School, Graduate Fields of Agriculture and Life Sciences, Field of Global Development, Ithaca, NY 14853-0001. Offers development policy (MPS); international agriculture and development (MPS); international development (MPS); international nutrition (MPS); international planning (MPS); international population (MPS); science and technology policy (MPS). *Degree requirements:* For master's, project paper. *Entrance requirements:* For master's, GRE General Test (recommended), 2 years of development experience, 2 letters of recommendation. Additional exam requirements/recommendations for international students: Required—TOEFL (minimum score 550 paper-based; 77 iBT). Electronic applications accepted.

Delaware Valley University, MBA Program, Doylestown, PA 18901-2697. Offers accounting (MBA); entrepreneurship (MBA); finance (MBA); food and agribusiness (MBA); general business (MBA); global executive leadership (MBA); human resource management (MBA); supply chain management (MBA). Part-time and evening/weekend programs available. Postbaccalaureate distance learning degree programs offered (no on-campus study). *Entrance requirements:* For master's, minimum undergraduate GPA of 3.0. Electronic applications accepted. *Expenses:* Contact institution.

Illinois State University, Graduate School, College of Applied Science and Technology, Department of Agriculture, Normal, IL 61790-2200. Offers agribusiness (MS). *Degree requirements:* For master's, thesis optional. *Entrance requirements:* For master's, GRE General Test, minimum GPA of 3.0 in last 60 hours. *Faculty research:* Engineering-economic system models for rural ethanol production facilities, development and evaluation of a propane-fueled, production scale, on-site thermal destruction system C-FAR 2007; field scale evaluation and technology transfer of economically, ecologically systems; sound liquid swine manure treatment and application.

Instituto Centroamericano de Administración de Empresas, Graduate Programs, La Garita, Costa Rica. Offers agribusiness management (MIAM); business administration (EMBA); finance (MBA); real estate management (MGREM); sustainable development (MBA); technology (MBA). *Degree requirements:* For master's, comprehensive exam, essay. *Entrance requirements:* For master's, GMAT or GRE General Test, fluency in Spanish, interview, letters of recommendation, minimum 1 year of work experience. Additional exam requirements/recommendations for international students: Recommended—TOEFL. Electronic applications accepted. *Faculty research:* Competitiveness, production.

Iowa State University of Science and Technology, Department of Economics, Ames, IA 50011. Offers agricultural economics (MS, PhD); economics (MS, PhD); JD/MS; JD/PhD. JD/MS and JD/PhD offered jointly with Drake University and The University of Iowa. *Degree requirements:* For master's, thesis or alternative; for doctorate, thesis/dissertation. *Entrance requirements:* For master's and doctorate, GRE General Test. Additional exam requirements/recommendations for international students: Required—TOEFL (minimum score 570 paper-based; 88 iBT), IELTS (minimum score 6.5). Electronic applications accepted.

Iowa State University of Science and Technology, Program in Agricultural Economics, Ames, IA 50011. Offers MS, PhD. *Degree requirements:* For master's, thesis or alternative; for doctorate, thesis/dissertation. *Entrance requirements:* For master's and doctorate, GRE General Test. Additional exam requirements/recommendations for international students: Required—TOEFL (minimum score 570 paper-based; 88 iBT), IELTS (minimum score 6.5). Electronic applications accepted.

Iowa State University of Science and Technology, Program in Seed Technology and Business, Ames, IA 50011. Offers MS. *Degree requirements:* For master's, thesis or alternative. *Entrance requirements:* For master's, resume, 3 letters of recommendation. Additional exam requirements/recommendations for international students: Required—TOEFL (minimum score 570 paper-based; 85 iBT), IELTS (minimum score 6.5). Electronic applications accepted.

Kansas State University, Graduate School, College of Agriculture, Department of Agricultural Economics, Manhattan, KS 66506. Offers MAB, MS, PhD. Part-time programs available. Postbaccalaureate distance learning degree programs offered (minimal on-campus study). *Faculty:* 28 full-time (3 women), 5 part-time/adjunct (1 woman). *Students:* 35 full-time (16 women), 77 part-time (22 women); includes 10 minority (3 Black or African American, non-Hispanic/Latino; 1 American Indian or Alaska Native, non-Hispanic/Latino; 1 Asian, non-Hispanic/Latino; 5 Hispanic/Latino), 22 international. Average age 30. 86 applicants, 47% accepted, 22 enrolled. In 2014, 29 master's, 3 doctorates awarded. Terminal master's awarded for partial completion of doctoral program. *Degree requirements:* For master's, thesis or alternative, oral exam; for doctorate, thesis/dissertation, preliminary exams. *Entrance requirements:* For master's and doctorate, GRE General Test. Additional exam requirements/recommendations for international students: Required—TOEFL (minimum score 550 paper-based). *Application deadline:* For fall admission, 6/1 priority date for domestic students, 2/1 priority date for international students; for spring admission, 10/1 priority date for domestic students, 8/1 priority date for international students. Applications are

processed on a rolling basis. Application fee: $50 ($75 for international students). Electronic applications accepted. *Financial support:* In 2014–15, 34 students received support, including 26 research assistantships (averaging $20,738 per year), 4 teaching assistantships with partial tuition reimbursements available (averaging $18,955 per year); Federal Work-Study, institutionally sponsored loans, scholarships/grants, and unspecified assistantships also available. Support available to part-time students. Financial award application deadline: 3/1; financial award applicants required to submit FAFSA. *Faculty research:* Livestock marketing, biofuels research, natural resources, agribusiness industry, international development and trade. *Total annual research expenditures:* $2.9 million. *Unit head:* Dr. Allen Featherstone, Head, 785-532-4441, Fax: 785-532-6925, E-mail: afeather@ksu.edu. *Application contact:* Dr. Jeff Peterson, Director, 785-477-0924, Fax: 785-532-6925, E-mail: jpeters@agecon.ksu.edu. Website: http://www.ageconomics.ksu.edu/

Louisiana State University and Agricultural & Mechanical College, Graduate School, College of Agriculture, Department of Agricultural Economics and Agribusiness, Baton Rouge, LA 70803. Offers MS, PhD. *Faculty:* 14 full-time (0 women). *Students:* 32 full-time (14 women), 4 part-time (2 women); includes 5 minority (3 Black or African American, non-Hispanic/Latino; 2 Hispanic/Latino), 23 international. Average age 32. 19 applicants, 74% accepted, 4 enrolled. In 2014, 8 master's, 8 doctorates awarded. *Degree requirements:* For master's, thesis (for some programs); for doctorate, thesis/dissertation. *Entrance requirements:* For master's and doctorate, GRE General Test, minimum GPA of 3.0. Additional exam requirements/recommendations for international students: Required—TOEFL (minimum score 550 paper-based; 79 iBT), IELTS (minimum score 6.5), or PTE (minimum score 59). *Application deadline:* For fall admission, 1/25 priority date for domestic students, 5/15 for international students; for spring admission, 10/15 for international students. Applications are processed on a rolling basis. Application fee: $50 ($70 for international students). Electronic applications accepted. *Financial support:* In 2014–15, 33 students received support, including 3 fellowships (averaging $19,893 per year), 26 research assistantships with partial tuition reimbursements available (averaging $18,379 per year); teaching assistantships with partial tuition reimbursements available, Federal Work-Study, institutionally sponsored loans, scholarships/grants, health care benefits, tuition waivers (full and partial), and unspecified assistantships also available. Support available to part-time students. Financial award applicants required to submit FAFSA. *Faculty research:* Natural and environmental economics, agribusiness, marketing, production economics, community economics, rural development. *Total annual research expenditures:* $59,230. *Unit head:* Dr. Gail L. Cramer, Head, 225-578-3282, Fax: 225-578-2716, E-mail: gcramer@agctr.lsu.edu. *Application contact:* Dr. Richard Kazmierczak, Graduate Coordinator, 225-578-2712, Fax: 225-578-2716, E-mail: rkazmierczak@agcenter.lsu.edu.
Website: http://www.agecon.lsu.edu/

McGill University, Faculty of Graduate and Postdoctoral Studies, Faculty of Agricultural and Environmental Sciences, Department of Agricultural Economics, Montréal, QC H3A 2T5, Canada. Offers M Sc.

Michigan State University, The Graduate School, College of Agriculture and Natural Resources, Department of Agricultural, Food, and Resource Economics, East Lansing, MI 48824. Offers agricultural economics (MS, PhD); agricultural, food, and resource economics (MS, PhD). *Entrance requirements:* Additional exam requirements/recommendations for international students: Required—TOEFL (minimum score 550 paper-based), Michigan State University ELT (minimum score 85), Michigan English Language Assessment Battery (minimum score 83). Electronic applications accepted.

Mississippi State University, College of Agriculture and Life Sciences, Department of Agricultural Economics, Mississippi State, MS 39762. Offers agribusiness management (MABM); agriculture (MS), including agricultural economics. MABM offered jointly with College of Business. Part-time programs available. *Faculty:* 22 full-time (2 women). *Students:* 13 full-time (3 women), 6 part-time (3 women), 10 international. Average age 26. 21 applicants, 57% accepted, 9 enrolled. In 2014, 7 master's awarded. *Degree requirements:* For master's, comprehensive exam, thesis (for some programs), thesis defense. *Entrance requirements:* For master's, GRE, minimum GPA of 3.0. Additional exam requirements/recommendations for international students: Required—TOEFL (minimum score 575 paper-based; 84 iBT); Recommended—IELTS (minimum score 7). *Application deadline:* For fall admission, 7/1 for domestic students, 5/1 for international students; for spring admission, 11/1 for domestic students, 9/1 for international students. Applications are processed on a rolling basis. Application fee: $60. Electronic applications accepted. *Expenses:* Tuition, state resident: full-time $7140; part-time $783 per credit hour. Tuition, nonresident: full-time $18,478; part-time $2043 per credit hour. *Financial support:* In 2014–15, 7 research assistantships with full tuition reimbursements (averaging $13,906 per year) were awarded; career-related internships or fieldwork, Federal Work-Study, institutionally sponsored loans, and unspecified assistantships also available. Financial award application deadline: 4/1; financial award applicants required to submit FAFSA. *Faculty research:* Production economics, policy, resource economics, international trade, agribusiness management. *Unit head:* Dr. Steven C. Turner, Professor and Head, 662-325-2049, Fax: 662-325-8777, E-mail: turner@aegcon.msstate.edu. *Application contact:* Dr. Barry Barnett, Professor and Graduate Coordinator, 662-325-0128, Fax: 662-325-8777, E-mail: bjb11@msstate.edu.
Website: http://www.agecon.msstate.edu/

New Mexico State University, College of Agricultural, Consumer and Environmental Sciences, Department of Agricultural Economics and Agricultural Business, Las Cruces, NM 88003-8001. Offers agribusiness (MBA); economic development (DED); water science management (MS). Part-time programs available. *Faculty:* 7 full-time (1 woman). *Students:* 10 full-time (4 women), 2 part-time (0 women); includes 3 minority (all Hispanic/Latino), 5 international. Average age 34. 11 applicants, 45% accepted, 2 enrolled. In 2014, 6 master's awarded. *Degree requirements:* For master's, thesis (for some programs); for doctorate, comprehensive exam, thesis/dissertation. *Entrance requirements:* For master's, GRE; GMAT (for MBA), previous course work in intermediate microeconomics, intermediate macroeconomics, college-level calculus, statistics; for doctorate, previous course work in intermediate microeconomics, intermediate macroeconomics, college-level calculus, statistics, related MS or equivalent, minimum GPA of 3.0. Additional exam requirements/recommendations for international students: Required—TOEFL (minimum score 550 paper-based; 79 iBT), IELTS (minimum score 6.5). *Application deadline:* For fall admission, 7/1 priority date for domestic and international students; for spring admission, 11/1 priority date for domestic and international students. Applications are processed on a rolling basis. Application fee: $40 ($50 for international students). Electronic applications accepted. *Expenses:* Tuition, state resident: full-time $3969; part-time $220.50 per credit hour. Tuition, nonresident: full-time $13,838; part-time $768.80 per credit hour. *Required fees:* $853; $47.40 per credit hour. *Financial support:* In 2014–15, 7 students received support, including 2 research assistantships (averaging $13,551 per year), 3 teaching assistantships (averaging $15,374 per year); career-related internships or fieldwork, Federal Work-Study, scholarships/grants, traineeships, health care benefits, and unspecified assistantships also available. Support available to part-time students. Financial award application deadline: 3/1. *Faculty research:* Natural resource policy, production economics and farm/ranch management, agribusiness and marketing,

international marketing and trade, agricultural risk management. *Total annual research expenditures:* $902,899. *Unit head:* Dr. Terry Crawford, Interim Head, 575-646-3215, Fax: 575-646-3808, E-mail: crawford@nmsu.edu. *Application contact:* Dr. L. Allen Torell, Graduate Committee Chair, 575-646-4732, Fax: 575-646-3808, E-mail: atorell@nmsu.edu.
Website: http://aces.nmsu.edu/academics/aeab/

North Carolina Agricultural and Technical State University, School of Graduate Studies, School of Agriculture and Environmental Sciences, Department of Agribusiness, Applied Economics, and Agriscience Education, Greensboro, NC 27411. Offers agricultural economics (MS); agricultural education (MS). *Accreditation:* NCATE. Part-time and evening/weekend programs available. *Degree requirements:* For master's, comprehensive exam, thesis or alternative, qualifying exam. *Entrance requirements:* For master's, GRE General Test, minimum GPA of 3.0. *Faculty research:* Aid for small farmers, agricultural technology resources, labor force mobility, agrology.

North Carolina State University, Graduate School, College of Agriculture and Life Sciences, Program in Agricultural and Resource Economics, Raleigh, NC 27695. Offers MS. Part-time programs available. *Degree requirements:* For master's, thesis. *Entrance requirements:* Additional exam requirements/recommendations for international students: Required—TOEFL. Electronic applications accepted. *Faculty research:* Resource economics, international economics, labor economics, econometrics, environmental economics.

North Dakota State University, College of Graduate and Interdisciplinary Studies, College of Agriculture, Food Systems, and Natural Resources, Department of Agribusiness and Applied Economics, Fargo, ND 58108. Offers agribusiness and applied economics (MS); international agribusiness (MS). Part-time programs available. *Degree requirements:* For master's, thesis. *Entrance requirements:* For master's, minimum GPA of 3.0. Additional exam requirements/recommendations for international students: Required—TOEFL (minimum score 525 paper-based; 79 iBT). Electronic applications accepted. *Faculty research:* Agribusiness, transportation, marketing, microeconomics, trade.

Northwest Missouri State University, Graduate School, Melvin and Valorie Booth College of Business and Professional Studies, School of Agricultural Sciences, Program in Agricultural Economics, Maryville, MO 64468-6001. Offers MBA. *Degree requirements:* For master's, comprehensive exam. *Entrance requirements:* For master's, GMAT, GRE, minimum GPA of 2.5. Additional exam requirements/ recommendations for international students: Required—TOEFL (minimum score 550 paper-based). *Application deadline:* For fall admission, 7/1 for domestic and international students; for spring admission, 12/1 for domestic students, 11/15 for international students. Applications are processed on a rolling basis. Application fee: $0 ($50 for international students). *Expenses:* Tuition, state resident: full-time $4464; part-time $346 per credit hour. Tuition, nonresident: full-time $8920; part-time $593 per credit hour. *Required fees:* $1763; $98 per credit hour. *Financial support:* Research assistantships with full tuition reimbursements available. Financial award application deadline: 4/1; financial award applicants required to submit FAFSA. *Unit head:* Dr. Naveen Musunuru, Program Director, 660-562-1341.
Website: http://www.nwmissouri.edu/graduate/mba/agricultureemphasis.htm

The Ohio State University, Graduate School, College of Food, Agricultural, and Environmental Sciences, Department of Agricultural, Environmental, and Development Economics, Columbus, OH 43210. Offers MS, PhD. *Faculty:* 21. *Students:* 84 full-time (39 women), 3 part-time (2 women); includes 10 minority (3 Black or African American, non-Hispanic/Latino; 5 Asian, non-Hispanic/Latino; 1 Hispanic/Latino; 1 Two or more races, non-Hispanic/Latino), 55 international. Average age 27. In 2014, 20 master's, 16 doctorates awarded. *Degree requirements:* For master's, thesis optional; for doctorate, thesis/dissertation. *Entrance requirements:* For master's, GRE General Test (recommended minimum score: 600 quantitative, 500 verbal), minimum undergraduate GPA of 3.1 (recommended); for doctorate, GRE General Test (minimum score: 700 quantitative, 600 verbal), minimum GPA of 3.3 undergraduate, 3.5 graduate (recommended). Additional exam requirements/recommendations for international students: Required—TOEFL (minimum score 600 paper-based; 100 IBT) for PhD; Recommended—TOEFL (minimum score 550 paper-based; 80 iBT). *Application deadline:* For fall admission, 12/15 priority date for domestic students, 11/30 priority date for international students; for winter admission, 12/1 for domestic students, 11/1 for international students; for spring admission, 3/1 for domestic students, 2/1 for international students. Applications are processed on a rolling basis. Application fee: $60 ($70 for international students). Electronic applications accepted. *Financial support:* Fellowships with tuition reimbursements, research assistantships with tuition reimbursements, teaching assistantships with tuition reimbursements, Federal Work-Study, and institutionally sponsored loans available. Support available to part-time students. *Unit head:* Dr. Ian Sheldon, Graduate Studies Committee Chair, 614-292-2194, E-mail: sheldon.1@osu.edu. *Application contact:* Susan K. Miller, Graduate Program Coordinator, 614-292-4429, E-mail: aedgradservices@osu.edu.
Website: http://aede.osu.edu/

Oklahoma State University, College of Agricultural Science and Natural Resources, Department of Agricultural Economics, Stillwater, OK 74078. Offers M Ag, MS, PhD. *Faculty:* 33 full-time (6 women). *Students:* 46 full-time (17 women), 13 part-time (7 women); includes 1 minority (Two or more races, non-Hispanic/Latino), 28 international. Average age 28. 60 applicants, 42% accepted, 14 enrolled. In 2014, 16 master's, 3 doctorates awarded. *Degree requirements:* For master's, thesis or report, oral exam; for doctorate, comprehensive exam, thesis/dissertation. *Entrance requirements:* For master's and doctorate, GRE or GMAT. Additional exam requirements/ recommendations for international students: Required—TOEFL (minimum score 550 paper-based; 79 iBT). *Application deadline:* For fall admission, 3/1 priority date for international students; for spring admission, 8/1 priority date for international students. Applications are processed on a rolling basis. Application fee: $40 ($75 for international students). Electronic applications accepted. *Expenses:* Tuition, state resident: full-time $4488; part-time $187 per credit hour. Tuition, nonresident: full-time $18,360; part-time $765 per credit hour. *Required fees:* $2413; $100.55 per credit hour. Tuition and fees vary according to campus/location. *Financial support:* In 2014–15, 40 research assistantships (averaging $16,945 per year), 4 teaching assistantships (averaging $16,005 per year) were awarded; career-related internships or fieldwork, Federal Work-Study, scholarships/grants, health care benefits, tuition waivers (partial), and unspecified assistantships also available. Support available to part-time students. Financial award application deadline: 3/1; financial award applicants required to submit FAFSA. *Faculty research:* Marketing and agribusiness, production and farm management, policy and natural resources, community and rural development, international trade and development. *Unit head:* Dr. Mike Woods, Department Head, 405-744-6161, Fax: 405-744-8210, E-mail: mike.woods@okstate.edu. *Application contact:* Dr. Chanjin Chung, Graduate Coordinator, 405-744-6084, Fax: 405-744-8210, E-mail: agecgrad@okstate.edu.
Website: http://agecon.okstate.edu

Penn State University Park, Graduate School, College of Agricultural Sciences, Department of Agricultural Economics, Sociology, and Education, University Park, PA 16802. Offers agricultural and extension education (M Ed, MS, PhD, Certificate);

agricultural, environmental and regional economics (MS, PhD); applied youth, family and community education (M Ed); community and economic development (MPS); rural sociology (MS, PhD). *Unit head:* Dr. Richard T. Roush, Dean, 814-865-2541, Fax: 814-865-3103, E-mail: rtr10@psu.edu. *Application contact:* Lori A. Stania, Director, Graduate Student Services, 814-867-5278, Fax: 814-863-4627, E-mail: gswww@psu.edu.
Website: http://aese.psu.edu/

Purdue University, Graduate School, College of Agriculture, Department of Agricultural Economics, West Lafayette, IN 47907. Offers agricultural economics (MS, PhD); food and agricultural business (EMBA). Part-time programs available. Terminal master's awarded for partial completion of doctoral program. *Degree requirements:* For master's, thesis (for some programs); for doctorate, thesis/dissertation. *Entrance requirements:* For master's and doctorate, GRE General Test, minimum undergraduate GPA of 3.0 or equivalent. Additional exam requirements/recommendations for international students: Required—TOEFL (minimum score 550 paper-based; 77 iBT). Electronic applications accepted. *Faculty research:* Marketing, international trade, policy and development, production, resources.

Rutgers, The State University of New Jersey, New Brunswick, Graduate School-New Brunswick, Program in Food and Business Economics, Piscataway, NJ 08854-8097. Offers MS. *Degree requirements:* For master's, comprehensive exam, thesis or alternative. *Entrance requirements:* Additional exam requirements/recommendations for international students: Required—TOEFL. Electronic applications accepted. *Faculty research:* Science policy, land use, nutrition policy, food industry, international development.

South Carolina State University, College of Graduate and Professional Studies, Department of Business Administration, Orangeburg, SC 29117-0001. Offers agribusiness (MBA). Part-time and evening/weekend programs available. *Faculty:* 6 full-time (0 women). *Students:* 16 full-time (7 women), 4 part-time (0 women); all minorities (all Black or African American, non-Hispanic/Latino). Average age 26. 16 applicants, 88% accepted, 14 enrolled. In 2014, 6 master's awarded. *Degree requirements:* For master's, comprehensive exam, business plan. *Entrance requirements:* For master's, GMAT, minimum GPA of 2.8. Additional exam requirements/recommendations for international students: Required—TOEFL. *Application deadline:* For fall admission, 6/15 for domestic and international students; for spring admission, 11/1 for domestic and international students. Applications are processed on a rolling basis. Application fee: $25. Electronic applications accepted. *Expenses:* Tuition, state resident: full-time $7290; part-time $405 per credit. Tuition, nonresident: full-time $17,058; part-time $948 per credit. *Required fees:* $2798; $155 per credit hour. *Financial support:* Fellowships, research assistantships, career-related internships or fieldwork, Federal Work-Study, institutionally sponsored loans, and unspecified assistantships available. Financial award application deadline: 6/1. *Unit head:* Dr. Matthew Guah, Chair, 803-516-4834, Fax: 803-536-8078, E-mail: mguah@scsu.edu. *Application contact:* Ellen R. Ricoma, MBA Program Director, 803-533-3777, Fax: 803-516-4651, E-mail: ericoma1@scsu.edu.

Southern Illinois University Carbondale, Graduate School, College of Agriculture, Department of Agribusiness Economics, Carbondale, IL 62901-4701. Offers MS, MBA/MS. Part-time programs available. *Faculty:* 6 full-time (1 woman). *Students:* 9 full-time (1 woman), 3 part-time (0 women); includes 1 minority (Black or African American, non-Hispanic/Latino), 6 international. Average age 29. 12 applicants, 42% accepted, 4 enrolled. In 2014, 1 master's awarded. *Degree requirements:* For master's, thesis. *Entrance requirements:* For master's, minimum GPA of 2.7. Additional exam requirements/recommendations for international students: Required—TOEFL (minimum score 550 paper-based; 80 iBT). *Application deadline:* For fall admission, 7/1 priority date for domestic students. Applications are processed on a rolling basis. Application fee: $0. *Expenses:* Tuition, state resident: full-time $10,176; part-time $1153 per credit. Tuition, nonresident: full-time $20,814; part-time $1744 per credit. *Required fees:* $7092; $394 per credit. $2364 per semester. *Financial support:* Fellowships with tuition reimbursements, research assistantships with tuition reimbursements, teaching assistantships with tuition reimbursements, Federal Work-Study, institutionally sponsored loans, and tuition waivers (full) available. Support available to part-time students. Financial award application deadline: 3/15. *Faculty research:* Agricultural finance and credit, agribusiness management, resource use, rural area economic development, marketing and price analysis. *Unit head:* Jeff Beaulieu, Chairperson, 618-453-2421, E-mail: jbeau@siu.edu. *Application contact:* Nancy McCalla, Administrative Clerk, 618-453-2421, Fax: 618-453-1708, E-mail: monicar@siu.edu.

Texas A&M University, College of Agriculture and Life Sciences, Department of Agricultural Economics, College Station, TX 77843. Offers agribusiness and managerial economics (PhD); agricultural economics (M Agr, MS, PhD). Part-time programs available. *Faculty:* 27. *Students:* 136 full-time (60 women), 15 part-time (6 women); includes 15 minority (6 Asian, non-Hispanic/Latino; 9 Hispanic/Latino), 80 international. Average age 28. 128 applicants, 73% accepted, 51 enrolled. In 2014, 29 master's, 15 doctorates awarded. Terminal master's awarded for partial completion of doctoral program. *Degree requirements:* For master's, comprehensive exam (for some programs), thesis (for some programs); for doctorate, comprehensive exam, thesis/dissertation. *Entrance requirements:* For master's and doctorate, GRE General Test. Additional exam requirements/recommendations for international students: Required—TOEFL. *Application deadline:* For fall admission, 3/1 for domestic students; for spring admission, 8/1 for domestic students. Applications are processed on a rolling basis. Application fee: $50 ($90 for international students). Electronic applications accepted. *Expenses:* Tuition, state resident: full-time $4078; part-time $226.55 per credit hour. Tuition, nonresident: full-time $10,594; part-time $577.55 per credit hour. *Required fees:* $2813; $237.70 per credit hour. $278.50 per semester. Tuition and fees vary according to degree level and student level. *Financial support:* In 2014–15, 116 students received support, including 12 fellowships with full and partial tuition reimbursements available (averaging $7,946 per year), 22 research assistantships with full and partial tuition reimbursements available (averaging $6,322 per year), 35 teaching assistantships with full and partial tuition reimbursements available (averaging $5,782 per year); career-related internships or fieldwork, institutionally sponsored loans, scholarships/grants, traineeships, health care benefits, tuition waivers (full and partial), and unspecified assistantships also available. Support available to part-time students. Financial award application deadline: 3/1; financial award applicants required to submit FAFSA. *Faculty research:* Production economics, agricultural finance, resources, marketing and policy, agribusiness. *Unit head:* Dr. C. Parr Rosson, III, Professor and Head, 979-845-2116, Fax: 979-847-9378, E-mail: prosson@tamu.edu. *Application contact:* Shelly Peacock, Program Coordinator, 979-845-5222, Fax: 979-862-1563, E-mail: shellypeacock@tamu.edu.
Website: http://agecon.tamu.edu/

Texas Tech University, Graduate School, College of Agricultural Sciences and Natural Resources, Department of Agricultural and Applied Economics, Lubbock, TX 79409-2132. Offers agribusiness (MAB); agricultural and applied economics (MS, PhD); JD/MS. Part-time programs available. *Faculty:* 17 full-time (2 women), 2 part-time/adjunct (0 women). *Students:* 45 full-time (19 women), 9 part-time (3 women); includes 2 minority (both Hispanic/Latino), 22 international. Average age 28. 45 applicants, 80% accepted, 18 enrolled. In 2014, 6 master's, 1 doctorate awarded. Terminal master's awarded for partial completion of doctoral program. *Degree requirements:* For master's, thesis or alternative; for doctorate, comprehensive exam, thesis/dissertation. *Entrance requirements:* For master's and doctorate, GRE General Test, formal approval from departmental committee. Additional exam requirements/recommendations for international students: Required—TOEFL (minimum score 550 paper-based; 79 iBT). *Application deadline:* For fall admission, 6/1 priority date for domestic students, 1/15 priority date for international students; for spring admission, 9/1 priority date for domestic students, 6/15 priority date for international students. Applications are processed on a rolling basis. Application fee: $60. Electronic applications accepted. *Expenses:* Tuition, state resident: full-time $6310; part-time $262.92 per credit hour. Tuition, nonresident: full-time $14,998; part-time $624.92 per credit hour. *Required fees:* $2701; $36.50 per credit. $912.50 per semester. Tuition and fees vary according to course load. *Financial support:* In 2014–15, 38 students received support, including 35 fellowships (averaging $3,516 per year), 20 research assistantships (averaging $18,180 per year); teaching assistantships, institutionally sponsored loans, scholarships/grants, health care benefits, and unspecified assistantships also available. Financial award application deadline: 5/1; financial award applicants required to submit FAFSA. *Faculty research:* Economics of the United States cotton and textile industries, natural resource management in semi-arid climates, commodity policy analysis, international trade in agricultural products, agribusiness analysis. *Total annual research expenditures:* $623,743. *Unit head:* Dr. Phillip N. Johnson, Chair, 806-834-0474, Fax: 806-742-1099, E-mail: phil.johnson@ttu.edu. *Application contact:* Dr. Tom Knight, Graduate Adviser, 806-742-2821, Fax: 806-742-1099, E-mail: tom.knight@ttu.edu.
Website: http://www.aaec.ttu.edu

Tropical Agriculture Research and Higher Education Center, Graduate School, Turrialba, Costa Rica. Offers agribusiness management (MS); agroforestry systems (PhD); development practices (MS); ecological agriculture (MS); environmental socioeconomics (MS); forestry in tropical and subtropical zones (PhD); integrated watershed management (MS); international sustainable tourism (MS); management and conservation of tropical rainforests and biodiversity (MS); tropical agriculture (PhD); tropical agroforestry (MS). *Entrance requirements:* For master's, GRE, 2 years of related professional experience, letters of recommendation; for doctorate, GRE, 4 letters of recommendation, letter of support from employing organization, master's degree in agronomy, biological sciences, forestry, natural resources or related field. Additional exam requirements/recommendations for international students: Required—TOEFL (minimum score 550 paper-based). Electronic applications accepted. *Faculty research:* Biodiversity in fragmented landscapes, ecosystem management, integrated pest management, environmental livestock production, biotechnology carbon balances in diverse land uses.

Tuskegee University, Graduate Programs, College of Agriculture, Environment and Nutrition Sciences, Department of Agricultural and Environmental Sciences, Program in Agricultural and Resource Economics, Tuskegee, AL 36088. Offers MS. *Degree requirements:* For master's, thesis. *Entrance requirements:* For master's, GRE General Test. Additional exam requirements/recommendations for international students: Required—TOEFL (minimum score 500 paper-based). *Expenses: Tuition:* Full-time $18,560; part-time $1542 per credit hour. *Required fees:* $2910; $1455 per semester.

Universidad del Este, Graduate School, Carolina, PR 00984. Offers accounting (MBA); adult education (M Ed); agribusiness (MBA); criminal justice and criminology (MA); curriculum and instruction - early education (M Ed); curriculum and instruction - elementary (M Ed); curriculum and instruction - English (M Ed); curriculum and instruction - Spanish (M Ed); human resources (MBA); information security management (MBA); information technology and Web business development (MBA); management (MBA); public policy (MPA); social work (MA), including clinical social work; special education (M Ed); strategic leadership (MBA).

Université Laval, Faculty of Agricultural and Food Sciences, Department of Agricultural Economics and Consumer Sciences, Program in Agricultural Economics, Québec, QC G1K 7P4, Canada. Offers M Sc. Part-time programs available. *Degree requirements:* For master's, thesis (for some programs). *Entrance requirements:* For master's, knowledge of French. Electronic applications accepted.

University of Alberta, Faculty of Graduate Studies and Research, Department of Rural Economy, Edmonton, AB T6G 2E1, Canada. Offers agricultural economics (M Ag, M Sc, PhD); forest economics (M Ag, M Sc, PhD); rural sociology (M Ag, M Sc); MBA/M Ag. Part-time programs available. *Degree requirements:* For doctorate, thesis/dissertation. *Entrance requirements:* Additional exam requirements/recommendations for international students: Required—TOEFL. *Faculty research:* Agroforestry, development, extension education, marketing and trade, natural resources and environment, policy, production economics.

The University of Arizona, College of Agriculture and Life Sciences, Department of Agricultural and Resource Economics, Tucson, AZ 85721. Offers MS. *Degree requirements:* For master's, thesis or alternative. *Entrance requirements:* For master's, GRE General Test, 3 letters of recommendation, minimum GPA of 3.0. Additional exam requirements/recommendations for international students: Required—TOEFL (minimum score 550 paper-based; 79 iBT). Electronic applications accepted. *Faculty research:* Natural resources, international development trade, production and marketing, agricultural policy, rural development.

University of Arkansas, Graduate School, Dale Bumpers College of Agricultural, Food and Life Sciences, Department of Agricultural Economics, Fayetteville, AR 72701-1201. Offers MS. *Degree requirements:* For master's, thesis optional. Electronic applications accepted.

The University of British Columbia, Faculty of Land and Food Systems, Agricultural Economics Program, Vancouver, BC V6T 1Z1, Canada. Offers agricultural economics (M Sc); food and resource economics (MFRE). Part-time programs available. *Degree requirements:* For master's, thesis. *Entrance requirements:* Additional exam requirements/recommendations for international students: Required—TOEFL (minimum score 577 paper-based; 90 iBT), IELTS (minimum score 6.5). Electronic applications accepted. *Faculty research:* International development, natural resources and environmental economics, marketing and trade, agribusiness, food market analysis, applied econometrics.

University of California, Berkeley, Graduate Division, College of Natural Resources, Department of Agricultural and Resource Economics, Berkeley, CA 94720-1500. Offers PhD. *Degree requirements:* For doctorate, thesis/dissertation, qualifying exam. *Entrance requirements:* For doctorate, GRE General Test, minimum GPA of 3.0, 3 letters of recommendation. *Faculty research:* Agricultural economics and policy, environmental and resource economics and policy, international agricultural development and trade.

University of California, Davis, Graduate Studies, Program in Agricultural and Resource Economics, Davis, CA 95616. Offers MS, PhD, MBA/MS. Terminal master's awarded for partial completion of doctoral program. *Degree requirements:* For master's, thesis optional; for doctorate, thesis/dissertation. *Entrance requirements:* For master's, GRE General Test, minimum GPA of 3.0; for doctorate, GRE General Test, minimum GPA of 3.3. Additional exam requirements/recommendations for international students: Required—TOEFL (minimum score 550 paper-based). Electronic applications accepted.

Faculty research: Applied microeconomics, international trade, development, econometrics, environmental economics.

University of California, Santa Barbara, Graduate Division, Donald Bren School of Environmental Science and Management, Santa Barbara, CA 93106-5131. Offers economics and environmental science (PhD); environmental science and management (MESM, PhD); technology and society (PhD). *Degree requirements:* For master's, thesis; for doctorate, thesis/dissertation. *Entrance requirements:* For master's and doctorate, GRE. Additional exam requirements/recommendations for international students: Required—TOEFL (minimum score 550 paper-based; 80 iBT), IELTS (minimum score 7). Electronic applications accepted. *Faculty research:* Coastal marine resources management, conservation planning, corporate environmental management, economics and politics of the environment, energy and climate, pollution prevention and remediation, water resources management.

University of Connecticut, Graduate School, College of Agriculture and Natural Resources, Department of Agricultural and Resource Economics, Storrs, CT 06269. Offers MS, PhD. Terminal master's awarded for partial completion of doctoral program. *Degree requirements:* For master's, comprehensive exam; for doctorate, thesis/dissertation. *Entrance requirements:* For master's and doctorate, GRE General Test. Additional exam requirements/recommendations for international students: Required—TOEFL (minimum score 550 paper-based). Electronic applications accepted. *Faculty research:* Food marketing, international agricultural development.

University of Delaware, College of Agriculture and Natural Resources, Department of Food and Resource Economics, Newark, DE 19716. Offers agricultural and resource economics (MS); agricultural education (MA); operations research (MS); statistics (MS). Part-time programs available. *Degree requirements:* For master's, thesis. *Entrance requirements:* For master's, GRE General Test, 3 letters of recommendation. Additional exam requirements/recommendations for international students: Required—TOEFL (minimum score 550 paper-based). Electronic applications accepted. *Faculty research:* Experimental economics, environmental and resource economics, land use, law and economics.

University of Florida, Graduate School, College of Agricultural and Life Sciences, Department of Food and Resource Economics, Gainesville, FL 32611. Offers agribusiness (MS); food and resource economics (MAB, MS, PhD); hydrologic sciences (MS, PhD); toxicology (MS, PhD); tropical conservation and developement (MAB, MS, PhD). Part-time programs available. *Faculty:* 32 full-time (9 women). *Students:* 56 full-time (27 women), 15 part-time (7 women); includes 9 minority (2 Black or African American, non-Hispanic/Latino; 2 Asian, non-Hispanic/Latino; 5 Hispanic/Latino), 45 international. Average age 29. 57 applicants, 40% accepted, 13 enrolled. In 2014, 25 master's, 8 doctorates awarded. *Degree requirements:* For master's, comprehensive exam, thesis; for doctorate, comprehensive exam, thesis/dissertation. *Entrance requirements:* For master's, GRE Total Minimum 300 overall, 145 on quantitative, Minimum GPA of 3.0, minimum B grade in prerequisites; for doctorate, GRE Total Minimum 305 overall, 150 on quantitative, Minimum GPA of 3.0, minimum B grade in prerequisites. Additional exam requirements/recommendations for international students: Required—TOEFL (minimum score 550 paper-based; 80 iBT), IELTS (minimum score 6). *Application deadline:* For fall admission, 2/1 priority date for domestic and international students. Applications are processed on a rolling basis. Application fee: $30. Electronic applications accepted. *Financial support:* In 2014–15, 22 students received support, including 2 fellowships (averaging $18,000 per year), 14 research assistantships (averaging $16,550 per year), 15 teaching assistantships (averaging $16,550 per year); scholarships/grants, health care benefits, and unspecified assistantships also available. Financial award application deadline: 2/1. *Faculty research:* Economics of agriculture marketing, production, international trade, and policy; environmental and resource economics, development economics. *Total annual research expenditures:* $756,254. *Unit head:* Dr. Spiro Stefanou, PhD, Professor and Chair, 352-294-7625, Fax: 352-846-0988, E-mail: sstefanou@ufl.edu. *Application contact:* Dr. Jessica Herman, Graduate Student Services Coordinator, 352-294-7622, Fax: 352-846-0988, E-mail: jherman@ufl.edu.
Website: http://www.fred.ifas.ufl.edu/

University of Georgia, College of Agricultural and Environmental Sciences, Department of Agricultural and Applied Economics, Athens, GA 30602. Offers agricultural economics (MAE, MS, PhD); environmental economics (MS). *Degree requirements:* For master's, thesis (MS); for doctorate, thesis/dissertation. *Entrance requirements:* For master's and doctorate, GRE General Test. Electronic applications accepted.

University of Guelph, Graduate Studies, College of Management and Economics, MBA Program, Guelph, ON N1G 2W1, Canada. Offers food and agribusiness management (MBA); hospitality and tourism management (MBA). Part-time and evening/weekend programs available. Postbaccalaureate distance learning degree programs offered (minimal on-campus study). *Entrance requirements:* For master's, minimum B-average, minimum of 3 years of relevant work experience. Additional exam requirements/recommendations for international students: Required—TOEFL (minimum score 550 paper-based). Electronic applications accepted. *Faculty research:* Marketing, operations management, business policy, financial management, organizational behavior.

University of Guelph, Graduate Studies, Ontario Agricultural College, Department of Food, Agricultural and Resource Economics, Guelph, ON N1G 2W1, Canada. Offers agricultural economics (M Sc, PhD); MA/M Sc. Part-time programs available. *Degree requirements:* For master's, thesis; for doctorate, comprehensive exam, thesis/dissertation. *Entrance requirements:* For master's, minimum B- average during previous 2 years of course work; for doctorate, minimum B standing in recognized master's degree. Additional exam requirements/recommendations for international students: Required—TOEFL (minimum score 550 paper-based), IELTS (minimum score 6.5). Electronic applications accepted. *Faculty research:* Agricultural policy, agribusiness, environmental economics, agricultural marketing, production economics.

University of Idaho, College of Graduate Studies, College of Agricultural and Life Sciences, Department of Agricultural Economics and Rural Sociology, Moscow, ID 83844-2334. Offers agricultural economics (MS); applied economics (MS), including agribusiness, agricultural economics, applied economics, natural resources. *Faculty:* 9 full-time. *Students:* 8 full-time, 1 part-time. Average age 27. In 2014, 4 master's awarded. *Entrance requirements:* For master's, minimum GPA of 2.8. *Application deadline:* For fall admission, 8/1 for domestic students; for spring admission, 12/15 for domestic students. Applications are processed on a rolling basis. Application fee: $60. Electronic applications accepted. *Expenses:* Tuition, state resident: full-time $4784; part-time $280.50 per credit hour. Tuition, nonresident: full-time $18,314; part-time $957.50 per credit hour. *Required fees:* $2000; $58.50 per credit hour. Tuition and fees vary according to program. *Financial support:* Research assistantships and teaching assistantships available. Financial award applicants required to submit FAFSA. *Faculty research:* Crops: potatoes, blue grass; livestock: beef, dairy; rural and community development; natural resources and the environment; farm and ranch management. *Unit head:* Dr. Cathy Roheim, Department Head, 208-885-6262, Fax: 208-885-5759, E-mail: cdarby@uidaho.edu. *Application contact:* Sean Scoggin, Graduate Recruitment Coordinator, 208-885-4001, Fax: 208-885-4406, E-mail: graduateadmissions@uidaho.edu. Website: http://www.cals.uidaho.edu/aers/

University of Illinois at Urbana–Champaign, Graduate College, College of Agricultural, Consumer and Environmental Sciences, Department of Agricultural and Consumer Economics, Champaign, IL 61820. Offers agricultural and applied economics (MS, PhD). *Students:* 68 full-time (31 women). Application fee: $70 ($90 for international students). *Unit head:* Paul N. Ellinger, Head, 217-333-5503, Fax: 217-333-5538, E-mail: pellinge@illinois.edu. *Application contact:* Pamela S. Splittstoesser, Graduate Studies Assistant, 217-333-1830, Fax: 217-244-7088, E-mail: splttsts@illinois.edu.
Website: http://ace.illinois.edu/

University of Kentucky, Graduate School, College of Agriculture, Food and Environment, Program in Agricultural Economics, Lexington, KY 40506-0032. Offers MS, PhD. *Degree requirements:* For master's, comprehensive exam, thesis optional; for doctorate, comprehensive exam, thesis/dissertation. *Entrance requirements:* For master's, GRE General Test, minimum undergraduate GPA of 2.75; for doctorate, GRE General Test, minimum graduate GPA of 3.0. Additional exam requirements/recommendations for international students: Required—TOEFL (minimum score 550 paper-based). Electronic applications accepted. *Faculty research:* Food and agricultural marketing, agricultural and food policy, natural resources and environment, rural economic development.

University of Maine, Graduate School, College of Natural Sciences, Forestry, and Agriculture, School of Economics, Orono, ME 04469. Offers economics (MA); financial economics (MA); resource economics and policy (MS). Part-time programs available. *Faculty:* 15 full-time (4 women). *Students:* 18 full-time (8 women), 2 part-time (1 woman), 8 international. Average age 27. 41 applicants, 66% accepted, 12 enrolled. In 2014, 10 master's awarded. *Degree requirements:* For master's, thesis (for some programs). *Entrance requirements:* For master's, GRE General Test. Additional exam requirements/recommendations for international students: Required—TOEFL. *Application deadline:* For fall admission, 2/1 priority date for domestic students; for spring admission, 10/1 for domestic students. Applications are processed on a rolling basis. Application fee: $65. Electronic applications accepted. *Expenses:* Tuition, state resident: part-time $658 per credit hour. Tuition, nonresident: part-time $1550 per credit hour. *Financial support:* In 2014–15, 11 students received support, including 4 research assistantships (averaging $14,600 per year), 6 teaching assistantships with full tuition reimbursements available (averaging $14,600 per year); career-related internships or fieldwork, Federal Work-Study, institutionally sponsored loans, scholarships/grants, and tuition waivers (full and partial) also available. Support available to part-time students. Financial award application deadline: 3/1. *Faculty research:* Energy, food safety, transportation, education, economic development. *Total annual research expenditures:* $2.6 million. *Unit head:* Dr. Mario Teisl, Director, 207-581-3151, Fax: 207-581-4278. *Application contact:* Scott G. Delcourt, Assistant Vice President for Graduate Studies and Senior Associate Dean, 207-581-3291, Fax: 207-581-3232, E-mail: graduate@maine.edu.
Website: http://umaine.edu/soe/

University of Manitoba, Faculty of Graduate Studies, Faculty of Agricultural and Food Sciences, Department of Agribusiness and Agricultural Economics, Winnipeg, MB R3T 2N2, Canada. Offers agribusiness (M Sc, PhD). *Degree requirements:* For master's, thesis or alternative; for doctorate, thesis/dissertation.

University of Maryland, College Park, Academic Affairs, College of Agriculture and Natural Resources, Department of Agricultural and Resource Economics, College Park, MD 20742. Offers agriculture economics (MS, PhD); resource economics (MS, PhD). Part-time and evening/weekend programs available. *Degree requirements:* For master's, variable foreign language requirement, thesis optional, oral exam; for doctorate, variable foreign language requirement, oral dissertation defense. *Entrance requirements:* For master's, GRE General Test, minimum GPA of 3.0, course work in microeconomics and calculus, 3 letters of recommendation; for doctorate, GRE General Test. Additional exam requirements/recommendations for international students: Required—TOEFL. Electronic applications accepted. *Faculty research:* Agricultural development, international trade, agricultural marketing, econometrics, farm management and production economics.

University of Massachusetts Amherst, Graduate School, College of Social and Behavioral Sciences, Department of Resource Economics, Amherst, MA 01003. Offers MS, PhD. Part-time programs available. *Faculty:* 17 full-time (6 women). *Students:* 21 full-time (8 women), 4 part-time (2 women), 10 international. Average age 28. 43 applicants, 40% accepted, 10 enrolled. In 2014, 7 master's, 3 doctorates awarded. Terminal master's awarded for partial completion of doctoral program. *Degree requirements:* For master's, thesis or alternative; for doctorate, comprehensive exam, thesis/dissertation. *Entrance requirements:* For master's and doctorate, GRE General Test. Additional exam requirements/recommendations for international students: Required—TOEFL (minimum score 550 paper-based; 80 iBT), IELTS (minimum score 6.5). *Application deadline:* For fall admission, 2/1 for domestic and international students. Applications are processed on a rolling basis. Application fee: $75. Electronic applications accepted. *Expenses:* Tuition, state resident: full-time $1980; part-time $110 per credit. Tuition, nonresident: full-time $14,644; part-time $414 per credit. *Required fees:* $11,417. One-time fee: $357. *Financial support:* Fellowships with full and partial tuition reimbursements, research assistantships with full and partial tuition reimbursements, teaching assistantships with full and partial tuition reimbursements, career-related internships or fieldwork, Federal Work-Study, scholarships/grants, traineeships, health care benefits, tuition waivers (full and partial), and unspecified assistantships available. Support available to part-time students. Financial award application deadline: 2/1; financial award applicants required to submit FAFSA. *Unit head:* Dr. John Spraggon, Graduate Program Director, 413-545-5732, Fax: 413-545-5853. *Application contact:* Lindsay DeSantis, Supervisor of Admissions, 413-545-0722, Fax: 413-577-0010, E-mail: gradadm@grad.umass.edu.
Website: http://www.umass.edu/resec/

University of Missouri, Office of Research and Graduate Studies, College of Agriculture, Food and Natural Resources, Department of Agricultural and Applied Economics, Columbia, MO 65211. Offers agricultural economics (MS, PhD); conservation biology (Graduate Certificate). *Faculty:* 23 full-time (3 women), 3 part-time/adjunct (1 woman). *Students:* 31 full-time (12 women), 17 part-time (6 women); includes 2 minority (both Black or African American, non-Hispanic/Latino), 23 international. Average age 31. 57 applicants, 33% accepted, 14 enrolled. In 2014, 6 master's, 6 doctorates, 1 other advanced degree awarded. *Degree requirements:* For doctorate, comprehensive exam, thesis/dissertation. *Entrance requirements:* For master's and doctorate, GRE General Test, minimum GPA of 3.0. Additional exam requirements/recommendations for international students: Required—TOEFL (minimum score 550 paper-based; 80 iBT). *Application deadline:* For fall admission, 2/15 priority date for domestic students, 2/15 for international students; for winter admission, 9/15 for domestic and international students. Applications are processed on a rolling basis. Application fee: $55 ($75 for international students). Electronic applications accepted. *Financial support:* Fellowships, research assistantships with tuition reimbursements, teaching assistantships with tuition reimbursements, Federal Work-Study, institutionally sponsored loans, scholarships/grants, health care benefits, and unspecified

assistantships available. Financial award application deadline: 3/1; financial award applicants required to submit FAFSA. *Faculty research:* Agribusiness management, contracting and strategy; collective action and cooperative theory; econometrics and price analysis; entrepreneurship; environmental and natural resource economics; food, biofuel and agricultural policy and regulation; international development; regional economics and rural development policy; science policy and innovation; sustainable agriculture and applied ethics. *Unit head:* Dr. Joe Parcell, Department Chair, 573-882-0870, E-mail: parcellj@missouri.edu. *Application contact:* Jody Pestle, Administrative Assistant, 573-882-3747, E-mail: pestlej@missouri.edu.
Website: http://dass.missouri.edu/agecon/grad/

University of Nebraska–Lincoln, Graduate College, College of Agricultural Sciences and Natural Resources, Department of Agricultural Economics, Lincoln, NE 68588. Offers agribusiness (MBA); agricultural economics (MS, PhD); community development (M Ag). *Degree requirements:* For master's, thesis optional; for doctorate, comprehensive exam, thesis/dissertation. *Entrance requirements:* For master's and doctorate, GRE General Test. Additional exam requirements/recommendations for international students: Required—TOEFL (minimum score 550 paper-based). Electronic applications accepted. *Faculty research:* Marketing and agribusiness, production economics, resource law, international trade and development, rural policy and revitalization.

University of Nevada, Reno, Graduate School, College of Agriculture, Biotechnology and Natural Resources, Department of Resource Economics, Reno, NV 89557. Offers MS, PhD. Terminal master's awarded for partial completion of doctoral program. *Degree requirements:* For master's, thesis optional; for doctorate, thesis/dissertation. *Entrance requirements:* For master's, GRE General Test, minimum GPA of 2.75; for doctorate, GRE General Test, minimum GPA of 3.0. Additional exam requirements/recommendations for international students: Required—TOEFL (minimum score 500 paper-based; 61 iBT), IELTS (minimum score 6). Electronic applications accepted. *Faculty research:* Econometrics, environmental valuation, natural resource and environmental policy analysis, public lands management.

University of Puerto Rico, Mayagüez Campus, Graduate Studies, College of Agricultural Sciences, Department of Agricultural Economics, Mayagüez, PR 00681-9000. Offers MS. Part-time programs available. *Faculty:* 6 full-time (3 women), 1 part-time/adjunct (0 women). *Students:* 12 full-time (5 women), 1 (woman) part-time. 7 applicants, 100% accepted, 4 enrolled. In 2014, 1 master's awarded. *Degree requirements:* For master's, comprehensive exam, thesis. *Entrance requirements:* For master's, bachelor's degree in agricultural economics or its equivalent. *Application deadline:* For fall admission, 2/15 for domestic and international students; for spring admission, 9/15 for domestic and international students. Applications are processed on a rolling basis. Application fee: $25. *Expenses: Tuition,* area resident: Full-time $2466; part-time $822 per credit. *International tuition:* $6371 full-time. *Required fees:* $1095; $1095 per year. Tuition and fees vary according to course level, course load and reciprocity agreements. *Financial support:* In 2014–15, 16 students received support, including 9 research assistantships with tuition reimbursements available (averaging $8,249 per year), 10 teaching assistantships with tuition reimbursements available (averaging $4,290 per year); fellowships with full tuition reimbursements available, Federal Work-Study, institutionally sponsored loans, and unspecified assistantships also available. *Faculty research:* Farm management, agricultural development, agrimarketing, natural resource economics. *Unit head:* Dr. Alwin J. Jimenez, Director, 787-265-3855 Ext. 3116, Fax: 787-265-3860, E-mail: alwin.jimenez@upr.edu. *Application contact:* Margarita Olivencia, Secretary, 787-832-4040 Ext. 2471, Fax: 787-265-3860, E-mail: margarita.olivencia@upr.edu.
Website: http://agricultura.uprm.edu/economia/

University of Saskatchewan, College of Graduate Studies and Research, College of Agriculture, Department of Agricultural Economics, Saskatoon, SK S7N 5A2, Canada. Offers M Ag, M Sc, MA, PhD, PGD. *Degree requirements:* For master's, thesis; for doctorate, comprehensive exam (for some programs), thesis/dissertation. *Entrance requirements:* Additional exam requirements/recommendations for international students: Required—TOEFL (minimum score 80 iBT); Recommended—IELTS (minimum score 6.5).

University of Saskatchewan, College of Graduate Studies and Research, Edwards School of Business, Program in Business Administration, Saskatoon, SK S7N 5A2, Canada. Offers agribusiness management (MBA); biotechnology management (MBA); health services management (MBA); indigenous management (MBA); international business management (MBA).

University of Vermont, Graduate College, College of Agriculture and Life Sciences, Department of Community Development and Applied Economics, Burlington, VT 05405. Offers community development and applied economics (MS); public administration (MPA). *Degree requirements:* For master's, thesis. *Entrance requirements:* For master's, GRE General Test. Additional exam requirements/recommendations for international students: Required—TOEFL (minimum score 550 paper-based; 80 iBT). Electronic applications accepted. *Faculty research:* Agricultural production and marketing.

University of Wisconsin–Madison, Graduate School, College of Agricultural and Life Sciences, Department of Agricultural and Applied Economics, Madison, WI 53706. Offers MA, MS, PhD. Part-time programs available. *Degree requirements:* For doctorate, thesis/dissertation, preliminary exams. *Entrance requirements:* For master's and doctorate, GRE General Test. Additional exam requirements/recommendations for international students: Required—TOEFL (minimum score 580 paper-based; 92 iBT). Electronic applications accepted. *Expenses:* Tuition, state resident: full-time $10,723; part-time $745 per credit. Tuition, nonresident: full-time $24,054; part-time $1578 per credit. *Required fees:* $374 per semester. Tuition and fees vary according to course load, program and reciprocity agreements. *Faculty research:* Environmental and resource economics, international development, community economics, energy economics, agricultural technology, food systems, markets and trade.

University of Wyoming, College of Agriculture and Natural Resources, Department of Agricultural and Applied Economics, Laramie, WY 82071. Offers MS. Part-time programs available. *Degree requirements:* For master's, thesis (for some programs). *Entrance requirements:* For master's, GRE General Test, minimum GPA of 3.0. Additional exam requirements/recommendations for international students: Required—TOEFL. Electronic applications accepted. *Faculty research:* Farm management, agricultural markets, water economics, community development, agricultural business.

Virginia Polytechnic Institute and State University, Graduate School, College of Agriculture and Life Sciences, Blacksburg, VA 24061. Offers agricultural and applied economics (MS); agricultural and life sciences (MS); animal and poultry science (MS, PhD); crop and soil environmental sciences (MS, PhD); dairy science (MS); entomology (PhD); horticulture (MS, PhD); human nutrition, foods and exercise (MS, PhD); life sciences (MS, PhD); plant pathology, physiology and weed science (PhD). *Faculty:* 242 full-time (69 women), 1 (woman) part-time/adjunct. *Students:* 400 full-time (225 women), 100 part-time (64 women); includes 60 minority (25 Black or African American, non-Hispanic/Latino; 16 Asian, non-Hispanic/Latino; 8 Hispanic/Latino; 11 Two or more races, non-Hispanic/Latino), 121 international. Average age 29. 444 applicants, 37% accepted, 132 enrolled. In 2014, 70 master's, 46 doctorates awarded. *Degree requirements:* For master's, comprehensive exam (for some programs), thesis (for some programs); for doctorate, comprehensive exam (for some programs), thesis/dissertation (for some programs). *Entrance requirements:* For master's and doctorate, GRE/GMAT (may vary by department). Additional exam requirements/recommendations for international students: Required—TOEFL (minimum score 550 paper-based). *Application deadline:* For fall admission, 8/1 for domestic students, 4/1 for international students; for spring admission, 1/1 for domestic students, 9/1 for international students. Applications are processed on a rolling basis. Application fee: $75. Electronic applications accepted. *Expenses:* Tuition, state resident: full-time $11,656; part-time $647.50 per credit hour. Tuition, nonresident: full-time $23,351; part-time $1297.25 per credit hour. *Required fees:* $2533; $465.75 per semester. Tuition and fees vary according to course load, campus/location and program. *Financial support:* In 2014–15, 274 research assistantships with full tuition reimbursements (averaging $21,739 per year), 91 teaching assistantships with full tuition reimbursements (averaging $22,005 per year) were awarded. Financial award application deadline: 3/1; financial award applicants required to submit FAFSA. *Total annual research expenditures:* $42.1 million. *Unit head:* Dr. Alan L. Grant, Dean, 540-231-4152, Fax: 540-231-4163, E-mail: algrant@vt.edu. *Application contact:* Sheila Norman, Administrative Assistant, 540-231-4152, Fax: 540-231-4163, E-mail: snorman@vt.edu.
Website: http://www.cals.vt.edu/

Washington State University, College of Agricultural, Human, and Natural Resource Sciences, School of Economic Sciences, Pullman, WA 99164-6210. Offers agricultural economics (PhD); economics (PhD). Programs offered at the Pullman campus. *Faculty:* 25 full-time (7 women). *Students:* 74 full-time (25 women), 3 part-time (1 woman); includes 2 minority (1 Black or African American, non-Hispanic/Latino; 1 American Indian or Alaska Native, non-Hispanic/Latino), 50 international. Average age 29. 99 applicants, 33% accepted, 17 enrolled. In 2014, 4 master's, 15 doctorates awarded. Terminal master's awarded for partial completion of doctoral program. *Degree requirements:* For master's, comprehensive exam (for some programs), thesis (for some programs), oral exam; for doctorate, comprehensive exam, thesis/dissertation, oral exam, written exam, qualifying exams. *Entrance requirements:* For master's and doctorate, GRE, minimum GPA of 3.0, 3 letters of recommendation. Additional exam requirements/recommendations for international students: Required—TOEFL (minimum score 550 paper-based). *Application deadline:* For fall admission, 2/15 priority date for domestic students, 2/1 priority date for international students. Applications are processed on a rolling basis. Application fee: $75. Electronic applications accepted. *Expenses:* Tuition, state resident: full-time $11,768. Tuition, nonresident: full-time $25,200. *Required fees:* $960. Tuition and fees vary according to program. *Financial support:* In 2014–15, 59 students received support, including 30 research assistantships with full and partial tuition reimbursements available (averaging $13,794 per year), 25 teaching assistantships with full and partial tuition reimbursements available (averaging $14,198 per year); career-related internships or fieldwork, Federal Work-Study, institutionally sponsored loans, tuition waivers (partial), and teaching associateships also available. Financial award application deadline: 4/1; financial award applicants required to submit FAFSA. *Faculty research:* Agricultural economics, econometrics, natural resource and environmental economics, industrial organization, health economics. *Total annual research expenditures:* $1.9 million. *Unit head:* Dr. H. Alan Love, Director, 509-335-3548, Fax: 509-335-1173, E-mail: a.love@wsu.edu. *Application contact:* Danielle K. Engelhardt, Graduate Coordinator, 509-335-5555, E-mail: dkbishop@wsu.edu.
Website: http://cahnrs-cms.wsu.edu/ses/Pages/default.aspx

West Texas A&M University, College of Agriculture, Science and Engineering, Department of Agricultural Sciences, Emphasis in Agricultural Business and Economics, Canyon, TX 79016-0001. Offers MS. Part-time programs available. *Degree requirements:* For master's, comprehensive exam, thesis optional. *Entrance requirements:* For master's, GRE General Test. Additional exam requirements/recommendations for international students: Required—TOEFL (minimum score 550 paper-based). Electronic applications accepted. *Faculty research:* Utilizing expected revenue in selecting optimal marketing alternatives for fixed resource cow/calf operators in the Texas panhandle.

West Virginia University, Davis College of Agriculture, Forestry and Consumer Sciences, Division of Resource Management and Sustainable Development, Program in Agricultural and Resource Economics, Morgantown, WV 26506. Offers MS. Part-time programs available. *Degree requirements:* For master's, thesis optional. *Entrance requirements:* For master's, GRE General Test, minimum GPA of 2.5, 1 calculus course. Additional exam requirements/recommendations for international students: Required—TOEFL. *Faculty research:* Agricultural production and marketing, rural development, mineral and energy economics, economic development.

Applied Economics

Auburn University, Graduate School, Interdepartmental Programs, Interdepartmental Program in Applied Economics, Auburn University, AL 36849. Offers PhD. *Faculty:* 23 full-time (5 women). *Students:* 27 full-time (13 women), 1 (woman) part-time; includes 3 minority (all Black or African American, non-Hispanic/Latino), 24 international. Average age 29. 20 applicants, 90% accepted, 9 enrolled. In 2014, 5 doctorates awarded. *Expenses:* Tuition, state resident: full-time $8586; part-time $477 per credit hour. Tuition, nonresident: full-time $25,758; part-time $1431 per credit hour. *Required fees:* $804 per semester. Tuition and fees vary according to degree level and program. *Unit head:* Henry Kinuucan, Graduate Program Officer, 334-844-5614, E-mail: kinnuhw@auburn.edu. *Application contact:* Dr. George Flowers, Dean of the Graduate School, 334-844-2125.

Buffalo State College, State University of New York, The Graduate School, Faculty of Natural and Social Sciences, Department of Economics and Finance, Buffalo, NY 14222-1095. Offers applied economics (MA). *Degree requirements:* For master's,

project. *Entrance requirements:* Additional exam requirements/recommendations for international students: Required—TOEFL (minimum score 550 paper-based).

Clemson University, Graduate School, College of Business and Behavioral Science, Department of Economics, Clemson, SC 29634. Offers applied economics (PhD), including applied economics, applied economics and statistics; applied economics and statistics (MS, PhD); economics (MA, PhD). Part-time programs available. *Faculty:* 23 full-time (2 women), 5 part-time/adjunct (2 women). *Students:* 90 full-time (29 women), 17 part-time (4 women); includes 7 minority (2 Black or African American, non-Hispanic/Latino; 1 Hispanic/Latino; 4 Two or more races, non-Hispanic/Latino), 64 international. Average age 27. 234 applicants, 60% accepted, 51 enrolled. In 2014, 42 master's, 10 doctorates awarded. Terminal master's awarded for partial completion of doctoral program. *Degree requirements:* For master's, thesis (for some programs); for doctorate, comprehensive exam, thesis/dissertation. *Entrance requirements:* For master's, GRE General Test or GMAT, intermediate microeconomic theory; multivariate calculus; for doctorate, GRE General Test, intermediate microeconomic theory; multivariate calculus. Additional exam requirements/recommendations for international students: Required—TOEFL. *Application deadline:* For fall admission, 1/15 priority date for domestic and international students; for spring admission, 9/15 for international students. Application fee: $80 ($90 for international students). Electronic applications accepted. *Expenses:* Expenses: Contact institution. *Financial support:* In 2014–15, 21 students received support, including 26 fellowships with partial tuition reimbursements available (averaging $4,923 per year), 15 teaching assistantships with partial tuition reimbursements available (averaging $21,128 per year); research assistantships with partial tuition reimbursements available, career-related internships or fieldwork, institutionally sponsored loans, scholarships/grants, health care benefits, and unspecified assistantships also available. Support available to part-time students. Financial award applicants required to submit FAFSA. *Faculty research:* Applied price theory, industrial organization, international economics, labor economics, public economics. *Total annual research expenditures:* $66,305. *Unit head:* Dr. Raymond Sauer, Interim Chair, 864-656-3969, Fax: 864-656-4192, E-mail: sauerr@clemson.edu. *Application contact:* Dr. Curtis J. Simon, Director of Graduate Programs, 864-656-3966, Fax: 864-656-4192, E-mail: cjsmn@clemson.edu.
Website: http://economics.clemson.edu/

Cornell University, Graduate School, Graduate Fields of Agriculture and Life Sciences, Field of Applied Economics and Management, Ithaca, NY 14853-0001. Offers agricultural finance (MS, PhD); applied econometrics and qualitative analysis (MS, PhD); economics of development (MS, PhD); environmental economics (MS, PhD); environmental management (MPS); farm management and production economics (MS, PhD); marketing and food distribution (MS, PhD); public policy analysis (MS, PhD); resource economics (PhD). *Entrance requirements:* For master's and doctorate, GRE. Additional exam requirements/recommendations for international students: Required—TOEFL.

Cornell University, Graduate School, Graduate Fields of Arts and Sciences, Field of Economics, Ithaca, NY 14853-0001. Offers applied economics (PhD); basic analytical economics (PhD); econometrics and economic statistics (PhD); economic development and planning (PhD); economic theory (PhD); industrial organization and control (PhD); international economics (PhD); labor economics (PhD); monetary and macro economics (PhD); public finance (PhD). *Degree requirements:* For doctorate, comprehensive exam, thesis/dissertation. *Entrance requirements:* For doctorate, GRE General Test, 3 letters of recommendation. Additional exam requirements/recommendations for international students: Required—TOEFL (minimum score 550 paper-based; 77 iBT). Electronic applications accepted. *Faculty research:* Learning and games, economics of education, political economy, transfer payments, time series and nonparametrics.

DePaul University, Charles H. Kellstadt Graduate School of Business, Chicago, IL 60604. Offers accountancy (M Acc, MS, MSA); applied economics (MBA); banking (MBA); behavioral finance (MBA); brand and product management (MBA); business development (MBA); business information technology (MS); business strategy and decision-making (MBA); computational finance (MS); consumer insights (MBA); corporate finance (MBA); economic policy analysis (MS); entrepreneurship (MBA, MS); finance (MBA, MS); financial analysis (MBA); general business (MBA); health sector management (MBA); hospitality leadership (MBA); hospitality leadership and operational performance (MS); human resource management (MBA); human resources (MS); investment management (MBA); leadership and change management (MBA); management accounting (MBA); marketing (MBA, MS); marketing analysis (MS); marketing strategy and planning (MBA); operations management (MBA); organizational diversity (MBA); real estate (MS); real estate finance and investment (MBA); revenue management (MBA); sports management (MBA); strategic global marketing (MBA); strategy, execution and valuation (MBA); sustainable management (MBA, MS); taxation (MS); wealth management (MS); JD/MBA. *Accreditation:* AACSB. Part-time and evening/weekend programs available. Postbaccalaureate distance learning degree programs offered (no on-campus study). *Entrance requirements:* For master's, GMAT, 2 letters of recommendation, resume, essay, official transcripts. Additional exam requirements/recommendations for international students: Required—TOEFL (minimum score 550 paper-based; 80 iBT). Electronic applications accepted. *Expenses:* Contact institution.

East Carolina University, Graduate School, Thomas Harriot College of Arts and Sciences, Department of Economics, Greenville, NC 27858-4353. Offers applied and resource economics (MS). Part-time programs available. *Degree requirements:* For master's, one foreign language, comprehensive exam. *Entrance requirements:* For master's, GRE General Test. Additional exam requirements/recommendations for international students: Required—TOEFL. *Expenses:* Tuition, state resident: full-time $4223. Tuition, nonresident: full-time $16,540. *Required fees:* $2184.

Georgia Southern University, Jack N. Averitt College of Graduate Studies, College of Business Administration, Program in Applied Economics, Statesboro, GA 30460. Offers MS, Graduate Certificate. Part-time and evening/weekend programs available. Postbaccalaureate distance learning degree programs offered (no on-campus study). *Students:* 1 full-time (0 women), 41 part-time (11 women); includes 10 minority (3 Black or African American, non-Hispanic/Latino; 1 Asian, non-Hispanic/Latino; 5 Hispanic/Latino; 1 Two or more races, non-Hispanic/Latino). Average age 37. 29 applicants, 34% accepted, 3 enrolled. In 2014, 12 master's awarded. *Entrance requirements:* For master's, GRE or GMAT, minimum GPA of 3.0. Additional exam requirements/recommendations for international students: Required—TOEFL (minimum score 550 paper-based; 80 iBT), IELTS (minimum score 6). *Application deadline:* For fall admission, 3/1 for domestic and international students; for spring admission, 10/1 priority date for domestic students, 10/1 for international students. Applications are processed on a rolling basis. Application fee: $50. Electronic applications accepted. *Expenses:* Tuition, state resident: full-time $7236; part-time $277 per semester hour. Tuition, nonresident: full-time $27,118; part-time $1105 per semester hour. *Required fees:* $2092. *Financial support:* Application deadline: 4/15. *Faculty research:* Analytical capabilities in economic development, financial economics, regulatory issues, market analysis, economic development. *Unit head:* Dr. Gordon Smith, Graduate Program Director, 912-478-2357, Fax: 912-478-0710, E-mail: gsmith@georgiasouthern.edu.

Website: http://coba.georgiasouthern.edu/dfe/graduate/master-of-science-in-applied-economics/

HEC Montreal, School of Business Administration, Master of Science Programs in Administration, Program in Applied Economics, Montréal, QC H3T 2A7, Canada. Offers M Sc. Most courses are given in French. *Students:* 16 full-time (13 women). 14 applicants, 71% accepted, 4 enrolled. In 2014, 10 master's awarded. *Degree requirements:* For master's, one foreign language, thesis. *Entrance requirements:* For master's, Test de francais international (TFI) with minimum score of 850 (for those who have never studied in French), BBA, undergraduate degree in another field, degree deemed equivalent by program director and minimum GPA of 3.0 on 4.3 scale. *Application deadline:* For fall admission, 3/15 for domestic and international students; for winter admission, 9/15 for domestic and international students. Application fee: $83 Canadian dollars. Electronic applications accepted. *Financial support:* Research assistantships, teaching assistantships, and scholarships/grants available. Financial award application deadline: 9/2. *Unit head:* Dr. Anne Bourhis, Director, 514-340-6873, Fax: 514-340-6880, E-mail: anne.bourhis@hec.ca. *Application contact:* Marianne de Moura, Administrative Director, 514-340-7106, Fax: 514-340-6411, E-mail: marianne.de-moura@hec.ca.
Website: http://www.hec.ca/programmes_formations/msc/options/economie_appliquee/index.html

Johns Hopkins University, Zanvyl Krieger School of Arts and Sciences, Advanced Academic Programs, Program in Applied Economics, Washington, DC 20036. Offers MA. Part-time and evening/weekend programs available. *Degree requirements:* For master's, thesis (for some programs). *Entrance requirements:* For master's, minimum GPA of 3.0, coursework in microeconomics and macroeconomics. Additional exam requirements/recommendations for international students: Required—TOEFL (minimum score 100 iBT). Electronic applications accepted.

Mississippi State University, College of Business, Department of Finance and Economics, Mississippi State, MS 39762. Offers applied economics (PhD); business administration (PhD); economics (MA). PhD in applied economics offered jointly with Department of Agricultural Economics. Part-time programs available. *Faculty:* 16 full-time (7 women), 1 part-time/adjunct (0 women). *Students:* 7 full-time (3 women), all international. Average age 31. 8 applicants. In 2014, 2 doctorates awarded. Terminal master's awarded for partial completion of doctoral program. *Degree requirements:* For master's, comprehensive exam, thesis optional; for doctorate, comprehensive exam, thesis/dissertation, written and oral exams. *Entrance requirements:* For master's, GRE, previously completed intermediate microeconomics and macroeconomics; for doctorate, GRE, BS with minimum GPA of 3.0 cumulative and over last 60 hours of undergraduate work and 3.25 on all graduate work. Additional exam requirements/recommendations for international students: Required—TOEFL (minimum score 575 paper-based; 84 iBT); Recommended—IELTS (minimum score 6.5). *Application deadline:* For fall admission, 7/1 for domestic students, 5/1 for international students; for spring admission, 11/1 for domestic students, 10/1 for international students. Applications are processed on a rolling basis. Application fee: $60. Electronic applications accepted. *Expenses:* Tuition, state resident: full-time $7140; part-time $783 per credit hour. Tuition, nonresident: full-time $18,478; part-time $2043 per credit hour. *Financial support:* Federal Work-Study, scholarships/grants, health care benefits, and unspecified assistantships available. Financial award application deadline: 4/1; financial award applicants required to submit FAFSA. *Faculty research:* Economics development, mergers, event studies, economic education, bank performance. *Total annual research expenditures:* $1.4 million. *Unit head:* Dr. Mike Highfield, Department Head, 662-325-3928, Fax: 662-325-1977, E-mail: mhighfield@msstate.edu. *Application contact:* Dr. Randy Campbell, Associate Professor/Graduate Coordinator, Economics, 662-325-1516, Fax: 662-325-1977, E-mail: mhighfield@msstate.edu.
Website: http://www.business.msstate.edu/programs/fe/index.php

New York University, Graduate School of Arts and Science, Department of Economics, New York, NY 10012-1019. Offers applied economic analysis (Advanced Certificate); economics (MA, PhD); JD/MA; MD/PhD. Part-time and evening/weekend programs available. *Faculty:* 35 full-time (2 women). *Students:* 214 full-time (77 women), 21 part-time (7 women); includes 15 minority (13 Asian, non-Hispanic/Latino; 2 Hispanic/Latino), 173 international. Average age 27. 1,531 applicants, 16% accepted, 88 enrolled. In 2014, 83 master's, 18 doctorates awarded. Terminal master's awarded for partial completion of doctoral program. *Degree requirements:* For master's, thesis; for doctorate, one foreign language, thesis/dissertation, 4 qualifying exams. *Entrance requirements:* For master's and doctorate, GRE General Test. Additional exam requirements/recommendations for international students: Required—TOEFL. *Application deadline:* For fall admission, 12/18 priority date for domestic students, 12/18 for international students. Application fee: $100. *Financial support:* Fellowships with tuition reimbursements, research assistantships with tuition reimbursements, teaching assistantships with tuition reimbursements, Federal Work-Study, institutionally sponsored loans, scholarships/grants, health care benefits, and unspecified assistantships available. Financial award application deadline: 12/18; financial award applicants required to submit FAFSA. *Faculty research:* Economic theory, experimental economics, growth and development, macroeconomics and finance, international trade and international finance. *Unit head:* Alessandro Lizzeri, Chair, 212-998-8900, Fax: 212-995-4186, E-mail: admissions@econ.nyu.edu. *Application contact:* Tim Cogley, Director of Graduate Studies, PhD Programs, 212-998-8900, Fax: 212-995-4186, E-mail: admissions@econ.nyu.edu.
Website: http://www.econ.nyu.edu/

North Carolina Agricultural and Technical State University, School of Graduate Studies, School of Agriculture and Environmental Sciences, Department of Agribusiness, Applied Economics, and Agriscience Education, Greensboro, NC 27411. Offers agricultural economics (MS); agricultural education (MS). *Accreditation:* NCATE. Part-time and evening/weekend programs available. *Degree requirements:* For master's, comprehensive exam, thesis or alternative, qualifying exam. *Entrance requirements:* For master's, GRE General Test, minimum GPA of 3.0. *Faculty research:* Aid for small farmers, agricultural technology resources, labor force mobility, agrology.

Ohio University, Graduate College, College of Arts and Sciences, Department of Economics, Athens, OH 45701-2979. Offers applied economics (MA); financial economics (MFE). Part-time and evening/weekend programs available. *Degree requirements:* For master's, thesis or alternative. *Entrance requirements:* For master's, GRE or GMAT (recommended), minimum GPA of 3.0. Additional exam requirements/recommendations for international students: Required—TOEFL (minimum score 550 paper-based; 80 iBT) or IELTS (minimum score 6.5). Electronic applications accepted. *Faculty research:* Macroeconomics, public finance, international economics and finance, monetary theory, healthcare economics.

Old Dominion University, Strome College of Business, MBA Program, Norfolk, VA 23529. Offers business and economic forecasting (MBA); financial analysis and valuation (MBA); health sciences administration (MBA); information technology and enterprise integration (MBA); international business (MBA); maritime and port management (MBA); public administration (MBA). *Accreditation:* AACSB. Part-time and evening/weekend programs available. Postbaccalaureate distance learning degree programs offered (no on-campus study). *Faculty:* 83 full-time (19 women), 5 part-time/

adjunct (2 women). *Students:* 37 full-time (24 women), 86 part-time (40 women); includes 22 minority (9 Black or African American, non-Hispanic/Latino; 5 Asian, non-Hispanic/Latino; 2 Hispanic/Latino; 6 Two or more races, non-Hispanic/Latino), 13 international. Average age 29. 200 applicants, 37% accepted, 54 enrolled. In 2014, 61 degrees awarded. *Entrance requirements:* For master's, GMAT, GRE, letter of reference, resume, essay. Additional exam requirements/recommendations for international students: Required—TOEFL (minimum score 550 paper-based; 80 iBT). *Application deadline:* For fall admission, 6/1 priority date for domestic students, 4/15 priority date for international students; for spring admission, 11/1 priority date for domestic students, 10/1 priority date for international students; for summer admission, 3/1 priority date for domestic students, 2/1 priority date for international students. Applications are processed on a rolling basis. Application fee: $50. Electronic applications accepted. *Expenses:* Expenses: Contact institution. *Financial support:* In 2014–15, 47 students received support, including 94 research assistantships with partial tuition reimbursements available (averaging $8,900 per year); career-related internships or fieldwork, scholarships/grants, and unspecified assistantships also available. Support available to part-time students. Financial award application deadline: 2/15; financial award applicants required to submit FAFSA. *Faculty research:* International business, buyer behavior, financial markets, strategy, operations research, maritime and transportation economics. *Unit head:* Dr. Kiran Karaude, Graduate Program Director, 757-683-3585, Fax: 757-683-5750, E-mail: mbainfo@odu.edu. *Application contact:* Sandi Phillips, MBA Program Assistant, 757-683-3585, Fax: 757-683-5750, E-mail: mbainfo@odu.edu.
Website: http://www.odu.edu/mba/

Portland State University, Graduate Studies, College of Liberal Arts and Sciences, Department of Economics, Portland, OR 97207-0751. Offers applied economics (MA, MS); general economics (MA, MS). Part-time programs available. *Faculty:* 14 full-time (2 women), 6 part-time/adjunct (4 women). *Students:* 13 full-time (4 women), 1 (woman) part-time, 4 international. Average age 28. 23 applicants, 39% accepted, 7 enrolled. In 2014, 10 master's awarded. *Degree requirements:* For master's, thesis optional; for doctorate, one foreign language, thesis/dissertation. *Entrance requirements:* For master's, minimum GPA of 3.0 in economic course work and overall; course work in calculus. Additional exam requirements/recommendations for international students: Required—TOEFL (minimum score 550 paper-based; 80 iBT). *Application deadline:* For fall admission, 2/1 for domestic and international students; for winter admission, 9/1 for domestic and international students; for spring admission, 12/5 for domestic and international students. Applications are processed on a rolling basis. Application fee: $50. *Expenses:* Tuition, state resident: part-time $222 per credit. Tuition, nonresident: part-time $527 per credit. *Required fees:* $22 per contact hour. $100 per quarter. Tuition and fees vary according to program. *Financial support:* In 2014–15, 10 teaching assistantships with full tuition reimbursements (averaging $6,570 per year) were awarded; career-related internships or fieldwork, Federal Work-Study, and unspecified assistantships also available. Support available to part-time students. Financial award application deadline: 3/1; financial award applicants required to submit FAFSA. *Faculty research:* NAFTA, economies of transition, economics of Eastern Europe, artificial intelligence, comparative economic systems. *Total annual research expenditures:* $407,002. *Unit head:* Dr. Thomas Potiowsky, Chair, 503-725-2288, Fax: 503-725-3945, E-mail: potiowskyt@pdx.edu. *Application contact:* Margie Port, Office Coordinator, 503-725-3974, Fax: 503-725-3945, E-mail: mport@pdx.edu.
Website: http://www.pdx.edu/econ/

Roosevelt University, Graduate Division, College of Arts and Sciences, Department of Economics, Chicago, IL 60605. Offers applied economics (MA); economics (MA). Part-time and evening/weekend programs available. *Degree requirements:* For master's, thesis or alternative. *Entrance requirements:* For master's, minimum GPA of 2.7. *Faculty research:* Labor, gender issues, international trade and development, entrepreneurship, political economy and money.

St. Cloud State University, School of Graduate Studies, College of Social Sciences, Department of Economics, Program in Applied Economics, St. Cloud, MN 56301-4498. Offers MS.

San Jose State University, Graduate Studies and Research, College of Social Sciences, Department of Economics, San Jose, CA 95192-0001. Offers applied economics (MA); economics (MA). Part-time programs available. *Degree requirements:* For master's, comprehensive exam, thesis optional. *Entrance requirements:* For master's, GRE, minimum GPA of 3.0. Electronic applications accepted.

Southern Methodist University, Dedman College of Humanities and Sciences, Department of Economics, Dallas, TX 75205. Offers applied economics (MA); applied economics and predictive analytics (MS); economics (PhD); law and economics (MA). Part-time and evening/weekend programs available. Terminal master's awarded for partial completion of doctoral program. *Degree requirements:* For master's, thesis, oral qualifying exam; for doctorate, thesis/dissertation, written exams. *Entrance requirements:* For master's, GRE General Test or GMAT, 12 hours of course work in economics, minimum GPA of 3.0, previous course work in calculus and statistics; for doctorate, GRE General Test, minimum GPA of 3.0; 3 semesters of course work in calculus; 1 semester each of course work in statistics and linear algebra. Additional exam requirements/recommendations for international students: Required—TOEFL (minimum score 550 paper-based). Electronic applications accepted. *Faculty research:* Economic theory, game theory, econometrics, international trade, labor.

Texas Tech University, Graduate School, College of Agricultural Sciences and Natural Resources, Department of Agricultural and Applied Economics, Lubbock, TX 79409-2132. Offers agribusiness (MAB); agricultural and applied economics (MS, PhD); JD/MS. Part-time programs available. *Faculty:* 17 full-time (2 women), 2 part-time/adjunct (0 women). *Students:* 45 full-time (19 women), 9 part-time (3 women); includes 2 minority (both Hispanic/Latino), 22 international. Average age 28. 45 applicants, 80% accepted, 18 enrolled. In 2014, 6 master's, 1 doctorate awarded. Terminal master's awarded for partial completion of doctoral program. *Degree requirements:* For master's, thesis or alternative; for doctorate, comprehensive exam, thesis/dissertation. *Entrance requirements:* For master's and doctorate, GRE General Test, formal approval from departmental committee. Additional exam requirements/recommendations for international students: Required—TOEFL (minimum score 550 paper-based; 79 iBT). *Application deadline:* For fall admission, 6/1 priority date for domestic students, 1/15 priority date for international students; for spring admission, 9/1 priority date for domestic students, 6/15 priority date for international students. Applications are processed on a rolling basis. Application fee: $60. Electronic applications accepted. *Expenses:* Tuition, state resident: full-time $6310; part-time $262.92 per credit hour. Tuition, nonresident: full-time $14,998; part-time $624.92 per credit hour. *Required fees:* $2701; $36.50 per credit. $912.50 per semester. Tuition and fees vary according to course load. *Financial support:* In 2014–15, 38 students received support, including 35 fellowships (averaging $3,516 per year), 20 research assistantships (averaging $18,180 per year); teaching assistantships, institutionally sponsored loans, scholarships/grants, health care benefits, and unspecified assistantships also available. Financial award application deadline: 5/1; financial award applicants required to submit FAFSA. *Faculty research:* Economics of the United States cotton and textile industries, natural resource management in semi-arid climates, commodity policy analysis, international trade in agricultural products, agribusiness analysis. *Total annual research expenditures:* $623,743. *Unit head:* Dr. Phillip N. Johnson, Chair, 806-834-0474, Fax: 806-742-1099, E-mail: phil.johnson@ttu.edu. *Application contact:* Dr. Tom Knight, Graduate Adviser, 806-742-2821, Fax: 806-742-1099, E-mail: tom.knight@ttu.edu.
Website: http://www.aaec.ttu.edu

Thomas Jefferson University, Jefferson School of Population Health, Philadelphia, PA 19107. Offers applied health economics and outcomes research (MS, PhD, Certificate); behavioral health science (PhD); health policy (MS, Certificate); healthcare quality and safety (MS, PhD); healthcare quality and safety management (MS); population health (Certificate); public health (MPH, Certificate). Part-time and evening/weekend programs available. Postbaccalaureate distance learning degree programs offered (no on-campus study). *Faculty:* 9 full-time (5 women), 14 part-time/adjunct (6 women). *Students:* 251 part-time (155 women); includes 60 minority (23 Black or African American, non-Hispanic/Latino; 1 American Indian or Alaska Native, non-Hispanic/Latino; 30 Asian, non-Hispanic/Latino; 4 Hispanic/Latino; 2 Two or more races, non-Hispanic/Latino). 169 applicants, 71% accepted, 66 enrolled. Terminal master's awarded for partial completion of doctoral program. *Degree requirements:* For master's, thesis; for doctorate, comprehensive exam, thesis/dissertation. *Entrance requirements:* For master's, GRE or other graduate entrance exam (MCAT, LSAT, DAT, etc.), two letters of recommendation, curriculum vitae, transcripts from all undergraduate and graduate institutions; for doctorate, GRE (taken within the last 5 years), three letters of recommendation, curriculum vitae, transcripts from all undergraduate and graduate institutions. Additional exam requirements/recommendations for international students: Required—TOEFL. *Application deadline:* For fall admission, 7/1 for domestic and international students; for spring admission, 11/1 for domestic and international students. Applications are processed on a rolling basis. Application fee: $25. Electronic applications accepted. *Financial support:* In 2014–15, 3 students received support. Federal Work-Study and scholarships/grants available. *Faculty research:* Applied health economics and outcomes research, behavioral and health sciences, chronic disease management, health policy, healthcare quality and patient safety, wellness and prevention. *Unit head:* Dr. Caroline Golab, Associate Dean, Academic and Student Affairs, 215-503-8467, Fax: 215-923-6939, E-mail: caroline.golab@jefferson.edu. *Application contact:* April L. Smith, Admissions/Programs Coordinator, 215-503-5305, Fax: 215-923-6939, E-mail: april.smith@jefferson.edu.
Website: http://www.jefferson.edu/population_health/

University of California, Santa Cruz, Division of Graduate Studies, Division of Social Sciences, Program in Applied Economics and Finance, Santa Cruz, CA 95064. Offers MS. *Degree requirements:* For master's, thesis or alternative, project. *Entrance requirements:* For master's, GRE General Test, GRE Subject Test. Additional exam requirements/recommendations for international students: Required—TOEFL (minimum score 550 paper-based; 83 iBT); Recommended—IELTS (minimum score 8). Electronic applications accepted. *Faculty research:* Economic decision-making skills for the design and operation of complex institutional systems.

University of Cincinnati, Graduate School, Carl H. Lindner College of Business, Program in Applied Economics, Cincinnati, OH 45221. Offers MA. Part-time and evening/weekend programs available. *Faculty:* 12 full-time (4 women), 2 part-time/adjunct (1 woman). *Students:* 30 full-time (10 women), 3 part-time (1 woman); includes 3 minority (1 Black or African American, non-Hispanic/Latino; 2 Hispanic/Latino), 13 international. Average age 27. 47 applicants, 70% accepted, 22 enrolled. In 2014, 16 master's awarded. *Degree requirements:* For master's, thesis optional. *Entrance requirements:* For master's, GRE General Test or GMAT, intermediate micro, macro theory, statistics, calculus. Additional exam requirements/recommendations for international students: Required—TOEFL (minimum score 577 paper-based; 90 iBT), IELTS (minimum score 6.5). *Application deadline:* For fall admission, 3/15 priority date for domestic and international students. Applications are processed on a rolling basis. Application fee: $65 ($70 for international students). Electronic applications accepted. *Financial support:* In 2014–15, 13 students received support, including 13 teaching assistantships with full tuition reimbursements available (averaging $4,500 per year); career-related internships or fieldwork, scholarships/grants, tuition waivers (partial), and unspecified assistantships also available. Financial award application deadline: 3/15. *Faculty research:* Econometrics, labor markets, pollution markets, transportation, urban economics. *Unit head:* Dr. David Szymanski, Dean, 513-556-7001, Fax: 513-556-4891, E-mail: david.szymanski@uc.edu. *Application contact:* Dr. Debashis Pal, Academic Director, 513-556-2630, E-mail: debashis.pal@uc.edu.

University of Georgia, College of Agricultural and Environmental Sciences, Department of Agricultural and Applied Economics, Athens, GA 30602. Offers agricultural economics (MAE, MS, PhD); environmental economics (MS). *Degree requirements:* For master's, thesis (MS); for doctorate, thesis/dissertation. *Entrance requirements:* For master's and doctorate, GRE General Test. Electronic applications accepted.

University of Houston, College of Liberal Arts and Social Sciences, Department of Economics, Houston, TX 77204. Offers applied economics (MA); economics (MA, PhD). Terminal master's awarded for partial completion of doctoral program. *Degree requirements:* For master's, thesis optional; for doctorate, comprehensive exam, thesis/dissertation. *Entrance requirements:* For master's and doctorate, GRE General Test, minimum GPA of 3.0, statement of purpose, three letters of recommendation. Additional exam requirements/recommendations for international students: Required—TOEFL (minimum score 550 paper-based; 79 iBT), IELTS (minimum score 6.5). Electronic applications accepted. *Faculty research:* Econometrics, labor economics, international economics.

University of Idaho, College of Graduate Studies, College of Agricultural and Life Sciences, Department of Agricultural Economics and Rural Sociology, Moscow, ID 83844-2334. Offers agricultural economics (MS); applied economics (MS), including agribusiness, agricultural economics, applied economics, natural resources. *Faculty:* 9 full-time. *Students:* 8 full-time, 1 part-time. Average age 27. In 2014, 4 master's awarded. *Entrance requirements:* For master's, minimum GPA of 2.8. *Application deadline:* For fall admission, 8/1 for domestic students; for spring admission, 12/15 for domestic students. Applications are processed on a rolling basis. Application fee: $60. Electronic applications accepted. *Expenses:* Tuition, state resident: full-time $4784; part-time $280.50 per credit hour. Tuition, nonresident: full-time $18,314; part-time $957.50 per credit hour. *Required fees:* $2000; $58.50 per credit hour. Tuition and fees vary according to program. *Financial support:* Research assistantships and teaching assistantships available. Financial award applicants required to submit FAFSA. *Faculty research:* Crops: potatoes, blue grass; livestock: beef, dairy; rural and community development; natural resources and the environment; farm and ranch management. *Unit head:* Dr. Cathy Roheim, Department Head, 208-885-6262, Fax: 208-885-5759, E-mail: cdarby@uidaho.edu. *Application contact:* Sean Scoggin, Graduate Recruitment Coordinator, 208-885-4001, Fax: 208-885-4406, E-mail: graduateadmissions@uidaho.edu.
Website: http://www.cals.uidaho.edu/aers/

University of Illinois at Urbana–Champaign, Graduate College, College of Agricultural, Consumer and Environmental Sciences, Department of Agricultural and Consumer Economics, Champaign, IL 61820. Offers agricultural and applied economics

(MS, PhD). *Students:* 68 full-time (31 women). Application fee: $70 ($90 for international students). *Unit head:* Paul N. Ellinger, Head, 217-333-5503, Fax: 217-333-5538, E-mail: pellinge@illinois.edu. *Application contact:* Pamela S. Splittstoesser, Graduate Studies Assistant, 217-333-1830, Fax: 217-244-7088, E-mail: splttsts@illinois.edu.
Website: http://ace.illinois.edu/

University of Massachusetts Boston, College of Liberal Arts, Program in Applied Economics, Boston, MA 02125-3393. Offers MA. *Expenses:* Tuition, state resident: full-time $2590; part-time $108 per credit. Tuition, nonresident: full-time $9758; part-time $406.50 per credit. Tuition and fees vary according to course load and program. *Unit head:* Dr. Donna Kuizenga, Dean, College of Liberal Arts, 617-287-6500, E-mail: donna.kuizenga@umb.edu. *Application contact:* Peggy Roldan Patel, Graduate Admissions Coordinator, 617-287-6400, Fax: 617-287-6236, E-mail: bos.gadm@dpc.umassp.edu.

University of Michigan, Horace H. Rackham School of Graduate Studies, College of Literature, Science, and the Arts, Department of Economics, Program in Applied Economics, Ann Arbor, MI 48109. Offers AM. Part-time programs available. *Entrance requirements:* For master's, GRE General Test. Additional exam requirements/recommendations for international students: Required—TOEFL (minimum score 600 paper-based). *Faculty research:* Econometric analysis transition, macro.

University of Minnesota, Twin Cities Campus, Graduate School, College of Food, Agricultural and Natural Resource Sciences, Applied Economics Graduate Program, Saint Paul, MN 55108. Offers MS, PhD. Terminal master's awarded for partial completion of doctoral program. *Degree requirements:* For master's, comprehensive exam, thesis; for doctorate, comprehensive exam, thesis/dissertation. *Entrance requirements:* For master's and doctorate, GRE, minimum GPA of 3.0 (preferred). Additional exam requirements/recommendations for international students: Required—TOEFL (minimum score 550 paper-based; 79 iBT), IELTS (minimum score 6.5). Electronic applications accepted. *Faculty research:* Consumer behavior, household and labor, policy analysis and health, production and marketing, resource and environmental, trade and development.

University of Nevada, Reno, Graduate School, College of Agriculture, Biotechnology and Natural Resources, Department of Resource Economics, Reno, NV 89557. Offers MS, PhD. Terminal master's awarded for partial completion of doctoral program. *Degree requirements:* For master's, thesis optional; for doctorate, thesis/dissertation. *Entrance requirements:* For master's, GRE General Test, minimum GPA of 2.75; for doctorate, GRE General Test, minimum GPA of 3.0. Additional exam requirements/recommendations for international students: Required—TOEFL (minimum score 500 paper-based; 61 iBT), IELTS (minimum score 6). Electronic applications accepted. *Faculty research:* Econometrics, environmental valuation, natural resource and environmental policy analysis, public lands management.

University of New Brunswick Fredericton, School of Graduate Studies, Faculty of Arts, Department of Economics, Fredericton, NB E3B 5A3, Canada. Offers applied economics and finance (M Sc); economics (MA). M Sc offered on Saint John campus. *Faculty:* 13 full-time (2 women), 2 part-time/adjunct (0 women). *Students:* 20 full-time (9 women), 11 part-time (5 women). In 2014, 5 master's awarded. *Entrance requirements:* For master's, minimum GPA of 3.0. Additional exam requirements/recommendations for international students: Required—TWE (minimum score 4), TOEFL (minimum score 580 paper-based) or IELTS (minimum score 7). *Application deadline:* For fall admission, 1/31 for domestic and international students; for winter admission, 1/15 for domestic students, 1/15 priority date for international students; for spring admission, 1/31 for domestic and international students. Applications are processed on a rolling basis. Application fee: $50 Canadian dollars. Electronic applications accepted. *Financial support:* Fellowships, research assistantships, teaching assistantships, scholarships/grants, health care benefits, and unspecified assistantships available. Financial award application deadline: 1/31. *Faculty research:* Epidemiology and population health, micro/macro economics, economics of transportation, regional development, health economics, econometrics. *Unit head:* Dr. Yuri Yevdokimov, Director of Graduate Studies, 506-447-3221, Fax: 506-453-4514, E-mail: yuri@unb.ca. *Application contact:* Allison Johnson-Sacobie, Graduate Secretary, 506-453-4828, Fax: 506-453-4514, E-mail: asacobie@unb.ca.
Website: http://go.unb.ca/gradprograms

The University of North Carolina at Greensboro, Graduate School, Bryan School of Business and Economics, Department of Economics, Program in Applied Economics, Greensboro, NC 27412-5001. Offers MA, MA/PhD. *Degree requirements:* For master's, comprehensive exam, thesis or alternative. *Entrance requirements:* For master's, GRE. Additional exam requirements/recommendations for international students: Required—TOEFL. Electronic applications accepted.

University of North Dakota, Graduate School, College of Business and Public Administration, Applied Economics Program, Grand Forks, ND 58202. Offers MSAE. Part-time programs available. Postbaccalaureate distance learning degree programs offered (minimal on-campus study). *Degree requirements:* For master's, comprehensive exam, thesis or alternative. *Entrance requirements:* For master's, GRE General Test. Additional exam requirements/recommendations for international students: Required—TOEFL (minimum score 550 paper-based; 79 iBT), IELTS (minimum score 6.5). Electronic applications accepted.

University of Oklahoma, College of Arts and Sciences, Department of Economics, Norman, OK 73019. Offers applied economics (MA); economics (PhD); managerial economics (MA). *Faculty:* 17 full-time (5 women), 1 part-time/adjunct (0 women). *Students:* 33 full-time (11 women), 41 part-time (7 women); includes 14 minority (6 Black or African American, non-Hispanic/Latino; 1 American Indian or Alaska Native, non-Hispanic/Latino; 3 Asian, non-Hispanic/Latino; 3 Hispanic/Latino; 1 Two or more races, non-Hispanic/Latino), 12 international. Average age 30. 39 applicants, 56% accepted, 12 enrolled. In 2014, 26 master's, 1 doctorate awarded. Terminal master's awarded for partial completion of doctoral program. *Degree requirements:* For master's, comprehensive exam, thesis; for doctorate, 2 foreign languages, comprehensive exam, thesis/dissertation. *Entrance requirements:* For master's, GRE, minimum GPA of 3.0; for doctorate, GRE, minimum GPA of 3.0; intermediate micro and macro economics; calculus I and II. Additional exam requirements/recommendations for international students: Required—TOEFL (minimum score 79 iBT). *Application deadline:* For fall admission, 1/15 for domestic and international students; for spring admission, 9/1 for domestic and international students. Applications are processed on a rolling basis. Application fee: $50 ($100 for international students). Electronic applications accepted. *Expenses:* Tuition, state resident: full-time $4394; part-time $183.10 per credit hour. Tuition, nonresident: full-time $16,970; part-time $707.10 per credit hour. *Required fees:* $2892; $109.95 per credit hour. $126.50 per semester. *Financial support:* In 2014–15, 25 students received support, including 24 teaching assistantships with partial tuition reimbursements available (averaging $14,245 per year); scholarships/grants and unspecified assistantships also available. Financial award application deadline: 6/1; financial award applicants required to submit FAFSA. *Faculty research:* Development economics, growth, industrial organization, international economics, public economics. *Total annual research expenditures:* $203,224. *Unit head:* Dr. Gary Hoover, Professor/Department Chair, 405-325-5857, Fax: 405-325-5842, E-mail: gary.hoover@ou.edu. *Application contact:* Dr. Benjamin Keen, Associate Professor and Graduate Liaison, 405-325-5900, Fax: 405-325-5842, E-mail: ben.keen@ou.edu.
Website: http://cas.ou.edu/economics

University of Pennsylvania, Wharton School, Program in Applied Economics, Philadelphia, PA 19104. Offers PhD.

University of Regina, Faculty of Graduate Studies and Research, Faculty of Arts, Department of Economics, Regina, SK S4S 0A2, Canada. Offers applied economics and policy analysis (MA). Part-time programs available. *Faculty:* 13 full-time (4 women), 6 part-time/adjunct (1 woman). *Students:* 12 full-time (7 women), 5 part-time (1 woman). 45 applicants, 31% accepted. In 2014, 6 master's awarded. *Degree requirements:* For master's, thesis (for some programs), research project. *Entrance requirements:* For master's, writing sample on approved topic. Additional exam requirements/recommendations for international students: Required—TOEFL (minimum score 580 paper-based; 80 iBT), IELTS (minimum score 6.5), PTE (minimum score 59). *Application deadline:* For fall admission, 3/1 for domestic and international students. Application fee: $100. Electronic applications accepted. *Expenses: Tuition, area resident:* Full-time $4900 Canadian dollars; part-time $837.65 Canadian dollars per semester. *International tuition:* $7900 Canadian dollars full-time. *Required fees:* $396 Canadian dollars; $86.90 Canadian dollars per semester. *Financial support:* In 2014–15, 1 fellowship (averaging $6,000 per year), 5 teaching assistantships (averaging $2,427 per year) were awarded; research assistantships and scholarships/grants also available. *Unit head:* Dr. Hafiz Akhand, Department Head, 306-585-4179, Fax: 306-585-4815, E-mail: hafiz.akhand@uregina.ca. *Application contact:* Dr. Stuart Wilson, Acting Graduate Coordinator, 306-337-2230, Fax: 306-585-4815, E-mail: stuart.wilson@uregina.ca.
Website: http://www.uregina.ca/arts/economics

University of Vermont, Graduate College, College of Agriculture and Life Sciences, Department of Community Development and Applied Economics, Burlington, VT 05405. Offers community development and applied economics (MS); public administration (MPA). *Degree requirements:* For master's, thesis. *Entrance requirements:* For master's, GRE General Test. Additional exam requirements/recommendations for international students: Required—TOEFL (minimum score 550 paper-based; 80 iBT). Electronic applications accepted. *Faculty research:* Agricultural production and marketing.

University of Wisconsin–Madison, Graduate School, College of Agricultural and Life Sciences, Department of Agricultural and Applied Economics, Madison, WI 53706. Offers MA, MS, PhD. Part-time programs available. *Degree requirements:* For doctorate, thesis/dissertation, preliminary exams. *Entrance requirements:* For master's and doctorate, GRE General Test. Additional exam requirements/recommendations for international students: Required—TOEFL (minimum score 580 paper-based; 92 iBT). Electronic applications accepted. *Expenses:* Tuition, state resident: full-time $10,723; part-time $745 per credit. Tuition, nonresident: full-time $24,054; part-time $1578 per credit. *Required fees:* $374 per semester. Tuition and fees vary according to course load, program and reciprocity agreements. *Faculty research:* Environmental and resource economics, international development, community economics, energy economics, agricultural technology, food systems, markets and trade.

University of Wyoming, College of Agriculture and Natural Resources, Department of Agricultural and Applied Economics, Laramie, WY 82071. Offers MS. Part-time programs available. *Degree requirements:* For master's, thesis (for some programs). *Entrance requirements:* For master's, GRE General Test, minimum GPA of 3.0. Additional exam requirements/recommendations for international students: Required—TOEFL. Electronic applications accepted. *Faculty research:* Farm management, agricultural markets, water economics, community development, agricultural business.

Utah State University, School of Graduate Studies, College of Business and College of Agriculture, Department of Economics, Program in Applied Economics, Logan, UT 84322. Offers MS. Part-time programs available. *Degree requirements:* For master's, thesis optional. *Entrance requirements:* For master's, GRE General Test, minimum GPA of 3.0.

Virginia Polytechnic Institute and State University, Graduate School, College of Agriculture and Life Sciences, Blacksburg, VA 24061. Offers agricultural and applied economics (MS); agricultural and life sciences (MS); animal and poultry science (MS, PhD); crop and soil environmental sciences (MS, PhD); dairy science (MS); entomology (PhD); horticulture (MS, PhD); human nutrition, foods and exercise (MS, PhD); life sciences (MS, PhD); plant pathology, physiology and weed science (PhD). *Faculty:* 242 full-time (69 women), 1 (woman) part-time/adjunct. *Students:* 400 full-time (225 women), 100 part-time (64 women); includes 60 minority (25 Black or African American, non-Hispanic/Latino; 16 Asian, non-Hispanic/Latino; 8 Hispanic/Latino; 11 Two or more races, non-Hispanic/Latino), 121 international. Average age 29. 444 applicants, 37% accepted, 132 enrolled. In 2014, 70 master's, 46 doctorates awarded. *Degree requirements:* For master's, comprehensive exam (for some programs), thesis (for some programs); for doctorate, comprehensive exam (for some programs), thesis/dissertation (for some programs). *Entrance requirements:* For master's and doctorate, GRE/GMAT (may vary by department). Additional exam requirements/recommendations for international students: Required—TOEFL (minimum score 550 paper-based). *Application deadline:* For fall admission, 8/1 for domestic students, 4/1 for international students; for spring admission, 1/1 for domestic students, 9/1 for international students. Applications are processed on a rolling basis. Application fee: $75. Electronic applications accepted. *Expenses:* Tuition, state resident: full-time $11,656; part-time $647.50 per credit hour. Tuition, nonresident: full-time $23,351; part-time $1297.25 per credit hour. *Required fees:* $2533; $465.75 per semester. Tuition and fees vary according to course load, campus/location and program. *Financial support:* In 2014–15, 274 research assistantships with full tuition reimbursements (averaging $21,739 per year), 91 teaching assistantships with full tuition reimbursements (averaging $22,005 per year) were awarded. Financial award application deadline: 3/1; financial award applicants required to submit FAFSA. *Total annual research expenditures:* $42.1 million. *Unit head:* Dr. Alan L. Grant, Dean, 540-231-4152, Fax: 540-231-4163, E-mail: algrant@vt.edu. *Application contact:* Sheila Norman, Administrative Assistant, 540-231-4152, Fax: 540-231-4163, E-mail: snorman@vt.edu.
Website: http://www.cals.vt.edu/

Western Kentucky University, Graduate Studies, Gordon Ford College of Business, Program in Applied Economics, Bowling Green, KY 42101. Offers MA.

★ **Western Michigan University,** Graduate College, College of Arts and Sciences, Department of Economics, Kalamazoo, MI 49008. Offers applied economics (MA, PhD). *Degree requirements:* For master's, thesis; for doctorate, thesis/dissertation. *Application deadline:* For fall admission, 2/15 for domestic students. *Financial support:* Application deadline: 2/15. *Application contact:* Admissions and Orientation, 269-387-2000, Fax: 269-387-2096.

See Display on page 849 and Close-Up on page 853.

Wright State University, School of Graduate Studies, Raj Soin College of Business, Department of Economics, Program in Social and Applied Economics, Dayton, OH 45435. Offers MS.

Economic Development

Albany State University, College of Arts and Humanities, Albany, GA 31705-2717. Offers English education (M Ed); public administration (MPA), including community and economic development administration, criminal justice administration, general administration, health administration and policy, human resources management, public policy, water resources management; social work (MSW). Part-time programs available. *Degree requirements:* For master's, comprehensive exam, professional portfolio (for MPA), internship, capstone report. *Entrance requirements:* For master's, GRE, MAT, minimum GPA of 3.0, official transcript, pre-medical record/certificate of immunization, letters of reference. Electronic applications accepted. *Faculty research:* HIV prevention for minority students.

The American University in Cairo, School of Business, New Cairo, Egypt. Offers business administration (MBA, Diploma); economics (MA); economics in international development (MA); finance (MS). Part-time programs available. *Faculty:* 19 full-time (3 women), 2 part-time/adjunct (0 women). *Students:* 69 full-time (24 women), 88 part-time (43 women), 3 international. 221 applicants, 47% accepted, 48 enrolled. In 2014, 90 master's awarded. *Degree requirements:* For master's, comprehensive exam (for some programs), thesis (for some programs). *Entrance requirements:* For master's, GMAT, GRE. Additional exam requirements/recommendations for international students: Required—TOEFL (minimum score 450 paper-based; 45 iBT), IELTS (minimum score 5). *Application deadline:* For fall admission, 2/1 priority date for domestic and international students; for spring admission, 10/1 priority date for domestic and international students. Applications are processed on a rolling basis. Application fee: $52. Electronic applications accepted. Tuition and fees vary according to course load and program. *Financial support:* Fellowships with partial tuition reimbursements, scholarships/grants, and tuition waivers (partial) available. Financial award application deadline: 7/1; financial award applicants required to submit CSS PROFILE. *Faculty research:* Marketing and quality management, banking operations management, economics, finance. *Unit head:* Dr. AbdelKrim Seghir, Dean, 20-22615-3290, E-mail: kseghir@aucegypt.edu. *Application contact:* Maha Hegazi, Assistant Director or Graduate Admissions, 20-22615-1462, E-mail: mahahegazi@aucegypt.edu.
Website: http://www.aucegypt.edu/Business/Pages/default.aspx

The Catholic University of America, School of Business and Economics, Washington, DC 20064. Offers accounting (MS); business analysis (MS); integral economic development management (MA); integral economic development policy (MA); international political economics (MA). Part-time programs available. *Faculty:* 21 full-time (7 women), 25 part-time/adjunct (4 women). *Students:* 56 full-time (37 women), 13 part-time (6 women); includes 23 minority (11 Black or African American, non-Hispanic/Latino; 5 Asian, non-Hispanic/Latino; 7 Hispanic/Latino), 21 international. Average age 27. 92 applicants, 64% accepted, 40 enrolled. In 2014, 30 master's awarded. *Degree requirements:* For master's, comprehensive exam. *Entrance requirements:* For master's, GRE General Test, statement of purpose, official copies of academic transcripts, three letters of recommendation. Additional exam requirements/recommendations for international students: Required—TOEFL (minimum score 580 paper-based). *Application deadline:* For fall admission, 7/15 priority date for domestic students, 7/1 for international students; for spring admission, 11/15 priority date for domestic students, 11/1 for international students. Applications are processed on a rolling basis. Application fee: $55. Electronic applications accepted. *Expenses: Tuition:* Full-time $40,200; part-time $1600 per credit hour. *Required fees:* $400; $195 per semester. One-time fee: $425. *Financial support:* Fellowships, research assistantships, teaching assistantships, Federal Work-Study, scholarships/grants, tuition waivers (full and partial), and unspecified assistantships available. Financial award application deadline: 2/1; financial award applicants required to submit FAFSA. *Faculty research:* Integrity of the marketing process, economics of energy and the environment, emerging markets, social change, international finance and economic development. *Total annual research expenditures:* $105,784. *Unit head:* Dr. Andrew V. Abela, Chair, 202-319-5235, Fax: 202-319-4426, E-mail: abela@cua.edu. *Application contact:* Director of Graduate Admissions, 202-319-5057, Fax: 202-319-6533, E-mail: cua-admissions@cua.edu.
Website: http://business.cua.edu/

Claremont Graduate University, Graduate Programs, School of Social Science, Policy and Evaluation, Department of Economics, Claremont, CA 91711-6160. Offers business and financial economics (MA, PhD); economic development (Certificate); international and development economics (PhD); international economics policy and development (MA); international money and finance (PhD); neuroeconomics and behavioral economics (PhD); political economy and public policy (MA); public choice and public economics (PhD); MBA/PhD. Part-time programs available. *Faculty:* 9 full-time (2 women), 1 part-time/adjunct (0 women). *Students:* 107 full-time (33 women), 35 part-time (15 women); includes 22 minority (3 Black or African American, non-Hispanic/Latino; 11 Asian, non-Hispanic/Latino; 6 Hispanic/Latino; 2 Two or more races, non-Hispanic/Latino), 73 international. Average age 32. In 2014, 15 master's, 11 doctorates awarded. *Entrance requirements:* For master's and doctorate, GRE General Test or GMAT. Additional exam requirements/recommendations for international students: Required—TOEFL (minimum score 550 paper-based; 80 iBT). *Application deadline:* For fall admission, 2/1 priority date for domestic and international students. Applications are processed on a rolling basis. Application fee: $80. Electronic applications accepted. *Expenses: Tuition:* Full-time $41,784; part-time $1741 per credit. *Required fees:* $600; $300 per semester. *Financial support:* Fellowships, research assistantships, teaching assistantships, Federal Work-Study, institutionally sponsored loans, and scholarships/grants available. Support available to part-time students. Financial award application deadline: 2/15; financial award applicants required to submit FAFSA. *Faculty research:* International and financial economics, law and economics, regulation, public choice economics. *Unit head:* Heather Campbell, Chair, 909-621-8689, E-mail: heather.campbell@cgu.edu. *Application contact:* Annekah Hall, Assistant Director of Admissions, 909-607-3371, E-mail: annekah.hall@cgu.edu.
Website: http://www.cgu.edu/pages/466.asp

Cleveland State University, College of Graduate Studies, Maxine Goodman Levin College of Urban Affairs, Program in Environmental Studies, Cleveland, OH 44115. Offers environmental nonprofit management (MAES); environmental planning (MAES); geographic information systems (Certificate); policy and administration (MAES); sustainable economic development (MAES); urban economic development (Certificate); urban real estate development and finance (Certificate); JD/MAES. Part-time and evening/weekend programs available. *Faculty:* 23 full-time (11 women), 23 part-time/adjunct (6 women). *Students:* 2 full-time (both women), 5 part-time (3 women); includes 1 minority (Hispanic/Latino). Average age 34. 4 applicants, 25% accepted. In 2014, 4 master's awarded. *Degree requirements:* For master's, thesis or alternative, exit project. *Entrance requirements:* For master's, GRE General Test (minimum score: verbal and quantitative combined 40th percentile, analytical writing 4.0), minimum GPA of 3.0. Additional exam requirements/recommendations for international students: Required—

TOEFL (minimum score 525 paper-based; 65 iBT), IELTS, or ITEP. *Application deadline:* For fall admission, 7/15 priority date for domestic students, 5/15 for international students; for spring admission, 11/1 for international students. Applications are processed on a rolling basis. Application fee: $30. Electronic applications accepted. *Expenses:* Expenses: $9,615 full-time, in-state tuition and fees. *Financial support:* In 2014–15, 4 students received support, including 3 research assistantships with full and partial tuition reimbursements available (averaging $7,200 per year); career-related internships or fieldwork, scholarships/grants, traineeships, and unspecified assistantships also available. Support available to part-time students. Financial award application deadline: 3/1; financial award applicants required to submit FAFSA. *Faculty research:* Environmental policy and administration, environmental planning, geographic information systems (GIS), urban sustainability planning and management, energy policy, land re-use. *Unit head:* Dr. Sanda Kaufman, Director, 216-687-2367, Fax: 216-687-9342, E-mail: s.kaufman@csuohio.edu. *Application contact:* David Arrighi, Graduate Academic Advisor, 216-523-7522, Fax: 216-687-5398, E-mail: urbanprograms@csuohio.edu.
Website: http://urban.csuohio.edu/academics/graduate/maes/

Cleveland State University, College of Graduate Studies, Maxine Goodman Levin College of Urban Affairs, Program in Public Administration, Cleveland, OH 44115. Offers city management (MPA); economic development (MPA); healthcare administration (MPA); local and urban management (Certificate); non-profit management (MPA, Certificate); public financial management (MPA); public management (MPA); urban economic development (Certificate); JD/MPA. *Accreditation:* NASPAA. Part-time and evening/weekend programs available. *Faculty:* 23 full-time (11 women), 23 part-time/adjunct (6 women). *Students:* 16 full-time (11 women), 64 part-time (40 women); includes 23 minority (19 Black or African American, non-Hispanic/Latino; 3 Hispanic/Latino; 1 Two or more races, non-Hispanic/Latino), 3 international. Average age 36. 67 applicants, 51% accepted, 13 enrolled. In 2014, 41 master's awarded. *Degree requirements:* For master's, thesis or alternative, capstone course. *Entrance requirements:* For master's, GRE General Test (minimum scores in 40th percentile verbal and quantitative, 4.0 writing), minimum GPA of 3.0. Additional exam requirements/recommendations for international students: Required—TOEFL (minimum score 525 paper-based; 65 iBT), IELTS, or ITEP. *Application deadline:* For fall admission, 7/15 priority date for domestic students, 5/15 for international students; for spring admission, 11/1 for international students. Applications are processed on a rolling basis. Application fee: $30. Electronic applications accepted. *Expenses:* Expenses: $9,615 full-time, in-state tuition and fees. *Financial support:* In 2014–15, 16 students received support, including 4 research assistantships with full and partial tuition reimbursements available (averaging $7,200 per year), 3 teaching assistantships with full and partial tuition reimbursements available (averaging $2,400 per year); career-related internships or fieldwork, scholarships/grants, traineeships, and unspecified assistantships also available. Support available to part-time students. Financial award application deadline: 3/1; financial award applicants required to submit FAFSA. *Faculty research:* City management, nonprofit management, health care administration, public management, economic development. *Unit head:* Dr. Nicholas Zingale, Director, 216-802-3398, Fax: 216-687-9342, E-mail: n.zingale@csuohio.edu. *Application contact:* David Arrighi, Graduate Academic Advisor, 216-523-7522, Fax: 216-687-5398, E-mail: urbanprograms@csuohio.edu.
Website: http://urban.csuohio.edu/academics/graduate/mpa/

Cleveland State University, College of Graduate Studies, Maxine Goodman Levin College of Urban Affairs, Program in Urban Planning, Design, and Development, Cleveland, OH 44115. Offers economic development (MUPDD); environmental sustainability (MUPDD); geographic information systems (MUPDD, Certificate); historic preservation (MUPDD); housing and neighborhood development (MUPDD); urban economic development (Certificate); urban real estate development and finance (MUPDD, Certificate); JD/MUPDD. *Accreditation:* ACSP. Part-time and evening/weekend programs available. *Faculty:* 23 full-time (11 women), 23 part-time/adjunct (6 women). *Students:* 11 full-time (5 women), 25 part-time (10 women); includes 8 minority (2 Black or African American, non-Hispanic/Latino; 1 Asian, non-Hispanic/Latino; 2 Hispanic/Latino; 3 Two or more races, non-Hispanic/Latino), 3 international. Average age 38. 48 applicants, 56% accepted, 5 enrolled. In 2014, 16 master's awarded. *Degree requirements:* For master's, thesis or alternative, planning studio. *Entrance requirements:* For master's, GRE General Test (minimum score: 50th percentile combined verbal and quantitative, 4.0 analytical writing), minimum GPA of 3.0. Additional exam requirements/recommendations for international students: Required—TOEFL (minimum score 525 paper-based; 65 iBT), IELTS, or ITEP. *Application deadline:* For fall admission, 7/15 priority date for domestic students, 5/15 for international students; for spring admission, 11/1 for international students. Applications are processed on a rolling basis. Application fee: $30. Electronic applications accepted. *Expenses:* Expenses: $9,615 full-time, in-state tuition and fees. *Financial support:* In 2014–15, 10 students received support, including 7 research assistantships with full and partial tuition reimbursements available (averaging $5,600 per year), 2 teaching assistantships with full and partial tuition reimbursements available (averaging $2,000 per year); career-related internships or fieldwork, Federal Work-Study, scholarships/grants, tuition waivers, and unspecified assistantships also available. Support available to part-time students. Financial award application deadline: 3/1; financial award applicants required to submit FAFSA. *Faculty research:* Housing and neighborhood development, urban housing policy, environmental sustainability, economic development, GIS and planning decision support. *Unit head:* Dr. Dennis Keating, Director, 216-687-2298, Fax: 216-687-2013, E-mail: w.keating@csuohio.edu. *Application contact:* David Arrighi, Graduate Academic Advisor, 216-523-7522, Fax: 216-687-5398, E-mail: urbanprograms@csuohio.edu.
Website: http://urban.csuohio.edu/academics/graduate/mupdd/

Cleveland State University, College of Graduate Studies, Maxine Goodman Levin College of Urban Affairs, Program in Urban Studies, Cleveland, OH 44115. Offers community and neighborhood development (MS); economic development (MS); law and public policy (MS); public finance (MS); urban economic development (Certificate); urban policy analysis (MS); urban real estate development (MS); urban real estate development and finance (Certificate). Part-time and evening/weekend programs available. *Faculty:* 23 full-time (11 women), 23 part-time/adjunct (6 women). *Students:* 5 full-time (1 woman), 8 part-time (2 women); includes 1 minority (Black or African American, non-Hispanic/Latino). Average age 34. 21 applicants, 29% accepted, 4 enrolled. In 2014, 4 master's awarded. *Degree requirements:* For master's, thesis or alternative, exit project. *Entrance requirements:* For master's, GRE General Test (minimum score: verbal and quantitative combined 40th percentile, analytical writing 4.0), minimum GPA of 3.0. Additional exam requirements/recommendations for international students: Required—TOEFL (minimum score 525 paper-based; 65 iBT),

IELTS, or ITEP. *Application deadline:* For fall admission, 1/15 priority date for domestic students, 1/15 for international students. Applications are processed on a rolling basis. Application fee: $30. Electronic applications accepted. *Expenses:* Expenses: $9,615 full-time, in-state tuition and fees. *Financial support:* In 2014–15, 4 students received support, including 3 research assistantships with full and partial tuition reimbursements available (averaging $7,200 per year), 2 teaching assistantships with full and partial tuition reimbursements available (averaging $4,800 per year); career-related internships or fieldwork, scholarships/grants, traineeships, and unspecified assistantships also available. Support available to part-time students. Financial award application deadline: 3/1; financial award applicants required to submit FAFSA. *Faculty research:* Environmental issues, economic development, urban and public policy, public management. *Unit head:* Dr. Brian Mikelbank, Director, 216-875-9980, Fax: 216-687-9342, E-mail: b.mikelbank@csuohio.edu. *Application contact:* David Arrighi, Graduate Academic Advisor, 216-523-7522, Fax: 216-687-5398, E-mail: urbanprograms@csuohio.edu.
Website: http://urban.csuohio.edu/academics/graduate/msus/

Concordia University, School of Graduate Studies, Faculty of Arts and Science, School of Community and Public Affairs, Montréal, QC H3G 1M8, Canada. Offers community economic development (Diploma).

Cornell University, Graduate School, Graduate Fields of Agriculture and Life Sciences, Field of Applied Economics and Management, Ithaca, NY 14853-0001. Offers agricultural finance (MS, PhD); applied econometrics and qualitative analysis (MS, PhD); economics of development (MS, PhD); environmental economics (MS, PhD); environmental management (MPS); farm management and production economics (MS, PhD); marketing and food distribution (MS, PhD); public policy analysis (MS, PhD); resource economics (PhD). *Entrance requirements:* For master's and doctorate, GRE. Additional exam requirements/recommendations for international students: Required—TOEFL.

Cornell University, Graduate School, Graduate Fields of Architecture, Art and Planning, Field of City and Regional Planning, Ithaca, NY 14853-0001. Offers city and regional planning (MRP, PhD); environmental planning and design (MRP, PhD); historic preservation planning (MA); international development planning (MRP, PhD); planning theory and systems analysis (MRP, PhD); regional economics and development planning (MRP, PhD); regional science (MRP, PhD); social and health systems planning (MRP, PhD); urban and regional theory (MRP, PhD); urban planning history (MRP, PhD). *Accreditation:* ACSP (one or more programs are accredited). *Degree requirements:* For master's, thesis (MA); for doctorate, comprehensive exam, thesis/dissertation. *Entrance requirements:* For master's and doctorate, GRE General Test, 2 letters of recommendation. Additional exam requirements/recommendations for international students: Required—TOEFL (minimum score 600 paper-based; 77 iBT). Electronic applications accepted. *Faculty research:* Land use planning, economic development, international development, historic preservation, community development.

Cornell University, Graduate School, Graduate Fields of Arts and Sciences, Field of Economics, Ithaca, NY 14853-0001. Offers applied economics (PhD); basic analytical economics (PhD); econometrics and economic statistics (PhD); economic development and planning (PhD); economic theory (PhD); industrial organization and control (PhD); international economics (PhD); labor economics (PhD); monetary and macro economics (PhD); public finance (PhD). *Degree requirements:* For doctorate, comprehensive exam, thesis/dissertation. *Entrance requirements:* For doctorate, GRE General Test, 3 letters of recommendation. Additional exam requirements/recommendations for international students: Required—TOEFL (minimum score 550 paper-based; 77 iBT). Electronic applications accepted. *Faculty research:* Learning and games, economics of education, political economy, transfer payments, time series and nonparametrics.

East Carolina University, Graduate School, Thomas Harriot College of Arts and Sciences, Department of Geography, Planning, and Environment, Greenville, NC 27858-4353. Offers economic development (Certificate); geographic information science and technology (Certificate); geography (MA), including geography, planning, rural development. Part-time and evening/weekend programs available. *Degree requirements:* For master's, one foreign language, comprehensive exam, thesis optional. *Entrance requirements:* For master's, GRE General Test. Additional exam requirements/recommendations for international students: Required—TOEFL. *Expenses:* Tuition, state resident: full-time $4223. Tuition, nonresident: full-time $16,540. *Required fees:* $2184.

Eastern University, School of Leadership and Development, St. Davids, PA 19087-3696. Offers economic development (MBA), including international development, urban development (MA, MBA); international development (MA), including global development, urban development (MA, MBA); nonprofit management (MS); organizational leadership (MA); M Div/MBA. Part-time and evening/weekend programs available. Postbaccalaureate distance learning degree programs offered (minimal on-campus study). *Faculty:* 6 full-time (3 women), 19 part-time/adjunct (8 women). *Students:* 112 full-time (62 women), 49 part-time (27 women); includes 36 minority (19 Black or African American, non-Hispanic/Latino; 2 American Indian or Alaska Native, non-Hispanic/Latino; 5 Asian, non-Hispanic/Latino; 7 Hispanic/Latino; 1 Native Hawaiian or other Pacific Islander, non-Hispanic/Latino; 2 Two or more races, non-Hispanic/Latino), 15 international. Average age 33. 62 applicants, 90% accepted, 46 enrolled. In 2014, 106 master's awarded. *Degree requirements:* For master's, thesis (for some programs). *Entrance requirements:* For master's, GMAT (for MBA), minimum GPA of 2.5. Additional exam requirements/recommendations for international students: Required—TOEFL (minimum score 550 paper-based; 79 iBT). *Application deadline:* For fall admission, 8/14 for domestic students. Applications are processed on a rolling basis. Application fee: $35. Application fee is waived when completed online. *Expenses:* Expenses: Contact institution. *Financial support:* In 2014–15, 131 students received support, including 3 fellowships with partial tuition reimbursements available (averaging $2,500 per year), 7 research assistantships with partial tuition reimbursements available (averaging $1,500 per year); scholarships/grants and unspecified assistantships also available. Financial award application deadline: 3/15; financial award applicants required to submit FAFSA. *Faculty research:* Micro-level economic development, China welfare and economic development, macroethics, micro- and macro-level economic development in transitional economics, organizational effectiveness. *Unit head:* Beth Birmingham, Chair, 610-341-4380. *Application contact:* Lindsey Perry, Enrollment Counselor, 484-581-1311, Fax: 484-581-1276, E-mail: lperry@eastern.edu.
Website: http://www.eastern.edu/academics/programs/school-leadership-and-development

East Tennessee State University, School of Graduate Studies, College of Arts and Sciences, Department of Political Science, International Affairs and Public Administration, Johnson City, TN 37614. Offers economic development (Postbaccalaureate Certificate); not-for-profit administration (MPA); planning and development (MPA); public financial management (MPA); urban planning (Postbaccalaureate Certificate). Part-time programs available. *Faculty:* 7 full-time (2 women), 1 part-time/adjunct (0 women). *Students:* 19 full-time (5 women), 9 part-time (4 women); includes 3 minority (2 Black or African American, non-Hispanic/Latino; 1 Hispanic/Latino), 6 international. Average age 29. 48 applicants, 33% accepted, 10 enrolled. In 2014, 7 master's, 1 other advanced degree awarded. *Degree requirements:*

For master's, internship. *Entrance requirements:* For master's, GRE General Test, three letters of recommendation; for Postbaccalaureate Certificate, GRE General Test. Additional exam requirements/recommendations for international students: Required—TOEFL (minimum score 550 paper-based; 79 iBT). *Application deadline:* For fall admission, 6/1 for domestic students, 4/29 for international students; for spring admission, 11/1 for domestic students, 9/30 for international students. Application fee: $35 ($45 for international students). Electronic applications accepted. *Financial support:* In 2014–15, 16 students received support, including 16 research assistantships with full tuition reimbursements available (averaging $6,000 per year), 4 teaching assistantships with full tuition reimbursements available (averaging $6,000 per year); career-related internships or fieldwork, institutionally sponsored loans, scholarships/grants, and unspecified assistantships also available. Financial award application deadline: 7/1; financial award applicants required to submit FAFSA. *Faculty research:* Labor issues, presidency, public law in American politics, East Asian politics, European politics, Middle Eastern politics, development in comparative politics, international political economy, international relations, world politics in international affairs. *Unit head:* Dr. Andrew Battista, Chair, 423-439-4217, Fax: 423-439-4348, E-mail: battista@etsu.edu. *Application contact:* Angela Edwards, Graduate Specialist, 423-439-4703, Fax: 423-439-5624, E-mail: edwardag@etsu.edu.
Website: http://www.etsu.edu/cas/polisci/

Florida Atlantic University, College of Design and Social Inquiry, School of Urban and Regional Planning, Boca Raton, FL 33431-0991. Offers economic development and tourism (Certificate); environmental planning (Certificate); sustainable community planning (Certificate); urban and regional planning (MURP); visual planning technology (Certificate). *Accreditation:* ACSP. Part-time and evening/weekend programs available. *Entrance requirements:* For master's, GRE General Test, minimum GPA of 3.0. Additional exam requirements/recommendations for international students: Required—TOEFL (minimum score 500 paper-based; 61 iBT), IELTS (minimum score 6). *Expenses:* Tuition, state resident: full-time $7396; part-time $369.82 per credit hour. Tuition, nonresident: full-time $19,392; part-time $1024.81 per credit hour. Tuition and fees vary according to course load. *Faculty research:* Growth management, urban design, computer applications/geographical information systems, environmental planning.

Fordham University, Graduate School of Arts and Sciences, Program in International Political Economy and Development, New York, NY 10458. Offers MA, Certificate. Part-time and evening/weekend programs available. *Students:* 33 full-time (17 women), 16 part-time (6 women); includes 3 minority (2 Asian, non-Hispanic/Latino; 1 Hispanic/Latino), 13 international. Average age 27. 181 applicants, 52% accepted, 24 enrolled. In 2014, 29 master's, 6 other advanced degrees awarded. *Degree requirements:* For master's, comprehensive exam. *Entrance requirements:* For master's, GRE General Test. Additional exam requirements/recommendations for international students: Required—TOEFL (minimum score 600 paper-based). *Application deadline:* For fall admission, 1/4 priority date for domestic students; for spring admission, 11/1 for domestic students. Application fee: $70. Electronic applications accepted. *Financial support:* In 2014–15, 16 students received support, including 2 fellowships with full and partial tuition reimbursements available (averaging $11,965 per year), 16 research assistantships with full and partial tuition reimbursements available (averaging $16,050 per year); career-related internships or fieldwork, institutionally sponsored loans, tuition waivers (full and partial), and unspecified assistantships also available. Financial award application deadline: 1/4; financial award applicants required to submit FAFSA. *Faculty research:* International economics, comparative international politics, international banking and finance, international development, emerging markets and country risk analysis. *Unit head:* Dr. Henry Schwalbenberg, Chair, 718-817-3866, Fax: 718-817-3518. *Application contact:* Bernadette Valentino-Morrison, Director of Graduate Admissions, 718-817-4419, Fax: 718-817-3566, E-mail: valentinomor@fordham.edu.

Georgetown University, Graduate School of Arts and Sciences, Department of Economics, Washington, DC 20057. Offers econometrics (PhD); economic development (PhD); economic theory (PhD); industrial organization (PhD); international macro and finance (PhD); international trade (PhD); labor economics (PhD); macroeconomics (PhD); public economics and political economy (PhD); MA/PhD; MS/MA. *Degree requirements:* For doctorate, comprehensive exam, thesis/dissertation. *Entrance requirements:* For doctorate, GRE General Test. Additional exam requirements/recommendations for international students: Required—TOEFL. *Faculty research:* International economics, economic development.

Georgia Institute of Technology, Graduate Studies, College of Architecture, School of City and Regional Planning, Atlanta, GA 30332-0001. Offers city and regional planning (PhD); economic development (MCRP); environmental planning and management (MCRP); geographic information systems (MCRP); land and community development (MCRP); land use planning (MCRP); transportation (MCRP); urban design (MCRP); MCP/MSCE. *Accreditation:* ACSP. *Degree requirements:* For master's, thesis, internship. *Entrance requirements:* For master's, GRE General Test, minimum GPA of 2.7. Additional exam requirements/recommendations for international students: Required—TOEFL. Electronic applications accepted. *Expenses:* Tuition, state resident: full-time $12,344; part-time $515 per credit hour. Tuition, nonresident: full-time $27,600; part-time $1150 per credit hour. *Required fees:* $1196 per term. Part-time tuition and fees vary according to course load.

Georgia State University, Andrew Young School of Policy Studies, Department of Public Management and Policy, Atlanta, GA 30303. Offers criminal justice (MPA); disaster management (Certificate); disaster policy (MPA); environmental policy (PhD); health policy (PhD); management and finance (MPA); nonprofit management (MPA, Certificate); nonprofit policy (MPA); planning and economic development (MPP, Certificate); policy analysis and evaluation (MPA), including planning and economic development; public and nonprofit management (PhD); public finance and budgeting (PhD), including science and technology policy, urban and regional economic development; public finance policy (MPA), including social policy; public health (MPA). *Accreditation:* NASPAA (one or more programs are accredited). Part-time programs available. *Faculty:* 14 full-time (7 women). *Students:* 136 full-time (80 women), 85 part-time (47 women); includes 81 minority (60 Black or African American, non-Hispanic/Latino; 7 Asian, non-Hispanic/Latino; 11 Hispanic/Latino; 3 Two or more races, non-Hispanic/Latino), 25 international. Average age 30. 269 applicants, 59% accepted, 64 enrolled. In 2014, 80 master's, 7 other advanced degrees awarded. Terminal master's awarded for partial completion of doctoral program. *Degree requirements:* For master's, thesis optional; for doctorate, comprehensive exam, thesis/dissertation. *Entrance requirements:* For master's and doctorate, GRE. Additional exam requirements/recommendations for international students: Required—TOEFL (minimum score 603 paper-based; 100 iBT) or IELTS (minimum score 7). *Application deadline:* For fall admission, 2/15 for domestic and international students; for spring admission, 10/1 for domestic and international students. Application fee: $50. Electronic applications accepted. *Expenses:* Tuition, state resident: full-time $6516; part-time $362 per credit hour. Tuition, nonresident: full-time $22,014; part-time $1223 per credit hour. *Required fees:* $2128 per semester. Tuition and fees vary according to course load and program. *Financial support:* In 2014–15, fellowships (averaging $8,194 per year), research assistantships (averaging $8,068 per year), teaching assistantships (averaging $3,600

per year) were awarded; institutionally sponsored loans, scholarships/grants, health care benefits, and unspecified assistantships also available. Financial award application deadline: 2/1. *Faculty research:* Public budgeting and finance, public management, nonprofit management, performance measurement and management, urban development. *Unit head:* Dr. Gregory Burr Lewis, Chair and Professor, 404-413-0114, Fax: 404-413-0104, E-mail: glewis@gsu.edu. *Application contact:* Charisma Parker, Admissions Coordinator, 404-413-0030, Fax: 404-413-0023, E-mail: cparker28@gsu.edu.
Website: http://aysps.gsu.edu/pmap/

Indiana University Bloomington, School of Public and Environmental Affairs, Public Affairs Programs, Bloomington, IN 47405. Offers economic development (MPA); energy (MPA); environmental policy (PhD); environmental policy and natural resource management (MPA); information systems (MPA); international development (MPA); local government management (MPA); nonprofit management (MPA, Certificate); policy analysis (MPA); public budgeting and financial management (Certificate); public finance (PhD); public financial administration (MPA); public management (MPA, PhD, Certificate); public policy analysis (PhD); social entrepreneurship (Certificate); specialized public affairs (MPA); sustainability and sustainable development (MPA); JD/MPA; MPA/MA; MPA/MIS; MPA/MLS; MSES/MPA. *Accreditation:* NASPAA (one or more programs are accredited). Part-time programs available. *Degree requirements:* For master's, capstone, internship; for doctorate, comprehensive exam, thesis/dissertation. *Entrance requirements:* For master's, GRE General Test or GMAT, official transcripts, 3 letters of recommendation, resume, personal statement; for doctorate, GRE General Test, official transcripts, 3 letters of recommendation, statement of purpose. Additional exam requirements/recommendations for international students: Required—TOEFL (minimum score 600 paper-based; 96 iBT); Recommended—IELTS (minimum score 7). Electronic applications accepted. *Faculty research:* International development, environmental policy and resource management, policy analysis, public finance, public management, urban management, nonprofit management, energy policy, social policy, public finance.

New Mexico State University, College of Business, Department of Economics, Applied Statistics and International Business, Las Cruces, NM 88003. Offers applied statistics (MS); economic development (DED); economics (MA). Part-time programs available. *Faculty:* 19 full-time (7 women). *Students:* 46 full-time (17 women), 27 part-time (15 women); includes 28 minority (2 Black or African American, non-Hispanic/Latino; 3 Asian, non-Hispanic/Latino; 23 Hispanic/Latino), 28 international. Average age 34. 80 applicants, 53% accepted, 20 enrolled. In 2014, 19 master's, 2 doctorates, 12 other advanced degrees awarded. Terminal master's awarded for partial completion of doctoral program. *Degree requirements:* For master's, comprehensive exam, thesis or alternative; for doctorate, comprehensive exam, thesis/dissertation, internship. *Entrance requirements:* For master's, minimum GPA of 3.0; for doctorate, appropriate master's degree, minimum GPA of 3.0. Additional exam requirements/recommendations for international students: Required—TOEFL (minimum score 550 paper-based; 79 iBT), IELTS (minimum score 6.5). *Application deadline:* For fall admission, 3/1 priority date for domestic and international students. Applications are processed on a rolling basis. Application fee: $40 ($50 for international students). Electronic applications accepted. *Expenses:* Tuition, state resident: full-time $3969; part-time $220.50 per credit hour. Tuition, nonresident: full-time $13,838; part-time $768.80 per credit hour. *Required fees:* $853; $47.40 per credit hour. *Financial support:* In 2014–15, 47 students received support, including 6 research assistantships (averaging $12,398 per year), 20 teaching assistantships (averaging $12,479 per year); career-related internships or fieldwork, Federal Work-Study, scholarships/grants, traineeships, health care benefits, and unspecified assistantships also available. Support available to part-time students. Financial award application deadline: 3/1. *Faculty research:* Public utilities, environment, linear models, biological sampling, public policy, economic development, energy, regional economics. *Unit head:* Dr. Richard V. Adkisson, Head, 575-646-4988, Fax: 575-646-1915, E-mail: radkisso@nmsu.edu. *Application contact:* 575-646-2113, Fax: 575-646-1915.
Website: http://business.nmsu.edu/departments/economics

Northeastern University, College of Professional Studies, Boston, MA 02115-5096. Offers applied nutrition (MS); commerce and economic development (MS); corporate and organizational communication (MS); digital media (MPS); geographic information technology (MPS); global studies and international affairs (MS); homeland security (MA); human services (MS); informatics (MPS); leadership (MS); nonprofit management (MS); project management (MS); regulatory affairs for drugs, biologics, and medical devices (MS); regulatory affairs of food and food industries (MS); respiratory care leadership (MS); technical communication (MS). Postbaccalaureate distance learning degree programs offered (no on-campus study).

State University of New York Empire State College, School for Graduate Studies, Program in Community and Economic Development, Saratoga Springs, NY 12866-4391. Offers MA. Part-time and evening/weekend programs available. Postbaccalaureate distance learning degree programs offered (minimal on-campus study). *Degree requirements:* For master's, thesis, final project. *Entrance requirements:* For master's, undergraduate-level courses in statistics and macroeconomics, bachelor's degree from regionally-accredited college/university. Additional exam requirements/recommendations for international students: Required—TOEFL (minimum score 600 paper-based). Electronic applications accepted. *Faculty research:* Business history, applied business statistics, labor/management relations, American social problems and business, effect of government economic policies on business.

Troy University, Graduate School, College of Business, Program in Business Administration, Troy, AL 36082. Offers accounting (EMBA, MBA); criminal justice (EMBA); finance (MBA); general management (EMBA, MBA); healthcare management (EMBA); information systems (EMBA, MBA); international economic development (MBA). *Accreditation:* ACBSP. Part-time and evening/weekend programs available. *Faculty:* 19 full-time (4 women), 2 part-time/adjunct (0 women). *Students:* 105 full-time (55 women), 239 part-time (123 women); includes 175 minority (114 Black or African American, non-Hispanic/Latino; 4 American Indian or Alaska Native, non-Hispanic/Latino; 40 Asian, non-Hispanic/Latino; 8 Hispanic/Latino; 1 Native Hawaiian or other Pacific Islander, non-Hispanic/Latino; 8 Two or more races, non-Hispanic/Latino). Average age 29. 281 applicants, 63% accepted, 35 enrolled. In 2014, 218 master's awarded. *Degree requirements:* For master's, minimum GPA of 3.0, capstone course, research course. *Entrance requirements:* For master's, GMAT (minimum score 500) or GRE (minimum score 900 on old exam or 294 on new exam), bachelor's degree; minimum undergraduate GPA of 2.5 or 3.0 on last 30 semester hours, letter of recommendation. Additional exam requirements/recommendations for international students: Required—TOEFL (minimum score 523 paper-based; 70 iBT), IELTS (minimum score 6). *Application deadline:* Applications are processed on a rolling basis. Application fee: $50. *Expenses:* Tuition, state resident: full-time $6570; part-time $365 per credit hour. Tuition, nonresident: full-time $13,140; part-time $730 per credit hour. *Required fees:* $365 per credit hour. *Unit head:* Dr. Bob Wheatley, Director, Graduate Business Programs, 334-670-3194, Fax: 334-670-3599, E-mail: rwheat@troy.edu. *Application contact:* Jessica A. Kimbro, Director of Graduate Admissions, 334-670-3178, E-mail: jacord@troy.edu.

Université de Sherbrooke, Faculty of Administration, PhD Program in Economic Development, Sherbrooke, QC J1K 2R1, Canada. Offers PhD. *Degree requirements:* For doctorate, one foreign language, comprehensive exam, thesis/dissertation, advanced English as a second language. *Entrance requirements:* For doctorate, letters of recommendation, work experience, formal training. *Faculty research:* Impact analysis of economical policies; productivity, competitivity and international commerce; macroeconometric modelisation; environmental economy.

University of Central Arkansas, Graduate School, College of Liberal Arts, Department of Geography, Conway, AR 72035-0001. Offers community and economic development (MS); geographic information systems (MGIS, Certificate). Part-time programs available. Postbaccalaureate distance learning degree programs offered (minimal on-campus study). *Entrance requirements:* Additional exam requirements/recommendations for international students: Required—TOEFL (minimum score 550 paper-based). Electronic applications accepted.

University of Central Arkansas, Graduate School, College of Liberal Arts, Program in Community and Economic Development, Conway, AR 72035-0001. Offers community and economic development (MS); geographic and information systems (MGIS, Graduate Certificate). Part-time programs available. Postbaccalaureate distance learning degree programs offered (minimal on-campus study). *Degree requirements:* For master's, comprehensive exam, thesis. *Entrance requirements:* For master's, GRE General Test, minimum GPA of 2.7. Additional exam requirements/recommendations for international students: Required—TOEFL (minimum score 550 paper-based). Electronic applications accepted. *Expenses:* Contact institution.

University of Colorado Denver, College of Architecture and Planning, Program in Urban and Regional Planning, Denver, CO 80217. Offers economic and community development planning (MURP); land use and environmental planning (MURP); urban place making (MURP). *Accreditation:* ACSP. Part-time programs available. *Students:* 84 full-time (39 women), 9 part-time (4 women); includes 14 minority (1 Black or African American, non-Hispanic/Latino; 1 American Indian or Alaska Native, non-Hispanic/Latino; 1 Asian, non-Hispanic/Latino; 7 Hispanic/Latino; 4 Two or more races, non-Hispanic/Latino), 5 international. Average age 30. 149 applicants, 64% accepted, 44 enrolled. In 2014, 57 master's awarded. *Degree requirements:* For master's, thesis, minimum of 51 semester hours. *Entrance requirements:* For master's, GRE (for students with an undergraduate GPA below 3.0), sample of writing or work project; statement of interest; resume; three letters of recommendation. Additional exam requirements/recommendations for international students: Required—TOEFL (minimum score 75 iBT). *Application deadline:* For fall admission, 2/1 priority date for domestic students, 1/1 priority date for international students; for spring admission, 10/1 for domestic students. Application fee: $50 ($75 for international students). Electronic applications accepted. *Expenses:* Expenses: Contact institution. *Financial support:* In 2014–15, 18 students received support. Fellowships, research assistantships, teaching assistantships, Federal Work-Study, institutionally sponsored loans, scholarships/grants, and traineeships available. Financial award application deadline: 4/1; financial award applicants required to submit FAFSA. *Faculty research:* Physical planning, environmental planning, economic development planning. *Unit head:* Jeremy Nemeth, Associate Professor/Chair/Director, 303-315-0069, E-mail: jeremy.nemeth@ucdenver.edu. *Application contact:* Rachael Kuroiwa, Manager of Admissions and Outreach, 303-315-2325, E-mail: rachael.kuroiwa@ucdenver.edu.
Website: http://www.ucdenver.edu/academics/colleges/ArchitecturePlanning/Academics/DegreePrograms/MURP/Pages/MURP.aspx

University of Houston–Victoria, School of Business Administration, Victoria, TX 77901-4450. Offers accounting (MBA); economic development and entrepreneurship (MS); finance (GMBA, MBA); general business (MBA); international business (MBA); management (GMBA, MBA); marketing (MBA). *Accreditation:* AACSB. Part-time and evening/weekend programs available. Postbaccalaureate distance learning degree programs offered (minimal on-campus study). *Entrance requirements:* For master's, GMAT. Additional exam requirements/recommendations for international students: Required—TOEFL (minimum score 550 paper-based). Electronic applications accepted. *Faculty research:* Economic development, marketing, finance.

University of Massachusetts Lowell, College of Fine Arts, Humanities and Social Sciences, Program in Regional Economic and Social Development, Lowell, MA 01854. Offers MA, Graduate Certificate. Part-time programs available. *Entrance requirements:* For master's, GRE. Electronic applications accepted.

University of Miami, Graduate School, School of Business Administration, Department of Economics, Coral Gables, FL 33124. Offers economic development (MA, PhD); environmental economics (PhD); human resource economics (MA, PhD); international economics (MA, PhD); macroeconomics (PhD). Students admitted every two years in the fall semester. Terminal master's awarded for partial completion of doctoral program. *Degree requirements:* For master's, comprehensive exam; for doctorate, comprehensive exam, thesis/dissertation. *Entrance requirements:* For master's and doctorate, GRE General Test, minimum GPA of 3.0. Additional exam requirements/recommendations for international students: Required—TOEFL (minimum score 550 paper-based). *Faculty research:* International economics/trade, applied microeconomics, development.

The University of North Carolina at Greensboro, Graduate School, College of Arts and Sciences, Department of Geography, Greensboro, NC 27412-5001. Offers applied geography (MA); geographic information science (Certificate); geography (PhD); urban and economic development (Certificate). *Degree requirements:* For master's, comprehensive exam, thesis or alternative. *Entrance requirements:* For master's, GRE General Test. Additional exam requirements/recommendations for international students: Required—TOEFL. Electronic applications accepted.

The University of North Carolina at Greensboro, Graduate School, College of Arts and Sciences, Department of Political Science, Greensboro, NC 27412-5001. Offers nonprofit management (Certificate); public affairs (MPA); urban and economic development (Certificate). *Accreditation:* NASPAA. *Degree requirements:* For master's, comprehensive exam. *Entrance requirements:* For master's, GRE General Test. Additional exam requirements/recommendations for international students: Required—TOEFL. Electronic applications accepted. *Faculty research:* U.S. Constitution, Canadian parliament, public management, ethical challenge of public service.

University of Pennsylvania, School of Arts and Sciences, Fels Institute of Government, Philadelphia, PA 19104. Offers economic development and growth (Certificate); government administration (MGA); nonprofit administration (Certificate); organization dynamics (MS); politics (Certificate); public administration (MPA); public finance (Certificate). Part-time and evening/weekend programs available. *Students:* 62 full-time (32 women), 75 part-time (45 women); includes 31 minority (17 Black or African American, non-Hispanic/Latino; 6 Asian, non-Hispanic/Latino; 4 Hispanic/Latino; 4 Two or more races, non-Hispanic/Latino), 20 international. 445 applicants, 24% accepted, 47 enrolled. In 2014, 56 master's, 31 other advanced degrees awarded. *Entrance requirements:* For master's, GRE, GMAT, or LSAT. Additional exam requirements/recommendations for international students: Required—TOEFL, IELTS. *Application deadline:* For fall admission, 1/15 for domestic students. Applications are processed on a rolling basis. Application fee: $70. *Financial support:* Fellowships, institutionally

sponsored loans, and scholarships/grants available. Financial award application deadline: 1/15; financial award applicants required to submit FAFSA. *Unit head:* John J. Mulhern, Executive Director, 215-898-2600, E-mail: david_thornburgh@sas.upenn.edu. *Application contact:* 215-746-6684, Fax: 215-898-6238, E-mail: felsinstitute@sas.upenn.edu.
Website: http://www.fels.upenn.edu/

University of Puerto Rico, Río Piedras Campus, Graduate School of Planning, San Juan, PR 00931-3300. Offers economic planning systems (MP); environmental planning (MP); social policy and planning (MP); urban and territorial planning (MP). *Accreditation:* ACSP. Part-time programs available. *Degree requirements:* For master's, comprehensive exam, thesis, planning project defense. *Entrance requirements:* For master's, PAEG, GRE, minimum GPA of 3.0, 2 letters of recommendation. *Faculty research:* Municipalities, historic Atlas, Puerto Rico, economic future.

University of Southern California, Graduate School, Dana and David Dornsife College of Letters, Arts and Sciences, Department of Economics, Los Angeles, CA 90089. Offers economic development programming (MA, PhD); mathematical finance (MS); M Pl/MA; MA/JD. Terminal master's awarded for partial completion of doctoral program. *Degree requirements:* For master's, comprehensive exam; for doctorate, comprehensive exam, thesis/dissertation. *Entrance requirements:* For master's and doctorate, GRE. Additional exam requirements/recommendations for international students: Required—TOEFL (minimum score 93 iBT). Electronic applications accepted. *Faculty research:* Macro theory, development economics, econometrics.

University of Southern Mississippi, Graduate School, College of Science and Technology, Department of Economic and Workforce Development, Hattiesburg, MS 39406-0001. Offers economic development (MS); human capital development (PhD); workforce training and development (MS). Part-time and evening/weekend programs available. *Degree requirements:* For master's, comprehensive exam, thesis optional, internships; for doctorate, comprehensive exam, thesis/dissertation. *Entrance requirements:* For master's, GMAT or GRE General Test, minimum GPA of 2.75 in last 60 hours; for doctorate, GMAT or GRE General Test, minimum GPA of 3.5. Additional exam requirements/recommendations for international students: Required—TOEFL, IELTS. Electronic applications accepted. *Faculty research:* Economic development, international studies, geography.

University of Waterloo, Graduate Studies, Faculty of Environment, Program in Local Economic Development, Waterloo, ON N2L 3G1, Canada. Offers MAES. Part-time programs available. *Degree requirements:* For master's, internship, research paper. Electronic applications accepted.

Vanderbilt University, Graduate School, Department of Economics, Nashville, TN 37240-1001. Offers economic development (MA); economics (PhD). *Faculty:* 31 full-time (6 women). *Students:* 128 full-time (53 women), 2 part-time (1 woman); includes 13 minority (1 Black or African American, non-Hispanic/Latino; 4 Asian, non-Hispanic/Latino; 6 Hispanic/Latino; 2 Two or more races, non-Hispanic/Latino), 90 international. Average age 26. 589 applicants, 29% accepted, 44 enrolled. In 2014, 40 master's, 6 doctorates awarded. Terminal master's awarded for partial completion of doctoral program. *Degree requirements:* For master's, thesis or alternative; for doctorate, thesis/dissertation, final and qualifying exams. *Entrance requirements:* For master's and doctorate, GRE General Test, GRE Subject Test (recommended). Additional exam requirements/recommendations for international students: Required—TOEFL (minimum score 570 paper-based; 88 iBT). *Application deadline:* For fall admission, 1/15 for domestic and international students; for spring admission, 11/1 for domestic students. Applications are processed on a rolling basis. Electronic applications accepted. *Expenses: Tuition:* Full-time $42,768; part-time $1782 per credit hour. *Required fees:* $422. One-time fee: $30 full-time. *Financial support:* Fellowships with full and partial tuition reimbursements, teaching assistantships with full and partial tuition reimbursements, career-related internships or fieldwork, Federal Work-Study, institutionally sponsored loans, scholarships/grants, and health care benefits available. Financial award application deadline: 1/15; financial award applicants required to submit CSS PROFILE or FAFSA. *Faculty research:* Economic theory, applied fields, developmental economics, environmental economics, health economics and policy. *Unit head:* Dr. William Collins, Chair, 615-322-3428, Fax: 615-343-8495, E-mail: william.collins@vanderbilt.edu. *Application contact:* Kathleen Finn, Assistant to the Director of Graduate Studies, 615-322-3419, Fax: 615-343-8495, E-mail: kathleen.finn@vanderbilt.edu.
Website: http://www.vanderbilt.edu/econ/

Washington University in St. Louis, Brown School of Social Work, St. Louis, MO 63130-4899. Offers affordable housing and mixed-income community management (Certificate); American Indian and Alaska native (MSW); children, youth and families (MSW); health (MSW); individualized (MSW), including health; mental health (MSW); older adults and aging societies (MSW); public health (MPH), including epidemiology/biostatistics, global health, health policy analysis, urban design; social and economic development (MSW); social work (MSW, PhD), including management (MSW), policy (MSW), research (MSW), sexual health and education (MSW), social entrepreneurship (MSW), system dynamics (MSW); violence and injury prevention (Certificate); JD/MSW; M Arch/MSW; MPH/MBA; MSW/M Div; MSW/MAPS; MSW/MBA; MSW/MPH. MSW/M Div and MSW/MAPS offered in partnership with Eden Theological Seminary. *Accreditation:* CSWE (one or more programs are accredited). *Faculty:* 42 full-time (24 women), 81 part-time/adjunct (49 women). *Students:* 272 full-time (229 women); includes 138 minority (47 Black or African American, non-Hispanic/Latino; 11 American Indian or Alaska Native, non-Hispanic/Latino; 54 Asian, non-Hispanic/Latino; 19 Hispanic/Latino; 7 Two or more races, non-Hispanic/Latino), 47 international. Average age 26. 817 applicants, 62% accepted, 303 enrolled. In 2014, 239 master's, 5 doctorates awarded. *Degree requirements:* For master's, 60 credit hours (MSW), 52 credit hours (MPH); practicum; for doctorate, comprehensive exam, thesis/dissertation. *Entrance requirements:* For master's, For public health: GRE, GMAT, LSAT, or MCAT, minimum GPA of 3.0; for doctorate, GRE, MA or MSW. Additional exam requirements/recommendations for international students: Required—TOEFL (minimum score 100 iBT) or IELTS. *Application deadline:* For fall admission, 3/1 priority date for domestic and international students. Applications are processed on a rolling basis. Application fee: $40. Electronic applications accepted. *Expenses:* Expenses: The tuition rate for new full-time MSW students for the 2015-2016 academic year is $38,234 per year. The tuition rate for new full-time MPH students for the 2015-2016 academic year is $33,132 per year. *Financial support:* In 2014–15, 301 students received support. Fellowships, research assistantships, Federal Work-Study, institutionally sponsored loans, scholarships/grants, health care benefits, tuition waivers (partial), and unspecified assistantships available. Support available to part-time students. Financial award application deadline: 3/1; financial award applicants required to submit FAFSA. *Faculty research:* Mental health services, social development, child welfare, at-risk teens, autism, environmental health, health policy, health communications, obesity, gender and sexuality, violence and injury prevention, chronic disease prevention, poverty, older adults/aging societies, civic engagement, school social work, program evaluation, health disparities. *Unit head:* Jamie L. Adkisson, Director of Recruitment & Admissions, 314-935-3524, Fax: 314-935-4859, E-mail: jadkisson@wustl.edu. *Application contact:* Cate M. Valentine, Admissions Counselor, 314-935-8879, Fax: 314-935-4859, E-mail: cvalentine@wustl.edu. Website: http://brownschool.wustl.edu

Wayne State University, College of Liberal Arts and Sciences, Department of Political Science, Detroit, MI 48202. Offers political science (MA, PhD); public administration (MPA), including economic development policy and management, health and human services policy and management, human and fiscal resource management, nonprofit policy and management, organizational behavior and management, urban and metropolitan policy and management; JD/MA. *Accreditation:* NASPAA. *Students:* 56 full-time (25 women), 78 part-time (49 women); includes 41 minority (28 Black or African American, non-Hispanic/Latino; 4 Asian, non-Hispanic/Latino; 5 Hispanic/Latino; 4 Two or more races, non-Hispanic/Latino), 12 international. Average age 34. 153 applicants, 41% accepted, 34 enrolled. In 2014, 30 master's, 5 doctorates awarded. *Degree requirements:* For master's, comprehensive exam; for doctorate, thesis/dissertation. *Entrance requirements:* For master's, GRE General Test, substantial undergraduate preparation in the social sciences (recommended); for doctorate, GRE General Test, 3 letters of recommendation; autobiography; interview. Additional exam requirements/recommendations for international students: Required—TOEFL (minimum score 550 paper-based; 79 iBT), TWE (minimum score 5.5), Michigan English Language Assessment Battery (minimum score 85); Recommended—IELTS (minimum score 6.5). *Application deadline:* For fall admission, 5/1 priority date for domestic and international students; for winter admission, 10/1 priority date for domestic students, 9/1 priority date for international students; for spring admission, 2/1 priority date for domestic students, 1/1 priority date for international students. Applications are processed on a rolling basis. Application fee: $0. Electronic applications accepted. *Expenses:* Tuition, state resident: full-time $10,294; part-time $571.90 per credit hour. Tuition, nonresident: full-time $29,730; part-time $1238.75 per credit hour. *Required fees:* $1365; $43.50 per credit hour. $291.10 per semester. Tuition and fees vary according to course load and program. *Financial support:* In 2014–15, 41 students received support, including 4 fellowships with tuition reimbursements available (averaging $14,146 per year), 13 teaching assistantships with tuition reimbursements available (averaging $16,838 per year); research assistantships with tuition reimbursements available, scholarships/grants, health care benefits, and unspecified assistantships also available. Financial award application deadline: 3/31; financial award applicants required to submit FAFSA. *Faculty research:* American politics and public policy, comparative politics and international relations, political theory, public administration, urban politics. *Unit head:* Dr. Daniel Geller, Chair, 313-577-6328, Fax: 313-993-3435, E-mail: dgeller@wayne.edu. *Application contact:* Dr. Sharon Lean, Graduate Director, E-mail: gradpolisci@wayne.edu.
Website: http://clas.wayne.edu/politicalscience/

Wayne State University, College of Liberal Arts and Sciences, Department of Urban Studies and Planning, Detroit, MI 48202. Offers economic development (Graduate Certificate); urban studies and planning (MUP). *Accreditation:* ACSP. Evening/weekend programs available. *Students:* 16 full-time (6 women), 43 part-time (22 women); includes 23 minority (19 Black or African American, non-Hispanic/Latino; 1 Asian, non-Hispanic/Latino; 2 Hispanic/Latino; 1 Two or more races, non-Hispanic/Latino), 6 international. Average age 29. 74 applicants, 38% accepted, 19 enrolled. In 2014, 21 master's awarded. *Degree requirements:* For master's, thesis or essay. *Entrance requirements:* For degree, graduate degree or actively pursuing a graduate degree at WSU; personal statement of interest. Additional exam requirements/recommendations for international students: Required—TOEFL (minimum score 550 paper-based; 79 iBT), TWE (minimum score 5.5), Michigan English Language Assessment Battery (minimum score 85); Recommended—IELTS (minimum score 6.5). *Application deadline:* For fall admission, 6/1 priority date for domestic students, 5/1 priority date for international students; for winter admission, 10/1 priority date for domestic students, 9/1 priority date for international students; for spring admission, 2/1 priority date for domestic students, 1/1 priority date for international students. Applications are processed on a rolling basis. Application fee: $0. Electronic applications accepted. *Expenses:* Tuition, state resident: full-time $10,294; part-time $571.90 per credit hour. Tuition, nonresident: full-time $29,730; part-time $1238.75 per credit hour. *Required fees:* $1365; $43.50 per credit hour. $291.10 per semester. Tuition and fees vary according to course load and program. *Financial support:* In 2014–15, 11 students received support, including 1 research assistantship (averaging $16,508 per year); scholarships/grants and unspecified assistantships also available. Financial award application deadline: 3/31; financial award applicants required to submit FAFSA. *Unit head:* Dr. Kami Pothukuchi, Interim Chair, 313-577-4296, E-mail: k.pothukuchi@wayne.edu. *Application contact:* Dr. Robin Boyle, 313-577-2701, E-mail: dusp@wayne.edu.
Website: http://clas.wayne.edu/dusp/

Western Illinois University, School of Graduate Studies, College of Business and Technology, Department of Economics and Decision Sciences, Macomb, IL 61455-1390. Offers community development (Certificate); economics (MA). Part-time programs available. *Students:* 19 full-time (6 women), 2 part-time (0 women); includes 4 minority (3 Black or African American, non-Hispanic/Latino; 1 Two or more races, non-Hispanic/Latino), 13 international. Average age 28. 38 applicants, 63% accepted, 10 enrolled. In 2014, 22 master's awarded. *Degree requirements:* For master's, thesis or alternative. *Entrance requirements:* Additional exam requirements/recommendations for international students: Required—TOEFL (minimum score 550 paper-based; 80 iBT). *Application deadline:* Applications are processed on a rolling basis. Application fee: $30. Electronic applications accepted. *Financial support:* In 2014–15, 6 students received support, including 1 research assistantship with full tuition reimbursement available (averaging $7,544 per year), 8 teaching assistantships with full tuition reimbursements available (averaging $8,688 per year). Financial award applicants required to submit FAFSA. *Unit head:* Dr. Tej Kaul, Chairperson, 309-298-1153. *Application contact:* Dr. Nancy Parsons, Assistant Director of Graduate Studies, 309-298-1806, Fax: 309-298-2345, E-mail: grad-office@wiu.edu.
Website: http://wiu.edu/econ

West Virginia University, College of Business and Economics, Division of Economics and Finance, Morgantown, WV 26506. Offers business analysis (MA); developmental financial economics (PhD); environmental and resource economics (PhD); international economics (PhD); mathematical economics (MA); monetary economics (PhD); public finance (PhD); public policy (MA); regional and urban economics (PhD); statistics and economics (MA). Terminal master's awarded for partial completion of doctoral program. *Degree requirements:* For master's, thesis optional; for doctorate, comprehensive exam, thesis/dissertation. *Entrance requirements:* For master's and doctorate, GRE General Test, minimum GPA of 3.0; course work in intermediate microeconomics, intermediate macroeconomics, calculus, and statistics. Additional exam requirements/recommendations for international students: Required—TOEFL. Electronic applications accepted. *Faculty research:* Financial economics, regional/urban development, public economics, international trade/international finance/development economics, monetary economics.

Economic Development

Williams College, Graduate Programs, Williamstown, MA 01267. Offers development economics (MA); history of art (MA). MA in history of art offered jointly with Sterling and Francine Clark Art Institute. *Degree requirements:* For master's, 2 foreign languages, symposium paper and lecture. *Entrance requirements:* For master's, GRE General Test. Additional exam requirements/recommendations for international students: Recommended—TOEFL. Electronic applications accepted.

Yale University, Graduate School of Arts and Sciences, Department of Economics, Program in International and Development Economics, New Haven, CT 06520. Offers MA. *Entrance requirements:* For master's, GRE General Test.

Economics

Albany State University, College of Arts and Humanities, Albany, GA 31705-2717. Offers English education (M Ed); public administration (MPA), including community and economic development administration, criminal justice administration, general administration, health administration and policy, human resources management, public policy, water resources management; social work (MSW). Part-time programs available. *Degree requirements:* For master's, comprehensive exam, professional portfolio (for MPA), internship, capstone report. *Entrance requirements:* For master's, GRE, MAT, minimum GPA of 3.0, official transcript, pre-medical record/certificate of immunization, letters of reference. Electronic applications accepted. *Faculty research:* HIV prevention for minority students.

American University, School of International Service, Washington, DC 20016-8071. Offers comparative and regional studies (Certificate); cross-cultural communication (Certificate); development management (MS); ethics, peace, and global affairs (MA); European studies (Certificate); global environmental policy (MA, Certificate); global information technology (Certificate); international affairs (MA), including comparative and international disability policy, comparative and regional studies, international economic relations, international politics, natural resources and sustainable development, U.S. foreign policy; international communication (MA, Certificate); international development (MA, Certificate); international economic policy (Certificate); international economic relations (Certificate); international media (MA); international peace and conflict resolution (MA, Certificate); international politics (Certificate); international relations (PhD); international service (MIS); peacebuilding (Certificate); social enterprise (MA); the Americas (Certificate); United States foreign policy (Certificate); JD/MA. Part-time and evening/weekend programs available. Postbaccalaureate distance learning degree programs offered (no on-campus study). *Faculty:* 112 full-time (43 women), 59 part-time/adjunct (27 women). *Students:* 545 full-time (335 women), 443 part-time (271 women); includes 231 minority (82 Black or African American, non-Hispanic/Latino; 8 American Indian or Alaska Native, non-Hispanic/Latino; 51 Asian, non-Hispanic/Latino; 81 Hispanic/Latino; 2 Native Hawaiian or other Pacific Islander, non-Hispanic/Latino; 7 Two or more races, non-Hispanic/Latino), 120 international. Average age 28. 1,991 applicants, 70% accepted, 365 enrolled. In 2014, 426 master's, 9 doctorates, 6 other advanced degrees awarded. Terminal master's awarded for partial completion of doctoral program. *Degree requirements:* For master's, one foreign language, comprehensive exam, thesis or alternative; for doctorate, one foreign language, comprehensive exam, thesis/dissertation. *Entrance requirements:* For master's, GRE, transcripts, resume, 2 letters of recommendation, statement of purpose; for doctorate, GRE, transcripts, resume, 3 letters of recommendation, statement of purpose. Additional exam requirements/recommendations for international students: Required—TOEFL (minimum score 600 paper-based; 100 iBT). *Application deadline:* For fall admission, 1/15 for domestic students; for spring admission, 10/1 for domestic students, 9/15 for international students. Application fee: $50. Electronic applications accepted. *Financial support:* Application deadline: 1/15. *Unit head:* Dr. James Goldgeier, Dean, 202-885-1603, Fax: 202-885-2494, E-mail: goldgeier@american.edu. *Application contact:* Jia Jiang, Associate Director, Graduate Education Enrollment, 202-885-1689, Fax: 202-885-1109, E-mail: jiang@american.edu.
Website: http://www.american.edu/sis/

The American University in Cairo, School of Business, New Cairo, Egypt. Offers business administration (MBA, Diploma); economics (MA); economics in international development (MA); finance (MS). Part-time programs available. *Faculty:* 19 full-time (3 women), 2 part-time/adjunct (0 women). *Students:* 69 full-time (24 women), 88 part-time (43 women), 3 international. 221 applicants, 47% accepted, 48 enrolled. In 2014, 90 master's awarded. *Degree requirements:* For master's, comprehensive exam (for some programs), thesis (for some programs). *Entrance requirements:* For master's, GMAT, GRE. Additional exam requirements/recommendations for international students: Required—TOEFL (minimum score 450 paper-based; 45 iBT), IELTS (minimum score 5). *Application deadline:* For fall admission, 2/1 priority date for domestic and international students; for spring admission, 10/1 priority date for domestic and international students. Applications are processed on a rolling basis. Application fee: $52. Electronic applications accepted. Tuition and fees vary according to course load and program. *Financial support:* Fellowships with partial tuition reimbursements, scholarships/grants, and tuition waivers (partial) available. Financial award application deadline: 7/1; financial award applicants required to submit CSS PROFILE. *Faculty research:* Marketing and quality management, banking operations management, economics, finance. *Unit head:* Dr. AbdelKrim Seghir, Dean, 20-22615-3290, E-mail: kseghir@aucegypt.edu. *Application contact:* Maha Hegazi, Assistant Director or Graduate Admissions, 20-22615-1462, E-mail: mahahegazi@aucegypt.edu.
Website: http://www.aucegypt.edu/Business/Pages/default.aspx

American University of Armenia, Graduate Programs, Yerevan, Armenia. Offers business administration (MBA); computer and information science (MS), including business management, design and manufacturing, energy (ME, MS), industrial engineering and systems management; economics (MS); industrial engineering and systems management (ME), including business, computer aided design/manufacturing, energy (ME, MS), information technology; law (LL M); political science and international affairs (MPSIA); public health (MPH); teaching English as a foreign language (MA). Part-time and evening/weekend programs available. *Degree requirements:* For master's, thesis (for some programs), capstone/project. *Entrance requirements:* For master's, GRE, GMAT, or LSAT. Additional exam requirements/recommendations for international students: Recommended—TOEFL (minimum score 79 iBT), IELTS (minimum score 6.5). *Faculty research:* Microfinance, finance (rural/development, international, corporate), firm life cycle theory, TESOL, language proficiency testing, public policy, administrative law, economic development, cryptography, artificial intelligence, energy efficiency/renewable energy, computer-aided design/manufacturing, health financing, tuberculosis control, mother/child health, preventive ophthalmology, post-earthquake psychopathological investigations, tobacco control, environmental health risk assessments.

American University of Beirut, Graduate Programs, Faculty of Arts and Sciences, Beirut, Lebanon. Offers anthropology (MA); Arab and Middle Eastern history (PhD); Arabic language and literature (MA, PhD); archaeology (MA); biology (MS); cell and molecular biology (PhD); chemistry (MS); clinical psychology (MA); computational sciences (MS); computer science (MS); economics (MA); English language (MA); English literature (MA); environmental policy planning (MS); financial economics (MAFE); geology (MS); history (MA); mathematics (MA, MS); media studies (MA); Middle Eastern studies (MA); physics (MS); political studies (MA); psychology (MA); public administration (MA); sociology (MA); statistics (MA, MS); theoretical physics (PhD); transnational American studies (MA). Part-time programs available. *Faculty:* 107 full-time (32 women), 6 part-time/adjunct (2 women). *Students:* 230 full-time (161 women), 209 part-time (146 women). Average age 26. 261 applicants, 70% accepted, 83 enrolled. In 2014, 68 master's, 2 doctorates awarded. *Degree requirements:* For master's, one foreign language, comprehensive exam, thesis (for some programs); for doctorate, one foreign language, comprehensive exam, thesis/dissertation. *Entrance requirements:* For master's, GRE (for some MA/MS programs), letter of recommendation; for doctorate, GRE, letters of recommendation. Additional exam requirements/recommendations for international students: Required—TOEFL (minimum score 600 paper-based; 97 iBT), IELTS (minimum score 7). *Application deadline:* For fall admission, 4/1 for domestic and international students; for spring admission, 11/1 for domestic and international students. Application fee: $50. Electronic applications accepted. *Expenses: Tuition:* Full-time $15,462; part-time $859 per credit. *Required fees:* $692. Tuition and fees vary according to course load and program. *Financial support:* Research assistantships, career-related internships or fieldwork, institutionally sponsored loans, scholarships/grants, health care benefits, and unspecified assistantships available. Financial award application deadline: 2/4; financial award applicants required to submit FAFSA. *Faculty research:* Determinants of language proficiency among Arab learners of English as a foreign language; opinion mining, information retrieval, runtime verification, high performance computing; solar and fuel cells, self-organizing systems, heterocyclic chemistry, air and water chemistry; complex analysis, harmonic analysis, number theory; social and political psychology, clinical psychology; thin films physics and technology; theory of soft matter; religious and ethnic conflict; sports and politics. *Total annual research expenditures:* $966,000. *Unit head:* Dr. Patrick McGreevy, Dean, 961-1374374 Ext. 3800, Fax: 961-1744461, E-mail: pm07@aub.edu.lb. *Application contact:* Dr. Salim Kanaan, Director, Admissions Office, 961-1350000 Ext. 2590, Fax: 961-1750775, E-mail: sk00@aub.edu.lb.
Website: http://www.aub.edu.lb/fas/

Andrews University, School of Graduate Studies, School of Business, Graduate Programs in Business, Berrien Springs, MI 49104. Offers MBA, MSA. *Faculty:* 11 full-time (4 women), 2 part-time/adjunct (both women). *Students:* 14 full-time (9 women), 64 part-time (36 women); includes 30 minority (12 Black or African American, non-Hispanic/Latino; 5 Asian, non-Hispanic/Latino; 12 Hispanic/Latino; 1 Native Hawaiian or other Pacific Islander, non-Hispanic/Latino), 31 international. Average age 33. 109 applicants, 45% accepted, 27 enrolled. In 2014, 14 master's awarded. *Entrance requirements:* For master's, GMAT. Additional exam requirements/recommendations for international students: Required—TOEFL (minimum score 550 paper-based). Application fee: $40. Tuition and fees vary according to course level. *Unit head:* Dr. Leonard K. Gashugi, Chair, 769-471-3429, E-mail: gashugi@andrews.edu. *Application contact:* Monica Wringer, Supervisor of Graduate Admission, 800-253-2874, Fax: 269-471-6321, E-mail: graduate@andrews.edu.

Arizona State University at the Tempe campus, W. P. Carey School of Business, Department of Economics, Tempe, AZ 85287-9801. Offers PhD. *Degree requirements:* For doctorate, comprehensive exam, thesis/dissertation, interactive Program of Study (iPOS) submitted before completing 50 percent of required credit hours. *Entrance requirements:* For doctorate, GRE, minimum GPA of 3.0 in last 2 years of work leading to bachelor's degree, 3 letters of recommendation, resume/curriculum vitae, letter of intent, thesis (if applicable), official university transcripts, personal statement. Additional exam requirements/recommendations for international students: Required—TOEFL (minimum score 550 paper-based; 80 iBT), IELTS (minimum score 6.5). Electronic applications accepted. *Faculty research:* Macroeconomics, general equilibrium, business cycles, monetary policy, environmental economics, applied econometrics, economic theory, game theory, procurement and auctions, industrial organization, labor economics, marketing, consumer choice behavior.

Assumption College, Department of Business Studies, Worcester, MA 01609-1296. Offers accounting (MBA); business administration (CAGS); finance/economics (MBA); frontline management (CGS); general business (MBA); human resources (MBA); international business (MBA); management (MBA); marketing (MBA); nonprofit leadership (MBA, CGS); organizational communication (CGS). Part-time and evening/weekend programs available. *Faculty:* 6 full-time (2 women), 16 part-time/adjunct (6 women). *Students:* 39 full-time (20 women), 135 part-time (76 women); includes 28 minority (11 Black or African American, non-Hispanic/Latino; 1 American Indian or Alaska Native, non-Hispanic/Latino; 4 Asian, non-Hispanic/Latino; 10 Hispanic/Latino; 1 Native Hawaiian or other Pacific Islander, non-Hispanic/Latino; 1 Two or more races, non-Hispanic/Latino), 3 international. Average age 30. 53 applicants, 57% accepted, 18 enrolled. In 2014, 57 master's awarded. *Degree requirements:* For master's, thesis, capstone. *Entrance requirements:* For master's and other advanced degree, 3 letters of recommendation, resume, essay. Additional exam requirements/recommendations for international students: Required—TOEFL (minimum score 540 paper-based; 76 iBT), IELTS (minimum score 6). *Application deadline:* For fall admission, 10/1 for domestic and international students; for winter admission, 2/1 for domestic and international students; for spring admission, 4/1 for domestic and international students. Applications are processed on a rolling basis. Application fee: $30. Electronic applications accepted. *Expenses: Tuition:* Full-time $10,620; part-time $590 per credit. *Required fees:* $20 per term. Full-time tuition and fees vary according to course load and program. *Financial support:* In 2014–15, 23 students received support. Tuition waivers (full and partial), unspecified assistantships, and institutional discounts available. Financial award application deadline: 5/1; financial award applicants required to submit FAFSA. *Faculty*

research: Workplace diversity, dynamics of team interaction, utilization of leased employees, experiential learning project on due diligence market for prostheses. *Unit head:* Eric Drouart, Director, 508-767-7457, E-mail: edrouart@assumption.edu. *Application contact:* Dr. Landy Johnson, Director of Operations for Graduate and Professional Studies, 508-767-7666, Fax: 508-767-7030, E-mail: graduate@assumption.edu.
Website: http://graduate.assumption.edu/mba/assumption-mba

Auburn University, Graduate School, College of Liberal Arts, Department of Economics, Auburn University, AL 36849. Offers MS. Part-time programs available. *Faculty:* 16 full-time (4 women), 2 part-time/adjunct (0 women). *Students:* 11 full-time (3 women), 8 part-time (3 women); includes 1 minority (Hispanic/Latino), 7 international. Average age 26. 48 applicants, 50% accepted, 8 enrolled. In 2014, 9 master's awarded. *Degree requirements:* For master's, thesis. *Entrance requirements:* For master's, GMAT, GRE General Test. Additional exam requirements/recommendations for international students: Required—TOEFL. *Application deadline:* For fall admission, 7/7 for domestic students; for spring admission, 11/24 for domestic students. Applications are processed on a rolling basis. Application fee: $50 ($60 for international students). Electronic applications accepted. *Expenses:* Tuition, state resident: full-time $8586; part-time $477 per credit hour. Tuition, nonresident: full-time $25,758; part-time $1431 per credit hour. *Required fees:* $804 per semester. Tuition and fees vary according to degree level and program. *Financial support:* Teaching assistantships, career-related internships or fieldwork, and Federal Work-Study available. Support available to part-time students. Financial award application deadline: 3/15; financial award applicants required to submit FAFSA. *Unit head:* Dr. Michael Stern, Interim Chair, 334-844-2982. *Application contact:* Dr. George Flowers, Dean of the Graduate School, 334-844-2125.
Website: http://www.cla.auburn.edu/economics/

Bard College, Levy Economics Institute, Annandale-on-Hudson, NY 12504. Offers economic theory and policy (MS).

Baruch College of the City University of New York, Zicklin School of Business, Department of Economics and Finance, Program in Economics, New York, NY 10010-5585. Offers MBA. Part-time and evening/weekend programs available. *Entrance requirements:* For master's, GMAT, 2 letters of recommendation, resume, 2 years of work experience. Additional exam requirements/recommendations for international students: Required—TOEFL (minimum score 590 paper-based), TWE (minimum score 5).

Baylor University, Graduate School, Hankamer School of Business, Department of Economics, Waco, TX 76798. Offers MS Eco. *Entrance requirements:* For master's, GMAT or GRE General Test. *Faculty research:* Econometrics, international economics, economic development, comparative economic systems, computational economics, health economics, economics of education, monetary economics.

Binghamton University, State University of New York, Graduate School, School of Arts and Sciences, Department of Economics, Vestal, NY 13850. Offers economics (MA, PhD); economics and finance (MA, PhD). *Faculty:* 23 full-time (6 women), 3 part-time/adjunct (0 women). *Students:* 41 full-time (16 women), 24 part-time (10 women); includes 2 minority (1 Black or African American, non-Hispanic/Latino; 1 Native Hawaiian or other Pacific Islander, non-Hispanic/Latino), 58 international. Average age 27. 130 applicants, 69% accepted, 24 enrolled. In 2014, 9 master's, 4 doctorates awarded. Terminal master's awarded for partial completion of doctoral program. *Degree requirements:* For doctorate, comprehensive exam, thesis/dissertation. *Entrance requirements:* For master's and doctorate, GRE General Test. Additional exam requirements/recommendations for international students: Required—TOEFL (minimum score 550 paper-based; 80 iBT). *Application deadline:* For fall admission, 8/1 priority date for domestic and international students. Applications are processed on a rolling basis. Application fee: $75. Electronic applications accepted. *Expenses:* Tuition, state resident: full-time $7776; part-time $432 per credit. Tuition, nonresident: full-time $15,138; part-time $841 per credit. *Required fees:* $1754; $213 per credit. Tuition and fees vary according to degree level and program. *Financial support:* In 2014–15, 34 students received support, including 1 research assistantship with full tuition reimbursement available (averaging $15,000 per year), 29 teaching assistantships with full tuition reimbursements available (averaging $15,000 per year); career-related internships or fieldwork, Federal Work-Study, institutionally sponsored loans, scholarships/grants, health care benefits, tuition waivers (full and partial), and unspecified assistantships also available. Financial award application deadline: 2/15; financial award applicants required to submit FAFSA. *Unit head:* Dr. Florenz Plassmann, Chairperson, 607-777-4304, E-mail: fplass@binghamton.edu. *Application contact:* Kishan Zuber, Recruiting and Admissions Coordinator, 607-777-2151, Fax: 607-777-2501, E-mail: kzuber@binghamton.edu.

Boston College, Graduate School of Arts and Sciences, Department of Economics, Chestnut Hill, MA 02467-3800. Offers PhD. *Faculty:* 35 full-time. *Students:* 79 full-time (23 women); includes 4 minority (2 Asian, non-Hispanic/Latino; 2 Hispanic/Latino), 58 international. 372 applicants, 9% accepted, 14 enrolled. In 2014, 12 doctorates awarded. *Degree requirements:* For doctorate, comprehensive exam, thesis/dissertation. *Entrance requirements:* For doctorate, GRE General Test, GRE Subject Test. Additional exam requirements/recommendations for international students: Required—TOEFL (minimum score 600 paper-based; 100 iBT), IELTS (minimum score 7). *Application deadline:* For fall admission, 1/2 for domestic and international students. Application fee: $75. Electronic applications accepted. *Financial support:* In 2014–15, 79 students received support, including fellowships with full tuition reimbursements available (averaging $20,500 per year), research assistantships with full tuition reimbursements available (averaging $21,000 per year), teaching assistantships with full tuition reimbursements available (averaging $21,000 per year); Federal Work-Study, scholarships/grants, health care benefits, and unspecified assistantships also available. Support available to part-time students. Financial award application deadline: 3/1; financial award applicants required to submit FAFSA. *Faculty research:* Economic theory, macroeconomics, microeconomics, econometrics, development economics, industrial organization, labor economics, international economics, public sector economics, monetary economics and finance, urban economics. *Unit head:* Dr. Donald Cox, Chairperson, 617-552-3670, E-mail: donald.cox@bc.edu. *Application contact:* Dr. Dick Tresch, Graduate Program Director, 617-552-3683, E-mail: richard.tresch@bc.edu.
Website: http://bc.edu/economics

Boston University, Graduate School of Arts and Sciences, Department of Economics, Boston, MA 02215. Offers economic policy (MAEP); economics (MAPE); MBA/MA. *Students:* 239 full-time (100 women), 23 part-time (17 women); includes 8 minority (5 Asian, non-Hispanic/Latino; 3 Hispanic/Latino), 201 international. Average age 26. 1,291 applicants, 44% accepted, 125 enrolled. In 2014, 177 master's, 19 doctorates awarded. Terminal master's awarded for partial completion of doctoral program. *Degree requirements:* For master's, one foreign language, comprehensive exam; for doctorate, one foreign language, comprehensive exam, thesis/dissertation, qualifying exam. *Entrance requirements:* For master's, GRE General Test, 2 letters of recommendation; for doctorate, GRE General Test, 3 letters of recommendation. Additional exam requirements/recommendations for international students: Required—TOEFL (minimum score 550 paper-based; 84 iBT). *Application deadline:* For fall admission, 1/5 for domestic and international students. Application fee: $80. Electronic applications

accepted. *Expenses: Tuition:* Full-time $45,686; part-time $1428 per credit hour. *Required fees:* $660; $60 per semester. Tuition and fees vary according to program. *Financial support:* In 2014–15, 127 students received support, including 20 fellowships with full tuition reimbursements available (averaging $20,500 per year), 15 research assistantships with full tuition reimbursements available (averaging $20,500 per year), 27 teaching assistantships with full tuition reimbursements available (averaging $20,500 per year); Federal Work-Study, scholarships/grants, and health care benefits also available. Financial award application deadline: 1/5. *Unit head:* Barton Lipman, Chairman, 617-353-2995, Fax: 617-353-4449, E-mail: blipman@bu.edu. *Application contact:* Andrew Campolieto, Graduate Program Administrator, 617-353-4454, Fax: 617-353-4449, E-mail: acamp@bu.edu.
Website: http://www.bu.edu/econ/

Boston University, Metropolitan College, Department of Administrative Sciences, Boston, MA 02215. Offers banking and financial services management (MSM); business continuity in emergency management (MSM); financial economics (MSAS); innovation and technology (MSAS); insurance management (MSM); international marketing management (MSM); project management (MS). *Accreditation:* AACSB. Part-time and evening/weekend programs available. Postbaccalaureate distance learning degree programs offered (no on-campus study). *Faculty:* 15 full-time (3 women), 22 part-time/adjunct (3 women). *Students:* 214 full-time (111 women), 619 part-time (325 women); includes 146 minority (52 Black or African American, non-Hispanic/Latino; 1 American Indian or Alaska Native, non-Hispanic/Latino; 38 Asian, non-Hispanic/Latino; 43 Hispanic/Latino; 2 Native Hawaiian or other Pacific Islander, non-Hispanic/Latino; 10 Two or more races, non-Hispanic/Latino), 268 international. Average age 32. 593 applicants, 69% accepted, 260 enrolled. In 2014, 163 master's awarded. *Degree requirements:* For master's, thesis optional. *Entrance requirements:* For master's, 1 year of work experience, minimum GPA of 3.0. Additional exam requirements/recommendations for international students: Required—TOEFL (minimum score 84 iBT). *Application deadline:* Applications are processed on a rolling basis. Application fee: $80. Electronic applications accepted. *Expenses:* Expenses: $800 per credit part-time; student services fees: $60 per semester; technology fee of $60 per credit (for online courses). *Financial support:* In 2014–15, 15 students received support, including 14 research assistantships (averaging $8,400 per year); career-related internships or fieldwork, Federal Work-Study, and unspecified assistantships also available. *Faculty research:* International business, innovative process. *Unit head:* Dr. John Sullivan, Chair, 617-353-3016, E-mail: adminsc@bu.edu. *Application contact:* Fiona Niven, Administrative Sciences Department, 617-353-3016, E-mail: adminsc@bu.edu.
Website: http://www.bu.edu/met/academic-community/departments/administrative-sciences/

Bowling Green State University, Graduate College, College of Business Administration, Department of Economics, Bowling Green, OH 43403. Offers MA. Part-time programs available. *Degree requirements:* For master's, thesis or alternative. *Entrance requirements:* For master's, GRE General Test. Additional exam requirements/recommendations for international students: Required—TOEFL. Electronic applications accepted. *Faculty research:* Labor economics, monetary economics, economic education, mathematical economics.

Brandeis University, International Business School (IBS), Master of Arts in International Economics and Finance Program, Waltham, MA 02454-9110. Offers business economics (MA). *Faculty:* 29 full-time (10 women), 27 part-time/adjunct (3 women). *Students:* 150 full-time (77 women); includes 134 minority (10 Black or African American, non-Hispanic/Latino; 111 Asian, non-Hispanic/Latino; 13 Hispanic/Latino), 108 international. Average age 23. 899 applicants, 20% accepted, 69 enrolled. In 2014, 79 master's awarded. *Entrance requirements:* For master's, GMAT or GRE. Additional exam requirements/recommendations for international students: Required—TOEFL (minimum score 577 paper-based; 90 iBT), IELTS (minimum score 7), PTE (minimum score 61). *Application deadline:* For fall admission, 11/1 priority date for domestic and international students; for winter admission, 1/15 priority date for domestic and international students; for spring admission, 3/15 priority date for domestic and international students; for summer admission, 5/15 for domestic and international students. Application fee: $55. Electronic applications accepted. *Expenses:* Expenses: $45,748 annually, one-time orientation fee $44, graduate activity fee $40 per term. *Financial support:* In 2014–15, 112 students received support. Institutionally sponsored loans and scholarships/grants available. Financial award application deadline: 3/15; financial award applicants required to submit FAFSA. *Faculty research:* International economic policy analysis, macroeconomics, econometrics, business economics, economic development. *Unit head:* Bruce Magid, Dean, 781-736-4663. *Application contact:* Brittany Leclerc, Senior Admissions Coordinator, 781-736-2252, Fax: 781-736-2263, E-mail: admission@lemberg.brandeis.edu.
Website: http://www.brandeis.edu/global/ma

Brandeis University, International Business School (IBS), PhD in International Economics and Finance Program, Waltham, MA 02454-9110. Offers global trade (PhD); macroeconomics (PhD). *Faculty:* 5 full-time (2 women). *Students:* 30 full-time (16 women); includes 19 minority (2 Black or African American, non-Hispanic/Latino; 15 Asian, non-Hispanic/Latino; 2 Hispanic/Latino), 22 international. Average age 32. 103 applicants, 17% accepted. In 2014, 3 doctorates awarded. *Degree requirements:* For doctorate, thesis/dissertation. *Entrance requirements:* Additional exam requirements/recommendations for international students: Required—TOEFL (minimum score 577 paper-based; 90 iBT), IELTS (minimum score 7), PTE (minimum score 61). *Application deadline:* For winter admission, 1/15 priority date for domestic and international students. Application fee: $55. *Expenses:* Expenses: $45,748 annually for first three years of program. *Financial support:* In 2014–15, 25 students received support, including 11 fellowships (averaging $9,545 per year); institutionally sponsored loans, scholarships/grants, and health care benefits also available. Financial award application deadline: 1/15; financial award applicants required to submit FAFSA. *Faculty research:* Global business, global trade, global finance, macroeconomics, development and institutions. *Unit head:* Bruce Magid, Dean, 781-736-4663. *Application contact:* Brittany Leclerc, Senior Admissions Coordinator, 781-736-2252, Fax: 781-736-2263, E-mail: admission@lemberg.brandeis.edu.
Website: https://www.brandeis.edu/global/academics/phd/

Brock University, Faculty of Graduate Studies, Faculty of Social Sciences, Program in Business Economics, St. Catharines, ON L2S 3A1, Canada. Offers MBE. *Degree requirements:* For master's, thesis or alternative. *Entrance requirements:* For master's, honours degree. Additional exam requirements/recommendations for international students: Required—TOEFL (minimum score 550 paper-based; 80 iBT), IELTS (minimum score 6.5), TWE (minimum score 4). Electronic applications accepted. *Faculty research:* Microeconomic theory, macroeconomics, econometrics, applied econometrics, economic development.

Brooklyn College of the City University of New York, School of Business, Brooklyn, NY 11210-2889. Offers accounting (MS); business administration (MS), including economic analysis, general business, global business and finance. Part-time and evening/weekend programs available. *Degree requirements:* For master's, comprehensive exam, thesis or alternative. *Entrance requirements:* For master's, GMAT, 2 letters of recommendation. Additional exam requirements/recommendations

for international students: Required—TOEFL (minimum score 550 paper-based; 79 iBT). Electronic applications accepted. *Faculty research:* Econometrics, environmental economics, microeconomics, macroeconomics, taxation.

Brown University, Graduate School, Department of Economics, Providence, RI 02912. Offers PhD. Terminal master's awarded for partial completion of doctoral program. *Degree requirements:* For doctorate, thesis/dissertation. *Entrance requirements:* For doctorate, GRE General Test.

Buffalo State College, State University of New York, The Graduate School, Faculty of Natural and Social Sciences, Department of Economics and Finance, Buffalo, NY 14222-1095. Offers applied economics (MA). *Degree requirements:* For master's, project. *Entrance requirements:* Additional exam requirements/recommendations for international students: Required—TOEFL (minimum score 550 paper-based).

California Lutheran University, Graduate Studies, School of Management, Thousand Oaks, CA 91360-2787. Offers business (IMBA); computer science (MS); econometrics (MBA); economics (MS); entrepreneurship (MBA, Certificate); finance (MBA, Certificate); financial planning (MBA, Certificate); information systems and technology (MS); information technology management (MBA, Certificate); international business (MBA, Certificate); management and organization behavior (MBA); management and organizational behavior (Certificate); marketing (MBA, Certificate); microeconomics (MBA); nonprofit and social enterprise (MBA). Part-time and evening/weekend programs available. Postbaccalaureate distance learning degree programs offered (no on-campus study). *Faculty:* 35 full-time (13 women), 44 part-time/adjunct (13 women). *Students:* 385 full-time (171 women), 256 part-time (109 women); includes 118 minority (15 Black or African American, non-Hispanic/Latino; 2 American Indian or Alaska Native, non-Hispanic/Latino; 25 Asian, non-Hispanic/Latino; 65 Hispanic/Latino; 1 Native Hawaiian or other Pacific Islander, non-Hispanic/Latino; 10 Two or more races, non-Hispanic/Latino), 320 international. Average age 32. 620 applicants, 69% accepted, 120 enrolled. In 2014, 317 master's awarded. *Entrance requirements:* For master's, GMAT, interview, minimum GPA of 3.0. *Application deadline:* Applications are processed on a rolling basis. Application fee: $50. *Expenses:* Expenses: Contact institution. *Unit head:* Dr. Gerhard Apfelthaler, Dean, 805-493-3360. *Application contact:* 805-493-3325, Fax: 805-493-3861, E-mail: clugrad@callutheran.edu.
Website: http://www.callutheran.edu/business/

California State Polytechnic University, Pomona, Program in Economics, Pomona, CA 91768-2557. Offers MS. Part-time programs available. *Students:* 7 full-time (2 women), 33 part-time (9 women); includes 17 minority (1 Black or African American, non-Hispanic/Latino; 6 Asian, non-Hispanic/Latino; 10 Hispanic/Latino), 13 international. Average age 28. 53 applicants, 74% accepted, 19 enrolled. In 2014, 20 master's awarded. *Degree requirements:* For master's, thesis or alternative. *Entrance requirements:* For master's, GRE General Test. *Application deadline:* For fall admission, 5/1 priority date for domestic students; for winter admission, 10/15 priority date for domestic students; for spring admission, 1/20 priority date for domestic students. Applications are processed on a rolling basis. Application fee: $55. Electronic applications accepted. *Expenses:* Tuition, state resident: full-time $6738. Tuition, nonresident: full-time $12,300. *Required fees:* $1400. *Financial support:* In 2014–15, 9 students received support. Federal Work-Study and institutionally sponsored loans available. Support available to part-time students. Financial award application deadline: 3/2; financial award applicants required to submit FAFSA. *Unit head:* Dr. Gregory Hunter, Graduate Coordinator, 909-869-4888, Fax: 909-869-6987, E-mail: gwhunter@cpp.edu.
Website: http://www.cpp.edu/~class/economics/graduate-students/

California State University, East Bay, Office of Academic Programs and Graduate Studies, College of Business and Economics, Economics Department, Hayward, CA 94542-3000. Offers MA. Part-time and evening/weekend programs available. *Degree requirements:* For master's, comprehensive exam, project or thesis. *Entrance requirements:* For master's, GMAT, minimum GPA of 2.75 during previous 2 years of course work. Additional exam requirements/recommendations for international students: Required—TOEFL (minimum score 580 paper-based; 92 iBT). *Application deadline:* For fall admission, 6/30 for domestic and international students. Applications are processed on a rolling basis. Application fee: $55. Electronic applications accepted. *Expenses:* Tuition, state resident: full-time $7830; part-time $1302 per credit hour. Tuition, nonresident: full-time $16,368. *Required fees:* $327 per quarter. Tuition and fees vary according to course load and program. *Financial support:* Career-related internships or fieldwork, Federal Work-Study, and institutionally sponsored loans available. Support available to part-time students. Financial award application deadline: 3/2; financial award applicants required to submit FAFSA. *Unit head:* Prof. Jed DeVaro, Chair, 510-885-3289, E-mail: jed.devaro@csueastbay.edu. *Application contact:* Christian Roessler, Graduate Program Director, 510-885-2858, E-mail: christian.roessler@csueastbay.edu.
Website: http://www20.csueastbay.edu/cbe/departments/economics/

California State University, Fullerton, Graduate Studies, College of Business and Economics, Department of Economics, Fullerton, CA 92834-9480. Offers MA, MBA. Part-time programs available. *Students:* 25 full-time (8 women), 9 part-time (2 women); includes 8 minority (1 Black or African American, non-Hispanic/Latino; 4 Asian, non-Hispanic/Latino; 3 Hispanic/Latino), 15 international. Average age 27. 40 applicants, 55% accepted, 10 enrolled. In 2014, 16 master's awarded. *Degree requirements:* For master's, thesis. *Entrance requirements:* For master's, GMAT, GRE General Test. Application fee: $55. *Financial support:* Career-related internships or fieldwork, Federal Work-Study, institutionally sponsored loans, and scholarships/grants available. Support available to part-time students. Financial award application deadline: 3/1; financial award applicants required to submit FAFSA. *Faculty research:* Environmental and natural resource issues. *Unit head:* Dr. David Wong, Chair, 657-278-3821. *Application contact:* Admissions/Applications, 657-278-2371.

California State University, Long Beach, Graduate Studies, College of Liberal Arts, Department of Economics, Long Beach, CA 90840. Offers economics (MA); global logistics (MA). Part-time programs available. *Degree requirements:* For master's, comprehensive exam or thesis. *Entrance requirements:* For master's, GRE General Test, GRE Subject Test, minimum GPA of 3.0. Electronic applications accepted. *Faculty research:* Trade and development, economic forecasting, resource economics.

California State University, Los Angeles, Graduate Studies, College of Business and Economics, Department of Economics and Statistics, Los Angeles, CA 90032-8530. Offers analytical quantitative economics (MA); business economics (MA, MBA, MS); economics (MA). Part-time and evening/weekend programs available. *Degree requirements:* For master's, comprehensive exam or thesis. *Entrance requirements:* For master's, GMAT, minimum GPA of 2.5 during previous 2 years of course work. Additional exam requirements/recommendations for international students: Required—TOEFL (minimum score 550 paper-based). Electronic applications accepted. *Expenses:* Tuition, state resident: full-time $6738; part-time $3609 per year. Tuition, nonresident: full-time $15,666; part-time $8073 per year. Tuition and fees vary according to course load, degree level and program.

California University of Management and Sciences, Graduate Programs, Anaheim, CA 92801. Offers business administration (MBA, DBA); computer information systems (MS); economics (MS); international business (MS); sports management (MS).

Carleton University, Faculty of Graduate Studies, Faculty of Public Affairs and Management, Department of Economics, Ottawa, ON K1S 5B6, Canada. Offers MA, PhD. PhD program offered jointly with University of Ottawa. *Degree requirements:* For master's, thesis optional; for doctorate, comprehensive exam, thesis/dissertation. *Entrance requirements:* For master's, honors degree; for doctorate, master's degree. Additional exam requirements/recommendations for international students: Required—TOEFL. *Faculty research:* Monetary economics, economic development, public economics, industrial organization, international trade.

Carleton University, Faculty of Graduate Studies, Faculty of Public Affairs and Management, Institute of Political Economy, Ottawa, ON K1S 5B6, Canada. Offers MA, PhD. *Degree requirements:* For master's, thesis optional. *Entrance requirements:* For master's, honors degree. Additional exam requirements/recommendations for international students: Required—TOEFL. *Faculty research:* Relationships between economy and politics as they affect the political, social and cultural life of societies; historical processes whereby social change is located in the interaction of the economic, political and cultural, and ideological moments of social life.

Carnegie Mellon University, Tepper School of Business, Program in Economics, Pittsburgh, PA 15213-3891. Offers PhD. *Degree requirements:* For doctorate, thesis/dissertation. *Entrance requirements:* For doctorate, GMAT, GRE General Test. *Faculty research:* Research allocation under asymmetric information, monetary theory, estimation of rational expectations models.

The Catholic University of America, School of Business and Economics, Washington, DC 20064. Offers accounting (MS); business analysis (MS); integral economic development management (MA); integral economic development policy (MA); international political economics (MA). Part-time programs available. *Faculty:* 21 full-time (7 women), 25 part-time/adjunct (4 women). *Students:* 56 full-time (37 women), 13 part-time (6 women); includes 23 minority (11 Black or African American, non-Hispanic/Latino; 5 Asian, non-Hispanic/Latino; 7 Hispanic/Latino), 21 international. Average age 27. 92 applicants, 64% accepted, 40 enrolled. In 2014, 30 master's awarded. *Degree requirements:* For master's, comprehensive exam. *Entrance requirements:* For master's, GRE General Test, statement of purpose, official copies of academic transcripts, three letters of recommendation. Additional exam requirements/recommendations for international students: Required—TOEFL (minimum score 580 paper-based). *Application deadline:* For fall admission, 7/15 priority date for domestic students, 7/1 for international students; for spring admission, 11/15 priority date for domestic students, 11/1 for international students. Applications are processed on a rolling basis. Application fee: $55. Electronic applications accepted. *Expenses: Tuition:* Full-time $40,200; part-time $1600 per credit hour. *Required fees:* $400; $195 per semester. One-time fee: $425. *Financial support:* Fellowships, research assistantships, teaching assistantships, Federal Work-Study, scholarships/grants, tuition waivers (full and partial), and unspecified assistantships available. Financial award application deadline: 2/1; financial award applicants required to submit FAFSA. *Faculty research:* Integrity of the marketing process, economics of energy and the environment, emerging markets, social change, international finance and economic development. *Total annual research expenditures:* $105,784. *Unit head:* Dr. Andrew V. Abela, Chair, 202-319-5235, Fax: 202-319-4426, E-mail: abela@cua.edu. *Application contact:* Director of Graduate Admissions, 202-319-5057, Fax: 202-319-6533, E-mail: cua-admissions@cua.edu.
Website: http://business.cua.edu/

Central European University, Graduate Studies, Department of Economics, Budapest, Hungary. Offers economic policy in global markets (MA); economics (MA, PhD); law and economics (MA). *Faculty:* 12 full-time (0 women), 18 part-time/adjunct (2 women). *Students:* 122 full-time (54 women). Average age 26. 210 applicants, 36% accepted, 52 enrolled. In 2014, 32 master's, 2 doctorates awarded. *Degree requirements:* For master's, one foreign language, thesis; for doctorate, one foreign language, comprehensive exam, thesis/dissertation. *Entrance requirements:* For master's and doctorate, interview. Additional exam requirements/recommendations for international students: Required—TOEFL (minimum score 570 paper-based); Recommended—IELTS (minimum score 6.5). *Application deadline:* For fall admission, 1/24 for domestic and international students. Application fee: $40. Electronic applications accepted. *Expenses: Tuition:* Full-time 12,000 euros. *Required fees:* 200 euros. One-time fee: 500 euros full-time. *Financial support:* In 2014–15, 107 fellowships (averaging $6,100 per year) were awarded; career-related internships or fieldwork, scholarships/grants, health care benefits, and tuition waivers also available. *Faculty research:* Organizational economics, political economy, development economics and microeconomic theory, social norms and law. *Unit head:* Gabor Kezdi, Head, 36 1 327-3000 Ext. 2201, E-mail: econdept@ceu.hu. *Application contact:* Zsuzsanna Jaszberenyi, Admissions Officer, 361-324-3009, Fax: 367-327-3211, E-mail: admissions@ceu.hu.
Website: http://economics.ceu.hu/

Central European University, Graduate Studies, Department of Legal Studies, Budapest, Hungary. Offers comparative Constitutional law (LL M); human rights (LL M, MA); international business law (LL M); law and economics (LL M, MA); legal studies (SJD). *Faculty:* 12 full-time (5 women), 18 part-time/adjunct (3 women). *Students:* 86 full-time (48 women). Average age 28. 275 applicants, 32% accepted, 61 enrolled. In 2014, 48 master's, 3 doctorates awarded. Terminal master's awarded for partial completion of doctoral program. *Degree requirements:* For master's, one foreign language, thesis; for doctorate, one foreign language, comprehensive exam, thesis/dissertation. *Entrance requirements:* For master's and doctorate, LSAT. Additional exam requirements/recommendations for international students: Required—TOEFL (minimum score 570 paper-based); Recommended—IELTS (minimum score 6.5). *Application deadline:* For fall admission, 1/24 for domestic and international students. Application fee: $40. Electronic applications accepted. *Expenses:* Expenses: Contact institution. *Financial support:* In 2014–15, 86 students received support, including 86 fellowships with full and partial tuition reimbursements available (averaging $6,100 per year); career-related internships or fieldwork, institutionally sponsored loans, scholarships/grants, and tuition waivers (full and partial) also available. Financial award application deadline: 1/5. *Faculty research:* Institutional, Constitutional and human rights in European Union law; biomedical law and reproductive rights; data protection law; Islamic banking and finance. *Unit head:* Dr. Renata Uitz, Head of Department, 36 1 327-3201, Fax: 361-327-3198, E-mail: legalst@ceu.hu. *Application contact:* Zsuzsanna Jaszberenyi, Department Coordinator, 361-327-3272, Fax: 361-327-3198, E-mail: admissions@ceu.edu.
Website: http://legal.ceu.hu/

Central Michigan University, College of Graduate Studies, College of Business Administration, Department of Economics, Mount Pleasant, MI 48859. Offers MA. Part-time programs available. *Degree requirements:* For master's, thesis or alternative. Electronic applications accepted. *Faculty research:* Economic development, industrial organization, international trade, monetary theory, public choice/labor.

City College of the City University of New York, Graduate School, College of Liberal Arts and Science, Division of Social Science, Department of Economics, New York, NY 10031-9198. Offers MA. Part-time programs available. *Degree requirements:* For master's, comprehensive exam, proficiency in a foreign language or advanced statistics. *Entrance requirements:* Additional exam requirements/recommendations for international students: Required—TOEFL (minimum score 550 paper-based; 79 iBT).

Electronic applications accepted. *Faculty research:* International economics, health, banking.

Claremont Graduate University, Graduate Programs, School of Social Science, Policy and Evaluation, Department of Economics, Claremont, CA 91711-6160. Offers business and financial economics (MA, PhD); economic development (Certificate); international and development economics (PhD); international economics policy and development (MA); international money and finance (PhD); neuroeconomics and behavioral economics (PhD); political economy and public policy (MA); public choice and public economics (PhD); MBA/PhD. Part-time programs available. *Faculty:* 9 full-time (2 women), 1 part-time/adjunct (0 women). *Students:* 107 full-time (33 women), 35 part-time (15 women); includes 22 minority (3 Black or African American, non-Hispanic/Latino; 11 Asian, non-Hispanic/Latino; 6 Hispanic/Latino; 2 Two or more races, non-Hispanic/Latino), 73 international. Average age 32. In 2014, 15 master's, 11 doctorates awarded. *Entrance requirements:* For master's and doctorate, GRE General Test or GMAT. Additional exam requirements/recommendations for international students: Required—TOEFL (minimum score 550 paper-based; 80 iBT). *Application deadline:* For fall admission, 2/1 priority date for domestic and international students. Applications are processed on a rolling basis. Application fee: $80. Electronic applications accepted. *Expenses: Tuition:* Full-time $41,784; part-time $1741 per credit. *Required fees:* $600; $300 per semester. *Financial support:* Fellowships, research assistantships, teaching assistantships, Federal Work-Study, institutionally sponsored loans, and scholarships/grants available. Support available to part-time students. Financial award application deadline: 2/15; financial award applicants required to submit FAFSA. *Faculty research:* International and financial economics, law and economics, regulation, public choice economics. *Unit head:* Heather Campbell, Chair, 909-621-8689, E-mail: heather.campbell@cgu.edu. *Application contact:* Annekah Hall, Assistant Director of Admissions, 909-607-3371, E-mail: annekah.hall@cgu.edu.
Website: http://www.cgu.edu/pages/466.asp

Claremont Graduate University, Graduate Programs, School of Social Science, Policy and Evaluation, Department of Politics and Policy, Claremont, CA 91711-6160. Offers American politics (MA, PhD); comparative politics (PhD); international political economy (MA); international studies (MA); political philosophy (PhD); political science (PhD); politics, economics and business (MA); public policy (MA, PhD); world politics (PhD); MBA/PhD. Part-time programs available. *Faculty:* 7 full-time (5 women), 2 part-time/adjunct (0 women). *Students:* 112 full-time (38 women), 39 part-time (9 women); includes 37 minority (7 Black or African American, non-Hispanic/Latino; 1 American Indian or Alaska Native, non-Hispanic/Latino; 12 Asian, non-Hispanic/Latino; 14 Hispanic/Latino; 1 Native Hawaiian or other Pacific Islander, non-Hispanic/Latino; 2 Two or more races, non-Hispanic/Latino), 30 international. Average age 34. In 2014, 22 master's, 12 doctorates awarded. Terminal master's awarded for partial completion of doctoral program. *Entrance requirements:* For master's and doctorate, GRE General Test. Additional exam requirements/recommendations for international students: Required—TOEFL (minimum score 550 paper-based; 80 iBT). *Application deadline:* For fall admission, 2/1 priority date for domestic and international students. Applications are processed on a rolling basis. Application fee: $80. Electronic applications accepted. *Expenses: Tuition:* Full-time $41,784; part-time $1741 per credit. *Required fees:* $600; $300 per semester. *Financial support:* Fellowships, research assistantships, teaching assistantships, Federal Work-Study, institutionally sponsored loans, and scholarships/grants available. Support available to part-time students. Financial award application deadline: 2/15; financial award applicants required to submit FAFSA. *Faculty research:* Environmental policy, international debt, global democratization, Third World development, public sector discrimination. *Unit head:* Heather Campbell, Chair, 909-621-8689, E-mail: heather.campbell@cgu.edu. *Application contact:* Annekah Hall, Assistant Director of Admissions, 909-607-3371, E-mail: annekah.hall@cgu.edu.
Website: http://www.cgu.edu/pages/458.asp

Claremont Graduate University, Graduate Programs, School of Social Science, Policy and Evaluation, Program in Politics, Economics, and Business, Claremont, CA 91711-6160. Offers MA. Part-time programs available. *Students:* 8 full-time (2 women), 1 (woman) part-time; includes 2 minority (1 Asian, non-Hispanic/Latino; 1 Two or more races, non-Hispanic/Latino), 3 international. Average age 25. In 2014, 2 master's awarded. *Entrance requirements:* For master's, GRE General Test. Additional exam requirements/recommendations for international students: Required—TOEFL (minimum score 550 paper-based; 80 iBT). *Application deadline:* For fall admission, 2/1 priority date for domestic and international students. Applications are processed on a rolling basis. Application fee: $80. Electronic applications accepted. *Expenses: Tuition:* Full-time $41,784; part-time $1741 per credit. *Required fees:* $600; $300 per semester. *Financial support:* Federal Work-Study, institutionally sponsored loans, and scholarships/grants available. Support available to part-time students. Financial award application deadline: 2/15; financial award applicants required to submit FAFSA. *Unit head:* Stewart Donaldson, Dean, 909-607-8235, E-mail: stewart.donaldson@cgu.edu. *Application contact:* Annekah Hall, Assistant Director of Admissions, 909-607-3371, E-mail: annekah.hall@cgu.edu.
Website: http://www.cgu.edu/dpe

Clark Atlanta University, School of Business Administration, Department of Economics, Atlanta, GA 30314. Offers MA. Part-time programs available. *Faculty:* 2 full-time (0 women). *Students:* 2 full-time (1 woman), 1 (woman) part-time; includes 1 minority (Black or African American, non-Hispanic/Latino), 1 international. Average age 26. 2 applicants, 50% accepted, 1 enrolled. *Degree requirements:* For master's, thesis optional. *Entrance requirements:* For master's, GRE General Test, minimum GPA of 2.5. Additional exam requirements/recommendations for international students: Required—TOEFL (minimum score 500 paper-based; 61 iBT). *Application deadline:* For fall admission, 4/1 for domestic and international students; for spring admission, 11/1 for domestic and international students. Applications are processed on a rolling basis. Application fee: $40 ($55 for international students). Electronic applications accepted. *Expenses: Tuition:* Full-time $14,904; part-time $828 per credit hour. *Required fees:* $746; $373 per semester. *Financial support:* Career-related internships or fieldwork, Federal Work-Study, scholarships/grants, and unspecified assistantships available. Support available to part-time students. Financial award application deadline: 4/30; financial award applicants required to submit FAFSA. *Faculty research:* Minority energy demand. *Unit head:* Dr. Young Kim, Chairperson, 404-880-8450, E-mail: ykim@cau.edu. *Application contact:* Michelle Clark-Davis, Graduate Program Admissions, 404-880-6605, E-mail: cauadmissions@cau.edu.

Clark University, Graduate School, Department of Economics, Worcester, MA 01610-1477. Offers PhD. *Faculty:* 8 full-time (3 women), 1 (woman) part-time/adjunct. *Students:* 35 full-time (19 women), 3 part-time (0 women), 32 international. Average age 31. 47 applicants, 57% accepted, 7 enrolled. In 2014, 5 doctorates awarded. *Degree requirements:* For doctorate, thesis/dissertation. *Entrance requirements:* For doctorate, GRE General Test. Additional exam requirements/recommendations for international students: Required—TOEFL. *Application deadline:* For fall admission, 2/1 priority date for domestic students. Applications are processed on a rolling basis. Application fee: $75. *Expenses: Tuition:* Full-time $40,380; part-time $1262 per credit hour. *Required fees:* $30. *Financial support:* In 2014–15, fellowships with full and partial tuition reimbursements (averaging $12,240 per year), 2 research assistantships with full and partial tuition reimbursements (averaging $12,240 per year), 9 teaching assistantships with full and partial tuition reimbursements (averaging $12,240 per year) were awarded; career-related internships or fieldwork, institutionally sponsored loans, and tuition waivers (full and partial) also available. *Faculty research:* Public finance, economic development, industrial organization, international finance and trade, environmental regulation. *Total annual research expenditures:* $175,000. *Unit head:* Dr. Jacqueline Geoghegan, Chair, 508-793-7709. *Application contact:* Cindy Rice, Managerial Secretary, 508-793-7226, Fax: 508-793-8849, E-mail: crice@clarku.edu.
Website: http://www.clarku.edu/departments/economics/graduate/index.cfm

Clemson University, Graduate School, College of Business and Behavioral Science, Department of Economics, Clemson, SC 29634. Offers applied economics (PhD), including applied economics, applied economics and statistics; applied economics and statistics (MS, PhD); economics (MA, PhD). Part-time programs available. *Faculty:* 23 full-time (2 women), 5 part-time/adjunct (2 women). *Students:* 90 full-time (29 women), 17 part-time (4 women); includes 7 minority (2 Black or African American, non-Hispanic/Latino; 1 Hispanic/Latino; 4 Two or more races, non-Hispanic/Latino), 64 international. Average age 27. 234 applicants, 60% accepted, 51 enrolled. In 2014, 42 master's, 10 doctorates awarded. Terminal master's awarded for partial completion of doctoral program. *Degree requirements:* For master's, thesis (for some programs); for doctorate, comprehensive exam, thesis/dissertation. *Entrance requirements:* For master's, GRE General Test or GMAT, intermediate microeconomic theory; multivariate calculus; for doctorate, GRE General Test, intermediate microeconomic theory; multivariate calculus. Additional exam requirements/recommendations for international students: Required—TOEFL. *Application deadline:* For fall admission, 1/15 priority date for domestic and international students; for spring admission, 9/15 for international students. Application fee: $80 ($90 for international students). Electronic applications accepted. *Expenses:* Expenses: Contact institution. *Financial support:* In 2014–15, 21 students received support, including 26 fellowships with partial tuition reimbursements available (averaging $4,923 per year), 15 teaching assistantships with partial tuition reimbursements available (averaging $21,128 per year); research assistantships with partial tuition reimbursements available, career-related internships or fieldwork, institutionally sponsored loans, scholarships/grants, health care benefits, and unspecified assistantships also available. Support available to part-time students. Financial award applicants required to submit FAFSA. *Faculty research:* Applied price theory, industrial organization, international economics, labor economics, public economics. *Total annual research expenditures:* $66,305. *Unit head:* Dr. Raymond Sauer, Interim Chair, 864-656-3969, Fax: 864-656-4192, E-mail: sauerr@clemson.edu. *Application contact:* Dr. Curtis J. Simon, Director of Graduate Programs, 864-656-3966, Fax: 864-656-4192, E-mail: cjsmn@clemson.edu.
Website: http://economics.clemson.edu/

Cleveland State University, College of Graduate Studies, College of Liberal Arts and Social Sciences, Department of Economics, Cleveland, OH 44115. Offers MA. Part-time and evening/weekend programs available. *Faculty:* 6 full-time (1 woman). *Students:* 15 full-time (2 women), 12 part-time (3 women); includes 7 minority (3 Black or African American, non-Hispanic/Latino; 4 Asian, non-Hispanic/Latino), 6 international. Average age 29. 69 applicants, 49% accepted. In 2014, 11 master's awarded. *Entrance requirements:* For master's, minimum GPA of 2.75; coursework in micro theory, macro theory, statistics, and calculus. Additional exam requirements/recommendations for international students: Required—TOEFL (minimum score 515 paper-based; 65 iBT), IELTS. *Application deadline:* For fall admission, 8/20 priority date for domestic students, 5/20 priority date for international students. Applications are processed on a rolling basis. Application fee: $30. Electronic applications accepted. *Expenses:* Tuition, state resident: full-time $9566; part-time $531 per credit hour. Tuition, nonresident: full-time $17,980; part-time $999 per credit hour. *Required fees:* $25 per semester. Tuition and fees vary according to degree level and program. *Financial support:* In 2014–15, 4 students received support, including 4 research assistantships with full and partial tuition reimbursements available (averaging $5,500 per year); teaching assistantships with full tuition reimbursements available, scholarships/grants, and unspecified assistantships also available. Financial award application deadline: 4/30. *Faculty research:* Labor economics, health economics, energy, environment, economics of law, organization theory, industrial organization, international economics, macro economics, monetary economics. *Unit head:* Dr. Myong-Hun Chang, Chairperson, 216-687-4523, Fax: 216-687-9206, E-mail: m.chang@csuohio.edu. *Application contact:* Glenda Carbaugh, Administrative Secretary, 216-687-4520, Fax: 216-687-9206, E-mail: g.carbaugh@csuohio.edu.
Website: http://www.csuohio.edu/class/economics/economics

Cleveland State University, College of Graduate Studies, Maxine Goodman Levin College of Urban Affairs, Program in Urban Planning, Design, and Development, Cleveland, OH 44115. Offers economic development (MUPDD); environmental sustainability (MUPDD); geographic information systems (MUPDD, Certificate); historic preservation (MUPDD); housing and neighborhood development (MUPDD); urban economic development (Certificate); urban real estate development and finance (MUPDD, Certificate); JD/MUPDD. *Accreditation:* ACSP. Part-time and evening/weekend programs available. *Faculty:* 23 full-time (11 women), 23 part-time/adjunct (6 women). *Students:* 11 full-time (5 women), 25 part-time (10 women); includes 8 minority (2 Black or African American, non-Hispanic/Latino; 1 Asian, non-Hispanic/Latino; 2 Hispanic/Latino; 3 Two or more races, non-Hispanic/Latino), 3 international. Average age 38. 48 applicants, 56% accepted, 5 enrolled. In 2014, 16 master's awarded. *Degree requirements:* For master's, thesis or alternative, planning studio. *Entrance requirements:* For master's, GRE General Test (minimum score: 50th percentile combined verbal and quantitative, 4.0 analytical writing), minimum GPA of 3.0. Additional exam requirements/recommendations for international students: Required—TOEFL (minimum score 525 paper-based; 65 iBT), IELTS, or ITEP. *Application deadline:* For fall admission, 7/15 priority date for domestic students, 5/15 for international students; for spring admission, 11/1 for international students. Applications are processed on a rolling basis. Application fee: $30. Electronic applications accepted. *Expenses:* Expenses: $9,615 full-time, in-state tuition and fees. *Financial support:* In 2014–15, 10 students received support, including 7 research assistantships with full and partial tuition reimbursements available (averaging $5,600 per year), 2 teaching assistantships with full and partial tuition reimbursements available (averaging $2,000 per year); career-related internships or fieldwork, Federal Work-Study, scholarships/grants, tuition waivers, and unspecified assistantships also available. Support available to part-time students. Financial award application deadline: 3/1; financial award applicants required to submit FAFSA. *Faculty research:* Housing and neighborhood development, urban housing policy, environmental sustainability, economic development, GIS and planning decision support. *Unit head:* Dr. Dennis Keating, Director, 216-687-2298, Fax: 216-687-2013, E-mail: w.keating@csuohio.edu. *Application contact:* David Arrighi, Graduate Academic Advisor, 216-523-7522, Fax: 216-687-5398, E-mail: urbanprograms@csuohio.edu.
Website: http://urban.csuohio.edu/academics/graduate/mupdd/

Cleveland State University, College of Graduate Studies, Maxine Goodman Levin College of Urban Affairs, Program in Urban Studies, Cleveland, OH 44115. Offers community and neighborhood development (MS); economic development (MS); law and public policy (MS); public finance (MS); urban economic development (Certificate);

urban policy analysis (MS); urban real estate development (MS); urban real estate development and finance (Certificate). Part-time and evening/weekend programs available. *Faculty:* 23 full-time (11 women), 23 part-time/adjunct (6 women). *Students:* 5 full-time (1 woman), 8 part-time (2 women); includes 1 minority (Black or African American, non-Hispanic/Latino). Average age 34. 21 applicants, 29% accepted, 4 enrolled. In 2014, 4 master's awarded. *Degree requirements:* For master's, thesis or alternative, exit project. *Entrance requirements:* For master's, GRE General Test (minimum score: verbal and quantitative combined 40th percentile, analytical writing 4.0), minimum GPA of 3.0. Additional exam requirements/recommendations for international students: Required—TOEFL (minimum score 525 paper-based; 65 iBT), IELTS, or ITEP. *Application deadline:* For fall admission, 1/15 priority date for domestic students, 1/15 for international students. Applications are processed on a rolling basis. Application fee: $30. Electronic applications accepted. *Expenses:* Expenses: $9,615 full-time, in-state tuition and fees. *Financial support:* In 2014–15, 4 students received support, including 3 research assistantships with full and partial tuition reimbursements available (averaging $7,200 per year), 2 teaching assistantships with full and partial tuition reimbursements available (averaging $4,800 per year); career-related internships or fieldwork, scholarships/grants, traineeships, and unspecified assistantships also available. Support available to part-time students. Financial award application deadline: 3/1; financial award applicants required to submit FAFSA. *Faculty research:* Environmental issues, economic development, urban and public policy, public management. *Unit head:* Dr. Brian Mikelbank, Director, 216-875-9980, Fax: 216-687-9342, E-mail: b.mikelbank@csuohio.edu. *Application contact:* David Arrighi, Graduate Academic Advisor, 216-523-7522, Fax: 216-687-5398, E-mail: urbanprograms@csuohio.edu.
Website: http://urban.csuohio.edu/academics/graduate/msus/

Colorado State University, Graduate School, College of Liberal Arts, Department of Economics, Fort Collins, CO 80523-1771. Offers MA, PhD. Part-time programs available. *Faculty:* 17 full-time (7 women). *Students:* 35 full-time (10 women), 29 part-time (8 women); includes 5 minority (2 Black or African American, non-Hispanic/Latino; 2 Hispanic/Latino; 1 Two or more races, non-Hispanic/Latino), 22 international. Average age 30. 100 applicants, 71% accepted, 20 enrolled. In 2014, 9 master's, 2 doctorates awarded. Terminal master's awarded for partial completion of doctoral program. *Degree requirements:* For master's, variable foreign language requirement, thesis or alternative; for doctorate, variable foreign language requirement, comprehensive exam, thesis/dissertation. *Entrance requirements:* For master's, GRE General Test (minimum score 1150 verbal and quantitative, 700 quantitative), minimum GPA of 3.3, 3 letters of recommendation, background in economics, transcripts, statement of purpose; for doctorate, GRE General Test (combined minimum score of 1150 on Verbal and Quantitative sections with at least 700 on Quantitative section), minimum GPA of 3.3, 3 letters of recommendation, statement of purpose, background in economics, transcripts. Additional exam requirements/recommendations for international students: Required—TOEFL. *Application deadline:* For fall admission, 1/31 priority date for domestic students. Applications are processed on a rolling basis. Application fee: $50. Electronic applications accepted. *Expenses:* Tuition, state resident: full-time $9348; part-time $519 per credit. Tuition, nonresident: full-time $22,916; part-time $1273 per credit. *Required fees:* $1584. *Financial support:* In 2014–15, 21 students received support, including 1 research assistantship (averaging $14,986 per year), 20 teaching assistantships with full tuition reimbursements available (averaging $16,550 per year); career-related internships or fieldwork, Federal Work-Study, institutionally sponsored loans, scholarships/grants, traineeships, and unspecified assistantships also available. Financial award application deadline: 3/1; financial award applicants required to submit FAFSA. *Faculty research:* Regional and development economics, political economy, international trade and investment, public finance, labor markets. *Total annual research expenditures:* $247,293. *Unit head:* Dr. Steven J. Shulman, Professor and Chair, 970-491-6940, Fax: 970-491-2925, E-mail: steven.shulman@colostate.edu. *Application contact:* Robert Kling, Graduate Contact, 970-491-5598, Fax: 970-491-2925, E-mail: robert.kling@colostate.edu.
Website: http://economics.colostate.edu/

Columbia University, Graduate School of Arts and Sciences, New York, NY 10027. Offers African-American studies (MA); American studies (MA); anthropology (MA, PhD); art history and archaeology (MA, PhD); astronomy (PhD); biological sciences (PhD); biotechnology (MA); chemical physics (PhD); chemistry (PhD); classical studies (MA, PhD); classics (MA, PhD); climate and society (MA); earth and environmental sciences (PhD); East Asia: regional studies (MA); East Asian languages and cultures (MA, PhD); ecology, evolution and environmental biology (MA), including conservation biology; ecology, evolution, and environmental biology (PhD), including ecology and evolutionary biology, evolutionary primatology; economics (PhD); English and comparative literature (MA, PhD); French and Romance philology (MA, PhD); Germanic languages (MA, PhD); global French studies (MA); Hispanic cultural studies (MA); history (PhD); history and literature (MA); human rights studies (MA); Islamic studies (MA); Italian (MA, PhD); Japanese pedagogy (MA); Jewish studies (MA); Latin America and the Caribbean: regional studies (MA); Latin American and Iberian cultures (PhD); mathematics (MA, PhD), including finance (MA); medieval and Renaissance studies (MA); Middle Eastern, South Asian, and African studies (MA, PhD); modern art: critical and curatorial studies (MA); modern European studies (MA); museum anthropology (MA); music (DMA, PhD); oral history (MA); philosophical foundations of physics (MA); philosophy (MA, PhD); physics (PhD); political science (MA, PhD); psychology (PhD); quantitative methods in the social sciences (MA); religion (MA, PhD); Russia, Eurasia and East Europe: regional studies (MA); Russian translation (MA); Slavic cultures (MA); Slavic languages (MA, PhD); sociology (MA, PhD); South Asian studies (MA); statistics (MA, PhD); theatre (PhD); JD/PhD; MA/MS; MD/PhD; MPA/MA. Dual-degree programs require admission to both Graduate School of Arts and Sciences and another Columbia school. Part-time and evening/weekend programs available. Terminal master's awarded for partial completion of doctoral program. *Degree requirements:* For master's, thesis (for some programs); for doctorate, comprehensive exam, thesis/dissertation. *Entrance requirements:* For master's and doctorate, GRE General Test, GRE Subject Test (for some programs). Electronic applications accepted. *Faculty research:* Humanities, natural sciences, social sciences.

Columbia University, Graduate School of Business, Doctoral Program in Business, New York, NY 10027. Offers business (PhD), including accounting, decision, risk, and operations, finance and economics, management, marketing. *Accreditation:* AACSB. *Degree requirements:* For doctorate, comprehensive exam, thesis/dissertation, major field exam, research paper, thesis proposal. *Entrance requirements:* For doctorate, GMAT or GRE (finance), 2 letters of reference, resume. Additional exam requirements/recommendations for international students: Required—TOEFL. Electronic applications accepted. *Expenses:* Contact institution. *Faculty research:* Human decision making and behavioral research; real estate market and mortgage defaults; financial crisis and corporate governance; international business; security analysis and accounting.

Columbia University, Graduate School of Business, MBA Program, New York, NY 10027. Offers accounting (MBA); decision, risk, and operations (MBA); entrepreneurship (MBA); finance and economics (MBA); healthcare and pharmaceutical management (MBA); human resource management (MBA); international business (MBA); leadership and ethics (MBA); management (MBA); marketing (MBA); media (MBA); private equity (MBA); real estate (MBA); social enterprise (MBA); value investing (MBA); DDS/MBA; JD/MBA; MBA/MIA; MBA/MPH; MBA/MS; MD/MBA. *Entrance requirements:* For master's, GMAT, 2 letters of recommendation. Additional exam requirements/recommendations for international students: Required—TOEFL. Electronic applications accepted. *Expenses:* Contact institution. *Faculty research:* Human decision making and behavioral research; real estate market and mortgage defaults; financial crisis and corporate governance; international business; security analysis and accounting.

Concordia University, School of Graduate Studies, Faculty of Arts and Science, Department of Economics, Montréal, QC H3G 1M8, Canada. Offers MA, PhD, Diploma. *Degree requirements:* For master's, thesis or alternative, research paper; for doctorate, one foreign language, comprehensive exam, thesis/dissertation, research seminar. *Entrance requirements:* For master's and doctorate, honors degree in economics or equivalent. *Faculty research:* Trade and industrial adjustment, tax policy and reform, environmental policy, economics of migration, economics of telecommunications.

Copenhagen Business School, Graduate Programs, Copenhagen, Denmark. Offers business administration (Exec MBA, MBA, PhD); business administration and information systems (M Sc); business, language and culture (M Sc); economics and business administration (M Sc); health management (MHM); international business and politics (M Sc); public administration (MPA); shipping and logistics (Exec MBA); technology, market and organization (MBA).

Cornell University, Graduate School, Graduate Fields of Architecture, Art and Planning, Field of Regional Science, Ithaca, NY 14853-0001. Offers environmental studies (MA, MS, PhD); international spatial problems (MA, MS, PhD); location theory (MA, MS, PhD); multiregional economic analysis (MA, MS, PhD); peace science (MA, MS, PhD); planning methods (MA, MS, PhD); urban and regional economics (MA, MS, PhD). Terminal master's awarded for partial completion of doctoral program. *Degree requirements:* For master's, thesis; for doctorate, comprehensive exam, thesis/dissertation. *Entrance requirements:* For master's and doctorate, GRE General Test, 2 letters of recommendation. Additional exam requirements/recommendations for international students: Required—TOEFL (minimum score 600 paper-based; 77 iBT). Electronic applications accepted. *Faculty research:* Urban and regional growth, spatial economics, formation of spatial patterns by socioeconomic systems, non-linear dynamics and complex systems, environmental-economic systems.

Cornell University, Graduate School, Graduate Fields of Arts and Sciences, Field of Economics, Ithaca, NY 14853-0001. Offers applied economics (PhD); basic analytical economics (PhD); econometrics and economic statistics (PhD); economic development and planning (PhD); economic theory (PhD); industrial organization and control (PhD); international economics (PhD); labor economics (PhD); monetary and macro economics (PhD); public finance (PhD). *Degree requirements:* For doctorate, comprehensive exam, thesis/dissertation. *Entrance requirements:* For doctorate, GRE General Test, 3 letters of recommendation. Additional exam requirements/recommendations for international students: Required—TOEFL (minimum score 550 paper-based; 77 iBT). Electronic applications accepted. *Faculty research:* Learning and games, economics of education, political economy, transfer payments, time series and nonparametrics.

Dalhousie University, Faculty of Science, Department of Economics, Halifax, NS B3H 4R2, Canada. Offers MA, MDE, PhD. *Degree requirements:* For master's, thesis; for doctorate, thesis/dissertation. *Entrance requirements:* For master's and doctorate, GRE (recommended). Additional exam requirements/recommendations for international students: Required—TOEFL, IELTS, CANTEST, CAEL, or Michigan English Language Assessment Battery. Electronic applications accepted. *Faculty research:* Applied econometrics, industrial organization, labor and income distribution, economic theory (micro and macro), resource economics (fishing, forestry).

DePaul University, Charles H. Kellstadt Graduate School of Business, Chicago, IL 60604. Offers accountancy (M Acc, MS, MSA); applied economics (MBA); banking (MBA); behavioral finance (MBA); brand and product management (MBA); business development (MBA); business information technology (MS); business strategy and decision-making (MBA); computational finance (MS); consumer insights (MBA); corporate finance (MBA); economic policy analysis (MS); entrepreneurship (MBA, MS); finance (MBA, MS); financial analysis (MBA); general business (MBA); health sector management (MBA); hospitality leadership (MBA); hospitality leadership and operational performance (MS); human resource management (MBA); human resources (MS); investment management (MBA); leadership and change management (MBA); management accounting (MBA); marketing (MBA, MS); marketing analysis (MS); marketing strategy and planning (MBA); operations management (MBA); organizational diversity (MBA); real estate (MS); real estate finance and investment (MBA); revenue management (MBA); sports management (MBA); strategic global marketing (MBA); strategy, execution and valuation (MBA); sustainable management (MBA, MS); taxation (MS); wealth management (MS); JD/MBA. *Accreditation:* AACSB. Part-time and evening/weekend programs available. Postbaccalaureate distance learning degree programs offered (no on-campus study). *Entrance requirements:* For master's, GMAT, 2 letters of recommendation, resume, essay, official transcripts. Additional exam requirements/recommendations for international students: Required—TOEFL (minimum score 550 paper-based; 80 iBT). Electronic applications accepted. *Expenses:* Contact institution.

DePaul University, College of Liberal Arts and Social Sciences, Chicago, IL 60614. Offers Arabic (MA); Chinese (MA); English (MA); French (MA); German (MA); history (MA); interdisciplinary studies (MA, MS); international public service (MS); international studies (MA); Italian (MA); Japanese (MA); leadership and policy studies (MS); liberal studies (MA); new media studies (MA); nonprofit management (MNM); public administration (MPA); public health (MPH); public service management (MS); social work (MSW); sociology (MA); Spanish (MA); sustainable urban development (MA); women and gender studies (MA); writing and publishing (MA); writing, rhetoric, and discourse (MA); MA/PhD. Part-time and evening/weekend programs available. Postbaccalaureate distance learning degree programs offered (no on-campus study). Terminal master's awarded for partial completion of doctoral program. *Degree requirements:* For master's, variable foreign language requirement, comprehensive exam (for some programs), thesis (for some programs). Electronic applications accepted.

Drexel University, LeBow College of Business, Program in Business Administration, Philadelphia, PA 19104-2875. Offers business administration (MBA, PhD, APC), including accounting (MBA, PhD), decision sciences (PhD), economics (MBA, PhD), finance (MBA, PhD), legal studies (MBA), management (MBA), marketing (MBA, PhD), organizational sciences (PhD), quantitative methods (MBA), strategic management (PhD). *Accreditation:* AACSB. Part-time and evening/weekend programs available. Postbaccalaureate distance learning degree programs offered (minimal on-campus study). Terminal master's awarded for partial completion of doctoral program. *Entrance requirements:* For master's, GMAT, minimum GPA of 2.75; for doctorate, GMAT. Additional exam requirements/recommendations for international students: Required—TOEFL. Electronic applications accepted. *Faculty research:* Decision support systems, individual and group behavior, operations research, techniques and strategy.

Duke University, Graduate School, Department of Economics, Durham, NC 27708. Offers AM, PhD, JD/AM. Spring admission applies to AM program only. *Degree*

requirements: For doctorate, thesis/dissertation. *Entrance requirements:* For master's and doctorate, GRE General Test. Additional exam requirements/recommendations for international students: Required—TOEFL (minimum score 577 paper-based; 90 iBT) or IELTS (minimum score 7). Electronic applications accepted. *Expenses: Tuition:* Full-time $45,760; part-time $2765 per credit. *Required fees:* $978. Full-time tuition and fees vary according to program.

Duke University, Graduate School, Program in Economics and Computation, Durham, NC 27708-0097. Offers MS. *Entrance requirements:* For master's, GRE General Test. Additional exam requirements/recommendations for international students: Required—TOEFL (minimum score 577 paper-based; 90 iBT) or IELTS (minimum score 7). *Expenses: Tuition:* Full-time $45,760; part-time $2765 per credit. *Required fees:* $978. Full-time tuition and fees vary according to program.

Duke University, Graduate School, Program in Statistical and Economic Modeling, Durham, NC 27708. Offers econometrics (MS); financial economics (MS). Program offered jointly by the Departments of Statistical Science and Economics. *Entrance requirements:* For master's, GRE General Test. Additional exam requirements/recommendations for international students: Required—TOEFL (minimum score 577 paper-based; 90 iBT) or IELTS (minimum score 7). Electronic applications accepted. *Expenses: Tuition:* Full-time $45,760; part-time $2765 per credit. *Required fees:* $978. Full-time tuition and fees vary according to program.

Eastern Illinois University, Graduate School, College of Sciences, Department of Economics, Charleston, IL 61920. Offers MA. Part-time and evening/weekend programs available. *Faculty:* 6. *Students:* 16 full-time (6 women), 11 part-time (5 women); includes 2 minority (both Asian, non-Hispanic/Latino), 19 international. Average age 27. 50 applicants, 58% accepted, 10 enrolled. In 2014, 3 master's awarded. *Degree requirements:* For master's, comprehensive exam (for some programs), thesis (for some programs). *Entrance requirements:* For master's, GMAT or GRE. Additional exam requirements/recommendations for international students: Required—TOEFL (minimum score 500 paper-based; 61 iBT), IELTS (minimum score 6). *Application deadline:* For fall admission, 5/15 for domestic and international students; for spring admission, 10/15 for domestic and international students. Applications are processed on a rolling basis. Application fee: $30. Electronic applications accepted. *Expenses:* Tuition, state resident: full-time $3113; part-time $283 per credit hour. Tuition, nonresident: full-time $7469; part-time $679 per credit hour. *Required fees:* $2287; $96 per credit hour. Tuition and fees vary according to course load. *Financial support:* In 2014–15, 16 students received support, including 1 fellowship with full tuition reimbursement available (averaging $7,830 per year), 3 teaching assistantships with full tuition reimbursements available (averaging $7,830 per year); career-related internships or fieldwork, Federal Work-Study, and unspecified assistantships also available. Support available to part-time students. Financial award application deadline: 3/1; financial award applicants required to submit FAFSA. *Unit head:* Ali Moshtagh, Department Chair, 217-581-2916, E-mail: amoshtagh@eiu.edu. *Application contact:* Mukti Upadhyay, Graduate Coordinator, 217-581-3812, E-mail: mpupadhyay@eiu.edu. Website: http://www.eiu.edu/economicgrad/index.php

Eastern Michigan University, Graduate School, College of Arts and Sciences, Department of Economics, Ypsilanti, MI 48197. Offers MA, Graduate Certificate. Part-time and evening/weekend programs available. Postbaccalaureate distance learning degree programs offered (minimal on-campus study). *Faculty:* 10 full-time (1 woman). *Students:* 23 full-time (9 women), 27 part-time (5 women); includes 10 minority (7 Black or African American, non-Hispanic/Latino; 2 Asian, non-Hispanic/Latino; 1 Two or more races, non-Hispanic/Latino), 16 international. Average age 31. 40 applicants, 68% accepted, 16 enrolled. In 2014, 18 master's, 1 other advanced degree awarded. *Degree requirements:* For master's, thesis or alternative. *Entrance requirements:* Additional exam requirements/recommendations for international students: Required—TOEFL. *Application deadline:* Applications are processed on a rolling basis. Application fee: $45. *Financial support:* Fellowships, research assistantships with full tuition reimbursements, teaching assistantships with full tuition reimbursements, career-related internships or fieldwork, Federal Work-Study, institutionally sponsored loans, scholarships/grants, tuition waivers (partial), and unspecified assistantships available. Support available to part-time students. Financial award applicants required to submit FAFSA. *Unit head:* Dr. Thomas Venner, Interim Department Head, 734-487-3395, Fax: 734-487-9666, E-mail: tom.venner@emich.edu. *Application contact:* Dr. David Crary, Director of Graduate Programs, 734-487-0001, Fax: 734-487-9666, E-mail: dcrary@emich.edu. Website: http://www.emich.edu/economics

Emory University, Laney Graduate School, Department of Economics, Atlanta, GA 30322-1100. Offers PhD. *Degree requirements:* For doctorate, comprehensive exam, thesis/dissertation. *Entrance requirements:* For doctorate, GRE General Test. Additional exam requirements/recommendations for international students: Recommended—TOEFL. Electronic applications accepted. *Faculty research:* Applied microeconomics, econometrics, public choice, macroeconomics, law and economics.

Florida Atlantic University, College of Business, Department of Economics, Boca Raton, FL 33431-0991. Offers MS. Part-time and evening/weekend programs available. *Degree requirements:* For master's, thesis optional. *Entrance requirements:* For master's, GMAT, GRE General Test, minimum GPA of 3.0. Additional exam requirements/recommendations for international students: Required—TOEFL (minimum score 600 paper-based; 61 iBT), IELTS (minimum score 6). *Expenses:* Tuition, state resident: full-time $7396; part-time $369.82 per credit hour. Tuition, nonresident: full-time $19,392; part-time $1024.81 per credit hour. Tuition and fees vary according to course load. *Faculty research:* International trade and finance, decision-making, monetary conditions, economic fluctuations and growth.

Florida International University, College of Arts and Sciences, Department of Economics, Miami, FL 33199. Offers MA, PhD. Part-time and evening/weekend programs available. *Degree requirements:* For master's, thesis or alternative; for doctorate, comprehensive exam, thesis/dissertation. *Entrance requirements:* For master's, GRE, minimum GPA of 3.0, letters of recommendation; for doctorate, GRE General Test, 3 letters of recommendation, minimum GPA of 3.0. Additional exam requirements/recommendations for international students: Required—TOEFL (minimum score 550 paper-based; 80 iBT). Electronic applications accepted. *Faculty research:* Economic development, international economics, urban/regional economics, Latin American economics.

Florida State University, The Graduate School, College of Social Sciences and Public Policy, Department of Economics, Tallahassee, FL 32306-2180. Offers MS, PhD, JD/MS. Part-time programs available. *Faculty:* 30 full-time (5 women), 1 part-time/adjunct (0 women). *Students:* 62 full-time (18 women), 4 part-time (1 woman); includes 11 minority (3 Black or African American, non-Hispanic/Latino; 1 Asian, non-Hispanic/Latino; 4 Hispanic/Latino; 3 Two or more races, non-Hispanic/Latino), 8 international. Average age 26. 156 applicants, 53% accepted, 30 enrolled. In 2014, 34 master's, 5 doctorates awarded. Terminal master's awarded for partial completion of doctoral program. *Degree requirements:* For master's, thesis (for some programs), applied project (for some programs); for doctorate, comprehensive exam, thesis/dissertation, dissertation prospectus, workshops. *Entrance requirements:* For master's, GRE General Test, minimum upper-division undergraduate GPA of 3.0, 3.4 on graduate work; minimum 1

course each in statistics and calculus; principles and sufficient upper-level economics courses; for doctorate, GRE General Test, minimum upper-division undergraduate GPA of 3.0, graduate 3.4; minimum 1 course each in statistics and linear algebra, 2 in calculus. Additional exam requirements/recommendations for international students: Required—TOEFL (minimum score 90 iBT). *Application deadline:* For fall admission, 2/15 priority date for domestic and international students. Applications are processed on a rolling basis. Application fee: $30. Electronic applications accepted. *Expenses:* Tuition, state resident: part-time $403.51 per credit hour. Tuition, nonresident: part-time $1004.85 per credit hour. *Required fees:* $75.81 per credit hour. One-time fee: $20 part-time. Tuition and fees vary according to campus/location. *Financial support:* In 2014–15, 50 students received support, including 12 fellowships with full tuition reimbursements available (averaging $25,000 per year), 6 research assistantships with full tuition reimbursements available (averaging $19,000 per year), 21 teaching assistantships with full tuition reimbursements available (averaging $19,000 per year); scholarships/grants, tuition waivers (partial), and unspecified assistantships also available. Financial award application deadline: 2/15; financial award applicants required to submit FAFSA. *Faculty research:* Industrial organization, experimental/behavioral, public/urban, law and economics, macroeconomics and financial. *Total annual research expenditures:* $650,000. *Unit head:* Dr. R. Mark Isaac, Chairman, 850-644-5001, Fax: 850-644-4535, E-mail: misaac@fsu.edu. *Application contact:* Dr. Thomas W. Zuehlke, Graduate Director, 850-644-5001, Fax: 850-644-4535, E-mail: tzuehlke@fsu.edu. Website: http://www.coss.fsu.edu/economics/

Fordham University, Graduate School of Arts and Sciences, Department of Economics, New York, NY 10458. Offers MA, PhD. Part-time and evening/weekend programs available. *Faculty:* 22 full-time (4 women). *Students:* 51 full-time (20 women), 20 part-time (7 women); includes 3 minority (2 Asian, non-Hispanic/Latino; 1 Hispanic/Latino), 28 international. Average age 32. 141 applicants, 51% accepted, 15 enrolled. In 2014, 20 master's, 5 doctorates awarded. Terminal master's awarded for partial completion of doctoral program. *Degree requirements:* For master's, comprehensive exam; for doctorate, comprehensive exam, thesis/dissertation. *Entrance requirements:* For master's and doctorate, GRE General Test. Additional exam requirements/recommendations for international students: Required—TOEFL (minimum score 600 paper-based). *Application deadline:* For fall admission, 1/4 priority date for domestic students; for spring admission, 11/1 for domestic students. Application fee: $70. Electronic applications accepted. *Financial support:* In 2014–15, 29 students received support, including 3 fellowships with full and partial tuition reimbursements available (averaging $28,975 per year), 25 teaching assistantships with full and partial tuition reimbursements available (averaging $22,240 per year); career-related internships or fieldwork, institutionally sponsored loans, tuition waivers (full and partial), and unspecified assistantships also available. Financial award application deadline: 1/4; financial award applicants required to submit FAFSA. *Faculty research:* Developmental economics, econometrics. *Total annual research expenditures:* $129,000. *Unit head:* Dr. Ralf Hepp, Associate Chair for Graduate Studies, 718-817-4066, Fax: 718-817-3518, E-mail: hepp@fordham.edu. *Application contact:* Bernadette Valentino-Morrison, Director of Graduate Admissions, 718-817-4419, Fax: 718-817-3566, E-mail: valentinomor@fordham.edu.

Fordham University, Graduate School of Arts and Sciences, Program in International Political Economy and Development, New York, NY 10458. Offers MA, Certificate. Part-time and evening/weekend programs available. *Students:* 33 full-time (17 women), 16 part-time (6 women); includes 3 minority (2 Asian, non-Hispanic/Latino; 1 Hispanic/Latino), 13 international. Average age 27. 181 applicants, 52% accepted, 24 enrolled. In 2014, 29 master's, 6 other advanced degrees awarded. *Degree requirements:* For master's, comprehensive exam. *Entrance requirements:* For master's, GRE General Test. Additional exam requirements/recommendations for international students: Required—TOEFL (minimum score 600 paper-based). *Application deadline:* For fall admission, 1/4 priority date for domestic students; for spring admission, 11/1 for domestic students. Application fee: $70. Electronic applications accepted. *Financial support:* In 2014–15, 16 students received support, including 2 fellowships with full and partial tuition reimbursements available (averaging $11,965 per year), 16 research assistantships with full and partial tuition reimbursements available (averaging $16,050 per year); career-related internships or fieldwork, institutionally sponsored loans, tuition waivers (full and partial), and unspecified assistantships also available. Financial award application deadline: 1/4; financial award applicants required to submit FAFSA. *Faculty research:* International economics, comparative international politics, international banking and finance, international development, emerging markets and country risk analysis. *Unit head:* Dr. Henry Schwalbenberg, Chair, 718-817-3866, Fax: 718-817-3518. *Application contact:* Bernadette Valentino-Morrison, Director of Graduate Admissions, 718-817-4419, Fax: 718-817-3566, E-mail: valentinomor@fordham.edu.

George Mason University, College of Humanities and Social Sciences, Department of Economics, Fairfax, VA 22030. Offers MA, PhD, Graduate Certificate. *Faculty:* 32 full-time (3 women), 12 part-time/adjunct (1 woman). *Students:* 143 full-time (40 women), 81 part-time (19 women); includes 27 minority (2 Black or African American, non-Hispanic/Latino; 6 Asian, non-Hispanic/Latino; 14 Hispanic/Latino; 5 Two or more races, non-Hispanic/Latino), 33 international. Average age 29. 289 applicants, 52% accepted, 70 enrolled. In 2014, 46 master's, 8 doctorates awarded. *Degree requirements:* For master's, thesis optional, 2 comprehensive exams; for doctorate, comprehensive exam, thesis/dissertation, 2 preliminary exams, field exams. *Entrance requirements:* For master's, GRE General Test, expanded goals statement; 2 letters of recommendation; undergraduate degree; intermediate microeconomics and macroeconomics; 1 semester of calculus; for doctorate, GRE General Test, 2 letters of recommendation; expanded goals statement; undergraduate degree; intermediate microeconomics and macroeconomics; 1 year of calculus and statistics; 1 semester of matrix algebra and econometrics; for Graduate Certificate, GRE General Test, expanded goals statement; 2 letters of recommendation; undergraduate degree; intermediate microeconomics and macroeconomics; at least 1 semester of calculus. Additional exam requirements/recommendations for international students: Required—TOEFL (minimum score 570 paper-based; 80 iBT), IELTS (minimum score 6.5), PTE. *Application deadline:* For fall admission, 3/15 priority date for domestic students. Application fee: $65 ($80 for international students). Electronic applications accepted. *Expenses:* Tuition, state resident: full-time $9794; part-time $408 per credit hour. Tuition, nonresident: full-time $26,978; part-time $1124 per credit hour. *Required fees:* $2820; $118 per credit hour. Tuition and fees vary according to course load and program. *Financial support:* In 2014–15, 89 students received support, including 20 fellowships (averaging $3,079 per year), 67 research assistantships with full and partial tuition reimbursements available (averaging $15,571 per year), 25 teaching assistantships with full and partial tuition reimbursements available (averaging $7,801 per year); career-related internships or fieldwork, Federal Work-Study, scholarships/grants, unspecified assistantships, and health care benefits (for full-time research or teaching assistantship recipients) also available. Support available to part-time students. Financial award application deadline: 3/1; financial award applicants required to submit FAFSA. *Faculty research:* Neuroeconomics, experimental economics (computer-based). *Total annual research expenditures:* $1.9 million. *Unit head:* Daniel Houser, Director/Professor/Chair, 703-993-4856, Fax: 703-993-4851, E-mail: dhouser@gmu.edu. *Application contact:* Mary

Jackson, Graduate Coordinator, 703-993-1135, Fax: 703-993-1133, E-mail: mjacksoq@gmu.edu. Website: http://economics.gmu.edu

Georgetown University, Graduate School of Arts and Sciences, Department of Economics, Washington, DC 20057. Offers econometrics (PhD); economic development (PhD); economic theory (PhD); industrial organization (PhD); international macro and finance (PhD); international trade (PhD); labor economics (PhD); macroeconomics (PhD); public economics and political economy (PhD); MA/PhD; MS/MA. *Degree requirements:* For doctorate, comprehensive exam, thesis/dissertation. *Entrance requirements:* For doctorate, GRE General Test. Additional exam requirements/ recommendations for international students: Required—TOEFL. *Faculty research:* International economics, economic development.

The George Washington University, Columbian College of Arts and Sciences, Department of Economics, Washington, DC 20052. Offers MA, PhD. Part-time and evening/weekend programs available. *Faculty:* 24 full-time (7 women). *Students:* 44 full-time (21 women), 62 part-time (21 women); includes 8 minority (1 Black or African American, non-Hispanic/Latino; 6 Asian, non-Hispanic/Latino; 1 Hispanic/Latino), 75 international. Average age 30. 527 applicants, 21% accepted, 12 enrolled. In 2014, 20 master's, 7 doctorates awarded. Terminal master's awarded for partial completion of doctoral program. *Degree requirements:* For master's, comprehensive exam, thesis or alternative; for doctorate, thesis/dissertation, general exam. *Entrance requirements:* For master's and doctorate, GRE General Test, minimum GPA of 3.0. Additional exam requirements/recommendations for international students: Required—TOEFL (minimum score 550 paper-based; 80 iBT). *Application deadline:* For fall admission, 1/15 priority date for domestic and international students; for spring admission, 9/1 for international students. Applications are processed on a rolling basis. Application fee: $75. Electronic applications accepted. *Financial support:* In 2014–15, 25 students received support. Fellowships with full tuition reimbursements available, teaching assistantships with tuition reimbursements available, and Federal Work-Study available. Financial award application deadline: 1/15. *Unit head:* Barry R. Chiswick, Chair, 202-994-8680, E-mail: brchis@gwu.edu. *Application contact:* Information Contact, 202-994-6150, Fax: 202-994-6147, E-mail: econgrad@gwu.edu.
Website: http://www.gwu.edu/~econ/

Georgia Institute of Technology, Graduate Studies, Ivan Allen College of Liberal Arts, School of Economics, Atlanta, GA 30332-0001. Offers MS, PhD. Part-time programs available. *Students:* 29 full-time (12 women), 5 part-time (3 women); includes 5 minority (1 Black or African American, non-Hispanic/Latino; 3 Asian, non-Hispanic/Latino; 1 Two or more races, non-Hispanic/Latino), 16 international. Average age 27. 72 applicants, 46% accepted, 18 enrolled. In 2014, 21 master's awarded. Terminal master's awarded for partial completion of doctoral program. *Degree requirements:* For master's, thesis; for doctorate, comprehensive exam, thesis/dissertation, teach two undergraduate courses. *Entrance requirements:* For master's, GRE, http://www.econ.gatech.edu/prospective/degrees-offered/ms-econ; for doctorate, GRE, http://www.econ.gatech.edu/prospective/degrees-offered/ds-econ. Additional exam requirements/recommendations for international students: Required—TOEFL (minimum score 550 paper-based; 79 iBT). *Application deadline:* For fall admission, 2/15 priority date for domestic and international students. Applications are processed on a rolling basis. Application fee: $75. Electronic applications accepted. *Expenses:* Tuition, state resident: full-time $12,344; part-time $515 per credit hour. Tuition, nonresident: full-time $27,600; part-time $1150 per credit hour. *Required fees:* $1196 per term. Part-time tuition and fees vary according to course load. *Financial support:* In 2014–15, 2 research assistantships, 1 teaching assistantship were awarded; fellowships, career-related internships or fieldwork, Federal Work-Study, institutionally sponsored loans, tuition waivers (partial), and unspecified assistantships also available. Support available to part-time students. Financial award application deadline: 5/1. *Faculty research:* Land use patterns in developing countries, office automation and productivity, dynamic modeling of financial markets. *Total annual research expenditures:* $131,537. *Unit head:* Vivek Ghosal, Director, 404-894-4910, E-mail: vivekghosal@gatech.edu. *Application contact:* Tony Gallego, Graduate Coordinator, 404-894-4917, E-mail: tony@econ.gatech.edu.
Website: http://www.econ.gatech.edu

Georgia State University, Andrew Young School of Policy Studies, Department of Economics, Atlanta, GA 30302-3992. Offers economics (MA); environmental economics (PhD); experimental economics (PhD); labor economics (PhD); policy (MA); public finance (PhD); urban and regional economics (PhD). MA offered through the College of Arts and Sciences. Part-time programs available. *Faculty:* 27 full-time (5 women). *Students:* 111 full-time (42 women), 15 part-time (4 women); includes 20 minority (8 Black or African American, non-Hispanic/Latino; 3 Asian, non-Hispanic/Latino; 8 Hispanic/Latino; 1 Two or more races, non-Hispanic/Latino), 67 international. Average age 29. 182 applicants, 41% accepted, 33 enrolled. In 2014, 47 master's, 7 doctorates awarded. Terminal master's awarded for partial completion of doctoral program. *Degree requirements:* For master's, thesis optional; for doctorate, comprehensive exam, thesis/dissertation. *Entrance requirements:* For master's, GRE; for doctorate, GRE. Additional exam requirements/recommendations for international students: Required—TOEFL (minimum score 603 paper-based; 100 iBT) or IELTS (minimum score 7). *Application deadline:* For fall admission, 2/15 for domestic and international students; for spring admission, 10/1 for domestic and international students. Application fee: $50. Electronic applications accepted. *Expenses:* Tuition, state resident: full-time $6516; part-time $362 per credit hour. Tuition, nonresident: full-time $22,014; part-time $1223 per credit hour. *Required fees:* $2128 per semester. Tuition and fees vary according to course load and program. *Financial support:* In 2014–15, fellowships with full tuition reimbursements (averaging $11,333 per year), research assistantships with full tuition reimbursements (averaging $9,788 per year), teaching assistantships with full tuition reimbursements (averaging $3,000 per year) were awarded; career-related internships or fieldwork also available. Financial award application deadline: 2/15. *Faculty research:* Public, experimental, urban/environmental, labor, and health economics. *Unit head:* Dr. Sally Wallace, Department Chair, 404-413-0046, Fax: 404-413-0145, E-mail: swallace@gsu.edu. *Application contact:* Charisma Parker, Admissions Coordinator, 404-413-0030, Fax: 404-413-0023, E-mail: cparker28@gsu.edu.
Website: http://economics.gsu.edu/

Georgia State University, College of Education, Department of Middle-Secondary Education and Instructional Technology, Atlanta, GA 30302-3083. Offers curriculum and instruction (Ed D); English education (MAT); mathematics education (M Ed, MAT); middle level education (MAT); reading, language and literacy education (M Ed, MAT), including reading instruction (M Ed); science education (M Ed, MAT), including biology (MAT), broad field science (MAT), chemistry (MAT), earth science (MAT), physics (MAT); social studies education (M Ed, MAT), including economics (MAT), geography (MAT), history (MAT), political science (MAT); teaching and learning (PhD), including language and literacy, mathematics education, music education, science education, social studies education, teaching and teacher education. *Accreditation:* NCATE. Part-time and evening/weekend programs available. Postbaccalaureate distance learning degree programs offered (minimal on-campus study). *Faculty:* 20 full-time (16 women). *Students:* 155 full-time (112 women), 101 part-time (70 women); includes 112 minority (82 Black or African American, non-Hispanic/Latino; 10 Asian, non-Hispanic/Latino; 12 Hispanic/Latino; 8 Two or more races, non-Hispanic/Latino), 3 international. Average age 32. 155 applicants, 61% accepted, 65 enrolled. *Degree requirements:* For master's, comprehensive exam (for some programs), thesis or alternative, exit portfolio; for doctorate, comprehensive exam, thesis/dissertation. *Entrance requirements:* For master's, GRE; GACE I (for initial teacher preparation programs), baccalaureate degree or equivalent, resume, goals statement, two letters of recommendation, minimum undergraduate GPA of 2.5; proof of initial teacher certification in the content area (for M Ed); for doctorate, GRE, resume, goals statement, writing sample, two letters of recommendation, minimum graduate GPA of 3.3, interview. Additional exam requirements/recommendations for international students: Required—TOEFL (minimum score 550 paper-based; 79 iBT) or IELTS (minimum score 6.5). *Application deadline:* For fall admission, 1/15 priority date for domestic and international students; for spring admission, 10/1 for domestic and international students. Application fee: $50. Electronic applications accepted. *Expenses:* Tuition, state resident: full-time $6516; part-time $362 per credit hour. Tuition, nonresident: full-time $22,014; part-time $1223 per credit hour. *Required fees:* $2128 per semester. Tuition and fees vary according to course load and program. *Financial support:* In 2014–15, fellowships with full tuition reimbursements (averaging $19,667 per year), research assistantships with full tuition reimbursements (averaging $5,436 per year), teaching assistantships with full tuition reimbursements (averaging $2,779 per year) were awarded; career-related internships or fieldwork, Federal Work-Study, scholarships/grants, health care benefits, tuition waivers (full and partial), and unspecified assistantships also available. Financial award application deadline: 3/15. *Faculty research:* Teacher education in language and literacy, mathematics, science, and social studies in urban middle and secondary school settings; learning technologies in school, community, and corporate settings; multicultural education and education for social justice; urban education; international education. *Unit head:* Dr. Dana L. Fox, Chair, 404-413-8060, Fax: 404-413-8063, E-mail: dfox@gsu.edu. *Application contact:* Bobbie Turner, Administrative Coordinator I, 404-413-8405, Fax: 404-413-8063, E-mail: bnturner@gsu.edu.
Website: http://mse.education.gsu.edu/

The Graduate Center, City University of New York, Graduate Studies, Program in Economics, New York, NY 10016-4039. Offers PhD. *Degree requirements:* For doctorate, thesis/dissertation. *Entrance requirements:* For doctorate, GRE General Test. Additional exam requirements/recommendations for international students: Required—TOEFL. Electronic applications accepted.

Harvard University, Graduate School of Arts and Sciences, Committee on Business Economics, Cambridge, MA 02138. Offers PhD. *Degree requirements:* For doctorate, thesis/dissertation. *Entrance requirements:* For doctorate, GMAT or GRE General Test. Additional exam requirements/recommendations for international students: Required—TOEFL.

Harvard University, Graduate School of Arts and Sciences, Department of Economics, Cambridge, MA 02138. Offers PhD. *Degree requirements:* For doctorate, thesis/dissertation, oral exam. *Entrance requirements:* For doctorate, GRE General Test, GRE Subject Test. Additional exam requirements/recommendations for international students: Required—TOEFL. *Faculty research:* Industrial organization, macromonetary issues, international economics.

Hawai`i Pacific University, College of Business Administration, Program in Business Administration, Honolulu, HI 96813. Offers accounting (MBA); economics (MBA); finance (MBA); hospitality and tourism management (MBA); human resource management (MBA); information systems (MBA); international business (MBA); management (MBA); marketing (MBA); organizational change and development (MBA). Part-time and evening/weekend programs available. Postbaccalaureate distance learning degree programs offered. *Faculty:* 11 full-time (5 women), 1 part-time/adjunct (0 women). *Students:* 153 full-time (67 women), 63 part-time (36 women); includes 130 minority (12 Black or African American, non-Hispanic/Latino; 58 Asian, non-Hispanic/Latino; 22 Hispanic/Latino; 8 Native Hawaiian or other Pacific Islander, non-Hispanic/Latino; 30 Two or more races, non-Hispanic/Latino). Average age 31. 102 applicants, 58% accepted, 47 enrolled. In 2014, 119 master's awarded. *Entrance requirements:* For master's, GMAT or GRE. Additional exam requirements/recommendations for international students: Recommended—TOEFL (minimum score 550 paper-based; 80 iBT), TWE (minimum score 5). *Application deadline:* For fall admission, 2/15 priority date for domestic students; for spring admission, 10/15 priority date for domestic students. Applications are processed on a rolling basis. Application fee: $50. Electronic applications accepted. *Expenses: Tuition:* Full-time $15,570; part-time $865 per credit. *Required fees:* $13. One-time fee: $50. Tuition and fees vary according to course load and program. *Financial support:* In 2014–15, 41 students received support. Research assistantships, career-related internships or fieldwork, Federal Work-Study, scholarships/grants, tuition waivers, and unspecified assistantships available. Financial award application deadline: 3/1; financial award applicants required to submit FAFSA. *Faculty research:* Business model innovation, impact of Disney's movies on Norwegian tourism, Thailand hotel management, Bali as a vacation destination, deceptive doctrine and psychological advertising. *Unit head:* Dr. Deborah Crown, Dean, 808-544-0275, Fax: 808-544-0283, E-mail: dcrown@hpu.edu. *Application contact:* Danny Lam, Assistant Director of Graduate Admissions, 808-543-8034, Fax: 808-544-0280, E-mail: grad@hpu.edu.
Website: http://www.hpu.edu/CBA/Graduate/MBA/index.html

Howard University, Graduate School, Department of Economics, Washington, DC 20059-0002. Offers MA, PhD. Part-time programs available. *Degree requirements:* For master's, comprehensive exam, thesis optional; for doctorate, one foreign language, comprehensive exam, thesis/dissertation. *Entrance requirements:* For master's, GRE General Test, minimum GPA of 3.0; for doctorate, GRE General Test, master's degree in economics or related field, minimum GPA of 3.0. Electronic applications accepted. *Faculty research:* Economic development, international trade, urban rentalization.

Hunter College of the City University of New York, Graduate School, School of Arts and Sciences, Department of Economics, New York, NY 10065-5085. Offers accounting (MS); economics (MA, PhD). Part-time and evening/weekend programs available. *Faculty:* 2 full-time (0 women), 3 part-time/adjunct (1 woman). *Students:* 6 full-time (4 women), 29 part-time (16 women); includes 14 minority (1 Black or African American, non-Hispanic/Latino; 6 Asian, non-Hispanic/Latino; 7 Hispanic/Latino), 6 international. Average age 32. 20 applicants, 55% accepted, 6 enrolled. In 2014, 14 master's awarded. *Degree requirements:* For master's, research paper or thesis. *Entrance requirements:* For master's, GMAT or GRE General Test, minimum GPA of 3.0, 18 credits of undergraduate course work in economics (9 in mathematics), 2 letters of recommendation (1 from department member). Additional exam requirements/ recommendations for international students: Required—TOEFL. *Application deadline:* For fall admission, 4/1 for domestic students, 2/1 for international students; for spring admission, 11/1 for domestic students, 9/1 for international students. *Financial support:* Fellowships, research assistantships, teaching assistantships, career-related internships or fieldwork, Federal Work-Study, institutionally sponsored loans, and tuition waivers (partial) available. Support available to part-time students. *Faculty research:* Earnings of immigrants and minority groups, taxation and the regional economy. *Unit head:* Dr. Partha Deb, Director of Graduate Studies, 212-772-5435, E-mail: partha.deb@hunter.cuny.edu. *Application contact:* Randall Filer, Professor/Advisor,

212-772-5399, Fax: 212-772-5398, E-mail: grad.econadvisor@hunter.cuny.edu.
Website: http://econ.hunter.cuny.edu/

Illinois State University, Graduate School, College of Arts and Sciences, Department of Economics, Normal, IL 61790-2200. Offers MA, MS. *Degree requirements:* For master's, thesis or alternative. *Entrance requirements:* For master's, GRE General Test, minimum GPA of 2.6 in last 60 hours of course work. *Faculty research:* Community/ economic development; the social, economic and educational correlates of rural school closure; Stevenson Center Americorps project.

Indiana University Bloomington, University Graduate School, College of Arts and Sciences, Department of Economics, Bloomington, IN 47405-7104. Offers PhD. *Faculty:* 21 full-time (5 women). *Students:* 81 full-time (26 women); includes 2 minority (1 Asian, non-Hispanic/Latino; 1 Hispanic/Latino), 59 international. Average age 29. 176 applicants, 13% accepted, 22 enrolled. In 2014, 7 doctorates awarded. Terminal master's awarded for partial completion of doctoral program. *Degree requirements:* For doctorate, comprehensive exam, thesis/dissertation, main field exam, two supporting fields, 3rd-year paper, tool skill classes, dissertation proposal presentation, oral defense of dissertation. *Entrance requirements:* For doctorate, GRE General Test, three semesters of calculus, semester of linear algebra, semester of statistics or probability. Additional exam requirements/recommendations for international students: Required—TOEFL (minimum score 600 paper-based; 100 iBT); Recommended—IELTS (minimum score 6.5). *Application deadline:* For fall admission, 1/15 priority date for domestic students, 12/1 priority date for international students. Applications are processed on a rolling basis. Application fee: $55 ($65 for international students). Electronic applications accepted. *Financial support:* Fellowships with full tuition reimbursements, research assistantships with full tuition reimbursements, teaching assistantships with full tuition reimbursements, institutionally sponsored loans, health care benefits, and unspecified assistantships available. *Faculty research:* Macroeconomics, microeconomic theory, econometrics, experimental economics, economic growth. *Unit head:* Prof. Michael Kaganovich, Chair, 812-855-6160, Fax: 812-855-3736, E-mail: mkaganov@indiana.edu. *Application contact:* Chris Cunningham, Graduate Services Assistant, 812-855-8453, Fax: 812-855-3736, E-mail: rcunning@indiana.edu.
Website: http://www.iub.edu/~econweb/

Indiana University–Purdue University Indianapolis, School of Liberal Arts, Department of Economics, Indianapolis, IN 46202. Offers MA, MA/MA. *Faculty:* 16 full-time (3 women). *Students:* 24 full-time (9 women), 6 part-time (1 woman); includes 2 minority (1 Black or African American, non-Hispanic/Latino; 1 Asian, non-Hispanic/ Latino), 20 international. Average age 27. 45 applicants, 33% accepted, 12 enrolled. In 2014, 8 master's awarded. *Entrance requirements:* For master's, GRE, minimum GPA of 3.0; courses in economic theory, statistics, and calculus. Additional exam requirements/ recommendations for international students: Required—TOEFL (minimum score 600 paper-based). *Application deadline:* For fall admission, 2/1 priority date for domestic and international students. Application fee: $55 ($65 for international students). *Financial support:* Fellowships with partial tuition reimbursements, research assistantships with partial tuition reimbursements, teaching assistantships, career-related internships or fieldwork, and health care benefits available. *Faculty research:* Charitable giving. *Unit head:* Steve Russell, Chair, 317-278-7214, E-mail: shrusse@iupui.edu. *Application contact:* Dana Ward, Information Contact, 317-274-4756, E-mail: dmward@iupui.edu.
Website: http://www.iupui.edu/~econ/

Instituto Tecnologico de Santo Domingo, Graduate School, Area of Humanities and Social Sciences, Santo Domingo, Dominican Republic. Offers accounting (Certificate); adult education (Certificate); applied linguistics (MA); economics (MA); education (M Ed); educational psychology (MA, Certificate); gender and development (MA, Certificate); humanistic studies (MA); international marketing management (Certificate); international relations in the Caribbean basin (Certificate); intervention systems in family therapy (MA); linguistic and literary communication (Certificate); pedagogical support (MA); social science education (M Ed); sustainable human development (MA); terminal illness and death psychology (Certificate); youth and adult education (M Ed).

Instituto Tecnológico y de Estudios Superiores de Monterrey, Campus Ciudad de México, School of Business Administration, Ciudad de Mexico, Mexico. Offers business administration (EMBA, MBA, PhD); economy (MBA); finance (MBA). EMBA program offered jointly with The University of Texas at Austin. Part-time and evening/weekend programs available. Postbaccalaureate distance learning degree programs offered (minimal on-campus study). *Entrance requirements:* For master's and doctorate, Instituto entrance exam. Additional exam requirements/recommendations for international students: Required—TOEFL.

Iowa State University of Science and Technology, Department of Economics, Ames, IA 50011. Offers agricultural economics (MS, PhD); economics (MS, PhD); JD/MS; JD/ PhD. JD/MS and JD/PhD offered jointly with Drake University and The University of Iowa. *Degree requirements:* For master's, thesis or alternative; for doctorate, thesis/ dissertation. *Entrance requirements:* For master's and doctorate, GRE General Test. Additional exam requirements/recommendations for international students: Required—TOEFL (minimum score 570 paper-based; 88 iBT), IELTS (minimum score 6.5). Electronic applications accepted.

Johns Hopkins University, Zanvyl Krieger School of Arts and Sciences, Department of Economics, Baltimore, MD 21218-2699. Offers PhD. Terminal master's awarded for partial completion of doctoral program. *Degree requirements:* For doctorate, comprehensive exam, thesis/dissertation. *Entrance requirements:* For doctorate, GRE General Test. Additional exam requirements/recommendations for international students: Required—TOEFL (minimum score 600 paper-based), IELTS. Electronic applications accepted. *Faculty research:* General economic theory, econometrics and mathematical economics, trade and development, game theory, urban economics.

Kansas State University, Graduate School, College of Arts and Sciences, Department of Economics, Manhattan, KS 66506. Offers MA, PhD. *Faculty:* 14 full-time (3 women), 2 part-time/adjunct (0 women). *Students:* 36 full-time (15 women), 3 part-time (1 woman); includes 4 minority (all Black or African American, non-Hispanic/Latino), 26 international. Average age 25. 57 applicants, 33% accepted, 6 enrolled. In 2014, 16 master's, 4 doctorates awarded. Terminal master's awarded for partial completion of doctoral program. *Degree requirements:* For master's, comprehensive exam (for some programs), thesis optional, 30 credit hours, including thesis/report or qualifying exams; for doctorate, comprehensive exam, thesis/dissertation, 90 credit hours. *Entrance requirements:* For master's, GRE (highly recommended), minimum GPA of 3.0; course work in microeconomics, macroeconomics, calculus and statistics; for doctorate, GRE (highly recommended), course work in microeconomics, macroeconomics, and calculus. Additional exam requirements/recommendations for international students: Required—TOEFL (minimum score 550 paper-based; 79 iBT), IELTS (minimum score 6.5), TWE (minimum score 5), PTE (minimum score 58). *Application deadline:* For fall admission, 1/1 priority date for domestic and international students; for spring admission, 8/1 priority date for domestic and international students. Applications are processed on a rolling basis. Application fee: $50 ($75 for international students). Electronic applications accepted. *Financial support:* In 2014–15, 26 teaching assistantships with full tuition reimbursements (averaging $15,125 per year) were awarded; institutionally sponsored loans, scholarships/grants, and unspecified assistantships also available. Financial award application deadline: 2/1; financial award applicants required to submit FAFSA. *Faculty research:* Macroeconomics, microeconomics and labor economics, development and growth, international economics, industrial organization. *Unit head:* Dr. William Blankenau, Head, 785-532-6340, Fax: 785-532-6919, E-mail: blankenw@ksu.edu. *Application contact:* Dr. Philip Gayle, Director of Graduate Studies, 785-532-4581, Fax: 785-532-6919, E-mail: gaylep@ksu.edu.
Website: http://www.k-state.edu/economics/

Kent State University, College of Business Administration, Master of Arts Program in Economics, Kent, OH 44242-0001. Offers MA. Part-time programs available. *Faculty:* 13 full-time (4 women). *Students:* 47 full-time (24 women), 4 part-time (1 woman); includes 3 minority (1 Black or African American, non-Hispanic/Latino; 1 Native Hawaiian or other Pacific Islander, non-Hispanic/Latino; 1 Two or more races, non-Hispanic/Latino), 40 international. Average age 24. 34 applicants, 100% accepted, 18 enrolled. In 2014, 28 master's awarded. *Entrance requirements:* For master's, GMAT or GRE General Test, minimum GPA of 2.75. Additional exam requirements/recommendations for international students: Required—TOEFL (minimum score 550 paper-based; 80 iBT). *Application deadline:* For fall admission, 4/1 priority date for domestic students, 4/1 for international students; for spring admission, 12/1 for domestic students, 10/15 for international students; for summer admission, 5/1 for domestic and international students. Applications are processed on a rolling basis. Application fee: $45 ($70 for international students). Electronic applications accepted. *Expenses:* Tuition, state resident: full-time $8730; part-time $485 per credit hour. Tuition, nonresident: full-time $14,886; part-time $827 per credit hour. Tuition and fees vary according to campus/location and program. *Financial support:* In 2014–15, 6 students received support, including 6 research assistantships with full tuition reimbursements available (averaging $8,000 per year); fellowships and Federal Work-Study also available. Financial award application deadline: 4/1; financial award applicants required to submit FAFSA. *Faculty research:* Macro and microeconomic theory, labor economics, international economics, quantitative methods. *Unit head:* Dr. Donald R. Williams, Chair and Professor, 330-672-2366, Fax: 330-672-9808, E-mail: dwilliam@kent.edu. *Application contact:* Louise M. Ditchey, Administrative Director, 330-672-2282, Fax: 330-672-7303, E-mail: gradbus@kent.edu.
Website: http://business.kent.edu/degrees/masters-programs

Lakehead University, Graduate Studies, Faculty of Social Sciences and Humanities, Department of Economics, Thunder Bay, ON P7B 5E1, Canada. Offers MA. Part-time and evening/weekend programs available. *Degree requirements:* For master's, thesis or comprehensive exams, research papers. *Entrance requirements:* For master's, minimum B average. Additional exam requirements/recommendations for international students: Required—TOEFL. *Faculty research:* Public finance, economic history, mathematical economics, quantitative economics.

Lehigh University, College of Business and Economics, Department of Economics, Bethlehem, PA 18015. Offers economics (MS). *Faculty:* 14 full-time (3 women), 1 (woman) part-time/adjunct. *Students:* 37 full-time (19 women), 4 part-time (2 women); includes 1 minority (Two or more races, non-Hispanic/Latino), 29 international. Average age 26. 139 applicants, 41% accepted, 14 enrolled. In 2014, 16 master's, 3 doctorates awarded. Terminal master's awarded for partial completion of doctoral program. *Degree requirements:* For master's, thesis optional; for doctorate, comprehensive exam, thesis/ dissertation, proposal defense. *Entrance requirements:* For master's and doctorate, GMAT or GRE General Test. Additional exam requirements/recommendations for international students: Required—TOEFL (minimum score 600 paper-based; 94 iBT). *Application deadline:* For fall admission, 7/15 for domestic students, 5/1 for international students; for spring admission, 12/1 for domestic students. Applications are processed on a rolling basis. Application fee: $100. Electronic applications accepted. *Financial support:* In 2014–15, 18 students received support, including 2 fellowships (averaging $26,000 per year), 1 research assistantship with full tuition reimbursement available (averaging $18,000 per year), 13 teaching assistantships with full tuition reimbursements available (averaging $18,000 per year); scholarships/grants, health care benefits, tuition waivers (full and partial), and unspecified assistantships also available. Financial award application deadline: 1/15. *Faculty research:* Public finance, investments, applied econometrics, labor economics, health economics. *Total annual research expenditures:* $522,300. *Unit head:* Dr. James Dearden, Chair, 610-758-5129, Fax: 610-758-4677, E-mail: jad8@lehigh.edu. *Application contact:* Michael Tarantino, Director of Recruitment and Admissions, 610-758-3418, Fax: 610-758-5283, E-mail: mgt215@lehigh.edu.
Website: http://www4.lehigh.edu/business/academics/depts/economics

Louisiana State University and Agricultural & Mechanical College, Graduate School, E. J. Ourso College of Business, Department of Economics, Baton Rouge, LA 70803. Offers MS, PhD. *Faculty:* 14 full-time (2 women). *Students:* 30 full-time (15 women); includes 2 minority (1 Black or African American, non-Hispanic/Latino; 1 Asian, non-Hispanic/Latino), 22 international. Average age 28. 54 applicants, 41% accepted, 8 enrolled. In 2014, 8 master's, 3 doctorates awarded. Terminal master's awarded for partial completion of doctoral program. *Degree requirements:* For doctorate, thesis/ dissertation. *Entrance requirements:* For master's and doctorate, GRE General Test, minimum GPA of 3.0. Additional exam requirements/recommendations for international students: Required—TOEFL (minimum score 550 paper-based; 79 IBT), IELTS (minimum score 6.5), or PTE (minimum score 59). *Application deadline:* For fall admission, 1/1 priority date for domestic students, 5/15 for international students; for spring admission, 10/15 for domestic and international students. Applications are processed on a rolling basis. Application fee: $50 ($70 for international students). *Financial support:* In 2014–15, 29 students received support, including 1 fellowship (averaging $17,427 per year), 14 research assistantships with full and partial tuition reimbursements available (averaging $17,214 per year), 13 teaching assistantships with full and partial tuition reimbursements available (averaging $15,981 per year); Federal Work-Study, scholarships/grants, health care benefits, and unspecified assistantships also available. Support available to part-time students. Financial award application deadline: 6/15; financial award applicants required to submit FAFSA. *Faculty research:* Microeconomics, macroeconomics, econometrics, industrial organization, public finance, labor. *Total annual research expenditures:* $1.5 million. *Unit head:* Dr. Robert Newman, Chair, 225-578-5211, Fax: 225-578-3807, E-mail: eonewm@lsu.edu. *Application contact:* Dr. Doug McMillan, Graduate Director, 225-578-3798, Fax: 225-578-3807, E-mail: eodoug@lsu.edu.
Website: http://www.business.lsu.edu/economics

Louisiana Tech University, Graduate School, College of Business, Department of Economics and Finance, Ruston, LA 71272. Offers finance (MBA); finance and economics (DBA). Part-time programs available. *Degree requirements:* For doctorate, thesis/dissertation. *Entrance requirements:* For master's and doctorate, GMAT. *Application deadline:* For fall admission, 7/29 for domestic students; for spring admission, 2/3 for domestic students. Application fee: $20 ($30 for international students). *Financial support:* Fellowships, research assistantships, and teaching assistantships available. Financial award application deadline: 2/1. *Unit head:* Dr. Otis Gilley, Director, 318-257-4140, Fax: 318-257-4253, E-mail: gilley@latech.edu. *Application contact:* Marilyn J. Robinson, Assistant to the Dean, 318-257-2924, Fax: 318-257-4487. Website: http://www.business.latech.edu/econ_fin/

Economics

Loyola University Chicago, Graduate School of Business, MBA Programs, Chicago, IL 60611. Offers accounting (MBA); business ethics (MBA); derivative markets (MBA); economics (MBA); entrepreneurship (MBA); executive business administration (MBA); finance (MBA); healthcare management (MBA); human resources management (MBA); information systems management (MBA); intercontinental (MBA); international business (MBA); marketing (MBA); operations management (MBA); risk management (MBA); JD/MBA; MBA/MSA; MBA/MSF; MBA/MSHR; MBA/MSN; MBA/MSP; MBA/MSSCM; MSIMC/MBA. Part-time and evening/weekend programs available. *Faculty:* 76 full-time (20 women), 10 part-time/adjunct (4 women). *Students:* 101 full-time (42 women), 335 part-time (159 women); includes 94 minority (26 Black or African American, non-Hispanic/Latino; 1 American Indian or Alaska Native, non-Hispanic/Latino; 35 Asian, non-Hispanic/Latino; 23 Hispanic/Latino; 9 Two or more races, non-Hispanic/Latino), 47 international. Average age 32. 490 applicants, 49% accepted, 127 enrolled. In 2014, 225 master's awarded. *Entrance requirements:* For master's, GMAT or GRE, a completed application, official transcripts, two letters of recommendation, a statement of purpose, resume. Additional exam requirements/recommendations for international students: Required—TOEFL (minimum score 90 iBT) or IELTS (minimum score 6.5). *Application deadline:* For fall admission, 7/15 for domestic and international students; for winter admission, 10/1 for domestic and international students; for spring admission, 1/15 for domestic and international students; for summer admission, 4/1 for domestic and international students. Applications are processed on a rolling basis. Application fee: $50. Electronic applications accepted. Application fee is waived when completed online. *Expenses:* Tuition: Full-time $17,370; part-time $965 per credit. *Required fees:* $138 per semester. *Financial support:* Scholarships/grants and unspecified assistantships available. *Faculty research:* Social enterprise and responsibility, emerging markets, supply chain management, risk management. *Unit head:* Katherine Acles, Assistant Dean for Graduate Programs, 312-915-6124, Fax: 312-915-7207, E-mail: kacles@luc.edu. *Application contact:* Lauren Griffin, Enrollment Advisor, Quinlan School of Business Graduate Programs, 312-915-6124, Fax: 312-915-7207, E-mail: lgriffin3@luc.edu.

Marquette University, Graduate School of Management, Department of Economics, Milwaukee, WI 53201-1881. Offers business economics (MSAE); financial economics (MSAE); international economics (MSAE); marketing research (MSAE); real estate economics (MSAE). Part-time and evening/weekend programs available. *Degree requirements:* For master's, comprehensive exam, professional project. *Entrance requirements:* For master's, GMAT or GRE General Test. Additional exam requirements/recommendations for international students: Required—TOEFL (minimum score 550 paper-based; 88 iBT), IELTS (minimum score 6.5), PTE. Electronic applications accepted. *Faculty research:* Monetary and fiscal policy in open economy, housing and regional migration, political economy of taxation and state/local government.

Marquette University, Graduate School of Management, Executive MBA Program, Milwaukee, WI 53201-1881. Offers economics (MBA); finance (MBA); human resources (MBA); international business (MBA); management information systems (MBA); marketing (MBA); operations and supply chain management (MBA); sports business (MBA). *Accreditation:* AACSB. *Degree requirements:* For master's, international trip. *Entrance requirements:* For master's, GMAT or GRE, two letters of recommendation, official transcripts from current and previous colleges/universities. Additional exam requirements/recommendations for international students: Required—TOEFL (minimum score 550 paper-based; 88 iBT), IELTS (minimum score 6.5), PTE. Electronic applications accepted. *Expenses:* Contact institution. *Faculty research:* International trade and finance, customer relationship management, consumer satisfaction, customer service.

Marquette University, Graduate School of Management, Program in Business Administration, Milwaukee, WI 53201-1881. Offers business administration (MBA); economics (MBA); entrepreneurship (Certificate); finance (MBA); human resources (MBA); international business (MBA); management information systems (MBA); marketing (MBA); operations and supply chain management (MBA); sports business (MBA); JD/MBA; MBA/MA; MBA/MSN. *Accreditation:* AACSB. Part-time and evening/weekend programs available. *Degree requirements:* For Certificate, business plan. *Entrance requirements:* For master's, GMAT or GRE, letters of recommendation. Additional exam requirements/recommendations for international students: Required—TOEFL (minimum score 550 paper-based; 88 iBT), IELTS (minimum score 6.5), PTE. Electronic applications accepted. *Faculty research:* Ethics in the professions, services marketing, technology impact on decision-making, mentoring.

Massachusetts Institute of Technology, School of Humanities, Arts, and Social Sciences, Department of Economics, Cambridge, MA 02139. Offers SM, PhD. *Faculty:* 30 full-time (5 women), 1 part-time/adjunct (0 women). *Students:* 127 full-time (35 women); includes 17 minority (1 Black or African American, non-Hispanic/Latino; 10 Asian, non-Hispanic/Latino; 3 Hispanic/Latino; 3 Two or more races, non-Hispanic/Latino), 70 international. Average age 27. 798 applicants, 5% accepted, 24 enrolled. In 2014, 3 master's, 20 doctorates awarded. Terminal master's awarded for partial completion of doctoral program. *Degree requirements:* For doctorate, comprehensive exam, thesis/dissertation. *Entrance requirements:* For doctorate, GRE General Test. Additional exam requirements/recommendations for international students: Required—TOEFL (minimum score 600 paper-based; 100 iBT), IELTS (minimum score 7). *Application deadline:* For fall admission, 12/15 for domestic and international students. Application fee: $75. Electronic applications accepted. *Expenses: Tuition:* Full-time $44,720; part-time $699 per unit. *Required fees:* $296. *Financial support:* In 2014–15, 103 students received support, including 59 fellowships (averaging $40,900 per year), 6 research assistantships (averaging $37,900 per year), 36 teaching assistantships (averaging $44,100 per year); Federal Work-Study, institutionally sponsored loans, scholarships/grants, health care benefits, and unspecified assistantships also available. Financial award application deadline: 4/15; financial award applicants required to submit FAFSA. *Faculty research:* Macroeconomics, international economics, development economics, political economy, industrial organization, labor economics; public finance, environmental economics, health economics, econometrics, economic theory, financial economics. *Total annual research expenditures:* $8.8 million. *Unit head:* Prof. Whitney Newey, Department Head, 617-253-3907. *Application contact:* Graduate Administrator, 617-253-8787, Fax: 617-253-1330, E-mail: econ-admit@mit.edu. Website: http://economics.mit.edu/

McGill University, Faculty of Graduate and Postdoctoral Studies, Faculty of Arts, Department of Economics, Montréal, QC H3A 2T5, Canada. Offers economics (MA, PhD); social statistics (MA).

McMaster University, School of Graduate Studies, Faculty of Social Sciences, Department of Economics, Hamilton, ON L8S 4M2, Canada. Offers MA, PhD. Part-time programs available. *Degree requirements:* For doctorate, comprehensive exam, thesis/dissertation. *Entrance requirements:* For master's, GRE (recommended), honors BA in economics; for doctorate, GRE (recommended), B+ average in a master's degree. Additional exam requirements/recommendations for international students: Required—TOEFL (minimum score 580 paper-based). *Faculty research:* Applied microeconomics, econometrics, health economics, labor economics, public finance.

Memorial University of Newfoundland, School of Graduate Studies, Department of Economics, St. John's, NL A1C 5S7, Canada. Offers MA. *Degree requirements:* For master's, thesis optional. *Entrance requirements:* For master's, honors degree (minimum 2nd class standing). *Faculty research:* Public sector economics, natural resource economics.

Miami University, Farmer School of Business, Department of Economics, Oxford, OH 45056. Offers MA. *Students:* 15 full-time (6 women); includes 3 minority (2 Hispanic/Latino; 1 Two or more races, non-Hispanic/Latino), 3 international. Average age 23. In 2014, 2 master's awarded. *Entrance requirements:* For master's, GRE or GMAT, minimum undergraduate GPA of 3.0 overall; completion of the following courses with minimum C grade: intermediate-level courses in microeconomic and macroeconomic theory, at least one course in calculus, and at least one course in statistics; three letters of recommendation. Additional exam requirements/recommendations for international students: Recommended—TOEFL (minimum score 80 iBT), IELTS (minimum score 6.5), TSE (minimum score 54). *Application deadline:* For fall admission, 2/15 for domestic students, 12/1 for international students. Application fee: $50. Electronic applications accepted. *Expenses:* Tuition, state resident: full-time $12,887; part-time $537 per credit hour. Tuition, nonresident: full-time $28,449; part-time $1186 per credit hour. *Required fees:* $530; $24 per credit hour. $30 per quarter. Part-time tuition and fees vary according to course load and program. *Financial support:* Fellowships with full and partial tuition reimbursements, research assistantships with full and partial tuition reimbursements, and teaching assistantships with full and partial tuition reimbursements available. Financial award application deadline: 2/15; financial award applicants required to submit FAFSA. *Unit head:* George Davis, Chair, 513-529-2836, E-mail: davisgk@miamioh.edu. *Application contact:* Dr. Melissa Thomasson, Director of Graduate Studies, 513-529-2858, E-mail: menketl@miamioh.edu. Website: http://www.MiamiOH.edu/economics

Michigan State University, The Graduate School, College of Social Science, Department of Economics, East Lansing, MI 48824. Offers MA, PhD. *Entrance requirements:* Additional exam requirements/recommendations for international students: Required—TOEFL. Electronic applications accepted.

Middle Tennessee State University, College of Graduate Studies, Jennings A. Jones College of Business, Department of Economics and Finance, Murfreesboro, TN 37132. Offers economics (MA, PhD). Part-time and evening/weekend programs available. Postbaccalaureate distance learning degree programs offered. *Faculty:* 19 full-time (3 women), 1 part-time/adjunct (0 women). *Students:* 29 full-time (9 women), 11 part-time (3 women); includes 4 minority (3 Black or African American, non-Hispanic/Latino; 1 Asian, non-Hispanic/Latino), 16 international. 133 applicants, 44% accepted. In 2014, 9 master's, 6 doctorates awarded. *Degree requirements:* For master's, comprehensive exam, thesis optional; for doctorate, comprehensive exam, thesis/dissertation. *Entrance requirements:* For master's and doctorate, GRE. Additional exam requirements/recommendations for international students: Required—TOEFL (minimum score 525 paper-based; 71 iBT) or IELTS (minimum score 6). *Application deadline:* For fall admission, 6/1 for domestic and international students. Applications are processed on a rolling basis. Application fee: $30. Electronic applications accepted. *Financial support:* In 2014–15, 23 students received support. Tuition waivers available. Support available to part-time students. Financial award application deadline: 4/1; financial award applicants required to submit FAFSA. *Unit head:* Dr. Charles L. Baum, II, Chair, 615-898-2527, Fax: 615-898-5596, E-mail: charles.baum@mtsu.edu. *Application contact:* Dr. Michael D. Allen, Vice Provost for Research/Dean, 615-898-2840, Fax: 615-904-8020, E-mail: michael.allen@mtsu.edu.

Mississippi State University, College of Business, Department of Finance and Economics, Mississippi State, MS 39762. Offers applied economics (PhD); business administration (PhD); economics (MA). PhD in applied economics offered jointly with Department of Agricultural Economics. Part-time programs available. *Faculty:* 16 full-time (7 women), 1 part-time/adjunct (0 women). *Students:* 7 full-time (3 women), all international. Average age 31. 8 applicants. In 2014, 2 doctorates awarded. Terminal master's awarded for partial completion of doctoral program. *Degree requirements:* For master's, comprehensive exam, thesis optional; for doctorate, comprehensive exam, thesis/dissertation, written and oral exams. *Entrance requirements:* For master's, GRE, previously completed intermediate microeconomics and macroeconomics; for doctorate, GRE, BS with minimum GPA of 3.0 cumulative and over last 60 hours of undergraduate work and 3.25 on all graduate work. Additional exam requirements/recommendations for international students: Required—TOEFL (minimum score 575 paper-based; 84 iBT); Recommended—IELTS (minimum score 6.5). *Application deadline:* For fall admission, 7/1 for domestic students, 5/1 for international students; for spring admission, 11/1 for domestic students, 10/1 for international students. Applications are processed on a rolling basis. Application fee: $60. Electronic applications accepted. *Expenses:* Tuition, state resident: full-time $7140; part-time $783 per credit hour. Tuition, nonresident: full-time $18,478; part-time $2043 per credit hour. *Financial support:* Federal Work-Study, scholarships/grants, health care benefits, and unspecified assistantships available. Financial award application deadline: 4/1; financial award applicants required to submit FAFSA. *Faculty research:* Economics development, mergers, event studies, economic education, bank performance. *Total annual research expenditures:* $1.4 million. *Unit head:* Dr. Mike Highfield, Department Head, 662-325-3928, Fax: 662-325-1977, E-mail: mhighfield@msstate.edu. *Application contact:* Dr. Randy Campbell, Associate Professor/Graduate Coordinator, Economics, 662-325-1516, Fax: 662-325-1977, E-mail: mhighfield@msstate.edu. Website: http://www.business.msstate.edu/programs/fe/index.php

Morgan State University, School of Graduate Studies, College of Liberal Arts, Department of Economics, Baltimore, MD 21251. Offers MA. *Degree requirements:* For master's, comprehensive exam. *Entrance requirements:* For master's, GRE. Additional exam requirements/recommendations for international students: Required—TOEFL (minimum score 550 paper-based).

Murray State University, College of Business and Public Affairs, Program in Economics, Murray, KY 42071. Offers MS. Part-time programs available. *Entrance requirements:* For master's, GRE General Test or GMAT, economics minor or equivalent, students may be conditionally admitted and fulfill undergraduate requirements. Additional exam requirements/recommendations for international students: Required—TOEFL. *Faculty research:* Economic education, public finance, economic development, banking, telecommunications systems management.

New Mexico State University, College of Business, Department of Economics, Applied Statistics and International Business, Las Cruces, NM 88003. Offers applied statistics (MS); economic development (DED); economics (MA). Part-time programs available. *Faculty:* 19 full-time (7 women). *Students:* 46 full-time (17 women), 27 part-time (15 women); includes 28 minority (2 Black or African American, non-Hispanic/Latino; 3 Asian, non-Hispanic/Latino; 23 Hispanic/Latino), 28 international. Average age 34. 80 applicants, 53% accepted, 20 enrolled. In 2014, 19 master's, 2 doctorates, 12 other advanced degrees awarded. Terminal master's awarded for partial completion of doctoral program. *Degree requirements:* For master's, comprehensive exam, thesis or alternative; for doctorate, comprehensive exam, thesis/dissertation, internship. *Entrance requirements:* For master's, minimum GPA of 3.0; for doctorate, appropriate master's degree, minimum GPA of 3.0. Additional exam requirements/recommendations for

international students: Required—TOEFL (minimum score 550 paper-based; 79 iBT), IELTS (minimum score 6.5). *Application deadline:* For fall admission, 3/1 priority date for domestic and international students. Applications are processed on a rolling basis. Application fee: $40 ($50 for international students). Electronic applications accepted. *Expenses:* Tuition, state resident: full-time $3969; part-time $220.50 per credit hour. Tuition, nonresident: full-time $13,838; part-time $768.80 per credit hour. *Required fees:* $853; $47.40 per credit hour. *Financial support:* In 2014–15, 47 students received support, including 6 research assistantships (averaging $12,398 per year), 20 teaching assistantships (averaging $12,479 per year); career-related internships or fieldwork, Federal Work-Study, scholarships/grants, traineeships, health care benefits, and unspecified assistantships also available. Support available to part-time students. Financial award application deadline: 3/1. *Faculty research:* Public utilities, environment, linear models, biological sampling, public policy, economic development, energy, regional economics. *Unit head:* Dr. Richard V. Adkisson, Head, 575-646-4988, Fax: 575-646-1915, E-mail: radkisso@nmsu.edu. *Application contact:* 575-646-2113, Fax: 575-646-1915.
Website: http://business.nmsu.edu/departments/economics

The New School, The New School for Social Research, Department of Economics, New York, NY 10003. Offers economics (M Phil, MA, MS, DS Sc, PhD); global finance (MS); global political economy and finance (MA). Part-time and evening/weekend programs available. Terminal master's awarded for partial completion of doctoral program. *Degree requirements:* For master's, exam; for doctorate, one foreign language, thesis/dissertation, qualifying exam. *Entrance requirements:* For master's, GRE General Test; for doctorate, GRE General Test, MA. Additional exam requirements/recommendations for international students: Required—TOEFL (minimum score 600 paper-based; 100 iBT). Electronic applications accepted. *Faculty research:* Heterodox, history of economic thought, post-Keynesian, global political economy and finance.

New York University, Graduate School of Arts and Science, Department of Economics, New York, NY 10012-1019. Offers applied economic analysis (Advanced Certificate); economics (MA, PhD); JD/MA; MD/PhD. Part-time and evening/weekend programs available. *Faculty:* 35 full-time (2 women). *Students:* 214 full-time (77 women), 21 part-time (7 women); includes 15 minority (13 Asian, non-Hispanic/Latino; 2 Hispanic/Latino), 173 international. Average age 27. 1,531 applicants, 16% accepted, 88 enrolled. In 2014, 83 master's, 18 doctorates awarded. Terminal master's awarded for partial completion of doctoral program. *Degree requirements:* For master's, thesis; for doctorate, one foreign language, thesis/dissertation, 4 qualifying exams. *Entrance requirements:* For master's and doctorate, GRE General Test. Additional exam requirements/recommendations for international students: Required—TOEFL. *Application deadline:* For fall admission, 12/18 priority date for domestic students, 12/18 for international students. Application fee: $100. *Financial support:* Fellowships with tuition reimbursements, research assistantships with tuition reimbursements, teaching assistantships with tuition reimbursements, Federal Work-Study, institutionally sponsored loans, scholarships/grants, health care benefits, and unspecified assistantships available. Financial award application deadline: 12/18; financial award applicants required to submit FAFSA. *Faculty research:* Economic theory, experimental economics, growth and development, macroeconomics and finance, international trade and international finance. *Unit head:* Alessandro Lizzeri, Chair, 212-998-8900, Fax: 212-995-4186, E-mail: admissions@econ.nyu.edu. *Application contact:* Tim Cogley, Director of Graduate Studies, PhD Programs, 212-998-8900, Fax: 212-995-4186, E-mail: admissions@econ.nyu.edu.
Website: http://www.econ.nyu.edu/

New York University, Leonard N. Stern School of Business, Department of Economics, New York, NY 10012-1019. Offers MBA, PhD. *Faculty research:* Applied macroeconomics, macroeconomics and macroeconomic policy, international financial markets, international trade and business, game theory.

North Carolina State University, Graduate School, Poole College of Management and College of Agriculture and Life Sciences, Program in Economics, Raleigh, NC 27695. Offers M Econ, MA, PhD. Part-time programs available. Terminal master's awarded for partial completion of doctoral program. *Degree requirements:* For master's, thesis (for some programs); for doctorate, thesis/dissertation. *Entrance requirements:* For master's and doctorate, GRE General Test. Additional exam requirements/recommendations for international students: Required—TOEFL. Electronic applications accepted. *Faculty research:* Endogenous growth modeling, generalized methods of moments estimation, integration and trade, agricultural policy, path dependence and network externalities.

Northeastern University, College of Social Sciences and Humanities, Boston, MA 02115. Offers criminology and criminal justice (MSCJ); criminology and justice policy (PhD); economics (MA, PhD); English (MA, PhD); law and public policy (MS, PhD); political science (MA, PhD); public administration (MPA); public history (MA); security and resilience studies (MS); sociology (MA, PhD); urban and regional policy (MS); world history (MA, PhD). *Degree requirements:* For doctorate, variable foreign language requirement, comprehensive exam, thesis/dissertation. *Entrance requirements:* For master's and doctorate, GRE. Additional exam requirements/recommendations for international students: Required—TOEFL, IELTS. Electronic applications accepted.

Northern Illinois University, Graduate School, College of Liberal Arts and Sciences, Department of Economics, De Kalb, IL 60115-2854. Offers MA, PhD. Part-time programs available. *Faculty:* 15 full-time (3 women). *Students:* 25 full-time (5 women), 8 part-time (4 women); includes 4 minority (all Black or African American, non-Hispanic/Latino), 25 international. Average age 32. 84 applicants, 37% accepted, 8 enrolled. In 2014, 4 master's, 5 doctorates awarded. Terminal master's awarded for partial completion of doctoral program. *Degree requirements:* For master's, comprehensive exam, thesis or alternative; for doctorate, thesis/dissertation, candidacy exam, dissertation defense, research seminar. *Entrance requirements:* For master's, GRE General Test, minimum GPA of 2.75; for doctorate, GRE General Test, minimum GPA of 2.75 (undergraduate), 3.2 (graduate). Additional exam requirements/recommendations for international students: Required—TOEFL (minimum score 550 paper-based). *Application deadline:* For fall admission, 6/1 for domestic students, 5/1 for international students; for spring admission, 11/1 for domestic students, 10/1 for international students. Applications are processed on a rolling basis. Application fee: $40. Electronic applications accepted. *Financial support:* In 2014–15, 29 teaching assistantships with full tuition reimbursements were awarded; fellowships with full tuition reimbursements, research assistantships with full tuition reimbursements, career-related internships or fieldwork, Federal Work-Study, scholarships/grants, tuition waivers (full), and unspecified assistantships also available. Support available to part-time students. Financial award applicants required to submit FAFSA. *Faculty research:* Unemployment, behavior under uncertainty, effect of debt on compensation and capital utilization, racial inequality of earnings. *Unit head:* Dr. Virginia Wilcox-Gok, Chair, 815-753-6974, Fax: 815-753-1019, E-mail: vlw@niu.edu. *Application contact:* Dr. Jeremy Groves, Director, Graduate Studies, 815-753-6957.
Website: http://www.niu.edu/econ/

Northwestern University, The Graduate School, Judd A. and Marjorie Weinberg College of Arts and Sciences, Department of Economics, Evanston, IL 60208. Offers PhD, JD/PhD. Admissions and degrees offered through The Graduate School. *Degree requirements:* For doctorate, thesis/dissertation, preliminary written exam. *Entrance requirements:* For doctorate, GRE General Test. Additional exam requirements/recommendations for international students: Required—TOEFL. *Faculty research:* Organization of industry, behavior of labor markets, effects of monetary policy, theory of markets.

Northwestern University, The Graduate School, Kellogg School of Management, Department of Managerial Economics and Decision Sciences, Evanston, IL 60208. Offers PhD. Admissions and degree offered through The Graduate School. *Degree requirements:* For doctorate, comprehensive exam, thesis/dissertation. *Entrance requirements:* For doctorate, GMAT or GRE General Test. Additional exam requirements/recommendations for international students: Required—TOEFL. Electronic applications accepted. *Faculty research:* Competitive strategy and organization, managerial economics, decision sciences, game theory, operations management.

Oakland University, Graduate Study and Lifelong Learning, School of Business Administration, Department of Economics, Rochester, MI 48309-4401. Offers Certificate.

The Ohio State University, Graduate School, College of Arts and Sciences, Division of Social and Behavioral Sciences, Department of Economics, Columbus, OH 43210. Offers MA, PhD. *Faculty:* 29. *Students:* 82 full-time (24 women), 1 part-time (0 women); includes 5 minority (1 Black or African American, non-Hispanic/Latino; 3 Asian, non-Hispanic/Latino; 1 Hispanic/Latino), 65 international. Average age 27. In 2014, 25 master's, 8 doctorates awarded. *Degree requirements:* For doctorate, thesis/dissertation. *Entrance requirements:* For doctorate, GRE. Additional exam requirements/recommendations for international students: Required—TOEFL (minimum score 550 paper-based; 79 iBT), Michigan English Language Assessment Battery (minimum score 82); Recommended—IELTS (minimum score 7). *Application deadline:* For fall admission, 11/30 priority date for domestic and international students; for winter admission, 12/1 for domestic students, 11/1 for international students; for spring admission, 3/1 for domestic students, 2/1 for international students. Applications are processed on a rolling basis. Application fee: $60 ($70 for international students). Electronic applications accepted. *Financial support:* Fellowships with tuition reimbursements, research assistantships with tuition reimbursements, teaching assistantships with tuition reimbursements, Federal Work-Study, and institutionally sponsored loans available. Support available to part-time students. *Unit head:* Dr. David Blau, Chair, 614-292-6701, Fax: 614-292-3906, E-mail: blau.12@osu.edu. *Application contact:* Graduate and Professional Admissions, 614-292-9444, Fax: 614-292-3895, E-mail: gpadmissions@osu.edu.
Website: https://economics.osu.edu/

Ohio University, Graduate College, College of Arts and Sciences, Department of Economics, Athens, OH 45701-2979. Offers applied economics (MA); financial economics (MFE). Part-time and evening/weekend programs available. *Degree requirements:* For master's, thesis or alternative. *Entrance requirements:* For master's, GRE or GMAT (recommended), minimum GPA of 3.0. Additional exam requirements/recommendations for international students: Required—TOEFL (minimum score 550 paper-based; 80 iBT) or IELTS (minimum score 6.5). Electronic applications accepted. *Faculty research:* Macroeconomics, public finance, international economics and finance, monetary theory, healthcare economics.

Oklahoma State University, Spears School of Business, Department of Economics and Legal Studies in Business, Stillwater, OK 74078. Offers MS, PhD. Part-time programs available. *Faculty:* 21 full-time (6 women), 4 part-time/adjunct (2 women). *Students:* 10 full-time (2 women), 10 part-time (3 women); includes 1 minority (American Indian or Alaska Native, non-Hispanic/Latino), 14 international. Average age 31. 47 applicants, 34% accepted, 6 enrolled. In 2014, 6 master's, 1 doctorate awarded. *Degree requirements:* For master's, thesis or alternative; for doctorate, comprehensive exam, thesis/dissertation. *Entrance requirements:* For master's and doctorate, GRE or GMAT. Additional exam requirements/recommendations for international students: Required—TOEFL (minimum score 550 paper-based; 79 iBT). *Application deadline:* For fall admission, 3/1 priority date for international students; for spring admission, 8/1 priority date for international students. Applications are processed on a rolling basis. Application fee: $40 ($75 for international students). Electronic applications accepted. *Expenses:* Tuition, state resident: full-time $4488; part-time $187 per credit hour. Tuition, nonresident: full-time $18,360; part-time $765 per credit hour. *Required fees:* $2413; $100.55 per credit hour. Tuition and fees vary according to campus/location. *Financial support:* In 2014–15, 21 teaching assistantships (averaging $18,585 per year) were awarded; research assistantships, career-related internships or fieldwork, Federal Work-Study, scholarships/grants, health care benefits, tuition waivers (partial), and unspecified assistantships also available. Support available to part-time students. Financial award application deadline: 3/1; financial award applicants required to submit FAFSA. *Faculty research:* Economics and legal studies in business, regional economic modeling/econometrics, urban/regional economics, monetary economics, international trade/finance/development, environmental economics. *Unit head:* Dr. Lee Adkins, Head, 405-744-5195, Fax: 405-744-5180, E-mail: lee.adkins@okstate.edu. *Application contact:* Dr. Mary Gade, Graduate Coordinator, 405-744-5197, Fax: 405-744-5180, E-mail: mary.gade@okstate.edu.
Website: http://spears.okstate.edu/ecls

Old Dominion University, Strome College of Business, Program in Economics, Norfolk, VA 23529. Offers MA. Part-time and evening/weekend programs available. *Faculty:* 11 full-time (1 woman). *Students:* 17 full-time (7 women), 16 part-time (8 women); includes 6 minority (4 Black or African American, non-Hispanic/Latino; 1 Asian, non-Hispanic/Latino; 1 Two or more races, non-Hispanic/Latino), 11 international. Average age 29. 50 applicants, 76% accepted, 26 enrolled. In 2014, 9 master's awarded. *Degree requirements:* For master's, comprehensive exam, thesis optional, independent research. *Entrance requirements:* For master's, GMAT or GRE General Test, minimum GPA of 2.5. Additional exam requirements/recommendations for international students: Required—TOEFL (minimum score 520 paper-based; 79 iBT). *Application deadline:* For fall admission, 8/1 priority date for domestic students, 4/15 for international students; for spring admission, 11/1 priority date for domestic students, 10/1 for international students. Applications are processed on a rolling basis. Application fee: $50. Electronic applications accepted. *Expenses:* Expenses: Contact institution. *Financial support:* In 2014–15, 8 students received support, including 8 research assistantships with partial tuition reimbursements available (averaging $3,200 per year); unspecified assistantships also available. Financial award application deadline: 8/1; financial award applicants required to submit FAFSA. *Faculty research:* International economics, transportation, public economics, macroeconomics, econometrics. *Unit head:* Dr. David Duden Selover, Graduate Program Director, 757-683-3541, Fax: 757-638-5639, E-mail: dselover@odu.edu. *Application contact:* Dr. Ali Ardalan, Associate Dean, 757-683-3520, Fax: 757-683-4076, E-mail: aardalan@odu.edu.
Website: http://www.odu.edu/business/departments/economics

Oregon State University, College of Agricultural Sciences, Program in Applied Economics, Corvallis, OR 97331. Offers MA, MS, PhD. Part-time programs available. *Faculty:* 15 full-time (3 women), 7 part-time/adjunct (0 women). *Students:* 36 full-time (16 women), 6 part-time (3 women); includes 3 minority (1 Asian, non-Hispanic/Latino; 1

Hispanic/Latino; 1 Two or more races, non-Hispanic/Latino), 15 international. Average age 30. 101 applicants, 25% accepted, 9 enrolled. In 2014, 9 master's, 3 doctorates awarded. Terminal master's awarded for partial completion of doctoral program. *Degree requirements:* For master's, thesis (for some programs); for doctorate, thesis/dissertation. *Entrance requirements:* For master's and doctorate, GRE General Test, minimum GPA of 3.0 in last 90 hours. Additional exam requirements/recommendations for international students: Required—TOEFL (minimum score 90 iBT). *Application deadline:* For fall admission, 1/15 for domestic and international students. Application fee: $60. *Expenses:* Tuition, state resident: full-time $11,907; part-time $189 per credit hour. Tuition, nonresident: full-time $19,953; part-time $441 per credit hour. *Required fees:* $1472; $449 per term. One-time fee: $350. Tuition and fees vary according to course load and program. *Financial support:* Fellowships, research assistantships, teaching assistantships, career-related internships or fieldwork, Federal Work-Study, and institutionally sponsored loans available. Support available to part-time students. Financial award application deadline: 2/1. *Faculty research:* Marine economics, environmental economics, effects of global climate change on agriculture, efficiency of agricultural markets, analysis of aquaculture development. *Unit head:* Dr. Steven Buccola, Director of Applied Economics Program, 541-737-1410. *Application contact:* Tjodie Richardson, Applied Economics Advisor, 541-737-1399, E-mail: tjrichardson@oregonstate.edu.
Website: http://oregonstate.edu/aecgradprogram/

Penn State University Park, Graduate School, College of the Liberal Arts, Department of Economics, University Park, PA 16802. Offers MA, PhD. *Unit head:* Dr. Susan Welch, Dean, 814-865-7691, Fax: 814-863-2085, E-mail: swelch@psu.edu. *Application contact:* Lori A. Stania, Director, Graduate Student Services, 814-867-5278, Fax: 814-863-4627, E-mail: gswww@psu.edu.
Website: http://econ.la.psu.edu/

Pepperdine University, School of Public Policy, Malibu, CA 90263. Offers American politics (MPP); economics (MPP); international relations (MPP); public policy (MPP); state and local policy (MPP). *Faculty:* 6 full-time (2 women), 7 part-time/adjunct (1 woman). *Students:* 74 full-time (42 women), 10 part-time (5 women); includes 22 minority (11 Black or African American, non-Hispanic/Latino; 3 American Indian or Alaska Native, non-Hispanic/Latino; 3 Asian, non-Hispanic/Latino; 2 Hispanic/Latino; 1 Native Hawaiian or other Pacific Islander, non-Hispanic/Latino; 2 Two or more races, non-Hispanic/Latino), 21 international. 157 applicants, 65% accepted, 32 enrolled. In 2014, 52 master's awarded. *Entrance requirements:* For master's, GRE or GMAT, 2 letters of recommendation, resume, two essays. Additional exam requirements/recommendations for international students: Required—TOEFL. *Application deadline:* For fall admission, 6/15 for domestic students. Applications are processed on a rolling basis. Application fee: $50. Electronic applications accepted. *Financial support:* Institutionally sponsored loans and scholarships/grants available. Financial award application deadline: 5/1; financial award applicants required to submit FAFSA. *Unit head:* Dr. James R. Wilburn, Dean, School of Public Policy, 310-506-7490, Fax: 310-506-7494, E-mail: james.wilburn@pepperdine.edu. *Application contact:* Melinda E. van Hemert, Director of Recruitment and Career Services, 310-506-7492, Fax: 310-506-7494, E-mail: melinda.vanhemert@pepperdine.edu.
Website: http://publicpolicy.pepperdine.edu/

Peru State College, Graduate Programs, Program in Organizational Management, Peru, NE 68421. Offers MS. Program offered online only. Part-time programs available. Postbaccalaureate distance learning degree programs offered (no on-campus study). *Degree requirements:* For master's, thesis (for some programs). *Expenses:* Contact institution. *Faculty research:* Emotional intelligence.

Portland State University, Graduate Studies, College of Liberal Arts and Sciences, Department of Economics, Portland, OR 97207-0751. Offers applied economics (MA, MS); general economics (MA, MS). Part-time programs available. *Faculty:* 14 full-time (2 women), 6 part-time/adjunct (4 women). *Students:* 13 full-time (4 women), 1 (woman) part-time, 4 international. Average age 28. 23 applicants, 39% accepted, 7 enrolled. In 2014, 10 master's awarded. *Degree requirements:* For master's, thesis optional; for doctorate, one foreign language, thesis/dissertation. *Entrance requirements:* For master's, minimum GPA of 3.0 in economic course work and overall; course work in calculus. Additional exam requirements/recommendations for international students: Required—TOEFL (minimum score 550 paper-based; 80 iBT). *Application deadline:* For fall admission, 2/1 for domestic and international students; for winter admission, 9/1 for domestic and international students; for spring admission, 12/5 for domestic and international students. Applications are processed on a rolling basis. Application fee: $50. *Expenses:* Tuition, state resident: part-time $222 per credit. Tuition, nonresident: part-time $527 per credit. *Required fees:* $22 per contact hour. $100 per quarter. Tuition and fees vary according to program. *Financial support:* In 2014–15, 10 teaching assistantships with full tuition reimbursements (averaging $6,570 per year) were awarded; career-related internships or fieldwork, Federal Work-Study, and unspecified assistantships also available. Support available to part-time students. Financial award application deadline: 3/1; financial award applicants required to submit FAFSA. *Faculty research:* NAFTA, economies of transition, economics of Eastern Europe, artificial intelligence, comparative economic systems. *Total annual research expenditures:* $407,002. *Unit head:* Dr. Thomas Potiowsky, Chair, 503-725-2288, Fax: 503-725-3945, E-mail: potiowskyt@pdx.edu. *Application contact:* Margie Port, Office Coordinator, 503-725-3974, Fax: 503-725-3945, E-mail: mport@pdx.edu.
Website: http://www.pdx.edu/econ/

Portland State University, Graduate Studies, College of Liberal Arts and Sciences, Systems Science Program, Portland, OR 97207-0751. Offers computational intelligence (Certificate); computer modeling and simulation (Certificate); systems science (MS); systems science/anthropology (PhD); systems science/business administration (PhD); systems science/civil engineering (PhD); systems science/economics (PhD); systems science/engineering management (PhD); systems science/general (PhD); systems science/mathematical sciences (PhD); systems science/mechanical engineering (PhD); systems science/psychology (PhD); systems science/sociology (PhD). *Faculty:* 2 full-time (0 women), 1 part-time/adjunct (0 women). *Students:* 6 full-time (2 women), 29 part-time (8 women); includes 6 minority (1 Black or African American, non-Hispanic/Latino; 1 American Indian or Alaska Native, non-Hispanic/Latino; 1 Asian, non-Hispanic/Latino; 3 Hispanic/Latino). Average age 41. 32 applicants, 19% accepted, 6 enrolled. In 2014, 10 master's, 3 doctorates awarded. *Degree requirements:* For master's, comprehensive exam (for some programs), thesis optional; for doctorate, variable foreign language requirement, comprehensive exam (for some programs), thesis/dissertation. *Entrance requirements:* For master's, GRE/GMAT (recommended), minimum GPA of 3.0 undergraduate or graduate work, 2 letters of recommendation, statement of interest; for doctorate, GMAT, GRE General Test, minimum GPA of 3.0 undergraduate, 3.25 graduate; 2 letters of recommendation; statement of interest. Additional exam requirements/recommendations for international students: Required—TOEFL (minimum score 550 paper-based; 80 iBT). *Application deadline:* For fall admission, 1/15 for domestic and international students; for spring admission, 11/1 for domestic students. Application fee: $50. Electronic applications accepted. *Expenses:* Tuition, state resident: part-time $222 per credit. Tuition, nonresident: part-time $527 per credit. *Required fees:* $22 per contact hour. $100 per quarter. Tuition and fees vary according to program. *Financial support:* In 2014–15, 1 research assistantship with full and partial tuition reimbursement (averaging $2,358 per year) was awarded; teaching assistantships with full and partial tuition reimbursements, career-related internships or fieldwork, Federal Work-Study, scholarships/grants, and unspecified assistantships also available. Support available to part-time students. Financial award application deadline: 3/1; financial award applicants required to submit FAFSA. *Faculty research:* Systems theory and methodology, artificial intelligence neural networks, information theory, nonlinear dynamics/chaos, modeling and simulation. *Total annual research expenditures:* $137,833. *Unit head:* Prof. Wayne Wakeland, PhD, Chair, 503-725-4975, E-mail: wakeland@pdx.edu.
Website: http://www.pdx.edu/sysc/

Princeton University, Graduate School, Department of Economics, Princeton, NJ 08544-1019. Offers PhD. *Degree requirements:* For doctorate, thesis/dissertation. *Entrance requirements:* For doctorate, GRE General Test, GRE Subject Test (recommended), working knowledge of multivariate calculus and matrix algebra. Additional exam requirements/recommendations for international students: Required—TOEFL (minimum score 600 paper-based). Electronic applications accepted.

Princeton University, Graduate School, Program in Population Studies, Princeton, NJ 08544-1019. Offers demography (PhD, Certificate); economics and demography (PhD); public affairs and demography (PhD); sociology and demography (PhD). *Degree requirements:* For doctorate, thesis/dissertation. *Entrance requirements:* For doctorate, GRE General Test. Additional exam requirements/recommendations for international students: Required—TOEFL (minimum score 600 paper-based). Electronic applications accepted. *Faculty research:* Models, fertility, infant and child mortality, migration.

Purdue University, Graduate School, Krannert School of Management, Doctoral Program in Economics, West Lafayette, IN 47907-2056. Offers PhD. *Degree requirements:* For doctorate, comprehensive exam, thesis/dissertation, dissertation proposal in 3rd year of study. *Entrance requirements:* For doctorate, GRE, two semesters of calculus, one semester of linear algebra. Additional exam requirements/recommendations for international students: Required—TOEFL (minimum score 575 paper-based); Recommended—TWE. Electronic applications accepted. *Faculty research:* Econometrics, experimental economics, international economics, macroeconomic theory, industrial organization.

Rice University, Graduate Programs, School of Social Sciences, Department of Economics, Houston, TX 77251-1892. Offers MA, PhD. *Degree requirements:* For doctorate, comprehensive exam, thesis/dissertation. *Entrance requirements:* For doctorate, GRE. Additional exam requirements/recommendations for international students: Required—TOEFL (minimum score 600 paper-based; 90 iBT). Electronic applications accepted.

Roosevelt University, Graduate Division, College of Arts and Sciences, Department of Economics, Chicago, IL 60605. Offers applied economics (MA); economics (MA). Part-time and evening/weekend programs available. *Degree requirements:* For master's, thesis or alternative. *Entrance requirements:* For master's, minimum GPA of 2.7. *Faculty research:* Labor, gender issues, international trade and development, entrepreneurship, political economy and money.

Rutgers, The State University of New Jersey, Newark, Graduate School, Program in Economics, Newark, NJ 07102. Offers MA. *Entrance requirements:* For master's, GRE, minimum undergraduate B average.

Rutgers, The State University of New Jersey, Newark, Rutgers Business School–Newark and New Brunswick, Doctoral Programs in Management, Newark, NJ 07102. Offers accounting (PhD); accounting information systems (PhD); economics (PhD); finance (PhD); individualized study (PhD); information technology (PhD); international business (PhD); management science (PhD); marketing science (PhD); organizational management (PhD); science, technology and management (PhD); supply chain management (PhD). *Degree requirements:* For doctorate, comprehensive exam, thesis/dissertation. *Entrance requirements:* For doctorate, GRE or GMAT. Additional exam requirements/recommendations for international students: Required—TOEFL (minimum score 550 paper-based; 79 iBT). Electronic applications accepted.

Rutgers, The State University of New Jersey, New Brunswick, Graduate School-New Brunswick, Program in Economics, Piscataway, NJ 08854-8097. Offers MA, PhD. Terminal master's awarded for partial completion of doctoral program. *Degree requirements:* For master's, comprehensive exam (for some programs), thesis or alternative; for doctorate, comprehensive exam, thesis/dissertation. *Entrance requirements:* For master's and doctorate, GRE General Test. Additional exam requirements/recommendations for international students: Required—TOEFL. Electronic applications accepted. *Faculty research:* Econometrics, microeconomics, macroeconomics, economichistory.

St. Cloud State University, School of Graduate Studies, College of Social Sciences, Department of Economics, St. Cloud, MN 56301-4498. Offers applied economics (MS); public and nonprofit institutions (MS). Part-time programs available. *Degree requirements:* For master's, thesis or alternative. *Entrance requirements:* For master's, GRE General Test, minimum GPA of 2.75. Additional exam requirements/recommendations for international students: Recommended—TOEFL (minimum score 550 paper-based), IELTS (minimum score 6.5). Electronic applications accepted.

San Diego State University, Graduate and Research Affairs, College of Arts and Letters, Department of Economics, San Diego, CA 92182. Offers MA. *Entrance requirements:* For master's, GRE General Test, 2 letters of recommendation. Additional exam requirements/recommendations for international students: Required—TOEFL. Electronic applications accepted. *Faculty research:* Financing public education, demand for alternative fuel vehicles, economics of the Gold Rush, interdependence of equity and economic efficiency, economics of welfare.

San Francisco State University, Division of Graduate Studies, College of Business, Department of Economics, San Francisco, CA 94132-1722. Offers MA. *Expenses:* Tuition, state resident: full-time $6738. Tuition, nonresident: full-time $17,898; part-time $372 per credit hour. *Required fees:* $498 per semester. *Unit head:* Dr. Sudip Chattopadhyay, Chair, 415-338-1839, E-mail: sudip@sfsu.edu. *Application contact:* Dr. Lisa Takeyama, Graduate Coordinator, 415-338-2499, E-mail: takeyama@sfsu.edu.
Website: http://cob6.sfsu.edu/cob/economics

San Jose State University, Graduate Studies and Research, College of Social Sciences, Department of Economics, San Jose, CA 95192-0001. Offers applied economics (MA); economics (MA). Part-time programs available. *Degree requirements:* For master's, comprehensive exam, thesis optional. *Entrance requirements:* For master's, GRE, minimum GPA of 3.0. Electronic applications accepted.

Simon Fraser University, Office of Graduate Studies, Faculty of Arts and Social Sciences, Department of Economics, Burnaby, BC V5A 1S6, Canada. Offers MA, PhD. *Degree requirements:* For master's, thesis (for some programs); for doctorate, comprehensive exam, thesis/dissertation. *Entrance requirements:* For master's, GRE, minimum GPA of 3.0 (on scale of 4.33), or 3.33 based on last 60 credits of undergraduate courses; for doctorate, GRE, minimum GPA of 3.5 (on scale of 4.33). Additional exam requirements/recommendations for international students: Recommended—TOEFL (minimum score 580 paper-based; 93 iBT), IELTS (minimum

score 7), TWE (minimum score 5). *Faculty research:* Industrial organization, international trade, econometrics, labor, macroeconomics.

South Dakota State University, Graduate School, College of Agriculture and Biological Sciences, Department of Economics, Brookings, SD 57007. Offers MS. *Degree requirements:* For master's, comprehensive exam, thesis (for some programs), oral exam. *Entrance requirements:* For master's, minimum GPA of 2.75. Additional exam requirements/recommendations for international students: Required—TOEFL (minimum score 550 paper-based; 79 iBT). *Faculty research:* Sustainable agriculture, rural finance, grain and livestock marketing, agricultural policy, applied economics.

Southern Illinois University Carbondale, Graduate School, College of Liberal Arts, Department of Economics, Carbondale, IL 62901-4701. Offers MA, MS, PhD. *Faculty:* 9 full-time (0 women). *Students:* 42 full-time (11 women), 8 part-time (0 women); includes 6 minority (4 Black or African American, non-Hispanic/Latino; 1 Asian, non-Hispanic/Latino; 1 Hispanic/Latino), 29 international. 68 applicants, 43% accepted, 15 enrolled. In 2014, 5 master's, 7 doctorates awarded. *Degree requirements:* For master's, thesis; for doctorate, thesis/dissertation. *Entrance requirements:* For master's, GRE General Test, minimum GPA of 2.7; for doctorate, GRE General Test, minimum GPA of 3.25. Additional exam requirements/recommendations for international students: Required—TOEFL. *Application deadline:* Applications are processed on a rolling basis. Application fee: $50. *Expenses:* Tuition, state resident: full-time $10,176; part-time $1153 per credit. Tuition, nonresident: full-time $20,814; part-time $1744 per credit. *Required fees:* $7092; $394 per credit. $2364 per semester. *Financial support:* In 2014–15, 23 students received support, including 2 fellowships with full tuition reimbursements available, 2 research assistantships with full tuition reimbursements available, 17 teaching assistantships with full tuition reimbursements available; Federal Work-Study, institutionally sponsored loans, and tuition waivers (full) also available. Support available to part-time students. *Faculty research:* Advanced economic theory, applied microeconomics, economic development, finance, international economics, monetary theory and policy. *Unit head:* Dr. Subhash C. Sharma, Chairperson, 618-453-5082, E-mail: sharma@siu.edu. *Application contact:* Monica Russell, Administrative Clerk, 618-453-5085, E-mail: monicar@siu.edu.
Website: http://economics.siuc.edu/

Southern Illinois University Edwardsville, Graduate School, School of Business, Department of Economics and Finance, Edwardsville, IL 62026. Offers MA, MS. Part-time and evening/weekend programs available. *Faculty:* 11 full-time (0 women). *Students:* 12 full-time (5 women), 7 part-time (3 women); includes 4 minority (3 Black or African American, non-Hispanic/Latino; 1 Asian, non-Hispanic/Latino), 7 international. 24 applicants, 50% accepted. In 2014, 7 master's awarded. *Degree requirements:* For master's, thesis or alternative, final exam, portfolio. *Entrance requirements:* For master's, GMAT or GRE. Additional exam requirements/recommendations for international students: Required—TOEFL (minimum score 550 paper-based; 79 iBT), IELTS (minimum score 6.5). *Application deadline:* For fall admission, 7/24 for domestic students, 7/15 for international students; for spring admission, 12/11 for domestic students, 11/15 for international students; for summer admission, 4/29 for domestic students, 4/15 for international students. Applications are processed on a rolling basis. Application fee: $30. Electronic applications accepted. *Expenses:* Tuition, state resident: full-time $5026. Tuition, nonresident: full-time $12,566. *International tuition:* $25,136 full-time. *Required fees:* $1682. Tuition and fees vary according to course load, campus/location and program. *Financial support:* In 2014–15, 9 students received support, including 1 fellowship with full tuition reimbursement available (averaging $8,370 per year), 1 research assistantship with full tuition reimbursement available, 7 teaching assistantships with full tuition reimbursements available; institutionally sponsored loans, scholarships/grants, and unspecified assistantships also available. Financial award application deadline: 3/1; financial award applicants required to submit FAFSA. *Unit head:* Dr. Ayse Evrensel, Chair, 618-650-2542, E-mail: aevrens@siue.edu. *Application contact:* Melissa K Mace, Assistant Director of Admissions for Graduate and International Recruitment, 618-650-2756, Fax: 618-650-3618, E-mail: mmace@siue.edu.
Website: http://www.siue.edu/business/economicsandfinance/

Southern Methodist University, Dedman College of Humanities and Sciences, Department of Economics, Dallas, TX 75205. Offers applied economics (MA); applied economics and predictive analytics (MS); economics (PhD); law and economics (MA). Part-time and evening/weekend programs available. Terminal master's awarded for partial completion of doctoral program. *Degree requirements:* For master's, thesis, oral qualifying exam; for doctorate, thesis/dissertation, written exams. *Entrance requirements:* For master's, GRE General Test or GMAT, 12 hours of course work in economics, minimum GPA of 3.0, previous course work in calculus and statistics; for doctorate, GRE General Test, minimum GPA of 3.0; 3 semesters of course work in calculus; 1 semester each of course work in statistics and linear algebra. Additional exam requirements/recommendations for international students: Required—TOEFL (minimum score 550 paper-based). Electronic applications accepted. *Faculty research:* Economic theory, game theory, econometrics, international trade, labor.

Stanford University, School of Humanities and Sciences, Department of Economics, Stanford, CA 94305-9991. Offers PhD. *Degree requirements:* For doctorate, thesis/dissertation, oral exam. *Entrance requirements:* For doctorate, GRE General Test. Additional exam requirements/recommendations for international students: Required—TOEFL. Electronic applications accepted. *Expenses: Tuition:* Full-time $44,184; part-time $982 per credit hour. *Required fees:* $191.

State University of New York College of Environmental Science and Forestry, Program in Environmental Science, Syracuse, NY 13210-2779. Offers biophysical and ecological economics (MPS); coupled natural and human systems (MPS); ecosystem restoration (MPS); environmental and community land planning (MPS, MS); environmental and natural resources policy (PhD); environmental communication and participatory processes (PhD); environmental monitoring and modeling (MPS); environmental policy and democratic processes (MPS, MS); water and wetland resource studies (MPS, MS). Part-time programs available. *Degree requirements:* For master's, thesis (for some programs); for doctorate, comprehensive exam, thesis/dissertation. *Entrance requirements:* For master's and doctorate, GRE General Test, minimum GPA of 3.0. Additional exam requirements/recommendations for international students: Required—TOEFL (minimum score 550 paper-based; 80 iBT), IELTS (minimum score 6). *Faculty research:* Environmental education/communications, water resources, land resources, waste management.

Stony Brook University, State University of New York, Graduate School, College of Arts and Sciences, Department of Economics, Stony Brook, NY 11794. Offers MA, PhD. *Faculty:* 14 full-time (3 women), 4 part-time/adjunct (1 woman). *Students:* 72 full-time (32 women); includes 1 minority (Asian, non-Hispanic/Latino), 68 international. Average age 28. 230 applicants, 32% accepted, 24 enrolled. In 2014, 16 master's, 5 doctorates awarded. *Degree requirements:* For doctorate, comprehensive exam, thesis/dissertation. *Entrance requirements:* For master's and doctorate, GRE General Test. Additional exam requirements/recommendations for international students: Required—TOEFL. *Application deadline:* For fall admission, 1/15 for domestic students; for spring admission, 10/1 for domestic students. Application fee: $100. *Expenses:* Tuition, state resident: full-time $10,370; part-time $432 per credit. Tuition, nonresident: full-time $20,190; part-time $841 per credit. *Required fees:* $1431. *Financial support:* In 2014–15, 23 teaching assistantships were awarded; fellowships and research assistantships also available. *Faculty research:* Economic theory, game theory, econometrics, macroeconomics, applied microeconomics. *Total annual research expenditures:* $67,456. *Unit head:* Dr. Sandro Brusco, Co-Chair, 631-632-7540, Fax: 631-632-7516, E-mail: sandro.brusco@stonybrook.edu. *Application contact:* Maryann Calvacca, Coordinator, 631-632-7537, E-mail: graduate_economics@stonybrook.edu.
Website: http://www.sunysb.edu/economics/

Suffolk University, College of Arts and Sciences, Department of Economics, Boston, MA 02108-2770. Offers economic policy (MSEP); economics (MSE); international economics (MSIE); JD/MSIE. Part-time and evening/weekend programs available. *Faculty:* 5 full-time (2 women), 1 part-time/adjunct (0 women). *Students:* 4 full-time (3 women), 16 part-time (3 women); includes 5 minority (1 Black or African American, non-Hispanic/Latino; 4 Asian, non-Hispanic/Latino), 7 international. Average age 30. 48 applicants, 71% accepted, 19 enrolled. In 2014, 12 master's awarded. *Entrance requirements:* For master's, GRE General Test or GMAT, 2 letters of recommendation, resume. Additional exam requirements/recommendations for international students: Required—TOEFL (minimum score 550 paper-based; 80 iBT). *Application deadline:* For fall admission, 6/15 priority date for domestic students, 6/15 for international students; for spring admission, 11/1 priority date for domestic students, 11/1 for international students. Applications are processed on a rolling basis. Application fee: $50. Electronic applications accepted. *Expenses:* Expenses: Contact institution. *Financial support:* In 2014–15, 16 students received support, including 15 fellowships (averaging $5,912 per year); career-related internships or fieldwork, Federal Work-Study, and institutionally sponsored loans also available. Support available to part-time students. Financial award application deadline: 4/1; financial award applicants required to submit FAFSA. *Faculty research:* Travel demands, decisions in multinational firms and in research production in higher education, charitable giving of fair tax, smoking, fair tax. *Unit head:* In-Mee Baek, Chairperson, 617-573-8376, Fax: 617-994-4216, E-mail: ibaek@beaconhill.org. *Application contact:* Cory Meyers, Director of Graduate Admissions, 617-573-8302, Fax: 617-305-1733, E-mail: grad.admission@suffolk.edu.
Website: http://www.suffolk.edu/economics

Syracuse University, Maxwell School of Citizenship and Public Affairs, Joint Program in Economics and International Relations, Syracuse, NY 13244. Offers MA/MA. *Students:* 2 full-time (1 woman). Average age 26. 13 applicants, 85% accepted, 3 enrolled. *Entrance requirements:* Additional exam requirements/recommendations for international students: Required—TOEFL (minimum score 100 iBT). *Application deadline:* For fall admission, 2/1 priority date for domestic and international students. Application fee: $75. Electronic applications accepted. *Expenses: Tuition:* Part-time $1341 per credit. *Financial support:* Fellowships with full tuition reimbursements, research assistantships with full and partial tuition reimbursements, and teaching assistantships with full and partial tuition reimbursements available. Financial award application deadline: 1/1. *Unit head:* Dr. Stuart Brown, Program Contact, 315-443-7097, Fax: 315-443-3385, E-mail: ssbrown@maxwell.syr.edu. *Application contact:* Christine Omolino, Associate Director, 315-443-4000, Fax: 315-443-3423, E-mail: comolino@syr.edu.
Website: http://www.maxwell.syr.edu/

Syracuse University, Maxwell School of Citizenship and Public Affairs, Program in Economics, Syracuse, NY 13244. Offers MA, PhD. *Students:* 51 full-time (19 women), 4 part-time (3 women); includes 7 minority (3 Black or African American, non-Hispanic/Latino; 3 Asian, non-Hispanic/Latino; 1 Hispanic/Latino), 40 international. Average age 27. 263 applicants, 34% accepted, 14 enrolled. In 2014, 35 master's, 5 doctorates awarded. *Degree requirements:* For doctorate, comprehensive exam, thesis/dissertation. *Entrance requirements:* For master's and doctorate, GRE General Test. Additional exam requirements/recommendations for international students: Required—TOEFL (minimum score 100 iBT). *Application deadline:* For fall admission, 2/1 priority date for domestic and international students. Applications are processed on a rolling basis. Application fee: $75. Electronic applications accepted. *Expenses: Tuition:* Part-time $1341 per credit. *Financial support:* Fellowships with full tuition reimbursements, research assistantships with full and partial tuition reimbursements, and teaching assistantships with full and partial tuition reimbursements available. Financial award application deadline: 1/1. *Faculty research:* International economics, labor economics, public finance, urban economics. *Unit head:* Dr. William Horace, Chair, 315-443-3612, Fax: 315-443-3717. *Application contact:* Laura Sauta, Recruiting Contact, 315-443-2414, E-mail: lsauta@maxwell.syr.edu.
Website: http://www.maxwell.syr.edu/econ/

Teachers College, Columbia University, Graduate Faculty of Education, Department of Education Policy and Social Analysis, Program in Economics and Education, New York, NY 10027. Offers Ed M, MA, PhD. *Faculty:* 4 full-time, 1 part-time/adjunct. *Students:* 39 full-time (28 women), 72 part-time (44 women); includes 14 minority (5 Black or African American, non-Hispanic/Latino; 6 Asian, non-Hispanic/Latino; 2 Hispanic/Latino; 1 Two or more races, non-Hispanic/Latino), 86 international. Average age 29. 130 applicants, 42% accepted, 29 enrolled. In 2014, 24 master's, 6 doctorates awarded. *Degree requirements:* For master's, thesis; for doctorate, one foreign language, comprehensive exam, thesis/dissertation. *Entrance requirements:* For doctorate, GRE. *Application deadline:* For fall admission, 12/15 for domestic students; for spring admission, 11/1 for domestic students. Applications are processed on a rolling basis. Application fee: $65. Electronic applications accepted. *Expenses: Tuition:* Full-time $33,552; part-time $1398 per credit. *Required fees:* $418 per semester. *Financial support:* Career-related internships or fieldwork, Federal Work-Study, institutionally sponsored loans, and tuition waivers (full and partial) available. Support available to part-time students. Financial award application deadline: 2/1; financial award applicants required to submit FAFSA. *Faculty research:* Education and economic growth, efficiency in education, training in education, labor and education policy, economic status of immigrant groups. *Unit head:* Prof. Thomas Bailey, Program Coordinator, 212-678-3091, E-mail: tbailey@tc.edu. *Application contact:* Deanna Ghozati, Assistant Director of Admission, 212-678-4018, Fax: 212-678-4171, E-mail: ghozati@tc.edu.
Website: http://www.tc.columbia.edu/epsa/economics/

Temple University, College of Liberal Arts, Department of Economics, Philadelphia, PA 19122-6096. Offers MA, PhD. Part-time and evening/weekend programs available. *Faculty:* 18 full-time (2 women), 4 part-time/adjunct (2 women). *Students:* 46 full-time (18 women), 9 part-time (3 women); includes 4 minority (2 Black or African American, non-Hispanic/Latino; 2 Asian, non-Hispanic/Latino), 26 international. 81 applicants, 43% accepted, 13 enrolled. In 2014, 12 master's, 7 doctorates awarded. *Entrance requirements:* For master's and doctorate, GRE, minimum GPA of 3.0, 3 letters of recommendation. Additional exam requirements/recommendations for international students: Required—TOEFL (minimum score 550 paper-based; 79 iBT). *Application deadline:* For fall admission, 3/1 for domestic students, 12/15 for international students; for spring admission, 11/1 for domestic students, 8/1 for international students. Application fee: $60. Electronic applications accepted. *Expenses:* Tuition, state resident: full-time $14,490; part-time $805 per credit hour. Tuition, nonresident: full-time $19,850; part-time $1103 per credit hour. *Required fees:* $690. Full-time tuition and fees vary according to class time, course load, degree level, campus/location and program.

Economics

Financial support: Application deadline: 1/15; applicants required to submit FAFSA. *Faculty research:* Applied econometrics, health economics, labor economics, macroeconomic theory, microeconomic theory. *Unit head:* Dr. Michael L. Leeds, Graduate Director, 215-204-8030, E-mail: micheal.leeds@temple.edu. *Application contact:* Linda Wyatt, Graduate Program Coordinator, 215-204-6638, E-mail: ldwyatt@temple.edu.
Website: http://www.cla.temple.edu/economics/

Texas A&M University, College of Liberal Arts, Department of Economics, College Station, TX 77843. Offers MS, PhD. Part-time programs available. *Faculty:* 24. *Students:* 232 full-time (103 women), 16 part-time (8 women); includes 14 minority (1 Black or African American, non-Hispanic/Latino; 6 Asian, non-Hispanic/Latino; 5 Hispanic/Latino; 2 Two or more races, non-Hispanic/Latino), 210 international. Average age 26. 339 applicants, 45% accepted, 99 enrolled. In 2014, 65 master's, 15 doctorates awarded. Terminal master's awarded for partial completion of doctoral program. *Degree requirements:* For master's, comprehensive exam, thesis optional; for doctorate, comprehensive exam, thesis/dissertation. *Entrance requirements:* For master's and doctorate, GRE General Test. Additional exam requirements/recommendations for international students: Required—TOEFL. *Application deadline:* For fall admission, 3/1 priority date for domestic students; for winter admission, 8/1 priority date for domestic students; for spring admission, 11/1 priority date for domestic students. Applications are processed on a rolling basis. Application fee: $50 ($90 for international students). Electronic applications accepted. *Expenses:* Tuition, state resident: full-time $4078; part-time $226.55 per credit hour. Tuition, nonresident: full-time $10,594; part-time $577.55 per credit hour. *Required fees:* $2813; $237.70 per credit hour. $278.50 per semester. Tuition and fees vary according to degree level and student level. *Financial support:* In 2014–15, 104 students received support, including 9 fellowships with full and partial tuition reimbursements available (averaging $19,760 per year), 35 research assistantships with full and partial tuition reimbursements available (averaging $7,061 per year), 25 teaching assistantships with full and partial tuition reimbursements available (averaging $7,594 per year); career-related internships or fieldwork, institutionally sponsored loans, scholarships/grants, traineeships, health care benefits, tuition waivers (full and partial), and unspecified assistantships also available. Support available to part-time students. Financial award application deadline: 2/1; financial award applicants required to submit FAFSA. *Faculty research:* Tax policy, state tax, labor, international economics, macroeconomics. *Unit head:* Dr. Timothy Gronberg, Head, 979-845-7351, E-mail: tjg@econmail.tamu.edu. *Application contact:* Dr. Dennis W. Jansen, Director of Doctoral Program, 979-845-7351, Fax: 979-847-8557, E-mail: d-jansen@tamu.edu.
Website: http://econweb.tamu.edu/

Texas Tech University, Graduate School, College of Arts and Sciences, Department of Economics, Lubbock, TX 79409-1014. Offers MA, PhD, MPA/MA. *Faculty:* 12 full-time (1 woman). *Students:* 45 full-time (20 women), 2 part-time (0 women); includes 1 minority (Hispanic/Latino), 39 international. Average age 33. 67 applicants, 55% accepted, 9 enrolled. In 2014, 3 master's, 8 doctorates awarded. Terminal master's awarded for partial completion of doctoral program. *Degree requirements:* For master's, variable foreign language requirement, comprehensive exam (for some programs), thesis (for some programs); for doctorate, variable foreign language requirement, comprehensive exam, thesis/dissertation. *Entrance requirements:* Additional exam requirements/recommendations for international students: Required—TOEFL (minimum score 550 paper-based; 79 iBT). *Application deadline:* For fall admission, 6/1 priority date for domestic students, 1/15 priority date for international students; for spring admission, 9/1 priority date for domestic students, 6/15 priority date for international students. Applications are processed on a rolling basis. Application fee: $60. Electronic applications accepted. *Expenses:* Tuition, state resident: full-time $6310; part-time $262.92 per credit hour. Tuition, nonresident: full-time $14,998; part-time $624.92 per credit hour. *Required fees:* $2701; $36.50 per credit. $912.50 per semester. Tuition and fees vary according to course load. *Financial support:* In 2014–15, 39 students received support, including 37 fellowships (averaging $1,268 per year), 1 research assistantship (averaging $14,450 per year), 32 teaching assistantships (averaging $14,416 per year); scholarships/grants and unspecified assistantships also available. Financial award application deadline: 3/1; financial award applicants required to submit FAFSA. *Faculty research:* Industrial organization, labor economics, public finance, monetary economics, international economics. *Total annual research expenditures:* $3,700. *Unit head:* Dr. Klaus G. Becker, Associate Professor/Chair, 806-834-7275, Fax: 806-742-1137, E-mail: klaus.becker@ttu.edu. *Application contact:* Rosie Carrillo, Coordinator, 806-742-2201, E-mail: rosie.carrillo@ttu.edu.
Website: http://www.depts.ttu.edu/economics/

Tufts University, Graduate School of Arts and Sciences, Department of Economics, Medford, MA 02155. Offers MS. Part-time programs available. *Faculty:* 26 full-time (9 women), 16 part-time/adjunct (6 women). *Students:* 35 full-time (19 women), 27 international. Average age 23. 200 applicants, 51% accepted, 24 enrolled. In 2014, 24 master's awarded. *Degree requirements:* For master's, thesis optional. *Entrance requirements:* For master's, GRE General Test. Additional exam requirements/recommendations for international students: Required—TOEFL (minimum score 550 paper-based; 80 iBT), IELTS (minimum score 6.5). *Application deadline:* For fall admission, 2/15 for domestic and international students. Applications are processed on a rolling basis. Application fee: $75. Electronic applications accepted. *Expenses: Tuition:* Full-time $45,590; part-time $1161 per credit hour. *Required fees:* $782. Full-time tuition and fees vary according to degree level, program and student level. Part-time tuition and fees vary according to course load. *Financial support:* Teaching assistantships with full and partial tuition reimbursements, Federal Work-Study, scholarships/grants, tuition waivers (partial), and unspecified assistantships available. Financial award application deadline: 5/15; financial award applicants required to submit FAFSA. *Unit head:* Dr. Gilbert Metcalf, Graduate Program Director. *Application contact:* Office of Graduate Admissions, 617-627-3395, E-mail: gradadmissions@tufts.edu.
Website: http://ase.tufts.edu/econ

Tulane University, School of Liberal Arts, Department of Economics, New Orleans, LA 70118-5669. Offers MA, PhD. *Degree requirements:* For master's, thesis or alternative; for doctorate, one foreign language, thesis/dissertation. *Entrance requirements:* For master's, GRE General Test, minimum B average in undergraduate course work; for doctorate, GRE General Test. Additional exam requirements/recommendations for international students: Required—TOEFL. Electronic applications accepted. *Expenses: Tuition:* Full-time $46,326; part-time $2574 per credit hour. *Required fees:* $1980; $44.50 per credit hour. $550 per term. Tuition and fees vary according to course load and program. *Faculty research:* Economic development, public finance, labor economics, international and regional economics, industrial organization.

Universidad de las Américas Puebla, Division of Graduate Studies, School of Social Sciences, Program in Economics, Puebla, Mexico. Offers economics (MA); finance (M Adm). Part-time and evening/weekend programs available. *Degree requirements:* For master's, one foreign language, thesis. *Faculty research:* Economic models (mathematics), industrial organization, assets and values market.

Université de Moncton, Faculty of Arts and Social Sciences, Department of Economics, Moncton, NB E1A 3E9, Canada. Offers MA. *Degree requirements:* For master's, one foreign language, thesis. *Entrance requirements:* For master's, minimum GPA of 3.0. *Faculty research:* Free trade, public finance, small and medium size businesses, regional development, demography and development.

Université de Montréal, Faculty of Arts and Sciences, Department of Economic Sciences, Montréal, QC H3C 3J7, Canada. Offers economics (M Sc, PhD); mathematical and computational finance (M Sc). *Degree requirements:* For master's, one foreign language, thesis; for doctorate, one foreign language, thesis/dissertation, general exam. Electronic applications accepted. *Faculty research:* Applied and economic theory, public choice, international trade, labor economics, industrial organization.

Université de Sherbrooke, Faculty of Administration, Program in Economics, Sherbrooke, QC J1K 2R1, Canada. Offers M Sc. Terminal master's awarded for partial completion of doctoral program. *Degree requirements:* For master's, one foreign language, thesis. *Entrance requirements:* For master's, minimum GPA of 3.0 (on 4.3 scale). Electronic applications accepted. *Faculty research:* Poverty and inequality analysis, wellbeing analysis, international trade, econometrics.

Université de Sherbrooke, Faculty of Letters and Human Sciences, Department of Economics, Sherbrooke, QC J1K 2R1, Canada. Offers MA. *Degree requirements:* For master's, thesis. *Faculty research:* Economic development, public finance, macroeconomics.

Université du Québec à Montréal, Graduate Programs, Program in Economics, Montréal, QC H3C 3P8, Canada. Offers M Sc, PhD. Part-time programs available. *Degree requirements:* For master's, thesis; for doctorate, thesis/dissertation. *Entrance requirements:* For master's, appropriate bachelor's degree or equivalent, proficiency in French; for doctorate, appropriate master's degree or equivalent, proficiency in French.

Université Laval, Faculty of Social Sciences, Department of Economics, Programs in Economics, Québec, QC G1K 7P4, Canada. Offers MA, PhD. Terminal master's awarded for partial completion of doctoral program. *Degree requirements:* For master's, thesis (for some programs); for doctorate, comprehensive exam, thesis/dissertation. *Entrance requirements:* For master's and doctorate, knowledge of French. Electronic applications accepted.

University at Albany, State University of New York, College of Arts and Sciences, Department of Economics, Albany, NY 12222-0001. Offers economic forcasting (MA); economics (MA, PhD). Part-time programs available. Terminal master's awarded for partial completion of doctoral program. *Degree requirements:* For doctorate, one foreign language, thesis/dissertation. *Entrance requirements:* For doctorate, GRE General Test, GRE Subject Test. Additional exam requirements/recommendations for international students: Required—TOEFL (minimum score 550 paper-based). Electronic applications accepted. *Faculty research:* Expectations of inflation and interest rates, diffusion of new technology, labor markets in developing countries, government deficits and international exchange markets.

University at Albany, State University of New York, Nelson A. Rockefeller College of Public Affairs and Policy, Department of Public Administration and Policy, Albany, NY 12222-0001. Offers financial management and public economics (MPA); financial market regulation (MPA); health policy (MPA); healthcare management (MPA); homeland security (MPA); human resources management (MPA); information strategy and management (MPA); local government management (MPA); nonprofit management (MPA); nonprofit management and leadership (Certificate); organizational behavior and theory (MPA, PhD); planning and policy analysis (CAS); policy analytic methods (MPA); politics and administration (PhD); public finance (PhD); public management (PhD); public policy (PhD); public sector management (Certificate); women and public policy (Certificate); JD/MPA. JD/MPA offered jointly with Albany Law School. *Accreditation:* NASPAA (one or more programs are accredited). *Degree requirements:* For doctorate, one foreign language, thesis/dissertation. *Entrance requirements:* For doctorate, GRE General Test. Additional exam requirements/recommendations for international students: Required—TOEFL (minimum score 550 paper-based). Electronic applications accepted.

University at Buffalo, the State University of New York, Graduate School, College of Arts and Sciences, Department of Economics, Buffalo, NY 14260. Offers economics (MA, MS, PhD); financial economics (Certificate); health services (Certificate); information and Internet economics (Certificate); international economics (Certificate); law and regulation (Certificate); urban and regional economics (Certificate). Part-time programs available. *Faculty:* 18 full-time (3 women), 6 part-time/adjunct (2 women). *Students:* 121 full-time (51 women), 2 part-time (0 women); includes 15 minority (3 Black or African American, non-Hispanic/Latino; 8 Asian, non-Hispanic/Latino; 1 Hispanic/Latino; 3 Native Hawaiian or other Pacific Islander, non-Hispanic/Latino), 89 international. Average age 27. 339 applicants, 51% accepted, 39 enrolled. In 2014, 58 master's, 3 doctorates, 2 other advanced degrees awarded. Terminal master's awarded for partial completion of doctoral program. *Degree requirements:* For master's, comprehensive exam; for doctorate, comprehensive exam, thesis/dissertation, field and theory exams. *Entrance requirements:* For master's, GRE General Test or GMAT; for doctorate, GRE General Test. Additional exam requirements/recommendations for international students: Required—TOEFL (minimum score 550 paper-based; 79 iBT), TWE. *Application deadline:* For fall admission, 1/15 priority date for domestic and international students. Applications are processed on a rolling basis. Application fee: $75. Electronic applications accepted. *Financial support:* In 2014–15, 3 fellowships with full tuition reimbursements (averaging $13,262 per year), 1 research assistantship with full tuition reimbursement (averaging $13,525 per year), 20 teaching assistantships with full tuition reimbursements (averaging $13,430 per year) were awarded; Federal Work-Study, health care benefits, and unspecified assistantships also available. Financial award application deadline: 2/1; financial award applicants required to submit FAFSA. *Faculty research:* Human capital, international economics, econometrics, applied economics, urban economics, economic growth and development. *Unit head:* Dr. Isaac Ehrlich, Chair, 716-645-8670, Fax: 716-645-2127, E-mail: mgtehrl@buffalo.edu. *Application contact:* Dr. Nagesh Revankar, Director of Graduate Studies, 716-645-2121 Ext. 428, Fax: 716-645-2127, E-mail: ecorevan@buffalo.edu.
Website: http://www.economics.buffalo.edu/

The University of Akron, Graduate School, Buchtel College of Arts and Sciences, Department of Economics, Akron, OH 44325. Offers MA. Part-time programs available. *Faculty:* 6 full-time (3 women), 2 part-time/adjunct (both women). *Students:* 15 full-time (8 women), 2 part-time (0 women); includes 1 minority (Asian, non-Hispanic/Latino), 11 international. Average age 27. 16 applicants, 75% accepted, 7 enrolled. In 2014, 7 master's awarded. *Degree requirements:* For master's, thesis optional. *Entrance requirements:* For master's, minimum GPA of 2.75, three letters of recommendation (preferably from academics), statement of purpose, resume. Additional exam requirements/recommendations for international students: Required—TOEFL (minimum score 550 paper-based; 79 iBT), IELTS (minimum score 6.5), GRE. *Application deadline:* For fall admission, 2/15 priority date for domestic and international students; for spring admission, 10/15 priority date for domestic and international students. Application fee: $45 ($70 for international students). Electronic applications accepted. *Expenses:* Tuition, state resident: full-time $7578; part-time $421 per credit hour. Tuition, nonresident: full-time $12,977; part-time $721 per credit hour. *Required fees:*

$1388; $35 per credit hour. Tuition and fees vary according to course load. *Financial support:* In 2014–15, 7 teaching assistantships with full tuition reimbursements were awarded. *Faculty research:* Regional economic performance, effects of addiction on labor market outcomes, programmatic assessment, regional trading arrangements, agriculture production in early twentieth-century South. *Total annual research expenditures:* $44,209. *Unit head:* Dr. Michael Nelson, Chair, 330-972-7939, E-mail: nelson2@uakron.edu. *Application contact:* Dr. Sucharita Ghosh, Director of Graduate Studies, 330-972-7549, E-mail: sghosh@uakron.edu.
Website: http://www.uakron.edu/economics/

The University of Alabama, Graduate School, Manderson Graduate School of Business, Economics, Finance and Legal Studies Department, Tuscaloosa, AL 35487. Offers economics (MA, PhD); finance (MS, PhD). *Faculty:* 29 full-time (3 women). *Students:* 55 full-time (18 women), 11 part-time (3 women); includes 10 minority (5 Black or African American, non-Hispanic/Latino; 2 Asian, non-Hispanic/Latino; 2 Hispanic/Latino; 1 Two or more races, non-Hispanic/Latino), 24 international. Average age 28. 257 applicants, 24% accepted, 19 enrolled. In 2014, 43 master's, 13 doctorates awarded. Terminal master's awarded for partial completion of doctoral program. *Degree requirements:* For master's, comprehensive exam (MA), thesis (MS); for doctorate, comprehensive exam, thesis/dissertation. *Entrance requirements:* For master's, GMAT, GRE; for doctorate, GRE or GMAT. Additional exam requirements/recommendations for international students: Required—TOEFL (minimum score 550 paper-based; 79 iBT). *Application deadline:* For fall admission, 7/1 priority date for domestic students, 1/15 for international students; for spring admission, 11/1 priority date for domestic students, 6/1 for international students. Applications are processed on a rolling basis. Application fee: $50 ($60 for international students). Electronic applications accepted. *Expenses:* Tuition, state resident: full-time $9826. Tuition, nonresident: full-time $24,950. *Financial support:* In 2014–15, 43 students received support, including 24 research assistantships with full and partial tuition reimbursements available (averaging $15,000 per year), 19 teaching assistantships with full and partial tuition reimbursements available (averaging $15,000 per year); fellowships, Federal Work-Study, institutionally sponsored loans, and unspecified assistantships also available. Financial award application deadline: 1/15. *Faculty research:* Taxation, futures market, monetary theory and policy, income distribution. *Total annual research expenditures:* $76,848. *Unit head:* Prof. Matthew T. Holt, Department Head, 205-348-8980, E-mail: mtholt@cba.ua.edu. *Application contact:* Debra F. Wheatley, Graduate Programs Secretary, 205-348-6683, Fax: 205-348-0590, E-mail: dwheatle@cba.ua.edu.
Website: http://www.cba.ua.edu/

University of Alaska Fairbanks, School of Management, Department of Economics, Fairbanks, AK 99775-6080. Offers resource and applied economics (MS). Part-time programs available. *Faculty:* 7 full-time (1 woman). *Students:* 8 full-time (6 women), 7 part-time (4 women); includes 2 minority (1 Asian, non-Hispanic/Latino; 1 Hispanic/Latino), 1 international. Average age 29. 9 applicants, 56% accepted, 4 enrolled. In 2014, 6 master's awarded. *Degree requirements:* For master's, comprehensive exam, oral defense of project or thesis. *Entrance requirements:* For master's, bachelor's degree from accredited institution with minimum cumulative undergraduate and major GPA of 3.0, intermediate microeconomics, intermediate macroeconomics, basic statistics, calculus. Additional exam requirements/recommendations for international students: Required—TOEFL (minimum score 550 paper-based; 79 iBT), IELTS (minimum score 6.5). *Application deadline:* For fall admission, 3/1 priority date for domestic students, 3/1 for international students; for spring admission, 9/1 priority date for domestic students, 9/1 for international students. Applications are processed on a rolling basis. Application fee: $60. Electronic applications accepted. *Expenses:* Tuition, state resident: full-time $7614; part-time $423 per credit. Tuition, nonresident: full-time $15,552; part-time $864 per credit. Tuition and fees vary according to course level, course load and reciprocity agreements. *Financial support:* In 2014–15, 7 teaching assistantships with full tuition reimbursements (averaging $14,820 per year) were awarded; fellowships with full tuition reimbursements, research assistantships with full tuition reimbursements, career-related internships or fieldwork, Federal Work-Study, scholarships/grants, health care benefits, and unspecified assistantships also available. Support available to part-time students. Financial award application deadline: 2/15; financial award applicants required to submit FAFSA. *Faculty research:* Statistics; resource and agriculture economics; oil, gas, and energy; sustainability; public land management. *Total annual research expenditures:* $4,000. *Unit head:* Jungho Baek, Economics Program Director, 907-474-2754, Fax: 907-474-5219, E-mail: jbaek3@alaska.edu. *Application contact:* Mary Kreta, Director of Admissions, 907-474-7500, Fax: 907-474-7097, E-mail: admissions@uaf.edu.
Website: http://www.uaf.edu/som/degrees/graduate/

University of Alberta, Faculty of Graduate Studies and Research, Department of Economics, Edmonton, AB T6G 2E1, Canada. Offers economics (MA, PhD); economics and finance (MA); environmental and natural resource economics (PhD). Part-time programs available. *Degree requirements:* For doctorate, thesis/dissertation. *Entrance requirements:* For master's and doctorate, GRE. Additional exam requirements/recommendations for international students: Required—TOEFL. *Faculty research:* Public finance, international trade, industrial organization, Pacific Rim economics, monetary economics.

The University of Arizona, Eller College of Management, Department of Economics, Tucson, AZ 85721. Offers MA, PhD, JD/MA, JD/PhD. Terminal master's awarded for partial completion of doctoral program. *Degree requirements:* For master's, comprehensive exam; for doctorate, thesis/dissertation. *Entrance requirements:* For doctorate, GRE General Test, 3 letters of recommendation. Additional exam requirements/recommendations for international students: Required—TOEFL (minimum score 550 paper-based; 79 iBT). Electronic applications accepted. *Faculty research:* Applied microeconomics, experimental economics, economic history, microeconomic theory, property rights, industrial organization.

University of Arkansas, Graduate School, Sam M. Walton College of Business Administration, Department of Economics, Fayetteville, AR 72701-1201. Offers MA, PhD. *Degree requirements:* For doctorate, variable foreign language requirement, thesis/dissertation. *Entrance requirements:* For master's and doctorate, GRE General Test.

The University of British Columbia, Faculty of Arts and Faculty of Graduate Studies, Department of Economics, Vancouver, BC V6T 1Z1, Canada. Offers MA, PhD. *Degree requirements:* For master's, thesis (for some programs); for doctorate, comprehensive exam, thesis/dissertation. *Entrance requirements:* For master's and doctorate, GRE General Test. Additional exam requirements/recommendations for international students: Required—TOEFL (minimum score 550 paper-based; 80 iBT). Electronic applications accepted. *Faculty research:* Economic theory, international economics, labor economics, public finance, economic development.

University of Calgary, Faculty of Graduate Studies, Faculty of Arts, Department of Economics, Calgary, AB T2N 1N4, Canada. Offers MA, PhD. Part-time and evening/weekend programs available. *Degree requirements:* For master's, thesis (for some programs); for doctorate, thesis/dissertation, candidacy exam. *Entrance requirements:* Additional exam requirements/recommendations for international students: Required—

TOEFL. *Faculty research:* Energy economics, public finance/public choice, resource economics, international trade, monetary economics.

University of California, Berkeley, Graduate Division, College of Letters and Science, Department of Economics, Berkeley, CA 94720-1500. Offers PhD, JD/MA. *Degree requirements:* For doctorate, thesis/dissertation, field exams, oral qualifying exam. *Entrance requirements:* For doctorate, GRE General Test, minimum GPA of 3.0, 3 letters of recommendation. Additional exam requirements/recommendations for international students: Required—TOEFL.

University of California, Davis, Graduate Studies, Program in Economics, Davis, CA 95616. Offers MA, PhD. Terminal master's awarded for partial completion of doctoral program. *Degree requirements:* For master's, comprehensive exam (for some programs), thesis (for some programs); for doctorate, thesis/dissertation. *Entrance requirements:* For master's, GRE General Test, minimum GPA of 3.0; for doctorate, GRE General Test, minimum GPA of 3.25. Additional exam requirements/recommendations for international students: Required—TOEFL (minimum score 550 paper-based). Electronic applications accepted. *Faculty research:* Applied microeconomics, macroeconomics, international studies, economic theory, economic history.

University of California, Irvine, School of Social Sciences, Department of Economics, Irvine, CA 92697. Offers economics (MA, PhD); public choice (MA, PhD); transportation economics (MA, PhD). *Students:* 81 full-time (26 women), 3 part-time (0 women); includes 16 minority (7 Asian, non-Hispanic/Latino; 3 Hispanic/Latino; 6 Two or more races, non-Hispanic/Latino), 21 international. Average age 28. 233 applicants, 21% accepted, 19 enrolled. In 2014, 7 master's, 12 doctorates awarded. *Degree requirements:* For doctorate, thesis/dissertation. *Entrance requirements:* For master's and doctorate, GRE General Test, minimum GPA of 3.0. Additional exam requirements/recommendations for international students: Required—TOEFL (minimum score 550 paper-based). *Application deadline:* For fall admission, 1/15 priority date for domestic and international students. Applications are processed on a rolling basis. Application fee: $90 ($110 for international students). Electronic applications accepted. *Financial support:* Fellowships, research assistantships with full tuition reimbursements, teaching assistantships, institutionally sponsored loans, traineeships, health care benefits, and unspecified assistantships available. Financial award application deadline: 3/1; financial award applicants required to submit FAFSA. *Faculty research:* Econometrics, urban economics, applied microeconomics. *Unit head:* Prof. Jan Brueckner, Chair, 949-824-0083, E-mail: jkbrueck@uci.edu. *Application contact:* Michelle Garfinkel, Director of Graduate Studies, 949-824-3190, E-mail: mrgarfin@uci.edu.
Website: http://www.economics.uci.edu/

University of California, Los Angeles, Graduate Division, College of Letters and Science, Department of Economics, Los Angeles, CA 90095. Offers MA, PhD. Terminal master's awarded for partial completion of doctoral program. *Degree requirements:* For master's, comprehensive exam; for doctorate, thesis/dissertation, oral and written qualifying exams. *Entrance requirements:* For doctorate, GRE General Test, bachelor's degree; minimum undergraduate GPA of 3.0 (or its equivalent if letter grade system not used). Additional exam requirements/recommendations for international students: Required—TOEFL. Electronic applications accepted.

University of California, Los Angeles, Graduate Division, UCLA Anderson School of Management, Los Angeles, CA 90095-1481. Offers accounting (PhD); Asia Pacific (EMBA); business administration (EMBA, MBA); decisions, operations and technology management (PhD); finance (PhD); financial engineering (MFE); global economics and management (PhD); management and organizations (PhD); marketing (PhD); strategy and policy (PhD); DDS/MBA; MBA/JD; MBA/MD; MBA/MLAS; MBA/MLIS; MBA/MN; MBA/MPH; MBA/MPP; MBA/MSCS. *Accreditation:* AACSB. Part-time and evening/weekend programs available. *Faculty:* 98 full-time (18 women), 61 part-time/adjunct (6 women). *Students:* 820 full-time (272 women), 1,145 part-time (322 women); includes 673 minority (42 Black or African American, non-Hispanic/Latino; 470 Asian, non-Hispanic/Latino; 67 Hispanic/Latino; 6 Native Hawaiian or other Pacific Islander, non-Hispanic/Latino; 88 Two or more races, non-Hispanic/Latino), 465 international. Average age 31. 6,471 applicants, 24% accepted, 895 enrolled. In 2014, 777 master's, 9 doctorates awarded. *Degree requirements:* For master's, comprehensive exam, field study consulting project; thesis/dissertation (for MFE); for doctorate, comprehensive exam, thesis/dissertation, oral and written qualifying exams. *Entrance requirements:* For master's, GMAT or GRE General Test, 4-year bachelor's degree or equivalent; recommendation letters (1 for MBA, 2 for MFE); essays (1 for MBA, 2 for MFE); interview (by invitation only for MBA); minimum eight years of work experience with at least three years at a management level (for EMBA); for doctorate, GMAT or GRE General Test, bachelor's degree from college or university of fully-recognized standing; minimum B average during junior and senior years of undergraduate years; statement of purpose; three recommendation letters. Additional exam requirements/recommendations for international students: Required—TOEFL (minimum score 560 paper-based, 87 iBT) or IELTS. *Application deadline:* For fall admission, 10/6 priority date for domestic and international students; for winter admission, 1/5 for domestic and international students; for spring admission, 4/12 for domestic and international students. Applications are processed on a rolling basis. Application fee: $200. Electronic applications accepted. *Expenses:* Expenses: $51,159 in-state, $56,159 out-of-state (for MBA); $39,540 (for FEMBA); $69,379 (for EMBA); $52,500 (for GEMBA); $57,268 (for MFE); $30,746 (for PhD). *Financial support:* In 2014–15, 564 students received support, including 470 fellowships (averaging $25,596 per year), 8 research assistantships with partial tuition reimbursements available (averaging $2,418 per year), 83 teaching assistantships with partial tuition reimbursements available (averaging $3,464 per year); career-related internships or fieldwork, institutionally sponsored loans, and scholarships/grants also available. Support available to part-time students. Financial award application deadline: 4/15; financial award applicants required to submit FAFSA. *Faculty research:* Asset pricing, decision-making, behavioral finance, international finance and economics, global macroeconomics. *Total annual research expenditures:* $325,000. *Unit head:* Dr. Judy D. Olian, Dean and John E. Anderson Chair in Management, 310-825-7982, Fax: 310-206-2073, E-mail: judy.olian@anderson.ucla.edu. *Application contact:* Alex Lawrence, Assistant Dean, MBA Admissions and Financial Aid, 310-825-6944, Fax: 310-825-8582, E-mail: mba.admissions@anderson.ucla.edu.
Website: http://www.anderson.ucla.edu/

University of California, Riverside, Graduate Division, Department of Economics, Riverside, CA 92521-0102. Offers MA, PhD. Terminal master's awarded for partial completion of doctoral program. *Degree requirements:* For master's, comprehensive exam; for doctorate, thesis/dissertation, qualifying exams. *Entrance requirements:* For master's and doctorate, GRE General Test, minimum GPA of 3.2. Additional exam requirements/recommendations for international students: Required—TOEFL (minimum score 550 paper-based; 80 iBT). Electronic applications accepted. *Expenses:* Tuition, state resident: full-time $5399. Tuition, nonresident: full-time $10,433. *Faculty research:* Advanced political economy; resource and environmental economics; advanced econometrics; labor economics; advanced microeconomics theory; advanced macroeconomics theory; development economics; economic history; international trade theory; money, credit and business cycles; public economics.

Economics

University of California, San Diego, Graduate Division, Department of Economics, La Jolla, CA 92093. Offers PhD. *Students:* 128 full-time (45 women), 2 part-time (1 woman); includes 16 minority (13 Asian, non-Hispanic/Latino; 3 Hispanic/Latino), 52 international. 827 applicants, 11% accepted, 24 enrolled. In 2014, 13 doctorates awarded. *Degree requirements:* For doctorate, comprehensive exam, thesis/dissertation. *Entrance requirements:* For doctorate, GRE General Test, minimum GPA of 3.5. Additional exam requirements/recommendations for international students: Required—TOEFL (minimum score 550 paper-based; 80 iBT), IELTS. *Application deadline:* For fall admission, 1/15 for domestic students. Application fee: $90 ($110 for international students). Electronic applications accepted. *Expenses:* Tuition, state resident: full-time $11,220; part-time $5610 per quarter. Tuition, nonresident: full-time $26,322; part-time $13,161 per quarter. *Required fees:* $570 per quarter. Tuition and fees vary according to program. *Financial support:* Fellowships, research assistantships, teaching assistantships, and scholarships/grants available. Financial award application deadline: 2/1; financial award applicants required to submit FAFSA. *Faculty research:* Microfoundations of macroeconomics, econometric model specification and testing, industrial organization. *Unit head:* James E. Rauch, Chair, 858-534-1055, E-mail: econchair@ucsd.edu. *Application contact:* Brittany Bender, Graduate Coordinator, 858-822-3502, E-mail: econ-phdadmissions@ucsd.edu. Website: http://economics.ucsd.edu

University of California, Santa Barbara, Graduate Division, College of Letters and Sciences, Division of Social Sciences, Department of Economics, Santa Barbara, CA 93106-9210. Offers econometrics (PhD); economics (MA, PhD); environmental and natural resources (PhD); experimental and behavioral economics (PhD); labor economics (PhD); macroeconomic theory and policy (PhD); mathematical economics (PhD); public finance (PhD); MA/PhD. Terminal master's awarded for partial completion of doctoral program. *Degree requirements:* For master's, comprehensive exam; for doctorate, comprehensive exam, thesis/dissertation. *Entrance requirements:* For master's and doctorate, GRE General Test, 3 letters of recommendation, statement of purpose, personal achievements/contributions statement, resume/curriculum vitae, transcripts for post-secondary institutions attended. Additional exam requirements/recommendations for international students: Required—TOEFL (minimum score 550 paper-based; 80 iBT), IELTS (minimum score 7). Electronic applications accepted. *Faculty research:* Labor economics, econometrics, macroeconomic theory and policy, environmental and natural resources economics, experimental and behavioral economics.

University of California, Santa Barbara, Graduate Division, College of Letters and Sciences, Division of Social Sciences, Department of Global and International Studies, Santa Barbara, CA 93106-7065. Offers global culture, ideology, and religion (MA); global government, civil society, and human rights (MA); global studies (PhD); political economy, sustainable development, and the environment (MA). *Degree requirements:* For master's, one foreign language, thesis, 2 years of a second language. *Entrance requirements:* For master's, GRE, 2 years of a second language with minimum B grade in the final term, 3 letters of recommendation, resume/curriculum vitae, personal statement, writing sample. Additional exam requirements/recommendations for international students: Required—TOEFL (minimum score 600 paper-based; 94 iBT), IELTS (minimum score 7). Electronic applications accepted. *Faculty research:* Global culture, ideology, and religion; global governance, civil society, and human rights; political economy, sustainable development and the environment.

University of California, Santa Barbara, Graduate Division, Donald Bren School of Environmental Science and Management, Santa Barbara, CA 93106-5131. Offers economics and environmental science (PhD); environmental science and management (MESM, PhD); technology and society (PhD). *Degree requirements:* For master's, thesis; for doctorate, thesis/dissertation. *Entrance requirements:* For master's and doctorate, GRE. Additional exam requirements/recommendations for international students: Required—TOEFL (minimum score 550 paper-based; 80 iBT), IELTS (minimum score 7). Electronic applications accepted. *Faculty research:* Coastal marine resources management, conservation planning, corporate environmental management, economics and politics of the environment, energy and climate, pollution prevention and remediation, water resources management.

University of California, Santa Cruz, Division of Graduate Studies, Division of Social Sciences, Program in International Economics, Santa Cruz, CA 95064. Offers PhD. *Degree requirements:* For doctorate, thesis/dissertation, 4 field exams, field papers, econometrics project, qualifying exams. *Entrance requirements:* For doctorate, GRE General Test. Additional exam requirements/recommendations for international students: Required—TOEFL (minimum score 550 paper-based; 83 iBT); Recommended—IELTS (minimum score 8). Electronic applications accepted. *Faculty research:* Current and emerging issues in taxation, industrial policy, environmental regulation, market structure, labor economics focus on behavior and adjustment in an interdependent world economy.

University of Central Arkansas, Graduate School, College of Liberal Arts, Program in Community and Economic Development, Conway, AR 72035-0001. Offers community and economic development (MS); geographic and information systems (MGIS, Graduate Certificate). Part-time programs available. Postbaccalaureate distance learning degree programs offered (minimal on-campus study). *Degree requirements:* For master's, comprehensive exam, thesis. *Entrance requirements:* For master's, GRE General Test, minimum GPA of 2.7. Additional exam requirements/recommendations for international students: Required—TOEFL (minimum score 550 paper-based). Electronic applications accepted. *Expenses:* Contact institution.

University of Chicago, Booth School of Business, Full-Time MBA Program, Chicago, IL 60637. Offers accounting (MBA); analytic finance (MBA); analytic management (MBA); econometrics and statistics (MBA); economics (MBA); entrepreneurship (MBA); finance (MBA); general management (MBA); health administration and policy (Certificate); human resource management (MBA); international business (MBA); managerial and organizational behavior (MBA); marketing management (MBA); operations management (MBA); strategic management (MBA); MBA/AM; MBA/JD; MBA/MA; MBA/MD; MBA/MPP. Accreditation: AACSB. *Students:* 1,171 full-time (412 women), 15 part-time (6 women). Terminal master's awarded for partial completion of doctoral program. *Entrance requirements:* For master's, GMAT, 2 letters of recommendation, 3 essays, resume, interview. Additional exam requirements/recommendations for international students: Required—TOEFL (minimum score 600 paper-based; 104 iBT), IELTS. *Application deadline:* For fall admission, 10/12 priority date for domestic and international students; for winter admission, 1/4 for domestic and international students; for spring admission, 4/4 for domestic and international students. Electronic applications accepted. *Expenses:* Expenses: Contact institution. *Financial support:* Fellowships available. Financial award applicants required to submit FAFSA. *Unit head:* Stacey Kole, Deputy Dean, 773-702-7121. *Application contact:* Kurt Ahlm, Associate Dean of Student Recruitment and Admissions, 773-702-7369, Fax: 773-702-9085, E-mail: admissions@chicagobooth.edu. Website: http://chicagobooth.edu/

University of Chicago, Division of the Social Sciences, Department of Economics, Chicago, IL 60637. Offers PhD. *Students:* 189 full-time (39 women); includes 14 minority (7 Asian, non-Hispanic/Latino; 3 Hispanic/Latino; 4 Two or more races, non-Hispanic/Latino), 135 international. 612 applicants, 15% accepted, 35 enrolled. In 2014, 17 doctorates awarded. *Degree requirements:* For doctorate, one foreign language, thesis/dissertation, written exams in 2 fields. *Entrance requirements:* For doctorate, GRE General Test. Additional exam requirements/recommendations for international students: Required—TOEFL (minimum score 104 iBT), IELTS (minimum score 7). *Application deadline:* For fall admission, 12/15 for domestic and international students. Application fee: $135. Electronic applications accepted. *Expenses: Tuition:* Full-time $46,899. *Required fees:* $347. *Financial support:* In 2014–15, 30 students received support, including 19 fellowships with full tuition reimbursements available (averaging $24,000 per year); Federal Work-Study, institutionally sponsored loans, scholarships/grants, health care benefits, and tuition waivers (full) also available. Financial award application deadline: 12/15. *Unit head:* Prof. John List, Chair. *Application contact:* Office of the Dean of Students, 773-702-8415, E-mail: admissions@ssd.uchicago.edu. Website: http://economics.uchicago.edu

University of Cincinnati, Graduate School, Carl H. Lindner College of Business, PhD Programs, Cincinnati, OH 45221. Offers accounting (PhD); economics (PhD); finance (PhD); information systems (PhD); management (PhD); marketing (PhD); operations and business analytics (PhD). *Faculty:* 72 full-time (18 women). *Students:* 39 full-time (16 women); includes 4 minority (1 American Indian or Alaska Native, non-Hispanic/Latino; 2 Asian, non-Hispanic/Latino; 1 Hispanic/Latino), 18 international. Average age 32. 86 applicants, 15% accepted, 10 enrolled. In 2014, 6 doctorates awarded. *Degree requirements:* For doctorate, comprehensive exam, thesis/dissertation. *Entrance requirements:* For doctorate, GMAT, GRE, transcripts, essays, resume, letters of recommendation. Additional exam requirements/recommendations for international students: Required—TOEFL (minimum score 600 paper-based; 100 iBT), IELTS (minimum score 6.5). *Application deadline:* For fall admission, 1/15 for domestic and international students. Application fee: $65 ($70 for international students). Electronic applications accepted. *Expenses:* Expenses: Contact institution. *Financial support:* In 2014–15, 33 students received support, including 25 research assistantships with full and partial tuition reimbursements available (averaging $23,250 per year); scholarships/grants, tuition waivers (full and partial), and unspecified assistantships also available. Financial award application deadline: 1/15; financial award applicants required to submit FAFSA. *Unit head:* Dr. Suzanne Masterson, Director, 513-556-7125, Fax: 513-556-5499, E-mail: suzanne.masterson@uc.edu. *Application contact:* Angel Elvin, Assistant Director, 513-556-7190, Fax: 513-558-7006, E-mail: angel.elvin@uc.edu. Website: http://www.business.uc.edu/phd

University of Cincinnati, Graduate School, McMicken College of Arts and Sciences, Department of Economics, Cincinnati, OH 45221. Offers applied economics (MA); labor and employment relations (MALER). Part-time and evening/weekend programs available. Electronic applications accepted.

University of Colorado Boulder, Graduate School, College of Arts and Sciences, Department of Economics, Boulder, CO 80309. Offers MA, PhD. *Faculty:* 27 full-time (5 women). *Students:* 68 full-time (20 women), 2 part-time (0 women); includes 11 minority (1 American Indian or Alaska Native, non-Hispanic/Latino; 5 Asian, non-Hispanic/Latino; 2 Hispanic/Latino; 3 Two or more races, non-Hispanic/Latino), 19 international. Average age 29. 115 applicants, 52% accepted, 16 enrolled. In 2014, 16 master's, 9 doctorates awarded. Terminal master's awarded for partial completion of doctoral program. *Degree requirements:* For master's, comprehensive exam, thesis or alternative; for doctorate, comprehensive exam, thesis/dissertation, preliminary exam. *Entrance requirements:* For master's, GRE General Test, minimum undergraduate GPA of 2.75; for doctorate, GRE General Test. Additional exam requirements/recommendations for international students: Required—TOEFL. *Application deadline:* For fall admission, 1/15 for domestic students, 12/1 for international students. Applications are processed on a rolling basis. Application fee: $50 ($70 for international students). Electronic applications accepted. *Financial support:* In 2014–15, 180 students received support, including 10 fellowships (averaging $3,588 per year), 3 research assistantships with full and partial tuition reimbursements available (averaging $39,171 per year), 62 teaching assistantships with full and partial tuition reimbursements available (averaging $37,664 per year); institutionally sponsored loans, scholarships/grants, health care benefits, and unspecified assistantships also available. Financial award application deadline: 2/1; financial award applicants required to submit FAFSA. *Faculty research:* Economics, microeconomics, labor economics, economic studies: developing countries, economics of the environment. *Total annual research expenditures:* $467,636. Website: http://www.colorado.edu/Economics/graduate/index.html

University of Colorado Denver, Business School, Program in Finance, Denver, CO 80217. Offers economics (MS); finance (MS); financial analysis and management (MS); financial and commodities risk management (MS); risk management and insurance (MS); MS/MA; MS/MBA. Part-time and evening/weekend programs available. *Students:* 71 full-time (23 women), 30 part-time (9 women); includes 14 minority (1 Black or African American, non-Hispanic/Latino; 6 Asian, non-Hispanic/Latino; 6 Hispanic/Latino; 1 Two or more races, non-Hispanic/Latino), 26 international. Average age 29. 114 applicants, 61% accepted, 20 enrolled. In 2014, 43 master's awarded. *Degree requirements:* For master's, 30 semester hours (18 of required core courses, 9 of finance electives, and 3 of free elective). *Entrance requirements:* For master's, GMAT, essay, resume, two letters of recommendation, financial statements (for international students). Additional exam requirements/recommendations for international students: Required—TOEFL (minimum score 537 paper-based; 75 iBT); Recommended—IELTS (minimum score 6.5). *Application deadline:* For fall admission, 4/15 priority date for domestic students, 3/15 priority date for international students; for spring admission, 10/15 priority date for domestic students, 9/15 priority date for international students; for summer admission, 2/15 priority date for domestic students, 1/15 priority date for international students. Applications are processed on a rolling basis. Application fee: $50 ($75 for international students). Electronic applications accepted. *Expenses:* Expenses: Contact institution. *Financial support:* In 2014–15, 21 students received support. Teaching assistantships, Federal Work-Study, institutionally sponsored loans, scholarships/grants, and traineeships available. Financial award application deadline: 4/1; financial award applicants required to submit FAFSA. *Faculty research:* Corporate governance, debt maturity policies, regulation and financial markets, option management strategies. *Unit head:* Jian Yang, Director of the Finance Program, 303-315-8423, E-mail: jian.yang@ucdenver.edu. *Application contact:* Shelly Townley, Director of Graduate Admissions, 303-315-8202, E-mail: shelly.townley@ucdenver.edu. Website: http://www.ucdenver.edu/academics/colleges/business/degrees/ms/finance/Pages/Finance.aspx

University of Colorado Denver, College of Liberal Arts and Sciences, Department of Economics, Denver, CO 80217. Offers MA. Part-time and evening/weekend programs available. *Faculty:* 11 full-time (1 woman), 3 part-time/adjunct (2 women). *Students:* 31 full-time (8 women), 11 part-time (5 women); includes 6 minority (1 Asian, non-Hispanic/Latino; 4 Hispanic/Latino; 1 Two or more races, non-Hispanic/Latino), 6 international. Average age 29. 69 applicants, 55% accepted, 11 enrolled. In 2014, 16 master's awarded. *Degree requirements:* For master's, thesis or alternative, 30 credit hours, including 21 of core courses and 9 of electives. *Entrance requirements:* For master's, GRE General Test, 15 hours of course work in economics, minimum GPA of 2.5, three letters of recommendation, calculus and statistics course completion. Additional exam

requirements/recommendations for international students: Required—TOEFL (minimum score 537 paper-based; 75 iBT); Recommended—IELTS (minimum score 6.5). *Application deadline:* For fall admission, 6/1 priority date for domestic and international students; for spring admission, 11/1 priority date for domestic and international students. Applications are processed on a rolling basis. Application fee: $50 ($75 for international students). Electronic applications accepted. *Financial support:* Fellowships, research assistantships, teaching assistantships, Federal Work-Study, institutionally sponsored loans, scholarships/grants, traineeships, and unspecified assistantships available. Financial award application deadline: 4/1; financial award applicants required to submit FAFSA. *Faculty research:* Economic/income inequality, poverty and mobility measurement; international finance and monetary policy; economics of philanthropy; history of economic thought; health and labor economics. *Unit head:* Dr. Buhong Zheng, Department Chair, 303-315-2034, Fax: 303-315-2048, E-mail: buhong.zheng@ucdenver.edu. *Application contact:* Brian Duncan, Graduate Admissions Advisor, 303-315-2041, E-mail: brian.duncan@ucdenver.edu. Website: http://www.ucdenver.edu/academics/colleges/CLAS/Departments/economics/Programs/MasterofArts/Pages/Overview.aspx

University of Connecticut, Graduate School, College of Liberal Arts and Sciences, Department of Economics, Storrs, CT 06269-1063. Offers MA, PhD. Terminal master's awarded for partial completion of doctoral program. *Degree requirements:* For master's, comprehensive exam; for doctorate, thesis/dissertation. *Entrance requirements:* For master's and doctorate, GRE General Test, GRE Subject Test. Additional exam requirements/recommendations for international students: Required—TOEFL (minimum score 550 paper-based). Electronic applications accepted.

University of Delaware, Alfred Lerner College of Business and Economics, Department of Economics, Newark, DE 19716. Offers economic education (PhD); economics (MA, MS, PhD); economics for entrepreneurship and educators (MA); MA/MBA. Part-time programs available. *Degree requirements:* For master's, comprehensive exam, thesis (for some programs), mathematics review exam, research project; for doctorate, comprehensive exam, thesis/dissertation, field exam. *Entrance requirements:* For master's, GMAT or GRE General Test, minimum GPA of 2.5; for doctorate, GRE General Test, minimum GPA of 3.5 in graduate economics course work. Additional exam requirements/recommendations for international students: Required—TOEFL (minimum score 550 paper-based). Electronic applications accepted. *Faculty research:* Applied quantitative economics, industrial organization, resource economics, monetary economics, labor economics.

University of Denver, Division of Arts, Humanities and Social Sciences, Department of Economics, Denver, CO 80208. Offers MA. Part-time programs available. *Faculty:* 9 full-time (3 women). *Students:* 11 full-time (2 women), 6 part-time (1 woman); includes 2 minority (both Hispanic/Latino), 6 international. Average age 25. 38 applicants, 79% accepted, 7 enrolled. In 2014, 10 master's awarded. *Degree requirements:* For master's, thesis. *Entrance requirements:* For master's, GRE General Test, bachelor's degree with major or minor in economics, 20 quarter hours of economics coursework, or departmental waiver; transcripts, personal statement, three letters of recommendation. Additional exam requirements/recommendations for international students: Required—TOEFL (minimum score 550 paper-based; 80 iBT). *Application deadline:* For fall admission, 3/1 priority date for domestic and international students. Applications are processed on a rolling basis. Application fee: $65. Electronic applications accepted. *Expenses:* Expenses: $1,199 per credit hour. *Financial support:* In 2014–15, 8 students received support, including 4 teaching assistantships with full and partial tuition reimbursements available (averaging $12,500 per year); career-related internships or fieldwork, Federal Work-Study, scholarships/grants, and unspecified assistantships also available. Support available to part-time students. Financial award application deadline: 2/15; financial award applicants required to submit FAFSA. *Faculty research:* Trade and policy effects on economic development; income distribution, inequality, and the macroeconomy; history of economic thought; the Chinese economy; problems of neo-liberalism. *Unit head:* Dr. Tracy Mott, Chair, 303-871-2569, E-mail: tracy.mott@du.edu. *Application contact:* Information Contact, 303-871-2685, E-mail: econ04@denver.du.edu.
Website: http://www.du.edu/ahss/economics/index.html

University of Florida, Graduate School, Warrington College of Business Administration, Hough Graduate School of Business, Department of Economics, Gainesville, FL 32611. Offers MA, PhD. *Faculty:* 12 full-time (0 women), 3 part-time/adjunct (2 women). *Students:* 9 full-time (3 women), 1 (woman) part-time; includes 4 minority (2 Black or African American, non-Hispanic/Latino; 1 Asian, non-Hispanic/Latino; 1 Hispanic/Latino), 4 international. 1 applicant. In 2014, 4 master's, 5 doctorates awarded. Terminal master's awarded for partial completion of doctoral program. *Degree requirements:* For master's, thesis optional; for doctorate, comprehensive exam, thesis/dissertation. *Entrance requirements:* For master's and doctorate, GMAT (minimum score of 465) or GRE General Test, minimum GPA of 3.0. Additional exam requirements/recommendations for international students: Required—TOEFL (minimum score 550 paper-based; 80 iBT), IELTS (minimum score 6). *Application deadline:* For fall admission, 2/1 for domestic and international students. Applications are processed on a rolling basis. Application fee: $30. Electronic applications accepted. *Financial support:* In 2014–15, 4 fellowships, 2 research assistantships, 7 teaching assistantships were awarded; unspecified assistantships also available. Financial award applicants required to submit FAFSA. *Faculty research:* Econometrics, international economics, industrial organization, public finance, economic theory. *Unit head:* Roger D. Blair, PhD, Professor and Chair, 352-392-0179, Fax: 352-392-7860, E-mail: blair@warrington.ufl.edu. *Application contact:* Steve Slutsky, PhD, Professor and Graduate Coordinator, 352-392-8106, Fax: 352-392-7860, E-mail: steven.slutsky@warrington.ufl.edu.

University of Georgia, Terry College of Business, Department of Economics, Athens, GA 30602. Offers MA, PhD. *Degree requirements:* For master's, thesis; for doctorate, thesis/dissertation. *Entrance requirements:* For master's and doctorate, GRE General Test. Electronic applications accepted.

University of Guelph, Graduate Studies, College of Management and Economics, Department of Economics, Guelph, ON N1G 2W1, Canada. Offers MA, PhD. Part-time programs available. *Degree requirements:* For master's, thesis or alternative; for doctorate, comprehensive exam, thesis/dissertation. *Entrance requirements:* For master's, minimum B+ average during previous 2 years of course work; for doctorate, minimum A- average, MA in economics. Additional exam requirements/recommendations for international students: Required—TOEFL (minimum score 550 paper-based; 89 iBT), IELTS (minimum score 6.5). Electronic applications accepted. *Faculty research:* Resource and environmental economics, econometrics, labor economics, micro and macro economics.

University of Hawaii at Manoa, Graduate Division, College of Social Sciences, Department of Economics, Honolulu, HI 96822. Offers MA, PhD. Part-time programs available. Terminal master's awarded for partial completion of doctoral program. *Degree requirements:* For master's, thesis optional; for doctorate, comprehensive exam, thesis/dissertation. *Entrance requirements:* For master's and doctorate, GRE General Test. Additional exam requirements/recommendations for international students: Required—TOEFL (minimum score 500 paper-based; 61 iBT), IELTS (minimum score 5). *Faculty research:* Trade, development, demography, labor, resource economics.

University of Houston, College of Liberal Arts and Social Sciences, Department of Economics, Houston, TX 77204. Offers applied economics (MA); economics (MA, PhD). Terminal master's awarded for partial completion of doctoral program. *Degree requirements:* For master's, thesis optional; for doctorate, comprehensive exam, thesis/dissertation. *Entrance requirements:* For master's and doctorate, GRE General Test, minimum GPA of 3.0, statement of purpose, three letters of recommendation. Additional exam requirements/recommendations for international students: Required—TOEFL (minimum score 550 paper-based; 79 iBT), IELTS (minimum score 6.5). Electronic applications accepted. *Faculty research:* Econometrics, labor economics, international economics.

University of Illinois at Chicago, Graduate College, College of Liberal Arts and Sciences, Department of Economics, Chicago, IL 60607-7128. Offers MA, PhD, MBA/MA. *Faculty:* 20 full-time (4 women), 3 part-time/adjunct (2 women). *Students:* 56 full-time (29 women), 21 part-time (5 women); includes 10 minority (7 Asian, non-Hispanic/Latino; 3 Hispanic/Latino), 42 international. Average age 30. 203 applicants, 22% accepted, 14 enrolled. In 2014, 14 master's, 5 doctorates awarded. Terminal master's awarded for partial completion of doctoral program. *Degree requirements:* For master's, comprehensive exam; for doctorate, thesis/dissertation. *Entrance requirements:* For master's and doctorate, GRE General Test, minimum GPA of 2.75. Additional exam requirements/recommendations for international students: Required—TOEFL. *Application deadline:* For fall admission, 1/15 priority date for domestic and international students; for spring admission, 11/1 for domestic and international students. Applications are processed on a rolling basis. Application fee: $60. Electronic applications accepted. *Expenses:* Tuition, state resident: full-time $11,254; part-time $468 per credit hour. Tuition, nonresident: full-time $23,252; part-time $968 per credit hour. *Required fees:* $1217 per term. Part-time tuition and fees vary according to course load, degree level and program. *Financial support:* In 2014–15, 2 fellowships with full tuition reimbursements were awarded; research assistantships with full tuition reimbursements, teaching assistantships with full tuition reimbursements, career-related internships or fieldwork, Federal Work-Study, traineeships, tuition waivers (full), and unspecified assistantships also available. Financial award application deadline: 1/15; financial award applicants required to submit FAFSA. *Faculty research:* International, labor, and urban economics. *Total annual research expenditures:* $74,000. *Unit head:* Prof. Steven Rivkin, Head, 312-413-2368, Fax: 312-996-3344, E-mail: sgrivkin@uic.edu. *Application contact:* Prof. Robert Kaestner, Director of Graduate Studies, 312-996-5214, E-mail: kaestner@uic.edu.
Website: http://www.uic.edu/depts/econ/

University of Illinois at Urbana–Champaign, Graduate College, College of Liberal Arts and Sciences, Department of Economics, Champaign, IL 61820. Offers economics (MS, PhD); policy economics (MS). *Students:* 259 (106 women). Terminal master's awarded for partial completion of doctoral program. Application fee: $70 ($90 for international students). *Unit head:* Martin Perry, Interim Head, 217-244-3108, Fax: 217-244-6678, E-mail: mkperry@illinois.edu. *Application contact:* Carol Banks, Office Support Specialist, 217-333-0120, Fax: 217-244-6678, E-mail: cbanks@illinois.edu.
Website: http://www.economics.illinois.edu/

The University of Iowa, Henry B. Tippie College of Business, Department of Economics, Iowa City, IA 52242-1316. Offers PhD. *Faculty:* 19 full-time (4 women), 7 part-time/adjunct (2 women). *Students:* 28 full-time (14 women); includes 1 minority (Asian, non-Hispanic/Latino), 17 international. Average age 30. 147 applicants, 12% accepted, 9 enrolled. In 2014, 7 doctorates awarded. *Degree requirements:* For doctorate, comprehensive exam, thesis/dissertation. *Entrance requirements:* For doctorate, GRE General Test. Additional exam requirements/recommendations for international students: Recommended—TOEFL (minimum score 100 iBT), IELTS (minimum score 7). *Application deadline:* For fall admission, 1/15 priority date for domestic and international students. Applications are processed on a rolling basis. Application fee: $60 ($100 for international students). Electronic applications accepted. *Financial support:* In 2014–15, 28 students received support, including 1 fellowship with full tuition reimbursement available (averaging $18,080 per year), 1 research assistantship with partial tuition reimbursement available (averaging $9,040 per year), 27 teaching assistantships with full and partial tuition reimbursements available (averaging $18,080 per year); institutionally sponsored loans, scholarships/grants, health care benefits, and unspecified assistantships also available. Financial award application deadline: 1/15. *Faculty research:* Political economy, macroeconomics, econometrics, game theory, economic development. *Unit head:* Prof. John Solow, Director/Executive Officer, 319-335-0829, Fax: 319-335-1956, E-mail: john-solow@uiowa.edu. *Application contact:* Renea L. Jay, PhD Program Coordinator, 319-335-0830, Fax: 319-335-1956, E-mail: renea-jay@uiowa.edu.
Website: http://tippie.uiowa.edu/economics/

The University of Kansas, Graduate Studies, College of Liberal Arts and Sciences, Department of Economics, Lawrence, KS 66045. Offers MA, PhD, JD/MA. Part-time programs available. *Faculty:* 17 full-time, 3 part-time/adjunct. *Students:* 60 full-time (20 women), 2 part-time (1 woman); includes 4 minority (1 Black or African American, non-Hispanic/Latino; 2 Asian, non-Hispanic/Latino; 1 Two or more races, non-Hispanic/Latino), 47 international. Average age 28. 155 applicants, 39% accepted, 13 enrolled. In 2014, 15 master's, 9 doctorates awarded. Terminal master's awarded for partial completion of doctoral program. *Degree requirements:* For master's, comprehensive exam, thesis optional; for doctorate, thesis/dissertation, qualifying exams. *Entrance requirements:* For doctorate, GRE. Additional exam requirements/recommendations for international students: Required—TOEFL, IELTS. *Application deadline:* For fall admission, 2/1 priority date for domestic and international students; for winter admission, 5/1 priority date for domestic and international students; for spring admission, 11/1 priority date for domestic and international students. Applications are processed on a rolling basis. Application fee: $55 ($65 for international students). Electronic applications accepted. *Financial support:* Fellowships with full tuition reimbursements, research assistantships with full tuition reimbursements, teaching assistantships with full tuition reimbursements, institutionally sponsored loans, scholarships/grants, health care benefits, and unspecified assistantships available. Financial award application deadline: 2/1. *Faculty research:* Macroeconomics, econometrics, industrial organization, microeconomics, economic development, international economics, financial economics. *Unit head:* Joseph Sicilian, Chair, 785-864-2842, Fax: 785-864-5270, E-mail: jsic@ku.edu. *Application contact:* Michelle Huslig-Lowrance, Graduate Secretary, 785-864-2841, E-mail: econgrad@ku.edu.
Website: http://www.economics.ku.edu/

University of Kentucky, Graduate School, Gatton College of Business and Economics, Program in Economics, Lexington, KY 40506-0032. Offers MS, PhD. *Degree requirements:* For master's, comprehensive exam; for doctorate, comprehensive exam, thesis/dissertation. *Entrance requirements:* For master's, GMAT, minimum undergraduate GPA of 2.75; for doctorate, GMAT, minimum undergraduate GPA of 3.0. Additional exam requirements/recommendations for international students: Required—TOEFL (minimum score 550 paper-based). Electronic applications accepted. *Faculty research:* Public economics, international economics and economic development, labor economics, environmental economics, industrial economics.

Economics

University of Lethbridge, School of Graduate Studies, Lethbridge, AB T1K 3M4, Canada. Offers addictions counseling (M Sc); agricultural biotechnology (M Sc); agricultural studies (M Sc, MA); anthropology (MA); archaeology (M Sc, MA); art (MA, MFA); biochemistry (M Sc); biological sciences (M Sc); biomolecular science (PhD); biosystems and biodiversity (PhD); Canadian studies (MA); chemistry (M Sc); computer science (M Sc); computer science and geographical information science (M Sc); counseling (MC); counseling psychology (M Ed); dramatic arts (MA); earth, space, and physical science (PhD); economics (MA); education (MA); educational leadership (M Ed); English (MA); environmental science (M Sc); evolution and behavior (PhD); exercise science (M Sc); French (MA); French/German (MA); French/Spanish (MA); general education (M Ed); geography (M Sc, MA); German (MA); health sciences (M Sc); individualized multidisciplinary (M Sc, MA); kinesiology (M Sc, MA); management (M Sc), including accounting, finance, general management, human resource management and labor relations, information systems, international management, marketing, policy and strategy; mathematics (M Sc); modern languages (MA); music (M Mus, MA); Native American studies (MA); neuroscience (M Sc, PhD); new media (MA, MFA); nursing (M Sc, MN); philosophy (MA); physics (M Sc); political science (MA); psychology (M Sc, MA); religious studies (MA); sociology (MA); theatre and dramatic arts (MFA); theoretical and computational science (PhD); urban and regional studies (MA); women and gender studies (MA). Part-time and evening/weekend programs available. *Faculty:* 358. *Students:* 445 full-time (243 women), 116 part-time (72 women). Average age 31. 351 applicants, 26% accepted, 87 enrolled. In 2014, 129 master's, 13 doctorates awarded. *Degree requirements:* For master's, thesis (for some programs); for doctorate, comprehensive exam, thesis/dissertation. *Entrance requirements:* For master's, GMAT (for M Sc in management), bachelor's degree in related field, minimum GPA of 3.0 during previous 20 graded semester courses, 2 years' teaching or related experience (M Ed); for doctorate, master's degree, minimum graduate GPA of 3.5. Additional exam requirements/recommendations for international students: Required—TOEFL. Application fee: $100 Canadian dollars. *Financial support:* Fellowships, research assistantships, teaching assistantships, scholarships/grants, health care benefits, and unspecified assistantships available. *Faculty research:* Movement and brain plasticity, gibberellin physiology, photosynthesis, carbon cycling, molecular properties of main-group ring components. *Application contact:* School of Graduate Studies, 403-329-5194, E-mail: sgsinquiries@uleth.ca.
Website: http://www.uleth.ca/graduatestudies/

University of Maine, Graduate School, College of Natural Sciences, Forestry, and Agriculture, School of Economics, Orono, ME 04469. Offers economics (MA); financial economics (MA); resource economics and policy (MS). Part-time programs available. *Faculty:* 15 full-time (4 women). *Students:* 18 full-time (8 women), 2 part-time (1 woman), 8 international. Average age 27. 41 applicants, 66% accepted, 12 enrolled. In 2014, 10 master's awarded. *Degree requirements:* For master's, thesis (for some programs). *Entrance requirements:* For master's, GRE General Test. Additional exam requirements/recommendations for international students: Required—TOEFL. *Application deadline:* For fall admission, 2/1 priority date for domestic students; for spring admission, 10/1 for domestic students. Applications are processed on a rolling basis. Application fee: $65. Electronic applications accepted. *Expenses:* Tuition, state resident: part-time $658 per credit hour. Tuition, nonresident: part-time $1550 per credit hour. *Financial support:* In 2014–15, 11 students received support, including 4 research assistantships (averaging $14,600 per year), 6 teaching assistantships with full tuition reimbursements available (averaging $14,600 per year); career-related internships or fieldwork, Federal Work-Study, institutionally sponsored loans, scholarships/grants, and tuition waivers (full and partial) also available. Support available to part-time students. Financial award application deadline: 3/1. *Faculty research:* Energy, food safety, transportation, education, economic development. *Total annual research expenditures:* $2.6 million. *Unit head:* Dr. Mario Teisl, Director, 207-581-3151, Fax: 207-581-4278. *Application contact:* Scott G. Delcourt, Assistant Vice President for Graduate Studies and Senior Associate Dean, 207-581-3291, Fax: 207-581-3232, E-mail: graduate@maine.edu.
Website: http://umaine.edu/soe/

The University of Manchester, School of Arts, Histories and Cultures, Manchester, United Kingdom. Offers anthropology, media and performance (PhD); applied theatre professional (PhD); archaeology (PhD); art history and visual studies (PhD); arts management and cultural policy (PhD); classics and ancient history (PhD); composition (PhD); creative writing (PhD); drama (PhD); economic and social history (PhD); electroacoustic composition (PhD); English and American studies (PhD); history (PhD); humanitarianism and conflict response (PhD); museology (PhD); music (PhD); musicology (PhD); religions and theology (PhD).

University of Manitoba, Faculty of Graduate Studies, Faculty of Arts, Department of Economics, Winnipeg, MB R3T 2N2, Canada. Offers MA, PhD. *Degree requirements:* For master's, thesis or alternative; for doctorate, one foreign language, thesis/dissertation.

University of Maryland, Baltimore County, The Graduate School, College of Arts, Humanities and Social Sciences, Department of Economics, Program in Economic Policy Analysis, Baltimore, MD 21250. Offers MA. Part-time programs available. *Faculty:* 25 full-time (9 women), 3 part-time/adjunct (1 woman). *Students:* 6 full-time (3 women), 11 part-time (4 women); includes 2 minority (both Black or African American, non-Hispanic/Latino), 7 international. Average age 26. 14 applicants, 36% accepted, 1 enrolled. In 2014, 9 master's awarded. *Degree requirements:* For master's, comprehensive exam, capstone research project. *Entrance requirements:* For master's, GRE General Test, undergraduate coursework in economic theory, econometrics, calculus. Additional exam requirements/recommendations for international students: Required—TOEFL. *Application deadline:* For fall admission, 7/1 priority date for domestic students, 3/1 priority date for international students; for spring admission, 1/1 priority date for domestic students, 9/15 priority date for international students. Applications are processed on a rolling basis. Application fee: $45. Electronic applications accepted. *Expenses:* Tuition, state resident: part-time $557. Tuition, nonresident: part-time $922. *Required fees:* $122 per semester. One-time fee: $200 part-time. *Financial support:* In 2014–15, 6 students received support, including 5 research assistantships with full and partial tuition reimbursements available (averaging $12,560 per year), 1 teaching assistantship with partial tuition reimbursement available (averaging $6,500 per year); Federal Work-Study, health care benefits, tuition waivers (full and partial), and unspecified assistantships also available. Support available to part-time students. Financial award application deadline: 4/15; financial award applicants required to submit FAFSA. *Faculty research:* International trade policy analysis, health and hospital policy evaluation, environmental policy analysis, economics of education, economic growth and development. *Total annual research expenditures:* $28,539. *Unit head:* Dr. David F. Mitch, Chair, 410-455-2157, Fax: 410-455-1054, E-mail: mitch@umbc.edu. *Application contact:* Dr. Tim H. Gindling, Graduate Program Director, 410-455-3629, Fax: 410-455-1054, E-mail: econ-masters@umbc.edu.
Website: http://www.umbc.edu/economics/grad_intro.html

University of Maryland, Baltimore County, The Graduate School, College of Arts, Humanities and Social Sciences, Department of Public Policy, Program in Public Policy, Baltimore, MD 21250. Offers economics (PhD); educational policy (MPP); evaluation and analytical methods (MPP); health policy (MPP); policy history (PhD); public management (MPP, PhD); urban policy (MPP, PhD). Part-time and evening/weekend programs available. *Faculty:* 9 full-time (3 women), 1 part-time/adjunct (0 women). *Students:* 50 full-time (29 women), 68 part-time (39 women); includes 28 minority (15 Black or African American, non-Hispanic/Latino; 8 Asian, non-Hispanic/Latino; 3 Hispanic/Latino; 1 Native Hawaiian or other Pacific Islander, non-Hispanic/Latino; 1 Two or more races, non-Hispanic/Latino), 9 international. Average age 35. 71 applicants, 58% accepted, 25 enrolled. In 2014, 23 master's, 13 doctorates awarded. Terminal master's awarded for partial completion of doctoral program. *Degree requirements:* For master's, thesis optional, public analysis paper; for doctorate, comprehensive exam, thesis/dissertation, comprehensive and field qualifying exams. *Entrance requirements:* For master's and doctorate, GRE General Test, 3 academic letters of reference, transcripts, resume, research paper. Additional exam requirements/recommendations for international students: Required—TOEFL (minimum score 550 paper-based; 80 iBT). *Application deadline:* For fall admission, 1/15 priority date for domestic students, 1/1 priority date for international students; for spring admission, 11/1 priority date for domestic students, 5/1 priority date for international students. Applications are processed on a rolling basis. Application fee: $50. Electronic applications accepted. *Expenses:* Expenses: $679 per credit resident; $1,114 non-resident. *Financial support:* In 2014–15, 26 students received support, including 1 fellowship with full tuition reimbursement available (averaging $12,000 per year), 25 research assistantships with full tuition reimbursements available (averaging $20,000 per year); career-related internships or fieldwork, Federal Work-Study, scholarships/grants, health care benefits, and unspecified assistantships also available. Support available to part-time students. Financial award application deadline: 1/15; financial award applicants required to submit FAFSA. *Faculty research:* Health policy, education policy, urban policy, public management, evaluation and analytical methods. *Unit head:* Dr. Donald F. Norris, Director, 410-455-1455, E-mail: norris@umbc.edu. *Application contact:* Sally F. Helms, Administrator of Academic Affairs, 410-455-3202, Fax: 410-455-1172, E-mail: gradpubpol@umbc.edu.
Website: http://www.umbc.edu/pubpol

University of Maryland, College Park, Academic Affairs, College of Behavioral and Social Sciences, Department of Economics, College Park, MD 20742. Offers MA, PhD. Part-time and evening/weekend programs available. Terminal master's awarded for partial completion of doctoral program. *Degree requirements:* For master's, comprehensive exam, thesis optional; for doctorate, comprehensive exam, thesis/dissertation, exams. *Entrance requirements:* For master's, GRE General Test, minimum GPA of 3.0, course work in calculus and mathematics, 3 letters of recommendation; for doctorate, GRE General Test, calculus background. Additional exam requirements/recommendations for international students: Required—TOEFL. Electronic applications accepted. *Faculty research:* International economics, natural resource and environmental economics, forecasting and policy analysis, economic growth, demography of inequality.

University of Maryland, College Park, Academic Affairs, College of Behavioral and Social Sciences, Department of Government and Politics, College Park, MD 20742. Offers American politics (PhD); comparative politics (PhD); international relations (PhD); political economy (PhD); political theory (PhD). Part-time and evening/weekend programs available. *Degree requirements:* For doctorate, comprehensive exam, thesis/dissertation, written exams in 2 fields. *Entrance requirements:* For doctorate, GRE General Test, minimum GPA of 3.5, writing sample. Additional exam requirements/recommendations for international students: Required—TOEFL. Electronic applications accepted. *Faculty research:* International development/conflict, international security, post-communist society, public service, dynamics of conflict and conflict resolution.

University of Massachusetts Amherst, Graduate School, College of Social and Behavioral Sciences, Department of Economics, Amherst, MA 01003. Offers MA, PhD. Part-time programs available. *Faculty:* 30 full-time (8 women). *Students:* 72 full-time (29 women), 9 part-time (4 women); includes 10 minority (2 Asian, non-Hispanic/Latino; 5 Hispanic/Latino; 3 Two or more races, non-Hispanic/Latino), 45 international. Average age 31. 164 applicants, 13% accepted, 9 enrolled. In 2014, 6 master's, 10 doctorates awarded. Terminal master's awarded for partial completion of doctoral program. *Degree requirements:* For master's, thesis or alternative; for doctorate, comprehensive exam, thesis/dissertation. *Entrance requirements:* For master's and doctorate, GRE General Test. Additional exam requirements/recommendations for international students: Required—TOEFL (minimum score 550 paper-based; 80 iBT), IELTS (minimum score 6.5). *Application deadline:* For fall admission, 1/15 for domestic and international students. Applications are processed on a rolling basis. Application fee: $75. Electronic applications accepted. *Expenses:* Tuition, state resident: full-time $1980; part-time $110 per credit. Tuition, nonresident: full-time $14,644; part-time $414 per credit. *Required fees:* $11,417. One-time fee: $357. *Financial support:* Fellowships with full and partial tuition reimbursements, research assistantships with full and partial tuition reimbursements, teaching assistantships with full and partial tuition reimbursements, career-related internships or fieldwork, Federal Work-Study, scholarships/grants, traineeships, health care benefits, tuition waivers (full and partial), and unspecified assistantships available. Support available to part-time students. Financial award application deadline: 1/15; financial award applicants required to submit FAFSA. *Unit head:* Dr. Mwangi wa Githinji, Graduate Program Director, 413-545-2082, Fax: 413-545-2921, E-mail: gradinfo@econs.umass.edu. *Application contact:* Lindsay DeSantis, Supervisor of Admissions, 413-545-0722, Fax: 413-577-0010, E-mail: gradadm@grad.umass.edu.
Website: http://www.umass.edu/economics/

University of Massachusetts Lowell, College of Fine Arts, Humanities and Social Sciences, Program in Regional Economic and Social Development, Lowell, MA 01854. Offers MA, Graduate Certificate. Part-time programs available. *Entrance requirements:* For master's, GRE. Electronic applications accepted.

University of Memphis, Graduate School, Fogelman College of Business and Economics, Department of Economics, Memphis, TN 38152. Offers MA, PhD. Part-time programs available. *Faculty:* 9 full-time (1 woman). *Students:* 6 full-time (0 women), 4 part-time (2 women); includes 2 minority (both Two or more races, non-Hispanic/Latino), 3 international. Average age 31. 6 applicants, 67% accepted. In 2014, 10 master's awarded. *Degree requirements:* For master's, comprehensive exam, thesis or alternative; for doctorate, comprehensive exam, thesis/dissertation. *Entrance requirements:* For master's, GMAT or GRE General Test, previous course work in statistics, intermediate micro and macro theory; for doctorate, GMAT, interview, minimum GPA of 3.4. *Application deadline:* For fall admission, 8/1 for domestic students; for spring admission, 12/1 for domestic students. Application fee: $35 ($60 for international students). *Financial support:* In 2014–15, 3 students received support. Research assistantships with full tuition reimbursements available, teaching assistantships with full tuition reimbursements available, Federal Work-Study, scholarships/grants, and unspecified assistantships available. Financial award application deadline: 2/15; financial award applicants required to submit FAFSA. *Faculty research:* Tax research, medical economics, law and economics, labor economics, U.S. and Japanese economic relations. *Unit head:* Dr. William Smith, Interim Chair, 901-678-2785, E-mail: wtsmith@memphis.edu. *Application contact:* Dr. Pinaki Bose, Master's

Program Coordinator, 901-678-5528, Fax: 901-678-4705, E-mail: psbose@memphis.edu. Website: http://economics.memphis.edu/

University of Memphis, Graduate School, Fogelman College of Business and Economics, Program in Business Administration, Memphis, TN 38152. Offers accounting (MBA, PhD); economics (PhD); executive business administration (MBA); finance (PhD); management (PhD); marketing (MS); marketing and supply chain management (PhD); real estate development (MS); JD/MBA. *Accreditation:* AACSB. *Faculty:* 44 full-time (9 women), 5 part-time/adjunct (0 women). *Students:* 238 full-time (101 women), 315 part-time (113 women); includes 146 minority (80 Black or African American, non-Hispanic/Latino; 1 American Indian or Alaska Native, non-Hispanic/Latino; 46 Asian, non-Hispanic/Latino; 13 Hispanic/Latino; 2 Native Hawaiian or other Pacific Islander, non-Hispanic/Latino; 4 Two or more races, non-Hispanic/Latino), 104 international. Average age 32. 302 applicants, 61% accepted, 102 enrolled. In 2014, 182 master's, 12 doctorates awarded. *Degree requirements:* For master's, comprehensive exam; for doctorate, comprehensive exam, thesis/dissertation. *Entrance requirements:* For master's, GMAT, resume; for doctorate, GMAT, interview, minimum GPA of 3.4, resume, letter of recommendation. Additional exam requirements/recommendations for international students: Required—TOEFL (minimum score 550 paper-based). *Application deadline:* For fall admission, 8/1 for domestic students; for spring admission, 12/1 for domestic students. Application fee: $35 ($60 for international students). *Financial support:* In 2014–15, 164 students received support. Research assistantships with full tuition reimbursements available, teaching assistantships with full tuition reimbursements available, career-related internships or fieldwork, Federal Work-Study, scholarships/grants, and unspecified assistantships available. Financial award application deadline: 2/15; financial award applicants required to submit FAFSA. *Faculty research:* Competitive business strategy, finance microstructures, supply chain management innovations, health care economics, litigation risks and corporate audits. *Unit head:* Dr. Rajiv Grover, Dean, 901-678-3759, E-mail: rgrover@memphis.edu. *Application contact:* Dr. Carol V. Danehower, Associate Dean, 901-678-5402, Fax: 901-678-3579, E-mail: fcbegp@memphis.edu.
Website: http://www.memphis.edu/fcbe/grad_programs.php

University of Miami, Graduate School, School of Business Administration, Department of Economics, Coral Gables, FL 33124. Offers economic development (MA, PhD); environmental economics (PhD); human resource economics (MA, PhD); international economics (MA, PhD); macroeconomics (PhD). Students admitted every two years in the fall semester. Terminal master's awarded for partial completion of doctoral program. *Degree requirements:* For master's, comprehensive exam; for doctorate, comprehensive exam, thesis/dissertation. *Entrance requirements:* For master's and doctorate, GRE General Test, minimum GPA of 3.0. Additional exam requirements/recommendations for international students: Required—TOEFL (minimum score 550 paper-based). *Faculty research:* International economics/trade, applied microeconomics, development.

University of Michigan, Horace H. Rackham School of Graduate Studies, College of Literature, Science, and the Arts, Department of Economics, Ann Arbor, MI 48109. Offers applied economics (AM); economics (AM, PhD); public policy and economics (PhD); social work and economics (PhD); JD/PhD; MPP/AM. Terminal master's awarded for partial completion of doctoral program. *Degree requirements:* For doctorate, comprehensive exam, thesis/dissertation, oral defense of dissertation; preliminary exams in microeconomics, macroeconomics, and 2 fields. *Entrance requirements:* For master's and doctorate, GRE General Test. Additional exam requirements/recommendations for international students: Required—TOEFL (minimum score 600 paper-based; 100 iBT). Electronic applications accepted. *Faculty research:* Econometric analysis, finance, industrial organization, international trade, public finance, economic development, economic history, health, labor, natural resources, population studies, macro theory, micro theory.

University of Michigan, School of Social Work, Interdisciplinary Program in Social Work and Social Science, Ann Arbor, MI 48109-1106. Offers social work and anthropology (PhD); social work and economics (PhD); social work and political science (PhD); social work and psychology (PhD); social work and sociology (PhD). Programs offered through the Horace H. Rackham School of Graduate Studies. *Faculty:* 57 full-time (33 women), 6 part-time/adjunct (4 women). *Students:* 64 full-time (46 women); includes 24 minority (7 Black or African American, non-Hispanic/Latino; 11 Asian, non-Hispanic/Latino; 6 Hispanic/Latino), 6 international. Average age 32. 108 applicants, 9% accepted, 9 enrolled. In 2014, 11 doctorates awarded. *Degree requirements:* For doctorate, thesis/dissertation, oral defense of dissertation, preliminary exam. *Entrance requirements:* For doctorate, GRE General Test. Additional exam requirements/recommendations for international students: Required—TOEFL. *Application deadline:* For fall admission, 12/1 for domestic and international students. Application fee: $75 ($90 for international students). *Financial support:* In 2014–15, 64 students received support, including 20 fellowships with full tuition reimbursements available (averaging $15,200 per year), 7 research assistantships with full tuition reimbursements available (averaging $18,971 per year), 19 teaching assistantships with full tuition reimbursements available (averaging $18,971 per year); career-related internships or fieldwork, Federal Work-Study, scholarships/grants, traineeships, health care benefits, tuition waivers (full and partial), and unspecified assistantships also available. Financial award application deadline: 12/1; financial award applicants required to submit FAFSA. *Faculty research:* Substance abuse, child welfare, mental health, poverty, aging. *Total annual research expenditures:* $4.1 million. *Unit head:* Dr. Berit Ingersoll-Dayton, Director, 734-763-5768, Fax: 734-615-3192, E-mail: bid@umich.edu. *Application contact:* Graduate Coordinator, 734-647-2554, Fax: 734-615-3192, E-mail: ssw.phd.info@umich.edu.
Website: http://www.ssw.umich.edu/doctoral

University of Minnesota, Twin Cities Campus, Graduate School, College of Liberal Arts, Department of Economics, Minneapolis, MN 55455. Offers PhD. *Faculty:* 19 full-time (3 women), 4 part-time/adjunct (1 woman). *Students:* 118 full-time (26 women), 3 part-time (1 woman); includes 5 minority (3 Asian, non-Hispanic/Latino; 2 Hispanic/Latino), 90 international. Average age 27. 376 applicants, 13% accepted, 22 enrolled. In 2014, 19 doctorates awarded. *Degree requirements:* For doctorate, thesis/dissertation, preliminary exams. *Entrance requirements:* For doctorate, GRE General Test. Additional exam requirements/recommendations for international students: Required—TOEFL (minimum score 100 iBT), IELTS (minimum score 7). *Application deadline:* For fall admission, 12/11 priority date for domestic and international students. Application fee: $75 ($95 for international students). Electronic applications accepted. *Financial support:* In 2014–15, 90 students received support, including 13 fellowships with full tuition reimbursements available (averaging $22,500 per year), 3 research assistantships with full tuition reimbursements available (averaging $16,000 per year), 74 teaching assistantships with full tuition reimbursements available (averaging $15,500 per year); scholarships/grants and unspecified assistantships also available. Financial award application deadline: 12/11. *Faculty research:* Econometrics, macro and monetary economics, mathematical economics, industrial organization, applied micro theory. *Unit head:* Prof. Christopher Phelan, Chair, 612-625-6353, Fax: 612-624-0209. *Application contact:* Prof. Timothy Kehoe, Director of Graduate Studies, 612-625-6833, Fax: 612-624-0209, E-mail: econdgs@umn.edu. Website: http://www.econ.umn.edu/

University of Mississippi, Graduate School, College of Liberal Arts, Department of Economics, University, MS 38677. Offers MA, PhD. Electronic applications accepted.

University of Missouri, Office of Research and Graduate Studies, College of Arts and Science, Department of Economics, Columbia, MO 65211. Offers MA, PhD, JD/MA. *Faculty:* 23 full-time (6 women), 2 part-time/adjunct (both women). *Students:* 47 full-time (13 women), 20 part-time (7 women); includes 2 minority (1 Asian, non-Hispanic/Latino; 1 Two or more races, non-Hispanic/Latino), 56 international. Average age 27. 137 applicants, 35% accepted, 17 enrolled. In 2014, 11 master's, 4 doctorates awarded. Terminal master's awarded for partial completion of doctoral program. *Degree requirements:* For doctorate, comprehensive exam, thesis/dissertation. *Entrance requirements:* For master's, GRE General Test (minimum score 700 quantitative, 400 verbal), minimum GPA of 3.0; bachelor's degree in any field; for doctorate, GRE General Test (minimum score 700 quantitative, 400 verbal), minimum GPA of 3.0. Additional exam requirements/recommendations for international students: Required—TOEFL (minimum score 550 paper-based; 79 iBT), IELTS (minimum score 6). *Application deadline:* For fall admission, 1/1 priority date for domestic and international students; for winter admission, 10/1 priority date for domestic and international students; for spring admission, 3/1 for domestic students. Application fee: $55 ($75 for international students). Electronic applications accepted. *Financial support:* In 2014–15, 2 fellowships with full and partial tuition reimbursements, 6 research assistantships with full tuition reimbursements, 51 teaching assistantships with full tuition reimbursements were awarded; institutionally sponsored loans, health care benefits, and unspecified assistantships also available. *Faculty research:* Monetary economics, econometrics, macroeconomics, public economics, industrial organization, game theory, labor economics, microeconomic theory, teacher labor markets, international trade. *Unit head:* Dr. David Mandy, Department Chair, 573-882-1763, E-mail: mandyd@missouri.edu. *Application contact:* Lynne Riddell, Administrative Assistant, 573-884-7989, E-mail: riddelll@missouri.edu.
Website: http://economics.missouri.edu/graduate/index.shtml

University of Missouri–Kansas City, College of Arts and Sciences, Department of Economics, Kansas City, MO 64110-2499. Offers MA, PhD. PhD (interdisciplinary) offered through the School of Graduate Studies. Part-time and evening/weekend programs available. *Faculty:* 10 full-time (2 women), 3 part-time/adjunct (0 women). *Students:* 37 full-time (15 women), 29 part-time (5 women); includes 18 minority (12 Black or African American, non-Hispanic/Latino; 2 Asian, non-Hispanic/Latino; 3 Hispanic/Latino; 1 Two or more races, non-Hispanic/Latino), 29 international. Average age 30. 79 applicants, 27% accepted, 15 enrolled. In 2014, 36 master's awarded. *Degree requirements:* For doctorate, comprehensive exam, thesis/dissertation. *Entrance requirements:* For master's, GRE or minimum undergraduate GPA of 2.5; for doctorate, GRE, master's degree in economics or equivalent. Additional exam requirements/recommendations for international students: Required—TOEFL (minimum score 550 paper-based; 80 iBT). *Application deadline:* For fall admission, 2/1 priority date for domestic and international students; for spring admission, 9/1 priority date for domestic and international students. Applications are processed on a rolling basis. Application fee: $45 ($50 for international students). Electronic applications accepted. *Financial support:* In 2014–15, 6 research assistantships with partial tuition reimbursements (averaging $15,117 per year), 21 teaching assistantships with partial tuition reimbursements (averaging $13,768 per year) were awarded; career-related internships or fieldwork, Federal Work-Study, institutionally sponsored loans, and tuition waivers (full and partial) also available. Support available to part-time students. Financial award application deadline: 3/1; financial award applicants required to submit FAFSA. *Faculty research:* International trade, general theory, institutions/utilities, forensic economics, human resources. *Unit head:* Stephanie Kelton, Chair, 816-235-1314, Fax: 816-238-2836, E-mail: sturgeonj@umkc.edu. *Application contact:* Linwood Tauheed, Graduate Advisor, 816-235-1314, E-mail: tauheedl@umkc.edu.
Website: http://cas.umkc.edu/econ/

University of Missouri–St. Louis, College of Arts and Sciences, Department of Economics, St. Louis, MO 63121. Offers MA. Part-time and evening/weekend programs available. *Faculty:* 12 full-time (5 women), 1 part-time/adjunct (0 women). *Students:* 10 full-time (5 women), 9 part-time (3 women); includes 4 minority (1 Black or African American, non-Hispanic/Latino; 2 Asian, non-Hispanic/Latino; 1 Hispanic/Latino), 4 international. Average age 28. 12 applicants, 92% accepted, 4 enrolled. In 2014, 5 master's awarded. *Entrance requirements:* For master's, GRE General Test, 2 letters of recommendation. Additional exam requirements/recommendations for international students: Required—TOEFL (minimum score 550 paper-based; 79 iBT), IELTS (minimum score 6.5). *Application deadline:* For fall admission, 7/1 priority date for domestic and international students; for spring admission, 12/1 priority date for domestic and international students. Applications are processed on a rolling basis. Application fee: $50 ($40 for international students). Electronic applications accepted. *Expenses:* Tuition, state resident: full-time $7364; part-time $409.10 per hour. Tuition, nonresident: full-time $18,153; part-time $1008.50 per hour. *Financial support:* In 2014–15, 1 teaching assistantship with full and partial tuition reimbursement (averaging $7,500 per year) was awarded; research assistantships also available. Financial award applicants required to submit FAFSA. *Faculty research:* Health economics, public policy analysis, econometrics, public choice, telecommunications and forensic economics. *Unit head:* Dr. Donald Kridel, Director of Graduate Studies, 314-516-5351, Fax: 314-516-5562, E-mail: kridel@umsl.edu. *Application contact:* 314-516-5458, Fax: 314-516-6996, E-mail: gradadm@umsl.edu.
Website: http://www.umsl.edu/~econ/

The University of Montana, Graduate School, College of Humanities and Sciences, Department of Economics, Missoula, MT 59812-0002. Offers MA. *Degree requirements:* For master's, thesis. *Entrance requirements:* For master's, GRE General Test. Additional exam requirements/recommendations for international students: Required—TOEFL (minimum score 525 paper-based). *Faculty research:* Resource economics, public policy, environmental economics, economic development, regional economics.

University of Nebraska at Omaha, Graduate Studies, College of Business Administration, Department of Economics, Omaha, NE 68182. Offers MA, MS. Part-time and evening/weekend programs available. *Faculty:* 10 full-time (2 women). *Students:* 34 full-time (9 women), 40 part-time (13 women); includes 12 minority (2 Black or African American, non-Hispanic/Latino; 6 Asian, non-Hispanic/Latino; 1 Hispanic/Latino; 3 Two or more races, non-Hispanic/Latino), 32 international. Average age 29. 70 applicants, 43% accepted, 17 enrolled. In 2014, 23 master's awarded. *Degree requirements:* For master's, comprehensive exam, thesis (for some programs). *Entrance requirements:* For master's, minimum GPA of 2.7, official transcripts. Additional exam requirements/recommendations for international students: Required—TOEFL, IELTS, PTE. *Application deadline:* For fall admission, 7/15 priority date for domestic and international students; for spring admission, 12/1 priority date for domestic and international students; for summer admission, 4/15 for domestic and international students. Applications are processed on a rolling basis. Application fee: $45. Electronic applications accepted. *Financial support:* In 2014–15, 6 students received support, including 3 research assistantships with tuition reimbursements available, 3 teaching assistantships with tuition reimbursements available; Federal Work-Study, scholarships/grants, and unspecified assistantships also available. Support available to part-time students.

Economics

Financial award application deadline: 3/1; financial award applicants required to submit FAFSA. *Unit head:* Dr. Christopher Decker, Chairperson, 402-554-2341, E-mail: graduate@unomaha.edu. *Application contact:* Dr. Donald Baum, Graduate Program Chair, 402-554-2341, E-mail: graduate@unomaha.edu.

University of Nebraska–Lincoln, Graduate College, College of Business Administration, Department of Economics, Lincoln, NE 68588. Offers MA, PhD, JD/MA. *Degree requirements:* For master's, thesis optional; for doctorate, comprehensive exam, thesis/dissertation. *Entrance requirements:* For master's and doctorate, GRE General Test. Additional exam requirements/recommendations for international students: Required—TOEFL (minimum score 550 paper-based). Electronic applications accepted. *Faculty research:* Applied microeconomics, economic education, international trade and finance, public finance, regional and institutional economics.

University of Nevada, Las Vegas, Graduate College, College of Business, Department of Economics, Las Vegas, NV 89154-6005. Offers MA, MA/MS. Part-time and evening/weekend programs available. *Faculty:* 6 full-time (1 woman), 1 part-time/adjunct (0 women). *Students:* 12 full-time (4 women), 15 part-time (3 women); includes 8 minority (2 Black or African American, non-Hispanic/Latino; 1 American Indian or Alaska Native, non-Hispanic/Latino; 2 Asian, non-Hispanic/Latino; 1 Hispanic/Latino; 2 Two or more races, non-Hispanic/Latino), 3 international. Average age 31. 16 applicants, 88% accepted, 9 enrolled. In 2014, 12 master's awarded. *Degree requirements:* For master's, thesis, oral defense of thesis. *Entrance requirements:* For master's, GRE General Test or GMAT. Additional exam requirements/recommendations for international students: Required—TOEFL (minimum score 550 paper-based; 80 iBT), IELTS (minimum score 7). *Application deadline:* For fall admission, 6/15 for domestic students, 5/1 for international students; for spring admission, 11/15 for domestic students, 10/1 for international students. Application fee: $60 ($95 for international students). Electronic applications accepted. *Financial support:* In 2014–15, 10 students received support, including 1 research assistantship with partial tuition reimbursement available (averaging $10,000 per year), 9 teaching assistantships with partial tuition reimbursements available (averaging $10,000 per year); institutionally sponsored loans, scholarships/grants, health care benefits, and unspecified assistantships also available. Financial award application deadline: 3/1. *Faculty research:* Labor economics/industrial organization; real estate economics; macroeconomics and credit markets; urban, regional and environmental economics; public finance/public policy. *Total annual research expenditures:* $62,078. *Unit head:* Dr. Mary Riddel, Chair/Professor, 702-895-2792, Fax: 702-895-1354, E-mail: mary.riddel@unlv.edu. *Application contact:* Graduate College Admissions Evaluator, 702-895-3320, Fax: 702-895-4180, E-mail: gradcollege@unlv.edu.
Website: http://business.unlv.edu/economics/

University of Nevada, Reno, Graduate School, College of Business Administration, Department of Economics, Reno, NV 89557. Offers MA, MS. *Degree requirements:* For master's, thesis. *Entrance requirements:* For master's, GMAT or GRE, minimum GPA of 2.75. Additional exam requirements/recommendations for international students: Required—TOEFL (minimum score 500 paper-based; 61 iBT), IELTS (minimum score 6). Electronic applications accepted. *Faculty research:* Applied microeconomics, public finance, development, labor.

University of New Brunswick Fredericton, School of Graduate Studies, Faculty of Arts, Department of Economics, Fredericton, NB E3B 5A3, Canada. Offers applied economics and finance (M Sc); economics (MA). M Sc offered on Saint John campus. *Faculty:* 13 full-time (2 women), 2 part-time/adjunct (0 women). *Students:* 20 full-time (9 women), 11 part-time (5 women). In 2014, 5 master's awarded. *Entrance requirements:* For master's, minimum GPA of 3.0. Additional exam requirements/recommendations for international students: Required—TWE (minimum score 4), TOEFL (minimum score 580 paper-based) or IELTS (minimum score 7). *Application deadline:* For fall admission, 1/31 for domestic and international students; for winter admission, 1/15 for domestic students, 1/15 priority date for international students; for spring admission, 1/31 for domestic and international students. Applications are processed on a rolling basis. Application fee: $50 Canadian dollars. Electronic applications accepted. *Financial support:* Fellowships, research assistantships, teaching assistantships, scholarships/grants, health care benefits, and unspecified assistantships available. Financial award application deadline: 1/31. *Faculty research:* Epidemiology and population health, micro/macro economics, economics of transportation, regional development, health economics, econometrics. *Unit head:* Dr. Yuri Yevdokimov, Director of Graduate Studies, 506-447-3221, Fax: 506-453-4514, E-mail: yuri@unb.ca. *Application contact:* Allison Johnson-Sacobie, Graduate Secretary, 506-453-4828, Fax: 506-453-4514, E-mail: asacobie@unb.ca.
Website: http://go.unb.ca/gradprograms

University of New Hampshire, Graduate School, Peter T. Paul College of Business and Economics, Department of Economics, Durham, NH 03824. Offers MA, PhD. Part-time programs available. *Faculty:* 13 full-time (2 women). *Students:* 20 full-time (9 women), 3 part-time (1 woman), 13 international. Average age 27. 63 applicants, 44% accepted, 10 enrolled. In 2014, 15 master's, 5 doctorates awarded. Terminal master's awarded for partial completion of doctoral program. *Degree requirements:* For master's, thesis or alternative; for doctorate, one foreign language, thesis/dissertation. *Entrance requirements:* For master's and doctorate, GRE General Test. Additional exam requirements/recommendations for international students: Required—TOEFL (minimum score 550 paper-based; 80 iBT). *Application deadline:* For fall admission, 6/1 priority date for domestic students, 4/1 for international students; for spring admission, 11/1 for domestic students. Applications are processed on a rolling basis. Application fee: $65. Electronic applications accepted. *Expenses:* Tuition, state resident: full-time $13,500; part-time $750 per credit hour. Tuition, nonresident: full-time $26,460; part-time $1110 per credit hour. *Required fees:* $1788; $447 per semester. *Financial support:* In 2014–15, 20 students received support, including 1 fellowship, 16 teaching assistantships; research assistantships, career-related internships or fieldwork, Federal Work-Study, scholarships/grants, and tuition waivers (full and partial) also available. Support available to part-time students. Financial award application deadline: 2/15. *Faculty research:* Labor economics, international development, econometrics, finance, political economy. *Unit head:* Dr. Jim Wibble, Chair, 603-862-3324. *Application contact:* Wendy Harris, Administrative Assistant, 603-862-3326, E-mail: econ.info@unh.edu.
Website: http://paulcollege.unh.edu/academics/graduate-programs/ma-phd-economics

University of New Mexico, Graduate School, College of Arts and Sciences, Program in Economics, Albuquerque, NM 87131-2039. Offers econometrics (MA); economic theory (MA); environmental/natural resource economics (MA, PhD); international/development and sustainability economics (MA, PhD); public economics (MA, PhD). Part-time programs available. *Faculty:* 12 full-time (7 women). *Students:* 40 full-time (13 women), 5 part-time (2 women); includes 8 minority (2 Black or African American, non-Hispanic/Latino; 1 Asian, non-Hispanic/Latino; 4 Hispanic/Latino; 1 Two or more races, non-Hispanic/Latino), 20 international. Average age 32. 69 applicants, 33% accepted, 12 enrolled. In 2014, 7 master's, 4 doctorates awarded. Terminal master's awarded for partial completion of doctoral program. *Degree requirements:* For master's, comprehensive exam, thesis (for some programs); for doctorate, comprehensive exam, thesis/dissertation. *Entrance requirements:* For master's and doctorate, GRE General Test, 3 letters of recommendation, letter of intent, curriculum vitae. Additional exam

requirements/recommendations for international students: Required—TOEFL (minimum score 520 paper-based; 68 iBT). *Application deadline:* For fall admission, 3/1 priority date for domestic students, 3/1 for international students. Applications are processed on a rolling basis. Application fee: $50. Electronic applications accepted. *Financial support:* In 2014–15, 47 students received support, including 3 fellowships with tuition reimbursements available (averaging $6,858 per year), 13 research assistantships with tuition reimbursements available (averaging $6,858 per year), 15 teaching assistantships with tuition reimbursements available (averaging $7,396 per year); career-related internships or fieldwork, Federal Work-Study, scholarships/grants, health care benefits, and unspecified assistantships also available. Support available to part-time students. Financial award application deadline: 3/1; financial award applicants required to submit FAFSA. *Faculty research:* Core theory, econometrics, public finance, international/development economics, labor/human resource economics, environmental/natural resource economics. *Total annual research expenditures:* $388,864. *Unit head:* Dr. Janie Chermak, Chair, 505-277-2037, Fax: 505-277-9445, E-mail: jchermak@unm.edu. *Application contact:* Jeff Newcomer Miller, Academic Advisor, 505-277-3056, Fax: 505-277-9445, E-mail: econgrad@unm.edu.
Website: http://econ.unm.edu

University of New Orleans, Graduate School, College of Business Administration, Department of Economics and Finance, Program in Financial Economics, New Orleans, LA 70148. Offers PhD. Terminal master's awarded for partial completion of doctoral program. *Degree requirements:* For doctorate, one foreign language, comprehensive exam, thesis/dissertation, general exams. *Entrance requirements:* For doctorate, GRE General Test, minimum GPA of 3.0. Additional exam requirements/recommendations for international students: Required—TOEFL (minimum score 550 paper-based; 79 iBT). Electronic applications accepted. *Faculty research:* Urban and regional economics, economic development, monetary theory and policy, international finance.

The University of North Carolina at Chapel Hill, Graduate School, College of Arts and Sciences, Department of Economics, Chapel Hill, NC 27599. Offers MS, PhD. Terminal master's awarded for partial completion of doctoral program. *Degree requirements:* For master's, comprehensive exam, thesis or alternative; for doctorate, comprehensive exam, thesis/dissertation. *Entrance requirements:* For master's, GRE General Test, minimum GPA of 3.0; for doctorate, GRE General Test, minimum GPA of 3.5. Additional exam requirements/recommendations for international students: Required—TOEFL (minimum score 550 paper-based). Electronic applications accepted. *Faculty research:* Health economics, micro theory/IO, labor economics, economic history, financial econometrics.

The University of North Carolina at Charlotte, Belk College of Business, Department of Economics, Charlotte, NC 28223-0001. Offers MS. Part-time and evening/weekend programs available. *Faculty:* 18 full-time (6 women), 1 part-time/adjunct (0 women). *Students:* 19 full-time (6 women), 18 part-time (3 women); includes 9 minority (3 Black or African American, non-Hispanic/Latino; 2 Asian, non-Hispanic/Latino; 4 Hispanic/Latino), 8 international. Average age 27. 44 applicants, 84% accepted, 11 enrolled. In 2014, 25 master's awarded. *Degree requirements:* For master's, thesis or project. *Entrance requirements:* For master's, GRE General Test, GMAT, minimum undergraduate GPA of 3.0 in major, 2.8 overall. Additional exam requirements/recommendations for international students: Required—TOEFL (minimum score 557 paper-based; 83 iBT). *Application deadline:* For fall admission, 7/15 priority date for domestic students, 5/1 priority date for international students; for spring admission, 11/15 priority date for domestic students, 10/1 priority date for international students. Applications are processed on a rolling basis. Application fee: $75. Electronic applications accepted. *Expenses:* Tuition, state resident: full-time $4008. Tuition, nonresident: full-time $16,295. *Required fees:* $2755. Tuition and fees vary according to course load and program. *Financial support:* Career-related internships or fieldwork, institutionally sponsored loans, scholarships/grants, and unspecified assistantships available. Support available to part-time students. Financial award application deadline: 4/1; financial award applicants required to submit FAFSA. *Faculty research:* Health care, taxation, energy, economic growth, monetary policy. *Total annual research expenditures:* $18,199. *Unit head:* Dr. Rob Roy McGregor, Program Director, 704-687-7639, Fax: 704-687-6442, E-mail: rrmcgreg@uncc.edu. *Application contact:* Kathy B. Giddings, Director of Graduate Admissions, 704-687-5503, Fax: 704-687-1668, E-mail: gradadm@uncc.edu.
Website: http://www.belkcollege.uncc.edu/economics/

The University of North Carolina at Greensboro, Graduate School, Bryan School of Business and Economics, Department of Economics, Program in Economics, Greensboro, NC 27412-5001. Offers PhD. *Degree requirements:* For doctorate, comprehensive exam, thesis/dissertation. *Entrance requirements:* Additional exam requirements/recommendations for international students: Required—TOEFL. Electronic applications accepted.

University of North Florida, Coggin College of Business, MBA Program, Jacksonville, FL 32224. Offers accounting (MBA); construction management (MBA); e-commerce (MBA); economics (MBA); finance (MBA); human resource management (MBA); international business (MBA); logistics (MBA); management applications (MBA). *Accreditation:* AACSB. Part-time and evening/weekend programs available. *Faculty:* 19 full-time (5 women), 1 part-time/adjunct (0 women). *Students:* 96 full-time (38 women), 189 part-time (70 women); includes 48 minority (18 Black or African American, non-Hispanic/Latino; 9 Asian, non-Hispanic/Latino; 14 Hispanic/Latino; 7 Two or more races, non-Hispanic/Latino), 29 international. Average age 29. 208 applicants, 36% accepted, 51 enrolled. In 2014, 121 master's awarded. *Entrance requirements:* For master's, GMAT or GRE, U.S. bachelor's degree from regionally-accredited university or equivalent foreign degree. Additional exam requirements/recommendations for international students: Required—TOEFL (minimum score 550 paper-based; 79 iBT). *Application deadline:* For fall admission, 7/1 priority date for domestic students, 5/1 for international students; for spring admission, 11/1 priority date for domestic students, 10/1 for international students. Application fee: $30. *Expenses:* Tuition, state resident: full-time $9794; part-time $408.10 per credit hour. Tuition, nonresident: full-time $22,383; part-time $932.61 per credit hour. *Required fees:* $2047; $85.29 per credit hour. Tuition and fees vary according to course load and program. *Financial support:* In 2014–15, 35 students received support, including 1 research assistantship (averaging $2,340 per year); teaching assistantships, Federal Work-Study, and tuition waivers (partial) also available. Support available to part-time students. Financial award application deadline: 4/1; financial award applicants required to submit FAFSA. *Faculty research:* Performance measures, costing, and inventory issues in logistics and supply chain management; inter-organizational systems; international management and marketing practices; e-commerce; organizational learning and socialization processes. *Total annual research expenditures:* $3,750. *Application contact:* Cheryl Campbell, Graduate Advisor, 904-620-2575, Fax: 904-620-2832, E-mail: coggin.students@unf.edu.
Website: http://www.unf.edu/graduateschool/academics/programs/MBA.aspx

University of North Texas, Robert B. Toulouse School of Graduate Studies, Denton, TX 76203-5459. Offers accounting (MS); applied anthropology (MA, MS); applied behavior analysis (Certificate); applied geography (MA); applied technology and performance improvement (M Ed, MS); art education (MA); art history (MA); art museum education (Certificate); arts leadership (Certificate); audiology (Au D); behavior analysis

(MS); behavioral science (PhD); biochemistry and molecular biology (MS); biology (MA, MS); biomedical engineering (MS); business analysis (MS); chemistry (MS); clinical health psychology (PhD); communication studies (MA, MS); computer engineering (MS); computer science (MS); counseling (M Ed, MS), including clinical mental health counseling (MS), college and university counseling, elementary school counseling, secondary school counseling; creative writing (MA); criminal justice (MS); curriculum and instruction (M Ed); decision sciences (MBA); design (MA, MFA), including fashion design (MFA), innovation studies, interior design (MFA); early childhood studies (MS); economics (MS); educational leadership (M Ed, Ed D); educational psychology (MS, PhD), including family studies (MS), gifted and talented (MS), human development (MS), learning and cognition (MS), research, measurement and evaluation (MS); electrical engineering (MS); emergency management (MPA); engineering technology (MS); English (MA); English as a second language (MA); environmental science (MS); finance (MBA, MS); financial management (MPA); French (MA); health services management (MBA); higher education (M Ed, Ed D); history (MA, MS); hospitality management (MS); human resources management (MPA); information science (MS); information systems (PhD); information technologies (MBA); interdisciplinary studies (MA, MS); international studies (MA); international sustainable tourism (MS); jazz studies (MM); journalism (MA, MJ, Graduate Certificate), including interactive and virtual digital communication (Graduate Certificate), narrative journalism (Graduate Certificate), public relations (Graduate Certificate); kinesiology (MS); linguistics (MA); local government management (MPA); logistics (PhD); logistics and supply chain management (MBA); long-term care, senior housing, and aging services (MA); management (PhD); marketing (MBA); mathematics (MA, MS); mechanical and energy engineering (MS, PhD); music (MA), including ethnomusicology, music theory, musicology, performance; music composition (PhD); music education (MM Ed, PhD); nonprofit management (MPA); operations and supply chain management (MBA); performance (MM, DMA); philosophy (MA); political science (MA); professional and technical communication (MA); radio, television and film (MA, MFA); rehabilitation counseling (Certificate); sociology (MA); Spanish (MA); special education (M Ed); speech-language pathology (MA); strategic management (MBA); studio art (MFA); teaching (M Ed); MBA/MS. Part-time and evening/weekend programs available. Postbaccalaureate distance learning degree programs offered. *Faculty:* 651 full-time (215 women), 233 part-time/adjunct (139 women). *Students:* 3,040 full-time (1,598 women), 3,401 part-time (2,097 women); includes 1,740 minority (533 Black or African American, non-Hispanic/Latino; 15 American Indian or Alaska Native, non-Hispanic/Latino; 286 Asian, non-Hispanic/Latino; 746 Hispanic/Latino; 3 Native Hawaiian or other Pacific Islander, non-Hispanic/Latino; 157 Two or more races, non-Hispanic/Latino), 1,145 international. Terminal master's awarded for partial completion of doctoral program. *Degree requirements:* For master's, variable foreign language requirement, comprehensive exam (for some programs), thesis (for some programs); for doctorate, variable foreign language requirement, comprehensive exam (for some programs), thesis/dissertation; for other advanced degree, variable foreign language requirement, comprehensive exam (for some programs). *Entrance requirements:* For master's and doctorate, GRE, GMAT. Additional exam requirements/recommendations for international students: Required—TOEFL (minimum score 550 paper-based; 79 iBT). *Application deadline:* For fall admission, 7/15 for domestic students, 3/15 for international students; for spring admission, 11/15 for domestic students, 9/15 for international students; for summer admission, 5/1 for domestic students. Applications are processed on a rolling basis. Application fee: $60. Electronic applications accepted. *Expenses:* Tuition, state resident: full-time $5450; part-time $3633 per year. Tuition, nonresident: full-time $11,966; part-time $7977 per year. *Required fees:* $1301; $398 per credit hour. $685 per semester. Tuition and fees vary according to program and reciprocity agreements. *Financial support:* Fellowships with partial tuition reimbursements, research assistantships with partial tuition reimbursements, teaching assistantships, career-related internships or fieldwork, Federal Work-Study, institutionally sponsored loans, scholarships/grants, health care benefits, and library assistantships available. Support available to part-time students. Financial award applicants required to submit FAFSA. *Unit head:* Mark Wardell, Dean, 940-565-2383, E-mail: mark.wardell@unt.edu. *Application contact:* Toulouse School of Graduate Studies, 940-565-2383, Fax: 940-565-2141, E-mail: gradsch@unt.edu. Website: http://tsgs.unt.edu/

University of Notre Dame, Graduate School, College of Arts and Letters, Division of Social Science, Department of Economics and Econometrics, Notre Dame, IN 46556. Offers MA, PhD. Terminal master's awarded for partial completion of doctoral program. *Degree requirements:* For master's, comprehensive exam (for some programs), thesis optional; for doctorate, thesis/dissertation, candidacy exam. *Entrance requirements:* For doctorate, GRE General Test. Additional exam requirements/recommendations for international students: Required—TOEFL (minimum score 600 paper-based; 80 iBT). Electronic applications accepted.

University of Oklahoma, College of Arts and Sciences, Department of Economics, Norman, OK 73019. Offers applied economics (MA); economics (PhD); managerial economics (MA). *Faculty:* 17 full-time (5 women), 1 part-time/adjunct (0 women). *Students:* 33 full-time (11 women), 41 part-time (7 women); includes 14 minority (6 Black or African American, non-Hispanic/Latino; 1 American Indian or Alaska Native, non-Hispanic/Latino; 3 Asian, non-Hispanic/Latino; 3 Hispanic/Latino; 1 Two or more races, non-Hispanic/Latino), 12 international. Average age 30. 39 applicants, 56% accepted, 12 enrolled. In 2014, 26 master's, 1 doctorate awarded. Terminal master's awarded for partial completion of doctoral program. *Degree requirements:* For master's, comprehensive exam, thesis; for doctorate, 2 foreign languages, comprehensive exam, thesis/dissertation. *Entrance requirements:* For master's, GRE, minimum GPA of 3.0; for doctorate, GRE, minimum GPA of 3.0; intermediate micro and macro economics; calculus I and II. Additional exam requirements/recommendations for international students: Required—TOEFL (minimum score 79 iBT). *Application deadline:* For fall admission, 1/15 for domestic and international students; for spring admission, 9/1 for domestic and international students. Applications are processed on a rolling basis. Application fee: $50 ($100 for international students). Electronic applications accepted. *Expenses:* Tuition, state resident: full-time $4394; part-time $183.10 per credit hour. Tuition, nonresident: full-time $16,970; part-time $707.10 per credit hour. *Required fees:* $2892; $109.95 per credit hour. $126.50 per semester. *Financial support:* In 2014–15, 25 students received support, including 24 teaching assistantships with partial tuition reimbursements available (averaging $14,245 per year); scholarships/grants and unspecified assistantships also available. Financial award application deadline: 6/1; financial award applicants required to submit FAFSA. *Faculty research:* Development economics, growth, industrial organization, international economics, public economics. *Total annual research expenditures:* $203,224. *Unit head:* Dr. Gary Hoover, Professor/Department Chair, 405-325-5857, Fax: 405-325-5842, E-mail: gary.hoover@ou.edu. *Application contact:* Dr. Benjamin Keen, Associate Professor and Graduate Liaison, 405-325-5900, Fax: 405-325-5842, E-mail: ben.keen@ou.edu. Website: http://cas.ou.edu/economics

University of Oregon, Graduate School, College of Arts and Sciences, Department of Economics, Eugene, OR 97403. Offers MA, MS, PhD. Terminal master's awarded for partial completion of doctoral program. *Degree requirements:* For master's, thesis or alternative; for doctorate, thesis/dissertation, qualifying exam. *Entrance requirements:* For master's and doctorate, GRE General Test, minimum GPA of 3.0. Additional exam

requirements/recommendations for international students: Required—TOEFL. *Faculty research:* Labor economics, macroeconomics, international economics, industrial organization, public finance.

University of Ottawa, Faculty of Graduate and Postdoctoral Studies, Faculty of Social Sciences, Department of Economics, Ottawa, ON K1N 6N5, Canada. Offers MA, PhD. PhD offered jointly with Carleton University. Part-time programs available. *Degree requirements:* For master's, thesis or alternative; for doctorate, comprehensive exam, thesis/dissertation. *Entrance requirements:* For master's, honors bachelor's degree or equivalent, minimum B average; for doctorate, master's degree, minimum B+ average. Electronic applications accepted. *Faculty research:* Public economics, industrial organizations, monetary economics, international economics, economic development.

University of Pennsylvania, School of Arts and Sciences, Graduate Group in Economics, Philadelphia, PA 19104. Offers AM, PhD, JD/AM, JD/PhD. *Faculty:* 42 full-time (5 women), 4 part-time/adjunct (0 women). *Students:* 117 full-time (28 women), 1 (woman) part-time; includes 7 minority (1 Black or African American, non-Hispanic/Latino; 4 Asian, non-Hispanic/Latino; 1 Hispanic/Latino; 1 Two or more races, non-Hispanic/Latino), 92 international. 800 applicants, 10% accepted, 24 enrolled. In 2014, 14 master's, 20 doctorates awarded. *Degree requirements:* For doctorate, thesis/dissertation. *Entrance requirements:* For doctorate, GRE General Test. Additional exam requirements/recommendations for international students: Required—TOEFL. *Application deadline:* For fall admission, 12/1 priority date for domestic students. Application fee: $70. Electronic applications accepted. *Financial support:* Institutionally sponsored loans, scholarships/grants, traineeships, health care benefits, and unspecified assistantships available. Financial award application deadline: 12/15. *Faculty research:* Economic theory, econometrics, international economics, monetary/macroeconomics, applied microeconomics, empirical microeconomics. *Unit head:* Dr. Ralph M. Rosen, Associate Dean for Graduate Studies, 215-898-7156, Fax: 215-573-8068, E-mail: grad-dean@sas.upenn.edu. *Application contact:* Arts and Sciences Graduate Admissions, 215-573-5816, Fax: 215-573-8068, E-mail: gdasadmis@sas.upenn.edu. Website: http://economics.sas.upenn.edu/graduate-program

University of Pittsburgh, Dietrich School of Arts and Sciences, Department of Economics, Pittsburgh, PA 15260. Offers PhD. *Faculty:* 23 full-time (5 women). *Students:* 50 full-time (21 women); includes 31 minority (28 Asian, non-Hispanic/Latino; 3 Hispanic/Latino). Average age 28. 362 applicants, 12% accepted, 9 enrolled. In 2014, 6 doctorates awarded. *Degree requirements:* For doctorate, comprehensive exam, thesis/dissertation, comprehensive research paper. *Entrance requirements:* For doctorate, GRE, 3 letters of recommendation. Additional exam requirements/recommendations for international students: Required—TOEFL (minimum score 90 iBT), IELTS (minimum score 7). *Application deadline:* For fall admission, 1/15 for domestic and international students. Application fee: $50. Electronic applications accepted. *Expenses:* Expenses: $23,158 full-time in-state; $37,478 full-time out-of-state. *Financial support:* In 2014–15, 44 students received support, including 16 fellowships with full tuition reimbursements available (averaging $21,262 per year), 5 research assistantships with full tuition reimbursements available (averaging $17,800 per year), 23 teaching assistantships with full tuition reimbursements available (averaging $17,800 per year); institutionally sponsored loans, scholarships/grants, traineeships, health care benefits, and unspecified assistantships also available. Financial award application deadline: 1/15. *Faculty research:* Game theory, experimental economics, econometrics, labor, international trade. *Unit head:* Dr. Frank Giarratani, Department Chair, 412-648-1741, Fax: 412-648-1793, E-mail: frankg@pitt.edu. *Application contact:* Amy M. Linn, Graduate Program Administrator, 412-648-1399, Fax: 412-648-1793, E-mail: amlinn@pitt.edu. Website: http://www.econ.pitt.edu/

University of Pittsburgh, Dietrich School of Arts and Sciences, Program in Computational Modeling and Simulation, Pittsburgh, PA 15260. Offers bioengineering (PhD); biological science (PhD); civil and environmental engineering (PhD); computer science (PhD); economics (PhD); industrial engineering (PhD); mathematics (PhD); mechanical engineering and materials science (PhD); physics and astronomy (PhD); psychology (PhD); statistics (PhD). Part-time programs available. *Faculty:* 4 full-time (0 women). *Students:* 5 full-time (2 women), 1 part-time (0 women), 5 international. Average age 22. 14 applicants, 14% accepted, 2 enrolled. *Degree requirements:* For doctorate, comprehensive exam, thesis/dissertation, preliminary exam. *Entrance requirements:* For doctorate, GRE, statement of purpose, transcripts for all college-level institutions attended, three letters of reference. Additional exam requirements/recommendations for international students: Required—TOEFL (minimum score 90 iBT), IELTS (minimum score 7). *Application deadline:* For fall admission, 2/21 for domestic and international students. Applications are processed on a rolling basis. Application fee: $0 ($50 for international students). Electronic applications accepted. *Expenses:* Tuition, state resident: full-time $20,742; part-time $838 per credit. Tuition, nonresident: full-time $33,960; part-time $1389 per credit. *Required fees:* $800; $205 per term. Tuition and fees vary according to program. *Financial support:* In 2014–15, 5 students received support, including 3 fellowships with tuition reimbursements available (averaging $25,500 per year), 2 research assistantships with tuition reimbursements available (averaging $26,000 per year). *Unit head:* Kathleen Blee, Associate Dean, Graduate Studies and Research, 412-624-3939, Fax: 412-624-6855. *Application contact:* Dave R. Carmen, Administrative Secretary, 412-624-6094, Fax: 412-624-6855, E-mail: drc41@pitt.edu. Website: http://cmsp.pitt.edu/

University of Pittsburgh, Graduate School of Public and International Affairs, Master of Public and International Affairs Program, Pittsburgh, PA 15260. Offers international political economy (MPIA); security and intelligence studies (MPIA); JD/MPIA; MBA/MPIA; MID/MPIA; MPA/MPIA; MPH/MPIA; MPIA/MSW; MSIS/MPIA. Part-time and evening/weekend programs available. *Faculty:* 34 full-time (12 women), 11 part-time/adjunct (3 women). *Students:* 145 full-time (63 women), 8 part-time (5 women); includes 18 minority (6 Black or African American, non-Hispanic/Latino; 3 Asian, non-Hispanic/Latino; 8 Hispanic/Latino; 1 Two or more races, non-Hispanic/Latino), 26 international. Average age 26. 251 applicants, 87% accepted, 64 enrolled. In 2014, 85 master's awarded. *Degree requirements:* For master's, thesis optional, internship, capstone seminar. *Entrance requirements:* For master's, GRE General Test or GMAT, 2 letters of recommendation, resume; undergraduate transcripts, personal statement. Additional exam requirements/recommendations for international students: Required—TOEFL (minimum score 550 paper-based; 80 iBT); Recommended—IELTS (minimum score 7), TWE (minimum score 4). *Application deadline:* For fall admission, 2/1 for domestic students, 1/15 for international students; for spring admission, 11/1 for domestic students, 8/1 for international students. Application fee: $50. Electronic applications accepted. *Expenses:* Tuition, state resident: full-time $20,742; part-time $838 per credit. Tuition, nonresident: full-time $33,960; part-time $1389 per credit. *Required fees:* $800; $205 per term. Tuition and fees vary according to program. *Financial support:* In 2014–15, 45 students received support, including 8 fellowships (averaging $15,000 per year); scholarships/grants, unspecified assistantships, and student employment also available. Financial award application deadline: 2/1. *Faculty research:* International political economy, international security and intelligence, transnational organized crime,

international trade, international finance, globalization, terrorism, multinational corporations and the global economy, human rights, human trafficking, gender and development, diplomacy. *Total annual research expenditures:* $640,844. *Unit head:* Dr. Michael Kenney, Director, International Affairs and International Development Divisions, 412-648-7921, Fax: 412-648-2605, E-mail: mkenney@pitt.edu. *Application contact:* Kelly C. McDevitt, Graduate Enrollment Counselor, 412-648-7640, Fax: 412-648-7641, E-mail: mcdevitt@pitt.edu.
Website: http://www.gspia.pitt.edu/

University of Puerto Rico, Río Piedras Campus, College of Social Sciences, Department of Economics, San Juan, PR 00931-3300. Offers MA. Part-time programs available. *Degree requirements:* For master's, comprehensive exam, thesis. *Entrance requirements:* For master's, GRE, PAEG, interview, minimum GPA of 3.0, letter of recommendation.

University of Regina, Faculty of Graduate Studies and Research, Johnson-Shoyama Graduate School of Public Policy, Regina, SK S4S 0A2, Canada. Offers economic analysis for public policy (Master's Certificate); health administration (MHA); health systems management (Master's Certificate); public management (MPA, Master's Certificate); public policy (MPA, MPP, PhD); public policy analysis (Master's Certificate). Part-time programs available. *Faculty:* 8 full-time (4 women), 12 part-time/adjunct (3 women). *Students:* 60 full-time (33 women), 109 part-time (66 women). 133 applicants, 35% accepted. In 2014, 26 master's, 1 doctorate, 13 other advanced degrees awarded. *Degree requirements:* For master's, thesis (for some programs); for doctorate, thesis/dissertation. *Entrance requirements:* For doctorate, master's degree, intended research program in an area of public policy. Additional exam requirements/recommendations for international students: Required—TOEFL (minimum score 580 paper-based; 80 iBT), IELTS (minimum score 6.5), PTE (minimum score 59). *Application deadline:* For fall admission, 2/1 for domestic and international students. Application fee: $100. Electronic applications accepted. *Expenses:* Expenses: $4,304.85 per semester of full time study (for MHA), $2,588.85 (for MPA), $1,450.35 (for MPP); $1,450.35 (for PhD). *Financial support:* In 2014–15, 11 fellowships (averaging $6,000 per year), 15 teaching assistantships (averaging $2,435 per year) were awarded; research assistantships, career-related internships or fieldwork, and scholarships/grants also available. Financial award application deadline: 6/15. *Faculty research:* Governance and administration, public finance, public policy analysis, non-governmental organizations and alternative service delivery, micro-economics for policy analysis. *Unit head:* Dr. Kathleen McNutt, Executive Director, Main Campus, 306-585-4759, Fax: 306-585-5461, E-mail: kathy.mcnutt@uregina.ca. *Application contact:* Constance Heshka-Argue, Manager, Main Campus, 306-585-5462, Fax: 306-585-5461, E-mail: connie.heska-argue@uregina.ca.
Website: http://www.schoolofpublicpolicy.sk.ca/

University of Rhode Island, Graduate School, College of the Environment and Life Sciences, Department of Environmental and Natural Resource Economics, Kingston, RI 02881. Offers MESM, MS, PhD. Part-time programs available. *Faculty:* 7 full-time (2 women). *Students:* 23 full-time (7 women), 7 part-time (3 women), 14 international. In 2014, 7 master's, 2 doctorates awarded. *Degree requirements:* For master's, comprehensive exam (for some programs), thesis optional; for doctorate, comprehensive exam, thesis/dissertation. *Entrance requirements:* For master's and doctorate, GRE, 3 letters of recommendation. Additional exam requirements/recommendations for international students: Required—TOEFL (minimum score 550 paper-based). *Application deadline:* For fall admission, 7/15 for domestic students, 2/1 for international students; for spring admission, 11/15 for domestic students, 7/15 for international students. Application fee: $65. Electronic applications accepted. *Expenses:* Tuition, state resident: full-time $11,532; part-time $641 per credit. Tuition, nonresident: full-time $23,606; part-time $1311 per credit. *Required fees:* $1442; $39 per credit. $35 per semester. One-time fee: $155. *Financial support:* In 2014–15, 2 research assistantships (averaging $9,750 per year) were awarded. Financial award application deadline: 7/15; financial award applicants required to submit FAFSA. *Faculty research:* Policy simulation, policy actions, experimental economics. *Total annual research expenditures:* $573,796. *Unit head:* Dr. James Opaluch, Chair, 401-874-4590, Fax: 401-874-4766, E-mail: jimo@uri.edu. *Application contact:* Graduate Admission, 401-874-2872, E-mail: gradadm@etal.uri.edu.
Website: http://web.uri.edu/enre/

University of Rochester, School of Arts and Sciences, Department of Economics, Rochester, NY 14627. Offers MS, PhD. *Faculty:* 19 full-time (6 women). *Students:* 50 full-time (13 women); includes 1 minority (Asian, non-Hispanic/Latino), 39 international. 374 applicants, 16% accepted, 8 enrolled. In 2014, 14 master's, 12 doctorates awarded. *Degree requirements:* For doctorate, thesis/dissertation, qualifying exam. *Entrance requirements:* For doctorate, GRE General Test, GRE Subject Test (strongly recommended). Additional exam requirements/recommendations for international students: Required—TOEFL. *Application deadline:* For fall admission, 1/1 priority date for domestic students. Application fee: $60. Electronic applications accepted. *Expenses: Tuition:* Full-time $46,150; part-time $1442 per credit hour. *Required fees:* $504. *Financial support:* Fellowships, research assistantships, teaching assistantships, and tuition waivers (full and partial) available. Financial award application deadline: 1/1. *Unit head:* Michael Wolkoff, Deputy Chair, 585-275-5279. *Application contact:* Jenna Wernert, Coordinator of Graduate Studies, 585-275-8625, E-mail: jenna.scott@rochester.edu.
Website: http://www.econ.rochester.edu/

University of San Francisco, College of Arts and Sciences, Economics Program, San Francisco, CA 94117-1080. Offers MA, MS, MS/MBA. Part-time and evening/weekend programs available. *Faculty:* 6 full-time (2 women), 4 part-time/adjunct (0 women). *Students:* 34 full-time (18 women), 4 part-time (1 woman); includes 8 minority (2 Black or African American, non-Hispanic/Latino; 4 Asian, non-Hispanic/Latino; 2 Hispanic/Latino), 23 international. Average age 27. 99 applicants, 60% accepted, 11 enrolled. In 2014, 20 master's awarded. *Degree requirements:* For master's, comprehensive exam, thesis or alternative. *Entrance requirements:* For master's, GRE General Test (recommended), BA in economics (preferred). Additional exam requirements/recommendations for international students: Required—TOEFL. *Application deadline:* For fall admission, 3/1 for domestic students. Applications are processed on a rolling basis. Application fee: $55 ($65 for international students). *Expenses: Tuition:* Full-time $21,762; part-time $1209 per credit hour. Tuition and fees vary according to degree level, campus/location and program. *Financial support:* In 2014–15, 8 students received support. Fellowships, teaching assistantships, and career-related internships or fieldwork available. Financial award application deadline: 3/2; financial award applicants required to submit FAFSA. *Faculty research:* Economic development, forecasting and planning, labor markets, Pacific Rim, financial markets. *Unit head:* Barbara Pena, Associate Director, 415-422-2711, Fax: 415-422-5784. *Application contact:* Mark Landerghini, Information Contact, 415-422-5101, Fax: 415-422-2217, E-mail: asgraduate@usfca.edu.
Website: http://www.usfca.edu/artsci/csg/

University of Saskatchewan, College of Graduate Studies and Research, College of Arts and Science, Department of Economics, Saskatoon, SK S7N 5A2, Canada. Offers MA, Diploma. *Degree requirements:* For master's, thesis (for some programs). *Entrance requirements:* Additional exam requirements/recommendations for international students: Required—TOEFL (minimum score 80 iBT); Recommended—IELTS (minimum score 6.5). Electronic applications accepted.

University of South Africa, College of Economic and Management Sciences, Pretoria, South Africa. Offers accounting (D Admin, D Com); accounting science (DA); auditing (D Admin, D Com); business administration (M Tech); business economics (D Admin); business leadership (DBL); business management (D Admin, D Com); economic management analysis (M Tech); economics (D Admin, D Com, PhD); human resource development (M Tech); industrial psychology (D Admin, D Com, PhD); logistics (D Com); marketing (M Tech); public administration (D Admin, D Com, DPA, PhD); public management (M Tech); quantitative management (D Admin, D Com); real estate (M Tech); statistics (D Admin, PhD); tourism management (D Admin, D Com); transport economics (D Admin, D Com).

University of South Carolina, The Graduate School, Darla Moore School of Business, Doctoral Program in Business Administration, Columbia, SC 29208. Offers business administration (PhD); economics (PhD). *Degree requirements:* For doctorate, thesis/dissertation, qualifying and comprehensive exams. *Entrance requirements:* For doctorate, GRE or GMAT. Additional exam requirements/recommendations for international students: Required—TOEFL (minimum score 600 paper-based; 100 iBT), IELTS (minimum score 7). Electronic applications accepted. *Expenses:* Contact institution. *Faculty research:* International competitiveness of U.S. textiles, international compensation, exchange rates, international finance.

University of South Carolina, The Graduate School, Darla Moore School of Business, Master of Arts in Economics Program, Columbia, SC 29208. Offers MA, JD/MA. *Degree requirements:* For master's, thesis optional. *Entrance requirements:* For master's, GMAT or GRE General Test. Additional exam requirements/recommendations for international students: Required—TOEFL (minimum score 100 iBT); Recommended—IELTS. Electronic applications accepted. *Faculty research:* Monetary theory, labor economics, international economics, industrial organization.

University of Southern California, Graduate School, Dana and David Dornsife College of Letters, Arts and Sciences, Department of Economics, Los Angeles, CA 90089. Offers economic development programming (MA, PhD); mathematical finance (MS); M Pl/MA; MA/JD. Terminal master's awarded for partial completion of doctoral program. *Degree requirements:* For master's, comprehensive exam; for doctorate, comprehensive exam, thesis/dissertation. *Entrance requirements:* For master's and doctorate, GRE. Additional exam requirements/recommendations for international students: Required—TOEFL (minimum score 93 iBT). Electronic applications accepted. *Faculty research:* Macro theory, development economics, econometrics.

University of Southern Mississippi, Graduate School, College of Science and Technology, Department of Economic and Workforce Development, Hattiesburg, MS 39406-0001. Offers economic development (MS); human capital development (PhD); workforce training and development (MS). Part-time and evening/weekend programs available. *Degree requirements:* For master's, comprehensive exam, thesis optional, internships; for doctorate, comprehensive exam, thesis/dissertation. *Entrance requirements:* For master's, GMAT or GRE General Test, minimum GPA of 2.75 in last 60 hours; for doctorate, GMAT or GRE General Test, minimum GPA of 3.5. Additional exam requirements/recommendations for international students: Required—TOEFL, IELTS. Electronic applications accepted. *Faculty research:* Economic development, international studies, geography.

University of South Florida, College of Arts and Sciences, Department of Economics, Tampa, FL 33620-9951. Offers MA, PhD. Part-time and evening/weekend programs available. *Faculty:* 10 full-time (2 women). *Students:* 25 full-time (12 women), 14 part-time (4 women); includes 7 minority (3 Black or African American, non-Hispanic/Latino; 1 Asian, non-Hispanic/Latino; 3 Hispanic/Latino), 9 international. Average age 28. 60 applicants, 50% accepted, 16 enrolled. In 2014, 10 master's, 4 doctorates awarded. *Degree requirements:* For master's, comprehensive exam, oral exam; for doctorate, comprehensive exam, thesis/dissertation. *Entrance requirements:* For master's, GRE General Test (within the past five years with minimum preferred scores in the 65th percentile for both verbal and quantitative), minimum GPA of 3.0 in last 60 hours of course work; minimum B grade in calculus, statistics, undergraduate-level intermediate microeconomics, and undergraduate-level intermediate macroeconomics; for doctorate, GRE General Test (within the past five years with minimum preferred scores in the 65th percentile for both verbal and quantitative), minimum GPA of 3.0 in last 60 hours of undergraduate and graduate coursework; minimum B grade in calculus (two courses), statistics, undergraduate intermediate-level microeconomics and undergraduate intermediate-level macroeconomics. Additional exam requirements/recommendations for international students: Required—TOEFL (minimum score 550 paper-based; 79 iBT) or IELTS (minimum score 6.5). *Application deadline:* For fall admission, 6/1 for domestic students, 1/2 for international students; for spring admission, 10/15 for domestic students, 6/1 for international students. Applications are processed on a rolling basis. Application fee: $30. *Financial support:* In 2014–15, 16 students received support, including 1 research assistantship (averaging $13,082 per year), 15 teaching assistantships with tuition reimbursements available (averaging $11,393 per year); unspecified assistantships also available. Financial award application deadline: 2/1; financial award applicants required to submit FAFSA. *Faculty research:* Applied microeconomics, health economics, industrial organization, development economics, public economics. *Total annual research expenditures:* $45,820. *Unit head:* Dr. Bradley Kamp, Associate Professor and Chairperson, 813-974-6549, Fax: 813-974-6510, E-mail: bkamp@usf.edu. *Application contact:* Dr. Michael Loewy, Associate Professor and Graduate Director, 813-974-6532, Fax: 813-974-6510, E-mail: mloewy@usf.edu.
Website: http://www.economics.usf.edu

The University of Tennessee, Graduate School, College of Arts and Sciences, Department of Sociology, Knoxville, TN 37996. Offers criminology (MA, PhD); energy, environment, and resource policy (MA, PhD); political economy (MA, PhD). Part-time programs available. *Degree requirements:* For master's, thesis or alternative; for doctorate, thesis/dissertation. *Entrance requirements:* For master's, GRE General Test, minimum GPA of 3.0; for doctorate, GRE General Test, minimum GPA of 3.5. Additional exam requirements/recommendations for international students: Required—TOEFL. Electronic applications accepted.

The University of Tennessee, Graduate School, College of Business Administration, Department of Economics, Knoxville, TN 37996. Offers MA, PhD. *Degree requirements:* For master's, thesis or alternative; for doctorate, thesis/dissertation. *Entrance requirements:* For master's and doctorate, GRE General Test or GMAT, minimum GPA of 2.7. Additional exam requirements/recommendations for international students: Required—TOEFL. Electronic applications accepted.

The University of Texas at Arlington, Graduate School, College of Business, Economics Department, Arlington, TX 76019. Offers MA. Part-time and evening/weekend programs available. *Degree requirements:* For master's, thesis optional. *Entrance requirements:* For master's, GMAT or GRE. Additional exam requirements/recommendations for international students: Required—TOEFL (minimum score 550 paper-based; 79 iBT).

The University of Texas at Austin, Graduate School, College of Liberal Arts, Department of Economics, Austin, TX 78712-1111. Offers MA, MS Econ, PhD. Part-time programs available. *Degree requirements:* For master's, thesis; for doctorate, comprehensive exam, thesis/dissertation. *Entrance requirements:* For master's and doctorate, GRE General Test, minimum GPA of 3.5 (based on upper-division undergraduate and graduate course work). Additional exam requirements/ recommendations for international students: Required—TOEFL. Electronic applications accepted. *Faculty research:* Industrial organization, game theory, monetary economics, labor economics, public economics.

The University of Texas at Dallas, School of Economic, Political and Policy Sciences, Program in Economics, Richardson, TX 75080. Offers MS, PhD. Part-time and evening/ weekend programs available. *Faculty:* 9 full-time (4 women), 1 part-time/adjunct (0 women). *Students:* 41 full-time (17 women), 17 part-time (5 women); includes 16 minority (4 Black or African American, non-Hispanic/Latino; 6 Asian, non-Hispanic/ Latino; 5 Hispanic/Latino; 1 Two or more races, non-Hispanic/Latino), 23 international. Average age 28. 113 applicants, 39% accepted, 25 enrolled. In 2014, 20 master's, 2 doctorates awarded. *Degree requirements:* For master's, internship; for doctorate, thesis/dissertation. *Entrance requirements:* For master's, GRE (minimum combined verbal and quantitative score of 1200), minimum GPA of 3.0 in upper-level course work in field; for doctorate, GRE (minimum combined verbal and quantitative score of 1200, writing 4.5), minimum GPA of 3.25 in upper-level and graduate course work in field. Additional exam requirements/recommendations for international students: Required— TOEFL (minimum score 550 paper-based). *Application deadline:* For fall admission, 7/ 15 for domestic students, 5/1 priority date for international students; for spring admission, 11/15 for domestic students, 9/1 priority date for international students. Applications are processed on a rolling basis. Application fee: $50 ($100 for international students). Electronic applications accepted. *Expenses:* Tuition, state resident: full-time $11,940; part-time $663 per credit. Tuition, nonresident: full-time $22,282; part-time $1238 per credit. *Financial support:* In 2014–15, 31 students received support, including 3 research assistantships with partial tuition reimbursements available (averaging $13,300 per year), 16 teaching assistantships with partial tuition reimbursements available (averaging $11,872 per year); career-related internships or fieldwork, Federal Work-Study, institutionally sponsored loans, scholarships/grants, and unspecified assistantships also available. Support available to part-time students. Financial award application deadline: 4/30; financial award applicants required to submit FAFSA. *Faculty research:* Bargaining and negotiation, experimental economics, judgment and decision-making, game theory, terrorism. *Unit head:* Dr. Daniel G. Arce, Program Head, 972-883-6857, Fax: 972-883-2735, E-mail: darce@utdallas.edu. *Application contact:* Judy Du, Graduate Program Administrator, 972-883-4964, Fax: 972-883-2735, E-mail: judy.du@utdallas.edu.
Website: http://www.utdallas.edu/epps/economics/

The University of Texas at Dallas, School of Economic, Political and Policy Sciences, Program in Public Policy and Political Economy, Richardson, TX 75080. Offers international political economy (MS); public policy (MPP); public policy and political economy (PhD). Part-time and evening/weekend programs available. *Faculty:* 14 full-time (1 woman), 1 part-time/adjunct (0 women). *Students:* 41 full-time (13 women), 35 part-time (16 women); includes 22 minority (6 Black or African American, non-Hispanic/ Latino; 1 American Indian or Alaska Native, non-Hispanic/Latino; 8 Asian, non-Hispanic/ Latino; 7 Hispanic/Latino), 21 international. Average age 36. 52 applicants, 60% accepted, 12 enrolled. In 2014, 18 master's, 3 doctorates awarded. *Degree requirements:* For doctorate, thesis/dissertation. *Entrance requirements:* For master's and doctorate, GRE General Test, minimum GPA of 3.0 in upper-level course work in field. Additional exam requirements/recommendations for international students: Required—TOEFL (minimum score 550 paper-based). *Application deadline:* For fall admission, 7/15 for domestic students, 5/1 priority date for international students; for spring admission, 11/15 for domestic students, 9/1 priority date for international students. Applications are processed on a rolling basis. Application fee: $50 ($100 for international students). Electronic applications accepted. *Expenses:* Tuition, state resident: full-time $11,940; part-time $663 per credit. Tuition, nonresident: full-time $22,282; part-time $1238 per credit. *Financial support:* In 2014–15, 49 students received support, including 4 research assistantships with partial tuition reimbursements available (averaging $12,070 per year), 15 teaching assistantships with partial tuition reimbursements available (averaging $11,790 per year); career-related internships or fieldwork, Federal Work-Study, institutionally sponsored loans, scholarships/grants, and unspecified assistantships also available. Support available to part-time students. Financial award application deadline: 4/30; financial award applicants required to submit FAFSA. *Faculty research:* Ethnicity, community and local public good provision; community mental health policy; Texas Schools Project; biological and chemical arms control; cross-disciplinary applications of quantitative methodology. *Unit head:* Dr. Jennifer Holmes, Program Head, 972-883-6843, Fax: 972-883-6297, E-mail: jholmes@utdallas.edu. *Application contact:* Betsy Albritton, Graduate Program Administrator, 972-883-6406, Fax: 972-883-6297, E-mail: pppe@utdallas.edu.
Website: http://www.utdallas.edu/epps/public-policy-and-political-economy/

The University of Texas at El Paso, Graduate School, College of Business Administration, Department of Economics and Finance, El Paso, TX 79968-0001. Offers economics (MS). Part-time and evening/weekend programs available. *Degree requirements:* For master's, thesis optional, at least 24 credit hours with minimum cumulative GPA of 3.0. *Entrance requirements:* For master's, GRE, undergraduate degree from accredited college or university. Additional exam requirements/ recommendations for international students: Required—TOEFL. Electronic applications accepted. *Faculty research:* Border economics, public utility economics, urban economics, international economics, applied econometrics.

The University of Texas at San Antonio, College of Business, Department of Economics, San Antonio, TX 78249-0617. Offers business economics (MBA); economics (MA). Part-time and evening/weekend programs available. *Faculty:* 7 full-time (2 women), 4 part-time/adjunct (1 woman). *Students:* 11 full-time (2 women), 6 part-time (2 women); includes 4 minority (all Hispanic/Latino), 4 international. Average age 30. 1,825 applicants, 1% accepted, 9 enrolled. In 2014, 6 master's awarded. *Degree requirements:* For master's, comprehensive exam, thesis optional. *Entrance requirements:* For master's, GMAT or GRE, transcripts, statement of purpose. Additional exam requirements/recommendations for international students: Required—TOEFL (minimum score 550 paper-based; 79 iBT), IELTS (minimum score 6.5). *Application deadline:* For fall admission, 7/1 for domestic students, 4/1 for international students; for spring admission, 11/1 for domestic students, 9/1 for international students. Applications are processed on a rolling basis. Application fee: $45 ($80 for international students). Electronic applications accepted. *Expenses:* Tuition, state resident: full-time $4671; part-time $260 per credit hour. Tuition, nonresident: full-time $18,022; part-time $1001 per credit hour. *Faculty research:* Game theory, international trade, monetary policy, panel data, exchange and interest rates. *Unit head:* Dr. Kenneth E. Weiher, Department Chair, 210-458-4315, Fax: 210-458-5837, E-mail: kweiher@utsa.edu. *Application contact:* Katherine Pope, Economics Graduate Advisor of Record, 210-458-7316, Fax: 210-458-4398, E-mail: katherine.pope@utsa.edu.
Website: http://business.utsa.edu/economics/

The University of Toledo, College of Graduate Studies, College of Languages, Literature and Social Sciences, Department of Economics, Toledo, OH 43606-3390. Offers applied econometric specialization (MA); economics (MA). Part-time programs available. *Degree requirements:* For master's, comprehensive exam, paper or thesis. *Entrance requirements:* For master's, GRE General Test, minimum cumulative GPA of 2.7 on all previous academic work, three letters of recommendation, statement of purpose, transcripts from all prior institutions attended. Additional exam requirements/ recommendations for international students: Required—TOEFL (minimum score 550 paper-based; 80 iBT). Electronic applications accepted. *Faculty research:* Economic development.

The University of Toledo, College of Graduate Studies, Judith Herb College of Education, Department of Curriculum and Instruction, Toledo, OH 43606-3390. Offers art education (ME); career and technical education (ME, Ed S); curriculum and instruction (ME, PhD, Ed S); early childhood education (Ed S); education and anthropology (MAE); education and biology (MES); education and chemistry (MES); education and classics (MAE); education and economics (MAE); education and English (MAE); education and French (MAE); education and geology (MES); education and German (MAE); education and history (MAE); education and mathematics (MAE, MES); education and physics (MES); education and political science (MAE); education and sociology (MAE); education and Spanish (MAE); educational media (PhD); educational technology (ME); educational technology: virtual educator (Certificate); elementary education (PhD); English as a second language (MAE); gifted and talented education (PhD); middle childhood education (ME); secondary education (ME, PhD); special education (PhD). *Accreditation:* NCATE. Part-time and evening/weekend programs available. *Degree requirements:* For master's, comprehensive exam, thesis or alternative; for doctorate, comprehensive exam, thesis/dissertation; for other advanced degree, thesis optional. *Entrance requirements:* For master's, doctorate, and other advanced degree, minimum cumulative GPA of 2.7 for all previous academic work, letters of recommendation. Additional exam requirements/recommendations for international students: Required—TOEFL (minimum score 550 paper-based; 80 iBT). Electronic applications accepted.

University of Toronto, School of Graduate Studies, Faculty of Arts and Science, Department of Economics, Toronto, ON M5S 2J7, Canada. Offers economics (MA, PhD); financial economics (MFE); JD/MA; JD/PhD. Part-time programs available. *Degree requirements:* For doctorate, comprehensive exam, thesis/dissertation. *Entrance requirements:* For master's, GRE (for applicants without a degree from a Canadian university), minimum B average in final year, 2 letters of reference; for doctorate, GRE (for applicants without a degree from a Canadian university), master's degree in economics, minimum B+ average, 3 letters of reference. Additional exam requirements/recommendations for international students: Required—TOEFL (minimum 580 paper-based; 93 iBT), IELTS (minimum score 7), TWE (minimum score 5), or Michigan English Language Assessment Battery (minimum score 85). Electronic applications accepted.

University of Utah, Graduate School, College of Social and Behavioral Science, Department of Economics, Salt Lake City, UT 84112. Offers econometrics (M Stat); economics (M Phil, MA, MS, PhD). Part-time programs available. *Faculty:* 18 full-time (4 women), 3 part-time/adjunct (1 woman). *Students:* 65 full-time (24 women), 41 part-time (10 women); includes 10 minority (2 Black or African American, non-Hispanic/Latino; 3 Asian, non-Hispanic/Latino; 4 Hispanic/Latino; 1 Two or more races, non-Hispanic/ Latino), 49 international. Average age 33. 153 applicants, 25% accepted, 24 enrolled. In 2014, 21 master's, 6 doctorates awarded. Terminal master's awarded for partial completion of doctoral program. *Degree requirements:* For master's, thesis or alternative, exam, oral presentation, research project; for doctorate, comprehensive exam, thesis/dissertation, qualifying exams. *Entrance requirements:* For master's, GRE General Test; GRE Subject Test (for M Stat), undergraduate course work in economics, minimum GPA of 3.0; for doctorate, GRE General Test, minimum GPA of 3.0, course work in calculus and statistics. Additional exam requirements/recommendations for international students: Required—TOEFL (minimum score 500 paper-based; 61 iBT) or IELTS (minimum score 6). *Application deadline:* For fall admission, 2/1 priority date for domestic and international students. Application fee: $55 ($65 for international students). Electronic applications accepted. *Financial support:* In 2014–15, 33 students received support, including 2 fellowships with full tuition reimbursements available (averaging $13,000 per year), 2 research assistantships with full tuition reimbursements available (averaging $16,750 per year), 29 teaching assistantships with full tuition reimbursements available (averaging $13,000 per year); scholarships/grants, health care benefits, and unspecified assistantships also available. Financial award application deadline: 2/1. *Faculty research:* Economic doctrines, economic history, labor and gender, development, international, environmental and natural resources, health economics. Total annual research expenditures: $20,000. *Unit head:* Dr. Thomas Maloney, Chair, 801-581-7481, Fax: 801-585-5649, E-mail: maloney@economics.utah.edu. *Application contact:* Jill Wilson, Academic Advisor, 801-581-7481, Fax: 801-585-5649, E-mail: jill.wilson@economics.utah.edu.
Website: http://www.economics.utah.edu

University of Utah, Graduate School, Interdepartmental Program in Statistics, Salt Lake City, UT 84112-1107. Offers biostatistics (M Stat); econometrics (M Stat); educational psychology (M Stat); mathematics (M Stat); sociology (M Stat). Part-time programs available. *Students:* 61 full-time (34 women), 45 part-time (13 women); includes 18 minority (3 Black or African American, non-Hispanic/Latino; 10 Asian, non-Hispanic/Latino; 3 Hispanic/Latino; 2 Two or more races, non-Hispanic/Latino), 30 international. Average age 32. 50 applicants, 70% accepted, 27 enrolled. In 2014, 18 master's awarded. *Degree requirements:* For master's, comprehensive exam (for some programs), projects. *Entrance requirements:* For master's, GRE General Test (for all but biostatistics); GRE Subject Test (for mathematics), minimum GPA of 3.0; course work in calculus, matrix theory, statistics. Additional exam requirements/recommendations for international students: Required—TOEFL (minimum score 500 paper-based; 61 iBT). *Application deadline:* For fall admission, 7/1 for domestic students, 4/1 for international students. Applications are processed on a rolling basis. Application fee: $55 ($65 for international students). Electronic applications accepted. *Financial support:* In 2014–15, 10 students received support, including 10 research assistantships with full and partial tuition reimbursements available (averaging $1,000 per year); career-related internships or fieldwork, scholarships/grants, and unspecified assistantships also available. *Faculty research:* Biostatistics, sociology, economics, educational psychology, mathematics. *Unit head:* Xiaoming Sheng, Chair, University Statistics Committee, 801-213-3729, E-mail: xiaoming.sheng@utah.edu. *Application contact:* Laura Egbert, Coordinator, 801-585-6853, E-mail: laura.egbert@utah.edu.
Website: http://www.mstat.utah.edu

University of Victoria, Faculty of Graduate Studies, Faculty of Social Sciences, Department of Economics, Victoria, BC V8W 2Y2, Canada. Offers MA, PhD. Part-time programs available. *Degree requirements:* For master's, comprehensive exam (for some programs), thesis optional; for doctorate, comprehensive exam, thesis/dissertation, candidacy exam. *Entrance requirements:* For master's and doctorate, GRE. Additional exam requirements/recommendations for international students: Required—TOEFL (minimum score 575 paper-based), IELTS (minimum score 7). Electronic applications

accepted. *Faculty research:* Industrial organization, cost/benefit, applied economics, econometrics, airline economics, health economics.

University of Virginia, College and Graduate School of Arts and Sciences, Department of Economics, Charlottesville, VA 22903. Offers MA, PhD. *Faculty:* 30 full-time (4 women), 2 part-time/adjunct (0 women). *Students:* 95 full-time (28 women), 3 part-time (1 woman); includes 5 minority (1 Black or African American, non-Hispanic/Latino; 3 Asian, non-Hispanic/Latino; 1 Two or more races, non-Hispanic/Latino), 57 international. Average age 27. 542 applicants, 7% accepted, 20 enrolled. In 2014, 13 master's, 12 doctorates awarded. *Degree requirements:* For master's, comprehensive exam (for some programs), thesis (for some programs), thesis or comprehensive exam; for doctorate, comprehensive exam, thesis/dissertation. *Entrance requirements:* For master's and doctorate, GRE General Test. Additional exam requirements/recommendations for international students: Required—TOEFL (minimum score 600 paper-based; 90 iBT), IELTS (minimum score 7). *Application deadline:* For fall admission, 4/1 for domestic and international students. Applications are processed on a rolling basis. Application fee: $60. Electronic applications accepted. *Expenses:* Tuition, state resident: full-time $14,164; part-time $349 per credit hour. Tuition, nonresident: full-time $23,722; part-time $1300 per credit hour. *Required fees:* $2514. *Financial support:* Fellowships, research assistantships, teaching assistantships, and tuition waivers (full and partial) available. Financial award application deadline: 2/1; financial award applicants required to submit FAFSA. *Faculty research:* Macroeconomics, public economics, labor, industrial organization, economic history. *Unit head:* Sarah Turner, Chair, 434-924-3177, Fax: 434-982-2904, E-mail: econ@virginia.edu. *Application contact:* Federico Ciliberto, Director of Graduate Studies, 434-924-3177, Fax: 434-982-2904, E-mail: ciliberto@virginia.edu.
Website: http://economics.virginia.edu/

University of Washington, Graduate School, College of Arts and Sciences, Department of Economics, Seattle, WA 98195. Offers PhD. Terminal master's awarded for partial completion of doctoral program. *Degree requirements:* For doctorate, comprehensive exam, thesis/dissertation. *Entrance requirements:* For doctorate, GRE General Test, minimum GPA of 3.0. Additional exam requirements/recommendations for international students: Required—TOEFL. Electronic applications accepted. *Faculty research:* Microeconomic theory; macroeconomic theory; econometrics; natural resource economics; international, development, and industrial organization.

University of Washington, Graduate School, School of Public Health, Department of Health Services, Seattle, WA 98195. Offers clinical research (MS); community-oriented public health practice (MPH); evaluative sciences and statistics (PhD); health behavior and social determinants of health (PhD); health economics (PhD); health informatics and health information management (MHIHIM); health services (MS, PhD); health services administration (EMHA, MHA); health systems and policy (MPH); health systems research (PhD); maternal and child health (MPH); social and behavioral sciences (MPH); JD/MHA; MHA/MBA; MHA/MD; MHA/MPA; MPH/JD; MPH/MD; MPH/MN; MPH/MPA; MPH/MS; MPH/MSD; MPH/MSW; MPH/PhD. Postbaccalaureate distance learning degree programs offered (minimal on-campus study). *Faculty:* 63 full-time (33 women), 62 part-time/adjunct (37 women). *Students:* 124 full-time (100 women), 19 part-time (15 women); includes 48 minority (7 Black or African American, non-Hispanic/Latino; 3 American Indian or Alaska Native, non-Hispanic/Latino; 26 Asian, non-Hispanic/Latino; 11 Hispanic/Latino; 1 Native Hawaiian or other Pacific Islander, non-Hispanic/Latino), 3 international. Average age 30. 292 applicants, 56% accepted, 66 enrolled. In 2014, 56 master's, 3 doctorates awarded. Terminal master's awarded for partial completion of doctoral program. *Degree requirements:* For master's, thesis (for some programs), practicum (MPH); for doctorate, comprehensive exam, thesis/dissertation. *Entrance requirements:* For master's and doctorate, GRE General Test, minimum GPA of 3.0. Additional exam requirements/recommendations for international students: Required—TOEFL (minimum score 580 paper-based; 92 iBT), IELTS (minimum score 7). *Application deadline:* For fall admission, 1/1 for domestic students, 11/1 for international students. Application fee: 85 Albanian leks. Electronic applications accepted. *Expenses:* Expenses: $17,703 state resident tuition and fees, $34,827 non-resident (for MPH); $17,037 state resident tuition and fees, $29,511 non-resident (for MS and PhD). *Financial support:* In 2014–15, 45 students received support, including 12 fellowships with full and partial tuition reimbursements available (averaging $22,000 per year), 9 research assistantships with full and partial tuition reimbursements available (averaging $18,700 per year), 9 teaching assistantships with full and partial tuition reimbursements available (averaging $4,575 per year); institutionally sponsored loans, traineeships, and health care benefits also available. Financial award application deadline: 2/28; financial award applicants required to submit FAFSA. *Faculty research:* Public health practice, health promotion and disease prevention, maternal and child health, organizational behavior and culture, health policy. *Unit head:* Dr. Larry Kessler, Chair, 206-543-2930. *Application contact:* Kitty A. Andert, MPH/MS/PhD Programs Manager, 206-616-2926, Fax: 206-543-3964, E-mail: hservmph@u.washington.edu.
Website: http://depts.washington.edu/hserv/

University of Waterloo, Graduate Studies, Faculty of Arts, Department of Economics, Waterloo, ON N2L 3G1, Canada. Offers MA, PhD. Part-time programs available. *Entrance requirements:* For master's, honors degree, minimum B average. Additional exam requirements/recommendations for international students: Required—TOEFL, TWE. Electronic applications accepted. *Faculty research:* Applied microeconomics, applied macroeconomics, public finance, international trade and finance, wage inflation and consumer problems.

The University of Western Ontario, Faculty of Graduate Studies, Social Sciences Division, Department of Economics, London, ON N6A 5B8, Canada. Offers MA, PhD. *Degree requirements:* For doctorate, thesis/dissertation. *Entrance requirements:* For master's, GRE, honours BA with B+ average. Additional exam requirements/recommendations for international students: Required—TOEFL.

University of Windsor, Faculty of Graduate Studies, Faculty of Science, Department of Economics, Windsor, ON N9B 3P4, Canada. Offers MA. Part-time programs available. *Degree requirements:* For master's, thesis or alternative. *Entrance requirements:* For master's, minimum B average. Additional exam requirements/recommendations for international students: Required—TOEFL (minimum score 560 paper-based). Electronic applications accepted. *Faculty research:* International trade, economic growth, microeconomic theory.

University of Wisconsin–Madison, Graduate School, College of Letters and Science, Department of Economics, Madison, WI 53706-1380. Offers PhD. *Degree requirements:* For doctorate, thesis/dissertation. *Entrance requirements:* For doctorate, GRE General Test, 3 semesters of course work in calculus, 1 semester of course work in algebra and mathematics/statistics. Electronic applications accepted. *Expenses:* Tuition, state resident: full-time $10,723; part-time $745 per credit. Tuition, nonresident: full-time $24,054; part-time $1578 per credit. *Required fees:* $374 per semester. Tuition and fees vary according to course load, program and reciprocity agreements.

University of Wisconsin–Milwaukee, Graduate School, College of Letters and Sciences, Department of Economics, Milwaukee, WI 53201-0413. Offers MA, PhD. *Degree requirements:* For master's, comprehensive exam; for doctorate, comprehensive exam, thesis/dissertation. *Entrance requirements:* For master's, GRE General Test; for doctorate, GRE General Test, GRE Subject Test, minimum GPA of 3.0. Additional exam requirements/recommendations for international students: Required—TOEFL (minimum score 550 paper-based; 79 iBT), IELTS (minimum score 6.5).

University of Wyoming, College of Business, Department of Economics and Finance, Program in Economics, Laramie, WY 82071. Offers MS, PhD. Part-time programs available. *Degree requirements:* For master's, thesis; for doctorate, comprehensive exam, thesis/dissertation. *Entrance requirements:* For master's, GRE General Test or GMAT, minimum GPA of 3.0; for doctorate, GRE General Test, minimum GPA of 3.0. Additional exam requirements/recommendations for international students: Required—TOEFL (minimum score 525 paper-based). *Faculty research:* Resource and environmental economics, industrial organization, regulation.

University of Wyoming, College of Business, Department of Economics and Finance, Program in Economics and Finance, Laramie, WY 82071. Offers MS. *Degree requirements:* For master's, thesis. *Entrance requirements:* For master's, GRE, minimum GPA of 3.0. Additional exam requirements/recommendations for international students: Required—TOEFL (minimum score 540 paper-based; 76 iBT). *Faculty research:* Financial economics.

Utah State University, School of Graduate Studies, College of Business and College of Agriculture, Department of Economics, Logan, UT 84322. Offers applied economics (MS); economics (MA, MS, PhD). Terminal master's awarded for partial completion of doctoral program. *Degree requirements:* For master's, thesis (for some programs); for doctorate, comprehensive exam, thesis/dissertation. *Entrance requirements:* For master's, GRE General Test, GMAT, minimum GPA of 3.0, TOEFL for international; for doctorate, GRE General Test, minimum GPA of 3.0, TOEFL. Additional exam requirements/recommendations for international students: Required—TOEFL. Electronic applications accepted. *Faculty research:* Resource economics, economic theory, international trade, industrial organization, development.

Vanderbilt University, Graduate School, Department of Economics, Nashville, TN 37240-1001. Offers economic development (MA); economics (PhD). *Faculty:* 31 full-time (6 women). *Students:* 128 full-time (53 women), 2 part-time (1 woman); includes 13 minority (1 Black or African American, non-Hispanic/Latino; 4 Asian, non-Hispanic/Latino; 6 Hispanic/Latino; 2 Two or more races, non-Hispanic/Latino), 90 international. Average age 26. 589 applicants, 29% accepted, 44 enrolled. In 2014, 40 master's, 6 doctorates awarded. Terminal master's awarded for partial completion of doctoral program. *Degree requirements:* For master's, thesis or alternative; for doctorate, thesis/dissertation, final and qualifying exams. *Entrance requirements:* For master's and doctorate, GRE General Test, GRE Subject Test (recommended). Additional exam requirements/recommendations for international students: Required—TOEFL (minimum score 570 paper-based; 88 iBT). *Application deadline:* For fall admission, 1/15 for domestic and international students; for spring admission, 11/1 for domestic students. Applications are processed on a rolling basis. Electronic applications accepted. *Expenses: Tuition:* Full-time $42,768; part-time $1782 per credit hour. *Required fees:* $422. One-time fee: $30 full-time. *Financial support:* Fellowships with full and partial tuition reimbursements, teaching assistantships with full and partial tuition reimbursements, career-related internships or fieldwork, Federal Work-Study, institutionally sponsored loans, scholarships/grants, and health care benefits available. Financial award application deadline: 1/15; financial award applicants required to submit CSS PROFILE or FAFSA. *Faculty research:* Economic theory, applied fields, developmental economics, environmental economics, health economics and policy. *Unit head:* Dr. William Collins, Chair, 615-322-3428, Fax: 615-343-8495, E-mail: william.collins@vanderbilt.edu. *Application contact:* Kathleen Finn, Assistant to the Director of Graduate Studies, 615-322-3419, Fax: 615-343-8495, E-mail: kathleen.finn@vanderbilt.edu.
Website: http://www.vanderbilt.edu/econ/

Vanderbilt University, Vanderbilt Law School, Nashville, TN 37203. Offers law (LL M, JD); law and economics (PhD); JD/M Div; JD/MA; JD/MBA; JD/MD; JD/MPP; JD/MTS; JD/PhD; LL M/MA. *Accreditation:* ABA. *Degree requirements:* For doctorate, comprehensive exam (for some programs), thesis/dissertation (for some programs), 72 hours of coursework and research (for PhD). *Entrance requirements:* For master's, foreign law degree; for doctorate, GRE (for PhD), LSAT, advanced undergraduate economics (for PhD). Additional exam requirements/recommendations for international students: Required—TOEFL. Electronic applications accepted. *Expenses:* Contact institution.

Virginia Commonwealth University, Graduate School, School of Business, Program in Economics, Richmond, VA 23284-9005. Offers MA. *Degree requirements:* For master's, thesis optional. *Entrance requirements:* For master's, GRE General Test (preferred) or GMAT. Additional exam requirements/recommendations for international students: Required—TOEFL (minimum score 600 paper-based; 100 iBT). Electronic applications accepted.

Virginia Polytechnic Institute and State University, Graduate School, College of Science, Blacksburg, VA 24061. Offers biological sciences (MS, PhD); biomedical technology development and management (MS); chemistry (MS, PhD); economics (MA, PhD); geosciences (MS, PhD); mathematics (MS, PhD); physics (MS, PhD); psychology (MS, PhD); statistics (MS, PhD). *Faculty:* 274 full-time (75 women), 3 part-time/adjunct (all women). *Students:* 544 full-time (212 women), 29 part-time (12 women); includes 54 minority (14 Black or African American, non-Hispanic/Latino; 9 Asian, non-Hispanic/Latino; 16 Hispanic/Latino; 15 Two or more races, non-Hispanic/Latino), 243 international. Average age 27. 1,105 applicants, 22% accepted, 104 enrolled. In 2014, 83 master's, 67 doctorates awarded. *Median time to degree:* Of those who began their doctoral program in fall 2006, 54% received their degree in 8 years or less. *Degree requirements:* For master's, comprehensive exam (for some programs), thesis (for some programs); for doctorate, comprehensive exam (for some programs), thesis/dissertation (for some programs). *Entrance requirements:* For master's and doctorate, GRE/GMAT (may vary by department). Additional exam requirements/recommendations for international students: Required—TOEFL (minimum score 550 paper-based). *Application deadline:* For fall admission, 8/1 for domestic students, 4/1 for international students; for spring admission, 1/1 for domestic students, 9/1 for international students. Applications are processed on a rolling basis. Application fee: $75. Electronic applications accepted. *Expenses:* Tuition, state resident: full-time $11,656; part-time $647.50 per credit hour. Tuition, nonresident: full-time $23,351; part-time $1297.25 per credit hour. *Required fees:* $2533; $465.75 per semester. Tuition and fees vary according to course load, campus/location and program. *Financial support:* In 2014–15, 1 fellowship with full tuition reimbursement (averaging $5,938 per year), 143 research assistantships with full tuition reimbursements (averaging $22,569 per year), 355 teaching assistantships with full tuition reimbursements (averaging $21,476 per year) were awarded. Financial award application deadline: 3/1; financial award applicants required to submit FAFSA. *Total annual research expenditures:* $24.3 million. *Unit head:* Dr. Lay Nam Chang, Dean, 540-231-5422, Fax: 540-231-3380, E-mail: laynam@vt.edu. *Application contact:* Diane Stearns, Assistant to the Dean, 540-231-7515, Fax: 540-231-3380, E-mail: dstearns@vt.edu.
Website: http://www.science.vt.edu/

Virginia State University, College of Graduate Studies, College of Humanities and Social Sciences, Department of Political Science, Public Administration and Economics, Petersburg, VA 23806-0001. Offers economics (MA). *Degree requirements:* For master's, thesis optional. *Entrance requirements:* For master's, GRE General Test.

Washington State University, College of Agricultural, Human, and Natural Resource Sciences, School of Economic Sciences, Pullman, WA 99164-6210. Offers agricultural economics (PhD); economics (PhD). Programs offered at the Pullman campus. *Faculty:* 25 full-time (7 women). *Students:* 74 full-time (25 women), 3 part-time (1 woman); includes 2 minority (1 Black or African American, non-Hispanic/Latino; 1 American Indian or Alaska Native, non-Hispanic/Latino), 50 international. Average age 29. 99 applicants, 33% accepted, 17 enrolled. In 2014, 4 master's, 15 doctorates awarded. Terminal master's awarded for partial completion of doctoral program. *Degree requirements:* For master's, comprehensive exam (for some programs), thesis (for some programs), oral exam; for doctorate, comprehensive exam, thesis/dissertation, oral exam, written exam, qualifying exams. *Entrance requirements:* For master's and doctorate, GRE, minimum GPA of 3.0, 3 letters of recommendation. Additional exam requirements/recommendations for international students: Required—TOEFL (minimum score 550 paper-based). *Application deadline:* For fall admission, 2/15 priority date for domestic students, 2/1 priority date for international students. Applications are processed on a rolling basis. Application fee: $75. Electronic applications accepted. *Expenses:* Tuition, state resident: full-time $11,768. Tuition, nonresident: full-time $25,200. *Required fees:* $960. Tuition and fees vary according to program. *Financial support:* In 2014–15, 59 students received support, including 30 research assistantships with full and partial tuition reimbursements available (averaging $13,794 per year), 25 teaching assistantships with full and partial tuition reimbursements available (averaging $14,198 per year); career-related internships or fieldwork, Federal Work-Study, institutionally sponsored loans, tuition waivers (partial), and teaching associateships also available. Financial award application deadline: 4/1; financial award applicants required to submit FAFSA. *Faculty research:* Agricultural economics, econometrics, natural resource and environmental economics, industrial organization, health economics. *Total annual research expenditures:* $1.9 million. *Unit head:* Dr. H. Alan Love, Director, 509-335-3548, Fax: 509-335-1173, E-mail: a.love@wsu.edu. *Application contact:* Danielle K. Engelhardt, Graduate Coordinator, 509-335-5555, E-mail: dkbishop@wsu.edu.
Website: http://cahnrs-cms.wsu.edu/ses/Pages/default.aspx

Washington University in St. Louis, Graduate School of Arts and Sciences, Department of Economics, St. Louis, MO 63130-4899. Offers PhD. Terminal master's awarded for partial completion of doctoral program. *Degree requirements:* For doctorate, one foreign language, thesis/dissertation. *Entrance requirements:* For doctorate, GRE General Test. Additional exam requirements/recommendations for international students: Required—TOEFL. Electronic applications accepted. *Faculty research:* Economic theory, industrial organization, political economy, public economics, macroeconomics, public finance, development economics.

Wayne State University, College of Liberal Arts and Sciences, Department of Economics, Detroit, MI 48202. Offers health economics (MA, PhD); industrial organization (MA, PhD); international economics (MA, PhD); labor and human resources (MA, PhD); JD/MA. *Faculty:* 13 full-time (3 women). *Students:* 46 full-time (15 women), 10 part-time (3 women); includes 13 minority (8 Black or African American, non-Hispanic/Latino; 4 Asian, non-Hispanic/Latino; 1 Two or more races, non-Hispanic/Latino), 24 international. Average age 32. 95 applicants, 34% accepted, 11 enrolled. In 2014, 10 master's, 4 doctorates awarded. *Degree requirements:* For master's, comprehensive exam, thesis optional; for doctorate, thesis/dissertation, oral examination on research, completion of course work in quantitative methods, final lecture. *Entrance requirements:* For master's, minimum upper-division GPA of 3.0, prior coursework in intermediate microeconomic and macroeconomic theory, statistics, and elementary calculus; for doctorate, GRE, minimum upper-division GPA of 3.0, prior coursework in intermediate microeconomic and macroeconomic theory, statistics, two courses in calculus, three letters of recommendation from officials or teaching staff at institution(s) most recently attended. Additional exam requirements/recommendations for international students: Required—TOEFL (minimum score 550 paper-based; 79 iBT), TWE (minimum score 5.5), Michigan English Language Assessment Battery (minimum score 85); Recommended—IELTS (minimum score 6.5). *Application deadline:* For fall admission, 5/1 for domestic and international students; for winter admission, 10/1 priority date for domestic students, 9/1 for international students; for spring admission, 1/1 priority date for domestic students, 1/1 for international students. Applications are processed on a rolling basis. Application fee: $0. Electronic applications accepted. *Expenses:* Tuition, state resident: full-time $10,294; part-time $571.90 per credit hour. Tuition, nonresident: full-time $29,730; part-time $1238.75 per credit hour. *Required fees:* $1365; $43.50 per credit hour. $291.10 per semester. Tuition and fees vary according to course load and program. *Financial support:* In 2014–15, 26 students received support, including 2 fellowships with tuition reimbursements available (averaging $16,000 per year), 1 research assistantship with tuition reimbursement available (averaging $22,011 per year), 17 teaching assistantships with tuition reimbursements available (averaging $17,117 per year); scholarships/grants, health care benefits, and unspecified assistantships also available. Support available to part-time students. Financial award application deadline: 3/31; financial award applicants required to submit FAFSA. *Faculty research:* Health economics, international economics, macro economics, urban and labor economics, econometrics. *Unit head:* Dr. Stephen J. Spurr, Professor and Chair, 313-577-3232, Fax: 313-577-9564, E-mail: sspurr@wayne.edu. *Application contact:* Dr. Allen Charles Goodman, Graduate Director, 313-577-3235, Fax: 313-577-9564, E-mail: allen.goodman@wayne.edu.
Website: http://clas.wayne.edu/economics/

Western Illinois University, School of Graduate Studies, College of Business and Technology, Department of Economics and Decision Sciences, Macomb, IL 61455-1390. Offers community development (Certificate); economics (MA). Part-time programs available. *Students:* 19 full-time (6 women), 2 part-time (0 women); includes 4 minority (3 Black or African American, non-Hispanic/Latino; 1 Two or more races, non-Hispanic/Latino), 13 international. Average age 28. 38 applicants, 63% accepted, 10 enrolled. In 2014, 22 master's awarded. *Degree requirements:* For master's, thesis or alternative. *Entrance requirements:* Additional exam requirements/recommendations for international students: Required—TOEFL (minimum score 550 paper-based; 80 iBT). *Application deadline:* Applications are processed on a rolling basis. Application fee: $30. Electronic applications accepted. *Financial support:* In 2014–15, 6 students received support, including 1 research assistantship with full tuition reimbursement available (averaging $7,544 per year), 8 teaching assistantships with full tuition reimbursements available (averaging $8,688 per year). Financial award applicants required to submit FAFSA. *Unit head:* Dr. Tej Kaul, Chairperson, 309-298-1153. *Application contact:* Dr. Nancy Parsons, Assistant Director of Graduate Studies, 309-298-1806, Fax: 309-298-2345, E-mail: grad-office@wiu.edu.
Website: http://wiu.edu/econ

 Western Michigan University, Graduate College, College of Arts and Sciences, Department of Economics, Kalamazoo, MI 49008. Offers applied economics (MA, PhD). *Degree requirements:* For master's, thesis; for doctorate, thesis/dissertation. *Application deadline:* For fall admission, 2/15 for domestic students. *Financial support:* Application deadline: 2/15. *Application contact:* Admissions and Orientation, 269-387-2000, Fax: 269-387-2096.
See Display below and Close-Up on page 853.

West Texas A&M University, College of Business, Department of Accounting, Economics, and Finance, Program in Finance and Economics, Canyon, TX 79016-0001. Offers MS. Part-time and evening/weekend programs available. Postbaccalaureate distance learning degree programs offered (minimal on-campus study). *Degree requirements:* For master's, comprehensive exam, thesis optional. *Entrance requirements:* For master's, GMAT. Additional exam requirements/recommendations for international students: Required—TOEFL (minimum score 550 paper-based). Electronic applications accepted. *Faculty research:* International trade composition, cycle of poverty, trade effects in Asian countries, structural problems in Japanese economy, reform and the US sugar program-Nebraska.

West Virginia University, College of Business and Economics, Division of Economics and Finance, Morgantown, WV 26506. Offers business analysis (MA); developmental financial economics (PhD); environmental and resource economics (PhD); international economics (PhD); mathematical economics (MA); monetary economics (PhD); public finance (PhD); public policy (MA); regional and urban economics (PhD); statistics and economics (MA). Terminal master's awarded for partial completion of doctoral program. *Degree requirements:* For master's, thesis optional; for doctorate, comprehensive exam, thesis/dissertation. *Entrance requirements:* For master's and doctorate, GRE General Test, minimum GPA of 3.0; course work in intermediate microeconomics, intermediate macroeconomics, calculus, and statistics. Additional exam requirements/recommendations for international students: Required—TOEFL. Electronic applications accepted. *Faculty research:* Financial economics, regional/urban development, public economics, international trade/international finance/development economics, monetary economics.

Wichita State University, Graduate School, W. Frank Barton School of Business, Department of Economics, Wichita, KS 67260. Offers business economics (MA); economic analysis (MA). Part-time and evening/weekend programs available. *Unit head:* Dr. Jen-Chi Cheng, Chair, 316-978-3220, Fax: 316-978-3845, E-mail: jenchi.cheng@wichita.edu. *Application contact:* Jordan Oleson, Admissions Coordinator, 316-978-3095, Fax: 316-978-3253, E-mail: jordan.oleson@wichita.edu. Website: http://www.wichita.edu/econ

Wilfrid Laurier University, Faculty of Graduate and Postdoctoral Studies, School of Business and Economics, Department of Business, Waterloo, ON N2L 3C5, Canada. Offers accounting (PhD); finance (M Fin); financial economics (PhD); marketing (PhD); operations and supply chain management (PhD); organizational behavior and human resource management (M Sc); organizational behaviour and human resource management (PhD); supply chain management (M Sc); technology management (EMTM). *Accreditation:* AACSB. Part-time and evening/weekend programs available. *Degree requirements:* For master's, thesis optional; for doctorate, comprehensive exam, thesis/dissertation. *Entrance requirements:* For master's, GMAT, 4-year honors degree with minimum B+ average; for doctorate, GMAT, master's degree, minimum B+ average. Additional exam requirements/recommendations for international students: Required—TOEFL (minimum score 89 iBT). Electronic applications accepted. *Faculty research:* Financial economics, management and organizational behavior, operations and supply chain management.

Wilfrid Laurier University, Faculty of Graduate and Postdoctoral Studies, School of Business and Economics, Department of Economics, Waterloo, ON N2L 3C5, Canada. Offers MA. *Entrance requirements:* For master's, honors BA or the equivalent in economics, minimum B average in undergraduate course work. Additional exam requirements/recommendations for international students: Required—TOEFL (minimum score 89 iBT). Electronic applications accepted. *Faculty research:* Economic forecasting, economic policy analysis, industry and market studies, financial economics, strategic planning, public policy and business.

Wilfrid Laurier University, Faculty of Graduate and Postdoctoral Studies, School of International Policy and Governance, Global Governance Program, Waterloo, ON N2L 3C5, Canada. Offers conflict and security (PhD); global environment (PhD); global justice and human rights (PhD); global political economy (PhD); global social governance (PhD); multilateral institutions and diplomacy (PhD). Offered jointly with University of Waterloo. *Degree requirements:* For doctorate, thesis/dissertation. *Entrance requirements:* For doctorate, MA in political science, history, economics, international development studies, international peace studies, globalization studies, environmental studies or related field with minimum A-. Additional exam requirements/recommendations for international students: Required—TOEFL (minimum score 89 iBT). Electronic applications accepted. *Faculty research:* Global political economy, global environment, conflict and security, global justice and human rights, multilateral institutions and diplomacy.

Wright State University, School of Graduate Studies, Raj Soin College of Business, Department of Economics, Dayton, OH 45435. Offers business economics (MBA); social and applied economics (MS); MBA/MS. *Entrance requirements:* For master's, GRE General Test. Additional exam requirements/recommendations for international students: Required—TOEFL.

Yale University, Graduate School of Arts and Sciences, Department of Economics, New Haven, CT 06520. Offers economics (PhD); international and development economics (MA). *Degree requirements:* For doctorate, thesis/dissertation. *Entrance requirements:* For master's, GRE General Test; for doctorate, GRE General Test, GRE Subject Test. *Faculty research:* Economic history of Western Europe, environmental economics, economic growth and development.

York University, Faculty of Graduate Studies, Faculty of Liberal Arts and Professional Studies, Program in Economics, Toronto, ON M3J 1P3, Canada. Offers MA, PhD. Part-time programs available. *Degree requirements:* For doctorate, comprehensive exam, thesis/dissertation. Electronic applications accepted.

Youngstown State University, Graduate School, College of Liberal Arts and Social Sciences, Department of Economics, Youngstown, OH 44555-0001. Offers economics (MA); financial economics (MA). Part-time programs available. *Degree requirements:* For master's, comprehensive exam, thesis optional. *Entrance requirements:* For master's, minimum GPA of 2.7, 21 hours in economics. Additional exam requirements/recommendations for international students: Required—TOEFL. *Faculty research:* Forecasting, applied econometrics, labor economics, applied macroeconomics, industrial organization.

International Economics

Claremont Graduate University, Graduate Programs, School of Social Science, Policy and Evaluation, Department of Economics, Claremont, CA 91711-6160. Offers business and financial economics (MA, PhD); economic development (Certificate); international and development economics (PhD); international economics policy and development (MA); international money and finance (PhD); neuroeconomics and behavioral economics (PhD); political economy and public policy (MA); public choice and public economics (PhD); MBA/PhD. Part-time programs available. *Faculty:* 9 full-time (2 women), 1 part-time/adjunct (0 women). *Students:* 107 full-time (33 women), 35 part-time (15 women); includes 22 minority (3 Black or African American, non-Hispanic/Latino; 11 Asian, non-Hispanic/Latino; 6 Hispanic/Latino; 2 Two or more races, non-Hispanic/Latino), 73 international. Average age 32. In 2014, 15 master's, 11 doctorates awarded. *Entrance requirements:* For master's and doctorate, GRE General Test or GMAT. Additional exam requirements/recommendations for international students: Required—TOEFL (minimum score 550 paper-based; 80 iBT). *Application deadline:* For fall admission, 2/1 priority date for domestic and international students. Applications are processed on a rolling basis. Application fee: $80. Electronic applications accepted. *Expenses: Tuition:* Full-time $41,784; part-time $1741 per credit. *Required fees:* $600; $300 per semester. *Financial support:* Fellowships, research assistantships, teaching assistantships, Federal Work-Study, institutionally sponsored loans, and scholarships/grants available. Support available to part-time students. Financial award application deadline: 2/15; financial award applicants required to submit FAFSA. *Faculty research:* International and financial economics, law and economics, regulation, public choice economics. *Unit head:* Heather Campbell, Chair, 909-621-8689, E-mail: heather.campbell@cgu.edu. *Application contact:* Annekah Hall, Assistant Director of Admissions, 909-607-3371, E-mail: annekah.hall@cgu.edu.
Website: http://www.cgu.edu/pages/466.asp

Cleveland State University, College of Graduate Studies, College of Liberal Arts and Social Sciences, Department of Political Science, Cleveland, OH 44115. Offers global interactions (MA), including global business interactions, global political interactions. *Students:* 13 full-time (5 women), 14 part-time (7 women); includes 11 minority (5 Black or African American, non-Hispanic/Latino; 1 Asian, non-Hispanic/Latino; 2 Hispanic/Latino; 3 Two or more races, non-Hispanic/Latino), 3 international. Average age 32. 8 applicants, 100% accepted, 6 enrolled. In 2014, 11 master's awarded. *Degree requirements:* For master's, internship, exit project. *Entrance requirements:* For master's, minimum undergraduate GPA of 3.0 or GRE (50th percentile or above); two letters of recommendation; undergraduate degree in economics, political science, international relations, or a related discipline; completion of undergraduate macro and micro economics course. Additional exam requirements/recommendations for international students: Required—TOEFL (minimum score 520 paper-based). Application fee: $30. *Expenses:* Expenses: $9,615 full-time, in-state tuition and fees. *Unit head:* Dr. Rodger M. Govea, Associate Professor/Chairperson, 216-687-4554, E-mail: r.govea@csuohio.edu. *Application contact:* Deborah L. Brown, Interim Assistant Director, Graduate Admissions, 216-523-7572, Fax: 216-687-5400, E-mail: d.l.brown@csuohio.edu.
Website: http://www.csuohio.edu/class/politicalscience/

Fordham University, Gabelli School of Business, New York, NY 10023. Offers accounting (MBA); communications and media management (MBA); executive business administration (EMBA), including management; finance (MBA); global finance (MS); information systems (MBA, MS); management systems (MBA); marketing (MBA); media management (MS); taxation (MS); taxation and public accountancy (MTA); JD/MBA; MBA/MIM; MS/MBA. MBA/MIM offered jointly with Thunderbird School of Global Management. *Accreditation:* AACSB. Part-time and evening/weekend programs available. *Faculty:* 131 full-time (61 women), 61 part-time/adjunct (13 women). *Students:* 1,233 full-time (708 women), 588 part-time (274 women); includes 1,032 minority (73 Black or African American, non-Hispanic/Latino; 7 American Indian or Alaska Native, non-Hispanic/Latino; 846 Asian, non-Hispanic/Latino; 103 Hispanic/Latino; 3 Native Hawaiian or other Pacific Islander, non-Hispanic/Latino), 53 international. Average age 28. 3,701 applicants, 51% accepted, 718 enrolled. In 2014, 916 master's awarded. *Degree requirements:* For master's, Internships - required for MSQF, recommended for MBA, optional for most other programs. *Entrance requirements:* For master's, GMAT/GRE, 2 letters of recommendation, resume, 2 essays, transcripts. Additional exam requirements/recommendations for international students: Required—TOEFL (minimum score 600 paper-based; 100 iBT). *Application deadline:* For fall admission, 6/1 priority date for domestic students, 5/1 priority date for international students; for winter admission, 11/1 for domestic students, 10/1 priority date for international students; for spring admission, 11/1 priority date for domestic students, 2/1 priority date for international students; for summer admission, 3/1 priority date for domestic students. Applications are processed on a rolling basis. Application fee: $130. Electronic applications accepted. *Expenses:* Expenses: $1,306 per credit. *Financial support:* In 2014–15, 53 students received support, including fellowships (averaging $25,838 per year); research assistantships, career-related internships or fieldwork, institutionally sponsored loans, scholarships/grants, and unspecified assistantships also available. Support available to part-time students. Financial award application deadline: 6/15; financial award applicants required to submit FAFSA. *Unit head:* Dr. Donna Rapaccioli, Dean, 212-636-6165, Fax: 212-307-1779, E-mail: rapaccioli@fordham.edu. *Application contact:* Patricia Caffrey, Director of Admissions and Financial Aid, 212-636-6200, Fax: 212-636-7076, E-mail: admissionsgb@fordham.edu.
Website: http://www.fordham.edu/info/20451/graduate_business

Fordham University, Graduate School of Arts and Sciences, Program in International Political Economy and Development, New York, NY 10458. Offers MA, Certificate. Part-time and evening/weekend programs available. *Students:* 33 full-time (17 women), 16 part-time (6 women); includes 3 minority (2 Asian, non-Hispanic/Latino; 1 Hispanic/Latino), 13 international. Average age 27. 181 applicants, 52% accepted, 24 enrolled. In 2014, 29 master's, 6 other advanced degrees awarded. *Degree requirements:* For master's, comprehensive exam. *Entrance requirements:* For master's, GRE General Test. Additional exam requirements/recommendations for international students: Required—TOEFL (minimum score 600 paper-based). *Application deadline:* For fall admission, 1/4 priority date for domestic students; for spring admission, 11/1 for domestic students. Application fee: $70. Electronic applications accepted. *Financial support:* In 2014–15, 16 students received support, including 2 fellowships with full and partial tuition reimbursements available (averaging $11,965 per year), 16 research assistantships with full and partial tuition reimbursements available (averaging $16,050 per year); career-related internships or fieldwork, institutionally sponsored loans, tuition waivers (full and partial), and unspecified assistantships also available. Financial award application deadline: 1/4; financial award applicants required to submit FAFSA. *Faculty research:* International economics, comparative international politics, international

banking and finance, international development, emerging markets and country risk analysis. *Unit head:* Dr. Henry Schwalbenberg, Chair, 718-817-3866, Fax: 718-817-3518. *Application contact:* Bernadette Valentino-Morrison, Director of Graduate Admissions, 718-817-4419, Fax: 718-817-3566, E-mail: valentinomor@fordham.edu.

Johns Hopkins University, Paul H. Nitze School of Advanced International Studies, Washington, DC 20036. Offers international development (MA, Certificate), including international economics (MA); international economics and finance (MA); international public policy (MIPP); international relations (PhD); international studies (Certificate); Japan studies (MA), including international economics; Korea studies (MA), including international economics; South Asia studies (MA), including international economics; Southeast Asia studies (MA), including international economics; JD/MA; MBA/MA; MHS/MA. Terminal master's awarded for partial completion of doctoral program. *Degree requirements:* For master's, 4-6 international economics courses, 5-6 functional or regional concentration courses, 2 core examinations, proficiency in language other than native language, capstone project; for doctorate, 2 foreign languages, thesis/dissertation, 3 comprehensive exams, economics, quantitative and qualitative course, dissertation prospectus and defense. *Entrance requirements:* For master's, GMAT or GRE General Test, previous course work in economics, foreign language, undergraduate degree; for doctorate, GRE General Test, master's degree. Additional exam requirements/recommendations for international students: Required—TOEFL (minimum score 600 paper-based; 100 iBT) or IELTS (minimum score 7). Electronic applications accepted. *Expenses:* Contact institution. *Faculty research:* Regional studies, international relations, international economics, energy and environment, international development.

The New School, The New School for Social Research, Department of Economics, New York, NY 10003. Offers economics (M Phil, MA, MS, DS Sc, PhD); global finance (MS); global political economy and finance (MA). Part-time and evening/weekend programs available. Terminal master's awarded for partial completion of doctoral program. *Degree requirements:* For master's, exam; for doctorate, one foreign language, thesis/dissertation, qualifying exam. *Entrance requirements:* For master's, GRE General Test; for doctorate, GRE General Test, MA. Additional exam requirements/recommendations for international students: Required—TOEFL (minimum score 600 paper-based; 100 iBT). Electronic applications accepted. *Faculty research:* Heterodox, history of economic thought, post-Keynesian, global political economy and finance.

University of Miami, Graduate School, School of Business Administration, Department of Economics, Coral Gables, FL 33124. Offers economic development (MA, PhD); environmental economics (PhD); human resource economics (MA, PhD); international economics (MA, PhD); macroeconomics (PhD). Students admitted every two years in the fall semester. Terminal master's awarded for partial completion of doctoral program. *Degree requirements:* For master's, comprehensive exam; for doctorate, comprehensive exam, thesis/dissertation. *Entrance requirements:* For master's and doctorate, GRE General Test, minimum GPA of 3.0. Additional exam requirements/recommendations for international students: Required—TOEFL (minimum score 550 paper-based). *Faculty research:* International economics/trade, applied microeconomics, development.

University of New Mexico, Graduate School, College of Arts and Sciences, Program in Economics, Albuquerque, NM 87131-2039. Offers econometrics (MA); economic theory (MA); environmental/natural resource economics (MA, PhD); international/development and sustainability economics (MA, PhD); public economics (MA, PhD). Part-time programs available. *Faculty:* 12 full-time (7 women). *Students:* 40 full-time (13 women), 5 part-time (2 women); includes 8 minority (2 Black or African American, non-Hispanic/Latino; 1 Asian, non-Hispanic/Latino; 4 Hispanic/Latino; 1 Two or more races, non-Hispanic/Latino), 20 international. Average age 32. 69 applicants, 33% accepted, 12 enrolled. In 2014, 7 master's, 4 doctorates awarded. Terminal master's awarded for partial completion of doctoral program. *Degree requirements:* For master's, comprehensive exam, thesis (for some programs); for doctorate, comprehensive exam, thesis/dissertation. *Entrance requirements:* For master's and doctorate, GRE General Test, 3 letters of recommendation, letter of intent, curriculum vitae. Additional exam requirements/recommendations for international students: Required—TOEFL (minimum score 520 paper-based; 68 iBT). *Application deadline:* For fall admission, 3/1 priority date for domestic students, 3/1 for international students. Applications are processed on a rolling basis. Application fee: $50. Electronic applications accepted. *Financial support:* In 2014–15, 47 students received support, including 3 fellowships with tuition reimbursements available (averaging $6,858 per year), 13 research assistantships with tuition reimbursements available (averaging $6,858 per year), 15 teaching assistantships with tuition reimbursements available (averaging $7,396 per year); career-related internships or fieldwork, Federal Work-Study, scholarships/grants, health care benefits, and unspecified assistantships also available. Support available to part-time students. Financial award application deadline: 3/1; financial award applicants required to submit FAFSA. *Faculty research:* Core theory, econometrics, public finance, international/development economics, labor/human resource economics, environmental/natural resource economics. *Total annual research expenditures:* $388,864. *Unit head:* Dr. Janie Chermak, Chair, 505-277-2037, Fax: 505-277-9445, E-mail: jchermak@unm.edu. *Application contact:* Jeff Newcomer Miller, Academic Advisor, 505-277-3056, Fax: 505-277-9445, E-mail: econgrad@unm.edu.
Website: http://econ.unm.edu

Valparaiso University, Graduate School, Program in International Economics and Finance, Valparaiso, IN 46383. Offers MS. Part-time and evening/weekend programs available. *Students:* 30 full-time (13 women), 3 part-time (2 women); includes 1 minority (Black or African American, non-Hispanic/Latino), 32 international. Average age 24. In 2014, 33 master's awarded. *Entrance requirements:* For master's, 1 semester of college-level calculus; 1 statistics or quantitative methods class; 2 semesters of introductory economics (course content in introductory economics must include both introductory microeconomics and macroeconomics) ; 1 introductory accounting course; minimum undergraduate GPA of 3.0; 2 letters of recommendation. Additional exam requirements/recommendations for international students: Required—TOEFL (minimum score 550 paper-based; 80 iBT), IELTS (minimum score 6). Application fee: $30 ($50 for international students). *Expenses: Tuition:* Full-time $10,710; part-time $595 per credit hour. *Required fees:* $378; $101 per term. Tuition and fees vary according to course load and program. *Financial support:* Available to part-time students. Applicants required to submit FAFSA. *Unit head:* Dr. Jennifer A. Ziegler, Dean, Graduate School and Continuing Education, 219-464-5313, Fax: 219-464-5381, E-mail: jennifer.ziegler@valpo.edu. *Application contact:* Jessica Choquette, Graduate Admissions Specialist, 219-464-5313, Fax: 219-464-5381, E-mail: jessica.ziegler@valpo.edu.
Website: http://www.valpo.edu/grad/ief/

Wayne State University, College of Liberal Arts and Sciences, Department of Economics, Detroit, MI 48202. Offers health economics (MA, PhD); industrial organization (MA, PhD); international economics (MA, PhD); labor and human resources (MA, PhD); JD/MA. *Faculty:* 13 full-time (3 women). *Students:* 46 full-time (15 women), 10 part-time (3 women); includes 13 minority (8 Black or African American, non-Hispanic/Latino; 4 Asian, non-Hispanic/Latino; 1 Two or more races, non-Hispanic/Latino), 24 international. Average age 32. 95 applicants, 34% accepted, 11 enrolled. In 2014, 10 master's, 4 doctorates awarded. *Degree requirements:* For master's, comprehensive exam, thesis optional; for doctorate, thesis/dissertation, oral examination on research, completion of course work in quantitative methods, final lecture. *Entrance requirements:* For master's, minimum upper-division GPA of 3.0, prior coursework in intermediate microeconomic and macroeconomic theory, statistics, and elementary calculus; for doctorate, GRE, minimum upper-division GPA of 3.0, prior coursework in intermediate microeconomic and macroeconomic theory, statistics, two courses in calculus, three letters of recommendation from officials or teaching staff at institution(s) most recently attended. Additional exam requirements/recommendations for international students: Required—TOEFL (minimum score 550 paper-based; 79 iBT), TWE (minimum score 5.5), Michigan English Language Assessment Battery (minimum score 85); Recommended—IELTS (minimum score 6.5). *Application deadline:* For fall admission, 5/1 for domestic and international students; for winter admission, 10/1 priority date for domestic students, 9/1 for international students; for spring admission, 1/1 priority date for domestic students, 1/1 for international students. Applications are processed on a rolling basis. Application fee: $0. Electronic applications accepted. *Expenses:* Tuition, state resident: full-time $10,294; part-time $571.90 per credit hour. Tuition, nonresident: full-time $29,730; part-time $1238.75 per credit hour. *Required fees:* $1365; $43.50 per credit hour. $291.10 per semester. Tuition and fees vary according to course load and program. *Financial support:* In 2014–15, 26 students received support, including 2 fellowships with tuition reimbursements available (averaging $16,000 per year), 1 research assistantship with tuition reimbursement available (averaging $22,011 per year), 17 teaching assistantships with tuition reimbursements available (averaging $17,117 per year); scholarships/grants, health care benefits, and unspecified assistantships also available. Support available to part-time students. Financial award application deadline: 3/31; financial award applicants required to submit FAFSA. *Faculty research:* Health economics, international economics, macro economics, urban and labor economics, econometrics. *Unit head:* Dr. Stephen J. Spurr, Professor and Chair, 313-577-3232, Fax: 313-577-9564, E-mail: sspurr@wayne.edu. *Application contact:* Dr. Allen Charles Goodman, Graduate Director, 313-577-3235, Fax: 313-577-9564, E-mail: allen.goodman@wayne.edu.
Website: http://clas.wayne.edu/economics/

West Virginia University, College of Business and Economics, Division of Economics and Finance, Morgantown, WV 26506. Offers business analysis (MA); developmental financial economics (PhD); environmental and resource economics (PhD); international economics (PhD); mathematical economics (MA); monetary economics (PhD); public finance (PhD); public policy (MA); regional and urban economics (PhD); statistics and economics (MA). Terminal master's awarded for partial completion of doctoral program. *Degree requirements:* For master's, thesis optional; for doctorate, comprehensive exam, thesis/dissertation. *Entrance requirements:* For master's and doctorate, GRE General Test, minimum GPA of 3.0; course work in intermediate microeconomics, intermediate macroeconomics, calculus, and statistics. Additional exam requirements/recommendations for international students: Required—TOEFL. Electronic applications accepted. *Faculty research:* Financial economics, regional/urban development, public economics, international trade/international finance/development economics, monetary economics.

Wilfrid Laurier University, Faculty of Graduate and Postdoctoral Studies, School of International Policy and Governance, International Public Policy Program, Waterloo, ON N2L 3C5, Canada. Offers global governance (MIPP); human security (MIPP); international economic relations (MIPP); international environmental policy (MIPP). Offered jointly with University of Waterloo. *Entrance requirements:* For master's, honours BA with minimum B average. Additional exam requirements/recommendations for international students: Required—TOEFL (minimum score 89 iBT). Electronic applications accepted. *Faculty research:* International environmental policy, international economic relations, human security, global governance.

Yale University, Graduate School of Arts and Sciences, Department of Economics, Program in International and Development Economics, New Haven, CT 06520. Offers MA. *Entrance requirements:* For master's, GRE General Test.

Mineral Economics

Colorado School of Mines, Graduate School, Division of Economics and Business, Golden, CO 80401. Offers engineering and technology management (MS); mineral economics (PhD); operations research and engineering (PhD). Part-time programs available. *Faculty:* 11 full-time (3 women), 24 part-time/adjunct (4 women). *Students:* 114 full-time (21 women), 22 part-time (5 women); includes 17 minority (3 Black or African American, non-Hispanic/Latino; 4 Asian, non-Hispanic/Latino; 8 Hispanic/Latino; 2 Two or more races, non-Hispanic/Latino), 36 international. Average age 30. 172 applicants, 66% accepted, 62 enrolled. In 2014, 60 master's, 4 doctorates awarded. *Degree requirements:* For master's, thesis (for some programs); for doctorate, comprehensive exam, thesis/dissertation. *Entrance requirements:* For master's and doctorate, GRE General Test. Additional exam requirements/recommendations for international students: Required—TOEFL (minimum score 550 paper-based; 80 iBT). *Application deadline:* For fall admission, 12/15 priority date for domestic and international students; for spring admission, 9/1 priority date for domestic and international students. Application fee: $50 ($70 for international students). Electronic applications accepted. *Financial support:* In 2014–15, 45 students received support, including 4 fellowships with full tuition reimbursements available (averaging $21,120 per year), 8 research assistantships with full tuition reimbursements available (averaging $21,120 per year), 23 teaching assistantships with full tuition reimbursements available (averaging $21,120 per year); scholarships/grants, health care benefits, and unspecified assistantships also available. Financial award application deadline: 1/15; financial award applicants required to submit FAFSA. *Faculty research:* International trade, resource and environmental economics, energy economics, operations research. *Total annual research expenditures:* $371,588. *Unit head:* Dr. Michael Walls, Interim Director, 303-

Mineral Economics

273-3492, Fax: 303-273-3416, E-mail: mwalls@mines.edu. *Application contact:* Kathleen Martin, Program Assistant, 303-273-3482, Fax: 303-273-3416, E-mail: kmartin@mines.edu.
Website: http://econbus.mines.edu

Michigan Technological University, Graduate School, School of Business and Economics, Houghton, MI 49931. Offers accounting (MS); applied natural resource economics (MS); business administration (MBA). *Accreditation:* AACSB. Part-time programs available. *Faculty:* 25 full-time, 1 part-time/adjunct. *Students:* 22 full-time (7 women), 18 part-time (6 women); includes 2 minority (1 Black or African American, non-Hispanic/Latino; 1 Hispanic/Latino), 13 international. Average age 31. 112 applicants, 38% accepted, 19 enrolled. In 2014, 24 master's awarded. *Degree requirements:* For master's, comprehensive exam (for some programs), thesis (for some programs). *Entrance requirements:* For master's, GMAT/GRE (recommended minimum score in the 50th percentile), statement of purpose, official transcripts, 2 letters of recommendation, resume/curriculum vitae. Additional exam requirements/recommendations for international students: Required—TOEFL or IELTS. *Application deadline:* Applications are processed on a rolling basis. Electronic applications accepted. *Expenses:* Tuition, state resident: full-time $14,769; part-time $820.50 per credit. Tuition, nonresident: full-time $14,769; part-time $820.50 per credit. *Required fees:* $248; $248 per year. Tuition and fees vary according to course load and program. *Financial support:* In 2014–15, 19 students received support, including 1 fellowship with full and partial tuition reimbursement available (averaging $13,824 per year), 3 teaching assistantships with full and partial tuition reimbursements available (averaging $13,824 per year); career-related internships or fieldwork, Federal Work-Study, scholarships/grants, health care benefits, unspecified assistantships, and cooperative program also available. Financial award applicants required to submit FAFSA. *Faculty research:* Natural resource and mineral economics, entrepreneurship, management of technology and innovation. *Unit head:* Dr. Eugene Klippel, Dean, 906-487-2668, Fax: 906-487-1863, E-mail: reklippe@mtu.edu. *Application contact:* Carol T. Wingerson, Administrative Aide, 906-487-2328, Fax: 906-487-2284, E-mail: gradadms@mtu.edu.
Website: http://www.mtu.edu/business/

The University of Texas at Austin, Graduate School, Cockrell School of Engineering, Department of Petroleum and Geosystems Engineering, Program in Energy and Earth Resources, Austin, TX 78712-1111. Offers MA. *Degree requirements:* For master's, thesis, seminar. *Entrance requirements:* For master's, GRE General Test. Additional exam requirements/recommendations for international students: Required—TOEFL. Electronic applications accepted.

WESTERN MICHIGAN
Department of Economics

 For more information, visit http://petersons.to/westernmichiganeconomics

WESTERN MICHIGAN UNIVERSITY
College of Arts and Sciences
Department of Economics

Programs of Study

The Department of Economics at Western Michigan University offers graduate programs in applied economics that prepare students for careers in academic and non-academic settings. Students graduate with the theoretical foundation, research skills, and professional acumen to obtain rewarding positions as economists.

According to the Bureau of Labor Statistics, employment for economists is expected to grow 14 percent from 2012 to 2022. This growth stems from businesses' increasing reliance on quantitative methods and economic analysis to evaluate and forecast a variety of economic trends. Increased competition, additional financial regulations, and a more complex global economy are also fueling this growth. Private industry, particularly in scientific, professional, and management consulting services, is expected to have higher demand for economists.

Master of Arts (M.A.) in Applied Economics: The M.A. in Applied Economics program provides students with a solid foundation in economic analysis and the ability to use theory to solve contemporary problems. The 30-credit hour curriculum includes thesis and non-thesis options. The non-thesis option consists of six core and four elective courses. Students can use electives to complete concentrations in economic development or econometrics/statistics. The thesis option contains 24 credit hours of courses and 6 credit hours of thesis work.

Doctor of Philosophy (Ph.D.) in Applied Economics: The Ph.D. in Applied Economics program is ideal for students interested in becoming high-level economists in nonacademic settings. Students with M.A. degrees in economics or solid undergraduate training in economics, mathematics, and statistics typically earn their degrees in four years. The program's 75-credit hour curriculum consists of the following components:

- Core courses
- A comprehensive exam (in microeconomics or macroeconomics theory)
- Specialization in two fields
- Advanced courses
- Workshops
- An internship (or an additional field)
- Dissertation work

Field specialization involves taking a sequence of two courses in two specialty areas. Workshops provide in-depth understanding of empirical and theoretical economics, experience in designing and implementing research projects, and familiarity with a variety of applied economic research. Internships involve analyzing economic problems and writing reports about the solutions. Dissertation work includes conducting original research that emphasizes application of economic theory, use of econometric methodology, and solutions to real-world problems.

Research Opportunities

The Department of Economics offers graduate students many opportunities to conduct innovative research. Students assist faculty members with research that addresses emerging and long-standing issues. Through class assignments, thesis work, and dissertation work, students also conduct original research to examine economic problems.

Faculty mentoring, research grants, research seminars, and other resources help students acquire the research skills and experience that employers value.

Faculty members in the Department of Economics actively engage in research that advances the discipline and solves real-world problems. Core research areas include the following:

- Econometrics
- Economic development
- Environmental economics
- Industrial organization
- International economics
- Labor economics
- Macroeconomics
- Microeconomics
- Monetary economics

Financial Aid

Economics graduate students at Western Michigan University may qualify for several financial aid opportunities, including scholarships, fellowships (master's and doctoral), teaching and research assistantships, doctoral associateships, research and travel grants, and federal loans. Additional potential funding sources include fellowships, associateships, and scholarships from external sources; loans from private lenders; and employer tuition assistance.

Costs

Graduate tuition for the 2015–16 academic year is $530.31 per credit hour for Michigan residents and $1,123.24 per credit hour for nonresidents.

Housing

Graduate students may apply to any housing options on campus or may seek off-campus housing options.

Faculty

Graduate faculty members are prolific researchers, accomplished teachers, and skillful economists. For example, Professor Jean Kimmel has research interests in child care, female employment, labor economics, motherhood wage gap, and wage determination. She has published numerous articles and reports in journals and other publications. Prior to joining the Department of Economics, she was a senior economist at the W. E. Upjohn Institute of Employment Research. Information about other professors in the department is available online at http://www.wmich.edu/economics/directory.

The University

Founded in 1903, Western Michigan University is a public research institution located in Kalamazoo, Michigan, in the Midwestern region of the United States, with an enrollment of approximately 24,000

students. The University offers 147 bachelor's, 73 master's, and 30 doctoral programs.

Western Michigan University consistently receives top rankings for excellence in education and research. The Carnegie Foundation designated the university as one of the country's 147 public research universities. *U.S. News & World Report* has ranked it as one of the top national universities for 24 consecutive years. *The Princeton Review* consistently rates the university as one of the best colleges in the Midwest.

Location

The University's location in Kalamazoo provides many learning and social opportunities. With more than 325,000 residents, Kalamazoo is the sixth-largest metropolitan area in Michigan and one of the 150 largest in the nation. It has the cultural, recreational, and entertainment opportunities of larger cities.

Kalamazoo is also within proximity of the Midwest's diverse offerings. Students can venture 20 minutes outside of the city to farm country or catch a train to Chicago, Illinois, the nation's third-largest city.

Graduate Student Life

Western Michigan University is a student-centered, supportive, and inclusive learning community where students from more than 100 countries thrive academically, professionally, and socially. The University's beautiful, park-like campus has many features including a first-rate aviation campus, high-tech science complex, and modern student recreation center as well as one of the country's top ten performing arts centers.

The University provides extensive academic resources, co-curricular activities, recreational options, and support services. Academic services include tutoring, writing assistance, lecture series, and research seminars. Support services include career services, child care, disability services, diversity and inclusion programs, faith and spiritual development, health and counseling services, and on-campus housing.

Co-curricular activities include the Graduate Student Association, 400 student organizations, community-service projects, and student media. Recreational and entertainment opportunities consist of concerts, comedy events, cultural events, movies, fitness programs, intramural sports, and open recreation.

Applying

Applicants must provide general information, including educational history details, and must also request official transcripts be sent to the University. The application deadline for the fall semester is April 1 and August 1 for the spring semester. A resume or curriculum vitae (CV) is required and must be submitted within the online application system. While this program does not require a graduate test, international applicants may have to provide evidence of English language proficiency. There is a $50 nonrefundable application fee for domestic applicants and $100 for international applicants. More information can be found in the online application.

Correspondence and Information

Admissions and Orientation
Department of Economics
College of Arts and Sciences
Western Michigan University
1903 West Michigan Avenue
Kalamazoo, Michigan 49008
United States
Phone: 269-387-2000
Fax: 269-387-2096
Website: http://wmich.edu/economics

Section 20
Family and Consumer Sciences

This section contains a directory of institutions offering graduate work in family and consumer sciences, followed by an in-depth entry submitted by an institution that chose to prepare a detailed program description. Additional information about programs listed in the directory but not augmented by an in-depth entry may be obtained by writing directly to the dean of a graduate school or chair of a department at the address given in the directory.

For programs offering related work, see also in this book *Economics, Psychology and Counseling,* and *Sociology, Anthropology, and Archaeology.* In another guide in this series:

Graduate Programs in Business, Education, Health, Information Studies, Law & Social Work
See *Social Work*

CONTENTS

Program Directories

Displays and Close-Ups

See also:

Family and Consumer Sciences-General

Alabama Agricultural and Mechanical University, School of Graduate Studies, College of Agricultural, Life and Natural Sciences, Department of Family and Consumer Sciences, Huntsville, AL 35811. Offers family and consumer sciences (MS); food science (MS, PhD). Part-time and evening/weekend programs available. *Degree requirements:* For master's, comprehensive exam, thesis optional; for doctorate, one foreign language, thesis/dissertation. *Entrance requirements:* For master's, GRE General Test; for doctorate, GRE General Test, MS. Additional exam requirements/recommendations for international students: Required—TOEFL (minimum score 500 paper-based; 61 iBT). Electronic applications accepted. *Faculty research:* Food biotechnology, nutrition, food microbiology, food engineering, food chemistry.

Appalachian State University, Cratis D. Williams Graduate School, Department of Family and Consumer Sciences, Boone, NC 28608. Offers child development: birth through kindergarten (MA). Part-time programs available. Postbaccalaureate distance learning degree programs offered (no on-campus study). *Degree requirements:* For master's, comprehensive exam, thesis optional. *Entrance requirements:* For master's, GRE General Test, 3 letters of recommendation. Additional exam requirements/recommendations for international students: Required—TOEFL (minimum score 550 paper-based; 79 iBT), IELTS (minimum score 6.5). Electronic applications accepted. *Faculty research:* Food antioxidants, preschool curriculum, children with special needs, family child care, FCS curriculum content.

Ball State University, Graduate School, College of Applied Science and Technology, Department of Family and Consumer Sciences, Muncie, IN 47306-1099. Offers dietetics (MS); family and consumer science (MS). *Faculty:* 9 full-time (8 women), 2 part-time/adjunct (1 woman). *Students:* 32 full-time (28 women), 31 part-time (25 women); includes 5 minority (1 Black or African American, non-Hispanic/Latino; 4 Asian, non-Hispanic/Latino, 5 international. Average age 25. 47 applicants, 68% accepted, 22 enrolled. In 2014, 28 master's awarded. *Entrance requirements:* For master's, resume. Application fee: $25 ($35 for international students). *Financial support:* In 2014–15, 11 students received support, including 4 research assistantships with partial tuition reimbursements available (averaging $11,446 per year), 4 teaching assistantships with partial tuition reimbursements available (averaging $10,696 per year); unspecified assistantships also available. Financial award application deadline: 3/1. *Faculty research:* Maternal and infant nutrition, nutrition education. *Unit head:* Dr. Jay Kandiah, Head, 765-285-5922, Fax: 765-285-2314, E-mail: jkandiah@bsu.edu. *Application contact:* Dr. Scott Hall, Program Director, 765-285-5943, Fax: 765-285-2314, E-mail: sshall@bsu.edu.
Website: http://www.bsu.edu/fcs/

Bowling Green State University, Graduate College, College of Education and Human Development, School of Family and Consumer Sciences, Bowling Green, OH 43403. Offers food and nutrition (MFCS); human development and family studies (MFCS). Part-time programs available. *Degree requirements:* For master's, thesis. *Entrance requirements:* For master's, GRE General Test, minimum GPA of 3.0. Additional exam requirements/recommendations for international students: Required—TOEFL. Electronic applications accepted. *Faculty research:* Public health, wellness, social issues and policies, ethnic foods, nutrition and aging.

California State University, Fresno, Division of Graduate Studies, College of Agricultural Sciences and Technology, Department of Child, Family and Consumer Sciences, Fresno, CA 93740-8027. Offers family and consumer sciences (MS). Currently not accepting applications. Part-time and evening/weekend programs available. *Degree requirements:* For master's, thesis (for some programs). *Entrance requirements:* For master's, GRE General Test, minimum GPA of 3.0 in last 60 hours. Additional exam requirements/recommendations for international students: Required—TOEFL. Electronic applications accepted.

California State University, Long Beach, Graduate Studies, College of Health and Human Services, Department of Family and Consumer Sciences, Long Beach, CA 90840. Offers family and consumer sciences (MA); nutritional science (MS), including food science, hospitality foodservice and hotel management, nutritional science. Part-time and evening/weekend programs available. *Degree requirements:* For master's, comprehensive exam or thesis. *Entrance requirements:* For master's, GRE (MS), minimum GPA of 3.0. Electronic applications accepted. *Faculty research:* School uniforms, consumer complaining behavior, nutrition and fitness education and behavior change, curriculum change, teaching experience of interns.

California State University, Northridge, Graduate Studies, College of Health and Human Development, Department of Family and Consumer Sciences, Northridge, CA 91330. Offers MS. Part-time and evening/weekend programs available. *Students:* 98 full-time (88 women), 78 part-time (73 women); includes 72 minority (11 Black or African American, non-Hispanic/Latino; 23 Asian, non-Hispanic/Latino; 33 Hispanic/Latino; 5 Two or more races, non-Hispanic/Latino), 21 international. Average age 31. *Degree requirements:* For master's, thesis, project, or comprehensive exam. *Entrance requirements:* For master's, GRE General Test or minimum GPA of 3.0. Additional exam requirements/recommendations for international students: Required—TOEFL. *Application deadline:* For fall admission, 11/30 for domestic students. Application fee: $55. *Expenses: Required fees:* $12,402. *Financial support:* Teaching assistantships, career-related internships or fieldwork, Federal Work-Study, and institutionally sponsored loans available. Financial award application deadline: 3/1. *Unit head:* Dr. Sandra B. Chong, Chair, 818-677-3051.
Website: http://www.csun.edu/hhd/fcs/

Central Michigan University, College of Graduate Studies, College of Education and Human Services, Department of Human Environmental Studies, Mount Pleasant, MI 48859. Offers apparel product development and merchandising technology (MS); gerontology (Graduate Certificate); human development and family studies (MA); nutrition and dietetics (MS). Part-time and evening/weekend programs available. *Degree requirements:* For master's, thesis or alternative. Electronic applications accepted. *Faculty research:* Human growth and development, family studies and human sexuality, human nutrition and dietetics, apparel and textile retailing, computer-aided design for apparel.

Central Washington University, Graduate Studies and Research, College of Education and Professional Studies, Department of Family and Consumer Sciences, Ellensburg, WA 98926. Offers career and technical education (MS); family and consumer sciences education (MS); family studies (MS). Part-time programs available. *Degree requirements:* For master's, thesis or alternative. *Entrance requirements:* For master's, minimum GPA of 3.0. Additional exam requirements/recommendations for international students: Required—TOEFL (minimum score 550 paper-based; 79 iBT). Electronic applications accepted.

East Carolina University, Graduate School, College of Education, Department of Elementary and Middle Grades Education, Greenville, NC 27858-4353. Offers elementary education (MA Ed, MAT); English education (MAT); family and consumer science (MAT); health education (MAT); Hispanic studies (MAT); history education (MAT); middle grades education (MA Ed, MAT); music education (MAT); science education (MAT); special education (MAT), including general curriculum; vocational education (MAT). *Accreditation:* NCATE. Part-time and evening/weekend programs available. Postbaccalaureate distance learning degree programs offered (no on-campus study). *Degree requirements:* For master's, comprehensive exam, thesis optional. *Entrance requirements:* For master's, GRE or MAT, minimum GPA of 2.5, bachelor's degree in related field, teaching license (MA Ed). Additional exam requirements/recommendations for international students: Required—TOEFL. *Application deadline:* For fall admission, 6/1 priority date for domestic students. Applications are processed on a rolling basis. Application fee: $70. *Expenses:* Tuition, state resident: full-time $4223. Tuition, nonresident: full-time $16,540. *Required fees:* $2184. *Financial support:* Federal Work-Study available. Support available to part-time students. Financial award application deadline: 6/1. *Unit head:* Dr. Ann Bullock, Chair, 252-328-1126, E-mail: bullockv@ecu.edu. *Application contact:* Dean of Graduate School, 252-328-6012, Fax: 252-328-6071, E-mail: gradschool@ecu.edu.
Website: http://www.ecu.edu/cs-educ/elmid/index.cfm

East Carolina University, Graduate School, College of Human Ecology, Department of Child Development and Family Relations, Greenville, NC 27858-4353. Offers birth through kindergarten education (MA Ed); child development and family relations (MS); family and consumer sciences (MA Ed); marriage and family therapy (MS); medical family therapy (PhD). *Accreditation:* AAMFT/COAMFTE. Part-time programs available. *Degree requirements:* For master's, comprehensive exam, thesis optional. *Expenses:* Tuition, state resident: full-time $4223. Tuition, nonresident: full-time $16,540. *Required fees:* $2184. *Faculty research:* Child care quality, mental health delivery systems for children, family violence.

Eastern Illinois University, Graduate School, Lumpkin College of Business and Applied Sciences, School of Family and Consumer Sciences, Program in Family and Consumer Sciences, Charleston, IL 61920. Offers MS. Part-time and evening/weekend programs available. Postbaccalaureate distance learning degree programs offered (minimal on-campus study). *Faculty:* 23. *Students:* 49 full-time (44 women), 32 part-time (28 women); includes 34 minority (29 Black or African American, non-Hispanic/Latino; 1 American Indian or Alaska Native, non-Hispanic/Latino; 3 Hispanic/Latino; 1 Two or more races, non-Hispanic/Latino). Average age 30. 69 applicants, 65% accepted, 22 enrolled. In 2014, 33 master's awarded. *Degree requirements:* For master's, comprehensive exam (for some programs), thesis (for some programs). *Entrance requirements:* For master's, GMAT or GRE. Additional exam requirements/recommendations for international students: Required—TOEFL (minimum score 500 paper-based; 61 iBT), IELTS (minimum score 6). *Application deadline:* For fall admission, 5/15 for domestic and international students; for spring admission, 10/15 for domestic and international students. Applications are processed on a rolling basis. Application fee: $30. Electronic applications accepted. *Expenses:* Tuition, state resident: full-time $3113; part-time $283 per credit hour. Tuition, nonresident: full-time $7469; part-time $679 per credit hour. *Required fees:* $2287; $96 per credit hour. Tuition and fees vary according to course load. *Financial support:* In 2014–15, 27 students received support, including 2 research assistantships with full tuition reimbursements available (averaging $7,830 per year), 4 teaching assistantships with full tuition reimbursements available (averaging $7,830 per year); career-related internships or fieldwork, Federal Work-Study, and unspecified assistantships also available. Support available to part-time students. Financial award application deadline: 3/1; financial award applicants required to submit FAFSA. *Unit head:* Linda Simpson, Interim Chair School of Family and Consumer Sciences, 217-581-2315, Fax: 217-581-6090, E-mail: ldsimpson@eiu.edu. *Application contact:* Lisa Moyer, Graduate Coordinator, 217-581-8584, Fax: 217-581-6090, E-mail: lmmoyer@eiu.edu.
Website: http://www.eiu.edu/famscigrad/

Florida State University, The Graduate School, College of Human Sciences, Tallahassee, FL 32306-1490. Offers MS, PhD. *Accreditation:* AAMFT/COAMFTE. Part-time programs available. *Faculty:* 39 full-time (26 women). *Students:* 141 full-time (88 women), 18 part-time (13 women); includes 39 minority (16 Black or African American, non-Hispanic/Latino; 2 Asian, non-Hispanic/Latino; 16 Hispanic/Latino; 1 Native Hawaiian or other Pacific Islander, non-Hispanic/Latino; 4 Two or more races, non-Hispanic/Latino), 24 international. 243 applicants, 50% accepted, 59 enrolled. In 2014, 57 master's, 15 doctorates awarded. *Degree requirements:* For master's, comprehensive exam (for some programs), thesis optional; for doctorate, thesis/dissertation. *Entrance requirements:* For master's, GRE General Test, minimum upper-division GPA of 3.0; for doctorate, GRE General Test, minimum upper-division GPA of 3.0, master's degree. Additional exam requirements/recommendations for international students: Required—TOEFL (minimum score 550 paper-based; 80 iBT). *Application deadline:* For fall admission, 7/1 for domestic and international students; for spring admission, 11/1 for domestic and international students; for summer admission, 4/1 for domestic and international students. Applications are processed on a rolling basis. Application fee: $30. Electronic applications accepted. *Expenses:* Tuition, state resident: part-time $403.51 per credit hour. Tuition, nonresident: part-time $1004.85 per credit hour. *Required fees:* $75.81 per credit hour. One-time fee: $20 part-time. Tuition and fees vary according to campus/location. *Financial support:* In 2014–15, 114 students received support, including 6 fellowships with partial tuition reimbursements available (averaging $2,362 per year), 27 research assistantships with full tuition reimbursements available (averaging $4,835 per year), 95 teaching assistantships with full tuition reimbursements available (averaging $10,311 per year); career-related internships or fieldwork, Federal Work-Study, institutionally sponsored loans, scholarships/grants, and unspecified assistantships also available. Financial award application deadline: 1/15; financial award applicants required to submit FAFSA. *Faculty research:* Body composition, functional food, chronic disease and aging response; food safety, food allergy, and safety/quality detection methods; sports nutrition, energy balance and human performance; families at risk, relational interventions, parenting, martial process and family therapy; merchandising and product development. *Total annual research expenditures:* $1.3 million. *Unit head:* Dr. Michael D. Delp, Dean, 850-644-1281, Fax: 850-644-0700, E-mail: mdelp@fsu.edu. *Application contact:* Tara L. Hartman, Academic Program Specialist, 850-644-7221, Fax: 850-644-0700, E-mail: thartman@fsu.edu.
Website: http://www.chs.fsu.edu/

Fontbonne University, Graduate Programs, Department of Human Environmental Sciences, St. Louis, MO 63105-3098. Offers family and consumer sciences (MA). *Degree requirements:* For master's, action paper/presentation portfolio. *Entrance*

requirements: For master's, minimum GPA of 3.0. *Faculty research:* Early intervention, public policy: children and families, program designer.

Illinois State University, Graduate School, College of Applied Science and Technology, Department of Family and Consumer Sciences, Normal, IL 61790-2200. Offers MA, MS. *Degree requirements:* For master's, thesis or alternative. *Entrance requirements:* For master's, GRE General Test, minimum GPA of 2.8 in last 60 hours of course work. *Faculty research:* Graduate practicum assistantships, startup for Jump Start of McLean County grant, providing low-income preschool children with early literacy experiences, generations of Hope-ICI replication.

Indiana State University, College of Graduate and Professional Studies, College of Arts and Sciences, Department of Family and Consumer Sciences, Terre Haute, IN 47809. Offers dietetics (MS); family and consumer sciences education (MS); inter-area option (MS). *Accreditation:* AND. Part-time programs available. *Degree requirements:* For master's, thesis optional. Electronic applications accepted.

Iowa State University of Science and Technology, Program in Family and Consumer Sciences, Ames, IA 50011. Offers MFCS. *Degree requirements:* For master's, thesis or alternative. *Entrance requirements:* For master's, GRE General Test. Additional exam requirements/recommendations for international students: Required—TOEFL (minimum score 550 paper-based; 79 iBT), IELTS (minimum score 6.5). Electronic applications accepted.

Kansas State University, Graduate School, College of Human Ecology, Manhattan, KS 66506. Offers MS, PhD, Graduate Certificate. Part-time programs available. Postbaccalaureate distance learning degree programs offered. *Faculty:* 64 full-time (41 women), 10 part-time/adjunct (7 women). *Students:* 172 full-time (124 women), 250 part-time (176 women); includes 83 minority (28 Black or African American, non-Hispanic/Latino; 5 American Indian or Alaska Native, non-Hispanic/Latino; 10 Asian, non-Hispanic/Latino; 28 Hispanic/Latino; 4 Native Hawaiian or other Pacific Islander, non-Hispanic/Latino; 8 Two or more races, non-Hispanic/Latino), 43 international. Average age 33. 319 applicants, 40% accepted, 91 enrolled. In 2014, 98 master's, 19 doctorates, 29 other advanced degrees awarded. *Degree requirements:* For master's, residency; for doctorate, thesis/dissertation, residency. *Application deadline:* For fall admission, 2/1 priority date for domestic and international students; for spring admission, 8/1 priority date for domestic and international students. Applications are processed on a rolling basis. Application fee: $50 ($75 for international students). Electronic applications accepted. *Financial support:* In 2014–15, 71 research assistantships (averaging $13,454 per year), 50 teaching assistantships with full and partial tuition reimbursements (averaging $13,202 per year) were awarded; career-related internships or fieldwork, Federal Work-Study, institutionally sponsored loans, scholarships/grants, and tuition waivers (full) also available. Support available to part-time students. Financial award application deadline: 3/1; financial award applicants required to submit FAFSA. *Faculty research:* Apparel and textiles, food service and hospitality management, life span human development, family life education and consultation, marriage and family therapy. *Total annual research expenditures:* $12.4 million. *Unit head:* Dr. John Buckwalter, Dean, 785-532-5500, Fax: 785-532-5504, E-mail: jbb3@ksu.edu. *Application contact:* Mary Anne Andrews, Director, Academic and Student Services, 785-532-5500, Fax: 785-532-5504, E-mail: mandrews@ksu.edu.
Website: http://www.he.k-state.edu/

Lamar University, College of Graduate Studies, College of Education and Human Development, Department of Family and Consumer Sciences, Beaumont, TX 77710. Offers MS. Part-time and evening/weekend programs available. *Faculty:* 7 full-time (6 women). *Students:* 15 full-time (all women), 12 part-time (10 women); includes 7 minority (3 Black or African American, non-Hispanic/Latino; 1 Asian, non-Hispanic/Latino; 3 Hispanic/Latino), 2 international. Average age 29. 124 applicants, 47% accepted. In 2014, 8 master's awarded. *Degree requirements:* For master's, thesis optional. *Entrance requirements:* For master's, GRE General Test. Additional exam requirements/recommendations for international students: Required—TOEFL (minimum score 550 paper-based; 79 iBT), IELTS (minimum score 6.5). *Application deadline:* For fall admission, 8/10 for domestic students, 7/1 for international students; for spring admission, 1/5 for domestic students, 12/1 for international students. Applications are processed on a rolling basis. Application fee: $25 ($50 for international students). *Expenses:* Tuition, state resident: full-time $5724; part-time $1908 per semester. Tuition, nonresident: full-time $12,240; part-time $4080 per semester. *Required fees:* $1940; $318 per credit hour. *Financial support:* In 2014–15, 3 students received support, including 3 teaching assistantships (averaging $5,000 per year); fellowships, research assistantships, career-related internships or fieldwork, Federal Work-Study, and institutionally sponsored loans also available. Support available to part-time students. Financial award application deadline: 4/1. *Faculty research:* Maternal and infant nutrition, eating disorders, sports nutrition, human sexuality, family violence. *Unit head:* Dr. Greg Thompson, Chair, 409-880-8663, Fax: 409-880-8666. *Application contact:* Melissa Gallien, Director, Admissions and Academic Services, 409-880-8888, Fax: 409-880-7419, E-mail: gradmissions@lamar.edu.
Website: http://education.lamar.edu/family-and-consumer-sciences

Louisiana State University and Agricultural & Mechanical College, Graduate School, College of Agriculture, School of Human Ecology, Baton Rouge, LA 70803. Offers MS, PhD. Part-time programs available. *Faculty:* 17 full-time (13 women). *Students:* 15 full-time (13 women), 7 part-time (all women); includes 9 minority (7 Black or African American, non-Hispanic/Latino; 1 Asian, non-Hispanic/Latino; 1 Hispanic/Latino), 8 international. Average age 33. 3 applicants, 33% accepted, 1 enrolled. In 2014, 1 master's, 4 doctorates awarded. *Degree requirements:* For master's, thesis; for doctorate, thesis/dissertation. *Entrance requirements:* For master's and doctorate, GRE General Test, minimum GPA of 3.0. Additional exam requirements/recommendations for international students: Required—TOEFL (minimum score 550 paper-based; 79 IBT), IELTS (minimum score 6.5), or PTE (minimum score 59). *Application deadline:* For fall admission, 1/25 priority date for domestic students, 5/15 for international students; for spring admission, 10/15 for international students. Applications are processed on a rolling basis. Application fee: $50 ($70 for international students). Electronic applications accepted. *Financial support:* In 2014–15, 17 students received support, including 7 research assistantships with full and partial tuition reimbursements available (averaging $17,000 per year), 5 teaching assistantships with full and partial tuition reimbursements available (averaging $11,000 per year); fellowships with full and partial tuition reimbursements available, career-related internships or fieldwork, Federal Work-Study, institutionally sponsored loans, scholarships/grants, health care benefits, and unspecified assistantships also available. Support available to part-time students. Financial award application deadline: 4/15; financial award applicants required to submit FAFSA. *Faculty research:* Nutrition for optimum health, textile and apparel production development, children's relationships with parents and caregivers, contextual influences on families. *Total annual research expenditures:* $25,533. *Unit head:* Dr. Jenna Kuttruff, Interim Director, 225-578-5748, Fax: 225-578-6709, E-mail: jkutt1@lsu.edu. *Application contact:* Melinda Mooney, Coordinator, 225-578-2448, E-mail: mmooney@agcenter.lsu.edu.
Website: http://www.huec.lsu.edu

Louisiana Tech University, Graduate School, College of Applied and Natural Sciences, School of Human Ecology, Ruston, LA 71272. Offers nutrition and dietetics (MS). Part-time programs available. *Degree requirements:* For master's, thesis or alternative, Registered Dietician Exam eligibility. *Entrance requirements:* For master's, GRE General Test. *Application deadline:* For fall admission, 7/29 priority date for domestic students; for spring admission, 2/3 for domestic students. Applications are processed on a rolling basis. Application fee: $20 ($30 for international students). *Financial support:* Fellowships, research assistantships, career-related internships or fieldwork, and Federal Work-Study available. Financial award application deadline: 2/1. *Unit head:* Dr. Amy Yates, Director, 318-257-3727, Fax: 318-257-4014. *Application contact:* Dr. Amy Yates, Director, 318-257-3727, Fax: 318-257-4014.
Website: http://ans.latech.edu/human-ecology.html

New Mexico State University, College of Agricultural, Consumer and Environmental Sciences, Department of Family and Consumer Sciences, Las Cruces, NM 88003. Offers family and child science (MS); family and consumer science education (MS); food science and technology (MS); human nutrition and dietetic science (MS); marriage and family therapy (MS). Part-time programs available. *Faculty:* 12 full-time (10 women). *Students:* 26 full-time (17 women), 10 part-time (8 women); includes 23 minority (1 Black or African American, non-Hispanic/Latino; 1 Asian, non-Hispanic/Latino; 21 Hispanic/Latino), 2 international. Average age 30. 19 applicants, 58% accepted, 10 enrolled. In 2014, 19 master's awarded. *Degree requirements:* For master's, comprehensive exam (for some programs), thesis (for some programs), oral exam. *Entrance requirements:* For master's, GRE, 3 letters of reference, resume, letter of interest. Additional exam requirements/recommendations for international students: Required—TOEFL (minimum score 550 paper-based; 79 iBT), IELTS (minimum score 6.5). *Application deadline:* For fall admission, 3/1 priority date for domestic and international students; for spring admission, 11/30 for domestic and international students. Applications are processed on a rolling basis. Application fee: $40 ($50 for international students). Electronic applications accepted. *Expenses:* Tuition, state resident: full-time $3969; part-time $220.50 per credit hour. Tuition, nonresident: full-time $13,838; part-time $768.80 per credit hour. *Required fees:* $853; $47.40 per credit hour. *Financial support:* In 2014–15, 24 students received support, including 2 fellowships (averaging $3,970 per year), 7 teaching assistantships (averaging $12,196 per year); career-related internships or fieldwork, Federal Work-Study, scholarships/grants, traineeships, health care benefits, and unspecified assistantships also available. Support available to part-time students. Financial award application deadline: 3/1. *Faculty research:* Food product analysis, childhood obesity, couple relationship education, military families, Latino college students. *Total annual research expenditures:* $448,204. *Unit head:* Dr. Esther Lynn Devall, Head, 575-646-3936, Fax: 575-646-1889, E-mail: edevall@nmsu.edu. *Application contact:* Dr. Margaret Ann Bock, Graduate Program Contact, 575-646-1178, Fax: 575-646-1889, E-mail: abock@nmsu.edu.
Website: http://aces.nmsu.edu/academics/fcs

North Carolina Central University, College of Behavioral and Social Sciences, Department of Human Sciences, Durham, NC 27707-3129. Offers family and consumer sciences (MS). Part-time and evening/weekend programs available. *Degree requirements:* For master's, one foreign language, comprehensive exam, thesis. *Entrance requirements:* For master's, GRE, minimum GPA of 3.0 in major, 2.5 overall. Additional exam requirements/recommendations for international students: Required—TOEFL.

North Dakota State University, College of Graduate and Interdisciplinary Studies, College of Human Development and Education, School of Education, Program in Family and Consumer Sciences Education, Fargo, ND 58108. Offers M Ed, MS. *Accreditation:* NCATE. Part-time programs available. *Degree requirements:* For master's, comprehensive exam, thesis or alternative. *Entrance requirements:* For master's, MAT. Additional exam requirements/recommendations for international students: Required—TOEFL. *Faculty research:* Needs of beginning teachers, learning styles and achievement, school-level variables and curriculum change.

The Ohio State University, Graduate School, College of Education and Human Ecology, Department of Human Sciences, Columbus, OH 43210. Offers consumer sciences (MS, PhD); human development and family science (PhD); human nutrition (MS, PhD); kinesiology (MA, PhD). Part-time programs available. *Faculty:* 55. *Students:* 116 full-time (73 women), 7 part-time (4 women); includes 20 minority (10 Black or African American, non-Hispanic/Latino; 1 American Indian or Alaska Native, non-Hispanic/Latino; 4 Asian, non-Hispanic/Latino; 4 Hispanic/Latino; 1 Two or more races, non-Hispanic/Latino), 31 international. Average age 28. In 2014, 17 master's, 16 doctorates awarded. *Degree requirements:* For master's, thesis optional; for doctorate, thesis/dissertation. *Entrance requirements:* For master's and doctorate, GRE. Additional exam requirements/recommendations for international students: Required—TOEFL (minimum score 550 paper-based; 79 iBT), Michigan English Language Assessment Battery (minimum score 82); Recommended—IELTS (minimum score 7). *Application deadline:* For fall admission, 12/1 priority date for domestic and international students; for winter admission, 12/1 for domestic students, 11/1 for international students; for spring admission, 3/1 for domestic students, 2/1 for international students. Applications are processed on a rolling basis. Application fee: $60 ($70 for international students). Electronic applications accepted. *Financial support:* Fellowships with tuition reimbursements, research assistantships with tuition reimbursements, teaching assistantships with tuition reimbursements, Federal Work-Study, and institutionally sponsored loans available. Support available to part-time students. *Unit head:* Dr. Carl M. Maresh, Chair, E-mail: maresh.15@osu.edu. *Application contact:* Graduate and Professional Admissions, 614-292-9444, Fax: 614-292-3895, E-mail: gpadmissions@osu.edu.
Website: http://ehe.osu.edu/human-sciences/

Ohio University, Graduate College, Gladys W. and David H. Patton College of Education and Human Services, Department of Human and Consumer Sciences Education, Athens, OH 45701-2979. Offers apparel, textiles, and merchandising (MS). Part-time programs available. *Degree requirements:* For master's, comprehensive exam (for some programs), thesis. *Entrance requirements:* For master's, GRE. Additional exam requirements/recommendations for international students: Required—TOEFL (minimum score 550 paper-based; 80 iBT) or IELTS (minimum score 6.5). Electronic applications accepted.

Oklahoma State University, College of Human Sciences, Department of Human Development and Family Science, Stillwater, OK 74078. Offers human development and family science (MS, PhD), including family financial planning (MS), human environmental sciences; marriage and family therapy (MS). *Accreditation:* AAMFT/COAMFTE (one or more programs are accredited). Postbaccalaureate distance learning degree programs offered. *Faculty:* 27 full-time (18 women), 9 part-time/adjunct (8 women). *Students:* 25 full-time (19 women), 45 part-time (39 women); includes 18 minority (7 Black or African American, non-Hispanic/Latino; 2 Asian, non-Hispanic/Latino; 1 Hispanic/Latino; 8 Two or more races, non-Hispanic/Latino), 2 international. Average age 30. 72 applicants, 33% accepted, 14 enrolled. In 2014, 24 master's, 3 doctorates awarded. *Degree requirements:* For master's, thesis (for some programs); for doctorate, comprehensive exam, thesis/dissertation. *Entrance requirements:* For master's and doctorate, GRE or GMAT. Additional exam requirements/recommendations for international students: Required—TOEFL (minimum score 550 paper-based; 79 iBT). *Application deadline:* For fall admission, 3/1 priority date for

international students; for spring admission, 8/1 priority date for international students. Applications are processed on a rolling basis. Application fee: $40 ($75 for international students). Electronic applications accepted. *Expenses:* Tuition, state resident: full-time $4488; part-time $187 per credit hour. Tuition, nonresident: full-time $18,360; part-time $765 per credit hour. *Required fees:* $2413; $100.55 per credit hour. Tuition and fees vary according to campus/location. *Financial support:* In 2014–15, 35 research assistantships (averaging $11,436 per year), 24 teaching assistantships (averaging $10,007 per year) were awarded; career-related internships or fieldwork, Federal Work-Study, scholarships/grants, health care benefits, tuition waivers (partial), and unspecified assistantships also available. Support available to part-time students. Financial award application deadline: 3/1; financial award applicants required to submit FAFSA. *Faculty research:* Family relations and child development, consequences of adolescent parenting, family stress and coping, impacts of sexual abuse on families, children's social cognition and self-competence, gerontology and health care. *Unit head:* Dr. Jennifer Hayes-Grudo, Department Head, 405-744-5360, Fax: 405-744-6344, E-mail: jennifer.hays.grudo@okstate.edu. *Application contact:* Dr. Brandt Gardner, Graduate Coordinator, 405-744-8360, Fax: 405-744-6344, E-mail: brandt.gardner@okstate.edu.
Website: http://humansciences.okstate.edu/hdfs/

Prairie View A&M University, College of Agriculture and Human Sciences, Prairie View, TX 77446-0519. Offers interdisciplinary human sciences (MS). Part-time and evening/weekend programs available. *Faculty:* 4 full-time (1 woman). *Students:* 54 full-time (47 women), 42 part-time (33 women); includes 88 minority (84 Black or African American, non-Hispanic/Latino; 1 Asian, non-Hispanic/Latino; 2 Hispanic/Latino; 1 Two or more races, non-Hispanic/Latino), 1 international. Average age 36. 42 applicants, 98% accepted, 35 enrolled. In 2014, 19 master's awarded. *Degree requirements:* For master's, comprehensive exam, thesis (for some programs), field placement. *Entrance requirements:* For master's, GRE General Test, minimum GPA of 2.45. Additional exam requirements/recommendations for international students: Required—TOEFL (minimum score 550 paper-based; 79 iBT). *Application deadline:* For fall admission, 7/1 priority date for domestic students, 6/1 priority date for international students; for spring admission, 11/1 priority date for domestic students, 10/1 priority date for international students; for summer admission, 3/1 priority date for domestic students, 2/1 priority date for international students. Applications are processed on a rolling basis. Application fee: $50. *Expenses:* Expenses: $6,686 tuition and fees. *Financial support:* In 2014–15, 10 research assistantships were awarded; career-related internships or fieldwork, Federal Work-Study, institutionally sponsored loans, scholarships/grants, tuition waivers (partial), and unspecified assistantships also available. Support available to part-time students. Financial award application deadline: 4/1; financial award applicants required to submit FAFSA. *Faculty research:* Domestic violence prevention, water quality, food growth regulators, wetland dynamics, biochemistry, obesity and nutrition, family therapy. *Unit head:* Dr. Alton Johnson, Dean, 936-261-5125, E-mail: abjohnson@pvamu.edu. *Application contact:* Pauline Walker, Administrative Assistant II, 936-261-3521, Fax: 936-261-3529, E-mail: pmwalker@pvamu.edu.

Purdue University, Graduate School, College of Health and Human Sciences, West Lafayette, IN 47907. Offers MS, Au D, PhD. Part-time programs available. *Degree requirements:* For doctorate, thesis/dissertation. *Entrance requirements:* Additional exam requirements/recommendations for international students: Required—TOEFL. Electronic applications accepted.

Queens College of the City University of New York, Division of Graduate Studies, Mathematics and Natural Sciences Division, Department of Family, Nutrition and Exercise Sciences, Flushing, NY 11367-1597. Offers home economics (MS Ed); physical education and exercise sciences (MS Ed). Part-time and evening/weekend programs available. *Degree requirements:* For master's, research project. *Entrance requirements:* For master's, minimum GPA of 3.0. Additional exam requirements/recommendations for international students: Required—TOEFL.

Sam Houston State University, College of Health Sciences, Department of Family and Consumer Sciences, Huntsville, TX 77341. Offers dietetics (MS); family and consumer sciences (MS). Part-time and evening/weekend programs available. *Faculty:* 5 full-time (4 women). *Students:* 22 full-time (20 women), 4 part-time (all women); includes 3 minority (1 Asian, non-Hispanic/Latino; 1 Hispanic/Latino; 1 Two or more races, non-Hispanic/Latino), 1 international. Average age 27. 12 applicants, 92% accepted, 12 enrolled. In 2014, 12 master's awarded. *Degree requirements:* For master's, comprehensive exam, thesis optional, internship. *Entrance requirements:* For master's, GRE General Test, letters of recommendation, personal statement, writing sample. Additional exam requirements/recommendations for international students: Required—TOEFL (minimum score 550 paper-based; 79 iBT), IELTS (minimum score 6.5). *Application deadline:* For fall admission, 8/1 for domestic students, 6/25 for international students; for spring admission, 12/1 for domestic students, 11/12 for international students; for summer admission, 5/15 for domestic students, 4/9 for international students. Applications are processed on a rolling basis. Application fee: $45 ($75 for international students). Electronic applications accepted. *Expenses:* Tuition, state resident: full-time $2286; part-time $254 per credit hour. Tuition, nonresident: full-time $5544; part-time $616 per credit hour. *Required fees:* $440 per semester. Tuition and fees vary according to course load and campus/location. *Financial support:* In 2014–15, 6 research assistantships (averaging $3,601 per year) were awarded; career-related internships or fieldwork, Federal Work-Study, scholarships/grants, tuition waivers (partial), and unspecified assistantships also available. Support available to part-time students. Financial award application deadline: 3/15; financial award applicants required to submit FAFSA. *Unit head:* Dr. Janice White, Chair/Professor, 936-294-1184, Fax: 936-294-4204, E-mail: hec_jhw@shsu.edu. *Application contact:* Dr. Valencia Browning-Keen, Graduate Advisor/Professor, 936-294-1245, Fax: 936-294-4204, E-mail: vbk001@shsu.edu.
Website: http://www.shsu.edu/academics/health-sciences/family-and-consumer-sciences/

San Francisco State University, Division of Graduate Studies, College of Health and Social Sciences, Department of Consumer and Family Studies/Dietetics, San Francisco, CA 94132-1722. Offers MA. Part-time programs available. *Application deadline:* Applications are processed on a rolling basis. *Expenses:* Tuition, state resident: full-time $6738. Tuition, nonresident: full-time $17,898; part-time $372 per credit hour. *Required fees:* $498 per semester. *Unit head:* Dr. Nancy Rabolt, Chair, 415-338-2060, E-mail: nrabolt@sfsu.edu. *Application contact:* Kelly Vuong, Academic Office Coordinator, 415-405-3529, E-mail: kvuong@sfsu.edu.
Website: http://cfsd.sfsu.edu/

South Carolina State University, College of Graduate and Professional Studies, Department of Family and Consumer Sciences, Orangeburg, SC 29117-0001. Offers individual and family development (MS). Part-time and evening/weekend programs available. *Faculty:* 3 full-time (all women). *Students:* 4 full-time (3 women), 6 part-time (all women); all minorities (all Black or African American, non-Hispanic/Latino). Average age 28. 5 applicants, 100% accepted, 4 enrolled. In 2014, 10 master's awarded. *Degree requirements:* For master's, comprehensive exam, thesis optional, departmental qualifying exam. *Entrance requirements:* For master's, GRE, MAT, or NTE, minimum GPA of 2.7. *Application deadline:* For fall admission, 6/15 priority date for domestic students, 6/15 for international students; for spring admission, 11/1 for domestic and international students. Applications are processed on a rolling basis. Application fee: $25. Electronic applications accepted. *Expenses:* Tuition, state resident: full-time $7290; part-time $405 per credit. Tuition, nonresident: full-time $17,058; part-time $948 per credit. *Required fees:* $2798; $155 per credit hour. *Financial support:* Fellowships and institutionally sponsored loans available. Financial award application deadline: 6/1. *Unit head:* Dr. Ethel G. Jones, Chair, 803-536-8958, Fax: 803-533-3268, E-mail: egjones@scsu.edu. *Application contact:* Curtis Foskey, Coordinator of Graduate Admission, 803-536-8419, Fax: 803-536-8812, E-mail: cfoskey@scsu.edu.

South Dakota State University, Graduate School, College of Education and Human Sciences, Department of Consumer Sciences, Brookings, SD 57007. Offers family financial planning (MS); merchandising (MS). *Entrance requirements:* For master's, resume. Additional exam requirements/recommendations for international students: Required—TOEFL (minimum score 525 paper-based).

Stephen F. Austin State University, Graduate School, College of Education, Department of Human Sciences, Nacogdoches, TX 75962. Offers MS. *Degree requirements:* For master's, comprehensive exam, thesis or alternative. *Entrance requirements:* For master's, GRE General Test. Additional exam requirements/recommendations for international students: Required—TOEFL. *Faculty research:* Consumer economics, nutrition education, clothing and textiles, family, interior design.

Tennessee State University, The School of Graduate Studies and Research, College of Agriculture, Human and Natural Sciences, Nashville, TN 37209-1561. Offers agricultural sciences (MS), including agribusiness, agricultural and extension education, animal science, plant and soil science; biological sciences (MS, PhD); biotechnology (PhD); chemistry (MS). Part-time and evening/weekend programs available. *Degree requirements:* For master's, thesis. *Entrance requirements:* For master's, GRE General Test, GRE Subject Test, MAT. *Faculty research:* Small farm economics, ornamental horticulture, beef cattle production, rural elderly.

Texas A&M University–Kingsville, College of Graduate Studies, Dick and Mary Lewis Kleberg College of Agriculture, Natural Resources and Human Sciences, Department of Human Sciences, Kingsville, TX 78363. Offers MS. *Faculty:* 1 full-time (0 women), 1 (woman) part-time/adjunct. *Students:* 12 full-time (all women), 11 part-time (10 women); includes 12 minority (3 Asian, non-Hispanic/Latino; 9 Hispanic/Latino), 2 international. Average age 26. 7 applicants, 71% accepted, 3 enrolled. In 2014, 16 master's awarded. *Degree requirements:* For master's, variable foreign language requirement, comprehensive exam, thesis (for some programs). *Entrance requirements:* For master's, GRE, MAT, GMAT. Additional exam requirements/recommendations for international students: Required—TOEFL (minimum score 550 paper-based; 79 iBT). *Application deadline:* For fall admission, 8/1 for domestic students, 6/1 for international students; for spring admission, 12/15 for domestic students, 10/1 for international students; for summer admission, 5/15 for domestic students, 4/1 for international students. Applications are processed on a rolling basis. Application fee: $35 ($50 for international students). Electronic applications accepted. *Financial support:* In 2014–15, 6 students received support. Career-related internships or fieldwork, Federal Work-Study, institutionally sponsored loans, scholarships/grants, tuition waivers (full and partial), and unspecified assistantships available. Support available to part-time students. Financial award application deadline: 5/15; financial award applicants required to submit FAFSA. *Faculty research:* Mexican-American families, abuse in families, nontraditional students. *Unit head:* Dr. Kathleen Rees, Department Chair, 361-593-2357, Fax: 361-593-2230, E-mail: kathleen.rees@tamuk.edu. *Application contact:* Dr. Mohamed Abdelrahman, Dean of Graduate Students, 361-593-2809, E-mail: mohamed.abdelrahman@tamuk.edu.

Texas Southern University, College of Liberal Arts and Behavioral Sciences, Department of Human Services and Consumer Sciences, Houston, TX 77004-4584. Offers MS. Part-time and evening/weekend programs available. *Degree requirements:* For master's, comprehensive exam, thesis (for some programs). *Entrance requirements:* For master's, GRE General Test, minimum GPA of 2.5. Additional exam requirements/recommendations for international students: Required—TOEFL. Electronic applications accepted. *Faculty research:* Food radiation/food for space travel, adolescent parenting, gerontology/grandparenting.

Texas State University, The Graduate College, College of Applied Arts, School of Family and Consumer Sciences, Program in Merchandising and Consumer Studies, San Marcos, TX 78666. Offers MS. Part-time programs available. *Faculty:* 2 full-time (both women). *Students:* 11 full-time (10 women), 1 (woman) part-time; includes 8 minority (2 Black or African American, non-Hispanic/Latino; 6 Hispanic/Latino), 2 international. Average age 25. 15 applicants, 87% accepted, 9 enrolled. *Degree requirements:* For master's, thesis optional. *Entrance requirements:* For master's, GRE (preferred), bachelor's degree; minimum GPA of 3.0 on last 60 hours of undergraduate coursework. Additional exam requirements/recommendations for international students: Required—TOEFL (minimum score 550 paper-based). *Application deadline:* For fall admission, 6/15 for domestic students, 6/1 for international students; for spring admission, 10/15 for domestic students, 10/1 for international students; for summer admission, 4/15 for domestic students, 3/15 for international students. Application fee: $40 ($90 for international students). Electronic applications accepted. *Expenses:* Expenses: $8,834 (tuition and fees combined). *Financial support:* In 2014–15, 6 students received support, including 4 research assistantships (averaging $12,169 per year), 2 teaching assistantships (averaging $9,040 per year); scholarships/grants also available. Financial award application deadline: 3/1. *Unit head:* Dr. Maria E. Canabal, School Director, 512-245-2155, Fax: 512-245-3829, E-mail: mc57@txstate.edu. *Application contact:* Dr. Elizabeth Russell, Graduate Adviser, 512-245-2155, Fax: 512-245-3829, E-mail: er15@txstate.edu.
Website: http://www.fcs.txstate.edu/degrees-programs/fm/fm_grad.html

Texas Tech University, Graduate School, College of Human Sciences, Lubbock, TX 79409-1162. Offers MS, PhD, JD/MS. Part-time programs available. Postbaccalaureate distance learning degree programs offered (minimal on-campus study). *Faculty:* 97 full-time (68 women), 14 part-time/adjunct (11 women). *Students:* 315 full-time (201 women), 147 part-time (113 women); includes 83 minority (20 Black or African American, non-Hispanic/Latino; 3 American Indian or Alaska Native, non-Hispanic/Latino; 7 Asian, non-Hispanic/Latino; 46 Hispanic/Latino; 7 Two or more races, non-Hispanic/Latino), 128 international. Average age 31. 316 applicants, 58% accepted, 124 enrolled. In 2014, 74 master's, 27 doctorates awarded. Terminal master's awarded for partial completion of doctoral program. *Degree requirements:* For master's, comprehensive exam, thesis (for some programs); for doctorate, comprehensive exam, thesis/dissertation. *Entrance requirements:* Additional exam requirements/recommendations for international students: Required—TOEFL. *Application deadline:* For fall admission, 6/1 priority date for domestic students, 1/15 priority date for international students; for spring admission, 9/1 priority date for domestic students, 6/15 priority date for international students. Applications are processed on a rolling basis. Application fee: $60. Electronic applications accepted. *Expenses:* Expenses: Contact institution. *Financial support:* In 2014–15, 329 students received support, including 321 fellowships (averaging $4,205 per year), 40 research assistantships (averaging $18,374 per year), 147 teaching assistantships (averaging $13,904 per year); institutionally sponsored loans, scholarships/grants, and unspecified assistantships also available.

Financial award application deadline: 2/1; financial award applicants required to submit FAFSA. *Faculty research:* Retirement planning and living, obesity, addiction and recovery sciences. *Total annual research expenditures:* $2.7 million. *Unit head:* Dr. Linda C. Hoover, Dean, 806-742-3031, Fax: 806-742-1849, E-mail: linda.hoover@ttu.edu. *Application contact:* Prof. Mitzi Lauderdale, Associate Dean for Students, 806-834-0529, Fax: 806-742-1849, E-mail: mitzi.lauderdale@ttu.edu. Website: http://www.hs.ttu.edu

Tufts University, Graduate School of Arts and Sciences, Eliot-Pearson Department of Child Study and Human Development, Medford, MA 02155. Offers child study and human development (MA, PhD); early childhood education (MAT). Part-time programs available. *Faculty:* 13 full-time (10 women), 22 part-time/adjunct (18 women). *Students:* 68 full-time (62 women), 31 part-time (24 women); includes 21 minority (6 Black or African American, non-Hispanic/Latino; 7 Asian, non-Hispanic/Latino; 4 Hispanic/Latino; 4 Two or more races, non-Hispanic/Latino), 11 international. Average age 28. 122 applicants, 58% accepted, 29 enrolled. In 2014, 42 master's, 3 doctorates awarded. *Degree requirements:* For master's, thesis (for some programs); for doctorate, thesis/dissertation. *Entrance requirements:* For master's and doctorate, GRE General Test. Additional exam requirements/recommendations for international students: Required—TOEFL (minimum score 550 paper-based; 80 iBT), IELTS (minimum score 6.5). *Application deadline:* For fall admission, 12/1 priority date for domestic and international students. Applications are processed on a rolling basis. Application fee: $75. Electronic applications accepted. *Expenses:* Tuition: Full-time $45,590; part-time $1161 per credit hour. *Required fees:* $782. Full-time tuition and fees vary according to degree level, program and student level. Part-time tuition and fees vary according to course load. *Financial support:* Fellowships, research assistantships with full and partial tuition reimbursements, teaching assistantships with full and partial tuition reimbursements, Federal Work-Study, scholarships/grants, tuition waivers (partial), and unspecified assistantships available. Support available to part-time students. Financial award application deadline: 5/15; financial award applicants required to submit FAFSA. *Unit head:* Dr. David Henry Feldman, Graduate Program Director. *Application contact:* Office of Graduate Admissions, 617-627-3395, E-mail: gradadmissions@tufts.edu. Website: http://ase.tufts.edu/epcd

The University of Alabama, Graduate School, College of Human Environmental Sciences, Tuscaloosa, AL 35487. Offers MA, MS, MSHES, PhD. Part-time and evening/weekend programs available. Postbaccalaureate distance learning degree programs offered (no on-campus study). *Faculty:* 48 full-time (36 women), 3 part-time/adjunct (2 women). *Students:* 181 full-time (130 women), 344 part-time (253 women); includes 129 minority (89 Black or African American, non-Hispanic/Latino; 2 American Indian or Alaska Native, non-Hispanic/Latino; 3 Asian, non-Hispanic/Latino; 23 Hispanic/Latino; 12 Two or more races, non-Hispanic/Latino), 4 international. Average age 32. 343 applicants, 70% accepted, 188 enrolled. In 2014, 247 master's, 3 doctorates awarded. *Degree requirements:* For doctorate, thesis/dissertation. *Entrance requirements:* For master's, GRE General Test or MAT (minimum score: 50th percentile), minimum GPA of 3.0; for doctorate, GRE General Test or MAT, minimum GPA of 3.0. *Application deadline:* For fall admission, 7/6 for domestic students. Applications are processed on a rolling basis. Application fee: $50 ($60 for international students). Electronic applications accepted. *Expenses:* Tuition, state resident: full-time $9826. Tuition, nonresident: full-time $24,950. *Financial support:* In 2014–15, 2 research assistantships with full tuition reimbursements (averaging $9,000 per year) were awarded; fellowships with tuition reimbursements, teaching assistantships with full tuition reimbursements, career-related internships or fieldwork, Federal Work-Study, institutionally sponsored loans, and scholarships/grants also available. *Faculty research:* Students' use of credit, determinants of income differential: comparing Asians with blacks and whites, expenditure patterns of Chinese, racial and ethnic differences in the likelihood of charitable contributions, health insurance coverage and precautionary behavior savings. *Total annual research expenditures:* $75,179. *Unit head:* Dr. Milla D. Boschung, Dean, 205-348-6250, Fax: 205-348-1786, E-mail: mboschun@ches.ua.edu. *Application contact:* Patrick D. Fuller, Admissions Officer, 205-348-5923, Fax: 205-348-0400, E-mail: patrick.d.fuller@ua.edu. Website: http://www.ches.ua.edu/

University of Alberta, Faculty of Graduate Studies and Research, Department of Human Ecology, Edmonton, AB T6G 2E1, Canada. Offers family ecology and practice (M Sc, PhD); textiles and clothing (M Sc, MA, PhD). Postbaccalaureate distance learning degree programs offered (no on-campus study). *Degree requirements:* For master's, thesis (for some programs); for doctorate, comprehensive exam, thesis/dissertation. *Entrance requirements:* For master's and doctorate, minimum GPA of 7.0 on a 9.0 scale. Additional exam requirements/recommendations for international students: Required—TOEFL (minimum score 580 paper-based). *Faculty research:* Families and aging, family and child poverty, paid and unpaid work of families, textiles and clothing, parent-child relationships.

The University of Arizona, College of Agriculture and Life Sciences, School of Family and Consumer Sciences, Tucson, AZ 85721. Offers MS, PhD. Part-time programs available. *Entrance requirements:* For master's and doctorate, GRE General Test, minimum GPA of 3.0. Additional exam requirements/recommendations for international students: Required—TOEFL (minimum score 550 paper-based; 79 iBT). Electronic applications accepted. *Faculty research:* Interpersonal relationships, human development, retailing management, consumer behaviors.

University of Arkansas, Graduate School, Dale Bumpers College of Agricultural, Food and Life Sciences, School of Human Environmental Sciences, Fayetteville, AR 72701-1201. Offers MS. Part-time programs available. Postbaccalaureate distance learning degree programs offered (minimal on-campus study). *Degree requirements:* For master's, comprehensive exam, thesis (for some programs). Electronic applications accepted.

University of Central Arkansas, Graduate School, College of Health and Behavioral Sciences, Department of Family and Consumer Sciences, Conway, AR 72035-0001. Offers MS. Part-time and evening/weekend programs available. Postbaccalaureate distance learning degree programs offered (minimal on-campus study). *Degree requirements:* For master's, comprehensive exam, thesis optional. *Entrance requirements:* For master's, GRE General Test, minimum GPA of 2.7. Additional exam requirements/recommendations for international students: Required—TOEFL (minimum score 550 paper-based). Electronic applications accepted. *Expenses:* Contact institution. *Faculty research:* Neurology, developmental disabilities, diet consequences.

University of Central Oklahoma, The Jackson College of Graduate Studies, College of Education and Professional Studies, Department of Human Environmental Sciences, Edmond, OK 73034-5209. Offers family and child studies (MS), including family life education, infant/child specialist, marriage and family therapy; nutrition-food management (MS). Part-time programs available. *Degree requirements:* For master's, comprehensive exam (for some programs), thesis (for some programs). *Entrance requirements:* For master's, GRE, essay, physical, CPR and First Aid training. Additional exam requirements/recommendations for international students: Required—TOEFL (minimum score 550 paper-based; 79 iBT), IELTS (minimum score 6.5). Electronic applications accepted.

University of Florida, Graduate School, College of Agricultural and Life Sciences, Department of Family, Youth, and Community Sciences, Gainesville, FL 32611. Offers community studies (MS); family and youth development (MS); family, youth and community sciences (MS); nonprofit organization development (MS). Part-time programs available. Postbaccalaureate distance learning degree programs offered (no on-campus study). *Faculty:* 21 full-time (11 women), 4 part-time/adjunct (2 women). *Students:* 14 full-time (11 women), 31 part-time (27 women); includes 9 minority (1 Black or African American, non-Hispanic/Latino; 1 American Indian or Alaska Native, non-Hispanic/Latino; 1 Asian, non-Hispanic/Latino; 6 Hispanic/Latino), 4 international. 34 applicants, 65% accepted, 19 enrolled. In 2014, 11 master's awarded. *Degree requirements:* For master's, comprehensive exam (for some programs), thesis (for some programs). *Entrance requirements:* For master's, GRE General Test, minimum GPA of 3.0. Additional exam requirements/recommendations for international students: Required—TOEFL (minimum score 550 paper-based; 80 iBT), IELTS (minimum score 6). *Application deadline:* For fall admission, 2/1 for domestic and international students; for spring admission, 10/15 for domestic and international students. Applications are processed on a rolling basis. Application fee: $30. Electronic applications accepted. *Financial support:* In 2014–15, 1 research assistantship, 9 teaching assistantships were awarded; fellowships also available. Financial award applicants required to submit FAFSA. *Faculty research:* Adolescent risk behaviors, family risk and resilience, family financial management, community-based organizations/interventions, nutrition and wellness. *Total annual research expenditures:* $712,782. *Unit head:* Traci Irani, PhD, Professor and Interim Chair, 352-273-3446, E-mail: irani@ufl.edu. *Application contact:* Gregg Henderschiedt, Academic Coordinator, Graduate Program, 352-273-3514, Fax: 352-392-8196, E-mail: ghenderschiedt@ufl.edu. Website: http://fycs.ifas.ufl.edu/

University of Georgia, College of Family and Consumer Sciences, Athens, GA 30602. Offers MAT, MFCS, MS, PhD. *Degree requirements:* For doctorate, thesis/dissertation. *Entrance requirements:* For master's and doctorate, GRE General Test. Electronic applications accepted.

University of Houston, College of Technology, Department of Human Development and Consumer Science, Houston, TX 77204. Offers future studies in commerce (MS); human resources development (MS). Part-time programs available. *Degree requirements:* For master's, project or thesis. *Entrance requirements:* For master's, GMAT, MAT. Additional exam requirements/recommendations for international students: Required—TOEFL (minimum score 550 paper-based; 79 iBT). Electronic applications accepted.

University of Louisiana at Monroe, Graduate School, College of Arts, Education, and Sciences, School of Education, Program in Curriculum and Instruction, Monroe, LA 71209-0001. Offers art education (M Ed); biology education (M Ed); chemistry education (M Ed); curriculum and instruction (Ed D); early childhood education (M Ed); earth science education (M Ed); educational leadership (M Ed); elementary education (1-5) (M Ed); English as a second language (M Ed); English education (M Ed); family and consumer education (M Ed); French education (M Ed); history education (M Ed); math education (M Ed); middle school education (M Ed); music education (M Ed); reading education (K-12) (M Ed); Spanish education (M Ed); special education - academically gifted (M Ed); special education - early intervention (M Ed); special education - educational diagnostician (M Ed); special education - mild/moderate disabilities (M Ed); speech education (M Ed). *Accreditation:* NCATE. *Degree requirements:* For master's, comprehensive exam (for some programs), thesis; for doctorate, thesis/dissertation, internships. *Entrance requirements:* For master's, GRE General Test; for doctorate, GRE General Test, minimum undergraduate GPA of 2.75, graduate 3.25. Additional exam requirements/recommendations for international students: Required—TOEFL (minimum score 500 paper-based; 61 iBT). Electronic applications accepted.

University of Manitoba, Faculty of Graduate Studies, Faculty of Human Ecology, Winnipeg, MB R3T 2N2, Canada. Offers M Sc. *Degree requirements:* For master's, thesis.

University of Maryland, College Park, Academic Affairs, School of Public Health, Department of Family Science, College Park, MD 20742. Offers family studies (PhD); marriage and family therapy (MS); maternal and child health (PhD). *Accreditation:* AAMFT/COAMFTE. Part-time and evening/weekend programs available. *Degree requirements:* For master's, thesis or alternative; for doctorate, comprehensive exam, thesis/dissertation, oral defense. *Entrance requirements:* For master's, GRE General Test, minimum GPA of 3.0, 3 letters of recommendation; for doctorate, GRE General Test, minimum GPA of 3.0, 3 letters of recommendation, research sample. Electronic applications accepted. *Faculty research:* Family life quality, interracial couples, child support, homeless families, family and child well-being.

University of Memphis, Graduate School, University College, Memphis, TN 38152. Offers liberal studies (MALS); merchandising and consumer science (MS), including consumer science and education; strategic leadership (MPS). Part-time and evening/weekend programs available. *Faculty:* 3 full-time (1 woman), 1 (woman) part-time/adjunct. *Students:* 24 full-time (10 women), 128 part-time (90 women); includes 94 minority (86 Black or African American, non-Hispanic/Latino; 1 Asian, non-Hispanic/Latino; 2 Hispanic/Latino; 5 Two or more races, non-Hispanic/Latino). Average age 39. 62 applicants, 82% accepted, 8 enrolled. In 2014, 52 master's awarded. *Degree requirements:* For master's, comprehensive exam, thesis (for some programs). *Entrance requirements:* For master's, MAT, GRE General Test (for MS), interview (MALS). Additional exam requirements/recommendations for international students: Required—TOEFL (minimum score 550 paper-based). *Application deadline:* For fall admission, 7/1 for domestic students, 5/1 for international students; for spring admission, 11/1 for domestic students, 9/15 for international students. Applications are processed on a rolling basis. Application fee: $35 ($60 for international students). Electronic applications accepted. *Financial support:* In 2014–15, 123 students received support. Research assistantships with full tuition reimbursements available, teaching assistantships with tuition reimbursements available, Federal Work-Study, scholarships/grants, and unspecified assistantships available. Financial award application deadline: 2/15; financial award applicants required to submit FAFSA. *Faculty research:* Media ethics, history of psychiatry, public relations. *Unit head:* Dr. Dan Lattimore, Dean, 901-678-2991. *Application contact:* Dr. Herbert McCree, Coordinator of Graduate Studies, 901-678-4171, Fax: 901-678-3363, E-mail: hmccree@memphis.edu. Website: http://www.memphis.edu/univcoll/

University of Missouri, Office of Research and Graduate Studies, College of Human Environmental Sciences, Columbia, MO 65211. Offers MA, MS, PhD, Certificate. Part-time programs available. *Faculty:* 39 full-time (24 women), 1 (woman) part-time/adjunct. *Students:* 152 full-time (116 women), 137 part-time (95 women); includes 39 minority (17 Black or African American, non-Hispanic/Latino; 7 Asian, non-Hispanic/Latino; 7 Hispanic/Latino; 8 Two or more races, non-Hispanic/Latino), 45 international. Average age 33. 146 applicants, 46% accepted, 47 enrolled. In 2014, 27 master's, 8 doctorates, 3 other advanced degrees awarded. *Degree requirements:* For doctorate, thesis/dissertation. *Entrance requirements:* For master's and doctorate, GRE General Test, minimum GPA of 3.0. Additional exam requirements/recommendations for international students: Required—TOEFL. *Application deadline:* Applications are processed on a rolling basis. Application fee: $55 ($75 for international students). *Financial support:*

Family and Consumer Sciences-General

Fellowships with tuition reimbursements, research assistantships with tuition reimbursements, teaching assistantships with tuition reimbursements, institutionally sponsored loans, scholarships/grants, traineeships, health care benefits, and unspecified assistantships available. Support available to part-time students. *Unit head:* Dr. Stephen R. Jorgensen, Dean, 573-882-6227, E-mail: jorgensens@missouri.edu. *Application contact:* Carla J. Beckmann, Coordinator of Student Services and Records, 573-882-6423, E-mail: jeromebeckmannc@missouri.edu. Website: http://hes.missouri.edu/

University of Nebraska–Lincoln, Graduate College, College of Education and Human Sciences, Department of Child, Youth and Family Studies, Lincoln, NE 68588. Offers child development/early childhood education (MS, PhD); child, youth and family studies (MS); family and consumer sciences education (MS, PhD); family financial planning (MS); family science (MS, PhD); gerontology (PhD); human sciences (PhD), including child, youth and family studies, gerontology, medical family therapy; marriage and family therapy (MS); medical family therapy (PhD); youth development (MS). *Accreditation:* AAMFT/COAMFTE (one or more programs are accredited). Postbaccalaureate distance learning degree programs offered. *Degree requirements:* For master's, thesis optional. *Entrance requirements:* For master's, GRE. Additional exam requirements/recommendations for international students: Required—TOEFL (minimum score 550 paper-based). Electronic applications accepted. *Faculty research:* Marriage and family therapy, child development/early childhood education, family financial management.

University of Northwestern–St. Paul, Master of Arts in Human Services Program, St. Paul, MN 55113-1598. Offers family studies (MAHS). Part-time and evening/weekend programs available. Postbaccalaureate distance learning degree programs offered (no on-campus study). *Application deadline:* Applications are processed on a rolling basis. Electronic applications accepted. *Expenses:* Expenses: $490 per credit. Website: https://www.unwsp.edu/web/graduate-studies/master-of-arts-in-human-services

University of Puerto Rico, Río Piedras Campus, College of Education, Program in Family Ecology and Nutrition, San Juan, PR 00931-3300. Offers M Ed. Part-time programs available. *Degree requirements:* For master's, thesis. *Entrance requirements:* For master's, PAEG or GRE, minimum GPA of 3.0, letter of recommendation.

University of South Africa, College of Agriculture and Environmental Sciences, Pretoria, South Africa. Offers agriculture (MS); consumer science (MCS); environmental management (MA, MS, PhD); environmental science (MA, MS, PhD); geography (MA, MS, PhD); horticulture (M Tech); human ecology (MHE); life sciences (MS); nature conservation (M Tech).

The University of Tennessee, Graduate School, College of Education, Health and Human Sciences, Program in Human Ecology, Knoxville, TN 37996. Offers child and family studies (PhD); community health (PhD); nutrition science (PhD); retailing and consumer sciences (PhD); textile science (PhD). *Degree requirements:* For doctorate, thesis/dissertation. *Entrance requirements:* For doctorate, GRE General Test, minimum GPA of 2.7. Additional exam requirements/recommendations for international students: Required—TOEFL. Electronic applications accepted.

The University of Tennessee at Martin, Graduate Programs, College of Agriculture and Applied Sciences, Department of Family and Consumer Sciences, Martin, TN 38238-1000. Offers dietetics (MSFCS); general family and consumer sciences (MSFCS). Part-time programs available. *Faculty:* 7. *Students:* 34 part-time (30 women); includes 9 minority (6 Black or African American, non-Hispanic/Latino; 2 Hispanic/Latino; 1 Two or more races, non-Hispanic/Latino). 33 applicants, 82% accepted, 18 enrolled. In 2014, 9 master's awarded. *Degree requirements:* For master's, comprehensive exam, thesis optional. *Entrance requirements:* For master's, GRE General Test, minimum GPA of 2.5. Additional exam requirements/recommendations for international students: Required—TOEFL (minimum score 525 paper-based; 71 iBT). *Application deadline:* For fall admission, 7/27 priority date for domestic and international students; for spring admission, 12/17 priority date for domestic and international students. Applications are processed on a rolling basis. Application fee: $30 ($130 for international students). Electronic applications accepted. *Financial support:* In 2014–15, 3 teaching assistantships with full tuition reimbursements (averaging $6,960 per year) were awarded; research assistantships, scholarships/grants, and unspecified assistantships also available. Support available to part-time students. Financial award application deadline: 2/15; financial award applicants required to submit FAFSA. *Faculty research:* Children with developmental disabilities, regional food product development and marketing, parent education. *Unit head:* Dr. Lisa LeBleu, Coordinator, 731-881-7116, Fax: 731-881-7106, E-mail: llebleu@utm.edu. *Application contact:* Jolene L. Cunningham, Student Services Specialist, 731-881-7012, Fax: 731-881-7499, E-mail: jcunningham@utm.edu. Website: http://www.utm.edu/departments/caas/fcs/index.php

The University of Texas at Austin, Graduate School, College of Natural Sciences, School of Human Ecology, Austin, TX 78712-1111. Offers human development and family sciences (MA, PhD); nutritional sciences (MA, PhD), including nutrition (MA), nutritional sciences (PhD); textile and apparel technology (MS). *Degree requirements:* For master's, thesis; for doctorate, thesis/dissertation. *Entrance requirements:* For master's and doctorate, GRE General Test. Electronic applications accepted.

University of Wisconsin–Madison, Graduate School, School of Human Ecology, Madison, WI 53706. Offers consumer behavior and family economics (MS, PhD); design studies (MFA, MS, PhD); human development and family studies (MS, PhD). Terminal master's awarded for partial completion of doctoral program. *Degree requirements:* For master's, thesis (for some programs); for doctorate, comprehensive exam, thesis/dissertation. *Entrance requirements:* For master's, GRE General Test, portfolio (design studies), 3 letters of recommendation; for doctorate, GRE General Test. Additional exam requirements/recommendations for international students: Required—TOEFL (minimum score 580 paper-based; 92 iBT). Electronic applications accepted. *Expenses:* Tuition, state resident: full-time $10,723; part-time $745 per credit. Tuition, nonresident: full-time $24,054; part-time $1578 per credit. *Required fees:* $374 per semester. Tuition and fees vary according to course load, program and reciprocity agreements.

University of Wisconsin–Stevens Point, College of Professional Studies, School of Health Promotion and Human Development, Program in Human and Community Resources, Stevens Point, WI 54481-3897. Offers MS. Part-time programs available. *Degree requirements:* For master's, thesis or alternative. *Entrance requirements:* For master's, minimum GPA of 2.75.

Utah State University, School of Graduate Studies, Emma Eccles Jones College of Education and Human Services, Department of Family, Consumer, and Human Development, Logan, UT 84322. Offers family and human development (MFHD); family, consumer, and human development (MS, PhD), including adolescence/youth (MS), adult development/aging (MS), consumer science (MS), infancy/childhood (MS), marriage and family relations (MS), marriage and family therapy (MS). *Accreditation:* AAMFT/COAMFTE (one or more programs are accredited). Part-time and evening/weekend programs available. Postbaccalaureate distance learning degree programs offered (minimal on-campus study). *Degree requirements:* For master's, thesis; for doctorate, comprehensive exam, thesis/dissertation, competencies. *Entrance requirements:* For master's, GRE General Test or MAT, minimum GPA of 3.0, 3 letters of recommendation; for doctorate, GRE, minimum GPA of 3.0, 3 letters of recommendation. Additional exam requirements/recommendations for international students: Required—TOEFL. Electronic applications accepted. *Faculty research:* Marriage and family relations, adolescent problem behavior, family financial management, early literacy, mental health in the elderly, parent child attachment.

Western Michigan University, Graduate College, College of Education and Human Development, Department of Family and Consumer Sciences, Kalamazoo, MI 49008. Offers career and technical education (MA); family and consumer sciences (MA). *Application deadline:* For fall admission, 2/15 for domestic students. *Financial support:* Application deadline: 2/15. *Application contact:* Admissions and Orientation, 269-387-2000, Fax: 269-387-2096.

Child and Family Studies

Arizona State University at the Tempe campus, College of Liberal Arts and Sciences, School of Social and Family Dynamics, Tempe, AZ 85287-3701. Offers family and human development (MS, PhD); infant-family practice (MAS); marriage and family therapy (MAS); sociology (MA, PhD). Terminal master's awarded for partial completion of doctoral program. *Degree requirements:* For master's, thesis or alternative, interactive Program of Study (iPOS) submitted before completing 50 percent of required credit hours; for doctorate, thesis/dissertation, interactive Program of Study (iPOS) submitted before completing 50 percent of required credit hours. *Entrance requirements:* For master's and doctorate, GRE, minimum GPA of 3.0 or equivalent in last 2 years of work leading to bachelor's degree. Additional exam requirements/recommendations for international students: Required—TOEFL, IELTS, or PTE. Electronic applications accepted. *Expenses:* Contact institution.

Asbury University, School of Graduate and Professional Studies, Master of Social Work Program, Wilmore, KY 40390-1198. Offers child and family services (MSW). *Accreditation:* CSWE. *Degree requirements:* For master's, comprehensive exam, 954 praticum hours completed in agency. *Entrance requirements:* For master's, prerequisite courses in psychology, sociology, and statistics. Additional exam requirements/recommendations for international students: Required—TOEFL. Electronic applications accepted. *Expenses:* Contact institution. *Faculty research:* Integration of faith and practice, survivors of family violence, program evaluation, cross-cultural counseling.

Assumption College, Counseling Psychology Program, Worcester, MA 01609-1296. Offers child and family interventions (MA); cognitive-behavioral therapies (MA); counseling psychology (CAGS); general psychology (MA). Part-time and evening/weekend programs available. *Faculty:* 5 full-time (2 women), 9 part-time/adjunct (2 women). *Students:* 48 full-time (37 women), 35 part-time (33 women); includes 10 minority (3 Black or African American, non-Hispanic/Latino; 3 Asian, non-Hispanic/Latino; 2 Hispanic/Latino; 2 Two or more races, non-Hispanic/Latino), 3 international. Average age 27. 78 applicants, 60% accepted, 15 enrolled. In 2014, 42 master's, 2 other advanced degrees awarded. *Degree requirements:* For master's, comprehensive exam, internship, practicum; for CAGS, comprehensive exam. *Entrance requirements:* For master's, 3 letters of recommendation, resume, essay, psychology prerequisite coursework; for CAGS, 3 letters of recommendation, resume, interview, essay, master's degree in counseling psychology or mental health counseling. Additional exam requirements/recommendations for international students: Required—TOEFL (minimum score 540 paper-based; 76 iBT), IELTS (minimum score 6). *Application deadline:* For fall admission, 3/6 for domestic and international students; for winter admission, 2/1 for domestic students; for spring admission, 10/3 for domestic and international students; for summer admission, 2/6 for domestic and international students. Application fee: $30. Electronic applications accepted. *Expenses: Tuition:* Full-time $10,620; part-time $590 per credit. *Required fees:* $20 per term. Full-time tuition and fees vary according to course load and program. *Financial support:* In 2014–15, 21 students received support, including 16 fellowships with full tuition reimbursements available; tuition waivers (full and partial), unspecified assistantships, and institutional discounts also available. Financial award application deadline: 3/7; financial award applicants required to submit FAFSA. *Faculty research:* Mood disorders, adjustment to life-threatening illness, perception of movement, socioemotional development of young children, discovery versus disclosure. *Unit head:* Dr. Leonard A. Doerfler, Director, 508-767-7549, Fax: 508-767-7263, E-mail: doerfler@assumption.edu. *Application contact:* Dr. Landy Johnson, Director of Operations for Graduate and Professional Studies, 508-767-7666, Fax: 508-767-7030, E-mail: graduate@assumption.edu. Website: http://graduate.assumption.edu/counseling-psychology/masterofarts

Auburn University, Graduate School, College of Human Sciences, Department of Human Development and Family Studies, Auburn University, AL 36849. Offers MS, PhD. *Accreditation:* AAMFT/COAMFTE (one or more programs are accredited). Part-time programs available. *Faculty:* 18 full-time (10 women), 2 part-time/adjunct (both women). *Students:* 26 full-time (24 women), 16 part-time (9 women); includes 9 minority (6 Black or African American, non-Hispanic/Latino; 2 Asian, non-Hispanic/Latino; 1 Hispanic/Latino), 2 international. Average age 27. 46 applicants, 26% accepted, 11 enrolled. In 2014, 15 master's, 6 doctorates awarded. *Degree requirements:* For master's, thesis, oral exam; for doctorate, thesis/dissertation. *Entrance requirements:* For master's, GRE General Test; for doctorate, GRE General Test, master's degree. *Application deadline:* For fall admission, 7/7 for domestic students; for spring admission, 11/24 for domestic students. Applications are processed on a rolling basis. Application fee: $50 ($60 for international students). *Expenses:* Tuition, state resident: full-time $8586; part-time $477 per credit hour. Tuition, nonresident: full-time $25,758; part-time $1431 per credit hour. *Required fees:* $804 per semester. Tuition and fees vary according to degree level and program. *Financial support:* Research assistantships, teaching assistantships, and Federal Work-Study available. Support available to part-time students. Financial award application deadline: 3/15; financial award applicants required to submit FAFSA. *Faculty research:* Family influences on personality and social

development, parent-child relations, infancy, day care, parent education. *Unit head:* Dr. Joe F. Pittman, Jr., Head, 334-844-3242, E-mail: mbradbar@humsci.auburn.edu. *Application contact:* Dr. George Flowers, Dean of the Graduate School, 334-844-2125. Website: http://www.humsci.auburn.edu/hdfs/

Bank Street College of Education, Graduate School, Program in Child Life, New York, NY 10025. Offers MS. *Degree requirements:* For master's, thesis. *Entrance requirements:* For master's, interview, essays, 100 hours of volunteer experience in a child life setting. Additional exam requirements/recommendations for international students: Required—TOEFL (minimum score 600 paper-based; 100 iBT), IELTS (minimum score 7). *Faculty research:* Therapeutic play in child life setting, child advocacy, psychosocial and educational intervention with care of sick children.

Bank Street College of Education, Graduate School, Program in Infant and Family Development and Early Intervention, New York, NY 10025. Offers infant and family development (MS Ed); infant and family early childhood special and general education (MS Ed); infant and family/early childhood special education (Ed M). *Degree requirements:* For master's, thesis. *Entrance requirements:* For master's, interview, essays. Additional exam requirements/recommendations for international students: Required—TOEFL (minimum score 600 paper-based; 100 iBT), IELTS (minimum score 7). Electronic applications accepted. *Faculty research:* Early intervention, early attachment practice in infant and toddler childcare, parenting skills in adolescents.

Bowling Green State University, Graduate College, College of Education and Human Development, School of Family and Consumer Sciences, Bowling Green, OH 43403. Offers food and nutrition (MFCS); human development and family studies (MFCS). Part-time programs available. *Degree requirements:* For master's, thesis. *Entrance requirements:* For master's, GRE General Test, minimum GPA of 3.0. Additional exam requirements/recommendations for international students: Required—TOEFL. Electronic applications accepted. *Faculty research:* Public health, wellness, social issues and policies, ethnic foods, nutrition and aging.

Brandeis University, The Heller School for Social Policy and Management, Program in Public Policy, Waltham, MA 02454-9110. Offers aging (MPP); behavioral health (MPP); children, youth and families (MPP); general social policy (MPP); health (MPP); poverty alleviation and development (MPP); MPP/MA. *Degree requirements:* For master's, thesis. *Entrance requirements:* For master's, GRE, 3 letters of recommendation, statement of purpose, 3 to 5 years of professional experience. Additional exam requirements/recommendations for international students: Required—TOEFL (minimum score 600 paper-based; 100 iBT). Electronic applications accepted. *Faculty research:* Health and behavioral health, children and families, disabilities, aging policy, substance abuse, work, inequality and social change, women/gender, poverty alleviation.

Brandeis University, The Heller School for Social Policy and Management, Program in Social Policy, Waltham, MA 02454-9110. Offers assets and inequalities (PhD); children, youth and families (PhD); global health and development (PhD); health and behavioral health (PhD). *Degree requirements:* For doctorate, comprehensive exam, thesis/dissertation, qualifying paper, 2-year residency. *Entrance requirements:* For doctorate, GRE General Test, 3 letters of recommendation, statement of purpose, writing sample, at least 3-5 years of professional experience. Additional exam requirements/recommendations for international students: Required—TOEFL (minimum score 600 paper-based; 100 iBT). Electronic applications accepted. *Faculty research:* Health; mental health; substance abuse; children, youth, and families; aging; international and community development; disabilities; work and inequality; hunger and poverty.

Brigham Young University, Graduate Studies, College of Family, Home, and Social Sciences, Program in Marriage, Family and Human Development, Provo, UT 84602. Offers MS, PhD. *Accreditation:* AAMFT/COAMFTE. *Faculty:* 24 full-time (5 women). *Students:* 23 full-time (11 women); includes 1 minority (Two or more races, non-Hispanic/Latino), 4 international. Average age 30. 20 applicants, 35% accepted, 7 enrolled. In 2014, 1 master's, 2 doctorates awarded. *Degree requirements:* For master's, thesis; for doctorate, comprehensive exam, thesis/dissertation. *Entrance requirements:* For master's and doctorate, GRE General Test, minimum GPA of 3.0 in last 60 semester hours, letters of recommendation. Additional exam requirements/recommendations for international students: Required—TOEFL (minimum score 580 paper-based; 85 iBT), IELTS (minimum score 7). *Application deadline:* For fall admission, 1/10 for domestic and international students. Application fee: $50. Electronic applications accepted. *Expenses: Tuition:* Full-time $6310; part-time $371 per credit hour. Tuition and fees vary according to program and student's religious affiliation. *Financial support:* In 2014–15, 14 students received support, including 14 research assistantships with full and partial tuition reimbursements available (averaging $8,560 per year), 2 teaching assistantships with full and partial tuition reimbursements available (averaging $2,800 per year); scholarships/grants and unspecified assistantships also available. Financial award application deadline: 3/20. *Faculty research:* Family studies and family process, marriage, adolescence and emerging adulthood, adult development and aging, child development. *Unit head:* Dr. Dean M. Busby, Director, School of Life, 801-422-2069, Fax: 801-422-0230, E-mail: dean_busby@byu.edu. *Application contact:* Graduate Secretary, 801-422-2060, E-mail: mfhdgrad@byu.edu. Website: http://mfhd.byu.edu

Brock University, Faculty of Graduate Studies, Faculty of Social Sciences, Program in Child and Youth Studies, St. Catharines, ON L2S 3A1, Canada. Offers MA. Part-time programs available. *Degree requirements:* For master's, thesis. *Entrance requirements:* For master's, honors BA. Additional exam requirements/recommendations for international students: Required—TOEFL (minimum score 550 paper-based; 80 iBT), IELTS (minimum score 6.5), TWE (minimum score 4). Electronic applications accepted. *Faculty research:* Cognitive mechanisms, youth resilience, developmental disabilities, parent-child interactions and communication.

California State University, East Bay, Office of Academic Programs and Graduate Studies, College of Letters, Arts, and Social Sciences, Department of Social Work, Hayward, CA 94542-3000. Offers children, youth, and family services (MSW); community mental health services (MSW). *Accreditation:* CSWE. *Degree requirements:* For master's, comprehensive exam. *Entrance requirements:* For master's, minimum GPA of 2.8; courses in statistics and either human biology, physiology, or anatomy; liberal arts or social science baccalaureate degree; 3 letters of recommendation; personal statement; consent to criminal background check; student professional liability insurance. Additional exam requirements/recommendations for international students: Required—TOEFL (minimum score 550 paper-based). *Application deadline:* For fall admission, 3/15 for domestic and international students. Applications are processed on a rolling basis. Application fee: $55. Electronic applications accepted. *Expenses:* Tuition, state resident: full-time $7830; part-time $1302 per credit hour. Tuition, nonresident: full-time $16,368. *Required fees:* $327 per quarter. Tuition and fees vary according to course load and program. *Financial support:* Fellowships, career-related internships or fieldwork, Federal Work-Study, institutionally sponsored loans, and scholarships/grants available. Support available to part-time students. Financial award application deadline: 3/2; financial award applicants required to submit FAFSA. *Unit head:* Dr. Evaon Wong-Kim, Chair, 510-885-2148, E-mail: evaon@csueastbay.edu. *Application contact:* Dr. Donna Wiley, Interim Associate Vice President for Academic Programs and Graduate Studies, 510-885-3716, Fax: 510-885-4777, E-mail:

donna.wiley@csueastbay.edu. Website: http://www20.csueastbay.edu/class/departments/socialwork/

California State University, Los Angeles, Graduate Studies, College of Health and Human Services, Department of Child and Family Studies, Los Angeles, CA 90032-8530. Offers child development (MA). Part-time and evening/weekend programs available. *Degree requirements:* For master's, comprehensive exam, project or thesis. *Entrance requirements:* Additional exam requirements/recommendations for international students: Required—TOEFL (minimum score 500 paper-based). *Expenses:* Tuition, state resident: full-time $6738; part-time $3609 per year. Tuition, nonresident: full-time $15,666; part-time $8073 per year. Tuition and fees vary according to course load, degree level and program. *Faculty research:* Nutrition education, laundry product and fabric durability, computer usage in public school home economics.

California State University, San Marcos, College of Education, Health and Human Services, Program in Social Work, San Marcos, CA 92096-0001. Offers behavioral health (MSW); children, youth and families (MSW). *Degree requirements:* For master's, thesis, capstone project. *Expenses:* Expenses: $525 per unit. *Unit head:* Dr. Blake Beecher, Chair, 760-750-7373. *Application contact:* Admissions, 760-750-4848, Fax: 760-750-3248, E-mail: apply@csusm.edu. Website: http://www.csusm.edu/socialwork/

Capella University, Harold Abel School of Social and Behavioral Science, Master's Programs in Counseling, Minneapolis, MN 55402. Offers child and adolescent development (MS); general addiction counseling (MS); general marriage and family counseling/therapy (MS); general mental health counseling (MS); general school counseling (MS).

Central Michigan University, College of Graduate Studies, College of Education and Human Services, Department of Human Environmental Studies, Mount Pleasant, MI 48859. Offers apparel product development and merchandising technology (MS); gerontology (Graduate Certificate); human development and family studies (MA); nutrition and dietetics (MS). Part-time and evening/weekend programs available. *Degree requirements:* For master's, thesis or alternative. Electronic applications accepted. *Faculty research:* Human growth and development, family studies and human sexuality, human nutrition and dietetics, apparel and textile retailing, computer-aided design for apparel.

Central Washington University, Graduate Studies and Research, College of Education and Professional Studies, Department of Family and Consumer Sciences, Ellensburg, WA 98926. Offers career and technical education (MS); family and consumer sciences education (MS); family studies (MS). Part-time programs available. *Degree requirements:* For master's, thesis or alternative. *Entrance requirements:* For master's, minimum GPA of 3.0. Additional exam requirements/recommendations for international students: Required—TOEFL (minimum score 550 paper-based; 79 iBT). Electronic applications accepted.

Colorado State University, Graduate School, College of Health and Human Sciences, Department of Human Development and Family Studies, Fort Collins, CO 80523-1570. Offers MS, PhD. *Accreditation:* AAMFT/COAMFTE. *Faculty:* 16 full-time (12 women). *Students:* 33 full-time (29 women), 8 part-time (all women); includes 6 minority (1 Black or African American, non-Hispanic/Latino; 2 Asian, non-Hispanic/Latino; 3 Hispanic/Latino), 1 international. Average age 28. 72 applicants, 22% accepted, 12 enrolled. In 2014, 7 master's, 2 doctorates awarded. Terminal master's awarded for partial completion of doctoral program. *Degree requirements:* For master's, thesis; for doctorate, comprehensive exam, thesis/dissertation, competency exams. *Entrance requirements:* For master's, GRE General Test, transcript, 3 letters of recommendation, minimum GPA of 3.0, BS/BA, background in family studies, course work in human development, family studies, and statistics; for doctorate, GRE General Test, transcript, 3 letters of recommendation, minimum GPA of 3.0, BS/BA, background in family studies, course work in human development, family studies, and statistics. Additional exam requirements/recommendations for international students: Required—TOEFL (minimum score 550 paper-based; 80 iBT), IELTS. *Application deadline:* For fall admission, 1/2 for domestic and international students. Application fee: $50. Electronic applications accepted. *Expenses:* Tuition, state resident: full-time $9348; part-time $519 per credit. Tuition, nonresident: full-time $22,916; part-time $1273 per credit. *Required fees:* $1584. *Financial support:* In 2014–15, 31 students received support, including 1 fellowship (averaging $37,767 per year), 14 research assistantships with full tuition reimbursements available (averaging $9,223 per year), 16 teaching assistantships with full tuition reimbursements available (averaging $7,338 per year); scholarships/grants and unspecified assistantships also available. Financial award application deadline: 1/2; financial award applicants required to submit FAFSA. *Faculty research:* Risk, resilience and developmental psychopathology treatment; intervention and prevention science; emotion regulation and relational processes; adult development and aging. *Total annual research expenditures:* $1.7 million. *Unit head:* Dr. Lise Youngblade, Department Head, 970-491-3581, Fax: 970-491-7975, E-mail: lise.youngblade@colostate.edu. *Application contact:* Aimee Walker, Graduate Program Advisor, 970-491-3971, Fax: 970-491-7975, E-mail: aimee.walker@colostate.edu. Website: http://www.hdfs.chhs.colostate.edu/

Concordia University, School of Graduate Studies, Faculty of Arts and Science, Department of Education, Program in Child Study, Montréal, QC H3G 1M8, Canada. Offers MA. *Degree requirements:* For master's, one foreign language, thesis optional. *Entrance requirements:* For master's, minimum B average in undergraduate course work. *Faculty research:* Development and family relations, children and technology, cooperative learning strategies, exceptional children, second language acquisition.

Concordia University, St. Paul, College of Education and Science, St. Paul, MN 55104-5494. Offers criminal justice (MA); curriculum and instruction (MA Ed), including K-12 reading; differentiated instruction (MA Ed); early childhood education (MA Ed); educational leadership (MA Ed); educational technology (MA Ed); exercise science (MA); family life education (MA); forensic mental health (MA); K-12 principal licensure (Ed S); K-12 reading (Certificate); physical therapy (DPT); special education (MA Ed, Certificate), including autism spectrum disorder (MA Ed), emotional and behavioral disorders (MA Ed), learning disabilities (MA Ed); sports management (MA); superintendent (Ed S). *Accreditation:* NCATE. Part-time and evening/weekend programs available. Postbaccalaureate distance learning degree programs offered (minimal on-campus study). *Faculty:* 16 full-time (9 women), 122 part-time/adjunct (72 women). *Students:* 1,147 full-time (810 women), 118 part-time (84 women); includes 147 minority (71 Black or African American, non-Hispanic/Latino; 12 American Indian or Alaska Native, non-Hispanic/Latino; 28 Asian, non-Hispanic/Latino; 20 Hispanic/Latino; 1 Native Hawaiian or other Pacific Islander, non-Hispanic/Latino; 15 Two or more races, non-Hispanic/Latino), 47 international. Average age 34. 874 applicants, 64% accepted, 440 enrolled. In 2014, 348 master's, 85 other advanced degrees awarded. *Degree requirements:* For master's, thesis (for some programs); for doctorate, clinical internships; capstone projects; for other advanced degree, e-folio review of competencies. *Entrance requirements:* For master's, official transcripts from regionally-accredited institution stating the conferral of a bachelor's degree with minimum cumulative GPA of 3.0; personal statement; professional resume; practitioner in field through work or volunteerism; resume; for doctorate, GRE (taken within last five years),

bachelor's degree with minimum cumulative GPA of 3.0; 100 physical therapy observation hours; 2 letters of recommendation; for other advanced degree, at least three years of teaching experience, master's degree, valid MN teaching license. Additional exam requirements/recommendations for international students: Recommended—TOEFL (minimum score 547 paper-based; 78 iBT), IELTS (minimum score 6). *Application deadline:* For fall admission, 8/1 for domestic and international students; for spring admission, 12/1 for domestic and international students; for summer admission, 5/1 for domestic and international students. Applications are processed on a rolling basis. Application fee: $50. Electronic applications accepted. *Expenses: Tuition:* Full-time $4416; part-time $368 per credit. Tuition and fees vary according to degree level and program. *Financial support:* Applicants required to submit FAFSA. *Unit head:* Dr. Donald Helmstetter, Dean, 651-641-8227, Fax: 651-641-8807, E-mail: helmstetter@csp.edu. *Application contact:* Kimberly Craig, Associate Vice President, Cohort Enrollment Management, 651-603-6223, Fax: 651-603-6320, E-mail: craig@csp.edu.

Concordia University Wisconsin, Graduate Programs, Department of Education, Program in Family Studies, Mequon, WI 53097-2402. Offers MS Ed. *Degree requirements:* For master's, comprehensive exam, thesis or alternative. *Entrance requirements:* For master's, minimum GPA of 3.0. Additional exam requirements/recommendations for international students: Required—TOEFL.

Cornell University, Graduate School, Graduate Fields of Human Ecology, Field of Human Development, Ithaca, NY 14853-0001. Offers developmental psychology (MA, PhD), including cognitive development, developmental psychopathology, ecology of human development, social and personality development; human development and family studies (MA, PhD), including ecology of human development, family studies and the life course. *Degree requirements:* For doctorate, comprehensive exam, thesis/ dissertation, pre-doctoral research project, teaching experience. *Entrance requirements:* For doctorate, GRE General Test, 2 letters of recommendation. Additional exam requirements/recommendations for international students: Required—TOEFL (minimum score 550 paper-based; 77 iBT). Electronic applications accepted. *Faculty research:* Cognitive development, developmental psychopathology, ecology of human development, family studies and the life course, social and personality development.

Dallas Theological Seminary, Graduate Programs, Dallas, TX 75204-6499. Offers adult education (Th M); apologetics (Th M); Bible backgrounds (Th M); Bible translation (Th M); Biblical and theological studies (Certificate); biblical counseling (MA); biblical exegesis and linguistics (MA); biblical exposition (PhD); biblical studies (MA); Biblical theology (Th M); children's education (Th M); Christian education (MA, D Min); Christian leadership (MA); cross-cultural ministries (MA); educational administration (Th M); educational leadership (Th M); evangelism and discipleship (Th M); exposition of Biblical books (Th M); family life education (Th M); general studies (Th M); Hebrew and cognate studies (Th M); hermeneutics (Th M); historical theology (Th M); homiletics (Th M); intercultural ministries (Th M); Jesus studies (Th M); leadership studies (Th M); media and communication (MA); media arts (Th M); ministry (D Min); ministry with women (Th M); New Testament studies (Th M, PhD); Old Testament studies (Th M, PhD); parachurch ministries (Th M); pastoral care and counseling (Th M); pastoral theology and practice (Th M); philosophy (Th M); sacred theology (STM); spiritual formation (Th M); systematic theology (Th M); teaching in Christian institutions (Th M); theological studies (PhD); urban ministries (Th M); worship studies (Th M); youth education (Th M). *Accreditation:* ATS (one or more programs are accredited). Part-time programs available. Postbaccalaureate distance learning degree programs offered (no on-campus study). *Degree requirements:* For master's, variable foreign language requirement, thesis (for some programs); for doctorate, 2 foreign languages, thesis/dissertation. *Entrance requirements:* For master's, GRE or MAT (if minimum undergraduate cumulative GPA is below 2.5 or undergraduate degree is unaccredited). Additional exam requirements/recommendations for international students: Required—TOEFL (minimum score 575 paper-based; 85 iBT), TWE. Electronic applications accepted.

East Carolina University, Graduate School, College of Human Ecology, Department of Child Development and Family Relations, Greenville, NC 27858-4353. Offers birth through kindergarten education (MA Ed); child development and family relations (MS); family and consumer sciences (MA Ed); marriage and family therapy (MS); medical family therapy (PhD). *Accreditation:* AAMFT/COAMFTE. Part-time programs available. *Degree requirements:* For master's, comprehensive exam, thesis optional. *Expenses:* Tuition, state resident: full-time $4223. Tuition, nonresident: full-time $16,540. *Required fees:* $2184. *Faculty research:* Child care quality, mental health delivery systems for children, family violence.

Fairfield University, Graduate School of Education and Allied Professions, Fairfield, CT 06824. Offers applied behavior analysis (ATC); applied psychology (MA); clinical mental health counseling (MA, CAS); early childhood studies (ATC); educational technology (MA); elementary education (MA, CAS); family studies (MA); integration of spirituality and religion in counseling (ATC); marriage and family therapy (MA); school counseling (MA, CAS); school psychology (MA, CAS); school-based marriage and family therapy (ATC); secondary education (MA); special education (MA, CAS); substance abuse counseling (ATC); teaching (Certificate); teaching and foundations (MA, CAS); TESOL, world languages, and bilingual education (MA, CAS). *Accreditation:* NCATE. Part-time and evening/weekend programs available. *Faculty:* 23 full-time (19 women), 32 part-time/adjunct (25 women). *Students:* 148 full-time (131 women), 286 part-time (238 women); includes 81 minority (18 Black or African American, non-Hispanic/Latino; 1 American Indian or Alaska Native, non-Hispanic/Latino; 14 Asian, non-Hispanic/Latino; 39 Hispanic/Latino; 9 Two or more races, non-Hispanic/Latino), 13 international. Average age 34. 264 applicants, 54% accepted, 68 enrolled. In 2014, 142 master's awarded. *Degree requirements:* For master's, comprehensive exam. *Entrance requirements:* For master's, PRAXIS I (for certification programs), minimum GPA of 3.0, 2 recommendations, resume. Additional exam requirements/recommendations for international students: Required—TOEFL (minimum score 550 paper-based; 84 iBT) or IELTS (minimum score 7.5). *Application deadline:* For fall admission, 2/15 for international students; for spring admission, 10/1 for international students. Application fee: $60. Electronic applications accepted. *Expenses:* Expenses: $675 per credit hour. *Financial support:* In 2014–15, 55 students received support. Career-related internships or fieldwork and unspecified assistantships available. Financial award applicants required to submit FAFSA. *Faculty research:* Literacy, spirituality, special education, bilingual/multicultural education, mentoring and professional development. *Unit head:* Dr. Robert D. Hannafin, Dean, 203-254-4250, Fax: 203-254-4241, E-mail: rhannafin@fairfield.edu. *Application contact:* Marianne Gumpper, Director of Graduate and Continuing Studies Admission, 203-254-4184, Fax: 203-254-4073, E-mail: gradadmis@fairfield.edu.
Website: http://www.fairfield.edu/academics/schoolscollegescenters/graduateschoolofeducationalliedprofessions/graduateprograms/

Florida State University, The Graduate School, College of Human Sciences, Department of Family and Child Sciences, Tallahassee, FL 32306-1491. Offers family and child sciences (MS); family relations (PhD); marriage and family therapy (PhD). *Accreditation:* AAMFT/COAMFTE. Part-time programs available. *Faculty:* 14 full-time (10 women). *Students:* 28 full-time (20 women), 6 part-time (5 women); includes 12 minority (7 Black or African American, non-Hispanic/Latino; 4 Hispanic/Latino; 1 Two or

more races, non-Hispanic/Latino), 3 international. 39 applicants, 56% accepted, 16 enrolled. In 2014, 5 master's, 11 doctorates awarded. Terminal master's awarded for partial completion of doctoral program. *Degree requirements:* For master's, comprehensive exam, thesis optional; for doctorate, thesis/dissertation, preliminary examination; clinical examination (for marriage and family therapy). *Entrance requirements:* For master's and doctorate, GRE General Test, writing assessment, minimum GPA of 3.0. Additional exam requirements/recommendations for international students: Required—TOEFL (minimum score 80 iBT). *Application deadline:* For fall admission, 1/5 for domestic and international students; for spring admission, 11/1 priority date for domestic students, 10/1 priority date for international students. Applications are processed on a rolling basis. Application fee: $30. Electronic applications accepted. *Expenses:* Tuition, state resident: part-time $403.51 per credit hour. Tuition, nonresident: part-time $1004.85 per credit hour. *Required fees:* $75.81 per credit hour. One-time fee: $20 part-time. Tuition and fees vary according to campus/ location. *Financial support:* In 2014–15, 33 students received support, including 3 fellowships with partial tuition reimbursements available (averaging $1,094 per year), 6 research assistantships with partial tuition reimbursements available (averaging $6,942 per year), 34 teaching assistantships with full tuition reimbursements available (averaging $16,000 per year); career-related internships or fieldwork, Federal Work-Study, institutionally sponsored loans, scholarships/grants, health care benefits, and unspecified assistantships also available. Financial award application deadline: 1/5; financial award applicants required to submit FAFSA. *Faculty research:* Family therapy, parent-child relations, distressed families and foster care, marital processes, relational interventions, family structural complexity. *Unit head:* Dr. Lenore McWey, Interim Chair, 850-644-3217, Fax: 850-644-3439, E-mail: lmcwey@fsu.edu. *Application contact:* Donna Romano, Office Administrator, 850-644-3217, Fax: 850-644-3439, E-mail: dromano@fsu.edu.

Indiana University–Purdue University Indianapolis, School of Liberal Arts, Department of Sociology, Indianapolis, IN 46202. Offers family/gender studies (MA); medical sociology (MA); work/occupations (MA). *Faculty:* 17 full-time (8 women). *Students:* 9 full-time (7 women), 15 part-time (13 women); includes 3 minority (all Black or African American, non-Hispanic/Latino), 2 international. Average age 30. 16 applicants, 69% accepted, 6 enrolled. In 2014, 10 master's awarded. Application fee: $55 ($65 for international students). *Financial support:* Fellowships and teaching assistantships available. *Unit head:* Dr. Robert W. White, Chair, 317-278-5226, E-mail: rwwhite@iupui.edu. *Application contact:* Dr. Carrie E. Foote, Director of Graduate Studies, 317-274-8454, E-mail: foote@iupui.edu.
Website: http://liberalarts.iupui.edu/sociology/

Iowa State University of Science and Technology, Department of Human Development and Family Studies, Ames, IA 50011. Offers human development and family studies (MFCS, MS, PhD). *Accreditation:* AAMFT/COAMFTE. *Degree requirements:* For master's, thesis; for doctorate, thesis/dissertation. *Entrance requirements:* For master's and doctorate, GRE General Test. Additional exam requirements/recommendations for international students: Required—TOEFL (minimum score 550 paper-based; 79 iBT), IELTS (minimum score 6.5). Electronic applications accepted. *Faculty research:* Child development, early childhood education, family resource management and housing, life span studies.

Kansas State University, Graduate School, College of Human Ecology, Program in Human Ecology, Manhattan, KS 66506. Offers apparel and textiles (PhD); family life education and consultation (PhD); food service and hospitality management (PhD); lifespan and human development (PhD); marriage and family therapy (PhD); personal financial planning (PhD). *Students:* 51 full-time (31 women), 44 part-time (24 women); includes 20 minority (8 Black or African American, non-Hispanic/Latino; 1 American Indian or Alaska Native, non-Hispanic/Latino; 3 Asian, non-Hispanic/Latino; 4 Hispanic/ Latino; 1 Native Hawaiian or other Pacific Islander, non-Hispanic/Latino; 3 Two or more races, non-Hispanic/Latino), 17 international. Average age 39. 44 applicants, 39% accepted, 14 enrolled. In 2014, 17 doctorates awarded. *Degree requirements:* For doctorate, thesis/dissertation. *Application deadline:* For fall admission, 2/1 priority date for domestic and international students; for spring admission, 8/1 priority date for domestic and international students. Applications are processed on a rolling basis. Application fee: $50 ($75 for international students). Electronic applications accepted. *Financial support:* Application deadline: 3/1. *Total annual research expenditures:* $1.8 million. *Unit head:* Dr. John Buckwalter, Dean, 785-532-5500, Fax: 785-532-5504, E-mail: jbb3@ksu.edu. *Application contact:* Application Contact, 785-532-5500, Fax: 785-532-5504, E-mail: he@ksu.edu.

Kansas State University, Graduate School, College of Human Ecology, School of Family Studies and Human Services, Manhattan, KS 66506. Offers communication sciences and disorders (MS); conflict resolution (Graduate Certificate); early childhood education (MS); family and community service (MS); family studies (MS); life span human development (MS); marriage and family therapy (MS); personal financial planning (MS, Graduate Certificate); youth development (MS, Graduate Certificate). *Accreditation:* AAMFT/COAMFTE; ASHA. Part-time programs available. Postbaccalaureate distance learning degree programs offered (no on-campus study). *Faculty:* 39 full-time (26 women), 9 part-time/adjunct (7 women). *Students:* 69 full-time (57 women), 141 part-time (99 women); includes 48 minority (15 Black or African American, non-Hispanic/Latino; 3 American Indian or Alaska Native, non-Hispanic/ Latino; 3 Asian, non-Hispanic/Latino; 21 Hispanic/Latino; 2 Native Hawaiian or other Pacific Islander, non-Hispanic/Latino; 4 Two or more races, non-Hispanic/Latino), 3 international. Average age 31. 203 applicants, 38% accepted, 57 enrolled. In 2014, 48 master's, 28 other advanced degrees awarded. *Degree requirements:* For master's, comprehensive exam (for some programs), thesis optional. *Entrance requirements:* For master's, GRE, minimum GPA of 3.0 in last 2 years of undergraduate study. Additional exam requirements/recommendations for international students: Required—TOEFL (minimum score 600 paper-based). *Application deadline:* For fall admission, 2/1 priority date for domestic students, 1/1 priority date for international students; for spring admission, 10/1 priority date for domestic students, 8/1 priority date for international students; for summer admission, 2/1 priority date for domestic students, 12/1 priority date for international students. Applications are processed on a rolling basis. Application fee: $50 ($75 for international students). Electronic applications accepted. *Financial support:* In 2014–15, 25 research assistantships (averaging $10,000 per year), 9 teaching assistantships with full tuition reimbursements (averaging $10,000 per year) were awarded; unspecified assistantships also available. Financial award application deadline: 3/1. *Faculty research:* Health and security of military families, personal and family risk assessment and evaluation, disorders of communication and swallowing, families and health, financial decision-making. *Total annual research expenditures:* $8.4 million. *Unit head:* Dr. Dottie Durband, Director, 785-532-5510, Fax: 785-532-5505, E-mail: dottie@ksu.edu. *Application contact:* Connie Fechter, Administrative Specialist, 785-532-5510, Fax: 785-532-5505, E-mail: fechter@ksu.edu.
Website: http://www.he.k-state.edu/fshs/

Kent State University, Graduate School of Education, Health, and Human Services, School of Lifespan Development and Educational Sciences, Program in Human Development and Family Studies, Kent, OH 44242-0001. Offers MA. *Faculty:* 8 full-time (5 women), 15 part-time/adjunct (13 women). *Students:* 7 full-time (6 women), 9 part-

time (all women); includes 4 minority (all Black or African American, non-Hispanic/Latino), 1 international. 12 applicants, 25% accepted. In 2014, 2 master's awarded. *Degree requirements:* For master's, thesis optional. *Entrance requirements:* For master's, minimum undergraduate GPA of 3.0, 3 letters of reference, goals statement. Additional exam requirements/recommendations for international students: Required—TOEFL (minimum score 550 paper-based; 80 iBT). Application fee: $45 ($60 for international students). *Expenses:* Tuition, state resident: full-time $8730; part-time $485 per credit hour. Tuition, nonresident: full-time $14,886; part-time $827 per credit hour. Tuition and fees vary according to campus/location and program. *Financial support:* In 2014–15, 6 research assistantships (averaging $8,500 per year) were awarded. *Unit head:* Dr. Kelly Cighy, Coordinator, 330-672-2449, E-mail: kcichy@kent.edu. *Application contact:* Nancy Miller, Academic Program Director, Office of Graduate Student Services, 330-672-2576, Fax: 330-672-9162, E-mail: ogs@kent.edu.

Liberty University, School of Behavioral Sciences, Lynchburg, VA 24515. Offers advanced clinical skills (PhD); clinical mental health counseling (MA); counselor education and supervision (PhD); human services counseling (MA), including addictions and recovery, business, child and family law, Christian ministries, criminal justice, crisis response and trauma, executive leadership, health and wellness, life coaching, marriage and family, military resilience; marriage and family therapy (MA); military resilience (Certificate); professional counseling (MA). Part-time programs available. Postbaccalaureate distance learning degree programs offered (minimal on-campus study). *Students:* 3,009 full-time (2,433 women), 6,251 part-time (4,981 women); includes 2,959 minority (2,520 Black or African American, non-Hispanic/Latino; 49 American Indian or Alaska Native, non-Hispanic/Latino; 51 Asian, non-Hispanic/Latino; 97 Hispanic/Latino; 9 Native Hawaiian or other Pacific Islander, non-Hispanic/Latino; 233 Two or more races, non-Hispanic/Latino), 153 international. Average age 38. 6,645 applicants, 55% accepted, 2039 enrolled. In 2014, 2,410 master's, 11 doctorates, 2 other advanced degrees awarded. *Application deadline:* Applications are processed on a rolling basis. Application fee: $50. Electronic applications accepted. *Financial support:* Applicants required to submit FAFSA. *Unit head:* Dr. Ronald Hawkins, Founding Dean, School of Behavioral Sciences. *Application contact:* Jay Bridge, Director of Admissions, 800-424-9595, Fax: 800-628-7977, E-mail: gradadmissions@liberty.edu.

Loma Linda University, School of Science and Technology, Department of Counseling and Family Science, Loma Linda, CA 92350. Offers MA, MS, DMFT, PhD, Certificate, MA/Certificate. *Degree requirements:* For master's, comprehensive exam, thesis optional; for doctorate, comprehensive exam, thesis/dissertation (for some programs). *Entrance requirements:* For master's, minimum GPA of 3.0; for doctorate, GRE. Additional exam requirements/recommendations for international students: Required—TOEFL (minimum score 550 paper-based), MTELP. Electronic applications accepted.

Miami University, College of Education, Health and Society, Department of Family Studies and Social Work, Oxford, OH 45056. Offers MA. Part-time programs available. *Students:* 32 full-time (31 women), 1 (woman) part-time; includes 8 minority (7 Black or African American, non-Hispanic/Latino; 1 Two or more races, non-Hispanic/Latino). Average age 27. In 2014, 12 master's awarded. *Entrance requirements:* For master's, statement of goals and accomplishments; three letters of reference. Additional exam requirements/recommendations for international students: Recommended—TOEFL (minimum score 80 iBT), IELTS (minimum score 6.5), TSE (minimum score 54). *Application deadline:* For fall admission, 2/1 for domestic and international students. Application fee: $50. Electronic applications accepted. *Expenses:* Tuition, state resident: full-time $12,887; part-time $537 per credit hour. Tuition, nonresident: full-time $28,449; part-time $1186 per credit hour. *Required fees:* $530; $24 per credit hour. $30 per quarter. Part-time tuition and fees vary according to course load and program. *Financial support:* Research assistantships with full and partial tuition reimbursements and teaching assistantships with full and partial tuition reimbursements available. Financial award application deadline: 2/15; financial award applicants required to submit FAFSA. *Unit head:* Dr. Howard Karger, Professor and Chair, 513-529-2323, E-mail: kargerhj@miamioh.edu. *Application contact:* Kellie Bottoms, Graduate Secretary, 513-529-2323, E-mail: penninka@miamioh.edu. Website: http://www.MiamiOH.edu/fsw

Michigan State University, The Graduate School, College of Social Science, Department of Family and Child Ecology, East Lansing, MI 48824. Offers child development (MA); community services (MS); family and child ecology (PhD); family studies (MA); marriage and family therapy (MA); youth development (MA). *Accreditation:* AAMFT/COAMFTE (one or more programs are accredited). *Entrance requirements:* For master's, GRE General Test, minimum GPA of 3.0 in last 2 years of undergraduate course work, 3 letters of recommendation; for doctorate, GRE General Test, minimum GPA of 3.0, 3 letters of recommendation, background in behavioral sciences. Additional exam requirements/recommendations for international students: Required—TOEFL. Electronic applications accepted.

Mississippi State University, College of Agriculture and Life Sciences, School of Human Sciences, Mississippi State, MS 39762. Offers agricultural sciences (PhD), including agriculture and extension education; agriculture and extension education (MS); human development and family studies (MS, PhD). *Accreditation:* NCATE (one or more programs are accredited). Part-time programs available. *Faculty:* 23 full-time (13 women), 1 part-time/adjunct (0 women). *Students:* 26 full-time (20 women), 65 part-time (41 women); includes 19 minority (17 Black or African American, non-Hispanic/Latino; 1 Hispanic/Latino; 1 Two or more races, non-Hispanic/Latino), 3 international. Average age 36. 37 applicants, 68% accepted, 20 enrolled. In 2014, 11 master's, 4 doctorates awarded. *Degree requirements:* For master's, thesis optional, comprehensive oral or written exam. *Entrance requirements:* For master's, GRE, minimum GPA of 2.75 in last 4 semesters of course work; for doctorate, minimum GPA of 3.0 on prior graduate work. Additional exam requirements/recommendations for international students: Required—TOEFL (minimum score 477 paper-based; 53 iBT); Recommended—IELTS (minimum score 4.5). *Application deadline:* For fall admission, 7/1 for domestic students, 5/1 for international students; for spring admission, 11/1 for domestic students, 9/1 for international students. Applications are processed on a rolling basis. Application fee: $60. Electronic applications accepted. *Expenses:* Tuition, state resident: full-time $7140; part-time $783 per credit hour. Tuition, nonresident: full-time $18,478; part-time $2043 per credit hour. *Financial support:* In 2014–15, 13 research assistantships (averaging $12,363 per year), 2 teaching assistantships with full tuition reimbursements (averaging $13,088 per year) were awarded; Federal Work-Study, institutionally sponsored loans, and unspecified assistantships also available. Financial award application deadline: 4/1; financial award applicants required to submit FAFSA. *Faculty research:* Animal welfare, agroscience, information technology, learning styles, problem solving. *Unit head:* Dr. Michael Newman, Director and Professor, 662-325-2950, E-mail: mnewman@humansci.msstate.edu. *Application contact:* Dr. Tommy Phillips, Graduate Coordinator, 662-325-0655, E-mail: tphillips@humansci.msstate.edu. Website: http://www.humansci.msstate.edu

Missouri State University, Graduate College, College of Education, Department of Childhood Education and Family Studies, Program in Early Childhood and Family Development, Springfield, MO 65897. Offers MS. Part-time programs available. Postbaccalaureate distance learning degree programs offered. *Students:* 11 full-time (10

women), 40 part-time (39 women); includes 8 minority (3 Black or African American, non-Hispanic/Latino; 1 Asian, non-Hispanic/Latino; 2 Hispanic/Latino; 2 Two or more races, non-Hispanic/Latino), 4 international. Average age 31. 19 applicants, 95% accepted, 14 enrolled. In 2014, 6 master's awarded. *Entrance requirements:* For master's, GRE, minimum GPA of 3.0. Additional exam requirements/recommendations for international students: Required—TOEFL (minimum score 550 paper-based; 79 iBT). *Application deadline:* For fall admission, 7/20 priority date for domestic students, 5/1 for international students; for spring admission, 12/20 priority date for domestic students, 9/1 for international students. Applications are processed on a rolling basis. Application fee: $35 ($50 for international students). Electronic applications accepted. *Expenses:* Tuition, state resident: full-time $2250; part-time $250 per credit hour. Tuition, nonresident: full-time $4509; part-time $501 per credit hour. Tuition and fees vary according to course level, course load and program. *Financial support:* Federal Work-Study, institutionally sponsored loans, scholarships/grants, and unspecified assistantships available. Financial award application deadline: 3/31; financial award applicants required to submit FAFSA. *Unit head:* Dr. Joanna Brigden, Program Coordinator, 417-836-8403, Fax: 417-836-8900, E-mail: cefs@missouristate.edu. *Application contact:* Misty Stewart, Coordinator of Admissions and Recruitment, 417-836-5079, Fax: 417-836-6200, E-mail: mistystewart@missouristate.edu. Website: http://education.missouristate.edu/ecfd/

Montclair State University, The Graduate School, College of Education and Human Services, Doctoral Program in Family Studies, Montclair, NJ 07043-1624. Offers PhD. Part-time and evening/weekend programs available. *Students:* 11 full-time (9 women), 5 part-time (all women); includes 7 minority (1 Black or African American, non-Hispanic/Latino; 4 Hispanic/Latino; 2 Two or more races, non-Hispanic/Latino). Average age 35. 16 applicants, 38% accepted, 6 enrolled. *Degree requirements:* For doctorate, comprehensive exam, thesis/dissertation. *Entrance requirements:* For doctorate, GRE General Test, interview, 3 letters of recommendation, essay. Additional exam requirements/recommendations for international students: Required—TOEFL (minimum score 83 iBT), IELTS (minimum score 6.5). *Application deadline:* For fall admission, 2/1 for domestic students. Application fee: $60. Electronic applications accepted. *Expenses:* Tuition, state resident: full-time $9960; part-time $553.35 per credit. Tuition, nonresident: full-time $15,074; part-time $837.43 per credit. *Required fees:* $1595; $88.63 per credit. Tuition and fees vary according to degree level and program. *Financial support:* Federal Work-Study, scholarships/grants, and unspecified assistantships available. Support available to part-time students. Financial award application deadline: 3/1; financial award applicants required to submit FAFSA. *Unit head:* Dr. Ada Beth Cutler, Dean, 973-655-5167, E-mail: cutler@mail.montclair.edu. *Application contact:* Amy Aiello, Executive Director of The Graduate School, 973-655-5147, Fax: 973-655-7869, E-mail: graduate.school@montclair.edu. Website: http://www.montclair.edu/cehs/academics/departments/fcs/academic-programs/family-studies/

Montclair State University, The Graduate School, College of Education and Human Services, Program in Family and Child Studies, Montclair, NJ 07043-1624. Offers MA. Part-time and evening/weekend programs available. *Students:* 3 full-time (all women), 4 part-time (3 women); includes 4 minority (3 Black or African American, non-Hispanic/Latino; 1 Hispanic/Latino). Average age 32. 15 applicants, 47% accepted, 7 enrolled. In 2014, 9 master's awarded. *Degree requirements:* For master's, comprehensive exam, thesis or alternative. *Entrance requirements:* For master's, GRE General Test, essay, 2 letters of recommendation. Additional exam requirements/recommendations for international students: Required—TOEFL (minimum score 83 iBT), IELTS (minimum score 6.5). *Application deadline:* Applications are processed on a rolling basis. Application fee: $60. Electronic applications accepted. *Expenses:* Tuition, state resident: full-time $9960; part-time $553.35 per credit. Tuition, nonresident: full-time $15,074; part-time $837.43 per credit. *Required fees:* $1595; $88.63 per credit. Tuition and fees vary according to degree level and program. *Financial support:* Federal Work-Study, scholarships/grants, and unspecified assistantships available. Support available to part-time students. Financial award application deadline: 3/1; financial award applicants required to submit FAFSA. *Unit head:* Dr. Ada Beth Cutler, Dean, 973-655-5167, E-mail: cutler@mail.montclair.edu. *Application contact:* Amy Aiello, Executive Director of The Graduate School, 973-655-5147, Fax: 973-655-7869, E-mail: graduate.school@montclair.edu. Website: http://www.montclair.edu/graduate/programs-of-study/family-and-child-studies/

Montclair State University, The Graduate School, College of Humanities and Social Sciences, Adolescent Advocacy Certificate Program, Montclair, NJ 07043-1624. Offers Certificate. *Students:* 41 part-time (34 women); includes 30 minority (20 Black or African American, non-Hispanic/Latino; 1 American Indian or Alaska Native, non-Hispanic/Latino; 9 Hispanic/Latino). Average age 36. 17 applicants, 88% accepted, 15 enrolled. In 2014, 27 Certificates awarded. *Expenses:* Tuition, state resident: full-time $9960; part-time $553.35 per credit. Tuition, nonresident: full-time $15,074; part-time $837.43 per credit. *Required fees:* $1595; $88.63 per credit. Tuition and fees vary according to degree level and program. *Unit head:* Dr. Jason Dickinson, Coordinator. *Application contact:* Amy Aiello, Executive Director of The Graduate School, 973-655-5147, Fax: 973-655-7869, E-mail: graduate.school@montclair.edu.

Montclair State University, The Graduate School, College of Humanities and Social Sciences, Child Advocacy and Policy Certificate Program, Montclair, NJ 07043-1624. Offers Certificate. *Students:* Average age 35. In 2014, 54 Certificates awarded. *Expenses:* Tuition, state resident: full-time $9960; part-time $553.35 per credit. Tuition, nonresident: full-time $15,074; part-time $837.43 per credit. *Required fees:* $1595; $88.63 per credit. Tuition and fees vary according to degree level and program. *Unit head:* Dr. Jason Dickinson, Coordinator, 973-655-4188. *Application contact:* Amy Aiello, Executive Director of The Graduate School, 973-655-5147, Fax: 973-655-7869, E-mail: graduate.school@montclair.edu.

Mount Saint Vincent University, Graduate Programs, Department of Child and Youth Study, Halifax, NS B3M 2J6, Canada. Offers MA. Part-time and evening/weekend programs available. *Degree requirements:* For master's, thesis. *Entrance requirements:* For master's, bachelor's degree in related field, minimum B+ average, professional experience. Electronic applications accepted.

Mount Saint Vincent University, Graduate Programs, Department of Family Studies and Gerontology, Halifax, NS B3M 2J6, Canada. Offers MA. Part-time programs available. Postbaccalaureate distance learning degree programs offered (minimal on-campus study). *Degree requirements:* For master's, thesis. *Entrance requirements:* For master's, minimum GPA of 3.0; course work in statistics, research methods, family and social theories.

North Carolina Agricultural and Technical State University, School of Graduate Studies, School of Agriculture and Environmental Sciences, Department of Family and Consumer Sciences, Greensboro, NC 27411. Offers child development early education and family studies (MAT); family and consumer sciences (MAT); food and nutrition (MS). Part-time and evening/weekend programs available. *Degree requirements:* For master's, comprehensive exam, thesis or alternative, qualifying exam. *Entrance requirements:* For master's, GRE General Test, minimum GPA of 2.6.

North Dakota State University, College of Graduate and Interdisciplinary Studies, College of Human Development and Education, Department of Human Development and Family Science, Fargo, ND 58108. Offers couple and family therapy (MS); developmental science (PhD); family financial planning (MS, Certificate); gerontology (MS, PhD, Certificate); human development (MS, PhD). *Accreditation:* AAMFT/COAMFTE. Part-time and evening/weekend programs available. Postbaccalaureate distance learning degree programs offered (no on-campus study). *Degree requirements:* For master's, thesis or alternative; for doctorate, thesis/dissertation. *Entrance requirements:* Additional exam requirements/recommendations for international students: Required—TOEFL (minimum score 525 paper-based; 71 iBT). *Faculty research:* Family therapy, resilience, parenting, adolescent development, mental health.

See Display below and Close-Up on page 887.

Northern Illinois University, Graduate School, College of Health and Human Sciences, School of Family, Consumer and Nutrition Sciences, De Kalb, IL 60115-2854. Offers applied family and child studies (MS); nutrition and dietetics (MS). *Accreditation:* AAMFT/COAMFTE. Part-time programs available. *Faculty:* 16 full-time (14 women), 2 part-time/adjunct (1 woman). *Students:* 71 full-time (65 women), 15 part-time (all women); includes 18 minority (2 Black or African American, non-Hispanic/Latino; 1 American Indian or Alaska Native, non-Hispanic/Latino; 1 Asian, non-Hispanic/Latino; 11 Hispanic/Latino; 3 Two or more races, non-Hispanic/Latino), 4 international. Average age 26. 85 applicants, 54% accepted, 20 enrolled. In 2014, 32 master's awarded. *Degree requirements:* For master's, comprehensive exam, internship, thesis (nutrition and dietetics). *Entrance requirements:* For master's, GRE General Test, minimum GPA of 2.75. Additional exam requirements/recommendations for international students: Required—TOEFL (minimum score 550 paper-based). *Application deadline:* For fall admission, 6/1 for domestic students, 5/1 for international students; for spring admission, 11/1 for domestic students, 10/1 for international students. Applications are processed on a rolling basis. Application fee: $40. Electronic applications accepted. *Financial support:* In 2014–15, 9 research assistantships with full tuition reimbursements, 33 teaching assistantships with full tuition reimbursements were awarded; fellowships with full tuition reimbursements, career-related internships or fieldwork, Federal Work-Study, scholarships/grants, tuition waivers (full), and staff assistantships also available. Support available to part-time students. Financial award applicants required to submit FAFSA. *Faculty research:* Preliminary child development, hospitality administration in Asia, sports nutrition, eating disorders. *Unit head:* Dr. Thomas Pavkov, Chair, 815-753-6342, Fax: 815-753-1321, E-mail: tpavkov@niu.edu. *Application contact:* Graduate School Office, 815-753-0395, E-mail: gradsch@niu.edu. Website: http://www.fcns.niu.edu/

The Ohio State University, Graduate School, College of Education and Human Ecology, Department of Human Sciences, Columbus, OH 43210. Offers consumer sciences (MS, PhD); human development and family science (PhD); human nutrition (MS, PhD); kinesiology (MA, PhD). Part-time programs available. *Faculty:* 55. *Students:* 116 full-time (73 women), 7 part-time (4 women); includes 20 minority (10 Black or African American, non-Hispanic/Latino; 1 American Indian or Alaska Native, non-Hispanic/Latino; 4 Asian, non-Hispanic/Latino; 4 Hispanic/Latino; 1 Two or more races, non-Hispanic/Latino), 31 international. Average age 28. In 2014, 17 master's, 16 doctorates awarded. *Degree requirements:* For master's, thesis optional; for doctorate, thesis/dissertation. *Entrance requirements:* For master's and doctorate, GRE. Additional exam requirements/recommendations for international students: Required—TOEFL (minimum score 550 paper-based; 79 iBT), Michigan English Language Assessment Battery (minimum score 82); Recommended—IELTS (minimum score 7). *Application deadline:* For fall admission, 12/1 priority date for domestic and international students; for winter admission, 12/1 for domestic students, 11/1 for international students; for spring admission, 3/1 for domestic students, 2/1 for international students. Applications are processed on a rolling basis. Application fee: $60 ($70 for international students). Electronic applications accepted. *Financial support:* Fellowships with tuition reimbursements, research assistantships with tuition reimbursements, teaching assistantships with tuition reimbursements, Federal Work-Study, and institutionally sponsored loans available. Support available to part-time students. *Unit head:* Dr. Carl M. Maresh, Chair, E-mail: maresh.15@osu.edu. *Application contact:* Graduate and Professional Admissions, 614-292-9444, Fax: 614-292-3895, E-mail: gpadmissions@osu.edu.
Website: http://ehe.osu.edu/human-sciences/

Ohio University, Graduate College, College of Health Sciences and Professions, Department of Social and Public Health, Athens, OH 45701-2979. Offers early child development and family life (MS); family studies (MS); health administration (MHA); public health (MPH); social work (MSW). *Accreditation:* CEPH. Part-time and evening/weekend programs available. Postbaccalaureate distance learning degree programs offered (no on-campus study). *Degree requirements:* For master's, capstone (MPH). *Entrance requirements:* For master's, GMAT, GRE General Test, previous course work in accounting, management, and statistics, previous public health background (MHA, MPH). Additional exam requirements/recommendations for international students: Required—TOEFL (minimum score 550 paper-based; 80 iBT) or IELTS (minimum score 6.5). Electronic applications accepted. *Expenses:* Contact institution. *Faculty research:* Health care management, health policy, managed care, health behavior, disease prevention.

Oklahoma State University, College of Human Sciences, Department of Human Development and Family Science, Stillwater, OK 74078. Offers human development and family science (MS, PhD), including family financial planning (MS), human environmental sciences; marriage and family therapy (MS). *Accreditation:* AAMFT/COAMFTE (one or more programs are accredited). Postbaccalaureate distance learning degree programs offered. *Faculty:* 27 full-time (18 women), 9 part-time/adjunct (8 women). *Students:* 25 full-time (19 women), 45 part-time (39 women); includes 18 minority (7 Black or African American, non-Hispanic/Latino; 2 Asian, non-Hispanic/Latino; 1 Hispanic/Latino; 8 Two or more races, non-Hispanic/Latino), 2 international. Average age 30. 72 applicants, 33% accepted, 14 enrolled. In 2014, 24 master's, 3 doctorates awarded. *Degree requirements:* For master's, thesis (for some programs); for doctorate, comprehensive exam, thesis/dissertation. *Entrance requirements:* For master's and doctorate, GRE or GMAT. Additional exam requirements/recommendations for international students: Required—TOEFL (minimum score 550 paper-based; 79 iBT). *Application deadline:* For fall admission, 3/1 priority date for international students; for spring admission, 8/1 priority date for international students. Applications are processed on a rolling basis. Application fee: $40 ($75 for international students). Electronic applications accepted. *Expenses:* Tuition, state resident: full-time $4488; part-time $187 per credit hour. Tuition, nonresident: full-time $18,360; part-time $765 per credit hour. *Required fees:* $2413; $100.55 per credit hour. Tuition and fees vary according to campus/location. *Financial support:* In 2014–15, 35 research assistantships (averaging $11,436 per year), 24 teaching assistantships (averaging $10,007 per year) were awarded; career-related internships or fieldwork, Federal Work-Study, scholarships/grants, health care benefits, tuition waivers (partial), and unspecified assistantships also available. Support available to part-time students. Financial award application deadline: 3/1; financial award applicants required to submit FAFSA. *Faculty research:* Family relations and child development, consequences of adolescent parenting, family stress and coping, impacts of sexual abuse on families, children's social cognition and self-competence, gerontology and health care. *Unit head:* Dr. Jennifer Hayes-Grudo, Department Head, 405-744-5360, Fax: 405-744-6344,

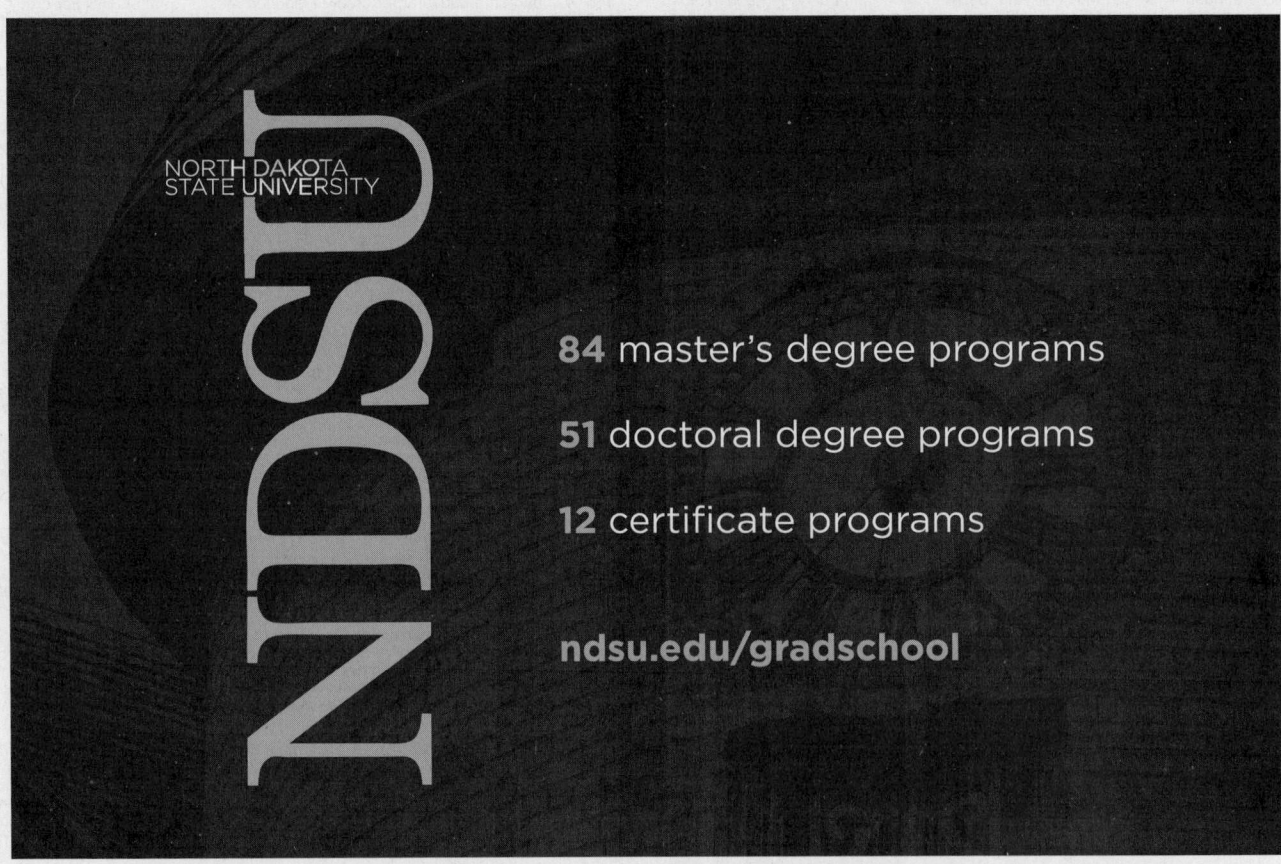

NORTH DAKOTA STATE UNIVERSITY

NDSU

84 master's degree programs

51 doctoral degree programs

12 certificate programs

ndsu.edu/gradschool

E-mail: jennifer.hays.grudo@okstate.edu. *Application contact:* Dr. Brandt Gardner, Graduate Coordinator, 405-744-8360, Fax: 405-744-6344, E-mail: brandt.gardner@okstate.edu.
Website: http://humansciences.okstate.edu/hdfs/

Oregon State University, College of Public Health and Human Sciences, Program in Human Development and Family Studies, Corvallis, OR 97331. Offers MS, PhD. Part-time programs available. *Faculty:* 15 full-time (12 women), 2 part-time/adjunct (1 woman). *Students:* 36 full-time (24 women); includes 12 minority (2 Black or African American, non-Hispanic/Latino; 2 American Indian or Alaska Native, non-Hispanic/Latino; 3 Asian, non-Hispanic/Latino; 4 Hispanic/Latino; 1 Two or more races, non-Hispanic/Latino), 5 international. Average age 32. 20 applicants, 45% accepted, 6 enrolled. In 2014, 2 master's, 3 doctorates awarded. *Entrance requirements:* For master's, GRE; for doctorate, GRE, master's degree (including thesis). Additional exam requirements/recommendations for international students: Required—TOEFL (minimum score 80 iBT), IELTS (minimum score 6.5). *Application deadline:* For fall admission, 4/15 for domestic students. Application fee: $60. *Expenses:* Tuition, state resident: full-time $11,907; part-time $189 per credit hour. Tuition, nonresident: full-time $19,953; part-time $441 per credit hour. *Required fees:* $1472; $449 per term. One-time fee: $350. Tuition and fees vary according to course load and program. *Financial support:* Fellowships, research assistantships, and teaching assistantships available. Financial award application deadline: 1/2. *Unit head:* Dr. Karen Hooker, Professor/Co-Director. *Application contact:* Kaycee Headley, Advisor, 541-737-4765, E-mail: kaycee.headley@oregonstate.edu.
Website: http://health.oregonstate.edu/degrees/graduate/hdfs

Oxford Graduate School, Graduate Programs, Dayton, TN 37321-6736. Offers family life education (M Litt); organizational leadership (M Litt); sociological integration of religion and society (D Phil).

Penn State University Park, Graduate School, College of Health and Human Development, Department of Human Development and Family Studies, University Park, PA 16802. Offers MS, PhD. *Unit head:* Dr. Ann C. Crouter, Dean, 814-865-1420, Fax: 814-865-3282, E-mail: ac1@psu.edu. *Application contact:* Lori A. Stania, Director, Graduate Student Services, 814-867-5278, Fax: 814-863-4627, E-mail: gswww@psu.edu.
Website: http://www.hhdev.psu.edu/hdfs/

Purdue University, Graduate School, College of Health and Human Sciences, Department of Child Development and Family Studies, West Lafayette, IN 47907. Offers developmental studies (MS, PhD); family studies (MS, PhD); marriage and family therapy (MS, PhD). *Accreditation:* AAMFT/COAMFTE (one or more programs are accredited). Part-time programs available. Terminal master's awarded for partial completion of doctoral program. *Degree requirements:* For master's, thesis; for doctorate, thesis/dissertation. *Entrance requirements:* For master's and doctorate, GRE General Test (minimum score 1000 combined verbal and quantitative), minimum undergraduate GPA of 3.0 or equivalent. Additional exam requirements/recommendations for international students: Required—TOEFL (minimum score 600 paper-based; 90 iBT), TWE (minimum score 4). Electronic applications accepted. *Faculty research:* Inclusion of children with special needs, families as learning environments, relationships in child care, work-family relations, AIDS prevention.

Purdue University Calumet, Graduate Studies Office, School of Liberal Arts and Social Sciences, Department of Behavioral Sciences, Hammond, IN 46323-2094. Offers child development and family studies (MS); marriage and family therapy (MS). *Accreditation:* AAMFT/COAMFTE. Part-time programs available. *Degree requirements:* For master's, thesis. *Entrance requirements:* For master's, GRE, interview. Additional exam requirements/recommendations for international students: Required—TOEFL. *Faculty research:* Substance abuse, sexual abuse, couple therapy, professional issues, adolescent therapy.

Roberts Wesleyan College, Program in Social Work, Rochester, NY 14624-1997. Offers child and family practice (MSW); mental health practice (MSW). *Accreditation:* CSWE. *Entrance requirements:* For master's, minimum GPA of 2.75. *Faculty research:* Religion and social work, family studies, values and ethics.

Sage Graduate School, School of Health Sciences, Department of Psychology, Program in Community Psychology, Troy, NY 12180-4115. Offers child care and children's services (MA). Part-time and evening/weekend programs available. *Faculty:* 4 full-time (3 women), 4 part-time/adjunct (3 women). *Students:* 1 (woman) full-time, 1 part-time (0 women). Average age 43. 7 applicants, 71% accepted, 1 enrolled. In 2014, 1 master's awarded. *Degree requirements:* For master's, thesis or alternative. *Entrance requirements:* For master's, minimum GPA of 2.75; 2 letters of reference; undergraduate courses in statistics, history, and systems of psychology; 3 other courses in behavioral science; resume. Additional exam requirements/recommendations for international students: Required—TOEFL (minimum score 550 paper-based). *Application deadline:* Applications are processed on a rolling basis. Application fee: $40. *Expenses: Tuition:* Full-time $12,240; part-time $680 per credit hour. *Financial support:* Fellowships, research assistantships, teaching assistantships, Federal Work-Study, scholarships/grants, and unspecified assistantships available. Support available to part-time students. Financial award application deadline: 3/1; financial award applicants required to submit FAFSA. *Unit head:* Dr. Patricia O'Connor, Associate Dean, School of Health Sciences, 518-244-2073, Fax: 518-244-4571, E-mail: oconnp@sage.edu. *Application contact:* Dr. Sybillyn Jennings, Professor and Chair, 518-244-2074, Fax: 518-244-4545, E-mail: jennis@sage.edu.

St. Cloud State University, School of Graduate Studies, School of Education, Department of Child and Family Studies, St. Cloud, MN 56301-4498. Offers MS. *Degree requirements:* For master's, thesis or alternative. *Entrance requirements:* For master's, GRE General Test, minimum GPA of 2.75. Additional exam requirements/recommendations for international students: Required—Michigan English Language Assessment Battery; Recommended—TOEFL (minimum score 550 paper-based), IELTS (minimum score 6.5). Electronic applications accepted.

San Diego State University, Graduate and Research Affairs, College of Education, Department of Child and Family Development, San Diego, CA 92182. Offers child development (MS). Part-time programs available. *Degree requirements:* For master's, thesis. *Entrance requirements:* For master's, GRE General Test, 3 letters of recommendation, interview. Additional exam requirements/recommendations for international students: Required—TOEFL. Electronic applications accepted.

San Jose State University, Graduate Studies and Research, Connie L. Lurie College of Education, Department of Child and Adolescent Development, San Jose, CA 95192-0001. Offers MA. Electronic applications accepted.

South Carolina State University, College of Graduate and Professional Studies, Department of Family and Consumer Sciences, Orangeburg, SC 29117-0001. Offers individual and family development (MS). Part-time and evening/weekend programs available. *Faculty:* 3 full-time (all women). *Students:* 4 full-time (3 women), 6 part-time (all women); all minorities (all Black or African American, non-Hispanic/Latino). Average age 28. 5 applicants, 100% accepted, 4 enrolled. In 2014, 10 master's awarded. *Degree requirements:* For master's, comprehensive exam, thesis optional, departmental

qualifying exam. *Entrance requirements:* For master's, GRE, MAT, or NTE, minimum GPA of 2.7. *Application deadline:* For fall admission, 6/15 priority date for domestic students, 6/15 for international students; for spring admission, 11/1 for domestic and international students. Applications are processed on a rolling basis. Application fee: $25. Electronic applications accepted. *Expenses:* Tuition, state resident: full-time $7290; part-time $405 per credit. Tuition, nonresident: full-time $17,058; part-time $948 per credit. *Required fees:* $2798; $155 per credit hour. *Financial support:* Fellowships and institutionally sponsored loans available. Financial award application deadline: 6/1. *Unit head:* Dr. Ethel G. Jones, Chair, 803-536-8958, Fax: 803-533-3268, E-mail: egjones@scsu.edu. *Application contact:* Curtis Foskey, Coordinator of Graduate Admission, 803-536-8419, Fax: 803-536-8812, E-mail: cfoskey@scsu.edu.

Spring Arbor University, School of Human Services, Spring Arbor, MI 49283-9799. Offers counseling (MAC); family studies (MAFS); nursing (MSN). Part-time and evening/weekend programs available. Postbaccalaureate distance learning degree programs offered (no on-campus study). *Entrance requirements:* For master's, bachelor's degree from regionally-accredited college or university, minimum GPA of 3.0 for at least the last two years of the bachelor's degree, at least two recommendations from professional/academic individuals. Additional exam requirements/recommendations for international students: Required—TOEFL (minimum score 600 paper-based). Electronic applications accepted.

State University of New York at Oswego, Graduate Studies, School of Education, Department of Vocational Teacher Preparation, Oswego, NY 13126. Offers agriculture (MS Ed); business and marketing (MS Ed); family and consumer sciences (MS Ed); health careers (MS Ed); technical education (MS Ed); trade education (MS Ed). *Accreditation:* NCATE. Part-time and evening/weekend programs available. *Degree requirements:* For master's, comprehensive exam, thesis or alternative. *Entrance requirements:* Additional exam requirements/recommendations for international students: Required—TOEFL (minimum score 560 paper-based).

Syracuse University, Falk College of Sport and Human Dynamics, Program in Child and Family Studies, Syracuse, NY 13244. Offers MA, MS, PhD. *Accreditation:* AAMFT/COAMFTE (one or more programs are accredited). Part-time programs available. *Students:* 27 full-time (23 women), 6 part-time (4 women); includes 6 minority (4 Black or African American, non-Hispanic/Latino; 1 American Indian or Alaska Native, non-Hispanic/Latino; 1 Asian, non-Hispanic/Latino), 13 international. Average age 33. 30 applicants, 40% accepted, 7 enrolled. In 2014, 3 master's, 6 doctorates awarded. *Degree requirements:* For master's, comprehensive exam (for some programs), thesis; for doctorate, comprehensive exam, thesis/dissertation. *Entrance requirements:* For master's and doctorate, GRE General Test. Additional exam requirements/recommendations for international students: Required—TOEFL (minimum score 100 iBT). *Application deadline:* For fall admission, 3/15 priority date for domestic and international students. Application fee: $75. Electronic applications accepted. *Expenses: Tuition:* Part-time $1341 per credit. *Financial support:* Fellowships with full tuition reimbursements, research assistantships with full and partial tuition reimbursements, teaching assistantships with full and partial tuition reimbursements, and tuition waivers available. Financial award application deadline: 1/1. *Unit head:* Dr. Rachel Razza., Graduate Program Director, 315-443-7377, Fax: 315-443-9402, E-mail: bbgump@syr.edu. *Application contact:* Felicia Otero, Information Contact, 315-443-5555, E-mail: falk@syr.edu.
Website: http://falk.syr.edu/ChildFamilyStudies/Default.aspx

Texas State University, The Graduate College, College of Applied Arts, School of Family and Consumer Sciences, Program in Family and Child Studies, San Marcos, TX 78666. Offers MS. Part-time programs available. *Faculty:* 4 full-time (all women), 1 (woman) part-time/adjunct. *Students:* 29 full-time (28 women), 22 part-time (all women); includes 13 minority (1 American Indian or Alaska Native, non-Hispanic/Latino; 1 Asian, non-Hispanic/Latino; 9 Hispanic/Latino; 2 Two or more races, non-Hispanic/Latino), 1 international. Average age 26. 43 applicants, 74% accepted, 17 enrolled. In 2014, 14 master's awarded. *Degree requirements:* For master's, thesis optional. *Entrance requirements:* For master's, GRE (minimum preferred combined score of 285 on the verbal/quantitative sections), minimum GPA of 3.0, three letters of reference, statement of interest and goals. Additional exam requirements/recommendations for international students: Required—TOEFL (minimum score 550 paper-based; 78 iBT). *Application deadline:* For fall admission, 3/1 priority date for domestic students, 3/1 for international students. Applications are processed on a rolling basis. Application fee: $40 ($90 for international students). *Expenses:* Expenses: $8,834 (tuition and fees combined). *Financial support:* In 2014–15, 27 students received support, including 8 research assistantships (averaging $11,346 per year), 5 teaching assistantships (averaging $11,030 per year); scholarships/grants and unspecified assistantships also available. Financial award application deadline: 4/1; financial award applicants required to submit FAFSA. *Faculty research:* Healthy marriage, strengthening families, Faces of Texas State. *Total annual research expenditures:* $737,110. *Unit head:* Dr. Maria E. Canabal, Chair, 512-245-2155, Fax: 512-245-3829, E-mail: mc57@txstate.edu. *Application contact:* Dr. Andrea Golato, Dean of the Graduate College, 512-245-2581, Fax: 512-245-8365, E-mail: er15@txstate.edu.
Website: http://www.fcs.txstate.edu/degrees-programs/fcd/fcdgrad.html

Texas Tech University, Graduate School, College of Human Sciences, Department of Human Development and Family Studies, Lubbock, TX 79409-1230. Offers MS, PhD. *Accreditation:* AAMFT/COAMFTE (one or more programs are accredited). Part-time programs available. *Faculty:* 23 full-time (20 women), 5 part-time/adjunct (all women). *Students:* 45 full-time (41 women), 52 part-time (41 women); includes 16 minority (2 Black or African American, non-Hispanic/Latino; 2 American Indian or Alaska Native, non-Hispanic/Latino; 11 Hispanic/Latino; 1 Two or more races, non-Hispanic/Latino), 14 international. Average age 34. 45 applicants, 58% accepted, 11 enrolled. In 2014, 9 master's, 2 doctorates awarded. *Degree requirements:* For master's, thesis; for doctorate, comprehensive exam, thesis/dissertation. *Entrance requirements:* For master's and doctorate, GRE General Test. Additional exam requirements/recommendations for international students: Required—TOEFL (minimum score 550 paper-based; 79 iBT). *Application deadline:* For fall admission, 6/1 priority date for domestic students, 1/15 priority date for international students; for spring admission, 9/1 priority date for domestic students, 6/15 priority date for international students. Applications are processed on a rolling basis. Application fee: $60. Electronic applications accepted. *Expenses:* Tuition, state resident: full-time $6310; part-time $262.92 per credit hour. Tuition, nonresident: full-time $14,998; part-time $624.92 per credit hour. *Required fees:* $2701; $36.50 per credit. $912.50 per semester. Tuition and fees vary according to course load. *Financial support:* In 2014–15, 54 students received support, including 53 fellowships (averaging $4,883 per year), 11 research assistantships (averaging $15,016 per year), 43 teaching assistantships (averaging $9,712 per year). Financial award application deadline: 4/15; financial award applicants required to submit FAFSA. *Faculty research:* Parenting, marital and premarital relationships, adolescent risky behaviors, life span, child development. *Total annual research expenditures:* $222,808. *Unit head:* Dr. Jean Pearson Scott, Chairperson, 806-834-6589, Fax: 806-742-0285, E-mail: jean.scott@ttu.edu. *Application contact:* Monya Castle, Graduate Secretary, 806-742-3000 Ext. 250, Fax: 806-742-0285, E-mail: monya.castle@ttu.edu. Website: http://www.depts.ttu.edu/hdfs

Child and Family Studies

Texas Woman's University, Graduate School, College of Professional Education, Department of Family Sciences, Denton, TX 76201. Offers child development (MS); counseling and development (MS); early childhood development and education (PhD); early childhood education (M Ed, MA, MS); family studies (MS, PhD); family therapy (MS, PhD). *Accreditation:* ACA (one or more programs are accredited). Part-time and evening/weekend programs available. Terminal master's awarded for partial completion of doctoral program. *Degree requirements:* For master's, comprehensive exam (for some programs), thesis (for some programs); for doctorate, comprehensive exam, thesis/dissertation. *Entrance requirements:* Additional exam requirements/ recommendations for international students: Required—TOEFL (minimum score 550 paper-based; 79 iBT). Electronic applications accepted. *Faculty research:* Parenting/ parent education, military families, play therapy, family sexuality, diversity, healthy relationships/healthy marriages, childhood obesity, male communication.

Towson University, Program in Child Life, Administration and Family Collaboration, Towson, MD 21252-0001. Offers MS. *Students:* 15 full-time (all women), 11 part-time (all women); includes 1 minority (Black or African American, non-Hispanic/Latino). *Entrance requirements:* For master's, bachelor's degree, minimum GPA of 3.0; minimum of 40 hours of volunteer or paid work experience with children with special health care needs in a child life department under the direct supervision of a Certified Child Life Specialist, essay, coursework verification form, volunteer/work experience verification form. Application fee: $45. Electronic applications accepted. *Unit head:* Prof. Lisa Martinelli Beasley, Graduate Program Director, 410-704-3766, E-mail: lmartinelli@towson.edu. *Application contact:* Alicia Arkell-Kleis, Information Contact, 410-704-6004, E-mail: grads@towson.edu.
Website: http://grad.towson.edu/program/master/fmst-ms/

Towson University, Program in Family-Professional Collaboration, Towson, MD 21252-0001. Offers Postbaccalaureate Certificate. *Students:* 17 full-time (all women), 13 part-time (all women); includes 3 minority (all Black or African American, non-Hispanic/ Latino). *Entrance requirements:* For degree, minimum GPA of 3.0; bachelor's degree; resume; interview with program director. *Application deadline:* Applications are processed on a rolling basis. Application fee: $45. Electronic applications accepted. *Unit head:* Dr. Karen Eskow, Graduate Program Director, 410-704-5851, E-mail: keskow@towson.edu. *Application contact:* Alicia Arkell-Kleis, Information Contact, 410-704-6004, Fax: 410-704-4675, E-mail: grads@towson.edu.
Website: http://grad.towson.edu/program/certificate/fmst-pbc/index.asp

Tufts University, Graduate School of Arts and Sciences, Eliot-Pearson Department of Child Study and Human Development, Medford, MA 02155. Offers child study and human development (MA, PhD); early childhood education (MAT). Part-time programs available. *Faculty:* 13 full-time (10 women), 22 part-time/adjunct (18 women). *Students:* 68 full-time (62 women), 31 part-time (24 women); includes 21 minority (6 Black or African American, non-Hispanic/Latino; 7 Asian, non-Hispanic/Latino; 4 Hispanic/Latino; 4 Two or more races, non-Hispanic/Latino), 11 international. Average age 28. 122 applicants, 58% accepted, 29 enrolled. In 2014, 42 master's, 3 doctorates awarded. *Degree requirements:* For master's, thesis (for some programs); for doctorate, thesis/ dissertation. *Entrance requirements:* For master's and doctorate, GRE General Test. Additional exam requirements/recommendations for international students: Required— TOEFL (minimum score 550 paper-based; 80 iBT), IELTS (minimum score 6.5). *Application deadline:* For fall admission, 12/1 priority date for domestic and international students. Applications are processed on a rolling basis. Application fee: $75. Electronic applications accepted. *Expenses:* Tuition: Full-time $45,590; part-time $1161 per credit hour. *Required fees:* $782. Full-time tuition and fees vary according to degree level, program and student level. Part-time tuition and fees vary according to course load. *Financial support:* Fellowships, research assistantships with full and partial tuition reimbursements, teaching assistantships with full and partial tuition reimbursements, Federal Work-Study, scholarships/grants, tuition waivers (partial), and unspecified assistantships available. Support available to part-time students. Financial award application deadline: 5/15; financial award applicants required to submit FAFSA. *Unit head:* Dr. David Henry Feldman, Graduate Program Director. *Application contact:* Office of Graduate Admissions, 617-627-3395, E-mail: gradadmissions@tufts.edu.
Website: http://ase.tufts.edu/epcd

The University of Akron, Graduate School, Buchtel College of Arts and Sciences, School of Family and Consumer Sciences, Akron, OH 44325. Offers child and family development (MA), including child development, family development; clothing, textiles and interiors (MA). Part-time and evening/weekend programs available. *Faculty:* 6 full-time (all women), 10 part-time/adjunct (6 women). *Students:* 6 full-time (5 women), 1 (woman) part-time; includes 1 minority (Black or African American, non-Hispanic/Latino). Average age 28. 8 applicants, 50% accepted, 3 enrolled. In 2014, 3 master's awarded. *Degree requirements:* For master's, comprehensive exam, thesis optional, oral exam. *Entrance requirements:* For master's, GRE, minimum GPA of 2.75, letters of recommendation, statement of purpose, resume. Additional exam requirements/ recommendations for international students: Required—TOEFL (minimum score 550 paper-based; 79 iBT), IELTS (minimum score 6.5). *Application deadline:* For fall admission, 3/1 priority date for domestic and international students; for spring admission, 10/1 priority date for domestic and international students. Application fee: $45 ($70 for international students). Electronic applications accepted. *Expenses:* Tuition, state resident: full-time $7578; part-time $421 per credit hour. Tuition, nonresident: full-time $12,977; part-time $721 per credit hour. *Required fees:* $1388; $35 per credit hour. Tuition and fees vary according to course load. *Financial support:* In 2014–15, 9 teaching assistantships with full tuition reimbursements were awarded. *Faculty research:* Nutritional health wellness/sports nutrition; historical/cultural aspects of clothing, textiles, interiors; family and consumer sciences (FCS) curriculum development; life span gender roles; families in international and historical perspectives. *Unit head:* Dr. Virginia Gunn, Interim Director, 330-972-7729, E-mail: vgunn@uakron.edu. *Application contact:* Dr. Pamela Schulze, Graduate Director, 330-972-7725, E-mail: schulze@uakron.edu.
Website: http://www.uakron.edu/fcs/

The University of Akron, Graduate School, College of Health Professions, School of Speech-Language Pathology and Audiology, Akron, OH 44325. Offers audiology (Au D); child life (MA); speech-language pathology (MA). *Accreditation:* ASHA. Part-time programs available. *Faculty:* 6 full-time (2 women), 29 part-time/adjunct (all women). *Students:* 141 full-time (125 women), 20 part-time (18 women); includes 9 minority (4 Black or African American, non-Hispanic/Latino; 1 Asian, non-Hispanic/Latino; 1 Hispanic/Latino; 3 Two or more races, non-Hispanic/Latino), 1 international. Average age 26. 374 applicants, 16% accepted, 56 enrolled. In 2014, 56 master's, 11 doctorates awarded. *Degree requirements:* For master's, thesis or written comprehensive exams; for doctorate, 2000 clock hours of clinical experience, academic and clinical competency-based exams. *Entrance requirements:* For master's, GRE, bachelor's degree in speech-language pathology, minimum GPA of 2.75, three letters of recommendation, statement of purpose, resume; for doctorate, GRE, minimum GPA of 3.0, three letters of recommendation, personal statement. Additional exam requirements/recommendations for international students: Required—TOEFL (minimum score 550 paper-based; 79 iBT), IELTS (minimum score 6.5). *Application deadline:* For fall admission, 1/1 for domestic and international students. Application fee: $45 ($70 for international students). Electronic applications accepted. *Expenses:* Tuition, state resident: full-time $7578; part-time $421 per credit hour. Tuition, nonresident: full-time $12,977; part-time $721 per credit hour. *Required fees:* $1388; $35 per credit hour. Tuition and fees vary according to course load. *Financial support:* In 2014–15, 34 fellowships with full and partial tuition reimbursements, 47 research assistantships with full and partial tuition reimbursements, 23 teaching assistantships with full and partial tuition reimbursements were awarded; unspecified assistantships also available. *Faculty research:* Auditory-verbal habilitation techniques, assistive technology for persons with cognitive challenges, traumatic brain injury issues for school-aged children, use of multi-media to train professionals in language/literacy for preschool populations, use of multi-media to teach at the university level. *Total annual research expenditures:* $374,917. *Unit head:* Dr. Kristina English, Interim Director, 330-972-6116, E-mail: ke3@uakron.edu. *Application contact:* Graduate Admissions Coordinator.
Website: http://www.uakron.edu/sslpa/

The University of Alabama, Graduate School, College of Human Environmental Sciences, Department of Human Development and Family Studies, Tuscaloosa, AL 35487. Offers MSHES. *Faculty:* 9 full-time (8 women), 1 (woman) part-time/adjunct. *Students:* 22 full-time (19 women), 4 part-time (all women); includes 5 minority (3 Black or African American, non-Hispanic/Latino; 1 American Indian or Alaska Native, non-Hispanic/Latino; 1 Asian, non-Hispanic/Latino), 1 international. Average age 26. 25 applicants, 64% accepted, 11 enrolled. In 2014, 9 master's awarded. *Degree requirements:* For master's, comprehensive exam (for some programs), thesis (for some programs). *Entrance requirements:* For master's, GRE General Test or MAT, minimum GPA of 3.0. Additional exam requirements/recommendations for international students: Required—TOEFL. *Application deadline:* For fall admission, 12/15 priority date for domestic and international students. Applications are processed on a rolling basis. Application fee: $50 ($60 for international students). Electronic applications accepted. *Expenses:* Tuition, state resident: full-time $9826. Tuition, nonresident: full-time $24,950. *Financial support:* In 2014–15, 8 students received support, including 3 research assistantships with full tuition reimbursements available (averaging $13,140 per year), 5 teaching assistantships (averaging $13,140 per year); career-related internships or fieldwork, Federal Work-Study, scholarships/grants, health care benefits, and unspecified assistantships also available. Financial award application deadline: 3/15. *Faculty research:* Parent/child relationships, preschool curricula and quality measures for child care programs, family strengths and adolescent behaviors, depression in mothers and infants, word association and word learning in young children, bullying behaviors in children, attachment parenting, medical play therapy, socialization of young children, impact of daily experiences on relationship quality, re-entry of service members into civilian roles. *Total annual research expenditures:* $5,470. *Unit head:* Dr. Carroll M. Tingle, Chair, 205-348-6158, Fax: 205-348-8153, E-mail: ctingle@ches.ua.edu. *Application contact:* Dr. Maria Hernandez-Reif, Professor, 205-348-5894, Fax: 205-348-8153, E-mail: mhernandez-reif@ches.ua.edu.
Website: http://www.ches.ua.edu/

The University of Arizona, College of Education, Department of Disability and Psychoeducational Studies, Tucson, AZ 85721. Offers counseling and mental health (MA), including rehabilitation counseling, school counseling; family studies and human development (M Ed); rehabilitation (MA, PhD); school counseling (M Ed); school psychology (PhD, Ed S); special education (MA, Ed D, PhD), including cross-categorical special education (MA), deaf and hard of hearing (MA), learning disabilities (MA), severe and multiple disabilities (MA), special education (Ed D, PhD), visual impairment (MA). *Accreditation:* CORE. Part-time programs available. Terminal master's awarded for partial completion of doctoral program. *Degree requirements:* For master's, comprehensive exam, thesis optional; for doctorate, comprehensive exam, thesis/ dissertation. *Entrance requirements:* For master's, statement of purpose; for doctorate, GRE General Test (minimum score 1100) or MAT, 3 letters of recommendation. Additional exam requirements/recommendations for international students: Required— TOEFL (minimum score 550 paper-based; 79 iBT).

University of Central Oklahoma, The Jackson College of Graduate Studies, College of Education and Professional Studies, Department of Human Environmental Sciences, Edmond, OK 73034-5209. Offers family and child studies (MS), including family life education, infant/child specialist, marriage and family therapy; nutrition-food management (MS). Part-time programs available. *Degree requirements:* For master's, comprehensive exam (for some programs), thesis (for some programs). *Entrance requirements:* For master's, GRE, essay, physical, CPR and First Aid training. Additional exam requirements/recommendations for international students: Required—TOEFL (minimum score 550 paper-based; 79 iBT), IELTS (minimum score 6.5). Electronic applications accepted.

University of Connecticut, Graduate School, College of Liberal Arts and Sciences, Department of Human Development and Family Studies, Storrs, CT 06269. Offers culture, health and human development (Graduate Certificate); human development and family studies (MA, PhD). *Accreditation:* AAMFT/COAMFTE (one or more programs are accredited). Terminal master's awarded for partial completion of doctoral program. *Degree requirements:* For master's, comprehensive exam; for doctorate, thesis/ dissertation. *Entrance requirements:* For doctorate, GRE General Test. Additional exam requirements/recommendations for international students: Required—TOEFL (minimum score 550 paper-based). Electronic applications accepted.

University of Delaware, College of Education and Human Development, Department of Human Development and Family Studies, Newark, DE 19716. Offers MS, PhD. Part-time programs available. Terminal master's awarded for partial completion of doctoral program. *Degree requirements:* For master's, thesis or alternative; for doctorate, comprehensive exam, thesis/dissertation. *Entrance requirements:* For master's and doctorate, GRE General Test, 3 letters of recommendation. Additional exam requirements/recommendations for international students: Required—TOEFL. Electronic applications accepted. *Faculty research:* Early childhood inclusive education, relationships, family risk and resilience, disability issues, program development and evaluation.

University of Denver, Morgridge College of Education, Denver, CO 80208. Offers child, family and school psychology (MA, Ed S); counseling psychology (PhD); curriculum and instruction (MA, PhD); curriculum instruction and teaching (Certificate); educational leadership and policy studies (MA, PhD); library and information science (MLIS). *Accreditation:* ALA; APA (one or more programs are accredited). Part-time and evening/ weekend programs available. Postbaccalaureate distance learning degree programs offered (no on-campus study). *Faculty:* 41 full-time (27 women), 62 part-time/adjunct (43 women). *Students:* 506 full-time (387 women), 325 part-time (237 women); includes 191 minority (50 Black or African American, non-Hispanic/Latino; 9 American Indian or Alaska Native, non-Hispanic/Latino; 21 Asian, non-Hispanic/Latino; 91 Hispanic/Latino; 3 Native Hawaiian or other Pacific Islander, non-Hispanic/Latino; 17 Two or more races, non-Hispanic/Latino), 23 international. Average age 32. 975 applicants, 73% accepted, 410 enrolled. In 2014, 234 master's, 38 doctorates, 178 other advanced degrees awarded. Terminal master's awarded for partial completion of doctoral program. *Degree requirements:* For master's, comprehensive exam; for doctorate, 2 foreign languages, comprehensive exam, thesis/dissertation. *Entrance requirements:* For master's and doctorate, GRE General Test or GMAT. Additional exam requirements/

recommendations for international students: Required—TOEFL (minimum score 550 paper-based; 80 iBT). *Application deadline:* Applications are processed on a rolling basis. Application fee: $65. Electronic applications accepted. *Expenses:* Expenses: $1,199 per credit hour. *Financial support:* In 2014–15, 674 students received support, including 43 research assistantships with full and partial tuition reimbursements available (averaging $9,090 per year), 80 teaching assistantships with full and partial tuition reimbursements available (averaging $6,084 per year); career-related internships or fieldwork, Federal Work-Study, institutionally sponsored loans, scholarships/grants, and unspecified assistantships also available. Support available to part-time students. Financial award application deadline: 2/15; financial award applicants required to submit FAFSA. *Faculty research:* Principal and teacher preparation, development and assessments, gifted education, service-learning, early childhood, mathematics education, access to higher education. *Unit head:* Dr. Karen Riley, Interim Dean, 303-871-3665, E-mail: karen.riley@du.edu. *Application contact:* Jodi Dye, Assistant Director of Admissions, 303-871-2510, E-mail: jodi.dye@du.edu.
Website: http://morgridge.du.edu/

University of Georgia, College of Education, Department of Elementary and Social Studies Education, Athens, GA 30602. Offers early childhood education (M Ed, MAT, PhD, Ed S), including child and family development (MAT); elementary education (PhD); middle school education (M Ed, PhD, Ed S); social studies education (M Ed, Ed D, PhD, Ed S). *Entrance requirements:* For master's and Ed S, GRE General Test or MAT; for doctorate, GRE General Test. Electronic applications accepted.

University of Georgia, College of Family and Consumer Sciences, Department of Human Development and Family Science, Athens, GA 30602. Offers child and family development (MS, PhD); early childhood education (MAT), including child and family development. *Accreditation:* AAMFT/COAMFTE (one or more programs are accredited). *Degree requirements:* For master's, thesis (MS); for doctorate, thesis/dissertation. *Entrance requirements:* For master's and doctorate, GRE General Test. Electronic applications accepted.

University of Guelph, Graduate Studies, College of Social and Applied Human Sciences, Department of Family Relations and Applied Nutrition, Guelph, ON N1G 2W1, Canada. Offers applied nutrition (MAN); family relations and human development (M Sc, PhD), including applied human nutrition, couple and family therapy (M Sc), family relations and human development. *Accreditation:* AAMFT/COAMFTE (one or more programs are accredited). Part-time programs available. *Degree requirements:* For master's, thesis (for some programs); for doctorate, comprehensive exam, thesis/dissertation. *Entrance requirements:* For master's, minimum B+ average; for doctorate, master's degree in family relations and human development or related field with a minimum B+ average or master's degree in applied human nutrition. Additional exam requirements/recommendations for international students: Required—TOEFL (minimum score 600 paper-based). Electronic applications accepted. *Faculty research:* Child and adolescent development, social gerontology, family roles and relations, couple and family therapy, applied human nutrition.

University of Illinois at Springfield, Graduate Programs, College of Education and Human Services, Program in Human Services, Springfield, IL 62703-5407. Offers alcohol and substance abuse (Graduate Certificate); alcoholism and substance abuse (MA); child and family services (MA); gerontology (MA); social services administration (MA). Part-time and evening/weekend programs available. Postbaccalaureate distance learning degree programs offered (no on-campus study). *Faculty:* 4 full-time (all women), 2 part-time/adjunct (0 women). *Students:* 11 full-time (all women), 69 part-time (60 women); includes 21 minority (17 Black or African American, non-Hispanic/Latino; 1 Asian, non-Hispanic/Latino; 1 Hispanic/Latino; 2 Two or more races, non-Hispanic/Latino). Average age 36. 53 applicants, 30% accepted, 16 enrolled. In 2014, 19 master's, 1 other advanced degree awarded. *Degree requirements:* For master's, internship; project or thesis. *Entrance requirements:* For master's, minimum undergraduate GPA of 3.0, 2 letters of recommendation, statement of intent. Additional exam requirements/recommendations for international students: Required—TOEFL (minimum score 500 paper-based; 61 iBT). Application fee: $60 ($75 for international students). Electronic applications accepted. *Expenses:* Tuition, state resident: full-time $7662; part-time $319.25 per credit hour. Tuition, nonresident: full-time $15,966; part-time $665.25 per credit hour. *Financial support:* In 2014–15, fellowships with full tuition reimbursements (averaging $9,900 per year), research assistantships with full tuition reimbursements (averaging $9,600 per year), teaching assistantships with full tuition reimbursements (averaging $9,600 per year) were awarded; career-related internships or fieldwork, Federal Work-Study, scholarships/grants, health care benefits, and unspecified assistantships also available. Support available to part-time students. Financial award application deadline: 11/15. *Unit head:* Dr. Carolyn Peck, Program Administrator, 217-206-7577, Fax: 217-206-6775, E-mail: peck.carolyn@uis.edu. *Application contact:* Dr. Lynn Pardie, Office of Graduate Studies, 800-252-8533, Fax: 217-206-7623, E-mail: lpard1@uis.edu.
Website: http://www.uis.edu/humanservices

University of Kentucky, Graduate School, College of Agriculture, Food and Environment, Program in Family Studies, Human Development, and Resource Management, Lexington, KY 40506-0032. Offers MS, PhD. *Accreditation:* AAMFT/COAMFTE. *Degree requirements:* For master's, comprehensive exam, thesis optional. *Entrance requirements:* For master's, GRE General Test, minimum undergraduate GPA of 2.75; for doctorate, GRE General Test, minimum undergraduate GPA of 3.0. Additional exam requirements/recommendations for international students: Required—TOEFL (minimum score 550 paper-based). Electronic applications accepted. *Faculty research:* Early childhood education, family therapy, family resource management and consumer studies, human development.

University of La Verne, College of Education and Organizational Leadership, Programs in Child Development/Child Life, La Verne, CA 91750-4443. Offers child development (MS); child life (MS). Part-time programs available. *Faculty:* 3 full-time (all women), 6 part-time/adjunct (all women). *Students:* 22 full-time (all women), 62 part-time (58 women); includes 42 minority (8 Black or African American, non-Hispanic/Latino; 5 Asian, non-Hispanic/Latino; 29 Hispanic/Latino), 3 international. Average age 30. In 2014, 27 master's awarded. *Entrance requirements:* For master's, minimum GPA of 3.0, 3 letters of reference, writing sample. Additional exam requirements/recommendations for international students: Required—TOEFL (minimum score 550 paper-based). *Application deadline:* Applications are processed on a rolling basis. Application fee: $50. *Expenses:* Expenses: Contact institution. *Financial support:* Institutionally sponsored loans, scholarships/grants, and unspecified assistantships available. Financial award application deadline: 3/2; financial award applicants required to submit FAFSA. *Unit head:* Laurie Schroeder, Chairperson, 909-448-4653, E-mail: lschroeder3@laverne.edu. *Application contact:* Christy Ranells, Program and Admission Specialist, 909-448-4644, Fax: 909-9712295, E-mail: cranells@laverne.edu.
Website: http://www.laverne.edu/education/

University of Manitoba, Faculty of Graduate Studies, Faculty of Human Ecology, Department of Family Social Sciences, Winnipeg, MB R3T 2N2, Canada. Offers M Sc. *Degree requirements:* For master's, thesis.

University of Maryland, College Park, Academic Affairs, School of Public Health, Department of Family Science, College Park, MD 20742. Offers family studies (PhD); marriage and family therapy (MS); maternal and child health (PhD). *Accreditation:* AAMFT/COAMFTE. Part-time and evening/weekend programs available. *Degree requirements:* For master's, thesis or alternative; for doctorate, comprehensive exam, thesis/dissertation, oral defense. *Entrance requirements:* For master's, GRE General Test, minimum GPA of 3.0, 3 letters of recommendation; for doctorate, GRE General Test, minimum GPA of 3.0, 3 letters of recommendation, research sample. Electronic applications accepted. *Faculty research:* Family life quality, interracial couples, child support, homeless families, family and child well-being.

University of Massachusetts Amherst, Graduate School, College of Education, Program in Education, Amherst, MA 01003. Offers bilingual/English as a second language/multicultural education (M Ed, Ed S); child study and early education (M Ed); children, families and schools (Ed D, Ed S); early childhood and elementary teacher education (M Ed); educational leadership (M Ed); educational policy and leadership (Ed D); higher education (M Ed); international education (M Ed); language, literacy and culture (Ed D); learning, media and technology (M Ed, Ed S); mathematics, science, and learning technologies (Ed D); psychometric methods, educational statistics and research methods (Ed D); reading and writing (M Ed); school counselor education (M Ed, Ed S); school psychology (Ed S); science education (Ed S); secondary teacher education (M Ed); social justice education (M Ed, Ed D, Ed S); special education (M Ed, Ed D, Ed S); teacher education and school improvement (Ed D, Ed S). *Accreditation:* NCATE. Part-time programs available. Postbaccalaureate distance learning degree programs offered (minimal on-campus study). *Faculty:* 99 full-time (57 women). *Students:* 353 full-time (252 women), 252 part-time (179 women); includes 113 minority (39 Black or African American, non-Hispanic/Latino; 5 American Indian or Alaska Native, non-Hispanic/Latino; 16 Asian, non-Hispanic/Latino; 42 Hispanic/Latino; 11 Two or more races, non-Hispanic/Latino), 104 international. Average age 34. 597 applicants, 53% accepted, 173 enrolled. In 2014, 161 master's, 37 doctorates, 26 other advanced degrees awarded. Terminal master's awarded for partial completion of doctoral program. *Degree requirements:* For doctorate, comprehensive exam, thesis/dissertation. *Entrance requirements:* Additional exam requirements/recommendations for international students: Required—TOEFL (minimum score 550 paper-based; 80 iBT), IELTS (minimum score 6.5). *Application deadline:* For fall admission, 1/2 for domestic and international students. Applications are processed on a rolling basis. Application fee: $75. Electronic applications accepted. *Expenses:* Tuition, state resident: full-time $1980; part-time $110 per credit. Tuition, nonresident: full-time $14,644; part-time $414 per credit. *Required fees:* $11,417. One-time fee: $357. *Financial support:* Fellowships with full and partial tuition reimbursements, research assistantships with full and partial tuition reimbursements, teaching assistantships with full and partial tuition reimbursements, career-related internships or fieldwork, Federal Work-Study, scholarships/grants, traineeships, health care benefits, tuition waivers (full and partial), and unspecified assistantships available. Support available to part-time students. Financial award application deadline: 1/2; financial award applicants required to submit FAFSA. *Unit head:* Dr. Linda L. Griffin, Graduate Program Director, 413-545-6984, Fax: 413-545-1523. *Application contact:* Lindsay DeSantis, Supervisor of Admissions, 413-545-0722, Fax: 413-577-0010, E-mail: gradadm@grad.umass.edu.
Website: http://www.umass.edu/education/

University of Minnesota, Twin Cities Campus, Graduate School, College of Education and Human Development, Department of Family Social Science, Minneapolis, MN 55455-0213. Offers marriage and family therapy (MA, PhD). *Accreditation:* AAMFT/COAMFTE (one or more programs are accredited). *Faculty:* 20 full-time (14 women). *Students:* 59 full-time (47 women), 26 part-time (21 women); includes 15 minority (1 Black or African American, non-Hispanic/Latino; 1 American Indian or Alaska Native, non-Hispanic/Latino; 5 Asian, non-Hispanic/Latino; 6 Hispanic/Latino; 2 Two or more races, non-Hispanic/Latino), 10 international. Average age 34. 73 applicants, 59% accepted, 34 enrolled. In 2014, 5 master's, 4 doctorates awarded. *Degree requirements:* For master's, thesis; for doctorate, thesis/dissertation. *Entrance requirements:* For master's and doctorate, GRE General Test, minimum undergraduate GPA of 3.0 (preferred). Additional exam requirements/recommendations for international students: Required—TOEFL. *Application deadline:* For fall admission, 12/15 for domestic students. Application fee: $75 ($95 for international students). *Financial support:* In 2014–15, 37 research assistantships (averaging $8,001 per year), 10 teaching assistantships (averaging $9,055 per year) were awarded; fellowships, career-related internships or fieldwork, Federal Work-Study, institutionally sponsored loans, and tuition waivers (partial) also available. Financial award application deadline: 6/30; financial award applicants required to submit FAFSA. *Faculty research:* Child adjustment in family context; families and culture; families and financial decisions; family formation and intergenerational studies; families, loss, and trauma; intimate family relationships. *Total annual research expenditures:* $2.3 million. *Unit head:* Dr. Lynne Borden, Head, 612-625-1900, Fax: 612-625-4227, E-mail: lmborden@umn.edu. *Application contact:* Dr. Jodi Dworkin, Director of Graduate Studies, 612-625-3732, Fax: 612-625-4227, E-mail: jdworkin@umn.edu.
Website: http://www.cehd.umn.edu/fsos/

University of Missouri, Office of Research and Graduate Studies, College of Human Environmental Sciences, Department of Human Development and Family Studies, Columbia, MO 65211. Offers MA, MS, PhD. *Faculty:* 12 full-time (6 women). *Students:* 41 full-time (32 women), 36 part-time (34 women); includes 18 minority (11 Black or African American, non-Hispanic/Latino; 4 Hispanic/Latino; 3 Two or more races, non-Hispanic/Latino), 7 international. Average age 29. 51 applicants, 61% accepted, 24 enrolled. In 2014, 14 master's, 6 doctorates awarded. *Entrance requirements:* For master's, GRE General Test, minimum GPA of 3.0. Additional exam requirements/recommendations for international students: Required—TOEFL (minimum score 550 paper-based; 80 iBT). *Application deadline:* For fall admission, 12/15 priority date for domestic and international students; for winter admission, 11/15 priority date for domestic and international students. Applications are processed on a rolling basis. Application fee: $55 ($75 for international students). Electronic applications accepted. *Financial support:* Fellowships, research assistantships, teaching assistantships, institutionally sponsored loans, scholarships/grants, health care benefits, and unspecified assistantships available. Support available to part-time students. *Faculty research:* Adolescent sexual risk taking, adolescent pregnancy prevention, marital structure and process, evaluation of research methodology, remarriage and stepfamilies, family obligations, family structure stereotyping, families and health, parent-child and teacher-child interaction, early head start evaluation, gender issues. *Unit head:* Dr. Lawrence Ganong, Department Co-Chair, 573-882-6852, E-mail: ganongl@missouri.edu. *Application contact:* Dr. Tyler Jamison, Director of Graduate Studies, 573-882-1301, E-mail: jamisontb@missouri.edu.
Website: http://hdfs.missouri.edu/

The University of Montana, Graduate School, Phyllis J. Washington College of Education and Human Sciences, Department of Counselor Education, Missoula, MT 59812-0002. Offers clinical mental health counseling (MA); counseling and supervision (Ed D); counselor education (Ed S); intercultural youth and family development (MA); school counseling (MA). *Accreditation:* ACA. *Degree requirements:* For doctorate, thesis/dissertation. *Entrance requirements:* For master's, doctorate, and Ed S, GRE

Child and Family Studies

General Test. Additional exam requirements/recommendations for international students: Required—TOEFL.

University of Nebraska–Lincoln, Graduate College, College of Education and Human Sciences, Department of Child, Youth and Family Studies, Lincoln, NE 68588. Offers child development/early childhood education (MS, PhD); child, youth and family studies (MS); family and consumer sciences education (MS, PhD); family financial planning (MS); family science (MS, PhD); gerontology (PhD); human sciences (PhD), including child, youth and family studies, gerontology, medical family therapy; marriage and family therapy (MS); medical family therapy (PhD); youth development (MS). *Accreditation:* AAMFT/COAMFTE (one or more programs are accredited). Postbaccalaureate distance learning degree programs offered. *Degree requirements:* For master's, thesis optional. *Entrance requirements:* For master's, GRE. Additional exam requirements/ recommendations for international students: Required—TOEFL (minimum score 550 paper-based). Electronic applications accepted. *Faculty research:* Marriage and family therapy, child development/early childhood education, family financial management.

University of Nevada, Reno, Graduate School, College of Education, Department of Human Development and Family Studies, Reno, NV 89557. Offers MS. *Degree requirements:* For master's, thesis optional. *Entrance requirements:* For master's, GRE General Test, minimum GPA of 2.75. Additional exam requirements/recommendations for international students: Required—TOEFL (minimum score 500 paper-based; 61 iBT), IELTS (minimum score 6). Electronic applications accepted. *Faculty research:* Early childhood/adolescent development, family studies.

University of New Hampshire, Graduate School, School of Health and Human Services, Department of Family Studies, Durham, NH 03824. Offers human development and family studies (MS); marriage and family therapy (MS). Program offered in fall only. *Accreditation:* AAMFT/COAMFTE. Part-time programs available. *Faculty:* 7 full-time (4 women). *Students:* 13 full-time (12 women), 6 part-time (5 women); includes 3 minority (1 Asian, non-Hispanic/Latino; 2 Hispanic/Latino). Average age 28. 7 applicants, 100% accepted, 6 enrolled. *Degree requirements:* For master's, thesis or alternative. *Entrance requirements:* For master's, GRE General Test. Additional exam requirements/recommendations for international students: Required—TOEFL (minimum score 550 paper-based; 80 iBT). *Application deadline:* For fall admission, 5/15 priority date for domestic students, 4/1 for international students. Applications are processed on a rolling basis. Application fee: $65. Electronic applications accepted. *Expenses:* Tuition, state resident: full-time $13,500; part-time $750 per credit hour. Tuition, nonresident: full-time $26,460; part-time $1110 per credit hour. *Required fees:* $1788; $447 per semester. *Financial support:* In 2014–15, 11 students received support, including 4 teaching assistantships; fellowships, research assistantships, career-related internships or fieldwork, Federal Work-Study, scholarships/grants, and tuition waivers (full and partial) also available. Support available to part-time students. Financial award application deadline: 2/15. *Unit head:* Kerry Kazura, Chairperson, 603-862-2135. *Application contact:* Matty Leighton, Administrative Assistant, 603-862-5021, E-mail: family.studies@unh.edu.
Website: http://www.chhs.unh.edu/hdfs

University of New Mexico, Graduate School, College of Education, Program in Family Studies, Albuquerque, NM 87131-2039. Offers family life education (MA); family relations (MA); family studies (PhD); human development in families (MA). Part-time and evening/weekend programs available. *Faculty:* 4 full-time (1 woman). *Students:* 13 full-time (11 women), 17 part-time (14 women); includes 22 minority (3 Black or African American, non-Hispanic/Latino; 3 American Indian or Alaska Native, non-Hispanic/ Latino; 1 Asian, non-Hispanic/Latino; 15 Hispanic/Latino), 1 international. Average age 36. 9 applicants, 56% accepted, 5 enrolled. In 2014, 2 master's, 1 doctorate awarded. *Degree requirements:* For master's, comprehensive exam, thesis (for some programs); for doctorate, comprehensive exam, thesis/dissertation. *Entrance requirements:* For master's, written paper, 3 letters of recommendation, personal statement; for doctorate, GRE General Test, written paper, 3 letters of recommendation, personal statement, interview. Additional exam requirements/recommendations for international students: Required—TOEFL (minimum score 550 paper-based). *Application deadline:* For fall admission, 3/15 priority date for domestic and international students; for spring admission, 10/15 priority date for domestic and international students. Applications are processed on a rolling basis. Application fee: $50. Electronic applications accepted. *Financial support:* In 2014–15, 20 students received support, including 1 fellowship (averaging $7,200 per year), 3 teaching assistantships with full and partial tuition reimbursements available (averaging $3,698 per year); unspecified assistantships also available. Financial award application deadline: 3/1; financial award applicants required to submit FAFSA. *Faculty research:* Home, community and school relations; multicultural issues; parent-child interactions; grandparents as primary caretakers for grandchildren; fathering; early childhood evaluation; early childhood development; globalization and indigenous cultures. *Unit head:* Dr. Ziarat Hossain, Program Coordinator, 505-277-4162, Fax: 505-277-8361, E-mail: zhossain@unm.edu. *Application contact:* Cynthia Salas, Department Administrator, 505-277-4535, Fax: 505-277-8361, E-mail: divbse@unm.edu.
Website: http://coe.unm.edu/departments/ifce/family-studies.html

University of North Alabama, College of Arts and Sciences, Department of Sociology and Family Studies, Florence, AL 35632. Offers family studies (MS). Part-time programs available. Postbaccalaureate distance learning degree programs offered (no on-campus study). *Faculty:* 3 full-time (2 women). *Students:* 3 full-time (all women). Average age 26. 4 applicants, 100% accepted, 4 enrolled. *Degree requirements:* For master's, project or thesis. *Entrance requirements:* For master's, GRE or MAT, three professional references. Additional exam requirements/recommendations for international students: Required—TOEFL (minimum score 550 paper-based; 79 iBT), IELTS (minimum score 6). *Application deadline:* For fall admission, 7/1 priority date for domestic and international students; for spring admission, 11/1 priority date for domestic and international students. Applications are processed on a rolling basis. Application fee: $25 ($50 for international students). Electronic applications accepted. *Expenses:* Tuition, state resident: full-time $5166; part-time $1722 per semester. Tuition, nonresident: full-time $10,332; part-time $3444 per semester. *Required fees:* $393.50 per semester. *Unit head:* Dr. Amber Paulk, Coordinator of Graduate Studies, 256-765-4855, E-mail: apaulk@una.edu. *Application contact:* Hillary N. Coats, Graduate Admissions Coordinator, 256-765-4447, E-mail: graduate@una.edu.
Website: https://www.una.edu/sociology/

The University of North Carolina at Greensboro, Graduate School, School of Health and Human Sciences, Department of Human Development and Family Studies, Greensboro, NC 27412-5001. Offers M Ed, MS, PhD. *Degree requirements:* For master's, one foreign language; for doctorate, one foreign language, thesis/dissertation. *Entrance requirements:* For master's and doctorate, GRE General Test. Additional exam requirements/recommendations for international students: Required—TOEFL. Electronic applications accepted. *Expenses:* Contact institution. *Faculty research:* Adolescent mothers, multi-handicapped, older adults.

University of North Texas, Robert B. Toulouse School of Graduate Studies, Denton, TX 76203-5459. Offers accounting (MS); applied anthropology (MA, MS); applied behavior analysis (Certificate); applied geography (MA); applied technology and performance improvement (M Ed, MS); art education (MA); art history (MA); art museum education (Certificate); arts leadership (Certificate); audiology (Au D); behavior analysis (MS); behavioral science (PhD); biochemistry and molecular biology (MS); biology (MA, MS); biomedical engineering (MS); business analysis (MS); chemistry (MS); clinical health psychology (PhD); communication studies (MA, MS); computer engineering (MS); computer science (MS); counseling (M Ed, MS), including clinical mental health counseling (MS), college and university counseling, elementary school counseling, secondary school counseling; creative writing (MA); criminal justice (MS); curriculum and instruction (M Ed); decision sciences (MBA); design (MA, MFA), including fashion design (MFA), innovation studies, interior design (MFA); early childhood studies (MS); economics (MS); educational leadership (M Ed, Ed D); educational psychology (MS, PhD), including family studies (MS), gifted and talented (MS), human development (MS), learning and cognition (MS), research, measurement and evaluation (MS); electrical engineering (MS); emergency management (MPA); engineering technology (MS); English (MA); English as a second language (MA); environmental science (MS); finance (MBA, MS); financial management (MPA); French (MA); health services management (MBA); higher education (M Ed, Ed D); history (MA, MS); hospitality management (MS); human resources management (MPA); information science (MS); information systems (PhD); information technologies (MBA); interdisciplinary studies (MA, MS); international studies (MA); international sustainable tourism (MS); jazz studies (MM); journalism (MA, MJ, Graduate Certificate), including interactive and virtual digital communication (Graduate Certificate), narrative journalism (Graduate Certificate), public relations (Graduate Certificate); kinesiology (MS); linguistics (MA); local government management (MPA); logistics (PhD); logistics and supply chain management (MBA); long-term care, senior housing, and aging services (MA); management (PhD); marketing (MBA); mathematics (MA, MS); mechanical and energy engineering (MS, PhD); music (MA), including ethnomusicology, music theory, musicology, performance; music composition (PhD); music education (MM Ed, PhD); nonprofit management (MPA); operations and supply chain management (MBA); performance (MM, DMA); philosophy (MA); political science (MA); professional and technical communication (MA); radio, television and film (MA, MFA); rehabilitation counseling (Certificate); sociology (MA); Spanish (MA); special education (M Ed); speech-language pathology (MA); strategic management (MBA); studio art (MFA); teaching (M Ed); MBA/MS. Part-time and evening/weekend programs available. Postbaccalaureate distance learning degree programs offered. *Faculty:* 651 full-time (215 women), 233 part-time/adjunct (139 women). *Students:* 3,040 full-time (1,598 women), 3,401 part-time (2,097 women); includes 1,740 minority (533 Black or African American, non-Hispanic/Latino; 15 American Indian or Alaska Native, non-Hispanic/Latino; 286 Asian, non-Hispanic/Latino; 746 Hispanic/Latino; 3 Native Hawaiian or other Pacific Islander, non-Hispanic/Latino; 157 Two or more races, non-Hispanic/Latino), 1,145 international. Terminal master's awarded for partial completion of doctoral program. *Degree requirements:* For master's, variable foreign language requirement, comprehensive exam (for some programs), thesis (for some programs); for doctorate, variable foreign language requirement, comprehensive exam (for some programs), thesis/dissertation; for other advanced degree, variable foreign language requirement, comprehensive exam (for some programs). *Entrance requirements:* For master's and doctorate, GRE, GMAT. Additional exam requirements/recommendations for international students: Required—TOEFL (minimum score 550 paper-based; 79 iBT). *Application deadline:* For fall admission, 7/15 for domestic students, 3/15 for international students; for spring admission, 11/15 for domestic students, 9/15 for international students; for summer admission, 5/1 for domestic students. Applications are processed on a rolling basis. Application fee: $60. Electronic applications accepted. *Expenses:* Tuition, state resident: full-time $5450; part-time $3633 per year. Tuition, nonresident: full-time $11,966; part-time $7977 per year. *Required fees:* $1301; $398 per credit hour. $685 per semester. Tuition and fees vary according to program and reciprocity agreements. *Financial support:* Fellowships with partial tuition reimbursements, research assistantships with partial tuition reimbursements, teaching assistantships, career-related internships or fieldwork, Federal Work-Study, institutionally sponsored loans, scholarships/grants, health care benefits, and library assistantships available. Support available to part-time students. Financial award applicants required to submit FAFSA. *Unit head:* Mark Wardell, Dean, 940-565-2383, E-mail: mark.wardell@unt.edu. *Application contact:* Toulouse School of Graduate Studies, 940-565-2383, Fax: 940-565-2141, E-mail: gradsch@unt.edu.
Website: http://tsgs.unt.edu/

University of Rhode Island, Graduate School, College of Human Science and Services, Department of Human Development and Family Studies, Kingston, RI 02881. Offers college student personnel (MS); human development and family studies (MS); marriage and family therapy (MS). *Accreditation:* AAMFT/COAMFTE. Part-time programs available. *Faculty:* 15 full-time (10 women). *Students:* 45 full-time (36 women), 11 part-time (9 women); includes 8 minority (5 Black or African American, non-Hispanic/ Latino; 1 Asian, non-Hispanic/Latino; 2 Hispanic/Latino), 2 international. In 2014, 21 master's awarded. *Degree requirements:* For master's, comprehensive exam (for some programs), thesis optional. *Entrance requirements:* For master's, GRE or MAT, 2 letters of recommendation; resume (for college student personnel specialization). Additional exam requirements/recommendations for international students: Required—TOEFL (minimum score 550 paper-based). *Application deadline:* For fall admission, 1/15 for domestic and international students. Application fee: $65. Electronic applications accepted. *Expenses:* Tuition, state resident: full-time $11,532; part-time $641 per credit. Tuition, nonresident: full-time $23,606; part-time $1311 per credit. *Required fees:* $1442; $39 per credit. $35 per semester. One-time fee: $155. *Financial support:* In 2014–15, 2 research assistantships (averaging $10,563 per year), 4 teaching assistantships (averaging $10,563 per year) were awarded. Financial award application deadline: 1/15; financial award applicants required to submit FAFSA. *Total annual research expenditures:* $256,058. *Unit head:* Dr. Karen McCurdy, Chair, 401-874-5960, Fax: 401-874-4020, E-mail: kmccurdy@uri.edu. *Application contact:* Graduate Admissions, 401-874-2872, E-mail: gradadm@etal.uri.edu.
Website: http://www.uri.edu/hss/hdf/

University of Southern California, Graduate School, School of Social Work, Los Angeles, CA 90089. Offers community organization, planning and administration (MSW); families and children (MSW); health (MSW); mental health (MSW); military social work and veterans services (MSW); older adults (MSW); public child welfare (MSW); school settings (MSW); social work (MSW, PhD); systems of mental illness recovery (MSW); work and life (MSW); JD/MSW; M Pl/MSW; MPA/MSW; MSW/MBA; MSW/MJCS; MSW/MS. *Accreditation:* CSWE (one or more programs are accredited). *Degree requirements:* For doctorate, comprehensive exam, thesis/dissertation, qualifying exam/publishable paper. *Entrance requirements:* For doctorate, GRE General Test. Additional exam requirements/recommendations for international students: Required—TOEFL (minimum score 600 paper-based; 100 iBT), ESL exam. Electronic applications accepted. *Faculty research:* Department of Defense Educational Activity, detection/treatment of depression among older adults, health/aging, psychosocial adaptation to extreme environments/man made disasters; mental health needs of older adults.

University of Southern Mississippi, Graduate School, College of Education and Psychology, Department of Child and Family Studies, Hattiesburg, MS 39406-0001. Offers child and family studies (MS); marriage and family therapy (MS). *Accreditation:* AAMFT/COAMFTE. Part-time programs available. *Degree requirements:* For master's,

comprehensive exam, thesis optional. *Entrance requirements:* For master's, GRE General Test, minimum GPA of 2.75 on last 60 hours. Additional exam requirements/recommendations for international students: Required—TOEFL. Electronic applications accepted. *Faculty research:* School food service, teen pregnancy, diet and cholesterol metabolism.

University of South Florida, College of Behavioral and Community Sciences, Department of Child and Family Studies, Tampa, FL 33620-9951. Offers applied behavior analysis (MA, PhD); child and adolescent behavioral health (MS), including developmental disabilities, leadership, translational research and evaluation, youth and behavioral health. *Accreditation:* ACA. *Faculty:* 15 full-time (9 women), 1 part-time/adjunct. *Students:* 54 full-time (44 women), 18 part-time (13 women); includes 24 minority (5 Black or African American, non-Hispanic/Latino; 4 Asian, non-Hispanic/Latino; 15 Hispanic/Latino), 2 international. Average age 25. 113 applicants, 38% accepted, 29 enrolled. In 2014, 29 master's awarded. *Degree requirements:* For master's, comprehensive exam, thesis; for doctorate, comprehensive exam, thesis/dissertation, Behavior Analyst Board Certification Exam. *Entrance requirements:* For master's, GRE General Test, minimum GPA of 3.0 in last 60 hours of coursework; three letters of recommendation; one-page narrative describing experience, interest, and career goals in applied behavior analysis; resume or curriculum vitae; for doctorate, GRE General Test (minimum preferred scores at or above the 40th percentile in verbal, quantitative, and analytical writing sections), master's degree in behavioral analysis or closely-related field; minimum GPA of 3.5 in graduate course work; three letters of recommendation; campus visit with faculty interview; personal statement; curriculum vitae; evidence of research experiences and expertise. Additional exam requirements/recommendations for international students: Required—TOEFL (minimum score 550 paper-based; 79 iBT) or IELTS (minimum score 6.5). *Application deadline:* For fall admission, 2/15 for domestic students, 1/2 for international students. Application fee: $30. *Financial support:* Unspecified assistantships available. *Faculty research:* Applied behavior analysis, autism, behavior management, behavioral intervention, children, developmental disabilities, experimental analysis of behavior, functional assessment, positive behavior support. *Total annual research expenditures:* $12 million. *Unit head:* Dr. Raymond G. Miltenberger, Professor/Director of Master's Program, 813-974-5079, Fax: 813-974-6115, E-mail: miltenbe@usf.edu. *Application contact:* Dr. Raymond G. Miltenberger, Professor/Director of Master's Program, 813-974-5079, Fax: 813-974-6115, E-mail: miltenbe@usf.edu.
Website: http://cfs.cbcs.usf.edu/

University of South Florida, Innovative Education, Tampa, FL 33620-9951. *Unit head:* Kathy Barnes, Interdisciplinary Programs Coordinator, 813-974-8031, Fax: 813-974-7061, E-mail: barnesk@usf.edu. *Application contact:* Karen Tylinski, Metro Initiatives, 813-974-9943, Fax: 813-974-7061, E-mail: ktylinsk@usf.edu.
Website: http://www.usf.edu/innovative-education/

The University of Tennessee, Graduate School, College of Education, Health and Human Sciences, Department of Child and Family Studies, Knoxville, TN 37996. Offers child and family studies (MS); early childhood education (MS). Part-time programs available. *Degree requirements:* For master's, thesis or alternative. *Entrance requirements:* For master's, GRE General Test, minimum GPA of 2.7. Additional exam requirements/recommendations for international students: Required—TOEFL. Electronic applications accepted.

The University of Tennessee, Graduate School, College of Education, Health and Human Sciences, Program in Human Ecology, Knoxville, TN 37996. Offers child and family studies (PhD); community health (PhD); nutrition science (PhD); retailing and consumer sciences (PhD); textile science (PhD). *Degree requirements:* For doctorate, thesis/dissertation. *Entrance requirements:* For doctorate, GRE General Test, minimum GPA of 2.7. Additional exam requirements/recommendations for international students: Required—TOEFL. Electronic applications accepted.

The University of Tennessee at Martin, Graduate Programs, College of Agriculture and Applied Sciences, Department of Family and Consumer Sciences, Martin, TN 38238-1000. Offers dietetics (MSFCS); general family and consumer sciences (MSFCS). Part-time programs available. *Faculty:* 7. *Students:* 34 part-time (30 women); includes 9 minority (6 Black or African American, non-Hispanic/Latino; 2 Hispanic/Latino; 1 Two or more races, non-Hispanic/Latino). 33 applicants, 82% accepted, 18 enrolled. In 2014, 9 master's awarded. *Degree requirements:* For master's, comprehensive exam, thesis optional. *Entrance requirements:* For master's, GRE General Test, minimum GPA of 2.5. Additional exam requirements/recommendations for international students: Required—TOEFL (minimum score 525 paper-based; 71 iBT). *Application deadline:* For fall admission, 7/27 priority date for domestic and international students; for spring admission, 12/17 priority date for domestic and international students. Applications are processed on a rolling basis. Application fee: $30 ($130 for international students). Electronic applications accepted. *Financial support:* In 2014–15, 3 teaching assistantships with full tuition reimbursements (averaging $6,960 per year) were awarded; research assistantships, scholarships/grants, and unspecified assistantships also available. Support available to part-time students. Financial award application deadline: 2/15; financial award applicants required to submit FAFSA. *Faculty research:* Children with developmental disabilities, regional food product development and marketing, parent education. *Unit head:* Dr. Lisa LeBleu, Coordinator, 731-881-7116, Fax: 731-881-7106, E-mail: llebleu@utm.edu. *Application contact:* Jolene L. Cunningham, Student Services Specialist, 731-881-7012, Fax: 731-881-7499, E-mail: jcunningham@utm.edu.
Website: http://www.utm.edu/departments/caas/fcs/index.php

The University of Texas at Austin, Graduate School, College of Natural Sciences, School of Human Ecology, Program in Human Development and Family Sciences, Austin, TX 78712-1111. Offers MA, PhD. *Degree requirements:* For master's, thesis; for doctorate, thesis/dissertation. *Entrance requirements:* For master's and doctorate, GRE General Test. Additional exam requirements/recommendations for international students: Required—TOEFL. Electronic applications accepted. *Faculty research:* Marriage and family relationships, parenting, impact of television on children, courtship, family policy.

The University of Texas at Dallas, School of Behavioral and Brain Sciences, Program in Psychological Sciences, Richardson, TX 75080. Offers early childhood disorders (MS); psychological sciences (MS, PhD). Part-time and evening/weekend programs available. *Faculty:* 13 full-time (8 women), 3 part-time/adjunct (all women). *Students:* 63 full-time (50 women), 15 part-time (12 women); includes 28 minority (7 Black or African American, non-Hispanic/Latino; 7 Asian, non-Hispanic/Latino; 12 Hispanic/Latino; 2 Two or more races, non-Hispanic/Latino), 9 international. Average age 28. 134 applicants, 32% accepted, 29 enrolled. In 2014, 33 master's, 8 doctorates awarded. *Degree requirements:* For master's, directed project or internship; for doctorate, thesis/dissertation. *Entrance requirements:* For master's and doctorate, GRE General Test, minimum GPA of 3.0 in upper-level course work. Additional exam requirements/recommendations for international students: Required—TOEFL (minimum score 550 paper-based). *Application deadline:* For fall admission, 7/15 for domestic students, 5/1 priority date for international students; for spring admission, 11/15 for domestic students, 9/1 priority date for international students. Applications are processed on a rolling basis. Application fee: $50 ($100 for international students). Electronic applications accepted.

Expenses: Tuition, state resident: full-time $11,940; part-time $663 per credit. Tuition, nonresident: full-time $22,282; part-time $1238 per credit. *Financial support:* In 2014–15, 52 students received support, including 3 research assistantships with partial tuition reimbursements available (averaging $17,238 per year), 15 teaching assistantships with partial tuition reimbursements available (averaging $17,109 per year); career-related internships or fieldwork, Federal Work-Study, scholarships/grants, and unspecified assistantships also available. Support available to part-time students. Financial award application deadline: 4/30; financial award applicants required to submit FAFSA. *Faculty research:* Neurocognitive development in young adulthood, infant learning, infant and toddler eye tracking, social aggression. *Unit head:* Dr. Candice Mills, Program Head, Psychological Sciences, 972-883-4475, Fax: 972-883-2491, E-mail: candice.mills@utdallas.edu. *Application contact:* Dr. Margaret Owen, Program Head, Early Childhood Disorders, 972-883-6876, Fax: 972-883-2491, E-mail: mowen@utdallas.edu.
Website: http://bbs.utdallas.edu/psysciphd/

University of Utah, Graduate School, College of Social and Behavioral Science, Department of Family and Consumer Studies, Salt Lake City, UT 84112-0080. Offers human development and social policy (MS). Part-time programs available. *Faculty:* 15 full-time (7 women), 2 part-time/adjunct (1 woman). *Students:* 11 full-time (10 women), 2 part-time (both women); includes 3 minority (all Asian, non-Hispanic/Latino). Average age 32. 12 applicants, 67% accepted, 7 enrolled. In 2014, 5 master's awarded. *Degree requirements:* For master's, comprehensive exam (for some programs), thesis (for some programs), thesis or project. *Entrance requirements:* For master's, GRE General Test, minimum undergraduate GPA of 3.0, courses in research methods and statistics. Additional exam requirements/recommendations for international students: Required—TOEFL (minimum score 550 paper-based). *Application deadline:* For fall admission, 2/1 priority date for domestic and international students. Applications are processed on a rolling basis. Application fee: $55 ($65 for international students). Electronic applications accepted. *Financial support:* In 2014–15, 4 students received support, including 4 teaching assistantships with full tuition reimbursements available (averaging $13,500 per year). Financial award application deadline: 2/1. *Faculty research:* Social, physical, educational and economic contexts of individuals, families and communities. *Unit head:* Prof. Robert Nathan Mayer, PhD, Chair, 801-581-7712, Fax: 801-581-5156, E-mail: robert.mayer@fcs.utah.edu. *Application contact:* Prof. Sonia Salari, PhD, Graduate Director, 801-581-5725, E-mail: sonia.salari@fcs.utah.edu.
Website: http://fcs.utah.edu/

University of Victoria, Faculty of Graduate Studies, Faculty of Human and Social Development, School of Child and Youth Care, Victoria, BC V8W 2Y2, Canada. Offers MA, PhD. Part-time programs available. *Degree requirements:* For master's, thesis. *Entrance requirements:* For master's, resume, professional references, sample of academic writing. Additional exam requirements/recommendations for international students: Required—TOEFL (minimum score 575 paper-based), IELTS (minimum score 7). Electronic applications accepted.

University of Wisconsin–Madison, Graduate School, School of Human Ecology, Program in Human Development and Family Studies, Madison, WI 53706-1380. Offers MS, PhD. Part-time programs available. Terminal master's awarded for partial completion of doctoral program. *Degree requirements:* For master's, thesis; for doctorate, comprehensive exam, thesis/dissertation. *Entrance requirements:* For master's, GRE General Test, 3 letters of recommendation; for doctorate, GRE General Test, MS or MA, 3 letters of recommendation. Additional exam requirements/recommendations for international students: Required—TOEFL (minimum score 580 paper-based; 92 iBT). Electronic applications accepted. *Expenses:* Tuition, state resident: full-time $10,723; part-time $745 per credit. Tuition, nonresident: full-time $24,054; part-time $1578 per credit. *Required fees:* $374 per semester. Tuition and fees vary according to course load, program and reciprocity agreements. *Faculty research:* Human development, adolescence, adulthood, prevention, intervention.

Utah State University, School of Graduate Studies, Emma Eccles Jones College of Education and Human Services, Department of Family, Consumer, and Human Development, Logan, UT 84322. Offers family and human development (MFHD); family, consumer, and human development (MS, PhD), including adolescence/youth (MS), adult development/aging (MS), consumer science (MS), infancy/childhood (MS), marriage and family relations (MS), marriage and family therapy (MS). *Accreditation:* AAMFT/COAMFTE (one or more programs are accredited). Part-time and evening/weekend programs available. Postbaccalaureate distance learning degree programs offered (minimal on-campus study). *Degree requirements:* For master's, thesis; for doctorate, comprehensive exam, thesis/dissertation, competencies. *Entrance requirements:* For master's, GRE General Test or MAT, minimum GPA of 3.0, 3 letters of recommendation; for doctorate, GRE, minimum GPA of 3.0, 3 letters of recommendation. Additional exam requirements/recommendations for international students: Required—TOEFL. Electronic applications accepted. *Faculty research:* Marriage and family relations, adolescent problem behavior, family financial management, early literacy, mental health in the elderly, parent child attachment.

Vanderbilt University, Peabody College, Department of Psychology and Human Development, Nashville, TN 37240-1001. Offers child studies (M Ed). *Accreditation:* APA. Part-time programs available. *Degree requirements:* For master's, comprehensive exam, thesis optional. *Entrance requirements:* For master's, GRE General Test. Additional exam requirements/recommendations for international students: Required—TOEFL (minimum score 550 paper-based; 80 iBT). Electronic applications accepted. *Expenses:* Tuition: Full-time $42,768; part-time $1782 per credit hour. *Required fees:* $422. One-time fee: $30 full-time. *Faculty research:* Child clinical psychology and developmental psychopathology; cognitive psychology, language and social development; educational and developmental neuroscience; quantitative methods and evaluation.

Walden University, Graduate Programs, School of Counseling, Minneapolis, MN 55401. Offers addiction counseling (MS), including addictions and public health, child and adolescent counseling, family studies and interventions, forensic counseling, general program (MS, PhD), trauma and crisis counseling; counselor education and supervision (PhD), including consultation, counseling and social change, forensic mental health counseling, general program (MS, PhD), trauma and crisis; marriage, couple, and family counseling (MS), including forensic counseling, general program (MS, PhD), trauma and crisis counseling; mental health counseling (MS), including forensic counseling, general program (MS, PhD), trauma and crisis counseling; school counseling (MS), including addiction counseling, crisis and trauma, general program (MS, PhD), military families and culture. Part-time and evening/weekend programs available. Postbaccalaureate distance learning degree programs offered (no on-campus study). *Faculty:* 77 full-time (62 women), 314 part-time/adjunct (215 women). *Students:* 1,835 full-time (1,558 women), 1,518 part-time (1,293 women); includes 1,521 minority (1,135 Black or African American, non-Hispanic/Latino; 13 American Indian or Alaska Native, non-Hispanic/Latino; 27 Asian, non-Hispanic/Latino; 234 Hispanic/Latino; 5 Native Hawaiian or other Pacific Islander, non-Hispanic/Latino; 107 Two or more races, non-Hispanic/Latino), 16 international. Average age 38. 684 applicants, 91% accepted, 610 enrolled. In 2014, 592 master's, 4 doctorates awarded. *Degree requirements:* For master's, residency, field experience, professional development plan, licensure plan; for

doctorate, thesis/dissertation, residency, practicum, internship. *Entrance requirements:* For master's, bachelor's degree or higher; minimum GPA of 2.5; official transcripts; goal statement (for some programs); access to computer and Internet; for doctorate, master's degree or higher; three years of related professional or academic experience (preferred); minimum GPA of 3.0; goal statement and current resume (for select programs); official transcripts; access to computer and Internet. Additional exam requirements/recommendations for international students: Required—TOEFL (minimum score 550 paper-based, 79 iBT), IELTS (minimum score 6.5), Michigan English Language Assessment Battery (minimum score 82), or PTE (minimum score 53). *Application deadline:* Applications are processed on a rolling basis. Application fee: $0. Electronic applications accepted. *Expenses: Tuition:* Full-time $11,925; part-time $500 per credit hour. *Required fees:* $647. *Financial support:* Federal Work-Study, scholarships/grants, unspecified assistantships, and family tuition reduction, active duty/veteran tuition reduction, group tuition reduction, interest-free payment plans, employee tuition reduction available. Support available to part-time students. Financial award applicants required to submit FAFSA. *Unit head:* Dr. Savitri Dixon-Saxon, Associate Dean, 866-492-5336. *Application contact:* Meghan M. Thomas, Vice President of Enrollment Management, 866-492-5336, E-mail: info@waldenu.edu.

Walden University, Graduate Programs, School of Social Work and Human Services, Minneapolis, MN 55401. Offers addictions (MSW); addictions and social work (DSW); children, families, and couples (MSW); clinical expertise (DSW); criminal justice (DSW); crisis and trauma (MSW); disaster, crisis, and intervention (DSW); forensic populations and settings (MSW); general program (MSW); human services (MS, PhD), including clinical social work (PhD), criminal justice, disaster, crisis and intervention, family studies and intervention strategies (PhD), family studies and interventions, general program, human services administration, public health, social policy analysis and planning; medical social work (MSW, DSW); military families and culture (MSW); policy practice (DSW); social work (PhD), including addictions and social work, clinical expertise, disaster, crisis and intervention (MS, PhD), family studies and interventions (MS, PhD), medical social work, policy practice, social work administration; social work administration (DSW). Part-time and evening/weekend programs available. Postbaccalaureate distance learning degree programs offered (no on-campus study). *Faculty:* 18 full-time (11 women), 236 part-time/adjunct (156 women). *Students:* 1,400 full-time (1,205 women), 884 part-time (759 women); includes 1,586 minority (1,373 Black or African American, non-Hispanic/Latino; 20 American Indian or Alaska Native, non-Hispanic/Latino; 16 Asian, non-Hispanic/Latino; 120 Hispanic/Latino; 57 Two or more races, non-Hispanic/Latino), 14 international. Average age 40. 892 applicants, 96% accepted, 826 enrolled. In 2014, 61 master's, 14 doctorates awarded. *Degree requirements:* For master's, residency (for some programs); for doctorate, thesis/dissertation, residency. *Entrance requirements:* For master's, bachelor's degree or higher; minimum GPA of 2.5; official transcripts; goal statement (for some programs); access to computer and Internet; for doctorate, master's degree or higher; three years of related professional or academic experience (preferred); minimum GPA of 3.0; goal statement and current resume (for select programs); official transcripts; access to computer and Internet. Additional exam requirements/recommendations for international students: Required—TOEFL (minimum score 550 paper-based, 79 iBT), IELTS (minimum score 6.5), Michigan English Language Assessment Battery (minimum score 82), or PTE (minimum score 53). *Application deadline:* Applications are processed on a rolling basis. Application fee: $0. Electronic applications accepted. *Expenses: Tuition:* Full-time $11,925; part-time $500 per credit hour. *Required fees:* $647. *Financial support:* Fellowships, Federal Work-Study, scholarships/grants, unspecified assistantships, and family tuition reduction, active duty/veteran tuition reduction, group tuition reduction, interest-free payment plans, employee tuition reduction available. Support available to part-time students. Financial award applicants required to submit FAFSA. *Unit head:* Dr. Savitri Dixon-Saxon, Associate Dean, 866-492-5336. *Application contact:* Meghan Thomas, Vice President of Enrollment Management, 866-492-5336, E-mail: info@waldenu.edu.

Website: http://www.waldenu.edu/colleges-schools/school-of-social-work-and-human-services/academic-programs

Washington University in St. Louis, Brown School of Social Work, St. Louis, MO 63130-4899. Offers affordable housing and mixed-income community management (Certificate); American Indian and Alaska native (MSW); children, youth and families (MSW); health (MSW); individualized (MSW), including health; mental health (MSW); older adults and aging societies (MSW); public health (MPH), including epidemiology/biostatistics, global health, health policy analysis, urban design; social and economic development (MSW); social work (MSW, PhD), including management (MSW), policy (MSW), research (MSW), sexual health and education (MSW), social entrepreneurship (MSW), system dynamics (MSW); violence and injury prevention (Certificate); JD/MSW; M Arch/MSW; MPH/MBA; MSW/M Div; MSW/MAPS; MSW/MBA; MSW/MPH. MSW/M Div and MSW/MAPS offered in partnership with Eden Theological Seminary. *Accreditation:* CSWE (one or more programs are accredited). *Faculty:* 42 full-time (24 women), 81 part-time/adjunct (49 women). *Students:* 272 full-time (229 women); includes 138 minority (47 Black or African American, non-Hispanic/Latino; 11 American Indian or Alaska Native, non-Hispanic/Latino; 54 Asian, non-Hispanic/Latino; 19 Hispanic/Latino; 7 Two or more races, non-Hispanic/Latino), 47 international. Average age 26. 817 applicants, 62% accepted, 303 enrolled. In 2014, 239 master's, 5 doctorates awarded. *Degree requirements:* For master's, 60 credit hours (MSW), 52 credit hours (MPH); practicum; for doctorate, comprehensive exam, thesis/dissertation. *Entrance requirements:* For master's, For public health: GRE, GMAT, LSAT, or MCAT, minimum GPA of 3.0; for doctorate, GRE, MA or MSW. Additional exam requirements/recommendations for international students: Required—TOEFL (minimum score 100 iBT) or IELTS. *Application deadline:* For fall admission, 3/1 priority date for domestic and international students. Applications are processed on a rolling basis. Application fee: $40. Electronic applications accepted. *Expenses:* Expenses: The tuition rate for new full-time MSW students for the 2015-2016 academic year is $38,234 per year. The tuition rate for new full-time MPH students for the 2015-2016 academic year is $33,132 per year. *Financial support:* In 2014–15, 301 students received support. Fellowships, research assistantships, Federal Work-Study, institutionally sponsored loans, scholarships/grants, health care benefits, tuition waivers (partial), and unspecified assistantships available. Support available to part-time students. Financial award application deadline: 3/1; financial award applicants required to submit FAFSA. *Faculty research:* Mental health services, social development, child welfare, at-risk teens, autism, environmental health, health policy, health communications, obesity, gender and sexuality, violence and injury prevention, chronic disease prevention, poverty, older adults/aging societies, civic engagement, school social work, program evaluation, health disparities. *Unit head:* Jamie L. Adkisson, Director of Recruitment & Admissions, 314-935-3524, Fax: 314-935-4859, E-mail: jadkisson@wustl.edu. *Application contact:* Cate M. Valentine, Admissions Counselor, 314-935-8879, Fax: 314-935-4859, E-mail: cvalentine@wustl.edu.
Website: http://brownschool.wustl.edu

West Virginia University, College of Human Resources and Education, Department of Technology, Learning and Culture, Program in Child Development and Family Studies, Morgantown, WV 26506. Offers MA. Part-time programs available. *Degree requirements:* For master's, thesis. *Entrance requirements:* For master's, GRE General Test, minimum GPA of 3.0; interview. Additional exam requirements/recommendations for international students: Required—TOEFL. Electronic applications accepted.

Wheelock College, Graduate Programs, Division of Child and Family Studies, Boston, MA 02215-4176. Offers family studies (MS); family support and parent education (MS); family, culture, and society (MS). Part-time programs available. Postbaccalaureate distance learning degree programs offered (minimal on-campus study). *Degree requirements:* For master's, comprehensive exam. Electronic applications accepted. *Faculty research:* Cross-cultural studies of parenting, effects of chronic illness on families, parenting education.

Child Development

Appalachian State University, Cratis D. Williams Graduate School, Department of Family and Consumer Sciences, Boone, NC 28608. Offers child development: birth through kindergarten (MA). Part-time programs available. Postbaccalaureate distance learning degree programs offered (no on-campus study). *Degree requirements:* For master's, comprehensive exam, thesis optional. *Entrance requirements:* For master's, GRE General Test, 3 letters of recommendation. Additional exam requirements/recommendations for international students: Required—TOEFL (minimum score 550 paper-based; 79 iBT), IELTS (minimum score 6.5). Electronic applications accepted. *Faculty research:* Food antioxidants, preschool curriculum, children with special needs, family child care, FCS curriculum content.

California State University, Los Angeles, Graduate Studies, College of Health and Human Services, Department of Child and Family Studies, Los Angeles, CA 90032-8530. Offers child development (MA). Part-time and evening/weekend programs available. *Degree requirements:* For master's, comprehensive exam, project or thesis. *Entrance requirements:* Additional exam requirements/recommendations for international students: Required—TOEFL (minimum score 500 paper-based). *Expenses:* Tuition, state resident: full-time $6738; part-time $3609 per year. Tuition, nonresident: full-time $15,666; part-time $8073 per year. Tuition and fees vary according to course load, degree level and program. *Faculty research:* Nutrition education, laundry product and fabric durability, computer usage in public school home economics.

California State University, San Bernardino, Graduate Studies, College of Social and Behavioral Sciences, Department of Psychology, Program in Child Development, San Bernardino, CA 92407-2397. Offers psychology-life span (MA). *Students:* 14 full-time (13 women), 13 part-time (all women); includes 14 minority (4 Black or African American, non-Hispanic/Latino; 10 Hispanic/Latino), 1 international. Average age 25. 25 applicants, 36% accepted, 9 enrolled. In 2014, 5 master's awarded. *Degree requirements:* For master's, comprehensive exam. *Entrance requirements:* Additional exam requirements/recommendations for international students: Required—TOEFL. *Application deadline:* For fall admission, 7/17 for domestic students. Application fee: $55. *Expenses:* Tuition, state resident: full-time $6738; part-time $1302 per term. Tuition, nonresident: full-time $17,898; part-time $248 per unit. *Required fees:* $365 per quarter. Tuition and fees vary according to degree level and program. *Unit head:* Dr. Sharon Ward, Director, 909-537-7304, E-mail: sward@csusb.edu. *Application contact:* Dr. Jeffrey Thompson, Dean of Graduate Studies, 909-537-5058, E-mail: jthompso@csusb.edu.

Chaminade University of Honolulu, Graduate Services, Program in Education, Honolulu, HI 96816-1578. Offers child development (M Ed); early childhood education (M Ed); educational leadership (M Ed); elementary education (MAT); instructional leadership (M Ed); Montessori education (M Ed); secondary education (MAT), including English, math, science, social studies; special education (MAT). Part-time and evening/weekend programs available. Postbaccalaureate distance learning degree programs offered (minimal on-campus study). *Degree requirements:* For master's, thesis or alternative. *Entrance requirements:* For master's, PRAXIS (for MAT only), minimum GPA of 2.75, 3 letters of recommendation. Additional exam requirements/recommendations for international students: Required—TOEFL (minimum score 550 paper-based). Electronic applications accepted. *Faculty research:* Peace and curriculum education.

East Carolina University, Graduate School, College of Human Ecology, Department of Child Development and Family Relations, Greenville, NC 27858-4353. Offers birth through kindergarten education (MA Ed); child development and family relations (MS); family and consumer sciences (MA Ed); marriage and family therapy (MS); medical family therapy (PhD). *Accreditation:* AAMFT/COAMFTE. Part-time programs available. *Degree requirements:* For master's, comprehensive exam, thesis optional. *Expenses:* Tuition, state resident: full-time $4223. Tuition, nonresident: full-time $16,540. *Required fees:* $2184. *Faculty research:* Child care quality, mental health delivery systems for children, family violence.

Erikson Institute, Academic Programs, Program in Child Development, Chicago, IL 60654. Offers MS. *Degree requirements:* For master's, comprehensive exam, internship. *Entrance requirements:* For master's, 3 letters of recommendation, minimum GPA of 2.75. Additional exam requirements/recommendations for international students: Required—TOEFL.

Kansas State University, Graduate School, College of Human Ecology, School of Family Studies and Human Services, Manhattan, KS 66506. Offers communication sciences and disorders (MS); conflict resolution (Graduate Certificate); early childhood education (MS); family and community service (MS); family studies (MS); life span human development (MS); marriage and family therapy (MS); personal financial planning (MS, Graduate Certificate); youth development (MS, Graduate Certificate). *Accreditation:* AAMFT/COAMFTE; ASHA. Part-time programs available. Postbaccalaureate distance learning degree programs offered (no on-campus study). *Faculty:* 39 full-time (26 women), 9 part-time/adjunct (7 women). *Students:* 69 full-time (57 women), 141 part-time (99 women); includes 48 minority (15 Black or African

American, non-Hispanic/Latino; 3 American Indian or Alaska Native, non-Hispanic/Latino; 3 Asian, non-Hispanic/Latino; 21 Hispanic/Latino; 2 Native Hawaiian or other Pacific Islander, non-Hispanic/Latino; 4 Two or more races, non-Hispanic/Latino), 3 international. Average age 31. 203 applicants, 38% accepted, 57 enrolled. In 2014, 48 master's, 28 other advanced degrees awarded. *Degree requirements:* For master's, comprehensive exam (for some programs), thesis optional. *Entrance requirements:* For master's, GRE, minimum GPA of 3.0 in last 2 years of undergraduate study. Additional exam requirements/recommendations for international students: Required—TOEFL (minimum score 600 paper-based). *Application deadline:* For fall admission, 2/1 priority date for domestic students, 1/1 priority date for international students; for spring admission, 10/1 priority date for domestic students, 8/1 priority date for international students; for summer admission, 2/1 priority date for domestic students, 12/1 priority date for international students. Applications are processed on a rolling basis. Application fee: $50 ($75 for international students). Electronic applications accepted. *Financial support:* In 2014–15, 25 research assistantships (averaging $10,000 per year), 9 teaching assistantships with full tuition reimbursements (averaging $10,000 per year) were awarded; unspecified assistantships also available. Financial award application deadline: 3/1. *Faculty research:* Health and security of military families, personal and family risk assessment and evaluation, disorders of communication and swallowing, families and health, financial decision-making. *Total annual research expenditures:* $8.4 million. *Unit head:* Dr. Dottie Durband, Director, 785-532-5510, Fax: 785-532-5505, E-mail: dottie@ksu.edu. *Application contact:* Connie Fechter, Administrative Specialist, 785-532-5510, Fax: 785-532-5505, E-mail: fechter@ksu.edu.
Website: http://www.he.k-state.edu/fshs/

Lee University, Graduate Studies in Counseling, Cleveland, TN 37320-3450. Offers holistic child development (MS); marriage and family therapy (MS); school counseling (MS). Part-time programs available. *Faculty:* 8 full-time (3 women), 4 part-time/adjunct (0 women). *Students:* 57 full-time (42 women), 25 part-time (19 women); includes 13 minority (8 Black or African American, non-Hispanic/Latino; 1 Asian, non-Hispanic/Latino; 4 Hispanic/Latino), 2 international. Average age 28. 45 applicants, 78% accepted, 30 enrolled. In 2014, 42 master's awarded. *Degree requirements:* For master's, variable foreign language requirement, comprehensive exam (for some programs), thesis (for some programs), internship. *Entrance requirements:* For master's, GRE General Test or MAT (waived if undergraduate GPA is greater than 3.0 or if applicant already has a graduate degree), minimum undergraduate GPA of 3.0, 3 letters of recommendation, interview, official transcripts, essay. Additional exam requirements/recommendations for international students: Required—TOEFL (minimum score 450 paper-based). *Application deadline:* For fall admission, 4/1 priority date for domestic and international students; for spring admission, 10/1 priority date for domestic and international students. Applications are processed on a rolling basis. Application fee: $25. *Expenses: Tuition:* Full-time $10,260; part-time $570 per credit hour. *Required fees:* $35 per semester. One-time fee: $25. Tuition and fees vary according to program. *Financial support:* In 2014–15, 26 students received support. Career-related internships or fieldwork, Federal Work-Study, institutionally sponsored loans, scholarships/grants, and unspecified assistantships available. Financial award application deadline: 3/1; financial award applicants required to submit FAFSA. *Unit head:* Dr. Trevor Milliron, Director, 423-614-8126, Fax: 423-614-8129, E-mail: tmilliron@leeuniversity.edu. *Application contact:* Vicki Glasscock, Graduate Admissions Director, 423-614-8059, E-mail: vglasscock@leeuniversity.edu.
Website: http://www.leeuniversity.edu/academics/graduate/counseling/

Michigan State University, The Graduate School, College of Social Science, Department of Family and Child Ecology, East Lansing, MI 48824. Offers child development (MA); community services (MS); family and child ecology (PhD); family studies (MA); marriage and family therapy (MA); youth development (MA). *Accreditation:* AAMFT/COAMFTE (one or more programs are accredited). *Entrance requirements:* For master's, GRE General Test, minimum GPA of 3.0 in last 2 years of undergraduate course work, 3 letters of recommendation; for doctorate, GRE General Test, minimum GPA of 3.0, 3 letters of recommendation, background in behavioral sciences. Additional exam requirements/recommendations for international students: Required—TOEFL. Electronic applications accepted.

Montclair State University, The Graduate School, College of Education and Human Services, Infant and Early Childhood Mental Health Certificate Program, Montclair, NJ 07043-1624. Offers Certificate. *Students:* Average age 41. In 2014, 1 Certificate awarded. *Expenses:* Tuition, state resident: full-time $9960; part-time $553.35 per credit. Tuition, nonresident: full-time $15,074; part-time $837.43 per credit. *Required fees:* $1595; $88.63 per credit. Tuition and fees vary according to degree level and program. *Unit head:* Dr. Gerard Costa, Coordinator, 973-655-6685, E-mail: costag@mail.montclair.edu. *Application contact:* Amy Aiello, Executive Director of The Graduate School, 973-655-5147, E-mail: graduate.school@montclair.edu.

Montclair State University, The Graduate School, College of Humanities and Social Sciences, MA Program in Child Advocacy and Policy, Montclair, NJ 07043-1624. Offers MA. Postbaccalaureate distance learning degree programs offered (no on-campus study). *Students:* Average age 32. In 2014, 42 master's awarded. *Degree requirements:* For master's, seminar. *Entrance requirements:* For master's, minimum GPA of 3.0 in undergraduate major, interview, writing sample. *Expenses:* Tuition, state resident: full-time $9960; part-time $553.35 per credit. Tuition, nonresident: full-time $15,074; part-time $837.43 per credit. *Required fees:* $1595; $88.63 per credit. Tuition and fees vary according to degree level and program. *Unit head:* Dr. Jason Dickinson, Coordinator, 973-655-4188. *Application contact:* Amy Aiello, Executive Director of The Graduate School, 973-655-5147, Fax: 973-655-7869, E-mail: graduate.school@montclair.edu.

North Carolina Agricultural and Technical State University, School of Graduate Studies, School of Agriculture and Environmental Sciences, Department of Family and Consumer Sciences, Greensboro, NC 27411. Offers child development early education and family studies (MAT); family and consumer sciences (MAT); food and nutrition (MS). Part-time and evening/weekend programs available. *Degree requirements:* For master's, comprehensive exam, thesis or alternative, qualifying exam. *Entrance requirements:* For master's, GRE General Test, minimum GPA of 2.6.

★ **North Dakota State University,** College of Graduate and Interdisciplinary Studies, College of Human Development and Education, Department of Human Development and Family Science, Fargo, ND 58108. Offers couple and family therapy (MS); developmental science (PhD); family financial planning (MS, Certificate); gerontology (MS, PhD, Certificate); human development (MS, PhD). *Accreditation:* AAMFT/COAMFTE. Part-time and evening/weekend programs available. Postbaccalaureate distance learning degree programs offered (no on-campus study). *Degree requirements:* For master's, thesis or alternative; for doctorate, thesis/dissertation. *Entrance requirements:* Additional exam requirements/recommendations for international students: Required—TOEFL (minimum score 525 paper-based; 71 iBT). *Faculty research:* Family therapy, resilience, parenting, adolescent development, mental health.

See Display on page 864 and Close-Up on page 887.

Ohio University, Graduate College, College of Health Sciences and Professions, Department of Social and Public Health, Athens, OH 45701-2979. Offers early child development and family life (MS); family studies (MS); health administration (MHA); public health (MPH); social work (MSW). *Accreditation:* CEPH. Part-time and evening/weekend programs available. Postbaccalaureate distance learning degree programs offered (no on-campus study). *Degree requirements:* For master's, capstone (MPH). *Entrance requirements:* For master's, GMAT, GRE General Test, previous course work in accounting, management, and statistics, previous public health background (MHA, MPH). Additional exam requirements/recommendations for international students: Required—TOEFL (minimum score 550 paper-based; 80 iBT) or IELTS (minimum score 6.5). Electronic applications accepted. *Expenses:* Contact institution. *Faculty research:* Health care management, health policy, managed care, health behavior, disease prevention.

Purdue University, Graduate School, College of Health and Human Sciences, Department of Child Development and Family Studies, West Lafayette, IN 47907. Offers developmental studies (MS, PhD); family studies (MS, PhD); marriage and family therapy (MS, PhD). *Accreditation:* AAMFT/COAMFTE (one or more programs are accredited). Part-time programs available. Terminal master's awarded for partial completion of doctoral program. *Degree requirements:* For master's, thesis; for doctorate, thesis/dissertation. *Entrance requirements:* For master's and doctorate, GRE General Test (minimum score 1000 combined verbal and quantitative), minimum undergraduate GPA of 3.0 or equivalent. Additional exam requirements/recommendations for international students: Required—TOEFL (minimum score 600 paper-based; 90 iBT), TWE (minimum score 4). Electronic applications accepted. *Faculty research:* Inclusion of children with special needs, families as learning environments, relationships in child care, work-family relations, AIDS prevention.

Purdue University Calumet, Graduate Studies Office, School of Liberal Arts and Social Sciences, Department of Behavioral Sciences, Hammond, IN 46323-2094. Offers child development and family studies (MS); marriage and family therapy (MS). *Accreditation:* AAMFT/COAMFTE. Part-time programs available. *Degree requirements:* For master's, thesis. *Entrance requirements:* For master's, GRE, interview. Additional exam requirements/recommendations for international students: Required—TOEFL. *Faculty research:* Substance abuse, sexual abuse, couple therapy, professional issues, adolescent therapy.

Rutgers, The State University of New Jersey, Camden, Graduate School of Arts and Sciences, Program in Childhood Studies, Camden, NJ 08102. Offers MA, PhD. Part-time and evening/weekend programs available. *Degree requirements:* For master's, comprehensive exam, thesis (for some programs), 30 credits; for doctorate, comprehensive exam, thesis/dissertation, 60 credits. *Entrance requirements:* For master's and doctorate, GRE, 3 letters of recommendation; statement of personal, professional and academic goals. Additional exam requirements/recommendations for international students: Required—TOEFL, IELTS. Electronic applications accepted. *Faculty research:* Children's consumer culture, moral development, development of personality and social relations, children's literature, commodification of childhood.

San Diego State University, Graduate and Research Affairs, College of Education, Department of Child and Family Development, San Diego, CA 92182. Offers child development (MS). Part-time programs available. *Degree requirements:* For master's, thesis. *Entrance requirements:* For master's, GRE General Test, 3 letters of recommendation, interview. Additional exam requirements/recommendations for international students: Required—TOEFL. Electronic applications accepted.

Sarah Lawrence College, Graduate Studies, Program in Child Development, Bronxville, NY 10708-5999. Offers MA. Part-time programs available. *Degree requirements:* For master's, thesis, fieldwork. *Entrance requirements:* For master's, minimum B average in undergraduate coursework. Additional exam requirements/recommendations for international students: Required—TOEFL. Electronic applications accepted.

Southern New Hampshire University, School of Education, Manchester, NH 03106-1045. Offers business education (M Ed); child development (M Ed); curriculum and instruction (M Ed), including education leadership, reading, special education, technology integration; education (M Ed); educational leadership (M Ed, Ed D); educational studies (M Ed); elementary education (M Ed); English (MAT); English for speakers of other languages (M Ed); reading and writing specialist (M Ed); school business administration (Certificate); secondary education (M Ed); special education (M Ed); technology integration specialist (M Ed). Part-time and evening/weekend programs available. Postbaccalaureate distance learning degree programs offered (no on-campus study). *Degree requirements:* For master's, comprehensive exam (for some programs), thesis or alternative. *Entrance requirements:* For master's, PRAXIS I, minimum GPA of 2.75. Additional exam requirements/recommendations for international students: Required—TOEFL (minimum score 550 paper-based). Electronic applications accepted. *Expenses:* Contact institution.

Texas Woman's University, Graduate School, College of Professional Education, Department of Family Sciences, Denton, TX 76201. Offers child development (MS); counseling and development (MS); early childhood development and education (PhD); early childhood education (M Ed, MA, MS); family studies (MS, PhD); family therapy (MS, PhD). *Accreditation:* ACA (one or more programs are accredited). Part-time and evening/weekend programs available. Terminal master's awarded for partial completion of doctoral program. *Degree requirements:* For master's, comprehensive exam (for some programs), thesis (for some programs); for doctorate, comprehensive exam, thesis/dissertation. *Entrance requirements:* Additional exam requirements/recommendations for international students: Required—TOEFL (minimum score 550 paper-based; 79 iBT). Electronic applications accepted. *Faculty research:* Parenting/parent education, military families, play therapy, family sexuality, diversity, healthy relationships/healthy marriages, childhood obesity, male communication.

Tufts University, Graduate School of Arts and Sciences, Eliot-Pearson Department of Child Study and Human Development, Medford, MA 02155. Offers child study and human development (MA, PhD); early childhood education (MAT). Part-time programs available. *Faculty:* 13 full-time (10 women), 22 part-time/adjunct (18 women). *Students:* 68 full-time (62 women), 31 part-time (24 women); includes 21 minority (6 Black or African American, non-Hispanic/Latino; 7 Asian, non-Hispanic/Latino; 4 Hispanic/Latino; 4 Two or more races, non-Hispanic/Latino), 11 international. Average age 28. 122 applicants, 58% accepted, 29 enrolled. In 2014, 42 master's, 3 doctorates awarded. *Degree requirements:* For master's, thesis (for some programs); for doctorate, thesis/dissertation. *Entrance requirements:* For master's and doctorate, GRE General Test. Additional exam requirements/recommendations for international students: Required—TOEFL (minimum score 550 paper-based; 80 iBT), IELTS (minimum score 6.5). *Application deadline:* For fall admission, 12/1 priority date for domestic and international students. Applications are processed on a rolling basis. Application fee: $75. Electronic applications accepted. *Expenses: Tuition:* Full-time $45,590; part-time $1161 per credit hour. *Required fees:* $782. Full-time tuition and fees vary according to degree level, program and student level. Part-time tuition and fees vary according to course load. *Financial support:* Fellowships, research assistantships with full and partial tuition reimbursements, teaching assistantships with full and partial tuition reimbursements, Federal Work-Study, scholarships/grants, tuition waivers (partial), and unspecified assistantships available. Support available to part-time students. Financial award

application deadline: 5/15; financial award applicants required to submit FAFSA. *Unit head:* Dr. David Henry Feldman, Graduate Program Director. *Application contact:* Office of Graduate Admissions, 617-627-3395, E-mail: gradadmissions@tufts.edu.
Website: http://ase.tufts.edu/epcd

The University of Akron, Graduate School, Buchtel College of Arts and Sciences, School of Family and Consumer Sciences, Akron, OH 44325. Offers child and family development (MA), including child development, family development; clothing, textiles and interiors (MA). Part-time and evening/weekend programs available. *Faculty:* 6 full-time (all women), 10 part-time/adjunct (6 women). *Students:* 6 full-time (5 women), 1 (woman) part-time; includes 1 minority (Black or African American, non-Hispanic/Latino). Average age 28. 8 applicants, 50% accepted, 3 enrolled. In 2014, 3 master's awarded. *Degree requirements:* For master's, comprehensive exam, thesis optional, oral exam. *Entrance requirements:* For master's, GRE, minimum GPA of 2.75, letters of recommendation, statement of purpose, resume. Additional exam requirements/recommendations for international students: Required—TOEFL (minimum score 550 paper-based; 79 iBT), IELTS (minimum score 6.5). *Application deadline:* For fall admission, 3/1 priority date for domestic and international students; for spring admission, 10/1 priority date for domestic and international students. Application fee: $45 ($70 for international students). Electronic applications accepted. *Expenses:* Tuition, state resident: full-time $7578; part-time $421 per credit hour. Tuition, nonresident: full-time $12,977; part-time $721 per credit hour. *Required fees:* $1388; $35 per credit hour. Tuition and fees vary according to course load. *Financial support:* In 2014–15, 9 teaching assistantships with full tuition reimbursements were awarded. *Faculty research:* Nutritional health wellness/sports nutrition; historical/cultural aspects of clothing, textiles, interiors; family and consumer sciences (FCS) curriculum development; life span gender roles; families in international and historical perspectives. *Unit head:* Dr. Virginia Gunn, Interim Director, 330-972-7729, E-mail: vgunn@uakron.edu. *Application contact:* Dr. Pamela Schulze, Graduate Director, 330-972-7725, E-mail: schulze@uakron.edu.
Website: http://www.uakron.edu/fcs/

University of California, Davis, Graduate Studies, Graduate Group in Child Development, Davis, CA 95616. Offers MS. *Degree requirements:* For master's, comprehensive exam (for some programs), thesis (for some programs). *Entrance requirements:* For master's, GRE General Test, minimum GPA of 3.0. Additional exam requirements/recommendations for international students: Required—TOEFL (minimum score 550 paper-based). Electronic applications accepted. *Faculty research:* Cognitive development, socio-emotional development, early childhood.

University of Florida, Graduate School, College of Agricultural and Life Sciences, Department of Family, Youth, and Community Sciences, Gainesville, FL 32611. Offers community studies (MS); family and youth development (MS); family, youth and community sciences (MS); nonprofit organization development (MS). Part-time programs available. Postbaccalaureate distance learning degree programs offered (no on-campus study). *Faculty:* 21 full-time (11 women), 4 part-time/adjunct (2 women). *Students:* 14 full-time (11 women), 31 part-time (27 women); includes 9 minority (1 Black or African American, non-Hispanic/Latino; 1 American Indian or Alaska Native, non-Hispanic/Latino; 1 Asian, non-Hispanic/Latino; 6 Hispanic/Latino), 4 international. 34 applicants, 65% accepted, 19 enrolled. In 2014, 11 master's awarded. *Degree requirements:* For master's, comprehensive exam (for some programs), thesis (for some programs). *Entrance requirements:* For master's, GRE General Test, minimum GPA of 3.0. Additional exam requirements/recommendations for international students: Required—TOEFL (minimum score 550 paper-based; 80 iBT), IELTS (minimum score 6). *Application deadline:* For fall admission, 2/1 for domestic and international students; for spring admission, 10/15 for domestic and international students. Applications are processed on a rolling basis. Application fee: $30. Electronic applications accepted. *Financial support:* In 2014–15, 1 research assistantship, 9 teaching assistantships were awarded; fellowships also available. Financial award applicants required to submit FAFSA. *Faculty research:* Adolescent risk behaviors, family risk and resilience, family financial management, community-based organizations/interventions, nutrition and wellness. *Total annual research expenditures:* $712,782. *Unit head:* Traci Irani, PhD, Professor and Interim Chair, 352-273-3446, E-mail: irani@ufl.edu. *Application contact:* Gregg Henderschiedt, Academic Coordinator, Graduate Program, 352-273-3514, Fax: 352-392-8196, E-mail: ghenderschiedt@ufl.edu.
Website: http://fycs.ifas.ufl.edu/

University of La Verne, College of Education and Organizational Leadership, Programs in Child Development/Child Life, La Verne, CA 91750-4443. Offers child development (MS); child life (MS). Part-time programs available. *Faculty:* 3 full-time (all women), 6 part-time/adjunct (all women). *Students:* 22 full-time (all women), 62 part-time (58 women); includes 42 minority (8 Black or African American, non-Hispanic/Latino; 5 Asian, non-Hispanic/Latino; 29 Hispanic/Latino), 3 international. Average age 30. In 2014, 27 master's awarded. *Entrance requirements:* For master's, minimum GPA of 3.0, 3 letters of reference, writing sample. Additional exam requirements/recommendations for international students: Required—TOEFL (minimum score 550 paper-based). *Application deadline:* Applications are processed on a rolling basis. Application fee: $50. *Expenses:* Expenses: Contact institution. *Financial support:* Institutionally sponsored loans, scholarships/grants, and unspecified assistantships available. Financial award application deadline: 3/2; financial award applicants required to submit FAFSA. *Unit head:* Laurie Schroeder, Chairperson, 909-448-4653, E-mail: lschroeder3@laverne.edu. *Application contact:* Christy Ranells, Program and Admission Specialist, 909-448-4644, Fax: 909-9712295, E-mail: cranells@laverne.edu.
Website: http://www.laverne.edu/education/

University of Minnesota, Twin Cities Campus, Graduate School, College of Education and Human Development, Institute of Child Development, Minneapolis, MN 55455-0213. Offers child psychology (MA, PhD); early childhood education (M Ed, MA, PhD); school psychology (MA, PhD). *Faculty:* 17 full-time (8 women). *Students:* 61 full-time (55 women), 15 part-time (14 women); includes 13 minority (4 Black or African American, non-Hispanic/Latino; 2 Asian, non-Hispanic/Latino; 6 Hispanic/Latino; 1 Two or more races, non-Hispanic/Latino), 5 international. Average age 28. 142 applicants, 32% accepted, 29 enrolled. In 2014, 77 master's, 8 doctorates awarded. Application fee: $75 ($95 for international students). *Financial support:* In 2014–15, 26 fellowships (averaging $20,013 per year), 13 research assistantships with full tuition reimbursements (averaging $10,984 per year), 17 teaching assistantships with full tuition reimbursements (averaging $8,929 per year) were awarded. *Faculty research:* Developmental affective and cognitive neuroscience; developmental psychopathology; intervention and prevention science; social and emotional development; cognitive, language, and perceptual development. *Total annual research expenditures:* $8 million. *Unit head:* Dr. Stephanie Carlson, Director, 612-625-6127, E-mail: smc@umn.edu. *Application contact:* Dr. Michael Maratsos, Director of Graduate Studies, 612-624-1027, E-mail: marat001@umn.edu.
Website: http://www.cehd.umn.edu/ICD

University of Nebraska–Lincoln, Graduate College, College of Education and Human Sciences, Department of Child, Youth and Family Studies, Lincoln, NE 68588. Offers child development/early childhood education (MS, PhD); child, youth and family studies (MS); family and consumer sciences education (MS, PhD); family financial planning (MS); family science (MS, PhD); gerontology (PhD); human sciences (PhD), including child, youth and family studies, gerontology, medical family therapy; marriage and family therapy (MS); medical family therapy (PhD); youth development (MS). *Accreditation:* AAMFT/COAMFTE (one or more programs are accredited). Postbaccalaureate distance learning degree programs offered. *Degree requirements:* For master's, thesis optional. *Entrance requirements:* For master's, GRE. Additional exam requirements/recommendations for international students: Required—TOEFL (minimum score 550 paper-based). Electronic applications accepted. *Faculty research:* Marriage and family therapy, child development/early childhood education, family financial management.

The University of North Carolina at Charlotte, College of Education, Department of Special Education and Child Development, Charlotte, NC 28223-0001. Offers academically gifted (Graduate Certificate); child and family studies (M Ed); special education (M Ed, PhD), including academically or intellectually gifted (M Ed), behavioral - emotional handicaps (M Ed), cross-categorical disabilities (M Ed), learning disabilities (M Ed), mental handicaps (M Ed), severe and profound handicaps (M Ed). Part-time programs available. *Faculty:* 26 full-time (20 women), 8 part-time/adjunct (6 women). *Students:* 18 full-time (17 women), 94 part-time (84 women); includes 12 minority (9 Black or African American, non-Hispanic/Latino; 1 Hispanic/Latino; 2 Two or more races, non-Hispanic/Latino). Average age 36. 94 applicants, 91% accepted, 72 enrolled. In 2014, 10 master's, 2 doctorates, 66 other advanced degrees awarded. Terminal master's awarded for partial completion of doctoral program. *Degree requirements:* For master's, thesis or alternative; for doctorate, comprehensive exam, thesis/dissertation, portfolio, qualifying exam. *Entrance requirements:* For master's, GRE or MAT; for doctorate, GRE or MAT, 3 letters of reference, resume or curriculum vitae, minimum GPA of 3.5, master's degree in special education or related field, 3 years of teaching experience. Additional exam requirements/recommendations for international students: Required—TOEFL (minimum score 557 paper-based; 83 iBT). *Application deadline:* For fall admission, 5/1 priority date for domestic students, 5/1 for international students; for spring admission, 10/1 priority date for domestic students, 10/1 for international students. Application fee: $75. Electronic applications accepted. *Expenses:* Tuition, state resident: full-time $4008. Tuition, nonresident: full-time $16,295. *Required fees:* $2755. Tuition and fees vary according to course load and program. *Financial support:* In 2014–15, 14 students received support, including 13 research assistantships (averaging $14,125 per year), 1 teaching assistantship (averaging $2,500 per year). Financial award application deadline: 4/1; financial award applicants required to submit FAFSA. *Faculty research:* Transition to adulthood and self-determination, teaching reading and other academic skills to students with disabilities, alternate assessment, early intervention, preschool education. *Total annual research expenditures:* $3.2 million. *Unit head:* Dr. Mary Lynne Calhoun, Dean, 704-687-8722, Fax: 704-687-2916. *Application contact:* Kathy B. Giddings, Director of Graduate Admissions, 704-687-5503, Fax: 704-687-1668, E-mail: gradadm@uncc.edu.
Website: http://education.uncc.edu/spcd/sped/special_ed.htm

The University of Tennessee at Martin, Graduate Programs, College of Agriculture and Applied Sciences, Department of Family and Consumer Sciences, Martin, TN 38238-1000. Offers dietetics (MSFCS); general family and consumer sciences (MSFCS). Part-time programs available. *Faculty:* 7. *Students:* 34 part-time (30 women); includes 9 minority (6 Black or African American, non-Hispanic/Latino; 2 Hispanic/Latino; 1 Two or more races, non-Hispanic/Latino). 33 applicants, 82% accepted, 18 enrolled. In 2014, 9 master's awarded. *Degree requirements:* For master's, comprehensive exam, thesis optional. *Entrance requirements:* For master's, GRE General Test, minimum GPA of 2.5. Additional exam requirements/recommendations for international students: Required—TOEFL (minimum score 525 paper-based; 71 iBT). *Application deadline:* For fall admission, 7/27 priority date for domestic and international students; for spring admission, 12/17 priority date for domestic and international students. Applications are processed on a rolling basis. Application fee: $30 ($130 for international students). Electronic applications accepted. *Financial support:* In 2014–15, 3 teaching assistantships with full tuition reimbursements (averaging $6,960 per year) were awarded; research assistantships, scholarships/grants, and unspecified assistantships also available. Support available to part-time students. Financial award application deadline: 2/15; financial award applicants required to submit FAFSA. *Faculty research:* Children with developmental disabilities, regional food product development and marketing, parent education. *Unit head:* Dr. Lisa LeBleu, Coordinator, 731-881-7116, Fax: 731-881-7106, E-mail: llebleu@utm.edu. *Application contact:* Jolene L. Cunningham, Student Services Specialist, 731-881-7012, Fax: 731-881-7499, E-mail: jcunningham@utm.edu.
Website: http://www.utm.edu/departments/caas/fcs/index.php

The University of Texas at Austin, Graduate School, College of Natural Sciences, School of Human Ecology, Austin, TX 78712-1111. Offers human development and family sciences (MA, PhD); nutritional sciences (MA, PhD), including nutrition (MA), nutritional sciences (PhD); textile and apparel technology (MS). *Degree requirements:* For master's, thesis; for doctorate, thesis/dissertation. *Entrance requirements:* For master's and doctorate, GRE General Test. Electronic applications accepted.

The University of West Alabama, School of Graduate Studies, College of Education, Departments of Instructional Leadership and Support/Curriculum and Instruction, Program in Early Childhood Education, Livingston, AL 35470. Offers early childhood development (Ed S); early childhood education (M Ed). *Accreditation:* NCATE. Part-time and evening/weekend programs available. Postbaccalaureate distance learning degree programs offered (no on-campus study). *Faculty:* 7 full-time (6 women), 25 part-time/adjunct (19 women). *Students:* 49 (all women); includes 25 minority (24 Black or African American, non-Hispanic/Latino; 1 Hispanic/Latino). Average age 36. 18 applicants, 89% accepted, 12 enrolled. In 2014, 11 master's, 8 Ed Ss awarded. *Degree requirements:* For master's, comprehensive exam, thesis optional. *Entrance requirements:* For master's, GRE General Test, MAT, minimum GPA of 2.75. Additional exam requirements/recommendations for international students: Required—TOEFL (minimum score 500 paper-based; 61 iBT). *Application deadline:* For fall admission, 8/12 for domestic students; for spring admission, 3/24 for domestic students. Applications are processed on a rolling basis. Application fee: $25. Electronic applications accepted. *Expenses:* Tuition, state resident: full-time $1902; part-time $317 per credit hour. Tuition, nonresident: full-time $3804; part-time $634 per credit hour. *Required fees:* $50 per semester. One-time fee: $65. Tuition and fees vary according to course load. *Financial support:* Teaching assistantships, career-related internships or fieldwork, Federal Work-Study, scholarships/grants, and unspecified assistantships available. Support available to part-time students. Financial award applicants required to submit FAFSA. *Unit head:* Dr. Jodie Winship, Chair of Curriculum and Instruction, 205-652-5415, Fax: 205-652-3706, E-mail: jwinship@uwa.edu. *Application contact:* Dr. Kathy Chandler, Dean of Graduate Studies, 205-652-3421, Fax: 205-652-3706, E-mail: kchandler@uwa.edu.
Website: http://www.uwa.edu/earlychildhoodeducationp3.aspx

University of Wyoming, College of Agriculture and Natural Resources, Department of Family and Consumer Sciences, Laramie, WY 82071. Offers early childhood development (MS); family and consumer sciences (MS); food science and human nutrition (MS). Part-time programs available. *Degree requirements:* For master's, thesis, project. *Entrance requirements:* For master's, GRE General Test or MCAT, minimum

GPA of 3.0. Additional exam requirements/recommendations for international students: Required—TOEFL (minimum score 540 paper-based; 76 iBT). Electronic applications accepted. *Faculty research:* Asthma, obesity and healthy weights, nutrition concerns of children with special health care needs, food product development, food safety, postpartum health, exercise nutrition.

Whittier College, Graduate Programs, Department of Education and Child Development, Whittier, CA 90608-0634. Offers educational administration (MA Ed); elementary education (MA Ed); secondary education (MA Ed). Part-time and evening/weekend programs available. *Degree requirements:* For master's, thesis. *Entrance requirements:* For master's, GRE General Test, MAT, minimum GPA of 3.5, academic writing sample.

Clothing and Textiles

Academy of Art University, Graduate Program, School of Fashion, San Francisco, CA 94105-3410. Offers fashion design (MFA); fashion merchandising (MFA); fashion textiles (MFA); knitwear (MFA). Part-time programs available. Postbaccalaureate distance learning degree programs offered (no on-campus study). *Faculty:* 22 full-time (15 women), 65 part-time/adjunct (47 women). *Students:* 468 full-time (408 women), 232 part-time (215 women); includes 186 minority (88 Black or African American, non-Hispanic/Latino; 1 American Indian or Alaska Native, non-Hispanic/Latino; 53 Asian, non-Hispanic/Latino; 31 Hispanic/Latino; 1 Native Hawaiian or other Pacific Islander, non-Hispanic/Latino; 12 Two or more races, non-Hispanic/Latino), 389 international. Average age 28. 239 applicants, 100% accepted, 115 enrolled. In 2014, 197 master's awarded. *Degree requirements:* For master's, final review. *Entrance requirements:* For master's, statement of intent; resume; portfolio/reel; official college transcripts. *Application deadline:* Applications are processed on a rolling basis. Application fee: $100. Electronic applications accepted. *Expenses: Tuition:* Part-time $910 per unit. *Financial support:* Career-related internships or fieldwork and Federal Work-Study available. Support available to part-time students. Financial award application deadline: 8/10; financial award applicants required to submit FAFSA. *Unit head:* 800-544-ARTS, E-mail: info@academyart.edu. *Application contact:* 800-544-ARTS, E-mail: info@academyart.edu.
Website: http://www.academyart.edu/fashion-school/index.html

Auburn University, Graduate School, College of Human Sciences, Department of Consumer Affairs, Auburn University, AL 36849. Offers apparel and textiles (MS); integrated textile and apparel science (PhD). Part-time programs available. *Faculty:* 15 full-time (all women). *Students:* 18 full-time (16 women), 6 part-time (all women); includes 4 minority (3 Black or African American, non-Hispanic/Latino; 1 Asian, non-Hispanic/Latino), 10 international. Average age 29. 18 applicants, 61% accepted, 9 enrolled. In 2014, 7 master's, 1 doctorate awarded. *Degree requirements:* For master's, thesis (for some programs). *Entrance requirements:* For master's, GRE General Test. *Application deadline:* For fall admission, 7/7 for domestic students; for spring admission, 11/24 for domestic students. Applications are processed on a rolling basis. Application fee: $50 ($60 for international students). Electronic applications accepted. *Expenses:* Tuition, state resident: full-time $8586; part-time $477 per credit hour. Tuition, nonresident: full-time $25,758; part-time $1431 per credit hour. *Required fees:* $804 per semester. Tuition and fees vary according to degree level and program. *Financial support:* Fellowships, research assistantships, teaching assistantships, career-related internships or fieldwork, and Federal Work-Study available. Support available to part-time students. Financial award application deadline: 3/15; financial award applicants required to submit FAFSA. *Faculty research:* Merchandising, consumer behavior, international marketing of textiles and apparel, apparel product development. *Total annual research expenditures:* $875,000. *Unit head:* Dr. Carol Warfield, Head, 334-844-1329, E-mail: cwarfiel@humsci.auburn.edu. *Application contact:* Dr. George Flowers, Dean of the Graduate School, 334-844-2125.

Central Michigan University, College of Graduate Studies, College of Education and Human Services, Department of Human Environmental Studies, Mount Pleasant, MI 48859. Offers apparel product development and merchandising technology (MS); gerontology (Graduate Certificate); human development and family studies (MA); nutrition and dietetics (MS). Part-time and evening/weekend programs available. *Degree requirements:* For master's, thesis or alternative. Electronic applications accepted. *Faculty research:* Human growth and development, family studies and human sexuality, human nutrition and dietetics, apparel and textile retailing, computer-aided design for apparel.

Cornell University, Graduate School, Graduate Fields of Human Ecology, Field of Fiber Science and Apparel Design, Ithaca, NY 14853. Offers apparel design (MA, MPS); fiber science (MS, PhD); polymer science (MS, PhD); textile science (MS, PhD). *Degree requirements:* For master's, thesis (MA, MS), project paper (MPS); for doctorate, comprehensive exam, thesis/dissertation. *Entrance requirements:* For master's, GRE General Test, 2 letters of recommendation, portfolio (for functional apparel design); for doctorate, GRE General Test, 2 letters of recommendation. Additional exam requirements/recommendations for international students: Required—TOEFL (minimum score 600 paper-based; 77 iBT). Electronic applications accepted. *Faculty research:* Apparel design, consumption, mass customization, 3-D body scanning.

Eastern Michigan University, Graduate School, College of Technology, School of Visual and Built Environments, Program in Apparel Textiles and Merchandising, Ypsilanti, MI 48197. Offers MS. Part-time and evening/weekend programs available. Postbaccalaureate distance learning degree programs offered (minimal on-campus study). *Students:* 1 (woman) full-time, 13 part-time (10 women); includes 6 minority (4 Black or African American, non-Hispanic/Latino; 1 Asian, non-Hispanic/Latino; 1 Two or more races, non-Hispanic/Latino), 5 international. Average age 29. 19 applicants, 53% accepted, 5 enrolled. In 2014, 11 master's awarded. *Entrance requirements:* Additional exam requirements/recommendations for international students: Required—TOEFL. *Application deadline:* Applications are processed on a rolling basis. Application fee: $45. *Financial support:* Fellowships, research assistantships with full tuition reimbursements, teaching assistantships with full tuition reimbursements, career-related internships or fieldwork, Federal Work-Study, institutionally sponsored loans, scholarships/grants, tuition waivers (partial), and unspecified assistantships available. Support available to part-time students. Financial award applicants required to submit FAFSA. *Application contact:* Dr. Subhas Ghosh, Program Coordinator, 734-487-1161, Fax: 734-487-7690, E-mail: subhas.ghosh@emich.edu.

Fashion Institute of Technology, School of Graduate Studies, Program in Fashion and Textile Studies, New York, NY 10001-5992. Offers MA. *Accreditation:* NASAD. *Degree requirements:* For master's, one foreign language, thesis, internship. *Entrance requirements:* For master's, GRE General Test or GRE Subject Test, previous course work in art history and chemistry, 4 semesters of a foreign language. Additional exam requirements/recommendations for international students: Required—TOEFL (minimum score 550 paper-based). Electronic applications accepted.
See Display on page 189 and Close-Up on page 199.

Georgia State University, College of Arts and Sciences, Ernest G. Welch School of Art and Design, Program in Studio Art, Atlanta, GA 30302-3083. Offers ceramics (MFA); drawing and painting (MFA); graphic design (MFA); interior design (MFA); photography (MFA); printmaking (MFA); sculpture (MFA); textiles (MFA). *Accreditation:* NASAD. *Degree requirements:* For master's, thesis. *Application deadline:* For fall admission, 1/6 for domestic and international students; for spring admission, 1/15 priority date for domestic and international students. Application fee: $50. Electronic applications accepted. *Expenses:* Tuition, state resident: full-time $6516; part-time $362 per credit hour. Tuition, nonresident: full-time $22,014; part-time $1223 per credit hour. *Required fees:* $2128 per semester. Tuition and fees vary according to course load and program. *Financial support:* In 2014–15, fellowships with full tuition reimbursements (averaging $11,000 per year), teaching assistantships with full tuition reimbursements (averaging $7,000 per year) were awarded; research assistantships, scholarships/grants, and unspecified assistantships also available. Financial award application deadline: 4/15. *Faculty research:* Advertising and typography, new media, traditional media, three-dimensional art, architectural and environmental design. *Unit head:* Michael White, Director, Welch School of Art and Design, 404-413-5221, Fax: 404-413-5261, E-mail: mwhite@gsu.edu. *Application contact:* Hubert Stanley Anderson, Director of Graduate Studies, 404-413-5229, Fax: 404-413-5261, E-mail: artgrad@gsu.edu.
Website: http://artdesign.gsu.edu/graduate/admissions/masters-of-fine-arts-in-studio/

Iowa State University of Science and Technology, Department of Apparel, Education Studies, and Hospitality Management, Ames, IA 50011. Offers family and consumer sciences education and studies (M Ed, MS, PhD); foodservice and lodging management (MFCS, MS, PhD); textiles and clothing (MFCS, MS, PhD). *Degree requirements:* For doctorate, thesis/dissertation. *Entrance requirements:* For master's and doctorate, GRE General Test. Additional exam requirements/recommendations for international students: Required—TOEFL (minimum score 550 paper-based; 79 iBT), IELTS (minimum score 6.5). Electronic applications accepted.

Iowa State University of Science and Technology, Program in Apparel, Merchandising, and Design, Ames, IA 50011. Offers MS, PhD. *Degree requirements:* For master's, thesis; for doctorate, thesis/dissertation. *Entrance requirements:* Additional exam requirements/recommendations for international students: Required—TOEFL (minimum score 550 paper-based; 79 iBT), IELTS (minimum score 6.5). Electronic applications accepted.

Kansas State University, Graduate School, College of Human Ecology, Department of Apparel, Textiles, and Interior Design, Manhattan, KS 66506. Offers apparel and textiles (MS), including design, general apparel and textiles, marketing, merchandising, product development. Postbaccalaureate distance learning degree programs offered (no on-campus study). *Faculty:* 12 full-time (9 women). *Students:* 4 full-time (all women), 13 part-time (12 women); includes 6 minority (4 Black or African American, non-Hispanic/Latino; 1 Asian, non-Hispanic/Latino; 1 Hispanic/Latino), 2 international. Average age 32. 7 applicants, 43% accepted, 1 enrolled. In 2014, 9 master's awarded. *Degree requirements:* For master's, comprehensive exam (for some programs), thesis (for some programs). *Entrance requirements:* For master's, GRE General Test (except for merchandising applicants), minimum undergraduate GPA of 3.0. Additional exam requirements/recommendations for international students: Required—TOEFL (minimum score 550 paper-based; 79 iBT), IELTS (minimum score 6.1). *Application deadline:* For fall admission, 1/1 priority date for domestic and international students; for spring admission, 8/1 priority date for domestic and international students; for summer admission, 12/1 priority date for domestic and international students. Applications are processed on a rolling basis. Application fee: $50 ($75 for international students). Electronic applications accepted. *Financial support:* In 2014–15, 7 students received support, including 1 fellowship (averaging $17,304 per year), 3 research assistantships (averaging $16,200 per year), 3 teaching assistantships with full tuition reimbursements available (averaging $14,053 per year); career-related internships or fieldwork, Federal Work-Study, institutionally sponsored loans, scholarships/grants, and unspecified assistantships also available. Support available to part-time students. Financial award application deadline: 2/1; financial award applicants required to submit FAFSA. *Faculty research:* Apparel marketing and consumer behavior, social and environmental responsibility, apparel design, new product development. *Total annual research expenditures:* $222,454. *Unit head:* Prof. Barbara G. Anderson, Head, 785-532-6993, Fax: 785-532-3796, E-mail: barbara@ksu.edu. *Application contact:* Gina Jackson, Application Contact, 785-532-6693, Fax: 785-532-3796, E-mail: gjackson@ksu.edu.
Website: http://www.he.k-state.edu/atid/

Kansas State University, Graduate School, College of Human Ecology, Program in Human Ecology, Manhattan, KS 66506. Offers apparel and textiles (PhD); family life education and consultation (PhD); food service and hospitality management (PhD); lifespan and human development (PhD); marriage and family therapy (PhD); personal financial planning (PhD). *Students:* 51 full-time (31 women), 44 part-time (24 women); includes 20 minority (8 Black or African American, non-Hispanic/Latino; 1 American Indian or Alaska Native, non-Hispanic/Latino; 3 Asian, non-Hispanic/Latino; 4 Hispanic/Latino; 1 Native Hawaiian or other Pacific Islander, non-Hispanic/Latino; 3 Two or more races, non-Hispanic/Latino), 17 international. Average age 39. 44 applicants, 39% accepted, 14 enrolled. In 2014, 17 doctorates awarded. *Degree requirements:* For doctorate, thesis/dissertation. *Application deadline:* For fall admission, 2/1 priority date for domestic and international students; for spring admission, 8/1 priority date for domestic and international students. Applications are processed on a rolling basis. Application fee: $50 ($75 for international students). Electronic applications accepted. *Financial support:* Application deadline: 3/1. *Total annual research expenditures:* $1.8 million. *Unit head:* Dr. John Buckwalter, Dean, 785-532-5500, Fax: 785-532-5504, E-mail: jbb3@ksu.edu. *Application contact:* Application Contact, 785-532-5500, Fax: 785-532-5504, E-mail: he@ksu.edu.

LIM College, MPS Program, New York, NY 10022-5268. Offers fashion marketing (MPS); fashion merchandising and retail management (MPS); visual merchandising (MPS).

Clothing and Textiles

North Carolina State University, Graduate School, College of Textiles, Program in Textile Technology Management, Raleigh, NC 27695. Offers PhD. *Degree requirements:* For doctorate, one foreign language, thesis/dissertation, cumulative exams. *Entrance requirements:* For doctorate, GRE or GMAT. Electronic applications accepted. *Faculty research:* Niche markets, supply chain, globalization, logistics.

North Dakota State University, College of Graduate and Interdisciplinary Studies, College of Human Development and Education, Department of Apparel, Design, and Hospitality Management, Fargo, ND 58108. Offers merchandising (MS, Certificate). Postbaccalaureate distance learning degree programs offered (no on-campus study). *Degree requirements:* For master's, practicum and/or thesis. Electronic applications accepted.

Ohio University, Graduate College, Gladys W. and David H. Patton College of Education and Human Services, Department of Human and Consumer Sciences Education, Athens, OH 45701-2979. Offers apparel, textiles, and merchandising (MS). Part-time programs available. *Degree requirements:* For master's, comprehensive exam (for some programs), thesis. *Entrance requirements:* For master's, GRE. Additional exam requirements/recommendations for international students: Required—TOEFL (minimum score 550 paper-based; 80 iBT) or IELTS (minimum score 6.5). Electronic applications accepted.

Oklahoma State University, College of Human Sciences, Department of Design, Housing and Merchandising, Stillwater, OK 74078. Offers MS, PhD. *Faculty:* 16 full-time (11 women). *Students:* 4 full-time (3 women), 9 part-time (6 women); includes 1 minority (Asian, non-Hispanic/Latino), 7 international. Average age 29. 14 applicants, 57% accepted, 7 enrolled. In 2014, 1 master's, 3 doctorates awarded. *Degree requirements:* For master's, thesis (for some programs); for doctorate, comprehensive exam, thesis/dissertation. *Entrance requirements:* For master's and doctorate, GRE or GMAT. Additional exam requirements/recommendations for international students: Required—TOEFL (minimum score 550 paper-based; 79 iBT). *Application deadline:* For fall admission, 3/1 priority date for international students; for spring admission, 8/1 priority date for international students. Applications are processed on a rolling basis. Application fee: $40 ($75 for international students). Electronic applications accepted. *Expenses:* Tuition, state resident: full-time $4488; part-time $187 per credit hour. Tuition, nonresident: full-time $18,360; part-time $765 per credit hour. *Required fees:* $2413; $100.55 per credit hour. Tuition and fees vary according to campus/location. *Financial support:* In 2014–15, 9 research assistantships (averaging $12,150 per year), 6 teaching assistantships (averaging $10,058 per year) were awarded; career-related internships or fieldwork, Federal Work-Study, scholarships/grants, health care benefits, tuition waivers (partial), and unspecified assistantships also available. Support available to part-time students. Financial award application deadline: 3/1; financial award applicants required to submit FAFSA. *Faculty research:* Environmental sciences design, housing and merchandising; creativity and physical environment; product development, production and evaluation; experimental learning and critical thinking; technology strategies and assessment; customer expectation and satisfaction. *Unit head:* Dr. Kathleen Robinette, Department Head, 405-744-5049, Fax: 405-744-6910, E-mail: kath.robinette@okstate.edu. *Application contact:* Dr. Christine Johnson, Associate Dean for Research and Graduate Studies, 405-744-1744, E-mail: christine.johnson@okstate.edu.
Website: http://humansciences.okstate.edu/dhm/

Oregon State University, College of Business, Program in Design and Human Environment, Corvallis, OR 97331. Offers MA, MS, PhD. Part-time programs available. *Faculty:* 7 full-time (all women). *Students:* 18 full-time (15 women), 4 part-time (2 women); includes 1 minority (Hispanic/Latino), 7 international. Average age 35. 31 applicants, 35% accepted, 5 enrolled. In 2014, 6 master's, 4 doctorates awarded. Terminal master's awarded for partial completion of doctoral program. *Degree requirements:* For master's, thesis or alternative; for doctorate, thesis/dissertation. *Entrance requirements:* For master's and doctorate, GRE General Test, minimum GPA of 3.0 in last 90 hours. Additional exam requirements/recommendations for international students: Required—TOEFL (minimum score 80 iBT), IELTS (minimum score 6.5). *Application deadline:* For fall admission, 8/1 priority date for domestic students, 4/1 for international students; for winter admission, 12/1 for domestic students, 7/1 for international students; for spring admission, 2/1 for domestic students, 10/1 for international students; for summer admission, 5/1 for domestic students, 1/1 for international students. Application fee: $60. *Expenses:* Tuition, state resident: full-time $11,907; part-time $189 per credit hour. Tuition, nonresident: full-time $19,953; part-time $441 per credit hour. *Required fees:* $1472; $449 per term. One-time fee: $350. Tuition and fees vary according to course load and program. *Financial support:* Research assistantships, teaching assistantships, career-related internships or fieldwork, Federal Work-Study, and institutionally sponsored loans available. Support available to part-time students. Financial award application deadline: 1/15. *Unit head:* Dr. Minjeong Kim, Associate Dean for School of Design and Human Environment, 541-737-3468. *Application contact:* Laura Scott, Advisor, 541-737-3796, E-mail: laura.scott@oregonstate.edu.
Website: http://business.oregonstate.edu/graduate-programs

Philadelphia University, School of Business Administration, Program in Global Fashion Enterprise, Philadelphia, PA 19144. Offers MS. Part-time programs available. *Entrance requirements:* For master's, GRE or GMAT, minimum GPA of 2.8, official transcripts, two letters of recommendation, essay. Additional exam requirements/recommendations for international students: Required—TOEFL (minimum score 550 paper-based; 79 iBT). Electronic applications accepted.

Savannah College of Art and Design, Graduate School, Program in Accessory Design, Savannah, GA 31402-3146. Offers MA, MFA. Part-time programs available. *Faculty:* 4 full-time (2 women). *Students:* 8 full-time (7 women), 2 part-time (1 woman); includes 4 minority (2 Black or African American, non-Hispanic/Latino; 1 Asian, non-Hispanic/Latino; 1 Hispanic/Latino), 2 international. Average age 25. 9 applicants, 67% accepted, 4 enrolled. In 2014, 1 master's awarded. *Degree requirements:* For master's, thesis (for some programs), final project (for MA); internship (for MFA). *Entrance requirements:* For master's, portfolio (submitted in digital format). Additional exam requirements/recommendations for international students: Required—TOEFL (minimum score 550 paper-based, 85 iBT), IELTS (minimum score 6.5), or ACTFL. *Application deadline:* For fall admission, 4/1 for domestic and international students. Applications are processed on a rolling basis. Application fee: $40. Electronic applications accepted. *Expenses: Tuition:* Full-time $34,605; part-time $3845 per course. One-time fee: $500. Tuition and fees vary according to course load. *Financial support:* Fellowships, career-related internships or fieldwork, Federal Work-Study, and scholarships/grants available. Financial award application deadline: 4/1; financial award applicants required to submit FAFSA. *Unit head:* Michael Fink, Dean, School of Fashion. *Application contact:* Jenny Jaquillard, Executive Director of Admissions, Recruitment and Events, 912-525-5100, Fax: 912-525-5985, E-mail: admission@scad.edu.
Website: http://www.scad.edu/academics/programs/accessory-design

South Dakota State University, Graduate School, College of Education and Human Sciences, Department of Apparel Merchandising and Interior Design, Brookings, SD 57007. Offers MFCS. Part-time and evening/weekend programs available. Postbaccalaureate distance learning degree programs offered. *Entrance requirements:* Additional exam requirements/recommendations for international students: Required—TOEFL (minimum score 550 paper-based; 79 iBT). *Faculty research:* Rural internet shopping, professional development in apparel merchandising, gender, aesthetics.

The University of Akron, Graduate School, Buchtel College of Arts and Sciences, School of Family and Consumer Sciences, Akron, OH 44325. Offers child and family development (MA), including child development, family development; clothing, textiles and interiors (MA). Part-time and evening/weekend programs available. *Faculty:* 6 full-time (all women), 10 part-time/adjunct (6 women). *Students:* 6 full-time (5 women), 1 (woman) part-time; includes 1 minority (Black or African American, non-Hispanic/Latino). Average age 28. 8 applicants, 50% accepted, 3 enrolled. In 2014, 3 master's awarded. *Degree requirements:* For master's, comprehensive exam, thesis optional, oral exam. *Entrance requirements:* For master's, GRE, minimum GPA of 2.75, letters of recommendation, statement of purpose, resume. Additional exam requirements/recommendations for international students: Required—TOEFL (minimum score 550 paper-based; 79 iBT), IELTS (minimum score 6.5). *Application deadline:* For fall admission, 3/1 priority date for domestic and international students; for spring admission, 10/1 priority date for domestic and international students. Application fee: $45 ($70 for international students). Electronic applications accepted. *Expenses:* Tuition, state resident: full-time $7578; part-time $421 per credit hour. Tuition, nonresident: full-time $12,977; part-time $721 per credit hour. *Required fees:* $1388; $35 per credit hour. Tuition and fees vary according to course load. *Financial support:* In 2014–15, 9 teaching assistantships with full tuition reimbursements were awarded. *Faculty research:* Nutritional health wellness/sports nutrition; historical/cultural aspects of clothing, textiles, interiors; family and consumer sciences (FCS) curriculum development; life span gender roles; families in international and historical perspectives. *Unit head:* Dr. Virginia Gunn, Interim Director, 330-972-7729, E-mail: vgunn@uakron.edu. *Application contact:* Dr. Pamela Schulze, Graduate Director, 330-972-7725, E-mail: schulze@uakron.edu.
Website: http://www.uakron.edu/fcs/

The University of Alabama, Graduate School, College of Human Environmental Sciences, Department of Clothing, Textiles, and Interior Design, Tuscaloosa, AL 35487. Offers apparel and textiles (MSHES). *Faculty:* 7 full-time (all women). *Students:* 1 (woman) full-time, 2 part-time (both women), 1 international. Average age 41. 1 applicant. In 2014, 1 master's awarded. *Degree requirements:* For master's, comprehensive exam, thesis optional. *Entrance requirements:* For master's, GRE General Test or MAT, minimum GPA of 3.0. *Application deadline:* For fall admission, 7/1 for domestic students; for spring admission, 10/30 for domestic students; for summer admission, 4/30 for domestic students. Applications are processed on a rolling basis. Application fee: $50 ($60 for international students). Electronic applications accepted. *Expenses:* Tuition, state resident: full-time $9826. Tuition, nonresident: full-time $24,950. *Financial support:* In 2014–15, 3 students received support, including 1 research assistantship with full tuition reimbursement available (averaging $12,000 per year), 2 teaching assistantships with partial tuition reimbursements available (averaging $6,000 per year); fellowships, career-related internships or fieldwork, Federal Work-Study, scholarships/grants, and health care benefits also available. Financial award application deadline: 4/15. *Faculty research:* Archeological and historic textiles and material culture analysis, textile science issues, scholarship of engagement in higher education, international marketing and trade with soft goods branding management, clothing choice relationships to sex role and self-concept development. *Unit head:* Dr. Shirley Foster, Interim Chair and Assistant Professor, 205-348-6176, Fax: 205-348-0022, E-mail: sfoster@ches.ua.edu. *Application contact:* Patrick D. Fuller, Admissions Officer, 205-348-5923, Fax: 205-348-0400, E-mail: patrick.d.fuller@ua.edu.
Website: http://www.ctd.ches.ua.edu/

University of Alberta, Faculty of Graduate Studies and Research, Department of Human Ecology, Edmonton, AB T6G 2E1, Canada. Offers family ecology and practice (M Sc, PhD); textiles and clothing (M Sc, MA, PhD). Postbaccalaureate distance learning degree programs offered (no on-campus study). *Degree requirements:* For master's, thesis (for some programs); for doctorate, comprehensive exam, thesis/dissertation. *Entrance requirements:* For master's and doctorate, minimum GPA of 7.0 on a 9.0 scale. Additional exam requirements/recommendations for international students: Required—TOEFL (minimum score 580 paper-based). *Faculty research:* Families and aging, family and child poverty, paid and unpaid work of families, textiles and clothing, parent-child relationships.

University of California, Davis, Graduate Studies, Graduate Group in Textiles, Davis, CA 95616. Offers MS. *Degree requirements:* For master's, comprehensive exam (for some programs), thesis (for some programs). *Entrance requirements:* For master's, GRE General Test, minimum GPA of 3.0. Additional exam requirements/recommendations for international students: Required—TOEFL (minimum score 550 paper-based). Electronic applications accepted. *Faculty research:* Fiber science, social psychology, consumer psychology, chemical and physical properties of fibrous and polymeric materials.

University of Delaware, College of Arts and Sciences, Department of Fashion and Apparel Studies, Newark, DE 19716. Offers MS.

University of Georgia, College of Family and Consumer Sciences, Department of Textiles, Merchandising, and Interiors, Athens, GA 30602. Offers historical/cultural aspects of dress and textiles (MS); interior environments (MS); merchandising/international trade (MS); textile analysis (PhD); textile chemical processes (PhD); textile products and standards (PhD); textile science (MS). *Degree requirements:* For master's, thesis; for doctorate, thesis/dissertation. *Entrance requirements:* For master's and doctorate, GRE General Test. Electronic applications accepted.

The University of Manchester, School of Materials, Manchester, United Kingdom. Offers advanced aerospace materials engineering (M Sc); advanced metallic systems (PhD); biomedical materials (M Phil, M Sc, PhD); ceramics and glass (M Phil, M Sc, PhD); composite materials (M Sc, PhD); corrosion and protection (M Phil, M Sc, PhD); materials (M Phil, PhD); metallic materials (M Phil, M Sc, PhD); nanostructural materials (M Phil, M Sc, PhD); paper science (M Phil, M Sc, PhD); polymer science and engineering (M Phil, M Sc, PhD); technical textiles (M Sc); textile design, fashion and management (M Phil, M Sc, PhD); textile science and technology (M Phil, M Sc, PhD); textiles (M Phil, PhD); textiles and fashion (M Ent).

University of Manitoba, Faculty of Graduate Studies, Faculty of Human Ecology, Department of Textile Sciences, Winnipeg, MB R3T 2N2, Canada. Offers M Sc. *Degree requirements:* For master's, thesis.

University of Minnesota, Twin Cities Campus, Graduate School, College of Design, Department of Design, Housing, and Apparel, Minneapolis, MN 55455-0213. Offers apparel (MA, MS, PhD); design communication (MA, MS, PhD); housing studies (MA, MS, PhD, Postbaccalaureate Certificate); interactive design (MFA); interior design (MA, MS, PhD). Part-time programs available. *Degree requirements:* For master's and Postbaccalaureate Certificate, comprehensive exam, thesis (for some programs); for doctorate, comprehensive exam, thesis/dissertation. *Entrance requirements:* For master's, GRE General Test, minimum GPA of 3.0 (preferred), portfolio, 3 letters of recommendation; for doctorate, GRE General Test, minimum GPA of 3.0 (preferred), portfolio, 3 letters of recommendation, writing sample; for Postbaccalaureate Certificate,

GRE General Test, minimum GPA of 3.0 (preferred). Additional exam requirements/recommendations for international students: Required—TOEFL (minimum score 550 paper-based; 79 iBT). Electronic applications accepted. *Faculty research:* Housing policy and community development; consumer behavior; interactive design; design history; social, cultural, and behavioral issues related to designed environments.

University of Missouri, Office of Research and Graduate Studies, College of Human Environmental Sciences, Department of Textile and Apparel Management, Columbia, MO 65211. Offers MA, MS, PhD. *Faculty:* 6 full-time (all women). *Students:* 16 full-time (13 women); includes 2 minority (1 Asian, non-Hispanic/Latino; 1 Two or more races, non-Hispanic/Latino), 8 international. Average age 31. 20 applicants, 30% accepted, 3 enrolled. *Entrance requirements:* For master's, GRE General Test, minimum GPA of 3.0. Additional exam requirements/recommendations for international students: Required—TOEFL (minimum score 550 paper-based; 79 iBT). *Application deadline:* For fall admission, 1/15 priority date for domestic and international students; for winter admission, 6/1 priority date for domestic and international students; for spring admission, 10/1 priority date for domestic and international students. Applications are processed on a rolling basis. Application fee: $55 ($75 for international students). Electronic applications accepted. *Financial support:* Fellowships with full and partial tuition reimbursements, research assistantships with full and partial tuition reimbursements, teaching assistantships with full and partial tuition reimbursements, institutionally sponsored loans, scholarships/grants, health care benefits, and unspecified assistantships available. Support available to part-time students. *Faculty research:* Sustainability and global initiatives, global supply chain and sourcing strategies, consumer behavior and branding, effect of socio-economic and demographic factors on household clothing expenditures, digital textile and apparel design, traditional textile production, historical dress worn in the American West. *Unit head:* Dr. Jana M. Hawley, Department Chair, 573-882-9638, E-mail: hawleyj@missouri.edu. *Application contact:* Jaime Mestres, Academic Advisor, 573-882-6425, E-mail: mestresj@missouri.edu.
Website: http://tam.missouri.edu/

University of Nebraska–Lincoln, Graduate College, College of Education and Human Sciences, Department of Textiles, Clothing and Design, Lincoln, NE 68588. Offers human sciences (PhD), including textiles, clothing and design (MS, PhD); merchandising (MS); textile history/quilt studies (MA); textile science (MS); textile-apparel (MA); textiles, clothing and design (MA, MS), including textiles, clothing and design (MS, PhD). Part-time programs available. Postbaccalaureate distance learning degree programs offered (minimal on-campus study). *Degree requirements:* For master's, thesis optional. *Entrance requirements:* For master's, GRE General Test. Additional exam requirements/recommendations for international students: Required—TOEFL (minimum score 550 paper-based). Electronic applications accepted. *Faculty research:* Merchandising, textile science, fiber arts, textile history, quilt studies.

University of Rhode Island, Graduate School, College of Human Science and Services, Department of Textiles, Fashion Merchandising and Design, Kingston, RI 02881. Offers MS. Part-time programs available. *Faculty:* 8 full-time (5 women). *Students:* 8 full-time (7 women), 6 part-time (all women). In 2014, 4 master's awarded. *Degree requirements:* For master's, comprehensive exam (for some programs), thesis optional. *Entrance requirements:* For master's, GRE, 2 letters of recommendation. Additional exam requirements/recommendations for international students: Required—TOEFL (minimum score 550 paper-based). *Application deadline:* For fall admission, 7/15 for domestic students, 2/1 for international students; for spring admission, 11/15 for domestic students, 7/15 for international students. Application fee: $65. Electronic

applications accepted. *Expenses:* Tuition, state resident: full-time $11,532; part-time $641 per credit. Tuition, nonresident: full-time $23,606; part-time $1311 per credit. *Required fees:* $1442; $39 per credit. $35 per semester. One-time fee: $155. *Financial support:* In 2014–15, 2 teaching assistantships with full and partial tuition reimbursements (averaging $7,130 per year) were awarded. Financial award application deadline: 2/1; financial award applicants required to submit FAFSA. *Unit head:* Dr. Susan Hannel, Chair, 401-874-2882, Fax: 401-874-2581, E-mail: susanhannel@uri.edu. *Application contact:* Dr. Linda Welters, Co-Chair, 401-874-4525, Fax: 401-874-2581, E-mail: lwelters@uri.edu.
Website: http://www.uri.edu/hss/tmd/

The University of Tennessee, Graduate School, College of Education, Health and Human Sciences, Department of Consumer and Industry Services Management, Program in Consumer Services Management, Knoxville, TN 37996. Offers retail and consumer sciences (MS); textile science (MS). Part-time programs available. *Degree requirements:* For master's, thesis or alternative. *Entrance requirements:* For master's, GRE General Test, minimum GPA of 2.7. Additional exam requirements/recommendations for international students: Required—TOEFL. Electronic applications accepted.

The University of Tennessee, Graduate School, College of Education, Health and Human Sciences, Program in Human Ecology, Knoxville, TN 37996. Offers child and family studies (PhD); community health (PhD); nutrition science (PhD); retailing and consumer sciences (PhD); textile science (PhD). *Degree requirements:* For doctorate, thesis/dissertation. *Entrance requirements:* For doctorate, GRE General Test, minimum GPA of 2.7. Additional exam requirements/recommendations for international students: Required—TOEFL. Electronic applications accepted.

Washington State University, College of Agricultural, Human, and Natural Resource Sciences, Department of Apparel, Merchandising, Design, and Textiles, Pullman, WA 99164-2020. Offers MA. Programs offered at the Pullman campus. Part-time programs available. *Students:* 9 full-time (all women); includes 2 minority (1 Asian, non-Hispanic/Latino; 1 Hispanic/Latino), 2 international. Average age 28. 16 applicants, 56% accepted, 5 enrolled. In 2014, 3 master's awarded. *Degree requirements:* For master's, comprehensive exam (for some programs), thesis, oral exam. *Entrance requirements:* For master's, minimum GPA of 3.0, 2 writing samples, 2 letters of recommendation. Additional exam requirements/recommendations for international students: Required—TOEFL, IELTS. *Application deadline:* For fall admission, 1/11 priority date for domestic students, 1/10 for international students; for spring admission, 7/1 for domestic and international students. Applications are processed on a rolling basis. Application fee: $75. Electronic applications accepted. *Expenses:* Tuition, state resident: full-time $11,768. Tuition, nonresident: full-time $25,200. *Required fees:* $960. Tuition and fees vary according to program. *Financial support:* In 2014–15, 1 research assistantship with full and partial tuition reimbursement (averaging $13,379 per year), 7 teaching assistantships with full and partial tuition reimbursements (averaging $13,379 per year) were awarded; career-related internships or fieldwork, Federal Work-Study, institutionally sponsored loans, scholarships/grants, health care benefits, and unspecified assistantships also available. Financial award application deadline: 2/15. *Faculty research:* Product development, supply chain management, cultural diversity, consumer behavior, functional design. *Total annual research expenditures:* $34,000. *Unit head:* Dr. Joan L. Ellis, Department Chair, 509-335-1233, Fax: 509-355-7299, E-mail: joan.ellis@wsu.edu. *Application contact:* Graduate School Admissions, 800-GRADWSU, Fax: 509-335-1949, E-mail: gradsch@wsu.edu.
Website: http://amdt.wsu.edu/

Consumer Economics

California State University, Long Beach, Graduate Studies, College of Health and Human Services, Department of Family and Consumer Sciences, Long Beach, CA 90840. Offers family and consumer sciences (MA); nutritional science (MS), including food science, hospitality foodservice and hotel management, nutritional science. Part-time and evening/weekend programs available. *Degree requirements:* For master's, comprehensive exam or thesis. *Entrance requirements:* For master's, GRE (MS), minimum GPA of 3.0. Electronic applications accepted. *Faculty research:* School uniforms, consumer complaining behavior, nutrition and fitness education and behavior change, curriculum change, teaching experience of interns.

Colorado State University, Graduate School, College of Health and Human Sciences, Department of Design and Merchandising, Fort Collins, CO 80523-1574. Offers MS. Part-time programs available. *Faculty:* 14 full-time (13 women). *Students:* 15 full-time (13 women), 11 part-time (all women); includes 3 minority (1 American Indian or Alaska Native, non-Hispanic/Latino; 1 Asian, non-Hispanic/Latino; 1 Two or more races, non-Hispanic/Latino), 3 international. Average age 31. 15 applicants, 80% accepted, 6 enrolled. In 2014, 4 master's awarded. *Degree requirements:* For master's, thesis or alternative. *Entrance requirements:* Additional exam requirements/recommendations for international students: Required—TOEFL (minimum score 550 paper-based; 80 iBT). *Application deadline:* For fall admission, 3/1 priority date for domestic and international students; for spring admission, 10/15 priority date for domestic and international students. Applications are processed on a rolling basis. Application fee: $50. Electronic applications accepted. *Expenses:* Tuition, state resident: full-time $9348; part-time $519 per credit. Tuition, nonresident: full-time $22,916; part-time $1273 per credit. *Required fees:* $1584. *Financial support:* In 2014–15, 11 students received support, including 5 research assistantships with partial tuition reimbursements available (averaging $10,728 per year), 6 teaching assistantships with partial tuition reimbursements available (averaging $8,940 per year); career-related internships or fieldwork, scholarships/grants, health care benefits, and unspecified assistantships also available. Financial award application deadline: 1/1. *Faculty research:* Consumer behavior, creativity and innovation, design/product development, social responsibility, social/cultural/historical aspects of the near environment. *Total annual research expenditures:* $59,934. *Unit head:* Dr. Nancy J. Miller, Professor and Department Head, 970-491-5811, Fax: 970-491-4855, E-mail: nancy.miller@colostate.edu. *Application contact:* Dr. Jennifer Ogle, Professor and Graduate Coordinator, 970-491-3794, Fax: 970-491-4855, E-mail: jennifer.ogle@colostate.edu.
Website: http://www.dm.chhs.colostate.edu/

Cornell University, Graduate School, Graduate Fields of Human Ecology, Field of Policy Analysis and Management, Ithaca, NY 14853-0001. Offers consumer policy (PhD); family and social welfare policy (PhD); health administration (MHA); health management and policy (PhD); public policy (PhD). *Degree requirements:* For master's, thesis; for doctorate, thesis/dissertation. *Entrance requirements:* For master's, GRE General Test or GMAT, 2 letters of recommendation; for doctorate, GRE General Test, 2

letters of recommendation. Additional exam requirements/recommendations for international students: Required—TOEFL (minimum score 550 paper-based; 77 iBT). Electronic applications accepted. *Faculty research:* Health policy, family policy, social welfare policy, program evaluation, consumer policy.

Indiana State University, College of Graduate and Professional Studies, College of Arts and Sciences, Department of Family and Consumer Sciences, Terre Haute, IN 47809. Offers dietetics (MS); family and consumer sciences education (MS); inter-area option (MS). *Accreditation:* AND. Part-time programs available. *Degree requirements:* For master's, thesis optional. Electronic applications accepted.

Iowa State University of Science and Technology, Department of Apparel, Education Studies, and Hospitality Management, Ames, IA 50011. Offers family and consumer sciences education and studies (M Ed, MS, PhD); foodservice and lodging management (MFCS, MS, PhD); textiles and clothing (MFCS, MS, PhD). *Degree requirements:* For doctorate, thesis/dissertation. *Entrance requirements:* For master's and doctorate, GRE General Test. Additional exam requirements/recommendations for international students: Required—TOEFL (minimum score 550 paper-based; 79 iBT), IELTS (minimum score 6.5). Electronic applications accepted.

Kansas State University, Graduate School, College of Human Ecology, Department of Human Nutrition, Manhattan, KS 66506. Offers human nutrition (MS, PhD); nutritional sciences (PhD); public health nutrition (PhD); public health physical activity (PhD); sensory analysis and consumer behavior (PhD). Part-time programs available. *Faculty:* 17 full-time (11 women), 11 part-time/adjunct (3 women). *Students:* 23 full-time (17 women), 6 part-time (3 women); includes 2 minority (both Asian, non-Hispanic/Latino), 15 international. Average age 30. 32 applicants, 31% accepted, 4 enrolled. In 2014, 5 master's, 2 doctorates awarded. *Degree requirements:* For master's, thesis or alternative, residency; for doctorate, thesis/dissertation, residency. *Entrance requirements:* For master's, GRE General Test, minimum undergraduate GPA of 3.0; for doctorate, GRE General Test, minimum graduate GPA of 3.0. Additional exam requirements/recommendations for international students: Required—TOEFL (minimum score 550 paper-based; 79 iBT), IELTS (minimum score 6.5). *Application deadline:* For fall admission, 2/1 priority date for domestic and international students; for spring admission, 8/1 priority date for domestic and international students. Applications are processed on a rolling basis. Application fee: $50 ($75 for international students). Electronic applications accepted. *Financial support:* In 2014–15, 29 students received support, including 16 research assistantships (averaging $15,711 per year), 6 teaching assistantships with full and partial tuition reimbursements available (averaging $10,167 per year); career-related internships or fieldwork, Federal Work-Study, institutionally sponsored loans, scholarships/grants, health care benefits, and tuition waivers (full) also available. Support available to part-time students. Financial award application deadline: 3/1; financial award applicants required to submit FAFSA. *Faculty research:* Cancer and immunology, obesity, sensory analysis and consumer behavior, nutrient metabolism, clinical and community interventions. *Total annual research expenditures:* $1.1 million.

Consumer Economics

Unit head: Dr. Mark Haub, Head, 785-532-5508, Fax: 785-532-3132, E-mail: haub@ksu.edu. *Application contact:* Janet Finney, Senior Administrative Specialist, 785-532-5508, Fax: 785-532-3132, E-mail: janetkay@ksu.edu.
Website: http://www.he.k-state.edu/hn/

Kansas State University, Graduate School, College of Human Ecology, Program in Human Ecology, Manhattan, KS 66506. Offers apparel and textiles (PhD); family life education and consultation (PhD); food service and hospitality management (PhD); lifespan and human development (PhD); marriage and family therapy (PhD); personal financial planning (PhD). *Students:* 51 full-time (31 women), 44 part-time (24 women); includes 20 minority (8 Black or African American, non-Hispanic/Latino; 1 American Indian or Alaska Native, non-Hispanic/Latino; 3 Asian, non-Hispanic/Latino; 4 Hispanic/Latino; 1 Native Hawaiian or other Pacific Islander, non-Hispanic/Latino; 3 Two or more races, non-Hispanic/Latino), 17 international. Average age 39. 44 applicants, 39% accepted, 14 enrolled. In 2014, 17 doctorates awarded. *Degree requirements:* For doctorate, thesis/dissertation. *Application deadline:* For fall admission, 2/1 priority date for domestic and international students; for spring admission, 8/1 priority date for domestic and international students. Applications are processed on a rolling basis. Application fee: $50 ($75 for international students). Electronic applications accepted. *Financial support:* Application deadline: 3/1. *Total annual research expenditures:* $1.8 million. *Unit head:* Dr. John Buckwalter, Dean, 785-532-5500, Fax: 785-532-5504, E-mail: jbb3@ksu.edu. *Application contact:* Application Contact, 785-532-5500, Fax: 785-532-5504, E-mail: he@ksu.edu.

North Carolina Agricultural and Technical State University, School of Graduate Studies, School of Agriculture and Environmental Sciences, Department of Family and Consumer Sciences, Greensboro, NC 27411. Offers child development early education and family studies (MAT); family and consumer sciences (MAT); food and nutrition (MS). Part-time and evening/weekend programs available. *Degree requirements:* For master's, comprehensive exam, thesis or alternative, qualifying exam. *Entrance requirements:* For master's, GRE General Test, minimum GPA of 2.6.

North Dakota State University, College of Graduate and Interdisciplinary Studies, College of Human Development and Education, Department of Human Development and Family Science, Program in Family Financial Planning, Fargo, ND 58108. Offers Certificate. Electronic applications accepted.

Ohio University, Graduate College, College of Health Sciences and Professions, School of Applied Health Sciences and Wellness, Program in Food and Nutrition, Athens, OH 45701-2979. Offers human and consumer sciences (MS).

Oklahoma State University, College of Human Sciences, Department of Human Development and Family Science, Stillwater, OK 74078. Offers human development and family science (MS, PhD), including family financial planning (MS), human environmental sciences; marriage and family therapy (MS). *Accreditation:* AAMFT/COAMFTE (one or more programs are accredited). Postbaccalaureate distance learning degree programs offered. *Faculty:* 27 full-time (18 women), 9 part-time/adjunct (8 women). *Students:* 25 full-time (19 women), 45 part-time (39 women); includes 18 minority (7 Black or African American, non-Hispanic/Latino; 2 Asian, non-Hispanic/Latino; 1 Hispanic/Latino; 8 Two or more races, non-Hispanic/Latino), 2 international. Average age 30. 72 applicants, 33% accepted, 14 enrolled. In 2014, 24 master's, 3 doctorates awarded. *Degree requirements:* For master's, thesis (for some programs); for doctorate, comprehensive exam, thesis/dissertation. *Entrance requirements:* For master's and doctorate, GRE or GMAT. Additional exam requirements/recommendations for international students: Required—TOEFL (minimum score 550 paper-based; 79 iBT). *Application deadline:* For fall admission, 3/1 priority date for international students; for spring admission, 8/1 priority date for international students. Applications are processed on a rolling basis. Application fee: $40 ($75 for international students). Electronic applications accepted. *Expenses:* Tuition, state resident: full-time $4488; part-time $187 per credit hour. Tuition, nonresident: full-time $18,360; part-time $765 per credit hour. *Required fees:* $2413; $100.55 per credit hour. Tuition and fees vary according to campus/location. *Financial support:* In 2014–15, 35 research assistantships (averaging $11,436 per year), 24 teaching assistantships (averaging $10,007 per year) were awarded; career-related internships or fieldwork, Federal Work-Study, scholarships/grants, health care benefits, tuition waivers (partial), and unspecified assistantships also available. Support available to part-time students. Financial award application deadline: 3/1; financial award applicants required to submit FAFSA. *Faculty research:* Family relations and child development, consequences of adolescent parenting, family stress and coping, impacts of sexual abuse on families, children's social cognition and self-competence, gerontology and health care. *Unit head:* Dr. Jennifer Hayes-Grudo, Department Head, 405-744-5360, Fax: 405-744-6344, E-mail: jennifer.hays.grudo@okstate.edu. *Application contact:* Dr. Brandt Gardner, Graduate Coordinator, 405-744-8360, Fax: 405-744-6344, E-mail: brandt.gardner@okstate.edu.
Website: http://humansciences.okstate.edu/hdfs/

Purdue University, Graduate School, College of Health and Human Sciences, Department of Consumer Sciences and Retailing, West Lafayette, IN 47907. Offers consumer behavior (MS, PhD); family and consumer economics (MS, PhD). Part-time programs available. *Degree requirements:* For master's, thesis, oral presentation, final examination; for doctorate, comprehensive exam, thesis/dissertation, oral presentation, final examination. *Entrance requirements:* For master's, GMAT or GRE General Test (minimum 50th percentile), minimum undergraduate GPA of 3.0 or equivalent; for doctorate, GMAT or GRE General Test (minimum 50th percentile), minimum undergraduate GPA of 3.0 or equivalent; master's degree with minimum GPA of 3.25 or equivalent. Additional exam requirements/recommendations for international students: Required—TOEFL (minimum score 550 paper-based; 77 iBT). Electronic applications accepted. *Faculty research:* Family financial resources, retail management and patronage, chemical analysis of textile dyes and finishes.

South Dakota State University, Graduate School, College of Education and Human Sciences, Department of Consumer Sciences, Brookings, SD 57007. Offers family financial planning (MS); merchandising (MS). *Entrance requirements:* For master's, resume. Additional exam requirements/recommendations for international students: Required—TOEFL (minimum score 525 paper-based).

State University of New York at Oswego, Graduate Studies, School of Education, Department of Vocational Teacher Preparation, Oswego, NY 13126. Offers agriculture (MS Ed); business and marketing (MS Ed); family and consumer sciences (MS Ed); health careers (MS Ed); technical education (MS Ed); trade education (MS Ed). *Accreditation:* NCATE. Part-time and evening/weekend programs available. *Degree requirements:* For master's, comprehensive exam, thesis or alternative. *Entrance requirements:* Additional exam requirements/recommendations for international students: Required—TOEFL (minimum score 560 paper-based).

Texas Tech University, Graduate School, College of Human Sciences, Department of Personal Financial Planning, Lubbock, TX 79409-1210. Offers MS, PhD, JD/MS. Part-time programs available. Postbaccalaureate distance learning degree programs offered (minimal on-campus study). *Faculty:* 12 full-time (5 women). *Students:* 86 full-time (31 women), 20 part-time (12 women); includes 25 minority (9 Black or African American, non-Hispanic/Latino; 2 Asian, non-Hispanic/Latino; 11 Hispanic/Latino; 3 Two or more

races, non-Hispanic/Latino), 37 international. Average age 30. 86 applicants, 76% accepted, 40 enrolled. In 2014, 18 master's, 3 doctorates awarded. Terminal master's awarded for partial completion of doctoral program. *Degree requirements:* For master's, thesis or alternative; for doctorate, comprehensive exam, thesis/dissertation. *Entrance requirements:* For doctorate, GRE, GMAT, or LSAT. Additional exam requirements/recommendations for international students: Required—TOEFL (minimum score 550 paper-based; 79 iBT). *Application deadline:* For fall admission, 6/1 priority date for domestic students, 1/15 priority date for international students; for spring admission, 9/1 priority date for domestic students, 6/15 priority date for international students. Applications are processed on a rolling basis. Application fee: $60. Electronic applications accepted. *Expenses:* Tuition, state resident: full-time $6310; part-time $262.92 per credit hour. Tuition, nonresident: full-time $14,998; part-time $624.92 per credit hour. *Required fees:* $2701; $36.50 per credit. $912.50 per semester. Tuition and fees vary according to course load. *Financial support:* In 2014–15, 81 students received support, including 79 fellowships (averaging $3,128 per year), 5 research assistantships (averaging $19,734 per year), 25 teaching assistantships (averaging $14,640 per year); scholarships/grants and unspecified assistantships also available. Financial award application deadline: 1/15; financial award applicants required to submit FAFSA. *Faculty research:* Financial literacy, retirement planning and living, financial risk tolerance, charitable financial planning, reverse mortgages. *Total annual research expenditures:* $118,082. *Unit head:* Dr. Vickie Hampton, Department Chair, 806-834-1824, Fax: 806-742-5033, E-mail: vickie.hampton@ttu.edu. *Application contact:* Dr. John Gilliam, Graduate Program Director, 806-834-8864, Fax: 806-742-5033, E-mail: john.gilliam@ttu.edu.
Website: http://www.pfp.ttu.edu

Université Laval, Faculty of Agricultural and Food Sciences, Department of Agricultural Economics and Consumer Sciences, Program in Consumer Sciences, Québec, QC G1K 7P4, Canada. Offers Diploma. Part-time programs available. *Entrance requirements:* For degree, knowledge of French and English. Electronic applications accepted.

The University of Alabama, Graduate School, College of Human Environmental Sciences, Department of Consumer Sciences, Tuscaloosa, AL 35487-0158. Offers MS. Part-time and evening/weekend programs available. Postbaccalaureate distance learning degree programs offered (minimal on-campus study). *Faculty:* 9 full-time (6 women), 2 part-time/adjunct (1 woman). *Students:* 10 full-time (5 women), 35 part-time (17 women); includes 8 minority (6 Black or African American, non-Hispanic/Latino; 1 American Indian or Alaska Native, non-Hispanic/Latino; 1 Hispanic/Latino). Average age 36. 27 applicants, 89% accepted, 23 enrolled. In 2014, 15 master's awarded. *Degree requirements:* For master's, capstone. *Entrance requirements:* For master's, GRE or GMAT (50th percentile or higher), minimum GPA of 3.0. Additional exam requirements/recommendations for international students: Required—TOEFL. *Application deadline:* For fall admission, 7/1 priority date for domestic and international students; for winter admission, 1/1 priority date for domestic and international students. Applications are processed on a rolling basis. Application fee: $50 ($60 for international students). Electronic applications accepted. *Expenses:* Tuition, state resident: full-time $9826. Tuition, nonresident: full-time $24,950. *Financial support:* In 2014–15, 1 research assistantship with full tuition reimbursement (averaging $13,000 per year), 1 teaching assistantship with full tuition reimbursement (averaging $13,000 per year) were awarded. Financial award application deadline: 3/15. *Faculty research:* Consumer economics, financial planning, policy evaluation, retirement preparedness, financial wellness. *Total annual research expenditures:* $39,709. *Unit head:* Dr. Milla D. Boschung, Chair, 205-348-6250, Fax: 205-348-3789, E-mail: mboschun@ches.ua.edu. *Application contact:* Rosemary Klein, Admissions Officer, 205-348-2897, Fax: 205-348-3789, E-mail: rfklein@ches.ua.edu.
Website: http://www.csm.ches.ua.edu/

University of Georgia, College of Family and Consumer Sciences, Department of Housing and Consumer Economics, Athens, GA 30602. Offers MS, PhD. Part-time programs available. *Degree requirements:* For master's, thesis; for doctorate, thesis/dissertation. *Entrance requirements:* For master's and doctorate, GRE General Test. Additional exam requirements/recommendations for international students: Required—TOEFL (minimum score 575 paper-based). Electronic applications accepted. *Faculty research:* Demographics, consumer decision-making, home ownership counseling, financial management, economics of divorce and poverty.

University of Guelph, Graduate Studies, College of Management and Economics, Department of Marketing and Consumer Studies, Guelph, ON N1G 2W1, Canada. Offers M Sc. *Degree requirements:* For master's, thesis. *Entrance requirements:* For master's, GMAT or GRE General Test, minimum B average during previous 2 years of course work. Additional exam requirements/recommendations for international students: Required—TOEFL (minimum score 575 paper-based). Electronic applications accepted. *Faculty research:* Marketing, quality management, consumer economics, housing and real estate management, problem gambling.

University of Idaho, College of Graduate Studies, College of Agricultural and Life Sciences, Margaret Ritchie School of Family and Consumer Sciences, Moscow, ID 83844-3183. Offers MS. *Faculty:* 7 full-time. *Students:* 11 full-time, 8 part-time. Average age 34. In 2014, 5 master's awarded. *Degree requirements:* For master's, thesis. *Entrance requirements:* For master's, minimum GPA of 2.8. *Application deadline:* For fall admission, 8/1 for domestic students; for spring admission, 12/15 for domestic students. Application fee: $60. *Expenses:* Tuition, state resident: full-time $4784; part-time $280.50 per credit hour. Tuition, nonresident: full-time $18,314; part-time $957.50 per credit hour. *Required fees:* $2000; $58.50 per credit hour. Tuition and fees vary according to program. *Financial support:* Research assistantships and teaching assistantships available. Financial award application deadline: 2/15. *Faculty research:* Food and nutrition; clothing, textiles and design; child, family and consumer studies; early childhood development. *Unit head:* Dr. Sonya Sue Meyer, Interim Chair, 208-885-6546, E-mail: famcon@uidaho.edu. *Application contact:* Sean Scoggin, Graduate Recruitment Coordinator, 208-885-4001, Fax: 208-885-4406, E-mail: graduateadmissions@uidaho.edu.
Website: http://www.uidaho.edu/fcs/

University of Illinois at Urbana–Champaign, Graduate College, College of Agricultural, Consumer and Environmental Sciences, Department of Agricultural and Consumer Economics, Champaign, IL 61820. Offers agricultural and applied economics (MS, PhD). *Students:* 68 full-time (31 women). Application fee: $70 ($90 for international students). *Unit head:* Paul N. Ellinger, Head, 217-333-5503, Fax: 217-333-5538, E-mail: pellinge@illinois.edu. *Application contact:* Pamela S. Splittstoesser, Graduate Studies Assistant, 217-333-1830, Fax: 217-244-7088, E-mail: splttsts@illinois.edu.
Website: http://ace.illinois.edu/

University of Missouri, Office of Research and Graduate Studies, College of Human Environmental Sciences, Department of Personal Financial Planning, Columbia, MO 65211. Offers MS, PhD, Certificate. *Faculty:* 4 full-time (3 women), 1 (woman) part-time/adjunct. *Students:* 8 full-time (4 women), 27 part-time (14 women); includes 7 minority (3 Black or African American, non-Hispanic/Latino; 2 Asian, non-Hispanic/Latino; 1 Hispanic/Latino; 1 Two or more races, non-Hispanic/Latino), 9 international. Average age 34. 22 applicants, 68% accepted, 12 enrolled. In 2014, 3 master's, 3 other

advanced degrees awarded. *Entrance requirements:* For master's, GRE General Test, minimum GPA of 3.0. Additional exam requirements/recommendations for international students: Required—TOEFL (minimum score 550 paper-based; 79 iBT). *Application deadline:* For fall admission, 2/1 priority date for domestic and international students; for winter admission, 10/1 priority date for domestic and international students. Applications are processed on a rolling basis. Application fee: $55 ($75 for international students). Electronic applications accepted. *Financial support:* Fellowships with full and partial tuition reimbursements, research assistantships with full and partial tuition reimbursements, teaching assistantships with full and partial tuition reimbursements, institutionally sponsored loans, scholarships/grants, health care benefits, and unspecified assistantships available. Support available to part-time students. *Faculty research:* Financial planning, expenditures, savings behavior and motives, later life financial and economic well-being, wealth accumulation and saving choices, financial risk tolerance, portfolio allocation, financial ratios, availability of credit to small businesses, consumer debt management, central policy issues, retirement preparation, household consumption patterns. *Unit head:* Dr. Robert O. Weagley, Department Chair, 573-882-9651, E-mail: weagleyr@missouri.edu. *Application contact:* Voronica Bonaparte, Business Support Specialist II, 573-882-7836, E-mail: bonapartev@missouri.edu.
Website: http://pfp.missouri.edu/

University of Nebraska–Lincoln, Graduate College, College of Education and Human Sciences, Department of Child, Youth and Family Studies, Lincoln, NE 68588. Offers child development/early childhood education (MS, PhD); child, youth and family studies (MS); family and consumer sciences education (MS, PhD); family financial planning (MS); family science (MS, PhD); gerontology (PhD); human sciences (PhD), including child, youth and family studies, gerontology, medical family therapy; marriage and family therapy (MS); medical family therapy (PhD); youth development (MS). *Accreditation:* AAMFT/COAMFTE (one or more programs are accredited). Postbaccalaureate distance learning degree programs offered. *Degree requirements:* For master's, thesis optional. *Entrance requirements:* For master's, GRE. Additional exam requirements/recommendations for international students: Required—TOEFL (minimum score 550 paper-based). Electronic applications accepted. *Faculty research:* Marriage and family therapy, child development/early childhood education, family financial management.

University of South Carolina, The Graduate School, College of Hospitality, Retail, and Sport Management, Department of Retailing, Columbia, SC 29208. Offers MR. Part-time programs available. *Degree requirements:* For master's, comprehensive exam, internship or thesis. *Entrance requirements:* For master's, GMAT or GRE General Test, minimum GPA of 3.0. Additional exam requirements/recommendations for international students: Required—TOEFL (minimum score 80 iBT). Electronic applications accepted. *Faculty research:* Retail technology, retail strategy, international retailing.

The University of Tennessee, Graduate School, College of Education, Health and Human Sciences, Department of Consumer and Industry Services Management, Program in Consumer Services Management, Knoxville, TN 37996. Offers retail and consumer sciences (MS); textile science (MS). Part-time programs available. *Degree requirements:* For master's, thesis or alternative. *Entrance requirements:* For master's, GRE General Test, minimum GPA of 2.7. Additional exam requirements/recommendations for international students: Required—TOEFL. Electronic applications accepted.

The University of Tennessee, Graduate School, College of Education, Health and Human Sciences, Program in Human Ecology, Knoxville, TN 37996. Offers child and family studies (PhD); community health (PhD); nutrition science (PhD); retailing and consumer sciences (PhD); textile science (PhD). *Degree requirements:* For doctorate, thesis/dissertation. *Entrance requirements:* For doctorate, GRE General Test, minimum GPA of 2.7. Additional exam requirements/recommendations for international students: Required—TOEFL. Electronic applications accepted.

University of Utah, Graduate School, College of Social and Behavioral Science, Department of Family and Consumer Studies, Salt Lake City, UT 84112-0080. Offers human development and social policy (MS). Part-time programs available. *Faculty:* 15 full-time (7 women), 2 part-time/adjunct (1 woman). *Students:* 11 full-time (10 women), 2 part-time (both women); includes 3 minority (all Asian, non-Hispanic/Latino). Average age 32. 12 applicants, 67% accepted, 7 enrolled. In 2014, 5 master's awarded. *Degree requirements:* For master's, comprehensive exam (for some programs), thesis (for some programs), thesis or project. *Entrance requirements:* For master's, GRE General Test, minimum undergraduate GPA of 3.0, courses in research methods and statistics. Additional exam requirements/recommendations for international students: Required—TOEFL (minimum score 550 paper-based). *Application deadline:* For fall admission, 2/1 priority date for domestic and international students. Applications are processed on a rolling basis. Application fee: $55 ($65 for international students). Electronic applications accepted. *Financial support:* In 2014–15, 4 students received support, including 4 teaching assistantships with full tuition reimbursements available (averaging $13,500 per year). Financial award application deadline: 2/1. *Faculty research:* Social, physical, educational and economic contexts of individuals, families and communities. *Unit head:* Prof. Robert Nathan Mayer, PhD, Chair, 801-581-7712, Fax: 801-581-5156, E-mail: robert.mayer@fcs.utah.edu. *Application contact:* Prof. Sonia Salari, PhD, Graduate Director, 801-581-5725, E-mail: sonia.salari@fcs.utah.edu.
Website: http://fcs.utah.edu/

University of Wisconsin–Madison, Graduate School, School of Human Ecology, Program in Consumer Behavior and Family Economics, Madison, WI 53706-1380. Offers MS, PhD. Terminal master's awarded for partial completion of doctoral program. *Degree requirements:* For master's, thesis optional; for doctorate, comprehensive exam, thesis/dissertation. *Entrance requirements:* For master's and doctorate, GRE General Test, 3 letters of recommendation. Additional exam requirements/recommendations for international students: Required—TOEFL (minimum score 580 paper-based; 92 iBT). Electronic applications accepted. *Expenses:* Tuition, state resident: full-time $10,723; part-time $745 per credit. Tuition, nonresident: full-time $24,054; part-time $1578 per credit. *Required fees:* $374 per semester. Tuition and fees vary according to course load, program and reciprocity agreements. *Faculty research:* Economic well-being of elderly, finance, financial planning, health care policy, consumer behavior.

University of Wyoming, College of Agriculture and Natural Resources, Department of Family and Consumer Sciences, Laramie, WY 82071. Offers early childhood development (MS); family and consumer sciences (MS); food science and human nutrition (MS). Part-time programs available. *Degree requirements:* For master's, thesis, project. *Entrance requirements:* For master's, GRE General Test or MCAT, minimum GPA of 3.0. Additional exam requirements/recommendations for international students: Required—TOEFL (minimum score 540 paper-based; 76 iBT). Electronic applications accepted. *Faculty research:* Asthma, obesity and healthy weights, nutrition concerns of children with special health care needs, food product development, food safety, postpartum health, exercise nutrition.

Utah State University, School of Graduate Studies, College of Agriculture, Department of Agricultural Systems Technology and Education, Logan, UT 84322. Offers agricultural systems technology (MS), including agricultural extension education, agricultural mechanization, international agricultural extension, secondary and postsecondary agricultural education; family and consumer sciences education (MS). Part-time programs available. Postbaccalaureate distance learning degree programs offered (minimal on-campus study). *Degree requirements:* For master's, comprehensive exam (for some programs), thesis (for some programs). *Entrance requirements:* For master's, GRE General Test, MAT, BS in agricultural education, agricultural extension, or related agricultural or science discipline; minimum GPA of 3.0. Additional exam requirements/recommendations for international students: Required—TOEFL. *Faculty research:* Extension and adult education; structures and environment; low-input agriculture; farm safety, systems, and mechanizations.

Gerontology

Adelphi University, Ruth S. Ammon School of Education, Program in Physical Education and Human Performance Science, Garden City, NY 11530-0701. Offers aging (Certificate); physical/educational human performance science (MA). Part-time and evening/weekend programs available. *Students:* 28 full-time (18 women), 26 part-time (10 women); includes 11 minority (2 Black or African American, non-Hispanic/Latino; 1 Asian, non-Hispanic/Latino; 7 Hispanic/Latino; 1 Two or more races, non-Hispanic/Latino). Average age 28. In 2014, 30 master's awarded. *Degree requirements:* For master's, internship. *Entrance requirements:* For master's, 3 letters of recommendation, resume. Additional exam requirements/recommendations for international students: Required—TOEFL (minimum score 550 paper-based; 80 iBT). *Application deadline:* For fall admission, 4/1 for international students; for spring admission, 11/1 for international students. Applications are processed on a rolling basis. Application fee: $50. Electronic applications accepted. *Financial support:* Career-related internships or fieldwork, Federal Work-Study, tuition waivers (full), and unspecified assistantships available. Financial award application deadline: 2/15; financial award applicants required to submit FAFSA. *Faculty research:* Physical education for the handicapped, sport sociology, sport pedagogy. *Unit head:* Dr. Ronald Feingold, Chair, 516-877-4764, E-mail: feingold@adelphi.edu. *Application contact:* Christine Murphy, Director of Admissions, 516-877-3050, Fax: 516-877-3039, E-mail: graduateadmissions@adelphi.edu.

Alliant International University–Los Angeles, California School of Professional Psychology, Program in Couple and Family Therapy, Alhambra, CA 91803-1360. Offers chemical dependency (MA); gerontology (MA); Latin American family therapy (MA). *Accreditation:* AAMFT/COAMFTE. Part-time and evening/weekend programs available. Terminal master's awarded for partial completion of doctoral program. *Degree requirements:* For master's, comprehensive exam, 50 hours of professional development activities. *Entrance requirements:* Additional exam requirements/recommendations for international students: Required—TOEFL (minimum score 550 paper-based). Electronic applications accepted. *Faculty research:* Foster care, therapy with minority couples, parenting, marriage, trauma.

Appalachian State University, Cratis D. Williams Graduate School, Department of Sociology, Boone, NC 28608. Offers gerontology (MA, Graduate Certificate); sociology (Graduate Certificate). Part-time and evening/weekend programs available. Postbaccalaureate distance learning degree programs offered (no on-campus study). *Degree requirements:* For master's, comprehensive exam, thesis or alternative. *Entrance requirements:* For master's, GRE General Test, 3 letters of recommendation. Additional exam requirements/recommendations for international students: Required— TOEFL (minimum score 570 paper-based; 79 iBT), IELTS (minimum score 6.5). Electronic applications accepted. *Faculty research:* Gerontology, demographics, sociology of aging, sociology of crime.

Arizona State University at the Tempe campus, College of Public Programs, School of Social Work, Phoenix, AZ 85004-0689. Offers advanced direct practice (MSW); assessment of integrative health modalities (Graduate Certificate); gerontology (Graduate Certificate); Latino cultural competency (Graduate Certificate); planning, administration and community practice (MSW); social work (PhD); trauma and bereavement (Graduate Certificate); MPA/MSW. *Accreditation:* CSWE (one or more programs are accredited). Part-time programs available. Terminal master's awarded for partial completion of doctoral program. *Degree requirements:* For master's, thesis or alternative, capstone project, interactive Program of Study (iPOS) submitted before completing 50 percent of required credit hours; for doctorate, comprehensive exam, thesis/dissertation, interactive Program of Study (iPOS) submitted before completing 50 percent of required credit hours. *Entrance requirements:* For master's, GRE or MAT, minimum GPA of 3.2 or equivalent in last 2 years of work leading to bachelor's degree; for doctorate, GRE, minimum GPA of 3.0 or equivalent in last 2 years of work leading to bachelor's degree, 3 letters of recommendation, resume, samples of professional writing, personal statement. Additional exam requirements/recommendations for international students: Required—TOEFL, IELTS, or PTE. Electronic applications accepted. *Expenses:* Contact institution.

Arkansas State University, Graduate School, College of Nursing and Health Professions, School of Nursing, State University, AR 72467. Offers aging studies (Certificate); health care management (Certificate); health sciences (MS); health sciences education (Certificate); nurse anesthesia (MSN); nursing (MSN); nursing practice (DNP). *Accreditation:* AANA/CANAEP (one or more programs are accredited). Part-time programs available. *Faculty:* 16 full-time (14 women). *Students:* 91 full-time (34 women), 121 part-time (107 women); includes 34 minority (23 Black or African American, non-Hispanic/Latino; 2 American Indian or Alaska Native, non-Hispanic/Latino; 2 Asian, non-Hispanic/Latino; 6 Hispanic/Latino; 1 Native Hawaiian or other Pacific Islander, non-Hispanic/Latino). Average age 33. 159 applicants, 38% accepted, 47 enrolled. In 2014, 96 master's awarded. *Degree requirements:* For master's and Certificate, comprehensive exam, thesis or alternative; for doctorate, comprehensive exam, thesis/dissertation. *Entrance requirements:* For master's, GRE General Test or MAT, appropriate bachelor's degree, current Arkansas nursing license, CPR certification, physical examination, professional liability insurance, critical care experience, ACLS Certification, PALS Certification, interview, immunization records,

personal goal statement, health assessment; for doctorate, GRE or MAT, NCLEX-RN Exam, appropriate master's degree, current Arkansas nursing license, CPR certification, physical examination, professional liability insurance, critical care experience, ACLS Certification, PALS Certification, interview, immunization records, personal goal statement, health assessment, TB skin test, background check; for Certificate, GRE or MAT, appropriate bachelor's degree, official transcripts, immunization records, proof of employment in healthcare, TB Skin Test, TB Mask Fit Test, CPR Certification. Additional exam requirements/recommendations for international students: Required—TOEFL (minimum score 550 paper-based; 79 iBT), IELTS (minimum score 6), PTE (minimum score 56). *Application deadline:* Applications are processed on a rolling basis. Electronic applications accepted. *Expenses:* Expenses: Contact institution. *Financial support:* In 2014–15, 11 students received support. Fellowships, career-related internships or fieldwork, scholarships/grants, and unspecified assistantships available. Financial award application deadline: 7/1; financial award applicants required to submit FAFSA. *Unit head:* Dr. Kathleen Wren, Chair of MSN Program, 870-972-3074, Fax: 870-972-2954, E-mail: kwren@astate.edu. *Application contact:* Vickey Ring, Graduate Admissions Coordinator, 870-972-3029, Fax: 870-972-3857, E-mail: vickeyring@astate.edu.
Website: http://www.astate.edu/college/conhp/departments/nursing/

Ball State University, Graduate School, College of Applied Science and Technology, Fisher Institute for Wellness and Gerontology, Program in Applied Gerontology, Muncie, IN 47306-1099. Offers MA. *Students:* 8 full-time (all women), 2 part-time (both women); includes 1 minority (Black or African American, non-Hispanic/Latino), 1 international. Average age 29. 4 applicants, 50% accepted, 1 enrolled. In 2014, 6 master's awarded. Application fee: $25 ($35 for international students). *Financial support:* In 2014–15, 3 students received support, including 5 research assistantships with partial tuition reimbursements available (averaging $9,800 per year). Financial award application deadline: 3/1. *Unit head:* Dr. Kathy Segrist, Interim Director, 765-285-1296, Fax: 765-285-8237, E-mail: ksegrist@bsu.edu.
Website: http://www.bsu.edu/wellness/

Bethel University, Graduate School, St. Paul, MN 55112-6999. Offers autism spectrum disorders (Certificate); business administration (MBA); communication (MA); counseling psychology (MA); educational leadership (Ed D); gerontology (MA); international baccalaureate education (Certificate); K-12 education (MA); literacy education (MA, Certificate); nurse educator (Certificate); nurse leader (Certificate); nurse-midwifery (MS); nursing (MS); physician assistant (MS); postsecondary teaching (Certificate); special education (MA); strategic leadership (MA); teaching (MA). Part-time and evening/weekend programs available. Postbaccalaureate distance learning degree programs offered (no on-campus study). *Faculty:* 13 full-time (7 women), 89 part-time/adjunct (43 women). *Students:* 739 full-time (484 women), 337 part-time (219 women); includes 175 minority (96 Black or African American, non-Hispanic/Latino; 2 American Indian or Alaska Native, non-Hispanic/Latino; 40 Asian, non-Hispanic/Latino; 20 Hispanic/Latino; 1 Native Hawaiian or other Pacific Islander, non-Hispanic/Latino; 16 Two or more races, non-Hispanic/Latino), 26 international. Average age 35. 1,354 applicants, 42% accepted, 421 enrolled. In 2014, 166 master's, 9 doctorates, 11 other advanced degrees awarded. *Degree requirements:* For master's, comprehensive exam (for some programs), thesis (for some programs); for doctorate, comprehensive exam, thesis/dissertation. *Entrance requirements:* Additional exam requirements/recommendations for international students: Required—TOEFL (minimum score 550 paper-based, 80 iBT) or IELTS. *Application deadline:* Applications are processed on a rolling basis. Application fee: $0. Electronic applications accepted. *Financial support:* Teaching assistantships, career-related internships or fieldwork, and scholarships/grants available. Support available to part-time students. Financial award applicants required to submit FAFSA. *Unit head:* Dick Crombie, Vice-President/Dean, 651-635-8000, Fax: 651-635-8004, E-mail: gs@bethel.edu. *Application contact:* Director of Admissions, 651-635-8000, Fax: 651-635-8004, E-mail: gs@bethel.edu.
Website: https://www.bethel.edu/graduate/

California State University, Fullerton, Graduate Studies, College of Humanities and Social Sciences, Program in Gerontology, Fullerton, CA 92834-9480. Offers MS. Part-time programs available. *Students:* 13 full-time (11 women), 16 part-time (14 women); includes 15 minority (3 Black or African American, non-Hispanic/Latino; 3 Asian, non-Hispanic/Latino; 8 Hispanic/Latino; 1 Two or more races, non-Hispanic/Latino). Average age 40. 13 applicants, 69% accepted, 9 enrolled. In 2014, 8 master's awarded. *Financial support:* Career-related internships or fieldwork, Federal Work-Study, institutionally sponsored loans, and scholarships/grants available. Financial award application deadline: 3/1; financial award applicants required to submit FAFSA. *Unit head:* Dr. Barbara Cherry, Coordinator, 657-278-3035. *Application contact:* Admissions/Applications, 657-278-2371.

California State University, Long Beach, Graduate Studies, College of Health and Human Services, Program in Gerontology, Long Beach, CA 90840. Offers MS. Part-time programs available. *Degree requirements:* For master's, thesis optional. Electronic applications accepted.

Capella University, School of Public Service Leadership, Master's Programs in Healthcare, Minneapolis, MN 55402. Offers criminal justice (MS); emergency management (MS); general public health (MPH); gerontology (MS); health administration (MHA); health care operations (MHA); health management policy (MPH); health policy (MHA); homeland security (MS); multidisciplinary human services (MS); public administration (MPA); public safety leadership (MS); social and community services (MS); social behavioral sciences (MPH); MS/MPA.

Central Michigan University, College of Graduate Studies, College of Education and Human Services, Department of Human Environmental Studies, Mount Pleasant, MI 48859. Offers apparel product development and merchandising technology (MS); gerontology (Graduate Certificate); human development and family studies (MA); nutrition and dietetics (MS). Part-time and evening/weekend programs available. *Degree requirements:* For master's, thesis or alternative. Electronic applications accepted. *Faculty research:* Human growth and development, family studies and human sexuality, human nutrition and dietetics, apparel and textile retailing, computer-aided design for apparel.

The College at Brockport, State University of New York, School of Education and Human Services, Greater Rochester Collaborative Master of Social Work Program, Brockport, NY 14420-2997. Offers gerontology (AGC); interdisciplinary health practice (MSW). Program offered jointly with Nazareth College of Rochester. *Accreditation:* CSWE. Part-time programs available. *Faculty:* 4 full-time (3 women), 4 part-time/adjunct (3 women). *Students:* 55 full-time (41 women), 146 part-time (124 women); includes 41 minority (24 Black or African American, non-Hispanic/Latino; 1 American Indian or Alaska Native, non-Hispanic/Latino; 4 Hispanic/Latino; 1 Native Hawaiian or other Pacific Islander, non-Hispanic/Latino; 11 Two or more races, non-Hispanic/Latino), 2 international. 186 applicants, 83% accepted, 115 enrolled. In 2014, 55 master's, 9 other advanced degrees awarded. *Degree requirements:* For master's, thesis or alternative. *Entrance requirements:* For master's, minimum GPA of 3.0, letters of recommendation, statement of objectives. Additional exam requirements/recommendations for international students: Required—TOEFL (minimum score 550 paper-based; 79 iBT), IELTS (minimum score 6.5). *Application deadline:* For fall admission, 1/15 priority date for domestic and international students; for summer admission, 1/15 priority date for domestic and international students. Application fee: $50. Electronic applications accepted. *Expenses:* Expenses: Contact institution. *Financial support:* Federal Work-Study, scholarships/grants, and unspecified assistantships available. Support available to part-time students. Financial award application deadline: 3/15; financial award applicants required to submit FAFSA. *Faculty research:* Care giving, child welfare, gerontological social work, home-school-community partnerships, domestic violence. *Unit head:* Dr. Jason Dauenhauer, Director, 585-395-8450, Fax: 585-395-8603, E-mail: grcmsw@brockport.edu. *Application contact:* Brad Snyder, Coordinator of Admissions, 585-395-3845, Fax: 585-395-8603, E-mail: bsynder@brockport.edu.
Website: http://www.brockport.edu/grcmsw

Concordia University Chicago, College of Graduate and Innovative Programs, Program in Gerontology, River Forest, IL 60305-1499. Offers MA. Part-time and evening/weekend programs available. *Degree requirements:* For master's, comprehensive exam, thesis. *Entrance requirements:* For master's, minimum GPA of 2.9. Additional exam requirements/recommendations for international students: Required—TOEFL (minimum score 550 paper-based). Electronic applications accepted.

East Carolina University, Graduate School, College of Human Ecology, School of Social Work, Greenville, NC 27858-4353. Offers gerontology (Certificate); social work (MSW); substance abuse (Certificate). *Accreditation:* CSWE. Postbaccalaureate distance learning degree programs offered (no on-campus study). *Degree requirements:* For master's, comprehensive exam. *Entrance requirements:* For master's, GRE or MAT. Additional exam requirements/recommendations for international students: Required—TOEFL. *Expenses:* Tuition, state resident: full-time $4223. Tuition, nonresident: full-time $16,540. *Required fees:* $2184. *Faculty research:* Social research, gerontology, women's issues, social services in schools, human behavior.

Eastern Illinois University, Graduate School, Lumpkin College of Business and Applied Sciences, School of Family and Consumer Sciences, Program in Aging Studies, Charleston, IL 61920. Offers MA. Part-time and evening/weekend programs available. *Faculty:* 23. *Students:* 8 full-time (7 women), 2 part-time (both women); includes 1 minority (Black or African American, non-Hispanic/Latino), 3 international. Average age 26. 11 applicants, 45% accepted, 3 enrolled. In 2014, 8 master's awarded. *Degree requirements:* For master's, comprehensive exam (for some programs), thesis (for some programs). *Entrance requirements:* For master's, GMAT or GRE. Additional exam requirements/recommendations for international students: Required—TOEFL (minimum score 500 paper-based; 61 iBT), IELTS (minimum score 6). *Application deadline:* For fall admission, 5/15 for domestic and international students; for spring admission, 10/15 for domestic and international students. Applications are processed on a rolling basis. Application fee: $30. Electronic applications accepted. *Expenses:* Tuition, state resident: full-time $3113; part-time $283 per credit hour. Tuition, nonresident: full-time $7469; part-time $679 per credit hour. *Required fees:* $2287; $96 per credit hour. Tuition and fees vary according to course load. *Financial support:* In 2014–15, 8 students received support, including 2 teaching assistantships with full tuition reimbursements available (averaging $8,010 per year); career-related internships or fieldwork, Federal Work-Study, and unspecified assistantships also available. Support available to part-time students. Financial award application deadline: 3/1; financial award applicants required to submit FAFSA. *Unit head:* Linda Simpson, Interim Department Chair, 217-581-2315, Fax: 217-581-6090, E-mail: ldsimpson@eiu.edu. *Application contact:* Jacquelyn Frank, Graduate Coordinator of Aging Studies, 217-581-7843, Fax: 217-581-6090, E-mail: jbfrank@eiu.edu.
Website: http://www.eiu.edu/ma_agingstudies/

Eastern Michigan University, Graduate School, College of Health and Human Services, School of Health Sciences, Programs in Gerontology and Dementia, Ypsilanti, MI 48197. Offers dementia (Graduate Certificate); gerontology (Graduate Certificate). *Students:* 4 part-time (all women). Average age 47. 6 applicants, 83% accepted. In 2014, 11 Graduate Certificates awarded. Application fee: $45. *Application contact:* Dr. Andrea Gossett Zakrajsek, Director, 734-487-3220, Fax: 734-487-4095, E-mail: azakrajs@emich.edu.

Fielding Graduate University, Graduate Programs, School of Human and Organization Development, Santa Barbara, CA 93105-3814. Offers comprehensive evidence-based coaching (Graduate Certificate); evidence based coaching for education leadership (Graduate Certificate); evidence based coaching for organization leadership (Graduate Certificate); evidence based coaching for personal development (Graduate Certificate); human and organizational systems (PhD), including aging, culture and society, information society and knowledge organizations, transformative learning for social justice; human development (PhD), including aging, culture and society, information society and knowledge organizations, transformative learning for social justice; nonprofit leadership (Graduate Certificate); organization consulting (Graduate Certificate); organizational development and leadership (MA). Postbaccalaureate distance learning degree programs offered (minimal on-campus study). *Faculty:* 19 full-time (12 women), 41 part-time/adjunct (20 women). *Students:* 273 full-time (196 women), 136 part-time (108 women); includes 115 minority (54 Black or African American, non-Hispanic/Latino; 3 American Indian or Alaska Native, non-Hispanic/Latino; 18 Asian, non-Hispanic/Latino; 21 Hispanic/Latino; 19 Two or more races, non-Hispanic/Latino), 1 international. Average age 49. 86 applicants, 99% accepted, 57 enrolled. In 2014, 18 master's, 65 doctorates, 123 other advanced degrees awarded. Terminal master's awarded for partial completion of doctoral program. *Degree requirements:* For master's, thesis or alternative; for doctorate, comprehensive exam, thesis/dissertation. *Entrance requirements:* For master's and Graduate Certificate, BA from regionally-accredited institution or equivalent; for doctorate, BA or MA from regionally-accredited institution or equivalent. *Application deadline:* For fall admission, 7/1 for domestic and international students; for spring admission, 9/1 for domestic and international students; for summer admission, 3/1 for domestic and international students. Application fee: $75. Electronic applications accepted. *Expenses: Tuition:* Full-time $25,650; part-time $2880 per course. Tuition and fees vary according to degree level and program. *Financial support:* In 2014–15, 57 students received support. Scholarships/grants, health care benefits, tuition waivers (partial), and unspecified assistantships available. Support available to part-time students. Financial award applicants required to submit FAFSA. *Unit head:* Dr. Gerald Porter, Provost and Senior Vice President, 805-898-2940, Fax: 805-687-9793, E-mail: gporter@fielding.edu. *Application contact:* Enrollment Coordinator, 800-340-1099 Ext. 4098, Fax: 805-687-9793, E-mail: hodadmissions@fielding.edu.
Website: http://www.fielding.edu/programs/hod/default.aspx

Georgia State University, College of Arts and Sciences, Gerontology Institute, Atlanta, GA 30302-3083. Offers MA, Certificate. Part-time programs available. *Faculty:* 4 full-time (all women). *Students:* 16 full-time (11 women), 20 part-time (17 women); includes 22 minority (19 Black or African American, non-Hispanic/Latino; 1 Asian, non-Hispanic/Latino; 1 Hispanic/Latino; 1 Two or more races, non-Hispanic/Latino). Average age 43. 16 applicants, 100% accepted, 14 enrolled. In 2014, 9 master's, 2 other advanced degrees awarded. *Degree requirements:* For master's, thesis (for some programs), internship/capstone project; for Certificate, thesis, internship. *Entrance requirements:* For master's, GRE. Additional exam requirements/recommendations for international students: Required—TOEFL. *Application deadline:* For fall admission, 4/15 for domestic and international students; for spring admission, 10/15 for domestic and international students. Applications are processed on a rolling basis. Application fee: $50. Electronic

applications accepted. *Expenses:* Tuition, state resident: full-time $6516; part-time $362 per credit hour. Tuition, nonresident: full-time $22,014; part-time $1223 per credit hour. *Required fees:* $2128 per semester. Tuition and fees vary according to course load and program. *Financial support:* In 2014–15, research assistantships with full tuition reimbursements (averaging $6,000 per year) were awarded; career-related internships or fieldwork, scholarships/grants, and unspecified assistantships also available. Financial award application deadline: 4/15. *Faculty research:* Long term care and assisted living, aging workforce, health disparities and aging, sexuality and relationships over the life course, caregiving and social relationships with age. *Unit head:* Dr. Elizabeth O. Burgess, Director, 404-413-5210, Fax: 404-413-5219, E-mail: eburgess@gsu.edu. *Application contact:* Dr. Candace L. Kemp, Director of Graduate Studies, 404-413-5210, Fax: 404-413-5219, E-mail: ckemp@gsu.edu.
Website: http://gerontology.gsu.edu/students/graduate/

Kansas State University, Graduate School, College of Human Ecology, Center on Aging, Manhattan, KS 66506. Offers gerontology (MS, Graduate Certificate). Part-time programs available. Postbaccalaureate distance learning degree programs offered (no on-campus study). *Faculty:* 5 full-time (4 women). *Students:* 1 full-time (0 women), 21 part-time (all women). 3 applicants, 100% accepted, 3 enrolled. In 2014, 18 master's awarded. *Degree requirements:* For master's, comprehensive exam. *Entrance requirements:* For master's, bachelor's degree with minimum GPA of 3.0 from college or university accredited by the cognizant regional accrediting agency. *Application deadline:* For fall admission, 2/1 priority date for domestic students, 1/1 for international students; for spring admission, 9/1 priority date for domestic students, 8/1 for international students; for summer admission, 2/1 priority date for domestic students, 12/1 for international students. Applications are processed on a rolling basis. Application fee: $50 ($75 for international students). Electronic applications accepted. *Financial support:* Teaching assistantships available. *Faculty research:* Long-term care, environments and aging, sexuality and aging, aging in rural America. *Unit head:* Dr. Gayle Marie Doll, Director, 785-532-5945, Fax: 785-532-5504, E-mail: gdoll@ksu.edu. *Application contact:* Pamela Kay Evans, Administrative Officer, 785-532-5945, Fax: 785-532-5504, E-mail: gerontology@k-state.edu.
Website: http://www.he.k-state.edu/aging/

Lakehead University, Graduate Studies, Department of History, Thunder Bay, ON P7B 5E1, Canada. Offers gerontology (MA); history (MA); women's studies (MA). Part-time programs available. *Degree requirements:* For master's, one foreign language, thesis. *Entrance requirements:* For master's, minimum B average. Additional exam requirements/recommendations for international students: Required—TOEFL. *Faculty research:* Canadian history, British history, Russian/German history, women's studies.

Lakehead University, Graduate Studies, Faculty of Education, Thunder Bay, ON P7B 5E1, Canada. Offers educational studies (PhD); gerontology (M Ed); women's studies (M Ed). Part-time and evening/weekend programs available. *Degree requirements:* For master's, project or thesis. *Entrance requirements:* For master's, minimum B average. Additional exam requirements/recommendations for international students: Required—TOEFL. *Faculty research:* Art education, AIDS education, language arts education, gerontology, women's studies.

Lakehead University, Graduate Studies, Faculty of Social Sciences and Humanities, Department of Sociology, Thunder Bay, ON P7B 5E1, Canada. Offers gerontology (MA); health services and policy research (MA); sociology (MA); women's studies (MA). Part-time and evening/weekend programs available. *Degree requirements:* For master's, research project or thesis. *Entrance requirements:* For master's, minimum B average. Additional exam requirements/recommendations for international students: Required—TOEFL. *Faculty research:* Sociology of medicine, cultural and social change, health human resources, gerontology, women's studies.

Lakehead University, Graduate Studies, Gerontology Collaborative Program-Northern Educational Center for Aging and Health, Thunder Bay, ON P7B 5E1, Canada. Offers gerontology (M Ed, M Sc, MA, MSW). Part-time programs available. *Degree requirements:* For master's, thesis (for some programs). *Entrance requirements:* Additional exam requirements/recommendations for international students: Required—TOEFL. *Faculty research:* Integrated health information systems.

Lakehead University, Graduate Studies, School of Kinesiology, Thunder Bay, ON P7B 5E1, Canada. Offers kinesiology (M Sc); kinesiology and gerontology (M Sc). Part-time programs available. *Degree requirements:* For master's, thesis. *Entrance requirements:* For master's, minimum B average. Additional exam requirements/recommendations for international students: Required—TOEFL. *Faculty research:* Social psychology and physical education, sport history, sports medicine, exercise physiology, gerontology.

Lakehead University, Graduate Studies, School of Social Work, Thunder Bay, ON P7B 5E1, Canada. Offers gerontology (MSW); social work (MSW); women's studies (MSW). Part-time programs available. *Degree requirements:* For master's, thesis or project. *Entrance requirements:* For master's, minimum B average. Additional exam requirements/recommendations for international students: Required—TOEFL. *Faculty research:* Clinical psychology, social work and practice theory, long-term care, health care for frail elderly, women's studies.

La Salle University, School of Nursing and Health Sciences, Program in Nursing, Philadelphia, PA 19141-1199. Offers adult gerontology primary care nurse practitioner (MSN, Certificate); adult health and illness clinical nurse specialist (MSN); adult-gerontology clinical nurse specialist (MSN, Certificate); clinical nurse leader (MSN); family primary care nurse practitioner (MSN, Certificate); gerontology (Certificate); nurse anesthetist (MSN, Certificate); nursing (MSN, Certificate); nursing administration (MSN, Certificate); nursing education (Certificate); nursing practice (DNP); nursing service administration (MSN); public health nursing (MSN, Certificate); school nursing (Certificate); MSN/MBA; MSN/MPH. *Accreditation:* AANA/CANAEP. Part-time programs available. Postbaccalaureate distance learning degree programs offered (minimal on-campus study). *Degree requirements:* For doctorate, minimum of 1,000 hours of post baccalaureate clinical practice supervised by preceptors. *Entrance requirements:* For master's, GRE, MAT, or GMAT (for students with BSN GPA of less than 3.2), baccalaureate degree in nursing from an NLNAC- or CCNE-accredited program or an MSN Bridge program; Pennsylvania RN license; 2 letters of reference; resume; statement of philosophy articulating professional values and future educational goal; 1 year of work experience as a registered nurse; for doctorate, GRE (waived for applicants with MSN cumulative GPA of 3.7 or above), MSN from nationally-accredited program or master's degree, MBA or MHA from nationally-accredited program; resume or curriculum vitae; 2 letters of reference; interview; for Certificate, GRE, MAT, or GMAT (for students with BSN GPA of less than 3.2, baccalaureate degree in nursing from an NLNAC- or CCNE-accredited program or an MSN Bridge program; Pennsylvania RN license; 2 letters of reference; resume; statement of philosophy articulating professional values and future educational goal; 1 year of work experience as a registered nurse. Additional exam requirements/recommendations for international students: Required—TOEFL. Electronic applications accepted. Application fee is waived when completed online. *Expenses:* Contact institution.

Lindenwood University, Graduate Programs, School of Accelerated Degree Programs, St. Charles, MO 63301-1695. Offers administration (MSA); business administration (MBA); communications (MA); criminal justice and administration (MS);

gerontology (MA); healthcare administration (MS); human resource management (MS); information technology (Certificate); managing information technology (MS); writing (MFA). Part-time and evening/weekend programs available. Postbaccalaureate distance learning degree programs offered (no on-campus study). *Faculty:* 22 full-time (9 women), 96 part-time/adjunct (34 women). *Students:* 811 full-time (488 women), 169 part-time (113 women); includes 374 minority (312 Black or African American, non-Hispanic/Latino; 6 American Indian or Alaska Native, non-Hispanic/Latino; 8 Asian, non-Hispanic/Latino; 26 Hispanic/Latino; 22 Two or more races, non-Hispanic/Latino), 25 international. Average age 35. 891 applicants, 65% accepted, 513 enrolled. In 2014, 498 master's awarded. *Degree requirements:* For master's, thesis (for some programs), minimum cumulative GPA of 3.0. *Entrance requirements:* For master's, interview, minimum GPA of 3.0. Additional exam requirements/recommendations for international students: Required—TOEFL (minimum score 550 paper-based; 80 iBT). *Application deadline:* For fall admission, 10/3 priority date for domestic and international students; for winter admission, 1/4 priority date for domestic and international students; for spring admission, 4/5 priority date for domestic and international students. Applications are processed on a rolling basis. Application fee: $30 ($100 for international students). Electronic applications accepted. *Expenses:* Tuition: Full-time $15,230; part-time $440 per credit hour. *Required fees:* $205 per semester. Tuition and fees vary according to course level, course load and degree level. *Financial support:* In 2014–15, 479 students received support. Career-related internships or fieldwork, institutionally sponsored loans, scholarships/grants, tuition waivers (partial), and unspecified assistantships available. Financial award application deadline: 6/30; financial award applicants required to submit FAFSA. *Unit head:* Dr. Gina Ganahl, Dean, 636-949-4501, Fax: 636-949-4505, E-mail: gganahl@lindenwood.edu. *Application contact:* Tyler Kostich, Director of Evening and Graduate Admissions, 636-949-4138, Fax: 636-949-4109, E-mail: adultadmissions@lindenwood.edu.
Website: http://www.lindenwood.edu/lead/

Marywood University, Academic Affairs, College of Health and Human Services, School of Social Work and Administrative Services, Program in Gerontology, Scranton, PA 18509-1598. Offers MS. Part-time programs available. *Students:* 1 (woman) full-time, all international. Average age 27. In 2014, 2 master's awarded. *Application deadline:* For fall admission, 4/1 for domestic students, 3/31 for international students; for spring admission, 11/1 for domestic students, 8/31 for international students. Applications are processed on a rolling basis. Application fee: $35. Electronic applications accepted. *Expenses:* Tuition: Part-time $775 per credit. *Required fees:* $688 per semester. Tuition and fees vary according to degree level and campus/location. *Financial support:* Application deadline: 6/30; applicants required to submit FAFSA. *Unit head:* Dr. Lloyd L. Lyter, Director, School of Social Work and Administrative Studies, 570-348-6282 Ext. 2388, E-mail: lyter@marywood.edu. *Application contact:* Tammy Manka, Assistant Director of Graduate Admissions, 570-348-6211 Ext. 2322, E-mail: tmanka@marywood.edu.
Website: http://www.marywood.edu/academics/gradcatalog/

McDaniel College, Graduate and Professional Studies, Program in Gerontology, Westminster, MD 21157-4390. Offers MS, Graduate Certificate. *Students:* 4 full-time (2 women), 9 part-time (7 women); includes 4 minority (2 Black or African American, non-Hispanic/Latino; 2 Hispanic/Latino). *Degree requirements:* For master's, portfolio. *Entrance requirements:* Additional exam requirements/recommendations for international students: Required—TOEFL (minimum score 79 iBT), IELTS (minimum score 6). *Application deadline:* Applications are processed on a rolling basis. Application fee: $75. Electronic applications accepted. *Financial support:* Application deadline: 3/1; applicants required to submit FAFSA. *Unit head:* Dr. Diane Martin, Coordinator, 410-386-4618, E-mail: dmartin@mcdaniel.edu. *Application contact:* Crystal L. Perry, Assistant Director, Graduate Enrollment Management, 410-857-2516, Fax: 410-857-2515, E-mail: cperry@mcdaniel.edu.

Miami University, College of Arts and Science, Department of Sociology and Gerontology, Oxford, OH 45056. Offers gerontology (MGS); population and social gerontology (MPSG); social gerontology (PhD). Part-time programs available. *Students:* 40 full-time (31 women), 7 part-time (6 women); includes 3 minority (1 Black or African American, non-Hispanic/Latino; 2 Asian, non-Hispanic/Latino), 15 international. Average age 32. In 2014, 8 master's, 5 doctorates awarded. *Entrance requirements:* For master's, GRE General Test; for doctorate, GRE, bachelor's degree; master's degree (or in process of completing master's degree); written professional statement; curriculum vitae/resume; three letters of recommendation. Additional exam requirements/recommendations for international students: Recommended—TOEFL (minimum score 80 iBT), IELTS (minimum score 6.5), TSE (minimum score 54). *Application deadline:* For fall admission, 2/1 for domestic and international students. Application fee: $50. Electronic applications accepted. *Expenses:* Tuition, state resident: full-time $12,887; part-time $537 per credit hour. Tuition, nonresident: full-time $28,449; part-time $1186 per credit hour. *Required fees:* $530; $24 per credit hour. $30 per quarter. Part-time tuition and fees vary according to course load and program. *Financial support:* Fellowships with full and partial tuition reimbursements, research assistantships with full and partial tuition reimbursements, and teaching assistantships with full and partial tuition reimbursements available. Financial award application deadline: 2/1; financial award applicants required to submit FAFSA. *Unit head:* Dr. Jennifer Kinney, Interim Chair, 513-529-2915, E-mail: kinneyjm@miamioh.edu. *Application contact:* Dr. Scott Brown, Director of Graduate Studies, 513-529-8325, E-mail: sbrow@miamioh.edu.
Website: http://www.MiamiOH.edu/sociology

Middle Tennessee State University, College of Graduate Studies, College of Liberal Arts, Program in Gerontology, Murfreesboro, TN 37132. Offers Graduate Certificate. Part-time and evening/weekend programs available. Postbaccalaureate distance learning degree programs offered. *Students:* 1 applicant, 100% accepted. In 2014, 1 Graduate Certificate awarded. *Entrance requirements:* Additional exam requirements/recommendations for international students: Required—TOEFL (minimum score 525 paper-based; 71 iBT) or IELTS (minimum score 6). *Application deadline:* For fall admission, 6/1 for domestic and international students. Applications are processed on a rolling basis. Application fee: $30. Electronic applications accepted. *Financial support:* Application deadline: 4/1. *Unit head:* Dr. Mark E. Byrnes, Dean, 615-898-2534, Fax: 615-904-8279, E-mail: mark.byrnes@mtsu.edu. *Application contact:* Dr. Michael D. Allen, Vice Provost for Research/Dean, 615-898-2840, Fax: 615-904-8020, E-mail: michael.allen@mtsu.edu.

Minnesota State University Mankato, College of Graduate Studies, College of Social and Behavioral Sciences, Program in Gerontology, Mankato, MN 56001. Offers MS, Certificate. *Students:* 3 full-time (2 women), 6 part-time (5 women). *Degree requirements:* For master's, comprehensive exam, thesis. *Entrance requirements:* For master's, GRE, minimum GPA of 3.0 during previous 2 years, letters of recommendation. Additional exam requirements/recommendations for international students: Required—TOEFL. *Application deadline:* For fall admission, 7/1 priority date for domestic students; for spring admission, 11/1 for domestic students. Applications are processed on a rolling basis. Application fee: $40. Electronic applications accepted. *Financial support:* Federal Work-Study and unspecified assistantships available. Support available to part-time students. Financial award application deadline: 3/15;

financial award applicants required to submit FAFSA. *Unit head:* Dr. Don Ebel, Director, 507-389-5188. *Application contact:* 507-389-2321, E-mail: grad@mnsu.edu.

Morehead State University, Graduate Programs, Caudill College of Arts, Humanities and Social Sciences, Department of Sociology, Social Work and Criminology, Morehead, KY 40351. Offers criminology (MA); general sociology (MA); gerontology (MA); sociology regional analysis (MA); sociology/chemical dependency (MA). Part-time and evening/weekend programs available. *Degree requirements:* For master's, comprehensive exam, thesis (for some programs). *Entrance requirements:* For master's, GRE General Test, minimum GPA of 3.0 in sociology, 2.75 overall; 18 hours of course work in sociology, writing sample. Additional exam requirements/recommendations for international students: Required—TOEFL (minimum score 500 paper-based). Electronic applications accepted. *Faculty research:* Death and dying; aging, drinking, and drugs; economic development; adult children of alcoholics.

Mount Saint Vincent University, Graduate Programs, Department of Family Studies and Gerontology, Halifax, NS B3M 2J6, Canada. Offers MA. Part-time programs available. Postbaccalaureate distance learning degree programs offered (minimal on-campus study). *Degree requirements:* For master's, thesis. *Entrance requirements:* For master's, minimum GPA of 3.0; course work in statistics, research methods, family and social theories.

New York University, College of Nursing, Doctor of Nursing Practice Program, New York, NY 10012-1019. Offers advanced practice nursing (DNP), including adult acute care, adult nurse practitioner/holistic nursing, adult nurse practitioner/palliative care nursing, adult primary care, adult primary care/geriatrics, family, geriatrics, mental health nursing, nurse-midwifery, pediatrics. Part-time and evening/weekend programs available. *Faculty:* 3 full-time (all women), 1 part-time/adjunct (0 women). *Students:* 4 full-time (all women), 34 part-time (30 women); includes 9 minority (3 Black or African American, non-Hispanic/Latino; 5 Asian, non-Hispanic/Latino; 1 Hispanic/Latino). Average age 40. 25 applicants, 88% accepted, 13 enrolled. In 2014, 6 doctorates awarded. *Degree requirements:* For doctorate, thesis/dissertation, capstone. *Entrance requirements:* For doctorate, MAT or GRE (either taken within past 5 years), MS, RN license, interview, Nurse Practitioner Certification. Additional exam requirements/recommendations for international students: Required—TOEFL (minimum score 90 iBT), IELTS (minimum score 7). *Application deadline:* For fall admission, 3/1 for domestic and international students. Applications are processed on a rolling basis. Application fee: $80. Electronic applications accepted. *Financial support:* In 2014–15, 12 students received support. Scholarships/grants available. Support available to part-time students. Financial award application deadline: 2/1; financial award applicants required to submit FAFSA. *Faculty research:* Workforce, LGBT, breast cancer, HIV, diabetes. *Unit head:* Dr. Rona Levin, Director, 212-998-5319, Fax: 212-995-3143, E-mail: rfl2039@nyu.edu. *Application contact:* Samantha Jaser, Assistant Director, Graduate Student Affairs and Admissions, 212-992-7653, Fax: 212-995-4302, E-mail: saj283@nyu.edu.

North Dakota State University, College of Graduate and Interdisciplinary Studies, College of Human Development and Education, Department of Human Development and Family Science, Program in Gerontology, Fargo, ND 58108. Offers MS, Certificate. Electronic applications accepted.

Northeastern Illinois University, College of Graduate Studies and Research, College of Arts and Sciences, Program in Gerontology, Chicago, IL 60625-4699. Offers MA. Part-time and evening/weekend programs available. *Degree requirements:* For master's, comprehensive exam, paper and project or thesis, practicum. *Entrance requirements:* For master's, 15 hours in social sciences (3 hours in gerontology), 1 course in research methods or statistics, minimum GPA of 2.75. Additional exam requirements/recommendations for international students: Required—TOEFL (minimum score 550 paper-based; 79 iBT). Electronic applications accepted. *Faculty research:* Later life development, cultural diversity, humanities and aging, elder abuse, AIDS and aging, computer training.

Oregon Health & Science University, School of Nursing, Program in Nursing Education, Portland, OR 97239-3098. Offers MN, MS, Post Master's Certificate.

Portland State University, Graduate Studies, College of Urban and Public Affairs, School of Community Health, Institute on Aging, Portland, OR 97207-0751. Offers Certificate. Part-time programs available. *Faculty:* 2 full-time (1 woman). *Students:* 8 part-time (all women); includes 1 minority (Asian, non-Hispanic/Latino), 1 international. Average age 41. In 2014, 10 Certificates awarded. *Application deadline:* For fall admission, 2/1 for domestic and international students. Applications are processed on a rolling basis. Application fee: $50. *Expenses:* Tuition, state resident: part-time $222 per credit. Tuition, nonresident: part-time $527 per credit. *Required fees:* $22 per contact hour. $100 per quarter. Tuition and fees vary according to program. *Financial support:* In 2014–15, 2 research assistantships with partial tuition reimbursements (averaging $2,527 per year) were awarded; career-related internships or fieldwork, Federal Work-Study, and unspecified assistantships also available. Support available to part-time students. Financial award application deadline: 3/1; financial award applicants required to submit FAFSA. *Total annual research expenditures:* $177,776. *Unit head:* Dr. Margaret Neal, Director, 503-725-3952, Fax: 503-725-5199, E-mail: nealm@pdx.edu. *Application contact:* Elizabeth Bull, Assistant to the Director, 503-725-4592, Fax: 503-725-5100, E-mail: bulle@pdx.edu.
Website: http://www.pdx.edu/ioa/

Sage Graduate School, School of Management, Program in Health Services Administration, Troy, NY 12180-4115. Offers dietetic internship (Certificate); gerontology (MS). Part-time and evening/weekend programs available. *Faculty:* 2 full-time (both women), 28 part-time/adjunct (21 women). *Students:* 8 full-time (6 women), 35 part-time (22 women); includes 9 minority (6 Black or African American, non-Hispanic/Latino; 2 Asian, non-Hispanic/Latino; 1 Hispanic/Latino), 1 international. Average age 33. 40 applicants, 43% accepted, 13 enrolled. In 2014, 10 master's awarded. *Entrance requirements:* For master's, minimum GPA of 2.75, resume, 2 letters of recommendation. Additional exam requirements/recommendations for international students: Required—TOEFL (minimum score 550 paper-based). Application fee: $40. *Expenses: Tuition:* Full-time $12,240; part-time $680 per credit hour. *Financial support:* Fellowships, research assistantships, Federal Work-Study, scholarships/grants, and unspecified assistantships available. Support available to part-time students. Financial award application deadline: 3/1; financial award applicants required to submit FAFSA. *Unit head:* Dr. Kimberly Fredericks, Associate Dean, School of Management, 518-292-1782, Fax: 518-292-1964, E-mail: fredek1@sage.edu. *Application contact:* Wendy D. Diefendorf, Director of Graduate and Adult Admission, 518-244-2443, Fax: 518-244-6880, E-mail: diefew@sage.edu.

St. Cloud State University, School of Graduate Studies, School of Health and Human Services, Program in Gerontology, St. Cloud, MN 56301-4498. Offers MS. Part-time programs available. *Degree requirements:* For master's, thesis or alternative. *Entrance requirements:* For master's, GRE General Test, minimum GPA of 2.75. Additional exam requirements/recommendations for international students: Required—Michigan English Language Assessment Battery; Recommended—TOEFL (minimum score 550 paper-based), IELTS (minimum score 6.5). Electronic applications accepted.

Saint Joseph's University, College of Arts and Sciences, Program in Gerontological Services, Philadelphia, PA 19131-1395. Offers gerontological services (MS); long-term care administration (MS). Part-time and evening/weekend programs available. *Faculty:* 2 part-time/adjunct (1 woman). *Students:* 3 full-time (all women), 12 part-time (10 women); includes 7 minority (5 Black or African American, non-Hispanic/Latino; 2 Hispanic/Latino), 1 international. Average age 33. 5 applicants, 100% accepted, 4 enrolled. In 2014, 6 master's awarded. *Entrance requirements:* For master's, 2 letters of recommendation, personal statement, resume. Additional exam requirements/recommendations for international students: Required—TOEFL (minimum score 550 paper-based; 80 iBT). *Application deadline:* For fall admission, 7/15 priority date for domestic students, 4/15 for international students; for winter admission, 1/15 for international students; for spring admission, 11/15 priority date for domestic students, 10/15 for international students. Applications are processed on a rolling basis. Application fee: $35. Electronic applications accepted. *Financial support:* Fellowships available. Financial award applicants required to submit FAFSA. *Unit head:* Dr. Catherine Murray, Director, 610-660-1805, E-mail: cmurray@sju.edu. *Application contact:* Elisabeth Woodward, Director of Marketing and Admissions, Graduate Arts and Sciences, 610-660-3131, Fax: 610-660-3230, E-mail: gradstudies@sju.edu.
Website: http://www.sju.edu/majors-programs/graduate-arts-sciences/masters/gerontological-services-ms

San Diego State University, Graduate and Research Affairs, College of Health and Human Services, Department of Gerontology, San Diego, CA 92182. Offers MS. Part-time and evening/weekend programs available. *Degree requirements:* For master's, thesis. *Entrance requirements:* For master's, GRE General Test. Additional exam requirements/recommendations for international students: Required—TOEFL. Electronic applications accepted.

San Francisco State University, Division of Graduate Studies, College of Health and Social Sciences, Gerontology Program, San Francisco, CA 94132-1722. Offers MA. Part-time programs available. *Application deadline:* Applications are processed on a rolling basis. *Expenses:* Tuition, state resident: full-time $6738. Tuition, nonresident: full-time $17,898; part-time $372 per credit hour. *Required fees:* $498 per semester. *Financial support:* Career-related internships or fieldwork and unspecified assistantships available. *Unit head:* Dr. Eileen F. Levy, Director, 415-405-4084, E-mail: efl@sfsu.edu. *Application contact:* Dr. Brian DeVries, Graduate Coordinator, 415-338-3559, E-mail: bdevries@sfsu.edu.
Website: http://socwork.sfsu.edu/gero

San Jose State University, Graduate Studies and Research, College of Applied Sciences and Arts, Department of Health Science, San Jose, CA 95192-0001. Offers applied social gerontology (Certificate); community health education (MPH). *Accreditation:* CEPH (one or more programs are accredited). Postbaccalaureate distance learning degree programs offered. *Entrance requirements:* For master's, GRE General Test. Electronic applications accepted. *Faculty research:* Behavioral science in occupational and health care settings, epidemiology in health care settings.

Simon Fraser University, Office of Graduate Studies, Faculty of Arts and Social Sciences, Department of Gerontology, Vancouver, BC V6B 5K3, Canada. Offers MA, PhD. Part-time programs available. *Degree requirements:* For master's, thesis or alternative, internship; for doctorate, comprehensive exam, thesis/dissertation. *Entrance requirements:* For master's, minimum GPA of 3.0 (on scale of 4.33), or 3.33 based on last 60 credits of undergraduate courses; for doctorate, minimum GPA of 3.5 (on scale of 4.33). Additional exam requirements/recommendations for international students: Recommended—TOEFL (minimum score 580 paper-based; 93 iBT), IELTS (minimum score 7), TWE (minimum score 5). Electronic applications accepted. *Faculty research:* Aging and the built environment, changing demography and lifestyles, health promotion/population health and aging, prevention of victimization and exploitation of older persons, technology and aging.

Slippery Rock University of Pennsylvania, Graduate Studies (Recruitment), College of Education, Department of Counseling and Development, Slippery Rock, PA 16057-1383. Offers clinical mental health counseling (MA), including addiction, adult, older adult, school and youth; student affairs (MA), including higher education; student affairs in higher education (MA), including college counseling. *Accreditation:* ACA; NCATE. Part-time and evening/weekend programs available. *Faculty:* 9 full-time (5 women). *Students:* 84 full-time (69 women), 16 part-time (13 women); includes 13 minority (8 Black or African American, non-Hispanic/Latino; 1 American Indian or Alaska Native, non-Hispanic/Latino; 2 Hispanic/Latino; 2 Two or more races, non-Hispanic/Latino), 1 international. Average age 29. 128 applicants, 51% accepted, 41 enrolled. In 2014, 45 master's awarded. *Degree requirements:* For master's, comprehensive exam, thesis (for some programs). *Entrance requirements:* For master's, GRE General Test or MAT, official transcripts, minimum GPA of 2.75 or 3.0 (depending on program), personal statement, three letters of recommendation, interview. Additional exam requirements/recommendations for international students: Required—TOEFL (minimum score 550 paper-based; 80 iBT). *Application deadline:* For fall admission, 1/15 priority date for domestic and international students. Application fee: $25 ($30 for international students). Electronic applications accepted. *Expenses:* Tuition, state resident: full-time $8172; part-time $454 per credit. Tuition, nonresident: full-time $12,258; part-time $681 per credit. *Required fees:* $2326; $200 per credit. Tuition and fees vary according to degree level and program. *Financial support:* Career-related internships or fieldwork, Federal Work-Study, institutionally sponsored loans, scholarships/grants, tuition waivers (partial), and unspecified assistantships available. Support available to part-time students. Financial award application deadline: 5/1; financial award applicants required to submit FAFSA. *Unit head:* Dr. Stacy Jacob, Graduate Coordinator, 724-738-2758, Fax: 724-738-4859, E-mail: stacy.jacob@sru.edu. *Application contact:* Brandi Weber-Mortimer, Director of Graduate Admissions, 724-738-2051, Fax: 724-738-2146, E-mail: graduate.admissions@sru.edu.
Website: http://srudss.ingeniuxondemand.com/academics/colleges-and-departments/coe/departments/counseling-and-development

Temple University, College of Health Professions and Social Work, Department of Nursing, Philadelphia, PA 19140. Offers adult-gerontology primary care (DNP); clinical nurse leader (MSN); family-individual across the lifespan (DNP); nurse educator (MSN); nursing (MSN, DNP). *Accreditation:* AACN. Part-time programs available. *Faculty:* 11 full-time (10 women). *Students:* 14 full-time (13 women), 66 part-time (54 women); includes 44 minority (27 Black or African American, non-Hispanic/Latino; 10 Asian, non-Hispanic/Latino; 6 Hispanic/Latino; 1 Two or more races, non-Hispanic/Latino). 14 applicants, 50% accepted, 5 enrolled. In 2014, 9 master's, 9 doctorates awarded. *Degree requirements:* For master's and doctorate, evidence based practice project. *Entrance requirements:* For master's and doctorate, GRE General Test or MAT, 2 letters of reference, RN license, interview, statement of purpose, resume. Additional exam requirements/recommendations for international students: Required—TOEFL (minimum score 600 paper-based; 100 iBT). *Application deadline:* For fall admission, 2/15 priority date for domestic students, 1/15 for international students; for spring admission, 10/15 for domestic students, 9/15 for international students. Applications are processed on a rolling basis. Application fee: $60. Electronic applications accepted. *Expenses:* Tuition, state resident: full-time $14,490; part-time $805 per credit hour. Tuition, nonresident: full-time $19,850; part-time $1103 per credit hour. *Required fees:* $690. Full-time tuition

and fees vary according to class time, course load, degree level, campus/location and program. *Financial support:* Federal Work-Study, scholarships/grants, traineeships, and tuition waivers available. Support available to part-time students. Financial award application deadline: 1/15. *Faculty research:* Health promotion, chronic illness, family support systems, primary care, health policy, community health services, evidence-based practice. *Unit head:* Dr. Jane Kurz, RN, Chair, 215-707-8327, E-mail: jane.kurz@temple.edu. *Application contact:* Audrey Scriven, Student Services Coordinator, 215-204-4618, E-mail: tunurse@temple.edu.

Texas State University, The Graduate College, College of Liberal Arts, Program in Dementia and Aging Studies, San Marcos, TX 78666. Offers MS. Part-time and evening/weekend programs available. *Faculty:* 14 full-time (7 women), 1 part-time/adjunct (0 women). *Degree requirements:* For master's, comprehensive exam, thesis optional. *Entrance requirements:* For master's, GRE (preferred), baccalaureate degree from regionally-accredited university with minimum GPA of 3.0 on last 60 undergraduate semester hours. Additional exam requirements/recommendations for international students: Required—TOEFL (minimum score 550 paper-based; 78 iBT). *Application deadline:* For fall admission, 7/15 for domestic students, 6/1 for international students; for spring admission, 10/15 for domestic students, 10/1 for international students; for summer admission, 4/15 for domestic students, 3/15 for international students. Application fee: $40 ($90 for international students). Electronic applications accepted. *Expenses:* Expenses: $8,834 (tuition and fees combined). *Financial support:* Research assistantships, teaching assistantships, career-related internships or fieldwork, Federal Work-Study, institutionally sponsored loans, scholarships/grants, and unspecified assistantships available. Support available to part-time students. Financial award application deadline: 4/1; financial award applicants required to submit FAFSA. *Faculty research:* Healthcare models, health services needs, Head Start. *Total annual research expenditures:* $47,502. *Unit head:* Dr. Patti Giuffre, Graduate Advisor, 512-245-8983, Fax: 512-245-8362, E-mail: pg07@txstate.edu. *Application contact:* Dr. Andrea Golato, Dean of Graduate School, 512-245-2581, Fax: 512-245-8365, E-mail: gradcollege@txstate.edu.
Website: http://www.soci.txstate.edu/

Towson University, Program in Applied Gerontology, Towson, MD 21252-0001. Offers MS, Postbaccalaureate Certificate. *Students:* 2 full-time (both women), 9 part-time (8 women); includes 2 minority (1 Black or African American, non-Hispanic/Latino; 1 Two or more races, non-Hispanic/Latino). *Entrance requirements:* For master's, bachelor's degree with minimum of 9 credits of upper-level related coursework, 2 letters of recommendation, minimum GPA of 3.0, essay; for Postbaccalaureate Certificate, minimum of 9 credits of upper-level related coursework, 2 letters of recommendation, minimum GPA of 3.0. *Application deadline:* Applications are processed on a rolling basis. Application fee: $45. Electronic applications accepted. *Financial support:* Application deadline: 4/1. *Unit head:* Dr. Mary Carter, Graduate Program Director, 410-704-4643, E-mail: mcarter@towson.edu. *Application contact:* Alicia Arkell-Kleis, Information Contact, 410-704-6004, E-mail: grads@towson.edu.
Website: http://grad.towson.edu/program/certificate/gero-pbc/index.asp

Université de Sherbrooke, Faculty of Letters and Human Sciences, Department of Psychology, Sherbrooke, QC J1K 2R1, Canada. Offers gerontology (MA). *Degree requirements:* For master's, thesis. *Faculty research:* Human relations.

Université Laval, Faculty of Medicine, Post-Professional Programs in Medical Studies, Québec, QC G1K 7P4, Canada. Offers anatomy–pathology (DESS); anesthesiology (DESS); cardiology (DESS); care of older people (Diploma); clinical research (DESS); community health (DESS); dermatology (DESS); diagnostic radiology (DESS); emergency medicine (Diploma); family medicine (DESS); general surgery (DESS); geriatrics (DESS); hematology (DESS); internal medicine (DESS); maternal and fetal medicine (Diploma); medical biochemistry (DESS); medical microbiology and infectious diseases (DESS); medical oncology (DESS); nephrology (DESS); neurology (DESS); neurosurgery (DESS); obstetrics and gynecology (DESS); ophthalmology (DESS); orthopedic surgery (DESS); oto-rhino-laryngology (DESS); palliative medicine (Diploma); pediatrics (DESS); plastic surgery (DESS); psychiatry (DESS); pulmonary medicine (DESS); radiology–oncology (DESS); thoracic surgery (DESS); urology (DESS). *Degree requirements:* For other advanced degree, comprehensive exam. *Entrance requirements:* For degree, knowledge of French. Electronic applications accepted.

The University of Akron, Graduate School, Buchtel College of Arts and Sciences, Department of Psychology, Akron, OH 44325. Offers adult development and aging (PhD); counseling psychology (MA, PhD); industrial/organizational psychology (MA, PhD); psychology (MA). *Accreditation:* APA (one or more programs are accredited). *Faculty:* 19 full-time (9 women), 3 part-time/adjunct (2 women). *Students:* 70 full-time (42 women), 17 part-time (13 women); includes 15 minority (3 Black or African American, non-Hispanic/Latino; 5 Asian, non-Hispanic/Latino; 5 Hispanic/Latino; 2 Two or more races, non-Hispanic/Latino), 3 international. Average age 26. 174 applicants, 2% accepted, 3 enrolled. In 2014, 13 master's, 12 doctorates awarded. Terminal master's awarded for partial completion of doctoral program. *Degree requirements:* For master's, thesis or specialty exam; for doctorate, one foreign language, comprehensive exam, thesis/dissertation. *Entrance requirements:* For master's, GRE General Test, minimum GPA of 2.75, 3.0 in psychology courses; three letters of recommendation; personal statement; curriculum vitae; for doctorate, GRE General Test, minimum graduate GPA of 3.25, three letters of recommendation, personal statement, statement of purpose, curriculum vitae. Additional exam requirements/recommendations for international students: Required—TOEFL (minimum score 550 paper-based; 79 iBT), IELTS (minimum score 6.5). *Application deadline:* For fall admission, 1/15 for domestic and international students. Application fee: $45 ($70 for international students). Electronic applications accepted. *Expenses:* Tuition, state resident: full-time $7578; part-time $421 per credit hour. Tuition, nonresident: full-time $12,977; part-time $721 per credit hour. *Required fees:* $1388; $35 per credit hour. Tuition and fees vary according to course load. *Financial support:* In 2014–15, 16 research assistantships with full tuition reimbursements, 46 teaching assistantships with full tuition reimbursements were awarded. *Faculty research:* Social cognitive determinants of behavior, the application of psychological principles to the workplace and career planning/development, the psychological processes of aging. *Total annual research expenditures:* $834,259. *Unit head:* Dr. Paul Levy, Chair, 330-972-8367, E-mail: plevy@uakron.edu.
Website: http://www.uakron.edu/psychology/

University of Arkansas at Little Rock, Graduate School, College of Education, School of Social Work, Program in Gerontology, Little Rock, AR 72204-1099. Offers Graduate Certificate. *Application deadline:* Applications are processed on a rolling basis. *Expenses:* Tuition, state resident: full-time $6000; part-time $300 per credit hour. Tuition, nonresident: full-time $13,800; part-time $690 per credit hour. *Required fees:* $1126; $603 per term. One-time fee: $40 full-time. *Financial support:* Research assistantships, career-related internships or fieldwork, Federal Work-Study, institutionally sponsored loans, and unspecified assistantships available. Support available to part-time students. *Unit head:* Dr. Carolyn Turturro, Coordinator, 501-569-8472, E-mail: clturturro@ualr.edu.
Website: http://ualr.edu/socialwork/home/programs/gerontology/graduate-certificate/

University of Central Missouri, The Graduate School, Warrensburg, MO 64093. Offers accountancy (MA); accounting (MBA); applied mathematics (MS); aviation safety (MA); biology (MS); business administration (MBA); career and technical education leadership (MS); college student personnel administration (MS); communication (MA); computer science (MS); counseling (MS); criminal justice (MS); educational leadership (Ed D); educational technology (MS); elementary and early childhood education (MSE); English (MA); environmental studies (MA); finance (MBA); history (MA); human services/educational technology (Ed S); human services/learning resources (Ed S); human services/professional counseling (Ed S); industrial hygiene (MS); industrial management (MS); information systems (MBA); information technology (MS); kinesiology (MS); library science and information services (MS); literacy education (MSE); marketing (MBA); mathematics (MS); music (MA); occupational safety management (MS); psychology (MS); rural family nursing (MS); school administration (MSE); social gerontology (MS); sociology (MA); special education (MSE); speech language pathology (MS); superintendency (Ed S); teaching (MAT); teaching English as a second language (MA); technology (MS); technology management (PhD); theatre (MA). Part-time programs available. *Faculty:* 314 full-time (137 women), 24 part-time/adjunct (14 women). *Students:* 1,624 full-time (542 women), 1,773 part-time (1,055 women); includes 194 minority (104 Black or African American, non-Hispanic/Latino; 6 American Indian or Alaska Native, non-Hispanic/Latino; 23 Asian, non-Hispanic/Latino; 41 Hispanic/Latino; 3 Native Hawaiian or other Pacific Islander, non-Hispanic/Latino; 17 Two or more races, non-Hispanic/Latino), 1,592 international. Average age 31. 2,800 applicants, 63% accepted, 1223 enrolled. In 2014, 796 master's, 81 other advanced degrees awarded. *Degree requirements:* For master's and Ed S, comprehensive exam (for some programs), thesis (for some programs). *Entrance requirements:* Additional exam requirements/recommendations for international students: Required—TOEFL (minimum score 550 paper-based; 79 iBT). *Application deadline:* For fall admission, 6/1 for domestic students; for spring admission, 10/1 for domestic and international students. Applications are processed on a rolling basis. Application fee: $30 ($75 for international students). Electronic applications accepted. *Expenses:* Tuition, state resident: full-time $6630; part-time $276.25 per credit hour. Tuition, nonresident: full-time $13,260; part-time $552.50 per credit hour. *Required fees:* $29 per credit hour. Tuition and fees vary according to campus/location. *Financial support:* In 2014–15, 118 students received support, including 271 research assistantships with full and partial tuition reimbursements available (averaging $7,500 per year), 109 teaching assistantships with full and partial tuition reimbursements available (averaging $7,500 per year); career-related internships or fieldwork, Federal Work-Study, scholarships/grants, and administrative and laboratory assistantships also available. Support available to part-time students. Financial award application deadline: 3/1; financial award applicants required to submit FAFSA. *Unit head:* Tina Church-Hockett, Director of Graduate School and International Admissions, 660-543-4621, Fax: 660-543-4778, E-mail: church@ucmo.edu. *Application contact:* Brittany Lawrence, Graduate Student Services Coordinator, 660-543-4621, Fax: 660-543-4778, E-mail: gradinfo@ucmo.edu.
Website: http://www.ucmo.edu/graduate/

University of Central Oklahoma, The Jackson College of Graduate Studies, College of Liberal Arts, Department of Sociology, Gerontology, and Substance Abuse Studies, Edmond, OK 73034-5209. Offers gerontology (MA); sociology (MA), including substance abuse studies. Part-time programs available. *Degree requirements:* For master's, variable foreign language requirement, comprehensive exam (for some programs), thesis (for some programs). *Entrance requirements:* For master's, GRE. Additional exam requirements/recommendations for international students: Required—TOEFL (minimum score 550 paper-based; 79 iBT), IELTS (minimum score 6.5). Electronic applications accepted.

University of Georgia, College of Public Health, Institute of Gerontology, Athens, GA 30602. Offers Certificate.

University of Hawaii at Manoa, John A. Burns School of Medicine, Center on Aging, Honolulu, HI 96822. Offers gerontology (Graduate Certificate). *Entrance requirements:* Additional exam requirements/recommendations for international students: Required—TOEFL (minimum score 550 paper-based; 79 iBT).

University of Illinois at Springfield, Graduate Programs, College of Education and Human Services, Program in Human Services, Springfield, IL 62703-5407. Offers alcohol and substance abuse (Graduate Certificate); alcoholism and substance abuse (MA); child and family services (MA); gerontology (MA); social services administration (MA). Part-time and evening/weekend programs available. Postbaccalaureate distance learning degree programs offered (no on-campus study). *Faculty:* 4 full-time (all women), 2 part-time/adjunct (0 women). *Students:* 11 full-time (all women), 69 part-time (60 women); includes 21 minority (17 Black or African American, non-Hispanic/Latino; 1 Asian, non-Hispanic/Latino; 1 Hispanic/Latino; 2 Two or more races, non-Hispanic/Latino). Average age 36. 53 applicants, 30% accepted, 16 enrolled. In 2014, 19 master's, 1 other advanced degree awarded. *Degree requirements:* For master's, internship; project or thesis. *Entrance requirements:* For master's, minimum undergraduate GPA of 3.0, 2 letters of recommendation, statement of intent. Additional exam requirements/recommendations for international students: Required—TOEFL (minimum score 500 paper-based; 61 iBT). Application fee: $60 ($75 for international students). Electronic applications accepted. *Expenses:* Tuition, state resident: full-time $7662; part-time $319.25 per credit hour. Tuition, nonresident: full-time $15,966; part-time $665.25 per credit hour. *Financial support:* In 2014–15, fellowships with full tuition reimbursements (averaging $9,900 per year), research assistantships with full tuition reimbursements (averaging $9,600 per year), teaching assistantships with full tuition reimbursements (averaging $9,600 per year) were awarded; career-related internships or fieldwork, Federal Work-Study, scholarships/grants, health care benefits, and unspecified assistantships also available. Support available to part-time students. Financial award application deadline: 11/15. *Unit head:* Dr. Carolyn Peck, Program Administrator, 217-206-7577, Fax: 217-206-6775, E-mail: peck.carolyn@uis.edu. *Application contact:* Dr. Lynn Pardie, Office of Graduate Studies, 800-252-8533, Fax: 217-206-7623, E-mail: lpard1@uis.edu.
Website: http://www.uis.edu/humanservices

University of Indianapolis, Graduate Programs, Center for Aging and Community, Indianapolis, IN 46227-3697. Offers gerontology (MS, Certificate). Part-time and evening/weekend programs available. Postbaccalaureate distance learning degree programs offered. *Faculty:* 4 full-time (2 women), 5 part-time/adjunct (4 women). *Students:* 2 full-time (both women), 30 part-time (24 women); includes 8 minority (4 Black or African American, non-Hispanic/Latino; 2 American Indian or Alaska Native, non-Hispanic/Latino; 2 Hispanic/Latino). Average age 38. In 2014, 12 master's awarded. *Degree requirements:* For master's, capstone course. *Entrance requirements:* For master's, 3 letters of recommendation. Additional exam requirements/recommendations for international students: Required—TOEFL (minimum score 550 paper-based). *Application deadline:* Applications are processed on a rolling basis. Application fee: $50. *Financial support:* Career-related internships or fieldwork, Federal Work-Study, scholarships/grants, and tuition waivers (full and partial) available. Support available to part-time students. *Unit head:* Dr. Ellen Miller, Interim Associate Provost for Research, Graduate Programs, and Academic Partnership, 317-791-5932, Fax: 317-791-5945, E-mail: emiller@uindy.edu. *Application contact:* Tamora Wolske, Academic Program

Director, 317-791-5930, Fax: 317-791-5945, E-mail: wolsketl@uindy.edu.
Website: http://cac.uindy.edu/masters/

University of Indianapolis, Graduate Programs, School of Nursing, Indianapolis, IN 46227-3697. Offers advanced practice nursing (DNP); family nurse practitioner (MSN); gerontological nurse practitioner (MSN); neonatal nurse practitioner (MSN); nurse-midwifery (MSN); nursing (MSN); nursing and health systems leadership (MSN); nursing education (MSN); women's health nurse practitioner (MSN); MBA/MSN. *Accreditation:* AACN; ACNM. *Faculty:* 13 full-time (12 women), 11 part-time/adjunct (all women). *Students:* 8 full-time (6 women), 290 part-time (275 women); includes 37 minority (23 Black or African American, non-Hispanic/Latino; 5 Asian, non-Hispanic/Latino; 2 Hispanic/Latino; 1 Native Hawaiian or other Pacific Islander, non-Hispanic/Latino; 6 Two or more races, non-Hispanic/Latino), 2 international. Average age 34. In 2014, 75 master's awarded. *Entrance requirements:* For master's, minimum GPA of 3.0, interview, letters of recommendation, resume, IN nursing license, 1 year of professional practice; for doctorate, graduate of NLNAC- or CCNE-accredited nursing program; MSN or MA with nursing major and minimum cumulative GPA of 3.25; unencumbered RN license with eligibility for licensure in Indiana; completion of graduate-level statistics course within last 5 years with minimum grade of B; resume; essay; official transcripts from all academic institutions. Additional exam requirements/recommendations for international students: Required—TOEFL (minimum score 550 paper-based). *Application deadline:* For fall admission, 8/1 for domestic students; for winter admission, 12/15 for domestic students; for spring admission, 4/15 for domestic students. Applications are processed on a rolling basis. Application fee: $60. Electronic applications accepted. *Financial support:* Federal Work-Study available. *Unit head:* Dr. Anne Thomas, Dean, 317-788-3206, E-mail: athomas@uindy.edu. *Application contact:* Sueann Meagher, Clinical Support Coordinator, 317-788-8005, Fax: 317-788-3542, E-mail: meaghers@uindy.edu.
Website: http://nursing.uindy.edu/

The University of Kansas, Graduate Studies, College of Liberal Arts and Sciences, Program in Gerontology, Lawrence, KS 66045. Offers MA, PhD, Graduate Certificate. *Faculty:* 4 full-time (2 women). *Students:* 3 full-time (all women); includes 2 minority (both Black or African American, non-Hispanic/Latino), 1 international. Average age 32. 6 applicants, 33% accepted, 2 enrolled. *Degree requirements:* For master's, thesis; for doctorate, comprehensive exam, thesis/dissertation, written preliminary exam. *Entrance requirements:* For master's and doctorate, GRE, 3 letters of reference, resume, personal statement, transcripts. Additional exam requirements/recommendations for international students: Required—TOEFL. *Application deadline:* For fall admission, 2/1 priority date for domestic and international students. Applications are processed on a rolling basis. Application fee: $55 ($65 for international students). Electronic applications accepted. *Financial support:* Fellowships with full tuition reimbursements, research assistantships with full tuition reimbursements, career-related internships or fieldwork, traineeships, and unspecified assistantships available. Financial award application deadline: 1/15. *Faculty research:* Communication and aging, work and retirement, cognitive aging, dementia, environmental gerontology. *Unit head:* David J. Ekerdt, Director, 785-864-4130, E-mail: dekerdt@ku.edu. *Application contact:* Corinne Butler, Graduate Admissions Contact, 785-864-9419, E-mail: cleg@ku.edu.
Website: http://www.gerontology.ku.edu/

University of Kentucky, Graduate School, College of Public Health, Program in Gerontology, Lexington, KY 40506-0032. Offers PhD, Graduate Certificate. *Degree requirements:* For doctorate, comprehensive exam, thesis/dissertation. *Entrance requirements:* For doctorate, GRE General Test, minimum undergraduate GPA of 2.75, graduate 3.0. Additional exam requirements/recommendations for international students: Required—TOEFL (minimum score 550 paper-based). Electronic applications accepted.

University of La Verne, College of Business and Public Management, Program in Gerontology, La Verne, CA 91750-4443. Offers geriatric care management (MS); gerontology (Certificate); gerontology administration (MS); health services management (MS). Part-time programs available. *Faculty:* 1 (woman) full-time, 3 part-time/adjunct (2 women). *Students:* 11 full-time (10 women), 14 part-time (13 women); includes 13 minority (4 Black or African American, non-Hispanic/Latino; 9 Hispanic/Latino), 4 international. Average age 43. In 2014, 12 master's awarded. *Entrance requirements:* For master's, bachelor's degree, preferred GPA of 2.75, 2 recommendations, personal statement. Additional exam requirements/recommendations for international students: Required—TOEFL (minimum score 550 paper-based). *Application deadline:* Applications are processed on a rolling basis. Application fee: $50. *Expenses:* Expenses: Contact institution. *Financial support:* Institutionally sponsored loans available. Financial award application deadline: 3/2; financial award applicants required to submit FAFSA. *Unit head:* Dr. Kathy Duncan, Program Director, 909-448-4415, E-mail: kduncan2@laverne.edu. *Application contact:* Barbara Cox, Program and Admissions Specialist, 909-593-3511 Ext. 4004, Fax: 909-9712295, E-mail: bcox@laverne.edu.
Website: http://laverne.edu/business-and-public-administration/healthadmin-gerontology/

University of Louisiana at Monroe, Graduate School, College of Health and Pharmaceutical Sciences, Department of Gerontology, Monroe, LA 71209-0001. Offers aging studies (MA); gerontology (CGS); program administration (MA). *Degree requirements:* For master's, thesis (for some programs), internship. *Entrance requirements:* For master's and CGS, GRE General Test, minimum cumulative undergraduate GPA of 2.75. Additional exam requirements/recommendations for international students: Required—TOEFL (minimum score 500 paper-based; 61 iBT). Electronic applications accepted.

University of Louisville, Graduate School, Raymond A. Kent School of Social Work, Louisville, KY 40292-0001. Offers marriage and family therapy (PMC), including mental health; social work (MSSW, PhD), including alcohol and drug counseling (MSSW), gerontology (MSSW), marriage and family (PhD), school social work (MSSW). *Accreditation:* AAMFT/COAMFTE; CSWE (one or more programs are accredited). Part-time and evening/weekend programs available. *Students:* 369 full-time (312 women), 101 part-time (89 women); includes 138 minority (95 Black or African American, non-Hispanic/Latino; 3 American Indian or Alaska Native, non-Hispanic/Latino; 5 Asian, non-Hispanic/Latino; 21 Hispanic/Latino; 14 Two or more races, non-Hispanic/Latino), 7 international. Average age 31. 425 applicants, 67% accepted, 176 enrolled. In 2014, 117 master's, 2 doctorates awarded. *Degree requirements:* For doctorate, comprehensive exam, thesis/dissertation. *Entrance requirements:* For master's, GRE or minimum GPA of 2.75; for doctorate, GRE General Test, interview, writing sample. Additional exam requirements/recommendations for international students: Required—TOEFL (minimum score 550 paper-based; 79 iBT). *Application deadline:* For fall admission, 7/31 for domestic and international students. Applications are processed on a rolling basis. Application fee: $60. Electronic applications accepted. *Expenses:* Tuition, state resident: full-time $11,326; part-time $630 per credit hour. Tuition, nonresident: full-time $23,568; part-time $1311 per credit hour. *Required fees:* $196. Tuition and fees vary according to program and reciprocity agreements. *Financial support:* Research assistantships with full tuition reimbursements, teaching assistantships with full tuition reimbursements, Federal Work-Study, institutionally sponsored loans, scholarships/grants, health care benefits, and unspecified assistantships available. Support available to part-time students. Financial award application deadline: 5/15; financial award applicants required to submit FAFSA. *Faculty research:* Child welfare, substance abuse, gerontology, family functioning, health behavior. *Total annual research expenditures:* $1.6 million. *Unit head:* Dr. Terry Singer, Dean, 502-852-6402, Fax: 502-852-0422, E-mail: terry.singer@louisville.edu. *Application contact:* Libby Leggett, Director, Graduate Admissions, 502-852-3101, Fax: 502-852-6536, E-mail: gradadm@louisville.edu.
Website: http://www.louisville.edu/kent

University of Maryland, Baltimore, Graduate School, Graduate Program in Life Sciences, Program in Gerontology, Baltimore, MD 21201. Offers PhD. *Students:* 6 full-time (5 women), 4 part-time (all women); includes 5 minority (3 Black or African American, non-Hispanic/Latino; 1 Hispanic/Latino; 1 Two or more races, non-Hispanic/Latino). Average age 31. 6 applicants, 67% accepted, 4 enrolled. In 2014, 1 doctorate awarded. *Degree requirements:* For doctorate, comprehensive exam, thesis/dissertation. *Entrance requirements:* For doctorate, GRE General Test. Additional exam requirements/recommendations for international students: Required—TOEFL (minimum score 550 paper-based; 80 iBT); Recommended—IELTS (minimum score 7). *Application deadline:* For fall admission, 1/15 for domestic and international students. Application fee: $75. Electronic applications accepted. *Financial support:* Fellowships and research assistantships available. Financial award application deadline: 3/1; financial award applicants required to submit FAFSA. *Unit head:* Dr. Denise Orwig, Professor and Program Director, 410-706-4926, E-mail: dorwig@epi.umaryland.edu. *Application contact:* Justine Golden, Coordinator, 410-706-1733, E-mail: jgolden@epi.umaryland.edu.
Website: http://www.gerontologyphd.umaryland.edu/

University of Maryland, Baltimore, School of Medicine, Department of Epidemiology and Public Health, Baltimore, MD 21201. Offers biostatistics (MS); clinical research (MS); epidemiology and preventive medicine (MPH, MS, PhD); gerontology (PhD); human genetics and genomic medicine (MS, PhD); molecular epidemiology (MS, PhD); toxicology (MS, PhD); JD/MS; MD/PhD; MS/PhD. *Accreditation:* CEPH. Part-time programs available. *Students:* 85 full-time (63 women), 64 part-time (40 women); includes 47 minority (28 Black or African American, non-Hispanic/Latino; 13 Asian, non-Hispanic/Latino; 4 Hispanic/Latino; 2 Two or more races, non-Hispanic/Latino), 22 international. Average age 31. 95 applicants, 46% accepted, 28 enrolled. In 2014, 23 master's, 7 doctorates awarded. *Degree requirements:* For doctorate, comprehensive exam, thesis/dissertation. *Entrance requirements:* For master's and doctorate, GRE General Test. Additional exam requirements/recommendations for international students: Required—TOEFL (minimum score 550 paper-based; 80 iBT); Recommended—IELTS (minimum score 7). *Application deadline:* For fall admission, 1/15 for domestic and international students. Application fee: $75. Electronic applications accepted. *Expenses:* Expenses: Contact institution. *Financial support:* In 2014–15, research assistantships with partial tuition reimbursements (averaging $26,000 per year) were awarded; fellowships, Federal Work-Study, scholarships/grants, and unspecified assistantships also available. Financial award application deadline: 3/1; financial award applicants required to submit FAFSA. *Unit head:* Dr. Laura Hungerford, Program Director, 410-706-8492, Fax: 410-706-4225. *Application contact:* Jessica Kelley, Program Coordinator, 410-706-8492, Fax: 410-706-4225, E-mail: jkelley@som.umaryland.edu.
Website: http://lifesciences.umaryland.edu/epidemiology/

University of Maryland, Baltimore County, The Graduate School, College of Arts, Humanities and Social Sciences, Doctoral Program in Gerontology at UMB/UMBC, Baltimore, MD 21201. Offers aging policy issues (PhD); epidemiology of aging (PhD); social, cultural, and behavioral sciences (PhD); MA/PhD; MS/PhD. Part-time programs available. *Faculty:* 17 part-time/adjunct (12 women). *Students:* 13 full-time (10 women), 12 part-time (10 women); includes 7 minority (5 Black or African American, non-Hispanic/Latino; 1 Asian, non-Hispanic/Latino; 1 Hispanic/Latino), 2 international. Average age 36. 16 applicants, 31% accepted, 4 enrolled. In 2014, 3 doctorates awarded. *Degree requirements:* For doctorate, comprehensive exam, thesis/dissertation. *Entrance requirements:* For doctorate, GRE General Test. Additional exam requirements/recommendations for international students: Required—TOEFL, TWE. *Application deadline:* For spring admission, 1/15 for domestic and international students. Application fee: $45. Electronic applications accepted. *Expenses:* Tuition, state resident: part-time $557. Tuition, nonresident: part-time $922. *Required fees:* $122 per semester. One-time fee: $200 part-time. *Financial support:* In 2014–15, 12 research assistantships with full tuition reimbursements (averaging $21,750 per year) were awarded; career-related internships or fieldwork, scholarships/grants, traineeships, health care benefits, and unspecified assistantships also available. Financial award application deadline: 2/1; financial award applicants required to submit FAFSA. *Faculty research:* Aging and health policy, behavioral aspects of aging, epidemiology of aging. *Total annual research expenditures:* $52.7 million. *Unit head:* Dr. Leslie Morgan, Co-Director, UMBC Campus, 410-455-2074, Fax: 410-455-1154, E-mail: lmorgan@umbc.edu. *Application contact:* Justine Golden, Academic Coordinator, 410-706-4926, Fax: 410-706-4433, E-mail: jgold002@umaryland.edu.
Website: http://www.gerontologyphd.umaryland.edu

University of Maryland, Baltimore County, The Graduate School, Erickson School of Aging Studies, Baltimore, MD 21228. Offers management of aging services (MA). *Faculty:* 3 full-time (0 women), 4 part-time/adjunct (0 women). *Students:* 18 full-time (12 women); includes 9 minority (8 Black or African American, non-Hispanic/Latino; 1 Hispanic/Latino). Average age 30. 23 applicants, 91% accepted, 18 enrolled. In 2014, 13 master's awarded. *Degree requirements:* For master's, thesis or alternative. *Entrance requirements:* For master's, essays. *Application deadline:* Applications are processed on a rolling basis. Application fee: $50. Electronic applications accepted. *Expenses:* Expenses: Contact institution. *Financial support:* In 2014–15, 15 students received support, including 1 teaching assistantship with tuition reimbursement available (averaging $21,600 per year). Financial award applicants required to submit FAFSA. *Faculty research:* Policy implications of entitlement programs, demographic impact of aging population, person-centered care for dementia, changing culture in long-term care. *Unit head:* Bill Holman, Graduate Program Director, 443-543-5603, E-mail: bholman@sagepointcare.org. *Application contact:* Michelle Howell, Administrative Assistant, 443-543-5607, E-mail: mhowell@umbc.edu.
Website: http://www.umbc.edu/erickson/

University of Massachusetts Boston, John W. McCormack Graduate School of Policy and Global Studies, Program in Gerontology, Boston, MA 02125-3393. Offers gerontology (MS, PhD, Certificate); gerontology research (MS); management of aging services (MS). Part-time programs available. *Degree requirements:* For doctorate, comprehensive exam, thesis/dissertation. *Entrance requirements:* For doctorate, GRE General Test, minimum GPA of 3.0. *Application deadline:* For fall admission, 2/1 for domestic students. *Expenses:* Tuition, state resident: full-time $2590; part-time $108 per credit. Tuition, nonresident: full-time $9758; part-time $406.50 per credit. Tuition and fees vary according to course load and program. *Financial support:* Research assistantships with full tuition reimbursements, teaching assistantships with full tuition reimbursements, career-related internships or fieldwork, Federal Work-Study, and

unspecified assistantships available. Support available to part-time students. Financial award application deadline: 3/1; financial award applicants required to submit FAFSA. *Faculty research:* Aging with a chronic disability, pension policy and social security system, elderly minorities, health services research, living arrangements. *Unit head:* Dr. Ellen Bruce, Director, 617-287-7300, E-mail: ellen.bruce@umb.edu. *Application contact:* Peggy Roldan Patel, Graduate Admissions Coordinator, 617-287-6400, Fax: 617-287-6236, E-mail: bos.gadm@dpc.umassp.edu.

University of Missouri, Office of Research and Graduate Studies, School of Social Work, Columbia, MO 65211. Offers gerontological social work (Certificate); military social work (Certificate); social work (MSW, PhD). *Accreditation:* CSWE. Part-time programs available. *Faculty:* 15 full-time (9 women). *Students:* 81 full-time (73 women), 128 part-time (113 women); includes 20 minority (9 Black or African American, non-Hispanic/Latino; 4 Hispanic/Latino; 7 Two or more races, non-Hispanic/Latino), 1 international. Average age 32. 151 applicants, 62% accepted, 63 enrolled. In 2014, 87 master's, 1 doctorate, 12 other advanced degrees awarded. *Entrance requirements:* For master's, GRE General Test, minimum GPA of 3.0. Additional exam requirements/recommendations for international students: Required—TOEFL (minimum score 500 paper-based; 61 iBT). *Application deadline:* For fall admission, 1/15 priority date for domestic and international students. Applications are processed on a rolling basis. Application fee: $55 ($75 for international students). Electronic applications accepted. *Financial support:* Fellowships with tuition reimbursements, research assistantships with tuition reimbursements, teaching assistantships with tuition reimbursements, institutionally sponsored loans, scholarships/grants, health care benefits, and unspecified assistantships available. Support available to part-time students. *Faculty research:* Assessment of risk and resiliency factors in trauma populations, retirement, child welfare, parenting education, adolescent mood disorders, gerontology, rural practice, employee empowerment and involvement, children and youth, field education, substance use disorders in women, child welfare services and organization, maternal and child health, youth development and community betterment, international social work issues, epidemiology, etiology, prevention of health risk behaviors. *Unit head:* Dr. Marjorie Sable, Director, 573-882-0914, E-mail: sablem@missouri.edu. *Application contact:* Crystal Null, Administrative Assistant, 573-884-9385, E-mail: nullc@missouri.edu.
Website: http://ssw.missouri.edu/

University of Missouri–St. Louis, College of Arts and Sciences, Program in Gerontology, St. Louis, MO 63121. Offers MS, Certificate. Part-time and evening/weekend programs available. *Faculty:* 4 part-time/adjunct (2 women). *Students:* 13 full-time (10 women), 14 part-time (all women); includes 6 minority (4 Black or African American, non-Hispanic/Latino; 2 Hispanic/Latino). Average age 41. 9 applicants, 33% accepted, 3 enrolled. In 2014, 4 master's, 2 other advanced degrees awarded. *Entrance requirements:* For master's, 3 letters of recommendation. Additional exam requirements/recommendations for international students: Required—TOEFL (minimum score 550 paper-based; 79 iBT), IELTS (minimum score 6.5). *Application deadline:* For fall admission, 7/1 priority date for domestic and international students; for spring admission, 12/1 priority date for domestic and international students. Applications are processed on a rolling basis. Application fee: $50 ($40 for international students). Electronic applications accepted. *Expenses:* Tuition, state resident: full-time $7364; part-time $409.10 per hour. Tuition, nonresident: full-time $18,153; part-time $1008.50 per hour. *Financial support:* In 2014–15, 1 research assistantship with full and partial tuition reimbursement (averaging $11,700 per year), 1 teaching assistantship (averaging $9,000 per year) were awarded; career-related internships or fieldwork and Federal Work-Study also available. Financial award applicants required to submit FAFSA. *Faculty research:* Health care policy, social support and stress, retirement policy health behavior, ethnic differences in aging. *Unit head:* Thomas Meuser, Director, 314-516-5421, Fax: 314-516-5210, E-mail: meusert@umsl.edu. *Application contact:* 314-516-5458, Fax: 314-516-6996, E-mail: gradadm@umsl.edu.
Website: http://www.umsl.edu/~socialwk/Gerontology/index.html

University of Missouri–St. Louis, College of Arts and Sciences, School of Social Work, St. Louis, MO 63121. Offers gerontology (MS, Certificate); long term care administration (Certificate); social work (MSW). *Accreditation:* CSWE. *Faculty:* 12 full-time (10 women), 8 part-time/adjunct (6 women). *Students:* 81 full-time (73 women), 69 part-time (59 women); includes 30 minority (24 Black or African American, non-Hispanic/Latino; 3 Asian, non-Hispanic/Latino; 1 Hispanic/Latino; 2 Two or more races, non-Hispanic/Latino). Average age 32. 174 applicants, 56% accepted, 57 enrolled. In 2014, 58 master's awarded. *Entrance requirements:* For master's, 3 letters of recommendation. Additional exam requirements/recommendations for international students: Required—TOEFL (minimum score 550 paper-based; 79 iBT), IELTS (minimum score 6.5). *Application deadline:* For fall admission, 3/1 for domestic and international students; for spring admission, 10/15 for domestic and international students. Application fee: $50 ($40 for international students). Electronic applications accepted. *Expenses:* Tuition, state resident: full-time $7364; part-time $409.10 per hour. Tuition, nonresident: full-time $18,153; part-time $1008.50 per hour. *Financial support:* In 2014–15, 2 research assistantships with full and partial tuition reimbursements (averaging $5,700 per year), 7 teaching assistantships with full and partial tuition reimbursements (averaging $5,786 per year) were awarded. Financial award applicants required to submit FAFSA. *Faculty research:* Family violence, child abuse/neglect, immigration, community economic development. *Unit head:* Dr. Baorong Guo, Graduate Program Director, 314-516-6364, Fax: 314-516-5816, E-mail: socialwork@umsl.edu. *Application contact:* 314-516-5458, Fax: 314-516-6996, E-mail: gradadm@umsl.edu.
Website: http://www.umsl.edu/~socialwk/

University of Nebraska at Omaha, Graduate Studies, College of Public Affairs and Community Service, Department of Gerontology, Omaha, NE 68182. Offers gerontology (Certificate); social gerontology (MA). Part-time and evening/weekend programs available. *Faculty:* 6 full-time (3 women). *Students:* 4 full-time (2 women), 23 part-time (22 women); includes 4 minority (1 Black or African American, non-Hispanic/Latino; 1 Asian, non-Hispanic/Latino; 2 Hispanic/Latino). Average age 36. 27 applicants, 63% accepted, 14 enrolled. In 2014, 4 master's, 9 other advanced degrees awarded. *Degree requirements:* For master's, comprehensive exam, thesis. *Entrance requirements:* For master's, minimum GPA of 3.0, official transcripts, 2 letters of recommendation; for Certificate, minimum GPA of 3.0, official transcripts, 3 letters of recommendation. Additional exam requirements/recommendations for international students: Required—TOEFL (minimum score 550 paper-based), IELTS (minimum score 5.5), PTE (minimum score 44). *Application deadline:* For fall admission, 7/1 for domestic students; for spring admission, 12/1 for domestic students. Applications are processed on a rolling basis. Application fee: $45. Electronic applications accepted. *Financial support:* Fellowships, career-related internships or fieldwork, Federal Work-Study, institutionally sponsored loans, scholarships/grants, and tuition waivers (partial) available. Support available to part-time students. Financial award application deadline: 3/1; financial award applicants required to submit FAFSA. *Unit head:* Dr. Julie Masters, Chairperson, 402-554-2341, E-mail: graduate@unomaha.edu. *Application contact:* Dr. Christopher Kelly, Graduate Program Chair, 402-554-2341, E-mail: graduate@unomaha.edu.

University of Nebraska–Lincoln, Graduate College, College of Education and Human Sciences, Department of Child, Youth and Family Studies, Lincoln, NE 68588. Offers child development/early childhood education (MS, PhD); child, youth and family studies (MS); family and consumer sciences education (MS, PhD); family financial planning (MS); family science (MS, PhD); gerontology (PhD); human sciences (PhD), including child, youth and family studies, gerontology, medical family therapy; marriage and family therapy (MS); medical family therapy (PhD); youth development (MS). *Accreditation:* AAMFT/COAMFTE (one or more programs are accredited). Postbaccalaureate distance learning degree programs offered. *Degree requirements:* For master's, thesis optional. *Entrance requirements:* For master's, GRE. Additional exam requirements/recommendations for international students: Required—TOEFL (minimum score 550 paper-based). Electronic applications accepted. *Faculty research:* Marriage and family therapy, child development/early childhood education, family financial management.

The University of North Carolina at Charlotte, College of Liberal Arts and Sciences, Interdisciplinary Liberal Arts and Sciences Programs, Charlotte, NC 28223-0001. Offers gerontology (MA, Graduate Certificate); Latin American studies (MA); liberal studies (MA); organizational psychology (PhD); public policy (PhD); women's studies (Graduate Certificate). *Faculty:* 6 full-time (3 women), 5 part-time/adjunct (all women). *Students:* 58 full-time (31 women), 55 part-time (45 women); includes 24 minority (15 Black or African American, non-Hispanic/Latino; 1 Asian, non-Hispanic/Latino; 6 Hispanic/Latino; 1 Native Hawaiian or other Pacific Islander, non-Hispanic/Latino; 1 Two or more races, non-Hispanic/Latino), 12 international. Average age 33. 96 applicants, 46% accepted, 29 enrolled. In 2014, 11 master's, 8 doctorates, 15 other advanced degrees awarded. Terminal master's awarded for partial completion of doctoral program. *Degree requirements:* For master's, thesis or alternative, comprehensive exam or project; for doctorate, thesis/dissertation. *Entrance requirements:* For master's, GRE General Test or MAT, minimum GPA of 3.0 during previous 2 years, 2.75 overall; for doctorate, GRE, letters of recommendation. Additional exam requirements/recommendations for international students: Required—TOEFL (minimum score 557 paper-based; 83 iBT). *Application deadline:* For fall admission, 5/1 priority date for domestic students, 5/1 for international students; for spring admission, 10/1 priority date for domestic students, 10/1 for international students. Applications are processed on a rolling basis. Application fee: $75. Electronic applications accepted. *Expenses:* Tuition, state resident: full-time $4008. Tuition, nonresident: full-time $16,295. *Required fees:* $2755. Tuition and fees vary according to course load and program. *Financial support:* In 2014–15, 24 students received support, including 20 research assistantships (averaging $10,400 per year), 4 teaching assistantships (averaging $8,250 per year); career-related internships or fieldwork, institutionally sponsored loans, scholarships/grants, and unspecified assistantships also available. Support available to part-time students. Financial award application deadline: 4/1; financial award applicants required to submit FAFSA. *Total annual research expenditures:* $15,045. *Unit head:* Dr. Nancy A. Gutierrez, Dean, 704-687-0081, Fax: 704-687-4347, E-mail: ngutierr@uncc.edu. *Application contact:* Kathy B. Giddings, Director of Graduate Admissions, 704-687-5503, Fax: 704-687-3279, E-mail: gradadm@uncc.edu.
Website: http://www.lbst.uncc.edu/

The University of North Carolina at Greensboro, Graduate School, School of Health and Human Sciences, Program in Gerontology, Greensboro, NC 27412-5001. Offers MS, Certificate, MS/MBA. Electronic applications accepted.

The University of North Carolina Wilmington, School of Health and Applied Human Sciences, Wilmington, NC 28403-3297. Offers applied gerontology (MS). Part-time programs available. Postbaccalaureate distance learning degree programs offered. *Faculty:* 19 full-time (10 women). *Students:* 2 full-time (both women), 3 part-time (all women); includes 1 minority (Black or African American, non-Hispanic/Latino). 4 applicants, 100% accepted, 2 enrolled. In 2014, 2 master's awarded. *Degree requirements:* For master's, comprehensive exam, thesis or alternative. *Entrance requirements:* For master's, GRE, minimum undergraduate B average. Additional exam requirements/recommendations for international students: Required—TOEFL (minimum score 79 iBT), IELTS. *Application deadline:* For fall admission, 6/15 for domestic students; for spring admission, 11/15 for domestic students; for summer admission, 3/15 for domestic students. Application fee: $60. *Expenses:* Tuition, state resident: full-time $3240. Tuition, nonresident: full-time $9208. *Required fees:* $1967. *Financial support:* Scholarships/grants and unspecified assistantships available. Support available to part-time students. Financial award applicants required to submit FAFSA. *Unit head:* Dr. Chris Lantz, Director, 910-962-2364, Fax: 910-962-7073, E-mail: lantzc@uncw.edu. *Application contact:* Dr. Elizabeth Fugate-Whitlock, Interim Program Coordinator, 910-962-7816, E-mail: whitlocke@uncw.edu.
Website: http://www.uncw.edu/shahs/

University of Northern Colorado, Graduate School, College of Natural and Health Sciences, School of Human Sciences, Program in Gerontology, Greeley, CO 80639. Offers MA. Part-time programs available. *Degree requirements:* For master's, comprehensive exam. *Entrance requirements:* For master's, GRE General Test or MAT, 2 letters of recommendation. Electronic applications accepted.

University of North Florida, Brooks College of Health, Department of Public Health, Jacksonville, FL 32224. Offers aging services (Certificate); community health (MPH); geriatric management (MSH); health administration (MHA); rehabilitation counseling (MS). *Accreditation:* CEPH. Part-time and evening/weekend programs available. *Faculty:* 19 full-time (13 women), 3 part-time/adjunct (2 women). *Students:* 142 full-time (102 women), 52 part-time (30 women); includes 55 minority (23 Black or African American, non-Hispanic/Latino; 10 Asian, non-Hispanic/Latino; 15 Hispanic/Latino; 7 Two or more races, non-Hispanic/Latino), 7 international. Average age 29. 275 applicants, 39% accepted, 72 enrolled. In 2014, 66 master's awarded. *Degree requirements:* For master's, thesis optional. *Entrance requirements:* For master's, GRE General Test (MSH, MS, MPH); GMAT or GRE General Test (MHA), minimum GPA of 3.0 in last 60 hours. Additional exam requirements/recommendations for international students: Required—TOEFL (minimum score 500 paper-based). *Application deadline:* For fall admission, 7/1 for domestic students, 5/1 for international students; for spring admission, 11/1 for domestic students, 10/1 for international students. Application fee: $30. Electronic applications accepted. *Expenses:* Tuition, state resident: full-time $9794; part-time $408.10 per credit hour. Tuition, nonresident: full-time $22,383; part-time $932.61 per credit hour. *Required fees:* $2047; $85.29 per credit hour. Tuition and fees vary according to course load and program. *Financial support:* In 2014–15, 34 students received support, including 2 teaching assistantships (averaging $2,000 per year); research assistantships, career-related internships or fieldwork, Federal Work-Study, scholarships/grants, and tuition waivers (partial) also available. Support available to part-time students. Financial award application deadline: 4/1; financial award applicants required to submit FAFSA. *Faculty research:* Dietary supplements; alcohol, tobacco, and other drug use prevention; turnover among health professionals; aging; psychosocial aspects of disabilities. *Total annual research expenditures:* $57,986. *Unit head:* Dr. Jeffrey Harrison, Chair, 904-620-1440, Fax: 904-620-2848, E-mail: jeffrey.harrison@unf.edu. *Application contact:* Dr. Heather Kenney, Director of Advising, 904-620-2810, Fax: 904-620-1030, E-mail: heather.kenney@unf.edu.
Website: http://www.unf.edu/brooks/public_health/

University of North Texas, Robert B. Toulouse School of Graduate Studies, Denton, TX 76203-5459. Offers accounting (MS); applied anthropology (MA, MS); applied behavior analysis (Certificate); applied geography (MA); applied technology and performance improvement (M Ed, MS); art education (MA); art history (MA); art museum education (Certificate); arts leadership (Certificate); audiology (Au D); behavior analysis (MS); behavioral science (PhD); biochemistry and molecular biology (MS); biology (MA, MS); biomedical engineering (MS); business analysis (MS); chemistry (MS); clinical health psychology (PhD); communication studies (MA, MS); computer engineering (MS); computer science (MS); counseling (M Ed, MS), including clinical mental health counseling (MS), college and university counseling, elementary school counseling, secondary school counseling; creative writing (MA); criminal justice (MS); curriculum and instruction (M Ed); decision sciences (MBA); design (MA, MFA), including fashion design (MFA), innovation studies, interior design (MFA); early childhood studies (MS); economics (MS); educational leadership (M Ed, Ed D); educational psychology (MS, PhD), including family studies (MS), gifted and talented (MS), human development (MS), learning and cognition (MS), research, measurement and evaluation (MS); electrical engineering (MS); emergency management (MPA); engineering technology (MS); English (MA); English as a second language (MA); environmental science (MS); finance (MBA, MS); financial management (MPA); French (MA); health services management (MBA); higher education (M Ed, Ed D); history (MA, MS); hospitality management (MS); human resources management (MPA); information science (MS); information systems (PhD); information technologies (MBA); interdisciplinary studies (MA, MS); international studies (MA); international sustainable tourism (MS); jazz studies (MM); journalism (MA, MJ, Graduate Certificate), including interactive and virtual digital communication (Graduate Certificate), narrative journalism (Graduate Certificate), public relations (Graduate Certificate); kinesiology (MS); linguistics (MA); local government management (MPA); logistics (PhD); logistics and supply chain management (MBA); long-term care, senior housing, and aging services (MA); management (PhD); marketing (MBA); mathematics (MA, MS); mechanical and energy engineering (MS, PhD); music (MA), including ethnomusicology, music theory, musicology, performance; music composition (PhD); music education (MM Ed, PhD); nonprofit management (MPA); operations and supply chain management (MBA); performance (MM, DMA); philosophy (MA); political science (MA); professional and technical communication (MA); radio, television and film (MA, MFA); rehabilitation counseling (Certificate); sociology (MA); Spanish (MA); special education (M Ed); speech-language pathology (MA); strategic management (MBA); studio art (MFA); teaching (M Ed); MBA/MS. Part-time and evening/weekend programs available. Postbaccalaureate distance learning degree programs offered. *Faculty:* 651 full-time (215 women), 233 part-time/adjunct (139 women). *Students:* 3,040 full-time (1,598 women), 3,401 part-time (2,097 women); includes 1,740 minority (533 Black or African American, non-Hispanic/Latino; 15 American Indian or Alaska Native, non-Hispanic/Latino; 286 Asian, non-Hispanic/Latino; 746 Hispanic/Latino; 3 Native Hawaiian or other Pacific Islander, non-Hispanic/Latino; 157 Two or more races, non-Hispanic/Latino), 1,145 international. Terminal master's awarded for partial completion of doctoral program. *Degree requirements:* For master's, variable foreign language requirement, comprehensive exam (for some programs), thesis (for some programs); for doctorate, variable foreign language requirement, comprehensive exam (for some programs), thesis/dissertation; for other advanced degree, variable foreign language requirement, comprehensive exam (for some programs). *Entrance requirements:* For master's and doctorate, GRE, GMAT. Additional exam requirements/recommendations for international students: Required—TOEFL (minimum score 550 paper-based; 79 iBT). *Application deadline:* For fall admission, 7/15 for domestic students, 3/15 for international students; for spring admission, 11/15 for domestic students, 9/15 for international students; for summer admission, 5/1 for domestic students. Applications are processed on a rolling basis. Application fee: $60. Electronic applications accepted. *Expenses:* Tuition, state resident: full-time $5450; part-time $3633 per year. Tuition, nonresident: full-time $11,966; part-time $7977 per year. *Required fees:* $1301; $398 per credit hour. $685 per semester. Tuition and fees vary according to program and reciprocity agreements. *Financial support:* Fellowships with partial tuition reimbursements, research assistantships with partial tuition reimbursements, teaching assistantships, career-related internships or fieldwork, Federal Work-Study, institutionally sponsored loans, scholarships/grants, health care benefits, and library assistantships available. Support available to part-time students. Financial award applicants required to submit FAFSA. *Unit head:* Mark Wardell, Dean, 940-565-2383, E-mail: mark.wardell@unt.edu. *Application contact:* Toulouse School of Graduate Studies, 940-565-2383, Fax: 940-565-2141, E-mail: gradsch@unt.edu. Website: http://tsgs.unt.edu/

University of Phoenix–Birmingham Campus, College of Health and Human Services, Birmingham, AL 35242. Offers education (MHA); gerontology (MHA); health administration (MHA); health care management (MBA); informatics (MHA); nursing (MSN); nursing/health care education (MSN); MSN/MBA; MSN/MHA.

University of Phoenix–Central Valley Campus, College of Nursing, Fresno, CA 93720-1562. Offers education (MHA); gerontology (MHA); health administration (MHA); nursing (MSN); MSN/MBA.

University of Phoenix–Charlotte Campus, College of Nursing, Charlotte, NC 28273-3409. Offers education (MHA); gerontology (MHA); health administration (MHA); informatics (MHA, MSN); nursing (MSN); nursing/health care education (MSN). Evening/weekend programs available. *Degree requirements:* For master's, thesis (for some programs). *Entrance requirements:* For master's, minimum undergraduate GPA of 2.5, 3 years work experience. Additional exam requirements/recommendations for international students: Required—TOEFL (minimum score 550 paper-based; 79 iBT). Electronic applications accepted.

University of Phoenix–Colorado Springs Downtown Campus, College of Nursing, Colorado Springs, CO 80903. Offers education (MHA); gerontology (MHA); health administration (MHA); nursing (MSN); MSN/MBA. Evening/weekend programs available. *Degree requirements:* For master's, thesis (for some programs). *Entrance requirements:* For master's, minimum undergraduate GPA of 2.5, 3 years of work experience, RN license. Additional exam requirements/recommendations for international students: Required—TOEFL (minimum score 550 paper-based; 79 iBT). Electronic applications accepted.

University of Phoenix–Des Moines Campus, College of Nursing, Des Moines, IA 50309. Offers education (MHA); gerontology (MHA); health administration (MHA, DHA); informatics (MHA, MSN); nursing (MSN, PhD); nursing/health care education (MSN).

University of Phoenix–Hawaii Campus, College of Nursing, Honolulu, HI 96813-4317. Offers education (MHA); family nurse practitioner (MSN); gerontology (MHA); health administration (MHA); nursing (MSN); nursing/health care education (MSN); MSN/MBA. Evening/weekend programs available. *Degree requirements:* For master's, thesis (for some programs). *Entrance requirements:* For master's, minimum undergraduate GPA of 2.5, 3 years of work experience, RN license. Additional exam requirements/recommendations for international students: Required—TOEFL (minimum score 550 paper-based; 79 iBT). Electronic applications accepted.

University of Phoenix–Washington D.C. Campus, College of Nursing, Washington, DC 20001. Offers education (MHA); gerontology (MHA); health administration (MHA, DHA); informatics (MHA, MSN); nursing (MSN, PhD); nursing/health care education (MSN); MSN/MBA; MSN/MHA.

University of Puerto Rico, Medical Sciences Campus, Graduate School of Public Health, Department of Human Development, Program in Gerontology, San Juan, PR 00936-5067. Offers MPH, Certificate. Part-time and evening/weekend programs available. *Entrance requirements:* For master's, GRE, previous course work in social sciences, biology, psychology, and algebra.

University of Regina, Faculty of Graduate Studies and Research, Faculty of Arts, Program in Gerontology, Regina, SK S4S 0A2, Canada. Offers M Sc, MA. Part-time programs available. *Students:* 3 full-time (2 women), 1 part-time (0 women). 4 applicants, 25% accepted. *Degree requirements:* For master's, thesis. *Entrance requirements:* Additional exam requirements/recommendations for international students: Required—TOEFL (minimum score 580 paper-based; 80 iBT), IELTS (minimum score 6.5), PTE (minimum score 59). *Application deadline:* For fall admission, 3/31 for domestic and international students. Application fee: $100. Electronic applications accepted. *Expenses: Tuition, area resident:* Full-time $4900 Canadian dollars; part-time $837.65 Canadian dollars per semester. *International tuition:* $7900 Canadian dollars full-time. *Required fees:* $396 Canadian dollars; $86.90 Canadian dollars per semester. *Financial support:* In 2014–15, 1 fellowship (averaging $6,000 per year), 1 teaching assistantship (averaging $2,427 per year) were awarded; research assistantships and scholarships/grants also available. Financial award application deadline: 6/15. *Faculty research:* Health economics and policy; aging, society, and human service work; end-of-life issues for human service workers; physiology of aging; ethical decision-making in kinesiology and health care administration. *Unit head:* Dr. Ronald Martin, Program Coordinator, 306-585-4515, Fax: 306-585-4880, E-mail: ron.martin@uregina.ca. *Application contact:* Dr. Thomas Bredohl, Associate Dean, Research and Graduate Studies, 306-585-5324, Fax: 306-585-5368, E-mail: thomas.bredohl@uregina.ca.

University of Rhode Island, Graduate School, College of Nursing, Kingston, RI 02881. Offers administration (MS); clinical nurse leader (MS); clinical specialist in gerontology (MS); clinical specialist in psychiatric/mental health (MS); family nurse practitioner (MS); gerontological nurse practitioner (MS); nursing (DNP, PhD); nursing education (MS). *Accreditation:* AACN; ACNM/ACME (one or more programs are accredited). Part-time programs available. *Faculty:* 27 full-time (26 women), 2 part-time/adjunct (1 woman). *Students:* 65 full-time (57 women), 77 part-time (69 women); includes 18 minority (12 Black or African American, non-Hispanic/Latino; 1 Asian, non-Hispanic/Latino; 4 Hispanic/Latino; 1 Two or more races, non-Hispanic/Latino), 4 international. In 2014, 25 master's, 5 doctorates awarded. *Degree requirements:* For master's, comprehensive exam; for doctorate, comprehensive exam, thesis/dissertation. *Entrance requirements:* For master's, GRE or MAT, 2 letters of recommendation, scholarly papers; for doctorate, GRE, 3 letters of recommendation, scholarly papers. Additional exam requirements/recommendations for international students: Required—TOEFL (minimum score 550 paper-based). *Application deadline:* For fall admission, 2/15 for domestic students, 2/1 for international students; for spring admission, 10/15 for domestic students, 7/15 for international students. Application fee: $65. Electronic applications accepted. *Expenses:* Tuition, state resident: full-time $11,532; part-time $641 per credit. Tuition, nonresident: full-time $23,606; part-time $1311 per credit. *Required fees:* $1442; $39 per credit. $35 per semester. One-time fee: $155. *Financial support:* In 2014–15, 1 research assistantship (averaging $16,300 per year), 7 teaching assistantships with full and partial tuition reimbursements (averaging $12,500 per year) were awarded. Financial award application deadline: 2/15; financial award applicants required to submit FAFSA. *Faculty research:* Group intervention for grieving women in prison, translating best practice in non-drug interventions for postoperative pain management, further development and testing of the pain assessment inventory, preschool motor and functional performance of two cohorts, neuroactivation of brain motor areas in preterm children. *Total annual research expenditures:* $1.2 million. *Unit head:* Dr. Mary Sullivan, Interim Dean, 401-874-5339, Fax: 401-874-2061, E-mail: mcsullivan@uri.edu. *Application contact:* Graduate Admission, 401-874-2872, E-mail: gradadm@etal.uri.edu. Website: http://www.uri.edu/nursing/

University of Saint Joseph, Program in Gerontology, West Hartford, CT 06117-2700. Offers Certificate. Part-time and evening/weekend programs available. *Entrance requirements:* For degree, 2 letters of recommendation, letter of intent. Electronic applications accepted. Application fee is waived when completed online. *Expenses: Tuition:* Part-time $700 per credit. *Required fees:* $42 per credit. Tuition and fees vary according to degree level, campus/location and program.

University of South Carolina, The Graduate School, Program in Gerontology, Columbia, SC 29208. Offers Certificate. Part-time programs available. *Degree requirements:* For Certificate, practicum. Electronic applications accepted.

University of Southern California, Graduate School, Davis School of Gerontology, Los Angeles, CA 90089. Offers aging services management (MASM); biology of aging (PhD); gerontology (MA, MS, PhD, Graduate Certificate); long term care administration (MLTCA); DDS/MS; JD/MS; M Pl/MS; MBA/MS; MHA/MS; MPA/MS; MS/MA; MS/MSW; Pharm D/MS. PhD in biology of aging offered jointly with Buck Institute for Research on Aging. Part-time programs available. Postbaccalaureate distance learning degree programs offered (no on-campus study). Terminal master's awarded for partial completion of doctoral program. *Degree requirements:* For master's, thesis or alternative; for doctorate, comprehensive exam, thesis/dissertation. *Entrance requirements:* For master's, GRE (recommended); for doctorate, GRE. Additional exam requirements/recommendations for international students: Recommended—TOEFL. Electronic applications accepted. *Faculty research:* Sex steroids and Alzheimer's disease, memory, cognition and brain plasticity, environment and injury prevention, antioxidants, stress and aging, inflammation and aging, euthanasia, caloric restriction and chemotherapy, biodemographic of aging, health outcomes research, families and intergenerational relatives, care-giving of elderly, biology, psychology, sociology, policy.

University of Southern California, Graduate School, School of Social Work, Los Angeles, CA 90089. Offers community organization, planning and administration (MSW); families and children (MSW); health (MSW); mental health (MSW); military social work and veterans services (MSW); older adults (MSW); public child welfare (MSW); school settings (MSW); social work (MSW, PhD); systems of mental illness recovery (MSW); work and life (MSW); JD/MSW; M Pl/MSW; MPA/MSW; MSW/MBA; MSW/MJCS; MSW/MS. *Accreditation:* CSWE (one or more programs are accredited). *Degree requirements:* For doctorate, comprehensive exam, thesis/dissertation, qualifying exam/publishable paper. *Entrance requirements:* For doctorate, GRE General Test. Additional exam requirements/recommendations for international students: Required—TOEFL (minimum score 600 paper-based; 100 iBT), ESL exam. Electronic applications accepted. *Faculty research:* Department of Defense Educational Activity, detection/treatment of depression among older adults, health/aging, psychosocial adaptation to extreme environments/man made disasters; mental health needs of older adults.

University of South Florida, College of Behavioral and Community Sciences, School of Aging Studies, Tampa, FL 33620-9951. Offers aging studies (PhD); gerontology (MA). Part-time and evening/weekend programs available. *Faculty:* 12 full-time (5 women).

Students: 25 full-time (21 women), 15 part-time (12 women); includes 11 minority (5 Black or African American, non-Hispanic/Latino; 1 Asian, non-Hispanic/Latino; 4 Hispanic/Latino; 1 Two or more races, non-Hispanic/Latino), 1 international. Average age 33. 29 applicants, 34% accepted, 7 enrolled. In 2014, 9 master's, 2 doctorates awarded. *Degree requirements:* For master's, comprehensive exam, thesis optional; for doctorate, comprehensive exam, thesis/dissertation. *Entrance requirements:* For master's, GRE General Test, minimum GPA of 3.0; for doctorate, GRE General Test (minimum preferred score of 580 verbal, 620 quantitative, and 5.0 in analytical writing on old scoring), minimum GPA of 3.25, three letters of recommendation, summary of career goals, single-authored writing sample. Additional exam requirements/recommendations for international students: Required—TOEFL (minimum score 600 paper-based), IELTS. *Application deadline:* For fall admission, 2/1 priority date for domestic students, 1/2 priority date for international students. Application fee: $30. Electronic applications accepted. *Financial support:* In 2014–15, 15 students received support, including 2 research assistantships with tuition reimbursements available (averaging $15,690 per year), 13 teaching assistantships with tuition reimbursements available (averaging $13,503 per year). Financial award application deadline: 2/3. *Faculty research:* Aging and mental health, public policy and long-term care, minority aging, care-giving, guardianship, cognitive aging, Alzheimer's disease. *Total annual research expenditures:* $428,601. *Unit head:* Dr. Cathy L. McEvoy, Director and Professor, 813-974-1940, Fax: 813-974-9754, E-mail: cmcevoy@usf.edu. *Application contact:* Brent Small, Professor, 813-974-9746, Fax: 813-974-9754, E-mail: bsmall@usf.edu.
Website: http://agingstudies.cbcs.usf.edu/aprog/

University of South Florida, Innovative Education, Tampa, FL 33620-9951. *Unit head:* Kathy Barnes, Interdisciplinary Programs Coordinator, 813-974-8031, Fax: 813-974-7061, E-mail: barnesk@usf.edu. *Application contact:* Karen Tylinski, Metro Initiatives, 813-974-9943, Fax: 813-974-7061, E-mail: ktylinsk@usf.edu.
Website: http://www.usf.edu/innovative-education

University of South Florida, Morsani College of Medicine and Graduate School, Graduate Programs in Medical Sciences, Tampa, FL 33620-9951. Offers aging and neuroscience (MSMS); allergy, immunology and infectious disease (PhD); anatomy (MSMS, PhD); athletic training (MSMS); bioinformatics and computational biology (MSBCB); biotechnology (MSB); clinical and translational research (MSMS, PhD); health informatics (MSHI, MSMS); health science (MSMS); interdisciplinary medical sciences (MSMS); medical microbiology and immunology (MSMS); metabolic and nutritional medicine (MSMS); molecular medicine (MSMS, PhD); molecular pharmacology and physiology (PhD); neurology (PhD); pathology and laboratory medicine (PhD); pharmacology and therapeutics (PhD); physiology and biophysics (PhD); women's health (MSMS). *Students:* 338 full-time (162 women), 36 part-time (25 women); includes 173 minority (43 Black or African American, non-Hispanic/Latino; 65 Asian, non-Hispanic/Latino; 58 Hispanic/Latino; 7 Two or more races, non-Hispanic/Latino), 24 international. Average age 26. 1,188 applicants, 41% accepted, 271 enrolled. In 2014, 216 master's awarded. Terminal master's awarded for partial completion of doctoral program. *Degree requirements:* For master's, comprehensive exam, thesis; for doctorate, comprehensive exam, thesis/dissertation. *Entrance requirements:* For master's, GRE General Test or GMAT, bachelor's degree or equivalent from regionally-accredited university with minimum GPA of 3.0 in upper-division sciences coursework; prerequisites in general biology, general chemistry, general physics, organic chemistry, quantitative analysis, and integral and differential calculus; for doctorate, GRE General Test (minimum score of 32nd percentile quantitative), bachelor's degree from regionally-accredited university with minimum GPA of 3.0 in upper-division sciences coursework; 3 letters of recommendation; personal interview; 1-2 page personal statement; prerequisites in biology, chemistry, physics, organic chemistry, quantitative analysis, and integral/differential calculus. Additional exam requirements/recommendations for international students: Required—TOEFL (minimum score 550 paper-based; 79 iBT) or IELTS (minimum score 6.5). *Application deadline:* For fall admission, 2/15 for domestic students, 1/2 for international students. Application fee: $30. *Expenses:* Expenses: Contact institution. *Faculty research:* Anatomy, biochemistry, cancer biology, cardiovascular disease, cell biology, immunology, microbiology, molecular biology, neuroscience, pharmacology, physiology. *Unit head:* Dr. Michael Barber, Professor and Associate Dean for Graduate and Postdoctoral Affairs, 813-974-9908, Fax: 813-974-4317, E-mail: mbarber@health.usf.edu. *Application contact:* Dr. Eric Bennett, Graduate Director, PhD Program in Medical Sciences, 813-974-1545, Fax: 813-974-4317, E-mail: esbennet@health.usf.edu.
Website: http://health.usf.edu/nocms/medicine/graduatestudies/

The University of Tennessee, Graduate School, College of Education, Health and Human Sciences, Program in Public Health, Knoxville, TN 37996. Offers community health education (MPH); gerontology (MPH); health planning/administration (MPH); MS/MPH. *Accreditation:* CEPH. *Degree requirements:* For master's, thesis optional. *Entrance requirements:* For master's, minimum GPA of 2.7. Additional exam requirements/recommendations for international students: Required—TOEFL. Electronic applications accepted.

The University of Toledo, College of Graduate Studies, College of Medicine and Life Sciences, Department of Public Health and Preventative Medicine, Toledo, OH 43606-3390. Offers biostatistics and epidemiology (Certificate); contemporary gerontological practice (Certificate); environmental and occupational health and safety (MPH); epidemiology (Certificate); global public health (Certificate); health promotion and education (MPH); industrial hygiene (MSOH); medical and health science teaching and learning (Certificate); occupational health (Certificate); public health administration (MPH); public health and emergency response (Certificate); public health epidemiology (MPH); public health nutrition (MPH); MD/MPH. Part-time and evening/weekend programs available. *Degree requirements:* For master's, thesis or alternative. *Entrance requirements:* For master's, GRE, minimum undergraduate GPA of 3.0, three letters of recommendation, statement of purpose, transcripts from all prior institutions attended, resume; for Certificate, minimum undergraduate GPA of 3.0, three letters of recommendation, statement of purpose, transcripts from all prior institutions attended, resume. Additional exam requirements/recommendations for international students: Required—TOEFL (minimum score 550 paper-based; 80 iBT), IELTS (minimum score 6.5). Electronic applications accepted.

University of Utah, Graduate School, College of Nursing, Gerontology Interdisciplinary Program, Salt Lake City, UT 84112. Offers MS, Certificate. *Accreditation:* AACN. Part-time and evening/weekend programs available. Postbaccalaureate distance learning degree programs offered (no on-campus study). *Students:* 9 full-time (8 women), 9 part-time (7 women); includes 4 minority (2 Black or African American, non-Hispanic/Latino; 1 American Indian or Alaska Native, non-Hispanic/Latino; 1 Hispanic/Latino), 1 international. Average age 42. 11 applicants, 91% accepted, 7 enrolled. In 2014, 2 master's awarded. *Degree requirements:* For master's, thesis or project. *Entrance requirements:* For master's, GRE General Test (if cumulative GPA is less than 3.2), minimum undergraduate GPA of 3.0. Additional exam requirements/recommendations for international students: Required—TOEFL (minimum score 500 paper-based; 85 iBT). *Application deadline:* For fall admission, 1/15 for domestic and international students. Applications are processed on a rolling basis. Application fee: $55 ($65 for international students). Electronic applications accepted. *Expenses:* Expenses: Contact institution.

Financial support: In 2014–15, 8 students received support, including 8 fellowships with partial tuition reimbursements available (averaging $5,040 per year), 1 teaching assistantship with partial tuition reimbursement available (averaging $20,250 per year); scholarships/grants and health care benefits also available. Support available to part-time students. Financial award application deadline: 1/15; financial award applicants required to submit FAFSA. *Faculty research:* Spousal bereavement, family caregiving, health promotion and self-care, geriatric care management, technology and aging. *Unit head:* Kara Dassel, Director, 801-585-7438, Fax: 801-587-7697, E-mail: kara.dassel@nurs.utah.edu. *Application contact:* Arminka Zeljkovic, Program Manager, 801-581-8198, Fax: 801-585-9705, E-mail: arminka.zeljkovic@nurs.utah.edu.
Website: http://www.nursing.utah.edu/gerontology/

University of West Florida, College of Professional Studies, Department of Health, Leisure, and Exercise Science, Community Health Education Program, Pensacola, FL 32514-5750. Offers aging studies (MS); health promotion and worksite wellness (MS); psychosocial (MS). Part-time and evening/weekend programs available. *Degree requirements:* For master's, thesis or alternative. *Entrance requirements:* For master's, GRE or MAT, official transcripts; minimum GPA of 3.0; letter of intent; three personal references. Additional exam requirements/recommendations for international students: Required—TOEFL (minimum score 550 paper-based).

University of Wisconsin–Milwaukee, Graduate School, School of Social Welfare, Department of Social Work, Milwaukee, WI 53201-0413. Offers applied gerontology (Certificate); marriage and family therapy (Certificate); non-profit management (Certificate); social work (MSW, PhD). *Accreditation:* CSWE. Part-time programs available. *Degree requirements:* For master's, thesis or alternative. *Entrance requirements:* For doctorate, GRE, bachelor's degree. Additional exam requirements/recommendations for international students: Required—TOEFL (minimum score 550 paper-based; 79 iBT), IELTS (minimum score 6.5). Electronic applications accepted.

Utica College, Graduate Certificate Program in Gerontology, Utica, NY 13502-4892. Offers Graduate Certificate. Part-time and evening/weekend programs available. *Faculty:* 1 (woman) full-time, 2 part-time/adjunct (both women). *Entrance requirements:* Additional exam requirements/recommendations for international students: Recommended—TOEFL (minimum score 525 paper-based). *Application deadline:* Applications are processed on a rolling basis. Electronic applications accepted. *Expenses:* Tuition: Full-time $33,216; part-time $706 per credit hour. *Required fees:* $520; $50 per course. Tuition and fees vary according to course load, degree level, campus/location and program. *Financial support:* Application deadline: 3/15; applicants required to submit FAFSA. *Unit head:* Dr. Sarah Burnett-Wo1le, Program Manager, 315-792-2576, E-mail: sburnet@utica.edu. *Application contact:* John D. Rowe, Director of Graduate Admissions, 315-792-3824, Fax: 315-792-3003, E-mail: jrowe@utica.edu.
Website: http://www.onlineuticacollege.com/programs/gerontology-certificate.asp

Valparaiso University, Graduate School, Programs in Liberal Studies, Concentration in Gerontology, Valparaiso, IN 46383. Offers MALS, Post-Master's Certificate, JD/MALS. Part-time and evening/weekend programs available. *Entrance requirements:* For master's, minimum GPA of 3.0. Additional exam requirements/recommendations for international students: Required—TOEFL (minimum score 550 paper-based; 80 iBT), IELTS (minimum score 6). *Application deadline:* Applications are processed on a rolling basis. Application fee: $30 ($50 for international students). Electronic applications accepted. *Expenses:* Tuition: Full-time $10,710; part-time $595 per credit hour. *Required fees:* $378; $101 per term. Tuition and fees vary according to course load and program. *Financial support:* Available to part-time students. Applicants required to submit FAFSA. *Unit head:* Dr. Jennifer A. Ziegler, Dean, Graduate School and Continuing Education, 219-464-5313, Fax: 219-464-5381, E-mail: jennifer.ziegler@valpo.edu. *Application contact:* Jessica Choquette, Graduate Admissions Specialist, 219-464-5313, Fax: 219-464-5381, E-mail: jessica.choquette@valpo.edu.
Website: http://www.valpo.edu/grad/mals/gerontology.pdf

Virginia Commonwealth University, Graduate School, School of Allied Health Professions, Department of Gerontology, Richmond, VA 23284-9005. Offers aging studies (CAS); gerontology (MS). Part-time programs available. *Entrance requirements:* For master's, GRE General Test or MAT. Additional exam requirements/recommendations for international students: Required—TOEFL (minimum score 600 paper-based; 100 iBT); Recommended—IELTS (minimum score 6.5). Electronic applications accepted. *Faculty research:* Alzheimer's disease, age-related alcoholism and suicide, pain perception, curriculum development and evaluation in gerontology/geriatrics.

Virginia Commonwealth University, Graduate School, School of Allied Health Professions, Doctoral Program in Health Related Sciences, Richmond, VA 23284-9005. Offers clinical laboratory sciences (PhD); gerontology (PhD); health administration (PhD); nurse anesthesia (PhD); occupational therapy (PhD); physical therapy (PhD); radiation sciences (PhD); rehabilitation leadership (PhD). *Entrance requirements:* For doctorate, GRE General Test or MAT, minimum GPA of 3.3 in master's degree. Additional exam requirements/recommendations for international students: Required—TOEFL (minimum score 600 paper-based; 100 iBT); Recommended—IELTS (minimum score 6.5). Electronic applications accepted.

Washington University in St. Louis, Brown School of Social Work, St. Louis, MO 63130-4899. Offers affordable housing and mixed-income community management (Certificate); American Indian and Alaska native (MSW); children, youth and families (MSW); health (MSW); individualized (MSW), including health; mental health (MSW); older adults and aging societies (MSW); public health (MPH), including epidemiology/biostatistics, global health, health policy analysis, urban design; social and economic development (MSW); social work (MSW, PhD), including management (MSW), policy (MSW), research (MSW), sexual health and education (MSW), social entrepreneurship (MSW), system dynamics (MSW); violence and injury prevention (Certificate); JD/MSW; M Arch/MSW; MPH/MBA; MSW/M Div; MSW/MAPS; MSW/MBA; MSW/MPH. MSW/M Div and MSW/MAPS offered in partnership with Eden Theological Seminary. *Accreditation:* CSWE (one or more programs are accredited). *Faculty:* 42 full-time (24 women), 81 part-time/adjunct (49 women). *Students:* 272 full-time (229 women); includes 138 minority (47 Black or African American, non-Hispanic/Latino; 11 American Indian or Alaska Native, non-Hispanic/Latino; 54 Asian, non-Hispanic/Latino; 19 Hispanic/Latino; 7 Two or more races, non-Hispanic/Latino), 47 international. Average age 26. 817 applicants, 62% accepted, 303 enrolled. In 2014, 239 master's, 5 doctorates awarded. *Degree requirements:* For master's, 60 credit hours (MSW), 52 credit hours (MPH); practicum; for doctorate, comprehensive exam, thesis/dissertation. *Entrance requirements:* For master's, For public health: GRE, GMAT, LSAT, or MCAT, minimum GPA of 3.0; for doctorate, GRE, MA or MSW. Additional exam requirements/recommendations for international students: Required—TOEFL (minimum score 100 iBT) or IELTS. *Application deadline:* For fall admission, 3/1 priority date for domestic and international students. Applications are processed on a rolling basis. Application fee: $40. Electronic applications accepted. *Expenses:* Expenses: The tuition rate for new full-time MSW students for the 2015-2016 academic year is $38,234 per year. The tuition rate for new full-time MPH students for the 2015-2016 academic year is $33,132 per year. *Financial support:* In 2014–15, 301 students received support. Fellowships, research assistantships, Federal Work-Study, institutionally sponsored loans,

scholarships/grants, health care benefits, tuition waivers (partial), and unspecified assistantships available. Support available to part-time students. Financial award application deadline: 3/1; financial award applicants required to submit FAFSA. *Faculty research:* Mental health services, social development, child welfare, at-risk teens, autism, environmental health, health policy, health communications, obesity, gender and sexuality, violence and injury prevention, chronic disease prevention, poverty, older adults/aging societies, civic engagement, school social work, program evaluation, health disparities. *Unit head:* Jamie L. Adkisson, Director of Recruitment & Admissions, 314-935-3524, Fax: 314-935-4859, E-mail: jadkisson@wustl.edu. *Application contact:* Cate M. Valentine, Admissions Counselor, 314-935-8879, Fax: 314-935-4859, E-mail: cvalentine@wustl.edu.
Website: http://brownschool.wustl.edu

Washington University in St. Louis, Graduate School of Arts and Sciences, Department of Psychology, St. Louis, MO 63130-4899. Offers aging and development (PhD); behavior, brain, and cognition (PhD); clinical psychology (PhD); social and personality psychology (PhD). *Accreditation:* APA. Terminal master's awarded for partial completion of doctoral program. *Degree requirements:* For doctorate, thesis/dissertation. *Entrance requirements:* For doctorate, GRE General Test. Additional exam requirements/recommendations for international students: Required—TOEFL. Electronic applications accepted.

Wayne State University, School of Social Work, Detroit, MI 48202. Offers alcohol and drug abuse studies (Certificate); disabilities (Certificate); gerontology (Certificate); social welfare research and evaluation (Certificate); social work (MSW, PhD); social work and gerontology (PhD); social work and infant mental health (MSW, PhD); social work practice with families and couples (Certificate). *Accreditation:* CSWE (one or more programs are accredited). Part-time and evening/weekend programs available. *Students:* 494 full-time (436 women), 131 part-time (106 women); includes 226 minority (175 Black or African American, non-Hispanic/Latino; 3 American Indian or Alaska Native, non-Hispanic/Latino; 6 Asian, non-Hispanic/Latino; 21 Hispanic/Latino; 2 Native Hawaiian or other Pacific Islander, non-Hispanic/Latino; 19 Two or more races, non-Hispanic/Latino), 20 international. Average age 31. 855 applicants, 35% accepted, 196 enrolled. In 2014, 292 master's, 1 doctorate, 24 other advanced degrees awarded. *Degree requirements:* For doctorate, thesis/dissertation. *Entrance requirements:* For master's, personal interest statement, resume, 3 references; for doctorate, GRE, MSW from a CSWE-accredited institution (or working towards one), resume, three letters of reference, personal statement, summary of relevant research and professional experience, writing sample, interview; for Certificate, MSW or actively enrolled in advanced portion of MSW program. Additional exam requirements/recommendations for international students: Required—TOEFL (minimum score 550 paper-based; 79 iBT), TWE (minimum score 5.5), Michigan English Language Assessment Battery (minimum score 85); Recommended—IELTS (minimum score 6.5). *Application deadline:* For fall admission, 10/1 priority date for domestic and international students. Application fee: $0. Electronic applications accepted. *Expenses:* Tuition, state resident: full-time $10,294; part-time $571.90 per credit hour. Tuition, nonresident: full-time $29,730; part-time $1238.75 per credit hour. *Required fees:* $1365; $43.50 per credit hour. $291.10 per semester. Tuition and fees vary according to course load and program. *Financial support:* In 2014–15, 98 students received support, including 4 fellowships with tuition reimbursements available (averaging $15,073 per year), 1 research assistantship with tuition reimbursement available (averaging $16,838 per year); scholarships/grants and unspecified assistantships also available. Financial award application deadline: 3/31; financial award applicants required to submit FAFSA. *Faculty research:* Child welfare, violence, adolescent dating, intimate partner and family violence, sexual assault, gerontology, long-term care, end of life issues, healthy aging, health care, behavioral health and infant mental health, community capacity building, innovation in community, leadership and policy. *Total annual research expenditures:* $539,866. *Unit head:* Dr. Cheryl E. Waites, Dean and Professor, 313-577-4400, E-mail: dv7029@wayne.edu. *Application contact:* Julie Alter-Kay, Director, Office of Admissions and Student Services, 313-577-4409, E-mail: ae8440@wayne.edu.
Website: http://socialwork.wayne.edu/

Webster University, College of Arts and Sciences, Department of Behavioral and Social Sciences, Program in Gerontology, St. Louis, MO 63119-3194. Offers MA. Part-time programs available. *Entrance requirements:* Additional exam requirements/recommendations for international students: Required—TOEFL.

Webster University, George Herbert Walker School of Business and Technology, Department of Business, St. Louis, MO 63119-3194. Offers business and organizational security management (MBA); decision support systems (MBA); environmental management (MBA); finance (MBA, MS); forensic accounting (MS); gerontology (MBA); human resources development (MBA); human resources management (MBA); information technology management (MBA); international business (MA, MBA); international relations (MBA); management and leadership (MBA); marketing (MBA); media communications (MBA); procurement and acquisitions management (MBA); Web services (MBA). *Accreditation:* ACBSP. Part-time and evening/weekend programs available. Postbaccalaureate distance learning degree programs offered (no on-campus study). *Degree requirements:* For master's, comprehensive exam (for some programs), thesis (for some programs). *Entrance requirements:* Additional exam requirements/recommendations for international students: Required—TOEFL.

Wichita State University, Graduate School, College of Health Professions, Department of Public Health Sciences, Wichita, KS 67260. Offers aging studies (MA). Part-time programs available. Postbaccalaureate distance learning degree programs offered (no on-campus study). *Unit head:* Dr. Suzanne Hawley, Chairperson, 316-978-3060, Fax: 316-978-3072, E-mail: suzanne.hawley@wichita.edu. *Application contact:* Jordan Oleson, Admissions Coordinator, 316-978-3095, Fax: 316-978-3253, E-mail: jordan.oleson@wichita.edu.
Website: http://www.wichita.edu/phs

Youngstown State University, Graduate School, College of Liberal Arts and Social Sciences, Program in Gerontology, Youngstown, OH 44555-0001. Offers MA. Part-time and evening/weekend programs available. Postbaccalaureate distance learning degree programs offered. *Degree requirements:* For master's, thesis optional. *Entrance requirements:* For master's, GRE, minimum GPA of 3.0, three letters of recommendation, letter of intent, resume or curriculum vitae, social statistics course at undergraduate or graduate level, minimum of 9 credit hours of aging-related coursework at undergraduate or graduate level.

NORTH DAKOTA STATE UNIVERSITY

College of Human Development and Education

 For more information, visit http://petersons.to/ndstatehumandevelopmenteducation

Programs of Study

The College of Human Development and Education at North Dakota State University educates and trains students who want to make a difference in others' lives. Its rigorous programs and innovative research focus on people and how they interact in educational, living, and work environments.

The college's fifteen master's and seven doctoral programs are provided through four departments:
- Apparel, Design, and Hospitality Management
- School of Education
- Health, Nutrition, and Exercise Sciences
- Human Development and Family Science

The college provides a student-focused, friendly community where students are actively involved in the learning process. As a result, they acquire the knowledge and skills to improve the lives of individuals within communities, families, and the workplace.

Online Master of Science (M.S.) program in Human Development and Family Science: The M.S. in Human Development and Family Science is a 36-credit, online program with three options: youth development, gerontology, and family financial planning.

The M.S. in Human Development and Family Science: Youth Development program trains individuals to develop and implement programs and services that promote the positive development of adolescents. The M.S. in Human Development and Family Science: Gerontology program provides in-depth knowledge of the social, physical, and mental changes associated with aging. The M.S. in Human Development and Family Science: Family Financial Planning program provides extensive knowledge of family and personal financial management and eligibility to take the CFP® Certification Examination.

Doctor of Philosophy (Ph.D.) programs in Human Development and Family Science: The College of Human Development and Education also offers Ph.D. programs in developmental science and couple and family therapy.

The 60-credit Ph.D. in Developmental Science program focuses on human development across the lifespan. It integrates the biological, cognitive, and socio-emotional aspects of development and incorporates the cultural, familial, institutional, and social contexts in which development occurs.

The 81-credit Ph.D. in Couple and Family Therapy program focuses on feminist and social justice principles. This foundation prepares students for clinical, research, and supervisory work with diverse and marginalized populations and communities.

Graduate programs in Health, Nutrition, and Exercise Sciences: The Department of Health, Nutrition, and Exercise Sciences offers six graduate programs, including the M.S. in Health, Nutrition, and Exercise Sciences and the Ph.D. in Exercise Science and Nutrition.

M.S. programs in Health, Nutrition, and Exercise Sciences prepare students for advanced positions in exercise science, health promotion, nutrition/dietetics, physical activity, and physical education teaching and coaching. There are three options: the 31-credit exercise and nutrition option; the 30-credit, online leadership in physical education and sport option; and the 36-credit, online dietetics option.

The 60-credit Ph.D. program in Exercise Science and Nutrition prepares students for leadership positions in community settings, government agencies, professional agencies and organizations, and universities.

Research

The College of Human Development and Education provides many resources and opportunities for students to engage in cutting-edge research, including state-of-the-art equipment, modern labs, and dedicated teachers.

Graduate students work closely with faculty members to investigate issues that impact human development, develop academic and grant-writing skills, and publish articles in periodicals. They coauthored more than twenty refereed journal articles and fifteen additional articles during the 2013–14 academic year.

Faculty members are dedicated to conducting research that improves people's lives and strengthens communities. Their accomplishments during the 2013–14 academic year include the following:
- Twenty-eight faculty members (47 percent) received external research funding.
- Forty tenured/tenure-track faculty members (68 percent) published refereed journal articles.
- Faculty members published 76 refereed journal articles (the highest total in the college's history).
- Faculty members made 23 presentations at international conferences in countries like Australia, Canada, Turkey, the United States, and other locations.

Financial Aid

Graduate students in the College of Human Development and Education may qualify for the following financial assistance programs: graduate assistantships (teaching or research), scholarships (from the University and private funders), grants, fellowships, loans (through federal programs or private lenders), military and veteran assistance, and employer tuition reimbursement programs.

Applicants should consult with their academic departments and the Office of Student Financial Services to learn about their financial aid options.

Cost of Study

The most current information on tuition and fees can be found online at https://www.ndsu.edu/bisonconnection/accounts/tuition.

Living and Housing Costs

Information about on-campus housing for graduate students can be found at www.ndsu.edu/reslife/general_apartment_information. While there is no specific residence hall for graduate students, they are able to live in the University apartments. There are also numerous housing options in the Fargo community.

North Dakota State University

The Faculty

Faculty members like James Deal, Ph.D. are accomplished teachers, scholars, and leaders. They bring cutting-edge research to their classrooms, serve on editorial boards of scholarly journals, and serve as officers of professional organizations, among other endeavors.

Professor Deal joined the Department of Human Development and Family Science in 1993. He has received several grants and published numerous articles in his areas of interest: whole family function, quantitative research methods, and personality development in children.

Student Life

Graduate students at North Dakota State University join a warm and opportunity-rich community where they can achieve their educational, personal, research, and social goals. Academic, wellness, and support resources include the following:

- Counseling Center
- Graduate Center for Writers
- Office of International Student and Study Abroad Services
- Office of Multicultural Programs
- Wallman Wellness Center

Additional amenities include banking services, childcare, on-campus housing, graphic services, and meeting rooms. Social resources include affinity groups, recreational programs, arts and culture, and student organizations.

Location

North Dakota State University is located on the eastern edge of North Dakota in Fargo, the state's largest community. With its sister city, Moorhead, Minnesota, directly across the Red River, Fargo is one of the largest metropolitan centers between Minneapolis and Seattle and offers a family-friendly environment with excellent schools, safe neighborhoods, and a low crime rate; an active arts and cultural scene, including a symphony, civic opera company, art museums, and community theater; and many places to shop and eat, including numerous restaurants, coffee shops, and a newly refurbished downtown district.

The University

Established in 1890, North Dakota State University is a student-focused, land-grant, research institution known nationally and internationally for excellence in education and research. Its vibrant campus community includes more than 14,700 students (approximately 2,200 of whom are graduate students), more than 1,000 faculty members and educators, and approximately 4,000 staff members. It offers students 100 undergraduate majors, 84 master's programs, and 51 doctoral programs.

According to the Carnegie Commission on Higher Education, North Dakota State University ranks among the top 108 universities in the country. The National Science Foundation also ranked a number of its programs among the top 100.

Correspondence and Information

College of Human Development and Education
Graduate School
North Dakota State University
Dept. 2820, P.O. Box 6050
Fargo, North Dakota 58108-6050
Phone: 701-231-7033
        800-608-6378 (toll-free)
E-mail: ndsu.grad.school@ndsu.edu
Website: www.ndsu.edu/gradschool
        facebook.com/ndsugradschool (Facebook)
        @NDSUGradSchool (Twitter)

The College of Human Development and Education offers graduate programs that focus on people. These nationally recognized programs conduct research and other scholarly activities that focus on individuals as they interact at work and in educational and living environments.

Section 21
Geography

This section contains a directory of institutions offering graduate work in geography. Additional information about programs listed in the directory may be obtained by writing directly to the dean of a graduate school or chair of a department at the address given in the directory.

For programs offering related work, see also in this book *Area and Cultural Studies* and *Humanities.* In another guide in this series:

Graduate Programs in the Physical Sciences, Mathematics, Agricultural Sciences, the Environment & Natural Resources
See *Geosciences*

CONTENTS

Program Directories

Geographic Information Systems

Acadia University, Faculty of Pure and Applied Science, Program in Applied Geomatics, Wolfville, NS B4P 2R6, Canada. Offers M Sc. Program offered jointly with Nova Scotia Community College. *Degree requirements:* For master's, thesis optional. *Entrance requirements:* Additional exam requirements/recommendations for international students: Required—TOEFL (minimum score 580 paper-based; 93 iBT), IELTS (minimum score 6.5).

Appalachian State University, Cratis D. Williams Graduate School, Department of Geography and Planning, Boone, NC 28608. Offers geography (MA), including geographic information science, planning. Part-time programs available. Postbaccalaureate distance learning degree programs offered (no on-campus study). *Degree requirements:* For master's, comprehensive exam, thesis or alternative. *Entrance requirements:* For master's, GRE General Test, 3 letters of recommendation. Additional exam requirements/recommendations for international students: Required—TOEFL (minimum score 570 paper-based; 79 iBT), IELTS (minimum score 6.5). Electronic applications accepted. *Faculty research:* Global change, climatology, production cartography, geographic information systems, North Carolina geography, Latin America.

Arizona State University at the Tempe campus, College of Liberal Arts and Sciences, School of Geographical Sciences and Urban Planning, Tempe, AZ 85287-5302. Offers geographic information systems (MAS); geographical information science (Graduate Certificate); geography (MA, PhD); transportation systems (Graduate Certificate); urban and environmental planning (MUEP); urban planning (PhD). Terminal master's awarded for partial completion of doctoral program. *Degree requirements:* For master's, thesis, interactive Program of Study (iPOS) submitted before completing 50 percent of required credit hours; for doctorate, comprehensive exam, thesis/dissertation, interactive Program of Study (iPOS) submitted before completing 50 percent of required credit hours. *Entrance requirements:* For master's and doctorate, GRE, minimum GPA of 3.0 or equivalent in last 2 years of work leading to bachelor's degree. Additional exam requirements/recommendations for international students: Required—TOEFL, IELTS, or PTE. Electronic applications accepted. *Expenses:* Contact institution.

Boston University, Graduate School of Arts and Sciences, Department of Earth and Environment, Boston, MA 02215. Offers earth sciences (MA, PhD); energy and environmental analysis (MA); environmental remote sensing and GIS (MA); geography and environment (MA, PhD); global development policy (MA); international relations and environmental policy (MA). *Students:* 67 full-time (31 women), 5 part-time (2 women); includes 6 minority (4 Asian, non-Hispanic/Latino; 2 Hispanic/Latino), 19 international. Average age 29. 213 applicants, 34% accepted, 16 enrolled. In 2014, 1 master's, 4 doctorates awarded. *Degree requirements:* For master's, comprehensive exam (for some programs), thesis (for some programs); for doctorate, comprehensive exam, thesis/dissertation. *Entrance requirements:* For master's and doctorate, GRE, 3 letters of recommendation, official transcripts, personal statement. Additional exam requirements/recommendations for international students: Required—TOEFL (minimum score 550 paper-based; 84 iBT). *Application deadline:* For fall admission, 1/31 for domestic and international students; for winter admission, 11/1 for domestic and international students. Application fee: $80. Electronic applications accepted. *Expenses: Tuition:* Full-time $45,686; part-time $1428 per credit hour. *Required fees:* $660; $60 per semester. Tuition and fees vary according to program. *Financial support:* In 2014–15, 59 students received support, including 2 fellowships with full tuition reimbursements available (averaging $20,500 per year), 25 research assistantships with full tuition reimbursements available (averaging $20,500 per year), 19 teaching assistantships with full tuition reimbursements available (averaging $20,500 per year); Federal Work-Study, scholarships/grants, traineeships, and health care benefits also available. Financial award application deadline: 1/31. *Faculty research:* Biogeosciences, climate and surface processes; energy, environment and society; geographical sciences; geology, geochemistry and geophysics. *Unit head:* Curtis Woodcock, Chair, 617-353-5746, E-mail: curtis@bu.edu. *Application contact:* Nora Watson, Graduate Program Coordinator, 617-353-2529, Fax: 617-353-8399, E-mail: norala31@bu.edu.
Website: http://www.bu.edu/earth/

Central Michigan University, College of Graduate Studies, College of Science and Technology, Department of Geography, Mount Pleasant, MI 48859. Offers geographic information sciences (MS). *Degree requirements:* For master's, thesis optional. *Entrance requirements:* For master's, GRE.

Chicago State University, School of Graduate and Professional Studies, College of Arts and Sciences, Department of Geography, Sociology, History, African-American Studies and Anthropology, Chicago, IL 60628. Offers geographic information systems (MA); geography (MA); history (MA). *Entrance requirements:* For master's, minimum GPA of 3.0.

Clark University, Graduate School, Department of International Development, Community, and Environment, Program in Geographic Information Science for Development and Environment, Worcester, MA 01610-1477. Offers MS. *Students:* 43 full-time (20 women), 4 part-time (1 woman); includes 3 minority (1 Black or African American, non-Hispanic/Latino; 1 Asian, non-Hispanic/Latino; 1 Two or more races, non-Hispanic/Latino), 28 international. Average age 25. 85 applicants, 75% accepted, 28 enrolled. In 2014, 22 master's awarded. *Degree requirements:* For master's, thesis. *Entrance requirements:* For master's, 3 references, resume or curriculum vitae. Additional exam requirements/recommendations for international students: Required—TOEFL (minimum score 575 paper-based; 90 iBT) or IELTS (minimum score 6.5). *Application deadline:* For fall admission, 1/15 for domestic students. Application fee: $75. *Expenses: Tuition:* Full-time $40,380; part-time $1262 per credit hour. *Required fees:* $30. *Financial support:* Fellowships with partial tuition reimbursements, research assistantships with partial tuition reimbursements, teaching assistantships with partial tuition reimbursements, institutionally sponsored loans, and scholarships/grants available. *Faculty research:* Land-use change, the effects of environmental influences on child health and development, quantitative methods, watershed management, brownfields redevelopment, human/environment interactions, biodiversity conservation, climate change. *Unit head:* Dr. Ellen Foley, Interim Director, 508-793-7201, Fax: 508-793-8820. *Application contact:* Paula Hall, Student and Academic Services Director, 508-793-7201, E-mail: eparadis@clarku.edu.
Website: http://clarku.edu/departments/idce/academicsGradGISDE.cfm

Cleveland State University, College of Graduate Studies, Maxine Goodman Levin College of Urban Affairs, Program in Environmental Studies, Cleveland, OH 44115. Offers environmental nonprofit management (MAES); environmental planning (MAES); geographic information systems (Certificate); policy and administration (MAES); sustainable economic development (MAES); urban economic development (Certificate); urban real estate development and finance (Certificate); JD/MAES. Part-time and evening/weekend programs available. *Faculty:* 23 full-time (11 women), 23 part-time/adjunct (6 women). *Students:* 2 full-time (both women), 5 part-time (3 women); includes 1 minority (Hispanic/Latino). Average age 34. 4 applicants, 25% accepted. In 2014, 4 master's awarded. *Degree requirements:* For master's, thesis or alternative, exit project. *Entrance requirements:* For master's, GRE General Test (minimum score: verbal and quantitative combined 40th percentile, analytical writing 4.0), minimum GPA of 3.0. Additional exam requirements/recommendations for international students: Required—TOEFL (minimum score 525 paper-based; 65 iBT), IELTS, or ITEP. *Application deadline:* For fall admission, 7/15 priority date for domestic students, 5/15 for international students; for spring admission, 11/1 for international students. Applications are processed on a rolling basis. Application fee: $30. Electronic applications accepted. *Expenses:* Expenses: $9,615 full-time, in-state tuition and fees. *Financial support:* In 2014–15, 4 students received support, including 3 research assistantships with full and partial tuition reimbursements available (averaging $7,200 per year); career-related internships or fieldwork, scholarships/grants, traineeships, and unspecified assistantships also available. Support available to part-time students. Financial award application deadline: 3/1; financial award applicants required to submit FAFSA. *Faculty research:* Environmental policy and administration, environmental planning, geographic information systems (GIS), urban sustainability planning and management, energy policy, land re-use. *Unit head:* Dr. Sanda Kaufman, Director, 216-687-2367, Fax: 216-687-9342, E-mail: s.kaufman@csuohio.edu. *Application contact:* David Arrighi, Graduate Academic Advisor, 216-523-7522, Fax: 216-687-5398, E-mail: urbanprograms@csuohio.edu.
Website: http://urban.csuohio.edu/academics/graduate/maes/

Cleveland State University, College of Graduate Studies, Maxine Goodman Levin College of Urban Affairs, Program in Urban Planning, Design, and Development, Cleveland, OH 44115. Offers economic development (MUPDD); environmental sustainability (MUPDD); geographic information systems (MUPDD, Certificate); historic preservation (MUPDD); housing and neighborhood development (MUPDD); urban economic development (Certificate); urban real estate development and finance (MUPDD, Certificate); JD/MUPDD. *Accreditation:* ACSP. Part-time and evening/weekend programs available. *Faculty:* 23 full-time (11 women), 23 part-time/adjunct (6 women). *Students:* 11 full-time (5 women), 25 part-time (10 women); includes 8 minority (2 Black or African American, non-Hispanic/Latino; 1 Asian, non-Hispanic/Latino; 2 Hispanic/Latino; 3 Two or more races, non-Hispanic/Latino), 3 international. Average age 38. 48 applicants, 56% accepted, 5 enrolled. In 2014, 16 master's awarded. *Degree requirements:* For master's, thesis or alternative, planning studio. *Entrance requirements:* For master's, GRE General Test (minimum score: 50th percentile combined verbal and quantitative, 4.0 analytical writing), minimum GPA of 3.0. Additional exam requirements/recommendations for international students: Required—TOEFL (minimum score 525 paper-based; 65 iBT), IELTS, or ITEP. *Application deadline:* For fall admission, 7/15 priority date for domestic students, 5/15 for international students; for spring admission, 11/1 for international students. Applications are processed on a rolling basis. Application fee: $30. Electronic applications accepted. *Expenses:* Expenses: $9,615 full-time, in-state tuition and fees. *Financial support:* In 2014–15, 10 students received support, including 7 research assistantships with full and partial tuition reimbursements available (averaging $5,600 per year), 2 teaching assistantships with full and partial tuition reimbursements available (averaging $2,000 per year); career-related internships or fieldwork, Federal Work-Study, scholarships/grants, tuition waivers, and unspecified assistantships also available. Support available to part-time students. Financial award application deadline: 3/1; financial award applicants required to submit FAFSA. *Faculty research:* Housing and neighborhood development, urban housing policy, environmental sustainability, economic development, GIS and planning decision support. *Unit head:* Dr. Dennis Keating, Director, 216-687-2298, Fax: 216-687-2013, E-mail: w.keating@csuohio.edu. *Application contact:* David Arrighi, Graduate Academic Advisor, 216-523-7522, Fax: 216-687-5398, E-mail: urbanprograms@csuohio.edu.
Website: http://urban.csuohio.edu/academics/graduate/mupdd/

The College of William and Mary, Faculty of Arts and Sciences, Department of Applied Science, Williamsburg, VA 23187-8795. Offers accelerator science (PhD); applied mathematics (PhD); applied mechanics (PhD); applied robotics (PhD); applied science (MS); interface, thin film and surface science (PhD); lasers and optics (PhD); magnetic resonance (PhD); nanotechnology (PhD); non-destructive evaluation (PhD); polymer chemistry (PhD); remote sensing (PhD). Part-time programs available. *Faculty:* 8 full-time (2 women), 2 part-time/adjunct (0 women). *Students:* 28 full-time (11 women), 5 part-time (2 women); includes 5 minority (2 Black or African American, non-Hispanic/Latino; 2 Asian, non-Hispanic/Latino; 1 Hispanic/Latino), 13 international. Average age 28. 32 applicants, 38% accepted, 7 enrolled. In 2014, 6 master's, 4 doctorates awarded. Terminal master's awarded for partial completion of doctoral program. *Degree requirements:* For master's, comprehensive exam, thesis; for doctorate, comprehensive exam, thesis/dissertation, 4 core courses. *Entrance requirements:* For master's and doctorate, GRE General Test, GRE Subject Test. Additional exam requirements/recommendations for international students: Required—TOEFL, TWE. *Application deadline:* For fall admission, 2/3 priority date for domestic students, 2/3 for international students; for spring admission, 10/15 priority date for domestic students, 10/14 for international students. Applications are processed on a rolling basis. Application fee: $45. Electronic applications accepted. *Financial support:* Fellowships, research assistantships, teaching assistantships, Federal Work-Study, health care benefits, tuition waivers (full), and unspecified assistantships available. Financial award application deadline: 4/15; financial award applicants required to submit FAFSA. *Faculty research:* Computational biology, non-destructive evaluation, neurophysiology, lasers and optics. *Total annual research expenditures:* $1.7 million. *Unit head:* Dr. Christopher Del Negro, Chair, 757-221-7808, Fax: 757-221-2050, E-mail: cadeln@wm.edu. *Application contact:* Lianne Rios Ashburne, Graduate Program Coordinator, 757-221-2563, Fax: 757-221-2050, E-mail: lrashburne@wm.edu.
Website: http://www.wm.edu/as/appliedscience

East Carolina University, Graduate School, Thomas Harriot College of Arts and Sciences, Department of Geography, Planning, and Environment, Greenville, NC 27858-4353. Offers economic development (Certificate); geographic information science and technology (Certificate); geography (MA), including geography, planning, rural development. Part-time and evening/weekend programs available. *Degree requirements:* For master's, one foreign language, comprehensive exam, thesis optional. *Entrance requirements:* For master's, GRE General Test. Additional exam requirements/recommendations for international students: Required—TOEFL. *Expenses:* Tuition, state resident: full-time $4223. Tuition, nonresident: full-time $16,540. *Required fees:* $2184.

Eastern Illinois University, Graduate School, College of Sciences, Department of Geology/Geography, Charleston, IL 61920. Offers MS. Part-time and evening/weekend

programs available. *Faculty:* 4. *Students:* 11 full-time (2 women), 2 part-time, 5 international. Average age 30. 17 applicants, 47% accepted, 3 enrolled. In 2014, 1 master's awarded. *Entrance requirements:* For master's, GMAT or GRE. Additional exam requirements/recommendations for international students: Required—TOEFL (minimum score 500 paper-based; 61 iBT), IELTS (minimum score 6). *Application deadline:* For fall admission, 5/15 for domestic and international students; for spring admission, 10/15 for domestic and international students. Applications are processed on a rolling basis. Application fee: $30. Electronic applications accepted. *Expenses:* Tuition, state resident: full-time $3113; part-time $283 per credit hour. Tuition, nonresident: full-time $7469; part-time $679 per credit hour. *Required fees:* $2287; $96 per credit hour. Tuition and fees vary according to course load. *Financial support:* In 2014–15, 3 students received support, including 1 teaching assistantship with full tuition reimbursement available (averaging $8,010 per year); career-related internships or fieldwork, Federal Work-Study, and unspecified assistantships also available. Support available to part-time students. Financial award application deadline: 3/1; financial award applicants required to submit FAFSA. *Unit head:* Michael Cornebise, Department Chair and Graduate Coordinator, 217-581-2626, Fax: 217-581-7141, E-mail: mwcornebise@eiu.edu. *Application contact:* Karen Gaines, Graduate Coordinator, 217-581-6235, Fax: 217-581-7141, E-mail: kfgaines@eiu.edu.
Website: http://www.eiu.edu/psm/index.php

Eastern Michigan University, Graduate School, College of Arts and Sciences, Department of Geography and Geology, Programs in Geographic Information Systems, Ypsilanti, MI 48197. Offers geographic information systems (MS); GIS educator (Graduate Certificate); GIS planning (MS); GIS professional (Graduate Certificate). *Students:* 10 full-time (4 women), 26 part-time (12 women); includes 2 minority (1 Black or African American, non-Hispanic/Latino; 1 Hispanic/Latino), 15 international. Average age 32. 23 applicants, 74% accepted, 15 enrolled. In 2014, 10 master's, 2 other advanced degrees awarded. Application fee: $45. *Application contact:* Dr. Hugh Semple, Program Advisor, 734-487-0218, Fax: 734-487-6979, E-mail: hsemple@emich.edu.

Elizabeth City State University, School of Mathematics, Science and Technology, Master of Science in Mathematics Program, Elizabeth City, NC 27909-7806. Offers applied mathematics (MS); community college teaching (MS); mathematics education (MS); remote sensing (MS). Part-time and evening/weekend programs available. *Degree requirements:* For master's, thesis. *Entrance requirements:* For master's, MAT and/or GRE, minimum GPA of 3.0, 3 letters of recommendation, two official transcripts from all undergraduate/graduate schools attended, typewritten one-page request for entry into program that includes description of student's educational preparation. Additional exam requirements/recommendations for international students: Required—TOEFL (minimum score 550 paper-based, 80 iBT) or IELTS (minimum score 6.5). Electronic applications accepted. *Faculty research:* Oceanic temperature effects, mathematics strategies in elementary schools, multimedia, Antarctic temperature mapping, computer networks, water quality, remote sensing, polar ice, satellite imagery.

Elmhurst College, Graduate Programs, Program in Applied Geospatial Sciences, Elmhurst, IL 60126-3296. Offers MS. Part-time and evening/weekend programs available. Postbaccalaureate distance learning degree programs offered (no on-campus study). *Faculty:* 2 part-time/adjunct (0 women). *Students:* 11 part-time (1 woman); includes 2 minority (both Hispanic/Latino). Average age 36. 21 applicants, 52% accepted, 11 enrolled. *Entrance requirements:* For master's, 3 recommendations, resume, statement of purpose. Additional exam requirements/recommendations for international students: Required—TOEFL (minimum score 550 paper-based; 79 iBT). *Application deadline:* Applications are processed on a rolling basis. Application fee: $0. Electronic applications accepted. *Expenses:* Expenses: Contact institution. *Financial support:* In 2014–15, 3 students received support. Scholarships/grants available. Support available to part-time students. Financial award application deadline: 6/1; financial award applicants required to submit FAFSA. *Application contact:* Timothy J. Panfil, Director of Enrollment Management, School for Professional Studies, 630-617-3300 Ext. 3256, Fax: 630-617-6471, E-mail: panfilt@elmhurst.edu.
Website: http://www.elmhurst.edu/applied_geospatial_sciences

Florida State University, The Graduate School, College of Social Sciences and Public Policy, Department of Geography, Tallahassee, FL 32306. Offers geographic information science (MS); geography (MA, MS, PhD). Part-time programs available. *Faculty:* 9 full-time (2 women), 2 part-time/adjunct (0 women). *Students:* 39 full-time (18 women), 8 part-time (4 women); includes 13 minority (2 Black or African American, non-Hispanic/Latino; 9 Asian, non-Hispanic/Latino; 2 Hispanic/Latino), 9 international. Average age 29. 38 applicants, 68% accepted, 16 enrolled. In 2014, 21 master's, 2 doctorates awarded. Terminal master's awarded for partial completion of doctoral program. *Degree requirements:* For master's, thesis (for some programs); for doctorate, comprehensive exam, thesis/dissertation. *Entrance requirements:* For master's, GRE General Test, minimum GPA of 3.0; for doctorate, GRE General Test, minimum GPA of 3.0. Additional exam requirements/recommendations for international students: Required—TOEFL. *Application deadline:* For fall admission, 1/15 priority date for domestic students, 12/15 priority date for international students; for spring admission, 11/1 priority date for domestic students, 9/15 priority date for international students. Applications are processed on a rolling basis. Application fee: $30. Electronic applications accepted. *Expenses:* Tuition, state resident: part-time $403.51 per credit hour. Tuition, nonresident: part-time $1004.85 per credit hour. *Required fees:* $75.81 per credit hour. One-time fee: $20 part-time. Tuition and fees vary according to campus/location. *Financial support:* In 2014–15, 53 students received support, including 17 research assistantships with full tuition reimbursements available (averaging $16,240 per year), 36 teaching assistantships with full tuition reimbursements available (averaging $16,240 per year); career-related internships or fieldwork, Federal Work-Study, institutionally sponsored loans, scholarships/grants, health care benefits, tuition waivers (full and partial), and unspecified assistantships also available. Financial award application deadline: 1/15; financial award applicants required to submit FAFSA. *Faculty research:* Society-nature interactions, geographic information science, environmental studies, hurricanes, remote sensing, urban, transportation. *Total annual research expenditures:* $163,316. *Unit head:* Prof. Victor Mesev, Chair, 850-645-2498, Fax: 850-644-5913, E-mail: vmesev@fsu.edu. *Application contact:* Prof. Tingting Zhao, Graduate Director, 850-645-8198, Fax: 850-644-5193, E-mail: tzhao@fsu.edu.
Website: http://www.coss.fsu.edu/geography

George Mason University, College of Science, Department of Geography and Geoinformation Science, Fairfax, VA 22030. Offers earth system science (MS); earth systems and geoinformation sciences (PhD); geographic and cartographic sciences (MS); geography and geoinformation science (Certificate); geoinformatics and geospatial intelligence (MS). *Faculty:* 17 full-time (4 women), 7 part-time/adjunct (0 women). *Students:* 54 full-time (17 women), 129 part-time (47 women); includes 33 minority (9 Black or African American, non-Hispanic/Latino; 2 American Indian or Alaska Native, non-Hispanic/Latino; 9 Asian, non-Hispanic/Latino; 8 Hispanic/Latino; 5 Two or more races, non-Hispanic/Latino), 25 international. Average age 35. 114 applicants, 55% accepted, 34 enrolled. In 2014, 17 master's, 10 doctorates, 15 other advanced degrees awarded. *Degree requirements:* For master's, thesis optional. *Entrance requirements:* For master's, GRE (waived for those who have earned a master's degree from U.S. institution), bachelor's degree with minimum GPA of 3.0; 2 copies of official transcripts; current resume; expanded goals statement; 3 letters of recommendation; for doctorate, GRE (waived for those who have earned a master's degree from U.S. institution), bachelor's degree with minimum GPA of 3.0; 2 copies of official transcripts; 3 letters of recommendation; resume; expanded goals statement; for Certificate, GRE (waived for those who have earned a master's degree from U.S. institution), baccalaureate degree with minimum GPA of 3.0; 2 official copies of transcripts; expanded goals statement; 3 letters of recommendation; resume. Additional exam requirements/recommendations for international students: Required—TOEFL (minimum score 570 paper-based; 80 iBT), IELTS (minimum score 6.5), PTE. *Application deadline:* For fall admission, 4/15 priority date for domestic students; for spring admission, 11/15 priority date for domestic students. Application fee: $65 ($80 for international students). Electronic applications accepted. *Expenses:* Tuition, state resident: full-time $9794; part-time $408 per credit hour. Tuition, nonresident: full-time $26,978; part-time $1124 per credit hour. *Required fees:* $2820; $118 per credit hour. Tuition and fees vary according to course load and program. *Financial support:* In 2014–15, 31 students received support, including 1 fellowship (averaging $9,302 per year), 23 research assistantships with full and partial tuition reimbursements available (averaging $16,864 per year), 8 teaching assistantships with full and partial tuition reimbursements available (averaging $13,392 per year); career-related internships or fieldwork, Federal Work-Study, scholarships/grants, unspecified assistantships, and health care benefits (for full-time research or teaching assistantship recipients) also available. Support available to part-time students. Financial award application deadline: 3/1; financial award applicants required to submit FAFSA. *Faculty research:* Global environment climate monitoring, gender and earth science, earth science education, remote sensing, planetary geology, hydrology, theoretical issues of geographic information data acquisition and processing. *Total annual research expenditures:* $2.2 million. *Unit head:* Anthony Stefanidis, Acting Chair, 703-993-9237, Fax: 703-993-9230, E-mail: astefani@gmu.edu. *Application contact:* Department of Geography and Geoinformation Sciences, 703-993-1210, Fax: 703-993-9299.
Website: http://ggs.gmu.edu/

Georgia Institute of Technology, Graduate Studies, College of Architecture, School of City and Regional Planning, Atlanta, GA 30332-0001. Offers city and regional planning (PhD); economic development (MCRP); environmental planning and management (MCRP); geographic information systems (MCRP); land and community development (MCRP); land use planning (MCRP); transportation (MCRP); urban design (MCRP); MCP/MSCE. *Accreditation:* ACSP. *Degree requirements:* For master's, thesis, internship. *Entrance requirements:* For master's, GRE General Test, minimum GPA of 2.7. Additional exam requirements/recommendations for international students: Required—TOEFL. Electronic applications accepted. *Expenses:* Tuition, state resident: full-time $12,344; part-time $515 per credit hour. Tuition, nonresident: full-time $27,600; part-time $1150 per credit hour. *Required fees:* $1196 per term. Part-time tuition and fees vary according to course load.

Georgia State University, College of Arts and Sciences, Department of Geosciences, Program in Geographic Information Systems, Atlanta, GA 30302-3083. Offers Certificate. Part-time programs available. *Entrance requirements:* For degree, GRE. Additional exam requirements/recommendations for international students: Required—TOEFL (minimum score 550 paper-based; 80 iBT). *Application deadline:* For fall admission, 4/15 for domestic and international students; for spring admission, 11/15 for domestic and international students. Electronic applications accepted. *Expenses:* Tuition, state resident: full-time $6516; part-time $362 per credit hour. Tuition, nonresident: full-time $22,014; part-time $1223 per credit hour. *Required fees:* $2128 per semester. Tuition and fees vary according to course load and program. *Financial support:* Career-related internships or fieldwork available. *Faculty research:* Geographic information science. *Unit head:* Dr. W. Crawford Elliott, Chair, 404-413-5756, E-mail: wcelliott@gsu.edu. *Application contact:* Dr. Jeremy Diem, Director of Graduate Studies, 404-413-5770, Fax: 404-413-5768, E-mail: jdiem@gsu.edu.
Website: http://geosciences.gsu.edu/grad-programs/

Idaho State University, Office of Graduate Studies, College of Science and Engineering, Department of Geosciences, Pocatello, ID 83209-8072. Offers geographic information science (MS); geology (MNS, MS); geology with emphasis in environmental geoscience (MS); geophysics/hydrology/geology (MS); geotechnology (Postbaccalaureate Certificate). Part-time programs available. *Degree requirements:* For master's, comprehensive exam, thesis, oral colloquium; for Postbaccalaureate Certificate, thesis optional, minimum 19 credits. *Entrance requirements:* For master's, GRE General Test (minimum 50th percentile in 2 sections), 3 letters of recommendation; for Postbaccalaureate Certificate, GRE General Test, 3 letters of recommendation, bachelor's degree, statement of goals. Additional exam requirements/recommendations for international students: Required—TOEFL (minimum score 550 paper-based; 80 iBT). Electronic applications accepted. *Faculty research:* Quantitative field mapping and sampling: microscopic, geochemical, and isotopic analysis of rocks, minerals and water; remote sensing, geographic information systems, and global positioning systems: environmental and watershed management; surficial and fluvial processes: landscape change; regional tectonics, structural geology; planetary geology.

Indiana University of Pennsylvania, School of Graduate Studies and Research, College of Humanities and Social Sciences, Department of Geography and Regional Planning, Geographic Information Science/Cartography Track, Indiana, PA 15705-1087. Offers MS. Part-time programs available. *Faculty:* 10 full-time (1 woman), 1 (woman) part-time/adjunct. *Students:* 7 full-time (1 woman). Average age 28. 8 applicants, 75% accepted, 3 enrolled. *Degree requirements:* For master's, thesis optional. *Entrance requirements:* Additional exam requirements/recommendations for international students: Required—TOEFL (minimum score 550 paper-based). *Application deadline:* Applications are processed on a rolling basis. Application fee: $50. Electronic applications accepted. *Financial support:* In 2014–15, 5 research assistantships with full and partial tuition reimbursements (averaging $3,564 per year) were awarded; career-related internships or fieldwork, Federal Work-Study, scholarships/grants, and unspecified assistantships also available. Financial award application deadline: 4/15; financial award applicants required to submit FAFSA. *Unit head:* Dr. Richard Hoch, Graduate Coordinator, 724-357-5990, E-mail: richard.hoch@iup.edu.
Website: http://www.iup.edu/upper.aspx?id-90827

Indiana University of Pennsylvania, School of Graduate Studies and Research, College of Humanities and Social Sciences, Department of Geography and Regional Planning, Program in Geographic Information Science and Geospatial Techniques, Indiana, PA 15705-1087. Offers Certificate. *Faculty:* 10 full-time (1 woman), 1 (woman) part-time/adjunct. In 2014, 4 Certificates awarded. *Entrance requirements:* Additional exam requirements/recommendations for international students: Required—TOEFL (minimum score 550 paper-based). *Application deadline:* Applications are processed on a rolling basis. Application fee: $50. Electronic applications accepted. *Financial support:* Application deadline: 4/15; applicants required to submit FAFSA. *Unit head:* Dr. Richard Hoch, Graduate Coordinator, 724-357-5990, E-mail: richard.hoch@iup.edu.
Website: http://www.iup.edu/upper.aspx?id-90827

Indiana University–Purdue University Indianapolis, School of Liberal Arts, Department of Geography, Indianapolis, IN 46202. Offers geographic information

systems (MS, Certificate). Part-time and evening/weekend programs available. *Faculty:* 5 full-time (1 woman). *Students:* 3 full-time (0 women), 14 part-time (8 women); includes 1 minority (Black or African American, non-Hispanic/Latino), 1 international. Average age 35. 17 applicants, 47% accepted, 6 enrolled. In 2014, 4 master's, 1 other advanced degree awarded. *Entrance requirements:* For master's, GRE (minimum verbal or quantitative score of 600, with the other score above 500), minimum GPA of 3.0; for Certificate, minimum GPA of 3.0. Additional exam requirements/recommendations for international students: Required—TOEFL (minimum score 550 paper-based), IELTS. *Application deadline:* Applications are processed on a rolling basis. Application fee: $60 ($63 for international students). Electronic applications accepted. Application fee is waived when completed online. *Expenses:* Expenses: Certificate: $5,876; MS: $11,752. *Financial support:* In 2014–15, 4 students received support. Fellowships with full tuition reimbursements available, research assistantships with full and partial tuition reimbursements available, health care benefits, and tuition waivers available. Financial award applicants required to submit FAFSA. *Faculty research:* Remote sensing, geographic information systems, epidemiology, public health, weather and climate, soils. *Unit head:* Dr. Daniel P. Johnson, Chair, 317-278-5536, Fax: 317-278-5220, E-mail: dpjohnso@iupui.edu. *Application contact:* Aniruddha Banerjee, Graduate Advisor, 317-274-3281, E-mail: geogdept@iupui.edu.
Website: http://liberalarts.iupui.edu/geography/

Johns Hopkins University, Zanvyl Krieger School of Arts and Sciences, Advanced Academic Programs, Program in Environmental Sciences and Policy, Washington, DC 20036. Offers energy policy and climate (MS); environmental sciences (MS); geographic information systems (MS, Certificate). Part-time and evening/weekend programs available. Postbaccalaureate distance learning degree programs offered (minimal on-campus study). *Degree requirements:* For master's, thesis (for some programs). *Entrance requirements:* For master's, minimum GPA of 3.0, coursework in chemistry and calculus. Additional exam requirements/recommendations for international students: Required—TOEFL (minimum score 100 iBT). Electronic applications accepted.

Michigan Technological University, Graduate School, School of Technology, Houghton, MI 49931. Offers integrated geospatial technology (MS). Part-time programs available. *Faculty:* 24 full-time, 5 part-time/adjunct. *Students:* 8 full-time, 10 part-time; includes 4 minority (1 Black or African American, non-Hispanic/Latino; 2 Asian, non-Hispanic/Latino; 1 Two or more races, non-Hispanic/Latino), 6 international. Average age 33. 48 applicants, 56% accepted, 7 enrolled. In 2014, 2 master's awarded. *Degree requirements:* For master's, thesis or comprehensive exam. *Entrance requirements:* For master's, GRE, statement of purpose, official transcripts, 2-3 letters of recommendation, resume/curriculum vitae. Additional exam requirements/recommendations for international students: Required—TOEFL (recommended score 79 iBT) or IELTS. *Application deadline:* Applications are processed on a rolling basis. Electronic applications accepted. *Expenses:* Tuition, state resident: full-time $14,769; part-time $820.50 per credit. Tuition, nonresident: full-time $14,769; part-time $820.50 per credit. *Required fees:* $248; $248 per year. Tuition and fees vary according to course load and program. *Financial support:* In 2014–15, 9 students received support, including 1 fellowship with full and partial tuition reimbursement available (averaging $13,824 per year); career-related internships or fieldwork, Federal Work-Study, scholarships/grants, and health care benefits also available. Financial award applicants required to submit FAFSA. *Faculty research:* Cybersecurity, medical image processing, sensory data fusion, architectural and archaeological laser scanning, high resolution remote sensing. *Total annual research expenditures:* $113,861. *Unit head:* Dr. James O. Frendewey, Dean, 906-487-2260, Fax: 906-487-2583, E-mail: jimf@mtu.edu. *Application contact:* Peggy A. Gorton, Executive Assistant, 906-487-2260, Fax: 906-487-2583, E-mail: pagorton@mtu.edu.
Website: http://www.mtu.edu/technology/

Millersville University of Pennsylvania, College of Graduate and Professional Studies, School of Science and Mathematics, Department of Earth Sciences, Program in Integrated Scientific Applications: GeoInformatics Option, Millersville, PA 17551-0302. Offers MS. Part-time and evening/weekend programs available. *Degree requirements:* For master's, thesis optional, internship, applied research. *Entrance requirements:* For master's, official transcript, minimum GPA of 2.75, three professional letters of recommendation, academic and professional goals statement, current resume. Additional exam requirements/recommendations for international students: Required—TOEFL (minimum score 500 paper-based, 65 iBT) or IELTS (minimum score 6). *Application deadline:* For fall admission, 1/15 priority date for domestic and international students; for winter admission, 6/1 priority date for domestic and international students; for spring admission, 10/1 priority date for domestic and international students. Applications are processed on a rolling basis. Application fee: $40. Electronic applications accepted. *Expenses:* Tuition, state resident: full-time $8172. Tuition, nonresident: full-time $12,258. *Required fees:* $2300. Tuition and fees vary according to course load and program. *Financial support:* Application deadline: 3/15; applicants required to submit FAFSA. *Faculty research:* Climatology and meteorology. *Total annual research expenditures:* $557,144. *Unit head:* Dr. Richard D. Clark, Chair, 717-872-3289, Fax: 717-871-4725, E-mail: richard.clark@millersville.edu. *Application contact:* Dr. Victor S. DeSantis, Dean of College of Graduate and Professional Studies/Associate Provost for Civic and Community Engagement, 717-871-7619, Fax: 717-871-7954, E-mail: victor.desantis@millersville.edu.
Website: http://www.millersville.edu/graduate/programs/masters-degree/msisa/geoinformatics.php

Minnesota State University Mankato, College of Graduate Studies, College of Social and Behavioral Sciences, Department of Geography, Mankato, MN 56001. Offers geography (MS); GIS (Certificate). Part-time programs available. *Students:* 4 full-time (0 women), 11 part-time (3 women). *Degree requirements:* For master's, one foreign language, comprehensive exam. *Entrance requirements:* For master's, GRE General Test (if GPA less than 2.8 for the last 2 years), minimum GPA of 3.0 during previous 2 years. *Application deadline:* For fall admission, 7/1 priority date for domestic students; for spring admission, 11/1 for domestic students. Applications are processed on a rolling basis. Application fee: $40. Electronic applications accepted. *Financial support:* Research assistantships, teaching assistantships with full tuition reimbursements, career-related internships or fieldwork, Federal Work-Study, institutionally sponsored loans, and unspecified assistantships available. Support available to part-time students. Financial award application deadline: 3/15; financial award applicants required to submit FAFSA. *Unit head:* Dr. Ginger Schmid, Chairperson, 507-389-2824. *Application contact:* 507-389-2321, E-mail: grad@mnsu.edu.
Website: http://sbs.mnsu.edu/geography/

Montclair State University, The Graduate School, College of Science and Mathematics, Geographic Information Science Certificate Program, Montclair, NJ 07043-1624. Offers Certificate. *Students:* Average age 30. In 2014, 1 Certificate awarded. *Expenses:* Tuition, state resident: full-time $9960; part-time $553.35 per credit. Tuition, nonresident: full-time $15,074; part-time $837.43 per credit. *Required fees:* $1595; $88.63 per credit. Tuition and fees vary according to degree level and program. *Unit head:* Dr. Danlin Yu, Coordinator, 973-655-4313, E-mail: yud@mail.montclair.edu. *Application contact:* Amy Aiello, Director of Graduate Admissions and Operations, 973-655-5147, Fax: 973-655-7869, E-mail: graduate.school@montclair.edu.

Naval Postgraduate School, Departments and Academic Groups, Department of Information Sciences, Monterey, CA 93943. Offers electronic warfare systems engineering (MS); information sciences (PhD); information systems and operations (MS); information technology management (MS); information warfare systems engineering (MS); knowledge superiority (Certificate); remote sensing intelligence (MS); system technology (command, control and communications) (MS). Program open only to commissioned officers of the United States and friendly nations and selected United States federal civilian employees. Part-time programs available. *Degree requirements:* For master's, thesis (for some programs); for doctorate, thesis/dissertation. *Faculty research:* Designing inter-organisational collectivities for dynamic fit: stability, manoeuvrability and application in disaster relief endeavours; system self-awareness and related methods for Improving the use and understanding of data within DoD; evaluating a macrocognition model of team collaboration using real-world data from the Haiti relief effort; cyber distortion in command and control; performance and QoS in service-based systems.

North Carolina State University, Graduate School, College of Natural Resources, Department of Parks, Recreation and Tourism Management, Raleigh, NC 27695. Offers natural resource management (MPRTM, MS); park and recreation management (MPRTM, MS); parks, recreation and tourism management (PhD); recreational sport management (MPRTM, MS); spatial information science (MPRTM, MS); tourism policy and development (MPRTM, MS). *Degree requirements:* For master's, thesis (for some programs); for doctorate, thesis/dissertation. *Entrance requirements:* For master's and doctorate, GRE General Test. Additional exam requirements/recommendations for international students: Required—TOEFL. Electronic applications accepted. *Faculty research:* Tourism policy and development, spatial information systems, natural resource management, recreational sports management, park and recreation management.

Northeastern University, College of Professional Studies, Boston, MA 02115-5096. Offers applied nutrition (MS); commerce and economic development (MS); corporate and organizational communication (MS); digital media (MPS); geographic information technology (MPS); global studies and international affairs (MS); homeland security (MA); human services (MS); informatics (MPS); leadership (MS); nonprofit management (MS); project management (MS); regulatory affairs for drugs, biologics, and medical devices (MS); regulatory affairs of food and food industries (MS); respiratory care leadership (MS); technical communication (MS). Postbaccalaureate distance learning degree programs offered (no on-campus study).

Northern Arizona University, Graduate College, College of Social and Behavioral Sciences, Department of Geography, Planning, and Recreation, Flagstaff, AZ 86011. Offers applied geospatial sciences (MS); community planning (Certificate); geographic information systems (Certificate). Postbaccalaureate distance learning degree programs offered. *Degree requirements:* For master's, thesis optional. *Entrance requirements:* For master's, GRE General Test. Additional exam requirements/recommendations for international students: Required—TOEFL (minimum score 550 paper-based; 80 iBT), IELTS (minimum score 7). Electronic applications accepted.

Northern Kentucky University, Office of Graduate Programs, College of Informatics, Department of Computer Science, Highland Heights, KY 41099. Offers computer science (MSCS); geographic information systems (Certificate); secure software engineering (Certificate). Part-time and evening/weekend programs available. *Faculty:* 6 full-time (0 women), 2 part-time/adjunct (0 women). *Students:* 5 full-time (1 woman), 21 part-time (4 women); includes 4 minority (1 Black or African American, non-Hispanic/Latino; 2 Asian, non-Hispanic/Latino; 1 Two or more races, non-Hispanic/Latino), 2 international. Average age 29. 33 applicants, 42% accepted, 8 enrolled. In 2014, 11 master's awarded. *Degree requirements:* For master's, thesis optional. *Entrance requirements:* For master's, GRE, minimum GPA of 3.0, at least 4 semesters of undergraduate study in computer science including intermediate computer programming and data structures, one year of calculus, one course in discrete mathematics. Additional exam requirements/recommendations for international students: Required—TOEFL (minimum score 550 paper-based; 79 iBT); Recommended—IELTS (minimum score 6.5). *Application deadline:* For fall admission, 8/1 for domestic students, 6/1 for international students; for spring admission, 12/1 for domestic students, 10/1 for international students; for summer admission, 5/1 for domestic students, 3/1 for international students. Applications are processed on a rolling basis. Application fee: $40. Electronic applications accepted. *Expenses: Tuition, area resident:* Part-time $518 per credit hour. Tuition, state resident: part-time $630 per credit hour. Tuition, nonresident: part-time $797 per credit hour. *Required fees:* $192 per semester. Tuition and fees vary according to course load, degree level, campus/location, program and reciprocity agreements. *Financial support:* In 2014–15, 4 students received support. Scholarships/grants and unspecified assistantships available. Financial award applicants required to submit FAFSA. *Faculty research:* Data privacy, data mining, wireless security, secure software engineering, secure networking. *Unit head:* Dr. Jeff Ward, Interim Director, 859-572-1453, E-mail: wardj1@nku.edu. *Application contact:* Alison Swanson, Graduate Admissions Coordinator, 859-572-6971, E-mail: swansona1@nku.edu.
Website: http://informatics.nku.edu/departments/computer-science.html

Northwest Missouri State University, Graduate School, College of Arts and Sciences, Department of History, Humanities, and Political Science, Program in Geographic Information Systems, Maryville, MO 64468-6001. Offers MS, Certificate. Part-time programs available. *Degree requirements:* For master's, comprehensive exam, thesis. *Entrance requirements:* For master's, GRE General Test, 2 letters of recommendation, writing sample, minimum undergraduate GPA of 2.5. Additional exam requirements/recommendations for international students: Required—TOEFL (minimum score 550 paper-based). *Application deadline:* For fall admission, 4/15 for domestic and international students. Application fee: $0 ($50 for international students). *Expenses:* Tuition, state resident: full-time $4464; part-time $346 per credit hour. Tuition, nonresident: full-time $8920; part-time $593 per credit hour. *Required fees:* $1763; $98 per credit hour. *Financial support:* Research assistantships with full tuition reimbursements available. Financial award application deadline: 4/1; financial award applicants required to submit FAFSA. *Unit head:* Dr. Patricia Drews, Head, 660-562-1273, E-mail: drews@nwmissouri.edu.

Saint Louis University, Graduate Education, College of Education and Public Service, Department of Public Policy Studies, St. Louis, MO 63103-2097. Offers geographic information systems (Certificate); organizational development (Certificate); public administration (MAPA); public policy analysis (PhD); urban affairs (MAUA); urban planning and real estate development (MUPRED). *Accreditation:* NASPAA. Part-time programs available. *Degree requirements:* For master's, comprehensive exam (for some programs), thesis (for some programs); for doctorate, comprehensive exam, thesis/dissertation, preliminary exams. *Entrance requirements:* For master's, GMAT, GRE General Test, or LSAT, letters of recommendation, resume; for doctorate, GMAT, GRE General Test, or LSAT, letters of recommendation, resumé, interview, transcripts, goal statement. Additional exam requirements/recommendations for international students: Required—TOEFL (minimum score 525 paper-based). Electronic applications accepted.

Faculty research: Urban politics, brown fields, e-government, and administration, evaluation research, community development, electronic government and governance.

Saint Mary's University of Minnesota, Schools of Graduate and Professional Programs, Graduate School of Business and Technology, Geographic Information Science Program, Winona, MN 55987-1399. Offers MS, Certificate.

Salisbury University, Program in Geographic Information Systems Management, Salisbury, MD 21801-6837. Offers MS. Part-time programs available. *Faculty:* 2 full-time (0 women). *Students:* 3 full-time (0 women), 4 part-time (1 woman). Average age 31. In 2014, 8 master's awarded. *Entrance requirements:* For master's, successful completion of required undergraduate coursework in mathematics and elementary statistics; professional resume; 3 letters of recommendation; personal statement. Additional exam requirements/recommendations for international students: Required—TOEFL (minimum score 550 paper-based; 79 iBT), IELTS (minimum score 6.5). *Application deadline:* For fall admission, 3/1 priority date for domestic and international students; for spring admission, 10/1 priority date for domestic and international students; for summer admission, 10/1 priority date for domestic and international students. Applications are processed on a rolling basis. Application fee: $65. Electronic applications accepted. *Expenses:* Expenses: $358 per credit hour for residents; $647 for non-residents; $78 fees. *Financial support:* In 2014–15, 2 teaching assistantships with full tuition reimbursements (averaging $9,000 per year) were awarded; institutionally sponsored loans and unspecified assistantships also available. Support available to part-time students. Financial award application deadline: 3/1; financial award applicants required to submit FAFSA. *Faculty research:* GIS and parallel processing, environmental hazards, GIS and public service, spatial statistics, land use change. *Unit head:* Dr. Michael Scott, Graduate Program Director, Geographic Information Systems Management, 410-543-6456, E-mail: msscott@salisbury.edu.
Website: http://www.salisbury.edu/gsr/gradstudies/GISpage

Sam Houston State University, College of Sciences, Department of Geography and Geology, Huntsville, TX 77341. Offers applied geographic information science (MS); geographic information science (Certificate). Part-time programs available. *Faculty:* 13 full-time (2 women), 1 part-time/adjunct (0 women). *Students:* 13 full-time (4 women), 17 part-time (5 women); includes 4 minority (2 Black or African American, non-Hispanic/Latino; 1 Hispanic/Latino; 1 Two or more races, non-Hispanic/Latino), 4 international. Average age 34. 15 applicants, 100% accepted, 9 enrolled. In 2014, 6 master's awarded. *Degree requirements:* For master's, comprehensive exam, thesis (for some programs). *Entrance requirements:* For master's, GRE General Test, letters of recommendation. Additional exam requirements/recommendations for international students: Required—TOEFL (minimum score 550 paper-based; 79 iBT), IELTS (minimum score 6.5). *Application deadline:* For fall admission, 8/1 for domestic students, 6/25 for international students; for spring admission, 12/1 for domestic students, 11/12 for international students; for summer admission, 5/15 for domestic students, 4/9 for international students. Applications are processed on a rolling basis. Application fee: $45 ($75 for international students). Electronic applications accepted. *Expenses:* Tuition, state resident: full-time $2286; part-time $254 per credit hour. Tuition, nonresident: full-time $5544; part-time $616 per credit hour. *Required fees:* $440 per semester. Tuition and fees vary according to course load and campus/location. *Financial support:* In 2014–15, 4 research assistantships (averaging $9,938 per year), 1 teaching assistantship (averaging $10,115 per year) were awarded; career-related internships or fieldwork, Federal Work-Study, scholarships/grants, tuition waivers (partial), and unspecified assistantships also available. Support available to part-time students. Financial award application deadline: 3/15; financial award applicants required to submit FAFSA. *Unit head:* Dr. Brian Cooper, Chair, 936-294-1566, Fax: 936-294-4203, E-mail: bjcooper@shsu.edu. *Application contact:* Dr. Falguni Mukherjee, Graduate Advisor, 936-294-1073, Fax: 936-294-4203, E-mail: fsm002@shsu.edu.
Website: http://www.shsu.edu/academics/geography-geology/

San Jose State University, Graduate Studies and Research, College of Social Sciences, Department of Geography, San Jose, CA 95192-0001. Offers geographic information science (Certificate); geography (MA). *Entrance requirements:* For master's, minimum GPA of 3.0. Electronic applications accepted.

State University of New York College of Environmental Science and Forestry, Department of Environmental Resources Engineering, Syracuse, NY 13210-2779. Offers ecological engineering (MPS, MS, PhD); environmental management (MPS); environmental resources engineering (MPS, MS, PhD); geospatial information science and engineering (MPS, MS, PhD); water resources engineering (MPS, MS, PhD). Part-time programs available. *Degree requirements:* For master's, thesis (for some programs); for doctorate, comprehensive exam, thesis/dissertation. *Entrance requirements:* For master's and doctorate, GRE General Test, minimum GPA of 3.0. Additional exam requirements/recommendations for international students: Required—TOEFL (minimum score 550 paper-based; 80 iBT), IELTS (minimum score 6). *Faculty research:* Ecological engineering, environmental resources engineering, geospatial information science and engineering, water resources engineering, environmental science.

Stony Brook University, State University of New York, Sustainability Studies Program, Stony Brook, NY 11794-3352. Offers geospatial sciences (Graduate Certificate). *Faculty:* 9 full-time (3 women), 8 part-time/adjunct (3 women). *Students:* 1 (woman) full-time, 4 part-time (2 women). Average age 30. In 2014, 1 Graduate Certificate awarded. *Entrance requirements:* For degree, personal statement, letters of recommendation, official transcripts. Additional exam requirements/recommendations for international students: Required—TOEFL. *Application deadline:* For fall admission, 8/1 for domestic students; for spring admission, 12/1 for domestic students; for summer admission, 5/15 for domestic students. Application fee: $100. *Expenses:* Tuition, state resident: full-time $10,370; part-time $432 per credit. Tuition, nonresident: full-time $20,190; part-time $841 per credit. *Required fees:* $1431. *Financial support:* In 2014–15, 1 teaching assistantship was awarded. *Total annual research expenditures:* $34,967. *Unit head:* Heidi Hutner, Director, 631-632-9404, Fax: 631-632-5375, E-mail: heidi.hutner@stonybrook.edu. *Application contact:* Ginny Clancy, Graduate Coordinator, 631-632-9404, Fax: 631-632-5375, E-mail: ginny.clancy@stonybrook.edu.
Website: http://www.stonybrook.edu/commcms/sustainability/

Texas State University, The Graduate College, College of Liberal Arts, Department of Geography, Program in Geographic Information Science, San Marcos, TX 78666. Offers MAG, PhD. Part-time and evening/weekend programs available. *Faculty:* 8 full-time (3 women). *Students:* 19 full-time (5 women), 12 part-time (7 women); includes 5 minority (2 Asian, non-Hispanic/Latino; 3 Hispanic/Latino), 10 international. Average age 33. 25 applicants, 60% accepted, 10 enrolled. In 2014, 13 master's, 3 doctorates awarded. *Degree requirements:* For master's, comprehensive exam; for doctorate, comprehensive exam, thesis/dissertation. *Entrance requirements:* For master's, GRE (minimum preferred score of 300 verbal and quantitative), baccalaureate degree from regionally-accredited institution with minimum GPA of 3.2 on last 60 hours of undergraduate course work; for doctorate, GRE (minimum preferred score of 303 verbal and quantitative), master's degree in geography or related field with minimum GPA of 3.5 on all graduate coursework. Additional exam requirements/recommendations for international students: Required—TOEFL (minimum score 550 paper-based; 78 iBT). *Application deadline:* For fall admission, 5/1 priority date for domestic students, 4/15 for international students; for spring admission, 10/15 for domestic students, 10/1 for international students. Applications are processed on a rolling basis. Application fee: $40 ($90 for international students). Electronic applications accepted. *Expenses:* Expenses: $8,834 (tuition and fees combined). *Financial support:* In 2014–15, 18 students received support, including 3 research assistantships (averaging $18,732 per year), 15 teaching assistantships (averaging $20,839 per year); career-related internships or fieldwork, Federal Work-Study, institutionally sponsored loans, and scholarships/grants also available. Support available to part-time students. Financial award application deadline: 4/1; financial award applicants required to submit FAFSA. *Faculty research:* Air pollution. *Total annual research expenditures:* $105,133. *Unit head:* Dr. David Butler, Graduate Adviser, 512-245-2618, Fax: 512-245-8353, E-mail: db25@txstate.edu. *Application contact:* Dr. Andrea Golato, Dean of Graduate School, 512-245-2581, Fax: 512-245-8365, E-mail: gradcollege@txstate.edu.
Website: http://www.geo.txstate.edu/

Université du Québec à Montréal, Graduate Programs, Program in Geographical Information Systems, Montréal, QC H3C 3P8, Canada. Offers Diploma. Part-time programs available. *Entrance requirements:* For degree, appropriate bachelor's degree or equivalent, proficiency in French.

Université Laval, Faculty of Administrative Sciences, Programs in Business Administration, Québec, QC G1K 7P4, Canada. Offers accounting (MBA); agri-food management (MBA); electronic business (MBA, Diploma); factory management and logistics (MBA); finance (MBA); firm management (MBA); geomatic management (MBA); information technology management (MBA); international management (MBA); management (MBA); management accounting (MBA, Diploma); marketing (MBA); modeling and organizational decision (MBA); occupational health and safety management (MBA); pharmacy management (MBA); social and environmental responsibility (MBA); technological entrepreneurship (Diploma). *Accreditation:* AACSB. Part-time and evening/weekend programs available. Postbaccalaureate distance learning degree programs offered (no on-campus study). *Entrance requirements:* For master's and Diploma, knowledge of French and English. Electronic applications accepted.

University at Buffalo, the State University of New York, Graduate School, College of Arts and Sciences, Department of Geography, Buffalo, NY 14260. Offers Canadian studies (Certificate); earth systems science (MA, MS); economic geography and business geographics (MS); environmental modeling and analysis (MA); geographic information science (MA, MS); geography (MA, PhD); GIS and environmental analysis (Certificate); health geography (MS); international trade (MA); transportation and business geographics (MA); urban and regional analysis (MA). Part-time programs available. *Faculty:* 18 full-time (9 women), 1 part-time/adjunct (0 women). *Students:* 87 full-time (37 women), 26 part-time (8 women); includes 78 minority (1 Black or African American, non-Hispanic/Latino; 74 Asian, non-Hispanic/Latino; 3 Hispanic/Latino). Average age 29. 167 applicants, 44% accepted, 32 enrolled. In 2014, 24 master's, 6 doctorates awarded. Terminal master's awarded for partial completion of doctoral program. *Degree requirements:* For master's, thesis (for some programs), project or portfolio; for doctorate, thesis/dissertation. *Entrance requirements:* For master's, GRE General Test, minimum GPA of 2.9; for doctorate, GRE General Test, minimum GPA of 3.0. Additional exam requirements/recommendations for international students: Required—TOEFL (minimum score 550 paper-based; 79 iBT). *Application deadline:* For fall admission, 5/1 priority date for domestic students, 3/10 priority date for international students; for spring admission, 11/1 priority date for domestic students, 9/1 priority date for international students. Applications are processed on a rolling basis. Application fee: $75. Electronic applications accepted. *Financial support:* In 2014–15, 13 students received support, including 8 fellowships with full tuition reimbursements available (averaging $5,500 per year), 13 teaching assistantships with full tuition reimbursements available (averaging $13,800 per year); research assistantships with full tuition reimbursements available, career-related internships or fieldwork, Federal Work-Study, institutionally sponsored loans, traineeships, health care benefits, and unspecified assistantships also available. Financial award application deadline: 1/10. *Faculty research:* International business and world trade, geographic information systems and cartography, transportation, urban and regional analysis, physical and environmental geography. *Total annual research expenditures:* $2.6 million. *Unit head:* Dr. Sharmistha Bagchi-Sen, Chairman, 716-645-0473, Fax: 716-645-2329, E-mail: geosbs@buffalo.edu. *Application contact:* Betsy Crooks, Graduate Secretary, 716-645-0471, Fax: 716-645-2329, E-mail: babraham@buffalo.edu.
Website: http://www.geog.buffalo.edu/

The University of Alabama, Graduate School, College of Arts and Sciences, Department of Geography, Tuscaloosa, AL 35487. Offers earth system science (MS); geographic information science (MS); planning (MS). Part-time programs available. *Faculty:* 14 full-time (1 woman), 1 (woman) part-time/adjunct. *Students:* 26 full-time (10 women), 5 part-time (2 women); includes 1 minority (Two or more races, non-Hispanic/Latino), 4 international. Average age 27. 19 applicants, 68% accepted, 10 enrolled. In 2014, 12 master's awarded. *Degree requirements:* For master's, comprehensive exam (for some programs), thesis (for some programs). *Entrance requirements:* For master's, GRE, minimum GPA of 3.0. Additional exam requirements/recommendations for international students: Required—TOEFL (minimum score 550 paper-based; 79 iBT). *Application deadline:* For fall admission, 2/15 priority date for domestic and international students; for spring admission, 10/1 priority date for domestic and international students. Applications are processed on a rolling basis. Application fee: $50 ($60 for international students). Electronic applications accepted. *Expenses:* Tuition, state resident: full-time $9826. Tuition, nonresident: full-time $24,950. *Financial support:* In 2014–15, 16 students received support, including fellowships with full tuition reimbursements available (averaging $15,000 per year), 4 research assistantships with full tuition reimbursements available (averaging $13,311 per year), 18 teaching assistantships with full tuition reimbursements available (averaging $13,311 per year); career-related internships or fieldwork, health care benefits, and unspecified assistantships also available. Financial award application deadline: 2/15. *Faculty research:* Earth system science; geographic information science; urban, regional and environmental planning; ecology. *Total annual research expenditures:* $393,294. *Unit head:* Dr. Douglas Sherman, Chair, 205-348-5047, Fax: 205-348-2278, E-mail: douglas.j.sherman@ua.edu. *Application contact:* Dr. Justin Hart, Assistant Professor, 205-348-5047, Fax: 205-348-2278, E-mail: hart013@ua.edu.
Website: http://geography.ua.edu

University of Alaska Fairbanks, College of Natural Sciences and Mathematics, Department of Geosciences, Fairbanks, AK 99775-5780. Offers geology (MS, PhD), including economic geology (PhD), petroleum geology (MS), quaternary geology (PhD), remote sensing (PhD), volcanology (PhD); geophysics (MS, PhD), including remote sensing geophysics, snow, ice, and permafrost geophysics (MS), solid-earth geophysics (MS). Part-time programs available. *Faculty:* 14 full-time (5 women), 1 part-time/adjunct (0 women). *Students:* 47 full-time (23 women), 15 part-time (8 women); includes 2 minority (1 Asian, non-Hispanic/Latino; 1 Two or more races, non-Hispanic/Latino), 16 international. Average age 29. 83 applicants, 18% accepted, 14 enrolled. In 2014, 14 master's, 10 doctorates awarded. *Degree requirements:* For master's, comprehensive exam, thesis, oral defense of thesis; for doctorate, comprehensive exam, thesis/

dissertation, defense of the dissertation. *Entrance requirements:* For master's, GRE General Test, bachelor's degree in geology, geophysics, or an appropriate physical science or engineering with minimum cumulative undergraduate and major GPA of 3.0; for doctorate, GRE General Test, minimum cumulative GPA of 3.0. Additional exam requirements/recommendations for international students: Required—TOEFL (minimum score 550 paper-based; 79 iBT), IELTS (minimum score 6.5). *Application deadline:* For fall admission, 6/1 for domestic students, 3/1 for international students; for spring admission, 10/15 for domestic students, 9/1 for international students. Applications are processed on a rolling basis. Application fee: $60. Electronic applications accepted. *Expenses:* Tuition, state resident: full-time $7614; part-time $423 per credit. Tuition, nonresident: full-time $15,552; part-time $864 per credit. Tuition and fees vary according to course level, course load and reciprocity agreements. *Financial support:* In 2014–15, 27 research assistantships with full tuition reimbursements (averaging $9,817 per year), 6 teaching assistantships with full tuition reimbursements (averaging $10,316 per year) were awarded; fellowships with full tuition reimbursements, Federal Work-Study, scholarships/grants, health care benefits, and unspecified assistantships also available. Support available to part-time students. Financial award application deadline: 2/15; financial award applicants required to submit FAFSA. *Faculty research:* Glacial surging, volcanology, geochronology, impact cratering, permafrost geophysics. *Unit head:* Dr. Paul McCarthy, Department Co-Chair, 907-474-7565, Fax: 907-474-5163, E-mail: geology@uaf.edu. *Application contact:* Mary Kreta, Director of Admissions, 907-474-7500, Fax: 907-474-7097, E-mail: admissions@uaf.edu.
Website: http://www.uaf.edu/geology/

The University of Arizona, College of Social and Behavioral Sciences, School of Geography and Development, Tucson, AZ 85721. Offers geographic information science (Certificate); geographic information systems technology (MA); geography (MA, PhD). Part-time programs available. Terminal master's awarded for partial completion of doctoral program. *Degree requirements:* For master's, thesis or additional course work; for doctorate, variable foreign language requirement, thesis/dissertation. *Entrance requirements:* For master's, GRE General Test, 2 letters of recommendation; for doctorate, GRE General Test, statement of purpose, 2 letters of recommendation, master's degree. Additional exam requirements/recommendations for international students: Required—TOEFL (minimum score 550 paper-based; 79 iBT). Electronic applications accepted. *Faculty research:* Population, Latin America, Anglo-America, the former Soviet Union, the Middle East.

University of Central Arkansas, Graduate School, College of Liberal Arts, Department of Geography, Conway, AR 72035-0001. Offers community and economic development (MS); geographic information systems (MGIS, Certificate). Part-time programs available. Postbaccalaureate distance learning degree programs offered (minimal on-campus study). *Entrance requirements:* Additional exam requirements/recommendations for international students: Required—TOEFL (minimum score 550 paper-based). Electronic applications accepted.

University of Central Arkansas, Graduate School, College of Liberal Arts, Program in Community and Economic Development, Conway, AR 72035-0001. Offers community and economic development (MS); geographic and information systems (MGIS, Graduate Certificate). Part-time programs available. Postbaccalaureate distance learning degree programs offered (minimal on-campus study). *Degree requirements:* For master's, comprehensive exam, thesis. *Entrance requirements:* For master's, GRE General Test, minimum GPA of 2.7. Additional exam requirements/recommendations for international students: Required—TOEFL (minimum score 550 paper-based). Electronic applications accepted. *Expenses:* Contact institution.

University of Colorado Denver, Business School, Program in Information Systems, Denver, CO 80217. Offers accounting and information systems audit and control (MS); business intelligence systems (MS); digital health entrepreneurship (MS); enterprise risk management (MS); enterprise technology management (MS); geographic information systems (MS); health information technology (MS); technology innovation and entrepreneurship (MS); Web and mobile computing (MS). Part-time and evening/weekend programs available. Postbaccalaureate distance learning degree programs offered (no on-campus study). *Students:* 72 full-time (22 women), 29 part-time (9 women); includes 18 minority (2 Black or African American, non-Hispanic/Latino; 12 Asian, non-Hispanic/Latino; 3 Hispanic/Latino; 1 Two or more races, non-Hispanic/Latino), 31 international. Average age 31. 81 applicants, 75% accepted, 24 enrolled. In 2014, 21 master's awarded. *Degree requirements:* For master's, 30 credit hours. *Entrance requirements:* For master's, GMAT, resume, essay, two letters of recommendation, financial statements (for international applicants). Additional exam requirements/recommendations for international students: Required—TOEFL (minimum score 525 paper-based; 71 iBT); Recommended—IELTS (minimum score 6.5). *Application deadline:* For fall admission, 4/15 priority date for domestic students, 3/15 priority date for international students; for spring admission, 10/15 priority date for domestic students, 9/15 priority date for international students; for summer admission, 2/15 priority date for domestic students, 1/15 priority date for international students. Applications are processed on a rolling basis. Application fee: $50 ($75 for international students). Electronic applications accepted. *Expenses:* Expenses: Contact institution. *Financial support:* In 2014–15, 21 students received support. Fellowships, research assistantships, teaching assistantships, Federal Work-Study, institutionally sponsored loans, scholarships/grants, and traineeships available. Financial award application deadline: 4/1; financial award applicants required to submit FAFSA. *Faculty research:* Human-computer interaction, expert systems, database management, electronic commerce, object-oriented software development. *Unit head:* Dr. Jahangir Karimi, Director of Information Systems Programs, 303-315-8430, E-mail: jahangir.karimi@ucdenver.edu. *Application contact:* Shelly Townley, Admissions Director, Graduate Programs, 303-315-8202, E-mail: shelly.townley@ucdenver.edu.
Website: http://www.ucdenver.edu/academics/colleges/business/degrees/ms/IS/Pages/Information-Systems.aspx

University of Colorado Denver, College of Engineering and Applied Science, Department of Civil Engineering, Denver, CO 80217. Offers civil engineering (EASPh D); civil engineering systems (PhD); environmental and sustainability engineering (MS, PhD); geographic information systems (MS); geotechnical engineering (MS, PhD); hydrology and hydraulics (MS, PhD); structural engineering (MS, PhD); transportation engineering (MS, PhD). Part-time and evening/weekend programs available. *Faculty:* 15 full-time (4 women), 11 part-time/adjunct (2 women). *Students:* 64 full-time (15 women), 43 part-time (8 women); includes 15 minority (3 Black or African American, non-Hispanic/Latino; 3 Asian, non-Hispanic/Latino; 6 Hispanic/Latino; 3 Two or more races, non-Hispanic/Latino), 34 international. Average age 32. 136 applicants, 54% accepted, 28 enrolled. In 2014, 35 master's, 9 doctorates awarded. *Degree requirements:* For master's, comprehensive exam, 30 credit hours, project or thesis; for doctorate, comprehensive exam, thesis/dissertation, 60 credit hours (30 of which are dissertation research). *Entrance requirements:* For master's, GRE, statement of purpose, transcripts, three references; for doctorate, GRE, statement of purpose, transcripts, references, letter of support from faculty stating willingness to serve as dissertation advisor and outlining plan for financial support. Additional exam requirements/recommendations for international students: Required—TOEFL (minimum score 537 paper-based; 75 iBT); Recommended—IELTS (minimum score 6.5). *Application deadline:* For fall admission, 5/1 for domestic students, 4/1 for international students; for spring admission, 10/1 for domestic students, 9/1 for international students; for summer admission, 2/15 for domestic students, 1/15 for international students. Application fee: $50 ($75 for international students). Electronic applications accepted. *Expenses:* Expenses: Contact institution. *Financial support:* In 2014–15, 26 students received support. Fellowships, research assistantships, teaching assistantships, career-related internships or fieldwork, Federal Work-Study, institutionally sponsored loans, scholarships/grants, traineeships, and unspecified assistantships available. Financial award application deadline: 4/1; financial award applicants required to submit FAFSA. *Faculty research:* Earthquake source physics, environmental biotechnology, hydrologic and hydraulic engineering, sustainability assessments, transportation energy use and greenhouse gas emissions. *Unit head:* Dr. Kevin Rens, Chair, 303-556-8017, E-mail: kevin.rens@ucdenver.edu. *Application contact:* Tammy Southern, Program Assistant, 303-556-6712, E-mail: tamara.southern@ucdenver.edu.
Website: http://www.ucdenver.edu/academics/colleges/Engineering/Programs/Civil-Engineering/Pages/CivilEngineering.aspx

University of Colorado Denver, College of Engineering and Applied Science, Master of Engineering Program, Denver, CO 80217-3364. Offers civil engineering (M Eng), including civil engineering, geographic information systems, transportation systems; electrical engineering (M Eng); mechanical engineering (M Eng). Part-time programs available. *Students:* 30 full-time (9 women), 20 part-time (7 women); includes 3 minority (1 Black or African American, non-Hispanic/Latino; 2 Hispanic/Latino), 8 international. Average age 34. 35 applicants, 83% accepted, 15 enrolled. In 2014, 14 master's awarded. *Degree requirements:* For master's, comprehensive exam, 27 credit hours of course work, 3 credit hours of report or thesis work. *Entrance requirements:* For master's, GRE (for those with GPA below 2.75), transcripts, references, statement of purpose. Additional exam requirements/recommendations for international students: Required—TOEFL (minimum score 537 paper-based; 75 iBT); Recommended—IELTS (minimum score 6.5). *Application deadline:* For fall admission, 4/1 for domestic students, 3/1 for international students; for spring admission, 10/1 for domestic students, 9/15 for international students. Applications are processed on a rolling basis. Application fee: $50 ($75 for international students). Electronic applications accepted. *Expenses:* Expenses: Contact institution. *Financial support:* In 2014–15, 4 students received support. Fellowships, research assistantships, teaching assistantships, Federal Work-Study, institutionally sponsored loans, scholarships/grants, traineeships, and unspecified assistantships available. Financial award application deadline: 4/1; financial award applicants required to submit FAFSA. *Faculty research:* Civil, electrical and mechanical engineering. *Unit head:* 303-556-2870, Fax: 303-556-2511, E-mail: engineering@ucdenver.edu. *Application contact:* Graduate School Admissions, 303-556-2704, E-mail: admissions@ucdenver.edu.
Website: http://www.ucdenver.edu/academics/colleges/Engineering/admissions/Masters/Pages/MastersAdmissions.aspx

University of Colorado Denver, College of Liberal Arts and Sciences, Department of Geography and Environmental Sciences, Denver, CO 80217. Offers environmental sciences (MS), including air quality, ecosystems, environmental health, environmental science education, geo-spatial analysis, hazardous waste, water quality. Part-time and evening/weekend programs available. *Faculty:* 11 full-time (4 women), 3 part-time/adjunct. *Students:* 39 full-time (29 women), 9 part-time (6 women); includes 6 minority (1 Black or African American, non-Hispanic/Latino; 1 Asian, non-Hispanic/Latino; 3 Hispanic/Latino; 1 Two or more races, non-Hispanic/Latino), 8 international. Average age 29. 40 applicants, 65% accepted, 14 enrolled. In 2014, 10 master's awarded. *Degree requirements:* For master's, thesis or alternative, 30 credits including 21 of core requirements and 9 of environmental science electives. *Entrance requirements:* For master's, GRE General Test, BA in one of the natural/physical sciences or engineering (or equivalent background); prerequisite coursework in calculus and physics (one semester each), general chemistry with lab and general biology with lab (two semesters each), three letters of recommendation. Additional exam requirements/recommendations for international students: Required—TOEFL (minimum score 537 paper-based; 75 iBT); Recommended—IELTS (minimum score 6.5). *Application deadline:* For fall admission, 1/20 for domestic and international students; for spring admission, 10/1 for domestic and international students. Application fee: $50 ($75 for international students). Electronic applications accepted. *Financial support:* In 2014–15, 4 students received support. Fellowships, research assistantships, teaching assistantships, Federal Work-Study, institutionally sponsored loans, scholarships/grants, and traineeships available. Financial award application deadline: 4/1; financial award applicants required to submit FAFSA. *Faculty research:* Air quality, environmental health, ecosystems, hazardous waste, water quality, geo-spatial analysis and environmental science education. *Unit head:* Dr. Frederick Chambers, Director of MS in Environmental Sciences Program, 303-556-2619, E-mail: frederick.chambers@ucdenver.edu. *Application contact:* Sue Eddleman, Program Assistant, 303-352-3698, E-mail: sue.eddleman@ucdenver.edu.
Website: http://www.ucdenver.edu/academics/colleges/CLAS/Departments/ges/Programs/MasterofScience/Pages/MasterofScience.aspx

University of Connecticut, Graduate School, College of Liberal Arts and Sciences, Department of Geography, Storrs, CT 06269. Offers geographic information systems (Certificate); geography (MS, PhD). *Degree requirements:* For master's, comprehensive exam; for doctorate, thesis/dissertation. *Entrance requirements:* For master's and doctorate, GRE General Test. Additional exam requirements/recommendations for international students: Required—TOEFL (minimum score 550 paper-based). Electronic applications accepted.

University of Denver, University College, Denver, CO 80208. Offers geographic information systems (Certificate); global affairs (Certificate), including translation studies, world history and culture; information and communications technology (MCIS), including geographic information systems, information systems security, project management (MCIS, Certificate), software design and programming, technology management, telecommunications technology, Web design and development; leadership and organizations (Certificate), including human capital in organizations, philanthropic leadership, project management (MCIS, Certificate), strategic innovation and change; organizational and professional communication (MPS), including alternative dispute resolution, organizational communication, organizational development and training, public relations and marketing; security management (MAS, Certificate), including emergency planning and response, information security (MAS), organizational security. Part-time and evening/weekend programs available. Postbaccalaureate distance learning degree programs offered (no on-campus study). *Faculty:* 8 full-time (4 women), 133 part-time/adjunct (46 women). *Students:* 54 full-time (21 women), 1,327 part-time (775 women); includes 272 minority (106 Black or African American, non-Hispanic/Latino; 6 American Indian or Alaska Native, non-Hispanic/Latino; 26 Asian, non-Hispanic/Latino; 108 Hispanic/Latino; 1 Native Hawaiian or other Pacific Islander, non-Hispanic/Latino; 25 Two or more races, non-Hispanic/Latino), 116 international. Average age 35. 768 applicants, 95% accepted, 620 enrolled. In 2014, 391 master's, 196 other advanced degrees awarded. *Degree requirements:* For master's, capstone project. *Entrance requirements:* For master's, transcripts, two letters of recommendation, personal statement, resume. Additional exam requirements/recommendations for international students: Required—TOEFL (minimum score 550

paper-based; 80 iBT). *Application deadline:* For fall admission, 6/21 priority date for domestic students, 5/1 priority date for international students; for winter admission, 9/14 priority date for domestic students, 9/19 priority date for international students; for spring admission, 1/11 for domestic students, 12/12 for international students; for summer admission, 3/29 priority date for domestic students, 3/6 priority date for international students. Applications are processed on a rolling basis. Application fee: $75. Electronic applications accepted. *Expenses:* Expenses: $959 per credit hour. *Financial support:* In 2014–15, 19 students received support. Applicants required to submit FAFSA. *Unit head:* Dr. Michael McGuire, Interim Dean, 303-871-3518, E-mail: mmcguire@du.edu. *Application contact:* Information Contact, 303-871-2291, E-mail: ucoladm@du.edu.
Website: http://www.universitycollege.du.edu/

University of Florida, Graduate School, College of Liberal Arts and Sciences, Department of Geography, Gainesville, FL 32611-7315. Offers applications of geographic technologies (MA, MS); geographic information systems (MA, MS, PhD); geography (MA, MS, PhD); hydrologic sciences (MS, PhD); tropical conservation and development (MA, MS, PhD); wetland sciences (MA, MS, PhD). *Faculty:* 12 full-time (4 women), 1 part-time/adjunct (0 women). *Students:* 35 full-time (16 women), 3 part-time (2 women); includes 5 minority (1 Black or African American, non-Hispanic/Latino; 4 Hispanic/Latino), 14 international. 55 applicants, 33% accepted, 8 enrolled. In 2014, 2 master's, 9 doctorates awarded. *Degree requirements:* For master's, thesis; for doctorate, comprehensive exam, thesis/dissertation. *Entrance requirements:* For master's and doctorate, GRE General Test, minimum GPA of 3.0. Additional exam requirements/recommendations for international students: Required—TOEFL (minimum score 550 paper-based; 80 iBT), IELTS (minimum score 6). *Application deadline:* For fall admission, 7/15 for domestic students, 6/15 for international students. Applications are processed on a rolling basis. Application fee: $30. Electronic applications accepted. *Financial support:* In 2014–15, 8 fellowships, 6 research assistantships, 22 teaching assistantships were awarded; career-related internships or fieldwork and unspecified assistantships also available. Financial award applicants required to submit FAFSA. *Faculty research:* Economic development, physical geography, hydrology, climatology, tropical agriculture. *Unit head:* Michael W. Binford, PhD, Chair and Professor, 352-294-7500, Fax: 352-392-8855, E-mail: mbinford@ufl.edu. *Application contact:* Corene Matyas, PhD, Associate Professor and Graduate Coordinator, 352-294-7508, Fax: 352-392-8855, E-mail: matyas@ufl.edu.
Website: http://geog.ufl.edu/

The University of Iowa, Graduate College, Program in Informatics, Iowa City, IA 52242-1316. Offers bioinformatics (MS, PhD); bioinformatics and computational biology (Certificate); geoinformatics (MS, PhD, Certificate); health informatics (MS, PhD, Certificate); information science (MS, PhD, Certificate). *Degree requirements:* For master's, thesis optional; for doctorate, comprehensive exam, thesis/dissertation. *Entrance requirements:* For master's and doctorate, GRE General Test, minimum GPA of 3.0. Additional exam requirements/recommendations for international students: Required—TOEFL (minimum score 550 paper-based; 81 iBT). Electronic applications accepted.

University of Lethbridge, School of Graduate Studies, Lethbridge, AB T1K 3M4, Canada. Offers addictions counseling (M Sc); agricultural biotechnology (M Sc); agricultural studies (M Sc, MA); anthropology (MA); archaeology (M Sc, MA); art (MA, MFA); biochemistry (M Sc); biological sciences (M Sc); biomolecular science (PhD); biosystems and biodiversity (PhD); Canadian studies (MA); chemistry (M Sc); computer science (M Sc); computer science and geographical information science (M Sc); counseling (MC); counseling psychology (M Ed); dramatic arts (MA); earth, space, and physical science (PhD); economics (MA); education (MA); educational leadership (M Ed); English (MA); environmental science (M Sc); evolution and behavior (PhD); exercise science (M Sc); French (MA); French/German (MA); French/Spanish (MA); general education (M Ed); geography (M Sc, MA); German (MA); health sciences (M Sc); individualized multidisciplinary (M Sc, MA); kinesiology (M Sc, MA); management (M Sc), including accounting, finance, general management, human resource management and labor relations, information systems, international management, marketing, policy and strategy; mathematics (M Sc); modern languages (MA); music (M Mus, MA); Native American studies (MA); neuroscience (M Sc, PhD); new media (MA, MFA); nursing (M Sc, MN); philosophy (MA); physics (M Sc); political science (MA); psychology (M Sc, MA); religious studies (MA); sociology (MA); theatre and dramatic arts (MFA); theoretical and computational science (PhD); urban and regional studies (MA); women and gender studies (MA). Part-time and evening/weekend programs available. *Faculty:* 358. *Students:* 445 full-time (243 women), 116 part-time (72 women). Average age 31. 351 applicants, 26% accepted, 87 enrolled. In 2014, 129 master's, 13 doctorates awarded. *Degree requirements:* For master's, thesis (for some programs); for doctorate, comprehensive exam, thesis/dissertation. *Entrance requirements:* For master's, GMAT (for M Sc in management), bachelor's degree in related field, minimum GPA of 3.0 during previous 20 graded semester courses, 2 years' teaching or related experience (M Ed); for doctorate, master's degree, minimum graduate GPA of 3.5. Additional exam requirements/recommendations for international students: Required—TOEFL. Application fee: $100 Canadian dollars. *Financial support:* Fellowships, research assistantships, teaching assistantships, scholarships/grants, health care benefits, and unspecified assistantships available. *Faculty research:* Movement and brain plasticity, gibberellin physiology, photosynthesis, carbon cycling, molecular properties of main-group ring components. *Application contact:* School of Graduate Studies, 403-329-5194, E-mail: sgsinquiries@uleth.ca.
Website: http://www.uleth.ca/graduatestudies/

University of Maine, Graduate School, College of Liberal Arts and Sciences, School of Computing and Information Science, Orono, ME 04469. Offers computer science (MS, PhD); geographic information systems (CGS); information systems (MS); spatial information science and engineering (MS, PhD). Part-time programs available. *Faculty:* 13 full-time (2 women). *Students:* 30 full-time (6 women), 9 part-time (2 women); includes 1 minority (Asian, non-Hispanic/Latino), 10 international. Average age 34. 46 applicants, 37% accepted, 3 enrolled. In 2014, 9 master's, 3 doctorates awarded. Terminal master's awarded for partial completion of doctoral program. *Degree requirements:* For master's, thesis (for some programs); for doctorate, comprehensive exam, thesis/dissertation. *Entrance requirements:* For master's and doctorate, GRE General Test, GRE Subject Test. Additional exam requirements/recommendations for international students: Required—TOEFL. *Application deadline:* For fall admission, 2/1 priority date for domestic students. Applications are processed on a rolling basis. Application fee: $65. Electronic applications accepted. *Expenses:* Tuition, state resident: part-time $658 per credit hour. Tuition, nonresident: part-time $1550 per credit hour. *Financial support:* In 2014–15, 18 students received support, including 3 fellowships (averaging $21,600 per year), 7 research assistantships with full tuition reimbursements available (averaging $14,600 per year), 8 teaching assistantships with full tuition reimbursements available (averaging $14,600 per year); career-related internships or fieldwork, Federal Work-Study, institutionally sponsored loans, and tuition waivers (full) also available. Financial award application deadline: 3/1. *Faculty research:* Geographic information science, virtual reality, robotics, sensor networks, ice sheet modeling. *Total annual research expenditures:* $436,973. *Unit head:* Dr. Max Egenhofer, Acting Director, 207-581-2114, Fax: 207-581-2206. *Application contact:* Scott G. Delcourt, Assistant Vice President for Graduate Studies and Senior Associate Dean, 207-581-3291, Fax: 207-581-3232, E-mail: graduate@maine.edu.
Website: http://umaine.edu/cis/

University of Maryland, Baltimore County, The Graduate School, College of Arts, Humanities and Social Sciences, Department of Geography and Environmental Systems, Program in Geographic Information Systems, Rockville, MD 20850. Offers MPS, Certificate. Part-time and evening/weekend programs available. *Faculty:* 13 part-time/adjunct (3 women). *Students:* 11 full-time (2 women), 29 part-time (9 women); includes 16 minority (4 Black or African American, non-Hispanic/Latino; 9 Asian, non-Hispanic/Latino; 3 Hispanic/Latino). Average age 36. 16 applicants, 88% accepted, 11 enrolled. In 2014, 5 master's, 1 Certificate awarded. *Entrance requirements:* Additional exam requirements/recommendations for international students: Required—TOEFL. *Application deadline:* For fall admission, 8/1 for domestic students, 6/1 for international students; for spring admission, 12/1 for domestic students, 11/1 for international students. Applications are processed on a rolling basis. Application fee: $50. Electronic applications accepted. *Expenses:* Tuition, state resident: part-time $557. Tuition, nonresident: part-time $922. *Required fees:* $122 per semester. One-time fee: $200 part-time. *Financial support:* In 2014–15, 1 teaching assistantship with full tuition reimbursement (averaging $14,000 per year) was awarded. *Faculty research:* Enterprise GIS. *Unit head:* Dr. Erwin Villiger, Program Director, 301-738-6087, E-mail: villiger@umbc.edu. *Application contact:* Ashley Waters, Program Coordinator, 301-738-6081, E-mail: awaters@umbc.edu.
Website: http://www.umbc.edu/gis

University of Memphis, Graduate School, College of Arts and Sciences, Department of Earth Sciences, Memphis, TN 38152. Offers archaeology (MS); earth sciences (PhD); geographic information systems (Graduate Certificate), including geographic information systems, GIS educator, GIS planning, GIS professional; geography (MA, MS); geology (MS); geophysics (MS); interdisciplinary (MS). Part-time and evening/weekend programs available. *Faculty:* 13 full-time (3 women), 2 part-time/adjunct (0 women). *Students:* 27 full-time (8 women), 26 part-time (7 women); includes 2 minority (1 Black or African American, non-Hispanic/Latino; 1 Asian, non-Hispanic/Latino), 19 international. Average age 32. 36 applicants, 69% accepted, 7 enrolled. In 2014, 7 master's, 5 doctorates awarded. Terminal master's awarded for partial completion of doctoral program. *Degree requirements:* For master's, comprehensive exam, thesis, seminar presentation; for doctorate, thesis/dissertation. *Entrance requirements:* For master's, GRE General Test, 3 letters of recommendation, statement of research interests; for doctorate, GRE General Test, 2 letters of recommendation, resume, personal statement. Additional exam requirements/recommendations for international students: Required—TOEFL (minimum score 550 paper-based). *Application deadline:* For fall admission, 1/31 for domestic students; for spring admission, 11/1 for domestic students. Applications are processed on a rolling basis. Application fee: $35 ($60 for international students). Electronic applications accepted. *Financial support:* In 2014–15, 18 students received support. Fellowships with full tuition reimbursements available, research assistantships with full tuition reimbursements available, teaching assistantships with full tuition reimbursements available, Federal Work-Study, scholarships/grants, and unspecified assistantships available. Financial award application deadline: 2/15; financial award applicants required to submit FAFSA. *Faculty research:* Hazards, active tectonics, geophysics, hydrology and water resources, spatial analysis. *Unit head:* Dr. M. Jerry Bartholomew, Chair, 901-678-4536, Fax: 901-678-4467, E-mail: jbrthlm1@memphis.edu. *Application contact:* Dr. Arlene Hill, Associate Professor and Graduate Program Coordinator, 901-678-4358, Fax: 901-678-2178, E-mail: dlarsen@memphis.edu.
Website: http://www.memphis.edu/des/

University of Minnesota, Twin Cities Campus, Graduate School, College of Food, Agricultural and Natural Resource Sciences, Program in Natural Resources Science and Management, St. Paul, MN 55108. Offers assessment, monitoring, and geospatial analysis (MS, PhD); economics, policy, management, and society (MS, PhD); forest hydrology and watershed management (MS, PhD); forest products (MS, PhD); forests: biology, ecology, conservation, and management (MS, PhD); natural resources science and management (MS, PhD); paper science and engineering (MS, PhD); recreation resources, tourism, and environmental education (MS, PhD); wildlife ecology and management (MS, PhD). Part-time programs available. *Faculty:* 65 full-time, 55 part-time/adjunct. *Students:* 65 full-time (30 women), 37 part-time (12 women); includes 3 minority (1 Black or African American, non-Hispanic/Latino; 1 American Indian or Alaska Native, non-Hispanic/Latino; 1 Asian, non-Hispanic/Latino), 11 international. 90 applicants, 44% accepted, 26 enrolled. In 2014, 17 master's, 5 doctorates awarded. Terminal master's awarded for partial completion of doctoral program. *Degree requirements:* For master's, comprehensive exam, thesis; for doctorate, comprehensive exam, thesis/dissertation. *Entrance requirements:* For master's and doctorate, GRE General Test. Additional exam requirements/recommendations for international students: Required—TOEFL (minimum score 550 paper-based; 79 iBT), IELTS (minimum score 6.5). *Application deadline:* For fall admission, 12/16 priority date for domestic and international students; for spring admission, 10/15 for domestic and international students. Applications are processed on a rolling basis. Application fee: $75 ($95 for international students). Electronic applications accepted. *Financial support:* In 2014–15, fellowships with full tuition reimbursements (averaging $40,000 per year), research assistantships with full tuition reimbursements (averaging $40,000 per year), teaching assistantships with full tuition reimbursements (averaging $40,000 per year) were awarded; scholarships/grants, health care benefits, tuition waivers (full and partial), and unspecified assistantships also available. *Faculty research:* Paper science, forestry, recreation resource management, wildlife ecology, environmental education, hydrology, conservation, tourism, economics, policy, watershed management, GIS, forest products. *Unit head:* Dr. Michael Kilgore, Director of Graduate Studies, 612-624-6298, E-mail: mkilgore@umn.edu. *Application contact:* Jennifer Welsh, Program Coordinator, 612-624-7683, Fax: 612-625-5212, E-mail: jwelsh@umn.edu.
Website: http://www.nrsm.umn.edu

University of Minnesota, Twin Cities Campus, Graduate School, College of Liberal Arts, Program in Geographic Information Science, Minneapolis, MN 55455-0213. Offers MGIS. Part-time programs available. *Degree requirements:* For master's, comprehensive exam, capstone project. *Entrance requirements:* For master's, minimum GPA of 3.0; course work in college-level math, statistics, and computer programming. Additional exam requirements/recommendations for international students: Required—TOEFL (minimum score 600 paper-based; 100 iBT). *Expenses:* Contact institution. *Faculty research:* Geographic information science and society, spatial analysis and modeling, spatial databases, remote sensing, geovisualization.

University of Missouri, Office of Research and Graduate Studies, College of Arts and Science, Department of Geography, Columbia, MO 65211. Offers geographic information science (Graduate Certificate); geography (MA). *Faculty:* 8 full-time (1 woman). *Students:* 11 full-time (6 women), 3 part-time (1 woman); includes 3 minority (1 Black or African American, non-Hispanic/Latino; 1 Asian, non-Hispanic/Latino; 1 Two or more races, non-Hispanic/Latino), 1 international. Average age 30. 24 applicants, 79% accepted, 9 enrolled. In 2014, 7 master's, 15 other advanced degrees awarded. *Degree requirements:* For master's, thesis or alternative. *Entrance requirements:* For master's, GRE General Test (minimum score 1000 verbal and quantitative), minimum GPA of 3.0.

Geographic Information Systems

Additional exam requirements/recommendations for international students: Required—TOEFL (minimum score 500 paper-based; 61 iBT). *Application deadline:* For fall admission, 1/15 priority date for domestic and international students; for winter admission, 10/1 for domestic students; for spring admission, 4/1 for domestic students. Applications are processed on a rolling basis. Application fee: $55 ($75 for international students). Electronic applications accepted. *Financial support:* Fellowships with full tuition reimbursements, research assistantships with full tuition reimbursements, teaching assistantships with full tuition reimbursements, institutionally sponsored loans, health care benefits, and unspecified assistantships available. *Faculty research:* Human geography, nature/society relationships, the physical environment, application of geographic information sciences. *Unit head:* Dr. Mike Urban, Department Chair, 573-884-2658, E-mail: urbanm@missouri.edu. *Application contact:* Dina Nichols, Administrative Assistant, 573-882-8370, E-mail: nicholsdi@missouri.edu.
Website: http://www.geog.missouri.edu/?q=grad/graduate-program

University of Nebraska at Omaha, Graduate Studies, College of Arts and Sciences, Department of Geography and Geology, Omaha, NE 68182. Offers geographic information science (Certificate); geography (MA). Part-time programs available. *Faculty:* 11 full-time (3 women). *Students:* 9 full-time (3 women), 20 part-time (5 women); includes 1 minority (Two or more races, non-Hispanic/Latino), 1 international. Average age 29. 15 applicants, 47% accepted, 4 enrolled. In 2014, 7 master's, 1 other advanced degree awarded. *Degree requirements:* For master's, comprehensive exam, thesis (for some programs). *Entrance requirements:* For master's, GRE, minimum GPA of 3.0, 15 undergraduate geography hours, transcripts, resume, statement of purpose, 2 letters of recommendation; for Certificate, minimum GPA of 3.0, transcripts, resume, statement of purpose, 2 letters of recommendation. Additional exam requirements/recommendations for international students: Required—TOEFL, IELTS, PTE. *Application deadline:* For fall admission, 7/1 priority date for domestic and international students; for spring admission, 12/1 priority date for domestic and international students; for summer admission, 5/1 for domestic and international students. Applications are processed on a rolling basis. Application fee: $45. Electronic applications accepted. *Financial support:* In 2014–15, 12 students received support, including 12 teaching assistantships with tuition reimbursements available; fellowships, research assistantships with tuition reimbursements available, Federal Work-Study, institutionally sponsored loans, scholarships/grants, tuition waivers (partial), and unspecified assistantships also available. Support available to part-time students. Financial award application deadline: 3/1; financial award applicants required to submit FAFSA. *Unit head:* Dr. Robert Schuster, Chairperson, 402-554-2341, E-mail: graduate@unomaha.edu. *Application contact:* Dr. Michael Peterson, Graduate Program Chair, 402-554-2341, E-mail: graduate@unomaha.edu.

University of New Hampshire, Graduate School, Interdisciplinary Programs, Program in Geospatial Science, Durham, NH 03824. Offers Postbaccalaureate Certificate. *Students:* 2 part-time (both women). Average age 31. 3 applicants, 100% accepted, 2 enrolled. In 2014, 2 Postbaccalaureate Certificates awarded. *Entrance requirements:* For degree, official transcripts, 2 letters of recommendation, personal statement/essay. Additional exam requirements/recommendations for international students: Required—TOEFL (minimum score 550 paper-based; 80 iBT). *Application deadline:* For fall admission, 7/1 for domestic students; for spring admission, 12/1 for domestic students. Applications are processed on a rolling basis. Application fee: $25. Electronic applications accepted. *Expenses:* Tuition, state resident: full-time $13,500; part-time $750 per credit hour. Tuition, nonresident: full-time $26,460; part-time $1110 per credit hour. *Required fees:* $1788; $447 per semester. *Financial support:* Fellowships, research assistantships, and teaching assistantships available. *Unit head:* Michael Routhier, Coordinator, 603-862-1792, E-mail: mike.routhier@unh.edu. *Application contact:* Sharon Andrews, Administrative Assistant, 603-862-3005, E-mail: college.teaching@unh.edu.
Website: http://gss.unh.edu/

University of New Haven, Graduate School, College of Arts and Sciences, Program in Environmental Science, West Haven, CT 06516-1916. Offers environmental ecology (MS); environmental education (MS); environmental geoscience (MS); environmental health and management (MS); environmental science (MS); geographical information systems (MS, Certificate). Part-time and evening/weekend programs available. *Degree requirements:* For master's, thesis optional, research project. *Entrance requirements:* Additional exam requirements/recommendations for international students: Required—TOEFL (minimum score 80 iBT), IELTS, PTE (minimum score 53). Electronic applications accepted. Application fee is waived when completed online. *Expenses: Tuition:* Full-time $22,248; part-time $824 per credit hour. *Required fees:* $45 per trimester. *Faculty research:* Mapping and assessing geological and living resources in Long Island Sound, geology, San Salvador Island, Bahamas.

University of North Alabama, College of Arts and Sciences, Department of Geography, Florence, AL 35632-0001. Offers geospatial science (MS). Part-time and evening/weekend programs available. *Faculty:* 7 full-time (2 women). *Students:* 8 full-time (1 woman), 2 part-time (0 women); includes 3 minority (2 Black or African American, non-Hispanic/Latino; 1 Asian, non-Hispanic/Latino), 1 international. Average age 28. 4 applicants, 50% accepted, 2 enrolled. In 2014, 4 master's awarded. *Degree requirements:* For master's, comprehensive exam (for some programs), thesis optional. *Entrance requirements:* For master's, GRE, 3 letters of recommendation, personal statement, letter of intent. Additional exam requirements/recommendations for international students: Required—TOEFL (minimum score 550 paper-based; 79 iBT), IELTS (minimum score 6). *Application deadline:* For fall admission, 7/1 for domestic and international students; for spring admission, 12/1 for domestic and international students. Applications are processed on a rolling basis. Application fee: $25 ($50 for international students). Electronic applications accepted. *Expenses:* Tuition, state resident: full-time $5166; part-time $1722 per semester. Tuition, nonresident: full-time $10,332; part-time $3444 per semester. *Required fees:* $393.50 per semester. *Financial support:* Applicants required to submit FAFSA. *Unit head:* Dr. Francis T. Koti, Chair, 256-765-4219, E-mail: ftkoti@una.edu. *Application contact:* Hillary N. Coats, Graduate Admissions Coordinator, 256-765-4447, E-mail: graduate@una.edu.
Website: http://www.una.edu/geography/

The University of North Carolina at Charlotte, College of Liberal Arts and Sciences, Department of Geography and Earth Sciences, Charlotte, NC 28223-0001. Offers earth sciences (MS); geography (MA), including community planning, geographic location science and technologies, location analysis, transportation studies, urban regional analysis; geography and urban regional analysis (PhD). Part-time and evening/weekend programs available. *Faculty:* 30 full-time (10 women), 1 part-time/adjunct (0 women). *Students:* 42 full-time (25 women), 29 part-time (14 women); includes 4 minority (2 Black or African American, non-Hispanic/Latino; 1 Hispanic/Latino; 1 Native Hawaiian or other Pacific Islander, non-Hispanic/Latino), 17 international. Average age 31. 51 applicants, 76% accepted, 16 enrolled. In 2014, 17 master's, 3 doctorates awarded. Terminal master's awarded for partial completion of doctoral program. *Degree requirements:* For master's, comprehensive exam, thesis or alternative, project. *Entrance requirements:* For master's, GRE General Test or MAT, Doppelt Mathematical Reasoning Test, minimum GPA of 3.0 in undergraduate major, 2.75 overall. Additional exam requirements/recommendations for international students: Required—TOEFL (minimum score 557 paper-based; 83 iBT). *Application deadline:* For fall admission, 4/1 for domestic and international students; for spring admission, 10/1 for domestic and international students. Application fee: $75. Electronic applications accepted. *Expenses:* Tuition, state resident: full-time $4008. Tuition, nonresident: full-time $16,295. *Required fees:* $2755. Tuition and fees vary according to course load and program. *Financial support:* In 2014–15, 38 students received support, including 10 research assistantships (averaging $10,140 per year), 28 teaching assistantships (averaging $8,748 per year); career-related internships or fieldwork, institutionally sponsored loans, scholarships/grants, and unspecified assistantships also available. Support available to part-time students. Financial award application deadline: 4/1; financial award applicants required to submit FAFSA. *Faculty research:* Improving geographic knowledge discovery and spatial reasoning with mobile and Web-based geographical information systems; an in-house supercomputing cluster for multi-scale science and collaborative research; feedback between a generalist pathogen, hosts and heterogeneous environments at multiple spatial and temporal scales. *Total annual research expenditures:* $620,703. *Unit head:* Dr. Craig Allan, Chair, 704-687-5999, Fax: 704-687-3182, E-mail: cjallan@uncc.edu. *Application contact:* Kathy B. Giddings, Director of Graduate Admissions, 704-687-5503, Fax: 704-687-1668, E-mail: gradadm@uncc.edu.
Website: https://geoearth.uncc.edu/

The University of North Carolina at Greensboro, Graduate School, College of Arts and Sciences, Department of Geography, Greensboro, NC 27412-5001. Offers applied geography (MA); geographic information science (Certificate); geography (PhD); urban and economic development (Certificate). *Degree requirements:* For master's, comprehensive exam, thesis or alternative. *Entrance requirements:* For master's, GRE General Test. Additional exam requirements/recommendations for international students: Required—TOEFL. Electronic applications accepted.

University of Pennsylvania, School of Design, Department of City and Regional Planning, Philadelphia, PA 19104. Offers city and regional planning (PhD); city planning (MCP); GIS and spatial analysis (Certificate); land preservation (Certificate); urban design (Certificate); urban redevelopment (Certificate); urban spatial analytics (MUSA). *Accreditation:* ACSP (one or more programs are accredited). *Faculty:* 15 full-time (6 women), 6 part-time/adjunct (0 women). *Students:* 158 full-time (87 women), 9 part-time (8 women); includes 32 minority (3 Black or African American, non-Hispanic/Latino; 15 Asian, non-Hispanic/Latino; 6 Hispanic/Latino; 1 Native Hawaiian or other Pacific Islander, non-Hispanic/Latino; 7 Two or more races, non-Hispanic/Latino), 62 international. 475 applicants, 46% accepted, 75 enrolled. In 2014, 89 master's, 3 other advanced degrees awarded. *Degree requirements:* For doctorate, thesis/dissertation, 20 approved courses, 4 seminars, 2 methods courses, writing and presentation/scholarly preparation, qualifying examination, final defense. *Entrance requirements:* For master's, GRE General Test; for doctorate, GRE General Test, writing sample. Additional exam requirements/recommendations for international students: Required—TOEFL, IELTS. *Application deadline:* For fall admission, 1/14 priority date for domestic and international students. Application fee: $80. Electronic applications accepted. *Financial support:* Fellowships, research assistantships, teaching assistantships, institutionally sponsored loans, scholarships/grants, and health care benefits available. Financial award application deadline: 2/15; financial award applicants required to submit FAFSA. *Faculty research:* Growth management, transportation planning, urban simulation modeling, housing, development planning. *Unit head:* Marilyn Jordan Taylor, Dean, 215-898-6520, E-mail: mjtaylor@design.upenn.edu. *Application contact:* Office of Admissions and Financial Aid, 215-898-6520, E-mail: admissions@design.upenn.edu.
Website: http://www.design.upenn.edu/city-regional-planning/graduate/work

University of Pittsburgh, Dietrich School of Arts and Sciences, Department of Geology and Planetary Science, Pittsburgh, PA 15260-3332. Offers geographical information systems and remote sensing (Pro-MS); geology and planetary science (MS, PhD). Part-time programs available. *Faculty:* 9 full-time (3 women), 4 part-time/adjunct (0 women). *Students:* 38 full-time (16 women), 1 international. Average age 29. 58 applicants, 34% accepted, 11 enrolled. In 2014, 3 master's, 1 doctorate awarded. *Degree requirements:* For master's, thesis, oral thesis defense; for doctorate, comprehensive exam, thesis/dissertation, oral dissertation defense. *Entrance requirements:* For master's and doctorate, GRE General Test. Additional exam requirements/recommendations for international students: Required—TOEFL (minimum score 90 iBT), IELTS (minimum score 7). *Application deadline:* For fall admission, 1/15 priority date for domestic and international students. Applications are processed on a rolling basis. Application fee: $50. Electronic applications accepted. *Expenses:* Tuition, state resident: full-time $20,742; part-time $838 per credit. Tuition, nonresident: full-time $33,960; part-time $1389 per credit. *Required fees:* $800; $205 per term. Tuition and fees vary according to program. *Financial support:* In 2014–15, 3 students received support, including 5 fellowships with full tuition reimbursements available (averaging $25,966 per year), 8 research assistantships with full and partial tuition reimbursements available (averaging $14,350 per year), 5 teaching assistantships with full and partial tuition reimbursements available (averaging $7,600 per year); career-related internships or fieldwork, Federal Work-Study, institutionally sponsored loans, scholarships/grants, health care benefits, and tuition waivers also available. Support available to part-time students. Financial award application deadline: 1/15; financial award applicants required to submit FAFSA. *Faculty research:* Tectonic, volcanic and surface processes, planetary science and astrobiology, paleoclimatology and environmental change, environmental geochemistry and biogeochemistry, energy geosciences, hydrologic processes. *Total annual research expenditures:* $2.1 million. *Unit head:* Dr. Mark Abbott, Chair, 412-624-8783, Fax: 412-624-3914, E-mail: mabbott1@pitt.edu. *Application contact:* Dr. Josef Werne, Director of Graduate Studies, 412-624-8775, Fax: 412-624-3914, E-mail: jwerne@pitt.edu.
Website: http://www.geology.pitt.edu/

University of Redlands, College of Arts and Sciences, Program in Geographic Information Systems, Redlands, CA 92373-0999. Offers MS. *Entrance requirements:* For master's, 2 years of professional experience using GIS or 2 university-level GIS courses plus internship, minimum undergraduate GPA of 3.0, 2 letters of recommendation. Additional exam requirements/recommendations for international students: Required—TOEFL (minimum score 550 paper-based); Recommended—IELTS (minimum score 5.5). Electronic applications accepted. *Expenses:* Contact institution.

University of Southern California, Graduate School, Dana and David Dornsife College of Letters, Arts and Sciences, Spatial Sciences Institute, Los Angeles, CA 90089. Offers geographic information science and technology (MS, Graduate Certificate). Part-time and evening/weekend programs available. Postbaccalaureate distance learning degree programs offered (minimal on-campus study). Terminal master's awarded for partial completion of doctoral program. *Degree requirements:* For master's, thesis. *Entrance requirements:* For master's, GRE. Additional exam requirements/recommendations for international students: Required—TOEFL. Electronic applications accepted. *Faculty research:* Geocoding, geocomputation, GIS, environmental exposure estimation, spatial data accuracy and uncertainty.

University of South Florida, College of Arts and Sciences, Department of Geography, Tampa, FL 33620-9951. Offers environmental geography (MA); environmental science and policy (MS); geographic information science and spatial analysis (MA); geography and environmental science and policy (PhD); human geography (MA); urban and

regional planning (MURP). Part-time and evening/weekend programs available. *Students:* 15 full-time (9 women), 12 part-time (4 women); includes 11 minority (4 Black or African American, non-Hispanic/Latino; 5 Hispanic/Latino; 2 Two or more races, non-Hispanic/Latino), 2 international. Average age 32. 39 applicants, 62% accepted, 9 enrolled. In 2014, 10 master's awarded. *Degree requirements:* For master's, comprehensive exam, thesis (for some programs); for doctorate, comprehensive exam, thesis/dissertation. *Entrance requirements:* For master's, GRE General Test (within the last 5 years), minimum GPA of 3.0 for last 60 credits of undergraduate degree, letter of intent, two letters of recommendation (three for MS); for doctorate, GRE General Test (within the last 5 years), minimum GPA of 3.2 for all academic work prior to admission, letter of intent, two letters of recommendation. Additional exam requirements/recommendations for international students: Required—TOEFL (minimum score 550 paper-based; 79 iBT) or IELTS (minimum score 6.5) for MA and MURP; TOEFL (minimum score 600 paper-based) for MS and PhD. *Application deadline:* For fall admission, 2/15 for domestic students, 1/2 for international students; for spring admission, 10/15 for domestic students, 6/1 for international students. Application fee: $30. *Financial support:* In 2014–15, 28 students received support, including 3 research assistantships (averaging $12,345 per year), 25 teaching assistantships with tuition reimbursements available (averaging $12,807 per year); unspecified assistantships also available. Financial award application deadline: 3/1. *Faculty research:* Geography: human geography, environmental geography, geographic information science and spatial analysis, urban geography, social theory; environmental science, policy, and planning: water resources, wildlife ecology, Karst and wetland environments, natural hazards, soil contamination, meteorology and climatology, environmental sustainability and policy, urban and regional planning. *Total annual research expenditures:* $89,465. *Unit head:* Dr. Jayajit Chakraborty, Professor and Chair, Geography Division, 813-974-8188, Fax: 813-974-5911, E-mail: jchakrab@usf.edu. *Application contact:* Dr. Jennifer Collins, Associate Professor and Graduate Program Coordinator, 813-974-4242, Fax: 813-974-5911, E-mail: collinsjm@usf.edu.
Website: http://gep.usf.edu/

University of South Florida, Innovative Education, Tampa, FL 33620-9951. *Unit head:* Kathy Barnes, Interdisciplinary Programs Coordinator, 813-974-8031, Fax: 813-974-7061, E-mail: barnesk@usf.edu. *Application contact:* Karen Tylinski, Metro Initiatives, 813-974-9943, Fax: 813-974-7061, E-mail: ktylinsk@usf.edu.
Website: http://www.usf.edu/innovative-education/

The University of Texas at Dallas, School of Economic, Political and Policy Sciences, Program in Geospatial Information Sciences, Richardson, TX 75080. Offers MS, PhD. Part-time and evening/weekend programs available. *Faculty:* 9 full-time (1 woman), 1 part-time/adjunct (0 women). *Students:* 40 full-time (15 women), 19 part-time (9 women); includes 12 minority (2 Black or African American, non-Hispanic/Latino; 4 Asian, non-Hispanic/Latino; 5 Hispanic/Latino; 1 Two or more races, non-Hispanic/Latino), 32 international. Average age 31. 79 applicants, 54% accepted, 14 enrolled. In 2014, 14 master's awarded. *Degree requirements:* For master's, thesis (for some programs), project or thesis; internship; for doctorate, comprehensive exam, thesis/dissertation. *Entrance requirements:* For master's and doctorate, GRE General Test, minimum GPA of 3.0 in upper-level coursework in field. Additional exam requirements/recommendations for international students: Required—TOEFL (minimum score 550 paper-based). *Application deadline:* For fall admission, 7/15 for domestic students, 5/1 priority date for international students; for spring admission, 11/15 for domestic students, 9/1 priority date for international students. Applications are processed on a rolling basis. Application fee: $50 ($100 for international students). Electronic applications accepted. *Expenses:* Tuition, state resident: full-time $11,940; part-time $663 per credit. Tuition, nonresident: full-time $22,282; part-time $1238 per credit. *Financial support:* In 2014–15, 26 students received support, including 5 fellowships (averaging $3,100 per year), 4 research assistantships with partial tuition reimbursements available (averaging $13,050 per year), 10 teaching assistantships with partial tuition reimbursements available (averaging $11,790 per year); career-related internships or fieldwork, Federal Work-Study, institutionally sponsored loans, scholarships/grants, and unspecified assistantships also available. Support available to part-time students. Financial award application deadline: 4/30; financial award applicants required to submit FAFSA. *Faculty research:* Urban and regional development, artificial intelligence techniques for geospatial investigation, improvement of current spatial analysis and modeling techniques, demographic studies. *Unit head:* Dr. Fang Qiu, Program Head, 972-883-4134, Fax: 972-883-2735, E-mail: ffqiu@utdallas.edu. *Application contact:* Dr. Daniel Griffith, Doctoral Advisor, 972-883-4950, Fax: 972-883-6297, E-mail: dagriffith@utdallas.edu.
Website: http://www.utdallas.edu/epps/geospatial-science/

The University of Toledo, College of Graduate Studies, College of Languages, Literature and Social Sciences, Department of Geography and Planning, Toledo, OH 43606-3390. Offers geographic information science and applied geographics (Certificate); geography and planning (MA); spatially-integrated social science (PhD). Part-time programs available. *Degree requirements:* For master's, comprehensive exam, thesis; for doctorate, thesis/dissertation. *Entrance requirements:* For master's and doctorate, GRE General Test, minimum cumulative point-hour ratio of 2.7 for all previous academic work, three letters of recommendation; for Certificate, minimum cumulative point-hour ratio of 2.7 for all previous academic work, three letters of recommendation. Additional exam requirements/recommendations for international students: Required—TOEFL (minimum score 550 paper-based; 80 iBT). Electronic applications accepted.

University of Utah, Graduate School, College of Social and Behavioral Science, Department of Geography, Salt Lake City, UT 84112-9155. Offers geographic information science (MS); geography (MA, MS, PhD). Part-time programs available. *Faculty:* 13 full-time (4 women), 9 part-time/adjunct (4 women). *Students:* 36 full-time (13 women), 17 part-time (4 women); includes 5 minority (1 Black or African American, non-Hispanic/Latino; 2 Asian, non-Hispanic/Latino; 2 Hispanic/Latino), 11 international. Average age 29. 66 applicants, 53% accepted, 19 enrolled. In 2014, 3 master's, 3 doctorates awarded. *Degree requirements:* For master's, variable foreign language requirement, thesis (for some programs), 6 research hours (for Geography MS) / skills portfolio (for MS in geographic information science); for doctorate, comprehensive exam, thesis/dissertation, 14 research hours / 2 consecutive full-time semesters. *Entrance requirements:* For master's, GRE General Test (not required for MS in geographic information science), minimum undergraduate GPA of 3.0; for doctorate, GRE General Test, minimum undergraduate GPA of 3.0. Additional exam requirements/recommendations for international students: Required—TOEFL (minimum score 550 paper-based; 80 iBT), IELTS (minimum score 6.5). *Application deadline:* For fall admission, 1/10 priority date for domestic and international students; for spring admission, 10/1 for domestic and international students. Application fee: $55 ($65 for international students). Electronic applications accepted. *Expenses:* Expenses: Contact institution. *Financial support:* In 2014–15, 26 students received support, including 3 fellowships with full tuition reimbursements available (averaging $24,000 per year), 10 research assistantships with full tuition reimbursements available (averaging $16,000 per year), 8 teaching assistantships with full tuition reimbursements available (averaging $15,000 per year); career-related internships or fieldwork, Federal Work-Study, scholarships/grants, health care benefits, and unspecified assistantships also available.

Financial award application deadline: 3/15; financial award applicants required to submit FAFSA. *Faculty research:* Urban-economic geography, earth system science, geographic information science and remote sensing, paleoenvironmental studies, hazards. *Total annual research expenditures:* $876,578. *Unit head:* Dr. Andrea R. Brunelle, Chair, 801-581-8218, Fax: 801-581-8219, E-mail: andrea.brunelle@geog.utah.edu. *Application contact:* Dr. Philip E. Dennison, Director of Graduate Studies, 801-581-8218, Fax: 801-581-8219, E-mail: dennison@geog.utah.edu.
Website: http://www.geog.utah.edu

University of West Georgia, College of Science and Mathematics, Department of Geosciences, Carrollton, GA 30118. Offers geographic information systems (Certificate). Part-time and evening/weekend programs available. Postbaccalaureate distance learning degree programs offered (no on-campus study). *Faculty:* 8 full-time (3 women). *Students:* 1 (woman) full-time, 6 part-time (4 women); includes 2 minority (both Black or African American, non-Hispanic/Latino). Average age 47. 7 applicants, 86% accepted, 4 enrolled. In 2014, 8 Certificates awarded. *Entrance requirements:* Additional exam requirements/recommendations for international students: Required—TOEFL (minimum score 523 paper-based; 69 iBT); Recommended—IELTS (minimum score 6). *Application deadline:* For fall admission, 5/1 for domestic students, 6/1 for international students; for spring admission, 11/15 for domestic students, 10/15 for international students. Applications are processed on a rolling basis. Application fee: $40. Electronic applications accepted. *Financial support:* Application deadline: 4/1; applicants required to submit FAFSA. *Unit head:* Dr. James R. Mayer, Chair, 678-839-4055, Fax: 678-839-4071, E-mail: jmayer@westga.edu. *Application contact:* Anita Bryant, Departmental Assistant, 678-839-6479, E-mail: abryant@westga.edu.
Website: http://www.westga.edu/~geosci/geoweb

University of Wisconsin–Madison, Graduate School, College of Letters and Science, Department of Geography, Madison, WI 53706-1380. Offers cartography and geographic information systems (MS); geographic information systems (Certificate); geography (MS, PhD). Part-time programs available. *Degree requirements:* For master's, thesis; for doctorate, thesis/dissertation; for Certificate, internship. *Entrance requirements:* For master's and doctorate, GRE General Test, minimum GPA of 3.25. Electronic applications accepted. *Expenses:* Tuition, state resident: full-time $10,723; part-time $745 per credit. Tuition, nonresident: full-time $24,054; part-time $1578 per credit. *Required fees:* $374 per semester. Tuition and fees vary according to course load, program and reciprocity agreements. *Faculty research:* Physical geography, urban/historical geography, people-environment, history of cartography, GIS.

University of Wisconsin–Milwaukee, Graduate School, School of Architecture and Urban Planning, Department of Urban Planning, Milwaukee, WI 53201-0413. Offers geographic information systems (Certificate); real estate development (Certificate); urban planning (MUP); M Arch/MUP; MPA/MUP; MUP/MS. *Accreditation:* ACSP. Part-time programs available. *Degree requirements:* For master's, comprehensive exam, thesis or alternative. *Entrance requirements:* For master's, GRE General Test. Additional exam requirements/recommendations for international students: Required—TOEFL (minimum score 550 paper-based; 79 iBT), IELTS (minimum score 6.5). Electronic applications accepted.

Virginia Commonwealth University, Graduate School, College of Humanities and Sciences, Wilder School of Government and Public Affairs, Department of Urban Studies and Planning, Program in Geographic Information Systems, Richmond, VA 23284-9005. Offers Certificate. *Entrance requirements:* Additional exam requirements/recommendations for international students: Required—TOEFL (minimum score 600 paper-based; 100 iBT); Recommended—IELTS (minimum score 6.5). Electronic applications accepted.

Virginia Polytechnic Institute and State University, Graduate School, College of Natural Resources and Environment, Blacksburg, VA 24061. Offers fisheries and wildlife (MS, PhD); forestry and forest products (MF, MS, PhD); geography (MS); geospatial and environmental analysis (PhD); natural resources (MNR). *Faculty:* 72 full-time (15 women), 1 part-time/adjunct (0 women). *Students:* 192 full-time (80 women), 87 part-time (45 women); includes 22 minority (5 Black or African American, non-Hispanic/Latino; 5 Asian, non-Hispanic/Latino; 11 Hispanic/Latino; 1 Two or more races, non-Hispanic/Latino), 46 international. Average age 31. 145 applicants, 59% accepted, 67 enrolled. In 2014, 99 master's, 12 doctorates awarded. *Degree requirements:* For master's, comprehensive exam (for some programs), thesis (for some programs); for doctorate, comprehensive exam (for some programs), thesis/dissertation (for some programs). *Entrance requirements:* For master's and doctorate, GRE/GMAT (may vary by department). Additional exam requirements/recommendations for international students: Required—TOEFL (minimum score 550 paper-based). *Application deadline:* For fall admission, 8/1 for domestic students, 4/1 for international students; for spring admission, 1/1 for domestic students, 9/1 for international students. Applications are processed on a rolling basis. Application fee: $75. Electronic applications accepted. *Expenses:* Tuition, state resident: full-time $11,656; part-time $647.50 per credit hour. Tuition, nonresident: full-time $23,351; part-time $1297.25 per credit hour. *Required fees:* $2533; $465.75 per semester. Tuition and fees vary according to course load, campus/location and program. *Financial support:* In 2014–15, 98 research assistantships with full tuition reimbursements (averaging $22,448 per year), 38 teaching assistantships with full tuition reimbursements (averaging $20,346 per year) were awarded. Financial award application deadline: 3/1; financial award applicants required to submit FAFSA. *Total annual research expenditures:* $15.1 million. *Unit head:* Dr. Paul M. Winistorfer, Dean, 540-231-5481, Fax: 540-231-7664, E-mail: pstorfer@vt.edu. *Application contact:* Arlice Banks, Executive Secretary to the Dean, 540-231-7051, Fax: 540-231-7664, E-mail: arbanks@vt.edu.
Website: http://cnre.vt.edu/

West Chester University of Pennsylvania, College of Business and Public Affairs, Department of Geography and Planning, West Chester, PA 19383. Offers geographic information systems (Certificate); geography (MA); urban and regional planning (MPA, Certificate). Part-time and evening/weekend programs available. Postbaccalaureate distance learning degree programs offered (no on-campus study). *Faculty:* 6 full-time (3 women). *Students:* 16 full-time (3 women), 9 part-time (5 women); includes 1 minority (Black or African American, non-Hispanic/Latino), 1 international. Average age 29. 18 applicants, 100% accepted, 10 enrolled. In 2014, 12 master's, 21 other advanced degrees awarded. *Degree requirements:* For master's, thesis optional, 33 credits or 11 courses: 5-6 required, 5-6 electives, thesis or independent research course; for Certificate, 18 credits or 6 courses. *Entrance requirements:* For master's and Certificate, minimum GPA of 2.8, resume, two letters of recommendation. Additional exam requirements/recommendations for international students: Required—TOEFL (minimum score 550 paper-based; 80 iBT). *Application deadline:* For fall admission, 4/15 priority date for domestic students, 3/15 for international students; for spring admission, 10/15 priority date for domestic students, 9/1 for international students. Applications are processed on a rolling basis. Application fee: $45. Electronic applications accepted. *Expenses:* Tuition, state resident: full-time $8172; part-time $454 per credit. Tuition, nonresident: full-time $12,258; part-time $681 per credit. *Required fees:* $2231; $110.78 per credit. Tuition and fees vary according to campus/location and program. *Financial support:* Unspecified assistantships available. Support available to part-time students.

Geographic Information Systems

Financial award application deadline: 2/15; financial award applicants required to submit FAFSA. *Faculty research:* Sustainability and environmental conservation, land use/suburban planning, geographic information systems, transportation planning, housing. *Unit head:* Dr. Dottie Ives Dewey, Chair/Graduate Coordinator for GIS Certificate Program, 610-436-2746, Fax: 610-436-2889, E-mail: divesdewey@wcupa.edu. *Application contact:* Dr. Matin Katirai, Graduate Coordinator, 610-436-2392, Fax: 610-436-2889, E-mail: mkatirai@wcupa.edu.
Website: http://www.wcupa.edu/_academics/sch_sba.geo/default.asp

Western Illinois University, School of Graduate Studies, College of Arts and Sciences, Department of Biological Sciences, Macomb, IL 61455-1390. Offers biological sciences (MS); environmental geographic information systems (Certificate); zoo and aquarium studies (Certificate). Part-time programs available. *Students:* 43 full-time (31 women), 27 part-time (21 women); includes 6 minority (1 Black or African American, non-Hispanic/Latino; 3 Hispanic/Latino; 2 Two or more races, non-Hispanic/Latino), 12 international. Average age 27. 46 applicants, 89% accepted, 30 enrolled. In 2014, 15 master's, 28 other advanced degrees awarded. *Degree requirements:* For master's, thesis or alternative. *Entrance requirements:* Additional exam requirements/recommendations for international students: Required—TOEFL (minimum score 550 paper-based; 80 iBT); Recommended—IELTS. *Application deadline:* Applications are processed on a rolling basis. Application fee: $30. Electronic applications accepted. *Financial support:* In 2014–15, 31 students received support, including 7 research assistantships with full tuition reimbursements available (averaging $7,544 per year), 24 teaching assistantships with full tuition reimbursements available (averaging $8,688 per year). Financial award applicants required to submit FAFSA. *Unit head:* Dr. Charles Lydeard, Chairperson, 309-298-1546. *Application contact:* Dr. Nancy Parsons, Associate Provost and Director of Graduate Studies, 309-298-1806, Fax: 309-298-2345, E-mail: grad-office@wiu.edu.
Website: http://wiu.edu/biology

Western Illinois University, School of Graduate Studies, College of Arts and Sciences, Department of Geography, Macomb, IL 61455-1390. Offers community development and planning (Certificate); geography (MA); GIS analysis (Certificate). Part-time programs available. *Students:* 12 full-time (5 women), 2 part-time (1 woman); includes 3 minority (2 Black or African American, non-Hispanic/Latino; 1 Hispanic/Latino). Average age 27. 14 applicants, 86% accepted, 6 enrolled. In 2014, 2 master's, 2 other advanced degrees awarded. *Degree requirements:* For master's, thesis or alternative. *Entrance requirements:* Additional exam requirements/recommendations for international students: Required—TOEFL (minimum score 550 paper-based; 80 iBT). *Application deadline:* Applications are processed on a rolling basis. Application fee: $30. Electronic applications accepted. *Financial support:* In 2014–15, 8 students received support, including 2 research assistantships with full tuition reimbursements available (averaging $7,544 per year), 6 teaching assistantships with full tuition reimbursements available (averaging $8,688 per year). Financial award applicants required to submit FAFSA. *Unit head:* Dr. Sam Thompson, Chairperson, 309-298-1648. *Application contact:* Dr. Nancy Parsons, Associate Provost and Director of Graduate School, 309-298-1806, Fax: 309-298-2345, E-mail: grad-office@wiu.edu.
Website: http://wiu.edu/geography

Western Michigan University, Graduate College, College of Arts and Sciences, Department of Geography, Kalamazoo, MI 49008. Offers geographic information science (Graduate Certificate); geography (MA). *Degree requirements:* For master's, thesis. *Application deadline:* For fall admission, 2/15 for domestic students. *Financial support:* Application deadline: 2/15. *Application contact:* Admissions and Orientation, 269-387-2000, Fax: 269-387-2096.

West Virginia University, Eberly College of Arts and Sciences, Department of Geology and Geography, Program in Geography, Morgantown, WV 26506. Offers energy and environmental resources (MA); geographic information systems (PhD); geography-regional development (PhD); GIS/cartographic analysis (MA); regional development (MA). Part-time programs available. *Degree requirements:* For master's, thesis, oral and written exams; for doctorate, comprehensive exam, thesis/dissertation, oral and written exams. *Entrance requirements:* For master's and doctorate, GRE General Test, minimum GPA of 3.0. Additional exam requirements/recommendations for international students: Required—TOEFL. Electronic applications accepted. *Faculty research:* Space, place and development, geographic information science, environmental geography.

Wilmington University, College of Technology, New Castle, DE 19720-6491. Offers geographic information systems (MS); information assurance (MS); information systems technologies (MS); Internet/Web design (MS); management and management information systems (MS). Part-time and evening/weekend programs available. *Faculty:* 5 full-time (2 women), 53 part-time/adjunct (14 women). *Students:* 674 full-time (197 women), 131 part-time (55 women); includes 48 minority (35 Black or African American, non-Hispanic/Latino; 3 American Indian or Alaska Native, non-Hispanic/Latino; 6 Asian, non-Hispanic/Latino; 4 Hispanic/Latino), 708 international. Average age 27. 679 applicants, 100% accepted, 423 enrolled. In 2014, 102 master's awarded. *Entrance requirements:* Additional exam requirements/recommendations for international students: Required—TOEFL (minimum score 500 paper-based). *Application deadline:* Applications are processed on a rolling basis. Application fee: $35. Electronic applications accepted. *Unit head:* Dr. Edward L. Guthrie, Dean, 302-356-6870. *Application contact:* Laura Morris, Director of Admissions, 877-967-5464, E-mail: infocenter@wilmu.edu.
Website: http://www.wilmu.edu/technology/

Geography

Appalachian State University, Cratis D. Williams Graduate School, Department of Geography and Planning, Boone, NC 28608. Offers geography (MA), including geographic information science, planning. Part-time programs available. Postbaccalaureate distance learning degree programs offered (no on-campus study). *Degree requirements:* For master's, comprehensive exam, thesis or alternative. *Entrance requirements:* For master's, GRE General Test, 3 letters of recommendation. Additional exam requirements/recommendations for international students: Required—TOEFL (minimum score 570 paper-based; 79 iBT), IELTS (minimum score 6.5). Electronic applications accepted. *Faculty research:* Global change, climatology, production cartography, geographic information systems, North Carolina geography, Latin America.

Arizona State University at the Tempe campus, College of Liberal Arts and Sciences, School of Geographical Sciences and Urban Planning, Tempe, AZ 85287-5302. Offers geographic information systems (MAS); geographical information science (Graduate Certificate); geography (MA, PhD); transportation systems (Graduate Certificate); urban and environmental planning (MUEP); urban planning (PhD). Terminal master's awarded for partial completion of doctoral program. *Degree requirements:* For master's, thesis, interactive Program of Study (iPOS) submitted before completing 50 percent of required credit hours; for doctorate, comprehensive exam, thesis/dissertation, interactive Program of Study (iPOS) submitted before completing 50 percent of required credit hours. *Entrance requirements:* For master's and doctorate, GRE, minimum GPA of 3.0 or equivalent in last 2 years of work leading to bachelor's degree. Additional exam requirements/recommendations for international students: Required—TOEFL, IELTS, or PTE. Electronic applications accepted. *Expenses:* Contact institution.

Auburn University, Graduate School, College of Sciences and Mathematics, Department of Geology and Geography, Auburn University, AL 36849. Offers geography (MS); geology (MS). Part-time programs available. *Faculty:* 14 full-time (3 women), 3 part-time/adjunct (1 woman). *Students:* 19 full-time (8 women), 10 part-time (3 women), 9 international. Average age 26. 26 applicants, 62% accepted, 9 enrolled. In 2014, 10 master's awarded. *Degree requirements:* For master's, computer language or geographic information systems, field camp. *Entrance requirements:* For master's, GRE General Test. *Application deadline:* For fall admission, 7/7 for domestic students; for spring admission, 11/24 for domestic students. Applications are processed on a rolling basis. Application fee: $50 ($60 for international students). Electronic applications accepted. *Expenses:* Tuition, state resident: full-time $8586; part-time $477 per credit hour. Tuition, nonresident: full-time $25,758; part-time $1431 per credit hour. *Required fees:* $804 per semester. Tuition and fees vary according to degree level and program. *Financial support:* Research assistantships, teaching assistantships, and Federal Work-Study available. Support available to part-time students. Financial award application deadline: 3/15; financial award applicants required to submit FAFSA. *Faculty research:* Empirical magma dynamics and melt migration, ore mineralogy, role of terrestrial plant biomass in deposition, metamorphic petrology and isotope geochemistry, reef development, crinoid topology. *Unit head:* Dr. Mark Steltenpohl, Interim Chair, 334-844-4893. *Application contact:* Dr. George Flowers, Dean of the Graduate School, 334-844-2125.

Ball State University, Graduate School, College of Sciences and Humanities, Department of Geography, Muncie, IN 47306-1099. Offers MS. *Faculty:* 6 full-time (2 women). *Students:* 2 full-time (both women), 7 part-time (3 women). Average age 25. 14 applicants, 43% accepted, 2 enrolled. In 2014, 2 master's awarded. Application fee: $50. *Financial support:* In 2014–15, 6 students received support, including 7 teaching assistantships with partial tuition reimbursements available (averaging $10,187 per year); unspecified assistantships also available. Financial award application deadline: 3/1. *Faculty research:* Remote sensing, tourism and recreation, Latin American urbanization. *Unit head:* Dr. Gopalan Venugopal, Chairman, 765-285-1776, E-mail: gvenugop@bsu.edu. *Application contact:* Dr. Christopher Airriess, Associate Provost for Research and Dean of the Graduate School, 765-285-1614, E-mail: cairriess@bsu.edu.
Website: http://www.bsu.edu/geography/

Binghamton University, State University of New York, Graduate School, School of Arts and Sciences, Department of Geography, Vestal, NY 13850. Offers MA. *Faculty:* 9 full-time (3 women), 4 part-time/adjunct (2 women). *Students:* 23 full-time (10 women), 11 part-time (4 women); includes 9 minority (2 Black or African American, non-Hispanic/Latino; 1 American Indian or Alaska Native, non-Hispanic/Latino; 1 Asian, non-Hispanic/Latino; 3 Hispanic/Latino; 2 Two or more races, non-Hispanic/Latino), 7 international. Average age 27. 26 applicants, 100% accepted, 12 enrolled. In 2014, 10 master's awarded. *Degree requirements:* For master's, one foreign language, thesis (for some programs). *Entrance requirements:* For master's, GRE General Test. Additional exam requirements/recommendations for international students: Required—TOEFL (minimum score 550 paper-based; 80 iBT). *Application deadline:* For fall admission, 5/15 priority date for domestic and international students; for spring admission, 10/15 priority date for domestic and international students. Applications are processed on a rolling basis. Application fee: $75. Electronic applications accepted. *Expenses:* Tuition, state resident: full-time $7776; part-time $432 per credit. Tuition, nonresident: full-time $15,138; part-time $841 per credit. *Required fees:* $1754; $213 per credit. Tuition and fees vary according to degree level and program. *Financial support:* In 2014–15, 13 students received support, including 8 teaching assistantships with full tuition reimbursements available (averaging $15,000 per year); career-related internships or fieldwork, Federal Work-Study, institutionally sponsored loans, scholarships/grants, health care benefits, tuition waivers (full and partial), and unspecified assistantships also available. Financial award application deadline: 2/15; financial award applicants required to submit FAFSA. *Unit head:* Dr. Norah Henry, Chairperson, 607-777-2755, E-mail: nhenry@binghamton.edu. *Application contact:* Kishan Zuber, Recruiting and Admissions Coordinator, 607-777-2151, Fax: 607-777-2501, E-mail: kzuber@binghamton.edu.

Boston University, Graduate School of Arts and Sciences, Department of Earth and Environment, Boston, MA 02215. Offers earth sciences (MA, PhD); energy and environmental analysis (MA); environmental remote sensing and GIS (MA); geography and environment (MA, PhD); global development policy (MA); international relations and environmental policy (MA). *Students:* 67 full-time (31 women), 5 part-time (2 women); includes 6 minority (4 Asian, non-Hispanic/Latino; 2 Hispanic/Latino), 19 international. Average age 29. 213 applicants, 34% accepted, 16 enrolled. In 2014, 1 master's, 4 doctorates awarded. *Degree requirements:* For master's, comprehensive exam (for some programs), thesis (for some programs); for doctorate, comprehensive exam, thesis/dissertation. *Entrance requirements:* For master's and doctorate, GRE, 3 letters of recommendation, official transcripts, personal statement. Additional exam requirements/recommendations for international students: Required—TOEFL (minimum score 550 paper-based; 84 iBT). *Application deadline:* For fall admission, 1/31 for domestic and international students; for winter admission, 11/1 for domestic and international students. Application fee: $80. Electronic applications accepted. *Expenses: Tuition:* Full-time $45,686; part-time $1428 per credit hour. *Required fees:* $660; $60 per semester. Tuition and fees vary according to program. *Financial support:* In 2014–15, 59 students received support, including 2 fellowships with full tuition reimbursements available (averaging $20,500 per year), 25 research assistantships with full tuition reimbursements available (averaging $20,500 per year), 19 teaching assistantships with full tuition reimbursements available (averaging $20,500 per year); Federal Work-Study, scholarships/grants, traineeships, and health care benefits also available. Financial award application deadline: 1/31. *Faculty research:* Biogeosciences, climate and surface

processes; energy, environment and society; geographical sciences; geology, geochemistry and geophysics. *Unit head:* Curtis Woodcock, Chair, 617-353-5746, E-mail: curtis@bu.edu. *Application contact:* Nora Watson, Graduate Program Coordinator, 617-353-2529, Fax: 617-353-8399, E-mail: norala31@bu.edu. Website: http://www.bu.edu/earth/

Brock University, Faculty of Graduate Studies, Faculty of Social Sciences, Program in Geography, St. Catharines, ON L2S 3A1, Canada. Offers MA. Part-time programs available. *Degree requirements:* For master's, thesis optional. *Entrance requirements:* For master's, honors degree. Additional exam requirements/recommendations for international students: Required—TOEFL (minimum score 550 paper-based; 80 iBT), IELTS (minimum score 6.5), TWE (minimum score 4).

California State University, East Bay, Office of Academic Programs and Graduate Studies, College of Letters, Arts, and Social Sciences, Department of Anthropology, Geography and Environmental Studies, Hayward, CA 94542-3000. Offers anthropology (MA); geography (MA). Part-time programs available. *Degree requirements:* For master's, variable foreign language requirement, project or thesis. *Entrance requirements:* For master's, minimum GPA of 3.0 in field. Additional exam requirements/recommendations for international students: Required—TOEFL (minimum score 550 paper-based). *Application deadline:* For fall admission, 6/30 for domestic and international students. Applications are processed on a rolling basis. Application fee: $55. Electronic applications accepted. *Expenses:* Tuition, state resident: full-time $7830; part-time $1302 per credit hour. Tuition, nonresident: full-time $16,368. *Required fees:* $327 per quarter. Tuition and fees vary according to course load and program. *Financial support:* Fellowships, teaching assistantships, career-related internships or fieldwork, Federal Work-Study, institutionally sponsored loans, and scholarships/grants available. Support available to part-time students. Financial award application deadline: 3/2; financial award applicants required to submit FAFSA. *Faculty research:* Sustainability, water resources, GIS, mapping. *Unit head:* Dr. David Larson, Chair, 510-885-3192, E-mail: david.larson@csueastbay.edu. *Application contact:* Prof. David Woo, Graduate Advisor for Geography, 510-885-3160, Fax: 510-885-2353, E-mail: david.woo@csueastbay.edu.
Website: http://www20.csueastbay.edu/class/departments/ages/index.html

California State University, Fullerton, Graduate Studies, College of Humanities and Social Sciences, Department of Geography, Fullerton, CA 92834-9480. Offers MA. Part-time programs available. *Students:* 5 full-time (3 women), 15 part-time (7 women); includes 5 minority (1 Asian, non-Hispanic/Latino; 4 Hispanic/Latino), 1 international. Average age 36. 7 applicants, 100% accepted, 4 enrolled. In 2014, 6 master's awarded. *Degree requirements:* For master's, comprehensive exam or thesis. *Entrance requirements:* For master's, minimum GPA of 3.0, 18 undergraduate credits in field. Application fee: $55. *Financial support:* Career-related internships or fieldwork, Federal Work-Study, institutionally sponsored loans, and scholarships/grants available. Support available to part-time students. Financial award application deadline: 3/1; financial award applicants required to submit FAFSA. *Faculty research:* Human geography, physical geography. *Unit head:* Dr. John Carroll, Chair, 657-278-3161. *Application contact:* Admissions/Applications, 657-278-2371.

California State University, Long Beach, Graduate Studies, College of Liberal Arts, Department of Geography, Long Beach, CA 90840. Offers MA. Part-time programs available. *Degree requirements:* For master's, thesis. Electronic applications accepted. *Faculty research:* Demography, geographic information systems, world landforms and societies.

California State University, Los Angeles, Graduate Studies, College of Natural and Social Sciences, Department of Geography and Urban Analysis, Los Angeles, CA 90032-8530. Offers geography (MA). Part-time and evening/weekend programs available. *Degree requirements:* For master's, one foreign language, comprehensive exam or thesis. *Entrance requirements:* Additional exam requirements/recommendations for international students: Required—TOEFL (minimum score 500 paper-based). Electronic applications accepted. *Expenses:* Tuition, state resident: full-time $6738; part-time $3609 per year. Tuition, nonresident: full-time $15,666; part-time $8073 per year. Tuition and fees vary according to course load, degree level and program. *Faculty research:* Technique focus-air photography, cartography, location analysis.

California State University, Northridge, Graduate Studies, College of Social and Behavioral Sciences, Department of Geography, Northridge, CA 91330. Offers MA. Part-time programs available. *Students:* 20 full-time (4 women), 33 part-time (21 women); includes 19 minority (3 Asian, non-Hispanic/Latino; 16 Hispanic/Latino), 3 international. Average age 32. *Degree requirements:* For master's, one foreign language, thesis. *Entrance requirements:* For master's, GRE General Test or minimum GPA of 3.0. Additional exam requirements/recommendations for international students: Required—TOEFL. *Application deadline:* For fall admission, 11/30 for domestic students. Application fee: $55. *Expenses: Required fees:* $12,402. *Financial support:* Teaching assistantships available. Financial award application deadline: 3/1. *Unit head:* Edward Jackiewicz, Chair, 818-677-3532. *Application contact:* Dr. Edward Jackiewicz, Graduate Advisor, 818-677-4565.
Website: http://www.csun.edu/csbs/departments/geography/index.html

Carleton University, Faculty of Graduate Studies, Faculty of Arts and Social Sciences, Department of Geography and Environmental Studies, Ottawa, ON K1S 5B6, Canada. Offers geography (M Sc, MA, PhD). *Degree requirements:* For master's, thesis, seminar; for doctorate, one foreign language, thesis/dissertation, 2 comprehensive exams. *Entrance requirements:* For master's, honors degree; for doctorate, master's degree in geography. Additional exam requirements/recommendations for international students: Required—TOEFL. *Faculty research:* Human dimensions of global environmental change, winter environments, population studies, historical geography, globalization.

Central Connecticut State University, School of Graduate Studies, College of Liberal Arts and Social Sciences, Department of Geography, New Britain, CT 06050-4010. Offers MS. Part-time and evening/weekend programs available. *Faculty:* 5 full-time (2 women). *Students:* 10 full-time (5 women), 24 part-time (12 women); includes 4 minority (1 Black or African American, non-Hispanic/Latino; 1 Hispanic/Latino; 2 Two or more races, non-Hispanic/Latino), 1 international. Average age 31. 16 applicants, 69% accepted, 10 enrolled. In 2014, 9 master's awarded. *Degree requirements:* For master's, comprehensive exam, thesis or alternative. *Entrance requirements:* For master's, minimum undergraduate GPA of 3.0, essay. Additional exam requirements/recommendations for international students: Required—TOEFL (minimum score 550 paper-based; 79 iBT). *Application deadline:* For fall admission, 6/1 for domestic students, 5/1 for international students; for spring admission, 11/1 for domestic and international students. Applications are processed on a rolling basis. Application fee: $50. Electronic applications accepted. *Expenses: Tuition, area resident:* Full-time $5730; part-time $534 per credit. Tuition, state resident: full-time $8596; part-time $534 per credit. Tuition, nonresident: full-time $15,964; part-time $548 per credit. *Required fees:* $4211; $215 per credit. *Financial support:* In 2014–15, 1 student received support, including 1 research assistantship; career-related internships or fieldwork, Federal Work-Study, scholarships/grants, and unspecified assistantships also available. Support

available to part-time students. Financial award application deadline: 3/1; financial award applicants required to submit FAFSA. *Faculty research:* Regional planning, environmental protection, tourism, computer mapping and geographic information systems. *Unit head:* Dr. Cynthia Pope, Chair, 860-832-2785, E-mail: popec@ccsu.edu. *Application contact:* Patricia Gardner, Associate Director of Graduate Studies, 860-832-2350, Fax: 860-832-2362, E-mail: graduateadmissions@ccsu.edu.
Website: http://www.ccsu.edu/geography/

Chicago State University, School of Graduate and Professional Studies, College of Arts and Sciences, Department of Geography, Sociology, History, African-American Studies and Anthropology, Chicago, IL 60628. Offers geographic information systems (MA); geography (MA); history (MA). *Entrance requirements:* For master's, minimum GPA of 3.0.

Clark University, Graduate School, School of Geography, Worcester, MA 01610-1477. Offers MS, PhD. *Faculty:* 16 full-time (5 women). *Students:* 56 full-time (27 women); includes 3 minority (1 Black or African American, non-Hispanic/Latino; 1 Asian, non-Hispanic/Latino; 1 Hispanic/Latino), 22 international. Average age 30. 120 applicants, 21% accepted, 21 enrolled. In 2014, 5 master's, 5 doctorates awarded. *Degree requirements:* For doctorate, thesis/dissertation. *Entrance requirements:* For doctorate, GRE General Test. Additional exam requirements/recommendations for international students: Required—TOEFL. *Application deadline:* For fall admission, 12/31 priority date for domestic and international students. Applications are processed on a rolling basis. Application fee: $75. *Expenses: Tuition:* Full-time $40,380; part-time $1262 per credit hour. *Required fees:* $30. *Financial support:* In 2014–15, 3 fellowships with full tuition reimbursements (averaging $16,015 per year), 11 research assistantships with full tuition reimbursements (averaging $16,015 per year), 16 teaching assistantships with full tuition reimbursements (averaging $16,015 per year) were awarded; career-related internships or fieldwork and tuition waivers (full) also available. *Faculty research:* Global environmental change, geographic information systems, natural and technological hazards, water resources, urbanization. *Total annual research expenditures:* $2.3 million. *Unit head:* Dr. Anthony Bebbington, Director, 508-793-7336. *Application contact:* Brenda Nikas-Hayes, Admission Coordinator, 508-793-7336, Fax: 508-793-8881, E-mail: geography@clarku.edu.
Website: http://www.clarku.edu/departments/geography/index.cfm

Concordia University, School of Graduate Studies, Faculty of Arts and Science, Department of Geography, Planning and Environment, Montréal, QC H3G 1M8, Canada. Offers environmental impact assessment (Diploma); geography, urban and environmental studies (M Sc).

Concordia University, School of Graduate Studies, Faculty of Arts and Science, Department of Political Science, Montréal, QC H3G 1M8, Canada. Offers political science (PhD); public policy and public administration (MA), including geography. *Degree requirements:* For master's, one foreign language, comprehensive exam, thesis optional, internship. *Entrance requirements:* For master's, honors degree or equivalent. Additional exam requirements/recommendations for international students: Required—TOEFL. *Faculty research:* International public policy and administration, Quebec public administration, public policy and social/political theory, geography and public policy, public administration and decision making.

Concord University, Graduate Studies, Athens, WV 24712-1000. Offers educational leadership and supervision (M Ed); geography (M Ed); health promotion (MA); reading specialist (M Ed); special education (M Ed); teaching (MAT). Part-time and evening/weekend programs available. Postbaccalaureate distance learning degree programs offered (no on-campus study). *Faculty:* 20 full-time (13 women), 5 part-time/adjunct (3 women). *Students:* 77 full-time (59 women), 225 part-time (175 women); includes 28 minority (26 Black or African American, non-Hispanic/Latino; 1 American Indian or Alaska Native, non-Hispanic/Latino; 1 Hispanic/Latino), 2 international. Average age 34. 185 applicants, 67% accepted, 104 enrolled. In 2014, 55 master's awarded. *Degree requirements:* For master's, thesis (for some programs). *Entrance requirements:* For master's, GRE or MAT, baccalaureate degree with minimum GPA of 2.5 from regionally-accredited institution; teaching license; 2 letters of recommendation; completed disposition assessment form. *Application deadline:* Applications are processed on a rolling basis. Application fee: $25. Electronic applications accepted. *Expenses:* Tuition, state resident: full-time $3447; part-time $383 per semester hour. Tuition, nonresident: full-time $6010; part-time $667 per semester hour. *Financial support:* Tuition waivers and unspecified assistantships available. Financial award applicants required to submit FAFSA. *Unit head:* Dr. Cheryl Barnes, Interim Director, 304-384-5148, E-mail: ctrull@concord.edu. *Application contact:* Wendy Bailey, Academic Program Associate, 304-384-6223, E-mail: baileyw@concord.edu.
Website: http://www.concord.edu/graduate

East Carolina University, Graduate School, Thomas Harriot College of Arts and Sciences, Department of Geography, Planning, and Environment, Greenville, NC 27858-4353. Offers economic development (Certificate); geographic information science and technology (Certificate); geography (MA), including geography, planning, rural development. Part-time and evening/weekend programs available. *Degree requirements:* For master's, one foreign language, comprehensive exam, thesis optional. *Entrance requirements:* For master's, GRE General Test. Additional exam requirements/recommendations for international students: Required—TOEFL. *Expenses:* Tuition, state resident: full-time $4223. Tuition, nonresident: full-time $16,540. *Required fees:* $2184.

Eastern Michigan University, Graduate School, College of Arts and Sciences, Department of Geography and Geology, Ypsilanti, MI 48197. Offers earth science education (MS); geographic information systems (MS, Graduate Certificate), including geographic information systems (MS), GIS educator (Graduate Certificate), GIS planning (MS), GIS professional (Graduate Certificate); geography and geology (Graduate Certificate), including water resources; historic preservation (MS), including heritage interpretation and tourism, historic preservation; urban and regional planning (MS). Part-time and evening/weekend programs available. Postbaccalaureate distance learning degree programs offered (minimal on-campus study). *Faculty:* 21 full-time (8 women). *Students:* 39 full-time (26 women), 82 part-time (47 women); includes 9 minority (4 Black or African American, non-Hispanic/Latino; 3 Hispanic/Latino; 2 Two or more races, non-Hispanic/Latino), 18 international. Average age 33. 81 applicants, 79% accepted, 39 enrolled. In 2014, 35 master's, 7 other advanced degrees awarded. *Entrance requirements:* Additional exam requirements/recommendations for international students: Required—TOEFL. *Application deadline:* Applications are processed on a rolling basis. Application fee: $45. *Financial support:* Fellowships, research assistantships with full tuition reimbursements, teaching assistantships with full tuition reimbursements, career-related internships or fieldwork, Federal Work-Study, institutionally sponsored loans, scholarships/grants, tuition waivers (partial), and unspecified assistantships available. Support available to part-time students. Financial award applicants required to submit FAFSA. *Unit head:* Dr. Richard Sambrook, Department Head, 734-487-0218, Fax: 734-487-6979, E-mail: rsambroo@emich.edu.
Website: http://www.emich.edu/geo/

Florida Atlantic University, Charles E. Schmidt College of Science, Department of Geosciences, Boca Raton, FL 33431-0991. Offers geography (MA); geology (MS);

geosciences (PhD). Part-time programs available. *Degree requirements:* For master's, thesis (for some programs). *Entrance requirements:* For master's, GRE General Test, minimum GPA of 3.0. Additional exam requirements/recommendations for international students: Required—TOEFL (minimum score 500 paper-based; 61 iBT), IELTS (minimum score 6). Electronic applications accepted. *Expenses:* Tuition, state resident: full-time $7396; part-time $369.82 per credit hour. Tuition, nonresident: full-time $19,392; part-time $1024.81 per credit hour. Tuition and fees vary according to course load. *Faculty research:* GIS applications, paleontology, hydrogeology, economic development.

Florida State University, The Graduate School, College of Social Sciences and Public Policy, Department of Geography, Tallahassee, FL 32306. Offers geographic information science (MS); geography (MA, MS, PhD). Part-time programs available. *Faculty:* 9 full-time (2 women), 2 part-time/adjunct (0 women). *Students:* 39 full-time (18 women), 8 part-time (4 women); includes 13 minority (2 Black or African American, non-Hispanic/Latino; 9 Asian, non-Hispanic/Latino; 2 Hispanic/Latino), 9 international. Average age 29. 38 applicants, 68% accepted, 16 enrolled. In 2014, 21 master's, 2 doctorates awarded. Terminal master's awarded for partial completion of doctoral program. *Degree requirements:* For master's, thesis (for some programs); for doctorate, comprehensive exam, thesis/dissertation. *Entrance requirements:* For master's, GRE General Test, minimum GPA of 3.0; for doctorate, GRE General Test, minimum GPA of 3.0. Additional exam requirements/recommendations for international students: Required—TOEFL. *Application deadline:* For fall admission, 1/15 priority date for domestic students, 12/15 priority date for international students; for spring admission, 11/1 priority date for domestic students, 9/15 priority date for international students. Applications are processed on a rolling basis. Application fee: $30. Electronic applications accepted. *Expenses:* Tuition, state resident: part-time $403.51 per credit hour. Tuition, nonresident: part-time $1004.85 per credit hour. *Required fees:* $75.81 per credit hour. One-time fee: $20 part-time. Tuition and fees vary according to campus/location. *Financial support:* In 2014–15, 53 students received support, including 17 research assistantships with full tuition reimbursements available (averaging $16,240 per year), 36 teaching assistantships with full tuition reimbursements available (averaging $16,240 per year); career-related internships or fieldwork, Federal Work-Study, institutionally sponsored loans, scholarships/grants, health care benefits, tuition waivers (full and partial), and unspecified assistantships also available. Financial award application deadline: 1/15; financial award applicants required to submit FAFSA. *Faculty research:* Society-nature interactions, geographic information science, environmental studies, hurricanes, remote sensing, urban, transportation. *Total annual research expenditures:* $163,316. *Unit head:* Prof. Victor Mesev, Chair, 850-645-2498, Fax: 850-644-5913, E-mail: vmesev@fsu.edu. *Application contact:* Prof. Tingting Zhao, Graduate Director, 850-645-8198, Fax: 850-644-5193, E-mail: tzhao@fsu.edu.
Website: http://www.coss.fsu.edu/geography

Fort Hays State University, Graduate School, College of Arts and Sciences, Department of Geosciences, Program in Geosciences, Hays, KS 67601-4099. Offers geography (MS); geology (MS). *Degree requirements:* For master's, comprehensive exam, thesis. *Entrance requirements:* For master's, GRE General Test. Additional exam requirements/recommendations for international students: Required—TOEFL (minimum score 550 paper-based). Electronic applications accepted. *Faculty research:* Cretaceous and late Cenozoic stratigraphy, sedimentation, paleontology.

George Mason University, College of Science, Department of Geography and Geoinformation Science, Fairfax, VA 22030. Offers earth system science (MS); earth systems and geoinformation sciences (PhD); geographic and cartographic sciences (MS); geography and geoinformation science (Certificate); geoinformatics and geospatial intelligence (MS). *Faculty:* 17 full-time (4 women), 7 part-time/adjunct (0 women). *Students:* 54 full-time (17 women), 129 part-time (47 women); includes 33 minority (9 Black or African American, non-Hispanic/Latino; 2 American Indian or Alaska Native, non-Hispanic/Latino; 9 Asian, non-Hispanic/Latino; 8 Hispanic/Latino; 5 Two or more races, non-Hispanic/Latino), 25 international. Average age 35. 114 applicants, 55% accepted, 34 enrolled. In 2014, 17 master's, 10 doctorates, 15 other advanced degrees awarded. *Degree requirements:* For master's, thesis optional. *Entrance requirements:* For master's, GRE (waived for those who have earned a master's degree from U.S. institution), bachelor's degree with minimum GPA of 3.0; 2 copies of official transcripts; current resume; expanded goals statement; 3 letters of recommendation; for doctorate, GRE (waived for those who have earned a master's degree from U.S. institution), bachelor's degree with minimum GPA of 3.0; 2 copies of official transcripts; 3 letters of recommendation; resume; expanded goals statement; for Certificate, GRE (waived for those who have earned a master's degree from U.S. institution), baccalaureate degree with minimum GPA of 3.0; 2 official copies of transcripts; expanded goals statement; 3 letters of recommendation; resume. Additional exam requirements/recommendations for international students: Required—TOEFL (minimum score 570 paper-based; 80 iBT), IELTS (minimum score 6.5), PTE. *Application deadline:* For fall admission, 4/15 priority date for domestic students; for spring admission, 11/15 priority date for domestic students. Application fee: $65 ($80 for international students). Electronic applications accepted. *Expenses:* Tuition, state resident: full-time $9794; part-time $408 per credit hour. Tuition, nonresident: full-time $26,978; part-time $1124 per credit hour. *Required fees:* $2820; $118 per credit hour. Tuition and fees vary according to course load and program. *Financial support:* In 2014–15, 31 students received support, including 1 fellowship (averaging $9,302 per year), 23 research assistantships with full and partial tuition reimbursements available (averaging $16,864 per year), 8 teaching assistantships with full and partial tuition reimbursements available (averaging $13,392 per year); career-related internships or fieldwork, Federal Work-Study, scholarships/grants, unspecified assistantships, and health care benefits (for full-time research or teaching assistantship recipients) also available. Support available to part-time students. Financial award application deadline: 3/1; financial award applicants required to submit FAFSA. *Faculty research:* Global environment climate monitoring, gender and earth science, earth science education, remote sensing, planetary geology, hydrology, theoretical issues of geographic information data acquisition and processing. *Total annual research expenditures:* $2.2 million. *Unit head:* Anthony Stefanidis, Acting Chair, 703-993-9237, Fax: 703-993-9230, E-mail: astefani@gmu.edu. *Application contact:* Department of Geography and Geoinformation Sciences, 703-993-1210, Fax: 703-993-9299.
Website: http://ggs.gmu.edu/

The George Washington University, Columbian College of Arts and Sciences, Department of Geography, Washington, DC 20052. Offers MA, Graduate Certificate. *Faculty:* 12 full-time (5 women). *Students:* 17 full-time (11 women), 12 part-time (8 women); includes 2 minority (1 Black or African American, non-Hispanic/Latino; 1 Hispanic/Latino), 7 international. Average age 26. 54 applicants, 89% accepted, 19 enrolled. In 2014, 10 master's awarded. *Degree requirements:* For master's, comprehensive exam, thesis or alternative. *Entrance requirements:* For master's, GRE General Test, BA in geography or related field, minimum GPA of 3.0. Additional exam requirements/recommendations for international students: Required—TOEFL (minimum score 550 paper-based; 80 iBT). *Application deadline:* For fall admission, 4/1 priority date for domestic students, 1/15 priority date for international students; for spring admission, 10/1 priority date for domestic students, 9/1 priority date for international students. Applications are processed on a rolling basis. Application fee: $75. Electronic applications accepted. *Financial support:* In 2014–15, 10 students received support. Fellowships with tuition reimbursements available, teaching assistantships with tuition reimbursements available, Federal Work-Study, institutionally sponsored loans, and tuition waivers available. Financial award application deadline: 1/15. *Unit head:* Dr. Marie Price, Chair, 202-994-6187. *Application contact:* Information Contact, 202-994-6185, Fax: 202-994-2484.
Website: http://www.gwu.edu/~geog/

Georgia State University, College of Arts and Sciences, Department of Geosciences, Program in Geography, Atlanta, GA 30302-3083. Offers MS. Part-time programs available. *Degree requirements:* For master's, one foreign language, thesis or alternative, written and oral exams. *Entrance requirements:* For master's, GRE General Test. Additional exam requirements/recommendations for international students: Required—TOEFL. *Application deadline:* For fall admission, 4/15 for domestic and international students; for spring admission, 10/15 for domestic and international students. Applications are processed on a rolling basis. Application fee: $50. Electronic applications accepted. *Expenses:* Tuition, state resident: full-time $6516; part-time $362 per credit hour. Tuition, nonresident: full-time $22,014; part-time $1223 per credit hour. *Required fees:* $2128 per semester. Tuition and fees vary according to course load and program. *Financial support:* Research assistantships with full tuition reimbursements and teaching assistantships with full tuition reimbursements available. *Faculty research:* Urban economics, biogeography, cartography, geographic information science. *Unit head:* Dr. W. Crawford Elliott, Chair, 404-413-5756, E-mail: wcelliott@gsu.edu. *Application contact:* Dr. Jeremy Diem, Director of Graduate Studies, 404-413-5770, E-mail: jdiem@gsu.edu.
Website: http://geosciences.gsu.edu/grad-programs/

Georgia State University, College of Education, Department of Middle-Secondary Education and Instructional Technology, Atlanta, GA 30302-3083. Offers curriculum and instruction (Ed D); English education (MAT); mathematics education (M Ed, MAT); middle level education (MAT); reading, language and literacy education (M Ed, MAT), including reading instruction (M Ed); science education (M Ed, MAT), including biology (MAT), broad field science (MAT), chemistry (MAT), earth science (MAT), physics (MAT); social studies education (M Ed, MAT), including economics (MAT), geography (MAT), history (MAT), political science (MAT); teaching and learning (PhD), including language and literacy, mathematics education, music education, science education, social studies education, teaching and teacher education. *Accreditation:* NCATE. Part-time and evening/weekend programs available. Postbaccalaureate distance learning degree programs offered (minimal on-campus study). *Faculty:* 20 full-time (16 women). *Students:* 155 full-time (112 women), 101 part-time (70 women); includes 112 minority (82 Black or African American, non-Hispanic/Latino; 10 Asian, non-Hispanic/Latino; 12 Hispanic/Latino; 8 Two or more races, non-Hispanic/Latino), 3 international. Average age 32. 155 applicants, 61% accepted, 65 enrolled. *Degree requirements:* For master's, comprehensive exam (for some programs), thesis or alternative, exit portfolio; for doctorate, comprehensive exam, thesis/dissertation. *Entrance requirements:* For master's, GRE; GACE I (for initial teacher preparation programs), baccalaureate degree or equivalent, resume, goals statement, two letters of recommendation, minimum undergraduate GPA of 2.5; proof of initial teacher certification in the content area (for M Ed); for doctorate, GRE, resume, goals statement, writing sample, two letters of recommendation, minimum graduate GPA of 3.3, interview. Additional exam requirements/recommendations for international students: Required—TOEFL (minimum score 550 paper-based; 79 iBT) or IELTS (minimum score 6.5). *Application deadline:* For fall admission, 1/15 priority date for domestic and international students; for spring admission, 10/1 for domestic and international students. Application fee: $50. Electronic applications accepted. *Expenses:* Tuition, state resident: full-time $6516; part-time $362 per credit hour. Tuition, nonresident: full-time $22,014; part-time $1223 per credit hour. *Required fees:* $2128 per semester. Tuition and fees vary according to course load and program. *Financial support:* In 2014–15, fellowships with full tuition reimbursements (averaging $19,667 per year), research assistantships with full tuition reimbursements (averaging $5,436 per year), teaching assistantships with full tuition reimbursements (averaging $2,779 per year) were awarded; career-related internships or fieldwork, Federal Work-Study, scholarships/grants, health care benefits, tuition waivers (full and partial), and unspecified assistantships also available. Financial award application deadline: 3/15. *Faculty research:* Teacher education in language and literacy, mathematics, science, and social studies in urban middle and secondary school settings; learning technologies in school, community, and corporate settings; multicultural education and education for social justice; urban education; international education. *Unit head:* Dr. Dana L. Fox, Chair, 404-413-8060, Fax: 404-413-8063, E-mail: dfox@gsu.edu. *Application contact:* Bobbie Turner, Administrative Coordinator I, 404-413-8405, Fax: 404-413-8063, E-mail: bnturner@gsu.edu.
Website: http://mse.education.gsu.edu/

Hunter College of the City University of New York, Graduate School, School of Arts and Sciences, Department of Geography, New York, NY 10065-5085. Offers MA, Certificate. Part-time and evening/weekend programs available. *Faculty:* 6 full-time (3 women). *Students:* 1 full-time (0 women), 48 part-time (20 women); includes 13 minority (2 Black or African American, non-Hispanic/Latino; 5 Asian, non-Hispanic/Latino; 6 Hispanic/Latino). Average age 32. 10 applicants, 70% accepted, 4 enrolled. In 2014, 7 master's, 8 other advanced degrees awarded. *Degree requirements:* For master's, comprehensive exam or thesis. *Entrance requirements:* For master's, GRE General Test, minimum B average in major, B- overall; 18 credits of course work in geography; 2 letters of recommendation; for Certificate, minimum B average in major, B- overall. Additional exam requirements/recommendations for international students: Required—TOEFL. *Application deadline:* For fall admission, 4/1 for domestic students; for spring admission, 11/1 for domestic students. Applications are processed on a rolling basis. *Financial support:* In 2014–15, 1 fellowship (averaging $3,000 per year), 2 research assistantships (averaging $10,000 per year), 10 teaching assistantships (averaging $6,000 per year) were awarded; career-related internships or fieldwork, Federal Work-Study, institutionally sponsored loans, and unspecified assistantships also available. Financial award application deadline: 3/1. *Faculty research:* Urban geography, economic geography, geographic information science, demographic methods, climate change. *Unit head:* Prof. Allan Frei, Chair, 212-772-5450, Fax: 212-772-5322, E-mail: afrei@hunter.cuny.edu. *Application contact:* Prof. Marianna Pavlovskaya, Graduate Adviser, 212-772-5320, Fax: 212-772-5268, E-mail: mpavlov@geo.hunter.cuny.edu.
Website: http://www.geo.hunter.cuny.edu/

Indiana State University, College of Graduate and Professional Studies, College of Arts and Sciences, Department of Geography, Geology and Anthropology, Terre Haute, IN 47809. Offers geography (MA); geology (MS); physical geography (PhD). *Degree requirements:* For master's, thesis or alternative; for doctorate, comprehensive exam, thesis/dissertation, departmental qualifying exam. *Entrance requirements:* For doctorate, GRE General Test. Additional exam requirements/recommendations for international students: Required—TOEFL (minimum score 550 paper-based). Electronic applications accepted.

Indiana University Bloomington, University Graduate School, College of Arts and Sciences, Department of Geography, Bloomington, IN 47405. Offers MA, MS, PhD. *Faculty:* 11 full-time (2 women), 13 part-time/adjunct (2 women). *Students:* 23 full-time

(10 women), 1 (woman) part-time; includes 3 minority (2 Asian, non-Hispanic/Latino; 1 Hispanic/Latino), 5 international. 44 applicants, 11% accepted, 4 enrolled. In 2014, 2 master's, 2 doctorates awarded. *Degree requirements:* For master's, comprehensive exam, thesis; for doctorate, comprehensive exam, thesis/dissertation. *Entrance requirements:* For master's and doctorate, GRE General Test, minimum GPA of 3.0. Additional exam requirements/recommendations for international students: Required—TOEFL (minimum score 620 paper-based; 105 iBT). *Application deadline:* For fall admission, 1/15 priority date for domestic students, 12/1 priority date for international students; for spring admission, 11/15 priority date for domestic students, 11/1 priority date for international students. Application fee: $55 ($65 for international students). Electronic applications accepted. *Financial support:* In 2014–15, 3 fellowships with full and partial tuition reimbursements (averaging $19,333 per year), 2 research assistantships with full tuition reimbursements (averaging $16,039 per year), 15 teaching assistantships with full tuition reimbursements (averaging $15,750 per year) were awarded; health care benefits also available. Financial award application deadline: 2/15; financial award applicants required to submit FAFSA. *Faculty research:* Statistical climatology, dendrochronology, land-change science, cultural and political ecology, cultural geography, economic geography, geographic information science, spatial data analysis and modeling. *Unit head:* Dr. Daniel Knudsen, Chair and Professor, 812-855-6303, Fax: 812-855-1661, E-mail: knudsen@indiana.edu. *Application contact:* Susan White, Graduate Secretary, 812-855-6303, Fax: 812-855-1661, E-mail: suswhite@indiana.edu.
Website: http://www.iub.edu/~geog/

Indiana University of Pennsylvania, School of Graduate Studies and Research, College of Humanities and Social Sciences, Department of Geography and Regional Planning, MA Program in Geography, Indiana, PA 15705-1087. Offers MA. Part-time programs available. *Faculty:* 10 full-time (1 woman), 1 (woman) part-time/adjunct. *Degree requirements:* For master's, thesis optional. *Entrance requirements:* For master's, GRE, 2 letters of recommendation. Additional exam requirements/recommendations for international students: Required—TOEFL (minimum score 540 paper-based). *Application deadline:* Applications are processed on a rolling basis. Application fee: $50. Electronic applications accepted. *Financial support:* Federal Work-Study, scholarships/grants, and unspecified assistantships available. Support available to part-time students. Financial award application deadline: 4/15; financial award applicants required to submit FAFSA. *Unit head:* Dr. Richard Hoch, Graduate Coordinator, 724-357-5990, E-mail: richard.hoch@iup.edu.
Website: http://www.iup.edu/upper.aspx?id-90827

Johns Hopkins University, G. W. C. Whiting School of Engineering, Department of Geography and Environmental Engineering, Baltimore, MD 21218-2699. Offers MA, MS, MSE, PhD. Terminal master's awarded for partial completion of doctoral program. *Degree requirements:* For master's, thesis (for some programs), 1-year full-time residency; for doctorate, comprehensive exam, thesis/dissertation, oral exam, 2-year full-time residency. *Entrance requirements:* For master's and doctorate, GRE General Test. Additional exam requirements/recommendations for international students: Required—TOEFL (minimum score 670 paper-based; 120 iBT); Recommended—IELTS. Electronic applications accepted. *Faculty research:* Environmental engineering; environmental chemistry; water resources engineering; systems analysis and economics for public decision-making; geomorphology, hydrology and ecology.

Kansas State University, Graduate School, College of Arts and Sciences, Department of Geography, Manhattan, KS 66506. Offers MA, PhD, Graduate Certificate. *Faculty:* 12 full-time (3 women), 1 part-time/adjunct (0 women). *Students:* 25 full-time (11 women), 16 part-time (7 women); includes 4 minority (1 Asian, non-Hispanic/Latino; 1 Hispanic/Latino; 1 Native Hawaiian or other Pacific Islander, non-Hispanic/Latino; 1 Two or more races, non-Hispanic/Latino), 9 international. Average age 30. 32 applicants, 47% accepted, 10 enrolled. In 2014, 5 master's, 2 doctorates, 4 other advanced degrees awarded. *Degree requirements:* For master's, thesis optional, oral exam; for doctorate, one foreign language, thesis/dissertation. *Entrance requirements:* For master's and doctorate, GRE General Test, minimum GPA of 3.0. *Application deadline:* For fall admission, 2/1 priority date for domestic and international students; for spring admission, 8/1 priority date for domestic and international students. Applications are processed on a rolling basis. Application fee: $50 ($75 for international students). Electronic applications accepted. *Financial support:* In 2014–15, 2 research assistantships (averaging $18,770 per year),*18 teaching assistantships with full tuition reimbursements (averaging $13,158 per year) were awarded; Federal Work-Study, institutionally sponsored loans, and scholarships/grants also available. Support available to part-time students. Financial award application deadline: 3/1; financial award applicants required to submit FAFSA. *Faculty research:* Human environment interaction, health and population, culture and landscape, physical geography, geospatial analysis and applications. *Total annual research expenditures:* $294,540. *Unit head:* Charles Martin, Head, 785-532-0136, Fax: 785-532-7310, E-mail: cwmgeog@ksu.edu. *Application contact:* Douglas Goodin, Director, 785-532-3411, Fax: 785-532-7310, E-mail: dgoodin@ksu.edu.
Website: http://www.k-state.edu/geography/

Kent State University, College of Arts and Sciences, Department of Geography, Kent, OH 44242-0001. Offers MA, PhD. Part-time programs available. *Faculty:* 14 full-time (5 women). *Students:* 37 full-time (12 women), 5 part-time (1 woman); includes 2 minority (1 Hispanic/Latino; 1 Two or more races, non-Hispanic/Latino), 10 international. Average age 33. 68 applicants, 65% accepted, 20 enrolled. In 2014, 9 master's, 2 doctorates awarded. *Degree requirements:* For master's, thesis; for doctorate, comprehensive exam, thesis/dissertation. *Entrance requirements:* For master's, minimum GPA of 2.75, transcript, statement of purpose, 3 letters of recommendation; for doctorate, minimum GPA of 3.5, transcript, 3 letters of recommendation. Additional exam requirements/recommendations for international students: Required—TOEFL (minimum score: paper-based 525, iBT 71), Michigan English Language Assessment Battery (minimum score of 75), IELTS (minimum score of 6.0), PTE Academic (minimum score of 48), or completion of ELS level 112 Intensive Program. *Application deadline:* For fall admission, 2/1 for domestic students; for spring admission, 7/1 for domestic students. Application fee: $45 ($70 for international students). Electronic applications accepted. *Expenses:* Tuition, state resident: full-time $8730; part-time $485 per credit hour. Tuition, nonresident: full-time $14,886; part-time $827 per credit hour. Tuition and fees vary according to campus/location and program. *Financial support:* Fellowships with full tuition reimbursements, research assistantships with full tuition reimbursements, teaching assistantships with full tuition reimbursements, career-related internships or fieldwork, Federal Work-Study, and unspecified assistantships available. Financial award application deadline: 2/1. *Unit head:* Dr. Mandy Munro-Stasiuk, Professor and Chair, 330-672-2045, Fax: 330-672-4304, E-mail: mmunrost@kent.edu. *Application contact:* Dr. Scott Sheridan, Professor and Graduate Coordinator, 330-672-2045, E-mail: geography@kent.edu.
Website: http://www.kent.edu/stark/geography

Louisiana State University and Agricultural & Mechanical College, Graduate School, College of Humanities and Social Sciences, Department of Geography and Anthropology, Baton Rouge, LA 70803. Offers geography (MA, MS); geography and anthropology (PhD). Part-time programs available. *Faculty:* 29 full-time (13 women).

Students: 72 full-time (37 women), 22 part-time (14 women); includes 6 minority (3 Black or African American, non-Hispanic/Latino; 3 Hispanic/Latino), 28 international. Average age 31. 69 applicants, 75% accepted, 17 enrolled. In 2014, 19 master's, 10 doctorates awarded. Terminal master's awarded for partial completion of doctoral program. *Degree requirements:* For master's, 2 foreign languages, thesis (for some programs); for doctorate, 2 foreign languages, thesis/dissertation. *Entrance requirements:* For master's and doctorate, GRE General Test, minimum GPA of 3.0. Additional exam requirements/recommendations for international students: Required—TOEFL (minimum score 550 paper-based; 79 IBT), IELTS (minimum score 6.5), or PTE (minimum score 59). *Application deadline:* For fall admission, 1/1 priority date for domestic students, 5/15 for international students; for spring admission, 10/15 for domestic and international students; for summer admission, 5/15 for domestic and international students. Applications are processed on a rolling basis. Application fee: $50 ($70 for international students). Electronic applications accepted. *Financial support:* In 2014–15, 73 students received support, including 2 fellowships with full tuition reimbursements available (averaging $23,675 per year), 24 research assistantships with full and partial tuition reimbursements available (averaging $15,302 per year), 31 teaching assistantships with full and partial tuition reimbursements available (averaging $12,842 per year); career-related internships or fieldwork, health care benefits, and unspecified assistantships also available. Financial award application deadline: 3/1; financial award applicants required to submit FAFSA. *Faculty research:* Cultural, coastal, climate, geographic information systems (geography); cultural, linguistics, archaeology (anthropology). *Total annual research expenditures:* $1.2 million. *Unit head:* Dr. Fahui Wang, Chair, 225-578-5942, Fax: 225-578-4420, E-mail: gachair@lsu.edu. *Application contact:* Dr. Robert Tague, Graduate Adviser, 225-578-6094, Fax: 225-578-4420, E-mail: rtague@lsu.edu.
Website: http://www.ga.lsu.edu/

Marshall University, Academic Affairs Division, College of Liberal Arts, Department of Geography, Huntington, WV 25755. Offers MA, MS, Certificate. *Students:* 8 full-time (4 women), 3 part-time (1 woman); includes 1 minority (Asian, non-Hispanic/Latino). Average age 36. In 2014, 3 master's awarded. *Degree requirements:* For master's, thesis optional. *Entrance requirements:* For master's, GRE General Test (for MS). Application fee: $40. *Unit head:* Dr. Joshua Hagen, Chairperson, 304-696-2505, E-mail: hagenj@marshall.edu. *Application contact:* Information Contact, 304-746-1907, Fax: 304-746-1902, E-mail: services@marshall.edu.

McGill University, Faculty of Graduate and Postdoctoral Studies, Faculty of Science, Department of Geography, Montréal, QC H3A 2T5, Canada. Offers geography (M Sc, MA, PhD); neo-tropical environment (MA, PhD); social statistics (MA).

McMaster University, School of Graduate Studies, Faculty of Science, School of Geography and Earth Sciences, Hamilton, ON L8S 4M2, Canada. Offers geochemistry (PhD); geology (M Sc, PhD); human geography (MA, PhD); physical geography (M Sc, PhD). Part-time programs available. Terminal master's awarded for partial completion of doctoral program. *Degree requirements:* For master's, thesis; for doctorate, comprehensive exam, thesis/dissertation. *Entrance requirements:* For master's, minimum B+ average. Additional exam requirements/recommendations for international students: Required—TOEFL (minimum score 550 paper-based).

Memorial University of Newfoundland, School of Graduate Studies, Department of Geography, St. John's, NL A1C 5S7, Canada. Offers M Sc, MA, PhD. *Degree requirements:* For master's, thesis; for doctorate, comprehensive exam, thesis/dissertation, seminar, oral defense of thesis. *Entrance requirements:* For master's, 2nd class degree; for doctorate, master's degree. Electronic applications accepted. *Faculty research:* Cultural/historical geography, physical geography, economic geography, cartography, geographical information systems.

Miami University, College of Arts and Science, Department of Geography, Oxford, OH 45056. Offers MA. *Students:* 11 full-time (5 women), 5 international. Average age 26. In 2014, 7 master's awarded. *Entrance requirements:* For master's, GRE (recommended), statement of research purpose; three letters of recommendation. Additional exam requirements/recommendations for international students: Recommended—TOEFL (minimum score 80 iBT), IELTS (minimum score 6.5), TSE (minimum score 54). *Application deadline:* For fall admission, 2/1 for domestic and international students. Application fee: $50. Electronic applications accepted. *Expenses:* Tuition, state resident: full-time $12,887; part-time $537 per credit hour. Tuition, nonresident: full-time $28,449; part-time $1186 per credit hour. *Required fees:* $530; $24 per credit hour. $30 per quarter. Part-time tuition and fees vary according to course load and program. *Financial support:* Fellowships with full and partial tuition reimbursements, research assistantships, teaching assistantships, and unspecified assistantships available. Financial award application deadline: 2/1; financial award applicants required to submit FAFSA. *Unit head:* Dr. Bruce D'Arcus, Department Chair/Associate Professor of Geography, 513-529-1521, E-mail: darcusb@miamioh.edu. *Application contact:* Department of Geography, 513-529-5010, E-mail: geography@miamioh.edu.
Website: http://www.MiamiOH.edu/geography/

Michigan State University, The Graduate School, College of Social Science, Department of Geography, East Lansing, MI 48824. Offers geographic information science (MS); geography (MS, PhD). *Degree requirements:* For master's, comprehensive exam, thesis (for some programs), presentation of poster/paper or oral defense of thesis; for doctorate, comprehensive exam, thesis/dissertation, presentation of poster/paper, presentation and defense of dissertation proposal, oral exam in defense of dissertation. *Entrance requirements:* Additional exam requirements/recommendations for international students: Required—TOEFL (minimum score 600 paper-based). Electronic applications accepted.

Minnesota State University Mankato, College of Graduate Studies, College of Social and Behavioral Sciences, Department of Geography, Mankato, MN 56001. Offers geography (MS); GIS (Certificate). Part-time programs available. *Students:* 4 full-time (0 women), 11 part-time (3 women). *Degree requirements:* For master's, one foreign language, comprehensive exam. *Entrance requirements:* For master's, GRE General Test (if GPA less than 2.8 for the last 2 years), minimum GPA of 3.0 during previous 2 years. *Application deadline:* For fall admission, 7/1 priority date for domestic students; for spring admission, 11/1 for domestic students. Applications are processed on a rolling basis. Application fee: $40. Electronic applications accepted. *Financial support:* Research assistantships, teaching assistantships with full tuition reimbursements, career-related internships or fieldwork, Federal Work-Study, institutionally sponsored loans, and unspecified assistantships available. Support available to part-time students. Financial award application deadline: 3/15; financial award applicants required to submit FAFSA. *Unit head:* Dr. Ginger Schmid, Chairperson, 507-389-2824. *Application contact:* 507-389-2321, E-mail: grad@mnsu.edu.
Website: http://sbs.mnsu.edu/geography/

Mississippi State University, College of Arts and Sciences, Department of Geosciences, Mississippi State, MS 39762. Offers applied meteorology (MS); broadcast meteorology (MS); earth and atmospheric science (PhD); environmental geoscience (MS); geography (MS); geology (MS); geospatial sciences (MS); professional meteorology/climatology (MS); teachers in geoscience (MS). Postbaccalaureate distance learning degree programs offered (no on-campus study). *Faculty:* 18 full-time (3 women), 1 part-time/adjunct (0 women). *Students:* 52 full-time (26 women), 210 part-

time (95 women); includes 23 minority (5 Black or African American, non-Hispanic/Latino; 4 Asian, non-Hispanic/Latino; 8 Hispanic/Latino; 2 Native Hawaiian or other Pacific Islander, non-Hispanic/Latino; 4 Two or more races, non-Hispanic/Latino), 8 international. Average age 33. 151 applicants, 75% accepted, 88 enrolled. In 2014, 106 master's, 5 doctorates awarded. *Degree requirements:* For master's, thesis (for some programs), comprehensive oral or written exam; for doctorate, thesis/dissertation, comprehensive oral or written exam. *Entrance requirements:* For master's, GRE (for on-campus applicants), minimum undergraduate GPA of 2.75; for doctorate, completed thesis-based MS with background in one department emphasis area. Additional exam requirements/recommendations for international students: Required—TOEFL (minimum score 477 paper-based; 53 iBT); Recommended—IELTS (minimum score 4.5). *Application deadline:* For fall admission, 7/1 for domestic students, 5/1 for international students; for spring admission, 11/1 for domestic students, 9/1 for international students. Applications are processed on a rolling basis. Application fee: $60. Electronic applications accepted. *Expenses:* Tuition, state resident: full-time $7140; part-time $783 per credit hour. Tuition, nonresident: full-time $18,478; part-time $2043 per credit hour. *Financial support:* In 2014–15, 9 research assistantships with full tuition reimbursements (averaging $23,177 per year), 29 teaching assistantships with full tuition reimbursements (averaging $14,483 per year) were awarded; Federal Work-Study, institutionally sponsored loans, scholarships/grants, tuition waivers (partial), and unspecified assistantships also available. Financial award application deadline: 4/1; financial award applicants required to submit FAFSA. *Faculty research:* Climatology, hydrogeology, sedimentology, meteorology. *Total annual research expenditures:* $2.7 million. *Unit head:* Dr. William Cooke, Interim Department Head, 662-325-3915, Fax: 662-325-9423, E-mail: whc5@geosci.msstate.edu. *Application contact:* Dr. Mike Brown, Associate Professor/Graduate Coordinator, 662-325-3915, Fax: 662-325-9423, E-mail: tina@gesci.msstate.edu.
Website: http://www.geosciences.msstate.edu

Missouri State University, Graduate College, College of Natural and Applied Sciences, Department of Geography, Geology, and Planning, Springfield, MO 65897. Offers geography, geology and planning (MNAS); secondary education (MS Ed), including earth science, physical geography. *Accreditation:* ACSP. Part-time and evening/weekend programs available. *Faculty:* 18 full-time (4 women), 1 part-time/adjunct (0 women). *Students:* 12 full-time (5 women), 12 part-time (8 women); includes 1 minority (Asian, non-Hispanic/Latino), 3 international. Average age 30. 16 applicants, 100% accepted, 9 enrolled. In 2014, 11 master's awarded. *Degree requirements:* For master's, comprehensive exam, thesis (for some programs). *Entrance requirements:* For master's, GRE General Test (MS, MNAS), minimum undergraduate GPA of 3.0 (MS, MNAS), 9-12 teacher certification (MS Ed). Additional exam requirements/recommendations for international students: Required—TOEFL (minimum score 550 paper-based; 79 iBT). *Application deadline:* For fall admission, 7/20 priority date for domestic students, 5/1 for international students; for spring admission, 12/20 priority date for domestic students, 9/1 for international students. Applications are processed on a rolling basis. Application fee: $35 ($50 for international students). Electronic applications accepted. *Expenses:* Tuition, state resident: full-time $2250; part-time $250 per credit hour. Tuition, nonresident: full-time $4509; part-time $501 per credit hour. Tuition and fees vary according to course level, course load and program. *Financial support:* In 2014–15, 3 research assistantships with full tuition reimbursements (averaging $11,574 per year), 12 teaching assistantships with full tuition reimbursements (averaging $9,365 per year) were awarded; career-related internships or fieldwork, Federal Work-Study, institutionally sponsored loans, scholarships/grants, and unspecified assistantships also available. Financial award application deadline: 3/31; financial award applicants required to submit FAFSA. *Faculty research:* Stratigraphy and ancient meteorite impacts, environmental geochemistry of karst, hyperspectral image processing, water quality, small town planning. *Unit head:* Dr. Thomas Plymate, Head, 417-836-5800, Fax: 417-836-6934, E-mail: tomplymate@missouristate.edu. *Application contact:* Misty Stewart, Coordinator of Graduate Recruitment, 417-836-6079, Fax: 417-836-6200, E-mail: mistystewart@missouristate.edu.
Website: http://geosciences.missouristate.edu/

New Mexico State University, College of Arts and Sciences, Department of Geography, Las Cruces, NM 88003. Offers MAG. Part-time programs available. *Faculty:* 6 full-time (2 women). *Students:* 11 full-time (4 women), 14 part-time (6 women); includes 12 minority (1 Black or African American, non-Hispanic/Latino; 11 Hispanic/Latino), 1 international. Average age 33. 7 applicants, 71% accepted, 4 enrolled. In 2014, 3 master's awarded. *Degree requirements:* For master's, comprehensive exam, thesis or residency paper. *Entrance requirements:* For master's, bachelor's degree in geography or related field. Additional exam requirements/recommendations for international students: Required—TOEFL (minimum score 550 paper-based; 79 iBT), IELTS (minimum score 6.5). *Application deadline:* For spring admission, 2/1 for domestic students, 2/1 priority date for international students. Applications are processed on a rolling basis. Application fee: $40 ($50 for international students). Electronic applications accepted. *Expenses:* Tuition, state resident: full-time $3969; part-time $220.50 per credit hour. Tuition, nonresident: full-time $13,838; part-time $768.80 per credit hour. *Required fees:* $853; $47.40 per credit hour. *Financial support:* In 2014–15, 10 students received support, including 1 research assistantship (averaging $8,788 per year), 6 teaching assistantships (averaging $16,295 per year); career-related internships or fieldwork, Federal Work-Study, scholarships/grants, traineeships, health care benefits, and unspecified assistantships also available. Support available to part-time students. Financial award application deadline: 3/1. *Faculty research:* Landscape ecology, land use, geomorphology, Latin America and the U.S.-Mexico border, geographic information systems, geographic education, biogeography, water resources research. *Total annual research expenditures:* $124,822. *Unit head:* Dr. Christopher Brown, Academic Department Head, 575-646-3509, Fax: 575-646-7430, E-mail: brownchr@nmsu.edu. *Application contact:* Dr. Daniel P. Dugas, Graduate Advisor, 575-646-1045, Fax: 575-646-7430, E-mail: ddugas@nmsu.edu.
Website: http://geography.nmsu.edu

Northeastern Illinois University, College of Graduate Studies and Research, College of Arts and Sciences, Program in Geography and Environmental Studies, Chicago, IL 60625-4699. Offers MA. Part-time and evening/weekend programs available. *Degree requirements:* For master's, comprehensive exam, thesis optional. *Entrance requirements:* For master's, undergraduate minor in geography or environmental studies, minimum GPA of 2.75. Additional exam requirements/recommendations for international students: Required—TOEFL (minimum score 550 paper-based; 79 iBT). Electronic applications accepted. *Faculty research:* Segregation and urbanization of minority groups in the Chicago area, scale dependence and parameterization in nonpoint source pollution modeling, ecological land classification and mapping, ecosystem restoration, soil-vegetation relationships.

Northern Arizona University, Graduate College, College of Social and Behavioral Sciences, Department of Geography, Planning, and Recreation, Flagstaff, AZ 86011. Offers applied geospatial sciences (MS); community planning (Certificate); geographic information systems (Certificate). Postbaccalaureate distance learning degree programs offered. *Degree requirements:* For master's, thesis optional. *Entrance requirements:* For master's, GRE General Test. Additional exam requirements/recommendations for international students: Required—TOEFL (minimum score 550 paper-based; 80 iBT), IELTS (minimum score 7). Electronic applications accepted.

Northern Illinois University, Graduate School, College of Liberal Arts and Sciences, Department of Geography, De Kalb, IL 60115-2854. Offers MS, PhD. Part-time programs available. *Faculty:* 8 full-time (2 women). *Students:* 18 full-time (4 women), 16 part-time (3 women); includes 3 minority (all Hispanic/Latino), 1 international. Average age 32. 31 applicants, 65% accepted, 10 enrolled. In 2014, 10 master's awarded. *Degree requirements:* For master's, comprehensive exam, thesis optional, research seminar. *Entrance requirements:* For master's, GRE General Test, minimum GPA of 2.75; for doctorate, master's degree. Additional exam requirements/recommendations for international students: Required—TOEFL (minimum score 550 paper-based). *Application deadline:* For fall admission, 2/1 priority date for domestic students, 5/1 for international students; for spring admission, 10/1 priority date for domestic students, 10/1 for international students. Applications are processed on a rolling basis. Application fee: $40. Electronic applications accepted. *Financial support:* In 2014–15, 3 research assistantships with full tuition reimbursements, 16 teaching assistantships with full tuition reimbursements were awarded; fellowships with full tuition reimbursements, career-related internships or fieldwork, Federal Work-Study, scholarships/grants, tuition waivers (full), and unspecified assistantships also available. Support available to part-time students. Financial award applicants required to submit FAFSA. *Faculty research:* Synoptic meteorology, human impacts on soil properties, plant-soil relationships, hydrological cycle, climate variability. *Unit head:* Dr. Andrew Krmenec, Chair, 815-753-6826, Fax: 815-753-6872, E-mail: akrmenec@niu.edu. *Application contact:* Dr. Michael Konen, Coordinator of Graduate Studies, 815-753-0631, E-mail: mkonen@niu.edu.
Website: http://globe.geog.niu.edu/

The Ohio State University, Graduate School, College of Arts and Sciences, Division of Social and Behavioral Sciences, Department of Geography, Columbus, OH 43210. Offers atmospheric sciences (MS, PhD); geography (MA, PhD). *Faculty:* 22. *Students:* 41 full-time (19 women), 2 part-time (both women); includes 1 minority (Hispanic/Latino), 21 international. Average age 29. In 2014, 8 master's, 11 doctorates awarded. *Degree requirements:* For doctorate, variable foreign language requirement, thesis/dissertation. *Entrance requirements:* For master's and doctorate, GRE. Additional exam requirements/recommendations for international students: Required—Michigan English Language Assessment Battery (minimum score 86); Recommended—TOEFL (minimum score 600 paper-based; 100 iBT), IELTS (minimum score 8). *Application deadline:* For fall admission, 12/13 priority date for domestic students, 11/30 priority date for international students; for winter admission, 12/1 for domestic students, 11/1 for international students; for spring admission, 3/1 for domestic students, 2/1 for international students. Applications are processed on a rolling basis. Application fee: $60 ($70 for international students). Electronic applications accepted. *Financial support:* Fellowships with tuition reimbursements, research assistantships with tuition reimbursements, teaching assistantships with tuition reimbursements, Federal Work-Study, and institutionally sponsored loans available. Support available to part-time students. *Unit head:* Dr. Daniel Sui, Chair, 614-688-5441, Fax: 614-292-6213, E-mail: sui.10@osu.edu. *Application contact:* Graduate and Professional Admissions, 614-292-9444, Fax: 614-292-3895, E-mail: gpadmissions@osu.edu.
Website: http://www.geography.osu.edu/

Ohio University, Graduate College, College of Arts and Sciences, Department of Geography, Athens, OH 45701-2979. Offers MA, MS. Part-time programs available. *Degree requirements:* For master's, thesis or alternative. *Entrance requirements:* For master's, GRE General Test, minimum GPA of 3.0. Additional exam requirements/recommendations for international students: Required—TOEFL (minimum score 600 paper-based; 100 iBT) or IELTS (minimum score 8). Electronic applications accepted. *Faculty research:* Environmental geography, cartography and geographic information systems, cultural ecology, area studies, historical geography.

Oklahoma State University, College of Arts and Sciences, Department of Geography, Stillwater, OK 74078. Offers MS, PhD. *Faculty:* 15 full-time (5 women), 1 part-time/adjunct (0 women). *Students:* 9 full-time (4 women), 33 part-time (11 women); includes 2 minority (1 Hispanic/Latino; 1 Two or more races, non-Hispanic/Latino), 11 international. Average age 32. 28 applicants, 50% accepted, 12 enrolled. In 2014, 3 master's, 3 doctorates awarded. *Degree requirements:* For master's, thesis or alternative; for doctorate, comprehensive exam, thesis/dissertation. *Entrance requirements:* For master's and doctorate, GRE. Additional exam requirements/recommendations for international students: Required—TOEFL (minimum score 550 paper-based; 79 iBT). *Application deadline:* For fall admission, 3/1 priority date for international students; for spring admission, 8/1 priority date for international students. Applications are processed on a rolling basis. Application fee: $40 ($75 for international students). Electronic applications accepted. *Expenses:* Tuition, state resident: full-time $4488; part-time $187 per credit hour. Tuition, nonresident: full-time $18,360; part-time $765 per credit hour. *Required fees:* $2413; $100.55 per credit hour. Tuition and fees vary according to campus/location. *Financial support:* In 2014–15, 5 research assistantships (averaging $16,116 per year), 21 teaching assistantships (averaging $17,836 per year) were awarded; career-related internships or fieldwork, Federal Work-Study, scholarships/grants, health care benefits, tuition waivers (partial), and unspecified assistantships also available. Support available to part-time students. Financial award application deadline: 3/1; financial award applicants required to submit FAFSA. *Faculty research:* Cultural ecology, resource management, historical/cultural geography, central Asia, geographic information systems. *Unit head:* Dr. Dale Lightfoot, Department Head, 405-744-6250, Fax: 405-744-5620, E-mail: d.lightfoot@okstate.edu. *Application contact:* Dr. Jonathan Comer, Professor/Coordinator of Graduate Studies, 405-744-6250, Fax: 405-744-5620, E-mail: jon.comer@okstate.edu.
Website: http://geog.okstate.edu

Oregon State University, College of Earth, Ocean, and Atmospheric Sciences, Program in Geography, Corvallis, OR 97331. Offers MA, MS, PhD. Part-time programs available. *Faculty:* 15 full-time (8 women), 4 part-time/adjunct (2 women). *Students:* 23 full-time (11 women), 4 part-time (2 women); includes 4 minority (1 Black or African American, non-Hispanic/Latino; 3 Hispanic/Latino), 4 international. Average age 31. 64 applicants, 22% accepted, 6 enrolled. In 2014, 4 master's, 1 doctorate awarded. Terminal master's awarded for partial completion of doctoral program. *Degree requirements:* For master's, variable foreign language requirement, thesis optional; for doctorate, one foreign language, thesis/dissertation. *Entrance requirements:* For master's and doctorate, GRE, minimum GPA of 3.0 in last 90 hours. Additional exam requirements/recommendations for international students: Required—TOEFL (minimum score 80 iBT), IELTS (minimum score 6.5). *Application deadline:* For fall admission, 1/5 for domestic students. Application fee: $60. *Expenses:* Tuition, state resident: full-time $11,907; part-time $189 per credit hour. Tuition, nonresident: full-time $19,953; part-time $441 per credit hour. *Required fees:* $1472; $449 per term. One-time fee: $350. Tuition and fees vary according to course load and program. *Financial support:* Fellowships, research assistantships, teaching assistantships, Federal Work-Study, and institutionally sponsored loans available. Support available to part-time students. Financial award application deadline: 1/5. *Faculty research:* Resources, physical geography, cartography, remote sensing. *Unit head:* Dr. Anita Grunder, Professor/Associate Dean for Academic Programs, 541-737-5189. *Application contact:* Lori

Hartline, Geography Advisor, 541-737-5188, E-mail: hartline@coas.oregonstate.edu. Website: http://ceoas.oregonstate.edu/academics/geography/

Penn State University Park, Graduate School, College of Earth and Mineral Sciences, Department of Geography, University Park, PA 16802. Offers MGIS, MS, PhD. *Unit head:* Dr. William E. Easterling, III, Dean, 814-865-7482, Fax: 814-863-7708, E-mail: wee2@psu.edu. *Application contact:* Lori A. Stania, Director, Graduate Student Services, 814-867-5278, Fax: 814-863-4627, E-mail: gswww@psu.edu. Website: http://www.geog.psu.edu/

Philadelphia University, College of Architecture and the Built Environment, Program in Geodesign, Philadelphia, PA 19144. Offers MS. Part-time programs available.

Portland State University, Graduate Studies, College of Liberal Arts and Sciences, Department of Geography, Portland, OR 97207-0751. Offers MA, MAT, MS, MST, PhD. Part-time programs available. *Faculty:* 9 full-time (2 women), 11 part-time/adjunct (3 women). *Students:* 21 full-time (8 women), 46 part-time (20 women); includes 5 minority (1 American Indian or Alaska Native, non-Hispanic/Latino; 3 Hispanic/Latino; 1 Two or more races, non-Hispanic/Latino). Average age 33. 49 applicants, 67% accepted, 23 enrolled. In 2014, 13 master's awarded. *Degree requirements:* For master's, thesis (for some programs). *Entrance requirements:* For master's, GRE General Test (minimum score of 297), geography degree with minimum GPA of 3.0 overall, 3 letters of recommendation. Additional exam requirements/recommendations for international students: Required—TOEFL (minimum score 550 paper-based; 80 iBT), IELTS (minimum score 6.5), PTE (minimum score 60). *Application deadline:* For fall admission, 1/15 priority date for domestic and international students. Applications are processed on a rolling basis. Application fee: $50. *Expenses:* Tuition, state resident: part-time $222 per credit. Tuition, nonresident: part-time $527 per credit. *Required fees:* $22 per contact hour. $100 per quarter. Tuition and fees vary according to program. *Financial support:* In 2014–15, 1 research assistantship with full tuition reimbursement (averaging $6,490 per year), 8 teaching assistantships with full and partial tuition reimbursements (averaging $5,717 per year) were awarded; career-related internships or fieldwork, Federal Work-Study, scholarships/grants, and unspecified assistantships also available. Support available to part-time students. Financial award application deadline: 3/1; financial award applicants required to submit FAFSA. *Faculty research:* Geographic information systems, natural lands, Latin American subsistence farming, climatic change, urban perspectives. *Total annual research expenditures:* $238,324. *Unit head:* Dr. Heejun Chang, Chair, 503-725-3162, Fax: 503-725-3166, E-mail: changh@pdx.edu. *Application contact:* Dr. Barbara Brower, Graduate Committee Chair, 503-725-8044, Fax: 503-725-3166, E-mail: browerb@pdx.edu. Website: http://www.pdx.edu/geography/

Queen's University at Kingston, School of Graduate Studies, Faculty of Arts and Sciences, Department of Geography, Kingston, ON K7L 3N6, Canada. Offers M Sc, MA, PhD. *Degree requirements:* For master's, thesis; for doctorate, comprehensive exam, thesis/dissertation. *Entrance requirements:* Additional exam requirements/recommendations for international students: Required—TOEFL. *Faculty research:* Urban and economic geography, historical-cultural geography, earth system science.

Rutgers, The State University of New Jersey, New Brunswick, Graduate School-New Brunswick, Program in Geography, Piscataway, NJ 08854-8097. Offers MA, MS, PhD. Terminal master's awarded for partial completion of doctoral program. *Degree requirements:* For master's, thesis or alternative; for doctorate, comprehensive exam, thesis/dissertation. *Entrance requirements:* For master's and doctorate, GRE General Test. Additional exam requirements/recommendations for international students: Required—TOEFL. *Faculty research:* Urban social theory, climate, political biology, hazards, economic development.

St. Cloud State University, School of Graduate Studies, College of Social Sciences, Department of Geography and Planning, St. Cloud, MN 56301-4498. Offers MS. *Degree requirements:* For master's, comprehensive exam (for some programs), thesis or alternative. *Entrance requirements:* For master's, GRE General Test, minimum GPA of 2.75. Additional exam requirements/recommendations for international students: Required—Michigan English Language Assessment Battery; Recommended—TOEFL (minimum score 550 paper-based), IELTS (minimum score 6.5). Electronic applications accepted.

Salem State University, School of Graduate Studies, Program in Geo-Information Science, Salem, MA 01970-5353. Offers MS. Part-time and evening/weekend programs available. *Degree requirements:* For master's, thesis optional. *Entrance requirements:* For master's, GRE or MAT. Additional exam requirements/recommendations for international students: Required—TOEFL (minimum score 550 paper-based; 80 iBT) or IELTS (minimum score 5.5).

San Diego State University, Graduate and Research Affairs, College of Arts and Letters, Department of Geography, San Diego, CA 92182. Offers MA, PhD. PhD offered jointly with University of California, Santa Barbara. *Degree requirements:* For master's, thesis; for doctorate, thesis/dissertation. *Entrance requirements:* For master's, GRE General Test, bachelor's degree in related field, 3 letters of recommendation. Additional exam requirements/recommendations for international students: Required—TOEFL. Electronic applications accepted. *Faculty research:* Physical geography, human geography, biogeography, environmental resources, geographic analysis.

San Francisco State University, Division of Graduate Studies, College of Science and Engineering, Department of Geography and Environment, San Francisco, CA 94132-1722. Offers MA, MS. *Expenses:* Tuition, state resident: full-time $6738. Tuition, nonresident: full-time $17,898; part-time $372 per credit hour. *Required fees:* $498 per semester. *Unit head:* Dr. Jerry Davis, Chair, 415-338-2983, Fax: 415-338-6243, E-mail: jerry@sfsu.edu. *Application contact:* Dr. Nancy Wilkinson, Graduate Coordinator, 415-338-1439, Fax: 415-338-6243, E-mail: nancyw@sfsu.edu. Website: http://geog.sfsu.edu/

San Jose State University, Graduate Studies and Research, College of Social Sciences, Department of Geography, San Jose, CA 95192-0001. Offers geographic information science (Certificate); geography (MA). *Entrance requirements:* For master's, minimum GPA of 3.0. Electronic applications accepted.

Shippensburg University of Pennsylvania, School of Graduate Studies, College of Education and Human Services, Department of Teacher Education, Shippensburg, PA 17257-2299. Offers curriculum and instruction (M Ed), including biology, early childhood education, elementary education, geography/earth science, history, mathematics, middle level education, modern languages; reading (M Ed). *Accreditation:* NCATE. Part-time and evening/weekend programs available. *Faculty:* 12 full-time (9 women), 3 part-time/adjunct (2 women). *Students:* 8 full-time (7 women), 66 part-time (53 women); includes 6 minority (2 Black or African American, non-Hispanic/Latino; 4 Hispanic/Latino), 1 international. Average age 30. 52 applicants, 75% accepted, 24 enrolled. In 2014, 29 master's awarded. *Degree requirements:* For master's, comprehensive exam (for some programs), thesis optional, practicum or internship; capstone seminar (for some programs). *Entrance requirements:* For master's, MAT or GRE (if GPA less than 2.75), interview, 3 letters of reference, questionnaire of teaching background and future goals, resume. Additional exam requirements/recommendations for international students: Required—TOEFL (minimum score 580 paper-based); Recommended—

IELTS (minimum score 6). *Application deadline:* For fall admission, 6/1 priority date for domestic students, 4/30 for international students; for spring admission, 9/1 priority date for domestic students, 9/30 for international students; for summer admission, 2/1 priority date for domestic students. Applications are processed on a rolling basis. Application fee: $45. Electronic applications accepted. *Expenses: Tuition, area resident:* Part-time $454 per credit. Tuition, state resident: part-time $454 per credit. Tuition, nonresident: part-time $681 per credit. *Required fees:* $133 per credit. *Financial support:* In 2014–15, 1 research assistantship with full tuition reimbursement (averaging $5,000 per year) was awarded; career-related internships or fieldwork, scholarships/grants, unspecified assistantships, and resident hall director and student payroll positions also available. Support available to part-time students. Financial award application deadline: 3/1; financial award applicants required to submit FAFSA. *Unit head:* Dr. Christine A. Royce, Chairperson, 717-477-1688, Fax: 717-477-4046, E-mail: caroyc@ship.edu. *Application contact:* Jeremy R. Goshorn, Assistant Dean of Graduate Admissions, 717-477-1231, Fax: 717-477-4016, E-mail: jrgoshorn@ship.edu. Website: http://www.ship.edu/teacher/

Simon Fraser University, Office of Graduate Studies, Faculty of Environment, Department of Geography, Burnaby, BC V5A 1S6, Canada. Offers M Sc, MA, PhD. *Degree requirements:* For master's, one foreign language, thesis; for doctorate, one foreign language, comprehensive exam, thesis/dissertation. *Entrance requirements:* For master's, minimum GPA of 3.0 (on scale of 4.33), or 3.33 based on last 60 credits of undergraduate courses; for doctorate, minimum GPA of 3.5 (on scale of 4.33). Additional exam requirements/recommendations for international students: Recommended—TOEFL (minimum score 580 paper-based; 93 iBT), IELTS (minimum score 7), TWE (minimum score 5). Electronic applications accepted. *Faculty research:* Theoretical and systematic aspects of geography, ginseng research, geographic information sciences, tourism and community planning, geomorphology.

South Dakota State University, Graduate School, College of Arts and Science, Department of Geography, Brookings, SD 57007. Offers MS. Part-time programs available. *Degree requirements:* For master's, thesis, oral exam. *Entrance requirements:* Additional exam requirements/recommendations for international students: Required—TOEFL (minimum score 525 paper-based; 71 iBT). *Faculty research:* Contemporary agriculture and rural land use, geography of Indian casino gambling, geography of illegal drug trade, geography of crop circles.

Southern Illinois University Carbondale, Graduate School, College of Liberal Arts, Department of Geography, Carbondale, IL 62901-4701. Offers MS, PhD. *Faculty:* 7 full-time (1 woman), 1 part-time/adjunct (0 women). *Students:* 13 full-time (11 women), 7 part-time (3 women); includes 1 minority (Hispanic/Latino), 5 international. Average age 27. 19 applicants, 53% accepted, 5 enrolled. In 2014, 8 master's awarded. *Degree requirements:* For master's, thesis; for doctorate, thesis/dissertation. *Entrance requirements:* For master's, minimum GPA of 2.7; for doctorate, minimum GPA of 3.25. Additional exam requirements/recommendations for international students: Required—TOEFL. *Application deadline:* Applications are processed on a rolling basis. Application fee: $50. *Expenses:* Tuition, state resident: full-time $10,176; part-time $1153 per credit. Tuition, nonresident: full-time $20,814; part-time $1744 per credit. *Required fees:* $7092; $394 per credit. $2364 per semester. *Financial support:* In 2014–15, 21 students received support, including 6 research assistantships with full tuition reimbursements available, 11 teaching assistantships with full tuition reimbursements available; fellowships with full tuition reimbursements available, career-related internships or fieldwork, Federal Work-Study, institutionally sponsored loans, and tuition waivers (full) also available. Support available to part-time students. Financial award application deadline: 4/1. *Faculty research:* Natural resources management emphasizing water resources and environmental quality of air, water, and land systems. *Unit head:* Dr. Justin Schoof, Chair, 618-453-6019, E-mail: jschoof@siu.edu. *Application contact:* Jennie Absher, Administrative Clerk, 618-536-3375, E-mail: jabsher@siu.edu. Website: http://cola.siu.edu/geography/graduate/index.php

Southern Illinois University Edwardsville, Graduate School, College of Arts and Sciences, Department of Geography, Edwardsville, IL 62026. Offers MS. Part-time and evening/weekend programs available. *Faculty:* 13 full-time (6 women). *Students:* 9 full-time (5 women), 14 part-time (2 women), 2 international. 13 applicants, 77% accepted. In 2014, 9 master's awarded. *Degree requirements:* For master's, thesis optional, final exam. *Entrance requirements:* For master's, GRE (for applicants with a GPA less than 2.8). Additional exam requirements/recommendations for international students: Required—TOEFL (minimum score 550 paper-based; 79 iBT), IELTS (minimum score 6.5). *Application deadline:* For fall admission, 7/24 for domestic students, 7/15 for international students; for spring admission, 12/11 for domestic students, 11/15 for international students; for summer admission, 4/29 for domestic students, 4/15 for international students. Applications are processed on a rolling basis. Application fee: $30. Electronic applications accepted. *Expenses:* Tuition, state resident: full-time $5026. Tuition, nonresident: full-time $12,566. *International tuition:* $25,136 full-time. *Required fees:* $1682. Tuition and fees vary according to course load, campus/location and program. *Financial support:* In 2014–15, 14 students received support, including 10 research assistantships with full tuition reimbursements available, 4 teaching assistantships with full tuition reimbursements available; fellowships with full tuition reimbursements available, career-related internships or fieldwork, scholarships/grants, and unspecified assistantships also available. Financial award application deadline: 3/1; financial award applicants required to submit FAFSA. *Unit head:* Dr. Gillian Acheson, Chair, 618-650-2090, E-mail: gacgeso@siue.edu. *Application contact:* Melissa K. Mace, Assistant Director of Admissions for Graduate and International Recruitment, 618-650-2756, Fax: 618-650-3618, E-mail: mmace@siue.edu. Website: http://www.siue.edu/artsandsciences/geography/

Syracuse University, Maxwell School of Citizenship and Public Affairs, Program in Geography, Syracuse, NY 13244. Offers MA, PhD. Part-time and evening/weekend programs available. *Students:* 26 full-time (10 women), 6 part-time (4 women); includes 4 minority (2 Black or African American, non-Hispanic/Latino; 1 Asian, non-Hispanic/Latino; 1 Hispanic/Latino), 9 international. Average age 29. 72 applicants, 36% accepted, 6 enrolled. In 2014, 6 master's, 9 doctorates awarded. *Degree requirements:* For master's, thesis or alternative; for doctorate, comprehensive exam, thesis/dissertation. *Entrance requirements:* For master's and doctorate, GRE General Test. Additional exam requirements/recommendations for international students: Required—TOEFL (minimum score 100 iBT). *Application deadline:* For fall admission, 1/5 priority date for domestic and international students. Application fee: $75. Electronic applications accepted. *Expenses: Tuition:* Part-time $1341 per credit. *Financial support:* Fellowships with full tuition reimbursements, research assistantships with full and partial tuition reimbursements, and teaching assistantships with full and partial tuition reimbursements available. Financial award application deadline: 1/1. *Unit head:* Dr. Jamie Winders, Chair, 315-443-2605, Fax: 315-443-4227. *Application contact:* Chris Chapman, Recruiting Contact, 315-443-2605, E-mail: cmchapma@maxwell.syr.edu. Website: http://www.maxwell.syr.edu/geo/

Temple University, College of Liberal Arts, Department of Geography and Urban Studies, Philadelphia, PA 19122-6096. Offers geography and urban studies (MA); urban studies (PhD). *Faculty:* 9 full-time (3 women), 1 (woman) part-time/adjunct. *Students:* 23 full-time (12 women), 4 part-time (2 women); includes 7 minority (5 Black or African

American, non-Hispanic/Latino; 1 Hispanic/Latino; 1 Two or more races, non-Hispanic/Latino), 3 international. 48 applicants, 38% accepted, 10 enrolled. In 2014, 6 master's, 2 doctorates awarded. *Degree requirements:* For master's, comprehensive exam, thesis or alternative. *Entrance requirements:* For master's, GRE General Test, minimum GPA of 3.0, 3 letters of recommendation; for doctorate, GRE, minimum GPA of 3.0, 3 letters of recommendation. Additional exam requirements/recommendations for international students: Required—TOEFL (minimum score 575 paper-based; 88 iBT). *Application deadline:* For fall admission, 1/15 for domestic students, 12/15 for international students; for spring admission, 10/15 for domestic students, 8/1 for international students. Applications are processed on a rolling basis. Application fee: $60. Electronic applications accepted. *Expenses:* Tuition, state resident: full-time $14,490; part-time $805 per credit hour. Tuition, nonresident: full-time $19,850; part-time $1103 per credit hour. *Required fees:* $690. Full-time tuition and fees vary according to class time, course load, degree level, campus/location and program. *Financial support:* Fellowships, teaching assistantships, career-related internships or fieldwork, Federal Work-Study, and tuition waivers (partial) available. Financial award application deadline: 1/15; financial award applicants required to submit FAFSA. *Faculty research:* Social justice, sustainability, globalization, geographic methods, urban processes. *Unit head:* Dr. C. Hamil Pearsall, Graduate Director, 215-204-3074, Fax: 215-204-7833, E-mail: hamil.pearsall@temple.edu. *Application contact:* Tycina Cousin, Coordinator, 215-204-7692, Fax: 215-204-7833, E-mail: tcousin@temple.edu.
Website: http://www.cla.temple.edu/gus/

Texas A&M University, College of Geosciences, Department of Geography, College Station, TX 77843. Offers MS, PhD. Part-time programs available. *Faculty:* 19. *Students:* 61 full-time (28 women), 19 part-time (15 women); includes 9 minority (2 Black or African American, non-Hispanic/Latino; 1 Asian, non-Hispanic/Latino; 6 Hispanic/Latino), 23 international. Average age 29. 130 applicants, 48% accepted, 27 enrolled. In 2014, 11 master's, 6 doctorates awarded. *Degree requirements:* For master's, thesis optional; for doctorate, thesis/dissertation. *Entrance requirements:* For master's and doctorate, GRE General Test. Additional exam requirements/recommendations for international students: Required—TOEFL. *Application deadline:* For fall admission, 3/1 priority date for domestic students; for spring admission, 10/1 for domestic students. Applications are processed on a rolling basis. Application fee: $50 ($90 for international students). Electronic applications accepted. *Expenses:* Tuition, state resident: full-time $4078; part-time $226.55 per credit hour. Tuition, nonresident: full-time $10,594; part-time $577.55 per credit hour. *Required fees:* $2813; $237.70 per credit hour. $278.50 per semester. Tuition and fees vary according to degree level and student level. *Financial support:* In 2014–15, 70 students received support, including 28 fellowships with full and partial tuition reimbursements available (averaging $3,112 per year), 27 research assistantships with full and partial tuition reimbursements available (averaging $6,045 per year), 25 teaching assistantships with full and partial tuition reimbursements available (averaging $7,330 per year); career-related internships or fieldwork, institutionally sponsored loans, scholarships/grants, traineeships, health care benefits, tuition waivers (full and partial), and unspecified assistantships also available. Support available to part-time students. Financial award application deadline: 3/1; financial award applicants required to submit FAFSA. *Faculty research:* Geomorphology, historical geography, urban-economic geography, geographic education and technology, human-environment interaction. *Unit head:* Dr. David M. Cairns, Department Head, 979-845-2783, E-mail: cairns@tamu.edu. *Application contact:* Gail Rowe, Academic Advisor II, 979-458-0895, Fax: 979-862-4487, E-mail: growe@geog.tamu.edu.
Website: http://geography.tamu.edu

Texas State University, The Graduate College, College of Liberal Arts, Department of Geography, Program in Geographic Education, San Marcos, TX 78666. Offers MAG, PhD. Part-time and evening/weekend programs available. *Faculty:* 6 full-time (1 woman). *Students:* 4 full-time (3 women), 7 part-time (6 women); includes 2 minority (both Hispanic/Latino), 1 international. Average age 37. 2 applicants, 50% accepted, 1 enrolled. In 2014, 4 doctorates awarded. *Degree requirements:* For master's, comprehensive exam, thesis (for some programs); for doctorate, comprehensive exam, thesis/dissertation. *Entrance requirements:* For master's, GRE (minimum preferred score of 300 verbal and quantitative), bachelor's degree from regionally-accredited institution with minimum GPA of 3.2 on last 60 hours of undergraduate course work; for doctorate, GRE General Test (minimum preferred score of 303 verbal and quantitative), master's degree in geography or related field with minimum GPA of 3.5 on all graduate coursework. Additional exam requirements/recommendations for international students: Required—TOEFL (minimum score 550 paper-based; 78 iBT). *Application deadline:* For fall admission, 5/1 priority date for domestic students, 4/15 for international students; for spring admission, 10/15 priority date for domestic students, 10/1 for international students. Applications are processed on a rolling basis. Application fee: $40 ($90 for international students). Electronic applications accepted. *Expenses:* Expenses: $8,834 (tuition and fees combined). *Financial support:* In 2014–15, 6 students received support, including 2 research assistantships (averaging $29,502 per year), 3 teaching assistantships (averaging $26,000 per year); career-related internships or fieldwork, Federal Work-Study, and institutionally sponsored loans also available. Support available to part-time students. Financial award application deadline: 4/1; financial award applicants required to submit FAFSA. *Total annual research expenditures:* $114,552. *Unit head:* Dr. David Butler, Graduate Adviser, 512-245-2170, Fax: 512-245-8353, E-mail: db25@txstate.edu. *Application contact:* Dr. Andrea Golato, Dean of Graduate School, 512-245-2581, Fax: 512-245-8365, E-mail: gradcollege@txstate.edu.
Website: http://www.geo.txstate.edu/

Texas State University, The Graduate College, College of Liberal Arts, Department of Geography, Program in Geography, San Marcos, TX 78666. Offers MAG, MS, PhD. Part-time programs available. *Faculty:* 16 full-time (5 women). *Students:* 35 full-time (14 women), 33 part-time (17 women); includes 11 minority (9 Hispanic/Latino; 2 Two or more races, non-Hispanic/Latino), 7 international. Average age 34. 43 applicants, 70% accepted, 18 enrolled. In 2014, 16 master's, 4 doctorates awarded. *Degree requirements:* For master's, comprehensive exam, thesis (for some programs); for doctorate, comprehensive exam, thesis/dissertation. *Entrance requirements:* For master's, GRE with minimum preferred verbal and quantitative score of 300 (for MAG), 303 (for MS), baccalaureate degree from regionally-accredited university; minimum GPA of 3.2 on last 60 undergraduate semester hours (for MAG), 3.4 (for MS); for doctorate, GRE (minimum preferred score of 303 verbal and quantitative), master's degree in geography or related field, minimum GPA of 3.5 in completed graduate course work. Additional exam requirements/recommendations for international students: Required—TOEFL (minimum score 550 paper-based; 78 iBT). *Application deadline:* For fall admission, 5/1 for domestic students, 4/15 for international students; for spring admission, 10/15 priority date for domestic students, 10/1 for international students. Applications are processed on a rolling basis. Application fee: $40 ($90 for international students). Electronic applications accepted. *Expenses:* Expenses: $8,834 (tuition and fees combined). *Financial support:* In 2014–15, 34 students received support, including 3 research assistantships (averaging $16,569 per year), 24 teaching assistantships (averaging $20,073 per year); career-related internships or fieldwork, Federal Work-Study, and institutionally sponsored loans also available. Support available to part-time students. Financial award application deadline: 4/1; financial award applicants required to submit FAFSA. *Faculty research:* Local to global SSC, land management impact. *Total annual research expenditures:* $97,699. *Unit head:* Dr. David Butler, Graduate Adviser, 512-245-2618, Fax: 512-245-8353, E-mail: db25@txstate.edu. *Application contact:* Dr. Andrea Golato, Dean of Graduate School, 512-245-2581, Fax: 512-245-8365, E-mail: gradcollege@txstate.edu.
Website: http://www.geo.txstate.edu/

Texas State University, The Graduate College, College of Liberal Arts, Department of Geography, Program in Land Management, San Marcos, TX 78666. Offers MAG. Part-time and evening/weekend programs available. *Faculty:* 3 full-time (0 women), 1 part-time/adjunct (0 women). *Students:* 1 part-time (0 women). Average age 39. In 2014, 2 master's awarded. *Degree requirements:* For master's, comprehensive exam. *Entrance requirements:* For master's, GRE General Test, minimum GPA of 3.0 in last 60 hours of course work, letter of interest, 2 letters of recommendation, curriculum vitae/resume. Additional exam requirements/recommendations for international students: Required—TOEFL (minimum score 550 paper-based; 78 iBT). *Application deadline:* For fall admission, 6/15 priority date for domestic students, 6/1 for international students; for spring admission, 10/15 priority date for domestic students, 10/1 for international students. Applications are processed on a rolling basis. Application fee: $40 ($90 for international students). Electronic applications accepted. *Financial support:* Research assistantships, teaching assistantships, career-related internships or fieldwork, Federal Work-Study, institutionally sponsored loans, and scholarships/grants available. Support available to part-time students. Financial award application deadline: 4/1; financial award applicants required to submit FAFSA. *Unit head:* Dr. David Butler, Graduate Adviser, 512-245-2170, Fax: 512-245-8353, E-mail: db25@txstate.edu. *Application contact:* Dr. Andrea Golato, Dean of Graduate School, 512-245-2581, Fax: 512-245-8365, E-mail: gradcollege@txstate.edu.
Website: http://www.geo.txstate.edu/

Texas Tech University, Graduate School, College of Arts and Sciences, Department of Geosciences, Lubbock, TX 79409-1053. Offers atmospheric science (MS); geography (MS); geosciences (MS, PhD). Part-time programs available. *Faculty:* 29 full-time (5 women), 4 part-time/adjunct (0 women). *Students:* 72 full-time (21 women), 9 part-time (5 women); includes 9 minority (1 Black or African American, non-Hispanic/Latino; 1 Asian, non-Hispanic/Latino; 5 Hispanic/Latino; 2 Two or more races, non-Hispanic/Latino), 9 international. Average age 27. 178 applicants, 17% accepted, 26 enrolled. In 2014, 20 master's, 1 doctorate awarded. *Degree requirements:* For master's, thesis; for doctorate, comprehensive exam, thesis/dissertation. *Entrance requirements:* For master's and doctorate, GRE General Test. Additional exam requirements/recommendations for international students: Required—TOEFL (minimum score 550 paper-based; 79 iBT). *Application deadline:* For fall admission, 6/1 priority date for domestic students, 1/15 priority date for international students; for spring admission, 9/1 priority date for domestic students, 6/15 priority date for international students. Applications are processed on a rolling basis. Application fee: $60. Electronic applications accepted. *Expenses:* Tuition, state resident: full-time $6310; part-time $262.92 per credit hour. Tuition, nonresident: full-time $14,998; part-time $624.92 per credit hour. *Required fees:* $2701; $36.50 per credit. $912.50 per semester. Tuition and fees vary according to course load. *Financial support:* In 2014–15, 71 students received support, including 58 fellowships (averaging $3,098 per year), 5 research assistantships (averaging $23,122 per year), 47 teaching assistantships (averaging $14,997 per year); Federal Work-Study, scholarships/grants, health care benefits, tuition waivers (partial), and unspecified assistantships also available. Financial award application deadline: 2/15; financial award applicants required to submit FAFSA. *Faculty research:* Geology, geophysics, geochemistry, geospatial technology, atmospheric sciences. *Total annual research expenditures:* $2.1 million. *Unit head:* Dr. Jeffrey A. Lee, Chairman, 806-834-8228, Fax: 806-742-0100, E-mail: jeff.lee@ttu.edu. *Application contact:* Dr. Callum Hetherington, Associate Professor, 806-834-3110, Fax: 806-724-0100, E-mail: callum.hetherington@ttu.edu.
Website: http://www.geosciences.ttu.edu

Towson University, Program in Geography and Environmental Planning, Towson, MD 21252-0001. Offers MA. Part-time and evening/weekend programs available. *Students:* 10 full-time (7 women), 19 part-time (8 women); includes 3 minority (2 Black or African American, non-Hispanic/Latino; 1 Asian, non-Hispanic/Latino), 3 international. *Degree requirements:* For master's, thesis optional. *Entrance requirements:* For master's, bachelor's degree with minimum of 9 credits of course work in geography, minimum GPA of 3.0 overall and in all geography courses, 2 letters of recommendation, essay. *Application deadline:* Applications are processed on a rolling basis. Application fee: $45. Electronic applications accepted. *Financial support:* Application deadline: 4/1. *Unit head:* Dr. Charles Schmitz, Graduate Program Director, 410-704-2966, E-mail: cschmitz@towson.edu. *Application contact:* Alicia Arkell-Kleis, Information Contact, 410-704-6004, Fax: 410-704-4675, E-mail: grads@towson.edu.
Website: http://grad.towson.edu/program/master/geog-ma/

Trent University, Graduate Studies, Program in Applications of Modeling in the Natural and Social Sciences, Peterborough, ON K9J 7B8, Canada. Offers applications of modeling in the natural and social sciences (MA); biology (M Sc, PhD); chemistry (M Sc); computer studies (M Sc); geography (M Sc, PhD); physics (M Sc). Part-time programs available. *Degree requirements:* For master's, thesis. *Entrance requirements:* For master's, honours degree. *Faculty research:* Computation of heat transfer, atmospheric physics, statistical mechanics, stress and coping, evolutionary ecology.

Trent University, Graduate Studies, Program in Environmental and Life Sciences and Program in Applications of Modeling in the Natural and Social Sciences, Department of Geography, Peterborough, ON K9J 7B8, Canada. Offers M Sc, PhD. Part-time programs available. *Degree requirements:* For master's, thesis; for doctorate, thesis/dissertation. *Entrance requirements:* For master's, honors degree; for doctorate, master's degree. *Faculty research:* Hydrometeorology, snow and ice, urban hydrology, fluvial geomorphology.

Université de Montréal, Faculty of Arts and Sciences, Department of Geography, Montréal, QC H3C 3J7, Canada. Offers environment and durable development (DESS); geography (M Sc, PhD, DESS). *Degree requirements:* For master's, 2 foreign languages, thesis (for some programs); for doctorate, 3 foreign languages, thesis/dissertation, general exam. *Entrance requirements:* For master's, bachelor's degree in related field; for doctorate, MA in geography or related field. Electronic applications accepted. *Faculty research:* Cartography, palynology, geomorphology, economic geography, regional and urban development.

Université de Sherbrooke, Faculty of Letters and Human Sciences, Department of Geography and Remote Sensing, Sherbrooke, QC J1K 2R1, Canada. Offers M Sc, PhD. *Degree requirements:* For master's, one foreign language, thesis; for doctorate, thesis/dissertation. *Faculty research:* Cartography.

Université du Québec à Montréal, Graduate Programs, Program in Geography, Montréal, QC H3C 3P8, Canada. Offers M Sc. Part-time programs available. *Degree requirements:* For master's, thesis optional. *Entrance requirements:* For master's, appropriate bachelor's degree or equivalent and proficiency in French.

Université Laval, Faculty of Forestry, Geography and Geomatics, Department of Geography, Program in Geographical Sciences, Québec, QC G1K 7P4, Canada. Offers

M Sc Geogr, PhD. Terminal master's awarded for partial completion of doctoral program. *Degree requirements:* For master's, thesis; for doctorate, comprehensive exam, thesis/dissertation. *Entrance requirements:* For master's, knowledge of French; for doctorate, knowledge of French, knowledge of a second language. Electronic applications accepted.

University at Albany, State University of New York, College of Arts and Sciences, Department of Geography and Planning, Program in Geography, Albany, NY 12222-0001. Offers MA. *Degree requirements:* For master's, thesis or alternative. *Entrance requirements:* Additional exam requirements/recommendations for international students: Required—TOEFL (minimum score 550 paper-based). Electronic applications accepted. *Faculty research:* Remote sensing, cultural/social geography, urban geography.

University at Buffalo, the State University of New York, Graduate School, College of Arts and Sciences, Department of Geography, Buffalo, NY 14260. Offers Canadian studies (Certificate); earth systems science (MA, MS); economic geography and business geographics (MS); environmental modeling and analysis (MA); geographic information science (MA, MS); geography (MA, PhD); GIS and environmental analysis (Certificate); health geography (MS); international trade (MA); transportation and business geographics (MA); urban and regional analysis (MA). Part-time programs available. *Faculty:* 18 full-time (9 women), 1 part-time/adjunct (0 women). *Students:* 87 full-time (37 women), 26 part-time (8 women); includes 78 minority (1 Black or African American, non-Hispanic/Latino; 74 Asian, non-Hispanic/Latino; 3 Hispanic/Latino). Average age 29. 167 applicants, 44% accepted, 32 enrolled. In 2014, 24 master's, 6 doctorates awarded. Terminal master's awarded for partial completion of doctoral program. *Degree requirements:* For master's, thesis (for some programs), project or portfolio; for doctorate, thesis/dissertation. *Entrance requirements:* For master's, GRE General Test, minimum GPA of 2.9; for doctorate, GRE General Test, minimum GPA of 3.0. Additional exam requirements/recommendations for international students: Required—TOEFL (minimum score 550 paper-based; 79 iBT). *Application deadline:* For fall admission, 5/1 priority date for domestic students, 3/10 priority date for international students; for spring admission, 11/1 priority date for domestic students, 9/1 priority date for international students. Applications are processed on a rolling basis. Application fee: $75. Electronic applications accepted. *Financial support:* In 2014–15, 13 students received support, including 8 fellowships with full tuition reimbursements available (averaging $5,500 per year), 13 teaching assistantships with full tuition reimbursements available (averaging $13,800 per year); research assistantships with full tuition reimbursements available, career-related internships or fieldwork, Federal Work-Study, institutionally sponsored loans, traineeships, health care benefits, and unspecified assistantships also available. Financial award application deadline: 1/10. *Faculty research:* International business and world trade, geographic information systems and cartography, transportation, urban and regional analysis, physical and environmental geography. *Total annual research expenditures:* $2.6 million. *Unit head:* Dr. Sharmistha Bagchi-Sen, Chairman, 716-645-0473, Fax: 716-645-2329, E-mail: geosbs@buffalo.edu. *Application contact:* Betsy Crooks, Graduate Secretary, 716-645-0471, Fax: 716-645-2329, E-mail: babraham@buffalo.edu.
Website: http://www.geog.buffalo.edu/

The University of Alabama, Graduate School, College of Arts and Sciences, Department of Geography, Tuscaloosa, AL 35487. Offers earth system science (MS); geographic information science (MS); planning (MS). Part-time programs available. *Faculty:* 14 full-time (1 woman), 1 (woman) part-time/adjunct. *Students:* 26 full-time (10 women), 5 part-time (2 women); includes 1 minority (Two or more races, non-Hispanic/Latino), 4 international. Average age 27. 19 applicants, 68% accepted, 10 enrolled. In 2014, 12 master's awarded. *Degree requirements:* For master's, comprehensive exam (for some programs), thesis (for some programs). *Entrance requirements:* For master's, GRE, minimum GPA of 3.0. Additional exam requirements/recommendations for international students: Required—TOEFL (minimum score 550 paper-based; 79 iBT). *Application deadline:* For fall admission, 2/15 priority date for domestic and international students; for spring admission, 10/1 priority date for domestic and international students. Applications are processed on a rolling basis. Application fee: $50 ($60 for international students). Electronic applications accepted. *Expenses:* Tuition, state resident: full-time $9826. Tuition, nonresident: full-time $24,950. *Financial support:* In 2014–15, 16 students received support, including fellowships with full tuition reimbursements available (averaging $15,000 per year), 4 research assistantships with full tuition reimbursements available (averaging $13,311 per year), 18 teaching assistantships with full tuition reimbursements available (averaging $13,311 per year); career-related internships or fieldwork, health care benefits, and unspecified assistantships also available. Financial award application deadline: 2/15. *Faculty research:* Earth system science; geographic information science; urban, regional and environmental planning; ecology. *Total annual research expenditures:* $393,294. *Unit head:* Dr. Douglas Sherman, Chair, 205-348-5047, Fax: 205-348-2278, E-mail: douglas.j.sherman@ua.edu. *Application contact:* Dr. Justin Hart, Assistant Professor, 205-348-5047, Fax: 205-348-2278, E-mail: hart013@ua.edu.
Website: http://geography.ua.edu

The University of Arizona, College of Social and Behavioral Sciences, School of Geography and Development, Tucson, AZ 85721. Offers geographic information science (Certificate); geographic information systems technology (MA); geography (MA, PhD). Part-time programs available. Terminal master's awarded for partial completion of doctoral program. *Degree requirements:* For master's, thesis or additional course work; for doctorate, variable foreign language requirement, thesis/dissertation. *Entrance requirements:* For master's, GRE General Test, 2 letters of recommendation; for doctorate, GRE General Test, statement of purpose, 2 letters of recommendation, master's degree. Additional exam requirements/recommendations for international students: Required—TOEFL (minimum score 550 paper-based; 79 iBT). Electronic applications accepted. *Faculty research:* Population, Latin America, Anglo-America, the former Soviet Union, the Middle East.

University of Arkansas, Graduate School, J. William Fulbright College of Arts and Sciences, Department of Geosciences, Program in Geography, Fayetteville, AR 72701-1201. Offers MA. Part-time programs available. *Degree requirements:* For master's, thesis. Electronic applications accepted.

The University of British Columbia, Faculty of Arts and Faculty of Graduate Studies, Department of Geography, Vancouver, BC V6T 1Z2, Canada. Offers M Sc, MA, PhD. Part-time programs available. Terminal master's awarded for partial completion of doctoral program. *Degree requirements:* For master's, thesis; for doctorate, comprehensive exam, thesis/dissertation. *Entrance requirements:* For master's and doctorate, minimum B average, 2nd class honors, upper division (class II, division I). Additional exam requirements/recommendations for international students: Required—TOEFL (minimum score 600 paper-based; 100 iBT). Electronic applications accepted. *Faculty research:* Earth system science, environmental geography, historical geography, social geography, urban geography.

University of Calgary, Faculty of Graduate Studies, Faculty of Arts, Department of Geography, Calgary, AB T2N 1N4, Canada. Offers M Sc, MA, MGIS, PhD. Part-time programs available. *Degree requirements:* For master's, thesis, departmental conference; for doctorate, thesis/dissertation, candidacy exam, departmental

conference. *Entrance requirements:* For master's, minimum undergraduate GPA of 3.0 during last 2 years; for doctorate, minimum GPA of 3.0 during previous 2 years, master's degree. Additional exam requirements/recommendations for international students: Required—TOEFL (minimum score 550 paper-based). Electronic applications accepted. *Faculty research:* Geographic information systems, remote sensing, geomorphology, earth system processes, urban and required environmental health research.

University of California, Berkeley, Graduate Division, College of Letters and Science, Department of Geography, Berkeley, CA 94720-1500. Offers PhD. *Degree requirements:* For doctorate, thesis/dissertation, qualifying exam. *Entrance requirements:* For doctorate, GRE General Test, minimum GPA of 3.0, 3 letters of recommendation. Electronic applications accepted.

University of California, Davis, Graduate Studies, Graduate Group in Geography, Davis, CA 95616. Offers MA, PhD. Terminal master's awarded for partial completion of doctoral program. *Degree requirements:* For master's, comprehensive exam (for some programs), thesis (for some programs); for doctorate, thesis/dissertation. *Entrance requirements:* For master's, GRE General Test, minimum GPA of 3.0; for doctorate, GRE General Test, master's degree, minimum GPA of 3.0. Additional exam requirements/recommendations for international students: Required—TOEFL (minimum score 550 paper-based). Electronic applications accepted. *Faculty research:* Cultural agrosystems, mountain society habitat and South Asia.

University of California, Los Angeles, Graduate Division, College of Letters and Science, Department of Geography, Los Angeles, CA 90095. Offers MA, PhD. Terminal master's awarded for partial completion of doctoral program. *Degree requirements:* For master's, thesis; for doctorate, thesis/dissertation, oral and written qualifying exams. *Entrance requirements:* For doctorate, GRE General Test, bachelor's degree; minimum undergraduate GPA of 3.3, 3.5 in graduate work (or its equivalent if letter grade system not used); writing sample. Additional exam requirements/recommendations for international students: Required—TOEFL. Electronic applications accepted.

University of California, Santa Barbara, Graduate Division, College of Letters and Sciences, Division of Mathematics, Life, and Physical Sciences, Department of Geography, Santa Barbara, CA 93106-4060. Offers cognitive science (PhD); geography (MA, PhD); global studies (PhD); quantitative methods in the social sciences (PhD); technology and society (PhD); transportation (PhD); MA/PhD. Terminal master's awarded for partial completion of doctoral program. *Degree requirements:* For master's, comprehensive exam (for some programs), thesis or alternative; for doctorate, comprehensive exam, thesis/dissertation, 1 quarter of teaching assistantship. *Entrance requirements:* For master's and doctorate, GRE (minimum combined verbal and quantitative scores of 1100 in old scoring system or 301 in new scoring system). Additional exam requirements/recommendations for international students: Required—TOEFL (minimum score 550 paper-based; 80 iBT), IELTS (minimum score 7). Electronic applications accepted. *Faculty research:* Earth system science; human environment relations; modeling, measurement, and computation.

University of Central Arkansas, Graduate School, College of Liberal Arts, Department of Geography, Conway, AR 72035-0001. Offers community and economic development (MS); geographic information systems (MGIS, Certificate). Part-time programs available. Postbaccalaureate distance learning degree programs offered (minimal on-campus study). *Entrance requirements:* Additional exam requirements/recommendations for international students: Required—TOEFL (minimum score 550 paper-based). Electronic applications accepted.

University of Cincinnati, Graduate School, McMicken College of Arts and Sciences, Department of Geography, Cincinnati, OH 45221. Offers MA, PhD. Terminal master's awarded for partial completion of doctoral program. *Degree requirements:* For master's, thesis optional; for doctorate, one foreign language, comprehensive exam, thesis/dissertation. *Entrance requirements:* For master's and doctorate, GRE General Test. Additional exam requirements/recommendations for international students: Required—TOEFL. Electronic applications accepted. *Faculty research:* Urban-economics, GIS, physical-environmental.

University of Colorado Boulder, Graduate School, College of Arts and Sciences, Department of Geography, Boulder, CO 80309. Offers MA, PhD. *Faculty:* 22 full-time (8 women). *Students:* 66 full-time (30 women), 5 part-time (2 women); includes 1 minority (Two or more races, non-Hispanic/Latino), 11 international. Average age 32. 133 applicants, 26% accepted, 13 enrolled. In 2014, 11 master's, 8 doctorates awarded. Terminal master's awarded for partial completion of doctoral program. *Degree requirements:* For master's, thesis; for doctorate, one foreign language, comprehensive exam, thesis/dissertation. *Entrance requirements:* For master's, GRE General Test, minimum undergraduate GPA of 3.0; for doctorate, GRE General Test. *Application deadline:* For fall admission, 12/1 for domestic and international students. Application fee: $50 ($70 for international students). Electronic applications accepted. *Financial support:* In 2014–15, 136 students received support, including 24 fellowships (averaging $10,666 per year), 11 research assistantships with full and partial tuition reimbursements available (averaging $30,408 per year), 40 teaching assistantships with full and partial tuition reimbursements available (averaging $35,618 per year); institutionally sponsored loans, scholarships/grants, health care benefits, and unspecified assistantships also available. Financial award application deadline: 1/15; financial award applicants required to submit FAFSA. *Faculty research:* Hydrology, physical geography, political geography, cultural geography, ecology. *Total annual research expenditures:* $23.3 million.
Website: http://geography.colorado.edu

University of Colorado Colorado Springs, College of Letters, Arts and Sciences, Department of Geography and Environmental Studies, Colorado Springs, CO 80933-7150. Offers MA. Part-time programs available. *Faculty:* 13 full-time (4 women), 5 part-time/adjunct (2 women). *Students:* 6 full-time (3 women), 11 part-time (5 women); includes 5 minority (1 Asian, non-Hispanic/Latino; 4 Hispanic/Latino). Average age 33. 10 applicants, 100% accepted, 9 enrolled. In 2014, 4 master's awarded. *Degree requirements:* For master's, comprehensive exam (for some programs), thesis (for some programs). *Entrance requirements:* For master's, GRE (recommended minimum combined score for the verbal and quantitative tests of 1000), minimum undergraduate GPA of 3.0, statement of intent (essay). Additional exam requirements/recommendations for international students: Recommended—TOEFL (minimum score 550 paper-based; 80 iBT). *Application deadline:* For fall admission, 2/1 priority date for domestic students, 2/1 for international students. Applications are processed on a rolling basis. Application fee: $60 ($100 for international students). *Expenses:* Tuition, state resident: full-time $9900; part-time $1892 per course. Tuition, nonresident: full-time $18,792; part-time $3375 per course. One-time fee: $100. Tuition and fees vary according to course load, program and reciprocity agreements. *Financial support:* In 2014–15, 10 students received support. Fellowships, Federal Work-Study, and scholarships/grants available. Support available to part-time students. Financial award application deadline: 3/1; financial award applicants required to submit FAFSA. *Faculty research:* Socio-ecological implications of conservation strategies, cultural geography, militarized spaces, geovisualization, geographic information systems, hydrology, biogeography, human-environment interactions, geomorphology, population. *Total annual research expenditures:* $160,127. *Unit head:* Dr. Kelli Klebe, Dean of the

Geography

Graduate School, 719-255-3779, Fax: 719-255-3045, E-mail: kklebe@uccs.edu. *Application contact:* Emily Skop, Program Assistant, 719-255-3789, E-mail: eskop@uccs.edu.
Website: http://www.uccs.edu/geography/

University of Connecticut, Graduate School, College of Liberal Arts and Sciences, Department of Geography, Storrs, CT 06269. Offers geographic information systems (Certificate); geography (MS, PhD). *Degree requirements:* For master's, comprehensive exam; for doctorate, thesis/dissertation. *Entrance requirements:* For master's and doctorate, GRE General Test. Additional exam requirements/recommendations for international students: Required—TOEFL (minimum score 550 paper-based). Electronic applications accepted.

University of Delaware, College of Earth, Ocean, and Environment, Department of Geography, Newark, DE 19716. Offers MA, MS, PhD. *Degree requirements:* For master's, thesis; for doctorate, thesis/dissertation. *Entrance requirements:* For master's and doctorate, GRE General Test. Additional exam requirements/recommendations for international students: Required—TOEFL. Electronic applications accepted. *Faculty research:* Permafrost, glaciers, climatology, physical geography, human geography.

University of Denver, Division of Natural Sciences and Mathematics, Department of Geography and the Environment, Denver, CO 80208. Offers MA, MS, PhD. Part-time programs available. *Faculty:* 13 full-time (4 women), 4 part-time/adjunct (2 women). *Students:* 3 full-time (all women), 52 part-time (17 women); includes 10 minority (2 Black or African American, non-Hispanic/Latino; 8 Hispanic/Latino), 2 international. Average age 32. 66 applicants, 50% accepted, 21 enrolled. In 2014, 22 master's, 3 doctorates awarded. Terminal master's awarded for partial completion of doctoral program. *Degree requirements:* For master's, comprehensive exam (for some programs), thesis or alternative; for doctorate, one foreign language, comprehensive exam, thesis/dissertation. *Entrance requirements:* For master's, GRE General Test, bachelor's degree, transcripts, personal statement, three letters of recommendation; for doctorate, GRE General Test, master's degree, transcripts, personal statement, three letters of recommendation. Additional exam requirements/recommendations for international students: Required—TOEFL (minimum score 570 paper-based; 88 iBT). *Application deadline:* For fall admission, 1/15 priority date for domestic and international students. Applications are processed on a rolling basis. Application fee: $65. Electronic applications accepted. *Expenses:* Expenses: $1,199 per credit hour. *Financial support:* In 2014–15, 51 students received support, including 15 teaching assistantships with full and partial tuition reimbursements available (averaging $16,972 per year); career-related internships or fieldwork, Federal Work-Study, institutionally sponsored loans, scholarships/grants, and unspecified assistantships also available. Support available to part-time students. Financial award application deadline: 2/15; financial award applicants required to submit FAFSA. *Faculty research:* Geomorphology, human-environment relationships, remote sensing and geovisualization, transportation, urbanization. *Total annual research expenditures:* $71,974. *Unit head:* Dr. Andrew Goetz, Chair, 303-871-2674, Fax: 303-871-2201, E-mail: agoetz@du.edu. *Application contact:* Amanda O'Connor, Assistant to the Chair, 303-871-2654, Fax: 303-871-2201, E-mail: amanda.oconnor@du.edu.
Website: http://www.du.edu/nsm/departments/geography/

University of Florida, Graduate School, College of Liberal Arts and Sciences, Department of Geography, Gainesville, FL 32611-7315. Offers applications of geographic technologies (MA, MS); geographic information systems (MA, MS, PhD); geography (MA, MS, PhD); hydrologic sciences (MS, PhD); tropical conservation and development (MA, MS, PhD); wetland sciences (MA, MS, PhD). *Faculty:* 12 full-time (4 women), 1 part-time/adjunct (0 women). *Students:* 35 full-time (16 women), 3 part-time (2 women); includes 5 minority (1 Black or African American, non-Hispanic/Latino; 4 Hispanic/Latino), 14 international. 55 applicants, 33% accepted, 8 enrolled. In 2014, 2 master's, 9 doctorates awarded. *Degree requirements:* For master's, thesis; for doctorate, comprehensive exam, thesis/dissertation. *Entrance requirements:* For master's and doctorate, GRE General Test, minimum GPA of 3.0. Additional exam requirements/recommendations for international students: Required—TOEFL (minimum score 550 paper-based; 80 iBT), IELTS (minimum score 6). *Application deadline:* For fall admission, 7/15 for domestic students, 6/15 for international students. Applications are processed on a rolling basis. Application fee: $30. Electronic applications accepted. *Financial support:* In 2014–15, 8 fellowships, 6 research assistantships, 22 teaching assistantships were awarded; career-related internships or fieldwork and unspecified assistantships also available. Financial award applicants required to submit FAFSA. *Faculty research:* Economic development, physical geography, hydrology, climatology, tropical agriculture. *Unit head:* Michael W. Binford, PhD, Chair and Professor, 352-294-7500, Fax: 352-392-8855, E-mail: mbinford@ufl.edu. *Application contact:* Corene Matyas, PhD, Associate Professor and Graduate Coordinator, 352-294-7508, Fax: 352-392-8855, E-mail: matyas@ufl.edu.
Website: http://geog.ufl.edu/

University of Georgia, Franklin College of Arts and Sciences, Department of Geography, Athens, GA 30602. Offers MA, MS, PhD. *Degree requirements:* For master's, one foreign language, thesis; for doctorate, one foreign language, thesis/dissertation. *Entrance requirements:* For master's and doctorate, GRE General Test. Electronic applications accepted.

University of Guelph, Graduate Studies, College of Social and Applied Human Sciences, Department of Geography, Guelph, ON N1G 2W1, Canada. Offers M Sc, MA, PhD. Part-time programs available. *Degree requirements:* For master's, thesis (for some programs); for doctorate, comprehensive exam, thesis/dissertation. *Entrance requirements:* For master's, minimum B average during previous 2 years of course work; for doctorate, minimum A- average. Additional exam requirements/recommendations for international students: Required—TOEFL (minimum score 550 paper-based). Electronic applications accepted. *Faculty research:* Rural resource evaluation, environmental analysis, biophysical process, rural settlement and land use, resource assessment.

University of Hawaii at Manoa, Graduate Division, College of Social Sciences, Department of Geography, Honolulu, HI 96822. Offers geography (MA, PhD); ocean policy (Graduate Certificate). Part-time programs available. *Degree requirements:* For master's, one foreign language, comprehensive exam, thesis; for doctorate, one foreign language, comprehensive exam, thesis/dissertation. *Entrance requirements:* For master's, GRE General Test; for doctorate, GRE General Test, sample of written work. Additional exam requirements/recommendations for international students: Required—TOEFL (minimum score 500 paper-based; 61 iBT), IELTS (minimum score 5). *Faculty research:* Physical geography, human geography, methodology.

University of Idaho, College of Graduate Studies, College of Science, Department of Geography, Moscow, ID 83844-3021. Offers MS, PhD. *Faculty:* 7 full-time, 1 part-time/adjunct. *Students:* 20 full-time, 11 part-time. Average age 32. In 2014, 3 master's, 1 doctorate awarded. *Degree requirements:* For doctorate, one foreign language, thesis/dissertation. *Entrance requirements:* For master's, minimum GPA of 2.8; for doctorate, minimum undergraduate GPA of 2.8, graduate 3.0. Additional exam requirements/recommendations for international students: Required—TOEFL. *Application deadline:* For fall admission, 8/1 for domestic students; for spring admission, 12/15 for domestic students. Applications are processed on a rolling basis. Application fee: $60. Electronic

applications accepted. *Expenses:* Tuition, state resident: full-time $4784; part-time $280.50 per credit hour. Tuition, nonresident: full-time $18,314; part-time $957.50 per credit hour. *Required fees:* $2000; $58.50 per credit hour. Tuition and fees vary according to program. *Financial support:* Research assistantships and teaching assistantships available. Financial award applicants required to submit FAFSA. *Faculty research:* Land cover land use changes, rural development, geographic trade models, climate change and effects on ecosystems, migration and regional development. *Unit head:* Dr. Karen S. Humes, Department Head, 208-885-6216, E-mail: geog@uidaho.edu. *Application contact:* Sean Scoggin, Graduate Recruitment Coordinator, 208-885-4001, Fax: 208-885-4406, E-mail: graduateadmissions@uidaho.edu.
Website: http://www.uidaho.edu/sci/geography

University of Illinois at Chicago, Graduate College, College of Liberal Arts and Sciences, Department of Anthropology, Program in Environmental and Urban Geography, Chicago, IL 60607-7128. Offers MA. Part-time programs available. *Students:* 1 full-time (0 women), 1 part-time (0 women); includes 1 minority (Hispanic/Latino). Average age 26. 2 applicants. *Degree requirements:* For master's, thesis. *Entrance requirements:* For master's, GRE General Test, minimum GPA of 2.75. Additional exam requirements/recommendations for international students: Required—TOEFL. *Application deadline:* For fall admission, 5/15 for domestic students, 2/15 for international students; for spring admission, 11/1 for domestic students, 7/15 for international students. Applications are processed on a rolling basis. Application fee: $60 ($50 for international students). Electronic applications accepted. *Expenses:* Tuition, state resident: full-time $11,254; part-time $468 per credit hour. Tuition, nonresident: full-time $23,252; part-time $968 per credit hour. *Required fees:* $1217 per term. Part-time tuition and fees vary according to course load, degree level and program. *Financial support:* Fellowships with full tuition reimbursements, research assistantships with full tuition reimbursements, teaching assistantships with full tuition reimbursements, Federal Work-Study, scholarships/grants, traineeships, tuition waivers (full), and unspecified assistantships available. Financial award application deadline: 3/1; financial award applicants required to submit FAFSA. *Unit head:* Dr. Brian Bauer, Director of Graduate Studies, 312-413-3731, E-mail: bsb@uic.edu. *Application contact:* Prof. John Monoghan, Director of Geographic Studies, 312-413-3570, E-mail: monaghan@uic.edu.
Website: http://anthropology.las.uic.edu/anthropology/graduate/degree-programs/environmental-and-urban-geography-(ma)

University of Illinois at Urbana–Champaign, Graduate College, College of Liberal Arts and Sciences, School of Earth, Society and Environment, Department of Geography and Geographic Information Science, Champaign, IL 61820. Offers MA, MS, PhD. *Students:* 35 (15 women). Application fee: $75 ($90 for international students). *Unit head:* Sara L. McLafferty, Head, 217-244-1771, Fax: 217-244-1785, E-mail: smclaff@illinois.edu. *Application contact:* Susan Etter, Office Support Specialist, 217-244-3488, Fax: 217-244-1785, E-mail: etter1@illinois.edu.
Website: http://www.geog.illinois.edu/

The University of Iowa, Graduate College, College of Liberal Arts and Sciences, Department of Geographical and Sustainability Sciences, Iowa City, IA 52242-1316. Offers MA, PhD, Certificate. *Degree requirements:* For master's, thesis optional, exam; for doctorate, comprehensive exam, thesis/dissertation. *Entrance requirements:* For master's and doctorate, GRE General Test, minimum GPA of 3.0. Additional exam requirements/recommendations for international students: Required—TOEFL (minimum score 550 paper-based; 81 iBT). Electronic applications accepted.

The University of Kansas, Graduate Studies, College of Liberal Arts and Sciences, Department of Geography, Lawrence, KS 66045-7613. Offers atmospheric science (MS); geography (MA, PhD); MUP/MA. Part-time programs available. *Faculty:* 23 full-time, 2 part-time/adjunct. *Students:* 69 full-time (22 women), 22 part-time (10 women); includes 9 minority (7 American Indian or Alaska Native, non-Hispanic/Latino; 2 Hispanic/Latino), 10 international. Average age 29. 52 applicants, 29% accepted, 10 enrolled. In 2014, 9 master's, 6 doctorates awarded. *Degree requirements:* For master's, comprehensive exam, thesis, thesis defense; for doctorate, one foreign language, comprehensive exam, thesis/dissertation, dissertation defense. *Entrance requirements:* For master's and doctorate, GRE General Test, 3 letters of reference, transcripts, statement of interests. Additional exam requirements/recommendations for international students: Required—TOEFL. *Application deadline:* For fall admission, 1/15 priority date for domestic and international students; for spring admission, 11/1 for domestic students, 10/1 for international students. Applications are processed on a rolling basis. Application fee: $55 ($65 for international students). Electronic applications accepted. *Financial support:* Fellowships with full tuition reimbursements, research assistantships with full tuition reimbursements, teaching assistantships with full and partial tuition reimbursements, and unspecified assistantships available. Financial award application deadline: 1/15. *Faculty research:* Physical geography, human/cultural/regional geography, geographic information science, atmospheric science. *Unit head:* Johannes Feddema, Chair, 785-864-5534, E-mail: feddema@ku.edu. *Application contact:* Beverly Koerner, Administrative Associate, 785-864-7706, E-mail: koerner@ku.edu.
Website: http://www.geog.ku.edu/

University of Kentucky, Graduate School, College of Arts and Sciences, Program in Geography, Lexington, KY 40506-0032. Offers MA, PhD. *Degree requirements:* For master's, comprehensive exam, thesis optional; for doctorate, one foreign language, comprehensive exam, thesis/dissertation. *Entrance requirements:* For master's, GRE General Test, minimum undergraduate GPA of 2.75; for doctorate, GRE General Test, minimum graduate GPA of 3.0. Additional exam requirements/recommendations for international students: Required—TOEFL (minimum score 550 paper-based). Electronic applications accepted. *Faculty research:* Cultural, industrial, medical, political, social, population, and transportation geography; geographic analysis; Third World (especially Southeast Asia theory); Eastern Europe.

University of Lethbridge, School of Graduate Studies, Lethbridge, AB T1K 3M4, Canada. Offers addictions counseling (M Sc); agricultural biotechnology (M Sc); agricultural studies (M Sc, MA); anthropology (MA); archaeology (M Sc, MA); art (MA, MFA); biochemistry (M Sc); biological sciences (M Sc); biomolecular science (PhD); biosystems and biodiversity (PhD); Canadian studies (MA); chemistry (M Sc); computer science (M Sc); computer science and geographical information science (M Sc); counseling (MC); counseling psychology (M Ed); dramatic arts (MA); earth, space, and physical science (PhD); economics (MA); education (MA); educational leadership (M Ed); English (MA); environmental science (M Sc); evolution and behavior (PhD); exercise science (M Sc); French (MA); French/German (MA); French/Spanish (MA); general education (M Ed); geography (M Sc, MA); German (MA); health sciences (M Sc); individualized multidisciplinary (M Sc, MA); kinesiology (M Sc, MA); management (M Sc), including accounting, finance, general management, human resource management and labor relations, information systems, international management, marketing, policy and strategy; mathematics (M Sc); modern languages (MA); music (M Mus, MA); Native American studies (MA); neuroscience (M Sc, PhD); new media (MA, MFA); nursing (M Sc, MN); philosophy (MA); physics (M Sc); political science (MA); psychology (M Sc, MA); religious studies (MA); sociology (MA); theatre and dramatic arts (MFA); theoretical and computational science (PhD); urban and

regional studies (MA); women and gender studies (MA). Part-time and evening/weekend programs available. *Faculty:* 358. *Students:* 445 full-time (243 women), 116 part-time (72 women). Average age 31. 351 applicants, 26% accepted, 87 enrolled. In 2014, 129 master's, 13 doctorates awarded. *Degree requirements:* For master's, thesis (for some programs); for doctorate, comprehensive exam, thesis/dissertation. *Entrance requirements:* For master's, GMAT (for M Sc in management), bachelor's degree in related field, minimum GPA of 3.0 during previous 20 graded semester courses, 2 years' teaching or related experience (M Ed); for doctorate, master's degree, minimum graduate GPA of 3.5. Additional exam requirements/recommendations for international students: Required—TOEFL. Application fee: $100 Canadian dollars. *Financial support:* Fellowships, research assistantships, teaching assistantships, scholarships/grants, health care benefits, and unspecified assistantships available. *Faculty research:* Movement and brain plasticity, gibberellin physiology, photosynthesis, carbon cycling, molecular properties of main-group ring components. *Application contact:* School of Graduate Studies, 403-329-5194, E-mail: sgsinquiries@uleth.ca.
Website: http://www.uleth.ca/graduatestudies/

University of Louisville, Graduate School, College of Arts and Sciences, Department of Geography and Geosciences, Louisville, KY 40292-0001. Offers applied geography (MS). Part-time programs available. *Students:* 11 full-time (5 women), 5 part-time (0 women); includes 2 minority (both Hispanic/Latino), 2 international. Average age 30. 10 applicants, 80% accepted, 7 enrolled. In 2014, 2 master's awarded. *Degree requirements:* For master's, thesis. *Entrance requirements:* For master's, GRE (minimum combined score of 1000), BA/BS with minimum cumulative GPA of 3.0. Additional exam requirements/recommendations for international students: Required—TOEFL (minimum score 550 paper-based; 79 iBT). *Application deadline:* For fall admission, 11/1 for domestic students, 5/1 priority date for international students; for spring admission, 4/1 for domestic students, 11/1 priority date for international students; for summer admission, 4/1 priority date for international students. Applications are processed on a rolling basis. Application fee: $60. Electronic applications accepted. *Expenses:* Tuition, state resident: full-time $11,326; part-time $630 per credit hour. Tuition, nonresident: full-time $23,568; part-time $1311 per credit hour. *Required fees:* $196. Tuition and fees vary according to program and reciprocity agreements. *Financial support:* Scholarships/grants available. Financial award application deadline: 4/1. *Faculty research:* Climatology and global climate change, physical geography, human geography, medical and population geography, geographic information systems, remote sensing and spatial statistics. *Unit head:* Dr. Keith R. Mountain, Chair, 502-852-2692, E-mail: krmoun01@gwise.louisville.edu. *Application contact:* Dr. Carol L. Hanchette, Director, Graduate Admissions, 502-852-2699, Fax: 502-852-4560, E-mail: carol.hanchette@louisville.edu.
Website: http://louisville.edu/geography/

The University of Manchester, School of Environment and Development, Manchester, United Kingdom. Offers architecture (M Phil, PhD); development policy and management (M Phil, PhD); human geography (M Phil, PhD); physical geography (M Phil, PhD); planning and landscape (M Phil, PhD).

The University of Manchester, School of Nursing, Midwifery and Social Work, Manchester, United Kingdom. Offers nursing (M Phil, PhD); social work (M Phil, PhD).

University of Manitoba, Faculty of Graduate Studies, Clayton H. Riddell Faculty of Environment, Earth, and Resources, Department of Environment and Geography, Winnipeg, MB R3T 2N2, Canada. Offers environment (M Env); environment and geography (M Sc); geography (MA, PhD). *Degree requirements:* For master's, thesis; for doctorate, one foreign language, thesis/dissertation.

University of Maryland, Baltimore County, The Graduate School, College of Arts, Humanities and Social Sciences, Department of Geography and Environmental Systems, Program in Geography and Environmental Systems, Baltimore, MD 21250. Offers MS, PhD. Part-time programs available. *Faculty:* 15 full-time (6 women), 11 part-time/adjunct (2 women). *Students:* 18 full-time (7 women), 14 part-time (10 women). Average age 30. 35 applicants, 51% accepted, 8 enrolled. In 2014, 6 master's, 3 doctorates awarded. Terminal master's awarded for partial completion of doctoral program. *Degree requirements:* For master's, thesis optional, annual faculty evaluation, research paper; for doctorate, comprehensive exam, thesis/dissertation, annual faculty evaluation, qualifying exams, proposal and dissertation defense. *Entrance requirements:* For master's and doctorate, GRE, minimum GPA of 3.0 overall, 3.3 in major. Additional exam requirements/recommendations for international students: Required—TOEFL (minimum score 550 paper-based; 80 iBT). *Application deadline:* For fall admission, 2/1 for domestic students, 1/1 for international students. Application fee: $50. Electronic applications accepted. *Expenses:* Tuition, state resident: part-time $557. Tuition, nonresident: part-time $922. *Required fees:* $122 per semester. One-time fee: $200 part-time. *Financial support:* In 2014–15, 19 students received support, including 4 research assistantships with full tuition reimbursements available (averaging $19,700 per year), 14 teaching assistantships with full tuition reimbursements available (averaging $19,700 per year); fellowships, scholarships/grants, traineeships, health care benefits, and unspecified assistantships also available. Financial award application deadline: 2/1. *Faculty research:* Watershed processes; climate and weather systems; ecology and biogeography; landscape ecology and land-use change; human geography, urban sustainability and environmental health; environmental policy; geographic information science and remote sensing. *Unit head:* Dr. Sandy Parker, Graduate Program Director, 410-455-2002, E-mail: eparker@umbc.edu. *Application contact:* Kathryn Nee, Coordinator of Domestic Admissions, 410-455-2944, E-mail: nee@umbc.edu.
Website: http://ges.umbc.edu/graduate/

University of Maryland, College Park, Academic Affairs, College of Behavioral and Social Sciences, Department of Geography, College Park, MD 20742. Offers MA, PhD, MA/MLS. Part-time and evening/weekend programs available. Terminal master's awarded for partial completion of doctoral program. *Degree requirements:* For master's, thesis, oral exam; for doctorate, comprehensive exam, thesis/dissertation. *Entrance requirements:* For master's, GRE General Test, minimum GPA of 3.0, 3 letters of recommendation; for doctorate, GRE General Test. Additional exam requirements/recommendations for international students: Required—TOEFL, TWE. Electronic applications accepted. *Faculty research:* Cartography and automated mapping, environmental systems analysis, metropolitan analysis and planning, historical and human geography, coastal geomorphology.

University of Massachusetts Amherst, Graduate School, College of Natural Sciences, Department of Geosciences, Program in Geography, Amherst, MA 01003. Offers MS. Part-time programs available. *Students:* 3 full-time (1 woman), 2 part-time (both women); includes 1 minority (Two or more races, non-Hispanic/Latino). Average age 37. 16 applicants, 19% accepted, 2 enrolled. In 2014, 1 master's awarded. *Degree requirements:* For master's, thesis or alternative. *Entrance requirements:* For master's, GRE General Test. Additional exam requirements/recommendations for international students: Required—TOEFL (minimum score 550 paper-based; 80 iBT), IELTS (minimum score 6.5). *Application deadline:* For fall admission, 2/1 for domestic and international students. Applications are processed on a rolling basis. Application fee: $75. Electronic applications accepted. *Expenses:* Tuition, state resident: full-time $1980; part-time $110 per credit. Tuition, nonresident: full-time $14,644; part-time $414 per credit. *Required fees:* $11,417. One-time fee: $357. *Financial support:* Fellowships with full and partial tuition reimbursements, research assistantships with full and partial tuition reimbursements, teaching assistantships with full and partial tuition reimbursements, career-related internships or fieldwork, Federal Work-Study, scholarships/grants, traineeships, health care benefits, tuition waivers (full and partial), and unspecified assistantships available. Support available to part-time students. Financial award application deadline: 2/1. *Unit head:* Dr. Stanley Stevens, Graduate Program Director, 413-545-2286, Fax: 413-545-1200. *Application contact:* Lindsay DeSantis, Supervisor of Admissions, 413-545-0722, Fax: 413-577-0010, E-mail: gradadm@grad.umass.edu.
Website: http://www.geo.umass.edu/

University of Memphis, Graduate School, College of Arts and Sciences, Department of Earth Sciences, Memphis, TN 38152. Offers archaeology (MS); earth sciences (PhD); geographic information systems (Graduate Certificate), including geographic information systems, GIS educator, GIS planning, GIS professional; geography (MA, MS); geology (MS); geophysics (MS); interdisciplinary (MS). Part-time and evening/weekend programs available. *Faculty:* 13 full-time (3 women), 2 part-time/adjunct (0 women). *Students:* 27 full-time (8 women), 26 part-time (7 women); includes 2 minority (1 Black or African American, non-Hispanic/Latino; 1 Asian, non-Hispanic/Latino), 19 international. Average age 32. 36 applicants, 69% accepted, 7 enrolled. In 2014, 7 master's, 5 doctorates awarded. Terminal master's awarded for partial completion of doctoral program. *Degree requirements:* For master's, comprehensive exam, thesis, seminar presentation; for doctorate, thesis/dissertation. *Entrance requirements:* For master's, GRE General Test, 3 letters of recommendation, statement of research interests; for doctorate, GRE General Test, 2 letters of recommendation, resume, personal statement. Additional exam requirements/recommendations for international students: Required—TOEFL (minimum score 550 paper-based). *Application deadline:* For fall admission, 1/31 for domestic students; for spring admission, 11/1 for domestic students. Applications are processed on a rolling basis. Application fee: $35 ($60 for international students). Electronic applications accepted. *Financial support:* In 2014–15, 18 students received support. Fellowships with full tuition reimbursements available, research assistantships with full tuition reimbursements available, teaching assistantships with full tuition reimbursements available, Federal Work-Study, scholarships/grants, and unspecified assistantships available. Financial award application deadline: 2/15; financial award applicants required to submit FAFSA. *Faculty research:* Hazards, active tectonics, geophysics, hydrology and water resources, spatial analysis. *Unit head:* Dr. M. Jerry Bartholomew, Chair, 901-678-4536, Fax: 901-678-4467, E-mail: jbrthlm1@memphis.edu. *Application contact:* Dr. Arlene Hill, Associate Professor and Graduate Program Coordinator, 901-678-4358, Fax: 901-678-2178, E-mail: dlarsen@memphis.edu.
Website: http://www.memphis.edu/des/

University of Miami, Graduate School, College of Arts and Sciences, Department of Geography and Regional Studies, Coral Gables, FL 33124. Offers geography (MA). Part-time programs available. *Degree requirements:* For master's, thesis. *Entrance requirements:* For master's, GRE, 3 letters of recommendation, official transcripts. Additional exam requirements/recommendations for international students: Required—TOEFL. Electronic applications accepted. *Faculty research:* Urbanization, globalization, environmental change.

University of Minnesota, Twin Cities Campus, Graduate School, College of Liberal Arts, Department of Geography, Environment and Society, Minneapolis, MN 55455. Offers MA, PhD. *Faculty:* 19 full-time (4 women), 15 part-time/adjunct (6 women). *Students:* 39 full-time (22 women); includes 3 minority (1 Black or African American, non-Hispanic/Latino; 1 Asian, non-Hispanic/Latino; 1 Two or more races, non-Hispanic/Latino), 12 international. 79 applicants, 20% accepted, 11 enrolled. In 2014, 2 master's, 9 doctorates awarded. *Degree requirements:* For master's, comprehensive exam, thesis or 3 papers; for doctorate, comprehensive exam, thesis/dissertation. *Entrance requirements:* For master's and doctorate, GRE General Test, minimum GPA of 3.5. Additional exam requirements/recommendations for international students: Required—TOEFL (minimum score 600 paper-based; 100 iBT), IELTS (minimum score 7), Michigan English Language Assessment Battery (minimum score 84). *Application deadline:* For fall admission, 12/15 for domestic and international students. Application fee: $75 ($95 for international students). Electronic applications accepted. *Expenses:* Expenses: Contact institution. *Financial support:* In 2014–15, 39 students received support, including 5 fellowships with full tuition reimbursements available (averaging $22,500 per year), 7 research assistantships with full and partial tuition reimbursements available (averaging $14,000 per year), 27 teaching assistantships with full and partial tuition reimbursements available (averaging $14,000 per year); career-related internships or fieldwork, scholarships/grants, traineeships, health care benefits, tuition waivers (full and partial), and unspecified assistantships also available. Financial award application deadline: 12/15. *Faculty research:* Geovisualization; geographic information systems; spatial analysis and modeling; spatial databases; remote sensing; biogeography; international labor migrations; political globalization and uneven development; governance, citizenship and justice; environmental change; culture, place and flow; nature and society; health geography; dendrochronology. *Total annual research expenditures:* $597,826. *Unit head:* Abdi I. Samatar, Chair, 612-625-6080, Fax: 612-624-1044, E-mail: samat001@umn.edu. *Application contact:* Sara C. Braun, Assistant Director of Graduate Studies, 612-625-6080, Fax: 612-624-1044, E-mail: willi046@umn.edu.
Website: http://www.geog.umn.edu/

University of Missouri, Office of Research and Graduate Studies, College of Arts and Science, Department of Geography, Columbia, MO 65211. Offers geographic information science (Graduate Certificate); geography (MA). *Faculty:* 8 full-time (1 woman). *Students:* 11 full-time (6 women), 3 part-time (1 woman); includes 3 minority (1 Black or African American, non-Hispanic/Latino; 1 Asian, non-Hispanic/Latino; 1 Two or more races, non-Hispanic/Latino), 1 international. Average age 30. 24 applicants, 79% accepted, 9 enrolled. In 2014, 7 master's, 15 other advanced degrees awarded. *Degree requirements:* For master's, thesis or alternative. *Entrance requirements:* For master's, GRE General Test (minimum score 1000 verbal and quantitative), minimum GPA of 3.0. Additional exam requirements/recommendations for international students: Required—TOEFL (minimum score 500 paper-based; 61 iBT). *Application deadline:* For fall admission, 1/15 priority date for domestic and international students; for winter admission, 10/1 for domestic students; for spring admission, 4/1 for domestic students. Applications are processed on a rolling basis. Application fee: $55 ($75 for international students). Electronic applications accepted. *Financial support:* Fellowships with full tuition reimbursements, research assistantships with full tuition reimbursements, teaching assistantships with full tuition reimbursements, institutionally sponsored loans, health care benefits, and unspecified assistantships available. *Faculty research:* Human geography, nature/society relationships, the physical environment, application of geographic information sciences. *Unit head:* Dr. Mike Urban, Department Chair, 573-884-2658, E-mail: urbanm@missouri.edu. *Application contact:* Dina Nichols, Administrative Assistant, 573-882-8370, E-mail: nicholsdi@missouri.edu.
Website: http://www.geog.missouri.edu/?q=grad/graduate-program

Geography

The University of Montana, Graduate School, College of Humanities and Sciences, Department of Geography, Missoula, MT 59812-0002. Offers community and environmental planning (MA); geography (MA, MS). *Entrance requirements:* For master's, GRE General Test. Additional exam requirements/recommendations for international students: Required—TOEFL.

University of Nebraska at Omaha, Graduate Studies, College of Arts and Sciences, Department of Geography and Geology, Omaha, NE 68182. Offers geographic information science (Certificate); geography (MA). Part-time programs available. *Faculty:* 11 full-time (3 women). *Students:* 9 full-time (3 women), 20 part-time (5 women); includes 1 minority (Two or more races, non-Hispanic/Latino), 1 international. Average age 29. 15 applicants, 47% accepted, 4 enrolled. In 2014, 7 master's, 1 other advanced degree awarded. *Degree requirements:* For master's, comprehensive exam, thesis (for some programs). *Entrance requirements:* For master's, GRE, minimum GPA of 3.0, 15 undergraduate geography hours, transcripts, resume, statement of purpose, 2 letters of recommendation; for Certificate, minimum GPA of 3.0, transcripts, resume, statement of purpose, 2 letters of recommendation. Additional exam requirements/recommendations for international students: Required—TOEFL, IELTS, PTE. *Application deadline:* For fall admission, 7/1 priority date for domestic and international students; for spring admission, 12/1 priority date for domestic and international students; for summer admission, 5/1 for domestic and international students. Applications are processed on a rolling basis. Application fee: $45. Electronic applications accepted. *Financial support:* In 2014–15, 12 students received support, including 12 teaching assistantships with tuition reimbursements available; fellowships, research assistantships with tuition reimbursements available, Federal Work-Study, institutionally sponsored loans, scholarships/grants, tuition waivers (partial), and unspecified assistantships also available. Support available to part-time students. Financial award application deadline: 3/1; financial award applicants required to submit FAFSA. *Unit head:* Dr. Robert Schuster, Chairperson, 402-554-2341, E-mail: graduate@unomaha.edu. *Application contact:* Dr. Michael Peterson, Graduate Program Chair, 402-554-2341, E-mail: graduate@unomaha.edu.

University of Nebraska–Lincoln, Graduate College, College of Arts and Sciences, Department of Anthropology and Geography, Program in Geography, Lincoln, NE 68588. Offers MA, PhD. *Degree requirements:* For master's, thesis optional; for doctorate, comprehensive exam, thesis/dissertation. *Entrance requirements:* For master's and doctorate, GRE General Test. Additional exam requirements/recommendations for international students: Required—TOEFL (minimum score 550 paper-based). Electronic applications accepted. *Faculty research:* Climatology, historical-cultural geography, geographic information systems/cartography/remote sensing, human geography, Great Plains studies.

University of Nevada, Reno, Graduate School, College of Science, Mackay School of Earth Sciences and Engineering, Department of Geography, Program in Geography, Reno, NV 89557. Offers MS, PhD. Terminal master's awarded for partial completion of doctoral program. *Degree requirements:* For master's, comprehensive exam, thesis; for doctorate, comprehensive exam, thesis/dissertation. *Entrance requirements:* For master's and doctorate, GRE General Test, minimum GPA of 2.75. Additional exam requirements/recommendations for international students: Required—TOEFL (minimum score 500 paper-based; 61 iBT), IELTS (minimum score 6). Electronic applications accepted. *Faculty research:* Natural resources, education, climatology, biogeography, ethnic/cultural geography.

University of New Mexico, Graduate School, College of Arts and Sciences, Program in Geography and Environmental Studies, Albuquerque, NM 87131-2039. Offers MS. Part-time programs available. *Faculty:* 6 full-time (2 women). *Students:* 11 full-time (3 women), 11 part-time (5 women); includes 8 minority (1 Black or African American, non-Hispanic/Latino; 1 American Indian or Alaska Native, non-Hispanic/Latino; 5 Hispanic/Latino; 1 Two or more races, non-Hispanic/Latino), 1 international. Average age 35. 14 applicants, 71% accepted, 6 enrolled. In 2014, 6 master's awarded. *Degree requirements:* For master's, comprehensive exam (for some programs), thesis (for some programs). *Entrance requirements:* For master's, GRE. Additional exam requirements/recommendations for international students: Required—TOEFL. *Application deadline:* For fall admission, 2/1 priority date for domestic students, 1/1 priority date for international students; for spring admission, 11/15 for domestic and international students. Application fee: $50. Electronic applications accepted. *Financial support:* In 2014–15, 10 students received support, including 6 research assistantships with full tuition reimbursements available (averaging $10,993 per year), 3 teaching assistantships with full tuition reimbursements available (averaging $10,034 per year); health care benefits and tuition waivers (full and partial) also available. Financial award applicants required to submit FAFSA. *Faculty research:* Geographic information science, environmental management. *Total annual research expenditures:* $94,525. *Unit head:* Dr. Scott M. Freundschuh, Chair, 505-277-0058, Fax: 505-277-3614, E-mail: sfreunds@unm.edu. *Application contact:* Dr. K. Maria D. Lane, Director of Graduate Studies, 505-277-4075, Fax: 505-277-3614, E-mail: mdlane@unm.edu. Website: http://geography.unm.edu

University of New Orleans, Graduate School, College of Liberal Arts, Department of Geography, New Orleans, LA 70148. Offers MA. *Entrance requirements:* For master's, GRE General Test. Additional exam requirements/recommendations for international students: Required—TOEFL (minimum score 550 paper-based; 79 iBT). Electronic applications accepted.

The University of North Carolina at Chapel Hill, Graduate School, College of Arts and Sciences, Department of Geography, Chapel Hill, NC 27599. Offers MA, PhD. *Degree requirements:* For master's, one foreign language, comprehensive exam, thesis; for doctorate, 2 foreign languages, comprehensive exam, thesis/dissertation. *Entrance requirements:* For master's and doctorate, GRE General Test, minimum GPA of 3.0. *Faculty research:* Geographic information systems, climatology, hydrology, population research, Latino immigration.

The University of North Carolina at Charlotte, College of Liberal Arts and Sciences, Department of Geography and Earth Sciences, Charlotte, NC 28223-0001. Offers earth sciences (MS); geography (MA), including community planning, geographic location science and technologies, location analysis, transportation studies, urban regional analysis; geography and urban regional analysis (PhD). Part-time and evening/weekend programs available. *Faculty:* 30 full-time (10 women), 1 part-time/adjunct (0 women). *Students:* 42 full-time (25 women), 29 part-time (14 women); includes 4 minority (2 Black or African American, non-Hispanic/Latino; 1 Hispanic/Latino; 1 Native Hawaiian or other Pacific Islander, non-Hispanic/Latino), 17 international. Average age 31. 51 applicants, 76% accepted, 16 enrolled. In 2014, 17 master's, 3 doctorates awarded. Terminal master's awarded for partial completion of doctoral program. *Degree requirements:* For master's, comprehensive exam, thesis or alternative, project. *Entrance requirements:* For master's, GRE General Test or MAT, Doppelt Mathematical Reasoning Test, minimum GPA of 3.0 in undergraduate major, 2.75 overall. Additional exam requirements/recommendations for international students: Required—TOEFL (minimum score 557 paper-based; 83 iBT). *Application deadline:* For fall admission, 4/1 for domestic and international students; for spring admission, 10/1 for domestic and international students. Application fee: $75. Electronic applications accepted. *Expenses:* Tuition, state resident: full-time $4008. Tuition, nonresident: full-time $16,295. *Required*

fees: $2755. Tuition and fees vary according to course load and program. *Financial support:* In 2014–15, 38 students received support, including 10 research assistantships (averaging $10,140 per year), 28 teaching assistantships (averaging $8,748 per year); career-related internships or fieldwork, institutionally sponsored loans, scholarships/grants, and unspecified assistantships also available. Support available to part-time students. Financial award application deadline: 4/1; financial award applicants required to submit FAFSA. *Faculty research:* Improving geographic knowledge discovery and spatial reasoning with mobile and Web-based geographical information systems; an in-house supercomputing cluster for multi-scale science and collaborative research; feedback between a generalist pathogen, hosts and heterogeneous environments at multiple spatial and temporal scales. *Total annual research expenditures:* $620,703. *Unit head:* Dr. Craig Allan, Chair, 704-687-5999, Fax: 704-687-3182, E-mail: cjallan@uncc.edu. *Application contact:* Kathy B. Giddings, Director of Graduate Admissions, 704-687-5503, Fax: 704-687-1668, E-mail: gradadm@uncc.edu. Website: https://geoearth.uncc.edu/

The University of North Carolina at Greensboro, Graduate School, College of Arts and Sciences, Department of Geography, Greensboro, NC 27412-5001. Offers applied geography (MA); geographic information science (Certificate); geography (PhD); urban and economic development (Certificate). *Degree requirements:* For master's, comprehensive exam, thesis or alternative. *Entrance requirements:* For master's, GRE General Test. Additional exam requirements/recommendations for international students: Required—TOEFL. Electronic applications accepted.

University of North Dakota, Graduate School, College of Arts and Sciences, Department of Geography, Grand Forks, ND 58202. Offers MA, MS. Part-time programs available. *Degree requirements:* For master's, comprehensive exam, thesis or alternative. *Entrance requirements:* For master's, minimum GPA of 3.0. Additional exam requirements/recommendations for international students: Required—TOEFL (minimum score 550 paper-based; 79 iBT), IELTS (minimum score 6.5). Electronic applications accepted. *Faculty research:* Regional and urban development, environmental geography, geographic education, geographic techniques.

University of Northern Iowa, Graduate College, College of Social and Behavioral Sciences, Department of Geography, Cedar Falls, IA 50614. Offers MA. Part-time programs available. *Students:* 8 full-time (3 women), 2 part-time (0 women), 6 international. 8 applicants, 38% accepted, 2 enrolled. In 2014, 3 master's awarded. *Degree requirements:* For master's, thesis or alternative. *Entrance requirements:* For master's, minimum GPA of 3.0; 2 letters of recommendation; brief statement about professional interests and career objectives. Additional exam requirements/recommendations for international students: Required—TOEFL (minimum score 500 paper-based; 61 iBT). *Application deadline:* For fall admission, 8/1 priority date for domestic students. Applications are processed on a rolling basis. Application fee: $50 ($70 for international students). Electronic applications accepted. *Expenses:* Tuition, state resident: full-time $7912; part-time $880 per credit. Tuition, nonresident: full-time $17,906; part-time $880 per credit. *Required fees:* $1101; $325.50 per credit. $465.63 per semester. Tuition and fees vary according to course load and program. *Financial support:* Career-related internships or fieldwork, Federal Work-Study, scholarships/grants, and tuition waivers (full and partial) available. Support available to part-time students. Financial award application deadline: 2/1. *Unit head:* Dr. Patrick P. Pease, Department Head/Associate Professor, 319-273-7117, Fax: 319-273-7103, E-mail: patrick.pease@uni.edu. *Application contact:* Laurie S. Russell, Record Analyst, 319-273-2623, Fax: 319-273-2885, E-mail: laurie.russell@uni.edu. Website: http://www.uni.edu/geography/

University of North Texas, Robert B. Toulouse School of Graduate Studies, Denton, TX 76203-5459. Offers accounting (MS); applied anthropology (MA, MS); applied behavior analysis (Certificate); applied geography (MA); applied technology and performance improvement (M Ed, MS); art education (MA); art history (MA); art museum education (Certificate); arts leadership (Certificate); audiology (Au D); behavior analysis (MS); behavioral science (PhD); biochemistry and molecular biology (MS); biology (MA, MS); biomedical engineering (MS); business analysis (MS); chemistry (MS); clinical health psychology (PhD); communication studies (MA, MS); computer engineering (MS); computer science (MS); counseling (M Ed, MS), including clinical mental health counseling (MS), college and university counseling, elementary school counseling, secondary school counseling; creative writing (MA); criminal justice (MS); curriculum and instruction (M Ed); decision sciences (MBA); design (MA, MFA), including fashion design (MFA), innovation studies, interior design (MFA); early childhood studies (MS); economics (MS); educational leadership (M Ed, Ed D); educational psychology (MS, PhD), including family studies (MS), gifted and talented (MS), human development (MS), learning and cognition (MS), research, measurement and evaluation (MS); electrical engineering (MS); emergency management (MPA); engineering technology (MS); English (MA); English as a second language (MA); environmental science (MS); finance (MBA, MS); financial management (MPA); French (MA); health services management (MBA); higher education (M Ed, Ed D); history (MA, MS); hospitality management (MS); human resources management (MPA); information science (MS); information systems (PhD); information technologies (MBA); interdisciplinary studies (MA, MS); international studies (MA); international sustainable tourism (MS); jazz studies (MM); journalism (MA, MJ, Graduate Certificate), including interactive and virtual digital communication (Graduate Certificate), narrative journalism (Graduate Certificate), public relations (Graduate Certificate); kinesiology (MS); linguistics (MA); local government management (MPA); logistics (PhD); logistics and supply chain management (MBA); long-term care, senior housing, and aging services (MA); management (PhD); marketing (MBA); mathematics (MA, MS); mechanical and energy engineering (MS, PhD); music (MA), including ethnomusicology, music theory, musicology, performance; music composition (PhD); music education (MM Ed, PhD); nonprofit management (MPA); operations and supply chain management (MBA); performance (MM, DMA); philosophy (MA); political science (MA); professional and technical communication (MA); radio, television and film (MA, MFA); rehabilitation counseling (Certificate); sociology (MA); Spanish (MA); special education (M Ed); speech-language pathology (MA); strategic management (MBA); studio art (MFA); teaching (M Ed); MBA/MS. Part-time and evening/weekend programs available. Postbaccalaureate distance learning degree programs offered. *Faculty:* 651 full-time (215 women), 233 part-time/adjunct (139 women). *Students:* 3,040 full-time (1,598 women), 3,401 part-time (2,097 women); includes 1,740 minority (533 Black or African American, non-Hispanic/Latino; 15 American Indian or Alaska Native, non-Hispanic/Latino; 286 Asian, non-Hispanic/Latino; 746 Hispanic/Latino; 3 Native Hawaiian or other Pacific Islander, non-Hispanic/Latino; 157 Two or more races, non-Hispanic/Latino), 1,145 international. Terminal master's awarded for partial completion of doctoral program. *Degree requirements:* For master's, variable foreign language requirement, comprehensive exam (for some programs), thesis (for some programs); for doctorate, variable foreign language requirement, comprehensive exam (for some programs), thesis/dissertation; for other advanced degree, variable foreign language requirement, comprehensive exam (for some programs). *Entrance requirements:* For master's and doctorate, GRE, GMAT. Additional exam requirements/recommendations for international students: Required—TOEFL (minimum score 550 paper-based; 79 iBT). *Application deadline:* For fall admission, 7/15 for domestic students, 3/15 for international students; for spring admission, 11/15 for domestic students, 9/15 for international students; for summer admission, 5/1 for

domestic students. Applications are processed on a rolling basis. Application fee: $60. Electronic applications accepted. *Expenses:* Tuition, state resident: full-time $5450; part-time $3633 per year. Tuition, nonresident: full-time $11,966; part-time $7977 per year. *Required fees:* $1301; $398 per credit hour. $685 per semester. Tuition and fees vary according to program and reciprocity agreements. *Financial support:* Fellowships with partial tuition reimbursements, research assistantships with partial tuition reimbursements, teaching assistantships, career-related internships or fieldwork, Federal Work-Study, institutionally sponsored loans, scholarships/grants, health care benefits, and library assistantships available. Support available to part-time students. Financial award applicants required to submit FAFSA. *Unit head:* Mark Wardell, Dean, 940-565-2383, E-mail: mark.wardell@unt.edu. *Application contact:* Toulouse School of Graduate Studies, 940-565-2383, Fax: 940-565-2141, E-mail: gradsch@unt.edu. Website: http://tsgs.unt.edu/

University of Oklahoma, College of Atmospheric and Geographic Sciences, Department of Geography and Environmental Sustainability, Norman, OK 73019. Offers environmental sustainability (MS); geography (MA, PhD). Part-time programs available. *Faculty:* 21 full-time (5 women), 2 part-time/adjunct (1 woman). *Students:* 18 full-time (8 women), 19 part-time (8 women); includes 4 minority (2 American Indian or Alaska Native, non-Hispanic/Latino; 1 Asian, non-Hispanic/Latino; 1 Hispanic/Latino), 9 international. Average age 32. 11 applicants, 27% accepted, 1 enrolled. In 2014, 3 master's, 3 doctorates awarded. Terminal master's awarded for partial completion of doctoral program. *Degree requirements:* For master's, comprehensive exam (for some programs), thesis (for some programs); for doctorate, one foreign language, comprehensive exam (for some programs), thesis/dissertation (for some programs), 4 required courses plus 4 elective courses. *Entrance requirements:* For master's, GRE, BA/BS in relevant area from accredited institution, minimum GPA of 3.0; for doctorate, MA/MS in relevant area from accredited institution, minimum GPA of 3.0. Additional exam requirements/recommendations for international students: Required—TOEFL (minimum score 79 iBT). *Application deadline:* For fall admission, 1/15 for domestic and international students; for spring admission, 11/1 for domestic and international students. Application fee: $50 ($100 for international students). Electronic applications accepted. *Expenses:* Tuition, state resident: full-time $4394; part-time $183.10 per credit hour. Tuition, nonresident: full-time $16,970; part-time $707.10 per credit hour. *Required fees:* $2892; $109.95 per credit hour. $126.50 per semester. *Financial support:* In 2014–15, 30 students received support, including 1 fellowship with full tuition reimbursement available (averaging $5,000 per year), 5 research assistantships with partial tuition reimbursements available (averaging $14,948 per year), 13 teaching assistantships with partial tuition reimbursements available (averaging $15,359 per year); career-related internships or fieldwork, Federal Work-Study, institutionally sponsored loans, scholarships/grants, traineeships, health care benefits, and unspecified assistantships also available. Financial award application deadline: 6/1; financial award applicants required to submit FAFSA. *Faculty research:* Land use land cover change, indigenous geography, physical and human geography, GIS and remote sensing, environmental sustainability and renewable energy, human-environment interactions, climate, climate change, climate variability, climate and water resources. *Total annual research expenditures:* $1 million. *Unit head:* Dr. Aondover Tarhule, Associate Professor and Chair, 405-325-0540, Fax: 405-325-6090, E-mail: atarhule@ou.edu. *Application contact:* Dr. Scott Greene, Professor and Graduate Liaison, 405-325-4319, Fax: 405-325-6090, E-mail: jgreene@ou.edu. Website: http://geography.ou.edu

University of Oregon, Graduate School, College of Arts and Sciences, Department of Geography, Eugene, OR 97403. Offers MA, MS, PhD. *Degree requirements:* For master's, one foreign language, thesis; for doctorate, one foreign language, thesis/dissertation. *Entrance requirements:* For master's and doctorate, GRE General Test, minimum GPA of 3.0. Additional exam requirements/recommendations for international students: Required—TOEFL. *Faculty research:* Place-name research, past climates, quaternary environments, plant diffusions, population redistributions.

University of Ottawa, Faculty of Graduate and Postdoctoral Studies, Faculty of Arts, Department of Geography, Ottawa, ON K1N 6N5, Canada. Offers M Geog, M Sc, MA, PhD. *Degree requirements:* For master's, one foreign language, thesis; for doctorate, one foreign language, comprehensive exam, thesis/dissertation. *Entrance requirements:* For master's, honors degree or equivalent, minimum B average; for doctorate, master's degree, minimum B+ average. Electronic applications accepted. *Faculty research:* The physical geography of cold environment; space, place and society, environmental change.

University of Prince Edward Island, Faculty of Arts, Charlottetown, PE C1A 4P3, Canada. Offers island studies (MA). Part-time programs available. *Degree requirements:* For master's, thesis. *Entrance requirements:* Additional exam requirements/recommendations for international students: Required—TOEFL (minimum score 550 paper-based; 80 iBT), Canadian Academic English Language Assessment, Michigan English Language Assessment Battery, Canadian Test of English for Scholars and Trainees. *Faculty research:* International island studies.

University of Regina, Faculty of Graduate Studies and Research, Faculty of Arts, Department of Geography, Regina, SK S4S 0A2, Canada. Offers M Sc, MA, PhD. Offered as a special case program. Part-time programs available. *Faculty:* 10 full-time (5 women), 4 part-time/adjunct (1 woman). *Students:* 2 full-time (1 woman), 1 part-time (0 women). 9 applicants, 11% accepted. In 2014, 2 master's awarded. *Degree requirements:* For master's, thesis; for doctorate, thesis/dissertation. *Entrance requirements:* Additional exam requirements/recommendations for international students: Required—TOEFL (minimum score 580 paper-based; 80 iBT), IELTS (minimum score 6.5), PTE (minimum score 59). *Application deadline:* For fall admission, 3/1 for domestic and international students; for winter admission, 10/1 for domestic and international students. Applications are processed on a rolling basis. Application fee: $100. Electronic applications accepted. *Expenses: Tuition, area resident:* Full-time $4900 Canadian dollars; part-time $837.65 Canadian dollars per semester. *International tuition:* $7900 Canadian dollars full-time. *Required fees:* $396 Canadian dollars; $86.90 Canadian dollars per semester. *Financial support:* Fellowships, research assistantships, teaching assistantships, and scholarships/grants available. Financial award application deadline: 6/15. *Faculty research:* Cultural, historical, economic, rural, urban, population, and prairie geography; thematic and atlas cartography; climatology and meteorology; geomorphology; biogeography. *Unit head:* Dr. Randy Widdis, Department Head and Graduate Coordinator, 306-585-4242, Fax: 306-585-4815, E-mail: randy.widdis@uregina.ca. Website: http://www.uregina.ca/arts/geography

University of Saskatchewan, College of Graduate Studies and Research, College of Arts and Science, Department of Geography, Saskatoon, SK S7N 5A2, Canada. Offers M Sc, MA, PhD. *Degree requirements:* For master's, thesis; for doctorate, comprehensive exam (for some programs), thesis/dissertation. *Entrance requirements:* Additional exam requirements/recommendations for international students: Required—TOEFL (minimum score 80 iBT); Recommended—IELTS (minimum score 6.5). Electronic applications accepted.

University of South Africa, College of Agriculture and Environmental Sciences, Pretoria, South Africa. Offers agriculture (MS); consumer science (MCS); environmental

management (MA, MS, PhD); environmental science (MA, MS, PhD); geography (MA, MS, PhD); horticulture (M Tech); human ecology (MHE); life sciences (MS); nature conservation (M Tech).

University of South Carolina, The Graduate School, College of Arts and Sciences, Department of Geography, Columbia, SC 29208. Offers geography (MA, MS, PhD); geography education (IMA). IMA and MAT offered in cooperation with the College of Education. Part-time programs available. *Degree requirements:* For master's, comprehensive exam, thesis (for some programs); for doctorate, comprehensive exam, thesis/dissertation. *Entrance requirements:* For master's, GRE General Test; for doctorate, GRE General Test, master's degree. Electronic applications accepted. *Faculty research:* Geographic information processing; economic, cultural, physical, and environmental geography.

University of Southern California, Graduate School, Dana and David Dornsife College of Letters, Arts and Sciences, Spatial Sciences Institute, Los Angeles, CA 90089. Offers geographic information science and technology (MS, Graduate Certificate). Part-time and evening/weekend programs available. Postbaccalaureate distance learning degree programs offered (minimal on-campus study). Terminal master's awarded for partial completion of doctoral program. *Degree requirements:* For master's, thesis. *Entrance requirements:* For master's, GRE. Additional exam requirements/recommendations for international students: Required—TOEFL. Electronic applications accepted. *Faculty research:* Geocoding, geocomputation, GIS, environmental exposure estimation, spatial data accuracy and uncertainty.

University of Southern Mississippi, Graduate School, College of Science and Technology, Department of Geography and Geology, Hattiesburg, MS 39406-0001. Offers geography (MS, PhD); geology (MS). Part-time programs available. *Degree requirements:* For master's, comprehensive exam, thesis (for some programs), internships; for doctorate, comprehensive exam, thesis/dissertation. *Entrance requirements:* For master's, GMAT, GRE General Test, minimum GPA of 3.0 for last 60 hours; for doctorate, GRE, minimum GPA of 3.5. Additional exam requirements/recommendations for international students: Required—TOEFL, IELTS. Electronic applications accepted. *Faculty research:* City and regional planning, geographic techniques, physical geography, human geography.

University of South Florida, College of Arts and Sciences, Department of Geography, Tampa, FL 33620-9951. Offers environmental geography (MA); environmental science and policy (MS); geographic information science and spatial analysis (MA); geography and environmental science and policy (PhD); human geography (MA); urban and regional planning (MURP). Part-time and evening/weekend programs available. *Students:* 15 full-time (9 women), 12 part-time (4 women); includes 11 minority (4 Black or African American, non-Hispanic/Latino; 5 Hispanic/Latino; 2 Two or more races, non-Hispanic/Latino), 2 international. Average age 32. 39 applicants, 62% accepted, 9 enrolled. In 2014, 10 master's awarded. *Degree requirements:* For master's, comprehensive exam, thesis (for some programs); for doctorate, comprehensive exam, thesis/dissertation. *Entrance requirements:* For master's, GRE General Test (within the last 5 years), minimum GPA of 3.0 for last 60 credits of undergraduate degree, letter of intent, two letters of recommendation (three for MS); for doctorate, GRE General Test (within the last 5 years), minimum GPA of 3.2 for all academic work prior to admission, letter of intent, two letters of recommendation. Additional exam requirements/recommendations for international students: Required—TOEFL (minimum score 550 paper-based; 79 iBT) or IELTS (minimum score 6.5) for MA and MURP; TOEFL (minimum score 600 paper-based) for MS and PhD. *Application deadline:* For fall admission, 2/15 for domestic students, 1/2 for international students; for spring admission, 10/15 for domestic students, 6/1 for international students. Application fee: $30. *Financial support:* In 2014–15, 28 students received support, including 3 research assistantships (averaging $12,345 per year), 25 teaching assistantships with tuition reimbursements available (averaging $12,807 per year); unspecified assistantships also available. Financial award application deadline: 3/1. *Faculty research:* Geography: human geography, environmental geography, geographic information science and spatial analysis, urban geography, social theory; environmental science, policy, and planning: water resources, wildlife ecology, Karst and wetland environments, natural hazards, soil contamination, meteorology and climatology, environmental sustainability and policy, urban and regional planning. *Total annual research expenditures:* $89,465. *Unit head:* Dr. Jayajit Chakraborty, Professor and Chair, Geography Division, 813-974-8188, Fax: 813-974-5911, E-mail: jchakrab@usf.edu. *Application contact:* Dr. Jennifer Collins, Associate Professor and Graduate Program Coordinator, 813-974-4242, Fax: 813-974-5911, E-mail: collinsjm@usf.edu. Website: http://gep.usf.edu/

University of South Florida, Innovative Education, Tampa, FL 33620-9951. *Unit head:* Kathy Barnes, Interdisciplinary Programs Coordinator, 813-974-8031, Fax: 813-974-7061, E-mail: barnesk@usf.edu. *Application contact:* Karen Tylinski, Metro Initiatives, 813-974-9943, Fax: 813-974-7061, E-mail: ktylinsk@usf.edu. Website: http://www.usf.edu/innovative-education/

The University of Tennessee, Graduate School, College of Arts and Sciences, Department of Geography, Knoxville, TN 37996. Offers MS, PhD. *Degree requirements:* For master's, thesis or alternative; for doctorate, thesis/dissertation. *Entrance requirements:* For master's and doctorate, GRE General Test, minimum GPA of 2.7. Additional exam requirements/recommendations for international students: Required—TOEFL. Electronic applications accepted.

The University of Texas at Austin, Graduate School, College of Liberal Arts, Department of Geography and the Environment, Austin, TX 78712-1111. Offers MA, PhD. *Degree requirements:* For master's, thesis or alternative; for doctorate, thesis/dissertation. *Entrance requirements:* For master's and doctorate, GRE General Test. Additional exam requirements/recommendations for international students: Required—TOEFL. Electronic applications accepted. *Faculty research:* Cultural and historical geography, environmental and physical geography, human-environment interactions, electronic technology and hypermedia, international area studies.

The University of Texas at Dallas, School of Economic, Political and Policy Sciences, Program in Geospatial Information Sciences, Richardson, TX 75080. Offers MS, PhD. Part-time and evening/weekend programs available. *Faculty:* 9 full-time (1 woman), 1 part-time/adjunct (0 women). *Students:* 40 full-time (15 women), 19 part-time (9 women); includes 12 minority (2 Black or African American, non-Hispanic/Latino; 4 Asian, non-Hispanic/Latino; 5 Hispanic/Latino; 1 Two or more races, non-Hispanic/Latino), 32 international. Average age 31. 79 applicants, 54% accepted, 14 enrolled. In 2014, 14 master's awarded. *Degree requirements:* For master's, thesis (for some programs), project or thesis; internship; for doctorate, comprehensive exam, thesis/dissertation. *Entrance requirements:* For master's and doctorate, GRE General Test, minimum GPA of 3.0 in upper-level coursework in field. Additional exam requirements/recommendations for international students: Required—TOEFL (minimum score 550 paper-based). *Application deadline:* For fall admission, 7/15 for domestic students, 5/1 priority date for international students; for spring admission, 11/15 for domestic students, 9/1 priority date for international students. Applications are processed on a rolling basis. Application fee: $50 ($100 for international students). Electronic applications accepted. *Expenses:* Tuition, state resident: full-time $11,940; part-time $663 per credit. Tuition,

nonresident: full-time $22,282; part-time $1238 per credit. *Financial support:* In 2014–15, 26 students received support, including 5 fellowships (averaging $3,100 per year), 4 research assistantships with partial tuition reimbursements available (averaging $13,050 per year), 10 teaching assistantships with partial tuition reimbursements available (averaging $11,790 per year); career-related internships or fieldwork, Federal Work-Study, institutionally sponsored loans, scholarships/grants, and unspecified assistantships also available. Support available to part-time students. Financial award application deadline: 4/30; financial award applicants required to submit FAFSA. *Faculty research:* Urban and regional development, artificial intelligence techniques for geospatial investigation, improvement of current spatial analysis and modeling techniques, demographic studies. *Unit head:* Dr. Fang Qiu, Program Head, 972-883-4134, Fax: 972-883-2735, E-mail: ffqiu@utdallas.edu. *Application contact:* Dr. Daniel Griffith, Doctoral Advisor, 972-883-4950, Fax: 972-883-6297, E-mail: dagriffith@utdallas.edu.
Website: http://www.utdallas.edu/epps/geospatial-science/

The University of Toledo, College of Graduate Studies, College of Languages, Literature and Social Sciences, Department of Geography and Planning, Toledo, OH 43606-3390. Offers geographic information science and applied geographics (Certificate); geography and planning (MA); spatially-integrated social science (PhD). Part-time programs available. *Degree requirements:* For master's, comprehensive exam, thesis; for doctorate, thesis/dissertation. *Entrance requirements:* For master's and doctorate, GRE General Test, minimum cumulative point-hour ratio of 2.7 for all previous academic work, three letters of recommendation; for Certificate, minimum cumulative point-hour ratio of 2.7 for all previous academic work, three letters of recommendation. Additional exam requirements/recommendations for international students: Required—TOEFL (minimum score 550 paper-based; 80 iBT). Electronic applications accepted.

University of Toronto, School of Graduate Studies, Faculty of Arts and Science, Department of Geography, Toronto, ON M5S 2J7, Canada. Offers geography (M Sc, MA, PhD); planning (M Sc Pl, MUDS, PhD); urban design (MUD). Part-time programs available. *Degree requirements:* For master's, thesis optional; for doctorate, thesis/dissertation. *Entrance requirements:* For master's, bachelor's degree or equivalent in geography or a closely related field, minimum B+ average in each of 2 final years of degree, 3 letters of reference; for doctorate, master of geography degree, minimum A- average. Additional exam requirements/recommendations for international students: Required—TOEFL (minimum score 580 paper-based; 93 iBT), TWE (minimum score 5). Electronic applications accepted. *Faculty research:* Spatial statistics, computer cartography, climatology, hydrology, biogeography.

University of Utah, Graduate School, College of Social and Behavioral Science, Department of Geography, Salt Lake City, UT 84112-9155. Offers geographic information science (MS); geography (MA, MS, PhD). Part-time programs available. *Faculty:* 13 full-time (4 women), 9 part-time/adjunct (4 women). *Students:* 36 full-time (13 women), 17 part-time (4 women); includes 5 minority (1 Black or African American, non-Hispanic/Latino; 2 Asian, non-Hispanic/Latino; 2 Hispanic/Latino), 11 international. Average age 29. 66 applicants, 53% accepted, 19 enrolled. In 2014, 3 master's, 3 doctorates awarded. *Degree requirements:* For master's, variable foreign language requirement, thesis (for some programs), 6 research hours (for Geography MS) / skills portfolio (for MS in geographic information science); for doctorate, comprehensive exam, thesis/dissertation, 14 research hours / 2 consecutive full-time semesters. *Entrance requirements:* For master's, GRE General Test (not required for MS in geographic information science), minimum undergraduate GPA of 3.0; for doctorate, GRE General Test, minimum undergraduate GPA of 3.0. Additional exam requirements/recommendations for international students: Required—TOEFL (minimum score 550 paper-based; 80 iBT), IELTS (minimum score 6.5). *Application deadline:* For fall admission, 1/10 priority date for domestic and international students; for spring admission, 10/1 for domestic and international students. Application fee: $55 ($65 for international students). Electronic applications accepted. *Expenses:* Expenses: Contact institution. *Financial support:* In 2014–15, 26 students received support, including 3 fellowships with full tuition reimbursements available (averaging $24,000 per year), 10 research assistantships with full tuition reimbursements available (averaging $16,000 per year), 8 teaching assistantships with full tuition reimbursements available (averaging $15,000 per year); career-related internships or fieldwork, Federal Work-Study, scholarships/grants, health care benefits, and unspecified assistantships also available. Financial award application deadline: 3/15; financial award applicants required to submit FAFSA. *Faculty research:* Urban-economic geography, earth system science, geographic information science and remote sensing, paleoenvironmental studies, hazards. *Total annual research expenditures:* $876,578. *Unit head:* Dr. Andrea R. Brunelle, Chair, 801-581-8218, Fax: 801-581-8219, E-mail: andrea.brunelle@geog.utah.edu. *Application contact:* Dr. Philip E. Dennison, Director of Graduate Studies, 801-581-8218, Fax: 801-581-8219, E-mail: dennison@geog.utah.edu.
Website: http://www.geog.utah.edu

University of Victoria, Faculty of Graduate Studies, Faculty of Social Sciences, Department of Geography, Victoria, BC V8W 2Y2, Canada. Offers M Sc, MA, PhD. Part-time programs available. *Degree requirements:* For master's, thesis; for doctorate, comprehensive exam, thesis/dissertation, candidacy exam. *Entrance requirements:* For master's, minimum B+ average in undergraduate course work; for doctorate, master's degree. Additional exam requirements/recommendations for international students: Required—TOEFL (minimum score 575 paper-based), IELTS (minimum score 7). Electronic applications accepted. *Faculty research:* Resources and protected areas, remote sensing and forestry, geographic information systems and cartography, urban regional planning, physical climatology.

University of Washington, Graduate School, College of Arts and Sciences, Department of Geography, Seattle, WA 98195. Offers MA, PhD. *Degree requirements:* For master's, thesis; for doctorate, thesis/dissertation. *Entrance requirements:* For master's and doctorate, GRE General Test. Additional exam requirements/recommendations for international students: Required—TOEFL. Electronic applications accepted. *Faculty research:* Globalization and social theory, nature and society, regional economic development, urban patterns and processes, geographic information systems.

University of Waterloo, Graduate Studies, Faculty of Environment, Department of Geography, Waterloo, ON N2L 3G1, Canada. Offers MA, PhD. MA, PhD offered jointly with Wilfrid Laurier University. *Degree requirements:* For master's, thesis optional; for doctorate, one foreign language, comprehensive exam, thesis/dissertation. *Entrance requirements:* For master's, honors degree, minimum B average; for doctorate, master's degree, minimum A- average. Additional exam requirements/recommendations for international students: Required—TOEFL, TWE. Electronic applications accepted. *Faculty research:* Urban economic geography; physical geography; resource management; cultural, regional, historical geography; spatial data.

The University of Western Ontario, Faculty of Graduate Studies, Social Sciences Division, Department of Geography, London, ON N6A 5B8, Canada. Offers M Sc, MA, PhD. *Degree requirements:* For master's, thesis; for doctorate, thesis/dissertation. *Entrance requirements:* For master's, GRE, honors degree, minimum B average; for doctorate, honors degree, minimum B average. Additional exam requirements/recommendations for international students: Required—TOEFL.

University of Wisconsin–Madison, Graduate School, College of Letters and Science, Department of Geography, Madison, WI 53706-1380. Offers cartography and geographic information systems (MS); geographic information systems (Certificate); geography (MS, PhD). Part-time programs available. *Degree requirements:* For master's, thesis; for doctorate, thesis/dissertation; for Certificate, internship. *Entrance requirements:* For master's and doctorate, GRE General Test, minimum GPA of 3.25. Electronic applications accepted. *Expenses:* Tuition, state resident: full-time $10,723; part-time $745 per credit. Tuition, nonresident: full-time $24,054; part-time $1578 per credit. *Required fees:* $374 per semester. Tuition and fees vary according to course load, program and reciprocity agreements. *Faculty research:* Physical geography, urban/historical geography, people-environment, history of cartography, GIS.

University of Wisconsin–Milwaukee, Graduate School, College of Letters and Sciences, Department of Geography, Milwaukee, WI 53201-0413. Offers MA, MS, PhD. *Degree requirements:* For master's, comprehensive exam, thesis; for doctorate, thesis/dissertation. *Entrance requirements:* For master's and doctorate, GRE. Additional exam requirements/recommendations for international students: Required—TOEFL (minimum score 550 paper-based; 79 iBT), IELTS (minimum score 6.5). Electronic applications accepted.

University of Wyoming, College of Arts and Sciences, Department of Geography, Laramie, WY 82071. Offers geography (MA, MP, MST); geography/water resources (MA); rural planning and natural resources (MP), including community and regional planning and natural resources. Postbaccalaureate distance learning degree programs offered (minimal on-campus study). *Degree requirements:* For master's, thesis optional. *Entrance requirements:* For master's, GRE General Test, minimum GPA of 3.0. Additional exam requirements/recommendations for international students: Required—TOEFL. Electronic applications accepted. *Faculty research:* Landscape ecology, landscape change, public land management, rural and small town planning, GIS.

Utah State University, School of Graduate Studies, College of Natural Resources, Department of Environment and Society, Logan, UT 84322. Offers bioregional planning (MS); geography (MA, MS); human dimensions of ecosystem science and management (MS, PhD); recreation resource management (MS, PhD). *Degree requirements:* For master's, comprehensive exam, thesis (for some programs). *Entrance requirements:* For master's and doctorate, GRE General Test, minimum GPA of 3.0. Additional exam requirements/recommendations for international students: Required—TOEFL. Electronic applications accepted. *Faculty research:* Geographic information systems/geographic and environmental education, bioregional planning, natural resource and environmental policy, outdoor recreation and tourism, natural resource and environmental management.

Virginia Polytechnic Institute and State University, Graduate School, College of Natural Resources and Environment, Blacksburg, VA 24061. Offers fisheries and wildlife (MS, PhD); forestry and forest products (MF, MS, PhD); geography (MS); geospatial and environmental analysis (PhD); natural resources (MNR). *Faculty:* 72 full-time (15 women), 1 part-time/adjunct (0 women). *Students:* 192 full-time (80 women), 87 part-time (45 women); includes 22 minority (5 Black or African American, non-Hispanic/Latino; 5 Asian, non-Hispanic/Latino; 11 Hispanic/Latino; 1 Two or more races, non-Hispanic/Latino), 46 international. Average age 31. 145 applicants, 59% accepted, 67 enrolled. In 2014, 99 master's, 12 doctorates awarded. *Degree requirements:* For master's, comprehensive exam (for some programs), thesis (for some programs); for doctorate, comprehensive exam (for some programs), thesis/dissertation (for some programs). *Entrance requirements:* For master's and doctorate, GRE/GMAT (may vary by department). Additional exam requirements/recommendations for international students: Required—TOEFL (minimum score 550 paper-based). *Application deadline:* For fall admission, 8/1 for domestic students, 4/1 for international students; for spring admission, 1/1 for domestic students, 9/1 for international students. Applications are processed on a rolling basis. Application fee: $75. Electronic applications accepted. *Expenses:* Tuition, state resident: full-time $11,656; part-time $647.50 per credit hour. Tuition, nonresident: full-time $23,351; part-time $1297.25 per credit hour. *Required fees:* $2533; $465.75 per semester. Tuition and fees vary according to course load, campus/location and program. *Financial support:* In 2014–15, 98 research assistantships with full tuition reimbursements (averaging $22,448 per year), 38 teaching assistantships with full tuition reimbursements (averaging $20,346 per year) were awarded. Financial award application deadline: 3/1; financial award applicants required to submit FAFSA. *Total annual research expenditures:* $15.1 million. *Unit head:* Dr. Paul M. Winistorfer, Dean, 540-231-5481, Fax: 540-231-7664, E-mail: pstorfer@vt.edu. *Application contact:* Arlice Banks, Executive Secretary to the Dean, 540-231-7051, Fax: 540-231-7664, E-mail: arbanks@vt.edu.
Website: http://cnre.vt.edu/

West Chester University of Pennsylvania, College of Business and Public Affairs, Department of Geography and Planning, West Chester, PA 19383. Offers geographic information systems (Certificate); geography (MA); urban and regional planning (MPA, Certificate). Part-time and evening/weekend programs available. Postbaccalaureate distance learning degree programs offered (no on-campus study). *Faculty:* 6 full-time (3 women). *Students:* 16 full-time (3 women), 9 part-time (5 women); includes 1 minority (Black or African American, non-Hispanic/Latino), 1 international. Average age 29. 18 applicants, 100% accepted, 10 enrolled. In 2014, 12 master's, 21 other advanced degrees awarded. *Degree requirements:* For master's, thesis optional, 33 credits or 11 courses: 5-6 required, 5-6 electives, thesis or independent research course; for Certificate, 18 credits or 6 courses. *Entrance requirements:* For master's and Certificate, minimum GPA of 2.8, resume, two letters of recommendation. Additional exam requirements/recommendations for international students: Required—TOEFL (minimum score 550 paper-based; 80 iBT). *Application deadline:* For fall admission, 4/15 priority date for domestic students, 3/15 for international students; for spring admission, 10/15 priority date for domestic students, 9/1 for international students. Applications are processed on a rolling basis. Application fee: $45. Electronic applications accepted. *Expenses:* Tuition, state resident: full-time $8172; part-time $454 per credit. Tuition, nonresident: full-time $12,258; part-time $681 per credit. *Required fees:* $2231; $110.78 per credit. Tuition and fees vary according to campus/location and program. *Financial support:* Unspecified assistantships available. Support available to part-time students. Financial award application deadline: 2/15; financial award applicants required to submit FAFSA. *Faculty research:* Sustainability and environmental conservation, land use/suburban planning, geographic information systems, transportation planning, housing. *Unit head:* Dr. Dottie Ives Dewey, Chair/Graduate Coordinator for GIS Certificate Program, 610-436-2746, Fax: 610-436-2889, E-mail: divesdewey@wcupa.edu. *Application contact:* Dr. Matin Katirai, Graduate Coordinator, 610-436-2392, Fax: 610-436-2889, E-mail: mkatirai@wcupa.edu.
Website: http://www.wcupa.edu/_academics/sch_sba.geo/default.asp

Western Illinois University, School of Graduate Studies, College of Arts and Sciences, Department of Geography, Macomb, IL 61455-1390. Offers community development and planning (Certificate); geography (MA); GIS analysis (Certificate). Part-time programs available. *Students:* 12 full-time (5 women), 2 part-time (1 woman); includes 3 minority (2 Black or African American, non-Hispanic/Latino; 1 Hispanic/Latino). Average

age 27. 14 applicants, 86% accepted, 6 enrolled. In 2014, 2 master's, 2 other advanced degrees awarded. *Degree requirements:* For master's, thesis or alternative. *Entrance requirements:* Additional exam requirements/recommendations for international students: Required—TOEFL (minimum score 550 paper-based; 80 iBT). *Application deadline:* Applications are processed on a rolling basis. Application fee: $30. Electronic applications accepted. *Financial support:* In 2014–15, 8 students received support, including 2 research assistantships with full tuition reimbursements available (averaging $7,544 per year), 6 teaching assistantships with full tuition reimbursements available (averaging $8,688 per year). Financial award applicants required to submit FAFSA. *Unit head:* Dr. Sam Thompson, Chairperson, 309-298-1648. *Application contact:* Dr. Nancy Parsons, Associate Provost and Director of Graduate School, 309-298-1806, Fax: 309-298-2345, E-mail: grad-office@wiu.edu.
Website: http://wiu.edu/geography

Western Michigan University, Graduate College, College of Arts and Sciences, Department of Geography, Kalamazoo, MI 49008. Offers geographic information science (Graduate Certificate); geography (MA). *Degree requirements:* For master's, thesis. *Application deadline:* For fall admission, 2/15 for domestic students. *Financial support:* Application deadline: 2/15. *Application contact:* Admissions and Orientation, 269-387-2000, Fax: 269-387-2096.

Western Michigan University, Graduate College, College of Arts and Sciences, Department of Interdisciplinary Arts and Sciences, Kalamazoo, MI 49008. Offers science education (MA, PhD), including biological sciences (PhD), chemistry (PhD), geosciences (PhD), physical geography (PhD), physics (PhD), science education (PhD). *Degree requirements:* For doctorate, thesis/dissertation. *Application deadline:* For fall admission, 2/15 for domestic students. *Financial support:* Application deadline: 2/15. *Application contact:* Admissions and Orientation, 269-387-2000, Fax: 269-387-2096.
Website: http://www.wmich.edu/science

Western Washington University, Graduate School, Huxley College of the Environment, Department of Environmental Studies, Program in Geography, Bellingham, WA 98225-5996. Offers MS. *Entrance requirements:* Additional exam requirements/recommendations for international students: Required—TOEFL (minimum score 567 paper-based). Electronic applications accepted.

West Virginia University, Eberly College of Arts and Sciences, Department of Geology and Geography, Program in Geography, Morgantown, WV 26506. Offers energy and environmental resources (MA); geographic information systems (PhD); geography-regional development (PhD); GIS/cartographic analysis (MA); regional development (MA). Part-time programs available. *Degree requirements:* For master's, thesis, oral and written exams; for doctorate, comprehensive exam, thesis/dissertation, oral and written exams. *Entrance requirements:* For master's and doctorate, GRE General Test, minimum GPA of 3.0. Additional exam requirements/recommendations for international students: Required—TOEFL. Electronic applications accepted. *Faculty research:* Space, place and development, geographic information science, environmental geography.

Wilfrid Laurier University, Faculty of Graduate and Postdoctoral Studies, Faculty of Arts, Department of Geography and Environmental Studies, Waterloo, ON N2L 3C5, Canada. Offers environmental and resource management (MA, MES, PhD); environmental science (M Sc, MES, PhD); geomatics (M Sc, MES, PhD); human geography (MES, PhD). Part-time programs available. *Degree requirements:* For master's, thesis optional; for doctorate, thesis/dissertation. *Entrance requirements:* For master's, honors BA in geography, minimum B average in undergraduate course work; honors BSc with minimum B+ or honors BES or BA in physical geography, environmental or earth sciences or the equivalent; for doctorate, MA in geography, minimum A- average. Additional exam requirements/recommendations for international students: Required—TOEFL (minimum score 89 iBT). Electronic applications accepted. *Faculty research:* Resources management, urban, economic, physical, cultural, earth surfaces, geomatics, historical, regional, spatial data handling.

York University, Faculty of Graduate Studies, Faculty of Liberal Arts and Professional Studies, Program in Geography, Toronto, ON M3J 1P3, Canada. Offers M Sc, MA, PhD. Part-time programs available. *Degree requirements:* For master's, thesis or alternative; for doctorate, comprehensive exam, thesis/dissertation. Electronic applications accepted.

Section 22
Military and Defense Studies

This section contains a directory of institutions offering graduate work in military and defense studies. Additional information about programs listed in the directory may be obtained by writing directly to the dean of a graduate school or chair of a department at the address given in the directory.

For programs offering related work, see also in this book *History* and *Political Science and International Affairs*.

CONTENTS

Program Directories

Military and Defense Studies

American Public University System, AMU/APU Graduate Programs, Charles Town, WV 25414. Offers accounting (MBA, MS); criminal justice (MA), including business administration, emergency and disaster management, general (MA, MS); educational leadership (M Ed); emergency and disaster management (MA); entrepreneurship (MBA); environmental policy and management (MS), including environmental planning, environmental sustainability, fish and wildlife management, general (MA, MS), global environmental management; finance (MBA); general (MBA); global business management (MBA); history (MA), including American history, ancient and classical history, European history, global history, public history; homeland security (MA), including business administration, counter-terrorism studies, criminal justice, cyber, emergency management and public health, intelligence studies, transportation security; homeland security resource allocation (MBA); humanities (MA); information technology (MS), including digital forensics, enterprise software development, information assurance and security, IT project management; information technology management (MBA); intelligence studies (MA), including criminal intelligence, cyber, general (MA, MS), homeland security, intelligence analysis, intelligence collection, intelligence management, intelligence operations, terrorism studies; international relations and conflict resolution (MA), including comparative and security issues, conflict resolution, international and transnational security issues, peacekeeping; legal studies (MA); management (MA), including defense management, general (MA, MS), human resource management, organizational leadership, public administration; marketing (MBA); military history (MA), including American military history, American Revolution, civil war, war since 1945, World War II; military studies (MA), including joint warfare, strategic leadership; national security studies (MA), including general (MA, MS), homeland security, regional security studies, security and intelligence analysis, terrorism studies; nonprofit management (MBA); political science (MA), including American politics and government, comparative government and development, general (MA, MS), international relations, public policy; psychology (MA); public administration (MPA), including disaster management, environmental policy, health policy, human resources, national security, organizational management, security management; public health (MPH); reverse logistics management (MA); school counseling (M Ed); security management (MA); space studies (MS), including aerospace science, general (MA, MS), planetary science; sports and health sciences (MS); teaching (M Ed), including curriculum and instruction for elementary teachers, elementary reading, English language learners, instructional leadership, online learning, special education; transportation and logistics management (MA), including general (MA, MS), maritime engineering management, reverse logistics management. Programs offered via distance learning only. Part-time and evening/weekend programs available. Postbaccalaureate distance learning degree programs offered (no on-campus study). *Faculty:* 426 full-time (236 women), 1,864 part-time/adjunct (880 women). *Students:* 475 full-time (215 women), 10,067 part-time (4,085 women); includes 3,462 minority (1,863 Black or African American, non-Hispanic/Latino; 74 American Indian or Alaska Native, non-Hispanic/Latino; 273 Asian, non-Hispanic/Latino; 831 Hispanic/Latino; 78 Native Hawaiian or other Pacific Islander, non-Hispanic/Latino; 343 Two or more races, non-Hispanic/Latino), 131 international. Average age 36. In 2014, 3,740 master's awarded. *Degree requirements:* For master's, comprehensive exam or practicum. *Entrance requirements:* For master's, official transcript showing earned bachelor's degree from institution accredited by recognized accrediting body. Additional exam requirements/recommendations for international students: Required—TOEFL (minimum score 550 paper-based), IELTS (minimum score 6.5). *Application deadline:* Applications are processed on a rolling basis. Application fee: $0. Electronic applications accepted. *Financial support:* Applicants required to submit FAFSA. *Faculty research:* Military history, criminal justice, management performance, national security. *Unit head:* Dr. Karan Powell, Executive Vice President and Provost, 877-468-6268, Fax: 304-724-3780. *Application contact:* Terry Grant, Vice President of Enrollment Management, 877-468-6268, Fax: 304-724-3780, E-mail: info@apus.edu.
Website: http://www.apus.edu

Austin Peay State University, College of Graduate Studies, College of Arts and Letters, Department of History and Philosophy, Clarksville, TN 37044. Offers military history (MA). Part-time programs available. Postbaccalaureate distance learning degree programs offered (minimal on-campus study). *Degree requirements:* For master's, comprehensive exam, thesis optional. *Entrance requirements:* For master's, GRE General Test, minimum undergraduate GPA of 2.75, 3 letters of recommendation, bachelor's degree. Additional exam requirements/recommendations for international students: Required—TOEFL (minimum score 500 paper-based). Electronic applications accepted. *Faculty research:* American Revolutionary War, American Civil War, World Wars I and II, the Cold War, German military history.

Bellevue University, Graduate School, College of Arts and Sciences, Bellevue, NE 68005-3098. Offers clinical counseling (MS); healthcare administration (MHA); human services (MA); international security and intelligence studies (MS); managerial communication (MA). Postbaccalaureate distance learning degree programs offered.

Columbia College, Master of Arts in Military Studies Program, Columbia, MO 65216-0002. Offers MA. Part-time and evening/weekend programs available. Postbaccalaureate distance learning degree programs offered (no on-campus study). *Faculty:* 3 part-time/adjunct (0 women). *Students:* 13 part-time (6 women); includes 2 minority (1 Black or African American, non-Hispanic/Latino; 1 American Indian or Alaska Native, non-Hispanic/Latino). Average age 38. 7 applicants, 100% accepted, 2 enrolled. In 2014, 2 master's awarded. *Degree requirements:* For master's, thesis. *Entrance requirements:* Additional exam requirements/recommendations for international students: Required—TOEFL (minimum score 550 paper-based; 61 iBT). *Application deadline:* For fall admission, 8/9 priority date for domestic and international students; for spring admission, 12/27 priority date for domestic and international students. Applications are processed on a rolling basis. Application fee: $55. Electronic applications accepted. *Expenses: Tuition:* Part-time $340 per credit hour. Tuition and fees vary according to campus/location. *Financial support:* Application deadline: 3/1; applicants required to submit FAFSA. *Unit head:* Dr. Brad Lookingbill, Graduate Program Coordinator, 573-875-7621, E-mail: bdlookingbill@ccis.edu. *Application contact:* Stephanie Johnson, Director of Admissions, 573-875-7343, Fax: 573-875-7506, E-mail: sjohnson@ccis.edu.
Website: http://www.ccis.edu/online/academics/degrees.asp?MAMS

East Carolina University, Graduate School, Thomas Harriot College of Arts and Sciences, Department of History, Greenville, NC 27858-4353. Offers American history (MA); Atlantic world (MA); European history (MA); history education (MA Ed); maritime studies (MA); military history (MA); public history (MA). Part-time and evening/weekend programs available. *Degree requirements:* For master's, one foreign language, comprehensive exam, thesis. *Entrance requirements:* For master's, GRE General Test, GRE Subject Test. Additional exam requirements/recommendations for international students: Required—TOEFL. *Expenses:* Tuition, state resident: full-time $4223. Tuition, nonresident: full-time $16,540. *Required fees:* $2184.

Embry-Riddle Aeronautical University–Prescott, College of Security and Intelligence, Prescott, AZ 86301-3720. Offers MS. Part-time programs available. *Faculty:* 4 full-time (1 woman), 1 part-time/adjunct (0 women). *Students:* 11 full-time (2 women), 2 part-time (1 woman); includes 2 minority (1 Black or African American, non-Hispanic/Latino; 1 Asian, non-Hispanic/Latino). Average age 27. 26 applicants, 81% accepted, 13 enrolled. *Degree requirements:* For master's, thesis or alternative. *Entrance requirements:* For master's, statement of objectives, references (two academic, one professional), resume. Additional exam requirements/recommendations for international students: Required—TOEFL (minimum score 550 paper-based; 79 iBT). *Application deadline:* For fall admission, 6/1 priority date for domestic students, 5/1 priority date for international students; for spring admission, 11/1 priority date for domestic students, 10/1 priority date for international students. Applications are processed on a rolling basis. Application fee: $50. Electronic applications accepted. *Expenses: Tuition:* Full-time $15,360; part-time $1280 per credit hour. *Required fees:* $1034. *Financial support:* Career-related internships or fieldwork, unspecified assistantships, and administrative assistantships available. *Faculty research:* New applications and storage methods that will prevent the leakage of sensitive information in the commercial world as well as in government. *Unit head:* Dr. Philip Jones, Dean, College of Security and Intelligence, 928-777-6992, E-mail: jonephil@erau.edu. *Application contact:* Graduate Admissions, 928-777-6600, E-mail: prescottgradinfo@erau.edu.
Website: http://prescott.erau.edu/degrees/master/security-intelligence/

George Mason University, College of Humanities and Social Sciences, Interdisciplinary Studies Program, Fairfax, VA 22030. Offers community college teaching (MAIS); computational social science (MAIS); energy and sustainability (MAIS); film and video studies (MAIS); folklore studies (MAIS); higher education administration (MAIS); neuroethics (MAIS); religion, culture and values (MAIS); social entrepreneurship (MAIS); war and military in society (MAIS); women and gender studies (MAIS). *Faculty:* 11 full-time (3 women), 4 part-time/adjunct (all women). *Students:* 22 full-time (13 women), 87 part-time (51 women); includes 31 minority (21 Black or African American, non-Hispanic/Latino; 2 Asian, non-Hispanic/Latino; 6 Hispanic/Latino; 2 Two or more races, non-Hispanic/Latino), 6 international. Average age 32. 75 applicants, 75% accepted, 28 enrolled. In 2014, 31 master's awarded. *Degree requirements:* For master's, project or thesis. *Entrance requirements:* For master's, 3 letters of recommendation; writing sample; official transcript; resume. Additional exam requirements/recommendations for international students: Required—TOEFL (minimum score 570 paper-based; 80 iBT), IELTS (minimum score 6.5), PTE. *Application deadline:* For fall admission, 3/1 priority date for domestic students; for spring admission, 10/15 for domestic students. Application fee: $65 ($80 for international students). Electronic applications accepted. *Expenses:* Tuition, state resident: full-time $9794; part-time $408 per credit hour. Tuition, nonresident: full-time $26,978; part-time $1124 per credit hour. *Required fees:* $2820; $118 per credit hour. Tuition and fees vary according to course load and program. *Financial support:* In 2014–15, 10 students received support, including 1 fellowship (averaging $6,935 per year), 2 research assistantships with full and partial tuition reimbursements available (averaging $6,499 per year), 8 teaching assistantships with full and partial tuition reimbursements available (averaging $8,271 per year); career-related internships or fieldwork, Federal Work-Study, scholarships/grants, unspecified assistantships, and health care benefits (for full-time research or teaching assistantship recipients) also available. Support available to part-time students. Financial award application deadline: 3/1; financial award applicants required to submit FAFSA. *Faculty research:* Combined English and folklore, religious and cultural studies (Christianity and Muslim society). *Unit head:* Meredith H. Lair, Director, 703-993-2159, Fax: 703-993-1251, E-mail: mlair@gmu.edu. *Application contact:* Lisa Struckmeyer, Administrative Coordinator, 703-993-8762, Fax: 703-993-5585, E-mail: lstruckm@gmu.edu.
Website: http://mais.gmu.edu

George Mason University, School of Policy, Government, and International Affairs, Program in International Security, Fairfax, VA 22030. Offers MA. *Expenses:* Tuition, state resident: full-time $9794; part-time $408 per credit hour. Tuition, nonresident: full-time $26,978; part-time $1124 per credit hour. *Required fees:* $2820; $118 per credit hour. Tuition and fees vary according to course load and program. *Unit head:* Elizabeth Sturtevant, Professor and Division Director of Literacy, 703-993-2052, Fax: 703-993-2013, E-mail: esturtev@gmu.edu. *Application contact:* Rabia Ghani, Program Manager for Literacy, 703-993-7611, Fax: 703-993-5300, E-mail: rghani@gmu.edu.

The George Washington University, Elliott School of International Affairs, Program in Security Policy Studies, Washington, DC 20052. Offers MA. Part-time programs available. *Students:* 88 full-time (22 women), 74 part-time (26 women); includes 32 minority (2 Black or African American, non-Hispanic/Latino; 13 Asian, non-Hispanic/Latino; 11 Hispanic/Latino; 6 Two or more races, non-Hispanic/Latino), 11 international. Average age 27. 372 applicants, 45 enrolled. In 2014, 50 master's awarded. *Degree requirements:* For master's, one foreign language, capstone project. *Entrance requirements:* For master's, GRE General Test, 2 semesters of introductory economics, 2 years of a modern foreign language or 1 semester of statistics. Additional exam requirements/recommendations for international students: Required—TOEFL (minimum score 100 iBT), IELTS (minimum score 7). *Application deadline:* For fall admission, 1/15 priority date for domestic and international students; for spring admission, 10/1 for domestic and international students. Application fee: $75. Electronic applications accepted. *Financial support:* In 2014–15, 22 students received support. Fellowships with partial tuition reimbursements available, Federal Work-Study, and scholarships/grants available. Financial award application deadline: 1/15; financial award applicants required to submit FAFSA. *Faculty research:* U.S. arms transfer policies, military balance in the Third World, U.S. foreign policy, technology and security policy. *Unit head:* Joanna Spear, Director, 202-994-7003, E-mail: security@gwu.edu. *Application contact:* Nicole A. Campbell, Director of Graduate Admissions, 202-994-7050, Fax: 202-994-9537, E-mail: esiagrad@gwu.edu.
Website: http://elliott.gwu.edu/academics/graduate/sps

Hawai`i Pacific University, College of Humanities and Social Sciences, Program in Diplomacy and Military Studies, Honolulu, HI 96813. Offers MA. *Faculty:* 4 full-time (0 women), 2 part-time/adjunct (0 women). *Students:* 59 full-time (23 women), 48 part-time (17 women); includes 46 minority (4 Black or African American, non-Hispanic/Latino; 1 American Indian or Alaska Native, non-Hispanic/Latino; 17 Asian, non-Hispanic/Latino; 13 Hispanic/Latino; 3 Native Hawaiian or other Pacific Islander, non-Hispanic/Latino; 8 Two or more races, non-Hispanic/Latino). Average age 33. 48 applicants, 58% accepted, 26 enrolled. In 2014, 12 master's awarded. *Application deadline:* For fall admission, 2/15 priority date for domestic students; for spring admission, 10/15 priority date for domestic students. Applications are processed on a rolling basis. Application

fee: $50. Electronic applications accepted. *Expenses: Tuition:* Full-time $15,570; part-time $865 per credit. *Required fees:* $13. One-time fee: $50. Tuition and fees vary according to course load and program. *Financial support:* In 2014–15, 8 students received support. Career-related internships or fieldwork, Federal Work-Study, scholarships/grants, tuition waivers, and unspecified assistantships available. Financial award application deadline: 3/1; financial award applicants required to submit FAFSA. *Unit head:* Dr. Russell Hart, Director, 808-544-8043, Fax: 808-544-1424, E-mail: rhart@hpu.edu. *Application contact:* Danny Lam, Assistant Director of Graduate Admissions, 808-543-8034, Fax: 808-544-0280, E-mail: grad@hpu.edu. Website: http://www.hpu.edu/CHSS/History/GraduateDegree/MADMS/MADMSmain.html

Henley-Putnam University, Master of Science Program in Intelligence Management, San Jose, CA 95131. Offers MS. Part-time programs available. Postbaccalaureate distance learning degree programs offered. *Faculty:* 19 part-time/adjunct (3 women). *Students:* 49 full-time (9 women), 81 part-time (15 women); includes 6 minority (3 Black or African American, non-Hispanic/Latino; 1 Asian, non-Hispanic/Latino; 2 Hispanic/Latino). Average age 35. 10 applicants, 100% accepted. In 2014, 23 master's awarded. *Degree requirements:* For master's, thesis. *Entrance requirements:* For master's, bachelor's degree from an institution accredited by an agency recognized by the U.S. Department of Education and/or the Council for Higher Education Accreditation; background check. Additional exam requirements/recommendations for international students: Required—TOEFL (minimum score 650 paper-based; 79 iBT); Recommended—IELTS (minimum score 7). *Application deadline:* Applications are processed on a rolling basis. *Expenses:* Expenses: Contact institution. *Financial support:* Scholarships/grants and unspecified assistantships available. *Unit head:* Barbara Burke, Associate Dean, 408-453-9900, E-mail: bburke@henley-putnam.edu. *Application contact:* Nancy Reggio, Director of Admissions, 888-852-8746, E-mail: nreggio@henley-putnam.edu. Website: http://www.henley-putnam.edu/programs/masters/intelligence-management.aspx

Henley-Putnam University, Master of Science Program in Strategic Security and Protection Management, San Jose, CA 95131. Offers extremist organizations (MS). Part-time programs available. Postbaccalaureate distance learning degree programs offered (no on-campus study). *Faculty:* 17 part-time/adjunct (2 women). *Students:* 21 full-time (0 women), 41 part-time (8 women); includes 5 minority (3 Black or African American, non-Hispanic/Latino; 1 American Indian or Alaska Native, non-Hispanic/Latino; 1 Hispanic/Latino). Average age 36. 6 applicants, 100% accepted, 6 enrolled. In 2014, 23 master's awarded. *Degree requirements:* For master's, comprehensive exam, thesis. *Entrance requirements:* For master's, bachelor's degree from institution accredited by an agency recognized by the U.S. Department of Education and/or the Council for Higher Education Accreditation, background check. Additional exam requirements/recommendations for international students: Required—TOEFL (minimum score 650 paper-based; 79 iBT; Recommended—IELTS. *Application deadline:* Applications are processed on a rolling basis. *Expenses:* Expenses: Contact institution. *Financial support:* Scholarships/grants and unspecified assistantships available. *Unit head:* Dr. Scott Catino, Associate Dean, 408-453-9900, E-mail: scatino@henley-putnam.edu. *Application contact:* Nancy Reggio, Director of Admissions, 888-852-8746, E-mail: nreggio@henley-putnam.edu.

Henley-Putnam University, Master of Science Program in Terrorism and Counterterrorism Studies, San Jose, CA 95131. Offers intelligence operations (MS); protective intelligence (MS). Part-time programs available. Postbaccalaureate distance learning degree programs offered (no on-campus study). *Faculty:* 22 part-time/adjunct (5 women). *Students:* 55 full-time (12 women), 72 part-time (18 women); includes 11 minority (5 Black or African American, non-Hispanic/Latino; 4 Asian, non-Hispanic/Latino; 2 Hispanic/Latino). Average age 35. 17 applicants, 100% accepted, 17 enrolled. In 2014, 23 master's awarded. *Degree requirements:* For master's, thesis. *Entrance requirements:* For master's, bachelor's degree from institution accredited by an agency recognized by the U.S. Department of Education and/or the Council for Higher Education Accreditation, background check. Additional exam requirements/recommendations for international students: Required—TOEFL (minimum score 650 paper-based; 79 iBT); Recommended—IELTS (minimum score 7). *Application deadline:* Applications are processed on a rolling basis. *Expenses:* Expenses: Contact institution. *Financial support:* Scholarships/grants and unspecified assistantships available. *Unit head:* Diane Maye, Associate Dean, 408-453-9900, E-mail: dmaye@henley-putnam.edu. *Application contact:* Nancy Reggio, Director of Admissions, 888-852-8746 Ext. 9928, E-mail: nreggio@henley-putnam.edu. Website: http://www.henley-putnam.edu/programs/masters/terrorism-and-counterterrorism-studies.aspx

The Institute of World Politics, Graduate Programs in National Security, Intelligence, and International Affairs, Washington, DC 20036. Offers American foreign policy (Certificate); comparative political culture (Certificate); counterintelligence (Certificate); democracy building (Certificate); intelligence (Certificate); international politics (Certificate); national security affairs (Certificate); public diplomacy and political warfare (Certificate); statecraft and national security affairs (MA); statecraft and world politics (MA); strategic intelligence studies (MA). Part-time and evening/weekend programs available. *Degree requirements:* For master's, comprehensive exam, thesis optional. *Entrance requirements:* For master's, GRE General Test. Additional exam requirements/recommendations for international students: Required—TOEFL. Electronic applications accepted. *Faculty research:* Intelligence, national security, statecraft.

Johns Hopkins University, School of Education, Master's Programs in Education, Baltimore, MD 21218-2699. Offers counseling (MS), including mental health counseling, school counseling; education (MS), including educational studies, gifted education, reading, school administration and supervision, technology for educators; elementary education (MAT); health professions (M Ed); intelligence analysis (MS); management (MS); secondary education (MAT); special education (MS), including early childhood special education, general special education studies, mild to moderate disabilities, severe disabilities. Part-time and evening/weekend programs available. Postbaccalaureate distance learning degree programs offered (no on-campus study). *Degree requirements:* For master's, comprehensive exam (for some programs), portfolio, capstone project and/or internship; PRAXIS II (for teacher preparation programs that lead to licensure). *Entrance requirements:* For master's, GRE (for full-time programs only); PRAXIS I or equivalent (for teacher preparation programs that lead to licensure), bachelor's degree from regionally- or nationally-accredited institution, minimum GPA of 3.0 in all previous programs of study, official transcripts from all post-secondary institutions attended, essay, curriculum vitae/resume, minimum of two letters of recommendation. Additional exam requirements/recommendations for international students: Required—TOEFL (minimum score 600 paper-based; 100 iBT) or IELTS (minimum score 7). Electronic applications accepted.

The Judge Advocate General's School, U.S. Army, Graduate Programs, Charlottesville, VA 22903-1781. Offers military law (LL M). Only active duty military lawyers attend this school. *Accreditation:* ABA. *Degree requirements:* For master's, thesis optional. *Entrance requirements:* For master's, active duty military lawyer, international military officer, or DOD civilian attorney, JD or LL B. *Faculty research:*

Criminal law, administrative and civil law, contract law, international law, legal research and writing.

Liberty University, Liberty Baptist Theological Seminary, Lynchburg, VA 24515. Offers Biblical studies (M Div, MAR, MTS, Th M); church history (M Div, MAR, MTS, Th M); discipleship (D Min); discipleship and church ministry (M Div, MAR, MCM); evangelism and church planting (M Div, MAR, MCM, D Min); global studies (M Div, MAR, MCM, MGS, Th M); homiletics (M Div, MAR, MCM, Th M, D Min); leadership (M Div, MAR, MCM, D Min); marketplace chaplaincy (M Div, MAR, MCM); ministry (D Min); pastoral counseling (M Div, MA, MAR, MCM, D Min), including addictions and recovery (MA), crisis response and trauma (MA), discipleship and church ministries (MA), leadership (MA), life coaching (MA), marketplace chaplaincy (MA), marriage and family (MA), military resilience (MA), pastoral counseling (MA); pastoral ministries (M Div, MAR, MCM); religious education (MRE); theology (M Div, MAR, MTS, Th M); theology and apologetics (PhD); worship (M Div, MAR, MCM, D Min). Part-time programs available. Postbaccalaureate distance learning degree programs offered (minimal on-campus study). *Students:* 2,865 full-time (781 women), 3,750 part-time (1,139 women); includes 1,742 minority (1,382 Black or African American, non-Hispanic/Latino; 22 American Indian or Alaska Native, non-Hispanic/Latino; 116 Asian, non-Hispanic/Latino; 105 Hispanic/Latino; 7 Native Hawaiian or other Pacific Islander, non-Hispanic/Latino; 110 Two or more races, non-Hispanic/Latino), 227 international. Average age 41. 5,446 applicants, 39% accepted, 1340 enrolled. In 2014, 1,969 master's, 126 doctorates, 75 other advanced degrees awarded. *Degree requirements:* For master's, 2 foreign languages, thesis (for some programs); for doctorate, 2 foreign languages, thesis/dissertation. *Entrance requirements:* For master's, minimum undergraduate GPA of 2.0; for doctorate, GRE General Test or MAT, minimum graduate GPA of 3.0. Additional exam requirements/recommendations for international students: Required—TOEFL (minimum score 600 paper-based; 100 iBT). *Application deadline:* For fall admission, 6/1 for domestic students; for spring admission, 11/1 for domestic students. Applications are processed on a rolling basis. Application fee: $50. Electronic applications accepted. *Expenses:* Expenses: Contact institution. *Financial support:* Teaching assistantships with tuition reimbursements, career-related internships or fieldwork, and Federal Work-Study available. Financial award applicants required to submit FAFSA. *Unit head:* Dr. David Hirschman, Acting Dean, 434-592-4140, Fax: 434-522-0415, E-mail: dwhirschman@liberty.edu. *Application contact:* Jay Bridge, Director of Graduate Admissions, 800-424-9595, Fax: 800-628-7977, E-mail: gradadmissions@liberty.edu. Website: http://www.liberty.edu/seminary/

Missouri State University, Graduate College; College of Humanities and Public Affairs, Department of Defense and Strategic Studies, Fairfax, VA 22031. Offers MS. Part-time programs available. *Faculty:* 2 full-time (0 women), 19 part-time/adjunct (5 women). *Students:* 24 full-time (11 women), 56 part-time (16 women); includes 10 minority (3 Black or African American, non-Hispanic/Latino; 2 Asian, non-Hispanic/Latino; 4 Hispanic/Latino; 1 Two or more races, non-Hispanic/Latino), 2 international. Average age 26. 53 applicants, 92% accepted, 39 enrolled. In 2014, 19 master's awarded. *Degree requirements:* For master's, comprehensive exam, thesis or alternative. *Entrance requirements:* For master's, GRE, minimum GPA of 2.75, 3 letters of recommendation. Additional exam requirements/recommendations for international students: Required—TOEFL (minimum score 550 paper-based; 79 iBT). *Application deadline:* For fall admission, 7/20 priority date for domestic students, 5/1 for international students; for spring admission, 12/20 priority date for domestic students, 9/1 for international students. Applications are processed on a rolling basis. Application fee: $35 ($50 for international students). Electronic applications accepted. *Expenses:* Tuition, state resident: full-time $2250; part-time $250 per credit hour. Tuition, nonresident: full-time $4509; part-time $501 per credit hour. Tuition and fees vary according to course level, course load and program. *Financial support:* Career-related internships or fieldwork, Federal Work-Study, institutionally sponsored loans, scholarships/grants, and unspecified assistantships available. Financial award application deadline: 3/31; financial award applicants required to submit FAFSA. *Faculty research:* Middle East, terrorism, arms control, U.S.-Soviet military balance, Strategic Defense Initiative. *Unit head:* Dr. Keith Payne, Head, 703-218-3565, Fax: 703-218-3568, E-mail: kbpayne@missouristate.edu. *Application contact:* Misty Stewart, Coordinator of Graduate Recruitment, 417-836-6079, Fax: 417-836-6200, E-mail: mistystewart@missouristate.edu. Website: http://dss.missouristate.edu

National Defense University, Industrial College of the Armed Forces, Washington, DC 20319-5066. Offers national resource strategy (MS). Open only to Department of Defense employees and specific federal agencies. *Degree requirements:* For master's, comprehensive exam. *Entrance requirements:* Additional exam requirements/recommendations for international students: Required—TOEFL. *Faculty research:* Industrial base and relation to national security, acquisition and relation to national security, resourcing the national security strategy.

National Defense University, Joint Advanced Warfighting School, Norfolk, AB 23511. Offers joint campaign planning and strategy (MS). Open only to Department of Defense employees and specific federal agencies. *Degree requirements:* For master's, thesis. *Entrance requirements:* For master's, Phase 1 JPME. *Faculty research:* Irregular warfare, national policy and strategy, international organizations and policies, modern military history and applications of lessons learned, historical military leadership relating to present-day environments.

National Defense University, National War College, Washington, DC 20319-5066. Offers national security strategy (MS). Open only to Department of Defense employees and specific federal agencies. *Degree requirements:* For master's, comprehensive exam. *Entrance requirements:* Additional exam requirements/recommendations for international students: Required—TOEFL. *Faculty research:* National security policy, regional security, US national security strategy, US military, strategy.

National Intelligence University, Graduate Program, Washington, DC 20340-5100. Offers MSSI. Open only to federal government employees. Part-time and evening/weekend programs available. *Degree requirements:* For master's, thesis. *Entrance requirements:* For master's, MAT, authorized nomination. *Faculty research:* Law and intelligence, intelligence and higher education, low-intensity conflict, intelligence information systems.

Naval Postgraduate School, Departments and Academic Groups, Department of Computer Science, Monterey, CA 93943. Offers computer science (MS, PhD); identity management and cyber security (MA); modeling of virtual environments and simulations (MS, PhD); software engineering (MS, PhD). Program only open to commissioned officers of the United States and friendly nations and selected United States federal civilian employees. Part-time programs available. Postbaccalaureate distance learning degree programs offered (minimal on-campus study). *Degree requirements:* For master's, thesis; for doctorate, thesis/dissertation.

Naval Postgraduate School, Departments and Academic Groups, Department of Defense Analysis, Monterey, CA 93943. Offers command and control (MS); communications (MS); defense analysis (MS), including astronautics; financial management (MS); information operations (MS); irregular warfare (MS); national security affairs (MS); operations analysis (MS); special operations (MA, MS), including

command and control (MS), communications (MS), financial management (MS), information operations (MS), irregular warfare (MS), national security affairs, operations analysis (MS), tactile missiles (MS), terrorist operations and financing (MS); tactile missiles (MS); terrorist operations and financing (MS). Program only open to commissioned officers of the United States and friendly nations and selected United States federal civilian employees. Part-time programs available. *Degree requirements:* For master's, thesis. *Faculty research:* CTF Global Ecco Project, Afghanistan endgames, core lab Philippines project, Defense Manpower Data Center (DMDC) data vulnerability.

Naval Postgraduate School, Departments and Academic Groups, Department of National Security Affairs, Monterey, CA 93943. Offers national security affairs (MA); security studies (MA), including civil-military relations, combating terrorism: policy and strategy, defense decision-making and planning, Europe and Eurasia, Far East, Southeast Asia, the Pacific, homeland security and defense, Middle East, South Asia, Sub-Saharan Africa, stabilization and reconstruction, western hemisphere. Program only open to commissioned officers of the United States and friendly nations and selected United States federal civilian employees. Part-time programs available. *Degree requirements:* For master's, thesis (for some programs). *Faculty research:* Privatizing welfare in the Middle East; social construction of Russia's resurgence; institutions, ethnicity and political mobilization in South Africa; Hezbollah; China's strategic interests in Cambodia.

Naval Postgraduate School, Departments and Academic Groups, Graduate School of Business and Public Policy, Monterey, CA 93943. Offers acquisition and contract management (MBA); business administration (EMBA, MBA); contract management (MS); defense business management (MBA); defense systems analysis (MS), including management; defense systems management (international) (MBA); financial management (MBA); information management (MBA); manpower systems analysis (MS); material logistics support management (MBA); program management (MS); resource planning and management for international defense (MBA); supply chain management (MBA); systems acquisition management (MBA); transportation management (MBA). Program only open to commissioned officers of the United States and friendly nations and selected United States federal civilian employees. *Accreditation:* AACSB; NASPAA. Part-time programs available. Postbaccalaureate distance learning degree programs offered (minimal on-campus study). *Degree requirements:* For master's, thesis (for some programs), terminal project/capstone (for some programs). *Faculty research:* U.S. and European public procurement policies for small and medium-sized enterprises, examining external validity criticisms in the choice of students as subjects in accounting experiment studies, assurance of learning in contract management education, contracting for cloud computing: opportunities and risks, NPS, Apple App Store as a business model supporting U. S. Navy requirements.

Naval Postgraduate School, Departments and Academic Groups, Undersea Warfare Academic Group, Monterey, CA 93943. Offers applied mathematics (MS); applied physics (MS); applied science (MS), including acoustics, operations research, physical oceanography, signal processing; electrical engineering (MS); engineering acoustics (MS, PhD); engineering science (MS), including electrical engineering, mechanical engineering; mechanical engineer (ME); mechanical engineering (MS, MSME); meteorology (MS); operations research (MS); physical oceanography (MS). Program only open to commissioned officers of the United States and friendly nations and selected United States federal civilian employees. Part-time programs available. *Degree requirements:* For master's, thesis. *Faculty research:* Unmanned/autonomous vehicles, sea mines and countermeasures, submarine warfare in the twentieth and twenty-first centuries.

Norwich University, College of Graduate and Continuing Studies, Master of Arts in Military History Program, Northfield, VT 05663. Offers MA. Evening/weekend programs available. Postbaccalaureate distance learning degree programs offered (minimal on-campus study). *Faculty:* 1 full-time (0 women), 18 part-time/adjunct (1 woman). *Students:* 85 full-time (13 women); includes 4 minority (1 American Indian or Alaska Native, non-Hispanic/Latino; 3 Two or more races, non-Hispanic/Latino). Average age 39. 55 applicants, 95% accepted, 44 enrolled. In 2014, 88 master's awarded. *Degree requirements:* For master's, thesis optional. *Entrance requirements:* For master's, minimum undergraduate GPA of 2.75. Additional exam requirements/recommendations for international students: Required—TOEFL (minimum score 550 paper-based; 80 iBT), IELTS (minimum score 6.5). *Application deadline:* For fall admission, 8/8 for domestic and international students; for winter admission, 11/7 for domestic and international students; for spring admission, 2/16 for domestic and international students; for summer admission, 5/18 for domestic and international students. Applications are processed on a rolling basis. Electronic applications accepted. *Expenses:* Expenses: Contact institution. *Financial support:* In 2014–15, 53 students received support. Scholarships/grants available. Financial award applicants required to submit FAFSA. *Unit head:* Dr. James Ehrman, Program Director, 802-485-2567, Fax: 802-485-2533. *Application contact:* Lars Nielsen, Associate Program Director, 802-485-2853, Fax: 802-485-2533, E-mail: lnielsen@norwich.edu.
Website: http://online.norwich.edu/degree-programs/masters/master-arts-military-history/overview

Royal Military College of Canada, Division of Graduate Studies and Research, Continuing Studies, Department of History, Kingston, ON K7K 7B4, Canada. Offers defense management and policy (MA); history (PhD); war studies (MA). *Degree requirements:* For master's, thesis. *Entrance requirements:* For master's, honours degree with second-class standing; for doctorate, master's degree. Electronic applications accepted.

School of Advanced Air and Space Studies, Program in Airpower Art and Science, Maxwell AFB, AL 36112-6424. Offers MA. Available to active duty military officers only. *Degree requirements:* For master's, comprehensive exam, thesis. *Entrance requirements:* For master's, less than 16 years total of active commissioned service; master's degree or undergraduate degree with a minimum GPA of 2.75. Additional exam requirements/recommendations for international students: Required—TOEFL. *Faculty research:* Military history, political science, international relations, social history, technology.

United States Army Command and General Staff College, Graduate Program, Fort Leavenworth, KS 66027-2301. Offers military art and science (MMAS). Only career military officers are selected to attend United States Army Command and General Staff College; Graduate Program is voluntary for first-year students, but mandatory for second-year students.

University of Calgary, Faculty of Graduate Studies, Centre for Military and Strategic Studies, Calgary, AB T2N 1N4, Canada. Offers MSS, PhD. PhD offered in special cases only. Part-time programs available. *Degree requirements:* For master's, thesis; for doctorate, comprehensive exam, thesis/dissertation. *Entrance requirements:* For master's, minimum GPA of 3.4. Additional exam requirements/recommendations for international students: Recommended—TOEFL (minimum score 550 paper-based). *Faculty research:* Military history, Israeli studies, strategic studies, int'l relations, Arctic security.

University of Colorado Denver, School of Public Affairs, Program in Public Affairs and Administration, Denver, CO 80127. Offers public administration (MPA), including domestic violence, emergency management and homeland security, environmental policy, management and law, homeland security and defense, local government, nonprofit management, public administration; public affairs (PhD). *Accreditation:* NASPAA. Part-time and evening/weekend programs available. Postbaccalaureate distance learning degree programs offered (no on-campus study). *Students:* 275 full-time (176 women), 140 part-time (93 women); includes 70 minority (7 Black or African American, non-Hispanic/Latino; 4 American Indian or Alaska Native, non-Hispanic/Latino; 9 Asian, non-Hispanic/Latino; 44 Hispanic/Latino; 2 Native Hawaiian or other Pacific Islander, non-Hispanic/Latino; 4 Two or more races, non-Hispanic/Latino), 19 international. Average age 34. 243 applicants, 71% accepted, 97 enrolled. In 2014, 127 master's, 5 doctorates awarded. *Degree requirements:* For master's, thesis or alternative, 36-39 credit hours; for doctorate, comprehensive exam, thesis/dissertation, minimum of 66 semester hours, including at least 30 hours of dissertation. *Entrance requirements:* For master's, GRE, GMAT or LSAT, resume, essay, transcripts, recommendations; for doctorate, GRE, resume, essay, transcripts, recommendations. Additional exam requirements/recommendations for international students: Required—TOEFL (minimum score 550 paper-based; 80 iBT); Recommended—IELTS (minimum score 6.5). *Application deadline:* For fall admission, 2/1 priority date for domestic students, 1/15 priority date for international students; for spring admission, 10/15 priority date for domestic students, 10/1 priority date for international students. Application fee: $50 ($75 for international students). Electronic applications accepted. *Expenses:* Expenses: Contact institution. *Financial support:* In 2014–15, 60 students received support. Fellowships with partial tuition reimbursements available, research assistantships with partial tuition reimbursements available, teaching assistantships with partial tuition reimbursements available, Federal Work-Study, institutionally sponsored loans, scholarships/grants, traineeships, and unspecified assistantships available. Financial award application deadline: 4/1; financial award applicants required to submit FAFSA. *Faculty research:* Housing, education and the social and economic issues of vulnerable populations; nonprofit governance and management; education finance, effectiveness and reform; P-20 education initiatives; municipal government accountability. *Unit head:* Dr. Christine Martell, Director of MPA Program, 303-315-2716, Fax: 303-315-2229, E-mail: christine.martell@ucdenver.edu. *Application contact:* Dawn Savage, Student Services Coordinator, 303-315-2743, Fax: 303-315-2229, E-mail: dawn.savage@ucdenver.edu.
Website: http://www.ucdenver.edu/academics/colleges/SPA/Academics/programs/PublicAffairsAdmin/Pages/index.aspx

University of Detroit Mercy, College of Liberal Arts and Education, Department of Criminal Justice and Human Services, Detroit, MI 48221. Offers criminal justice (MA); intelligence analysis (MS); security administration (MS).

University of Pittsburgh, Graduate School of Public and International Affairs, Master of Public and International Affairs Program, Pittsburgh, PA 15260. Offers international political economy (MPIA); security and intelligence studies (MPIA); JD/MPIA; MBA/MPIA; MID/MPIA; MPA/MPIA; MPH/MPIA; MPIA/MSW; MSIS/MPIA. Part-time and evening/weekend programs available. *Faculty:* 34 full-time (12 women), 11 part-time/adjunct (3 women). *Students:* 145 full-time (63 women), 8 part-time (5 women); includes 18 minority (6 Black or African American, non-Hispanic/Latino; 3 Asian, non-Hispanic/Latino; 8 Hispanic/Latino; 1 Two or more races, non-Hispanic/Latino), 26 international. Average age 26. 251 applicants, 87% accepted, 64 enrolled. In 2014, 85 master's awarded. *Degree requirements:* For master's, thesis optional, internship, capstone seminar. *Entrance requirements:* For master's, GRE General Test or GMAT, 2 letters of recommendation, resume; undergraduate transcripts, personal statement. Additional exam requirements/recommendations for international students: Required—TOEFL (minimum score 550 paper-based; 80 iBT); Recommended—IELTS (minimum score 7), TWE (minimum score 4). *Application deadline:* For fall admission, 2/1 for domestic students, 1/15 for international students; for spring admission, 11/1 for domestic students, 8/1 for international students. Application fee: $50. Electronic applications accepted. *Expenses:* Tuition, state resident: full-time $20,742; part-time $838 per credit. Tuition, nonresident: full-time $33,960; part-time $1389 per credit. *Required fees:* $800; $205 per term. Tuition and fees vary according to program. *Financial support:* In 2014–15, 45 students received support, including 8 fellowships (averaging $15,000 per year); scholarships/grants, unspecified assistantships, and student employment also available. Financial award application deadline: 2/1. *Faculty research:* International political economy, international security and intelligence, transnational organized crime, international trade, international finance, globalization, terrorism, multinational corporations and the global economy, human rights, human trafficking, gender and development, diplomacy. *Total annual research expenditures:* $640,844. *Unit head:* Dr. Michael Kenney, Director, International Affairs and International Development Divisions, 412-648-7921, Fax: 412-648-2605, E-mail: mkenney@pitt.edu. *Application contact:* Kelly C. McDevitt, Graduate Enrollment Counselor, 412-648-7640, Fax: 412-648-7641, E-mail: mcdevitt@pitt.edu.
Website: http://www.gspia.pitt.edu/

University of West Florida, College of Arts and Sciences: Arts, Department of History, Pensacola, FL 32514-5750. Offers history (MA); military history (MA); public history (MA). Part-time and evening/weekend programs available. *Degree requirements:* For master's, thesis or alternative. *Entrance requirements:* For master's, GRE (minimum score: verbal 500, writing 3.5) or MAT (minimum score 415), minimum GPA of 3.0, minimum 15 hours of upper-level history courses; official transcripts; letter of intent; writing sample (undergraduate research paper preferred). Additional exam requirements/recommendations for international students: Required—TOEFL (minimum score 550 paper-based).

National Security

American Public University System, AMU/APU Graduate Programs, Charles Town, WV 25414. Offers accounting (MBA, MS); criminal justice (MA), including business administration, emergency and disaster management, general (MA, MS); educational leadership (M Ed); emergency and disaster management (MA); entrepreneurship (MBA); environmental policy and management (MS), including environmental planning, environmental sustainability, fish and wildlife management, general (MA, MS), global environmental management; finance (MBA); general (MBA); global business management (MBA); history (MA), including American history, ancient and classical history, European history, global history, public history; homeland security (MA), including business administration, counter-terrorism studies, criminal justice, cyber, emergency management and public health, intelligence studies, transportation security; homeland security resource allocation (MBA); humanities (MA); information technology (MS), including digital forensics, enterprise software development, information assurance and security, IT project management; information technology management (MBA); intelligence studies (MA), including criminal intelligence, cyber, general (MA, MS), homeland security, intelligence analysis, intelligence collection, intelligence management, intelligence operations, terrorism studies; international relations and conflict resolution (MA), including comparative and security issues, conflict resolution, international and transnational security issues, peacekeeping; legal studies (MA); management (MA), including defense management, general (MA, MS), human resource management, organizational leadership, public administration; marketing (MBA); military history (MA), including American military history, American Revolution, civil war, war since 1945, World War II; military studies (MA), including joint warfare, strategic leadership; national security studies (MA), including general (MA, MS), homeland security, regional security studies, security and intelligence analysis, terrorism studies; nonprofit management (MBA); political science (MA), including American politics and government, comparative government and development, general (MA, MS), international relations, public policy; psychology (MA); public administration (MPA), including disaster management, environmental policy, health policy, human resources, national security, organizational management, security management; public health (MPH); reverse logistics management (MA); school counseling (M Ed); security management (MA); space studies (MS), including aerospace science, general (MA, MS), planetary science; sports and health sciences (MS); teaching (M Ed), including curriculum and instruction for elementary teachers, elementary reading, English language learners, instructional leadership, online learning, special education; transportation and logistics management (MA), including general (MA, MS), maritime engineering management, reverse logistics management. Programs offered via distance learning only. Part-time and evening/weekend programs available. Postbaccalaureate distance learning degree programs offered (no on-campus study). *Faculty:* 426 full-time (236 women), 1,864 part-time/adjunct (880 women). *Students:* 475 full-time (215 women), 10,067 part-time (4,085 women); includes 3,462 minority (1,863 Black or African American, non-Hispanic/Latino; 74 American Indian or Alaska Native, non-Hispanic/Latino; 273 Asian, non-Hispanic/Latino; 831 Hispanic/Latino; 78 Native Hawaiian or other Pacific Islander, non-Hispanic/Latino; 343 Two or more races, non-Hispanic/Latino), 131 international. Average age 36. In 2014, 3,740 master's awarded. *Degree requirements:* For master's, comprehensive exam or practicum. *Entrance requirements:* For master's, official transcript showing earned bachelor's degree from institution accredited by recognized accrediting body. Additional exam requirements/recommendations for international students: Required—TOEFL (minimum score 550 paper-based), IELTS (minimum score 6.5). *Application deadline:* Applications are processed on a rolling basis. Application fee: $0. Electronic applications accepted. *Financial support:* Applicants required to submit FAFSA. *Faculty research:* Military history, criminal justice, management performance, national security. *Unit head:* Dr. Karan Powell, Executive Vice President and Provost, 877-468-6268, Fax: 304-724-3780. *Application contact:* Terry Grant, Vice President of Enrollment Management, 877-468-6268, Fax: 304-724-3780, E-mail: info@apus.edu.
Website: http://www.apus.edu

Angelo State University, College of Graduate Studies, Department of Security Studies and Criminal Justice, San Angelo, TX 76909. Offers MS, MSS. Part-time and evening/weekend programs available. Postbaccalaureate distance learning degree programs offered (no on-campus study). *Degree requirements:* For master's, comprehensive exam. *Entrance requirements:* For master's, essay, letters of recommendation. Additional exam requirements/recommendations for international students: Required—TOEFL or IELTS. Electronic applications accepted.

Bellevue University, Graduate School, College of Arts and Sciences, Bellevue, NE 68005-3098. Offers clinical counseling (MS); healthcare administration (MHA); human services (MA); international security and intelligence studies (MS); managerial communication (MA). Postbaccalaureate distance learning degree programs offered.

California State University, San Bernardino, Graduate Studies, College of Social and Behavioral Sciences, National Security Studies Program, San Bernardino, CA 92407-2397. Offers MA. Part-time and evening/weekend programs available. *Students:* 19 full-time (4 women), 28 part-time (11 women); includes 20 minority (2 Black or African American, non-Hispanic/Latino; 5 Asian, non-Hispanic/Latino; 11 Hispanic/Latino; 2 Two or more races, non-Hispanic/Latino), 1 international. Average age 26. 18 applicants, 83% accepted, 10 enrolled. In 2014, 15 master's awarded. *Degree requirements:* For master's, comprehensive exam. *Entrance requirements:* Additional exam requirements/recommendations for international students: Required—TOEFL. *Application deadline:* For fall admission, 7/17 for domestic students. Application fee: $55. *Expenses:* Tuition, state resident: full-time $6738; part-time $1302 per term. Tuition, nonresident: full-time $17,898; part-time $248 per unit. *Required fees:* $365 per quarter. Tuition and fees vary according to degree level and program. *Unit head:* Dr. Mark Clark, Director, 909-537-5491, Fax: 909-537-7018, E-mail: mtclark@csusb.edu. *Application contact:* Dr. Jeffrey Thompson, Dean of Graduate Studies, 909-537-5058, E-mail: sjthompso@csusb.edu.

George Mason University, School of Policy, Government, and International Affairs, Program in Biodefense, Fairfax, VA 22030. Offers MS, PhD. *Expenses:* Tuition, state resident: full-time $9794; part-time $408 per credit hour. Tuition, nonresident: full-time $26,978; part-time $1124 per credit hour. *Required fees:* $2820; $118 per credit hour. Tuition and fees vary according to course load and program. *Unit head:* Elizabeth Sturtevant, Professor and Division Director of Literacy, 703-993-2052, Fax: 703-993-2013, E-mail: esturtev@gmu.edu. *Application contact:* Rabia Ghani, Program Manager for Literacy, 703-993-7611, Fax: 703-993-5300, E-mail: rghani@gmu.edu.

George Mason University, School of Policy, Government, and International Affairs, Program in International Security, Fairfax, VA 22030. Offers MA. *Expenses:* Tuition, state resident: full-time $9794; part-time $408 per credit hour. Tuition, nonresident: full-time $26,978; part-time $1124 per credit hour. *Required fees:* $2820; $118 per credit hour. Tuition and fees vary according to course load and program. *Unit head:* Elizabeth Sturtevant, Professor and Division Director of Literacy, 703-993-2052, Fax: 703-993-2013, E-mail: esturtev@gmu.edu. *Application contact:* Rabia Ghani, Program Manager for Literacy, 703-993-7611, Fax: 703-993-5300, E-mail: rghani@gmu.edu.

The George Washington University, Law School, Washington, DC 20052. Offers law (SJD); national security and US foreign relations (LL M). *Accreditation:* ABA. Part-time and evening/weekend programs available. *Faculty:* 90 full-time (37 women). *Students:* 1,539 full-time (791 women), 386 part-time (156 women); includes 461 minority (151 Black or African American, non-Hispanic/Latino; 10 American Indian or Alaska Native, non-Hispanic/Latino; 220 Asian, non-Hispanic/Latino; 72 Hispanic/Latino; 3 Native Hawaiian or other Pacific Islander, non-Hispanic/Latino; 5 Two or more races, non-Hispanic/Latino), 180 international. Average age 27. 258 applicants, 98% accepted, 162 enrolled. In 2014, 225 master's, 581 doctorates awarded. *Degree requirements:* For doctorate, thesis/dissertation (for some programs). *Entrance requirements:* For master's, JD or equivalent; for doctorate, LSAT (for JD), LL M or equivalent (for SJD). *Application deadline:* For fall admission, 3/1 for domestic students. Applications are processed on a rolling basis. Application fee: $75. *Expenses:* Expenses: Contact institution. *Financial support:* Research assistantships, career-related internships or fieldwork, Federal Work-Study, institutionally sponsored loans, scholarships/grants, and tuition waivers (full and partial) available. Support available to part-time students. Financial award application deadline: 3/1; financial award applicants required to submit CSS PROFILE or FAFSA. *Unit head:* Blake D. Morant, Dean, 202-994-6261, Fax: 202-994-5157. *Application contact:* Sophia Sim, Assistant Dean of Admissions and Financial Aid, 202-994-7230, Fax: 202-739-0624, E-mail: ssim@law.gwu.edu.
Website: http://www.law.gwu.edu/

Henley-Putnam University, Doctorate Program in Strategic Security, San Jose, CA 95131. Offers DSS. Part-time programs available. Postbaccalaureate distance learning degree programs offered (no on-campus study). *Faculty:* 13 part-time/adjunct (2 women). *Students:* 27 full-time (3 women), 58 part-time (12 women); includes 5 minority (2 Black or African American, non-Hispanic/Latino; 1 American Indian or Alaska Native, non-Hispanic/Latino; 1 Hispanic/Latino; 1 Native Hawaiian or other Pacific Islander, non-Hispanic/Latino). Average age 41. 14 applicants, 100% accepted. In 2014, 2 doctorates awarded. *Degree requirements:* For doctorate, thesis/dissertation. *Entrance requirements:* For doctorate, 5 years of strategic security experience; background check; interview with dean; copy of master's thesis; master's or bachelor's degree with equivalent of 30 graduate-level semester hours in strategic security or related field from accredited institution. Additional exam requirements/recommendations for international students: Required—TOEFL (minimum score 650 paper-based; 79 iBT); Recommended—IELTS (minimum score 7). *Application deadline:* Applications are processed on a rolling basis. *Expenses:* Expenses: Contact institution. *Financial support:* Scholarships/grants and unspecified assistantships available. *Unit head:* Dr. Scott Catino, Associate Dean, 408-453-9900 Ext., E-mail: scatino@henley-putnam.edu. *Application contact:* Nancy Reggio, Director of Admissions, 888-852-8746 Ext. 9928, E-mail: nreggio@henley-putnam.edu.
Website: http://www.henley-putnam.edu/programs/doctoral/strategic-security.aspx

Hult International Business School, Program in International Relations - Hult London Campus, London WC 1B 4JP, United Kingdom. Offers conflict resolution (MA); diplomacy (MA); international public law (MA); international relations (MA); Middle East international security (MA); politics (MA); security studies (MA); terrorism (MA); U.S. foreign policy (MA). Part-time programs available. *Entrance requirements:* Additional exam requirements/recommendations for international students: Required—TOEFL (minimum score 580 paper-based), TWE (minimum score 5). Electronic applications accepted. *Faculty research:* American foreign politics, Middle East, security studies.

The Institute of World Politics, Graduate Programs in National Security, Intelligence, and International Affairs, Washington, DC 20036. Offers American foreign policy (Certificate); comparative political culture (Certificate); counterintelligence (Certificate); democracy building (Certificate); intelligence (Certificate); international politics (Certificate); national security affairs (Certificate); public diplomacy and political warfare (Certificate); statecraft and national security affairs (MA); statecraft and world politics (MA); strategic intelligence studies (MA). Part-time and evening/weekend programs available. *Degree requirements:* For master's, comprehensive exam, thesis optional. *Entrance requirements:* For master's, GRE General Test. Additional exam requirements/recommendations for international students: Required—TOEFL. Electronic applications accepted. *Faculty research:* Intelligence, national security, statecraft.

Kansas State University, Graduate School, College of Arts and Sciences, Security Studies Program, Manhattan, KS 66506. Offers MA, PhD. Part-time programs available. *Faculty:* 17 full-time (3 women). *Students:* 8 full-time (1 woman), 48 part-time (10 women); includes 6 minority (3 Black or African American, non-Hispanic/Latino; 2 Hispanic/Latino; 1 Two or more races, non-Hispanic/Latino), 3 international. Average age 36. 45 applicants, 49% accepted, 14 enrolled. In 2014, 12 master's, 1 doctorate awarded. Terminal master's awarded for partial completion of doctoral program. *Degree requirements:* For doctorate, comprehensive exam, thesis/dissertation. *Entrance requirements:* For doctorate, GRE. Additional exam requirements/recommendations for international students: Required—TOEFL (minimum score 550 paper-based; 79 iBT), IELTS (minimum score 6.5), PTE (minimum score 58). *Application deadline:* For fall admission, 2/1 for domestic students, 1/1 for international students; for spring admission, 10/15 for domestic students, 8/1 for international students; for summer admission, 2/1 for domestic students. Application fee: $50 ($75 for international students). Electronic applications accepted. *Financial support:* Teaching assistantships with full tuition reimbursements available. Financial award application deadline: 4/1. *Faculty research:* International conflict and security, military history. *Unit head:* Dr. Andrew Long, Director, 785-532-0448, E-mail: aglong@ksu.edu. *Application contact:* Mary Reichert, Administrative Assistant, 785-532-3786, E-mail: securstu@ksu.edu.
Website: http://www.k-state.edu/securitystudies/

La Salle University, School of Arts and Sciences, Central and Eastern European Studies Program, Philadelphia, PA 19141-1199. Offers Central and Eastern European studies (MA); intelligence and security studies (Certificate). Part-time and evening/weekend programs available. *Degree requirements:* For master's, one foreign language, proficiency in one Central or Eastern European language; capstone seminar or thesis; for Certificate, one foreign language, evidence of reading knowledge of at least one of the languages of Central or Eastern Europe upon graduation. *Entrance requirements:* For master's and Certificate, bachelor's degree; 2 letters of recommendation. Additional exam requirements/recommendations for international students: Required—TOEFL. Electronic applications accepted. Application fee is waived when completed online. *Expenses:* Contact institution.

National Defense University, College of International Security Affairs, Washington, DC 20319-5066. Offers strategic security studies (MA), including conflict management, counterterrorism, homeland defense/ security, international security studies. Part-time

and evening/weekend programs available. *Degree requirements:* For master's, thesis. *Entrance requirements:* Additional exam requirements/recommendations for international students: Required—TOEFL.

National Defense University, National War College, Washington, DC 20319-5066. Offers national security strategy (MS). Open only to Department of Defense employees and specific federal agencies. *Degree requirements:* For master's, comprehensive exam. *Entrance requirements:* Additional exam requirements/recommendations for international students: Required—TOEFL. *Faculty research:* National security policy, regional security, US national security strategy, US military, strategy.

Naval Postgraduate School, Departments and Academic Groups, Department of Defense Analysis, Monterey, CA 93943. Offers command and control (MS); communications (MS); defense analysis (MS), including astronautics; financial management (MS); information operations (MS); irregular warfare (MS); national security affairs (MS); operations analysis (MS); special operations (MA, MS), including command and control (MS), communications (MS), financial management (MS), information operations (MS), irregular warfare (MS), national security affairs, operations analysis (MS), tactile missiles (MS), terrorist operations and financing (MS); tactile missiles (MS); terrorist operations and financing (MS). Program only open to commissioned officers of the United States and friendly nations and selected United States federal civilian employees. Part-time programs available. *Degree requirements:* For master's, thesis. *Faculty research:* CTF Global Ecco Project, Afghanistan endgames, core lab Philippines project, Defense Manpower Data Center (DMDC) data vulnerability.

Naval Postgraduate School, Departments and Academic Groups, Department of National Security Affairs, Monterey, CA 93943. Offers national security affairs (MA); security studies (MA), including civil-military relations, combating terrorism: policy and strategy, defense decision-making and planning, Europe and Eurasia, Far East, Southeast Asia, the Pacific, homeland security and defense, Middle East, South Asia, Sub-Saharan Africa, stabilization and reconstruction, western hemisphere. Program only open to commissioned officers of the United States and friendly nations and selected United States federal civilian employees. Part-time programs available. *Degree requirements:* For master's, thesis (for some programs). *Faculty research:* Privatizing welfare in the Middle East; social construction of Russia's resurgence; institutions, ethnicity and political mobilization in South Africa; Hezbollah; China's strategic interests in Cambodia.

Naval Postgraduate School, Departments and Academic Groups, Global Public Policy Academic Group, Monterey, CA 93943. Offers stability, security, and development in complex operations (Certificate). *Degree requirements:* For Certificate, certificate hybrid course (requiring short biographical essay and short introductory session with instructor during the distributed learning component). *Faculty research:* Implementing program budgeting in the Serbian Ministry of Defense, recognizing patterns of anomie that set the conditions for insurgency.

Naval War College, Program in National Security and Strategic Studies, Newport, RI 02841-1207. Offers MA. Program open only to full-time military personnel.

New Jersey City University, Graduate Studies and Continuing Education, College of Professional Studies, Program in National Security Studies, Jersey City, NJ 07305-1597. Offers civil security leadership (D Sc); national security studies (MS). Part-time programs available. *Faculty:* 2 full-time (0 women), 5 part-time/adjunct (0 women). *Students:* 17 full-time (5 women), 79 part-time (15 women); includes 40 minority (22 Black or African American, non-Hispanic/Latino; 6 Asian, non-Hispanic/Latino; 11 Hispanic/Latino; 1 Two or more races, non-Hispanic/Latino), 2 international. Average age 38. 39 applicants, 100% accepted, 34 enrolled. In 2014, 12 master's awarded. *Entrance requirements:* Additional exam requirements/recommendations for international students: Required—TOEFL (minimum score 79 iBT). Application fee: $50. *Expenses: Tuition, area resident:* Part-time $538 per credit. Tuition, state resident: part-time $538 per credit. Tuition, nonresident: part-time $948 per credit. *Unit head:* Dr. Tsung (Bill) Soo Hoo, Chair, 201-200-3492, E-mail: bsoohoo@njcu.edu. *Application contact:* Jose Balda, Director of Admission, E-mail: jbalda@njcu.edu.
Website: http://www.njcu.edu/grad/national-security-studies/

New York University, School of Continuing and Professional Studies, Center for Global Affairs, New York, NY 10012-1019. Offers global affairs (MS), including environment/energy policy, human rights and international law, international development and humanitarian assistance, international relations, peace building, private sector, transnational security; global energy (Advanced Certificate); peacebuilding (Advanced Certificate); transnational security (Advanced Certificate). Part-time and evening/weekend programs available. *Faculty:* 11 full-time (6 women), 32 part-time/adjunct (14 women). *Students:* 156 full-time (105 women), 136 part-time (86 women); includes 79 minority (24 Black or African American, non-Hispanic/Latino; 17 Asian, non-Hispanic/Latino; 37 Hispanic/Latino; 1 Two or more races, non-Hispanic/Latino), 66 international. Average age 28. 357 applicants, 72% accepted, 98 enrolled. In 2014, 144 master's awarded. *Degree requirements:* For master's, thesis. *Entrance requirements:* For master's, GRE or GMAT (only upon request), bachelor's degree, resume with relevant professional work, internship or volunteer experience, two letters of recommendation, statement of purpose. Additional exam requirements/recommendations for international students: Required—TOEFL (minimum score 600 paper-based; 100 iBT), IELTS (minimum score 7). *Application deadline:* For fall admission, 2/1 priority date for domestic and international students; for spring admission, 10/15 priority date for domestic students, 8/15 priority date for international students. Applications are processed on a rolling basis. Application fee: $150. Electronic applications accepted. *Financial support:* In 2014–15, 99 students received support, including 95 fellowships (averaging $2,218 per year); Federal Work-Study and scholarships/grants also available. Support available to part-time students. Financial award application deadline: 4/1; financial award applicants required to submit FAFSA. *Unit head:* Vera Jelinek, Divisional Dean and Clinical Associate Professor, 212-992-8380. *Application contact:* Office of Admissions, 212-998-7100, E-mail: sps.gradadmissions@nyu.edu.
Website: http://www.sps.nyu.edu/academics/departments/global-affairs.html

Stanford University, School of Humanities and Sciences, Program in International Policy Studies, Stanford, CA 94305-9991. Offers democracy, development, and rule of law (MA); energy, environment, and natural resources (MA); global health (MA); international political economy (MA); international security and cooperation (MA). *Degree requirements:* For master's, thesis optional. *Entrance requirements:* For master's, GRE General Test. Additional exam requirements/recommendations for international students: Required—TOEFL. Electronic applications accepted. *Expenses: Tuition:* Full-time $44,184; part-time $982 per credit hour. *Required fees:* $191.

Texas A&M University, Bush School of Government and Public Service, College Station, TX 77843. Offers homeland security (Certificate); international affairs (MIA, Certificate); national security affairs (Certificate); non-profit management (Certificate); public service and administration (MPSA). *Accreditation:* NASPAA. *Faculty:* 60. *Students:* 313 full-time (146 women), 12 part-time (2 women); includes 61 minority (13 Black or African American, non-Hispanic/Latino; 7 Asian, non-Hispanic/Latino; 32 Hispanic/Latino; 1 Native Hawaiian or other Pacific Islander, non-Hispanic/Latino; 8 Two or more races, non-Hispanic/Latino), 44 international. Average age 28. 298 applicants, 71% accepted, 143 enrolled. In 2014, 137 master's awarded. *Degree requirements:* For master's, summer internship. *Entrance requirements:* For master's, GRE (preferred) or GMAT. Additional exam requirements/recommendations for international students: Required—TOEFL (minimum score 550 paper-based; 80 iBT), IELTS (minimum score 6). *Application deadline:* For fall admission, 1/20 for domestic and international students. Application fee: $50 ($90 for international students). Electronic applications accepted. *Expenses:* Tuition, state resident: full-time $4078; part-time $226.55 per credit hour. Tuition, nonresident: full-time $10,594; part-time $577.55 per credit hour. *Required fees:* $2813; $237.70 per credit hour. $278.50 per semester. Tuition and fees vary according to degree level and student level. *Financial support:* In 2014–15, 407 students received support, including 26 fellowships with full and partial tuition reimbursements available (averaging $15,902 per year), 44 research assistantships with full and partial tuition reimbursements available (averaging $7,163 per year); career-related internships or fieldwork, institutionally sponsored loans, scholarships/grants, traineeships, health care benefits, tuition waivers (full and partial), and unspecified assistantships also available. Support available to part-time students. Financial award application deadline: 2/1; financial award applicants required to submit FAFSA. *Faculty research:* Public policy, Presidential studies, public leadership, economic policy, social policy. *Unit head:* Dr. Ryan Crocker, Dean, 979-862-8007, E-mail: rcrocker@tamu.edu. *Application contact:* Kathryn Meyer, Director of Recruitment and Admissions, 979-458-4767, Fax: 979-845-4155, E-mail: bushschooladmissions@tamu.edu.
Website: http://bush.tamu.edu/

Trinity Washington University, School of Business and Graduate Studies, Washington, DC 20017-1094. Offers business administration (MBA); communication (MA); international security studies (MA); organizational management (MSA), including federal program management, human resource management, nonprofit management, organizational development, public and community health. Part-time and evening/weekend programs available. *Degree requirements:* For master's, thesis (for some programs), capstone project (MSA). *Entrance requirements:* For master's, minimum GPA of 2.5. Additional exam requirements/recommendations for international students: Required—TOEFL (minimum score 550 paper-based).

Troy University, Graduate School, College of Arts and Sciences, Program in Public Administration, Troy, AL 36082. Offers government contracting (MPA); health care administration (MPA); justice administration (MPA); national security affairs (MPA); nonprofit management (MPA); public human resources management (MPA); public management (MPA). *Accreditation:* NASPAA. Part-time and evening/weekend programs available. Postbaccalaureate distance learning degree programs offered (no on-campus study). *Faculty:* 14 full-time (9 women), 8 part-time/adjunct (4 women). *Students:* 56 full-time (37 women), 255 part-time (154 women); includes 181 minority (157 Black or African American, non-Hispanic/Latino; 4 Asian, non-Hispanic/Latino; 14 Hispanic/Latino; 6 Two or more races, non-Hispanic/Latino). Average age 32. 182 applicants, 67% accepted, 64 enrolled. In 2014, 108 master's awarded. *Degree requirements:* For master's, capstone course with minimum B grade, minimum GPA of 3.0, admission to candidacy. *Entrance requirements:* For master's, GRE (minimum score of 920 on old exam or 294 on new exam), MAT (minimum score of 400) or GMAT (minimum score of 490), bachelor's degree; minimum undergraduate GPA of 2.5 or 3.0 on last 30 semester hours, letter of recommendation; essay, resume. Additional exam requirements/recommendations for international students: Required—TOEFL (minimum score 523 paper-based; 70 iBT), IELTS (minimum score 6). *Application deadline:* Applications are processed on a rolling basis. Application fee: $50. Electronic applications accepted. *Expenses:* Tuition, state resident: full-time $6570; part-time $365 per credit hour. Tuition, nonresident: full-time $13,140; part-time $730 per credit hour. *Required fees:* $365 per credit hour. *Financial support:* Available to part-time students. Applicants required to submit FAFSA. *Unit head:* Dr. Pamela Trump Dunning, Director, 334-808-6507, Fax: 334-670-5647, E-mail: pdunningl@troy.edu. *Application contact:* Jessica A. Kimbro, Director of Graduate Admissions, 334-670-3178, E-mail: jacord@troy.edu.

University of Central Florida, College of Sciences, Department of Political Science, Orlando, FL 32816. Offers political science (MA); security studies (PhD). Part-time and evening/weekend programs available. *Faculty:* 30 full-time (9 women), 10 part-time/adjunct (1 woman). *Students:* 36 full-time (18 women), 27 part-time (12 women); includes 12 minority (4 Black or African American, non-Hispanic/Latino; 5 Hispanic/Latino; 3 Two or more races, non-Hispanic/Latino), 5 international. Average age 31. 52 applicants, 77% accepted, 26 enrolled. In 2014, 12 master's awarded. *Degree requirements:* For master's, comprehensive exam, thesis; for doctorate, one foreign language, thesis/dissertation, oral qualifying examination. *Entrance requirements:* For master's, GRE General Test, minimum GPA of 3.0 in last 60 hours; for doctorate, GRE General Test, master's degree, three letters of reference, personal statement, writing sample, resume. Additional exam requirements/recommendations for international students: Required—TOEFL. *Application deadline:* For fall admission, 7/15 for domestic students; for spring admission, 12/1 for domestic students. Application fee: $30. Electronic applications accepted. *Expenses:* Tuition, state resident: part-time $288.16 per credit hour. Tuition, nonresident: part-time $1073.31 per credit hour. *Financial support:* In 2014–15, 13 students received support, including 3 fellowships with partial tuition reimbursements available (averaging $10,200 per year), 2 research assistantships with partial tuition reimbursements available (averaging $4,600 per year), 11 teaching assistantships with partial tuition reimbursements available (averaging $10,300 per year); career-related internships or fieldwork, Federal Work-Study, institutionally sponsored loans, tuition waivers (partial), and unspecified assistantships also available. Financial award application deadline: 3/1; financial award applicants required to submit FAFSA. *Faculty research:* Environment, presidential campaigning, term limits for elected officials. *Unit head:* Dr. Kerstin Hamann, Chair, 407-823-2085, Fax: 407-823-0051, E-mail: kerstin.hamann@ucf.edu. *Application contact:* Barbara Rodriguez Lamas, Director, Admissions and Student Services, 407-823-2766, Fax: 407-823-6442, E-mail: gradadmissions@ucf.edu.
Website: http://politicalscience.cos.ucf.edu/

University of New Haven, Graduate School, Henry C. Lee College of Criminal Justice and Forensic Sciences, National Security Program, West Haven, CT 06516-1916. Offers information protection and security (MS, Certificate); national security (MS, Certificate); national security administration (Certificate). Part-time and evening/weekend programs available. *Degree requirements:* For master's, thesis or alternative, research project or internship. *Entrance requirements:* Additional exam requirements/recommendations for international students: Required—TOEFL (minimum score 70 iBT), IELTS, or PTE (minimum score of 53). Electronic applications accepted. Application fee is waived when completed online. *Expenses: Tuition:* Full-time $22,248; part-time $824 per credit hour. *Required fees:* $45 per trimester.

Virginia Polytechnic Institute and State University, VT Online, Blacksburg, VA 24061. Offers advanced transportation systems (Certificate); aerospace engineering (MS); agricultural and life sciences (MSLFS); business information systems (Graduate Certificate); career and technical education (MS); civil engineering (MS); computer engineering (M Eng, MS); decision support systems (Graduate Certificate); eLearning leadership (MA); electrical engineering (M Eng, MS); engineering administration (MEA); environmental engineering (Certificate); environmental politics and policy (Graduate Certificate); environmental sciences and engineering (MS); foundations of political

analysis (Graduate Certificate); health product risk management (Graduate Certificate); industrial and systems engineering (MS); information policy and society (Graduate Certificate); information security (Graduate Certificate); information technology (MIT); instructional technology (MA); integrative STEM education (MA Ed); liberal arts (Graduate Certificate); life sciences: health product risk management (MS); natural resources (MNR, Graduate Certificate); networking (Graduate Certificate); nonprofit and nongovernmental organization management (Graduate Certificate); ocean engineering (MS); political science (MA); security studies (Graduate Certificate); software development (Graduate Certificate). *Expenses:* Tuition, state resident: full-time $11,656; part-time $647.50 per credit hour. Tuition, nonresident: full-time $23,351; part-time $1297.25 per credit hour. *Required fees:* $2533; $465.75 per semester. Tuition and fees vary according to course load, campus/location and program.

Western Michigan University Cooley Law School, Graduate Programs, Lansing, MI 48901-3038. Offers administrative law (public law) (JD); business transactions (JD); Canadian law practice (JD); Constitutional law and civil rights (public law) (JD); corporate law and finance (LL M); environmental law (public law) (JD); general practice (JD), including solo and small firm; homeland and national security law (LL M); insurance law (LL M); intellectual property (JD); intellectual property law (LL M); international law (JD); litigation (JD); self-directed (LL M, JD); tax law (LL M); taxation (JD); U.S. legal studies for foreign attorneys (LL M); JD/LL M; JD/MBA; JD/MPA; JD/MSW. *Accreditation:* ABA. Part-time and evening/weekend programs available. Postbaccalaureate distance learning degree programs offered (no on-campus study).

Faculty: 75 full-time (36 women), 127 part-time/adjunct (43 women). *Students:* 343 full-time (178 women), 1,537 part-time (826 women). *Degree requirements:* For master's, thesis optional; for doctorate, minimum of 3 credits of clinical experience. *Entrance requirements:* For master's, JD or LL B; for doctorate, LSAT. Additional exam requirements/recommendations for international students: Required—TOEFL (for US legal studies for foreign attorneys LL M program). *Application deadline:* For fall admission, 9/1 for domestic and international students; for winter admission, 1/1 for domestic and international students; for spring admission, 5/1 for domestic and international students. Applications are processed on a rolling basis. Application fee: $0. Electronic applications accepted. *Expenses: Tuition:* Full-time $44,950; part-time $1550 per credit hour. *Required fees:* $40; $40 per year. Tuition and fees vary according to degree level and student level. *Financial support:* Career-related internships or fieldwork, Federal Work-Study, scholarships/grants, traineeships, and unspecified assistantships available. Support available to part-time students. Financial award applicants required to submit FAFSA. *Faculty research:* Wrongful convictions, civil rights, environmental law, litigation techniques, data mining, intellectual property, practical and skills-based legal education. *Unit head:* Don LeDuc, President and Dean, 517-371-5140 Ext. 2009, Fax: 517-334-5152. *Application contact:* Mohammed S. Sohail, Acting Director of Admissions, 517-371-5140 Ext. 2233, Fax: 517-334-5718, E-mail: sohailm@cooley.edu.
Website: http://www.cooley.edu/gradprograms/index.html

Section 23
Political Science and International Affairs

This section contains a directory of institutions offering graduate work in political science and international affairs. Additional information about programs listed in the directory but not augmented by an in-depth entry may be obtained by writing directly to the dean of a graduate school or chair of a department at the address given in the directory.

For programs offering related work, see also in this book *Area and Cultural Studies, History, Language and Literature,* and *Public, Regional, and Industrial Affairs.* In another guide in this series:

Graduate Programs in Business, Education, Information Studies, Law & Social Work

See *International Business*

CONTENTS

Program Directories

International Affairs

Alliant International University–México City, School of Management, International Studies Division, Mexico City, Mexico. Offers international relations (MA). Part-time and evening/weekend programs available. *Degree requirements:* For master's, thesis. *Entrance requirements:* For master's, GRE, minimum GPA of 3.0. Additional exam requirements/recommendations for international students: Required—TOEFL (minimum score 550 paper-based; 80 iBT), TWE (minimum score 5). Electronic applications accepted. *Faculty research:* Economic history, comparative studies.

American Graduate School in Paris, Program in International Relations and Diplomacy, Paris, France. Offers MA, PhD.

American Public University System, AMU/APU Graduate Programs, Charles Town, WV 25414. Offers accounting (MBA, MS); criminal justice (MA), including business administration, emergency and disaster management, general (MA, MS); educational leadership (M Ed); emergency and disaster management (MA); entrepreneurship (MBA); environmental policy and management (MS), including environmental planning, environmental sustainability, fish and wildlife management, general (MA, MS), global environmental management; finance (MBA); general (MBA); global business management (MBA); history (MA), including American history, ancient and classical history, European history, global history, public history; homeland security (MA), including business administration, counter-terrorism studies, criminal justice, cyber, emergency management and public health, intelligence studies, transportation security; homeland security resource allocation (MBA); humanities (MA); information technology (MS), including digital forensics, enterprise software development, information assurance and security, IT project management; information technology management (MBA); intelligence studies (MA), including criminal intelligence, cyber, general (MA, MS), homeland security, intelligence analysis, intelligence collection, intelligence management, intelligence operations, terrorism studies; international relations and conflict resolution (MA), including comparative and security issues, conflict resolution, international and transnational security issues, peacekeeping; legal studies (MA); management (MA), including defense management, general (MA, MS), human resource management, organizational leadership, public administration; marketing (MBA); military history (MA), including American military history, American Revolution, civil war, war since 1945, World War II; military studies (MA), including joint warfare, strategic leadership; national security studies (MA), including general (MA, MS), homeland security, regional security studies, security and intelligence analysis, terrorism studies; nonprofit management (MBA); political science (MA), including American politics and government, comparative government and development, general (MA, MS), international relations, public policy; psychology (MA); public administration (MPA), including disaster management, environmental policy, health policy, human resources, national security, organizational management, security management; public health (MPH); reverse logistics management (MA); school counseling (M Ed); security management (MA); space studies (MS), including aerospace science, general (MA, MS), planetary science; sports and health sciences (MS); teaching (M Ed), including curriculum and instruction for elementary teachers, elementary reading, English language learners, instructional leadership, online learning, special education; transportation and logistics management (MA), including general (MA, MS), maritime engineering management, reverse logistics management. Programs offered via distance learning only. Part-time and evening/weekend programs available. Postbaccalaureate distance learning degree programs offered (no on-campus study). *Faculty:* 426 full-time (236 women), 1,864 part-time/adjunct (880 women). *Students:* 475 full-time (215 women), 10,067 part-time (4,085 women); includes 3,462 minority (1,863 Black or African American, non-Hispanic/Latino; 74 American Indian or Alaska Native, non-Hispanic/Latino; 273 Asian, non-Hispanic/Latino; 831 Hispanic/Latino; 78 Native Hawaiian or other Pacific Islander, non-Hispanic/Latino; 343 Two or more races, non-Hispanic/Latino), 131 international. Average age 36. In 2014, 3,740 master's awarded. *Degree requirements:* For master's, comprehensive exam or practicum. *Entrance requirements:* For master's, official transcript showing earned bachelor's degree from institution accredited by recognized accrediting body. Additional exam requirements/recommendations for international students: Required—TOEFL (minimum score 550 paper-based), IELTS (minimum score 6.5). *Application deadline:* Applications are processed on a rolling basis. Application fee: $0. Electronic applications accepted. *Financial support:* Applicants required to submit FAFSA. *Faculty research:* Military history, criminal justice, management performance, national security. *Unit head:* Dr. Karan Powell, Executive Vice President and Provost, 877-468-6268, Fax: 304-724-3780. *Application contact:* Terry Grant, Vice President of Enrollment Management, 877-468-6268, Fax: 304-724-3780, E-mail: info@apus.edu.
Website: http://www.apus.edu

American University, School of International Service, Washington, DC 20016-8071. Offers comparative and regional studies (Certificate); cross-cultural communication (Certificate); development management (MS); ethics, peace, and global affairs (MA); European studies (Certificate); global environmental policy (MA, Certificate); global information technology (Certificate); international affairs (MA), including comparative and international disability policy, comparative and regional studies, international economic relations, international politics, natural resources and sustainable development, U.S. foreign policy; international communication (MA, Certificate); international development (MA, Certificate); international economic policy (Certificate); international economic relations (Certificate); international media (MA); international peace and conflict resolution (MA, Certificate); international politics (Certificate); international relations (PhD); international service (MIS); peacebuilding (Certificate); social enterprise (MA); the Americas (Certificate); United States foreign policy (Certificate); JD/MA. Part-time and evening/weekend programs available. Postbaccalaureate distance learning degree programs offered (no on-campus study). *Faculty:* 112 full-time (43 women), 59 part-time/adjunct (27 women). *Students:* 545 full-time (335 women), 443 part-time (271 women); includes 231 minority (82 Black or African American, non-Hispanic/Latino; 8 American Indian or Alaska Native, non-Hispanic/Latino; 51 Asian, non-Hispanic/Latino; 81 Hispanic/Latino; 2 Native Hawaiian or other Pacific Islander, non-Hispanic/Latino; 7 Two or more races, non-Hispanic/Latino), 120 international. Average age 28. 1,991 applicants, 70% accepted, 365 enrolled. In 2014, 426 master's, 9 doctorates, 6 other advanced degrees awarded. Terminal master's awarded for partial completion of doctoral program. *Degree requirements:* For master's, one foreign language, comprehensive exam, thesis or alternative; for doctorate, one foreign language, comprehensive exam, thesis/dissertation. *Entrance requirements:* For master's, GRE, transcripts, resume, 2 letters of recommendation, statement of purpose; for doctorate, GRE, transcripts, resume, 3 letters of recommendation, statement of purpose. Additional exam requirements/recommendations for international students: Required—TOEFL (minimum score 600 paper-based; 100 iBT). *Application deadline:* For fall admission, 1/15 for domestic students; for spring admission, 10/1 for domestic students, 9/15 for international students. Application fee: $50. Electronic applications accepted. *Financial support:* Application deadline: 1/15. *Unit head:* Dr. James Goldgeier, Dean, 202-885-1603, Fax: 202-885-2494, E-mail: goldgeier@american.edu. *Application contact:* Jia Jiang, Associate Director, Graduate Education Enrollment, 202-885-1689, Fax: 202-885-1109, E-mail: jiang@american.edu.
Website: http://www.american.edu/sis/

The American University in Cairo, School of Global Affairs and Public Policy, Department of Public Policy and Administration, Cairo, Egypt. Offers global affairs (MGA); public administration (MPA, Diploma); public policy (MPP, Diploma). Tuition and fees vary according to course load and program.

American University of Armenia, Graduate Programs, Yerevan, Armenia. Offers business administration (MBA); computer and information science (MS), including business management, design and manufacturing, energy (ME, MS), industrial engineering and systems management; economics (MS); industrial engineering and systems management (ME), including business, computer aided design/manufacturing, energy (ME, MS), information technology; law (LL M); political science and international affairs (MPSIA); public health (MPH); teaching English as a foreign language (MA). Part-time and evening/weekend programs available. *Degree requirements:* For master's, thesis (for some programs), capstone/project. *Entrance requirements:* For master's, GRE, GMAT, or LSAT. Additional exam requirements/recommendations for international students: Recommended—TOEFL (minimum score 79 iBT), IELTS (minimum score 6.5). *Faculty research:* Microfinance, finance (rural/development, international, corporate), firm life cycle theory, TESOL, language proficiency testing, public policy, administrative law, economic development, cryptography, artificial intelligence, energy efficiency/renewable energy, computer-aided design/manufacturing, health financing, tuberculosis control, mother/child health, preventive ophthalmology, post-earthquake psychopathological investigations, tobacco control, environmental health risk assessments.

The American University of Paris, Graduate Programs, Paris, France. Offers cross-cultural and sustainable business management (MA); cultural translation (MA); global communications (MA); global communications and civil society (MA); international affairs (MA); international affairs, conflict resolution and civil society development (MA); Middle East and Islamic studies (MA); Middle East and Islamic studies and international affairs (MA); public policy and international affairs (MA); public policy and international law (MA). *Degree requirements:* For master's, thesis (for some programs). *Entrance requirements:* For master's, minimum undergraduate GPA of 3.0. Additional exam requirements/recommendations for international students: Recommended—TOEFL, IELTS. Electronic applications accepted.

Appalachian State University, Cratis D. Williams Graduate School, Department of Government and Justice Studies, Boone, NC 28608. Offers criminal justice (MS); political science (MA), including American government, environmental politics and policy analysis, international relations; public administration (MPA), including public management, town, city and county management. Part-time programs available. Postbaccalaureate distance learning degree programs offered (no on-campus study). *Degree requirements:* For master's, variable foreign language requirement, comprehensive exam, thesis optional. *Entrance requirements:* For master's, GRE General Test, 3 letters of recommendation. Additional exam requirements/recommendations for international students: Required—TOEFL (minimum score 570 paper-based; 79 iBT), IELTS (minimum score 6.5). Electronic applications accepted. *Faculty research:* Campaign finance, emerging democracies, bureaucratic politics, judicial behavior, administration of justice.

Arcadia University, Graduate Studies, Program in International Public Relations, Glenside, PA 19038-3295. Offers health communications (MA); new media marketing (MA). *Degree requirements:* For master's, thesis, internship.

Auburn University at Montgomery, College of Public Policy and Justice, Department of Political Science and Public Administration, Montgomery, AL 36124-4023. Offers international relations (MIR); nonprofit management and leadership (Certificate); political science (MPS); public administration (MPA); public administration and public policy (PhD); public health care administration and policy (Certificate). PhD offered jointly with Auburn University. *Accreditation:* NASPAA (one or more programs are accredited). Part-time and evening/weekend programs available. *Faculty:* 5 full-time (1 woman), 1 part-time/adjunct (0 women). *Students:* 9 full-time (7 women), 40 part-time (26 women); includes 16 minority (13 Black or African American, non-Hispanic/Latino; 1 American Indian or Alaska Native, non-Hispanic/Latino; 1 Hispanic/Latino; 1 Two or more races, non-Hispanic/Latino), 2 international. Average age 29. 20 applicants, 90% accepted, 12 enrolled. In 2014, 13 master's awarded. *Degree requirements:* For master's, comprehensive exam; for doctorate, thesis/dissertation. *Entrance requirements:* For master's, GRE General Test or MAT; for doctorate, GRE General Test. *Application deadline:* Applications are processed on a rolling basis. Electronic applications accepted. *Expenses:* Tuition, state resident: full-time $6264; part-time $348 per credit hour. Tuition, nonresident: full-time $14,094; part-time $783 per credit hour. *Financial support:* In 2014–15, 1 teaching assistantship was awarded; research assistantships, career-related internships or fieldwork, and scholarships/grants also available. Support available to part-time students. Financial award application deadline: 3/1; financial award applicants required to submit FAFSA. *Unit head:* Dr. Andrew Cortell, Department Head, 334-244-3622, E-mail: acortell@aum.edu.
Website: http://www.cla.auburn.edu/polisci/graduate-programs/phd-in-public-administration-and-public-policy/

Azusa Pacific University, School of Behavioral and Applied Sciences, Department of Higher Education and Organizational Leadership, Azusa, CA 91702-7000. Offers college student affairs (M Ed); global leadership (MA); organizational leadership (MA).

Baylor University, Graduate School, College of Arts and Sciences, Department of Political Science, Waco, TX 76798. Offers international studies (MA); political science (MA, PhD); public policy and administration (MPPA); JD/MPPA. Terminal master's awarded for partial completion of doctoral program. *Degree requirements:* For master's, variable foreign language requirement, comprehensive exam (for some programs), thesis (for some programs); for doctorate, variable foreign language requirement, comprehensive exam, thesis/dissertation. *Entrance requirements:* For master's and doctorate, GRE General Test. Additional exam requirements/recommendations for international students: Required—TOEFL. Electronic applications accepted.

Baylor University, Graduate School, Hankamer School of Business, Department of Economics, Waco, TX 76798. Offers MS Eco. *Entrance requirements:* For master's, GMAT or GRE General Test. *Faculty research:* Econometrics, international economics, economic development, comparative economic systems, computational economics, health economics, economics of education, monetary economics.

Boston University, Graduate School of Arts and Sciences, Frederick S. Pardee School of Global Studies, Boston, MA 02215. Offers international affairs (MA); international relations and environmental policy (MA); international relations and international communication (MA); international relations and religion (MA); international relations, mid-career (MA); Latin American studies (MA); MA/JD; MBA/MA. *Faculty:* 33 full-time (8 women), 10 part-time/adjunct (4 women). *Students:* 78 full-time (50 women), 15 part-time (11 women); includes 12 minority (3 Black or African American, non-Hispanic/Latino; 5 Asian, non-Hispanic/Latino; 3 Hispanic/Latino; 1 Two or more races, non-Hispanic/Latino), 26 international. Average age 25. 338 applicants, 68% accepted, 36 enrolled. In 2014, 51 master's awarded. *Degree requirements:* For master's, one foreign language, capstone. *Entrance requirements:* For master's, GRE General Test, 3 letters of recommendation, transcript of all prior college coursework, statement of purpose. Additional exam requirements/recommendations for international students: Required—TOEFL (minimum score 600 paper-based; 94 iBT). *Application deadline:* For fall admission, 4/15 for domestic and international students; for spring admission, 10/15 for domestic and international students. Applications are processed on a rolling basis. Application fee: $80. Electronic applications accepted. *Expenses: Tuition:* Full-time $45,686; part-time $1428 per credit hour. *Required fees:* $660; $60 per semester. Tuition and fees vary according to program. *Financial support:* In 2014–15, 21 students received support. Federal Work-Study, scholarships/grants, and unspecified assistantships available. Financial award application deadline: 1/3; financial award applicants required to submit FAFSA. *Faculty research:* International relations, area studies, political economy, global development policy, global climate. *Unit head:* Adil Najam, Dean, 617-353-9279, Fax: 617-353-9290, E-mail: psgs@bu.edu. *Application contact:* Michael Williams, Graduate Program Administrator, 617-353-9349, Fax: 617-353-9290, E-mail: psgsgrad@bu.edu.
Website: http://www.bu.edu/PardeeSchool

Brandeis University, Graduate School of Arts and Sciences, Graduate Program in Global Studies, Waltham, MA 02454-9110. Offers MA. Part-time programs available. *Degree requirements:* For master's, one foreign language, thesis, global economy requirement. *Entrance requirements:* For master's, GRE, official transcript(s), 2 recommendation letters, curriculum vitae or resume, statement of purpose, writing sample. Additional exam requirements/recommendations for international students: Required—TOEFL (minimum score 600 paper-based; 100 iBT); Recommended—IELTS (minimum score 7). Electronic applications accepted. *Faculty research:* Globalization, civil society and human rights, communications and media, culture and globalization, global and regional governance, global environment, global health, immigration, social justice and gender.

Brandeis University, International Business School (IBS), Master of Business Administration Program, Waltham, MA 02454-9110. Offers asset management (MBA); business economics (MBA); corporate finance (MBA); data analytics (MBA); international economic policy analysis (MBA); marketing (MBA); real estate (MBA); risk management (MBA); sustainability (MBA). *Faculty:* 29 full-time (10 women), 27 part-time/adjunct (3 women). *Students:* 92 full-time (33 women), 1 (woman) part-time; includes 75 minority (7 Black or African American, non-Hispanic/Latino; 65 Asian, non-Hispanic/Latino; 3 Hispanic/Latino), 80 international. Average age 27. 131 applicants, 67% accepted, 37 enrolled. In 2014, 42 master's awarded. *Entrance requirements:* For master's, GMAT or GRE. Additional exam requirements/recommendations for international students: Required—TOEFL (minimum score 577 paper-based; 90 iBT), IELTS (minimum score 7), PTE (minimum score 61). *Application deadline:* For fall admission, 11/1 priority date for domestic and international students; for winter admission, 1/15 priority date for domestic and international students; for spring admission, 3/15 priority date for domestic and international students; for summer admission, 5/15 for domestic and international students. Application fee: $55. Electronic applications accepted. *Expenses:* Expenses: $45,748 annually, one-time orientation fee $44, graduate activity fee $40 per term. *Financial support:* In 2014–15, 80 students received support. Institutionally sponsored loans and scholarships/grants available. Financial award application deadline: 3/15; financial award applicants required to submit FAFSA. *Faculty research:* Strategic alliances, IPO and venture capital financing, real estate, risk management, data analytics. *Unit head:* Bruce Magid, Dean, 781-736-4663. *Application contact:* Brittany Leclerc, Senior Admissions Coordinator, 781-736-2252, Fax: 781-736-2263, E-mail: admission@lemberg.brandeis.edu.

Brock University, Faculty of Graduate Studies, Faculty of Social Sciences, Program in Political Science, St. Catharines, ON L2S 3A1, Canada. Offers Canadian politics (MA); comparative politics (MA); international relations (MA); political theory or philosophy (MA); public policy (MA). Part-time programs available. *Degree requirements:* For master's, thesis optional. *Entrance requirements:* For master's, honors degree. Additional exam requirements/recommendations for international students: Required—TOEFL (minimum score 550 paper-based; 80 iBT), IELTS (minimum score 6.5), TWE (minimum score 4). Electronic applications accepted. *Faculty research:* Public administration reform, economic and social justice, politics of societies, Canadian politics, international relations.

Brooklyn College of the City University of New York, School of Humanities and Social Sciences, Department of Political Science, Brooklyn, NY 11210-2889. Offers international affairs (MA); political science (MA); urban policy and administration (MA). Part-time and evening/weekend programs available. *Degree requirements:* For master's, comprehensive exam (for some programs), thesis or alternative, foreign language exam (for international affairs program). *Entrance requirements:* For master's, 2 letters of recommendation, personal statement. Additional exam requirements/recommendations for international students: Required—TOEFL (minimum score 500 paper-based; 61 iBT). *Faculty research:* Ethics and politics, politics of criminal justice, Western Europe, international law and politics, labor politics.

California State University, Fresno, Division of Graduate Studies, College of Social Sciences, Department of Political Science, Program in International Relations, Fresno, CA 93740-8027. Offers MA. Part-time and evening/weekend programs available. *Degree requirements:* For master's, one foreign language, thesis or alternative. *Entrance requirements:* For master's, GRE General Test, minimum GPA of 3.0. Additional exam requirements/recommendations for international students: Required—TOEFL. Electronic applications accepted.

California State University, Stanislaus, College of Humanities and Social Sciences, Program in History (MA), Turlock, CA 95382. Offers history (MA); international relations (MA); secondary school teachers (MA). Part-time programs available. *Degree requirements:* For master's, comprehensive exam, thesis or alternative. *Entrance requirements:* For master's, GRE, minimum GPA of 3.0, personal statement. Additional exam requirements/recommendations for international students: Required—TOEFL (minimum score 575 paper-based). Electronic applications accepted. *Faculty research:* History of Ancient Greece, history and ecology of the Central Valley, acculturation and gender.

Carleton University, Faculty of Graduate Studies, Faculty of Public Affairs and Management, Norman Paterson School of International Affairs, Ottawa, ON K1S 5B6, Canada. Offers MA, PhD. Part-time programs available. *Degree requirements:* For master's, one foreign language, comprehensive exam, thesis optional. *Entrance requirements:* For master's, honors degree. Additional exam requirements/recommendations for international students: Required—TOEFL. *Faculty research:* International conflict, development, political economy, conflict analysis.

The Catholic University of America, School of Arts and Sciences, Department of Politics, Washington, DC 20064. Offers American government (MA, PhD); Congressional and Presidential studies (MA); international affairs (MA); international political economics (MA); political theory (MA, PhD); world politics (MA, PhD); MA/JD. Part-time programs available. *Faculty:* 14 full-time (2 women), 4 part-time/adjunct (0 women). *Students:* 23 full-time (7 women), 44 part-time (8 women); includes 9 minority (2 Black or African American, non-Hispanic/Latino; 1 American Indian or Alaska Native, non-Hispanic/Latino; 2 Asian, non-Hispanic/Latino; 2 Hispanic/Latino; 2 Two or more races, non-Hispanic/Latino), 5 international. Average age 31. 67 applicants, 69% accepted, 10 enrolled. In 2014, 22 master's, 7 doctorates awarded. *Degree requirements:* For master's, one foreign language, comprehensive exam, thesis or alternative; for doctorate, variable foreign language requirement, comprehensive exam, thesis/dissertation. *Entrance requirements:* For master's, GRE General Test, statement of purpose, official copies of academic transcripts, three letters of recommendation, minimum GPA of 3.0; for doctorate, GRE General Test, statement of purpose, official copies of academic transcripts, three letters of recommendation. Additional exam requirements/recommendations for international students: Required—TOEFL (minimum score 580 paper-based). *Application deadline:* For fall admission, 7/15 priority date for domestic students, 7/1 for international students; for spring admission, 11/15 priority date for domestic students, 11/1 for international students. Applications are processed on a rolling basis. Application fee: $55. Electronic applications accepted. *Expenses: Tuition:* Full-time $40,200; part-time $1600 per credit hour. *Required fees:* $400; $195 per semester. One-time fee: $425. *Financial support:* Fellowships, research assistantships, teaching assistantships, Federal Work-Study, scholarships/grants, tuition waivers (full and partial), and unspecified assistantships available. Financial award application deadline: 2/1; financial award applicants required to submit FAFSA. *Faculty research:* Political philosophy, American political institutions and processes, political economy, international relations, U.S. political leadership since 1789. *Unit head:* Dr. Dennis Coyle, Chair, 202-319-5813, Fax: 202-319-6289, E-mail: coyle@cua.edu. *Application contact:* Director of Graduate Admissions, 202-319-5057, Fax: 202-319-6533, E-mail: cua-admissions@cua.edu.
Website: http://politics.cua.edu/

The Catholic University of America, School of Business and Economics, Washington, DC 20064. Offers accounting (MS); business analysis (MS); integral economic development management (MA); integral economic development policy (MA); international political economics (MA). Part-time programs available. *Faculty:* 21 full-time (7 women), 25 part-time/adjunct (4 women). *Students:* 56 full-time (37 women), 13 part-time (6 women); includes 23 minority (11 Black or African American, non-Hispanic/Latino; 5 Asian, non-Hispanic/Latino; 7 Hispanic/Latino), 21 international. Average age 27. 92 applicants, 64% accepted, 40 enrolled. In 2014, 30 master's awarded. *Degree requirements:* For master's, comprehensive exam. *Entrance requirements:* For master's, GRE General Test, statement of purpose, official copies of academic transcripts, three letters of recommendation. Additional exam requirements/recommendations for international students: Required—TOEFL (minimum score 580 paper-based). *Application deadline:* For fall admission, 7/15 priority date for domestic students, 7/1 for international students; for spring admission, 11/15 priority date for domestic students, 11/1 for international students. Applications are processed on a rolling basis. Application fee: $55. Electronic applications accepted. *Expenses: Tuition:* Full-time $40,200; part-time $1600 per credit hour. *Required fees:* $400; $195 per semester. One-time fee: $425. *Financial support:* Fellowships, research assistantships, teaching assistantships, Federal Work-Study, scholarships/grants, tuition waivers (full and partial), and unspecified assistantships available. Financial award application deadline: 2/1; financial award applicants required to submit FAFSA. *Faculty research:* Integrity of the marketing process, economics of energy and the environment, emerging markets, social change, international finance and economic development. *Total annual research expenditures:* $105,784. *Unit head:* Dr. Andrew V. Abela, Chair, 202-319-5235, Fax: 202-319-4426, E-mail: abela@cua.edu. *Application contact:* Director of Graduate Admissions, 202-319-5057, Fax: 202-319-6533, E-mail: cua-admissions@cua.edu.
Website: http://business.cua.edu/

Central Connecticut State University, School of Graduate Studies, College of Liberal Arts and Social Sciences, Program in International Area Studies, New Britain, CT 06050-4010. Offers international studies (MS). Part-time and evening/weekend programs available. *Faculty:* 3 full-time (1 woman). *Students:* 6 full-time (3 women), 11 part-time (4 women); includes 5 minority (3 Black or African American, non-Hispanic/Latino; 2 Hispanic/Latino), 1 international. Average age 36. 16 applicants, 50% accepted, 5 enrolled. In 2014, 9 master's awarded. *Degree requirements:* For master's, comprehensive exam, thesis or alternative. *Entrance requirements:* For master's, minimum undergraduate GPA of 2.7, essay, resume. Additional exam requirements/recommendations for international students: Required—TOEFL (minimum score 550 paper-based; 79 iBT). *Application deadline:* For fall admission, 5/1 for domestic and international students; for spring admission, 11/1 for domestic and international students. Applications are processed on a rolling basis. Application fee: $50. Electronic applications accepted. *Expenses: Tuition, area resident:* Full-time $5730; part-time $534 per credit. Tuition, state resident: full-time $8596; part-time $534 per credit. Tuition, nonresident: full-time $15,964; part-time $548 per credit. *Required fees:* $4211; $215 per credit. *Financial support:* In 2014–15, 3 students received support. Application deadline: 3/1; applicants required to submit FAFSA. *Unit head:* Dr. Matthew Ciscel, Program Director, 860-832-2749, E-mail: iasmailbox@ccsu.edu. *Application contact:* Patricia Gardner, Associate Director of Graduate Studies, 860-832-2350, Fax: 860-832-2362, E-mail: graduateadmissions@ccsu.edu.

Central European University, Graduate Studies, Department of International Relations and European Studies, Budapest, Hungary. Offers MA, PhD. *Faculty:* 12 full-time (4 women), 2 part-time/adjunct (1 woman). *Students:* 74 full-time (40 women). Average age 28. 319 applicants, 23% accepted, 52 enrolled. In 2014, 45 master's, 2 doctorates awarded. *Degree requirements:* For master's, one foreign language, thesis; for doctorate, one foreign language, comprehensive exam, thesis/dissertation. *Entrance requirements:* For master's and doctorate, interview. Additional exam requirements/recommendations for international students: Required—TOEFL (minimum score 570 paper-based); Recommended—IELTS (minimum score 6.5). *Application deadline:* For fall admission, 1/24 for domestic and international students. Application fee: $40. Electronic applications accepted. *Expenses: Tuition:* Full-time 12,000 euros. *Required fees:* 200 euros. One-time fee: 500 euros full-time. *Financial support:* In 2014–15, 71 students received support, including 71 fellowships (averaging $6,100 per year); career-related internships or fieldwork, scholarships/grants, health care benefits, and tuition waivers also available. *Faculty research:* Political, economic and social influences of European integration; social, political, economic and cultural dynamics in Asia; varieties of transnational capitalisms; matters of development, North/South relations, and regions such as Africa, Asia, Latin America and the Pacific; ethnic and ideological civil wars; political violence; peace-building; third party intervention; conflict management; ethnic politics; diasporas and migration; nationalism, identity and foreign policy. *Unit head:* Matteo Fumagalli, Head, 36 1 327-3243 Ext. 2219, E-mail: fumagallim@ceu.hu.

International Affairs

Application contact: Zsuzsanna Jaszberenyi, Admissions Officer, 361-324-3009, Fax: 367-327-3211, E-mail: admissions@ceu.hu. Website: http://ires.ceu.hu/

Central Michigan University, Central Michigan University Global Campus, Program in Administration, Mount Pleasant, MI 48859. Offers acquisitions administration (MSA, Certificate); engineering management administration (MSA, Certificate); general administration (MSA, Certificate); health services administration (MSA, Certificate); human resources administration (MSA, Certificate); information resource management (MSA); information resource management administration (Certificate); international administration (MSA, Certificate); leadership (MSA, Certificate); philanthropy and fundraising administration (MSA, Certificate); public administration (MSA, Certificate); recreation and park administration (MSA); research administration (MSA, Certificate). Part-time and evening/weekend programs available. Postbaccalaureate distance learning degree programs offered (no on-campus study). *Students:* Average age 38. *Entrance requirements:* For master's, minimum GPA of 2.7 in major. *Application deadline:* Applications are processed on a rolling basis. Application fee: $50. Electronic applications accepted. *Financial support:* Scholarships/grants available. Support available to part-time students. Financial award applicants required to submit FAFSA. *Unit head:* Dr. Patricia Chase, Director, 989-774-6525, E-mail: chase1pb@cmich.edu. *Application contact:* 877-268-4636, E-mail: cmuglobal@cmich.edu.

Chapman University, Wilkinson College of Humanities and Social Sciences, International Studies Program, Orange, CA 92866. Offers MA. Part-time and evening/weekend programs available. *Students:* 20 full-time (15 women), 4 part-time (3 women); includes 11 minority (2 Black or African American, non-Hispanic/Latino; 1 American Indian or Alaska Native, non-Hispanic/Latino; 3 Asian, non-Hispanic/Latino; 4 Hispanic/Latino; 1 Native Hawaiian or other Pacific Islander, non-Hispanic/Latino), 5 international. Average age 27. 33 applicants, 67% accepted, 6 enrolled. In 2014, 12 master's awarded. *Entrance requirements:* For master's, GRE, minimum undergraduate GPA of 2.5. Additional exam requirements/recommendations for international students: Required—TOEFL (minimum score 550 paper-based; 80 iBT). *Application deadline:* Applications are processed on a rolling basis. Application fee: $60. Electronic applications accepted. *Financial support:* Fellowships, Federal Work-Study, and scholarships/grants available. Financial award applicants required to submit FAFSA. *Unit head:* Dr. Lynn Horton, Director, 714-997-6976, E-mail: horton@chapman.edu. Website: http://www.chapman.edu/wilkinson/intlStudies/

City College of the City University of New York, Graduate School, College of Liberal Arts and Science, Division of Social Science, Program in International Relations, New York, NY 10031-9198. Offers MA. Part-time programs available. *Degree requirements:* For master's, one foreign language, thesis. *Entrance requirements:* For master's, GRE, 3 letters of recommendation. Additional exam requirements/recommendations for international students: Required—TOEFL (minimum score 600 paper-based; 100 iBT). Electronic applications accepted. *Faculty research:* International finance, international economics, European diplomatic history, area studies, international politics and diplomacy.

Claremont Graduate University, Graduate Programs, School of Social Science, Policy and Evaluation, Department of Politics and Policy, Claremont, CA 91711-6160. Offers American politics (MA, PhD); comparative politics (PhD); international political economy (MA); international studies (MA); political philosophy (PhD); political science (PhD); politics, economics and business (MA); public policy (MA, PhD); world politics (PhD); MBA/PhD. Part-time programs available. *Faculty:* 7 full-time (5 women), 2 part-time/adjunct (0 women). *Students:* 112 full-time (38 women), 39 part-time (9 women); includes 37 minority (7 Black or African American, non-Hispanic/Latino; 1 American Indian or Alaska Native, non-Hispanic/Latino; 12 Asian, non-Hispanic/Latino; 14 Hispanic/Latino; 1 Native Hawaiian or other Pacific Islander, non-Hispanic/Latino; 2 Two or more races, non-Hispanic/Latino), 30 international. Average age 34. In 2014, 22 master's, 12 doctorates awarded. Terminal master's awarded for partial completion of doctoral program. *Entrance requirements:* For master's and doctorate, GRE General Test. Additional exam requirements/recommendations for international students: Required—TOEFL (minimum score 550 paper-based; 80 iBT). *Application deadline:* For fall admission, 2/1 priority date for domestic and international students. Applications are processed on a rolling basis. Application fee: $80. Electronic applications accepted. *Expenses: Tuition:* Full-time $41,784; part-time $1741 per credit. *Required fees:* $600; $300 per semester. *Financial support:* Fellowships, research assistantships, teaching assistantships, Federal Work-Study, institutionally sponsored loans, and scholarships/grants available. Support available to part-time students. Financial award application deadline: 2/15; financial award applicants required to submit FAFSA. *Faculty research:* Environmental policy, international debt, global democratization, Third World development, public sector discrimination. *Unit head:* Heather Campbell, Chair, 909-621-8689, E-mail: heather.campbell@cgu.edu. *Application contact:* Annekah Hall, Assistant Director of Admissions, 909-607-3371, E-mail: annekah.hall@cgu.edu. Website: http://www.cgu.edu/pages/458.asp

Cleveland State University, College of Graduate Studies, College of Liberal Arts and Social Sciences, Department of Political Science, Cleveland, OH 44115. Offers global interactions (MA), including global business interactions, global political interactions. *Students:* 13 full-time (5 women), 14 part-time (7 women); includes 11 minority (5 Black or African American, non-Hispanic/Latino; 1 Asian, non-Hispanic/Latino; 2 Hispanic/Latino; 3 Two or more races, non-Hispanic/Latino), 3 international. Average age 32. 8 applicants, 100% accepted, 6 enrolled. In 2014, 11 master's awarded. *Degree requirements:* For master's, internship, exit project. *Entrance requirements:* For master's, minimum undergraduate GPA of 3.0 or GRE (50th percentile or above); two letters of recommendation; undergraduate degree in economics, political science, international relations, or a related discipline; completion of undergraduate macro and micro economics course. Additional exam requirements/recommendations for international students: Required—TOEFL (minimum score 520 paper-based). Application fee: $30. *Expenses: Expenses:* $9,615 full-time, in-state tuition and fees. *Unit head:* Dr. Rodger M. Govea, Associate Professor/Chairperson, 216-687-4554, E-mail: r.govea@csuohio.edu. *Application contact:* Deborah L. Brown, Interim Assistant Director, Graduate Admissions, 216-523-7572, Fax: 216-687-5400, E-mail: d.l.brown@csuohio.edu.
Website: http://www.csuohio.edu/class/politicalscience/

Colorado School of Mines, Graduate School, Division of Liberal Arts and International Studies, Golden, CO 80401. Offers international political economy (Graduate Certificate); science and technology policy (Graduate Certificate). Part-time programs available. *Faculty:* 27 full-time (13 women), 12 part-time/adjunct (7 women). *Students:* 10 full-time (2 women), 3 part-time (0 women); includes 1 minority (Hispanic/Latino), 3 international. Average age 35. 11 applicants, 73% accepted, 3 enrolled. *Entrance requirements:* Additional exam requirements/recommendations for international students: Required—TOEFL (minimum score 550 paper-based; 80 iBT). *Application deadline:* For fall admission, 12/15 priority date for domestic and international students; for spring admission, 9/1 priority date for domestic and international students. Application fee: $50 ($70 for international students). Electronic applications accepted. *Financial support:* In 2014–15, 10 students received support, including fellowships with full tuition reimbursements available (averaging $21,120 per year), research assistantships with full tuition reimbursements available (averaging $21,120 per year),

10 teaching assistantships with full tuition reimbursements available (averaging $21,120 per year); scholarships/grants, health care benefits, and unspecified assistantships also available. Financial award application deadline: 12/15. *Total annual research expenditures:* $124,093. *Unit head:* Dr. Tina Gianquitto, Interim Department Head, 303-273-3754, Fax: 303-273-3751, E-mail: tinagian@mines.edu. *Application contact:* Jody Lowther, Program Assistant, 303-384-2509, Fax: 303-273-3751, E-mail: jlowther@mines.edu.
Website: http://lais.mines.edu

Columbia University, School of International and Public Affairs, Program in International Affairs, New York, NY 10027. Offers MIA, JD/MIA, MBA/MIA, MIA/MS, MPH/MIA, MSJ/MIA. *Degree requirements:* For master's, one foreign language. *Entrance requirements:* For master's, GRE General Test. Additional exam requirements/recommendations for international students: Required—TOEFL (minimum score 600 paper-based; 100 iBT). Electronic applications accepted.

Concordia University, School of Business and Professional Studies, Irvine, CA 92612-3299. Offers business administration: business practice (MBA); international studies (MA). Part-time and evening/weekend programs available. *Degree requirements:* For master's, capstone project or thesis. *Entrance requirements:* For master's, official college transcript(s), signed statement of intent, resume, two references, interview (MBA); passport photo, photocopies of valid U.S. passport, and college diploma (MAIS). Additional exam requirements/recommendations for international students: Required—TOEFL. Electronic applications accepted. *Expenses:* Contact institution.

Cornell University, Graduate School, Graduate Fields of Arts and Sciences, Field of Government, Ithaca, NY 14853-0001. Offers American politics (PhD); comparative politics (PhD); international relations (PhD); political methodology (PhD); political thought (PhD); public policy (PhD). *Degree requirements:* For doctorate, comprehensive exam, thesis/dissertation. *Entrance requirements:* For doctorate, GRE General Test, sample of written work, 3 letters of recommendation. Additional exam requirements/recommendations for international students: Required—TOEFL (minimum score 550 paper-based; 77 iBT). Electronic applications accepted. *Faculty research:* Political theory, American politics, comparative politics, international relations, methodology.

Creighton University, Graduate School, College of Arts and Sciences, Program in International Relations, Omaha, NE 68178-0001. Offers MA. Part-time and evening/weekend programs available. *Faculty:* 14 full-time (3 women). *Students:* 4 full-time (3 women), 8 part-time (4 women); includes 1 minority (Asian, non-Hispanic/Latino). Average age 28. 9 applicants, 78% accepted, 2 enrolled. In 2014, 8 master's awarded. *Degree requirements:* For master's, comprehensive exam, thesis optional. *Entrance requirements:* For master's, GRE General Test, 3 letters of recommendation. Additional exam requirements/recommendations for international students: Required—TOEFL (minimum score 550 paper-based; 80 iBT). *Application deadline:* For fall admission, 3/1 priority date for domestic and international students; for winter admission, 12/1 priority date for domestic students, 7/1 priority date for international students; for spring admission, 4/1 priority date for domestic students, 9/1 priority date for international students; for summer admission, 3/1 for domestic and international students. Applications are processed on a rolling basis. Application fee: $50. Electronic applications accepted. *Expenses: Tuition:* Full-time $14,040; part-time $780 per credit hour. *Required fees:* $153 per semester. Tuition and fees vary according to course load, campus/location, program, reciprocity agreements and student's religious affiliation. *Financial support:* In 2014–15, 4 fellowships with full and partial tuition reimbursements (averaging $11,240 per year) were awarded; health care benefits also available. Support available to part-time students. Financial award application deadline: 5/1; financial award applicants required to submit FAFSA. *Unit head:* Dr. Terry Clark, Chair, 402-280-4712, E-mail: tclark@creighton.edu. *Application contact:* Lindsay Johnson, Director of Graduate and Adult Recruitment, 402-280-2703, Fax: 402-280-2423, E-mail: gradschool@creighton.edu.

DePaul University, College of Liberal Arts and Social Sciences, Chicago, IL 60614. Offers Arabic (MA); Chinese (MA); English (MA); French (MA); German (MA); history (MA); interdisciplinary studies (MA, MS); international public service (MS); international studies (MA); Italian (MA); Japanese (MA); leadership and policy studies (MS); liberal studies (MA); new media studies (MA); nonprofit management (MNM); public administration (MPA); public health (MPH); public service management (MS); social work (MSW); sociology (MA); Spanish (MA); sustainable urban development (MA); women and gender studies (MA); writing and publishing (MA); writing, rhetoric, and discourse (MA); MA/PhD. Part-time and evening/weekend programs available. Postbaccalaureate distance learning degree programs offered (no on-campus study). Terminal master's awarded for partial completion of doctoral program. *Degree requirements:* For master's, variable foreign language requirement, comprehensive exam (for some programs), thesis (for some programs). Electronic applications accepted.

East Carolina University, Graduate School, Thomas Harriot College of Arts and Sciences, Program in International Studies, Greenville, NC 27858-4353. Offers MA. Part-time programs available. *Degree requirements:* For master's, one foreign language, thesis optional, international field experience. *Entrance requirements:* For master's, GRE General Test. Additional exam requirements/recommendations for international students: Required—TOEFL. *Expenses:* Tuition, state resident: full-time $4223. Tuition, nonresident: full-time $16,540. *Required fees:* $2184.

Embry-Riddle Aeronautical University–Daytona, Department of Security Studies and International Affairs, Daytona Beach, FL 32114-3900. Offers cybersecurity management and policy (MS); human security and resilience (MS). *Degree requirements:* For master's, capstone projects. *Entrance requirements:* Additional exam requirements/recommendations for international students: Required—TOEFL (minimum score 550 paper-based; 79 iBT). *Application deadline:* Applications are processed on a rolling basis. Application fee: $50. Electronic applications accepted. *Expenses: Tuition:* Full-time $15,360; part-time $1280 per credit hour. *Required fees:* $1334. *Financial support:* Research assistantships, teaching assistantships, career-related internships or fieldwork, and unspecified assistantships available. *Faculty research:* Cybersecurity education and curriculum, and the practice of digital forensics and information security; intelligence and homeland security, military intervention and nation building, and international relations theory; environmental and human security, resilience and their relationship to domestic and national security; African political culture and governance; military rule; regional cooperation; mass media and democratization. *Unit head:* James Ramsay, PhD, Professor of Homeland Security and Chair, Department of Security Studies and International Affairs, 386-226-7153, E-mail: james.ramsay@erau.edu. *Application contact:* International and Graduate Admissions, 386-226-6176, Fax: 386-226-7070, E-mail: graduate.admissions@erau.edu.
Website: http://daytonabeach.erau.edu/college-arts-sciences/security-studies/index.html

Embry-Riddle Aeronautical University–Worldwide, Department of Security, Emergency Response and Interdisciplinary Studies, Daytona Beach, FL 32114-3900. Offers MS. Part-time and evening/weekend programs available. Postbaccalaureate distance learning degree programs offered (no on-campus study). *Degree requirements:* For master's, capstone project. *Entrance requirements:* Additional exam requirements/

recommendations for international students: Required—TOEFL (minimum score 550 paper-based; 79 iBT). *Application deadline:* Applications are processed on a rolling basis. Application fee: $50. Electronic applications accepted. *Expenses: Tuition:* Full-time $6720; part-time $560 per credit hour. *Unit head:* Dr. James T. Schultz, Professor, College of Business, Dean, College of Arts & Sciences, 386-226-6970, E-mail: john.watret@erau.edu. *Application contact:* Admissions, 800-522-6787, Fax: 386-226-6984, E-mail: worldwide@erau.edu.

Fairleigh Dickinson University, Metropolitan Campus, University College: Arts, Sciences, and Professional Studies, School of History, Political and International Studies, Program in International Studies, Teaneck, NJ 07666-1914. Offers MA.

Florida International University, College of Arts and Sciences, Department of Politics and International Relations, Program in International Relations, Miami, FL 33199. Offers international relations (PhD); international studies (MA). Ph D program has fall admissions only. Part-time and evening/weekend programs available. *Degree requirements:* For master's, one foreign language, thesis optional; for doctorate, comprehensive exam, thesis/dissertation. *Entrance requirements:* For master's, GRE General Test, 2 letters of recommendation; for doctorate, GRE General Test, letter of intent; 2 letters of recommendation; minimum undergraduate GPA of 3.2 or equivalent, 3.5 for all combined graduate work. Additional exam requirements/recommendations for international students: Required—TOEFL (minimum score 550 paper-based; 80 iBT). Electronic applications accepted.

Florida State University, The Graduate School, College of Social Sciences and Public Policy, Program in International Affairs, Tallahassee, FL 32306-2161. Offers MA, MS, JD/MA, JD/MS. Part-time programs available. *Students:* 52 full-time (20 women), 19 part-time (8 women); includes 23 minority (9 Black or African American, non-Hispanic/Latino; 1 American Indian or Alaska Native, non-Hispanic/Latino; 4 Asian, non-Hispanic/Latino; 9 Hispanic/Latino). Average age 25. 65 applicants, 75% accepted, 23 enrolled. In 2014, 28 master's awarded. *Degree requirements:* For master's, one foreign language, comprehensive exam, thesis optional. *Entrance requirements:* For master's, GRE General Test, minimum GPA of 3.0. Additional exam requirements/recommendations for international students: Required—TOEFL (minimum score 550 paper-based; 80 iBT). *Application deadline:* For fall admission, 7/1 for domestic students; for spring admission, 7/1 for domestic students. Applications are processed on a rolling basis. Application fee: $30. *Expenses:* Tuition, state resident: part-time $403.51 per credit hour. Tuition, nonresident: part-time $1004.85 per credit hour. *Required fees:* $75.81 per credit hour. One-time fee: $20 part-time. Tuition and fees vary according to campus/location. *Financial support:* In 2014–15, 5 students received support, including 5 research assistantships with full tuition reimbursements available (averaging $5,000 per year); career-related internships or fieldwork, Federal Work-Study, institutionally sponsored loans, and unspecified assistantships also available. Financial award application deadline: 2/1; financial award applicants required to submit FAFSA. *Unit head:* Dr. Lee K. Metcalf, Director, 850-644-7327, Fax: 850-645-4981, E-mail: lmetcalf@fsu.edu. *Application contact:* Kaley Boggs, Academic Program Specialist, 850-644-4418, Fax: 850-645-4981, E-mail: plollie@fsu.edu.
Website: http://www.fsu.edu/~inaprog/

Fordham University, Graduate School of Arts and Sciences, Program in International Political Economy and Development, New York, NY 10458. Offers MA, Certificate. Part-time and evening/weekend programs available. *Students:* 33 full-time (17 women), 16 part-time (6 women); includes 3 minority (2 Asian, non-Hispanic/Latino; 1 Hispanic/Latino), 13 international. Average age 27. 181 applicants, 52% accepted, 24 enrolled. In 2014, 29 master's, 6 other advanced degrees awarded. *Degree requirements:* For master's, comprehensive exam. *Entrance requirements:* For master's, GRE General Test. Additional exam requirements/recommendations for international students: Required—TOEFL (minimum score 600 paper-based). *Application deadline:* For fall admission, 1/4 priority date for domestic students; for spring admission, 11/1 for domestic students. Application fee: $70. Electronic applications accepted. *Financial support:* In 2014–15, 16 students received support, including 2 fellowships with full and partial tuition reimbursements available (averaging $11,965 per year), 16 research assistantships with full and partial tuition reimbursements available (averaging $16,050 per year); career-related internships or fieldwork, institutionally sponsored loans, tuition waivers (full and partial), and unspecified assistantships also available. Financial award application deadline: 1/4; financial award applicants required to submit FAFSA. *Faculty research:* International economics, comparative international politics, international banking and finance, international development, emerging markets and country risk analysis. *Unit head:* Dr. Henry Schwalbenberg, Chair, 718-817-3866, Fax: 718-817-3518. *Application contact:* Bernadette Valentino-Morrison, Director of Graduate Admissions, 718-817-4419, Fax: 718-817-3566, E-mail: valentinomor@fordham.edu.

George Mason University, School of Policy, Government, and International Affairs, Program in International Commerce and Policy, Arlington, VA 22201. Offers MA. *Faculty:* 20 full-time (5 women), 11 part-time/adjunct (3 women). *Students:* 38 full-time (12 women), 94 part-time (42 women); includes 43 minority (13 Black or African American, non-Hispanic/Latino; 9 Asian, non-Hispanic/Latino; 18 Hispanic/Latino; 3 Two or more races, non-Hispanic/Latino), 6 international. Average age 30. 51 applicants, 78% accepted, 25 enrolled. In 2014, 84 master's awarded. *Degree requirements:* For master's, thesis or alternative. *Entrance requirements:* For master's, GRE/GMAT (for students seeking merit-based scholarships), bachelor's degree with minimum of GPA of 3.0; expanded goals statement; current resume; 2 official copies of transcripts; 2 letters of recommendation. Additional exam requirements/recommendations for international students: Required—TOEFL (minimum score 575 paper-based; 80 iBT), IELTS (minimum score 6.5), PTE. *Application deadline:* For fall admission, 6/1 priority date for domestic students, 5/1 priority date for international students; for spring admission, 12/1 priority date for domestic students, 11/1 priority date for international students. Applications are processed on a rolling basis. Application fee: $65 ($80 for international students). Electronic applications accepted. *Expenses:* Expenses: Contact institution. *Financial support:* Career-related internships or fieldwork, Federal Work-Study, scholarships/grants, unspecified assistantships, and health care benefits (for full-time research or teaching assistantship recipients) available. Support available to part-time students. Financial award application deadline: 3/1; financial award applicants required to submit FAFSA. *Unit head:* Kenneth Reinert, Director, 703-993-8212, Fax: 703-993-8215, E-mail: kreinert@gmu.edu. *Application contact:* Travis Major, Director of Graduate Admissions, 703-993-3183, Fax: 703-993-4876, E-mail: tmajor@gmu.edu.
Website: http://spgia.gmu.edu/programs/graduate-degrees/international-commerce-and-policy-icp/

Georgetown University, Graduate School of Arts and Sciences, Edmund A. Walsh School of Foreign Service, BMW Center for German and European Studies, Washington, DC 20057. Offers MA, MA/JD, MA/PhD. *Degree requirements:* For master's, 2 foreign languages, comprehensive exam. *Entrance requirements:* For master's, GRE General Test. Additional exam requirements/recommendations for international students: Required—TOEFL. Electronic applications accepted. *Faculty research:* Transatlantic relations, European Union, German and European Studies.

Georgetown University, Graduate School of Arts and Sciences, Edmund A. Walsh School of Foreign Service, Master of Science in Foreign Service Program, Washington, DC 20057. Offers MS, JD/MS, MA/MS, MBA/MS, MPP/MS. *Faculty:* 28 full-time (7 women), 41 part-time/adjunct (6 women). *Students:* 199 full-time (94 women); includes 42 minority (10 Black or African American, non-Hispanic/Latino; 1 American Indian or Alaska Native, non-Hispanic/Latino; 15 Asian, non-Hispanic/Latino; 6 Hispanic/Latino; 10 Two or more races, non-Hispanic/Latino), 62 international. Average age 27. 808 applicants. In 2014, 97 master's awarded. *Degree requirements:* For master's, one foreign language, comprehensive exam, internship. *Entrance requirements:* For master's, GRE General Test or GMAT (for students with undergraduate degree from English-speaking institution), one semester each of micro and macroeconomics with minimum B grade. Additional exam requirements/recommendations for international students: Required—TOEFL (minimum score 100 iBT) or IELTS (minimum score 7). *Application deadline:* For fall admission, 1/15 for domestic and international students. Application fee: $80. Electronic applications accepted. *Financial support:* In 2014–15, research assistantships (averaging $5,000 per year), teaching assistantships (averaging $5,000 per year) were awarded; career-related internships or fieldwork, scholarships/grants, and tuition waivers (partial) also available. Financial award application deadline: 1/15. *Faculty research:* International business diplomacy, political risk analysis, foreign policy decision-making, intercultural perspectives on contemporary issues. *Unit head:* Dr. Anthony Arend, Director, 202-687-5763. *Application contact:* MSFS Admissions, 202-687-5763, E-mail: msfsinfo@georgetown.edu.
Website: http://msfs.georgetown.edu/

Georgetown University, Graduate School of Arts and Sciences, School of Continuing Studies, Washington, DC 20057. Offers American studies (MALS); Catholic studies (MALS); classical civilizations (MALS); emergency and disaster management (MPS); ethics and the professions (MALS); hospitality management (MPS); human resources management (MPS); humanities (MALS); individualized study (MALS); international affairs (MALS); Islam and Muslim-Christian relations (MALS); journalism (MPS); liberal studies (DLS); literature and society (MALS); medieval and early modern European studies (MALS); public relations and corporate communications (MPS); real estate (MPS); religious studies (MALS); social and public policy (MALS); sports industry management (MPS); systems engineering management (MPS); technology management (MPS); the theory and practice of American democracy (MALS); urban and regional planning (MPS); visual culture (MALS). MPS in systems engineering management offered jointly with Stevens Institute of Technology. *Entrance requirements:* Additional exam requirements/recommendations for international students: Required—TOEFL.

Georgetown University, Law Center, Washington, DC 20001. Offers environmental law (LL M); global health law (LL M); global health law and international institutions (LL M); individualized study (LL M); international business and economic law (LL M); law (JD, SJD); national security law (LL M); securities and financial regulation (LL M); taxation (LL M); JD/LL M; JD/MA; JD/MBA; JD/MPH; JD/PhD. *Accreditation:* ABA. Part-time and evening/weekend programs available. *Degree requirements:* For master's, thesis; for doctorate, thesis/dissertation (for some programs). *Entrance requirements:* For master's, JD, LL B, or first law degree earned in country of origin; for doctorate, LSAT (for JD). Additional exam requirements/recommendations for international students: Required—TOEFL. *Expenses:* Contact institution. *Faculty research:* Constitutional law, legal history, jurisprudence.

The George Washington University, Elliott School of International Affairs, Program in International Affairs, Washington, DC 20052. Offers MA. Part-time programs available. *Faculty:* 66 full-time (18 women). *Students:* 212 full-time (117 women), 84 part-time (56 women); includes 67 minority (9 Black or African American, non-Hispanic/Latino; 1 American Indian or Alaska Native, non-Hispanic/Latino; 17 Asian, non-Hispanic/Latino; 33 Hispanic/Latino; 7 Two or more races, non-Hispanic/Latino), 65 international. Average age 26. 679 applicants, 133 enrolled. In 2014, 95 master's awarded. *Degree requirements:* For master's, one foreign language, capstone project. *Entrance requirements:* For master's, GRE General Test, 2 years of a modern foreign language, 2 semesters of introductory economics. Additional exam requirements/recommendations for international students: Required—TOEFL (minimum score 100 iBT), IELTS (minimum score 7). *Application deadline:* For fall admission, 1/15 priority date for domestic and international students; for spring admission, 10/1 for domestic students. Application fee: $75. Electronic applications accepted. *Financial support:* In 2014–15, 61 students received support. Fellowships with partial tuition reimbursements available and Federal Work-Study available. Financial award application deadline: 1/15; financial award applicants required to submit FAFSA. *Faculty research:* Area studies, international economics, national security policy studies, international economic development, Sino-Soviet studies. *Unit head:* Dr. Marcus King, Director, 202-994-7137, E-mail: maia@gwu.edu. *Application contact:* Nicole A. Campbell, Director of Graduate Admissions, 202-994-7050, Fax: 202-994-9537, E-mail: esiagrad@gwu.edu.
Website: http://elliott.gwu.edu/international-affairs-masters

The George Washington University, Elliott School of International Affairs, Program in International Policy and Practice, Washington, DC 20052. Offers MIPP. Part-time programs available. *Students:* 10 full-time (2 women), 24 part-time (10 women); includes 9 minority (4 Black or African American, non-Hispanic/Latino; 1 Asian, non-Hispanic/Latino; 3 Hispanic/Latino; 1 Two or more races, non-Hispanic/Latino), 4 international. Average age 39. 75 applicants, 13 enrolled. In 2014, 32 master's awarded. *Degree requirements:* For master's, one foreign language. *Entrance requirements:* For master's, GRE (recommended), advanced degree or 8 years of experience plus BA, introductory microeconomics and macroeconomics. Additional exam requirements/recommendations for international students: Required—TOEFL (minimum score 100 iBT), IELTS (minimum score 7). *Application deadline:* For fall admission, 1/15 priority date for domestic and international students; for spring admission, 10/1 for domestic and international students. Application fee: $75. Electronic applications accepted. *Financial support:* In 2014–15, 13 students received support. Fellowships with partial tuition reimbursements available, Federal Work-Study, and scholarships/grants available. Financial award application deadline: 1/15; financial award applicants required to submit FAFSA. *Unit head:* Prof. Matthew Levinger, Director, 202-994-9946, E-mail: mippgw@gwu.edu. *Application contact:* Nicole A. Campbell, Director of Graduate Admissions, 202-994-7050, Fax: 202-994-9537, E-mail: esiagrad@gwu.edu.
Website: http://elliott.gwu.edu/international-policy-and-practice

The George Washington University, Elliott School of International Affairs, Program in International Studies, Washington, DC 20052. Offers MIS. Part-time programs available. *Degree requirements:* For master's, one foreign language. *Entrance requirements:* For master's, 2 years (or equivalent) of a modern, spoken, foreign language; introductory microeconomics/macroeconomics coursework. Additional exam requirements/recommendations for international students: Required—TOEFL (minimum score 100 iBT), IELTS (minimum score 7). *Application deadline:* For fall admission, 1/15 priority date for domestic and international students; for spring admission, 10/1 for domestic students. Application fee: $75. Electronic applications accepted. *Financial support:* Fellowships with partial tuition reimbursements, Federal Work-Study, and scholarships/grants available. Financial award application deadline: 1/15; financial award applicants required to submit FAFSA. *Unit head:* Lisa Stephenson, Director, 202-994-7050, E-mail: esiagrad@gwu.edu. *Application contact:* Nicole A. Campbell, Director of Graduate Admissions, 202-994-7050, Fax: 202-994-9537, E-mail: esiagrad@gwu.edu.
Website: http://elliott.gwu.edu/international-studies-masters

International Affairs

The George Washington University, Law School, Washington, DC 20052. Offers law (SJD); national security and US foreign relations (LL M). *Accreditation:* ABA. Part-time and evening/weekend programs available. *Faculty:* 90 full-time (37 women). *Students:* 1,539 full-time (791 women), 386 part-time (156 women); includes 461 minority (151 Black or African American, non-Hispanic/Latino; 10 American Indian or Alaska Native, non-Hispanic/Latino; 220 Asian, non-Hispanic/Latino; 72 Hispanic/Latino; 3 Native Hawaiian or other Pacific Islander, non-Hispanic/Latino; 5 Two or more races, non-Hispanic/Latino), 180 international. Average age 27. 258 applicants, 98% accepted, 162 enrolled. In 2014, 225 master's, 581 doctorates awarded. *Degree requirements:* For doctorate, thesis/dissertation (for some programs). *Entrance requirements:* For master's, JD or equivalent; for doctorate, LSAT (for JD), LL M or equivalent (for SJD). *Application deadline:* For fall admission, 3/1 for domestic students. Applications are processed on a rolling basis. Application fee: $75. *Expenses:* Expenses: Contact institution. *Financial support:* Research assistantships, career-related internships or fieldwork, Federal Work-Study, institutionally sponsored loans, scholarships/grants, and tuition waivers (full and partial) available. Support available to part-time students. Financial award application deadline: 3/1; financial award applicants required to submit CSS PROFILE or FAFSA. *Unit head:* Blake D. Morant, Dean, 202-994-6261, Fax: 202-994-5157. *Application contact:* Sophia Sim, Assistant Dean of Admissions and Financial Aid, 202-994-7230, Fax: 202-739-0624, E-mail: ssim@law.gwu.edu.
Website: http://www.law.gwu.edu/

Georgia Institute of Technology, Graduate Studies, Ivan Allen College of Liberal Arts, Sam Nunn School of International Affairs, Atlanta, GA 30332-0001. Offers MS, PhD. Part-time programs available. *Students:* 38 full-time (20 women), 8 part-time (4 women); includes 11 minority (3 Black or African American, non-Hispanic/Latino; 4 Asian, non-Hispanic/Latino; 3 Hispanic/Latino; 1 Two or more races, non-Hispanic/Latino), 7 international. Average age 27. 52 applicants, 63% accepted, 11 enrolled. In 2014, 19 master's, 1 doctorate awarded. Terminal master's awarded for partial completion of doctoral program. *Degree requirements:* For master's, one foreign language, thesis optional, minimum 3.0 GPA, literacy in economics and technology; for doctorate, one foreign language, comprehensive exam, thesis/dissertation. *Entrance requirements:* For master's, GRE, http://www.iac.gatech.edu/academics/graduate-programs/ms-inta; for doctorate, GRE, http://www.iac.gatech.edu/academics/graduate-programs/dp-intast. Additional exam requirements/recommendations for international students: Required—TOEFL (minimum score 600 paper-based; 100 iBT). *Application deadline:* For fall admission, 1/15 priority date for domestic and international students. Applications are processed on a rolling basis. Application fee: $75. Electronic applications accepted. *Expenses:* Tuition, state resident: full-time $12,344; part-time $515 per credit hour. Tuition, nonresident: full-time $27,600; part-time $1150 per credit hour. *Required fees:* $1196 per term. Part-time tuition and fees vary according to course load. *Financial support:* Fellowships, research assistantships, teaching assistantships, career-related internships or fieldwork, Federal Work-Study, institutionally sponsored loans, tuition waivers (partial), and unspecified assistantships available. Support available to part-time students. Financial award application deadline: 5/1. *Faculty research:* International political economy, international security, Asian and European studies. *Total annual research expenditures:* $880,726. *Unit head:* Brian Woodall, Director, 404-894-1902, E-mail: brian.woodall@inta.gatech.edu. *Application contact:* Vince Pedicino, Graduate Coordinator, 404-894-1905, E-mail: vince.pedicino@inta.gatech.edu.
Website: http://www.inta.gatech.edu

Harvard University, Graduate School of Arts and Sciences, Department of Government, Cambridge, MA 02138. Offers political science (PhD), including American politics, comparative politics, international relations, political thought, quantitative methods. *Degree requirements:* For doctorate, one foreign language, thesis/dissertation, general exams. *Entrance requirements:* For doctorate, GRE General Test. Additional exam requirements/recommendations for international students: Required—TOEFL.

Harvard University, Law School, Professional Programs in Law, Cambridge, MA 02138. Offers international and comparative law (JD); law and business (JD); law and government (JD); law and social change (JD); law, science and technology (JD); JD/MALD; JD/MBA; JD/MPH; JD/MPP; JD/PhD. *Accreditation:* ABA. *Degree requirements:* For doctorate, 3rd-year paper. *Entrance requirements:* For doctorate, LSAT. *Faculty research:* Constitutional law, voting rights law, cyber law.

Hult International Business School, Program in International Relations - Hult London Campus, London WC 1B 4JP, United Kingdom. Offers conflict resolution (MA); diplomacy (MA); international public law (MA); international relations (MA); Middle East international security (MA); politics (MA); security studies (MA); terrorism (MA); U.S. foreign policy (MA). Part-time programs available. *Entrance requirements:* Additional exam requirements/recommendations for international students: Required—TOEFL (minimum score 580 paper-based), TWE (minimum score 5). Electronic applications accepted. *Faculty research:* American foreign politics, Middle East, security studies.

Hult International Business School, Program in International Relations - Hult San Francisco Campus, San Francisco, CA 94133. Offers MA.

Instituto Tecnologico de Santo Domingo, Graduate School, Area of Humanities and Social Sciences, Santo Domingo, Dominican Republic. Offers accounting (Certificate); adult education (Certificate); applied linguistics (MA); economics (MA); education (M Ed); educational psychology (MA, Certificate); gender and development (MA, Certificate); humanistic studies (MA); international marketing management (Certificate); international relations in the Caribbean basin (Certificate); intervention systems in family therapy (MA); linguistic and literary communication (Certificate); pedagogical support (MA); social science education (M Ed); sustainable human development (MA); terminal illness and death psychology (Certificate); youth and adult education (M Ed).

Instituto Tecnológico y de Estudios Superiores de Monterrey, Campus Ciudad Obregón, Program in International Relations, Ciudad Obregón, Mexico. Offers MIR.

Johns Hopkins University, Paul H. Nitze School of Advanced International Studies, Washington, DC 20036. Offers international development (MA, Certificate), including international economics (MA); international economics and finance (MA); international public policy (MIPP); international relations (PhD); international studies (Certificate); Japan studies (MA), including international economics; Korea studies (MA), including international economics; South Asia studies (MA), including international economics; Southeast Asia studies (MA), including international economics; JD/MA; MBA/MA; MHS/MA. Terminal master's awarded for partial completion of doctoral program. *Degree requirements:* For master's, 4-6 international economics courses, 5-6 functional or regional concentration courses, 2 core examinations, proficiency in language other than native language, capstone project; for doctorate, 2 foreign languages, thesis/dissertation, 3 comprehensive exams, economics, quantitative and qualitative course, dissertation prospectus and defense. *Entrance requirements:* For master's, GMAT or GRE General Test, previous course work in economics, foreign language, undergraduate degree; for doctorate, GRE General Test, master's degree. Additional exam requirements/recommendations for international students: Required—TOEFL (minimum score 600 paper-based; 100 iBT) or IELTS (minimum score 7). Electronic applications accepted. *Expenses:* Contact institution. *Faculty research:* Regional studies, international relations, international economics, energy and environment, international development.

Kansas State University, Graduate School, College of Arts and Sciences, Department of Political Science, Manhattan, KS 66506. Offers political science (MA), including international service, political science; public administration (MPA). Part-time programs available. *Faculty:* 16 full-time (4 women), 1 (woman) part-time/adjunct. *Students:* 24 full-time (15 women), 14 part-time (6 women); includes 7 minority (3 Black or African American, non-Hispanic/Latino; 1 Asian, non-Hispanic/Latino; 3 Hispanic/Latino), 4 international. Average age 29. 25 applicants, 68% accepted, 11 enrolled. In 2014, 20 master's awarded. *Degree requirements:* For master's, thesis or alternative. *Entrance requirements:* For master's, GRE (recommended), minimum GPA of 3.0. Additional exam requirements/recommendations for international students: Required—TOEFL (minimum score 550 paper-based). *Application deadline:* For fall admission, 2/1 priority date for domestic and international students; for spring admission, 8/1 priority date for domestic and international students. Applications are processed on a rolling basis. Application fee: $50 ($75 for international students). Electronic applications accepted. *Financial support:* In 2014–15, 10 teaching assistantships with tuition reimbursements (averaging $9,286 per year) were awarded; fellowships, research assistantships, career-related internships or fieldwork, Federal Work-Study, institutionally sponsored loans, and scholarships/grants also available. Support available to part-time students. Financial award application deadline: 3/1; financial award applicants required to submit FAFSA. *Faculty research:* Armed conflict, civil military relations, comparative public administration and policy, electoral competition, legislative studies. *Unit head:* Dr. Jeff Pickering, Head, 785-532-0454, Fax: 785-532-2339, E-mail: jjp@ksu.edu. *Application contact:* Dr. James Franke, Director, 785-532-0451, Fax: 785-532-2339, E-mail: jfranke@ksu.edu.
Website: http://www.k-state.edu/polsci/

Kennesaw State University, College of Humanities and Social Sciences, Program in International Policy Management, Kennesaw, GA 30144. Offers MS. Postbaccalaureate distance learning degree programs offered (minimal on-campus study). *Students:* 2 full-time (both women), 21 part-time (9 women); includes 6 minority (2 Black or African American, non-Hispanic/Latino; 3 Hispanic/Latino; 1 Two or more races, non-Hispanic/Latino), 1 international. Average age 33. 21 applicants, 71% accepted, 13 enrolled. In 2014, 6 master's awarded. *Degree requirements:* For master's, practicum or thesis. *Entrance requirements:* For master's, GRE, resume, letters of recommendation, writing sample. Additional exam requirements/recommendations for international students: Required—TOEFL (minimum score 550 paper-based; 80 iBT), IELTS (minimum score 6.5). *Application deadline:* For fall admission, 6/1 for domestic and international students. Application fee: $60. Electronic applications accepted. *Expenses:* Tuition, state resident: part-time $275 per semester hour. Tuition, nonresident: part-time $990 per semester hour. *Financial support:* In 2014–15, 2 research assistantships with full tuition reimbursements (averaging $8,000 per year) were awarded; unspecified assistantships also available. Financial award application deadline: 4/1; financial award applicants required to submit FAFSA. *Unit head:* Dr. Chien-Pin Li, Director, 470-578-6227, E-mail: msipm@kennesaw.edu. *Application contact:* Natalia Meneses, Program Coordinator, 470-578-6631, Fax: 470-578-9172, E-mail: nxm4943@kennesaw.edu.
Website: https://www.kennesaw.edu/msipm/

Lebanese American University, School of Arts and Sciences, Beirut, Lebanon. Offers computer science (MS); international affairs (MA).

Lesley University, Graduate School of Arts and Social Sciences, Cambridge, MA 02138-2790. Offers clinical mental health counseling (MA), including holistic counseling, school and community counseling, trauma studies; counseling psychology (MA, CAGS), including professional counseling (MA), school counseling (MA); creative writing (MFA); expressive therapies (MA, PhD, CAGS), including art (MA), clinical mental health counseling (MA), dance (MA), expressive therapies (MA), music (MA); independent studies (CAGS); independent study (MA); intercultural relations (MA, CAGS); interdisciplinary studies (MA), including individualized studies, integrative holistic health, mindfulness studies, peace and conflict transformation, trauma sensitive assessment, intervention, and consultation, women's studies; urban environmental leadership (MA). Part-time programs available. Postbaccalaureate distance learning degree programs offered (no on-campus study). *Faculty:* 35 full-time (25 women), 115 part-time/adjunct (90 women). *Students:* 420 full-time (379 women), 514 part-time (414 women); includes 142 minority (50 Black or African American, non-Hispanic/Latino; 5 American Indian or Alaska Native, non-Hispanic/Latino; 16 Asian, non-Hispanic/Latino; 48 Hispanic/Latino; 23 Two or more races, non-Hispanic/Latino), 46 international. Average age 33. In 2014, 475 master's, 11 doctorates, 4 other advanced degrees awarded. *Degree requirements:* For master's, internship, practicum, thesis (for expressive therapies); for doctorate, thesis/dissertation, arts apprenticeship, field placement; for CAGS, thesis, internship (for counseling psychology, expressive therapies). *Entrance requirements:* For master's, MAT (counseling psychology), interview, writing samples, art portfolio; for doctorate, GRE or MAT, interview, master's degree; for CAGS, interview, master's degree. Additional exam requirements/recommendations for international students: Required—TOEFL (minimum score 550 paper-based; 80 iBT). *Application deadline:* Applications are processed on a rolling basis. Application fee: $50. Electronic applications accepted. *Financial support:* Fellowships, career-related internships or fieldwork, Federal Work-Study, scholarships/grants, tuition waivers, and unspecified assistantships available. Financial award applicants required to submit FAFSA. *Faculty research:* Psychotherapy and culture; psychotherapy and psychological trauma; women's issues in art, teaching and psychotherapy; community-based art, psycho-spiritual inquiry. *Unit head:* Dr. Catherine Koverola, Dean, 617-349-8317, Fax: 617-349-8366, E-mail: koverola@lesley.edu. *Application contact:* Martha Sheehan, Director, Graduate Admissions, 888-LESLEYU, Fax: 617-349-8313, E-mail: info@lesley.edu.
Website: http://www.lesley.edu/graduate-school-of-arts-and-social-sciences/

Liberty University, Helms School of Government, Lynchburg, VA 24515. Offers criminal justice (MS); public policy (MA), including campaigns and elections, international affairs, Middle East affairs, public administration, public policy. Part-time programs available. Postbaccalaureate distance learning degree programs offered (no on-campus study). *Students:* 248 full-time (119 women), 522 part-time (209 women); includes 194 minority (157 Black or African American, non-Hispanic/Latino; 8 American Indian or Alaska Native, non-Hispanic/Latino; 7 Asian, non-Hispanic/Latino; 5 Hispanic/Latino; 1 Native Hawaiian or other Pacific Islander, non-Hispanic/Latino; 16 Two or more races, non-Hispanic/Latino), 14 international. Average age 34. 837 applicants, 55% accepted, 226 enrolled. In 2014, 65 degrees awarded. *Entrance requirements:* For master's, minimum undergraduate GPA of 3.0. Additional exam requirements/recommendations for international students: Required—TOEFL (minimum score 600 paper-based; 100 iBT). *Application deadline:* Applications are processed on a rolling basis. Application fee: $50. Electronic applications accepted. *Unit head:* Shawn D. Akers, Dean, 434-592-4986. *Application contact:* Jay Bridge, Director of Admissions, 800-424-9595, Fax: 800-628-7977, E-mail: gradadmissions@liberty.edu.

Liberty University, Liberty Baptist Theological Seminary, Lynchburg, VA 24515. Offers Biblical studies (M Div, MAR, MTS, Th M); church history (M Div, MAR, MTS, Th M); discipleship (D Min); discipleship and church ministry (M Div, MAR, MCM); evangelism and church planting (M Div, MAR, MCM, D Min); global studies (M Div, MAR, MCM,

MGS, Th M); homiletics (M Div, MAR, MCM, Th M, D Min); leadership (M Div, MAR, MCM, D Min); marketplace chaplaincy (M Div, MAR, MCM); ministry (D Min); pastoral counseling (M Div, MA, MAR, MCM, D Min), including addictions and recovery (MA), crisis response and trauma (MA), discipleship and church ministries (MA), leadership (MA), life coaching (MA), marketplace chaplaincy (MA), marriage and family (MA), military resilience (MA), pastoral counseling (MA); pastoral ministries (M Div, MAR, MCM); religious education (MRE); theology (M Div, MAR, MTS, Th M); theology and apologetics (PhD); worship (M Div, MAR, MCM, D Min). Part-time programs available. Postbaccalaureate distance learning degree programs offered (minimal on-campus study). *Students:* 2,865 full-time (781 women), 3,750 part-time (1,139 women); includes 1,742 minority (1,382 Black or African American, non-Hispanic/Latino; 22 American Indian or Alaska Native, non-Hispanic/Latino; 116 Asian, non-Hispanic/Latino; 105 Hispanic/Latino; 7 Native Hawaiian or other Pacific Islander, non-Hispanic/Latino; 110 Two or more races, non-Hispanic/Latino), 227 international. Average age 41. 5,446 applicants, 39% accepted, 1340 enrolled. In 2014, 1,969 master's, 126 doctorates, 75 other advanced degrees awarded. *Degree requirements:* For master's, 2 foreign languages, thesis (for some programs); for doctorate, 2 foreign languages, thesis/dissertation. *Entrance requirements:* For master's, minimum undergraduate GPA of 2.0; for doctorate, GRE General Test or MAT, minimum graduate GPA of 3.0. Additional exam requirements/recommendations for international students: Required—TOEFL (minimum score 600 paper-based; 100 iBT). *Application deadline:* For fall admission, 6/1 for domestic students; for spring admission, 11/1 for domestic students. Applications are processed on a rolling basis. Application fee: $50. Electronic applications accepted. *Expenses:* Expenses: Contact institution. *Financial support:* Teaching assistantships with tuition reimbursements, career-related internships or fieldwork, and Federal Work-Study available. Financial award applicants required to submit FAFSA. *Unit head:* Dr. David Hirschman, Acting Dean, 434-592-4140, Fax: 434-522-0415, E-mail: dwhirschman@liberty.edu. *Application contact:* Jay Bridge, Director of Graduate Admissions, 800-424-9595, Fax: 800-628-7977, E-mail: gradadmissions@liberty.edu. Website: http://www.liberty.edu/seminary/

Marquette University, Graduate School, College of Arts and Sciences, Department of History, Milwaukee, WI 53201-1881. Offers European history (MA, PhD); global studies (MA); United States history (MA, PhD). Part-time programs available. *Degree requirements:* For master's, comprehensive exam, essay, 2 classes of research seminars (6 hours); for doctorate, one foreign language, comprehensive exam, thesis/dissertation, 2 research seminars, dissertation seminar. *Entrance requirements:* For master's, GRE General Test, official transcripts from all current and previous colleges/universities except Marquette, one-page statement of purpose, three letters of recommendation from former teachers; for doctorate, GRE General Test, official transcripts from all current and previous colleges/universities except Marquette, one-page statement of purpose, three letters of recommendation from former teachers, writing sample. Additional exam requirements/recommendations for international students: Required—TOEFL (minimum score 530 paper-based). Electronic applications accepted. *Faculty research:* Children's history, Soviet and post-Soviet history, modern Ireland and Britain, Japan and martial arts, American Catholicism.

Marquette University, Graduate School, College of Arts and Sciences, Department of Political Science, Milwaukee, WI 53201-1881. Offers international affairs (MA); political science (MA); JD/MA; MA/MBA. Part-time programs available. *Degree requirements:* For master's, comprehensive exam, thesis optional. *Entrance requirements:* For master's, GRE General Test, official transcripts from all current and previous colleges/universities except Marquette, three letters of recommendation, statement of purpose. Additional exam requirements/recommendations for international students: Required—TOEFL (minimum score 530 paper-based). Electronic applications accepted. *Faculty research:* Public opinion and electoral behavior, public policy analysis, Congress and the Presidency, judicial behavior, political system transitions.

McMaster University, School of Graduate Studies, Faculty of Humanities and Faculty of Social Sciences, Institute on Globalization and the Human Condition, Hamilton, ON L8S 4M2, Canada. Offers globalization studies (MA).

McMaster University, School of Graduate Studies, Faculty of Social Sciences, Department of Political Science, Hamilton, ON L8S 4M2, Canada. Offers international relations (PhD); political science (MA); public and the global economy (MA); public policy (PhD); public policy and administration (MA). MA program in public policy and administration offered jointly with University of Guelph. Part-time programs available. *Degree requirements:* For master's, thesis or alternative. *Entrance requirements:* For master's, minimum B+ average. Additional exam requirements/recommendations for international students: Required—TOEFL (minimum score 580 paper-based). *Faculty research:* Organizational theory, internationalization of public policy, water resource policies, political interest intermediation, comparative politics.

Middlebury Institute of International Studies, Graduate School of International Policy and Management, Program in International Policy and Development, Monterey, CA 93940-2691. Offers MA. *Degree requirements:* For master's, one foreign language. *Entrance requirements:* For master's, minimum GPA of 3.0, proficiency in a foreign language. Additional exam requirements/recommendations for international students: Required—TOEFL (minimum score 550 paper-based; 80 iBT). *Application deadline:* For fall admission, 3/15 priority date for domestic and international students; for spring admission, 10/1 priority date for domestic and international students. Applications are processed on a rolling basis. Application fee: $50. Electronic applications accepted. *Expenses:* Tuition: Full-time $36,020; part-time $1715 per credit. *Required fees:* $53 per semester. *Financial support:* Application deadline: 3/15. *Unit head:* Edward J. Laurance, Chair, 831-647-4144, Fax: 831-647-4199, E-mail: elaurance@miis.edu. *Application contact:* 831-647-4123, Fax: 831-647-6405, E-mail: admit@miis.edu. Website: http://www.miis.edu/academics/programs/development-practice-policy/policy

Middle Tennessee State University, College of Graduate Studies, College of Liberal Arts, Department of Political Science, Murfreesboro, TN 37132. Offers international affairs (MA). Part-time and evening/weekend programs available. Postbaccalaureate distance learning degree programs offered. *Faculty:* 10 full-time (3 women), 1 (woman) part-time/adjunct. *Students:* 6 full-time (2 women), 7 part-time (4 women); includes 4 minority (1 Black or African American, non-Hispanic/Latino; 1 Asian, non-Hispanic/Latino; 1 Hispanic/Latino; 1 Two or more races, non-Hispanic/Latino). 19 applicants, 79% accepted. In 2014, 3 master's awarded. *Entrance requirements:* Additional exam requirements/recommendations for international students: Required—TOEFL (minimum score 525 paper-based; 71 iBT) or IELTS (minimum score 6). *Application deadline:* For fall admission, 6/1 for domestic and international students. Applications are processed on a rolling basis. Application fee: $30. Electronic applications accepted. *Financial support:* In 2014–15, 6 students received support. Application deadline: 4/1; applicants required to submit FAFSA. *Unit head:* Dr. Mark E. Byrnes, Dean, 615-898-2534, Fax: 615-904-8279, E-mail: mark.byrnes@mtsu.edu. *Application contact:* Dr. Michael D. Allen, Vice Provost for Research/Dean, 615-898-2840, Fax: 615-904-8020, E-mail: michael.allen@mtsu.edu.

Missouri State University, Graduate College, College of Humanities and Public Affairs, Department of Political Science, Program in Global Studies, Springfield, MO 65897. Offers MGS. Part-time programs available. *Students:* 19 full-time (7 women), 2 part-time (both women); includes 2 minority (1 Black or African American, non-Hispanic/Latino; 1

Hispanic/Latino), 8 international. Average age 25. 10 applicants, 90% accepted, 6 enrolled. In 2014, 15 master's awarded. *Degree requirements:* For master's, 2 foreign languages, comprehensive exam, thesis or alternative. *Entrance requirements:* For master's, GRE, minimum GPA of 3.0. Additional exam requirements/recommendations for international students: Required—TOEFL (minimum score 550 paper-based; 79 iBT). *Application deadline:* For fall admission, 7/20 priority date for domestic students, 5/1 for international students; for spring admission, 12/20 priority date for domestic students, 9/1 for international students. Applications are processed on a rolling basis. Application fee: $35 ($50 for international students). Electronic applications accepted. *Expenses:* Tuition, state resident: full-time $2250; part-time $250 per credit hour. Tuition, nonresident: full-time $4509; part-time $501 per credit hour. Tuition and fees vary according to course level, course load and program. *Financial support:* Federal Work-Study, institutionally sponsored loans, scholarships/grants, and unspecified assistantships available. Support available to part-time students. Financial award application deadline: 3/31; financial award applicants required to submit FAFSA. *Faculty research:* U.S.-China policy, Eastern European politics, South American political reform, landmine use policy. *Unit head:* Dr. Dennis Hickey, Program Director, 417-836-5850, Fax: 417-836-6655, E-mail: dennishickey@missouristate.edu. *Application contact:* Misty Stewart, Coordinator of Graduate Recruitment, 417-836-6079, Fax: 417-836-6200, E-mail: mistystewart@missouristate.edu. Website: http://polsci.missouristate.edu/mgs/

Morgan State University, School of Graduate Studies, College of Liberal Arts, Department of World Languages and International Studies, Baltimore, MD 21251. Offers international studies (MA). Part-time and evening/weekend programs available. *Degree requirements:* For master's, one foreign language, comprehensive exam, thesis. *Entrance requirements:* For master's, GRE. Additional exam requirements/recommendations for international students: Required—TOEFL (minimum score 550 paper-based).

New England College, Program in Management, Henniker, NH 03242-3293. Offers accounting (MSA); healthcare administration (MS); international relations (MA); marketing management (MS); nonprofit leadership (MS); project management (MS); strategic leadership (MS). Part-time and evening/weekend programs available. *Degree requirements:* For master's, independent research project. Electronic applications accepted.

The New School, The New School for Public Engagement, Program in International Affairs, New York, NY 10011. Offers MA, MS. Part-time and evening/weekend programs available. *Degree requirements:* For master's, thesis or practicum. *Entrance requirements:* Additional exam requirements/recommendations for international students: Required—TOEFL (minimum score 600 paper-based; 100 iBT). Electronic applications accepted.

New York University, Graduate School of Arts and Science, Department of Politics, New York, NY 10012-1019. Offers political campaign management (MA); politics (MA, PhD); JD/MA; MBA/MA. Part-time programs available. *Faculty:* 30 full-time (4 women). *Students:* 175 full-time (88 women), 68 part-time (31 women); includes 36 minority (3 Black or African American, non-Hispanic/Latino; 1 American Indian or Alaska Native, non-Hispanic/Latino; 18 Asian, non-Hispanic/Latino; 12 Hispanic/Latino; 2 Two or more races, non-Hispanic/Latino), 129 international. Average age 27. 670 applicants, 45% accepted, 80 enrolled. In 2014, 101 master's, 13 doctorates awarded. Terminal master's awarded for partial completion of doctoral program. *Degree requirements:* For master's, one foreign language, thesis or alternative; for doctorate, 2 foreign languages, comprehensive exam, thesis/dissertation. *Entrance requirements:* For master's and doctorate, GRE General Test. Additional exam requirements/recommendations for international students: Required—TOEFL. *Application deadline:* For fall admission, 12/18 priority date for domestic students, 12/18 for international students. Application fee: $100. *Financial support:* Fellowships with tuition reimbursements, teaching assistantships with tuition reimbursements, career-related internships or fieldwork, Federal Work-Study, and institutionally sponsored loans available. Financial award application deadline: 12/18; financial award applicants required to submit FAFSA. *Faculty research:* Comparative politics, democratic theory and practice, rational choice, political economy, international relations. *Unit head:* Sanford Gordon, Director of Graduate Studies, PhD Program, 212-998-8500, Fax: 212-995-4184, E-mail: politics.phd@nyu.edu. *Application contact:* Nicole Simonelli, Director of Graduate Studies, Master's Program, 212-998-8500, Fax: 212-995-4184, E-mail: politics.masters@nyu.edu. Website: http://www.nyu.edu/gsas/dept/politics/

New York University, School of Continuing and Professional Studies, Center for Global Affairs, New York, NY 10012-1019. Offers global affairs (MS), including environment/energy policy, human rights and international law, international development and humanitarian assistance, international relations, peace building, private sector, transnational security; global energy (Advanced Certificate); peacebuilding (Advanced Certificate); transnational security (Advanced Certificate). Part-time and evening/weekend programs available. *Faculty:* 11 full-time (6 women), 32 part-time/adjunct (14 women). *Students:* 156 full-time (105 women), 136 part-time (86 women); includes 79 minority (24 Black or African American, non-Hispanic/Latino; 17 Asian, non-Hispanic/Latino; 37 Hispanic/Latino; 1 Two or more races, non-Hispanic/Latino), 66 international. Average age 28. 357 applicants, 72% accepted, 98 enrolled. In 2014, 144 master's awarded. *Degree requirements:* For master's, thesis. *Entrance requirements:* For master's, GRE or GMAT (only upon request), bachelor's degree, resume with relevant professional work, internship or volunteer experience, two letters of recommendation, statement of purpose. Additional exam requirements/recommendations for international students: Required—TOEFL (minimum score 600 paper-based; 100 iBT), IELTS (minimum score 7). *Application deadline:* For fall admission, 2/1 priority date for domestic and international students; for spring admission, 10/15 priority date for domestic students, 8/15 priority date for international students. Applications are processed on a rolling basis. Application fee: $150. Electronic applications accepted. *Financial support:* In 2014–15, 99 students received support, including 95 fellowships (averaging $2,218 per year); Federal Work-Study and scholarships/grants also available. Support available to part-time students. Financial award application deadline: 4/1; financial award applicants required to submit FAFSA. *Unit head:* Vera Jelinek, Divisional Dean and Clinical Associate Professor, 212-992-8380. *Application contact:* Office of Admissions, 212-998-7100, E-mail: sps.gradadmissions@nyu.edu. Website: http://www.sps.nyu.edu/academics/departments/global-affairs.html

North Carolina State University, Graduate School, College of Humanities and Social Sciences, School of Public and International Affairs, Program in International Studies, Raleigh, NC 27695. Offers MIS. *Degree requirements:* For master's, thesis optional. *Entrance requirements:* For master's, GRE General Test, minimum GPA of 3.0 during previous 2 years. Electronic applications accepted. *Faculty research:* Global environmental policy and climate change, drug policy and the Caribbean, U.S. national security politics, local responses to globalization, the political economy of the European Union.

Northeastern University, College of Professional Studies, Boston, MA 02115-5096. Offers applied nutrition (MS); commerce and economic development (MS); corporate and organizational communication (MS); digital media (MPS); geographic information

technology (MPS); global studies and international affairs (MS); homeland security (MA); human services (MS); informatics (MPS); leadership (MS); nonprofit management (MS); project management (MS); regulatory affairs for drugs, biologics, and medical devices (MS); regulatory affairs of food and food industries (MS); respiratory care leadership (MS); technical communication (MS). Postbaccalaureate distance learning degree programs offered (no on-campus study).

Northwestern University, The Graduate School, Center for International and Comparative Studies, Evanston, IL 60208. Offers Certificate.

Northwestern University, Law School, Chicago, IL 60611-3069. Offers international human rights (LL M); law (JD); law and business (LL M); science law (MSL); tax (LL M in Tax); JD/LL M; JD/MBA; JD/PhD; LL M/Certificate. Executive LL M programs offered in Madrid (Spain), Seoul (South Korea), and Tel Aviv (Israel). *Accreditation:* ABA. *Entrance requirements:* For master's, law degree or equivalent, letter of recommendation, resume; for doctorate, LSAT, 1 letter of recommendation, resume. Additional exam requirements/recommendations for international students: Required—TOEFL. Electronic applications accepted. *Expenses:* Contact institution. *Faculty research:* Constitutional law, corporate law, international law, law and social policy, ethical studies.

Norwich University, College of Graduate and Continuing Studies, Master of Arts in Diplomacy Program, Northfield, VT 05663. Offers international commerce (MA); international conflict management (MA); international terrorism (MA). Evening/weekend programs available. Postbaccalaureate distance learning degree programs offered (minimal on-campus study). *Faculty:* 2 full-time (0 women), 21 part-time/adjunct (2 women). *Students:* 174 full-time (50 women); includes 36 minority (27 Black or African American, non-Hispanic/Latino; 6 Hispanic/Latino; 3 Two or more races, non-Hispanic/Latino). Average age 35. 87 applicants, 98% accepted, 65 enrolled. In 2014, 123 master's awarded. *Degree requirements:* For master's, comprehensive exam, thesis optional. *Entrance requirements:* For master's, minimum undergraduate GPA of 2.75. Additional exam requirements/recommendations for international students: Required—TOEFL (minimum score 550 paper-based; 80 iBT), IELTS (minimum score 6.5). *Application deadline:* For fall admission, 8/8 for domestic and international students; for winter admission, 11/7 for domestic and international students; for spring admission, 2/16 for domestic and international students; for summer admission, 5/18 for domestic and international students. Applications are processed on a rolling basis. Electronic applications accepted. *Expenses:* Expenses: Contact institution. *Financial support:* In 2014–15, 111 students received support. Scholarships/grants available. Financial award applicants required to submit FAFSA. *Unit head:* Dr. Lasha Tchantouridze, Program Director, 802-485-2095, Fax: 802-485-2533, E-mail: ltchanto@norwich.edu. *Application contact:* Fianna Verret, Associate Program Director, 802-485-2783, Fax: 802-485-2533, E-mail: fverret@norwich.edu.
Website: http://online.norwich.edu/degree-programs/masters/master-arts-diplomacy/overview

Ohio University, Graduate College, Center for International Studies, Program in Communications and Development Studies, Athens, OH 45701-2979. Offers MA. Part-time programs available. *Degree requirements:* For master's, one foreign language, thesis optional, internship. *Entrance requirements:* For master's, minimum GPA of 3.0. Additional exam requirements/recommendations for international students: Required—TOEFL (minimum score 550 paper-based; 80 iBT), IELTS (minimum score 6.5). Electronic applications accepted. *Faculty research:* National development processes, public relations and participatory research, audio and video production, health communication, urban development.

Oklahoma State University, Graduate College, Stillwater, OK 74078. Offers aerospace security (Graduate Certificate); bioenergy and sustainable technology (Graduate Certificate); business data mining (Graduate Certificate); business sustainability (Graduate Certificate); environmental science (MS); international studies (MS); non-profit management (Graduate Certificate); teaching English to speakers of other languages (Graduate Certificate); telecommunications management (MS). Programs are interdisciplinary. *Faculty:* 3 full-time (1 woman), 2 part-time/adjunct (1 woman). *Students:* 49 full-time (27 women), 94 part-time (45 women); includes 21 minority (3 Black or African American, non-Hispanic/Latino; 1 American Indian or Alaska Native, non-Hispanic/Latino; 3 Asian, non-Hispanic/Latino; 4 Hispanic/Latino; 10 Two or more races, non-Hispanic/Latino), 36 international. Average age 30. 385 applicants, 76% accepted, 55 enrolled. In 2014, 47 master's, 1 doctorate awarded. *Degree requirements:* For master's, thesis (for some programs); for doctorate, comprehensive exam, thesis/dissertation. *Entrance requirements:* For master's and doctorate, GRE or GMAT. Additional exam requirements/recommendations for international students: Required—TOEFL (minimum score 550 paper-based; 79 iBT). *Application deadline:* For fall admission, 3/1 priority date for international students; for spring admission, 8/1 priority date for international students. Applications are processed on a rolling basis. Application fee: $40 ($75 for international students). Electronic applications accepted. *Expenses:* Tuition, state resident: full-time $4488; part-time $187 per credit hour. Tuition, nonresident: full-time $18,360; part-time $765 per credit hour. *Required fees:* $2413; $100.55 per credit hour. Tuition and fees vary according to campus/location. *Financial support:* In 2014–15, 4 research assistantships (averaging $14,400 per year) were awarded; career-related internships or fieldwork, Federal Work-Study, scholarships/grants, health care benefits, tuition waivers (partial), and unspecified assistantships also available. Support available to part-time students. Financial award application deadline: 3/1; financial award applicants required to submit FAFSA. *Unit head:* Dr. Sheryl Tucker, Dean, 405-744-6368, Fax: 405-744-0355, E-mail: gradi@okstate.edu. *Application contact:* Dr. Susan Mathew, Coordinator of Admissions, 405-744-6368, Fax: 405-744-0355, E-mail: gradi@okstate.edu.
Website: http://gradcollege.okstate.edu/

Old Dominion University, College of Arts and Letters, Graduate Program in International Studies, Norfolk, VA 23529. Offers conflict and cooperation (MA, PhD); interdependence and transnationalism (MA, PhD); international cultural studies (MA, PhD); international political economy and development (MA, PhD); modeling and simulation (MA, PhD); U.S. foreign policy and international relations (MA, PhD). Part-time programs available. *Faculty:* 18 full-time (4 women). *Students:* 41 full-time (14 women), 46 part-time (23 women); includes 11 minority (5 Black or African American, non-Hispanic/Latino; 1 Asian, non-Hispanic/Latino; 2 Hispanic/Latino; 3 Two or more races, non-Hispanic/Latino), 24 international. Average age 35. 99 applicants, 54% accepted, 34 enrolled. In 2014, 10 master's, 9 doctorates awarded. Terminal master's awarded for partial completion of doctoral program. *Degree requirements:* For master's, one foreign language, comprehensive exam, thesis optional; for doctorate, one foreign language, comprehensive exam, thesis/dissertation. *Entrance requirements:* For master's, GRE General Test, sample of written work, 2 letters of recommendation; for doctorate, GRE General Test, sample of written work, 3 letters of recommendation. Additional exam requirements/recommendations for international students: Required—TOEFL (minimum score 570 paper-based). *Application deadline:* For fall admission, 1/15 for domestic and international students; for spring admission, 10/15 for domestic and international students. Application fee: $50. Electronic applications accepted. *Expenses:* Tuition, state resident: full-time $10,488; part-time $437 per credit. Tuition, nonresident: full-time $26,136; part-time $1089 per credit. *Required fees:* $64 per semester. One-time fee: $50. *Financial support:* In 2014–15, 20 students received support, including 2 fellowships (averaging $13,000 per year), 5 research assistantships with tuition reimbursements available (averaging $15,000 per year), 7 teaching assistantships with tuition reimbursements available (averaging $15,000 per year); career-related internships or fieldwork, institutionally sponsored loans, scholarships/grants, and unspecified assistantships also available. Support available to part-time students. Financial award application deadline: 2/15; financial award applicants required to submit FAFSA. *Faculty research:* U.S. foreign policy, international security, Transatlantic and Transpacific relations, transnational issues, international political economy and development. *Total annual research expenditures:* $330,391. *Unit head:* Dr. Regina Karp, Graduate Program Director, 757-683-5700, Fax: 757-683-5701, E-mail: rkarp@odu.edu. *Application contact:* Dr. David C. Earnest, Associate Dean, 757-683-6077, Fax: 757-683-5746, E-mail: dearnest@odu.edu.
Website: http://www.al.odu.edu/gpis/

Penn State University Park, Graduate School, School of International Affairs, University Park, PA 16802. Offers MIA. Part-time and evening/weekend programs available. Postbaccalaureate distance learning degree programs offered. *Students:* 57 full-time (31 women), 3 part-time (1 woman). Average age 24. 146 applicants, 71% accepted, 33 enrolled. *Entrance requirements:* Additional exam requirements/recommendations for international students: Required—TOEFL (minimum score 550 paper-based; 80 iBT), IELTS. *Application deadline:* Applications are processed on a rolling basis. Application fee: $65. Electronic applications accepted. *Financial support:* Fellowships, research assistantships, teaching assistantships, Federal Work-Study, scholarships/grants, traineeships, health care benefits, and unspecified assistantships available. Support available to part-time students. Financial award application deadline: 3/1; financial award applicants required to submit FAFSA. *Unit head:* James W. Houck, Interim Director, 814-863-1521, Fax: 814-863-7274, E-mail: jwh32@psu.edu. *Application contact:* Lori A. Stania, Director, Graduate Student Services, 814-867-5278, Fax: 814-863-4627, E-mail: gswww@psu.edu.
Website: http://www.sia.psu.edu/

Pepperdine University, School of Public Policy, Malibu, CA 90263. Offers American politics (MPP); economics (MPP); international relations (MPP); public policy (MPP); state and local policy (MPP). *Faculty:* 6 full-time (2 women), 7 part-time/adjunct (1 woman). *Students:* 74 full-time (42 women), 10 part-time (5 women); includes 22 minority (11 Black or African American, non-Hispanic/Latino; 3 American Indian or Alaska Native, non-Hispanic/Latino; 3 Asian, non-Hispanic/Latino; 2 Hispanic/Latino; 1 Native Hawaiian or other Pacific Islander, non-Hispanic/Latino; 2 Two or more races, non-Hispanic/Latino), 21 international. 157 applicants, 65% accepted, 32 enrolled. In 2014, 52 master's awarded. *Entrance requirements:* For master's, GRE or GMAT, 2 letters of recommendation, resume, two essays. Additional exam requirements/recommendations for international students: Required—TOEFL. *Application deadline:* For fall admission, 6/15 for domestic students. Applications are processed on a rolling basis. Application fee: $50. Electronic applications accepted. *Financial support:* Institutionally sponsored loans and scholarships/grants available. Financial award application deadline: 5/1; financial award applicants required to submit FAFSA. *Unit head:* Dr. James R. Wilburn, Dean, School of Public Policy, 310-506-7490, Fax: 310-506-7494, E-mail: james.wilburn@pepperdine.edu. *Application contact:* Melinda E. van Hemert, Director of Recruitment and Career Services, 310-506-7492, Fax: 310-506-7494, E-mail: melinda.vanhemert@pepperdine.edu.
Website: http://publicpolicy.pepperdine.edu/

Pontificia Universidad Catolica Madre y Maestra, Graduate School, Faculty of Social and Administrative Sciences, Santiago, Dominican Republic. Offers business administration (MBA), including business development, finance, international business, management skills (M Mgmt, MBA), marketing, operations, strategic cost management, strategy, tourist destination planning and management; law (LL M), including civil law, corporate business law, criminal law, international relations, real estate law; management (M Mgmt), including higher financial management, insurance program administration, management skills (M Mgmt, MBA); psychology (MA), including clinical child and adolescent psychology, forensic psychology; strategic human resources (EMBA).

Princeton University, Graduate School, Woodrow Wilson School of Public and International Affairs, Princeton, NJ 08544-1019. Offers public affairs (MPA, PhD); public policy (MPP); JD/MPA. JD/MPA offered jointly with Columbia University, New York University, Stanford University. Terminal master's awarded for partial completion of doctoral program. *Degree requirements:* For master's, internship; for doctorate, one foreign language, thesis/dissertation. *Entrance requirements:* For master's, GRE General Test, original policy memo; for doctorate, GRE General Test. Additional exam requirements/recommendations for international students: Required—TOEFL (minimum score 600 paper-based). Electronic applications accepted.

Queen's University at Kingston, School of Graduate Studies, Faculty of Arts and Sciences, Department of Political Studies, Kingston, ON K7L 3N6, Canada. Offers Canadian politics (PhD); comparative politics (PhD); gender and politics (PhD); international relations (PhD); political theory (PhD). *Degree requirements:* For master's, thesis or alternative; for doctorate, one foreign language, thesis/dissertation, qualifying exams. *Entrance requirements:* Additional exam requirements/recommendations for international students: Required—TOEFL (minimum score 600 paper-based). *Faculty research:* Canadian politics, comparative politics, political thought, international politics, women and politics.

Regent's University London, Webster Graduate School, London, United Kingdom. Offers business (MBA); finance (MS); human resources (MA); information technology management (MA); international business (MA); international non-governmental organizations (MA); international relations (MA); management and leadership (MA); marketing (MA). Part-time programs available.

Regent University, Graduate School, Robertson School of Government, Virginia Beach, VA 23464. Offers government (MA), including American government, international relations, political theory; public administration (MPA), including emergency management and homeland security, general public administration, nonprofit administration and faith-based organizations, public leadership and management. Part-time and evening/weekend programs available. Postbaccalaureate distance learning degree programs offered (minimal on-campus study). *Faculty:* 10 full-time (1 woman), 9 part-time/adjunct (2 women). *Students:* 34 full-time (15 women), 56 part-time (26 women); includes 21 minority (15 Black or African American, non-Hispanic/Latino; 6 Hispanic/Latino), 4 international. Average age 34. 106 applicants, 45% accepted, 33 enrolled. In 2014, 57 master's awarded. *Degree requirements:* For master's, thesis optional, internship. *Entrance requirements:* For master's, GRE General Test or LSAT, minimum undergraduate GPA of 3.0, writing sample, resume, interview, references. Additional exam requirements/recommendations for international students: Required—TOEFL (minimum score 577 paper-based). *Application deadline:* For fall admission, 5/1 priority date for domestic students; for spring admission, 11/1 priority date for domestic students. Applications are processed on a rolling basis. Application fee: $50. Electronic applications accepted. *Expenses:* Expenses: Contact institution. *Financial support:* Career-related internships or fieldwork, scholarships/grants, tuition waivers (full and partial), and unspecified assistantships available. Support available to part-time students. Financial award application deadline: 9/1; financial award applicants required

to submit FAFSA. *Faculty research:* Education reform, political character issues, social capital concerns, administrative ethics, Biblical law and public policy. *Unit head:* Dr. Eric Patterson, Dean, 757-352-4616, Fax: 757-352-4735, E-mail: epatterson@regent.edu. *Application contact:* Matthew Chadwick, Director of Enrollment Support Services, 800-373-5504, Fax: 757-352-4381, E-mail: admissions@regent.edu.
Website: http://www.regent.edu/government/

Richmond, The American International University in London, MA in International Relations Program, Richmond, United Kingdom. Offers MA. Part-time programs available. *Entrance requirements:* Additional exam requirements/recommendations for international students: Required—TOEFL, IELTS. Electronic applications accepted.

Rutgers, The State University of New Jersey, Camden, Graduate School of Arts and Sciences, Department of Public Policy and Administration, Camden, NJ 08102. Offers education policy and leadership (MPA); international public service and development (MPA); public management (MPA); JD/MPA; MPA/MA. *Accreditation:* NASPAA. Part-time and evening/weekend programs available. *Degree requirements:* For master's, directed study, research workshop, 42 credits. *Entrance requirements:* For master's, GRE General Test, GMAT or LSAT, 3 letters of recommendation; resume. Additional exam requirements/recommendations for international students: Required—TOEFL (minimum score 550 paper-based), IELTS. Electronic applications accepted. *Faculty research:* Nonprofit management, county and municipal administration, health and human services, government communication, administrative law, educational finance.

Rutgers, The State University of New Jersey, Newark, Graduate School, Division of Global Affairs, Newark, NJ 07102. Offers MS, PhD. Part-time and evening/weekend programs available. *Degree requirements:* For master's, one foreign language, thesis optional. *Entrance requirements:* For master's and doctorate, GRE General Test, minimum B average. Electronic applications accepted. *Faculty research:* International organizations, diplomacy, world history, international political economy, global environment.

Rutgers, The State University of New Jersey, Newark, Graduate School, Program in Political Science, Newark, NJ 07102. Offers American political system (MA); international relations (MA); JD/MA. Part-time and evening/weekend programs available. *Degree requirements:* For master's, comprehensive exam, thesis optional. *Entrance requirements:* For master's, GRE, minimum undergraduate B average. Electronic applications accepted. *Faculty research:* Policymaking and policy evaluation in the United States; government and politics in Europe, Middle East, Asia, Africa, and Latin America.

Rutgers, The State University of New Jersey, New Brunswick, Graduate School-New Brunswick, Department of Political Science, Piscataway, NJ 08854-8097. Offers American politics (PhD); comparative politics (PhD); international relations (PhD); political theory (PhD); public law (PhD); United Nations and global policy studies (MA); women and politics (PhD). *Degree requirements:* For doctorate, one foreign language, comprehensive exam, thesis/dissertation. *Entrance requirements:* For master's, bachelor's degree from accredited U.S. college or university or a comparable institution in another country; for doctorate, GRE General Test. Additional exam requirements/recommendations for international students: Required—TOEFL.

Rutgers, The State University of New Jersey, New Brunswick, Graduate School-New Brunswick, Program in Global and Comparative History, New Brunswick, NJ 08901. Offers MA. *Entrance requirements:* For master's, GRE, minimum GPA of 3.0, official transcripts, two letters of recommendation, 1-2 page personal statement, 10-15 page writing sample. Electronic applications accepted.

St. John's University, College of Professional Studies, Department of Mass Communications, Queens, NY 11439. Offers international communications (MS). Part-time and evening/weekend programs available. *Students:* 30 full-time (19 women), 14 part-time (11 women); includes 25 minority (15 Black or African American, non-Hispanic/Latino; 1 Asian, non-Hispanic/Latino; 6 Hispanic/Latino; 3 Two or more races, non-Hispanic/Latino), 11 international. Average age 25. 53 applicants, 92% accepted, 20 enrolled. In 2014, 25 master's awarded. *Degree requirements:* For master's, one foreign language, thesis optional. *Entrance requirements:* For master's, GRE, official transcript showing conferral of bachelor's degree, 2 letters of recommendation, proficiency in a foreign language, minimum GPA of 3.0. Additional exam requirements/recommendations for international students: Required—TOEFL (minimum score 600 paper-based; 100 iBT), IELTS (minimum score 7). *Application deadline:* For fall admission, 5/1 priority date for domestic and international students; for spring admission, 11/1 priority date for domestic and international students. Applications are processed on a rolling basis. Application fee: $70. Electronic applications accepted. *Expenses: Tuition:* Full-time $20,610; part-time $1145 per credit. *Required fees:* $170 per semester. *Unit head:* Prof. Richard Thomas, Chair, 718-990-7339, E-mail: thomasr@stjohns.edu. *Application contact:* Robert Medrano, Director of Graduate Admission, 718-990-1601, Fax: 718-990-5686, E-mail: gradhelp@stjohns.edu.
Website: http://www.stjohns.edu/academics/schools-and-colleges/college-professional-studies/programs-and-majors

St. John's University, St. John's College of Liberal Arts and Sciences, Department of Government and Politics, Queens, NY 11439. Offers government and politics (MA, Adv C), including government and politics (MA), international law and diplomacy (Adv C), public administration (Adv C); international law and diplomacy (Adv C); JD/MA; MA/MS. Part-time and evening/weekend programs available. *Students:* 34 full-time (21 women), 33 part-time (18 women); includes 26 minority (11 Black or African American, non-Hispanic/Latino; 1 Asian, non-Hispanic/Latino; 11 Hispanic/Latino; 3 Two or more races, non-Hispanic/Latino), 2 international. Average age 27. 76 applicants, 78% accepted, 26 enrolled. In 2014, 49 master's, 48 other advanced degrees awarded. *Degree requirements:* For master's, comprehensive exam, thesis optional. *Entrance requirements:* For master's, minimum GPA of 3.0, 18 undergraduate credits in government and politics. Additional exam requirements/recommendations for international students: Required—TOEFL (minimum score 600 paper-based; 100 iBT), IELTS (minimum score 7). *Application deadline:* For fall admission, 5/1 priority date for domestic and international students; for spring admission, 11/1 priority date for domestic and international students. Applications are processed on a rolling basis. Application fee: $70. Electronic applications accepted. *Expenses: Tuition:* Full-time $20,610; part-time $1145 per credit. *Required fees:* $170 per semester. *Financial support:* Research assistantships, career-related internships or fieldwork, and scholarships/grants available. Support available to part-time students. Financial award application deadline: 3/1; financial award applicants required to submit FAFSA. *Faculty research:* Presidential leadership, morality and politics, U.S. foreign policy, U.S. national security policy, New York state and local government and politics, state building and social policy, public opinion, campaigns and elections, education politics, North African politics, energy and European Union politics. *Unit head:* Dr. Diane Heith, Chair, 718-990-6329, E-mail: heithd@stjohns.edu. *Application contact:* Robert Medrano, Director of Graduate Admission, 718-990-1601, Fax: 718-990-5686, E-mail: gradhelp@stjohns.edu.

St. Mary's University, Graduate School, Department of Education, Program in Education, San Antonio, TX 78228-8507. Offers computer science (MA); education (MA); English literature and language (MA); international relations (MA); political science (MA). *Students:* 1 (woman) part-time; minority (Black or African American, non-Hispanic/

Latino). Average age 28. 12 applicants, 17% accepted. In 2014, 3 master's awarded. *Entrance requirements:* For master's, GRE or MAT, 200 X GPA + Average GRE [(Verbal + Quantitative)/2]= 1050; or 10 X GPA + MAT = 68. *Expenses: Tuition:* Full-time $15,070; part-time $800 per credit hour. *Required fees:* $156 per semester. *Faculty research:* Bronfenbrenner's ecological systems theory: implications for education today. *Unit head:* Dr. Dan Higgins, Department Chair, 210-436-3121, E-mail: dhiggins@stmarytx.edu.
Website: https://www.stmarytx.edu/academics/graduate/masters/education/

St. Mary's University, Graduate School, Graduate Department of International Relations, San Antonio, TX 78228-8507. Offers international conflict resolution (MA); security policy (MA); JD/MA. Part-time and evening/weekend programs available. Postbaccalaureate distance learning degree programs offered (no on-campus study). *Faculty:* 4 full-time (2 women), 1 part-time/adjunct (0 women). *Students:* 15 full-time (9 women), 64 part-time (21 women); includes 31 minority (5 Black or African American, non-Hispanic/Latino; 1 American Indian or Alaska Native, non-Hispanic/Latino; 6 Asian, non-Hispanic/Latino; 18 Hispanic/Latino; 1 Native Hawaiian or other Pacific Islander, non-Hispanic/Latino), 7 international. Average age 32. 54 applicants, 65% accepted, 25 enrolled. In 2014, 34 master's, 7 other advanced degrees awarded. *Degree requirements:* For master's, one foreign language, comprehensive exam, thesis optional, Demonstration of a working knowledge of a foreign language. *Entrance requirements:* For master's, GRE General Test, GPA x Verbal GRE Score = 450. Minimum writing score is 4.0. Additional exam requirements/recommendations for international students: Required—TOEFL (minimum score 550 paper-based; 80 iBT), IELTS (minimum score 6). *Application deadline:* Applications are processed on a rolling basis. Application fee: $0. Electronic applications accepted. *Expenses: Tuition:* Full-time $15,070; part-time $800 per credit hour. *Required fees:* $156 per semester. *Financial support:* In 2014–15, 4 research assistantships (averaging $7,000 per year) were awarded; Federal Work-Study, scholarships/grants, tuition waivers (full), unspecified assistantships, and grant for active-duty and retired military, DOD employees, and their spouses also available. Financial award application deadline: 3/31; financial award applicants required to submit FAFSA. *Faculty research:* World religions and global affairs; human security and conflict transformation; military, security, peacekeeping; development studies, sustainability and the environment; migration and immigration policy. *Unit head:* Dr. Aaron Tyler, Chair Graduate International Relations, 210-436-3111, Fax: 210-431-4336, E-mail: atyler@stmarytx.edu.
Website: https://www.stmarytx.edu/academics/graduate/masters/internationalrelations/

Salve Regina University, Program in International Relations, Newport, RI 02840-4192. Offers MA, Certificate. Part-time and evening/weekend programs available. Postbaccalaureate distance learning degree programs offered (no on-campus study). *Faculty:* 2 full-time (0 women), 3 part-time/adjunct (1 woman). *Students:* 7 full-time (4 women), 31 part-time (9 women); includes 2 minority (1 Black or African American, non-Hispanic/Latino; 1 Hispanic/Latino), 13 international. Average age 36. 11 applicants, 100% accepted, 11 enrolled. In 2014, 26 master's awarded. *Entrance requirements:* For master's, GMAT, GRE General Test, MAT or LSAT. Additional exam requirements/recommendations for international students: Required—TOEFL (minimum score 600 paper-based; 100 iBT) or IELTS. *Application deadline:* For fall admission, 3/15 priority date for domestic and international students; for spring admission, 9/15 priority date for domestic and international students. Applications are processed on a rolling basis. Application fee: $60. Electronic applications accepted. *Expenses: Tuition:* Full-time $8550; part-time $475 per credit. *Required fees:* $50 per term. Tuition and fees vary according to course level, course load and degree level. *Financial support:* Career-related internships or fieldwork and Federal Work-Study available. Support available to part-time students. Financial award application deadline: 3/1; financial award applicants required to submit FAFSA. *Unit head:* Dr. Symeon Giannakos, Director, 401-341-3177, E-mail: symeon.giannakos@salve.edu. *Application contact:* Nicole Ferreira, Associate Director of Graduate Admissions, 401-341-2462, Fax: 401-341-2973, E-mail: nicole.ferreira@salve.edu.
Website: http://www.salve.edu/graduate-studies/international-relations

San Francisco State University, Division of Graduate Studies, College of Liberal and Creative Arts, Department of International Relations, San Francisco, CA 94132-1722. Offers MA. *Expenses:* Tuition, state resident: full-time $6738. Tuition, nonresident: full-time $17,898; part-time $372 per credit hour. *Required fees:* $498 per semester. *Unit head:* Dr. Sophie Clavier, Chair, 415-338-7498, E-mail: sclavier@sfsu.edu. *Application contact:* Dr. Burcu Akan Ellis, Graduate Coordinator, 415-405-2694, E-mail: bellis@sfsu.edu.
Website: http://internationalrelations.sfsu.edu/

Schiller International University, Program in International Relations and Diplomacy, Paris, France. Offers MA. Part-time and evening/weekend programs available. *Degree requirements:* For master's, one foreign language, final comprehensive exam or thesis. *Entrance requirements:* For master's, undergraduate mathematics (strongly advised). Additional exam requirements/recommendations for international students: Required—TOEFL (minimum score 550 paper-based).

Seton Hall University, School of Diplomacy and International Relations, South Orange, NJ 07079-2697. Offers diplomacy (MA); post-conflict state reconstruction and sustainability (Graduate Certificate); JD/MA; MA/MA; MBA/MA; MPA/MA. Part-time and evening/weekend programs available. *Degree requirements:* For master's, thesis (for some programs). *Entrance requirements:* For master's, GRE, GMAT, or LSAT. Additional exam requirements/recommendations for international students: Required—TOEFL. Electronic applications accepted. *Faculty research:* International economics and development, global health, United Nations, conflict negotiation, foreign policy analysis, international security, energy politics, Eastern and Central Europe, Latin America, Africa, peacemaking, genocide prevention, international organizations, international political economy, U.S.-China relations, democratization, international law, research methods.

Simon Fraser University, Office of Graduate Studies, Faculty of Arts and Social Sciences, School for International Studies, Burnaby, BC V5A 1S6, Canada. Offers MA. *Entrance requirements:* Additional exam requirements/recommendations for international students: Required—TOEFL (minimum score 580 paper-based; 93 iBT), IELTS (minimum score 7), TWE (minimum score 5). Electronic applications accepted. *Faculty research:* Peace and security, international development, human rights and international law, governance and civil society.

SIT Graduate Institute, Graduate Programs, Master's Programs in Intercultural Service, Leadership, and Management, Brattleboro, VT 05302-0676. Offers conflict transformation (MA); intercultural service, leadership, and management (MA); international education (MA); sustainable development (MA). Postbaccalaureate distance learning degree programs offered (minimal on-campus study). *Students:* 28 full-time (20 women); includes 3 minority (1 American Indian or Alaska Native, non-Hispanic/Latino; 1 Asian, non-Hispanic/Latino; 1 Hispanic/Latino), 4 international. Average age 27. 730 applicants, 95% accepted, 164 enrolled. In 2014, 179 master's awarded. *Degree requirements:* For master's, one foreign language, thesis. *Entrance requirements:* For master's, 3 letters of reference. Additional exam requirements/recommendations for international students: Required—TOEFL, IELTS. *Application deadline:* Applications are processed on a rolling basis. Application fee: $50. *Financial*

support: Career-related internships or fieldwork, Federal Work-Study, institutionally sponsored loans, and scholarships/grants available. Financial award application deadline: 3/7; financial award applicants required to submit FAFSA. *Faculty research:* Intercultural communication, conflict resolution, international education, world issues, international affairs. *Unit head:* Dr. Daniel Yalowitz, SIT Graduate Institute Dean, 802-336-1616, Fax: 802-258-3500. *Application contact:* Information Contact, 800-336-1616, Fax: 802-258-3500, E-mail: admissions@sit.edu.
Website: http://www.sit.edu/graduate

Stanford University, School of Humanities and Sciences, Program in International Policy Studies, Stanford, CA 94305-9991. Offers democracy, development, and rule of law (MA); energy, environment, and natural resources (MA); global health (MA); international political economy (MA); international security and cooperation (MA). *Degree requirements:* For master's, thesis optional. *Entrance requirements:* For master's, GRE General Test. Additional exam requirements/recommendations for international students: Required—TOEFL. Electronic applications accepted. *Expenses: Tuition:* Full-time $44,184; part-time $982 per credit hour. *Required fees:* $191.

Syracuse University, Maxwell School of Citizenship and Public Affairs, Executive Master in International Relations Program, Syracuse, NY 13244. Offers MA. Part-time programs available. *Students:* 4 full-time (0 women), 2 international. Average age 35. 14 applicants, 71% accepted, 3 enrolled. In 2014, 4 master's awarded. *Entrance requirements:* For master's, work experience. Additional exam requirements/ recommendations for international students: Required—TOEFL (minimum score 100 iBT). *Application deadline:* For fall admission, 2/1 priority date for domestic and international students; for spring admission, 8/15 priority date for domestic and international students. Applications are processed on a rolling basis. Application fee: $75. Electronic applications accepted. *Expenses: Tuition:* Part-time $1341 per credit. *Financial support:* Application deadline: 2/1. *Unit head:* Prof. Steve Lux, Director, 315-443-4000. *Application contact:* Margaret Lane, Assistant Director, 315-443-8708, E-mail: melane@syr.edu.
Website: http://www.maxwell.syr.edu/exed/degree_programs/emir/overview/

Syracuse University, Maxwell School of Citizenship and Public Affairs, Joint Program in Economics and International Relations, Syracuse, NY 13244. Offers MA/MA. *Students:* 2 full-time (1 woman). Average age 26. 13 applicants, 85% accepted, 3 enrolled. *Entrance requirements:* Additional exam requirements/recommendations for international students: Required—TOEFL (minimum score 100 iBT). *Application deadline:* For fall admission, 2/1 priority date for domestic and international students. Application fee: $75. Electronic applications accepted. *Expenses: Tuition:* Part-time $1341 per credit. *Financial support:* Fellowships with full tuition reimbursements, research assistantships with full and partial tuition reimbursements, and teaching assistantships with full and partial tuition reimbursements available. Financial award application deadline: 1/1. *Unit head:* Dr. Stuart Brown, Program Contact, 315-443-7097, Fax: 315-443-3385, E-mail: ssbrown@maxwell.syr.edu. *Application contact:* Christine Omolino, Associate Director, 315-443-4000, Fax: 315-443-3423, E-mail: comolino@syr.edu.
Website: http://www.maxwell.syr.edu/

Syracuse University, Maxwell School of Citizenship and Public Affairs, Joint Program in International Relations/Public Administration, Syracuse, NY 13244. Offers MPA/MA. *Students:* 26 full-time (15 women), 1 part-time (0 women); includes 8 minority (2 Black or African American, non-Hispanic/Latino; 3 Asian, non-Hispanic/Latino; 2 Hispanic/Latino; 1 Two or more races, non-Hispanic/Latino), 3 international. Average age 27. 71 applicants, 72% accepted, 20 enrolled. *Entrance requirements:* Additional exam requirements/recommendations for international students: Required—TOEFL (minimum score 100 iBT). *Application deadline:* For fall admission, 2/1 for domestic and international students; for summer admission, 2/1 priority date for domestic and international students. Application fee: $75. Electronic applications accepted. *Expenses: Tuition:* Part-time $1341 per credit. *Financial support:* Fellowships with full tuition reimbursements, research assistantships with full and partial tuition reimbursements, and teaching assistantships with full and partial tuition reimbursements available. Financial award application deadline: 1/1; financial award applicants required to submit FAFSA. *Unit head:* Donald Planty, Chair and Ambassador, 315-443-2306. *Application contact:* Christine Omolino, 315-443-4000, E-mail: comolino@syr.eduu.
Website: http://www.maxwell.syr.edu/

Syracuse University, Maxwell School of Citizenship and Public Affairs, Program in Public Diplomacy, Syracuse, NY 13244. Offers MS/MA. *Students:* 22 full-time (13 women), 2 part-time (both women); includes 7 minority (4 Black or African American, non-Hispanic/Latino; 2 Hispanic/Latino; 1 Two or more races, non-Hispanic/Latino), 3 international. Average age 26. 37 applicants, 70% accepted, 12 enrolled. *Entrance requirements:* Additional exam requirements/recommendations for international students: Required—TOEFL (minimum score 100 iBT). *Application deadline:* For fall admission, 2/1 for domestic students, 2/1 priority date for international students. Application fee: $75. Electronic applications accepted. *Expenses: Tuition:* Part-time $1341 per credit. *Financial support:* Fellowships with full tuition reimbursements available. Financial award application deadline: 1/1. *Unit head:* Dr. Dennis Kinsey, Director, 315-443-1944, E-mail: publicdiplomacy@syr.edu. *Application contact:* Martha Coria, Program Contact, 315-443-5749, Fax: 315-443-1834, E-mail: pcgrad@syr.edu.
Website: http://www.maxwell.syr.edu/

Texas A&M University, Bush School of Government and Public Service, College Station, TX 77843. Offers homeland security (Certificate); international affairs (MIA, Certificate); national security affairs (Certificate); non-profit management (Certificate); public service and administration (MPSA). *Accreditation:* NASPAA. *Faculty:* 60. *Students:* 313 full-time (146 women), 12 part-time (2 women); includes 61 minority (13 Black or African American, non-Hispanic/Latino; 7 Asian, non-Hispanic/Latino; 32 Hispanic/Latino; 1 Native Hawaiian or other Pacific Islander, non-Hispanic/Latino; 8 Two or more races, non-Hispanic/Latino), 44 international. Average age 28. 298 applicants, 71% accepted, 143 enrolled. In 2014, 137 master's awarded. *Degree requirements:* For master's, summer internship. *Entrance requirements:* For master's, GRE (preferred) or GMAT. Additional exam requirements/recommendations for international students: Required—TOEFL (minimum score 550 paper-based; 80 iBT), IELTS (minimum score 6). *Application deadline:* For fall admission, 1/20 for domestic and international students. Application fee: $50 ($90 for international students). Electronic applications accepted. *Expenses:* Tuition, state resident: full-time $4078; part-time $226.55 per credit hour. Tuition, nonresident: full-time $10,594; part-time $577.55 per credit hour. *Required fees:* $2813; $237.70 per credit hour. $278.50 per semester. Tuition and fees vary according to degree level and student level. *Financial support:* In 2014–15, 407 students received support, including 26 fellowships with full and partial tuition reimbursements available (averaging $15,902 per year), 44 research assistantships with full and partial tuition reimbursements available (averaging $7,163 per year); career-related internships or fieldwork, institutionally sponsored loans, scholarships/grants, traineeships, health care benefits, tuition waivers (full and partial), and unspecified assistantships also available. Support available to part-time students. Financial award application deadline: 2/1; financial award applicants required to submit FAFSA. *Faculty research:* Public policy, Presidential studies, public leadership, economic policy, social policy. *Unit head:* Dr. Ryan Crocker, Dean, 979-862-8007, E-mail: rcrocker@tamu.edu. *Application contact:* Kathryn Meyer, Director of Recruitment and Admissions, 979-458-4767, Fax: 979-845-4155, E-mail: bushschooladmissions@tamu.edu.
Website: http://bush.tamu.edu/

Texas State University, The Graduate College, College of Liberal Arts, Department of Political Science, Program in Public Administration, San Marcos, TX 78666. Offers international relations (MPA); public finance administration (MPA); urban and environmental planning (MPA). *Accreditation:* NASPAA. Part-time and evening/weekend programs available. *Faculty:* 6 full-time (3 women), 1 (woman) part-time/adjunct. *Students:* 29 full-time (16 women), 67 part-time (30 women); includes 45 minority (7 Black or African American, non-Hispanic/Latino; 3 Asian, non-Hispanic/Latino; 31 Hispanic/Latino; 4 Two or more races, non-Hispanic/Latino), 2 international. Average age 33. 42 applicants, 83% accepted, 16 enrolled. In 2014, 39 master's awarded. *Degree requirements:* For master's, comprehensive 'exam, applied research project. *Entrance requirements:* For master's, The Public Administration program requires an official Graduate Record Exam (GRE) score to be submitted prior to admission consideration with with a preferred score of 297., baccalaureate degree from regionally-accredited university with minimum GPA of 3.0 on last 60 undergraduate semester hours. Additional exam requirements/recommendations for international students: Required—TOEFL (minimum score 550 paper-based; 78 iBT), TWE. *Application deadline:* For fall admission, 6/15 priority date for domestic students, 6/1 priority date for international students; for spring admission, 10/15 priority date for domestic students, 10/1 priority date for international students; for summer admission, 4/15 for domestic students, 3/15 for international students. Applications are processed on a rolling basis. Application fee: $40 ($90 for international students). Electronic applications accepted. *Expenses:* Expenses: $8,834 (tuition and fees combined). *Financial support:* In 2014–15, 42 students received support, including 3 research assistantships (averaging $10,708 per year), 1 teaching assistantship (averaging $12,464 per year); career-related internships or fieldwork, Federal Work-Study, institutionally sponsored loans, scholarships/grants, and unspecified assistantships also available. Support available to part-time students. Financial award application deadline: 4/1; financial award applicants required to submit FAFSA. *Unit head:* Dr. Thomas Longoria, Graduate Advisor, 512-245-7582, Fax: 512-245-7815, E-mail: tl28@txstate.edu. *Application contact:* Dr. Andrea Golato, Dean of Graduate School, 512-245-2581, Fax: 512-245-8365, E-mail: gradcollege@txstate.edu.
Website: http://www.polisci.txstate.edu/public_administration/

Texas State University, The Graduate College, College of Liberal Arts, Program in International Studies, San Marcos, TX 78666. Offers MA. *Students:* 11 full-time (6 women), 17 part-time (9 women); includes 9 minority (1 Black or African American, non-Hispanic/Latino; 1 Asian, non-Hispanic/Latino; 6 Hispanic/Latino; 1 Two or more races, non-Hispanic/Latino), 4 international. Average age 31. 16 applicants, 75% accepted, 4 enrolled. In 2014, 12 master's awarded. *Degree requirements:* For master's, comprehensive exam, thesis optional. *Entrance requirements:* For master's, GRE (preferred), minimum GPA of 3.0 in last 60 hours leading to bachelor's degree. Additional exam requirements/recommendations for international students: Required—TOEFL (minimum score 550 paper-based; 78 iBT). *Application deadline:* For fall admission, 6/15 priority date for domestic students, 6/1 for international students; for spring admission, 10/15 priority date for domestic students, 10/1 for international students; for summer admission, 4/15 for domestic students, 3/15 for international students. Applications are processed on a rolling basis. Application fee: $40 ($90 for international students). *Financial support:* In 2014–15, 21 students received support, including 2 research assistantships (averaging $11,855 per year), 4 teaching assistantships (averaging $12,152 per year); Federal Work-Study, institutionally sponsored loans, scholarships/grants, health care benefits, and unspecified assistantships also available. Support available to part-time students. Financial award application deadline: 4/1; financial award applicants required to submit FAFSA. *Unit head:* Dr. Dennis Dunn, Head, 512-245-2107, E-mail: dd05@txstate.edu. *Application contact:* Dr. Andrea Golato, Dean of Graduate School, 512-245-2581, Fax: 512-245-8365, E-mail: gradcollege@txstate.edu.
Website: http://www.txstate.edu/internationalstudies

Troy University, Graduate School, College of Arts and Sciences, Program in International Relations, Troy, AL 36082. Offers regional affairs (MS). Part-time and evening/weekend programs available. Postbaccalaureate distance learning degree programs offered (no on-campus study). *Faculty:* 13 full-time (1 woman), 12 part-time/adjunct (0 women). *Students:* 73 full-time (30 women), 265 part-time (86 women); includes 104 minority (44 Black or African American, non-Hispanic/Latino; 1 American Indian or Alaska Native, non-Hispanic/Latino; 16 Asian, non-Hispanic/Latino; 33 Hispanic/Latino; 10 Two or more races, non-Hispanic/Latino). Average age 32. 188 applicants, 88% accepted, 74 enrolled. In 2014, 130 master's awarded. *Degree requirements:* For master's, comprehensive exam (for some programs), thesis (for some programs), comprehensive exam or thesis, minimum GPA of 3.0, admission to candidacy, minimum B grade on research. *Entrance requirements:* For master's, GRE (minimum score of 920 on old exam or 294 on new exam), MAT (minimum score of 396) or GMAT (minimum score of 490), bachelor's degree; minimum undergraduate GPA of 2.5 or 3.0 on last 30 semester hours. Additional exam requirements/recommendations for international students: Required—TOEFL (minimum score 523 paper-based; 70 iBT), IELTS (minimum score 6). *Application deadline:* Applications are processed on a rolling basis. Application fee: $50. Electronic applications accepted. *Expenses:* Tuition, state resident: full-time $6570; part-time $365 per credit hour. Tuition, nonresident: full-time $13,140; part-time $730 per credit hour. *Required fees:* $365 per credit hour. *Financial support:* Available to part-time students. Applicants required to submit FAFSA. *Faculty research:* Elections, religion and world politics, terrorism. *Unit head:* Dr. Jonathon Harrington, Department Chairman, 334-670-5968, Fax: 334-670-5647, E-mail: jhharrington@troy.edu. *Application contact:* Jessica A. Kimbro, Director of Graduate Admissions, 334-670-3178, Fax: 334-670-3733, E-mail: jacord@troy.edu.

Tufts University, The Fletcher School of Law and Diplomacy, Medford, MA 02155. Offers LL M, MA, MALD, MIB, PhD, DVM/MA, JD/MALD, MALD/MA, MALD/MBA, MALD/MS, MD/MA. Postbaccalaureate distance learning degree programs offered (minimal on-campus study). *Degree requirements:* For master's, one foreign language, thesis; for doctorate, one foreign language, comprehensive exam, thesis/dissertation, dissertation defense. *Entrance requirements:* For master's and doctorate, GMAT or GRE General Test. Additional exam requirements/recommendations for international students: Required—TOEFL (minimum score 600 paper-based; 100 iBT), IELTS (minimum score 7). Electronic applications accepted. *Expenses:* Contact institution. *Faculty research:* Negotiation and conflict resolution, international organizations, international business and economic law, security studies, development economics.

United States International University, School of Arts and Sciences, Nairobi, Kenya. Offers counseling psychology (MA), including chemical dependency, health psychology; international relations (MA), including development studies, diplomacy and foreign policy, peace and conflict studies. Part-time and evening/weekend programs available. *Degree requirements:* For master's, thesis, practicum. *Entrance requirements:* For master's, GRE General Test, 2 letters of recommendation, resume. Additional exam requirements/recommendations for international students: Required—TOEFL. *Faculty research:* Trauma in children, African intellectualism, psychological assessment tools.

Universidad de las Americas, A.C., Program in International Organizations and Institutions, Mexico City, Mexico. Offers MA.

Universidad Nacional Pedro Henriquez Urena, Graduate School, Santo Domingo, Dominican Republic. Offers agricultural diversity (MS), including horticultural/fruit production, tropical animal production; conservation of monuments and cultural assets (M Arch); ecology and environment (MS); environmental engineering (MEE); international relations (MA); natural resource management (MS); political science (MA); project optimization (MPM); project feasibility (MPM); project management (MPM); sanitation engineering (ME); science for teachers (MS); tropical Caribbean architecture (M Arch).

Université de Montréal, Faculty of Arts and Sciences, Programs in International Studies, Montréal, QC H3C 3J7, Canada. Offers M Sc, DESS.

Université Laval, Québec Institute for Advanced International Studies, Program in International Relations, Québec, QC G1K 7P4, Canada. Offers MA, PhD. *Degree requirements:* For master's, thesis (for some programs). *Entrance requirements:* For master's, English exam, French exam. Electronic applications accepted.

University of Bridgeport, College of Public and International Affairs, Bridgeport, CT 06604. Offers East Asian and Pacific Rim studies (MA); global development and peace (MA); global media and communication studies (MA). Part-time and evening/weekend programs available. *Degree requirements:* For master's, thesis. *Entrance requirements:* Additional exam requirements/recommendations for international students: Recommended—TOEFL (minimum score 550 paper-based; 80 iBT), IELTS (minimum score 6.5).

The University of British Columbia, Institute of Asian Research, Vancouver, BC V6T 1Z2, Canada. Offers MAAPPS. *Degree requirements:* For master's, thesis optional. *Entrance requirements:* Additional exam requirements/recommendations for international students: Required—TOEFL (minimum score 600 paper-based; 100 iBT). Electronic applications accepted. *Faculty research:* Social cohesion, globalization, social safety nets, policy research, research and development alliances, knowledge-based workshops on Asia-Pacific studies.

University of California, Berkeley, Graduate Division, Haas School of Business and Program in International and Area Studies, MBA/MA Program in International and Area Studies, Berkeley, CA 94720-1500. Offers MBA/MA. *Accreditation:* AACSB. *Entrance requirements:* Additional exam requirements/recommendations for international students: Required—TOEFL (minimum score 570 paper-based; 68 iBT). Application fee: $200. *Financial support:* Fellowships with full tuition reimbursements, research assistantships, teaching assistantships with partial tuition reimbursements, career-related internships or fieldwork, scholarships/grants, and unspecified assistantships available. Financial award application deadline: 6/12; financial award applicants required to submit FAFSA. *Unit head:* Julia Hwang, Director, MBA Program, 510-642-1405, Fax: 510-643-6659, E-mail: julia_hwang@haas.berkeley.edu. *Application contact:* 510-642-1405, Fax: 510-643-6659.

University of California, Berkeley, Graduate Division, Program in International and Area Studies, Berkeley, CA 94720-1500. Offers MA, PhD, JD/MA, MBA/MA, MJ/MA.

University of California, San Diego, Graduate Division, Department of Political Science, La Jolla, CA 92093. Offers political science (PhD); political science and international affairs (PhD). *Students:* 76 full-time (22 women), 2 part-time (both women); includes 13 minority (all Asian, non-Hispanic/Latino), 7 international. 332 applicants, 10% accepted, 6 enrolled. In 2014, 11 doctorates awarded. *Degree requirements:* For doctorate, comprehensive exam, thesis/dissertation. *Entrance requirements:* For doctorate, GRE General Test. Additional exam requirements/recommendations for international students: Required—TOEFL (minimum score 600 paper-based; 100 iBT), IELTS. *Application deadline:* For fall admission, 12/10 for domestic students. Application fee: $90 ($110 for international students). Electronic applications accepted. *Expenses:* Tuition, state resident: full-time $11,220; part-time $5610 per quarter. Tuition, nonresident: full-time $26,322; part-time $13,161 per quarter. *Required fees:* $570 per quarter. Tuition and fees vary according to program. *Financial support:* Fellowships, research assistantships, teaching assistantships, and scholarships/grants available. Financial award applicants required to submit FAFSA. *Faculty research:* American politics, comparative politics, international relations, methodology, political theory. *Unit head:* Philip G. Roeder, Chair, 858-534-0721, E-mail: proeder@ucsd.edu. *Application contact:* Arturo Vazquez, Graduate Coordinator, 858-534-2705, E-mail: avazquez@ucsd.edu.
Website: http://polisci.ucsd.edu/

University of California, San Diego, Graduate Division, School of Global Policy and Strategy, Program in International Affairs, La Jolla, CA 92093. Offers MIA. *Faculty:* 33 full-time (9 women), 20 part-time/adjunct (4 women). *Students:* 240 full-time (120 women). Average age 24. 460 applicants, 120 enrolled. In 2014, 120 master's awarded. *Degree requirements:* For master's, one foreign language. *Entrance requirements:* For master's, GMAT or GRE General Test. Additional exam requirements/recommendations for international students: Required—TOEFL (minimum score 90 iBT), IELTS (minimum score 7). *Application deadline:* For fall admission, 1/15 for domestic and international students. Applications are processed on a rolling basis. Application fee: $50. Electronic applications accepted. *Expenses:* Tuition, state resident: full-time $11,220; part-time $5610 per quarter. Tuition, nonresident: full-time $26,322; part-time $13,161 per quarter. *Required fees:* $570 per quarter. Tuition and fees vary according to program. *Financial support:* In 2014–15, 140 students received support, including 60 fellowships with full and partial tuition reimbursements available (averaging $50,000 per year), 15 research assistantships with full tuition reimbursements available (averaging $20,000 per year), 20 teaching assistantships with full tuition reimbursements available (averaging $20,000 per year); career-related internships or fieldwork, scholarships/grants, and unspecified assistantships also available. Financial award application deadline: 3/1; financial award applicants required to submit FAFSA. *Unit head:* Sonja Steinbrech, Director of Enrollment, 858-534-7162, E-mail: ssteinbrech@ucsd.edu. *Application contact:* Admissions Representative, 858-534-5914, Fax: 858-534-1135, E-mail: gps-apply@uscd.edu.
Website: http://gps.ucsd.edu/academics/mia.html

University of California, Santa Barbara, Graduate Division, College of Letters and Sciences, Division of Humanities and Fine Arts, Department of English, Santa Barbara, CA 93106-3170. Offers English (PhD); European medieval studies (PhD); feminist studies (PhD); global studies (PhD); technology and society (PhD); translation studies (PhD); writing studies (PhD); MA/PhD. Terminal master's awarded for partial completion of doctoral program. *Degree requirements:* For doctorate, one foreign language, comprehensive exam, thesis/dissertation. *Entrance requirements:* For doctorate, GRE General Test, GRE Subject Test (English). Additional exam requirements/recommendations for international students: Required—TOEFL (minimum score 550 paper-based; 80 iBT), IELTS (minimum score 7). Electronic applications accepted. *Faculty research:* Medieval, Romantic and Victorian studies; gender studies and feminist theory; literature and the mind; American literature; literature and new media/information culture.

University of California, Santa Barbara, Graduate Division, College of Letters and Sciences, Division of Humanities and Fine Arts, Department of History, Santa Barbara, CA 93106-9410. Offers European medieval studies (PhD); global studies (PhD); public historical studies (PhD); technology and society (PhD); women's studies (PhD); MA/PhD. *Degree requirements:* For doctorate, variable foreign language requirement, comprehensive exam, thesis/dissertation. *Entrance requirements:* For doctorate, GRE. Additional exam requirements/recommendations for international students: Required—TOEFL (minimum score 550 paper-based; 80 iBT), IELTS (minimum score 7). Electronic applications accepted. *Faculty research:* Europe, United States, Latin America, Africa, Middle East, East Asia.

University of California, Santa Barbara, Graduate Division, College of Letters and Sciences, Division of Humanities and Fine Arts, Department of Religious Studies, Santa Barbara, CA 93106-3130. Offers ancient Mediterranean studies (PhD); cognitive science (PhD); European medieval studies (PhD); feminist studies (PhD); global studies (PhD); religious studies (MA, PhD); translation studies (PhD); MA/PhD. Terminal master's awarded for partial completion of doctoral program. *Degree requirements:* For master's, one foreign language, comprehensive exam (for some programs), thesis (for some programs), colloquium; for doctorate, 2 foreign languages, thesis/dissertation, methodology, colloquium. *Entrance requirements:* For master's and doctorate, GRE General Test. Additional exam requirements/recommendations for international students: Required—TOEFL (minimum score 550 paper-based; 80 iBT), IELTS (minimum score 7). Electronic applications accepted. *Faculty research:* Area studies; religious traditions; theory and method in the study of religion; religion, culture, and politics; spirituality and religious experience.

University of California, Santa Barbara, Graduate Division, College of Letters and Sciences, Division of Humanities and Fine Arts, Program in Comparative Literature, Santa Barbara, CA 93106-4130. Offers comparative literature (PhD); East Asian literatures (PhD); feminist studies (PhD); French (PhD); global studies (PhD); translation studies (PhD); MA/PhD. *Degree requirements:* For doctorate, 2 foreign languages, comprehensive exam, thesis/dissertation. *Entrance requirements:* For doctorate, GRE. Additional exam requirements/recommendations for international students: Required—TOEFL (minimum score 550 paper-based; 80 iBT), IELTS (minimum score 7). Electronic applications accepted. *Faculty research:* Comparative literary studies in global context, critical theory, translation studies, media technological studies, trauma studies.

University of California, Santa Barbara, Graduate Division, College of Letters and Sciences, Division of Mathematics, Life, and Physical Sciences, Department of Geography, Santa Barbara, CA 93106-4060. Offers cognitive science (PhD); geography (MA, PhD); global studies (PhD); quantitative methods in the social sciences (PhD); technology and society (PhD); transportation (PhD); MA/PhD. Terminal master's awarded for partial completion of doctoral program. *Degree requirements:* For master's, comprehensive exam (for some programs), thesis or alternative; for doctorate, comprehensive exam, thesis/dissertation, 1 quarter of teaching assistantship. *Entrance requirements:* For master's and doctorate, GRE (minimum combined verbal and quantitative scores of 1100 in old scoring system or 301 in new scoring system). Additional exam requirements/recommendations for international students: Required—TOEFL (minimum score 550 paper-based; 80 iBT), IELTS (minimum score 7). Electronic applications accepted. *Faculty research:* Earth system science; human environment relations; modeling, measurement, and computation.

University of California, Santa Barbara, Graduate Division, College of Letters and Sciences, Division of Social Sciences, Department of Global and International Studies, Santa Barbara, CA 93106-7065. Offers global culture, ideology, and religion (MA); global government, civil society, and human rights (MA); global studies (PhD); political economy, sustainable development, and the environment (MA). *Degree requirements:* For master's, one foreign language, thesis, 2 years of a second language. *Entrance requirements:* For master's, GRE, 2 years of a second language with minimum B grade in the final term, 3 letters of recommendation, resume/curriculum vitae, personal statement, writing sample. Additional exam requirements/recommendations for international students: Required—TOEFL (minimum score 600 paper-based; 94 iBT), IELTS (minimum score 7). Electronic applications accepted. *Faculty research:* Global culture, ideology, and religion; global governance, civil society, and human rights; political economy, sustainable development and the environment.

University of California, Santa Barbara, Graduate Division, College of Letters and Sciences, Division of Social Sciences, Department of Sociology, Santa Barbara, CA 93106-9430. Offers interdisciplinary emphasis: Black studies (PhD); interdisciplinary emphasis: environment and society (PhD); interdisciplinary emphasis: feminist studies (PhD); interdisciplinary emphasis: global studies (PhD); interdisciplinary emphasis: language, interaction and social organization (PhD); interdisciplinary emphasis: quantitative methods in social science (PhD); interdisciplinary emphasis: technology and society (PhD); sociology (PhD); MA/PhD. Terminal master's awarded for partial completion of doctoral program. *Degree requirements:* For doctorate, comprehensive exam, thesis/dissertation. *Entrance requirements:* For doctorate, GRE General Test. Additional exam requirements/recommendations for international students: Required—TOEFL (minimum score 550 paper-based; 80 iBT), IELTS (minimum score 7). Electronic applications accepted. *Faculty research:* Gender and sexualities, race/ethnicity, social movements, conversation analysis, global sociology.

University of California, Santa Cruz, Division of Graduate Studies, Division of Social Sciences, Program in International Economics, Santa Cruz, CA 95064. Offers PhD. *Degree requirements:* For doctorate, thesis/dissertation, 4 field exams, field papers, econometrics project, qualifying exams. *Entrance requirements:* For doctorate, GRE General Test. Additional exam requirements/recommendations for international students: Required—TOEFL (minimum score 550 paper-based; 83 iBT); Recommended—IELTS (minimum score 8). Electronic applications accepted. *Faculty research:* Current and emerging issues in taxation, industrial policy, environmental regulation, market structure, labor economics focus on behavior and adjustment in an interdependent world economy.

University of Central Oklahoma, The Jackson College of Graduate Studies, College of Liberal Arts, Department of Political Science, Edmond, OK 73034-5209. Offers international affairs (MA); political science (MA); public administration (MPA). Part-time programs available. *Degree requirements:* For master's, comprehensive exam (for some programs), thesis (for some programs). *Entrance requirements:* For master's, GRE, 18 undergraduate hours in political science. Additional exam requirements/recommendations for international students: Required—TOEFL (minimum score 550 paper-based; 79 iBT), IELTS (minimum score 6.5). Electronic applications accepted.

University of Chicago, Division of the Social Sciences, Committee on International Relations, Chicago, IL 60637. Offers MA. *Students:* 48 full-time (21 women); includes 7 minority (4 Asian, non-Hispanic/Latino; 3 Hispanic/Latino), 19 international. 200 applicants, 84% accepted, 45 enrolled. In 2014, 45 master's awarded. *Degree requirements:* For master's, thesis. *Entrance requirements:* For master's, GRE General Test. Additional exam requirements/recommendations for international students: Required—TOEFL (minimum score 104 iBT), IELTS (minimum score 7). *Application deadline:* For fall admission, 1/5 for domestic and international students. Application fee: $90. Electronic applications accepted. *Expenses: Tuition:* Full-time $46,899. *Required*

fees: $347. *Financial support:* In 2014–15, 36 students received support. Federal Work-Study, institutionally sponsored loans, and scholarships/grants available. Financial award application deadline: 1/5. *Unit head:* Prof. Mark Bradley, Chair, 773-702-8074. *Application contact:* Office of the Dean of Students, 773-702-8415, E-mail: admissions@ssd.uchicago.edu.
Website: http://cir.uchicago.edu

University of Colorado Boulder, Graduate School, College of Arts and Sciences, Department of Political Science, Boulder, CO 80309. Offers international affairs (MA); political science (MA, PhD); public policy (MA). *Faculty:* 26 full-time (8 women). *Students:* 53 full-time (20 women), 5 part-time (0 women); includes 6 minority (3 American Indian or Alaska Native, non-Hispanic/Latino; 1 Asian, non-Hispanic/Latino; 2 Hispanic/Latino), 5 international. Average age 30. 120 applicants, 26% accepted, 10 enrolled. In 2014, 11 master's, 4 doctorates awarded. Terminal master's awarded for partial completion of doctoral program. *Degree requirements:* For master's, comprehensive exam, thesis; for doctorate, one foreign language, thesis/dissertation. *Entrance requirements:* For master's, GRE General Test, minimum undergraduate GPA of 3.0; for doctorate, GRE General Test, minimum GPA of 3.5 (undergraduate), 3.0 (graduate). *Application deadline:* For fall admission, 12/15 for domestic and international students. Application fee: $50 ($60 for international students). Electronic applications accepted. *Financial support:* In 2014–15, 142 students received support, including 21 fellowships (averaging $2,782 per year), 1 research assistantship with full and partial tuition reimbursement available (averaging $39,356 per year), 49 teaching assistantships with full and partial tuition reimbursements available (averaging $38,468 per year); institutionally sponsored loans, scholarships/grants, health care benefits, and unspecified assistantships also available. Financial award application deadline: 12/31; financial award applicants required to submit FAFSA. *Faculty research:* Political science, democracy, comparative government, political economics/economy, international relations. *Total annual research expenditures:* $752,632.
Website: http://polsci.colorado.edu/

University of Colorado Denver, College of Liberal Arts and Sciences, Program in Humanities, Denver, CO 80217. Offers community health science (MSS); humanities (MH); international studies (MSS); philosophy and theory (MH); social justice (MSS); society and the environment (MSS); visual studies (MH); women's and gender studies (MSS). Part-time and evening/weekend programs available. *Faculty:* 1 full-time (0 women), 1 (woman) part-time/adjunct. *Students:* 49 full-time (37 women), 26 part-time (19 women); includes 14 minority (3 Black or African American, non-Hispanic/Latino; 1 American Indian or Alaska Native, non-Hispanic/Latino; 1 Asian, non-Hispanic/Latino; 6 Hispanic/Latino; 3 Two or more races, non-Hispanic/Latino), 1 international. Average age 35. 27 applicants, 63% accepted, 11 enrolled. In 2014, 16 master's awarded. *Degree requirements:* For master's, 36 credit hours, project or thesis. *Entrance requirements:* For master's, writing sample, statement of purpose/letter of intent, three letters of recommendation. Additional exam requirements/recommendations for international students: Required—TOEFL (minimum score 537 paper-based; 75 iBT); Recommended—IELTS (minimum score 6.5). *Application deadline:* For fall admission, 5/15 for domestic students, 5/15 priority date for international students; for spring admission, 10/15 for domestic students, 10/15 priority date for international students; for summer admission, 3/15 for domestic and international students. Application fee: $50 ($75 for international students). Electronic applications accepted. *Financial support:* In 2014–15, 4 students received support. Fellowships, research assistantships, teaching assistantships, Federal Work-Study, institutionally sponsored loans, scholarships/grants, and traineeships available. Financial award application deadline: 4/1; financial award applicants required to submit FAFSA. *Faculty research:* Women and gender in the classical Mediterranean, communication theory and democracy, relationship between psychology and philosophy. *Unit head:* Margaret Woodhull, Director of Humanities, 303-315-3568, E-mail: margaret.woodhull@ucdenver.edu. *Application contact:* Angela Beale, Program Assistant, 303-315-3565, E-mail: angela.beale@ucdenver.edu.
Website: http://www.ucdenver.edu/academics/colleges/CLAS/Programs/HumanitiesSocialSciences/Programs/Pages/MasterofHumanities.aspx

University of Connecticut, Graduate School, College of Liberal Arts and Sciences, Field of International Studies, Program in International Studies, Storrs, CT 06269. Offers MA. *Degree requirements:* For master's, comprehensive exam. *Entrance requirements:* For master's, GRE General Test. Additional exam requirements/recommendations for international students: Required—TOEFL (minimum score 550 paper-based). Electronic applications accepted.

University of Delaware, College of Arts and Sciences, Department of Political Science and International Relations, Newark, DE 19716. Offers MA, PhD. Terminal master's awarded for partial completion of doctoral program. *Degree requirements:* For master's, research paper; for doctorate, one foreign language, comprehensive exam, thesis/dissertation. *Entrance requirements:* For master's and doctorate, GRE General Test, minimum GPA of 3.2 in major, 3.0 overall. Additional exam requirements/recommendations for international students: Required—TOEFL (minimum score 600 paper-based). Electronic applications accepted. *Faculty research:* Social constructivism, international migration, international security, democratization, human rights.

University of Denver, Division of Arts, Humanities and Social Sciences, Department of Media, Film and Journalism Studies, Denver, CO 80208. Offers emergent digital practices (MA); international and intercultural communication (MA); strategic communication (MS); student designed emphasis (MA); video production (MA). Part-time programs available. *Faculty:* 14 full-time (8 women), 6 part-time/adjunct (2 women). *Students:* 24 full-time (17 women), 25 part-time (17 women); includes 10 minority (1 Asian, non-Hispanic/Latino; 4 Hispanic/Latino; 5 Two or more races, non-Hispanic/Latino), 4 international. Average age 27. 73 applicants, 89% accepted, 21 enrolled. In 2014, 17 master's awarded. *Degree requirements:* For master's, thesis (for some programs). *Entrance requirements:* For master's, GRE General Test, bachelor's degree, transcripts, personal statement, three letters of recommendation. Additional exam requirements/recommendations for international students: Required—TOEFL (minimum score 620 paper-based; 105 iBT). *Application deadline:* For fall admission, 2/15 priority date for domestic students, 1/1 priority date for international students. Applications are processed on a rolling basis. Application fee: $65. Electronic applications accepted. *Expenses:* Expenses: $1,199 per credit hour. *Financial support:* In 2014–15, 41 students received support, including 7 teaching assistantships with full and partial tuition reimbursements available (averaging $9,515 per year); career-related internships or fieldwork, Federal Work-Study, institutionally sponsored loans, scholarships/grants, and unspecified assistantships also available. Support available to part-time students. Financial award application deadline: 2/15; financial award applicants required to submit FAFSA. *Faculty research:* International and intercultural communication; media law; film history; youth, families, and social media; activist media. *Total annual research expenditures:* $50,000. *Unit head:* Dr. Lynn Schofield Clark, Chair, 303-871-3984, Fax: 303-871-4949, E-mail: lynn.clark@du.edu. *Application contact:* Information Contact, 303-871-2166, E-mail: mfjs@du.edu.
Website: http://www.du.edu/ahss/mfjs/index.html

University of Denver, Josef Korbel School of International Studies, Denver, CO 80208. Offers MA, PhD, Certificate. Part-time programs available. *Faculty:* 39 full-time (12 women), 21 part-time/adjunct (4 women). *Students:* 390 full-time (226 women), 36 part-time (15 women); includes 78 minority (12 Black or African American, non-Hispanic/Latino; 13 Asian, non-Hispanic/Latino; 42 Hispanic/Latino; 1 Native Hawaiian or other Pacific Islander, non-Hispanic/Latino; 10 Two or more races, non-Hispanic/Latino), 38 international. Average age 27. 754 applicants, 87% accepted, 187 enrolled. In 2014, 223 master's, 9 doctorates, 35 other advanced degrees awarded. *Degree requirements:* For master's, one foreign language, thesis (for some programs); for doctorate, one foreign language, comprehensive exam, thesis/dissertation, two extended research papers. *Entrance requirements:* For master's, GRE General Test, bachelor's degree, transcripts, two letters of recommendation, statement of purpose, resume or curriculum vitae; for doctorate, GRE General Test, master's degree, transcripts, three letters of recommendation, statement of purpose, resume or curriculum vitae, writing sample; for Certificate, bachelor's degree, transcripts, two letters of recommendation, statement of purpose, resume or curriculum vitae. Additional exam requirements/recommendations for international students: Required—TOEFL (minimum score 587 paper-based; 95 iBT). *Application deadline:* For fall admission, 1/15 priority date for domestic and international students; for winter admission, 11/1 for domestic and international students. Application fee: $65. Electronic applications accepted. *Expenses:* Expenses: $1,199 per credit hour. *Financial support:* In 2014–15, 228 students received support, including 3 teaching assistantships with full and partial tuition reimbursements available (averaging $2,201 per year); research assistantships, career-related internships or fieldwork, Federal Work-Study, institutionally sponsored loans, scholarships/grants, and unspecified assistantships also available. Support available to part-time students. Financial award application deadline: 2/15; financial award applicants required to submit FAFSA. *Faculty research:* Human rights and international security, international politics and economics, economic-social and political development, international technology analysis and management. *Unit head:* Christopher R. Hill, Dean, 303-871-2359, Fax: 303-871-2456, E-mail: christopher.r.hill@du.edu. *Application contact:* Brad Miller, Director of Graduate Admissions, 303-871-2989, Fax: 303-871-2124, E-mail: brad.miller@du.edu.
Website: http://www.du.edu/korbel/

University of Denver, University College, Denver, CO 80208. Offers geographic information systems (Certificate); global affairs (Certificate), including translation studies, world history and culture; information and communications technology (MCIS), including geographic information systems, information systems security, project management (MCIS, Certificate), software design and programming, technology management, telecommunications technology, Web design and development; leadership and organizations (Certificate), including human capital in organizations, philanthropic leadership, project management (MCIS, Certificate), strategic innovation and change; organizational and professional communication (MPS), including alternative dispute resolution, organizational communication, organizational development and training, public relations and marketing; security management (MAS, Certificate), including emergency planning and response, information security (MAS), organizational security. Part-time and evening/weekend programs available. Postbaccalaureate distance learning degree programs offered (no on-campus study). *Faculty:* 8 full-time (4 women), 133 part-time/adjunct (46 women). *Students:* 54 full-time (21 women), 1,327 part-time (775 women); includes 272 minority (106 Black or African American, non-Hispanic/Latino; 6 American Indian or Alaska Native, non-Hispanic/Latino; 26 Asian, non-Hispanic/Latino; 108 Hispanic/Latino; 1 Native Hawaiian or other Pacific Islander, non-Hispanic/Latino; 25 Two or more races, non-Hispanic/Latino), 116 international. Average age 35. 768 applicants, 95% accepted, 620 enrolled. In 2014, 391 master's, 196 other advanced degrees awarded. *Degree requirements:* For master's, capstone project. *Entrance requirements:* For master's, transcripts, two letters of recommendation, personal statement, resume. Additional exam requirements/recommendations for international students: Required—TOEFL (minimum score 550 paper-based; 80 iBT). *Application deadline:* For fall admission, 6/21 priority date for domestic students, 5/1 priority date for international students; for winter admission, 9/14 priority date for domestic students, 9/19 priority date for international students; for spring admission, 1/11 for domestic students, 12/12 for international students; for summer admission, 3/29 priority date for domestic students, 3/6 priority date for international students. Applications are processed on a rolling basis. Application fee: $75. Electronic applications accepted. *Expenses:* Expenses: $959 per credit hour. *Financial support:* In 2014–15, 19 students received support. Applicants required to submit FAFSA. *Unit head:* Dr. Michael McGuire, Interim Dean, 303-871-3518, E-mail: mmcguire@du.edu. *Application contact:* Information Contact, 303-871-2291, E-mail: ucoladm@du.edu.
Website: http://www.universitycollege.du.edu/

University of Florida, Graduate School, College of Liberal Arts and Sciences, Department of Political Science, Program in International Relations, Gainesville, FL 32611. Offers MA, MAT. *Students:* 7 full-time (5 women), 4 international. 32 applicants, 16% accepted, 1 enrolled. In 2014, 7 master's awarded. *Degree requirements:* For master's, comprehensive exam (for some programs), thesis optional. *Entrance requirements:* For master's, GRE General Test, minimum GPA of 3.0. Additional exam requirements/recommendations for international students: Required—TOEFL (minimum score 550 paper-based; 80 iBT), IELTS (minimum score 6). *Application deadline:* For fall admission, 3/1 priority date for domestic students, 3/1 for international students. Applications are processed on a rolling basis. Application fee: $30. Electronic applications accepted. *Financial support:* In 2014–15, 4 teaching assistantships were awarded. *Faculty research:* International relations theory, international political economy, feminist international relations, international security, international organization. *Unit head:* Ido Oren, PhD, Professor and Chair, 352-273-2393, Fax: 352-392-8127, E-mail: oren@ufl.edu. *Application contact:* Leslie Anderson, PhD, Graduate Coordinator, 352-273-3725, Fax: 352-392-8127, E-mail: landerso@ufl.edu.
Website: http://polisci.ufl.edu/

University of Georgia, School of Public and International Affairs, Department of International Affairs, Athens, GA 30602. Offers MA, MIP, PhD.

University of Hawaii at Manoa, Graduate Division, International Cultural Studies Graduate Certificate Program, Honolulu, HI 96822. Offers Graduate Certificate. Part-time programs available. *Entrance requirements:* For degree, GRE General Test. Additional exam requirements/recommendations for international students: Required—TOEFL (minimum score 540 paper-based; 76 iBT), IELTS (minimum score 5).

University of Indianapolis, Graduate Programs, College of Arts and Sciences, Department of History and Political Science, Indianapolis, IN 46227-3697. Offers history (MA); international relations (MA). Part-time and evening/weekend programs available. *Faculty:* 6 full-time (1 woman). *Students:* 4 full-time (3 women), 19 part-time (7 women); includes 2 minority (1 Hispanic/Latino; 1 Two or more races, non-Hispanic/Latino), 6 international. Average age 29. In 2014, 5 master's awarded. *Degree requirements:* For master's, thesis optional. *Entrance requirements:* For master's, GRE Subject Test, minimum GPA of 3.0, 3 letters of recommendation. Additional exam requirements/recommendations for international students: Required—TOEFL (minimum score 550 paper-based). *Application deadline:* Applications are processed on a rolling basis. Application fee: $30. Electronic applications accepted. *Financial support:* Federal Work-Study, scholarships/grants, and tuition waivers (full and partial) available. Support available to part-time students. Financial award application deadline: 5/1; financial award applicants required to submit FAFSA. *Unit head:* Dr. Lawrence Sondhaus,

Chairperson, 317-788-2196, Fax: 317-788-3480, E-mail: sondhaus@uindy.edu. *Application contact:* Linda Corn, Administrative Assistant, 317-788-3395, E-mail: lcorn@uindy.edu. Website: http://history.uindy.edu/

The University of Kansas, Graduate Studies, College of Liberal Arts and Sciences, Global and International Studies Program, Lawrence, KS 66045. Offers MA. Part-time and evening/weekend programs available. *Faculty:* 2 full-time, 11 part-time/adjunct. *Students:* 31 full-time (5 women), 20 part-time (7 women); includes 6 minority (3 Black or African American, non-Hispanic/Latino; 2 Asian, non-Hispanic/Latino; 1 Hispanic/Latino), 4 international. Average age 33. 46 applicants, 91% accepted, 23 enrolled. In 2014, 33 master's awarded. *Degree requirements:* For master's, one foreign language, thesis or exam. *Entrance requirements:* For master's, GRE, minimum GPA of 3.0, 3 letters of reference, curriculum vitae, reflective essay. Additional exam requirements/recommendations for international students: Required—TOEFL. *Application deadline:* For fall admission, 4/1 priority date for domestic and international students; for spring admission, 10/1 priority date for domestic and international students. Applications are processed on a rolling basis. Application fee: $55 ($65 for international students). Electronic applications accepted. *Financial support:* Scholarships/grants available. *Faculty research:* Globalization, environmental sociology, economic development, comparative government, international relations. *Unit head:* Johannes Feddema, Chair, 785-864-1120, E-mail: feddema@ku.edu. *Application contact:* Alyssa McDonald, Graduate Admissions Contact, 785-864-9814, E-mail: mcdonalda@ku.edu. Website: http://global.ku.edu/

University of Kentucky, Graduate School, Patterson School of Diplomacy and International Commerce, Lexington, KY 40506-0027. Offers MA. *Degree requirements:* For master's, one foreign language, comprehensive exam, statistics. *Entrance requirements:* For master's, GRE General Test, minimum undergraduate GPA of 3.0. Additional exam requirements/recommendations for international students: Required—TOEFL (minimum score 550 paper-based; 79 iBT). Electronic applications accepted. *Faculty research:* International relations, foreign and defense policy, cross-cultural negotiation, international science and technology, diplomacy, international economics and development, geopolitical modeling.

University of Maine, Graduate School, College of Liberal Arts and Sciences, School of Policy and International Affairs, Orono, ME 04469. Offers global policy (MA). *Faculty:* 1 (woman) full-time, 5 part-time/adjunct (1 woman). *Students:* 14 full-time (6 women), 2 part-time (1 woman), 4 international. Average age 27. 15 applicants, 73% accepted, 6 enrolled. In 2014, 13 master's awarded. *Entrance requirements:* For master's, GRE. Additional exam requirements/recommendations for international students: Required—TOEFL. *Application deadline:* Applications are processed on a rolling basis. Application fee: $65. Electronic applications accepted. *Expenses:* Tuition, state resident: part-time $658 per credit hour. Tuition, nonresident: part-time $1550 per credit hour. *Financial support:* In 2014–15, 3 students received support. Career-related internships or fieldwork, Federal Work-Study, scholarships/grants, and unspecified assistantships available. *Faculty research:* International environmental/climate change security, international political economy, political risk, foreign direct investment, developmental aid impact on extremism, developmental diplomacy. *Total annual research expenditures:* $10,000. *Unit head:* Capt. James Settele, Director, 207-581-3153, E-mail: james.settele@umit.maine.edu. *Application contact:* Scott G. Delcourt, Assistant Vice President for Graduate Studies and Senior Associate Dean, 207-581-3291, Fax: 207-581-3232, E-mail: graduate@maine.edu. Website: http://spia.umaine.edu/

The University of Manchester, School of Arts, Histories and Cultures, Manchester, United Kingdom. Offers anthropology, media and performance (PhD); applied theatre professional (PhD); archaeology (PhD); art history and visual studies (PhD); arts management and cultural policy (PhD); classics and ancient history (PhD); composition (PhD); creative writing (PhD); drama (PhD); economic and social history (PhD); electroacoustic composition (PhD); English and American studies (PhD); history (PhD); humanitarianism and conflict response (PhD); museology (PhD); music (PhD); musicology (PhD); religions and theology (PhD).

University of Massachusetts Boston, John W. McCormack Graduate School of Policy and Global Studies, Program in Global Governance and Human Security, Boston, MA 02125-3393. Offers MA. *Expenses:* Tuition, state resident: full-time $2590; part-time $108 per credit. Tuition, nonresident: full-time $9758; part-time $406.50 per credit. Tuition and fees vary according to course load and program. *Unit head:* Dr. Stephen Crosby, Dean, 617-287-5550, E-mail: stephen.crosby@umb.edu. *Application contact:* Peggy Roldan Patel, Graduate Admissions Coordinator, 617-287-6400, Fax: 617-287-6236, E-mail: bos.gadm@dpc.umassp.edu.

University of Miami, Graduate School, College of Arts and Sciences, Department of International Studies, Coral Gables, FL 33124. Offers MA, PhD. *Degree requirements:* For master's, one foreign language, comprehensive exam; for doctorate, one foreign language, comprehensive exam, thesis/dissertation. *Entrance requirements:* For master's, GRE General Test, minimum GPA of 3.0; for doctorate, GRE General Test. Additional exam requirements/recommendations for international students: Required—TOEFL. Electronic applications accepted. *Faculty research:* Latin American studies, international economics, international security and conflict, comparative development, international health policy.

University of Miami, Graduate School, Program in International Administration, Coral Gables, FL 33124. Offers MAIA. Part-time and evening/weekend programs available. *Degree requirements:* For master's, practicum. *Entrance requirements:* For master's, GRE General Test. Additional exam requirements/recommendations for international students: Required—TOEFL (minimum score 550 paper-based), IELTS (minimum score 6.5). Electronic applications accepted.

University of Michigan–Flint, College of Arts and Sciences, Program in Social Sciences, Flint, MI 48502-1950. Offers gender studies (MA); global studies (MA); U.S. history and politics (MA). Part-time programs available. *Faculty:* 14 full-time (8 women), 5 part-time/adjunct (3 women). *Students:* 1 (woman) full-time, 20 part-time (13 women); includes 8 minority (6 Black or African American, non-Hispanic/Latino; 1 Hispanic/Latino; 1 Two or more races, non-Hispanic/Latino). Average age 41. 8 applicants, 75% accepted, 3 enrolled. In 2014, 7 master's awarded. *Entrance requirements:* For master's, bachelor's degree from accredited institution, minimum overall GPA of 3.0. Additional exam requirements/recommendations for international students: Required—TOEFL (minimum score 84 iBT), IELTS (minimum score 6.5). *Application deadline:* For fall admission, 8/1 for domestic students, 5/1 for international students; for winter admission, 11/15 for domestic students, 9/1 for international students; for spring admission, 3/15 for domestic students, 1/1 for international students; for summer admission, 5/15 for domestic students. Applications are processed on a rolling basis. Application fee: $55. Electronic applications accepted. *Expenses:* Expenses: Contact institution. *Financial support:* Federal Work-Study, scholarships/grants, and unspecified assistantships available. Support available to part-time students. Financial award application deadline: 3/1; financial award applicants required to submit FAFSA. *Unit head:* Dr. Adam Lutzker, Interim Director, 810-762-3280, Fax: 810-762-3281, E-mail: alutzker@umflint.edu. *Application contact:* Bradley T. Maki, Director of Graduate

Admissions, 810-762-3171, Fax: 810-766-6789, E-mail: bmaki@umflint.edu. Website: http://www.umflint.edu/graduateprograms/social-sciences-ma

University of Northern British Columbia, Office of Graduate Studies, Prince George, BC V2N 4Z9, Canada. Offers business administration (Diploma); community health science (M Sc); disability management (MA); education (M Ed); first nations studies (MA); gender studies (MA); history (MA); interdisciplinary studies (MA); international studies (MA); mathematical, computer and physical sciences (M Sc); natural resources and environmental studies (M Sc, MA, MNRES, PhD); political science (MA); psychology (M Sc, PhD); social work (MSW). Part-time and evening/weekend programs available. Postbaccalaureate distance learning degree programs offered (no on-campus study). *Degree requirements:* For master's, thesis; for doctorate, thesis/dissertation. *Entrance requirements:* For master's, GRE, minimum B average in undergraduate course work; for doctorate, candidacy exam, minimum A average in graduate course work.

University of North Georgia, Department of Political Science and Criminal Justice, Dahlonega, GA 30597. Offers criminal justice (MS); international affairs (MAIA); public administration (MPA). Part-time and evening/weekend programs available. Postbaccalaureate distance learning degree programs offered (no on-campus study). *Degree requirements:* For master's, thesis optional, internship. *Entrance requirements:* For master's, GRE or GMAT, minimum undergraduate GPA of 2.5, 3 letters of recommendation. Additional exam requirements/recommendations for international students: Required—TOEFL (minimum score 550 paper-based; 79 iBT), IELTS (minimum score 6.5). Electronic applications accepted.

University of North Texas, Robert B. Toulouse School of Graduate Studies, Denton, TX 76203-5459. Offers accounting (MS); applied anthropology (MA, MS); applied behavior analysis (Certificate); applied geography (MA); applied technology and performance improvement (M Ed, MS); art education (MA); art history (MA); art museum education (Certificate); arts leadership (Certificate); audiology (Au D); behavior analysis (MS); behavioral science (PhD); biochemistry and molecular biology (MS); biology (MA, MS); biomedical engineering (MS); business analysis (MS); chemistry (MS); clinical health psychology (PhD); communication studies (MA, MS); computer engineering (MS); computer science (MS); counseling (M Ed, MS), including clinical mental health counseling (MS), college and university counseling, elementary school counseling, secondary school counseling; creative writing (MA); criminal justice (MS); curriculum and instruction (M Ed); decision sciences (MBA); design (MA, MFA), including fashion design (MFA), innovation studies, interior design (MFA); early childhood studies (MS); economics (MS); educational leadership (M Ed, Ed D); educational psychology (MS, PhD), including family studies (MS), gifted and talented (MS), human development (MS), learning and cognition (MS), research, measurement and evaluation (MS); electrical engineering (MS); emergency management (MPA); engineering technology (MS); English (MA); English as a second language (MA); environmental science (MS); finance (MBA, MS); financial management (MPA); French (MA); health services management (MBA); higher education (M Ed, Ed D); history (MA, MS); hospitality management (MS); human resources management (MPA); information science (MS); information systems (PhD); information technologies (MBA); interdisciplinary studies (MA, MS); international studies (MA); international sustainable tourism (MS); jazz studies (MM); journalism (MA, MJ, Graduate Certificate), including interactive and virtual digital communication (Graduate Certificate), narrative journalism (Graduate Certificate), public relations (Graduate Certificate); kinesiology (MS); linguistics (MA); local government management (MPA); logistics (PhD); logistics and supply chain management (MBA); long-term care, senior housing, and aging services (MA); management (PhD); marketing (MBA); mathematics (MA, MS); mechanical and energy engineering (MS, PhD); music (MA), including ethnomusicology, music theory, musicology, performance; music composition (PhD); music education (MM Ed, PhD); nonprofit management (MPA); operations and supply chain management (MBA); performance (MM, DMA); philosophy (MA); political science (MA); professional and technical communication (MA); radio, television and film (MA, MFA); rehabilitation counseling (Certificate); sociology (MA); Spanish (MA); special education (M Ed); speech-language pathology (MA); strategic management (MBA); studio art (MFA); teaching (M Ed); MBA/MS. Part-time and evening/weekend programs available. Postbaccalaureate distance learning degree programs offered. *Faculty:* 651 full-time (215 women), 233 part-time/adjunct (139 women). *Students:* 3,040 full-time (1,598 women), 3,401 part-time (2,097 women); includes 1,740 minority (533 Black or African American, non-Hispanic/Latino; 15 American Indian or Alaska Native, non-Hispanic/Latino; 286 Asian, non-Hispanic/Latino; 746 Hispanic/Latino; 3 Native Hawaiian or other Pacific Islander, non-Hispanic/Latino; 157 Two or more races, non-Hispanic/Latino), 1,145 international. Terminal master's awarded for partial completion of doctoral program. *Degree requirements:* For master's, variable foreign language requirement, comprehensive exam (for some programs), thesis (for some programs); for doctorate, variable foreign language requirement, comprehensive exam (for some programs), thesis/dissertation; for other advanced degree, variable foreign language requirement, comprehensive exam (for some programs). *Entrance requirements:* For master's and doctorate, GRE, GMAT. Additional exam requirements/recommendations for international students: Required—TOEFL (minimum score 550 paper-based; 79 iBT). *Application deadline:* For fall admission, 7/15 for domestic students, 3/15 for international students; for spring admission, 11/15 for domestic students, 9/15 for international students; for summer admission, 5/1 for domestic students. Applications are processed on a rolling basis. Application fee: $60. Electronic applications accepted. *Expenses:* Tuition, state resident: full-time $5450; part-time $3633 per year. Tuition, nonresident: full-time $11,966; part-time $7977 per year. *Required fees:* $1301; $398 per credit hour. $685 per semester. Tuition and fees vary according to program and reciprocity agreements. *Financial support:* Fellowships with partial tuition reimbursements, research assistantships with partial tuition reimbursements, teaching assistantships, career-related internships or fieldwork, Federal Work-Study, institutionally sponsored loans, scholarships/grants, health care benefits, and library assistantships available. Support available to part-time students. Financial award applicants required to submit FAFSA. *Unit head:* Mark Wardell, Dean, 940-565-2383, E-mail: mark.wardell@unt.edu. *Application contact:* Toulouse School of Graduate Studies, 940-565-2383, Fax: 940-565-2141, E-mail: gradsch@unt.edu. Website: http://tsgs.unt.edu/

University of Oklahoma, College of International Studies, Norman, OK 73019. Offers area studies (MAIS, Graduate Certificate), including global economics and development, global security studies (MAIS); global studies (MAIS, Graduate Certificate), including global economics and development, global security studies (MAIS). Part-time programs available. *Faculty:* 21 full-time (9 women), 1 (woman) part-time/adjunct. *Students:* 18 full-time (7 women), 5 part-time (4 women); includes 6 minority (1 American Indian or Alaska Native, non-Hispanic/Latino; 2 Hispanic/Latino; 3 Two or more races, non-Hispanic/Latino), 1 international. Average age 26. 29 applicants, 62% accepted, 11 enrolled. In 2014, 12 master's awarded. Terminal master's awarded for partial completion of doctoral program. *Degree requirements:* For master's, variable foreign language requirement, 36 credit hours; thesis, policy paper, or internship; for Graduate Certificate, 15 credit hours. *Entrance requirements:* For master's, GRE. Additional exam requirements/recommendations for international students: Required—TOEFL (minimum score 79 iBT). *Application deadline:* For fall admission, 2/15 for domestic and international students; for spring admission, 10/15 for domestic students, 9/1 for

international students. Application fee: $50 ($100 for international students). Electronic applications accepted. *Expenses:* Tuition, state resident: full-time $4394; part-time $183.10 per credit hour. Tuition, nonresident: full-time $16,970; part-time $707.10 per credit hour. *Required fees:* $2892; $109.95 per credit hour. $126.50 per semester. *Financial support:* In 2014–15, 17 students received support, including 1 fellowship with full tuition reimbursement available (averaging $6,000 per year), 4 research assistantships with partial tuition reimbursements available (averaging $13,500 per year), 6 teaching assistantships with partial tuition reimbursements available (averaging $13,447 per year); career-related internships or fieldwork, scholarships/grants, health care benefits, and unspecified assistantships also available. Financial award application deadline: 6/1; financial award applicants required to submit FAFSA. *Faculty research:* Area studies, including the Middle East, China, east and south Asia, Latin America, and Europe; political economy and development; international security; identity and nationalism; global history and culture. *Total annual research expenditures:* $6,369. *Unit head:* Dr. Mitchell Smith, Professor/Chair, 405-325-1584, Fax: 405-325-7738, E-mail: mps@ou.edu. *Application contact:* Katie Watkins, Academic Advisor, 405-325-2337, Fax: 405-325-7738, E-mail: mais@ou.edu.
Website: http://www.ou.edu/dias

University of Oregon, Graduate School, College of Arts and Sciences, Program in International Studies, Eugene, OR 97403. Offers MA. Part-time programs available. *Degree requirements:* For master's, one foreign language, thesis, internship. *Entrance requirements:* For master's, minimum GPA of 3.0. Additional exam requirements/recommendations for international students: Required—TOEFL. *Faculty research:* International development studies; environmental studies; cross-cultural communications; planning, public policy, and management; several world regions.

University of Pennsylvania, School of Arts and Sciences, Graduate Group in International Studies, Philadelphia, PA 19104. Offers AM. *Faculty:* 8 full-time (1 woman), 5 part-time/adjunct (1 woman). *Students:* 15 full-time (5 women), 1 part-time (0 women); includes 2 minority (1 Black or African American, non-Hispanic/Latino; 1 Two or more races, non-Hispanic/Latino), 8 international. In 2014, 60 master's awarded. Application fee: $70. *Unit head:* Dr. Ralph M. Rosen, Associate Dean for Graduate Studies, 215-898-7156, Fax: 215-573-8068, E-mail: grad-dean@sas.upenn.edu. *Application contact:* Arts and Sciences Graduate Admissions, 215-573-5816, Fax: 215-573-8068, E-mail: gdasadmis@sas.upenn.edu.
Website: http://www.sas.upenn.edu/graduate-division

University of Pittsburgh, Graduate School of Public and International Affairs, Doctoral Program in Public and International Affairs, Pittsburgh, PA 15260. Offers international affairs (PhD). *Accreditation:* NASPAA. *Faculty:* 34 full-time (12 women), 11 part-time/adjunct (3 women). *Students:* 32 full-time (15 women); includes 1 minority (Asian, non-Hispanic/Latino), 12 international. Average age 36. 72 applicants, 21% accepted, 7 enrolled. In 2014, 3 doctorates awarded. *Degree requirements:* For doctorate, comprehensive exam, thesis/dissertation, mid-term evaluation, preliminary exam, annual review. *Entrance requirements:* For doctorate, GRE or GMAT, 2 letters of recommendation, resume, undergraduate transcripts, personal statement, writing sample. Additional exam requirements/recommendations for international students: Required—TOEFL (minimum score 600 paper-based; 100 iBT); Recommended—IELTS (minimum score 7), TWE (minimum score 4). *Application deadline:* For fall admission, 1/15 for domestic and international students. Application fee: $50. Electronic applications accepted. *Expenses:* Tuition, state resident: full-time $20,742; part-time $838 per credit. Tuition, nonresident: full-time $33,960; part-time $1389 per credit. *Required fees:* $800; $205 per term. Tuition and fees vary according to program. *Financial support:* In 2014–15, 15 students received support, including 15 research assistantships (averaging $13,980 per year). Financial award application deadline: 1/15; financial award applicants required to submit FAFSA. *Faculty research:* International political economy, international development, public policy and management, international security. *Total annual research expenditures:* $640,844. *Unit head:* Dr. Nuno Themudo, Program Director, 412-648-7632, Fax: 412-648-7641, E-mail: themudo@pitt.edu. *Application contact:* Julie Korade, Doctoral Program Administrator/Graduate Enrollment Counselor, 412-648-7640, Fax: 412-648-7641, E-mail: korade@pitt.edu.
Website: http://www.gspia.pitt.edu/

University of Pittsburgh, Graduate School of Public and International Affairs, Master of Public Administration Program, Pittsburgh, PA 15260. Offers energy and environment (MPA); governance and international public management (MPA); policy research and analysis (MPA); public and nonprofit management (MPA); urban affairs and planning (MPA); JD/MPA; MPA/MID; MPA/MPIA; MPH/MPA; MSIS/MPA; MSW/MPA. Part-time and evening/weekend programs available. *Faculty:* 32 full-time (12 women), 13 part-time/adjunct (5 women). *Students:* 99 full-time (69 women), 15 part-time (10 women); includes 8 minority (5 Black or African American, non-Hispanic/Latino; 1 Asian, non-Hispanic/Latino; 1 Hispanic/Latino; 1 Two or more races, non-Hispanic/Latino), 52 international. Average age 26. 273 applicants, 70% accepted, 51 enrolled. In 2014, 50 master's awarded. *Degree requirements:* For master's, thesis optional, internship, capstone seminar. *Entrance requirements:* For master's, GRE General Test or GMAT, 2 letters of recommendation, resume; undergraduate transcripts, personal statement. Additional exam requirements/recommendations for international students: Required—TOEFL (minimum score 550 paper-based; 80 iBT); Recommended—IELTS (minimum score 7), TWE (minimum score 4). *Application deadline:* For fall admission, 2/1 for domestic students, 1/15 for international students; for spring admission, 11/1 for domestic students, 8/1 for international students. Application fee: $50. Electronic applications accepted. *Expenses:* Tuition, state resident: full-time $20,742; part-time $838 per credit. Tuition, nonresident: full-time $33,960; part-time $1389 per credit. *Required fees:* $800; $205 per term. Tuition and fees vary according to program. *Financial support:* In 2014–15, 17 students received support, including 3 fellowships (averaging $13,980 per year); scholarships/grants, unspecified assistantships, and student employment also available. Financial award application deadline: 2/1. *Faculty research:* Urban management, regional development, disaster response management, public program evaluation, comparative regional governance, nonprofit management, health policy, environmental policy, strategic management, human resources management. *Total annual research expenditures:* $640,844. *Unit head:* Dr. David Y. Miller, Director, 412-648-7606, Fax: 412-648-2605, E-mail: dymiller@pitt.edu. *Application contact:* Elizabeth A. Hruby, Graduate Enrollment Counselor, 412-648-7640, Fax: 412-648-7641, E-mail: eah44@pitt.edu.
Website: http://www.gspia.pitt.edu/

University of Pittsburgh, Graduate School of Public and International Affairs, Master of Public and International Affairs Program, Pittsburgh, PA 15260. Offers international political economy (MPIA); security and intelligence studies (MPIA); JD/MPIA; MBA/MPIA; MID/MPIA; MPA/MPIA; MPH/MPIA; MPIA/MSW; MSIS/MPIA. Part-time and evening/weekend programs available. *Faculty:* 34 full-time (12 women), 11 part-time/adjunct (3 women). *Students:* 145 full-time (63 women), 8 part-time (5 women); includes 18 minority (6 Black or African American, non-Hispanic/Latino; 3 Asian, non-Hispanic/Latino; 8 Hispanic/Latino; 1 Two or more races, non-Hispanic/Latino), 26 international. Average age 26. 251 applicants, 87% accepted, 64 enrolled. In 2014, 85 master's awarded. *Degree requirements:* For master's, thesis optional, internship, capstone seminar. *Entrance requirements:* For master's, GRE General Test or GMAT, 2 letters of recommendation, resume; undergraduate transcripts, personal statement. Additional exam requirements/recommendations for international students: Required—TOEFL (minimum score 550 paper-based; 80 iBT); Recommended—IELTS (minimum score 7), TWE (minimum score 4). *Application deadline:* For fall admission, 2/1 for domestic students, 1/15 for international students; for spring admission, 11/1 for domestic students, 8/1 for international students. Application fee: $50. Electronic applications accepted. *Expenses:* Tuition, state resident: full-time $20,742; part-time $838 per credit. Tuition, nonresident: full-time $33,960; part-time $1389 per credit. *Required fees:* $800; $205 per term. Tuition and fees vary according to program. *Financial support:* In 2014–15, 45 students received support, including 8 fellowships (averaging $15,000 per year); scholarships/grants, unspecified assistantships, and student employment also available. Financial award application deadline: 2/1. *Faculty research:* International political economy, international security and intelligence, transnational organized crime, international trade, international finance, globalization, terrorism, multinational corporations and the global economy, human rights, human trafficking, gender and development, diplomacy. *Total annual research expenditures:* $640,844. *Unit head:* Dr. Michael Kenney, Director, International Affairs and International Development Divisions, 412-648-7921, Fax: 412-648-2605, E-mail: mkenney@pitt.edu. *Application contact:* Kelly C. McDevitt, Graduate Enrollment Counselor, 412-648-7640, Fax: 412-648-7641, E-mail: mcdevitt@pitt.edu.
Website: http://www.gspia.pitt.edu/

University of Pittsburgh, Katz Graduate School of Business, MBA/Master of Public and International Affairs Joint Degree Program, Pittsburgh, PA 15260. Offers MBA/MPIA. *Accreditation:* AACSB. Part-time and evening/weekend programs available. *Faculty:* 53 full-time (12 women), 31 part-time/adjunct (9 women). *Students:* 2 full-time (both women); includes 1 minority (Asian, non-Hispanic/Latino). Average age 29. 2 applicants. *Entrance requirements:* Additional exam requirements/recommendations for international students: Required—TOEFL or IELTS. *Application deadline:* For fall admission, 4/1 priority date for domestic students, 2/1 priority date for international students. Application fee: $50. Electronic applications accepted. *Expenses:* Tuition, state resident: full-time $20,742; part-time $838 per credit. Tuition, nonresident: full-time $33,960; part-time $1389 per credit. *Required fees:* $800; $205 per term. Tuition and fees vary according to program. *Financial support:* Scholarships/grants available. Financial award application deadline: 6/1; financial award applicants required to submit FAFSA. *Faculty research:* Accounting systems/financial reporting, corporate finance, shopper marketing/consumer behavior, management information systems, organizational behavior and entrepreneurship. *Unit head:* William Valenta, Jr., Assistant Dean, MBA and Executive Programs, 412-648-1694, Fax: 412-648-1659, E-mail: valenta@pitt.edu. *Application contact:* Thomas Keller, Director of MBA Admissions, 412-648-1700, Fax: 412-648-1659, E-mail: mba@katz.pitt.edu.
Website: http://www.business.pitt.edu/katz/mba/academics/programs/mba-mpia.php

University of Pittsburgh, University Center for International Studies, Pittsburgh, PA 15260. Offers African studies (Certificate); Asian studies (Certificate); European Union studies (Certificate); global studies (Certificate); Latin American studies (Certificate); Russian and East European studies (Certificate); West European studies (Certificate). *Students:* 223 full-time (98 women), 11 part-time (1 woman); includes 97 minority (2 Black or African American, non-Hispanic/Latino; 41 Asian, non-Hispanic/Latino; 52 Hispanic/Latino; 2 Two or more races, non-Hispanic/Latino). Average age 31. In 2014, 72 Certificates awarded. *Degree requirements:* For Certificate, one foreign language, study abroad. *Application deadline:* Applications are processed on a rolling basis. *Expenses:* Tuition, state resident: full-time $20,742; part-time $838 per credit. Tuition, nonresident: full-time $33,960; part-time $1389 per credit. *Required fees:* $800; $205 per term. Tuition and fees vary according to program. *Unit head:* Dr. Ariel Armony, Director, 412-648-7374, Fax: 412-624-4672, E-mail: armony@pitt.edu. *Application contact:* Information Contact, 412-624-4141, E-mail: graduate@pitt.edu.
Website: http://www.ucis.pitt.edu

University of Rhode Island, Graduate School, College of Arts and Sciences, Department of Political Science, Kingston, RI 02881. Offers political science (MA), including American politics, comparative government, international relations, public policy; public policy and administration (MPA); MLIS/MPA. Part-time programs available. *Faculty:* 11 full-time (4 women). *Students:* 20 full-time (11 women), 28 part-time (21 women); includes 9 minority (4 Black or African American, non-Hispanic/Latino; 3 Asian, non-Hispanic/Latino; 2 Hispanic/Latino), 2 international. In 2014, 20 master's awarded. *Degree requirements:* For master's, comprehensive exam (for some programs), thesis optional. *Entrance requirements:* For master's, GRE, GMAT or MAT, 2 letters of recommendation. Additional exam requirements/recommendations for international students: Required—TOEFL (minimum score 550 paper-based). *Application deadline:* For fall admission, 2/1 for international students; for spring admission, 7/15 for international students. Application fee: $65. Electronic applications accepted. *Expenses:* Tuition, state resident: full-time $11,532; part-time $641 per credit. Tuition, nonresident: full-time $23,606; part-time $1311 per credit. *Required fees:* $1442; $39 per credit. $35 per semester. One-time fee: $155. *Financial support:* In 2014–15, 3 teaching assistantships with full and partial tuition reimbursements (averaging $12,675 per year) were awarded. Financial award application deadline: 7/15; financial award applicants required to submit FAFSA. *Unit head:* Dr. Brian Krueger, Department Chair, 401-874-4058, Fax: 401-874-4072, E-mail: bkrueger@uri.edu. *Application contact:* Dr. Robert Weygand, Director, 401-874-2124, Fax: 401-874-4072, E-mail: bobw@uri.edu.
Website: http://www.uri.edu/artsci/psc/

University of Rochester, School of Arts and Sciences, Department of History, Rochester, NY 14627. Offers American history (MA, PhD); European history (MA, PhD); global history (MA, PhD). *Faculty:* 18 full-time (4 women). *Students:* 30 full-time (8 women); includes 4 minority (1 Asian, non-Hispanic/Latino; 1 Hispanic/Latino; 2 Two or more races, non-Hispanic/Latino), 1 international. 32 applicants, 41% accepted, 7 enrolled. In 2014, 5 master's, 7 doctorates awarded. Terminal master's awarded for partial completion of doctoral program. *Degree requirements:* For master's, one foreign language, thesis or alternative; for doctorate, 2 foreign languages, thesis/dissertation, comprehensive oral exam, qualifying exam. *Entrance requirements:* For master's and doctorate, GRE General Test, sample of written work. Additional exam requirements/recommendations for international students: Required—TOEFL. *Application deadline:* For fall admission, 1/15 priority date for domestic students. Application fee: $60. Electronic applications accepted. *Expenses: Tuition:* Full-time $46,150; part-time $1442 per credit hour. *Required fees:* $504. *Financial support:* Fellowships, research assistantships, teaching assistantships, and tuition waivers (full and partial) available. Financial award application deadline: 1/15. *Unit head:* Matthew Lenoe, Chair, 585-275-9355. *Application contact:* Caleb Rood, Secretary, 585-275-2053.
Website: http://www.rochester.edu/College/HIS/

University of San Diego, College of Arts and Sciences, Program in International Relations, San Diego, CA 92110-2492. Offers MA, JD/MA. Part-time and evening/weekend programs available. *Faculty:* 5 full-time (2 women), 1 part-time/adjunct (0 women). *Students:* 13 full-time (4 women), 19 part-time (7 women); includes 9 minority (1 Black or African American, non-Hispanic/Latino; 2 Asian, non-Hispanic/Latino; 6 Hispanic/Latino). Average age 30. 48 applicants, 63% accepted, 12 enrolled. In 2014, 17 master's awarded. *Degree requirements:* For master's, comprehensive exam.

Entrance requirements: For master's, GRE General Test (minimum scores: 153 verbal/144 quantitative/4.5 analytical writing), minimum GPA of 3.2, 24 units in political science, history and/or economics. Additional exam requirements/recommendations for international students: Required—TOEFL (minimum score 580 paper-based; 83 iBT), TWE. *Application deadline:* For fall admission, 7/1 for domestic and international students; for spring admission, 12/1 for domestic and international students. Applications are processed on a rolling basis. Application fee: $45. Electronic applications accepted. *Financial support:* In 2014–15, 27 students received support. Federal Work-Study, institutionally sponsored loans, and unspecified assistantships available. Support available to part-time students. Financial award application deadline: 4/1; financial award applicants required to submit FAFSA. *Faculty research:* Comparative politics, international relations, international security, politics of intelligence, transnational crime. *Unit head:* Dr. Randy Willoughby, Graduate Program Director, 619-260-4014, Fax: 619-260-6840, E-mail: rwilloug@sandiego.edu. *Application contact:* Monica Mahon, Associate Director of Graduate Admissions, 619-260-4524, Fax: 619-260-4158, E-mail: grads@sandiego.edu.
Website: http://www.sandiego.edu/cas/mair/

University of San Francisco, College of Arts and Sciences, International Studies Program, San Francisco, CA 94117-1080. Offers MA. *Faculty:* 4 full-time (3 women), 3 part-time/adjunct (2 women). *Students:* 48 full-time (33 women), 37 part-time (24 women); includes 34 minority (7 Black or African American, non-Hispanic/Latino; 5 Asian, non-Hispanic/Latino; 17 Hispanic/Latino; 5 Two or more races, non-Hispanic/Latino), 17 international. Average age 27. 165 applicants, 79% accepted, 47 enrolled. In 2014, 28 master's awarded. *Application deadline:* For fall admission, 2/15 for domestic students. *Expenses: Tuition:* Full-time $21,762; part-time $1209 per credit hour. Tuition and fees vary according to degree level, campus/location and program. *Financial support:* In 2014–15, 14 students received support. *Unit head:* Lindsay Arentz, Administrative Director, 415-422-5122. *Application contact:* Mark Landerghini, Information Contact, 415-422-5101, Fax: 415-422-2217, E-mail: asgraduate@usfca.edu.
Website: http://www.usfca.edu/artsci/mais/

University of South Carolina, The Graduate School, College of Arts and Sciences, Department of Political Science, Program in International Studies, Columbia, SC 29208. Offers MA, PhD. Part-time programs available. Terminal master's awarded for partial completion of doctoral program. *Degree requirements:* For master's, one foreign language, thesis or alternative; for doctorate, one foreign language, comprehensive exam, thesis/dissertation. *Entrance requirements:* For master's, GRE General Test, minimum GPA of 3.3; for doctorate, GRE General Test, minimum GPA of 3.5. Additional exam requirements/recommendations for international students: Required—TOEFL. Electronic applications accepted. *Faculty research:* International relations, international organization, foreign policy, comparative politics.

University of Southern California, Graduate School, Annenberg School for Communication and Journalism, School of Communication, Program in Public Diplomacy, Los Angeles, CA 90089. Offers MPD. Part-time programs available. *Students:* 41 full-time (0 women), 3 part-time (0 women); includes 12 minority (3 Black or African American, non-Hispanic/Latino; 4 Asian, non-Hispanic/Latino; 5 Hispanic/Latino), 12 international. Average age 26. 60 applicants, 75% accepted, 18 enrolled. In 2014, 26 master's awarded. *Degree requirements:* For master's, thesis. *Entrance requirements:* For master's, GRE, resume, writing samples, statement of purpose, recommendation letters. Additional exam requirements/recommendations for international students: Required—TOEFL (minimum score 114 iBT) or IELTS (minimum score 8). *Application deadline:* For fall admission, 1/15 priority date for domestic and international students. Application fee: $85. Electronic applications accepted. *Financial support:* In 2014–15, 4 fellowships with partial tuition reimbursements (averaging $39,000 per year) were awarded; career-related internships or fieldwork, Federal Work-Study, and scholarships/grants also available. Support available to part-time students. Financial award application deadline: 1/15; financial award applicants required to submit FAFSA. *Unit head:* Dr. Nicholas Cull, Director, 213-821-4080, E-mail: cull@usc.edu. *Application contact:* Allyson Hill, Associate Dean for Admissions, 213-821-0770, Fax: 213-740-1933, E-mail: ascadm@usc.edu.
Website: http://www.annenberg.usc.edu/

University of Southern California, Graduate School, Dana and David Dornsife College of Letters, Arts and Sciences, Political Science and International Relations PhD Program, Los Angeles, CA 90089. Offers PhD. *Degree requirements:* For doctorate, variable foreign language requirement, comprehensive exam, thesis/dissertation. *Entrance requirements:* For doctorate, GRE (minimum score 1000). Additional exam requirements/recommendations for international students: Required—TOEFL (minimum score 600 paper-based; 100 iBT). Electronic applications accepted. *Faculty research:* American politics, foreign policy analysis, international political economy, race/ethics politics, security studies.

University of Southern California, Graduate School, School of Policy, Planning, and Development, Master of International Public Policy and Management Program, Los Angeles, CA 90089. Offers MPPM. Part-time programs available. *Entrance requirements:* Additional exam requirements/recommendations for international students: Required—TOEFL (minimum score 71 iBT). Electronic applications accepted. *Expenses:* Contact institution. *Faculty research:* International development, economic development, social policy problems, issues of developing countries, international and comparative.

University of Southern Mississippi, Graduate School, College of Arts and Letters, Department of Political Science, International Development, and International Affairs, Hattiesburg, MS 39406-0001. Offers international development (PhD); political science (MA, MS). Part-time and evening/weekend programs available. Postbaccalaureate distance learning degree programs offered. *Degree requirements:* For master's, comprehensive exam, thesis (for some programs); for doctorate, comprehensive exam, thesis/dissertation. *Entrance requirements:* For master's, GRE General Test, minimum GPA of 2.75 in last 2 years, 3.0 in field of study; for doctorate, GRE General Test, minimum GPA of 3.5. Additional exam requirements/recommendations for international students: Required—TOEFL, IELTS. *Faculty research:* American politics, international politics, political theory, comparative politics, public law.

University of South Florida, College of Arts and Sciences, Department of Government and International Affairs, Tampa, FL 33620-9951. Offers government (PhD); Latin American, Caribbean and Latino studies (MA); political science (MA), including comparative government and politics, international relations, public policy. Part-time and evening/weekend programs available. *Faculty:* 10 full-time (1 woman). *Students:* 56 full-time (29 women), 47 part-time (23 women); includes 18 minority (6 Black or African American, non-Hispanic/Latino; 1 Asian, non-Hispanic/Latino; 9 Hispanic/Latino; 2 Two or more races, non-Hispanic/Latino), 9 international. Average age 33. 73 applicants, 51% accepted, 25 enrolled. In 2014, 45 master's, 2 doctorates awarded. *Degree requirements:* For master's, comprehensive exam, thesis; for doctorate, comprehensive exam, thesis/dissertation. *Entrance requirements:* For master's, GRE General Test, minimum GPA of 3.0 in upper-division undergraduate course work; letters of recommendation (2 for MPA, 3 for MPS); 500-word personal statement and undergraduate background in political science or related fields (for MPS); one-page career statement (for MPA); for doctorate, GRE General Test, 500-word personal statement, three letters of recommendation, transcripts of MA/BA coursework, writing sample. Additional exam requirements/recommendations for international students: Required—TOEFL (minimum score 550 paper-based; 79 iBT) or IELTS (minimum score 6.5). *Application deadline:* For fall admission, 2/15 for domestic students, 1/2 for international students; for spring admission, 10/15 for domestic students, 6/1 for international students. Applications are processed on a rolling basis. Application fee: $30. Electronic applications accepted. *Financial support:* In 2014–15, 18 students received support, including 18 teaching assistantships with tuition reimbursements available (averaging $12,390 per year); unspecified assistantships also available. Financial award application deadline: 4/1. *Faculty research:* Citizenship and identity, social movements, global governance, American politics, public policy. *Unit head:* Dr. Steven Tauber, Associate Professor and Interim Chair, 813-974-2278, Fax: 813-974-0832, E-mail: stauber@usf.edu. *Application contact:* Dr. Bernd Reiter, Associate Professor and Director of Graduate Studies, 813-974-3583, Fax: 813-974-0832, E-mail: breiter@usf.edu.
Website: http://gia.usf.edu/

University of South Florida, Innovative Education, Tampa, FL 33620-9951. *Unit head:* Kathy Barnes, Interdisciplinary Programs Coordinator, 813-974-8031, Fax: 813-974-7061, E-mail: barnesk@usf.edu. *Application contact:* Karen Tylinski, Metro Initiatives, 813-974-9943, Fax: 813-974-7061, E-mail: ktylinsk@usf.edu.
Website: http://www.usf.edu/innovative-education/

University of the Pacific, McGeorge School of Law, Sacramento, CA 95817. Offers advocacy (JD); international water resources law (JSD); public policy and law (LL M); JD/MBA; JD/MPPA. *Accreditation:* ABA. Part-time and evening/weekend programs available. *Students:* 430 full-time (232 women), 169 part-time (84 women); includes 203 minority (19 Black or African American, non-Hispanic/Latino; 7 American Indian or Alaska Native, non-Hispanic/Latino; 93 Asian, non-Hispanic/Latino; 83 Hispanic/Latino; 1 Two or more races, non-Hispanic/Latino), 24 international. Average age 28. 1,144 applicants, 72% accepted, 156 enrolled. In 2014, 11 master's, 187 doctorates awarded. *Degree requirements:* For master's, thesis (for some programs); for doctorate, thesis/dissertation (for some programs). *Entrance requirements:* For master's, JD; for doctorate, LSAT (for JD), LL M (for JSD). Additional exam requirements/recommendations for international students: Required—TOEFL (minimum score 600 paper-based; 100 iBT). *Application deadline:* For fall admission, 3/15 priority date for domestic students. Applications are processed on a rolling basis. Application fee: $50. Electronic applications accepted. *Expenses:* Expenses: Contact institution. *Financial support:* Fellowships, research assistantships, teaching assistantships, career-related internships or fieldwork, Federal Work-Study, institutionally sponsored loans, and scholarships/grants available. Support available to part-time students. Financial award applicants required to submit FAFSA. *Faculty research:* International legal studies, public policy and law, advocacy, intellectual property law, taxation, criminal law. *Unit head:* Francis Jay Mootz, III, Dean, 916-739-7151, E-mail: jmootz@pacific.edu. *Application contact:* 916-739-7105, Fax: 916-739-7301, E-mail: mcgeorge@pacific.edu.
Website: http://www.mcgeorge.edu/

University of Toronto, School of Graduate Studies, Munk School of Global Affairs, Toronto, ON M5S 2J7, Canada. Offers European, Russian and Eurasian studies (MA); global affairs (MGA); JD/MA. *Entrance requirements:* For master's, GRE General Test, GMAT, or LSAT, Honours (4-year) BA or equivalent, minimum cumulative and final year GPA of 3.5. Additional exam requirements/recommendations for international students: Required—TOEFL (minimum score 100 iBT), TWE (minimum score 5). Electronic applications accepted.

University of Utah, Graduate School, College of Social and Behavioral Science, Department of Political Science, Program in Political Science, Salt Lake City, UT 84112. Offers American politics (MA, MS, PhD); comparative politics (MA, MS, PhD); international relations (MA, MS, PhD); political theory (MA, MS, PhD); public administration (MA, MS, PhD). *Faculty:* 32 full-time (7 women), 10 part-time/adjunct (3 women). *Students:* 67 full-time (25 women); includes 11 minority (1 Black or African American, non-Hispanic/Latino; 1 American Indian or Alaska Native, non-Hispanic/Latino; 4 Asian, non-Hispanic/Latino; 5 Two or more races, non-Hispanic/Latino), 9 international. Average age 34. 35 applicants, 71% accepted, 12 enrolled. In 2014, 6 master's, 6 doctorates awarded. Terminal master's awarded for partial completion of doctoral program. *Degree requirements:* For master's, variable foreign language requirement, thesis or research paper; for doctorate, comprehensive exam, thesis/dissertation. *Entrance requirements:* For master's and doctorate, GRE General Test, minimum GPA of 3.2. Additional exam requirements/recommendations for international students: Required—TOEFL (minimum score 580 paper-based; 61 iBT), IELTS (minimum score 6). *Application deadline:* For fall admission, 1/15 priority date for domestic and international students; for spring admission, 10/1 for domestic and international students. Application fee: $55 ($65 for international students). Electronic applications accepted. *Financial support:* In 2014–15, 4 students received support, including 2 fellowships with full tuition reimbursements available (averaging $15,250 per year), 14 teaching assistantships with full tuition reimbursements available (averaging $13,750 per year); career-related internships or fieldwork, scholarships/grants, health care benefits, and unspecified assistantships also available. Financial award application deadline: 1/15; financial award applicants required to submit FAFSA. *Faculty research:* International politics, comparative politics, political theory, American politics, public administration. *Total annual research expenditures:* $24,651. *Unit head:* Brent Steele, Chair, 801-587-7754, Fax: 801-585-6492, E-mail: brent.steele@utah.edu. *Application contact:* Mary Ann Underwood, Graduate Coordinator/Advisor, 801-581-8608, Fax: 801-585-6492, E-mail: maryann.underwood@poli-sci.utah.edu.
Website: http://www.poli-sci.utah.edu/

University of Utah, Graduate School, College of Social and Behavioral Science, Master of Science in International Affairs and Global Enterprise Program, Salt Lake City, UT 84112. Offers MS. Part-time programs available. *Students:* 15 full-time (8 women), 15 part-time (5 women); includes 7 minority (1 Black or African American, non-Hispanic/Latino; 5 Asian, non-Hispanic/Latino; 1 Hispanic/Latino), 6 international. Average age 30. 15 applicants, 80% accepted, 5 enrolled. In 2014, 15 master's awarded. *Degree requirements:* For master's, one foreign language, comprehensive exam, thesis optional, major research paper. *Entrance requirements:* For master's, GMAT, LSAT, or GRE, undergraduate coursework in statistics, microeconomics theory and macroeconomics theory. Additional exam requirements/recommendations for international students: Required—TOEFL (minimum score 600 paper-based; 100 iBT). *Application deadline:* For fall admission, 2/1 for domestic and international students; for spring admission, 9/1 for domestic and international students; for summer admission, 1/15 for domestic and international students. Application fee: $55 ($65 for international students). Electronic applications accepted. *Expenses:* Expenses: Contact institution. *Financial support:* In 2014–15, 2 students received support. Scholarships/grants and unspecified assistantships available. *Faculty research:* East Asian economies. *Unit head:* Dr. Stephen Reynolds, Director, 801-581-8620, Fax: 801-585-5081, E-mail: stephen.reynolds@csbs.utah.edu. *Application contact:* Elizabeth Henke, Program Manager, 801-585-7722, Fax: 801-587-7861, E-mail: elizabeth.henke@cppa.utah.edu.
Website: http://www.miage.utah.edu

International Affairs

University of Virginia, College and Graduate School of Arts and Sciences, Department of Politics, Program in Foreign Affairs, Charlottesville, VA 22903. Offers MA, PhD. *Students:* 33 full-time (15 women), 1 (woman) part-time; includes 4 minority (2 Asian, non-Hispanic/Latino; 1 Hispanic/Latino; 1 Two or more races, non-Hispanic/Latino), 10 international. Average age 30. 142 applicants, 17% accepted, 9 enrolled. In 2014, 5 master's, 5 doctorates awarded. *Degree requirements:* For master's, one foreign language, 2 research/statistics courses or thesis; for doctorate, variable foreign language requirement, thesis/dissertation, 2 research/statistics courses. *Entrance requirements:* For master's and doctorate, GRE General Test, long writing sample; 2 letters of recommendation. Additional exam requirements/recommendations for international students: Required—TOEFL (minimum score 600 paper-based; 90 iBT), IELTS (minimum score 7). *Application deadline:* For fall admission, 12/4 for domestic and international students. Applications are processed on a rolling basis. Application fee: $60. Electronic applications accepted. *Expenses:* Tuition, state resident: full-time $14,164; part-time $349 per credit hour. Tuition, nonresident: full-time $23,722; part-time $1300 per credit hour. *Required fees:* $2514. *Financial support:* Fellowships and teaching assistantships available. Financial award application deadline: 12/4; financial award applicants required to submit FAFSA. *Unit head:* David Leblang, Chair, 434-924-3192, Fax: 434-924-3359, E-mail: dal7w@virginia.edu. *Application contact:* Jeffery A. Jenkins, Director of Graduate Studies, 434-924-3192, Fax: 434-924-3359, E-mail: jaj7d@virginia.edu.
Website: http://politics.virginia.edu/

University of Washington, Graduate School, College of Arts and Sciences, Henry M. Jackson School of International Studies, International Studies PhD Program, Seattle, WA 98195. Offers PhD. *Degree requirements:* For doctorate, variable foreign language requirement, comprehensive exam, thesis/dissertation, research tutorial with capstone presentation; dissertation prospectus defense; final examination. *Entrance requirements:* For doctorate, GRE General Test, master's degree. Additional exam requirements/recommendations for international students: Required—TOEFL (minimum score 500 paper-based; 92 iBT), IELTS (minimum score 7).

University of Waterloo, Graduate Studies, Faculty of Arts, Department of Political Science, Global Governance Program, Waterloo, ON N2L 3G1, Canada. Offers MA, PhD. *Entrance requirements:* For doctorate, MA. Additional exam requirements/recommendations for international students: Required—TOEFL. Electronic applications accepted. *Faculty research:* Global political economy, global environment, peace and security, global justice and human rights, multilateral institutions and diplomacy.

University of Wyoming, College of Arts and Sciences, Program in International Studies, Laramie, WY 82071. Offers international peace corps (MA); international studies (MA). Part-time programs available. *Degree requirements:* For master's, one foreign language, thesis. *Entrance requirements:* For master's, GRE General Test, minimum GPA of 3.0. Additional exam requirements/recommendations for international students: Required—TOEFL (minimum score 525 paper-based). Electronic applications accepted. *Faculty research:* International political economy, comparative social institutions, foreign policy, economic development.

Virginia Polytechnic Institute and State University, Graduate School, College of Architecture and Urban Studies, Blacksburg, VA 24061. Offers architecture (MS Arch); architecture and design research (PhD); building/construction science and management (MS); creative technologies (MFA); environmental design and planning (PhD); landscape architecture (MLA); planning, governance, and globalization (PhD); public administration (MPA); public administration/public affairs (PhD, Certificate); public and international affairs (MPIA); urban and regional planning (MURP); MS/MA. *Accreditation:* ASLA (one or more programs are accredited). *Faculty:* 133 full-time (54 women), 2 part-time/adjunct (1 woman). *Students:* 316 full-time (166 women), 237 part-time (108 women); includes 104 minority (46 Black or African American, non-Hispanic/Latino; 1 American Indian or Alaska Native, non-Hispanic/Latino; 20 Asian, non-Hispanic/Latino; 21 Hispanic/Latino; 16 Two or more races, non-Hispanic/Latino), 108 international. Average age 32. 609 applicants, 50% accepted, 108 enrolled. In 2014, 155 master's, 29 doctorates awarded. *Degree requirements:* For master's, comprehensive exam (for some programs), thesis (for some programs); for doctorate, comprehensive exam (for some programs), thesis/dissertation (for some programs). *Entrance requirements:* For master's and doctorate, GRE/GMAT (may vary by department). Additional exam requirements/recommendations for international students: Required—TOEFL (minimum score 550 paper-based). *Application deadline:* For fall admission, 8/1 for domestic students, 4/1 for international students; for spring admission, 1/1 for domestic students, 9/1 for international students. Applications are processed on a rolling basis. Application fee: $75. Electronic applications accepted. *Expenses:* Tuition, state resident: full-time $11,656; part-time $647.50 per credit hour. Tuition, nonresident: full-time $23,351; part-time $1297.25 per credit hour. *Required fees:* $2533; $465.75 per semester. Tuition and fees vary according to course load, campus/location and program. *Financial support:* In 2014–15, 13 research assistantships with full tuition reimbursements (averaging $20,302 per year), 44 teaching assistantships with full tuition reimbursements (averaging $19,484 per year) were awarded. Financial award application deadline: 3/1; financial award applicants required to submit FAFSA. *Total annual research expenditures:* $3.2 million. *Unit head:* Dr. A. J. Davis, Dean, 540-231-6416, Fax: 540-231-6332, E-mail: davisa@vt.edu. *Application contact:* Christine Mattsson-Coon, Executive Assistant, 540-231-6416, Fax: 540-231-6332, E-mail: cmattsso@vt.edu.
Website: http://www.caus.vt.edu/

Walden University, Graduate Programs, School of Public Policy and Administration, Minneapolis, MN 55401. Offers criminal justice (MPA, MPP, MS, Graduate Certificate), including emergency management (MS, PhD), general program (MS, PhD), homeland security and policy coordination (MS, PhD), law and public policy (MS, PhD), policy analysis (MS, PhD), public management and leadership (MS, PhD), self-designed (MS), terrorism, mediation, and peace (MS, PhD); criminal justice leadership and executive management (MS), including emergency management (MS, PhD), general program (MS, PhD), homeland security and policy coordination (MS, PhD), law and public policy (MS, PhD), policy analysis (MS, PhD), public management and leadership (MS, PhD), self-designed, terrorism, mediation, and peace (MS, PhD); emergency management (MPA, MPP, MS), including criminal justice (MS, PhD), general program (MS, PhD), homeland security (MS), public management and leadership (MS, PhD), terrorism and emergency management (MS); general program (MPA, MPP); government management (Graduate Certificate); health policy (MPA, MPP); homeland security (Graduate Certificate); homeland security and policy coordination (MPA, MPP); international nongovernmental organizations (MPA, MPP); law and public policy (MPA, MPP); local government management for sustainable communities (MPA, MPP); nonprofit management (Graduate Certificate); nonprofit management and leadership (MPA, MPP, MS); online teaching in higher education (Post-Master's Certificate); policy analysis (MPA); public management and leadership (MPA, MPP, Graduate Certificate); public policy (Graduate Certificate); public policy and administration (PhD), including criminal justice (MS, PhD), emergency management (MS, PhD), general program (MS, PhD), health policy, homeland security and policy coordination (MS, PhD), international nongovernmental organizations, law and public policy (MS, PhD), local government management for sustainable communities, nonprofit management and leadership, policy analysis (MS, PhD), public management and leadership (MS, PhD), terrorism, mediation, and peace (MS, PhD); strategic planning and public policy (Graduate Certificate); terrorism, mediation, and peace (MPA, MPP). Part-time and evening/weekend programs available. Postbaccalaureate distance learning degree programs offered (no on-campus study). *Faculty:* 13 full-time (5 women), 151 part-time/adjunct (65 women). *Students:* 1,009 full-time (573 women), 1,632 part-time (954 women); includes 1,553 minority (1,307 Black or African American, non-Hispanic/Latino; 15 American Indian or Alaska Native, non-Hispanic/Latino; 38 Asian, non-Hispanic/Latino; 127 Hispanic/Latino; 66 Two or more races, non-Hispanic/Latino), 15 international. Average age 42. 665 applicants, 97% accepted, 616 enrolled. In 2014, 317 master's, 95 doctorates, 34 other advanced degrees awarded. *Degree requirements:* For doctorate, thesis/dissertation, residency. *Entrance requirements:* For master's, bachelor's degree or higher; minimum GPA of 2.5; official transcripts; goal statement (for some programs); access to computer and Internet; for doctorate, master's degree or higher; three years of related professional or academic experience (preferred); minimum GPA of 3.0; goal statement and current resume (for select programs); official transcripts; access to computer and Internet; for other advanced degree, relevant work experience; access to computer and Internet. Additional exam requirements/recommendations for international students: Required—TOEFL (minimum score 550 paper-based, 79 iBT), IELTS (minimum score 6.5), Michigan English Language Assessment Battery (minimum score 82), or PTE (minimum score 53). *Application deadline:* Applications are processed on a rolling basis. Application fee: $0. Electronic applications accepted. *Expenses: Tuition:* Full-time $11,925; part-time $500 per credit hour. *Required fees:* $647. *Financial support:* Fellowships, Federal Work-Study, scholarships/grants, unspecified assistantships, and family tuition reduction, active duty/veteran tuition reduction, group tuition reduction, interest-free payment plans, employee tuition reduction available. Support available to part-time students. Financial award applicants required to submit FAFSA. *Unit head:* Dr. Shana Garrett, Associate Dean, 866-492-5336. *Application contact:* Meghan Thomas, Vice President of Enrollment Management, 866-492-5336, E-mail: info@waldenu.edu.
Website: http://www.waldenu.edu/programs/colleges-schools/public-policy-and-administration

Webster University, College of Arts and Sciences, Department of History, Politics and International Relations, Program in International Relations, St. Louis, MO 63119-3194. Offers global international relations (MA); international relations (MA). Part-time and evening/weekend programs available. *Degree requirements:* For master's, thesis optional. *Faculty research:* International organizations, international political economy, politics of development, environmental law, Latin American law.

Webster University, George Herbert Walker School of Business and Technology, Department of Business, St. Louis, MO 63119-3194. Offers business and organizational security management (MBA); decision support systems (MBA); environmental management (MBA); finance (MBA, MS); forensic accounting (MS); gerontology (MBA); human resources development (MBA); human resources management (MBA); information technology management (MBA); international business (MA, MBA); international relations (MBA); management and leadership (MBA); marketing (MBA); media communications (MBA); procurement and acquisitions management (MBA); Web services (MBA). *Accreditation:* ACBSP. Part-time and evening/weekend programs available. Postbaccalaureate distance learning degree programs offered (no on-campus study). *Degree requirements:* For master's, comprehensive exam (for some programs), thesis (for some programs). *Entrance requirements:* Additional exam requirements/recommendations for international students: Required—TOEFL.

Western Michigan University, Graduate College, College of Arts and Sciences, Department of Political Science, Kalamazoo, MI 49008. Offers international development administration (MIDA), including Peace Corps; political science (MA, PhD). *Degree requirements:* For master's, thesis optional; for doctorate, thesis/dissertation. *Application deadline:* For fall admission, 2/15 for domestic students. *Financial support:* Application deadline: 2/15; applicants required to submit FAFSA. *Application contact:* Admissions and Orientation, 269-387-2000, Fax: 269-387-2096.

West Virginia University, Eberly College of Arts and Sciences, Department of Political Science, Morgantown, WV 26506. Offers American public policy and politics (MA); international and comparative public policy and politics (MA); political science (PhD); public policy analysis (PhD). Terminal master's awarded for partial completion of doctoral program. *Degree requirements:* For master's, thesis optional; for doctorate, comprehensive exam, thesis/dissertation. *Entrance requirements:* For master's, GRE General Test, minimum GPA of 2.75; for doctorate, GRE General Test, minimum GPA of 3.0. Additional exam requirements/recommendations for international students: Required—TOEFL. *Faculty research:* Public policy, research methods, foreign policy analysis, judicial politics, environmental and energy policy.

Wilfrid Laurier University, Faculty of Graduate and Postdoctoral Studies, Faculty of Arts, Department of Political Science, Waterloo, ON N2L 3C5, Canada. Offers Canadian political studies (MA); comparative politics/international relations (MA). Part-time programs available. *Degree requirements:* For master's, thesis optional. *Entrance requirements:* For master's, honors bachelor's degree or the equivalent in political science, minimum B average in undergraduate course work. Additional exam requirements/recommendations for international students: Required—TOEFL (minimum score 89 iBT). Electronic applications accepted. *Faculty research:* Political behavior/political psychology, Canadian political studies, comparative, politics/relations, public opinion and electoral studies, international.

Wilfrid Laurier University, Faculty of Graduate and Postdoctoral Studies, School of International Policy and Governance, Global Governance Program, Waterloo, ON N2L 3C5, Canada. Offers conflict and security (PhD); global environment (PhD); global justice and human rights (PhD); global political economy (PhD); global social governance (PhD); multilateral institutions and diplomacy (PhD). Offered jointly with University of Waterloo. *Degree requirements:* For doctorate, thesis/dissertation. *Entrance requirements:* For doctorate, MA in political science, history, economics, international development studies, international peace studies, globalization studies, environmental studies or related field with minimum A-. Additional exam requirements/recommendations for international students: Required—TOEFL (minimum score 89 iBT). Electronic applications accepted. *Faculty research:* Global political economy, global environment, conflict and security, global justice and human rights, multilateral institutions and diplomacy.

Wilfrid Laurier University, Faculty of Graduate and Postdoctoral Studies, School of International Policy and Governance, International Public Policy Program, Waterloo, ON N2L 3C5, Canada. Offers global governance (MIPP); human security (MIPP); international economic relations (MIPP); international environmental policy (MIPP). Offered jointly with University of Waterloo. *Entrance requirements:* For master's, honours BA with minimum B average. Additional exam requirements/recommendations for international students: Required—TOEFL (minimum score 89 iBT). Electronic applications accepted. *Faculty research:* International environmental policy, international economic relations, human security, global governance.

Wilfrid Laurier University, Laurier Brantford, Brantford, ON N3T 2Y3, Canada. Offers criminology (MA), including culture, crime and policy, international crime and justice,

media criminology. *Degree requirements:* For master's, thesis. *Entrance requirements:* For master's, honours bachelor's degree with major in criminology or equivalent degree; minimum B+ average in final year and in all criminology courses. Additional exam requirements/recommendations for international students: Required—TOEFL (minimum score 89 iBT). Electronic applications accepted.

Yale University, Graduate School of Arts and Sciences, Department of Economics, Program in International and Development Economics, New Haven, CT 06520. Offers MA. *Entrance requirements:* For master's, GRE General Test.

Yale University, Graduate School of Arts and Sciences, Graduate Program in Global Affairs, New Haven, CT 06520-8206. Offers MA, JD/MA, MBA/MA, MEM/MA, MF/MA, MFS/MA, MPH/MA. *Degree requirements:* For master's, one foreign language, summer internship or project. *Entrance requirements:* For master's, GRE General Test, professional experience and introductory coursework in microeconomics and macroeconomics (strongly preferred). Additional exam requirements/recommendations for international students: Required—TOEFL (minimum score 102 iBT) or IELTS (minimum score 7.5). Electronic applications accepted. *Expenses:* Contact institution. *Faculty research:* International security studies, global health, international economic development, political economy, policy.

York University, Faculty of Graduate Studies, Glendon Campus, Program in Public and International Affairs, Toronto, ON M3J 1P3, Canada. Offers MA.

International Development

American University, School of International Service, Washington, DC 20016-8071. Offers comparative and regional studies (Certificate); cross-cultural communication (Certificate); development management (MS); ethics, peace, and global affairs (MA); European studies (Certificate); global environmental policy (MA, Certificate); global information technology (Certificate); international affairs (MA), including comparative and international disability policy, comparative and regional studies, international economic relations, international politics, natural resources and sustainable development, U.S. foreign policy; international communication (MA, Certificate); international development (MA, Certificate); international economic policy (Certificate); international economic relations (Certificate); international media (MA); international peace and conflict resolution (MA, Certificate); international politics (Certificate); international relations (PhD); international service (MIS); peacebuilding (Certificate); social enterprise (MA); the Americas (Certificate); United States foreign policy (Certificate); JD/MA. Part-time and evening/weekend programs available. Postbaccalaureate distance learning degree programs offered (no on-campus study). *Faculty:* 112 full-time (43 women), 59 part-time/adjunct (27 women). *Students:* 545 full-time (335 women), 443 part-time (271 women); includes 231 minority (82 Black or African American, non-Hispanic/Latino; 8 American Indian or Alaska Native, non-Hispanic/Latino; 51 Asian, non-Hispanic/Latino; 81 Hispanic/Latino; 2 Native Hawaiian or other Pacific Islander, non-Hispanic/Latino; 7 Two or more races, non-Hispanic/Latino), 120 international. Average age 28. 1,991 applicants, 70% accepted, 365 enrolled. In 2014, 426 master's, 9 doctorates, 6 other advanced degrees awarded. Terminal master's awarded for partial completion of doctoral program. *Degree requirements:* For master's, one foreign language, comprehensive exam, thesis or alternative; for doctorate, one foreign language, comprehensive exam, thesis/dissertation. *Entrance requirements:* For master's, GRE, transcripts, resume, 2 letters of recommendation, statement of purpose; for doctorate, GRE, transcripts, resume, 3 letters of recommendation, statement of purpose. Additional exam requirements/recommendations for international students: Required—TOEFL (minimum score 600 paper-based; 100 iBT). *Application deadline:* For fall admission, 1/15 for domestic students; for spring admission, 10/1 for domestic students, 9/15 for international students. Application fee: $50. Electronic applications accepted. *Financial support:* Application deadline: 1/15. *Unit head:* Dr. James Goldgeier, Dean, 202-885-1603, Fax: 202-885-2494, E-mail: goldgeier@american.edu. *Application contact:* Jia Jiang, Associate Director, Graduate Education Enrollment, 202-885-1689, Fax: 202-885-1109, E-mail: jiang@american.edu.
Website: http://www.american.edu/sis/

Andrews University, School of Graduate Studies, College of Arts and Sciences, Department of Behavioral Science, Program in International Development, Berrien Springs, MI 49104. Offers MSA. Postbaccalaureate distance learning degree programs offered. *Faculty:* 10 full-time (2 women), 1 part-time/adjunct (0 women). *Students:* 15 full-time (11 women), 7 part-time (4 women); includes 13 minority (7 Black or African American, non-Hispanic/Latino; 2 American Indian or Alaska Native, non-Hispanic/Latino; 1 Asian, non-Hispanic/Latino; 2 Hispanic/Latino; 1 Two or more races, non-Hispanic/Latino), 6 international. Average age 31. 18 applicants, 39% accepted, 5 enrolled. In 2014, 1 master's awarded. *Entrance requirements:* For master's, GRE General Test. Additional exam requirements/recommendations for international students: Required—TOEFL (minimum score 550 paper-based). Application fee: $40. Tuition and fees vary according to course level. *Unit head:* Dr. Duane C. McBride, Director, 269-471-3152. *Application contact:* Monica Wringer, Supervisor of Graduate Admission, 800-253-2874, Fax: 269-471-6321, E-mail: graduate@andrews.edu.
Website: http://www.andrews.edu/grad/programs/community-and-international-development-off-campus.html

Athabasca University, Centre for Integrated Studies, Athabasca, AB T9S 3A3, Canada. Offers adult education (MA); community studies (MA); cultural studies (MA); educational studies (MA); global change (MA); work, organization, and leadership (MA). Part-time and evening/weekend programs available. Postbaccalaureate distance learning degree programs offered (no on-campus study). *Degree requirements:* For master's, project. *Entrance requirements:* Additional exam requirements/recommendations for international students: Required—TOEFL (minimum score 560 paper-based). Electronic applications accepted. *Faculty research:* Women's history, literature and culture studies, sustainable development, labor and education.

Clark University, Graduate School, Department of International Development, Community, and Environment, Program in International Development and Social Change, Worcester, MA 01610-1477. Offers MA. *Students:* 49 full-time (30 women), 6 part-time (2 women); includes 10 minority (6 Black or African American, non-Hispanic/Latino; 3 Asian, non-Hispanic/Latino; 1 Hispanic/Latino), 15 international. Average age 30. 136 applicants, 93% accepted, 28 enrolled. In 2014, 42 master's awarded. *Degree requirements:* For master's, thesis. *Entrance requirements:* For master's, 3 references, resume or curriculum vitae. Additional exam requirements/recommendations for international students: Required—TOEFL (minimum score 575 paper-based; 90 iBT) or IELTS (minimum score 6.5). *Application deadline:* For fall admission, 1/15 for domestic students. Application fee: $75. *Expenses: Tuition:* Full-time $40,380; part-time $1262 per credit hour. *Required fees:* $30. *Financial support:* Fellowships with partial tuition reimbursements, research assistantships with partial tuition reimbursements, teaching assistantships with partial tuition reimbursements, institutionally sponsored loans, and scholarships/grants available. *Faculty research:* Community action research, gender analysis, land-use planning, geographic information systems, HIV and AIDS, global health and social justice, environmental health, climate change and sustainability. *Unit head:* Dr. Ellen Foley, Advisor, 508-793-7201, Fax: 508-793-8820. *Application contact:* Erika Paradis, IDCE Graduate Admissions Office, 508-793-7201, E-mail: eparadis@clarku.edu.

Dalhousie University, Faculty of Arts and Social Science, Department of International Development Studies, Halifax, NS B3H 4R2, Canada. Offers MA. *Entrance requirements:* Additional exam requirements/recommendations for international students: Required—TOEFL, IELTS, CANTEST, CAEL, or Michigan English Language Assessment Battery. Electronic applications accepted.

Duke University, Sanford School of Public Policy, Master of International Development Policy Program, Durham, NC 27708-0237. Offers MIDP. *Faculty:* 14 full-time (5 women), 4 part-time/adjunct (0 women). *Students:* 75 full-time (37 women), 70 international. Average age 33. 143 applicants, 39 enrolled. In 2014, 60 master's awarded. *Degree requirements:* For master's, internship, master's project. *Entrance requirements:* For master's, minimum five years of professional experience in a development-related field. Additional exam requirements/recommendations for international students: Required—TOEFL (minimum score 577 paper-based; 90 iBT), IELTS (minimum score 7). *Application deadline:* For fall admission, 1/5 priority date for domestic and international students. Applications are processed on a rolling basis. Application fee: $80. Electronic applications accepted. *Expenses:* Expenses: Contact institution. *Financial support:* In 2014–15, 47 students received support, including teaching assistantships (averaging $4,000 per year); fellowships, research assistantships, scholarships/grants, tuition waivers (partial), and unspecified assistantships also available. Financial award application deadline: 1/5; financial award applicants required to submit FAFSA. *Unit head:* Dr. Corinne Krupp, Director of Graduate Studies, 919-613-9221, Fax: 919-684-2861, E-mail: midpinfo@duke.edu. *Application contact:* Cheryl Bailey, Senior Program Coordinator, 919-613-9281, Fax: 919-684-2861, E-mail: midinfo@duke.edu.
Website: http://dcid.sanford.duke.edu/academics/midp

Eastern University, School of Leadership and Development, St. Davids, PA 19087-3696. Offers economic development (MBA), including international development, urban development (MA, MBA); international development (MA), including global development, urban development (MA, MBA); nonprofit management (MS); organizational leadership (MA); M Div/MBA. Part-time and evening/weekend programs available. Postbaccalaureate distance learning degree programs offered (minimal on-campus study). *Faculty:* 6 full-time (3 women), 19 part-time/adjunct (8 women). *Students:* 112 full-time (62 women), 49 part-time (27 women); includes 36 minority (19 Black or African American, non-Hispanic/Latino; 2 American Indian or Alaska Native, non-Hispanic/Latino; 5 Asian, non-Hispanic/Latino; 7 Hispanic/Latino; 1 Native Hawaiian or other Pacific Islander, non-Hispanic/Latino; 2 Two or more races, non-Hispanic/Latino), 15 international. Average age 33. 62 applicants, 90% accepted, 46 enrolled. In 2014, 106 master's awarded. *Degree requirements:* For master's, thesis (for some programs). *Entrance requirements:* For master's, GMAT (for MBA), minimum GPA of 2.5. Additional exam requirements/recommendations for international students: Required—TOEFL (minimum score 550 paper-based; 79 iBT). *Application deadline:* For fall admission, 8/14 for domestic students. Applications are processed on a rolling basis. Application fee: $35. Application fee is waived when completed online. *Expenses:* Expenses: Contact institution. *Financial support:* In 2014–15, 131 students received support, including 3 fellowships with partial tuition reimbursements available (averaging $2,500 per year), 7 research assistantships with partial tuition reimbursements available (averaging $1,500 per year); scholarships/grants and unspecified assistantships also available. Financial award application deadline: 3/15; financial award applicants required to submit FAFSA. *Faculty research:* Micro-level economic development, China welfare and economic development, macroethics, micro- and macro-level economic development in transitional economics, organizational effectiveness. *Unit head:* Beth Birmingham, Chair, 610-341-4380. *Application contact:* Lindsey Perry, Enrollment Counselor, 484-581-1311, Fax: 484-581-1276, E-mail: lperry@eastern.edu.
Website: http://www.eastern.edu/academics/programs/school-leadership-and-development

Fordham University, Graduate School of Arts and Sciences, Program in International Political Economy and Development, New York, NY 10458. Offers MA, Certificate. Part-time and evening/weekend programs available. *Students:* 33 full-time (17 women), 16 part-time (6 women); includes 3 minority (2 Asian, non-Hispanic/Latino; 1 Hispanic/Latino), 13 international. Average age 27. 181 applicants, 52% accepted, 24 enrolled. In 2014, 29 master's, 6 other advanced degrees awarded. *Degree requirements:* For master's, comprehensive exam. *Entrance requirements:* For master's, GRE General Test. Additional exam requirements/recommendations for international students: Required—TOEFL (minimum score 600 paper-based). *Application deadline:* For fall admission, 1/4 priority date for domestic students; for spring admission, 11/1 for domestic students. Application fee: $70. Electronic applications accepted. *Financial support:* In 2014–15, 16 students received support, including 2 fellowships with full and partial tuition reimbursements available (averaging $11,965 per year), 16 research assistantships with full and partial tuition reimbursements available (averaging $16,050 per year); career-related internships or fieldwork, institutionally sponsored loans, tuition waivers (full and partial), and unspecified assistantships also available. Financial award application deadline: 1/4; financial award applicants required to submit FAFSA. *Faculty research:* International economics, comparative international politics, international banking and finance, international development, emerging markets and country risk analysis. *Unit head:* Dr. Henry Schwalbenberg, Chair, 718-817-3866, Fax: 718-817-3518. *Application contact:* Bernadette Valentino-Morrison, Director of Graduate Admissions, 718-817-4419, Fax: 718-817-3566, E-mail: valentinomor@fordham.edu.

The George Washington University, Columbian College of Arts and Sciences, Department of Anthropology, Washington, DC 20052. Offers anthropology (MA, PhD); international development (MA); medical antropology (MA); museum training (MA). Part-time and evening/weekend programs available. *Faculty:* 15 full-time (5 women). *Students:* 38 full-time (29 women), 7 part-time (5 women); includes 6 minority (1 Black or African American, non-Hispanic/Latino; 2 Hispanic/Latino; 3 Two or more races, non-Hispanic/Latino), 6 international. Average age 27. 98 applicants, 39% accepted, 15

enrolled. In 2014, 13 master's, 4 doctorates awarded. *Degree requirements:* For master's, one foreign language, comprehensive exam, thesis or alternative. *Entrance requirements:* For master's, GRE General Test, minimum GPA of 3.0. Additional exam requirements/recommendations for international students: Required—TOEFL (minimum score 550 paper-based; 80 iBT). *Application deadline:* For fall admission, 1/15 priority date for international students; for spring admission, 9/15 priority date for domestic students, 9/1 priority date for international students. Applications are processed on a rolling basis. Application fee: $75. Electronic applications accepted. *Financial support:* In 2014–15, 8 students received support. Fellowships, teaching assistantships, career-related internships or fieldwork, and Federal Work-Study available. Financial award application deadline: 1/15. *Unit head:* Richard Grinker, Chair, 202-994-6984, E-mail: rgrink@email.gwu.edu. *Application contact:* Information Contact, 202-994-6075, E-mail: anth@gwu.edu.
Website: http://anthropology.columbian.gwu.edu/

The George Washington University, Elliott School of International Affairs, Program in International Development Studies, Washington, DC 20052. Offers MA. Part-time programs available. *Students:* 79 full-time (64 women), 32 part-time (27 women); includes 31 minority (6 Black or African American, non-Hispanic/Latino; 7 Asian, non-Hispanic/Latino; 13 Hispanic/Latino; 5 Two or more races, non-Hispanic/Latino), 28 international. Average age 27. 287 applicants, 47 enrolled. In 2014, 33 master's awarded. *Degree requirements:* For master's, one foreign language, capstone project. *Entrance requirements:* For master's, GRE General Test, 2 years (or the equivalent) of a modern foreign language, introductory courses in microeconomics and macroeconomics. Additional exam requirements/recommendations for international students: Required—TOEFL (minimum score 100 iBT), IELTS (minimum score 7). *Application deadline:* For fall admission, 1/15 priority date for domestic and international students; for spring admission, 10/1 for domestic students. Application fee: $75. Electronic applications accepted. *Financial support:* In 2014–15, 27 students received support. Fellowships with partial tuition reimbursements available, Federal Work-Study, and scholarships/grants available. Financial award application deadline: 1/15; financial award applicants required to submit FAFSA. *Faculty research:* Development, anthropology, health and development, political science, education. *Unit head:* Prof. Sean Roberts, Director, 202-994-5767, E-mail: ids@gwu.edu. *Application contact:* Nicole A. Campbell, Director of Graduate Admissions, 202-994-7050, Fax: 202-994-9537, E-mail: esiagrad@gwu.edu.
Website: http://elliott.gwu.edu/international-development-studies

Harvard University, John F. Kennedy School of Government, Master in Public Administration/International Development Program, Cambridge, MA 02138. Offers MPAID. *Students:* 137 full-time (65 women); includes 15 minority (1 Black or African American, non-Hispanic/Latino; 8 Asian, non-Hispanic/Latino; 3 Hispanic/Latino; 3 Two or more races, non-Hispanic/Latino), 109 international. Average age 29. 278 applicants, 36% accepted, 65 enrolled. In 2014, 58 master's awarded. *Entrance requirements:* For master's, GMAT or GRE General Test (for joint Business School applicants), one course each in microeconomics and macroeconomics; two college-level calculus courses (one must contain multivariable calculus); bachelor's degree; 2-3 years of professional experience in development (strongly encouraged). Additional exam requirements/recommendations for international students: Required—TOEFL (minimum score 600 paper-based; 100 iBT). *Application deadline:* For fall admission, 12/1 for domestic students. Application fee: $100. Electronic applications accepted. *Financial support:* Fellowships, research assistantships, teaching assistantships, career-related internships or fieldwork, Federal Work-Study, institutionally sponsored loans, scholarships/grants, health care benefits, and unspecified assistantships available. Financial award application deadline: 2/6; financial award applicants required to submit CSS PROFILE or FAFSA. *Unit head:* Carol Finney, Director, 617-495-7799, E-mail: carol_finney@harvard.edu. *Application contact:* 617-495-2133, E-mail: mpaid_program@hks.harvard.edu.
Website: http://www.hks.harvard.edu/degrees/masters/mpa-id

Hope International University, School of Graduate and Professional Studies, Program in Business Administration, Fullerton, CA 92831-3138. Offers general management (MBA, MSM); international development (MBA, MSM); marketing management (MBA, MSM); non-profit management (MBA, MSM). Part-time programs available. Postbaccalaureate distance learning degree programs offered (no on-campus study). *Degree requirements:* For master's, comprehensive exam (for some programs), thesis (for some programs), project. *Entrance requirements:* For master's, minimum GPA of 3.0; 2 references. Additional exam requirements/recommendations for international students: Required—TOEFL (minimum score 550 paper-based; 86 iBT); Recommended—IELTS (minimum score 6.5). Electronic applications accepted. *Expenses:* Contact institution.

Indiana University Bloomington, School of Public and Environmental Affairs, Public Affairs Programs, Bloomington, IN 47405. Offers economic development (MPA); energy (MPA); environmental policy (PhD); environmental policy and natural resource management (MPA); information systems (MPA); international development (MPA); local government management (MPA); nonprofit management (MPA, Certificate); policy analysis (MPA); public budgeting and financial management (Certificate); public finance (PhD); public financial administration (MPA); public management (MPA, PhD, Certificate); public policy analysis (PhD); social entrepreneurship (Certificate); specialized public affairs (MPA); sustainability and sustainable development (MPA); JD/MPA; MPA/MA; MPA/MIS; MPA/MLS; MSES/MPA. *Accreditation:* NASPAA (one or more programs are accredited). Part-time programs available. *Degree requirements:* For master's, capstone, internship; for doctorate, comprehensive exam, thesis/dissertation. *Entrance requirements:* For master's, GRE General Test or GMAT, official transcripts, 3 letters of recommendation, resume, personal statement; for doctorate, GRE General Test, official transcripts, 3 letters of recommendation, statement of purpose. Additional exam requirements/recommendations for international students: Required—TOEFL (minimum score 600 paper-based; 96 iBT); Recommended—IELTS (minimum score 7). Electronic applications accepted. *Faculty research:* International development, environmental policy and resource management, policy analysis, public finance, public management, urban management, nonprofit management, energy policy, social policy, public finance.

John Brown University, Soderquist College of Business, Siloam Springs, AR 72761-2121. Offers global continuous improvement (MBA); higher education leadership (MS); leadership and ethics (MS). *Accreditation:* ACBSP. Part-time and evening/weekend programs available. Postbaccalaureate distance learning degree programs offered (minimal on-campus study). *Faculty:* 6 full-time (1 woman), 29 part-time/adjunct (8 women). *Students:* 23 full-time (13 women), 210 part-time (102 women); includes 41 minority (14 Black or African American, non-Hispanic/Latino; 5 American Indian or Alaska Native, non-Hispanic/Latino; 3 Asian, non-Hispanic/Latino; 11 Hispanic/Latino; 8 Two or more races, non-Hispanic/Latino), 3 international. Average age 34. 121 applicants, 98% accepted, 99 enrolled. *Entrance requirements:* For master's, MAT, GMAT or GRE (if undergraduate GPA is less than 3.0, recommendation forms from three people, 200-word essay describing professional plans and reason for seeking acceptance. Additional exam requirements/recommendations for international students: Required—TOEFL (minimum score 550 paper-based; 70 iBT). *Application deadline:*

Applications are processed on a rolling basis. Application fee: $35 ($100 for international students). Electronic applications accepted. *Expenses: Tuition:* Full-time $9576; part-time $532 per credit hour. *Financial support:* Fellowships with full tuition reimbursements, scholarships/grants, and unspecified assistantships available. Financial award applicants required to submit FAFSA. *Faculty research:* Ethical leadership. *Unit head:* Kai Togami, Program Director, 479-524-7370, E-mail: ktogami@jbu.edu. *Application contact:* Kent Shaffer, Graduate Business Representative, 479-631-4665, E-mail: kents@jbu.edu.
Website: http://www.jbu.edu/grad/business/

Johns Hopkins University, Paul H. Nitze School of Advanced International Studies, Washington, DC 20036. Offers international development (MA, Certificate), including international economics (MA); international economics and finance (MA); international public policy (MIPP); international relations (PhD); international studies (Certificate); Japan studies (MA), including international economics; Korea studies (MA), including international economics; South Asia studies (MA), including international economics; Southeast Asia studies (MA), including international economics; JD/MA; MBA/MA; MHS/MA. Terminal master's awarded for partial completion of doctoral program. *Degree requirements:* For master's, 4-6 international economics courses, 5-6 functional or regional concentration courses, 2 core examinations, proficiency in language other than native language, capstone project; for doctorate, 2 foreign languages, thesis/dissertation, 3 comprehensive exams, economics, quantitative and qualitative course, dissertation prospectus and defense. *Entrance requirements:* For master's, GMAT or GRE General Test, previous course work in economics, foreign language, undergraduate degree; for doctorate, GRE General Test, master's degree. Additional exam requirements/recommendations for international students: Required—TOEFL (minimum score 600 paper-based; 100 iBT) or IELTS (minimum score 7). Electronic applications accepted. *Expenses:* Contact institution. *Faculty research:* Regional studies, international relations, international economics, energy and environment, international development.

Kentucky State University, College of Professional Studies, Frankfort, KY 40601. Offers nursing (DNP); public administration (MPA), including human resource management, international development, management information systems, nonprofit management; special education (MA). Part-time and evening/weekend programs available. Postbaccalaureate distance learning degree programs offered (minimal on-campus study). *Faculty:* 10 full-time (5 women). *Students:* 20 full-time (16 women), 50 part-time (33 women); includes 45 minority (44 Black or African American, non-Hispanic/Latino; 1 Two or more races, non-Hispanic/Latino). Average age 34. 50 applicants, 82% accepted, 24 enrolled. In 2014, 24 master's awarded. *Degree requirements:* For master's, comprehensive exam, thesis optional; for doctorate, comprehensive exam. *Entrance requirements:* For master's, GMAT, GRE; for doctorate, RN license. Additional exam requirements/recommendations for international students: Required—TOEFL (minimum score 525 paper-based). *Application deadline:* Applications are processed on a rolling basis. Application fee: $30 ($100 for international students). Electronic applications accepted. *Expenses:* Tuition, state resident: full-time $7164; part-time $398 per credit hour. Tuition, nonresident: full-time $10,782; part-time $599 per credit hour. Tuition and fees vary according to course load. *Financial support:* In 2014–15, 4 students received support. Scholarships/grants and tuition waivers (partial) available. Financial award application deadline: 4/15; financial award applicants required to submit FAFSA. *Unit head:* Dr. Lorna Shaw-Berbick, Dean, 502-597-6443. *Application contact:* Dr. James Obielodan, Director of Graduate Studies, 502-597-4723, E-mail: james.obielodan@kysu.edu.
Website: http://kysu.edu/academics/college-of-professional-studies/

Lehigh University, College of Education, Program in Comparative and International Education, Bethlehem, PA 18015. Offers comparative and international education (MA, PhD); globalization and educational change (M Ed); international development in education (Certificate); TESOL (Certificate). Part-time and evening/weekend programs available. Postbaccalaureate distance learning degree programs offered (minimal on-campus study). *Faculty:* 4 full-time (2 women). *Students:* 28 full-time (23 women), 26 part-time (17 women); includes 2 minority (both Asian, non-Hispanic/Latino), 17 international. Average age 30. 73 applicants, 49% accepted, 17 enrolled. In 2014, 21 master's awarded. Terminal master's awarded for partial completion of doctoral program. *Degree requirements:* For master's, thesis (MA); for doctorate, comprehensive exam, thesis/dissertation. *Entrance requirements:* For master's, 2 letters of recommendation; for doctorate, GRE, transcripts, 2 letters of recommendation, essay. Additional exam requirements/recommendations for international students: Required—TOEFL (minimum score 600 paper-based; 93 iBT). *Application deadline:* For fall and spring admission, 2/1 for domestic and international students. Application fee: $65. Electronic applications accepted. *Expenses:* Expenses: $565 per credit; $200 internship fee (for some programs); $100 technology fee (for some programs); $75 printing fee. *Financial support:* Application deadline: 3/15; applicants required to submit FAFSA. *Faculty research:* Comparative education, rural education, gender equity in education, post-socialist education transformation, educational borrowing, comparing education systems, education policy and globalization, family-school relationships, China, international testing, social inequities. *Total annual research expenditures:* $19,351. *Unit head:* Dr. Iveta Silova, Program Director and Associate Professor, 610-758-5750, Fax: 610-758-6223, E-mail: ism207@lehigh.edu. *Application contact:* Sharon Y. Warden, Coordinator, 610-758-3256, Fax: 610-758-6223, E-mail: sy00@lehigh.edu.
Website: http://www.lehigh.edu/education/cie

Marymount California University, Program in Leadership and Global Development, Rancho Palos Verdes, CA 90275-6299. Offers MS.

McGill University, Faculty of Graduate and Postdoctoral Studies, Desautels Faculty of Management, Montréal, QC H3A 2T5, Canada. Offers administration (PhD); entrepreneurial studies (MBA); finance (MBA); general management (Post Master's Certificate); information systems (MBA); international business (MBA); international practicing management (MM); management (MBA); management for development (MBA); manufacturing management (MMM); marketing (MBA); operations management (MBA); public accountancy (Diploma); strategic management (MBA); MBA/LL B; MD/MBA. MMM offered jointly with Faculty of Engineering; PhD with Concordia University, HEC Montreal, Université de Montréal, Université du Québec à Montréal.

Middlebury Institute of International Studies, Graduate School of International Policy and Management, Program in International Policy and Development, Monterey, CA 93940-2691. Offers MA. *Degree requirements:* For master's, one foreign language. *Entrance requirements:* For master's, minimum GPA of 3.0, proficiency in a foreign language. Additional exam requirements/recommendations for international students: Required—TOEFL (minimum score 550 paper-based; 80 iBT). *Application deadline:* For fall admission, 3/15 priority date for domestic and international students; for spring admission, 10/1 priority date for domestic and international students. Applications are processed on a rolling basis. Application fee: $50. Electronic applications accepted. *Expenses: Tuition:* Full-time $36,020; part-time $1715 per credit. *Required fees:* $53 per semester. *Financial support:* Application deadline: 3/15. *Unit head:* Edward J. Laurance, Chair, 831-647-4144, Fax: 831-647-4199, E-mail: elaurance@miis.edu. *Application contact:* 831-647-4123, Fax: 831-647-6405, E-mail: admit@miis.edu.
Website: http://www.miis.edu/academics/programs/development-practice-policy/policy

New York University, School of Continuing and Professional Studies, Center for Global Affairs, New York, NY 10012-1019. Offers global affairs (MS), including environment/energy policy, human rights and international law, international development and humanitarian assistance, international relations, peace building, private sector, transnational security; global energy (Advanced Certificate); peacebuilding (Advanced Certificate); transnational security (Advanced Certificate). Part-time and evening/weekend programs available. *Faculty:* 11 full-time (6 women), 32 part-time/adjunct (14 women). *Students:* 156 full-time (105 women), 136 part-time (86 women); includes 79 minority (24 Black or African American, non-Hispanic/Latino; 17 Asian, non-Hispanic/Latino; 37 Hispanic/Latino; 1 Two or more races, non-Hispanic/Latino), 66 international. Average age 28. 357 applicants, 72% accepted, 98 enrolled. In 2014, 144 master's awarded. *Degree requirements:* For master's, thesis. *Entrance requirements:* For master's, GRE or GMAT (only upon request), bachelor's degree, resume with relevant professional work, internship or volunteer experience, two letters of recommendation, statement of purpose. Additional exam requirements/recommendations for international students: Required—TOEFL (minimum score 600 paper-based; 100 iBT), IELTS (minimum score 7). *Application deadline:* For fall admission, 2/1 priority date for domestic and international students; for spring admission, 10/15 priority date for domestic students, 8/15 priority date for international students. Applications are processed on a rolling basis. Application fee: $150. Electronic applications accepted. *Financial support:* In 2014–15, 99 students received support, including 95 fellowships (averaging $2,218 per year); Federal Work-Study and scholarships/grants also available. Support available to part-time students. Financial award application deadline: 4/1; financial award applicants required to submit FAFSA. *Unit head:* Vera Jelinek, Divisional Dean and Clinical Associate Professor, 212-992-8380. *Application contact:* Office of Admissions, 212-998-7100, E-mail: sps.gradadmissions@nyu.edu. Website: http://www.sps.nyu.edu/academics/departments/global-affairs.html

New York University, Steinhardt School of Culture, Education, and Human Development, Department of Humanities and Social Sciences in the Professions, Program in International Education, New York, NY 10003. Offers cross-cultural exchange and training (PhD); international development education (PhD); international education (MA, Advanced Certificate). Part-time programs available. *Faculty:* 5 full-time (3 women). *Students:* 76 full-time (68 women), 44 part-time (38 women); includes 36 minority (11 Black or African American, non-Hispanic/Latino; 9 Asian, non-Hispanic/Latino; 13 Hispanic/Latino; 3 Two or more races, non-Hispanic/Latino), 28 international. Average age 36. 220 applicants, 64% accepted, 38 enrolled. In 2014, 45 master's, 6 doctorates, 6 other advanced degrees awarded. *Degree requirements:* For master's, thesis (for some programs); for doctorate, thesis/dissertation. *Entrance requirements:* For doctorate, GRE General Test, interview; for Advanced Certificate, master's degree. Additional exam requirements/recommendations for international students: Required—TOEFL (minimum score 100 iBT). *Application deadline:* For fall admission, 12/1 priority date for domestic and international students; for spring admission, 10/1 for domestic and international students. Applications are processed on a rolling basis. Application fee: $75. Electronic applications accepted. *Financial support:* Fellowships with full and partial tuition reimbursements, career-related internships or fieldwork, Federal Work-Study, institutionally sponsored loans, and scholarships/grants available. Support available to part-time students. Financial award application deadline: 2/1; financial award applicants required to submit FAFSA. *Faculty research:* Civic education, ethnic identity among students and teachers, comparative education, education during emergencies, cross-cultural exchange. *Unit head:* Dr. Philip M. Hosay, Director, 212-998-5496, Fax: 212-995-4832, E-mail: pmh2@nyu.edu. *Application contact:* 212-998-5030, Fax: 212-995-4328, E-mail: steinhardt.gradadmissions@nyu.edu. Website: http://steinhardt.nyu.edu/humsocsci/international

Norwich University, College of Graduate and Continuing Studies, Master of Public Administration Program, Northfield, VT 05663. Offers fiscal management (MPA); international development and influence (MPA); policy analysis and analytics (MPA). Evening/weekend programs available. Postbaccalaureate distance learning degree programs offered (minimal on-campus study). *Faculty:* 13 part-time/adjunct (8 women). *Students:* 70 full-time (23 women); includes 9 minority (4 Black or African American, non-Hispanic/Latino; 1 American Indian or Alaska Native, non-Hispanic/Latino; 1 Native Hawaiian or other Pacific Islander, non-Hispanic/Latino; 3 Two or more races, non-Hispanic/Latino). Average age 38. 48 applicants, 100% accepted, 35 enrolled. In 2014, 79 master's awarded. *Entrance requirements:* For master's, minimum undergraduate GPA of 2.75. Additional exam requirements/recommendations for international students: Required—TOEFL (minimum score 550 paper-based; 80 iBT), IELTS (minimum score 6.5). *Application deadline:* For fall admission, 8/8 for domestic and international students; for winter admission, 11/7 for domestic and international students; for spring admission, 2/16 for domestic and international students; for summer admission, 5/18 for domestic and international students. Applications are processed on a rolling basis. Electronic applications accepted. *Expenses:* Expenses: Contact institution. *Financial support:* In 2014–15, 34 students received support. Scholarships/grants available. Financial award applicants required to submit FAFSA. *Faculty research:* Pre-employment investigations for public safety professionals, sustainability programs and policy implementation, innovative voting procedures. *Unit head:* Dr. Rosemarie Pelletier, Program Director, 802-485-2767, Fax: 802-485-2533, E-mail: rpellet2@norwich.edu. *Application contact:* Lars Nielsen, Associate Program Director, 802-485-2853, Fax: 802-485-2533, E-mail: lnielsen@norwich.edu. Website: http://online.norwich.edu/degree-programs/masters/master-public-administration/overview

Ohio University, Graduate College, Center for International Studies, Program in Development Studies, Athens, OH 45701-2979. Offers MA. Part-time programs available. *Degree requirements:* For master's, one foreign language, thesis optional. *Entrance requirements:* For master's, minimum GPA of 3.0. Additional exam requirements/recommendations for international students: Required—TOEFL (minimum score 550 paper-based; 80 iBT), IELTS (minimum score 6.5). Electronic applications accepted. *Faculty research:* Problems and issues in social, economic, political, health and environmental development.

Old Dominion University, College of Arts and Letters, Graduate Program in International Studies, Norfolk, VA 23529. Offers conflict and cooperation (MA, PhD); interdependence and transnationalism (MA, PhD); international cultural studies (MA, PhD); international political economy and development (MA, PhD); modeling and simulation (MA, PhD); U.S. foreign policy and international relations (MA, PhD). Part-time programs available. *Faculty:* 18 full-time (4 women). *Students:* 41 full-time (14 women), 46 part-time (23 women); includes 11 minority (5 Black or African American, non-Hispanic/Latino; 1 Asian, non-Hispanic/Latino; 2 Hispanic/Latino; 3 Two or more races, non-Hispanic/Latino), 24 international. Average age 35. 99 applicants, 54% accepted, 34 enrolled. In 2014, 10 master's, 9 doctorates awarded. Terminal master's awarded for partial completion of doctoral program. *Degree requirements:* For master's, one foreign language, comprehensive exam, thesis optional; for doctorate, one foreign language, comprehensive exam, thesis/dissertation. *Entrance requirements:* For master's, GRE General Test, sample of written work, 2 letters of recommendation; for doctorate, GRE General Test, sample of written work, 3 letters of recommendation. Additional exam requirements/recommendations for international students: Required—TOEFL (minimum score 570 paper-based). *Application deadline:* For fall admission, 1/

15 for domestic and international students; for spring admission, 10/15 for domestic and international students. Application fee: $50. Electronic applications accepted. *Expenses:* Tuition, state resident: full-time $10,488; part-time $437 per credit. Tuition, nonresident: full-time $26,136; part-time $1089 per credit. *Required fees:* $64 per semester. One-time fee: $50. *Financial support:* In 2014–15, 20 students received support, including 2 fellowships (averaging $13,000 per year), 5 research assistantships with tuition reimbursements available (averaging $15,000 per year), 7 teaching assistantships with tuition reimbursements available (averaging $15,000 per year); career-related internships or fieldwork, institutionally sponsored loans, scholarships/grants, and unspecified assistantships also available. Support available to part-time students. Financial award application deadline: 2/15; financial award applicants required to submit FAFSA. *Faculty research:* U.S. foreign policy, international security, Transatlantic and Transpacific relations, transnational issues, international political economy and development. *Total annual research expenditures:* $330,391. *Unit head:* Dr. Regina Karp, Graduate Program Director, 757-683-5700, Fax: 757-683-5701, E-mail: rkarp@odu.edu. *Application contact:* Dr. David C. Earnest, Associate Dean, 757-683-6077, Fax: 757-683-5746, E-mail: dearnest@odu.edu. Website: http://www.al.odu.edu/gpis/

Rutgers, The State University of New Jersey, Camden, Graduate School of Arts and Sciences, Department of Public Policy and Administration, Camden, NJ 08102. Offers education policy and leadership (MPA); international public service and development (MPA); public management (MPA); JD/MPA; MPA/MA. *Accreditation:* NASPAA. Part-time and evening/weekend programs available. *Degree requirements:* For master's, directed study, research workshop, 42 credits. *Entrance requirements:* For master's, GRE General Test, GMAT or LSAT, 3 letters of recommendation; resume. Additional exam requirements/recommendations for international students: Required—TOEFL (minimum score 550 paper-based), IELTS. Electronic applications accepted. *Faculty research:* Nonprofit management, county and municipal administration, health and human services, government communication, administrative law, educational finance.

Saint Mary's University, Faculty of Arts, International Development Studies Program, Halifax, NS B3H 3C3, Canada. Offers MA, Graduate Diploma. Part-time programs available. *Degree requirements:* For master's, thesis. *Entrance requirements:* For master's, honors degree. *Faculty research:* Dynamics of global development, gender and development, policy analysis, models and strategies for development, Latin American and Caribbean development.

Saint Mary's University of Minnesota, Schools of Graduate and Professional Programs, Graduate School of Business and Technology, International Development Program, Winona, MN 55987-1399. Offers MA. Postbaccalaureate distance learning degree programs offered (no on-campus study).

Stanford University, School of Humanities and Sciences, Program in International Policy Studies, Stanford, CA 94305-9991. Offers democracy, development, and rule of law (MA); energy, environment, and natural resources (MA); global health (MA); international political economy (MA); international security and cooperation (MA). *Degree requirements:* For master's, thesis optional. *Entrance requirements:* For master's, GRE General Test. Additional exam requirements/recommendations for international students: Required—TOEFL. Electronic applications accepted. *Expenses:* Tuition: Full-time $44,184; part-time $982 per credit hour. *Required fees:* $191.

Tufts University, The Fletcher School of Law and Diplomacy, Medford, MA 02155. Offers LL M, MA, MALD, MIB, PhD, DVM/MA, JD/MALD, MALD/MA, MALD/MBA, MALD/MS, MD/MA. Postbaccalaureate distance learning degree programs offered (minimal on-campus study). *Degree requirements:* For master's, one foreign language, thesis; for doctorate, one foreign language, comprehensive exam, thesis/dissertation, dissertation defense. *Entrance requirements:* For master's and doctorate, GMAT or GRE General Test. Additional exam requirements/recommendations for international students: Required—TOEFL (minimum score 600 paper-based; 100 iBT), IELTS (minimum score 7). Electronic applications accepted. *Expenses:* Contact institution. *Faculty research:* Negotiation and conflict resolution, international organizations, international business and economic law, security studies, development economics.

Tufts University, Graduate School of Arts and Sciences, Department of Urban and Environmental Policy and Planning, Medford, MA 02155. Offers community development (MA); environmental policy (MA); health and human welfare (MA); housing policy (MA); international environment/development policy (MA); public policy (MPP); MA/MS; MALD/MA. *Accreditation:* ACSP (one or more programs are accredited). Part-time programs available. *Faculty:* 13 full-time (5 women), 15 part-time/adjunct (8 women). *Students:* 62 full-time (43 women), 36 part-time (26 women); includes 24 minority (10 Black or African American, non-Hispanic/Latino; 7 Asian, non-Hispanic/Latino; 6 Hispanic/Latino; 1 Two or more races, non-Hispanic/Latino), 10 international. Average age 30. 119 applicants, 81% accepted, 32 enrolled. In 2014, 64 master's awarded. *Degree requirements:* For master's, thesis, internship. *Entrance requirements:* For master's, GRE General Test. Additional exam requirements/recommendations for international students: Required—TOEFL (minimum score 550 paper-based; 80 iBT), IELTS (minimum score 6.5). *Application deadline:* For fall admission, 1/15 for domestic and international students. Applications are processed on a rolling basis. Application fee: $75. Electronic applications accepted. *Expenses:* Expenses: Contact institution. *Financial support:* Teaching assistantships with partial tuition reimbursements, career-related internships or fieldwork, Federal Work-Study, scholarships/grants, tuition waivers (partial), and unspecified assistantships available. Support available to part-time students. Financial award application deadline: 1/15; financial award applicants required to submit FAFSA. *Unit head:* Dr. Weiping Wu, Graduate Program Director. *Application contact:* Office of Graduate Admissions, 617-627-3395, E-mail: gradadmissions@tufts.edu. Website: http://ase.tufts.edu/uep/

Tulane University, School of Law, The Payson Center for International Development, New Orleans, LA 70118. Offers international development (MS, PhD); law and development (LL M); JD/MS. Part-time programs available. Terminal master's awarded for partial completion of doctoral program. *Degree requirements:* For master's, comprehensive exam (for some programs), thesis optional; for doctorate, comprehensive exam, thesis/dissertation. *Entrance requirements:* For master's, GRE General Test, minimum 3.0 GPA in undergraduate course work; for doctorate, GRE. Additional exam requirements/recommendations for international students: Required—TOEFL (minimum score 600 paper-based; 90 iBT). Electronic applications accepted. *Expenses:* Contact institution. *Faculty research:* Poverty and inequality, sustainability, health and human development, GIS for development, monitoring and evaluation.

University of Florida, Graduate School, College of Liberal Arts and Sciences, Department of Political Science, Gainesville, FL 32611. Offers educational policy (PhD); international development policy and administration (MA, Certificate); international relations (MA, MAT); political campaigning (MA, Certificate); political science (MA, PhD); public affairs (MA, Certificate); tropical conservation and development (MA, PhD); JD/MA. *Faculty:* 25 full-time (9 women), 4 part-time/adjunct (1 woman). *Students:* 115 full-time (45 women), 19 part-time (7 women); includes 26 minority (12 Black or African American, non-Hispanic/Latino; 6 Asian, non-Hispanic/Latino; 8 Hispanic/Latino), 34 international. 136 applicants, 44% accepted, 22 enrolled. In 2014, 28 master's, 8

doctorates awarded. Terminal master's awarded for partial completion of doctoral program. *Degree requirements:* For master's, variable foreign language requirement, comprehensive exam (for some programs), thesis or alternative, internship (for some programs); for doctorate, variable foreign language requirement, comprehensive exam, thesis/dissertation. *Entrance requirements:* For master's and doctorate, GRE General Test 308 combined verbal/math, minimum GPA of 3.5. Additional exam requirements/recommendations for international students: Required—TOEFL (minimum score 550 paper-based; 80 iBT), IELTS (minimum score 6). *Application deadline:* For fall admission, 1/15 priority date for domestic students, 1/15 for international students. Applications are processed on a rolling basis. Application fee: $30. Electronic applications accepted. *Financial support:* In 2014–15, 13 fellowships, 13 research assistantships, 50 teaching assistantships were awarded; career-related internships or fieldwork, Federal Work-Study, institutionally sponsored loans, and unspecified assistantships also available. Financial award application deadline: 1/15; financial award applicants required to submit FAFSA. *Faculty research:* American electoral politics and political institutions, comparative democratization and development, theories of international relation, and political theory. *Total annual research expenditures:* $208,864. *Unit head:* Ido Oren, PhD, Professor and Chair, 352-273-2393, Fax: 352-392-8127, E-mail: oren@ufl.edu. *Application contact:* Leslie Anderson, PhD, Graduate Coordinator, 352-273-3725, Fax: 352-392-8127, E-mail: landerso@ufl.edu.
Website: http://polisci.ufl.edu/

University of Guelph, Graduate Studies, Collaborative International Development Studies, Guelph, ON N1G 2W1, Canada. Offers M Eng, M Sc, MA, MBA, PhD. Part-time programs available. *Degree requirements:* For master's, thesis (for some programs), seminar; for doctorate, comprehensive exam (for some programs), thesis/dissertation. *Entrance requirements:* For master's, honour's degree with courses in economics, social science, and empirical methods. *Faculty research:* Transformation of developing societies, regional differences, national and international processes of development, long-term change.

The University of Manchester, School of Environment and Development, Manchester, United Kingdom. Offers architecture (M Phil, PhD); development policy and management (M Phil, PhD); human geography (M Phil, PhD); physical geography (M Phil, PhD); planning and landscape (M Phil, PhD).

University of Massachusetts Boston, Graduate School of Global Inclusion and Social Development, Program in Global Inclusion and Social Development, Boston, MA 02125-3393. Offers MA, PhD. *Expenses:* Tuition, state resident: full-time $2590; part-time $108 per credit. Tuition, nonresident: full-time $9758; part-time $406.50 per credit. Tuition and fees vary according to course load and program. *Unit head:* Dr. Kristy Alster, Associate Provost, 617-287-5700, Fax: 617-287-5699, E-mail: kristine.alster@umb.edu. *Application contact:* Peggy Roldan Patel, Graduate Admissions Coordinator, 617-287-6400, Fax: 617-287-6236, E-mail: bos.gadm@dpc.umassp.edu.

University of Minnesota, Twin Cities Campus, Graduate School, Hubert H. Humphrey School of Public Affairs, Master of Development Practice in International Development Program, Minneapolis, MN 55455. Offers MDP. Program offered jointly with Interdisciplinary Center for the Study of Global Change (ICGC). *Students:* 15 full-time (8 women); includes 7 minority (3 Black or African American, non-Hispanic/Latino; 1 Asian, non-Hispanic/Latino; 3 Hispanic/Latino), 4 international. Average age 28. 87 applicants, 51% accepted, 15 enrolled. In 2014, 15 master's awarded. *Degree requirements:* For master's, thesis or alternative, international field experience. *Entrance requirements:* For master's, GRE. Additional exam requirements/recommendations for international students: Required—TOEFL (minimum score 600 paper-based; 100 iBT), IELTS (minimum score 7). *Application deadline:* For fall admission, 1/15 for domestic and international students. Applications are processed on a rolling basis. Application fee: $75 ($95 for international students). Electronic applications accepted. *Expenses:* Expenses: State resident full-time: $17,603 per year, nonresident full-time: $25,417 per year (6-16 credits per semester). *Financial support:* In 2014–15, 20 students received support, including fellowships with full and partial tuition reimbursements available (averaging $11,400 per year), research assistantships with full and partial tuition reimbursements available (averaging $26,000 per year). Financial award application deadline: 1/15. *Faculty research:* Policy analysis and management, health and education, natural sciences, social sciences, interdisciplinary research methods. *Unit head:* Laura Bloomberg, Associate Dean, 612-625-0608, Fax: 612-626-0002, E-mail: bloom004@umn.edu. *Application contact:* Amy Luitjens, Director of Admissions, 612-624-3800, Fax: 612-626-0002, E-mail: luitjens@umn.edu.
Website: http://www.hhh.umn.edu/degrees/mdp/

University of New Brunswick Fredericton, School of Graduate Studies, Policy Studies Program, Fredericton, NB E3B 5A3, Canada. Offers citizen engagement/dispute resolution (M Phil); community development (M Phil); international development (M Phil); leadership (M Phil); sustainability/environmental issues (M Phil); worldviews (M Phil). Part-time programs available. *Faculty:* 17 full-time (9 women), 1 part-time/adjunct (0 women). *Students:* 14 full-time (7 women), 4 part-time (3 women). In 2014, 3 master's awarded. *Degree requirements:* For master's, thesis, report. *Entrance requirements:* For master's, minimum GPA of 3.5. Additional exam requirements/recommendations for international students: Required—TWE (minimum score 5.5), TOEFL (minimum score 600 paper-based; 100 iBT) or IELTS (minimum score 7). *Application deadline:* Applications are processed on a rolling basis. Application fee: $50 Canadian dollars. Electronic applications accepted. *Financial support:* In 2014–15, 3 fellowships, research assistantships (averaging $5,600 per year), teaching assistantships (averaging $4,400 per year) were awarded. *Faculty research:* International development, worldviews, citizenship/dispute resolution, sustainability/environmental issues, leadership, community development. *Unit head:* Dr. Linda Eyre, Dean of Graduate Studies, 506-447-3044, Fax: 506-453-4817, E-mail: gradidst@unb.ca. *Application contact:* Janet Amirault, Graduate Secretary, 506-458-7558, Fax: 506-453-4817, E-mail: jamiraul@unb.ca.
Website: http://www.unb.ca/gradstudies/programs/mphil/index.html

University of New Hampshire, Graduate School, Interdisciplinary Programs, Program in Community Development Policy and Practice, Durham, NH 03824. Offers MA. *Students:* 8 part-time (4 women); includes 1 minority (Black or African American, non-Hispanic/Latino), 2 international. Average age 31. 3 applicants, 33% accepted. *Degree requirements:* For master's, project. *Entrance requirements:* Additional exam requirements/recommendations for international students: Required—TOEFL (minimum score 550 paper-based; 80 iBT). *Application deadline:* For fall admission, 2/15 for domestic students. Applications are processed on a rolling basis. Application fee: $65. Electronic applications accepted. *Expenses:* Tuition, state resident: full-time $13,500; part-time $750 per credit hour. Tuition, nonresident: full-time $26,460; part-time $1110 per credit hour. *Required fees:* $1788; $447 per semester. *Financial support:* In 2014–15, 6 students received support. Fellowships, research assistantships, teaching assistantships, and scholarships/grants available. *Unit head:* Michael Swack, Chairperson, 603-862-3201, Fax: 603-862-0275, E-mail: harry.richards@unh.edu. *Application contact:* Robin Husslage, Administrative Assistant, 603-862-1871, E-mail: college.teaching@unh.edu.
Website: http://carsey.unh.edu/macdpp

University of New Mexico, Graduate School, College of Arts and Sciences, Program in Economics, Albuquerque, NM 87131-2039. Offers econometrics (MA); economic theory (MA); environmental/natural resource economics (MA, PhD); international/development and sustainability economics (MA, PhD); public economics (MA, PhD). Part-time programs available. *Faculty:* 12 full-time (7 women). *Students:* 40 full-time (13 women), 5 part-time (2 women); includes 8 minority (2 Black or African American, non-Hispanic/Latino; 1 Asian, non-Hispanic/Latino; 4 Hispanic/Latino; 1 Two or more races, non-Hispanic/Latino), 20 international. Average age 32. 69 applicants, 33% accepted, 12 enrolled. In 2014, 7 master's, 4 doctorates awarded. Terminal master's awarded for partial completion of doctoral program. *Degree requirements:* For master's, comprehensive exam, thesis (for some programs); for doctorate, comprehensive exam, thesis/dissertation. *Entrance requirements:* For master's and doctorate, GRE General Test, 3 letters of recommendation, letter of intent, curriculum vitae. Additional exam requirements/recommendations for international students: Required—TOEFL (minimum score 520 paper-based; 68 iBT). *Application deadline:* For fall admission, 3/1 priority date for domestic students, 3/1 for international students. Applications are processed on a rolling basis. Application fee: $50. Electronic applications accepted. *Financial support:* In 2014–15, 47 students received support, including 3 fellowships with tuition reimbursements available (averaging $6,858 per year), 13 research assistantships with tuition reimbursements available (averaging $6,858 per year), 15 teaching assistantships with tuition reimbursements available (averaging $7,396 per year); career-related internships or fieldwork, Federal Work-Study, scholarships/grants, health care benefits, and unspecified assistantships also available. Support available to part-time students. Financial award application deadline: 3/1; financial award applicants required to submit FAFSA. *Faculty research:* Core theory, econometrics, public finance, international/development economics, labor/human resource economics, environmental/natural resource economics. *Total annual research expenditures:* $388,864. *Unit head:* Dr. Janie Chermak, Chair, 505-277-2037, Fax: 505-277-9445, E-mail: jchermak@unm.edu. *Application contact:* Jeff Newcomer Miller, Academic Advisor, 505-277-3056, Fax: 505-277-9445, E-mail: econgrad@unm.edu.
Website: http://econ.unm.edu

University of Ottawa, Faculty of Graduate and Postdoctoral Studies, Program in Globalization and International Development, Ottawa, ON K1N 6N5, Canada. Offers MA. *Degree requirements:* For master's, thesis or alternative. *Entrance requirements:* For master's, honours bachelor's degree or equivalent, minimum B average.

University of Pittsburgh, Graduate School of Public and International Affairs, Master of International Development Program, Pittsburgh, PA 15260. Offers human security (MID); nongovernmental organizations and civil society (MID); urban affairs and planning (MID); MID/JD; MID/MBA; MID/MPH; MID/MPIA; MID/MSIS; MID/MSW; MPA/MID. Part-time and evening/weekend programs available. *Faculty:* 34 full-time (12 women), 11 part-time/adjunct (3 women). *Students:* 60 full-time (43 women), 3 part-time (1 woman); includes 16 minority (3 Black or African American, non-Hispanic/Latino; 10 Asian, non-Hispanic/Latino; 2 Hispanic/Latino; 1 Two or more races, non-Hispanic/Latino), 7 international. Average age 26. 94 applicants, 86% accepted, 26 enrolled. In 2014, 27 master's awarded. *Degree requirements:* For master's, thesis optional, internship, capstone seminar. *Entrance requirements:* For master's, GRE General Test or GMAT, 2 letters of recommendation; undergraduate transcripts; resume; personal statement. Additional exam requirements/recommendations for international students: Required—TOEFL (minimum score 550 paper-based; 80 iBT); Recommended—IELTS (minimum score 7), TWE (minimum score 4). *Application deadline:* For fall admission, 2/1 for domestic students, 1/15 for international students; for spring admission, 11/1 for domestic students, 8/1 for international students. Application fee: $50. Electronic applications accepted. *Expenses:* Tuition, state resident: full-time $20,742; part-time $838 per credit. Tuition, nonresident: full-time $33,960; part-time $1389 per credit. *Required fees:* $800; $205 per term. Tuition and fees vary according to program. *Financial support:* In 2014–15, 26 students received support, including 1 fellowship (averaging $18,000 per year); scholarships/grants, unspecified assistantships, and student employment also available. Financial award application deadline: 2/1. *Faculty research:* Nongovernmental organizations, religion and civil society, international development, development economics and policy, human rights and development, humanitarian intervention, ethnic conflict and civil war, post-conflict peace-building, corruption and transnational governance, civil society and public affairs, political constraints on rural development. *Total annual research expenditures:* $640,844. *Unit head:* Dr. Paul J. Nelson, Director, 412-648-7645, Fax: 412-648-2605, E-mail: pjnelson@pitt.edu. *Application contact:* Elizabeth A. Hruby, Graduate Enrollment Counselor, 412-648-7640, Fax: 412-648-7641, E-mail: eah44@pitt.edu.
Website: http://www.gspia.pitt.edu/

University of Pittsburgh, Katz Graduate School of Business, MBA/Master of International Development Joint Degree Program, Pittsburgh, PA 15260. Offers MID/MBA. *Accreditation:* AACSB. Part-time and evening/weekend programs available. *Faculty:* 53 full-time (12 women), 31 part-time/adjunct (9 women). *Students:* 2 applicants. *Entrance requirements:* Additional exam requirements/recommendations for international students: Required—TOEFL (minimum score 600 paper-based; 100 iBT) or IELTS. *Application deadline:* For fall admission, 4/1 priority date for domestic students, 2/1 priority date for international students. Application fee: $50. Electronic applications accepted. *Expenses:* Tuition, state resident: full-time $20,742; part-time $838 per credit. Tuition, nonresident: full-time $33,960; part-time $1389 per credit. *Required fees:* $800; $205 per term. Tuition and fees vary according to program. *Financial support:* Scholarships/grants available. Financial award application deadline: 6/1; financial award applicants required to submit FAFSA. *Faculty research:* Accounting systems/financial reporting, corporate finance, shopper marketing/consumer behavior, management information systems, organizational behavior and entrepreneurship. *Unit head:* William Valenta, Jr., Assistant Dean, 412-648-1694, Fax: 412-648-1659, E-mail: valenta@pitt.edu. *Application contact:* Thomas Keller, Director of MBA Admissions, 412-648-1700, Fax: 412-648-1659, E-mail: mba@katz.pitt.edu.
Website: http://www.business.pitt.edu/katz/mba/academics/programs/mba-mid.php

University of San Francisco, College of Arts and Sciences, International and Development Economics Program, San Francisco, CA 94117-1080. Offers MA. *Faculty:* 6 full-time (2 women), 4 part-time/adjunct (0 women). *Students:* 34 full-time (16 women), 1 part-time (0 women); includes 6 minority (4 Black or African American, non-Hispanic/Latino; 1 Asian, non-Hispanic/Latino; 1 Hispanic/Latino), 12 international. Average age 27. 75 applicants, 83% accepted, 16 enrolled. In 2014, 17 master's awarded. *Application deadline:* For fall admission, 3/1 for domestic students. *Expenses: Tuition:* Full-time $21,762; part-time $1209 per credit hour. Tuition and fees vary according to degree level, campus/location and program. *Financial support:* In 2014–15, 27 students received support. *Unit head:* Barbara Pena, Associate Director, 415-422-2765, Fax: 415-422-6983. *Application contact:* Mark Landerghini, Information Contact, 415-422-5101, Fax: 415-422-6983, E-mail: asgraduate@usfca.edu.
Website: http://www.usfca.edu/artsci/idec/

University of Southern Mississippi, Graduate School, College of Arts and Letters, Department of Political Science, International Development, and International Affairs, Hattiesburg, MS 39406-0001. Offers international development (PhD); political science (MA, MS). Part-time and evening/weekend programs available. Postbaccalaureate

distance learning degree programs offered. *Degree requirements:* For master's, comprehensive exam, thesis (for some programs); for doctorate, comprehensive exam, thesis/dissertation. *Entrance requirements:* For master's, GRE General Test, minimum GPA of 2.75 in last 2 years, 3.0 in field of study; for doctorate, GRE General Test, minimum GPA of 3.5. Additional exam requirements/recommendations for international students: Required—TOEFL, IELTS. *Faculty research:* American politics, international politics, political theory, comparative politics, public law.

Walden University, Graduate Programs, School of Public Policy and Administration, Minneapolis, MN 55401. Offers criminal justice (MPA, MPP, MS, Graduate Certificate), including emergency management (MS, PhD), general program (MS, PhD), homeland security and policy coordination (MS, PhD), law and public policy (MS, PhD), policy analysis (MS, PhD), public management and leadership (MS, PhD), self-designed (MS), terrorism, mediation, and peace (MS, PhD); criminal justice leadership and executive management (MS), including emergency management (MS, PhD), general program (MS, PhD), homeland security and policy coordination (MS, PhD), law and public policy (MS, PhD), policy analysis (MS, PhD), public management and leadership (MS, PhD), self-designed, terrorism, mediation, and peace (MS, PhD); emergency management (MPA, MPP, MS), including criminal justice (MS, PhD), general program (MS, PhD), homeland security (MS), public management and leadership (MS, PhD), terrorism and emergency management (MS); general program (MPA, MPP); government management (Graduate Certificate); health policy (MPA, MPP); homeland security (Graduate Certificate); homeland security and policy coordination (MPA, MPP); international nongovernmental organizations (MPA, MPP); law and public policy (MPA, MPP); local government management for sustainable communities (MPA, MPP); nonprofit management (Graduate Certificate); nonprofit management and leadership (MPA, MPP, MS); online teaching in higher education (Post-Master's Certificate); policy analysis (MPA); public management and leadership (MPA, MPP, Graduate Certificate); public policy (Graduate Certificate); public policy and administration (PhD), including criminal justice (MS, PhD), emergency management (MS, PhD), general program (MS, PhD), health policy, homeland security and policy coordination (MS, PhD), international nongovernmental organizations, law and public policy (MS, PhD), local government management for sustainable communities, nonprofit management and leadership, policy analysis (MS, PhD), public management and leadership (MS, PhD), terrorism, mediation, and peace (MS, PhD); strategic planning and public policy (Graduate Certificate); terrorism, mediation, and peace (MPA, MPP). Part-time and evening/weekend programs available. Postbaccalaureate distance learning degree programs offered (no on-campus study). *Faculty:* 13 full-time (5 women), 151 part-time/adjunct (65 women). *Students:* 1,009 full-time (573 women), 1,632 part-time (954 women); includes 1,553 minority (1,307 Black or African American, non-Hispanic/Latino; 15 American Indian or Alaska Native, non-Hispanic/Latino; 38 Asian, non-Hispanic/Latino; 127 Hispanic/Latino; 66 Two or more races, non-Hispanic/Latino), 15 international. Average age 42. 665 applicants, 97% accepted, 616 enrolled. In 2014, 317 master's, 95 doctorates, 34 other advanced degrees awarded. *Degree requirements:* For doctorate, thesis/dissertation, residency. *Entrance requirements:* For master's, bachelor's degree or higher; minimum GPA of 2.5; official transcripts; goal statement (for some programs); access to computer and Internet; for doctorate, master's degree or higher; three years of related professional or academic experience (preferred); minimum GPA of 3.0; goal statement and current resume (for select programs); official transcripts; access to computer and Internet; for other advanced degree, relevant work experience; access to computer and Internet. Additional exam requirements/recommendations for international students: Required—TOEFL (minimum score 550 paper-based, 79 iBT), IELTS (minimum score 6.5), Michigan English Language Assessment Battery (minimum score 82), or PTE (minimum score 53). *Application deadline:* Applications are processed on a rolling basis. Application fee: $0. Electronic applications accepted. *Expenses: Tuition:* Full-time $11,925; part-time $500 per credit hour. *Required fees:* $647. *Financial support:* Fellowships, Federal Work-Study, scholarships/grants, unspecified assistantships, and family tuition reduction, active duty/veteran tuition reduction, group tuition reduction, interest-free payment plans, employee tuition reduction available. Support available to part-time students. Financial award applicants required to submit FAFSA. *Unit head:* Dr. Shana Garrett, Associate Dean, 866-492-5336. *Application contact:* Meghan Thomas, Vice President of Enrollment Management, 866-492-5336, E-mail: info@waldenu.edu.
Website: http://www.waldenu.edu/programs/colleges-schools/public-policy-and-administration

International Trade Policy

The George Washington University, Elliott School of International Affairs, Program in International Trade and Investment Policy, Washington, DC 20052. Offers MA. Part-time programs available. *Students:* 28 full-time (14 women), 15 part-time (7 women); includes 11 minority (1 Black or African American, non-Hispanic/Latino; 6 Asian, non-Hispanic/Latino; 3 Hispanic/Latino; 1 Two or more races, non-Hispanic/Latino), 15 international. Average age 27. 75 applicants, 14 enrolled. In 2014, 21 master's awarded. *Degree requirements:* For master's, one foreign language, capstone project. *Entrance requirements:* For master's, GRE General Test, 2 years of a modern foreign language, 2 semesters of introductory economics. Additional exam requirements/recommendations for international students: Required—TOEFL (minimum score 100 iBT), IELTS (minimum score 7). *Application deadline:* For fall admission, 1/15 priority date for domestic and international students; for spring admission, 10/1 for domestic students. Application fee: $75. Electronic applications accepted. *Financial support:* In 2014–15, 11 students received support. Fellowships with partial tuition reimbursements available, Federal Work-Study, and scholarships/grants available. Financial award application deadline: 1/15. *Unit head:* Prof. Michael Moore, Director, 202-994-5230, E-mail: itip@gwu.edu. *Application contact:* Nicole A. Campbell, Director of Graduate Admissions, 202-994-7050, Fax: 202-994-9537, E-mail: esiagrad@gwu.edu.
Website: http://elliott.gwu.edu/international-trade-investment-policy

Political Science

Acadia University, Faculty of Arts, Department of Political Science, Wolfville, NS B4P 2R6, Canada. Offers MA. *Degree requirements:* For master's, thesis. *Entrance requirements:* For master's, honors degree or equivalent. Additional exam requirements/recommendations for international students: Required—TOEFL (minimum score 580 paper-based; 93 iBT), IELTS (minimum score 6.5). *Faculty research:* Atlantic Canada, international relations and organization, human rights, Canadian politics, political thought, technology.

American Public University System, AMU/APU Graduate Programs, Charles Town, WV 25414. Offers accounting (MBA, MS); criminal justice (MA), including business administration, emergency and disaster management, general (MA, MS); educational leadership (M Ed); emergency and disaster management (MA); entrepreneurship (MBA); environmental policy and management (MS), including environmental planning, environmental sustainability, fish and wildlife management, general (MA, MS), global environmental management; finance (MBA); general (MBA); global business management (MBA); history (MA), including American history, ancient and classical history, European history, global history, public history; homeland security (MA), including business administration, counter-terrorism studies, criminal justice, cyber, emergency management and public health, intelligence studies, transportation security; homeland security resource allocation (MBA); humanities (MA); information technology (MS), including digital forensics, enterprise software development, information assurance and security, IT project management; information technology management (MBA); intelligence studies (MA), including criminal intelligence, cyber, general (MA, MS), homeland security, intelligence analysis, intelligence collection, intelligence management, intelligence operations, terrorism studies; international relations and conflict resolution (MA), including comparative and security issues, conflict resolution, international and transnational security issues, peacekeeping; legal studies (MA); management (MA), including defense management, general (MA, MS), human resource management, organizational leadership, public administration; marketing (MBA); military history (MA), including American military history, American Revolution, civil war, war since 1945, World War II; military studies (MA), including joint warfare, strategic leadership; national security studies (MA), including general (MA, MS), homeland security, regional security studies, security and intelligence analysis, terrorism studies; nonprofit management (MBA); political science (MA), including American politics and government, comparative government and development, general (MA, MS), international relations, public policy; psychology (MA); public administration (MPA), including disaster management, environmental policy, health policy, human resources, national security, organizational management, security management; public health (MPH); reverse logistics management (MA); school counseling (M Ed); security management (MA); space studies (MS), including aerospace science, general (MA, MS), planetary science; sports and health sciences (MS); teaching (M Ed), including curriculum and instruction for elementary teachers, elementary reading, English language learners, instructional leadership, online learning, special education; transportation and logistics management (MA), including general (MA, MS), maritime engineering management, reverse logistics management. Programs offered via distance learning only. Part-time and evening/weekend programs available. Postbaccalaureate distance learning degree programs offered (no on-campus study). *Faculty:* 426 full-time (236 women), 1,864 part-time/adjunct (880 women). *Students:* 475 full-time (215 women), 10,067 part-time (4,085 women); includes 3,462 minority (1,863 Black or African American, non-Hispanic/Latino; 74 American Indian or Alaska Native, non-Hispanic/Latino; 273 Asian, non-Hispanic/Latino; 831 Hispanic/Latino; 78 Native Hawaiian or other Pacific Islander, non-Hispanic/Latino; 343 Two or more races, non-Hispanic/Latino), 131 international. Average age 36. In 2014, 3,740 master's awarded. *Degree requirements:* For master's, comprehensive exam or practicum. *Entrance requirements:* For master's, official transcript showing earned bachelor's degree from institution accredited by recognized accrediting body. Additional exam requirements/recommendations for international students: Required—TOEFL (minimum score 550 paper-based), IELTS (minimum score 6.5). *Application deadline:* Applications are processed on a rolling basis. Application fee: $0. Electronic applications accepted. *Financial support:* Applicants required to submit FAFSA. *Faculty research:* Military history, criminal justice, management performance, national security. *Unit head:* Dr. Karan Powell, Executive Vice President and Provost, 877-468-6268, Fax: 304-724-3780. *Application contact:* Terry Grant, Vice President of Enrollment Management, 877-468-6268, Fax: 304-724-3780, E-mail: info@apus.edu.
Website: http://www.apus.edu

American University, School of Communication, Program in Political Communication, Washington, DC 20016-8001. Offers MA. Part-time and evening/weekend programs available. *Students:* 8 full-time (7 women), 2 part-time (both women); includes 3 minority (2 Black or African American, non-Hispanic/Latino; 1 Hispanic/Latino), 1 international. 33 applicants, 58% accepted, 8 enrolled. In 2014, 11 master's awarded. *Degree requirements:* For master's, comprehensive exam, thesis or alternative. *Entrance requirements:* For master's, GRE General Test. Additional exam requirements/recommendations for international students: Required—TOEFL (minimum score 600 paper-based; 100 iBT), IELTS (minimum score 7). *Application deadline:* For fall admission, 2/1 priority date for domestic students, 2/1 for international students; for spring admission, 11/15 for domestic students, 11/1 for international students. Applications are processed on a rolling basis. Application fee: $55. Electronic applications accepted. *Financial support:* In 2014–15, 3 research assistantships with full tuition reimbursements (averaging $15,000 per year) were awarded; career-related internships or fieldwork, Federal Work-Study, institutionally sponsored loans, scholarships/grants, tuition waivers (partial), and unspecified assistantships also available. Financial award application deadline: 2/1; financial award applicants required to submit FAFSA. *Faculty research:* Polling and public opinion, political polling, advocacy communication, entertainment and politics, communication research and management, political communication theory, campaign ethics. *Unit head:* Prof. Pallavi

Kumar, Division Director, 202-885-2047, Fax: 202-885-2099, E-mail: kumar@american.edu. *Application contact:* Sharmeen Ahsan-Bracciale, Graduate Admissions Office, 202-885-2040, Fax: 202-885-2019, E-mail: gradcomm@american.edu.
Website: http://www.american.edu/soc/communication/degrees/MA-POLC-SOC.cfm

American University, School of International Service, Washington, DC 20016-8071. Offers comparative and regional studies (Certificate); cross-cultural communication (Certificate); development management (MS); ethics, peace, and global affairs (MA); European studies (Certificate); global environmental policy (MA, Certificate); global information technology (Certificate); international affairs (MA), including comparative and international disability policy, comparative and regional studies, international economic relations, international politics, natural resources and sustainable development, U.S. foreign policy; international communication (MA, Certificate); international development (MA, Certificate); international economic policy (Certificate); international economic relations (Certificate); international media (MA); international peace and conflict resolution (MA, Certificate); international politics (Certificate); international relations (PhD); international service (MIS); peacebuilding (Certificate); social enterprise (MA); the Americas (Certificate); United States foreign policy (Certificate); JD/MA. Part-time and evening/weekend programs available. Postbaccalaureate distance learning degree programs offered (no on-campus study). *Faculty:* 112 full-time (43 women), 59 part-time/adjunct (27 women). *Students:* 545 full-time (335 women), 443 part-time (271 women); includes 231 minority (82 Black or African American, non-Hispanic/Latino; 8 American Indian or Alaska Native, non-Hispanic/Latino; 51 Asian, non-Hispanic/Latino; 81 Hispanic/Latino; 2 Native Hawaiian or other Pacific Islander, non-Hispanic/Latino; 7 Two or more races, non-Hispanic/Latino), 120 international. Average age 28. 1,991 applicants, 70% accepted, 365 enrolled. In 2014, 426 master's, 9 doctorates, 6 other advanced degrees awarded. Terminal master's awarded for partial completion of doctoral program. *Degree requirements:* For master's, one foreign language, comprehensive exam, thesis or alternative; for doctorate, one foreign language, comprehensive exam, thesis/dissertation. *Entrance requirements:* For master's, GRE, transcripts, resume, 2 letters of recommendation, statement of purpose; for doctorate, GRE, transcripts, resume, 3 letters of recommendation, statement of purpose. Additional exam requirements/recommendations for international students: Required—TOEFL (minimum score 600 paper-based; 100 iBT). *Application deadline:* For fall admission, 1/15 for domestic students; for spring admission, 10/1 for domestic students, 9/15 for international students. Application fee: $50. Electronic applications accepted. *Financial support:* Application deadline: 1/15. *Unit head:* Dr. James Goldgeier, Dean, 202-885-1603, Fax: 202-885-2494, E-mail: goldgeier@american.edu. *Application contact:* Jia Jiang, Associate Director, Graduate Education Enrollment, 202-885-1689, Fax: 202-885-1109, E-mail: jiang@american.edu.
Website: http://www.american.edu/sis/

The American University in Cairo, School of Humanities and Social Sciences, Department of Political Science, Cairo, Egypt. Offers MA. *Degree requirements:* For master's, thesis. *Entrance requirements:* Additional exam requirements/recommendations for international students: Required—English entrance exam and/or TOEFL. Electronic applications accepted. Tuition and fees vary according to course load and program. *Faculty research:* African and Middle East politics, international relations, development of human rights, international law.

American University of Armenia, Graduate Programs, Yerevan, Armenia. Offers business administration (MBA); computer and information science (MS), including business management, design and manufacturing, energy (ME, MS), industrial engineering and systems management; economics (MS); industrial engineering and systems management (ME), including business, computer aided design/manufacturing, energy (ME, MS), information technology; law (LL M); political science and international affairs (MPSIA); public health (MPH); teaching English as a foreign language (MA). Part-time and evening/weekend programs available. *Degree requirements:* For master's, thesis (for some programs), capstone/project. *Entrance requirements:* For master's, GRE, GMAT, or LSAT. Additional exam requirements/recommendations for international students: Recommended—TOEFL (minimum score 79 iBT), IELTS (minimum score 6.5). *Faculty research:* Microfinance, finance (rural/development, international, corporate), firm life cycle theory, TESOL, language proficiency testing, public policy, administrative law, economic development, cryptography, artificial intelligence, energy efficiency/renewable energy, computer-aided design/manufacturing, health financing, tuberculosis control, mother/child health, preventive ophthalmology, post-earthquake psychopathological investigations, tobacco control, environmental health risk assessments.

American University of Beirut, Graduate Programs, Faculty of Arts and Sciences, Beirut, Lebanon. Offers anthropology (MA); Arab and Middle Eastern history (PhD); Arabic language and literature (MA, PhD); archaeology (MA); biology (MS); cell and molecular biology (PhD); chemistry (MS); clinical psychology (MA); computational sciences (MS); computer science (MS); economics (MA); English language (MA); English literature (MA); environmental policy planning (MS); financial economics (MAFE); geology (MS); history (MA); mathematics (MA, MS); media studies (MA); Middle Eastern studies (MA); physics (MS); political studies (MA); psychology (MA); public administration (MA); sociology (MA); statistics (MA, MS); theoretical physics (PhD); transnational American studies (MA). Part-time programs available. *Faculty:* 107 full-time (32 women), 6 part-time/adjunct (2 women). *Students:* 230 full-time (161 women), 209 part-time (146 women). Average age 26. 261 applicants, 70% accepted, 83 enrolled. In 2014, 68 master's, 2 doctorates awarded. *Degree requirements:* For master's, one foreign language, comprehensive exam, thesis (for some programs); for doctorate, one foreign language, comprehensive exam, thesis/dissertation. *Entrance requirements:* For master's, GRE (for some MA/MS programs), letter of recommendation; for doctorate, GRE, letters of recommendation. Additional exam requirements/recommendations for international students: Required—TOEFL (minimum score 600 paper-based; 97 iBT), IELTS (minimum score 7). *Application deadline:* For fall admission, 4/1 for domestic and international students; for spring admission, 11/1 for domestic and international students. Application fee: $50. Electronic applications accepted. *Expenses: Tuition:* Full-time $15,462; part-time $859 per credit. *Required fees:* $692. Tuition and fees vary according to course load and program. *Financial support:* Research assistantships, career-related internships or fieldwork, institutionally sponsored loans, scholarships/grants, health care benefits, and unspecified assistantships available. Financial award application deadline: 2/4; financial award applicants required to submit FAFSA. *Faculty research:* Determinants of language proficiency among Arab learners of English as a foreign language; opinion mining, information retrieval, runtime verification, high performance computing; solar and fuel cells, self-organizing systems, heterocyclic chemistry, air and water chemistry; complex analysis, harmonic analysis, number theory; social and political psychology, clinical psychology; thin films physics and technology; theory of soft matter; religious and ethnic conflict; sports and politics. *Total annual research expenditures:* $966,000. *Unit head:* Dr. Patrick McGreevy, Dean, 961-1374374 Ext. 3800, Fax: 961-1744461, E-mail: pm07@aub.edu.lb. *Application contact:* Dr. Salim Kanaan, Director, Admissions Office, 961-1350000 Ext. 2590, Fax: 961-1750775, E-mail: sk00@aub.edu.lb.
Website: http://www.aub.edu.lb/fas/

Appalachian State University, Cratis D. Williams Graduate School, Department of Government and Justice Studies, Boone, NC 28608. Offers criminal justice (MS); political science (MA), including American government, environmental politics and policy analysis, international relations; public administration (MPA), including public management, town, city and county management. Part-time programs available. Postbaccalaureate distance learning degree programs offered (no on-campus study). *Degree requirements:* For master's, variable foreign language requirement, comprehensive exam, thesis optional. *Entrance requirements:* For master's, GRE General Test, 3 letters of recommendation. Additional exam requirements/recommendations for international students: Required—TOEFL (minimum score 570 paper-based; 79 iBT), IELTS (minimum score 6.5). Electronic applications accepted. *Faculty research:* Campaign finance, emerging democracies, bureaucratic politics, judicial behavior, administration of justice.

Arizona State University at the Tempe campus, College of Liberal Arts and Sciences, School of Politics and Global Studies, Tempe, AZ 85287-3902. Offers political science (MA, PhD). Part-time programs available. Terminal master's awarded for partial completion of doctoral program. *Degree requirements:* For master's, thesis or alternative, interactive Program of Study (iPOS) submitted before completing 50 percent of required credit hours; for doctorate, comprehensive exam, thesis/dissertation, interactive Program of Study (iPOS) submitted before completing 50 percent of required credit hours. *Entrance requirements:* For master's and doctorate, GRE, minimum GPA of 3.0 or equivalent in last 2 years of work leading to bachelor's degree. Additional exam requirements/recommendations for international students: Required—TOEFL, IELTS, or PTE. Electronic applications accepted.

Arkansas State University, Graduate School, College of Humanities and Social Sciences, Department of Political Science, State University, AR 72467. Offers political science (MA); political science education (SCCT); public administration (MPA). *Accreditation:* NASPAA (one or more programs are accredited). Part-time programs available. *Faculty:* 7 full-time (2 women). *Students:* 25 full-time (8 women), 153 part-time (86 women); includes 69 minority (50 Black or African American, non-Hispanic/Latino; 3 American Indian or Alaska Native, non-Hispanic/Latino; 3 Asian, non-Hispanic/Latino; 9 Hispanic/Latino; 4 Two or more races, non-Hispanic/Latino), 15 international. Average age 34. 184 applicants, 57% accepted, 69 enrolled. In 2014, 41 master's awarded. *Degree requirements:* For master's, comprehensive exam, thesis or alternative; for SCCT, comprehensive exam. *Entrance requirements:* For master's, GRE General Test or MAT, GMAT, appropriate bachelor's degree, letters of recommendation, official transcripts, immunization records, statement of purpose; for SCCT, GRE General Test or MAT, GMAT, interview, master's degree, official transcript, letters of recommendation, immunization records. Additional exam requirements/recommendations for international students: Required—TOEFL (minimum score 550 paper-based; 79 iBT), IELTS (minimum score 6), PTE (minimum score 56). *Application deadline:* For fall admission, 7/1 for domestic and international students; for spring admission, 11/15 for domestic students, 11/14 for international students. Applications are processed on a rolling basis. Application fee: $30 ($40 for international students). Electronic applications accepted. *Expenses:* Tuition, state resident: full-time $4392; part-time $244 per credit hour. Tuition, nonresident: full-time $8784; part-time $488 per credit hour. *International tuition:* $9484 full-time. *Required fees:* $1134; $63 per credit hour. $25 per term. Tuition and fees vary according to course load and program. *Financial support:* In 2014–15, 17 students received support. Teaching assistantships, career-related internships or fieldwork, scholarships/grants, and unspecified assistantships available. Financial award application deadline: 7/1; financial award applicants required to submit FAFSA. *Unit head:* Dr. William McLean, Chair, 870-972-3048, Fax: 870-972-2720, E-mail: wmclean@astate.edu. *Application contact:* Vickey Ring, Graduate Admissions Coordinator, 870-972-3029, Fax: 870-972-3857, E-mail: vickeyring@astate.edu.
Website: http://www.astate.edu/college/humanities-and-social-sciences/departments/political-science/

Ashland University, College of Arts and Sciences, Program in American History and Government, Ashland, OH 44805-3702. Offers MAHG. Part-time programs available. *Degree requirements:* For master's, capstone project or thesis. *Entrance requirements:* For master's, minimum undergraduate GPA of 2.75, 3.0 graduate. Electronic applications accepted. *Expenses:* Contact institution. *Faculty research:* American founding, United States Civil War, Progressive Era.

Auburn University, Graduate School, College of Liberal Arts, Department of Political Science, Auburn University, AL 36849. Offers public administration (MPA, PhD, Graduate Certificate); MPA/MCP. Part-time programs available. *Faculty:* 20 full-time (8 women), 7 part-time/adjunct (3 women). *Students:* 41 full-time (16 women), 49 part-time (22 women); includes 21 minority (all Black or African American, non-Hispanic/Latino), 9 international. Average age 35. 58 applicants, 48% accepted, 12 enrolled. In 2014, 21 master's, 4 doctorates, 3 other advanced degrees awarded. *Degree requirements:* For doctorate, thesis/dissertation. *Entrance requirements:* For master's, GRE General Test, minimum GPA of 3.0 in political science, 2.5 overall; for doctorate, GRE General Test. *Application deadline:* For fall admission, 7/7 for domestic students; for spring admission, 11/24 for domestic students. Applications are processed on a rolling basis. Application fee: $50 ($60 for international students). Electronic applications accepted. *Expenses:* Tuition, state resident: full-time $8586; part-time $477 per credit hour. Tuition, nonresident: full-time $25,758; part-time $1431 per credit hour. *Required fees:* $804 per semester. Tuition and fees vary according to degree level and program. *Financial support:* Fellowships, research assistantships, teaching assistantships, career-related internships or fieldwork, and Federal Work-Study available. Support available to part-time students. Financial award application deadline: 3/15; financial award applicants required to submit FAFSA. *Faculty research:* Policy evaluation, political economy, privatization, participation, election administration. *Total annual research expenditures:* $200,000. *Unit head:* Dr. Steve Brown, Chair, 334-844-5370. *Application contact:* Dr. George Flowers, Dean of the Graduate School, 334-844-2125.
Website: http://cla.auburn.edu/polisci/

Auburn University at Montgomery, College of Public Policy and Justice, Department of Political Science and Public Administration, Montgomery, AL 36124-4023. Offers international relations (MIR); nonprofit management and leadership (Certificate); political science (MPS); public administration (MPA); public administration and public policy (PhD); public health care administration and policy (Certificate). PhD offered jointly with Auburn University. *Accreditation:* NASPAA (one or more programs are accredited). Part-time and evening/weekend programs available. *Faculty:* 5 full-time (1 woman), 1 part-time/adjunct (0 women). *Students:* 9 full-time (7 women), 40 part-time (26 women); includes 16 minority (13 Black or African American, non-Hispanic/Latino; 1 American Indian or Alaska Native, non-Hispanic/Latino; 1 Hispanic/Latino; 1 Two or more races, non-Hispanic/Latino), 2 international. Average age 29. 20 applicants, 90% accepted, 12 enrolled. In 2014, 13 master's awarded. *Degree requirements:* For master's, comprehensive exam; for doctorate, thesis/dissertation. *Entrance requirements:* For master's, GRE General Test or MAT; for doctorate, GRE General Test. *Application deadline:* Applications are processed on a rolling basis. Electronic applications accepted. *Expenses:* Tuition, state resident: full-time $6264; part-time $348 per credit hour. Tuition, nonresident: full-time $14,094; part-time $783 per credit hour. *Financial*

support: In 2014–15, 1 teaching assistantship was awarded; research assistantships, career-related internships or fieldwork, and scholarships/grants also available. Support available to part-time students. Financial award application deadline: 3/1; financial award applicants required to submit FAFSA. *Unit head:* Dr. Andrew Cortell, Department Head, 334-244-3622, E-mail: acortell@aum.edu. Website: http://www.cla.auburn.edu/polisci/graduate-programs/phd-in-public-administration-and-public-policy/

Ball State University, Graduate School, College of Sciences and Humanities, Department of Political Science, Program in Political Science, Muncie, IN 47306-1099. Offers MA. *Students:* 7 full-time (3 women), 5 part-time (2 women); includes 1 minority (Black or African American, non-Hispanic/Latino), 2 international. Average age 30. 16 applicants, 75% accepted, 4 enrolled. In 2014, 4 master's awarded. Application fee: $50. *Financial support:* In 2014–15, 4 students received support, including 4 research assistantships with partial tuition reimbursements available (averaging $9,245 per year). Financial award application deadline: 3/1. *Faculty research:* Survey research, public policy. *Unit head:* Dr. Joseph Losco, Director, 765-285-8780, Fax: 765-285-5345, E-mail: jlosco@bsu.edu. *Application contact:* Dr. Gary Crawley, Associate Provost for Research and Dean of the Graduate School, 765-285-8785, E-mail: gcrawley@bsu.edu. Website: http://www.bsu.edu/poli-sci/

Baylor University, Graduate School, College of Arts and Sciences, Department of Political Science, Waco, TX 76798. Offers international studies (MA); political science (MA, PhD); public policy and administration (MPPA); JD/MPPA. Terminal master's awarded for partial completion of doctoral program. *Degree requirements:* For master's, variable foreign language requirement, comprehensive exam (for some programs), thesis (for some programs); for doctorate, variable foreign language requirement, comprehensive exam, thesis/dissertation. *Entrance requirements:* For master's and doctorate, GRE General Test. Additional exam requirements/recommendations for international students: Required—TOEFL. Electronic applications accepted.

Binghamton University, State University of New York, Graduate School, School of Arts and Sciences, Department of Political Science, Vestal, NY 13850. Offers MA, PhD. *Faculty:* 20 full-time (7 women), 2 part-time/adjunct (1 woman). *Students:* 24 full-time (7 women), 22 part-time (6 women); includes 5 minority (2 Black or African American, non-Hispanic/Latino; 1 American Indian or Alaska Native, non-Hispanic/Latino; 2 Hispanic/Latino), 18 international. Average age 30. 71 applicants, 35% accepted, 5 enrolled. In 2014, 14 master's, 4 doctorates awarded. Terminal master's awarded for partial completion of doctoral program. *Degree requirements:* For master's, comprehensive exam (for some programs), thesis (for some programs); for doctorate, variable foreign language requirement, comprehensive exam, thesis/dissertation. *Entrance requirements:* For master's and doctorate, GRE General Test. Additional exam requirements/recommendations for international students: Required—TOEFL (minimum score 550 paper-based; 80 iBT). *Application deadline:* For fall admission, 2/15 priority date for domestic and international students. Applications are processed on a rolling basis. Application fee: $75. Electronic applications accepted. *Expenses:* Tuition, state resident: full-time $7776; part-time $432 per credit. Tuition, nonresident: full-time $15,138; part-time $841 per credit. *Required fees:* $1754; $213 per credit. Tuition and fees vary according to degree level and program. *Financial support:* In 2014–15, 27 students received support, including 4 research assistantships with full tuition reimbursements available (averaging $15,000 per year), 19 teaching assistantships with full tuition reimbursements available (averaging $15,000 per year); career-related internships or fieldwork, Federal Work-Study, institutionally sponsored loans, scholarships/grants, health care benefits, tuition waivers (full), and unspecified assistantships also available. Financial award application deadline: 2/15; financial award applicants required to submit FAFSA. *Unit head:* Dr. Benjamin Fordham, Chairperson, 607-777-2946, E-mail: bfordham@binghamton.edu. *Application contact:* Kishan Zuber, Recruiting and Admissions Coordinator, 607-777-2151, Fax: 607-777-2501, E-mail: kzuber@binghamton.edu.

Boston College, Graduate School of Arts and Sciences, Department of Political Science, Chestnut Hill, MA 02467-3800. Offers MA, PhD. *Faculty:* 28 full-time. *Students:* 55 full-time (16 women); includes 2 minority (1 Asian, non-Hispanic/Latino; 1 Hispanic/Latino), 6 international. 168 applicants, 52% accepted, 15 enrolled. In 2014, 6 master's, 2 doctorates awarded. Terminal master's awarded for partial completion of doctoral program. *Degree requirements:* For master's, thesis or alternative; for doctorate, one foreign language, thesis/dissertation. *Entrance requirements:* For master's and doctorate, GRE General Test. Additional exam requirements/recommendations for international students: Required—TOEFL (minimum score 600 paper-based; 100 iBT), IELTS (minimum score 7). *Application deadline:* For fall admission, 1/2 for domestic and international students. Application fee: $75. Electronic applications accepted. *Financial support:* In 2014–15, fellowships with full tuition reimbursements (averaging $21,000 per year), research assistantships with full tuition reimbursements (averaging $21,000 per year), teaching assistantships with full tuition reimbursements (averaging $21,000 per year) were awarded; Federal Work-Study, scholarships/grants, health care benefits, tuition waivers (full and partial), and unspecified assistantships also available. Support available to part-time students. Financial award application deadline: 3/1; financial award applicants required to submit FAFSA. *Faculty research:* Political theory, American politics, international politics, comparative politics. *Unit head:* Dr. Susan Shell, Chairperson, 617-552-4161, E-mail: susan.shell@bc.edu. *Application contact:* Dr. Nasser Behnegar, Graduate Program Director, 617-552-1897, E-mail: nasser.behnegar@bc.edu. Website: http://www.bc.edu/polisci

Boston University, Graduate School of Arts and Sciences, Department of Political Science, Boston, MA 02215. Offers MA, PhD. *Students:* 51 full-time (25 women), 4 part-time (1 woman); includes 6 minority (2 Black or African American, non-Hispanic/Latino; 3 Asian, non-Hispanic/Latino; 1 Two or more races, non-Hispanic/Latino), 20 international. Average age 32. 97 applicants, 19% accepted, 9 enrolled. In 2014, 12 master's, 4 doctorates awarded. Terminal master's awarded for partial completion of doctoral program. *Degree requirements:* For master's, one foreign language; for doctorate, 2 foreign languages, comprehensive exam, thesis/dissertation. *Entrance requirements:* For master's and doctorate, GRE General Test, 3 letters of recommendation. Additional exam requirements/recommendations for international students: Required—TOEFL (minimum score 600 paper-based; 84 iBT). *Application deadline:* For fall admission, 12/1 for domestic and international students. Application fee: $80. Electronic applications accepted. *Expenses: Tuition:* Full-time $45,686; part-time $1428 per credit hour. *Required fees:* $660; $60 per semester. Tuition and fees vary according to program. *Financial support:* In 2014–15, 56 students received support, including 7 fellowships with full tuition reimbursements available (averaging $20,500 per year), 3 research assistantships with full tuition reimbursements available (averaging $20,500 per year), 11 teaching assistantships with full tuition reimbursements available (averaging $20,500 per year); career-related internships or fieldwork, Federal Work-Study, and health care benefits also available. Support available to part-time students. Financial award application deadline: 12/1. *Unit head:* Graham Wilson, Chairman, 617-353-2545, Fax: 617-353-5508, E-mail: gkwilson@bu.edu. *Application contact:* Nicole Rothenberg, Graduate Program

Coordinator, 617-353-2541, Fax: 617-353-5508, E-mail: pograd@bu.edu. Website: http://www.bu.edu/polisci/

Bowling Green State University, Graduate College, College of Arts and Sciences, Department of Political Science, Program in Political Science, Bowling Green, OH 43403. Offers MA/MA. *Entrance requirements:* Additional exam requirements/recommendations for international students: Required—TOEFL. Electronic applications accepted.

Brandeis University, Graduate School of Arts and Sciences, Department of Politics, Waltham, MA 02454-9110. Offers MA, PhD. *Faculty:* 14 full-time (3 women). *Students:* 15 full-time (6 women); includes 1 minority (Hispanic/Latino), 3 international. 120 applicants, 9% accepted, 5 enrolled. In 2014, 6 doctorates awarded. Terminal master's awarded for partial completion of doctoral program. *Degree requirements:* For master's, thesis or alternative, proseminar; for doctorate, one foreign language, comprehensive exam, thesis/dissertation, proseminar; teaching requirement; research tools requirement; qualifying exams. *Entrance requirements:* For master's and doctorate, GRE General Test, sample of written work, resume, 3 letters of recommendation, statement of purpose, transcript(s). Additional exam requirements/recommendations for international students: Required—TOEFL (minimum score 600 paper-based; 100 iBT), PTE (minimum score 68); Recommended—IELTS (minimum score 7). *Application deadline:* For fall admission, 1/15 priority date for domestic and international students. Application fee: $75. Electronic applications accepted. *Financial support:* In 2014–15, 8 fellowships with full tuition reimbursements (averaging $20,800 per year), 3 teaching assistantships with partial tuition reimbursements (averaging $3,200 per year) were awarded; Federal Work-Study, scholarships/grants, health care benefits, and tuition waivers (partial) also available. Financial award application deadline: 2/1; financial award applicants required to submit FAFSA. *Faculty research:* American institutions, international law and foreign policy, political theory, comparative politics, European politics. *Unit head:* Dr. Kerry Chase, Director of Graduate Studies, 781-736-2725, Fax: 781-736-2777, E-mail: chase@brandeis.edu. *Application contact:* Rosanne Colocouris, Department Administrator, 781-736-2755, Fax: 781-736-2777, E-mail: colocour@brandeis.edu. Website: http://www.brandeis.edu/gsas/programs/politics.html

Brigham Young University, Graduate Studies, Marriott School of Management, Master of Public Administration Program, Provo, UT 84602. Offers finance (MPA); human resources (MPA); local government (MPA); nonprofit management (MPA); JD/MPA. *Students:* 100 full-time (51 women); includes 15 minority (1 Black or African American, non-Hispanic/Latino; 4 Asian, non-Hispanic/Latino; 7 Hispanic/Latino; 3 Native Hawaiian or other Pacific Islander, non-Hispanic/Latino), 12 international. Average age 27. 86 applicants, 69% accepted, 46 enrolled. In 2014, 49 master's awarded. *Entrance requirements:* For master's, GRE or GMAT, minimum GPA of 3.0, MPA Excel prep course. Additional exam requirements/recommendations for international students: Required—TOEFL (minimum score 580 paper-based; 85 iBT). *Application deadline:* For fall admission, 2/1 for domestic and international students. Application fee: $50. Electronic applications accepted. *Expenses: Tuition:* Full-time $6310; part-time $371 per credit hour. Tuition and fees vary according to program and student's religious affiliation. *Financial support:* In 2014–15, 94 students received support. Career-related internships or fieldwork, institutionally sponsored loans, and scholarships/grants available. Financial award application deadline: 4/15; financial award applicants required to submit FAFSA. *Faculty research:* Taxes, budgeting, nonprofit, ethics, decision modeling, work balance, organizational behavior. *Unit head:* Dr. Jeffery Thompson, Director, 801-422-4221, Fax: 801-422-0311, E-mail: mpa@byu.edu. *Application contact:* Catherine Cooper, Associate Director, 801-422-4221, Fax: 801-422-0311, E-mail: mpa@byu.edu. Website: http://mpa.byu.edu

Brock University, Faculty of Graduate Studies, Faculty of Social Sciences, Program in Political Science, St. Catharines, ON L2S 3A1, Canada. Offers Canadian politics (MA); comparative politics (MA); international relations (MA); political theory or philosophy (MA); public policy (MA). Part-time programs available. *Degree requirements:* For master's, thesis optional. *Entrance requirements:* For master's, honors degree. Additional exam requirements/recommendations for international students: Required—TOEFL (minimum score 550 paper-based; 80 iBT), IELTS (minimum score 6.5), TWE (minimum score 4). Electronic applications accepted. *Faculty research:* Public administration reform, economic and social justice, politics of societies, Canadian politics, international relations.

Brooklyn College of the City University of New York, School of Humanities and Social Sciences, Department of Political Science, Brooklyn, NY 11210-2889. Offers international affairs (MA); political science (MA); urban policy and administration (MA). Part-time and evening/weekend programs available. *Degree requirements:* For master's, comprehensive exam (for some programs), thesis or alternative, foreign language exam (for international affairs program). *Entrance requirements:* For master's, 2 letters of recommendation, personal statement. Additional exam requirements/recommendations for international students: Required—TOEFL (minimum score 500 paper-based; 61 iBT). *Faculty research:* Ethics and politics, politics of criminal justice, Western Europe, international law and politics, labor politics.

Brown University, Graduate School, Department of Political Science, Providence, RI 02912. Offers PhD. *Degree requirements:* For doctorate, thesis/dissertation. *Entrance requirements:* For doctorate, GRE General Test.

California Polytechnic State University, San Luis Obispo, College of Liberal Arts, Department of Political Science, San Luis Obispo, CA 93407. Offers MPP. Part-time programs available. *Faculty:* 2 full-time (1 woman). *Students:* 11 full-time (5 women), 4 part-time (2 women); includes 6 minority (1 Asian, non-Hispanic/Latino; 4 Hispanic/Latino; 1 Two or more races, non-Hispanic/Latino). Average age 28. 23 applicants, 74% accepted, 9 enrolled. In 2014, 6 master's awarded. *Degree requirements:* For master's, comprehensive exam. *Application deadline:* For fall admission, 2/1 for domestic and international students. Application fee: $55. *Expenses:* Tuition, state resident: full-time $6738; part-time $3906 per year. Tuition, nonresident: full-time $15,666; part-time $8370 per year. *Required fees:* $3447; $1001 per quarter. One-time fee: $3447 full-time; $3003 part-time. *Financial support:* Fellowships, research assistantships, career-related internships or fieldwork, Federal Work-Study, and scholarships/grants available. Support available to part-time students. Financial award application deadline: 3/2; financial award applicants required to submit FAFSA. *Faculty research:* Public policy analysis, public finance, policy internship. *Unit head:* Dr. Elizabeth Lowham, Graduate Coordinator, 805-756-2919, Fax: 805-756-7168, E-mail: elowham@calpoly.edu. *Application contact:* Dr. James Maraviglia, Associate Vice Provost for Marketing and Enrollment Development, 805-756-2311, Fax: 805-756-5400, E-mail: admissions@calpoly.edu. Website: http://mpp.calpoly.edu/

California State University, Chico, Office of Graduate Studies, College of Behavioral and Social Sciences, Political Science Department, Program in Political Science, Chico, CA 95929-0722. Offers MA. Part-time programs available. *Faculty:* 10 full-time (5 women), 2 part-time/adjunct (1 woman). *Students:* 16 full-time (7 women), 14 part-time (6 women); includes 8 minority (2 Black or African American, non-Hispanic/Latino; 1 Asian, non-Hispanic/Latino; 5 Hispanic/Latino), 4 international. Average age 30. 24

applicants, 79% accepted, 12 enrolled. In 2014, 8 master's awarded. *Degree requirements:* For master's, thesis or comprehensive examination. *Entrance requirements:* For master's, 2 letters of recommendation, statement of purpose. Additional exam requirements/recommendations for international students: Required—TOEFL (minimum score 550 paper-based; 80 iBT), IELTS (minimum score 6.5), PTE (minimum score 59). *Application deadline:* For fall admission, 3/1 priority date for domestic students, 3/1 for international students; for spring admission, 9/15 priority date for domestic students, 9/15 for international students. Application fee: $55. Electronic applications accepted. *Expenses:* Tuition, state resident: full-time $7002. Tuition, nonresident: full-time $18,162. *Required fees:* $1530. Tuition and fees vary according to program. *Financial support:* Career-related internships or fieldwork available. Financial award application deadline: 3/1; financial award applicants required to submit FAFSA. *Unit head:* Dr. Ryan Patten, Chair, 530-898-6506, Fax: 530-898-6910, E-mail: rpatten@csuchico.edu. *Application contact:* Judy L. Rice, School of Graduate, International, and Interdisciplinary Studies, 530-898-5416, Fax: 530-898-3342, E-mail: jlrice@csuchico.edu.
Website: http://catalog.csuchico.edu/viewer/11/POLS/POLSNONEMA.html

California State University, Fullerton, Graduate Studies, College of Humanities and Social Sciences, Division of Politics, Administration, and Justice, Fullerton, CA 92834-9480. Offers political science (MA); public administration (MPA). *Accreditation:* NASPAA (one or more programs are accredited). Part-time programs available. *Students:* 20 full-time (8 women), 85 part-time (40 women); includes 62 minority (3 Black or African American, non-Hispanic/Latino; 18 Asian, non-Hispanic/Latino; 38 Hispanic/Latino; 1 Native Hawaiian or other Pacific Islander, non-Hispanic/Latino; 2 Two or more races, non-Hispanic/Latino), 6 international. Average age 30. 97 applicants, 59% accepted, 32 enrolled. In 2014, 34 master's awarded. *Degree requirements:* For master's, comprehensive exam, project or thesis. *Entrance requirements:* For master's, minimum GPA of 2.5 in last 60 units of course work, 12 units of course work in social sciences. Application fee: $55. *Financial support:* Career-related internships or fieldwork, Federal Work-Study, institutionally sponsored loans, and scholarships/grants available. Support available to part-time students. Financial award application deadline: 3/1; financial award applicants required to submit FAFSA. *Faculty research:* Emergency management plans. *Unit head:* Dr. Stephen Stambough, Chair, 657-278-2933. *Application contact:* Admissions/Applications, 657-278-2371.

California State University, Long Beach, Graduate Studies, College of Liberal Arts, Department of Political Science, Long Beach, CA 90840. Offers MA. Part-time programs available. *Degree requirements:* For master's, one foreign language, comprehensive exam or thesis. *Entrance requirements:* For master's, GRE General Test, minimum GPA of 3.0 in field. Electronic applications accepted. *Faculty research:* Social welfare policy, international political economy, Marxism, voting behavior.

California State University, Los Angeles, Graduate Studies, College of Natural and Social Sciences, Department of Political Science, Los Angeles, CA 90032-8530. Offers political science (MA); public administration (MS). Part-time and evening/weekend programs available. *Degree requirements:* For master's, comprehensive exam or thesis. *Entrance requirements:* Additional exam requirements/recommendations for international students: Required—TOEFL (minimum score 500 paper-based). Electronic applications accepted. *Expenses:* Tuition, state resident: full-time $6738; part-time $3609 per year. Tuition, nonresident: full-time $15,666; part-time $8073 per year. Tuition and fees vary according to course load, degree level and program. *Faculty research:* Government; public policy and law; international, political, and economic relations; comparative politics.

California State University, Northridge, Graduate Studies, College of Social and Behavioral Sciences, Department of Political Science, Northridge, CA 91330. Offers MA. *Students:* 9 full-time (5 women), 10 part-time (5 women); includes 8 minority (7 Hispanic/Latino; 1 Native Hawaiian or other Pacific Islander, non-Hispanic/Latino), 3 international. Average age 32. *Degree requirements:* For master's, comprehensive exam. *Entrance requirements:* For master's, GRE (if cumulative undergraduate GPA less than 3.0), 2 letters of recommendation. Additional exam requirements/recommendations for international students: Required—TOEFL. *Application deadline:* For fall admission, 11/30 for domestic students. Application fee: $55. *Expenses: Required fees:* $12,402. *Financial support:* Application deadline: 3/1. *Unit head:* Dr. Lawrence Becker, Chair, 818-677-3488.
Website: http://www.csun.edu/csbs/departments/political_science/index.html

California State University, Sacramento, Office of Graduate Studies, College of Social Sciences and Interdisciplinary Studies, Department of Government, Sacramento, CA 95819. Offers MA. Part-time programs available. *Degree requirements:* For master's, thesis, project or comprehensive exam; writing proficiency exam. *Entrance requirements:* For master's, GRE, minimum GPA of 3.0 during previous 2 years. Additional exam requirements/recommendations for international students: Required—TOEFL. Electronic applications accepted.

Carleton University, Faculty of Graduate Studies, Faculty of Public Affairs and Management, Department of Political Science, Ottawa, ON K1S 5B6, Canada. Offers MA, PhD. *Degree requirements:* For master's, one foreign language, comprehensive exam, thesis optional; for doctorate, one foreign language, comprehensive exam, thesis/dissertation. *Entrance requirements:* For master's, honors degree in political science, minimum B average; for doctorate, master's degree in political science. Additional exam requirements/recommendations for international students: Required—TOEFL. *Faculty research:* Canadian politics, comparative politics, international relations, public administration and policy analysis, political theory.

Carleton University, Faculty of Graduate Studies, Faculty of Public Affairs and Management, Institute of Political Economy, Ottawa, ON K1S 5B6, Canada. Offers MA, PhD. *Degree requirements:* For master's, thesis optional. *Entrance requirements:* For master's, honors degree. Additional exam requirements/recommendations for international students: Required—TOEFL. *Faculty research:* Relationships between economy and politics as they affect the political, social and cultural life of societies; historical processes whereby social change is located in the interaction of the economic, political and cultural, and ideological moments of social life.

Case Western Reserve University, School of Graduate Studies, Department of Political Science, Cleveland, OH 44106. Offers MA, PhD. *Faculty:* 9 full-time (5 women), 3 part-time/adjunct (0 women). *Students:* 2 full-time (1 woman); includes 1 minority (Black or African American, non-Hispanic/Latino). Average age 21. 9 applicants, 22% accepted, 2 enrolled. Terminal master's awarded for partial completion of doctoral program. *Degree requirements:* For master's, comprehensive exam; for doctorate, thesis/dissertation. *Entrance requirements:* For master's and doctorate, GRE General Test, undergraduate degree in political science, letters of recommendation, statement of objectives. Additional exam requirements/recommendations for international students: Required—TOEFL (minimum score 577 paper-based; 90 iBT); Recommended—IELTS (minimum score 7). *Application deadline:* For fall admission, 5/1 priority date for domestic students; for spring admission, 11/1 for domestic students. Applications are processed on a rolling basis. Application fee: $50. Electronic applications accepted. *Financial support:* Federal Work-Study and institutionally sponsored loans available. Financial award application deadline: 2/15; financial award applicants required to submit CSS PROFILE or FAFSA. *Faculty research:* American political institutions, elections and political parties both in the United States and abroad; legislative politics; international relations with an emphasis on international political economy; the development and decline of nation-states; the politics of gender; public policy and public organizations; research methods; comparative politics with regional concentrations including Western Europe, Africa, Central Asia and the Middle East. *Unit head:* Joseph White, Chairman, 216-368-2426, Fax: 216-368-4681, E-mail: joseph.white@case.edu. *Application contact:* Samantha Hill, Department Assistant, 216-368-2424, Fax: 216-368-4681, E-mail: samantha.hill@case.edu.
Website: http://politicalscience.case.edu/

The Catholic University of America, School of Arts and Sciences, Department of Politics, Washington, DC 20064. Offers American government (MA, PhD); Congressional and Presidential studies (MA); international affairs (MA); international political economics (MA); political theory (MA, PhD); world politics (MA, PhD); MA/JD. Part-time programs available. *Faculty:* 14 full-time (2 women), 4 part-time/adjunct (0 women). *Students:* 23 full-time (7 women), 44 part-time (8 women); includes 9 minority (2 Black or African American, non-Hispanic/Latino; 1 American Indian or Alaska Native, non-Hispanic/Latino; 2 Asian, non-Hispanic/Latino; 2 Hispanic/Latino; 2 Two or more races, non-Hispanic/Latino), 5 international. Average age 31. 67 applicants, 69% accepted, 10 enrolled. In 2014, 22 master's, 7 doctorates awarded. *Degree requirements:* For master's, one foreign language, comprehensive exam, thesis or alternative; for doctorate, variable foreign language requirement, comprehensive exam, thesis/dissertation. *Entrance requirements:* For master's, GRE General Test, statement of purpose, official copies of academic transcripts, three letters of recommendation, minimum GPA of 3.0; for doctorate, GRE General Test, statement of purpose, official copies of academic transcripts, three letters of recommendation. Additional exam requirements/recommendations for international students: Required—TOEFL (minimum score 580 paper-based). *Application deadline:* For fall admission, 7/15 priority date for domestic students, 7/1 for international students; for spring admission, 11/15 priority date for domestic students, 11/1 for international students. Applications are processed on a rolling basis. Application fee: $55. Electronic applications accepted. *Expenses: Tuition:* Full-time $40,200; part-time $1600 per credit hour. *Required fees:* $400; $195 per semester. One-time fee: $425. *Financial support:* Fellowships, research assistantships, teaching assistantships, Federal Work-Study, scholarships/grants, tuition waivers (full and partial), and unspecified assistantships available. Financial award application deadline: 2/1; financial award applicants required to submit FAFSA. *Faculty research:* Political philosophy, American political institutions and processes, political economy, international relations, U.S. political leadership since 1789. *Unit head:* Dr. Dennis Coyle, Chair, 202-319-5813, Fax: 202-319-6289, E-mail: coyle@cua.edu. *Application contact:* Director of Graduate Admissions, 202-319-5057, Fax: 202-319-6533, E-mail: cua-admissions@cua.edu.
Website: http://politics.cua.edu/

Central European University, Graduate Studies, Department of Political Science, Budapest, Hungary. Offers MA, PhD. *Faculty:* 16 full-time (2 women), 4 part-time/adjunct (2 women). *Students:* 126 full-time (44 women). Average age 27. 234 applicants, 22% accepted, 34 enrolled. In 2014, 44 master's, 10 doctorates awarded. *Degree requirements:* For master's, one foreign language, thesis; for doctorate, one foreign language, comprehensive exam, thesis/dissertation. *Entrance requirements:* For master's and doctorate, interview. Additional exam requirements/recommendations for international students: Required—TOEFL (minimum score 570 paper-based); Recommended—IELTS (minimum score 6.5). *Application deadline:* For fall admission, 1/24 for domestic and international students. Application fee: $40. Electronic applications accepted. *Expenses: Tuition:* Full-time 12,000 euros. *Required fees:* 200 euros. One-time fee: 500 euros full-time. *Financial support:* In 2014–15, 124 students received support, including 124 fellowships; career-related internships or fieldwork, scholarships/grants, health care benefits, and tuition waivers (full and partial) also available. *Faculty research:* Comparative and international political economy, public policy analysis, public understanding of genetics, legislation on abortion and euthanasia, democratization and elite change, rational choice theory, experimental economics (behavioral game theory), Cold War history, gender and politics. *Unit head:* Dorothee Bohle, Head, 36 1 235-6164, E-mail: bohled@ceu.hu. *Application contact:* Zsuzsanna Jaszberenyi, Admissions Officer, 361-324-3009, Fax: 367-327-3211, E-mail: admissions@ceu.hu.
Website: http://web.ceu.hu/polsci/

Central European University, Graduate Studies, Nationalism Studies Program, Budapest, Hungary. Offers MA. *Faculty:* 5 full-time (1 woman), 3 part-time/adjunct (1 woman). *Students:* 32 full-time (21 women). Average age 25. 127 applicants, 24% accepted, 26 enrolled. In 2014, 24 master's awarded. *Degree requirements:* For master's, one foreign language, thesis. *Entrance requirements:* For master's, interview. Additional exam requirements/recommendations for international students: Required—TOEFL (minimum score 570 paper-based); Recommended—IELTS (minimum score 6.5). *Application deadline:* For fall admission, 1/24 for domestic and international students. Application fee: $40. Electronic applications accepted. *Expenses: Tuition:* Full-time 12,000 euros. *Required fees:* 200 euros. One-time fee: 500 euros full-time. *Financial support:* In 2014–15, 32 students received support, including 32 fellowships (averaging $6,100 per year); scholarships/grants, health care benefits, and tuition waivers (full and partial) also available. *Faculty research:* Issues of territory, power, and identity; comparative welfare state studies; social history of social policy in Central and Eastern Europe; gender and ethnic aspects of old and new poverty; ethnic minorities, Jewish studies. *Unit head:* Dr. Szabolcs Pogonyi, Director, 36 1 327-3081. *Application contact:* Zsuzsanna Jaszberenyi, Admissions Officer, 361-324-3009, Fax: 367-327-3211, E-mail: admissions@ceu.hu.

Central Michigan University, Central Michigan University Global Campus, Program in Public Administration, Mount Pleasant, MI 48859. Offers general (MPA); public management (MPA); state and local government (MPA). *Accreditation:* NASPAA. Part-time and evening/weekend programs available. *Entrance requirements:* For master's, minimum GPA of 2.8. Additional exam requirements/recommendations for international students: Required—TOEFL. Electronic applications accepted. *Financial support:* Scholarships/grants available. Support available to part-time students. *Unit head:* Dr. Lawrence Sych, Program Director, 989-774-3316, E-mail: sych1l@cmich.edu. *Application contact:* 877-268-4636, E-mail: cmuglobal@cmich.edu.

Central Michigan University, College of Graduate Studies, College of Humanities and Social and Behavioral Sciences, Department of Political Science, Program in Political Science, Mount Pleasant, MI 48859. Offers American politics (MA), including American politics, comparative/international politics. Part-time programs available. *Degree requirements:* For master's, thesis or alternative. Electronic applications accepted.

Central Michigan University, College of Graduate Studies, College of Humanities and Social and Behavioral Sciences, Department of Political Science, Program in Public Administration, Mount Pleasant, MI 48859. Offers professional development in public administration (Graduate Certificate); public administration (MPA); public management (MPA); state and local government (MPA). Part-time programs available. *Degree requirements:* For master's, thesis or alternative. Electronic applications accepted.

Claremont Graduate University, Graduate Programs, School of Social Science, Policy and Evaluation, Department of Politics and Policy, Claremont, CA 91711-6160. Offers American politics (MA, PhD); comparative politics (PhD); international political economy (MA); international studies (MA); political philosophy (PhD); political science (PhD); politics, economics and business (MA); public policy (MA, PhD); world politics (PhD); MBA/PhD. Part-time programs available. *Faculty:* 7 full-time (5 women), 2 part-time/adjunct (0 women). *Students:* 112 full-time (38 women), 39 part-time (9 women); includes 37 minority (7 Black or African American, non-Hispanic/Latino; 1 American Indian or Alaska Native, non-Hispanic/Latino; 12 Asian, non-Hispanic/Latino; 14 Hispanic/Latino; 1 Native Hawaiian or other Pacific Islander, non-Hispanic/Latino; 2 Two or more races, non-Hispanic/Latino), 30 international. Average age 34. In 2014, 22 master's, 12 doctorates awarded. Terminal master's awarded for partial completion of doctoral program. *Entrance requirements:* For master's and doctorate, GRE General Test. Additional exam requirements/recommendations for international students: Required—TOEFL (minimum score 550 paper-based; 80 iBT). *Application deadline:* For fall admission, 2/1 priority date for domestic and international students. Applications are processed on a rolling basis. Application fee: $80. Electronic applications accepted. *Expenses: Tuition:* Full-time $41,784; part-time $1741 per credit. *Required fees:* $600; $300 per semester. *Financial support:* Fellowships, research assistantships, teaching assistantships, Federal Work-Study, institutionally sponsored loans, and scholarships/grants available. Support available to part-time students. Financial award application deadline: 2/15; financial award applicants required to submit FAFSA. *Faculty research:* Environmental policy, international debt, global democratization, Third World development, public sector discrimination. *Unit head:* Heather Campbell, Chair, 909-621-8689, E-mail: heather.campbell@cgu.edu. *Application contact:* Annekah Hall, Assistant Director of Admissions, 909-607-3371, E-mail: annekah.hall@cgu.edu.
Website: http://www.cgu.edu/pages/458.asp

Claremont Graduate University, Graduate Programs, School of Social Science, Policy and Evaluation, Program in Politics, Economics, and Business, Claremont, CA 91711-6160. Offers MA. Part-time programs available. *Students:* 8 full-time (2 women), 1 (woman) part-time; includes 2 minority (1 Asian, non-Hispanic/Latino; 1 Two or more races, non-Hispanic/Latino), 3 international. Average age 25. In 2014, 2 master's awarded. *Entrance requirements:* For master's, GRE General Test. Additional exam requirements/recommendations for international students: Required—TOEFL (minimum score 550 paper-based; 80 iBT). *Application deadline:* For fall admission, 2/1 priority date for domestic and international students. Applications are processed on a rolling basis. Application fee: $80. Electronic applications accepted. *Expenses: Tuition:* Full-time $41,784; part-time $1741 per credit. *Required fees:* $600; $300 per semester. *Financial support:* Federal Work-Study, institutionally sponsored loans, and scholarships/grants available. Support available to part-time students. Financial award application deadline: 2/15; financial award applicants required to submit FAFSA. *Unit head:* Stewart Donaldson, Dean, 909-607-8235, E-mail: stewart.donaldson@cgu.edu. *Application contact:* Annekah Hall, Assistant Director of Admissions, 909-607-3371, E-mail: annekah.hall@cgu.edu.
Website: http://www.cgu.edu/dpe

Clark Atlanta University, School of Arts and Sciences, Department of Political Science, Atlanta, GA 30314. Offers MA, PhD. Part-time programs available. *Faculty:* 5 full-time (0 women), 1 part-time/adjunct (0 women). *Students:* 11 full-time (6 women), 24 part-time (10 women); includes 31 minority (all Black or African American, non-Hispanic/Latino). Average age 38. 10 applicants, 50% accepted, 2 enrolled. In 2014, 1 master's, 2 doctorates awarded. Terminal master's awarded for partial completion of doctoral program. *Degree requirements:* For master's, one foreign language, comprehensive exam, thesis; for doctorate, 2 foreign languages, comprehensive exam, thesis/dissertation. *Entrance requirements:* For master's, GRE General Test, minimum GPA of 2.5; for doctorate, GRE General Test, minimum graduate GPA of 3.0. Additional exam requirements/recommendations for international students: Required—TOEFL (minimum score 500 paper-based; 61 iBT). *Application deadline:* For fall admission, 4/1 for domestic and international students; for spring admission, 11/1 for domestic and international students. Applications are processed on a rolling basis. Application fee: $40 ($55 for international students). *Expenses: Tuition:* Full-time $14,904; part-time $828 per credit hour. *Required fees:* $746; $373 per semester. *Financial support:* In 2014–15, 1 fellowship was awarded; scholarships/grants and unspecified assistantships also available. Financial award application deadline: 4/30; financial award applicants required to submit FAFSA. *Faculty research:* Public policy and education, rural politics, women and state economic programs, reconstruction after war in Africa, environmental policies. *Unit head:* Dr. Kurt Young, Chairperson, 404-880-8737, Fax: 404-880-8717, E-mail: kyoung@cau.edu. *Application contact:* Michelle Clark-Davis, Graduate Program Admissions, 404-880-6605, E-mail: cauadmissions@cau.edu.

The College of Saint Rose, Graduate Studies, School of Arts and Humanities, Program in History/Political Science, Albany, NY 12203-1419. Offers MA. Part-time and evening/weekend programs available. *Degree requirements:* For master's, final paper/project, thesis or comprehensive exam. *Entrance requirements:* For master's, minimum undergraduate GPA of 3.0, 12 undergraduate credits in US history and/or political science. Additional exam requirements/recommendations for international students: Required—TOEFL (minimum score 550 paper-based). Electronic applications accepted.

Colorado State University, Graduate School, College of Liberal Arts, Department of Political Science, Fort Collins, CO 80523-1782. Offers MA, PhD. Part-time programs available. *Faculty:* 15 full-time (6 women). *Students:* 18 full-time (10 women), 14 part-time (8 women); includes 2 minority (1 Asian, non-Hispanic/Latino; 1 Hispanic/Latino). Average age 29. 27 applicants, 67% accepted, 11 enrolled. In 2014, 10 master's, 2 doctorates awarded. *Degree requirements:* For master's, variable foreign language requirement, comprehensive exam (for some programs), thesis (for some programs); for doctorate, variable foreign language requirement, comprehensive exam (for some programs), thesis/dissertation (for some programs). *Entrance requirements:* For master's, GRE General Test (minimum score 1080 verbal and quantitative, 5.0 analytical), minimum GPA of 3.0, BA/BS, 3 letters of recommendation, transcripts, personal statement, interview; for doctorate, GRE General Test (minimum combined score of 1200 on Verbal and Quantitative sections, 5.0 analytical), minimum GPA of 3.5, 15-page writing sample, MA/MS or at least 24 credits in a master's program, 3 letters of recommendation, transcripts, personal statement, interview. Additional exam requirements/recommendations for international students: Required—TOEFL (minimum score 550 paper-based; 80 iBT). *Application deadline:* For fall admission, 2/15 priority date for domestic and international students; for spring admission, 10/15 priority date for domestic students, 8/1 priority date for international students. Applications are processed on a rolling basis. Application fee: $50. Electronic applications accepted. *Expenses:* Tuition, state resident: full-time $9348; part-time $519 per credit. Tuition, nonresident: full-time $22,916; part-time $1273 per credit. *Required fees:* $1584. *Financial support:* In 2014–15, 27 students received support, including 27 teaching assistantships with full tuition reimbursements available (averaging $14,914 per year); career-related internships or fieldwork, Federal Work-Study, institutionally sponsored loans, scholarships/grants, traineeships, and unspecified assistantships also available. Financial award application deadline: 3/1; financial award applicants required to submit FAFSA. *Faculty research:* Environmental politics and policy, international relations, politics of developing nations, state and local politics and administration, political behavior. *Total annual research expenditures:* $5,916. *Unit head:* Dr. Robert Duffy, Chair, 970-491-6225, Fax: 970-491-2490, E-mail: robert.duffy@colostate.edu. *Application contact:* Dr. Bradley MacDonald, Graduate Contact, 970-491-6943, Fax: 970-491-2490, E-mail: bradley.macdonald@colostate.edu.
Website: http://polisci.colostate.edu/

Columbia University, Graduate School of Arts and Sciences, New York, NY 10027. Offers African-American studies (MA); American studies (MA); anthropology (MA, PhD); art history and archaeology (MA, PhD); astronomy (PhD); biological sciences (PhD); biotechnology (MA); chemical physics (PhD); chemistry (PhD); classical studies (MA, PhD); classics (MA, PhD); climate and society (MA); earth and environmental sciences (PhD); East Asia: regional studies (MA); East Asian languages and cultures (MA, PhD); ecology, evolution and environmental biology (MA), including conservation biology; ecology, evolution, and environmental biology (PhD), including ecology and evolutionary biology, evolutionary primatology; economics (PhD); English and comparative literature (MA, PhD); French and Romance philology (MA, PhD); Germanic languages (MA, PhD); global French studies (MA); Hispanic cultural studies (MA); history (PhD); history and literature (MA); human rights studies (MA); Islamic studies (MA); Italian (MA, PhD); Japanese pedagogy (MA); Jewish studies (MA); Latin America and the Caribbean: regional studies (MA); Latin American and Iberian cultures (PhD); mathematics (MA, PhD), including finance (MA); medieval and Renaissance studies (MA); Middle Eastern, South Asian, and African studies (MA, PhD); modern art: critical and curatorial studies (MA); modern European studies (MA); museum anthropology (MA); music (DMA, PhD); oral history (MA); philosophical foundations of physics (MA); philosophy (MA, PhD); physics (PhD); political science (MA, PhD); psychology (PhD); quantitative methods in the social sciences (MA); religion (MA, PhD); Russia, Eurasia and East Europe: regional studies (MA); Russian translation (MA); Slavic cultures (MA); Slavic languages (MA, PhD); sociology (MA, PhD); South Asian studies (MA); statistics (MA, PhD); theatre (PhD); JD/PhD; MA/MS; MD/PhD; MPA/MA. Dual-degree programs require admission to both Graduate School of Arts and Sciences and another Columbia school. Part-time and evening/weekend programs available. Terminal master's awarded for partial completion of doctoral program. *Degree requirements:* For master's, thesis (for some programs); for doctorate, comprehensive exam, thesis/dissertation. *Entrance requirements:* For master's and doctorate, GRE General Test, GRE Subject Test (for some programs). Electronic applications accepted. *Faculty research:* Humanities, natural sciences, social sciences.

Concordia University, School of Graduate Studies, Faculty of Arts and Science, Department of Political Science, Montréal, QC H3G 1M8, Canada. Offers political science (PhD); public policy and public administration (MA), including geography. *Degree requirements:* For master's, one foreign language, comprehensive exam, thesis optional, internship. *Entrance requirements:* For master's, honors degree or equivalent. Additional exam requirements/recommendations for international students: Required—TOEFL. *Faculty research:* International public policy and administration, Quebec public administration, public policy and social/political theory, geography and public policy, public administration and decision making.

Converse College, School of Education and Graduate Studies, Program in Liberal Arts, Spartanburg, SC 29302-0006. Offers English (MLA); history (MLA); political science (MLA). *Degree requirements:* For master's, capstone paper. *Entrance requirements:* For master's, minimum GPA of 3.0, 2 recommendations.

Cornell University, Graduate School, Graduate Fields of Arts and Sciences, Field of Government, Ithaca, NY 14853-0001. Offers American politics (PhD); comparative politics (PhD); international relations (PhD); political methodology (PhD); political thought (PhD); public policy (PhD). *Degree requirements:* For doctorate, comprehensive exam, thesis/dissertation. *Entrance requirements:* For doctorate, GRE General Test, sample of written work, 3 letters of recommendation. Additional exam requirements/recommendations for international students: Required—TOEFL (minimum score 550 paper-based; 77 iBT). Electronic applications accepted. *Faculty research:* Political theory, American politics, comparative politics, international relations, methodology.

Dalhousie University, Faculty of Arts and Social Science, Department of Political Science, Halifax, NS B3H 4R2, Canada. Offers MA, PhD. *Entrance requirements:* Additional exam requirements/recommendations for international students: Required—TOEFL, IELTS, CANTEST, CAEL, or Michigan English Language Assessment Battery. Electronic applications accepted. *Faculty research:* Canadian political behavior and institutions, international politics, foreign policy, African politics, liberalism and modern political theory.

Dominican University of California, School of Arts, Humanities and Social Sciences, Humanities Program, San Rafael, CA 94901-2298. Offers applied music (MA); art history (MA); creative writing (MA); history (MA); literature (MA); philosophy (MA); political theory (MA); religion (MA); women and gender studies (MA). Part-time programs available. *Faculty:* 11 full-time (5 women), 5 part-time/adjunct (2 women). *Students:* 2 full-time (1 woman), 25 part-time (16 women); includes 7 minority (1 Black or African American, non-Hispanic/Latino; 1 American Indian or Alaska Native, non-Hispanic/Latino; 3 Hispanic/Latino; 2 Two or more races, non-Hispanic/Latino). Average age 46. 12 applicants, 83% accepted, 7 enrolled. *Degree requirements:* For master's, thesis or alternative. *Entrance requirements:* For master's, minimum GPA of 3.0, interview. Additional exam requirements/recommendations for international students: Required—TOEFL (minimum score 550 paper-based; 80 iBT), IELTS (minimum score 6.5). *Application deadline:* For fall admission, 5/15 priority date for domestic and international students; for spring admission, 11/15 priority date for domestic and international students. Applications are processed on a rolling basis. Electronic applications accepted. Application fee is waived when completed online. *Expenses:* Expenses: $935 per unit. *Financial support:* Scholarships/grants available. Support available to part-time students. Financial award application deadline: 3/2; financial award applicants required to submit FAFSA. *Unit head:* Dr. Laura Stivers, Acting Dean, 415-458-3734, E-mail: laura.stivers@dominican.edu. *Application contact:* Ryan Purtill, Director, 415-458-3748, Fax: 415-485-3214, E-mail: ryan.purtill@dominican.edu.
Website: http://www.dominican.edu/academics/ahss/graduate-program/index_html

Duke University, Graduate School, Department of Political Science, Durham, NC 27708. Offers AM, PhD, JD/AM. Terminal master's awarded for partial completion of doctoral program. *Degree requirements:* For doctorate, 2 foreign languages, thesis/dissertation. *Entrance requirements:* For master's and doctorate, GRE General Test. Additional exam requirements/recommendations for international students: Required—TOEFL (minimum score 577 paper-based; 90 iBT) or IELTS (minimum score 7). Electronic applications accepted. *Expenses: Tuition:* Full-time $45,760; part-time $2765 per credit. *Required fees:* $978. Full-time tuition and fees vary according to program.

East Carolina University, Graduate School, Thomas Harriot College of Arts and Sciences, Department of Political Science, Greenville, NC 27858-4353. Offers community health administration (Certificate); public administration (MPA); security studies (Certificate). *Accreditation:* NASPAA. Part-time and evening/weekend programs available. *Degree requirements:* For master's, one foreign language, comprehensive exam. *Entrance requirements:* For master's, GRE General Test. Additional exam requirements/recommendations for international students: Required—TOEFL.

Expenses: Tuition, state resident: full-time $4223. Tuition, nonresident: full-time $16,540. *Required fees:* $2184.

Eastern Illinois University, Graduate School, College of Sciences, Department of Political Science, Charleston, IL 61920. Offers MA. Part-time and evening/weekend programs available. *Faculty:* 8. *Students:* 16 full-time (10 women), 11 part-time (3 women); includes 5 minority (4 Black or African American, non-Hispanic/Latino; 1 Hispanic/Latino), 3 international. Average age 28. 20 applicants, 55% accepted, 9 enrolled. In 2014, 10 master's awarded. *Degree requirements:* For master's, comprehensive exam (for some programs), thesis (for some programs). *Entrance requirements:* For master's, GMAT or GRE. Additional exam requirements/recommendations for international students: Required—TOEFL (minimum score 500 paper-based; 61 iBT), IELTS (minimum score 6). *Application deadline:* For fall admission, 5/15 for domestic and international students; for spring admission, 10/15 for domestic and international students. Applications are processed on a rolling basis. Application fee: $30. Electronic applications accepted. *Expenses:* Tuition, state resident: full-time $3113; part-time $283 per credit hour. Tuition, nonresident: full-time $7469; part-time $679 per credit hour. *Required fees:* $2287; $96 per credit hour. Tuition and fees vary according to course load. *Financial support:* In 2014–15, 16 students received support, including 6 research assistantships with full tuition reimbursements available (averaging $8,010 per year), 1 teaching assistantship with full tuition reimbursement available (averaging $8,010 per year); career-related internships or fieldwork, Federal Work-Study, and unspecified assistantships also available. Support available to part-time students. Financial award application deadline: 3/1; financial award applicants required to submit FAFSA. *Unit head:* Richard Wandling, Department Chair, 217-581-2523, Fax: 217-581-2926, E-mail: rawandling@eiu.edu. *Application contact:* Malinda Mueller, Graduate Coordinator, 217-581-3022, Fax: 217-581-2926, E-mail: mamueller@eiu.edu.
Website: http://www.eiu.edu/poliscigrad/

Eastern Kentucky University, The Graduate School, College of Arts and Sciences, Department of Government, Program in Political Science, Richmond, KY 40475-3102. Offers MA. *Entrance requirements:* For master's, GRE General Test, minimum GPA of 2.5.

East Stroudsburg University of Pennsylvania, Graduate College, College of Arts and Sciences, Department of Political Science, East Stroudsburg, PA 18301-2999. Offers M Ed, MA. Part-time and evening/weekend programs available. *Degree requirements:* For master's, variable foreign language requirement, comprehensive exam, thesis or alternative. *Entrance requirements:* Additional exam requirements/recommendations for international students: Required—TOEFL (minimum score 560 paper-based; 83 iBT) or IELTS. Electronic applications accepted.

East Tennessee State University, School of Graduate Studies, College of Arts and Sciences, Department of Political Science, International Affairs and Public Administration, Johnson City, TN 37614. Offers economic development (Postbaccalaureate Certificate); not-for-profit administration (MPA); planning and development (MPA); public financial management (MPA); urban planning (Postbaccalaureate Certificate). Part-time programs available. *Faculty:* 7 full-time (2 women), 1 part-time/adjunct (0 women). *Students:* 19 full-time (5 women), 9 part-time (4 women); includes 3 minority (2 Black or African American, non-Hispanic/Latino; 1 Hispanic/Latino), 6 international. Average age 29. 48 applicants, 33% accepted, 10 enrolled. In 2014, 7 master's, 1 other advanced degree awarded. *Degree requirements:* For master's, internship. *Entrance requirements:* For master's, GRE General Test, three letters of recommendation; for Postbaccalaureate Certificate, GRE General Test. Additional exam requirements/recommendations for international students: Required—TOEFL (minimum score 550 paper-based; 79 iBT). *Application deadline:* For fall admission, 6/1 for domestic students, 4/29 for international students; for spring admission, 11/1 for domestic students, 9/30 for international students. Application fee: $35 ($45 for international students). Electronic applications accepted. *Financial support:* In 2014–15, 16 students received support, including 16 research assistantships with full tuition reimbursements available (averaging $6,000 per year), 4 teaching assistantships with full tuition reimbursements available (averaging $6,000 per year); career-related internships or fieldwork, institutionally sponsored loans, scholarships/grants, and unspecified assistantships also available. Financial award application deadline: 7/1; financial award applicants required to submit FAFSA. *Faculty research:* Labor issues, presidency, public law in American politics, East Asian politics, European politics, Middle Eastern politics, development in comparative politics, international political economy, international relations, world politics in international affairs. *Unit head:* Dr. Andrew Battista, Chair, 423-439-4217, Fax: 423-439-4348, E-mail: battista@etsu.edu. *Application contact:* Angela Edwards, Graduate Specialist, 423-439-4703, Fax: 423-439-5624, E-mail: edwardag@etsu.edu.
Website: http://www.etsu.edu/cas/polisci/

Emory University, Laney Graduate School, Department of Political Science, Atlanta, GA 30322-1100. Offers PhD. *Degree requirements:* For doctorate, comprehensive exam, thesis/dissertation. *Entrance requirements:* For doctorate, GRE General Test, minimum GPA of 3.0. Additional exam requirements/recommendations for international students: Required—TOEFL. Electronic applications accepted. *Faculty research:* Post-Soviet politics, comparative politics, international politics, judicial politics and methodology, American national political institutions.

Fairleigh Dickinson University, Metropolitan Campus, University College: Arts, Sciences, and Professional Studies, School of History, Political and International Studies, Program in Political Science, Teaneck, NJ 07666-1914. Offers MA.

Fayetteville State University, Graduate School, Department of Geography, History and Political Science, Fayetteville, NC 28301-4298. Offers history (MA). Part-time and evening/weekend programs available. *Faculty:* 13 full-time (4 women). *Students:* Average age 40. *Degree requirements:* For master's, comprehensive exam, internship. *Entrance requirements:* For master's, GRE General Test. *Application deadline:* For fall admission, 4/15 for domestic students; for spring admission, 10/15 for domestic students. Applications are processed on a rolling basis. Application fee: $40. Electronic applications accepted. *Unit head:* Dr. Adeguke Ademiluyi, Chairperson, 910-672-1137, E-mail: aademiluyi@uncfsu.edu. *Application contact:* Adeguke Ademiluyi, 910-672-1137, Fax: 910-672-1470, E-mail: aademiluyi@uncfsu.edu.

Florida Agricultural and Mechanical University, Division of Graduate Studies, Research, and Continuing Education, College of Social Sciences, Arts and Humanities, Department of History and Political Science, Program in Applied Social Science, Tallahassee, FL 32307-3200. Offers criminal justice (MASS); history (MASS); political science (MASS); public administration (MASS). Part-time programs available. *Degree requirements:* For master's, thesis optional. *Entrance requirements:* For master's, GRE General Test, minimum GPA of 3.0. *Faculty research:* Southern history, black history, election trends, Presidential history.

Florida Atlantic University, Dorothy F. Schmidt College of Arts and Letters, Department of Political Science, Boca Raton, FL 33431-0991. Offers MA. Part-time programs available. *Degree requirements:* For master's, one foreign language, thesis or alternative. *Entrance requirements:* For master's, GRE General Test, minimum GPA of 3.0 during last 60 hours of course work. Additional exam requirements/recommendations for international students: Required—TOEFL (minimum score 500 paper-based; 61 iBT), IELTS (minimum score 6). Electronic applications accepted. *Expenses:* Tuition, state resident: full-time $7396; part-time $369.82 per credit hour. Tuition, nonresident: full-time $19,392; part-time $1024.81 per credit hour. Tuition and fees vary according to course load. *Faculty research:* Public policy, comparative policy affecting women, Congress, international system, urban policy.

Florida International University, College of Arts and Sciences, Department of Politics and International Relations, Program of Political Science, Miami, FL 33199. Offers MA, PhD. Part-time and evening/weekend programs available. *Degree requirements:* For master's, one foreign language, thesis or alternative, research project; for doctorate, one foreign language, comprehensive exam, thesis/dissertation. *Entrance requirements:* For master's, GRE General Test, minimum GPA of 3.2, 2 letters of recommendation; for doctorate, GRE General Test, minimum GPA of 3.2 (undergraduate), 3.25 (graduate); 2 letters of recommendation; master's thesis or other major paper. Additional exam requirements/recommendations for international students: Required—TOEFL (minimum score 550 paper-based; 80 iBT). Electronic applications accepted.

Florida State University, The Graduate School, College of Social Sciences and Public Policy, Department of Political Science, Tallahassee, FL 32306-2230. Offers MA, MS, PhD. Part-time programs available. *Faculty:* 21 full-time (4 women), 1 part-time/adjunct (0 women). *Students:* 55 full-time (17 women), 28 part-time (12 women); includes 26 minority (6 Black or African American, non-Hispanic/Latino; 1 American Indian or Alaska Native, non-Hispanic/Latino; 1 Asian, non-Hispanic/Latino; 15 Hispanic/Latino; 3 Two or more races, non-Hispanic/Latino), 3 international. Average age 25. 86 applicants, 52% accepted, 25 enrolled. In 2014, 38 master's, 9 doctorates awarded. Terminal master's awarded for partial completion of doctoral program. *Degree requirements:* For master's, thesis optional; for doctorate, comprehensive exam, thesis/dissertation. *Entrance requirements:* For master's, GRE General Test, minimum undergraduate GPA of 3.0; for doctorate, GRE General Test, minimum graduate GPA of 3.5, undergraduate 3.0. Additional exam requirements/recommendations for international students: Required—TOEFL (minimum score 600 paper-based; 100 iBT). *Application deadline:* For fall admission, 1/15 priority date for domestic and international students. Applications are processed on a rolling basis. Application fee: $30. Electronic applications accepted. *Expenses:* Tuition, state resident: part-time $403.51 per credit hour. Tuition, nonresident: part-time $1004.85 per credit hour. *Required fees:* $75.81 per credit hour. One-time fee: $20 part-time. Tuition and fees vary according to campus/location. *Financial support:* In 2014–15, 38 students received support, including 2 fellowships with full tuition reimbursements available (averaging $20,000 per year), 31 research assistantships with full tuition reimbursements available (averaging $17,000 per year), 5 teaching assistantships with full tuition reimbursements available (averaging $17,000 per year); Federal Work-Study, institutionally sponsored loans, scholarships/grants, and unspecified assistantships also available. Financial award application deadline: 1/15; financial award applicants required to submit FAFSA. *Faculty research:* American government, international relations, comparative government, public policy. *Total annual research expenditures:* $130,000. *Unit head:* Dr. Mark Souva, Director of Graduate Studies, 850-644-7315, Fax: 850-644-1367, E-mail: msouva@fsu.edu. *Application contact:* Jeremiah J. Fisher, Academic Coordinator, 850-644-7305, Fax: 850-644-1367, E-mail: jeremiah.fisher@fsu.edu.
Website: http://www.polisci.fsu.edu

Fordham University, Graduate School of Arts and Sciences, Program in Elections and Campaign Management, New York, NY 10458. Offers MA. *Students:* 4 full-time (1 woman), 8 part-time (5 women), 1 international. Average age 29. 21 applicants, 90% accepted, 10 enrolled. In 2014, 17 master's awarded. Application fee: $70. *Unit head:* Dr. Costas Panagopoulos, Director, 718-817-3967, E-mail: cpanagopoulos@fordham.edu. *Application contact:* Bernadette Valentino-Morrison, Director of Graduate Admissions, 718-817-4419, Fax: 718-817-3566, E-mail: valentinomor@fordham.edu.
Website: http://www.fordham.edu/academics/programs_at_fordham_/elections__campaign_/

George Mason University, School of Policy, Government, and International Affairs, Program in Political Science, Fairfax, VA 22030. Offers MA, PhD. *Expenses:* Tuition, state resident: full-time $9794; part-time $408 per credit hour. Tuition, nonresident: full-time $26,978; part-time $1124 per credit hour. *Required fees:* $2820; $118 per credit hour. Tuition and fees vary according to course load and program. *Unit head:* Elizabeth Sturtevant, Professor and Division Director of Literacy, 703-993-2052, Fax: 703-993-2013, E-mail: esturtev@gmu.edu. *Application contact:* Rabia Ghani, Program Manager for Literacy, 703-993-7611, Fax: 703-993-5300, E-mail: rghani@gmu.edu.

George Mason University, School of Policy, Government, and International Affairs, Program in Public Administration, Fairfax, VA 22030. Offers administration of justice (Certificate); association management (Certificate); biodefense (MS, PhD); critical analysis and strategic response to terrorism (Certificate); emergency management and homeland security (Certificate); nonprofit management (Certificate); political science (MA, PhD); public administration (MPA); public management (Certificate). *Accreditation:* NASPAA (one or more programs are accredited). *Entrance requirements:* For degree, expanded goals statement; 3 letters of recommendation; official transcripts; resume. Additional exam requirements/recommendations for international students: Required—TOEFL, IELTS, PTE. Application fee: $65 ($80 for international students). Electronic applications accepted. *Expenses:* Expenses: Contact institution. *Financial support:* Fellowships, research assistantships with full and partial tuition reimbursements, teaching assistantships with full and partial tuition reimbursements, career-related internships or fieldwork, Federal Work-Study, scholarships/grants, and unspecified assistantships available. Support available to part-time students. Financial award application deadline: 3/1; financial award applicants required to submit FAFSA. *Application contact:* Peg Koback, Education Support Specialist, 703-993-3707, Fax: 703-993-1399, E-mail: mkoback@gmu.edu.
Website: http://pia.gmu.edu/

Georgetown University, Graduate School of Arts and Sciences, Department of Government, Program in Democracy and Governance, Washington, DC 20057. Offers MA.

Georgetown University, Graduate School of Arts and Sciences, School of Continuing Studies, Washington, DC 20057. Offers American studies (MALS); Catholic studies (MALS); classical civilizations (MALS); emergency and disaster management (MPS); ethics and the professions (MALS); hospitality management (MPS); human resources management (MPS); humanities (MALS); individualized study (MALS); international affairs (MALS); Islam and Muslim-Christian relations (MALS); journalism (MPS); liberal studies (DLS); literature and society (MALS); medieval and early modern European studies (MALS); public relations and corporate communications (MPS); real estate (MPS); religious studies (MALS); social and public policy (MALS); sports industry management (MPS); systems engineering management (MPS); technology management (MPS); the theory and practice of American democracy (MALS); urban and regional planning (MPS); visual culture (MALS). MPS in systems engineering management offered jointly with Stevens Institute of Technology. *Entrance requirements:* Additional exam requirements/recommendations for international students: Required—TOEFL.

The George Washington University, College of Professional Studies, Graduate School of Political Management, Program in Legislative Affairs, Washington, DC 20052. Offers MPS. Part-time and evening/weekend programs available. *Students:* 37 full-time (12 women), 49 part-time (15 women); includes 17 minority (10 Black or African American, non-Hispanic/Latino; 2 Asian, non-Hispanic/Latino; 2 Hispanic/Latino; 1 Native Hawaiian or other Pacific Islander, non-Hispanic/Latino; 2 Two or more races, non-Hispanic/Latino), 3 international. Average age 32. 70 applicants, 93% accepted, 51 enrolled. In 2014, 47 master's awarded. *Degree requirements:* For master's, comprehensive exam. *Entrance requirements:* For master's, GRE General Test, minimum GPA of 3.0. Additional exam requirements/recommendations for international students: Required—TOEFL (minimum score 550 paper-based). *Application deadline:* For fall admission, 4/1 priority date for domestic and international students; for spring admission, 10/1 priority date for domestic and international students. Applications are processed on a rolling basis. Application fee: $75. Electronic applications accepted. *Financial support:* Application deadline: 2/1. *Unit head:* Dr. Steven E. Billet, Director, 202-994-6000, E-mail: sbillet@gwu.edu. *Application contact:* Information Contact, 202-994-6000, Fax: 202-994-6006, E-mail: gspmmail@gwu.edu.
Website: http://www.gwu.edu/~gspm/academics/mala.shtml

The George Washington University, Columbian College of Arts and Sciences, Department of Political Science, Washington, DC 20052. Offers legal institutions and theory (MA); political science (MA). Part-time and evening/weekend programs available. *Faculty:* 30 full-time (9 women), 8 part-time/adjunct (2 women). *Students:* 44 full-time (16 women), 58 part-time (24 women); includes 12 minority (1 Black or African American, non-Hispanic/Latino; 6 Asian, non-Hispanic/Latino; 4 Hispanic/Latino; 1 Two or more races, non-Hispanic/Latino), 24 international. Average age 31. 396 applicants, 11% accepted, 14 enrolled. In 2014, 19 master's, 14 doctorates awarded. Terminal master's awarded for partial completion of doctoral program. *Degree requirements:* For master's, one foreign language, comprehensive exam, thesis or alternative; for doctorate, 2 foreign languages, thesis/dissertation, general exam. *Entrance requirements:* For master's and doctorate, GRE General Test, minimum GPA of 3.0. Additional exam requirements/recommendations for international students: Required—TOEFL (minimum score 550 paper-based; 80 iBT). *Application deadline:* For fall admission, 1/15 priority date for domestic students; for spring admission, 10/1 priority date for domestic students. Applications are processed on a rolling basis. Application fee: $75. Electronic applications accepted. *Financial support:* In 2014–15, 43 students received support. Fellowships with tuition reimbursements available, teaching assistantships with tuition reimbursements available, Federal Work-Study, and tuition waivers available. *Unit head:* Christopher J. Deering, Chair, 202-994-6564, E-mail: rocket@gwu.edu. *Application contact:* 202-994-6210, Fax: 202-994-6213, E-mail: askccas@gwu.edu.
Website: http://www.gwu.edu/~psc/

The George Washington University, Elliott School of International Affairs, Program in Security Policy Studies, Washington, DC 20052. Offers MA. Part-time programs available. *Students:* 88 full-time (22 women), 74 part-time (26 women); includes 32 minority (2 Black or African American, non-Hispanic/Latino; 13 Asian, non-Hispanic/Latino; 11 Hispanic/Latino; 6 Two or more races, non-Hispanic/Latino), 11 international. Average age 27. 372 applicants, 45 enrolled. In 2014, 50 master's awarded. *Degree requirements:* For master's, one foreign language, capstone project. *Entrance requirements:* For master's, GRE General Test, 2 semesters of introductory economics, 2 years of a modern foreign language or 1 semester of statistics. Additional exam requirements/recommendations for international students: Required—TOEFL (minimum score 100 iBT), IELTS (minimum score 7). *Application deadline:* For fall admission, 1/15 priority date for domestic and international students; for spring admission, 10/1 for domestic and international students. Application fee: $75. Electronic applications accepted. *Financial support:* In 2014–15, 22 students received support. Fellowships with partial tuition reimbursements available, Federal Work-Study, and scholarships/grants available. Financial award application deadline: 1/15; financial award applicants required to submit FAFSA. *Faculty research:* U.S. arms transfer policies, military balance in the Third World, U.S. foreign policy, technology and security policy. *Unit head:* Joanna Spear, Director, 202-994-7003, E-mail: security@gwu.edu. *Application contact:* Nicole A. Campbell, Director of Graduate Admissions, 202-994-7050, Fax: 202-994-9537, E-mail: esiagrad@gwu.edu.
Website: http://elliott.gwu.edu/academics/graduate/sps

Georgia Regents University, The Graduate School, Pamplin College of Arts, Humanities, and Social Sciences, Department of Political Science, Augusta, GA 30912. Offers MPA. Part-time and evening/weekend programs available. *Degree requirements:* For master's, comprehensive exam, thesis. *Entrance requirements:* For master's, GRE General Test. Electronic applications accepted. *Faculty research:* Political behavior, administrative law, political participation, human resources administration.

Georgia State University, College of Arts and Sciences, Department of Communication, Atlanta, GA 30302-3083. Offers film, video, and digital imaging (MA), including critical studies, production, screenwriting; human communication and social influence (MA); mass communication (MA); media and society (PhD); moving image studies (PhD); public communication (PhD); rhetoric and politics (PhD). Part-time programs available. *Faculty:* 35 full-time (18 women). *Students:* 102 full-time (51 women), 40 part-time (15 women); includes 37 minority (20 Black or African American, non-Hispanic/Latino; 4 Asian, non-Hispanic/Latino; 6 Hispanic/Latino; 7 Two or more races, non-Hispanic/Latino), 14 international. Average age 33. 154 applicants, 39% accepted, 30 enrolled. In 2014, 25 master's, 5 doctorates awarded. *Degree requirements:* For master's, variable foreign language requirement, thesis (for some programs); for doctorate, comprehensive exam, thesis/dissertation. *Entrance requirements:* For master's, GRE; for doctorate, GRE. Additional exam requirements/recommendations for international students: Required—TOEFL (minimum score 550 paper-based; 80 iBT), IELTS (minimum score 6.5). *Application deadline:* For fall admission, 2/10 for domestic and international students; for spring admission, 10/15 for domestic and international students. Application fee: $50. Electronic applications accepted. *Expenses:* Tuition, state resident: full-time $6516; part-time $362 per credit hour. Tuition, nonresident: full-time $22,014; part-time $1223 per credit hour. *Required fees:* $2128 per semester. Tuition and fees vary according to course load and program. *Financial support:* In 2014–15, fellowships with tuition reimbursements (averaging $15,000 per year), teaching assistantships with tuition reimbursements (averaging $15,000 per year) were awarded; career-related internships or fieldwork and unspecified assistantships also available. Financial award applicants required to submit FAFSA. *Faculty research:* New media, mass media and journalism, rhetoric, film and media studies, film production. *Unit head:* Dr. David Cheshier, Chair, 404-413-5649, Fax: 404-413-5634, E-mail: dcheshier@gsu.edu. *Application contact:* Dr. Jennifer Barker, Associate Professor, 404-413-5793, Fax: 404-413-5634, E-mail: jmbarker@gsu.edu.
Website: http://communication.gsu.edu

Georgia State University, College of Arts and Sciences, Department of Political Science, Atlanta, GA 30302-3083. Offers MA, PhD. Part-time and evening/weekend programs available. *Faculty:* 29 full-time (9 women). *Students:* 64 full-time (34 women), 25 part-time (10 women); includes 14 minority (10 Black or African American, non-Hispanic/Latino; 1 Hispanic/Latino; 3 Two or more races, non-Hispanic/Latino), 23 international. Average age 33. 62 applicants, 63% accepted, 19 enrolled. In 2014, 9 master's, 4 doctorates awarded. Terminal master's awarded for partial completion of doctoral program. *Degree requirements:* For master's, thesis (for some programs); for doctorate, one foreign language, comprehensive exam, thesis/dissertation. *Entrance requirements:* For master's and doctorate, GRE. Additional exam requirements/recommendations for international students: Required—TOEFL (minimum score 550 paper-based; 80 iBT) or IELTS (minimum score 6.5). *Application deadline:* For fall admission, 2/1 priority date for domestic and international students; for spring admission, 10/15 for domestic and international students. Applications are processed on a rolling basis. Application fee: $50. Electronic applications accepted. *Expenses:* Tuition, state resident: full-time $6516; part-time $362 per credit hour. Tuition, nonresident: full-time $22,014; part-time $1223 per credit hour. *Required fees:* $2128 per semester. Tuition and fees vary according to course load and program. *Financial support:* In 2014–15, fellowships with full tuition reimbursements (averaging $19,000 per year), research assistantships with full tuition reimbursements (averaging $14,000 per year), teaching assistantships with full tuition reimbursements (averaging $4,000 per year) were awarded; career-related internships or fieldwork and health care benefits also available. Financial award application deadline: 2/1. *Faculty research:* Political behavior and attitudes, judicial politics and policymaking, comparative democratization, international governance, national and international political institutions and structures. *Unit head:* Dr. Carrie Manning, Chair, 404-413-6162, Fax: 404-413-6156, E-mail: cmanning2@gsu.edu. *Application contact:* Dr. Amy Steigerwalt, Director of Graduate Studies, 404-413-6162, Fax: 404-413-6156, E-mail: asteigerwalt@gsu.edu.
Website: http://politicalscience.gsu.edu/home/graduate/degree-requirements/

Georgia State University, College of Education, Department of Middle-Secondary Education and Instructional Technology, Atlanta, GA 30302-3083. Offers curriculum and instruction (Ed D); English education (MAT); mathematics education (M Ed, MAT); middle level education (MAT); reading, language and literacy education (M Ed, MAT), including reading instruction (M Ed); science education (M Ed, MAT), including biology (MAT), broad field science (MAT), chemistry (MAT), earth science (MAT), physics (MAT); social studies education (M Ed, MAT), including economics (MAT), geography (MAT), history (MAT), political science (MAT); teaching and learning (PhD), including language and literacy, mathematics education, music education, science education, social studies education, teaching and teacher education. *Accreditation:* NCATE. Part-time and evening/weekend programs available. Postbaccalaureate distance learning degree programs offered (minimal on-campus study). *Faculty:* 20 full-time (16 women). *Students:* 155 full-time (112 women), 101 part-time (70 women); includes 112 minority (82 Black or African American, non-Hispanic/Latino; 10 Asian, non-Hispanic/Latino; 12 Hispanic/Latino; 8 Two or more races, non-Hispanic/Latino), 3 international. Average age 32. 155 applicants, 61% accepted, 65 enrolled. *Degree requirements:* For master's, comprehensive exam (for some programs), thesis or alternative, exit portfolio; for doctorate, comprehensive exam, thesis/dissertation. *Entrance requirements:* For master's, GRE; GACE I (for initial teacher preparation programs), baccalaureate degree or equivalent, resume, goals statement, two letters of recommendation, minimum undergraduate GPA of 2.5; proof of initial teacher certification in the content area (for M Ed); for doctorate, GRE, resume, goals statement, writing sample, two letters of recommendation, minimum graduate GPA of 3.3, interview. Additional exam requirements/recommendations for international students: Required—TOEFL (minimum score 550 paper-based; 79 iBT) or IELTS (minimum score 6.5). *Application deadline:* For fall admission, 1/15 priority date for domestic and international students; for spring admission, 10/1 for domestic and international students. Application fee: $50. Electronic applications accepted. *Expenses:* Tuition, state resident: full-time $6516; part-time $362 per credit hour. Tuition, nonresident: full-time $22,014; part-time $1223 per credit hour. *Required fees:* $2128 per semester. Tuition and fees vary according to course load and program. *Financial support:* In 2014–15, fellowships with full tuition reimbursements (averaging $19,667 per year), research assistantships with full tuition reimbursements (averaging $5,436 per year), teaching assistantships with full tuition reimbursements (averaging $2,779 per year) were awarded; career-related internships or fieldwork, Federal Work-Study, scholarships/grants, health care benefits, tuition waivers (full and partial), and unspecified assistantships also available. Financial award application deadline: 3/15. *Faculty research:* Teacher education in language and literacy, mathematics, science, and social studies in urban middle and secondary school settings; learning technologies in school, community, and corporate settings; multicultural education and education for social justice; urban education; international education. *Unit head:* Dr. Dana L. Fox, Chair, 404-413-8060, Fax: 404-413-8063, E-mail: dfox@gsu.edu. *Application contact:* Bobbie Turner, Administrative Coordinator I, 404-413-8405, Fax: 404-413-8063, E-mail: bnturner@gsu.edu.
Website: http://mse.education.gsu.edu/

Governors State University, College of Arts and Sciences, Program in Political and Justice Studies, University Park, IL 60484. Offers MA. Part-time and evening/weekend programs available. *Degree requirements:* For master's, thesis or alternative. *Entrance requirements:* For master's, bachelor's degree in related field.

The Graduate Center, City University of New York, Graduate Studies, Program in Political Science, New York, NY 10016-4039. Offers MA, PhD. Terminal master's awarded for partial completion of doctoral program. *Degree requirements:* For master's, one foreign language, thesis; for doctorate, one foreign language, thesis/dissertation. *Entrance requirements:* For master's and doctorate, GRE General Test. Additional exam requirements/recommendations for international students: Required—TOEFL. Electronic applications accepted.

Grambling State University, School of Graduate Studies and Research, College of Arts and Sciences, Department of Political Science and Public Administration, Grambling, LA 71270. Offers health services administration (MPA); human resource management (MPA); public management (MPA); state and local government (MPA). *Accreditation:* NASPAA. Part-time programs available. *Degree requirements:* For master's, comprehensive exam (for some programs), thesis optional. *Entrance requirements:* For master's, GRE, minimum GPA of 2.75 on last degree. Additional exam requirements/recommendations for international students: Required—TOEFL (minimum score 500 paper-based; 62 iBT). Electronic applications accepted.

Harvard University, Graduate School of Arts and Sciences, Committee on Political Economy and Government, Cambridge, MA 02138. Offers PhD. *Entrance requirements:* For doctorate, GRE General Test or GMAT. Additional exam requirements/recommendations for international students: Required—TOEFL.

Harvard University, Graduate School of Arts and Sciences, Department of Government, Cambridge, MA 02138. Offers political science (PhD), including American politics, comparative politics, international relations, political thought, quantitative methods. *Degree requirements:* For doctorate, one foreign language, thesis/dissertation, general exams. *Entrance requirements:* For doctorate, GRE General Test. Additional exam requirements/recommendations for international students: Required—TOEFL.

Harvard University, John F. Kennedy School of Government, Cambridge, MA 02138. Offers MPA, MPAID, MPP, PhD, JD/MPP, MBA/MPP, MD/MPP. *Students:* 893 full-time (397 women), 28 part-time (10 women); includes 203 minority (31 Black or African American, non-Hispanic/Latino; 1 American Indian or Alaska Native, non-Hispanic/

Latino; 69 Asian, non-Hispanic/Latino; 50 Hispanic/Latino; 1 Native Hawaiian or other Pacific Islander, non-Hispanic/Latino; 51 Two or more races, non-Hispanic/Latino), 402 international. Average age 30. 2,969 applicants, 31% accepted, 566 enrolled. In 2014, 513 master's awarded. *Degree requirements:* For doctorate, thesis/dissertation. *Entrance requirements:* For master's, GMAT or GRE General Test; for doctorate, GRE General Test. Additional exam requirements/recommendations for international students: Required—TOEFL (minimum score 600 paper-based; 100 iBT), TWE. *Application deadline:* For fall admission, 12/1 for domestic students. Application fee: $100. Electronic applications accepted. *Financial support:* Fellowships, research assistantships, teaching assistantships, career-related internships or fieldwork, Federal Work-Study, institutionally sponsored loans, scholarships/grants, and unspecified assistantships available. Support available to part-time students. Financial award application deadline: 2/26; financial award applicants required to submit CSS PROFILE or FAFSA. *Unit head:* Dr. David Ellwood, Dean, 617-495-1122. *Application contact:* 617-495-1155, Fax: 617-496-1165, E-mail: hks_admissions@harvard.edu.
Website: http://www.hks.harvard.edu/

Hillsdale College, Graduate School, Hillsdale, MI 49242-1298. Offers politics (MA, PhD).

Howard University, Graduate School, Department of Political Science, Program in Political Science, Washington, DC 20059-0002. Offers MA, PhD. *Degree requirements:* For master's, comprehensive exam. *Entrance requirements:* For master's, GRE General Test, minimum GPA of 3.0; for doctorate, GRE General Test, minimum GPA of 2.8.

Hult International Business School, Program in International Relations - Hult London Campus, London WC 1B 4JP, United Kingdom. Offers conflict resolution (MA); diplomacy (MA); international public law (MA); international relations (MA); Middle East international security (MA); politics (MA); security studies (MA); terrorism (MA); U.S. foreign policy (MA). Part-time programs available. *Entrance requirements:* Additional exam requirements/recommendations for international students: Required—TOEFL (minimum score 580 paper-based), TWE (minimum score 5). Electronic applications accepted. *Faculty research:* American foreign politics, Middle East, security studies.

Idaho State University, Office of Graduate Studies, College of Arts and Letters, Department of Political Science, Pocatello, ID 83209-8073. Offers political science (MA, DA); public administration (MPA). Part-time programs available. *Degree requirements:* For master's, comprehensive exam, thesis optional; for doctorate, comprehensive exam, thesis/dissertation, teaching internship. *Entrance requirements:* For master's, GRE General Test, minimum GPA of 3.0 in last 2 years of undergraduate study, 3 letters of recommendation; for doctorate, GRE General Test, major field of American politics, minimum GPA of 3.0 in last 2 years of undergraduate study, 3 letters of recommendation. Additional exam requirements/recommendations for international students: Required—TOEFL (minimum score 550 paper-based; 80 iBT). Electronic applications accepted. *Faculty research:* International affairs, environmental policy, decision making, Constitution, executive/legislative relations.

Illinois State University, Graduate School, College of Arts and Sciences, Department of Politics and Government, Normal, IL 61790-2200. Offers MA, MS. *Degree requirements:* For master's, thesis or alternative. *Entrance requirements:* For master's, GRE General Test, minimum GPA of 3.0 in last 60 hours of course work, 15 hours of course work in political science. *Faculty research:* Political tolerance in a democracy under external threats: a survey of public opinion.

Indiana State University, College of Graduate and Professional Studies, College of Arts and Sciences, Department of Political Science, Terre Haute, IN 47809. Offers political science (MA, MS); public administration (MPA). *Degree requirements:* For master's, thesis (for some programs). *Entrance requirements:* For master's, GRE or minimum undergraduate GPA of 2.75, 18 semester hours of course work in political science. Additional exam requirements/recommendations for international students: Required—TOEFL (minimum score 550 paper-based). Electronic applications accepted.

Indiana University Bloomington, University Graduate School, College of Arts and Sciences, Department of Political Science, Bloomington, IN 47405-7000. Offers MA, PhD. *Faculty:* 26 full-time (9 women). *Students:* 67 full-time (24 women); includes 7 minority (4 Black or African American, non-Hispanic/Latino; 1 Asian, non-Hispanic/Latino; 1 Hispanic/Latino; 1 Two or more races, non-Hispanic/Latino), 16 international. Average age 31. 111 applicants, 4% accepted, 4 enrolled. In 2014, 1 master's, 12 doctorates awarded. Terminal master's awarded for partial completion of doctoral program. *Degree requirements:* For master's, thesis, 30 credit hours; for doctorate, comprehensive exam, thesis/dissertation. *Entrance requirements:* For master's, GRE, personal statement, transcripts, 3 letters of recommendation; for doctorate, GRE, sample of written work, 3 letters of recommendation, personal statement. Additional exam requirements/recommendations for international students: Required—TOEFL (minimum score 640 paper-based; 112 iBT). *Application deadline:* For fall admission, 1/15 for domestic students, 12/1 for international students. Application fee: $55 ($65 for international students). Electronic applications accepted. *Financial support:* Fellowships with full tuition reimbursements, research assistantships with full tuition reimbursements, teaching assistantships with full tuition reimbursements, Federal Work-Study, institutionally sponsored loans, scholarships/grants, health care benefits, and unspecified assistantships available. Financial award application deadline: 2/25. *Faculty research:* American politics, international relations, public policy, political theory, comparative politics, theory and methodology. *Total annual research expenditures:* $291,773. *Unit head:* Russell Hanson, Chair, 812-855-1209, Fax: 812-855-2027, E-mail: hansonr@indiana.edu. *Application contact:* Amanda Campbell, Graduate Secretary, 812-855-1208, Fax: 812-855-2027, E-mail: acperry@indiana.edu.
Website: http://polisci.indiana.edu/

Indiana University–Purdue University Indianapolis, School of Liberal Arts, Department of Political Science, Indianapolis, IN 46202. Offers MA, Certificate. *Students:* 6 full-time (2 women), 5 part-time (1 woman); includes 1 minority (Black or African American, non-Hispanic/Latino), 1 international. Average age 27. 9 applicants, 67% accepted, 6 enrolled. In 2014, 3 master's awarded. *Unit head:* Dr. Scott Pegg, Chair, 317-278-5749, E-mail: smpegg@iupui.edu. *Application contact:* John McCormick, Director of Graduate Studies, 317-274-4066, E-mail: jmccormi@iupui.edu.
Website: http://liberalarts.iupui.edu/political_science/index.php/graduate/master_of_arts

Institute for Christian Studies, Graduate Programs, Toronto, ON M5T 1R4, Canada. Offers education (M Phil F, PhD); history of philosophy (M Phil F, PhD); philosophical aesthetics (M Phil F, PhD); philosophy of religion (M Phil F, PhD); political theory (M Phil F, PhD); systematic philosophy (M Phil F, PhD); theology (M Phil F, PhD); worldview studies (MWS). Part-time programs available. Postbaccalaureate distance learning degree programs offered (minimal on-campus study). *Degree requirements:* For master's, one foreign language, thesis; for doctorate, 2 foreign languages, thesis/dissertation. *Entrance requirements:* For master's and doctorate, philosophy background. Additional exam requirements/recommendations for international students: Required—TOEFL (minimum score 600 paper-based). *Faculty research:* Human rights, anthropology of self, medieval discourse, gender and body, post-modern thought; biblical hermeneutics, creational aesthetics, ecumenism, epistemology, political theory and public policy, relational psychotherapy.

The Institute of World Politics, Graduate Programs in National Security, Intelligence, and International Affairs, Washington, DC 20036. Offers American foreign policy (Certificate); comparative political culture (Certificate); counterintelligence (Certificate); democracy building (Certificate); intelligence (Certificate); international politics (Certificate); national security affairs (Certificate); public diplomacy and political warfare (Certificate); statecraft and national security affairs (MA); statecraft and world politics (MA); strategic intelligence studies (MA). Part-time and evening/weekend programs available. *Degree requirements:* For master's, comprehensive exam, thesis optional. *Entrance requirements:* For master's, GRE General Test. Additional exam requirements/recommendations for international students: Required—TOEFL. Electronic applications accepted. *Faculty research:* Intelligence, national security, statecraft.

Iowa State University of Science and Technology, Department of Political Science, Ames, IA 50011. Offers political science (MA); public administration (MPA); JD/MA. JD/MA offered jointly with Drake University. *Degree requirements:* For master's, thesis (for some programs). *Entrance requirements:* For master's, GRE General Test, GMAT or LSAT. Additional exam requirements/recommendations for international students: Required—TOEFL (minimum score 570 paper-based; 80 iBT), IELTS (minimum score 6.5). Electronic applications accepted.

Jackson State University, Graduate School, College of Liberal Arts, Department of Political Science, Jackson, MS 39217. Offers MA. Part-time and evening/weekend programs available. *Degree requirements:* For master's, comprehensive exam, thesis or alternative. *Entrance requirements:* For master's, GRE General Test. Additional exam requirements/recommendations for international students: Required—TOEFL (minimum score 520 paper-based; 67 iBT).

Jacksonville State University, College of Graduate Studies and Continuing Education, College of Arts and Sciences, Department of Political Science, Jacksonville, AL 36265-1602. Offers MPA. Part-time and evening/weekend programs available. *Faculty:* 8 full-time (2 women), 2 part-time/adjunct (1 woman). *Students:* 7 full-time (4 women), 35 part-time (21 women); includes 10 minority (9 Black or African American, non-Hispanic/Latino; 1 Hispanic/Latino), 1 international. Average age 30. 36 applicants, 58% accepted, 12 enrolled. In 2014, 29 master's awarded. *Degree requirements:* For master's, comprehensive exam, thesis (for some programs). *Entrance requirements:* For master's, GRE General Test or MAT. Additional exam requirements/recommendations for international students: Required—TOEFL (minimum score 61 iBT). *Application deadline:* Applications are processed on a rolling basis. Application fee: $35. Electronic applications accepted. *Financial support:* In 2014–15, 14 students received support. Available to part-time students. Application deadline: 4/1; applicants required to submit FAFSA. *Unit head:* Dr. Dan Krejci, Head, 256-782-5687, E-mail: dkrejci@jsu.edu. *Application contact:* Dr. Jean Pugliese, Associate Dean, 256-782-8278, Fax: 256-782-5321, E-mail: pugliese@jsu.edu.

James Madison University, The Graduate School, College of Arts and Letters, Department of Political Science, Program in Political Science, Harrisonburg, VA 22807. Offers political science (MA), including European Union policy studies. Part-time programs available. *Students:* 14 full-time (10 women); includes 6 minority (1 Asian, non-Hispanic/Latino; 5 Hispanic/Latino). Average age 28. 19 applicants, 100% accepted, 14 enrolled. In 2014, 11 master's awarded. *Application deadline:* For fall admission, 5/1 for domestic students; for spring admission, 9/1 for domestic students. Application fee: $55. Electronic applications accepted. *Expenses:* Tuition, state resident: full-time $7812; part-time $434 per credit hour. Tuition, nonresident: full-time $20,430; part-time $1135 per credit hour. *Financial support:* Application deadline: 3/1; applicants required to submit FAFSA. *Unit head:* Dr. Charles Blake, Academic Unit Head, 540-568-6149, E-mail: blakech@jmu.edu. *Application contact:* Lynette D. Michael, Director of Graduate Admissions and Student Records, 540-568-6131 Ext. 6395, Fax: 540-568-7860, E-mail: michaeld@jmu.edu.
Website: http://www.jmu.edu/eupolicystudies

Johns Hopkins University, Zanvyl Krieger School of Arts and Sciences, Advanced Academic Programs, Program in Government, Washington, DC 20036. Offers global security studies (MA); government (MA); national securities study (Certificate); nonprofit management (Certificate); public management (MA); research administration (MS); MA/MBA. Part-time and evening/weekend programs available. Postbaccalaureate distance learning degree programs offered (minimal on-campus study). *Degree requirements:* For master's, thesis. *Entrance requirements:* For master's, minimum GPA of 3.0. Additional exam requirements/recommendations for international students: Required—TOEFL (minimum score 100 iBT). Electronic applications accepted.

Johns Hopkins University, Zanvyl Krieger School of Arts and Sciences, Department of Political Science, Baltimore, MD 21218-2699. Offers MA, PhD. *Degree requirements:* For doctorate, one foreign language, comprehensive exam, thesis/dissertation. *Entrance requirements:* For doctorate, GRE General Test. Additional exam requirements/recommendations for international students: Required—TOEFL (minimum score 600 paper-based; 100 iBT), IELTS. Electronic applications accepted. *Faculty research:* American politics, comparative politics, international relations, political theory, urban politics.

Kansas State University, Graduate School, College of Arts and Sciences, Department of Political Science, Manhattan, KS 66506. Offers political science (MA), including international service, political science; public administration (MPA). Part-time programs available. *Faculty:* 16 full-time (4 women), 1 (woman) part-time/adjunct. *Students:* 24 full-time (15 women), 14 part-time (6 women); includes 7 minority (3 Black or African American, non-Hispanic/Latino; 1 Asian, non-Hispanic/Latino; 3 Hispanic/Latino), 4 international. Average age 29. 25 applicants, 68% accepted, 11 enrolled. In 2014, 20 master's awarded. *Degree requirements:* For master's, thesis or alternative. *Entrance requirements:* For master's, GRE (recommended), minimum GPA of 3.0. Additional exam requirements/recommendations for international students: Required—TOEFL (minimum score 550 paper-based). *Application deadline:* For fall admission, 2/1 priority date for domestic and international students; for spring admission, 8/1 priority date for domestic and international students. Applications are processed on a rolling basis. Application fee: $50 ($75 for international students). Electronic applications accepted. *Financial support:* In 2014–15, 10 teaching assistantships with tuition reimbursements (averaging $9,286 per year) were awarded; fellowships, research assistantships, career-related internships or fieldwork, Federal Work-Study, institutionally sponsored loans, and scholarships/grants also available. Support available to part-time students. Financial award application deadline: 3/1; financial award applicants required to submit FAFSA. *Faculty research:* Armed conflict, civil military relations, comparative public administration and policy, electoral competition, legislative studies. *Unit head:* Dr. Jeff Pickering, Head, 785-532-0454, Fax: 785-532-2339, E-mail: jjp@ksu.edu. *Application contact:* Dr. James Franke, Director, 785-532-0451, Fax: 785-532-2339, E-mail: jfranke@ksu.edu.
Website: http://www.k-state.edu/polsci/

Kaplan University, Davenport Campus, School of Legal Studies, Davenport, IA 52807-2095. Offers health care delivery (MS); pathway to paralegal (Postbaccalaureate Certificate); state and local government (MS). Part-time and evening/weekend programs available. Postbaccalaureate distance learning degree programs offered (no on-campus

study). *Entrance requirements:* Additional exam requirements/recommendations for international students: Required—TOEFL (minimum score 550 paper-based; 80 iBT).

Kent State University, College of Arts and Sciences, Department of Political Science, Kent, OH 44242-0001. Offers public administration (MPA). Part-time and evening/weekend programs available. Postbaccalaureate distance learning degree programs offered. *Faculty:* 20 full-time (5 women). *Students:* 45 full-time (19 women), 43 part-time (23 women); includes 8 minority (1 Black or African American, non-Hispanic/Latino; 1 Asian, non-Hispanic/Latino; 2 Hispanic/Latino; 4 Two or more races, non-Hispanic/Latino), 11 international. Average age 33. 107 applicants, 50% accepted, 38 enrolled. In 2014, 16 master's, 4 doctorates awarded. *Degree requirements:* For master's, thesis optional; for doctorate, 2 foreign languages, thesis/dissertation. *Entrance requirements:* For master's, GRE General Test, minimum GPA of 3.0, transcript, resume, statement of purpose, 3 letters of recommendation; for doctorate, GRE General Test, minimum GPA of 3.0, transcript, statement of purpose/intent, writing sample, 3 letters of recommendation. Additional exam requirements/recommendations for international students: Required—TOEFL (minimum score: paper-based 525, iBT 71), Michigan English Language Assessment Battery (minimum score of 75), IELTS (minimum score of 6.0), PTE Academic (minimum score of 48), or completion of ELS level 112 Intensive Program. *Application deadline:* For fall admission, 7/31 for domestic students; for spring admission, 11/15 for domestic students; for summer admission, 3/31 for domestic students. Application fee: $45 ($70 for international students). Electronic applications accepted. *Expenses:* Tuition, state resident: full-time $8730; part-time $485 per credit hour. Tuition, nonresident: full-time $14,886; part-time $827 per credit hour. Tuition and fees vary according to campus/location and program. *Financial support:* Research assistantships with full tuition reimbursements, teaching assistantships with full tuition reimbursements, career-related internships or fieldwork, Federal Work-Study, and unspecified assistantships available. Financial award application deadline: 2/1. *Unit head:* Dr. Andrew Barnes, Associate Professor and Chair, 330-672-2060, E-mail: abarnes3@kent.edu. *Application contact:* Dr. Michael Ensley, Graduate Coordinator, 330-672-2060, E-mail: polisci@kent.edu.
Website: http://www.kent.edu/stark/political-science

Lamar University, College of Graduate Studies, College of Arts and Sciences, Department of Political Science, Beaumont, TX 77710. Offers public administration (MPA). Part-time programs available. *Faculty:* 4 full-time (2 women). *Students:* 12 full-time (5 women), 9 part-time (6 women); includes 12 minority (8 Black or African American, non-Hispanic/Latino; 3 Hispanic/Latino; 1 Two or more races, non-Hispanic/Latino), 4 international. Average age 32. 7 applicants, 86% accepted, 3 enrolled. In 2014, 19 master's awarded. *Entrance requirements:* For master's, GRE General Test. Additional exam requirements/recommendations for international students: Required—TOEFL (minimum score 550 paper-based; 79 iBT), IELTS (minimum score 6.5). *Application deadline:* For fall admission, 8/10 for domestic students, 7/1 for international students; for spring admission, 1/5 for domestic students, 12/1 for international students. Applications are processed on a rolling basis. Application fee: $25 ($50 for international students). *Expenses:* Tuition, state resident: full-time $5724; part-time $1908 per semester. Tuition, nonresident: full-time $12,240; part-time $4080 per semester. *Required fees:* $1940; $318 per credit hour. *Financial support:* Fellowships, research assistantships, teaching assistantships, career-related internships or fieldwork, Federal Work-Study, and institutionally sponsored loans available. Financial award application deadline: 4/1. *Faculty research:* Political activities of administrators, administrative response to Hurricane Rita, budgeting, environmental politics, urban planning. *Unit head:* Dr. Terri Davis, Chair, 409-880-8285, Fax: 409-880-8710. *Application contact:* Melissa Gallien, Director, Admissions and Academic Services, 409-880-8888, Fax: 409-880-7419, E-mail: gradmissions@lamar.edu.
Website: http://artssciences.lamar.edu/political-science

Lehigh University, College of Arts and Sciences, Department of Political Science, Bethlehem, PA 18015. Offers politics and policy (MA), including political theory. Part-time programs available. *Faculty:* 12 full-time (6 women), 1 (woman) part-time/adjunct. *Students:* 11 full-time (7 women), 2 part-time (1 woman); includes 3 minority (1 Black or African American, non-Hispanic/Latino; 1 Hispanic/Latino; 1 Two or more races, non-Hispanic/Latino). Average age 23. 15 applicants, 67% accepted, 6 enrolled. In 2014, 13 master's awarded. *Degree requirements:* For master's, thesis optional, extended paper. *Entrance requirements:* Additional exam requirements/recommendations for international students: Required—TOEFL. *Application deadline:* For fall admission, 6/15 for domestic and international students. Applications are processed on a rolling basis. Application fee: $75. Electronic applications accepted. *Financial support:* In 2014–15, 6 students received support, including 5 fellowships with partial tuition reimbursements available, 2 teaching assistantships with full tuition reimbursements available; career-related internships or fieldwork, tuition waivers (partial), and unspecified assistantships also available. Financial award application deadline: 4/1. *Faculty research:* American politics and institutions, comparative politics, public policy, political theory. *Total annual research expenditures:* $580. *Unit head:* Dr. Richard K. Matthews, Chairman, 610-758-3343, Fax: 610-758-3348, E-mail: rm02@lehigh.edu. *Application contact:* Dr. Janet Laible, Director, Graduate Studies, 610-758-5879, Fax: 610-758-3348, E-mail: jml6@lehigh.edu.
Website: http://polisci.cas2.lehigh.edu/

Liberty University, Helms School of Government, Lynchburg, VA 24515. Offers criminal justice (MS); public policy (MA), including campaigns and elections, international affairs, Middle East affairs, public administration, public policy. Part-time programs available. Postbaccalaureate distance learning degree programs offered (no on-campus study). *Students:* 248 full-time (119 women), 522 part-time (209 women); includes 194 minority (157 Black or African American, non-Hispanic/Latino; 8 American Indian or Alaska Native, non-Hispanic/Latino; 7 Asian, non-Hispanic/Latino; 5 Hispanic/Latino; 1 Native Hawaiian or other Pacific Islander, non-Hispanic/Latino; 16 Two or more races, non-Hispanic/Latino), 14 international. Average age 34. 837 applicants, 55% accepted, 226 enrolled. In 2014, 65 degrees awarded. *Entrance requirements:* For master's, minimum undergraduate GPA of 3.0. Additional exam requirements/recommendations for international students: Required—TOEFL (minimum score 600 paper-based; 100 iBT). *Application deadline:* Applications are processed on a rolling basis. Application fee: $50. Electronic applications accepted. *Unit head:* Shawn D. Akers, Dean, 434-592-4986. *Application contact:* Jay Bridge, Director of Admissions, 800-424-9595, Fax: 800-628-7977, E-mail: gradadmissions@liberty.edu.

Louisiana State University and Agricultural & Mechanical College, Graduate School, College of Humanities and Social Sciences, Department of Political Science, Baton Rouge, LA 70803. Offers MA, PhD. *Faculty:* 24 full-time (5 women). *Students:* 38 full-time (15 women), 15 part-time (5 women); includes 8 minority (2 Black or African American, non-Hispanic/Latino; 1 American Indian or Alaska Native, non-Hispanic/Latino; 4 Hispanic/Latino; 1 Two or more races, non-Hispanic/Latino), 8 international. Average age 31. 44 applicants, 32% accepted, 8 enrolled. In 2014, 4 master's, 5 doctorates awarded. Terminal master's awarded for partial completion of doctoral program. *Degree requirements:* For master's, thesis or alternative; for doctorate, one foreign language, thesis/dissertation. *Entrance requirements:* For master's and doctorate, GRE General Test, minimum GPA of 3.0. Additional exam requirements/recommendations for international students: Required—TOEFL (minimum score 550 paper-based; 79 IBT), IELTS (minimum score 6.5), or PTE (minimum score 59). *Application deadline:* For fall admission, 1/1 priority date for domestic students, 5/15 for international students; for spring admission, 10/15 for domestic and international students; for summer admission, 5/15 for domestic and international students. Application fee: $50 ($70 for international students). Electronic applications accepted. *Financial support:* In 2014–15, 43 students received support, including 3 fellowships with full and partial tuition reimbursements available (averaging $35,894 per year), 3 research assistantships with full and partial tuition reimbursements available (averaging $16,167 per year), 24 teaching assistantships with full and partial tuition reimbursements available (averaging $12,160 per year); Federal Work-Study, institutionally sponsored loans, health care benefits, tuition waivers (full), and unspecified assistantships also available. Financial award application deadline: 3/1; financial award applicants required to submit FAFSA. *Faculty research:* American government and policy, political theory, international relations and comparative politics. *Total annual research expenditures:* $12,037. *Unit head:* Dr. William Clark, Chair, 225-578-2141, Fax: 225-578-2540, E-mail: poclark@lsu.edu. *Application contact:* Dr. James Garand, Graduate Advisor, 225-578-2548, Fax: 225-578-2540, E-mail: pogarand@lsu.edu.
Website: http://uiswcmsweb.prod.lsu.edu/hss/polisci/

Loyola University Chicago, Graduate School, Department of Political Science, Chicago, IL 60660. Offers MA, PhD. Part-time and evening/weekend programs available. *Faculty:* 19 full-time (4 women). *Students:* 31 full-time (14 women), 2 part-time (0 women); includes 3 minority (1 Black or African American, non-Hispanic/Latino; 2 Hispanic/Latino), 7 international. Average age 31. 61 applicants, 31% accepted, 12 enrolled. In 2014, 5 master's, 1 doctorate awarded. Terminal master's awarded for partial completion of doctoral program. *Degree requirements:* For master's, comprehensive exam, thesis or alternative; for doctorate, comprehensive exam, thesis/dissertation. *Entrance requirements:* For master's and doctorate, GRE General Test. Additional exam requirements/recommendations for international students: Required—TOEFL (minimum score 550 paper-based; 79 iBT). *Application deadline:* For fall admission, 6/1 for domestic and international students; for spring admission, 10/1 for domestic and international students. Applications are processed on a rolling basis. Electronic applications accepted. *Expenses: Tuition:* Full-time $17,370; part-time $965 per credit. *Required fees:* $138 per semester. *Financial support:* In 2014–15, 9 fellowships with full tuition reimbursements (averaging $18,000 per year), 9 research assistantships with full tuition reimbursements (averaging $18,000 per year) were awarded; Federal Work-Study, institutionally sponsored loans, scholarships/grants, tuition waivers (partial), and unspecified assistantships also available. Financial award application deadline: 2/15; financial award applicants required to submit FAFSA. *Faculty research:* American elections, parties and political institutions; comparative politics; foreign policy analysis; international relations theory; modern and contemporary political thought. *Unit head:* Prof. Peter Sanchez, Graduate Program Director, 773-508-8658, Fax: 773-508-3131, E-mail: psanche@luc.edu. *Application contact:* Ron Martin, Assistant Director of Enrollment Management, 312-915-8950, Fax: 312-915-8905, E-mail: gradapp@luc.edu.
Website: http://www.luc.edu/politicalscience/

Marquette University, Graduate School, College of Arts and Sciences, Department of Political Science, Milwaukee, WI 53201-1881. Offers international affairs (MA); political science (MA); JD/MA; MA/MBA. Part-time programs available. *Degree requirements:* For master's, comprehensive exam, thesis optional. *Entrance requirements:* For master's, GRE General Test, official transcripts from all current and previous colleges/universities except Marquette, three letters of recommendation, statement of purpose. Additional exam requirements/recommendations for international students: Required—TOEFL (minimum score 530 paper-based). Electronic applications accepted. *Faculty research:* Public opinion and electoral behavior, public policy analysis, Congress and the Presidency, judicial behavior, political system transitions.

Marshall University, Academic Affairs Division, College of Liberal Arts, Department of Political Science, Huntington, WV 25755. Offers MA, MPA. *Students:* 13 full-time (5 women), 6 part-time (5 women); includes 2 minority (both Hispanic/Latino), 1 international. Average age 28. In 2014, 5 master's awarded. *Degree requirements:* For master's, thesis optional. *Entrance requirements:* For master's, GRE General Test. Application fee: $40. *Unit head:* Dr. George Davis, Chair, 304-696-2766, Fax: 304-696-3245, E-mail: davg@marshall.edu. *Application contact:* Graduate Admissions, 304-746-1900, Fax: 304-746-1902, E-mail: services@marshall.edu.
Website: http://www.marshall.edu/polsci/

Massachusetts Institute of Technology, School of Humanities, Arts, and Social Sciences, Department of Political Science, Cambridge, MA 02139. Offers SM, PhD. *Faculty:* 29 full-time (8 women). *Students:* 64 full-time (27 women); includes 5 minority (1 Asian, non-Hispanic/Latino; 1 Hispanic/Latino; 3 Two or more races, non-Hispanic/Latino), 28 international. Average age 29. 463 applicants, 8% accepted, 15 enrolled. In 2014, 8 master's, 9 doctorates awarded. Terminal master's awarded for partial completion of doctoral program. *Degree requirements:* For master's, thesis, Maintain a GPA of 3.5 in all subjects applied toward fulfillment of the requirements for master's degree; for doctorate, one foreign language, comprehensive exam, thesis/dissertation. *Entrance requirements:* For master's and doctorate, GRE General Test. Additional exam requirements/recommendations for international students: Required—TOEFL (minimum score 600 paper-based; 100 iBT), IELTS (minimum score 7). *Application deadline:* For fall admission, 12/15 for domestic and international students. Application fee: $75. Electronic applications accepted. *Expenses: Tuition:* Full-time $44,720; part-time $699 per unit. *Required fees:* $296. *Financial support:* In 2014–15, 53 students received support, including 19 fellowships (averaging $35,700 per year), 27 research assistantships (averaging $34,100 per year), 14 teaching assistantships (averaging $36,900 per year); Federal Work-Study, institutionally sponsored loans, scholarships/grants, health care benefits, and unspecified assistantships also available. Financial award application deadline: 4/15; financial award applicants required to submit FAFSA. *Faculty research:* International relations, security studies, American politics, comparative politics, political economy, models and methods. *Total annual research expenditures:* $2.2 million. *Unit head:* Melissa Nobles, Department Head, 617-253-5262, Fax: 617-258-6164. *Application contact:* Graduate Administrator, 617-253-8336, Fax: 617-258-6164.
Website: http://web.mit.edu/polisci/

McGill University, Faculty of Graduate and Postdoctoral Studies, Faculty of Arts, Department of Political Science, Montréal, QC H3A 2T5, Canada. Offers MA, PhD.

McMaster University, School of Graduate Studies, Faculty of Social Sciences, Department of Political Science, Hamilton, ON L8S 4M2, Canada. Offers international relations (PhD); political science (MA); public and the global economy (MA); public policy (PhD); public policy and administration (MA). MA program in public policy and administration offered jointly with University of Guelph. Part-time programs available. *Degree requirements:* For master's, thesis or alternative. *Entrance requirements:* For master's, minimum B+ average. Additional exam requirements/recommendations for international students: Required—TOEFL (minimum score 580 paper-based). *Faculty research:* Organizational theory, internationalization of public policy, water resource policies, political interest intermediation, comparative politics.

Political Science

Memorial University of Newfoundland, School of Graduate Studies, Department of Political Science, St. John's, NL A1C 5S7, Canada. Offers MA. Part-time and evening/weekend programs available. *Degree requirements:* For master's, thesis optional. *Entrance requirements:* For master's, minimum 2nd class bachelor's degree. Electronic applications accepted. *Faculty research:* Comparative politics, Canadian government and politics, Newfoundland politics, and the politics of multi-level systems.

Miami University, College of Arts and Science, Department of Political Science, Oxford, OH 45056. Offers MA. *Students:* 8. In 2014, 14 master's awarded. *Entrance requirements:* Additional exam requirements/recommendations for international students: Recommended—TOEFL (minimum score 80 iBT), IELTS (minimum score 6.5), TSE (minimum score 54). *Application deadline:* For fall admission, 3/1 priority date for domestic and international students. Application fee: $50. Electronic applications accepted. *Expenses:* Tuition, state resident: full-time $12,887; part-time $537 per credit hour. Tuition, nonresident: full-time $28,449; part-time $1186 per credit hour. *Required fees:* $530; $24 per credit hour. $30 per quarter. Part-time tuition and fees vary according to course load and program. *Financial support:* Fellowships with full and partial tuition reimbursements, research assistantships with full and partial tuition reimbursements, and teaching assistantships with full and partial tuition reimbursements available. Financial award application deadline: 2/15; financial award applicants required to submit FAFSA. *Faculty research:* Constitutional rights and liberties, American foreign policy, world regional politics, public management, political philosophy, parties and interest groups, international law. *Unit head:* Dr. Patrick Haney, Interim Chair, 513-529-4321, E-mail: haneypk@miamioh.edu. *Application contact:* Dr. Cyril Daddieh, Professor and Graduate Studies Director, 513-529-2000, E-mail: daddieck@miamioh.edu.

Michigan State University, The Graduate School, College of Social Science, Department of Political Science, East Lansing, MI 48824. Offers political science (MA, PhD); public policy (MPP). *Degree requirements:* For master's, practicum; for doctorate, comprehensive exam, presentation of dissertation. *Entrance requirements:* Additional exam requirements/recommendations for international students: Required—TOEFL. Electronic applications accepted.

Middle Tennessee State University, College of Graduate Studies, College of Liberal Arts, Department of Political Science, Murfreesboro, TN 37132. Offers international affairs (MA). Part-time and evening/weekend programs available. Postbaccalaureate distance learning degree programs offered. *Faculty:* 10 full-time (3 women), 1 (woman) part-time/adjunct. *Students:* 6 full-time (2 women), 7 part-time (4 women); includes 4 minority (1 Black or African American, non-Hispanic/Latino; 1 Asian, non-Hispanic/Latino; 1 Hispanic/Latino; 1 Two or more races, non-Hispanic/Latino). 19 applicants, 79% accepted. In 2014, 3 master's awarded. *Entrance requirements:* Additional exam requirements/recommendations for international students: Required—TOEFL (minimum score 525 paper-based; 71 iBT) or IELTS (minimum score 6). *Application deadline:* For fall admission, 6/1 for domestic and international students. Applications are processed on a rolling basis. Application fee: $30. Electronic applications accepted. *Financial support:* In 2014–15, 6 students received support. Application deadline: 4/1; applicants required to submit FAFSA. *Unit head:* Dr. Mark E. Byrnes, Dean, 615-898-2534, Fax: 615-904-8279, E-mail: mark.byrnes@mtsu.edu. *Application contact:* Dr. Michael D. Allen, Vice Provost for Research/Dean, 615-898-2840, Fax: 615-904-8020, E-mail: michael.allen@mtsu.edu.

Midwestern State University, Billie Doris McAda Graduate School, Prothro-Yeager College of Humanities and Social Sciences, Department of Political Science, Wichita Falls, TX 76308. Offers MA. *Degree requirements:* For master's, one foreign language, comprehensive exam, thesis optional. *Entrance requirements:* For master's, GRE General Test/GMAT/MAT, bachelor's degree from regionally-accredited institution, minimum GPA of 3.0 on last 60 hours of undergraduate work. Additional exam requirements/recommendations for international students: Required—TOEFL (minimum score 550 paper-based). *Application deadline:* For fall admission, 7/1 priority date for domestic students, 4/1 for international students; for spring admission, 11/1 priority date for domestic students, 8/1 for international students. Applications are processed on a rolling basis. Application fee: $35 ($50 for international students). Electronic applications accepted. *Financial support:* Teaching assistantships with partial tuition reimbursements, career-related internships or fieldwork, Federal Work-Study, institutionally sponsored loans, scholarships/grants, and unspecified assistantships available. Support available to part-time students. Financial award application deadline: 3/1; financial award applicants required to submit FAFSA. *Faculty research:* American politics, political behavior, political research methods, conflict processes, Latin American politics. *Unit head:* Rebecca Tuck, Secretary, 940-397-4376, Fax: 940-397-4865, E-mail: rebecca.tuck@mwsu.edu.
Website: http://www.mwsu.edu/academics/libarts/politicalscience/

Mississippi College, Graduate School, College of Arts and Sciences, School of Humanities and Social Sciences, Department of History, Political Science, Administration of Justice, and Paralegal Studies, Clinton, MS 39058. Offers administration of justice (MSS); history (M Ed, MA, MSS); paralegal studies (Certificate); political science (MSS); social sciences (M Ed, MSS). Part-time programs available. *Degree requirements:* For master's, one foreign language, comprehensive exam, thesis (for some programs). *Entrance requirements:* For master's, GRE or NTE, minimum GPA of 2.5. Additional exam requirements/recommendations for international students: Recommended—TOEFL, IELTS. Electronic applications accepted.

Mississippi State University, College of Arts and Sciences, Department of Political Science and Public Administration, Mississippi State, MS 39762. Offers political science (MA); public policy and administration (MPPA, PhD). *Accreditation:* NASPAA (one or more programs are accredited). Evening/weekend programs available. Postbaccalaureate distance learning degree programs offered (no on-campus study). *Faculty:* 11 full-time (2 women), 1 part-time/adjunct (0 women). *Students:* 38 full-time (20 women), 41 part-time (24 women); includes 31 minority (26 Black or African American, non-Hispanic/Latino; 1 American Indian or Alaska Native, non-Hispanic/Latino; 3 Hispanic/Latino; 1 Two or more races, non-Hispanic/Latino), 3 international. Average age 30. 32 applicants, 63% accepted, 14 enrolled. In 2014, 28 master's, 5 doctorates awarded. *Degree requirements:* For master's, thesis optional, comprehensive oral or written exam; for doctorate, thesis/dissertation, comprehensive oral and written exam. *Entrance requirements:* For master's, GRE, minimum GPA of 3.0 on the last two years of undergraduate courses or graduate work; for doctorate, GRE General Test, minimum graduate GPA of 3.35. Additional exam requirements/recommendations for international students: Required—TOEFL (minimum score 600 paper-based; 100 iBT); Recommended—IELTS (minimum score 7.5). *Application deadline:* For fall admission, 8/1 priority date for domestic students, 5/1 for international students; for spring admission, 12/1 priority date for domestic students, 9/1 for international students. Applications are processed on a rolling basis. Application fee: $60. Electronic applications accepted. *Expenses:* Tuition, state resident: full-time $7140; part-time $783 per credit hour. Tuition, nonresident: full-time $18,478; part-time $2043 per credit hour. *Financial support:* In 2014–15, 1 research assistantship with full tuition reimbursement (averaging $9,250 per year), 9 teaching assistantships with full tuition reimbursements (averaging $8,993 per year) were awarded; Federal Work-Study, institutionally sponsored loans, scholarships/grants, and unspecified assistantships also available. Financial award application deadline: 4/1; financial award applicants required

to submit FAFSA. *Faculty research:* American politics, international relations, state and local government, comparative government, public administration. *Total annual research expenditures:* $807,000. *Unit head:* Dr. K. C. Morrison, Department Head, 662-325-2711, Fax: 662-325-2716, E-mail: kcmorrison@ps.msstate.edu. *Application contact:* Dr. Christine Rush, Graduate Coordinator, 662-325-2711, Fax: 662-325-2716, E-mail: clr449@msstate.edu.
Website: http://www.pspa.msstate.edu/

Missouri State University, Graduate College, College of Humanities and Public Affairs, Department of Political Science, Springfield, MO 65897. Offers global studies (MGS); public administration (MPA); public management (Certificate). Part-time programs available. *Faculty:* 14 full-time (2 women). *Students:* 36 full-time (13 women), 13 part-time (10 women); includes 4 minority (3 Black or African American, non-Hispanic/Latino; 1 Hispanic/Latino), 17 international. Average age 28. 22 applicants, 73% accepted, 11 enrolled. In 2014, 16 master's awarded. *Degree requirements:* For master's, variable foreign language requirement, comprehensive exam, thesis or alternative. *Entrance requirements:* For master's, GRE, minimum GPA of 3.0. Additional exam requirements/recommendations for international students: Required—TOEFL (minimum score 550 paper-based; 79 iBT). *Application deadline:* For fall admission, 7/20 priority date for domestic students, 5/1 for international students; for spring admission, 12/20 priority date for domestic students, 9/1 for international students. Applications are processed on a rolling basis. Application fee: $35 ($50 for international students). Electronic applications accepted. *Expenses:* Tuition, state resident: full-time $2250; part-time $250 per credit hour. Tuition, nonresident: full-time $4509; part-time $501 per credit hour. Tuition and fees vary according to course level, course load and program. *Financial support:* Career-related internships or fieldwork, Federal Work-Study, scholarships/grants, and unspecified assistantships available. Support available to part-time students. Financial award application deadline: 3/31; financial award applicants required to submit FAFSA. *Faculty research:* Public procurement; Missouri politics; international relations of East Asia, law of church and state. *Unit head:* Dr. George Connor, Acting Head, 417-836-5630, Fax: 417-836-6655, E-mail: georgeconnor@missouristate.edu. *Application contact:* Misty Stewart, Coordinator of Admissions and Recruitment, 417-836-6079, Fax: 417-836-6200, E-mail: mistystewart@missouristate.edu.
Website: http://polsci.missouristate.edu

Montclair State University, The Graduate School, College of Humanities and Social Sciences, MA Program in Law and Governance, Montclair, NJ 07043-1624. Offers conflict management and peace studies (MA); governance, compliance and regulation (MA); intellectual property (MA); law and governance (MA); legal management (MA). Part-time and evening/weekend programs available. *Faculty:* 13 full-time (6 women), 25 part-time/adjunct (8 women). *Students:* 11 full-time (6 women), 23 part-time (13 women); includes 17 minority (8 Black or African American, non-Hispanic/Latino; 2 Asian, non-Hispanic/Latino; 5 Hispanic/Latino; 2 Two or more races, non-Hispanic/Latino), 2 international. Average age 31. 32 applicants, 44% accepted, 10 enrolled. In 2014, 27 master's awarded. *Degree requirements:* For master's, thesis or comprehensive exam. *Entrance requirements:* For master's, GRE General Test, minimum cumulative GPA of 2.75 for undergraduate work, 2 letters of recommendation, essay. Additional exam requirements/recommendations for international students: Required—TOEFL (minimum score 83 iBT) or IELTS (minimum score 6.5). *Application deadline:* Applications are processed on a rolling basis. Application fee: $60. Electronic applications accepted. *Expenses:* Tuition, state resident: full-time $9960; part-time $553.35 per credit. Tuition, nonresident: full-time $15,074; part-time $837.43 per credit. *Required fees:* $1595; $88.63 per credit. Tuition and fees vary according to degree level and program. *Financial support:* In 2014–15, 1 research assistantship with full tuition reimbursement (averaging $7,000 per year) was awarded; Federal Work-Study, scholarships/grants, and unspecified assistantships also available. Support available to part-time students. Financial award application deadline: 3/1; financial award applicants required to submit FAFSA. *Unit head:* Dr. William Berlin, Chair, 973-655-7576, E-mail: berlinw@mail.montclair.edu. *Application contact:* Amy Aiello, Director of Graduate Admissions and Operations, 973-655-5147, Fax: 973-655-7869, E-mail: graduate.school@montclair.edu.
Website: http://www.montclair.edu/graduate/programs-of-study/law-and-governance/

New Mexico Highlands University, Graduate Studies, College of Arts and Sciences, Department of History, Political Science, and Languages and Culture, Las Vegas, NM 87701. Offers public affairs (MA), including historical and cross-cultural perspectives, history/political science, political and governmental processes. *Faculty:* 9 full-time (3 women), 1 part-time/adjunct (0 women). *Students:* 13 full-time (6 women), 12 part-time (1 woman); includes 15 minority (all Hispanic/Latino), 5 international. Average age 34. 12 applicants, 100% accepted, 4 enrolled. In 2014, 1 master's awarded. *Degree requirements:* For master's, comprehensive exam, thesis or alternative. *Entrance requirements:* Additional exam requirements/recommendations for international students: Required—TOEFL (minimum score 540 paper-based). *Application deadline:* For fall admission, 8/1 priority date for domestic students. Applications are processed on a rolling basis. Application fee: $15. *Financial support:* In 2014–15, 11 teaching assistantships were awarded; research assistantships, career-related internships or fieldwork, Federal Work-Study, institutionally sponsored loans, scholarships/grants, traineeships, tuition waivers (full and partial), and unspecified assistantships also available. Support available to part-time students. Financial award application deadline: 3/1. *Unit head:* Dr. Steven Williams, Associate Professor, 505-454-3435. *Application contact:* Diane Trujillo, Administrative Assistant, Graduate Studies, 505-454-3266, Fax: 505-426-2117, E-mail: dtrujillo@nmhu.edu.
Website: http://www.nmhu.edu/current-students/graduate/arts-and-sciences/history-political-science-languages-and-culture/

New Mexico State University, College of Arts and Sciences, Department of Government, Las Cruces, NM 88003-8001. Offers MA, MPA. *Accreditation:* NASPAA (one or more programs are accredited). Part-time and evening/weekend programs available. *Faculty:* 9 full-time (2 women). *Students:* 17 full-time (6 women), 18 part-time (11 women); includes 15 minority (all Hispanic/Latino), 1 international. Average age 31. 20 applicants, 65% accepted, 9 enrolled. In 2014, 23 master's awarded. *Degree requirements:* For master's, comprehensive exam (for some programs), thesis optional. *Entrance requirements:* For master's, GRE (if GPA less than 3.0), writing sample, 3 letters of recommendation, resume. Additional exam requirements/recommendations for international students: Required—TOEFL (minimum score 550 paper-based; 79 iBT), IELTS (minimum score 6.5). *Application deadline:* Applications are processed on a rolling basis. Application fee: $40 ($50 for international students). Electronic applications accepted. *Expenses:* Tuition, state resident: full-time $3969; part-time $220.50 per credit hour. Tuition, nonresident: full-time $13,838; part-time $768.80 per credit hour. *Required fees:* $853; $47.40 per credit hour. *Financial support:* In 2014–15, 16 students received support, including 2 research assistantships (averaging $6,098 per year), 9 teaching assistantships (averaging $12,197 per year); career-related internships or fieldwork, Federal Work-Study, scholarships/grants, health care benefits, and unspecified assistantships also available. Support available to part-time students. Financial award application deadline: 3/1. *Faculty research:* U.S.-Mexico border studies, public administration and policy, international relations, Latin America, American politics and theory. *Total annual research expenditures:* $14,992. *Unit head:* Dr. Neil Harvey, Acting Head, 575-646-4935, Fax: 575-646-2052, E-mail: nharvey@nmsu.edu.

Application contact: Dr. Yosef Lapid, Director, Master of Arts in Government Program, 575-646-4935, Fax: 575-646-2052, E-mail: ylapid@nmsu.edu.
Website: http://deptofgov.nmsu.edu

The New School, The New School for Social Research, Department of Political Science, New York, NY 10003. Offers M Phil, MA, DS Sc, PhD. Part-time programs available. Terminal master's awarded for partial completion of doctoral program. *Degree requirements:* For master's, thesis; for doctorate, one foreign language, comprehensive exam, thesis/dissertation, two methodology courses, PhD seminar, field seminars. *Entrance requirements:* For master's, GRE General Test; for doctorate, GRE General Test, MA. Additional exam requirements/recommendations for international students: Required—TOEFL (minimum score 600 paper-based; 100 iBT). Electronic applications accepted. *Faculty research:* Democratic transitions and institution; race, class and gender; immigration and incorporation.

New York University, Graduate School of Arts and Science, Department of Politics, New York, NY 10012-1019. Offers political campaign management (MA); politics (MA, PhD); JD/MA; MBA/MA. Part-time programs available. *Faculty:* 30 full-time (4 women). *Students:* 175 full-time (88 women), 68 part-time (31 women); includes 36 minority (3 Black or African American, non-Hispanic/Latino; 1 American Indian or Alaska Native, non-Hispanic/Latino; 18 Asian, non-Hispanic/Latino; 12 Hispanic/Latino; 2 Two or more races, non-Hispanic/Latino), 129 international. Average age 27. 670 applicants, 45% accepted, 80 enrolled. In 2014, 101 master's, 13 doctorates awarded. Terminal master's awarded for partial completion of doctoral program. *Degree requirements:* For master's, one foreign language, thesis or alternative; for doctorate, 2 foreign languages, comprehensive exam, thesis/dissertation. *Entrance requirements:* For master's and doctorate, GRE General Test. Additional exam requirements/recommendations for international students: Required—TOEFL. *Application deadline:* For fall admission, 12/18 priority date for domestic students, 12/18 for international students. Application fee: $100. *Financial support:* Fellowships with tuition reimbursements, teaching assistantships with tuition reimbursements, career-related internships or fieldwork, Federal Work-Study, and institutionally sponsored loans available. Financial award application deadline: 12/18; financial award applicants required to submit FAFSA. *Faculty research:* Comparative politics, democratic theory and practice, rational choice, political economy, international relations. *Unit head:* Sanford Gordon, Director of Graduate Studies, PhD Program, 212-998-8500, Fax: 212-995-4184, E-mail: politics.phd@nyu.edu. *Application contact:* Nicole Simonelli, Director of Graduate Studies, Master's Program, 212-998-8500, Fax: 212-995-4184, E-mail: politics.masters@nyu.edu.
Website: http://www.nyu.edu/gsas/dept/politics/

Northeastern Illinois University, College of Graduate Studies and Research, College of Arts and Sciences, Program in Political Science, Chicago, IL 60625-4699. Offers MA. Part-time and evening/weekend programs available. *Degree requirements:* For master's, comprehensive exam, thesis optional. *Entrance requirements:* For master's, minimum GPA of 2.75. Additional exam requirements/recommendations for international students: Required—TOEFL (minimum score 550 paper-based; 79 iBT). Electronic applications accepted. *Faculty research:* Chinese politics, Latin American democratization, Jewish feminism, administration and delegation.

Northeastern University, College of Social Sciences and Humanities, Boston, MA 02115. Offers criminology and criminal justice (MSCJ); criminology and justice policy (PhD); economics (MA, PhD); English (MA, PhD); law and public policy (MS, PhD); political science (MA, PhD); public administration (MPA); public history (MA); security and resilience studies (MS); sociology (MA, PhD); urban and regional policy (MS); world history (MA, PhD). *Degree requirements:* For doctorate, variable foreign language requirement, comprehensive exam, thesis/dissertation. *Entrance requirements:* For master's and doctorate, GRE. Additional exam requirements/recommendations for international students: Required—TOEFL, IELTS. Electronic applications accepted.

Northern Arizona University, Graduate College, College of Social and Behavioral Sciences, Department of Politics and International Affairs, Flagstaff, AZ 86011. Offers political science (MA, PhD); public administration (MPA); public management (Certificate). Part-time programs available. *Degree requirements:* For master's, comprehensive exam (for some programs), thesis optional; for doctorate, one foreign language, comprehensive exam, thesis/dissertation. *Entrance requirements:* For master's, GRE (minimum 70th percentile ranking in each testing area preferred); for doctorate, GRE (minimum score in 70th percentile in each testing area preferred). Additional exam requirements/recommendations for international students: Required—TOEFL (minimum score 550 paper-based; 80 iBT), IELTS (minimum score 7). Electronic applications accepted.

Northern Illinois University, Graduate School, College of Liberal Arts and Sciences, Department of Political Science, De Kalb, IL 60115-2854. Offers political science (MA, PhD); public administration (MPA). Part-time and evening/weekend programs available. *Faculty:* 24 full-time (5 women), 8 part-time/adjunct (2 women). *Students:* 74 full-time (24 women), 61 part-time (26 women); includes 16 minority (7 Black or African American, non-Hispanic/Latino; 2 Asian, non-Hispanic/Latino; 4 Hispanic/Latino; 3 Two or more races, non-Hispanic/Latino), 24 international. Average age 31. 107 applicants, 41% accepted, 25 enrolled. In 2014, 37 master's, 10 doctorates awarded. Terminal master's awarded for partial completion of doctoral program. *Degree requirements:* For master's, comprehensive exam, thesis optional; for doctorate, variable foreign language requirement, thesis/dissertation, candidacy exam, dissertation defense. *Entrance requirements:* For master's, GRE General Test, minimum GPA of 2.75, 9 hours of course work in political science; for doctorate, GRE General Test, minimum GPA of 2.75 (undergraduate), 3.2 (graduate); undergraduate major in related field. Additional exam requirements/recommendations for international students: Required—TOEFL (minimum score 550 paper-based). *Application deadline:* For fall admission, 3/1 priority date for domestic students, 5/1 for international students; for spring admission, 11/1 for domestic students, 10/1 for international students. Applications are processed on a rolling basis. Application fee: $40. Electronic applications accepted. *Financial support:* In 2014–15, 2 research assistantships with full tuition reimbursements, 20 teaching assistantships with full tuition reimbursements were awarded; fellowships with full tuition reimbursements, career-related internships or fieldwork, Federal Work-Study, scholarships/grants, tuition waivers (full), and unspecified assistantships also available. Support available to part-time students. Financial award applicants required to submit FAFSA. *Faculty research:* Terrorism and dynamics of trade, U.S. foreign policy, political economy of development, biopolitical theory, women and politics. *Unit head:* Dr. Matthew Streb, Chair, 815-753-7046, Fax: 815-753-6302, E-mail: mstreb@niu.edu. *Application contact:* Dr. Scot Schraufnagel, Director, Graduate Studies, 815-753-7054, E-mail: sschrauf@niu.edu.
Website: http://polisci.niu.edu/

Northwestern University, The Graduate School, Judd A. and Marjorie Weinberg College of Arts and Sciences, Department of Political Science, Evanston, IL 60208. Offers PhD, JD/PhD. Admissions and degrees offered through The Graduate School. Terminal master's awarded for partial completion of doctoral program. *Degree requirements:* For doctorate, thesis/dissertation, qualifying exams. *Entrance requirements:* For doctorate, GRE General Test, sample of written work. Additional exam requirements/recommendations for international students: Required—TOEFL. *Faculty research:* Formal theory/formal political economy, political economy of

development/state-business relations, labor market institutions and welfare policy, public opinion and political behavior, feminist political theory.

The Ohio State University, Graduate School, College of Arts and Sciences, Division of Social and Behavioral Sciences, Department of Political Science, Columbus, OH 43210. Offers PhD. *Faculty:* 30. *Students:* 70 full-time (26 women), 3 part-time (all women); includes 11 minority (1 Black or African American, non-Hispanic/Latino; 3 Asian, non-Hispanic/Latino; 7 Hispanic/Latino), 13 international. Average age 29. In 2014, 14 doctorates awarded. Terminal master's awarded for partial completion of doctoral program. *Degree requirements:* For doctorate, thesis/dissertation. *Entrance requirements:* For doctorate, GRE General Test. Additional exam requirements/recommendations for international students: Recommended—TOEFL (minimum score 600 paper-based; 100 iBT), IELTS (minimum score 8). *Application deadline:* For fall admission, 12/15 priority date for domestic students, 11/30 priority date for international students; for winter admission, 12/1 for domestic students, 11/1 for international students; for spring admission, 3/1 for domestic students, 2/1 for international students. Applications are processed on a rolling basis. Application fee: $60 ($70 for international students). Electronic applications accepted. *Financial support:* Fellowships with tuition reimbursements, research assistantships with tuition reimbursements, teaching assistantships with tuition reimbursements, Federal Work-Study, and institutionally sponsored loans available. Support available to part-time students. *Faculty research:* American, comparative, and international politics; political theory. *Unit head:* Dr. Richard Hermann, Chair, 614-292-2880, Fax: 614-292-1146, E-mail: hermann.1@osu.edu. *Application contact:* Graduate and Professional Admissions, 614-292-9444, Fax: 614-292-3895, E-mail: gpadmissions@osu.edu.
Website: http://polisci.osu.edu/

Ohio University, Graduate College, College of Arts and Sciences, Department of Political Science, Athens, OH 45701-2979. Offers MA. Part-time and evening/weekend programs available. *Degree requirements:* For master's, comprehensive exam, thesis or alternative. *Entrance requirements:* For master's, GRE General Test, minimum GPA of 3.0. Additional exam requirements/recommendations for international students: Required—TOEFL (minimum score 550 paper-based; 80 iBT) or IELTS (minimum score 6.5). Electronic applications accepted. *Faculty research:* International relations, Latin American politics, public policy, economic development, political theory.

Oklahoma State University, College of Arts and Sciences, Department of Political Science, Stillwater, OK 74078. Offers fire and emergency management administration (MS, PhD); political science (MA). *Faculty:* 21 full-time (7 women), 2 part-time/adjunct (0 women). *Students:* 11 full-time (5 women), 62 part-time (12 women); includes 14 minority (4 Black or African American, non-Hispanic/Latino; 7 Hispanic/Latino; 3 Two or more races, non-Hispanic/Latino), 4 international. Average age 39. 42 applicants, 40% accepted, 14 enrolled. In 2014, 20 master's awarded. *Degree requirements:* For master's, comprehensive exam, thesis or creative component; for doctorate, comprehensive exam, thesis/dissertation. *Entrance requirements:* For master's, GRE; for doctorate, GRE. Additional exam requirements/recommendations for international students: Required—TOEFL (minimum score 550 paper-based; 79 iBT). *Application deadline:* For fall admission, 3/1 priority date for international students; for spring admission, 8/1 priority date for international students. Applications are processed on a rolling basis. Application fee: $40 ($75 for international students). Electronic applications accepted. *Expenses:* Tuition, state resident: full-time $4488; part-time $187 per credit hour. Tuition, nonresident: full-time $18,360; part-time $765 per credit hour. *Required fees:* $2413; $100.55 per credit hour. Tuition and fees vary according to campus/location. *Financial support:* In 2014–15, 1 research assistantship (averaging $19,644 per year), 10 teaching assistantships (averaging $16,961 per year) were awarded; career-related internships or fieldwork, Federal Work-Study, scholarships/grants, health care benefits, tuition waivers (partial), and unspecified assistantships also available. Support available to part-time students. Financial award application deadline: 3/1; financial award applicants required to submit FAFSA. *Faculty research:* Fire and emergency management, environmental dispute resolution, voting and elections, women and politics, urban politics. *Unit head:* Dr. Anthony Brown, Interim Department Head, 405-744-0420, Fax: 405-744-6534, E-mail: anthony.brown@okstate.edu. *Application contact:* Dr. Rebekah Herrick, Interim Director of Graduate Studies, 405-744-8437, Fax: 405-744-6534, E-mail: rebekah.herrick@okstate.edu.
Website: http://polsci.okstate.edu

Penn State University Park, Graduate School, College of the Liberal Arts, Department of Political Science, University Park, PA 16802. Offers MA, PhD. *Unit head:* Dr. Susan Welch, Dean, 814-865-7691, Fax: 814-863-2085, E-mail: swelch@psu.edu. *Application contact:* Lori A. Stania, Director, Graduate Student Services, 814-867-5278, Fax: 814-863-4627, E-mail: gswww@psu.edu.
Website: http://polisci.la.psu.edu/

Pepperdine University, School of Public Policy, Malibu, CA 90263. Offers American politics (MPP); economics (MPP); international relations (MPP); public policy (MPP); state and local policy (MPP). *Faculty:* 6 full-time (2 women), 7 part-time/adjunct (1 woman). *Students:* 74 full-time (42 women), 10 part-time (5 women); includes 22 minority (11 Black or African American, non-Hispanic/Latino; 3 American Indian or Alaska Native, non-Hispanic/Latino; 3 Asian, non-Hispanic/Latino; 2 Hispanic/Latino; 1 Native Hawaiian or other Pacific Islander, non-Hispanic/Latino; 2 Two or more races, non-Hispanic/Latino), 21 international. 157 applicants, 65% accepted, 32 enrolled. In 2014, 52 master's awarded. *Entrance requirements:* For master's, GRE or GMAT, 2 letters of recommendation, resume, two essays. Additional exam requirements/recommendations for international students: Required—TOEFL. *Application deadline:* For fall admission, 6/15 for domestic students. Applications are processed on a rolling basis. Application fee: $50. Electronic applications accepted. *Financial support:* Institutionally sponsored loans and scholarships/grants available. Financial award application deadline: 5/1; financial award applicants required to submit FAFSA. *Unit head:* Dr. James R. Wilburn, Dean, School of Public Policy, 310-506-7490, Fax: 310-506-7494, E-mail: james.wilburn@pepperdine.edu. *Application contact:* Melinda E. van Hemert, Director of Recruitment and Career Services, 310-506-7492, Fax: 310-506-7494, E-mail: melinda.vanhemert@pepperdine.edu.
Website: http://publicpolicy.pepperdine.edu/

Portland State University, Graduate Studies, College of Urban and Public Affairs, Hatfield School of Government, Division of Political Science, Portland, OR 97207-0751. Offers MA, MAT, MS, MST, PhD. Part-time programs available. *Faculty:* 10 full-time (3 women), 3 part-time/adjunct (2 women). *Students:* 9 full-time (3 women), 7 part-time (1 woman); includes 2 minority (1 Hispanic/Latino; 1 Two or more races, non-Hispanic/Latino). Average age 32. 14 applicants, 29% accepted, 2 enrolled. In 2014, 5 master's awarded. *Degree requirements:* For master's, one foreign language, comprehensive exam, thesis; for doctorate, comprehensive exam, thesis/dissertation. *Entrance requirements:* For master's, GRE General Test or MAT, minimum GPA of 3.1, 2 letters of recommendation. Additional exam requirements/recommendations for international students: Required—TOEFL (minimum score 550 paper-based; 90 iBT). *Application deadline:* For fall admission, 4/1 priority date for domestic students, 3/1 priority date for international students; for spring admission, 11/1 for domestic and international students. Application fee: $50. *Expenses:* Tuition, state resident: part-time $222 per credit. Tuition, nonresident: part-time $527 per credit. *Required fees:* $22 per contact

hour. $100 per quarter. Tuition and fees vary according to program. *Financial support:* In 2014–15, 3 research assistantships with full and partial tuition reimbursements (averaging $3,890 per year), 2 teaching assistantships with full and partial tuition reimbursements (averaging $7,290 per year) were awarded; career-related internships or fieldwork, Federal Work-Study, and unspecified assistantships also available. Support available to part-time students. Financial award application deadline: 3/1; financial award applicants required to submit FAFSA. *Faculty research:* Congress, Presidency, political reform, international environment, hate speech. *Total annual research expenditures:* $326. *Unit head:* David Kinsella, Chair, 503-725-3035, Fax: 503-725-8444, E-mail: kinsella@pdx.edu. *Application contact:* Dr. Christopher Shortell, Associate Professor, 503-725-5139, E-mail: shortell@pdx.edu.
Website: http://www.pdx.edu/hatfieldschool/political-science

Princeton University, Graduate School, Department of Politics, Princeton, NJ 08544-1019. Offers political philosophy (PhD); politics (PhD). *Degree requirements:* For doctorate, comprehensive exam, thesis/dissertation, teaching experience. *Entrance requirements:* For doctorate, GRE General Test, sample of written work, letters of recommendation. Additional exam requirements/recommendations for international students: Required—TOEFL (minimum score 600 paper-based). Electronic applications accepted. *Faculty research:* American politics, comparative politics, formal and quantitative methods, international relations, public law, political theory.

Purdue University, Graduate School, College of Liberal Arts, Department of Political Science, West Lafayette, IN 47907. Offers MA, PhD. Part-time and evening/weekend programs available. Terminal master's awarded for partial completion of doctoral program. *Degree requirements:* For master's, comprehensive exam; for doctorate, comprehensive exam, thesis/dissertation. *Entrance requirements:* For master's and doctorate, GRE General Test (minimum score of 160 verbal, 600 on old scoring), minimum undergraduate GPA of 3.0. Additional exam requirements/recommendations for international students: Required—TOEFL (minimum score 600 paper-based; 90 iBT). Electronic applications accepted. *Faculty research:* International relations, political behavior and institutions, comparative politics, political theory, public policy.

Queen's University at Kingston, School of Graduate Studies, Faculty of Arts and Sciences, Department of Political Studies, Kingston, ON K7L 3N6, Canada. Offers Canadian politics (PhD); comparative politics (PhD); gender and politics (PhD); international relations (PhD); political theory (PhD). *Degree requirements:* For master's, thesis or alternative; for doctorate, one foreign language, thesis/dissertation, qualifying exams. *Entrance requirements:* Additional exam requirements/recommendations for international students: Required—TOEFL (minimum score 600 paper-based). *Faculty research:* Canadian politics, comparative politics, political thought, international politics, women and politics.

Regent University, Graduate School, Robertson School of Government, Virginia Beach, VA 23464. Offers government (MA), including American government, international relations, political theory; public administration (MPA), including emergency management and homeland security, general public administration, nonprofit administration and faith-based organizations, public leadership and management. Part-time and evening/weekend programs available. Postbaccalaureate distance learning degree programs offered (minimal on-campus study). *Faculty:* 10 full-time (1 woman), 9 part-time/adjunct (2 women). *Students:* 34 full-time (15 women), 56 part-time (26 women); includes 21 minority (15 Black or African American, non-Hispanic/Latino; 6 Hispanic/Latino), 4 international. Average age 34. 106 applicants, 45% accepted, 33 enrolled. In 2014, 57 master's awarded. *Degree requirements:* For master's, thesis optional, internship. *Entrance requirements:* For master's, GRE General Test or LSAT, minimum undergraduate GPA of 3.0, writing sample, resume, interview, references. Additional exam requirements/recommendations for international students: Required—TOEFL (minimum score 577 paper-based). *Application deadline:* For fall admission, 5/1 priority date for domestic students; for spring admission, 11/1 priority date for domestic students. Applications are processed on a rolling basis. Application fee: $50. Electronic applications accepted. *Expenses:* Expenses: Contact institution. *Financial support:* Career-related internships or fieldwork, scholarships/grants, tuition waivers (full and partial), and unspecified assistantships available. Support available to part-time students. Financial award application deadline: 9/1; financial award applicants required to submit FAFSA. *Faculty research:* Education reform, political character issues, social capital concerns, administrative ethics, Biblical law and public policy. *Unit head:* Dr. Eric Patterson, Dean, 757-352-4616, Fax: 757-352-4735, E-mail: epatterson@regent.edu. *Application contact:* Matthew Chadwick, Director of Enrollment Support Services, 800-373-5504, Fax: 757-352-4381, E-mail: admissions@regent.edu.
Website: http://www.regent.edu/government/

Rice University, Graduate Programs, School of Social Sciences, Department of Political Science, Houston, TX 77251-1892. Offers PhD. Terminal master's awarded for partial completion of doctoral program. *Degree requirements:* For doctorate, comprehensive exam, thesis/dissertation, 42 hours of coursework. *Entrance requirements:* For doctorate, GRE General Test. Additional exam requirements/recommendations for international students: Required—TOEFL (minimum score 600 paper-based; 90 iBT). Electronic applications accepted. *Faculty research:* Comparative government in Western Europe and the former Soviet Union, international relations, Congress and public policy in American government, minority politics.

Roosevelt University, Graduate Division, College of Arts and Sciences, Department of Political Science and Public Administration, Program in Political Science, Chicago, IL 60605. Offers MA. Part-time and evening/weekend programs available. *Degree requirements:* For master's, thesis or alternative. *Entrance requirements:* For master's, minimum GPA of 2.7. *Faculty research:* Metropolitan social movements, American politics, comparative politics, political theory.

Rutgers, The State University of New Jersey, Newark, Graduate School, Program in Political Science, Newark, NJ 07102. Offers American political system (MA); international relations (MA); JD/MA. Part-time and evening/weekend programs available. *Degree requirements:* For master's, comprehensive exam, thesis optional. *Entrance requirements:* For master's, GRE, minimum undergraduate B average. Electronic applications accepted. *Faculty research:* Policymaking and policy evaluation in the United States; government and politics in Europe, Middle East, Asia, Africa, and Latin America.

Rutgers, The State University of New Jersey, New Brunswick, Graduate School-New Brunswick, Department of Political Science, Piscataway, NJ 08854-8097. Offers American politics (PhD); comparative politics (PhD); international relations (PhD); political theory (PhD); public law (PhD); United Nations and global policy studies (MA); women and politics (PhD). *Degree requirements:* For doctorate, one foreign language, comprehensive exam, thesis/dissertation. *Entrance requirements:* For master's, bachelor's degree from accredited U.S. college or university or a comparable institution in another country; for doctorate, GRE General Test. Additional exam requirements/recommendations for international students: Required—TOEFL.

St. John's University, St. John's College of Liberal Arts and Sciences, Department of Government and Politics and Division of Library and Information Science, Program in Government and Library and Information Science, Queens, NY 11439. Offers MA/MS. Part-time and evening/weekend programs available. *Students:* 2 full-time (1 woman).

Average age 24. 3 applicants, 33% accepted, 1 enrolled. *Entrance requirements:* Additional exam requirements/recommendations for international students: Required—TOEFL (minimum score 600 paper-based; 100 iBT), IELTS (minimum score 7). *Application deadline:* For fall admission, 5/1 priority date for domestic and international students; for spring admission, 11/1 priority date for domestic and international students. Applications are processed on a rolling basis. Application fee: $70. Electronic applications accepted. *Expenses:* Tuition: Full-time $20,610; part-time $1145 per credit. *Required fees:* $170 per semester. *Financial support:* Research assistantships, career-related internships or fieldwork, and scholarships/grants available. Support available to part-time students. Financial award application deadline: 3/1; financial award applicants required to submit FAFSA. *Unit head:* Dr. Diane Heith, Chair, 718-990-6329, E-mail: heithd@stjohns.edu. *Application contact:* Robert Medrano, Director of Graduate Admission, 718-990-1601, Fax: 718-990-5686, E-mail: gradhelp@stjohns.edu.

St. John's University, St. John's College of Liberal Arts and Sciences, Department of Government and Politics, Program in Government and Politics, Queens, NY 11439. Offers government and politics (MA); public administration (Adv C); JD/MA. Part-time and evening/weekend programs available. *Students:* 34 full-time (13 women), 33 part-time (18 women); includes 26 minority (11 Black or African American, non-Hispanic/Latino; 1 Asian, non-Hispanic/Latino; 11 Hispanic/Latino; 3 Two or more races, non-Hispanic/Latino), 2 international. Average age 27. 76 applicants, 78% accepted, 26 enrolled. In 2014, 49 master's, 8 other advanced degrees awarded. *Degree requirements:* For master's, comprehensive exam, thesis optional. *Entrance requirements:* For master's, minimum GPA of 3.0, 18 credits at undergraduate level in government and politics. Additional exam requirements/recommendations for international students: Required—TOEFL (minimum score 600 paper-based; 100 iBT), IELTS (minimum score 7). *Application deadline:* For fall admission, 5/1 priority date for domestic and international students; for spring admission, 11/1 priority date for domestic and international students. Applications are processed on a rolling basis. Application fee: $70. Electronic applications accepted. *Expenses:* Tuition: Full-time $20,610; part-time $1145 per credit. *Required fees:* $170 per semester. *Financial support:* Research assistantships and scholarships/grants available. Support available to part-time students. Financial award application deadline: 3/1; financial award applicants required to submit FAFSA. *Unit head:* Dr. Diane Heith, Chair, 718-990-6329, E-mail: heithd@stjohns.edu. *Application contact:* Robert Medrano, Director of Graduate Admissions, 718-990-1601, Fax: 718-990-5686, E-mail: gradhelp@stjohns.edu.

Saint Louis University, Graduate Education, College of Arts and Sciences and Graduate Education, Department of Political Science, St. Louis, MO 63103-2097. Offers MA. Part-time programs available. *Entrance requirements:* For master's, GRE or LSAT, letters of recommendation, resume, writing sample. Additional exam requirements/recommendations for international students: Required—TOEFL (minimum score 525 paper-based). Electronic applications accepted. *Faculty research:* Part of Asia, Africa, Latin America, and Russia; international political economy; diplomacy and international organization; theories of democracy and justice; American political institutions.

St. Mary's University, Graduate School, Department of Education, Program in Education, San Antonio, TX 78228-8507. Offers computer science (MA); education (MA); English literature and language (MA); international relations (MA); political science (MA). *Students:* 1 (woman) part-time; minority (Black or African American, non-Hispanic/Latino). Average age 28. 12 applicants, 17% accepted. In 2014, 3 master's awarded. *Entrance requirements:* For master's, GRE or MAT, 200 X GPA + Average GRE [(Verbal + Quantitative)/2]= 1050; or 10 X GPA + MAT = 68. *Expenses: Tuition:* Full-time $15,070; part-time $800 per credit hour. *Required fees:* $156 per semester. *Faculty research:* Bronfenbrenner's ecological systems theory: implications for education today. *Unit head:* Dr. Dan Higgins, Department Chair, 210-436-3121, E-mail: dhiggins@stmarytx.edu.
Website: https://www.stmarytx.edu/academics/graduate/masters/education/

Sam Houston State University, College of Humanities and Social Sciences, Department of Political Science, Huntsville, TX 77341. Offers political science (MA); public administration (MPA). Part-time programs available. Postbaccalaureate distance learning degree programs offered (minimal on-campus study). *Faculty:* 16 full-time (6 women), 1 (woman) part-time/adjunct. *Students:* 9 full-time (4 women), 47 part-time (19 women); includes 19 minority (7 Black or African American, non-Hispanic/Latino; 1 Asian, non-Hispanic/Latino; 9 Hispanic/Latino; 2 Two or more races, non-Hispanic/Latino), 4 international. Average age 36. 29 applicants, 79% accepted, 19 enrolled. In 2014, 18 master's awarded. *Degree requirements:* For master's, comprehensive exam, thesis optional, internship. *Entrance requirements:* For master's, GRE General Test, GMAT, writing sample of scholarly work, letters of recommendation, statement of purpose, resume. Additional exam requirements/recommendations for international students: Required—TOEFL (minimum score 550 paper-based; 79 iBT), IELTS (minimum score 6.5). *Application deadline:* For fall admission, 8/1 for domestic students, 6/25 for international students; for spring admission, 12/1 for domestic students, 11/12 for international students; for summer admission, 5/15 for domestic students, 4/9 for international students. Applications are processed on a rolling basis. Application fee: $45 ($75 for international students). Electronic applications accepted. *Expenses:* Tuition, state resident: full-time $2286; part-time $254 per credit hour. Tuition, nonresident: full-time $5544; part-time $616 per credit hour. *Required fees:* $440 per semester. Tuition and fees vary according to course load and campus/location. *Financial support:* In 2014–15, 7 research assistantships (averaging $7,111 per year) were awarded; career-related internships or fieldwork, Federal Work-Study, scholarships/grants, tuition waivers (partial), and unspecified assistantships also available. Support available to part-time students. Financial award application deadline: 3/15; financial award applicants required to submit FAFSA. *Unit head:* Dr. Tamara Waggener, Chair, 936-294-1466, Fax: 936-294-4172, E-mail: pol_taw@shsu.edu. *Application contact:* Dr. Heather Evans, Advisor, 936-294-3378, Fax: 936-294-4172, E-mail: hke002@shsu.edu.
Website: http://www.shsu.edu/academics/political-science/graduate.html

San Diego State University, Graduate and Research Affairs, College of Arts and Letters, Department of Political Science, San Diego, CA 92182. Offers MA. Part-time programs available. *Degree requirements:* For master's, thesis. *Entrance requirements:* For master's, GRE General Test, minimum GPA of 3.0, 2 letters of reference. Additional exam requirements/recommendations for international students: Required—TOEFL. Electronic applications accepted.

San Francisco State University, Division of Graduate Studies, College of Liberal and Creative Arts, Department of Political Science, San Francisco, CA 94132-1722. Offers MA. *Expenses:* Tuition, state resident: full-time $6738. Tuition, nonresident: full-time $17,898; part-time $372 per credit hour. *Required fees:* $498 per semester. *Financial support:* Research assistantships and teaching assistantships available. *Unit head:* Dr. James Martel, Chair, 415-405-2162, Fax: 415-338-2391, E-mail: jmartel@sfsu.edu. *Application contact:* Prof. Nicole Watts, Graduate Coordinator, 415-405-2470, Fax: 415-338-2391, E-mail: nfwatts@sfsu.edu.
Website: http://politicalscience.sfsu.edu/

Simon Fraser University, Office of Graduate Studies, Faculty of Arts and Social Sciences, Department of Political Science, Burnaby, BC V5A 1S6, Canada. Offers MA, PhD. *Degree requirements:* For master's, thesis or alternative, field exams; for doctorate, one foreign language, comprehensive exam, thesis/dissertation. *Entrance*

requirements: For master's, minimum GPA of 3.0 (on scale of 4.33), or 3.33 based on last 60 credits of undergraduate courses; for doctorate, minimum GPA of 3.5 (on scale of 4.33). Additional exam requirements/recommendations for international students: Recommended—TOEFL (minimum score 580 paper-based; 93 iBT), IELTS (minimum score 7), TWE (minimum score 5). Electronic applications accepted. *Faculty research:* Political theory and methodology, Canadian politics, comparative politics, international relations, urban politics, public policy, and public administration.

Sonoma State University, School of Social Sciences, Department of Political Science, Rohnert Park, CA 94928. Offers administration of nonprofit agencies (Certificate); public administration (MPA). Part-time and evening/weekend programs available. *Degree requirements:* For master's, thesis or alternative. *Entrance requirements:* For master's, GRE General Test, minimum GPA of 3.0. Additional exam requirements/recommendations for international students: Required—TOEFL (minimum score 500 paper-based).

Southern Connecticut State University, School of Graduate Studies, School of Arts and Sciences, Department of Political Science, New Haven, CT 06515-1355. Offers MS. Part-time and evening/weekend programs available. *Degree requirements:* For master's, thesis or alternative. *Entrance requirements:* For master's, interview. Electronic applications accepted.

Southern Illinois University Carbondale, Graduate School, College of Liberal Arts, Department of Political Science, Program in Political Science, Carbondale, IL 62901-4701. Offers MA, PhD, JD/PhD. Part-time programs available. *Faculty:* 17 full-time (1 woman), 2 part-time/adjunct (0 women). *Students:* 19 full-time (5 women), 14 part-time (6 women); includes 4 minority (all Black or African American, non-Hispanic/Latino), 10 international. Average age 25. 28 applicants, 50% accepted, 8 enrolled. In 2014, 2 master's, 5 doctorates awarded. *Degree requirements:* For doctorate, thesis/dissertation. *Entrance requirements:* For master's, GRE General Test, minimum GPA of 2.7; for doctorate, GRE General Test, minimum GPA of 3.5. Additional exam requirements/recommendations for international students: Required—TOEFL. *Application deadline:* Applications are processed on a rolling basis. Application fee: $50. *Expenses:* Tuition, state resident: full-time $10,176; part-time $1153 per credit. Tuition, nonresident: full-time $20,814; part-time $1744 per credit. *Required fees:* $7092; $394 per credit. $2364 per semester. *Financial support:* In 2014–15, 3 fellowships with full tuition reimbursements, 5 research assistantships with full tuition reimbursements, 10 teaching assistantships with full tuition reimbursements were awarded; career-related internships or fieldwork, Federal Work-Study, institutionally sponsored loans, and tuition waivers (full) also available. Support available to part-time students. Financial award application deadline: 2/1. *Faculty research:* Public law, international relations, comparative government, American government. *Unit head:* Dr. Stephen Bloom, Director of Graduate Studies, 618-453-3183, E-mail: bloom@siu.edu. *Application contact:* Mary Kay Bledsoe, Office Systems Specialist, 618-453-3165, E-mail: polsgrad@siu.edu.

Southern University and Agricultural and Mechanical College, Graduate School, Nelson Mandela School of Public Policy and Urban Affairs, Department of Political Science and Geography, Baton Rouge, LA 70813. Offers social sciences (MA). *Degree requirements:* For master's, thesis. *Entrance requirements:* For master's, GMAT or GRE General Test, minimum GPA of 3.0. Additional exam requirements/recommendations for international students: Required—TOEFL. *Faculty research:* Redistricting, comparative studies, environmental politics, political geography, mayoral elections.

Stanford University, School of Humanities and Sciences, Department of Political Science, Stanford, CA 94305-9991. Offers PhD. Terminal master's awarded for partial completion of doctoral program. *Degree requirements:* For doctorate, one foreign language, thesis/dissertation, oral exam. *Entrance requirements:* For doctorate, GRE General Test. Additional exam requirements/recommendations for international students: Required—TOEFL. Electronic applications accepted. *Expenses: Tuition:* Full-time $44,184; part-time $982 per credit hour. *Required fees:* $191.

Stony Brook University, State University of New York, Graduate School, College of Arts and Sciences, Department of Political Science, Stony Brook, NY 11794. Offers political science (MA, PhD); public policy (MAPP); public policy and urban development (MA). Evening/weekend programs available. *Faculty:* 20 full-time (4 women), 8 part-time/adjunct (2 women). *Students:* 72 full-time (31 women), 12 part-time (6 women); includes 16 minority (3 Black or African American, non-Hispanic/Latino; 6 Asian, non-Hispanic/Latino; 7 Hispanic/Latino), 20 international. Average age 27. 138 applicants, 59% accepted, 43 enrolled. In 2014, 49 master's, 3 doctorates awarded. *Degree requirements:* For doctorate, thesis/dissertation. *Entrance requirements:* For master's and doctorate, GRE General Test. *Application deadline:* For fall admission, 1/15 for domestic students; for spring admission, 10/1 for domestic students. Application fee: $100. *Expenses:* Tuition, state resident: full-time $10,370; part-time $432 per credit. Tuition, nonresident: full-time $20,190; part-time $841 per credit. *Required fees:* $1431. *Financial support:* In 2014–15, 2 fellowships, 25 teaching assistantships were awarded; research assistantships also available. *Total annual research expenditures:* $96,098. *Unit head:* Dr. Jeffrey Segal, Chair, 631-632-7640, Fax: 631-632-4116, E-mail: jeffrey.segal@stonybrook.edu. *Application contact:* Dr. Matthew Lebo, Graduate Program Director, 631-632-7554, Fax: 631-632-4116, E-mail: matthew.lebo@stonybrook.edu.
Website: http://www.sunysb.edu/polsci/

Suffolk University, College of Arts and Sciences, Department of Government, Boston, MA 02108-2770. Offers international relations (MSPS); political science (MSPS); professional politics (MSPS, CAGS); MPA/MSPS. Part-time and evening/weekend programs available. *Faculty:* 7 full-time (2 women), 2 part-time/adjunct (1 woman). *Students:* 8 full-time (5 women), 7 part-time (2 women); includes 6 minority (2 Black or African American, non-Hispanic/Latino; 1 Asian, non-Hispanic/Latino; 3 Hispanic/Latino), 3 international. Average age 27. 30 applicants, 77% accepted, 16 enrolled. In 2014, 19 master's, 1 CAGS awarded. *Degree requirements:* For master's, thesis optional. *Entrance requirements:* For master's, GRE General Test or MAT, 2 letters of recommendation, resume. Additional exam requirements/recommendations for international students: Required—TOEFL (minimum score 550 paper-based; 80 iBT). *Application deadline:* For fall admission, 6/15 priority date for domestic students, 6/15 for international students; for spring admission, 11/1 priority date for domestic students, 11/1 for international students. Applications are processed on a rolling basis. Application fee: $50. Electronic applications accepted. *Expenses:* Expenses: Contact institution. *Financial support:* In 2014–15, 13 students received support, including 13 fellowships (averaging $6,793 per year); career-related internships or fieldwork, Federal Work-Study, and institutionally sponsored loans also available. Support available to part-time students. Financial award application deadline: 4/1; financial award applicants required to submit FAFSA. *Faculty research:* Political marketing, social movements and political parties, election administration, urban resilience, the regulatory state. *Unit head:* Brian Conley, Program Director, 617-994-6414, E-mail: bconley@suffolk.edu. *Application contact:* Cory Meyers, Director of Graduate Admissions, 617-573-8302, Fax: 617-305-1733, E-mail: grad.admission@suffolk.edu.
Website: http://www.cas.suffolk.edu/government

Sul Ross State University, School of Arts and Sciences, Department of Behavioral and Social Sciences, Program in Political Science, Alpine, TX 79832. Offers MA. Part-time and evening/weekend programs available. *Degree requirements:* For master's, thesis optional. *Entrance requirements:* For master's, GRE General Test, minimum undergraduate GPA of 2.5 in last 60 hours. *Faculty research:* Local government, state government, borderland studies, British studies.

Syracuse University, Maxwell School of Citizenship and Public Affairs, Program in E-Government Management and Leadership, Syracuse, NY 13244. Offers CAS. Part-time programs available. *Students:* 1 part-time (0 women); minority (Black or African American, non-Hispanic/Latino). Average age 59. 3 applicants, 100% accepted. In 2014, 6 CASs awarded. *Entrance requirements:* For degree, Syracuse degree program matriculation. Additional exam requirements/recommendations for international students: Required—TOEFL (minimum score 100 iBT). *Application deadline:* For fall admission, 2/1 priority date for domestic students; for spring admission, 8/15 priority date for domestic and international students. Applications are processed on a rolling basis. Application fee: $75. Electronic applications accepted. *Expenses: Tuition:* Part-time $1341 per credit. *Unit head:* Prof. Steve Lux, Director, 315-443-4000. *Application contact:* Margaret Lane, Director of Executive Education, 315-443-8708, E-mail: melane@syr.edu.
Website: http://www.maxwell.syr.edu/

Syracuse University, Maxwell School of Citizenship and Public Affairs, Program in Political Science, Syracuse, NY 13244. Offers MA, PhD. *Students:* 54 full-time (25 women), 7 part-time (2 women); includes 7 minority (1 Black or African American, non-Hispanic/Latino; 4 Asian, non-Hispanic/Latino; 1 Hispanic/Latino; 1 Two or more races, non-Hispanic/Latino), 27 international. Average age 31. 149 applicants, 22% accepted, 13 enrolled. In 2014, 10 master's, 6 doctorates awarded. *Degree requirements:* For doctorate, comprehensive exam, thesis/dissertation. *Entrance requirements:* For master's and doctorate, GRE General Test. Additional exam requirements/recommendations for international students: Required—TOEFL (minimum score 100 iBT). *Application deadline:* For fall admission, 2/1 priority date for domestic and international students. Application fee: $75. Electronic applications accepted. *Expenses: Tuition:* Part-time $1341 per credit. *Financial support:* Fellowships with full tuition reimbursements, research assistantships with full and partial tuition reimbursements, and teaching assistantships with full and partial tuition reimbursements available. Financial award application deadline: 1/1. *Unit head:* Dr. Thomas Keck, Chair, 315-443-2416, Fax: 315-443-9082. *Application contact:* Candy Brooks, Recruiting Contact, 315-443-2416, E-mail: cbrooks01@syr.edu.
Website: http://www.maxwell.syr.edu/psc/

Tarleton State University, College of Graduate Studies, College of Liberal and Fine Arts, Department of Social Sciences, Stephenville, TX 76402. Offers history (MA); political science (MA). Part-time and evening/weekend programs available. Postbaccalaureate distance learning degree programs offered (minimal on-campus study). *Degree requirements:* For master's, variable foreign language requirement, comprehensive exam, thesis optional. *Entrance requirements:* For master's, GRE General Test, minimum GPA of 3.0. Additional exam requirements/recommendations for international students: Required—TOEFL (minimum score 550 paper-based; 80 iBT). Electronic applications accepted.

Teachers College, Columbia University, Graduate Faculty of Education, Department of Education Policy and Social Analysis, Program in Politics and Education, New York, NY 10027. Offers Ed M, MA, Ed D, PhD. *Faculty:* 1 full-time, 2 part-time/adjunct. *Students:* 7 full-time (2 women), 21 part-time (17 women); includes 9 minority (5 Black or African American, non-Hispanic/Latino; 2 Asian, non-Hispanic/Latino; 1 Hispanic/Latino; 1 Two or more races, non-Hispanic/Latino), 4 international. Average age 34. 24 applicants, 50% accepted, 2 enrolled. In 2014, 15 master's awarded. *Degree requirements:* For master's, comprehensive exam, thesis or alternative; for doctorate, one foreign language, comprehensive exam, thesis/dissertation. *Entrance requirements:* For master's and doctorate, GRE. *Application deadline:* For fall admission, 12/15 for domestic students; for spring admission, 11/1 for domestic students. Application fee: $65. *Expenses: Tuition:* Full-time $33,552; part-time $1398 per credit. *Required fees:* $418 per semester. *Financial support:* Career-related internships or fieldwork, Federal Work-Study, institutionally sponsored loans, and tuition waivers (full and partial) available. Support available to part-time students. Financial award application deadline: 2/1. *Faculty research:* Urban and social programs in education. *Unit head:* Dr. Jeffrey Henig, Program Coordinator, 212-678-8313, E-mail: henig@tc.edu. *Application contact:* Debbie Lesperance, Assistant Director of Admission, 212-678-3710, Fax: 212-678-4171.
Website: http://www.tc.edu/epsa/Politics/

Temple University, College of Liberal Arts, Department of Political Science, Philadelphia, PA 19122-6096. Offers MA, PhD. Part-time programs available. *Faculty:* 20 full-time (4 women), 6 part-time/adjunct (3 women). *Students:* 46 full-time (20 women), 1 part-time (0 women); includes 8 minority (1 Black or African American, non-Hispanic/Latino; 4 Asian, non-Hispanic/Latino; 2 Hispanic/Latino; 1 Two or more races, non-Hispanic/Latino), 4 international. 33 applicants, 61% accepted, 9 enrolled. In 2014, 6 master's, 6 doctorates awarded. Terminal master's awarded for partial completion of doctoral program. *Degree requirements:* For master's, comprehensive exam; for doctorate, thesis/dissertation, preliminary and oral exams. *Entrance requirements:* For master's and doctorate, GRE General Test, minimum GPA of 3.0, 3 letters of recommendation. Additional exam requirements/recommendations for international students: Required—TOEFL (minimum score 600 paper-based; 100 iBT). *Application deadline:* For fall admission, 12/1 for domestic students, 12/15 for international students; for spring admission, 10/15 for domestic students, 8/1 for international students. Applications are processed on a rolling basis. Application fee: $60. Electronic applications accepted. *Expenses:* Tuition, state resident: full-time $14,490; part-time $805 per credit hour. Tuition, nonresident: full-time $19,850; part-time $1103 per credit hour. *Required fees:* $690. Full-time tuition and fees vary according to class time, course load, degree level, campus/location and program. *Financial support:* Fellowships, research assistantships, teaching assistantships with tuition reimbursements, career-related internships or fieldwork, Federal Work-Study, institutionally sponsored loans, scholarships/grants, and tuition waivers (partial) available. Financial award application deadline: 1/15; financial award applicants required to submit FAFSA. *Faculty research:* American politics, international relations, comparative politics, political theory, public policy. *Unit head:* Dr. Kevin Arceneaux, Graduate Director, 215-204-6950, Fax: 215-204-3770, E-mail: arceneau@temple.edu. *Application contact:* Tanya Taylor, Coordinator, 215-204-1469, Fax: 215-204-3770, E-mail: ttaylo01@temple.edu.
Website: http://www.cla.temple.edu/politicalscience/

Texas A&M International University, Office of Graduate Studies and Research, College of Arts and Sciences, Department of Humanities, Laredo, TX 78041-1900. Offers English (MA); Hispanic studies (PhD); history and political thought (MA); language, literature and translation (MA). *Degree requirements:* For master's, comprehensive exam (for some programs), thesis (for some programs). *Entrance requirements:* For master's, GRE General Test. Additional exam requirements/recommendations for international students: Required—TOEFL (minimum score 550 paper-based; 79 iBT).

Political Science

Texas A&M International University, Office of Graduate Studies and Research, College of Arts and Sciences, Department of Public Affairs and Social Research, Laredo, TX 78041-1900. Offers criminal justice (MS); history and political thought (MA); political science (MA); public administration (MPA). *Degree requirements:* For master's, comprehensive exam (for some programs), thesis (for some programs). *Entrance requirements:* For master's, GRE General Test. Additional exam requirements/recommendations for international students: Required—TOEFL (minimum score 550 paper-based; 79 iBT).

Texas A&M University, College of Liberal Arts, Department of Political Science, College Station, TX 77843. Offers MA, PhD. *Faculty:* 15. *Students:* 41 full-time (18 women), 5 part-time (4 women); includes 9 minority (1 Black or African American, non-Hispanic/Latino; 8 Hispanic/Latino), 10 international. Average age 28. 38 applicants, 21% accepted, 2 enrolled. In 2014, 2 master's, 9 doctorates awarded. *Degree requirements:* For doctorate, comprehensive exam, thesis/dissertation. *Entrance requirements:* For doctorate, GRE General Test, minimum GPA of 3.4. Additional exam requirements/recommendations for international students: Required—TOEFL. *Application deadline:* For fall admission, 12/20 for domestic and international students. Application fee: $50 ($90 for international students). Electronic applications accepted. *Expenses:* Tuition, state resident: full-time $4078; part-time $226.55 per credit hour. Tuition, nonresident: full-time $10,594; part-time $577.55 per credit hour. *Required fees:* $2813; $237.70 per credit hour. $278.50 per semester. Tuition and fees vary according to degree level and student level. *Financial support:* In 2014–15, 40 students received support, including 12 fellowships with full and partial tuition reimbursements available (averaging $11,535 per year), 30 research assistantships with full and partial tuition reimbursements available (averaging $7,495 per year), 10 teaching assistantships with full and partial tuition reimbursements available (averaging $8,833 per year); career-related internships or fieldwork, institutionally sponsored loans, scholarships/grants, traineeships, health care benefits, tuition waivers (full and partial), unspecified assistantships, and assistant lecturer positions also available. Support available to part-time students. Financial award application deadline: 12/20; financial award applicants required to submit FAFSA. *Faculty research:* American politics, international relations, comparative politics, political theory, public policy. *Unit head:* Dr. William Clark, Department Head, 979-845-2827, E-mail: wrclark@tamu.edu. *Application contact:* Dr. Alex C. Pacek, Director of Graduate Studies, 979-845-3229, Fax: 979-847-8924, E-mail: a-pacek@tamu.edu.
Website: http://politicalscience.tamu.edu/html/home.html

Texas A&M University–Central Texas, Graduate Studies and Research, Killeen, TX 76549. Offers accounting (MS); business administration (MBA); clinical mental health counseling (MS); criminal justice (MCJ); curriculum and instruction (M Ed); educational administration (M Ed); educational psychology - experimental psychology (MS); history (MA); human resource management (MS); information systems (MS); liberal studies (MS); management and leadership (MS); marriage and family therapy (MS); mathematics (MS); political science (MA); school counseling (M Ed); school psychology (Ed S).

Texas A&M University–Kingsville, College of Graduate Studies, College of Arts and Sciences, Program in History and Political Science, Kingsville, TX 78363. Offers MA, MS. *Students:* 1 (woman) part-time; minority (Hispanic/Latino). Average age 32. In 2014, 3 master's awarded. *Degree requirements:* For master's, variable foreign language requirement, comprehensive exam, thesis (for some programs). *Entrance requirements:* For master's, GRE, MAT, GMAT. Additional exam requirements/recommendations for international students: Required—TOEFL (minimum score 550 paper-based; 79 iBT). *Application deadline:* For fall admission, 8/15 for domestic students, 6/1 for international students; for spring admission, 12/15 for domestic students, 10/1 for international students; for summer admission, 5/15 for domestic students, 4/1 for international students. Applications are processed on a rolling basis. Application fee: $35 ($50 for international students). Electronic applications accepted. *Financial support:* Career-related internships or fieldwork, Federal Work-Study, institutionally sponsored loans, scholarships/grants, health care benefits, tuition waivers (full and partial), and unspecified assistantships available. Support available to part-time students. Financial award application deadline: 5/15; financial award applicants required to submit FAFSA. *Unit head:* Dr. Shannon Baker, Department Chair, 361-593-3594, Fax: 361-593-3502, E-mail: shannon.baker@tamuk.edu. *Application contact:* Dr. Mohamed Abdelrahman, Dean of Graduate Studies, 361-593-2809, E-mail: mohamed.abdelrahman@tamuk.edu.

Texas State University, The Graduate College, College of Liberal Arts, Department of Political Science, Program in Political Science, San Marcos, TX 78666. Offers MA. Part-time and evening/weekend programs available. *Faculty:* 11 full-time (3 women). *Students:* 22 full-time (7 women), 17 part-time (7 women); includes 64 minority (55 Black or African American, non-Hispanic/Latino; 8 Hispanic/Latino; 1 Two or more races, non-Hispanic/Latino), 1 international. Average age 29. 23 applicants, 78% accepted, 9 enrolled. In 2014, 16 master's awarded. *Degree requirements:* For master's, comprehensive exam, thesis (for some programs). *Entrance requirements:* For master's, GRE (preferred), baccalaureate degree in political science from regionally-accredited university with minimum GPA of 3.0 on last 60 undergraduate semester hours. Additional exam requirements/recommendations for international students: Required—TOEFL (minimum score 550 paper-based; 78 iBT). *Application deadline:* For fall admission, 6/15 priority date for domestic students, 6/1 priority date for international students; for spring admission, 10/15 priority date for domestic students, 10/1 priority date for international students. Applications are processed on a rolling basis. Application fee: $40 ($90 for international students). Electronic applications accepted. *Expenses:* Expenses: $8,834 (tuition and fees combined). *Financial support:* In 2014–15, 24 students received support, including 2 research assistantships (averaging $12,007 per year), 10 teaching assistantships (averaging $12,619 per year); career-related internships or fieldwork, Federal Work-Study, institutionally sponsored loans, scholarships/grants, and unspecified assistantships also available. Support available to part-time students. Financial award application deadline: 4/1; financial award applicants required to submit FAFSA. *Total annual research expenditures:* $15,815. *Unit head:* Dr. Cecilia Castillio, Graduate Adviser, 512-245-2143, Fax: 512-345-7815, E-mail: cr09@txstate.edu. *Application contact:* Dr. Andrea Golato, Dean of Graduate School, 512-245-2581, Fax: 512-245-8365, E-mail: gradcollege@txstate.edu.
Website: http://www.polisci.txstate.edu/

Texas Tech University, Graduate School, College of Arts and Sciences, Department of Political Science, Lubbock, TX 79409-1015. Offers political science (MA, PhD); public administration (MPA); JD/MPA; MPA/MA; MPA/MS. *Accreditation:* NASPAA (one or more programs are accredited). *Faculty:* 26 full-time (5 women), 3 part-time/adjunct (1 woman). *Students:* 48 full-time (15 women), 24 part-time (11 women); includes 16 minority (5 Black or African American, non-Hispanic/Latino; 1 Asian, non-Hispanic/Latino; 10 Hispanic/Latino), 7 international. Average age 29. 49 applicants, 53% accepted, 17 enrolled. In 2014, 21 master's, 2 doctorates awarded. *Degree requirements:* For master's, thesis or alternative; for doctorate, thesis/dissertation. *Entrance requirements:* For master's and doctorate, GRE General Test, 3 letters of reference. Additional exam requirements/recommendations for international students: Required—TOEFL (minimum score 550 paper-based; 79 iBT). *Application deadline:* For fall admission, 6/1 priority date for domestic students, 1/15 priority date for international

students; for spring admission, 9/1 priority date for domestic students, 6/15 priority date for international students. Applications are processed on a rolling basis. Application fee: $60. Electronic applications accepted. *Expenses:* Tuition, state resident: full-time $6310; part-time $262.92 per credit hour. Tuition, nonresident: full-time $14,998; part-time $624.92 per credit hour. *Required fees:* $2701; $36.50 per credit. $912.50 per semester. Tuition and fees vary according to course load. *Financial support:* In 2014–15, 46 students received support, including 40 fellowships (averaging $1,708 per year), 1 research assistantship (averaging $25,800 per year), 31 teaching assistantships (averaging $12,226 per year). Financial award application deadline: 4/15; financial award applicants required to submit FAFSA. *Faculty research:* State politics, American institutions and behavior, Asian politics, international and comparative political relations and economics, public administration and organizations. *Total annual research expenditures:* $77,245. *Unit head:* Dr. Dennis Patterson, Chair, 806-742-3121, Fax: 806-742-0850, E-mail: dennis.patterson@ttu.edu. *Application contact:* Dr. Frank Thames, Associate Chair, 806-742-4049, Fax: 806-742-0850, E-mail: frank.thames@ttu.edu. Website: http://www.depts.ttu.edu/politicalscience/

Texas Woman's University, Graduate School, College of Arts and Sciences, Department of History and Government, Denton, TX 76201. Offers government (MA); history (MA). Part-time and evening/weekend programs available. *Degree requirements:* For master's, comprehensive exam, thesis. *Entrance requirements:* For master's, minimum GPA of 3.25, written statement of purpose; 2 letters of reference. Additional exam requirements/recommendations for international students: Required—TOEFL (minimum score 550 paper-based; 79 iBT). Electronic applications accepted. *Faculty research:* U.S. history, politics, and law; global history, politics, and law; Latin American and Caribbean history; legal studies; women in history, politics, and law.

Tulane University, School of Liberal Arts, Department of Political Science, New Orleans, LA 70118-5669. Offers PhD. *Degree requirements:* For doctorate, 2 foreign languages, thesis/dissertation. *Entrance requirements:* For doctorate, GRE General Test. Additional exam requirements/recommendations for international students: Required—TOEFL. Electronic applications accepted. *Expenses:* Tuition: Full-time $46,326; part-time $2574 per credit hour. *Required fees:* $1980; $44.50 per credit hour. $550 per term. Tuition and fees vary according to course load and program.

Universidad Nacional Pedro Henriquez Urena, Graduate School, Santo Domingo, Dominican Republic. Offers agricultural diversity (MS), including horticultural/fruit production, tropical animal production; conservation of monuments and cultural assets (M Arch); ecology and environment (MS); environmental engineering (MEE); international relations (MA); natural resource management (MS); political science (MA); project optimization (MPM); project feasibility (MPM); project management (MPM); sanitation engineering (ME); science for teachers (MS); tropical Caribbean architecture (M Arch).

Université de Montréal, Faculty of Arts and Sciences, Department of Political Science, Montréal, QC H3C 3J7, Canada. Offers M Sc, PhD. *Degree requirements:* For master's, thesis; for doctorate, thesis/dissertation, general exam. *Entrance requirements:* For master's, minimum GPA of 2.8; for doctorate, master's degree, minimum GPA of 3.0. Electronic applications accepted.

Université du Québec à Montréal, Graduate Programs, Program in Political Science, Montréal, QC H3C 3P8, Canada. Offers MA, PhD. Part-time programs available. *Degree requirements:* For master's, thesis; for doctorate, thesis/dissertation. *Entrance requirements:* For master's, appropriate bachelor's degree or equivalent, proficiency in French; for doctorate, appropriate master's degree or equivalent, proficiency in French.

Université Laval, Faculty of Social Sciences, Department of Political Science, Program in Policy Analysis, Québec, QC G1K 7P4, Canada. Offers MA. *Degree requirements:* For master's, thesis (for some programs). *Entrance requirements:* For master's, knowledge of French, comprehension of written English. Electronic applications accepted.

Université Laval, Faculty of Social Sciences, Department of Political Science, Programs in Political Science, Québec, QC G1K 7P4, Canada. Offers MA, PhD. Terminal master's awarded for partial completion of doctoral program. *Degree requirements:* For master's, thesis (for some programs); for doctorate, comprehensive exam, thesis/dissertation. *Entrance requirements:* For master's, knowledge of French; for doctorate, knowledge of French, comprehension of written English. Electronic applications accepted.

University at Albany, State University of New York, Nelson A. Rockefeller College of Public Affairs and Policy, Department of Political Science, Albany, NY 12222-0001. Offers MA, PhD. *Degree requirements:* For doctorate, one foreign language, thesis/dissertation. *Entrance requirements:* For doctorate, GRE General Test. Additional exam requirements/recommendations for international students: Required—TOEFL (minimum score 550 paper-based). Electronic applications accepted.

University at Buffalo, the State University of New York, Graduate School, College of Arts and Sciences, Department of Political Science, Buffalo, NY 14260. Offers MA, PhD. *Faculty:* 14 full-time (3 women), 2 part-time/adjunct (0 women). *Students:* 25 full-time (12 women), 21 part-time (4 women); includes 9 minority (5 Black or African American, non-Hispanic/Latino; 3 Asian, non-Hispanic/Latino; 1 Native Hawaiian or other Pacific Islander, non-Hispanic/Latino), 1 international. Average age 29. 44 applicants, 75% accepted, 9 enrolled. In 2014, 4 master's, 4 doctorates awarded. Terminal master's awarded for partial completion of doctoral program. *Degree requirements:* For master's, thesis or alternative, paper, project, comprehensive exam, portfolio; for doctorate, comprehensive exam, thesis/dissertation. *Entrance requirements:* For master's, GRE General Test, minimum GPA of 3.0; for doctorate, GRE General Test, minimum GPA of 3.3. Additional exam requirements/recommendations for international students: Required—TOEFL (minimum score 550 paper-based; 79 iBT), IELTS (minimum score 6.5), PTE (minimum score 55). *Application deadline:* For fall admission, 8/1 priority date for domestic students, 3/1 for international students; for spring admission, 11/1 priority date for domestic students, 10/1 for international students. Applications are processed on a rolling basis. Application fee: $75. Electronic applications accepted. *Financial support:* In 2014–15, 12 students received support, including 12 teaching assistantships with full tuition reimbursements available (averaging $13,300 per year); fellowships with full tuition reimbursements available, research assistantships, career-related internships or fieldwork, Federal Work-Study, health care benefits, tuition waivers (partial), and unspecified assistantships also available. Financial award application deadline: 2/1; financial award applicants required to submit FAFSA. *Faculty research:* American politics, public law, comparative politics, international politics. *Unit head:* Dr. Harvey Palmer, Chairman, 716-645-8449, Fax: 716-645-2166, E-mail: hpalmer@buffalo.edu. *Application contact:* Mary E. O'Brien, Graduate Coordinator, 716-645-3441, Fax: 716-645-2166, E-mail: meobrien@buffalo.edu.
Website: http://polsci.buffalo.ed

The University of Akron, Graduate School, Buchtel College of Arts and Sciences, Department of Political Science, Akron, OH 44325. Offers applied politics (MAP); political science (MA); JD/MAP. Part-time programs available. *Faculty:* 10 full-time (1 woman), 11 part-time/adjunct (4 women). *Students:* 30 full-time (11 women), 7 part-time (1 woman); includes 5 minority (all Black or African American, non-Hispanic/Latino), 5 international. Average age 26. 33 applicants, 97% accepted, 17 enrolled. In 2014, 9

master's awarded. *Degree requirements:* For master's, comprehensive exam, essay, seminars (political science), portfolio (applied politics). *Entrance requirements:* For master's, GRE, minimum GPA of 3.0, three letters of recommendation (two of which must be from faculty members), statement of purpose. Additional exam requirements/recommendations for international students: Required—TOEFL (minimum score 550 paper-based; 79 iBT), IELTS (minimum score 6.5). *Application deadline:* For fall admission, 3/1 for domestic and international students; for spring admission, 12/1 for domestic and international students. Applications are processed on a rolling basis. Application fee: $45 ($70 for international students). Electronic applications accepted. *Expenses:* Tuition, state resident: full-time $7578; part-time $421 per credit hour. Tuition, nonresident: full-time $12,977; part-time $721 per credit hour. *Required fees:* $1388; $35 per credit hour. Tuition and fees vary according to course load. *Financial support:* In 2014–15, 1 research assistantship with full tuition reimbursement, 18 teaching assistantships with full tuition reimbursements were awarded; unspecified assistantships also available. *Faculty research:* Public opinion and public policy, international/comparative politics, the politics of criminal justice, conflict management. *Total annual research expenditures:* $249,604. *Unit head:* Dr. John Green, Interim Chair, 330-972-5182, E-mail: green@uakron.edu. *Application contact:* Dr. Nancy Marion, Graduate Director, 330-972-5551, E-mail: nmarion@uakron.edu.
Website: http://www.uakron.edu/polisci/

The University of Alabama, Graduate School, College of Arts and Sciences, Department of Political Science, Tuscaloosa, AL 35487. Offers political science (MA, PhD); public administration (MPA). Part-time programs available. *Faculty:* 16 full-time (5 women). *Students:* 58 full-time (15 women), 10 part-time (3 women); includes 15 minority (11 Black or African American, non-Hispanic/Latino; 2 Asian, non-Hispanic/Latino; 1 Hispanic/Latino; 1 Two or more races, non-Hispanic/Latino), 3 international. Average age 29. 59 applicants, 71% accepted, 21 enrolled. In 2014, 10 master's, 5 doctorates awarded. Terminal master's awarded for partial completion of doctoral program. *Degree requirements:* For master's, comprehensive exam, thesis optional; for doctorate, comprehensive exam, thesis/dissertation. *Entrance requirements:* For master's and doctorate, GRE, minimum undergraduate GPA of 3.0. Additional exam requirements/recommendations for international students: Required—TOEFL. *Application deadline:* For fall admission, 6/30 for domestic and international students; for spring admission, 10/15 for domestic students. Applications are processed on a rolling basis. Application fee: $50 ($60 for international students). Electronic applications accepted. *Expenses:* Tuition, state resident: full-time $9826. Tuition, nonresident: full-time $24,950. *Financial support:* In 2014–15, 15 students received support, including 3 fellowships with full tuition reimbursements available (averaging $15,000 per year), teaching assistantships with full tuition reimbursements available (averaging $12,500 per year); career-related internships or fieldwork and Federal Work-Study also available. Financial award application deadline: 2/15. *Faculty research:* American politics, comparative politics, international relations, public policy and administration, political theory. *Total annual research expenditures:* $43,562. *Unit head:* Dr. Richard C. Fording, Chair and Professor, 205-348-5981, Fax: 205-348-5298, E-mail: rcfording@as.ua.edu. *Application contact:* Dr. Douglas Gibler, Graduate Advisor, 205-348-5528, Fax: 205-348-5298, E-mail: dmgibler@bama.ua.edu.
Website: http://www.as.ua.edu/psc/

University of Alberta, Faculty of Graduate Studies and Research, Department of Political Science, Edmonton, AB T6G 2E1, Canada. Offers MA, PhD. Part-time programs available. *Degree requirements:* For master's, thesis (for some programs); for doctorate, one foreign language, thesis/dissertation. *Entrance requirements:* Additional exam requirements/recommendations for international students: Required—TOEFL. *Faculty research:* Canadian politics, international relations, globalization, classical and contemporary political theory, gender and politics.

The University of Arizona, College of Social and Behavioral Sciences, Department of Political Science, Tucson, AZ 85721. Offers MA, PhD. Terminal master's awarded for partial completion of doctoral program. *Degree requirements:* For master's, thesis or alternative; for doctorate, variable foreign language requirement, comprehensive exam, thesis/dissertation. *Entrance requirements:* For master's, GRE General Test, minimum GPA of 3.2, 3 letters of recommendation, writing sample; for doctorate, GRE General Test, minimum GPA of 3.2, 3 letters of recommendation, statement of purpose, writing sample. Additional exam requirements/recommendations for international students: Required—TOEFL (minimum score 550 paper-based; 79 iBT). Electronic applications accepted. *Faculty research:* Voting behavior, political participation, Soviet domestic and Sino-Soviet relations, presidential leadership and congressional behavior.

University of Arkansas, Graduate School, J. William Fulbright College of Arts and Sciences, Department of Political Science, Program in Political Science, Fayetteville, AR 72701-1201. Offers MA. *Degree requirements:* For master's, thesis or alternative. *Entrance requirements:* For master's, GRE General Test. Electronic applications accepted.

The University of British Columbia, Faculty of Arts and Faculty of Graduate Studies, Department of Political Science, Vancouver, BC V6T 1Z1, Canada. Offers MA, PhD. Part-time programs available. *Degree requirements:* For master's, thesis; for doctorate, comprehensive exam, thesis/dissertation. *Entrance requirements:* For master's, BA in political science; for doctorate, GRE, BA and MA in political science. Additional exam requirements/recommendations for international students: Required—TOEFL (minimum score 580 paper-based), TWE (minimum score 5). Electronic applications accepted. *Faculty research:* Canadian politics, international relations, political theory, comparative politics, public policy.

University of Calgary, Faculty of Graduate Studies, Faculty of Arts, Department of Political Science, Calgary, AB T2N 1N4, Canada. Offers MA, PhD. *Degree requirements:* For master's, thesis; for doctorate, one foreign language, comprehensive exam, thesis/dissertation, prospectus, oral and written candidacy exams. *Entrance requirements:* For master's, minimum GPA of 3.4; for doctorate, minimum GPA of 3.7. Additional exam requirements/recommendations for international students: Required—TOEFL (minimum score 620 paper-based). Electronic applications accepted. *Faculty research:* Canadian politics, international relations, comparative politics, theory, public policy.

University of California, Berkeley, Graduate Division, College of Letters and Science, Charles and Louise Travers Department of Political Science, Berkeley, CA 94720-1500. Offers PhD. *Degree requirements:* For doctorate, thesis/dissertation, oral qualifying exams. *Entrance requirements:* For doctorate, GRE General Test, minimum GPA of 3.0, 3 letters of recommendation. Electronic applications accepted.

University of California, Davis, Graduate Studies, Program in Political Science, Davis, CA 95616. Offers MA, PhD. Terminal master's awarded for partial completion of doctoral program. *Degree requirements:* For master's, thesis; for doctorate, thesis/dissertation. *Entrance requirements:* For master's and doctorate, GRE General Test, minimum GPA of 3.0, writing sample. Additional exam requirements/recommendations for international students: Required—TOEFL (minimum score 550 paper-based). Electronic applications accepted. *Faculty research:* American government and politics, political theory, comparative politics, international relations, public law.

University of California, Irvine, School of Social Sciences, Department of Political Science, Irvine, CA 92697. Offers political psychology (PhD); political sciences (PhD); public choice (PhD). *Students:* 65 full-time (27 women), 2 part-time (both women); includes 20 minority (1 Black or African American, non-Hispanic/Latino; 8 Asian, non-Hispanic/Latino; 8 Hispanic/Latino; 3 Two or more races, non-Hispanic/Latino), 5 international. Average age 30. 128 applicants, 21% accepted, 12 enrolled. In 2014, 8 doctorates awarded. *Degree requirements:* For doctorate, thesis/dissertation. *Entrance requirements:* For doctorate, GRE General Test, minimum GPA of 3.0. Additional exam requirements/recommendations for international students: Required—TOEFL (minimum score 550 paper-based). *Application deadline:* For fall admission, 1/15 priority date for domestic students, 1/15 for international students. Applications are processed on a rolling basis. Application fee: $90 ($110 for international students). Electronic applications accepted. *Financial support:* Fellowships, research assistantships with full tuition reimbursements, teaching assistantships, institutionally sponsored loans, traineeships, health care benefits, and unspecified assistantships available. Financial award application deadline: 3/1; financial award applicants required to submit FAFSA. *Faculty research:* Political behavior, political economy, international relations. *Unit head:* Dr. Louis DeSipio, Interim Chair, 949-824-4012, E-mail: ldesipio@uci.edu. *Application contact:* Marek Kaminski, Graduate Advisor, 949-824-2744, Fax: 949-824-8762, E-mail: marek.kaminski@uci.edu.
Website: http://www.polisci.uci.edu/

University of California, Los Angeles, Graduate Division, College of Letters and Science, Department of Political Science, Los Angeles, CA 90095. Offers MA, PhD. Terminal master's awarded for partial completion of doctoral program. *Degree requirements:* For master's, comprehensive exam; for doctorate, one foreign language, thesis/dissertation, oral and written qualifying exams. *Entrance requirements:* For doctorate, GRE General Test, bachelor's degree; minimum undergraduate GPA of 3.0 (or its equivalent if letter grade system not used); writing sample. Additional exam requirements/recommendations for international students: Required—TOEFL. Electronic applications accepted.

University of California, Riverside, Graduate Division, Department of Ethnic Studies, Riverside, CA 92521. Offers cultural politics and production (PhD); the state, law, and social transformation (PhD). *Faculty:* 15 full-time (9 women). *Students:* 18 full-time (13 women); includes 16 minority (5 Black or African American, non-Hispanic/Latino; 1 American Indian or Alaska Native, non-Hispanic/Latino; 2 Asian, non-Hispanic/Latino; 7 Hispanic/Latino; 1 Native Hawaiian or other Pacific Islander, non-Hispanic/Latino). Average age 30. 42 applicants, 19% accepted, 4 enrolled. Terminal master's awarded for partial completion of doctoral program. *Degree requirements:* For doctorate, variable foreign language requirement, comprehensive exam, thesis/dissertation. *Entrance requirements:* For doctorate, GRE, Writing Sample, Statement of Purpose, Personal History Statement, Letters of Recommendation (3). Additional exam requirements/recommendations for international students: Required—TOEFL (minimum score 550 paper-based; 80 iBT), Individual section score on IELTS must not be less than 6 in any section. Recommended—IELTS (minimum score 7). *Application deadline:* For fall admission, 1/5 priority date for domestic and international students. Applications are processed on a rolling basis. Application fee: $80 ($100 for international students). Electronic applications accepted. *Expenses:* Tuition, state resident: full-time $5399. Tuition, nonresident: full-time $10,433. *Financial support:* In 2014–15, 10 students received support, including 4 fellowships with full tuition reimbursements available (averaging $10,000 per year), 7 teaching assistantships with full tuition reimbursements available (averaging $18,000 per year); unspecified assistantships also available. Financial award application deadline: 1/5; financial award applicants required to submit FAFSA. *Faculty research:* The political economy of race, class, gender, sexuality, cultural production, the state, law, criminal justice and grass roots responses. *Unit head:* Dr. Dylan Rodriguez, Chair, 951-827-4707, E-mail: dylan.rodriguez@ucr.edu. *Application contact:* Trina B. Elerts, Graduate Program Coordinator, 951-827-1584, E-mail: trina.elerts@ucr.edu.
Website: http://www.ethnicstudies.ucr.edu

University of California, Riverside, Graduate Division, Department of Political Science, Riverside, CA 92521-0102. Offers MA, PhD. Part-time programs available. Terminal master's awarded for partial completion of doctoral program. *Degree requirements:* For master's, comprehensive exams or thesis; for doctorate, thesis/dissertation, qualifying exams. *Entrance requirements:* For master's and doctorate, GRE General Test, minimum GPA of 3.2. Additional exam requirements/recommendations for international students: Required—TOEFL (minimum score 550 paper-based; 80 iBT). Electronic applications accepted. *Expenses:* Tuition, state resident: full-time $5399. Tuition, nonresident: full-time $10,433. *Faculty research:* American politics, mass political behavior, comparative politics, international relations, political theory.

University of California, San Diego, Graduate Division, Department of Political Science, La Jolla, CA 92093. Offers political science (PhD); political science and international affairs (PhD). *Students:* 76 full-time (22 women), 2 part-time (both women); includes 13 minority (all Asian, non-Hispanic/Latino), 7 international. 332 applicants, 10% accepted, 6 enrolled. In 2014, 11 doctorates awarded. *Degree requirements:* For doctorate, comprehensive exam, thesis/dissertation. *Entrance requirements:* For doctorate, GRE General Test. Additional exam requirements/recommendations for international students: Required—TOEFL (minimum score 600 paper-based; 100 iBT), IELTS. *Application deadline:* For fall admission, 12/10 for domestic students. Application fee: $90 ($110 for international students). Electronic applications accepted. *Expenses:* Tuition, state resident: full-time $11,220; part-time $5610 per quarter. Tuition, nonresident: full-time $26,322; part-time $13,161 per quarter. *Required fees:* $570 per quarter. Tuition and fees vary according to program. *Financial support:* Fellowships, research assistantships, teaching assistantships, and scholarships/grants available. Financial award applicants required to submit FAFSA. *Faculty research:* American politics, comparative politics, international relations, methodology, political theory. *Unit head:* Philip G. Roeder, Chair, 858-534-0721, E-mail: proeder@ucsd.edu. *Application contact:* Arturo Vazquez, Graduate Coordinator, 858-534-2705, E-mail: avazquez@ucsd.edu.
Website: http://polisci.ucsd.edu/

University of California, San Diego, Graduate Division, School of Global Policy and Strategy, La Jolla, CA 92093. Offers international affairs (MAS, MIA); political science and international affairs (PhD); public policy (MPP). Part-time programs available. *Faculty:* 33 full-time (9 women), 20 part-time/adjunct (4 women). *Students:* 390 full-time, 6 part-time. Average age 26. 590 applicants, 165 enrolled. In 2014, 160 master's, 3 doctorates awarded. *Degree requirements:* For master's, one foreign language; for doctorate, thesis/dissertation. *Entrance requirements:* For master's, GMAT or GRE General Test; for doctorate, GRE General Test. Additional exam requirements/recommendations for international students: Required—TOEFL (minimum score 90 iBT), IELTS (minimum score 7). *Application deadline:* For fall admission, 1/15 for domestic and international students. Applications are processed on a rolling basis. Application fee: $50. Electronic applications accepted. *Expenses:* Tuition, state resident: full-time $11,220; part-time $5610 per quarter. Tuition, nonresident: full-time $26,322; part-time $13,161 per quarter. *Required fees:* $570 per quarter. Tuition and fees vary according to program. *Financial support:* In 2014–15, 140 students received

support, including 60 fellowships with full and partial tuition reimbursements available (averaging $50,000 per year), 15 research assistantships with full tuition reimbursements available (averaging $20,000 per year), 20 teaching assistantships with full tuition reimbursements available (averaging $20,000 per year); career-related internships or fieldwork, scholarships/grants, and unspecified assistantships also available. Financial award application deadline: 3/1; financial award applicants required to submit FAFSA. *Faculty research:* Public policy; international management, finance and trade; international development; international politics in Latin America, China, Korea, Japan, and Southeast Asia; international environmental policy. *Unit head:* Sonja Steinbrech, Director of Enrollment, 858-534-7162, E-mail: ssteinbrech@ucsd.edu. *Application contact:* Admissions Representative, 858-534-5914, Fax: 858-534-5914, E-mail: gps-apply@uscd.edu.
Website: http://gps.ucsd.edu

University of California, Santa Barbara, Graduate Division, College of Letters and Sciences, Division of Social Sciences, Department of Global and International Studies, Santa Barbara, CA 93106-7065. Offers global culture, ideology, and religion (MA); global government, civil society, and human rights (MA); global studies (PhD); political economy, sustainable development, and the environment (MA). *Degree requirements:* For master's, one foreign language, thesis, 2 years of a second language. *Entrance requirements:* For master's, GRE, 2 years of a second language with minimum B grade in the final term, 3 letters of recommendation, resume/curriculum vitae, personal statement, writing sample. Additional exam requirements/recommendations for international students: Required—TOEFL (minimum score 600 paper-based; 94 iBT), IELTS (minimum score 7). Electronic applications accepted. *Faculty research:* Global culture, ideology, and religion; global governance, civil society, and human rights; political economy, sustainable development and the environment.

University of California, Santa Barbara, Graduate Division, College of Letters and Sciences, Division of Social Sciences, Department of Political Science, Santa Barbara, CA 93106-9420. Offers PhD, MA/PhD. Terminal master's awarded for partial completion of doctoral program. *Degree requirements:* For doctorate, one foreign language, thesis/dissertation, 2 comprehensive exams or 1 exam and field paper. *Entrance requirements:* For doctorate, GRE General Test. Additional exam requirements/recommendations for international students: Required—TOEFL (minimum score 600 paper-based; 100 iBT), IELTS. Electronic applications accepted. *Faculty research:* American politics, comparative politics, international relations, political theory.

University of California, Santa Cruz, Division of Graduate Studies, Division of Social Sciences, Politics Department, Santa Cruz, CA 95064. Offers PhD. *Degree requirements:* For doctorate, qualifying exam. *Entrance requirements:* For doctorate, GRE. Additional exam requirements/recommendations for international students: Required—TOEFL (minimum score 550 paper-based; 83 iBT); Recommended—IELTS (minimum score 8). Electronic applications accepted. *Faculty research:* Political and social thought, political institutions, political economy, political and social forces.

University of Central Florida, College of Sciences, Department of Political Science, Orlando, FL 32816. Offers political science (MA); security studies (PhD). Part-time and evening/weekend programs available. *Faculty:* 30 full-time (9 women), 10 part-time/adjunct (1 woman). *Students:* 36 full-time (18 women), 27 part-time (12 women); includes 12 minority (4 Black or African American, non-Hispanic/Latino; 5 Hispanic/Latino; 3 Two or more races, non-Hispanic/Latino), 5 international. Average age 31. 52 applicants, 77% accepted, 26 enrolled. In 2014, 12 master's awarded. *Degree requirements:* For master's, comprehensive exam, thesis; for doctorate, one foreign language, thesis/dissertation, oral qualifying examination. *Entrance requirements:* For master's, GRE General Test, minimum GPA of 3.0 in last 60 hours; for doctorate, GRE General Test, master's degree, three letters of reference, personal statement, writing sample, resume. Additional exam requirements/recommendations for international students: Required—TOEFL. *Application deadline:* For fall admission, 7/15 for domestic students; for spring admission, 12/1 for domestic students. Application fee: $30. Electronic applications accepted. *Expenses:* Tuition, state resident: part-time $288.16 per credit hour. Tuition, nonresident: part-time $1073.31 per credit hour. *Financial support:* In 2014–15, 13 students received support, including 3 fellowships with partial tuition reimbursements available (averaging $10,200 per year), 2 research assistantships with partial tuition reimbursements available (averaging $4,600 per year), 11 teaching assistantships with partial tuition reimbursements available (averaging $10,300 per year); career-related internships or fieldwork, Federal Work-Study, institutionally sponsored loans, tuition waivers (partial), and unspecified assistantships also available. Financial award application deadline: 3/1; financial award applicants required to submit FAFSA. *Faculty research:* Environment, presidential campaigning, term limits for elected officials. *Unit head:* Dr. Kerstin Hamann, Chair, 407-823-2085, Fax: 407-823-0051, E-mail: kerstin.hamann@ucf.edu. *Application contact:* Barbara Rodriguez Lamas, Director, Admissions and Student Services, 407-823-2766, Fax: 407-823-6442, E-mail: gradadmissions@ucf.edu.
Website: http://politicalscience.cos.ucf.edu/

University of Central Oklahoma, The Jackson College of Graduate Studies, College of Liberal Arts, Department of Political Science, Edmond, OK 73034-5209. Offers international affairs (MA); political science (MA); public administration (MPA). Part-time programs available. *Degree requirements:* For master's, comprehensive exam (for some programs), thesis (for some programs). *Entrance requirements:* For master's, GRE, 18 undergraduate hours in political science. Additional exam requirements/recommendations for international students: Required—TOEFL (minimum score 550 paper-based; 79 iBT), IELTS (minimum score 6.5). Electronic applications accepted.

University of Chicago, Division of the Social Sciences, Department of Political Science, Chicago, IL 60637. Offers PhD. *Students:* 123 full-time (52 women); includes 42 minority (19 Black or African American, non-Hispanic/Latino; 1 American Indian or Alaska Native, non-Hispanic/Latino; 6 Asian, non-Hispanic/Latino; 10 Hispanic/Latino; 6 Two or more races, non-Hispanic/Latino), 32 international. 456 applicants, 8% accepted, 14 enrolled. In 2014, 16 doctorates awarded. *Degree requirements:* For doctorate, one foreign language, thesis/dissertation, exam, qualifying paper. *Entrance requirements:* For doctorate, GRE General Test. Additional exam requirements/recommendations for international students: Required—TOEFL (minimum score 104 iBT), IELTS (minimum score 7). *Application deadline:* For fall admission, 12/15 for domestic and international students. Application fee: $90. Electronic applications accepted. *Expenses: Tuition:* Full-time $46,899. *Required fees:* $347. *Financial support:* In 2014–15, 14 students received support, including 14 fellowships with full tuition reimbursements available (averaging $23,000 per year); career-related internships or fieldwork, Federal Work-Study, institutionally sponsored loans, scholarships/grants, and health care benefits also available. Financial award application deadline: 12/15. *Faculty research:* Political philosophy, international political economy, strategic studies, public policy and race relations, comparative politics (China, Middle East, Soviet Union, Africa, India, Japan). *Unit head:* Prof. Cathy Cohen, Chair. *Application contact:* Office of the Dean of Students, 773-702-8415, E-mail: admissions@ssd.uchicago.edu.
Website: http://political-science.uchicago.edu

University of Cincinnati, Graduate School, McMicken College of Arts and Sciences, Department of Political Science, Cincinnati, OH 45221. Offers MA, PhD. Terminal master's awarded for partial completion of doctoral program. *Degree requirements:* For master's, thesis (for some programs); for doctorate, thesis/dissertation. *Entrance requirements:* For master's and doctorate, GRE General Test, GRE Subject Test. Additional exam requirements/recommendations for international students: Required—TOEFL. Electronic applications accepted. *Faculty research:* International security, methodology, American politics, comparative politics.

University of Colorado Boulder, Graduate School, College of Arts and Sciences, Department of Political Science, Boulder, CO 80309. Offers international affairs (MA); political science (MA, PhD); public policy (MA). *Faculty:* 26 full-time (8 women). *Students:* 53 full-time (20 women), 5 part-time (0 women); includes 6 minority (3 American Indian or Alaska Native, non-Hispanic/Latino; 1 Asian, non-Hispanic/Latino; 2 Hispanic/Latino), 5 international. Average age 30. 120 applicants, 26% accepted, 10 enrolled. In 2014, 11 master's, 4 doctorates awarded. Terminal master's awarded for partial completion of doctoral program. *Degree requirements:* For master's, comprehensive exam, thesis; for doctorate, one foreign language, thesis/dissertation. *Entrance requirements:* For master's, GRE General Test, minimum undergraduate GPA of 3.0; for doctorate, GRE General Test, minimum GPA of 3.5 (undergraduate), 3.0 (graduate). *Application deadline:* For fall admission, 12/15 for domestic and international students. Application fee: $50 ($60 for international students). Electronic applications accepted. *Financial support:* In 2014–15, 142 students received support, including 21 fellowships (averaging $2,782 per year), 1 research assistantship with full and partial tuition reimbursement available (averaging $39,356 per year), 49 teaching assistantships with full and partial tuition reimbursements available (averaging $38,468 per year); institutionally sponsored loans, scholarships/grants, health care benefits, and unspecified assistantships also available. Financial award application deadline: 12/31; financial award applicants required to submit FAFSA. *Faculty research:* Political science, democracy, comparative government, political economics/economy, international relations. *Total annual research expenditures:* $752,632.
Website: http://polsci.colorado.edu/

University of Colorado Denver, College of Liberal Arts and Sciences, Department of Political Science, Denver, CO 80217. Offers MA. Part-time and evening/weekend programs available. *Faculty:* 13 full-time (4 women), 2 part-time/adjunct (0 women). *Students:* 61 full-time (27 women), 31 part-time (12 women); includes 25 minority (11 Black or African American, non-Hispanic/Latino; 5 American Indian or Alaska Native, non-Hispanic/Latino; 2 Asian, non-Hispanic/Latino; 7 Hispanic/Latino), 3 international. Average age 34. 24 applicants, 71% accepted, 11 enrolled. In 2014, 17 master's awarded. *Degree requirements:* For master's, project or thesis, minimum of 30 credit hours. *Entrance requirements:* For master's, 18 hours of course work in political science; minimum GPA of 3.0 (3.2 preferred); statement of purpose; academic writing sample. Additional exam requirements/recommendations for international students: Required—TOEFL (minimum score 537 paper-based; 75 iBT); Recommended—IELTS (minimum score 6.5). *Application deadline:* For fall admission, 3/1 for domestic students, 3/1 priority date for international students; for spring admission, 10/1 for domestic students, 10/1 priority date for international students. Application fee: $50 ($75 for international students). Electronic applications accepted. *Financial support:* In 2014–15, 4 students received support. Fellowships, research assistantships, teaching assistantships, Federal Work-Study, institutionally sponsored loans, scholarships/grants, and traineeships available. Financial award application deadline: 4/1; financial award applicants required to submit FAFSA. *Faculty research:* Indigenous peoples in the international legal and political arena; political developments in Europe and the former Soviet Union; early Chinese industrialization, modern Chinese political and economic development, and human rights; Congressional oversight and Congressional-executive relations. *Unit head:* Dr. Anthony Robinson, Chair, 303-556-2746, E-mail: tony.robinson@ucdenver.edu. *Application contact:* Political Science Department, 303-556-3556.
Website: http://www.ucdenver.edu/academics/colleges/CLAS/Departments/PoliticalScience/Programs/Masters/Pages/MasterofArts.aspx

University of Colorado Denver, School of Public Affairs, Program in Public Affairs and Administration, Denver, CO 80127. Offers public administration (MPA), including domestic violence, emergency management and homeland security, environmental policy, management and law, homeland security and defense, local government, nonprofit management, public administration; public affairs (PhD). *Accreditation:* NASPAA. Part-time and evening/weekend programs available. Postbaccalaureate distance learning degree programs offered (no on-campus study). *Students:* 275 full-time (176 women), 140 part-time (93 women); includes 70 minority (7 Black or African American, non-Hispanic/Latino; 4 American Indian or Alaska Native, non-Hispanic/Latino; 9 Asian, non-Hispanic/Latino; 44 Hispanic/Latino; 2 Native Hawaiian or other Pacific Islander, non-Hispanic/Latino; 4 Two or more races, non-Hispanic/Latino), 19 international. Average age 34. 243 applicants, 71% accepted, 97 enrolled. In 2014, 127 master's, 5 doctorates awarded. *Degree requirements:* For master's, thesis or alternative, 36-39 credit hours; for doctorate, comprehensive exam, thesis/dissertation, minimum of 66 semester hours, including at least 30 hours of dissertation. *Entrance requirements:* For master's, GRE, GMAT or LSAT, resume, essay, transcripts, recommendations; for doctorate, GRE, resume, essay, transcripts, recommendations. Additional exam requirements/recommendations for international students: Required—TOEFL (minimum score 550 paper-based; 80 iBT); Recommended—IELTS (minimum score 6.5). *Application deadline:* For fall admission, 2/1 priority date for domestic students, 1/15 priority date for international students; for spring admission, 10/15 priority date for domestic students, 10/1 priority date for international students. Application fee: $50 ($75 for international students). Electronic applications accepted. *Expenses:* Expenses: Contact institution. *Financial support:* In 2014–15, 60 students received support. Fellowships with partial tuition reimbursements available, research assistantships with partial tuition reimbursements available, teaching assistantships with partial tuition reimbursements available, Federal Work-Study, institutionally sponsored loans, scholarships/grants, traineeships, and unspecified assistantships available. Financial award application deadline: 4/1; financial award applicants required to submit FAFSA. *Faculty research:* Housing, education and the social and economic issues of vulnerable populations; nonprofit governance and management; education finance, effectiveness and reform; P-20 education initiatives; municipal government accountability. *Unit head:* Dr. Christine Martell, Director of MPA Program, 303-315-2716, Fax: 303-315-2229, E-mail: christine.martell@ucdenver.edu. *Application contact:* Dawn Savage, Student Services Coordinator, 303-315-2743, Fax: 303-315-2229, E-mail: dawn.savage@ucdenver.edu.
Website: http://www.ucdenver.edu/academics/colleges/SPA/Academics/programs/PublicAffairsAdmin/Pages/index.aspx

University of Connecticut, Graduate School, College of Liberal Arts and Sciences, Department of Political Science, Storrs, CT 06269. Offers MA, PhD. Terminal master's awarded for partial completion of doctoral program. *Degree requirements:* For master's, comprehensive exam; for doctorate, 2 foreign languages, thesis/dissertation. *Entrance requirements:* For master's and doctorate, GRE General Test. Additional exam requirements/recommendations for international students: Required—TOEFL (minimum score 550 paper-based). Electronic applications accepted.

University of Dallas, Braniff Graduate School of Liberal Arts, Institute of Philosophic Studies, Doctoral Program in Politics, Irving, TX 75062-4736. Offers PhD. *Degree*

requirements: For doctorate, 2 foreign languages, comprehensive exam, thesis/dissertation. *Entrance requirements:* For doctorate, GRE General Test. Additional exam requirements/recommendations for international students: Required—TOEFL. *Faculty research:* Classical, medieval, and modern political philosophy; American political thought and institutions; politics and literature.

University of Dallas, Braniff Graduate School of Liberal Arts, Master's Program in Politics, Irving, TX 75062-4736. Offers M Pol, MA. Part-time programs available. *Degree requirements:* For master's, one foreign language, comprehensive exam, thesis. *Entrance requirements:* For master's, GRE General Test. Additional exam requirements/recommendations for international students: Required—TOEFL. *Faculty research:* Classical, medieval, and modern political philosophy; American political thought and institutions; politics and literature.

University of Delaware, College of Arts and Sciences, Department of Political Science and International Relations, Newark, DE 19716. Offers MA, PhD. Terminal master's awarded for partial completion of doctoral program. *Degree requirements:* For master's, research paper; for doctorate, one foreign language, comprehensive exam, thesis/dissertation. *Entrance requirements:* For master's and doctorate, GRE General Test, minimum GPA of 3.2 in major, 3.0 overall. Additional exam requirements/recommendations for international students: Required—TOEFL (minimum score 600 paper-based). Electronic applications accepted. *Faculty research:* Social constructivism. international migration, international security, democratization, human rights.

University of Florida, Graduate School, College of Liberal Arts and Sciences, Department of Political Science, Gainesville, FL 32611. Offers educational policy (PhD); international development policy and administration (MA, Certificate); international relations (MA, MAT); political campaigning (MA, Certificate); political science (MA, PhD); public affairs (MA, Certificate); tropical conservation and development (MA, PhD); JD/MA. *Faculty:* 25 full-time (9 women), 4 part-time/adjunct (1 woman). *Students:* 115 full-time (45 women), 19 part-time (7 women); includes 26 minority (12 Black or African American, non-Hispanic/Latino; 6 Asian, non-Hispanic/Latino; 8 Hispanic/Latino), 34 international. 136 applicants, 44% accepted, 22 enrolled. In 2014, 28 master's, 8 doctorates awarded. Terminal master's awarded for partial completion of doctoral program. *Degree requirements:* For master's, variable foreign language requirement, comprehensive exam (for some programs), thesis or alternative, internship (for some programs); for doctorate, variable foreign language requirement, comprehensive exam, thesis/dissertation. *Entrance requirements:* For master's and doctorate, GRE General Test 308 combined verbal/math, minimum GPA of 3.5. Additional exam requirements/recommendations for international students: Required—TOEFL (minimum score 550 paper-based; 80 iBT), IELTS (minimum score 6). *Application deadline:* For fall admission, 1/15 priority date for domestic students, 1/15 for international students. Applications are processed on a rolling basis. Application fee: $30. Electronic applications accepted. *Financial support:* In 2014–15, 13 fellowships, 13 research assistantships, 50 teaching assistantships were awarded; career-related internships or fieldwork, Federal Work-Study, institutionally sponsored loans, and unspecified assistantships also available. Financial award application deadline: 1/15; financial award applicants required to submit FAFSA. *Faculty research:* American electoral politics and political institutions, comparative democratization and development, theories of international relation, and political theory. *Total annual research expenditures:* $208,864. *Unit head:* Ido Oren, PhD, Professor and Chair, 352-273-2393, Fax: 352-392-8127, E-mail: oren@ufl.edu. *Application contact:* Leslie Anderson, PhD, Graduate Coordinator, 352-273-3725, Fax: 352-392-8127, E-mail: landerso@ufl.edu.
Website: http://polisci.ufl.edu/

University of Georgia, School of Public and International Affairs, Program in Political Science, Athens, GA 30602. Offers MA, PhD. *Degree requirements:* For master's, one foreign language, thesis; for doctorate, one foreign language, thesis/dissertation. *Entrance requirements:* For master's and doctorate, GRE General Test. Electronic applications accepted.

University of Guelph, Graduate Studies, College of Social and Applied Human Sciences, Department of Political Science, Guelph, ON N1G 2W1, Canada. Offers comparative politics (MA); international development (MA); political science (MA); public policy and public administration (MA); the Americas (Canada emphasis) (MA). MA in public policy and public administration offered in collaboration with Department of Political Science of McMaster University. *Degree requirements:* For master's, thesis or paper. *Entrance requirements:* For master's, minimum B average during previous 2 years of course work, 4 year Honours Degree in Political Science. Additional exam requirements/recommendations for international students: Required—TOEFL. Electronic applications accepted. *Faculty research:* Political ethics, constitutional power.

University of Hawaii at Manoa, Graduate Division, College of Social Sciences, Department of Political Science, Honolulu, HI 96822. Offers MA, PhD. Part-time programs available. Terminal master's awarded for partial completion of doctoral program. *Degree requirements:* For master's, thesis optional; for doctorate, comprehensive exam, thesis/dissertation. *Entrance requirements:* Additional exam requirements/recommendations for international students: Required—TOEFL (minimum score 540 paper-based; 76 iBT), IELTS (minimum score 5). *Faculty research:* Asia/Pacific, political economy, human rights, futures, postmodernism.

University of Houston, College of Liberal Arts and Social Sciences, Department of Political Science, Houston, TX 77204. Offers political science (MA, PhD); public administration (MA). Part-time programs available. Terminal master's awarded for partial completion of doctoral program. *Degree requirements:* For master's, thesis optional; for doctorate, thesis/dissertation. *Entrance requirements:* For master's and doctorate, GRE. Additional exam requirements/recommendations for international students: Required—TOEFL (minimum score 550 paper-based; 79 iBT). *Faculty research:* American politics, political theory, judicial process, public policy, comparative politics.

University of Idaho, College of Graduate Studies, College of Letters, Arts and Social Sciences, The Martin School, Political Science Department, Moscow, ID 83844-3165. Offers political science (MA, PhD); public administration (MPA). *Faculty:* 6 full-time, 1 part-time/adjunct. *Students:* 7 full-time, 8 part-time. Average age 35. In 2014, 9 master's, 1 doctorate awarded. *Degree requirements:* For doctorate, thesis/dissertation. *Entrance requirements:* For master's, minimum GPA of 2.8; for doctorate, minimum undergraduate GPA of 2.8, 3.0 graduate. *Application deadline:* For fall admission, 8/1 for domestic students; for spring admission, 12/15 for domestic students. Applications are processed on a rolling basis. Application fee: $60. Electronic applications accepted. *Expenses:* Tuition, state resident: full-time $4784; part-time $280.50 per credit hour. Tuition, nonresident: full-time $18,314; part-time $957.50 per credit hour. *Required fees:* $2000; $58.50 per credit hour. Tuition and fees vary according to program. *Financial support:* Research assistantships and teaching assistantships available. Financial award applicants required to submit FAFSA. *Unit head:* Dr. Brian Ellison, Director, 208-885-6328. *Application contact:* Sean Scoggin, Graduate Recruitment Coordinator, 208-885-4001, Fax: 208-885-4406, E-mail: graduateadmissions@uidaho.edu.
Website: http://www.uidaho.edu/class/politicalscience

University of Illinois at Chicago, Graduate College, College of Liberal Arts and Sciences, Department of Political Science, Chicago, IL 60607-7128. Offers MA, PhD. Part-time programs available. *Faculty:* 16 full-time (7 women), 4 part-time/adjunct (1 woman). *Students:* 38 full-time (20 women), 14 part-time (7 women); includes 7 minority (2 Black or African American, non-Hispanic/Latino; 5 Hispanic/Latino), 13 international. Average age 31. 63 applicants, 37% accepted, 8 enrolled. In 2014, 4 master's, 4 doctorates awarded. Terminal master's awarded for partial completion of doctoral program. *Degree requirements:* For master's, thesis or comprehensive exam. *Entrance requirements:* For master's, GRE General Test, minimum GPA of 3.0. Additional exam requirements/recommendations for international students: Required—TOEFL. *Application deadline:* For fall admission, 3/15 for domestic students, 2/15 for international students. Applications are processed on a rolling basis. Application fee: $60. Electronic applications accepted. *Expenses:* Tuition, state resident: full-time $11,254; part-time $468 per credit hour. Tuition, nonresident: full-time $23,252; part-time $968 per credit hour. *Required fees:* $1217 per term. Part-time tuition and fees vary according to course load, degree level and program. *Financial support:* In 2014–15, 4 fellowships with full tuition reimbursements were awarded; research assistantships with full tuition reimbursements, teaching assistantships with full tuition reimbursements, Federal Work-Study, institutionally sponsored loans, scholarships/grants, traineeships, tuition waivers (full), and unspecified assistantships also available. Financial award application deadline: 3/15; financial award applicants required to submit FAFSA. *Faculty research:* Policy analysis/national urban politics and policy, electoral behavior. *Unit head:* Dennis R. Judd, Professor and Interim Head, 312-996-4421, Fax: 312-413-0440, E-mail: djudd@uic.edu. *Application contact:* Prof. Evan McKenzie, Director of Graduate Studies, 312-355-3782, E-mail: mckenzie@uic.edu.
Website: http://pols.las.uic.edu/

University of Illinois at Springfield, Graduate Programs, College of Public Affairs and Administration, Department of Political Science, Springfield, IL 62703-5407. Offers MA. Part-time and evening/weekend programs available. *Faculty:* 5 full-time (1 woman), 1 part-time/adjunct (0 women). *Students:* 14 full-time (5 women), 32 part-time (6 women); includes 9 minority (4 Black or African American, non-Hispanic/Latino; 1 Asian, non-Hispanic/Latino; 4 Hispanic/Latino), 1 international. Average age 30. 69 applicants, 51% accepted, 19 enrolled. In 2014, 11 master's awarded. *Degree requirements:* For master's, comprehensive exam, participant/observer case study, or thesis. *Entrance requirements:* For master's, minimum undergraduate GPA of 3.0. Additional exam requirements/recommendations for international students: Required—TOEFL (minimum score 500 paper-based; 61 iBT). *Application deadline:* Applications are processed on a rolling basis. Application fee: $60 ($75 for international students). Electronic applications accepted. *Expenses:* Tuition, state resident: full-time $7662; part-time $319.25 per credit hour. Tuition, nonresident: full-time $15,966; part-time $665.25 per credit hour. *Financial support:* In 2014–15, fellowships with full tuition reimbursements (averaging $9,900 per year), research assistantships with full tuition reimbursements (averaging $9,600 per year), teaching assistantships with full tuition reimbursements (averaging $9,600 per year) were awarded; career-related internships or fieldwork, Federal Work-Study, scholarships/grants, health care benefits, and unspecified assistantships also available. Support available to part-time students. Financial award application deadline: 11/15; financial award applicants required to submit FAFSA. *Unit head:* Dr. Richard Gilman-Opalsky, Program Administrator, 217-206-8328, E-mail: rgilm3@uis.edu. *Application contact:* Dr. Lynn Pardie, Office of Graduate Studies, 800-252-8533, Fax: 217-206-7623, E-mail: lpard1@uis.edu.
Website: http://www.uis.edu/politicalstudies/

University of Illinois at Urbana–Champaign, Graduate College, College of Liberal Arts and Sciences, Department of Political Science, Champaign, IL 61820. Offers MA, PhD, PhD/JD. *Students:* 48 (20 women). Application fee: $70 ($90 for international students). *Unit head:* William Bernhard, Head, 217-333-3881, Fax: 217-244-5712, E-mail: bernhard@illinois.edu. *Application contact:* Jeffery J. Mondak, Associate Professor, 217-333-3881, Fax: 217-244-5712, E-mail: jmondak@illinois.edu.
Website: http://www.pol.illinois.edu

The University of Iowa, Graduate College, College of Liberal Arts and Sciences, Department of Political Science, Iowa City, IA 52242-1316. Offers PhD. *Degree requirements:* For doctorate, comprehensive exam, thesis/dissertation. *Entrance requirements:* For doctorate, GRE General Test, minimum GPA of 3.0. Additional exam requirements/recommendations for international students: Required—TOEFL (minimum score 600 paper-based; 100 iBT). Electronic applications accepted.

The University of Kansas, Graduate Studies, College of Liberal Arts and Sciences, Department of Political Science, Lawrence, KS 66045. Offers MA, PhD. Part-time programs available. *Faculty:* 20 full-time, 3 part-time/adjunct. *Students:* 41 full-time (14 women), 9 part-time (2 women); includes 7 minority (2 Black or African American, non-Hispanic/Latino; 1 American Indian or Alaska Native, non-Hispanic/Latino; 1 Hispanic/Latino; 3 Two or more races, non-Hispanic/Latino), 5 international. Average age 32. 53 applicants, 55% accepted, 8 enrolled. In 2014, 7 master's, 5 doctorates awarded. Terminal master's awarded for partial completion of doctoral program. *Degree requirements:* For master's, comprehensive exam, thesis or alternative; for doctorate, comprehensive exam, thesis/dissertation, research and responsible scholarship skills. *Entrance requirements:* For master's, GRE General Test, 3 letters of recommendation, curriculum vitae, transcripts, personal statement; for doctorate, GRE General Test, 3 letters of recommendation, transcripts, personal statement, curriculum vitae. Additional exam requirements/recommendations for international students: Required—TOEFL. *Application deadline:* For fall admission, 4/15 priority date for domestic and international students. Application fee: $55 ($65 for international students). Electronic applications accepted. *Financial support:* Fellowships with full tuition reimbursements, research assistantships, teaching assistantships with full tuition reimbursements, scholarships/grants, health care benefits, and unspecified assistantships available. Financial award application deadline: 1/7. *Faculty research:* Latino politics, gender politics, Middle East and North African politics, American politics/voting behavior, environmental policy. *Unit head:* Don Haider-Markel, Chair, 785-864-9034, E-mail: dhmarkel@ku.edu. *Application contact:* Linda Pickerel, Graduate Coordinator, 785-864-3523, E-mail: lpicke@ku.edu.
Website: https://kups.ku.edu/

University of Kentucky, Graduate School, College of Arts and Sciences, Program in Political Science, Lexington, KY 40506-0032. Offers MA, PhD. *Degree requirements:* For master's, comprehensive exam, thesis optional; for doctorate, comprehensive exam, thesis/dissertation. *Entrance requirements:* For master's, GRE General Test, minimum undergraduate GPA of 2.75; for doctorate, GRE General Test, minimum graduate GPA of 3.0. Additional exam requirements/recommendations for international students: Required—TOEFL (minimum score 550 paper-based). Electronic applications accepted. *Faculty research:* International political economy, critical policy studies, regional conflict and integration, race and American politics, media studies.

University of Lethbridge, School of Graduate Studies, Lethbridge, AB T1K 3M4, Canada. Offers addictions counseling (M Sc); agricultural biotechnology (M Sc); agricultural studies (M Sc, MA); anthropology (MA); archaeology (M Sc, MA); art (MA, MFA); biochemistry (M Sc); biological sciences (M Sc); biomolecular science (PhD); biosystems and biodiversity (PhD); Canadian studies (MA); chemistry (M Sc); computer science (M Sc); computer science and geographical information science (M Sc); counseling (MC); counseling psychology (M Ed); dramatic arts (MA); earth, space, and physical science (PhD); economics (MA); education (MA); educational leadership (M Ed); English (MA); environmental science (M Sc); evolution and behavior (PhD);

exercise science (M Sc); French (MA); French/German (MA); French/Spanish (MA); general education (M Ed); geography (M Sc, MA); German (MA); health sciences (M Sc); individualized multidisciplinary (M Sc, MA); kinesiology (M Sc, MA); management (M Sc), including accounting, finance, general management, human resource management and labor relations, information systems, international management, marketing, policy and strategy; mathematics (M Sc); modern languages (MA); music (M Mus, MA); Native American studies (MA); neuroscience (M Sc, PhD); new media (MA, MFA); nursing (M Sc, MN); philosophy (MA); physics (M Sc); political science (MA); psychology (M Sc, MA); religious studies (MA); sociology (MA); theatre and dramatic arts (MFA); theoretical and computational science (PhD); urban and regional studies (MA); women and gender studies (MA). Part-time and evening/weekend programs available. *Faculty:* 358. *Students:* 445 full-time (243 women), 116 part-time (72 women). Average age 31. 351 applicants, 26% accepted, 87 enrolled. In 2014, 129 master's, 13 doctorates awarded. *Degree requirements:* For master's, thesis (for some programs); for doctorate, comprehensive exam, thesis/dissertation. *Entrance requirements:* For master's, GMAT (for M Sc in management), bachelor's degree in related field, minimum GPA of 3.0 during previous 20 graded semester courses, 2 years' teaching or related experience (M Ed); for doctorate, master's degree, minimum graduate GPA of 3.5. Additional exam requirements/recommendations for international students: Required—TOEFL. Application fee: $100 Canadian dollars. *Financial support:* Fellowships, research assistantships, teaching assistantships, scholarships/grants, health care benefits, and unspecified assistantships available. *Faculty research:* Movement and brain plasticity, gibberellin physiology, photosynthesis, carbon cycling, molecular properties of main-group ring components. *Application contact:* School of Graduate Studies, 403-329-5194, E-mail: sgsinquiries@uleth.ca.
Website: http://www.uleth.ca/graduatestudies/

University of Louisville, Graduate School, College of Arts and Sciences, Department of Political Science, Louisville, KY 40292-0001. Offers MA. Part-time and evening/weekend programs available. *Students:* 14 full-time (3 women), 2 part-time (1 woman); includes 2 minority (1 Hispanic/Latino; 1 Two or more races, non-Hispanic/Latino), 2 international. Average age 28. 9 applicants, 67% accepted, 4 enrolled. In 2014, 8 master's awarded. *Degree requirements:* For master's, thesis or directed research paper. *Entrance requirements:* For master's, GRE General Test, 2 academic letters of recommendation. Additional exam requirements/recommendations for international students: Required—TOEFL (minimum score 550 paper-based; 79 iBT). *Application deadline:* For fall admission, 8/1 for domestic students, 5/1 priority date for international students; for winter admission, 8/1 for domestic students; for spring admission, 12/1 for domestic students, 11/1 priority date for international students; for summer admission, 4/1 priority date for international students. Applications are processed on a rolling basis. Application fee: $60. Electronic applications accepted. *Expenses:* Tuition, state resident: full-time $11,326; part-time $630 per credit hour. Tuition, nonresident: full-time $23,568; part-time $1311 per credit hour. *Required fees:* $196. Tuition and fees vary according to program and reciprocity agreements. *Financial support:* Research assistantships available. Financial award application deadline: 6/1. *Faculty research:* International law, politics of east Asia, comparative political systems, environmental policy, international relations. *Unit head:* Dr. Rodger A. Payne, Chair, 502-852-3316, E-mail: r.payne@louisvile.edu. *Application contact:* Libby Leggett, Director, Graduate Admissions, 502-852-3101, Fax: 502-852-6536, E-mail: gradadm@louisville.edu.
Website: http://louisville.edu/politicalscience

The University of Manchester, School of Social Sciences, Manchester, United Kingdom. Offers ethnographic documentary (M Phil); interdisciplinary study of culture (PhD); philosophy (PhD); politics (PhD); social anthropology (PhD); social anthropology with visual media (PhD); social change (PhD); social statistics (PhD); sociology (PhD); visual anthropology (M Phil).

University of Manitoba, Faculty of Graduate Studies, Faculty of Arts, Department of Political Studies, Winnipeg, MB R3T 2N2, Canada. Offers political studies (MA); public administration (MPA). *Degree requirements:* For master's, one foreign language, thesis or alternative.

University of Maryland, College Park, Academic Affairs, College of Behavioral and Social Sciences, Department of Government and Politics, College Park, MD 20742. Offers American politics (PhD); comparative politics (PhD); international relations (PhD); political economy (PhD); political theory (PhD). Part-time and evening/weekend programs available. *Degree requirements:* For doctorate, comprehensive exam, thesis/dissertation, written exams in 2 fields. *Entrance requirements:* For doctorate, GRE General Test, minimum GPA of 3.5, writing sample. Additional exam requirements/recommendations for international students: Required—TOEFL. Electronic applications accepted. *Faculty research:* International development/conflict, international security, post-communist society, public service, dynamics of conflict and conflict resolution.

University of Massachusetts Amherst, Graduate School, College of Social and Behavioral Sciences, Department of Political Science, Amherst, MA 01003. Offers MA, PhD. Part-time programs available. *Faculty:* 55 full-time (24 women). *Students:* 53 full-time (27 women), 11 part-time (1 woman); includes 8 minority (3 Black or African American, non-Hispanic/Latino; 1 Asian, non-Hispanic/Latino; 4 Hispanic/Latino), 16 international. Average age 31. 95 applicants, 20% accepted, 10 enrolled. In 2014, 5 master's, 5 doctorates awarded. Terminal master's awarded for partial completion of doctoral program. *Degree requirements:* For master's, one foreign language, thesis or alternative; for doctorate, one foreign language, comprehensive exam, thesis/dissertation. *Entrance requirements:* For master's and doctorate, GRE General Test, writing sample, 3 letters of recommendation. Additional exam requirements/recommendations for international students: Required—TOEFL (minimum score 550 paper-based; 80 iBT), IELTS (minimum score 6.5). *Application deadline:* For fall admission, 1/15 for domestic and international students. Applications are processed on a rolling basis. Application fee: $75. Electronic applications accepted. *Expenses:* Tuition, state resident: full-time $1980; part-time $110 per credit. Tuition, nonresident: full-time $14,644; part-time $414 per credit. *Required fees:* $11,417. One-time fee: $357. *Financial support:* Fellowships with full and partial tuition reimbursements, research assistantships with full and partial tuition reimbursements, teaching assistantships with full and partial tuition reimbursements, career-related internships or fieldwork, Federal Work-Study, scholarships/grants, traineeships, health care benefits, tuition waivers (full and partial), and unspecified assistantships available. Support available to part-time students. Financial award application deadline: 1/15; financial award applicants required to submit FAFSA. *Unit head:* Dr. Tatishe Nteta, Graduate Program Director, 413-545-0410, Fax: 413-545-3349. *Application contact:* Lindsay DeSantis, Supervisor of Admissions, 413-545-0722, Fax: 413-577-0010, E-mail: gradadm@grad.umass.edu.
Website: http://www.umass.edu/polsci/

University of Memphis, Graduate School, College of Arts and Sciences, Department of Political Science, Memphis, TN 38152. Offers MA. *Faculty:* 6 full-time (3 women). *Students:* 11 full-time (4 women), 2 part-time (both women); includes 1 minority (Black or African American, non-Hispanic/Latino). Average age 28. 14 applicants, 86% accepted, 3 enrolled. In 2014, 4 master's awarded. *Degree requirements:* For master's, comprehensive exam, thesis or alternative, internship. *Entrance requirements:* For master's, GRE General Test or GMAT, minimum GPA of 3.0. *Application deadline:* For fall admission, 8/1 for domestic students; for spring admission, 12/1 for domestic students. Applications are processed on a rolling basis. Application fee: $35 ($60 for international students). *Financial support:* In 2014–15, 10 students received support. Research assistantships with full tuition reimbursements available, Federal Work-Study, scholarships/grants, and unspecified assistantships available. Financial award application deadline: 2/15; financial award applicants required to submit FAFSA. *Faculty research:* Political philosophy, comparative judicial studies, conflict studies, legislative studies, foreign policy. *Unit head:* Dr. Robert Blanton, Interim Chair, 901-678-2395, Fax: 901-678-2983, E-mail: rblanton@memphis.edu. *Application contact:* Dr. David Richards, Graduate Studies Coordinator, 901-678-3348, Fax: 901-678-2983, E-mail: drich1@memphis.edu.
Website: http://www.memphis.edu/polisci/

University of Miami, Graduate School, College of Arts and Sciences, Department of Political Science, Coral Gables, FL 33124. Offers MPA, MPA/JD, MPA/MPH. Part-time and evening/weekend programs available. *Degree requirements:* For master's, thesis optional. *Entrance requirements:* For master's, GRE General Test. Additional exam requirements/recommendations for international students: Required—TOEFL (minimum score 550 paper-based; 80 iBT). Electronic applications accepted. *Faculty research:* Financial management, non-profit management, human resource management, public service ethics, information technology management.

University of Michigan, Horace H. Rackham School of Graduate Studies, College of Literature, Science, and the Arts, Department of Political Science, Ann Arbor, MI 48109. Offers political science (PhD); political science and public policy (PhD); social work and political science (PhD). *Faculty:* 47 full-time (17 women), 10 part-time/adjunct (4 women). *Students:* 126 full-time (63 women); includes 26 minority (9 Black or African American, non-Hispanic/Latino; 7 Asian, non-Hispanic/Latino; 7 Hispanic/Latino; 3 Two or more races, non-Hispanic/Latino), 28 international. 322 applicants, 13% accepted, 18 enrolled. In 2014, 17 doctorates awarded. Terminal master's awarded for partial completion of doctoral program. *Degree requirements:* For doctorate, comprehensive exam, thesis/dissertation, oral defense of dissertation, preliminary exam. *Entrance requirements:* For doctorate, GRE General Test. Additional exam requirements/recommendations for international students: Required—TOEFL. *Application deadline:* For fall admission, 12/15 for domestic and international students. Application fee: $75 ($90 for international students). Electronic applications accepted. *Financial support:* In 2014–15, 23 fellowships with full tuition reimbursements (averaging $18,600 per year), 5 research assistantships with full tuition reimbursements (averaging $18,600 per year), 35 teaching assistantships with full tuition reimbursements (averaging $18,600 per year) were awarded; health care benefits, tuition waivers, and unspecified assistantships also available. Financial award application deadline: 12/15. *Faculty research:* Political theory, American politics, world politics, comparative politics, methodology, public law. *Unit head:* Nancy Burns, Chair, 734-764-6313, Fax: 734-764-3522. *Application contact:* Kathryn Cardenas, Graduate Program Coordinator, 734-764-6313, Fax: 734-764-3522, E-mail: kmcard@umich.edu.
Website: http://www.lsa.umich.edu/polisci

University of Michigan, School of Social Work, Interdisciplinary Program in Social Work and Social Science, Ann Arbor, MI 48109-1106. Offers social work and anthropology (PhD); social work and economics (PhD); social work and political science (PhD); social work and psychology (PhD); social work and sociology (PhD). Programs offered through the Horace H. Rackham School of Graduate Studies. *Faculty:* 57 full-time (33 women), 6 part-time/adjunct (4 women). *Students:* 64 full-time (46 women); includes 24 minority (7 Black or African American, non-Hispanic/Latino; 11 Asian, non-Hispanic/Latino; 6 Hispanic/Latino), 6 international. Average age 32. 108 applicants, 9% accepted, 9 enrolled. In 2014, 11 doctorates awarded. *Degree requirements:* For doctorate, thesis/dissertation, oral defense of dissertation, preliminary exam. *Entrance requirements:* For doctorate, GRE General Test. Additional exam requirements/recommendations for international students: Required—TOEFL. *Application deadline:* For fall admission, 12/1 for domestic and international students. Application fee: $75 ($90 for international students). *Financial support:* In 2014–15, 64 students received support, including 20 fellowships with full tuition reimbursements available (averaging $15,200 per year), 7 research assistantships with full tuition reimbursements available (averaging $18,971 per year), 19 teaching assistantships with full tuition reimbursements available (averaging $18,971 per year); career-related internships or fieldwork, Federal Work-Study, scholarships/grants, traineeships, health care benefits, tuition waivers (full and partial), and unspecified assistantships also available. Financial award application deadline: 12/1; financial award applicants required to submit FAFSA. *Faculty research:* Substance abuse, child welfare, mental health, poverty, aging. *Total annual research expenditures:* $4.1 million. *Unit head:* Dr. Berit Ingersoll-Dayton, Director, 734-763-5768, Fax: 734-615-3192, E-mail: bid@umich.edu. *Application contact:* Graduate Coordinator, 734-647-2554, Fax: 734-615-3192, E-mail: ssw.phd.info@umich.edu.
Website: http://www.ssw.umich.edu/doctoral

University of Michigan–Flint, College of Arts and Sciences, Program in Social Sciences, Flint, MI 48502-1950. Offers gender studies (MA); global studies (MA); U.S. history and politics (MA). Part-time programs available. *Faculty:* 14 full-time (8 women), 5 part-time/adjunct (3 women). *Students:* 1 (woman) full-time, 20 part-time (13 women); includes 8 minority (6 Black or African American, non-Hispanic/Latino; 1 Hispanic/Latino; 1 Two or more races, non-Hispanic/Latino). Average age 41. 8 applicants, 75% accepted, 3 enrolled. In 2014, 7 master's awarded. *Entrance requirements:* For master's, bachelor's degree from accredited institution, minimum overall GPA of 3.0. Additional exam requirements/recommendations for international students: Required—TOEFL (minimum score 84 iBT), IELTS (minimum score 6.5). *Application deadline:* For fall admission, 8/1 for domestic students, 5/1 for international students; for winter admission, 11/15 for domestic students, 9/1 for international students; for spring admission, 3/15 for domestic students, 1/1 for international students; for summer admission, 5/15 for domestic students. Applications are processed on a rolling basis. Application fee: $55. Electronic applications accepted. *Expenses:* Expenses: Contact institution. *Financial support:* Federal Work-Study, scholarships/grants, and unspecified assistantships available. Support available to part-time students. Financial award application deadline: 3/1; financial award applicants required to submit FAFSA. *Unit head:* Dr. Adam Lutzker, Interim Director, 810-762-3280, Fax: 810-762-3281, E-mail: alutzker@umflint.edu. *Application contact:* Bradley T. Maki, Director of Graduate Admissions, 810-762-3171, Fax: 810-766-6789, E-mail: bmaki@umflint.edu.
Website: http://www.umflint.edu/graduateprograms/social-sciences-ma

University of Minnesota, Twin Cities Campus, Graduate School, College of Liberal Arts, Department of Political Science, Minneapolis, MN 55455. Offers PhD. *Degree requirements:* For doctorate, thesis/dissertation, 1 foreign language or statistics. *Entrance requirements:* For doctorate, GRE. Additional exam requirements/recommendations for international students: Required—TOEFL; Recommended—IELTS. Electronic applications accepted. *Faculty research:* American politics, comparative politics, international relations, political theory, research methodology.

University of Mississippi, Graduate School, College of Liberal Arts, Department of Political Science, University, MS 38677. Offers MA, PhD. *Degree requirements:* For doctorate, thesis/dissertation. *Entrance requirements:* For master's, GRE General Test,

minimum GPA of 3.0; for doctorate, GRE General Test. Additional exam requirements/recommendations for international students: Required—TOEFL. Electronic applications accepted.

University of Missouri, Office of Research and Graduate Studies, College of Arts and Science, Department of Political Science, Columbia, MO 65211. Offers MA, PhD. *Faculty:* 20 full-time (4 women), 1 part-time/adjunct (0 women). *Students:* 63 full-time (25 women), 2 part-time (1 woman); includes 9 minority (2 Black or African American, non-Hispanic/Latino; 1 American Indian or Alaska Native, non-Hispanic/Latino; 2 Asian, non-Hispanic/Latino; 3 Hispanic/Latino; 1 Two or more races, non-Hispanic/Latino), 20 international. Average age 28. 44 applicants, 45% accepted, 13 enrolled. In 2014, 11 master's, 9 doctorates awarded. Terminal master's awarded for partial completion of doctoral program. *Degree requirements:* For doctorate, one foreign language, comprehensive exam, thesis/dissertation. *Entrance requirements:* For master's, GRE General Test (minimum combined score 1000 Verbal and Quantitative), minimum GPA of 3.0 in last 60 hours and in political science courses; at least 12 hours of upper-level course work in political science; for doctorate, GRE General Test (minimum combined score 1200 Verbal and Quantitative), minimum GPA of 3.0 in last 60 hours and in political science courses; at least 12 hours of upper-level course work in political science. Additional exam requirements/recommendations for international students: Required—TOEFL (minimum score 570 paper-based; 88 iBT). *Application deadline:* For fall admission, 2/1 priority date for domestic and international students; for winter admission, 10/1 for domestic and international students. Applications are processed on a rolling basis. Application fee: $55 ($75 for international students). Electronic applications accepted. *Financial support:* Fellowships with full and partial tuition reimbursements, research assistantships with full and partial tuition reimbursements, teaching assistantships with full tuition reimbursements, institutionally sponsored loans, health care benefits, and unspecified assistantships available. *Faculty research:* American politics, comparative politics, international relations, public policy and administration. *Unit head:* Dr. Cooper Drury, Department Chair, 573-884-6747, E-mail: drurya@missouri.edu. *Application contact:* Audra Jenkins, Graduate Studies Assistant, 573-882-2062, E-mail: jenkinsau@missouri.edu.
Website: http://politicalscience.missouri.edu/grad/index.shtml

University of Missouri–Kansas City, College of Arts and Sciences, Department of Political Science, Kansas City, MO 64110-2499. Offers MA. PhD (interdisciplinary) offered through the School of Graduate Studies. Part-time and evening/weekend programs available. *Faculty:* 7 full-time (4 women), 3 part-time/adjunct (0 women). *Students:* 1 (woman) full-time, 2 part-time (0 women). Average age 25. 10 applicants, 20% accepted, 1 enrolled. In 2014, 9 master's awarded. Terminal master's awarded for partial completion of doctoral program. *Degree requirements:* For master's, thesis optional. *Entrance requirements:* For master's, GRE, minimum GPA of 3.0, course work in political science, 2 letters of recommendation. Additional exam requirements/recommendations for international students: Required—TOEFL (minimum score 550 paper-based; 80 iBT). *Application deadline:* For fall admission, 4/1 priority date for domestic and international students; for spring admission, 11/1 priority date for domestic and international students. Applications are processed on a rolling basis. Application fee: $45 ($50 for international students). Electronic applications accepted. *Financial support:* In 2014–15, 1 teaching assistantship (averaging $11,200 per year) was awarded; career-related internships or fieldwork and institutionally sponsored loans also available. Financial award application deadline: 3/1; financial award applicants required to submit FAFSA. *Faculty research:* Sex and gender, Chinese politics, voting behavior, politics of Presidency and social security, public law. *Unit head:* Dr. Mona Lyne, Chair, 816-235-1383, Fax: 816-235-5594, E-mail: lynem@umkc.edu. *Application contact:* Tamera Byland, Director of Admissions, 816-235-1111, Fax: 816-235-5544, E-mail: admit@umkc.edu.
Website: http://cas.umkc.edu/polisci/

University of Missouri–St. Louis, College of Arts and Sciences, Department of Political Science, St. Louis, MO 63121. Offers American politics (MA); comparative politics (MA); international politics (MA); political process and behavior (MA); political science (PhD); public administration and public policy (MA); urban and regional politics (MA). Part-time and evening/weekend programs available. *Faculty:* 17 full-time (4 women), 6 part-time/adjunct (2 women). *Students:* 22 full-time (7 women), 35 part-time (20 women); includes 6 minority (5 Black or African American, non-Hispanic/Latino; 1 American Indian or Alaska Native, non-Hispanic/Latino), 5 international. Average age 35. 27 applicants, 63% accepted, 12 enrolled. In 2014, 6 master's, 3 doctorates awarded. Terminal master's awarded for partial completion of doctoral program. *Degree requirements:* For master's, thesis optional; for doctorate, thesis/dissertation. *Entrance requirements:* For master's, GRE General Test, 2 letters of recommendation; for doctorate, GRE General Test, 3 letters of recommendation. Additional exam requirements/recommendations for international students: Required—TOEFL (minimum score 550 paper-based; 79 iBT), IELTS (minimum score 6.5). *Application deadline:* For fall admission, 2/15 priority date for domestic and international students; for spring admission, 10/15 priority date for domestic and international students. Applications are processed on a rolling basis. Application fee: $50 ($40 for international students). Electronic applications accepted. *Expenses:* Tuition, state resident: full-time $7364; part-time $409.10 per hour. Tuition, nonresident: full-time $18,153; part-time $1008.50 per hour. *Financial support:* In 2014–15, 3 research assistantships with full and partial tuition reimbursements (averaging $10,800 per year), 10 teaching assistantships with full and partial tuition reimbursements (averaging $10,800 per year) were awarded; fellowships and career-related internships or fieldwork also available. Support available to part-time students. Financial award application deadline: 3/15; financial award applicants required to submit FAFSA. *Faculty research:* Public policy, urban politics and administration, American government. *Unit head:* Dr. David Kimball, Director of Graduate Studies, 314-516-5521, Fax: 314-516-5268, E-mail: umslpolisci@umsl.edu. *Application contact:* 314-516-5458, Fax: 314-516-6996, E-mail: gradadm@umsl.edu.
Website: http://www.umsl.edu/~polisci/

The University of Montana, Graduate School, College of Humanities and Sciences, Department of Political Science, Program in Political Science, Missoula, MT 59812-0002. Offers MA. *Degree requirements:* For master's, thesis. *Entrance requirements:* For master's, GRE General Test.

University of Nebraska at Omaha, Graduate Studies, College of Arts and Sciences, Department of Political Science, Omaha, NE 68182. Offers MS, Certificate. Part-time and evening/weekend programs available. Postbaccalaureate distance learning degree programs offered (no on-campus study). *Faculty:* 10 full-time (4 women). *Students:* 22 full-time (6 women), 70 part-time (32 women); includes 15 minority (6 Black or African American, non-Hispanic/Latino; 2 Asian, non-Hispanic/Latino; 7 Hispanic/Latino), 5 international. Average age 32. 53 applicants, 70% accepted, 26 enrolled. In 2014, 11 master's, 1 other advanced degree awarded. *Degree requirements:* For master's, comprehensive exam, thesis (for some programs). *Entrance requirements:* For master's, 15 undergraduate political science hours, minimum undergraduate GPA of 3.0, 2 letters of recommendation, official transcripts. Additional exam requirements/recommendations for international students: Required—TOEFL, IELTS, PTE. *Application deadline:* For fall admission, 7/15 priority date for domestic and international students; for spring admission, 11/15 priority date for domestic and international students; for summer

admission, 4/15 for domestic and international students. Applications are processed on a rolling basis. Application fee: $45. Electronic applications accepted. *Financial support:* In 2014–15, 2 students received support, including 2 teaching assistantships with tuition reimbursements available; fellowships, research assistantships with tuition reimbursements available, Federal Work-Study, scholarships/grants, tuition waivers (partial), and unspecified assistantships also available. Financial award application deadline: 3/1; financial award applicants required to submit FAFSA. *Unit head:* Dr. Randall Adkins, Chairperson, 402-554-2341, E-mail: graduate@unomaha.edu. *Application contact:* Dr. Gregory Petrow, Graduate Program Chair, 402-554-2341, E-mail: graduate@unomaha.edu.

University of Nebraska–Lincoln, Graduate College, College of Arts and Sciences, Department of Political Science, Lincoln, NE 68588. Offers political science (MA, PhD); public policy analysis (Graduate Certificate). *Degree requirements:* For master's, thesis optional; for doctorate, variable foreign language requirement, comprehensive exam, thesis/dissertation. *Entrance requirements:* For master's and doctorate, GRE General Test, writing sample. Additional exam requirements/recommendations for international students: Required—TOEFL (minimum score 600 paper-based). Electronic applications accepted. *Faculty research:* Public policy; comparative politics; international relations; political theory, behavior, and methodology; American politics.

University of Nevada, Las Vegas, Graduate College, College of Liberal Arts, Department of Political Science, Las Vegas, NV 89154-5029. Offers MA, PhD. Part-time programs available. *Faculty:* 11 full-time (3 women). *Students:* 14 full-time (3 women), 28 part-time (10 women); includes 11 minority (1 Black or African American, non-Hispanic/Latino; 2 Asian, non-Hispanic/Latino; 5 Hispanic/Latino; 3 Two or more races, non-Hispanic/Latino), 4 international. Average age 34. 23 applicants, 100% accepted, 15 enrolled. In 2014, 2 master's, 1 doctorate awarded. *Degree requirements:* For master's, comprehensive exam (for some programs), thesis (for some programs); for doctorate, comprehensive exam, thesis/dissertation, oral examination. *Entrance requirements:* For master's and doctorate, GRE General Test. Additional exam requirements/recommendations for international students: Required—TOEFL (minimum score 550 paper-based; 80 iBT), IELTS (minimum score 7). *Application deadline:* For fall admission, 2/1 for domestic students, 5/1 for international students; for spring admission, 10/1 for international students. Application fee: $60 ($95 for international students). Electronic applications accepted. *Financial support:* In 2014–15, 11 students received support, including 4 research assistantships with partial tuition reimbursements available (averaging $13,222 per year), 7 teaching assistantships with partial tuition reimbursements available (averaging $13,516 per year); institutionally sponsored loans, scholarships/grants, health care benefits, and unspecified assistantships also available. Financial award application deadline: 3/1. *Faculty research:* International political economy, religion and politics, democratization, international security and political violence, ancient political philosophy. *Unit head:* Dr. John Tuman, Chair/Associate Professor, 702-895-5258, Fax: 702-895-1065, E-mail: john.tuman@unlv.edu. *Application contact:* Graduate College Admissions Evaluator, 702-895-3320, Fax: 702-895-4180, E-mail: gradcollege@unlv.edu.
Website: http://liberalarts.unlv.edu/Political_Science/

University of Nevada, Reno, Graduate School, College of Liberal Arts, Department of Political Science, Program in Political Science, Reno, NV 89557. Offers MA, PhD. Terminal master's awarded for partial completion of doctoral program. *Degree requirements:* For master's, comprehensive exam, oral exam/thesis or professional paper; for doctorate, thesis/dissertation, 2 field exams, oral exam. *Entrance requirements:* For master's, GRE General Test, GMAT, LSAT, minimum GPA of 2.75; for doctorate, GRE General Test, GMAT, LSAT, minimum GPA of 3.0. Additional exam requirements/recommendations for international students: Required—TOEFL (minimum score 500 paper-based; 61 iBT), IELTS (minimum score 6). Electronic applications accepted. *Faculty research:* Analysis of political processes, institutions, and policies.

University of New Brunswick Fredericton, School of Graduate Studies, Faculty of Arts, Department of Political Science, Fredericton, NB E3B 5A3, Canada. Offers MA. Part-time programs available. *Faculty:* 7 full-time (2 women). *Students:* 9 full-time (5 women). In 2014, 1 master's awarded. *Degree requirements:* For master's, thesis (for some programs). *Entrance requirements:* For master's, minimum cumulative GPA of 3.3, 4-year bachelor's degree, or equivalent, in political science. Additional exam requirements/recommendations for international students: Required—TOEFL. *Application deadline:* For fall admission, 3/1 for domestic students; for winter admission, 1/15 priority date for domestic and international students. Applications are processed on a rolling basis. Application fee: $50 Canadian dollars. Electronic applications accepted. *Financial support:* Fellowships, research assistantships, and teaching assistantships available. *Faculty research:* Political theory, public policy, gender and politics, global political economy and Canadian politics. *Unit head:* Dr. Donald Wright, Director of Graduate Studies, 506-458-7494, Fax: 506-453-4755, E-mail: wrightd@unb.ca. *Application contact:* Zabrina Hamilton, Graduate Secretary, 506-453-4826, Fax: 506-453-4755, E-mail: zhamilto@unb.ca.
Website: http://go.unb.ca/gradprograms

University of New Hampshire, Graduate School, College of Liberal Arts, Department of Political Science, Program in Political Science, Durham, NH 03824. Offers political science (MA); sustainability (Postbaccalaureate Certificate). Part-time programs available. *Students:* 7 full-time (4 women), 9 part-time (4 women); includes 1 minority (Black or African American, non-Hispanic/Latino), 1 international. Average age 28. 14 applicants, 71% accepted, 4 enrolled. In 2014, 9 master's, 1 other advanced degree awarded. *Degree requirements:* For master's, thesis. *Entrance requirements:* For master's, GRE General Test. Additional exam requirements/recommendations for international students: Required—TOEFL (minimum score 550 paper-based; 80 iBT). *Application deadline:* For fall admission, 6/1 priority date for domestic students, 4/1 for international students; for spring admission, 12/1 for domestic students. Applications are processed on a rolling basis. Application fee: $65. Electronic applications accepted. *Expenses:* Tuition, state resident: full-time $13,500; part-time $750 per credit hour. Tuition, nonresident: full-time $26,460; part-time $1110 per credit hour. *Required fees:* $1788; $447 per semester. *Financial support:* In 2014–15, 5 students received support, including 4 teaching assistantships; fellowships, research assistantships, career-related internships or fieldwork, Federal Work-Study, scholarships/grants, and tuition waivers (full and partial) also available. Support available to part-time students. Financial award application deadline: 2/15. *Unit head:* Stacy VanDeever, Chairperson, 603-862-0167. *Application contact:* Tama Andrews, Administrative Assistant, 603-862-2321, E-mail: mpa.ma.political.science.grad@unh.edu.
Website: http://cola.unh.edu/political-science

University of New Mexico, Graduate School, College of Arts and Sciences, Program in Political Science, Albuquerque, NM 87131-2039. Offers MA, PhD. Part-time programs available. *Faculty:* 8 full-time (4 women). *Students:* 34 full-time (18 women), 3 part-time (2 women); includes 17 minority (1 Black or African American, non-Hispanic/Latino; 1 Asian, non-Hispanic/Latino; 15 Hispanic/Latino), 2 international. Average age 32. 38 applicants, 53% accepted, 14 enrolled. In 2014, 7 master's, 2 doctorates awarded. Terminal master's awarded for partial completion of doctoral program. *Degree requirements:* For master's, comprehensive exam, thesis optional; for doctorate, comprehensive exam, thesis/dissertation, field research paper, minimum cumulative

Political Science

GPA of 3.5. *Entrance requirements:* For master's and doctorate, GRE General Test, 3 letters of recommendation, writing sample, letter of intent. Additional exam requirements/recommendations for international students: Required—TOEFL. *Application deadline:* For fall admission, 1/15 priority date for domestic and international students. Application fee: $50. Electronic applications accepted. *Financial support:* In 2014–15, 31 students received support, including 7 fellowships with full tuition reimbursements available (averaging $19,000 per year), 1 research assistantship with full tuition reimbursement available (averaging $14,828 per year), 28 teaching assistantships with full tuition reimbursements available (averaging $14,828 per year); scholarships/grants, health care benefits, and unspecified assistantships also available. Financial award application deadline: 1/15; financial award applicants required to submit FAFSA. *Faculty research:* Latin American politics, American politics, comparative politics, public policy, international relations, methodology. *Total annual research expenditures:* $140,000. *Unit head:* Dr. William Stanley, Chair, 505-277-5104, Fax: 505-277-2821, E-mail: wstanley@unm.edu. *Application contact:* Shoshana Handel, Graduate Program Assistant, 505-277-5104, Fax: 505-277-2821, E-mail: shandel@unm.edu.
Website: http://polisci.unm.edu/index.html

University of New Orleans, Graduate School, College of Liberal Arts, Department of Political Science, New Orleans, LA 70148. Offers political science (MA, PhD); public administration (MPA). Evening/weekend programs available. *Degree requirements:* For master's, one foreign language, thesis or alternative; for doctorate, one foreign language, thesis/dissertation. *Entrance requirements:* For master's, GRE General Test; for doctorate, GRE General Test, GRE Subject Test. Additional exam requirements/recommendations for international students: Required—TOEFL (minimum score 550 paper-based; 79 iBT), IELTS (minimum score 6.5). Electronic applications accepted. *Faculty research:* Judicial politics, public policy, voting rights, Southern politics, presidential-congressional relations.

The University of North Carolina at Chapel Hill, Graduate School, College of Arts and Sciences, Department of Political Science, Chapel Hill, NC 27599. Offers Latin American studies (Certificate); political science (MA, PhD); trans-Atlantic studies (MA). *Degree requirements:* For master's, comprehensive exam; for doctorate, one foreign language, comprehensive exam, thesis/dissertation. *Entrance requirements:* For master's and doctorate, GRE General Test, minimum GPA of 3.0 recommended. Electronic applications accepted.

The University of North Carolina at Charlotte, College of Liberal Arts and Sciences, Department of Sociology, Charlotte, NC 28223-0001. Offers health research (MA); mathematical sociology and quantitative methods (MA); organizations, occupations, and work (MA); political sociology (MA); race and gender (MA); social psychology (MA); social theory (MA); sociology of education (MA); stratification (MA). Part-time and evening/weekend programs available. *Faculty:* 16 full-time (10 women). *Students:* 11 full-time (5 women), 2 part-time (0 women); includes 5 minority (4 Black or African American, non-Hispanic/Latino; 1 Hispanic/Latino), 1 international. Average age 29. 14 applicants, 71% accepted, 5 enrolled. In 2014, 6 master's awarded. *Degree requirements:* For master's, thesis or comprehensive exam. *Entrance requirements:* For master's, GRE or MAT, minimum GPA of 3.0 in last 2 years, 2.75 overall. Additional exam requirements/recommendations for international students: Required—TOEFL (minimum score 557 paper-based; 83 iBT). *Application deadline:* For fall admission, 4/15 for domestic and international students; for spring admission, 10/1 for domestic and international students. Application fee: $75. Electronic applications accepted. *Expenses:* Tuition, state resident: full-time $4008. Tuition, nonresident: full-time $16,295. *Required fees:* $2755. Tuition and fees vary according to course load and program. *Financial support:* In 2014–15, 10 students received support, including 5 research assistantships (averaging $10,400 per year), 5 teaching assistantships (averaging $9,200 per year); career-related internships or fieldwork, institutionally sponsored loans, scholarships/grants, and unspecified assistantships also available. Support available to part-time students. Financial award application deadline: 4/1; financial award applicants required to submit FAFSA. *Faculty research:* Impact of race on high school course selection; income inequality within the United States and cross-nationally; small group interaction, nonverbal behaviors, identity, emotions, gender, and expectations; mathematical models of social processes. *Total annual research expenditures:* $413,099. *Unit head:* Dr. Lisa Walker, Chair, 704-687-7825, Fax: 704-687-3091, E-mail: lisa.walker@uncc.edu. *Application contact:* Kathy B. Giddings, Director of Graduate Admissions, 704-687-5503, Fax: 704-687-1668, E-mail: gradadm@uncc.edu.
Website: http://sociology.uncc.edu/

The University of North Carolina at Greensboro, Graduate School, College of Arts and Sciences, Department of Political Science, Greensboro, NC 27412-5001. Offers nonprofit management (Certificate); public affairs (MPA); urban and economic development (Certificate). *Accreditation:* NASPAA. *Degree requirements:* For master's, comprehensive exam. *Entrance requirements:* For master's, GRE General Test. Additional exam requirements/recommendations for international students: Required—TOEFL. Electronic applications accepted. *Faculty research:* U.S. Constitution, Canadian parliament, public management, ethical challenge of public service.

University of Northern British Columbia, Office of Graduate Studies, Prince George, BC V2N 4Z9, Canada. Offers business administration (Diploma); community health science (M Sc); disability management (MA); education (M Ed); first nations studies (MA); gender studies (MA); history (MA); interdisciplinary studies (MA); international studies (MA); mathematical, computer and physical sciences (M Sc); natural resources and environmental studies (M Sc, MA, MNRES, PhD); political science (MA); psychology (M Sc, PhD); social work (MSW). Part-time and evening/weekend programs available. Postbaccalaureate distance learning degree programs offered (no on-campus study). *Degree requirements:* For master's, thesis; for doctorate, thesis/dissertation. *Entrance requirements:* For master's, GRE, minimum B average in undergraduate course work; for doctorate, candidacy exam, minimum A average in graduate course work.

University of North Texas, Robert B. Toulouse School of Graduate Studies, Denton, TX 76203-5459. Offers accounting (MS); applied anthropology (MA, MS); applied behavior analysis (Certificate); applied geography (MA); applied technology and performance improvement (M Ed, MS); art education (MA); art history (MA); art museum education (Certificate); arts leadership (Certificate); audiology (Au D); behavior analysis (MS); behavioral science (PhD); biochemistry and molecular biology (MS); biology (MA, MS); biomedical engineering (MS); business analysis (MS); chemistry (MS); clinical health psychology (PhD); communication studies (MA, MS); computer engineering (MS); computer science (MS); counseling (M Ed, MS), including clinical mental health counseling (MS), college and university counseling, elementary school counseling, secondary school counseling; creative writing (MA); criminal justice (MS); curriculum and instruction (M Ed); decision sciences (MBA); design (MA, MFA), including fashion design (MFA), innovation studies, interior design (MFA); early childhood studies (MS); economics (MS); educational leadership (M Ed, Ed D); educational psychology (MS, PhD), including family studies (MS), gifted and talented (MS), human development (MS), learning and cognition (MS), research, measurement and evaluation (MS); electrical engineering (MS); emergency management (MPA); engineering technology (MS); English (MA); English as a second language (MA); environmental science (MS); finance

(MBA, MS); financial management (MPA); French (MA); health services management (MBA); higher education (M Ed, Ed D); history (MA, MS); hospitality management (MS); human resources management (MPA); information science (MS); information systems (PhD); information technologies (MBA); interdisciplinary studies (MA, MS); international studies (MA); international sustainable tourism (MS); jazz studies (MM); journalism (MA, MJ, Graduate Certificate), including interactive and virtual digital communication (Graduate Certificate), narrative journalism (Graduate Certificate), public relations (Graduate Certificate); kinesiology (MS); linguistics (MA); local government management (MPA); logistics (PhD); logistics and supply chain management (MBA); long-term care, senior housing, and aging services (MA); management (PhD); marketing (MBA); mathematics (MA, MS); mechanical and energy engineering (MS, PhD); music (MA), including ethnomusicology, music theory, musicology, performance; music composition (PhD); music education (MM Ed, PhD); nonprofit management (MPA); operations and supply chain management (MBA); performance (MM, DMA); philosophy (MA); political science (MA); professional and technical communication (MA); radio, television and film (MA, MFA); rehabilitation counseling (Certificate); sociology (MA); Spanish (MA); special education (M Ed); speech-language pathology (MA); strategic management (MBA); studio art (MFA); teaching (M Ed); MBA/MS. Part-time and evening/weekend programs available. Postbaccalaureate distance learning degree programs offered. *Faculty:* 651 full-time (215 women), 233 part-time/adjunct (139 women). *Students:* 3,040 full-time (1,598 women), 3,401 part-time (2,097 women); includes 1,740 minority (533 Black or African American, non-Hispanic/Latino; 15 American Indian or Alaska Native, non-Hispanic/Latino; 286 Asian, non-Hispanic/Latino; 746 Hispanic/Latino; 3 Native Hawaiian or other Pacific Islander, non-Hispanic/Latino; 157 Two or more races, non-Hispanic/Latino), 1,145 international. Terminal master's awarded for partial completion of doctoral program. *Degree requirements:* For master's, variable foreign language requirement, comprehensive exam (for some programs), thesis (for some programs); for doctorate, variable foreign language requirement, comprehensive exam (for some programs), thesis/dissertation; for other advanced degree, variable foreign language requirement, comprehensive exam (for some programs). *Entrance requirements:* For master's and doctorate, GRE, GMAT. Additional exam requirements/recommendations for international students: Required—TOEFL (minimum score 550 paper-based; 79 iBT). *Application deadline:* For fall admission, 7/15 for domestic students, 3/15 for international students; for spring admission, 11/15 for domestic students, 9/15 for international students; for summer admission, 5/1 for domestic students. Applications are processed on a rolling basis. Application fee: $60. Electronic applications accepted. *Expenses:* Tuition, state resident: full-time $5450; part-time $3633 per year. Tuition, nonresident: full-time $11,966; part-time $7977 per year. *Required fees:* $1301; $398 per credit hour. $685 per semester. Tuition and fees vary according to program and reciprocity agreements. *Financial support:* Fellowships with partial tuition reimbursements, research assistantships with partial tuition reimbursements, teaching assistantships, career-related internships or fieldwork, Federal Work-Study, institutionally sponsored loans, scholarships/grants, health care benefits, and library assistantships available. Support available to part-time students. Financial award applicants required to submit FAFSA. *Unit head:* Mark Wardell, Dean, 940-565-2383, E-mail: mark.wardell@unt.edu. *Application contact:* Toulouse School of Graduate Studies, 940-565-2383, Fax: 940-565-2141, E-mail: gradsch@unt.edu.
Website: http://tsgs.unt.edu/

University of Notre Dame, Graduate School, College of Arts and Letters, Division of Social Science, Department of Political Science, Notre Dame, IN 46556. Offers PhD. *Degree requirements:* For doctorate, one foreign language, comprehensive exam, thesis/dissertation, candidacy exam. *Entrance requirements:* For doctorate, GRE General Test. Additional exam requirements/recommendations for international students: Required—TOEFL (minimum score 600 paper-based; 80 iBT). Electronic applications accepted. *Faculty research:* American government, comparative politics, international relations, political theory.

University of Oklahoma, College of Arts and Sciences, Department of Political Science, Program in Political Science, Norman, OK 73019. Offers MA, PhD. *Students:* 30 full-time (10 women), 10 part-time (4 women); includes 2 minority (1 Asian, non-Hispanic/Latino; 1 Hispanic/Latino), 5 international. Average age 31. 26 applicants, 46% accepted, 6 enrolled. In 2014, 7 master's, 4 doctorates awarded. Terminal master's awarded for partial completion of doctoral program. *Degree requirements:* For master's, comprehensive exam, thesis optional; for doctorate, comprehensive exam, thesis/dissertation. *Entrance requirements:* For master's and doctorate, GRE. Additional exam requirements/recommendations for international students: Required—TOEFL (minimum iBT score of 100) or IELTS. *Application deadline:* For fall admission, 2/1 for domestic and international students; for spring admission, 10/1 for domestic and international students. Application fee: $50 ($100 for international students). Electronic applications accepted. *Expenses:* Tuition, state resident: full-time $4394; part-time $183.10 per credit hour. Tuition, nonresident: full-time $16,970; part-time $707.10 per credit hour. *Required fees:* $2892; $109.95 per credit hour. $126.50 per semester. *Financial support:* In 2014–15, 32 students received support. Scholarships/grants, health care benefits, and unspecified assistantships available. Financial award application deadline: 6/1; financial award applicants required to submit FAFSA. *Faculty research:* American politics, comparative politics, international relations, public administration, public policy and political theory. *Unit head:* Prof. Tyler Johnson, Director of Graduate Programs, 405-325-1845, Fax: 405-325-0718, E-mail: pscgradprog@ou.edu. *Application contact:* Prof. Tyler Johnson, 405-325-1845, Fax: 405-325-0718, E-mail: pscgradprog@ou.edu.
Website: http://psc.ou.edu/graduate-programs

University of Oregon, Graduate School, College of Arts and Sciences, Department of Political Science, Eugene, OR 97403. Offers MA, MS, PhD. Terminal master's awarded for partial completion of doctoral program. *Degree requirements:* For master's, thesis or alternative; for doctorate, thesis/dissertation. *Entrance requirements:* For master's and doctorate, GRE General Test, minimum GPA of 3.0. Additional exam requirements/recommendations for international students: Required—TOEFL. *Faculty research:* Public policy, public choice, comparative politics, political economy, international relations.

University of Ottawa, Faculty of Graduate and Postdoctoral Studies, Faculty of Social Sciences, Department of Political Studies, Ottawa, ON K1N 6N5, Canada. Offers MA, PhD. *Degree requirements:* For master's, thesis or alternative, fluency in English and French; for doctorate, comprehensive exam, thesis/dissertation. *Entrance requirements:* For master's, honors bachelor's degree or equivalent, minimum B average; for doctorate, master's degree, minimum B+ average. Electronic applications accepted. *Faculty research:* Political thought and analysis of ideologies, Canadian and Québécois policies, international and comparative policies.

University of Pennsylvania, School of Arts and Sciences, Fels Institute of Government, Philadelphia, PA 19104. Offers economic development and growth (Certificate); government administration (MGA); nonprofit administration (Certificate); organization dynamics (MS); politics (Certificate); public administration (MPA); public finance (Certificate). Part-time and evening/weekend programs available. *Students:* 62 full-time (32 women), 75 part-time (45 women); includes 31 minority (17 Black or African American, non-Hispanic/Latino; 6 Asian, non-Hispanic/Latino; 4 Hispanic/Latino; 4 Two or more races, non-Hispanic/Latino), 20 international. 445 applicants, 24% accepted, 47

enrolled. In 2014, 56 master's, 31 other advanced degrees awarded. *Entrance requirements:* For master's, GRE, GMAT, or LSAT. Additional exam requirements/recommendations for international students: Required—TOEFL, IELTS. *Application deadline:* For fall admission, 1/15 for domestic students. Applications are processed on a rolling basis. Application fee: $70. *Financial support:* Fellowships, institutionally sponsored loans, and scholarships/grants available. Financial award application deadline: 1/15; financial award applicants required to submit FAFSA. *Unit head:* John J. Mulhern, Executive Director, 215-898-2600, E-mail: david_thornburgh@sas.upenn.edu. *Application contact:* 215-746-6684, Fax: 215-898-6238, E-mail: felsinstitute@sas.upenn.edu.
Website: http://www.fels.upenn.edu/

University of Pennsylvania, School of Arts and Sciences, Graduate Group in Political Science, Philadelphia, PA 19104. Offers AM, PhD, MGA/AM. *Faculty:* 32 full-time (11 women), 1 part-time/adjunct (0 women). *Students:* 61 full-time (23 women), 3 part-time (0 women); includes 10 minority (3 Black or African American, non-Hispanic/Latino; 1 Asian, non-Hispanic/Latino; 3 Hispanic/Latino; 3 Two or more races, non-Hispanic/Latino), 14 international. 326 applicants, 8% accepted, 7 enrolled. In 2014, 6 master's, 8 doctorates awarded. Terminal master's awarded for partial completion of doctoral program. *Degree requirements:* For doctorate, one foreign language, thesis/dissertation. *Entrance requirements:* For master's and doctorate, GRE General Test. Additional exam requirements/recommendations for international students: Required—TOEFL. *Application deadline:* For fall admission, 12/1 priority date for domestic students. Application fee: $70. Electronic applications accepted. *Financial support:* Fellowships, research assistantships, teaching assistantships, institutionally sponsored loans, scholarships/grants, traineeships, health care benefits, and unspecified assistantships available. Financial award application deadline: 12/15. *Unit head:* Dr. Ralph M. Rosen, Associate Dean for Graduate Studies, 215-898-7156, Fax: 215-573-8068, E-mail: grad-dean@sas.upenn.edu. *Application contact:* Arts and Sciences Graduate Admissions, 215-573-5816, Fax: 215-573-8068, E-mail: gdasadmis@sas.upenn.edu.
Website: http://www.sas.upenn.edu/polisci/content/graduate-program

University of Pittsburgh, Dietrich School of Arts and Sciences, Department of Political Science, Pittsburgh, PA 15260. Offers MA, PhD. *Faculty:* 25 full-time (8 women). *Students:* 49 full-time (17 women); includes 16 minority (5 Asian, non-Hispanic/Latino; 10 Hispanic/Latino; 1 Two or more races, non-Hispanic/Latino). Average age 30. 115 applicants, 27% accepted, 12 enrolled. In 2014, 9 master's, 7 doctorates awarded. Terminal master's awarded for partial completion of doctoral program. *Degree requirements:* For master's, comprehensive exam; for doctorate, comprehensive exam, thesis/dissertation. *Entrance requirements:* For master's and doctorate, GRE General Test, minimum QPA of 3.0. Additional exam requirements/recommendations for international students: Required—TOEFL. *Application deadline:* For fall admission, 1/8 for domestic and international students. Applications are processed on a rolling basis. Application fee: $50. Electronic applications accepted. *Expenses:* Tuition, state resident: full-time $20,742; part-time $838 per credit. Tuition, nonresident: full-time $33,960; part-time $1389 per credit. *Required fees:* $800; $205 per term. Tuition and fees vary according to program. *Financial support:* In 2014–15, 18 students received support, including 18 fellowships with full tuition reimbursements available (averaging $21,262 per year), 8 research assistantships with full tuition reimbursements available (averaging $13,980 per year), 14 teaching assistantships with full tuition reimbursements available (averaging $17,800 per year); tuition waivers (partial) also available. Financial award application deadline: 1/8. *Unit head:* Prof. Steven Finkel, Chairman, 412-648-7290, Fax: 412-648-7277, E-mail: finkel@pitt.edu. *Application contact:* Prof. Anibal Perez-Linan, Director of Graduate Students, 412-648-7250, Fax: 412-648-7277, E-mail: asp27@pitt.edu.
Website: http://www.polisci.pitt.edu/

University of Pittsburgh, Graduate School of Public and International Affairs, Master of Public and International Affairs Program, Pittsburgh, PA 15260. Offers international political economy (MPIA); security and intelligence studies (MPIA); JD/MPIA; MBA/MPIA; MID/MPIA; MPA/MPIA; MPH/MPIA; MPIA/MSW; MSIS/MPIA. Part-time and evening/weekend programs available. *Faculty:* 34 full-time (12 women), 11 part-time/adjunct (3 women). *Students:* 145 full-time (63 women), 8 part-time (5 women); includes 18 minority (6 Black or African American, non-Hispanic/Latino; 3 Asian, non-Hispanic/Latino; 8 Hispanic/Latino; 1 Two or more races, non-Hispanic/Latino), 26 international. Average age 26. 251 applicants, 87% accepted, 64 enrolled. In 2014, 85 master's awarded. *Degree requirements:* For master's, thesis optional, internship, capstone seminar. *Entrance requirements:* For master's, GRE General Test or GMAT, 2 letters of recommendation, resume; undergraduate transcripts, personal statement. Additional exam requirements/recommendations for international students: Required—TOEFL (minimum score 550 paper-based; 80 iBT); Recommended—IELTS (minimum score 7), TWE (minimum score 4). *Application deadline:* For fall admission, 2/1 for domestic students, 1/15 for international students; for spring admission, 11/1 for domestic students, 8/1 for international students. Application fee: $50. Electronic applications accepted. *Expenses:* Tuition, state resident: full-time $20,742; part-time $838 per credit. Tuition, nonresident: full-time $33,960; part-time $1389 per credit. *Required fees:* $800; $205 per term. Tuition and fees vary according to program. *Financial support:* In 2014–15, 45 students received support, including 8 fellowships (averaging $15,000 per year); scholarships/grants, unspecified assistantships, and student employment also available. Financial award application deadline: 2/1. *Faculty research:* International political economy, international security and intelligence, transnational organized crime, international trade, international finance, globalization, terrorism, multinational corporations and the global economy, human rights, human trafficking, gender and development, diplomacy. *Total annual research expenditures:* $640,844. *Unit head:* Dr. Michael Kenney, Director, International Affairs and International Development Divisions, 412-648-7921, Fax: 412-648-2605, E-mail: mkenney@pitt.edu. *Application contact:* Kelly C. McDevitt, Graduate Enrollment Counselor, 412-648-7640, Fax: 412-648-7641, E-mail: mcdevitt@pitt.edu.
Website: http://www.gspia.pitt.edu/

University of Regina, Faculty of Graduate Studies and Research, Faculty of Arts, Program in Social and Political Thought, Regina, SK S4S 0A2, Canada. Offers MA. Part-time programs available. *Students:* 2 full-time (0 women), 3 part-time (1 woman). 7 applicants, 57% accepted. In 2014, 1 master's awarded. *Degree requirements:* For master's, thesis. *Entrance requirements:* Additional exam requirements/recommendations for international students: Required—TOEFL (minimum score 580 paper-based; 80 iBT), IELTS (minimum score 6.5), PTE (minimum score 59). *Application deadline:* For fall admission, 3/30 for domestic and international students. Application fee: $100. Electronic applications accepted. *Expenses: Tuition, area resident:* Full-time $4900 Canadian dollars; part-time $837.65 Canadian dollars per semester. *International tuition:* $7900 Canadian dollars full-time. *Required fees:* $396 Canadian dollars; $86.90 Canadian dollars per semester. *Financial support:* In 2014–15, 1 teaching assistantship (averaging $2,427 per year) was awarded; fellowships, research assistantships, and scholarships/grants also available. Financial award application deadline: 6/15. *Faculty research:* Liberalism and freedom, neo-conservatism, Aristotle's ethics, Kant's ethical theory and political philosophy, Hegel's philosophy of right. *Unit head:* Dr. Lee Ward, Graduate Coordinator, 306-359-1259, E-mail: lee.ward@uregina.ca. *Application contact:* Doreen Thompson, Administrative Assistant, 306-585-4332, E-mail: doreen.thompson@uregina.ca.

University of Rhode Island, Graduate School, College of Arts and Sciences, Department of Political Science, Kingston, RI 02881. Offers political science (MA), including American politics, comparative government, international relations, public policy; public policy and administration (MPA); MLIS/MPA. Part-time programs available. *Faculty:* 11 full-time (4 women). *Students:* 20 full-time (11 women), 28 part-time (21 women); includes 9 minority (4 Black or African American, non-Hispanic/Latino; 3 Asian, non-Hispanic/Latino; 2 Hispanic/Latino), 2 international. In 2014, 20 master's awarded. *Degree requirements:* For master's, comprehensive exam (for some programs), thesis optional. *Entrance requirements:* For master's, GRE, GMAT or MAT, 2 letters of recommendation. Additional exam requirements/recommendations for international students: Required—TOEFL (minimum score 550 paper-based). *Application deadline:* For fall admission, 2/1 for international students; for spring admission, 7/15 for international students. Application fee: $65. Electronic applications accepted. *Expenses:* Tuition, state resident: full-time $11,532; part-time $641 per credit. Tuition, nonresident: full-time $23,606; part-time $1311 per credit. *Required fees:* $1442; $39 per credit. $35 per semester. One-time fee: $155. *Financial support:* In 2014–15, 3 teaching assistantships with full and partial tuition reimbursements (averaging $12,675 per year) were awarded. Financial award application deadline: 7/15; financial award applicants required to submit FAFSA. *Unit head:* Dr. Brian Krueger, Department Chair, 401-874-4058, Fax: 401-874-4072, E-mail: bkrueger@uri.edu. *Application contact:* Dr. Robert Weygand, Director, 401-874-2124, Fax: 401-874-4072, E-mail: bobw@uri.edu.
Website: http://www.uri.edu/artsci/psc/

University of Rochester, School of Arts and Sciences, Department of Political Science, Rochester, NY 14627. Offers PhD, MS/PhD. *Faculty:* 20 full-time (4 women). *Students:* 43 full-time (15 women); includes 2 minority (1 Asian, non-Hispanic/Latino; 1 Hispanic/Latino), 19 international. 101 applicants, 19% accepted, 6 enrolled. In 2014, 7 doctorates awarded. Terminal master's awarded for partial completion of doctoral program. *Degree requirements:* For doctorate, thesis/dissertation, qualifying exam. *Entrance requirements:* For doctorate, GRE General Test. Additional exam requirements/recommendations for international students: Required—TOEFL. *Application deadline:* For fall admission, 1/1 priority date for domestic students. Application fee: $60. *Expenses: Tuition:* Full-time $46,150; part-time $1442 per credit hour. *Required fees:* $504. *Financial support:* Fellowships, research assistantships, teaching assistantships, institutionally sponsored loans, scholarships/grants, and tuition waivers (full and partial) available. Financial award application deadline: 2/1. *Unit head:* Gretchen Helmke, Chair, 585-275-5236. *Application contact:* Pamm Ferguson, Administrator/Executive Assistant to the Chair, 585-275-5403.
Website: http://rochester.edu/college/psc/graduate/intro.php

University of Saskatchewan, College of Graduate Studies and Research, College of Arts and Science, Department of Political Studies, Saskatoon, SK S7N 5A2, Canada. Offers MA. *Degree requirements:* For master's, thesis. *Entrance requirements:* Additional exam requirements/recommendations for international students: Required—TOEFL (minimum score 80 iBT); Recommended—IELTS (minimum score 6.5). Electronic applications accepted.

University of South Africa, College of Human Sciences, Pretoria, South Africa. Offers adult education (M Ed); African languages (MA, PhD); African politics (MA, PhD); Afrikaans (MA, PhD); ancient history (MA, PhD); ancient Near Eastern studies (MA, PhD); anthropology (MA, PhD); applied linguistics (MA); Arabic (MA, PhD); archaeology (MA); art history (MA); Biblical archaeology (MA); Biblical studies (M Th, D Th, PhD); Christian spirituality (M Th, D Th); church history (M Th, D Th); classical studies (MA, PhD); clinical psychology (MA); communication (MA, PhD); comparative education (M Ed, Ed D); consulting psychology (D Admin, D Com, PhD); curriculum studies (M Ed, Ed D); development studies (M Admin, MA, D Admin, PhD); didactics (M Ed, Ed D); education (M Tech); education management (M Ed, Ed D); educational psychology (M Ed); English (MA); environmental education (M Ed); French (MA, PhD); German (MA, PhD); Greek (MA); guidance and counseling (M Ed); health studies (MA, PhD), including health sciences education (MA), health services management (MA), medical and surgical nursing science (critical care general) (MA), midwifery and neonatal nursing science (MA), trauma and emergency care (MA); history (MA, PhD); history of education (Ed D); inclusive education (M Ed, Ed D); information and communications technology policy and regulation (MA); information science (MA, MIS, PhD); international politics (MA, PhD); Islamic studies (MA, PhD); Italian (MA, PhD); Judaica (MA, PhD); linguistics (MA, PhD); mathematical education (M Ed); mathematics education (MA); missiology (M Th, D Th); modern Hebrew (MA, PhD); musicology (MA, MMus, D Mus, PhD); natural science education (M Ed); New Testament (M Th, D Th); Old Testament (D Th); pastoral therapy (M Th, D Th); philosophy (MA); philosophy of education (M Ed, Ed D); politics (MA, PhD); Portuguese (MA, PhD); practical theology (M Th, D Th); psychology (MA, MS, PhD); psychology of education (M Ed, Ed D); public health (MA); religious studies (MA, D Th, PhD); Romance languages (MA); Russian (MA, PhD); Semitic languages (MA, PhD); social behavior studies in HIV/AIDS (MA); social science (mental health) (MA); social science in development studies (MA); social science in psychology (MA); social science in social work (MA); social science in sociology (MA); social work (MSW, DSW, PhD); socio-education (M Ed, Ed D); sociolinguistics (MA); sociology (MA, PhD); Spanish (MA, PhD); systematic theology (M Th, D Th); TESOL (teaching English to speakers of other languages) (MA); theological ethics (M Th, D Th); theory of literature (MA, PhD); urban ministries (D Th); urban ministry (M Th).

University of South Carolina, The Graduate School, College of Arts and Sciences, Department of Political Science, Program in Political Science, Columbia, SC 29208. Offers MA, PhD. Part-time programs available. Terminal master's awarded for partial completion of doctoral program. *Degree requirements:* For master's, one foreign language, thesis; for doctorate, one foreign language, comprehensive exam, thesis/dissertation. *Entrance requirements:* For master's and doctorate, GRE General Test, minimum GPA of 3.5. Additional exam requirements/recommendations for international students: Required—TOEFL. Electronic applications accepted. *Faculty research:* American government and politics, comparative politics, political theory, international politics, public administration and policy.

The University of South Dakota, Graduate School, College of Arts and Sciences, Department of Political Science, Vermillion, SD 57069-2390. Offers American political institutions (PhD); American politics and public policy (MA); political science (EMPA, MA); public administration (MPA, PhD); public policy (PhD); JD/MA. *Accreditation:* NASPAA (one or more programs are accredited). Part-time programs available. Postbaccalaureate distance learning degree programs offered. *Degree requirements:* For master's, comprehensive exam, thesis (for some programs). *Entrance requirements:* For master's, GRE or LSAT (MPA), GRE General Test (MA), minimum GPA of 2.7. Additional exam requirements/recommendations for international students: Required—TOEFL (minimum score 550 paper-based; 79 iBT). Electronic applications accepted.

University of Southern California, Graduate School, Annenberg School for Communication and Journalism, School of Communication, Program in Public Diplomacy, Los Angeles, CA 90089. Offers MPD. Part-time programs available. *Students:* 41 full-time (0 women), 3 part-time (0 women); includes 12 minority (3 Black or African American, non-Hispanic/Latino; 4 Asian, non-Hispanic/Latino; 5 Hispanic/

Latino), 12 international. Average age 26. 60 applicants, 75% accepted, 18 enrolled. In 2014, 26 master's awarded. *Degree requirements:* For master's, thesis. *Entrance requirements:* For master's, GRE, resume, writing samples, statement of purpose, recommendation letters. Additional exam requirements/recommendations for international students: Required—TOEFL (minimum score 114 iBT) or IELTS (minimum score 8). *Application deadline:* For fall admission, 1/15 priority date for domestic and international students. Application fee: $85. Electronic applications accepted. *Financial support:* In 2014–15, 4 fellowships with partial tuition reimbursements (averaging $39,000 per year) were awarded; career-related internships or fieldwork, Federal Work-Study, and scholarships/grants also available. Support available to part-time students. Financial award application deadline: 1/15; financial award applicants required to submit FAFSA. *Unit head:* Dr. Nicholas Cull, Director, 213-821-4080, E-mail: cull@usc.edu. *Application contact:* Allyson Hill, Associate Dean for Admissions, 213-821-0770, Fax: 213-740-1933, E-mail: ascadm@usc.edu.
Website: http://www.annenberg.usc.edu

University of Southern California, Graduate School, Dana and David Dornsife College of Letters, Arts and Sciences, Political Science and International Relations PhD Program, Los Angeles, CA 90089. Offers PhD. *Degree requirements:* For doctorate, variable foreign language requirement, comprehensive exam, thesis/dissertation. *Entrance requirements:* For doctorate, GRE (minimum score 1000). Additional exam requirements/recommendations for international students: Required—TOEFL (minimum score 600 paper-based; 100 iBT). Electronic applications accepted. *Faculty research:* American politics, foreign policy analysis, international political economy, race/ethics politics, security studies.

University of Southern Mississippi, Graduate School, College of Arts and Letters, Department of Political Science, International Development, and International Affairs, Hattiesburg, MS 39406-0001. Offers international development (PhD); political science (MA, MS). Part-time and evening/weekend programs available. Postbaccalaureate distance learning degree programs offered. *Degree requirements:* For master's, comprehensive exam, thesis (for some programs); for doctorate, comprehensive exam, thesis/dissertation. *Entrance requirements:* For master's, GRE General Test, minimum GPA of 2.75 in last 2 years, 3.0 in field of study; for doctorate, GRE General Test, minimum GPA of 3.5. Additional exam requirements/recommendations for international students: Required—TOEFL, IELTS. *Faculty research:* American politics, international politics, political theory, comparative politics, public law.

University of South Florida, College of Arts and Sciences, Department of Government and International Affairs, Tampa, FL 33620-9951. Offers government (PhD); Latin American, Caribbean and Latino studies (MA); political science (MA), including comparative government and politics, international relations, public policy. Part-time and evening/weekend programs available. *Faculty:* 10 full-time (1 woman). *Students:* 56 full-time (29 women), 47 part-time (23 women); includes 18 minority (6 Black or African American, non-Hispanic/Latino; 1 Asian, non-Hispanic/Latino; 9 Hispanic/Latino; 2 Two or more races, non-Hispanic/Latino), 9 international. Average age 33. 73 applicants, 51% accepted, 25 enrolled. In 2014, 45 master's, 2 doctorates awarded. *Degree requirements:* For master's, comprehensive exam, thesis; for doctorate, comprehensive exam, thesis/dissertation. *Entrance requirements:* For master's, GRE General Test, minimum GPA of 3.0 in upper-division undergraduate course work; letters of recommendation (2 for MPA, 3 for MPS); 500-word personal statement and undergraduate background in political science or related fields (for MPS); one-page career statement (for MPA); for doctorate, GRE General Test, 500-word personal statement, three letters of recommendation, transcripts of MA/BA coursework, writing sample. Additional exam requirements/recommendations for international students: Required—TOEFL (minimum score 550 paper-based; 79 iBT) or IELTS (minimum score 6.5). *Application deadline:* For fall admission, 2/15 for domestic students, 1/2 for international students; for spring admission, 10/15 for domestic students, 6/1 for international students. Applications are processed on a rolling basis. Application fee: $30. Electronic applications accepted. *Financial support:* In 2014–15, 18 students received support, including 18 teaching assistantships with tuition reimbursements available (averaging $12,390 per year); unspecified assistantships also available. Financial award application deadline: 4/1. *Faculty research:* Citizenship and identity, social movements, global governance, American politics, public policy. *Unit head:* Dr. Steven Tauber, Associate Professor and Interim Chair, 813-974-2278, Fax: 813-974-0832, E-mail: stauber@usf.edu. *Application contact:* Dr. Bernd Reiter, Associate Professor and Director of Graduate Studies, 813-974-3583, Fax: 813-974-0832, E-mail: breiter@usf.edu.
Website: http://gia.usf.edu/

University of South Florida, Innovative Education, Tampa, FL 33620-9951. *Unit head:* Kathy Barnes, Interdisciplinary Programs Coordinator, 813-974-8031, Fax: 813-974-7061, E-mail: barnesk@usf.edu. *Application contact:* Karen Tylinski, Metro Initiatives, 813-974-9943, Fax: 813-974-7061, E-mail: ktylinsk@usf.edu.
Website: http://www.usf.edu/innovative-education/

The University of Tennessee, Graduate School, College of Arts and Sciences, Department of Political Science, Program in Political Science, Knoxville, TN 37996. Offers MA, PhD. Part-time programs available. *Degree requirements:* For master's, thesis or alternative; for doctorate, one foreign language, thesis/dissertation. *Entrance requirements:* For master's and doctorate, GRE General Test, minimum GPA of 2.7. Additional exam requirements/recommendations for international students: Required—TOEFL. Electronic applications accepted.

The University of Tennessee, Graduate School, College of Arts and Sciences, Department of Sociology, Knoxville, TN 37996. Offers criminology (MA, PhD); energy, environment, and resource policy (MA, PhD); political economy (MA, PhD). Part-time programs available. *Degree requirements:* For master's, thesis or alternative; for doctorate, thesis/dissertation. *Entrance requirements:* For master's, GRE General Test, minimum GPA of 3.0; for doctorate, GRE General Test, minimum GPA of 3.5. Additional exam requirements/recommendations for international students: Required—TOEFL. Electronic applications accepted.

The University of Texas at Arlington, Graduate School, College of Liberal Arts, Department of Political Science, Arlington, TX 76019. Offers MA. Part-time and evening/weekend programs available. *Degree requirements:* For master's, comprehensive exam, thesis optional. *Entrance requirements:* For master's, GRE, minimum GPA of 3.0 in last 60 hours of course work. Additional exam requirements/recommendations for international students: Required—TOEFL (minimum score 550 paper-based). Electronic applications accepted.

The University of Texas at Austin, Graduate School, College of Liberal Arts, Department of Government, Austin, TX 78712-1111. Offers MA, PhD, PhD/JD. *Degree requirements:* For master's, thesis; for doctorate, comprehensive exam, thesis/dissertation. *Entrance requirements:* For master's and doctorate, GRE General Test. Electronic applications accepted.

The University of Texas at Brownsville, Graduate Studies, College of Liberal Arts, Department of Government, Brownsville, TX 78520-4991. Offers MPPM. Part-time and evening/weekend programs available. *Degree requirements:* For master's, comprehensive exam (for some programs), thesis optional, professional report. *Entrance requirements:* For master's, 2 letters of recommendation, one of which should be academic; resume. Additional exam requirements/recommendations for international students: Required—TOEFL (minimum score 550 paper-based; 77 iBT). Electronic applications accepted.

The University of Texas at Dallas, School of Economic, Political and Policy Sciences, Program in Political Science, Richardson, TX 75080. Offers Constitutional law (MA); legislative studies (MA); political science (MA, PhD). Part-time and evening/weekend programs available. *Faculty:* 12 full-time (2 women). *Students:* 32 full-time (16 women), 25 part-time (12 women); includes 14 minority (4 Black or African American, non-Hispanic/Latino; 1 American Indian or Alaska Native, non-Hispanic/Latino; 3 Asian, non-Hispanic/Latino; 6 Hispanic/Latino), 7 international. Average age 32. 33 applicants, 42% accepted, 14 enrolled. In 2014, 15 master's, 2 doctorates awarded. Terminal master's awarded for partial completion of doctoral program. *Degree requirements:* For master's, thesis optional, independent study; for doctorate, thesis/dissertation, practicum research. *Entrance requirements:* For master's, GRE (minimum combined verbal and quantitative score of 1100), minimum undergraduate GPA of 3.0; for doctorate, GRE (minimum combined verbal and quantitative score of 1200, writing 4.5), minimum undergraduate GPA of 3.2. Additional exam requirements/recommendations for international students: Required—TOEFL (minimum score 550 paper-based). *Application deadline:* For fall admission, 7/15 for domestic students, 5/1 priority date for international students; for spring admission, 11/15 for domestic students, 9/1 priority date for international students. Applications are processed on a rolling basis. Application fee: $50 ($100 for international students). Electronic applications accepted. *Expenses:* Tuition, state resident: full-time $11,940; part-time $663 per credit. Tuition, nonresident: full-time $22,282; part-time $1238 per credit. *Financial support:* In 2014–15, 22 students received support, including 18 teaching assistantships with partial tuition reimbursements available (averaging $12,161 per year); research assistantships with partial tuition reimbursements available, career-related internships or fieldwork, Federal Work-Study, institutionally sponsored loans, and scholarships/grants also available. Support available to part-time students. Financial award application deadline: 4/30; financial award applicants required to submit FAFSA. *Faculty research:* Terrorism and democratic stability, redistricting and representation, trust and social exchange, how economic ideas impact political thought and public policy. *Unit head:* Dr. Jennifer Holmes, Program Head, 972-883-6843, Fax: 972-883-2735, E-mail: jholmes@utdallas.edu. *Application contact:* Cheryl Berry, Graduate Program Administrator, 972-883-2932, Fax: 972-883-2735, E-mail: politicalscience@utdallas.edu.
Website: http://www.utdallas.edu/epps/political-science/

The University of Texas at Dallas, School of Economic, Political and Policy Sciences, Program in Public Policy and Political Economy, Richardson, TX 75080. Offers international political economy (MS); public policy (MPP); public policy and political economy (PhD). Part-time and evening/weekend programs available. *Faculty:* 14 full-time (1 woman), 1 part-time/adjunct (0 women). *Students:* 41 full-time (13 women), 35 part-time (16 women); includes 22 minority (6 Black or African American, non-Hispanic/Latino; 1 American Indian or Alaska Native, non-Hispanic/Latino; 8 Asian, non-Hispanic/Latino; 7 Hispanic/Latino), 21 international. Average age 36. 52 applicants, 60% accepted, 12 enrolled. In 2014, 18 master's, 3 doctorates awarded. *Degree requirements:* For doctorate, thesis/dissertation. *Entrance requirements:* For master's and doctorate, GRE General Test, minimum GPA of 3.0 in upper-level course work in field. Additional exam requirements/recommendations for international students: Required—TOEFL (minimum score 550 paper-based). *Application deadline:* For fall admission, 7/15 for domestic students, 5/1 priority date for international students; for spring admission, 11/15 for domestic students, 9/1 priority date for international students. Applications are processed on a rolling basis. Application fee: $50 ($100 for international students). Electronic applications accepted. *Expenses:* Tuition, state resident: full-time $11,940; part-time $663 per credit. Tuition, nonresident: full-time $22,282; part-time $1238 per credit. *Financial support:* In 2014–15, 49 students received support, including 4 research assistantships with partial tuition reimbursements available (averaging $12,070 per year), 15 teaching assistantships with partial tuition reimbursements available (averaging $11,790 per year); career-related internships or fieldwork, Federal Work-Study, institutionally sponsored loans, scholarships/grants, and unspecified assistantships also available. Support available to part-time students. Financial award application deadline: 4/30; financial award applicants required to submit FAFSA. *Faculty research:* Ethnicity, community and local public good provision; community mental health policy; Texas Schools Project; biological and chemical arms control; cross-disciplinary applications of quantitative methodology. *Unit head:* Dr. Jennifer Holmes, Program Head, 972-883-6843, Fax: 972-883-6297, E-mail: jholmes@utdallas.edu. *Application contact:* Betsy Albritton, Graduate Program Administrator, 972-883-6406, Fax: 972-883-6297, E-mail: pppe@utdallas.edu.
Website: http://www.utdallas.edu/epps/public-policy-and-political-economy/

The University of Texas at El Paso, Graduate School, College of Liberal Arts, Department of Political Science, El Paso, TX 79968-0001. Offers MA. Part-time and evening/weekend programs available. *Degree requirements:* For master's, thesis optional. *Entrance requirements:* For master's, GRE, letters of recommendation, personal statement, transcripts. Additional exam requirements/recommendations for international students: Required—TOEFL; Recommended—IELTS. Electronic applications accepted. *Faculty research:* Democracy and democratization, political institutions, regional integration, international security, presidential and legislative politics.

The University of Texas at San Antonio, College of Liberal and Fine Arts, Department of Political Science and Geography, San Antonio, TX 78249-0617. Offers political science (MA). Part-time and evening/weekend programs available. *Faculty:* 9 full-time (4 women). *Students:* 10 full-time (5 women), 13 part-time (4 women); includes 11 minority (1 Asian, non-Hispanic/Latino; 9 Hispanic/Latino; 1 Two or more races, non-Hispanic/Latino), 3 international. Average age 29. 28 applicants, 71% accepted, 14 enrolled. In 2014, 14 master's awarded. *Degree requirements:* For master's, comprehensive exam (for some programs), thesis optional. *Entrance requirements:* For master's, GRE General Test or LSAT, 18 semester credit hours in upper-division undergraduate or graduate-level courses in political science or directly-related fields in the social or behavioral sciences, 3 letters of recommendation, statement of purpose. Additional exam requirements/recommendations for international students: Required—TOEFL (minimum score 550 paper-based; 79 iBT), IELTS (minimum score 6.5). *Application deadline:* For fall admission, 7/1 for domestic students, 4/1 for international students; for spring admission, 11/1 for domestic students, 9/1 for international students. Application fee: $45 ($80 for international students). *Expenses:* Tuition, state resident: full-time $4671; part-time $260 per credit hour. Tuition, nonresident: full-time $18,022; part-time $1001 per credit hour. *Financial support:* Applicants required to submit FAFSA. *Faculty research:* Minority representation and legislation, comparative welfare policy, strategic conflict in India and Pakistan, homeland security, global governance, American political behavior. *Unit head:* Dr. Mansour El-Kikhia, Chair, 210-458-5600, Fax: 210-458-4629, E-mail: mansour.elkikhia@utsa.edu. *Application contact:* Dr. James Calder, Graduate Advisor of Record, 210-458-7671, Fax: 210-458-7671, E-mail: james.calder@utsa.edu.
Website: http://colfa.utsa.edu/Polisci/

The University of Texas at Tyler, College of Arts and Sciences, Department of Political Science, Tyler, TX 75799-0001. Offers MA. Part-time and evening/weekend programs available. *Degree requirements:* For master's, comprehensive exam, thesis optional. *Entrance requirements:* Additional exam requirements/recommendations for international students: Required—TOEFL. *Faculty research:* American politics, comparative politics, international relations, political theory and philosophy.

The University of Texas of the Permian Basin, Office of Graduate Studies, College of Arts and Sciences, Department of Social Sciences, Odessa, TX 79762-0001. Offers criminal justice administration (MS); political science (MPA). Part-time and evening/weekend programs available. *Degree requirements:* For master's, comprehensive exam (for some programs), thesis (for some programs). *Entrance requirements:* For master's, GRE General Test. Additional exam requirements/recommendations for international students: Required—TOEFL (minimum score 550 paper-based).

The University of Toledo, College of Graduate Studies, College of Languages, Literature and Social Sciences, Department of Political Science and Public Administration, Toledo, OH 43606-3390. Offers health care policy and administration (Certificate); management of non-profit organizations (Certificate); municipal administration (Certificate); political science (MA); public administration (MPA); JD/MPA. *Accreditation:* NASPAA. Part-time programs available. *Degree requirements:* For master's, comprehensive exam (for some programs), thesis. *Entrance requirements:* For master's, GRE General Test, minimum cumulative point-hour ratio of 2.7 (3.0 for MPA) for all previous academic work, three letters of recommendation, statement of purpose, transcripts from all prior institutions attended; for Certificate, minimum cumulative point-hour ratio of 2.7 for all previous academic work, three letters of recommendation, statement of purpose, transcripts from all prior institutions attended. Additional exam requirements/recommendations for international students: Required—TOEFL (minimum score 550 paper-based; 80 iBT). Electronic applications accepted. *Faculty research:* Economic development, health care, Third World, criminal justice, Eastern Europe.

University of Toronto, School of Graduate Studies, Faculty of Arts and Science, Department of Political Science, Toronto, ON M5S 2J7, Canada. Offers MA, PhD, JD/MA, JD/PhD. Part-time programs available. *Degree requirements:* For master's, thesis optional; for doctorate, one foreign language, thesis/dissertation, reading competency in a language other than English. *Entrance requirements:* For master's, 3 letters of recommendation, writing sample, statement of scholarly intent, minimum cumulative GPA of B+ in a four-year bachelor's program including B+ average over five to eight suitably-distributed full-year political science courses; for doctorate, 4 letters of recommendation, writing sample, minimum A- in most recent political science (or equivalent) degree. Additional exam requirements/recommendations for international students: Required—TOEFL (minimum score 580 paper-based; 93 iBT), TWE (minimum score 5). Electronic applications accepted.

University of Utah, Graduate School, College of Humanities, Program in Middle East Studies, Salt Lake City, UT 84112. Offers Arabic (MA, PhD); Hebrew (MA); history (MA, PhD); Persian (MA, PhD); political science (MA, PhD). *Students:* 1 full-time (0 women), 8 part-time (3 women); includes 1 minority (Asian, non-Hispanic/Latino), 3 international. Average age 40. In 2014, 5 master's, 1 doctorate awarded. Terminal master's awarded for partial completion of doctoral program. *Degree requirements:* For master's, 2 foreign languages, comprehensive exam, thesis optional; for doctorate, 3 foreign languages, comprehensive exam, thesis/dissertation. *Entrance requirements:* For master's, GRE General Test, minimum GPA of 3.2; for doctorate, GRE General Test, MA in Middle East studies or equivalent, minimum GPA of 3.2. Additional exam requirements/recommendations for international students: Required—TOEFL (minimum score 580 paper-based; 92 iBT); Recommended—IELTS (minimum score 7). *Application deadline:* For fall admission, 1/15 priority date for domestic and international students. Application fee: $55 ($65 for international students). Electronic applications accepted. *Financial support:* In 2014–15, 5 students received support, including 2 teaching assistantships with full tuition reimbursements available (averaging $13,500 per year); fellowships and unspecified assistantships also available. Financial award application deadline: 1/15. *Faculty research:* Islamic studies; Middle Eastern history; political science; Judaic studies; anthropology; Arabic, Persian, Hebrew, and Turkish language and literature. *Unit head:* Johanna Watzinger-Tharp, Director, 801-581-7148, Fax: 801-581-6105, E-mail: j.tharp@utah.edu. *Application contact:* Kellie Hubbard, Academic Advisor, 801-581-5362, Fax: 801-581-6105, E-mail: kellie.hubbard@utah.edu.
Website: http://www.mec.utah.edu

University of Utah, Graduate School, College of Social and Behavioral Science, Department of Political Science, Program in Political Science, Salt Lake City, UT 84112. Offers American politics (MA, MS, PhD); comparative politics (MA, MS, PhD); international relations (MA, MS, PhD); political theory (MA, MS, PhD); public administration (MA, MS, PhD). *Faculty:* 32 full-time (7 women), 10 part-time/adjunct (3 women). *Students:* 67 full-time (25 women); includes 11 minority (1 Black or African American, non-Hispanic/Latino; 1 American Indian or Alaska Native, non-Hispanic/Latino; 4 Asian, non-Hispanic/Latino; 5 Two or more races, non-Hispanic/Latino), 9 international. Average age 34. 35 applicants, 71% accepted, 12 enrolled. In 2014, 6 master's, 6 doctorates awarded. Terminal master's awarded for partial completion of doctoral program. *Degree requirements:* For master's, variable foreign language requirement, thesis or research paper; for doctorate, comprehensive exam, thesis/dissertation. *Entrance requirements:* For master's and doctorate, GRE General Test, minimum GPA of 3.2. Additional exam requirements/recommendations for international students: Required—TOEFL (minimum score 580 paper-based; 61 iBT), IELTS (minimum score 6). *Application deadline:* For fall admission, 1/15 priority date for domestic and international students; for spring admission, 10/1 for domestic and international students. Application fee: $55 ($65 for international students). Electronic applications accepted. *Financial support:* In 2014–15, 4 students received support, including 2 fellowships with full tuition reimbursements available (averaging $15,250 per year), 14 teaching assistantships with full tuition reimbursements available (averaging $13,750 per year); career-related internships or fieldwork, scholarships/grants, health care benefits, and unspecified assistantships also available. Financial award application deadline: 1/15; financial award applicants required to submit FAFSA. *Faculty research:* International politics, comparative politics, political theory, American politics, public administration. *Total annual research expenditures:* $24,651. *Unit head:* Brent Steele, Chair, 801-587-7754, Fax: 801-585-6492, E-mail: brent.steele@utah.edu. *Application contact:* Mary Ann Underwood, Graduate Coordinator/Advisor, 801-581-8608, Fax: 801-585-6492, E-mail: maryann.underwood@poli-sci.utah.edu.
Website: http://www.poli-sci.utah.edu/

University of Victoria, Faculty of Graduate Studies, Faculty of Social Sciences, Department of Political Science, Victoria, BC V8W 2Y2, Canada. Offers MA, PhD. Part-time programs available. *Degree requirements:* For master's, thesis; for doctorate, thesis/dissertation, candidacy exam. *Entrance requirements:* For master's, minimum B+ average in last 2 years of undergraduate course work. Additional exam requirements/recommendations for international students: Required—TOEFL (minimum score 600 paper-based). Electronic applications accepted. *Faculty research:* Political theory, political parties, international political economy, comparative public policy, British Columbian politics.

University of Virginia, College and Graduate School of Arts and Sciences, Department of Politics, Program in Government, Charlottesville, VA 22903. Offers MA, PhD, JD/MA, MBA/MA. *Students:* 34 full-time (10 women); includes 1 minority (Hispanic/Latino), 5 international. Average age 28. 72 applicants, 21% accepted, 7 enrolled. In 2014, 3 master's, 7 doctorates awarded. *Degree requirements:* For master's, 2 research/statistics courses or thesis; for doctorate, variable foreign language requirement, thesis/dissertation, 2 research/statistics courses. *Entrance requirements:* For master's and doctorate, GRE General Test, long writing sample; 2 letters of recommendation. Additional exam requirements/recommendations for international students: Required—TOEFL (minimum score 600 paper-based; 90 iBT), IELTS (minimum score 7). *Application deadline:* For fall admission, 12/4 for domestic and international students. Applications are processed on a rolling basis. Application fee: $60. Electronic applications accepted. *Expenses:* Tuition, state resident: full-time $14,164; part-time $349 per credit hour. Tuition, nonresident: full-time $23,722; part-time $1300 per credit hour. *Required fees:* $2514. *Financial support:* Fellowships and teaching assistantships available. Financial award application deadline: 12/4; financial award applicants required to submit FAFSA. *Unit head:* David Leblang, Chair, 434-924-3192, Fax: 434-924-3159, E-mail: dal7w@virginia.edu. *Application contact:* Jeffery A. Jenkins, Director of Graduate Studies, 434-924-3192, Fax: 434-924-3159, E-mail: jaj7d@virginia.edu.
Website: http://politics.virginia.edu/

University of Washington, Graduate School, College of Arts and Sciences, Department of Political Science, Seattle, WA 98195. Offers MA, PhD. *Degree requirements:* For doctorate, thesis/dissertation. *Entrance requirements:* For master's and doctorate, GRE General Test, minimum GPA of 3.0. Additional exam requirements/recommendations for international students: Required—TOEFL. Electronic applications accepted. *Faculty research:* American politics, comparative politics, international relations, political theory, political economy.

University of Waterloo, Graduate Studies, Faculty of Arts, Department of Political Science, Global Governance Program, Waterloo, ON N2L 3G1, Canada. Offers MA, PhD. *Entrance requirements:* For doctorate, MA. Additional exam requirements/recommendations for international students: Required—TOEFL. Electronic applications accepted. *Faculty research:* Global political economy, global environment, peace and security, global justice and human rights, multilateral institutions and diplomacy.

The University of Western Ontario, Faculty of Graduate Studies, Social Sciences Division, Department of Political Science, London, ON N6A 5B8, Canada. Offers MA, MPA, PhD. Part-time programs available. *Degree requirements:* For master's, thesis; for doctorate, comprehensive exam, thesis/dissertation. *Entrance requirements:* For master's, minimum B average, honors BA in political science or equivalent, sample of written work; for doctorate, MA in political science or equivalent. *Faculty research:* Political theory, Canadian politics, local government, comparative politics, international relations.

University of West Florida, College of Arts and Sciences: Arts, Department of Government, Pensacola, FL 32514-5750. Offers political science (MA), including public administration, security and diplomacy. Part-time and evening/weekend programs available. *Degree requirements:* For master's, thesis or alternative. *Entrance requirements:* For master's, GRE, official transcripts; minimum GPA of 3.0; 500-word writing sample in form of letter of intent; resume. Additional exam requirements/recommendations for international students: Required—TOEFL (minimum score 550 paper-based). *Faculty research:* Political campaigns, elections, law enforcement, growth management.

University of Windsor, Faculty of Graduate Studies, Faculty of Arts and Social Sciences, Department of Political Science, Windsor, ON N9B 3P4, Canada. Offers MA. Part-time programs available. *Entrance requirements:* For master's, minimum B+ average. Additional exam requirements/recommendations for international students: Required—TOEFL (minimum score 600 paper-based). Electronic applications accepted. *Faculty research:* Canadian politics and government, local government, comparative political Canadian public administration, public policy.

University of Wisconsin–Madison, Graduate School, College of Letters and Science, Department of Political Science, Madison, WI 53706-1380. Offers PhD. *Degree requirements:* For doctorate, thesis/dissertation. *Entrance requirements:* For doctorate, GRE General Test. Electronic applications accepted. *Expenses:* Tuition, state resident: full-time $10,723; part-time $745 per credit. Tuition, nonresident: full-time $24,054; part-time $1578 per credit. *Required fees:* $374 per semester. Tuition and fees vary according to course load, program and reciprocity agreements. *Faculty research:* Comparative politics, American politics, international relations, political theory, political methodology.

University of Wisconsin–Milwaukee, Graduate School, College of Letters and Sciences, Department of Political Science, Milwaukee, WI 53201-0413. Offers MA, PhD. *Degree requirements:* For master's, thesis or alternative; for doctorate, one foreign language, thesis/dissertation. *Entrance requirements:* For master's and doctorate, GRE General Test, minimum GPA of 3.0. Additional exam requirements/recommendations for international students: Required—TOEFL (minimum score 550 paper-based; 79 iBT), IELTS (minimum score 6.5). Electronic applications accepted.

University of Wyoming, College of Arts and Sciences, Department of Political Science, Program in Political Science, Laramie, WY 82071. Offers MA. Part-time programs available. *Degree requirements:* For master's, thesis or alternative. *Entrance requirements:* For master's, GRE General Test, bachelor's degree in political science, minimum GPA of 3.0. Additional exam requirements/recommendations for international students: Required—TOEFL (minimum score 525 paper-based). Electronic applications accepted. *Faculty research:* American government, public law, judicial politics, political theory, international relations.

Utah State University, School of Graduate Studies, College of Humanities, Arts and Social Sciences, Department of Political Science, Logan, UT 84322. Offers MA, MS. Part-time programs available. *Degree requirements:* For master's, one foreign language, thesis. *Entrance requirements:* For master's, GRE General Test, minimum GPA of 3.0. Additional exam requirements/recommendations for international students: Required—TOEFL. *Faculty research:* Political parties; social choice; international political economics; foreign policy; politics, markets, and public policy.

Vanderbilt University, Graduate School, Department of Political Science, Nashville, TN 37240-1001. Offers MA, MAT, PhD. *Faculty:* 26 full-time (11 women), 1 part-time/adjunct (0 women). *Students:* 39 full-time (17 women); includes 5 minority (1 Black or African American, non-Hispanic/Latino; 1 Asian, non-Hispanic/Latino; 2 Hispanic/Latino; 1 Two or more races, non-Hispanic/Latino), 10 international. Average age 28. 156 applicants, 13% accepted, 7 enrolled. In 2014, 5 master's, 7 doctorates awarded. Terminal master's awarded for partial completion of doctoral program. *Degree requirements:* For master's, thesis; for doctorate, thesis/dissertation, final and qualifying exams. *Entrance requirements:* For master's and doctorate, GRE General Test, writing sample. Additional exam requirements/recommendations for international students: Required—TOEFL (minimum score 570 paper-based; 88 iBT). *Application deadline:* For fall admission, 1/15 for domestic and international students. Electronic applications accepted. *Expenses: Tuition:* Full-time $42,768; part-time $1782 per credit hour. *Required fees:* $422. One-time fee: $30 full-time. *Financial support:* Fellowships with

full tuition reimbursements, research assistantships with full tuition reimbursements, teaching assistantships with full tuition reimbursements, Federal Work-Study, institutionally sponsored loans, scholarships/grants, and health care benefits available. Financial award application deadline: 1/15; financial award applicants required to submit CSS PROFILE or FAFSA. *Faculty research:* American politics, comparative politics, international politics, political theory, political culture and life. *Unit head:* Dr. Cindy Kam, Director of Graduate Studies, 615-322-4946, Fax: 615-343-6003, E-mail: cindy.d.kam@vanderbilt.edu. *Application contact:* Darlene Davidson, Administrative Assistant, 615-322-6222, Fax: 615-343-6003, E-mail: darlene.l.davidson@vanderbilt.edu.
Website: http://www.vanderbilt.edu/political-science/

Villanova University, Graduate School of Liberal Arts and Sciences, Department of Political Science, Villanova, PA 19085-1699. Offers MA. Part-time and evening/weekend programs available. Postbaccalaureate distance learning degree programs offered (minimal on-campus study). *Faculty:* 6. *Students:* 24 full-time (10 women), 5 part-time (2 women); includes 6 minority (1 Black or African American, non-Hispanic/Latino; 5 Hispanic/Latino), 1 international. Average age 28. 16 applicants, 75% accepted, 7 enrolled. In 2014, 21 master's awarded. *Degree requirements:* For master's, comprehensive exam (for some programs). *Entrance requirements:* For master's, GRE, minimum GPA of 3.0. Additional exam requirements/recommendations for international students: Required—TOEFL. *Application deadline:* For fall admission, 5/1 priority date for international students; for spring admission, 10/15 for international students. Applications are processed on a rolling basis. Application fee: $50. Electronic applications accepted. *Financial support:* Research assistantships, scholarships/grants, and unspecified assistantships available. Financial award applicants required to submit FAFSA. *Unit head:* Dr. Markus Kreuzer, Director, 610-519-4710.
Website: http://www.psc.villanova.edu/gradwww.htm

Virginia Commonwealth University, Graduate School, College of Humanities and Sciences, Wilder School of Government and Public Affairs, Richmond, VA 23284-9005. Offers MA, MPA, MS, MURP, PhD, CASR, CCJA, CPM, CURP, Certificate, Graduate Certificate, JD/MURP, MSW/Certificate.

Virginia Polytechnic Institute and State University, Graduate School, College of Liberal Arts and Human Sciences, Blacksburg, VA 24061. Offers career and technical education (MS Ed, Ed D, PhD, Ed S); communication (MA); counselor education (MA Ed, Ed D, PhD, Ed S); creative writing (MFA); curriculum and instruction (MA Ed, Ed D, PhD, Ed S); educational leadership and policy studies (MA Ed, Ed D, PhD, Ed S); educational research and evaluation (PhD); English (MA); foreign languages, cultures, and literatures (MA); higher education and student affairs (MA Ed); history (MA); human development (MS, PhD); material culture and public humanities (MA); philosophy (MA); political science (MA); rhetoric and writing (PhD); science and technology studies (MS, PhD); social, political, ethical, and cultural thought (PhD); sociology (MS, PhD); theater arts (MFA). *Faculty:* 421 full-time (216 women), 2 part-time/adjunct (both women). *Students:* 642 full-time (437 women), 537 part-time (344 women); includes 235 minority (132 Black or African American, non-Hispanic/Latino; 2 American Indian or Alaska Native, non-Hispanic/Latino; 27 Asian, non-Hispanic/Latino; 52 Hispanic/Latino; 1 Native Hawaiian or other Pacific Islander, non-Hispanic/Latino; 21 Two or more races, non-Hispanic/Latino), 81 international. Average age 34. 890 applicants, 46% accepted, 303 enrolled. In 2014, 342 master's, 96 doctorates, 33 other advanced degrees awarded. *Degree requirements:* For master's, comprehensive exam (for some programs), thesis (for some programs); for doctorate, comprehensive exam (for some programs), thesis/dissertation (for some programs). *Entrance requirements:* For master's and doctorate, GRE/GMAT (may vary by department). Additional exam requirements/recommendations for international students: Required—TOEFL (minimum score 550 paper-based). *Application deadline:* For fall admission, 8/1 for domestic students, 4/1 for international students; for spring admission, 1/1 for domestic students, 9/1 for international students. Applications are processed on a rolling basis. Application fee: $75. Electronic applications accepted. *Expenses:* Tuition, state resident: full-time $11,656; part-time $647.50 per credit hour. Tuition, nonresident: full-time $23,351; part-time $1297.25 per credit hour. *Required fees:* $2533; $465.75 per semester. Tuition and fees vary according to course load, campus/location and program. *Financial support:* In 2014–15, 19 research assistantships with full tuition reimbursements (averaging $22,141 per year), 231 teaching assistantships with full tuition reimbursements (averaging $19,470 per year) were awarded. Financial award application deadline: 3/1; financial award applicants required to submit FAFSA. *Total annual research expenditures:* $6.5 million. *Unit head:* Elizabeth Spiller, Dean, 540-231-6779, Fax: 540-231-7157, E-mail: espiller@vt.edu. *Application contact:* Melissa Elliott, Executive Assistant, 540-231-6779, Fax: 540-231-7157, E-mail: elliott1@vt.edu.
Website: http://www.clahs.vt.edu/

Virginia Polytechnic Institute and State University, VT Online, Blacksburg, VA 24061. Offers advanced transportation systems (Certificate); aerospace engineering (MS); agricultural and life sciences (MSLFS); business information systems (Graduate Certificate); career and technical education (MS); civil engineering (MS); computer engineering (M Eng, MS); decision support systems (Graduate Certificate); eLearning leadership (MA); electrical engineering (M Eng, MS); engineering administration (MEA); environmental engineering (Certificate); environmental politics and policy (Graduate Certificate); environmental sciences and engineering (MS); foundations of political analysis (Graduate Certificate); health product risk management (Graduate Certificate); industrial and systems engineering (MS); information policy and society (Graduate Certificate); information security (Graduate Certificate); information technology (MIT); instructional technology (MA); integrative STEM education (MA Ed); liberal arts (Graduate Certificate); life sciences: health product risk management (MS); natural resources (MNR, Graduate Certificate); networking (Graduate Certificate); nonprofit and nongovernmental organization management (Graduate Certificate); ocean engineering (MS); political science (MA); security studies (Graduate Certificate); software development (Graduate Certificate). *Expenses:* Tuition, state resident: full-time $11,656; part-time $647.50 per credit hour. Tuition, nonresident: full-time $23,351; part-time $1297.25 per credit hour. *Required fees:* $2533; $465.75 per semester. Tuition and fees vary according to course load, campus/location and program.

Washington State University, College of Liberal Arts, School of Politics, Philosophy and Public Affairs, Pullman, WA 99164-4880. Offers bioethics (Graduate Certificate); political science (MA, PhD); public affairs (MPA). MPA, MA, and PhD programs also offered at the Vancouver campus; Graduate Certificate offered through Global (online) campus. Postbaccalaureate distance learning degree programs offered (no on-campus study). *Students:* 33 full-time (13 women), 15 part-time (9 women); includes 9 minority (1 Black or African American, non-Hispanic/Latino; 1 American Indian or Alaska Native, non-Hispanic/Latino; 1 Asian, non-Hispanic/Latino; 5 Hispanic/Latino; 1 Two or more races, non-Hispanic/Latino), 4 international. Average age 30. 52 applicants, 54% accepted, 16 enrolled. In 2014, 12 master's, 2 doctorates, 6 other advanced degrees awarded. Terminal master's awarded for partial completion of doctoral program. *Degree requirements:* For master's, comprehensive exam (for some programs), thesis, oral exam; for doctorate, comprehensive exam, thesis/dissertation, oral exam, written exam. *Entrance requirements:* For master's, GRE General Test, minimum GPA of 3.0; for doctorate, GRE General Test, minimum GPA of 3.5. Additional exam requirements/recommendations for international students: Required—TOEFL. *Application deadline:* For fall admission, 2/1 for domestic and international students; for spring admission, 11/1 for domestic students, 7/1 for international students. Application fee: $75. Electronic applications accepted. *Expenses:* Tuition, state resident: full-time $11,768. Tuition, nonresident: full-time $25,200. *Required fees:* $960. Tuition and fees vary according to program. *Financial support:* In 2014–15, 34 students received support, including 2 research assistantships with full and partial tuition reimbursements available (averaging $14,411 per year), 21 teaching assistantships with full and partial tuition reimbursements available (averaging $14,120 per year). Financial award application deadline: 2/1; financial award applicants required to submit FAFSA. *Faculty research:* Political psychology and image theory, grass roots environmental policy, federal juvenile policy. *Unit head:* Dr. Thomas Preston, Professor/Director, 509-335-5225, Fax: 509-335-7990, E-mail: tpreston@wsu.edu. *Application contact:* Bonnie Kemper, Graduate and Student Records Coordinator, 509-335-2545, Fax: 509-335-1949, E-mail: bkemper@wsu.edu.
Website: http://libarts.wsu.edu/pppa/

Washington University in St. Louis, Graduate School of Arts and Sciences, Department of Political Science, St. Louis, MO 63130-4899. Offers PhD. *Degree requirements:* For doctorate, thesis/dissertation. *Entrance requirements:* For doctorate, GRE General Test. Additional exam requirements/recommendations for international students: Required—TOEFL. Electronic applications accepted. *Faculty research:* American politics, comparative politics, formal theory, international politics, law and courts, normative theory, political methodology.

Washington University in St. Louis, Graduate School of Arts and Sciences, Program in Political Economy and Public Policy, St. Louis, MO 63130-4899. Offers MA. *Degree requirements:* For master's, thesis or alternative. *Entrance requirements:* For master's, GRE General Test. Electronic applications accepted.

Wayne State University, College of Liberal Arts and Sciences, Department of Political Science, Detroit, MI 48202. Offers political science (MA, PhD); public administration (MPA), including economic development policy and management, health and human services policy and management, human and fiscal resource management, nonprofit policy and management, organizational behavior and management, urban and metropolitan policy and management; JD/MA. *Accreditation:* NASPAA. *Students:* 56 full-time (25 women), 78 part-time (49 women); includes 41 minority (28 Black or African American, non-Hispanic/Latino; 4 Asian, non-Hispanic/Latino; 5 Hispanic/Latino; 4 Two or more races, non-Hispanic/Latino), 12 international. Average age 34. 153 applicants, 41% accepted, 34 enrolled. In 2014, 30 master's, 5 doctorates awarded. *Degree requirements:* For master's, comprehensive exam; for doctorate, thesis/dissertation. *Entrance requirements:* For master's, GRE General Test, substantial undergraduate preparation in the social sciences (recommended); for doctorate, GRE General Test, 3 letters of recommendation; autobiography; interview. Additional exam requirements/recommendations for international students: Required—TOEFL (minimum score 550 paper-based; 79 iBT), TWE (minimum score 5.5), Michigan English Language Assessment Battery (minimum score 85); Recommended—IELTS (minimum score 6.5). *Application deadline:* For fall admission, 5/1 priority date for domestic and international students; for winter admission, 10/1 priority date for domestic students, 9/1 priority date for international students; for spring admission, 2/1 priority date for domestic students, 1/1 priority date for international students. Applications are processed on a rolling basis. Application fee: $0. Electronic applications accepted. *Expenses:* Tuition, state resident: full-time $10,294; part-time $571.90 per credit hour. Tuition, nonresident: full-time $29,730; part-time $1238.75 per credit hour. *Required fees:* $1365; $43.50 per credit hour. $291.10 per semester. Tuition and fees vary according to course load and program. *Financial support:* In 2014–15, 41 students received support, including 4 fellowships with tuition reimbursements available (averaging $14,146 per year), 13 teaching assistantships with tuition reimbursements available (averaging $16,838 per year); research assistantships with tuition reimbursements available, scholarships/grants, health care benefits, and unspecified assistantships also available. Financial award application deadline: 3/31; financial award applicants required to submit FAFSA. *Faculty research:* American politics and public policy, comparative politics and international relations, political theory, public administration, urban politics. *Unit head:* Dr. Daniel Geller, Chair, 313-577-6328, Fax: 313-993-3435, E-mail: dgeller@wayne.edu. *Application contact:* Dr. Sharon Lean, Graduate Director, E-mail: gradpolisci@wayne.edu.
Website: http://clas.wayne.edu/politicalscience/

Western Illinois University, School of Graduate Studies, College of Arts and Sciences, Department of Political Science, Macomb, IL 61455-1390. Offers MA. Part-time programs available. *Students:* 24 full-time (6 women), 4 part-time (1 woman); includes 10 minority (8 Black or African American, non-Hispanic/Latino; 1 Hispanic/Latino; 1 Two or more races, non-Hispanic/Latino), 6 international. Average age 28. 18 applicants, 72% accepted, 10 enrolled. In 2014, 11 master's awarded. *Degree requirements:* For master's, comprehensive exam, thesis or alternative. *Entrance requirements:* Additional exam requirements/recommendations for international students: Required—TOEFL (minimum score 550 paper-based; 80 iBT). *Application deadline:* Applications are processed on a rolling basis. Application fee: $30. Electronic applications accepted. *Financial support:* In 2014–15, 14 students received support, including 7 research assistantships with full tuition reimbursements available (averaging $7,544 per year), 9 teaching assistantships with full tuition reimbursements available (averaging $8,688 per year). Financial award applicants required to submit FAFSA. *Unit head:* Dr. Keith Boeckelman, Chairperson, 309-298-1055. *Application contact:* Dr. Nancy Parsons, Associate Provost and Director of Graduate Studies, 309-298-1806, Fax: 309-298-2345, E-mail: grad-office@wiu.edu.
Website: http://www.wiu.edu/cas/Political_Science/

Western Kentucky University, Graduate Studies, Potter College of Arts and Letters, Department of Political Science, Bowling Green, KY 42101. Offers MPA. *Accreditation:* NASPAA. Part-time and evening/weekend programs available. *Degree requirements:* For master's, comprehensive exam, final exam. *Entrance requirements:* For master's, GRE General Test, minimum GPA of 2.75. Additional exam requirements/recommendations for international students: Required—TOEFL (minimum score 555 paper-based; 79 iBT). *Faculty research:* Role of non-profits, comparative policy analysis, social welfare policy, rural administration, ethics and bureaucracy.

Western Michigan University, Graduate College, College of Arts and Sciences, Department of Political Science, Kalamazoo, MI 49008. Offers international development administration (MIDA), including Peace Corps; political science (MA, PhD). *Degree requirements:* For master's, thesis optional; for doctorate, thesis/dissertation. *Application deadline:* For fall admission, 2/15 for domestic students. *Financial support:* Application deadline: 2/15; applicants required to submit FAFSA. *Application contact:* Admissions and Orientation, 269-387-2000, Fax: 269-387-2096.

Western Washington University, Graduate School, College of Humanities and Social Sciences, Department of Political Science, Bellingham, WA 98225-5996. Offers MA. Part-time programs available. *Degree requirements:* For master's, comprehensive exam, thesis (for some programs). *Entrance requirements:* For master's, GRE General Test, minimum GPA of 3.0 in last 60 semester hours or last 90 quarter hours. Additional exam requirements/recommendations for international students: Required—TOEFL

(minimum score 567 paper-based). Electronic applications accepted. *Faculty research:* Elections, environment, identity, international relations.

West Virginia University, Eberly College of Arts and Sciences, Department of Political Science, Morgantown, WV 26506. Offers American public policy and politics (MA); international and comparative public policy and politics (MA); political science (PhD); public policy analysis (PhD). Terminal master's awarded for partial completion of doctoral program. *Degree requirements:* For master's, thesis optional; for doctorate, comprehensive exam, thesis/dissertation. *Entrance requirements:* For master's, GRE General Test, minimum GPA of 2.75; for doctorate, GRE General Test, minimum GPA of 3.0. Additional exam requirements/recommendations for international students: Required—TOEFL. *Faculty research:* Public policy, research methods, foreign policy analysis, judicial politics, environmental and energy policy.

Wilfrid Laurier University, Faculty of Graduate and Postdoctoral Studies, Faculty of Arts, Department of Political Science, Waterloo, ON N2L 3C5, Canada. Offers Canadian political studies (MA); comparative politics/international relations (MA). Part-time programs available. *Entrance requirements:* For master's, honors bachelor's degree or the equivalent in political science, minimum B average in undergraduate course work. Additional exam requirements/recommendations for international students: Required—TOEFL (minimum score 89 iBT). Electronic applications accepted. *Faculty research:* Political behavior/political psychology, Canadian political studies, comparative, politics/relations, public opinion and electoral studies, international.

Wilfrid Laurier University, Faculty of Graduate and Postdoctoral Studies, School of International Policy and Governance, Global Governance Program, Waterloo, ON N2L 3C5, Canada. Offers conflict and security (PhD); global environment (PhD); global justice and human rights (PhD); global political economy (PhD); global social governance (PhD); multilateral institutions and diplomacy (PhD). Offered jointly with University of Waterloo. *Degree requirements:* For doctorate, thesis/dissertation. *Entrance requirements:* For doctorate, MA in political science, history, economics, international development studies, international peace studies, globalization studies,

environmental studies or related field with minimum A-. Additional exam requirements/recommendations for international students: Required—TOEFL (minimum score 89 iBT). Electronic applications accepted. *Faculty research:* Global political economy, global environment, conflict and security, global justice and human rights, multilateral institutions and diplomacy.

Wilfrid Laurier University, Faculty of Graduate and Postdoctoral Studies, School of International Policy and Governance, International Public Policy Program, Waterloo, ON N2L 3C5, Canada. Offers global governance (MIPP); human security (MIPP); international economic relations (MIPP); international environmental policy (MIPP). Offered jointly with University of Waterloo. *Entrance requirements:* For master's, honours BA with minimum B average. Additional exam requirements/recommendations for international students: Required—TOEFL (minimum score 89 iBT). Electronic applications accepted. *Faculty research:* International environmental policy, international economic relations, human security, global governance.

Yale University, Graduate School of Arts and Sciences, Department of Political Science, New Haven, CT 06520. Offers PhD. *Degree requirements:* For doctorate, one foreign language, thesis/dissertation. *Entrance requirements:* For doctorate, GRE General Test. *Faculty research:* U.N. and international security.

York University, Faculty of Graduate Studies, Faculty of Liberal Arts and Professional Studies, Program in Political Science, Toronto, ON M3J 1P3, Canada. Offers MA, PhD. Part-time programs available. *Degree requirements:* For master's, thesis or alternative; for doctorate, one foreign language, comprehensive exam, thesis/dissertation. Electronic applications accepted.

York University, Faculty of Graduate Studies, Program in Social and Political Thought, Toronto, ON M3J 1P3, Canada. Offers MA, PhD. Part-time programs available. *Degree requirements:* For master's, one foreign language, thesis or alternative, oral exams; for doctorate, one foreign language, comprehensive exam, thesis/dissertation. Electronic applications accepted.

Section 24
Psychology and Counseling

This section contains a directory of institutions offering graduate work in psychology and counseling, followed by in-depth entries submitted by institutions that chose to prepare detailed program descriptions. Additional information about programs listed in the directory but not augmented by an in-depth entry may be obtained by writing directly to the dean of a graduate school or chair of a department at the address given in the directory.

For programs offering related work, see also in this book *Criminology and Forensics, Family and Consumer Sciences,* and *Sociology, Anthropology, and Archaeology.* In the other guides in this series:

Graduate Programs in the Biological/Biomedical Sciences & Health-Related Medical Professions

See *Biological and Biomedical Sciences; Genetics, Developmental Biology, and Reproductive Biology; Neuroscience and Neurobiology; Nursing (Psychiatric Nursing); Pharmacy and Pharmaceutical Sciences; Pharmacology and Toxicology;* and *Public Health*

Graduate Programs in Business, Education, Information Studies, Law & Social Work

See *Education* and *Social Work*

CONTENTS

Program Directories

Displays and Close-Ups

See also:

Psychology—General

Abilene Christian University, Graduate School, College of Arts and Sciences, Department of Psychology, Program in Psychology, Abilene, TX 79699-9100. Offers MS. *Students:* 3 full-time (2 women); includes 1 minority (Hispanic/Latino). 14 applicants, 21% accepted, 2 enrolled. In 2014, 1 master's awarded. *Degree requirements:* For master's, comprehensive exam, thesis. *Entrance requirements:* Additional exam requirements/recommendations for international students: Required—TOEFL (minimum score 550 paper-based; 90 iBT), IELTS (minimum score 6.5), PTE. *Application deadline:* For fall admission, 3/1 priority date for domestic students; for spring admission, 11/1 for domestic students. Applications are processed on a rolling basis. Application fee: $50. Electronic applications accepted. *Expenses: Tuition:* Full-time $18,228; part-time $1016 per credit hour. *Financial support:* In 2014–15, 1 student received support. Federal Work-Study available. Support available to part-time students. Financial award application deadline: 4/1; financial award applicants required to submit FAFSA. *Unit head:* Dr. Robert McKelvain, Graduate Director, 325-674-2286, Fax: 325-674-6968, E-mail: mckelvainr@acu.edu. *Application contact:* Corey Patterson, Director of Graduate Admission and Recruiting, 325-674-6566, Fax: 325-674-6717, E-mail: gradinfo@acu.edu.

Acadia University, Faculty of Pure and Applied Science, Department of Psychology, Wolfville, NS B4P 2R6, Canada. Offers clinical psychology (M Sc). *Degree requirements:* For master's, thesis. *Entrance requirements:* For master's, GRE General Test, GRE Subject Test, honors degree or equivalent. Additional exam requirements/recommendations for international students: Required—TOEFL (minimum score 580 paper-based; 93 iBT), IELTS (minimum score 6.5). *Faculty research:* Social psychology, job stress, psychotherapy, cognition perception, development.

Adelphi University, Derner Institute of Advanced Psychological Studies, Garden City, NY 11530-0701. Offers clinical psychology (PhD); general psychology (MA); mental health counseling (MA); school psychology (MA). *Accreditation:* APA (one or more programs are accredited). Part-time programs available. *Faculty:* 24 full-time (13 women), 51 part-time/adjunct (26 women). *Students:* 211 full-time (172 women), 72 part-time (60 women); includes 72 minority (14 Black or African American, non-Hispanic/Latino; 14 Asian, non-Hispanic/Latino; 39 Hispanic/Latino; 5 Two or more races, non-Hispanic/Latino), 20 international. Average age 29. 418 applicants, 43% accepted, 87 enrolled. In 2014, 73 master's, 29 doctorates awarded. *Degree requirements:* For master's, comprehensive exam; for doctorate, thesis/dissertation, research (second-year), 1-year internship. *Entrance requirements:* For master's, 3 letters of recommendation, minimum GPA of 3.0; for doctorate, GRE General Test, GRE Subject Test, interview; resume; undergraduate course work in psychology, experimental psychology, statistics, developmental psychology, and abnormal psychology. Additional exam requirements/recommendations for international students: Required—TOEFL (minimum score 550 paper-based; 80 iBT). *Application deadline:* For fall admission, 4/1 priority date for domestic students, 5/1 priority date for international students; for spring admission, 11/1 priority date for international students. Application fee: $50. Electronic applications accepted. *Expenses:* Expenses: Contact institution. *Financial support:* Research assistantships, career-related internships or fieldwork, Federal Work-Study, institutionally sponsored loans, and unspecified assistantships available. Financial award application deadline: 2/15; financial award applicants required to submit FAFSA. *Faculty research:* Psychoanalytic processes, trauma and resilience, personality disorders, program evaluation, psychotherapy process. *Unit head:* Dr. Jacques P. Barber, Dean, 516-877-4803, E-mail: jcmuran@adelphi.edu. *Application contact:* Christine Murphy, Director of Admissions, 516-877-3050, Fax: 516-877-3039, E-mail: graduateadmissions@adelphi.edu.
Website: http://derner.adelphi.edu/

See Display below and Close-Up on page 1205.

⭐ **Adler University,** Programs in Psychology, Chicago, IL 60602. Offers advanced Adlerian psychotherapy (Certificate); art therapy (MA); clinical neuropsychology (Certificate); clinical psychology (Psy D); community psychology (MA); counseling and organizational psychology (MA); counseling psychology (MA); criminology (MA); emergency management leadership (MA); forensic psychology (MA); marriage and family counseling (MA); marriage and family therapy (Certificate); military psychology (MA); nonprofit management (MA); organizational psychology (MA); police psychology (MA); public policy and administration (MA); rehabilitation counseling (MA); sport and health psychology (MA); substance abuse counseling (Certificate); Psy D/Certificate; Psy D/MACAT; Psy D/MACP; Psy D/MAMFC; Psy D/MASAC. *Accreditation:* APA. Part-time and evening/weekend programs available. Postbaccalaureate distance learning degree programs offered (minimal on-campus study). Terminal master's awarded for partial completion of doctoral program. *Degree requirements:* For master's, thesis or alternative, oral exam, practicum; for doctorate, thesis/dissertation, clinical exam, internship, oral exam, practicum, written qualifying exam. *Entrance requirements:* For master's, 12 semester hours in psychology, minimum GPA of 3.0; for doctorate, 18 semester hours in psychology, minimum GPA of 3.25; for Certificate, appropriate master's or doctoral degree. Additional exam requirements/recommendations for international students: Required—TOEFL (minimum score 550 paper-based; 79 iBT). Electronic applications accepted.

See Display on next page and Close-Up on page 1207.

Alabama Agricultural and Mechanical University, School of Graduate Studies, School of Education, Department of Counseling and Special Education, Huntsville, AL 35811. Offers communicative disorders (M Ed, MS); psychology and counseling (MS, Ed S), including clinical psychology (MS), counseling and guidance, counseling psychology (MS), personnel management (MS), psychometry (MS), school psychology (MS); special education (M Ed, MS). *Accreditation:* CORE; NCATE. Part-time and evening/weekend programs available. *Degree requirements:* For master's, comprehensive exam. *Entrance requirements:* For master's, GRE General Test. Additional exam requirements/recommendations for international students: Required—TOEFL (minimum score 500 paper-based; 61 iBT). *Faculty research:* Increasing numbers of minorities in special education and speech-language pathology.

Alliant International University–Fresno, California School of Professional Psychology, Fresno, CA 93727. Offers MA, PhD, Psy D, MA/PhD, Psy D/MA. *Accreditation:* APA. *Degree requirements:* For doctorate, comprehensive exam, thesis/dissertation. *Entrance requirements:* For doctorate, minimum GPA of 3.0, letters of recommendation, essay, interview. Additional exam requirements/recommendations for international students: Required—TOEFL (minimum score 550 paper-based), TWE (minimum score 5). Electronic applications accepted. *Faculty research:* Parent-child relationships, LGBT families, social justice, women's health, neurocognitive functioning.

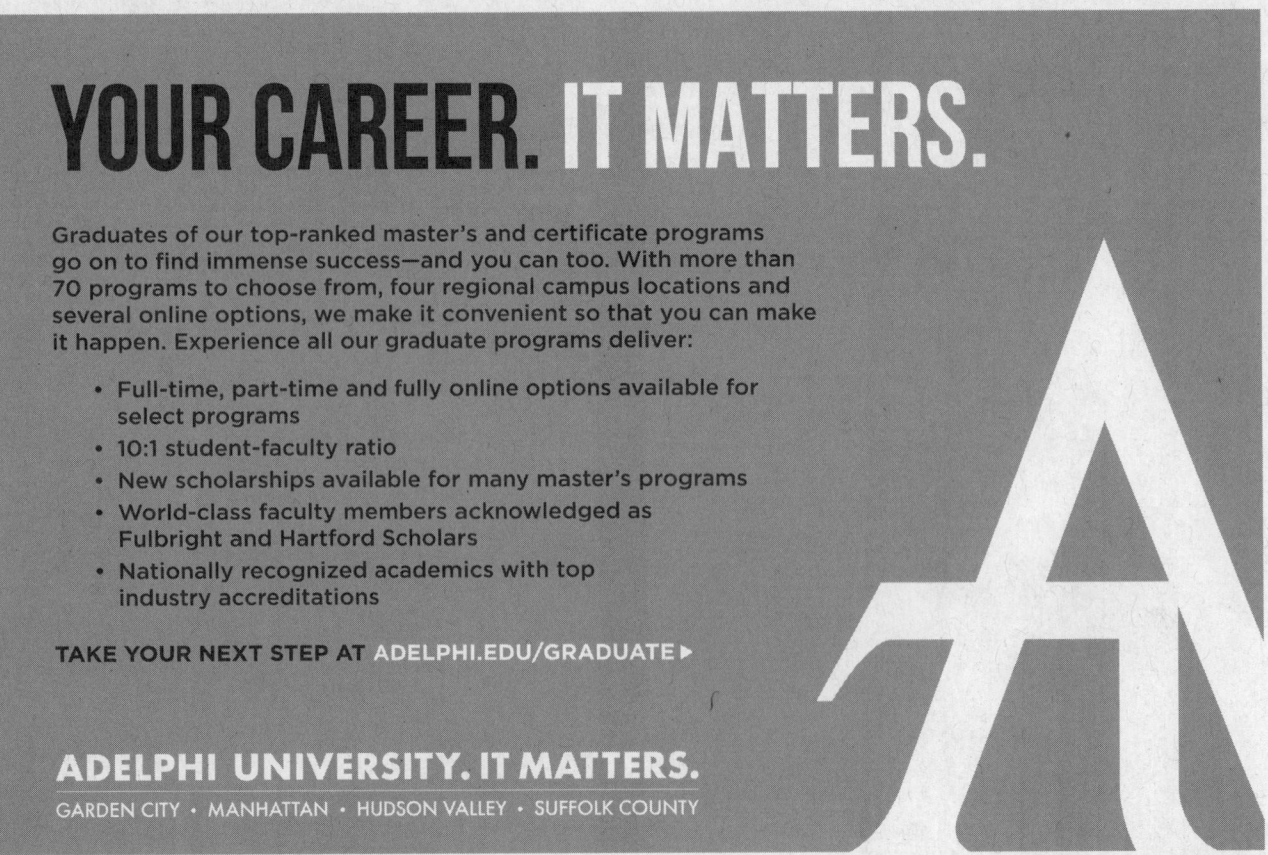

Alliant International University–Los Angeles, California School of Professional Psychology, Alhambra, CA 91803-1360. Offers MA, PhD, Psy D. *Accreditation:* APA. *Degree requirements:* For doctorate, comprehensive exam, thesis/dissertation. *Entrance requirements:* For doctorate, interview, minimum GPA of 3.0 in psychology and overall, letters of recommendation. Additional exam requirements/recommendations for international students: Required—TOEFL (minimum score 600 paper-based), TWE (minimum score 5). Electronic applications accepted. *Faculty research:* Family therapy, multi-cultural psychology, post-traumatic stress, assessment, community mental health.

Alliant International University–Sacramento, California School of Professional Psychology, Sacramento, CA 95833. Offers MA, Psy D. Part-time programs available. *Degree requirements:* For doctorate, comprehensive exam, thesis/dissertation. *Entrance requirements:* For master's and doctorate, minimum GPA of 3.0, recommendations, essay. Additional exam requirements/recommendations for international students: Required—TOEFL (minimum score 600 paper-based), TWE (minimum score 5). Electronic applications accepted. *Faculty research:* International research testing a model of health behavior change for the developing world, immigration stress, addiction, issues facing LGBTQI community life.

Alliant International University–San Diego, California School of Professional Psychology, San Diego, CA 92131-1799. Offers MA, MS, PhD, Psy D. *Accreditation:* APA. Part-time programs available. Terminal master's awarded for partial completion of doctoral program. *Degree requirements:* For master's, practicum; for doctorate, comprehensive exam, thesis/dissertation, internship or practicum. *Entrance requirements:* For master's and doctorate, minimum GPA of 3.0, essay, letters of recommendation, interview. Additional exam requirements/recommendations for international students: Required—TOEFL (minimum score 550 paper-based; 80 iBT), TWE (minimum score 5). *Faculty research:* Couples therapy, depression, multicultural and international issues, evidence-based practice, neuropsychology of autism, ADHD.

Alliant International University–San Francisco, California School of Professional Psychology, San Francisco, CA 94133-1221. Offers MA, Post-Doctoral MS, PhD, Psy D, Certificate. *Accreditation:* APA (one or more programs are accredited). *Degree requirements:* For doctorate, comprehensive exam, thesis/dissertation, internship. *Entrance requirements:* For master's and doctorate, minimum GPA of 3.0, recommendations, essay, interview. Additional exam requirements/recommendations for international students: Required—TOEFL (minimum score 550 paper-based; 80 iBT), TWE (minimum score 5). Electronic applications accepted. *Faculty research:* Multicultural issues, lesbian/gay/bisexual/transgender issues, health psychology, family systems, substance abuse.

American International College, School of Graduate and Adult Education, Graduate Psychology Department, General Psychology Program, Springfield, MA 01109-3189. Offers MA. Part-time and evening/weekend programs available. *Students:* 1 part-time (0 women); minority (Black or African American, non-Hispanic/Latino). Average age 25. 1 applicant, 100% accepted, 1 enrolled. *Entrance requirements:* For master's, bachelor's degree with minimum GPA of 2.75. Additional exam requirements/recommendations for international students: Required—TOEFL. *Application deadline:* Applications are processed on a rolling basis. Application fee: $50. Electronic applications accepted. *Expenses:* Expenses: $795 per credit; registration fee $30 per term. *Financial support:* Application deadline: 4/1; applicants required to submit FAFSA. *Unit head:* Dr. Lina Racicot, Director, 413-205-3909, Fax: 413-205-3943, E-mail: lina.racicot@aic.edu. *Application contact:* Kerry Barnes, Director of Graduate Admissions, 413-205-3703, Fax: 413-205-3051, E-mail: kerry.barnes@aic.edu.
Website: http://www.aic.edu/academics/graduate

American Public University System, AMU/APU Graduate Programs, Charles Town, WV 25414. Offers accounting (MBA, MS); criminal justice (MA), including business administration, emergency and disaster management, general (MA, MS); educational leadership (M Ed); emergency and disaster management (MA); entrepreneurship (MBA); environmental policy and management (MS), including environmental planning, environmental sustainability, fish and wildlife management, general (MA, MS), global environmental management; finance (MBA); general (MBA); global business management (MBA); history (MA), including American history, ancient and classical history, European history, global history, public history; homeland security (MA), including business administration, counter-terrorism studies, criminal justice, cyber, emergency management and public health, intelligence studies, transportation security; homeland security resource allocation (MBA); humanities (MA); information technology (MS), including digital forensics, enterprise software development, information assurance and security, IT project management; information technology management (MBA); intelligence studies (MA), including criminal intelligence, cyber, general (MA, MS), homeland security, intelligence analysis, intelligence collection, intelligence management, intelligence operations, terrorism studies; international relations and conflict resolution (MA), including comparative and security issues, conflict resolution, international and transnational security issues, peacekeeping; legal studies (MA); management (MA), including defense management, general (MA, MS), human resource management, organizational leadership, public administration; marketing (MBA); military history (MA), including American military history, American Revolution, civil war, war since 1945, World War II; military studies (MA), including joint warfare, strategic leadership; national security studies (MA), including general (MA, MS), homeland security, regional security studies, security and intelligence analysis, terrorism studies; nonprofit management (MBA); political science (MA), including American politics and government, comparative government and development, general (MA, MS), international relations, public policy; psychology (MA); public administration (MPA), including disaster management, environmental policy, health policy, human resources, national security, organizational management, security management; public health (MPH); reverse logistics management (MA); school counseling (M Ed); security management (MA); space studies (MS), including aerospace science, general (MA, MS), planetary science; sports and health sciences (MS); teaching (M Ed), including curriculum and instruction for elementary teachers, elementary reading, English language learners, instructional leadership, online learning, special education; transportation and logistics management (MA), including general (MA, MS), maritime engineering management, reverse logistics management. Programs offered via distance learning only. Part-time and evening/weekend programs available. Postbaccalaureate distance learning degree programs offered (no on-campus study). *Faculty:* 426 full-time (236 women), 1,864 part-time/adjunct (880 women). *Students:* 475 full-time (215 women), 10,067 part-time (4,085 women); includes 3,462 minority (1,863 Black or African American, non-Hispanic/Latino; 74 American Indian or Alaska Native, non-Hispanic/Latino; 273 Asian, non-Hispanic/Latino; 831 Hispanic/Latino; 78 Native Hawaiian or other Pacific Islander, non-Hispanic/Latino; 343 Two or more races, non-Hispanic/Latino), 131 international. Average age 36. In 2014, 3,740 master's awarded. *Degree requirements:* For master's, comprehensive exam or practicum. *Entrance requirements:* For master's, official transcript showing earned bachelor's degree from institution accredited by recognized accrediting body. Additional exam requirements/recommendations for international students: Required—TOEFL (minimum score 550 paper-based), IELTS (minimum score 6.5). *Application deadline:* Applications are processed on a rolling basis. Application fee: $0. Electronic applications accepted. *Financial support:* Applicants required to submit FAFSA. *Faculty research:* Military history, criminal justice, management performance, national security. *Unit head:* Dr. Karan Powell, Executive Vice President and Provost, 877-468-6268, Fax: 304-724-3780. *Application contact:* Terry Grant, Vice President of Enrollment Management, 877-468-6268, Fax: 304-724-3780, E-mail: info@apus.edu.
Website: http://www.apus.edu

Psychology—General

The American University in Cairo, School of Humanities and Social Sciences, Department of Sociology, Anthropology, Psychology, and Egyptology, Cairo, Egypt. Offers Egyptology and Coptology (MA); psychology (MA); sociology and anthropology (MA). *Degree requirements:* For master's, one foreign language, thesis. *Entrance requirements:* Additional exam requirements/recommendations for international students: Required—English entrance exam and/or TOEFL. Electronic applications accepted. Tuition and fees vary according to course load and program. *Faculty research:* Development, gender, sociopolitical economic formulations, social science indigenization, Arab world.

American University of Beirut, Graduate Programs, Faculty of Arts and Sciences, Beirut, Lebanon. Offers anthropology (MA); Arab and Middle Eastern history (PhD); Arabic language and literature (MA, PhD); archaeology (MA); biology (MS); cell and molecular biology (PhD); chemistry (MS); clinical psychology (MA); computational sciences (MS); computer science (MS); economics (MA); English language (MA); English literature (MA); environmental policy planning (MS); financial economics (MAFE); geology (MS); history (MA); mathematics (MA, MS); media studies (MA); Middle Eastern studies (MA); physics (MS); political studies (MA); psychology (MA); public administration (MA); sociology (MA); statistics (MA, MS); theoretical physics (PhD); transnational American studies (MA). Part-time programs available. *Faculty:* 107 full-time (32 women), 6 part-time/adjunct (2 women). *Students:* 230 full-time (161 women), 209 part-time (146 women). Average age 26. 261 applicants, 70% accepted, 83 enrolled. In 2014, 68 master's, 2 doctorates awarded. *Degree requirements:* For master's, one foreign language, comprehensive exam, thesis (for some programs); for doctorate, one foreign language, comprehensive exam, thesis/dissertation. *Entrance requirements:* For master's, GRE (for some MA/MS programs), letter of recommendation; for doctorate, GRE, letters of recommendation. Additional exam requirements/recommendations for international students: Required—TOEFL (minimum score 600 paper-based; 97 iBT), IELTS (minimum score 7). *Application deadline:* For fall admission, 4/1 for domestic and international students; for spring admission, 11/1 for domestic and international students. Application fee: $50. Electronic applications accepted. *Expenses: Tuition:* Full-time $15,462; part-time $859 per credit. *Required fees:* $692. Tuition and fees vary according to course load and program. *Financial support:* Research assistantships, career-related internships or fieldwork, institutionally sponsored loans, scholarships/grants, health care benefits, and unspecified assistantships available. Financial award application deadline: 2/4; financial award applicants required to submit FAFSA. *Faculty research:* Determinants of language proficiency among Arab learners of English as a foreign language; opinion mining, information retrieval, runtime verification, high performance computing; solar and fuel cells, self-organizing systems, heterocyclic chemistry, air and water chemistry; complex analysis, harmonic analysis, number theory; social and political psychology, clinical psychology; thin films physics and technology; theory of soft matter; religious and ethnic conflict; sports and politics. *Total annual research expenditures:* $966,000. *Unit head:* Dr. Patrick McGreevy, Dean, 961-1374374 Ext. 3800, Fax: 961-1744461, E-mail: pm07@aub.edu.lb. *Application contact:* Dr. Salim Kanaan, Director, Admissions Office, 961-1350000 Ext. 2590, Fax: 961-1750775, E-mail: sk00@aub.edu.lb. Website: http://www.aub.edu.lb/fas/

Andrews University, School of Graduate Studies, School of Education, Department of Graduate Psychology and Counseling, Berrien Springs, MI 49104. Offers community counseling (MA), including clinical mental health counseling, community counseling; counseling psychology (PhD); educational and developmental psychology (MA, Ed D, PhD), including educational and developmental psychology (MA), educational psychology (Ed D, PhD); school counseling (MA); school psychology (Ed S); special education (MS). *Accreditation:* ACA (one or more programs are accredited). Part-time programs available. *Faculty:* 12 full-time (5 women), 2 part-time/adjunct (0 women). *Students:* 79 full-time (60 women), 14 part-time (12 women); includes 33 minority (18 Black or African American, non-Hispanic/Latino; 1 American Indian or Alaska Native, non-Hispanic/Latino; 5 Asian, non-Hispanic/Latino; 7 Hispanic/Latino; 2 Two or more races, non-Hispanic/Latino), 21 international. Average age 35. 75 applicants, 48% accepted, 18 enrolled. In 2014, 14 master's, 2 doctorates, 7 other advanced degrees awarded. Terminal master's awarded for partial completion of doctoral program. *Degree requirements:* For master's, thesis optional; for doctorate, thesis/dissertation. *Entrance requirements:* For master's, GRE Subject Test, minimum GPA of 2.6; for doctorate, GRE General Test, MA, minimum GPA of 3.5, sample of research. Additional exam requirements/recommendations for international students: Required—TOEFL (minimum score 550 paper-based). *Application deadline:* Applications are processed on a rolling basis. Application fee: $40. Tuition and fees vary according to course level. *Faculty research:* Testing methods, temperament, African-American studies, counseling process, multicultural issues. *Unit head:* Dr. Rudi Bailey, Chair, 269-471-3473. *Application contact:* Monica Wringer, Supervisor of Graduate Admission, 800-253-2874, Fax: 269-471-6321, E-mail: graduate@andrews.edu.

Angelo State University, College of Graduate Studies, College of Arts and Sciences, Department of Psychology, Sociology and Social Work, San Angelo, TX 76909. Offers psychology (MS), including applied psychology, counseling psychology, industrial and organizational psychology. Part-time and evening/weekend programs available. *Degree requirements:* For master's, comprehensive exam, thesis optional. *Entrance requirements:* For master's, GRE General Test (for industrial and organizational psychology only), essay, letters of recommendation (for industrial and organizational psychology only). Additional exam requirements/recommendations for international students: Required—TOEFL or IELTS. Electronic applications accepted.

Antioch University Los Angeles, Graduate Programs, Program in Psychology, Culver City, CA 90230. Offers clinical psychology (MA); psychology (MA). Part-time programs available. *Degree requirements:* For master's, thesis (for some programs), internship. *Entrance requirements:* For master's, interview. Additional exam requirements/recommendations for international students: Required—TOEFL. *Faculty research:* Creativity and humor, ethnic humor, adult development, Jungian theory, psychoanalytic theory.

Antioch University Midwest, Graduate Programs, Individualized Liberal and Professional Studies Program, Yellow Springs, OH 45387-1609. Offers liberal and professional studies (MA), including counseling, creative writing, education, liberal studies, management, modern literature, psychology, visual arts. Part-time and evening/weekend programs available. Postbaccalaureate distance learning degree programs offered (minimal on-campus study). *Degree requirements:* For master's, thesis or alternative. *Entrance requirements:* For master's, resume, goal statement, interview. Electronic applications accepted. *Expenses:* Contact institution.

Antioch University Seattle, Graduate Programs, Program in Psychology, Seattle, WA 98121-1814. Offers counseling (MA); psychology (MA, Psy D). Part-time and evening/weekend programs available. *Degree requirements:* For master's, internship; for doctorate, thesis/dissertation. Electronic applications accepted. *Faculty research:* Trauma and post-traumatic stress disorders, workplace harassment and violence, multicultural issues and diversity.

Appalachian State University, Cratis D. Williams Graduate School, Department of Psychology, Boone, NC 28608. Offers clinical health psychology (MA); general experimental psychology (MA); industrial and organizational psychology (MA); MA/SSP.

Part-time programs available. *Degree requirements:* For master's, comprehensive exam, thesis optional, exit exam. *Entrance requirements:* For master's, GRE General Test, 3 letters of recommendation. Additional exam requirements/recommendations for international students: Required—TOEFL (minimum score 550 paper-based; 79 iBT) or IELTS (minimum score 6.5). Electronic applications accepted. *Faculty research:* Eating disorders, school-based consultations, organizational behavior management, brain mechanisms of sound localization, parenting styles.

Arcadia University, Graduate Studies, Department of Psychology, Glenside, PA 19038-3295. Offers community counseling (MACP); school counseling (MACP). Part-time programs available. *Degree requirements:* For master's, practicum. *Entrance requirements:* For master's, GRE General Test or MAT. *Expenses:* Contact institution.

Arcadia University, Graduate Studies, School of Education, Glenside, PA 19038-3295. Offers art education (M Ed); computer education (CAS); curriculum (CAS); curriculum studies (M Ed); early childhood education (M Ed, CAS), including individualized (M Ed), master teacher (M Ed), research in child development (M Ed); educational leadership (M Ed, Ed D, CAS); elementary education (M Ed, CAS); English education (MA Ed); environmental education (MA Ed, CAS); history education (MA Ed); instructional technology (M Ed); language arts (M Ed, CAS); library science (M Ed); mathematics education (M Ed, MA Ed, CAS); music education (MA Ed); psychology (MA Ed); reading (M Ed, CAS); science education (M Ed, CAS); secondary education (M Ed, CAS); special education (M Ed, Ed D, CAS); theater arts (MA Ed); written communication (MA Ed). *Accreditation:* NASAD. Part-time and evening/weekend programs available. Postbaccalaureate distance learning degree programs offered (minimal on-campus study). Electronic applications accepted. *Expenses:* Contact institution.

Argosy University, Atlanta, College of Psychology and Behavioral Sciences, Atlanta, GA 30328. Offers clinical psychology (MA, Psy D, Postdoctoral Respecialization Certificate), including child and family psychology (Psy D), general adult clinical (Psy D), health psychology (Psy D), neuropsychology/geropsychology (Psy D); community counseling (MA), including marriage and family therapy; counselor education and supervision (Ed D); forensic psychology (MA); industrial organizational psychology (MA); marriage and family therapy (Certificate); sport-exercise psychology (MA). *Accreditation:* APA.

Argosy University, Chicago, College of Psychology and Behavioral Sciences, Chicago, IL 60601. Offers clinical psychology (MA, Psy D), including child and adolescent psychology (Psy D), client-centered and experiential psychotherapies (Psy D), diversity and multicultural psychology (Psy D), family psychology (Psy D), forensic psychology (Psy D), health psychology (Psy D), neuropsychology (Psy D), organizational consulting (Psy D), psychoanalytic psychology (Psy D), psychology and spirituality (Psy D); community counseling (MA); counseling psychology (Ed D), including counselor education and supervision; counselor education and supervision (Ed D); industrial organizational psychology (MA). *Accreditation:* APA (one or more programs are accredited). Postbaccalaureate distance learning degree programs offered (minimal on-campus study).

Argosy University, Dallas, College of Psychology and Behavioral Sciences, Farmers Branch, TX 75244. Offers MA, Ed D, Psy D.

Argosy University, Denver, College of Psychology and Behavioral Sciences, Denver, CO 80231. Offers clinical mental health counseling (MA); clinical psychology (MA, Psy D); counseling psychology (Ed D); counselor education and supervision (Ed D); forensic psychology (MA); industrial organizational psychology (MA); marriage and family therapy (MA, DMFT).

Argosy University, Hawai`i, College of Psychology and Behavioral Sciences, Honolulu, HI 96813. Offers MA, MS, Ed D, Psy D, Certificate, Postdoctoral Respecialization Certificate. *Accreditation:* APA.

Argosy University, Inland Empire, College of Psychology and Behavioral Sciences, Ontario, CA 91761. Offers clinical psychology/marriage and family therapy (MA); counseling psychology (Ed D); counseling psychology/marriage and family therapy (MA); forensic psychology (MA); industrial organizational psychology (MA); sport-exercise psychology (MA).

Argosy University, Los Angeles, College of Psychology and Behavioral Sciences, Santa Monica, CA 90045. Offers clinical psychology/marriage and family therapy (MA); counseling psychology (Ed D); counseling psychology/marriage and family therapy (MA); forensic psychology (MA).

Argosy University, Nashville, College of Psychology and Behavioral Sciences, Nashville, TN 37214. Offers counselor education and supervision (Ed D); mental health counseling (MA).

Argosy University, Orange County, College of Psychology and Behavioral Sciences, Orange, CA 92868. Offers MA, Ed D, Psy D. *Accreditation:* APA. Part-time and evening/weekend programs available. *Degree requirements:* For master's, comprehensive exam; for doctorate, comprehensive exam, thesis/dissertation. *Entrance requirements:* For master's and doctorate, 3 letters of recommendation, interview, resume. Additional exam requirements/recommendations for international students: Required—TOEFL. Electronic applications accepted. *Faculty research:* The psychological aspects of infertility medicine, depression, psychoanalytic therapy, experiential approaches to teaching.

Argosy University, Phoenix, College of Psychology and Behavioral Sciences, Phoenix, AZ 85021. Offers MA, Psy D.

Argosy University, Salt Lake City, College of Psychology and Behavioral Sciences, Draper, UT 84020. Offers counseling psychology (Ed D); counselor education and supervision (Ed D); forensic psychology (MA); marriage and family therapy (MA, DMFT); mental health counseling (MA).

Argosy University, San Diego, College of Psychology and Behavioral Sciences, San Diego, CA 92108. Offers clinical psychology/marriage and family therapy (MA); counseling psychology (Ed D); counseling psychology/marriage and family therapy (MA); forensic psychology (MA).

Argosy University, San Francisco Bay Area, College of Psychology and Behavioral Sciences, Alameda, CA 94501. Offers clinical psychology (MA, Psy D); counseling psychology (MA, Ed D); forensic psychology (MA); sport-exercise psychology (MA). *Accreditation:* APA (one or more programs are accredited).

Argosy University, Sarasota, College of Psychology and Behavioral Sciences, Sarasota, FL 34235. Offers community counseling (MA); counseling psychology (Ed D); counselor education and supervision (Ed D); forensic psychology (MA); marriage and family therapy (MA); mental health counseling (MA); pastoral community counseling (Ed D).

Argosy University, Schaumburg, College of Behavioral Sciences, Schaumburg, IL 60173-5403. Offers clinical mental health counseling (MA); forensic psychology (MA, Post-Graduate Certificate); industrial organizational psychology (MA); sport-exercise psychology (MA). *Accreditation:* ACA; APA.

Argosy University, Seattle, College of Psychology and Behavioral Sciences, Seattle, WA 98121. Offers MA, Ed D, Psy D, Postdoctoral Respecialization Certificate.

Argosy University, Tampa, College of Psychology and Behavioral Sciences, Tampa, FL 33607. Offers clinical psychology (MA, Psy D), including clinical psychology; counselor education and supervision (Ed D); industrial organizational psychology (MA); marriage and family therapy (MA); mental health counseling (MA).

Argosy University, Twin Cities, College of Psychology and Behavioral Sciences, Eagan, MN 55121. Offers clinical psychology (MA, Psy D), including child and family psychology (Psy D), forensic psychology (Psy D), health and neuropsychology (Psy D), trauma (Psy D); forensic counseling (Post-Graduate Certificate); forensic psychology (MA); industrial organizational psychology (MA); marriage and family therapy (MA, DMFT), including forensic counseling (MA). *Accreditation:* AAMFT; AAMFT/COAMFTE; APA.

Argosy University, Washington DC, College of Psychology and Behavioral Sciences, Arlington, VA 22209. Offers clinical psychology (MA, Psy D), including child and family psychology (Psy D), diversity and multicultural psychology (Psy D), forensic psychology (Psy D), health and neuropsychology (Psy D); community counseling (MA); counseling psychology (Ed D), including counselor education and supervision; counselor education and supervision (Ed D); forensic psychology (MA). *Accreditation:* APA.

Arizona State University at the Tempe campus, College of Liberal Arts and Sciences, Department of Psychology, Tempe, AZ 85287-1104. Offers applied behavior analysis (MS); behavioral neuroscience (PhD); clinical psychology (PhD); cognitive science (PhD); developmental psychology (PhD); quantitative psychology (PhD); social psychology (PhD). *Accreditation:* APA. *Degree requirements:* For doctorate, comprehensive exam, thesis/dissertation, interactive Program of Study (iPOS) submitted before completing 50 percent of required credit hours. *Entrance requirements:* For doctorate, GRE General Test, GRE Subject Test, minimum GPA of 3.0 or equivalent in last 2 years of work leading to bachelor's degree. Additional exam requirements/ recommendations for international students: Required—TOEFL, IELTS, or PTE. Electronic applications accepted.

Arizona State University at the Tempe campus, New College of Interdisciplinary Arts and Sciences, Program in Psychology, Phoenix, AZ 85069-7100. Offers MS. Part-time and evening/weekend programs available. *Degree requirements:* For master's, thesis or applied project, interactive Program of Study (iPOS) submitted before completing 50 percent of required credit hours. *Entrance requirements:* For master's, GRE, bachelor's degree in psychology or related field; minimum cumulative GPA of 3.0; successful completion of undergraduate statistics and research methods courses; three letters of recommendation from faculty; personal statement of research interests and goals. Additional exam requirements/recommendations for international students: Required—TOEFL, IELTS, or PTE. Electronic applications accepted. *Faculty research:* Emotion; stress; social identity, intergroup relations and prejudice; psychology and the legal system; discursive psychology; cognitive neuroscience, bilingualism and cognition; social psychology and bullying; health related decision-making; psychophysiology; attention, eye-tracking and natural behavior.

Arkansas Tech University, College of Arts and Humanities, Russellville, AR 72801. Offers English (M Ed, MA); history (MA); liberal arts (MLA); multi-media journalism (MA); psychology (MS); teaching English as a second language (MA). Part-time programs available. *Students:* 70 full-time (39 women), 105 part-time (72 women); includes 20 minority (3 Black or African American, non-Hispanic/Latino; 2 American Indian or Alaska Native, non-Hispanic/Latino; 1 Asian, non-Hispanic/Latino; 10 Hispanic/Latino; 4 Two or more races, non-Hispanic/Latino), 51 international. Average age 30. In 2014, 63 master's awarded. *Degree requirements:* For master's, comprehensive exam (for some programs), thesis (for some programs), project. *Entrance requirements:* For master's, GRE General Test or GMAT. Additional exam requirements/recommendations for international students: Required—TOEFL (minimum score 550 paper-based; 79 iBT), IELTS (minimum score 6). *Application deadline:* For fall admission, 3/1 priority date for domestic students, 5/1 priority date for international students; for spring admission, 10/1 priority date for domestic and international students. Applications are processed on a rolling basis. Application fee: $25 ($75 for international students). Electronic applications accepted. *Expenses:* Tuition, state resident: full-time $6264; part-time $261 per credit hour. Tuition, nonresident: full-time $12,528; part-time $522 per credit hour. *Required fees:* $423 per semester. Tuition and fees vary according to course load. *Financial support:* In 2014–15, research assistantships with full tuition reimbursements (averaging $4,800 per year), teaching assistantships with full tuition reimbursements (averaging $4,800 per year) were awarded; career-related internships or fieldwork, Federal Work-Study, scholarships/grants, health care benefits, and unspecified assistantships also available. Support available to part-time students. Financial award application deadline: 4/15; financial award applicants required to submit FAFSA. *Unit head:* Dr. Jeffrey Woods, Dean, 479-968-0274, Fax: 479-964-0812, E-mail: jwoods@atu.edu. *Application contact:* Dr. Mary B. Gunter, Dean of Graduate College, 479-968-0398, Fax: 479-964-0542, E-mail: gradcollege@atu.edu.
Website: http://www.atu.edu/humanities/

Assumption College, Counseling Psychology Program, Worcester, MA 01609-1296. Offers child and family interventions (MA); cognitive-behavioral therapies (MA); counseling psychology (CAGS); general psychology (MA). Part-time and evening/ weekend programs available. *Faculty:* 5 full-time (2 women), 9 part-time/adjunct (2 women). *Students:* 48 full-time (37 women), 35 part-time (33 women); includes 10 minority (3 Black or African American, non-Hispanic/Latino; 3 Asian, non-Hispanic/ Latino; 2 Hispanic/Latino; 2 Two or more races, non-Hispanic/Latino), 3 international. Average age 27. 78 applicants, 60% accepted, 15 enrolled. In 2014, 42 master's, 2 other advanced degrees awarded. *Degree requirements:* For master's, comprehensive exam, internship, practicum; for CAGS, comprehensive exam. *Entrance requirements:* For master's, 3 letters of recommendation, resume, essay, psychology prerequisite coursework; for CAGS, 3 letters of recommendation, resume, interview, essay, master's degree in counseling psychology or mental health counseling. Additional exam requirements/recommendations for international students: Required—TOEFL (minimum score 540 paper-based; 76 iBT), IELTS (minimum score 6). *Application deadline:* For fall admission, 3/6 for domestic and international students; for winter admission, 2/1 for domestic students; for spring admission, 10/3 for domestic and international students; for summer admission, 2/6 for domestic and international students. Application fee: $30. Electronic applications accepted. *Expenses: Tuition:* Full-time $10,620; part-time $590 per credit. *Required fees:* $20 per term. Full-time tuition and fees vary according to course load and program. *Financial support:* In 2014–15, 21 students received support, including 16 fellowships with full tuition reimbursements available; tuition waivers (full and partial), unspecified assistantships, and institutional discounts also available. Financial award application deadline: 3/7; financial award applicants required to submit FAFSA. *Faculty research:* Mood disorders, adjustment to life-threatening illness, perception of movement, socioemotional development of young children, discovery versus disclosure. *Unit head:* Dr. Leonard A. Doerfler, Director, 508-767-7549, Fax: 508-767-7263, E-mail: doerfler@assumption.edu. *Application contact:* Dr. Landy Johnson, Director of Operations for Graduate and Professional Studies, 508-767-7666, Fax: 508-767-7030, E-mail: graduate@assumption.edu.
Website: http://graduate.assumption.edu/counseling-psychology/masterofarts

Auburn University, Graduate School, College of Liberal Arts, Department of Psychology, Auburn University, AL 36849. Offers applied behavior analysis in developmental disabilities (MS); clinical psychology (PhD); experimental psychology (PhD); industrial/organizational psychology (PhD). *Accreditation:* APA (one or more programs are accredited). Part-time programs available. *Faculty:* 23 full-time (9 women), 2 part-time/adjunct (both women). *Students:* 49 full-time (34 women), 47 part-time (31 women); includes 13 minority (6 Black or African American, non-Hispanic/Latino; 3 Asian, non-Hispanic/Latino; 4 Hispanic/Latino), 5 international. Average age 27. 328 applicants, 10% accepted, 23 enrolled. In 2014, 22 master's, 5 doctorates awarded. *Degree requirements:* For doctorate, thesis/dissertation. *Entrance requirements:* For master's, GRE General Test, GRE Subject Test, minimum GPA of 3.25 in psychology, 3.0 overall; for doctorate, GRE General Test, GRE Subject Test. *Application deadline:* For fall admission, 7/7 for domestic students; for spring admission, 11/24 for domestic students. Applications are processed on a rolling basis. Application fee: $50 ($60 for international students). Electronic applications accepted. *Expenses:* Tuition, state resident: full-time $8586; part-time $477 per credit hour. Tuition, nonresident: full-time $25,758; part-time $1431 per credit hour. *Required fees:* $804 per semester. Tuition and fees vary according to degree level and program. *Financial support:* Research assistantships, teaching assistantships, and Federal Work-Study available. Support available to part-time students. Financial award application deadline: 3/15; financial award applicants required to submit FAFSA. *Faculty research:* Clinical psychology, learning, industrial psychology, organizational psychology. *Total annual research expenditures:* $200,000. *Unit head:* Dr. Peter Chen, Head, 334-844-4412. *Application contact:* Dr. George Flowers, Dean of the Graduate School, 334-844-2125.

Auburn University at Montgomery, College of Arts and Sciences, Department of Psychology, Montgomery, AL 36124-4023. Offers clinical psychology (MS). Part-time and evening/weekend programs available. *Faculty:* 6 full-time (2 women). *Students:* 14 full-time (12 women), 8 part-time (5 women); includes 3 minority (all Black or African American, non-Hispanic/Latino), 2 international. Average age 29. 13 applicants, 92% accepted, 10 enrolled. In 2014, 6 master's awarded. *Degree requirements:* For master's, comprehensive exam, thesis optional. *Entrance requirements:* For master's, GRE General Test or MAT. *Application deadline:* Applications are processed on a rolling basis. Electronic applications accepted. *Expenses:* Tuition, state resident: full-time $6264; part-time $348 per credit hour. Tuition, nonresident: full-time $14,094; part-time $783 per credit hour. *Financial support:* In 2014–15, 6 teaching assistantships were awarded; career-related internships or fieldwork and scholarships/grants also available. Support available to part-time students. Financial award application deadline: 3/1; financial award applicants required to submit FAFSA. *Faculty research:* Community service, diagnosis, behavior modification. *Unit head:* Dr. Glen Ray, Acting Head, 334-244-3690, Fax: 334-244-3826, E-mail: gray@aum.edu. *Application contact:* Tonya Sexton, Administrative Associate, 334-244-3306, Fax: 334-244-3826, E-mail: tsexton1@aum.edu.
Website: http://sciences.aum.edu/departments/psychology

Austin Peay State University, College of Graduate Studies, College of Behavioral and Health Sciences, Department of Psychology, Clarksville, TN 37044. Offers industrial-organizational psychology (MA); mental health counseling (MS); school counseling (MS). Part-time programs available. Postbaccalaureate distance learning degree programs offered (no on-campus study). *Degree requirements:* For master's, comprehensive exam, thesis (for some programs). *Entrance requirements:* For master's, GRE General Test, minimum undergraduate GPA of 2.5, 3 letters of recommendation, bachelor's degree. Additional exam requirements/recommendations for international students: Required—TOEFL (minimum score 500 paper-based). Electronic applications accepted.

Avila University, Department of Psychology, Kansas City, MO 64145-1698. Offers counseling psychology (MS). Part-time and evening/weekend programs available. *Faculty:* 7 full-time (6 women), 14 part-time/adjunct (8 women). *Students:* 131 full-time (104 women), 24 part-time (20 women); includes 54 minority (38 Black or African American, non-Hispanic/Latino; 2 American Indian or Alaska Native, non-Hispanic/ Latino; 1 Asian, non-Hispanic/Latino; 10 Hispanic/Latino; 3 Two or more races, non-Hispanic/Latino), 1 international. Average age 33. 75 applicants, 61% accepted, 34 enrolled. In 2014, 37 master's awarded. *Degree requirements:* For master's, thesis optional, capstone project. *Entrance requirements:* For master's, bachelor's degree, minimum GPA of 3.0 in all previous undergraduate and graduate coursework, 2 letters of recommendation, letter of intent, resume. Additional exam requirements/ recommendations for international students: Required—TOEFL (minimum score 80 iBT). *Application deadline:* Applications are processed on a rolling basis. Application fee: $0. Electronic applications accepted. *Expenses: Tuition:* Full-time $8604; part-time $478 per credit hour. *Required fees:* $684; $38 per credit hour. Tuition and fees vary according to program. *Financial support:* In 2014–15, 15 students received support, including 6 research assistantships with full and partial tuition reimbursements available; career-related internships or fieldwork, scholarships/grants, and unspecified assistantships also available. Support available to part-time students. Financial award applicants required to submit FAFSA. *Faculty research:* Emotional regulation, embodied cognition, mindful wellness, trauma and restorative justice, psychophysiology of public speaking anxiety. *Unit head:* Aaron R. Coffey, Director of Graduate Psychology Enrollment Management, 816-501-0419, Fax: 816-501-2455, E-mail: aaron.coffey@avila.edu. *Application contact:* Metra Augustin, Graduate Admissions Advisor, 816-501-2968, Fax: 816-501-2455, E-mail: gradpsych@avila.edu.
Website: http://www.avila.edu/psychology/

Azusa Pacific University, School of Behavioral and Applied Sciences, Department of Graduate Psychology, Azusa, CA 91702-7000. Offers clinical psychology (MA, Psy D), including family therapy (MA). *Accreditation:* APA (one or more programs are accredited). Part-time and evening/weekend programs available. *Degree requirements:* For master's, comprehensive exam, 250 hours of clinical experience, individual and group therapy. *Entrance requirements:* For master's, interview, minimum GPA of 3.0, Minnesota Multiphasic Personality Inventory. Additional exam requirements/ recommendations for international students: Required—TOEFL (minimum score 600 paper-based).

Ball State University, Graduate School, College of Sciences and Humanities, Department of Psychological Science, Muncie, IN 47306-1099. Offers clinical psychology (MA); cognitive and social processes (MA). *Faculty:* 9 full-time (5 women), 2 part-time/adjunct (1 woman). *Students:* 28 full-time (21 women), 2 part-time (both women). Average age 23. 39 applicants, 41% accepted, 14 enrolled. In 2014, 15 master's awarded. Application fee: $50. *Financial support:* In 2014–15, 26 students received support, including 5 research assistantships with partial tuition reimbursements available (averaging $9,366 per year), 22 teaching assistantships with partial tuition reimbursements available (averaging $9,593 per year); unspecified assistantships also available. Financial award application deadline: 3/1. *Unit head:* Dr. Bernard Whitley, Chairman, 765-285-1690, Fax: 765-285-8980, E-mail: bwhitley@bsu.edu. *Application contact:* Dr. Kerri Pickel, Graduate Program Director, 765-285-1711, Fax: 765-285-8980, E-mail: kpickel@bsu.edu.
Website: http://www.bsu.edu/psysc/

Barry University, College of Arts and Sciences, Department of Psychology, Miami Shores, FL 33161-6695. Offers clinical psychology (MS); school psychology (MS, SSP). Part-time and evening/weekend programs available. *Degree requirements:* For

master's, thesis, practicum. *Entrance requirements:* For master's, GRE General Test, minimum GPA of 3.0, course work in psychology. Electronic applications accepted. *Faculty research:* Closed head injury, memory and aging, infant/mother interaction, evolutionary aspects of behavior, gender roles.

Baylor University, Graduate School, College of Arts and Sciences, Department of Psychology and Neuroscience, Program in Psychology, Waco, TX 76798. Offers MA, PhD. Terminal master's awarded for partial completion of doctoral program. *Degree requirements:* For master's, thesis; for doctorate, comprehensive exam, thesis/dissertation. *Entrance requirements:* For master's and doctorate, GRE General Test. Additional exam requirements/recommendations for international students: Required—TOEFL. *Faculty research:* Animal learning/behavior, psychopharmacology, memory and cognition, health psychology, psychology of religion.

Binghamton University, State University of New York, Graduate School, School of Arts and Sciences, Department of Psychology, Vestal, NY 13850. Offers behavioral neuroscience (PhD); clinical psychology (PhD); cognitive and behavioral science (PhD). *Accreditation:* APA. *Faculty:* 33 full-time (14 women), 9 part-time/adjunct (4 women). *Students:* 45 full-time (32 women), 43 part-time (29 women); includes 13 minority (5 Black or African American, non-Hispanic/Latino; 1 American Indian or Alaska Native, non-Hispanic/Latino; 4 Asian, non-Hispanic/Latino; 3 Hispanic/Latino), 3 international. Average age 28. 327 applicants, 7% accepted, 14 enrolled. In 2014, 11 doctorates awarded. Terminal master's awarded for partial completion of doctoral program. *Degree requirements:* For doctorate, comprehensive exam (for some programs), thesis/dissertation. *Entrance requirements:* For doctorate, GRE General Test. Additional exam requirements/recommendations for international students: Required—TOEFL (minimum score 550 paper-based; 80 iBT). *Application deadline:* Applications are processed on a rolling basis. Application fee: $75. Electronic applications accepted. *Expenses:* Tuition, state resident: full-time $7776; part-time $432 per credit. Tuition, nonresident: full-time $15,138; part-time $841 per credit. *Required fees:* $1754; $213 per credit. Tuition and fees vary according to degree level and program. *Financial support:* In 2014–15, 69 students received support, including 15 research assistantships with full tuition reimbursements available (averaging $17,500 per year), 40 teaching assistantships with full tuition reimbursements available (averaging $17,500 per year); career-related internships or fieldwork, Federal Work-Study, institutionally sponsored loans, scholarships/grants, health care benefits, tuition waivers (full and partial), and unspecified assistantships also available. Financial award application deadline: 2/15; financial award applicants required to submit FAFSA. *Unit head:* Dr. Peter C. Gerhardstein, Chair, 607-777-4387, E-mail: gerhard@binghamton.edu. *Application contact:* Kishan Zuber, Recruiting and Admissions Coordinator, 607-777-2151, Fax: 607-777-2501, E-mail: kzuber@binghamton.edu.

Biola University, Rosemead School of Psychology, La Mirada, CA 90639-0001. Offers clinical psychology (PhD, Psy D). *Accreditation:* APA. *Faculty:* 24. *Students:* 122 full-time (87 women), 13 part-time (10 women); includes 57 minority (6 Black or African American, non-Hispanic/Latino; 30 Asian, non-Hispanic/Latino; 20 Hispanic/Latino; 1 Two or more races, non-Hispanic/Latino), 2 international. 96 applicants, 41% accepted, 21 enrolled. In 2014, 19 doctorates awarded. *Degree requirements:* For doctorate, comprehensive exam, thesis/dissertation. *Entrance requirements:* For doctorate, GRE General Test, interview, 30 undergraduate semester hours of credits in psychology, minimum GPA of 3.0. Additional exam requirements/recommendations for international students: Required—TOEFL (minimum score 600 paper-based; 100 iBT). *Application deadline:* For fall admission, 1/15 priority date for domestic students, 1/15 for international students. Application fee: $65. Electronic applications accepted. *Expenses:* Expenses: Contact institution. *Financial support:* Scholarships/grants and unspecified assistantships available. Financial award applicants required to submit FAFSA. *Faculty research:* Integration of psychology and theology, psychology of child/adolescent, psychology of marriage, psychology of gender, psychology of trauma, psychology of forensics, multi-cultural studies and mental health. *Unit head:* Dr. Clark Campbell, Dean, 562-903-4867, Fax: 562-903-4864. *Application contact:* Jon Garcia, Graduate Admissions Counselor, 562-903-4752, E-mail: graduate.admissions@biola.edu.
Website: http://www.rosemead.edu/

Boston College, Graduate School of Arts and Sciences, Department of Psychology, Chestnut Hill, MA 02467-3800. Offers MA, PhD. *Faculty:* 18 full-time. *Students:* 29 full-time (20 women); includes 4 minority (1 Asian, non-Hispanic/Latino; 2 Hispanic/Latino; 1 Two or more races, non-Hispanic/Latino), 7 international. 278 applicants, 4% accepted, 7 enrolled. In 2014, 8 master's, 1 doctorate awarded. *Degree requirements:* For doctorate, thesis/dissertation, fieldwork. *Entrance requirements:* For master's, GRE General Test; for doctorate, GRE General Test, GRE Subject Test. Additional exam requirements/recommendations for international students: Required—TOEFL (minimum score 600 paper-based; 100 iBT). *Application deadline:* For fall admission, 1/2 for domestic and international students. Application fee: $75. Electronic applications accepted. *Financial support:* In 2014–15, fellowships with full tuition reimbursements (averaging $22,500 per year), research assistantships with full tuition reimbursements (averaging $22,500 per year), teaching assistantships with full tuition reimbursements (averaging $22,500 per year) were awarded; career-related internships or fieldwork, health care benefits, and unspecified assistantships also available. Support available to part-time students. Financial award application deadline: 3/1; financial award applicants required to submit FAFSA. *Faculty research:* Behavioral neuroscience, cognitive neuroscience, developmental psychology, quantitative psychology and social psychology. *Unit head:* Dr. Ellen Winner, Chairperson, 617-552-4100, E-mail: winner@bc.edu. *Application contact:* Dr. Scott Slotnick, Graduate Program Director, 617-552-4100, E-mail: slotnics@bc.edu.
Website: http://www.bc.edu/psychology

Boston Graduate School of Psychoanalysis, BGSP-New Jersey, Brookline, MA 02446-4602. Offers psychoanalysis (MA); psychoanalytic counseling (MA). Programs offered in conjunction with Academic of Clinical and Applied Psychoanalysis in Livingston, NJ.

Boston Graduate School of Psychoanalysis, New York Graduate School of Psychoanalysis, New York, NY 10011. Offers MA. Part-time programs available. *Degree requirements:* For master's, thesis. *Entrance requirements:* For master's, interview, BA, writing sample, letters of recommendation. Additional exam requirements/recommendations for international students: Required—TOEFL.

Boston University, Graduate School of Arts and Sciences, Department of Psychological and Brain Sciences, Boston, MA 02215. Offers MA, PhD. *Accreditation:* APA (one or more programs are accredited). *Students:* 102 full-time (75 women), 9 part-time (5 women); includes 20 minority (2 Black or African American, non-Hispanic/Latino; 10 Asian, non-Hispanic/Latino; 7 Hispanic/Latino; 1 Two or more races, non-Hispanic/Latino), 13 international. Average age 26. 1,093 applicants, 10% accepted, 42 enrolled. In 2014, 82 master's, 22 doctorates awarded. Terminal master's awarded for partial completion of doctoral program. *Degree requirements:* For master's, one foreign language, comprehensive exam; for doctorate, one foreign language, comprehensive exam, thesis/dissertation. *Entrance requirements:* For master's and doctorate, GRE General Test, GRE Subject Test (recommended), three letters of recommendation. Additional exam requirements/recommendations for international students: Required—TOEFL (minimum score 84 iBT). *Application deadline:* For fall admission, 12/1 for domestic and international students. Application fee: $80. Electronic applications accepted. *Expenses: Tuition:* Full-time $45,686; part-time $1428 per credit hour. *Required fees:* $660; $60 per semester. Tuition and fees vary according to program. *Financial support:* In 2014–15, 76 students received support, including 9 fellowships with full tuition reimbursements available (averaging $20,500 per year), 35 research assistantships with full tuition reimbursements available (averaging $20,500 per year), 24 teaching assistantships with full tuition reimbursements available (averaging $20,500 per year); career-related internships or fieldwork, Federal Work-Study, health care benefits, and unspecified assistantships also available. Support available to part-time students. Financial award application deadline: 12/1; financial award applicants required to submit FAFSA. *Unit head:* David Somers, Chairman, 617-358-1372, Fax: 617-353-6933, E-mail: somers@bu.edu. *Application contact:* Martin Gastmann, Assistant Director of Admissions and Financial Aid, 617-353-2696, Fax: 617-358-5492, E-mail: grs@bu.edu.
Website: http://www.bu.edu/psych/

Boston University, School of Medicine, Division of Graduate Medical Sciences, Program in Mental Health Counseling and Behavioral Medicine, Boston, MA 02215. Offers MA. *Expenses: Tuition:* Full-time $45,686; part-time $1428 per credit hour. *Required fees:* $660; $60 per semester. Tuition and fees vary according to program. *Faculty research:* HIV/AIDS, trauma, behavioral medicine (obesity, breast cancer), neurosciences, autism, serious mental illness, sports psychology. *Unit head:* Dr. Stephen Brady, Director, 617-414-2320, Fax: 617-414-2323, E-mail: sbrady@bu.edu. *Application contact:* Bernice Mark, Administrative Assistant, 617-414-2328, E-mail: nicey@bu.edu.
Website: http://www.bumc.bu.edu/mhbm/

Bowling Green State University, Graduate College, College of Arts and Sciences, Department of Psychology, Bowling Green, OH 43403. Offers clinical psychology (MA, PhD); developmental psychology (MA, PhD); experimental psychology (MA, PhD); industrial/organizational psychology (MA, PhD); quantitative psychology (MA, PhD). *Accreditation:* APA (one or more programs are accredited). *Degree requirements:* For doctorate, thesis/dissertation. *Entrance requirements:* For doctorate, GRE General Test, GRE Subject Test. Additional exam requirements/recommendations for international students: Required—TOEFL. Electronic applications accepted. *Faculty research:* Personnel psychology, developmental-mathematical models, behavioral medication, brain process, child/adolescent social cognition.

Brandeis University, Graduate School of Arts and Sciences, Department of Psychology, Waltham, MA 02454-9110. Offers brain, body and behavior (PhD); cognitive neuroscience (PhD); general psychology (MA); social/developmental psychology (PhD). Part-time programs available. Terminal master's awarded for partial completion of doctoral program. *Degree requirements:* For master's, thesis; for doctorate, thesis/dissertation, research reports. *Entrance requirements:* For master's and doctorate, GRE General Test; GRE Subject Test (recommended), 3 letters of recommendation, statement of purpose, transcript(s), resume. Additional exam requirements/recommendations for international students: Required—TOEFL (minimum score 600 paper-based; 100 iBT), PTE (minimum score 68); Recommended—IELTS (minimum score 7). Electronic applications accepted. *Faculty research:* Cognitive neuroscience, social developmental psychology, motor control, visual perception, taste physiology and psychophysics, memory, learning, aging, child development, aggression, emotion, personality and cognition in adulthood and old age, social relations and health, stereotypes, nonverbal communication.

Brandeis University, Graduate School of Arts and Sciences, Joint Master's Programs in Women's and Gender Studies, Waltham, MA 02454-9110. Offers anthropology and women's and gender studies (MA); English and women's and gender studies (MA); history and women's and gender studies (MA); Near Eastern and Judaic studies and women's and gender studies (MA); psychology and women's and gender studies (MA); public policy and women's and gender studies (MA); social policy and women's and gender studies (MA); sociology and women's and gender studies (MA); sustainable international development and women's/gender studies (MA). *Degree requirements:* For master's, thesis. *Entrance requirements:* For master's, GRE, sample of written work, resume, statement of purpose, transcript(s), letters of recommendation. Additional exam requirements/recommendations for international students: Required—TOEFL (minimum score 600 paper-based; 100 iBT), PTE (minimum score 68); Recommended—IELTS (minimum score 7). Electronic applications accepted. *Faculty research:* Anthropology, English, history, music, Near Eastern and Judaic studies, public policy, psychology, sociology, and sustainable international development.

Brandman University, School of Arts and Sciences, Irvine, CA 92618. Offers psychology (MA), including counseling, marriage and family therapy.

Brenau University, Sydney O. Smith Graduate School, College of Health and Science, Gainesville, GA 30501. Offers family nurse practitioner (MSN); nurse educator (MSN); nursing management (MSN); occupational therapy (MS); psychology (MS). *Accreditation:* AOTA. Part-time and evening/weekend programs available. *Degree requirements:* For master's, comprehensive exam (for some programs), thesis (for some programs), clinical practicum hours. *Entrance requirements:* For master's, GRE General Test or MAT (for some programs), interview, writing sample, references (for some programs). Additional exam requirements/recommendations for international students: Required—TOEFL (minimum score 500 paper-based; 61 iBT); Recommended—IELTS (minimum score 5). Electronic applications accepted. *Expenses:* Contact institution.

Bridgewater State University, College of Graduate Studies, School of Arts and Sciences, Department of Psychology, Bridgewater, MA 02325-0001. Offers MA. Part-time and evening/weekend programs available. *Entrance requirements:* For master's, GRE General Test.

Brigham Young University, Graduate Studies, College of Family, Home, and Social Sciences, Department of Psychology, Provo, UT 84602. Offers behavioral neuroscience (PhD); clinical psychology (PhD); general psychology (MS). *Accreditation:* APA (one or more programs are accredited). *Faculty:* 29 full-time (6 women), 2 part-time/adjunct (1 woman). *Students:* 60 full-time (34 women); includes 6 minority (1 American Indian or Alaska Native, non-Hispanic/Latino; 3 Asian, non-Hispanic/Latino; 2 Hispanic/Latino), 3 international. Average age 26. 57 applicants, 25% accepted, 9 enrolled. In 2014, 6 master's, 17 doctorates awarded. *Degree requirements:* For master's, thesis; for doctorate, comprehensive exam, thesis/dissertation, publishable paper. *Entrance requirements:* For master's and doctorate, GRE General Test, minimum GPA of 3.0 in last 60 hours of upper-division course work. Additional exam requirements/recommendations for international students: Required—TOEFL. *Application deadline:* For fall admission, 12/1 for domestic and international students. Application fee: $50. Electronic applications accepted. *Expenses: Tuition:* Full-time $6310; part-time $371 per credit hour. Tuition and fees vary according to program and student's religious affiliation. *Financial support:* In 2014–15, 43 students received support, including 27 research assistantships with partial tuition reimbursements available (averaging $10,000 per year), 11 teaching assistantships with partial tuition reimbursements available (averaging $10,000 per year); fellowships, career-related internships or fieldwork, scholarships/grants, tuition waivers (partial), and unspecified assistantships also available. Financial award application deadline: 5/31. *Faculty research:* Psychotherapy

process, Alzheimer's disease/dementia, psychology and law, health, psychology, developmental. *Total annual research expenditures:* $1 million. *Unit head:* Dr. Dawson Hedges, Chair, 801-422-6357, Fax: 801-422-0602, E-mail: dawson_hedges@byu.edu. *Application contact:* Leesa D. Scott, Coordinator of Student Programs, 801-422-4560, Fax: 801-422-0602, E-mail: leesa_scott@byu.edu.
Website: http://psychology.byu.edu/

Brock University, Faculty of Graduate Studies, Faculty of Social Sciences, Program in Psychology, St. Catharines, ON L2S 3A1, Canada. Offers behavioral neuroscience (MA, PhD); life span development (MA, PhD); social personality (MA, PhD). Part-time programs available. *Degree requirements:* For master's, thesis; for doctorate, thesis/dissertation. *Entrance requirements:* For master's, GRE, honors degree; for doctorate, GRE, master's degree. Additional exam requirements/recommendations for international students: Required—TOEFL (minimum score 550 paper-based; 80 iBT), IELTS (minimum score 6.5), TWE (minimum score 4). Electronic applications accepted. *Faculty research:* Social personality, behavioral neuroscience, life-span development.

Brooklyn College of the City University of New York, School of Natural and Behavioral Sciences, Department of Psychology, Brooklyn, NY 11210-2889. Offers experimental psychology (MA); industrial and organizational psychology (MA), including human relations, organizational behavior; mental health counseling (MA); psychology (PhD). Part-time programs available. *Degree requirements:* For master's, comprehensive exam, thesis (for some programs). *Entrance requirements:* For master's, minimum GPA of 3.0, 2 letters of recommendation, essay; for doctorate, GRE. Additional exam requirements/recommendations for international students: Required—TOEFL (minimum score 520 paper-based; 69 iBT). Electronic applications accepted.

Brown University, Graduate School, Department of Cognitive, Linguistic and Psychological Sciences, Providence, RI 02912. Offers cognitive science (Sc M, PhD); linguistics (AM, PhD); psychology (PhD). *Degree requirements:* For master's, one foreign language, thesis or alternative; for doctorate, 2 foreign languages, thesis/dissertation.

Bucknell University, Graduate Studies, College of Arts and Sciences, Department of Psychology, Lewisburg, PA 17837. Offers MS. *Degree requirements:* For master's, thesis. *Entrance requirements:* For master's, GRE General Test, GRE Subject Test, minimum GPA of 3.0. Additional exam requirements/recommendations for international students: Required—TOEFL (minimum score 600 paper-based).

California Coast University, School of Behavioral Science, Santa Ana, CA 92701. Offers psychology (MS). Postbaccalaureate distance learning degree programs offered (no on-campus study).

California Institute of Integral Studies, School of Consciousness and Transformation, San Francisco, CA 94103. Offers anthropology and social change (MA, PhD); creative inquiry/interdisciplinary arts (MFA); East-West psychology (MA, PhD); philosophy and religion (MA, PhD), including Asian and comparative studies, ecology, spirituality, and religion, philosophy, cosmology, and consciousness, women's spirituality; transformative leadership (MA); transformative studies (PhD); writing and consciousness (MFA). Part-time and evening/weekend programs available. Postbaccalaureate distance learning degree programs offered (no on-campus study). *Students:* 385 full-time (256 women), 102 part-time (71 women); includes 124 minority (31 Black or African American, non-Hispanic/Latino; 3 American Indian or Alaska Native, non-Hispanic/Latino; 19 Asian, non-Hispanic/Latino; 39 Hispanic/Latino; 1 Native Hawaiian or other Pacific Islander, non-Hispanic/Latino; 31 Two or more races, non-Hispanic/Latino), 53 international. Average age 43. 196 applicants, 92% accepted, 125 enrolled. In 2014, 75 master's, 41 doctorates awarded. Terminal master's awarded for partial completion of doctoral program. *Degree requirements:* For master's, thesis optional; for doctorate, comprehensive exam, thesis/dissertation, 1 foreign language (for Asian comparative studies). *Entrance requirements:* For master's, minimum GPA of 3.0, letters of recommendation, writing sample; for doctorate, master's degree, minimum GPA of 3.0, letters of recommendation, writing sample. Additional exam requirements/recommendations for international students: Required—TOEFL. *Application deadline:* For fall admission, 2/1 priority date for domestic and international students; for spring admission, 10/15 priority date for domestic and international students. Applications are processed on a rolling basis. Application fee: $65. Electronic applications accepted. *Expenses: Tuition:* Full-time $18,270; part-time $1015 per credit. *Required fees:* $85 per semester hour. *Financial support:* In 2014–15, 445 students received support, including 5 research assistantships (averaging $800 per year), 28 teaching assistantships (averaging $825 per year); career-related internships or fieldwork, Federal Work-Study, and scholarships/grants also available. Support available to part-time students. Financial award application deadline: 4/15; financial award applicants required to submit FAFSA. *Faculty research:* Ecology and sustainability, philosophy and religion, East-West psychology, integrative health, social and cultural anthropology, transformative leadership. *Application contact:* David Townes, Senior Admissions Counselor, 415-575-6152, Fax: 415-575-1268, E-mail: admissions@ciis.edu.
Website: http://www.ciis.edu/

California Institute of Integral Studies, School of Professional Psychology and Health, San Francisco, CA 94103. Offers clinical psychology (Psy D); community mental health (MA); drama therapy (MA); expressive arts therapy (MA); integral counseling psychology (MA); integrative health studies (MA); psychological studies (MA); somatic psychology (MA). *Accreditation:* APA. Part-time and evening/weekend programs available. *Students:* 522 full-time (397 women), 105 part-time (83 women); includes 155 minority (27 Black or African American, non-Hispanic/Latino; 3 American Indian or Alaska Native, non-Hispanic/Latino; 31 Asian, non-Hispanic/Latino; 62 Hispanic/Latino; 3 Native Hawaiian or other Pacific Islander, non-Hispanic/Latino; 29 Two or more races, non-Hispanic/Latino), 49 international. Average age 34. 351 applicants, 86% accepted, 175 enrolled. In 2014, 168 master's, 24 doctorates awarded. *Degree requirements:* For doctorate, comprehensive exam, thesis/dissertation. *Entrance requirements:* For master's, minimum GPA of 3.0, letters of recommendation, writing sample; for doctorate, GRE, MA in psychology or social work with appropriate practical experience for advanced standing, or BA with a minimum GPA of 3.1; letters of recommendation; writing sample. Additional exam requirements/recommendations for international students: Required—TOEFL. *Application deadline:* For fall admission, 2/1 priority date for domestic and international students; for spring admission, 10/15 priority date for domestic and international students. Applications are processed on a rolling basis. Application fee: $65. Electronic applications accepted. *Expenses: Tuition:* Full-time $18,270; part-time $1015 per credit. *Required fees:* $85 per semester hour. *Financial support:* In 2014–15, 464 students received support, including 5 research assistantships with tuition reimbursements available (averaging $800 per year), 36 teaching assistantships with tuition reimbursements available (averaging $825 per year); career-related internships or fieldwork, Federal Work-Study, and scholarships/grants also available. Support available to part-time students. Financial award application deadline: 4/15; financial award applicants required to submit FAFSA. *Faculty research:* Transpersonal psychology, somatic psychology, expressive arts therapy, drama therapy, community mental health, ecopsychology, integrative health. *Application contact:* David Townes, Senior Admissions Counselor, 415-575-6152, Fax: 415-575-1268, E-mail: admissions@ciis.edu.

California Lutheran University, Graduate Studies, Department of Psychology, Thousand Oaks, CA 91360-2787. Offers clinical psychology (MS, Psy D); marital and family therapy (MS). Part-time programs available. *Faculty:* 12 full-time (6 women), 19 part-time/adjunct (14 women). *Students:* 156 full-time (133 women), 28 part-time (25 women); includes 85 minority (5 Black or African American, non-Hispanic/Latino; 1 American Indian or Alaska Native, non-Hispanic/Latino; 6 Asian, non-Hispanic/Latino; 67 Hispanic/Latino; 2 Native Hawaiian or other Pacific Islander, non-Hispanic/Latino; 4 Two or more races, non-Hispanic/Latino), 6 international. Average age 31. 201 applicants, 57% accepted, 56 enrolled. In 2014, 64 master's awarded. *Degree requirements:* For master's, thesis or comprehensive exams; for doctorate, internship. *Entrance requirements:* For master's, GRE General Test, interview, minimum GPA of 3.0; for doctorate, GRE General Test. *Application deadline:* For fall admission, 1/15 priority date for domestic and international students. Applications are processed on a rolling basis. Application fee: $50. *Unit head:* Dr. Richard Holigrock, Dean, 805-493-3675. *Application contact:* 805-493-3325, Fax: 805-493-3861, E-mail: clugrad@callutheran.edu.

California Polytechnic State University, San Luis Obispo, College of Liberal Arts, Department of Psychology and Child Development, San Luis Obispo, CA 93407. Offers psychology (MS). Part-time programs available. *Faculty:* 2 full-time (1 woman), 2 part-time/adjunct (both women). *Students:* 29 full-time (27 women), 7 part-time (6 women); includes 14 minority (1 Black or African American, non-Hispanic/Latino; 2 Asian, non-Hispanic/Latino; 6 Hispanic/Latino; 5 Two or more races, non-Hispanic/Latino), 1 international. Average age 28. 54 applicants, 26% accepted, 12 enrolled. In 2014, 14 master's awarded. *Degree requirements:* For master's, comprehensive exam (for some programs), thesis (for some programs). *Application deadline:* For fall admission, 12/1 for domestic and international students. Application fee: $55. Electronic applications accepted. *Expenses:* Tuition, state resident: full-time $6738; part-time $3906 per year. Tuition, nonresident: full-time $15,666; part-time $8370 per year. *Required fees:* $3447; $1001 per quarter. One-time fee: $3447 full-time; $3003 part-time. *Financial support:* Fellowships, research assistantships, career-related internships or fieldwork, Federal Work-Study, and institutionally sponsored loans available. Support available to part-time students. Financial award application deadline: 3/2; financial award applicants required to submit FAFSA. *Faculty research:* Eating disorders, mood disorders, neuropsychology, forensic psychology, group therapy. *Unit head:* Dr. Kelly Moreno, Graduate Coordinator, 805-756-2805, Fax: 805-756-1134, E-mail: kmoreno@calpoly.edu. *Application contact:* Dr. James Maraviglia, Associate Vice Provost for Marketing and Enrollment Development, 805-756-2311, Fax: 805-756-5400, E-mail: admissions@calpoly.edu.
Website: http://psycd.calpoly.edu/graduate/?pid-3

California State Polytechnic University, Pomona, Program in Psychology, Pomona, CA 91768-2557. Offers MS. Part-time programs available. *Students:* 30 full-time (24 women); includes 21 minority (1 American Indian or Alaska Native, non-Hispanic/Latino; 3 Asian, non-Hispanic/Latino; 14 Hispanic/Latino; 3 Two or more races, non-Hispanic/Latino), 1 international. Average age 24. 80 applicants, 19% accepted, 14 enrolled. In 2014, 13 master's awarded. *Degree requirements:* For master's, thesis or alternative. *Application deadline:* For fall admission, 4/15 for domestic students. Applications are processed on a rolling basis. Application fee: $55. Electronic applications accepted. *Expenses:* Tuition, state resident: full-time $6738. Tuition, nonresident: full-time $12,300. *Required fees:* $1400. *Financial support:* Application deadline: 3/2. *Unit head:* Dr. Jeffery Mio, Director of Graduate Studies, 909-869-3899, Fax: 909-869-4930, E-mail: jsmio@cpp.edu.
Website: http://www.cpp.edu/~class/psychology-sociology/psychology/masters-program.shtml

California State University, Chico, Office of Graduate Studies, College of Behavioral and Social Sciences, Department of Psychology, Program in Psychological Science, Chico, CA 95929-0722. Offers MA. *Students:* 9 full-time (5 women), 12 part-time (7 women); includes 7 minority (1 Asian, non-Hispanic/Latino; 6 Hispanic/Latino). Average age 28. 26 applicants, 38% accepted, 7 enrolled. In 2014, 15 master's awarded. *Degree requirements:* For master's, thesis. *Entrance requirements:* For master's, GRE General Test or MAT, 3 letters of recommendation, three departmental recommendation forms, statement of purpose. Additional exam requirements/recommendations for international students: Required—TOEFL (minimum score 550 paper-based; 80 iBT), IELTS (minimum score 6.5), PTE (minimum score 59). *Application deadline:* For fall admission, 3/1 for domestic and international students. Application fee: $55. Electronic applications accepted. *Expenses:* Tuition, state resident: full-time $7002. Tuition, nonresident: full-time $18,162. *Required fees:* $1530. Tuition and fees vary according to program. *Financial support:* Research assistantships available. Financial award application deadline: 3/1; financial award applicants required to submit FAFSA. *Unit head:* Dr. Brian Oppy, Chair, 530-898-5147, Fax: 530-898-4740, E-mail: psy@csuchico.edu. *Application contact:* Judy L. Rice, Graduate Admissions Coordinator, 530-898-5416, Fax: 530-898-3342, E-mail: jlrice@csuchico.edu.
Website: http://www.csuchico.edu/psy/graduate/psyScience.shtml

California State University, Dominguez Hills, College of Natural and Behavioral Sciences, Program in Psychology, Carson, CA 90747-0001. Offers clinical psychology (MA). Part-time and evening/weekend programs available. *Faculty:* 2 full-time (both women), 5 part-time/adjunct (3 women). *Students:* 37 full-time (29 women), 18 part-time (12 women); includes 39 minority (4 Black or African American, non-Hispanic/Latino; 1 American Indian or Alaska Native, non-Hispanic/Latino; 3 Asian, non-Hispanic/Latino; 28 Hispanic/Latino; 3 Two or more races, non-Hispanic/Latino). Average age 31. 52 applicants, 50% accepted, 17 enrolled. In 2014, 17 master's awarded. Terminal master's awarded for partial completion of doctoral program. *Degree requirements:* For master's, comprehensive exam, thesis optional. *Entrance requirements:* For master's, GRE General Test or MAT, interview, minimum GPA of 3.0, prerequisite psychology courses. Additional exam requirements/recommendations for international students: Required—TOEFL (minimum score 550 paper-based). *Application deadline:* For fall admission, 3/1 for domestic and international students. Application fee: $55. Electronic applications accepted. *Expenses:* Tuition, state resident: full-time $6738; part-time $3960 per year. Tuition, nonresident: full-time $13,434; part-time $8370 per year. *Required fees:* $623; $623 per year. *Faculty research:* Culture and health, neuropsychology and HIV, psychohistory of the Holocaust, community and adolescents, malingering. *Unit head:* Dr. Karen Wilson, Program Coordinator, 310-243-3642, E-mail: kmason@csudh.edu. *Application contact:* Dr. Karen I. Mason, Coordinator, 310-243-3642, Fax: 310-516-3642, E-mail: kmason@csudh.edu.
Website: http://www4.csudh.edu/psychology/

California State University, Fresno, Division of Graduate Studies, College of Science and Mathematics, Department of Psychology, Fresno, CA 93740-8027. Offers MA, MS. *Degree requirements:* For master's, thesis. *Entrance requirements:* For master's, GRE General Test, GRE Subject Test, minimum GPA of 3.0. Additional exam requirements/recommendations for international students: Required—TOEFL. Electronic applications accepted. *Faculty research:* Oncology prediction, parenting stress, wellness, aging and memory, retrieval inhibition, anger, minority mental health.

California State University, Fullerton, Graduate Studies, College of Humanities and Social Sciences, Department of Psychology, Fullerton, CA 92834-9480. Offers clinical/

community psychology (MS); psychology (MA). Part-time programs available. *Students:* 83 full-time (57 women), 16 part-time (7 women); includes 45 minority (1 Black or African American, non-Hispanic/Latino; 9 Asian, non-Hispanic/Latino; 31 Hispanic/Latino; 4 Two or more races, non-Hispanic/Latino), 9 international. Average age 25. 110 applicants, 35% accepted, 37 enrolled. In 2014, 28 master's awarded. *Degree requirements:* For master's, thesis. *Entrance requirements:* For master's, GRE General Test, GRE Subject Test, undergraduate major in psychology or related field. Application fee: $55. *Financial support:* Career-related internships or fieldwork, Federal Work-Study, institutionally sponsored loans, and scholarships/grants available. Support available to part-time students. Financial award application deadline: 3/1; financial award applicants required to submit FAFSA. *Unit head:* Dr. Jack Mearns, Chair, 657-278-3514. *Application contact:* Admissions/Applications, 657-278-2371.

California State University, Long Beach, Graduate Studies, College of Liberal Arts, Department of Psychology, Long Beach, CA 90840. Offers human factors (MS); industrial/organizational psychology (MS); psychology (MA). Part-time and evening/weekend programs available. *Degree requirements:* For master's, comprehensive exam, thesis. *Entrance requirements:* For master's, GRE General Test, GRE Subject Test. Electronic applications accepted. *Faculty research:* Physiological psychology, social and personality psychology, community-clinical psychology, industrial-organizational psychology, developmental psychology.

California State University, Los Angeles, Graduate Studies, College of Natural and Social Sciences, Department of Psychology, Los Angeles, CA 90032-8530. Offers MA, MS. Part-time and evening/weekend programs available. *Degree requirements:* For master's, comprehensive exam or thesis. *Entrance requirements:* Additional exam requirements/recommendations for international students: Required—TOEFL (minimum score 500 paper-based). Electronic applications accepted. *Expenses:* Tuition, state resident: full-time $6738; part-time $3609 per year. Tuition, nonresident: full-time $15,666; part-time $8073 per year. Tuition and fees vary according to course load, degree level and program. *Faculty research:* Binaural resolution of the size of an acoustic array, response and generalization of matching to sample in children.

California State University, Northridge, Graduate Studies, College of Social and Behavioral Sciences, Department of Psychology, Northridge, CA 91330. Offers clinical psychology (MA); general-experimental psychology (MA); human factors and applied experimental psychology (MA). *Students:* 46 full-time (32 women), 16 part-time (10 women); includes 27 minority (3 Black or African American, non-Hispanic/Latino; 2 Asian, non-Hispanic/Latino; 20 Hispanic/Latino; 2 Two or more races, non-Hispanic/Latino). Average age 26. *Degree requirements:* For master's, thesis. *Entrance requirements:* For master's, GRE General Test, GRE Subject Test, minimum GPA of 3.0, letters of recommendation. Additional exam requirements/recommendations for international students: Required—TOEFL. *Application deadline:* For fall admission, 11/30 for domestic students. Application fee: $55. *Expenses: Required fees:* $12,402. *Financial support:* Application deadline: 3/1. *Unit head:* Jill Razani, Chair, 818-677-3506.
Website: http://www.csun.edu/csbs/departments/psychology/index.html

California State University, Sacramento, Office of Graduate Studies, College of Social Sciences and Interdisciplinary Studies, Department of Psychology, Sacramento, CA 95819. Offers applied behavior analysis (MA); counseling psychology (MA); industrial/organizational psychology (MA). Part-time programs available. *Degree requirements:* For master's, thesis, writing proficiency exam. *Entrance requirements:* For master's, GRE, minimum GPA of 3.0 during previous 2 years. Additional exam requirements/recommendations for international students: Required—TOEFL. Electronic applications accepted.

California State University, San Bernardino, Graduate Studies, College of Social and Behavioral Sciences, Department of Psychology, San Bernardino, CA 92407-2397. Offers child development (MA), including psychology-life span; clinical/counseling psychology (MS), including clinical psychology; general/experimental psychology (MA); industrial/organizational psychology (MS), including organizational psychology. *Students:* 59 full-time (46 women), 25 part-time (14 women); includes 46 minority (6 Black or African American, non-Hispanic/Latino; 4 Asian, non-Hispanic/Latino; 31 Hispanic/Latino; 5 Two or more races, non-Hispanic/Latino), 5 international. Average age 26. 202 applicants, 20% accepted, 33 enrolled. In 2014, 25 master's awarded. *Degree requirements:* For master's, comprehensive exam, thesis (for some programs). *Entrance requirements:* Additional exam requirements/recommendations for international students: Required—TOEFL. *Application deadline:* For fall admission, 7/17 for domestic students. Application fee: $55. *Expenses:* Tuition, state resident: full-time $6738; part-time $1302 per term. Tuition, nonresident: full-time $17,898; part-time $248 per unit. *Required fees:* $365 per quarter. Tuition and fees vary according to degree level and program. *Financial support:* Fellowships, research assistantships, and teaching assistantships available. *Faculty research:* Perceptual development, human memory, psychopharmacology, psychology of women, language acquisition. *Unit head:* Dr. Robert Ricco, Chair, 909-537-5485, Fax: 909-537-7003, E-mail: rricco@csusb.edu. *Application contact:* Dr. Jeffrey Thompson, Dean of Graduate Studies, 909-537-5058, E-mail: jthompso@csusb.edu.
Website: http://psychology.csusb.edu/

California State University, San Marcos, College of Humanities, Arts, Behavioral and Social Sciences, Program in Psychology, San Marcos, CA 92096-0001. Offers MA. *Students:* 26 full-time (21 women), 8 part-time (5 women); includes 14 minority (1 Black or African American, non-Hispanic/Latino; 1 Asian, non-Hispanic/Latino; 12 Hispanic/Latino), 1 international. Average age 26. *Degree requirements:* For master's, thesis. *Entrance requirements:* For master's, GRE General Test, GRE Subject Test in psychology (recommended), 3 letters of recommendation. Additional exam requirements/recommendations for international students: Required—TOEFL (minimum score 550 paper-based). *Application deadline:* For fall admission, 2/1 for domestic students. Application fee: $55. Electronic applications accepted. *Expenses:* Tuition, state resident: full-time $6738. *Required fees:* $1692. Tuition and fees vary according to program. *Financial support:* Research assistantships and teaching assistantships available. *Faculty research:* Psychopharmacology, recovery from major surgery, computer literacy in children, neuropsychology of hemispheric differences, conservation psychology. *Unit head:* Dr. Nancy Caine, Graduate Program Coordinator, Psychology, 760-750-4102, E-mail: mschusta@csusm.edu. *Application contact:* Admissions, 760-750-4848, Fax: 760-750-3248, E-mail: apply@csusm.edu.
Website: http://www.csusm.edu/psychology/maprogram/

California State University, Stanislaus, College of Human and Health Sciences, Program in Psychology (MA/MS), Turlock, CA 95382. Offers behavior analysis (MS); counseling psychology (MS); psychology (MA). Part-time programs available. *Degree requirements:* For master's, thesis. *Entrance requirements:* For master's, GRE, minimum GPA of 3.0, 3 letters of reference, 16 psychology prerequisites, personal statement. Additional exam requirements/recommendations for international students: Required—TOEFL (minimum score 550 paper-based). Electronic applications accepted. *Faculty research:* Hedonic tone judgment, syntax and autism, early literacy assessment and native and non-native languages.

Cambridge College, School of Psychology and Counseling, Cambridge, MA 02138-5304. Offers addiction counseling (M Ed); alcohol and drug counseling (Certificate); counseling psychology (M Ed, CAGS); counseling psychology: forensic counseling (M Ed); marriage and family therapy (M Ed); mental health and addiction counseling (M Ed); mental health counseling (M Ed); mental health counseling for school guidance counselors (Post Master's Certificate); psychological studies (M Ed); school adjustment and mental health counseling (M Ed); school adjustment, mental health and addiction counseling (M Ed); school guidance counselor (M Ed); trauma studies (Certificate). Part-time and evening/weekend programs available. *Degree requirements:* For master's and other advanced degree, thesis, practicum/internship. *Entrance requirements:* For master's, resume, 2 professional references; for other advanced degree, official transcripts, documents for transfer credit evaluation, resume, written personal statement/essay, 2 professional references, health insurance, immunizations form. Additional exam requirements/recommendations for international students: Required—TOEFL (minimum score 550 paper-based; 79 iBT), Michigan English Language Assessment Battery (minimum score 85); Recommended—IELTS (minimum score 6). Electronic applications accepted. *Expenses:* Contact institution. *Faculty research:* Trauma, drug and alcohol counseling, cross-cultural issues, school counseling, trauma in schools.

Cameron University, Office of Graduate Studies, Program in Behavioral Sciences, Lawton, OK 73505-6377. Offers MS. Part-time and evening/weekend programs available. *Degree requirements:* For master's, comprehensive exam, thesis optional. *Entrance requirements:* Additional exam requirements/recommendations for international students: Required—TOEFL (minimum score 550 paper-based). Electronic applications accepted. *Faculty research:* Student burnout, attention deficit hyperactivity disorder, group decision making, counseling outcomes, smoking cessation.

Capella University, Harold Abel School of Social and Behavioral Science, Doctoral Programs in Psychology, Minneapolis, MN 55402. Offers addiction psychology (PhD); clinical psychology (Psy D); educational psychology (PhD); general advanced studies in human behavior (PhD); general psychology (PhD); industrial/organizational psychology (PhD); school psychology (Psy D).

Capella University, Harold Abel School of Social and Behavioral Science, Master's Programs in Psychology, Minneapolis, MN 55402. Offers applied behavior analysis (MS); clinical psychology (MS); counseling psychology (MS); educational psychology (MS); evaluation, research, and measurement (MS); general advanced studies in human behavior (MS); general psychology (MS); industrial/organizational psychology (MS); leadership coaching psychology (MS); school psychology (MS); sport psychology (MS).

Cardinal Stritch University, College of Arts and Sciences, Department of Psychology, Milwaukee, WI 53217-3985. Offers clinical psychology (MA). Part-time and evening/weekend programs available. *Degree requirements:* For master's, thesis, portfolio, clinical practicum. *Entrance requirements:* For master's, GRE General Test, GRE Subject Test (psychology), interview, minimum GPA of 3.0, 3 letters of recommendation.

Carleton University, Faculty of Graduate Studies, Faculty of Arts and Social Sciences, Department of Psychology, Ottawa, ON K1S 5B6, Canada. Offers neuroscience (M Sc); psychology (MA, PhD). Part-time programs available. *Degree requirements:* For master's, thesis; for doctorate, comprehensive exam, thesis/dissertation. *Entrance requirements:* For master's, honors degree; for doctorate, GRE, master's degree. Additional exam requirements/recommendations for international students: Required—TOEFL. *Faculty research:* Behavioral neuroscience, social and personality psychology, cognitive/perception, developmental psychology, computer user research and evaluation, forensic psychology, health psychology.

Carlos Albizu University, Graduate Programs, San Juan, PR 00901. Offers clinical psychology (MS, PhD, Psy D); general psychology (PhD); industrial/organizational psychology (MS, PhD); speech and language pathology (MS). *Accreditation:* APA (one or more programs are accredited). Part-time and evening/weekend programs available. Terminal master's awarded for partial completion of doctoral program. *Degree requirements:* For master's, one foreign language, comprehensive exam, thesis; for doctorate, one foreign language, comprehensive exam, thesis/dissertation, written qualifying exams. *Entrance requirements:* For master's, GRE General Test or EXADEP, interview; minimum GPA of 2.8 (industrial/organizational psychology); for doctorate, GRE General Test or EXADEP, interview; minimum GPA of 3.0 (PhD in industrial/organizational psychology and clinical psychology), 3.25 (Psy D). *Faculty research:* Psychotherapeutic techniques for Hispanics, psychology of the aged, school dropouts, stress, violence.

Carlos Albizu University, Miami Campus, Graduate Programs, Miami, FL 33172-2209. Offers clinical psychology (Psy D); entrepreneurship (MBA); exceptional student education (MS); human services (PhD); industrial/organizational psychology (MS); marriage and family therapy (MS); mental health counseling (MS); nonprofit management (MBA); organizational management (MBA); psychology (MS); school counseling (MS); teaching English as a second language (MS). *Accreditation:* APA. Part-time and evening/weekend programs available. Postbaccalaureate distance learning degree programs offered (minimal on-campus study). *Faculty:* 25 full-time (20 women), 29 part-time/adjunct (15 women). *Students:* 431 full-time (343 women), 264 part-time (225 women); includes 586 minority (45 Black or African American, non-Hispanic/Latino; 1 American Indian or Alaska Native, non-Hispanic/Latino; 8 Asian, non-Hispanic/Latino; 530 Hispanic/Latino; 2 Two or more races, non-Hispanic/Latino), 14 international. Average age 33. 189 applicants, 69% accepted, 111 enrolled. In 2014, 177 master's, 28 doctorates awarded. Terminal master's awarded for partial completion of doctoral program. *Degree requirements:* For master's, one foreign language, comprehensive exam, integrative project (MBA), research project (exceptional student education, teaching English as a second language); for doctorate, one foreign language, comprehensive exam, internship, project. *Entrance requirements:* For master's, 3 letters of recommendation, interview, minimum GPA of 3.0, resume, statement of purpose, official transcripts; for doctorate, 3 letters of recommendation, minimum GPA of 3.0, resume, interview, statement of purpose, official transcripts. Additional exam requirements/recommendations for international students: Required—Michigan Test of English Language Proficiency. *Application deadline:* For fall admission, 4/1 priority date for domestic students, 5/1 priority date for international students; for spring admission, 11/1 priority date for domestic students, 9/1 priority date for international students. Applications are processed on a rolling basis. Application fee: $50. Electronic applications accepted. *Expenses:* Expenses: $570 per credit (for master's programs); $750 per credit (for doctoral programs). *Financial support:* In 2014–15, 72 students received support. Federal Work-Study, scholarships/grants, and tuition discounts available. Financial award application deadline: 6/1; financial award applicants required to submit FAFSA. *Faculty research:* Psychotherapy, forensic psychology, neuropsychology, marketing strategy, entrepreneurship, special education. *Unit head:* Dr. Irene M. Bravo, Interim Provost, 305-593-1223 Ext. 3120, Fax: 305-592-7930, E-mail: ibravo@albizu.edu. *Application contact:* Vanessa Almendarez, Administrative Assistant, 305-593-1223 Ext. 3137, Fax: 305-593-1854, E-mail: valmendarez@albizu.edu.

Carnegie Mellon University, Dietrich College of Humanities and Social Sciences, Department of Psychology, Pittsburgh, PA 15213-3891. Offers cognitive neuroscience (PhD); cognitive psychology (PhD); developmental psychology (PhD); social/personality/health psychology (PhD). *Degree requirements:* For doctorate, comprehensive exam, thesis/dissertation. *Entrance requirements:* For doctorate, GRE General Test. Additional exam requirements/recommendations for international students: Required—TOEFL. *Faculty research:* Artificial intelligence, stress and the immune system, children's learning strategies, neural basis of cognition.

Case Western Reserve University, School of Graduate Studies, Psychological Sciences Department, Cleveland, OH 44106. Offers clinical psychology (PhD); communication sciences (MA, PhD), including speech-language pathology; experimental psychology (PhD). *Accreditation:* APA (one or more programs are accredited). Part-time programs available. *Faculty:* 17 full-time (12 women), 16 part-time/adjunct (7 women). *Students:* 74 full-time (63 women), 2 part-time (both women); includes 14 minority (4 Black or African American, non-Hispanic/Latino; 5 Asian, non-Hispanic/Latino; 1 Hispanic/Latino; 4 Two or more races, non-Hispanic/Latino). Average age 26. 415 applicants, 4% accepted, 16 enrolled. In 2014, 15 master's, 7 doctorates awarded. Terminal master's awarded for partial completion of doctoral program. *Degree requirements:* For master's, comprehensive exam, thesis optional; for doctorate, thesis/dissertation, internship. *Entrance requirements:* For doctorate, GRE General Test, GRE Subject Test, personal statement; curriculum vitae. Additional exam requirements/recommendations for international students: Required—TOEFL (minimum score 577 paper-based; 90 iBT); Recommended—IELTS (minimum score 7). *Application deadline:* For fall admission, 12/1 priority date for domestic students. Application fee: $50. Electronic applications accepted. *Financial support:* Fellowships, research assistantships, teaching assistantships, and tuition waivers (full and partial) available. Financial award application deadline: 12/1. *Faculty research:* Adolescent suicide, cognitive processing, repressive responses, visual perception, impact of HIV infection, neuropsychology; traumatic brain injury, phonological disorders, child language disorders, communication problems in the aged and Alzheimer's patients, cleft palate, voice disorders. *Unit head:* Dr. Lee Thompson, Chair, 216-368-2685, Fax: 216-368-4891, E-mail: cwrupsych@gmail.com. *Application contact:* Dr. James C. Overholser, Director of Clinical Training, 216-368-2686, Fax: 216-368-4891, E-mail: cwrupsych@gmail.com.
Website: http://psychsciences.case.edu/

Castleton State College, Division of Graduate Studies, Department of Psychology, Castleton, VT 05735. Offers forensic psychology (MA). *Degree requirements:* For master's, thesis. *Entrance requirements:* For master's, GRE General Test, minimum undergraduate GPA of 3.5, previous course work in research methodology and statistics. Additional exam requirements/recommendations for international students: Required—TOEFL. *Faculty research:* Psychology and law, juvenile delinquency, criminal psychology, correctional psychology, police psychology.

The Catholic University of America, School of Arts and Sciences, Department of Psychology, Washington, DC 20064. Offers applied experimental psychology (PhD); clinical psychology (PhD); general psychology (MA); human factors (MA); MA/JD. *Accreditation:* APA (one or more programs are accredited). Part-time programs available. *Faculty:* 13 full-time (6 women), 7 part-time/adjunct (2 women). *Students:* 37 full-time (26 women), 42 part-time (33 women); includes 17 minority (1 Black or African American, non-Hispanic/Latino; 3 Asian, non-Hispanic/Latino; 7 Hispanic/Latino; 6 Two or more races, non-Hispanic/Latino), 3 international. Average age 28. 263 applicants, 14% accepted, 19 enrolled. In 2014, 19 master's, 6 doctorates awarded. *Degree requirements:* For master's, comprehensive exam, thesis (for some programs); for doctorate, comprehensive exam, thesis/dissertation. *Entrance requirements:* For master's, GRE General Test, statement of purpose, official copies of academic transcripts, three letters of recommendation; for doctorate, GRE General Test, GRE Subject Test, statement of purpose, official copies of academic transcripts, three letters of recommendation. Additional exam requirements/recommendations for international students: Required—TOEFL (minimum score 580 paper-based). *Application deadline:* For fall admission, 7/15 priority date for domestic students, 7/1 for international students; for spring admission, 11/15 priority date for domestic students, 11/1 for international students. Applications are processed on a rolling basis. Application fee: $55. Electronic applications accepted. *Expenses: Tuition:* Full-time $40,200; part-time $1600 per credit hour. *Required fees:* $400; $195 per semester. One-time fee: $425. *Financial support:* Fellowships, research assistantships, teaching assistantships, Federal Work-Study, scholarships/grants, tuition waivers (full and partial), and unspecified assistantships available. Financial award application deadline: 2/1; financial award applicants required to submit FAFSA. *Faculty research:* Clinical psychology, applied cognitive science, psychopathology, cognitive neuroscience, psychotherapy. *Total annual research expenditures:* $1.2 million. *Unit head:* Dr. Marc M. Sebrechts, Chair, 202-319-5750, Fax: 202-319-6263, E-mail: sebrechts@cua.edu. *Application contact:* Director of Graduate Admissions, 202-319-5057, Fax: 202-319-6533, E-mail: cua-admissions@cua.edu.
Website: http://psychology.cua.edu/

Central Connecticut State University, School of Graduate Studies, College of Liberal Arts and Social Sciences, Department of Psychology, New Britain, CT 06050-4010. Offers community psychology (MA); general psychology (MA); health psychology (MA). Part-time and evening/weekend programs available. *Faculty:* 15 full-time (9 women). *Students:* 16 full-time (13 women), 18 part-time (14 women); includes 8 minority (2 Black or African American, non-Hispanic/Latino; 2 Asian, non-Hispanic/Latino; 4 Hispanic/Latino), 2 international. Average age 28. 27 applicants, 41% accepted, 6 enrolled. In 2014, 13 master's awarded. *Degree requirements:* For master's, comprehensive exam, thesis or alternative. *Entrance requirements:* For master's, minimum undergraduate GPA of 2.75, 3.0 in psychology courses; letters of recommendation. Additional exam requirements/recommendations for international students: Required—TOEFL (minimum score 550 paper-based; 79 iBT). *Application deadline:* For fall admission, 5/1 for domestic and international students; for spring admission, 11/1 for domestic and international students. Applications are processed on a rolling basis. Application fee: $50. Electronic applications accepted. *Expenses: Tuition, area resident:* Full-time $5730; part-time $534 per credit. Tuition, state resident: full-time $8596; part-time $534 per credit. Tuition, nonresident: full-time $15,964; part-time $548 per credit. *Required fees:* $4211; $215 per credit. *Financial support:* In 2014–15, 8 students received support, including 5 research assistantships; career-related internships or fieldwork, Federal Work-Study, scholarships/grants, and unspecified assistantships also available. Support available to part-time students. Financial award application deadline: 3/1; financial award applicants required to submit FAFSA. *Faculty research:* Clinical psychology, general psychology, child development, cognitive development, drugs/behavior. *Unit head:* Dr. Carolyn Fallahi, Chair, 860-832-3100, E-mail: fallahic@ccsu.edu. *Application contact:* Patricia Gardner, Associate Director of Graduate Studies, 860-832-2350, Fax: 860-832-2362, E-mail: graduateadmissions@ccsu.edu.
Website: http://web.ccsu.edu/psychology/

Central Michigan University, College of Graduate Studies, College of Humanities and Social and Behavioral Sciences, Department of Psychology, Mount Pleasant, MI 48859. Offers clinical psychology (PhD); experimental psychology (MS, PhD), including applied experimental psychology (PhD), experimental psychology (MS); industrial and organizational psychology (MA, PhD), including industrial and organizational psychology, occupational health psychology (PhD); neuroscience (MS, PhD); school psychology (PhD, S Psy S), including psychological services (S Psy S), school psychology (PhD). *Accreditation:* APA (one or more programs are accredited). Terminal master's awarded for partial completion of doctoral program. *Degree requirements:* For master's, thesis or alternative; for doctorate, thesis/dissertation; for S Psy S, thesis. *Entrance requirements:* For doctorate, GRE. Electronic applications accepted. *Faculty research:* Experimental psychology, clinical psychology, industrial/organizational psychology, school psychology, neuroscience.

Central Washington University, Graduate Studies and Research, College of the Sciences, Department of Psychology, Ellensburg, WA 98926. Offers experimental psychology (MS); mental health counseling (MS); school counseling (M Ed); school psychology (M Ed). Evening/weekend programs available. *Degree requirements:* For master's, thesis. *Entrance requirements:* For master's, GRE General Test, minimum GPA of 3.0. Additional exam requirements/recommendations for international students: Required—TOEFL (minimum score 550 paper-based; 79 iBT). Electronic applications accepted.

Chestnut Hill College, School of Graduate Studies, Division of Psychology, Philadelphia, PA 19118-2693. Offers clinical and counseling psychology (MS, CAS), including addictions treatment, child and adolescent therapy, marriage and family therapy (MS, Psy D, CAS), trauma studies, treatment of autism spectrum disorders; clinical psychology (Psy D), including marriage and family therapy (MS, Psy D, CAS), psychological assessment. Part-time and evening/weekend programs available. *Faculty:* 11 full-time (6 women), 35 part-time/adjunct (25 women). *Students:* 200 full-time (153 women), 136 part-time (113 women); includes 69 minority (38 Black or African American, non-Hispanic/Latino; 7 Asian, non-Hispanic/Latino; 21 Hispanic/Latino; 3 Two or more races, non-Hispanic/Latino), 3 international. Average age 32. 291 applicants, 54% accepted, 85 enrolled. In 2014, 121 master's, 21 doctorates, 7 other advanced degrees awarded. *Degree requirements:* For master's, thesis optional, practica; for doctorate, comprehensive exam, thesis/dissertation, internship, practica, clinical competency exam. *Entrance requirements:* For master's, GRE General Test, writing sample, letters of recommendation; for doctorate, GRE General Test, master's degree in counseling/clinical psychology or closely-related field, official transcripts, letters of recommendation, statement of professional goals, writing sample; for CAS, GRE General Test, official transcripts, letters of recommendation, statement of professional goals, writing sample. Additional exam requirements/recommendations for international students: Required—TOEFL (minimum score 500 paper-based), IELTS (mnimum score 6.0), or TWE (minimum score 22). *Application deadline:* For fall admission, 7/1 for domestic and international students; for spring admission, 11/1 for domestic and international students; for summer admission, 4/1 for domestic and international students. Applications are processed on a rolling basis. Application fee: $55. *Expenses:* Expenses: Contact institution. *Financial support:* Unspecified assistantships available. *Faculty research:* Lifespan development, trauma and sexual abuse, cultural diversity, family psychology and family therapy, psychodynamic therapy. *Unit head:* Dr. Cheryll Rothery, Chair, 215-248-7023, Fax: 215-248-3619, E-mail: rotheryc@chc.edu. *Application contact:* Amy Boorse, Assistant Director of Graduate Admissions, 215-248-7097, Fax: 215-248-7161, E-mail: gradadmissions@chc.edu.
Website: http://www.chc.edu/Graduate/Programs/PsyD/

The Chicago School of Professional Psychology, Program in Business Psychology, Chicago, IL 60610. Offers business psychology (PhD); industrial and organizational business psychology (Psy D); industrial and organizational psychology (MA); organizational leadership (MA, PhD). *Degree requirements:* For doctorate, thesis/dissertation optional. *Entrance requirements:* For doctorate, GRE. Additional exam requirements/recommendations for international students: Required—TOEFL.

The Chicago School of Professional Psychology at Irvine, Program in Psychology, Irvine, CA 92612. Offers generalist (Psy D); psychodynamic psychotherapy (Psy D).

The Chicago School of Professional Psychology at Westwood, Program in Psychology, Los Angeles, CA 90024. Offers generalist (Psy D); psychodynamic psychotherapy (Psy D).

The Chicago School of Professional Psychology: Online, Program in International Psychology, Chicago, IL 60654. Offers PhD.

The Chicago School of Professional Psychology: Online, Program in Psychology, Chicago, IL 60654. Offers child and adolescent psychology (MA); generalist (MA); gerontology (MA); international psychology (MA); organizational leadership (MA); sport and exercise psychology (MA).

The Citadel, The Military College of South Carolina, Citadel Graduate College, Department of Psychology, Charleston, SC 29409. Offers psychology (MA), including clinical counseling; school psychology (Ed S), including school psychology. Part-time and evening/weekend programs available. *Degree requirements:* For master's, comprehensive exam, thesis optional; for Ed S, comprehensive exam, thesis, internship. *Entrance requirements:* For master's, GRE (minimum score of 297, 150 on the verbal reasoning and 141 on the quantitative reasoning section) or MAT (minimum score of 410), minimum undergraduate GPA of 3.0; 2 letters of reference; for Ed S, GRE (minimum score of 297, 150 on the verbal reasoning and 141 on the quantitative reasoning section) or MAT (minimum score of 410), minimum undergraduate or graduate GPA of 3.0; 2 letters of reference. Additional exam requirements/recommendations for international students: Required—TOEFL (minimum score 550 paper-based). Electronic applications accepted. *Faculty research:* Ostracism and social exclusion, bullying, social concerns of special-needs children, childhood obesity, phantom limb pain, validation of psychological tests, perfectionism, school-based interventions with at-risk children.

City College of the City University of New York, Graduate School, College of Liberal Arts and Science, Division of Social Science, Department of Psychology, New York, NY 10031-9198. Offers clinical psychology (PhD); experimental cognition (PhD); general psychology (MA); mental health counseling (MA). PhD program offered jointly with Graduate School and University Center of the City University of New York. *Accreditation:* APA (one or more programs are accredited). Part-time programs available. *Degree requirements:* For master's, one foreign language, comprehensive exam, thesis. *Entrance requirements:* For master's, GRE. Additional exam requirements/recommendations for international students: Required—TOEFL (minimum score 550 paper-based; 79 iBT). Electronic applications accepted. *Faculty research:* Social/personality psychology, physiological psychology, cognition and development.

Claremont Graduate University, Graduate Programs, School of Social Science, Policy and Evaluation, Department of Psychology, Claremont, CA 91711-6160. Offers advanced study in evaluation (Certificate); cognitive psychology (MA, PhD); developmental psychology (MA, PhD); evaluation and applied research methods (MA, PhD); health behavior research and evaluation (MA, PhD); human resource development and evaluation (MA); industrial/organizational psychology (MA, PhD); organizational behavior (MA, PhD); organizational psychology (MA, PhD); social psychology (MA, PhD); MBA/PhD. Part-time programs available. *Faculty:* 18 full-time (7 women), 1 part-time/adjunct (0 women). *Students:* 256 full-time (160 women), 70 part-

time (50 women); includes 93 minority (17 Black or African American, non-Hispanic/Latino; 3 American Indian or Alaska Native, non-Hispanic/Latino; 26 Asian, non-Hispanic/Latino; 30 Hispanic/Latino; 17 Two or more races, non-Hispanic/Latino), 35 international. Average age 30. In 2014, 56 master's, 15 doctorates, 7 other advanced degrees awarded. Terminal master's awarded for partial completion of doctoral program. *Entrance requirements:* For master's and doctorate, GRE General Test. Additional exam requirements/recommendations for international students: Required—TOEFL (minimum score 550 paper-based; 80 iBT). *Application deadline:* For fall admission, 1/15 priority date for domestic and international students. Applications are processed on a rolling basis. Application fee: $80. Electronic applications accepted. *Expenses: Tuition:* Full-time $41,784; part-time $1741 per credit. *Required fees:* $600; $300 per semester. *Financial support:* Fellowships, research assistantships, teaching assistantships, Federal Work-Study, institutionally sponsored loans, scholarships/grants, and tuition waivers (full and partial) available. Support available to part-time students. Financial award application deadline: 2/15; financial award applicants required to submit FAFSA. *Faculty research:* Social intervention, diversity in organizations, eyewitness memory, aging and cognition, drug policy. *Unit head:* William Crano, Chair, 909-621-8084, E-mail: william.crano@cgu.edu. *Application contact:* Annekah Hall, Assistant Director of Admissions, 909-607-3371, E-mail: annekah.hall@cgu.edu.
Website: http://www.cgu.edu/pages/502.asp

Clayton State University, School of Graduate Studies, College of Arts and Sciences, Program in Psychology, Morrow, GA 30260-0285. Offers applied developmental psychology (MS); clinical psychology (MS). *Entrance requirements:* For master's, GRE, 2 official transcripts; 3 letters of recommendation; statement of purpose; on-campus interview; background check. Additional exam requirements/recommendations for international students: Required—TOEFL (minimum score 550 paper-based). Electronic applications accepted.

Clemson University, Graduate School, College of Business and Behavioral Science, Department of Psychology, Program in Human Factors Psychology, Clemson, SC 29634. Offers PhD. *Students:* 15 full-time (8 women), 2 part-time (0 women); includes 2 minority (both Two or more races, non-Hispanic/Latino). Average age 28. 37 applicants, 14% accepted, 4 enrolled. In 2014, 2 doctorates awarded. *Degree requirements:* For doctorate, thesis/dissertation. *Entrance requirements:* For doctorate, GRE General Test. Additional exam requirements/recommendations for international students: Required—TOEFL. *Application deadline:* For fall admission, 1/15 for domestic students. Applications are processed on a rolling basis. Application fee: $70 ($80 for international students). Electronic applications accepted. *Expenses:* Expenses: Contact institution. *Financial support:* In 2014–15, 14 students received support, including 6 fellowships with full and partial tuition reimbursements available (averaging $5,000 per year), 14 teaching assistantships with partial tuition reimbursements available (averaging $20,000 per year); research assistantships with partial tuition reimbursements available, career-related internships or fieldwork, institutionally sponsored loans, scholarships/grants, health care benefits, and unspecified assistantships also available. Support available to part-time students. *Faculty research:* Transportation safety, human factors in health care, human-computer interaction, ergonomics, vision and visual performance. *Unit head:* Dr. Patrick Raymark, Chair, 864-656-4715, Fax: 864-656-0358, E-mail: praymar@clemson.edu. *Application contact:* Dr. Lee Gugerty, Professor, 864-656-4467, Fax: 864-656-0358, E-mail: gugerty@clemson.edu.
Website: http://www.clemson.edu/psych

Cleveland State University, College of Graduate Studies, College of Sciences and Health Professions, Department of Psychology, Cleveland, OH 44115. Offers MA, PhD, Psy S. *Accreditation:* APA. *Faculty:* 9 full-time (3 women), 14 part-time/adjunct (5 women). *Students:* 61 full-time (44 women), 38 part-time (29 women); includes 16 minority (10 Black or African American, non-Hispanic/Latino; 3 Asian, non-Hispanic/Latino; 3 Hispanic/Latino), 1 international. Average age 28. 155 applicants, 48% accepted, 45 enrolled. In 2014, 41 master's, 1 doctorate, 14 other advanced degrees awarded. Terminal master's awarded for partial completion of doctoral program. *Degree requirements:* For master's, comprehensive exam (for some programs), thesis (for some programs); for doctorate, comprehensive exam, thesis/dissertation; for Psy S, internship. *Entrance requirements:* For master's and doctorate, GRE General Test. Additional exam requirements/recommendations for international students: Required—TOEFL (minimum score 525 paper-based). *Application deadline:* For fall admission, 2/1 priority date for domestic and international students. Application fee: $30. Electronic applications accepted. *Expenses:* Tuition, state resident: full-time $9566; part-time $531 per credit hour. Tuition, nonresident: full-time $17,980; part-time $999 per credit hour. *Required fees:* $25 per semester. Tuition and fees vary according to degree level and program. *Financial support:* In 2014–15, 40 students received support, including 4 research assistantships with full tuition reimbursements available (averaging $15,500 per year), 4 teaching assistantships with full tuition reimbursements available (averaging $15,500 per year); career-related internships or fieldwork, Federal Work-Study, scholarships/grants, tuition waivers (partial), and unspecified assistantships also available. Financial award application deadline: 3/1; financial award applicants required to submit FAFSA. *Faculty research:* Cognition and language, neuropsychological functioning and assessment, academic and behavioral interventions for schoolchildren, dementia care giving, emotional regulation. *Total annual research expenditures:* $68,057. *Unit head:* Dr. Kathleen M. McNamara, Chairperson, 216-687-2545, Fax: 216-687-9294, E-mail: k.mcnamara@csuohio.edu. *Application contact:* Barbara E. Durfey, Administrative Secretary, 216-687-2544, Fax: 216-687-9294, E-mail: b.durfey@csuohio.edu.
Website: http://www.csuohio.edu/sciences/dept/psychology/

The College at Brockport, State University of New York, School of Science and Mathematics, Department of Psychology, Brockport, NY 14420-2997. Offers MA. Part-time programs available. *Faculty:* 14 full-time (11 women), 1 (woman) part-time/adjunct. *Students:* 20 full-time (12 women), 4 part-time (2 women); includes 4 minority (1 Asian, non-Hispanic/Latino; 2 Hispanic/Latino; 1 Two or more races, non-Hispanic/Latino). 23 applicants, 43% accepted, 9 enrolled. In 2014, 3 master's awarded. *Degree requirements:* For master's, thesis optional. *Entrance requirements:* For master's, GRE General Test, letters of recommendation, interview, minimum GPA of 3.0. Additional exam requirements/recommendations for international students: Required—TOEFL (minimum score 550 paper-based; 79 iBT), IELTS (minimum score 6.5). *Application deadline:* For fall admission, 4/1 priority date for domestic and international students. Application fee: $50. Electronic applications accepted. *Financial support:* In 2014–15, 3 teaching assistantships with full tuition reimbursements (averaging $6,000 per year) were awarded; Federal Work-Study, scholarships/grants, and unspecified assistantships also available. Support available to part-time students. Financial award application deadline: 3/15; financial award applicants required to submit FAFSA. *Faculty research:* Positive psychology, decision-making and applied behavior analysis, family processes and close relationships, cognition and neuropsychology, social/personality and industrial/organizational psychology. *Unit head:* Dr. Melissa M. Brown, Chairperson, 585-395-2488, Fax: 585-395-2116, E-mail: mmbrown@brockport.edu. *Application contact:* Dr. Sara Margolin, Graduate Director, 585-395-2908, Fax: 585-395-2116, E-mail: smargoli@brockport.edu.
Website: http://www.brockport.edu/math/grad/

College of Saint Elizabeth, Department of Psychology, Morristown, NJ 07960-6989. Offers counseling psychology (MA); forensic psychology (MA); mental health counseling (Certificate); student affairs in higher education (Certificate). Part-time programs available. *Degree requirements:* For master's, thesis or alternative. *Entrance requirements:* For master's, minimum GPA of 3.0, BA in psychology (preferred), 12 credits of course work in psychology. Additional exam requirements/recommendations for international students: Required—TOEFL. Electronic applications accepted.

College of St. Joseph, Graduate Programs, Division of Psychology and Human Services, Rutland, VT 05701-3899. Offers alcohol and substance abuse counseling (MS); clinical mental health counseling (MS); clinical psychology (MS); community counseling (MS); school guidance counseling (MS). Part-time and evening/weekend programs available. *Degree requirements:* For master's, comprehensive exam, thesis optional. *Entrance requirements:* For master's, official college transcripts; 2 letters of reference. Additional exam requirements/recommendations for international students: Required—TOEFL (minimum score 550 paper-based). Electronic applications accepted.

Colorado State University, Graduate School, College of Natural Sciences, Department of Psychology, Fort Collins, CO 80523-1876. Offers psychology (MS, PhD). *Accreditation:* APA. *Faculty:* 27 full-time (16 women), 1 part-time/adjunct (0 women). *Students:* 65 full-time (45 women), 66 part-time (43 women); includes 19 minority (4 Asian, non-Hispanic/Latino; 11 Hispanic/Latino; 4 Two or more races, non-Hispanic/Latino), 3 international. Average age 29. 111 applicants, 32% accepted, 34 enrolled. In 2014, 23 master's, 16 doctorates awarded. Terminal master's awarded for partial completion of doctoral program. *Degree requirements:* For master's, comprehensive exam (for some programs), thesis; for doctorate, comprehensive exam, thesis/dissertation. *Entrance requirements:* For master's, GRE General Test, GRE Subject Test (minimum scores within 50th percentile), minimum GPA of 3.2; for doctorate, GRE General Test, GRE Subject Test (minimum scores within 50th percentile), minimum GPA of 3.6. Additional exam requirements/recommendations for international students: Required—TOEFL (minimum score 550 paper-based; 80 iBT). *Application deadline:* For fall admission, 12/1 priority date for domestic and international students; for spring admission, 1/1 for domestic and international students. Applications are processed on a rolling basis. Application fee: $50. Electronic applications accepted. *Expenses:* Tuition, state resident: full-time $9348; part-time $519 per credit. Tuition, nonresident: full-time $22,916; part-time $1273 per credit. *Required fees:* $1584. *Financial support:* In 2014–15, 63 students received support, including 1 fellowship with tuition reimbursement available (averaging $9,115 per year), 10 research assistantships with full tuition reimbursements available (averaging $10,780 per year), 52 teaching assistantships with full tuition reimbursements available (averaging $13,176 per year); scholarships/grants, health care benefits, and unspecified assistantships also available. Financial award application deadline: 1/15; financial award applicants required to submit FAFSA. *Faculty research:* Lifespan development, health psychology, vocational psychology, substance use and abuse. *Total annual research expenditures:* $4.5 million. *Unit head:* Dr. Evelinn Borrayo, Director of Training, 970-491-3550, Fax: 970-491-1032, E-mail: evelinn.borrayo@colostate.edu. *Application contact:* Ginger Lacey-Gill, Administrative Assistant III, 970-491-6363, Fax: 970-491-1032, E-mail: ginger.lacy-gill@colostate.edu.
Website: http://www.colostate.edu/Depts/Psychology/

Columbia University, Graduate School of Arts and Sciences, New York, NY 10027. Offers African-American studies (MA); American studies (MA); anthropology (MA, PhD); art history and archaeology (MA, PhD); astronomy (PhD); biological sciences (PhD); biotechnology (MA); chemical physics (PhD); chemistry (PhD); classical studies (MA, PhD); classics (MA, PhD); climate and society (MA); earth and environmental sciences (PhD); East Asia: regional studies (MA); East Asian languages and cultures (MA, PhD); ecology, evolution and environmental biology (MA), including conservation biology; ecology, evolution, and environmental biology (PhD), including ecology and evolutionary biology, evolutionary primatology; economics (PhD); English and comparative literature (MA, PhD); French and Romance philology (MA, PhD); Germanic languages (MA, PhD); global French studies (MA); Hispanic cultural studies (MA); history (PhD); history and literature (MA); human rights studies (MA); Islamic studies (MA); Italian (MA, PhD); Japanese pedagogy (MA); Jewish studies (MA); Latin America and the Caribbean: regional studies (MA); Latin American and Iberian cultures (PhD); mathematics (MA, PhD), including finance (MA); medieval and Renaissance studies (MA); Middle Eastern, South Asian, and African studies (MA, PhD); modern art: critical and curatorial studies (MA); modern European studies (MA); museum anthropology (MA); music (DMA, PhD); oral history (MA); philosophical foundations of physics (MA); philosophy (MA, PhD); physics (PhD); political science (MA, PhD); psychology (PhD); quantitative methods in the social sciences (MA); religion (MA, PhD); Russia, Eurasia and East Europe: regional studies (MA); Russian translation (MA); Slavic cultures (MA); Slavic languages (MA, PhD); sociology (MA, PhD); South Asian studies (MA); statistics (MA, PhD); theatre (PhD); JD/PhD; MA/MS; MD/PhD; MPA/MA. Dual-degree programs require admission to both Graduate School of Arts and Sciences and another Columbia school. Part-time and evening/weekend programs available. Terminal master's awarded for partial completion of doctoral program. *Degree requirements:* For master's, thesis (for some programs); for doctorate, comprehensive exam, thesis/dissertation. *Entrance requirements:* For master's and doctorate, GRE General Test, GRE Subject Test (for some programs). Electronic applications accepted. *Faculty research:* Humanities, natural sciences, social sciences.

Concordia University, School of Graduate Studies, Faculty of Arts and Science, Department of Psychology, Program in Psychology (General), Montréal, QC H3G 1M8, Canada. Offers MA, PhD. *Degree requirements:* For master's, comprehensive exam, thesis; for doctorate, comprehensive exam, thesis/dissertation. *Entrance requirements:* For master's, GRE General Test, GRE Subject Test, honors degree in psychology or equivalent; for doctorate, master's degree in psychology. *Faculty research:* Appetitive motivation and drug dependence, human information processing, psychology of physical activity.

Concordia University Chicago, College of Graduate and Innovative Programs, Program in Psychology, River Forest, IL 60305-1499. Offers MA. Part-time and evening/weekend programs available. *Degree requirements:* For master's, comprehensive exam, thesis optional. *Entrance requirements:* For master's, minimum GPA of 2.9. Additional exam requirements/recommendations for international students: Required—TOEFL (minimum score 550 paper-based). Electronic applications accepted. *Faculty research:* Lutheran high school counseling research.

Concordia University Wisconsin, Graduate Programs, Department of Psychology, Mequon, WI 53097-2402. Offers professional counseling (MPC).

Connecticut College, Department of Psychology, New London, CT 06320-4196. Offers behavioral medicine/health psychology (MA); clinical psychology (MA); neuroscience/psychobiology (MA); social/personality psychology (MA). Part-time programs available. *Students:* 4 full-time (2 women), 3 part-time (2 women). Average age 30. 7 applicants, 29% accepted, 2 enrolled. *Degree requirements:* For master's, thesis. *Entrance requirements:* For master's, GRE General Test, statistics course. Additional exam requirements/recommendations for international students: Required—TOEFL (minimum score 600 paper-based). *Application deadline:* For fall admission, 2/1 for domestic and international students. Application fee: $60. *Expenses: Tuition:* Full-time $12,120. *Financial support:* Tuition remission available. Financial award application deadline: 2/

1; financial award applicants required to submit CSS PROFILE or FAFSA. *Unit head:* Dr. Ruth Grahn, Chair, 860-439-2387, Fax: 860-439-5300, E-mail: ruth.grahn@conncoll.edu. *Application contact:* Nancy M. MacLeod, Academic Department Assistant, 860-439-2330, Fax: 860-439-5300, E-mail: nancy.macleod@conncoll.edu.

Cornell University, Graduate School, Graduate Fields of Arts and Sciences, Field of Psychology, Ithaca, NY 14853-0001. Offers biopsychology (PhD); human experimental psychology (PhD); personality and social psychology (PhD). *Degree requirements:* For doctorate, comprehensive exam, thesis/dissertation, 2 semesters of teaching experience. *Entrance requirements:* For doctorate, GRE General Test, 3 letters of recommendation. Additional exam requirements/recommendations for international students: Required—TOEFL (minimum score 550 paper-based; 77 iBT). Electronic applications accepted. *Faculty research:* Sensory and perceptual systems, social cognition, cognitive development, quantitative and computational modeling, behavioral neuroscience.

Dalhousie University, Faculty of Science, Department of Psychology, Halifax, NS B3H 4R2, Canada. Offers clinical psychology (PhD); psychology (M Sc, PhD); psychology/neuroscience (M Sc, PhD). *Degree requirements:* For master's, thesis; for doctorate, thesis/dissertation. *Entrance requirements:* For doctorate, GRE General Test. Additional exam requirements/recommendations for international students: Required—TOEFL, IELTS, CANTEST, CAEL, or Michigan English Language Assessment Battery. Electronic applications accepted. *Faculty research:* Physiological psychology, psychology of learning, learning and behavior, forensic clinical health psychology, development perception and cognition.

Dartmouth College, Arts and Sciences Graduate Programs, Department of Psychological and Brain Sciences, Hanover, NH 03755. Offers cognitive neuroscience (PhD); psychology (PhD). *Faculty:* 20 full-time (5 women), 7 part-time/adjunct (3 women). *Students:* 37 full-time (20 women); includes 7 minority (1 American Indian or Alaska Native, non-Hispanic/Latino; 3 Asian, non-Hispanic/Latino; 3 Hispanic/Latino), 10 international. Average age 27. 121 applicants, 6% accepted, 4 enrolled. In 2014, 3 doctorates awarded. *Degree requirements:* For doctorate, thesis/dissertation. *Entrance requirements:* For doctorate, GRE General Test, GRE Subject Test. Additional exam requirements/recommendations for international students: Required—TOEFL. *Application deadline:* For fall admission, 1/15 priority date for domestic students. Application fee: $50. *Financial support:* Fellowships with full tuition reimbursements, research assistantships with full tuition reimbursements, teaching assistantships, institutionally sponsored loans, traineeships, tuition waivers (full), and unspecified assistantships available. *Faculty research:* Behavioral neuroscience, cognitive neuroscience, cognitive science, social/personality psychology. *Unit head:* Dr. Jay Hull, Chair, 603-646-2098, Fax: 603-646-1419. *Application contact:* Nancy Tenney, Department Administrator, 603-646-2781, E-mail: nancy.tenney@dartmouth.edu. Website: http://www.dartmouth.edu/~psych/graduate/

DePaul University, College of Science and Health, Chicago, IL 60614. Offers applied mathematics (MS); applied statistics (MS); biological sciences (MA, MS); chemistry (MS); mathematics education (MA); mathematics for teaching (MS); nursing (MS); nursing practice (DNP); physics (MS); psychology (MS); pure mathematics (MS); science education (MS); MA/PhD. Electronic applications accepted.

Drexel University, College of Arts and Sciences, Department of Psychology, Philadelphia, PA 19104-2875. Offers clinical psychology (PhD), including clinical psychology, forensic psychology, health psychology, neuropsychology; law-psychology (PhD); psychology (MS); JD/PhD. *Accreditation:* APA (one or more programs are accredited). *Degree requirements:* For doctorate, thesis/dissertation, internship. *Entrance requirements:* For doctorate, GRE General Test. Additional exam requirements/recommendations for international students: Required—TOEFL. Electronic applications accepted. *Expenses:* Contact institution. *Faculty research:* Neurosciences, rehabilitation psychology, cognitive science, neurological assessment.

Duke University, Graduate School, Department of Psychology and Neuroscience, Durham, NC 27708. Offers biological psychology (PhD); clinical psychology (PhD); cognitive psychology (PhD); developmental psychology (PhD); experimental psychology (PhD); health psychology (PhD); human social development (PhD); JD/MA. *Accreditation:* APA (one or more programs are accredited). *Degree requirements:* For doctorate, thesis/dissertation. *Entrance requirements:* For doctorate, GRE General Test. Additional exam requirements/recommendations for international students: Required—TOEFL (minimum score 577 paper-based; 90 iBT) or IELTS (minimum score 7). Electronic applications accepted. *Expenses: Tuition:* Full-time $45,760; part-time $2765 per credit. *Required fees:* $978. Full-time tuition and fees vary according to program.

Duquesne University, Graduate School of Liberal Arts, Department of Psychology, Pittsburgh, PA 15282-0001. Offers clinical psychology (PhD). *Accreditation:* APA. *Faculty:* 13 full-time (7 women). *Students:* 46 full-time (28 women), 1 (woman) part-time; includes 5 minority (1 Black or African American, non-Hispanic/Latino; 1 Asian, non-Hispanic/Latino; 2 Hispanic/Latino; 1 Two or more races, non-Hispanic/Latino), 7 international. Average age 30. 180 applicants, 4% accepted, 8 enrolled. In 2014, 5 doctorates awarded. *Degree requirements:* For doctorate, comprehensive exam, thesis/dissertation. *Entrance requirements:* For doctorate, GRE General Test, MA in psychology. Additional exam requirements/recommendations for international students: Required—TOEFL. *Application deadline:* For fall admission, 12/15 for domestic and international students. Electronic applications accepted. *Expenses: Tuition:* Full-time $18,882; part-time $1049 per credit. *Required fees:* $1800; $100 per credit. Tuition and fees vary according to program. *Financial support:* In 2014–15, 26 teaching assistantships with full tuition reimbursements (averaging $17,000 per year) were awarded; career-related internships or fieldwork, scholarships/grants, tuition waivers (partial), and unspecified assistantships also available. Financial award application deadline: 5/1. *Faculty research:* Emotion, language motivation, imagination, development. *Unit head:* Dr. Leswin Laubscher, Chair, 412-396-6520, E-mail: laubscherl@duq.edu. *Application contact:* Linda Rendulic, Assistant to the Dean, 412-396-6400, Fax: 412-396-5265, E-mail: rendulic@duq.edu. Website: http://www.duq.edu/academics/schools/liberal-arts/graduate-school/programs/clinical-psychology

East Central University, School of Graduate Studies, Department of Psychology, Ada, OK 74820. Offers MSPS. Part-time and evening/weekend programs available. *Entrance requirements:* For master's, GRE General Test, MAT. Electronic applications accepted.

Eastern Illinois University, Graduate School, College of Sciences, Department of Psychology, Charleston, IL 61920. Offers clinical psychology (MA); school psychology (SSP). Part-time and evening/weekend programs available. *Faculty:* 13. *Students:* 37 full-time (23 women), 13 part-time (8 women); includes 4 minority (2 Black or African American, non-Hispanic/Latino; 1 Hispanic/Latino; 1 Two or more races, non-Hispanic/Latino), 3 international. Average age 24. 85 applicants, 21% accepted, 15 enrolled. In 2014, 5 master's, 5 other advanced degrees awarded. *Degree requirements:* For master's, comprehensive exam, thesis; for SSP, thesis. *Entrance requirements:* For master's and SSP, GMAT or GRE. Additional exam requirements/recommendations for international students: Required—TOEFL (minimum score 500 paper-based; 61 iBT), IELTS (minimum score 6). *Application deadline:* For fall admission, 5/15 for domestic

and international students; for spring admission, 10/15 for domestic and international students. Applications are processed on a rolling basis. Application fee: $30. Electronic applications accepted. *Expenses:* Tuition, state resident: full-time $3113; part-time $283 per credit hour. Tuition, nonresident: full-time $7469; part-time $679 per credit hour. *Required fees:* $2287; $96 per credit hour. Tuition and fees vary according to course load. *Financial support:* In 2014–15, 41 students received support, including 4 research assistantships with full tuition reimbursements available (averaging $8,100 per year), 8 teaching assistantships with full tuition reimbursements available (averaging $8,010 per year); career-related internships or fieldwork, Federal Work-Study, and unspecified assistantships also available. Support available to part-time students. Financial award application deadline: 3/1; financial award applicants required to submit FAFSA. *Unit head:* Assege Haile Mariam, Interim Department Chair, 217-581-6615, Fax: 217-581-6764, E-mail: ahailemariam@eiu.edu. *Application contact:* Department of Psychology, 217-581-2127, Fax: 217-581-6764, E-mail: psych@eiu.edu. Website: http://www.eiu.edu/psych/index.php

Eastern Kentucky University, The Graduate School, College of Arts and Sciences, Department of Psychology, Richmond, KY 40475-3102. Offers clinical psychology (MS); industrial/organizational psychology (MS); school psychology (Psy S). Part-time programs available. *Entrance requirements:* For master's and Psy S, GRE General Test, minimum GPA of 2.5. *Faculty research:* Autism, social psychology, parenting, assessment of depression/anxiety, reading.

Eastern Michigan University, Graduate School, College of Arts and Sciences, Department of Psychology, Ypsilanti, MI 48197. Offers clinical psychology (MS); experimental psychology (MS). *Accreditation:* APA. *Faculty:* 22 full-time (13 women). *Students:* 53 full-time (44 women), 44 part-time (31 women); includes 13 minority (1 Black or African American, non-Hispanic/Latino; 1 American Indian or Alaska Native, non-Hispanic/Latino; 5 Asian, non-Hispanic/Latino; 2 Hispanic/Latino; 4 Two or more races, non-Hispanic/Latino), 4 international. Average age 27. 248 applicants, 19% accepted, 33 enrolled. In 2014, 30 master's, 5 doctorates awarded. *Degree requirements:* For master's, 600-hour practicum; for doctorate, 1500-hour practicum; 2000-hour internship. *Entrance requirements:* For master's and doctorate, GRE. *Application deadline:* For fall admission, 2/15 for domestic students. Application fee: $45. *Financial support:* Fellowships available. *Unit head:* Dr. Carol Freedman-Doan, Department Head, 734-487-1155, Fax: 734-487-6553, E-mail: cfreedman@emich.edu.

Eastern Washington University, Graduate Studies, College of Social and Behavioral Sciences and Social Work, Department of Psychology, Cheney, WA 99004-2431. Offers clinical psychology (MS); experimental psychology (MS); psychology (MS). *Degree requirements:* For master's, comprehensive exam, thesis or alternative. *Entrance requirements:* For master's, GRE General Test, minimum GPA of 3.0.

East Tennessee State University, School of Graduate Studies, College of Arts and Sciences, Department of Psychology, Johnson City, TN 37614. Offers PhD. *Faculty:* 17 full-time (8 women). *Students:* 36 full-time (22 women), 7 part-time (3 women); includes 4 minority (3 Black or African American, non-Hispanic/Latino; 1 Two or more races, non-Hispanic/Latino). Average age 28. 162 applicants, 9% accepted, 10 enrolled. In 2014, 8 doctorates awarded. Terminal master's awarded for partial completion of doctoral program. *Degree requirements:* For doctorate, thesis/dissertation, externship. *Entrance requirements:* For doctorate, GRE General Test, minimum GPA of 3.0, three letters of recommendation, interview. Additional exam requirements/recommendations for international students: Required—TOEFL (minimum score 550 paper-based; 79 iBT). *Application deadline:* For fall admission, 2/1 for domestic and international students. Application fee: $35 ($45 for international students). Electronic applications accepted. *Financial support:* In 2014–15, 34 students received support, including 33 research assistantships with full tuition reimbursements available (averaging $11,000 per year), 3 teaching assistantships with full tuition reimbursements available (averaging $12,000 per year); career-related internships or fieldwork, institutionally sponsored loans, scholarships/grants, and unspecified assistantships also available. Financial award application deadline: 7/1; financial award applicants required to submit FAFSA. *Faculty research:* Women's issues, prenatal stress, childhood obesity, suicide prevention, behavioral pediatrics, self-control, substance dependence, violence. *Unit head:* Dr. Wallace Dixon, Chair, 423-439-4461, Fax: 423-439-5695, E-mail: dixonw@etsu.edu. *Application contact:* Angela Edwards, Graduate Specialist, 423-439-4703, Fax: 423-439-5624, E-mail: edwardag@etsu.edu. Website: http://www.etsu.edu/cas/psychology/

Emory University, Laney Graduate School, Department of Psychology, Atlanta, GA 30322-1100. Offers clinical psychology (PhD); cognition and development (PhD); neuroscience and animal behavior (PhD). *Accreditation:* APA. *Degree requirements:* For doctorate, comprehensive exam, thesis/dissertation. *Entrance requirements:* For doctorate, GRE General Test, minimum GPA of 3.25. Additional exam requirements/recommendations for international students: Required—TOEFL. Electronic applications accepted. *Faculty research:* Neuroscience and animal behavior; adult and child psychopathology, cognition development assessment.

Emporia State University, Program in Psychology, Emporia, KS 66801-5415. Offers general psychology (MS); industrial/organizational psychology (MS). Part-time programs available. *Faculty:* 8 full-time (4 women). *Students:* 19 full-time (11 women), 9 part-time (5 women); includes 6 minority (1 Black or African American, non-Hispanic/Latino; 1 American Indian or Alaska Native, non-Hispanic/Latino; 2 Hispanic/Latino; 2 Two or more races, non-Hispanic/Latino), 3 international. 14 applicants, 100% accepted, 9 enrolled. In 2014, 8 master's awarded. *Degree requirements:* For master's, comprehensive exam or thesis, internship. *Entrance requirements:* For master's, GRE General Test or MAT, essay exam, appropriate bachelor's degree, letters of recommendation. Additional exam requirements/recommendations for international students: Required—TOEFL (minimum score 520 paper-based; 68 iBT). *Application deadline:* For fall admission, 6/1 priority date for domestic students; for spring admission, 10/1 for domestic students. Applications are processed on a rolling basis. Application fee: $30 ($75 for international students). Electronic applications accepted. *Expenses:* Tuition, state resident: part-time $227 per credit hour. Tuition, nonresident: part-time $706 per credit hour. *Required fees:* $75 per credit hour. Tuition and fees vary according to campus/location. *Financial support:* In 2014–15, 13 teaching assistantships with full tuition reimbursements (averaging $7,344 per year) were awarded; career-related internships or fieldwork, Federal Work-Study, institutionally sponsored loans, health care benefits, and unspecified assistantships also available. Financial award application deadline: 3/15; financial award applicants required to submit FAFSA. *Faculty research:* Driving under the influence (DUI) personality, lifestyles and imposter phenomenon. *Unit head:* Dr. Brian W. Schrader, Chair, 620-341-5317, E-mail: bschrade@emporia.edu. *Application contact:* Mary Sewell, Admissions Coordinator, 800-950-GRAD, Fax: 620-341-5909, E-mail: msewell@emporia.edu.

Evangel University, Department of Behavioral Sciences, Springfield, MO 65802. Offers clinical mental health counseling (MS). Part-time programs available. *Faculty:* 4 full-time (3 women), 2 part-time/adjunct (0 women). *Students:* 33 full-time (22 women), 20 part-time (12 women); includes 7 minority (2 Black or African American, non-Hispanic/Latino; 4 Hispanic/Latino; 1 Two or more races, non-Hispanic/Latino). Average age 35. 15 applicants, 93% accepted, 12 enrolled. In 2014, 18 master's awarded. *Degree requirements:* For master's, comprehensive exam, thesis optional. *Entrance*

requirements: For master's, GRE General Test or MAT, minimum undergraduate GPA of 3.0, undergraduate major or minor in psychology. Additional exam requirements/recommendations for international students: Required—TOEFL (minimum score 550 paper-based). *Application deadline:* For fall admission, 7/15 priority date for domestic students, 8/1 for international students; for spring admission, 11/15 priority date for domestic students, 12/1 for international students. Applications are processed on a rolling basis. Application fee: $25. Electronic applications accepted. *Financial support:* In 2014–15, 6 students received support. Career-related internships or fieldwork, scholarships/grants, and unspecified assistantships available. Support available to part-time students. Financial award application deadline: 4/1; financial award applicants required to submit FAFSA. *Unit head:* Christine Arnzen, Program Coordinator, 417-865-2815 Ext. 8618, E-mail: arnzenc@evangel.edu. *Application contact:* Matt Petry, Admissions Representative, Graduate Studies, 417-865-2815 Ext. 7229, Fax: 417-575-5484, E-mail: petrym@evangel.edu.
Website: https://www.evangel.edu/departments/behavioral-social-sciences/about-the-department/

Fairleigh Dickinson University, College at Florham, Maxwell Becton College of Arts and Sciences, Department of Psychology, Madison, NJ 07940-1099. Offers clinical mental health counseling (MA); counseling (MA); industrial/organizational psychology (MA); organizational behavior (MA, Certificate), including organizational behavior (MA), organizational leadership (Certificate); MA/MBA.

Fairleigh Dickinson University, Metropolitan Campus, University College: Arts, Sciences, and Professional Studies, School of Psychology, Teaneck, NJ 07666-1914. Offers clinical psychology (MA, PhD); clinical psychopharmacology (MA); forensic psychology (MA); general-theoretical psychology (MA, Certificate); school psychology (MA, Psy D). *Accreditation:* APA (one or more programs are accredited).

Fayetteville State University, Graduate School, Program in Psychology, Fayetteville, NC 28301-4298. Offers MA. Part-time and evening/weekend programs available. *Faculty:* 13 full-time (6 women). *Students:* 27 full-time (25 women), 4 part-time (3 women); includes 20 minority (9 Black or African American, non-Hispanic/Latino; 2 Asian, non-Hispanic/Latino; 3 Hispanic/Latino; 6 Two or more races, non-Hispanic/Latino). Average age 32. 13 applicants, 100% accepted, 13 enrolled. In 2014, 11 master's awarded. *Degree requirements:* For master's, comprehensive exam, internship. *Application deadline:* For fall admission, 4/15 for domestic students. Applications are processed on a rolling basis. Application fee: $40. Electronic applications accepted. *Faculty research:* Psychopathology and psychotherapy, psychological assessment, psychological disorders and behaviors, cognitive, psychophysiology, social epidemiology. *Unit head:* Dr. Timothy O. Moore, Interim Chair, 910-672-1413, Fax: 910-672-1043, E-mail: tmoore40@uncfsu.edu. *Application contact:* 910-672-1413, Fax: 910-672-1043, E-mail: tmoore40@uncfsu.edu.

Fielding Graduate University, Graduate Programs, School of Psychology, Santa Barbara, CA 93105-3814. Offers clinical psychology (PhD, Graduate Certificate), including forensic psychology (PhD), health psychology (PhD), neuropsychology (PhD), parent-infant mental health (PhD), violence prevention and control (PhD); clinical psychology respecialization (Post-Doctoral Certificate); media psychology (MA, PhD), including forensic psychology (PhD); neuropsychology (Post-Doctoral Certificate). *Accreditation:* APA. Postbaccalaureate distance learning degree programs offered (minimal on-campus study). *Faculty:* 33 full-time (21 women), 40 part-time/adjunct (20 women). *Students:* 502 full-time (366 women), 79 part-time (62 women); includes 186 minority (69 Black or African American, non-Hispanic/Latino; 8 American Indian or Alaska Native, non-Hispanic/Latino; 23 Asian, non-Hispanic/Latino; 62 Hispanic/Latino; 1 Native Hawaiian or other Pacific Islander, non-Hispanic/Latino; 23 Two or more races, non-Hispanic/Latino), 4 international. Average age 45. 215 applicants, 56% accepted, 78 enrolled. In 2014, 15 master's, 54 doctorates, 9 other advanced degrees awarded. Terminal master's awarded for partial completion of doctoral program. *Degree requirements:* For master's, thesis or alternative, capstone project; for doctorate, comprehensive exam, thesis/dissertation. *Entrance requirements:* For master's, BA from regionally-accredited institution or equivalent, minimum GPA of 2.5; for doctorate, BA or MA from regionally-accredited institution or equivalent, writing sample, minimum GPA of 3.0. *Application deadline:* For fall admission, 3/6 for domestic students, 2/6 for international students; for spring admission, 11/1 for domestic and international students; for summer admission, 3/1 for domestic students, 2/1 for international students. Application fee: $75. Electronic applications accepted. *Expenses: Tuition:* Full-time $25,650; part-time $2880 per course. Tuition and fees vary according to degree level and program. *Financial support:* In 2014–15, 88 students received support, including 14 teaching assistantships (averaging $1,200 per year); scholarships/grants, health care benefits, tuition waivers (partial), and unspecified assistantships also available. Support available to part-time students. *Unit head:* Dr. Gerald Porter, Provost and Senior Vice President, 805-898-2940, E-mail: gporter@fielding.edu. *Application contact:* Enrollment Coordinator, 800-340-1099 Ext. 4098, Fax: 805-687-9793, E-mail: psyadmissions@fielding.edu.
Website: http://www.fielding.edu/programs/psy/default.aspx

Fisk University, Division of Graduate Studies, Department of Psychology, Nashville, TN 37208-3051. Offers clinical psychology (MA); psychology (MA). *Degree requirements:* For master's, thesis. *Entrance requirements:* For master's, GRE General Test, GRE Subject Test, minimum GPA of 3.0. Electronic applications accepted. *Faculty research:* Ethnic and gender identity, development, female adolescent development, juvenile delinquency prevention.

Florida Agricultural and Mechanical University, Division of Graduate Studies, Research, and Continuing Education, College of Social Sciences, Arts and Humanities, Department of Psychology, Tallahassee, FL 32307-3200. Offers community psychology (MS). *Degree requirements:* For master's, thesis. *Entrance requirements:* For master's, GRE General Test, minimum GPA of 3.0. Additional exam requirements/recommendations for international students: Required—TOEFL.

Florida Atlantic University, Charles E. Schmidt College of Science, Department of Psychology, Boca Raton, FL 33431-0991. Offers experimental psychology (PhD); psychology (MA). Terminal master's awarded for partial completion of doctoral program. *Degree requirements:* For master's, one foreign language, thesis or alternative; for doctorate, one foreign language, comprehensive exam, thesis/dissertation. *Entrance requirements:* For master's and doctorate, GRE General Test, minimum GPA of 3.0 during previous 2 years. Additional exam requirements/recommendations for international students: Required—TOEFL (minimum score 500 paper-based; 61 iBT), IELTS (minimum score 6). Electronic applications accepted. *Expenses:* Tuition, state resident: full-time $7396; part-time $369.82 per credit hour. Tuition, nonresident: full-time $19,392; part-time $1024.81 per credit hour. Tuition and fees vary according to course load. *Faculty research:* Cognition, psychobiology, developmental psychology, social psychology, neuroscience.

Florida Institute of Technology, Graduate Programs, College of Psychology and Liberal Arts, Melbourne, FL 32901-6975. Offers MA, MS, PhD, Psy D. Part-time programs available. *Faculty:* 33 full-time (15 women), 6 part-time/adjunct (3 women). *Students:* 279 full-time (212 women), 23 part-time (19 women); includes 70 minority (15 Black or African American, non-Hispanic/Latino; 1 American Indian or Alaska Native, non-Hispanic/Latino; 17 Asian, non-Hispanic/Latino; 27 Hispanic/Latino; 10 Two or more races, non-Hispanic/Latino), 21 international. Average age 28. 557 applicants, 38% accepted, 134 enrolled. In 2014, 50 master's, 30 doctorates awarded. Terminal master's awarded for partial completion of doctoral program. *Degree requirements:* For master's, comprehensive exam, thesis or final exam; for doctorate, comprehensive exam, thesis/dissertation optional, internship, full-time resident of school for 4 years (8 semesters, 3 summers), student review. *Entrance requirements:* For master's, GRE General Test, minimum GPA of 3.0, 2 letters of recommendation, resume, statement of objectives; for doctorate, GRE General Test, GRE Subject Test, 3 letters of recommendation, minimum GPA of 3.2, resume, statement of objectives. Additional exam requirements/recommendations for international students: Required—TOEFL (minimum score 550 paper-based; 79 iBT). *Application deadline:* For fall admission, 4/1 for international students; for spring admission, 9/30 for international students. Applications are processed on a rolling basis. Electronic applications accepted. *Expenses: Tuition:* Part-time $1179 per credit hour. Tuition and fees vary according to campus/location. *Financial support:* In 2014–15, 13 research assistantships with full and partial tuition reimbursements (averaging $8,990 per year), 2 teaching assistantships with full and partial tuition reimbursements (averaging $5,002 per year) were awarded; career-related internships or fieldwork, institutionally sponsored loans, tuition waivers (partial), unspecified assistantships, and tuition remissions also available. Support available to part-time students. Financial award application deadline: 3/1; financial award applicants required to submit FAFSA. *Total annual research expenditures:* $135,099. *Unit head:* Dr. Mary Beth Kenkel, Dean, 321-674-8142, Fax: 321-674-7105, E-mail: mkenkel@fit.edu. *Application contact:* Cheryl A. Brown, Associate Director of Graduate Admissions, 321-674-7581, Fax: 321-723-9468, E-mail: cbrown@fit.edu.
Website: http://cpla.fit.edu

Florida International University, College of Arts and Sciences, Department of Psychology, Miami, FL 33199. Offers behavioral analysis (MS); clinical science (PhD); counseling psychology (MS); developmental science (MS, PhD); legal psychology (PhD); organizational psychology (MS, PhD). Program has fall admissions only. Part-time and evening/weekend programs available. Terminal master's awarded for partial completion of doctoral program. *Degree requirements:* For master's, thesis; for doctorate, comprehensive exam, thesis/dissertation. *Entrance requirements:* For master's, GRE General Test, minimum GPA of 3.0, resume, 3 letters of recommendation; for doctorate, GRE General Test, 3 letters of recommendation, resume, letter of intent, two writing samples, minimum GPA of 3.0. Additional exam requirements/recommendations for international students: Required—TOEFL (minimum score 550 paper-based; 80 iBT). Electronic applications accepted. *Faculty research:* Legal psychology, organizational and industrial psychology, child behavior psychology.

Florida State University, The Graduate School, College of Arts and Sciences, Department of Psychology, Tallahassee, FL 32306-4301. Offers applied behavior analysis (MS); clinical psychology (PhD); cognitive psychology (PhD); developmental psychology (PhD); neuroscience (PhD); social psychology (PhD). *Accreditation:* APA (one or more programs are accredited). *Faculty:* 42 full-time (17 women). *Students:* 159 full-time (104 women), 5 part-time (3 women); includes 29 minority (10 Black or African American, non-Hispanic/Latino; 1 American Indian or Alaska Native, non-Hispanic/Latino; 5 Asian, non-Hispanic/Latino; 13 Hispanic/Latino), 2 international. Average age 26. 647 applicants, 9% accepted, 37 enrolled. In 2014, 30 master's, 15 doctorates awarded. Terminal master's awarded for partial completion of doctoral program. *Degree requirements:* For master's, comprehensive exam (for some programs), thesis (for some programs); for doctorate, comprehensive exam, thesis/dissertation. *Entrance requirements:* For master's, GRE General Test, minimum GPA of 3.0; for doctorate, GRE General Test. Additional exam requirements/recommendations for international students: Required—TOEFL (minimum score 550 paper-based; 80 iBT). Application fee: $30. Electronic applications accepted. *Expenses:* Tuition, state resident: part-time $403.51 per credit hour. Tuition, nonresident: part-time $1004.85 per credit hour. *Required fees:* $75.81 per credit hour. One-time fee: $20 part-time. Tuition and fees vary according to campus/location. *Financial support:* In 2014–15, 159 students received support, including 25 fellowships with full tuition reimbursements available (averaging $20,000 per year), 88 research assistantships with full tuition reimbursements available (averaging $20,000 per year), 46 teaching assistantships with full tuition reimbursements available (averaging $17,775 per year); career-related internships or fieldwork, Federal Work-Study, institutionally sponsored loans, scholarships/grants, traineeships, health care benefits, tuition waivers (partial), and unspecified assistantships also available. Financial award applicants required to submit FAFSA. *Total annual research expenditures:* $6.1 million. *Unit head:* Dr. Jeanette Taylor, Chairman, 850-644-2040, Fax: 850-644-7739, E-mail: taylor@psy.fsu.edu. *Application contact:* Cherie P. Miller, Graduate Program Assistant, 850-644-2499, Fax: 850-644-7739, E-mail: grad-info@psy.fsu.edu.
Website: http://www.psy.fsu.edu/

Fordham University, Graduate School of Arts and Sciences, Department of Psychology, New York, NY 10458. Offers applied developmental psychology (PhD); applied psychological methods (MS); clinical psychology (PhD); psychometrics (PhD). *Faculty:* 25 full-time (8 women), 3 part-time/adjunct (2 women). *Students:* 94 full-time (68 women), 32 part-time (21 women); includes 28 minority (5 Black or African American, non-Hispanic/Latino; 1 American Indian or Alaska Native, non-Hispanic/Latino; 14 Asian, non-Hispanic/Latino; 8 Hispanic/Latino), 15 international. Average age 31. 720 applicants, 6% accepted, 20 enrolled. In 2014, 14 master's, 23 doctorates awarded. Terminal master's awarded for partial completion of doctoral program. *Degree requirements:* For master's, comprehensive exam; for doctorate, comprehensive exam, thesis/dissertation. *Entrance requirements:* For doctorate, GRE General Test, GRE Subject Test. Additional exam requirements/recommendations for international students: Required—TOEFL (minimum score 600 paper-based). *Application deadline:* For fall admission, 12/14 for domestic students. Application fee: $70. Electronic applications accepted. *Financial support:* In 2014–15, 73 students received support, including 11 fellowships with full and partial tuition reimbursements available (averaging $24,775 per year), 9 research assistantships with full and partial tuition reimbursements available (averaging $20,643 per year), 27 teaching assistantships with full and partial tuition reimbursements available (averaging $17,762 per year); career-related internships or fieldwork, institutionally sponsored loans, tuition waivers (full and partial), and unspecified assistantships also available. Financial award application deadline: 12/14; financial award applicants required to submit FAFSA. *Total annual research expenditures:* $2.8 million. *Unit head:* Dr. Barry Rosenfeld, Chair, 718-817-3794, Fax: 718-817-3785, E-mail: wertz@fordham.edu. *Application contact:* Bernadette Valentino-Morrison, Director of Graduate Admissions, 718-817-4419, Fax: 718-817-3566, E-mail: valentinomor@fordham.edu.

Fort Hays State University, Graduate School, College of Arts and Sciences, Department of Psychology, Hays, KS 67601-4099. Offers psychology (MS); school psychology (Ed S). *Degree requirements:* For master's and Ed S, comprehensive exam, thesis. *Entrance requirements:* For master's, GRE General Test. Additional exam requirements/recommendations for international students: Required—TOEFL (minimum score 550 paper-based). Electronic applications accepted. *Faculty research:* Memory, learning, motivation, clinical and experimental psychology, history and systems of psychological stressors in rural environments.

Framingham State University, Continuing Education, Program in Counseling Psychology, Framingham, MA 01701-9101. Offers MA. Part-time and evening/weekend programs available.

Francis Marion University, Graduate Programs, Department of Psychology, Florence, SC 29502-0547. Offers applied psychology (MS), including clinical/counseling psychology, school psychology; school psychology (SSP). Part-time and evening/weekend programs available. *Faculty:* 6 full-time (2 women), 4 part-time/adjunct (all women). *Students:* 35 full-time (30 women), 11 part-time (all women); includes 9 minority (7 Black or African American, non-Hispanic/Latino; 2 Asian, non-Hispanic/Latino) 1 international. Average age 26. 43 applicants, 100% accepted, 16 enrolled. In 2014, 15 master's, 6 other advanced degrees awarded. *Degree requirements:* For master's, internship. *Entrance requirements:* For master's, GRE General Test, official transcripts, two letters of recommendation, written statement. *Application deadline:* For fall admission, 2/15 for domestic and international students; for spring admission, 10/15 for domestic and international students. Applications are processed on a rolling basis. Application fee: $35. Electronic applications accepted. *Expenses:* Tuition, state resident: full-time $9472; part-time $473.60 per credit hour. Tuition, nonresident: full-time $18,944; part-time $947.20 per credit hour. *Required fees:* $14 per credit hour. $107 per semester. Tuition and fees vary according to course load and program. *Financial support:* In 2014–15, 4 teaching assistantships (averaging $7,750 per year) were awarded; career-related internships or fieldwork, scholarships/grants, and unspecified assistantships also available. Support available to part-time students. Financial award application deadline: 3/1; financial award applicants required to submit FAFSA. *Faculty research:* Parenting and family relationships, child development, applied behavioral analysis, post-traumatic stress disorder, clinical psychology in adults. *Unit head:* Dr. William Wattles, Chair, 843-661-1641, Fax: 843-661-1628. *Application contact:* Sharekka Bridges, Administrative Assistant, 843-661-1641, Fax: 843-661-1628. Website: http://www.fmarion.edu/academics/psychology

Frostburg State University, Graduate School, College of Liberal Arts and Sciences, Department of Psychology, Frostburg, MD 21532-1099. Offers counseling psychology (MS). Part-time and evening/weekend programs available. *Degree requirements:* For master's, internship. *Entrance requirements:* For master's, GRE General Test or MAT, interview, minimum GPA of 3.0, resume. Additional exam requirements/recommendations for international students: Required—TOEFL. Electronic applications accepted.

Gardner-Webb University, Graduate School, School of Psychology, Boiling Springs, NC 28017. Offers mental health counseling (MA); school counseling (MA). Part-time and evening/weekend programs available. *Faculty:* 5 full-time (4 women). *Students:* 18 full-time (16 women), 54 part-time (46 women); includes 14 minority (10 Black or African American, non-Hispanic/Latino; 1 Asian, non-Hispanic/Latino; 3 Hispanic/Latino). Average age 31. 113 applicants, 27% accepted, 30 enrolled. In 2014, 22 master's awarded. *Degree requirements:* For master's, comprehensive exam. *Entrance requirements:* For master's, GRE General Test, MAT, minimum GPA of 2.7. *Application deadline:* For fall admission, 7/1 priority date for domestic students. Applications are processed on a rolling basis. Application fee: $40. Electronic applications accepted. *Expenses:* Tuition: Part-time $406 per credit hour. Tuition and fees vary according to program. *Financial support:* Unspecified assistantships available. *Unit head:* Dr. David Carscaddon, Chair, 704-406-4437, Fax: 704-406-4329, E-mail: dcarscaddon@gardner-webb.edu. *Application contact:* Office of Graduate Admissions, 877-498-4723, Fax: 704-406-3895, E-mail: gradinfo@gardner-webb.edu.

Geneva College, Master of Arts in Counseling Program, Beaver Falls, PA 15010-3599. Offers clinical mental health counseling (MA); marriage and family counseling (MA); school counseling (MA). *Accreditation:* ACA. Part-time and evening/weekend programs available. *Faculty:* 6 full-time (2 women), 7 part-time/adjunct (3 women). *Students:* 53 full-time (42 women), 42 part-time (31 women); includes 8 minority (all Black or African American, non-Hispanic/Latino). Average age 34. 42 applicants, 74% accepted, 27 enrolled. In 2014, 29 master's awarded. *Degree requirements:* For master's, 50-60 credits (depending on program), practicum, internship. *Entrance requirements:* For master's, minimum GPA of 3.0 (preferred), 3 letters of recommendation, essay on career goals, resume of educational and professional experiences. Additional exam requirements/recommendations for international students: Required—TOEFL. *Application deadline:* For fall admission, 9/1 for domestic students; for spring admission, 1/10 for domestic students. Applications are processed on a rolling basis. Electronic applications accepted. *Expenses:* Expenses: Contact institution. *Financial support:* In 2014–15, 5 students received support. Research assistantships, teaching assistantships, career-related internships or fieldwork, and unspecified assistantships available. Financial award application deadline: 8/1; financial award applicants required to submit FAFSA. *Faculty research:* Blended family counseling; premarital and newlywed couples; religion in clinical supervision; conceptual mapping in research, supervision, and clinical work; Factor Analytic Study of the ROSI (Recovery Oriented System Indicators). *Unit head:* Dr. Shannon Shiderly, Program Director, 724-847-6649, Fax: 724-847-6101, E-mail: slshider@geneva.edu. *Application contact:* Marina Frazier, Graduate Program Manager, 724-847-6697, E-mail: counseling@geneva.edu. Website: http://www.geneva.edu/page/grad_counseling

George Mason University, College of Humanities and Social Sciences, Department of Psychology, Fairfax, VA 22030. Offers applied developmental psychology (Certificate); cognitive and behavioral neuroscience (MA); human factors/applied cognition (MA); industrial/organizational psychology (MA, PhD); school psychology (MA). *Accreditation:* APA. *Faculty:* 43 full-time (22 women), 13 part-time/adjunct (8 women). *Students:* 167 full-time (114 women), 48 part-time (34 women); includes 41 minority (7 Black or African American, non-Hispanic/Latino; 8 Asian, non-Hispanic/Latino; 21 Hispanic/Latino; 1 Native Hawaiian or other Pacific Islander, non-Hispanic/Latino; 4 Two or more races, non-Hispanic/Latino), 10 international. Average age 27. 833 applicants, 14% accepted, 75 enrolled. In 2014, 49 master's, 17 doctorates, 10 other advanced degrees awarded. *Degree requirements:* For master's, comprehensive exam, thesis (for biopsychology); for doctorate, comprehensive exam, thesis/dissertation, 2nd year project. *Entrance requirements:* For master's, GRE, 2 official transcripts; goals statement; 15 undergraduate credits in concentration for which the applicant is applying; for doctorate, GRE, 3 letters of recommendation; resume; goals statement; minimum GPA of 3.0 overall for last 60 undergraduate credits, 3.25 in psychology courses; 15 undergraduate credits in concentration for which the applicant is applying; 2 official transcripts; for Certificate, GRE, 2 official transcripts; expanded goals statement; 3 letters of recommendation. Additional exam requirements/recommendations for international students: Required—TOEFL (minimum score 570 paper-based; 80 iBT), IELTS (minimum score 6.5), PTE. Application fee: $65 ($80 for international students). Electronic applications accepted. *Expenses:* Tuition, state resident: full-time $9794; part-time $408 per credit hour. Tuition, nonresident: full-time $26,978; part-time $1124 per credit hour. *Required fees:* $2820; $118 per credit hour. Tuition and fees vary according to course load and program. *Financial support:* In 2014–15, 130 students received support, including 6 fellowships (averaging $6,576 per year), 84 research assistantships with full and partial tuition reimbursements available (averaging $15,356 per year), 63 teaching assistantships with full and partial tuition reimbursements available (averaging $13,274 per year); career-related internships or fieldwork, Federal

Work-Study, scholarships/grants, tuition waivers (partial), unspecified assistantships, and health care benefits (for full-time research or teaching assistantship recipients) also available. Support available to part-time students. Financial award application deadline: 3/1; financial award applicants required to submit FAFSA. *Faculty research:* Applied developmental psychology, biopsychology, clinical psychology, human factors/applied cognition psychology, industrial/organizational psychology, school psychology. *Total annual research expenditures:* $5.2 million. *Unit head:* Reeshad Dalal, Department Chair, 703-993-9487, Fax: 703-993-1359, E-mail: rdalal@gmu.edu. *Application contact:* Adam Winsler, Associate Chair of Graduate Studies, 703-993-1881, Fax: 703-993-1359, E-mail: awinsler@gmu.edu. Website: http://psychology.gmu.edu

Georgetown University, Graduate School of Arts and Sciences, Department of Psychology, Washington, DC 20057. Offers PhD, JD/MPP. *Degree requirements:* For doctorate, thesis/dissertation. *Entrance requirements:* For doctorate, GRE General Test, GRE Subject Test. Additional exam requirements/recommendations for international students: Required—TOEFL.

The George Washington University, Columbian College of Arts and Sciences, Department of Psychology, Washington, DC 20052. Offers applied social psychology (PhD); clinical psychology (PhD); cognitive neuroscience (PhD). *Accreditation:* APA. Part-time and evening/weekend programs available. *Faculty:* 24 full-time (14 women), 1 (woman) part-time/adjunct. *Students:* 46 full-time (33 women), 24 part-time (15 women); includes 19 minority (7 Black or African American, non-Hispanic/Latino; 3 Asian, non-Hispanic/Latino; 8 Hispanic/Latino; 1 Two or more races, non-Hispanic/Latino), 8 international. Average age 28. 513 applicants, 3% accepted, 14 enrolled. In 2014, 10 doctorates awarded. *Degree requirements:* For doctorate, thesis/dissertation or alternative, general exam. *Entrance requirements:* For doctorate, GRE General Test, minimum GPA of 3.0. Additional exam requirements/recommendations for international students: Required—TOEFL (minimum score 550 paper-based; 80 iBT). *Application deadline:* For fall admission, 1/15 for domestic and international students. Application fee: $75. *Financial support:* In 2014–15, 62 students received support. Fellowships with tuition reimbursements available, teaching assistantships with tuition reimbursements available, career-related internships or fieldwork, Federal Work-Study, and tuition waivers available. *Unit head:* Dr. Paul Poppen, Chair, 202-994-6324, E-mail: pjp@gwu.edu. *Application contact:* Information Contact, 202-994-6320, Fax: 202-994-1602, E-mail: psydept@gwu.edu. Website: http://psychology.columbian.gwu.edu/

The George Washington University, Columbian College of Arts and Sciences, Program in Professional Psychology, Washington, DC 20052. Offers MA, Psy D, Graduate Certificate. *Accreditation:* APA. *Faculty:* 6 full-time (2 women). *Students:* 113 full-time (89 women), 109 part-time (82 women); includes 40 minority (14 Black or African American, non-Hispanic/Latino; 8 Asian, non-Hispanic/Latino; 14 Hispanic/Latino; 1 Native Hawaiian or other Pacific Islander, non-Hispanic/Latino; 3 Two or more races, non-Hispanic/Latino), 8 international. Average age 28. 578 applicants, 27% accepted, 85 enrolled. In 2014, 50 master's, 40 doctorates, 13 other advanced degrees awarded. *Entrance requirements:* For doctorate, GRE General Test, interview, minimum GPA of 3.0. Additional exam requirements/recommendations for international students: Required—TOEFL (minimum score 550 paper-based; 80 iBT). *Application deadline:* For fall admission, 12/1 priority date for domestic students. Applications are processed on a rolling basis. Application fee: $75. Electronic applications accepted. *Financial support:* Fellowships with partial tuition reimbursements available. *Unit head:* Dr. Loring Ingraham, Director, 202-496-4712, Fax: 202-496-6263, E-mail: ingraham@gwu.edu. *Application contact:* 202-994-6210, Fax: 202-994-6213, E-mail: askccas@gwu.edu. Website: http://www.gwu.edu/~psyd/

Georgia Institute of Technology, Graduate Studies, College of Sciences, School of Psychology, Atlanta, GA 30332-0001. Offers MS, PhD. Part-time programs available. *Students:* 81 full-time (45 women), 8 part-time (4 women); includes 16 minority (2 Black or African American, non-Hispanic/Latino; 5 Asian, non-Hispanic/Latino; 6 Hispanic/Latino; 3 Two or more races, non-Hispanic/Latino), 9 international. Average age 27. 186 applicants, 17% accepted, 15 enrolled. In 2014, 10 master's, 12 doctorates awarded. Terminal master's awarded for partial completion of doctoral program. *Degree requirements:* For master's, thesis; for doctorate, thesis/dissertation. *Entrance requirements:* For master's and doctorate, GRE General Test, GRE Subject Test, http://www.psychology.gatech.edu/graduate/prospectivestudents/prospectivestudents_ar.php. Additional exam requirements/recommendations for international students: Required—TOEFL (minimum score 550 paper-based; 79 iBT). *Application deadline:* For fall admission, 1/1 for domestic and international students. Applications are processed on a rolling basis. Application fee: $75. Electronic applications accepted. *Expenses:* Tuition, state resident: full-time $12,344; part-time $515 per credit hour. Tuition, nonresident: full-time $27,600; part-time $1150 per credit hour. *Required fees:* $1196 per term. Part-time tuition and fees vary according to course load. *Financial support:* Fellowships, research assistantships, teaching assistantships, career-related internships or fieldwork, Federal Work-Study, institutionally sponsored loans, tuition waivers (partial), and unspecified assistantships available. Support available to part-time students. Financial award application deadline: 5/1. *Faculty research:* Experimental, industrial-organizational, and engineering psychology; cognitive aging and processes; leadership; human factors. *Total annual research expenditures:* $2.7 million. *Unit head:* Paul Verhaeghen, Director, 404-894-0963, E-mail: paul.verhaeghen@psych.gatech.edu. *Application contact:* Jan Westbrook, Graduate Coordinator, 404-894-0886, E-mail: jan.westbrook@psych.gatech.edu. Website: http://www.psychology.gatech.edu

Georgia Regents University, The Graduate School, College of Science and Mathematics, Department of Psychology, Augusta, GA 30912. Offers MS. Part-time programs available. *Degree requirements:* For master's, thesis optional, written/oral exam. *Entrance requirements:* For master's, GRE General Test, minimum GPA of 2.5, bachelor's degree in psychology or equivalent course work. *Faculty research:* Developmental, cognitive, gender and aging issues, consumer behavior, conditioned taste aversions, circadian rhythms, use of slang and offensive language.

Georgia Southern University, Jack N. Averitt College of Graduate Studies, College of Liberal Arts and Social Sciences, Program in Psychology, Statesboro, GA 30460. Offers MS, Psy D. *Students:* 58 full-time (39 women), 10 part-time (6 women); includes 21 minority (7 Black or African American, non-Hispanic/Latino; 2 Asian, non-Hispanic/Latino; 11 Hispanic/Latino; 1 Two or more races, non-Hispanic/Latino). Average age 27. 73 applicants, 40% accepted, 20 enrolled. In 2014, 16 master's, 1 doctorate awarded. Terminal master's awarded for partial completion of doctoral program. *Degree requirements:* For master's, comprehensive exam, thesis (for some programs), terminal exam; for doctorate, comprehensive exam, thesis/dissertation, clinical qualifying exam, practicum, internship. *Entrance requirements:* For master's, GRE General Test, minimum GPA of 3.0, introductory courses in psychology and statistics, letters of recommendation; for doctorate, GRE General Test; GRE Subject Test (if no undergraduate degree in psychology), minimum undergraduate GPA of 3.25; 3 letters of reference; statement of purpose. Additional exam requirements/recommendations for international students: Required—TOEFL (minimum score 550 paper-based; 80 iBT), IELTS (minimum score 6). *Application deadline:* For fall admission, 1/15 priority date for

domestic students, 1/15 for international students. Applications are processed on a rolling basis. Application fee: $50. Electronic applications accepted. *Expenses:* Tuition, state resident: full-time $7236; part-time $277 per semester hour. Tuition, nonresident: full-time $27,118; part-time $1105 per semester hour. *Required fees:* $2092. *Financial support:* In 2014–15, 52 students received support, including fellowships with partial tuition reimbursements available (averaging $12,000 per year), research assistantships with partial tuition reimbursements available (averaging $7,200 per year), teaching assistantships with partial tuition reimbursements available (averaging $7,200 per year); career-related internships or fieldwork, Federal Work-Study, scholarships/grants, tuition waivers (partial), and unspecified assistantships also available. Support available to part-time students. Financial award application deadline: 4/15; financial award applicants required to submit FAFSA. *Faculty research:* Clinical psychology, cognitive psychology, social psychology, developmental psychology, teaching and psychology, social judgment and behavior, psychology of religion. *Unit head:* Dr. Michael Nielsen, Graduate Director, 912-478-5539, Fax: 912-478-0751, E-mail: mnielsen@georgiasouthern.edu.
Website: http://class.georgiasouthern.edu/psychology/

Georgia State University, College of Arts and Sciences, Department of Psychology, Atlanta, GA 30302-3083. Offers clinical (PhD); cognitive sciences (PhD); community (PhD); developmental (PhD); neuropsychology and behavioral neuroscience (PhD). *Accreditation:* APA. *Faculty:* 29 full-time (17 women). *Students:* 116 full-time (95 women), 2 part-time (both women); includes 30 minority (10 Black or African American, non-Hispanic/Latino; 9 Asian, non-Hispanic/Latino; 6 Hispanic/Latino; 5 Two or more races, non-Hispanic/Latino), 10 international. Average age 28. 577 applicants, 7% accepted, 27 enrolled. In 2014, 16 doctorates awarded. *Degree requirements:* For doctorate, comprehensive exam, thesis/dissertation, residency year (for clinical only). *Entrance requirements:* For doctorate, GRE. Additional exam requirements/recommendations for international students: Required—TOEFL (minimum score 550 paper-based; 80 iBT). *Application deadline:* For fall admission, 12/1 for domestic and international students. Application fee: $50. Electronic applications accepted. *Expenses:* Tuition, state resident: full-time $6516; part-time $362 per credit hour. Tuition, nonresident: full-time $22,014; part-time $1223 per credit hour. *Required fees:* $2128 per semester. Tuition and fees vary according to course load and program. *Financial support:* In 2014–15, fellowships with full tuition reimbursements (averaging $19,282 per year), research assistantships with full tuition reimbursements (averaging $5,173 per year), teaching assistantships with full tuition reimbursements (averaging $6,389 per year) were awarded; scholarships/grants, traineeships, health care benefits, and unspecified assistantships also available. *Faculty research:* Clinical psychology, developmental psychology, community psychology, neuropsychology and behavioral neuroscience, cognitive sciences. *Unit head:* Dr. Lisa Armistead, Chair, 404-413-6205, Fax: 404-413-6207, E-mail: lparmistead@gsu.edu. *Application contact:* Dr. Lindsey Cohen, Director of Graduate Studies, 404-413-6263, Fax: 404-413-6207, E-mail: llcohen@gsu.edu.
Website: http://psychology.gsu.edu/graduate/areas-of-study/

Golden Gate University, Ageno School of Business, San Francisco, CA 94105-2968. Offers accounting (MBA); business administration (EMBA, MBA, PMBA, DBA); finance (MBA, MS, Certificate); financial planning (MS, Certificate); healthcare information systems (Certificate); human resource management (MBA, MS); human resources management (Certificate); information systems (MS); information technology (MBA); information technology management (Certificate); integrated marketing and communications (MS, Certificate); international business (MBA); management (MBA); marketing (MBA, MS, Certificate); operations supply chain management (Certificate); psychology (MA, Certificate); public administration (EMPA); public relations (MS, Certificate); technical market analysis (Certificate); JD/MBA. Part-time and evening/weekend programs available. *Degree requirements:* For doctorate, thesis/dissertation, qualifying examination. *Entrance requirements:* For master's, GMAT (MBA), minimum GPA of 2.5 (MS). Additional exam requirements/recommendations for international students: Required—TOEFL (minimum score 550 paper-based; 79 iBT). Electronic applications accepted. *Expenses:* Contact institution.

Governors State University, College of Education, Program in Psychology, University Park, IL 60484. Offers MA. Part-time and evening/weekend programs available. *Degree requirements:* For master's, thesis or alternative, practicum. *Entrance requirements:* For master's, GRE or MAT.

The Graduate Center, City University of New York, Graduate Studies, Program in Psychology, New York, NY 10016-4039. Offers basic applied neurocognition (PhD); biopsychology (PhD); clinical psychology (PhD); developmental psychology (PhD); environmental psychology (PhD); experimental psychology (PhD); industrial psychology (PhD); learning processes (PhD); neuropsychology (PhD); psychology (PhD); social personality (PhD). *Degree requirements:* For doctorate, one foreign language, thesis/dissertation. *Entrance requirements:* For doctorate, GRE General Test. Additional exam requirements/recommendations for international students: Required—TOEFL. Electronic applications accepted.

Grand Canyon University, College of Doctoral Studies, Phoenix, AZ 85017-1097. Offers business administration (DBA); general psychology (PhD), including cognition and instruction, industrial and organizational psychology; organizational leadership (Ed D, PhD), including behavioral health (PhD), education and effective schools (PhD), higher education (PhD), instructional leadership (PhD), organizational development (Ed D). *Degree requirements:* For doctorate, comprehensive exam, thesis/dissertation. *Entrance requirements:* For doctorate, minimum GPA of 3.4 on earned advanced degree from regionally-accredited institution; transcripts; goals statement.

Hampton University, School of Liberal Arts, Hampton, VA 23668. Offers MS. Part-time programs available. *Faculty:* 9 full-time (5 women). *Students:* 9 full-time (5 women); all minorities (all Black or African American, non-Hispanic/Latino). Average age 27. 13 applicants, 85% accepted, 9 enrolled. *Degree requirements:* For master's, thesis. *Entrance requirements:* For master's, GRE, TOEFL or IELTS. Additional exam requirements/recommendations for international students: Required—TOEFL (minimum score 525 paper-based), IELTS (minimum score 6.5). *Application deadline:* For fall admission, 6/1 priority date for domestic students, 4/1 priority date for international students; for spring admission, 11/1 priority date for domestic students, 9/1 priority date for international students; for summer admission, 4/1 priority date for domestic and international students. Application fee: $35. Electronic applications accepted. *Expenses:* Expenses: Contact institution. *Financial support:* Unspecified assistantships available. Financial award application deadline: 6/30; financial award applicants required to submit FAFSA. *Faculty research:* Marriage and family studies, violence prevention, racial identity and race relations, learning styles, psychosocial factors influencing health. *Unit head:* Dr. Candice M. Wallace, Assistant Professor, 757-727-5041.

Hardin-Simmons University, Graduate School, Cynthia Ann Parker College of Liberal Arts, Department of Psychology, Abilene, TX 79698-0001. Offers clinical counseling and marriage and family therapy (MA). Part-time programs available. *Faculty:* 5 full-time (3 women). *Students:* 20 full-time (18 women), 2 part-time (1 woman); includes 2 minority (both Hispanic/Latino). Average age 24. In 2014, 7 master's awarded. *Degree requirements:* For master's, comprehensive exam, clinical experience, project. *Entrance requirements:* For master's, 21 semester hours of course work in psychology (18 in upper-division classes); minimum undergraduate GPA of 3.0 in major, 2.7 overall; writing sample; letters of recommendation. Additional exam requirements/recommendations for international students: Required—TOEFL (minimum score 550 paper-based; 75 iBT). *Application deadline:* For fall admission, 8/15 priority date for domestic students, 4/1 for international students; for spring admission, 1/5 priority date for domestic students, 9/1 for international students. Applications are processed on a rolling basis. Application fee: $50. *Expenses: Tuition:* Full-time $12,060; part-time $670 per credit hour. *Required fees:* $325; $110 per semester. Tuition and fees vary according to program. *Financial support:* In 2014–15, 17 students received support, including 20 fellowships (averaging $677 per year); career-related internships or fieldwork and scholarships/grants also available. Support available to part-time students. Financial award application deadline: 6/30; financial award applicants required to submit FAFSA. *Faculty research:* Spirituality in marriage, intimacy and sexuality in marriage, sex education in the church, role of faith in marital satisfaction, family stress management. *Unit head:* Dr. John Eric Swenson III, Department Head, 325-670-1488, Fax: 325-670-1458, E-mail: johneric.swenson@hsutx.edu. *Application contact:* Dr. Nancy Kucinski, Dean of Graduate Studies, 325-670-1298, Fax: 325-670-1564, E-mail: gradoff@hsutx.edu.
Website: http://www.hsutx.edu/academics/cap/graduate/fampsych

Harvard University, Graduate School of Arts and Sciences, Department of Psychology, Cambridge, MA 02138. Offers psychology (PhD), including behavior and decision analysis, cognition, developmental psychology, experimental psychology, personality, psychobiology, psychopathology; social psychology (PhD). *Accreditation:* APA. *Degree requirements:* For doctorate, thesis/dissertation, general exams. *Entrance requirements:* For doctorate, GRE General Test. Additional exam requirements/recommendations for international students: Required—TOEFL.

Hofstra University, College of Liberal Arts and Sciences, Programs in Psychology, Hempstead, NY 11549. Offers applied organizational psychology (PhD); clinical psychology (PhD); industrial/organizational psychology (MA); school-community psychology (Psy D). Part-time and evening/weekend programs available. *Students:* 226 full-time (146 women), 14 part-time (9 women); includes 42 minority (7 Black or African American, non-Hispanic/Latino; 2 American Indian or Alaska Native, non-Hispanic/Latino; 11 Asian, non-Hispanic/Latino; 17 Hispanic/Latino; 1 Native Hawaiian or other Pacific Islander, non-Hispanic/Latino; 4 Two or more races, non-Hispanic/Latino), 20 international. Average age 27. 313 applicants, 40% accepted, 67 enrolled. In 2014, 40 master's, 30 doctorates awarded. *Degree requirements:* For master's, comprehensive exam, thesis (for some programs), internship, minimum GPA of 3.0; for doctorate, comprehensive exam, thesis/dissertation, 1st year qualifying examination, 2nd year research project, successful practicum/externship placements, written presentation and successful oral defense of dissertation, completion of full-time internship. *Entrance requirements:* For master's, GRE General Test, minimum GPA of 3.0, essay, interview; for doctorate, GRE General Test, GRE Subject Test (psychology), 3 letters of recommendation, interview, essay, curriculum vitae. Additional exam requirements/recommendations for international students: Required—TOEFL (minimum score 550 paper-based; 80 iBT). *Application deadline:* For fall admission, 12/15 for domestic and international students. Application fee: $70 ($75 for international students). Electronic applications accepted. *Expenses: Tuition:* Full-time $20,610; part-time $1145 per credit hour. *Required fees:* $970; $165 per term. Tuition and fees vary according to program. *Financial support:* In 2014–15, 139 students received support, including 118 fellowships with full and partial tuition reimbursements available (averaging $7,236 per year), 7 research assistantships with full and partial tuition reimbursements available (averaging $5,788 per year); Federal Work-Study, institutionally sponsored loans, scholarships/grants, health care benefits, tuition waivers (full and partial), and diversity and endowed scholarships also available. Support available to part-time students. Financial award applicants required to submit FAFSA. *Faculty research:* Cognitive behavioral therapy for anxiety disorders, autism spectrum disorders, parent child interaction training (PCIT), positive organizational behavior, personnel selection and decision-making. *Unit head:* Dr. Keith Shafritz, Chairperson, 516-463-4856, Fax: 516-463-6052, E-mail: psykms@hofstra.edu. *Application contact:* Sunil Samuel, Assistant Vice President of Admissions, 516-463-4723, Fax: 516-463-4664, E-mail: graduateadmission@hofstra.edu.
Website: http://www.hofstra.edu/hclas

Hood College, Graduate School, Programs in Human Sciences, Frederick, MD 21701-8575. Offers human sciences (MA), including psychology; thanatology (MA, Certificate). Part-time and evening/weekend programs available. *Degree requirements:* For master's, comprehensive exam, capstone/research project. *Entrance requirements:* For master's, minimum GPA of 2.75. Additional exam requirements/recommendations for international students: Required—TOEFL (minimum score 575 paper-based; 89 iBT), IELTS (minimum score 6.5). Electronic applications accepted. Application fee is waived when completed online. *Faculty research:* Mind-body medicine and multicultural healing, the New Orleans jazz funeral, death practices in African-American culture, bereavement theories and gender differences, Piaget's theory of cognitive development as a formal mathematical model.

Houston Baptist University, College of Education and Behavioral Sciences, Program in Psychology, Houston, TX 77074-3298. Offers MAP. Part-time and evening/weekend programs available. *Faculty:* 5 full-time (4 women), 6 part-time/adjunct (all women). *Students:* 51 full-time (44 women), 73 part-time (61 women); includes 73 minority (48 Black or African American, non-Hispanic/Latino; 10 Asian, non-Hispanic/Latino; 13 Hispanic/Latino; 2 Two or more races, non-Hispanic/Latino), 2 international. Average age 31. 137 applicants, 19% accepted, 16 enrolled. In 2014, 33 master's awarded. *Degree requirements:* For master's, comprehensive exam, thesis. *Entrance requirements:* For master's, GRE, minimum GPA of 2.5, two recommendations, resume, bachelor's degree, transcript. Additional exam requirements/recommendations for international students: Required—TOEFL. *Application deadline:* For fall admission, 8/1 for domestic students, 6/1 for international students; for winter admission, 10/1 for domestic and international students; for spring admission, 12/1 for domestic students, 10/1 for international students; for summer admission, 5/1 for domestic students, 3/1 for international students. Applications are processed on a rolling basis. Application fee: $0. Electronic applications accepted. *Expenses:* Expenses: $1,500 per 3 credit hours (36 hour program); fees: $875 per semester. *Financial support:* In 2014–15, 2 students received support. Federal Work-Study and scholarships/grants available. Support available to part-time students. Financial award application deadline: 4/1; financial award applicants required to submit FAFSA. *Faculty research:* Drug and alcohol abuse in relation to delinquency, mental health and school factors, chronic stress, coping strategies. *Unit head:* Dr. Renata Nero, Chair, 281-649-3171, Fax: 281-649-3361, E-mail: rnero@hbu.edu. *Application contact:* Grace Rosales, Administrative Assistant to the Dean, 281-649-3131, E-mail: grosales@hbu.edu.
Website: http://www.hbu.edu/MAP

Howard University, Graduate School, Department of Psychology, Washington, DC 20059-0002. Offers clinical psychology (PhD); developmental psychology (PhD); experimental psychology (PhD); neuropsychology (PhD); personality psychology (PhD); psychology (MS); social psychology (PhD). *Accreditation:* APA (one or more programs are accredited). Part-time programs available. *Degree requirements:* For master's,

thesis; for doctorate, comprehensive exam, thesis/dissertation, qualifying exam. *Entrance requirements:* For master's, GRE General Test, minimum GPA of 2.5, bachelor's degree in psychology or related field; for doctorate, GRE General Test, minimum GPA of 3.0. *Faculty research:* Personality and psychophysiology, educational and social development of African-American children, child and adult psychopathology.

Humboldt State University, Academic Programs, College of Professional Studies, Department of Psychology, Arcata, CA 95521-8299. Offers psychology (MA), including academic research, counseling, school psychology. *Students:* 52 full-time (42 women), 6 part-time (3 women); includes 22 minority (15 Hispanic/Latino; 7 Two or more races, non-Hispanic/Latino). Average age 27. 73 applicants, 47% accepted, 24 enrolled. In 2014, 15 master's awarded. *Degree requirements:* For master's, thesis. *Entrance requirements:* For master's, appropriate bachelor's degree, minimum GPA of 2.5. Additional exam requirements/recommendations for international students: Required—TOEFL (minimum score 500 paper-based). *Application deadline:* For fall admission, 2/1 for domestic students, 2/15 for international students. Applications are processed on a rolling basis. Application fee: $55. *Expenses:* Tuition, state resident: full-time $6738; part-time $3906 per year. Tuition, nonresident: full-time $13,434; part-time $6138 per year. *Required fees:* $1690; $1266 per year. Tuition and fees vary according to program. *Financial support:* Career-related internships or fieldwork available. Financial award application deadline: 3/1; financial award applicants required to submit FAFSA. *Faculty research:* School psychology, counseling, eating disorders, mood induction, depression. *Unit head:* Dr. Gregg Gold, Chair, 707-826-3740, Fax: 707-826-4993, E-mail: gjg14@humboldt.edu. *Application contact:* Dr. Chris Aberson, Coordinator, 707-826-3670, Fax: 707-826-4993, E-mail: cla18@humboldt.edu.
Website: http://www2.humboldt.edu/psychology/programs-child/graduate-programs-psychology

Hunter College of the City University of New York, Graduate School, School of Arts and Sciences, Department of Psychology, New York, NY 10065-5085. Offers MA. Part-time and evening/weekend programs available. *Faculty:* 5 full-time (1 woman), 1 (woman) part-time/adjunct. *Students:* 2 full-time (both women), 25 part-time (17 women); includes 9 minority (1 Black or African American, non-Hispanic/Latino; 1 American Indian or Alaska Native, non-Hispanic/Latino; 5 Asian, non-Hispanic/Latino; 2 Hispanic/Latino). Average age 27. 109 applicants, 31% accepted, 10 enrolled. In 2014, 30 master's awarded. *Degree requirements:* For master's, comprehensive exam, thesis. *Entrance requirements:* For master's, GRE General Test, minimum 12 credits of course work in psychology, including statistics and experimental psychology; 2 letters of recommendation. Additional exam requirements/recommendations for international students: Required—TOEFL. *Application deadline:* For fall admission, 4/1 for domestic students, 2/1 for international students; for spring admission, 11/1 for domestic students, 9/1 for international students. Applications are processed on a rolling basis. *Financial support:* Federal Work-Study, scholarships/grants, and tuition waivers (partial) available. Support available to part-time students. *Faculty research:* Personality, cognitive and linguistic development, hormonal and neural control of behavior, gender and culture, social cognition of health and attitudes. *Unit head:* Dr. Vanya Quinones-Jenab, Chairperson, 212-772-5550, Fax: 212-772-5620, E-mail: psychadv@hunter.cuny.edu. *Application contact:* Milena Solo, Graduate Admissions Director, 212-772-4288, Fax: 212-650-3336, E-mail: milena.solo@hunter.cuny.edu.
Website: http://maxweber.hunter.cuny.edu/psych/

Idaho State University, Office of Graduate Studies, College of Arts and Letters, Department of Psychology, Pocatello, ID 83209-8112. Offers clinical psychology (PhD); experimental psychology (PhD). *Accreditation:* APA. Part-time programs available. *Degree requirements:* For doctorate, comprehensive exam, thesis/dissertation, 1 year full-time clinical internship. *Entrance requirements:* For doctorate, GRE General Test, GRE Subject Test, MS in psychology, recommendation from Clinical Admissions Committee. Additional exam requirements/recommendations for international students: Required—TOEFL (minimum score 550 paper-based; 80 iBT). Electronic applications accepted. *Faculty research:* Substance abuse, sexual decision making, trauma, behavioral pharmacology, developmental psychopathology, working memory and strategies, goal setting, person perception, developmental psychobiology, parent-child interactions.

Illinois Institute of Technology, Graduate College, Lewis College of Human Sciences, Department of Psychology, Chicago, IL 60616. Offers clinical psychology (PhD); industrial and organizational psychology (PhD); personnel and human resource development (MS); rehabilitation and mental health counseling (MS); rehabilitation counseling education (PhD). *Accreditation:* APA (one or more programs are accredited); CORE. Part-time and evening/weekend programs available. *Faculty:* 22 full-time (11 women), 3 part-time/adjunct (2 women). *Students:* 187 full-time (139 women), 11 part-time (8 women); includes 28 minority (5 Black or African American, non-Hispanic/Latino; 1 American Indian or Alaska Native, non-Hispanic/Latino; 7 Asian, non-Hispanic/Latino; 12 Hispanic/Latino; 3 Two or more races, non-Hispanic/Latino), 19 international. Average age 30. 293 applicants, 32% accepted, 38 enrolled. In 2014, 27 master's, 4 doctorates awarded. Terminal master's awarded for partial completion of doctoral program. *Degree requirements:* For master's, thesis (for some programs); for doctorate, comprehensive exam, thesis/dissertation, 107 credit hours minimum, 1 yr full-time internship, comprehensive exam, dissertation and oral defense. *Entrance requirements:* For master's, GRE General Test (minimum score 298 Quantitative and Verbal, 3.0 Analytical Writing), minimum gpa 3.0/4.0; 3 letters of recommendation. Applicants for master's degree programs should have a bachelor's degree from an accredited institution and meet the minimum standards listed above. The exception is the masters in Rehabilitation and Mental Health Counseling; for doctorate, GRE General Test (minimum score 298 Quantitative and Verbal, 3.0 Analytical Writing), Prerequisite to admission to doctoral programs are a bachelor's or master's degree from an accredited institution, superior academic records in both undergraduate and graduate programs, and favorable academic recommendations. GRE results are required for all psychology doctoral programs. Additional exam requirements/recommendations for international students: Required—TOEFL (minimum score 550 paper-based; 80 iBT). *Application deadline:* For fall admission, 1/15 for domestic and international students. Application fee: $50. Electronic applications accepted. *Expenses: Tuition:* Full-time $22,500; part-time $1250 per credit hour. *Required fees:* $30 per course. $260 per semester. One-time fee: $235. Tuition and fees vary according to course load and program. *Financial support:* Fellowships with full and partial tuition reimbursements, research assistantships with full and partial tuition reimbursements, career-related internships or fieldwork, Federal Work-Study, institutionally sponsored loans, scholarships/grants, traineeships, health care benefits, tuition waivers (partial), and unspecified assistantships available. Support available to part-time students. Financial award application deadline: 1/15; financial award applicants required to submit FAFSA. *Faculty research:* Clinical psychology, rehabilitation and mental health counseling, industrial organizational psychology. *Unit head:* Ronald Landis, Chair, 312-567-6467, Fax: 312-567-3493, E-mail: rlandis@iit.edu. *Application contact:* Rishab Malhotra, Director, Graduate Admissions, 866-472-3448, Fax: 312-567-3138, E-mail: inquiry.grad@iit.edu.
Website: http://iit.edu/psych/

Illinois State University, Graduate School, College of Arts and Sciences, Department of Psychology, Normal, IL 61790-2200. Offers psychology (MA, MS), including clinical psychology, counseling psychology, developmental psychology, educational psychology, experimental psychology, measurement-evaluation, organizational-industrial psychology; school psychology (PhD, SSP). *Accreditation:* APA. *Degree requirements:* For master's, thesis or alternative; for doctorate, variable foreign language requirement, thesis/dissertation, 2 terms of residency, internship, practicum. *Entrance requirements:* For master's, GRE General Test, GRE Subject Test, minimum GPA of 3.0 in last 60 hours of course work; for doctorate, GRE General Test. *Faculty research:* Comprehensive evaluation system for the central region professional development grant, Illinois school psychology internship consortium, for children's sake.

Immaculata University, College of Graduate Studies, Department of Psychology, Immaculata, PA 19345. Offers clinical mental health counseling (MA); clinical psychology (Psy D); forensic psychology (Graduate Certificate); integrative psychotherapy (Graduate Certificate); neuropsychology (Graduate Certificate); psychodynamic psychotherapy (Graduate Certificate); psychological testing (Graduate Certificate); school counseling (MA, Graduate Certificate); school psychology (MA). *Accreditation:* APA. Part-time and evening/weekend programs available. Terminal master's awarded for partial completion of doctoral program. *Degree requirements:* For master's, comprehensive exam, thesis optional; for doctorate, comprehensive exam, thesis/dissertation. *Entrance requirements:* For master's, GRE General Test or MAT, minimum GPA of 3.0; for doctorate, GRE General Test or MAT, minimum GPA of 3.5. Additional exam requirements/recommendations for international students: Required—TOEFL, IELTS. Electronic applications accepted. *Faculty research:* Supervision ethics, psychology of teaching, gender.

Indiana State University, College of Graduate and Professional Studies, College of Arts and Sciences, Department of Psychology, Terre Haute, IN 47809. Offers clinical psychology (Psy D); general psychology (MA, MS). *Accreditation:* APA (one or more programs are accredited). Terminal master's awarded for partial completion of doctoral program. *Degree requirements:* For master's, thesis (for some programs); for doctorate, comprehensive exam, thesis/dissertation, internship, professional research project. *Entrance requirements:* For master's, GRE General Test, 12 semester hours of course work in psychology, minimum GPA of 2.75; for doctorate, GRE General Test, minimum GPA of 3.0. Additional exam requirements/recommendations for international students: Required—TOEFL (minimum score 550 paper-based). Electronic applications accepted.

Indiana University Bloomington, University Graduate School, College of Arts and Sciences, Department of Psychological and Brain Sciences, Bloomington, IN 47405. Offers clinical science (PhD); cognitive neuroscience (PhD); cognitive psychology (PhD); developmental psychology (PhD); methods of behavior (PhD); molecular systems neuroscience (PhD); social psychology (PhD). *Accreditation:* APA. *Faculty:* 54 full-time (15 women). *Students:* 95 full-time (56 women); includes 19 minority (4 Black or African American, non-Hispanic/Latino; 7 Asian, non-Hispanic/Latino; 7 Hispanic/Latino; 1 Two or more races, non-Hispanic/Latino), 16 international. Average age 24. 364 applicants, 10% accepted, 20 enrolled. In 2014, 9 doctorates awarded. *Degree requirements:* For doctorate, comprehensive exam, 90 credit hours, 2 advanced statistics/methods courses, 2 written research projects, the teaching of psychology course, teaching 1 semester of undergraduate methods course, qualifying examination, minor or a second major, first-year research seminar course, dissertation defense, written dissertation. *Entrance requirements:* For doctorate, GRE. Additional exam requirements/recommendations for international students: Required—TOEFL (minimum score 550 paper-based; 79 iBT). *Application deadline:* For fall admission, 12/1 for domestic and international students. Application fee: $55 ($65 for international students). Electronic applications accepted. *Financial support:* Fellowships with full tuition reimbursements, research assistantships with full tuition reimbursements, teaching assistantships with full tuition reimbursements, career-related internships or fieldwork, scholarships/grants, traineeships, health care benefits, and unspecified assistantships available. *Faculty research:* Clinical science, cognitive neuroscience, cognitive psychology, developmental psychology, mechanisms of behavior, molecular and systems neuroscience, social psychology. *Unit head:* Dr. William Hetrick, Chair, 812-855-2012, Fax: 812-855-4691, E-mail: whetrick@indiana.edu. *Application contact:* Dale Sengelaub, Graduate Admissions, 812-855-9149, Fax: 812-855-4691, E-mail: psychgrd@indiana.edu.
Website: http://www.psych.indiana.edu

Indiana University of Pennsylvania, School of Graduate Studies and Research, College of Natural Sciences and Mathematics, Department of Psychology, Indiana, PA 15705-1087. Offers clinical psychology (Psy D); psychology (MA). *Accreditation:* APA (one or more programs are accredited). Part-time programs available. *Faculty:* 12 full-time (7 women). *Students:* 52 full-time (38 women), 20 part-time (17 women); includes 12 minority (4 Asian, non-Hispanic/Latino; 4 Hispanic/Latino; 4 Two or more races, non-Hispanic/Latino), 3 international. Average age 26. 236 applicants, 14% accepted, 15 enrolled. In 2014, 9 master's, 12 doctorates awarded. Terminal master's awarded for partial completion of doctoral program. *Degree requirements:* For doctorate, comprehensive exam, thesis/dissertation, internship, practicum. *Entrance requirements:* For doctorate, GRE General Test, minimum GPA of 3.0, interview, 3 letters of recommendation. Additional exam requirements/recommendations for international students: Required—TOEFL (minimum score 540 paper-based). *Application deadline:* Applications are processed on a rolling basis. Application fee: $50. Electronic applications accepted. *Financial support:* In 2014–15, 6 fellowships with full tuition reimbursements (averaging $1,695 per year), 48 research assistantships with full and partial tuition reimbursements (averaging $3,765 per year), 2 teaching assistantships with partial tuition reimbursements (averaging $23,305 per year) were awarded; career-related internships or fieldwork, Federal Work-Study, scholarships/grants, and unspecified assistantships also available. Support available to part-time students. Financial award application deadline: 4/15; financial award applicants required to submit FAFSA. *Unit head:* Dr. Raymond Pavloski, Chairperson, 724-357-2426, E-mail: pavloski@iup.edu. *Application contact:* Dr. David LaPorte, Graduate Coordinator, 724-357-2426, E-mail: laporte@iup.edu.
Website: http://www.iup.edu/psychology

Indiana University–Purdue University Indianapolis, School of Science, Department of Psychology, Indianapolis, IN 46202-3275. Offers clinical psychology (MS); industrial/organizational psychology (MS); psychobiology of addictions (PhD). *Accreditation:* APA (one or more programs are accredited). *Faculty:* 25 full-time (13 women), 2 part-time/adjunct (both women). *Students:* 51 full-time (34 women), 9 part-time (6 women); includes 10 minority (3 Black or African American, non-Hispanic/Latino; 5 Asian, non-Hispanic/Latino; 1 Hispanic/Latino; 1 Two or more races, non-Hispanic/Latino), 2 international. Average age 28. 189 applicants, 10% accepted, 19 enrolled. In 2014, 15 master's, 4 doctorates awarded. Terminal master's awarded for partial completion of doctoral program. *Degree requirements:* For master's, thesis; for doctorate, thesis/dissertation. *Entrance requirements:* For master's, GRE General Test, minimum undergraduate GPA of 3.0; for doctorate, GRE General Test, GRE Subject Test (clinical psychology), minimum undergraduate GPA of 3.2. Additional exam requirements/recommendations for international students: Required—TOEFL (minimum score 567 paper-based; 86 iBT), IELTS (minimum score 6.5). *Application deadline:* For fall admission, 12/1 priority date for domestic and international students. Application fee: $60. Electronic applications accepted. *Financial support:* In 2014–15, 3 fellowships with

partial tuition reimbursements (averaging $22,500 per year) were awarded; research assistantships with partial tuition reimbursements, teaching assistantships with partial tuition reimbursements, career-related internships or fieldwork, Federal Work-Study, institutionally sponsored loans, traineeships, health care benefits, and unspecified assistantships also available. Financial award application deadline: 3/1; financial award applicants required to submit FAFSA. *Faculty research:* Severe mental illness, health psychology, neurological research, alcoholism and psychopathology, functional activities within organizations. *Unit head:* Dr. Peggy S. Stockdale, Chair, 317-278-3838, E-mail: pstockda@iupui.edu. *Application contact:* Heather Sissons, Office Manager and Graduate Coordinator, 317-274-6945, E-mail: hsissons@iupui.edu. Website: http://www.psych.iupui.edu/

Inter American University of Puerto Rico, Metropolitan Campus, Graduate Programs, Program in Psychology, San Juan, PR 00919-1293. Offers counseling psychology (MA, PhD); industrial/organizational psychology (MA, PhD); labor relations (MA); school psychology (MA, PhD). *Degree requirements:* For master's, comprehensive exam. *Entrance requirements:* For master's, GRE or EXADEP, interview. Electronic applications accepted.

Inter American University of Puerto Rico, San Germán Campus, Graduate Studies Center, Program in Psychology, San Germán, PR 00683-5008. Offers counseling psychology (MA, PhD); school psychology (MA, PhD). Part-time and evening/weekend programs available. *Degree requirements:* For master's, comprehensive exam, thesis; for doctorate, comprehensive exam, thesis/dissertation. *Entrance requirements:* For master's, GRE General Test or EXADEP, minimum GPA of 3.0; for doctorate, GRE, EXADEP or MAT, minimum GPA of 3.0.

Iona College, School of Arts and Science, Department of Psychology, New Rochelle, NY 10801-1890. Offers general-experimental psychology (MA); human resources (Certificate); industrial-organizational psychology (MA); mental health counseling (MA); organizational behavior (Certificate); psychology (MA); school psychology (MA). Part-time programs available. *Faculty:* 8 full-time (3 women), 5 part-time/adjunct (3 women). *Students:* 41 full-time (30 women), 33 part-time (22 women); includes 29 minority (12 Black or African American, non-Hispanic/Latino; 2 Asian, non-Hispanic/Latino; 15 Hispanic/Latino), 1 international. Average age 24. 65 applicants, 85% accepted, 22 enrolled. In 2014, 38 master's awarded. *Degree requirements:* For master's, thesis (for some programs), literature review (for some programs). *Entrance requirements:* For master's, BA in psychology including 3 credits in psychology statistics and 3 credits in experimental research methods; or 9 credits in psychology including 3 credits in psychology statistics,3 credits in psychology research methods and 3 credits of upper-level coursework. Additional exam requirements/recommendations for international students: Required—TOEFL (minimum score 550 paper-based), IELTS (minimum score 6.5). *Application deadline:* For fall admission, 8/15 for domestic students, 5/1 for international students; for spring admission, 1/15 for domestic students, 9/1 for international students. Applications are processed on a rolling basis. Application fee: $50. Electronic applications accepted. *Expenses: Tuition:* Part-time $985 per credit. *Required fees:* $245 per term. *Financial support:* In 2014–15, 6 students received support, including 1 research assistantship with partial tuition reimbursement available (averaging $8,000 per year); tuition waivers (partial) and unspecified assistantships also available. Support available to part-time students. Financial award application deadline: 4/15; financial award applicants required to submit FAFSA. *Faculty research:* Non-suicidal self-injury, trauma response, performance appraisal and evaluation, diversity infusion, assessment and treatment of sexual offenders. *Unit head:* Patricia Oswald, PhD, Chair, 914-633-7788, E-mail: poswald@iona.edu. *Application contact:* Amanda St. Bernard, Assistant Director, Graduate Admissions, 914-633-2440, Fax: 914-633-2277, E-mail: astbernard@iona.edu.

Website: http://www.iona.edu/Academics/School-of-Arts-Science/Departments/Psychology/Graduate-Programs.aspx

Iowa State University of Science and Technology, Department of Psychology, Ames, IA 50011. Offers cognitive psychology (PhD); counseling psychology (PhD); social psychology (PhD). *Accreditation:* APA. *Entrance requirements:* For doctorate, GRE General Test, GRE Subject Test (psychology), 3 letters of recommendation. Additional exam requirements/recommendations for international students: Required—TOEFL (minimum score 560 paper-based; 79 iBT), IELTS (minimum score 6.5). Electronic applications accepted. *Faculty research:* Counseling psychology, cognitive psychology, social psychology, health psychology, psychology and public policy.

Jackson State University, Graduate School, College of Liberal Arts, Department of Psychology, Jackson, MS 39217. Offers clinical psychology (PhD). *Accreditation:* APA. *Degree requirements:* For doctorate, comprehensive exam, thesis/dissertation. *Entrance requirements:* For doctorate, MAT, GRE. Additional exam requirements/recommendations for international students: Required—TOEFL (minimum score 520 paper-based; 67 iBT).

See Display below and Close-Up on page 1209.

Jacksonville State University, College of Graduate Studies and Continuing Education, College of Arts and Sciences, Department of Psychology, Jacksonville, AL 36265-1602. Offers MS. Part-time and evening/weekend programs available. *Faculty:* 4 full-time (3 women). *Students:* 14 full-time (10 women), 2 part-time (1 woman). Average age 28. 26 applicants, 38% accepted, 8 enrolled. In 2014, 7 master's awarded. *Degree requirements:* For master's, comprehensive exam, thesis (for some programs). *Entrance requirements:* For master's, GRE General Test or MAT. Additional exam requirements/recommendations for international students: Required—TOEFL (minimum score 500 paper-based; 61 iBT). *Application deadline:* Applications are processed on a rolling basis. Application fee: $35. Electronic applications accepted. *Financial support:* In 2014–15, 7 students received support. Available to part-time students. Application deadline: 4/1; applicants required to submit FAFSA. *Unit head:* Dr. Paige McKerchar, Interim Department Head, 256-782-5808, E-mail: pmckerchar@jsu.edu. *Application contact:* Dr. Jean Pugliese, Associate Dean, 256-782-8278, Fax: 256-782-5321, E-mail: pugliese@jsu.edu.

James Madison University, The Graduate School, College of Health and Behavioral Sciences, Department of Graduate Psychology, Harrisonburg, VA 22807. Offers assessment and measurement (PhD); clinical and school psychology (Psy D); clinical mental health counseling (MA, Ed S); college student personnel administration (M Ed); counseling and supervision (PhD); psychological sciences (MA), including behavior analysis; school psychology (MA, Ed S). *Accreditation:* ACA (one or more programs are accredited); APA (one or more programs are accredited). Part-time and evening/weekend programs available. *Faculty:* 68 full-time (39 women), 8 part-time/adjunct (3 women). *Students:* 137 full-time (97 women), 33 part-time (23 women); includes 30 minority (18 Black or African American, non-Hispanic/Latino; 2 Asian, non-Hispanic/Latino; 7 Hispanic/Latino; 3 Two or more races, non-Hispanic/Latino), 6 international. Average age 28. 422 applicants, 23% accepted, 69 enrolled. In 2014, 49 master's, 13 doctorates, 15 other advanced degrees awarded. *Degree requirements:* For doctorate, thesis/dissertation; for Ed S, thesis. *Application deadline:* For fall admission, 2/1 for domestic students; for spring admission, 9/1 for domestic students. Application fee: $55. Electronic applications accepted. *Expenses:* Tuition, state resident: full-time $7812; part-time $434 per credit hour. Tuition, nonresident: full-time $20,430; part-time $1135 per credit hour. *Financial support:* In 2014–15, 125 students received support, including 10 fellowships, 3 teaching assistantships with full tuition reimbursements available (averaging $8,837 per year); career-related internships or fieldwork, Federal Work-Study, and 99 assistantships (averaging $7530), 13 doctoral assistantships also

Jackson State University® (JSU) is a diverse, technologically-advanced university designated by the Carnegie Foundation as a research-intensive university. JSU offers more than 90 bachelor's, master's, and doctoral degree programs ranging from Art to Urban Studies. The Clinical Psychology Doctoral Program at JSU has been accredited by the American Psychological Association since 2003.

Learn more at: http://www.jsums.edu/psychology/graduate

available. Financial award application deadline: 3/1; financial award applicants required to submit FAFSA. *Unit head:* Dr. Robin D. Anderson, Academic Unit Head, 540-568-3293, Fax: 540-568-3322, E-mail: ander2rd@jmu.edu. *Application contact:* Lynette D. Michael, Director of Graduate Admissions and Student Records, 540-568-6131 Ext. 6395, Fax: 540-568-7860, E-mail: michaeld@jmu.edu.
Website: http://www.psyc.jmu.edu/gradpsyc/

John F. Kennedy University, Graduate School of Holistic Studies, Department of Integral Studies, Program in Integral Psychology, Pleasant Hill, CA 94523-4817. Offers dream studies (Certificate); integral psychology (MA); life coaching (Certificate). Part-time and evening/weekend programs available.

John F. Kennedy University, Graduate School of Professional Psychology, Pleasant Hill, CA 94523-4817. Offers MA, Psy D, Certificate. *Accreditation:* APA. Part-time and evening/weekend programs available. *Degree requirements:* For master's, thesis or alternative. *Entrance requirements:* For master's, interview. Additional exam requirements/recommendations for international students: Required—TOEFL.

Johns Hopkins University, Zanvyl Krieger School of Arts and Sciences, Department of Psychological and Brain Sciences, Baltimore, MD 21218. Offers PhD. *Degree requirements:* For doctorate, thesis/dissertation, research project, teaching experience. *Entrance requirements:* For doctorate, GRE General Test. Additional exam requirements/recommendations for international students: Required—TOEFL (minimum score 600 paper-based; 100 iBT), IELTS (minimum score 7). Electronic applications accepted. *Faculty research:* Biopsychology, cognitive psychology, cognitive neuroscience, developmental psychology, neurobiology.

Kansas State University, Graduate School, College of Arts and Sciences, Department of Psychological Sciences, Manhattan, KS 66506. Offers MS, PhD. Part-time programs available. *Faculty:* 16 full-time (5 women), 5 part-time/adjunct (2 women). *Students:* 50 full-time (25 women), 27 part-time (18 women); includes 9 minority (2 Black or African American, non-Hispanic/Latino; 3 Asian, non-Hispanic/Latino; 2 Hispanic/Latino; 2 Two or more races, non-Hispanic/Latino), 3 international. Average age 27. 117 applicants, 23% accepted, 22 enrolled. In 2014, 10 master's, 5 doctorates awarded. *Degree requirements:* For master's, thesis or alternative; for doctorate, thesis/dissertation, preliminary exam. *Entrance requirements:* For master's, GRE General Test, minimum undergraduate GPA of 3.0; for doctorate, GRE General Test, minimum GPA of 3.0. Additional exam requirements/recommendations for international students: Required—TOEFL (minimum score 600 paper-based). *Application deadline:* For fall admission, 1/15 priority date for domestic and international students; for spring admission, 8/1 for domestic and international students. Applications are processed on a rolling basis. Application fee: $50 ($75 for international students). Electronic applications accepted. *Financial support:* In 2014–15, 8 research assistantships (averaging $17,635 per year), 22 teaching assistantships with full tuition reimbursements (averaging $12,675 per year) were awarded; career-related internships or fieldwork, institutionally sponsored loans, and scholarships/grants also available. Support available to part-time students. Financial award application deadline: 3/1; financial award applicants required to submit FAFSA. *Faculty research:* Personal and occupational health, neurological bases of drug use and abuse, measurement and reduction of prejudice, judgment and decision-making, visual perception. *Total annual research expenditures:* $922,093. *Unit head:* Prof. Michael Young, Head, 785-532-0602, Fax: 785-532-5401, E-mail: michaelyoung@ksu.edu. *Application contact:* Prof. Gary L. Brase, Director, 785-532-0609, Fax: 785-532-5401, E-mail: gbrase@ksu.edu.
Website: http://www.k-state.edu/psych

Kean University, College of Humanities and Social Sciences, Program in Psychology, Union, NJ 07083. Offers human behavior and organizational psychology (MA); psychological services (MA). Part-time programs available. *Faculty:* 16 full-time (13 women). *Students:* 28 full-time (25 women), 24 part-time (13 women); includes 23 minority (12 Black or African American, non-Hispanic/Latino; 3 Asian, non-Hispanic/Latino; 7 Hispanic/Latino; 1 Two or more races, non-Hispanic/Latino), 1 international. Average age 29. 35 applicants, 89% accepted, 15 enrolled. In 2014, 22 master's awarded. *Degree requirements:* For master's, comprehensive exam, research component, two semesters of advanced seminar. *Entrance requirements:* For master's, GRE General Test, minimum GPA of 3.0; official transcripts from all institutions attended; two letters of recommendation; professional resume/curriculum vitae; 12 credits in behavioral sciences on the undergraduate level. Additional exam requirements/recommendations for international students: Required—TOEFL (minimum score 79 iBT). *Application deadline:* For fall admission, 6/1 for domestic and international students; for spring admission, 12/1 for domestic and international students. Applications are processed on a rolling basis. Application fee: $75 ($150 for international students). Electronic applications accepted. *Expenses:* Tuition, state resident: full-time $12,461; part-time $607 per credit. Tuition, nonresident: full-time $16,889; part-time $744 per credit. *Required fees:* $3141; $143 per credit. Tuition and fees vary according to course load, degree level and program. *Financial support:* In 2014–15, 3 research assistantships with full tuition reimbursements (averaging $3,742 per year) were awarded; scholarships/grants and unspecified assistantships also available. Financial award applicants required to submit FAFSA. *Unit head:* Dr. Muriel Singer, Program Coordinator, 908-737-5886, E-mail: msinger@kean.edu. *Application contact:* Reenat Hasan, Admissions Counselor, 908-737-7134, Fax: 908-737-7135, E-mail: rhasan@exchange.kean.edu.
Website: http://grad.kean.edu/masters-programs/psychological-services

Keiser University, MS in Psychology Program, Ft. Lauderdale, FL 33309. Offers MS.

Keiser University, PhD in Psychology Program, Ft. Lauderdale, FL 33309. Offers PhD.

Kent State University, College of Arts and Sciences, Department of Psychological Sciences, Kent, OH 44242-0001. Offers clinical psychology (MA, PhD); experimental psychology (MA, PhD). *Accreditation:* APA (one or more programs are accredited). Part-time programs available. *Faculty:* 28 full-time (15 women). *Students:* 90 full-time (64 women), 1 part-time (0 women); includes 8 minority (4 Black or African American, non-Hispanic/Latino; 2 Asian, non-Hispanic/Latino; 2 Hispanic/Latino), 5 international. Average age 27. 858 applicants, 5% accepted, 31 enrolled. In 2014, 10 master's, 21 doctorates awarded. Terminal master's awarded for partial completion of doctoral program. *Degree requirements:* For master's, thesis; for doctorate, thesis/dissertation. *Entrance requirements:* For master's, GRE General Test, minimum GPA of 3.0, transcript, resume, statement of purpose, 3 letters of recommendation; for doctorate, GRE General Test, minimum GPA of 3.0, transcript, resume, statement of purpose, writing sample, 3 letters of recommendation. Additional exam requirements/recommendations for international students: Required—TOEFL (minimum score: paper-based 525, iBT 71), Michigan English Language Assessment Battery (minimum score of 75), IELTS (minimum score of 6.0), PTE Academic (minimum score of 48), or completion of ELS level 112 Intensive Program. *Application deadline:* For fall admission, 12/15 for domestic students, 1/1 for international students. Application fee: $45 ($70 for international students). Electronic applications accepted. *Expenses:* Tuition, state resident: full-time $8730; part-time $485 per credit hour. Tuition, nonresident: full-time $14,886; part-time $827 per credit hour. Tuition and fees vary according to campus/location and program. *Financial support:* Research assistantships with full tuition reimbursements, teaching assistantships with full tuition reimbursements, career-related internships or fieldwork, Federal Work-Study, and unspecified assistantships available. Financial award application deadline: 1/1. *Unit head:* Dr. Maria Zaragoza, Professor and Chair, 330-672-2018, E-mail: mzaragoz@kent.edu. *Application contact:* Dr. John Updegraff, Associate Professor and Graduate Coordinator, 330-672-2166, Fax: 330-672-3786, E-mail: jupdegr1@kent.edu.
Website: http://www.kent.edu/psychology/graduate-programs

Lakehead University, Graduate Studies, Department of Psychology, Thunder Bay, ON P7B 5E1, Canada. Offers clinical psychology (PhD); experimental psychology (MA). Part-time and evening/weekend programs available. *Degree requirements:* For master's, thesis optional; for doctorate, thesis/dissertation, 2 comprehensive exams, internship. *Entrance requirements:* For master's, GRE, honors degree in psychology, advanced course work in statistics, minimum B average; for doctorate, GRE, minimum B average. Additional exam requirements/recommendations for international students: Required—TOEFL. *Faculty research:* Chaos theory, health psychology, counseling psychology, gerontology, women's studies.

Lamar University, College of Graduate Studies, College of Arts and Sciences, Department of Psychology, Beaumont, TX 77710. Offers clinical psychology (MS); industrial/organizational psychology (MS). Part-time programs available. *Faculty:* 7 full-time (4 women). *Students:* 14 full-time (10 women), 8 part-time (5 women); includes 6 minority (2 Black or African American, non-Hispanic/Latino; 3 Hispanic/Latino; 1 Two or more races, non-Hispanic/Latino), 1 international. Average age 25. 14 applicants, 71% accepted, 4 enrolled. In 2014, 7 master's awarded. *Degree requirements:* For master's, thesis, practicum. *Entrance requirements:* For master's, GRE General Test, minimum GPA of 2.75 in last 60 hours of undergraduate course work. Additional exam requirements/recommendations for international students: Required—TOEFL (minimum score 550 paper-based; 79 iBT), IELTS (minimum score 6.5). *Application deadline:* For fall admission, 8/10 for domestic students, 7/1 for international students; for spring admission, 1/5 for domestic students, 12/1 for international students. Application fee: $25 ($50 for international students). *Expenses:* Tuition, state resident: full-time $5724; part-time $1908 per semester. Tuition, nonresident: full-time $12,240; part-time $4080 per semester. *Required fees:* $1940; $318 per credit hour. *Financial support:* In 2014–15, 12 students received support, including 3 teaching assistantships (averaging $4,500 per year); fellowships, research assistantships, career-related internships or fieldwork, Federal Work-Study, scholarships/grants, and tuition waivers (partial) also available. Support available to part-time students. Financial award application deadline: 4/1. *Faculty research:* Groupthink, health psychology, school psychology, behavioral neuroscience. *Unit head:* Dr. Edythe E Kirk, Interim Chair, 409-880-8285, Fax: 409-880-1710. *Application contact:* Melissa Gallien, Director, Admissions and Academic Services, 409-880-8888, Fax: 409-880-7419, E-mail: gradmissions@lamar.edu.
Website: http://artssciences.lamar.edu/psychology

La Salle University, School of Arts and Sciences, Program in Clinical Psychology, Philadelphia, PA 19141-1199. Offers child clinical psychology (Psy D); clinical health psychology (Psy D); clinical psychology (MA); general practice psychology (Psy D). *Accreditation:* AAMFT/COAMFTE. Part-time and evening/weekend programs available. Terminal master's awarded for partial completion of doctoral program. *Degree requirements:* For doctorate, comprehensive exam, thesis/dissertation. *Entrance requirements:* For doctorate, GRE (minimum scores of 148 on both the Verbal Reasoning and Quantitative Reasoning sections strongly recommended); GRE Subject Test in psychology for those entering with bachelor's degree, baccalaureate degree from accredited institution with major in psychology or related discipline; minimum undergraduate GPA of 3.0, 3.2 graduate; three letters of recommendation; statement of interest and intent; curriculum vitae or resume; personal interview. Additional exam requirements/recommendations for international students: Required—TOEFL. Electronic applications accepted. Application fee is waived when completed online. *Expenses:* Contact institution.

Laurentian University, School of Graduate Studies and Research, Programme in Psychology, Sudbury, ON P3E 2C6, Canada. Offers applied psychology (MA); experimental psychology (MA).

Lehigh University, College of Arts and Sciences, Department of Psychology, Bethlehem, PA 18015. Offers MS, PhD. *Faculty:* 15 full-time (10 women). *Students:* 18 full-time (14 women), 2 part-time (1 woman); includes 1 minority (Asian, non-Hispanic/Latino), 5 international. Average age 27. 87 applicants, 11% accepted, 5 enrolled. In 2014, 6 master's, 1 doctorate awarded. Terminal master's awarded for partial completion of doctoral program. *Degree requirements:* For master's, thesis; for doctorate, comprehensive exam, thesis/dissertation. *Entrance requirements:* For master's and doctorate, GRE General Test. Additional exam requirements/recommendations for international students: Required—TOEFL. *Application deadline:* For fall admission, 1/1 for domestic and international students. Application fee: $75. Electronic applications accepted. *Financial support:* In 2014–15, 16 students received support, including 1 fellowship with full tuition reimbursement available (averaging $26,500 per year), 3 research assistantships with full tuition reimbursements available (averaging $19,500 per year), 12 teaching assistantships with full tuition reimbursements available (averaging $19,500 per year); scholarships/grants, tuition waivers (full and partial), and unspecified assistantships also available. Financial award application deadline: 1/1. *Faculty research:* Cognition, memory, language, and their development; prosocial cognition, emotion, and action; conflict and cooperation between and within groups; self-control of cognition and emotion; optimizing developmental and relational outcomes. *Total annual research expenditures:* $323,581. *Unit head:* Dr. Gordon Moskowitz, Chairperson, 610-758-3624, Fax: 610-758-6277, E-mail: gbm4@lehigh.edu. *Application contact:* Dr. Dominic Packer, Program Director, 610-758-3630, Fax: 610-758-6277, E-mail: inpsy@lehigh.edu.
Website: http://psychology.cas2.lehigh.edu/

Lesley University, Graduate School of Arts and Social Sciences, Cambridge, MA 02138-2790. Offers clinical mental health counseling (MA), including holistic counseling, school and community counseling, trauma studies; counseling psychology (MA, CAGS), including professional counseling (MA), school counseling (MA); creative writing (MFA); expressive therapies (MA, PhD, CAGS), including art (MA), clinical mental health counseling (MA), dance (MA), expressive therapies (MA), music (MA); independent studies (CAGS); independent study (MA); intercultural relations (MA, CAGS); interdisciplinary studies (MA), including individualized studies, integrative holistic health, mindfulness studies, peace and conflict transformation, trauma sensitive assessment, intervention, and consultation, women's studies; urban environmental leadership (MA). Part-time programs available. Postbaccalaureate distance learning degree programs offered (no on-campus study). *Faculty:* 35 full-time (25 women), 115 part-time/adjunct (90 women). *Students:* 420 full-time (379 women), 514 part-time (414 women); includes 142 minority (50 Black or African American, non-Hispanic/Latino; 5 American Indian or Alaska Native, non-Hispanic/Latino; 16 Asian, non-Hispanic/Latino; 48 Hispanic/Latino; 23 Two or more races, non-Hispanic/Latino), 46 international. Average age 33. In 2014, 475 master's, 11 doctorates, 4 other advanced degrees awarded. *Degree requirements:* For master's, internship, practicum, thesis (for expressive therapies); for doctorate, thesis/dissertation, arts apprenticeship, field placement; for CAGS, thesis, internship (for counseling psychology, expressive therapies). *Entrance requirements:* For master's, MAT (counseling psychology), interview, writing samples, art portfolio; for doctorate,

GRE or MAT, interview, master's degree; for CAGS, interview, master's degree. Additional exam requirements/recommendations for international students: Required—TOEFL (minimum score 550 paper-based; 80 iBT). *Application deadline:* Applications are processed on a rolling basis. Application fee: $50. Electronic applications accepted. *Financial support:* Fellowships, career-related internships or fieldwork, Federal Work-Study, scholarships/grants, tuition waivers, and unspecified assistantships available. Financial award applicants required to submit FAFSA. *Faculty research:* Psychotherapy and culture; psychotherapy and psychological trauma; women's issues in art, teaching and psychotherapy; community-based art, psycho-spiritual inquiry. *Unit head:* Dr. Catherine Koverola, Dean, 617-349-8317, Fax: 617-349-8366, E-mail: koverola@lesley.edu. *Application contact:* Martha Sheehan, Director, Graduate Admissions, 888-LESLEYU, Fax: 617-349-8313, E-mail: info@lesley.edu.
Website: http://www.lesley.edu/graduate-school-of-arts-and-social-sciences/

LeTourneau University, Graduate Programs, Longview, TX 75607-7001. Offers business administration (MBA); counseling (MA); curriculum and instruction (M Ed); education administration (M Ed); engineering (ME, MS); engineering management (MEM); health care administration (MS); marriage and family therapy (MA); psychology (MA); strategic leadership (MSL); teacher leadership (M Ed); teaching and learning (M Ed). Part-time programs available. Postbaccalaureate distance learning degree programs offered (no on-campus study). *Faculty:* 14 full-time (4 women), 41 part-time/adjunct (18 women). *Students:* 58 full-time (37 women), 359 part-time (289 women); includes 140 minority (78 Black or African American, non-Hispanic/Latino; 2 American Indian or Alaska Native, non-Hispanic/Latino; 4 Asian, non-Hispanic/Latino; 40 Hispanic/Latino; 16 Two or more races, non-Hispanic/Latino), 11 international. Average age 38. 199 applicants, 73% accepted, 130 enrolled. In 2014, 139 master's awarded. *Degree requirements:* For master's, thesis (for some programs). *Entrance requirements:* For master's, GRE (for engineering and psychology programs). Additional exam requirements/recommendations for international students: Required—TOEFL. *Application deadline:* For fall admission, 8/22 for domestic students, 8/29 for international students; for winter admission, 10/10 for domestic students; for spring admission, 1/2 for domestic students, 1/10 for international students; for summer admission, 5/1 for domestic and international students. Applications are processed on a rolling basis. Electronic applications accepted. Application fee is waived when completed online. *Financial support:* In 2014–15, 11 students received support, including 16 research assistantships (averaging $11,621 per year); institutionally sponsored loans and unspecified assistantships also available. Financial award applicants required to submit FAFSA. *Application contact:* Chris Fontaine, Assistant Vice President for Global Campus Admissions, 903-233-4312, E-mail: chrisfontaine@letu.edu.
Website: http://www.letu.edu

Lewis & Clark College, Graduate School of Education and Counseling, Department of Counseling Psychology, Portland, OR 97219-7899. Offers marriage, couple and family therapy (MA, MS); professional mental health counseling (MA, MS); professional mental health counseling–addictions (MA, MS); psychological and cultural studies (MA, MS); school psychology (Ed S). *Accreditation:* AAMFT/COAMFTE; ACA. Part-time and evening/weekend programs available. *Degree requirements:* For master's, thesis proposal (MS). *Entrance requirements:* For master's, GRE General Test, minimum undergraduate GPA of 2.75. Additional exam requirements/recommendations for international students: Required—TOEFL (minimum score 575 paper-based). Electronic applications accepted.

Lipscomb University, Department of Graduate Psychology and Counseling, Nashville, TN 37204-3951. Offers clinical mental health counseling (MS); counseling psychology (Certificate); marriage and family therapy (MMFT); psychology (MS). Part-time and evening/weekend programs available. *Faculty:* 11 full-time (3 women), 6 part-time/adjunct (2 women). *Students:* 90 full-time (70 women), 40 part-time (32 women); includes 36 minority (25 Black or African American, non-Hispanic/Latino; 1 American Indian or Alaska Native, non-Hispanic/Latino; 2 Asian, non-Hispanic/Latino; 6 Hispanic/Latino; 2 Two or more races, non-Hispanic/Latino), 1 international. Average age 29. In 2014, 66 master's awarded. *Degree requirements:* For master's, thesis (for some programs), practicum, internship, capstone. *Entrance requirements:* For master's, GRE, resume, 3 reference letters, transcripts, goals statement. Additional exam requirements/recommendations for international students: Required—TOEFL (minimum score 570 paper-based; 80 iBT). *Application deadline:* For fall admission, 7/1 for domestic students; for spring admission, 11/1 for domestic students. Applications are processed on a rolling basis. Application fee: $50 ($75 for international students). Electronic applications accepted. *Expenses:* Expenses: $898 per credit hour. *Financial support:* Scholarships/grants and unspecified assistantships available. Financial award applicants required to submit FAFSA. *Faculty research:* Cognitive psychology, neuroscience, health psychology, grief issues. *Unit head:* Dr. Shanna Ray, Director/Professor of Psychology, 615-966-5833, E-mail: shanna.ray@lipscomb.edu. *Application contact:* Kathi Johnson, Recruiting and Marketing Coordinator, 615-966-5237, E-mail: kathi.johnson@lipscomb.edu.
Website: http://www.lipscomb.edu/psychology/graduate-programs

Loma Linda University, School of Science and Technology, Department of Psychology, Loma Linda, CA 92350. Offers PhD, Psy D. *Accreditation:* APA. *Degree requirements:* For doctorate, comprehensive exam, thesis/dissertation. *Entrance requirements:* For doctorate, GRE General Test. Additional exam requirements/recommendations for international students: Required—TOEFL (minimum score 550 paper-based), MTELP. Electronic applications accepted.

Louisiana State University and Agricultural & Mechanical College, Graduate School, College of Humanities and Social Sciences, Department of Psychology, Baton Rouge, LA 70803. Offers biological psychology (MA, PhD); clinical psychology (MA, PhD); cognitive psychology (MA, PhD); developmental psychology (MA, PhD); school psychology (MA, PhD). PhD programs offered jointly with Southeastern Louisiana University. *Accreditation:* APA (one or more programs are accredited). *Faculty:* 22 full-time (10 women). *Students:* 67 full-time (54 women), 30 part-time (21 women); includes 13 minority (4 Black or African American, non-Hispanic/Latino; 3 Asian, non-Hispanic/Latino; 3 Hispanic/Latino; 3 Two or more races, non-Hispanic/Latino), 3 international. Average age 27. 221 applicants, 10% accepted, 22 enrolled. In 2014, 13 master's, 18 doctorates awarded. Terminal master's awarded for partial completion of doctoral program. *Degree requirements:* For master's, thesis; for doctorate, thesis/dissertation, 1-year internship. *Entrance requirements:* For master's and doctorate, GRE General Test, minimum GPA of 3.0. Additional exam requirements/recommendations for international students: Required—TOEFL (minimum score 550 paper-based; 79 IBT), IELTS (minimum score 6.5), or PTE (minimum score 59). *Application deadline:* For fall admission, 1/1 priority date for domestic students, 5/15 for international students; for spring admission, 10/15 for domestic and international students; for summer admission, 5/15 for domestic students, 5/5 for international students. Applications are processed on a rolling basis. Application fee: $50 ($70 for international students). Electronic applications accepted. *Financial support:* In 2014–15, 90 students received support, including 2 fellowships (averaging $15,763 per year), 8 research assistantships with partial tuition reimbursements available (averaging $16,669 per year), 49 teaching assistantships with partial tuition reimbursements available (averaging $13,003 per year); career-related internships or fieldwork, Federal Work-Study, institutionally sponsored loans, scholarships/grants, health care benefits, and tuition waivers (full and partial) also available. Financial award applicants required to submit FAFSA. *Faculty research:* Clinical psychology, autism, anxiety, addition, neuropsychology, school psychology, cognitive psychology, experimental psychology. *Total annual research expenditures:* $986,140. *Unit head:* Dr. Robert Matthews, Chair, 225-578-8745, Fax: 225-578-4125, E-mail: psmath@lsu.edu. *Application contact:* Dr. Jason Hicks, Coordinator of Graduate Studies, 225-578-4109, Fax: 225-578-4125, E-mail: jhicks@lsu.edu.
Website: http://www.lsu.edu/psychology/graduate.html

Louisiana Tech University, Graduate School, College of Education, Department of Psychology and Behavioral Sciences, Ruston, LA 71272. Offers counseling and guidance (MA); counseling psychology (PhD); industrial and organizational psychology (MA, PhD). *Accreditation:* APA (one or more programs are accredited). Part-time programs available. *Degree requirements:* For master's, thesis or alternative; for doctorate, thesis/dissertation. *Entrance requirements:* For master's and doctorate, GRE General Test. *Application deadline:* For fall admission, 7/29 for domestic students; for spring admission, 2/3 for domestic students. Application fee: $20 ($30 for international students). *Financial support:* Fellowships, research assistantships, teaching assistantships, and career-related internships or fieldwork available. Financial award application deadline: 2/1. *Unit head:* Dr. Donna Thomas, Chair, 318-257-5066, Fax: 318-257-2379, E-mail: dthomas@latech.edu. *Application contact:* Dr. Cathy Stockton, Associate Dean of Graduate Studies, 318-257-3229, Fax: 318-257-2379, E-mail: cstock@latech.edu.
Website: http://www.latech.edu/education/psychology/

Loyola University Chicago, Graduate School, Department of Psychology, Chicago, IL 60660. Offers applied social psychology (MA, PhD); clinical psychology (MA, PhD); developmental psychology (MA, PhD). *Accreditation:* APA (one or more programs are accredited). *Faculty:* 27 full-time (12 women), 1 part-time/adjunct (0 women). *Students:* 79 full-time (66 women), 4 part-time (all women); includes 23 minority (8 Black or African American, non-Hispanic/Latino; 5 Asian, non-Hispanic/Latino; 7 Hispanic/Latino; 3 Two or more races, non-Hispanic/Latino), 5 international. Average age 29. 369 applicants, 7% accepted, 13 enrolled. In 2014, 8 master's, 11 doctorates awarded. Terminal master's awarded for partial completion of doctoral program. *Degree requirements:* For master's, comprehensive exam, thesis; for doctorate, comprehensive exam, thesis/dissertation. *Entrance requirements:* For master's and doctorate, GRE General Test. *Application deadline:* For fall admission, 1/15 for domestic students. Application fee: $50. Electronic applications accepted. Application fee is waived when completed online. *Expenses: Tuition:* Full-time $17,370; part-time $965 per credit. *Required fees:* $138 per semester. *Financial support:* In 2014–15, 7 fellowships with full tuition reimbursements (averaging $12,000 per year), 24 research assistantships with full tuition reimbursements (averaging $12,000 per year), 10 teaching assistantships with full tuition reimbursements (averaging $12,000 per year) were awarded; career-related internships or fieldwork, Federal Work-Study, scholarships/grants, and traineeships also available. Financial award applicants required to submit FAFSA. *Faculty research:* Cognitive development, hearing and vision, attitude and prejudice, child and family, AIDS and health promotion. *Total annual research expenditures:* $2.5 million. *Unit head:* Dr. Scott Tindale, Chair, 773-508-3014, E-mail: rtindal@luc.edu. *Application contact:* Ron Martin, Assistant Director of Enrollment Management, 312-915-8950, Fax: 312-915-8905, E-mail: gradapp@luc.edu.
Website: http://www.luc.edu/psychology/

Loyola University Maryland, Graduate Programs, Loyola College of Arts and Sciences, Department of Psychology, Baltimore, MD 21210-2699. Offers clinical psychology (MS, Psy D, CAS); counseling psychology (MS, CAS). *Accreditation:* APA. Part-time and evening/weekend programs available. *Degree requirements:* For master's, comprehensive exam, thesis; for doctorate, thesis/dissertation. *Entrance requirements:* For master's, GRE, essay, 3 letters of recommendation, transcript. Additional exam requirements/recommendations for international students: Required—TOEFL (minimum score 550 paper-based). Electronic applications accepted.

Madonna University, Department of Psychology, Livonia, MI 48150-1173. Offers clinical psychology (MSCP). Part-time and evening/weekend programs available. *Degree requirements:* For master's, thesis or alternative. *Entrance requirements:* Additional exam requirements/recommendations for international students: Required—TOEFL. Electronic applications accepted.

Mansfield University of Pennsylvania, Graduate Studies, Program in Organizational Leadership, Mansfield, PA 16933. Offers MA. Postbaccalaureate distance learning degree programs offered.

Marietta College, Program in Psychology, Marietta, OH 45750-4000. Offers MAP. Part-time programs available. *Faculty:* 5 part-time/adjunct (2 women). *Students:* 10 full-time (6 women), 1 (woman) part-time; includes 1 minority (Black or African American, non-Hispanic/Latino), 1 international. Average age 24. 15 applicants, 67% accepted, 4 enrolled. In 2014, 1 master's awarded. *Degree requirements:* For master's, thesis. *Entrance requirements:* For master's, GRE, transcripts, essay, two letters of recommendation. *Application deadline:* Applications are processed on a rolling basis. *Expenses:* Expenses: $13,050. *Financial support:* Unspecified assistantships available. *Unit head:* Dr. Chris Klein, Director, 740-376-4795, E-mail: clk002@marietta.edu.

Marist College, Graduate Programs, School of Social and Behavioral Sciences, Poughkeepsie, NY 12601-1387. Offers education (M Ed, MA); mental health counseling (MA); school psychology (MA, Adv C). Part-time and evening/weekend programs available. *Degree requirements:* For master's, thesis optional. *Entrance requirements:* For master's, GRE General Test, letters of recommendation, minimum undergraduate GPA of 3.0, interview. Additional exam requirements/recommendations for international students: Required—TOEFL (minimum score 550 paper-based; 80 iBT); Recommended—IELTS (minimum score 6.5). Electronic applications accepted. *Faculty research:* AIDS prevention, educational intervention, humanistic counseling research, aging and development, neuroimaging.

Marquette University, Graduate School, College of Arts and Sciences, Department of Psychology, Milwaukee, WI 53201-1881. Offers PhD. *Accreditation:* APA. Terminal master's awarded for partial completion of doctoral program. *Degree requirements:* For doctorate, thesis/dissertation, internship, qualifying exam. *Entrance requirements:* For doctorate, GRE General Test, sample of scholarly writing, official transcripts from all current and previous colleges/universities except Marquette, personal statement, three letters of reference. Additional exam requirements/recommendations for international students: Required—TOEFL (minimum score 530 paper-based). Electronic applications accepted. *Faculty research:* Mental imagery, moral development, organizational behavior, depression, psychotherapy outcomes.

Marshall University, Academic Affairs Division, College of Liberal Arts, Department of Psychology, Huntington, WV 25755. Offers clinical psychology (Certificate); psychology (MA, Psy D). *Accreditation:* APA. *Students:* 97 full-time (78 women), 18 part-time (11 women); includes 6 minority (3 Black or African American, non-Hispanic/Latino; 2 Hispanic/Latino; 1 Two or more races, non-Hispanic/Latino), 1 international. Average age 27. In 2014, 34 master's, 8 doctorates awarded. *Degree requirements:* For

master's, thesis optional. *Entrance requirements:* For master's, GRE General Test or MAT. *Application deadline:* For fall admission, 3/1 for domestic students; for spring admission, 11/1 for domestic students. Application fee: $40. *Financial support:* Teaching assistantships with tuition reimbursements available. *Unit head:* Dr. Marianna Linz, Chair, 304-696-2774, E-mail: linz@marshall.edu. *Application contact:* Graduate Admissions, 304-746-1900, Fax: 304-746-1902, E-mail: services@marshall.edu.

Martin University, Division of Psychology, Indianapolis, IN 46218-3867. Offers community psychology (MS). Part-time and evening/weekend programs available. *Degree requirements:* For master's, thesis. *Entrance requirements:* For master's, GRE General Test, GRE Subject Test.

Marywood University, Academic Affairs, Reap College of Education and Human Development, Department of Psychology and Counseling, Program in Psychology, Scranton, PA 18509-1598. Offers clinical services (MA); general theoretical psychology (MA). Part-time programs available. *Students:* 37 full-time (27 women), 6 part-time (4 women); includes 1 minority (Two or more races, non-Hispanic/Latino), 1 international. Average age 25. In 2014, 32 master's awarded. *Application deadline:* For fall admission, 4/1 for domestic students, 3/30 for international students; for spring admission, 11/1 for domestic students, 8/31 for international students. Applications are processed on a rolling basis. Application fee: $35. Electronic applications accepted. *Expenses:* Tuition: Part-time $775 per credit. *Required fees:* $688 per semester. Tuition and fees vary according to degree level and campus/location. *Financial support:* Application deadline: 6/30; applicants required to submit FAFSA. *Unit head:* Dr. C. Estelle Campenni, Coordinator, 570-348-6211 Ext. 2320, E-mail: campenni@marywood.edu. *Application contact:* Tammy Manka, Associate Director of Graduate Admissions, 570-348-6211 Ext. 2322, E-mail: tmanka@marywood.edu.
Website: http://www.marywood.edu/psychology/psychology-ma/

Massachusetts School of Professional Psychology, Graduate Programs, Boston, MA 02132. Offers applied psychology in higher education student personnel administration (MA); clinical psychology (Psy D); counseling psychology (MA); counseling psychology and community mental health (MA); counseling psychology and global mental health (MA); executive coaching (Graduate Certificate); forensic and counseling psychology (MA); leadership psychology (Psy D); organizational psychology (MA); primary care psychology (MA); respecialization in clinical psychology (Certificate); school psychology (Psy D); MA/CAGS. *Accreditation:* APA. *Degree requirements:* For master's, comprehensive exam (for some programs); for doctorate, thesis/dissertation (for some programs). Electronic applications accepted.

McGill University, Faculty of Graduate and Postdoctoral Studies, Faculty of Medicine, Department of Psychiatry, Montréal, QC H3A 2T5, Canada. Offers M Sc.

McGill University, Faculty of Graduate and Postdoctoral Studies, Faculty of Science, Department of Psychology, Montréal, QC H3A 2T5, Canada. Offers clinical psychology (PhD); experimental psychology (M Sc, MA, PhD). *Accreditation:* APA (one or more programs are accredited).

McMaster University, School of Graduate Studies, Faculty of Science, Department of Psychology, Hamilton, ON L8S 4M2, Canada. Offers M Sc, PhD. *Degree requirements:* For doctorate, comprehensive exam, thesis/dissertation. *Entrance requirements:* For doctorate, GRE General Test, honors degree, minimum B+ average. Additional exam requirements/recommendations for international students: Required—TOEFL (minimum score 550 paper-based).

McNeese State University, Doré School of Graduate Studies, Burton College of Education, Department of Psychology, Lake Charles, LA 70609. Offers addiction treatment (MA); applied behavior analysis (MA); counseling psychology (MA); general/experimental psychology (MA). Evening/weekend programs available. *Entrance requirements:* For master's, GRE.

Medaille College, Programs in Psychology, Buffalo, NY 14214-2695. Offers clinical psychology (Psy D); marriage and family therapy (MA); mental health counseling (MA); psychology (MA). Part-time and evening/weekend programs available. *Degree requirements:* For master's, comprehensive exam (for some programs), thesis (for some programs). *Entrance requirements:* For master's, GRE General Test (psychology), minimum GPA of 2.75 (psychology). Additional exam requirements/recommendations for international students: Required—TOEFL (minimum score 550 paper-based). Electronic applications accepted. *Faculty research:* Schizophrenia, Parkinson's Disease, eyewitness testimony, methodology.

Memorial University of Newfoundland, School of Graduate Studies, Department of Psychology, St. John's, NL A1C 5S7, Canada. Offers applied social psychology (MASP); experimental psychology (M Sc, PhD). Part-time programs available. *Degree requirements:* For master's, workterms (MASP), thesis (M Sc); for doctorate, comprehensive exam, thesis/dissertation, oral thesis defense. *Entrance requirements:* For master's, GRE, honors bachelor's degree of high second class standing or equivalent; for doctorate, GRE, master's or honors degree. Additional exam requirements/recommendations for international students: Recommended—TOEFL. Electronic applications accepted. *Faculty research:* Behavioral neuroscience, cognition, theory and research on abnormal behavior.

Mercy College, School of Social and Behavioral Sciences, Program in Psychology, Dobbs Ferry, NY 10522-1189. Offers MS. Part-time and evening/weekend programs available. Postbaccalaureate distance learning degree programs offered (no on-campus study). *Students:* 22 full-time (15 women), 34 part-time (29 women); includes 38 minority (11 Black or African American, non-Hispanic/Latino; 2 Asian, non-Hispanic/Latino; 20 Hispanic/Latino; 1 Native Hawaiian or other Pacific Islander, non-Hispanic/Latino; 4 Two or more races, non-Hispanic/Latino), 1 international. Average age 34. 65 applicants, 51% accepted, 23 enrolled. In 2014, 12 master's awarded. *Degree requirements:* For master's, thesis (for some programs), written comprehensive exam or 6-credit thesis. *Entrance requirements:* For master's, essay, interview, resume, letter of recommendation, undergraduate transcript with minimum GPA of 3.0. Additional exam requirements/recommendations for international students: Required—TOEFL (minimum score 600 paper-based; 100 iBT), IELTS (minimum score 8). *Application deadline:* For fall admission, 8/1 for international students. Applications are processed on a rolling basis. Application fee: $40. Electronic applications accepted. *Expenses:* Tuition: Full-time $14,952; part-time $814 per credit. *Required fees:* $600; $150 per semester. Tuition and fees vary according to course load, degree level and program. *Financial support:* Career-related internships or fieldwork, Federal Work-Study, scholarships/grants, and unspecified assistantships available. Support available to part-time students. Financial award applicants required to submit FAFSA. *Unit head:* Dr. Karol Dean, Interim Dean, School of Social and Behavioral Sciences, 914-674-7517, E-mail: kdean@mercy.edu. *Application contact:* Allison Gurdineer, Senior Director of Admissions, 877-637-2946, Fax: 914-674-7382, E-mail: admissions@mercy.edu.
Website: https://www.mercy.edu/degrees-programs/ms-psychology

Metropolitan State University, College of Health, Community and Professional Studies, St. Paul, MN 55106-5000. Offers advanced dental therapy (MS); leadership and management (MSN); nurse educator (MSN); nursing (DNP); psychology (MA). *Accreditation:* AACN. Part-time programs available. *Degree requirements:* For master's, thesis or alternative; for doctorate, thesis/dissertation or alternative. *Entrance*

requirements: For master's, GRE General Test, minimum GPA of 3.0, RN license, BS/BA; for doctorate, minimum GPA of 3.0; RN license, MSN. Additional exam requirements/recommendations for international students: Required—TOEFL (minimum score 550 paper-based). *Faculty research:* Women's health, gerontology.

Miami University, College of Arts and Science, Department of Psychology, Oxford, OH 45056. Offers MA, PhD. *Accreditation:* APA (one or more programs are accredited). *Students:* 68 full-time (48 women); includes 11 minority (1 Black or African American, non-Hispanic/Latino; 5 Asian, non-Hispanic/Latino; 4 Hispanic/Latino; 1 Two or more races, non-Hispanic/Latino), 8 international. Average age 27. In 2014, 12 master's, 13 doctorates awarded. *Degree requirements:* For doctorate, comprehensive exam, thesis/dissertation. *Entrance requirements:* For master's and doctorate, GRE General Test, personal statement; three letters of recommendation; bachelor's degree with background in psychology, at least one course in mathematics, statistics, and one laboratory course in psychology. Additional exam requirements/recommendations for international students: Required—TOEFL (minimum score 80 iBT); Recommended—IELTS (minimum score 6.5), TSE (minimum score 54). *Application deadline:* For fall admission, 11/1 for domestic and international students. Application fee: $50. Electronic applications accepted. *Expenses:* Tuition, state resident: full-time $12,887; part-time $537 per credit hour. Tuition, nonresident: full-time $28,449; part-time $1186 per credit hour. *Required fees:* $530; $24 per credit hour. $30 per quarter. Part-time tuition and fees vary according to course load and program. *Financial support:* Fellowships with full and partial tuition reimbursements, research assistantships with full and partial tuition reimbursements, and teaching assistantships with full and partial tuition reimbursements available. *Unit head:* Dr. Margaret Wright, Professor and Interim Chair, 513-529-2406, E-mail: wrightmo@miamioh.edu. *Application contact:* Pam Turner, Senior Graduate Program Assistant, 513-529-7224, E-mail: turnerpr@miamioh.edu.
Website: http://www.MiamiOH.edu/psychology/

Michigan School of Professional Psychology, MA and Psy D Programs in Clinical Psychology, Farmington Hills, MI 48334. Offers MA, Psy D. Part-time programs available. *Faculty:* 9 full-time (4 women), 18 part-time/adjunct (15 women). *Students:* 93 full-time (68 women), 57 part-time (45 women); includes 31 minority (22 Black or African American, non-Hispanic/Latino; 5 Asian, non-Hispanic/Latino; 2 Hispanic/Latino; 2 Two or more races, non-Hispanic/Latino), 1 international. Average age 25. 150 applicants, 53% accepted, 60 enrolled. In 2014, 50 master's, 13 doctorates awarded. *Degree requirements:* For master's, practicum; for doctorate, comprehensive exam, thesis/dissertation, internship, practicum. *Entrance requirements:* For master's, undergraduate degree from accredited institution with minimum GPA of 2.5; major in psychology, social work, or counseling; for doctorate, GRE General Test, undergraduate degree from accredited institution with minimum GPA of 2.5; graduate degree in psychology, social work, or counseling from accredited institution with minimum GPA of 3.25; graduate-level practicum. Additional exam requirements/recommendations for international students: Required—TOEFL (minimum score 550 paper-based; 79 iBT). *Application deadline:* Applications are processed on a rolling basis. Application fee: $75. Electronic applications accepted. *Expenses: Tuition:* Full-time $28,504; part-time $12,147 per year. *Required fees:* $435 per semester. One-time fee: $75. Tuition and fees vary according to course load, degree level, program and student level. *Financial support:* In 2014–15, 6 students received support, including 3 research assistantships (averaging $1,200 per year), 4 teaching assistantships (averaging $1,200 per year); career-related internships or fieldwork, institutionally sponsored loans, scholarships/grants, and unspecified assistantships also available. Support available to part-time students. Financial award application deadline: 6/30; financial award applicants required to submit FAFSA. *Faculty research:* Qualitative research, existential, phenomenological psychology, multicultural, humanistic. *Unit head:* Dr. Lee Bach, Program Director, 248-476-1122, Fax: 248-476-1125. *Application contact:* Tori Holmes, Coordinator of Admissions and Student Engagement, 248-476-1122 Ext. 117, Fax: 248-476-1125, E-mail: tholmes@mispp.edu. Website: http://www.mispp.edu

Michigan State University, The Graduate School, College of Social Science, Department of Psychology, East Lansing, MI 48824. Offers MA, PhD. *Accreditation:* APA (one or more programs are accredited). *Entrance requirements:* Additional exam requirements/recommendations for international students: Required—TOEFL (minimum score 550 paper-based), Michigan State University ELT (minimum score 85), Michigan English Language Assessment Battery (minimum score 83). Electronic applications accepted.

Middle Tennessee State University, College of Graduate Studies, College of Behavioral and Health Sciences, Department of Psychology, Murfreesboro, TN 37132. Offers clinical psychology (MA); experimental psychology (MA); industrial/organizational psychology (MA); psychology (MA, Ed S); quantitative psychology (MA); school psychology (MA). Part-time and evening/weekend programs available. Postbaccalaureate distance learning degree programs offered. *Faculty:* 37 full-time (14 women), 3 part-time/adjunct (2 women). *Students:* 66 full-time (54 women), 47 part-time (37 women); includes 15 minority (8 Black or African American, non-Hispanic/Latino; 1 American Indian or Alaska Native, non-Hispanic/Latino; 2 Asian, non-Hispanic/Latino; 3 Hispanic/Latino; 1 Two or more races, non-Hispanic/Latino), 1 international. 225 applicants, 84% accepted. In 2014, 37 master's awarded. *Degree requirements:* For master's, comprehensive exam, thesis. *Entrance requirements:* For master's, GRE. Additional exam requirements/recommendations for international students: Required—TOEFL (minimum score 525 paper-based; 71 iBT) or IELTS (minimum score 6). *Application deadline:* For fall admission, 6/1 for domestic and international students. Applications are processed on a rolling basis. Application fee: $30. Electronic applications accepted. *Financial support:* In 2014–15, 38 students received support. Tuition waivers available. Support available to part-time students. Financial award application deadline: 4/1; financial award applicants required to submit FAFSA. *Faculty research:* Health psychology, industrial/organizational psychology, experimental psychology. *Unit head:* Dr. Greg Schmidt, Chair, 615-898-2706, Fax: 615-898-5027, E-mail: greg.schmidt@mtsu.edu. *Application contact:* Dr. Michael D. Allen, Vice Provost for Research/Dean, 615-898-2840, Fax: 615-904-8020, E-mail: michael.allen@mtsu.edu.

Millersville University of Pennsylvania, College of Graduate and Professional Studies, School of Education, Department of Psychology, Millersville, PA 17551-0302. Offers clinical psychology (MS); school counseling (M Ed); school psychology (MS). Part-time programs available. *Faculty:* 17 full-time (12 women), 10 part-time/adjunct (8 women). *Students:* 87 full-time (73 women), 51 part-time (36 women); includes 14 minority (4 Black or African American, non-Hispanic/Latino; 7 Hispanic/Latino; 3 Two or more races, non-Hispanic/Latino). Average age 26. 90 applicants, 73% accepted, 33 enrolled. In 2014, 29 master's awarded. *Degree requirements:* For master's, comprehensive exam, thesis optional. *Entrance requirements:* For master's, GRE, 3 letters of recommendation, interview (in-person), goal statement, official transcripts. Additional exam requirements/recommendations for international students: Required—TOEFL (minimum score 500 paper-based, 65 iBT) or IELTS (minimum score 6). *Application deadline:* For fall admission, 1/15 for domestic and international students; for winter admission, 6/1 for domestic and international students; for spring admission, 10/1 for domestic and international students. Application fee: $40. Electronic applications accepted. *Expenses:* Tuition, state resident: full-time $8172. Tuition, nonresident: full-

time $12,258. *Required fees:* $2300. Tuition and fees vary according to course load and program. *Financial support:* In 2014–15, 39 students received support, including 39 research assistantships with full tuition reimbursements available (averaging $4,590 per year); institutionally sponsored loans and unspecified assistantships also available. Support available to part-time students. Financial award application deadline: 3/15; financial award applicants required to submit FAFSA. *Faculty research:* Correlates of creativity, mindfulness training with special needs children, preference assessments with young children, memory and aging, contingency management and behavioral economics. *Unit head:* Dr. Frederick S. Foster-Clark, Chair, 717-871-7301, Fax: 717-871-7946, E-mail: frederick.foster-clark@millersville.edu. *Application contact:* Dr. Victor S. DeSantis, Dean of College of Graduate and Professional Studies/Associate Provost for Civic and Community Engagement, 717-871-7619, Fax: 717-871-7954, E-mail: victor.desantis@millersville.edu.
Website: http://www.millersville.edu/psychology/

Minnesota State University Mankato, College of Graduate Studies, College of Social and Behavioral Sciences, Department of Psychology, Mankato, MN 56001. Offers clinical psychology (MA); industrial/organizational psychology (MA); school psychology (Psy D). Part-time programs available. *Students:* 47 full-time (38 women), 11 part-time (9 women). *Degree requirements:* For master's, one foreign language, comprehensive exam, thesis (for some programs). *Entrance requirements:* For master's, GRE General Test, GRE Subject Test (clinical psychology), minimum GPA of 3.0 during previous 2 years, 3 letters of reference. Additional exam requirements/recommendations for international students: Required—TOEFL. *Application deadline:* For fall admission, 1/1 priority date for domestic students. Applications are processed on a rolling basis. Application fee: $40. Electronic applications accepted. *Financial support:* Research assistantships, teaching assistantships with full tuition reimbursements, career-related internships or fieldwork, Federal Work-Study, institutionally sponsored loans, and unspecified assistantships available. Support available to part-time students. Financial award application deadline: 3/15; financial award applicants required to submit FAFSA. *Faculty research:* Professional competency in hospitals, mood disturbance, 360-degree feedback, employee selection, planning fallacy. *Unit head:* Dr. Jeff Buchanan, Chairperson, 507-389-2724. *Application contact:* 507-389-2321, E-mail: grad@mnsu.edu.
Website: http://www.mnsu.edu/psych/

Mississippi State University, College of Arts and Sciences, Department of Psychology, Mississippi State, MS 39762. Offers applied cognitive science (PhD); clinical psychology (MS); experimental psychology (MS). *Faculty:* 19 full-time (7 women), 1 part-time/adjunct (0 women). *Students:* 36 full-time (23 women); includes 5 minority (2 Black or African American, non-Hispanic/Latino; 2 Asian, non-Hispanic/Latino; 1 Two or more races, non-Hispanic/Latino), 4 international. Average age 26. 64 applicants, 36% accepted, 20 enrolled. In 2014, 7 master's, 1 doctorate awarded. Terminal master's awarded for partial completion of doctoral program. *Degree requirements:* For master's, comprehensive exam, thesis; for doctorate, thesis/dissertation, qualifying exam, comprehensive written and oral exam. *Entrance requirements:* For master's, GRE General Test, minimum GPA of 2.75 on last two years of undergraduate courses; for doctorate, GRE General Test, proficiency in at least 1 computer language, minimum GPA of 3.0. Additional exam requirements/recommendations for international students: Required—TOEFL (minimum score 477 paper-based; 53 iBT); Recommended—IELTS (minimum score 4.5). *Application deadline:* For fall admission, 1/15 priority date for domestic students, 5/1 for international students; for spring admission, 11/1 priority date for domestic students, 9/1 for international students. Applications are processed on a rolling basis. Application fee: $60. Electronic applications accepted. *Expenses:* Tuition, state resident: full-time $7140; part-time $783 per credit hour. Tuition, nonresident: full-time $18,478; part-time $2043 per credit hour. *Financial support:* In 2014–15, 6 research assistantships with full tuition reimbursements (averaging $12,729 per year), 18 teaching assistantships with full tuition reimbursements (averaging $8,808 per year) were awarded; career-related internships or fieldwork, Federal Work-Study, institutionally sponsored loans, scholarships/grants, and unspecified assistantships also available. Financial award application deadline: 4/1; financial award applicants required to submit FAFSA. *Faculty research:* Personality type, alcoholism, blindness and low vision, mental retardation, language comprehension. *Total annual research expenditures:* $1.1 million. *Unit head:* Dr. Mitchell E. Berman, Department Head, 662-325-3202, Fax: 662-325-7212, E-mail: mberman@psychology.msstate.edu. *Application contact:* Dr. Deborah Eakin, Graduate Coordinator, 662-325-3202, Fax: 662-325-7212, E-mail: grad@psychology.msstate.edu.
Website: http://www.psychology.msstate.edu/

Missouri State University, Graduate College, College of Health and Human Services, Department of Psychology, Springfield, MO 65897. Offers clinical psychology (MS); experimental (MS). *Faculty:* 25 full-time (11 women), 4 part-time/adjunct (0 women). *Students:* 55 full-time (41 women), 7 part-time (5 women); includes 10 minority (3 Black or African American, non-Hispanic/Latino; 3 Asian, non-Hispanic/Latino; 4 Hispanic/Latino), 3 international. Average age 25. 119 applicants, 24% accepted, 23 enrolled. In 2014, 22 master's awarded. *Degree requirements:* For master's, comprehensive exam, thesis. *Entrance requirements:* For master's, GRE General Test, GRE Subject Test, minimum GPA of 3.25 in major, 3.0 overall; 20 hours of course work in psychology. Additional exam requirements/recommendations for international students: Required—TOEFL (minimum score 550 paper-based; 79 iBT). *Application deadline:* For fall admission, 3/1 priority date for domestic and international students. Application fee: $35 ($50 for international students). Electronic applications accepted. *Expenses:* Tuition, state resident: full-time $2250; part-time $250 per credit hour. Tuition, nonresident: full-time $4509; part-time $501 per credit hour. Tuition and fees vary according to course level, course load and program. *Financial support:* In 2014–15, 5 research assistantships with full tuition reimbursements (averaging $8,450 per year), 6 teaching assistantships with full tuition reimbursements (averaging $8,450 per year) were awarded; career-related internships or fieldwork, Federal Work-Study, institutionally sponsored loans, scholarships/grants, and unspecified assistantships also available. Financial award application deadline: 3/31; financial award applicants required to submit FAFSA. *Faculty research:* Work-family conflict, child forensic psychology, sports psychology, body image assessment, visual learning. *Unit head:* Dr. Robert Jones, Interim Head, 417-836-5797, Fax: 417-836-8330, E-mail: psychology@missouristate.edu. *Application contact:* Misty Stewart, Coordinator of Graduate Recruitment, 417-836-6079, Fax: 417-836-6200, E-mail: mistystewart@missouristate.edu.
Website: http://psychology.missouristate.edu/

Monmouth University, The Graduate School, Department of Psychology, West Long Branch, NJ 07764-1898. Offers mental health counseling (MS); professional counseling (PMC); psychological counseling (MA), including addiction studies, psychological counseling. *Accreditation:* ACA. Part-time and evening/weekend programs available. *Faculty:* 8 full-time (4 women), 11 part-time/adjunct (8 women). *Students:* 146 full-time (126 women), 111 part-time (94 women); includes 50 minority (10 Black or African American, non-Hispanic/Latino; 2 American Indian or Alaska Native, non-Hispanic/Latino; 7 Asian, non-Hispanic/Latino; 27 Hispanic/Latino; 4 Two or more races, non-Hispanic/Latino), 1 international. Average age 27. 96 applicants, 96% accepted, 59 enrolled. In 2014, 75 master's awarded. *Degree requirements:* For master's, comprehensive exam (for some programs), thesis optional, fieldwork. *Entrance requirements:* For master's, GRE, minimum GPA of 3.0 overall, 12 credits in psychology or closely-related field, two Monmouth University psychological counseling recommendation forms, essay form; for PMC, degree or current enrollment in CACREP-accredited master's program in counseling with minimum cumulative GPA of 3.0. Additional exam requirements/recommendations for international students: Required—TOEFL (minimum score 550 paper-based; 79 iBT), IELTS (minimum score 5), Michigan English Language Assessment Battery (minimum score 77) or Certificate of Advanced English (minimum score B2). *Application deadline:* For fall admission, 7/15 priority date for domestic students, 6/1 for international students; for spring admission, 11/15 priority date for domestic students, 11/1 for international students. Applications are processed on a rolling basis. Application fee: $50. Electronic applications accepted. *Expenses: Tuition:* Full-time $18,072; part-time $1004 per credit. *Required fees:* $157 per semester. *Financial support:* In 2014–15, 211 students received support, including 195 fellowships (averaging $3,010 per year), 13 research assistantships (averaging $11,728 per year); career-related internships or fieldwork, scholarships/grants, and unspecified assistantships also available. Support available to part-time students. Financial award applicants required to submit FAFSA. *Faculty research:* Violent crime, single parenting, the African-American male, counseling older women, successful behavior for under-achieving youth. *Unit head:* Dr. Stephanie Hall, Program Director, 732-571-3570, Fax: 732-923-4661, E-mail: shall@monmouth.edu. *Application contact:* Andrea Thompson, Graduate Admission Counselor, 732-571-3452, Fax: 732-263-5123, E-mail: gradadm@monmouth.edu.
Website: http://www.monmouth.edu/psychological_counseling

Montana State University, The Graduate School, College of Letters and Science, Department of Psychology, Bozeman, MT 59717. Offers MS. Part-time programs available. *Degree requirements:* For master's, comprehensive exam, thesis (for some programs). *Entrance requirements:* For master's, GRE General Test. Additional exam requirements/recommendations for international students: Required—TOEFL (minimum score 550 paper-based). Electronic applications accepted. *Faculty research:* Psychological study of social cognitive, neuro and eating behaviors.

Montana State University Billings, College of Arts and Sciences, Department of Psychology, Billings, MT 59101. Offers MS. Part-time programs available. *Degree requirements:* For master's, thesis optional. *Entrance requirements:* For master's, GRE General Test, 3 letters of recommendation, resume. *Application deadline:* For fall admission, 3/15 for domestic students, 7/15 for international students; for spring admission, 12/1 for international students. Applications are processed on a rolling basis. Application fee: $40. *Financial support:* Teaching assistantships with partial tuition reimbursements, career-related internships or fieldwork, Federal Work-Study, institutionally sponsored loans, scholarships/grants, tuition waivers (partial), and unspecified assistantships available. Support available to part-time students. Financial award application deadline: 5/1; financial award applicants required to submit FAFSA. *Unit head:* Dr. Mike Havens, Chair, 406-657-2248, E-mail: mhavens@msubillings.edu. *Application contact:* David M. Sullivan, Graduate Studies Counselor, 406-657-2053, Fax: 406-657-2299, E-mail: dsullivan@msubillings.edu.

Montclair State University, The Graduate School, College of Humanities and Social Sciences, Program in Psychology, Montclair, NJ 07043-1624. Offers MA. Part-time and evening/weekend programs available. *Students:* 22 full-time (13 women), 10 part-time (4 women); includes 6 minority (1 Black or African American, non-Hispanic/Latino; 2 Asian, non-Hispanic/Latino; 2 Hispanic/Latino; 1 Two or more races, non-Hispanic/Latino), 2 international. Average age 26. 67 applicants, 28% accepted, 11 enrolled. In 2014, 8 master's awarded. *Degree requirements:* For master's, thesis. *Entrance requirements:* For master's, GRE General Test, 2 letters of recommendation, essay. Additional exam requirements/recommendations for international students: Required—TOEFL (minimum score 83 iBT), IELTS (minimum score 6.5). *Application deadline:* Applications are processed on a rolling basis. Application fee: $60. Electronic applications accepted. *Expenses:* Tuition, state resident: full-time $9960; part-time $553.35 per credit. Tuition, nonresident: full-time $15,074; part-time $837.43 per credit. *Required fees:* $1595; $88.63 per credit. Tuition and fees vary according to degree level and program. *Financial support:* Application deadline: 3/1; applicants required to submit FAFSA. *Faculty research:* Information processing, cerebral lateralization, hedonics. *Unit head:* Dr. Peter Vietze, Chairperson, 973-655-5201. *Application contact:* Amy Aiello, Executive Director of The Graduate School, 973-655-5147, Fax: 973-655-7869, E-mail: graduate.school@montclair.edu.
Website: http://www.montclair.edu/graduate/programs-of-study/psychology/

Morehead State University, Graduate Programs, College of Science and Technology, Department of Psychology, Morehead, KY 40351. Offers clinical/counseling psychology (MS); general/experimental psychology (MS). Part-time and evening/weekend programs available. *Degree requirements:* For master's, comprehensive exam, thesis optional. *Entrance requirements:* For master's, GRE General Test, 18 undergraduate hours in psychology, minimum GPA of 3.0, 3 letters of recommendation. Additional exam requirements/recommendations for international students: Required—TOEFL (minimum score 500 paper-based). Electronic applications accepted. *Faculty research:* Mood induction effects, serotonin receptor activity, stress, perceptual processes.

Morgan State University, School of Graduate Studies, College of Liberal Arts, Department of Psychology, Baltimore, MD 21251. Offers psychometrics (MS, PhD). *Entrance requirements:* For master's and doctorate, GRE.

Mount Aloysius College, Program in Psychology, Cresson, PA 16630-1999. Offers MS. *Entrance requirements:* For master's, GRE General Test. Additional exam requirements/recommendations for international students: Recommended—TOEFL.

Mount Holyoke College, Department of Psychology and Education, South Hadley, MA 01075. Offers MA.

Murray State University, College of Humanities and Fine Arts, Program in Psychology, Murray, KY 42071. Offers clinical psychology (MA, MS); psychology (MA, MS). Part-time programs available. *Degree requirements:* For master's, one foreign language, comprehensive exam (for some programs), thesis. *Entrance requirements:* For master's, GRE General Test. Additional exam requirements/recommendations for international students: Required—TOEFL.

National Louis University, College of Arts and Sciences, Chicago, IL 60603. Offers adult education (Ed D); counseling and human services (MS); language and academic development (M Ed, Certificate); psychology (MA, PhD, Certificate); public policy (MA); written communication (MS, Certificate). Part-time and evening/weekend programs available. Postbaccalaureate distance learning degree programs offered (minimal on-campus study). *Degree requirements:* For master's and Certificate, comprehensive exam (for some programs), thesis (for some programs); for doctorate, thesis/dissertation. *Entrance requirements:* For master's, MAT or GRE, 3 professional or academic references, interview, minimum GPA of 3.0; for doctorate, GRE General Test, MAT, or Watson-Glaser Critical Thinking Appraisal, three professional or academic references, statement of academic and professional goals, 3 years of experience in field, interview, master's degree, resume, writing sample; for Certificate, GRE, MAT, or Watson-Glaser Critical Thinking Appraisal, three professional or academic references, statement of academic and professional goals, interview, minimum GPA of 3.0.

Additional exam requirements/recommendations for international students: Required—Department of Language Studies Assessment or TOEFL (minimum score 550 paper-based; 79 iBT). Electronic applications accepted.

National University, Academic Affairs, College of Letters and Sciences, La Jolla, CA 92037-1011. Offers applied linguistics (MA); biology (MS); counseling psychology (MA), including licensed professional clinical counseling; marriage and family therapy; creative writing (MFA); English (MA), including Gothic studies, rhetoric; film studies (MA); forensic and crime science (Certificate); forensic studies (MFS), including criminalistics, investigation; history (MA); human behavior (MA); mathematics for educators (MS); performance psychology (MA); strategic communications (MA). Part-time and evening/weekend programs available. Postbaccalaureate distance learning degree programs offered (no on-campus study). *Faculty:* 69 full-time (34 women), 100 part-time/adjunct (55 women). *Students:* 727 full-time (532 women), 349 part-time (240 women); includes 505 minority (128 Black or African American, non-Hispanic/Latino; 5 American Indian or Alaska Native, non-Hispanic/Latino; 52 Asian, non-Hispanic/Latino; 260 Hispanic/Latino; 9 Native Hawaiian or other Pacific Islander, non-Hispanic/Latino; 51 Two or more races, non-Hispanic/Latino), 4 international. Average age 34. In 2014, 569 master's awarded. *Degree requirements:* For master's, thesis (for some programs). *Entrance requirements:* For master's, interview, minimum GPA of 2.5. Additional exam requirements/recommendations for international students: Required—TOEFL (minimum score 550 paper-based; 79 iBT), IELTS (minimum score 6). *Application deadline:* Applications are processed on a rolling basis. Application fee: $60 ($65 for international students). Electronic applications accepted. *Expenses: Tuition:* Full-time $14,184; part-time $1773 per course. *Financial support:* Career-related internships or fieldwork, institutionally sponsored loans, scholarships/grants, and tuition waivers (partial) available. Support available to part-time students. Financial award application deadline: 6/30; financial award applicants required to submit FAFSA. *Unit head:* College of Letters and Sciences, 800-628-8648, E-mail: cols@nu.edu. *Application contact:* Frank Rojas, Interim Vice President for Enrollment Services, 800-628-8648, E-mail: advisor@nu.edu.
Website: http://www.nu.edu/OurPrograms/CollegeOfLettersAndSciences.html

New Mexico Highlands University, Graduate Studies, College of Arts and Sciences, Department of Social and Behavioral Sciences, Las Vegas, NM 87701. Offers psychology (MS), including clinical psychology/counseling, general psychology; public affairs (MA), including applied sociology; Southwest studies (MA), including anthropology. Part-time programs available. *Faculty:* 11 full-time (5 women), 3 part-time/adjunct (all women). *Students:* 24 full-time (16 women), 19 part-time (14 women); includes 27 minority (3 Black or African American, non-Hispanic/Latino; 1 American Indian or Alaska Native, non-Hispanic/Latino; 23 Hispanic/Latino), 2 international. Average age 33. 45 applicants, 33% accepted, 15 enrolled. In 2014, 7 master's awarded. *Degree requirements:* For master's, comprehensive exam, thesis or alternative. *Entrance requirements:* For master's, minimum undergraduate GPA of 3.0. Additional exam requirements/recommendations for international students: Required—TOEFL (minimum score 540 paper-based). *Application deadline:* For fall admission, 8/1 priority date for domestic students. Applications are processed on a rolling basis. Application fee: $15. *Financial support:* In 2014–15, 34 teaching assistantships were awarded; career-related internships or fieldwork, Federal Work-Study, institutionally sponsored loans, scholarships/grants, tuition waivers (full and partial), and unspecified assistantships also available. Support available to part-time students. Financial award application deadline: 3/1; financial award applicants required to submit FAFSA. *Faculty research:* Southwest Native American resettlement development, community-level interventions, neurochemistry of personality, comparative criminal justice, social theory and activism. *Unit head:* Dr. Tom Ward, Program Coordinator, 505-454-3196, E-mail: tsward@nmhu.edu. *Application contact:* Diane Trujillo, Administrative Assistant for Graduate Studies, 505-454-3266, Fax: 505-426-2117, E-mail: dtrujillo@nmhu.edu.

New Mexico State University, College of Arts and Sciences, Department of Psychology, Las Cruces, NM 88003-8001. Offers cognitive psychology (PhD); engineering psychology (PhD); experimental psychology (MA); social psychology (PhD). Part-time programs available. *Faculty:* 11 full-time (3 women). *Students:* 31 full-time (15 women), 5 part-time (2 women); includes 7 minority (2 Asian, non-Hispanic/Latino; 3 Hispanic/Latino; 2 Two or more races, non-Hispanic/Latino), 5 international. Average age 29. 56 applicants, 27% accepted, 10 enrolled. In 2014, 6 master's, 5 doctorates awarded. *Degree requirements:* For master's, thesis; for doctorate, comprehensive exam, thesis/dissertation, work-related experience (teaching or internship). *Entrance requirements:* For master's, GRE General Test, letters of recommendation, curriculum vitae, personal statement; for doctorate, GRE General Test, letters of recommendation, master's thesis, curriculum vitae, personal statement. Additional exam requirements/recommendations for international students: Required—TOEFL (minimum score 550 paper-based; 79 iBT), IELTS (minimum score 6.5). *Application deadline:* For fall admission, 2/1 priority date for domestic students, 2/1 for international students. Applications are processed on a rolling basis. Application fee: $40 ($50 for international students). Electronic applications accepted. *Expenses:* Tuition, state resident: full-time $3969; part-time $220.50 per credit hour. Tuition, nonresident: full-time $13,838; part-time $768.80 per credit hour. *Required fees:* $853; $47.40 per credit hour. *Financial support:* In 2014–15, 34 students received support, including 7 fellowships (averaging $3,970 per year), 4 research assistantships (averaging $14,330 per year), 20 teaching assistantships (averaging $9,979 per year); career-related internships or fieldwork, Federal Work-Study, scholarships/grants, traineeships, health care benefits, and unspecified assistantships also available. Support available to part-time students. Financial award application deadline: 3/1. *Faculty research:* Engineering, cognitive, and social psychology; human/computer interaction; cognitive science. *Total annual research expenditures:* $184,443. *Unit head:* Dr. Dominic A. Simon, Academic Department Head, 575-646-2502, Fax: 575-646-6212, E-mail: domsimon@nmsu.edu. *Application contact:* Dr. Laura J. Madson, Chair of Graduate Committee, 575-646-6207, Fax: 575-646-6212, E-mail: lmadson@nmsu.edu.
Website: http://psych.nmsu.edu

The New School, The New School for Social Research, Department of Psychology, New York, NY 10011. Offers clinical psychology (PhD); cognitive, social and developmental psychology (PhD); general psychology (MA). *Accreditation:* APA (one or more programs are accredited). Part-time programs available. Terminal master's awarded for partial completion of doctoral program. *Degree requirements:* For master's, comprehensive exam (for some programs), thesis (for some programs); for doctorate, thesis/dissertation, qualifying exam. *Entrance requirements:* For master's, GRE General Test; for doctorate, GRE General Test, MA. Additional exam requirements/recommendations for international students: Required—TOEFL (minimum score 600 paper-based; 100 iBT). Electronic applications accepted. *Faculty research:* Consciousness, memory, language, perceptions, psychopathology.

New York University, Graduate School of Arts and Science, Department of Psychology, New York, NY 10012-1019. Offers cognition and perception (PhD); community psychology (PhD); general psychology (MA); industrial/organizational psychology (MA); psychotherapy and psychoanalysis (Advanced Certificate); social/personality psychology (PhD). Part-time programs available. *Students:* 270 full-time (183 women), 162 part-time (115 women); includes 92 minority (14 Black or African American, non-Hispanic/Latino; 36 Asian, non-Hispanic/Latino; 33 Hispanic/Latino; 9

Two or more races, non-Hispanic/Latino), 114 international. Average age 31. 874 applicants, 46% accepted, 153 enrolled. In 2014, 102 master's, 9 doctorates, 10 other advanced degrees awarded. Terminal master's awarded for partial completion of doctoral program. *Degree requirements:* For master's, comprehensive exam, thesis or alternative; for doctorate, thesis/dissertation. *Entrance requirements:* For master's and doctorate, GRE General Test. Additional exam requirements/recommendations for international students: Required—TOEFL. *Application deadline:* For fall admission, 12/12 for domestic and international students. Application fee: $100. *Financial support:* Fellowships with tuition reimbursements, research assistantships with tuition reimbursements, teaching assistantships with tuition reimbursements, career-related internships or fieldwork, Federal Work-Study, institutionally sponsored loans, scholarships/grants, traineeships, health care benefits, and unspecified assistantships available. Financial award application deadline: 12/12; financial award applicants required to submit FAFSA. *Faculty research:* Vision, memory, social cognition, social and cognitive development, relationships. *Unit head:* Gabriele Oettingen, Director of Graduate Studies, PhD Program, 212-998-7900, Fax: 212-995-4018, E-mail: psychq@psych.nyu.edu. *Application contact:* Adrienne Gans, Director of Graduate Studies, MA Program, 212-998-7900, Fax: 212-995-4018, E-mail: psychq@psych.nyu.edu.
Website: http://www.psych.nyu.edu/

New York University, Steinhardt School of Culture, Education, and Human Development, Department of Applied Psychology, Programs in Educational and Developmental Psychology, New York, NY 10003. Offers developmental psychology (PhD); human development and social intervention (MA); psychology and social intervention (PhD). *Accreditation:* APA (one or more programs are accredited). Part-time programs available. *Faculty:* 24 full-time (16 women). *Students:* 54 full-time (44 women), 6 part-time (all women); includes 23 minority (7 Black or African American, non-Hispanic/Latino; 5 Asian, non-Hispanic/Latino; 10 Hispanic/Latino; 1 Two or more races, non-Hispanic/Latino), 10 international. Average age 27. 137 applicants, 26% accepted, 13 enrolled. In 2014, 16 master's, 4 doctorates awarded. *Degree requirements:* For master's, thesis (for some programs); for doctorate, thesis/dissertation. *Entrance requirements:* For doctorate, GRE General Test, interview. Additional exam requirements/recommendations for international students: Required—TOEFL. *Application deadline:* For fall admission, 12/1 priority date for domestic and international students. Applications are processed on a rolling basis. Application fee: $75. Electronic applications accepted. *Financial support:* Teaching assistantships with partial tuition reimbursements, career-related internships or fieldwork, Federal Work-Study, institutionally sponsored loans, and tuition waivers (partial) available. Support available to part-time students. Financial award application deadline: 2/1; financial award applicants required to submit FAFSA. *Faculty research:* Schools and communities, self-regulation and academic achievement, intervention and social change, trauma and resilience, cognition. *Unit head:* Prof. Clancy Blair, Director, 212-998-5853, Fax: 212-995-4358, E-mail: clancy.blair@nyu.edu. *Application contact:* 212-998-5030, Fax: 212-995-4328, E-mail: steinhardt.gradadmissions@nyu.edu.
Website: http://steinhardt.nyu.edu/appsych

Norfolk State University, School of Graduate Studies, School of Liberal Arts, Department of Psychology, Norfolk, VA 23504. Offers community/clinical psychology (MA); psychology (Psy D). Psy D offered through the Virginia Consortium for Professional Psychology. Part-time programs available. *Degree requirements:* For master's, comprehensive exam, thesis or alternative; for doctorate, comprehensive exam, thesis/dissertation. *Entrance requirements:* For master's, minimum GPA of 2.7.

North Carolina Central University, College of Behavioral and Social Sciences, Department of Psychology, Durham, NC 27707-3129. Offers MA. Part-time and evening/weekend programs available. *Degree requirements:* For master's, one foreign language, comprehensive exam, thesis. *Entrance requirements:* For master's, GRE, minimum GPA of 3.0 in major, 2.5 overall. Additional exam requirements/recommendations for international students: Required—TOEFL. *Faculty research:* Aggression, hypertension, faces, anger, teaching.

North Carolina State University, Graduate School, College of Humanities and Social Sciences, Department of Psychology, Raleigh, NC 27695. Offers developmental psychology (PhD); ergonomics and experimental psychology (PhD); industrial/organizational psychology (PhD); psychology in the public interest (PhD); school psychology (PhD). *Accreditation:* APA. *Degree requirements:* For doctorate, comprehensive exam, thesis/dissertation. *Entrance requirements:* For doctorate, GRE General Test, GRE Subject Test (industrial/organizational psychology), MAT (recommended), minimum GPA of 3.0 in major. Electronic applications accepted. *Faculty research:* Cognitive and social development (human factors, families, the workplace, community issues and health, aging).

Northcentral University, Graduate Studies, Prescott Valley, AZ 86314. Offers business (MBA, DBA, PhD, Post-Master's Certificate, Postbaccalaureate Certificate); education (M Ed, Ed D, PhD, Ed S, Post-Master's Certificate, Postbaccalaureate Certificate); marriage and family therapy (MA, PhD, Post-Master's Certificate, Postbaccalaureate Certificate); psychology (MA, PhD, Post-Master's Certificate, Postbaccalaureate Certificate). Part-time and evening/weekend programs available. Postbaccalaureate distance learning degree programs offered (no on-campus study). *Faculty:* 128 full-time (79 women), 378 part-time/adjunct (178 women). *Students:* 3,058 full-time (1,942 women), 10,343 part-time (6,423 women); includes 5,141 minority (3,568 Black or African American, non-Hispanic/Latino; 122 American Indian or Alaska Native, non-Hispanic/Latino; 257 Asian, non-Hispanic/Latino; 684 Hispanic/Latino; 61 Native Hawaiian or other Pacific Islander, non-Hispanic/Latino; 449 Two or more races, non-Hispanic/Latino). Average age 46. In 2014, 331 master's, 166 doctorates, 25 other advanced degrees awarded. *Entrance requirements:* For master's, bachelor's degree from regionally- or nationally-accredited institution, current resume or curriculum vitae, statement of intent, interview, and background check (for marriage and family therapy); for doctorate, post-baccalaureate master's degree and/or doctoral degree from nationally- or regionally-accredited academic institution; for other advanced degree, bachelor's-level or higher degree from accredited institution or university (for Post-Baccalaureate Certificate); master's and/or doctoral degree from regionally- or nationally-accredited academic institution (for Post-Master's Certificate). Additional exam requirements/recommendations for international students: Required—TOEFL (minimum score 95 iBT), IELTS (minimum score 6) or PTE (minimum score 65). *Application deadline:* Applications are processed on a rolling basis. Application fee: $0. Electronic applications accepted. *Expenses: Tuition:* Full-time $15,330; part-time $2550 per course. *Required fees:* $2550 per course. *Financial support:* Scholarships/grants available. *Faculty research:* Business management, curriculum and instruction, educational leadership, health psychology, organizational behavior. *Unit head:* Dr. Jim Dorris, Interim Provost and Chief Academic Officer, 888-327-2877, Fax: 928-759-6381, E-mail: provost@ncu.edu. *Application contact:* Ken Boutelle, Vice President, Enrollment Services, 480-253-3535, E-mail: kboutelle@ncu.edu.

North Dakota State University, College of Graduate and Interdisciplinary Studies, College of Science and Mathematics, Department of Psychology, Fargo, ND 58108. Offers clinical psychology (MS); cognitive and visual neuroscience (PhD); health and social psychology (PhD); psychology (MS). *Degree requirements:* For master's, thesis;

for doctorate, thesis/dissertation. *Entrance requirements:* For master's and doctorate, GRE General Test, GRE Subject Test. Additional exam requirements/recommendations for international students: Required—TOEFL (minimum score 525 paper-based; 71 iBT). Electronic applications accepted. *Faculty research:* Cognition science, neuropsychology, group behavior, applied behavior analysis, behavior therapy.

Northeastern State University, College of Education, Department of Psychology and Counseling, Tahlequah, OK 74464-2399. Offers counseling psychology (MS); school counseling (M Ed); substance abuse counseling (MS). Part-time and evening/weekend programs available. *Faculty:* 12 full-time (6 women), 4 part-time/adjunct (2 women). *Students:* 80 full-time (67 women), 70 part-time (61 women); includes 47 minority (8 Black or African American, non-Hispanic/Latino; 21 American Indian or Alaska Native, non-Hispanic/Latino; 1 Asian, non-Hispanic/Latino; 5 Hispanic/Latino; 12 Two or more races, non-Hispanic/Latino), 2 international. Average age 34. In 2014, 43 master's awarded. *Degree requirements:* For master's, thesis (for some programs), written and oral examinations. *Entrance requirements:* For master's, GRE, minimum GPA of 2.5. Application fee: $25. *Expenses:* Tuition, state resident: part-time $178.75 per credit hour. Tuition, nonresident: part-time $451.75 per credit hour. *Required fees:* $37.40 per credit hour. *Financial support:* Teaching assistantships, career-related internships or fieldwork, and Federal Work-Study available. Financial award application deadline: 3/1. *Unit head:* Dr. Kenny Paris, Department Chair of Psychology and Counseling, 918-444-3021, E-mail: parisk@nsuok.edu. *Application contact:* Margie Railey, Administrative Assistant, 918-456-5511 Ext. 2093, Fax: 918-458-2061, E-mail: railey@nsouk.edu.
Website: https://academics.nsuok.edu/education/EducationHome/COEDepartments/PsychologyCounseling.aspx

Northern Arizona University, Graduate College, College of Social and Behavioral Sciences, Department of Psychology, Flagstaff, AZ 86011. Offers clinical health psychology (MA); general psychology (MA); teaching psychology (MA). Part-time programs available. *Degree requirements:* For master's, comprehensive exam (for some programs), thesis (for some programs), oral defense. *Entrance requirements:* For master's, GRE General Test. Additional exam requirements/recommendations for international students: Required—TOEFL (minimum score 550 paper-based; 80 iBT), IELTS (minimum score 7). Electronic applications accepted.

Northern Illinois University, Graduate School, College of Liberal Arts and Sciences, Department of Psychology, De Kalb, IL 60115-2854. Offers MA, PhD. *Accreditation:* APA (one or more programs are accredited). *Faculty:* 26 full-time (11 women), 5 part-time/adjunct (1 woman). *Students:* 115 full-time (86 women), 10 part-time (4 women); includes 16 minority (5 Black or African American, non-Hispanic/Latino; 1 American Indian or Alaska Native, non-Hispanic/Latino; 8 Hispanic/Latino; 2 Two or more races, non-Hispanic/Latino), 7 international. Average age 29. 418 applicants, 11% accepted, 19 enrolled. In 2014, 20 master's, 23 doctorates awarded. *Degree requirements:* For master's, comprehensive exam, thesis optional; for doctorate, thesis/dissertation, candidacy exam, dissertation defense. *Entrance requirements:* For master's, GRE General Test, minimum GPA of 3.0 for last 2 years of undergraduate work; for doctorate, GRE General Test, minimum undergraduate GPA of 2.75, graduate 3.2; master's degree with research thesis. Additional exam requirements/recommendations for international students: Required—TOEFL (minimum score 550 paper-based). *Application deadline:* For fall admission, 3/1 for domestic students, 5/1 for international students; for spring admission, 11/1 for domestic students, 10/1 for international students. Applications are processed on a rolling basis. Application fee: $40. Electronic applications accepted. *Financial support:* In 2014–15, 27 research assistantships with full tuition reimbursements, 66 teaching assistantships with full tuition reimbursements were awarded; fellowships with full tuition reimbursements, career-related internships or fieldwork, Federal Work-Study, scholarships/grants, tuition waivers (full), and staff assistantships also available. Support available to part-time students. Financial award applicants required to submit FAFSA. *Faculty research:* Neglect syndrome, ADHD, workplace discrimination, adolescent suicide, social dilemmas. *Unit head:* Dr. Gregory A. Waas, Chair, 815-753-7065, E-mail: gwaas@niu.edu. *Application contact:* Dr. James V. Corwin, Director, Graduate Studies, 815-753-7088, E-mail: jcorwin@niu.edu.
Website: http://www.niu.edu/psyc/

Northern Michigan University, Office of Graduate Education and Research, College of Arts and Sciences, Department of Psychology, Marquette, MI 49855-5301. Offers applied behavior analysis (MS); performance improvement (Graduate Certificate); psychology (MS); training and performance improvement (MS). Part-time programs available. *Faculty:* 8 full-time (3 women), 1 part-time/adjunct. *Students:* 32 full-time (17 women), 17 part-time (10 women); includes 9 minority (2 Black or African American, non-Hispanic/Latino; 3 American Indian or Alaska Native, non-Hispanic/Latino; 3 Hispanic/Latino; 1 Two or more races, non-Hispanic/Latino). Average age 29. 38 applicants, 55% accepted, 13 enrolled. In 2014, 7 master's, 14 other advanced degrees awarded. *Degree requirements:* For master's, thesis (for some programs). *Entrance requirements:* For master's, minimum GPA of 3.0; bachelor's degree preferably in psychology; undergraduate course on introduction to psychology; undergraduate course on statistics; personal statement; 3 letters of recommendation. Additional exam requirements/recommendations for international students: Required—TOEFL (minimum score 550 paper-based; 79 iBT), IELTS (minimum score 6.5). *Application deadline:* For fall admission, 7/1 for domestic students; for winter admission, 11/15 for domestic students; for spring admission, 3/17 for domestic students. Applications are processed on a rolling basis. Application fee: $50. Electronic applications accepted. *Expenses:* Tuition, state resident: full-time $7716; part-time $441 per credit hour. Tuition, nonresident: full-time $10,812; part-time $634.50 per credit hour. *Required fees:* $31.88 per semester. Tuition and fees vary according to course load, degree level and program. *Financial support:* In 2014–15, teaching assistantships with full tuition reimbursements (averaging $8,898 per year) were awarded; Federal Work-Study, institutionally sponsored loans, scholarships/grants, and unspecified assistantships also available. Support available to part-time students. Financial award application deadline: 3/1; financial award applicants required to submit FAFSA. *Faculty research:* Emotion and cognition, neuropsychopharmacology, sensation and perception, behavior analysis, developmental psychology. *Unit head:* Dr. Paul Andronis, Department Head, 906-227-2935, E-mail: pandroni@nmu.edu. *Application contact:* Dr. Brian Cherry, Assistant Provost of Graduate Education and Research, 906-227-2300, Fax: 906-227-2315, E-mail: graduate@nmu.edu.
Website: http://psychology.nmu.edu

Northwestern State University of Louisiana, Graduate Studies and Research, Department of Psychology, Natchitoches, LA 71497. Offers clinical psychology (MS). *Degree requirements:* For master's, comprehensive exam, thesis or alternative. *Entrance requirements:* For master's, GRE General Test, GRE Subject Test, minimum undergraduate GPA of 2.5. Additional exam requirements/recommendations for international students: Required—TOEFL. Electronic applications accepted.

Northwestern University, The Graduate School, Judd A. and Marjorie Weinberg College of Arts and Sciences, Department of Psychology, Evanston, IL 60208. Offers brain, behavior and cognition (PhD); clinical psychology (PhD); cognitive psychology (PhD); personality psychology (PhD); social psychology (PhD); JD/PhD. Admissions and degrees offered through The Graduate School. *Accreditation:* APA (one or more programs are accredited). Part-time programs available. *Degree requirements:* For doctorate, thesis/dissertation. *Entrance requirements:* For doctorate, GRE General Test, GRE Subject Test. Additional exam requirements/recommendations for international students: Required—TOEFL. Electronic applications accepted. *Faculty research:* Memory and higher order cognition, anxiety and depression, effectiveness of psychotherapy, social cognition, molecular basis of memory.

Northwest Missouri State University, Graduate School, College of Education and Human Services, Department of Psychology and Sociology, Maryville, MO 64468-6001. Offers guidance and counseling (MS Ed); sport and exercise psychology (MS). Part-time programs available. *Degree requirements:* For master's, comprehensive exam, thesis. *Entrance requirements:* For master's, GRE General Test, minimum undergraduate GPA of 2.5, 3.0 in major; writing sample. Additional exam requirements/recommendations for international students: Required—TOEFL (minimum score 550 paper-based). *Application deadline:* For fall admission, 3/1 for domestic and international students. Applications are processed on a rolling basis. Application fee: $0 ($50 for international students). Electronic applications accepted. *Expenses:* Tuition, state resident: full-time $4464; part-time $346 per credit hour. Tuition, nonresident: full-time $8920; part-time $593 per credit hour. *Required fees:* $1763; $98 per credit hour. *Financial support:* Research assistantships with full tuition reimbursements, teaching assistantships with full tuition reimbursements, and unspecified assistantships available. Financial award application deadline: 4/1; financial award applicants required to submit FAFSA. *Unit head:* Dr. Rochelle Hiatt, Chairperson, 660-562-1287.
Website: http://www.nwmissouri.edu/behavioralsciences/

Northwest University, College of Social and Behavioral Sciences, Kirkland, WA 98033. Offers counseling psychology (MA, Psy D); international community development (MA). Evening/weekend programs available. *Faculty:* 5 full-time (2 women), 17 part-time/adjunct (5 women). *Students:* 223 full-time (185 women), 55 part-time (41 women); includes 74 minority (13 Black or African American, non-Hispanic/Latino; 3 American Indian or Alaska Native, non-Hispanic/Latino; 30 Asian, non-Hispanic/Latino; 15 Hispanic/Latino; 1 Native Hawaiian or other Pacific Islander, non-Hispanic/Latino; 12 Two or more races, non-Hispanic/Latino), 6 international. Average age 37. 122 applicants, 80% accepted, 62 enrolled. In 2014, 56 master's, 3 doctorates awarded. *Entrance requirements:* For master's, 3 character references. Additional exam requirements/recommendations for international students: Required—TOEFL (minimum score 580 paper-based). *Application deadline:* For fall admission, 12/1 priority date for domestic and international students; for spring admission, 4/1 priority date for domestic and international students. Applications are processed on a rolling basis. Application fee: $75. *Expenses:* Expenses: Contact institution. *Financial support:* In 2014–15, 13 students received support. Career-related internships or fieldwork, health care benefits, and international student scholarships available. Financial award application deadline: 6/30. *Unit head:* Dr. Matt Nelson, Dean, 425-889-5328, E-mail: matt.nelson@northwestu.edu. *Application contact:* Daniela Zuniga, Enrollment Counselor, College of Social and Behavioral Sciences, 425-889-5249, E-mail: daniela.zuniga@northwestu.edu.
Website: http://www.northwestu.edu/social_behavioral

Notre Dame de Namur University, Division of Academic Affairs, College of Arts and Sciences, Department of Clinical Psychology and Gerontology, Belmont, CA 94002-1908. Offers clinical psychology (MS); clinical psychology: marital and family therapy (MS). Part-time programs available. *Degree requirements:* For master's, thesis. *Entrance requirements:* For master's, interview, minimum GPA of 2.5. Additional exam requirements/recommendations for international students: Required—TOEFL (minimum score 550 paper-based; 79 iBT). Electronic applications accepted.

Nova Southeastern University, Center for Psychological Studies, Fort Lauderdale, FL 33314-7796. Offers clinical psychology (PhD, Psy D); counseling (MS); general psychology (MS); mental health counseling (MS); school counseling (MS). *Accreditation:* APA (one or more programs are accredited). Postbaccalaureate distance learning degree programs offered. *Faculty:* 50 full-time (19 women), 119 part-time/adjunct (69 women). *Students:* 1,827 (1,560 women); includes 842 minority (289 Black or African American, non-Hispanic/Latino; 2 American Indian or Alaska Native, non-Hispanic/Latino; 45 Asian, non-Hispanic/Latino; 478 Hispanic/Latino; 28 Two or more races, non-Hispanic/Latino), 41 international. Average age 31. 1,186 applicants, 51% accepted, 398 enrolled. In 2014, 344 master's, 117 doctorates, 10 other advanced degrees awarded. Terminal master's awarded for partial completion of doctoral program. *Degree requirements:* For master's, comprehensive exam, 3 practica; for doctorate, thesis/dissertation, clinical internship, competency exam; for Psy S, comprehensive exam, internship. *Entrance requirements:* For doctorate, GRE General Test, GRE Subject Test (recommended), minimum undergraduate GPA of 3.0; for Psy S, GRE General Test. Additional exam requirements/recommendations for international students: Required—TOEFL (minimum score 550 paper-based). *Application deadline:* Applications are processed on a rolling basis. Application fee: $50. Electronic applications accepted. *Expenses:* Expenses: Contact institution. *Financial support:* In 2014–15, 15 research assistantships, 68 teaching assistantships (averaging $4,800 per year) were awarded; career-related internships or fieldwork, Federal Work-Study, institutionally sponsored loans, scholarships/grants, and unspecified assistantships also available. Support available to part-time students. Financial award application deadline: 4/1. *Faculty research:* Clinical and child clinical psychology, geriatrics, interpersonal violence. *Unit head:* Karen Grosby, EdD, Dean, 954-262-5701, Fax: 954-262-3859, E-mail: grosby@nova.edu. *Application contact:* Carlos Perez, Enrollment Management, 954-262-5790, Fax: 954-262-3893, E-mail: cpsinfo@cps.nova.edu.
Website: http://www.cps.nova.edu/

The Ohio State University, Graduate School, College of Arts and Sciences, Division of Social and Behavioral Sciences, Department of Psychology, Columbus, OH 43210. Offers behavioral neuroscience (PhD); clinical psychology (PhD); cognitive psychology (PhD); developmental psychology (PhD); intellectual and developmental disabilities psychology (PhD); quantitative psychology (PhD); social psychology (PhD). *Accreditation:* APA. *Faculty:* 55. *Students:* 158 full-time (91 women); includes 26 minority (6 Black or African American, non-Hispanic/Latino; 2 American Indian or Alaska Native, non-Hispanic/Latino; 7 Asian, non-Hispanic/Latino; 9 Hispanic/Latino; 2 Two or more races, non-Hispanic/Latino), 23 international. Average age 27. In 2014, 12 doctorates awarded. *Degree requirements:* For doctorate, thesis/dissertation. *Entrance requirements:* For doctorate, GRE General Test. Additional exam requirements/recommendations for international students: Required—TOEFL (minimum score 600 paper-based; 100 iBT); Recommended—IELTS (minimum score 8). *Application deadline:* For fall admission, 12/1 for domestic and international students. Applications are processed on a rolling basis. Application fee: $60 ($70 for international students). Electronic applications accepted. *Financial support:* Fellowships with tuition reimbursements, research assistantships with tuition reimbursements, and teaching assistantships with tuition reimbursements available. *Unit head:* Dr. Richard Petty, Chair, 614-292-1640, E-mail: petty.1@osu.edu. *Application contact:* Graduate and Professional Admissions, 614-292-9444, Fax: 614-292-3895, E-mail: gpadmissions@osu.edu.
Website: http://www.psy.ohio-state.edu/

Ohio University, Graduate College, College of Arts and Sciences, Department of Psychology, Athens, OH 45701-2979. Offers clinical psychology (MS, PhD);

experimental psychology (MA, PhD); organizational psychology (MA, PhD). *Accreditation:* APA (one or more programs are accredited). *Degree requirements:* For doctorate, one foreign language, comprehensive exam, thesis/dissertation. *Entrance requirements:* For doctorate, GRE General Test, GRE Subject Test. Additional exam requirements/recommendations for international students: Required—TOEFL (minimum score 550 paper-based; 80 iBT) or IELTS (minimum score 6.5). Electronic applications accepted. *Faculty research:* Health, cognitive, child clinical, and social psychology.

Oklahoma State University, College of Arts and Sciences, Department of Psychology, Stillwater, OK 74078. Offers clinical psychology (PhD); general psychology (MS); lifespan development psychology (PhD). *Accreditation:* APA (one or more programs are accredited). *Faculty:* 31 full-time (16 women), 3 part-time/adjunct (2 women). *Students:* 39 full-time (27 women), 18 part-time (12 women); includes 12 minority (1 Black or African American, non-Hispanic/Latino; 5 American Indian or Alaska Native, non-Hispanic/Latino; 1 Hispanic/Latino; 1 Native Hawaiian or other Pacific Islander, non-Hispanic/Latino; 4 Two or more races, non-Hispanic/Latino), 2 international. Average age 27. 218 applicants, 7% accepted, 9 enrolled. In 2014, 9 master's, 9 doctorates awarded. *Degree requirements:* For master's, thesis or alternative; for doctorate, comprehensive exam, thesis/dissertation. *Entrance requirements:* For master's and doctorate, GRE General Test. Additional exam requirements/recommendations for international students: Required—TOEFL (minimum score 550 paper-based; 79 iBT). *Application deadline:* For fall admission, 3/1 priority date for international students; for spring admission, 8/1 priority date for international students. Applications are processed on a rolling basis. Application fee: $40 ($75 for international students). Electronic applications accepted. *Expenses:* Tuition, state resident: full-time $4488; part-time $187 per credit hour. Tuition, nonresident: full-time $18,360; part-time $765 per credit hour. *Required fees:* $2413; $100.55 per credit hour. Tuition and fees vary according to campus/location. *Financial support:* In 2014–15, 14 research assistantships (averaging $14,585 per year), 46 teaching assistantships (averaging $13,749 per year) were awarded; career-related internships or fieldwork, Federal Work-Study, scholarships/grants, health care benefits, tuition waivers (partial), and unspecified assistantships also available. Support available to part-time students. Financial award application deadline: 3/1; financial award applicants required to submit FAFSA. *Unit head:* Dr. Thad Leffingwell, Department Head, 405-744-7494, Fax: 405-744-8067, E-mail: thad.leffingwell@okstate.edu. *Application contact:* Patricia Alexander, Graduate Advisor, 405-744-7591, Fax: 405-744-8967, E-mail: patricia.alexander@okstate.edu.
Website: http://psychology.okstate.edu

Old Dominion University, College of Sciences, Doctoral Program in Psychology, Norfolk, VA 23529. Offers applied experimental psychology (PhD); human factors psychology (PhD). *Faculty:* 22 full-time (7 women). *Students:* 35 full-time (16 women), 17 part-time (13 women); includes 8 minority (3 Black or African American, non-Hispanic/Latino; 5 Hispanic/Latino), 3 international. Average age 27. 82 applicants, 30% accepted, 7 enrolled. In 2014, 5 doctorates awarded. *Degree requirements:* For doctorate, thesis/dissertation, candidacy exam. *Entrance requirements:* For doctorate, GRE General Test, GRE Subject Test, 3 recommendation letters. Additional exam requirements/recommendations for international students: Required—TOEFL. *Application deadline:* For winter admission, 1/5 for domestic and international students. Application fee: $50. Electronic applications accepted. *Expenses:* Tuition, state resident: full-time $10,488; part-time $437 per credit. Tuition, nonresident: full-time $26,136; part-time $1089 per credit. *Required fees:* $64 per semester. One-time fee: $50. *Financial support:* In 2014–15, 42 students received support, including 4 research assistantships with full tuition reimbursements available (averaging $17,500 per year), 38 teaching assistantships with full tuition reimbursements available (averaging $17,500 per year). Financial award application deadline: 1/15. *Faculty research:* Human factors, industrial psychology, organizational psychology, applied experimental (health, developmental, quantitative). *Total annual research expenditures:* $978,563. *Unit head:* Dr. Bryan E. Porter, Graduate Program Director, 757-683-4458, Fax: 757-683-5087, E-mail: bporter@odu.edu. *Application contact:* William Heffelfinger, Director of Graduate Admissions, 757-683-5554, Fax: 757-683-3255, E-mail: gradadmit@odu.edu.
Website: http://sci.odu.edu/psychology/

Old Dominion University, College of Sciences, Master of Science in Psychology Program, Norfolk, VA 23529. Offers MS. Part-time programs available. *Faculty:* 22 full-time (7 women). *Students:* 12 full-time (11 women), 5 part-time (all women); includes 4 minority (2 Black or African American, non-Hispanic/Latino; 2 Hispanic/Latino), 2 international. Average age 27. 67 applicants, 13% accepted, 7 enrolled. In 2014, 13 master's awarded. *Degree requirements:* For master's, comprehensive exam, thesis. *Entrance requirements:* For master's, GRE General Test, minimum GPA of 3.0 in major, previous course work in psychology. Additional exam requirements/recommendations for international students: Required—TOEFL. *Application deadline:* For fall admission, 5/15 for domestic and international students. Applications are processed on a rolling basis. Application fee: $50. Electronic applications accepted. *Expenses:* Tuition, state resident: full-time $10,488; part-time $437 per credit. Tuition, nonresident: full-time $26,136; part-time $1089 per credit. *Required fees:* $64 per semester. One-time fee: $50. *Financial support:* In 2014–15, 11 students received support, including 2 research assistantships with full tuition reimbursements available (averaging $12,000 per year), 9 teaching assistantships with full tuition reimbursements available (averaging $12,000 per year); career-related internships or fieldwork, scholarships/grants, and tuition waivers (partial) also available. Financial award application deadline: 2/15; financial award applicants required to submit FAFSA. *Faculty research:* Social psychology, developmental psychology, physiopsychology, clinical psychology, industrial/organizational psychology. *Unit head:* Dr. James M. Henson, Graduate Program Director, 757-683-5761, Fax: 757-683-5087, E-mail: jhenson@odu.edu. *Application contact:* William Heffelfinger, Director of Graduate Admissions, 757-683-5554, Fax: 757-683-3255, E-mail: gradadmit@odu.edu.
Website: http://sci.odu.edu/psychology/academics/ms.shtml

Our Lady of the Lake University of San Antonio, School of Professional Studies, Program in Psychology, San Antonio, TX 78207-4689. Offers counseling psychology (MS, Psy D); marriage and family therapy (MS); school psychology (MS). *Accreditation:* APA (one or more programs are accredited). Part-time and evening/weekend programs available. *Degree requirements:* For master's, comprehensive exam, thesis optional, practicum; for doctorate, thesis/dissertation, internship, qualifying exam. *Entrance requirements:* For master's and doctorate, GRE General Test or MAT, interview. Additional exam requirements/recommendations for international students: Required—TOEFL. Electronic applications accepted. *Faculty research:* Marriage and family therapy, supervision, cross-cultural counseling, violence.

Pace University, Dyson College of Arts and Sciences, Department of Psychology, Program in Psychology, New York, NY 10038. Offers MA. Part-time and evening/weekend programs available. *Students:* 22 full-time (19 women), 6 part-time (4 women); includes 9 minority (1 Black or African American, non-Hispanic/Latino; 2 Asian, non-Hispanic/Latino; 5 Hispanic/Latino; 1 Two or more races, non-Hispanic/Latino), 6 international. Average age 25. 67 applicants, 52% accepted, 18 enrolled. In 2014, 11 master's awarded. *Entrance requirements:* For master's, GRE, two letters of recommendation, resume, statement of purpose, all official transcripts. Additional exam requirements/recommendations for international students: Required—TOEFL (minimum score 100 iBT). *Application deadline:* For fall admission, 8/1 priority date for domestic students, 6/1 for international students; for spring admission, 12/1 for domestic students, 10/1 for international students. Applications are processed on a rolling basis. Application fee: $70. Electronic applications accepted. *Expenses: Tuition:* Part-time $1120 per credit. *Required fees:* $266 per semester. Tuition and fees vary according to course load, degree level and program. *Unit head:* Dr. Barbara Mowder, Director of Graduate Psychology Programs, 212-346-1556, E-mail: bmowder@pace.edu. *Application contact:* Susan Ford-Goldschein, Director of Graduate Admissions, 212-346-1531, Fax: 212-346-1585, E-mail: gradnyc@pace.edu.
Website: http://www.pace.edu/dyson/academic-departments-and-programs/psychology—-nyc/graduate-programs

Pacifica Graduate Institute, Graduate Programs, Carpinteria, CA 93013. Offers clinical psychology (PhD); counseling psychology (MA); depth psychology (MA, PhD); mythological studies (MA, PhD). Terminal master's awarded for partial completion of doctoral program. *Degree requirements:* For master's, thesis (for some programs), practicum; for doctorate, comprehensive exam, thesis/dissertation, internship. *Entrance requirements:* For master's, resume, 3 letters of recommendation, writing sample, interview; for doctorate, resumé, 4 letters of recommendation, writing sample, interview. Additional exam requirements/recommendations for international students: Required—TOEFL. *Faculty research:* Imaginal and archetypal theory; post-Colonial psychoanalytic and Jungian theory; myth literature as it applies to the theory and practice of psychology.

Pacific University, School of Professional Psychology, Forest Grove, OR 97116-1797. Offers clinical psychology (MS, Psy D); counseling psychology (MA). *Accreditation:* APA (one or more programs are accredited). Part-time programs available. *Degree requirements:* For master's, comprehensive exam (for some programs), thesis (for some programs); for doctorate, comprehensive exam, thesis/dissertation. *Entrance requirements:* For master's, course work in introductory psychology, statistics, and abnormal psychology; minimum GPA of 3.0; for doctorate, GRE General Test, minimum GPA of 3.0, undergraduate course work in psychology, minimum GPA of 3.1 in last 2 years. Additional exam requirements/recommendations for international students: Required—TOEFL (minimum score 600 paper-based). Electronic applications accepted. *Expenses:* Contact institution. *Faculty research:* Neuropsychological assessment, assessment and treatment of anxiety, forensic psychology, cross-cultural psychology, child and adolescent psychopathology.

Palo Alto University, MS in Psychology (PhD Prep) Program, Palo Alto, CA 94304. Offers MS. Part-time programs available. Postbaccalaureate distance learning degree programs offered (minimal on-campus study). *Faculty:* 3 part-time/adjunct (2 women). *Students:* 35 part-time (27 women); includes 16 minority (3 Black or African American, non-Hispanic/Latino; 1 American Indian or Alaska Native, non-Hispanic/Latino; 6 Asian, non-Hispanic/Latino; 6 Hispanic/Latino). Average age 31. 26 applicants, 96% accepted, 20 enrolled. In 2014, 10 master's awarded. *Degree requirements:* For master's, online program with a 1-week on-campus intensive. *Entrance requirements:* For master's, undergraduate degree in psychology with minimum GPA of 3.3. Additional exam requirements/recommendations for international students: Required—TOEFL. *Application deadline:* For fall admission, 6/30 priority date for domestic and international students. Applications are processed on a rolling basis. Application fee: $40. Electronic applications accepted. *Expenses:* Expenses: Contact institution. *Financial support:* In 2014–15, 1 student received support. Federal Work-Study and scholarships/grants available. Financial award application deadline: 1/15; financial award applicants required to submit FAFSA. *Unit head:* Dr. Kristel Nazzal, Associate Director, 650-417-2022, E-mail: knazzal@paloaltou.edu. *Application contact:* Deanna Berger, Assistant Director of Admissions, 650-417-2023, E-mail: dberger@paloaltou.edu.
Website: http://www.paloaltou.edu/graduate-programs/masters-degree-programs/ms-psychology-phd-prep

Palo Alto University, PhD in Clinical Psychology Program, Palo Alto, CA 94304. Offers PhD, JD/PhD, MBA/PhD. *Accreditation:* APA. *Faculty:* 32 full-time (20 women), 27 part-time/adjunct (16 women). *Students:* 410 full-time (320 women), 19 part-time (14 women); includes 118 minority (20 Black or African American, non-Hispanic/Latino; 1 American Indian or Alaska Native, non-Hispanic/Latino; 55 Asian, non-Hispanic/Latino; 31 Hispanic/Latino; 2 Native Hawaiian or other Pacific Islander, non-Hispanic/Latino; 9 Two or more races, non-Hispanic/Latino), 22 international. Average age 29. 237 applicants, 58% accepted, 82 enrolled. In 2014, 65 doctorates awarded. *Degree requirements:* For doctorate, comprehensive exam, thesis/dissertation, 2000-hour clinical internship. *Entrance requirements:* For doctorate, GRE General Test, undergraduate or graduate degree in psychology or related area; 4 course prerequisites: biopsychology, abnormal psychology, developmental psychology, and statistics. Additional exam requirements/recommendations for international students: Required—TOEFL, IELTS. *Application deadline:* For fall admission, 12/2 priority date for domestic and international students. Applications are processed on a rolling basis. Application fee: $50. Electronic applications accepted. *Expenses:* Expenses: Contact institution. *Financial support:* In 2014–15, 45 students received support, including fellowships (averaging $7,500 per year), research assistantships (averaging $4,000 per year), teaching assistantships (averaging $3,000 per year); Federal Work-Study and scholarships/grants also available. Financial award application deadline: 1/15; financial award applicants required to submit FAFSA. *Faculty research:* Forensic psychology, LGBT psychology, trauma, diversity and community mental health, neuropsychology. *Unit head:* Dr. Rowena Gomez, Director of Clinical Training, 650-433-3823, E-mail: rgomez@paloaltou.edu. *Application contact:* Eirian Williams, Vice President of Enrollment Management, 800-818-6136, E-mail: admissions@paloaltou.edu.
Website: http://www.paloaltou.edu/graduate-programs/phd-programs/phd-clinical-psychology

Penn State Harrisburg, Graduate School, School of Behavioral Sciences and Education, Middletown, PA 17057-4898. Offers applied behavior analysis (MA); applied clinical psychology (MA); applied psychological research (MA); community psychology and social change (MA); health education (M Ed); literacy education (M Ed); teaching and curriculum (M Ed); training and development (M Ed). Part-time and evening/weekend programs available. *Unit head:* Dr. Mukund S. Kulkarni, Chancellor, 717-948-6105, Fax: 717-948-6452, E-mail: msk5@psu.edu. *Application contact:* Robert W. Coffman, Jr., Director of Enrollment Management, Admissions, 717-948-6250, Fax: 717-948-6325, E-mail: ric1@psu.edu.
Website: http://harrisburg.psu.edu/behavioral-sciences-and-education/

Penn State University Park, Graduate School, College of the Liberal Arts, Department of Psychology, University Park, PA 16802. Offers MPS, MS, PhD. *Accreditation:* APA (one or more programs are accredited). *Unit head:* Dr. Susan Welch, Dean, 814-865-7691, Fax: 814-863-2085, E-mail: swelch@psu.edu. *Application contact:* Lori A. Stania, Director, Graduate Student Services, 814-867-5278, Fax: 814-863-4627, E-mail: gswww@psu.edu.
Website: http://psych.la.psu.edu/

Pepperdine University, Graduate School of Education and Psychology, Division of Psychology, Doctor of Psychology Program, Malibu, CA 90263. Offers Psy D. Part-time and evening/weekend programs available. *Students:* 106 full-time (89 women), 40 part-time (33 women); includes 53 minority (11 Black or African American, non-Hispanic/Latino; 1 American Indian or Alaska Native, non-Hispanic/Latino; 12 Asian, non-

Psychology—General

Hispanic/Latino; 26 Hispanic/Latino; 2 Native Hawaiian or other Pacific Islander, non-Hispanic/Latino; 1 Two or more races, non-Hispanic/Latino), 4 international. In 2014, 26 doctorates awarded. *Entrance requirements:* For doctorate, GRE General Test, GRE Subject Test (psychology), autobiographical statement of three to ten typed pages, brief resume of professional experience, two recommendations. Additional exam requirements/recommendations for international students: Required—TOEFL. *Application deadline:* For fall admission, 11/15 for domestic students. Application fee: $55. *Unit head:* Dr. Helen Williams, Dean, 310-568-5600, E-mail: helen.williams@pepperdine.edu. *Application contact:* Deanna Schwartz, Psychology Admissions Manager, 310-568-5777, E-mail: deanna.lazaro@pepperdine.edu. Website: http://gsep.pepperdine.edu/doctorate-clinical-psychology/

Pepperdine University, Graduate School of Education and Psychology, Division of Psychology, MA Program in Psychology, Malibu, CA 90263. Offers MA. Part-time and evening/weekend programs available. *Students:* 48 full-time (40 women), 96 part-time (75 women); includes 47 minority (13 Black or African American, non-Hispanic/Latino; 10 Asian, non-Hispanic/Latino; 19 Hispanic/Latino; 1 Native Hawaiian or other Pacific Islander, non-Hispanic/Latino; 4 Two or more races, non-Hispanic/Latino), 5 international. In 2014, 84 master's awarded. *Entrance requirements:* For master's, GRE (taken within last five years) or MAT (taken within last two years), two professional recommendations, two- to five-page typed personal statement. Additional exam requirements/recommendations for international students: Required—TOEFL. *Application deadline:* For fall admission, 6/1 for domestic students; for spring admission, 10/1 for domestic students. Applications are processed on a rolling basis. Application fee: $55. *Financial support:* Research assistantships and teaching assistantships available. Financial award application deadline: 7/1; financial award applicants required to submit FAFSA. *Unit head:* Dr. Helen Williams, Dean, 310-568-5600, E-mail: helen.williams@pepperdine.edu. *Application contact:* Deanna Schwartz, Psychology Admissions Manager, 310-568-5777, E-mail: deanna.lazaro@pepperdine.edu. Website: http://gsep.pepperdine.edu/masters-psychology/

 **Philadelphia College of Osteopathic Medicine,** Graduate and Professional Programs, Department of Psychology, Philadelphia, PA 19131. Offers applied behavior analysis (Certificate); clinical health psychology (Post-Doctoral Certificate); clinical neuropsychology (Post-Doctoral Certificate); clinical psychology (Psy D); mental health counseling (MS); organizational development and leadership (MS); psychology (Certificate); school psychology (MS, Psy D, Ed S). *Accreditation:* APA. *Faculty:* 19 full-time (11 women), 122 part-time/adjunct (58 women). *Students:* 395 (304 women); includes 80 minority (49 Black or African American, non-Hispanic/Latino; 13 Asian, non-Hispanic/Latino; 7 Hispanic/Latino; 11 Two or more races, non-Hispanic/Latino). 345 applicants, 47% accepted, 113 enrolled. In 2014, 72 master's, 42 doctorates, 17 other advanced degrees awarded. Terminal master's awarded for partial completion of doctoral program. *Degree requirements:* For master's, comprehensive exam (for some programs), thesis (for some programs); for doctorate, comprehensive exam, thesis/dissertation. *Entrance requirements:* For master's, GRE or MAT, minimum GPA of 3.0; bachelor's degree from regionally-accredited college or university; for doctorate, PRAXIS II (for Psy D in school psychology), minimum undergraduate GPA of 3.0; for other advanced degree, GRE (for Ed S). Additional exam requirements/recommendations for international students: Required—TOEFL (minimum score 79 iBT). *Application deadline:* For fall admission, 3/1 priority date for domestic students. Applications are processed on a rolling basis. Application fee: $50. Electronic applications accepted. *Financial support:* In 2014–15, 28 teaching assistantships were awarded; Federal Work-Study, institutionally sponsored loans, and scholarships/grants also available. Financial award application deadline: 3/15; financial award applicants required to submit FAFSA. *Faculty research:* Adult and childhood anxiety and ADHD; coping with chronic illness; primary care psychology/integrated health care; applied behavior analysis; psychological, educational, and neuropsychological assessment. *Total annual research expenditures:* $533,489. *Unit head:* Dr. Robert DiTomasso, Chairman, 215-871-6442, Fax: 215-871-6458, E-mail: robertd@pcom.edu. *Application contact:* Kari A. Shotwell, Director of Admissions, 215-871-6700, Fax: 215-871-6719, E-mail: karis@pcom.edu.

See Display on this page and Close-Up on page 1211.

Pittsburg State University, Graduate School, College of Education, Department of Psychology and Counseling, Program in Psychology, Pittsburg, KS 66762. Offers MS. *Degree requirements:* For master's, thesis or alternative. *Entrance requirements:* For master's, GRE General Test, minimum GPA of 2.8.

Pontifical Catholic University of Puerto Rico, College of Graduate Studies in Behavioral Science and Community Affairs, Ponce, PR 00717-0777. Offers clinical psychology (PhD, Psy D); clinical social work (MSW); criminology (MA); industrial psychology (PhD); psychology (PhD); public administration (MSS); rehabilitation counseling (MA). Part-time and evening/weekend programs available. *Degree requirements:* For master's, thesis; for doctorate, comprehensive exam, thesis/dissertation. *Entrance requirements:* For master's, EXADEP, GRE General Test, 3 letters of recommendation, interview, minimum GPA of 2.75.

Pontificia Universidad Catolica Madre y Maestra, Graduate School, Faculty of Social and Administrative Sciences, Santiago, Dominican Republic. Offers business administration (MBA), including business development, finance, international business, management skills (M Mgmt, MBA), marketing, operations, strategic cost management, strategy, tourist destination planning and management; law (LL M), including civil law, corporate business law, criminal law, international relations, real estate law; management (M Mgmt), including higher financial management, insurance program administration, management skills (M Mgmt, MBA); psychology (MA), including clinical child and adolescent psychology, forensic psychology; strategic human resources (EMBA).

Portland State University, Graduate Studies, College of Liberal Arts and Sciences, Department of Psychology, Portland, OR 97207-0751. Offers MA, MS, PhD. *Faculty:* 18 full-time (8 women), 17 part-time/adjunct (6 women). *Students:* 48 full-time (35 women), 5 part-time (4 women); includes 8 minority (1 American Indian or Alaska Native, non-Hispanic/Latino; 1 Asian, non-Hispanic/Latino; 4 Hispanic/Latino; 2 Two or more races, non-Hispanic/Latino), 1 international. Average age 30. 196 applicants, 8% accepted, 15 enrolled. In 2014, 7 master's, 10 doctorates awarded. *Degree requirements:* For master's, variable foreign language requirement, thesis; for doctorate, variable foreign language requirement, comprehensive exam, thesis/dissertation. *Entrance requirements:* Additional exam requirements/recommendations for international students: Required—TOEFL (minimum score 550 paper-based). *Application deadline:* For fall admission, 12/15 for domestic and international students. Application fee: $50. *Expenses:* Tuition, state resident: part-time $222 per credit. Tuition, nonresident: part-time $527 per credit. *Required fees:* $22 per contact hour. $100 per quarter. Tuition and fees vary according to program. *Financial support:* In 2014–15, 10 research assistantships with full and partial tuition reimbursements (averaging $9,821 per year), 29 teaching assistantships with full and partial tuition reimbursements (averaging $10,138 per year) were awarded; career-related internships or fieldwork, Federal Work-Study, scholarships/grants, tuition waivers (partial), and unspecified assistantships also available. Support available to part-time students. Financial award application deadline:

3/1; financial award applicants required to submit FAFSA. *Faculty research:* Organizational psychology, work and the family, quantitative psychology, decision-making, psychosocial factors affecting health. *Total annual research expenditures:* $2.3 million. *Unit head:* Dr. Ellen Skinner, Chair, 503-725-3966, Fax: 503-725-3904, E-mail: skinnere@pdx.edu. *Application contact:* 503-725-3511, Fax: 503-725-5525.
Website: http://www.pdx.edu/psy/

Portland State University, Graduate Studies, College of Liberal Arts and Sciences, Systems Science Program, Portland, OR 97207-0751. Offers computational intelligence (Certificate); computer modeling and simulation (Certificate); systems science (MS); systems science/anthropology (PhD); systems science/business administration (PhD); systems science/civil engineering (PhD); systems science/economics (PhD); systems science/engineering management (PhD); systems science/general (PhD); systems science/mathematical sciences (PhD); systems science/mechanical engineering (PhD); systems science/psychology (PhD); systems science/sociology (PhD). *Faculty:* 2 full-time (0 women), 1 part-time/adjunct (0 women). *Students:* 6 full-time (2 women), 29 part-time (8 women); includes 6 minority (1 Black or African American, non-Hispanic/Latino; 1 American Indian or Alaska Native, non-Hispanic/Latino; 1 Asian, non-Hispanic/Latino; 3 Hispanic/Latino). Average age 41. 32 applicants, 19% accepted, 6 enrolled. In 2014, 10 master's, 3 doctorates awarded. *Degree requirements:* For master's, comprehensive exam (for some programs), thesis optional; for doctorate, variable foreign language requirement, comprehensive exam (for some programs), thesis/dissertation. *Entrance requirements:* For master's, GRE/GMAT (recommended), minimum GPA of 3.0 undergraduate or graduate work, 2 letters of recommendation, statement of interest; for doctorate, GMAT, GRE General Test, minimum GPA of 3.0 undergraduate, 3.25 graduate; 2 letters of recommendation; statement of interest. Additional exam requirements/recommendations for international students: Required—TOEFL (minimum score 550 paper-based; 80 iBT). *Application deadline:* For fall admission, 1/15 for domestic and international students; for spring admission, 11/1 for domestic students. Application fee: $50. Electronic applications accepted. *Expenses:* Tuition, state resident: part-time $222 per credit. Tuition, nonresident: part-time $527 per credit. *Required fees:* $22 per contact hour. $100 per quarter. Tuition and fees vary according to program. *Financial support:* In 2014–15, 1 research assistantship with full and partial tuition reimbursement (averaging $2,358 per year) was awarded; teaching assistantships with full and partial tuition reimbursements, career-related internships or fieldwork, Federal Work-Study, scholarships/grants, and unspecified assistantships also available. Support available to part-time students. Financial award application deadline: 3/1; financial award applicants required to submit FAFSA. *Faculty research:* Systems theory and methodology, artificial intelligence neural networks, information theory, nonlinear dynamics/chaos, modeling and simulation. *Total annual research expenditures:* $137,833. *Unit head:* Prof. Wayne Wakeland, PhD, Chair, 503-725-4975, E-mail: wakeland@pdx.edu.
Website: http://www.pdx.edu/sysc/

Princeton University, Graduate School, Department of Psychology, Princeton, NJ 08544-1019. Offers neuroscience (PhD); psychology (PhD). *Degree requirements:* For doctorate, thesis/dissertation. *Entrance requirements:* For doctorate, GRE General Test, GRE Subject Test. Additional exam requirements/recommendations for international students: Required—TOEFL (minimum score 550 paper-based). Electronic applications accepted.

Purdue University, Graduate School, College of Health and Human Sciences, Department of Psychological Sciences, West Lafayette, IN 47907. Offers behavioral neuroscience (PhD); clinical psychology (PhD); cognitive psychology (PhD); industrial/organizational psychology (PhD); mathematical and computational cognitive science (PhD). *Accreditation:* APA. Terminal master's awarded for partial completion of doctoral program. *Degree requirements:* For doctorate, thesis/dissertation. *Entrance requirements:* For doctorate, GRE General Test, minimum undergraduate GPA of 3.0 or equivalent. Additional exam requirements/recommendations for international students: Required—TOEFL (minimum score 550 paper-based; 77 iBT); Recommended—TWE. Electronic applications accepted. *Faculty research:* Career development of women in science, development of friendships during childhood and adolescence, social competence, human information processing.

Queens College of the City University of New York, Division of Graduate Studies, Mathematics and Natural Sciences Division, Department of Psychology, Flushing, NY 11367-1597. Offers clinical behavioral applications in mental health settings (MA); psychology (MA). Part-time programs available. *Degree requirements:* For master's, comprehensive exam, thesis or alternative. *Entrance requirements:* For master's, GRE, minimum GPA of 3.0. Additional exam requirements/recommendations for international students: Required—TOEFL.

Queen's University at Kingston, School of Graduate Studies, Faculty of Arts and Sciences, Department of Psychology, Kingston, ON K7L 3N6, Canada. Offers brain behavior and cognitive science (MA, PhD); clinical psychology (MA, PhD); developmental psychology (MA, PhD); social personality psychology (MA, PhD). *Degree requirements:* For master's, thesis; for doctorate, comprehensive exam, thesis/dissertation. *Entrance requirements:* For master's and doctorate, GRE General Test. Additional exam requirements/recommendations for international students: Required—TOEFL. *Faculty research:* Human development, social, personality, behavioral neuroscience, forensic.

Radford University, College of Graduate and Professional Studies, College of Humanities and Behavioral Sciences, Department of Psychology, Radford, VA 24142. Offers counseling psychology (Psy D); psychology (MA, MS), including clinical psychology, experimental psychology (MA), industrial/organizational psychology (MS), industrial/organizational psychology (MA); school psychology (Ed S). *Faculty:* 18 full-time (10 women), 1 (woman) part-time/adjunct. *Students:* 68 full-time (47 women), 11 part-time (9 women); includes 5 minority (2 Black or African American, non-Hispanic/Latino; 2 Asian, non-Hispanic/Latino; 1 Hispanic/Latino). Average age 24. 171 applicants, 49% accepted, 38 enrolled. In 2014, 27 master's, 3 doctorates, 9 other advanced degrees awarded. *Application deadline:* For fall admission, 12/1 for international students. Applications are processed on a rolling basis. Application fee: $50. Electronic applications accepted. *Expenses:* Tuition, state resident: full-time $7187; part-time $299 per credit hour. Tuition, nonresident: full-time $16,394; part-time $683 per credit hour. *Required fees:* $2974; $125 per credit hour. Tuition and fees vary according to course load and program. *Financial support:* In 2014–15, 59 students received support, including 10 fellowships with full tuition reimbursements available (averaging $13,800 per year), 30 research assistantships (averaging $5,560 per year), 16 teaching assistantships with partial tuition reimbursements available (averaging $10,438 per year). Financial award application deadline: 3/1; financial award applicants required to submit FAFSA. *Unit head:* Dr. Hilary M. Lips, Chair, 540-831-5387, Fax: 540-831-6113, E-mail: hlips@radford.edu. *Application contact:* Rebecca Conner, Director, Graduate Enrollment, 540-831-6296, Fax: 540-831-6061, E-mail: gradcollege@radford.edu.
Website: http://www.radford.edu/content/chbs/home/psychology.html

Rhode Island College, School of Graduate Studies, Faculty of Arts and Sciences, Department of Psychology, Providence, RI 02908-1991. Offers health psychology (CGS); psychology (MA). Part-time and evening/weekend programs available. *Faculty:* 5 full-time (2 women). *Students:* 2 full-time (both women), 9 part-time (4 women); includes 3 minority (1 Asian, non-Hispanic/Latino; 2 Hispanic/Latino). Average age 31. In 2014, 5 master's awarded. *Degree requirements:* For master's, comprehensive exam. *Entrance requirements:* For master's, GRE, 3 letters of recommendation. Additional exam requirements/recommendations for international students: Recommended—TOEFL (minimum score 550 paper-based; 79 iBT). *Application deadline:* For fall admission, 3/1 for domestic students; for spring admission, 11/1 for domestic students. Applications are processed on a rolling basis. Application fee: $50. *Expenses:* Tuition, state resident: full-time $8928; part-time $372 per credit hour. Tuition, nonresident: full-time $17,376; part-time $724 per credit hour. *Required fees:* $602; $22 per credit. $72 per term. *Financial support:* Teaching assistantships with full tuition reimbursements, Federal Work-Study, scholarships/grants, health care benefits, and unspecified assistantships available. Support available to part-time students. Financial award application deadline: 5/15; financial award applicants required to submit FAFSA. *Unit head:* Dr. Randi Kim, Chair, 401-456-8015. *Application contact:* Graduate Studies, 401-456-8700.
Website: http://www.ric.edu/psychology/index.php

Rice University, Graduate Programs, School of Humanities, Department of Religious Studies, Houston, TX 77251-1892. Offers African religions (PhD); African-American religions (PhD); contemplative studies (PhD); ghosticism, esotericism, mysticism (PhD); Islam (PhD); Jewish thought and philosophy (PhD); modern Christianity in thought and popular culture (PhD); psychology of religion (PhD); the Bible and beyond (PhD). *Degree requirements:* For doctorate, 2 foreign languages, comprehensive exam, thesis/dissertation. *Entrance requirements:* For doctorate, GRE, letters of recommendation, writing sample. Additional exam requirements/recommendations for international students: Required—TOEFL (minimum score 600 paper-based; 90 iBT). Electronic applications accepted. *Faculty research:* Origins and historical development of Islam, history of Christianity, the study of comparative religion, African-American religion, religion and culture.

Rice University, Graduate Programs, School of Social Sciences, Department of Psychology, Houston, TX 77251-1892. Offers cognitive sciences (MA, PhD); industrial-organizational/social psychology (MA, PhD); psychology (MA, PhD). Terminal master's awarded for partial completion of doctoral program. *Degree requirements:* For master's, thesis; for doctorate, thesis/dissertation. *Entrance requirements:* For doctorate, GRE General Test, minimum GPA of 3.0. Additional exam requirements/recommendations for international students: Required—TOEFL. Electronic applications accepted. *Faculty research:* Cognitive, cognitive neuropsychology, human factors, human-computer interaction, industrial-organizational psychology.

Richmont Graduate University, School of Psychology, Atlanta, GA 30327. Offers Christian psychological studies (MS).

Rivier University, School of Graduate Studies, Department of Psychology, Nashua, NH 03060. Offers clinical psychology (MS); experimental psychology (MS).

Rochester Institute of Technology, Graduate Enrollment Services, College of Liberal Arts, Psychology Department, Rochester, NY 14623-5604. Offers engineering psychology (Advanced Certificate); experimental psychology (MS); school psychology (MS, Advanced Certificate). Part-time programs available. *Students:* 32 full-time (25 women), 8 part-time (3 women); includes 6 minority (3 Black or African American, non-Hispanic/Latino; 3 Hispanic/Latino), 5 international. Average age 26. 73 applicants, 40% accepted, 10 enrolled. In 2014, 6 master's, 1 other advanced degree awarded. *Degree requirements:* For master's, thesis. *Entrance requirements:* For master's, GRE and TOEFL, IELTS, or PTE for non-native English speakers, recommended minimum GPA of 3.0. Additional exam requirements/recommendations for international students: Required—PTE (minimum score 58), TOEFL (minimum score 550 paper-based; 79 iBT) or IELTS (minimum score 6.5). *Application deadline:* For fall admission, 2/15 priority date for domestic and international students; for winter admission, 11/1 for domestic and international students; for spring admission, 12/15 priority date for domestic and international students. Applications are processed on a rolling basis. Application fee: $60. Electronic applications accepted. *Expenses:* Expenses: $1,673 per credit hour. *Financial support:* In 2014–15, 13 students received support. Research assistantships with partial tuition reimbursements available, teaching assistantships with partial tuition reimbursements available, career-related internships or fieldwork, Federal Work-Study, institutionally sponsored loans, scholarships/grants, and unspecified assistantships available. Support available to part-time students. Financial award applicants required to submit FAFSA. *Unit head:* Dr. Andrew Herbert, Graduate Program Director, 585-475-4554, E-mail: amhgss@rit.edu. *Application contact:* Diane Ellison, Associate Vice President, Graduate Enrollment Services, 585-475-2229, Fax: 585-475-7164, E-mail: gradinfo@rit.edu.
Website: http://www.rit.edu/cla/psychology/

Roosevelt University, Graduate Division, College of Arts and Sciences, Department of Psychology, Program in Clinical Psychology, Chicago, IL 60605. Offers MA, Psy D.

Rosalind Franklin University of Medicine and Science, College of Health Professions, Department of Psychology, North Chicago, IL 60064-3095. Offers clinical counseling (MS); psychology (MS, PhD). *Accreditation:* APA. Terminal master's awarded for partial completion of doctoral program. *Degree requirements:* For master's, capstone experience. *Entrance requirements:* For master's, minimum GPA of 3.0, bachelor's degree (preferably in related subject); for doctorate, GRE, minimum GPA of 3.0, bachelor's or master's degree. Additional exam requirements/recommendations for international students: Required—TOEFL. *Faculty research:* Anxiety, pain, psychopathy, epilepsy, neuropsychology.

Rowan University, Graduate School, College of Science and Mathematics, Department of Psychology, Glassboro, NJ 08028-1701. Offers MA, CAGS. *Faculty:* 13 full-time (8 women), 11 part-time/adjunct (9 women). *Students:* 26 full-time (21 women), 54 part-time (48 women); includes 9 minority (3 Black or African American, non-Hispanic/Latino; 1 American Indian or Alaska Native, non-Hispanic/Latino; 5 Hispanic/Latino). Average age 29. 79 applicants, 48% accepted, 28 enrolled. In 2014, 23 master's awarded. *Application deadline:* For fall admission, 6/1 for domestic students; for spring admission, 11/1 for domestic students; for summer admission, 2/15 for domestic students. Applications are processed on a rolling basis. Application fee: $65. Electronic applications accepted. *Expenses: Tuition, area resident:* Part-time $648 per credit. Tuition, state resident: part-time $648 per credit. Tuition, nonresident: part-time $648 per credit. *Required fees:* $145 per credit. Tuition and fees vary according to degree level, campus/location, program and student level. *Unit head:* Dr. Horacio Sosa, Dean, College of Graduate and Continuing Education, 856-256-4747, Fax: 856-256-5638, E-mail: sosa@rowan.edu. *Application contact:* Admissions and Enrollment Services, 856-256-5435, Fax: 856-256-5637, E-mail: cgceadmissions@rowan.edu.

Rutgers, The State University of New Jersey, Camden, Graduate School of Arts and Sciences, Program in Psychology, Camden, NJ 08102. Offers MA. Part-time and evening/weekend programs available. *Degree requirements:* For master's, thesis, 30 credits. *Entrance requirements:* For master's, GRE, 3 letters of recommendation; statement of personal, professional, and academic goals; prerequisite course work in introductory psychology, statistics and experimental psychology. Additional exam requirements/recommendations for international students: Required—TOEFL, IELTS.

Electronic applications accepted. *Faculty research:* Cognitive psychology, sexuality, health psychology, personality psychology, clinical psychology.

Rutgers, The State University of New Jersey, Newark, Graduate School, Program in Psychology, Newark, NJ 07102. Offers cognitive neuroscience (PhD); cognitive science (PhD); perception (PhD); psychobiology (PhD); social cognition (PhD). *Degree requirements:* For doctorate, comprehensive exam, thesis/dissertation. *Entrance requirements:* For doctorate, GRE General Test, GRE Subject Test, minimum undergraduate B average. Electronic applications accepted. *Faculty research:* Visual perception (luminance, motion), neuroendocrine mechanisms in behavior (reproduction, pain), attachment theory, connectionist modeling of cognition.

Rutgers, The State University of New Jersey, New Brunswick, Graduate School-New Brunswick, Program in Psychology, Piscataway, NJ 08854-8097. Offers behavioral neuroscience (PhD); clinical psychology (PhD); cognitive psychology (PhD); interdisciplinary health psychology (PhD); social psychology (PhD). *Accreditation:* APA. *Degree requirements:* For doctorate, comprehensive exam, thesis/dissertation. *Entrance requirements:* For doctorate, GRE General Test, 3 letters of recommendation. Additional exam requirements/recommendations for international students: Required—TOEFL (minimum score 577 paper-based). Electronic applications accepted. *Faculty research:* Learning and memory, behavioral ecology, hormones and behavior, psychopharmacology, anxiety disorders.

Sage Graduate School, School of Health Sciences, Department of Psychology, Troy, NY 12180-4115. Offers community psychology (MA), including child care and children's services, community counseling, community health education, community psychology, general psychology; counseling and community psychology (MA); forensic mental health (MS, Certificate). Part-time and evening/weekend programs available. *Faculty:* 4 full-time (3 women), 4 part-time/adjunct (3 women). *Students:* 48 full-time (39 women), 40 part-time (33 women); includes 19 minority (10 Black or African American, non-Hispanic/Latino; 1 American Indian or Alaska Native, non-Hispanic/Latino; 1 Asian, non-Hispanic/Latino; 4 Hispanic/Latino; 3 Two or more races, non-Hispanic/Latino). Average age 29. 94 applicants, 57% accepted, 21 enrolled. In 2014, 16 master's awarded. *Degree requirements:* For master's, thesis or alternative. *Entrance requirements:* For master's, GRE General Test. Additional exam requirements/recommendations for international students: Required—TOEFL (minimum score 550 paper-based). *Application deadline:* Applications are processed on a rolling basis. Application fee: $40. *Expenses: Tuition:* Full-time $12,240; part-time $680 per credit hour. *Financial support:* Fellowships, research assistantships, Federal Work-Study, scholarships/grants, and unspecified assistantships available. Support available to part-time students. Financial award application deadline: 3/1; financial award applicants required to submit FAFSA. *Faculty research:* Effectiveness of arts integration programs in elementary and secondary schools, literacy-based substance abuse program, outcome evaluation of program to increase college entry among urban youth. *Unit head:* Dr. Patricia O'Connor, Interim Dean, School of Health Sciences, 518-244-2073, Fax: 518-244-4571, E-mail: oconnp@sage.edu. *Application contact:* Dr. Sybillyn Jennings, Department Chair, 518-244-2074, Fax: 518-244-4545, E-mail: jennis@sage.edu.

St. Cloud State University, School of Graduate Studies, School of Education, Department of Educational Leadership and Higher Education, St. Cloud, MN 56301. Offers college counseling and student development (MS); higher education administration (MS, Ed D); rehabilitation counseling (MS); school counseling (MS). *Degree requirements:* For master's, thesis or alternative; for doctorate, comprehensive exam, thesis/dissertation. *Entrance requirements:* For master's, GRE General Test (for some programs), minimum GPA of 2.75; for doctorate, GRE General Test. Additional exam requirements/recommendations for international students: Required—Michigan English Language Assessment Battery; Recommended—TOEFL (minimum score 550 paper-based), IELTS (minimum score 6.5). Electronic applications accepted.

St. John's University, St. John's College of Liberal Arts and Sciences, Department of Psychology, Queens, NY 11439. Offers clinical psychology (MA, PhD), including clinical psychology (MA), clinical psychology-child (PhD), clinical psychology-general (PhD); general experimental psychology (MA); school psychology (MS, Psy D). *Accreditation:* APA (one or more programs are accredited). Part-time and evening/weekend programs available. *Students:* 169 full-time (133 women), 53 part-time (43 women); includes 67 minority (16 Black or African American, non-Hispanic/Latino; 18 Asian, non-Hispanic/Latino; 31 Hispanic/Latino; 2 Two or more races, non-Hispanic/Latino), 4 international. Average age 27. 552 applicants, 22% accepted, 65 enrolled. In 2014, 45 master's, 34 doctorates awarded. *Degree requirements:* For master's, comprehensive exam, thesis optional; for doctorate, comprehensive exam, thesis/dissertation, internship. *Entrance requirements:* For master's, GRE, minimum GPA of 3.0, 2 writing samples, transcripts, 3 letters of recommendation, personal essay, 24 credits in psychology or related field, bachelor's degree; for doctorate, GRE General Test, GRE Subject Test, 3 letters of recommendation, 2 writing samples, personal statement. Additional exam requirements/recommendations for international students: Required—TOEFL (minimum score 600 paper-based; 100 iBT), IELTS (minimum score 7). *Application deadline:* For fall admission, 1/15 priority date for domestic and international students; for spring admission, 11/1 priority date for domestic and international students. Applications are processed on a rolling basis. Application fee: $70. Electronic applications accepted. *Expenses:* Expenses: Contact institution. *Financial support:* Fellowships, research assistantships, career-related internships or fieldwork, scholarships/grants, and unspecified assistantships available. Support available to part-time students. Financial award application deadline: 3/1; financial award applicants required to submit FAFSA. *Faculty research:* Clinical psychology, school psychology, developmental psychopathology, risky behaviors and health, cognitive behavior treatments for trauma, assessment and treatment of anger problems, development of mathematical reasoning, personality disorders and depression. *Unit head:* Dr. William Chaplin, Chair, 718-990-5541, E-mail: chaplinw@stjohns.edu. *Application contact:* Robert Medrano, Director of Graduate Admissions, 718-990-1601, Fax: 718-990-5686, E-mail: gradhelp@stjohns.edu.

Saint Joseph's University, College of Arts and Sciences, Department of Criminal Justice, Philadelphia, PA 19131-1395. Offers administration/police executive (MS); behavior analysis (MS, Post-Master's Certificate); criminal justice (MS); criminology (MS); federal law (MS); intelligence and crime (MS); probation, parole, and corrections (MS). Part-time and evening/weekend programs available. Postbaccalaureate distance learning degree programs offered (no on-campus study). *Faculty:* 6 full-time (4 women), 42 part-time/adjunct (16 women). *Students:* 31 full-time (21 women), 401 part-time (276 women); includes 158 minority (104 Black or African American, non-Hispanic/Latino; 7 Asian, non-Hispanic/Latino; 31 Hispanic/Latino; 16 Two or more races, non-Hispanic/Latino), 3 international. Average age 32. 226 applicants, 68% accepted, 115 enrolled. In 2014, 188 master's awarded. *Degree requirements:* For master's, thesis. *Entrance requirements:* For master's, GRE General Test or minimum GPA of 3.0, 2 letters of recommendation, personal statement, resume, official transcripts. Additional exam requirements/recommendations for international students: Required—TOEFL (minimum score 550 paper-based; 80 iBT). *Application deadline:* For fall admission, 7/15 priority date for domestic students, 4/15 for international students; for winter admission, 1/15 for international students; for spring admission, 11/15 priority date for domestic students, 10/15 for international students. Applications are processed on a rolling basis.

Application fee: $35. Electronic applications accepted. *Financial support:* In 2014–15, 8 students received support. Career-related internships or fieldwork and unspecified assistantships available. Financial award applicants required to submit FAFSA. *Faculty research:* Housing mobility and the intergenerational transmission of neighborhood poverty, fair trade. *Total annual research expenditures:* $17,309. *Unit head:* Sylvia DeSantis, Director. *Application contact:* Elisabeth Woodward, Director of Marketing and Admissions, Graduate Arts and Sciences, 610-660-3131, Fax: 610-660-3131, E-mail: gradstudies@sju.edu.
Website: http://www.sju.edu/majors-programs/graduate-arts-sciences/masters/criminal-justice-ms

Saint Joseph's University, College of Arts and Sciences, Department of Psychology, Philadelphia, PA 19131-1395. Offers MS. Evening/weekend programs available. *Faculty:* 4 full-time (2 women), 1 (woman) part-time/adjunct. *Students:* 23 full-time (13 women); includes 5 minority (2 Black or African American, non-Hispanic/Latino; 3 Hispanic/Latino). Average age 23. 72 applicants, 25% accepted, 18 enrolled. In 2014, 12 master's awarded. *Entrance requirements:* For master's, GRE General Test, 2 letters of recommendation, official transcripts, personal statement. Additional exam requirements/recommendations for international students: Required—TOEFL (minimum score 550 paper-based; 80 iBT). *Application deadline:* For fall admission, 3/1 priority date for domestic and international students; for winter admission, 1/15 for international students; for spring admission, 11/15 for domestic students, 10/15 for international students. Electronic applications accepted. *Financial support:* In 2014–15, 9 students received support. Teaching assistantships and unspecified assistantships available. Financial award applicants required to submit FAFSA. *Faculty research:* Improving outcomes of severe disorders of consciousness. *Total annual research expenditures:* $20,967. *Unit head:* Dr. Jodi Mindell, Director, 610-660-1806, E-mail: jmindell@sju.edu. *Application contact:* Elisabeth Woodward, Director of Marketing and Admissions, Graduate Arts and Sciences, 610-660-3131, Fax: 610-660-3230, E-mail: gradstudies@sju.edu.
Website: http://www.sju.edu/academics/cas/grad/psychology

Saint Louis University, Graduate Education, College of Arts and Sciences and Graduate Education, Department of Psychology, St. Louis, MO 63103-2097. Offers clinical psychology (MS-R, PhD); experimental psychology (MS-R, PhD); industrial-organizational psychology (PhD); psychology (PhD). *Accreditation:* APA (one or more programs are accredited). Part-time programs available. *Degree requirements:* For master's, comprehensive exam, thesis; for doctorate, thesis/dissertation, clinical internship (for clinical psychology PhD). *Entrance requirements:* For master's, GRE General Test, interview, letters of recommendation, resume; for doctorate, GRE General Test, interview, letters of recommendation, resumé, transcripts, goal statement. Additional exam requirements/recommendations for international students: Required—TOEFL (minimum score 550 paper-based). Electronic applications accepted. *Faculty research:* Violence and trauma; neural basis of learning and memory function; eating disorders; body image and health behavior; prejudice, stereotyping, and victimization; memory, cognitive aging and language processing.

Saint Mary's University, Faculty of Science, Department of Psychology, Halifax, NS B3H 3C3, Canada. Offers applied psychology (M Sc, PhD), including industrial/organizational psychology (M Sc). Part-time programs available. *Degree requirements:* For master's, thesis, 500-hour internship; for doctorate, comprehensive exam, thesis/dissertation, research project. *Entrance requirements:* For master's and doctorate, GRE General Test. *Faculty research:* Assessment, health psychology, social psychology, cognition.

Salem State University, School of Graduate Studies, Program in Counseling and Psychological Services, Salem, MA 01970-5353. Offers MS, Graduate Certificate. Part-time and evening/weekend programs available. *Entrance requirements:* For master's, GRE or MAT. Additional exam requirements/recommendations for international students: Required—TOEFL (minimum score 550 paper-based; 80 iBT) or IELTS (minimum score 5.5).

Sam Houston State University, College of Humanities and Social Sciences, Department of Psychology and Philosophy, Huntsville, TX 77341. Offers psychology (MA, PhD, SSP), including clinical psychology (MA, PhD), psychology (MA), school psychology (SSP). *Accreditation:* APA. Part-time programs available. *Faculty:* 27 full-time (9 women), 2 part-time/adjunct (0 women). *Students:* 74 full-time (58 women), 38 part-time (33 women); includes 12 minority (2 Black or African American, non-Hispanic/Latino; 1 American Indian or Alaska Native, non-Hispanic/Latino; 1 Asian, non-Hispanic/Latino; 5 Hispanic/Latino; 3 Two or more races, non-Hispanic/Latino), 8 international. Average age 27. 155 applicants, 32% accepted, 33 enrolled. In 2014, 25 master's, 9 doctorates awarded. Terminal master's awarded for partial completion of doctoral program. *Degree requirements:* For master's, comprehensive exam, thesis optional; for doctorate, comprehensive exam, thesis/dissertation. *Entrance requirements:* For master's, GRE General Test, personal statement, letters of recommendation; for doctorate, GRE General Test, GRE Subject Test (advanced psychology), personal essay, letters of recommendation, resume. Additional exam requirements/recommendations for international students: Required—TOEFL (minimum score 550 paper-based; 79 iBT), IELTS (minimum score 6.5). *Application deadline:* For fall admission, 12/1 priority date for domestic students, 6/25 for international students; for spring admission, 12/1 for domestic students, 11/12 for international students. Applications are processed on a rolling basis. Application fee: $45 ($75 for international students). Electronic applications accepted. *Expenses:* Tuition, state resident: full-time $2286; part-time $254 per credit hour. Tuition, nonresident: full-time $5544; part-time $616 per credit hour. *Required fees:* $440 per semester. Tuition and fees vary according to course load and campus/location. *Financial support:* In 2014–15, 61 research assistantships (averaging $9,562 per year), 7 teaching assistantships (averaging $11,088 per year) were awarded; career-related internships or fieldwork, Federal Work-Study, scholarships/grants, tuition waivers (partial), and unspecified assistantships also available. Support available to part-time students. Financial award application deadline: 3/15; financial award applicants required to submit FAFSA. *Unit head:* Dr. D. Christopher Wilson, Chair, 936-294-3052, Fax: 936-294-3798, E-mail: wilson@shsu.edu. *Application contact:* Dr. Jeffrey Anastasi, Assistant Professor/Coordinator of Master of Arts in Psychology Programs, 936-294-3049, Fax: 936-294-3798, E-mail: jeff.anastasi@shsu.edu.
Website: http://www.shsu.edu/~psy_www/

San Diego State University, Graduate and Research Affairs, College of Sciences, Department of Psychology, San Diego, CA 92182. Offers clinical psychology (MS, PhD); industrial and organizational psychology (MS); program evaluation (MS); psychology (MA). PhD offered jointly with University of California, San Diego. *Accreditation:* APA (one or more programs are accredited). Terminal master's awarded for partial completion of doctoral program. *Degree requirements:* For master's, thesis, oral exam; for doctorate, thesis/dissertation. *Entrance requirements:* For master's, GRE General Test, GRE Subject Test, 3 letters of recommendation; for doctorate, GRE General Test, GRE Subject Test, minimum GPA of 3.0, 3 letters of recommendation. Additional exam requirements/recommendations for international students: Required—TOEFL. Electronic applications accepted.

San Francisco State University, Division of Graduate Studies, College of Science and Engineering, Department of Psychology, San Francisco, CA 94132-1722. Offers industrial/organizational psychology (MS); school psychology (Credential); social psychology (MA). *Expenses:* Tuition, state resident: full-time $6738. Tuition, nonresident: full-time $17,898; part-time $372 per credit hour. *Required fees:* $498 per semester. *Financial support:* Teaching assistantships available. Financial award application deadline: 3/1. *Unit head:* Dr. Jeffrey Cookston, Chair, 415-338-2167, Fax: 415-338-2398, E-mail: cookston@sfsu.edu. *Application contact:* Dr. Ryan Howell, Graduate Program Coordinator, 415-405-2140, Fax: 415-338-2398, E-mail: rhowell@sfsu.edu.
Website: http://psychology.sfsu.edu/graduate/application.html

San Jose State University, Graduate Studies and Research, College of Social Sciences, Department of Psychology, San Jose, CA 95192-0001. Offers clinical psychology (MS); experimental psychology (MA); industrial/organizational psychology (MS); psychology (MA). *Degree requirements:* For master's, comprehensive exam, thesis (for some programs). *Entrance requirements:* For master's, GRE General Test, minimum GPA of 3.0. Electronic applications accepted. *Faculty research:* Drug and alcohol abuse, neurohormonal mechanisms in motion sickness, behavior modification, sleep research, genetics.

Saybrook University, LIOS MA Residential Programs, Kirkland, WA 98033. Offers leadership and organization development (MA); psychology counseling (MA). *Degree requirements:* For master's, thesis (for some programs), oral exams. *Entrance requirements:* For master's, bachelor's degree from an accredited university or college. Additional exam requirements/recommendations for international students: Recommended—TOEFL, IELTS, TWE.

Saybrook University, School of Psychology and Interdisciplinary Inquiry, San Francisco, CA 94111-1920. Offers human science (MA, PhD), including consciousness and spirituality, humanistic and transpersonal psychology, integrative health studies, organizational systems, social transformation; organizational systems (MA, PhD), including consciousness and spirituality, humanistic and transpersonal psychology, integrative health studies, leadership of sustainable systems (MA), organizational systems, social transformation; psychology (MA, PhD), including consciousness and spirituality, creativity studies (MA), humanistic and transpersonal psychology, integrative health studies, Jungian studies, marriage and family therapy (MA), organizational systems, social transformation. Postbaccalaureate distance learning degree programs offered (minimal on-campus study). Terminal master's awarded for partial completion of doctoral program. *Degree requirements:* For master's, thesis or alternative; for doctorate, thesis/dissertation. *Entrance requirements:* Additional exam requirements/recommendations for international students: Required—TOEFL (minimum score 580 paper-based; 93 iBT). Electronic applications accepted. *Faculty research:* Humanistic theory, health studies, organizational systems, consciousness and spirituality, social transformation.

The School of Professional Psychology at Forest Institute, Graduate Programs, Springfield, MO 65807. Offers applied behavior analysis (MS); clinical psychology (MA, Psy D); counseling psychology (MA); marriage and family therapy (MA, PGC). *Accreditation:* AAMFT/COAMFTE; APA (one or more programs are accredited). Part-time and evening/weekend programs available. Terminal master's awarded for partial completion of doctoral program. *Degree requirements:* For master's, thesis, practicum; for doctorate, comprehensive exam, thesis/dissertation, internship, practicum. *Entrance requirements:* For master's, GRE General Test, interview, minimum GPA of 3.0, 12 hours in psychology; for doctorate, GRE General Test (minimum combined Verbal and Quantitative score of 1000, Analytic Writing 4.0), interview, minimum GPA of 3.0, 18 hours in psychology. Additional exam requirements/recommendations for international students: Required—TOEFL (minimum score 550 paper-based). Electronic applications accepted. *Faculty research:* Forensics/corrections, marriage and family therapy, child and adolescent, integrated health care, neuropsychology.

The Seattle School of Theology and Psychology, Graduate Programs, Seattle, WA 98121. Offers Christian studies (MA); counseling psychology (MA); divinity (M Div). Part-time programs available. *Entrance requirements:* For master's, MAT.

Seattle University, College of Arts and Sciences, Department of Psychology, Seattle, WA 98122-1090. Offers existential and phenomenological therapeutic psychology (MA Psych). *Faculty:* 7 full-time (2 women), 5 part-time/adjunct (4 women). *Students:* 40 full-time (29 women), 5 part-time (2 women); includes 7 minority (1 Black or African American, non-Hispanic/Latino; 1 Asian, non-Hispanic/Latino; 1 Hispanic/Latino; 4 Two or more races, non-Hispanic/Latino), 3 international. Average age 31. 62 applicants, 48% accepted, 20 enrolled. In 2014, 22 master's awarded. *Degree requirements:* For master's, thesis optional. *Entrance requirements:* For master's, interview, minimum GPA of 3.0, previous undergraduate course work in psychology, experience (paid or volunteer) in counseling or human services. *Application deadline:* For fall admission, 1/15 for domestic and international students. Application fee: $55. Electronic applications accepted. *Financial support:* In 2014–15, 9 students received support. Career-related internships or fieldwork and Federal Work-Study available. Support available to part-time students. Financial award applicants required to submit FAFSA. *Faculty research:* Interpersonal relations, psychotherapy, qualitative research, trauma, philosophy and psychology. *Unit head:* Dr. Kevin Krycka, Director of Graduate Programs, 206-296-5398, Fax: 206-296-2141, E-mail: krycka@seattleu.edu. *Application contact:* Janet Shandley, Associate Dean of Graduate Admissions, 206-296-5900, Fax: 206-298-5656, E-mail: grad_admissions@seattleu.edu.
Website: http://www.seattleu.edu/artsci/departments/psychology/

Seton Hall University, College of Arts and Sciences, Department of Psychology, South Orange, NJ 07079-2697. Offers experimental psychology (non-thesis) (MS), including data visualization and analysis. Part-time and evening/weekend programs available. *Faculty:* 12 full-time (7 women). *Students:* 20 full-time (11 women); includes 4 minority (1 Black or African American, non-Hispanic/Latino; 2 Asian, non-Hispanic/Latino; 1 Hispanic/Latino), 1 international. Average age 25. 31 applicants, 81% accepted, 12 enrolled. In 2014, 11 master's awarded. *Degree requirements:* For master's, thesis optional. *Entrance requirements:* For master's, GRE, minimum of 18 credits in psychology with at least a 3.0 (or B) GPA. Additional exam requirements/recommendations for international students: Required—TOEFL. *Application deadline:* For fall admission, 7/1 priority date for domestic and international students. Applications are processed on a rolling basis. Application fee: $75. Electronic applications accepted. *Financial support:* Research assistantships, teaching assistantships with full tuition reimbursements, career-related internships or fieldwork, Federal Work-Study, scholarships/grants, and unspecified assistantships available. Financial award applicants required to submit FAFSA. *Faculty research:* Behavioral neuroscience, cognitive psychology, social psychology, perception/motor skills, memory, depression, anxiety. *Unit head:* Dr. Amy Hunter, Chair, 973-761-9485, E-mail: amy.hunter@shu.edu. *Application contact:* Dr. Kelly Goedert, Director of Graduate Studies, 973-275-2703, Fax: 973-275-5829, E-mail: kelly.goedert@shu.edu.
Website: http://www.shu.edu/academics/artsci/psychology/index.cfm

Seton Hall University, College of Education and Human Services, Department of Professional Psychology and Family Therapy, South Orange, NJ 07079-2697. Offers counseling psychology (MA, PhD), including counseling psychology (PhD), school counseling (MA); marriage and family therapy (MS, Ed S, Professional Diploma); psychological studies (MA), including individualized, marriage and family therapy, sports and exercise psychology; school and community psychology (MA). *Accreditation:* APA. Part-time and evening/weekend programs available. Postbaccalaureate distance learning degree programs offered (minimal on-campus study). Terminal master's awarded for partial completion of doctoral program. *Degree requirements:* For master's, comprehensive exam, case study; for doctorate, comprehensive exam, thesis/dissertation, internship; for other advanced degree, comprehensive exam, internship. *Entrance requirements:* For master's, GRE or MAT; for doctorate, GRE, interview; for other advanced degree, GRE or MAT, interview. *Faculty research:* Counseling process, ethics, family systems, child pathology.

Shippensburg University of Pennsylvania, School of Graduate Studies, College of Arts and Sciences, Department of Psychology, Shippensburg, PA 17257-2299. Offers MS. Part-time and evening/weekend programs available. *Faculty:* 8 full-time (4 women). *Students:* 10 full-time (6 women), 15 part-time (7 women); includes 3 minority (1 Black or African American, non-Hispanic/Latino; 1 American Indian or Alaska Native, non-Hispanic/Latino; 1 Two or more races, non-Hispanic/Latino), 1 international. Average age 24. 34 applicants, 74% accepted, 11 enrolled. In 2014, 6 master's awarded. *Degree requirements:* For master's, comprehensive exam (for some programs), thesis (for research track); field experience (for applied track); competency exam (for general/reading track). *Entrance requirements:* For master's, minimum GPA of 2.75, 1 course in statistics, 9 undergraduate credit hours in psychology, supplemental form with personal goals statement. Additional exam requirements/recommendations for international students: Required—TOEFL (minimum score 580 paper-based); Recommended—IELTS (minimum score 6). *Application deadline:* For fall admission, 3/1 priority date for domestic students, 4/30 for international students; for spring admission, 11/1 priority date for domestic students, 9/30 for international students. Applications are processed on a rolling basis. Application fee: $45. Electronic applications accepted. *Expenses: Tuition, area resident:* Part-time $454 per credit. Tuition, state resident: part-time $454 per credit. Tuition, nonresident: part-time $681 per credit. *Required fees:* $133 per credit. *Financial support:* In 2014–15, 12 research assistantships with full tuition reimbursements (averaging $5,000 per year) were awarded; career-related internships or fieldwork, scholarships/grants, unspecified assistantships, and resident hall director and student payroll positions also available. Support available to part-time students. Financial award application deadline: 3/1; financial award applicants required to submit FAFSA. *Unit head:* Dr. Kathryn M. Potoczak, Program Coordinator, 717-477-1372, Fax: 717-477-4057, E-mail: kmpoto@ship.edu. *Application contact:* Jeremy R. Goshorn, Assistant Dean of Graduate Admissions, 717-477-1231, Fax: 717-477-4016, E-mail: jrgoshorn@ship.edu.
Website: http://www.ship.edu/psychology/

Simon Fraser University, Office of Graduate Studies, Faculty of Arts and Social Sciences, Department of Psychology, Burnaby, BC V5A 1S6, Canada. Offers MA, PhD. *Accreditation:* APA (one or more programs are accredited). *Degree requirements:* For master's, thesis; for doctorate, comprehensive exam, thesis/dissertation, clinical training (for some programs). *Entrance requirements:* For master's, GRE General Test, GRE Subject Test (psychology), minimum GPA of 3.0 (on scale of 4.33), or 3.33 based on last 60 credits of undergraduate courses; for doctorate, GRE General Test, GRE Subject Test (psychology), minimum GPA of 3.5 (on scale of 4.33). Additional exam requirements/recommendations for international students: Recommended—TOEFL (minimum score 580 paper-based; 93 iBT), IELTS (minimum score 7), TWE (minimum score 5). Electronic applications accepted. *Expenses:* Contact institution. *Faculty research:* Cognitive and neural sciences; developmental, law and forensic psychology; social history; quantitative and theoretical psyhcology; clinical sciences.

Sofia University, Hybrid: Face-to-Face/Online Programs, Palo Alto, CA 94303. Offers counseling psychology (MA); psychology (PhD), including transpersonal psychology; spiritual guidance (MA); transpersonal psychology (MA, Certificate); women's spirituality (MA, Certificate). Postbaccalaureate distance learning degree programs offered (minimal on-campus study). *Entrance requirements:* For master's, bachelor's degree; for doctorate, bachelor's degree; master's degree. Electronic applications accepted.

Sofia University, Residential Programs, Palo Alto, CA 94303. Offers clinical psychology (Psy D); counseling psychology (MA); transpersonal psychology (MA, PhD). Part-time and evening/weekend programs available. Terminal master's awarded for partial completion of doctoral program. *Degree requirements:* For doctorate, thesis/dissertation. *Entrance requirements:* For master's, bachelor's degree; for doctorate, bachelor's degree; master's degree (for some programs). Electronic applications accepted.

Southeastern Baptist Theological Seminary, Graduate and Professional Programs, Wake Forest, NC 27588-1889. Offers advanced biblical studies (M Div); Christian education (M Div, MACE); Christian ethics (PhD); Christian ministry (M Div); Christian planting (M Div); church music (MACM); counseling (MACO); evangelism (PhD); language (M Div); ministry (D Min); New Testament (PhD); Old Testament (PhD); philosophy (PhD); theology (Th M, PhD); women's studies (M Div). *Accreditation:* ACIPE; ATS (one or more programs are accredited). *Degree requirements:* For master's, thesis (for some programs), oral exam; for doctorate, thesis/dissertation, fieldwork. *Entrance requirements:* For master's, Cooperative English Test, minimum GPA of 2.0, M Div or equivalent (Th M); for doctorate, GRE General Test or MAT, Cooperative English Test, M Div or equivalent, 3 years of professional experience.

Southeastern Louisiana University, College of Arts, Humanities and Social Sciences, Department of Psychology, Hammond, LA 70402. Offers MA. Part-time programs available. *Faculty:* 8 full-time (5 women). *Students:* 22 full-time (19 women), 15 part-time (11 women); includes 5 minority (1 Black or African American, non-Hispanic/Latino; 1 Asian, non-Hispanic/Latino; 2 Hispanic/Latino; 1 Two or more races, non-Hispanic/Latino). Average age 25. In 2014, 2 master's awarded. *Degree requirements:* For master's, comprehensive exam, thesis, 38 hours of psychology course work including core courses in statistics, social psychology, cognition, and physiological psychology. *Entrance requirements:* For master's, GRE (minimum combined score 950), 18 hours of psychology/educational psychology; at least three hours each of statistics course/experimental lab; minimum GPA of 3.0; three letters of reference. Additional exam requirements/recommendations for international students: Required—TOEFL (minimum score 500 paper-based; 61 iBT). *Application deadline:* For fall admission, 7/15 priority date for domestic students, 6/1 priority date for international students; for spring admission, 12/1 priority date for domestic students, 10/1 priority date for international students. Applications are processed on a rolling basis. Application fee: $20 ($30 for international students). Electronic applications accepted. *Financial support:* In 2014–15, 19 research assistantships (averaging $8,652 per year) were awarded; career-related internships or fieldwork, Federal Work-Study, institutionally sponsored loans, scholarships/grants, and traineeships also available. Support available to part-time students. Financial award application deadline: 5/1; financial award applicants required to submit FAFSA. *Faculty research:* Evolutionary psychology, development of religion, health behaviors and violence exposure, performance assessment, social cognition, intergroup processes, stigma of eating and other psychological disorders. *Total annual research expenditures:* $33,752. *Unit head:* Dr. Susan Coats, Interim Department Head,

985-549-2154, Fax: 985-549-6892, E-mail: jworthen@selu.edu. *Application contact:* Sandra Meyers, Graduate Admissions Analyst, 985-549-5620, Fax: 985-549-5632, E-mail: admissions@selu.edu.
Website: http://www.selu.edu/acad_research/depts/psyc

Southern Adventist University, School of Education and Psychology, Collegedale, TN 37315-0370. Offers clinical mental health counseling (MS); inclusive education (MS Ed); instructional leadership (MS Ed); literacy education (MS Ed); outdoor teacher education (MS Ed); school counseling (MS). *Accreditation:* NCATE. Part-time and evening/weekend programs available. *Degree requirements:* For master's, comprehensive exam (for some programs), thesis optional, position paper (MS), portfolio (MS Ed in outdoor teacher education). *Entrance requirements:* For master's, interview (MS); 9 semester hours of upper-division course work in psychology or related field, including 1 course in psychology research or statistics; 9 semester hours of education (MS Ed). Additional exam requirements/recommendations for international students: Required—TOEFL (minimum score 600 paper-based; 100 iBT). Electronic applications accepted.

Southern California Seminary, Graduate and Professional Programs, El Cajon, CA 92019. Offers Biblical studies (MABS); counseling psychology (MACP); marriage and family therapy (MAMFT); psychology (Psy D); religious studies (MRS); theology (M Div). Part-time and evening/weekend programs available. Postbaccalaureate distance learning degree programs offered (minimal on-campus study). *Degree requirements:* For master's, thesis (for some programs); for doctorate, thesis/dissertation. *Entrance requirements:* For doctorate, master's degree in psychology. Additional exam requirements/recommendations for international students: Required—TOEFL (minimum score 550 paper-based). Electronic applications accepted.

Southern Connecticut State University, School of Graduate Studies, School of Arts and Sciences, Department of Psychology, New Haven, CT 06515-1355. Offers MA. Part-time and evening/weekend programs available. *Degree requirements:* For master's, thesis or alternative. *Entrance requirements:* For master's, interview, previous course work in psychology. Electronic applications accepted.

Southern Illinois University Carbondale, Graduate School, College of Education and Human Services, Program in Behavior Analysis and Therapy, Carbondale, IL 62901-4701. Offers MS. *Students:* 44 full-time (32 women), 81 part-time (63 women); includes 12 minority (9 Black or African American, non-Hispanic/Latino; 1 Asian, non-Hispanic/Latino; 2 Hispanic/Latino), 2 international. 85 applicants, 53% accepted, 38 enrolled. In 2014, 26 master's awarded. Application fee: $50. *Expenses:* Tuition, state resident: full-time $10,176; part-time $1153 per credit. Tuition, nonresident: full-time $20,814; part-time $1744 per credit. *Required fees:* $7092; $394 per credit. $2364 per semester. *Unit head:* Dr. Mark Dixon, Coordinator, 618-536-7704, E-mail: mdixon@siu.edu. *Application contact:* Char Burrell, Administrative Clerk, 618-453-6411, E-mail: cburrell@siu.edu.
Website: http://www.bat.siuc.edu/

Southern Illinois University Carbondale, Graduate School, College of Liberal Arts, Department of Psychology, Carbondale, IL 62901-4701. Offers clinical psychology (PhD); counseling psychology (PhD); experimental psychology (MA, MS). *Accreditation:* APA (one or more programs are accredited). *Faculty:* 27 full-time (14 women), 1 part-time/adjunct (0 women). *Students:* 70 full-time (46 women), 35 part-time (20 women); includes 10 minority (8 Black or African American, non-Hispanic/Latino; 2 Asian, non-Hispanic/Latino), 12 international. 274 applicants, 11% accepted, 20 enrolled. In 2014, 10 master's, 10 doctorates awarded. *Degree requirements:* For master's, thesis; for doctorate, thesis/dissertation. *Entrance requirements:* For master's, GRE General Test, GRE Subject Test, minimum GPA of 2.7; for doctorate, GRE General Test, GRE Subject Test, minimum GPA of 3.25. Additional exam requirements/recommendations for international students: Required—TOEFL. *Application deadline:* For fall admission, 3/1 priority date for domestic students. Applications are processed on a rolling basis. Application fee: $50. *Expenses:* Tuition, state resident: full-time $10,176; part-time $1153 per credit. Tuition, nonresident: full-time $20,814; part-time $1744 per credit. *Required fees:* $7092; $394 per credit. $2364 per semester. *Financial support:* In 2014–15, 82 students received support, including 14 fellowships with full tuition reimbursements available, 23 research assistantships with full tuition reimbursements available, 22 teaching assistantships with full tuition reimbursements available; Federal Work-Study, institutionally sponsored loans, and tuition waivers (full) also available. *Faculty research:* Developmental neuropsychology; smoking, affect, and cognition; personality measurement; vocational psychology; program evaluation. *Unit head:* Dr. Meera Komarraju, Chair, 618-453-3529, E-mail: meerak@siu.edu. *Application contact:* Stacia Werner, Office Specialist, 618-453-3564, E-mail: gradpsych@siu.edu.
Website: http://psychology.siuc.edu/

Southern Illinois University Edwardsville, Graduate School, School of Education, Health, and Human Behavior, Department of Psychology, Edwardsville, IL 62026. Offers clinical child and school psychology (MS); clinical psychology (MA); industrial-organizational psychology (MA); school psychology (SD). Part-time and evening/weekend programs available. *Faculty:* 22 full-time (9 women). *Students:* 50 full-time (40 women), 26 part-time (21 women); includes 9 minority (4 Black or African American, non-Hispanic/Latino; 1 Hispanic/Latino; 4 Two or more races, non-Hispanic/Latino), 2 international. 130 applicants, 22% accepted. In 2014, 28 master's, 8 other advanced degrees awarded. *Degree requirements:* For master's, thesis (for some programs), research paper; for SD, thesis. *Entrance requirements:* For master's, GRE. Additional exam requirements/recommendations for international students: Required—TOEFL (minimum score 550 paper-based; 79 iBT), IELTS (minimum score 6.5). *Application deadline:* For fall and spring admission, 2/1 for domestic and international students. Application fee: $30. Electronic applications accepted. *Expenses:* Tuition, state resident: full-time $5026. Tuition, nonresident: full-time $12,566. *International tuition:* $25,136 full-time. *Required fees:* $1682. Tuition and fees vary according to course load, campus/location and program. *Financial support:* In 2014–15, 50 students received support, including 1 fellowship with full tuition reimbursement available (averaging $8,370 per year), 23 research assistantships with full tuition reimbursements available, 26 teaching assistantships with full tuition reimbursements available; institutionally sponsored loans, scholarships/grants, and unspecified assistantships also available. Financial award application deadline: 3/1; financial award applicants required to submit FAFSA. *Unit head:* Dr. Paul Rose, Chair, 618-650-2202, E-mail: prose@siue.edu. *Application contact:* Melissa K. Mace, Assistant Director of Admissions for Graduate and International Recruitment, 618-650-2756, Fax: 618-650-3618, E-mail: mmace@siue.edu.
Website: http://www.siue.edu/education/psychology/graduate

Southern Methodist University, Dedman College of Humanities and Sciences, Department of Psychology, Dallas, TX 75275. Offers clinical psychology (PhD). *Accreditation:* APA. Terminal master's awarded for partial completion of doctoral program. *Degree requirements:* For doctorate, comprehensive exam, thesis/dissertation, oral exam, practicum, research presentation and publication. *Entrance requirements:* For doctorate, GRE General Test, minimum GPA of 3.4. Additional exam requirements/recommendations for international students: Required—TOEFL (minimum score 550 paper-based). Electronic applications accepted. *Faculty research:* Experimental, social, developmental, and cognitive psychology; anger/violence; mood disorders; depression and anxiety; family assessment and development; chronic pain and mental health.

Southern Nazarene University, College of Professional and Graduate Studies, Department of Psychology and Counseling, Bethany, OK 73008. Offers counseling psychology (MA, MSCP); marital and family therapy (MA). *Degree requirements:* For master's, thesis optional. *Entrance requirements:* For master's, English proficiency exam, minimum GPA of 3.0 in last 60 hours/major, 2.7 overall.

Southern New Hampshire University, School of Arts and Sciences, Manchester, NH 03106-1045. Offers community mental health (Graduate Certificate); community mental health and mental health counseling (MS); fiction and nonfiction (MFA); teaching English as a foreign language (MS). Part-time and evening/weekend programs available. *Degree requirements:* For master's, one foreign language, thesis. *Entrance requirements:* For master's, minimum GPA of 2.75 (for MS in teaching English as a foreign language), 3.0 (for MFA). Additional exam requirements/recommendations for international students: Required—TOEFL (minimum score 550 paper-based; 79 iBT), IELTS (minimum score 6.5), TWE (minimum score 5). Electronic applications accepted. *Expenses:* Contact institution. *Faculty research:* Action research, state of the art practice in behavioral health services, wraparound approaches to working with youth, learning styles.

Southern Oregon University, Graduate Studies, Department of Psychology, Ashland, OR 97520. Offers MHC. Part-time programs available. Postbaccalaureate distance learning degree programs offered (minimal on-campus study). *Faculty:* 13 full-time (7 women), 10 part-time/adjunct (6 women). *Students:* 38 full-time (27 women), 3 part-time (2 women); includes 3 minority (1 American Indian or Alaska Native, non-Hispanic/Latino; 1 Asian, non-Hispanic/Latino; 1 Hispanic/Latino), 2 international. Average age 34. 61 applicants, 49% accepted, 21 enrolled. In 2014, 19 master's awarded. *Degree requirements:* For master's, thesis, portfolio, oral defense. *Entrance requirements:* For master's, GRE General Test, minimum cumulative GPA of 3.0 in the last 90 quarter credits (60 semester credits) of undergraduate coursework. Additional exam requirements/recommendations for international students: Required—TOEFL (minimum score 540 paper-based; 76 iBT), IELTS (minimum score 6), ELPT (minimum score 964) or ELS (minimum score 112). *Application deadline:* For fall admission, 7/31 priority date for domestic and international students; for winter admission, 11/15 priority date for domestic and international students; for spring admission, 1/7 priority date for domestic and international students. Applications are processed on a rolling basis. Application fee: $50. Electronic applications accepted. *Expenses:* Tuition, state resident: full-time $10,225; part-time $1515 per quarter. Tuition, nonresident: full-time $12,782; part-time $1894 per quarter. *Required fees:* $1395; $261 per quarter. *Financial support:* In 2014–15, 2 students received support, including 2 research assistantships with partial tuition reimbursements available; career-related internships or fieldwork, institutionally sponsored loans, scholarships/grants, and unspecified assistantships also available. *Unit head:* Dr. Josie Wilson, Graduate Program Coordinator, 541-552-6946, E-mail: jwilson@sou.edu. *Application contact:* Lori Courtney, Graduate Coordinator, 541-552-6947, E-mail: courtney@sou.edu.
Website: http://www.sou.edu/psychology/mhc

Southern University and Agricultural and Mechanical College, Graduate School, College of Sciences, Department of Psychology, Baton Rouge, LA 70813. Offers rehabilitation counseling (MS). *Degree requirements:* For master's, comprehensive exam, thesis optional. *Entrance requirements:* For master's, GMAT or GRE General Test. Additional exam requirements/recommendations for international students: Required—TOEFL (minimum score 525 paper-based). *Faculty research:* Cultural diversity, professional preparation and participation of minorities, needs and satisfaction of students with disabilities, prediction model for rehabilitation outcome, diabetes.

Southwestern College, Program in Psychodrama and Action Methods, Santa Fe, NM 87502-4788. Offers Certificate. *Entrance requirements:* For degree, 3 letters of reference.

Spalding University, Graduate Studies, Kosair College of Health and Natural Sciences, School of Professional Psychology, Louisville, KY 40203-2188. Offers clinical psychology (MA, Psy D). *Accreditation:* APA (one or more programs are accredited). Part-time programs available. *Faculty:* 8 full-time (4 women), 11 part-time/adjunct (6 women). *Students:* 122 full-time (99 women), 55 part-time (41 women); includes 20 minority (5 Black or African American, non-Hispanic/Latino; 5 Asian, non-Hispanic/Latino; 4 Hispanic/Latino; 1 Native Hawaiian or other Pacific Islander, non-Hispanic/Latino; 5 Two or more races, non-Hispanic/Latino), 2 international. Average age 29. 151 applicants, 33% accepted, 30 enrolled. In 2014, 25 master's, 23 doctorates awarded. Terminal master's awarded for partial completion of doctoral program. *Degree requirements:* For master's, comprehensive exam; for doctorate, thesis/dissertation. *Entrance requirements:* For master's and doctorate, GRE General Test, 18 hours of undergraduate course work in psychology, interview, letters of recommendation, writing sample, autobiographical statement. Additional exam requirements/recommendations for international students: Required—TOEFL (minimum score 535 paper-based). *Application deadline:* For fall admission, 1/15 priority date for domestic and international students. Application fee: $30. *Financial support:* In 2014–15, 56 research assistantships (averaging $2,920 per year) were awarded; career-related internships or fieldwork, scholarships/grants, and unspecified assistantships also available. Financial award application deadline: 3/30; financial award applicants required to submit FAFSA. *Faculty research:* Substance abuse, prayer research, end-of-life issues, complementary and alternative medicine, research methodology and statistical inference. *Unit head:* Dr. Steven Katsikas, Chair, 502-873-4459, E-mail: skatsikas@spalding.edu. *Application contact:* Elizabeth A. Simpson, Administrative Assistant, 502-585-7127, Fax: 502-585-7159, E-mail: esimpson@spalding.edu.

Stanford University, School of Humanities and Sciences, Department of Psychology, Stanford, CA 94305-9991. Offers PhD. *Degree requirements:* For doctorate, thesis/dissertation, oral exam. *Entrance requirements:* For doctorate, GRE General Test, GRE Subject Test. Additional exam requirements/recommendations for international students: Required—TOEFL. Electronic applications accepted. *Expenses: Tuition:* Full-time $44,184; part-time $982 per credit hour. *Required fees:* $191.

State University of New York at New Paltz, Graduate School, School of Liberal Arts and Sciences, Department of Psychology, New Paltz, NY 12561. Offers mental health counseling (MS, AC); psychology (MA); school counseling (MS). Part-time and evening/weekend programs available. *Faculty:* 7 full-time (5 women), 1 (woman) part-time/adjunct. *Students:* 39 full-time (31 women), 23 part-time (16 women); includes 12 minority (1 Black or African American, non-Hispanic/Latino; 3 Asian, non-Hispanic/Latino; 4 Hispanic/Latino; 4 Two or more races, non-Hispanic/Latino), 1 international. Average age 28. 75 applicants, 61% accepted, 23 enrolled. In 2014, 30 master's awarded. *Degree requirements:* For master's, comprehensive exam, thesis. *Entrance requirements:* For master's, GRE General Test, minimum GPA of 3.0. Additional exam requirements/recommendations for international students: Required—TOEFL (minimum score 550 paper-based; 80 iBT), IELTS (minimum score 6.5). *Application deadline:* For fall admission, 2/1 priority date for domestic and international students; for spring admission, 11/15 priority date for domestic and international students. Application fee: $50. Electronic applications accepted. *Financial support:* In 2014–15, 6 teaching assistantships with partial tuition reimbursements (averaging $5,000 per year) were awarded. Financial award application deadline: 8/1. *Faculty research:* Disaster mental health, women's objectification, mate selection, cultural psychology, achievement

motivation. *Unit head:* Dr. Glenn Geher, Chair, 845-257-3091, E-mail: geherg@newpaltz.edu. *Application contact:* Dr. Melanie Hill, Coordinator, 845-257-3475, E-mail: hillm@newpaltz.edu.
Website: http://www.newpaltz.edu/psychology/

State University of New York at Plattsburgh, School of Arts and Sciences, Department of Psychology, Plattsburgh, NY 12901-2681. Offers school psychology (MA, CAS). Part-time programs available. *Students:* 13 full-time (all women), 7 part-time (5 women); includes 1 minority (Hispanic/Latino), 1 international. Average age 25. *Entrance requirements:* For master's, GRE General Test, minimum GPA of 3.0. Additional exam requirements/recommendations for international students: Required—TOEFL. *Application deadline:* For fall admission, 2/15 priority date for domestic students. Applications are processed on a rolling basis. Application fee: $75. *Financial support:* Federal Work-Study available. Support available to part-time students. Financial award application deadline: 4/15; financial award applicants required to submit FAFSA. *Faculty research:* Alzheimer's disease, adolescent behavior, intellectual assessment, learning disabilities, reading skill acquisition. *Unit head:* Dr. Laci Charette, Program Coordinator, 518-564-3385, E-mail: charetlm@plattsburgh.edu. *Application contact:* Betsy Kane, Director, Graduate Admissions, 518-564-4723, Fax: 518-564-4722, E-mail: bkane002@plattsburgh.edu.

Stephen F. Austin State University, Graduate School, College of Liberal Arts, Department of Psychology, Nacogdoches, TX 75962. Offers MA. *Degree requirements:* For master's, comprehensive exam, thesis. *Entrance requirements:* For master's, GRE General Test. Additional exam requirements/recommendations for international students: Required—TOEFL.

Stony Brook University, State University of New York, Graduate School, College of Arts and Sciences, Department of Psychology, Stony Brook, NY 11794. Offers clinical psychology (PhD); cognitive/experimental psychology (PhD); integrative neuroscience (PhD); psychology (MA); social and health psychology (PhD). *Accreditation:* APA (one or more programs are accredited). *Faculty:* 31 full-time (15 women), 3 part-time/adjunct (2 women). *Students:* 93 full-time (72 women), 1 (woman) part-time; includes 17 minority (3 Black or African American, non-Hispanic/Latino; 7 Asian, non-Hispanic/Latino; 5 Hispanic/Latino; 2 Two or more races, non-Hispanic/Latino), 12 international. Average age 27. 419 applicants, 7% accepted, 14 enrolled. In 2014, 24 master's, 14 doctorates awarded. *Degree requirements:* For doctorate, thesis/dissertation. *Entrance requirements:* For doctorate, GRE General Test, GRE Subject Test. Additional exam requirements/recommendations for international students: Required—TOEFL. *Application deadline:* For fall admission, 1/15 for domestic students; for spring admission, 10/1 for domestic students. Application fee: $100. *Expenses:* Tuition, state resident: full-time $10,370; part-time $432 per credit. Tuition, nonresident: full-time $20,190; part-time $841 per credit. *Required fees:* $1431. *Financial support:* In 2014–15, 4 fellowships, 8 research assistantships, 55 teaching assistantships were awarded; career-related internships or fieldwork also available. *Faculty research:* Behavior therapy, memory and cognition, child and family studies, quantitative methods, health psychology. *Total annual research expenditures:* $3.1 million. *Unit head:* Dr. Arthur Samuel, Chair, 631-632-7808, Fax: 631-632-7876, E-mail: arthur.samuel@stonybrook.edu. *Application contact:* Marilynn Wollmuth, Coordinator, 631-632-7855, Fax: 631-632-7876, E-mail: marilyn.wollmuth@stonybrook.edu.
Website: http://www.psychology.sunysb.edu/psychology/

Suffolk University, College of Arts and Sciences, Department of Psychology, Boston, MA 02108-2770. Offers clinical psychology (PhD); college admission counseling (Certificate); mental health counseling (MS, CAGS); school counseling (MS, CAGS). *Accreditation:* APA. *Faculty:* 14 full-time (6 women), 6 part-time/adjunct (4 women). *Students:* 61 full-time (52 women), 39 part-time (33 women); includes 23 minority (6 Black or African American, non-Hispanic/Latino; 7 Asian, non-Hispanic/Latino; 8 Hispanic/Latino; 2 Two or more races, non-Hispanic/Latino), 6 international. Average age 27. 384 applicants, 18% accepted, 33 enrolled. In 2014, 33 master's, 21 doctorates, 6 other advanced degrees awarded. *Degree requirements:* For doctorate, thesis/dissertation, practicum. *Entrance requirements:* For doctorate, GRE General Test or MAT, 2 letters of recommendation, resume. Additional exam requirements/recommendations for international students: Required—TOEFL (minimum score 550 paper-based; 80 iBT). *Application deadline:* For fall admission, 12/15 for domestic and international students. Applications are processed on a rolling basis. Application fee: $50. Electronic applications accepted. *Expenses:* Expenses: Contact institution. *Financial support:* In 2014–15, 62 students received support, including 60 fellowships (averaging $16,231 per year); career-related internships or fieldwork, Federal Work-Study, and institutionally sponsored loans also available. Support available to part-time students. Financial award application deadline: 4/1; financial award applicants required to submit FAFSA. *Faculty research:* Assessing exposure in the context of a family-based cognitive behavioral treatment for pediatric OCD, a mindfulness approach to designing and testing the efficacy of a new sexual revictimization prevention program for college women, olfaction and decision-making in substance-dependent individuals, the role of experiential avoidance in Generalized Anxiety Disorder, ego development as a predictor of dogmatism and intolerance in the political right and left. *Unit head:* Dr. Gary Fireman, Chairperson, 617-305-6368, Fax: 617-367-2924, E-mail: gfireman@suffolk.edu. *Application contact:* Cory Meyers, Director of Graduate Admissions, 617-573-8302, Fax: 617-305-1733, E-mail: grad.admission@suffolk.edu.
Website: http://www.suffolk.edu/college/departments/9912.php

Sul Ross State University, School of Arts and Sciences, Department of Behavioral and Social Sciences, Program in Psychology, Alpine, TX 79832. Offers clinical psychology (MA); general psychology (MA). *Entrance requirements:* For master's, GRE General Test, minimum GPA of 2.5 in last 60 hours of undergraduate work.

Temple University, College of Liberal Arts, Department of Psychology, Philadelphia, PA 19122-6096. Offers psychology (PhD); psychology neuroscience (PhD). *Accreditation:* APA. *Faculty:* 34 full-time (17 women), 17 part-time/adjunct (12 women). *Students:* 94 full-time (72 women), 1 part-time (0 women); includes 14 minority (4 Black or African American, non-Hispanic/Latino; 5 Asian, non-Hispanic/Latino; 5 Hispanic/Latino), 4 international. 576 applicants, 5% accepted, 14 enrolled. In 2014, 18 doctorates awarded. *Degree requirements:* For doctorate, thesis/dissertation. *Entrance requirements:* For doctorate, GRE General Test, minimum GPA of 3.0, 2 letters of recommendation. Additional exam requirements/recommendations for international students: Required—TOEFL (minimum score 620 paper-based; 105 iBT). *Application deadline:* For fall admission, 12/1 for domestic students, 12/15 for international students. Application fee: $60. Electronic applications accepted. *Expenses:* Tuition, state resident: full-time $14,490; part-time $805 per credit hour. Tuition, nonresident: full-time $19,850; part-time $1103 per credit hour. *Required fees:* $690. Full-time tuition and fees vary according to class time, course load, degree level, campus/location and program. *Financial support:* Fellowships, research assistantships, teaching assistantships, career-related internships or fieldwork, Federal Work-Study, institutionally sponsored loans, and unspecified assistantships available. Financial award application deadline: 12/15; financial award applicants required to submit FAFSA. *Faculty research:* Behavioral and cognitive neuroscience, cognitive and social development, psychopathology: study and treatment, social cognition and decision-making. *Unit head:* Dr. Robert Weisberg, Graduate Director, 215-204-7567, Fax: 215-204-5539, E-mail: weisberg@temple.edu. *Application contact:* Vanessa Allen-Smith, Graduate Coordinator, 215-204-7667, Fax: 215-204-5539, E-mail: vallens@temple.edu.
Website: http://www.cla.temple.edu/psychology/

Tennessee State University, The School of Graduate Studies and Research, College of Education, Department of Psychology, Nashville, TN 37209-1561. Offers counseling psychology (MS, PhD); professional school counseling (MS); psychology (MS, PhD); school psychology (MS, PhD). *Accreditation:* APA. *Degree requirements:* For doctorate, thesis/dissertation (for some programs). *Entrance requirements:* For master's, GRE General Test or MAT; for doctorate, GRE General Test or MAT, minimum GPA of 3.25, work experience. Electronic applications accepted.

Texas A&M International University, Office of Graduate Studies and Research, College of Arts and Sciences, Department of Psychology and Communication, Laredo, TX 78041-1900. Offers counseling psychology (MACP); psychology (MS). *Degree requirements:* For master's, thesis (for some programs). *Entrance requirements:* For master's, GRE General Test. Additional exam requirements/recommendations for international students: Required—TOEFL (minimum score 550 paper-based; 79 iBT).

Texas A&M University, College of Liberal Arts, Department of Psychology, College Station, TX 77843. Offers behavioral and cellular neuroscience (PhD); clinical psychology (PhD); cognitive psychology (PhD); developmental psychology (PhD); industrial/organizational psychology (PhD); psychology (MS); social psychology (PhD). *Accreditation:* APA (one or more programs are accredited). *Faculty:* 35. *Students:* 82 full-time (45 women), 15 part-time (12 women); includes 30 minority (6 Black or African American, non-Hispanic/Latino; 6 Asian, non-Hispanic/Latino; 18 Hispanic/Latino), 11 international. Average age 28. 375 applicants, 5% accepted, 8 enrolled. In 2014, 8 master's, 16 doctorates awarded. *Degree requirements:* For doctorate, comprehensive exam (for some programs), thesis/dissertation. *Entrance requirements:* For doctorate, GRE General Test. Additional exam requirements/recommendations for international students: Required—TOEFL. *Application deadline:* For fall admission, 1/5 for domestic and international students. Application fee: $50 ($90 for international students). Electronic applications accepted. *Expenses:* Tuition, state resident: full-time $4078; part-time $226.55 per credit hour. Tuition, nonresident: full-time $10,594; part-time $577.55 per credit hour. *Required fees:* $2813; $237.70 per credit hour. $278.50 per semester. Tuition and fees vary according to degree level and student level. *Financial support:* In 2014–15, 84 students received support, including 25 fellowships with full and partial tuition reimbursements available (averaging $17,037 per year), 20 research assistantships with full and partial tuition reimbursements available (averaging $8,269 per year), 57 teaching assistantships with full and partial tuition reimbursements available (averaging $7,431 per year); career-related internships or fieldwork, institutionally sponsored loans, scholarships/grants, traineeships, health care benefits, tuition waivers (full and partial), and unspecified assistantships also available. Support available to part-time students. Financial award application deadline: 1/5; financial award applicants required to submit FAFSA. *Unit head:* Dr. Doug Woods, Head, 979-845-2540, E-mail: dowoods@tamu.edu. *Application contact:* Dr. Charles D. Samuelson, Director of Graduate Studies, 979-845-0880, Fax: 979-845-4727, E-mail: c-samuelson@tamu.edu.
Website: http://psychology.tamu.edu

Texas A&M University–Corpus Christi, College of Graduate Studies, College of Liberal Arts, Program in Psychology, Corpus Christi, TX 78412-5503. Offers MA. Part-time and evening/weekend programs available. *Students:* 21 full-time (17 women), 9 part-time (5 women); includes 9 minority (1 American Indian or Alaska Native, non-Hispanic/Latino; 8 Hispanic/Latino), 1 international. Average age 29. 50 applicants, 54% accepted, 14 enrolled. In 2014, 21 master's awarded. *Degree requirements:* For master's, comprehensive exam, thesis (for some programs). *Entrance requirements:* For master's, GRE General Test (taken within 5 years), minimum graduate GPA of 3.0, essay (500-1000 words), 2 letters of evaluation. Additional exam requirements/recommendations for international students: Required—TOEFL (minimum score 550 paper-based; 79 iBT), IELTS (minimum score 6.5). *Application deadline:* For fall admission, 4/1 priority date for domestic and international students; for spring admission, 11/15 for domestic students, 9/1 for international students. Applications are processed on a rolling basis. Application fee: $50 ($70 for international students). Electronic applications accepted. *Financial support:* In 2014–15, 14 students received support. Research assistantships, teaching assistantships, career-related internships or fieldwork, Federal Work-Study, institutionally sponsored loans, scholarships/grants, health care benefits, and unspecified assistantships available. Support available to part-time students. Financial award application deadline: 3/15; financial award applicants required to submit FAFSA. *Unit head:* Dr. Amy Houlihan, Chair, 361-825-2971, E-mail: amy.houlihan@tamucc.edu. *Application contact:* Graduate Admissions Coordinator, 361-825-2177, Fax: 361-825-2755, E-mail: gradweb@tamucc.edu.
Website: http://cla.tamucc.edu/psychology/pages/graduate.html

Texas A&M University–Kingsville, College of Graduate Studies, College of Arts and Sciences, Department of Psychology and Sociology, Program in Psychology, Kingsville, TX 78363. Offers MA, MS, PhD. *Students:* 28 full-time (20 women), 13 part-time (10 women); includes 34 minority (4 Black or African American, non-Hispanic/Latino; 1 American Indian or Alaska Native, non-Hispanic/Latino; 28 Hispanic/Latino; 1 Two or more races, non-Hispanic/Latino), 2 international. Average age 29. 19 applicants, 95% accepted, 8 enrolled. In 2014, 5 master's awarded. *Degree requirements:* For master's, variable foreign language requirement, comprehensive exam, thesis (for some programs); for doctorate, one foreign language, comprehensive exam, thesis/dissertation. *Entrance requirements:* For master's, GRE, MAT, GMAT. Additional exam requirements/recommendations for international students: Required—TOEFL (minimum score 550 paper-based; 79 iBT). *Application deadline:* For fall admission, 8/15 for domestic students, 6/1 for international students; for spring admission, 12/15 for domestic students, 10/1 for international students; for summer admission, 5/15 for domestic students, 4/1 for international students. Applications are processed on a rolling basis. Application fee: $35 ($50 for international students). Electronic applications accepted. *Financial support:* In 2014–15, 9 students received support, including 1 research assistantship (averaging $5,326 per year), 2 teaching assistantships (averaging $8,216 per year); career-related internships or fieldwork, Federal Work-Study, institutionally sponsored loans, scholarships/grants, health care benefits, tuition waivers (full and partial), and unspecified assistantships also available. Support available to part-time students. Financial award application deadline: 5/1; financial award applicants required to submit FAFSA. *Unit head:* Dr. Richard Miller, Department Chair, 361-593-4181, E-mail: richard.miller@tamuk.edu. *Application contact:* Dr. Lloyd Dempster, Graduate Coordinator, E-mail: lloyd.dempster@tamuk. Edu.

Texas A&M University–Texarkana, Graduate Studies and Research, College of Health and Behavioral Sciences, Texarkana, TX 75505-5518. Offers counseling psychology (MS). Part-time and evening/weekend programs available. *Degree requirements:* For master's, comprehensive exam (for some programs), thesis or alternative. *Entrance requirements:* For master's, minimum GPA of 3.0 in last 60 hours of bachelor's degree. Additional exam requirements/recommendations for international students: Required—TOEFL. Electronic applications accepted.

Texas Christian University, College of Science and Engineering, Department of Psychology, Fort Worth, TX 76129. Offers developmental trauma (MS); experimental

psychology (MA, MS, PhD), including behavioral neuroscience (MS), cognition (MS), learning (MS), social (MS). *Faculty:* 12 full-time (5 women), 2 part-time/adjunct (1 woman). *Students:* 28 full-time (14 women); includes 1 minority (Hispanic/Latino), 3 international. Average age 27. 37 applicants, 22% accepted, 8 enrolled. In 2014, 2 master's, 6 doctorates awarded. Terminal master's awarded for partial completion of doctoral program. *Degree requirements:* For master's, thesis; for doctorate, thesis/dissertation. *Entrance requirements:* For master's and doctorate, GRE General Test. Additional exam requirements/recommendations for international students: Required—TOEFL. *Application deadline:* For fall admission, 2/1 for domestic and international students; for spring admission, 12/1 for domestic students. Application fee: $60 ($0 for international students). Electronic applications accepted. *Expenses: Tuition:* Full-time $22,860; part-time $1270 per credit hour. *Financial support:* In 2014–15, 23 students received support, including 23 teaching assistantships with full tuition reimbursements available (averaging $19,750 per year); scholarships/grants and tuition waivers also available. Financial award application deadline: 2/1; financial award applicants required to submit FAFSA. *Faculty research:* Neuroscience, human and animal learning, cognition, development, experimental social psychology. *Unit head:* Dr. Mauricio Papini, Chair, 817-257-7410, Fax: 817-257-7681, E-mail: m.papini@tcu.edu. *Application contact:* Cindy Hayes, Administrative Assistant, 817-257-7410, Fax: 817-257-7681, E-mail: c.hayes@tcu.edu.
Website: http://www.psy.tcu.edu/gradpro.html

Texas Southern University, College of Liberal Arts and Behavioral Sciences, Department of Psychology, Houston, TX 77004-4584. Offers MA. Electronic applications accepted.

Texas State University, The Graduate College, College of Liberal Arts, Program in Psychological Research, San Marcos, TX 78666. Offers MA. *Faculty:* 15 full-time (9 women), 1 part-time/adjunct (0 women). *Students:* 32 full-time (17 women), 1 (woman) part-time; includes 8 minority (2 Black or African American, non-Hispanic/Latino; 1 Asian, non-Hispanic/Latino; 4 Hispanic/Latino; 1 Two or more races, non-Hispanic/Latino), 1 international. Average age 26. 35 applicants, 51% accepted, 10 enrolled. *Degree requirements:* For master's, comprehensive exam, thesis optional. *Entrance requirements:* For master's, GRE General Test, baccalaureate degree from regionally-accredited university with minimum GPA of 3.0 on last 60 undergraduate semester hours. Additional exam requirements/recommendations for international students: Required—TOEFL (minimum score 550 paper-based; 78 iBT). *Application deadline:* For fall admission, 4/30 for domestic and international students. Applications are processed on a rolling basis. Application fee: $40 ($90 for international students). Electronic applications accepted. *Expenses:* Expenses: $8,834 (tuition and fees combined). *Financial support:* In 2014–15, 27 students received support, including 3 research assistantships (averaging $10,082 per year), 23 teaching assistantships (averaging $9,912 per year); Federal Work-Study, institutionally sponsored loans, scholarships/grants, health care benefits, and unspecified assistantships also available. Support available to part-time students. Financial award application deadline: 4/1; financial award applicants required to submit FAFSA. *Faculty research:* Cross-cultural study, stress and alcohol. *Total annual research expenditures:* $3,503. *Unit head:* Dr. Reiko Graham, Graduate Advisor, 512-245-6806, Fax: 512-245-3153, E-mail: rg30@txstate.edu. *Application contact:* Dr. Andrea Golato, Dean of Graduate College, 512-245-2581, Fax: 512-245-8365, E-mail: gradcollege@txstate.edu.
Website: http://www.psych.txstate.edu/

Texas Tech University, Graduate School, College of Arts and Sciences, Department of Psychological Sciences, Lubbock, TX 79409-2051. Offers clinical psychology (PhD); counseling psychology (MA, PhD); general experimental psychology (MA, PhD); psychology (MA). *Accreditation:* APA (one or more programs are accredited). *Faculty:* 32 full-time (14 women), 1 part-time/adjunct (0 women). *Students:* 96 full-time (60 women), 18 part-time (16 women); includes 25 minority (4 Black or African American, non-Hispanic/Latino; 5 Asian, non-Hispanic/Latino; 14 Hispanic/Latino; 2 Two or more races, non-Hispanic/Latino), 6 international. Average age 27. 281 applicants, 17% accepted, 24 enrolled. In 2014, 12 master's, 16 doctorates awarded. *Degree requirements:* For doctorate, comprehensive exam, thesis/dissertation, 100 credit hours of organized courses, research credits, and practica. *Entrance requirements:* For master's, GRE General Test, GRE Subject Test, essays; for doctorate, GRE General Test, essays. Additional exam requirements/recommendations for international students: Required—TOEFL (minimum score 550 paper-based; 79 iBT). *Application deadline:* For fall admission, 6/1 priority date for domestic students, 1/15 priority date for international students; for spring admission, 9/1 priority date for domestic students, 6/15 priority date for international students. Applications are processed on a rolling basis. Application fee: $60. Electronic applications accepted. *Expenses:* Tuition, state resident: full-time $6310; part-time $262.92 per credit hour. Tuition, nonresident: full-time $14,998; part-time $624.92 per credit hour. *Required fees:* $2701; $36.50 per credit. $912.50 per semester. Tuition and fees vary according to course load. *Financial support:* In 2014–15, 102 students received support, including 101 fellowships (averaging $4,037 per year), 23 research assistantships (averaging $13,150 per year), 72 teaching assistantships (averaging $10,753 per year). Financial award application deadline: 4/15; financial award applicants required to submit FAFSA. *Faculty research:* Health psychology, addictive behaviors, depression and suicide risk, sexuality/sexual risk behaviors/HIV, neuroscience/neuroimaging. *Total annual research expenditures:* $345,735. *Unit head:* Dr. Lee M. Cohen, Professor and Chair, 806-834-2530, Fax: 806-742-0818, E-mail: lee.cohen@ttu.edu. *Application contact:* Kay Hill, Admissions Coordinator, 806-742-3711 Ext. 222, Fax: 806-742-0818, E-mail: kay.hill@ttu.edu.
Website: http://www.depts.ttu.edu/psy/

Texas Woman's University, Graduate School, College of Arts and Sciences, Department of Psychology and Philosophy, Denton, TX 76201. Offers counseling psychology (MA, PhD); school psychology (PhD, SSP). *Accreditation:* APA (one or more programs are accredited). Terminal master's awarded for partial completion of doctoral program. *Degree requirements:* For master's, comprehensive exam (for some programs), thesis (for some programs); for doctorate, comprehensive exam, thesis/dissertation, internship, residency. *Entrance requirements:* For master's, GRE (preferred minimum score 153 [500 old version] Verbal, 144 [500 old version] Quantitative, 4 Analytical), BA/BS or 18 hours in psychology; minimum GPA of 3.0, 3.5 in psychology classes; 3 letters of reference; curriculum vitae; essays; for doctorate, GRE (preferred minimum score 153 [500 old version] Verbal, 144 [500 old version] Quantitative, 4 Analytical), 3 letters of reference, minimum GPA of 3.0 overall and 3.5 in psychology classes, MA in psychology or related discipline with thesis, curriculum vitae, essays. Additional exam requirements/recommendations for international students: Required—TOEFL (minimum score 550 paper-based; 79 iBT). Electronic applications accepted. *Faculty research:* Women's anger, school neuropsychological theory and assessment, body image dysfunction, traumatic stress, classical ethics, mental health and behavioral needs of adolescents in alternative education.

Tiffin University, Program in Psychology, Tiffin, OH 44883-2161. Offers MS.

Touro College, Graduate School of Psychology, New York, NY 10006. Offers general psychology (MS); industrial/organizational psychology (MS); mental health counseling (MS); school counseling (MS); school psychology (MS). *Students:* 101 full-time (80 women), 81 part-time (66 women); includes 76 minority (41 Black or African American,

non-Hispanic/Latino; 1 American Indian or Alaska Native, non-Hispanic/Latino; 8 Asian, non-Hispanic/Latino; 26 Hispanic/Latino), 2 international. *Unit head:* Dr. Richard Waxman, Dean, 212-242-4668 Ext. 6077, E-mail: richard.waxman@touro.edu.
Website: http://gsp.touro.edu/

Tufts University, Graduate School of Arts and Sciences, Department of Psychology, Medford, MA 02155. Offers cognitive science (PhD); psychology (MS, PhD). *Students:* 36 full-time (28 women), 4 part-time (3 women); includes 9 minority (2 Black or African American, non-Hispanic/Latino; 4 Asian, non-Hispanic/Latino; 1 Hispanic/Latino; 2 Two or more races, non-Hispanic/Latino), 7 international. Average age 28. 174 applicants, 9% accepted, 5 enrolled. In 2014, 5 master's, 6 doctorates awarded. Terminal master's awarded for partial completion of doctoral program. *Degree requirements:* For master's, thesis; for doctorate, one foreign language, thesis/dissertation. *Entrance requirements:* For master's and doctorate, GRE General Test, GRE Subject Test. Additional exam requirements/recommendations for international students: Required—TOEFL (minimum score 550 paper-based; 80 iBT), IELTS (minimum score 6.5). *Application deadline:* For fall admission, 12/15 for domestic and international students. Applications are processed on a rolling basis. Application fee: $75. Electronic applications accepted. *Expenses: Tuition:* Full-time $45,590; part-time $1161 per credit hour. *Required fees:* $782. Full-time tuition and fees vary according to degree level, program and student level. Part-time tuition and fees vary according to course load. *Financial support:* Fellowships, research assistantships with full tuition reimbursements, teaching assistantships with full tuition reimbursements, Federal Work-Study, scholarships/grants, tuition waivers (partial), and unspecified assistantships available. Support available to part-time students. Financial award application deadline: 12/15. *Unit head:* Dr. Holly Taylor, Graduate Program Director. *Application contact:* Office of Graduate Admissions, 617-627-3395, E-mail: gradadmissions@tufts.edu.
Website: http://ase.tufts.edu/psychology

Tulane University, School of Science and Engineering, Department of Psychology, New Orleans, LA 70118-5669. Offers MS, PhD. *Accreditation:* APA (one or more programs are accredited). Terminal master's awarded for partial completion of doctoral program. *Degree requirements:* For master's, variable foreign language requirement, thesis; for doctorate, thesis/dissertation. *Entrance requirements:* For master's, GRE General Test, minimum B average in undergraduate course work; for doctorate, GRE General Test. Additional exam requirements/recommendations for international students: Required—TOEFL. Electronic applications accepted. *Expenses: Tuition:* Full-time $46,326; part-time $2574 per credit hour. *Required fees:* $1980; $44.50 per credit hour. $550 per term. Tuition and fees vary according to course load and program. *Faculty research:* Hormones and behavior, aggression, personnel selection, cognitive development, stereotyping, diabetes.

Uniformed Services University of the Health Sciences, F. Edward Hebert School of Medicine, Graduate Programs in the Biomedical Sciences and Public Health, Department of Medical and Clinical Psychology, Bethesda, MD 20814. Offers clinical psychology (PhD); medical psychology (PhD). PhD in clinical psychology available to active duty military only. *Accreditation:* APA. Terminal master's awarded for partial completion of doctoral program. *Degree requirements:* For doctorate, comprehensive exam, thesis/dissertation, qualifying exam. *Entrance requirements:* For doctorate, GRE General Test, minimum GPA of 3.0, U.S. citizenship. Additional exam requirements/recommendations for international students: Required—TOEFL. Electronic applications accepted. *Faculty research:* Addictive and appetitive behavior, psychopharmacology, stress and eating, obesity, health.

Union College, Graduate Programs, Department of Psychology, Barbourville, KY 40906-1499. Offers clinical psychology (MA); counseling psychology (MA); school psychology (MA).

Union Institute & University, Graduate Programs in Psychology, Cincinnati, OH 45206-1925. Offers clinical psychology (Psy D). Psy D offered in Ohio and Vermont. Postbaccalaureate distance learning degree programs offered (minimal on-campus study). *Faculty:* 9 full-time (7 women), 8 part-time/adjunct (4 women). *Students:* 66 full-time (45 women), 21 part-time (16 women); includes 13 minority (5 Black or African American, non-Hispanic/Latino; 2 American Indian or Alaska Native, non-Hispanic/Latino; 1 Asian, non-Hispanic/Latino; 4 Hispanic/Latino; 1 Native Hawaiian or other Pacific Islander, non-Hispanic/Latino). Average age 38. Terminal master's awarded for partial completion of doctoral program. *Degree requirements:* For master's, thesis, internship; for doctorate, thesis/dissertation, internship, practicum. *Entrance requirements:* For master's and doctorate, transcripts, letters of recommendation, essay. *Application deadline:* Applications are processed on a rolling basis. Application fee: $50. Electronic applications accepted. *Expenses: Tuition:* Full-time $26,640; part-time $719 per credit hour. *Required fees:* $216; $54 per semester. Part-time tuition and fees vary according to course load, degree level and program. *Financial support:* Federal Work-Study available. Financial award applicants required to submit FAFSA. *Unit head:* Dr. Bill Lax, Dean, 802-254-0152, E-mail: bill.lax@myunion.edu. *Application contact:* Director of Admissions, 888-828-8575.

Universidad de las Americas, A.C., Program in Psychology, Mexico City, Mexico. Offers family therapy (MA).

Universidad de las Américas Puebla, Division of Graduate Studies, School of Social Sciences, Program in Psychology, Puebla, Mexico. Offers MA. Part-time and evening/weekend programs available. *Degree requirements:* For master's, one foreign language, thesis. *Entrance requirements:* For master's, minimum B+ average. *Faculty research:* Testing, social hemispheric specialization, clinical psychology.

Université de Montréal, Faculty of Arts and Sciences, Department of Psychology, Montréal, QC H3C 3J7, Canada. Offers M Sc, PhD. Terminal master's awarded for partial completion of doctoral program. *Degree requirements:* For master's, one foreign language, thesis; for doctorate, one foreign language, thesis/dissertation, general exam. Electronic applications accepted. *Faculty research:* Vision, marital counseling, memory.

Université de Sherbrooke, Faculty of Letters and Human Sciences, Department of Psychology, Sherbrooke, QC J1K 2R1, Canada. Offers gerontology (MA). *Degree requirements:* For master's, thesis. *Faculty research:* Human relations.

Université du Québec à Montréal, Graduate Programs, Program in Psychology, Montréal, QC H3C 3P8, Canada. Offers D Ps, PhD. Programs offered jointly with Université du Québec à Trois-Rivières. Part-time programs available. *Degree requirements:* For doctorate, thesis/dissertation. *Entrance requirements:* For doctorate, appropriate master's degree or equivalent, proficiency in French.

Université du Québec à Trois-Rivières, Graduate Programs, Program in Psychology, Trois-Rivières, QC G9A 5H7, Canada. Offers PhD, Certificate. Part-time programs available. *Degree requirements:* For doctorate, thesis/dissertation. *Entrance requirements:* For doctorate, appropriate master's degree, proficiency in French. *Faculty research:* Child and family development, gerontology, mental health.

Université Laval, Faculty of Social Sciences, School of Psychology, Programs in Psychology, Québec, QC G1K 7P4, Canada. Offers clinical psychology (PhD); community psychology (PhD); psychology (PhD, Psy D). *Degree requirements:* For doctorate, comprehensive exam, thesis/dissertation. *Entrance requirements:* For

doctorate, comprehension of written English, knowledge of French, interview. Electronic applications accepted.

University at Albany, State University of New York, College of Arts and Sciences, Department of Psychology, Albany, NY 12222-0001. Offers behavioral neuroscience (PhD); clinical psychology (PhD); cognitive psychology (PhD); industrial/organizational psychology (MA, PhD); social-personality psychology (PhD). *Accreditation:* APA (one or more programs are accredited). *Degree requirements:* For doctorate, thesis/dissertation. *Entrance requirements:* For doctorate, GRE General Test, GRE Subject Test. Additional exam requirements/recommendations for international students: Required—TOEFL (minimum score 550 paper-based). Electronic applications accepted.

University at Buffalo, the State University of New York, Graduate School, College of Arts and Sciences, Department of Psychology, Buffalo, NY 14260. Offers MA, PhD. *Accreditation:* APA (one or more programs are accredited). *Faculty:* 25 full-time (8 women), 13 part-time/adjunct (2 women). *Students:* 88 full-time (60 women), 3 part-time (1 woman); includes 14 minority (1 Black or African American, non-Hispanic/Latino; 1 American Indian or Alaska Native, non-Hispanic/Latino; 6 Asian, non-Hispanic/Latino; 6 Hispanic/Latino), 3 international. Average age 27. 278 applicants, 15% accepted, 21 enrolled. In 2014, 11 master's, 9 doctorates awarded. Terminal master's awarded for partial completion of doctoral program. *Degree requirements:* For master's, project; for doctorate, thesis/dissertation. *Entrance requirements:* For master's and doctorate, GRE General Test. Additional exam requirements/recommendations for international students: Required—TOEFL (minimum score 550 paper-based; 79 iBT). *Application deadline:* For fall admission, 12/1 for domestic and international students. Application fee: $75. Electronic applications accepted. *Financial support:* In 2014–15, 56 students received support, including 1 fellowship with full tuition reimbursement available (averaging $13,500 per year), 13 research assistantships with full tuition reimbursements available (averaging $13,700 per year), 42 teaching assistantships with full tuition reimbursements available (averaging $13,700 per year); career-related internships or fieldwork, institutionally sponsored loans, scholarships/grants, and tuition waivers (full and partial) also available. Financial award application deadline: 12/1; financial award applicants required to submit FAFSA. *Faculty research:* Neural, endocrine, and molecular bases of behavior; adult mood and anxiety disorders; relationship dysfunction; attention deficit/hyperactivity disorder; psycho-linguistics. *Total annual research expenditures:* $7.9 million. *Unit head:* Dr. Stephen T. Tiffany, Chair, 716-645-0244, Fax: 716-645-3801, E-mail: chairpsych@buffalo.edu. *Application contact:* Mary Wlodarczyk, Admissions Officer, 716-645-8617, Fax: 716-645-3801, E-mail: psych@buffalo.edu.
Website: http://www.psychology.buffalo.edu/

The University of Akron, Graduate School, Buchtel College of Arts and Sciences, Department of Psychology, Akron, OH 44325. Offers adult development and aging (PhD); counseling psychology (MA, PhD); industrial/organizational psychology (MA, PhD); psychology (MA). *Accreditation:* APA (one or more programs are accredited). *Faculty:* 19 full-time (9 women), 3 part-time/adjunct (2 women). *Students:* 70 full-time (42 women), 17 part-time (13 women); includes 15 minority (3 Black or African American, non-Hispanic/Latino; 5 Asian, non-Hispanic/Latino; 5 Hispanic/Latino; 2 Two or more races, non-Hispanic/Latino), 3 international. Average age 26. 174 applicants, 2% accepted, 3 enrolled. In 2014, 13 master's, 12 doctorates awarded. Terminal master's awarded for partial completion of doctoral program. *Degree requirements:* For master's, thesis or specialty exam; for doctorate, one foreign language, comprehensive exam, thesis/dissertation. *Entrance requirements:* For master's, GRE General Test, minimum GPA of 2.75, 3.0 in psychology courses; three letters of recommendation; personal statement; curriculum vitae; for doctorate, GRE General Test, minimum graduate GPA of 3.25, three letters of recommendation, personal statement, statement of purpose, curriculum vitae. Additional exam requirements/recommendations for international students: Required—TOEFL (minimum score 550 paper-based; 79 iBT), IELTS (minimum score 6.5). *Application deadline:* For fall admission, 1/15 for domestic and international students. Application fee: $45 ($70 for international students). Electronic applications accepted. *Expenses:* Tuition, state resident: full-time $7578; part-time $421 per credit hour. Tuition, nonresident: full-time $12,977; part-time $721 per credit hour. Required fees: $1388; $35 per credit hour. Tuition and fees vary according to course load. *Financial support:* In 2014–15, 16 research assistantships with full tuition reimbursements, 46 teaching assistantships with full tuition reimbursements were awarded. *Faculty research:* Social cognitive determinants of behavior, the application of psychological principles to the workplace and career planning/development, the psychological processes of aging. *Total annual research expenditures:* $834,259. *Unit head:* Dr. Paul Levy, Chair, 330-972-8367, E-mail: plevy@uakron.edu.
Website: http://www.uakron.edu/psychology/

The University of Alabama, Graduate School, College of Arts and Sciences, Department of Psychology, Tuscaloosa, AL 35487. Offers clinical psychology (PhD); experimental psychology (PhD). *Accreditation:* APA. *Faculty:* 33 full-time (19 women), 2 part-time/adjunct (both women). *Students:* 88 full-time (64 women), 13 part-time (10 women); includes 14 minority (1 Black or African American, non-Hispanic/Latino; 4 Asian, non-Hispanic/Latino; 7 Hispanic/Latino; 2 Two or more races, non-Hispanic/Latino), 9 international. Average age 27. 318 applicants, 8% accepted, 19 enrolled. In 2014, 20 doctorates awarded. *Degree requirements:* For doctorate, thesis/dissertation, internship (for clinical psychology). *Entrance requirements:* For doctorate, GRE. Additional exam requirements/recommendations for international students: Required—TOEFL (minimum score 550 paper-based). *Application deadline:* For fall admission, 12/1 for domestic and international students. Application fee: $50 ($60 for international students). Electronic applications accepted. *Expenses:* Tuition, state resident: full-time $9826. Tuition, nonresident: full-time $24,950. *Financial support:* In 2014–15, 73 students received support, including 12 fellowships with full tuition reimbursements available (averaging $17,000 per year), 40 research assistantships with full and partial tuition reimbursements available (averaging $12,744 per year), 34 teaching assistantships with full and partial tuition reimbursements available (averaging $13,824 per year); career-related internships or fieldwork, institutionally sponsored loans, scholarships/grants, health care benefits, and unspecified assistantships also available. Financial award application deadline: 12/1. *Faculty research:* Cognitive development/disability, child clinical, psychology and law, health/aging, social psychology. *Total annual research expenditures:* $2.9 million. *Unit head:* Dr. Beverly E. Thorn, Chair, 205-348-1913, Fax: 205-348-8648, E-mail: bthorn@ua.edu. *Application contact:* Mary Beth Hubbard, Information Contact, 205-348-1919, Fax: 205-348-8648, E-mail: mbhubbard@as.ua.edu.
Website: http://www.psychology.ua.edu

The University of Alabama at Birmingham, College of Arts and Sciences, Program in Psychology, Birmingham, AL 35294. Offers behavioral neuroscience (PhD); lifespan developmental psychology (PhD); medical/clinical psychology (PhD); psychology (MA). *Accreditation:* APA (one or more programs are accredited). *Students:* 69 full-time (51 women), 2 part-time (both women); includes 14 minority (2 Black or African American, non-Hispanic/Latino; 2 Asian, non-Hispanic/Latino; 4 Hispanic/Latino; 6 Two or more races, non-Hispanic/Latino), 4 international. Average age 26. In 2014, 8 master's, 15 doctorates awarded. *Entrance requirements:* For master's and doctorate, GRE General

Test, letters of recommendation. *Application deadline:* Applications are processed on a rolling basis. Electronic applications accepted. *Expenses:* Tuition, state resident: full-time $7090; part-time $370 per credit hour. Tuition, nonresident: full-time $16,072; part-time $869 per credit hour. Full-time tuition and fees vary according to course load and program. *Financial support:* Fellowships, research assistantships, and teaching assistantships available. *Faculty research:* Biological basis of behavior structure, function of the nervous system. *Unit head:* Dr. Karlene K. Ball, Chair, 205-934-2610, Fax: 205-975-2295, E-mail: psych-dept@uab.edu. *Application contact:* Susan Noblitt Banks, Director of Graduate School Operations, 205-934-8227, Fax: 205-934-8413, E-mail: gradschool@uab.edu.
Website: http://www.uab.edu/cas/psychology/graduate

The University of Alabama in Huntsville, School of Graduate Studies, College of Liberal Arts, Department of Psychology, Huntsville, AL 35899. Offers industrial/organizational psychology (MA); psychology (MA). Part-time and evening/weekend programs available. *Degree requirements:* For master's, comprehensive exam, thesis or alternative, oral and written exams. *Entrance requirements:* For master's, GRE General Test, 15 hours of course work in psychology, minimum GPA of 3.25, sample of written work. Additional exam requirements/recommendations for international students: Required—TOEFL (minimum score 500 paper-based; 80 iBT), IELTS (minimum score 6.5). Electronic applications accepted. *Faculty research:* Virtual teams and teamwork, eyewitness identification, aging and memory, psychology of natural disasters and emergency preparedness, pain and pain management research.

University of Alaska Anchorage, College of Arts and Sciences, Department of Psychology, Anchorage, AK 99508. Offers clinical psychology (MS); clinical-community psychology with rural-indigenous emphasis (PhD). Part-time programs available. *Degree requirements:* For master's, thesis. *Entrance requirements:* For master's, GRE General Test, GRE Subject Test, interview, references; for doctorate, interview, bachelor's or master's degree in psychology. Additional exam requirements/recommendations for international students: Required—TOEFL (minimum score 550 paper-based). *Faculty research:* Substance abuse, childhood autism, biofeedback, psychological assessment, mental health in Native Alaskans.

University of Alaska Fairbanks, College of Liberal Arts, Department of Psychology, Fairbanks, AK 99775-6480. Offers clinical-community psychology (PhD), including rural cross-cultural emphasis. Program offered jointly with University of Alaska Anchorage. *Faculty:* 9 full-time (5 women). *Students:* 4 full-time (3 women), 16 part-time (10 women); includes 4 minority (1 Asian, non-Hispanic/Latino; 1 Hispanic/Latino; 2 Two or more races, non-Hispanic/Latino), 1 international. Average age 30. 8 applicants, 63% accepted, 5 enrolled. In 2014, 1 doctorate awarded. *Degree requirements:* For doctorate, comprehensive exam, thesis/dissertation, oral defense of dissertation. *Entrance requirements:* For doctorate, bachelor's degree from accredited institution with minimum cumulative undergraduate and major GPA of 3.0; criminal background check; interview; course work in abnormal psychology, statistics, and research methods. Additional exam requirements/recommendations for international students: Required—TOEFL (minimum score 550 paper-based; 80 iBT), IELTS (minimum score 6.5). *Application deadline:* For fall admission, 1/15 for domestic and international students. Application fee: $60. Electronic applications accepted. *Expenses:* Tuition, state resident: full-time $7614; part-time $423 per credit. Tuition, nonresident: full-time $15,552; part-time $864 per credit. Tuition and fees vary according to course level, course load and reciprocity agreements. *Financial support:* In 2014–15, 12 teaching assistantships with full tuition reimbursements (averaging $13,286 per year) were awarded; fellowships with full tuition reimbursements, research assistantships with full tuition reimbursements, career-related internships or fieldwork, Federal Work-Study, scholarships/grants, health care benefits, and unspecified assistantships also available. Support available to part-time students. Financial award application deadline: 7/1; financial award applicants required to submit FAFSA. *Faculty research:* Clinical and community psychology; rural, indigenous, and cultural psychology. *Unit head:* Dr. David Webster, Doctoral Program Director, 907-474-7007, Fax: 907-474-5781, E-mail: fypsych@uaf.edu. *Application contact:* Mary Kreta, Director of Admissions, 907-474-7500, Fax: 907-474-7097, E-mail: admissions@uaf.edu.
Website: http://www.uaf.edu/psych/

University of Alberta, Faculty of Graduate Studies and Research, Department of Psychology, Edmonton, AB T6G 2E1, Canada. Offers M Sc, MA, PhD. Terminal master's awarded for partial completion of doctoral program. *Degree requirements:* For master's, thesis (for some programs); for doctorate, thesis/dissertation. *Entrance requirements:* For master's and doctorate, GRE. Additional exam requirements/recommendations for international students: Required—TOEFL (minimum score 550 paper-based). Electronic applications accepted. *Faculty research:* Animal behavior processes; cognitive, social and perceptual processes; development and aging; neuroscience.

The University of Arizona, College of Science, Department of Psychology, Tucson, AZ 85721. Offers MA, PhD. *Accreditation:* APA (one or more programs are accredited). *Degree requirements:* For doctorate, comprehensive exam, thesis/dissertation. *Entrance requirements:* For master's, GRE General Test, 3 letters of recommendation, statement of purpose; for doctorate, GRE General Test, 3 letters of recommendation. Additional exam requirements/recommendations for international students: Required—TOEFL (minimum score 550 paper-based; 79 iBT). Electronic applications accepted. *Faculty research:* Cognitive neuroscience, aging, law and psychology, psycholinguistics, family psychology.

University of Arkansas, Graduate School, J. William Fulbright College of Arts and Sciences, Department of Psychology, Fayetteville, AR 72701-1201. Offers MA, PhD. *Accreditation:* APA (one or more programs are accredited). *Degree requirements:* For master's, thesis; for doctorate, variable foreign language requirement, thesis/dissertation. *Entrance requirements:* For doctorate, GRE General Test, GRE Subject Test. Electronic applications accepted.

University of Arkansas at Little Rock, Graduate School, College of Social Sciences and Communication, Department of Psychology, Little Rock, AR 72204-1099. Offers applied psychology (MAP). Part-time and evening/weekend programs available. *Entrance requirements:* For master's, GRE General Test, minimum GPA of 2.7. *Application deadline:* Applications are processed on a rolling basis. *Expenses:* Tuition, state resident: full-time $6000; part-time $300 per credit hour. Tuition, nonresident: full-time $13,800; part-time $690 per credit hour. Required fees: $1126; $603 per term. One-time fee: $40 full-time. *Financial support:* Fellowships with tuition reimbursements, research assistantships with tuition reimbursements, teaching assistantships with tuition reimbursements, career-related internships or fieldwork, Federal Work-Study, institutionally sponsored loans, and unspecified assistantships available. Support available to part-time students. *Faculty research:* Psychological methods and theories in business industry, government, and organizations; personnel program evaluation; training; affirmative action; organizational analysis and development. *Unit head:* Dr. Amanda Nolen, Interim Chair, 501-569-3171, Fax: 501-569-3047, E-mail: alnolen@ualr.edu. *Application contact:* Dr. Robert J. Hines, Program Coordinator, 501-569-3527, E-mail: rjhines@ualr.edu.
Website: http://ualr.edu/psychology/

Psychology—General

The University of British Columbia, Faculty of Arts and Faculty of Graduate Studies, Department of Psychology, Vancouver, BC V6T 1Z4, Canada. Offers behavioral neuroscience (MA, PhD); clinical psychology (MA, PhD); cognitive science (MA, PhD); developmental psychology (MA, PhD); health psychology (MA, PhD); quantitative methods (MA, PhD); social/personality psychology (MA, PhD). *Accreditation:* APA (one or more programs are accredited). Terminal master's awarded for partial completion of doctoral program. *Degree requirements:* For master's, thesis; for doctorate, comprehensive exam, thesis/dissertation. *Entrance requirements:* For master's and doctorate, GRE General Test. Additional exam requirements/recommendations for international students: Required—TOEFL (minimum score 550 paper-based; 80 iBT). Electronic applications accepted. *Faculty research:* Clinical, developmental, social/personality, cognition, behavioral neuroscience.

University of Calgary, Faculty of Graduate Studies, Faculty of Arts, Department of Psychology, Calgary, AB T2N 1N4, Canada. Offers clinical psychology (M Sc, PhD); psychology (M Sc, PhD). *Degree requirements:* For master's, thesis; for doctorate, thesis/dissertation. *Entrance requirements:* For master's, GRE General Test, bachelor's degree in psychology, minimum GPA of 3.4. Additional exam requirements/recommendations for international students: Required—TOEFL (minimum score 550 paper-based). Electronic applications accepted. *Faculty research:* Cognition and cognitive development, social psychology, theoretical psychology, perception, aging.

University of California, Berkeley, Graduate Division, College of Letters and Science, Department of Psychology, Berkeley, CA 94720-1500. Offers PhD. *Accreditation:* APA. *Degree requirements:* For doctorate, thesis/dissertation, qualifying exam. *Entrance requirements:* For doctorate, GRE General Test, GRE Subject Test, minimum GPA of 3.0, 3 letters of recommendation. Electronic applications accepted.

University of California, Davis, Graduate Studies, Program in Psychology, Davis, CA 95616. Offers PhD. *Degree requirements:* For doctorate, thesis/dissertation. *Entrance requirements:* For doctorate, GRE General Test, GRE Subject Test, minimum GPA of 3.0. Additional exam requirements/recommendations for international students: Required—TOEFL (minimum score 550 paper-based). Electronic applications accepted. *Faculty research:* Social personality, perception, cognition, psychobiology.

University of California, Irvine, School of Social Ecology, Department of Psychology and Social Behavior, Irvine, CA 92697. Offers PhD. *Students:* 57 full-time (40 women); includes 22 minority (2 Black or African American, non-Hispanic/Latino; 8 Asian, non-Hispanic/Latino; 7 Hispanic/Latino; 5 Two or more races, non-Hispanic/Latino). Average age 27. 142 applicants, 13% accepted, 14 enrolled. In 2014, 12 doctorates awarded. *Degree requirements:* For doctorate, thesis/dissertation, research project. *Entrance requirements:* For doctorate, GRE General Test, minimum GPA of 3.0. Additional exam requirements/recommendations for international students: Required—TOEFL (minimum score 550 paper-based). *Application deadline:* For fall admission, 12/15 priority date for domestic and international students. Applications are processed on a rolling basis. Application fee: $90 ($110 for international students). Electronic applications accepted. *Financial support:* Fellowships, research assistantships with full tuition reimbursements, teaching assistantships, institutionally sponsored loans, traineeships, health care benefits, and unspecified assistantships available. Financial award application deadline: 3/1; financial award applicants required to submit FAFSA. *Faculty research:* Psychosocial development in children, adolescents, and adults; gerontology, childhood behavior disorders, and developmental psychopathology; sex differences; attitude change; social psychology. *Unit head:* Linda J. Levine, Department Chair, 949-824-7692, Fax: 949-824-3002, E-mail: llevine@uci.edu. *Application contact:* Roxane C. Silver, Graduate Advisors, 949-824-2192, Fax: 949-824-3002, E-mail: rsilver@uci.edu. Website: http://psb.soceco.uci.edu/

University of California, Irvine, School of Social Sciences, Department of Cognitive Science, Irvine, CA 92697. Offers psychology (PhD). *Students:* 48 full-time (20 women); 4 part-time (3 women); includes 10 minority (6 Asian, non-Hispanic/Latino; 2 Hispanic/Latino; 2 Two or more races, non-Hispanic/Latino), 5 international. Average age 27. 128 applicants, 17% accepted, 17 enrolled. In 2014, 16 doctorates awarded. *Degree requirements:* For doctorate, thesis/dissertation. *Entrance requirements:* For doctorate, GRE General Test, minimum GPA of 3.0. Additional exam requirements/recommendations for international students: Required—TOEFL (minimum score 550 paper-based). *Application deadline:* For fall admission, 1/15 priority date for domestic and international students. Applications are processed on a rolling basis. Application fee: $90 ($110 for international students). Electronic applications accepted. *Financial support:* Fellowships, research assistantships with full tuition reimbursements, teaching assistantships, institutionally sponsored loans, traineeships, health care benefits, and unspecified assistantships available. Financial award application deadline: 3/1; financial award applicants required to submit FAFSA. *Faculty research:* Mathematical psychology, visual and auditory perception, cognitive development, problem solving, experimental psychology. *Unit head:* Prof. Ramesh Srinivasan, Department Chair, 949-824-2969, E-mail: r.srinivasan@uci.edu. *Application contact:* Geoff Iverson, Graduate Director, 949-824-4053, E-mail: giverson@uci.edu. Website: http://www.cogsci.uci.edu/cs_graduates

University of California, Los Angeles, Graduate Division, College of Letters and Science, Department of Psychology, Los Angeles, CA 90034. Offers MA, PhD. *Accreditation:* APA (one or more programs are accredited). Terminal master's awarded for partial completion of doctoral program. *Degree requirements:* For master's, comprehensive exam; for doctorate, thesis/dissertation, oral and written qualifying exams, teaching experience. *Entrance requirements:* For doctorate, GRE General Test, GRE Subject Test (psychology), bachelor's degree; minimum undergraduate GPA of 3.0 (or its equivalent if letter grade system not used); interview. Additional exam requirements/recommendations for international students: Required—TOEFL. Electronic applications accepted.

University of California, Merced, Graduate Division, School of Social Sciences, Humanities and Arts, Merced, CA 95343. Offers cognitive and information sciences (MA, PhD); psychology (MA, PhD); social sciences (MA, PhD); world cultures (MA, PhD). *Faculty:* 89 full-time (40 women). *Students:* 114 full-time (79 women), 2 part-time (1 woman); includes 43 minority (3 Black or African American, non-Hispanic/Latino; 1 American Indian or Alaska Native, non-Hispanic/Latino; 10 Asian, non-Hispanic/Latino; 24 Hispanic/Latino; 1 Native Hawaiian or other Pacific Islander, non-Hispanic/Latino; 4 Two or more races, non-Hispanic/Latino), 13 international. Average age 32. 127 applicants, 34% accepted, 22 enrolled. In 2014, 3 master's, 11 doctorates awarded. *Degree requirements:* For master's, variable foreign language requirement, comprehensive exam, thesis; for doctorate, variable foreign language requirement, comprehensive exam, thesis/dissertation. *Entrance requirements:* For master's and doctorate, GRE. Additional exam requirements/recommendations for international students: Required—TOEFL (minimum score 550 paper-based; 68 iBT); Recommended—IELTS. *Application deadline:* For fall admission, 1/15 for domestic and international students. Application fee: $80 ($100 for international students). Electronic applications accepted. *Expenses:* Tuition, state resident: full-time $11,220; part-time $2805 per semester. *Required fees:* $1940; $970 per semester hour. *Financial support:* In 2014–15, 29 fellowships with full and partial tuition reimbursements (averaging $7,056 per year) were awarded; scholarships/grants also available. *Faculty research:* Psychology, political science, social inequality, interdisciplinary, humanities, cognitive

sciences. *Unit head:* Dr. Mark Aldenderfer, Dean, 209-228-7843, Fax: 209-228-4007, E-mail: maldenderfer@ucmerced.edu. *Application contact:* Tsu Ya, Graduate Admissions and Academic Services Manager, 209-228-4521, Fax: 209-228-6906, E-mail: tya@ucmerced.edu.

University of California, Riverside, Graduate Division, Department of Psychology, Riverside, CA 92521-0102. Offers MA, PhD. *Accreditation:* APA. *Degree requirements:* For doctorate, comprehensive exam, thesis/dissertation, 3 quarters of teaching experience, qualifying exams. *Entrance requirements:* For doctorate, GRE General Test, minimum GPA of 3.2. Additional exam requirements/recommendations for international students: Required—TOEFL (minimum score 550 paper-based; 80 iBT). Electronic applications accepted. *Expenses:* Tuition, state resident: full-time $5399. Tuition, nonresident: full-time $10,433. *Faculty research:* Neuroscience, personality and social psychology, developmental psychology, cognition, health psychology, quantitative psychology.

University of California, San Diego, Graduate Division, Department of Psychology, La Jolla, CA 92093. Offers PhD. *Students:* 50 full-time (22 women), 1 (woman) part-time; includes 10 minority (1 Black or African American, non-Hispanic/Latino; 1 American Indian or Alaska Native, non-Hispanic/Latino; 7 Asian, non-Hispanic/Latino; 1 Hispanic/Latino), 5 international. 305 applicants, 6% accepted, 10 enrolled. In 2014, 13 doctorates awarded. *Degree requirements:* For doctorate, comprehensive exam, thesis/dissertation, 7 quarters of teaching assistantship. *Entrance requirements:* For doctorate, GRE General Test, minimum GPA of 3.0. Additional exam requirements/recommendations for international students: Required—TOEFL (minimum score 550 paper-based; 80 iBT), IELTS (minimum score 7). *Application deadline:* For fall admission, 12/4 for domestic students. Application fee: $90 ($110 for international students). Electronic applications accepted. *Expenses:* Tuition, state resident: full-time $11,220; part-time $5610 per quarter. Tuition, nonresident: full-time $26,322; part-time $13,161 per quarter. *Required fees:* $570 per quarter. Tuition and fees vary according to program. *Financial support:* Fellowships, research assistantships, teaching assistantships, scholarships/grants, and unspecified assistantships available. Financial award applicants required to submit FAFSA. *Faculty research:* Cognitive and behavioral neuroscience, cognitive psychology, developmental psychology, sensation and perception, social psychology. *Unit head:* Victor Ferreira, Chair, 858-534-6303. *Application contact:* Rachael Lapidis, Graduate Coordinator, 858-534-3002, E-mail: psycphdinfo@ucsd.edu. Website: http://psychology.ucsd.edu/

University of California, Santa Barbara, Graduate Division, College of Letters and Sciences, Division of Mathematics, Life, and Physical Sciences, Department of Psychological and Brain Sciences, Santa Barbara, CA 93106-9660. Offers cognitive science (PhD); psychology (PhD); quantitative methods in the social sciences (PhD); technology and society (PhD). Terminal master's awarded for partial completion of doctoral program. *Degree requirements:* For doctorate, comprehensive exam, thesis/dissertation, teaching assistant training, progress report, papers, mini-convention presentation, 1 quarter of student teaching or teaching assistant class with section lab, continued participation in research and weekly area meetings. *Entrance requirements:* For doctorate, GRE General Test. Additional exam requirements/recommendations for international students: Required—TOEFL (minimum score 550 paper-based; 80 iBT) or IELTS (minimum score 7). Electronic applications accepted. *Faculty research:* Social psychology; developmental and evolutionary psychology; neuroscience and behavior; cognition, perception and cognitive neuroscience.

University of California, Santa Cruz, Division of Graduate Studies, Division of Social Sciences, Department of Psychology, Santa Cruz, CA 95064. Offers PhD. *Degree requirements:* For doctorate, thesis/dissertation, qualifying exam, seminars. *Entrance requirements:* For doctorate, GRE General Test. Additional exam requirements/recommendations for international students: Required—TOEFL (minimum score 550 paper-based; 83 iBT); Recommended—IELTS (minimum score 8). Electronic applications accepted. *Faculty research:* Cognitive psychology, developmental psychology, social psychology.

University of Central Arkansas, Graduate School, College of Health and Behavioral Sciences, Department of Counseling and Psychology, Conway, AR 72035-0001. Offers community counseling (MS); counseling psychology (MS); school psychology (MS, PhD, PMC). *Accreditation:* APA. Terminal master's awarded for partial completion of doctoral program. *Degree requirements:* For master's, comprehensive exam, thesis optional, internship; for doctorate, comprehensive exam, thesis/dissertation, internship. *Entrance requirements:* For master's, GRE General Test, minimum GPA of 2.75; for doctorate, GRE General Test, minimum GPA of 3.25. Additional exam requirements/recommendations for international students: Required—TOEFL (minimum score 550 paper-based). Electronic applications accepted.

University of Central Florida, College of Sciences, Department of Psychology, Orlando, FL 32816. Offers applied experimental and human factors psychology (PhD); clinical psychology (MA); industrial/organizational psychology (MS, PhD). *Accreditation:* APA. Part-time and evening/weekend programs available. *Faculty:* 51 full-time (22 women), 8 part-time/adjunct (3 women). *Students:* 151 full-time (97 women), 15 part-time (9 women); includes 36 minority (6 Black or African American, non-Hispanic/Latino; 10 Asian, non-Hispanic/Latino; 16 Hispanic/Latino; 4 Two or more races, non-Hispanic/Latino), 2 international. Average age 27. 447 applicants, 17% accepted, 42 enrolled. In 2014, 53 master's, 11 doctorates awarded. *Degree requirements:* For doctorate, thesis/dissertation, candidacy exam. *Entrance requirements:* For master's, GRE General Test, minimum GPA of 3.0 in last 60 hours. Additional exam requirements/recommendations for international students: Required—TOEFL. *Application deadline:* For fall admission, 2/15 for domestic students. Application fee: $30. Electronic applications accepted. *Expenses:* Tuition, state resident: part-time $288.16 per credit hour. Tuition, nonresident: part-time $1073.31 per credit hour. *Financial support:* In 2014–15, 103 students received support, including 39 fellowships with partial tuition reimbursements available (averaging $7,000 per year), 35 research assistantships with partial tuition reimbursements available (averaging $11,809 per year), 62 teaching assistantships with partial tuition reimbursements available (averaging $9,800 per year); career-related internships or fieldwork, Federal Work-Study, institutionally sponsored loans, tuition waivers (partial), and unspecified assistantships also available. Financial award application deadline: 3/1; financial award applicants required to submit FAFSA. *Faculty research:* Professional ethical decision-making, electronic selection systems, psychometrics. *Unit head:* Dr. Jeffrey E. Cassisi, Chair, 407-823-4201, E-mail: jeffrey.cassisi@ucf.edu. *Application contact:* Barbara Rodriguez Lamas, Director, Admissions and Student Services, 407-823-2766, Fax: 407-823-6442, E-mail: gradadmissions@ucf.edu. Website: http://psychology.cos.ucf.edu/

University of Central Missouri, The Graduate School, Warrensburg, MO 64093. Offers accountancy (MA); accounting (MBA); applied mathematics (MS); aviation safety (MA); biology (MS); business administration (MBA); career and technical education leadership (MS); college student personnel administration (MS); communication (MA); computer science (MS); counseling (MS); criminal justice (MS); educational leadership (Ed D); educational technology (MS); elementary and early childhood education (MSE); English (MA); environmental studies (MA); finance (MBA); history (MA); human services/

educational technology (Ed S); human services/learning resources (Ed S); human services/professional counseling (Ed S); industrial hygiene (MS); industrial management (MS); information systems (MBA); information technology (MS); kinesiology (MS); library science and information services (MS); literacy education (MSE); marketing (MBA); mathematics (MS); music (MA); occupational safety management (MS); psychology (MS); rural family nursing (MS); school administration (MSE); social gerontology (MS); sociology (MA); special education (MSE); speech language pathology (MS); superintendency (Ed S); teaching (MAT); teaching English as a second language (MA); technology (MS); technology management (PhD); theatre (MA). Part-time programs available. *Faculty:* 314 full-time (137 women), 24 part-time/adjunct (14 women). *Students:* 1,624 full-time (542 women), 1,773 part-time (1,055 women); includes 194 minority (104 Black or African American, non-Hispanic/Latino; 6 American Indian or Alaska Native, non-Hispanic/Latino; 23 Asian, non-Hispanic/Latino; 41 Hispanic/Latino; 3 Native Hawaiian or other Pacific Islander, non-Hispanic/Latino; 17 Two or more races, non-Hispanic/Latino), 1,592 international. Average age 31. 2,800 applicants, 63% accepted, 1223 enrolled. In 2014, 796 master's, 81 other advanced degrees awarded. *Degree requirements:* For master's and Ed S, comprehensive exam (for some programs), thesis (for some programs). *Entrance requirements:* Additional exam requirements/recommendations for international students: Required—TOEFL (minimum score 550 paper-based; 79 iBT). *Application deadline:* For fall admission, 6/1 for domestic students; for spring admission, 10/1 for domestic and international students. Applications are processed on a rolling basis. Application fee: $30 ($75 for international students). Electronic applications accepted. *Expenses:* Tuition, state resident: full-time $6630; part-time $276.25 per credit hour. Tuition, nonresident: full-time $13,260; part-time $552.50 per credit hour. *Required fees:* $29 per credit hour. Tuition and fees vary according to campus/location. *Financial support:* In 2014–15, 118 students received support, including 271 research assistantships with full and partial tuition reimbursements available (averaging $7,500 per year), 109 teaching assistantships with full and partial tuition reimbursements available (averaging $7,500 per year); career-related internships or fieldwork, Federal Work-Study, scholarships/grants, and administrative and laboratory assistantships also available. Support available to part-time students. Financial award application deadline: 3/1; financial award applicants required to submit FAFSA. *Unit head:* Tina Church-Hockett, Director of Graduate School and International Admissions, 660-543-4621, Fax: 660-543-4778, E-mail: church@ucmo.edu. *Application contact:* Brittany Lawrence, Graduate Student Services Coordinator, 660-543-4621, Fax: 660-543-4778, E-mail: gradinfo@ucmo.edu. Website: http://www.ucmo.edu/graduate/

University of Central Oklahoma, The Jackson College of Graduate Studies, College of Education and Professional Studies, Department of Psychology, Edmond, OK 73034-5209. Offers counseling psychology (MA); experimental psychology (MA); forensic psychology (MA); general psychology (MA); school psychology (MA). *Degree requirements:* For master's, thesis (for some programs). *Entrance requirements:* For master's, GRE. Additional exam requirements/recommendations for international students: Required—TOEFL (minimum score 550 paper-based; 79 iBT), IELTS (minimum score 6.5). Electronic applications accepted. *Faculty research:* Psychopharmacology, computer psychometrics, health psychology research.

University of Chicago, Division of the Social Sciences, Department of Psychology, Chicago, IL 60637. Offers PhD. *Students:* 52 full-time (34 women); includes 9 minority (1 Black or African American, non-Hispanic/Latino; 1 American Indian or Alaska Native, non-Hispanic/Latino; 2 Asian, non-Hispanic/Latino; 4 Hispanic/Latino; 1 Two or more races, non-Hispanic/Latino), 12 international. 305 applicants, 6% accepted, 8 enrolled. In 2014, 7 doctorates awarded. *Degree requirements:* For doctorate, one foreign language, thesis/dissertation, exams. *Entrance requirements:* For doctorate, GRE General Test. Additional exam requirements/recommendations for international students: Required—TOEFL (minimum score 104 iBT), IELTS (minimum score 7). *Application deadline:* For fall admission, 12/15 for domestic and international students. Application fee: $90. Electronic applications accepted. *Expenses: Tuition:* Full-time $46,899. *Required fees:* $347. *Financial support:* In 2014–15, 8 students received support, including 8 fellowships with full tuition reimbursements available (averaging $23,000 per year); career-related internships or fieldwork, Federal Work-Study, institutionally sponsored loans, scholarships/grants, and health care benefits also available. Financial award application deadline: 12/15. *Unit head:* Prof. Susan C. Levine, Chair. *Application contact:* Office of the Dean of Students, 773-702-8415, E-mail: admissions@ssd.uchicago.edu.
Website: http://psychology.uchicago.edu

University of Cincinnati, Graduate School, McMicken College of Arts and Sciences, Department of Psychology, Cincinnati, OH 45221. Offers clinical psychology (PhD); experimental psychology (PhD). *Accreditation:* APA. *Degree requirements:* For doctorate, comprehensive exam, thesis/dissertation. *Entrance requirements:* For doctorate, GRE General Test. Additional exam requirements/recommendations for international students: Required—TOEFL. *Faculty research:* Neuropsychology, human factors, health.

University of Colorado Boulder, Graduate School, College of Arts and Sciences, Department of Psychology and Neuroscience, Boulder, CO 80309. Offers MA, PhD. *Accreditation:* APA (one or more programs are accredited). *Faculty:* 42 full-time (15 women). *Students:* 110 full-time (62 women), 2 part-time (both women); includes 9 minority (3 Asian, non-Hispanic/Latino; 6 Hispanic/Latino), 2 international. Average age 29. 666 applicants, 3% accepted, 20 enrolled. In 2014, 24 master's, 23 doctorates awarded. Terminal master's awarded for partial completion of doctoral program. *Degree requirements:* For master's, comprehensive exam; for doctorate, thesis/dissertation. *Entrance requirements:* For master's, GRE General Test, minimum undergraduate GPA of 2.75; for doctorate, GRE General Test. *Application deadline:* For fall admission, 12/1 for domestic and international students. Application fee: $50 ($70 for international students). Electronic applications accepted. *Financial support:* In 2014–15, 194 students received support, including 23 fellowships (averaging $15,560 per year), 26 research assistantships with full and partial tuition reimbursements available (averaging $32,843 per year), 56 teaching assistantships with full and partial tuition reimbursements available (averaging $34,256 per year); institutionally sponsored loans, scholarships/grants, health care benefits, and unspecified assistantships also available. Financial award application deadline: 1/1; financial award applicants required to submit FAFSA. *Faculty research:* Behavioral/experimental psychology, cognitive development/processes, clinical psychology. *Total annual research expenditures:* $15.7 million.
Website: http://psych.colorado.edu/

University of Colorado Colorado Springs, College of Letters, Arts and Sciences, Department of Psychology, Colorado Springs, CO 80933-7150. Offers MA, PhD. *Accreditation:* APA. Part-time programs available. *Faculty:* 15 full-time (6 women), 16 part-time/adjunct (9 women). *Students:* 30 full-time (26 women), 27 part-time (21 women); includes 7 minority (2 Black or African American, non-Hispanic/Latino; 1 American Indian or Alaska Native, non-Hispanic/Latino; 3 Hispanic/Latino; 1 Two or more races, non-Hispanic/Latino), 3 international. Average age 30. 144 applicants, 27% accepted, 19 enrolled. In 2014, 4 master's, 5 doctorates awarded. *Degree requirements:* For master's, thesis; for doctorate, comprehensive exam, thesis/dissertation. *Entrance requirements:* For master's, GRE, BA in psychology or equivalent background; minimum

GPA of 3.0; for doctorate, GRE (minimum score of 1200 cumulative on the Verbal and Quantitative sections, or above the 50th percentile using the new GRE scoring), minimum overall GPA of 3.0 in all undergraduate courses, 3.5 on graduate coursework. Additional exam requirements/recommendations for international students: Required— TOEFL (minimum score 550 paper-based; 80 iBT), IELTS (minimum score 6). *Application deadline:* For fall admission, 1/1 for domestic and international students. Applications are processed on a rolling basis. Application fee: $60 ($100 for international students). *Expenses:* Expenses: Contact institution. *Financial support:* In 2014–15, 41 students received support, including 6 fellowships (averaging $2,300 per year), 7 research assistantships (averaging $2,800 per year); teaching assistantships, career-related internships or fieldwork, Federal Work-Study, and scholarships/grants also available. Support available to part-time students. Financial award application deadline: 3/1; financial award applicants required to submit FAFSA. *Faculty research:* Attention, emotion, neuroscience, adult development, relationship attachment style, attraction, event-related brain potentials, human adaptation from trauma, behavioral genetics, personality disorders, adolescent development, memory and executive function across the life span, early detection of Alzheimer's disease, psychometrics, differential attitudes toward and etiology of sexual abusers, clinical psychology, behavioral gerontology, forensic neuropsychology. *Total annual research expenditures:* $1.3 million. *Unit head:* Dr. Michael Kisley, Director, Graduate Training, 719-255-4177, Fax: 719-255-4166, E-mail: mkisley@uccs.edu. *Application contact:* Dr. David Dubois, Graduate Student Advisor, 719-255-4500, Fax: 719-255-4166, E-mail: ddubois@uccs.edu.
Website: http://www.uccs.edu/~psych/

University of Connecticut, Graduate School, College of Liberal Arts and Sciences, Department of Psychology, Storrs, CT 06269. Offers behavioral neuroscience (PhD); biopsychology (PhD); clinical psychology (MA, PhD); cognition and instruction (PhD); developmental psychology (MA, PhD); ecological psychology (PhD); experimental psychology (PhD); general psychology (MA, PhD); health psychology (Graduate Certificate); industrial/organizational psychology (PhD); language and cognition (PhD); neuroscience (PhD); occupational health psychology (Graduate Certificate); social psychology (MA, PhD). *Accreditation:* APA. Terminal master's awarded for partial completion of doctoral program. *Degree requirements:* For master's, comprehensive exam; for doctorate, thesis/dissertation. *Entrance requirements:* For master's and doctorate, GRE General Test, GRE Subject Test. Additional exam requirements/recommendations for international students: Required—TOEFL (minimum score 550 paper-based). Electronic applications accepted.

University of Dallas, Braniff Graduate School of Liberal Arts, Program in Psychology, Irving, TX 75062-4736. Offers M Psych, MA. Part-time programs available. *Degree requirements:* For master's, one foreign language, comprehensive exam (for some programs), thesis (for some programs). *Entrance requirements:* Additional exam requirements/recommendations for international students: Required—TOEFL.

University of Delaware, College of Arts and Sciences, Department of Psychology, Newark, DE 19716. Offers behavioral neuroscience (PhD); clinical psychology (PhD); cognitive psychology (PhD); social psychology (PhD). *Accreditation:* APA. *Degree requirements:* For doctorate, thesis/dissertation. *Entrance requirements:* For doctorate, GRE General Test. Additional exam requirements/recommendations for international students: Required—TOEFL (minimum score 600 paper-based). Electronic applications accepted. *Faculty research:* Emotion development, neural and cognitive aspects of memory, neural control of feeding, intergroup relations, social cognition and communication.

University of Denver, Division of Arts, Humanities and Social Sciences, Department of Psychology, Denver, CO 80208. Offers affective/social psychology (PhD); clinical child psychology (PhD); cognitive psychology (PhD); developmental psychology (PhD). *Accreditation:* APA. *Faculty:* 25 full-time (11 women), 4 part-time/adjunct (2 women). *Students:* 21 full-time (18 women), 5 part-time (all women); includes 7 minority (2 Black or African American, non-Hispanic/Latino; 3 Asian, non-Hispanic/Latino; 1 Hispanic/Latino; 1 Two or more races, non-Hispanic/Latino), 3 international. Average age 28. 348 applicants, 5% accepted, 6 enrolled. In 2014, 9 doctorates awarded. Terminal master's awarded for partial completion of doctoral program. *Degree requirements:* For doctorate, variable foreign language requirement, comprehensive exam (for some programs), thesis/dissertation. *Entrance requirements:* For doctorate, GRE General Test, master's degree, transcripts, biographical statement, three letters of recommendation. Additional exam requirements/recommendations for international students: Required—TOEFL (minimum score 550 paper-based; 80 iBT). *Application deadline:* For fall admission, 12/1 priority date for domestic and international students. Application fee: $65. Electronic applications accepted. *Expenses:* Expenses: $1,199 per credit hour. *Financial support:* In 2014–15, 26 students received support, including 13 research assistantships with full and partial tuition reimbursements available (averaging $12,821 per year), 20 teaching assistantships with full and partial tuition reimbursements available (averaging $15,333 per year); Federal Work-Study, institutionally sponsored loans, scholarships/grants, and unspecified assistantships also available. Support available to part-time students. Financial award application deadline: 2/15; financial award applicants required to submit FAFSA. *Faculty research:* Developmental cognitive neuroscience, social and emotional processes, child and adolescent development, clinical child psychology, cognitive psychology. *Total annual research expenditures:* $3 million. *Unit head:* Dr. George Potts, Chair, 303-871-3717, Fax: 303-871-4747, E-mail: gpotts@du.edu. *Application contact:* Paula Houghtaling, Graduate Program Administrator, 303-871-3803, Fax: 303-871-4747, E-mail: phoughta@du.edu.
Website: http://www.du.edu/ahss/psychology/index.html

University of Denver, Graduate School of Professional Psychology, Denver, CO 80208. Offers forensic psychology (MA); international disaster psychology (MA); sport and performance psychology (MA). *Accreditation:* APA. *Faculty:* 18 full-time (9 women), 23 part-time/adjunct (9 women). *Students:* 205 full-time (148 women), 51 part-time (38 women); includes 57 minority (11 Black or African American, non-Hispanic/Latino; 1 American Indian or Alaska Native, non-Hispanic/Latino; 15 Asian, non-Hispanic/Latino; 21 Hispanic/Latino; 9 Two or more races, non-Hispanic/Latino), 12 international. Average age 27. 720 applicants, 31% accepted, 102 enrolled. In 2014, 90 master's, 32 doctorates awarded. *Degree requirements:* For master's, comprehensive exam (for some programs); for doctorate, comprehensive exam (for some programs), paper, clinical internship. *Entrance requirements:* For master's and doctorate, GRE General Test, transcripts, resume, two letters of recommendation, essay. Additional exam requirements/recommendations for international students: Required—TOEFL (minimum score 550 paper-based; 80 iBT). *Application deadline:* For fall admission, 12/1 priority date for domestic and international students. Application fee: $65. Electronic applications accepted. *Expenses:* Expenses: $1,199 per credit hour. *Financial support:* In 2014–15, 76 students received support, including 33 teaching assistantships with full and partial tuition reimbursements available (averaging $3,042 per year); career-related internships or fieldwork, Federal Work-Study, institutionally sponsored loans, scholarships/grants, unspecified assistantships, and clinical assistantships also available. Support available to part-time students. Financial award application deadline: 2/15; financial award applicants required to submit FAFSA. *Unit head:* Dr. Shelly Smith-Acuna, Dean, 303-871-3880, E-mail: shelly.smith-acuna@du.edu. *Application contact:*

Psychology—General

Admissions Counselor, 303-871-3736, Fax: 303-871-7656, E-mail: gsppinfo@du.edu.
Website: http://www.du.edu/gspp/

University of Detroit Mercy, College of Liberal Arts and Education, Department of Psychology, Detroit, MI 48221. Offers clinical psychology (MA, PhD); industrial/organizational psychology (MA); school psychology (Spec). *Accreditation:* APA. Evening/weekend programs available. *Degree requirements:* For doctorate, departmental qualifying exam. *Faculty research:* Gerontology.

University of Florida, Graduate School, College of Liberal Arts and Sciences, Department of Psychology, Gainesville, FL 32661-2250. Offers counseling psychology (PhD); psychology (MA, MS, PhD), including psychology (PhD), women's and gender studies (PhD); JD/PhD. *Faculty:* 29 full-time (11 women), 9 part-time/adjunct (4 women). *Students:* 108 full-time (80 women), 11 part-time (8 women); includes 24 minority (6 Black or African American, non-Hispanic/Latino; 1 American Indian or Alaska Native, non-Hispanic/Latino; 7 Asian, non-Hispanic/Latino; 10 Hispanic/Latino), 16 international. 279 applicants, 10% accepted, 13 enrolled. In 2014, 13 master's, 18 doctorates awarded. *Degree requirements:* For master's, comprehensive exam, thesis or alternative; for doctorate, comprehensive exam, thesis/dissertation. *Entrance requirements:* For master's and doctorate, GRE General Test, minimum GPA of 3.0. Additional exam requirements/recommendations for international students: Required—TOEFL (minimum score 550 paper-based; 80 iBT), IELTS (minimum score 6). *Application deadline:* For fall admission, 12/1 priority date for domestic students, 12/1 for international students. Applications are processed on a rolling basis. Application fee: $30. Electronic applications accepted. *Financial support:* In 2014–15, 15 fellowships, 11 research assistantships, 72 teaching assistantships were awarded; career-related internships or fieldwork and unspecified assistantships also available. Financial award application deadline: 12/9; financial award applicants required to submit FAFSA. *Faculty research:* Behavior analysis, behavioral and cognitive neuroscience, counseling, developmental psychology, social psychology. *Total annual research expenditures:* $1.8 million. *Unit head:* Neil E. Rowland, PhD, Chair, 352-273-2127, Fax: 352-392-7985, E-mail: nrowland@ufl.edu. *Application contact:* Main Office Information Contact, 352-392-0601, Fax: 352-392-7985, E-mail: psych-info@ufl.edu.
Website: http://www.psych.ufl.edu/

University of Florida, Graduate School, College of Public Health and Health Professions, Department of Clinical and Health Psychology, Gainesville, FL 32610-0165. Offers clinical and translational science (PhD); clnical and health psychology (PhD); psychology (MA, MS). *Accreditation:* APA (one or more programs are accredited). *Faculty:* 22 full-time (10 women), 12 part-time/adjunct (4 women). *Students:* 95 full-time (64 women), 14 part-time (13 women); includes 22 minority (10 Black or African American, non-Hispanic/Latino; 1 American Indian or Alaska Native, non-Hispanic/Latino; 3 Asian, non-Hispanic/Latino; 8 Hispanic/Latino), 2 international. 323 applicants, 5% accepted, 12 enrolled. In 2014, 13 master's, 13 doctorates awarded. *Degree requirements:* For doctorate, comprehensive exam, thesis/dissertation, pre-doctoral internship. *Entrance requirements:* For master's and doctorate, GRE General Test, minimum GPA of 3.0. Additional exam requirements/recommendations for international students: Required—TOEFL (minimum score 550 paper-based; 80 iBT), IELTS (minimum score 6). *Application deadline:* For fall admission, 12/1 for domestic and international students. Application fee: $30. Electronic applications accepted. *Financial support:* In 2014–15, 8 teaching assistantships were awarded; career-related internships or fieldwork, Federal Work-Study, institutionally sponsored loans, scholarships/grants, and unspecified assistantships also available. Financial award application deadline: 12/1; financial award applicants required to submit FAFSA. *Faculty research:* Clinical child and pediatric psychology, medical psychology, neuropsychology, health promotion and aging. *Unit head:* William W. Latimer, PhD, Professor and Chair, 352-273-6556, Fax: 352-273-6156, E-mail: wwlatimer@phhp.ufl.edu. *Application contact:* Office of Admissions, 352-392-1365, E-mail: webrequests@admissions.ufl.edu.
Website: http://www.phhp.ufl.edu/chp/

University of Georgia, Franklin College of Arts and Sciences, Department of Psychology, Athens, GA 30602. Offers MS, PhD. *Accreditation:* APA (one or more programs are accredited). *Degree requirements:* For master's, thesis; for doctorate, one foreign language, thesis/dissertation. *Entrance requirements:* For master's and doctorate, GRE General Test. Additional exam requirements/recommendations for international students: Required—TOEFL. Electronic applications accepted.

University of Guelph, Graduate Studies, College of Social and Applied Human Sciences, Department of Psychology, Guelph, ON N1G 2W1, Canada. Offers applied social psychology (MA, PhD); clinical psychology: applied development emphasis (PhD); clinical psychology: applied developmental emphasis (MA); industrial/organizational psychology (MA, PhD); neuroscience and applied cognitive science (MA, PhD). *Degree requirements:* For master's, thesis; for doctorate, comprehensive exam, thesis/dissertation. *Entrance requirements:* For master's, GRE General Test, GRE Subject Test, minimum B+ average during previous 2 years of course work; for doctorate, GRE General Test, GRE Subject Test, minimum A- average. Additional exam requirements/recommendations for international students: Required—TOEFL (minimum score 89 iBT). Electronic applications accepted. *Faculty research:* Organizational psychology, reading comprehension and mathematical ability, drug addiction and relapse, gender issues and culture, memory, clinical psychology.

University of Hartford, College of Arts and Sciences, Department of Psychology, West Hartford, CT 06117-1599. Offers clinical practices (MA, Psy D), including clinical practices (Psy D), psychology (MA); general experimental psychology (MA); organizational behavior (MS); school psychology (MS). *Accreditation:* APA. Part-time programs available. *Degree requirements:* For master's, comprehensive exam, thesis (for some programs). *Entrance requirements:* For master's, GRE General Test, GRE Subject Test, minimum GPA of 3.0; for doctorate, GRE General Test, GRE Subject Test. Additional exam requirements/recommendations for international students: Required—TOEFL (minimum score 550 paper-based). Electronic applications accepted. *Expenses:* Contact institution.

University of Hawaii at Manoa, Graduate Division, College of Social Sciences, Department of Psychology, Honolulu, HI 96822. Offers clinical psychology (PhD); community and cultural psychology (PhD); community and culture (MA); psychology (MA, PhD, Graduate Certificate). *Accreditation:* APA (one or more programs are accredited). Part-time programs available. Terminal master's awarded for partial completion of doctoral program. *Degree requirements:* For master's, comprehensive exam, thesis; for doctorate, comprehensive exam, thesis/dissertation. *Entrance requirements:* For master's and doctorate, GRE General Test, GRE Subject Test. Additional exam requirements/recommendations for international students: Required—TOEFL (minimum score 600 paper-based; 100 iBT), IELTS (minimum score 7). *Faculty research:* Cross-cultural psychology, health psychology, marine mammals, child/adult psychopathology.

University of Houston, College of Liberal Arts and Social Sciences, Department of Psychology, Houston, TX 77204. Offers clinical psychology (PhD); developmental psychology (PhD); industrial/organizational psychology (PhD); psychology (MA); social psychology (PhD). *Accreditation:* APA (one or more programs are accredited). *Degree requirements:* For master's, comprehensive exam, thesis; for doctorate, comprehensive exam, thesis/dissertation. *Entrance requirements:* For master's, GRE General Test, career statement, 3 letters of recommendation; for doctorate, GRE General Test, 3 letters of recommendation. Additional exam requirements/recommendations for international students: Required—TOEFL (minimum score 550 paper-based; 79 iBT). Electronic applications accepted. *Faculty research:* Health psychology, depression, child/family process, organizational effectiveness, close relationships.

University of Houston–Clear Lake, School of Human Sciences and Humanities, Programs in Human Sciences, Houston, TX 77058-1002. Offers behavioral sciences (MA), including criminology, cross cultural studies, general psychology, sociology; clinical psychology (MA); criminology (MA); cross cultural studies (MA); family therapy (MA); fitness and human performance (MA); school psychology (MA). *Accreditation:* AAMFT/COAMFTE. Part-time and evening/weekend programs available. Postbaccalaureate distance learning degree programs offered (minimal on-campus study). *Degree requirements:* For master's, thesis or alternative. *Entrance requirements:* For master's, GRE General Test. Additional exam requirements/recommendations for international students: Required—TOEFL (minimum score 550 paper-based). Electronic applications accepted. *Faculty research:* Smoking cessation, adolescent sexuality, white collar crime, serial murder, human factors/human computer interaction.

University of Houston–Victoria, School of Arts and Sciences, Program in Psychology, Victoria, TX 77901-4450. Offers counseling psychology (MA); forensic psychology (MA); school psychology (MA). Part-time and evening/weekend programs available. Postbaccalaureate distance learning degree programs offered (minimal on-campus study). *Degree requirements:* For master's, project or thesis. *Entrance requirements:* For master's, GRE General Test. Additional exam requirements/recommendations for international students: Required—TOEFL (minimum score 550 paper-based). Electronic applications accepted.

University of Idaho, College of Graduate Studies, College of Letters, Arts and Social Sciences, Department of Psychology and Communication Studies, Moscow, ID 83844-3043. Offers psychology (MS). *Faculty:* 12 full-time, 3 part-time/adjunct. *Students:* 15 full-time, 14 part-time. Average age 29. In 2014, 5 master's awarded. *Entrance requirements:* For master's, GRE, minimum GPA of 2.8. *Application deadline:* For fall admission, 8/1 for domestic students; for spring admission, 12/15 for domestic students. Applications are processed on a rolling basis. Application fee: $60. Electronic applications accepted. *Expenses:* Tuition, state resident: full-time $4784; part-time $280.50 per credit hour. Tuition, nonresident: full-time $18,314; part-time $957.50 per credit hour. *Required fees:* $2000; $58.50 per credit hour. Tuition and fees vary according to program. *Financial support:* Fellowships, research assistantships, and teaching assistantships available. Financial award applicants required to submit FAFSA. *Faculty research:* Clinical, experimental, and cognitive psychology. *Unit head:* Dr. Todd Thorsteinson, Chair, 208-885-6324, E-mail: seanm@uidaho.edu. *Application contact:* Sean Scoggin, Graduate Recruitment Coordinator, 208-885-4001, Fax: 208-885-4406, E-mail: graduateadmissions@uidaho.edu.
Website: http://www.uidaho.edu/class/psychcomm

University of Illinois at Chicago, Graduate College, College of Liberal Arts and Sciences, Department of Psychology, Chicago, IL 60607-7128. Offers MA, PhD. *Accreditation:* APA. *Faculty:* 37 full-time (17 women), 10 part-time/adjunct (4 women). *Students:* 93 full-time (60 women), 4 part-time (all women); includes 20 minority (4 Black or African American, non-Hispanic/Latino; 7 Asian, non-Hispanic/Latino; 5 Hispanic/Latino; 4 Two or more races, non-Hispanic/Latino), 4 international. Average age 28. 524 applicants, 6% accepted, 16 enrolled. In 2014, 18 master's, 16 doctorates awarded. *Degree requirements:* For doctorate, thesis/dissertation, departmental qualifying exam. *Entrance requirements:* For doctorate, GRE General Test, minimum GPA of 2.75. Additional exam requirements/recommendations for international students: Required—TOEFL. *Application deadline:* For fall admission, 1/1 for domestic and international students. Application fee: $60. Electronic applications accepted. *Expenses:* Expenses: $16,066 in-state; $28,064 out-of-state. *Financial support:* In 2014–15, 4 fellowships with full tuition reimbursements were awarded; research assistantships with full tuition reimbursements, teaching assistantships with full tuition reimbursements, career-related internships or fieldwork, Federal Work-Study, institutionally sponsored loans, scholarships/grants, traineeships, tuition waivers (full), and unspecified assistantships also available. Financial award application deadline: 1/1; financial award applicants required to submit FAFSA. *Faculty research:* Cognition, behavioral neuroscience, community and prevention research, social and personality. *Unit head:* Prof. Mitchell F. Roitman, Director of Graduate Studies, 312-996-3113, E-mail: mroitman@uic.edu. *Application contact:* Admissions Committee, 312-996-2434.
Website: https://home.psch.uic.edu/

University of Illinois at Urbana–Champaign, Graduate College, College of Liberal Arts and Sciences, Department of Psychology, Champaign, IL 61820. Offers MA, MS, PhD. *Accreditation:* APA (one or more programs are accredited). *Students:* 138 (87 women). Application fee: $70 ($90 for international students). *Unit head:* Dr. David Irwin, Head, 217-333-0632, Fax: 217-244-5876, E-mail: irwin@illinois.edu. *Application contact:* Ashley Ramm, Office Support Specialist, 217-333-2169, Fax: 217-244-5876, E-mail: aramm@illinois.edu.
Website: http://www.psych.illinois.edu/

University of Indianapolis, Graduate Programs, School of Psychological Sciences, Indianapolis, IN 46227-3697. Offers clinical psychology (Psy D); clinical psychology/mental health counseling (MA). *Accreditation:* APA. *Faculty:* 14 full-time (7 women), 7 part-time/adjunct (5 women). *Students:* 115 full-time (96 women), 58 part-time (51 women); includes 24 minority (4 Black or African American, non-Hispanic/Latino; 10 Asian, non-Hispanic/Latino; 8 Hispanic/Latino; 2 Two or more races, non-Hispanic/Latino), 5 international. Average age 26. In 2014, 43 master's, 20 doctorates awarded. *Degree requirements:* For master's, practicum; for doctorate, comprehensive exam, thesis/dissertation, 1200 hours of clinical practicum, 2000-hour internship. *Entrance requirements:* For master's, GRE, 3 letters of recommendation; for doctorate, GRE, minimum GPA of 3.0, 18 hours of course work in psychology, 3 letters of recommendation. Additional exam requirements/recommendations for international students: Required—TOEFL (minimum score 550 paper-based). *Application deadline:* For fall admission, 2/25 for domestic students. Application fee: $50. *Financial support:* Federal Work-Study available. *Unit head:* Dr. Anita Jones Thomas, Dean, 317-788-3353, Fax: 317-788-2120, E-mail: thomasaj@uindy.edu. *Application contact:* School of Psychological Sciences, 317-788-3353, E-mail: psych@uindy.edu.
Website: http://psych.uindy.edu/

The University of Iowa, Graduate College, College of Education, Department of Psychological and Quantitative Foundations, Iowa City, IA 52242-1316. Offers counseling psychology (PhD); educational measurement and statistics (MA, PhD); educational psychology (MA, PhD); school psychology (PhD, Ed S). *Accreditation:* APA. *Degree requirements:* For master's, thesis optional, exam; for doctorate, comprehensive exam, thesis/dissertation; for Ed S, exam. *Entrance requirements:* For master's, doctorate, and Ed S, GRE General Test, minimum GPA of 3.0. Additional exam requirements/recommendations for international students: Required—TOEFL (minimum score 550 paper-based; 81 iBT). Electronic applications accepted.

The University of Iowa, Graduate College, College of Liberal Arts and Sciences, Department of Psychology, Iowa City, IA 52242-1316. Offers MA, PhD. *Degree requirements:* For master's, thesis optional, exam; for doctorate, comprehensive exam, thesis/dissertation. *Entrance requirements:* For master's and doctorate, GRE General Test, minimum GPA of 3.0. Additional exam requirements/recommendations for international students: Required—TOEFL (minimum score 550 paper-based; 81 iBT). Electronic applications accepted.

The University of Kansas, Graduate Studies, College of Liberal Arts and Sciences, Department of Applied Behavioral Science, Lawrence, KS 66045. Offers applied behavioral science (MA); behavioral psychology (PhD). *Faculty:* 17 full-time. *Students:* 40 full-time (30 women); includes 7 minority (4 Black or African American, non-Hispanic/Latino; 3 Two or more races, non-Hispanic/Latino), 1 international. Average age 28. 87 applicants, 15% accepted, 13 enrolled. In 2014, 3 master's, 8 doctorates awarded. Terminal master's awarded for partial completion of doctoral program. *Degree requirements:* For master's, thesis; for doctorate, thesis/dissertation, comprehensive oral and written exams, journal reviews. *Entrance requirements:* For master's and doctorate, minimum GPA of 3.0, curriculum vitae, 3 letters of recommendation, personal statement. Additional exam requirements/recommendations for international students: Required—TOEFL. *Application deadline:* For fall admission, 12/15 priority date for domestic students, 12/15 for international students. Applications are processed on a rolling basis. Application fee: $55 ($65 for international students). Electronic applications accepted. *Financial support:* Fellowships, research assistantships with full and partial tuition reimbursements, teaching assistantships with full and partial tuition reimbursements, career-related internships or fieldwork, traineeships, tuition waivers (full), and unspecified assistantships available. Financial award application deadline: 12/15; financial award applicants required to submit CSS PROFILE or FAFSA. *Faculty research:* Organizational behavioral management, community health and development, early childhood education and intervention, developmental disabilities, behavioral economics of choice. *Unit head:* Dr. Edward K. Morris, Chair, 785-864-0519, E-mail: ekm@ku.edu. *Application contact:* Andrea Noltner, Office Manager, 785-864-0503, E-mail: anoltner@ku.edu.
Website: http://www.absc.ku.edu

The University of Kansas, Graduate Studies, College of Liberal Arts and Sciences, Department of Psychology, Lawrence, KS 66045. Offers clinical child psychology (MA, PhD); clinical health and rehabilitation (PhD); cognitive psychology (PhD); developmental psychology (PhD); quantitative psychology (PhD); social psychology (MA). *Accreditation:* APA (one or more programs are accredited). *Faculty:* 36 full-time, 3 part-time/adjunct. *Students:* 81 full-time (49 women), 1 (woman) part-time; includes 12 minority (4 Black or African American, non-Hispanic/Latino; 5 Asian, non-Hispanic/Latino; 1 Hispanic/Latino; 2 Two or more races, non-Hispanic/Latino), 13 international. Average age 29. 194 applicants, 10% accepted, 9 enrolled. In 2014, 17 master's, 13 doctorates awarded. *Degree requirements:* For doctorate, variable foreign language requirement, comprehensive exam, thesis/dissertation. *Entrance requirements:* For doctorate, GRE General Test, minimum GPA of 3.0; undergraduate degree with 15 hours of course work in psychology, curriculum vitae, writing sample (clinical program only). Additional exam requirements/recommendations for international students: Required—TOEFL. *Application deadline:* For fall admission, 12/1 for domestic and international students. Application fee: $55 ($65 for international students). Electronic applications accepted. *Financial support:* In 2014–15, 1 fellowship with full tuition reimbursement (averaging $12,750 per year), 4 research assistantships with partial tuition reimbursements (averaging $12,980 per year), 70 teaching assistantships with partial tuition reimbursements (averaging $12,750 per year) were awarded; career-related internships or fieldwork, Federal Work-Study, scholarships/grants, health care benefits, and unspecified assistantships also available. Financial award application deadline: 12/1; financial award applicants required to submit FAFSA. *Faculty research:* Origins, correlates and treatment of depression; health and emotion; concentration on topics related to prejudice, stereotyping, and intergroup relations; memory, cognitive development, language, perception, attention, aging; psychometric methods, item response theory, structural equation modeling. *Unit head:* Ruth Anne Atchley, Chair, 785-864-4131. *Application contact:* Cathy O'Keefe, Graduate Officer, 785-864-4195, Fax: 785-864-5596, E-mail: cokeefe@ku.edu.
Website: http://www.psych.ku.edu/

University of Kentucky, Graduate School, College of Arts and Sciences, Program in Psychology, Lexington, KY 40506-0032. Offers MA, PhD. *Accreditation:* APA (one or more programs are accredited). *Degree requirements:* For master's, comprehensive exam, thesis; for doctorate, comprehensive exam, thesis/dissertation. *Entrance requirements:* For master's, GRE General Test, minimum undergraduate GPA of 2.75; for doctorate, GRE General Test, minimum graduate GPA of 3.0. Additional exam requirements/recommendations for international students: Required—TOEFL (minimum score 550 paper-based). Electronic applications accepted. *Faculty research:* Psychopharmacology and teratology, behavioral neuroscience, social psychology, cognitive psychology, development and developmental psychobiology.

University of La Verne, College of Arts and Sciences, Department of Psychology, La Verne, CA 91750-4443. Offers clinical psychology (Psy D); marriage and family therapy (MS). *Accreditation:* APA (one or more programs are accredited). Part-time programs available. *Faculty:* 14 full-time (8 women), 11 part-time/adjunct (6 women). *Students:* 66 full-time (57 women), 89 part-time (74 women); includes 87 minority (11 Black or African American, non-Hispanic/Latino; 11 Asian, non-Hispanic/Latino; 62 Hispanic/Latino; 3 Two or more races, non-Hispanic/Latino), 1 international. Average age 29. In 2014, 48 master's, 6 doctorates awarded. *Degree requirements:* For master's, thesis, competency exam, fieldwork, culminating project; for doctorate, thesis/dissertation, clinical practica, clinical internship, competency exams, personal psychotherapy. *Entrance requirements:* For master's, minimum undergraduate GPA of 3.0, 3 letters of recommendation, interview, curriculum vitae; for doctorate, GRE, minimum GPA of 3.3 undergraduate, 3.5 graduate; 3 recommendations; interview; curriculum vitae. Additional exam requirements/recommendations for international students: Required—TOEFL (minimum score 600 paper-based; 100 iBT); Recommended—IELTS (minimum score 6.5). *Application deadline:* Applications are processed on a rolling basis. *Expenses:* Expenses: Contact institution. *Financial support:* Career-related internships or fieldwork, institutionally sponsored loans, and scholarships/grants available. Financial award application deadline: 3/2; financial award applicants required to submit FAFSA. *Unit head:* Dr. Glenn Gamst, Department Chair, 909-448-4176, E-mail: ggamst@laverne.edu. *Application contact:* Christy Ranells, Associate Director of Admission, 909-448-4644, Fax: 909-9712295, E-mail: cranells@laverne.edu.
Website: http://laverne.edu/psychology/

University of Lethbridge, School of Graduate Studies, Lethbridge, AB T1K 3M4, Canada. Offers addictions counseling (M Sc); agricultural biotechnology (M Sc); agricultural studies (M Sc, MA); anthropology (MA); archaeology (M Sc, MA); art (MA, MFA); biochemistry (M Sc); biological sciences (M Sc); biomolecular science (PhD); biosystems and biodiversity (PhD); Canadian studies (MA); chemistry (M Sc); computer science (M Sc); computer science and geographical information science (M Sc); counseling (MC); counseling psychology (M Ed); dramatic arts (MA); earth, space, and physical science (PhD); economics (MA); education (MA); educational leadership (M Ed); English (MA); environmental science (M Sc); evolution and behavior (PhD); exercise science (M Sc); French (MA); French/German (MA); French/Spanish (MA); general education (M Ed); geography (M Sc, MA); German (MA); health sciences (M Sc); individualized multidisciplinary (M Sc, MA); kinesiology (M Sc, MA); management (M Sc), including accounting, finance, general management, human resource management and labor relations, information systems, international management, marketing, policy and strategy; mathematics (M Sc); modern languages (MA); music (M Mus, MA); Native American studies (MA); neuroscience (M Sc, PhD); new media (MA, MFA); nursing (M Sc, MN); philosophy (MA); physics (M Sc); political science (MA); psychology (M Sc, MA); religious studies (MA); sociology (MA); theatre and dramatic arts (MFA); theoretical and computational science (PhD); urban and regional studies (MA); women and gender studies (MA). Part-time and evening/weekend programs available. *Faculty:* 358. *Students:* 445 full-time (243 women), 116 part-time (72 women). Average age 31. 351 applicants, 26% accepted, 87 enrolled. In 2014, 129 master's, 13 doctorates awarded. *Degree requirements:* For master's, thesis (for some programs); for doctorate, comprehensive exam, thesis/dissertation. *Entrance requirements:* For master's, GMAT (for M Sc in management), bachelor's degree in related field, minimum GPA of 3.0 during previous 20 graded semester courses, 2 years' teaching or related experience (M Ed); for doctorate, master's degree, minimum graduate GPA of 3.5. Additional exam requirements/recommendations for international students: Required—TOEFL. Application fee: $100 Canadian dollars. *Financial support:* Fellowships, research assistantships, teaching assistantships, scholarships/grants, health care benefits, and unspecified assistantships available. *Faculty research:* Movement and brain plasticity, gibberellin physiology, photosynthesis, carbon cycling, molecular properties of main-group ring components. *Application contact:* School of Graduate Studies, 403-329-5194, E-mail: sgsinquiries@uleth.ca.
Website: http://www.uleth.ca/graduatestudies

University of Louisiana at Lafayette, College of Liberal Arts, Department of Psychology, Program in Psychology, Lafayette, LA 70504. Offers MS. *Degree requirements:* For master's, comprehensive exam, thesis (for some programs). *Entrance requirements:* For master's, GRE General Test. Additional exam requirements/recommendations for international students: Required—TOEFL (minimum score 550 paper-based).

University of Louisiana at Monroe, Graduate School, College of Business and Social Sciences, Department of Psychology, Monroe, LA 71209-0001. Offers forensic psychology (MS); general psychology (MS); psychometrics (MS). Part-time and evening/weekend programs available. Postbaccalaureate distance learning degree programs offered (no on-campus study). *Degree requirements:* For master's, comprehensive exam, thesis optional. *Entrance requirements:* For master's, GRE General Test, minimum GPA of 2.75. Additional exam requirements/recommendations for international students: Required—TOEFL (minimum score 500 paper-based; 61 iBT). Electronic applications accepted.

University of Louisville, Graduate School, College of Arts and Sciences, Department of Psychological and Brain Sciences, Louisville, KY 40292-0001. Offers clinical psychology (PhD); experimental psychology (PhD). *Accreditation:* APA. *Students:* 65 full-time (46 women); includes 10 minority (4 Black or African American, non-Hispanic/Latino; 1 Asian, non-Hispanic/Latino; 4 Hispanic/Latino; 1 Two or more races, non-Hispanic/Latino), 3 international. Average age 28. 179 applicants, 1% accepted, 1 enrolled. In 2014, 2 doctorates awarded. *Degree requirements:* For doctorate, thesis/dissertation, preliminary exam, research, internship. *Entrance requirements:* For doctorate, GRE General Test. Additional exam requirements/recommendations for international students: Required—TOEFL. *Application deadline:* For fall admission, 12/1 for domestic students, 5/1 priority date for international students; for spring admission, 11/1 for international students; for summer admission, 4/1 for international students. Applications are processed on a rolling basis. Application fee: $60. Electronic applications accepted. *Expenses:* Tuition, state resident: full-time $11,326; part-time $630 per credit hour. Tuition, nonresident: full-time $23,568; part-time $1311 per credit hour. *Required fees:* $196. Tuition and fees vary according to program and reciprocity agreements. *Financial support:* Fellowships, teaching assistantships, and career-related internships or fieldwork available. *Faculty research:* Health psychology, geropsychology, psychopathology, cognitive and development sciences, vision and hearing sciences. *Unit head:* Dr. Suzanne Meeks, Chair, 502-852-6068, Fax: 502-852-8904, E-mail: smeeks@louisville.edu. *Application contact:* Libby Leggett, Director, Graduate Admissions, 502-852-3101, Fax: 502-852-6536, E-mail: gradadm@louisville.edu.
Website: http://louisville.edu/psychology

University of Maine, Graduate School, College of Liberal Arts and Sciences, Department of Psychology, Orono, ME 04469. Offers psychological sciences (PhD). *Accreditation:* APA (one or more programs are accredited). *Faculty:* 27 full-time (10 women), 26 part-time/adjunct (11 women). *Students:* 30 full-time (19 women), 1 (woman) part-time; includes 3 minority (1 American Indian or Alaska Native, non-Hispanic/Latino; 2 Hispanic/Latino), 1 international. Average age 29. 181 applicants, 3% accepted, 6 enrolled. In 2014, 1 master's, 6 doctorates awarded. *Degree requirements:* For master's, thesis; for doctorate, comprehensive exam, thesis/dissertation. *Entrance requirements:* For master's and doctorate, GRE General Test, GRE Subject Test. Additional exam requirements/recommendations for international students: Required—TOEFL. *Application deadline:* For fall admission, 12/1 priority date for domestic students. Applications are processed on a rolling basis. Application fee: $65. Electronic applications accepted. *Expenses:* Tuition, state resident: part-time $658 per credit hour. Tuition, nonresident: part-time $1550 per credit hour. *Financial support:* In 2014–15, 24 students received support, including 1 fellowship with full tuition reimbursement available (averaging $25,000 per year), 3 research assistantships with full tuition reimbursements available (averaging $14,600 per year), 19 teaching assistantships with full tuition reimbursements available (averaging $14,600 per year); Federal Work-Study, institutionally sponsored loans, and tuition waivers (full and partial) also available. Financial award application deadline: 3/1. *Faculty research:* Social development, hypertension and aging, attitude change, self-confidence in achievement situations, health psychology. *Total annual research expenditures:* $130,883. *Unit head:* Dr. Michael Robbins, Chair, 207-581-2051, Fax: 207-581-6128. *Application contact:* Scott G. Delcourt, Assistant Vice President for Graduate Studies and Senior Associate Dean, 207-581-3291, Fax: 207-581-3232, E-mail: graduate@maine.edu.
Website: http://www.umaine.edu/psychology/

The University of Manchester, School of Psychological Sciences, Manchester, United Kingdom. Offers audiology (M Phil, PhD); clinical psychology (M Phil, PhD, Psy D); psychology (M Phil, PhD).

University of Manitoba, Faculty of Graduate Studies, Faculty of Arts, Department of Psychology, Winnipeg, MB R3T 2N2, Canada. Offers clinical psychology (PhD); psychology (MA, PhD); school psychology (MA). *Degree requirements:* For master's, thesis; for doctorate, one foreign language, thesis/dissertation. *Entrance requirements:* For master's and doctorate, GRE General Test.

University of Maryland, Baltimore County, The Graduate School, College of Arts, Humanities and Social Sciences, Department of Psychology, Baltimore, MD 21250. Offers applied developmental psychology (PhD); human services psychology (MA,

PhD); industrial organizational psychology (MPS). *Accreditation:* APA (one or more programs are accredited). *Faculty:* 31 full-time (17 women), 37 part-time/adjunct (16 women). *Students:* 170 full-time (142 women), 53 part-time (42 women); includes 79 minority (35 Black or African American, non-Hispanic/Latino; 19 Asian, non-Hispanic/Latino; 20 Hispanic/Latino; 2 Native Hawaiian or other Pacific Islander, non-Hispanic/Latino; 3 Two or more races, non-Hispanic/Latino). Average age 27. 410 applicants, 39% accepted, 91 enrolled. In 2014, 30 master's, 14 doctorates awarded. Terminal master's awarded for partial completion of doctoral program. *Degree requirements:* For master's, thesis or alternative; for doctorate, comprehensive exam, thesis/dissertation. *Entrance requirements:* For master's, GRE General Test; for doctorate, GRE General Test, GRE Subject Test, minimum GPA of 3.0. Additional exam requirements/recommendations for international students: Required—TOEFL. *Application deadline:* For fall admission, 12/1 for domestic and international students. Application fee: $50. Electronic applications accepted. *Expenses:* Tuition, state resident: part-time $557. Tuition, nonresident: part-time $922. *Required fees:* $122 per semester. One-time fee: $200 part-time. *Financial support:* In 2014–15, 2 students received support, including 1 fellowship with full and partial tuition reimbursement available (averaging $22,000 per year), 33 research assistantships with full and partial tuition reimbursements available (averaging $18,300 per year), 32 teaching assistantships with full and partial tuition reimbursements available (averaging $15,450 per year); career-related internships or fieldwork, Federal Work-Study, health care benefits, tuition waivers (full and partial), and unspecified assistantships also available. Financial award application deadline: 3/1; financial award applicants required to submit FAFSA. *Faculty research:* Prevention and treatment of behavior problems, early intervention, cultural contexts, applications to education, behavioral medicine. *Total annual research expenditures:* $2.3 million. *Unit head:* Dr. Christopher Murphy, Chair, 410-455-2415, Fax: 410-455-1055, E-mail: chmurphy@umbc.edu. *Application contact:* Nicole Mooney, Program Management Specialist, 410-455-2567, Fax: 410-455-1055, E-mail: psycdept@umbc.edu.

University of Maryland, College Park, Academic Affairs, College of Behavioral and Social Sciences, Department of Psychology, College Park, MD 20742. Offers clinical psychology (PhD); developmental psychology (PhD); experimental psychology (PhD); industrial psychology (MA, MS, PhD); social psychology (PhD). *Accreditation:* APA (one or more programs are accredited). *Degree requirements:* For master's, thesis; for doctorate, variable foreign language requirement, comprehensive exam, thesis/dissertation. *Entrance requirements:* For master's and doctorate, GRE General Test, GRE Subject Test, minimum GPA of 3.5, research and/or work experience, 3 letters of recommendation. Electronic applications accepted. *Faculty research:* Social stereotyping and prejudice, anxiety disorders, auditory neuroethology, counseling and social psychology.

University of Massachusetts Amherst, Graduate School, College of Natural Sciences, Department of Psychological and Brain Sciences, Amherst, MA 01003. Offers clinical psychology (MS, PhD); cognitive psychology (MS, PhD); developmental science (MS, PhD); psychology of peace and violence (MS, PhD); social psychology (MS, PhD). *Accreditation:* APA (one or more programs are accredited). *Faculty:* 62 full-time (31 women). *Students:* 47 full-time (32 women), 14 part-time (11 women); includes 12 minority (2 Black or African American, non-Hispanic/Latino; 6 Asian, non-Hispanic/Latino; 3 Hispanic/Latino; 1 Two or more races, non-Hispanic/Latino), 9 international. Average age 27. 317 applicants, 7% accepted, 11 enrolled. In 2014, 12 master's, 10 doctorates awarded. Terminal master's awarded for partial completion of doctoral program. *Degree requirements:* For master's, thesis; for doctorate, comprehensive exam, thesis/dissertation. *Entrance requirements:* For master's and doctorate, GRE General Test, 3 letters of recommendation. Additional exam requirements/recommendations for international students: Required—TOEFL (minimum score 550 paper-based; 80 iBT), IELTS (minimum score 6.5). *Application deadline:* For fall admission, 12/1 for domestic and international students. Applications are processed on a rolling basis. Application fee: $75. Electronic applications accepted. *Expenses:* Tuition, state resident: full-time $1980; part-time $110 per credit. Tuition, nonresident: full-time $14,644; part-time $414 per credit. *Required fees:* $11,417. One-time fee: $357. *Financial support:* Fellowships with full and partial tuition reimbursements, research assistantships with full and partial tuition reimbursements, teaching assistantships with full and partial tuition reimbursements, career-related internships or fieldwork, Federal Work-Study, scholarships/grants, traineeships, health care benefits, tuition waivers (full and partial), and unspecified assistantships available. Support available to part-time students. Financial award application deadline: 12/1. *Unit head:* Dr. Michael Constantino, Graduate Program Director, 413-545-2503, Fax: 413-545-0996. *Application contact:* Lindsay DeSantis, Supervisor of Admissions, 413-545-0722, Fax: 413-577-0010, E-mail: gradadm@grad.umass.edu.
Website: http://www.psych.umass.edu/

University of Massachusetts Dartmouth, Graduate School, College of Arts and Sciences, Department of Psychology, North Dartmouth, MA 02747-2300. Offers MA, Post-Master's Certificate. Part-time programs available. *Faculty:* 17 full-time (11 women), 9 part-time/adjunct (2 women). *Students:* 36 full-time (22 women), 38 part-time (23 women); includes 10 minority (2 Black or African American, non-Hispanic/Latino; 1 Asian, non-Hispanic/Latino; 7 Hispanic/Latino), 1 international. Average age 29. 102 applicants, 39% accepted, 25 enrolled. In 2014, 26 master's awarded. *Degree requirements:* For master's, comprehensive exam (for some programs), thesis (for some programs), written thesis or exam. *Entrance requirements:* For master's, GRE, statement of purpose (minimum of 300 words), resume, 3 letters of recommendation, official transcripts; for Post-Master's Certificate, statement of purpose (minimum of 300 words), resume, 3 letters of recommendation, official transcripts. Additional exam requirements/recommendations for international students: Required—TOEFL (minimum score 533 paper-based; 72 iBT), IELTS (minimum score 6). *Application deadline:* For fall admission, 2/1 priority date for domestic students, 1/1 priority date for international students; for spring admission, 12/20 priority date for domestic students, 11/20 priority date for international students. Applications are processed on a rolling basis. Application fee: $60. Electronic applications accepted. *Expenses:* Tuition, state resident: full-time $2071; part-time $86.29 per credit. Tuition, nonresident: full-time $8099; part-time $337.46 per credit. *Required fees:* $16,520; $712.33 per credit. Tuition and fees vary according to course load and reciprocity agreements. *Financial support:* In 2014–15, 1 research assistantship with partial tuition reimbursement (averaging $6,000 per year), 2 teaching assistantships with full tuition reimbursements (averaging $12,000 per year) were awarded; career-related internships or fieldwork, Federal Work-Study, and unspecified assistantships also available. Support available to part-time students. Financial award application deadline: 3/1; financial award applicants required to submit FAFSA. *Faculty research:* Nonverbal communication, behavioral medicine, learning, social and developmental psychology, child neuropsychology, counseling, clinical research, psychotherapy. *Total annual research expenditures:* $516,000. *Unit head:* Dr. Judith Sims-Knight, Graduate Program Director, Research Psychology, 508-999-8382, Fax: 508-999-9169, E-mail: jsimsknight@umassd.edu. *Application contact:* Steven Briggs, Director of Marketing and Recruitment for Graduate Studies, 508-999-8604, Fax: 508-999-8183, E-mail: graduate@umassd.edu.
Website: http://www.umassd.edu/cas/psychology/

University of Massachusetts Lowell, College of Fine Arts, Humanities and Social Sciences, Department of Psychology, Lowell, MA 01854. Offers community social psychology (MA). Part-time programs available. *Degree requirements:* For master's, thesis optional. *Entrance requirements:* For master's, GRE General Test or MAT. Electronic applications accepted. *Faculty research:* Domestic violence, youth sports, teen pregnancy, substance abuse, family and work roles.

University of Memphis, Graduate School, College of Arts and Sciences, Department of Psychology, Memphis, TN 38152-3230. Offers psychology (MS), including general psychology; school psychology (MA); MS/PhD. *Faculty:* 26 full-time (10 women), 4 part-time/adjunct (0 women). *Students:* 96 full-time (66 women), 20 part-time (12 women); includes 19 minority (11 Black or African American, non-Hispanic/Latino; 4 Asian, non-Hispanic/Latino; 1 Hispanic/Latino; 3 Two or more races, non-Hispanic/Latino), 10 international. Average age 28. 298 applicants, 14% accepted, 15 enrolled. In 2014, 18 master's, 13 doctorates awarded. *Degree requirements:* For master's, comprehensive exam (for some programs), thesis (for some programs), 37 credit hours (MA); 33 credit hours with thesis or 36 with exam (MS); for doctorate, comprehensive exam (for some programs), thesis/dissertation, 80 semester hours, major area paper; clinical: 1-year placement and 1-year internship; internship (for school psychology). *Entrance requirements:* For master's, GRE; for doctorate, GRE (minimum combined score of 1100), minimum GPA of 2.75, 18 hours of undergraduate psychology courses, transcripts, personal statement, letters of recommendation; for Ed S, GRE (minimum combined score of 1100), minimum GPA of 2.75, 18 hours of undergraduate psychology courses, letters of recommendation. Additional exam requirements/recommendations for international students: Required—TOEFL (minimum score 550 paper-based; 79 iBT). *Application deadline:* For fall admission, 12/5 for domestic students. Applications are processed on a rolling basis. Application fee: $35 ($60 for international students). Electronic applications accepted. *Financial support:* In 2014–15, 66 students received support. Fellowships with full tuition reimbursements available, research assistantships with full tuition reimbursements available, teaching assistantships with full tuition reimbursements available, Federal Work-Study, scholarships/grants, tuition waivers (partial), and unspecified assistantships available. Financial award application deadline: 2/15; financial award applicants required to submit FAFSA. *Faculty research:* Clinical health; school, child and family psychology; psychotherapy; cognitive and behavioral neuroscience; industrial-organizational psychology. *Unit head:* Dr. Robert Cohen, Coordinator of Graduate Programs, 901-678-4679, Fax: 901-678-2579, E-mail: rcohen@memphis.edu. *Application contact:* Lynell Connable, Graduate Secretary, 901-678-4340, Fax: 901-678-2579, E-mail: dconnabl@memphis.edu.
Website: http://www.memphis.edu/psychology

University of Miami, Graduate School, College of Arts and Sciences, Department of Psychology, Coral Gables, FL 33124. Offers adult clinical (PhD); behavioral neuroscience (PhD); child clinical (PhD); developmental psychology (PhD); health clinical (PhD); psychology (MS). *Accreditation:* APA (one or more programs are accredited). *Degree requirements:* For doctorate, comprehensive exam, thesis/dissertation. *Entrance requirements:* For doctorate, GRE General Test, minimum GPA of 3.5. Additional exam requirements/recommendations for international students: Required—TOEFL. Electronic applications accepted. *Faculty research:* Behavioral factors in cardiovascular disease and cancer adult psychopathology, developmental disabilities, social and emotional development, mechanisms of coping.

University of Michigan, Horace H. Rackham School of Graduate Studies, College of Literature, Science, and the Arts, Department of Psychology, Ann Arbor, MI 48109. Offers biopsychology (PhD); clinical science (PhD); cognition and cognitive neuroscience (PhD); developmental psychology (PhD); personality and social contexts (PhD); social psychology (PhD). *Accreditation:* APA. *Faculty:* 57 full-time (27 women), 31 part-time/adjunct (17 women). *Students:* 118 full-time (80 women); includes 58 minority (15 Black or African American, non-Hispanic/Latino; 1 American Indian or Alaska Native, non-Hispanic/Latino; 15 Asian, non-Hispanic/Latino; 25 Hispanic/Latino; 2 Two or more races, non-Hispanic/Latino), 12 international. Average age 27. 687 applicants, 7% accepted, 25 enrolled. In 2014, 36 doctorates awarded. *Degree requirements:* For doctorate, comprehensive exam, thesis/dissertation, oral defense of dissertation, preliminary exam. *Entrance requirements:* For doctorate, GRE General Test. Additional exam requirements/recommendations for international students: Required—TOEFL. *Application deadline:* For fall admission, 12/1 for domestic and international students. Application fee: $75 ($90 for international students). Electronic applications accepted. *Financial support:* In 2014–15, 82 students received support, including 45 fellowships with full tuition reimbursements available (averaging $21,600 per year), 16 research assistantships with full tuition reimbursements available (averaging $28,450 per year), 50 teaching assistantships with full tuition reimbursements available (averaging $26,200 per year); career-related internships or fieldwork also available. Financial award application deadline: 4/15. *Unit head:* Prof. Patricia Reuter-Lorenz, Department Chair, 734-764-7429. *Application contact:* Danielle Joanette, Psychology Student Academic Affairs, 731-764-2580, Fax: 734-615-7584, E-mail: psych.saa@umich.edu.
Website: http://www.lsa.umich.edu/psych/

University of Michigan, Horace H. Rackham School of Graduate Studies, College of Literature, Science, and the Arts, Department of Women's Studies, Ann Arbor, MI 48109. Offers English and women's studies (PhD); history and women's studies (PhD); LGBTQ studies (Certificate); psychology and women's studies (PhD); women's studies (Certificate). *Faculty:* 36 full-time. *Students:* 58 full-time (48 women). 119 applicants, 8% accepted, 6 enrolled. In 2014, 7 doctorates, 4 other advanced degrees awarded. *Degree requirements:* For doctorate, variable foreign language requirement, comprehensive exam (for some programs), thesis/dissertation. *Entrance requirements:* For doctorate, GRE General Test, previous undergraduate coursework in women's studies. *Application deadline:* For fall admission, 12/1 for domestic and international students. Application fee: $75 ($90 for international students). Electronic applications accepted. *Financial support:* In 2014–15, fellowships with full tuition reimbursements (averaging $18,000 per year), research assistantships with full tuition reimbursements (averaging $18,000 per year), teaching assistantships with full tuition reimbursements (averaging $18,000 per year) were awarded; scholarships/grants, health care benefits, tuition waivers (full), and unspecified assistantships also available. *Faculty research:* LGBTQ studies, sexuality studies, feminist science studies, global feminism, health studies, international studies, cultural studies. *Unit head:* Lilia Cortina, Director of Graduate Studies, 734-763-2047, Fax: 734-647-4943, E-mail: lilia@umich.edu. *Application contact:* Aimee Germain, Graduate Program Coordinator, 734-763-2047, Fax: 734-647-4943, E-mail: wsdgradinquiry@umich.edu.
Website: http://www.lsa.umich.edu/women/

University of Michigan, Horace H. Rackham School of Graduate Studies, Combined Program in Education and Psychology, Ann Arbor, MI 48109. Offers PhD. *Accreditation:* Teacher Education Accreditation Council. *Faculty:* 17 part-time/adjunct (9 women). *Students:* 37 full-time (24 women); includes 20 minority (10 Black or African American, non-Hispanic/Latino; 2 Asian, non-Hispanic/Latino; 3 Hispanic/Latino; 5 Two or more races, non-Hispanic/Latino), 5 international. Average age 27. 95 applicants, 8% accepted, 6 enrolled. In 2014, 5 doctorates awarded. *Degree requirements:* For doctorate, thesis/dissertation, independent research project, preliminary exam, oral defense of dissertation. *Entrance requirements:* For doctorate, GRE General Test with Analytical Writing Test. Additional exam requirements/recommendations for

international students: Required—TOEFL (minimum score 600 paper-based; 100 iBT). *Application deadline:* For fall admission, 12/1 for domestic and international students. Application fee: $75. Electronic applications accepted. *Expenses:* Expenses: Contact institution. *Financial support:* In 2014–15, 34 students received support, including 20 fellowships with full tuition reimbursements available (averaging $27,806 per year), 6 research assistantships with full tuition reimbursements available (averaging $28,448 per year), 8 teaching assistantships with full tuition reimbursements available (averaging $31,564 per year); institutionally sponsored loans, scholarships/grants, health care benefits, tuition waivers (full and partial), and unspecified assistantships also available. Financial award application deadline: 12/1. *Faculty research:* Human development in context of schools, families, communities; cognitive and learning sciences; motivation and self-regulated learning; culture, ethnicity, social and class influences on learning and motivation. *Unit head:* Dr. Robert J. Jagers, Director, 734-647-0626, Fax: 734-615-2164, E-mail: rjagers@umich.edu. *Application contact:* Janie Knieper, Administrative Specialist, 734-763-0680, Fax: 734-615-2164, E-mail: cpep@umich.edu.
Website: http://www.soe.umich.edu/academics/doctoral_programs/ep/

University of Michigan, School of Social Work, Interdisciplinary Program in Social Work and Social Science, Ann Arbor, MI 48109-1106. Offers social work and anthropology (PhD); social work and economics (PhD); social work and political science (PhD); social work and psychology (PhD); social work and sociology (PhD). Programs offered through the Horace H. Rackham School of Graduate Studies. *Faculty:* 57 full-time (33 women), 6 part-time/adjunct (4 women). *Students:* 64 full-time (46 women); includes 24 minority (7 Black or African American, non-Hispanic/Latino; 11 Asian, non-Hispanic/Latino; 6 Hispanic/Latino), 6 international. Average age 32. 108 applicants, 9% accepted, 9 enrolled. In 2014, 11 doctorates awarded. *Degree requirements:* For doctorate, thesis/dissertation, oral defense of dissertation, preliminary exam. *Entrance requirements:* For doctorate, GRE General Test. Additional exam requirements/recommendations for international students: Required—TOEFL. *Application deadline:* For fall admission, 12/1 for domestic and international students. Application fee: $75 ($90 for international students). *Financial support:* In 2014–15, 64 students received support, including 20 fellowships with full tuition reimbursements available (averaging $15,200 per year), 7 research assistantships with full tuition reimbursements available (averaging $18,971 per year), 19 teaching assistantships with full tuition reimbursements available (averaging $18,971 per year); career-related internships or fieldwork, Federal Work-Study, scholarships/grants, traineeships, health care benefits, tuition waivers (full and partial), and unspecified assistantships also available. Financial award application deadline: 12/1; financial award applicants required to submit FAFSA. *Faculty research:* Substance abuse, child welfare, mental health, poverty, aging. *Total annual research expenditures:* $4.1 million. *Unit head:* Dr. Berit Ingersoll-Dayton, Director, 734-763-5768, Fax: 734-615-3192, E-mail: bid@umich.edu. *Application contact:* Graduate Coordinator, 734-647-2554, Fax: 734-615-3192, E-mail: ssw.phd.info@umich.edu.
Website: http://www.ssw.umich.edu/doctoral

University of Minnesota, Twin Cities Campus, Graduate School, College of Liberal Arts, Department of Psychology, Minneapolis, MN 55455-0213. Offers biological psychopathology (PhD); clinical psychology (PhD); cognitive and biological psychology (PhD); counseling psychology (PhD); industrial/organizational psychology (PhD); personality, individual differences, and behavior genetics (PhD); quantitative/psychometric methods (PhD); school psychology (PhD); social psychology (PhD). *Accreditation:* APA. *Degree requirements:* For doctorate, comprehensive exam, thesis/dissertation. *Entrance requirements:* For doctorate, GRE General Test, GRE Subject Test (recommended), 12 credits of upper-level psychology courses, including a course in statistics or psychological measurement. Additional exam requirements/recommendations for international students: Required—TOEFL (minimum score 79 iBT).

University of Mississippi, Graduate School, College of Liberal Arts, Department of Psychology, University, MS 38677. Offers clinical psychology (PhD); experimental psychology (PhD); psychology (MA). *Accreditation:* APA (one or more programs are accredited). *Degree requirements:* For master's, thesis; for doctorate, thesis/dissertation. *Entrance requirements:* For master's, GRE General Test, minimum GPA of 3.0; for doctorate, GRE General Test. Additional exam requirements/recommendations for international students: Required—TOEFL. Electronic applications accepted.

University of Missouri, Office of Research and Graduate Studies, College of Arts and Science, Department of Psychological Sciences, Columbia, MO 65211. Offers MA, MS, PhD. *Accreditation:* APA (one or more programs are accredited). *Faculty:* 41 full-time (13 women), 4 part-time/adjunct (3 women). *Students:* 82 full-time (51 women), 3 part-time (2 women); includes 12 minority (3 Black or African American, non-Hispanic/Latino; 4 Asian, non-Hispanic/Latino; 3 Hispanic/Latino; 2 Two or more races, non-Hispanic/Latino), 9 international. Average age 27. 282 applicants, 7% accepted, 18 enrolled. In 2014, 14 master's, 13 doctorates awarded. Terminal master's awarded for partial completion of doctoral program. *Degree requirements:* For doctorate, comprehensive exam, thesis/dissertation. *Entrance requirements:* For master's, GRE General Test, minimum GPA of 3.0; for doctorate, GRE General Test; GRE Subject Test (strongly recommended), minimum GPA of 3.0. Additional exam requirements/recommendations for international students: Required—TOEFL (minimum score 500 paper-based; 61 iBT). *Application deadline:* For fall admission, 12/1 priority date for domestic and international students. Applications are processed on a rolling basis. Application fee: $55 ($75 for international students). Electronic applications accepted. *Financial support:* Fellowships with full tuition reimbursements, research assistantships with full tuition reimbursements, teaching assistantships with full tuition reimbursements, career-related internships or fieldwork, institutionally sponsored loans, traineeships, health care benefits, and unspecified assistantships available. *Faculty research:* Clinical psychology, cognition and neuroscience, developmental psychology, quantitative psychology and social/personality psychology, child clinical and developmental psychology. *Unit head:* Dr. Ann Bettencourt, Department Chair, 573-823-2628, E-mail: bettencourta@missouri.edu. *Application contact:* Kristina Bradley, Office Support Assistant IV, 573-882-0838, E-mail: bradleykm@missouri.edu.
Website: http://psychology.missouri.edu/grad

University of Missouri–Kansas City, College of Arts and Sciences, Department of Psychology, Kansas City, MO 64110-2499. Offers clinical psychology (PhD); community psychology (PhD); health psychology (PhD); psychology (MA). PhD (interdisciplinary) offered through the School of Graduate Studies. *Accreditation:* APA. *Faculty:* 10 full-time (7 women), 2 part-time/adjunct (1 woman). *Students:* 21 full-time (14 women), 10 part-time (6 women); includes 5 minority (1 Asian, non-Hispanic/Latino; 4 Hispanic/Latino). Average age 32. 109 applicants, 6% accepted, 6 enrolled. In 2014, 4 master's, 7 doctorates awarded. Terminal master's awarded for partial completion of doctoral program. *Degree requirements:* For master's, thesis; for doctorate, comprehensive exam, thesis/dissertation, residency. *Entrance requirements:* For master's, GRE, minimum GPA of 3.5, letter of recommendation; for doctorate, GRE, minimum GPA of 3.25. Additional exam requirements/recommendations for international students: Required—TOEFL (minimum score 550 paper-based; 80 iBT). *Application deadline:* For fall admission, 1/15 for domestic and international students. Applications are processed on a rolling basis. Application fee: $45 ($50 for international students). Electronic applications accepted. *Financial support:* In 2014–15, 8 research assistantships (averaging $11,229 per year), 20 teaching assistantships (averaging $12,015 per year) were awarded; career-related internships or fieldwork, Federal Work-Study, and institutionally sponsored loans also available. Support available to part-time students. Financial award application deadline: 3/1; financial award applicants required to submit FAFSA. *Faculty research:* HIV/AIDS research group, psycho-oncology, sensory and cognitive neuroscience, cognitive psychophysiology, obesity and related metabolic disorders. *Unit head:* Dr. Jennifer Lundgren, Department Chair, 816-235-5384, Fax: 816-235-1062, E-mail: lundgrenj@umkc.edu. *Application contact:* Dr. Cathy Rawlings, Director, Graduate Programs, 816-235-1318, Fax: 816-235-1062, E-mail: psychology@umkc.edu.
Website: http://cas.umkc.edu/psyc

University of Missouri–St. Louis, College of Arts and Sciences, Department of Psychology, St. Louis, MO 63121. Offers behavioral neuroscience (MA, PhD); clinical psychology (PhD); clinical psychology respecialization (Certificate); industrial/organizational psychology (MA, PhD); trauma studies (Certificate). *Accreditation:* APA (one or more programs are accredited). Evening/weekend programs available. *Faculty:* 20 full-time (12 women), 5 part-time/adjunct (0 women). *Students:* 61 full-time (39 women), 17 part-time (15 women); includes 8 minority (3 Black or African American, non-Hispanic/Latino; 1 American Indian or Alaska Native, non-Hispanic/Latino; 1 Asian, non-Hispanic/Latino; 3 Hispanic/Latino). Average age 27. 232 applicants, 8% accepted, 14 enrolled. In 2014, 17 master's, 15 doctorates awarded. Terminal master's awarded for partial completion of doctoral program. *Degree requirements:* For master's, thesis; for doctorate, thesis/dissertation. *Entrance requirements:* For master's, GRE General Test, 3 letters of recommendation; for doctorate, GRE General Test, GRE Subject Test, 3 letters of recommendation. Additional exam requirements/recommendations for international students: Required—TOEFL (minimum score 550 paper-based; 79 iBT), IELTS (minimum score 6.5). *Application deadline:* For fall admission, 12/15 for domestic and international students. Application fee: $50 ($40 for international students). Electronic applications accepted. *Expenses:* Tuition, state resident: full-time $7364; part-time $409.10 per hour. Tuition, nonresident: full-time $18,153; part-time $1008.50 per hour. *Financial support:* In 2014–15, 8 research assistantships with full and partial tuition reimbursements (averaging $10,600 per year), 25 teaching assistantships with full and partial tuition reimbursements (averaging $9,422 per year) were awarded; fellowships with full tuition reimbursements also available. Financial award applicants required to submit FAFSA. *Faculty research:* Bereavement and loss, neuroscience, post-traumatic stress disorder, conflict and negotiation, social psychology. *Unit head:* Dr. Brian Vandenberg, Chair, 314-516-5391, Fax: 314-516-5392, E-mail: umslpsychology@msx.umsl.edu. *Application contact:* 314-516-5458, Fax: 314-516-6996, E-mail: gradadm@umsl.edu.
Website: http://www.umsl.edu/divisions/artscience/psychology/

The University of Montana, Graduate School, College of Humanities and Sciences, Department of Psychology, Missoula, MT 59812-0002. Offers clinical psychology (PhD); experimental psychology (PhD), including animal behavior psychology, developmental psychology; school psychology (MA, PhD, Ed S). *Accreditation:* APA (one or more programs are accredited). Terminal master's awarded for partial completion of doctoral program. *Degree requirements:* For master's, thesis; for doctorate, thesis/dissertation. *Entrance requirements:* For master's, doctorate, and Ed S, GRE General Test. Additional exam requirements/recommendations for international students: Required—TOEFL.

University of Nebraska at Omaha, Graduate Studies, College of Arts and Sciences, Department of Psychology, Omaha, NE 68182. Offers industrial/organizational psychology (MS); psychology (MS, PhD); school psychology (MS, Ed S). Part-time programs available. *Faculty:* 19 full-time (8 women). *Students:* 66 full-time (52 women), 53 part-time (33 women); includes 10 minority (2 Black or African American, non-Hispanic/Latino; 2 Asian, non-Hispanic/Latino; 6 Hispanic/Latino). Average age 26. 178 applicants, 31% accepted, 51 enrolled. In 2014, 20 master's, 6 doctorates, 10 other advanced degrees awarded. *Degree requirements:* For master's, comprehensive exam, thesis (for some programs); for doctorate, comprehensive exam, thesis/dissertation. *Entrance requirements:* For master's and doctorate, GRE, minimum GPA of 3.0, official transcripts, 3 letters of recommendation, statement of purpose, writing sample, resume. Additional exam requirements/recommendations for international students: Required—TOEFL, IELTS, PTE. *Application deadline:* For fall admission, 1/5 for domestic and international students. Application fee: $45. Electronic applications accepted. *Financial support:* In 2014–15, 42 students received support, including 16 research assistantships with tuition reimbursements available, 26 teaching assistantships with tuition reimbursements available; fellowships with tuition reimbursements available, career-related internships or fieldwork, Federal Work-Study, institutionally sponsored loans, scholarships/grants, tuition waivers (partial), and unspecified assistantships also available. Support available to part-time students. Financial award application deadline: 3/1; financial award applicants required to submit FAFSA. *Unit head:* Dr. Brigette Ryalls, Chairperson, 402-554-2341, E-mail: graduate@unomaha.edu. *Application contact:* Dr. Joseph Brown, Graduate Program Chair, 402-554-2341, E-mail: graduate@unomaha.edu.

University of Nebraska–Lincoln, Graduate College, College of Arts and Sciences, Department of Psychology, Lincoln, NE 68588. Offers biopsychology (PhD); clinical psychology (PhD); cognitive psychology (PhD); developmental psychology (PhD); psychology (MA); social/personality psychology (PhD); JD/MA; JD/PhD. *Accreditation:* APA (one or more programs are accredited). *Degree requirements:* For master's, thesis optional; for doctorate, comprehensive exam, thesis/dissertation. *Entrance requirements:* For master's and doctorate, GRE General Test. Additional exam requirements/recommendations for international students: Required—TOEFL (minimum score 550 paper-based). Electronic applications accepted. *Faculty research:* Law and psychology, rural mental health, chronic mental illness, neuropsychology, child clinical psychology.

University of Nevada, Las Vegas, Graduate College, College of Liberal Arts, Department of Psychology, Las Vegas, NV 89154-5030. Offers MA, PhD. *Accreditation:* APA. Part-time programs available. *Faculty:* 10 full-time (2 women), 4 part-time/adjunct (3 women). *Students:* 57 full-time (39 women), 8 part-time (6 women); includes 9 minority (1 Black or African American, non-Hispanic/Latino; 1 American Indian or Alaska Native, non-Hispanic/Latino; 1 Asian, non-Hispanic/Latino; 5 Hispanic/Latino; 1 Two or more races, non-Hispanic/Latino), 5 international. Average age 29. 93 applicants, 13% accepted, 8 enrolled. In 2014, 9 master's, 14 doctorates awarded. Terminal master's awarded for partial completion of doctoral program. *Degree requirements:* For master's, comprehensive exam, thesis, oral defense of dissertation; for doctorate, comprehensive exam, thesis/dissertation, oral defense of dissertation. *Entrance requirements:* For master's and doctorate, GRE General and Subject Tests. Additional exam requirements/recommendations for international students: Required—TOEFL (minimum score 550 paper-based; 80 iBT), IELTS (minimum score 7). *Application deadline:* For fall admission, 12/1 for domestic students, 5/1 for international students; for spring admission, 10/1 for international students. Application fee: $60 ($95 for international students). Electronic applications accepted. *Financial support:* In 2014–15, 55 students received support, including 1 fellowship with full tuition reimbursement available

(averaging $20,000 per year), 13 research assistantships with partial tuition reimbursements available (averaging $13,231 per year), 41 teaching assistantships with partial tuition reimbursements available (averaging $14,293 per year); institutionally sponsored loans, scholarships/grants, health care benefits, and unspecified assistantships also available. Financial award application deadline: 3/1. *Faculty research:* School absenteeism and selective autism, dementia and schizophrenia, biomarkers for mental disorders, infant cognition, sports psychology. *Total annual research expenditures:* $513,046. *Unit head:* Dr. Christopher Kearney, Chair/Professor, 702-895-0183, Fax: 702-895-0195, E-mail: chris.kearney@unlv.edu. *Application contact:* Graduate College Admissions Evaluator, 702-895-3320, Fax: 702-895-4180, E-mail: gradcollege@unlv.edu.
Website: http://psychology.unlv.edu/

University of Nevada, Reno, Graduate School, College of Liberal Arts, Department of Psychology, Reno, NV 89557. Offers behavior analysis (MA, PhD); clinical psychology (MA, PhD); cognitive brain science (MA, PhD). *Accreditation:* APA (one or more programs are accredited). Terminal master's awarded for partial completion of doctoral program. *Degree requirements:* For master's, thesis optional; for doctorate, thesis/dissertation. *Entrance requirements:* For master's, GRE General Test, GRE Subject Test, minimum GPA of 2.75; for doctorate, GRE General Test, GRE Subject Test, minimum GPA of 3.0. Additional exam requirements/recommendations for international students: Required—TOEFL (minimum score 500 paper-based; 61 iBT), IELTS (minimum score 6). Electronic applications accepted. *Faculty research:* Cognitive psychology, social psychological theory, animal and human intelligence, psychotherapy outcome, perception.

University of New Brunswick Fredericton, School of Graduate Studies, Faculty of Arts, Department of Psychology, Fredericton, NB E3B 5A3, Canada. Offers MA, PhD. Part-time programs available. *Faculty:* 14 full-time (8 women), 4 part-time/adjunct (1 woman). *Students:* 33 full-time (30 women), 3 part-time (all women). In 2014, 6 doctorates awarded. *Degree requirements:* For doctorate, comprehensive exam, thesis/dissertation. *Entrance requirements:* For master's, BA (Honors) in psychology or equivalent research experience; for doctorate, minimum GPA of 3.7. Additional exam requirements/recommendations for international students: Required—TOEFL (minimum score 600 paper-based). *Application deadline:* For fall admission, 1/15 for domestic and international students; for winter admission, 1/15 priority date for domestic and international students. Applications are processed on a rolling basis. Application fee: $50 Canadian dollars. Electronic applications accepted. *Financial support:* Fellowships, research assistantships, and teaching assistantships available. Financial award application deadline: 1/15. *Faculty research:* Brain-behavior relationships, cognitive science, social psychology, marginalized groups, human sexuality, sport and exercise psychology, child and adolescent development, health psychology. *Unit head:* Dr. Heather Sears, Director of Graduate Studies, 506-458-7122, Fax: 506-447-3063, E-mail: hsears@unb.ca. *Application contact:* Jessica Carter, Graduate Secretary, 506-453-4707, Fax: 506-447-3063, E-mail: j.carter4@unb.ca.
Website: http://go.unb.ca/gradprograms

University of New Brunswick Saint John, Department of Psychology, Saint John, NB E2L 4L5, Canada. Offers clinical psychology (PhD); experimental psychology (MA, PhD). Part-time programs available. *Faculty:* 9 full-time (4 women). *Students:* 16 full-time (9 women). In 2014, 3 master's awarded. *Degree requirements:* For master's, thesis. *Entrance requirements:* For master's, GRE General and Subject Tests, honors thesis; minimum GPA of 3.7. Additional exam requirements/recommendations for international students: Required—TOEFL (minimum score 550 paper-based), TWE. *Application deadline:* For fall admission, 1/15 priority date for domestic students. Application fee: $50. Electronic applications accepted. *Financial support:* In 2014–15, 6 fellowships, 5 research assistantships, 16 teaching assistantships were awarded; unspecified assistantships also available. Support available to part-time students. Financial award application deadline: 2/1. *Faculty research:* Forensic psychology, peer relationships and social skills, polygraph techniques, addictions, attachment and social adjustment, neuroscience, optical illusions, graphical perception, associative learning in animals, bio-psychology. *Unit head:* Dr. Lisa Best, Director of Graduate Studies, 506-648-5562, Fax: 506-648-5780, E-mail: lbest@unb.ca. *Application contact:* Laura Galbraith, Secretary, 506-648-5640, Fax: 506-648-5780, E-mail: galbral@unb.ca.
Website: http://go.unb.ca/gradprograms

University of New Hampshire, Graduate School, College of Liberal Arts, Department of Psychology, Durham, NH 03824. Offers PhD. *Faculty:* 19 full-time (8 women). *Students:* 23 full-time (14 women), 8 part-time (6 women); includes 4 minority (1 Asian, non-Hispanic/Latino; 1 Hispanic/Latino; 2 Two or more races, non-Hispanic/Latino), 1 international. Average age 31. 68 applicants, 4% accepted, 3 enrolled. In 2014, 4 doctorates awarded. *Degree requirements:* For doctorate, thesis/dissertation. *Entrance requirements:* For doctorate, GRE General Test, GRE Subject Test. Additional exam requirements/recommendations for international students: Required—TOEFL (minimum score 550 paper-based; 80 iBT). *Application deadline:* For fall admission, 6/15 priority date for domestic students, 4/15 for international students; for spring admission, 12/1 for domestic students. Applications are processed on a rolling basis. Application fee: $65. Electronic applications accepted. *Expenses:* Tuition, state resident: full-time $13,500; part-time $750 per credit hour. Tuition, nonresident: full-time $26,460; part-time $1110 per credit hour. *Required fees:* $1788; $447 per semester. *Financial support:* In 2014–15, 27 students received support, including 1 fellowship, 26 teaching assistantships; research assistantships, career-related internships or fieldwork, Federal Work-Study, scholarships/grants, and tuition waivers (full and partial) also available. Support available to part-time students. Financial award application deadline: 2/15. *Faculty research:* History of psychology; cognition and perception; learning, developmental, physiological, and social psychology. *Unit head:* Dr. William Stein, Chairperson, 603-862-2823. *Application contact:* Robin Scholefield, Administrative Assistant, 603-862-2369, E-mail: psychology.ph.d@unh.edu.
Website: http://cola.unh.edu/psychology

University of New Mexico, Graduate School, College of Arts and Sciences, Program in Psychology, Albuquerque, NM 87131-2039. Offers behavioral neuroscience (PhD); clinical psychology (PhD); cognitive neuroimaging (PhD); developmental psychology (PhD); evolution (PhD); health psychology (PhD); quantitative methodology (PhD). *Faculty:* 25 full-time (9 women), 1 (woman) part-time/adjunct. *Students:* 66 full-time (44 women), 12 part-time (6 women); includes 23 minority (2 Black or African American, non-Hispanic/Latino; 2 American Indian or Alaska Native, non-Hispanic/Latino; 4 Asian, non-Hispanic/Latino; 13 Hispanic/Latino; 2 Two or more races, non-Hispanic/Latino), 1 international. Average age 33. 135 applicants, 10% accepted, 13 enrolled. In 2014, 10 doctorates awarded. *Degree requirements:* For doctorate, comprehensive exam, thesis/dissertation. *Entrance requirements:* For doctorate, GRE General Test, GRE Subject Test (psychology), minimum GPA of 3.0. Additional exam requirements/recommendations for international students: Required—TOEFL (minimum score 550 paper-based; 79 iBT), IELTS (minimum score 6.5). *Application deadline:* For fall admission, 12/15 priority date for domestic and international students. Applications are processed on a rolling basis. Application fee: $50. Electronic applications accepted. *Financial support:* In 2014–15, 62 students received support, including 8 fellowships (averaging $13,124 per year), 37 research assistantships with full and partial tuition reimbursements available (averaging $11,655 per year), 67 teaching assistantships with full and partial tuition reimbursements available (averaging $13,600 per year); career-related internships or fieldwork, Federal Work-Study, institutionally sponsored loans, scholarships/grants, health care benefits, tuition waivers (partial), and unspecified assistantships also available. Financial award application deadline: 3/1; financial award applicants required to submit FAFSA. *Faculty research:* Addiction, cognition, brain and behavior, developmental, evolutionary, functioning neuroimaging, health psychology, learning and memory, neuroscience. *Unit head:* Dr. Jane Ellen Smith, Department Chair, 505-277-4121, Fax: 505-277-1394. *Application contact:* Rikk Murphy, Graduate Program Coordinator, 505-277-5009, Fax: 505-277-1394, E-mail: advising@unm.edu.
Website: http://psych.unm.edu

University of New Orleans, Graduate School, College of Sciences, Department of Psychology, New Orleans, LA 70148. Offers MS, PhD. *Degree requirements:* For doctorate, thesis/dissertation. *Entrance requirements:* For doctorate, GRE General Test, minimum GPA of 3.0, 21 hours of course work in psychology. Additional exam requirements/recommendations for international students: Required—TOEFL (minimum score 550 paper-based; 79 iBT), IELTS. Electronic applications accepted. *Faculty research:* Biofeedback, visual and auditory perception, psychopharmacology, neuropeptides.

The University of North Carolina at Chapel Hill, Graduate School, College of Arts and Sciences, Department of Psychology, Chapel Hill, NC 27599-3270. Offers behavioral neuroscience psychology (PhD); clinical psychology (PhD); cognitive psychology (PhD); developmental psychology (PhD); quantitative psychology (PhD); social psychology (PhD). *Accreditation:* APA. *Degree requirements:* For doctorate, comprehensive exam, thesis/dissertation. *Entrance requirements:* For doctorate, GRE General Test, minimum GPA of 3.0. Additional exam requirements/recommendations for international students: Required—TOEFL (minimum score 550 paper-based; 79 iBT), IELTS (minimum score 7). Electronic applications accepted. *Faculty research:* Expressed emotion, cognitive development, social cognitive neuroscience, human memory personality.

The University of North Carolina at Charlotte, College of Liberal Arts and Sciences, Department of Psychology, Charlotte, NC 28223-0001. Offers clinical/community psychology (MA); cognitive sciences (Graduate Certificate); health psychology (PhD); industrial/organizational psychology (MA). Part-time programs available. *Faculty:* 31 full-time (17 women), 1 part-time/adjunct (0 women). *Students:* 42 full-time (35 women), 31 part-time (26 women); includes 18 minority (5 Black or African American, non-Hispanic/Latino; 2 Asian, non-Hispanic/Latino; 9 Hispanic/Latino; 2 Two or more races, non-Hispanic/Latino), 1 international. Average age 28. 243 applicants, 16% accepted, 25 enrolled. In 2014, 9 master's, 5 doctorates, 1 other advanced degree awarded. Terminal master's awarded for partial completion of doctoral program. *Degree requirements:* For master's, thesis; for doctorate, thesis/dissertation. *Entrance requirements:* For master's, GRE General Test, GRE Subject Test, minimum GPA of 3.0 in undergraduate major, 2.8 overall, letters of recommendation; for doctorate, GRE General Test, minimum GPA of 3.5, letters of recommendation. Additional exam requirements/recommendations for international students: Required—TOEFL (minimum score 557 paper-based; 83 iBT). *Application deadline:* For fall admission, 5/1 for domestic and international students. Application fee: $75. Electronic applications accepted. *Expenses:* Tuition, state resident: full-time $4008. Tuition, nonresident: full-time $16,295. *Required fees:* $2755. Tuition and fees vary according to course load and program. *Financial support:* In 2014–15, 33 students received support, including 16 research assistantships (averaging $15,239 per year), 17 teaching assistantships (averaging $12,809 per year); career-related internships or fieldwork, Federal Work-Study, institutionally sponsored loans, and scholarships/grants also available. Support available to part-time students. Financial award application deadline: 4/1; financial award applicants required to submit FAFSA. *Faculty research:* Neuropsychology of information processing, perception and human performance, computer-based applications in research and instruction, interventions to facilitate team effectiveness, post-traumatic psychological growth. *Total annual research expenditures:* $327,551. *Unit head:* Dr. Fary Cachelin, Chair, 704-687-1319, Fax: 704-687-1317, E-mail: fcacheli@uncc.edu. *Application contact:* Kathy B. Giddings, Director of Graduate Admissions, 704-687-5503, Fax: 704-687-1668, E-mail: gradadm@uncc.edu.
Website: http://psych.uncc.edu/graduate-programs

The University of North Carolina at Greensboro, Graduate School, College of Arts and Sciences, Department of Psychology, Greensboro, NC 27412-5001. Offers clinical psychology (MA, PhD); cognitive psychology (MA, PhD); developmental psychology (MA, PhD); social psychology (MA, PhD). *Accreditation:* APA (one or more programs are accredited). Terminal master's awarded for partial completion of doctoral program. *Degree requirements:* For master's, comprehensive exam, thesis; for doctorate, one foreign language, thesis/dissertation, preliminary exam. *Entrance requirements:* For master's and doctorate, GRE General Test. Additional exam requirements/recommendations for international students: Required—TOEFL. Electronic applications accepted. *Faculty research:* Sensory and perceptual determinants; evoked potential: disorders, deafness, and development.

The University of North Carolina Wilmington, College of Arts and Sciences, Department of Psychology, Wilmington, NC 28403-3297. Offers MA. Part-time programs available. *Faculty:* 31 full-time (18 women). *Students:* 40 full-time (31 women), 41 part-time (31 women); includes 7 minority (1 Black or African American, non-Hispanic/Latino; 1 Asian, non-Hispanic/Latino; 5 Hispanic/Latino), 2 international. 120 applicants, 36% accepted, 29 enrolled. In 2014, 26 master's awarded. *Degree requirements:* For master's, comprehensive exam, thesis. *Entrance requirements:* For master's, GRE General Test, GRE Subject Test, minimum B average in undergraduate major. Additional exam requirements/recommendations for international students: Required—TOEFL (minimum score 79 iBT), IELTS. *Application deadline:* For fall admission, 1/15 for domestic students. Applications are processed on a rolling basis. Application fee: $60. *Expenses:* Tuition, state resident: full-time $3240. Tuition, nonresident: full-time $9208. *Required fees:* $1967. *Financial support:* Career-related internships or fieldwork and Federal Work-Study available. Financial award application deadline: 3/15; financial award applicants required to submit FAFSA. *Unit head:* Dr. Rich Ogle, Chair, 910-962-7753, Fax: 910-962-7010, E-mail: ogler@uncw.edu. *Application contact:* Dr. Christine Hughes, Graduate Coordinator, 910-962-7795, Fax: 910-962-7010, E-mail: hughesc@uncw.edu.
Website: http://www.uncw.edu/psy/grad/

University of North Dakota, Graduate School, College of Arts and Sciences, Department of Psychology, Grand Forks, ND 58202. Offers clinical psychology (PhD); counseling psychology (PhD); experimental psychology (PhD); forensic psychology (MA, MS); psychology (MA). *Accreditation:* APA (one or more programs are accredited). *Degree requirements:* For master's, thesis, final exam; for doctorate, comprehensive exam, thesis/dissertation, internship, final exam. *Entrance requirements:* For master's, GRE General Test, GRE Subject Test, minimum GPA of 3.0; for doctorate, GRE General Test, GRE Subject Test, minimum GPA of 3.5. Additional exam requirements/recommendations for international students: Required—TOEFL (minimum score 550 paper-based; 79 iBT), IELTS (minimum score 6.5). Electronic applications accepted. *Faculty research:* Developmental psychology, clinical social psychology, educational psychology, personality disorders.

University of Northern British Columbia, Office of Graduate Studies, Prince George, BC V2N 4Z9, Canada. Offers business administration (Diploma); community health science (M Sc); disability management (MA); education (M Ed); first nations studies (MA); gender studies (MA); history (MA); interdisciplinary studies (MA); international studies (MA); mathematical, computer and physical sciences (M Sc); natural resources and environmental studies (M Sc, MA, MNRES, PhD); political science (MA); psychology (M Sc, PhD); social work (MSW). Part-time and evening/weekend programs available. Postbaccalaureate distance learning degree programs offered (no on-campus study). *Degree requirements:* For master's, thesis; for doctorate, thesis/dissertation. *Entrance requirements:* For master's, GRE, minimum B average in undergraduate course work; for doctorate, candidacy exam, minimum A average in graduate course work.

University of Northern Colorado, Graduate School, College of Education and Behavioral Sciences, School of Psychological Sciences, Greeley, CO 80639. Offers MA, PhD. Part-time programs available. *Degree requirements:* For master's, comprehensive exam, thesis or alternative; for doctorate, comprehensive exam, thesis/dissertation. *Entrance requirements:* For master's and doctorate, GRE General Test, letters of recommendation. Electronic applications accepted.

University of Northern Iowa, Graduate College, College of Social and Behavioral Sciences, Department of Psychology, Cedar Falls, IA 50614. Offers MA. Part-time programs available. *Students:* 17 full-time (12 women), 10 part-time (3 women); includes 5 minority (2 Black or African American, non-Hispanic/Latino; 2 American Indian or Alaska Native, non-Hispanic/Latino; 1 Two or more races, non-Hispanic/Latino), 4 international. 55 applicants, 20% accepted, 8 enrolled. In 2014, 8 master's awarded. *Degree requirements:* For master's, comprehensive exam, thesis. *Entrance requirements:* For master's, GRE, minimum GPA of 3.0, 3 letters of recommendation. Additional exam requirements/recommendations for international students: Required—TOEFL (minimum score 500 paper-based; 61 iBT). *Application deadline:* For fall admission, 4/30 for domestic students. Applications are processed on a rolling basis. Application fee: $50 ($70 for international students). Electronic applications accepted. *Expenses:* Tuition, state resident: full-time $7912; part-time $880 per credit. Tuition, nonresident: full-time $17,906; part-time $880 per credit. *Required fees:* $1101; $325.50 per credit. $465.63 per semester. Tuition and fees vary according to course load and program. *Financial support:* Career-related internships or fieldwork, Federal Work-Study, and tuition waivers (full and partial) available. Support available to part-time students. Financial award application deadline: 2/1. *Unit head:* Dr. Eric Hiris, Department Head, 319-273-2303, Fax: 319-273-6188, E-mail: eric.hiris@uni.edu. *Application contact:* Laurie S. Russell, Record Analyst, 319-273-2623, Fax: 319-273-2885, E-mail: laurie.russell@uni.edu.
Website: http://www.uni.edu/psych/

University of North Florida, College of Arts and Sciences, Department of Psychology, Jacksonville, FL 32224. Offers counseling psychology (MAC); general psychology (MA). Part-time and evening/weekend programs available. *Faculty:* 21 full-time (11 women). *Students:* 29 full-time (18 women), 7 part-time (6 women); includes 8 minority (2 Black or African American, non-Hispanic/Latino; 5 Hispanic/Latino; 1 Two or more races, non-Hispanic/Latino), 1 international. Average age 25. 87 applicants, 30% accepted, 16 enrolled. In 2014, 7 master's awarded. *Degree requirements:* For master's, comprehensive exam, thesis optional, practicum. *Entrance requirements:* For master's, GRE General Test, 2 letters of recommendation, minimum GPA of 3.0 in last 60 hours of course work. Additional exam requirements/recommendations for international students: Required—TOEFL (minimum score 500 paper-based; 61 iBT). *Application deadline:* For fall admission, 6/1 priority date for domestic students, 4/1 for international students. Applications are processed on a rolling basis. Application fee: $30. Electronic applications accepted. *Expenses:* Tuition, state resident: full-time $9794; part-time $408.10 per credit hour. Tuition, nonresident: full-time $22,383; part-time $932.61 per credit hour. *Required fees:* $2047; $85.29 per credit hour. Tuition and fees vary according to course load and program. *Financial support:* In 2014–15, 10 students received support, including 5 teaching assistantships (averaging $4,182 per year); research assistantships, Federal Work-Study, scholarships/grants, and tuition waivers (partial) also available. Financial award application deadline: 4/1; financial award applicants required to submit FAFSA. *Faculty research:* Sensory perception, social cognition, sexual behavior, evolutionary psychology, psychology and law. *Total annual research expenditures:* $68,180. *Unit head:* Dr. Michael Toglia, Chair, 904-620-1624, E-mail: m.toglia@unf.edu. *Application contact:* Dr. Amanda Pascale, Director, The Graduate School, 904-620-1360, Fax: 904-620-1362, E-mail: graduateschool@unf.edu.
Website: http://www.unf.edu/coas/psychology/

University of North Texas, Robert B. Toulouse School of Graduate Studies, Denton, TX 76203-5459. Offers accounting (MS); applied anthropology (MA, MS); applied behavior analysis (Certificate); applied geography (MA); applied technology and performance improvement (M Ed, MS); art education (MA); art history (MA); art museum education (Certificate); arts leadership (Certificate); audiology (Au D); behavior analysis (MS); behavioral science (PhD); biochemistry and molecular biology (MS); biology (MA, MS); biomedical engineering (MS); business analysis (MS); chemistry (MS); clinical health psychology (PhD); communication studies (MA, MS); computer engineering (MS); computer science (MS); counseling (M Ed, MS), including clinical mental health counseling (MS), college and university counseling, elementary school counseling, secondary school counseling; creative writing (MA); criminal justice (MS); curriculum and instruction (M Ed); decision sciences (MBA); design (MA, MFA), including fashion design (MFA), innovation studies, interior design (MFA); early childhood studies (MS); economics (MS); educational leadership (M Ed, Ed D); educational psychology (MS, PhD), including family studies (MS), gifted and talented (MS), human development (MS), learning and cognition (MS), research, measurement and evaluation (MS); electrical engineering (MS); emergency management (MPA); engineering technology (MS); English (MA); English as a second language (MA); environmental science (MS); finance (MBA, MS); financial management (MPA); French (MA); health services management (MBA); higher education (M Ed, Ed D); history (MA, MS); hospitality management (MS); human resources management (MPA); information science (MS); information systems (PhD); information technologies (MBA); interdisciplinary studies (MA, MS); international studies (MA); international sustainable tourism (MS); jazz studies (MM); journalism (MA, MJ, Graduate Certificate), including interactive and virtual digital communication (Graduate Certificate), narrative journalism (Graduate Certificate), public relations (Graduate Certificate); kinesiology (MS); linguistics (MA); local government management (MPA); logistics (PhD); logistics and supply chain management (MBA); long-term care, senior housing, and aging services (MA); management (PhD); marketing (MBA); mathematics (MA, MS); mechanical and energy engineering (MS, PhD); music (MA), including ethnomusicology, music theory, musicology, performance; music composition (PhD); music education (MM Ed, PhD); nonprofit management (MPA); operations and supply chain management (MBA); performance (MM, DMA); philosophy (MA); political science (MA); professional and technical communication (MA); radio, television and film (MA, MFA); rehabilitation counseling (Certificate); sociology (MA); Spanish (MA); special education (M Ed); speech-language pathology (MA); strategic management (MBA); studio art (MFA); teaching (M Ed); MBA/MS. Part-time and evening/weekend programs available. Postbaccalaureate distance learning degree programs offered. *Faculty:* 651 full-time (215 women), 233 part-time/adjunct (139 women). *Students:* 3,040 full-time (1,598 women), 3,401 part-time (2,097 women); includes 1,740 minority (533 Black or African American, non-Hispanic/Latino; 15 American Indian or Alaska Native, non-Hispanic/Latino; 286 Asian, non-Hispanic/Latino; 746 Hispanic/Latino; 3 Native Hawaiian or other Pacific Islander, non-Hispanic/Latino; 157 Two or more races, non-Hispanic/Latino), 1,145 international. Terminal master's awarded for partial completion of doctoral program. *Degree requirements:* For master's, variable foreign language requirement, comprehensive exam (for some programs), thesis (for some programs); for doctorate, variable foreign language requirement, comprehensive exam (for some programs), thesis/dissertation; for other advanced degree, variable foreign language requirement, comprehensive exam (for some programs). *Entrance requirements:* For master's and doctorate, GRE, GMAT. Additional exam requirements/recommendations for international students: Required—TOEFL (minimum score 550 paper-based; 79 iBT). *Application deadline:* For fall admission, 7/15 for domestic students, 3/15 for international students; for spring admission, 11/15 for domestic students, 9/15 for international students; for summer admission, 5/1 for domestic students. Applications are processed on a rolling basis. Application fee: $60. Electronic applications accepted. *Expenses:* Tuition, state resident: full-time $5450; part-time $3633 per year. Tuition, nonresident: full-time $11,966; part-time $7977 per year. *Required fees:* $1301; $398 per credit hour. $685 per semester. Tuition and fees vary according to program and reciprocity agreements. *Financial support:* Fellowships with partial tuition reimbursements, research assistantships with partial tuition reimbursements, teaching assistantships, career-related internships or fieldwork, Federal Work-Study, institutionally sponsored loans, scholarships/grants, health care benefits, and library assistantships available. Support available to part-time students. Financial award applicants required to submit FAFSA. *Unit head:* Mark Wardell, Dean, 940-565-2383, E-mail: mark.wardell@unt.edu. *Application contact:* Toulouse School of Graduate Studies, 940-565-2383, Fax: 940-565-2141, E-mail: gradsch@unt.edu.
Website: http://tsgs.unt.edu/

University of Notre Dame, Graduate School, College of Arts and Letters, Division of Social Science, Department of Psychology, Notre Dame, IN 46556. Offers cognitive psychology (PhD); counseling psychology (PhD); developmental psychology (PhD); quantitative psychology (PhD). *Accreditation:* APA. *Degree requirements:* For doctorate, comprehensive exam, thesis/dissertation, candidacy exam. *Entrance requirements:* For doctorate, GRE General Test, GRE Subject Test (strongly recommended). Additional exam requirements/recommendations for international students: Required—TOEFL (minimum score 600 paper-based; 80 iBT). Electronic applications accepted. *Faculty research:* Cognitive and socio-emotional development, statistical methods and quantitative models applicable to psychology, interpersonal relations, life span development and developmental delay, childhood depression, structural equation and dynamical systems.

University of Oklahoma, College of Arts and Sciences, Department of Psychology, Norman, OK 73019. Offers organizational dynamics (MA), including human resource management, technical project management; psychology (MS), including industrial and organizational psychology, psychology. Part-time and evening/weekend programs available. *Faculty:* 25 full-time (12 women). *Students:* 51 full-time (30 women), 48 part-time (22 women); includes 19 minority (3 Black or African American, non-Hispanic/Latino; 2 American Indian or Alaska Native, non-Hispanic/Latino; 6 Asian, non-Hispanic/Latino; 3 Hispanic/Latino; 1 Native Hawaiian or other Pacific Islander, non-Hispanic/Latino; 4 Two or more races, non-Hispanic/Latino), 3 international. Average age 30. 136 applicants, 14% accepted, 18 enrolled. In 2014, 15 master's, 13 doctorates awarded. Terminal master's awarded for partial completion of doctoral program. *Degree requirements:* For master's, comprehensive exam (for some programs), thesis (for some programs); for doctorate, thesis/dissertation. *Entrance requirements:* Additional exam requirements/recommendations for international students: Required—TOEFL (minimum score 79 iBT). *Application deadline:* For fall admission, 1/1 for domestic and international students; for spring admission, 11/1 for domestic and international students. Application fee: $50 ($100 for international students). Electronic applications accepted. *Expenses:* Tuition, state resident: full-time $4394; part-time $183.10 per credit hour. Tuition, nonresident: full-time $16,970; part-time $707.10 per credit hour. *Required fees:* $2892; $109.95 per credit hour. $126.50 per semester. *Financial support:* In 2014–15, 65 students received support, including 11 fellowships with full tuition reimbursements available (averaging $2,455 per year), 4 research assistantships with partial tuition reimbursements available (averaging $13,937 per year), 43 teaching assistantships with partial tuition reimbursements available (averaging $15,058 per year); unspecified assistantships also available. Financial award application deadline: 6/1; financial award applicants required to submit FAFSA. *Faculty research:* Leading for creativity, innovation, ethical behavior, health and well-being, decision-making and risk, organizational behavior, teamwork, research methodology, ethics, leadership. *Total annual research expenditures:* $881,449. *Unit head:* Dr. Jorge Mendoza, Chair, 405-325-4511, Fax: 405-325-4737, E-mail: jmendoza@ou.edu. *Application contact:* Kathryn Paine, Graduate Admissions Coordinator, 405-325-4512, Fax: 405-325-4737, E-mail: kpaine@ou.edu.
Website: http://www.ou.edu/cas/psychology

University of Oregon, Graduate School, College of Arts and Sciences, Department of Psychology, Eugene, OR 97403. Offers clinical psychology (PhD); cognitive psychology (MA, MS, PhD); developmental psychology (MA, MS, PhD); physiological psychology (MA, MS, PhD); psychology (MA, MS, PhD); social/personality psychology (MA, MS, PhD). *Accreditation:* APA (one or more programs are accredited). Terminal master's awarded for partial completion of doctoral program. *Degree requirements:* For doctorate, thesis/dissertation. *Entrance requirements:* For master's, GRE General Test, minimum GPA of 3.0; for doctorate, GRE General Test. Additional exam requirements/recommendations for international students: Required—TOEFL.

University of Ottawa, Faculty of Graduate and Postdoctoral Studies, Faculty of Social Sciences, School of Psychology, Ottawa, ON K1N 6N5, Canada. Offers PhD. *Degree requirements:* For doctorate, thesis/dissertation. *Entrance requirements:* For doctorate, minimum B+ average. Electronic applications accepted. *Faculty research:* Behavioral neuroscience, social psychology, developmental psychology, cognition.

University of Pennsylvania, School of Arts and Sciences, Graduate Group in Psychology, Philadelphia, PA 19104. Offers PhD. *Accreditation:* APA. *Faculty:* 59 full-time (19 women), 15 part-time/adjunct (4 women). *Students:* 64 full-time (39 women); includes 12 minority (4 Asian, non-Hispanic/Latino; 4 Hispanic/Latino; 4 Two or more races, non-Hispanic/Latino), 13 international. 594 applicants, 4% accepted, 12 enrolled. In 2014, 10 doctorates awarded. *Degree requirements:* For doctorate, thesis/dissertation. *Entrance requirements:* For doctorate, GRE General Test, GRE Subject Test. Additional exam requirements/recommendations for international students: Required—TOEFL. *Application deadline:* For fall admission, 12/1 priority date for domestic students. Application fee: $70. Electronic applications accepted. *Financial support:* In 2014–15, 10 fellowships, 2 research assistantships, 20 teaching assistantships were awarded; institutionally sponsored loans, scholarships/grants, traineeships, health care benefits, and unspecified assistantships also available. Financial award application deadline: 12/15. *Faculty research:* Cognitive psychology, sensation and perception, biological psychology, clinical psychology, social psychology. *Unit head:* Dr. Ralph M. Rosen, Associate Dean for Graduate Studies, 215-898-7156,

Fax: 215-573-8068, E-mail: grad-dean@sas.upenn.edu. *Application contact:* Arts and Sciences Graduate Admissions, 215-573-5816, Fax: 215-573-8068, E-mail: gdasadmis@sas.upenn.edu.
Website: http://psychology.sas.upenn.edu/graduate

University of Philosophical Research, Master's in Transformational Psychology Program, Los Angeles, CA 90027. Offers MA. *Degree requirements:* For master's, thesis. Electronic applications accepted.

University of Phoenix–Birmingham Campus, College of Social and Behavioral Science, Birmingham, AL 35242. Offers administration of justice and security (MS); psychology (MS).

University of Phoenix–Jersey City Campus, College of Social Services, Jersey City, NJ 07310. Offers psychology (MS). Postbaccalaureate distance learning degree programs offered.

University of Phoenix–Online Campus, College of Social Science, Phoenix, AZ 85034-7209. Offers mediation (Certificate); psychology (MS), including behavioral health, industrial-organizational, psychology. Evening/weekend programs available. Postbaccalaureate distance learning degree programs offered. *Entrance requirements:* Additional exam requirements/recommendations for international students: Required—TOEFL, TOEIC (Test of English as an International Communication), Berlitz Online English Proficiency Exam, PTE, or IELTS. Electronic applications accepted. *Expenses:* Contact institution.

University of Phoenix–Philadelphia Campus, College of Social Services, Wayne, PA 19087-2121. Offers psychology (MS). Evening/weekend programs available. *Degree requirements:* For master's, thesis (for some programs). *Entrance requirements:* For master's, minimum undergraduate GPA of 2.5, 3 years work experience. Additional exam requirements/recommendations for international students: Required—TOEFL (minimum score 550 paper-based; 79 iBT). Electronic applications accepted.

University of Phoenix–Phoenix Campus, College of Social Sciences, Tempe, AZ 85282-2371. Offers counseling (MS), including clinical mental health counseling, community counseling, counseling, marriage, family and child therapy; psychology (MS). Evening/weekend programs available. Postbaccalaureate distance learning degree programs offered. *Entrance requirements:* Additional exam requirements/recommendations for international students: Required—TOEFL, TOEIC (Test of English as an International Communication), Berlitz Online English Proficiency Exam, PTE, or IELTS. Electronic applications accepted. *Expenses:* Contact institution.

University of Phoenix–Southern Arizona Campus, College of Social Sciences, Tucson, AZ 85711. Offers psychology (MS). Evening/weekend programs available. *Degree requirements:* For master's, thesis (for some programs). *Entrance requirements:* For master's, minimum undergraduate GPA of 2.5, 3 years of work experience, RN license. Additional exam requirements/recommendations for international students: Required—TOEFL (minimum score 550 paper-based; 79 iBT). Electronic applications accepted.

University of Phoenix–Southern California Campus, College of Social Sciences, Costa Mesa, CA 92626. Offers counseling (MS), including counseling, marriage, family and child therapy; psychology (MS), including behavioral health. Evening/weekend programs available. Postbaccalaureate distance learning degree programs offered. *Entrance requirements:* Additional exam requirements/recommendations for international students: Required—TOEFL, TOEIC (Test of English as an International Communication), Berlitz Online English Proficiency Exam, PTE, or IELTS. Electronic applications accepted. *Expenses:* Contact institution.

University of Phoenix–Washington D.C. Campus, College of Social Sciences, Washington, DC 20001. Offers industrial/organizational psychology (PhD); psychology (MS).

University of Pittsburgh, Dietrich School of Arts and Sciences, Department of Psychology, Pittsburgh, PA 15260. Offers MS, PhD. *Accreditation:* APA (one or more programs are accredited). *Faculty:* 45 full-time (21 women), 6 part-time/adjunct (3 women). *Students:* 94 full-time (76 women); includes 24 minority (3 Black or African American, non-Hispanic/Latino; 1 American Indian or Alaska Native, non-Hispanic/Latino; 13 Asian, non-Hispanic/Latino; 6 Hispanic/Latino; 1 Two or more races, non-Hispanic/Latino), 9 international. Average age 25. 507 applicants, 6% accepted, 22 enrolled. In 2014, 22 master's, 9 doctorates awarded. Terminal master's awarded for partial completion of doctoral program. *Degree requirements:* For master's, comprehensive exam, thesis; for doctorate, comprehensive exam, thesis/dissertation. *Entrance requirements:* For doctorate, GRE General Test, minimum GPA of 3.0. Additional exam requirements/recommendations for international students: Required—TOEFL (minimum score 550 paper-based; 90 iBT) or IELTS (minimum score 7). *Application deadline:* For fall admission, 12/1 for domestic and international students. Application fee: $50. Electronic applications accepted. *Expenses:* Tuition, state resident: full-time $20,742; part-time $838 per credit. Tuition, nonresident: full-time $33,960; part-time $1389 per credit. *Required fees:* $800; $205 per term. Tuition and fees vary according to program. *Financial support:* In 2014–15, 89 students received support, including 23 fellowships with full tuition reimbursements available (averaging $21,262 per year), 30 research assistantships with full tuition reimbursements available (averaging $16,000 per year), 33 teaching assistantships with full tuition reimbursements available (averaging $17,130 per year); career-related internships or fieldwork, scholarships/grants, traineeships, health care benefits, and unspecified assistantships also available. Financial award application deadline: 12/1. *Faculty research:* Behavioral medicine and psychoneuroimmunology; learning, reasoning and memory; psychopathology and behavioral problems; social cognition; social influence and group processes; social and cognitive development. *Total annual research expenditures:* $16.5 million. *Unit head:* Dr. Daniel S. Shaw, Chairman, 412-624-4501, Fax: 412-624-4428, E-mail: casey@pitt.edu. *Application contact:* Loranna Sayre-Nath, Graduate Program Coordinator, 412-624-4502, Fax: 412-624-4428, E-mail: psygrad@pitt.edu.
Website: http://www.psychology.pitt.edu/

University of Pittsburgh, Dietrich School of Arts and Sciences, Program in Computational Modeling and Simulation, Pittsburgh, PA 15260. Offers bioengineering (PhD); biological science (PhD); civil and environmental engineering (PhD); computer science (PhD); economics (PhD); industrial engineering (PhD); mathematics (PhD); mechanical engineering and materials science (PhD); physics and astronomy (PhD); psychology (PhD); statistics (PhD). Part-time programs available. *Faculty:* 4 full-time (0 women). *Students:* 5 full-time (2 women), 1 part-time (0 women), 5 international. Average age 22. 14 applicants, 14% accepted, 2 enrolled. *Degree requirements:* For doctorate, comprehensive exam, thesis/dissertation, preliminary exam. *Entrance requirements:* For doctorate, GRE, statement of purpose, transcripts for all college-level institutions attended, three letters of reference. Additional exam requirements/recommendations for international students: Required—TOEFL (minimum score 90 iBT), IELTS (minimum score 7). *Application deadline:* For fall admission, 2/21 for domestic and international students. Applications are processed on a rolling basis. Application fee: $0 ($50 for international students). Electronic applications accepted. *Expenses:* Tuition, state resident: full-time $20,742; part-time $838 per credit. Tuition, nonresident: full-time $33,960; part-time $1389 per credit. *Required fees:* $800; $205 per term. Tuition and fees vary according to program. *Financial support:* In 2014–15, 5 students received support, including 3 fellowships with tuition reimbursements available (averaging $25,500 per year), 2 research assistantships with tuition reimbursements available (averaging $26,000 per year). *Unit head:* Kathleen Blee, Associate Dean, Graduate Studies and Research, 412-624-3939, Fax: 412-624-6855. *Application contact:* Dave R. Carmen, Administrative Secretary, 412-624-6094, Fax: 412-624-6855, E-mail: drc41@pitt.edu.
Website: http://cmsp.pitt.edu/

University of Puerto Rico, Río Piedras Campus, College of Social Sciences, Department of Psychology, San Juan, PR 00931-3300. Offers clinical psychology (MA); industrial organizational psychology (MA); investigative academic psychology (MA); psychology (PhD); social-community psychology (MA). Part-time programs available. *Degree requirements:* For master's, comprehensive exam, thesis; for doctorate, comprehensive exam, thesis/dissertation, internship. *Entrance requirements:* For master's, GRE or PAEG, interview, minimum GPA of 3.0; for doctorate, GRE or PAEG, interview, master's degree, minimum GPA of 3.0. *Faculty research:* Intervention on depressed Latino youth, biosychosocial training.

University of Regina, Faculty of Graduate Studies and Research, Faculty of Arts, Department of Psychology, Regina, SK S4S 0A2, Canada. Offers clinical psychology (MA, PhD); experimental and applied psychology (MA, PhD). *Faculty:* 20 full-time (9 women), 7 part-time/adjunct (5 women). *Students:* 57 full-time (46 women). 81 applicants, 25% accepted. In 2014, 12 master's, 4 doctorates awarded. *Degree requirements:* For master's, thesis; for doctorate, comprehensive exam, thesis/dissertation. *Entrance requirements:* For master's, GRE General Test; for doctorate, GRE General Test and GRE Subject Test (optional for those with a master's degree from a Canadian university). Additional exam requirements/recommendations for international students: Required—TOEFL (minimum score 580 paper-based; 80 iBT), IELTS (minimum score 6.5), PTE (minimum score 59). *Application deadline:* For fall admission, 1/15 for domestic and international students. Application fee: $100. Electronic applications accepted. *Expenses: Tuition, area resident:* Full-time $4900 Canadian dollars; part-time $837.65 Canadian dollars per semester. *International tuition:* $7900 Canadian dollars full-time. *Required fees:* $396 Canadian dollars; $86.90 Canadian dollars per semester. *Financial support:* In 2014–15, 17 fellowships (averaging $6,588 per year), 1 research assistantship (averaging $5,500 per year), 27 teaching assistantships (averaging $2,471 per year) were awarded; career-related internships or fieldwork and scholarships/grants also available. Financial award application deadline: 6/15. *Faculty research:* Clinical, experimental, cognitive, and applied psychology; post-traumatic stress disorder, anxiety, and panic disorder; traumatic brain injury; chronic pain; perception and memory. *Unit head:* Dr. Richard MacLennan, Department Head, 306-585-4458, Fax: 306-585-5429, E-mail: richard.maclennan@uregina.ca.
Website: http://www.uregina.ca/arts/psychology

University of Rhode Island, Graduate School, College of Arts and Sciences, Department of Psychology, Kingston, RI 02881. Offers behavioral science (PhD); clinical psychology (MA, PhD); school psychology (MS, PhD). *Accreditation:* APA (one or more programs are accredited). Part-time programs available. *Faculty:* 19 full-time (10 women), 1 part-time/adjunct (0 women). *Students:* 108 full-time (83 women), 32 part-time (25 women); includes 34 minority (21 Black or African American, non-Hispanic/Latino; 2 American Indian or Alaska Native, non-Hispanic/Latino; 3 Asian, non-Hispanic/Latino; 7 Hispanic/Latino; 1 Two or more races, non-Hispanic/Latino), 7 international. In 2014, 20 master's awarded. *Degree requirements:* For master's, comprehensive exam, thesis optional; for doctorate, thesis/dissertation. *Entrance requirements:* For master's and doctorate, GRE, 3 letters of recommendation. Additional exam requirements/recommendations for international students: Required—TOEFL (minimum score 550 paper-based). *Application deadline:* For fall admission, 12/1 for domestic and international students. Application fee: $65. Electronic applications accepted. *Expenses:* Tuition, state resident: full-time $11,532; part-time $641 per credit. Tuition, nonresident: full-time $23,606; part-time $1311 per credit. *Required fees:* $1442; $39 per credit. $35 per semester. One-time fee: $155. *Financial support:* In 2014–15, 10 research assistantships with full and partial tuition reimbursements (averaging $12,774 per year), 23 teaching assistantships with full and partial tuition reimbursements (averaging $12,892 per year) were awarded. Financial award application deadline: 12/1; financial award applicants required to submit FAFSA. *Total annual research expenditures:* $22,461. *Unit head:* Dr. Su Boatright-Horowitz, Interim Chair, 401-874-4231, Fax: 401-874-2157, E-mail: ugpsych@aol.com. *Application contact:* Graduate Admission, 401-874-2872, E-mail: gradadm@etal.uri.edu.
Website: http://www.uri.edu/artsci/psy/

University of Rochester, School of Arts and Sciences, Department of Clinical and Social Sciences in Psychology, Rochester, NY 14627. Offers clinical psychology (PhD); developmental psychology (PhD); social-personality psychology (PhD). *Accreditation:* APA. *Faculty:* 14 full-time (7 women). *Students:* 46 full-time (37 women), 1 (woman) part-time; includes 6 minority (2 Asian, non-Hispanic/Latino; 3 Hispanic/Latino; 1 Two or more races, non-Hispanic/Latino), 6 international. 326 applicants, 4% accepted, 6 enrolled. In 2014, 9 doctorates awarded. Terminal master's awarded for partial completion of doctoral program. *Degree requirements:* For doctorate, thesis/dissertation, qualifying exam. *Entrance requirements:* For doctorate, GRE General Test. Additional exam requirements/recommendations for international students: Required—TOEFL. *Application deadline:* For fall admission, 12/15 priority date for domestic students. Application fee: $60. *Expenses: Tuition:* Full-time $46,150; part-time $1442 per credit hour. *Required fees:* $504. *Financial support:* Fellowships, research assistantships, teaching assistantships, career-related internships or fieldwork, and tuition waivers (full and partial) available. Financial award application deadline: 2/1. *Faculty research:* Clinical psychology, social-personality psychology, developmental psychology, human motivation. *Unit head:* Loisa Bennetto, Chair, 585-275-8712. *Application contact:* April Engram, Academic Coordinator/Analyst, 585-275-8704.
Website: http://www.psych.rochester.edu/csp/

University of Saint Francis, Graduate School, Department of Psychology and Counseling, Fort Wayne, IN 46808-3994. Offers clinical mental health counseling (MS, Post Master's Certificate); pastoral counseling (MS, Post Master's Certificate); psychology (MS); rehabilitation counseling (MS, Post Master's Certificate); school counseling (MS Ed). Part-time and evening/weekend programs available. *Faculty:* 3 full-time (1 woman). *Students:* 29 full-time (22 women), 20 part-time (all women); includes 10 minority (7 Black or African American, non-Hispanic/Latino; 2 Hispanic/Latino; 1 Two or more races, non-Hispanic/Latino), 1 international. Average age 32. 21 applicants, 90% accepted, 16 enrolled. In 2014, 23 master's awarded. *Entrance requirements:* For master's, minimum undergraduate GPA of 3.0; undergraduate coursework in psychology. Additional exam requirements/recommendations for international students: Required—TOEFL or IELTS. *Application deadline:* For fall admission, 7/1 for domestic students; for spring admission, 11/1 for domestic students. Applications are processed on a rolling basis. Application fee: $0. Electronic applications accepted. *Expenses:* Expenses: $830 per credit hour. *Financial support:* In 2014–15, 5 students received support. Federal Work-Study, scholarships/grants, and unspecified assistantships

available. Support available to part-time students. Financial award application deadline: 3/10; financial award applicants required to submit FAFSA. *Unit head:* Dr. John Brinkman, Associate Professor/Chair, Department of Psychology and Counseling, 260-399-7700 Ext. 8425, Fax: 260-399-8170, E-mail: jbrinkman@sf.edu. *Application contact:* Kyle Richardson, Enrollment Specialist, 260-399-7700 Ext. 6310, Fax: 260-399-8152, E-mail: krichardson@sf.edu.
Website: http://psychology.sf.edu/

University of Saint Mary, Graduate Programs, Program in Psychology, Leavenworth, KS 66048-5082. Offers MA. Part-time and evening/weekend programs available. *Degree requirements:* For master's, thesis. *Entrance requirements:* For master's, minimum undergraduate GPA of 2.75. *Application deadline:* Applications are processed on a rolling basis. Application fee: $25. *Unit head:* Dr. David Greene, Chair, 913-758-6105. *Application contact:* Dr. Les Hemphill, Director, 913-319-3015, E-mail: hemphill48@stmary.edu.
Website: http://www.stmary.edu/success/Grad-Program/Master-of-Arts-Psychology.aspx

University of St. Thomas, Graduate Studies, Graduate School of Professional Psychology, St. Paul, MN 55105-1096. Offers counseling psychology (MA, Psy D); family therapy (Certificate). *Accreditation:* APA. Part-time and evening/weekend programs available. *Degree requirements:* For master's, comprehensive exam, practicum; for doctorate, comprehensive exam, thesis/dissertation, qualifying exam, practicum, internship. *Entrance requirements:* For master's, GRE, minimum GPA of 2.75, letters of recommendation, personal statement; for doctorate, GRE, minimum GPA of 3.2, letters of recommendation, personal statement. Additional exam requirements/recommendations for international students: Required—TOEFL (minimum score 550 paper-based; 80 iBT). *Expenses:* Contact institution. *Faculty research:* Elderly, neuropsychology, anxiety, family, therapist expertise, business of practice, religion and psychology, early attachment, relationship of science and practice in psychotherapy.

University of Saskatchewan, College of Graduate Studies and Research, College of Arts and Science, Department of Psychology, Saskatoon, SK S7N 5A2, Canada. Offers MA, PhD. *Degree requirements:* For master's, thesis; for doctorate, comprehensive exam (for some programs), thesis/dissertation. *Entrance requirements:* Additional exam requirements/recommendations for international students: Required—TOEFL (minimum score 80 iBT); Recommended—IELTS (minimum score 6.5). Electronic applications accepted.

University of South Africa, College of Human Sciences, Pretoria, South Africa. Offers adult education (M Ed); African languages (MA, PhD); African politics (MA, PhD); Afrikaans (MA, PhD); ancient history (MA, PhD); ancient Near Eastern studies (MA, PhD); anthropology (MA, PhD); applied linguistics (MA); Arabic (MA, PhD); archaeology (MA); art history (MA); Biblical archaeology (MA); Biblical studies (M Th, D Th, PhD); Christian spirituality (M Th, D Th); church history (M Th, D Th); classical studies (MA, PhD); clinical psychology (MA); communication (MA, PhD); comparative education (M Ed, Ed D); consulting psychology (D Admin, D Com, PhD); curriculum studies (M Ed, Ed D); development studies (M Admin, MA, D Admin, PhD); didactics (M Ed, Ed D); education (M Tech); education management (M Ed, Ed D); educational psychology (M Ed); English (MA); environmental education (M Ed); French (MA, PhD); German (MA, PhD); Greek (MA); guidance and counseling (M Ed); health studies (MA, PhD), including health sciences education (MA), health services management (MA), medical and surgical nursing science (critical care general) (MA), midwifery and neonatal nursing science (MA), trauma and emergency care (MA); history (MA, PhD); history of education (Ed D); inclusive education (M Ed, Ed D); information and communications technology policy and regulation (MA); information science (MA, MIS, PhD); international politics (MA, PhD); Islamic studies (MA, PhD); Italian (MA, PhD); Judaica (MA, PhD); linguistics (MA, PhD); mathematical education (M Ed); mathematics education (MA); missiology (M Th, D Th); modern Hebrew (MA, PhD); musicology (MA, MMus, D Mus, PhD); natural science education (M Ed); New Testament (M Th, D Th); Old Testament (D Th); pastoral therapy (M Th, D Th); philosophy (MA); philosophy of education (M Ed, Ed D); politics (MA, PhD); Portuguese (MA, PhD); practical theology (M Th, D Th); psychology (MA, MS, PhD); psychology of education (M Ed, Ed D); public health (MA); religious studies (MA, D Th, PhD); Romance languages (MA); Russian (MA, PhD); Semitic languages (MA, PhD); social behavior studies in HIV/AIDS (MA); social science (mental health) (MA); social science in development studies (MA); social science in psychology (MA); social science in social work (MA); social science in sociology (MA); social work (MSW, DSW, PhD); socio-education (M Ed, Ed D); sociolinguistics (MA); sociology (MA, PhD); Spanish (MA, PhD); systematic theology (M Th, D Th); TESOL (teaching English to speakers of other languages) (MA); theological ethics (M Th, D Th); theory of literature (MA, PhD); urban ministries (D Th); urban ministry (M Th).

University of South Carolina, The Graduate School, College of Arts and Sciences, Department of Psychology, Columbia, SC 29208. Offers clinical/community psychology (MA, PhD), including clinical/community psychology (PhD), general psychology (MA); experimental psychology (MA, PhD); school psychology (PhD). *Accreditation:* APA (one or more programs are accredited). Terminal master's awarded for partial completion of doctoral program. *Degree requirements:* For master's, thesis; for doctorate, comprehensive exam, thesis/dissertation. *Entrance requirements:* For master's and doctorate, GRE General Test. Additional exam requirements/recommendations for international students: Required—TOEFL. Electronic applications accepted. *Faculty research:* Developmental cognitive neuroscience, alcohol and drug addictions, reading and language processing, child and family, prevention.

The University of South Dakota, Graduate School, College of Arts and Sciences, Department of Psychology, Vermillion, SD 57069-2390. Offers clinical psychology (MA, PhD); human factors (MA, PhD). *Accreditation:* APA (one or more programs are accredited). *Degree requirements:* For master's, comprehensive exam, thesis; for doctorate, comprehensive exam, thesis/dissertation. *Entrance requirements:* For master's, GRE, minimum GPA of 2.7; for doctorate, GRE General Test, GRE Subject Test, minimum GPA of 2.7. Additional exam requirements/recommendations for international students: Required—TOEFL (minimum score 550 paper-based; 79 iBT). Electronic applications accepted. *Faculty research:* Human-computer interactions, perceptual-cognitive processing, medical psychology, depression, moral psychology.

University of Southern California, Graduate School, Dana and David Dornsife College of Letters, Arts and Sciences, Department of Psychology, Los Angeles, CA 90089. Offers brain and cognitive science (PhD); clinical science (PhD); developmental psychology (PhD); human behavior (MHB); quantitative methods (PhD); social psychology (PhD). *Accreditation:* APA. *Degree requirements:* For doctorate, comprehensive exam, thesis/dissertation, one-year internship (for clinical science students). *Entrance requirements:* For doctorate, GRE. Additional exam requirements/recommendations for international students: Recommended—TOEFL (minimum score 600 paper-based; 100 iBT). Electronic applications accepted. *Faculty research:* Affective neuroscience; children and families; vision, culture and ethnicity; intergroup relations; aggression and violence; language and reading development; substance abuse.

University of Southern Mississippi, Graduate School, College of Education and Psychology, Department of Psychology, Hattiesburg, MS 39406-0001. Offers clinical psychology (PhD); counseling psychology (MS, PhD); experimental psychology (PhD);

school psychology (PhD). *Accreditation:* APA (one or more programs are accredited). Terminal master's awarded for partial completion of doctoral program. *Degree requirements:* For master's, comprehensive exam, thesis; for doctorate, comprehensive exam, thesis/dissertation. *Entrance requirements:* For master's, GRE General Test, minimum GPA of 3.0; for doctorate, GRE General Test, interview, minimum GPA of 3.5. Additional exam requirements/recommendations for international students: Required—TOEFL, IELTS. *Faculty research:* Psychopathology, alcohol and drug abuse, child clinical psychology, parenting, suicide, career/vocational, marine mammal, cognition, psychological psychology, behavioral interventions, positive psychology, anger/aggression, diversity issues.

University of South Florida, College of Arts and Sciences, Department of Psychology, Tampa, FL 33620-9951. Offers clinical psychology (PhD); cognitive and neural sciences (PhD); industrial-organizational psychology (PhD). *Accreditation:* APA. *Faculty:* 33 full-time (15 women), 1 part-time/adjunct. *Students:* 96 full-time (68 women), 18 part-time (11 women); includes 25 minority (2 Black or African American, non-Hispanic/Latino; 9 Asian, non-Hispanic/Latino; 10 Hispanic/Latino; 4 Two or more races, non-Hispanic/Latino), 12 international. Average age 28. 513 applicants, 5% accepted, 19 enrolled. In 2014, 16 doctorates awarded. *Degree requirements:* For doctorate, comprehensive exam, thesis/dissertation, internship. *Entrance requirements:* For doctorate, GRE General Test (minimum recommended verbal and quantitative scores each above the 50th percentile), minimum upper-division GPA of 3.4, three letters of recommendation, personal goals statement. Additional exam requirements/recommendations for international students: Required—TOEFL (minimum score 550 paper-based; 79 iBT) or IELTS (minimum score 6.5). *Application deadline:* For fall admission, 12/1 for domestic and international students. Application fee: $30. Electronic applications accepted. *Expenses:* Expenses: Contact institution. *Financial support:* In 2014–15, 75 students received support, including 18 research assistantships with tuition reimbursements available (averaging $14,727 per year), 57 teaching assistantships with tuition reimbursements available (averaging $14,543 per year); tuition waivers (partial) and unspecified assistantships also available. Financial award applicants required to submit FAFSA. *Faculty research:* Clinical, cognitive, neuroscience, social, and industrial/organizational. *Total annual research expenditures:* $1.7 million. *Unit head:* Dr. Toru Shimizu, Chairperson, 813-974-0352, Fax: 813-974-4617, E-mail: shimizu@usf.edu. *Application contact:* Dr. Joseph Vandello, Associate Professor and Graduate Program Director, 813-974-0362, Fax: 813-974-4617, E-mail: vandello@usf.edu.
Website: http://psychology.usf.edu/

University of South Florida, St. Petersburg, College of Arts and Sciences, St. Petersburg, FL 33701. Offers digital journalism and design (MA); environmental science and policy (MA, MS); Florida studies (MLA); journalism and media studies (MA); liberal studies (MLA); psychology (MA). Part-time programs available. Postbaccalaureate distance learning degree programs offered (no on-campus study). *Degree requirements:* For master's, comprehensive exam, thesis or project. *Entrance requirements:* For master's, GRE, LSAT, MCAT (varies by program), letter of intent, 3 letters of recommendation, writing samples, bachelor's degree from regionally-accredited institution with minimum GPA of 3.0 overall or in upper two years. Additional exam requirements/recommendations for international students: Required—TOEFL (minimum score 550 paper-based; 79 iBT); Recommended—IELTS. Electronic applications accepted.

The University of Tennessee, Graduate School, College of Arts and Sciences, Department of Psychology, Knoxville, TN 37996. Offers clinical psychology (PhD); experimental psychology (MA, PhD); psychology (MA). *Accreditation:* APA (one or more programs are accredited). Terminal master's awarded for partial completion of doctoral program. *Degree requirements:* For master's, thesis; for doctorate, thesis/dissertation. *Entrance requirements:* For master's and doctorate, GRE General Test, GRE Subject Test, minimum GPA of 2.7. Additional exam requirements/recommendations for international students: Required—TOEFL. Electronic applications accepted.

The University of Tennessee at Chattanooga, Program in Psychology, Chattanooga, TN 37403. Offers industrial/organizational psychology (MS); research psychology (MS). Part-time and evening/weekend programs available. *Faculty:* 10 full-time (4 women), 1 part-time/adjunct (0 women). *Students:* 38 full-time (20 women), 4 part-time (2 women); includes 3 minority (1 American Indian or Alaska Native, non-Hispanic/Latino; 2 Hispanic/Latino), 1 international. Average age 25. 54 applicants, 57% accepted, 18 enrolled. In 2014, 22 master's awarded. *Degree requirements:* For master's, comprehensive exam (for some programs), thesis (for some programs), practicum (industrial/organizational psychology). *Entrance requirements:* For master's, GRE General Test, minimum GPA of 2.5 on all undergraduate coursework or 3.0 in senior year. Additional exam requirements/recommendations for international students: Required—TOEFL (minimum score 550 paper-based; 79 iBT), IELTS (minimum score 6). *Application deadline:* For fall admission, 6/13 priority date for domestic students, 6/1 for international students; for spring admission, 10/15 priority date for domestic students, 10/1 for international students. Applications are processed on a rolling basis. Application fee: $30 ($35 for international students). Electronic applications accepted. *Expenses:* Tuition, state resident: full-time $7708; part-time $428 per credit hour. Tuition, nonresident: full-time $23,826; part-time $1323 per credit hour. *Required fees:* $1708; $252 per credit hour. *Financial support:* In 2014–15, 19 research assistantships with tuition reimbursements (averaging $5,800 per year), 6 teaching assistantships with tuition reimbursements (averaging $5,982 per year) were awarded; career-related internships or fieldwork, scholarships/grants, and unspecified assistantships also available. Support available to part-time students. Financial award applicants required to submit FAFSA. *Faculty research:* Decision processes, philosophical psychology, memory, social cognition, employee selection. *Total annual research expenditures:* $180,611. *Unit head:* Dr. Brian O'Leary, Department Head, 423-425-4283, Fax: 423-425-4284, E-mail: brian-o'leary@utc.edu. *Application contact:* Dr. J. Randy Walker, Interim Dean of Graduate Studies, 423-425-4478, Fax: 423-425-5223, E-mail: randy-walker@utc.edu.
Website: http://www.utc.edu/Academic/Psychology/

The University of Texas at Arlington, Graduate School, College of Science, Department of Psychology, Arlington, TX 76019. Offers experimental psychology (PhD); health psychology (PhD); industrial organizational psychology (MS); psychology (MS). Part-time programs available. Terminal master's awarded for partial completion of doctoral program. *Degree requirements:* For master's, comprehensive exam or thesis; for doctorate, thesis/dissertation (for some programs). *Entrance requirements:* For master's and doctorate, GRE General Test, minimum GPA of 3.0 in last 60 hours of course work. Additional exam requirements/recommendations for international students: Required—TOEFL (minimum score 550 paper-based).

The University of Texas at Austin, Graduate School, College of Liberal Arts, Department of Psychology, Austin, TX 78712-1111. Offers behavioral neuroscience (PhD); clinical psychology (PhD); cognitive systems (PhD); developmental psychology (PhD); individual differences and evolutionary psychology (PhD); perceptual systems (PhD); social psychology (PhD). *Accreditation:* APA. *Degree requirements:* For doctorate, thesis/dissertation. *Entrance requirements:* For doctorate, GRE General Test. Electronic applications accepted. *Faculty research:* Behavioral neuroscience, sensory

neuroscience, evolutionary psychology, cognitive processes in psychopathology, cognitive processes and their development.

The University of Texas at Brownsville, Graduate Studies, College of Liberal Arts, Department of Behavioral Sciences, Brownsville, TX 78520-4991. Offers psychology (MA); sociology (MAIS). Part-time and evening/weekend programs available. *Degree requirements:* For master's, comprehensive exam (for some programs), thesis optional, capstone experience. *Entrance requirements:* For master's, GRE General Test, letters of recommendation. Additional exam requirements/recommendations for international students: Required—TOEFL (minimum score 550 paper-based; 77 iBT). Electronic applications accepted.

The University of Texas at Dallas, School of Behavioral and Brain Sciences, Program in Psychological Sciences, Richardson, TX 75080. Offers early childhood disorders (MS); psychological sciences (MS, PhD). Part-time and evening/weekend programs available. *Faculty:* 13 full-time (8 women), 3 part-time/adjunct (all women). *Students:* 63 full-time (50 women), 15 part-time (12 women); includes 28 minority (7 Black or African American, non-Hispanic/Latino; 7 Asian, non-Hispanic/Latino; 12 Hispanic/Latino; 2 Two or more races, non-Hispanic/Latino), 9 international. Average age 28. 134 applicants, 32% accepted, 29 enrolled. In 2014, 33 master's, 8 doctorates awarded. *Degree requirements:* For master's, directed project or internship; for doctorate, thesis/dissertation. *Entrance requirements:* For master's and doctorate, GRE General Test, minimum GPA of 3.0 in upper-level course work. Additional exam requirements/recommendations for international students: Required—TOEFL (minimum score 550 paper-based). *Application deadline:* For fall admission, 7/15 for domestic students, 5/1 priority date for international students; for spring admission, 11/15 for domestic students, 9/1 priority date for international students. Applications are processed on a rolling basis. Application fee: $50 ($100 for international students). Electronic applications accepted. *Expenses:* Tuition, state resident: full-time $11,940; part-time $663 per credit. Tuition, nonresident: full-time $22,282; part-time $1238 per credit. *Financial support:* In 2014–15, 52 students received support, including 3 research assistantships with partial tuition reimbursements available (averaging $17,238 per year), 15 teaching assistantships with partial tuition reimbursements available (averaging $17,109 per year); career-related internships or fieldwork, Federal Work-Study, scholarships/grants, and unspecified assistantships also available. Support available to part-time students. Financial award application deadline: 4/30; financial award applicants required to submit FAFSA. *Faculty research:* Neurocognitive development in young adulthood, infant learning, infant and toddler eye tracking, social aggression. *Unit head:* Dr. Candice Mills, Program Head, Psychological Sciences, 972-883-4475, Fax: 972-883-2491, E-mail: candice.mills@utdallas.edu. *Application contact:* Dr. Margaret Owen, Program Head, Early Childhood Disorders, 972-883-6876, Fax: 972-883-2491, E-mail: mowen@utdallas.edu.
Website: http://bbs.utdallas.edu/psysciphd/

The University of Texas at El Paso, Graduate School, College of Liberal Arts, Department of Psychology, El Paso, TX 79968-0001. Offers clinical psychology (MA); experimental psychology (MA); psychology (PhD). Part-time and evening/weekend programs available. *Degree requirements:* For master's, thesis; for doctorate, thesis/dissertation. *Entrance requirements:* For master's, GRE, letters of recommendation; for doctorate, GRE, statement of purpose, letters of recommendation. Additional exam requirements/recommendations for international students: Required—TOEFL; Recommended—IELTS. Electronic applications accepted.

The University of Texas at San Antonio, College of Liberal and Fine Arts, Department of Psychology, San Antonio, TX 78249-0617. Offers MS, PhD. Part-time programs available. *Faculty:* 13 full-time (5 women), 2 part-time/adjunct (1 woman). *Students:* 31 full-time (19 women), 11 part-time (4 women); includes 19 minority (3 Black or African American, non-Hispanic/Latino; 15 Hispanic/Latino; 1 Two or more races, non-Hispanic/Latino), 2 international. Average age 27. 58 applicants, 59% accepted, 22 enrolled. In 2014, 10 master's awarded. *Degree requirements:* For master's, comprehensive exam, thesis or alternative; for doctorate, comprehensive exam, thesis/dissertation. *Entrance requirements:* For master's, TOEFL - Paper-based 500 IBT 79 IELTS - Paper-based 6.5, GRE, minimum GPA of 3.2 in last 60 hours and in all psychology courses; 18 hours of psychology courses including, inferential statistics and research methods; two letters of recommendation; statement of purpose; for doctorate, TOEFL - Paper-based 500 IBT 79 IELTS - Paper-based 6.5, GRE, master's degree with minimum GPA of 3.5, three letters of recommendation, statement of purpose. Additional exam requirements/recommendations for international students: Required—TOEFL (minimum score 550 paper-based; 79 iBT), IELTS (minimum score 6.5). *Application deadline:* For fall admission, 6/1 for domestic students, 4/1 for international students; for spring admission, 11/1 for domestic students, 9/1 for international students. Application fee: $45 ($80 for international students). Electronic applications accepted. *Expenses:* Expenses: $8,143. *Financial support:* In 2014–15, 11 students received support, including 6 research assistantships with full tuition reimbursements available (averaging $25,000 per year), 5 teaching assistantships (averaging $9,200 per year); tuition waivers (partial) also available. *Faculty research:* Social psychology, cognitive psychology, developmental psychology, industrial/organizational psychology, biopsychology. *Total annual research expenditures:* $6.7 million. *Unit head:* Dr. Robert W. Fuhrman, Department Chair, 210-458-7352, Fax: 210-458-5728, E-mail: robert.fuhrman@utsa.edu. *Application contact:* Dr. Rebecca Weston, Graduate Advisor of Record, 210-458-6432, Fax: 210-458-5728, E-mail: rebecca.weston@utsa.edu.
Website: http://colfa.utsa.edu/psychology

The University of Texas at Tyler, College of Education and Psychology, Department of Psychology and Counseling, Tyler, TX 75799-0001. Offers clinical psychology (MS), including neuropsychology, school psychology; counseling psychology (MA), including general, marriage and family; interdisciplinary studies (MSIS); school counseling (MA). Part-time and evening/weekend programs available. *Degree requirements:* For master's, comprehensive exam, thesis optional. *Entrance requirements:* For master's, GRE General Test, minimum GPA of 3.0. Additional exam requirements/recommendations for international students: Required—TOEFL. Electronic applications accepted. *Faculty research:* Neuropsychology, child abuse, psychometric properties of psychological instruments, maternal behavior, clinical practice issues, victimization of women, post-traumatic stress disorder.

The University of Texas of the Permian Basin, Office of Graduate Studies, College of Arts and Sciences, Department of Psychology, Odessa, TX 79762-0001. Offers applied research psychology (MA); clinical psychology (MA). Part-time and evening/weekend programs available. *Degree requirements:* For master's, comprehensive exam, thesis, practicum. *Entrance requirements:* For master's, GRE General Test, 3 letters of recommendation. Additional exam requirements/recommendations for international students: Required—TOEFL (minimum score 550 paper-based).

The University of Texas–Pan American, College of Social and Behavioral Sciences, Department of Psychology and Anthropology, Edinburg, TX 78539. Offers anthropology (MAIS); psychology (MA), including clinical psychology, experimental psychology. Part-time and evening/weekend programs available. *Degree requirements:* For master's, comprehensive exam, thesis optional, internship. *Entrance requirements:* For master's, GRE, letters of recommendation. Additional exam requirements/recommendations for international students: Required—TOEFL. Electronic applications accepted. *Expenses:*

Tuition, state resident: full-time $4187; part-time $232.60 per credit hour. Tuition, nonresident: full-time $10,857; part-time $603.16 per credit hour. *Required fees:* $782; $27.50 per credit hour. $143.35 per semester. *Faculty research:* Biofeedback, acculturation, health, stress/trauma, neuropsychological assessment, false memories, children's theory of mind.

University of the Incarnate Word, Extended Academic Programs, Programs in Psychology, San Antonio, TX 78209-6397. Offers educational psychology (MS); industrial and organizational psychology (MS). *Faculty:* 1 full-time (0 women), 17 part-time/adjunct (7 women). *Students:* 7 part-time (4 women); includes 1 minority (Hispanic/Latino). Average age 36. 9 applicants, 33% accepted, 1 enrolled. *Expenses: Tuition:* Part-time $815 per credit hour. *Required fees:* $86 per credit hour. *Unit head:* Dr. Cyndi Porter, Vice President, 877-603-1130, E-mail: porter@uiwtx.edu. *Application contact:* Julie Weber, Director of Marketing and Recruitment, 210-318-1876, Fax: 210-829-2756, E-mail: eapadmission@uiwtx.edu.

University of the Pacific, College of the Pacific, Department of Psychology, Stockton, CA 95211-0197. Offers MA. *Students:* 14 part-time (10 women); includes 4 minority (1 Asian, non-Hispanic/Latino; 2 Hispanic/Latino; 1 Two or more races, non-Hispanic/Latino), 1 international. Average age 24. 28 applicants, 43% accepted, 6 enrolled. In 2014, 2 master's awarded. *Degree requirements:* For master's, thesis. *Entrance requirements:* For master's, GRE General Test. Additional exam requirements/recommendations for international students: Required—TOEFL (minimum score 475 paper-based). *Application deadline:* For fall admission, 3/1 priority date for domestic students. Applications are processed on a rolling basis. Application fee: $75. *Financial support:* In 2014–15, 13 teaching assistantships were awarded; institutionally sponsored loans also available. Support available to part-time students. Financial award application deadline: 3/1; financial award applicants required to submit FAFSA. *Unit head:* Dr. Scott Jensen, Chairperson, 209-946-7320, E-mail: sjensen@pacific.edu. *Application contact:* Information Contact, 209-946-2133.

University of the Rockies, Graduate Programs, Colorado Springs, CO 80903. Offers MA, Psy D.

University of the West, Department of Psychology, Rosemead, CA 91770. Offers Buddhist psychology (MA); multicultural counseling (MA). Part-time and evening/weekend programs available. *Degree requirements:* For master's, fieldwork; comprehensive exam or thesis.

The University of Toledo, College of Graduate Studies, College of Languages, Literature and Social Sciences, Department of Psychology, Toledo, OH 43606-3390. Offers clinical psychology (MA, PhD); experimental psychology (MA, PhD). *Accreditation:* APA. *Degree requirements:* For master's, comprehensive exam, thesis; for doctorate, comprehensive exam, thesis/dissertation. *Entrance requirements:* For master's and doctorate, GRE General Test, GRE Subject Test, minimum cumulative point-hour ratio of 2.7 for all previous academic work, three letters of recommendation, statement of purpose, transcripts from all prior institutions attended. Additional exam requirements/recommendations for international students: Required—TOEFL (minimum score 550 paper-based; 80 iBT). Electronic applications accepted. *Faculty research:* Neural taste response.

University of Toronto, School of Graduate Studies, Faculty of Arts and Science, Department of Psychology, Toronto, ON M5S 2J7, Canada. Offers MA, PhD. *Degree requirements:* For master's, thesis; for doctorate, thesis/dissertation, oral exam. *Entrance requirements:* For master's, minimum A- average in last two years, 6 full courses in psychology, laboratory experience; for doctorate, minimum A- average, research experience. Additional exam requirements/recommendations for international students: Required—TOEFL (minimum score 580 paper-based; 93 iBT), TWE (minimum score 5). Electronic applications accepted.

The University of Tulsa, Graduate School, Kendall College of Arts and Sciences, Department of Psychology, Tulsa, OK 74104-3189. Offers clinical psychology (MA, PhD); industrial/organizational psychology (MA, PhD); JD/MA. *Accreditation:* APA (one or more programs are accredited). Part-time programs available. *Faculty:* 13 full-time (5 women). *Students:* 51 full-time (36 women), 16 part-time (11 women); includes 14 minority (1 Black or African American, non-Hispanic/Latino; 3 American Indian or Alaska Native, non-Hispanic/Latino; 4 Asian, non-Hispanic/Latino; 6 Hispanic/Latino), 5 international. Average age 27. 213 applicants, 16% accepted, 19 enrolled. In 2014, 26 master's, 2 doctorates awarded. Terminal master's awarded for partial completion of doctoral program. *Degree requirements:* For doctorate, comprehensive exam, thesis/dissertation. *Entrance requirements:* For master's and doctorate, GRE General Test. Additional exam requirements/recommendations for international students: Required—TOEFL (minimum score 577 paper-based; 91 iBT), IELTS (minimum score 6.5). Application fee: $55. Electronic applications accepted. *Expenses: Tuition:* Full-time $20,160; part-time $1120 per credit hour. *Required fees:* $6 per credit hour. Tuition and fees vary according to course level and course load. *Financial support:* In 2014–15, 64 students received support, including 12 fellowships with full and partial tuition reimbursements available (averaging $11,693 per year), 18 research assistantships with full and partial tuition reimbursements available (averaging $14,578 per year), 39 teaching assistantships with full and partial tuition reimbursements available (averaging $11,758 per year); career-related internships or fieldwork, Federal Work-Study, scholarships/grants, health care benefits, tuition waivers (full and partial), and unspecified assistantships also available. Support available to part-time students. Financial award application deadline: 2/1; financial award applicants required to submit FAFSA. *Faculty research:* Traumatic stress studies, randomized control trials of exposure treatments, pain modulation, neuropsychological assessment of health/mental health, psychological assessment, psychometrics, ethics, longitudinal assessment of child development, trauma and journalism, MMPI studies, personnel testing and selection, training, performance appraisal, organizational development, job attitudes and motivation, leadership. *Total annual research expenditures:* $944,778. *Unit head:* Dr. John McNulty, Chairperson, 918-631-2835, Fax: 918-631-2833, E-mail: john-mcnulty@utulsa.edu. *Application contact:* Graduate School, 918-631-2336, Fax: 918-631-2156, E-mail: grad@utulsa.edu.
Website: http://artsandsciences.utulsa.edu/academics/departments-schools/psychology/

University of Utah, Graduate School, College of Social and Behavioral Science, Department of Psychology, Salt Lake City, UT 84112. Offers clinical psychology (PhD); psychology (PhD). *Accreditation:* APA. *Faculty:* 29 full-time (14 women), 8 part-time/adjunct (4 women). *Students:* 54 full-time (39 women), 5 part-time (2 women); includes 6 minority (1 Black or African American, non-Hispanic/Latino; 3 Asian, non-Hispanic/Latino; 2 Hispanic/Latino), 1 international. Average age 28. 359 applicants, 7% accepted, 18 enrolled. In 2014, 12 doctorates awarded. *Degree requirements:* For doctorate, thesis/dissertation. *Entrance requirements:* For doctorate, GRE General Test. Additional exam requirements/recommendations for international students: Required—TOEFL (minimum score 500 paper-based). *Application deadline:* For fall admission, 12/15 for domestic and international students. Application fee: $55 ($65 for international students). Electronic applications accepted. *Financial support:* In 2014–15, 56 students received support, including 2 fellowships with full tuition reimbursements available (averaging $15,000 per year), 17 research assistantships with full tuition

reimbursements available (averaging $15,000 per year), 37 teaching assistantships with full tuition reimbursements available (averaging $15,000 per year); career-related internships or fieldwork and health care benefits also available. Financial award applicants required to submit FAFSA. *Faculty research:* Cognitive neuroscience, health, social cognition, psychopathology, cognitive and social development. *Total annual research expenditures:* $1.9 million. *Unit head:* Dr. Carol Sansone, Chair, 801-581-8925, Fax: 801-581-5841, E-mail: carol.sansone@psych.utah.edu. *Application contact:* Nancy Seegmiller, Program Manager, 801-581-8925, Fax: 801-581-5841, E-mail: nancy.seegmiller@psych.utah.edu.
Website: http://www.psych.utah.edu/

University of Vermont, Graduate College, College of Arts and Sciences, Department of Psychology, Burlington, VT 05405. Offers clinical psychology (PhD); psychology (PhD). *Accreditation:* APA. *Degree requirements:* For doctorate, thesis/dissertation. *Entrance requirements:* For doctorate, GRE General Test, writing sample (for clinical psychology). Additional exam requirements/recommendations for international students: Required—TOEFL (minimum score 550 paper-based; 80 iBT). Electronic applications accepted.

University of Victoria, Faculty of Graduate Studies, Faculty of Social Sciences, Department of Psychology, Victoria, BC V8W 2Y2, Canada. Offers clinical psychology (PhD); clinical psychology (neuropsychology) (M Sc); cognition and brain science (M Sc, PhD); experimental neuropsychology (M Sc, PhD); individualized study (M Sc, PhD); life span development psychology (PhD); life span developmental psychology (M Sc); social psychology (M Sc, PhD). *Accreditation:* APA (one or more programs are accredited). *Degree requirements:* For master's, thesis; for doctorate, thesis/dissertation, candidacy exam. *Entrance requirements:* For master's and doctorate, GRE General Test. Additional exam requirements/recommendations for international students: Required—TOEFL (minimum score 600 paper-based). Electronic applications accepted. *Faculty research:* Life span development psychology and aging, behavioral neuroscience, cognitive psychology, behavioral psychology, environmental psychology.

University of Virginia, College and Graduate School of Arts and Sciences, Department of Psychology, Charlottesville, VA 22903. Offers MA, PhD. *Accreditation:* APA (one or more programs are accredited). *Faculty:* 29 full-time (10 women), 1 part-time/adjunct (0 women). *Students:* 73 full-time (48 women); includes 14 minority (2 Black or African American, non-Hispanic/Latino; 6 Asian, non-Hispanic/Latino; 5 Hispanic/Latino; 1 Two or more races, non-Hispanic/Latino), 6 international. Average age 27. 583 applicants, 5% accepted, 15 enrolled. In 2014, 16 master's, 15 doctorates awarded. *Degree requirements:* For master's, pre-dissertation research project; for doctorate, comprehensive exam, thesis/dissertation. *Entrance requirements:* For master's and doctorate, GRE General Test, 3 or more letters of recommendation. Additional exam requirements/recommendations for international students: Required—TOEFL (minimum score 600 paper-based; 90 iBT), IELTS (minimum score 7). *Application deadline:* For fall admission, 12/1 for domestic and international students. Applications are processed on a rolling basis. Application fee: $60. Electronic applications accepted. *Expenses:* Tuition, state resident: full-time $14,164; part-time $349 per credit hour. Tuition, nonresident: full-time $23,722; part-time $1300 per credit hour. *Required fees:* $2514. *Financial support:* Fellowships, research assistantships, and teaching assistantships available. Financial award applicants required to submit FAFSA. *Unit head:* Dave Hill, Chair, 434-982-4750, Fax: 434-982-4766, E-mail: psy-dept@virginia.edu. *Application contact:* Robert Emery, Director of Graduate Studies, 434-982-4750, Fax: 434-982-4766, E-mail: psy-dept@virginia.edu.
Website: http://cacsprd.web.virginia.edu/Psych/Graduates

University of Washington, Graduate School, College of Arts and Sciences, Department of Psychology, Seattle, WA 98195. Offers animal behavior (PhD); child psychology (PhD); clinical psychology (PhD); cognition and perception (PhD); developmental psychology (PhD); quantitative psychology (PhD); social psychology and personality (PhD). *Accreditation:* APA. *Degree requirements:* For doctorate, thesis/dissertation. *Entrance requirements:* For doctorate, GRE General Test, minimum GPA of 3.0. Electronic applications accepted. *Faculty research:* Addictive behaviors, artificial intelligence, child psychopathology, mechanisms and development of vision, physiology of ingestive behaviors.

University of Waterloo, Graduate Studies, Faculty of Arts, Department of Psychology, Waterloo, ON N2L 3G1, Canada. Offers MA, MA Sc, PhD. Terminal master's awarded for partial completion of doctoral program. *Degree requirements:* For master's, thesis (for some programs); for doctorate, thesis/dissertation. *Entrance requirements:* For master's, GRE, honors degree in psychology, minimum B average; for doctorate, GRE, master's degree in psychology, minimum B average. Additional exam requirements/recommendations for international students: Required—TOEFL, TWE. Electronic applications accepted. *Faculty research:* Memory and attention, attitudes and behavior in the workplace, object recognition, judgment and decision making, communication and knowledge in toddlers.

The University of Western Ontario, Faculty of Graduate Studies, Biosciences Division, Department of Psychology, London, ON N6A 5B8, Canada. Offers MA, PhD. *Degree requirements:* For master's, thesis; for doctorate, thesis/dissertation. *Entrance requirements:* For master's, minimum B average during last 2 years; for doctorate, MA in psychology. Additional exam requirements/recommendations for international students: Required—TOEFL. *Faculty research:* Clinical, applied and social/personality psychology; psychobiology; cognitive processes.

University of West Florida, College of Arts and Sciences: Arts, Department of Psychology, Pensacola, FL 32514-5750. Offers counseling (MA); counseling-licensed mental health counselor (MA); general psychology (MA); industrial-organizational (MA). Part-time programs available. *Degree requirements:* For master's, thesis (for some programs). *Entrance requirements:* For master's, GRE, official transcripts; minimum GPA of 3.0; writing sample; three letters of reference; field experience or skill sets; oral interview (for counseling specialization). Additional exam requirements/recommendations for international students: Required—TOEFL (minimum score 550 paper-based). *Faculty research:* Prose recall, brain imaging, peak performance, biofeedback and pain control, comparable worth.

University of West Georgia, College of Social Sciences, Department of Psychology, Carrollton, GA 30118. Offers integrative health studies (Certificate); psychology (MA); psychology: consciousness and society (PhD). Part-time programs available. *Faculty:* 16 full-time (5 women). *Students:* 65 full-time (37 women), 31 part-time (14 women); includes 17 minority (10 Black or African American, non-Hispanic/Latino; 1 Asian, non-Hispanic/Latino; 5 Hispanic/Latino; 1 Two or more races, non-Hispanic/Latino), 5 international. Average age 36. 49 applicants, 49% accepted, 17 enrolled. In 2014, 23 master's, 1 doctorate awarded. Terminal master's awarded for partial completion of doctoral program. *Degree requirements:* For master's, one foreign language, comprehensive exam, thesis optional; for doctorate, comprehensive exam, thesis/dissertation, 60 hours of course work, including 30 hours of required courses. *Entrance requirements:* For master's, GRE General Test, interview, minimum GPA of 2.5; for doctorate, GRE or MAT, interview; for Certificate, BA, interview. Additional exam requirements/recommendations for international students: Required—TOEFL (minimum score 523 paper-based; 69 iBT); Recommended—IELTS (minimum score 6). *Application deadline:* For fall admission, 7/17 for domestic students; for spring admission, 9/16 for domestic students. Applications are processed on a rolling basis. Application fee: $40. Electronic applications accepted. *Financial support:* In 2014–15, 1 student received support, including 12 research assistantships with full tuition reimbursements available (averaging $3,000 per year), 15 teaching assistantships with full tuition reimbursements available (averaging $4,500 per year); career-related internships or fieldwork, tuition waivers (full), and unspecified assistantships also available. Support available to part-time students. Financial award application deadline: 4/1; financial award applicants required to submit FAFSA. *Faculty research:* Creativity, inspiration and consciousness; parapsychology; spirituality of children; feminism and culture; mind/body connection. *Total annual research expenditures:* $30,000. *Unit head:* Dr. Donadrian Rice, Interim Chair, 678-839-0612, Fax: 678-839-0611, E-mail: drice@westga.edu. *Application contact:* Trish Wells, Graduate Studies Associate, 678-839-5170, Fax: 678-839-5171, E-mail: pwells@westga.edu.
Website: http://www.westga.edu/psydept/

University of Windsor, Faculty of Graduate Studies, Faculty of Arts and Social Sciences, Department of Psychology, Windsor, ON N9B 3P4, Canada. Offers adult clinical (MA, PhD); applied social psychology (MA, PhD); child clinical (MA, PhD); clinical neuropsychology (MA, PhD). *Accreditation:* APA (one or more programs are accredited). *Degree requirements:* For master's, thesis; for doctorate, comprehensive exam, thesis/dissertation. *Entrance requirements:* For master's, GRE General Test, GRE Subject Test in psychology, minimum B average; for doctorate, GRE General Test, GRE Subject Test in psychology, master's degree. Additional exam requirements/recommendations for international students: Required—TOEFL (minimum score 600 paper-based). Electronic applications accepted. *Faculty research:* Gambling, suicidology, emotional competence, psychotherapy and trauma.

University of Wisconsin–Eau Claire, College of Arts and Sciences, Department of Psychology, Eau Claire, WI 54702-4004. Offers school psychology (MSE, Ed S). Part-time programs available. *Degree requirements:* For master's, comprehensive exam, thesis, National Certified School Psychologist Professional Exam, written exam, externship. *Entrance requirements:* For master's, GRE, minimum undergraduate GPA of 3.0; courses in exceptional children and youth, statistics, psychopathology, and theories of counseling. Additional exam requirements/recommendations for international students: Required—TOEFL (minimum score 79 iBT).

University of Wisconsin–La Crosse, Graduate Studies, College of Liberal Studies, Department of Psychology, La Crosse, WI 54601-3742. Offers school psychology (MS Ed, Ed S). *Faculty:* 4 full-time (2 women). *Students:* 23 full-time (19 women), 6 part-time (5 women); includes 1 minority (Hispanic/Latino). Average age 24. 51 applicants, 35% accepted, 12 enrolled. In 2014, 11 master's, 14 Ed Ss awarded. *Degree requirements:* For master's, thesis, seminar, or comprehensive exams. *Entrance requirements:* For master's and Ed S, GRE. Additional exam requirements/recommendations for international students: Required—TOEFL (minimum score 550 paper-based; 79 iBT). *Application deadline:* For fall admission, 1/31 for domestic and international students. Electronic applications accepted. *Financial support:* In 2014–15, 6 research assistantships were awarded; Federal Work-Study, scholarships/grants, and health care benefits also available. Support available to part-time students. *Unit head:* Dr. Betsy Morgan, Chair, 608-785-6885, E-mail: bmorgan@uwlax.edu. *Application contact:* Brandon Schaller, Senior Graduate Student Status Examiner, 608-785-8941, E-mail: admissions@uwlax.edu.
Website: http://www.uwlax.edu/school-psychology/

University of Wisconsin–Madison, Graduate School, College of Letters and Science, Department of Psychology, Madison, WI 53706-1380. Offers biology of brain and behavior (PhD); clinical psychology (PhD); cognitive neurosciences (PhD); developmental psychology (PhD); perception (PhD); psychology (PhD); social and personality psychology (PhD). *Accreditation:* APA. *Degree requirements:* For doctorate, comprehensive exam, thesis/dissertation. *Entrance requirements:* For doctorate, GRE General Test, minimum undergraduate GPA of 3.0. Additional exam requirements/recommendations for international students: Required—TOEFL. Electronic applications accepted. *Expenses:* Tuition, state resident: full-time $10,723; part-time $745 per credit. Tuition, nonresident: full-time $24,054; part-time $1578 per credit. *Required fees:* $374 per semester. Tuition and fees vary according to course load, program and reciprocity agreements.

University of Wisconsin–Milwaukee, Graduate School, College of Letters and Sciences, Department of Psychology, Milwaukee, WI 53201-0413. Offers clinical psychology (MS, PhD); psychology (MS, PhD). *Accreditation:* APA (one or more programs are accredited). *Degree requirements:* For master's, thesis; for doctorate, variable foreign language requirement, thesis/dissertation. *Entrance requirements:* For master's and doctorate, GRE General Test, GRE Subject Test. Additional exam requirements/recommendations for international students: Required—TOEFL (minimum score 550 paper-based; 79 iBT), IELTS (minimum score 6.5). Electronic applications accepted.

University of Wisconsin–Oshkosh, Graduate Studies, College of Letters and Science, Department of Psychology, Oshkosh, WI 54901. Offers experimental psychology (MS); industrial/organizational psychology (MS). *Degree requirements:* For master's, thesis. *Entrance requirements:* For master's, GRE, 10 semester hours of undergraduate course work in psychology. Additional exam requirements/recommendations for international students: Required—TOEFL (minimum score 550 paper-based; 79 iBT). Electronic applications accepted. *Faculty research:* Performance evaluation, training, biological bases of behavior, tactile perception, aging.

University of Wisconsin–Whitewater, School of Graduate Studies, College of Letters and Sciences, Department of Psychology, Whitewater, WI 53190-1790. Offers education specialist (Ed S); educational specialist (MSE). Part-time and evening/weekend programs available. Postbaccalaureate distance learning degree programs offered (no on-campus study). *Degree requirements:* For master's, comprehensive exam or thesis. *Entrance requirements:* For master's, MAT or GRE, interview, minimum GPA of 3.0, 3 letters of recommendation. Additional exam requirements/recommendations for international students: Required—TOEFL (minimum score 550 paper-based; 80 iBT), IELTS (minimum score 6). Electronic applications accepted. *Faculty research:* School violence/youth violence; anger/aggression interventions; women's mental health; pedagogy of empathy, social psychology, and personality.

University of Wyoming, College of Arts and Sciences, Department of Psychology, Laramie, WY 82071. Offers MA, MS, PhD. *Accreditation:* APA (one or more programs are accredited). Terminal master's awarded for partial completion of doctoral program. *Degree requirements:* For master's, thesis; for doctorate, comprehensive exam, thesis/dissertation. *Entrance requirements:* For master's and doctorate, GRE General Test, GRE Subject Test, minimum GPA of 3.0. Additional exam requirements/recommendations for international students: Required—TOEFL. *Faculty research:* Child development, health psychology, psychology and law, social psychology, mood/anxiety disorders.

Utah State University, School of Graduate Studies, Emma Eccles Jones College of Education and Human Services, Department of Psychology, Logan, UT 84322. Offers clinical/counseling/school psychology (PhD); research and evaluation methodology (PhD); school counseling (MS); school psychology (MS). *Accreditation:* APA (one or

more programs are accredited). Part-time and evening/weekend programs available. Postbaccalaureate distance learning degree programs offered (no on-campus study). Terminal master's awarded for partial completion of doctoral program. *Degree requirements:* For master's, thesis (for some programs); for doctorate, thesis/dissertation. *Entrance requirements:* For master's, GRE General Test (school psychology), MAT (school counseling), minimum GPA of 3.5; for doctorate, GRE General Test, minimum GPA of 3.5. Additional exam requirements/recommendations for international students: Required—TOEFL. *Faculty research:* Hearing loss detection in infancy, ADHD, eating disorders, domestic violence, neuropsychology, bilingual/Spanish speaking students/parents.

Valdosta State University, Department of Psychology and Counseling, Valdosta, GA 31698. Offers school counseling (M Ed, Ed S). Part-time and evening/weekend programs available. *Faculty:* 14 full-time (8 women). *Students:* 13 full-time (all women), 18 part-time (16 women); includes 9 minority (8 Black or African American, non-Hispanic/Latino; 1 Two or more races, non-Hispanic/Latino). Average age 25. 20 applicants, 55% accepted, 11 enrolled. In 2014, 7 master's awarded. *Degree requirements:* For master's, thesis or alternative, comprehensive written and/or oral exams; for Ed S, thesis. *Entrance requirements:* For master's and Ed S, GRE General Test or MAT. Additional exam requirements/recommendations for international students: Required—TOEFL (minimum score 523 paper-based). *Application deadline:* For fall admission, 7/1 for domestic and international students; for spring admission, 11/15 for domestic and international students. Applications are processed on a rolling basis. Application fee: $35. Electronic applications accepted. *Expenses:* Tuition, state resident: part-time $236 per credit hour. Tuition, nonresident: part-time $850 per credit hour. *Required fees:* $1032 per semester. *Financial support:* In 2014–15, 5 students received support, including 2 research assistantships with full tuition reimbursements available (averaging $3,652 per year); institutionally sponsored loans and unspecified assistantships also available. Support available to part-time students. Financial award application deadline: 7/1; financial award applicants required to submit FAFSA. *Unit head:* Dr. David Monetti, Chair, 229-333-5930, Fax: 229-259-5576. *Application contact:* Jessica Powers, Coordinator of Graduate Admissions, 229-333-5694, Fax: 229-245-3853, E-mail: jldevane@valdosta.edu.
Website: http://www.valdosta.edu/colleges/education/psychology-and-counseling/welcome.php

Valparaiso University, Graduate School, Department of Psychology, Valparaiso, IN 46383. Offers clinical mental health counseling (MA); JD/MA. Part-time and evening/weekend programs available. *Faculty:* 10 part-time/adjunct (5 women). *Students:* 38 full-time (32 women), 6 part-time (all women); includes 5 minority (1 Black or African American, non-Hispanic/Latino; 2 Hispanic/Latino; 2 Two or more races, non-Hispanic/Latino). Average age 28. In 2014, 21 master's awarded. *Degree requirements:* For master's, thesis or alternative, internship. *Entrance requirements:* For master's, minimum GPA of 3.0; 15 credits in the social/behavioral sciences (psychology, sociology, human development, etc.) with minimum GPA of 3.0; course in introductory psychology; recent statistics course with minimum B average. Additional exam requirements/recommendations for international students: Required—TOEFL (minimum score 550 paper-based; 80 iBT), IELTS (minimum score 6). *Application deadline:* Applications are processed on a rolling basis. Application fee: $30 ($50 for international students). Electronic applications accepted. *Expenses: Tuition:* Full-time $10,710; part-time $595 per credit hour. *Required fees:* $378; $101 per term. Tuition and fees vary according to course load and program. *Financial support:* Career-related internships or fieldwork, traineeships, and unspecified assistantships available. Support available to part-time students. Financial award applicants required to submit FAFSA. *Faculty research:* Environmental psychology, human sexuality, developmental psychopathology, social psychology. *Unit head:* Dr. David Simpson, Director of Graduate Programs, 219-464-6941, Fax: 219-464-6878, E-mail: david.simpson@valpo.edu. *Application contact:* Jessica Choquette, Graduate Admissions Specialist, 219-464-5313, Fax: 219-464-5381, E-mail: jessica.choquette@valpo.edu.
Website: http://www.valpo.edu/psychology/graduate/index.php

Vanderbilt University, Graduate School, Program in Psychological Sciences, Nashville, TN 37240-1001. Offers MA, MS, PhD. *Accreditation:* APA (one or more programs are accredited). *Faculty:* 48 full-time (19 women), 1 (woman) part-time/adjunct. *Students:* 84 full-time (60 women); includes 11 minority (3 Black or African American, non-Hispanic/Latino; 5 Asian, non-Hispanic/Latino; 3 Hispanic/Latino), 13 international. Average age 27. 21 applicants, 100% accepted, 11 enrolled. In 2014, 11 master's, 9 doctorates awarded. *Degree requirements:* For doctorate, comprehensive exam, thesis/dissertation, final and qualifying exams. *Entrance requirements:* For doctorate, GRE General Test, GRE Subject Test. Additional exam requirements/recommendations for international students: Required—TOEFL (minimum score 570 paper-based; 88 iBT). *Application deadline:* For fall admission, 12/15 for domestic and international students. Electronic applications accepted. *Expenses: Tuition:* Full-time $42,768; part-time $1782 per credit hour. *Required fees:* $422. One-time fee: $30 full-time. *Financial support:* Fellowships with full and partial tuition reimbursements, research assistantships with full and partial tuition reimbursements, teaching assistantships with full and partial tuition reimbursements, career-related internships or fieldwork, Federal Work-Study, institutionally sponsored loans, scholarships/grants, traineeships, and health care benefits available. Financial award application deadline: 1/15; financial award applicants required to submit CSS PROFILE or FAFSA. *Faculty research:* Clinical, cognitive, developmental, and social psychology; neuroscience; vision; behavior. *Unit head:* Dr. Daniel T. Levin, Director of Graduate Studies for the Psychology of Human Development in Peabody College, 615-322-1518, Fax: 615-343-9494, E-mail: daniel.t.levin@vanderbilt.edu. *Application contact:* Dr. Rene Marois, Director of Graduate Studies for Psychological Studies in the College of Arts and Science, 615-322-1779, Fax: 615-343-5027, E-mail: r.marois@vanderbilt.edu.
Website: http://peabody.vanderbilt.edu/departments/psych/

Vanderbilt University, Peabody College, Department of Psychology and Human Development, Nashville, TN 37240-1001. Offers child studies (M Ed). *Accreditation:* APA. Part-time programs available. *Degree requirements:* For master's, comprehensive exam, thesis optional. *Entrance requirements:* For master's, GRE General Test. Additional exam requirements/recommendations for international students: Required—TOEFL (minimum score 550 paper-based; 80 iBT). Electronic applications accepted. *Expenses: Tuition:* Full-time $42,768; part-time $1782 per credit hour. *Required fees:* $422. One-time fee: $30 full-time. *Faculty research:* Child clinical psychology and developmental psychopathology; cognitive psychology, language and social development; educational and developmental neuroscience; quantitative methods and evaluation.

Villanova University, Graduate School of Liberal Arts and Sciences, Department of Psychology, Villanova, PA 19085-1699. Offers MS. Part-time and evening/weekend programs available. *Faculty:* 12. *Students:* 52 full-time (33 women); includes 6 minority (3 Asian, non-Hispanic/Latino; 3 Hispanic/Latino), 2 international. Average age 26. 122 applicants, 73% accepted, 18 enrolled. In 2014, 18 master's awarded. *Degree requirements:* For master's, thesis. *Entrance requirements:* For master's, GRE General Test, minimum GPA of 3.0, statement of goals. Additional exam requirements/recommendations for international students: Required—TOEFL. *Application deadline:* For fall admission, 3/1 for domestic students, 5/1 priority date for international students; for spring admission, 11/15 for domestic students, 10/15 priority date for international students; for summer admission, 5/1 for domestic students. Applications are processed on a rolling basis. Application fee: $50. Electronic applications accepted. *Financial support:* Research assistantships, scholarships/grants, and unspecified assistantships available. Financial award applicants required to submit FAFSA. *Unit head:* Dr. Michael Brown, Director, 610-519-4720.
Website: http://www1.villanova.edu/villanova/artsci/psychology/graduate.html

Virginia Commonwealth University, Graduate School, College of Humanities and Sciences, Department of Psychology, Program in General Psychology, Richmond, VA 23284-9005. Offers biopsychology (PhD); developmental psychology (PhD); social psychology (PhD). *Degree requirements:* For doctorate, thesis/dissertation. *Entrance requirements:* For doctorate, GRE General Test. Additional exam requirements/recommendations for international students: Required—TOEFL (minimum score 600 paper-based; 100 iBT); Recommended—IELTS (minimum score 6.5). Electronic applications accepted. *Faculty research:* Biopsychology, developmental and social psychology.

Virginia Polytechnic Institute and State University, Graduate School, College of Science, Blacksburg, VA 24061. Offers biological sciences (MS, PhD); biomedical technology development and management (MS); chemistry (MS, PhD); economics (MA, PhD); geosciences (MS, PhD); mathematics (MS, PhD); physics (MS, PhD); psychology (MS, PhD); statistics (MS, PhD). *Faculty:* 274 full-time (75 women), 3 part-time/adjunct (all women). *Students:* 544 full-time (212 women), 29 part-time (12 women); includes 54 minority (14 Black or African American, non-Hispanic/Latino; 9 Asian, non-Hispanic/Latino; 16 Hispanic/Latino; 15 Two or more races, non-Hispanic/Latino), 243 international. Average age 27. 1,105 applicants, 22% accepted, 104 enrolled. In 2014, 83 master's, 67 doctorates awarded. *Median time to degree:* Of those who began their doctoral program in fall 2006, 54% received their degree in 8 years or less. *Degree requirements:* For master's, comprehensive exam (for some programs), thesis (for some programs); for doctorate, comprehensive exam (for some programs), thesis/dissertation (for some programs). *Entrance requirements:* For master's and doctorate, GRE/GMAT (may vary by department). Additional exam requirements/recommendations for international students: Required—TOEFL (minimum score 550 paper-based). *Application deadline:* For fall admission, 8/1 for domestic students, 4/1 for international students; for spring admission, 1/1 for domestic students, 9/1 for international students. Applications are processed on a rolling basis. Application fee: $75. Electronic applications accepted. *Expenses:* Tuition, state resident: full-time $11,656; part-time $647.50 per credit hour. Tuition, nonresident: full-time $23,351; part-time $1297.25 per credit hour. *Required fees:* $2533; $465.75 per semester. Tuition and fees vary according to course load, campus/location and program. *Financial support:* In 2014–15, 1 fellowship with full tuition reimbursement (averaging $5,938 per year), 143 research assistantships with full tuition reimbursements (averaging $22,569 per year), 355 teaching assistantships with full tuition reimbursements (averaging $21,476 per year) were awarded. Financial award application deadline: 3/1; financial award applicants required to submit FAFSA. *Total annual research expenditures:* $24.3 million. *Unit head:* Dr. Lay Nam Chang, Dean, 540-231-5422, Fax: 540-231-3380, E-mail: laynam@vt.edu. *Application contact:* Diane Stearns, Assistant to the Dean, 540-231-7515, Fax: 540-231-3380, E-mail: dstearns@vt.edu.
Website: http://www.science.vt.edu/

Virginia State University, College of Graduate Studies, College of Natural and Health Sciences, Department of Psychology, Petersburg, VA 23806-0001. Offers behavioral and community health sciences (PhD); clinical health psychology (PhD); clinical psychology (MS); general psychology (MS). *Degree requirements:* For master's, one foreign language, thesis. *Entrance requirements:* For master's, GRE General Test.

Wake Forest University, Graduate School of Arts and Sciences, Department of Psychology, Winston-Salem, NC 27109. Offers MA. *Degree requirements:* For master's, one foreign language, comprehensive exam, thesis. *Entrance requirements:* For master's, GRE General Test. Additional exam requirements/recommendations for international students: Required—TOEFL (minimum score 79 iBT). Electronic applications accepted. *Faculty research:* Developmental, social, personality, experimental, and physiological psychology.

Walden University, Graduate Programs, School of Psychology, Minneapolis, MN 55401. Offers clinical psychology (MS), including counseling, general program; forensic psychology (MS), including forensic psychology in the community, general program, mental health applications, program planning and evaluation in forensic settings, psychology and legal systems; organizational psychology and development (Postbaccalaureate Certificate); psychology (MS, PhD), including applied psychology (MS), clinical psychology (PhD), counseling psychology (PhD), crisis management and response (MS), educational psychology, forensic psychology (PhD), general psychology (MS), general psychology research (PhD), health psychology, leadership development and coaching (MS), psychology of culture (MS), psychology, public administration, and social change (MS), social psychology, terrorism and security (MS); psychology respecialization (Post-Doctoral Certificate); teaching online (Post-Master's Certificate). Part-time and evening/weekend programs available. Postbaccalaureate distance learning degree programs offered (no on-campus study). *Faculty:* 56 full-time (36 women), 351 part-time/adjunct (201 women). *Students:* 2,757 full-time (2,202 women), 1,466 part-time (1,148 women); includes 1,849 minority (1,299 Black or African American, non-Hispanic/Latino; 37 American Indian or Alaska Native, non-Hispanic/Latino; 74 Asian, non-Hispanic/Latino; 315 Hispanic/Latino; 8 Native Hawaiian or other Pacific Islander, non-Hispanic/Latino; 116 Two or more races, non-Hispanic/Latino), 28 international. Average age 41. 913 applicants, 97% accepted, 851 enrolled. In 2014, 602 master's, 204 doctorates, 19 other advanced degrees awarded. Terminal master's awarded for partial completion of doctoral program. *Degree requirements:* For master's, thesis optional; for doctorate, thesis/dissertation, residency. *Entrance requirements:* For master's, bachelor's degree or higher; minimum GPA of 2.5; official transcripts; goal statement (for some programs); access to computer and Internet; for doctorate, master's degree or higher; three years of related professional or academic experience (preferred); minimum GPA of 3.0; goal statement and current resume (for select programs); official transcripts; access to computer and Internet; for other advanced degree, relevant work experience; access to computer and Internet. Additional exam requirements/recommendations for international students: Required—TOEFL (minimum score 550 paper-based, 79 iBT), IELTS (minimum score 6.5), Michigan English Language Assessment Battery (minimum score 82), or PTE (minimum score 53). *Application deadline:* Applications are processed on a rolling basis. Application fee: $0. Electronic applications accepted. *Expenses: Tuition:* Full-time $11,925; part-time $500 per credit hour. *Required fees:* $647. *Financial support:* Fellowships, Federal Work-Study, scholarships/grants, unspecified assistantships, and family tuition reduction, active duty/veteran tuition reduction, group tuition reduction, interest-free payment plans, employee tuition reduction available. Support available to part-time students. Financial award applicants required to submit FAFSA. *Unit head:* Dr. Marilyn Powell, Associate Dean, 866-492-5366. *Application contact:* Meghan Thomas, Vice President of

Enrollment Management, 866-492-5336, E-mail: info@waldenu.edu.
Website: http://www.waldenu.edu/programs/colleges-schools/psychology

Washburn University, College of Arts and Sciences, Department of Psychology, Topeka, KS 66621. Offers clinical psychology (MA). Part-time programs available. *Faculty:* 7 full-time (3 women). *Students:* 22 full-time (17 women), 4 part-time (3 women); includes 2 minority (both Hispanic/Latino). Average age 29. 21 applicants, 71% accepted, 11 enrolled. In 2014, 6 master's awarded. *Degree requirements:* For master's, comprehensive exam (for some programs), thesis or alternative. *Entrance requirements:* For master's, GRE General Test, 15 hours of undergraduate course work in psychology. Additional exam requirements/recommendations for international students: Required—TOEFL (minimum score 80 iBT). *Application deadline:* For fall admission, 3/15 for domestic and international students; for spring admission, 12/1 for domestic and international students. Electronic applications accepted. *Expenses:* Tuition, state resident: full-time $6120; part-time $340 per credit hour. Tuition, nonresident: full-time $12,456; part-time $692 per credit hour. *Required fees:* $86; $43 per semester. Tuition and fees vary according to program. *Financial support:* Unspecified assistantships available. *Faculty research:* Metacognition, anxiety disorders, auditory perception, sports performance psychology, ADHD. *Unit head:* Dr. Cindy Turk, Chair, 785-670-1565, Fax: 785-670-1239, E-mail: cindy.turk@washburn.edu. *Application contact:* Kris Klima, Director of Admissions, 785-670-1030, Fax: 785-670-1113, E-mail: admissions@washburn.edu.
Website: http://www.washburn.edu/academics/college-schools/arts-sciences/departments/psychology/

Washington College, Graduate Programs, Department of Psychology, Chestertown, MD 21620-1197. Offers MA. Part-time and evening/weekend programs available. *Degree requirements:* For master's, thesis optional. *Entrance requirements:* For master's, GRE General Test, minimum GPA of 3.0 in undergraduate coursework with significant coursework in psychology.

Washington State University, College of Liberal Arts, Department of Psychology, Pullman, WA 99164. Offers clinical psychology (PhD); experimental psychology (PhD). Program applications must be made through the Pullman campus. *Accreditation:* APA (one or more programs are accredited). *Students:* 58 full-time (40 women), 5 part-time (3 women); includes 10 minority (1 Black or African American, non-Hispanic/Latino; 1 American Indian or Alaska Native, non-Hispanic/Latino; 2 Asian, non-Hispanic/Latino; 3 Hispanic/Latino; 3 Two or more races, non-Hispanic/Latino), 2 international. Average age 28. 236 applicants, 8% accepted, 12 enrolled. In 2014, 7 master's, 6 doctorates awarded. *Degree requirements:* For doctorate, comprehensive exam, thesis/dissertation, oral exam, written exam. *Entrance requirements:* For doctorate, GRE General Test, three letters of reference; summary data form; at least 18 credits of study in psychology; at least one course in statistics and research methodology; official transcripts; minimum cumulative undergraduate GPA of 3.0 or master's degree in psychology. Additional exam requirements/recommendations for international students: Required—TOEFL, IELTS. *Application deadline:* For fall admission, 12/1 priority date for domestic and international students. Application fee: $75. Electronic applications accepted. *Expenses:* Tuition, state resident: full-time $11,768. Tuition, nonresident: full-time $25,200. *Required fees:* $960. Tuition and fees vary according to program. *Financial support:* In 2014–15, 31 students received support, including 5 research assistantships with full and partial tuition reimbursements available (averaging $13,870 per year), 46 teaching assistantships with full and partial tuition reimbursements available (averaging $13,890 per year); fellowships, career-related internships or fieldwork, Federal Work-Study, institutionally sponsored loans, and unspecified assistantships also available. Financial award application deadline: 2/15; financial award applicants required to submit FAFSA. *Faculty research:* Adult psychopathology and therapy, child psychopathology, neuropsychology, health psychology. *Unit head:* Dr. David K. Marcus, Director of Clinical Training, 509-335-7750, Fax: 509-335-5043, E-mail: david.marcus@wsu.edu. *Application contact:* Graduate School Admissions, 800-GRADWSU, Fax: 509-335-1949, E-mail: gradsch@wsu.edu.
Website: https://psychology.wsu.edu/

Washington University in St. Louis, Graduate School of Arts and Sciences, Department of Philosophy, Program in Philosophy-Neuroscience-Psychology, St. Louis, MO 63130-4899. Offers PhD. *Degree requirements:* For doctorate, thesis/dissertation. *Entrance requirements:* For doctorate, GRE General Test, sample of written work. Additional exam requirements/recommendations for international students: Required—TOEFL. Electronic applications accepted. *Faculty research:* Philosophy of mind and language with a special emphasis on the philosophical dimensions of psychology, neuroscience, and linguistics.

Washington University in St. Louis, Graduate School of Arts and Sciences, Department of Psychology, St. Louis, MO 63130-4899. Offers aging and development (PhD); behavior, brain, and cognition (PhD); clinical psychology (PhD); social and personality psychology (PhD). *Accreditation:* APA. Terminal master's awarded for partial completion of doctoral program. *Degree requirements:* For doctorate, thesis/dissertation. *Entrance requirements:* For doctorate, GRE General Test. Additional exam requirements/recommendations for international students: Required—TOEFL. Electronic applications accepted.

Wayne State University, College of Liberal Arts and Sciences, Department of Psychology, Detroit, MI 48202. Offers behavioral and cognitive neuroscience (PhD); clinical psychology (PhD); cognitive, developmental and social psychology (PhD); industrial and organizational psychology (MA); social psychology (PhD). Doctoral programs admit for fall only. *Accreditation:* APA (one or more programs are accredited). *Faculty:* 37 full-time (13 women), 8 part-time/adjunct (4 women). *Students:* 107 full-time (74 women), 28 part-time (16 women); includes 19 minority (8 Black or African American, non-Hispanic/Latino; 2 Asian, non-Hispanic/Latino; 5 Hispanic/Latino; 4 Two or more races, non-Hispanic/Latino), 10 international. Average age 28. 397 applicants, 11% accepted, 25 enrolled. In 2014, 24 master's, 18 doctorates awarded. Terminal master's awarded for partial completion of doctoral program. *Degree requirements:* For master's, thesis (for some programs); for doctorate, thesis/dissertation, training assignments. *Entrance requirements:* For master's, GRE General Test, minimum undergraduate upper-division cumulative GPA of 3.0, courses in introductory psychology and statistics, two letters of recommendation, professional statement; for doctorate, GRE General Test, bachelor's, master's, or other advanced degree; at least three letters of recommendation; statement of purpose. Additional exam requirements/recommendations for international students: Required—TOEFL (minimum score 550 paper-based; 79 iBT), TWE (minimum score 5.5), Michigan English Language Assessment Battery (minimum score 85); Recommended—IELTS (minimum score 6.5). *Application deadline:* For fall admission, 12/1 for domestic and international students; for winter admission, 10/15 for domestic students, 9/1 for international students; for spring admission, 3/15 for domestic students, 1/1 for international students. Application fee: $0. Electronic applications accepted. *Expenses:* Tuition, state resident: full-time $10,294; part-time $571.90 per credit hour. Tuition, nonresident: full-time $29,730; part-time $1238.75 per credit hour. *Required fees:* $1365; $43.50 per credit hour. $291.10 per semester. Tuition and fees vary according to course load and program. *Financial support:* In 2014–15, 91 students received support, including 8 fellowships with tuition reimbursements available (averaging $15,983 per year), 12 research assistantships with tuition reimbursements available (averaging $17,862 per year), 49 teaching assistantships with tuition reimbursements available (averaging $16,838 per year); scholarships/grants, health care benefits, and unspecified assistantships also available. Financial award application deadline: 3/31; financial award applicants required to submit FAFSA. *Faculty research:* Neuroscience, including functional cognitive imaging, neural physiology, behavioral pharmacology, and neurobehavioral teratology; cognitive and neurochemical processes associated with aging, drug addiction and neurological disorders to studies of the neural circuits that underlie learning, emotion, and weight regulation; the life-long developmental plasticity of the neurobiological processes of behavior; neuropsychology; child clinical psychology; health psychology; community psychology. *Total annual research expenditures:* $2.1 million. *Unit head:* Boris Baltes, PhD, Chair/Professor, 313-577-2800, Fax: 313-577-7636, E-mail: b.baltes@wayne.edu. *Application contact:* Alia Allen, Academic Services Officer, 313-577-2823, E-mail: aallen@wayne.edu.
Website: http://clas.wayne.edu/psychology/

West Chester University of Pennsylvania, College of Arts and Sciences, Department of Psychology, West Chester, PA 19383. Offers clinical mental health (Certificate); clinical psychology (MA); general psychology (MA); industrial psychology (MA). Part-time and evening/weekend programs available. *Faculty:* 14 full-time (11 women), 6 part-time/adjunct (4 women). *Students:* 74 full-time (46 women), 23 part-time (13 women); includes 12 minority (7 Black or African American, non-Hispanic/Latino; 1 Asian, non-Hispanic/Latino; 2 Hispanic/Latino; 2 Two or more races, non-Hispanic/Latino), 5 international. Average age 27. 158 applicants, 56% accepted, 42 enrolled. In 2014, 37 master's, 2 other advanced degrees awarded. *Degree requirements:* For master's, comprehensive exam, thesis (for some programs). *Entrance requirements:* For master's, GRE General Test, minimum GPA of 3.0, psychology 3.25; three letters of reference. Additional exam requirements/recommendations for international students: Required—TOEFL (minimum score 550 paper-based; 80 iBT). *Application deadline:* For fall admission, 4/15 priority date for domestic students, 3/15 for international students; for spring admission, 10/15 priority date for domestic students, 9/1 for international students. Applications are processed on a rolling basis. Application fee: $45. Electronic applications accepted. *Expenses:* Tuition, state resident: full-time $8172; part-time $454 per credit. Tuition, nonresident: full-time $12,258; part-time $681 per credit. *Required fees:* $2231; $110.78 per credit. Tuition and fees vary according to campus/location and program. *Financial support:* Unspecified assistantships available. Support available to part-time students. Financial award application deadline: 2/15; financial award applicants required to submit FAFSA. *Faculty research:* Stress, coping, and resilience; preventative interventions; workplace stress; organizational leadership; eating disorders; schizophrenia; diversity; cognition; animal behavior. *Unit head:* Dr. Loretta Rieser-Danner, Chairperson, 610-436-3106, E-mail: lrieser-danner@wcupa.edu. *Application contact:* Dr. Vanessa Johnson, Graduate Coordinator, 610-436-2749, E-mail: vjohnson@wcupa.edu.
Website: http://www.wcupa.edu/_academics/sch_cas.psy/

Western Carolina University, Graduate School, College of Education and Allied Professions, Department of Psychology, Cullowhee, NC 28723. Offers general psychology (MA); school psychology (MA). Part-time programs available. *Degree requirements:* For master's, comprehensive exam, thesis. *Entrance requirements:* For master's, GRE General Test, appropriate undergraduate degree, interview, 3 letters of recommendation. Additional exam requirements/recommendations for international students: Required—TOEFL (minimum score 550 paper-based; 79 iBT). *Faculty research:* Five-factor model of personality, evolutionary psychology, stress and worry, body image and physical attractiveness, moral decision-making, memory, learning styles.

Western Illinois University, School of Graduate Studies, College of Arts and Sciences, Department of Psychology, Macomb, IL 61455-1390. Offers clinical/community mental health (MS); general psychology (MS); psychology (MS, SSP); school psychology (SSP). Part-time programs available. *Students:* 28 full-time (19 women), 10 part-time (5 women); includes 1 minority (Hispanic/Latino), 5 international. Average age 26. 69 applicants, 46% accepted, 12 enrolled. In 2014, 18 master's, 6 other advanced degrees awarded. *Degree requirements:* For master's, comprehensive exam (for some programs), thesis or alternative. *Entrance requirements:* For master's and SSP, GRE General Test. Additional exam requirements/recommendations for international students: Required—TOEFL (minimum score 550 paper-based; 80 iBT). *Application deadline:* Applications are processed on a rolling basis. Application fee: $30. Electronic applications accepted. *Financial support:* In 2014–15, 41 students received support, including 14 research assistantships with full tuition reimbursements available (averaging $7,544 per year), 34 teaching assistantships with full tuition reimbursements available (averaging $8,688 per year). Financial award applicants required to submit FAFSA. *Unit head:* Dr. Karen Sears, Interim Chairperson, 309-298-1593. *Application contact:* Dr. Nancy Parsons, Associate Provost and Director of Graduate Studies, 309-298-1806, Fax: 309-298-2345, E-mail: grad-office@wiu.edu.
Website: http://wiu.edu/psychology

Western Kentucky University, Graduate Studies, College of Education and Behavioral Sciences, Department of Psychology, Bowling Green, KY 42101. Offers clinical psychology (MA); experimental psychology (MA); general psychology (MA); industrial/organizational psychology (MA); school psychology (Ed S). *Degree requirements:* For master's, comprehensive exam, thesis (for some programs); for Ed S, thesis, oral exam. *Entrance requirements:* For master's, GRE General Test; for Ed S, GRE General Test, minimum GPA of 3.5. Additional exam requirements/recommendations for international students: Required—TOEFL (minimum score 555 paper-based; 79 iBT). *Faculty research:* Neural regeneration, enhancing mobility in the elderly, improvement in visual processing in older adults, lifespan development.

Western Michigan University, Graduate College, College of Arts and Sciences, Department of Psychology, Kalamazoo, MI 49008. Offers behavior analysis (MA, PhD); clinical psychology (PhD); industrial/organizational behavior management (MA). *Accreditation:* APA (one or more programs are accredited). *Degree requirements:* For master's, variable foreign language requirement, thesis; for doctorate, 2 foreign languages, comprehensive exam, thesis/dissertation. *Application deadline:* For fall admission, 2/15 for domestic students. *Financial support:* Application deadline: 2/15. *Application contact:* Admissions and Orientation, 269-387-2000, Fax: 269-387-2096.

Western Washington University, Graduate School, College of Humanities and Social Sciences, Department of Psychology, Bellingham, WA 98225-5996. Offers experimental psychology (MS); mental health counseling (MS); school counseling (M Ed). *Accreditation:* ACA (one or more programs are accredited). *Degree requirements:* For master's, comprehensive exam, thesis (for some programs). *Entrance requirements:* For master's, GRE General Test, minimum GPA of 3.0 in last 60 semester hours or last 90 quarter hours. Additional exam requirements/recommendations for international students: Required—TOEFL (minimum score 567 paper-based). *Faculty research:* Social, cognitive, behavioral neuroscience, counseling/clinical, developmental.

Westfield State University, Division of Graduate and Continuing Education, Department of Psychology, Westfield, MA 01086. Offers applied behavior analysis (MA); mental health counseling (MA); school guidance (MA). Part-time and evening/weekend programs available. *Degree requirements:* For master's, comprehensive exam.

Entrance requirements: For master's, GRE General Test, MAT, minimum undergraduate GPA of 2.7.

West Texas A&M University, College of Education and Social Sciences, Department of Psychology, Sociology and Social Work, Canyon, TX 79016-0001. Offers psychology (MA); social work (MS). Part-time and evening/weekend programs available. *Degree requirements:* For master's, comprehensive exam, thesis optional. *Entrance requirements:* For master's, GRE General Test, 3 letters of recommendation; interview; minimum GPA of 3.25 in psychology, 3.0 overall. Additional exam requirements/recommendations for international students: Required—TOEFL (minimum score 550 paper-based). Electronic applications accepted. *Faculty research:* Application of sociological principles to historical and contemporary analyses of social systems.

West Virginia University, Eberly College of Arts and Sciences, Department of Psychology, Morgantown, WV 26506. Offers behavior analysis (PhD); clinical psychology (MA, PhD); development psychology (PhD); psychology (MS). *Accreditation:* APA (one or more programs are accredited). Part-time programs available. Terminal master's awarded for partial completion of doctoral program. *Degree requirements:* For master's, thesis optional; for doctorate, comprehensive exam, thesis/dissertation. *Entrance requirements:* For master's and doctorate, GRE General Test, minimum GPA of 3.0. Additional exam requirements/recommendations for international students: Required—TOEFL. *Faculty research:* Adult and child clinical psychology, behavioral assessment and therapy, child and adolescent behavior, life span development, experimental and applied behavior analysis.

Wheaton College, Graduate School, Department of Psychology, Wheaton, IL 60187-5593. Offers clinical mental health counseling (MA); clinical psychology (MA, Psy D); counseling ministries (MA); marriage and family therapy (MA). *Accreditation:* APA (one or more programs are accredited). *Students:* 104 full-time (78 women), 22 part-time (14 women); includes 25 minority (13 Black or African American, non-Hispanic/Latino; 8 Asian, non-Hispanic/Latino; 2 Hispanic/Latino; 2 Two or more races, non-Hispanic/Latino), 8 international. Average age 27. 141 applicants, 74% accepted, 64 enrolled. In 2014, 47 master's, 16 doctorates awarded. Terminal master's awarded for partial completion of doctoral program. *Degree requirements:* For master's, thesis or alternative; for doctorate, thesis/dissertation, internship. *Entrance requirements:* For master's, GRE General Test, 18 hours of course work in psychology; for doctorate, GRE General Test. Additional exam requirements/recommendations for international students: Required—TOEFL (minimum score 550 paper-based; 80 iBT), IELTS (minimum score 6.5), TOEFL (minimum score 600 paper-based; 90 iBT) or IELTS (minimum score 7.5) for Psy D. *Application deadline:* For fall admission, 3/1 priority date for domestic students, 1/1 for international students. Applications are processed on a rolling basis. Application fee: $30. *Financial support:* In 2014–15, 3 research assistantships (averaging $4,800 per year) were awarded; career-related internships or fieldwork, Federal Work-Study, scholarships/grants, and unspecified assistantships also available. Financial award application deadline: 3/1; financial award applicants required to submit FAFSA. *Unit head:* Dr. Terri Watson, Associate Dean of Psychology, 630-752-5104. *Application contact:* Dusty Di Santo, Director of Graduate Admissions, 630-752-5195, Fax: 630-752-7047, E-mail: graduate.admissions@wheaton.edu.
Website: http://www.wheaton.edu/academics/departments/psychology

Wichita State University, Graduate School, Fairmount College of Liberal Arts and Sciences, Department of Psychology, Wichita, KS 67260. Offers clinical (PhD); community (PhD); human factors (PhD). *Accreditation:* APA. Part-time programs available. *Unit head:* Dr. Alex Chaparro, Chair, 316-978-3170, Fax: 316-978-3006, E-mail: alex.chaparro@wichita.edu. *Application contact:* Jordan Oleson, Admissions Coordinator, 316-978-3095, Fax: 316-978-3253, E-mail: jordan.oleson@wichita.edu.
Website: http://www.wichita.edu/psychology

Widener University, School of Human Service Professions, Institute for Graduate Clinical Psychology, Law-Psychology Program, Chester, PA 19013-5792. Offers JD/Psy D. Electronic applications accepted.

Wilfrid Laurier University, Faculty of Graduate and Postdoctoral Studies, Faculty of Science, Department of Psychology, Waterloo, ON N2L 3C5, Canada. Offers behavioral neuroscience (M Sc, PhD); cognitive neuroscience (M Sc, PhD); community psychology (MA, PhD); social and developmental psychology (MA, PhD). Part-time programs available. *Degree requirements:* For master's, thesis; for doctorate, thesis/dissertation. *Entrance requirements:* For master's, GRE General Test, honors BA or the equivalent in psychology, minimum B average in undergraduate course work; for doctorate, GRE General Test, master's degree, minimum A- average. Additional exam requirements/recommendations for international students: Required—TOEFL (minimum score 89 iBT). Electronic applications accepted. *Faculty research:* Brain and cognition, community psychology, social and developmental psychology.

William Carey University, School of Psychology and Counseling, Hattiesburg, MS 39401-5499. Offers counseling psychology (MS). Part-time programs available. *Entrance requirements:* For master's, GRE, PRAXIS, MAT, minimum GPA of 2.5. Additional exam requirements/recommendations for international students: Required—TOEFL (minimum score 550 paper-based). *Expenses:* Contact institution. *Faculty research:* Addiction prevention, psychometric measurement, crisis counseling, gerontology.

Winthrop University, College of Arts and Sciences, Department of Psychology, Rock Hill, SC 29733. Offers MS, SSP. *Degree requirements:* For master's and SSP, comprehensive exam. *Entrance requirements:* For master's, GRE General Test, interview, minimum GPA of 3.0, 3 letters of recommendation, 15 hours of psychology courses in specified subject areas. Electronic applications accepted.

Wisconsin School of Professional Psychology, Program in Clinical Psychology, Milwaukee, WI 53225-4960. Offers MA, Psy D. *Accreditation:* APA. Part-time and evening/weekend programs available. Terminal master's awarded for partial completion of doctoral program. *Degree requirements:* For master's, candidacy exam, 500 hours of supervised clinical practica; for doctorate, thesis/dissertation, 1 year clinical intern and practicum experience (2000 hrs), candidacy and clinical exams. *Entrance requirements:* For master's, GRE General Test, GRE Subject Test, bachelor's degree in psychology, writing sample; for doctorate, GRE General Test, GRE Subject Test, master's degree in clinical psychology or equivalent, writing sample. *Faculty research:* Violence prevention, psychology of women, forensic psychology, custody evaluation, aging, harm reduction in AODA.

Wright Institute, Doctoral Program in Clinical Psychology, Berkeley, CA 94704-1796. Offers Psy D. *Accreditation:* APA. *Degree requirements:* For doctorate, comprehensive exam, thesis/dissertation. *Entrance requirements:* For doctorate, GRE General Test, statistics, human development, theories of personality or abnormal psychology. Additional exam requirements/recommendations for international students: Required—TOEFL (minimum score 600 paper-based). Electronic applications accepted. *Faculty research:* Time-limited dynamic psychotherapy; mindfulness/ACT; psychotherapy integration; empathy, altruism and survivor guilt; culturally-informed practice.

Wright State University, School of Graduate Studies, College of Science and Mathematics, Department of Psychology, Dayton, OH 45435. Offers human factors and industrial/organizational psychology (MS, PhD). *Degree requirements:* For master's, thesis; for doctorate, thesis/dissertation. *Entrance requirements:* For master's, GRE General Test. Additional exam requirements/recommendations for international students: Required—TOEFL.

Wright State University, School of Professional Psychology, Dayton, OH 45435. Offers clinical psychology (Psy D). *Accreditation:* APA. *Degree requirements:* For doctorate, thesis/dissertation. *Entrance requirements:* For doctorate, GRE General Test, GRE Subject Test. Additional exam requirements/recommendations for international students: Required—TOEFL. *Expenses:* Contact institution.

Xavier University, College of Social Sciences, Health and Education, Department of Psychology, Cincinnati, OH 45207. Offers clinical psychology (Psy D); industrial-organizational psychology (MA). *Accreditation:* APA (one or more programs are accredited). *Faculty:* 16 full-time (9 women), 7 part-time/adjunct (3 women). *Students:* 89 full-time (67 women), 38 part-time (24 women); includes 18 minority (4 Black or African American, non-Hispanic/Latino; 7 Asian, non-Hispanic/Latino; 4 Hispanic/Latino; 3 Two or more races, non-Hispanic/Latino), 1 international. Average age 26. 235 applicants, 26% accepted, 35 enrolled. In 2014, 29 master's, 15 doctorates awarded. *Degree requirements:* For master's, one foreign language, comprehensive exam, thesis, internship; for doctorate, one foreign language, comprehensive exam, thesis/dissertation, internship. *Entrance requirements:* For master's, GRE, official transcript; 3 letters of recommendation; for doctorate, GRE General Test; GRE Subject Test in psychology (if no undergraduate degree in psychology), bachelor's or master's degree; 18 semester hours of psychology coursework; minimum GPA of 3.0; work and research experience; official transcript; 3 letters of recommendation; statement of purpose. Additional exam requirements/recommendations for international students: Required—TOEFL (minimum score 550 paper-based; 79 iBT), IELTS (minimum score 6.5). *Application deadline:* For fall admission, 12/1 for domestic and international students. Application fee: $35. Electronic applications accepted. *Expenses:* Expenses: $600 per credit hour (for MA); $760 per credit hour (for Psy D). *Financial support:* In 2014–15, 62 students received support, including 26 research assistantships with partial tuition reimbursements available, 4 teaching assistantships with partial tuition reimbursements available; career-related internships or fieldwork, traineeships, and unspecified assistantships also available. Financial award application deadline: 3/1; financial award applicants required to submit FAFSA. *Faculty research:* Older adults, clinical child and adolescent issues, personnel selection and employee behavior, at-risk youth, sexual abuse. *Unit head:* Dr. Karl Stukenberg, Chair, 513-745-1041, Fax: 513-745-3327, E-mail: stukenb@xavier.edu. *Application contact:* Margaret Maybury, Director, Academic Programs, 513-745-1053, Fax: 513-745-3347, E-mail: maybury@xavier.edu.
Website: http://www.xavier.edu/psychology-grad/

Yale University, Graduate School of Arts and Sciences, Department of Psychology, New Haven, CT 06520. Offers behavioral neuroscience (PhD); clinical psychology (PhD); cognitive psychology (PhD); developmental psychology (PhD); social/personality psychology (PhD). *Accreditation:* APA. *Degree requirements:* For doctorate, thesis/dissertation. *Entrance requirements:* For doctorate, GRE General Test.

Yeshiva University, Ferkauf Graduate School of Psychology, New York, NY 10033-3201. Offers MA, PhD, Psy D. *Accreditation:* APA (one or more programs are accredited). Part-time programs available. *Degree requirements:* For doctorate, comprehensive exam, thesis/dissertation. *Entrance requirements:* For master's and doctorate, GRE General Test.

York University, Faculty of Graduate Studies, Faculty of Health, Program in Psychology, Toronto, ON M3J 1P3, Canada. Offers MA, PhD. *Accreditation:* APA (one or more programs are accredited). Part-time programs available. *Degree requirements:* For master's, thesis, practicum; for doctorate, thesis/dissertation, practicum. *Entrance requirements:* For master's, GRE. Electronic applications accepted.

Youngstown State University, Graduate School, College of Liberal Arts and Social Sciences, Department of Psychology, Youngstown, OH 44555-0001. Offers applied behavior analysis (MS).

Addictions/Substance Abuse Counseling

Adler Graduate School, Program in Adlerian Counseling and Psychotherapy, Richfield, MN 55423. Offers Adlerian studies (MA); art therapy (MA); clinical counseling (MA); co-occurring substance abuse and mental health disorders (MA); marriage and family therapy (MA); school counseling (MA). Part-time and evening/weekend programs available. *Faculty:* 7 full-time (6 women), 68 part-time/adjunct (49 women). *Students:* 368 part-time (283 women); includes 61 minority (41 Black or African American, non-Hispanic/Latino; 4 American Indian or Alaska Native, non-Hispanic/Latino; 8 Asian, non-Hispanic/Latino; 8 Hispanic/Latino). Average age 40. In 2014, 90 master's awarded. *Degree requirements:* For master's, thesis or alternative, 500-700 hour internship (depending on license choice). *Entrance requirements:* For master's, personal goal statement, three letters of reference, resume or work history, official transcripts. *Application deadline:* Applications are processed on a rolling basis. Application fee: $50. Electronic applications accepted. *Expenses: Tuition:* Full-time $6060; part-time $505 per credit. *Financial support:* Career-related internships or fieldwork and tuition waivers available. Support available to part-time students. Financial award applicants required to submit FAFSA. *Unit head:* Dr. Dan Haugen, President, 612-767-7048, Fax: 612-861-7559, E-mail: haugen@alfredadler.edu. *Application contact:* Evelyn B. Haas, Director of Admissions, 612-767-7044, Fax: 612-861-7559, E-mail: ev@alfredadler.edu.

★ **Adler University,** Programs in Psychology, Chicago, IL 60602. Offers advanced Adlerian psychotherapy (Certificate); art therapy (MA); clinical neuropsychology (Certificate); clinical psychology (Psy D); community psychology (MA); counseling and organizational psychology (MA); counseling psychology (MA); criminology (MA); emergency management leadership (MA); forensic psychology (MA); marriage and family counseling (MA); marriage and family therapy (Certificate); military psychology (MA); nonprofit management (MA); organizational psychology (MA); police psychology (MA); public policy and administration (MA);

rehabilitation counseling (MA); sport and health psychology (MA); substance abuse counseling (Certificate); Psy D/Certificate; Psy D/MACAT; Psy D/MACP; Psy D/MAMFC; Psy D/MASAC. *Accreditation:* APA. Part-time and evening/weekend programs available. Postbaccalaureate distance learning degree programs offered (minimal on-campus study). Terminal master's awarded for partial completion of doctoral program. *Degree requirements:* For master's, thesis or alternative, oral exam, practicum; for doctorate, thesis/dissertation, clinical exam, internship, oral exam, practicum, written qualifying exam. *Entrance requirements:* For master's, 12 semester hours in psychology, minimum GPA of 3.0; for doctorate, 18 semester hours in psychology, minimum GPA of 3.25; for Certificate, appropriate master's or doctoral degree. Additional exam requirements/recommendations for international students: Required—TOEFL (minimum score 550 paper-based; 79 iBT). Electronic applications accepted.

See Display on page 969 and Close-Up on page 1207.

Alliant International University–Los Angeles, California School of Professional Psychology, Program in Couple and Family Therapy, Alhambra, CA 91803-1360. Offers chemical dependency (MA); gerontology (MA); Latin American family therapy (MA). *Accreditation:* AAMFT/COAMFTE. Part-time and evening/weekend programs available. Terminal master's awarded for partial completion of doctoral program. *Degree requirements:* For master's, comprehensive exam, 50 hours of professional development activities. *Entrance requirements:* Additional exam requirements/recommendations for international students: Required—TOEFL (minimum score 550 paper-based). Electronic applications accepted. *Faculty research:* Foster care, therapy with minority couples, parenting, marriage, trauma.

Antioch University New England, Graduate School, Department of Applied Psychology, Program in Clinical Mental Health Counseling, Keene, NH 03431-3552. Offers clinical mental health counseling (MA); substance abuse counseling (MA). *Accreditation:* ACA. *Degree requirements:* For master's, internship, practicum. *Entrance requirements:* For master's, previous course work and work experience in psychology. Additional exam requirements/recommendations for international students: Required—TOEFL (minimum score 550 paper-based). Electronic applications accepted. *Expenses:* Contact institution. *Faculty research:* Multicultural issues in field supervision.

Argosy University, Hawai`i, College of Psychology and Behavioral Sciences, Program in Substance Abuse Counseling, Honolulu, HI 96813. Offers Certificate.

Arkansas State University, Graduate School, College of Nursing and Health Professions, Department of Social Work, State University, AR 72467. Offers addiction studies (Certificate); social work (MSW). *Accreditation:* CSWE. Part-time programs available. *Faculty:* 7 full-time (5 women). *Students:* 30 full-time (21 women), 37 part-time (33 women); includes 26 minority (24 Black or African American, non-Hispanic/Latino; 2 Hispanic/Latino). Average age 32. 64 applicants, 66% accepted, 40 enrolled. In 2014, 29 master's awarded. *Degree requirements:* For master's and Certificate, comprehensive exam, thesis (for some programs). *Entrance requirements:* For master's and Certificate, GRE or MAT, appropriate bachelor's degree, letters of reference, personal statement, resume, official transcript, immunization records. Additional exam requirements/recommendations for international students: Required—TOEFL (minimum score 550 paper-based; 79 iBT), IELTS (minimum score 6), PTE (minimum score 56). *Application deadline:* For fall admission, 3/1 for domestic and international students; for spring admission, 10/1 for domestic and international students. Applications are processed on a rolling basis. Application fee: $30 ($40 for international students). Electronic applications accepted. *Expenses:* Expenses: Contact institution. *Financial support:* In 2014–15, 2 students received support. Career-related internships or fieldwork, scholarships/grants, and unspecified assistantships available. Financial award application deadline: 7/1; financial award applicants required to submit FAFSA. *Unit head:* Dr. Loretta Brewer, Interim Chair, 870-972-3984, Fax: 870-972-3987, E-mail: lbrewer@astate.edu. *Application contact:* Vickey Ring, Graduate Admissions Coordinator, 870-972-3029, Fax: 870-972-3857, E-mail: vickeyring@astate.edu.
Website: http://www.astate.edu/college/conhp/departments/social-work/

Cambridge College, School of Psychology and Counseling, Cambridge, MA 02138-5304. Offers addiction counseling (M Ed); alcohol and drug counseling (Certificate); counseling psychology (M Ed, CAGS); counseling psychology: forensic counseling (M Ed); marriage and family therapy (M Ed); mental health and addiction counseling (M Ed); mental health counseling (M Ed); mental health counseling for school guidance counselors (Post Master's Certificate); psychological studies (M Ed); school adjustment and mental health counseling (M Ed); school adjustment, mental health and addiction counseling (M Ed); school guidance counselor (M Ed); trauma studies (Certificate). Part-time and evening/weekend programs available. *Degree requirements:* For master's and other advanced degree, thesis, practicum/internship. *Entrance requirements:* For master's, resume, 2 professional references; for other advanced degree, official transcripts, documents for transfer credit evaluation, resume, written personal statement/essay, 2 professional references, health insurance, immunizations form. Additional exam requirements/recommendations for international students: Required—TOEFL (minimum score 550 paper-based; 79 iBT), Michigan English Language Assessment Battery (minimum score 85); Recommended—IELTS (minimum score 6). Electronic applications accepted. *Expenses:* Contact institution. *Faculty research:* Trauma, drug and alcohol counseling, cross-cultural issues, school counseling, trauma in schools.

Capella University, Harold Abel School of Social and Behavioral Science, Doctoral Programs in Psychology, Minneapolis, MN 55402. Offers addiction psychology (PhD); clinical psychology (Psy D); educational psychology (PhD); general advanced studies in human behavior (PhD); general psychology (PhD); industrial/organizational psychology (PhD); school psychology (Psy D).

Capella University, Harold Abel School of Social and Behavioral Science, Master's Programs in Counseling, Minneapolis, MN 55402. Offers child and adolescent development (MS); general addiction counseling (MS); general marriage and family counseling/therapy (MS); general mental health counseling (MS); general school counseling (MS).

Carlow University, College of Leadership and Social Change, Program in Alcohol and Drug Counseling, Pittsburgh, PA 15213. Offers Certificate. Part-time and evening/weekend programs available. Postbaccalaureate distance learning degree programs offered (no on-campus study). *Students:* 1 (woman) full-time, 2 part-time (both women); all minorities (2 Black or African American, non-Hispanic/Latino; 1 Hispanic/Latino). Average age 30. 4 applicants, 75% accepted, 1 enrolled. In 2014, 4 Certificates awarded. *Entrance requirements:* Additional exam requirements/recommendations for international students: Required—TOEFL. *Application deadline:* Applications are processed on a rolling basis. Electronic applications accepted. Application fee is waived when completed online. *Expenses: Tuition:* Full-time $9750; part-time $785 per credit. Part-time tuition and fees vary according to degree level and program. *Unit head:* Dr. Joseph M. Roberts, Chair, Department of Psychology and Counseling, 412-575-6331, E-mail: jmroberts@carlow.edu. *Application contact:* Dr. Kathleen A. Chrisman, Associate Director, Graduate Admissions, 412-578-8812, Fax: 412-578-6321, E-mail: kachrisman@carlow.edu.
Website: http://www.carlow.edu/Alcohol_and_Drug_Counseling_Certificate_.aspx

Carlow University, College of Leadership and Social Change, Program in Professional Counseling, Pittsburgh, PA 15213-3165. Offers drug and alcohol counseling (MS); professional counseling (MS, Certificate); school counseling (MS); school counselor (Certificate). Part-time and evening/weekend programs available. *Students:* 177 full-time (149 women), 35 part-time (31 women); includes 45 minority (29 Black or African American, non-Hispanic/Latino; 2 Asian, non-Hispanic/Latino; 7 Hispanic/Latino; 7 Two or more races, non-Hispanic/Latino). Average age 31. 90 applicants, 96% accepted, 42 enrolled. In 2014, 56 master's awarded. *Entrance requirements:* For master's, personal essay; resume or curriculum vitae; three recommendations; official transcripts; interview; minimum undergraduate GPA of 3.0; undergraduate courses in statistics, abnormal psychology, and personality theory; undergraduate work or work experience in the helping professions. Additional exam requirements/recommendations for international students: Required—TOEFL (minimum score 550 paper-based). Application fee is waived when completed online. *Expenses: Tuition:* Full-time $9750; part-time $785 per credit. Part-time tuition and fees vary according to degree level and program. *Unit head:* Dr. Joseph Roberts, Director, Master in Professional Counseling Program, 412-575-6331, E-mail: jmroberts@carlow.edu. *Application contact:* Dr. Kathleen A. Chrisman, Associate Director, Graduate Admissions, 412-578-8812, Fax: 412-578-8822, E-mail: kachrisman@carlow.edu.
Website: http://www.carlow.edu/Master_of_Science_in_Professional_Counseling.aspx

Chestnut Hill College, School of Graduate Studies, Division of Psychology, Program in Clinical and Counseling Psychology, Philadelphia, PA 19118-2693. Offers addictions treatment (MS, CAS); child and adolescent therapy (MS, CAS); marriage and family therapy (MS, CAS); trauma studies (MS, CAS); treatment of autism spectrum disorders (MS, CAS). Part-time and evening/weekend programs available. *Faculty:* 4 full-time (3 women), 34 part-time/adjunct (24 women). *Students:* 88 full-time (73 women), 136 part-time (113 women); includes 41 minority (27 Black or African American, non-Hispanic/Latino; 1 Asian, non-Hispanic/Latino; 12 Hispanic/Latino; 1 Two or more races, non-Hispanic/Latino), 2 international. Average age 33. 119 applicants, 98% accepted, 70 enrolled. In 2014, 1,021 master's, 7 other advanced degrees awarded. *Degree requirements:* For master's, thesis optional, practica. *Entrance requirements:* For master's, GRE General Test, writing sample, letters of recommendation. Additional exam requirements/recommendations for international students: Required—TOEFL (minimum score 500 paper-based), IELTS (mnimum score 6.0), or TWE (minimum score 22). *Application deadline:* For fall admission, 7/1 for domestic and international students; for spring admission, 11/1 for domestic and international students; for summer admission, 4/1 for domestic and international students. Applications are processed on a rolling basis. Application fee: $55. Electronic applications accepted. *Expenses:* Expenses: Contact institution. *Financial support:* Unspecified assistantships available. *Faculty research:* Play therapy, eating disorders, addictions, group psychology and group therapy, health psychology. *Unit head:* Dr. Cheryll Rothery, Chair, Psychology Division, 215-248-7023, Fax: 215-248-3619, E-mail: rotheryc@chc.edu. *Application contact:* Amy Boorse, Assistant Director of Graduate Admissions, 215-248-7097, Fax: 215-248-7161, E-mail: gradadmissions@chc.edu.
Website: http://www.chc.edu/Graduate/Programs/Masters/Clinical_and_Counseling_Psychology/

Cleveland State University, College of Graduate Studies, College of Education and Human Services, Department of Counseling, Administration, Supervision and Adult Learning (CASAL), Cleveland, OH 44115. Offers adult learning and development (M Ed); chemical dependency counseling (Certificate); clinical mental health counseling (M Ed); early childhood mental health counseling (Certificate); educational administration and supervision (M Ed); organizational leadership (M Ed); school administration (Ed S); school counseling (M Ed). *Accreditation:* ACA (one or more programs are accredited). Part-time and evening/weekend programs available. *Faculty:* 15 full-time (8 women), 19 part-time/adjunct (10 women). *Students:* 76 full-time (59 women), 214 part-time (174 women); includes 110 minority (93 Black or African American, non-Hispanic/Latino; 3 Asian, non-Hispanic/Latino; 13 Hispanic/Latino; 1 Two or more races, non-Hispanic/Latino), 9 international. Average age 34. 57 applicants, 93% accepted, 51 enrolled. In 2014, 99 master's, 4 Certificates awarded. *Degree requirements:* For master's, comprehensive exam (for some programs), thesis optional, internship. *Entrance requirements:* For master's, GRE General Test or MAT, letter of recommendation and minimum GPA of 2.75 (for counseling); 2 letters of recommendation and interviews (for organizational leadership). Additional exam requirements/recommendations for international students: Required—TOEFL (minimum score 525 paper-based), IELTS (minimum score 6). *Application deadline:* For fall admission, 6/21 for domestic students, 5/15 for international students; for spring admission, 8/31 for domestic students, 11/1 for international students. Application fee: $30. Electronic applications accepted. *Expenses:* Tuition, state resident: full-time $9566; part-time $531 per credit hour. Tuition, nonresident: full-time $17,980; part-time $999 per credit hour. *Required fees:* $25 per semester. Tuition and fees vary according to degree level and program. *Financial support:* In 2014–15, 19 students received support, including 10 research assistantships with full and partial tuition reimbursements available (averaging $11,882 per year), 5 teaching assistantships with full and partial tuition reimbursements available (averaging $11,882 per year); scholarships/grants and unspecified assistantships also available. Support available to part-time students. *Faculty research:* Education law, career development, bullying, psychopharmacology, counseling and spirituality. *Total annual research expenditures:* $225,821. *Unit head:* Dr. Ann L. Bauer, Chairperson, 216-687-4582, Fax: 216-687-5378, E-mail: a.l.bauer@csuohio.edu. *Application contact:* Deborah L. Brown, Interim Assistant Director, Graduate Admissions, 216-523-7572, Fax: 216-687-5400, E-mail: d.l.brown@csuohio.edu.
Website: http://www.csuohio.edu/cehs/departments/CASAL/casal_dept.html

The College of New Jersey, Graduate Studies, School of Education, Department of Counselor Education, Program in Community Counseling: Substance Abuse and Addiction Specialization, Ewing, NJ 08628. Offers MA, Certificate. Part-time programs available. *Students:* 1 (woman) full-time, 3 part-time (all women); includes 1 minority (Black or African American, non-Hispanic/Latino). 3 applicants, 67% accepted, 1 enrolled. In 2014, 1 other advanced degree awarded. *Degree requirements:* For master's, comprehensive exam. *Entrance requirements:* For master's, GRE, minimum GPA of 3.0 in field or 2.75 overall; for Certificate, previous master's degree or higher. Additional exam requirements/recommendations for international students: Required—TOEFL. *Application deadline:* For fall admission, 2/1 for domestic students; for spring admission, 10/1 for domestic students. Application fee: $75. Electronic applications accepted. *Financial support:* Tuition waivers (partial) and unspecified assistantships available. Financial award application deadline: 5/1; financial award applicants required to submit FAFSA. *Unit head:* Dr. Marion Cavallaro, Coordinator, 609-771-2406, Fax: 609-637-5166, E-mail: cavallar@tcnj.edu. *Application contact:* Susan L. Hydro, Director of Graduate and Intersession Programs, 609-771-2300, Fax: 609-637-5105, E-mail: graduate@tcnj.edu.

College of St. Joseph, Graduate Programs, Division of Psychology and Human Services, Program in Alcohol and Substance Abuse Counseling, Rutland, VT 05701-3899. Offers MS. Part-time programs available. *Degree requirements:* For master's, comprehensive exam. *Entrance requirements:* For master's, official college transcripts; 2 letters of reference. Additional exam requirements/recommendations for international

students: Required—TOEFL (minimum score 550 paper-based). Electronic applications accepted.

Coppin State University, Division of Graduate Studies, Division of Arts and Sciences, Department of Applied Psychology and Rehabilitation Counseling, Program in Alcohol and Substance Abuse Counseling, Baltimore, MD 21216-3698. Offers MS. Part-time programs available. *Degree requirements:* For master's, comprehensive exam (for some programs), thesis optional, internship, clinical requirement. *Entrance requirements:* For master's, GRE General Test, interview, minimum GPA of 3.0.

East Carolina University, Graduate School, College of Allied Health Sciences, Department of Addictions and Rehabilitation Studies, Greenville, NC 27858-4353. Offers military and trauma counseling (Certificate); rehabilitation and career counseling (MS); rehabilitation counseling (Certificate); rehabilitation counseling and administration (PhD); substance abuse and clinical counseling (MS); substance abuse counseling (Certificate); vocational evaluation (Certificate). *Accreditation:* CORE. Part-time and evening/weekend programs available. *Degree requirements:* For master's, comprehensive exam, thesis or alternative, internship. *Entrance requirements:* For master's, GRE General Test or MAT. Additional exam requirements/recommendations for international students: Required—TOEFL. *Application deadline:* For fall admission, 3/1 priority date for domestic students; for spring admission, 10/1 priority date for domestic students. Applications are processed on a rolling basis. Application fee: $50. *Expenses:* Tuition, state resident: full-time $4223. Tuition, nonresident: full-time $16,540. *Required fees:* $2184. *Financial support:* Research assistantships with partial tuition reimbursements, teaching assistantships with partial tuition reimbursements, Federal Work-Study, and scholarships/grants available. Support available to part-time students. Financial award application deadline: 3/1. *Unit head:* Dr. Paul Toriello, Chair, 252-744-6292, E-mail: toriellop@ecu.edu.
Website: http://www.ecu.edu/rehb/

East Carolina University, Graduate School, College of Human Ecology, School of Social Work, Greenville, NC 27858-4353. Offers gerontology (Certificate); social work (MSW); substance abuse (Certificate). *Accreditation:* CSWE. Postbaccalaureate distance learning degree programs offered (no on-campus study). *Degree requirements:* For master's, comprehensive exam. *Entrance requirements:* For master's, GRE or MAT. Additional exam requirements/recommendations for international students: Required—TOEFL. *Expenses:* Tuition, state resident: full-time $4223. Tuition, nonresident: full-time $16,540. *Required fees:* $2184. *Faculty research:* Social research, gerontology, women's issues, social services in schools, human behavior.

Fairfield University, Graduate School of Education and Allied Professions, Fairfield, CT 06824. Offers applied behavior analysis (ATC); applied psychology (MA); clinical mental health counseling (MA, CAS); early childhood studies (ATC); educational technology (MA); elementary education (MA, CAS); family studies (MA); integration of spirituality and religion in counseling (ATC); marriage and family therapy (MA); school counseling (MA, CAS); school psychology (MA, CAS); school-based marriage and family therapy (ATC); secondary education (MA); special education (MA, CAS); substance abuse counseling (ATC); teaching (Certificate); teaching and foundations (MA, CAS); TESOL, world languages, and bilingual education (MA, CAS). *Accreditation:* NCATE. Part-time and evening/weekend programs available. *Faculty:* 23 full-time (19 women), 32 part-time/adjunct (25 women). *Students:* 148 full-time (131 women), 286 part-time (238 women); includes 81 minority (18 Black or African American, non-Hispanic/Latino; 1 American Indian or Alaska Native, non-Hispanic/Latino; 14 Asian, non-Hispanic/Latino; 39 Hispanic/Latino; 9 Two or more races, non-Hispanic/Latino), 13 international. Average age 34. 264 applicants, 54% accepted, 68 enrolled. In 2014, 142 master's awarded. *Degree requirements:* For master's, comprehensive exam. *Entrance requirements:* For master's, PRAXIS I (for certification programs), minimum GPA of 3.0, 2 recommendations, resume. Additional exam requirements/recommendations for international students: Required—TOEFL (minimum score 550 paper-based; 84 iBT) or IELTS (minimum score 7.5). *Application deadline:* For fall admission, 2/15 for international students; for spring admission, 10/1 for international students. Application fee: $60. Electronic applications accepted. *Expenses:* Expenses: $675 per credit hour. *Financial support:* In 2014–15, 55 students received support. Career-related internships or fieldwork and unspecified assistantships available. Financial award applicants required to submit FAFSA. *Faculty research:* Literacy, spirituality, special education, bilingual/multicultural education, mentoring and professional development. *Unit head:* Dr. Robert D. Hannafin, Dean, 203-254-4250, Fax: 203-254-4241, E-mail: rhannafin@fairfield.edu. *Application contact:* Marianne Gumpper, Director of Graduate and Continuing Studies Admission, 203-254-4184, Fax: 203-254-4073, E-mail: gradadmis@fairfield.edu.
Website: http://www.fairfield.edu/academics/schoolscollegescenters/graduateschoolofeducationalliedprofessions/graduateprograms/

The George Washington University, Graduate School of Education and Human Development, Department of Counseling and Human Development, Program in Rehabilitation Counseling, Washington, DC 20052. Offers autism spectrum disorder (MA Ed/HD); substance abuse and psychiatric disabilities (MA Ed/HD); traumatic brain injury (MA Ed/HD). *Accreditation:* CORE. Postbaccalaureate distance learning degree programs offered. *Students:* 10 full-time (8 women), 21 part-time (14 women); includes 10 minority (7 Black or African American, non-Hispanic/Latino; 2 Asian, non-Hispanic/Latino; 1 Two or more races, non-Hispanic/Latino), 2 international. Average age 31. 27 applicants, 89% accepted, 10 enrolled. In 2014, 17 master's awarded. *Entrance requirements:* For master's, GRE or MAT, two letters of recommendation, 1- to 2-page statement of purpose, official transcripts from all instiutions attended, resume. Additional exam requirements/recommendations for international students: Required—TOEFL or IELTS. Electronic applications accepted. *Unit head:* Dr. Kenneth C. Hergenrather, Director, 202-994-1334, E-mail: hergenkc@gwu.edu. *Application contact:* Sarah Lang, Director of Graduate Admissions, 202-994-1447, Fax: 202-994-7207, E-mail: slang@gwu.edu.
Website: http://gsehd.gwu.edu/rehabilitation-counseling-masters

Governors State University, College of Health Professions, Program in Addictions Studies, University Park, IL 60484. Offers MHS. Part-time and evening/weekend programs available. *Degree requirements:* For master's, comprehensive exam, thesis or alternative, internship. *Entrance requirements:* For master's, minimum undergraduate GPA of 2.5; 9 hours of course work in behavioral sciences; 6 hours of course work in biological sciences or chemistry, statistics or research methods.

Grand Canyon University, College of Nursing and Health Sciences, Phoenix, AZ 85017-1097. Offers addiction counseling (MS); health care administration (MS); health care informatics (MS); marriage and family therapy (MS); professional counseling (MS); public health (MS). Part-time and evening/weekend programs available. Postbaccalaureate distance learning degree programs offered (no on-campus study). *Entrance requirements:* For master's, undergraduate degree with minimum GPA of 2.8. Additional exam requirements/recommendations for international students: Required—TOEFL (minimum score 575 paper-based; 90 iBT), IELTS (minimum score 7).

Hazelden Graduate School of Addiction Studies, Graduate Programs, Center City, MN 55012. Offers addiction counseling (MA, Certificate). Part-time programs available. *Entrance requirements:* Additional exam requirements/recommendations for international students: Required—TOEFL.

Indiana University Northwest, College of Arts and Sciences, Gary, IN 46408-1197. Offers clinical counseling (MS), including drug and alcohol counseling; liberal studies (MLS). *Students:* 7 full-time (5 women), 23 part-time (18 women); includes 15 minority (13 Black or African American, non-Hispanic/Latino; 2 Hispanic/Latino). 10 applicants, 80% accepted, 5 enrolled. In 2014, 2 master's awarded. *Unit head:* Robert Mucci, Graduate Program Director, 219-980-6607, E-mail: rmucci@iun.edu.
Website: http://www.iun.edu/coas/

Indiana University–Purdue University Indianapolis, School of Science, Department of Psychology, Indianapolis, IN 46202-3275. Offers clinical psychology (MS); industrial/organizational psychology (MS); psychobiology of addictions (PhD). *Accreditation:* APA (one or more programs are accredited). *Faculty:* 25 full-time (13 women), 2 part-time/adjunct (both women). *Students:* 51 full-time (34 women), 9 part-time (6 women); includes 10 minority (3 Black or African American, non-Hispanic/Latino; 5 Asian, non-Hispanic/Latino; 1 Hispanic/Latino; 1 Two or more races, non-Hispanic/Latino), 2 international. Average age 28. 189 applicants, 10% accepted, 19 enrolled. In 2014, 15 master's, 4 doctorates awarded. Terminal master's awarded for partial completion of doctoral program. *Degree requirements:* For master's, thesis; for doctorate, thesis/dissertation. *Entrance requirements:* For master's, GRE General Test, minimum undergraduate GPA of 3.0; for doctorate, GRE General Test, GRE Subject Test (clinical psychology), minimum undergraduate GPA of 3.2. Additional exam requirements/recommendations for international students: Required—TOEFL (minimum score 567 paper-based; 86 iBT), IELTS (minimum score 6.5). *Application deadline:* For fall admission, 12/1 priority date for domestic and international students. Application fee: $60. Electronic applications accepted. *Financial support:* In 2014–15, 3 fellowships with partial tuition reimbursements (averaging $22,500 per year) were awarded; research assistantships with partial tuition reimbursements, teaching assistantships with partial tuition reimbursements, career-related internships or fieldwork, Federal Work-Study, institutionally sponsored loans, traineeships, health care benefits, and unspecified assistantships also available. Financial award application deadline: 3/1; financial award applicants required to submit FAFSA. *Faculty research:* Severe mental illness, health psychology, neurological research, alcoholism and psychopathology, functional activities within organizations. *Unit head:* Dr. Peggy S. Stockdale, Chair, 317-278-3838, E-mail: pstockda@iupui.edu. *Application contact:* Heather Sissons, Office Manager and Graduate Coordinator, 317-274-6945, E-mail: hsissons@iupui.edu.
Website: http://www.psych.iupui.edu/

Indiana Wesleyan University, Graduate School, College of Arts and Sciences, Marion, IN 46953. Offers addictions counseling (MS); clinical mental health counseling (MS); community counseling (MS); marriage and family therapy (MS); school counseling (MS); student development counseling and administration (MS). *Accreditation:* ACA. Part-time programs available. *Degree requirements:* For master's, thesis or alternative. *Entrance requirements:* For master's, GRE General Test. Additional exam requirements/recommendations for international students: Required—TOEFL. Electronic applications accepted. *Expenses:* Contact institution. *Faculty research:* Community counseling, multicultural counseling, addictions.

Johns Hopkins University, Bloomberg School of Public Health, Department of Mental Health, Baltimore, MD 21218-2699. Offers children's mental health services (PhD); drug dependence epidemiology (PhD); mental health (MHS, Dr PH); psychiatric epidemiology (PhD). *Degree requirements:* For master's, thesis (for some programs); for doctorate, thesis/dissertation, 1-year full-time residency, oral and written exams. *Entrance requirements:* For master's, GRE General Test, MCAT, 3 letters of recommendation, curriculum vitae; for doctorate, GRE General Test, MCAT or GMAT, 3 letters of recommendation, curriculum vitae. Additional exam requirements/recommendations for international students: Required—TOEFL (minimum score 600 paper-based; 100 iBT). Electronic applications accepted. *Faculty research:* Etiology, development and prevention of aggressive and antisocial behavior; epidemiology of mental disorders; genetic epidemiology of mental disorders; brain and behavior.

Johnson State College, Program in Counseling, Johnson, VT 05656. Offers college counseling (MA); school guidance counseling (MA); substance abuse and mental health counseling (MA). Part-time programs available. *Degree requirements:* For master's, comprehensive exam. *Entrance requirements:* For master's, interview. Additional exam requirements/recommendations for international students: Required—TOEFL. *Expenses: Tuition, area resident:* Part-time $511 per credit. Tuition, state resident: part-time $767 per credit. Tuition, nonresident: part-time $1103 per credit.

Kean University, Nathan Weiss Graduate College, Program in Counselor Education, Union, NJ 07083. Offers alcohol and drug abuse counseling (MA); clinical mental health counseling (MA); school counseling (MA). *Accreditation:* ACA; NCATE. Part-time programs available. *Faculty:* 8 full-time (6 women). *Students:* 120 full-time (92 women), 144 part-time (122 women); includes 111 minority (47 Black or African American, non-Hispanic/Latino; 4 Asian, non-Hispanic/Latino; 58 Hispanic/Latino; 2 Two or more races, non-Hispanic/Latino), 2 international. Average age 32. 195 applicants, 48% accepted, 59 enrolled. In 2014, 62 master's awarded. *Degree requirements:* For master's, practicum, internship, portfolio. *Entrance requirements:* For master's, minimum GPA of 3.0, 2 letters of recommendation, personal statement, resume. Additional exam requirements/recommendations for international students: Required—TOEFL (minimum score 550 paper-based; 79 iBT). *Application deadline:* For fall admission, 3/2 for domestic and international students; for spring admission, 10/31 for domestic and international students. Applications are processed on a rolling basis. Application fee: $75 ($150 for international students). Electronic applications accepted. *Expenses:* Tuition, state resident: full-time $12,461; part-time $607 per credit. Tuition, nonresident: full-time $16,889; part-time $744 per credit. *Required fees:* $3141; $143 per credit. Tuition and fees vary according to course load, degree level and program. *Financial support:* In 2014–15, 14 research assistantships with full tuition reimbursements (averaging $3,742 per year) were awarded; scholarships/grants and unspecified assistantships also available. Financial award applicants required to submit FAFSA. *Unit head:* Dr. J. Barry Mascari, Program Coordinator, 908-737-5954, E-mail: jmascari@kean.edu. *Application contact:* Steven Koch, Admissions Counselor, 908-737-7136, Fax: 908-737-7135, E-mail: skoch@kean.edu.
Website: http://grad.kean.edu/counseling

Lenoir-Rhyne University, Graduate Programs, School of Education, Program in Human Services, Hickory, NC 28601. Offers management (MA); substance abuse (MA); vocational strategies (MA). Part-time programs available. Postbaccalaureate distance learning degree programs offered (no on-campus study). *Faculty:* 1 (woman) full-time. *Students:* 3 full-time (all women), 4 part-time (all women); includes 2 minority (both Black or African American, non-Hispanic/Latino). Average age 38. *Degree requirements:* For master's, comprehensive exam. *Entrance requirements:* For master's, GRE General Test or MAT, essay; minimum GPA of 2.7 undergraduate, 3.0 graduate. Additional exam requirements/recommendations for international students: Required—TOEFL (minimum score 600 paper-based). Application fee: $35. Electronic applications accepted. *Expenses: Tuition:* Full-time $9000; part-time $500 per credit hour. Tuition and fees vary according to program. *Unit head:* Dr. Amy Wood, Coordinator, 828-328-7728, Fax: 828-328-7368, E-mail: amy.wood@lr.edu. *Application contact:* Mary Ann Gosnell, Associate

Director of Enrollment Management Graduate Studies and Adult Learners, 828-328-7111, E-mail: admission@lr.edu.
Website: http://www.lr.edu/academics/programs/human-services

Lewis & Clark College, Graduate School of Education and Counseling, Department of Counseling Psychology, Program in Professional Mental Health Counseling–Addictions, Portland, OR 97219-7899. Offers MA, MS. Part-time and evening/weekend programs available. *Degree requirements:* For master's, thesis (MS). *Entrance requirements:* For master's, GRE General Test, minimum undergraduate GPA of 2.75. Additional exam requirements/recommendations for international students: Required—TOEFL (minimum score 575 paper-based). Electronic applications accepted.

Liberty University, Liberty Baptist Theological Seminary, Lynchburg, VA 24515. Offers Biblical studies (M Div, MAR, MTS, Th M); church history (M Div, MAR, MTS, Th M); discipleship (D Min); discipleship and church ministry (M Div, MAR, MCM); evangelism and church planting (M Div, MAR, MCM, D Min); global studies (M Div, MAR, MCM, MGS, Th M); homiletics (M Div, MAR, MCM, Th M, D Min); leadership (M Div, MAR, MCM, D Min); marketplace chaplaincy (M Div, MAR, MCM); ministry (D Min); pastoral counseling (M Div, MA, MAR, MCM, D Min), including addictions and recovery (MA), crisis response and trauma (MA), discipleship and church ministries (MA), leadership (MA), life coaching (MA), marketplace chaplaincy (MA), marriage and family (MA), military resilience (MA), pastoral counseling (MA); pastoral ministries (M Div, MAR, MCM); religious education (MRE); theology (M Div, MAR, MTS, Th M); theology and apologetics (PhD); worship (M Div, MAR, MCM, D Min). Part-time programs available. Postbaccalaureate distance learning degree programs offered (minimal on-campus study). *Students:* 2,865 full-time (781 women), 3,750 part-time (1,139 women); includes 1,742 minority (1,382 Black or African American, non-Hispanic/Latino; 22 American Indian or Alaska Native, non-Hispanic/Latino; 116 Asian, non-Hispanic/Latino; 105 Hispanic/Latino; 7 Native Hawaiian or other Pacific Islander, non-Hispanic/Latino; 110 Two or more races, non-Hispanic/Latino), 227 international. Average age 41. 5,446 applicants, 39% accepted, 1340 enrolled. In 2014, 1,969 master's, 126 doctorates, 75 other advanced degrees awarded. *Degree requirements:* For master's, 2 foreign languages, thesis (for some programs); for doctorate, 2 foreign languages, thesis/dissertation. *Entrance requirements:* For master's, minimum undergraduate GPA of 2.0; for doctorate, GRE General Test or MAT, minimum graduate GPA of 3.0. Additional exam requirements/recommendations for international students: Required—TOEFL (minimum score 600 paper-based; 100 iBT). *Application deadline:* For fall admission, 6/1 for domestic students; for spring admission, 11/1 for domestic students. Applications are processed on a rolling basis. Application fee: $50. Electronic applications accepted. *Expenses:* Expenses: Contact institution. *Financial support:* Teaching assistantships with tuition reimbursements, career-related internships or fieldwork, and Federal Work-Study available. Financial award applicants required to submit FAFSA. *Unit head:* Dr. David Hirschman, Acting Dean, 434-592-4140, Fax: 434-522-0415, E-mail: dwhirschman@liberty.edu. *Application contact:* Jay Bridge, Director of Graduate Admissions, 800-424-9595, Fax: 800-628-7977, E-mail: gradadmissions@liberty.edu. Website: http://www.liberty.edu/seminary/

Liberty University, School of Behavioral Sciences, Lynchburg, VA 24515. Offers advanced clinical skills (PhD); clinical mental health counseling (MA); counselor education and supervision (PhD); human services counseling (MA), including addictions and recovery, business, child and family law, Christian ministries, criminal justice, crisis response and trauma, executive leadership, health and wellness, life coaching, marriage and family, military resilience; marriage and family therapy (MA); military resilience (Certificate); professional counseling (MA). Part-time programs available. Postbaccalaureate distance learning degree programs offered (minimal on-campus study). *Students:* 3,009 full-time (2,433 women), 6,251 part-time (4,981 women); includes 2,959 minority (2,520 Black or African American, non-Hispanic/Latino; 49 American Indian or Alaska Native, non-Hispanic/Latino; 51 Asian, non-Hispanic/Latino; 97 Hispanic/Latino; 9 Native Hawaiian or other Pacific Islander, non-Hispanic/Latino; 233 Two or more races, non-Hispanic/Latino), 153 international. Average age 38. 6,645 applicants, 55% accepted, 2039 enrolled. In 2014, 2,410 master's, 11 doctorates, 2 other advanced degrees awarded. *Application deadline:* Applications are processed on a rolling basis. Application fee: $50. Electronic applications accepted. *Financial support:* Applicants required to submit FAFSA. *Unit head:* Dr. Ronald Hawkins, Founding Dean, School of Behavioral Sciences. *Application contact:* Jay Bridge, Director of Admissions, 800-424-9595, Fax: 800-628-7977, E-mail: gradadmissions@liberty.edu.

Maryville University of Saint Louis, College of Health Professions, Program in Rehabilitation Counseling, St. Louis, MO 63141-7299. Offers marriage and family therapy (MARC); music therapy (MARC); substance abuse (MARC). *Accreditation:* CORE. Part-time and evening/weekend programs available. *Faculty:* 3 full-time (1 woman), 3 part-time/adjunct (all women). *Students:* 9 full-time (all women), 25 part-time (23 women); includes 5 minority (4 Black or African American, non-Hispanic/Latino; 1 Two or more races, non-Hispanic/Latino). Average age 32. In 2014, 24 master's awarded. *Degree requirements:* For master's, internship, seminar. *Entrance requirements:* For master's, minimum cumulative GPA of 3.0, 2 letters of recommendation, interview. Additional exam requirements/recommendations for international students: Required—TOEFL (minimum score 550 paper-based). *Application deadline:* For fall admission, 1/15 for domestic students; for spring admission, 10/1 for domestic students. Application fee: $40 ($60 for international students). Electronic applications accepted. Application fee is waived when completed online. *Expenses:* Tuition: Full-time $24,694; part-time $755 per credit hour. Part-time tuition and fees vary according to course load and degree level. *Financial support:* Career-related internships or fieldwork, Federal Work-Study, and campus employment available. Financial award application deadline: 3/1; financial award applicants required to submit FAFSA. *Unit head:* Dr. Michael Kiener, Director, 314-529-9443, Fax: 314-529-9495, E-mail: mkiener@maryville.edu. *Application contact:* Crystal Jacobsmeyer, Assistant Director, Graduate Enrollment Advising, 314-529-9654, Fax: 314-529-9927, E-mail: cjacobsmeyer@maryville.edu.
Website: http://www.maryville.edu/hp/rehabilitation-counseling/

McNeese State University, Doré School of Graduate Studies, Burton College of Education, Department of Psychology, Lake Charles, LA 70609. Offers addiction treatment (MA); applied behavior analysis (MA); counseling psychology (MA); general/experimental psychology (MA). Evening/weekend programs available. *Entrance requirements:* For master's, GRE.

Monmouth University, The Graduate School, Department of Psychology, West Long Branch, NJ 07764-1898. Offers mental health counseling (MS); professional counseling (PMC); psychological counseling (MA), including addiction studies, psychological counseling. *Accreditation:* ACA. Part-time and evening/weekend programs available. *Faculty:* 8 full-time (4 women), 11 part-time/adjunct (8 women). *Students:* 146 full-time (126 women), 111 part-time (94 women); includes 50 minority (10 Black or African American, non-Hispanic/Latino; 2 American Indian or Alaska Native, non-Hispanic/Latino; 7 Asian, non-Hispanic/Latino; 27 Hispanic/Latino; 4 Two or more races, non-Hispanic/Latino), 1 international. Average age 27. 96 applicants, 96% accepted, 59 enrolled. In 2014, 75 master's awarded. *Degree requirements:* For master's, comprehensive exam (for some programs), thesis optional, fieldwork. *Entrance requirements:* For master's, GRE, minimum GPA of 3.0 overall, 12 credits in psychology or closely-related field, two Monmouth University psychological counseling recommendation forms, essay form; for PMC, degree or current enrollment in CACREP-accredited master's program in counseling with minimum cumulative GPA of 3.0. Additional exam requirements/recommendations for international students: Required—TOEFL (minimum score 550 paper-based; 79 iBT), IELTS (minimum score 5), Michigan English Language Assessment Battery (minimum score 77) or Certificate of Advanced English (minimum score B2). *Application deadline:* For fall admission, 7/15 priority date for domestic students, 6/1 for international students; for spring admission, 11/15 priority date for domestic students, 11/1 for international students. Applications are processed on a rolling basis. Application fee: $50. Electronic applications accepted. *Expenses:* Tuition: Full-time $18,072; part-time $1004 per credit. *Required fees:* $157 per semester. *Financial support:* In 2014–15, 211 students received support, including 195 fellowships (averaging $3,010 per year), 13 research assistantships (averaging $11,728 per year); career-related internships or fieldwork, scholarships/grants, and unspecified assistantships also available. Support available to part-time students. Financial award applicants required to submit FAFSA. *Faculty research:* Violent crime, single parenting, the African-American male, counseling older women, successful behavior for under-achieving youth. *Unit head:* Dr. Stephanie Hall, Program Director, 732-571-3570, Fax: 732-923-4661, E-mail: shall@monmouth.edu. *Application contact:* Andrea Thompson, Graduate Admission Counselor, 732-571-3452, Fax: 732-263-5123, E-mail: gradadm@monmouth.edu.
Website: http://www.monmouth.edu/psychological_counseling

Montclair State University, The Graduate School, College of Education and Human Services, Certified Alcohol and Drug Counselor Certificate Program, Montclair, NJ 07043-1624. Offers Certificate. *Students:* Average age 33. In 2014, 5 Certificates awarded. *Expenses:* Tuition, state resident: full-time $9960; part-time $553.35 per credit. Tuition, nonresident: full-time $15,074; part-time $837.43 per credit. *Required fees:* $1595; $88.63 per credit. Tuition and fees vary according to degree level and program. *Unit head:* Dr. Suzanne McCotter, Coordinator, 973-655-5381. *Application contact:* Amy Aiello, Executive Director of The Graduate School, 973-655-5147, E-mail: graduate.school@montclair.edu.

New York Institute of Technology, School of Health Professions, Department of Interdisciplinary Health Sciences, Old Westbury, NY 11568-8000. Offers alcohol and substance abuse counseling (AC); clinical nutrition (MS). Part-time and evening/weekend programs available. Postbaccalaureate distance learning degree programs offered (minimal on-campus study). *Degree requirements:* For master's, comprehensive exam, thesis (for some programs). *Entrance requirements:* For master's, minimum QPA of 2.85. Additional exam requirements/recommendations for international students: Required—TOEFL (minimum score 550 paper-based; 79 iBT), IELTS (minimum score 6). Electronic applications accepted. *Faculty research:* Diabetes prevention and treatment, college students' health behavior, online education in health sciences, autism, mental health and aging.

Northeastern State University, College of Education, Department of Psychology and Counseling, Tahlequah, OK 74464-2399. Offers counseling psychology (MS); school counseling (M Ed); substance abuse counseling (MS). Part-time and evening/weekend programs available. *Faculty:* 12 full-time (6 women), 4 part-time/adjunct (2 women). *Students:* 80 full-time (67 women), 70 part-time (61 women); includes 47 minority (8 Black or African American, non-Hispanic/Latino; 21 American Indian or Alaska Native, non-Hispanic/Latino; 1 Asian, non-Hispanic/Latino; 5 Hispanic/Latino; 12 Two or more races, non-Hispanic/Latino), 2 international. Average age 34. In 2014, 43 master's awarded. *Degree requirements:* For master's, thesis (for some programs), written and oral examinations. *Entrance requirements:* For master's, GRE, minimum GPA of 2.5. Application fee: $25. *Expenses:* Tuition, state resident: part-time $178.75 per credit hour. Tuition, nonresident: part-time $451.75 per credit hour. *Required fees:* $37.40 per credit hour. *Financial support:* Teaching assistantships, career-related internships or fieldwork, and Federal Work-Study available. Financial award application deadline: 3/1. *Unit head:* Dr. Kenny Paris, Department Chair of Psychology and Counseling, 918-444-3021, E-mail: parisk@nsuok.edu. *Application contact:* Margie Railey, Administrative Assistant, 918-456-5511 Ext. 2093, Fax: 918-458-2061, E-mail: railey@nsouk.edu. Website: https://academics.nsuok.edu/education/EducationHome/COEDepartments/PsychologyCounseling.aspx

Northwest Nazarene University, Graduate Studies, Program in Social Work, Nampa, ID 83686-5897. Offers addiction studies (MSW); clinical mental health practice (MSW); management, community planning and social administration (MSW); medical social work (MSW). *Accreditation:* CSWE. Part-time programs available. Postbaccalaureate distance learning degree programs offered (no on-campus study). *Faculty:* 10 full-time (6 women), 5 part-time/adjunct (4 women). *Students:* 129 full-time (97 women), 33 part-time (29 women); includes 23 minority (3 Black or African American, non-Hispanic/Latino; 1 American Indian or Alaska Native, non-Hispanic/Latino; 12 Hispanic/Latino; 7 Two or more races, non-Hispanic/Latino). Average age 27. 152 applicants, 54% accepted, 73 enrolled. In 2014, 54 master's awarded. *Degree requirements:* For master's, comprehensive exam. *Application deadline:* Applications are processed on a rolling basis. Application fee: $50. Electronic applications accepted. *Unit head:* Dr. Lawanna Lancaster, Director, 208-467-8679, E-mail: msw@nnu.edu. *Application contact:* Jodie Engel, Program Assistant, 208-467-8679, Fax: 208-467-8879, E-mail: jrodriguez-engel@nnu.edu.

Pace University, Dyson College of Arts and Sciences, Department of Psychology, Program in Mental Health Counseling, New York, NY 10038. Offers loss and grief counseling (MS); mental health (MS, PhD); substance abuse (MS). Offered at Pleasantville, NY location only. Part-time and evening/weekend programs available. *Students:* 92 full-time (77 women), 53 part-time (40 women); includes 53 minority (15 Black or African American, non-Hispanic/Latino; 1 American Indian or Alaska Native, non-Hispanic/Latino; 9 Asian, non-Hispanic/Latino; 20 Hispanic/Latino; 8 Two or more races, non-Hispanic/Latino), 4 international. Average age 29. 80 applicants, 81% accepted, 36 enrolled. In 2014, 58 master's awarded. *Degree requirements:* For master's, comprehensive exam, qualifying exams, internship. *Entrance requirements:* For master's, GRE, resume, personal statement, two letters of reference, official transcripts, interview. Additional exam requirements/recommendations for international students: Required—TOEFL (minimum score 100 iBT). *Application deadline:* For fall admission, 8/1 priority date for domestic students, 6/1 for international students; for spring admission, 12/1 priority date for domestic students, 10/1 for international students. Applications are processed on a rolling basis. Application fee: $70. Electronic applications accepted. *Expenses:* Tuition: Part-time $1120 per credit. *Required fees:* $266 per semester. Tuition and fees vary according to course load, degree level and program. *Financial support:* Research assistantships, teaching assistantships, career-related internships or fieldwork, Federal Work-Study, and tuition waivers (partial) available. Financial award applicants required to submit FAFSA. *Unit head:* Dr. Ross Robak, Psychology Department Chair/Director, Graduate Program in Counseling, 914-773-3786, E-mail: rrobak@pace.edu. *Application contact:* Susan Ford-Goldschein, Director of Graduate Admissions, 914-422-4283, Fax: 914-422-4287, E-mail: gradwp@pace.edu.
Website: http://www.pace.edu/academics/graduate-students/degrees/mental-health-counseling-ms

Addictions/Substance Abuse Counseling

Palm Beach Atlantic University, School of Education and Behavioral Studies, West Palm Beach, FL 33416-4708. Offers counseling psychology (MS), including addictions/mental health, general counseling, marriage and family therapy, mental health counseling, school guidance counseling. Part-time and evening/weekend programs available. *Faculty:* 9 full-time (3 women), 14 part-time/adjunct (8 women). *Students:* 286 full-time (237 women), 30 part-time (25 women); includes 151 minority (60 Black or African American, non-Hispanic/Latino; 5 Asian, non-Hispanic/Latino; 73 Hispanic/Latino; 13 Two or more races, non-Hispanic/Latino), 5 international. Average age 34. 111 applicants, 78% accepted, 75 enrolled. In 2014, 98 master's awarded. *Entrance requirements:* For master's, GRE or MAT and MMPI-2, minimum GPA of 3.0. Additional exam requirements/recommendations for international students: Required—TOEFL (minimum score 550 paper-based; 79 iBT). *Application deadline:* For fall admission, 7/15 priority date for domestic students; for spring admission, 11/15 priority date for domestic students. Applications are processed on a rolling basis. Application fee: $50. Electronic applications accepted. *Expenses: Tuition:* Part-time $510 per credit hour. *Financial support:* In 2014–15, 16 students received support. Tuition waivers and Employee Education grants available. Financial award application deadline: 5/1; financial award applicants required to submit FAFSA. *Unit head:* Dr. Gene Sale, Program Director, 561-803-2352. *Application contact:* Graduate Admissions, 888-468-6722, E-mail: grad@pba.edu.
Website: http://www.pba.edu/graduate-counseling-program

Post University, Program in Human Services, Waterbury, CT 06723-2540. Offers human services (MS); human services/alcohol and drug counseling (MS); human services/clinical counseling (MS); human services/non-profit management (MS). Part-time and evening/weekend programs available. Postbaccalaureate distance learning degree programs offered.

Saint Mary's University of Minnesota, Schools of Graduate and Professional Programs, Graduate School of Health and Human Services, Counseling and Psychological Services Program, Winona, MN 55987-1399. Offers addiction studies (Certificate); counseling and psychological services (MA).

Salve Regina University, Holistic Graduate Programs, Newport, RI 02840-4192. Offers expressive and creative arts (CAGS, CGS); holistic counseling (MA); holistic leadership (MA, CAGS, CGS); holistic leadership and change management (CAGS); holistic studies (CGS); substance abuse and treatment (CAGS); substance abuse foundations in holistic studies (CGS). Part-time and evening/weekend programs available. *Faculty:* 2 full-time (both women), 10 part-time/adjunct (7 women). *Students:* 18 full-time (16 women), 65 part-time (57 women); includes 7 minority (1 Black or African American, non-Hispanic/Latino; 1 American Indian or Alaska Native, non-Hispanic/Latino; 1 Asian, non-Hispanic/Latino; 3 Hispanic/Latino; 1 Two or more races, non-Hispanic/Latino). Average age 41. 27 applicants, 100% accepted, 26 enrolled. In 2014, 16 master's, 5 other advanced degrees awarded. *Degree requirements:* For master's, internship, project. *Entrance requirements:* For master's, GMAT, GRE General Test, or MAT. Additional exam requirements/recommendations for international students: Required—TOEFL (minimum score 600 paper-based; 100 iBT) or IELTS. *Application deadline:* For fall admission, 3/15 priority date for domestic and international students; for spring admission, 9/15 priority date for domestic and international students. Applications are processed on a rolling basis. Application fee: $60. Electronic applications accepted. *Expenses: Tuition:* Full-time $8550; part-time $475 per credit. *Required fees:* $50 per term. Tuition and fees vary according to course level, course load and degree level. *Financial support:* Career-related internships or fieldwork and Federal Work-Study available. Support available to part-time students. Financial award application deadline: 3/1; financial award applicants required to submit FAFSA. *Unit head:* Dr. Nancy Gordon, Director, 401-341-3290, E-mail: nancy.gordon@salve.edu. *Application contact:* Nicole Ferreira, Associate Director of Graduate Admissions, 401-341-2462, Fax: 401-341-2973, E-mail: nicole.ferreira@salve.edu.
Website: http://www.salve.edu/graduate-studies/holistic-studies

Salve Regina University, Program in Rehabilitation Counseling, Newport, RI 02840-4192. Offers mental health (CAGS), including rehabilitation counseling; rehabilitation counseling (MA); substance abuse (CGS), including foundations in rehabilitation counseling. *Accreditation:* CORE. Part-time and evening/weekend programs available. *Faculty:* 1 (woman) full-time, 8 part-time/adjunct (3 women). *Students:* 6 full-time (5 women), 64 part-time (53 women); includes 17 minority (9 Black or African American, non-Hispanic/Latino; 3 American Indian or Alaska Native, non-Hispanic/Latino; 5 Hispanic/Latino). Average age 37. 23 applicants, 100% accepted, 22 enrolled. In 2014, 14 master's, 4 other advanced degrees awarded. *Entrance requirements:* For master's, GMAT, GRE General Test or MAT. Additional exam requirements/recommendations for international students: Required—TOEFL (minimum score 600 paper-based; 100 iBT) or IELTS. *Application deadline:* For fall admission, 3/15 priority date for domestic and international students; for spring admission, 9/15 priority date for domestic and international students. Applications are processed on a rolling basis. Application fee: $60. Electronic applications accepted. *Expenses: Tuition:* Full-time $8550; part-time $475 per credit. *Required fees:* $50 per term. Tuition and fees vary according to course level, course load and degree level. *Financial support:* Career-related internships or fieldwork and Federal Work-Study available. Support available to part-time students. Financial award application deadline: 3/1; financial award applicants required to submit FAFSA. *Unit head:* Dr. Judith Drew, Director, 401-341-3189, E-mail: judith.drew@salve.edu. *Application contact:* Nicole Ferreira, Associate Director of Graduate Admissions, 401-341-2462, Fax: 401-341-2973, E-mail: nicole.ferreira@salve.edu.
Website: http://www.salve.edu/graduate-studies/rehabilitation-counseling

Slippery Rock University of Pennsylvania, Graduate Studies (Recruitment), College of Education, Department of Counseling and Development, Slippery Rock, PA 16057-1383. Offers clinical mental health counseling (MA), including addiction, adult, older adult, school and youth; student affairs (MA), including higher education; student affairs in higher education (MA), including college counseling. *Accreditation:* ACA; NCATE. Part-time and evening/weekend programs available. *Faculty:* 9 full-time (5 women). *Students:* 84 full-time (69 women), 16 part-time (13 women); includes 13 minority (8 Black or African American, non-Hispanic/Latino; 1 American Indian or Alaska Native, non-Hispanic/Latino; 2 Hispanic/Latino; 2 Two or more races, non-Hispanic/Latino), 1 international. Average age 29. 128 applicants, 51% accepted, 41 enrolled. In 2014, 45 master's awarded. *Degree requirements:* For master's, comprehensive exam, thesis (for some programs). *Entrance requirements:* For master's, GRE General Test or MAT, official transcripts, minimum GPA of 2.75 or 3.0 (depending on program), personal statement, three letters of recommendation, interview. Additional exam requirements/recommendations for international students: Required—TOEFL (minimum score 550 paper-based; 80 iBT). *Application deadline:* For fall admission, 1/15 priority date for domestic and international students. Application fee: $25 ($30 for international students). Electronic applications accepted. *Expenses:* Tuition, state resident: full-time $8172; part-time $454 per credit. Tuition, nonresident: full-time $12,258; part-time $681 per credit. *Required fees:* $2326; $200 per credit. Tuition and fees vary according to degree level and program. *Financial support:* Career-related internships or fieldwork, Federal Work-Study, institutionally sponsored loans, scholarships/grants, tuition waivers (partial), and unspecified assistantships available. Support available to part-time students. Financial award application deadline: 5/1; financial award applicants required to submit FAFSA. *Unit head:* Dr. Stacy Jacob, Graduate Coordinator, 724-738-2758, Fax: 724-738-4859, E-mail: stacy.jacob@sru.edu. *Application contact:* Brandi Weber-Mortimer, Director of Graduate Admissions, 724-738-2051, Fax: 724-738-2146, E-mail: graduate.admissions@sru.edu.
Website: http://srudss.ingeniuxondemand.com/academics/colleges-and-departments/coe/departments/counseling-and-development

Springfield College, Graduate Programs, Programs in Rehabilitation Counseling and Services, Springfield, MA 01109-3797. Offers alcohol and substance abuse services (M Ed); psychiatric rehabilitation and substance abuse counseling (M Ed). *Accreditation:* CORE (one or more programs are accredited). Part-time programs available. *Degree requirements:* For master's, comprehensive exam. *Entrance requirements:* Additional exam requirements/recommendations for international students: Required—TOEFL (minimum score 550 paper-based); Recommended—IELTS (minimum score 6). *Application deadline:* For fall admission, 1/15 for domestic and international students; for winter admission, 11/1 for international students; for spring admission, 11/1 for domestic and international students. Applications are processed on a rolling basis. Application fee: $50. Electronic applications accepted. *Financial support:* Fellowships with partial tuition reimbursements, teaching assistantships with partial tuition reimbursements, career-related internships or fieldwork, Federal Work-Study, institutionally sponsored loans, and unspecified assistantships available. Financial award application deadline: 3/1; financial award applicants required to submit FAFSA. *Unit head:* Deborah Cook, Director, 413-748-3321, E-mail: dcook@springfieldcollege.edu. *Application contact:* Mary DeAngelo, Director of Enrollment Management, 413-748-3136, Fax: 413-748-3694, E-mail: mdeangel@spfldcol.edu.

Stony Brook University, State University of New York, Stony Brook University Medical Center, Health Sciences Center, School of Medicine, Program in Public Health, Stony Brook, NY 11794. Offers community health (MPH); evaluation sciences (MPH); family violence (MPH); health communication (Certificate); health economics (MPH); population health (MPH); substance abuse (MPH). *Accreditation:* CEPH. *Students:* 46 full-time (35 women), 18 part-time (16 women); includes 29 minority (5 Black or African American, non-Hispanic/Latino; 14 Asian, non-Hispanic/Latino; 10 Hispanic/Latino), 4 international. Average age 29. 168 applicants, 46% accepted, 31 enrolled. In 2014, 23 master's awarded. *Entrance requirements:* For master's, GRE, 3 references, bachelor's degree from accredited college or university with minimum GPA of 3.0, essays, interview. Additional exam requirements/recommendations for international students: Required—TOEFL (minimum score 85 iBT). *Application deadline:* For fall admission, 6/1 for domestic students, 3/15 for international students. Application fee: $100. Electronic applications accepted. *Expenses:* Tuition, state resident: full-time $10,370; part-time $432 per credit. Tuition, nonresident: full-time $20,190; part-time $841 per credit. *Required fees:* $1431. *Financial support:* Fellowships available. *Faculty research:* Population health, health service research, health economics. *Unit head:* Dr. Lisa A. Benz Scott, Director, 631-444-9396, Fax: 631-444-3480, E-mail: lisa.benzscott@stonybrook.edu. *Application contact:* Senior Academic Coordinator, 631-444-9396, Fax: 631-444-3480, E-mail: joanmarie.maniaci@stonybrook.edu.
Website: http://publichealth.stonybrookmedicine.edu/

Syracuse University, Falk College of Sport and Human Dynamics, Program in Addiction Studies, Syracuse, NY 13244. Offers CAS. Part-time programs available. *Students:* 1 part-time (0 women). Average age 30. 2 applicants, 100% accepted. In 2014, 10 CASs awarded. *Entrance requirements:* Additional exam requirements/recommendations for international students: Required—TOEFL (minimum score 100 iBT). *Application deadline:* For fall admission, 3/15 priority date for domestic and international students; for spring admission, 11/15 priority date for domestic and international students. Application fee: $75. Electronic applications accepted. *Expenses: Tuition:* Part-time $1341 per credit. *Financial support:* Application deadline: 1/1. *Unit head:* Dr. Brooks Gump, Graduate Program Director, 315-443-2208, E-mail: bbgump@syr.edu. *Application contact:* Felicia Otero, Director of College Admissions, 315-443-5555, Fax: 315-443-2562, E-mail: falk@syr.edu.
Website: http://falk.syr.edu/HealthWellness/Addiction_CAS.aspx

Troy University, Graduate School, College of Education, Program in Counseling and Psychology, Troy, AL 36082. Offers agency counseling (Ed S); clinical mental health (MS); community counseling (MS, Ed S); corrections counseling (MS); rehabilitation counseling (MS); school psychology (MS, Ed S); school psychometry (MS); social service counseling (MS); student affairs counseling (MS); substance abuse counseling (MS). *Accreditation:* ACA; CORE; NCATE. Part-time and evening/weekend programs available. *Faculty:* 41 full-time (18 women), 32 part-time/adjunct (18 women). *Students:* 358 full-time (286 women), 503 part-time (425 women); includes 572 minority (481 Black or African American, non-Hispanic/Latino; 3 American Indian or Alaska Native, non-Hispanic/Latino; 5 Asian, non-Hispanic/Latino; 62 Hispanic/Latino; 21 Two or more races, non-Hispanic/Latino). Average age 34. 248 applicants, 86% accepted, 139 enrolled. In 2014, 212 master's, 4 other advanced degrees awarded. *Degree requirements:* For master's, comprehensive exam, thesis. *Entrance requirements:* For master's, GRE (minimum score of 850 on old exam or 290 on new exam), GMAT (minimum score of 380), or MAT (minimum score of 385), bachelor's degree; minimum undergraduate GPA of 2.5 or 3.0 on last 30 semester hours, letter of recommendation. Additional exam requirements/recommendations for international students: Required—TOEFL (minimum score 523 paper-based; 70 iBT), IELTS (minimum score 6). *Application deadline:* Applications are processed on a rolling basis. Application fee: $50. Electronic applications accepted. *Expenses:* Tuition, state resident: full-time $6570; part-time $365 per credit hour. Tuition, nonresident: full-time $13,140; part-time $730 per credit hour. *Required fees:* $365 per credit hour. *Unit head:* Dr. Andrew Creamer, Chair, 334-670-3350, Fax: 334-670-3291, E-mail: acreamer@troy.edu. *Application contact:* Jessica A. Kimbro, Director of Graduate Admissions, 334-670-3178, E-mail: jacord@troy.edu.

United States International University, School of Arts and Sciences, Nairobi, Kenya. Offers counseling psychology (MA), including chemical dependency, health psychology; international relations (MA), including development studies, diplomacy and foreign policy, peace and conflict studies. Part-time and evening/weekend programs available. *Degree requirements:* For master's, thesis, practicum. *Entrance requirements:* For master's, GRE General Test, 2 letters of recommendation, resume. Additional exam requirements/recommendations for international students: Required—TOEFL. *Faculty research:* Trauma in children, African intellectualism, psychological assessment tools.

Universidad Central del Caribe, Program in Substance Abuse Counseling, Bayamón, PR 00960-6032. Offers MHS.

University of Arkansas at Pine Bluff, School of Arts and Sciences, Pine Bluff, AR 71601-2799. Offers addiction studies (MS).

University of California, Berkeley, UC Berkeley Extension, Certificate Programs in Behavioral and Health Sciences, Berkeley, CA 94720-1500. Offers alcohol and drug abuse studies (Certificate).

University of Central Oklahoma, The Jackson College of Graduate Studies, College of Liberal Arts, Department of Sociology, Gerontology, and Substance Abuse Studies, Edmond, OK 73034-5209. Offers gerontology (MA); sociology (MA), including substance

abuse studies. Part-time programs available. *Degree requirements:* For master's, variable foreign language requirement, comprehensive exam (for some programs), thesis (for some programs). *Entrance requirements:* For master's, GRE. Additional exam requirements/recommendations for international students: Required—TOEFL (minimum score 550 paper-based; 79 iBT), IELTS (minimum score 6.5). Electronic applications accepted.

University of Detroit Mercy, College of Liberal Arts and Education, Department of Counseling and Addiction Studies, Program in Addiction Studies, Detroit, MI 48221. Offers Certificate. Part-time programs available.

University of Detroit Mercy, College of Liberal Arts and Education, Department of Counseling and Addiction Studies, Program in Counseling, Detroit, MI 48221. Offers addiction counseling (MA); community counseling (MA); school counseling (MA). *Accreditation:* ACA; Teacher Education Accreditation Council. Part-time and evening/weekend programs available. *Degree requirements:* For master's, thesis or alternative. *Entrance requirements:* For master's, minimum GPA of 2.75.

University of Illinois at Springfield, Graduate Programs, College of Education and Human Services, Program in Human Services, Springfield, IL 62703-5407. Offers alcohol and substance abuse (Graduate Certificate); alcoholism and substance abuse (MA); child and family services (MA); gerontology (MA); social services administration (MA). Part-time and evening/weekend programs available. Postbaccalaureate distance learning degree programs offered (no on-campus study). *Faculty:* 4 full-time (all women), 2 part-time/adjunct (0 women). *Students:* 11 full-time (all women), 69 part-time (60 women); includes 21 minority (17 Black or African American, non-Hispanic/Latino; 1 Asian, non-Hispanic/Latino; 1 Hispanic/Latino; 2 Two or more races, non-Hispanic/Latino). Average age 36. 53 applicants, 30% accepted, 16 enrolled. In 2014, 19 master's, 1 other advanced degree awarded. *Degree requirements:* For master's, internship; project or thesis. *Entrance requirements:* For master's, minimum undergraduate GPA of 3.0, 2 letters of recommendation, statement of intent. Additional exam requirements/recommendations for international students: Required—TOEFL (minimum score 500 paper-based; 61 iBT). Application fee: $60 ($75 for international students). Electronic applications accepted. *Expenses:* Tuition, state resident: full-time $7662; part-time $319.25 per credit hour. Tuition, nonresident: full-time $15,966; part-time $665.25 per credit hour. *Financial support:* In 2014–15, fellowships with full tuition reimbursements (averaging $9,900 per year), research assistantships with full tuition reimbursements (averaging $9,600 per year), teaching assistantships with full tuition reimbursements (averaging $9,600 per year) were awarded; career-related internships or fieldwork, Federal Work-Study, scholarships/grants, health care benefits, and unspecified assistantships also available. Support available to part-time students. Financial award application deadline: 11/15. *Unit head:* Dr. Carolyn Peck, Program Administrator, 217-206-7577, Fax: 217-206-6775, E-mail: peck.carolyn@uis.edu. *Application contact:* Dr. Lynn Pardie, Office of Graduate Studies, 800-252-8533, Fax: 217-206-7623, E-mail: lpard1@uis.edu.
Website: http://www.uis.edu/humanservices

University of Lethbridge, School of Graduate Studies, Lethbridge, AB T1K 3M4, Canada. Offers addictions counseling (M Sc); agricultural biotechnology (M Sc); agricultural studies (M Sc, MA); anthropology (MA); archaeology (M Sc, MA); art (MA, MFA); biochemistry (M Sc); biological sciences (M Sc); biomolecular science (PhD); biosystems and biodiversity (PhD); Canadian studies (MA); chemistry (M Sc); computer science (M Sc); computer science and geographical information science (M Sc); counseling (MC); counseling psychology (M Ed); dramatic arts (MA); earth, space, and physical science (PhD); economics (MA); education (MA); educational leadership (M Ed); English (MA); environmental science (M Sc); evolution and behavior (PhD); exercise science (M Sc); French (MA); French/German (MA); French/Spanish (MA); general education (M Ed); geography (M Sc, MA); German (MA); health sciences (M Sc); individualized multidisciplinary (M Sc, MA); kinesiology (M Sc, MA); management (M Sc), including accounting, finance, general management, human resource management and labor relations, information systems, international management, marketing, policy and strategy; mathematics (M Sc); modern languages (MA); music (M Mus, MA); Native American studies (MA); neuroscience (M Sc, PhD); new media (MA, MFA); nursing (M Sc, MN); philosophy (MA); physics (M Sc); political science (MA); psychology (M Sc, MA); religious studies (MA); sociology (MA); theatre and dramatic arts (MFA); theoretical and computational science (PhD); urban and regional studies (MA); women and gender studies (MA). Part-time and evening/weekend programs available. *Faculty:* 358. *Students:* 445 full-time (243 women), 116 part-time (72 women). Average age 31. 351 applicants, 26% accepted, 87 enrolled. In 2014, 129 master's, 13 doctorates awarded. *Degree requirements:* For master's, thesis (for some programs); for doctorate, comprehensive exam, thesis/dissertation. *Entrance requirements:* For master's, GMAT (for M Sc in management), bachelor's degree in related field, minimum GPA of 3.0 during previous 20 graded semester courses, 2 years' teaching or related experience (M Ed); for doctorate, master's degree, minimum graduate GPA of 3.5. Additional exam requirements/recommendations for international students: Required—TOEFL. Application fee: $100 Canadian dollars. *Financial support:* Fellowships, research assistantships, teaching assistantships, scholarships/grants, health care benefits, and unspecified assistantships available. *Faculty research:* Movement and brain plasticity, gibberellin physiology, photosynthesis, carbon cycling, molecular properties of main-group ring components. *Application contact:* School of Graduate Studies, 403-329-5194, E-mail: sgsinquiries@uleth.ca.
Website: http://www.uleth.ca/graduatestudies/

University of Louisville, Graduate School, Raymond A. Kent School of Social Work, Louisville, KY 40292-0001. Offers marriage and family therapy (PMC), including mental health; social work (MSSW, PhD), including alcohol and drug counseling (MSSW), gerontology (MSSW), marriage and family (PhD), school social work (MSSW). *Accreditation:* AAMFT/COAMFTE; CSWE (one or more programs are accredited). Part-time and evening/weekend programs available. *Students:* 369 full-time (312 women), 101 part-time (89 women); includes 138 minority (95 Black or African American, non-Hispanic/Latino; 3 American Indian or Alaska Native, non-Hispanic/Latino; 5 Asian, non-Hispanic/Latino; 21 Hispanic/Latino; 14 Two or more races, non-Hispanic/Latino), 7 international. Average age 31. 425 applicants, 67% accepted, 176 enrolled. In 2014, 117 master's, 2 doctorates awarded. *Degree requirements:* For doctorate, comprehensive exam, thesis/dissertation. *Entrance requirements:* For master's, GRE or minimum GPA of 2.75; for doctorate, GRE General Test, interview, writing sample. Additional exam requirements/recommendations for international students: Required—TOEFL (minimum score 550 paper-based; 79 iBT). *Application deadline:* For fall admission, 7/31 for domestic and international students. Applications are processed on a rolling basis. Application fee: $60. Electronic applications accepted. *Expenses:* Tuition, state resident: full-time $11,326; part-time $630 per credit hour. Tuition, nonresident: full-time $23,568; part-time $1311 per credit hour. *Required fees:* $196. Tuition and fees vary according to program and reciprocity agreements. *Financial support:* Research assistantships with full tuition reimbursements, teaching assistantships with full tuition reimbursements, Federal Work-Study, institutionally sponsored loans, scholarships/grants, health care benefits, and unspecified assistantships available. Support available to part-time students. Financial award application deadline: 5/15; financial award applicants required to submit FAFSA. *Faculty research:* Child welfare, substance abuse,

gerontology, family functioning, health behavior. *Total annual research expenditures:* $1.6 million. *Unit head:* Dr. Terry Singer, Dean, 502-852-6402, Fax: 502-852-0422, E-mail: terry.singer@louisville.edu. *Application contact:* Libby Leggett, Director, Graduate Admissions, 502-852-3101, Fax: 502-852-6536, E-mail: gradadm@louisville.edu.
Website: http://www.louisville.edu/kent

University of Mary, Liffrig Family School of Education and Behavioral Sciences, Department of Behavioral Sciences, Bismarck, ND 58504-9652. Offers addiction counseling (MSC); clinical mental health counseling (MSC); military families (MSC); school counseling (MSC); student affairs (MSC). Part-time programs available. Postbaccalaureate distance learning degree programs offered (minimal on-campus study). *Degree requirements:* For master's, thesis, internship. *Entrance requirements:* For master's, coursework/experience in psychology, statistics, minimum GPA of 3.0. Additional exam requirements/recommendations for international students: Required—TOEFL (minimum score 500 paper-based; 71 iBT). *Application deadline:* For fall admission, 8/1 priority date for domestic students. Application fee: $40. *Expenses:* Tuition: Full-time $4772; part-time $530.25 per credit hour. *Required fees:* $20 per credit hour. Tuition and fees vary according to degree level and program. *Financial support:* Application deadline: 8/1; applicants required to submit FAFSA. *Application contact:* Jeanette Shaeffer, Accelerated and Distance Education Administrative Assistant, 701-355-8128, Fax: 701-255-7687, E-mail: jgschae@umary.edu.

University of Nevada, Las Vegas, Graduate College, College of Education, Department of Educational and Clinical Studies, Las Vegas, NV 89154-3066. Offers addiction studies (Advanced Certificate); counselor education (MS), including clinical mental health; educational and clinical studies (M Ed); mental health counseling (Advanced Certificate); special education (PhD); PhD/JD. Part-time and evening/weekend programs available. *Faculty:* 18 full-time (10 women), 12 part-time/adjunct (10 women). *Students:* 164 full-time (140 women), 206 part-time (167 women); includes 142 minority (39 Black or African American, non-Hispanic/Latino; 17 Asian, non-Hispanic/Latino; 62 Hispanic/Latino; 1 Native Hawaiian or other Pacific Islander, non-Hispanic/Latino; 23 Two or more races, non-Hispanic/Latino), 26 international. Average age 34. 184 applicants, 83% accepted, 117 enrolled. In 2014, 121 master's, 6 doctorates awarded. *Degree requirements:* For master's, comprehensive exam (for some programs), thesis (for some programs); for Advanced Certificate, thesis (for some programs). *Entrance requirements:* Additional exam requirements/recommendations for international students: Required—TOEFL (minimum score 550 paper-based; 80 iBT), IELTS (minimum score 7). *Application deadline:* For fall admission, 3/1 for domestic students, 5/1 for international students; for spring admission, 9/1 for domestic students, 10/1 for international students; for summer admission, 3/15 for domestic students. Application fee: $60 ($95 for international students). Electronic applications accepted. *Financial support:* In 2014–15, 32 students received support, including 6 research assistantships with partial tuition reimbursements available (averaging $10,708 per year), 26 teaching assistantships with partial tuition reimbursements available (averaging $14,792 per year); institutionally sponsored loans, scholarships/grants, health care benefits, and unspecified assistantships also available. Financial award application deadline: 3/1. *Faculty research:* Multicultural issues in counseling, academic interventions for students with disabilities, establishment of pro-social skills in young children with severe disabilities, inclusive strategies for students with disabilities, language and literacy for English language learners. *Total annual research expenditures:* $343,782. *Unit head:* Dr. Thomas Pierce, Interim Chair/Associate Professor, 702-895-1104, Fax: 702-895-5550, E-mail: tom.pierce@unlv.edu. *Application contact:* Graduate College Admissions Evaluator, 702-895-3320, Fax: 702-895-4180, E-mail: gradcollege@unlv.edu.
Website: http://education.unlv.edu/ecs/

The University of North Carolina at Charlotte, College of Education, Department of Counseling, Charlotte, NC 28223-0001. Offers counseling (MA, PhD, Graduate Certificate); play therapy (Postbaccalaureate Certificate); school counseling (MA); substance abuse counseling (Postbaccalaureate Certificate). *Accreditation:* ACA. Part-time and evening/weekend programs available. Postbaccalaureate distance learning degree programs offered (no on-campus study). *Faculty:* 10 full-time (5 women), 7 part-time/adjunct (all women). *Students:* 115 full-time (96 women), 87 part-time (70 women); includes 51 minority (41 Black or African American, non-Hispanic/Latino; 1 American Indian or Alaska Native, non-Hispanic/Latino; 2 Asian, non-Hispanic/Latino; 6 Hispanic/Latino; 1 Two or more races, non-Hispanic/Latino), 2 international. Average age 31. 221 applicants, 52% accepted, 74 enrolled. In 2014, 42 master's, 5 doctorates, 38 other advanced degrees awarded. Terminal master's awarded for partial completion of doctoral program. *Degree requirements:* For master's, thesis; for doctorate, thesis/dissertation. *Entrance requirements:* For master's, GRE or MAT; for doctorate, GRE. Additional exam requirements/recommendations for international students: Required—TOEFL (minimum score 557 paper-based; 83 iBT). *Application deadline:* For fall admission, 12/1 for domestic and international students; for spring admission, 11/1 for domestic students, 10/1 for international students. Applications are processed on a rolling basis. Application fee: $75. Electronic applications accepted. *Expenses:* Tuition, state resident: full-time $4008. Tuition, nonresident: full-time $16,295. *Required fees:* $2755. Tuition and fees vary according to course load and program. *Financial support:* In 2014–15, 11 students received support, including 2 research assistantships (averaging $18,166 per year), 9 teaching assistantships (averaging $5,333 per year); career-related internships or fieldwork, institutionally sponsored loans, scholarships/grants, unspecified assistantships, and administrative assistantships also available. Support available to part-time students. Financial award application deadline: 4/1; financial award applicants required to submit FAFSA. *Total annual research expenditures:* $60,684. *Unit head:* Dr. Henry Harris, Chair, 704-687-8971, Fax: 704-687-1636, E-mail: srfurr@uncc.edu. *Application contact:* Kathy B. Giddings, Director of Graduate Admissions, 704-687-5503, Fax: 704-687-1668, E-mail: gradadm@uncc.edu.
Website: http://education.uncc.edu/counseling/

University of Oklahoma, College of Liberal Studies, Norman, OK 73019. Offers administrative leadership (MA Ed); liberal studies (MA), including human and health services administration, museum studies; prevention science (MPS). Part-time programs available. Postbaccalaureate distance learning degree programs offered (no on-campus study). *Faculty:* 14 full-time (8 women), 3 part-time/adjunct (1 woman). *Students:* 65 full-time (33 women), 600 part-time (301 women); includes 184 minority (57 Black or African American, non-Hispanic/Latino; 37 American Indian or Alaska Native, non-Hispanic/Latino; 8 Asian, non-Hispanic/Latino; 44 Hispanic/Latino; 3 Native Hawaiian or other Pacific Islander, non-Hispanic/Latino; 35 Two or more races, non-Hispanic/Latino), 1 international. Average age 35. 217 applicants, 97% accepted, 141 enrolled. In 2014, 155 master's, 5 other advanced degrees awarded. Terminal master's awarded for partial completion of doctoral program. *Degree requirements:* For master's, comprehensive exam (for some programs), thesis optional, practicum (for museum studies only); for Graduate Certificate, comprehensive exam (for some programs), thesis optional. *Entrance requirements:* For master's and Graduate Certificate, minimum cumulative GPA of 3.0 in previous undergraduate/graduate coursework. Additional exam requirements/recommendations for international students: Required—TOEFL (minimum score 79 iBT). *Application deadline:* For fall admission, 7/1 for domestic and international students; for winter admission, 12/1 for domestic and international

students; for spring admission, 5/1 for domestic and international students. Application fee: $50 ($100 for international students). Electronic applications accepted. *Expenses:* Tuition, state resident: full-time $4394; part-time $183.10 per credit hour. Tuition, nonresident: full-time $16,970; part-time $707.10 per credit hour. *Required fees:* $2892; $109.95 per credit hour. $126.50 per semester. *Financial support:* In 2014–15, 107 students received support. Career-related internships or fieldwork, Federal Work-Study, institutionally sponsored loans, scholarships/grants, health care benefits, and tuition waivers (partial) available. Support available to part-time students. Financial award application deadline: 6/1; financial award applicants required to submit FAFSA. *Faculty research:* Race, crime, and class inequality; human trafficking; textual analysis and early Christianity; drug policy implementation; professionalism in police practice; service-learning; Chinese cultural studies. *Unit head:* Dr. James Pappas, Dean/Vice President of OU Outreach, 405-325-6361, Fax: 405-325-7132, E-mail: jpappas@ou.edu. *Application contact:* Missy Heinze, Recruitment Coordinator, 405-325-0559, Fax: 405-325-7132, E-mail: mheinze@ou.edu.
Website: http://www.ou.edu/cls/

The University of South Dakota, Graduate School, College of Arts and Sciences, Program in Administrative Studies, Vermillion, SD 57069-2390. Offers alcohol and drug studies (MSA); criminal justice (MSA); health services administration (MSA); human resource management (MSA); interdisciplinary (MSA); long term care administration (MSA); organizational leadership (MSA). Part-time and evening/weekend programs available. Postbaccalaureate distance learning degree programs offered (no on-campus study). *Degree requirements:* For master's, thesis or alternative. *Entrance requirements:* For master's, 3 years of work or experience, minimum GPA of 2.7, resume. Additional exam requirements/recommendations for international students: Required—TOEFL (minimum score 550 paper-based; 79 iBT). Electronic applications accepted.

The University of South Dakota, Graduate School, School of Health Sciences, Vermillion, SD 57069-2390. Offers addiction studies (MA); alcohol and drug studies (Graduate Certificate); occupational therapy (MS); physical therapy (DPT); physician assistant studies (MS); social work (MSW). Part-time programs available. *Entrance requirements:* For master's, GRE General Test, GRE Subject Test. *Faculty research:* Occupational therapy, physical therapy, vision, pediatrics, geriatrics.

University of Southern Maine, College of Management and Human Service, School of Education and Human Development, Program in Counselor Education, Portland, ME 04104-9300. Offers clinical mental health counseling (MS); counseling (CAS); culturally responsive practices in education and human development (CGS); mental health rehabilitation technician/community (CGS); rehabilitation counseling (MS); school counseling (MS); substance abuse counseling (CGS). *Accreditation:* ACA (one or more programs are accredited); CORE; Teacher Education Accreditation Council. Part-time and evening/weekend programs available. *Faculty:* 6 full-time (4 women), 3 part-time/adjunct (2 women). *Students:* 60 full-time (44 women), 82 part-time (67 women); includes 8 minority (2 Black or African American, non-Hispanic/Latino; 1 American Indian or Alaska Native, non-Hispanic/Latino; 1 Asian, non-Hispanic/Latino; 2 Hispanic/Latino; 2 Two or more races, non-Hispanic/Latino). Average age 36. 76 applicants, 75% accepted, 44 enrolled. In 2014, 35 master's, 8 other advanced degrees awarded. *Degree requirements:* For master's, comprehensive exam, thesis or alternative; for other advanced degree, thesis or alternative. *Entrance requirements:* For master's, GRE General Test or MAT, interview; for other advanced degree, master's degree. Additional exam requirements/recommendations for international students: Required—TOEFL (minimum score 550 paper-based; 79 iBT). *Application deadline:* For fall admission, 11/15 for domestic students. Application fee: $65. Electronic applications accepted. *Expenses: Tuition, area resident:* Full-time $6840; part-time $380 per credit hour. Tuition, state resident: full-time $10,260; part-time $570 per credit hour. Tuition, nonresident: full-time $18,468; part-time $1026 per credit hour. *Required fees:* $830; $83 per credit hour. Tuition and fees vary according to course load and program. *Financial support:* Research assistantships, career-related internships or fieldwork, Federal Work-Study, institutionally sponsored loans, scholarships/grants, and unspecified assistantships available. Support available to part-time students. Financial award application deadline: 3/1; financial award applicants required to submit FAFSA. *Faculty research:* Counselor licensure, group dynamics, counseling theories, healthy adaptation, counselor educator well-being. *Unit head:* Adele Baruch, Program Coordinator, 207-780-5317, E-mail: abaruch@usm.maine.edu. *Application contact:* Mary Sloan, Assistant Dean of Graduate Studies and Director of Graduate Admissions, 207-780-4386, E-mail: gradstudies@usm.maine.edu.
Website: http://usm.maine.edu/counselor-education

University of South Florida, College of Behavioral and Community Sciences, Department of Rehabilitation and Mental Health Counseling, Tampa, FL 33620-9951. Offers addictions and substance abuse counseling (MA); marriage and family therapy (MA). *Accreditation:* CORE. Part-time and evening/weekend programs available. *Faculty:* 5 full-time (3 women), 1 part-time/adjunct (0 women). *Students:* 63 full-time (52 women), 54 part-time (50 women); includes 32 minority (9 Black or African American, non-Hispanic/Latino; 3 Asian, non-Hispanic/Latino; 18 Hispanic/Latino; 1 Native Hawaiian or other Pacific Islander, non-Hispanic/Latino; 1 Two or more races, non-Hispanic/Latino), 1 international. Average age 30. 52 applicants, 67% accepted, 25 enrolled. In 2014, 41 master's awarded. *Degree requirements:* For master's, comprehensive exam, thesis optional. *Entrance requirements:* For master's, GRE General Test, three letters of recommendation, personal statement of intent, on-campus interview, undergraduate statistics or research methods course. Additional exam requirements/recommendations for international students: Required—TOEFL (minimum score 550 paper-based; 79 iBT) or IELTS (minimum score 6.5). *Application deadline:* For fall admission, 2/15 for domestic students, 1/2 for international students; for spring admission, 10/15 for domestic students, 6/1 for international students. Application fee: $30. Electronic applications accepted. *Total annual research expenditures:* $233,747. *Unit head:* Dr. Tennyson Wright, Chair and Associate Professor, 813-974-2963, Fax: 813-974-8080, E-mail: tjwright@usf.edu. *Application contact:* Dr. Gary DuDell, Instructor and Director of Graduate Studies, 813-974-1257, Fax: 813-974-8080, E-mail: gdudell@usf.edu.
Website: http://rmhc.cbcs.usf.edu/

Viterbo University, Master of Science in Mental Health Counseling Program, La Crosse, WI 54601-4797. Offers addiction counseling (MS); child and adolescent counseling (MS); complementary health and wellness counseling (MS). Part-time and evening/weekend programs available. *Faculty:* 3 full-time (1 woman), 6 part-time/adjunct (3 women). *Students:* 52 full-time (43 women), 10 part-time (8 women); includes 6 minority (2 Black or African American, non-Hispanic/Latino; 1 Asian, non-Hispanic/Latino; 3 Two or more races, non-Hispanic/Latino), 1 international. Average age 33. 41 applicants, 51% accepted, 20 enrolled. In 2014, 12 master's awarded. *Degree requirements:* For master's, comprehensive exam, thesis, 54 credits of core program courses; 6 elective credits; minimum GPA of 3.0; action research project; practicum/internship experience. *Entrance requirements:* For master's, MAT, BS in a human service or social science discipline; prerequisite coursework in general psychology, behavior disorders/abnormal psychology, and research methods/statistics; minimum undergraduate cumulative GPA of 3.0; background check; personal statement; undergraduate transcripts; interview. Additional exam requirements/recommendations for international students: Required—TOEFL (minimum score 525 paper-based). *Application deadline:* For fall admission, 3/15 priority date for domestic students, 7/31 priority date for international students. Applications are processed on a rolling basis. Application fee: $50. Electronic applications accepted. Application fee is waived when completed online. *Expenses:* Expenses: $475 per credit. *Financial support:* Applicants required to submit FAFSA. *Faculty research:* Supervision, recovery substance abuse, culture, counseling theory, health and wellness. *Unit head:* Dr. Debra A. Murray, Program Director, 608-796-3720, E-mail: damurray@viterbo.edu. *Application contact:* Dr. Debra A. Murray, Program Director, 608-796-3720, E-mail: damurray@viterbo.edu.
Website: http://www.viterbo.edu/master-science-mental-health-counseling

Walden University, Graduate Programs, School of Counseling, Minneapolis, MN 55401. Offers addiction counseling (MS), including addictions and public health, child and adolescent counseling, family studies and interventions, forensic counseling, general program (MS, PhD), trauma and crisis counseling; counselor education and supervision (PhD), including consultation, counseling and social change, forensic mental health counseling, general program (MS, PhD), trauma and crisis; marriage, couple, and family counseling (MS), including forensic counseling, general program (MS, PhD), trauma and crisis counseling; mental health counseling (MS), including forensic counseling, general program (MS, PhD), trauma and crisis counseling; school counseling (MS), including addiction counseling, crisis and trauma, general program (MS, PhD), military families and culture. Part-time and evening/weekend programs available. Postbaccalaureate distance learning degree programs offered (no on-campus study). *Faculty:* 77 full-time (62 women), 314 part-time/adjunct (215 women). *Students:* 1,835 full-time (1,558 women), 1,518 part-time (1,293 women); includes 1,521 minority (1,135 Black or African American, non-Hispanic/Latino; 13 American Indian or Alaska Native, non-Hispanic/Latino; 27 Asian, non-Hispanic/Latino; 234 Hispanic/Latino; 5 Native Hawaiian or other Pacific Islander, non-Hispanic/Latino; 107 Two or more races, non-Hispanic/Latino), 16 international. Average age 38. 684 applicants, 91% accepted, 610 enrolled. In 2014, 592 master's, 4 doctorates awarded. *Degree requirements:* For master's, residency, field experience, professional development plan, licensure plan; for doctorate, thesis/dissertation, residency, practicum, internship. *Entrance requirements:* For master's, bachelor's degree or higher; minimum GPA of 2.5; official transcripts; goal statement (for some programs); access to computer and Internet; for doctorate, master's degree or higher; three years of related professional or academic experience (preferred); minimum GPA of 3.0; goal statement and current resume (for select programs); official transcripts; access to computer and Internet. Additional exam requirements/recommendations for international students: Required—TOEFL (minimum score 550 paper-based, 79 iBT), IELTS (minimum score 6.5), Michigan English Language Assessment Battery (minimum score 82), or PTE (minimum score 53). *Application deadline:* Applications are processed on a rolling basis. Application fee: $0. Electronic applications accepted. *Expenses: Tuition:* Full-time $11,925; part-time $500 per credit hour. *Required fees:* $647. *Financial support:* Federal Work-Study, scholarships/grants, unspecified assistantships, and family tuition reduction, active duty/veteran tuition reduction, group tuition reduction, interest-free payment plans, employee tuition reduction available. Support available to part-time students. Financial award applicants required to submit FAFSA. *Unit head:* Dr. Savitri Dixon-Saxon, Associate Dean, 866-492-5336. *Application contact:* Meghan M. Thomas, Vice President of Enrollment Management, 866-492-5336, E-mail: info@waldenu.edu.

Walden University, Graduate Programs, School of Social Work and Human Services, Minneapolis, MN 55401. Offers addictions (MSW); addictions and social work (DSW); children, families, and couples (MSW); clinical expertise (DSW); criminal justice (DSW); crisis and trauma (MSW); disaster, crisis, and intervention (DSW); forensic populations and settings (MSW); general program (MSW); human services (MS, PhD), including clinical social work (PhD), criminal justice, disaster, crisis and intervention, family studies and intervention strategies (PhD), family studies and interventions, general program, human services administration, public health, social policy analysis and planning; medical social work (MSW, DSW); military families and culture (MSW); policy practice (DSW); social work (PhD), including addictions and social work, clinical expertise, disaster, crisis and intervention (MS, PhD), family studies and interventions (MS, PhD), medical social work, policy practice, social work administration; social work administration (DSW). Part-time and evening/weekend programs available. Postbaccalaureate distance learning degree programs offered (no on-campus study). *Faculty:* 18 full-time (11 women), 236 part-time/adjunct (156 women). *Students:* 1,400 full-time (1,205 women), 884 part-time (759 women); includes 1,586 minority (1,373 Black or African American, non-Hispanic/Latino; 20 American Indian or Alaska Native, non-Hispanic/Latino; 16 Asian, non-Hispanic/Latino; 120 Hispanic/Latino; 57 Two or more races, non-Hispanic/Latino), 14 international. Average age 40. 892 applicants, 96% accepted, 826 enrolled. In 2014, 61 master's, 14 doctorates awarded. *Degree requirements:* For master's, residency (for some programs); for doctorate, thesis/dissertation, residency. *Entrance requirements:* For master's, bachelor's degree or higher; minimum GPA of 2.5; official transcripts; goal statement (for some programs); access to computer and Internet; for doctorate, master's degree or higher; three years of related professional or academic experience (preferred); minimum GPA of 3.0; goal statement and current resume (for select programs); official transcripts; access to computer and Internet. Additional exam requirements/recommendations for international students: Required—TOEFL (minimum score 550 paper-based, 79 iBT), IELTS (minimum score 6.5), Michigan English Language Assessment Battery (minimum score 82), or PTE (minimum score 53). *Application deadline:* Applications are processed on a rolling basis. Application fee: $0. Electronic applications accepted. *Expenses: Tuition:* Full-time $11,925; part-time $500 per credit hour. *Required fees:* $647. *Financial support:* Fellowships, Federal Work-Study, scholarships/grants, unspecified assistantships, and family tuition reduction, active duty/veteran tuition reduction, group tuition reduction, interest-free payment plans, employee tuition reduction available. Support available to part-time students. Financial award applicants required to submit FAFSA. *Unit head:* Dr. Savitri Dixon-Saxon, Associate Dean, 866-492-5336. *Application contact:* Meghan Thomas, Vice President of Enrollment Management, 866-492-5336, E-mail: info@waldenu.edu.
Website: http://www.waldenu.edu/colleges-schools/school-of-social-work-and-human-services/academic-programs

Washburn University, School of Applied Studies, Department of Human Services, Topeka, KS 66621. Offers addiction counseling (MA). Evening/weekend programs available. *Faculty:* 4 full-time (3 women). *Students:* 20 full-time (15 women), 5 part-time (4 women). Average age 43. In 2014, 3 master's awarded. *Entrance requirements:* For master's, minimum GPA of 3.0 in last 60 hours of coursework. Additional exam requirements/recommendations for international students: Required—TOEFL (minimum score 80 iBT). *Application deadline:* For fall admission, 5/1 for domestic students. Application fee: $35. *Expenses:* Tuition, state resident: full-time $6120; part-time $340 per credit hour. Tuition, nonresident: full-time $12,456; part-time $692 per credit hour. *Required fees:* $86; $43 per semester. Tuition and fees vary according to program. *Financial support:* Career-related internships or fieldwork, Federal Work-Study, institutionally sponsored loans, and scholarships/grants available. Financial award applicants required to submit FAFSA. *Faculty research:* Professional identity development in students, expressive therapeutic writing, prevention, community mental health, agency professional development, behavioral analysis, group living among the

elderly, ethical identity development, higher education pedagogy, Morita therapy/anxiety disorders, ecological/contextual healing, post-trauma. *Unit head:* Dr. Brian Ogawa, Chair, 785-670-2116, Fax: 785-670-1027, E-mail: brian.ogawa@washburn.edu. Website: http://www.washburn.edu/academics/college-schools/applied-studies/departments/human-services/

Waynesburg University, Graduate and Professional Studies, Canonsburg, PA 15370. Offers business (MBA), including energy management, finance, health systems, human resources, leadership, market development; counseling (MA), including addictions

counseling, clinical mental health; education (M Ed, MAT), including autism (M Ed), curriculum and instruction (M Ed), educational leadership (M Ed), online teaching (M Ed); nursing (MSN), including administration, education, informatics; nursing practice (DNP); special education (M Ed); technology (M Ed); MSN/MBA. *Accreditation:* AACN. Part-time and evening/weekend programs available. *Degree requirements:* For doctorate, thesis/dissertation. *Entrance requirements:* Additional exam requirements/recommendations for international students: Required—TOEFL. Electronic applications accepted.

Applied Behavior Analysis

Antioch University New England, Graduate School, Department of Applied Psychology, Program in Autism Spectrum Disorders, Keene, NH 03431-3552. Offers applied behavior analysis (Certificate); applied behavior analysis internship (Certificate); autism spectrum disorders (Certificate). *Entrance requirements:* Additional exam requirements/recommendations for international students: Required—TOEFL (minimum score 550 paper-based).

Antioch University New England, Graduate School, Department of Education, Experienced Educators Program, Keene, NH 03431-3552. Offers foundations of education (M Ed), including applied behavioral analysis, autism spectrum disorders, educating for sustainability, next-generation learning using technology, problem-based learning using critical skills, teacher leadership; principal certification (PMC). *Degree requirements:* For master's, thesis, practicum. *Entrance requirements:* For master's, previous course work and work experience in education. Additional exam requirements/recommendations for international students: Required—TOEFL (minimum score 550 paper-based). Electronic applications accepted. *Expenses:* Contact institution. *Faculty research:* Classroom action research, school restructuring, problem-based learning, brain-based learning.

Arizona State University at the Tempe campus, College of Liberal Arts and Sciences, Department of Psychology, Tempe, AZ 85287-1104. Offers applied behavior analysis (MS); behavioral neuroscience (PhD); clinical psychology (PhD); cognitive science (PhD); developmental psychology (PhD); quantitative psychology (PhD); social psychology (PhD). *Accreditation:* APA. *Degree requirements:* For doctorate, comprehensive exam, thesis/dissertation, interactive Program of Study (iPOS) submitted before completing 50 percent of required credit hours. *Entrance requirements:* For doctorate, GRE General Test, GRE Subject Test, minimum GPA of 3.0 or equivalent in last 2 years of work leading to bachelor's degree. Additional exam requirements/recommendations for international students: Required—TOEFL, IELTS, or PTE. Electronic applications accepted.

Auburn University, Graduate School, College of Liberal Arts, Department of Psychology, Auburn University, AL 36849. Offers applied behavior analysis in developmental disabilities (MS); clinical psychology (PhD); experimental psychology (PhD); industrial/organizational psychology (PhD). *Accreditation:* APA (one or more programs are accredited). Part-time programs available. *Faculty:* 23 full-time (9 women), 2 part-time/adjunct (both women). *Students:* 49 full-time (34 women), 47 part-time (31 women); includes 13 minority (6 Black or African American, non-Hispanic/Latino; 3 Asian, non-Hispanic/Latino; 4 Hispanic/Latino), 5 international. Average age 27. 328 applicants, 10% accepted, 23 enrolled. In 2014, 22 master's, 5 doctorates awarded. *Degree requirements:* For doctorate, thesis/dissertation. *Entrance requirements:* For master's, GRE General Test, GRE Subject Test, minimum GPA of 3.25 in psychology, 3.0 overall; for doctorate, GRE General Test, GRE Subject Test. *Application deadline:* For fall admission, 7/7 for domestic students; for spring admission, 11/24 for domestic students. Applications are processed on a rolling basis. Application fee: $50 ($60 for international students). Electronic applications accepted. *Expenses:* Tuition, state resident: full-time $8586; part-time $477 per credit hour. Tuition, nonresident: full-time $25,758; part-time $1431 per credit hour. *Required fees:* $804 per semester. Tuition and fees vary according to degree level and program. *Financial support:* Research assistantships, teaching assistantships, and Federal Work-Study available. Support available to part-time students. Financial award application deadline: 3/15; financial award applicants required to submit FAFSA. *Faculty research:* Clinical psychology, learning, industrial psychology, organizational psychology. *Total annual research expenditures:* $200,000. *Unit head:* Dr. Peter Chen, Head, 334-844-4412. *Application contact:* Dr. George Flowers, Dean of the Graduate School, 334-844-2125.

Ball State University, Graduate School, Teachers College, Department of Special Education, Muncie, IN 47306-1099. Offers applied behavior analysis (MA); special education (MA, MAE, Ed D, Ed S). *Accreditation:* NCATE. *Faculty:* 18 full-time (13 women), 26 part-time/adjunct (21 women). *Students:* 227 full-time (201 women), 997 part-time (890 women); includes 98 minority (54 Black or African American, non-Hispanic/Latino; 8 American Indian or Alaska Native, non-Hispanic/Latino; 15 Asian, non-Hispanic/Latino; 16 Hispanic/Latino; 3 Native Hawaiian or other Pacific Islander, non-Hispanic/Latino; 2 Two or more races, non-Hispanic/Latino), 55 international. Average age 30. 674 applicants, 85% accepted, 402 enrolled. In 2014, 370 master's, 3 doctorates, 217 other advanced degrees awarded. *Degree requirements:* For doctorate, thesis/dissertation; for Ed S, thesis. *Entrance requirements:* For doctorate, GRE General Test, interview, minimum graduate GPA of 3.2; for Ed S, GRE General Test. Application fee: $50. *Financial support:* In 2014–15, 6 students received support, including 6 research assistantships with partial tuition reimbursements available (averaging $10,112 per year), 2 teaching assistantships with partial tuition reimbursements available (averaging $7,250 per year); unspecified assistantships also available. Financial award application deadline: 3/1. *Faculty research:* Language development and utilization in the handicapped (preschool through adult). *Unit head:* Dr. John Merbler, Chairperson, 765-285-5700, Fax: 765-285-4280, E-mail: jmerbler@bsu.edu. *Application contact:* Dr. Robert Morris, Associate Provost for Research and Dean of the Graduate School, 765-285-1300, E-mail: rmorris@bsu.edu.
Website: http://www.bsu.edu/teachers/departments/sped/

Baylor University, Graduate School, School of Education, Department of Educational Psychology, Waco, TX 76798-7301. Offers applied behavior analysis (MS Ed); educational psychology (MA, PhD); exceptionalities (PhD); learning and development (PhD); measurement (PhD); school psychology (Ed S). *Accreditation:* NCATE. *Degree requirements:* For master's, thesis optional; for doctorate, comprehensive exam, thesis/dissertation; for Ed S, comprehensive exam, thesis or alternative. *Entrance requirements:* For master's, minimum GPA of 3.0; for doctorate, GRE General Test, master's degree; for Ed S, GRE General Test. Additional exam requirements/recommendations for international students: Required—TOEFL. Electronic applications accepted. *Faculty research:* Individual differences, quantitative methods, gifted and

talented, special education, school psychology, autism, applied behavior analysis, learning, human development.

Bay Path University, Program in Education, Longmeadow, MA 01106-2292. Offers applied behavior analysis (MS Ed); moderate disabilities 5-12 (MS Ed); moderate disabilities PreK-8 (MS Ed); severe disabilities PreK-12 (MS Ed); special education (MS Ed, Ed S). Part-time and evening/weekend programs available. Postbaccalaureate distance learning degree programs offered. *Students:* 55 full-time (50 women), 252 part-time (224 women); includes 42 minority (15 Black or African American, non-Hispanic/Latino; 3 American Indian or Alaska Native, non-Hispanic/Latino; 5 Asian, non-Hispanic/Latino; 13 Hispanic/Latino; 1 Native Hawaiian or other Pacific Islander, non-Hispanic/Latino; 5 Two or more races, non-Hispanic/Latino). Average age 32. 176 applicants, 88% accepted, 137 enrolled. In 2014, 68 master's, 18 Ed Ss awarded. *Degree requirements:* For master's, six 3-credit courses and one 12-credit practicum for a total of 30 credits. *Application deadline:* Applications are processed on a rolling basis. Application fee: $45. Electronic applications accepted. Application fee is waived when completed online. *Expenses:* Expenses: Contact institution. *Financial support:* In 2014–15, 10 students received support. Scholarships/grants available. Financial award applicants required to submit FAFSA. *Unit head:* Dr. Liz Fleming, Director/Founding Dean, 413-565-1332. *Application contact:* Diane Ranaldi, Dean of Graduate Admissions, 413-565-1332, Fax: 413-565-1250, E-mail: dranaldi@baypath.edu. Website: http://graduate.baypath.edu/Graduate-Programs/Programs-On-Campus/MS-Programs/Education-Special-Education

Caldwell University, Graduate Studies, Division of Applied Behavior Analysis, Caldwell, NJ 07006-6195. Offers MA, PhD, Post-Master's Certificate. Part-time programs available. *Faculty:* 5 full-time (3 women), 3 part-time/adjunct (all women). *Students:* 12 full-time (10 women), 92 part-time (87 women); includes 20 minority (4 Black or African American, non-Hispanic/Latino; 1 American Indian or Alaska Native, non-Hispanic/Latino; 2 Asian, non-Hispanic/Latino; 12 Hispanic/Latino; 1 Two or more races, non-Hispanic/Latino), 2 international. Average age 34. 61 applicants, 48% accepted, 26 enrolled. In 2014, 22 master's, 4 doctorates awarded. Terminal master's awarded for partial completion of doctoral program. *Degree requirements:* For master's, comprehensive exam; for doctorate, comprehensive exam, thesis/dissertation. *Entrance requirements:* For master's, GRE, MAT; for doctorate, GRE, MAT, ABA Certification. Additional exam requirements/recommendations for international students: Required—TOEFL (minimum score 580 paper-based). *Application deadline:* For fall admission, 7/1 for domestic and international students; for spring admission, 12/1 for domestic and international students. Applications are processed on a rolling basis. Application fee: $40. Electronic applications accepted. *Expenses: Tuition:* Part-time $930 per credit. *Financial support:* In 2014–15, 5 teaching assistantships with partial tuition reimbursements were awarded. Financial award applicants required to submit FAFSA. *Faculty research:* Autism research. *Unit head:* Dr. Sharon Reeve, Department Chair/Co-Coordinator, 973-618-3315, Fax: 973-615-3580, E-mail: sreeve@caldwell.edu. *Application contact:* Vilma Mueller, Director of Graduate Studies, 973-618-3544, E-mail: graduate@caldwell.edu.

California State University, Sacramento, Office of Graduate Studies, College of Social Sciences and Interdisciplinary Studies, Department of Psychology, Sacramento, CA 95819. Offers applied behavior analysis (MA); counseling psychology (MA); industrial/organizational psychology (MA). Part-time programs available. *Degree requirements:* For master's, thesis, writing proficiency exam. *Entrance requirements:* For master's, GRE, minimum GPA of 3.0 during previous 2 years. Additional exam requirements/recommendations for international students: Required—TOEFL. Electronic applications accepted.

California State University, Stanislaus, College of Human and Health Sciences, Program in Psychology (MA/MS), Turlock, CA 95382. Offers behavior analysis (MS); counseling psychology (MS); psychology (MA). Part-time programs available. *Degree requirements:* For master's, thesis. *Entrance requirements:* For master's, GRE, minimum GPA of 3.0, 3 letters of reference, 16 psychology prerequisites, personal statement. Additional exam requirements/recommendations for international students: Required—TOEFL (minimum score 550 paper-based). Electronic applications accepted. *Faculty research:* Hedonic tone judgment, syntax and autism, early literacy assessment and native and non-native languages.

Capella University, Harold Abel School of Social and Behavioral Science, Master's Programs in Psychology, Minneapolis, MN 55402. Offers applied behavior analysis (MS); clinical psychology (MS); counseling psychology (MS); educational psychology (MS); evaluation, research, and measurement (MS); general advanced studies in human behavior (MS); general psychology (MS); industrial/organizational psychology (MS); leadership coaching psychology (MS); school psychology (MS); sport psychology (MS).

The Chicago School of Professional Psychology, Program in Applied Behavior Analysis, Chicago, IL 60610. Offers MS, PhD. *Degree requirements:* For master's, thesis, practicum; for doctorate, thesis/dissertation, practicum. *Entrance requirements:* For doctorate, GRE. Additional exam requirements/recommendations for international students: Required—TOEFL.

The Chicago School of Professional Psychology at Downtown Los Angeles, Program in Applied Behavior Analysis, Los Angeles, CA 90017. Offers Psy D.

The Chicago School of Professional Psychology at Downtown Los Angeles, Program in Clinical Psychology, Los Angeles, CA 90017. Offers applied behavior analysis (MA); clinical psychology (Psy D); marital and family therapy (MA).

Drexel University, Goodwin College of Professional Studies, School of Education, Philadelphia, PA 19104-2875. Offers applied behavior analysis (MS); creativity and innovation (MS); education improvement and transformation (MS); educational administration (MS); educational leadership and management (Ed D); educational leadership development and learning technologies (PhD); global and international

education (MS); higher education (MS); human resources development (MS); learning technologies (MS); mathematics, learning and teaching (MS); special education (MS); teaching, learning and curriculum (MS). Part-time and evening/weekend programs available. Postbaccalaureate distance learning degree programs offered (no on-campus study). *Degree requirements:* For doctorate, thesis/dissertation. *Entrance requirements:* For doctorate, GRE or GMAT. Additional exam requirements/recommendations for international students: Required—TOEFL, IELTS. Electronic applications accepted. Application fee is waived when completed online. *Expenses:* Contact institution. *Faculty research:* Leadership development, mathematics education, literacy, autism, educational technology.

Eastern University, Department of Counseling Psychology, St. Davids, PA 19087-3696. Offers applied behavior analysis (MA); counseling (MA); school counseling (MA, Certificate); school psychology (MS, Certificate). Part-time programs available. *Faculty:* 6 full-time (3 women), 8 part-time/adjunct (6 women). *Students:* 61 full-time (49 women), 102 part-time (85 women); includes 51 minority (44 Black or African American, non-Hispanic/Latino; 1 American Indian or Alaska Native, non-Hispanic/Latino; 4 Hispanic/Latino; 2 Two or more races, non-Hispanic/Latino), 2 international. Average age 30. 117 applicants, 77% accepted, 68 enrolled. In 2014, 68 master's awarded. *Degree requirements:* For master's, internship. *Entrance requirements:* For master's, minimum GPA of 2.8 (3.0 for school psychology). Additional exam requirements/recommendations for international students: Required—TOEFL (minimum score 550 paper-based; 79 iBT). *Application deadline:* For fall admission, 6/15 for domestic students, 5/30 for international students. Applications are processed on a rolling basis. Application fee: $35. Electronic applications accepted. Application fee is waived when completed online. *Expenses: Tuition:* Full-time $15,600; part-time $650 per credit. *Required fees:* $30; $27.50 per semester. One-time fee: $50. Tuition and fees vary according to course load, degree level and program. *Financial support:* In 2014–15, 21 students received support, including 6 research assistantships with partial tuition reimbursements available (averaging $8,115 per year); scholarships/grants and unspecified assistantships also available. Financial award application deadline: 3/15. *Unit head:* Dr. Susan Edgar-Smith, Co-Chair, 610-341-4379. *Application contact:* Katelyn Ambrose, Enrollment Counselor, 610-225-5564, Fax: 610-341-1585, E-mail: kambrose@eastern.edu.
Website: http://www.eastern.edu/academics/programs/counseling-psychology-department

Endicott College, Van Loan School of Graduate and Professional Studies, Program in Autism and Applied Behavior Analysis, Beverly, MA 01915-2096. Offers M Ed, PhD. Part-time programs available. *Faculty:* 7 full-time (2 women), 28 part-time/adjunct (19 women). *Students:* 7 full-time (all women), 101 part-time (91 women); includes 11 minority (3 Black or African American, non-Hispanic/Latino; 5 Asian, non-Hispanic/Latino; 2 Hispanic/Latino; 1 Two or more races, non-Hispanic/Latino), 3 international. Average age 31. 34 applicants, 62% accepted, 18 enrolled. In 2014, 19 master's awarded. *Degree requirements:* For master's, thesis; for doctorate, thesis/dissertation, qualifying examination. *Entrance requirements:* For master's, MAT or GRE, undergraduate transcript, two recommendations, personal statement. Additional exam requirements/recommendations for international students: Required—TOEFL. *Application deadline:* Applications are processed on a rolling basis. Application fee: $50. Electronic applications accepted. *Financial support:* Applicants required to submit FAFSA. *Faculty research:* ABA intervention for autism, behavioral assessment, evidence-based treatments. *Unit head:* Dr. Mary Jane Weiss, Director of Autism and Applied Behavior Analysis, 978-232-2199, E-mail: mweiss@endicott.edu. *Application contact:* Ian Menchini, Director, Graduate Enrollment and Advising, 978-232-5292, Fax: 978-232-3000, E-mail: imenchin@endicott.edu.
Website: http://www.endicott.edu/VanLoan/Institute-Behavioral-Studies/Degree-Programs/Master-Ed-Autism-ABA.aspx

Fairfield University, Graduate School of Education and Allied Professions, Fairfield, CT 06824. Offers applied behavior analysis (ATC); applied psychology (MA); clinical mental health counseling (MA, CAS); early childhood studies (ATC); educational technology (MA); elementary education (MA, CAS); family studies (MA); integration of spirituality and religion in counseling (ATC); marriage and family therapy (MA); school counseling (MA, CAS); school psychology (MA, CAS); school-based marriage and family therapy (ATC); secondary education (MA); special education (MA, CAS); substance abuse counseling (ATC); teaching (Certificate); teaching and foundations (MA, CAS); TESOL, world languages, and bilingual education (MA, CAS). *Accreditation:* NCATE. Part-time and evening/weekend programs available. *Faculty:* 23 full-time (19 women), 32 part-time/adjunct (25 women). *Students:* 148 full-time (131 women), 286 part-time (238 women); includes 81 minority (18 Black or African American, non-Hispanic/Latino; 1 American Indian or Alaska Native, non-Hispanic/Latino; 14 Asian, non-Hispanic/Latino; 39 Hispanic/Latino; 9 Two or more races, non-Hispanic/Latino), 13 international. Average age 34. 264 applicants, 54% accepted, 68 enrolled. In 2014, 142 master's awarded. *Degree requirements:* For master's, comprehensive exam. *Entrance requirements:* For master's, PRAXIS I (for certification programs), minimum GPA of 3.0, 2 recommendations, resume. Additional exam requirements/recommendations for international students: Required—TOEFL (minimum score 550 paper-based; 84 iBT) or IELTS (minimum score 7.5). *Application deadline:* For fall admission, 2/15 for international students; for spring admission, 10/1 for international students. Application fee: $60. Electronic applications accepted. *Expenses:* Expenses: $675 per credit hour. *Financial support:* In 2014–15, 55 students received support. Career-related internships or fieldwork and unspecified assistantships available. Financial award applicants required to submit FAFSA. *Faculty research:* Literacy, spirituality, special education, bilingual/multicultural education, mentoring and professional development. *Unit head:* Dr. Robert D. Hannafin, Dean, 203-254-4250, Fax: 203-254-4241, E-mail: rhannafin@fairfield.edu. *Application contact:* Marianne Gumpper, Director of Graduate and Continuing Studies Admission, 203-254-4184, Fax: 203-254-4073, E-mail: gradadmis@fairfield.edu.
Website: http://www.fairfield.edu/academics/schoolscollegescenters/graduateschoolofeducationalliedprofessions/graduateprograms/

Florida Institute of Technology, Graduate Programs, College of Psychology and Liberal Arts, Program in Applied Behavior Analysis and Organizational Behavior Management, Melbourne, FL 32901-6975. Offers MS. *Students:* 14 full-time (11 women), 1 part-time (0 women); includes 3 minority (1 Asian, non-Hispanic/Latino; 1 Hispanic/Latino; 1 Two or more races, non-Hispanic/Latino), 2 international. Average age 27. 31 applicants, 35% accepted, 6 enrolled. In 2014, 5 master's awarded. *Degree requirements:* For master's, comprehensive exam, thesis or alternative, capstone project. *Entrance requirements:* For master's, GRE General Test, 3 letters of recommendation, resume, statement of objectives. *Expenses: Tuition:* Part-time $1179 per credit hour. Tuition and fees vary according to campus/location. *Unit head:* Dr. Mary Beth Kenkel, Dean, 321-674-8142, E-mail: mkenkel@fit.edu. *Application contact:* Cheryl A. Brown, Associate Director of Graduate Admissions, 321-674-7581, Fax: 321-723-9468, E-mail: cbrown@fit.edu.
Website: http://cpla.fit.edu/programs.php

Florida Institute of Technology, Graduate Programs, College of Psychology and Liberal Arts, Program in Behavior Analysis, Melbourne, FL 32901-6975. Offers PhD. Evening/weekend programs available. *Students:* 9 full-time (6 women), 1 (woman) part-time; includes 2 minority (1 Black or African American, non-Hispanic/Latino; 1 Hispanic/Latino). Average age 30. 23 applicants, 48% accepted, 4 enrolled. In 2014, 2 doctorates awarded. *Degree requirements:* For doctorate, comprehensive exam, thesis/dissertation (for some programs). *Entrance requirements:* For doctorate, GRE General Test, 3 letters of recommendation, resume, statement of objectives, minimum GPA of 3.6. *Expenses: Tuition:* Part-time $1179 per credit hour. Tuition and fees vary according to campus/location. *Unit head:* Dr. Mary Beth Kenkel, Dean, 321-674-8142, E-mail: mkenkel@fit.edu. *Application contact:* Cheryl A. Brown, Associate Director of Graduate Admissions, 321-674-7581, Fax: 321-723-9468, E-mail: cbrown@fit.edu.
Website: http://www.fit.edu/programs/9147/phd-behavior-analysis#.VT_Wqk10ypo

Florida Institute of Technology, Graduate Programs, College of Psychology and Liberal Arts, Program in Professional Behavior Analysis, Melbourne, FL 32901-6975. Offers MA. *Accreditation:* APA. Part-time programs available. *Students:* 56 full-time (41 women), 1 (woman) part-time; includes 20 minority (1 Black or African American, non-Hispanic/Latino; 1 American Indian or Alaska Native, non-Hispanic/Latino; 9 Asian, non-Hispanic/Latino; 8 Hispanic/Latino; 1 Two or more races, non-Hispanic/Latino). Average age 27. 85 applicants, 68% accepted, 54 enrolled. Terminal master's awarded for partial completion of doctoral program. *Degree requirements:* For master's, comprehensive exam (for some programs), thesis (for some programs). *Entrance requirements:* Additional exam requirements/recommendations for international students: Required—TOEFL (minimum score 550 paper-based; 79 iBT). *Application deadline:* For fall admission, 4/1 for international students; for spring admission, 9/30 for international students. Applications are processed on a rolling basis. Application fee: $0. Electronic applications accepted. *Expenses: Tuition:* Part-time $1179 per credit hour. Tuition and fees vary according to campus/location. *Financial support:* Career-related internships or fieldwork, institutionally sponsored loans, tuition waivers (partial), unspecified assistantships, and tuition remissions available. Support available to part-time students. Financial award application deadline: 3/1; financial award applicants required to submit FAFSA. *Faculty research:* Addictions, neuropsychology, child abuse, assessment, psychological trauma. *Unit head:* Dr. Mary Beth Kenkel, Dean, 321-674-8142, Fax: 321-674-7105, E-mail: mkenkel@fit.edu. *Application contact:* Cheryl A. Brown, Associate Director of Graduate Admissions, 321-674-7581, Fax: 321-723-9468, E-mail: cbrown@fit.edu.
Website: http://www.fit.edu/programs/8146/ma-professional-behavior-analysis#.VUIxk010ypo

Florida International University, College of Arts and Sciences, Department of Psychology, Miami, FL 33199. Offers behavioral analysis (MS); clinical science (PhD); counseling psychology (MS); developmental science (MS, PhD); legal psychology (PhD); organizational psychology (MS, PhD). Program has fall admissions only. Part-time and evening/weekend programs available. Terminal master's awarded for partial completion of doctoral program. *Degree requirements:* For master's, thesis; for doctorate, comprehensive exam, thesis/dissertation. *Entrance requirements:* For master's, GRE General Test, minimum GPA of 3.0, resume, 3 letters of recommendation; for doctorate, GRE General Test, 3 letters of recommendation, resume, letter of intent, two writing samples, minimum GPA of 3.0. Additional exam requirements/recommendations for international students: Required—TOEFL (minimum score 550 paper-based; 80 iBT). Electronic applications accepted. *Faculty research:* Legal psychology, organizational and industrial psychology, child behavior psychology.

Florida State University, The Graduate School, College of Arts and Sciences, Department of Psychology, Program in Applied Behavior Analysis, Tallahassee, FL 32306. Offers MS. *Faculty:* 4 full-time (2 women). *Students:* 34 full-time (30 women); includes 7 minority (3 Black or African American, non-Hispanic/Latino; 4 Hispanic/Latino). Average age 25. 68 applicants, 38% accepted, 17 enrolled. In 2014, 17 master's awarded. *Degree requirements:* For master's, comprehensive exam. *Entrance requirements:* For master's, GRE General Test, minimum GPA of 3.0. Additional exam requirements/recommendations for international students: Required—TOEFL (minimum score 550 paper-based; 80 iBT). *Application deadline:* For fall admission, 1/15 for domestic and international students. Application fee: $30. Electronic applications accepted. *Expenses:* Expenses: Contact institution. *Financial support:* In 2014–15, 34 students received support, including research assistantships with full tuition reimbursements available (averaging $20,000 per year), 34 teaching assistantships with full tuition reimbursements available (averaging $17,775 per year); career-related internships or fieldwork, Federal Work-Study, institutionally sponsored loans, and unspecified assistantships also available. Financial award application deadline: 1/15; financial award applicants required to submit FAFSA. *Unit head:* Dr. Jon Bailey, Head, 850-644-1877, Fax: 850-645-7518, E-mail: bailey@psy.fsu.edu. *Application contact:* Cherie P. Miller, Graduate Program Assistant, 850-644-2499, Fax: 850-644-7739, E-mail: grad-info@psy.fsu.edu.
Website: http://www.psy.fsu.edu/

Georgian Court University, School of Arts and Sciences, Lakewood, NJ 08701-2697. Offers applied behavior analysis (MA); Catholic school leadership (Certificate); clinical mental health counseling (MA); holistic health studies (MA, Certificate); homeland security (MS); parish administration (Certificate); pastoral ministry (Certificate); professional counseling (Certificate); religious education (Certificate); school psychology (MA, Certificate); theology (MA, Certificate). Part-time and evening/weekend programs available. *Faculty:* 19 full-time (9 women), 9 part-time/adjunct (4 women). *Students:* 87 full-time (74 women), 127 part-time (110 women); includes 47 minority (14 Black or African American, non-Hispanic/Latino; 2 Asian, non-Hispanic/Latino; 23 Hispanic/Latino; 8 Two or more races, non-Hispanic/Latino). Average age 34. In 2014, 68 master's, 11 other advanced degrees awarded. *Degree requirements:* For master's, comprehensive exam (for some programs), thesis (for some programs). *Entrance requirements:* For master's, GRE, MAT, or NTE/PRAXIS, 3 letters of recommendation. Additional exam requirements/recommendations for international students: Required—TOEFL (minimum score 550 paper-based). *Application deadline:* For fall admission, 8/1 priority date for domestic students, 4/1 for international students; for spring admission, 1/1 priority date for domestic students, 7/1 for international students. Applications are processed on a rolling basis. Application fee: $40. Electronic applications accepted. *Expenses: Tuition:* Full-time $19,752; part-time $823 per credit. *Required fees:* $948; $243 per semester hour. Tuition and fees vary according to campus/location and program. *Financial support:* Scholarships/grants, health care benefits, and unspecified assistantships available. Financial award application deadline: 4/15; financial award applicants required to submit FAFSA. *Unit head:* Dr. Rita Kipp, Dean, 732-987-2493, Fax: 732-987-2007, E-mail: rkipp@georgian.edu. *Application contact:* Patrick Givens, Interim Director of Enrollment Management, 732-987-2736, Fax: 732-987-2084, E-mail: graduateadmissions@georgian.edu.
Website: http://www.georgian.edu/arts_sciences/index.htm

Hofstra University, School of Education, Specialized Programs in Education, Hempstead, NY 11549. Offers applied behavior analysis (Advanced Certificate); early childhood special education (MS Ed, Advanced Certificate); gifted education (Advanced Certificate); inclusive early childhood special education (MS Ed); inclusive elementary special education (MS Ed); inclusive secondary special education (MS Ed); secondary education generalist (MS Ed), including students with disabilties 7-12; special education

(MS Ed, Advanced Certificate); special education assessment and diagnosis (Advanced Certificate); special education generalist (MS Ed), including extension in secondary education; teaching students with severe or multiple disabilities (Advanced Certificate). Part-time and evening/weekend programs available. Postbaccalaureate distance learning degree programs offered (no on-campus study). *Students:* 114 full-time (90 women), 248 part-time (174 women); includes 90 minority (53 Black or African American, non-Hispanic/Latino; 2 American Indian or Alaska Native, non-Hispanic/Latino; 6 Asian, non-Hispanic/Latino; 27 Hispanic/Latino; 2 Two or more races, non-Hispanic/Latino), 2 international. Average age 32. 229 applicants, 92% accepted, 101 enrolled. In 2014, 126 master's, 8 doctorates, 42 other advanced degrees awarded. *Degree requirements:* For master's, one foreign language, comprehensive exam (for some programs), thesis (for some programs), electronic portfolio, capstone course, internship, practicum, student teaching, seminars, minimum GPA of 3.0; for doctorate, one foreign language, comprehensive exam, thesis/dissertation, qualifying hearing. *Entrance requirements:* For master's, GRE, interview, letters of recommendation, portfolio, essay, certification; for doctorate, GRE or MAT, interview, resume, essay, master's degree, 3 letters of recommendation, writing sample; for Advanced Certificate, GRE, interview, letters of recommendation, essay, professional experience, resume, master's degree. Additional exam requirements/recommendations for international students: Required—TOEFL (minimum score 550 paper-based; 80 iBT). *Application deadline:* Applications are processed on a rolling basis. Application fee: $70 ($75 for international students). Electronic applications accepted. *Expenses: Tuition:* Full-time $20,610; part-time $1145 per credit hour. *Required fees:* $970; $165 per term. Tuition and fees vary according to program. *Financial support:* In 2014–15, 220 students received support, including 99 fellowships with full and partial tuition reimbursements available (averaging $3,592 per year), 6 research assistantships with full and partial tuition reimbursements available (averaging $11,432 per year); Federal Work-Study, institutionally sponsored loans, scholarships/grants, and tuition waivers (full and partial) also available. Support available to part-time students. Financial award applicants required to submit FAFSA. *Faculty research:* Collaborative consultation, charter schools in urban and suburban districts, energy expenditures in physical activities, research literacy practices of immigrant and urban youth, universal design for learning. *Unit head:* Dr. Elfreda Blue, Chairperson, 516-463-5762, Fax: 516-463-6184, E-mail: cprevb@hofstra.edu. *Application contact:* Sunil Samuel, Assistant Vice President of Admissions, 516-463-4723, Fax: 516-463-4664, E-mail: graduateadmission@hofstra.edu.
Website: http://www.hofstra.edu/education/

James Madison University, The Graduate School, College of Health and Behavioral Sciences, Department of Graduate Psychology, Harrisonburg, VA 22807. Offers assessment and measurement (PhD); clinical and school psychology (Psy D); clinical mental health counseling (MA, Ed S); college student personnel administration (M Ed); counseling and supervision (PhD); psychological sciences (MA), including behavior analysis; school psychology (MA, Ed S). *Accreditation:* ACA (one or more programs are accredited); APA (one or more programs are accredited). Part-time and evening/weekend programs available. *Faculty:* 68 full-time (39 women), 8 part-time/adjunct (3 women). *Students:* 137 full-time (97 women), 33 part-time (23 women); includes 30 minority (18 Black or African American, non-Hispanic/Latino; 2 Asian, non-Hispanic/Latino; 7 Hispanic/Latino; 3 Two or more races, non-Hispanic/Latino), 6 international. Average age 28. 422 applicants, 23% accepted, 69 enrolled. In 2014, 49 master's, 13 doctorates, 15 other advanced degrees awarded. *Degree requirements:* For doctorate, thesis/dissertation; for Ed S, thesis. *Application deadline:* For fall admission, 2/1 for domestic students; for spring admission, 9/1 for domestic students. Application fee: $55. Electronic applications accepted. *Expenses:* Tuition, state resident: full-time $7812; part-time $434 per credit hour. Tuition, nonresident: full-time $20,430; part-time $1135 per credit hour. *Financial support:* In 2014–15, 125 students received support, including 10 fellowships, 3 teaching assistantships with full tuition reimbursements available (averaging $8,837 per year); career-related internships or fieldwork, Federal Work-Study, and 99 assistantships (averaging $7530), 13 doctoral assistantships also available. Financial award application deadline: 3/1; financial award applicants required to submit FAFSA. *Unit head:* Dr. Robin D. Anderson, Academic Unit Head, 540-568-3293, Fax: 540-568-3322, E-mail: ander2rd@jmu.edu. *Application contact:* Lynette D. Michael, Director of Graduate Admissions and Student Records, 540-568-6131 Ext. 6395, Fax: 540-568-7860, E-mail: michaeld@jmu.edu.
Website: http://www.psyc.jmu.edu/gradpsyc/

Johns Hopkins University, School of Education, Certificate Programs in Education, Baltimore, MD 21218-2699. Offers advanced methods for differentiated instruction and inclusive education (Certificate); applied behavior analysis (Certificate); counseling (CAGS); data-based decision making and organizational improvement (Certificate); early intervention/preschool special education specialist (Certificate); education leadership for independent schools (Certificate); education of students with autism and other pervasive developmental disorders (Certificate); evidence-based teaching in the health professions (Certificate); gifted education (Certificate); K-8 mathematics lead-teacher (Certificate); K-8 STEM education lead-teacher (Certificate); leadership for school, family, and community collaboration (Certificate); leadership in technology integration (Certificate); mental health counseling (Certificate); mind, brain, and teaching (Certificate); school administration and supervision (Certificate); urban education (Certificate). Part-time and evening/weekend programs available. Postbaccalaureate distance learning degree programs offered (no on-campus study). *Entrance requirements:* For degree, bachelor's degree from regionally- or nationally-accredited institution (master's for some programs), minimum GPA of 3.0 in all previous programs of study, official transcripts from all post-secondary institutions attended, essay, curriculum vitae/resume, minimum of two letters of recommendation. Additional exam requirements/recommendations for international students: Required—TOEFL (minimum score 600 paper-based; 100 iBT) or IELTS (minimum score 7). Electronic applications accepted.

Johnson State College, Graduate Program in Education, Johnson, VT 05656. Offers applied behavior analysis (MA Ed), including applied behavior analysis; curriculum and instruction (MA Ed); literacy (MA Ed); secondary education (MA Ed); special education (MA Ed). Part-time programs available. *Degree requirements:* For master's, comprehensive exam, thesis or alternative. *Entrance requirements:* For master's, interview. Additional exam requirements/recommendations for international students: Required—TOEFL. Electronic applications accepted. *Expenses: Tuition, area resident:* Part-time $511 per credit. Tuition, state resident: part-time $767 per credit. Tuition, nonresident: part-time $1103 per credit.

Lipscomb University, Program in Education, Nashville, TN 37204-3951. Offers applied behavior analysis (MS, Certificate); collaborative professional learning (M Ed, Ed S); educational leadership (M Ed, Ed S); English language learning (M Ed, Ed S); instructional coaching (Certificate); instructional practice (M Ed); learning organizations and strategic change (Ed D); professional learning and coaching in mathematics (M Ed, Ed S); reading specialty (M Ed, Ed S); special education (M Ed); teaching, learning, and leading (M Ed); technology integration (M Ed); technology integration specialist (Certificate). *Accreditation:* NCATE. Part-time and evening/weekend programs available. Postbaccalaureate distance learning degree programs offered (no on-campus study). *Faculty:* 22 full-time (16 women), 27 part-time/adjunct (17 women). *Students:*

168 full-time (128 women), 456 part-time (365 women); includes 114 minority (70 Black or African American, non-Hispanic/Latino; 1 American Indian or Alaska Native, non-Hispanic/Latino; 11 Asian, non-Hispanic/Latino; 25 Hispanic/Latino; 1 Native Hawaiian or other Pacific Islander, non-Hispanic/Latino; 6 Two or more races, non-Hispanic/Latino). Average age 32. In 2014, 195 master's, 34 doctorates, 80 other advanced degrees awarded. *Degree requirements:* For master's, comprehensive exam, portfolio, research project and presentation; for doctorate, practical capstone project in experiential setting. *Entrance requirements:* For master's, MAT (minimum score 31) or GRE General Test (minimum score 294), 2 reference letters, goals statement, writing sample, interview; for doctorate, MAT or GRE General Test, 3 reference letters, artifact of demonstrated academic excellence, written personal statements, interview. Additional exam requirements/recommendations for international students: Required—TOEFL (minimum score 570 paper-based; 80 iBT). *Application deadline:* For fall admission, 8/29 priority date for domestic students; for spring admission, 1/15 priority date for domestic students. Applications are processed on a rolling basis. Application fee: $50 ($75 for international students). *Expenses:* Expenses: $898 per credit hour. *Financial support:* Scholarships/grants, unspecified assistantships, and parterships with local school districts available. Financial award applicants required to submit FAFSA. *Faculty research:* Facilitative learning styles, leadership, student assessment, interactive multimedia inclusion, learning organizations and strategic change. *Unit head:* Dr. Deborah Boyd, Director of Graduate Studies, 615-966-6263, E-mail: deborah.boyd@lipscomb.edu. *Application contact:* Kristin Baese, Director of Enrollment and Outreach, 615-966-5173 Ext. 6081, E-mail: kristin.baese@lipscomb.edu.
Website: http://www.lipscomb.edu/education/graduate-programs

Long Island University–LIU Brooklyn, School of Education, Brooklyn, NY 11201-8423. Offers applied behavior analysis (Advanced Certificate); bilingual education in urban settings (Advanced Certificate); bilingual school counselor (Advanced Certificate); childhood/early childhood urban education (MS Ed); early childhood urban education (MS Ed, Advanced Certificate); educational leadership (Advanced Certificate); marriage and family therapy (Advanced Certificate); school counselor (MS Ed, Advanced Certificate); teaching English to speakers of other languages (TESOL) (MS Ed). *Accreditation:* Teacher Education Accreditation Council. Part-time and evening/weekend programs available. *Faculty:* 20 full-time (14 women), 47 part-time/adjunct (34 women). *Students:* 224 full-time (183 women), 604 part-time (472 women); includes 551 minority (302 Black or African American, non-Hispanic/Latino; 3 American Indian or Alaska Native, non-Hispanic/Latino; 42 Asian, non-Hispanic/Latino; 189 Hispanic/Latino; 15 Two or more races, non-Hispanic/Latino), 10 international. Average age 36. 353 applicants, 61% accepted, 129 enrolled. In 2014, 213 master's, 16 other advanced degrees awarded. *Degree requirements:* For master's, thesis optional, electronic portfolio. *Entrance requirements:* For master's, 2 letters of recommendation; GPA requirement varies by program; some programs require interview, personal statement, writing assessment; for Advanced Certificate, 2 letters of recommendation, GPA requirement varies by program; interview; personal statement. Additional exam requirements/recommendations for international students: Required—TOEFL (minimum score 500 paper-based). *Application deadline:* For fall admission, 5/1 for international students; for spring admission, 11/1 for international students. Applications are processed on a rolling basis. Electronic applications accepted. *Expenses: Tuition:* Part-time $1132 per credit. *Required fees:* $434 per semester. *Financial support:* Career-related internships or fieldwork, scholarships/grants, tuition waivers (partial), and unspecified assistantships available. Support available to part-time students. Financial award applicants required to submit FAFSA. *Faculty research:* The intersection between race and gender in diverse women's leadership and health outcomes, selective mutism, risk factors among juvenile sex offenders and their reintegration into the school system, infant development, theoretical orientation in clinical practice. *Unit head:* Dr. Amy Patraka Ginsberg, Acting Dean (2015-2016), 718-488-1055, E-mail: amy.ginsberg@liu.edu. *Application contact:* Chanelle Lester, Director of Graduate Admissions, 718-780-4321, Fax: 718-780-6110, E-mail: chanelle.lester@liu.edu.
Website: http://www.liu.edu/Brooklyn/Academics/School-of-Education

McNeese State University, Doré School of Graduate Studies, Burton College of Education, Department of Psychology, Lake Charles, LA 70609. Offers addiction treatment (MA); applied behavior analysis (MA); counseling psychology (MA); general/experimental psychology (MA). Evening/weekend programs available. *Entrance requirements:* For master's, GRE.

Monmouth University, The Graduate School, School of Education, West Long Branch, NJ 07764-1898. Offers applied behavioral analysis (Certificate); autism (Certificate); initial certification (MAT), including elementary level, K-12, secondary level; principal/school administrator (MS Ed); principal/supervisor (MS Ed); school counseling (MS Ed); special education (MS Ed), including autism, learning disabilities teacher-consultant, teacher of students with disabilities, teaching in inclusive settings; speech-language pathology (MS Ed); student affairs and college counseling (MS Ed); teaching English to speakers of other languages (TESOL) (Certificate). *Accreditation:* NCATE. Part-time and evening/weekend programs available. Postbaccalaureate distance learning degree programs offered (no on-campus study). *Faculty:* 19 full-time (15 women), 23 part-time/adjunct (18 women). *Students:* 146 full-time (120 women), 166 part-time (137 women); includes 44 minority (11 Black or African American, non-Hispanic/Latino; 4 Asian, non-Hispanic/Latino; 24 Hispanic/Latino; 1 Native Hawaiian or other Pacific Islander, non-Hispanic/Latino; 4 Two or more races, non-Hispanic/Latino). Average age 28. 448 applicants, 45% accepted, 136 enrolled. In 2014, 130 master's awarded. *Entrance requirements:* For master's, GRE taken within last 5 years (for MS Ed in speech-language pathology); SAT (minimum combined score of 1660 in 3 sections), ACT (23), GRE (minimum score of 4.0 on analytical writing section and minimum combined score of 310 on quantitative and verbal sections), or passing scores on 3 parts of Core Academic Skills Educators, minimum GPA of 3.0 in major; 2 letters of recommendation (for some programs); resume, personal statement or essay (depending on program). Additional exam requirements/recommendations for international students: Required—TOEFL (minimum score 550 paper-based; 79 iBT), IELTS (minimum score 6), Michigan English Language Assessment Battery (minimum score 77) or Certificate of Advanced English (minimum score B2). *Application deadline:* For fall admission, 7/15 priority date for domestic students, 7/1 for international students; for spring admission, 11/15 priority date for domestic students, 11/1 for international students. Applications are processed on a rolling basis. Application fee: $50. Electronic applications accepted. *Expenses: Tuition:* Full-time $18,072; part-time $1004 per credit. *Required fees:* $157 per semester. *Financial support:* In 2014–15, 275 students received support, including 236 fellowships (averaging $3,652 per year), 29 research assistantships (averaging $10,276 per year); career-related internships or fieldwork, scholarships/grants, and unspecified assistantships also available. Support available to part-time students. Financial award applicants required to submit FAFSA. *Faculty research:* Multicultural literacy, science and mathematics teaching strategies, teacher as reflective practitioner, children with disabilities. *Unit head:* Dr. John E. Henning, Dean of The School of Education, 732-263-5513, Fax: 732-263-5277. *Application contact:* Jessica Kimball, Graduate Admission Counselor, 732-571-3452, Fax: 732-263-5123, E-mail: gradadm@monmouth.edu.
Website: http://www.monmouth.edu/academics/schools/education/default.asp

Mount Aloysius College, Program in Behavioral Specialist Consulting, Cresson, PA 16630-1999. Offers MS. Evening/weekend programs available. *Entrance requirements:*

Applied Behavior Analysis

For master's, GRE or overall GPA above 3.2, two letters of recommendation; official undergraduate transcript(s); undergraduate statistics course; undergraduate research methods course (highly recommended).

National University, Academic Affairs, School of Education, La Jolla, CA 92037-1011. Offers applied behavior analysis (Certificate); applied school leadership (MS); autism (Certificate); best practices (Certificate); e-teaching and learning (Certificate); early childhood education (Certificate); education (MA), including best practices (M Ed, MA), e-teaching and learning (M Ed, MA), education technology, teacher leadership (M Ed, MA), teaching and learning in a global society (M Ed, MA), teaching mathematics (M Ed, MA); education with preliminary multiple or single subject (M Ed), including best practices (M Ed, MA), e-teaching and learning (M Ed, MA), educational technology (M Ed, MA), teacher leadership (M Ed, MA), teaching and learning in a global society (M Ed, MA), teaching mathematics (M Ed, MA); educational administration (MS); educational and instructional technology (MS); educational counseling (MS); educational technology (Certificate); higher education administration (MS); innovative school leadership (MS); instructional leadership (MS); juvenile justice special education (MS); reading (Certificate); school psychology (MS); special education (MS), including deaf and hard-of-hearing, mild/moderate disabilities, moderate/severe disabilities; teacher leadership (Certificate); teaching (MA), including applied behavioral analysis, autism, best practices (M Ed, MA), e-teaching and learning (M Ed, MA), early childhood education, educational technology (M Ed, MA), reading, special education, teacher leadership (M Ed, MA), teaching and learning in a global society (M Ed, MA), teaching mathematics (M Ed, MA); teaching mathematics (Certificate). Part-time and evening/weekend programs available. Postbaccalaureate distance learning degree programs offered (no on-campus study). *Faculty:* 83 full-time (50 women), 309 part-time/adjunct (188 women). *Students:* 2,563 full-time (1,811 women), 1,992 part-time (1,374 women); includes 2,016 minority (363 Black or African American, non-Hispanic/Latino; 22 American Indian or Alaska Native, non-Hispanic/Latino; 273 Asian, non-Hispanic/Latino; 1,188 Hispanic/Latino; 27 Native Hawaiian or other Pacific Islander, non-Hispanic/Latino; 143 Two or more races, non-Hispanic/Latino), 2 international. Average age 34. In 2014, 1,813 master's awarded. *Degree requirements:* For master's, thesis (for some programs). *Entrance requirements:* For master's, interview, minimum GPA of 2.5. Additional exam requirements/recommendations for international students: Required—TOEFL (minimum score 550 paper-based; 79 iBT), IELTS (minimum score 6). *Application deadline:* Applications are processed on a rolling basis. Application fee: $60 ($65 for international students). Electronic applications accepted. *Expenses: Tuition:* Full-time $14,184; part-time $1773 per course. *Financial support:* Career-related internships or fieldwork, institutionally sponsored loans, scholarships/grants, and tuition waivers (partial) available. Support available to part-time students. Financial award application deadline: 6/30. *Faculty research:* Teacher education, special education, educational effectiveness, teaching abroad, school counseling. *Unit head:* School of Education, 800-628-8648, E-mail: soe@nu.edu. *Application contact:* Frank Rojas, Vice President for Enrollment Services, 800-628-8648, E-mail: advisor@nu.edu. Website: http://www.nu.edu/OurPrograms/SchoolOfEducation.html

Northern Michigan University, Office of Graduate Education and Research, College of Arts and Sciences, Department of Psychology, Marquette, MI 49855-5301. Offers applied behavior analysis (MS); performance improvement (Graduate Certificate); psychology (MS); training and performance improvement (MS). Part-time programs available. *Faculty:* 8 full-time (3 women), 1 part-time/adjunct. *Students:* 32 full-time (17 women), 17 part-time (10 women); includes 9 minority (2 Black or African American, non-Hispanic/Latino; 3 American Indian or Alaska Native, non-Hispanic/Latino; 3 Hispanic/Latino; 1 Two or more races, non-Hispanic/Latino). Average age 29. 38 applicants, 55% accepted, 13 enrolled. In 2014, 7 master's, 14 other advanced degrees awarded. *Degree requirements:* For master's, thesis (for some programs). *Entrance requirements:* For master's, minimum GPA of 3.0; bachelor's degree preferably in psychology; undergraduate course on introduction to psychology; undergraduate course on statistics; personal statement; 3 letters of recommendation. Additional exam requirements/recommendations for international students: Required—TOEFL (minimum score 550 paper-based; 79 iBT), IELTS (minimum score 6.5). *Application deadline:* For fall admission, 7/1 for domestic students; for winter admission, 11/15 for domestic students; for spring admission, 3/17 for domestic students. Applications are processed on a rolling basis. Application fee: $50. Electronic applications accepted. *Expenses:* Tuition, state resident: full-time $7716; part-time $441 per credit hour. Tuition, nonresident: full-time $10,812; part-time $634.50 per credit hour. *Required fees:* $31.88 per semester. Tuition and fees vary according to course load, degree level and program. *Financial support:* In 2014–15, teaching assistantships with full tuition reimbursements (averaging $8,898 per year) were awarded; Federal Work-Study, institutionally sponsored loans, scholarships/grants, and unspecified assistantships also available. Support available to part-time students. Financial award application deadline: 3/1; financial award applicants required to submit FAFSA. *Faculty research:* Emotion and cognition, neuropsychopharmacology, sensation and perception, behavior analysis, developmental psychology. *Unit head:* Dr. Paul Andronis, Department Head, 906-227-2935, E-mail: pandroni@nmu.edu. *Application contact:* Dr. Brian Cherry, Assistant Provost of Graduate Education and Research, 906-227-2300, Fax: 906-227-2315, E-mail: graduate@nmu.edu.
Website: http://psychology.nmu.edu

Oklahoma City University, Petree College of Arts and Sciences, Programs in Education, Oklahoma City, OK 73106-1402. Offers applied behavioral studies (M Ed); early childhood education (M Ed), including Montessori education. Part-time and evening/weekend programs available. *Faculty:* 1 full-time, 1 part-time/adjunct. *Students:* 21 full-time (18 women), 26 part-time (all women); includes 12 minority (7 Black or African American, non-Hispanic/Latino; 1 American Indian or Alaska Native, non-Hispanic/Latino; 1 Asian, non-Hispanic/Latino; 2 Hispanic/Latino; 1 Two or more races, non-Hispanic/Latino), 6 international. Average age 33. 33 applicants, 70% accepted, 15 enrolled. In 2014, 5 master's awarded. *Entrance requirements:* For master's, bachelor's degree from accredited institution, minimum GPA of 3.0, essay, recommendation letters. Additional exam requirements/recommendations for international students: Required—TOEFL (minimum score 550 paper-based; 80 iBT). *Application deadline:* Applications are processed on a rolling basis. Application fee: $50. Electronic applications accepted. *Expenses: Tuition:* Part-time $936 per credit hour. *Required fees:* $115 per credit hour. One-time fee: $250. Tuition and fees vary according to course load, degree level, program and student's religious affiliation. *Financial support:* In 2014–15, 14 students received support. Career-related internships or fieldwork, Federal Work-Study, institutionally sponsored loans, scholarships/grants, and tuition waivers available. Support available to part-time students. Financial award application deadline: 6/1; financial award applicants required to submit FAFSA. *Faculty research:* Adult literacy, cognition, reading strategies. *Unit head:* Dr. Lois Lawler-Brown, Chair, 405-208-5374, Fax: 405-208-6012, E-mail: llbrown@okcu.edu. *Application contact:* Michael Harrington, Director of Graduate Admissions, 800-633-7242, Fax: 405-208-5916, E-mail: gadmissions@okcu.edu.
Website: http://www.okcu.edu/petree/education/graduate.aspx

Oklahoma State University, College of Education, School of Applied Health and Educational Psychology, Stillwater, OK 74078. Offers applied behavioral studies (Ed D); applied health and educational psychology (MS, PhD, Ed S). *Accreditation:* APA (one or more programs are accredited). Part-time programs available. *Faculty:* 41 full-time (22 women), 15 part-time/adjunct (10 women). *Students:* 178 full-time (119 women), 130 part-time (94 women); includes 80 minority (14 Black or African American, non-Hispanic/Latino; 14 American Indian or Alaska Native, non-Hispanic/Latino; 4 Asian, non-Hispanic/Latino; 24 Hispanic/Latino; 24 Two or more races, non-Hispanic/Latino), 10 international. Average age 30. 237 applicants, 37% accepted, 66 enrolled. In 2014, 84 master's, 33 doctorates awarded. *Degree requirements:* For master's, thesis (for some programs); for doctorate, comprehensive exam, thesis/dissertation. *Entrance requirements:* For master's and doctorate, GRE or GMAT. Additional exam requirements/recommendations for international students: Required—TOEFL (minimum score 550 paper-based; 79 iBT). *Application deadline:* For fall admission, 3/1 priority date for international students; for spring admission, 8/1 priority date for international students. Applications are processed on a rolling basis. Application fee: $40 ($75 for international students). Electronic applications accepted. *Expenses:* Tuition, state resident: full-time $4488; part-time $187 per credit hour. Tuition, nonresident: full-time $18,360; part-time $765 per credit hour. *Required fees:* $2413; $100.55 per credit hour. Tuition and fees vary according to campus/location. *Financial support:* In 2014–15, 30 research assistantships (averaging $9,530 per year), 70 teaching assistantships (averaging $9,677 per year) were awarded; career-related internships or fieldwork, Federal Work-Study, scholarships/grants, health care benefits, tuition waivers (partial), and unspecified assistantships also available. Support available to part-time students. Financial award application deadline: 3/1; financial award applicants required to submit FAFSA. *Unit head:* Dr. Aric Warren, Head, 405-744-6040, Fax: 405-744-6779, E-mail: aric.warren@okstate.edu.
Website: http://education.okstate.edu/sahep

Penn State Harrisburg, Graduate School, School of Behavioral Sciences and Education, Middletown, PA 17057-4898. Offers applied behavior analysis (MA); applied clinical psychology (MA); applied psychological research (MA); community psychology and social change (MA); health education (M Ed); literacy education (M Ed); teaching and curriculum (M Ed); training and development (M Ed). Part-time and evening/weekend programs available. *Unit head:* Dr. Mukund S. Kulkarni, Chancellor, 717-948-6105, Fax: 717-948-6452, E-mail: msk5@psu.edu. *Application contact:* Robert W. Coffman, Jr., Director of Enrollment Management, Admissions, 717-948-6250, Fax: 717-948-6325, E-mail: ric1@psu.edu.
Website: http://harrisburg.psu.edu/behavioral-sciences-and-education/

★ **Philadelphia College of Osteopathic Medicine,** Graduate and Professional Programs, Department of Psychology, Philadelphia, PA 19131. Offers applied behavior analysis (Certificate); clinical health psychology (Post-Doctoral Certificate); clinical neuropsychology (Post-Doctoral Certificate); clinical psychology (Psy D); mental health counseling (MS); organizational development and leadership (MS); psychology (Certificate); school psychology (MS, Psy D, Ed S). *Accreditation:* APA. *Faculty:* 19 full-time (11 women), 122 part-time/adjunct (58 women). *Students:* 395 (304 women); includes 80 minority (49 Black or African American, non-Hispanic/Latino; 13 Asian, non-Hispanic/Latino; 7 Hispanic/Latino; 11 Two or more races, non-Hispanic/Latino). 345 applicants, 47% accepted, 113 enrolled. In 2014, 72 master's, 42 doctorates, 17 other advanced degrees awarded. Terminal master's awarded for partial completion of doctoral program. *Degree requirements:* For master's, comprehensive exam (for some programs), thesis (for some programs); for doctorate, comprehensive exam, thesis/dissertation. *Entrance requirements:* For master's, GRE or MAT, minimum GPA of 3.0; bachelor's degree from regionally-accredited college or university; for doctorate, PRAXIS II (for Psy D in school psychology), minimum undergraduate GPA of 3.0; for other advanced degree, GRE (for Ed S). Additional exam requirements/recommendations for international students: Required—TOEFL (minimum score 79 iBT). *Application deadline:* For fall admission, 3/1 priority date for domestic students. Applications are processed on a rolling basis. Application fee: $50. Electronic applications accepted. *Financial support:* In 2014–15, 28 teaching assistantships were awarded; Federal Work-Study, institutionally sponsored loans, and scholarships/grants also available. Financial award application deadline: 3/15; financial award applicants required to submit FAFSA. *Faculty research:* Adult and childhood anxiety and ADHD; coping with chronic illness; primary care psychology/integrated health care; applied behavior analysis; psychological, educational, and neuropsychological assessment. Total annual research expenditures: $533,489. *Unit head:* Dr. Robert DiTomasso, Chairman, 215-871-6442, Fax: 215-871-6458, E-mail: robertd@pcom.edu. *Application contact:* Kari A. Shotwell, Director of Admissions, 215-871-6700, Fax: 215-871-6719, E-mail: karis@pcom.edu.

See Display on page 990 and Close-Up on page 1211.

Regis College, School of Nursing, Science and Health Professions, Weston, MA 02493. Offers applied behavior analysis (MS); biomedical sciences (MS); health administration (MS); nurse practitioner (Certificate); nursing (MS, DNP); nursing education (Certificate). Part-time and evening/weekend programs available. *Degree requirements:* For master's, thesis. *Entrance requirements:* For master's, GRE General Test or MAT, minimum GPA of 3.0; for doctorate, MAT or GRE if GPA from master's lower than 3.5. Additional exam requirements/recommendations for international students: Required—TOEFL (minimum score 550 paper-based). Electronic applications accepted. *Faculty research:* Health policy, education, aging, job satisfaction, psychiatric nursing, critical thinking.

Rowan University, Graduate School, College of Science and Mathematics, Program in Applied Behavioral Analysis, Glassboro, NJ 08028-1701. Offers MA, CAGS. *Faculty:* 2 full-time (both women). *Students:* 3 full-time (2 women), 50 part-time (44 women); includes 6 minority (2 Black or African American, non-Hispanic/Latino; 1 American Indian or Alaska Native, non-Hispanic/Latino; 3 Hispanic/Latino). Average age 30. 32 applicants, 41% accepted, 7 enrolled. In 2014, 58 master's awarded. *Entrance requirements:* For master's, GRE General Test. Additional exam requirements/recommendations for international students: Required—TOEFL. *Application deadline:* For fall admission, 2/15 for domestic students; for summer admission, 2/15 for domestic students. Application fee: $65. *Expenses: Tuition, area resident:* Part-time $648 per credit. Tuition, state resident: part-time $648 per credit. Tuition, nonresident: part-time $648 per credit. *Required fees:* $145 per credit. Tuition and fees vary according to degree level, campus/location, program and student level. *Unit head:* Dr. Horacio Sosa, Vice President, Global Learning and Partnerships, 856-256-4747, Fax: 856-256-5638, E-mail: sosa@rowan.edu. *Application contact:* Admissions and Enrollment Services, 856-256-4747, Fax: 856-256-5637, E-mail: globaladmissions@rowan.edu.

Sage Graduate School, Esteves School of Education, Program in Applied Behavior Analysis and Autism, Troy, NY 12180-4115. Offers MS, Post Master's Certificate. Part-time and evening/weekend programs available. *Faculty:* 10 full-time (5 women), 13 part-time/adjunct (all women). *Students:* 36 full-time (32 women), 115 part-time (103 women); includes 28 minority (6 Black or African American, non-Hispanic/Latino; 1 American Indian or Alaska Native, non-Hispanic/Latino; 2 Asian, non-Hispanic/Latino; 14 Hispanic/Latino; 1 Native Hawaiian or other Pacific Islander, non-Hispanic/Latino; 4 Two or more races, non-Hispanic/Latino). Average age 29. 211 applicants, 42% accepted, 62 enrolled. In 2014, 75 master's, 4 other advanced degrees awarded. *Entrance requirements:* Additional exam requirements/recommendations for international students: Required—TOEFL (minimum score 550 paper-based).

Application deadline: Applications are processed on a rolling basis. Application fee: $40. *Expenses: Tuition:* Full-time $12,240; part-time $680 per credit hour. *Financial support:* Federal Work-Study, scholarships/grants, tuition waivers (partial), and unspecified assistantships available. Support available to part-time students. Financial award applicants required to submit FAFSA. *Unit head:* Dr. Lori Quigley, Dean, Esteves School of Education, 518-244-2326, Fax: 518-244-4571, E-mail: l.quigley@sage.edu. *Application contact:* Dr. Dana Reineke, Director, Center for Applied Behavior Analysis, 518-244-6873, Fax: 518-244-6880, E-mail: caba@sage.edu.
Website: http://www.sage.edu/academics/education/programs/aba_autism/

St. Cloud State University, School of Graduate Studies, School of Health and Human Services, Department of Counseling and Community Psychology, Program in Applied Behavior Analysis, St. Cloud, MN 56301-4498. Offers MS. Part-time programs available. Postbaccalaureate distance learning degree programs offered (no on-campus study). *Degree requirements:* For master's, comprehensive exam (for some programs), thesis or alternative. *Entrance requirements:* For master's, GRE General Test, minimum GPA of 2.75. Additional exam requirements/recommendations for international students: Required—Michigan English Language Assessment Battery; Recommended—TOEFL (minimum score 550 paper-based), IELTS (minimum score 6.5).

Saint Peter's University, Graduate Programs in Education, Jersey City, NJ 07306-5997. Offers director of school counseling services (Certificate); educational leadership (MA Ed, Ed D); higher education (Ed D); middle school mathematics (Certificate); professional/associate counselor (Certificate); reading (MA Ed); school business administrator (Certificate); school counseling (MA, Certificate); special education (MA Ed, Certificate), including applied behavioral analysis (MA Ed), literacy (MA Ed), teacher of students with disabilities (Certificate); teaching (MA Ed, Certificate), including 6-8 middle school education, K-12 secondary education, K-5 elementary education. *Accreditation:* Teacher Education Accreditation Council. Part-time and evening/weekend programs available. *Degree requirements:* For master's, comprehensive exam; for doctorate, comprehensive exam, thesis/dissertation. *Entrance requirements:* For master's and doctorate, GRE or MAT. Additional exam requirements/recommendations for international students: Required—TOEFL. Electronic applications accepted.

The School of Professional Psychology at Forest Institute, Graduate Programs, Springfield, MO 65807. Offers applied behavior analysis (MS); clinical psychology (MA, Psy D); counseling psychology (MA); marriage and family therapy (MA, PGC). *Accreditation:* AAMFT/COAMFTE; APA (one or more programs are accredited). Part-time and evening/weekend programs available. Terminal master's awarded for partial completion of doctoral program. *Degree requirements:* For master's, thesis, practicum; for doctorate, comprehensive exam, thesis/dissertation, internship, practicum. *Entrance requirements:* For master's, GRE General Test, interview, minimum GPA of 3.0, 12 hours in psychology; for doctorate, GRE General Test (minimum combined Verbal and Quantitative score of 1000, Analytic Writing 4.0), interview, minimum GPA of 3.0, 18 hours in psychology. Additional exam requirements/recommendations for international students: Required—TOEFL (minimum score 550 paper-based). Electronic applications accepted. *Faculty research:* Forensics/corrections, marriage and family therapy, child and adolescent, integrated health care, neuropsychology.

Shenandoah University, College of Arts and Sciences, Winchester, VA 22601-5195. Offers applied behavior analysis (MS). Part-time programs available. *Faculty:* 1 full-time (0 women), 2 part-time/adjunct (1 woman). *Students:* 19 full-time (all women), 4 part-time (3 women); includes 1 minority (Black or African American, non-Hispanic/Latino). Average age 29. 16 applicants, 94% accepted, 13 enrolled. *Degree requirements:* For master's, minimum of 37 credit hours, including 21 in coursework, 12 of supervised practical experience, and 4 for capstone project. *Entrance requirements:* For master's, minimum GPA of 3.0 in undergraduate work with bachelor's degree preferably in psychology, education, special education, social work, speech pathology or a similar discipline; essay or writing sample. Additional exam requirements/recommendations for international students: Required—TOEFL (minimum score 550 paper-based; 79 iBT), IELTS (minimum score 6.5), Sakae Institute of Study Abroad (SISA) test (minimum score 15). *Application deadline:* For fall admission, 7/15 for domestic and international students. Application fee: $30. Electronic applications accepted. *Expenses: Tuition:* Full-time $19,512; part-time $813 per credit hour. *Required fees:* $365 per term. Tuition and fees vary according to course level, course load and program. *Faculty research:* Behavior analysis as it pertains to problems with child welfare; developmental disabilities and consultation on matters of human performance in business, education, and human services. *Unit head:* Calvin Allen, PhD, Dean, 540-665-4587, Fax: 540-665-4644, E-mail: callen@su.edu. *Application contact:* Andrew Woodall, Executive Director of Recruitment and Admissions, 540-665-4581, Fax: 540-665-4627, E-mail: admit@su.edu.

Simmons College, College of Arts and Sciences, Boston, MA 02115. Offers behavior analysis (MS, PhD, Ed S); educational leadership (MS Ed); elementary, middle or high school teacher (MAT); general and special education (MAT); public policy (MPP); special education (MS Ed, Ed S), including assistive technology, language and literacy, moderate and severe disabilities; teaching English as a second language (MA, CAGS); MA/MA; MA/MS. Part-time programs available. *Faculty:* 16 full-time (12 women), 1 (woman) part-time/adjunct. *Students:* 51 full-time (40 women), 85 part-time (73 women); includes 18 minority (6 Black or African American, non-Hispanic/Latino; 1 Asian, non-Hispanic/Latino; 9 Hispanic/Latino; 2 Two or more races, non-Hispanic/Latino), 2 international. 56 applicants, 84% accepted, 17 enrolled. In 2014, 306 master's, 11 doctorates awarded. Terminal master's awarded for partial completion of doctoral program. *Degree requirements:* For master's, thesis (for some programs). *Entrance requirements:* For master's, GRE. Additional exam requirements/recommendations for international students: Required—TOEFL (minimum score 600 paper-based; 100 iBT). *Application deadline:* For fall admission, 8/1 for domestic and international students; for spring admission, 12/15 for domestic and international students; for summer admission, 5/1 for domestic and international students. Applications are processed on a rolling basis. Application fee: $35. Electronic applications accepted. *Expenses:* Expenses: Contact institution. *Financial support:* Fellowships with partial tuition reimbursements, teaching assistantships with partial tuition reimbursements, and scholarships/grants available. Financial award applicants required to submit FAFSA. *Unit head:* Dr. Renee White, Dean, 617-521-2079. *Application contact:* Patricia Flaherty, Director, Graduate Studies Admission, 617-521-3902, Fax: 617-521-3058, E-mail: gsa@simmons.edu.
Website: http://www.simmons.edu/gradstudies/

Spalding University, Graduate Studies, Kosair College of Health and Natural Sciences, Program in Applied Behavior Analysis, Louisville, KY 40203-2188. Offers MS. *Faculty:* 3 full-time (1 woman). *Students:* 32 full-time (23 women), 1 (woman) part-time; includes 2 minority (1 Black or African American, non-Hispanic/Latino; 1 Asian, non-Hispanic/Latino). Average age 30. 32 applicants, 56% accepted, 18 enrolled. In 2014, 4 master's awarded. *Entrance requirements:* For master's, GRE or MAT, autobiographical statement, letters of recommendation, writing sample, transcripts, interview. Additional exam requirements/recommendations for international students: Required—TOEFL (minimum score 535 paper-based). *Application deadline:* For fall admission, 4/17 priority date for domestic students. Application fee: $30. *Financial support:* In 2014–15, 2 research assistantships (averaging $2,550 per year) were awarded; unspecified assistantships also available. Financial award application deadline: 3/30; financial award applicants required to submit FAFSA. *Unit head:* Dr. Erick Dubuque, Director, 502-873-4193, E-mail: edubaque@spalding.edu. *Application contact:* Debbie Pierce, Administrative Assistant, 502-873-4309, E-mail: dpierce@spalding.edu.

Teachers College, Columbia University, Graduate Faculty of Education, Department of Health and Behavioral Studies, Program in Applied Behavior Analysis, New York, NY 10027. Offers MA, Ed D, PhD. *Faculty:* 7 full-time, 13 part-time/adjunct. *Students:* 6 full-time (5 women), 75 part-time (72 women); includes 22 minority (7 Black or African American, non-Hispanic/Latino; 9 Asian, non-Hispanic/Latino; 6 Hispanic/Latino), 15 international. Average age 26. 65 applicants, 62% accepted, 23 enrolled. In 2014, 15 master's, 5 doctorates awarded. *Degree requirements:* For doctorate, comprehensive exam, thesis/dissertation. *Entrance requirements:* For doctorate, writing sample. *Application deadline:* For fall admission, 1/15 priority date for domestic students; for spring admission, 11/15 for domestic students. Applications are processed on a rolling basis. Application fee: $65. Electronic applications accepted. *Expenses: Tuition:* Full-time $33,552; part-time $1398 per credit. *Required fees:* $418 per semester. *Financial support:* Applicants required to submit FAFSA. *Faculty research:* Communication skills, academic skills (reading and math), behavior problems, cultural differences, transition support services and teacher preparation for individuals with autism. *Unit head:* Dr. Douglas Greer, Program Coordinator, 212-678-3880, E-mail: rdg13@columbia.edu. *Application contact:* Elizabeth Puleio, Admissions Contact, 212-678-3710.
Website: http://www.tc.columbia.edu/hbs/SpecialEd/

Tennessee Technological University, College of Graduate Studies, College of Education, Department of Curriculum and Instruction, Program in Exceptional Learning, Cookeville, TN 38505. Offers applied behavior analysis (PhD); literacy (PhD); program planning and evaluation (PhD); STEM education (PhD). Part-time and evening/weekend programs available. *Students:* 10 full-time (8 women), 25 part-time (18 women); includes 2 minority (both Two or more races, non-Hispanic/Latino), 2 international. 14 applicants, 64% accepted, 6 enrolled. In 2014, 6 doctorates awarded. *Degree requirements:* For doctorate, comprehensive exam, thesis/dissertation. *Entrance requirements:* For doctorate, GRE, minimum GPA of 3.0. Additional exam requirements/recommendations for international students: Required—TOEFL (minimum score 550 paper-based; 79 iBT), IELTS (minimum score 5.5), PTE (minimum score 53), or TOEIC (Test of English as an International Communication). *Application deadline:* For fall admission, 8/1 for domestic students, 5/1 for international students; for spring admission, 12/1 for domestic students, 10/1 for international students. Applications are processed on a rolling basis. Application fee: $35 ($40 for international students). Electronic applications accepted. *Expenses:* Tuition, state resident: full-time $9783; part-time $492 per credit hour. Tuition, nonresident: full-time $24,071; part-time $1179 per credit hour. *Financial support:* In 2014–15, 4 fellowships (averaging $8,000 per year), 10 research assistantships (averaging $12,000 per year), 1 teaching assistantship (averaging $12,000 per year) were awarded. Financial award application deadline: 4/1. *Unit head:* Dr. Lisa Zagumny, Director, 931-372-3078, Fax: 931-372-3517, E-mail: lzagumny@tntech.edu. *Application contact:* Shelia K. Kendrick, Coordinator of Graduate Studies, 931-372-3808, Fax: 931-372-3497, E-mail: skendrick@tntech.edu.
Website: https://www.tntech.edu/education/elphd/

The University of Kansas, Graduate Studies, College of Liberal Arts and Sciences, Department of Applied Behavioral Science, Lawrence, KS 66045. Offers applied behavioral science (MA); behavioral psychology (PhD). *Faculty:* 17 full-time. *Students:* 40 full-time (30 women); includes 7 minority (4 Black or African American, non-Hispanic/Latino; 3 Two or more races, non-Hispanic/Latino), 1 international. Average age 28. 87 applicants, 15% accepted, 13 enrolled. In 2014, 3 master's, 8 doctorates awarded. Terminal master's awarded for partial completion of doctoral program. *Degree requirements:* For master's, thesis; for doctorate, thesis/dissertation, comprehensive oral and written exams, journal reviews. *Entrance requirements:* For master's and doctorate, minimum GPA of 3.0, curriculum vitae, 3 letters of recommendation, personal statement. Additional exam requirements/recommendations for international students: Required—TOEFL. *Application deadline:* For fall admission, 12/15 priority date for domestic students, 12/15 for international students. Applications are processed on a rolling basis. Application fee: $55 ($65 for international students). Electronic applications accepted. *Financial support:* Fellowships, research assistantships with full and partial tuition reimbursements, teaching assistantships with full and partial tuition reimbursements, career-related internships or fieldwork, traineeships, tuition waivers (full), and unspecified assistantships available. Financial award application deadline: 12/15; financial award applicants required to submit CSS PROFILE or FAFSA. *Faculty research:* Organizational behavioral management, community health and development, early childhood education and intervention, developmental disabilities, behavioral economics of choice. *Unit head:* Dr. Edward K. Morris, Chair, 785-864-0519, E-mail: ekm@ku.edu. *Application contact:* Andrea Noltner, Office Manager, 785-864-0503, E-mail: anoltner@ku.edu.
Website: http://www.absc.ku.edu

University of North Florida, College of Education and Human Services, Department of Exceptional, Deaf, and Interpreter Education, Jacksonville, FL 32224. Offers American Sign Language/English interpreting (M Ed); applied behavior analysis (M Ed); autism (M Ed); deaf education (M Ed); disability services (M Ed); exceptional student education (M Ed). *Accreditation:* NCATE. Part-time and evening/weekend programs available. *Faculty:* 11 full-time (9 women), 4 part-time/adjunct (all women). *Students:* 26 full-time (21 women), 52 part-time (44 women); includes 15 minority (9 Black or African American, non-Hispanic/Latino; 2 Asian, non-Hispanic/Latino; 3 Hispanic/Latino; 1 Two or more races, non-Hispanic/Latino), 2 international. Average age 32. 39 applicants, 51% accepted, 15 enrolled. In 2014, 51 master's awarded. *Entrance requirements:* For master's, GRE General Test, minimum GPA of 3.0 in last 60 hours, interview, 3 letters of recommendation. Additional exam requirements/recommendations for international students: Required—TOEFL (minimum score 500 paper-based). *Application deadline:* For fall admission, 7/1 priority date for domestic students, 5/1 for international students; for spring admission, 11/1 priority date for domestic students, 10/1 for international students. Application fee: $30. Electronic applications accepted. *Expenses:* Tuition, state resident: full-time $9794; part-time $408.10 per credit hour. Tuition, nonresident: full-time $22,383; part-time $932.61 per credit hour. *Required fees:* $2047; $85.29 per credit hour. Tuition and fees vary according to course load and program. *Financial support:* In 2014–15, 19 students received support, including 1 research assistantship (averaging $4,524 per year); teaching assistantships, career-related internships or fieldwork, Federal Work-Study, scholarships/grants, tuition waivers (partial), and unspecified assistantships also available. Support available to part-time students. Financial award application deadline: 4/1; financial award applicants required to submit FAFSA. *Faculty research:* Transition, integrating technology into teacher education, written language development, professional school development, learning strategies. *Total annual research expenditures:* $816,202. *Unit head:* Dr. Karen Patterson, Chair, 904-620-2930, Fax: 904-620-3895, E-mail: karen.patterson@unf.edu. *Application contact:* Dr. Amanda Pascale, Director, The Graduate School, 904-620-1360, Fax: 904-620-1362, E-mail: graduateschool@unf.edu.
Website: http://www.unf.edu/coehs/edie/

University of North Texas, Robert B. Toulouse School of Graduate Studies, Denton, TX 76203-5459. Offers accounting (MS); applied anthropology (MA, MS); applied

behavior analysis (Certificate); applied geography (MA); applied technology and performance improvement (M Ed, MS); art education (MA); art history (MA); art museum education (Certificate); arts leadership (Certificate); audiology (Au D); behavior analysis (MS); behavioral science (PhD); biochemistry and molecular biology (MS); biology (MA, MS); biomedical engineering (MS); business analysis (MS); chemistry (MS); clinical health psychology (PhD); communication studies (MA, MS); computer engineering (MS); computer science (MS); counseling (M Ed, MS), including clinical mental health counseling (MS), college and university counseling, elementary school counseling, secondary school counseling; creative writing (MA); criminal justice (MS); curriculum and instruction (M Ed); decision sciences (MBA); design (MA, MFA), including fashion design (MFA), innovation studies, interior design (MFA); early childhood studies (MS); economics (MS); educational leadership (M Ed, Ed D); educational psychology (MS, PhD), including family studies (MS), gifted and talented (MS), human development (MS), learning and cognition (MS), research, measurement and evaluation (MS); electrical engineering (MS); emergency management (MPA); engineering technology (MS); English (MA); English as a second language (MA); environmental science (MS); finance (MBA, MS); financial management (MPA); French (MA); health services management (MBA); higher education (M Ed, Ed D); history (MA, MS); hospitality management (MS); human resources management (MPA); information science (MS); information systems (PhD); information technologies (MBA); interdisciplinary studies (MA, MS); international studies (MA); international sustainable tourism (MS); jazz studies (MM); journalism (MA, MJ, Graduate Certificate), including interactive and virtual digital communication (Graduate Certificate), narrative journalism (Graduate Certificate), public relations (Graduate Certificate); kinesiology (MS); linguistics (MA); local government management (MPA); logistics (PhD); logistics and supply chain management (MBA); long-term care, senior housing, and aging services (MA); management (PhD); marketing (MBA); mathematics (MA, MS); mechanical and energy engineering (MS, PhD); music (MA), including ethnomusicology, music theory, musicology, performance; music composition (PhD); music education (MM Ed, PhD); nonprofit management (MPA); operations and supply chain management (MBA); performance (MM, DMA); philosophy (MA); political science (MA); professional and technical communication (MA); radio, television and film (MA, MFA); rehabilitation counseling (Certificate); sociology (MA); Spanish (MA); special education (M Ed); speech-language pathology (MA); strategic management (MBA); studio art (MFA); teaching (M Ed); MBA/MS. Part-time and evening/weekend programs available. Postbaccalaureate distance learning degree programs offered. *Faculty:* 651 full-time (215 women), 233 part-time/adjunct (139 women). *Students:* 3,040 full-time (1,598 women), 3,401 part-time (2,097 women); includes 1,740 minority (533 Black or African American, non-Hispanic/Latino; 15 American Indian or Alaska Native, non-Hispanic/Latino; 286 Asian, non-Hispanic/Latino; 746 Hispanic/Latino; 3 Native Hawaiian or other Pacific Islander, non-Hispanic/Latino; 157 Two or more races, non-Hispanic/Latino), 1,145 international. Terminal master's awarded for partial completion of doctoral program. *Degree requirements:* For master's, variable foreign language requirement, comprehensive exam (for some programs), thesis (for some programs); for doctorate, variable foreign language requirement, comprehensive exam (for some programs), thesis/dissertation; for other advanced degree, variable foreign language requirement, comprehensive exam (for some programs). *Entrance requirements:* For master's and doctorate, GRE, GMAT. Additional exam requirements/recommendations for international students: Required—TOEFL (minimum score 550 paper-based; 79 iBT). *Application deadline:* For fall admission, 7/15 for domestic students, 3/15 for international students; for spring admission, 11/15 for domestic students, 9/15 for international students; for summer admission, 5/1 for domestic students. Applications are processed on a rolling basis. Application fee: $60. Electronic applications accepted. *Expenses:* Tuition, state resident: full-time $5450; part-time $3633 per year. Tuition, nonresident: full-time $11,966; part-time $7977 per year. *Required fees:* $1301; $398 per credit hour. $685 per semester. Tuition and fees vary according to program and reciprocity agreements. *Financial support:* Fellowships with partial tuition reimbursements, research assistantships with partial tuition reimbursements, teaching assistantships, career-related internships or fieldwork, Federal Work-Study, institutionally sponsored loans, scholarships/grants, health care benefits, and library assistantships available. Support available to part-time students. Financial award applicants required to submit FAFSA. *Unit head:* Mark Wardell, Dean, 940-565-2383, E-mail: mark.wardell@unt.edu. *Application contact:* Toulouse School of Graduate Studies, 940-565-2383, Fax: 940-565-2141, E-mail: gradsch@unt.edu.
Website: http://tsgs.unt.edu/

University of Pittsburgh, School of Education, Department of Instruction and Learning, Program in Special Education, Pittsburgh, PA 15260. Offers applied behavior analysis (M Ed); early intervention (M Ed); general special education (M Ed); special education (Ed D); special education teacher preparation (M Ed); vision studies (M Ed). Part-time and evening/weekend programs available. *Faculty:* 27 full-time (17 women), 76 part-time/adjunct (57 women). *Students:* 79 full-time (75 women), 78 part-time (74 women); includes 13 minority (5 Black or African American, non-Hispanic/Latino; 2 Asian, non-Hispanic/Latino; 3 Hispanic/Latino; 3 Two or more races, non-Hispanic/Latino), 2 international. Average age 30. 68 applicants, 88% accepted, 48 enrolled. In 2014, 69 master's, 4 doctorates awarded. *Degree requirements:* For master's, thesis; for doctorate, thesis/dissertation. *Entrance requirements:* For master's, PRAXIS I; for doctorate, GRE General Test. Additional exam requirements/recommendations for international students: Required—TOEFL. *Application deadline:* For fall admission, 2/1 priority date for domestic students; for spring admission, 11/1 priority date for domestic students. Applications are processed on a rolling basis. Application fee: $50. *Expenses:* Tuition, state resident: full-time $20,742; part-time $838 per credit. Tuition, nonresident: full-time $33,960; part-time $1389 per credit. *Required fees:* $800; $205 per term. Tuition and fees vary according to program. *Financial support:* In 2014–15, fellowships with full and partial tuition reimbursements (averaging $20,500 per year), research assistantships with full and partial tuition reimbursements (averaging $17,800 per year), teaching assistantships with full and partial tuition reimbursements (averaging $17,800 per year) were awarded; career-related internships or fieldwork, Federal Work-Study, and tuition waivers (partial) also available. Support available to part-time students. Financial award application deadline: 3/15; financial award applicants required to submit FAFSA. *Unit head:* Dr. Richard Donato, Chairman, 412-624-7248, Fax: 412-648-7081, E-mail: donato@pitt.edu. *Application contact:* Norma Ann McMichael, Graduate Enrollment Manager, 412-648-2230, Fax: 412-648-1899, E-mail: soeinfo@pitt.edu.
Website: http://www.education.pitt.edu/AcademicDepartments/InstructionLearning/Programs/GeneralSpecialEducation.aspx

University of Saint Joseph, Department of Special Education, West Hartford, CT 06117-2700. Offers applied behavior analysis (Postbaccalaureate Certificate); autism and applied behavior analysis (MS); autism spectrum disorders (Postbaccalaureate Certificate); special education (MA). Part-time and evening/weekend programs available. *Degree requirements:* For master's, thesis. Electronic applications accepted. Application fee is waived when completed online. *Expenses: Tuition:* Part-time $700 per credit. *Required fees:* $42 per credit. Tuition and fees vary according to degree level, campus/location and program.

University of Southern Maine, College of Management and Human Service, School of Education and Human Development, Program in Educational Psychology, Portland, ME 04104-9300. Offers applied behavior analysis (MS, CGS); response to intervention: academic (CGS); response to intervention: behavior (CGS). Part-time and evening/weekend programs available. *Faculty:* 2 full-time (1 woman), 3 part-time/adjunct (1 woman). *Students:* 1 (woman) full-time, 26 part-time (17 women); includes 3 minority (1 Black or African American, non-Hispanic/Latino; 1 American Indian or Alaska Native, non-Hispanic/Latino; 1 Native Hawaiian or other Pacific Islander, non-Hispanic/Latino). Average age 33. 16 applicants, 69% accepted, 10 enrolled. In 2014, 18 master's, 6 other advanced degrees awarded. *Entrance requirements:* For master's, GRE or MAT. Additional exam requirements/recommendations for international students: Required—TOEFL (minimum score 550 paper-based; 79 iBT). *Application deadline:* For fall admission, 5/1 priority date for domestic students; for spring admission, 10/15 priority date for domestic students. Applications are processed on a rolling basis. Application fee: $65. Electronic applications accepted. *Expenses: Tuition, area resident:* Full-time $6840; part-time $380 per credit hour. Tuition, state resident: full-time $10,260; part-time $570 per credit hour. Tuition, nonresident: full-time $18,468; part-time $1026 per credit hour. *Required fees:* $830; $83 per credit hour. Tuition and fees vary according to course load and program. *Financial support:* Federal Work-Study, institutionally sponsored loans, scholarships/grants, and unspecified assistantships available. Support available to part-time students. Financial award application deadline: 3/1. *Faculty research:* Applied behavior analysis, functional behavioral analysis, positive behavioral interventions and supports. *Unit head:* Dr. Rachel Brown, Program Director, 207-228-8322, E-mail: rbrown@usm.maine.edu. *Application contact:* Mary Sloan, Assistant Dean of Graduate Studies and Director of Graduate Admissions, 207-780-4812, E-mail: gradstudies@usm.maine.edu.
Website: http://usm.maine.edu/educational-psychology

University of South Florida, College of Behavioral and Community Sciences, Department of Child and Family Studies, Tampa, FL 33620-9951. Offers applied behavior analysis (MA, PhD); child and adolescent behavioral health (MS), including developmental disabilities, leadership, translational research and evaluation, youth and behavioral health. *Accreditation:* ACA. *Faculty:* 15 full-time (9 women), 1 part-time/adjunct. *Students:* 54 full-time (44 women), 18 part-time (13 women); includes 24 minority (5 Black or African American, non-Hispanic/Latino; 4 Asian, non-Hispanic/Latino; 15 Hispanic/Latino), 2 international. Average age 25. 113 applicants, 38% accepted, 29 enrolled. In 2014, 29 master's awarded. *Degree requirements:* For master's, comprehensive exam, thesis; for doctorate, comprehensive exam, thesis/dissertation, Behavior Analyst Board Certification Exam. *Entrance requirements:* For master's, GRE General Test, minimum GPA of 3.0 in last 60 hours of coursework; three letters of recommendation; one-page narrative describing experience, interest, and career goals in applied behavior analysis; resume or curriculum vitae; for doctorate, GRE General Test (minimum preferred scores at or above the 40th percentile in verbal, quantitative, and analytical writing sections), master's degree in behavioral analysis or closely-related field; minimum GPA of 3.5 in graduate course work; three letters of recommendation; campus visit with faculty interview; personal statement; curriculum vitae; evidence of research experiences and expertise. Additional exam requirements/recommendations for international students: Required—TOEFL (minimum score 550 paper-based; 79 iBT) or IELTS (minimum score 6.5). *Application deadline:* For fall admission, 2/15 for domestic students, 1/2 for international students. Application fee: $30. *Financial support:* Unspecified assistantships available. *Faculty research:* Applied behavior analysis, autism, behavior management, behavioral intervention, children, developmental disabilities, experimental analysis of behavior, functional assessment, positive behavior support. *Total annual research expenditures:* $12 million. *Unit head:* Dr. Raymond G. Miltenberger, Professor/Director of Master's Program, 813-974-5079, Fax: 813-974-6115, E-mail: miltenbe@usf.edu. *Application contact:* Dr. Raymond G. Miltenberger, Professor/Director of Master's Program, 813-974-5079, Fax: 813-974-6115, E-mail: miltenbe@usf.edu.
Website: http://cfs.cbcs.usf.edu/

The University of Texas at San Antonio, College of Education and Human Development, Department of Educational Psychology, San Antonio, TX 78207. Offers applied behavioral analysis (Certificate); digital learning design (Certificate); language acquisition and bilingual psychoeducational assessment (Certificate); school psychology (MA). Part-time programs available. *Faculty:* 10 full-time (7 women), 1 (woman) part-time/adjunct. *Students:* 37 full-time (30 women), 38 part-time (33 women); includes 48 minority (5 Black or African American, non-Hispanic/Latino; 1 Asian, non-Hispanic/Latino; 41 Hispanic/Latino; 1 Native Hawaiian or other Pacific Islander, non-Hispanic/Latino), 1 international. Average age 27. 46 applicants, 89% accepted, 20 enrolled. In 2014, 17 master's awarded. *Degree requirements:* For master's, comprehensive exam, thesis (for some programs). *Entrance requirements:* For master's, GRE, bachelor's degree with 18 credit hours in field of study or in another appropriate field of study, two letters of recommendation, statement of purpose; for Certificate, 18 hours in psychology, sociology, education, or anything related (for applied behavioral analysis); minimum GPA of 2.7 in last 30 hours (for language acquisition and bilingual psychoeducational assessment). Additional exam requirements/recommendations for international students: Required—TOEFL (minimum score 550 paper-based; 79 iBT), IELTS (minimum score 6.5). *Application deadline:* For fall admission, 7/1 for domestic students, 4/1 for international students; for spring admission, 11/1 for domestic students, 9/1 for international students; for summer admission, 3/1 for international students. Applications are processed on a rolling basis. Application fee: $45 ($80 for international students). Electronic applications accepted. *Expenses:* Tuition, state resident: full-time $4671; part-time $260 per credit hour. Tuition, nonresident: full-time $18,022; part-time $1001 per credit hour. *Financial support:* In 2014–15, 9 research assistantships (averaging $2,829 per year) were awarded. Financial award application deadline: 3/5; financial award applicants required to submit FAFSA. *Faculty research:* Teacher consultation and culturally responsive school psychology practices, youth mentoring, cross-age peer mentoring, adolescent connectedness, pair counseling. *Unit head:* Dr. Jeremy Sullivan, Department Chair, 210-458-2408, Fax: 210-458-2019, E-mail: jeremy.sullivan@utsa.edu. *Application contact:* Dr. John Pruiett, Development Specialist, 210-458-2721, Fax: 210-458-2019, E-mail: johnny.pruiett@utsa.edu.
Website: http://education.utsa.edu/educational_psychology

Western New England University, College of Arts and Sciences, Program in Behavior Analysis, Springfield, MA 01119. Offers applied behavior analysis (MS); behavior analysis (PhD). Part-time programs available. *Students:* 145 part-time (121 women); includes 15 minority (3 Black or African American, non-Hispanic/Latino; 1 American Indian or Alaska Native, non-Hispanic/Latino; 4 Asian, non-Hispanic/Latino; 6 Hispanic/Latino; 1 Two or more races, non-Hispanic/Latino), 7 international. Average age 26. In 2014, 20 master's, 1 doctorate awarded. *Degree requirements:* For doctorate, thesis/dissertation. *Entrance requirements:* For master's, GRE, official transcript, personal statement, resume, three letters of recommendation; for doctorate, GRE, master's degree in behavior analysis with minimum GPA of 3.6, official transcript, personal statement, resume, three letters of recommendation. Additional exam requirements/recommendations for international students: Required—TOEFL (minimum score 79 iBT). *Application deadline:* For fall admission, 1/15 for domestic and international students. Application fee: $30. Electronic applications accepted. *Financial support:* Fellowships with full and partial tuition reimbursements available. Support available to part-time students. Financial award application deadline: 4/15; financial award applicants required to submit FAFSA. *Unit head:* Dr. Gregory Hanley, Director of the

PhD Program in Behavioral Analysis/Professor, 413-796-2367, E-mail: ghanley@wne.edu. *Application contact:* Matthew Fox, Director of Admissions for Graduate Students and Adult Learners, 413-782-1517, Fax: 413-782-1777, E-mail: study@wne.edu.
Website: http://www1.wne.edu/artsandsciences/index.cfm?selection-doc.6317

Westfield State University, Division of Graduate and Continuing Education, Department of Psychology, Westfield, MA 01086. Offers applied behavior analysis (MA); mental health counseling (MA); school guidance (MA). Part-time and evening/weekend programs available. *Degree requirements:* For master's, comprehensive exam. *Entrance requirements:* For master's, GRE General Test, MAT, minimum undergraduate GPA of 2.7.

Wright State University, School of Graduate Studies, College of Liberal Arts, Program in Applied Behavioral Science, Dayton, OH 45435. Offers criminal justice and social problems (MA); international and comparative politics (MA). *Degree requirements:* For master's, thesis optional. *Entrance requirements:* Additional exam requirements/recommendations for international students: Required—TOEFL. *Faculty research:* Training and development, criminal justice and social problems, community systems, human factors, industrial/organizational psychology.

Youngstown State University, Graduate School, College of Liberal Arts and Social Sciences, Department of Psychology, Youngstown, OH 44555-0001. Offers applied behavior analysis (MS).

Applied Psychology

Angelo State University, College of Graduate Studies, College of Arts and Sciences, Department of Psychology, Sociology and Social Work, San Angelo, TX 76909. Offers psychology (MS), including applied psychology, counseling psychology, industrial and organizational psychology. Part-time and evening/weekend programs available. *Degree requirements:* For master's, comprehensive exam, thesis optional. *Entrance requirements:* For master's, GRE General Test (for industrial and organizational psychology only), essay, letters of recommendation (for industrial and organizational psychology only). Additional exam requirements/recommendations for international students: Required—TOEFL or IELTS. Electronic applications accepted.

Antioch University New England, Graduate School, Department of Applied Psychology, Keene, NH 03431-3552. Offers autism spectrum disorders (Certificate), including applied behavioral analysis internship, autism spectrum disorders; clinical mental health counseling (MA), including clinical mental health counseling, substance abuse counseling; dance/movement therapy and counseling (M Ed, MA, PMC); marriage and family therapy (MA, PhD, Certificate). *Degree requirements:* For master's, internship, practicum. *Entrance requirements:* For master's, previous course work and work experience in psychology. Additional exam requirements/recommendations for international students: Required—TOEFL (minimum score 550 paper-based). Electronic applications accepted. *Expenses:* Contact institution. *Faculty research:* Diversity, descendents of survivors of the Holocaust and American slavery.

Arizona State University at the Tempe campus, Ira A. Fulton Schools of Engineering, The Polytechnic School, Applied Psychology Program, Mesa, AZ 85212. Offers MS. Part-time programs available. Terminal master's awarded for partial completion of doctoral program. *Degree requirements:* For master's, thesis or applied project with oral defense and exam; interactive Program of Study (iPOS) submitted before completing 50 percent of required credit hours. *Entrance requirements:* For master's, GRE, minimum GPA of 3.0 or equivalent in last 2 years of work leading to bachelor's degree. Additional exam requirements/recommendations for international students: Required—TOEFL, IELTS, or PTE. Electronic applications accepted.

Athabasca University, Graduate Centre for Applied Psychology, Athabasca, AB T9S 3A3, Canada. Offers art therapy (MC); career counseling (MC); counseling (Advanced Certificate); counseling psychology (MC); school counseling (MC).

Boston College, Lynch Graduate School of Education, Program in Applied Developmental and Educational Psychology, Chestnut Hill, MA 02467-3800. Offers MA, PhD. Part-time and evening/weekend programs available. Terminal master's awarded for partial completion of doctoral program. *Degree requirements:* For master's, comprehensive exam; for doctorate, comprehensive exam, thesis/dissertation. *Entrance requirements:* For master's and doctorate, GRE General Test. Additional exam requirements/recommendations for international students: Required—TOEFL (minimum score 100 iBT). Electronic applications accepted. *Faculty research:* Cognitive learning and culture, effects of social policy reform on children and families, psychosocial trauma, human rights and international justice, positive youth development, children and adolescents living in poverty.

California State University, Chico, Office of Graduate Studies, College of Behavioral and Social Sciences, Department of Psychology, Program in Applied Psychology, Chico, CA 95929-0722. Offers MA. *Students:* 19 full-time (15 women), 1 (woman) part-time; includes 2 minority (both Hispanic/Latino), 1 international. Average age 27. 32 applicants, 47% accepted, 7 enrolled. In 2014, 12 master's awarded. *Degree requirements:* For master's, thesis or comprehensive exam. *Entrance requirements:* For master's, GRE General Test or MAT, 3 letters of recommendation, three departmental recommendation forms, statement of purpose. Additional exam requirements/recommendations for international students: Required—TOEFL (minimum score 550 paper-based; 80 iBT), IELTS (minimum score 6.5). *Application deadline:* For fall admission, 3/1 for domestic and international students. Application fee: $55. Electronic applications accepted. *Expenses:* Tuition, state resident: full-time $7002. Tuition, nonresident: full-time $18,162. *Required fees:* $1530. Tuition and fees vary according to program. *Financial support:* Application deadline: 3/1; applicants required to submit FAFSA. *Unit head:* Dr. Brian Oppy, Chair, 530-898-5147, Fax: 530-898-4740, E-mail: psy@csuchico.edu. *Application contact:* Judy L. Rice, Graduate Admissions Coordinator, 530-898-5416, Fax: 530-898-3342, E-mail: jlrice@csuchico.edu.
Website: http://catalog.csuchico.edu/viewer/12/PSYC/PSYCNONEMA.html

California State University, Northridge, Graduate Studies, College of Social and Behavioral Sciences, Department of Psychology, Northridge, CA 91330. Offers clinical psychology (MA); general-experimental psychology (MA); human factors and applied experimental psychology (MA). *Students:* 46 full-time (32 women), 16 part-time (10 women); includes 27 minority (3 Black or African American, non-Hispanic/Latino; 2 Asian, non-Hispanic/Latino; 20 Hispanic/Latino; 2 Two or more races, non-Hispanic/Latino). Average age 26. *Degree requirements:* For master's, thesis. *Entrance requirements:* For master's, GRE General Test, GRE Subject Test, minimum GPA of 3.0, letters of recommendation. Additional exam requirements/recommendations for international students: Required—TOEFL. *Application deadline:* For fall admission, 11/30 for domestic students. Application fee: $55. *Expenses: Required fees:* $12,402. *Financial support:* Application deadline: 3/1. *Unit head:* Jill Razani, Chair, 818-677-3506.
Website: http://www.csun.edu/csbs/departments/psychology/index.html

The Catholic University of America, School of Arts and Sciences, Department of Psychology, Washington, DC 20064. Offers applied experimental psychology (PhD); clinical psychology (PhD); general psychology (MA); human factors (MA); MA/JD. *Accreditation:* APA (one or more programs are accredited). Part-time programs available. *Faculty:* 13 full-time (6 women), 7 part-time/adjunct (2 women). *Students:* 37 full-time (26 women), 42 part-time (33 women); includes 17 minority (1 Black or African American, non-Hispanic/Latino; 3 Asian, non-Hispanic/Latino; 7 Hispanic/Latino; 6 Two or more races, non-Hispanic/Latino), 3 international. Average age 28. 263 applicants, 14% accepted, 19 enrolled. In 2014, 19 master's, 6 doctorates awarded. *Degree requirements:* For master's, comprehensive exam, thesis (for some programs); for doctorate, comprehensive exam, thesis/dissertation. *Entrance requirements:* For master's, GRE General Test, statement of purpose, official copies of academic transcripts, three letters of recommendation; for doctorate, GRE General Test, GRE Subject Test, statement of purpose, official copies of academic transcripts, three letters of recommendation. Additional exam requirements/recommendations for international students: Required—TOEFL (minimum score 580 paper-based). *Application deadline:* For fall admission, 7/15 priority date for domestic students, 7/1 for international students; for spring admission, 11/15 priority date for domestic students, 11/1 for international students. Applications are processed on a rolling basis. Application fee: $55. Electronic applications accepted. *Expenses: Tuition:* Full-time $40,200; part-time $1600 per credit hour. *Required fees:* $400; $195 per semester. One-time fee: $425. *Financial support:* Fellowships, research assistantships, teaching assistantships, Federal Work-Study, scholarships/grants, tuition waivers (full and partial), and unspecified assistantships available. Financial award application deadline: 2/1; financial award applicants required to submit FAFSA. *Faculty research:* Clinical psychology, applied cognitive science, psychopathology, cognitive neuroscience, psychotherapy. *Total annual research expenditures:* $1.2 million. *Unit head:* Dr. Marc M. Sebrechts, Chair, 202-319-5750, Fax: 202-319-6263, E-mail: sebrechts@cua.edu. *Application contact:* Director of Graduate Admissions, 202-319-5057, Fax: 202-319-6533, E-mail: cua-admissions@cua.edu.
Website: http://psychology.cua.edu/

Central Michigan University, College of Graduate Studies, College of Humanities and Social and Behavioral Sciences, Department of Psychology, Program in Experimental Psychology, Mount Pleasant, MI 48859. Offers applied experimental psychology (PhD); experimental psychology (MS). Part-time programs available. *Degree requirements:* For master's, thesis or alternative; for doctorate, thesis/dissertation. Electronic applications accepted. *Faculty research:* Behavioral neuroscience, human development, perception and cognition, social/personal problem solving, psychophysiology.

The Chicago School of Professional Psychology: Online, Program in Applied Industrial and Organizational Psychology, Chicago, IL 60654. Offers MA, Certificate.

Clayton State University, School of Graduate Studies, College of Arts and Sciences, Program in Psychology, Morrow, GA 30260-0285. Offers applied developmental psychology (MS); clinical psychology (MS). *Entrance requirements:* For master's, GRE, 2 official transcripts; 3 letters of recommendation; statement of purpose; on-campus interview; background check. Additional exam requirements/recommendations for international students: Required—TOEFL (minimum score 550 paper-based). Electronic applications accepted.

Clemson University, Graduate School, College of Business and Behavioral Science, Department of Psychology, Program in Applied Psychology, Clemson, SC 29634. Offers MS. *Students:* 3 full-time (1 woman), 2 part-time (1 woman), 1 international. Average age 28. 40 applicants, 3% accepted, 1 enrolled. In 2014, 7 master's awarded. *Degree requirements:* For master's, thesis, internship. *Entrance requirements:* For master's, GRE General Test. Additional exam requirements/recommendations for international students: Required—TOEFL. *Application deadline:* For fall admission, 1/15 for domestic students. Application fee: $70 ($80 for international students). Electronic applications accepted. *Expenses:* Expenses: Contact institution. *Financial support:* In 2014–15, 1 student received support, including 1 teaching assistantship with partial tuition reimbursement available (averaging $16,000 per year); fellowships with full and partial tuition reimbursements available, research assistantships with partial tuition reimbursements available, career-related internships or fieldwork, institutionally sponsored loans, scholarships/grants, health care benefits, and unspecified assistantships also available. Support available to part-time students. Financial award applicants required to submit FAFSA. *Faculty research:* Personnel selection and evaluation, occupational health, motivation and decision-making, human factors, transportation safety. *Unit head:* Dr. Patrick Raymark, Chair, 864-656-4715, Fax: 864-656-0358, E-mail: praymar@clemson.edu. *Application contact:* Dr. Robert Sinclair, Graduate Program Coordinator, 864-656-3931, Fax: 864-656-0358, E-mail: rsincla@clemson.edu.
Website: http://www.clemson.edu/psych/grad/ms-psych/

DEREE - The American College of Greece, Graduate Programs, Athens, Greece. Offers applied psychology (MS); communication (MA); leadership (MS); marketing (MS).

Eastern Washington University, Graduate Studies, College of Social and Behavioral Sciences and Social Work, Program in Mental Health Counseling, Cheney, WA 99004-2431. Offers applied psychology (MS); mental health counseling (MS).

Eastern Washington University, Graduate Studies, College of Social and Behavioral Sciences and Social Work, Program in School Counseling, Cheney, WA 99004-2431. Offers applied psychology (MS); school counseling (MS). *Accreditation:* ACA. *Degree requirements:* For master's, comprehensive exam, thesis or alternative. *Entrance requirements:* For master's, GRE General Test, minimum GPA of 3.0.

Fairfield University, Graduate School of Education and Allied Professions, Fairfield, CT 06824. Offers applied behavior analysis (ATC); applied psychology (MA); clinical mental health counseling (MA, CAS); early childhood studies (ATC); educational technology (MA); elementary education (MA, CAS); family studies (MA); integration of spirituality and religion in counseling (ATC); marriage and family therapy (MA); school counseling (MA, CAS); school psychology (MA, CAS); school-based marriage and family therapy (ATC); secondary education (MA); special education (MA, CAS); substance abuse counseling (ATC); teaching (Certificate); teaching and foundations (MA, CAS); TESOL, world languages, and bilingual education (MA, CAS). *Accreditation:* NCATE. Part-time

and evening/weekend programs available. *Faculty:* 23 full-time (19 women), 32 part-time/adjunct (25 women). *Students:* 148 full-time (131 women), 286 part-time (238 women); includes 81 minority (18 Black or African American, non-Hispanic/Latino; 1 American Indian or Alaska Native, non-Hispanic/Latino; 14 Asian, non-Hispanic/Latino; 39 Hispanic/Latino; 9 Two or more races, non-Hispanic/Latino), 13 international. Average age 34. 264 applicants, 54% accepted, 68 enrolled. In 2014, 142 master's awarded. *Degree requirements:* For master's, comprehensive exam. *Entrance requirements:* For master's, PRAXIS I (for certification programs), minimum GPA of 3.0, 2 recommendations, resume. Additional exam requirements/recommendations for international students: Required—TOEFL (minimum score 550 paper-based; 84 iBT) or IELTS (minimum score 7.5). *Application deadline:* For fall admission, 2/15 for international students; for spring admission, 10/1 for international students. Application fee: $60. Electronic applications accepted. *Expenses:* Expenses: $675 per credit hour. *Financial support:* In 2014–15, 55 students received support. Career-related internships or fieldwork and unspecified assistantships available. Financial award applicants required to submit FAFSA. *Faculty research:* Literacy, spirituality, special education, bilingual/multicultural education, mentoring and professional development. *Unit head:* Dr. Robert D. Hannafin, Dean, 203-254-4250, Fax: 203-254-4241, E-mail: rhannafin@fairfield.edu. *Application contact:* Marianne Gumpper, Director of Graduate and Continuing Studies Admission, 203-254-4184, Fax: 203-254-4073, E-mail: gradadmis@fairfield.edu.
Website: http://www.fairfield.edu/academics/schoolscollegescenters/graduateschoolofeducationalliedprofessions/graduateprograms/

Fordham University, Graduate School of Arts and Sciences, Department of Psychology, Program in Applied Developmental Psychology, New York, NY 10458. Offers PhD. *Students:* 21 full-time (18 women), 9 part-time (6 women); includes 6 minority (2 Black or African American, non-Hispanic/Latino; 3 Asian, non-Hispanic/Latino; 1 Hispanic/Latino), 7 international. Average age 31. 29 applicants, 21% accepted, 5 enrolled. In 2014, 8 doctorates awarded. *Degree requirements:* For doctorate, comprehensive exam, thesis/dissertation. *Entrance requirements:* For doctorate, GRE General Test, GRE Subject Test. Additional exam requirements/recommendations for international students: Required—TOEFL (minimum score 600 paper-based). *Application deadline:* For fall admission, 12/14 for domestic students. Application fee: $70. Electronic applications accepted. *Financial support:* In 2014–15, 15 students received support, including 1 fellowship with tuition reimbursement available (averaging $24,890 per year), 1 research assistantship with tuition reimbursement available (averaging $22,240 per year), 10 teaching assistantships with tuition reimbursements available (averaging $20,223 per year); career-related internships or fieldwork, institutionally sponsored loans, tuition waivers (full and partial), and unspecified assistantships also available. Financial award application deadline: 12/14. *Faculty research:* Development of citizenship, impact of participation in community service, impact of poverty on children, development of moral reasoning and behavior. *Unit head:* Dr. Barry Rosenfeld, Director, 718-817-3794, Fax: 718-817-3785, E-mail: tyip@fordham.edu. *Application contact:* Bernadette Valentino-Morrison, Director of Graduate Admissions, 718-817-4419, Fax: 718-817-3566, E-mail: valentinomor@fordham.edu.

Fordham University, Graduate School of Arts and Sciences, Department of Psychology, Program in Applied Psychological Methods, New York, NY 10458. Offers MS. *Students:* 4 full-time (2 women), 7 part-time (4 women); includes 3 minority (1 Asian, non-Hispanic/Latino; 2 Hispanic/Latino), 2 international. Average age 27. 35 applicants, 51% accepted, 4 enrolled. *Degree requirements:* For master's, three-credit one-semester internship. *Entrance requirements:* For master's, GRE General Test. *Application deadline:* For fall admission, 1/4 priority date for domestic students, 1/4 for international students; for spring admission, 10/31 for domestic and international students. Application fee: $70. *Unit head:* Dr. Barry Rosenfeld, Department Chair, 718-817-3794, E-mail: arasmussen@fordham.edu. *Application contact:* Bernadette Valentino-Morrison, Director of Graduate Admissions, 718-817-4419, Fax: 718-817-3566, E-mail: valentinomor@fordham.edu.

Francis Marion University, Graduate Programs, Department of Psychology, Florence, SC 29502-0547. Offers applied psychology (MS), including clinical/counseling psychology, school psychology; school psychology (SSP). Part-time and evening/weekend programs available. *Faculty:* 6 full-time (2 women), 4 part-time/adjunct (all women). *Students:* 35 full-time (30 women), 11 part-time (all women); includes 9 minority (7 Black or African American, non-Hispanic/Latino; 2 Asian, non-Hispanic/Latino), 1 international. Average age 26. 43 applicants, 100% accepted, 16 enrolled. In 2014, 15 master's, 6 other advanced degrees awarded. *Degree requirements:* For master's, internship. *Entrance requirements:* For master's, GRE General Test, official transcripts, two letters of recommendation, written statement. *Application deadline:* For fall admission, 2/15 for domestic and international students; for spring admission, 10/15 for domestic and international students. Applications are processed on a rolling basis. Application fee: $35. Electronic applications accepted. *Expenses:* Tuition, state resident: full-time $9472; part-time $473.60 per credit hour. Tuition, nonresident: full-time $18,944; part-time $947.20 per credit hour. *Required fees:* $14 per credit hour. $107 per semester. Tuition and fees vary according to course load and program. *Financial support:* In 2014–15, 4 teaching assistantships (averaging $7,750 per year) were awarded; career-related internships or fieldwork, scholarships/grants, and unspecified assistantships also available. Support available to part-time students. Financial award application deadline: 3/1; financial award applicants required to submit FAFSA. *Faculty research:* Parenting and family relationships, child development, applied behavioral analysis, post-traumatic stress disorder, clinical psychology in adults. *Unit head:* Dr. William Wattles, Chair, 843-661-1641, Fax: 843-661-1628. *Application contact:* Sharekka Bridges, Administrative Assistant, 843-661-1641, Fax: 843-661-1628.
Website: http://www.fmarion.edu/academics/psychology

George Mason University, College of Humanities and Social Sciences, Department of Psychology, Fairfax, VA 22030. Offers applied developmental psychology (Certificate); cognitive and behavioral neuroscience (MA); human factors/applied cognition (MA); industrial/organizational psychology (MA, PhD); school psychology (MA). *Accreditation:* APA. *Faculty:* 43 full-time (22 women), 13 part-time/adjunct (8 women). *Students:* 167 full-time (114 women), 48 part-time (34 women); includes 41 minority (7 Black or African American, non-Hispanic/Latino; 8 Asian, non-Hispanic/Latino; 21 Hispanic/Latino; 1 Native Hawaiian or other Pacific Islander, non-Hispanic/Latino; 4 Two or more races, non-Hispanic/Latino), 10 international. Average age 27. 833 applicants, 14% accepted, 75 enrolled. In 2014, 49 master's, 17 doctorates, 10 other advanced degrees awarded. *Degree requirements:* For master's, comprehensive exam, thesis (for biopsychology); for doctorate, comprehensive exam, thesis/dissertation, 2nd year project. *Entrance requirements:* For master's, GRE, 2 official transcripts; goals statement; 15 undergraduate credits in concentration for which the applicant is applying; for doctorate, GRE, 3 letters of recommendation; resume; goals statement; minimum GPA of 3.0 overall for last 60 undergraduate credits, 3.25 in psychology courses; 15 undergraduate credits in concentration for which the applicant is applying; 2 official transcripts; for Certificate, GRE, 2 official transcripts; expanded goals statement; 3 letters of recommendation. Additional exam requirements/recommendations for international students: Required—TOEFL (minimum score 570 paper-based; 80 iBT), IELTS (minimum score 6.5), PTE. Application fee: $65 ($80 for international students). Electronic applications accepted. *Expenses:* Tuition, state resident: full-time $9794; part-time $408 per credit hour. Tuition, nonresident: full-time $26,978; part-time $1124 per credit hour. *Required fees:* $2820; $118 per credit hour. Tuition and fees vary according to course load and program. *Financial support:* In 2014–15, 130 students received support, including 6 fellowships (averaging $6,576 per year), 84 research assistantships with full and partial tuition reimbursements available (averaging $15,356 per year), 63 teaching assistantships with full and partial tuition reimbursements available (averaging $13,274 per year); career-related internships or fieldwork, Federal Work-Study, scholarships/grants, tuition waivers (partial), unspecified assistantships, and health care benefits (for full-time research or teaching assistantship recipients) also available. Support available to part-time students. Financial award application deadline: 3/1; financial award applicants required to submit FAFSA. *Faculty research:* Applied developmental psychology, biopsychology, clinical psychology, human factors/applied cognition psychology, industrial/organizational psychology, school psychology. *Total annual research expenditures:* $5.2 million. *Unit head:* Reeshad Dalal, Department Chair, 703-993-9487, Fax: 703-993-1359, E-mail: rdalal@gmu.edu. *Application contact:* Adam Winsler, Associate Chair of Graduate Studies, 703-993-1881, Fax: 703-993-1359, E-mail: awinsler@gmu.edu.
Website: http://psychology.gmu.edu

The George Washington University, Columbian College of Arts and Sciences, Department of Psychology, Washington, DC 20052. Offers applied social psychology (PhD); clinical psychology (PhD); cognitive neuroscience (PhD). *Accreditation:* APA. Part-time and evening/weekend programs available. *Faculty:* 24 full-time (14 women), 1 (woman) part-time/adjunct. *Students:* 46 full-time (33 women), 24 part-time (15 women); includes 19 minority (7 Black or African American, non-Hispanic/Latino; 3 Asian, non-Hispanic/Latino; 8 Hispanic/Latino; 1 Two or more races, non-Hispanic/Latino), 8 international. Average age 28. 513 applicants, 3% accepted, 14 enrolled. In 2014, 10 doctorates awarded. *Degree requirements:* For doctorate, thesis/dissertation or alternative, general exam. *Entrance requirements:* For doctorate, GRE General Test, minimum GPA of 3.0. Additional exam requirements/recommendations for international students: Required—TOEFL (minimum score 550 paper-based; 80 iBT). *Application deadline:* For fall admission, 1/15 for domestic and international students. Application fee: $75. *Financial support:* In 2014–15, 62 students received support. Fellowships with tuition reimbursements available, teaching assistantships with tuition reimbursements available, career-related internships or fieldwork, Federal Work-Study, and tuition waivers available. *Unit head:* Dr. Paul Poppen, Chair, 202-994-6324, E-mail: pjp@gwu.edu. *Application contact:* Information Contact, 202-994-6320, Fax: 202-994-1602, E-mail: psydept@gwu.edu.
Website: http://psychology.columbian.gwu.edu/

Laurentian University, School of Graduate Studies and Research, Programme in Psychology, Sudbury, ON P3E 2C6, Canada. Offers applied psychology (MA); experimental psychology (MA).

Loras College, Graduate Division, Program in Applied Psychology, Dubuque, IA 52004-0178. Offers MA. Part-time and evening/weekend programs available. *Degree requirements:* For master's, comprehensive exam, thesis (for some programs). *Entrance requirements:* For master's, Ohio State University Psychological Test or GRE General Test, minimum undergraduate GPA of 2.75.

Loyola University Chicago, Graduate School, Department of Psychology, Program in Applied Social Psychology, Chicago, IL 60660. Offers MA, PhD. *Faculty:* 7 full-time (2 women), 1 (woman) part-time/adjunct. *Students:* 22 full-time (17 women), 1 (woman) part-time; includes 8 minority (3 Black or African American, non-Hispanic/Latino; 1 Asian, non-Hispanic/Latino; 1 Hispanic/Latino; 3 Two or more races, non-Hispanic/Latino), 3 international. Average age 29. 89 applicants, 19% accepted, 5 enrolled. In 2014, 3 master's, 4 doctorates awarded. Terminal master's awarded for partial completion of doctoral program. *Degree requirements:* For master's, thesis; for doctorate, comprehensive exam, thesis/dissertation, internship. *Entrance requirements:* For master's and doctorate, GRE General Test, sample of written work. Additional exam requirements/recommendations for international students: Required—TOEFL. *Application deadline:* For fall admission, 1/15 for domestic and international students. Application fee: $50. Electronic applications accepted. Application fee is waived when completed online. *Expenses: Tuition:* Full-time $17,370; part-time $965 per credit. *Required fees:* $138 per semester. *Financial support:* In 2014–15, 1 fellowship with tuition reimbursement (averaging $16,000 per year), 5 research assistantships with tuition reimbursements (averaging $16,000 per year), 1 teaching assistantship with tuition reimbursement (averaging $16,000 per year) were awarded; career-related internships or fieldwork, Federal Work-Study, and scholarships/grants also available. Financial award application deadline: 12/15; financial award applicants required to submit FAFSA. *Faculty research:* Program evaluation, attitudes and prejudice, psychological well-being, self esteem and relationships, groups and organizations. *Total annual research expenditures:* $150,000. *Unit head:* Dr. Scott Tindale, Director, 773-508-3014. *Application contact:* Ron Martin, Assistant Director of Enrollment Management, 312-915-8950, Fax: 312-915-8905, E-mail: gradapp@luc.edu.

Lynn University, College of Arts and Sciences, Boca Raton, FL 33431-5598. Offers applied psychology (MS); criminal justice administration (MS); emergency planning and administration (MS). Part-time and evening/weekend programs available. Postbaccalaureate distance learning degree programs offered (no on-campus study). *Faculty:* 4 full-time (2 women), 10 part-time/adjunct (8 women). *Students:* 77 full-time (58 women), 36 part-time (21 women); includes 23 minority (12 Black or African American, non-Hispanic/Latino; 2 Asian, non-Hispanic/Latino; 9 Hispanic/Latino), 11 international. Average age 32. 103 applicants, 96% accepted, 71 enrolled. In 2014, 27 master's awarded. *Degree requirements:* For master's, comprehensive exam (for some programs), thesis (for some programs). *Entrance requirements:* For master's, bachelor's degree from accredited institution, resume, letter of recommendation, essay of professional goals, official transcripts. Additional exam requirements/recommendations for international students: Required—TOEFL (minimum score 550 paper-based; 80 iBT), IELTS (minimum score 6.5). *Application deadline:* For fall admission, 8/17 for domestic students, 8/3 for international students; for spring admission, 12/15 for domestic students, 11/24 for international students; for summer admission, 4/17 for domestic students, 4/6 for international students. Applications are processed on a rolling basis. Application fee: $45. Electronic applications accepted. *Expenses: Tuition:* Full-time $16,200; part-time $675 per credit hour. Tuition and fees vary according to class time, course load, degree level and program. *Financial support:* In 2014–15, 33 students received support. Career-related internships or fieldwork, Federal Work-Study, scholarships/grants, tuition waivers (full and partial), and unspecified assistantships available. Support available to part-time students. Financial award application deadline: 3/1; financial award applicants required to submit FAFSA. *Faculty research:* Terrorism, criminological theory, corrections, emergency planning, counseling. *Unit head:* Dr. Katrina Carter-Tellison, Dean, 561-237-7412, E-mail: kcartertellison@lynn.edu. *Application contact:* Steven Pruitt, Director of Graduate Admission, 561-237-7834, Fax: 561-237-7100, E-mail: admissionpm@lynn.edu.
Website: http://www.lynn.edu/academics/colleges/arts-and-sciences/

Massachusetts School of Professional Psychology, Graduate Programs, Boston, MA 02132. Offers applied psychology in higher education student personnel

administration (MA); clinical psychology (Psy D); counseling psychology (MA); counseling psychology and community mental health (MA); counseling psychology and global mental health (MA); executive coaching (Graduate Certificate); forensic and counseling psychology (MA); leadership psychology (Psy D); organizational psychology (MA); primary care psychology (MA); respecialization in clinical psychology (Certificate); school psychology (Psy D); MA/CAGS. *Accreditation:* APA. *Degree requirements:* For master's, comprehensive exam (for some programs); for doctorate, thesis/dissertation (for some programs). Electronic applications accepted.

New York University, Steinhardt School of Culture, Education, and Human Development, Department of Applied Psychology, New York, NY 10003. Offers counseling (PhD, Advanced Certificate), including counseling and guidance (Advanced Certificate), counseling psychology (PhD), LGBT health, education, and social services (Advanced Certificate); educational and developmental psychology (MA, PhD), including developmental psychology (PhD), human development and social intervention (MA), psychology and social intervention (PhD); Advanced Certificate/MPH; MA/Advanced Certificate. *Accreditation:* APA (one or more programs are accredited). Part-time programs available. *Faculty:* 37 full-time (25 women), 38 part-time/adjunct (25 women). *Students:* 189 full-time (154 women), 47 part-time (40 women); includes 96 minority (30 Black or African American, non-Hispanic/Latino; 21 Asian, non-Hispanic/Latino; 42 Hispanic/Latino; 3 Two or more races, non-Hispanic/Latino), 21 international. Average age 28. 800 applicants, 32% accepted, 87 enrolled. In 2014, 103 master's, 11 doctorates awarded. Terminal master's awarded for partial completion of doctoral program. *Degree requirements:* For master's, thesis (for some programs); for doctorate, thesis/dissertation. *Entrance requirements:* For doctorate, GRE General Test, interview. Additional exam requirements/recommendations for international students: Required—TOEFL (minimum score 100 iBT). *Application deadline:* For fall admission, 12/1 priority date for domestic and international students. Applications are processed on a rolling basis. Application fee: $75. Electronic applications accepted. *Financial support:* Fellowships with full and partial tuition reimbursements, research assistantships with full and partial tuition reimbursements, teaching assistantships with full and partial tuition reimbursements, career-related internships or fieldwork, Federal Work-Study, institutionally sponsored loans, scholarships/grants, tuition waivers (partial), and unspecified assistantships available. Support available to part-time students. Financial award application deadline: 2/1; financial award applicants required to submit FAFSA. *Faculty research:* Applied measurement and research methods, health and human development, social and emotional development, cultural contexts and immigration. *Unit head:* Dr. LaRue Allen, Chairperson, 212-998-5076, Fax: 212-995-4358, E-mail: larue.allen@nyu.edu. *Application contact:* 212-998-5030, Fax: 212-995-4328, E-mail: steinhardt.gradadmissions@nyu.edu.
Website: http://steinhardt.nyu.edu/appsych/

Oklahoma State University, College of Education, School of Applied Health and Educational Psychology, Stillwater, OK 74078. Offers applied behavioral studies (Ed D); applied health and educational psychology (MS, PhD, Ed S). *Accreditation:* APA (one or more programs are accredited). Part-time programs available. *Faculty:* 41 full-time (22 women), 15 part-time/adjunct (10 women). *Students:* 178 full-time (119 women), 130 part-time (94 women); includes 80 minority (14 Black or African American, non-Hispanic/Latino; 14 American Indian or Alaska Native, non-Hispanic/Latino; 4 Asian, non-Hispanic/Latino; 24 Hispanic/Latino; 24 Two or more races, non-Hispanic/Latino), 10 international. Average age 30. 237 applicants, 37% accepted, 66 enrolled. In 2014, 84 master's, 33 doctorates awarded. *Degree requirements:* For master's, thesis (for some programs); for doctorate, comprehensive exam, thesis/dissertation. *Entrance requirements:* For master's and doctorate, GRE or GMAT. Additional exam requirements/recommendations for international students: Required—TOEFL (minimum score 550 paper-based; 79 iBT). *Application deadline:* For fall admission, 3/1 priority date for international students; for spring admission, 8/1 priority date for international students. Applications are processed on a rolling basis. Application fee: $40 ($75 for international students). Electronic applications accepted. *Expenses:* Tuition, state resident: full-time $4488; part-time $187 per credit hour. Tuition, nonresident: full-time $18,360; part-time $765 per credit hour. *Required fees:* $2413; $100.55 per credit hour. Tuition and fees vary according to campus/location. *Financial support:* In 2014–15, 30 research assistantships (averaging $9,530 per year), 70 teaching assistantships (averaging $9,677 per year) were awarded; career-related internships or fieldwork, Federal Work-Study, scholarships/grants, health care benefits, tuition waivers (partial), and unspecified assistantships also available. Support available to part-time students. Financial award application deadline: 3/1; financial award applicants required to submit FAFSA. *Unit head:* Dr. Aric Warren, Head, 405-744-6040, Fax: 405-744-6779, E-mail: aric.warren@okstate.edu.
Website: http://education.okstate.edu/sahep

Old Dominion University, College of Sciences, Doctoral Program in Psychology, Norfolk, VA 23529. Offers applied experimental psychology (PhD); human factors psychology (PhD). *Faculty:* 22 full-time (7 women). *Students:* 35 full-time (16 women), 17 part-time (13 women); includes 8 minority (3 Black or African American, non-Hispanic/Latino; 5 Hispanic/Latino), 3 international. Average age 27. 82 applicants, 30% accepted, 7 enrolled. In 2014, 5 doctorates awarded. *Degree requirements:* For doctorate, thesis/dissertation, candidacy exam. *Entrance requirements:* For doctorate, GRE General Test, GRE Subject Test, 3 recommendation letters. Additional exam requirements/recommendations for international students: Required—TOEFL. *Application deadline:* For winter admission, 1/5 for domestic and international students. Application fee: $50. Electronic applications accepted. *Expenses:* Tuition, state resident: full-time $10,488; part-time $437 per credit. Tuition, nonresident: full-time $26,136; part-time $1089 per credit. *Required fees:* $64 per semester. One-time fee: $50. *Financial support:* In 2014–15, 42 students received support, including 4 research assistantships with full tuition reimbursements available (averaging $17,500 per year), 38 teaching assistantships with full tuition reimbursements available (averaging $17,500 per year). Financial award application deadline: 1/15. *Faculty research:* Human factors, industrial psychology, organizational psychology, applied experimental (health, developmental, quantitative). *Total annual research expenditures:* $978,563. *Unit head:* Dr. Bryan E. Porter, Graduate Program Director, 757-683-4458, Fax: 757-683-5087, E-mail: bporter@odu.edu. *Application contact:* William Heffelfinger, Director of Graduate Admissions, 757-683-5554, Fax: 757-683-3255, E-mail: gradadmit@odu.edu.
Website: http://sci.odu.edu/psychology/

Penn State Harrisburg, Graduate School, School of Behavioral Sciences and Education, Middletown, PA 17057-4898. Offers applied behavior analysis (MA); applied clinical psychology (MA); applied psychological research (MA); community psychology and social change (MA); health education (M Ed); literacy education (M Ed); teaching and curriculum (M Ed); training and development (M Ed). Part-time and evening/weekend programs available. *Unit head:* Dr. Mukund S. Kulkarni, Chancellor, 717-948-6105, Fax: 717-948-6452, E-mail: msk5@psu.edu. *Application contact:* Robert W. Coffman, Jr., Director of Enrollment Management, Admissions, 717-948-6250, Fax: 717-948-6325, E-mail: ric1@psu.edu.
Website: http://harrisburg.psu.edu/behavioral-sciences-and-education/

Rider University, College of Liberal Arts, Education, and Sciences, Lawrenceville, NJ 08648-3001. Offers applied psychology (MA); business communication (MA). Part-time and evening/weekend programs available. *Entrance requirements:* For master's, official transcripts, current resume, two professional letters of recommendation, statement of aims and objectives, personal interview by invitation of faculty. Additional exam requirements/recommendations for international students: Required—TOEFL (minimum score 550 paper-based). Electronic applications accepted.

Rutgers, The State University of New Jersey, New Brunswick, Graduate School of Applied and Professional Psychology, Piscataway, NJ 08854. Offers Psy M, Psy D. *Accreditation:* APA (one or more programs are accredited). *Degree requirements:* For doctorate, comprehensive exam, thesis/dissertation, 1 year internship. *Entrance requirements:* For doctorate, GRE General Test, GRE Subject Test, bachelor's degree in psychology or equivalent. Additional exam requirements/recommendations for international students: Required—TOEFL. Electronic applications accepted. *Expenses:* Contact institution. *Faculty research:* Organizational psychology, behavior modification, long- and short-term dynamic therapy, school psychology, addictive behaviors.

Sacred Heart University, Graduate Programs, College of Arts and Sciences, Department of Psychology, Fairfield, CT 06825-1000. Offers applied psychology (MS), including applied psychology. Part-time and evening/weekend programs available. Postbaccalaureate distance learning degree programs offered (no on-campus study). *Faculty:* 11 full-time (10 women), 1 (woman) part-time/adjunct. *Students:* 15 full-time (9 women), 104 part-time (78 women); includes 25 minority (8 Black or African American, non-Hispanic/Latino; 3 Asian, non-Hispanic/Latino; 11 Hispanic/Latino; 3 Two or more races, non-Hispanic/Latino). Average age 33. 45 applicants, 56% accepted, 18 enrolled. In 2014, 50 master's awarded. *Degree requirements:* For master's, comprehensive exam, thesis optional. *Entrance requirements:* For master's, minimum overall GPA of 3.0, bachelor's degree from accredited college or university. Additional exam requirements/recommendations for international students: Required—PTE; Recommended—TOEFL (minimum score 570 paper-based; 80 iBT), IELTS (minimum score 6.5). *Application deadline:* Applications are processed on a rolling basis. Application fee: $60. Electronic applications accepted. *Expenses:* *Tuition:* Full-time $24,559; part-time $649 per credit. *Financial support:* Unspecified assistantships available. Financial award applicants required to submit FAFSA. *Unit head:* Rachel Bowman, Interim Chair/Associate Professor, 203-396-8243, E-mail: bowmanr@sacredheart.edu. *Application contact:* Kathy Dilks, Executive Director of Graduate Admissions, 203-365-7916, Fax: 203-365-4732, E-mail: gradstudies@sacredheart.edu.
Website: http://www.sacredheart.edu/academics/collegeofartssciences/academicdepartments/psychology/mastersinappliedpsychology/

Saint Mary's University, Faculty of Science, Department of Psychology, Halifax, NS B3H 3C3, Canada. Offers applied psychology (M Sc, PhD), including industrial/organizational psychology (M Sc). Part-time programs available. *Degree requirements:* For master's, thesis, 500-hour internship; for doctorate, comprehensive exam, thesis/dissertation, research project. *Entrance requirements:* For master's and doctorate, GRE General Test. *Faculty research:* Assessment, health psychology, social psychology, cognition.

Teachers College, Columbia University, Graduate Faculty of Education, Department of Health and Behavioral Studies, Program in Applied Educational Psychology-School Psychology, New York, NY 10027. Offers Ed M, MA, Ed D, PhD. *Accreditation:* APA (one or more programs are accredited). *Faculty:* 5 full-time. *Students:* 37 full-time (32 women), 41 part-time (37 women); includes 12 minority (3 Black or African American, non-Hispanic/Latino; 2 Asian, non-Hispanic/Latino; 6 Hispanic/Latino; 1 Two or more races, non-Hispanic/Latino), 5 international. Average age 26. 123 applicants, 33% accepted, 21 enrolled. In 2014, 59 master's, 5 doctorates awarded. *Degree requirements:* For master's, project; for doctorate, comprehensive exam, thesis/dissertation. *Entrance requirements:* For master's, GRE General Test (for Ed M); for doctorate, GRE General Test. *Application deadline:* For fall admission, 12/15 for domestic students. Application fee: $65. *Expenses:* *Tuition:* Full-time $33,552; part-time $1398 per credit. *Required fees:* $418 per semester. *Financial support:* Fellowships, research assistantships, career-related internships or fieldwork, Federal Work-Study, institutionally sponsored loans, and tuition waivers (full and partial) available. Support available to part-time students. Financial award application deadline: 2/1; financial award applicants required to submit FAFSA. *Faculty research:* Psychoeducational assessment, observation and concept acquisition in young children, reading, mathematical thinking, memory. *Unit head:* Prof. Marla Brassard, Chair, 212-678-3368, E-mail: brassard@tc.edu. *Application contact:* Peter Shon, Assistant Director of Admission, 212-678-3305, Fax: 212-678-4171, E-mail: shon@exchange.tc.columbia.edu.
Website: http://www.tc.edu/hbs/SchoolPsych/

University of Arkansas at Little Rock, Graduate School, College of Social Sciences and Communication, Department of Psychology, Little Rock, AR 72204-1099. Offers applied psychology (MAP). Part-time and evening/weekend programs available. *Entrance requirements:* For master's, GRE General Test, minimum GPA of 2.7. *Application deadline:* Applications are processed on a rolling basis. *Expenses:* Tuition, state resident: full-time $6000; part-time $300 per credit hour. Tuition, nonresident: full-time $13,800; part-time $690 per credit hour. *Required fees:* $1126; $603 per term. One-time fee: $40 full-time. *Financial support:* Fellowships with tuition reimbursements, research assistantships with tuition reimbursements, teaching assistantships with tuition reimbursements, career-related internships or fieldwork, Federal Work-Study, institutionally sponsored loans, and unspecified assistantships available. Support available to part-time students. *Faculty research:* Psychological methods and theories in business industry, government, and organizations; personnel program evaluation; training; affirmative action; organizational analysis and development. *Unit head:* Dr. Amanda Nolen, Interim Chair, 501-569-3171, Fax: 501-569-3047, E-mail: alnolen@ualr.edu. *Application contact:* Dr. Robert J. Hines, Program Coordinator, 501-569-3527, E-mail: rjhines@ualr.edu.
Website: http://ualr.edu/psychology/

University of Baltimore, Graduate School, Yale Gordon College of Arts and Sciences, Program in Applied Psychology, Baltimore, MD 21201-5779. Offers counseling psychology (MS). Part-time and evening/weekend programs available. *Degree requirements:* For master's, thesis optional. *Entrance requirements:* For master's, GRE, minimum GPA of 3.0. Additional exam requirements/recommendations for international students: Required—TOEFL (minimum score 550 paper-based). Electronic applications accepted. *Expenses:* Contact institution. *Faculty research:* Participatory decision-making, counter-productive workplace behavior, organizational consulting, substance abuse treatment, cognitive functioning in head injured.

University of Calgary, Faculty of Graduate Studies, Werklund School of Education, Division of Applied Psychology, Calgary, AB T2N 1N4, Canada. Offers counseling psychology (M Sc, MC, PhD); school and applied child psychology (M Ed, M Sc, PhD). Part-time programs available. *Degree requirements:* For master's, thesis (for some programs), final oral exam; for doctorate, thesis/dissertation, candidacy exam, final oral exam. *Entrance requirements:* For master's, minimum GPA of 3.0, 3 letters of reference; for doctorate, minimum GPA of 3.5, 3 letters of reference. *Faculty research:* Counselor education, family life studies, learning and cognition.

Applied Psychology

University of Central Florida, College of Sciences, Department of Psychology, Program in Applied Experimental and Human Factors Psychology, Orlando, FL 32816. Offers MA, PhD. *Students:* 40 full-time (26 women), 7 part-time (4 women); includes 10 minority (1 Black or African American, non-Hispanic/Latino; 3 Asian, non-Hispanic/Latino; 3 Hispanic/Latino; 3 Two or more races, non-Hispanic/Latino), 1 international. Average age 29. 48 applicants, 19% accepted, 7 enrolled. In 2014, 9 master's, 6 doctorates awarded. *Degree requirements:* For doctorate, thesis/dissertation, departmental candidacy exam. *Entrance requirements:* For doctorate, GRE General Test, minimum GPA of 3.2 in last 60 hours or master's qualifying exam. Additional exam requirements/recommendations for international students: Required—TOEFL. *Application deadline:* For fall admission, 2/1 for domestic students. Application fee: $30. Electronic applications accepted. *Expenses:* Tuition, state resident: part-time $288.16 per credit hour. Tuition, nonresident: part-time $1073.31 per credit hour. *Financial support:* In 2014–15, 36 students received support, including 18 fellowships with partial tuition reimbursements available (averaging $8,200 per year), 15 research assistantships with partial tuition reimbursements available (averaging $13,400 per year), 18 teaching assistantships with partial tuition reimbursements available (averaging $10,100 per year); career-related internships or fieldwork, Federal Work-Study, institutionally sponsored loans, tuition waivers (partial), and unspecified assistantships also available. Financial award application deadline: 3/1; financial award applicants required to submit FAFSA. *Faculty research:* Visual performance, team training, controls/displays, synthetic speech, alarms/warning. *Unit head:* Dr. Mustapha Mouloua, Program Director, 407-823-2910, E-mail: mustapha.mouloua@ucf.edu. *Application contact:* Barbara Rodriguez Lamas, Director, Admissions and Student Services, 407-823-2766, Fax: 407-823-6442, E-mail: gradadmissions@ucf.edu. Website: http://psychology.cos.ucf.edu/graduate/

University of Guelph, Graduate Studies, College of Social and Applied Human Sciences, Department of Psychology, Guelph, ON N1G 2W1, Canada. Offers applied social psychology (MA, PhD); clinical psychology: applied development emphasis (PhD); clinical psychology: applied developmental emphasis (MA); industrial/organizational psychology (MA, PhD); neuroscience and applied cognitive science (MA, PhD). *Degree requirements:* For master's, thesis; for doctorate, comprehensive exam, thesis/dissertation. *Entrance requirements:* For master's, GRE General Test, GRE Subject Test, minimum B+ average during previous 2 years of course work; for doctorate, GRE General Test, GRE Subject Test, minimum A- average. Additional exam requirements/recommendations for international students: Required—TOEFL (minimum score 89 iBT). Electronic applications accepted. *Faculty research:* Organizational psychology, reading comprehension and mathematical ability, drug addiction and relapse, gender issues and culture, memory, clinical psychology.

University of Maryland, Baltimore County, The Graduate School, College of Arts, Humanities and Social Sciences, Department of Psychology, Program in Applied Developmental Psychology, Baltimore, MD 21250. Offers PhD. *Faculty:* 8 full-time (5 women), 11 part-time/adjunct (4 women). *Students:* 25 full-time (24 women); includes 8 minority (1 Black or African American, non-Hispanic/Latino; 6 Asian, non-Hispanic/Latino; 1 Hispanic/Latino). Average age 27. 30 applicants, 37% accepted, 4 enrolled. In 2014, 4 doctorates awarded. *Degree requirements:* For doctorate, comprehensive exam, thesis/dissertation. *Entrance requirements:* For doctorate, GRE General Test, minimum GPA of 3.0. Additional exam requirements/recommendations for international students: Required—TOEFL. *Application deadline:* For fall admission, 1/9 for domestic and international students. Application fee: $50. Electronic applications accepted. *Expenses:* Tuition, state resident: part-time $557. Tuition, nonresident: part-time $922. *Required fees:* $122 per semester. One-time fee: $200 part-time. *Financial support:* In 2014–15, 3 fellowships with full and partial tuition reimbursements (averaging $16,795 per year), 2 research assistantships with full and partial tuition reimbursements (averaging $19,890 per year), 11 teaching assistantships with full and partial tuition reimbursements (averaging $16,795 per year) were awarded; career-related internships or fieldwork, Federal Work-Study, health care benefits, and unspecified assistantships also available. Financial award application deadline: 3/1; financial award applicants required to submit FAFSA. *Faculty research:* Early intervention and development, schooling and development, cultural aspects of development, development in high risk children, social-emotional development. *Total annual research expenditures:* $154,339. *Unit head:* Dr. Susan Sonnenschein, Director, 410-455-2361, Fax: 410-455-1055, E-mail: sonnenschein@umbc.edu. *Application contact:* Nicole Mooney, Program Management Specialist, 410-455-2567, Fax: 410-455-1055, E-mail: psycdept@umbc.edu. Website: http://www.umbc.edu/gradschool/programs/psych_appdev.html

University of Pennsylvania, Graduate School of Education, Division of Applied Psychology and Human Development, Philadelphia, PA 19104. Offers M Phil, MS Ed, PhD. Part-time programs available. *Students:* 187 full-time (159 women), 9 part-time (8 women); includes 75 minority (32 Black or African American, non-Hispanic/Latino; 21 Asian, non-Hispanic/Latino; 14 Hispanic/Latino; 8 Two or more races, non-Hispanic/Latino), 57 international. 375 applicants, 64% accepted, 149 enrolled. In 2014, 119 master's, 3 doctorates awarded. Terminal master's awarded for partial completion of doctoral program. *Degree requirements:* For master's, exam; for doctorate, thesis/dissertation, exam. *Entrance requirements:* For master's, GRE General Test; for doctorate, GRE General Test, GRE Subject Test. *Application deadline:* For fall admission, 12/15 priority date for domestic students. Applications are processed on a rolling basis. Application fee: $70. Electronic applications accepted. *Expenses:* Expenses: Contact institution. *Financial support:* Fellowships, research assistantships, institutionally sponsored loans, scholarships/grants, traineeships, health care benefits, and unspecified assistantships available. *Faculty research:* Multivariate analysis, therapeutic intervention at a preschool level, actuarial systems for assessment of children. *Unit head:* Dr. Andrew Porter, Dean, 215-898-7014. *Application contact:* 215-898-6415, Fax: 215-746-6884, E-mail: admissions@gse.upenn.edu. Website: http://www.gse.upenn.edu

University of Pennsylvania, School of Arts and Sciences, College of Liberal and Professional Studies, Philadelphia, PA 19104. Offers applied geosciences (MSAG); applied positive psychology (MAP); chemical sciences (MCS); environmental studies (MES); individualized study (MLA); liberal arts (M Phil); medical physics (MMP); organization dynamics (M Phil). *Students:* 143 full-time (77 women), 322 part-time (179 women); includes 96 minority (33 Black or African American, non-Hispanic/Latino; 1 American Indian or Alaska Native, non-Hispanic/Latino; 24 Asian, non-Hispanic/Latino; 21 Hispanic/Latino; 17 Two or more races, non-Hispanic/Latino), 61 international. 461 applicants, 42% accepted, 132 enrolled. In 2014, 176 master's awarded. *Application deadline:* For fall admission, 12/1 priority date for domestic students. Application fee: $70. Electronic applications accepted. *Unit head:* Nora Lewis, Vice Dean, Professional and Liberal Education, 215-898-7326, E-mail: nlewis@sas.upenn.edu. *Application contact:* 215-898-7326, E-mail: lps@sas.upenn.edu. Website: http://www.sas.upenn.edu/lps/graduate

University of Pittsburgh, School of Education, Department of Psychology in Education, Program in Applied Developmental Psychology, Pittsburgh, PA 15260. Offers M Ed, MS, PhD. Part-time and evening/weekend programs available. *Faculty:* 17 full-time (10 women), 13 part-time/adjunct (10 women). *Students:* 48 full-time (45 women), 25 part-time (22 women); includes 20 minority (9 Black or African American, non-Hispanic/Latino; 4 Asian, non-Hispanic/Latino; 4 Hispanic/Latino; 3 Two or more races, non-Hispanic/Latino), 8 international. Average age 29. 100 applicants, 64% accepted, 38 enrolled. In 2014, 28 master's, 1 doctorate awarded. *Degree requirements:* For master's, thesis. *Entrance requirements:* For doctorate, GRE. Additional exam requirements/recommendations for international students: Required—TOEFL. *Application deadline:* For fall admission, 2/1 for domestic students, 2/1 priority date for international students; for spring admission, 7/1 priority date for international students. Applications are processed on a rolling basis. Application fee: $50. Electronic applications accepted. *Expenses:* Tuition, state resident: full-time $20,742; part-time $838 per credit. Tuition, nonresident: full-time $33,960; part-time $1389 per credit. *Required fees:* $800; $205 per term. Tuition and fees vary according to program. *Financial support:* In 2014–15, fellowships with full and partial tuition reimbursements (averaging $20,500 per year), research assistantships with full and partial tuition reimbursements (averaging $17,800 per year), teaching assistantships with full and partial tuition reimbursements (averaging $17,800 per year) were awarded; tuition waivers (partial) also available. Support available to part-time students. Financial award applicants required to submit FAFSA. *Unit head:* Dr. Carl N. Johnson, Chairman, 412-624-6942, Fax: 412-624-7231, E-mail: johnson@pitt.edu. *Application contact:* Maggie Sikora, Graduate Enrollment Manager, 412-648-2230, Fax: 412-648-1899, E-mail: soeinfo@pitt.edu.

University of Regina, Faculty of Graduate Studies and Research, Faculty of Arts, Department of Psychology, Regina, SK S4S 0A2, Canada. Offers clinical psychology (MA, PhD); experimental and applied psychology (MA, PhD). *Faculty:* 20 full-time (9 women), 7 part-time/adjunct (5 women). *Students:* 57 full-time (46 women). 81 applicants, 25% accepted. In 2014, 12 master's, 4 doctorates awarded. *Degree requirements:* For master's, thesis; for doctorate, comprehensive exam, thesis/dissertation. *Entrance requirements:* For master's, GRE General Test; for doctorate, GRE General Test and GRE Subject Test (optional for those with a master's degree from a Canadian university). Additional exam requirements/recommendations for international students: Required—TOEFL (minimum score 580 paper-based; 80 iBT), IELTS (minimum score 6.5), PTE (minimum score 59). *Application deadline:* For fall admission, 1/15 for domestic and international students. Application fee: $100. Electronic applications accepted. *Expenses:* Tuition, area resident: Full-time $4900 Canadian dollars; part-time $837.65 Canadian dollars per semester. *International tuition:* $7900 Canadian dollars full-time. *Required fees:* $396 Canadian dollars; $86.90 Canadian dollars per semester. *Financial support:* In 2014–15, 17 fellowships (averaging $6,588 per year), 1 research assistantship (averaging $5,500 per year), 27 teaching assistantships (averaging $2,471 per year) were awarded; career-related internships or fieldwork and scholarships/grants also available. Financial award application deadline: 6/15. *Faculty research:* Clinical, experimental, cognitive, and applied psychology; post-traumatic stress disorder, anxiety, and panic disorder; traumatic brain injury; chronic pain; perception and memory. *Unit head:* Dr. Richard MacLennan, Department Head, 306-585-4458, Fax: 306-585-5429, E-mail: richard.maclennan@uregina.ca. Website: http://www.uregina.ca/arts/psychology

University of South Carolina Aiken, Program in Applied Clinical Psychology, Aiken, SC 29801. Offers MS. Part-time programs available. *Faculty:* 8 full-time (7 women). *Students:* 21 full-time (15 women), 12 part-time (9 women); includes 3 minority (1 Black or African American, non-Hispanic/Latino; 1 Asian, non-Hispanic/Latino; 1 Two or more races, non-Hispanic/Latino). Average age 24. 57 applicants, 32% accepted, 13 enrolled. In 2014, 13 master's awarded. *Degree requirements:* For master's, thesis. *Entrance requirements:* For master's, GRE General Test. Additional exam requirements/recommendations for international students: Required—TOEFL (minimum score 550 paper-based; 80 iBT). *Application deadline:* For fall admission, 4/1 priority date for domestic and international students. Applications are processed on a rolling basis. Application fee: $45. Electronic applications accepted. *Expenses:* Tuition, state resident: full-time $12,024; part-time $501 per credit hour. Tuition, nonresident: full-time $25,770; part-time $1073.75 per credit hour. *Required fees:* $9 per credit hour. $25 per semester. Full-time tuition and fees vary according to course load. *Financial support:* In 2014–15, 23 students received support, including 20 research assistantships with partial tuition reimbursements available (averaging $1,750 per year), 3 teaching assistantships with partial tuition reimbursements available (averaging $1,100 per year); career-related internships or fieldwork, Federal Work-Study, scholarships/grants, tuition waivers (partial), and unspecified assistantships also available. Financial award application deadline: 3/15; financial award applicants required to submit FAFSA. *Faculty research:* Learning and motivation, addictive behaviors, neuroscience, childhood disorders, social and personality psychology. *Unit head:* Dr. Jane Stafford, Director, 803-641-3358, Fax: 803-641-3720, E-mail: jstafford@usca.edu. *Application contact:* Dan Robb, Associate Vice Chancellor for Enrollment Management, 803-641-3487, Fax: 803-641-3727, E-mail: danr@usca.edu. Website: http://web.usca.edu/psychology/programs-and-courses/master-of-science.dot?

The University of Tennessee, Graduate School, College of Education, Health and Human Sciences, Department of Educational Psychology and Counseling, Knoxville, TN 37996. Offers adult education (MS); applied educational psychology (MS); collaborative learning (Ed D); college student personnel (MS); mental health counseling (MS); rehabilitation counseling (MS); school counseling (MS). *Accreditation:* ACA (one or more programs are accredited); CORE (one or more programs are accredited); NCATE. Part-time and evening/weekend programs available. *Degree requirements:* For master's, thesis optional. *Entrance requirements:* For master's, GRE General Test, minimum GPA of 2.7. Additional exam requirements/recommendations for international students: Required—TOEFL. Electronic applications accepted.

The University of Texas at El Paso, Graduate School, College of Liberal Arts, Department of Sociology and Anthropology, El Paso, TX 79968-0001. Offers applied anthropology (Certificate); applied social sciences (Certificate); sociology (MA). Part-time and evening/weekend programs available. *Degree requirements:* For master's, thesis. *Entrance requirements:* For master's, GRE General Test, minimum GPA of 3.0. Additional exam requirements/recommendations for international students: Required—TOEFL. Electronic applications accepted. *Faculty research:* U.S.-Mexico border, social inequality, immigration, Chicano culture, Mexico.

The University of Texas of the Permian Basin, Office of Graduate Studies, College of Arts and Sciences, Department of Psychology, Odessa, TX 79762-0001. Offers applied research psychology (MA); clinical psychology (MA). Part-time and evening/weekend programs available. *Degree requirements:* For master's, comprehensive exam, thesis, practicum. *Entrance requirements:* For master's, GRE General Test, 3 letters of recommendation. Additional exam requirements/recommendations for international students: Required—TOEFL (minimum score 550 paper-based).

University of Windsor, Faculty of Graduate Studies, Faculty of Arts and Social Sciences, Department of Psychology, Windsor, ON N9B 3P4, Canada. Offers adult clinical (MA, PhD); applied social psychology (MA, PhD); child clinical (MA, PhD); clinical neuropsychology (MA, PhD). *Accreditation:* APA (one or more programs are accredited). *Degree requirements:* For master's, thesis; for doctorate, comprehensive

exam, thesis/dissertation. *Entrance requirements:* For master's, GRE General Test, GRE Subject Test in psychology, minimum B average; for doctorate, GRE General Test, GRE Subject Test in psychology, master's degree. Additional exam requirements/recommendations for international students: Required—TOEFL (minimum score 600 paper-based). Electronic applications accepted. *Faculty research:* Gambling, suicidology, emotional competence, psychotherapy and trauma.

University of Wisconsin–Stout, Graduate School, College of Human Development, Program in Applied Psychology, Menomonie, WI 54751. Offers MS. Part-time programs available. *Degree requirements:* For master's, thesis. *Entrance requirements:* For master's, GRE General Test, GRE Subject Test, minimum GPA of 3.0, 15 semester credits of undergraduate course work in psychology, 8 semester credits in research methods and statistics. Additional exam requirements/recommendations for international students: Required—TOEFL (minimum score 500 paper-based; 61 iBT). *Application deadline:* For fall admission, 2/1 priority date for domestic and international students; for spring admission, 10/1 priority date for domestic and international students. Application fee: $45. Electronic applications accepted. *Financial support:* Research assistantships with partial tuition reimbursements, teaching assistantships with tuition reimbursements, Federal Work-Study, scholarships/grants, tuition waivers (partial), and unspecified assistantships available. Support available to part-time students. Financial award application deadline: 5/1; financial award applicants required to submit FAFSA. *Faculty research:* Health complementary therapies, motivation, group dynamics, social reasoning, stress. *Unit head:* Dr. Kristina Gorbatenko-Roth, Director, 715-232-2451, Fax: 715-232-5303, E-mail: gorbatenkok@uwstout.edu. *Application contact:* Anne E. Johnson, Graduate Student Evaluator (Admissions and Assistantship Coordinator), 715-232-1322, Fax: 715-232-2413, E-mail: johnsona@uwstout.edu.
Website: http://www3.uwstout.edu/programs/msap/index.cfm

Walden University, Graduate Programs, School of Psychology, Minneapolis, MN 55401. Offers clinical psychology (MS), including counseling, general program; forensic psychology (MS), including forensic psychology in the community, general program, mental health applications, program planning and evaluation in forensic settings, psychology and legal systems; organizational psychology and development (Postbaccalaureate Certificate); psychology (MS, PhD), including applied psychology (MS), clinical psychology (PhD), counseling psychology (PhD), crisis management and response (MS), educational psychology, forensic psychology (PhD), general psychology (MS), general psychology research (PhD), health psychology, leadership development and coaching (MS), psychology of culture (MS), psychology, public administration, and social change (MS), social psychology, terrorism and security (MS); psychology respecialization (Post-Doctoral Certificate); teaching online (Post-Master's Certificate). Part-time and evening/weekend programs available. Postbaccalaureate distance learning degree programs offered (no on-campus study). *Faculty:* 56 full-time (36 women), 351 part-time/adjunct (201 women). *Students:* 2,757 full-time (2,202 women), 1,466 part-time (1,148 women); includes 1,849 minority (1,299 Black or African American, non-Hispanic/Latino; 37 American Indian or Alaska Native, non-Hispanic/Latino; 74 Asian, non-Hispanic/Latino; 315 Hispanic/Latino; 8 Native Hawaiian or other Pacific Islander, non-Hispanic/Latino; 116 Two or more races, non-Hispanic/Latino), 28 international. Average age 41. 913 applicants, 97% accepted, 851 enrolled. In 2014, 602 master's, 204 doctorates, 19 other advanced degrees awarded. Terminal master's awarded for partial completion of doctoral program. *Degree requirements:* For master's, thesis optional; for doctorate, thesis/dissertation, residency. *Entrance requirements:* For master's, bachelor's degree or higher; minimum GPA of 2.5; official transcripts; goal statement (for some programs); access to computer and Internet; for doctorate, master's degree or higher; three years of related professional or academic experience (preferred); minimum GPA of 3.0; goal statement and current resume (for select programs); official transcripts; access to computer and Internet; for other advanced degree, relevant work experience; access to computer and Internet. Additional exam requirements/recommendations for international students: Required—TOEFL (minimum score 550 paper-based, 79 iBT), IELTS (minimum score 6.5), Michigan English Language Assessment Battery (minimum score 82), or PTE (minimum score 53). *Application deadline:* Applications are processed on a rolling basis. Application fee: $0. Electronic applications accepted. *Expenses: Tuition:* Full-time $11,925; part-time $500 per credit hour. *Required fees:* $647. *Financial support:* Fellowships, Federal Work-Study, scholarships/grants, unspecified assistantships, and family tuition reduction, active duty/veteran tuition reduction, group tuition reduction, interest-free payment plans, employee tuition reduction available. Support available to part-time students. Financial award applicants required to submit FAFSA. *Unit head:* Dr. Marilyn Powell, Associate Dean, 866-492-5366. *Application contact:* Meghan Thomas, Vice President of Enrollment Management, 866-492-5336, E-mail: info@waldenu.edu.
Website: http://www.waldenu.edu/programs/colleges-schools/psychology

Clinical Psychology

Abilene Christian University, Graduate School, College of Arts and Sciences, Department of Psychology, Program in Clinical Psychology, Abilene, TX 79699-9100. Offers MS. Part-time programs available. *Students:* 12 full-time (11 women), 2 part-time (0 women); includes 6 minority (3 Black or African American, non-Hispanic/Latino; 1 Asian, non-Hispanic/Latino; 2 Hispanic/Latino), 1 international. 32 applicants, 34% accepted, 7 enrolled. In 2014, 5 master's awarded. *Degree requirements:* For master's, thesis, practicum. *Entrance requirements:* Additional exam requirements/recommendations for international students: Required—TOEFL (minimum score 550 paper-based; 90 iBT), IELTS (minimum score 6.5), PTE. *Application deadline:* For fall admission, 3/1 priority date for domestic students; for spring admission, 11/1 for domestic students. Applications are processed on a rolling basis. Application fee: $50. Electronic applications accepted. *Expenses: Tuition:* Full-time $18,228; part-time $1016 per credit hour. *Financial support:* In 2014–15, 11 students received support. Career-related internships or fieldwork and Federal Work-Study available. Support available to part-time students. Financial award application deadline: 4/1; financial award applicants required to submit FAFSA. *Unit head:* Dr. Robert McKelvain, Graduate Director, 325-674-2286, Fax: 325-674-6968, E-mail: mckelvainr@acu.edu. *Application contact:* Corey Patterson, Director of Graduate Admission and Recruiting, 325-674-6566, Fax: 325-674-6717, E-mail: gradinfo@acu.edu.

Acadia University, Faculty of Pure and Applied Science, Department of Psychology, Wolfville, NS B4P 2R6, Canada. Offers clinical psychology (M Sc). *Degree requirements:* For master's, thesis. *Entrance requirements:* For master's, GRE General Test, GRE Subject Test, honors degree or equivalent. Additional exam requirements/recommendations for international students: Required—TOEFL (minimum score 580 paper-based; 93 iBT), IELTS (minimum score 6.5). *Faculty research:* Social psychology, job stress, psychotherapy, cognition perception, development.

Adelphi University, Derner Institute of Advanced Psychological Studies, Program in Clinical Psychology, Garden City, NY 11530-0701. Offers PhD. *Students:* 76 full-time (61 women), 20 part-time (14 women); includes 15 minority (3 Black or African American, non-Hispanic/Latino; 7 Asian, non-Hispanic/Latino; 4 Hispanic/Latino; 1 Two or more races, non-Hispanic/Latino), 8 international. Average age 31. In 2014, 22 doctorates awarded. *Degree requirements:* For doctorate, thesis/dissertation, research (second-year), 1-year internship. *Entrance requirements:* For doctorate, GRE General Test, GRE Subject Test, interview; resume; undergraduate course work in psychology, experimental psychology, statistics, developmental psychology, and abnormal psychology. Additional exam requirements/recommendations for international students: Required—TOEFL (minimum score 550 paper-based; 80 iBT). *Application deadline:* For fall admission, 1/15 priority date for domestic and international students. Application fee: $50. Electronic applications accepted. *Financial support:* Research assistantships with full and partial tuition reimbursements, teaching assistantships, career-related internships or fieldwork, Federal Work-Study, institutionally sponsored loans, and unspecified assistantships available. Financial award application deadline: 2/15; financial award applicants required to submit FAFSA. *Unit head:* Dr. J. Christopher Muran, Associate Dean, 516-877-4803, E-mail: jcmuran@adelphi.edu. *Application contact:* Christine Murphy, Director of Admissions, 516-877-3050, Fax: 516-877-3039, E-mail: graduateadmissions@adelphi.edu.
Website: http://derner.adelphi.edu/psychology/doctoral-program/

Adler Graduate School, Program in Adlerian Counseling and Psychotherapy, Richfield, MN 55423. Offers Adlerian studies (MA); art therapy (MA); clinical counseling (MA); co-occurring substance abuse and mental health disorders (MA); marriage and family therapy (MA); school counseling (MA). Part-time and evening/weekend programs available. *Faculty:* 7 full-time (6 women), 68 part-time/adjunct (49 women). *Students:* 368 part-time (283 women); includes 61 minority (41 Black or African American, non-Hispanic/Latino; 4 American Indian or Alaska Native, non-Hispanic/Latino; 8 Asian, non-Hispanic/Latino; 8 Hispanic/Latino). Average age 40. In 2014, 90 master's awarded. *Degree requirements:* For master's, thesis or alternative, 500-700 hour internship (depending on license choice). *Entrance requirements:* For master's, personal goal statement, three letters of reference, resume or work history, official transcripts. *Application deadline:* Applications are processed on a rolling basis. Application fee: $50. Electronic applications accepted. *Expenses: Tuition:* Full-time $6060; part-time $505 per credit. *Financial support:* Career-related internships or fieldwork and tuition waivers available. Support available to part-time students. Financial award applicants required to submit FAFSA. *Unit head:* Dr. Dan Haugen, President, 612-767-7048, Fax: 612-861-7559, E-mail: haugen@alfredadler.edu. *Application contact:* Evelyn B. Haas, Director of Admissions, 612-767-7044, Fax: 612-861-7559, E-mail: ev@alfredadler.edu.

★ **Adler University,** Programs in Psychology, Chicago, IL 60602. Offers advanced Adlerian psychotherapy (Certificate); art therapy (MA); clinical neuropsychology (Certificate); clinical psychology (Psy D); community psychology (MA); counseling and organizational psychology (MA); counseling psychology (MA); criminology (MA); emergency management leadership (MA); forensic psychology (MA); marriage and family counseling (MA); marriage and family therapy (Certificate); military psychology (MA); nonprofit management (MA); organizational psychology (MA); police psychology (MA); public policy and administration (MA); rehabilitation counseling (MA); sport and health psychology (MA); substance abuse counseling (Certificate); Psy D/Certificate; Psy D/MACAT; Psy D/MACP; Psy D/MAMFC; Psy D/MASAC. *Accreditation:* APA. Part-time and evening/weekend programs available. Postbaccalaureate distance learning degree programs offered (minimal on-campus study). Terminal master's awarded for partial completion of doctoral program. *Degree requirements:* For master's, thesis or alternative, oral exam, practicum; for doctorate, thesis/dissertation, clinical exam, internship, oral exam, practicum, written qualifying exam. *Entrance requirements:* For master's, 12 semester hours in psychology, minimum GPA of 3.0; for doctorate, 18 semester hours in psychology, minimum GPA of 3.25; for Certificate, appropriate master's or doctoral degree. Additional exam requirements/recommendations for international students: Required—TOEFL (minimum score 550 paper-based; 79 iBT). Electronic applications accepted.

See Display on page 969 and Close-Up on page 1207.

Alabama Agricultural and Mechanical University, School of Graduate Studies, School of Education, Department of Counseling and Special Education, Huntsville, AL 35811. Offers communicative disorders (M Ed, MS); psychology and counseling (MS, Ed S), including clinical psychology (MS), counseling and guidance, counseling psychology (MS), personnel management (MS), psychometry (MS), school psychology (MS); special education (M Ed, MS). *Accreditation:* CORE; NCATE. Part-time and evening/weekend programs available. *Degree requirements:* For master's, comprehensive exam. *Entrance requirements:* For master's, GRE General Test. Additional exam requirements/recommendations for international students: Required—TOEFL (minimum score 500 paper-based; 61 iBT). *Faculty research:* Increasing numbers of minorities in special education and speech-language pathology.

Alliant International University–Fresno, California School of Professional Psychology, PhD Program in Clinical Psychology, Fresno, CA 93727. Offers PhD. *Degree requirements:* For doctorate, comprehensive exam, thesis/dissertation. *Entrance requirements:* For doctorate, minimum GPA of 3.0 in both psychology and overall, letters of recommendation, interview. Additional exam requirements/recommendations for international students: Required—TOEFL (minimum score 550 paper-based; 80 iBT), TWE (minimum score 5). Electronic applications accepted. *Faculty research:* Teaching of psychology, ecosystemic child psychology, cultural competence, neuro-cognitive processes.

Alliant International University–Fresno, California School of Professional Psychology, Psy D Program in Clinical Psychology, Fresno, CA 93727. Offers Psy D. *Accreditation:* APA. *Degree requirements:* For doctorate, comprehensive exam, thesis/dissertation. *Entrance requirements:* For doctorate, minimum GPA of 3.0 in both psychology and overall, letters of recommendation, interview. Additional exam requirements/recommendations for international students: Required—TOEFL (minimum score 550 paper-based; 80 iBT), TWE (minimum score 5). Electronic applications accepted. *Faculty research:* Psychodynamic correlates of self-care behavior, women's health and development, gay and lesbian issues, child development and abuse, trauma.

Alliant International University–Los Angeles, California School of Professional Psychology, PhD Program in Clinical Psychology, Alhambra, CA 91803-1360. Offers

Clinical Psychology

PhD. *Accreditation:* APA. *Degree requirements:* For doctorate, comprehensive exam, thesis/dissertation. *Entrance requirements:* For doctorate, interview, minimum GPA of 3.0 in both psychology and overall. Additional exam requirements/recommendations for international students: Required—TOEFL (minimum score 600 paper-based), TWE (minimum score 5). Electronic applications accepted. *Faculty research:* Multicultural and community clinical psychology, health and chronic disease, individual and family psychology, pediatric neuropsychology.

Alliant International University–Los Angeles, California School of Professional Psychology, Psy D Program in Clinical Psychology, Alhambra, CA 91803-1360. Offers clinical health psychology (Psy D); family/child and couple clinical psychology (Psy D); multi-interest option (Psy D); multicultural community-clinical psychology (Psy D). *Accreditation:* APA. *Degree requirements:* For doctorate, comprehensive exam, thesis/dissertation. *Entrance requirements:* For doctorate, interview, minimum GPA of 3.0 in both psychology and overall. Additional exam requirements/recommendations for international students: Required—TOEFL (minimum score 600 paper-based), TWE. Electronic applications accepted. *Faculty research:* Child and family psychology, multicultural and community psychology, acculturation, lesbian and gay issues, women's health.

Alliant International University–Sacramento, California School of Professional Psychology, Program in Clinical Psychology, Sacramento, CA 95833. Offers Psy D. *Degree requirements:* For doctorate, comprehensive exam, thesis/dissertation, internship. *Entrance requirements:* For doctorate, minimum GPA of 3.0, letters of recommendation, interview. Additional exam requirements/recommendations for international students: Required—TOEFL (minimum score 600 paper-based; 80 iBT), TWE (minimum score 5). Electronic applications accepted. *Faculty research:* Creating and testing evidence-based interventions for underserved minority populations with cardiovascular disease and cancer, substance abuse treatment and relapse prediction, cultural diversity, personality disorders, trauma.

Alliant International University–San Diego, California School of Professional Psychology, Organizational Psychology Division, San Diego, CA 92131-1799. Offers clinical/industrial organizational psychology (PhD); consulting psychology (PhD); industrial/organizational psychology (MA, MS, PhD); leadership (PhD). Part-time and evening/weekend programs available. Terminal master's awarded for partial completion of doctoral program. *Degree requirements:* For doctorate, comprehensive exam, thesis/dissertation, internship/practicum. *Entrance requirements:* For master's and doctorate, minimum GPA of 3.0, recommendations, essay, interview. Additional exam requirements/recommendations for international students: Required—TOEFL (minimum score 550 paper-based; 80 iBT), TWE (minimum score 5). Electronic applications accepted. *Faculty research:* Cultural diversity in the workplace, work motivation, personnel and performance management, organizational diagnosis.

Alliant International University–San Diego, California School of Professional Psychology, PhD Program in Clinical Psychology, San Diego, CA 92131-1799. Offers PhD. *Accreditation:* APA. *Degree requirements:* For doctorate, comprehensive exam, thesis/dissertation, internship. *Entrance requirements:* For doctorate, interview, minimum GPA of 3.0, recommendations, essay, interview. Additional exam requirements/recommendations for international students: Required—TOEFL (minimum score 600 paper-based; 80 iBT), TWE (minimum score 5). Electronic applications accepted. *Faculty research:* Pediatric child clinical psychology, neuro-psychological assessment, ADHD, effect of alcohol and abstinence on the central nervous system.

Alliant International University–San Diego, California School of Professional Psychology, Psy D Program in Clinical Psychology, San Diego, CA 92131-1799. Offers Psy D. *Accreditation:* APA. *Degree requirements:* For doctorate, comprehensive exam, thesis/dissertation, internship. *Entrance requirements:* For doctorate, minimum GPA of 3.0, recommendations, essay, interview. Additional exam requirements/recommendations for international students: Required—TOEFL (minimum score 550 paper-based; 80 iBT), TWE (minimum score 5). Electronic applications accepted. *Faculty research:* Forensic psychology, health psychology, family and child psychology, cultural competency in mental health services, women's health.

Alliant International University–San Francisco, California School of Forensic Studies, San Francisco, CA 94133-1221. Offers applied criminology (MS), including victimology; clinical forensic psychology (PhD, Psy D). *Degree requirements:* For doctorate, comprehensive exam, thesis/dissertation, internship. *Entrance requirements:* For master's, minimum GPA of 3.0, recommendations, essay; for doctorate, minimum GPA of 3.0, recommendations, essay, interview. Additional exam requirements/recommendations for international students: Required—TOEFL (minimum score 550 paper-based; 80 iBT), TWE (minimum score 5). *Faculty research:* Post-traumatic stress disorder, correctional mental health.

Alliant International University–San Francisco, California School of Professional Psychology, PhD Program in Clinical Psychology, San Francisco, CA 94133-1221. Offers PhD. *Degree requirements:* For doctorate, comprehensive exam, thesis/dissertation, internship. *Entrance requirements:* For doctorate, minimum GPA of 3.0, recommendations, essay, interview. Additional exam requirements/recommendations for international students: Required—TOEFL (minimum score 550 paper-based; 80 iBT), TWE (minimum score 5). Electronic applications accepted. *Faculty research:* Social model of disability, feminist models of clinical training, post-traumatic stress disorder, gay and lesbian parents and their children, psychology of women.

Alliant International University–San Francisco, California School of Professional Psychology, Psy D Program in Clinical Psychology, San Francisco, CA 94133-1221. Offers Psy D, Certificate. *Accreditation:* APA (one or more programs are accredited). *Degree requirements:* For doctorate, comprehensive exam, thesis/dissertation, internship. *Entrance requirements:* For doctorate, minimum GPA of 3.0, recommendations, essay, interview. Additional exam requirements/recommendations for international students: Required—TOEFL (minimum score 550 paper-based; 80 iBT), TWE (minimum score 5). Electronic applications accepted. *Faculty research:* Health psychology, family and child psychology, social justice, multicultural and community psychology, gender issues.

American International College, School of Graduate and Adult Education, Graduate Psychology Department, Clinical Psychology Program, Springfield, MA 01109-3189. Offers MA. Part-time and evening/weekend programs available. *Faculty:* 2 full-time (1 woman), 3 part-time/adjunct (1 woman). *Students:* 17 full-time (15 women), 27 part-time (21 women); includes 13 minority (7 Black or African American, non-Hispanic/Latino; 2 American Indian or Alaska Native, non-Hispanic/Latino; 1 Asian, non-Hispanic/Latino; 3 Hispanic/Latino). Average age 29. 29 applicants, 79% accepted, 8 enrolled. In 2014, 19 master's awarded. Terminal master's awarded for partial completion of doctoral program. *Degree requirements:* For master's, thesis or alternative, practicum. *Entrance requirements:* For master's, graduate of accredited four-year college with minimum B average. Additional exam requirements/recommendations for international students: Required—TOEFL, IELTS. *Application deadline:* For fall admission, 4/15 for domestic and international students; for spring admission, 10/15 for international students. Applications are processed on a rolling basis. Application fee: $50. Electronic applications accepted. *Expenses:* Expenses: $795 per credit; registration fee $30 per term. *Financial support:* Career-related internships or fieldwork available. Financial award application deadline: 4/1; financial award applicants required to submit FAFSA. *Unit head:* Dr. Lina Racicot, Director, 413-205-3909, Fax: 413-205-3943, E-mail: lina.racicot@aic.edu. *Application contact:* Kerry Barnes, Director of Graduate Admissions, 413-205-3703, Fax: 413-205-3051, E-mail: kerry.barnes@aic.edu. Website: http://www.aic.edu/academics/graduate

American University of Beirut, Graduate Programs, Faculty of Arts and Sciences, Beirut, Lebanon. Offers anthropology (MA); Arab and Middle Eastern history (PhD); Arabic language and literature (MA, PhD); archaeology (MA); biology (MS); cell and molecular biology (PhD); chemistry (MS); clinical psychology (MA); computational sciences (MS); computer science (MS); economics (MA); English language (MA); English literature (MA); environmental policy planning (MS); financial economics (MAFE); geology (MS); history (MA); mathematics (MA, MS); media studies (MA); Middle Eastern studies (MA); physics (MS); political studies (MA); psychology (MA); public administration (MA); sociology (MA); statistics (MA, MS); theoretical physics (PhD); transnational American studies (MA). Part-time programs available. *Faculty:* 107 full-time (32 women), 6 part-time/adjunct (2 women). *Students:* 230 full-time (161 women), 209 part-time (146 women). Average age 26. 261 applicants, 70% accepted, 83 enrolled. In 2014, 68 master's, 2 doctorates awarded. *Degree requirements:* For master's, one foreign language, comprehensive exam, thesis (for some programs); for doctorate, one foreign language, comprehensive exam, thesis/dissertation. *Entrance requirements:* For master's, GRE (for some MA/MS programs), letter of recommendation; for doctorate, GRE, letters of recommendation. Additional exam requirements/recommendations for international students: Required—TOEFL (minimum score 600 paper-based; 97 iBT), IELTS (minimum score 7). *Application deadline:* For fall admission, 4/1 for domestic and international students; for spring admission, 11/1 for domestic and international students. Application fee: $50. Electronic applications accepted. *Expenses: Tuition:* Full-time $15,462; part-time $859 per credit. *Required fees:* $692. Tuition and fees vary according to course load and program. *Financial support:* Research assistantships, career-related internships or fieldwork, institutionally sponsored loans, scholarships/grants, health care benefits, and unspecified assistantships available. Financial award application deadline: 2/4; financial award applicants required to submit FAFSA. *Faculty research:* Determinants of language proficiency among Arab learners of English as a foreign language; opinion mining, information retrieval, runtime verification, high performance computing; solar and fuel cells, self-organizing systems, heterocyclic chemistry, air and water chemistry; complex analysis, harmonic analysis, number theory; social and political psychology, clinical psychology; thin films physics and technology; theory of soft matter; religious and ethnic conflict; sports and politics. *Total annual research expenditures:* $966,000. *Unit head:* Dr. Patrick McGreevy, Dean, 961-1374374 Ext. 3800, Fax: 961-1744461, E-mail: pm07@aub.edu.lb. *Application contact:* Dr. Salim Kanaan, Director, Admissions Office, 961-1350000 Ext. 2590, Fax: 961-1750775, E-mail: sk00@aub.edu.lb. Website: http://www.aub.edu.lb/fas/

Andrews University, School of Graduate Studies, School of Education, Department of Graduate Psychology and Counseling, Program in Community Counseling, Berrien Springs, MI 49104. Offers clinical mental health counseling (MA); community counseling (MA). *Students:* 24 full-time (17 women), 1 (woman) part-time; includes 9 minority (5 Black or African American, non-Hispanic/Latino; 1 American Indian or Alaska Native, non-Hispanic/Latino; 1 Asian, non-Hispanic/Latino; 2 Hispanic/Latino), 5 international. Average age 32. 27 applicants, 56% accepted, 10 enrolled. In 2014, 4 master's awarded. *Degree requirements:* For master's, thesis optional. *Entrance requirements:* For master's, GRE. Additional exam requirements/recommendations for international students: Required—TOEFL (minimum score 550 paper-based). Application fee: $40. Tuition and fees vary according to course level. *Unit head:* Dr. Nancy Carbonell, Coordinator, 269-471-3472. *Application contact:* Monica Wringer, Supervisor of Graduate Admission, 800-253-2874, Fax: 269-471-6321, E-mail: graduate@andrews.edu.

Antioch University Los Angeles, Graduate Programs, Program in Psychology, Culver City, CA 90230. Offers clinical psychology (MA); psychology (MA). Part-time programs available. *Degree requirements:* For master's, thesis (for some programs), internship. *Entrance requirements:* For master's, interview. Additional exam requirements/recommendations for international students: Required—TOEFL. *Faculty research:* Creativity and humor, ethnic humor, adult development, Jungian theory, psychoanalytic theory.

Antioch University New England, Graduate School, Department of Applied Psychology, Program in Clinical Mental Health Counseling, Keene, NH 03431-3552. Offers clinical mental health counseling (MA); substance abuse counseling (MA). *Accreditation:* ACA. *Degree requirements:* For master's, internship, practicum. *Entrance requirements:* For master's, previous course work and work experience in psychology. Additional exam requirements/recommendations for international students: Required—TOEFL (minimum score 550 paper-based). Electronic applications accepted. *Expenses:* Contact institution. *Faculty research:* Multicultural issues in field supervision.

Antioch University New England, Graduate School, Department of Clinical Psychology, Keene, NH 03431-3552. Offers Psy D. *Accreditation:* APA. *Degree requirements:* For doctorate, thesis/dissertation, internship, practicum. *Entrance requirements:* For doctorate, GRE General Test, GRE Subject Test, previous course work in psychology, work sample. Additional exam requirements/recommendations for international students: Required—TOEFL (minimum score 550 paper-based). *Expenses:* Contact institution. *Faculty research:* Psychotherapy outcome and process in private practice, neuropsychiatric evaluations, effects of trauma on adults, supervision, clinical training evaluation.

Antioch University Santa Barbara, Program in Clinical Psychology, Santa Barbara, CA 93101-1581. Offers MA, Psy D. *Entrance requirements:* Additional exam requirements/recommendations for international students: Required—TOEFL (minimum score 550 paper-based). *Application deadline:* Applications are processed on a rolling basis. Application fee: $60. Electronic applications accepted. *Unit head:* Dr. Sharleen O'Brien, Director of Clinical Training, 805-962-8179 Ext. 320, Fax: 805-962-4786, E-mail: sdolan@antioch.edu.

Appalachian State University, Cratis D. Williams Graduate School, Department of Human Development and Psychological Counseling, Boone, NC 28608. Offers clinical mental health counseling (MA); college student development (MA); marriage and family therapy (MA); school counseling (MA). *Accreditation:* AAMFT/COAMFTE; ACA; NCATE. Part-time programs available. *Degree requirements:* For master's, comprehensive exam (for some programs), thesis optional, internships. *Entrance requirements:* For master's, GRE General Test, 3 letters of recommendation. Additional exam requirements/recommendations for international students: Required—TOEFL (minimum score 570 paper-based; 79 iBT), IELTS (minimum score 6.5). Electronic applications accepted. *Faculty research:* Multicultural counseling, addictions counseling, play therapy, expressive arts, child and adolescent therapy, sexual abuse counseling.

Appalachian State University, Cratis D. Williams Graduate School, Department of Psychology, Boone, NC 28608. Offers clinical health psychology (MA); general experimental psychology (MA); industrial and organizational psychology (MA); MA/SSP. Part-time programs available. *Degree requirements:* For master's, comprehensive

exam, thesis optional, exit exam. *Entrance requirements:* For master's, GRE General Test, 3 letters of recommendation. Additional exam requirements/recommendations for international students: Required—TOEFL (minimum score 550 paper-based; 79 iBT) or IELTS (minimum score 6.5). Electronic applications accepted. *Faculty research:* Eating disorders, school-based consultations, organizational behavior management, brain mechanisms of sound localization, parenting styles.

Argosy University, Atlanta, College of Psychology and Behavioral Sciences, Atlanta, GA 30328. Offers clinical psychology (MA, Psy D, Postdoctoral Respecialization Certificate), including child and family psychology (Psy D), general adult clinical (Psy D), health psychology (Psy D), neuropsychology/geropsychology (Psy D); community counseling (MA), including marriage and family therapy; counselor education and supervision (Ed D); forensic psychology (MA); industrial organizational psychology (MA); marriage and family therapy (Certificate); sport-exercise psychology (MA). *Accreditation:* APA.

Argosy University, Chicago, College of Psychology and Behavioral Sciences, Doctoral Program in Clinical Psychology, Chicago, IL 60601. Offers child and adolescent psychology (Psy D); client-centered and experiential psychotherapies (Psy D); diversity and multicultural psychology (Psy D); family psychology (Psy D); forensic psychology (Psy D); health psychology (Psy D); neuropsychology (Psy D); organizational consulting (Psy D); psychoanalytic psychology (Psy D); psychology and spirituality (Psy D). *Accreditation:* APA.

Argosy University, Chicago, College of Psychology and Behavioral Sciences, Master's Program in Clinical Psychology, Chicago, IL 60601. Offers MA.

Argosy University, Dallas, College of Psychology and Behavioral Sciences, Program in Clinical Psychology, Farmers Branch, TX 75244. Offers MA, Psy D.

Argosy University, Denver, College of Psychology and Behavioral Sciences, Denver, CO 80231. Offers clinical mental health counseling (MA); clinical psychology (MA, Psy D); counseling psychology (Ed D); counselor education and supervision (Ed D); forensic psychology (MA); industrial organizational psychology (MA); marriage and family therapy (MA, DMFT).

Argosy University, Hawai`i, College of Psychology and Behavioral Sciences, Program in Clinical Psychology, Honolulu, HI 96813. Offers clinical psychology (MA, Psy D, Postdoctoral Respecialization Certificate), including child and family clinical practice (Psy D), diversity in clinical practice (Psy D). *Accreditation:* APA.

Argosy University, Inland Empire, College of Psychology and Behavioral Sciences, Ontario, CA 91761. Offers clinical psychology/marriage and family therapy (MA); counseling psychology (Ed D); counseling psychology/marriage and family therapy (MA); forensic psychology (MA); industrial organizational psychology (MA); sport-exercise psychology (MA).

Argosy University, Los Angeles, College of Psychology and Behavioral Sciences, Santa Monica, CA 90045. Offers clinical psychology/marriage and family therapy (MA); counseling psychology (Ed D); counseling psychology/marriage and family therapy (MA); forensic psychology (MA).

Argosy University, Orange County, College of Psychology and Behavioral Sciences, Program in Clinical Psychology, Orange, CA 92868. Offers child and adolescent psychology (Psy D); forensic psychology (Psy D); marriage and family therapy (MA). *Accreditation:* APA.

Argosy University, Phoenix, College of Psychology and Behavioral Sciences, Program in Clinical Psychology, Phoenix, AZ 85021. Offers clinical psychology (MA); neuropsychology (Psy D); sports-exercise psychology (Psy D). *Accreditation:* APA (one or more programs are accredited).

Argosy University, San Diego, College of Psychology and Behavioral Sciences, San Diego, CA 92108. Offers clinical psychology/marriage and family therapy (MA); counseling psychology (Ed D); counseling psychology/marriage and family therapy (MA); forensic psychology (MA).

Argosy University, San Francisco Bay Area, College of Psychology and Behavioral Sciences, Alameda, CA 94501. Offers clinical psychology (MA, Psy D); counseling psychology (MA, Ed D); forensic psychology (MA); sport-exercise psychology (MA). *Accreditation:* APA (one or more programs are accredited).

Argosy University, Schaumburg, Illinois School of Professional Psychology at Argosy University Schaumburg, Schaumburg, IL 60173-5403. Offers clinical psychology (MA, Psy D).

Argosy University, Seattle, College of Psychology and Behavioral Sciences, Program in Clinical Psychology, Seattle, WA 98121. Offers MA, Psy D, Postdoctoral Respecialization Certificate.

Argosy University, Tampa, College of Psychology and Behavioral Sciences, Program in Clinical Psychology, Tampa, FL 33607. Offers clinical psychology (MA, Psy D), including child and adolescent psychology (Psy D), geropsychology (Psy D), marriage/ couples and family therapy (Psy D), neuropsychology (Psy D). *Accreditation:* APA.

Argosy University, Twin Cities, College of Psychology and Behavioral Sciences, Eagan, MN 55121. Offers clinical psychology (MA, Psy D), including child and family psychology (Psy D), forensic psychology (Psy D), health and neuropsychology (Psy D), trauma (Psy D); forensic counseling (Post-Graduate Certificate); forensic psychology (MA); industrial organizational psychology (MA); marriage and family therapy (MA, DMFT), including forensic counseling (MA). *Accreditation:* AAMFT; AAMFT/COAMFTE; APA.

Argosy University, Washington DC, College of Psychology and Behavioral Sciences, Arlington, VA 22209. Offers clinical psychology (MA, Psy D), including child and family psychology (Psy D), diversity and multicultural psychology (Psy D), forensic psychology (Psy D), health and neuropsychology (Psy D); community counseling (MA); counseling psychology (Ed D), including counselor education and supervision; counselor education and supervision (Ed D); forensic psychology (MA). *Accreditation:* APA.

Arizona State University at the Tempe campus, College of Liberal Arts and Sciences, Department of Psychology, Tempe, AZ 85287-1104. Offers applied behavior analysis (MS); behavioral neuroscience (PhD); clinical psychology (PhD); cognitive science (PhD); developmental psychology (PhD); quantitative psychology (PhD); social psychology (PhD). *Accreditation:* APA. *Degree requirements:* For doctorate, comprehensive exam, thesis/dissertation, interactive Program of Study (iPOS) submitted before completing 50 percent of required credit hours. *Entrance requirements:* For doctorate, GRE General Test, GRE Subject Test, minimum GPA of 3.0 or equivalent in last 2 years of work leading to bachelor's degree. Additional exam requirements/ recommendations for international students: Required—TOEFL, IELTS, or PTE. Electronic applications accepted.

Arkansas State University, Graduate School, College of Education and Behavioral Science, Department of Psychology and Counseling, State University, AR 72467. Offers clinical mental health counseling (Certificate); college student personnel services (MS); psychology and counseling (Ed S); rehabilitation counseling (MRC); school counseling (MSE); student affairs (Certificate). *Accreditation:* ACA (one or more programs are accredited); CORE (one or more programs are accredited); NCATE. Part-time programs

available. *Faculty:* 15 full-time (9 women). *Students:* 57 full-time (36 women), 51 part-time (38 women); includes 21 minority (19 Black or African American, non-Hispanic/ Latino; 1 Hispanic/Latino; 1 Two or more races, non-Hispanic/Latino), 1 international. Average age 30. 102 applicants, 54% accepted, 48 enrolled. In 2014, 22 master's, 22 other advanced degrees awarded. *Degree requirements:* For master's and other advanced degree, comprehensive exam, thesis or alternative. *Entrance requirements:* For master's, GRE General Test or MAT (for MSE), appropriate bachelor's degree, interview, letters of reference, official transcripts, immunization records, written statement, 2-3 page autobiography; for other advanced degree, GRE General Test, interview, master's degree, letters of reference, official transcript, personal statement, immunization records. Additional exam requirements/recommendations for international students: Required—TOEFL (minimum score 550 paper-based; 79 iBT), IELTS (minimum score 6), PTE (minimum score 56). *Application deadline:* Applications are processed on a rolling basis. Application fee: $30 ($40 for international students). Electronic applications accepted. *Expenses:* Tuition, state resident: full-time $4392; part-time $244 per credit hour. Tuition, nonresident: full-time $8784; part-time $488 per credit hour. *International tuition:* $9484 full-time. *Required fees:* $1134; $63 per credit hour. $25 per term. Tuition and fees vary according to course load and program. *Financial support:* In 2014–15, 8 students received support. Teaching assistantships, career-related internships or fieldwork, scholarships/grants, and unspecified assistantships available. Financial award application deadline: 7/1; financial award applicants required to submit FAFSA. *Unit head:* Dr. Kris Biondolillo, Interim Chair, 870-972-3064, Fax: 870-972-3962, E-mail: kdbiondo@astate.edu. *Application contact:* Vickey Ring, Graduate Admissions Coordinator, 870-972-3029, Fax: 870-972-3857, E-mail: vickeyring@astate.edu.
Website: http://www.astate.edu/college/education/departments/psychology-and-counseling/index.dot

Auburn University at Montgomery, College of Arts and Sciences, Department of Psychology, Montgomery, AL 36124-4023. Offers clinical psychology (MS). Part-time and evening/weekend programs available. *Faculty:* 6 full-time (2 women). *Students:* 14 full-time (12 women), 8 part-time (5 women); includes 3 minority (all Black or African American, non-Hispanic/Latino), 2 international. Average age 29. 13 applicants, 92% accepted, 10 enrolled. In 2014, 6 master's awarded. *Degree requirements:* For master's, comprehensive exam, thesis optional. *Entrance requirements:* For master's, GRE General Test or MAT. *Application deadline:* Applications are processed on a rolling basis. Electronic applications accepted. *Expenses:* Tuition, state resident: full-time $6264; part-time $348 per credit hour. Tuition, nonresident: full-time $14,094; part-time $783 per credit hour. *Financial support:* In 2014–15, 6 teaching assistantships were awarded; career-related internships or fieldwork and scholarships/grants also available. Support available to part-time students. Financial award application deadline: 3/1; financial award applicants required to submit FAFSA. *Faculty research:* Community service, diagnosis, behavior modification. *Unit head:* Dr. Glen Ray, Acting Head, 334-244-3690, Fax: 334-244-3826, E-mail: gray@aum.edu. *Application contact:* Tonya Sexton, Administrative Associate, 334-244-3306, Fax: 334-244-3826, E-mail: tsexton1@aum.edu.
Website: http://sciences.aum.edu/departments/psychology

Azusa Pacific University, School of Behavioral and Applied Sciences, Department of Graduate Psychology, Azusa, CA 91702-7000. Offers clinical psychology (MA, Psy D), including family therapy (MA). *Accreditation:* APA (one or more programs are accredited). Part-time and evening/weekend programs available. *Degree requirements:* For master's, comprehensive exam, 250 hours of clinical experience, individual and group therapy. *Entrance requirements:* For master's, interview, minimum GPA of 3.0, Minnesota Multiphasic Personality Inventory. Additional exam requirements/ recommendations for international students: Required—TOEFL (minimum score 600 paper-based).

Ball State University, Graduate School, College of Sciences and Humanities, Department of Psychological Science, Program in Clinical Psychology, Muncie, IN 47306-1099. Offers MA. *Students:* 12 full-time (11 women), 2 part-time (both women). Average age 22. 27 applicants, 30% accepted, 6 enrolled. In 2014, 8 master's awarded. *Entrance requirements:* For master's, GRE General Test, interview. Application fee: $50. *Financial support:* In 2014–15, 15 students received support, including 3 research assistantships with partial tuition reimbursements available (averaging $9,610 per year), 9 teaching assistantships with partial tuition reimbursements available (averaging $9,628 per year). Financial award application deadline: 3/1. *Unit head:* Dr. Kerri Pickel, Program Director, 765-285-1711, Fax: 765-285-8980, E-mail: kpickel@bsu.edu.
Website: http://www.bsu.edu/psysc/

Barry University, College of Arts and Sciences, Department of Psychology, Miami Shores, FL 33161-6695. Offers clinical psychology (MS); school psychology (MS, SSP). Part-time and evening/weekend programs available. *Degree requirements:* For master's, thesis, practicum. *Entrance requirements:* For master's, GRE General Test, minimum GPA of 3.0, course work in psychology. Electronic applications accepted. *Faculty research:* Closed head injury, memory and aging, infant/mother interaction, evolutionary aspects of behavior, gender roles.

Baylor University, Graduate School, College of Arts and Sciences, Department of Psychology and Neuroscience, Program in Clinical Psychology, Waco, TX 76798. Offers Psy D. *Accreditation:* APA. Terminal master's awarded for partial completion of doctoral program. *Degree requirements:* For doctorate, comprehensive exam, thesis/ dissertation. *Entrance requirements:* For doctorate, GRE General Test, interview. Electronic applications accepted. *Faculty research:* Hypnosis/behavioral medicine, drug and alcohol, pediatric psychology, marital communication, religion and mental health.

Bay Path University, Program in Clinical Mental Health Counseling, Longmeadow, MA 01106-2292. Offers MS. Program also offered in Sturbridge and Burlington, MA. Part-time programs available. *Students:* 52 full-time (50 women), 58 part-time (55 women); includes 26 minority (10 Black or African American, non-Hispanic/Latino; 1 Asian, non-Hispanic/Latino; 13 Hispanic/Latino; 2 Two or more races, non-Hispanic/Latino), 2 international. Average age 32. 72 applicants, 83% accepted, 45 enrolled. In 2014, 10 master's awarded. *Degree requirements:* For master's, practicum, internship. *Application deadline:* Applications are processed on a rolling basis. Application fee: $45. Electronic applications accepted. Application fee is waived when completed online. *Financial support:* In 2014–15, 35 students received support. Applicants required to submit FAFSA. *Unit head:* Dr. Mark Benander, Interim Director, 413-565-1332. *Application contact:* Diane Ranaldi, Dean of Graduate Admissions, 413-565-1332, Fax: 413-565-1250, E-mail: dranaldi@baypath.edu.
Website: http://graduate.baypath.edu/graduate-programs/programs-on-campus/ms-programs/clinical-mental-health

Benedictine University, Graduate Programs, Program in Clinical Psychology, Lisle, IL 60532-0900. Offers MS. Part-time programs available. *Degree requirements:* For master's, comprehensive exam, internship. *Entrance requirements:* For master's, MAT. Additional exam requirements/recommendations for international students: Required—TOEFL (minimum score 550 paper-based). Electronic applications accepted.

Binghamton University, State University of New York, Graduate School, School of Arts and Sciences, Department of Psychology, Specialization in Clinical Psychology,

Vestal, NY 13850. Offers PhD. *Accreditation:* APA. *Students:* 20 full-time (16 women), 24 part-time (18 women); includes 4 minority (2 Black or African American, non-Hispanic/Latino; 2 Hispanic/Latino), 1 international. Average age 28. 256 applicants, 3% accepted, 7 enrolled. In 2014, 5 doctorates awarded. *Degree requirements:* For doctorate, comprehensive exam, thesis/dissertation. *Entrance requirements:* For doctorate, GRE General Test. Additional exam requirements/recommendations for international students: Required—TOEFL (minimum score 550 paper-based; 80 iBT). *Application deadline:* For fall admission, 12/15 priority date for domestic and international students. Applications are processed on a rolling basis. Application fee: $75. Electronic applications accepted. *Expenses:* Tuition, state resident: full-time $7776; part-time $432 per credit. Tuition, nonresident: full-time $15,138; part-time $841 per credit. *Required fees:* $1754; $213 per credit. Tuition and fees vary according to degree level and program. *Financial support:* In 2014–15, 30 students received support, including 9 research assistantships with full tuition reimbursements available (averaging $17,500 per year), 13 teaching assistantships with full tuition reimbursements available (averaging $17,500 per year); career-related internships or fieldwork, Federal Work-Study, institutionally sponsored loans, scholarships/grants, traineeships, health care benefits, tuition waivers (full and partial), and unspecified assistantships also available. Financial award application deadline: 2/15; financial award applicants required to submit FAFSA. *Unit head:* Dr. Brandon E. Gibb, Program Coordinator, 607-777-2511, E-mail: bgibb@binghamton.edu. *Application contact:* Kishan Zuber, Recruiting and Admissions Coordinator, 607-777-2151, Fax: 607-777-2501, E-mail: kzuber@binghamton.edu.

Biola University, Rosemead School of Psychology, La Mirada, CA 90639-0001. Offers clinical psychology (PhD, Psy D). *Accreditation:* APA. *Faculty:* 24. *Students:* 122 full-time (87 women), 13 part-time (10 women); includes 57 minority (6 Black or African American, non-Hispanic/Latino; 30 Asian, non-Hispanic/Latino; 20 Hispanic/Latino; 1 Two or more races, non-Hispanic/Latino), 2 international. 96 applicants, 41% accepted, 21 enrolled. In 2014, 19 doctorates awarded. *Degree requirements:* For doctorate, comprehensive exam, thesis/dissertation. *Entrance requirements:* For doctorate, GRE General Test, interview, 30 undergraduate semester hours of credits in psychology, minimum GPA of 3.0. Additional exam requirements/recommendations for international students: Required—TOEFL (minimum score 600 paper-based; 100 iBT). *Application deadline:* For fall admission, 1/15 priority date for domestic students, 1/15 for international students. Application fee: $65. Electronic applications accepted. *Expenses:* Expenses: Contact institution. *Financial support:* Scholarships/grants and unspecified assistantships available. Financial award applicants required to submit FAFSA. *Faculty research:* Integration of psychology and theology, psychology of child/adolescent, psychology of marriage, psychology of gender, psychology of trauma, psychology of forensics, multi-cultural studies and mental health. *Unit head:* Dr. Clark Campbell, Dean, 562-903-4867, Fax: 562-903-4864. *Application contact:* Jon Garcia, Graduate Admissions Counselor, 562-903-4752, E-mail: graduate.admissions@biola.edu.
Website: http://www.rosemead.edu/

Bowling Green State University, Graduate College, College of Arts and Sciences, Department of Psychology, Bowling Green, OH 43403. Offers clinical psychology (MA, PhD); developmental psychology (MA, PhD); experimental psychology (MA, PhD); industrial/organizational psychology (MA, PhD); quantitative psychology (MA, PhD). *Accreditation:* APA (one or more programs are accredited). *Degree requirements:* For doctorate, thesis/dissertation. *Entrance requirements:* For doctorate, GRE General Test, GRE Subject Test. Additional exam requirements/recommendations for international students: Required—TOEFL. Electronic applications accepted. *Faculty research:* Personnel psychology, developmental-mathematical models, behavioral medication, brain process, child/adolescent social cognition.

Bradley University, Graduate School, College of Education and Health Sciences, Department of Leadership in Education, Human Services, and Counseling, Peoria, IL 61625-0002. Offers human development counseling (MA), including clinical mental health counseling, school counseling; leadership in educational administration (MA); non-profit leadership (MA). *Accreditation:* ACA; NCATE. Part-time and evening/weekend programs available. *Faculty:* 8 full-time (5 women), 5 part-time/adjunct (2 women). *Students:* 43 full-time (34 women), 35 part-time (30 women); includes 4 minority (1 Black or African American, non-Hispanic/Latino; 1 American Indian or Alaska Native, non-Hispanic/Latino; 2 Asian, non-Hispanic/Latino), 1 international. 42 applicants, 71% accepted, 21 enrolled. In 2014, 26 master's awarded. *Degree requirements:* For master's, comprehensive exam, thesis optional. *Entrance requirements:* For master's, GRE General Test or MAT, interview, 3 letters of recommendation. Additional exam requirements/recommendations for international students: Required—TOEFL (minimum score 550 paper-based; 79 iBT), IELTS (minimum score 6.5). *Application deadline:* For fall admission, 5/15 priority date for domestic and international students; for spring admission, 10/15 priority date for domestic and international students. Applications are processed on a rolling basis. Application fee: $40 ($50 for international students). Electronic applications accepted. *Expenses: Tuition:* Full-time $14,580; part-time $810 per credit. *Required fees:* $224. Full-time tuition and fees vary according to course load. *Financial support:* In 2014–15, 6 research assistantships with full and partial tuition reimbursements (averaging $19,640 per year) were awarded; career-related internships or fieldwork, scholarships/grants, tuition waivers (partial), and unspecified assistantships also available. Support available to part-time students. Financial award application deadline: 4/1. *Unit head:* Dr. Christopher Rybak, Chair, 309-677-3193, E-mail: cjr@bradley.edu. *Application contact:* Kayla Carroll, Director of International Admissions and Student Services, 309-677-2375, E-mail: klcarroll@fsmail.bradley.edu.

Brigham Young University, Graduate Studies, College of Family, Home, and Social Sciences, Department of Psychology, Provo, UT 84602. Offers behavioral neuroscience (PhD); clinical psychology (PhD); general psychology (MS). *Accreditation:* APA (one or more programs are accredited). *Faculty:* 29 full-time (6 women), 2 part-time/adjunct (1 woman). *Students:* 60 full-time (34 women); includes 6 minority (1 American Indian or Alaska Native, non-Hispanic/Latino; 3 Asian, non-Hispanic/Latino; 2 Hispanic/Latino), 3 international. Average age 26. 57 applicants, 25% accepted, 9 enrolled. In 2014, 6 master's, 17 doctorates awarded. *Degree requirements:* For master's, thesis; for doctorate, comprehensive exam, thesis/dissertation, publishable paper. *Entrance requirements:* For master's and doctorate, GRE General Test, minimum GPA of 3.0 in last 60 hours of upper-division course work. Additional exam requirements/recommendations for international students: Required—TOEFL. *Application deadline:* For fall admission, 12/1 for domestic and international students. Application fee: $50. Electronic applications accepted. *Expenses: Tuition:* Full-time $6310; part-time $371 per credit hour. Tuition and fees vary according to program and student's religious affiliation. *Financial support:* In 2014–15, 43 students received support, including 27 research assistantships with partial tuition reimbursements available (averaging $10,000 per year), 11 teaching assistantships with partial tuition reimbursements available (averaging $10,000 per year); fellowships, career-related internships or fieldwork, scholarships/grants, tuition waivers (partial), and unspecified assistantships also available. Financial award application deadline: 5/31. *Faculty research:* Psychotherapy process, Alzheimer's disease/dementia, psychology and law, health, psychology, developmental. *Total annual research expenditures:* $1 million. *Unit head:* Dr. Dawson Hedges, Chair, 801-422-6357, Fax: 801-422-0602, E-mail: dawson_hedges@byu.edu. *Application contact:* Leesa D. Scott, Coordinator of Student Programs, 801-422-4560, Fax: 801-422-0602, E-mail: leesa_scott@byu.edu. Website: http://psychology.byu.edu/

California Institute of Integral Studies, School of Professional Psychology and Health, San Francisco, CA 94103. Offers clinical psychology (Psy D); community mental health (MA); drama therapy (MA); expressive arts therapy (MA); integral counseling psychology (MA); integrative health studies (MA); psychological studies (MA); somatic psychology (MA). *Accreditation:* APA. Part-time and evening/weekend programs available. *Students:* 522 full-time (397 women), 105 part-time (83 women); includes 155 minority (27 Black or African American, non-Hispanic/Latino; 3 American Indian or Alaska Native, non-Hispanic/Latino; 31 Asian, non-Hispanic/Latino; 62 Hispanic/Latino; 3 Native Hawaiian or other Pacific Islander, non-Hispanic/Latino; 29 Two or more races, non-Hispanic/Latino), 49 international. Average age 34. 351 applicants, 86% accepted, 175 enrolled. In 2014, 168 master's, 24 doctorates awarded. *Degree requirements:* For doctorate, comprehensive exam, thesis/dissertation. *Entrance requirements:* For master's, minimum GPA of 3.0, letters of recommendation, writing sample; for doctorate, GRE, MA in psychology or social work with appropriate practical experience for advanced standing, or BA with a minimum GPA of 3.1; letters of recommendation; writing sample. Additional exam requirements/recommendations for international students: Required—TOEFL. *Application deadline:* For fall admission, 2/1 priority date for domestic and international students; for spring admission, 10/15 priority date for domestic and international students. Applications are processed on a rolling basis. Application fee: $65. Electronic applications accepted. *Expenses: Tuition:* Full-time $18,270; part-time $1015 per credit. *Required fees:* $85 per semester hour. *Financial support:* In 2014–15, 464 students received support, including 5 research assistantships with tuition reimbursements available (averaging $800 per year), 36 teaching assistantships with tuition reimbursements available (averaging $825 per year); career-related internships or fieldwork, Federal Work-Study, and scholarships/grants also available. Support available to part-time students. Financial award application deadline: 4/15; financial award applicants required to submit FAFSA. *Faculty research:* Transpersonal psychology, somatic psychology, expressive arts therapy, drama therapy, community mental health, ecopsychology, integrative health. *Application contact:* David Townes, Senior Admissions Counselor, 415-575-6152, Fax: 415-575-1268, E-mail: admissions@ciis.edu.

California Lutheran University, Graduate Studies, Department of Psychology, Thousand Oaks, CA 91360-2787. Offers clinical psychology (MS, Psy D); marital and family therapy (MS). Part-time programs available. *Faculty:* 12 full-time (6 women), 19 part-time/adjunct (14 women). *Students:* 156 full-time (133 women), 28 part-time (25 women); includes 85 minority (5 Black or African American, non-Hispanic/Latino; 1 American Indian or Alaska Native, non-Hispanic/Latino; 6 Asian, non-Hispanic/Latino; 67 Hispanic/Latino; 2 Native Hawaiian or other Pacific Islander, non-Hispanic/Latino; 4 Two or more races, non-Hispanic/Latino), 6 international. Average age 31. 201 applicants, 57% accepted, 56 enrolled. In 2014, 64 master's awarded. *Degree requirements:* For master's, thesis or comprehensive exams; for doctorate, internship. *Entrance requirements:* For master's, GRE General Test, interview, minimum GPA of 3.0; for doctorate, GRE General Test. *Application deadline:* For fall admission, 1/15 priority date for domestic and international students. Applications are processed on a rolling basis. Application fee: $50. *Unit head:* Dr. Richard Holigrock, Dean, 805-493-3675. *Application contact:* 805-493-3325, Fax: 805-493-3861, E-mail: clugrad@callutheran.edu.

California State University, Dominguez Hills, College of Natural and Behavioral Sciences, Program in Psychology, Carson, CA 90747-0001. Offers clinical psychology (MA). Part-time and evening/weekend programs available. *Faculty:* 2 full-time (both women), 5 part-time/adjunct (3 women). *Students:* 37 full-time (29 women), 18 part-time (12 women); includes 39 minority (4 Black or African American, non-Hispanic/Latino; 1 American Indian or Alaska Native, non-Hispanic/Latino; 3 Asian, non-Hispanic/Latino; 28 Hispanic/Latino; 3 Two or more races, non-Hispanic/Latino). Average age 31. 52 applicants, 50% accepted, 17 enrolled. In 2014, 17 master's awarded. Terminal master's awarded for partial completion of doctoral program. *Degree requirements:* For master's, comprehensive exam, thesis optional. *Entrance requirements:* For master's, GRE General Test or MAT, interview, minimum GPA of 3.0, prerequisite psychology courses. Additional exam requirements/recommendations for international students: Required—TOEFL (minimum score 550 paper-based). *Application deadline:* For fall admission, 3/1 for domestic and international students. Application fee: $55. Electronic applications accepted. *Expenses:* Tuition, state resident: full-time $6738; part-time $3960 per year. Tuition, nonresident: full-time $13,434; part-time $8370 per year. *Required fees:* $623; $623 per year. *Faculty research:* Culture and health, neuropsychology and HIV, psychohistory of the Holocaust, community and adolescents, malingering. *Unit head:* Dr. Karen Wilson, Program Coordinator, 310-243-3642, E-mail: kmason@csudh.edu. *Application contact:* Dr. Karen I. Mason, Coordinator, 310-243-3642, Fax: 310-516-3642, E-mail: kmason@csudh.edu.
Website: http://www4.csudh.edu/psychology/

California State University, Fullerton, Graduate Studies, College of Humanities and Social Sciences, Department of Psychology, Fullerton, CA 92834-9480. Offers clinical/community psychology (MS); psychology (MA). Part-time programs available. *Students:* 83 full-time (57 women), 16 part-time (7 women); includes 45 minority (1 Black or African American, non-Hispanic/Latino; 9 Asian, non-Hispanic/Latino; 31 Hispanic/Latino; 4 Two or more races, non-Hispanic/Latino), 9 international. Average age 25. 110 applicants, 35% accepted, 37 enrolled. In 2014, 28 master's awarded. *Degree requirements:* For master's, thesis. *Entrance requirements:* For master's, GRE General Test, GRE Subject Test, undergraduate major in psychology or related field. Application fee: $55. *Financial support:* Career-related internships or fieldwork, Federal Work-Study, institutionally sponsored loans, and scholarships/grants available. Support available to part-time students. Financial award application deadline: 3/1; financial award applicants required to submit FAFSA. *Unit head:* Dr. Jack Mearns, Chair, 657-278-3514. *Application contact:* Admissions/Applications, 657-278-2371.

California State University, Northridge, Graduate Studies, College of Social and Behavioral Sciences, Department of Psychology, Northridge, CA 91330. Offers clinical psychology (MA); general-experimental psychology (MA); human factors and applied experimental psychology (MA). *Students:* 46 full-time (32 women), 16 part-time (10 women); includes 27 minority (3 Black or African American, non-Hispanic/Latino; 2 Asian, non-Hispanic/Latino; 20 Hispanic/Latino; 2 Two or more races, non-Hispanic/Latino). Average age 26. *Degree requirements:* For master's, thesis. *Entrance requirements:* For master's, GRE General Test, GRE Subject Test, minimum GPA of 3.0, letters of recommendation. Additional exam requirements/recommendations for international students: Required—TOEFL. *Application deadline:* For fall admission, 11/30 for domestic students. Application fee: $55. *Expenses: Required fees:* $12,402. *Financial support:* Application deadline: 3/1. *Unit head:* Jill Razani, Chair, 818-677-3506.
Website: http://www.csun.edu/csbs/departments/psychology/index.html

California State University, San Bernardino, Graduate Studies, College of Social and Behavioral Sciences, Department of Psychology, Program in Clinical/Counseling Psychology, San Bernardino, CA 92407-2397. Offers clinical psychology (MS). *Students:* 20 part-time (18 women); includes 15 minority (4 Black or African American,

non-Hispanic/Latino; 1 Asian, non-Hispanic/Latino; 10 Hispanic/Latino). Average age 26. 94 applicants, 12% accepted, 11 enrolled. In 2014, 13 master's awarded. *Entrance requirements:* Additional exam requirements/recommendations for international students: Required—TOEFL. *Application deadline:* For fall admission, 7/17 for domestic students. Application fee: $55. *Expenses:* Tuition, state resident: full-time $6738; part-time $1302 per term. Tuition, nonresident: full-time $17,898; part-time $248 per unit. *Required fees:* $365 per quarter. Tuition and fees vary according to degree level and program. *Financial support:* Application deadline: 3/1. *Unit head:* Dr. Robert Ricco, Chair, 909-537-5485, Fax: 909-537-7003, E-mail: rricco@csusb.edu. *Application contact:* Stacy Brooks, Graduate Secretary, 909-537-5570, Fax: 909-537-7003, E-mail: sbrooks@csusb.edu.

Capella University, Harold Abel School of Social and Behavioral Science, Doctoral Programs in Psychology, Minneapolis, MN 55402. Offers addiction psychology (PhD); clinical psychology (Psy D); educational psychology (PhD); general advanced studies in human behavior (PhD); general psychology (PhD); industrial/organizational psychology (PhD); school psychology (Psy D).

Capella University, Harold Abel School of Social and Behavioral Science, Master's Programs in Psychology, Minneapolis, MN 55402. Offers applied behavior analysis (MS); clinical psychology (MS); counseling psychology (MS); educational psychology (MS); evaluation, research, and measurement (MS); general advanced studies in human behavior (MS); general psychology (MS); industrial/organizational psychology (MS); leadership coaching psychology (MS); school psychology (MS); sport psychology (MS).

Cardinal Stritch University, College of Arts and Sciences, Department of Psychology, Milwaukee, WI 53217-3985. Offers clinical psychology (MA). Part-time and evening/weekend programs available. *Degree requirements:* For master's, thesis, portfolio, clinical practicum. *Entrance requirements:* For master's, GRE General Test, GRE Subject Test (psychology), interview, minimum GPA of 3.0, 3 letters of recommendation.

Carlos Albizu University, Graduate Programs, San Juan, PR 00901. Offers clinical psychology (MS, PhD, Psy D); general psychology (PhD); industrial/organizational psychology (MS, PhD); speech and language pathology (MS). *Accreditation:* APA (one or more programs are accredited). Part-time and evening/weekend programs available. Terminal master's awarded for partial completion of doctoral program. *Degree requirements:* For master's, one foreign language, comprehensive exam, thesis; for doctorate, one foreign language, comprehensive exam, thesis/dissertation, written qualifying exams. *Entrance requirements:* For master's, GRE General Test or EXADEP, interview; minimum GPA of 2.8 (industrial/organizational psychology); for doctorate, GRE General Test or EXADEP, interview; minimum GPA of 3.0 (PhD in industrial/organizational psychology and clinical psychology), 3.25 (Psy D). *Faculty research:* Psychotherapeutic techniques for Hispanics, psychology of the aged, school dropouts, stress, violence.

Carlos Albizu University, Miami Campus, Graduate Programs, Miami, FL 33172-2209. Offers clinical psychology (Psy D); entrepreneurship (MBA); exceptional student education (MS); human services (PhD); industrial/organizational psychology (MS); marriage and family therapy (MS); mental health counseling (MS); nonprofit management (MBA); organizational management (MBA); psychology (MS); school counseling (MS); teaching English as a second language (MS). *Accreditation:* APA. Part-time and evening/weekend programs available. Postbaccalaureate distance learning degree programs offered (minimal on-campus study). *Faculty:* 25 full-time (20 women), 29 part-time/adjunct (15 women). *Students:* 431 full-time (343 women), 264 part-time (225 women); includes 586 minority (45 Black or African American, non-Hispanic/Latino; 1 American Indian or Alaska Native, non-Hispanic/Latino; 8 Asian, non-Hispanic/Latino; 530 Hispanic/Latino; 2 Two or more races, non-Hispanic/Latino), 14 international. Average age 33. 189 applicants, 69% accepted, 111 enrolled. In 2014, 177 master's, 28 doctorates awarded. Terminal master's awarded for partial completion of doctoral program. *Degree requirements:* For master's, one foreign language, comprehensive exam, integrative project (MBA), research project (exceptional student education, teaching English as a second language); for doctorate, one foreign language, comprehensive exam, internship, project. *Entrance requirements:* For master's, 3 letters of recommendation, interview, minimum GPA of 3.0, resume, statement of purpose, official transcripts; for doctorate, 3 letters of recommendation, minimum GPA of 3.0, resume, interview, statement of purpose, official transcripts. Additional exam requirements/recommendations for international students: Required—Michigan Test of English Language Proficiency. *Application deadline:* For fall admission, 4/1 priority date for domestic students, 5/1 priority date for international students; for spring admission, 11/1 priority date for domestic students, 9/1 priority date for international students. Applications are processed on a rolling basis. Application fee: $50. Electronic applications accepted. *Expenses:* Expenses: $570 per credit (for master's programs); $750 per credit (for doctoral programs). *Financial support:* In 2014–15, 72 students received support. Federal Work-Study, scholarships/grants, and tuition discounts available. Financial award application deadline: 6/1; financial award applicants required to submit FAFSA. *Faculty research:* Psychotherapy, forensic psychology, neuropsychology, marketing strategy, entrepreneurship, special education. *Unit head:* Dr. Irene M. Bravo, Interim Provost, 305-593-1223 Ext. 3120, Fax: 305-592-7930, E-mail: ibravo@albizu.edu. *Application contact:* Vanessa Almendarez, Administrative Assistant, 305-593-1223 Ext. 3137, Fax: 305-593-1854, E-mail: valmendarez@albizu.edu.

Case Western Reserve University, School of Graduate Studies, Psychological Sciences Department, Program in Clinical Psychology, Cleveland, OH 44106. Offers PhD. *Accreditation:* APA. Part-time programs available. *Faculty:* 12 full-time (7 women), 6 part-time/adjunct (2 women). *Students:* 28 full-time (20 women); includes 2 minority (1 Black or African American, non-Hispanic/Latino; 1 Hispanic/Latino). Average age 27. 165 applicants, 4% accepted, 5 enrolled. In 2014, 6 doctorates awarded. *Degree requirements:* For doctorate, thesis/dissertation, internship. *Entrance requirements:* For doctorate, GRE General Test, GRE Subject Test, personal statement; curriculum vitae; three letters of recommendation. Additional exam requirements/recommendations for international students: Required—TOEFL (minimum score 577 paper-based; 90 iBT); Recommended—IELTS (minimum score 7). *Application deadline:* For fall admission, 12/1 priority date for domestic students. Application fee: $50. Electronic applications accepted. *Financial support:* Fellowships, research assistantships, and teaching assistantships available. Financial award application deadline: 12/1; financial award applicants required to submit FAFSA. *Faculty research:* Pediatric psychology, family functioning, depression, geriatric psychopathology, creativity and play. *Unit head:* Dr. Lee Thompson, Chair, 216-368-6477, E-mail: lee.thompson@case.edu. *Application contact:* Dr. James C. Overholser, Director of Clinical Training, 216-368-2686, Fax: 216-368-4891, E-mail: cwrupsych@gmail.com.
Website: http://psychsciences.case.edu/graduate/

The Catholic University of America, School of Arts and Sciences, Department of Psychology, Washington, DC 20064. Offers applied experimental psychology (PhD); clinical psychology (PhD); general psychology (MA); human factors (MA); MA/JD. *Accreditation:* APA (one or more programs are accredited). Part-time programs available. *Faculty:* 13 full-time (6 women), 7 part-time/adjunct (2 women). *Students:* 37 full-time (26 women), 42 part-time (33 women); includes 17 minority (1 Black or African American, non-Hispanic/Latino; 3 Asian, non-Hispanic/Latino; 7 Hispanic/Latino; 6 Two or more races, non-Hispanic/Latino), 3 international. Average age 28. 263 applicants, 14% accepted, 19 enrolled. In 2014, 19 master's, 6 doctorates awarded. *Degree requirements:* For master's, comprehensive exam, thesis (for some programs); for doctorate, comprehensive exam, thesis/dissertation. *Entrance requirements:* For master's, GRE General Test, statement of purpose, official copies of academic transcripts, three letters of recommendation; for doctorate, GRE General Test, GRE Subject Test, statement of purpose, official copies of academic transcripts, three letters of recommendation. Additional exam requirements/recommendations for international students: Required—TOEFL (minimum score 580 paper-based). *Application deadline:* For fall admission, 7/15 priority date for domestic students, 7/1 for international students; for spring admission, 11/15 priority date for domestic students, 11/1 for international students. Applications are processed on a rolling basis. Application fee: $55. Electronic applications accepted. *Expenses: Tuition:* Full-time $40,200; part-time $1600 per credit hour. *Required fees:* $400; $195 per semester. One-time fee: $425. *Financial support:* Fellowships, research assistantships, teaching assistantships, Federal Work-Study, scholarships/grants, tuition waivers (full and partial), and unspecified assistantships available. Financial award application deadline: 2/1; financial award applicants required to submit FAFSA. *Faculty research:* Clinical psychology, applied cognitive science, psychopathology, cognitive neuroscience, psychotherapy. *Total annual research expenditures:* $1.2 million. *Unit head:* Dr. Marc M. Sebrechts, Chair, 202-319-5750, Fax: 202-319-6263, E-mail: sebrechts@cua.edu. *Application contact:* Director of Graduate Admissions, 202-319-5057, Fax: 202-319-6533, E-mail: cua-admissions@cua.edu.
Website: http://psychology.cua.edu/

Central Michigan University, College of Graduate Studies, College of Humanities and Social and Behavioral Sciences, Department of Psychology, Program in Clinical Psychology, Mount Pleasant, MI 48859. Offers PhD. *Accreditation:* APA. *Degree requirements:* For doctorate, thesis/dissertation. *Entrance requirements:* For doctorate, GRE. Electronic applications accepted. *Faculty research:* Applied youth development; emotional processes, personality disorders, and assessment; influence of affective variables on cognitive performance; post-traumatic stress disorder and panic disorder; validation of clinical inferences from psychological tests.

Chestnut Hill College, School of Graduate Studies, Division of Psychology, Program in Clinical and Counseling Psychology, Philadelphia, PA 19118-2693. Offers addictions treatment (MS, CAS); child and adolescent therapy (MS, CAS); marriage and family therapy (MS, CAS); trauma studies (MS, CAS); treatment of autism spectrum disorders (MS, CAS). Part-time and evening/weekend programs available. *Faculty:* 4 full-time (3 women), 34 part-time/adjunct (24 women). *Students:* 88 full-time (73 women), 136 part-time (113 women); includes 41 minority (27 Black or African American, non-Hispanic/Latino; 1 Asian, non-Hispanic/Latino; 12 Hispanic/Latino; 1 Two or more races, non-Hispanic/Latino), 2 international. Average age 33. 119 applicants, 98% accepted, 70 enrolled. In 2014, 1,021 master's, 7 other advanced degrees awarded. *Degree requirements:* For master's, thesis optional, practica. *Entrance requirements:* For master's, GRE General Test, writing sample, letters of recommendation. Additional exam requirements/recommendations for international students: Required—TOEFL (minimum score 500 paper-based), IELTS (mnimum score 6.0), or TWE (minimum score 22). *Application deadline:* For fall admission, 7/1 for domestic and international students; for spring admission, 11/1 for domestic and international students; for summer admission, 4/1 for domestic and international students. Applications are processed on a rolling basis. Application fee: $55. Electronic applications accepted. *Expenses:* Expenses: Contact institution. *Financial support:* Unspecified assistantships available. *Faculty research:* Play therapy, eating disorders, addictions, group psychology and group therapy, health psychology. *Unit head:* Dr. Cheryll Rothery, Chair, Psychology Division, 215-248-7023, Fax: 215-248-3619, E-mail: rotheryc@chc.edu. *Application contact:* Amy Boorse, Assistant Director of Graduate Admissions, 215-248-7097, Fax: 215-248-7161, E-mail: gradadmissions@chc.edu.
Website: http://www.chc.edu/Graduate/Programs/Masters/Clinical_and_Counseling_Psychology/

Chestnut Hill College, School of Graduate Studies, Division of Psychology, Program in Clinical Psychology, Philadelphia, PA 19118-2693. Offers marriage and family therapy (Psy D); psychological assessment (Psy D). *Accreditation:* APA. Part-time and evening/weekend programs available. *Faculty:* 7 full-time (4 women), 1 (woman) part-time/adjunct. *Students:* 112 full-time (80 women); includes 28 minority (11 Black or African American, non-Hispanic/Latino; 6 Asian, non-Hispanic/Latino; 9 Hispanic/Latino; 2 Two or more races, non-Hispanic/Latino), 1 international. Average age 30. 172 applicants, 23% accepted, 15 enrolled. In 2014, 21 doctorates awarded. *Degree requirements:* For doctorate, comprehensive exam, thesis/dissertation, internship, practica, clinical competency exam. *Entrance requirements:* For doctorate, GRE General Test, letters of recommendation, writing sample, master's degree in clinical/counseling psychology or closely-related field. Additional exam requirements/recommendations for international students: Required—TOEFL (minimum score 500 paper-based), IELTS (mnimum score 6.0), or TWE (minimum score 22). *Application deadline:* For fall admission, 7/1 for domestic and international students; for spring admission, 11/1 for domestic and international students; for summer admission, 4/1 for domestic and international students. Applications are processed on a rolling basis. Application fee: $60. Electronic applications accepted. *Expenses:* Expenses: $985 per credit hour. *Financial support:* Unspecified assistantships available. *Faculty research:* Psychological testing and assessment, GLBT issues, autism and developmental disorders, stepfamilies, gender issues. *Unit head:* Dr. Cheryll Rothery, Chair, Division of Psychology, 215-248-7023, Fax: 215-248-3619, E-mail: rotheryc@chc.edu. *Application contact:* Eileen Webb, Director of Psy D Admissions, 215-248-7077, Fax: 215-248-3619, E-mail: profpsyc@chc.edu.
Website: http://www.chc.edu/Graduate/Programs/

The Chicago School of Professional Psychology, Program in Clinical Forensic Psychology, Chicago, IL 60610. Offers Psy D. *Degree requirements:* For doctorate, thesis/dissertation. *Entrance requirements:* For doctorate, GRE. Additional exam requirements/recommendations for international students: Required—TOEFL, IELTS.

The Chicago School of Professional Psychology, Program in Clinical Psychology, Chicago, IL 60610. Offers Psy D. *Accreditation:* APA. *Degree requirements:* For doctorate, comprehensive exam, thesis/dissertation. *Entrance requirements:* For doctorate, GRE, 18 hours of psychology credit (including courses in statistics, normal psychology and human development); minimum GPA of 3.2. Additional exam requirements/recommendations for international students: Required—TOEFL. Electronic applications accepted.

The Chicago School of Professional Psychology at Downtown Los Angeles, Program in Clinical Forensic Psychology, Los Angeles, CA 90017. Offers Psy D.

The Chicago School of Professional Psychology at Downtown Los Angeles, Program in Clinical Psychology, Los Angeles, CA 90017. Offers applied behavior analysis (MA); clinical psychology (Psy D); marital and family therapy (MA).

The Chicago School of Professional Psychology at Grayslake, Program in Clinical Counseling Psychology, Chicago, IL 60610. Offers counseling (MA), including child and

adolescent treatment, generalist, health psychology, Latino mental health, supervision and leadership in mental health, treatment of addiction disorders.

The Chicago School of Professional Psychology at Irvine, Program in Clinical Forensic Psychology, Irvine, CA 92612. Offers Psy D.

The Chicago School of Professional Psychology at Westwood, Program in Clinical Psychology, Los Angeles, CA 90024. Offers marital and family therapy (MA).

City College of the City University of New York, Graduate School, College of Liberal Arts and Science, Division of Social Science, Department of Psychology, New York, NY 10031-9198. Offers clinical psychology (PhD); experimental cognition (PhD); general psychology (MA); mental health counseling (MA). PhD program offered jointly with Graduate School and University Center of the City University of New York. *Accreditation:* APA (one or more programs are accredited). Part-time programs available. *Degree requirements:* For master's, one foreign language, comprehensive exam, thesis. *Entrance requirements:* For master's, GRE. Additional exam requirements/recommendations for international students: Required—TOEFL (minimum score 550 paper-based; 79 iBT). Electronic applications accepted. *Faculty research:* Social/personality psychology, physiological psychology, cognition and development.

Clark University, Graduate School, Hiatt School of Psychology, Program in Clinical Psychology, Worcester, MA 01610-1477. Offers PhD. *Accreditation:* APA. *Students:* 21 full-time (17 women), 1 (woman) part-time; includes 5 minority (1 Black or African American, non-Hispanic/Latino; 1 American Indian or Alaska Native, non-Hispanic/Latino; 3 Hispanic/Latino). Average age 30. In 2014, 3 doctorates awarded. *Degree requirements:* For doctorate, thesis/dissertation. *Entrance requirements:* For doctorate, GRE General Test. Additional exam requirements/recommendations for international students: Required—TOEFL. *Application deadline:* For fall admission, 12/15 priority date for domestic and international students. Applications are processed on a rolling basis. Application fee: $50. *Expenses: Tuition:* Full-time $40,380; part-time $1262 per credit hour. *Required fees:* $30. *Financial support:* In 2014–15, fellowships with full tuition reimbursements (averaging $16,015 per year), research assistantships with full tuition reimbursements (averaging $16,015 per year), teaching assistantships with full tuition reimbursements (averaging $16,015 per year) were awarded; tuition waivers (full) also available. *Faculty research:* Marital relations and interventions, adult emotional development, Latino men and depression, violence prevention. *Total annual research expenditures:* $650,000. *Unit head:* Dr. Esteban Cardemil, Chair, 508-793-7274, E-mail: ecardemil@clarku.edu. *Application contact:* Kelly Boulay, Departmental Administrator, 508-793-7274, Fax: 508-793-7265, E-mail: psychology@clarku.edu.
Website: http://www.clarku.edu/departments/psychology/grad/clinical/index.cfm

Clayton State University, School of Graduate Studies, College of Arts and Sciences, Program in Psychology, Morrow, GA 30260-0285. Offers applied developmental psychology (MS); clinical psychology (MS). *Entrance requirements:* For master's, GRE, 2 official transcripts; 3 letters of recommendation; statement of purpose; on-campus interview; background check. Additional exam requirements/recommendations for international students: Required—TOEFL (minimum score 550 paper-based). Electronic applications accepted.

College of St. Joseph, Graduate Programs, Division of Psychology and Human Services, Program in Clinical Mental Health Counseling, Rutland, VT 05701-3899. Offers MS. Part-time programs available. *Degree requirements:* For master's, comprehensive exam. *Entrance requirements:* For master's, official college transcripts; 2 letters of reference. Additional exam requirements/recommendations for international students: Required—TOEFL (minimum score 550 paper-based). Electronic applications accepted.

College of St. Joseph, Graduate Programs, Division of Psychology and Human Services, Program in Clinical Psychology, Rutland, VT 05701-3899. Offers MS. Part-time and evening/weekend programs available. *Degree requirements:* For master's, comprehensive exam, thesis optional. *Entrance requirements:* For master's, official college transcripts; 2 letters of reference. Additional exam requirements/recommendations for international students: Required—TOEFL (minimum score 550 paper-based). Electronic applications accepted.

College of Staten Island of the City University of New York, Graduate Programs, Division of Humanities and Social Sciences, Clinical Mental Health Counseling Program, Staten Island, NY 10314-6600. Offers MA. *Faculty:* 5 full-time (all women), 6 part-time/adjunct (4 women). *Students:* 62 full-time (51 women). Average age 27. 83 applicants, 35% accepted, 19 enrolled. In 2014, 19 master's awarded. *Degree requirements:* For master's, comprehensive exam, practicum, three internship courses. *Entrance requirements:* For master's, BA/BS; minimum GPA of 3.0; 15-19 undergraduate credits in psychology; two letters of recommendation; statement of intent; 1-2 page statement of intent detailing interest in the field, background information, academic and related experience, field placements, and the reasons the student chose this field of study. Additional exam requirements/recommendations for international students: Required—TOEFL (minimum score 600 paper-based; 100 iBT), IELTS (minimum score 7). *Application deadline:* For fall admission, 3/10 for domestic and international students. Application fee: $125. *Expenses:* Tuition, state resident: full-time $9650; part-time $405 per credit. Tuition, nonresident: full-time $17,880; part-time $745 per credit. *Required fees:* $141.10 per semester. Tuition and fees vary according to program. *Financial support:* In 2014–15, 37 students received support. Career-related internships or fieldwork, Federal Work-Study, and scholarships/grants available. Support available to part-time students. Financial award applicants required to submit FAFSA. *Unit head:* Dr. Frances Melendez, Graduate Program Coordinator, 718-982-3960, Fax: 718-982-4114, E-mail: frances.melendez@csi.cuny.edu. *Application contact:* Sasha Spence, Assistant Director for Graduate Admissions, 718-982-2019, Fax: 718-982-2500, E-mail: sasha.spence@csi.cuny.edu.
Website: http://csivc.csi.cuny.edu/psy/files/MHC.html

Concordia University, School of Graduate Studies, Faculty of Arts and Science, Department of Psychology, Program in Psychology (Clinical), Montréal, QC H3G 1M8, Canada. Offers MA, PhD, Certificate. *Accreditation:* APA (one or more programs are accredited). *Degree requirements:* For master's, comprehensive exam, thesis; for doctorate, comprehensive exam, thesis/dissertation. *Entrance requirements:* For master's, GRE General Test, GRE Subject Test, honors degree in psychology or equivalent; for doctorate, master's degree in psychology. *Faculty research:* Developmental-clinical psychology, sensory deficits, sexual dysfunction.

Connecticut College, Department of Psychology, New London, CT 06320-4196. Offers behavioral medicine/health psychology (MA); clinical psychology (MA); neuroscience/psychobiology (MA); social/personality psychology (MA). Part-time programs available. *Students:* 4 full-time (2 women), 3 part-time (2 women). Average age 30. 7 applicants, 29% accepted, 2 enrolled. *Degree requirements:* For master's, thesis. *Entrance requirements:* For master's, GRE General Test, statistics course. Additional exam requirements/recommendations for international students: Required—TOEFL (minimum score 600 paper-based). *Application deadline:* For fall admission, 2/1 for domestic and international students. Application fee: $60. *Expenses: Tuition:* Full-time $12,120. *Financial support:* Tuition remission available. Financial award application deadline: 2/1; financial award applicants required to submit CSS PROFILE or FAFSA. *Unit head:* Dr. Ruth Grahn, Chair, 860-439-2387, Fax: 860-439-5300, E-mail: ruth.grahn@conncoll.edu. *Application contact:* Nancy M. MacLeod, Academic Department Assistant, 860-439-2330, Fax: 860-439-5300, E-mail: nancy.macleod@conncoll.edu.

Dalhousie University, Faculty of Science, Department of Psychology, Halifax, NS B3H 4R2, Canada. Offers clinical psychology (PhD); psychology (M Sc, PhD); psychology/neuroscience (M Sc, PhD). *Degree requirements:* For master's, thesis; for doctorate, thesis/dissertation. *Entrance requirements:* For doctorate, GRE General Test. Additional exam requirements/recommendations for international students: Required—TOEFL, IELTS, CANTEST, CAEL, or Michigan English Language Assessment Battery. Electronic applications accepted. *Faculty research:* Physiological psychology, psychology of learning, learning and behavior, forensic clinical health psychology, development perception and cognition.

DePaul University, College of Education, Chicago, IL 60614. Offers bilingual bicultural education (M Ed, MA); counseling (M Ed, MA), including clinical mental health counseling, college student development, school counseling; curriculum studies (M Ed, MA, Ed D); early childhood education (M Ed, MA, Ed D); educating adults (MA); educational leadership (M Ed, MA, Ed D), including administration and supervision (M Ed, MA), principal preparation (M Ed, MA); elementary education (MA); mathematics education (MA); mathematics for teaching (MS); middle school mathematics education (MS); reading specialist (M Ed, MA); secondary education (M Ed); social and cultural foundations in education (MA); special education (M Ed, MA); world languages education (M Ed, MA). Part-time and evening/weekend programs available. Postbaccalaureate distance learning degree programs offered (no on-campus study). *Degree requirements:* For doctorate, thesis/dissertation. Electronic applications accepted.

Drexel University, College of Arts and Sciences, Department of Psychology, Clinical Psychology Program, Philadelphia, PA 19104-2875. Offers clinical psychology (PhD); forensic psychology (PhD); health psychology (PhD); neuropsychology (PhD). *Accreditation:* APA. Terminal master's awarded for partial completion of doctoral program. *Degree requirements:* For doctorate, thesis/dissertation, qualifying exam. *Entrance requirements:* For doctorate, GRE General Test, GRE Subject Test, minimum GPA of 3.0. Electronic applications accepted. *Expenses:* Contact institution. *Faculty research:* Cognitive behavioral therapy, stress and coping, eating disorders, substance abuse, developmental disabilities.

Drexel University, College of Arts and Sciences, Department of Psychology, Program in Law-Psychology, Philadelphia, PA 19104-2875. Offers JD/PhD. Electronic applications accepted. *Expenses:* Contact institution. *Faculty research:* Mental health law issues, professional ethics, social science applications to law.

Duke University, Graduate School, Department of Psychology and Neuroscience, Durham, NC 27708. Offers biological psychology (PhD); clinical psychology (PhD); cognitive psychology (PhD); developmental psychology (PhD); experimental psychology (PhD); health psychology (PhD); human social development (PhD); JD/MA. *Accreditation:* APA (one or more programs are accredited). *Degree requirements:* For doctorate, thesis/dissertation. *Entrance requirements:* For doctorate, GRE General Test. Additional exam requirements/recommendations for international students: Required—TOEFL (minimum score 577 paper-based; 90 iBT) or IELTS (minimum score 7). Electronic applications accepted. *Expenses: Tuition:* Full-time $45,760; part-time $2765 per credit. *Required fees:* $978. Full-time tuition and fees vary according to program.

Duquesne University, Graduate School of Liberal Arts, Department of Psychology, Pittsburgh, PA 15282-0001. Offers clinical psychology (PhD). *Accreditation:* APA. *Faculty:* 13 full-time (7 women). *Students:* 46 full-time (28 women), 1 (woman) part-time; includes 5 minority (1 Black or African American, non-Hispanic/Latino; 1 Asian, non-Hispanic/Latino; 2 Hispanic/Latino; 1 Two or more races, non-Hispanic/Latino), 7 international. Average age 30. 180 applicants, 4% accepted, 8 enrolled. In 2014, 5 doctorates awarded. *Degree requirements:* For doctorate, comprehensive exam, thesis/dissertation. *Entrance requirements:* For doctorate, GRE General Test, MA in psychology. Additional exam requirements/recommendations for international students: Required—TOEFL. *Application deadline:* For fall admission, 12/15 for domestic and international students. Electronic applications accepted. *Expenses: Tuition:* Full-time $18,882; part-time $1049 per credit. *Required fees:* $1800; $100 per credit. Tuition and fees vary according to program. *Financial support:* In 2014–15, 26 teaching assistantships with full tuition reimbursements (averaging $17,000 per year) were awarded; career-related internships or fieldwork, scholarships/grants, tuition waivers (partial), and unspecified assistantships also available. Financial award application deadline: 5/1. *Faculty research:* Emotion, language motivation, imagination, development. *Unit head:* Dr. Leswin Laubscher, Chair, 412-396-6520, E-mail: laubscherl@duq.edu. *Application contact:* Linda Rendulic, Assistant to the Dean, 412-396-6400, Fax: 412-396-5265, E-mail: rendulic@duq.edu.
Website: http://www.duq.edu/academics/schools/liberal-arts/graduate-school/programs/clinical-psychology

Duquesne University, School of Education, Department of Counseling, Psychology, and Special Education, Program in Counselor Education, Pittsburgh, PA 15282-0001. Offers clinical mental health counseling (MS Ed, Post-Master's Certificate); counselor education and supervision (Ed D); counselor licensure (Post-Master's Certificate); marriage and family counseling (MS Ed); school counseling (MS Ed). *Accreditation:* ACA (one or more programs are accredited). Part-time and evening/weekend programs available. *Faculty:* 9 full-time (4 women). *Students:* 165 full-time (122 women), 21 part-time (18 women); includes 38 minority (26 Black or African American, non-Hispanic/Latino; 1 American Indian or Alaska Native, non-Hispanic/Latino; 2 Asian, non-Hispanic/Latino; 4 Hispanic/Latino; 5 Two or more races, non-Hispanic/Latino), 6 international. Average age 30. 207 applicants, 43% accepted, 57 enrolled. In 2014, 42 master's, 4 doctorates awarded. *Degree requirements:* For master's, thesis optional; for doctorate, thesis/dissertation. *Entrance requirements:* For master's, letters of recommendation, essay, interview, bachelor's degree; for doctorate, GRE, letters of recommendation, essay, interview, master's degree; for Post-Master's Certificate, GRE, letters of recommendation, essay, interview, bachelor's/master's degree. Additional exam requirements/recommendations for international students: Required—TOEFL (minimum score 550 paper-based), IELTS (minimum score 7). *Application deadline:* For fall admission, 3/1 for domestic students; for spring admission, 9/1 for domestic students. Applications are processed on a rolling basis. Application fee: $0. Electronic applications accepted. *Expenses: Tuition:* Full-time $18,882; part-time $1049 per credit. *Required fees:* $1800; $100 per credit. Tuition and fees vary according to program. *Financial support:* Research assistantships, teaching assistantships, and Federal Work-Study available. Support available to part-time students. *Unit head:* Dr. Jered Kolbert, Professor/Director, 412-396-4471, Fax: 412-396-1340, E-mail: kolbertj@duq.edu. *Application contact:* Michael Dolinger, Director of Student and Academic Services, 412-396-6647, Fax: 412-396-5585, E-mail: dolingerm@duq.edu.
Website: http://www.duq.edu/academics/schools/education/graduate-programs-education/ms-ed-counselor-education

East Carolina University, Graduate School, Thomas Harriot College of Arts and Sciences, Department of Psychology, Program in Health Psychology, Greenville, NC 27858-4353. Offers clinical health psychology (PhD); occupational health psychology

(PhD); pediatric school psychology (PhD). *Entrance requirements:* For doctorate, GRE. *Expenses:* Tuition, state resident: full-time $4223. Tuition, nonresident: full-time $16,540. *Required fees:* $2184.

Eastern Illinois University, Graduate School, College of Sciences, Department of Psychology, Charleston, IL 61920. Offers clinical psychology (MA); school psychology (SSP). Part-time and evening/weekend programs available. *Faculty:* 13. *Students:* 37 full-time (23 women), 13 part-time (8 women); includes 4 minority (2 Black or African American, non-Hispanic/Latino; 1 Hispanic/Latino; 1 Two or more races, non-Hispanic/Latino), 3 international. Average age 24. 85 applicants, 21% accepted, 15 enrolled. In 2014, 5 master's, 5 other advanced degrees awarded. *Degree requirements:* For master's, comprehensive exam, thesis; for SSP, thesis. *Entrance requirements:* For master's and SSP, GMAT or GRE. Additional exam requirements/recommendations for international students: Required—TOEFL (minimum score 500 paper-based; 61 iBT), IELTS (minimum score 6). *Application deadline:* For fall admission, 5/15 for domestic and international students; for spring admission, 10/15 for domestic and international students. Applications are processed on a rolling basis. Application fee: $30. Electronic applications accepted. *Expenses:* Tuition, state resident: full-time $3113; part-time $283 per credit hour. Tuition, nonresident: full-time $7469; part-time $679 per credit hour. *Required fees:* $2287; $96 per credit hour. Tuition and fees vary according to course load. *Financial support:* In 2014–15, 41 students received support, including 4 research assistantships with full tuition reimbursements available (averaging $8,100 per year), 8 teaching assistantships with full tuition reimbursements available (averaging $8,010 per year); career-related internships or fieldwork, Federal Work-Study, and unspecified assistantships also available. Support available to part-time students. Financial award application deadline: 3/1; financial award applicants required to submit FAFSA. *Unit head:* Assege Haile Mariam, Interim Department Chair, 217-581-6615, Fax: 217-581-6764, E-mail: ahailemariam@eiu.edu. *Application contact:* Department of Psychology, 217-581-2127, Fax: 217-581-6764, E-mail: psych@eiu.edu.
Website: http://www.eiu.edu/psych/index.php

Eastern Kentucky University, The Graduate School, College of Arts and Sciences, Department of Psychology, Richmond, KY 40475-3102. Offers clinical psychology (MS); industrial/organizational psychology (MS); school psychology (Psy S). Part-time programs available. *Entrance requirements:* For master's and Psy S, GRE General Test, minimum GPA of 2.5. *Faculty research:* Autism, social psychology, parenting, assessment of depression/anxiety, reading.

Eastern Michigan University, Graduate School, College of Arts and Sciences, Department of Psychology, Ypsilanti, MI 48197. Offers clinical psychology (MS); experimental psychology (MS). *Accreditation:* APA. *Faculty:* 22 full-time (13 women). *Students:* 53 full-time (44 women), 44 part-time (31 women); includes 13 minority (1 Black or African American, non-Hispanic/Latino; 1 American Indian or Alaska Native, non-Hispanic/Latino; 5 Asian, non-Hispanic/Latino; 2 Hispanic/Latino; 4 Two or more races, non-Hispanic/Latino), 4 international. Average age 27. 248 applicants, 19% accepted, 33 enrolled. In 2014, 30 master's, 5 doctorates awarded. *Degree requirements:* For master's, 600-hour practicum; for doctorate, 1500-hour practicum; 2000-hour internship. *Entrance requirements:* For master's and doctorate, GRE. *Application deadline:* For fall admission, 2/15 for domestic students. Application fee: $45. *Financial support:* Fellowships available. *Unit head:* Dr. Carol Freedman-Doan, Department Head, 734-487-1155, Fax: 734-487-6553, E-mail: cfreedman@emich.edu.

Eastern Virginia Medical School, The Virginia Consortium Program in Clinical Psychology, Norfolk, VA 23501-1980. Offers Psy D. Program offered jointly with The College of William and Mary, Norfolk State University, and Old Dominion University. *Entrance requirements:* For doctorate, GRE, BS in behavioral sciences or equivalent. Additional exam requirements/recommendations for international students: Required—TOEFL. *Expenses:* Contact institution.

Eastern Washington University, Graduate Studies, College of Social and Behavioral Sciences and Social Work, Department of Psychology, Cheney, WA 99004-2431. Offers clinical psychology (MS); experimental psychology (MS); psychology (MS). *Degree requirements:* For master's, comprehensive exam, thesis or alternative. *Entrance requirements:* For master's, GRE General Test, minimum GPA of 3.0.

Edinboro University of Pennsylvania, Department of Counseling, School Psychology and Special Education, Edinboro, PA 16444. Offers counseling (MA), including art therapy, clinical mental health counseling, college counseling, rehabilitation counseling, school counseling; educational psychology (M Ed); school psychology (Ed S); special education (M Ed), including autism, behavior management. Part-time and evening/weekend programs available. *Degree requirements:* For master's, thesis or alternative, competency exam; for Ed S, thesis or alternative. *Entrance requirements:* For master's and Ed S, GRE or MAT, minimum QPA of 2.5. Electronic applications accepted.

Emory University, Laney Graduate School, Department of Psychology, Atlanta, GA 30322-1100. Offers clinical psychology (PhD); cognition and development (PhD); neuroscience and animal behavior (PhD). *Accreditation:* APA. *Degree requirements:* For doctorate, comprehensive exam, thesis/dissertation. *Entrance requirements:* For doctorate, GRE General Test, minimum GPA of 3.25. Additional exam requirements/recommendations for international students: Required—TOEFL. Electronic applications accepted. *Faculty research:* Neuroscience and animal behavior; adult and child psychopathology, cognition development assessment.

Emporia State University, Program in Clinical Psychology, Emporia, KS 66801-5415. Offers MS. Part-time programs available. *Students:* 18 full-time (11 women), 2 part-time (1 woman); includes 6 minority (2 Black or African American, non-Hispanic/Latino; 1 Asian, non-Hispanic/Latino; 2 Hispanic/Latino; 1 Two or more races, non-Hispanic/Latino), 3 international. 8 applicants, 100% accepted, 4 enrolled. In 2014, 7 master's awarded. *Degree requirements:* For master's, comprehensive exam, clinical internship. *Entrance requirements:* For master's, GRE or MAT, 24 hours of course work in undergraduate psychology, 3 letters of recommendation. Additional exam requirements/recommendations for international students: Required—TOEFL (minimum score 520 paper-based; 68 iBT). *Application deadline:* For fall admission, 8/15 for domestic students. Applications are processed on a rolling basis. Application fee: $30 ($75 for international students). Electronic applications accepted. *Expenses:* Tuition, state resident: part-time $227 per credit hour. Tuition, nonresident: part-time $706 per credit hour. *Required fees:* $75 per credit hour. Tuition and fees vary according to campus/location. *Financial support:* Career-related internships or fieldwork, Federal Work-Study, institutionally sponsored loans, health care benefits, and unspecified assistantships available. Support available to part-time students. Financial award application deadline: 3/15; financial award applicants required to submit FAFSA. *Unit head:* Dr. Brian W. Schrader, Chair, 620-341-5317, E-mail: schrade@emporia.edu. *Application contact:* Mary Sewell, Admissions Coordinator, 800-950-GRAD, Fax: 620-341-5909, E-mail: msewell@emporia.edu.

Evangel University, Department of Behavioral Sciences, Springfield, MO 65802. Offers clinical mental health counseling (MS). Part-time programs available. *Faculty:* 4 full-time (3 women), 2 part-time/adjunct (0 women). *Students:* 33 full-time (22 women), 20 part-time (12 women); includes 7 minority (2 Black or African American, non-Hispanic/Latino; 4 Hispanic/Latino; 1 Two or more races, non-Hispanic/Latino). Average age 35. 15 applicants, 93% accepted, 12 enrolled. In 2014, 18 master's awarded. *Degree requirements:* For master's, comprehensive exam, thesis optional. *Entrance requirements:* For master's, GRE General Test or MAT, minimum undergraduate GPA of 3.0, undergraduate major or minor in psychology. Additional exam requirements/recommendations for international students: Required—TOEFL (minimum score 550 paper-based). *Application deadline:* For fall admission, 7/15 priority date for domestic students, 8/1 for international students; for spring admission, 11/15 priority date for domestic students, 12/1 for international students. Applications are processed on a rolling basis. Application fee: $25. Electronic applications accepted. *Financial support:* In 2014–15, 6 students received support. Career-related internships or fieldwork, scholarships/grants, and unspecified assistantships available. Support available to part-time students. Financial award application deadline: 4/1; financial award applicants required to submit FAFSA. *Unit head:* Christine Arnzen, Program Coordinator, 417-865-2815 Ext. 8618, E-mail: arnzenc@evangel.edu. *Application contact:* Matt Petry, Admissions Representative, Graduate Studies, 417-865-2815 Ext. 7229, Fax: 417-575-5484, E-mail: petrym@evangel.edu.
Website: https://www.evangel.edu/departments/behavioral-social-sciences/about-the-department/

Fairfield University, Graduate School of Education and Allied Professions, Fairfield, CT 06824. Offers applied behavior analysis (ATC); applied psychology (MA); clinical mental health counseling (MA, CAS); early childhood studies (ATC); educational technology (MA); elementary education (MA, CAS); family studies (MA); integration of spirituality and religion in counseling (ATC); marriage and family therapy (MA); school counseling (MA, CAS); school psychology (MA, CAS); school-based marriage and family therapy (ATC); secondary education (MA); special education (MA, CAS); substance abuse counseling (ATC); teaching (Certificate); teaching and foundations (MA, CAS); TESOL, world languages, and bilingual education (MA, CAS). *Accreditation:* NCATE. Part-time and evening/weekend programs available. *Faculty:* 23 full-time (19 women), 32 part-time/adjunct (25 women). *Students:* 148 full-time (131 women), 286 part-time (238 women); includes 81 minority (18 Black or African American, non-Hispanic/Latino; 1 American Indian or Alaska Native, non-Hispanic/Latino; 14 Asian, non-Hispanic/Latino; 39 Hispanic/Latino; 9 Two or more races, non-Hispanic/Latino), 13 international. Average age 34. 264 applicants, 54% accepted, 68 enrolled. In 2014, 142 master's awarded. *Degree requirements:* For master's, comprehensive exam. *Entrance requirements:* For master's, PRAXIS I (for certification programs), minimum GPA of 3.0, 2 recommendations, resume. Additional exam requirements/recommendations for international students: Required—TOEFL (minimum score 550 paper-based; 84 iBT) or IELTS (minimum score 7.5). *Application deadline:* For fall admission, 2/15 for international students; for spring admission, 10/1 for international students. Application fee: $60. Electronic applications accepted. *Expenses:* Expenses: $675 per credit hour. *Financial support:* In 2014–15, 55 students received support. Career-related internships or fieldwork and unspecified assistantships available. Financial award applicants required to submit FAFSA. *Faculty research:* Literacy, spirituality, special education, bilingual/multicultural education, mentoring and professional development. *Unit head:* Dr. Robert D. Hannafin, Dean, 203-254-4250, Fax: 203-254-4241, E-mail: rhannafin@fairfield.edu. *Application contact:* Marianne Gumpper, Director of Graduate and Continuing Studies Admission, 203-254-4184, Fax: 203-254-4073, E-mail: gradadmis@fairfield.edu.
Website: http://www.fairfield.edu/academics/schoolscollegescenters/graduateschoolofeducationalliedprofessions/graduateprograms/

Fairleigh Dickinson University, College at Florham, Maxwell Becton College of Arts and Sciences, Department of Psychology, Program in Clinical Mental Health Counseling, Madison, NJ 07940-1099. Offers MA. *Accreditation:* ACA.

Fairleigh Dickinson University, Metropolitan Campus, University College: Arts, Sciences, and Professional Studies, School of Psychology, Program in Clinical Psychology, Teaneck, NJ 07666-1914. Offers MA, PhD. *Accreditation:* APA.

Fairleigh Dickinson University, Metropolitan Campus, University College: Arts, Sciences, and Professional Studies, School of Psychology, Program in Clinical Psychopharmacology, Teaneck, NJ 07666-1914. Offers MA.

Fielding Graduate University, Graduate Programs, School of Psychology, Santa Barbara, CA 93105-3814. Offers clinical psychology (PhD, Graduate Certificate), including forensic psychology (PhD), health psychology (PhD), neuropsychology (PhD), parent-infant mental health (PhD), violence prevention and control (PhD); clinical psychology respecialization (Post-Doctoral Certificate); media psychology (MA, PhD), including forensic psychology (PhD); neuropsychology (Post-Doctoral Certificate). *Accreditation:* APA. Postbaccalaureate distance learning degree programs offered (minimal on-campus study). *Faculty:* 33 full-time (21 women), 40 part-time/adjunct (20 women). *Students:* 502 full-time (366 women), 79 part-time (62 women); includes 186 minority (69 Black or African American, non-Hispanic/Latino; 8 American Indian or Alaska Native, non-Hispanic/Latino; 23 Asian, non-Hispanic/Latino; 62 Hispanic/Latino; 1 Native Hawaiian or other Pacific Islander, non-Hispanic/Latino; 23 Two or more races, non-Hispanic/Latino), 4 international. Average age 45. 215 applicants, 56% accepted, 78 enrolled. In 2014, 15 master's, 54 doctorates, 9 other advanced degrees awarded. Terminal master's awarded for partial completion of doctoral program. *Degree requirements:* For master's, thesis or alternative, capstone project; for doctorate, comprehensive exam, thesis/dissertation. *Entrance requirements:* For master's, BA from regionally-accredited institution or equivalent, minimum GPA of 2.5; for doctorate, BA or MA from regionally-accredited institution or equivalent, writing sample, minimum GPA of 3.0. *Application deadline:* For fall admission, 3/6 for domestic students, 2/6 for international students; for spring admission, 11/1 for domestic and international students; for summer admission, 3/1 for domestic students, 2/1 for international students. Application fee: $75. Electronic applications accepted. *Expenses:* Tuition: Full-time $25,650; part-time $2880 per course. Tuition and fees vary according to degree level and program. *Financial support:* In 2014–15, 88 students received support, including 14 teaching assistantships (averaging $1,200 per year); scholarships/grants, health care benefits, tuition waivers (partial), and unspecified assistantships also available. Support available to part-time students. *Unit head:* Dr. Gerald Porter, Provost and Senior Vice President, 805-898-2940, E-mail: gporter@fielding.edu. *Application contact:* Enrollment Coordinator, 800-340-1099 Ext. 4098, Fax: 805-687-9793, E-mail: psyadmissions@fielding.edu.
Website: http://www.fielding.edu/programs/psy/default.aspx

Fisk University, Division of Graduate Studies, Department of Psychology, Nashville, TN 37208-3051. Offers clinical psychology (MA); psychology (MA). *Degree requirements:* For master's, thesis. *Entrance requirements:* For master's, GRE General Test, GRE Subject Test, minimum GPA of 3.0. Electronic applications accepted. *Faculty research:* Ethnic and gender identity, development, female adolescent development, juvenile delinquency prevention.

Florida International University, College of Arts and Sciences, Department of Psychology, Miami, FL 33199. Offers behavioral analysis (MS); clinical science (PhD); counseling psychology (MS); developmental science (MS, PhD); legal psychology (PhD); organizational psychology (MS, PhD). Program has fall admissions only. Part-time and evening/weekend programs available. Terminal master's awarded for partial completion of doctoral program. *Degree requirements:* For master's, thesis; for doctorate, comprehensive exam, thesis/dissertation. *Entrance requirements:* For

master's, GRE General Test, minimum GPA of 3.0, resume, 3 letters of recommendation; for doctorate, GRE General Test, 3 letters of recommendation, resume, letter of intent, two writing samples, minimum GPA of 3.0. Additional exam requirements/recommendations for international students: Required—TOEFL (minimum score 550 paper-based; 80 iBT). Electronic applications accepted. *Faculty research:* Legal psychology, organizational and industrial psychology, child behavior psychology.

Florida International University, College of Education, Department of Leadership and Professional Studies, Miami, FL 33199. Offers adult education and human resource development (MS, Ed D); counseling (MS), including rehabilitation counseling, school counseling; counselor education (MS), including clinical mental health counseling; educational administration and supervision (Ed D); educational leadership (MS, Certificate, Ed S); higher education (Ed D); higher education administration (MS); recreation and sport management (MS), including recreation and sport management, recreational therapy; school psychology (Ed S); urban education (MS), including instruction in urban settings, learning technologies, multicultural/bilingual, multicultural/TESOL, urban education. Part-time and evening/weekend programs available. *Degree requirements:* For doctorate, thesis/dissertation. *Entrance requirements:* For master's, minimum GPA of 3.0; for doctorate and other advanced degree, GRE General Test. Additional exam requirements/recommendations for international students: Required—TOEFL (minimum score 550 paper-based; 80 iBT), IELTS (minimum score 6.3). Electronic applications accepted.

Florida State University, The Graduate School, College of Arts and Sciences, Department of Psychology, Program in Clinical Psychology, Tallahassee, FL 32306. Offers PhD. *Accreditation:* APA. *Faculty:* 11 full-time (5 women). *Students:* 55 full-time (41 women), 3 part-time (2 women); includes 10 minority (2 Black or African American, non-Hispanic/Latino; 1 American Indian or Alaska Native, non-Hispanic/Latino; 3 Asian, non-Hispanic/Latino; 4 Hispanic/Latino), 1 international. Average age 25. 322 applicants, 4% accepted, 9 enrolled. In 2014, 4 doctorates awarded. Terminal master's awarded for partial completion of doctoral program. *Degree requirements:* For doctorate, comprehensive exam, thesis/dissertation, independent project. *Entrance requirements:* For doctorate, GRE General Test, minimum GPA of 3.3, research experience, letters of recommendation. Additional exam requirements/recommendations for international students: Required—TOEFL (minimum score 550 paper-based; 80 iBT). *Application deadline:* For fall admission, 12/1 for domestic and international students. Application fee: $30. Electronic applications accepted. *Expenses:* Tuition, state resident: part-time $403.51 per credit hour. Tuition, nonresident: part-time $1004.85 per credit hour. *Required fees:* $75.81 per credit hour. One-time fee: $20 part-time. Tuition and fees vary according to campus/location. *Financial support:* In 2014–15, 55 students received support, including 7 fellowships with full tuition reimbursements available (averaging $20,000 per year), 41 research assistantships with full tuition reimbursements available (averaging $20,000 per year), 7 teaching assistantships with full tuition reimbursements available (averaging $17,775 per year); career-related internships or fieldwork, Federal Work-Study, institutionally sponsored loans, scholarships/grants, traineeships, health care benefits, tuition waivers (partial), and unspecified assistantships also available. Financial award application deadline: 12/1; financial award applicants required to submit FAFSA. *Faculty research:* Antisocial behavior, depression, addictive behavior, developmental psychopathology, anxiety. *Total annual research expenditures:* $2.1 million. *Unit head:* Dr. Pamela Keel, Director, 850-644-7243, Fax: 850-644-7739, E-mail: keel@psy.fsu.edu. *Application contact:* Cherie P. Miller, Graduate Program Assistant, 850-644-2499, Fax: 850-644-7739, E-mail: grad-info@psy.fsu.edu.
Website: http://www.psy.fsu.edu/

Fordham University, Graduate School of Arts and Sciences, Department of Psychology, Program in Clinical Psychology, New York, NY 10458. Offers PhD. *Students:* 56 full-time (40 women), 13 part-time (9 women); includes 15 minority (3 Black or African American, non-Hispanic/Latino; 1 American Indian or Alaska Native, non-Hispanic/Latino; 6 Asian, non-Hispanic/Latino; 5 Hispanic/Latino), 3 international. Average age 30. 629 applicants, 2% accepted, 9 enrolled. In 2014, 12 doctorates awarded. Terminal master's awarded for partial completion of doctoral program. *Degree requirements:* For doctorate, comprehensive exam, thesis/dissertation, clinical internship. *Entrance requirements:* For doctorate, GRE General Test, GRE Subject Test. Additional exam requirements/recommendations for international students: Required—TOEFL (minimum score 600 paper-based). *Application deadline:* For fall admission, 12/14 for domestic students. Application fee: $70. Electronic applications accepted. *Financial support:* In 2014–15, 32 students received support, including 5 fellowships with full and partial tuition reimbursements available (averaging $24,353 per year), 4 research assistantships with full and partial tuition reimbursements available (averaging $19,446 per year), 8 teaching assistantships with full and partial tuition reimbursements available (averaging $15,083 per year); career-related internships or fieldwork, institutionally sponsored loans, tuition waivers (full and partial), and unspecified assistantships also available. Financial award application deadline: 12/14. *Total annual research expenditures:* $1.9 million. *Unit head:* Dr. Barry Rosenfeld, Director, 718-817-3794, Fax: 718-817-3785, E-mail: riveramindt@fordham.edu. *Application contact:* Bernadette Valentino-Morrison, Director of Graduate Admissions, 718-817-4419, Fax: 718-817-3566, E-mail: valentinomor@fordham.edu.

Franciscan University of Steubenville, Graduate Programs, Department of Clinical Mental Health Counseling, Steubenville, OH 43952-1763. Offers MA. Part-time programs available. *Faculty:* 3 full-time (1 woman), 6 part-time/adjunct (3 women). *Students:* 38 full-time (28 women), 14 part-time (13 women); includes 14 minority (2 Black or African American, non-Hispanic/Latino; 9 Hispanic/Latino; 3 Two or more races, non-Hispanic/Latino). Average age 31. 39 applicants, 69% accepted, 22 enrolled. In 2014, 22 master's awarded. *Degree requirements:* For master's, case presentation, integrative paper. *Entrance requirements:* For master's, GRE General Test or MAT for those with a GPA below 3.0, minimum undergraduate GPA of 2.5. Additional exam requirements/recommendations for international students: Required—TOEFL. *Application deadline:* For fall admission, 7/1 for domestic students, 4/30 for international students; for spring admission, 12/15 for domestic students, 9/30 for international students. Applications are processed on a rolling basis. Application fee: $20. Electronic applications accepted. Application fee is waived when completed online. *Expenses: Tuition:* Full-time $12,330; part-time $685 per credit. *Required fees:* $288; $16 per credit. One-time fee: $170 full-time. Tuition and fees vary according to course load and program. *Financial support:* Career-related internships or fieldwork, Federal Work-Study, and scholarships/grants available. Support available to part-time students. Financial award application deadline: 7/1; financial award applicants required to submit FAFSA. *Unit head:* Dr. Christin Jungers, Program Director, 740-284-7220. *Application contact:* Mark McGuire, Director of Graduate Enrollment, 800-783-6220, Fax: 740-284-5456, E-mail: mmcguire@franciscan.edu.
Website: http://www.franciscan.edu/cmhc/

Francis Marion University, Graduate Programs, Department of Psychology, Florence, SC 29502-0547. Offers applied psychology (MS), including clinical/counseling psychology, school psychology; school psychology (SSP). Part-time and evening/weekend programs available. *Faculty:* 6 full-time (2 women), 4 part-time/adjunct (all women). *Students:* 35 full-time (30 women), 11 part-time (all women); includes 9 minority (7 Black or African American, non-Hispanic/Latino; 2 Asian, non-Hispanic/Latino), 1 international. Average age 26. 43 applicants, 100% accepted, 16 enrolled. In 2014, 15 master's, 6 other advanced degrees awarded. *Degree requirements:* For master's, internship. *Entrance requirements:* For master's, GRE General Test, official transcripts, two letters of recommendation, written statement. *Application deadline:* For fall admission, 2/15 for domestic and international students; for spring admission, 10/15 for domestic and international students. Applications are processed on a rolling basis. Application fee: $35. Electronic applications accepted. *Expenses:* Tuition, state resident: full-time $9472; part-time $473.60 per credit hour. Tuition, nonresident: full-time $18,944; part-time $947.20 per credit hour. *Required fees:* $14 per credit hour. $107 per semester. Tuition and fees vary according to course load and program. *Financial support:* In 2014–15, 4 teaching assistantships (averaging $7,750 per year) were awarded; career-related internships or fieldwork, scholarships/grants, and unspecified assistantships also available. Support available to part-time students. Financial award application deadline: 3/1; financial award applicants required to submit FAFSA. *Faculty research:* Parenting and family relationships, child development, applied behavioral analysis, post-traumatic stress disorder, clinical psychology in adults. *Unit head:* Dr. William Wattles, Chair, 843-661-1641, Fax: 843-661-1628. *Application contact:* Sharekka Bridges, Administrative Assistant, 843-661-1641, Fax: 843-661-1628.
Website: http://www.fmarion.edu/academics/psychology

Fuller Theological Seminary, Graduate Programs, Pasadena, CA 91182. Offers Christian leadership (MACL); clinical psychology (PhD, Psy D); family studies (MA); global leadership (MA); global ministries (D Min); global ministries (Korean language) (D Min); intercultural studies (MA, Th M, PhD); intercultural studies (Korean language) (MA); marital and family therapy (MS); marriage and family enrichment (Certificate); ministry (M Div, D Min); missiology (D Miss); missiology (Korean language) (Th M); theology (MA, Th M, PhD), including evangelism (MA), family life education (MA), pastoral ministry (MA), recovery ministry (MA), worship music ministry (MA), worship, theology, and the arts (MA), youth, family, and culture (MA); theology and ministry (MA).

Gallaudet University, The Graduate School, Washington, DC 20002-3625. Offers ASL/English bilingual early childhood education: birth to 5 (Certificate); audiology (Au D); clinical psychology (PhD); critical studies in the education of deaf learners (PhD); deaf and hard of hearing infants, toddlers, and their families (Certificate); deaf education (Ed S); deaf education: advanced studies (MA); deaf education: special programs (MA); deaf history (Certificate); deaf studies (MA, Certificate); educating deaf students with disabilities (Certificate); education: teacher preparation (MA), including deaf education, early childhood education and deaf education, elementary education and deaf education, secondary education and deaf education; educational neuroscience (PhD); hearing, speech and language sciences (MS, PhD); international development (MA); interpretation (MA, PhD), including combined interpreting practice and research (MA), interpreting research (MA); linguistics (MA, PhD); mental health counseling (MA); peer mentoring (Certificate); public administration (MPA); school counseling (MA); school psychology (Psy S); sign language teaching (MA); social work (MSW); speech-language pathology (MS). Part-time programs available. *Students:* 325 full-time (251 women), 118 part-time (90 women); includes 91 minority (41 Black or African American, non-Hispanic/Latino; 1 American Indian or Alaska Native, non-Hispanic/Latino; 14 Asian, non-Hispanic/Latino; 25 Hispanic/Latino; 10 Two or more races, non-Hispanic/Latino), 28 international. Average age 30. 617 applicants, 42% accepted, 171 enrolled. In 2014, 145 master's, 21 doctorates, 8 other advanced degrees awarded. Terminal master's awarded for partial completion of doctoral program. *Degree requirements:* For master's, comprehensive exam (for some programs), thesis optional; for doctorate, comprehensive exam, thesis/dissertation. *Entrance requirements:* For master's and doctorate, GRE General Test or MAT, letters of recommendation, interviews, goals statement, American Sign Language proficiency interview, written English competency. Additional exam requirements/recommendations for international students: Required—TOEFL. *Application deadline:* For fall admission, 2/15 for domestic students. Applications are processed on a rolling basis. Application fee: $75. Electronic applications accepted. *Expenses: Tuition:* Full-time $15,956; part-time $886.45 per credit hour. *Required fees:* $3404; $263 per semester. *Financial support:* Fellowships, research assistantships, teaching assistantships, career-related internships or fieldwork, Federal Work-Study, scholarships/grants, tuition waivers (partial), and unspecified assistantships available. Support available to part-time students. Financial award applicants required to submit FAFSA. *Faculty research:* Signing math dictionaries, telecommunications access, cancer genetics, linguistics, visual language and visual learning, integrated quantum materials, deaf legal discourse, advance recruitment and retention in geosciences. *Unit head:* Dr. Gaurav Mathur, Interim Dean, Graduate School and Continuing Studies, 202-250-2380, Fax: 202-651-5027, E-mail: gaurav.mathur@gallaudet.edu. *Application contact:* Wednesday Luria, Coordinator of Prospective Graduate Student Services, 202-651-5400, Fax: 202-651-5295, E-mail: graduate.school@gallaudet.edu.
Website: http://www.gallaudet.edu/x26696.xml

Gannon University, School of Graduate Studies, College of Humanities, Education, and Social Sciences, School of Humanities, Program in Clinical Mental Health Counseling, Erie, PA 16541-0001. Offers MS. *Accreditation:* ACA. Part-time and evening/weekend programs available. *Degree requirements:* For master's, thesis, internship. *Entrance requirements:* For master's, GRE, minimum GPA of 2.8, PA child abuse clearances. Additional exam requirements/recommendations for international students: Required—TOEFL (minimum score 79 iBT). Electronic applications accepted. *Faculty research:* Student learning outcomes in CACREP clinical mental health counselor education, affective forecasting and counseling outcomes in clinical mental health counseling.

Geneva College, Master of Arts in Counseling Program, Beaver Falls, PA 15010-3599. Offers clinical mental health counseling (MA); marriage and family counseling (MA); school counseling (MA). *Accreditation:* ACA. Part-time and evening/weekend programs available. *Faculty:* 6 full-time (2 women), 7 part-time/adjunct (3 women). *Students:* 53 full-time (42 women), 42 part-time (31 women); includes 8 minority (all Black or African American, non-Hispanic/Latino). Average age 34. 42 applicants, 74% accepted, 27 enrolled. In 2014, 29 master's awarded. *Degree requirements:* For master's, 50-60 credits (depending on program), practicum, internship. *Entrance requirements:* For master's, minimum GPA of 3.0 (preferred), 3 letters of recommendation, essay on career goals, resume of educational and professional experiences. Additional exam requirements/recommendations for international students: Required—TOEFL. *Application deadline:* For fall admission, 9/1 for domestic students; for spring admission, 1/10 for domestic students. Applications are processed on a rolling basis. Electronic applications accepted. *Expenses:* Expenses: Contact institution. *Financial support:* In 2014–15, 5 students received support. Research assistantships, teaching assistantships, career-related internships or fieldwork, and unspecified assistantships available. Financial award application deadline: 8/1; financial award applicants required to submit FAFSA. *Faculty research:* Blended family counseling; premarital and newlywed couples; religion in clinical supervision; conceptual mapping in research, supervision, and clinical work; Factor Analytic Study of the ROSI (Recovery Oriented System Indicators). *Unit head:* Dr. Shannon Shiderly, Program Director, 724-847-6649, Fax: 724-847-6101, E-mail: slshider@geneva.edu. *Application contact:* Marina Frazier, Graduate Program Manager, 724-847-6697, E-mail: counseling@geneva.edu.
Website: http://www.geneva.edu/page/grad_counseling

George Fox University, College of Education, Graduate Department of Counseling, Newberg, OR 97132-2697. Offers clinical mental health counseling (MA); marriage, couple and family counseling (MA, Certificate); mental health trauma (Certificate); school counseling (MA, Certificate); school psychology (Certificate, Ed S). Part-time programs available. *Degree requirements:* For master's, clinical project. *Entrance requirements:* For master's, MAT or GRE, bachelor's degree from regionally-accredited college or university, minimum cumulative GPA of 3.0, 1 professional and 1 academic reference, resume, on-campus interview, official transcripts. Additional exam requirements/recommendations for international students: Required—TOEFL (minimum score 577 paper-based; 90 iBT), IELTS (minimum score 7). Electronic applications accepted. *Expenses:* Contact institution.

George Fox University, Program in Clinical Psychology, Newberg, OR 97132-2697. Offers Psy D. *Accreditation:* APA. *Degree requirements:* For doctorate, thesis/dissertation, internship. *Entrance requirements:* For doctorate, GRE General Test, bachelor's degree from regionally-accredited university or college, minimum undergraduate GPA of 3.0 during previous 2 years, interview, official transcripts. Additional exam requirements/recommendations for international students: Required—TOEFL (minimum score 577 paper-based; 90 iBT), IELTS (minimum score 7). Electronic applications accepted. *Expenses:* Contact institution. *Faculty research:* Psychological assessment, impact of psychological services on medical outcome, spirituality and wellness, effectiveness of clinical training and supervision, shame.

The George Washington University, Columbian College of Arts and Sciences, Department of Psychology, Washington, DC 20052. Offers applied social psychology (PhD); clinical psychology (PhD); cognitive neuroscience (PhD). *Accreditation:* APA. Part-time and evening/weekend programs available. *Faculty:* 24 full-time (14 women), 1 (woman) part-time/adjunct. *Students:* 46 full-time (33 women), 24 part-time (15 women); includes 19 minority (7 Black or African American, non-Hispanic/Latino; 3 Asian, non-Hispanic/Latino; 8 Hispanic/Latino; 1 Two or more races, non-Hispanic/Latino), 8 international. Average age 28. 513 applicants, 3% accepted, 14 enrolled. In 2014, 10 doctorates awarded. *Degree requirements:* For doctorate, thesis/dissertation or alternative, general exam. *Entrance requirements:* For doctorate, GRE General Test, minimum GPA of 3.0. Additional exam requirements/recommendations for international students: Required—TOEFL (minimum score 550 paper-based; 80 iBT). *Application deadline:* For fall admission, 1/15 for domestic and international students. Application fee: $75. *Financial support:* In 2014–15, 62 students received support. Fellowships with tuition reimbursements available, teaching assistantships with tuition reimbursements available, career-related internships or fieldwork, Federal Work-Study, and tuition waivers available. *Unit head:* Dr. Paul Poppen, Chair, 202-994-6324, E-mail: pjp@gwu.edu. *Application contact:* Information Contact, 202-994-6320, Fax: 202-994-1602, E-mail: psydept@gwu.edu.
Website: http://psychology.columbian.gwu.edu/

The George Washington University, Graduate School of Education and Human Development, Department of Counseling and Human Development, Program in Clinical Mental Health Counseling, Washington, DC 20052. Offers MA. *Students:* 38 full-time (33 women), 12 part-time (10 women); includes 10 minority (6 Black or African American, non-Hispanic/Latino; 1 Asian, non-Hispanic/Latino; 3 Hispanic/Latino), 5 international. Average age 28. 111 applicants, 50% accepted, 22 enrolled. In 2014, 14 master's awarded. *Degree requirements:* For master's, internship. *Entrance requirements:* For master's, GRE or MAT, two letters of recommendation, 1- to 2-page statement of purpose, official transcripts from all institutions attended, resume. Additional exam requirements/recommendations for international students: Required—TOEFL or IELTS. *Financial support:* Fellowships available. *Unit head:* Dr. Sylvia Marotta, Professor, 202-994-6642, E-mail: syl@gwu.edu. *Application contact:* Sarah Lang, Director of Graduate Admissions, 202-994-1447, Fax: 202-994-7207, E-mail: slang@gwu.edu.
Website: http://gsehd.gwu.edu/clinical-mental-health-counseling-masters

Georgian Court University, School of Arts and Sciences, Lakewood, NJ 08701-2697. Offers applied behavior analysis (MA); Catholic school leadership (Certificate); clinical mental health counseling (MA); holistic health studies (MA, Certificate); homeland security (MS); parish administration (Certificate); pastoral ministry (Certificate); professional counseling (Certificate); religious education (Certificate); school psychology (MA, Certificate); theology (MA, Certificate). Part-time and evening/weekend programs available. *Faculty:* 19 full-time (9 women), 9 part-time/adjunct (4 women). *Students:* 87 full-time (74 women), 127 part-time (110 women); includes 47 minority (14 Black or African American, non-Hispanic/Latino; 2 Asian, non-Hispanic/Latino; 23 Hispanic/Latino; 8 Two or more races, non-Hispanic/Latino). Average age 34. In 2014, 68 master's, 11 other advanced degrees awarded. *Degree requirements:* For master's, comprehensive exam (for some programs), thesis (for some programs). *Entrance requirements:* For master's, GRE, MAT, or NTE/PRAXIS, 3 letters of recommendation. Additional exam requirements/recommendations for international students: Required—TOEFL (minimum score 550 paper-based). *Application deadline:* For fall admission, 8/1 priority date for domestic students, 4/1 for international students; for spring admission, 1/1 priority date for domestic students, 7/1 for international students. Applications are processed on a rolling basis. Application fee: $40. Electronic applications accepted. *Expenses: Tuition:* Full-time $19,752; part-time $823 per credit. *Required fees:* $948; $243 per semester hour. Tuition and fees vary according to campus/location and program. *Financial support:* Scholarships/grants, health care benefits, and unspecified assistantships available. Financial award application deadline: 4/15; financial award applicants required to submit FAFSA. *Unit head:* Dr. Rita Kipp, Dean, 732-987-2493, Fax: 732-987-2007, E-mail: rkipp@georgian.edu. *Application contact:* Patrick Givens, Interim Director of Enrollment Management, 732-987-2736, Fax: 732-987-2084, E-mail: graduateadmissions@georgian.edu.
Website: http://www.georgian.edu/arts_sciences/index.htm

Georgia State University, College of Arts and Sciences, Department of Psychology, Atlanta, GA 30302-3083. Offers clinical (PhD); cognitive sciences (PhD); community (PhD); developmental (PhD); neuropsychology and behavioral neuroscience (PhD). *Accreditation:* APA. *Faculty:* 29 full-time (17 women). *Students:* 116 full-time (95 women), 2 part-time (both women); includes 30 minority (10 Black or African American, non-Hispanic/Latino; 9 Asian, non-Hispanic/Latino; 6 Hispanic/Latino; 5 Two or more races, non-Hispanic/Latino), 10 international. Average age 28. 577 applicants, 7% accepted, 27 enrolled. In 2014, 16 doctorates awarded. *Degree requirements:* For doctorate, comprehensive exam, thesis/dissertation, residency year (for clinical only). *Entrance requirements:* For doctorate, GRE. Additional exam requirements/recommendations for international students: Required—TOEFL (minimum score 550 paper-based; 80 iBT). *Application deadline:* For fall admission, 12/1 for domestic and international students. Application fee: $50. Electronic applications accepted. *Expenses:* Tuition, state resident: full-time $6516; part-time $362 per credit hour. Tuition, nonresident: full-time $22,014; part-time $1223 per credit hour. *Required fees:* $2128 per semester. Tuition and fees vary according to course load and program. *Financial support:* In 2014–15, fellowships with full tuition reimbursements (averaging $19,282 per year), research assistantships with full tuition reimbursements (averaging $5,173 per year), teaching assistantships with full tuition reimbursements (averaging $6,389 per year) were awarded; scholarships/grants, traineeships, health care benefits, and unspecified assistantships also available. *Faculty research:* Clinical psychology,

developmental psychology, community psychology, neuropsychology and behavioral neuroscience, cognitive sciences. *Unit head:* Dr. Lisa Armistead, Chair, 404-413-6205, Fax: 404-413-6207, E-mail: lparmistead@gsu.edu. *Application contact:* Dr. Lindsey Cohen, Director of Graduate Studies, 404-413-6263, Fax: 404-413-6207, E-mail: llcohen@gsu.edu.
Website: http://psychology.gsu.edu/graduate/areas-of-study/

Grace College, Department of Counseling and Interpersonal Relations, Winona Lake, IN 46590-1294. Offers clinical mental health counseling (MA). *Accreditation:* ACA. Part-time programs available. *Degree requirements:* For master's, comprehensive exam, portfolio, internships. *Entrance requirements:* For master's, GRE, references, background check, interview, minimum GPA of 3.0. Additional exam requirements/recommendations for international students: Required—TOEFL. Electronic applications accepted. Application fee is waived when completed online. *Faculty research:* Trauma and sexual abuse.

The Graduate Center, City University of New York, Graduate Studies, Program in Psychology, New York, NY 10016-4039. Offers basic applied neurocognition (PhD); biopsychology (PhD); clinical psychology (PhD); developmental psychology (PhD); environmental psychology (PhD); experimental psychology (PhD); industrial psychology (PhD); learning processes (PhD); neuropsychology (PhD); psychology (PhD); social personality (PhD). *Degree requirements:* For doctorate, one foreign language, thesis/dissertation. *Entrance requirements:* For doctorate, GRE General Test. Additional exam requirements/recommendations for international students: Required—TOEFL. Electronic applications accepted.

Hawai`i Pacific University, College of Humanities and Social Sciences, Program in Clinical Mental Health Counseling, Honolulu, HI 96813. Offers MA. Part-time and evening/weekend programs available. *Faculty:* 5 full-time (2 women), 4 part-time/adjunct (2 women). *Students:* 33 full-time (23 women), 1 (woman) part-time; includes 16 minority (3 Black or African American, non-Hispanic/Latino; 2 Asian, non-Hispanic/Latino; 5 Hispanic/Latino; 6 Two or more races, non-Hispanic/Latino). Average age 27. 49 applicants, 49% accepted, 15 enrolled. In 2014, 10 master's awarded. *Entrance requirements:* For master's, GRE (Verbal and Quantitative), minimum cumulative undergraduate GPA of 3.0; 500-word personal statement of professional goals which addresses why the applicant wishes to pursue a mental health counseling graduate degree and description of the applicant's personal and professional goals. *Application deadline:* For fall admission, 2/15 priority date for domestic students. Applications are processed on a rolling basis. Application fee: $50. Electronic applications accepted. *Expenses: Tuition:* Full-time $15,570; part-time $865 per credit. *Required fees:* $13. One-time fee: $50. Tuition and fees vary according to course load and program. *Financial support:* In 2014–15, 17 students received support. Career-related internships or fieldwork, Federal Work-Study, scholarships/grants, tuition waivers, and unspecified assistantships available. Financial award application deadline: 3/1; financial award applicants required to submit FAFSA. *Unit head:* Dr. Michael Erickson, Department Chair, 808-356-5211, Fax: 808-544-1424, E-mail: merickson@hpu.edu. *Application contact:* Danny Lam, Assistant Director of Graduate Admissions, 808-543-8034, Fax: 808-544-0280, E-mail: grad@hpu.edu.
Website: http://www.hpu.edu/CHSS/Psychology/MA_CHMC/index.html

Hodges University, Graduate Programs, Naples, FL 34119. Offers accounting (M Acc); business administration (MBA); clinical mental health counseling (MS); health services administration (MS); information systems management (MIS); legal studies (MS); management (MSM). Part-time and evening/weekend programs available. Postbaccalaureate distance learning degree programs offered (no on-campus study). *Faculty:* 17 full-time (10 women), 4 part-time/adjunct (2 women). *Students:* 71 full-time (56 women), 133 part-time (109 women); includes 86 minority (26 Black or African American, non-Hispanic/Latino; 8 Asian, non-Hispanic/Latino; 51 Hispanic/Latino; 1 Two or more races, non-Hispanic/Latino). Average age 35. 48 applicants, 100% accepted, 48 enrolled. In 2014, 63 master's awarded. *Degree requirements:* For master's, comprehensive exam (for some programs), thesis (for some programs). *Entrance requirements:* For master's, essay. Additional exam requirements/recommendations for international students: Recommended—TOEFL. *Application deadline:* Applications are processed on a rolling basis. Application fee: $50. Electronic applications accepted. *Financial support:* Federal Work-Study and scholarships/grants available. Financial award application deadline: 7/9; financial award applicants required to submit FAFSA. *Unit head:* Dr. David Borofsky, President, 239-513-1122, Fax: 239-598-6253, E-mail: dborofsky@hodges.edu. *Application contact:* Brent Passey, Chief Admissions Officer, 239-513-1122, Fax: 239-598-6253, E-mail: bpassey@hodges.edu.

Hofstra University, College of Liberal Arts and Sciences, Programs in Psychology, Hempstead, NY 11549. Offers applied organizational psychology (PhD); clinical psychology (PhD); industrial/organizational psychology (MA); school-community psychology (Psy D). Part-time and evening/weekend programs available. *Students:* 226 full-time (146 women), 14 part-time (9 women); includes 42 minority (7 Black or African American, non-Hispanic/Latino; 2 American Indian or Alaska Native, non-Hispanic/Latino; 11 Asian, non-Hispanic/Latino; 17 Hispanic/Latino; 1 Native Hawaiian or other Pacific Islander, non-Hispanic/Latino; 4 Two or more races, non-Hispanic/Latino), 20 international. Average age 27. 313 applicants, 40% accepted, 67 enrolled. In 2014, 40 master's, 30 doctorates awarded. *Degree requirements:* For master's, comprehensive exam, thesis (for some programs), internship, minimum GPA of 3.0; for doctorate, comprehensive exam, thesis/dissertation, 1st year qualifying examination, 2nd year research project, successful practicum/externship placements, written presentation and successful oral defense of dissertation, completion of full-time internship. *Entrance requirements:* For master's, GRE General Test, minimum GPA of 3.0, essay, interview; for doctorate, GRE General Test, GRE Subject Test (psychology), 3 letters of recommendation, interview, essay, curriculum vitae. Additional exam requirements/recommendations for international students: Required—TOEFL (minimum score 550 paper-based; 80 iBT). *Application deadline:* For fall admission, 12/15 for domestic and international students. Application fee: $70 ($75 for international students). Electronic applications accepted. *Expenses: Tuition:* Full-time $20,610; part-time $1145 per credit hour. *Required fees:* $970; $165 per term. Tuition and fees vary according to program. *Financial support:* In 2014–15, 139 students received support, including 118 fellowships with full and partial tuition reimbursements available (averaging $7,236 per year), 7 research assistantships with full and partial tuition reimbursements available (averaging $5,788 per year); Federal Work-Study, institutionally sponsored loans, scholarships/grants, health care benefits, tuition waivers (full and partial), and diversity and endowed scholarships also available. Support available to part-time students. Financial award applicants required to submit FAFSA. *Faculty research:* Cognitive behavioral therapy for anxiety disorders, autism spectrum disorders, parent child interaction training (PCIT), positive organizational behavior, personnel selection and decision-making. *Unit head:* Dr. Keith Shafritz, Chairperson, 516-463-4856, Fax: 516-463-6052, E-mail: psykms@hofstra.edu. *Application contact:* Sunil Samuel, Assistant Vice President of Admissions, 516-463-4723, Fax: 516-463-4664, E-mail: graduateadmission@hofstra.edu.
Website: http://www.hofstra.edu/hclas

Howard University, Graduate School, Department of Psychology, Washington, DC 20059-0002. Offers clinical psychology (PhD); developmental psychology (PhD);

experimental psychology (PhD); neuropsychology (PhD); personality psychology (PhD); psychology (MS); social psychology (PhD). *Accreditation:* APA (one or more programs are accredited). Part-time programs available. *Degree requirements:* For master's, thesis; for doctorate, comprehensive exam, thesis/dissertation, qualifying exam. *Entrance requirements:* For master's, GRE General Test, minimum GPA of 2.5, bachelor's degree in psychology or related field; for doctorate, GRE General Test, minimum GPA of 3.0. *Faculty research:* Personality and psychophysiology, educational and social development of African-American children, child and adult psychopathology.

Husson University, Graduate Programs in Counseling and Human Relations, Bangor, ME 04401-2999. Offers clinical mental health counseling (MS); human relations (MS); pastoral counseling (MS); school counseling (MS). Part-time and evening/weekend programs available. *Faculty:* 3 full-time (2 women), 2 part-time/adjunct (both women). *Students:* 39 full-time (33 women), 25 part-time (20 women); includes 3 minority (2 Black or African American, non-Hispanic/Latino; 1 Two or more races, non-Hispanic/Latino), 2 international. Average age 34. 55 applicants, 69% accepted, 32 enrolled. In 2014, 19 master's awarded. *Degree requirements:* For master's, comprehensive exam (for some programs), thesis optional. *Entrance requirements:* For master's, GRE or MAT, BS with minimum GPA of 3.0, letters of recommendation, interview. Additional exam requirements/recommendations for international students: Required—TOEFL (minimum score 550 paper-based; 80 iBT). *Application deadline:* For fall admission, 2/1 for domestic students. Applications are processed on a rolling basis. Application fee: $50. Electronic applications accepted. *Expenses:* Expenses: Contact institution. *Financial support:* In 2014–15, 1 student received support. Federal Work-Study, scholarships/grants, and unspecified assistantships available. Financial award application deadline: 4/15; financial award applicants required to submit FAFSA. *Faculty research:* Challenges and rewards of counseling practice in rural, small town and neighborhood settings. *Unit head:* Dr. Deborah Drew, Director, Graduate Counseling Programs, 207-992-4912, Fax: 207-992-4952, E-mail: drewd@husson.edu. *Application contact:* Kristen Card, Director of Graduate Admissions, 207-404-5660, Fax: 207-941-7935, E-mail: cardk@husson.edu.
Website: http://www.husson.edu/human-relations

Idaho State University, Office of Graduate Studies, College of Arts and Letters, Department of Psychology, Program in Clinical Psychology, Pocatello, ID 83209-8112. Offers PhD. *Degree requirements:* For doctorate, comprehensive exam, thesis/dissertation, 1 year full-time clinical internship. *Entrance requirements:* For doctorate, GRE General Test, GRE Subject Test, MS in psychology. Additional exam requirements/recommendations for international students: Required—TOEFL (minimum score 550 paper-based; 80 iBT). Electronic applications accepted. *Faculty research:* Pre-adolescent behavior, substance abuse training, trauma related problems.

Illinois Institute of Technology, Graduate College, Lewis College of Human Sciences, Department of Psychology, Chicago, IL 60616. Offers clinical psychology (PhD); industrial and organizational psychology (PhD); personnel and human resource development (MS); rehabilitation and mental health counseling (MS); rehabilitation counseling education (PhD). *Accreditation:* APA (one or more programs are accredited); CORE. Part-time and evening/weekend programs available. *Faculty:* 22 full-time (11 women), 3 part-time/adjunct (2 women). *Students:* 187 full-time (139 women), 11 part-time (8 women); includes 28 minority (5 Black or African American, non-Hispanic/Latino; 1 American Indian or Alaska Native, non-Hispanic/Latino; 7 Asian, non-Hispanic/Latino; 12 Hispanic/Latino; 3 Two or more races, non-Hispanic/Latino), 19 international. Average age 30. 293 applicants, 32% accepted, 38 enrolled. In 2014, 27 master's, 4 doctorates awarded. Terminal master's awarded for partial completion of doctoral program. *Degree requirements:* For master's, thesis (for some programs); for doctorate, comprehensive exam, thesis/dissertation, 107 credit hours minimum, 1 yr full-time internship, comprehensive exam, dissertation and oral defense. *Entrance requirements:* For master's, GRE General Test (minimum score 298 Quantitative and Verbal, 3.0 Analytical Writing), minimum gpa 3.0/4.0; 3 letters of recommendation. Applicants for master's degree programs should have a bachelor's degree from an accredited institution and meet the minimum standards listed above. The exception is the masters in Rehabilitation and Mental Health Counseling; for doctorate, GRE General Test (minimum score 298 Quantitative and Verbal, 3.0 Analytical Writing), Prerequisite to admission to doctoral programs are a bachelor's or master's degree from an accredited institution, superior academic records in both undergraduate and graduate programs, and favorable academic recommendations. GRE results are required for all psychology doctoral programs. Additional exam requirements/recommendations for international students: Required—TOEFL (minimum score 550 paper-based; 80 iBT). *Application deadline:* For fall admission, 1/15 for domestic and international students. Application fee: $50. Electronic applications accepted. *Expenses: Tuition:* Full-time $22,500; part-time $1250 per credit hour. *Required fees:* $30 per course. $260 per semester. One-time fee: $235. Tuition and fees vary according to course load and program. *Financial support:* Fellowships with full and partial tuition reimbursements, research assistantships with full and partial tuition reimbursements, career-related internships or fieldwork, Federal Work-Study, institutionally sponsored loans, scholarships/grants, traineeships, health care benefits, tuition waivers (partial), and unspecified assistantships available. Support available to part-time students. Financial award application deadline: 1/15; financial award applicants required to submit FAFSA. *Faculty research:* Clinical psychology, rehabilitation and mental health counseling, industrial organizational psychology. *Unit head:* Ronald Landis, Chair, 312-567-6467, Fax: 312-567-3493, E-mail: rlandis@iit.edu. *Application contact:* Rishab Malhotra, Director, Graduate Admissions, 866-472-3448, Fax: 312-567-3138, E-mail: inquiry.grad@iit.edu.
Website: http://iit.edu/psych/

Illinois State University, Graduate School, College of Arts and Sciences, Department of Psychology, Normal, IL 61790-2200. Offers psychology (MA, MS), including clinical psychology, counseling psychology, developmental psychology, educational psychology, experimental psychology, measurement-evaluation, organizational-industrial psychology; school psychology (PhD, SSP). *Accreditation:* APA. *Degree requirements:* For master's, thesis or alternative; for doctorate, variable foreign language requirement, thesis/dissertation, 2 terms of residency, internship, practicum. *Entrance requirements:* For master's, GRE General Test, GRE Subject Test, minimum GPA of 3.0 in last 60 hours of course work; for doctorate, GRE General Test. *Faculty research:* Comprehensive evaluation system for the central region professional development grant, Illinois school psychology internship consortium, for children's sake.

Immaculata University, College of Graduate Studies, Department of Psychology, Immaculata, PA 19345. Offers clinical mental health counseling (MA); clinical psychology (Psy D); forensic psychology (Graduate Certificate); integrative psychotherapy (Graduate Certificate); neuropsychology (Graduate Certificate); psychodynamic psychotherapy (Graduate Certificate); psychological testing (Graduate Certificate); school counseling (MA, Graduate Certificate); school psychology (MA). *Accreditation:* APA. Part-time and evening/weekend programs available. Terminal master's awarded for partial completion of doctoral program. *Degree requirements:* For master's, comprehensive exam, thesis optional; for doctorate, comprehensive exam, thesis/dissertation. *Entrance requirements:* For master's, GRE General Test or MAT, minimum GPA of 3.0; for doctorate, GRE General Test or MAT, minimum GPA of 3.5. Additional exam requirements/recommendations for international students: Required—TOEFL, IELTS. Electronic applications accepted. *Faculty research:* Supervision ethics, psychology of teaching, gender.

Indiana State University, College of Graduate and Professional Studies, College of Arts and Sciences, Department of Psychology, Terre Haute, IN 47809. Offers clinical psychology (Psy D); general psychology (MA, MS). *Accreditation:* APA (one or more programs are accredited). Terminal master's awarded for partial completion of doctoral program. *Degree requirements:* For master's, thesis (for some programs); for doctorate, comprehensive exam, thesis/dissertation, internship, professional research project. *Entrance requirements:* For master's, GRE General Test, 12 semester hours of course work in psychology, minimum GPA of 2.75; for doctorate, GRE General Test, minimum GPA of 3.0. Additional exam requirements/recommendations for international students: Required—TOEFL (minimum score 550 paper-based). Electronic applications accepted.

Indiana University of Pennsylvania, School of Graduate Studies and Research, College of Education and Educational Technology, Department of Counseling, Program in Clinical Mental Health Counseling, Indiana, PA 15705-1087. Offers MA. Part-time and evening/weekend programs available. *Faculty:* 12 full-time (10 women), 6 part-time/adjunct (4 women). *Students:* 72 full-time (54 women), 32 part-time (23 women); includes 15 minority (12 Black or African American, non-Hispanic/Latino; 1 Asian, non-Hispanic/Latino; 1 Hispanic/Latino; 1 Two or more races, non-Hispanic/Latino). Average age 31. 121 applicants, 50% accepted, 45 enrolled. In 2014, 1 master's awarded. *Entrance requirements:* For master's, minimum undergraduate GPA of 2.8. Additional exam requirements/recommendations for international students: Required—TOEFL (minimum score 540 paper-based). *Application deadline:* For fall admission, 3/17 priority date for domestic students. Electronic applications accepted. *Financial support:* In 2014–15, 21 research assistantships with full and partial tuition reimbursements (averaging $1,567 per year) were awarded; fellowships with full tuition reimbursements, career-related internships or fieldwork, Federal Work-Study, scholarships/grants, and unspecified assistantships also available. Financial award application deadline: 4/15; financial award applicants required to submit FAFSA. *Unit head:* Dr. Robert Witchel, Program Coordinator, 724-357-2306, E-mail: bwitchel@iup.edu. *Application contact:* Claire Dandeneau, Program Coordinator, 724-357-4534, E-mail: cdanden@iup.edu.

Indiana University of Pennsylvania, School of Graduate Studies and Research, College of Natural Sciences and Mathematics, Department of Psychology, Program in Clinical Psychology, Indiana, PA 15705-1087. Offers Psy D. *Accreditation:* APA. Part-time programs available. *Faculty:* 12 full-time (7 women). *Students:* 52 full-time (38 women), 20 part-time (17 women); includes 12 minority (4 Asian, non-Hispanic/Latino; 4 Hispanic/Latino; 4 Two or more races, non-Hispanic/Latino), 3 international. Average age 26. 236 applicants, 14% accepted, 15 enrolled. In 2014, 12 doctorates awarded. *Degree requirements:* For doctorate, comprehensive exam, thesis/dissertation, internship, practicum. *Entrance requirements:* For doctorate, GRE General Test, minimum GPA of 3.0, 3 letters of recommendation, interview. Additional exam requirements/recommendations for international students: Required—TOEFL (minimum score 540 paper-based). *Application deadline:* For fall admission, 12/15 priority date for domestic students. Application fee: $50. Electronic applications accepted. *Financial support:* In 2014–15, 6 fellowships with full tuition reimbursements (averaging $1,695 per year), 48 research assistantships with full and partial tuition reimbursements (averaging $3,765 per year), 2 teaching assistantships with partial tuition reimbursements (averaging $23,305 per year) were awarded; career-related internships or fieldwork, Federal Work-Study, scholarships/grants, and unspecified assistantships also available. Financial award application deadline: 4/15; financial award applicants required to submit FAFSA. *Unit head:* Dr. David LaPorte, Graduate Coordinator, 724-357-2426, E-mail: laporte@iup.edu.
Website: http://www.iup.edu/upper.aspx?id=89119

Indiana University–Purdue University Indianapolis, School of Science, Department of Psychology, Indianapolis, IN 46202-3275. Offers clinical psychology (MS); industrial/organizational psychology (MS); psychobiology of addictions (PhD). *Accreditation:* APA (one or more programs are accredited). *Faculty:* 25 full-time (13 women), 2 part-time/adjunct (both women). *Students:* 51 full-time (34 women), 9 part-time (6 women); includes 10 minority (3 Black or African American, non-Hispanic/Latino; 5 Asian, non-Hispanic/Latino; 1 Hispanic/Latino; 1 Two or more races, non-Hispanic/Latino), 2 international. Average age 28. 189 applicants, 10% accepted, 19 enrolled. In 2014, 15 master's, 4 doctorates awarded. Terminal master's awarded for partial completion of doctoral program. *Degree requirements:* For master's, thesis; for doctorate, thesis/dissertation. *Entrance requirements:* For master's, GRE General Test, minimum undergraduate GPA of 3.0; for doctorate, GRE General Test, GRE Subject Test (clinical psychology), minimum undergraduate GPA of 3.2. Additional exam requirements/recommendations for international students: Required—TOEFL (minimum score 567 paper-based; 86 iBT), IELTS (minimum score 6.5). *Application deadline:* For fall admission, 12/1 priority date for domestic and international students. Application fee: $60. Electronic applications accepted. *Financial support:* In 2014–15, 3 fellowships with partial tuition reimbursements (averaging $22,500 per year) were awarded; research assistantships with partial tuition reimbursements, teaching assistantships with partial tuition reimbursements, career-related internships or fieldwork, Federal Work-Study, institutionally sponsored loans, traineeships, health care benefits, and unspecified assistantships also available. Financial award application deadline: 3/1; financial award applicants required to submit FAFSA. *Faculty research:* Severe mental illness, health psychology, neurological research, alcoholism and psychopathology, functional activities within organizations. *Unit head:* Dr. Peggy S. Stockdale, Chair, 317-278-3838, E-mail: pstockda@iupui.edu. *Application contact:* Heather Sissons, Office Manager and Graduate Coordinator, 317-274-6945, E-mail: hsissons@iupui.edu.
Website: http://www.psych.iupui.edu/

The Institute for the Psychological Sciences, Program in Clinical Psychology, Arlington, VA 30327. Offers MS, Psy D. Part-time programs available. *Degree requirements:* For master's, comprehensive exam; for doctorate, comprehensive exam, thesis/dissertation. *Entrance requirements:* For master's and doctorate, GRE. Additional exam requirements/recommendations for international students: Required—TOEFL.

Jackson State University, Graduate School, College of Liberal Arts, Department of Psychology, Jackson, MS 39217. Offers clinical psychology (PhD). *Accreditation:* APA. *Degree requirements:* For doctorate, comprehensive exam, thesis/dissertation. *Entrance requirements:* For doctorate, MAT, GRE. Additional exam requirements/recommendations for international students: Required—TOEFL (minimum score 520 paper-based; 67 iBT).

See Display on page 982 and Close-Up on page 1209.

James Madison University, The Graduate School, College of Health and Behavioral Sciences, Department of Graduate Psychology, Clinical Mental Health Counseling Program, Harrisonburg, VA 22807. Offers MA, Ed S. *Accreditation:* ACA (one or more programs are accredited). Part-time and evening/weekend programs available. *Students:* 57 full-time (40 women), 13 part-time (10 women); includes 15 minority (11 Black or African American, non-Hispanic/Latino; 3 Hispanic/Latino; 1 Two or more races, non-Hispanic/Latino), 1 international. Average age 28. 256 applicants, 21% accepted, 18 enrolled. In 2014, 30 master's, 8 other advanced degrees awarded. *Degree requirements:* For Ed S, comprehensive exam, thesis. *Application deadline:* For fall

admission, 2/1 for domestic students. Application fee: $55. Electronic applications accepted. *Expenses:* Tuition, state resident: full-time $7812; part-time $434 per credit hour. Tuition, nonresident: full-time $20,430; part-time $1135 per credit hour. *Financial support:* In 2014–15, 14 students received support. Career-related internships or fieldwork, Federal Work-Study, and 13 assistantships (averaging $7530), 1 service assistantship (averaging $7530) available. Financial award application deadline: 3/1; financial award applicants required to submit FAFSA. *Unit head:* Dr. Robin Anderson, Department Head, 540-568-3293, E-mail: ander2rd@jmu.edu. *Application contact:* Lynette D. Michael, Director of Graduate Admissions and Student Records, 540-568-6131 Ext. 6395, Fax: 540-568-7860, E-mail: michaeld@jmu.edu.
Website: http://psyc.jmu.edu/counseling/clinical/

James Madison University, The Graduate School, College of Health and Behavioral Sciences, Department of Graduate Psychology, Combined-Integrated Program in Clinical and School Psychology, Harrisonburg, VA 22807. Offers Psy D. Part-time and evening/weekend programs available. *Students:* 23 full-time (15 women); includes 4 minority (3 Black or African American, non-Hispanic/Latino; 1 Two or more races, non-Hispanic/Latino), 2 international. Average age 28. 32 applicants, 19% accepted, 6 enrolled. In 2014, 9 doctorates awarded. *Degree requirements:* For doctorate, thesis/dissertation. *Application deadline:* For fall admission, 2/1 for domestic students. Application fee: $55. Electronic applications accepted. *Expenses:* Tuition, state resident: full-time $7812; part-time $434 per credit hour. Tuition, nonresident: full-time $20,430; part-time $1135 per credit hour. *Financial support:* In 2014–15, 18 students received support, including 1 fellowship; teaching assistantships, unspecified assistantships, and 17 doctoral assistantships (averaging $14,790) also available. Financial award application deadline: 3/1; financial award applicants required to submit FAFSA. *Unit head:* Dr. Gregg R. Henriques, Graduate Program Director, 540-568-7857, E-mail: henrigg@jmu.edu. *Application contact:* Lynette D. Michael, Director of Graduate Admissions and Student Records, 540-568-6131 Ext. 6395, Fax: 540-568-7860, E-mail: michaeld@jmu.edu.
Website: http://www.psyc.jmu.edu/cipsyd/

John Brown University, Graduate Counseling Programs, Siloam Springs, AR 72761-2121. Offers clinical mental health counseling (MS); marriage and family therapy (MS); play therapy (Graduate Certificate); school counseling (MS). *Accreditation:* NCATE. Part-time and evening/weekend programs available. *Faculty:* 5 full-time (0 women), 19 part-time/adjunct (6 women). *Students:* 104 full-time (82 women), 100 part-time (75 women); includes 46 minority (15 Black or African American, non-Hispanic/Latino; 4 American Indian or Alaska Native, non-Hispanic/Latino; 3 Asian, non-Hispanic/Latino; 19 Hispanic/Latino; 5 Two or more races, non-Hispanic/Latino). Average age 33. 102 applicants, 84% accepted, 71 enrolled. *Degree requirements:* For master's, practica or internships. *Entrance requirements:* For master's, GRE (minimum score of 300), recommendation forms from three people, 200-word essay describing professional plans and reason for seeking acceptance. Additional exam requirements/recommendations for international students: Required—TOEFL (minimum score 550 paper-based; 70 iBT). *Application deadline:* Applications are processed on a rolling basis. Application fee: $35 ($100 for international students). Electronic applications accepted. *Expenses:* Expenses: $532 per credit hour. *Financial support:* Fellowships, institutionally sponsored loans, scholarships/grants, and unspecified assistantships available. Financial award applicants required to submit FAFSA. *Unit head:* Dr. John V. Carmack, Program Director, 479-524-8630, E-mail: jcarmack@jbu.edu. *Application contact:* Nikki Rader, Graduate Counseling Representative, 479-524-7425, E-mail: nikki@jbu.edu.
Website: http://www.jbu.edu/

Johns Hopkins University, Bloomberg School of Public Health, Department of Mental Health, Baltimore, MD 21218-2699. Offers children's mental health services (PhD); drug dependence epidemiology (PhD); mental health (MHS, Dr PH); psychiatric epidemiology (PhD). *Degree requirements:* For master's, thesis (for some programs); for doctorate, thesis/dissertation, 1-year full-time residency, oral and written exams. *Entrance requirements:* For master's, GRE General Test, MCAT, 3 letters of recommendation, curriculum vitae; for doctorate, GRE General Test, MCAT or GMAT, 3 letters of recommendation, curriculum vitae. Additional exam requirements/recommendations for international students: Required—TOEFL (minimum score 600 paper-based; 100 iBT). Electronic applications accepted. *Faculty research:* Etiology, development and prevention of aggressive and antisocial behavior; epidemiology of mental disorders; genetic epidemiology of mental disorders; brain and behavior.

Kean University, Nathan Weiss Graduate College, Program in Combined School and Clinical Psychology, Union, NJ 07083. Offers Psy D. Part-time programs available. *Faculty:* 7 full-time (3 women). *Students:* 19 full-time (14 women), 9 part-time (8 women); includes 4 minority (2 Black or African American, non-Hispanic/Latino; 1 Asian, non-Hispanic/Latino; 1 Hispanic/Latino), 1 international. Average age 29. *Degree requirements:* For doctorate, comprehensive exam, thesis/dissertation, externship. *Entrance requirements:* For doctorate, GRE General Test, GRE Subject Test in psychology (taken within last 5 years), minimum undergraduate GPA of 3.3, graduate 3.5; 3 letters of recommendation; personal interview; prerequisite coursework in theories of personality, abnormal psychology, tests and measurements, statistics, and experimental psychology; personal statement. Additional exam requirements/recommendations for international students: Required—TOEFL (minimum score 550 paper-based; 79 iBT). *Application deadline:* For fall admission, 2/2 for domestic and international students. Applications are processed on a rolling basis. Application fee: $75 ($150 for international students). Electronic applications accepted. *Expenses:* Expenses: Contact institution. *Financial support:* In 2014–15, 5 research assistantships with full tuition reimbursements were awarded; scholarships/grants and unspecified assistantships also available. Financial award applicants required to submit FAFSA. *Unit head:* Dr. Jennifer Block-Lerner, Program Coordinator, 908-737-5864, E-mail: jlerner@kean.edu. *Application contact:* Reenat Hasan, Admissions Counselor, 908-737-7134, Fax: 908-737-7135, E-mail: hasanr@kean.edu.
Website: http://grad.kean.edu/doctoral-programs/combined-school-and-clinical-psychology

Kean University, Nathan Weiss Graduate College, Program in Counselor Education, Union, NJ 07083. Offers alcohol and drug abuse counseling (MA); clinical mental health counseling (MA); school counseling (MA). *Accreditation:* ACA; NCATE. Part-time programs available. *Faculty:* 8 full-time (6 women). *Students:* 120 full-time (92 women), 144 part-time (122 women); includes 111 minority (47 Black or African American, non-Hispanic/Latino; 4 Asian, non-Hispanic/Latino; 58 Hispanic/Latino; 2 Two or more races, non-Hispanic/Latino), 2 international. Average age 32. 195 applicants, 48% accepted, 59 enrolled. In 2014, 62 master's awarded. *Degree requirements:* For master's, practicum, internship, portfolio. *Entrance requirements:* For master's, minimum GPA of 3.0, 2 letters of recommendation, personal statement, resume. Additional exam requirements/recommendations for international students: Required—TOEFL (minimum score 550 paper-based; 79 iBT). *Application deadline:* For fall admission, 3/2 for domestic and international students; for spring admission, 10/31 for domestic and international students. Applications are processed on a rolling basis. Application fee: $75 ($150 for international students). Electronic applications accepted. *Expenses:* Tuition, state resident: full-time $12,461; part-time $607 per credit. Tuition, nonresident:

full-time $16,889; part-time $744 per credit. *Required fees:* $3141; $143 per credit. Tuition and fees vary according to course load, degree level and program. *Financial support:* In 2014–15, 14 research assistantships with full tuition reimbursements (averaging $3,742 per year) were awarded; scholarships/grants and unspecified assistantships also available. Financial award applicants required to submit FAFSA. *Unit head:* Dr. J. Barry Mascari, Program Coordinator, 908-737-5954, E-mail: jmascari@kean.edu. *Application contact:* Steven Koch, Admissions Counselor, 908-737-7136, Fax: 908-737-7135, E-mail: skoch@kean.edu.
Website: http://grad.kean.edu/counseling

Kent State University, College of Arts and Sciences, Department of Psychological Sciences, Kent, OH 44242-0001. Offers clinical psychology (MA, PhD); experimental psychology (MA, PhD). *Accreditation:* APA (one or more programs are accredited). Part-time programs available. *Faculty:* 28 full-time (15 women). *Students:* 90 full-time (64 women), 1 part-time (0 women); includes 8 minority (4 Black or African American, non-Hispanic/Latino; 2 Asian, non-Hispanic/Latino; 2 Hispanic/Latino), 5 international. Average age 27. 858 applicants, 5% accepted, 31 enrolled. In 2014, 10 master's, 21 doctorates awarded. Terminal master's awarded for partial completion of doctoral program. *Degree requirements:* For master's, thesis; for doctorate, thesis/dissertation. *Entrance requirements:* For master's, GRE General Test, minimum GPA of 3.0, transcript, resume, statement of purpose, 3 letters of recommendation; for doctorate, GRE General Test, minimum GPA of 3.0, transcript, resume, statement of purpose, writing sample, 3 letters of recommendation. Additional exam requirements/recommendations for international students: Required—TOEFL (minimum score: paper-based 525, iBT 71), Michigan English Language Assessment Battery (minimum score of 75), IELTS (minimum score of 6.0), PTE Academic (minimum score of 48), or completion of ELS level 112 Intensive Program. *Application deadline:* For fall admission, 12/15 for domestic students, 1/1 for international students. Application fee: $45 ($70 for international students). Electronic applications accepted. *Expenses:* Tuition, state resident: full-time $8730; part-time $485 per credit hour. Tuition, nonresident: full-time $14,886; part-time $827 per credit hour. Tuition and fees vary according to campus/location and program. *Financial support:* Research assistantships with full tuition reimbursements, teaching assistantships with full tuition reimbursements, career-related internships or fieldwork, Federal Work-Study, and unspecified assistantships available. Financial award application deadline: 1/1. *Unit head:* Dr. Maria Zaragoza, Professor and Chair, 330-672-2018, E-mail: mzaragoz@kent.edu. *Application contact:* Dr. John Updegraff, Associate Professor and Graduate Coordinator, 330-672-2166, Fax: 330-672-3786, E-mail: jupdegr1@kent.edu.
Website: http://www.kent.edu/psychology/graduate-programs

Lakehead University, Graduate Studies, Department of Psychology, Thunder Bay, ON P7B 5E1, Canada. Offers clinical psychology (PhD); experimental psychology (MA). Part-time and evening/weekend programs available. *Degree requirements:* For master's, thesis optional; for doctorate, thesis/dissertation, 2 comprehensive exams, internship. *Entrance requirements:* For master's, GRE, honors degree in psychology, advanced course work in statistics, minimum B average; for doctorate, GRE, minimum B average. Additional exam requirements/recommendations for international students: Required—TOEFL. *Faculty research:* Chaos theory, health psychology, counseling psychology, gerontology, women's studies.

Lamar University, College of Graduate Studies, College of Arts and Sciences, Department of Psychology, Beaumont, TX 77710. Offers clinical psychology (MS); industrial/organizational psychology (MS). Part-time programs available. *Faculty:* 7 full-time (4 women). *Students:* 14 full-time (10 women), 8 part-time (5 women); includes 6 minority (2 Black or African American, non-Hispanic/Latino; 3 Hispanic/Latino; 1 Two or more races, non-Hispanic/Latino), 1 international. Average age 25. 14 applicants, 71% accepted, 4 enrolled. In 2014, 7 master's awarded. *Degree requirements:* For master's, thesis, practicum. *Entrance requirements:* For master's, GRE General Test, minimum GPA of 2.75 in last 60 hours of undergraduate course work. Additional exam requirements/recommendations for international students: Required—TOEFL (minimum score 550 paper-based; 79 iBT), IELTS (minimum score 6.5). *Application deadline:* For fall admission, 8/10 for domestic students, 7/1 for international students; for spring admission, 1/5 for domestic students, 12/1 for international students. Application fee: $25 ($50 for international students). *Expenses:* Tuition, state resident: full-time $5724; part-time $1908 per semester. Tuition, nonresident: full-time $12,240; part-time $4080 per semester. *Required fees:* $1940; $318 per credit hour. *Financial support:* In 2014–15, 12 students received support, including 3 teaching assistantships (averaging $4,500 per year); fellowships, research assistantships, career-related internships or fieldwork, Federal Work-Study, scholarships/grants, and tuition waivers (partial) also available. Support available to part-time students. Financial award application deadline: 4/1. *Faculty research:* Groupthink, health psychology, school psychology, behavioral neuroscience. *Unit head:* Dr. Edythe E Kirk, Interim Chair, 409-880-8285, Fax: 409-880-1710. *Application contact:* Melissa Gallien, Director, Admissions and Academic Services, 409-880-8888, Fax: 409-880-7419, E-mail: gradmissions@lamar.edu.
Website: http://artssciences.lamar.edu/psychology

Lamar University, College of Graduate Studies, College of Education and Human Development, Department of Counseling and Special Populations, Beaumont, TX 77710. Offers clinical mental health counseling (M Ed); school counseling (M Ed); special education (M Ed), including special education. *Faculty:* 21 full-time (16 women), 19 part-time/adjunct (15 women). *Students:* 12 full-time (11 women), 1,402 part-time (1,280 women); includes 618 minority (311 Black or African American, non-Hispanic/Latino; 5 American Indian or Alaska Native, non-Hispanic/Latino; 7 Asian, non-Hispanic/Latino; 273 Hispanic/Latino; 22 Two or more races, non-Hispanic/Latino), 7 international. Average age 37. 804 applicants, 88% accepted, 201 enrolled. In 2014, 412 master's awarded. *Entrance requirements:* Additional exam requirements/recommendations for international students: Required—TOEFL (minimum score 550 paper-based; 79 iBT), IELTS (minimum score 6.5). *Application deadline:* For fall admission, 8/10 for domestic students, 7/1 for international students; for spring admission, 1/5 for domestic students, 12/1 for international students. Applications are processed on a rolling basis. Application fee: $25 ($50 for international students). *Expenses:* Tuition, state resident: full-time $5724; part-time $1908 per semester. Tuition, nonresident: full-time $12,240; part-time $4080 per semester. *Required fees:* $1940; $318 per credit hour. *Unit head:* Dr. Carl J. Sheperis, Chair, 409-880-8978, Fax: 409-880-2263. *Application contact:* Melissa Gallien, Director, Admissions and Academic Services, 409-880-8888, Fax: 409-880-7419, E-mail: gradmissions@lamar.edu.
Website: http://education.lamar.edu/counseling-and-special-populations

La Salle University, School of Arts and Sciences, Program in Clinical Psychology, Philadelphia, PA 19141-1199. Offers child clinical psychology (Psy D); clinical health psychology (Psy D); clinical psychology (MA); general practice psychology (Psy D). *Accreditation:* AAMFT/COAMFTE. Part-time and evening/weekend programs available. Terminal master's awarded for partial completion of doctoral program. *Degree requirements:* For doctorate, comprehensive exam, thesis/dissertation. *Entrance requirements:* For doctorate, GRE (minimum scores of 148 on both the Verbal Reasoning and Quantitative Reasoning sections strongly recommended); GRE Subject Test in psychology for those entering with bachelor's degree, baccalaureate degree from accredited institution with major in psychology or related discipline; minimum

undergraduate GPA of 3.0, 3.2 graduate; three letters of recommendation; statement of interest and intent; curriculum vitae or resume; personal interview. Additional exam requirements/recommendations for international students: Required—TOEFL. Electronic applications accepted. Application fee is waived when completed online. *Expenses:* Contact institution.

La Salle University, School of Arts and Sciences, Program in Counseling and Family Therapy, Philadelphia, PA 19141-1199. Offers industrial/organizational management and human resources (MA); marriage and family therapy (MA); pastoral counseling (MA); professional clinical counseling (MA). *Accreditation:* APA. Part-time and evening/weekend programs available. *Degree requirements:* For master's, comprehensive exam. *Entrance requirements:* For master's, GRE or MAT (waived for applicants that already possess a master's degree in any field or for applicants that have a cumulative GPA of 3.5 or higher), minimum of 15 hours in psychology, counseling, or marriage and family studies; minimum GPA of 3.0; three letters of recommendation; personal statement; work experience (paid or volunteer). Additional exam requirements/recommendations for international students: Required—TOEFL. Electronic applications accepted. Application fee is waived when completed online. *Expenses:* Contact institution. *Faculty research:* Cognitive therapy, attribution theory, work habits, single parent families, treatment of addictions.

Lenoir-Rhyne University, Graduate Programs, School of Counseling, Programs in Counseling, Hickory, NC 28601. Offers clinical mental health counseling (MA). Part-time and evening/weekend programs available. *Faculty:* 6 full-time (4 women). *Students:* 73 full-time (62 women), 91 part-time (73 women); includes 25 minority (18 Black or African American, non-Hispanic/Latino; 1 Asian, non-Hispanic/Latino; 4 Hispanic/Latino; 2 Two or more races, non-Hispanic/Latino). Average age 32. In 2014, 34 master's awarded. *Degree requirements:* For master's, comprehensive exam, thesis optional. *Entrance requirements:* For master's, GRE General Test or MAT, writing sample; minimum undergraduate GPA of 2.7, graduate 3.0. Additional exam requirements/recommendations for international students: Required—TOEFL (minimum score 600 paper-based). *Application deadline:* Applications are processed on a rolling basis. Application fee: $35. Electronic applications accepted. *Expenses: Tuition:* Full-time $9000; part-time $500 per credit hour. Tuition and fees vary according to program. *Financial support:* Career-related internships or fieldwork available. Financial award application deadline: 3/1; financial award applicants required to submit FAFSA. *Unit head:* Dr. Amy Wood, Coordinator, 828-328-7728, Fax: 828-328-7368, E-mail: amy.wood@lr.edu. *Application contact:* Mary Ann Gosnell, 828-328-7111, E-mail: admission@lr.edu.
Website: http://www.lr.edu/academics/programs/clinical-mental-health-and-school-counseling

Lesley University, Graduate School of Arts and Social Sciences, Cambridge, MA 02138-2790. Offers clinical mental health counseling (MA), including holistic counseling, school and community counseling, trauma studies; counseling psychology (MA, CAGS), including professional counseling (MA), school counseling (MA); creative writing (MFA); expressive therapies (MA, PhD, CAGS), including art (MA), clinical mental health counseling (MA), dance (MA), expressive therapies (MA), music (MA); independent studies (CAGS); independent study (MA); intercultural relations (MA, CAGS); interdisciplinary studies (MA), including individualized studies, integrative holistic health, mindfulness studies, peace and conflict transformation, trauma sensitive assessment, intervention, and consultation, women's studies; urban environmental leadership (MA). Part-time programs available. Postbaccalaureate distance learning degree programs offered (no on-campus study). *Faculty:* 35 full-time (25 women), 115 part-time/adjunct (90 women). *Students:* 420 full-time (379 women), 514 part-time (414 women); includes 142 minority (50 Black or African American, non-Hispanic/Latino; 5 American Indian or Alaska Native, non-Hispanic/Latino; 16 Asian, non-Hispanic/Latino; 48 Hispanic/Latino; 23 Two or more races, non-Hispanic/Latino), 46 international. Average age 33. In 2014, 475 master's, 11 doctorates, 4 other advanced degrees awarded. *Degree requirements:* For master's, internship, practicum, thesis (for expressive therapies); for doctorate, thesis/dissertation, arts apprenticeship, field placement; for CAGS, thesis, internship (for counseling psychology, expressive therapies). *Entrance requirements:* For master's, MAT (counseling psychology), interview, writing samples, art portfolio; for doctorate, GRE or MAT, interview, master's degree; for CAGS, interview, master's degree. Additional exam requirements/recommendations for international students: Required—TOEFL (minimum score 550 paper-based; 80 iBT). *Application deadline:* Applications are processed on a rolling basis. Application fee: $50. Electronic applications accepted. *Financial support:* Fellowships, career-related internships or fieldwork, Federal Work-Study, scholarships/grants, tuition waivers, and unspecified assistantships available. Financial award applicants required to submit FAFSA. *Faculty research:* Psychotherapy and culture; psychotherapy and psychological trauma; women's issues in art, teaching and psychotherapy; community-based art, psycho-spiritual inquiry. *Unit head:* Dr. Catherine Koverola, Dean, 617-349-8317, Fax: 617-349-8366, E-mail: koverola@lesley.edu. *Application contact:* Martha Sheehan, Director, Graduate Admissions, 888-LESLEYU, Fax: 617-349-8313, E-mail: info@lesley.edu.
Website: http://www.lesley.edu/graduate-school-of-arts-and-social-sciences/

Lewis University, College of Arts and Sciences, Program in Clinical Mental Health Counseling, Romeoville, IL 60446. Offers child and adolescent counseling (MA); mental health counseling (MA). Part-time and evening/weekend programs available. *Students:* 19 full-time (16 women), 45 part-time (43 women); includes 20 minority (7 Black or African American, non-Hispanic/Latino; 3 Asian, non-Hispanic/Latino; 9 Hispanic/Latino; 1 Two or more races, non-Hispanic/Latino), 1 international. Average age 28. In 2014, 27 master's awarded. *Degree requirements:* For master's, comprehensive exam, thesis optional, practicum, internship. *Entrance requirements:* For master's, 15 hours of psychology, including statistics or research; 2 letters of recommendation; minimum GPA of 3.0 in last 60 hours; interview. Additional exam requirements/recommendations for international students: Required—TOEFL (minimum score 550 paper-based; 80 iBT). *Application deadline:* For fall admission, 5/1 priority date for international students; for spring admission, 11/15 priority date for international students. Applications are processed on a rolling basis. Application fee: $40. Electronic applications accepted. *Financial support:* Federal Work-Study, scholarships/grants, tuition waivers, and unspecified assistantships available. Financial award application deadline: 5/1; financial award applicants required to submit FAFSA. *Faculty research:* Cognitive development, attitude formation, juvenile delinquency, gender issues, work-family conflict. *Unit head:* Dr. Katherine Helm-Lewis, Director, 815-838-0500 Ext. 5604, Fax: 815-836-5032, E-mail: helmka@lewisu.edu. *Application contact:* Nancy Hanley, Information Contact, 815-838-0500 Ext. 5604, E-mail: hanleyna@lewisu.edu.
Website: http://www.lewisu.edu/academics/grad.htm/

Liberty University, School of Behavioral Sciences, Lynchburg, VA 24515. Offers advanced clinical skills (PhD); clinical mental health counseling (MA); counselor education and supervision (PhD); human services counseling (MA), including addictions and recovery, business, child and family law, Christian ministries, criminal justice, crisis response and trauma, executive leadership, health and wellness, life coaching, marriage and family, military resilience; marriage and family therapy (MA); military resilience (Certificate); professional counseling (MA). Part-time programs available. Postbaccalaureate distance learning degree programs offered (minimal on-campus study). *Students:* 3,009 full-time (2,433 women), 6,251 part-time (4,981 women); includes 2,959 minority (2,520 Black or African American, non-Hispanic/Latino; 49 American Indian or Alaska Native, non-Hispanic/Latino; 51 Asian, non-Hispanic/Latino; 97 Hispanic/Latino; 9 Native Hawaiian or other Pacific Islander, non-Hispanic/Latino; 233 Two or more races, non-Hispanic/Latino), 153 international. Average age 38. 6,645 applicants, 55% accepted, 2039 enrolled. In 2014, 2,410 master's, 11 doctorates, 2 other advanced degrees awarded. *Application deadline:* Applications are processed on a rolling basis. Application fee: $50. Electronic applications accepted. *Financial support:* Applicants required to submit FAFSA. *Unit head:* Dr. Ronald Hawkins, Founding Dean, School of Behavioral Sciences. *Application contact:* Jay Bridge, Director of Admissions, 800-424-9595, Fax: 800-628-7977, E-mail: gradadmissions@liberty.edu.

Lipscomb University, Department of Graduate Psychology and Counseling, Nashville, TN 37204-3951. Offers clinical mental health counseling (MS); counseling psychology (Certificate); marriage and family therapy (MMFT); psychology (MS). Part-time and evening/weekend programs available. *Faculty:* 11 full-time (3 women), 6 part-time/adjunct (2 women). *Students:* 90 full-time (70 women), 40 part-time (32 women); includes 36 minority (25 Black or African American, non-Hispanic/Latino; 1 American Indian or Alaska Native, non-Hispanic/Latino; 2 Asian, non-Hispanic/Latino; 6 Hispanic/Latino; 2 Two or more races, non-Hispanic/Latino), 1 international. Average age 29. In 2014, 66 master's awarded. *Degree requirements:* For master's, thesis (for some programs), practicum, internship, capstone. *Entrance requirements:* For master's, GRE, resume, 3 reference letters, transcripts, goals statement. Additional exam requirements/recommendations for international students: Required—TOEFL (minimum score 570 paper-based; 80 iBT). *Application deadline:* For fall admission, 7/1 for domestic students; for spring admission, 11/1 for domestic students. Applications are processed on a rolling basis. Application fee: $50 ($75 for international students). Electronic applications accepted. *Expenses:* Expenses: $898 per credit hour. *Financial support:* Scholarships/grants and unspecified assistantships available. Financial award applicants required to submit FAFSA. *Faculty research:* Cognitive psychology, neuroscience, health psychology, grief issues. *Unit head:* Dr. Shanna Ray, Director/Professor of Psychology, 615-966-5833, E-mail: shanna.ray@lipscomb.edu. *Application contact:* Kathi Johnson, Recruiting and Marketing Coordinator, 615-966-5237, E-mail: kathi.johnson@lipscomb.edu.
Website: http://www.lipscomb.edu/psychology/graduate-programs

Lock Haven University of Pennsylvania, College of Business, Information Systems and Human Services, Lock Haven, PA 17745-2390. Offers clinical mental health counseling (MS); sport science (MS). Postbaccalaureate distance learning degree programs offered (no on-campus study). *Degree requirements:* For master's, thesis. *Entrance requirements:* For master's, minimum undergraduate GPA of 3.0. Additional exam requirements/recommendations for international students: Required—TOEFL. Electronic applications accepted.

Long Island University–LIU Brooklyn, Richard L. Conolly College of Liberal Arts and Sciences, Brooklyn, NY 11201-8423. Offers clinical psychology (PhD). Part-time and evening/weekend programs available. *Faculty:* 53 full-time (22 women), 33 part-time/adjunct (18 women). *Students:* 342 full-time (242 women), 227 part-time (62 women); includes 262 minority (132 Black or African American, non-Hispanic/Latino; 36 Asian, non-Hispanic/Latino; 77 Hispanic/Latino; 17 Two or more races, non-Hispanic/Latino), 73 international. Average age 31. 867 applicants, 42% accepted, 149 enrolled. In 2014, 187 master's, 8 doctorates, 3 other advanced degrees awarded. *Degree requirements:* For doctorate, thesis/dissertation. *Entrance requirements:* For master's, 2 letters of recommendation; for doctorate, GRE Subject Test. Additional exam requirements/recommendations for international students: Required—TOEFL (minimum score 550 paper-based). *Application deadline:* For fall admission, 5/1 for international students; for spring admission, 11/1 for international students. Applications are processed on a rolling basis. Application fee: $50. Electronic applications accepted. *Expenses: Tuition:* Part-time $1132 per credit. *Required fees:* $434 per semester. *Financial support:* In 2014–15, 31 research assistantships with partial tuition reimbursements (averaging $1,500 per year), 60 teaching assistantships with full tuition reimbursements (averaging $4,000 per year) were awarded; fellowships, career-related internships or fieldwork, scholarships/grants, tuition waivers (partial), and unspecified assistantships also available. Support available to part-time students. Financial award application deadline: 8/1; financial award applicants required to submit FAFSA. *Unit head:* Dr. David Cohen, Dean, 718-488-1003. *Application contact:* Edward Dettling, Director of Graduate Admissions, 718-488-1011, Fax: 718-797-2399, E-mail: admissions@brooklyn.liu.edu.

Long Island University–LIU Post, College of Education, Information and Technology, Brookville, NY 11548-1300. Offers adolescence education (MS); art education (MS); childhood education (MS); childhood education literacy B-6 (MS); childhood/special education (MS); clinical mental health counseling (AC); early childhood education (MS); early childhood education/childhood education (MS); education (MS Ed); educational leadership (AC); educational technology (MS); information systems (MS); information technology education (MS); informational studies (PhD); public library administration (AC); student with disabilities, 7-12 generalist (AC); teaching students with speech language disabilities (MA). *Accreditation:* Teacher Education Accreditation Council. Part-time and evening/weekend programs available. *Faculty:* 62 full-time (35 women), 131 part-time/adjunct (49 women). *Students:* 422 full-time (359 women), 732 part-time (564 women); includes 257 minority (109 Black or African American, non-Hispanic/Latino; 31 Asian, non-Hispanic/Latino; 104 Hispanic/Latino; 1 Native Hawaiian or other Pacific Islander, non-Hispanic/Latino; 12 Two or more races, non-Hispanic/Latino), 44 international. Average age 31. 1,130 applicants, 65% accepted, 368 enrolled. In 2014, 366 master's, 17 doctorates, 140 other advanced degrees awarded. Terminal master's awarded for partial completion of doctoral program. *Degree requirements:* For master's, comprehensive exam (for some programs), thesis (for some programs); for doctorate, comprehensive exam, thesis/dissertation; for AC, internship. *Entrance requirements:* For master's, GRE (for some programs if GPA less than 3.0). Additional exam requirements/recommendations for international students: Required—TOEFL (minimum score 550 paper-based; 79 iBT), IELTS (minimum score 6.5). *Application deadline:* Applications are processed on a rolling basis. Application fee: $50. Electronic applications accepted. *Expenses:* Expenses: $1,132 per credit, $1,153 for speech language pathology (for master's programs); $1,505 per credit (for doctoral programs); $867 in fees for 12+ credits per term, $434 for less than 12 credits. *Financial support:* Career-related internships or fieldwork and Federal Work-Study available. Support available to part-time students. Financial award application deadline: 5/15; financial award applicants required to submit CSS PROFILE or FAFSA. *Total annual research expenditures:* $97,964. *Unit head:* Dr. Barbara Garii, Dean, 516-299-2210, Fax: 516-299-4167, E-mail: barbara.garii@liu.edu. *Application contact:* Carol Zerah, Director of Graduate and International Admissions, 516-299-2900 Ext. 3952, Fax: 516-299-3952, E-mail: enroll@cwpost.liu.edu.

Louisiana State University and Agricultural & Mechanical College, Graduate School, College of Humanities and Social Sciences, Department of Psychology, Baton Rouge, LA 70803. Offers biological psychology (MA, PhD); clinical psychology (MA, PhD); cognitive psychology (MA, PhD); developmental psychology (MA, PhD); school psychology (MA, PhD). PhD programs offered jointly with Southeastern Louisiana University. *Accreditation:* APA (one or more programs are accredited). *Faculty:* 22 full-

time (10 women). *Students:* 67 full-time (54 women), 30 part-time (21 women); includes 13 minority (4 Black or African American, non-Hispanic/Latino; 3 Asian, non-Hispanic/Latino; 3 Hispanic/Latino; 3 Two or more races, non-Hispanic/Latino), 3 international. Average age 27. 221 applicants, 10% accepted, 22 enrolled. In 2014, 13 master's, 18 doctorates awarded. Terminal master's awarded for partial completion of doctoral program. *Degree requirements:* For master's, thesis; for doctorate, thesis/dissertation, 1-year internship. *Entrance requirements:* For master's and doctorate, GRE General Test, minimum GPA of 3.0. Additional exam requirements/recommendations for international students: Required—TOEFL (minimum score 550 paper-based; 79 IBT), IELTS (minimum score 6.5), or PTE (minimum score 59). *Application deadline:* For fall admission, 1/1 priority date for domestic students, 5/15 for international students; for spring admission, 10/15 for domestic and international students; for summer admission, 5/15 for domestic students, 5/5 for international students. Applications are processed on a rolling basis. Application fee: $50 ($70 for international students). Electronic applications accepted. *Financial support:* In 2014–15, 90 students received support, including 2 fellowships (averaging $15,763 per year), 8 research assistantships with partial tuition reimbursements available (averaging $16,669 per year), 49 teaching assistantships with partial tuition reimbursements available (averaging $13,003 per year); career-related internships or fieldwork, Federal Work-Study, institutionally sponsored loans, scholarships/grants, health care benefits, and tuition waivers (full and partial) also available. Financial award applicants required to submit FAFSA. *Faculty research:* Clinical psychology, autism, anxiety, addition, neuropsychology, school psychology, cognitive psychology, experimental psychology. *Total annual research expenditures:* $986,140. *Unit head:* Dr. Robert Matthews, Chair, 225-578-8745, Fax: 225-578-4125, E-mail: psmath@lsu.edu. *Application contact:* Dr. Jason Hicks, Coordinator of Graduate Studies, 225-578-4109, Fax: 225-578-4125, E-mail: jhicks@lsu.edu.
Website: http://www.lsu.edu/psychology/graduate.html

Loyola University Chicago, Graduate School, Department of Psychology, Program in Clinical Psychology, Chicago, IL 60660. Offers MA, PhD. *Accreditation:* APA. *Faculty:* 9 full-time (7 women). *Students:* 36 full-time (30 women); includes 11 minority (3 Black or African American, non-Hispanic/Latino; 4 Asian, non-Hispanic/Latino; 4 Hispanic/Latino). Average age 27. 257 applicants, 2% accepted, 6 enrolled. In 2014, 4 master's, 1 doctorate awarded. Terminal master's awarded for partial completion of doctoral program. *Degree requirements:* For master's, thesis; for doctorate, comprehensive exam, thesis/dissertation. *Entrance requirements:* For doctorate, GRE General Test, GRE Subject Test, letters of recommendation, personal statement, curriculum vitae, transcript. Additional exam requirements/recommendations for international students: Recommended—TOEFL. *Application deadline:* For fall admission, 12/1 for domestic students. Electronic applications accepted. Application fee is waived when completed online. *Expenses: Tuition:* Full-time $17,370; part-time $965 per credit. *Required fees:* $138 per semester. *Financial support:* In 2014–15, 22 students received support, including 7 fellowships with full tuition reimbursements available (averaging $18,000 per year), 11 research assistantships with full tuition reimbursements available (averaging $18,000 per year), 5 teaching assistantships with full tuition reimbursements available (averaging $18,000 per year); career-related internships or fieldwork, scholarships/grants, and unspecified assistantships also available. Financial award application deadline: 12/1. *Faculty research:* Child and family, AIDS, ethics and professional practice, psychotherapy, stress and coping, positive youth development, pediatric psychology, adolescence, inner city youth, emerging adulthood, mental health services, exposure to violence, obesity, spina bifida, asthma. *Unit head:* Dr. Grayson Holmbeck, Director, 773-508-2967, Fax: 773-508-8713, E-mail: gholmbe@luc.edu. *Application contact:* Jacquie Hamilton, Senior Secretary, 773-508-2974, Fax: 773-508-8713, E-mail: jhamilt@luc.edu.
Website: http://www.luc.edu/psychology/clinical.shtml

Loyola University Maryland, Graduate Programs, Loyola College of Arts and Sciences, Department of Psychology, Program in Clinical Psychology, Baltimore, MD 21210-2699. Offers MS, Psy D, CAS. *Accreditation:* APA. Part-time and evening/weekend programs available. *Degree requirements:* For master's, comprehensive exam, thesis; for doctorate, thesis/dissertation. *Entrance requirements:* For master's, doctorate, and CAS, GRE General Test, GRE Subject Test (recommended), transcripts, essay, 3 letters of recommendation. Additional exam requirements/recommendations for international students: Required—TOEFL (minimum score 550 paper-based). Electronic applications accepted.

Loyola University New Orleans, College of Social Sciences, Department of Counseling, New Orleans, LA 70118-6195. Offers clinical mental health counseling (MS). Part-time and evening/weekend programs available. *Faculty:* 5 full-time (2 women), 4 part-time/adjunct (3 women). *Students:* 23 full-time (21 women), 50 part-time (44 women); includes 9 minority (4 Black or African American, non-Hispanic/Latino; 3 Asian, non-Hispanic/Latino; 1 Hispanic/Latino; 1 Two or more races, non-Hispanic/Latino), 1 international. Average age 27. 48 applicants, 46% accepted, 18 enrolled. In 2014, 16 master's awarded. *Degree requirements:* For master's, comprehensive exam, minimum GPA of 3.0 in counseling coursework. *Entrance requirements:* For master's, GRE, resume, transcripts, letters of recommendation, objective statement, degree from regionally-accredited institution, interview, writing sample. Additional exam requirements/recommendations for international students: Required—TOEFL (minimum score 550 paper-based; 79 iBT). *Application deadline:* For fall admission, 2/15 priority date for domestic and international students; for spring admission, 9/15 priority date for domestic and international students. Applications are processed on a rolling basis. Application fee: $0. Electronic applications accepted. *Financial support:* Research assistantships, career-related internships or fieldwork, Federal Work-Study, and tuition waivers (partial) available. Support available to part-time students. Financial award application deadline: 5/1; financial award applicants required to submit FAFSA. *Faculty research:* Counseling theory, spirituality issues, group counseling, multicultural applications. *Unit head:* Dr. Christine H. Ebrahim, Chair, 504-864-7840, Fax: 504-864-7844, E-mail: counselingdept@loyno.edu. *Application contact:* Dianna Whitfield, Department Assistant, 504-864-7840, Fax: 504-864-7844, E-mail: counselingdept@loyno.edu.
Website: http://css.loyno.edu/counseling

Lynchburg College, Graduate Studies, M Ed Program in Clinical Mental Health Counseling, Lynchburg, VA 24501-3199. Offers M Ed. *Accreditation:* ACA. Part-time and evening/weekend programs available. *Faculty:* 4 full-time (2 women), 2 part-time/adjunct (1 woman). *Students:* 31 full-time (29 women), 13 part-time (11 women); includes 10 minority (7 Black or African American, non-Hispanic/Latino; 1 American Indian or Alaska Native, non-Hispanic/Latino; 1 Hispanic/Latino; 1 Two or more races, non-Hispanic/Latino), 1 international. Average age 29. In 2014, 14 master's awarded. *Degree requirements:* For master's, counseling internship. *Entrance requirements:* For master's, GRE, minimum GPA of 3.0 (preferred), official transcripts (bachelor's, others as relevant), three letters of recommendation, career goals statement. Additional exam requirements/recommendations for international students: Required—TOEFL (minimum score 550 paper-based; 79 iBT), IELTS (minimum score 6.5). *Application deadline:* For fall admission, 7/31 for domestic students, 6/1 for international students; for spring admission, 11/30 for domestic students, 10/15 for international students. Applications are processed on a rolling basis. Application fee: $30. Electronic applications accepted.

Application fee is waived when completed online. *Financial support:* Fellowships, research assistantships, Federal Work-Study, scholarships/grants, health care benefits, and unspecified assistantships available. Support available to part-time students. Financial award application deadline: 7/31; financial award applicants required to submit FAFSA. *Unit head:* Dr. Michael Williams, Assistant Professor and Program Director, Counselor Education, 434-544-8150, Fax: 434-544-8150, E-mail: williams.ma1@lynchburg.edu. *Application contact:* Christine Priller, Executive Assistant, Graduate Studies, 434-544-8383, Fax: 434-544-8483, E-mail: gradstudies@lynchburg.edu.
Website: http://www.lynchburg.edu/graduate/master-of-education-in-counselor-education/clinical-mental-health-counseling

Madonna University, Department of Psychology, Livonia, MI 48150-1173. Offers clinical psychology (MSCP). Part-time and evening/weekend programs available. *Degree requirements:* For master's, thesis or alternative. *Entrance requirements:* Additional exam requirements/recommendations for international students: Required—TOEFL. Electronic applications accepted.

Marquette University, Graduate School, College of Education, Department of Counselor Education and Counseling Psychology, Milwaukee, WI 53201-1881. Offers clinical mental health counseling (MS); community counseling (MA); counseling psychology (PhD); school counseling (MA). Part-time programs available. Terminal master's awarded for partial completion of doctoral program. *Degree requirements:* For master's, comprehensive exam, thesis (for some programs); for doctorate, thesis/dissertation, qualifying exam. *Entrance requirements:* For master's, GRE General Test or MAT, official transcripts from all current and previous colleges/universities except Marquette, three letters of recommendation, statement of purpose; for doctorate, GRE General Test, MAT, sample of written work, official transcripts from all current and previous colleges/universities except Marquette, three letters of recommendation, statement of purpose, resume/curriculum vitae. Additional exam requirements/recommendations for international students: Required—TOEFL (minimum score 530 paper-based). *Faculty research:* Ethical and legal issues in education, anxiety disorders, multicultural counseling, child psychopathology, group counseling and dynamics.

Marshall University, Academic Affairs Division, College of Liberal Arts, Department of Psychology, Huntington, WV 25755. Offers clinical psychology (Certificate); psychology (MA, Psy D). *Accreditation:* APA. *Students:* 97 full-time (78 women), 18 part-time (11 women); includes 6 minority (3 Black or African American, non-Hispanic/Latino; 2 Hispanic/Latino; 1 Two or more races, non-Hispanic/Latino), 1 international. Average age 27. In 2014, 34 master's, 8 doctorates awarded. *Degree requirements:* For master's, thesis optional. *Entrance requirements:* For master's, GRE General Test or MAT. *Application deadline:* For fall admission, 3/1 for domestic students; for spring admission, 11/1 for domestic students. Application fee: $40. *Financial support:* Teaching assistantships with tuition reimbursements available. *Unit head:* Dr. Marianna Linz, Chair, 304-696-2774, E-mail: linz@marshall.edu. *Application contact:* Graduate Admissions, 304-746-1900, Fax: 304-746-1902, E-mail: services@marshall.edu.

Marymount University, School of Education and Human Services, Program in Counseling, Arlington, VA 22207-4299. Offers clinical mental health counseling (MA); counseling (Certificate); pastoral and spiritual care (MA); pastoral counseling (MA); school counseling (MA). *Accreditation:* ACA (one or more programs are accredited). Part-time and evening/weekend programs available. *Faculty:* 8 full-time (4 women), 7 part-time/adjunct (6 women). *Students:* 87 full-time (74 women), 44 part-time (37 women); includes 40 minority (14 Black or African American, non-Hispanic/Latino; 1 American Indian or Alaska Native, non-Hispanic/Latino; 6 Asian, non-Hispanic/Latino; 16 Hispanic/Latino; 3 Two or more races, non-Hispanic/Latino), 6 international. Average age 29. 87 applicants, 77% accepted, 42 enrolled. In 2014, 51 master's awarded. *Entrance requirements:* For master's, GRE, 2 letters of recommendation, interview, resume, personal statement; for Certificate, master's degree in counseling. Additional exam requirements/recommendations for international students: Required—TOEFL (minimum score 600 paper-based; 96 iBT), IELTS (minimum score 6.5). *Application deadline:* For fall admission, 2/3 priority date for domestic students, 7/1 for international students; for spring admission, 10/5 for domestic students. Application fee: $40. Electronic applications accepted. *Expenses: Tuition:* Part-time $885 per credit. *Required fees:* $10 per credit. One-time fee: $220 part-time. Tuition and fees vary according to program. *Financial support:* In 2014–15, 13 students received support, including 2 research assistantships with full and partial tuition reimbursements available, 1 teaching assistantship with full and partial tuition reimbursement available; career-related internships or fieldwork, Federal Work-Study, scholarships/grants, and unspecified assistantships also available. Support available to part-time students. Financial award applicants required to submit FAFSA. *Unit head:* Dr. Lisa Jackson-Cherry, Director, 703-284-1633, Fax: 703-284-5708, E-mail: lisa.jackson-cherry@marymount.edu. *Application contact:* Francesca Reed, Director, Graduate Admissions, 703-284-5901, Fax: 703-527-3815, E-mail: grad.admissions@marymount.edu.
Website: http://www.marymount.edu/Academics/School-of-Education-Human-Services/Graduate-Programs/Counseling-(M-A-)

Marywood University, Academic Affairs, Reap College of Education and Human Development, Department of Psychology and Counseling, Program in Clinical Psychology, Scranton, PA 18509-1598. Offers Psy D. *Accreditation:* APA. Part-time programs available. *Students:* 39 full-time (28 women), 9 part-time (all women); includes 6 minority (1 Black or African American, non-Hispanic/Latino; 4 Asian, non-Hispanic/Latino; 1 Hispanic/Latino), 1 international. Average age 26. In 2014, 12 doctorates awarded. *Application deadline:* For fall admission, 1/8 for domestic and international students. Applications are processed on a rolling basis. Application fee: $35. Electronic applications accepted. *Expenses:* Expenses: $875 per credit. *Financial support:* Application deadline: 6/30; applicants required to submit FAFSA. *Unit head:* Dr. David Renjilian, Director of Clinical Training, 570-348-6211 Ext. 2697, E-mail: renjilian@marywood.edu. *Application contact:* Tammy Manka, Associate Director of Graduate Admissions, 570-348-6211 Ext. 2322, E-mail: tmanka@marywood.edu.
Website: http://www.marywood.edu/psyd/

Marywood University, Academic Affairs, Reap College of Education and Human Development, Department of Psychology and Counseling, Program in Psychology, Scranton, PA 18509-1598. Offers clinical services (MA); general theoretical psychology (MA). Part-time programs available. *Students:* 37 full-time (27 women), 6 part-time (4 women); includes 1 minority (Two or more races, non-Hispanic/Latino), 1 international. Average age 25. In 2014, 32 master's awarded. *Application deadline:* For fall admission, 4/1 for domestic students, 3/30 for international students; for spring admission, 11/1 for domestic students, 8/31 for international students. Applications are processed on a rolling basis. Application fee: $35. Electronic applications accepted. *Expenses: Tuition:* Part-time $775 per credit. *Required fees:* $688 per semester. Tuition and fees vary according to degree level and campus/location. *Financial support:* Application deadline: 6/30; applicants required to submit FAFSA. *Unit head:* Dr. C. Estelle Campenni, Coordinator, 570-348-6211 Ext. 2320, E-mail: campenni@marywood.edu. *Application contact:* Tammy Manka, Associate Director of Graduate Admissions, 570-348-6211 Ext. 2322, E-mail: tmanka@marywood.edu.
Website: http://www.marywood.edu/psychology/psychology-ma/

Clinical Psychology

Massachusetts School of Professional Psychology, Graduate Programs, Boston, MA 02132. Offers applied psychology in higher education student personnel administration (MA); clinical psychology (Psy D); counseling psychology (MA); counseling psychology and community mental health (MA); counseling psychology and global mental health (MA); executive coaching (Graduate Certificate); forensic and counseling psychology (MA); leadership psychology (Psy D); organizational psychology (MA); primary care psychology (MA); respecialization in clinical psychology (Certificate); school psychology (Psy D); MA/CAGS. *Accreditation:* APA. *Degree requirements:* For master's, comprehensive exam (for some programs); for doctorate, thesis/dissertation (for some programs). Electronic applications accepted.

McGill University, Faculty of Graduate and Postdoctoral Studies, Faculty of Science, Department of Psychology, Montréal, QC H3A 2T5, Canada. Offers clinical psychology (PhD); experimental psychology (M Sc, MA, PhD). *Accreditation:* APA (one or more programs are accredited).

McKendree University, Graduate Programs, Master of Arts Program in Clinical Mental Health Counseling, Lebanon, IL 62254-1299. Offers MA. Part-time and evening/weekend programs available. *Degree requirements:* For master's, comprehensive exam, internship. *Entrance requirements:* For master's, official transcripts from each college or university attended, minimum undergraduate GPA of 3.0, three letters of recommendation, personal statement, completion of six undergraduate credit hours in a behavior science, curriculum vitae or resume. Electronic applications accepted.

Medaille College, Programs in Psychology, Buffalo, NY 14214-2695. Offers clinical psychology (Psy D); marriage and family therapy (MA); mental health counseling (MA); psychology (MA). Part-time and evening/weekend programs available. *Degree requirements:* For master's, comprehensive exam (for some programs), thesis (for some programs). *Entrance requirements:* For master's, GRE General Test (psychology), minimum GPA of 2.75 (psychology). Additional exam requirements/recommendations for international students: Required—TOEFL (minimum score 550 paper-based). Electronic applications accepted. *Faculty research:* Schizophrenia, Parkinson's Disease, eyewitness testimony, methodology.

Mercer University, Graduate Studies, Cecil B. Day Campus, College of Continuing and Professional Studies, Macon, GA 31207. Offers certified rehabilitation counseling (MS); clinical mental health (MS); counselor education and supervision (PhD); human services (MS); organizational leadership (MS); public safety leadership (MS); school counseling (MS). Part-time and evening/weekend programs available. Postbaccalaureate distance learning degree programs offered (minimal on-campus study). *Faculty:* 15 full-time (6 women), 23 part-time/adjunct (15 women). *Students:* 132 full-time (110 women), 230 part-time (184 women); includes 198 minority (167 Black or African American, non-Hispanic/Latino; 1 American Indian or Alaska Native, non-Hispanic/Latino; 10 Asian, non-Hispanic/Latino; 14 Hispanic/Latino; 3 Native Hawaiian or other Pacific Islander, non-Hispanic/Latino; 3 Two or more races, non-Hispanic/Latino), 3 international. Average age 32. In 2014, 126 master's, 1 doctorate awarded. *Degree requirements:* For master's, comprehensive exam (for some programs), thesis (for some programs); for doctorate, thesis/dissertation. *Entrance requirements:* For master's and doctorate, GRE or MAT. Additional exam requirements/recommendations for international students: Recommended—TOEFL (minimum score 550 paper-based; 80 iBT), IELTS (minimum score 6.5). *Application deadline:* For fall admission, 7/1 priority date for domestic and international students; for spring admission, 11/1 priority date for domestic and international students; for summer admission, 4/1 priority date for domestic and international students. Application fee: $35. Electronic applications accepted. Tuition and fees vary according to class time, degree level, campus/location and program. *Unit head:* Dr. Priscilla R. Danheiser, Dean, 678-547-6028, E-mail: danheiser_p@mercer.edu. *Application contact:* Carmen C. Jones, Associate Director of Admissions, 678-547-6346, E-mail: jones_c@mercer.edu.
Website: http://penfield.mercer.edu/programs/graduate-professional/

Messiah College, Program in Counseling, Mechanicsburg, PA 17055. Offers clinical mental health counseling (MAC); counseling (CAGS); marriage, couple, and family counseling (MAC); school counseling (MAC). *Accreditation:* ACA. Part-time programs available. Postbaccalaureate distance learning degree programs offered (no on-campus study). *Entrance requirements:* For master's, minimum undergraduate cumulative GPA of 3.0, 2 recommendations, resume or curriculum vitae, interview; for CAGS, bachelor's degree, minimum undergraduate cumulative GPA of 3.0, essay, two recommendations, resume or curriculum vitae, interview. Electronic applications accepted.

Michigan School of Professional Psychology, MA and Psy D Programs in Clinical Psychology, Farmington Hills, MI 48334. Offers MA, Psy D. Part-time programs available. *Faculty:* 9 full-time (4 women), 18 part-time/adjunct (15 women). *Students:* 93 full-time (68 women), 57 part-time (45 women); includes 31 minority (22 Black or African American, non-Hispanic/Latino; 5 Asian, non-Hispanic/Latino; 2 Hispanic/Latino; 2 Two or more races, non-Hispanic/Latino), 1 international. Average age 25. 150 applicants, 53% accepted, 60 enrolled. In 2014, 50 master's, 13 doctorates awarded. *Degree requirements:* For master's, practicum; for doctorate, comprehensive exam, thesis/dissertation, internship, practicum. *Entrance requirements:* For master's, undergraduate degree from accredited institution with minimum GPA of 2.5; major in psychology, social work, or counseling; for doctorate, GRE General Test, undergraduate degree from accredited institution with minimum GPA of 2.5; graduate degree in psychology, social work, or counseling from accredited institution with minimum GPA of 3.25; graduate-level practicum. Additional exam requirements/recommendations for international students: Required—TOEFL (minimum score 550 paper-based; 79 iBT). *Application deadline:* Applications are processed on a rolling basis. Application fee: $75. Electronic applications accepted. *Expenses:* Tuition: Full-time $28,504; part-time $12,147 per year. *Required fees:* $435 per semester. One-time fee: $75. Tuition and fees vary according to course load, degree level, program and student level. *Financial support:* In 2014–15, 6 students received support, including 3 research assistantships (averaging $1,200 per year), 4 teaching assistantships (averaging $1,200 per year); career-related internships or fieldwork, institutionally sponsored loans, scholarships/grants, and unspecified assistantships also available. Support available to part-time students. Financial award application deadline: 6/30; financial award applicants required to submit FAFSA. *Faculty research:* Qualitative research, existential, phenomenological psychology, multicultural, humanistic. *Unit head:* Dr. Lee Bach, Program Director, 248-476-1122, Fax: 248-476-1125. *Application contact:* Tori Holmes, Coordinator of Admissions and Student Engagement, 248-476-1122 Ext. 117, Fax: 248-476-1125, E-mail: tholmes@mispp.edu.
Website: http://www.mispp.edu

Middle Tennessee State University, College of Graduate Studies, College of Behavioral and Health Sciences, Department of Psychology, Murfreesboro, TN 37132. Offers clinical psychology (MA); experimental psychology (MA); industrial/organizational psychology (MA); psychology (MA, Ed S); quantitative psychology (MA); school psychology (MA). Part-time and evening/weekend programs available. Postbaccalaureate distance learning degree programs offered. *Faculty:* 37 full-time (14 women), 3 part-time/adjunct (2 women). *Students:* 66 full-time (54 women), 47 part-time (37 women); includes 15 minority (8 Black or African American, non-Hispanic/Latino; 1 American Indian or Alaska Native, non-Hispanic/Latino; 2 Asian, non-Hispanic/Latino; 3 Hispanic/Latino; 1 Two or more races, non-Hispanic/Latino), 1 international. 225 applicants, 84% accepted. In 2014, 37 master's awarded. *Degree requirements:* For

master's, comprehensive exam, thesis. *Entrance requirements:* For master's, GRE. Additional exam requirements/recommendations for international students: Required—TOEFL (minimum score 525 paper-based; 71 iBT) or IELTS (minimum score 6). *Application deadline:* For fall admission, 6/1 for domestic and international students. Applications are processed on a rolling basis. Application fee: $30. Electronic applications accepted. *Financial support:* In 2014–15, 38 students received support. Tuition waivers available. Support available to part-time students. Financial award application deadline: 4/1; financial award applicants required to submit FAFSA. *Faculty research:* Health psychology, industrial/organizational psychology, experimental psychology. *Unit head:* Dr. Greg Schmidt, Chair, 615-898-2706, Fax: 615-898-5027, E-mail: greg.schmidt@mtsu.edu. *Application contact:* Dr. Michael D. Allen, Vice Provost for Research/Dean, 615-898-2840, Fax: 615-904-8020, E-mail: michael.allen@mtsu.edu.

Midwestern State University, Billie Doris McAda Graduate School, Prothro-Yeager College of Humanities and Social Sciences, Department of Psychology, Wichita Falls, TX 76308. Offers clinical/counseling psychology (MA). Part-time and evening/weekend programs available. *Degree requirements:* For master's, one foreign language, comprehensive exam, thesis optional. *Entrance requirements:* For master's, GRE General Test, 3 recommendation forms. Additional exam requirements/recommendations for international students: Required—TOEFL (minimum score 550 paper-based). *Application deadline:* For fall admission, 7/1 priority date for domestic students, 4/1 for international students; for spring admission, 11/1 priority date for domestic students, 8/1 for international students. Applications are processed on a rolling basis. Application fee: $35 ($50 for international students). Electronic applications accepted. *Financial support:* Teaching assistantships with partial tuition reimbursements, career-related internships or fieldwork, Federal Work-Study, institutionally sponsored loans, scholarships/grants, tuition waivers (partial), and unspecified assistantships available. Support available to part-time students. Financial award application deadline: 3/1; financial award applicants required to submit FAFSA. *Faculty research:* Child assessment and treatment outcomes, Christianity as it relates to psychology, treatment of behavioral/emotional problems in childhood, people struggling with HIV/AIDS, educational psychology. *Unit head:* Barbara Waddell, Secretary, 940-397-4340, Fax: 940-397-4682, E-mail: barbara.waddell@mwsu.edu. *Application contact:* Barbara Waddell, Secretary, 940-397-4340, Fax: 940-397-4682, E-mail: barbara.waddell@mwsu.edu.
Website: http://www.mwsu.edu/academics/libarts/psychology/index

Midwestern University, Downers Grove Campus, College of Health Sciences, Illinois Campus, Program in Clinical Psychology, Downers Grove, IL 60515-1235. Offers MA, Psy D. *Degree requirements:* For doctorate, thesis/dissertation, qualifying examination. *Entrance requirements:* For master's and doctorate, GRE, minimum overall GPA of 2.75, 3 letters of recommendation. Additional exam requirements/recommendations for international students: Required—TOEFL.

Midwestern University, Glendale Campus, College of Health Sciences, Arizona Campus, Program in Clinical Psychology, Glendale, AZ 85308. Offers Psy D. *Accreditation:* APA.

Millersville University of Pennsylvania, College of Graduate and Professional Studies, School of Education, Department of Psychology, Program in Clinical Psychology, Millersville, PA 17551-0302. Offers MS. Part-time programs available. *Faculty:* 17 full-time (12 women), 10 part-time/adjunct (8 women). *Students:* 44 full-time (37 women), 22 part-time (17 women); includes 8 minority (1 Black or African American, non-Hispanic/Latino; 4 Hispanic/Latino; 3 Two or more races, non-Hispanic/Latino). Average age 26. 48 applicants, 71% accepted, 12 enrolled. In 2014, 16 master's awarded. *Degree requirements:* For master's, comprehensive exam, thesis optional, internship. *Entrance requirements:* For master's, GRE, 3 letters of recommendation; interview (in-person); official transcripts; goal statement. Additional exam requirements/recommendations for international students: Required—TOEFL (minimum score 500 paper-based, 65 iBT) or IELTS (minimum score 6). *Application deadline:* For fall admission, 1/15 for domestic and international students; for winter admission, 6/1 for domestic and international students; for spring admission, 10/1 for domestic and international students. Application fee: $40. Electronic applications accepted. *Expenses:* Tuition, state resident: full-time $8172. Tuition, nonresident: full-time $12,258. *Required fees:* $2300. Tuition and fees vary according to course load and program. *Financial support:* In 2014–15, 17 students received support, including 17 research assistantships with full tuition reimbursements available (averaging $4,547 per year); institutionally sponsored loans and unspecified assistantships also available. Support available to part-time students. Financial award application deadline: 3/15; financial award applicants required to submit FAFSA. *Faculty research:* Cognitive-behavioral treatment, counselor training and supervision, child social-emotional development, empirically supported treatments and evidence-based practices, humanistic/existential therapy, animal assisted therapy. *Unit head:* Dr. Claudia J. Haferkamp, Director, 717-871-7301, Fax: 717-871-7946, E-mail: claudia.haferkamp@millersville.edu. *Application contact:* Dr. Victor S. DeSantis, Dean of College of Graduate and Professional Studies/Associate Provost for Civic and Community Engagement, 717-871-7619, Fax: 717-871-7954, E-mail: victor.desantis@millersville.edu.
Website: http://www.millersville.edu/psychology/graduate/clinical-psychology/

Minnesota State University Mankato, College of Graduate Studies, College of Social and Behavioral Sciences, Department of Psychology, Mankato, MN 56001. Offers clinical psychology (MA); industrial/organizational psychology (MA); school psychology (Psy D). Part-time programs available. *Students:* 47 full-time (38 women), 11 part-time (9 women). *Degree requirements:* For master's, one foreign language, comprehensive exam, thesis (for some programs). *Entrance requirements:* For master's, GRE General Test, GRE Subject Test (clinical psychology), minimum GPA of 3.0 during previous 2 years, 3 letters of reference. Additional exam requirements/recommendations for international students: Required—TOEFL. *Application deadline:* For fall admission, 1/1 priority date for domestic students. Applications are processed on a rolling basis. Application fee: $40. Electronic applications accepted. *Financial support:* Research assistantships, teaching assistantships with full tuition reimbursements, career-related internships or fieldwork, Federal Work-Study, institutionally sponsored loans, and unspecified assistantships available. Support available to part-time students. Financial award application deadline: 3/15; financial award applicants required to submit FAFSA. *Faculty research:* Professional competency in hospitals, mood disturbance, 360-degree feedback, employee selection, planning fallacy. *Unit head:* Dr. Jeff Buchanan, Chairperson, 507-389-2724. *Application contact:* 507-389-2321, E-mail: grad@mnsu.edu.
Website: http://www.mnsu.edu/psych/

Mississippi State University, College of Arts and Sciences, Department of Psychology, Mississippi State, MS 39762. Offers applied cognitive science (PhD); clinical psychology (MS); experimental psychology (MS). *Faculty:* 19 full-time (7 women), 1 part-time/adjunct (0 women). *Students:* 36 full-time (23 women); includes 5 minority (2 Black or African American, non-Hispanic/Latino; 2 Asian, non-Hispanic/Latino; 1 Two or more races, non-Hispanic/Latino), 4 international. Average age 26. 64 applicants, 36% accepted, 20 enrolled. In 2014, 7 master's, 1 doctorate awarded. Terminal master's awarded for partial completion of doctoral program. *Degree*

requirements: For master's, comprehensive exam, thesis; for doctorate, thesis/dissertation, qualifying exam, comprehensive written and oral exam. *Entrance requirements:* For master's, GRE General Test, minimum GPA of 2.75 on last two years of undergraduate courses; for doctorate, GRE General Test, proficiency in at least 1 computer language, minimum GPA of 3.0. Additional exam requirements/recommendations for international students: Required—TOEFL (minimum score 477 paper-based; 53 iBT); Recommended—IELTS (minimum score 4.5). *Application deadline:* For fall admission, 1/15 priority date for domestic students, 5/1 for international students; for spring admission, 11/1 priority date for domestic students, 9/1 for international students. Applications are processed on a rolling basis. Application fee: $60. Electronic applications accepted. *Expenses:* Tuition, state resident: full-time $7140; part-time $783 per credit hour. Tuition, nonresident: full-time $18,478; part-time $2043 per credit hour. *Financial support:* In 2014–15, 6 research assistantships with full tuition reimbursements (averaging $12,729 per year), 18 teaching assistantships with full tuition reimbursements (averaging $8,808 per year) were awarded; career-related internships or fieldwork, Federal Work-Study, institutionally sponsored loans, scholarships/grants, and unspecified assistantships also available. Financial award application deadline: 4/1; financial award applicants required to submit FAFSA. *Faculty research:* Personality type, alcoholism, blindness and low vision, mental retardation, language comprehension. *Total annual research expenditures:* $1.1 million. *Unit head:* Dr. Mitchell E. Berman, Department Head, 662-325-3202, Fax: 662-325-7212, E-mail: mberman@psychology.msstate.edu. *Application contact:* Dr. Deborah Eakin, Graduate Coordinator, 662-325-3202, Fax: 662-325-7212, E-mail: grad@psychology.msstate.edu.
Website: http://www.psychology.msstate.edu/

Mississippi State University, College of Education, Department of Counseling and Educational Psychology, Mississippi State, MS 39762. Offers college/postsecondary student counseling and personnel services (PhD); counselor education (MS), including clinical mental health, college counseling, rehabilitation, school counseling, student affairs in higher education; counselor education/student counseling and guidance services (PhD); education (Ed S), including counselor education, school psychology (PhD, Ed S); educational psychology (MS, PhD), including general education psychology (MS), general educational psychology (PhD), psychometry (MS), school psychology (PhD, Ed S). *Accreditation:* ACA (one or more programs are accredited); APA; CORE (one or more programs are accredited); NCATE. Part-time programs available. Postbaccalaureate distance learning degree programs offered (minimal on-campus study). *Faculty:* 21 full-time (15 women), 2 part-time/adjunct (both women). *Students:* 124 full-time (95 women), 72 part-time (63 women); includes 59 minority (48 Black or African American, non-Hispanic/Latino; 2 American Indian or Alaska Native, non-Hispanic/Latino; 6 Asian, non-Hispanic/Latino; 2 Hispanic/Latino; 1 Two or more races, non-Hispanic/Latino), 1 international. Average age 32. 138 applicants, 57% accepted, 53 enrolled. In 2014, 55 master's, 10 doctorates, 10 other advanced degrees awarded. Terminal master's awarded for partial completion of doctoral program. *Degree requirements:* For master's, comprehensive exam, thesis optional; for doctorate, thesis/dissertation, comprehensive oral and written exam. *Entrance requirements:* For master's, GRE (taken within the last five years), BS with minimum GPA of 2.75 on last 60 hours; for doctorate, GRE, MS from CACREP- or CORE-accredited program in counseling; for Ed S, GRE, MS in counseling or related field, minimum GPA of 3.3 on all graduate work. Additional exam requirements/recommendations for international students: Required—TOEFL (minimum score 550 paper-based; 79 iBT); Recommended—IELTS (minimum score 6.5). *Application deadline:* For fall admission, 2/1 priority date for domestic and international students. Applications are processed on a rolling basis. Application fee: $60. Electronic applications accepted. *Expenses:* Tuition, state resident: full-time $7140; part-time $783 per credit hour. Tuition, nonresident: full-time $18,478; part-time $2043 per credit hour. *Financial support:* In 2014–15, 3 research assistantships (averaging $9,800 per year), 9 teaching assistantships with full tuition reimbursements (averaging $8,401 per year) were awarded; career-related internships or fieldwork, Federal Work-Study, institutionally sponsored loans, and unspecified assistantships also available. Financial award application deadline: 2/1; financial award applicants required to submit FAFSA. *Faculty research:* HIV/AIDS in college population, substance abuse in youth and college students, ADHD and conduct disorders in youth, assessment and identification of early childhood disabilities, assessment and vocational transition of the disabled. *Unit head:* Dr. David Morse, Professor and Interim Head, 662-325-3426, Fax: 662-325-3263, E-mail: dmorse@colled.msstate.edu. *Application contact:* Dr. Charles Palmer, Graduate Coordinator, Counselor Education, 662-325-7917, Fax: 662-325-3263, E-mail: cpalmer@colled.msstate.edu.
Website: http://www.cep.msstate.edu/

Missouri State University, Graduate College, College of Health and Human Services, Department of Psychology, Springfield, MO 65897. Offers clinical psychology (MS); experimental (MS). *Faculty:* 25 full-time (11 women), 4 part-time/adjunct (0 women). *Students:* 55 full-time (41 women), 7 part-time (5 women); includes 10 minority (3 Black or African American, non-Hispanic/Latino; 3 Asian, non-Hispanic/Latino; 4 Hispanic/Latino), 3 international. Average age 25. 119 applicants, 24% accepted, 23 enrolled. In 2014, 22 master's awarded. *Degree requirements:* For master's, comprehensive exam, thesis. *Entrance requirements:* For master's, GRE General Test, GRE Subject Test, minimum GPA of 3.25 in major, 3.0 overall; 20 hours of course work in psychology. Additional exam requirements/recommendations for international students: Required—TOEFL (minimum score 550 paper-based; 79 iBT). *Application deadline:* For fall admission, 3/1 priority date for domestic and international students. Application fee: $35 ($50 for international students). Electronic applications accepted. *Expenses:* Tuition, state resident: full-time $2250; part-time $250 per credit hour. Tuition, nonresident: full-time $4509; part-time $501 per credit hour. Tuition and fees vary according to course level, course load and program. *Financial support:* In 2014–15, 5 research assistantships with full tuition reimbursements (averaging $8,450 per year), 6 teaching assistantships with full tuition reimbursements (averaging $8,450 per year) were awarded; career-related internships or fieldwork, Federal Work-Study, institutionally sponsored loans, scholarships/grants, and unspecified assistantships also available. Financial award application deadline: 3/31; financial award applicants required to submit FAFSA. *Faculty research:* Work-family conflict, child forensic psychology, sports psychology, body image assessment, visual learning. *Unit head:* Dr. Robert Jones, Interim Head, 417-836-5797, Fax: 417-836-8330, E-mail: psychology@missouristate.edu. *Application contact:* Misty Stewart, Coordinator of Graduate Recruitment, 417-836-6079, Fax: 417-836-6200, E-mail: mistystewart@missouristate.edu.
Website: http://psychology.missouristate.edu/

Montclair State University, The Graduate School, College of Humanities and Social Sciences, Program in Clinical Psychology, Montclair, NJ 07043-1624. Offers MA. Part-time and evening/weekend programs available. *Students:* 12 full-time (9 women), 8 part-time (all women); includes 14 minority (4 Black or African American, non-Hispanic/Latino; 2 Asian, non-Hispanic/Latino; 7 Hispanic/Latino; 1 Two or more races, non-Hispanic/Latino). Average age 26. 94 applicants, 32% accepted, 17 enrolled. In 2014, 31 master's awarded. *Entrance requirements:* For master's, GRE General Test, 2 letters of recommendation, essay. Additional exam requirements/recommendations for international students: Required—TOEFL (minimum score 83 iBT), IELTS (minimum score 6.5). *Application deadline:* Applications are processed on a rolling basis. Application fee: $60. Electronic applications accepted. *Expenses:* Tuition, state resident: full-time $9960; part-time $553.35 per credit. Tuition, nonresident: full-time $15,074; part-time $837.43 per credit. *Required fees:* $1595; $88.63 per credit. Tuition and fees vary according to degree level and program. *Financial support:* Federal Work-Study, scholarships/grants, and unspecified assistantships available. Support available to part-time students. Financial award application deadline: 3/1; financial award applicants required to submit FAFSA. *Faculty research:* Community psychology, infant cognitive development. *Unit head:* Dr. Peter Vietze, Chairperson, 973-655-5201. *Application contact:* Amy Aiello, Director of Admissions and Operations, 973-655-5147, Fax: 973-655-7869, E-mail: graduate.school@montclair.edu.
Website: http://www.montclair.edu/chss/psychology/graduate-programs/ma-clinical-psychology-child/

Morehead State University, Graduate Programs, College of Science and Technology, Department of Psychology, Morehead, KY 40351. Offers clinical/counseling psychology (MS); general/experimental psychology (MS). Part-time and evening/weekend programs available. *Degree requirements:* For master's, comprehensive exam, thesis optional. *Entrance requirements:* For master's, GRE General Test, 18 undergraduate hours in psychology, minimum GPA of 3.0, 3 letters of recommendation. Additional exam requirements/recommendations for international students: Required—TOEFL (minimum score 500 paper-based). Electronic applications accepted. *Faculty research:* Mood induction effects, serotonin receptor activity, stress, perceptual processes.

Mount Mary University, Graduate Division, Program in Counseling, Milwaukee, WI 53222-4597. Offers clinical mental health counseling (MS, Certificate); school counseling (MS, Certificate). Part-time and evening/weekend programs available. *Faculty:* 5 full-time (all women), 14 part-time/adjunct (12 women). *Students:* 97 full-time (90 women), 31 part-time (28 women); includes 46 minority (29 Black or African American, non-Hispanic/Latino; 1 American Indian or Alaska Native, non-Hispanic/Latino; 1 Asian, non-Hispanic/Latino; 8 Hispanic/Latino; 1 Native Hawaiian or other Pacific Islander, non-Hispanic/Latino; 6 Two or more races, non-Hispanic/Latino), 1 international. Average age 32. 64 applicants, 59% accepted, 18 enrolled. In 2014, 43 master's, 2 other advanced degrees awarded. *Degree requirements:* For master's, comprehensive exam, thesis or alternative. *Entrance requirements:* For master's, minimum GPA of 3.0. Additional exam requirements/recommendations for international students: Required—TOEFL (minimum score 550 paper-based, 80 iBT) or IELTS (minimum score 6.5). *Application deadline:* For fall admission, 5/1 for domestic and international students; for spring admission, 10/1 for domestic and international students; for summer admission, 4/15 for domestic and international students. Applications are processed on a rolling basis. Application fee: $50 ($0 for international students). Electronic applications accepted. *Expenses:* Expenses: Contact institution. *Financial support:* Career-related internships or fieldwork, Federal Work-Study, and unspecified assistantships available. Support available to part-time students. Financial award application deadline: 5/1; financial award applicants required to submit FAFSA. *Faculty research:* Cognitive behavioral interventions for depression, eating disorders and compliance. *Unit head:* Dr. Carrie King, Graduate Program Director, 414-258-4810 Ext. 318, E-mail: kingc@mtmary.edu. *Application contact:* Dr. Douglas J. Mickelson, Dean for Graduate Education, 414-256-1252, Fax: 414-256-0167, E-mail: mickelsd@mtmary.edu.
Website: http://www.mtmary.edu/majors-programs/graduate/counseling/index.html

Murray State University, College of Humanities and Fine Arts, Program in Psychology, Murray, KY 42071. Offers clinical psychology (MA, MS); psychology (MA, MS). Part-time programs available. *Degree requirements:* For master's, one foreign language, comprehensive exam (for some programs), thesis. *Entrance requirements:* For master's, GRE General Test. Additional exam requirements/recommendations for international students: Required—TOEFL.

National University, Academic Affairs, College of Letters and Sciences, La Jolla, CA 92037-1011. Offers applied linguistics (MA); biology (MS); counseling psychology (MA), including licensed professional clinical counseling, marriage and family therapy; creative writing (MFA); English (MA), including Gothic studies, rhetoric; film studies (MA); forensic and crime science (Certificate); forensic studies (MFS), including criminalistics, investigation; history (MA); human behavior (MA); mathematics for educators (MS); performance psychology (MA); strategic communications (MA). Part-time and evening/weekend programs available. Postbaccalaureate distance learning degree programs offered (no on-campus study). *Faculty:* 69 full-time (34 women), 100 part-time/adjunct (55 women). *Students:* 727 full-time (532 women), 349 part-time (240 women); includes 505 minority (128 Black or African American, non-Hispanic/Latino; 5 American Indian or Alaska Native, non-Hispanic/Latino; 52 Asian, non-Hispanic/Latino; 260 Hispanic/Latino; 9 Native Hawaiian or other Pacific Islander, non-Hispanic/Latino; 51 Two or more races, non-Hispanic/Latino), 4 international. Average age 34. In 2014, 569 master's awarded. *Degree requirements:* For master's, thesis (for some programs). *Entrance requirements:* For master's, interview, minimum GPA of 2.5. Additional exam requirements/recommendations for international students: Required—TOEFL (minimum score 550 paper-based; 79 iBT), IELTS (minimum score 6). *Application deadline:* Applications are processed on a rolling basis. Application fee: $60 ($65 for international students). Electronic applications accepted. *Expenses: Tuition:* Full-time $14,184; part-time $1773 per course. *Financial support:* Career-related internships or fieldwork, institutionally sponsored loans, scholarships/grants, and tuition waivers (partial) available. Support available to part-time students. Financial award application deadline: 6/30; financial award applicants required to submit FAFSA. *Unit head:* College of Letters and Sciences, 800-628-8648, E-mail: cols@nu.edu. *Application contact:* Frank Rojas, Interim Vice President for Enrollment Services, 800-628-8648, E-mail: advisor@nu.edu.
Website: http://www.nu.edu/OurPrograms/CollegeOfLettersAndSciences.html

New Mexico Highlands University, Graduate Studies, College of Arts and Sciences, Department of Social and Behavioral Sciences, Las Vegas, NM 87701. Offers psychology (MS), including clinical psychology/counseling, general psychology; public affairs (MA), including applied sociology; Southwest studies (MA), including anthropology. Part-time programs available. *Faculty:* 11 full-time (5 women), 3 part-time/adjunct (all women). *Students:* 24 full-time (16 women), 19 part-time (14 women); includes 27 minority (3 Black or African American, non-Hispanic/Latino; 1 American Indian or Alaska Native, non-Hispanic/Latino; 23 Hispanic/Latino), 2 international. Average age 33. 45 applicants, 33% accepted, 15 enrolled. In 2014, 7 master's awarded. *Degree requirements:* For master's, comprehensive exam, thesis or alternative. *Entrance requirements:* For master's, minimum undergraduate GPA of 3.0. Additional exam requirements/recommendations for international students: Required—TOEFL (minimum score 540 paper-based). *Application deadline:* For fall admission, 8/1 priority date for domestic students. Applications are processed on a rolling basis. Application fee: $15. *Financial support:* In 2014–15, 34 teaching assistantships were awarded; career-related internships or fieldwork, Federal Work-Study, institutionally sponsored loans, scholarships/grants, tuition waivers (full and partial), and unspecified assistantships available. Support available to part-time students. Financial award application deadline: 3/1; financial award applicants required to submit FAFSA. *Faculty research:* Southwest Native American resettlement development, community-level interventions, neurochemistry of personality, comparative criminal justice, social theory

and activism. *Unit head:* Dr. Tom Ward, Program Coordinator, 505-454-3196, E-mail: tsward@nmhu.edu. *Application contact:* Diane Trujillo, Administrative Assistant for Graduate Studies, 505-454-3266, Fax: 505-426-2117, E-mail: dtrujillo@nmhu.edu.

The New School, The New School for Social Research, Department of Psychology, New York, NY 10011. Offers clinical psychology (PhD); cognitive, social and developmental psychology (PhD); general psychology (MA). *Accreditation:* APA (one or more programs are accredited). Part-time programs available. Terminal master's awarded for partial completion of doctoral program. *Degree requirements:* For master's, comprehensive exam (for some programs), thesis (for some programs); for doctorate, thesis/dissertation, qualifying exam. *Entrance requirements:* For master's, GRE General Test; for doctorate, GRE General Test, MA. Additional exam requirements/recommendations for international students: Required—TOEFL (minimum score 600 paper-based; 100 iBT). Electronic applications accepted. *Faculty research:* Consciousness, memory, language, perceptions, psychopathology.

Norfolk State University, School of Graduate Studies, School of Liberal Arts, Department of Psychology, Program in Community/Clinical Psychology, Norfolk, VA 23504. Offers MA. *Degree requirements:* For master's, comprehensive exam, thesis or alternative. *Entrance requirements:* For master's, minimum GPA of 2.7.

North Dakota State University, College of Graduate and Interdisciplinary Studies, College of Science and Mathematics, Department of Psychology, Fargo, ND 58108. Offers clinical psychology (MS); cognitive and visual neuroscience (PhD); health and social psychology (PhD); psychology (MS). *Degree requirements:* For master's, thesis; for doctorate, thesis/dissertation. *Entrance requirements:* For master's and doctorate, GRE General Test, GRE Subject Test. Additional exam requirements/recommendations for international students: Required—TOEFL (minimum score 525 paper-based; 71 iBT). Electronic applications accepted. *Faculty research:* Cognition science, neuropsychology, group behavior, applied behavior analysis, behavior therapy.

Northern Arizona University, Graduate College, College of Social and Behavioral Sciences, Department of Psychology, Flagstaff, AZ 86011. Offers clinical health psychology (MA); general psychology (MA); teaching psychology (MA). Part-time programs available. *Degree requirements:* For master's, comprehensive exam (for some programs), thesis (for some programs), oral defense. *Entrance requirements:* For master's, GRE General Test. Additional exam requirements/recommendations for international students: Required—TOEFL (minimum score 550 paper-based; 80 iBT), IELTS (minimum score 7). Electronic applications accepted.

Northern Kentucky University, Office of Graduate Programs, College of Education and Human Services, Clinical Mental Health Counseling Program, Highland Heights, KY 41099. Offers MS. *Accreditation:* ACA. Part-time and evening/weekend programs available. *Faculty:* 7 full-time (3 women), 2 part-time/adjunct (1 woman). *Students:* 30 full-time (28 women), 30 part-time (27 women); includes 5 minority (all Black or African American, non-Hispanic/Latino). Average age 29. 40 applicants, 60% accepted, 14 enrolled. In 2014, 19 master's awarded. *Degree requirements:* For master's, comprehensive exam. *Entrance requirements:* For master's, GRE or MAT. Additional exam requirements/recommendations for international students: Required—TOEFL (minimum score 550 paper-based; 79 iBT); Recommended—IELTS (minimum score 6.5). *Application deadline:* For fall admission, 2/1 priority date for domestic students, 6/1 priority date for international students; for spring admission, 11/1 for domestic students, 10/1 for international students; for summer admission, 2/1 priority date for domestic students, 6/1 priority date for international students. Application fee: $40. Electronic applications accepted. *Expenses: Tuition, area resident:* Part-time $518 per credit hour. Tuition, state resident: part-time $630 per credit hour. Tuition, nonresident: part-time $797 per credit hour. *Required fees:* $192 per semester. Tuition and fees vary according to course load, degree level, campus/location, program and reciprocity agreements. *Financial support:* In 2014–15, 7 students received support. Applicants required to submit FAFSA. *Faculty research:* Preferences for college counseling, accreditation, partner violence prevention, data-based school counseling, creativity in counseling. *Unit head:* Dr. Greg Hatchett, Program Director, 859-572-6195, Fax: 859-572-6592, E-mail: hatchettg@nku.edu. *Application contact:* Alison Swanson, Graduate Admissions Coordinator, 859-572-6971, E-mail: swansona1@nku.edu.
Website: http://coehs.nku.edu/gradprograms/counseling/clinicalmentalhealthcounseling.html

Northern State University, MS Ed Program in Counseling, Aberdeen, SD 57401-7198. Offers clinical mental health counseling (MS Ed); school counseling (MS Ed). *Accreditation:* NCATE. Part-time programs available. Postbaccalaureate distance learning degree programs offered (minimal on-campus study). *Faculty:* 3 full-time (2 women), 2 part-time/adjunct (0 women). *Students:* 32 full-time (20 women), 25 part-time (20 women); includes 1 minority (Black or African American, non-Hispanic/Latino). Average age 25. 30 applicants, 90% accepted, 22 enrolled. In 2014, 22 master's awarded. *Degree requirements:* For master's, comprehensive exam, thesis optional. *Entrance requirements:* For master's, minimum GPA of 2.75. Additional exam requirements/recommendations for international students: Required—TOEFL (minimum score 550 paper-based; 78 iBT), IELTS (minimum score 6). *Application deadline:* For fall admission, 8/15 for domestic and international students; for spring admission, 12/15 for domestic and international students. Applications are processed on a rolling basis. Application fee: $35. Electronic applications accepted. *Expenses:* Tuition, state resident: full-time $1817; part-time $202 per credit hour. Tuition, nonresident: full-time $3846; part-time $428 per credit hour. *Required fees:* $1072; $120 per credit hour. One-time fee: $35. *Financial support:* In 2014–15, 1 student received support, including 5 teaching assistantships with partial tuition reimbursements available (averaging $6,478 per year); career-related internships or fieldwork, Federal Work-Study, institutionally sponsored loans, scholarships/grants, and unspecified assistantships also available. Support available to part-time students. Financial award application deadline: 3/1; financial award applicants required to submit FAFSA. *Unit head:* Dr. Constance Geier, Dean of Education, 605-626-2558, Fax: 605-626-7190, E-mail: connie.geier@northern.edu. *Application contact:* Tammy K. Griffith, Program Assistant, 605-626-2558, Fax: 605-626-7190, E-mail: tammy.griffith@northern.edu.

Northwestern State University of Louisiana, Graduate Studies and Research, Department of Psychology, Natchitoches, LA 71497. Offers clinical psychology (MS). *Degree requirements:* For master's, comprehensive exam, thesis or alternative. *Entrance requirements:* For master's, GRE General Test, GRE Subject Test, minimum undergraduate GPA of 2.5. Additional exam requirements/recommendations for international students: Required—TOEFL. Electronic applications accepted.

Northwestern University, The Graduate School, Judd A. and Marjorie Weinberg College of Arts and Sciences, Department of Psychology, Evanston, IL 60208. Offers brain, behavior and cognition (PhD); clinical psychology (PhD); cognitive psychology (PhD); personality psychology (PhD); social psychology (PhD); JD/PhD. Admissions and degrees offered through The Graduate School. *Accreditation:* APA (one or more programs are accredited). Part-time programs available. *Degree requirements:* For doctorate, thesis/dissertation. *Entrance requirements:* For doctorate, GRE General Test, GRE Subject Test. Additional exam requirements/recommendations for international students: Required—TOEFL. Electronic applications accepted. *Faculty research:*

Memory and higher order cognition, anxiety and depression, effectiveness of psychotherapy, social cognition, molecular basis of memory.

Northwestern University, The Graduate School and Feinberg School of Medicine, Program in Clinical Psychology, Evanston, IL 60208. Offers clinical psychology (PhD), including clinical neuropsychology. Admissions and degree offered through The Graduate School. *Accreditation:* APA. *Degree requirements:* For doctorate, thesis/dissertation, clinical internship. *Entrance requirements:* For doctorate, GRE General Test, GRE Subject Test, minimum GPA of 3.2, course work in psychology. Additional exam requirements/recommendations for international students: Required—TOEFL. *Faculty research:* Cancer and cardiovascular risk reduction, evaluation of mental health services and policy, neuropsychological assessment, outcome of psychotherapy, cognitive therapy, pediatric and clinical child psychology.

Northwest Nazarene University, Graduate Studies, Program in Social Work, Nampa, ID 83686-5897. Offers addiction studies (MSW); clinical mental health practice (MSW); management, community planning and social administration (MSW); medical social work (MSW). *Accreditation:* CSWE. Part-time programs available. Postbaccalaureate distance learning degree programs offered (no on-campus study). *Faculty:* 10 full-time (6 women), 5 part-time/adjunct (4 women). *Students:* 129 full-time (97 women), 33 part-time (29 women); includes 23 minority (3 Black or African American, non-Hispanic/Latino; 1 American Indian or Alaska Native, non-Hispanic/Latino; 12 Hispanic/Latino; 7 Two or more races, non-Hispanic/Latino). Average age 27. 152 applicants, 54% accepted, 73 enrolled. In 2014, 54 master's awarded. *Degree requirements:* For master's, comprehensive exam. *Application deadline:* Applications are processed on a rolling basis. Application fee: $50. Electronic applications accepted. *Unit head:* Dr. Lawanna Lancaster, Director, 208-467-8679, E-mail: msw@nnu.edu. *Application contact:* Jodie Engel, Program Assistant, 208-467-8679, Fax: 208-467-8879, E-mail: jrodriguez-engel@nnu.edu.

Notre Dame de Namur University, Division of Academic Affairs, College of Arts and Sciences, Department of Clinical Psychology and Gerontology, Program in Clinical Psychology, Belmont, CA 94002-1908. Offers MS. Part-time programs available. *Degree requirements:* For master's, thesis. *Entrance requirements:* Additional exam requirements/recommendations for international students: Required—TOEFL (minimum score 550 paper-based; 79 iBT). Electronic applications accepted.

Nova Southeastern University, Center for Psychological Studies, Fort Lauderdale, FL 33314-7796. Offers clinical psychology (PhD, Psy D); counseling (MS); general psychology (MS); mental health counseling (MS); school counseling (MS). *Accreditation:* APA (one or more programs are accredited). Postbaccalaureate distance learning degree programs offered. *Faculty:* 50 full-time (19 women), 119 part-time/adjunct (69 women). *Students:* 1,827 (1,560 women); includes 842 minority (289 Black or African American, non-Hispanic/Latino; 2 American Indian or Alaska Native, non-Hispanic/Latino; 45 Asian, non-Hispanic/Latino; 478 Hispanic/Latino; 28 Two or more races, non-Hispanic/Latino), 41 international. Average age 31. 1,186 applicants, 51% accepted, 398 enrolled. In 2014, 344 master's, 117 doctorates, 10 other advanced degrees awarded. Terminal master's awarded for partial completion of doctoral program. *Degree requirements:* For master's, comprehensive exam, 3 practica; for doctorate, thesis/dissertation, clinical internship, competency exam; for Psy S, comprehensive exam, internship. *Entrance requirements:* For doctorate, GRE General Test, GRE Subject Test (recommended), minimum undergraduate GPA of 3.0; for Psy S, GRE General Test. Additional exam requirements/recommendations for international students: Required—TOEFL (minimum score 550 paper-based). *Application deadline:* Applications are processed on a rolling basis. Application fee: $50. Electronic applications accepted. *Expenses:* Expenses: Contact institution. *Financial support:* In 2014–15, 15 research assistantships, 68 teaching assistantships (averaging $4,800 per year) were awarded; career-related internships or fieldwork, Federal Work-Study, institutionally sponsored loans, scholarships/grants, and unspecified assistantships also available. Support available to part-time students. Financial award application deadline: 4/1. *Faculty research:* Clinical and child clinical psychology, geriatrics, interpersonal violence. *Unit head:* Karen Grosby, EdD, Dean, 954-262-5701, Fax: 954-262-3859, E-mail: grosby@nova.edu. *Application contact:* Carlos Perez, Enrollment Management, 954-262-5790, Fax: 954-262-3893, E-mail: cpsinfo@cps.nova.edu.
Website: http://www.cps.nova.edu

The Ohio State University, Graduate School, College of Arts and Sciences, Division of Social and Behavioral Sciences, Department of Psychology, Columbus, OH 43210. Offers behavioral neuroscience (PhD); clinical psychology (PhD); cognitive psychology (PhD); developmental psychology (PhD); intellectual and developmental disabilities psychology (PhD); quantitative psychology (PhD); social psychology (PhD). *Accreditation:* APA. *Faculty:* 55. *Students:* 158 full-time (91 women); includes 26 minority (6 Black or African American, non-Hispanic/Latino; 2 American Indian or Alaska Native, non-Hispanic/Latino; 7 Asian, non-Hispanic/Latino; 9 Hispanic/Latino; 2 Two or more races, non-Hispanic/Latino), 23 international. Average age 27. In 2014, 12 doctorates awarded. *Degree requirements:* For doctorate, thesis/dissertation. *Entrance requirements:* For doctorate, GRE General Test. Additional exam requirements/recommendations for international students: Required—TOEFL (minimum score 600 paper-based; 100 iBT); Recommended—IELTS (minimum score 8). *Application deadline:* For fall admission, 12/1 for domestic and international students. Applications are processed on a rolling basis. Application fee: $60 ($70 for international students). Electronic applications accepted. *Financial support:* Fellowships with tuition reimbursements, research assistantships with tuition reimbursements, and teaching assistantships with tuition reimbursements available. *Unit head:* Dr. Richard Petty, Chair, 614-292-1640, E-mail: petty.1@osu.edu. *Application contact:* Graduate and Professional Admissions, 614-292-9444, Fax: 614-292-3895, E-mail: gpadmissions@osu.edu.
Website: http://www.psy.ohio-state.edu/

Ohio University, Graduate College, College of Arts and Sciences, Department of Psychology, Program in Clinical Psychology, Athens, OH 45701-2979. Offers MS, PhD. *Accreditation:* APA. *Degree requirements:* For doctorate, one foreign language, comprehensive exam, thesis/dissertation. *Entrance requirements:* For doctorate, GRE General Test, GRE Subject Test, minimum graduate GPA of 3.4. Additional exam requirements/recommendations for international students: Required—TOEFL. *Faculty research:* Health psychology, child clinical psychology, psychotherapy outcomes.

Oklahoma State University, College of Arts and Sciences, Department of Psychology, Stillwater, OK 74078. Offers clinical psychology (PhD); general psychology (MS); lifespan development psychology (PhD). *Accreditation:* APA (one or more programs are accredited). *Faculty:* 31 full-time (16 women), 3 part-time/adjunct (2 women). *Students:* 39 full-time (27 women), 18 part-time (12 women); includes 12 minority (1 Black or African American, non-Hispanic/Latino; 5 American Indian or Alaska Native, non-Hispanic/Latino; 1 Hispanic/Latino; 1 Native Hawaiian or other Pacific Islander, non-Hispanic/Latino; 4 Two or more races, non-Hispanic/Latino), 2 international. Average age 27. 218 applicants, 7% accepted, 9 enrolled. In 2014, 9 master's, 9 doctorates awarded. *Degree requirements:* For master's, thesis or alternative; for doctorate, comprehensive exam, thesis/dissertation. *Entrance requirements:* For master's and doctorate, GRE General Test. Additional exam requirements/recommendations for international students: Required—TOEFL (minimum score 550 paper-based; 79 iBT).

Application deadline: For fall admission, 3/1 priority date for international students; for spring admission, 8/1 priority date for international students. Applications are processed on a rolling basis. Application fee: $40 ($75 for international students). Electronic applications accepted. *Expenses:* Tuition, state resident: full-time $4488; part-time $187 per credit hour. Tuition, nonresident: full-time $18,360; part-time $765 per credit hour. *Required fees:* $2413; $100.55 per credit hour. Tuition and fees vary according to campus/location. *Financial support:* In 2014–15, 14 research assistantships (averaging $14,585 per year), 46 teaching assistantships (averaging $13,749 per year) were awarded; career-related internships or fieldwork, Federal Work-Study, scholarships/grants, health care benefits, tuition waivers (partial), and unspecified assistantships also available. Support available to part-time students. Financial award application deadline: 3/1; financial award applicants required to submit FAFSA. *Unit head:* Dr. Thad Leffingwell, Department Head, 405-744-7494, Fax: 405-744-8067, E-mail: thad.leffingwell@okstate.edu. *Application contact:* Patricia Alexander, Graduate Advisor, 405-744-7591, Fax: 405-744-8967, E-mail: patricia.alexander@okstate.edu.
Website: http://psychology.okstate.edu

Old Dominion University, College of Sciences, Virginia Consortium Program in Clinical Psychology, Norfolk, VA 23504. Offers PhD. Program offered jointly with Eastern Virginia Medical School and Norfolk State University. *Faculty:* 22 full-time (10 women), 4 part-time/adjunct (1 woman). *Students:* 23 full-time (17 women), 9 part-time (7 women); includes 11 minority (7 Black or African American, non-Hispanic/Latino; 1 Asian, non-Hispanic/Latino; 2 Hispanic/Latino; 1 Native Hawaiian or other Pacific Islander, non-Hispanic/Latino), 1 international. Average age 29. 76 applicants, 9% accepted, 6 enrolled. In 2014, 7 doctorates awarded. *Degree requirements:* For doctorate, comprehensive exam, thesis/dissertation, internship. *Entrance requirements:* For doctorate, GRE General Test. Additional exam requirements/recommendations for international students: Required—TOEFL. *Application deadline:* For fall admission, 12/1 for domestic and international students. Application fee: $65. *Expenses:* Expenses: Contact institution. *Financial support:* In 2014–15, 2 fellowships with partial tuition reimbursements (averaging $15,000 per year), 6 research assistantships with partial tuition reimbursements (averaging $7,500 per year), 4 teaching assistantships with partial tuition reimbursements (averaging $8,000 per year) were awarded; career-related internships or fieldwork, scholarships/grants, and unspecified assistantships also available. Financial award application deadline: 12/1; financial award applicants required to submit FAFSA. *Faculty research:* Coping with stress, minority and women's issues, neuropsychology, assessment, alcohol abuse, health psychology. *Unit head:* Dr. Robin Lewis, Graduate Program Director, 757-683-4439, Fax: 757-683-5087, E-mail: rlewis@odu.edu. *Application contact:* Eileen O'Neill, Coordinator, 757-451-7733, Fax: 757-823-8919, E-mail: exoneill@odu.edu.
Website: http://sci.odu.edu/vcpcp/

Pace University, Dyson College of Arts and Sciences, Department of Psychology, Program in School-Clinical Child Psychology, New York, NY 10038. Offers school psychology (MS Ed); school-clinical psychology (Psy D). *Accreditation:* APA (one or more programs are accredited). *Students:* 85 full-time (71 women), 42 part-time (34 women); includes 29 minority (6 Black or African American, non-Hispanic/Latino; 12 Asian, non-Hispanic/Latino; 8 Hispanic/Latino; 1 Native Hawaiian or other Pacific Islander, non-Hispanic/Latino; 2 Two or more races, non-Hispanic/Latino), 10 international. Average age 27. 232 applicants, 36% accepted, 39 enrolled. In 2014, 11 master's, 23 doctorates awarded. Terminal master's awarded for partial completion of doctoral program. *Degree requirements:* For master's, comprehensive exam, qualifying exams, internship; for doctorate, comprehensive exam, qualifying exams, externship, internship, project. *Entrance requirements:* For master's, GRE General Test, GRE Subject Test, interview, 3 letters of recommendation, resume, personal statement; for doctorate, GRE General Test, GRE Subject Test (psychology), interview, transcripts, 3 letters of recommendation. Additional exam requirements/recommendations for international students: Required—TOEFL (minimum score 100 iBT). *Application deadline:* For fall admission, 1/15 priority date for domestic students, 11/15 for international students. Applications are processed on a rolling basis. Application fee: $70. Electronic applications accepted. *Expenses: Tuition:* Part-time $1120 per credit. *Required fees:* $266 per semester. Tuition and fees vary according to course load, degree level and program. *Financial support:* Research assistantships, teaching assistantships, career-related internships or fieldwork, Federal Work-Study, and tuition waivers (partial) available. Support available to part-time students. Financial award applicants required to submit FAFSA. *Unit head:* Dr. Barbara Mowder, Director of Graduate Psychology Programs, 212-346-1556, E-mail: bmowder@pace.edu. *Application contact:* Susan Ford-Goldschein, Director of Graduate Admissions, 212-346-1660, Fax: 212-346-1585, E-mail: gradnyc@pace.edu.
Website: http://www.pace.edu/dyson/academic-departments-and-programs/psychology—-nyc/graduate-programs

Pacifica Graduate Institute, Graduate Programs, Carpinteria, CA 93013. Offers clinical psychology (PhD); counseling psychology (MA); depth psychology (MA, PhD); mythological studies (MA, PhD). Terminal master's awarded for partial completion of doctoral program. *Degree requirements:* For master's, thesis (for some programs), practicum; for doctorate, comprehensive exam, thesis/dissertation, internship. *Entrance requirements:* For master's, resume, 3 letters of recommendation, writing sample, interview; for doctorate, resumé, 4 letters of recommendation, writing sample, interview. Additional exam requirements/recommendations for international students: Required—TOEFL. *Faculty research:* Imaginal and archetypal theory; post-Colonial psychoanalytic and Jungian theory; myth literature as it applies to the theory and practice of psychology.

Palo Alto University, PGSP-Stanford Psy D Consortium Program, Palo Alto, CA 94304. Offers Psy D. Program offered jointly with Stanford University. *Accreditation:* APA. *Faculty:* 16 full-time (12 women), 31 part-time/adjunct (22 women). *Students:* 155 full-time (129 women), 4 part-time (all women); includes 47 minority (5 Black or African American, non-Hispanic/Latino; 25 Asian, non-Hispanic/Latino; 14 Hispanic/Latino; 3 Two or more races, non-Hispanic/Latino), 3 international. Average age 29. 339 applicants, 17% accepted, 32 enrolled. In 2014, 29 doctorates awarded. *Degree requirements:* For doctorate, comprehensive exam, thesis/dissertation, 2000-hour clinical internship. *Entrance requirements:* For doctorate, GRE General Test (minimum overall score 1200); GRE Subject Test in psychology (highly recommended), undergraduate degree in psychology or related area with minimum GPA of 3.3. Additional exam requirements/recommendations for international students: Required—TOEFL, IELTS. *Application deadline:* For fall admission, 12/2 priority date for domestic and international students. Applications are processed on a rolling basis. Application fee: $50. Electronic applications accepted. *Expenses:* Expenses: Contact institution. *Financial support:* In 2014–15, 48 students received support, including fellowships (averaging $4,000 per year), research assistantships (averaging $1,000 per year), teaching assistantships (averaging $3,000 per year); Federal Work-Study and scholarships/grants also available. Financial award application deadline: 1/15; financial award applicants required to submit FAFSA. *Unit head:* Dr. Steve Smith, Co-Director of Clinical Training, PGSP-Stanford Psy D Consortium, E-mail: stevesmith@paloaltou.edu. *Application contact:* Dr. Kimberly Hill, Co-Director of Clinical Training, PGSP-Stanford Psy D Consortium, 650-725-5582, E-mail: khill@paloaltou.edu.
Website: http://www.paloaltou.edu/graduate-programs/pgsp-psyd-stanford-consortium

Palo Alto University, PhD in Clinical Psychology Program, Palo Alto, CA 94304. Offers PhD, JD/PhD, MBA/PhD. *Accreditation:* APA. *Faculty:* 32 full-time (20 women), 27 part-time/adjunct (16 women). *Students:* 410 full-time (320 women), 19 part-time (14 women); includes 118 minority (20 Black or African American, non-Hispanic/Latino; 1 American Indian or Alaska Native, non-Hispanic/Latino; 55 Asian, non-Hispanic/Latino; 31 Hispanic/Latino; 2 Native Hawaiian or other Pacific Islander, non-Hispanic/Latino; 9 Two or more races, non-Hispanic/Latino), 22 international. Average age 29. 237 applicants, 58% accepted, 82 enrolled. In 2014, 65 doctorates awarded. *Degree requirements:* For doctorate, comprehensive exam, thesis/dissertation, 2000-hour clinical internship. *Entrance requirements:* For doctorate, GRE General Test, undergraduate or graduate degree in psychology or related area; 4 course prerequisites: biopsychology, abnormal psychology, developmental psychology, and statistics. Additional exam requirements/recommendations for international students: Required—TOEFL, IELTS. *Application deadline:* For fall admission, 12/2 priority date for domestic and international students. Applications are processed on a rolling basis. Application fee: $50. Electronic applications accepted. *Expenses:* Expenses: Contact institution. *Financial support:* In 2014–15, 45 students received support, including fellowships (averaging $7,500 per year), research assistantships (averaging $4,000 per year), teaching assistantships (averaging $3,000 per year); Federal Work-Study and scholarships/grants also available. Financial award application deadline: 1/15; financial award applicants required to submit FAFSA. *Faculty research:* Forensic psychology, LGBT psychology, trauma, diversity and community mental health, neuropsychology. *Unit head:* Dr. Rowena Gomez, Director of Clinical Training, 650-433-3823, E-mail: rgomez@paloaltou.edu. *Application contact:* Eirian Williams, Vice President of Enrollment Management, 800-818-6136, E-mail: admissions@paloaltou.edu.
Website: http://www.paloaltou.edu/graduate-programs/phd-programs/phd-clinical-psychology

Penn State Harrisburg, Graduate School, School of Behavioral Sciences and Education, Middletown, PA 17057-4898. Offers applied behavior analysis (MA); applied clinical psychology (MA); applied psychological research (MA); community psychology and social change (MA); health education (M Ed); literacy education (M Ed); teaching and curriculum (M Ed); training and development (M Ed). Part-time and evening/weekend programs available. *Unit head:* Dr. Mukund S. Kulkarni, Chancellor, 717-948-6105, Fax: 717-948-6452, E-mail: msk5@psu.edu. *Application contact:* Robert W. Coffman, Jr., Director of Enrollment Management, Admissions, 717-948-6250, Fax: 717-948-6325, E-mail: ric1@psu.edu.
Website: http://harrisburg.psu.edu/behavioral-sciences-and-education/

Pepperdine University, Graduate School of Education and Psychology, Division of Psychology, MA Program in Clinical Psychology (Day Format), Malibu, CA 90263. Offers marriage and family therapy (MA). *Students:* 305 full-time (256 women), 292 part-time (246 women); includes 213 minority (57 Black or African American, non-Hispanic/Latino; 1 American Indian or Alaska Native, non-Hispanic/Latino; 36 Asian, non-Hispanic/Latino; 98 Hispanic/Latino; 5 Native Hawaiian or other Pacific Islander, non-Hispanic/Latino; 16 Two or more races, non-Hispanic/Latino), 17 international. In 2014, 187 master's awarded. *Entrance requirements:* For master's, GRE (taken within last five years) or MAT (taken within last two years), two professional recommendations, two- to five-page typed personal statement. Additional exam requirements/recommendations for international students: Required—TOEFL. *Application deadline:* For fall admission, 2/1 for domestic students. Application fee: $55. *Unit head:* Dr. Helen Williams, Dean, 310-568-5600, E-mail: helen.williams@pepperdine.edu. *Application contact:* Deanna Schwartz, Psychology Admissions Manager, 310-568-5777, E-mail: deanna.lazaro@pepperdine.edu.
Website: http://gsep.pepperdine.edu/masters-clinical-psychology-mft-day/

★ **Philadelphia College of Osteopathic Medicine,** Graduate and Professional Programs, Department of Psychology, Philadephia, PA 19131. Offers applied behavior analysis (Certificate); clinical health psychology (Post-Doctoral Certificate); clinical neuropsychology (Post-Doctoral Certificate); clinical psychology (Psy D); mental health counseling (MS); organizational development and leadership (MS); psychology (Certificate); school psychology (MS, Psy D, Ed S). *Accreditation:* APA. *Faculty:* 19 full-time (11 women), 122 part-time/adjunct (58 women). *Students:* 395 (304 women); includes 80 minority (49 Black or African American, non-Hispanic/Latino; 13 Asian, non-Hispanic/Latino; 7 Hispanic/Latino; 11 Two or more races, non-Hispanic/Latino). 345 applicants, 47% accepted, 113 enrolled. In 2014, 72 master's, 42 doctorates, 17 other advanced degrees awarded. Terminal master's awarded for partial completion of doctoral program. *Degree requirements:* For master's, comprehensive exam (for some programs), thesis (for some programs); for doctorate, comprehensive exam, thesis/dissertation. *Entrance requirements:* For master's, GRE or MAT, minimum GPA of 3.0; bachelor's degree from regionally-accredited college or university; for doctorate, PRAXIS II (for Psy D in school psychology), minimum undergraduate GPA of 3.0; for other advanced degree, GRE (for Ed S). Additional exam requirements/recommendations for international students: Required—TOEFL (minimum score 79 iBT). *Application deadline:* For fall admission, 3/1 priority date for domestic students. Applications are processed on a rolling basis. Application fee: $50. Electronic applications accepted. *Financial support:* In 2014–15, 28 teaching assistantships were awarded; Federal Work-Study, institutionally sponsored loans, and scholarships/grants also available. Financial award application deadline: 3/15; financial award applicants required to submit FAFSA. *Faculty research:* Adult and childhood anxiety and ADHD; coping with chronic illness; primary care psychology/integrated health care; applied behavior analysis; psychological, educational, and neuropsychological assessment. *Total annual research expenditures:* $533,489. *Unit head:* Dr. Robert DiTomasso, Chairman, 215-871-6442, Fax: 215-871-6458, E-mail: robertd@pcom.edu. *Application contact:* Kari A. Shotwell, Director of Admissions, 215-871-6700, Fax: 215-871-6719, E-mail: karis@pcom.edu.

See Display on page 990 and Close-Up on page 1211.

Plymouth State University, College of Graduate Studies, Graduate Studies in Education, Certificate of Advanced Graduate Studies Programs, Plymouth, NH 03264-1595. Offers clinical mental health counseling (CAGS); educational leadership (CAGS); higher education (CAGS); school psychology (CAGS). Part-time and evening/weekend programs available.

Plymouth State University, College of Graduate Studies, Graduate Studies in Education, Program in Science, Plymouth, NH 03264-1595. Offers applied meteorology (MS); biology (MS); clinical mental health counseling (MS); environmental science and policy (MS); science education (MS).

Point Park University, School of Arts and Sciences, Department of Humanities and Human Sciences, Pittsburgh, PA 15222-1984. Offers clinical-community psychology (MA).

Ponce Health Sciences University, Program in Clinical Psychology, Ponce, PR 00732-7004. Offers PhD, Psy D. *Accreditation:* APA. *Faculty:* 16 full-time (10 women), 10 part-time/adjunct (5 women). *Students:* 255 full-time (211 women); all minorities (all Hispanic/Latino). Average age 27. 92 applicants, 64% accepted, 47 enrolled. In 2014, 20 doctorates awarded. *Degree requirements:* For doctorate, one foreign language, comprehensive exam, thesis/dissertation, internship. *Entrance requirements:* For

doctorate, GRE General Test or EXADEP, proficiency in Spanish and English; 2 letters of recommendation; minimum undergraduate GPA of 2.7, graduate 3.0; criminal background check. *Application deadline:* For fall admission, 3/16 for domestic and international students. Application fee: $75. *Expenses: Tuition:* Full-time $44,476. *Required fees:* $950. One-time fee: $690 full-time. Full-time tuition and fees vary according to course level, course load, degree level, program and student level. *Financial support:* In 2014–15, 83,123 students received support. Scholarships/grants available. Financial award application deadline: 4/30; financial award applicants required to submit FAFSA. *Unit head:* Dr. Jose Pons, Head, 787-840-2575, E-mail: jpons@psm.edu. *Application contact:* Maria Colon, Admissions Officer, 787-840-2575 Ext. 2143, E-mail: mcolon@psm.edu.

Pontifical Catholic University of Puerto Rico, College of Graduate Studies in Behavioral Science and Community Affairs, Program in Clinical Psychology, Ponce, PR 00717-0777. Offers PhD, Psy D. Part-time and evening/weekend programs available. *Degree requirements:* For doctorate, comprehensive exam, thesis/dissertation. *Entrance requirements:* For doctorate, EXADEP, minimum GPA of 2.75.

Pontificia Universidad Catolica Madre y Maestra, Graduate School, Faculty of Social and Administrative Sciences, Santiago, Dominican Republic. Offers business administration (MBA), including business development, finance, international business, management skills (M Mgmt, MBA), marketing, operations, strategic cost management, strategy, tourist destination planning and management; law (LL M), including civil law, corporate business law, criminal law, international relations, real estate law; management (M Mgmt), including higher financial management, insurance program administration, management skills (M Mgmt, MBA); psychology (MA), including clinical child and adolescent psychology, forensic psychology; strategic human resources (EMBA).

Prairie View A&M University, College of Arts and Sciences, Department of Biology, Prairie View, TX 77446-0519. Offers bio-environmental toxicology (MS); biology (MS). Part-time and evening/weekend programs available. In 2014, 8 master's awarded. *Degree requirements:* For master's, comprehensive exam, thesis optional. *Entrance requirements:* For master's, GRE General Test. Additional exam requirements/recommendations for international students: Required—TOEFL. *Application deadline:* For fall admission, 7/1 for domestic and international students; for spring admission, 11/1 for domestic and international students. Applications are processed on a rolling basis. Electronic applications accepted. *Expenses:* Tuition, state resident: full-time $4134; part-time $248.68 per credit hour. Tuition, nonresident: full-time $11,051; part-time $632.97 per credit hour. *Required fees:* $2552; $475.10 per credit hour. *Financial support:* In 2014–15, teaching assistantships (averaging $13,440 per year) were awarded; Federal Work-Study and unspecified assistantships also available. Financial award application deadline: 4/1; financial award applicants required to submit FAFSA. *Faculty research:* Genomics, hypertension, control of gene express, proteins, ligands that interact with hormone receptors, prostate cancer, renin-angiotensin yeast metabolism. *Unit head:* Dr. Harriette Howard-Lee Block, Head, 936-261-3160, Fax: 936-261-3179, E-mail: hlblock@pvamu.edu. *Application contact:* Dr. Seab A. Smith, Associate Professor, 936-261-3169, Fax: 936-261-3179, E-mail: sasmith@pvamu.edu.

Prairie View A&M University, College of Juvenile Justice and Psychology, Prairie View, TX 77446-0519. Offers clinical adolescent psychology (PhD); juvenile forensic psychology (MSJFP); juvenile justice (MSJJ, PhD). Part-time and evening/weekend programs available. *Faculty:* 8 full-time (4 women). *Students:* 27 full-time (24 women), 33 part-time (27 women); includes 49 minority (48 Black or African American, non-Hispanic/Latino; 1 Two or more races, non-Hispanic/Latino), 9 international. Average age 34. 43 applicants, 77% accepted, 22 enrolled. In 2014, 9 master's, 1 doctorate awarded. *Degree requirements:* For master's, comprehensive exam (for some programs), thesis (for some programs); for doctorate, comprehensive exam, thesis/dissertation. *Entrance requirements:* For master's, GRE, minimum GPA of 2.75; for doctorate, GRE, previous course work in clinical adolescent psychology, minimum GPA of 3.5. Additional exam requirements/recommendations for international students: Required—TOEFL (minimum score 550 paper-based; 79 iBT). *Application deadline:* For fall admission, 7/1 priority date for domestic students, 6/1 priority date for international students; for spring admission, 11/1 priority date for domestic students, 10/1 priority date for international students; for summer admission, 3/1 priority date for domestic students, 2/1 priority date for international students. Applications are processed on a rolling basis. Application fee: $50. *Expenses:* Expenses: $6,686 tuition and fees. *Financial support:* Career-related internships or fieldwork, Federal Work-Study, institutionally sponsored loans, tuition waivers (full and partial), and unspecified assistantships available. Support available to part-time students. Financial award application deadline: 3/1; financial award applicants required to submit FAFSA. *Faculty research:* Juvenile justice, juvenile forensic psychology, teen court, graduate education, capital punishment. *Unit head:* Dr. Tamara L. Brown, Dean, 936-261-5206, Fax: 936-261-5253, E-mail: tlbrown@pvamu.edu. *Application contact:* Pauline Walker, Executive Secretary, Graduate Program, 936-261-3521, Fax: 936-261-3529, E-mail: pmwalker@pvamu.edu.

Purdue University, Graduate School, College of Health and Human Sciences, Department of Psychological Sciences, West Lafayette, IN 47907. Offers behavioral neuroscience (PhD); clinical psychology (PhD); cognitive psychology (PhD); industrial/organizational psychology (PhD); mathematical and computational cognitive science (PhD). *Accreditation:* APA. Terminal master's awarded for partial completion of doctoral program. *Degree requirements:* For doctorate, thesis/dissertation. *Entrance requirements:* For doctorate, GRE General Test, minimum undergraduate GPA of 3.0 or equivalent. Additional exam requirements/recommendations for international students: Required—TOEFL (minimum score 550 paper-based; 77 iBT); Recommended—TWE. Electronic applications accepted. *Faculty research:* Career development of women in science, development of friendships during childhood and adolescence, social competence, human information processing.

Queens College of the City University of New York, Division of Graduate Studies, Mathematics and Natural Sciences Division, Department of Psychology, Flushing, NY 11367-1597. Offers clinical behavioral applications in mental health settings (MA); psychology (MA). Part-time programs available. *Degree requirements:* For master's, comprehensive exam, thesis or alternative. *Entrance requirements:* For master's, GRE, minimum GPA of 3.0. Additional exam requirements/recommendations for international students: Required—TOEFL.

Queen's University at Kingston, School of Graduate Studies, Faculty of Arts and Sciences, Department of Psychology, Kingston, ON K7L 3N6, Canada. Offers brain behavior and cognitive science (MA, PhD); clinical psychology (MA, PhD); developmental psychology (MA, PhD); social personality psychology (MA, PhD). *Degree requirements:* For master's, thesis; for doctorate, comprehensive exam, thesis/dissertation. *Entrance requirements:* For master's and doctorate, GRE General Test. Additional exam requirements/recommendations for international students: Required—TOEFL. *Faculty research:* Human development, social, personality, behavioral neuroscience, forensic.

Radford University, College of Graduate and Professional Studies, College of Education and Human Development, Department of Counselor Education, Radford, VA 24142. Offers clinical mental health counseling (MS); school counseling (MS). *Accreditation:* ACA; NCATE. Part-time and evening/weekend programs available. *Faculty:* 6 full-time (4 women), 4 part-time/adjunct (3 women). *Students:* 60 full-time (47 women), 15 part-time (13 women); includes 10 minority (4 Black or African American, non-Hispanic/Latino; 1 Asian, non-Hispanic/Latino; 2 Hispanic/Latino; 3 Two or more races, non-Hispanic/Latino), 2 international. Average age 27. 71 applicants, 77% accepted, 28 enrolled. In 2014, 27 master's awarded. *Degree requirements:* For master's, comprehensive exam, thesis optional. *Entrance requirements:* For master's, GRE or MAT, minimum GPA of 2.75, 3 letters of reference, personal essay, resume, official transcripts. Additional exam requirements/recommendations for international students: Required—TOEFL (minimum score 550 paper-based; 79 iBT), IELTS (minimum score 6.5). *Application deadline:* For fall admission, 2/15 priority date for domestic students, 12/1 for international students; for spring admission, 7/1 for international students. Applications are processed on a rolling basis. Application fee: $50. Electronic applications accepted. *Expenses:* Tuition, state resident: full-time $7187; part-time $299 per credit hour. Tuition, nonresident: full-time $16,394; part-time $683 per credit hour. *Required fees:* $2974; $125 per credit hour. Tuition and fees vary according to course load and program. *Financial support:* In 2014–15, 16 students received support, including 13 research assistantships (averaging $8,481 per year), 3 teaching assistantships with partial tuition reimbursements available (averaging $11,000 per year); career-related internships or fieldwork, Federal Work-Study, institutionally sponsored loans, scholarships/grants, and unspecified assistantships also available. Financial award application deadline: 3/1; financial award applicants required to submit FAFSA. *Unit head:* Dr. Nadine Hartig, Chair, 540-831-5214, Fax: 540-831-6755, E-mail: vgoad4@radford.edu. *Application contact:* Rebecca Conner, Director, Graduate Enrollment, 540-831-6296, Fax: 540-831-6061, E-mail: gradcollege@radford.edu.
Website: http://www.radford.edu/content/cehd/home/counselor-education.html

Radford University, College of Graduate and Professional Studies, College of Humanities and Behavioral Sciences, Department of Psychology, Program in Psychology, Radford, VA 24142. Offers clinical psychology (MA, MS); experimental psychology (MA); industrial/organizational psychology (MA, MS). Part-time programs available. *Faculty:* 14 full-time (7 women). *Students:* 47 full-time (29 women); includes 3 minority (2 Asian, non-Hispanic/Latino; 1 Hispanic/Latino). Average age 24. 117 applicants, 40% accepted, 25 enrolled. In 2014, 27 master's awarded. *Degree requirements:* For master's, comprehensive exam, thesis (for some programs). *Entrance requirements:* For master's, GRE, minimum GPA of 3.0; 3 letters of reference; essay, resume, official transcripts. Additional exam requirements/recommendations for international students: Required—TOEFL (minimum score 550 paper-based; 79 iBT), IELTS (minimum score 6.5). *Application deadline:* For fall admission, 2/15 priority date for domestic students, 12/1 for international students; for spring admission, 7/1 for international students. Applications are processed on a rolling basis. Application fee: $50. Electronic applications accepted. *Expenses:* Tuition, state resident: full-time $7187; part-time $299 per credit hour. Tuition, nonresident: full-time $16,394; part-time $683 per credit hour. *Required fees:* $2974; $125 per credit hour. Tuition and fees vary according to course load and program. *Financial support:* In 2014–15, 39 students received support, including 22 research assistantships (averaging $5,946 per year), 15 teaching assistantships with partial tuition reimbursements available (averaging $10,467 per year); career-related internships or fieldwork, institutionally sponsored loans, scholarships/grants, and unspecified assistantships also available. Financial award application deadline: 3/1; financial award applicants required to submit FAFSA. *Faculty research:* Social cognition and interpersonal relationships, relationship between one's self-concept and social interactions, creativity and innovation, organizational politics and ethical decision-making, victimization in childhood. *Unit head:* Dr. Hilary M. Lips, Chair, 540-831-5361, Fax: 540-831-6113, E-mail: hlips@radford.edu. *Application contact:* Rebecca Conner, Director, Graduate Enrollment, 540-831-6296, Fax: 540-831-6061, E-mail: gradcollege@radford.edu.
Website: http://www.radford.edu/content/chbs/home/psychology/programs.html

Regent University, Graduate School, School of Psychology and Counseling, Virginia Beach, VA 23464-9800. Offers clinical psychology (Psy D); counseling (MA), including clinical mental health counseling, marriage, couple, and family counseling, school counseling; counseling studies (CAGS); counselor education and supervision (PhD); human services counseling (MA); M Div/MA; M Ed/MA; MBA/MA. PhD program offered online only. *Accreditation:* ACA; APA (one or more programs are accredited). Part-time and evening/weekend programs available. Postbaccalaureate distance learning degree programs offered (minimal on-campus study). *Faculty:* 29 full-time (15 women), 45 part-time/adjunct (29 women). *Students:* 257 full-time (211 women), 288 part-time (225 women); includes 156 minority (121 Black or African American, non-Hispanic/Latino; 2 American Indian or Alaska Native, non-Hispanic/Latino; 10 Asian, non-Hispanic/Latino; 23 Hispanic/Latino), 29 international. Average age 35. 681 applicants, 38% accepted, 170 enrolled. In 2014, 127 master's, 34 doctorates awarded. *Degree requirements:* For master's, thesis or alternative, internship, practicum, written competency exam; for doctorate, thesis/dissertation or alternative. *Entrance requirements:* For master's, GRE General Test (including writing exam), minimum undergraduate GPA of 2.75, 3 recommendations, resume, transcripts, writing sample; for doctorate, GRE General Test (including writing exam), GRE Subject Test, minimum undergraduate GPA of 3.0, graduate 3.5; 10-15 minute VHS tape demonstrating counseling skills; writing sample; 3 recommendations; resume. Additional exam requirements/recommendations for international students: Required—TOEFL (minimum score 577 paper-based). *Application deadline:* For fall admission, 4/1 priority date for domestic students; for spring admission, 11/1 priority date for domestic students. Applications are processed on a rolling basis. Application fee: $50. Electronic applications accepted. *Expenses:* Expenses: Contact institution. *Financial support:* Research assistantships with full and partial tuition reimbursements, teaching assistantships with full and partial tuition reimbursements, career-related internships or fieldwork, scholarships/grants, and tuition waivers (full and partial) available. Support available to part-time students. Financial award application deadline: 9/1; financial award applicants required to submit FAFSA. *Faculty research:* Marriage enrichment, AIDS counseling, troubled youth, faith and learning, trauma. *Unit head:* Dr. William Hathaway, Dean, 757-352-4294, Fax: 757-352-4282, E-mail: willhat@regent.edu. *Application contact:* Matthew Chadwick, Director of Enrollment Support Services, 800-373-5504, Fax: 757-352-4381, E-mail: admissions@regent.edu.
Website: http://www.regent.edu/psychology/

Rivier University, School of Graduate Studies, Department of Psychology, Nashua, NH 03060. Offers clinical psychology (MS); experimental psychology (MS).

Roger Williams University, Feinstein College of Arts and Sciences, Bristol, RI 02809. Offers clinical psychology (MA); forensic psychology (MA). Part-time and evening/weekend programs available. Postbaccalaureate distance learning degree programs offered (minimal on-campus study). *Faculty:* 7 full-time (3 women). *Students:* 35 full-time (28 women), 1 (woman) part-time; includes 5 minority (1 Black or African American, non-Hispanic/Latino; 1 Asian, non-Hispanic/Latino; 2 Hispanic/Latino; 1 Two or more races, non-Hispanic/Latino), 2 international. Average age 23. 118 applicants, 58% accepted, 20 enrolled. In 2014, 21 master's awarded. *Degree requirements:* For master's, thesis optional, internship. *Entrance requirements:* For master's, GRE, 3 letters of recommendation. Additional exam requirements/recommendations for international students: Required—TOEFL (minimum score 85 iBT), IELTS. *Application deadline:*

Applications are processed on a rolling basis. Application fee: $50. Electronic applications accepted. *Expenses:* Expenses: $14,724. *Financial support:* In 2014–15, 5 research assistantships (averaging $5,000 per year) were awarded. Financial award application deadline: 6/15; financial award applicants required to submit FAFSA. *Unit head:* Robert Eisinger, Dean, 401-254-3149, E-mail: reisinger@rwu.edu. *Application contact:* Lori Vales, Director of Graduate Admissions, 401-254-6200, Fax: 401-254-3557, E-mail: gradadmit@rwu.edu.
Website: http://www.rwu.edu/academics/schools/fcas/

Roosevelt University, Graduate Division, College of Arts and Sciences, Department of Psychology, Program in Clinical Professional Psychology, Chicago, IL 60605. Offers MA. *Accreditation:* APA.

Rowan University, Graduate School, College of Science and Mathematics, Program in Clinical Mental Health Counseling, Glassboro, NJ 08028-1701. Offers MA, CAGS. Part-time and evening/weekend programs available. *Faculty:* 3 full-time (1 woman), 7 part-time/adjunct (3 women). *Students:* 23 full-time (19 women), 4 part-time (2 women); includes 3 minority (1 Black or African American, non-Hispanic/Latino; 2 Hispanic/Latino). Average age 26. 45 applicants, 49% accepted, 14 enrolled. In 2014, 26 master's awarded. *Entrance requirements:* For master's, GRE General Test. Additional exam requirements/recommendations for international students: Required—TOEFL. *Application deadline:* For fall admission, 2/15 for domestic students. Application fee: $65. *Expenses: Tuition, area resident:* Part-time $648 per credit. Tuition, state resident: part-time $648 per credit. Tuition, nonresident: part-time $648 per credit. *Required fees:* $145 per credit. Tuition and fees vary according to degree level, campus/location, program and student level. *Financial support:* Career-related internships or fieldwork, Federal Work-Study, and unspecified assistantships available. Support available to part-time students. *Unit head:* Dr. Horacio Sosa, Vice President, Global Learning and Partnerships, 856-256-4747, Fax: 856-256-5638, E-mail: sosa@rowan.edu. *Application contact:* Admissions and Enrollment Services, 856-256-4747, Fax: 856-256-5637, E-mail: globaladmissions@rowan.edu.

Rutgers, The State University of New Jersey, New Brunswick, Graduate School-New Brunswick, Program in Psychology, Piscataway, NJ 08854-8097. Offers behavioral neuroscience (PhD); clinical psychology (PhD); cognitive psychology (PhD); interdisciplinary health psychology (PhD); social psychology (PhD). *Accreditation:* APA. *Degree requirements:* For doctorate, comprehensive exam, thesis/dissertation. *Entrance requirements:* For doctorate, GRE General Test, 3 letters of recommendation. Additional exam requirements/recommendations for international students: Required—TOEFL (minimum score 577 paper-based). Electronic applications accepted. *Faculty research:* Learning and memory, behavioral ecology, hormones and behavior, psychopharmacology, anxiety disorders.

Rutgers, The State University of New Jersey, New Brunswick, Graduate School of Applied and Professional Psychology, Department of Clinical Psychology, Piscataway, NJ 08854-8097. Offers Psy M, Psy D. *Accreditation:* APA (one or more programs are accredited). *Degree requirements:* For doctorate, comprehensive exam, thesis/dissertation, 1 year internship. *Entrance requirements:* For doctorate, GRE General Test, GRE Subject Test, bachelor's degree in psychology or equivalent. Additional exam requirements/recommendations for international students: Required—TOEFL. Electronic applications accepted. *Expenses:* Contact institution. *Faculty research:* Long- and short-term dynamic therapy, community psychology, cognitive-behavioral therapy: anxiety and depressive disorders, addictive behaviors: eating disorders and alcoholism.

St. John's University, St. John's College of Liberal Arts and Sciences, Department of Psychology, Program in Clinical Psychology, Queens, NY 11439. Offers clinical psychology-child (PhD); clinical psychology-general (PhD). *Accreditation:* APA. *Students:* 36 full-time (26 women), 17 part-time (16 women); includes 14 minority (4 Black or African American, non-Hispanic/Latino; 6 Asian, non-Hispanic/Latino; 3 Hispanic/Latino; 1 Two or more races, non-Hispanic/Latino). Average age 27. 329 applicants, 5% accepted, 9 enrolled. In 2014, 9 doctorates awarded. *Degree requirements:* For doctorate, comprehensive exam, thesis/dissertation, internship, practicum. *Entrance requirements:* For doctorate, GRE General Test, GRE Subject Test, 24 credits of undergraduate course work in psychology, 2 writing samples, 3 letters of recommendation, personal statement, bachelor's degree, transcript. Additional exam requirements/recommendations for international students: Required—TOEFL (minimum score 600 paper-based; 100 iBT), IELTS (minimum score 7). *Application deadline:* For fall admission, 1/15 priority date for domestic and international students. Applications are processed on a rolling basis. Application fee: $70. Electronic applications accepted. *Expenses:* Expenses: Contact institution. *Financial support:* Fellowships, research assistantships, career-related internships or fieldwork, and scholarships/grants available. Support available to part-time students. Financial award application deadline: 3/1; financial award applicants required to submit FAFSA. *Faculty research:* Cognitive-behavioral therapy, sucking cessation pedagogical research and implicit attitudes. *Unit head:* Dr. Jeffrey S. Nevid, Director, 718-990-1548, E-mail: nevidj@stjohns.edu. *Application contact:* Robert Medrano, Director of Graduate Admission, 718-990-1601, Fax: 718-990-5686, E-mail: gradhelp@stjohns.edu.

St. John's University, The School of Education, Department of Human Services and Counseling, Program in Clinical Mental Health Counseling, Queens, NY 11439. Offers MS Ed, Adv C. Part-time and evening/weekend programs available. *Students:* 48 full-time (43 women), 27 part-time (20 women); includes 37 minority (10 Black or African American, non-Hispanic/Latino; 8 Asian, non-Hispanic/Latino; 17 Hispanic/Latino; 2 Two or more races, non-Hispanic/Latino), 1 international. Average age 28. 57 applicants, 84% accepted, 14 enrolled. In 2014, 23 master's awarded. *Degree requirements:* For master's, internship, state examination. *Entrance requirements:* For master's, bachelor's degree from an accredited college or university, minimum GPA of 3.0, 2 letters of recommendation, interview, 18 credits in behavioral and social science. Additional exam requirements/recommendations for international students: Required—TOEFL (minimum score 600 paper-based; 100 iBT), IELTS (minimum score 7). *Application deadline:* For fall admission, 4/1 for domestic students, 4/1 priority date for international students; for spring admission, 11/1 for domestic students, 11/1 priority date for international students. Applications are processed on a rolling basis. Application fee: $70. Electronic applications accepted. *Expenses: Tuition:* Full-time $20,610; part-time $1145 per credit. *Required fees:* $170 per semester. *Financial support:* Research assistantships and career-related internships or fieldwork available. Support available to part-time students. Financial award application deadline: 3/1; financial award applicants required to submit FAFSA. *Unit head:* Dr. E. Francine Guastello, Chair, 718-990-1475, E-mail: guastelf@stjohns.edu. *Application contact:* Dr. Kelly K. Ronayne, Associate Dean for Graduate Admissions, 718-990-2304, Fax: 718-990-2343, E-mail: graded@stjohns.edu.

Saint Louis University, Graduate Education, College of Arts and Sciences and Graduate Education, Department of Psychology, St. Louis, MO 63103-2097. Offers clinical psychology (MS-R, PhD); experimental psychology (MS-R, PhD); industrial-organizational psychology (PhD); psychology (PhD). *Accreditation:* APA (one or more programs are accredited). Part-time programs available. *Degree requirements:* For master's, comprehensive exam, thesis; for doctorate, thesis/dissertation, clinical internship (for clinical psychology PhD). *Entrance requirements:* For master's, GRE General Test, interview, letters of recommendation, resume; for doctorate, GRE General Test, interview, letters of recommendation, resumé, transcripts, goal statement.

Additional exam requirements/recommendations for international students: Required—TOEFL (minimum score 550 paper-based). Electronic applications accepted. *Faculty research:* Violence and trauma; neural basis of learning and memory function; eating disorders; body image and health behavior; prejudice, stereotyping, and victimization; memory, cognitive aging and language processing.

Saint Michael's College, Graduate Programs, Program in Clinical Psychology, Colchester, VT 05439. Offers MA. Part-time and evening/weekend programs available. *Degree requirements:* For master's, thesis or alternative, internship, practicum, research seminar. *Entrance requirements:* For master's, GRE General Test, GRE Subject Test, undergraduate major in psychology or related area, minimum 12 credits in psychology, minimum GPA of 3.0. *Application deadline:* For fall admission, 6/1 priority date for domestic students. Applications are processed on a rolling basis. Application fee: $35. Electronic applications accepted. *Expenses: Tuition:* Part-time $590 per credit hour. *Financial support:* Teaching assistantships with partial tuition reimbursements, career-related internships or fieldwork, Federal Work-Study, scholarships/grants, tuition waivers (partial), and unspecified assistantships available. Financial award application deadline: 5/1; financial award applicants required to submit FAFSA. *Faculty research:* Psychodynamic psychotherapy, family therapy, philosophical foundations of clinical psychology. *Unit head:* Dr. Ronald B. Miller, Director, 802-654-2206, Fax: 802-654-2664, E-mail: rmiller@smcvt.edu. *Application contact:* Lindsay A. Damici, Marketing Communications Manager, 802-654-2556, Fax: 802-654-2732.
Website: http://www.smcvt.edu/graduate-programs/academic-programs/clinical-psychology.aspx

Sam Houston State University, College of Humanities and Social Sciences, Department of Psychology and Philosophy, Huntsville, TX 77341. Offers psychology (MA, PhD, SSP), including clinical psychology (MA, PhD), psychology (MA), school psychology (SSP). *Accreditation:* APA. Part-time programs available. *Faculty:* 27 full-time (9 women), 2 part-time/adjunct (0 women). *Students:* 74 full-time (58 women), 38 part-time (33 women); includes 12 minority (2 Black or African American, non-Hispanic/Latino; 1 American Indian or Alaska Native, non-Hispanic/Latino; 1 Asian, non-Hispanic/Latino; 5 Hispanic/Latino; 3 Two or more races, non-Hispanic/Latino), 8 international. Average age 27. 155 applicants, 32% accepted, 33 enrolled. In 2014, 25 master's, 9 doctorates awarded. Terminal master's awarded for partial completion of doctoral program. *Degree requirements:* For master's, comprehensive exam, thesis optional; for doctorate, comprehensive exam, thesis/dissertation. *Entrance requirements:* For master's, GRE General Test, personal statement, letters of recommendation; for doctorate, GRE General Test, GRE Subject Test (advanced psychology), personal essay, letters of recommendation, resume. Additional exam requirements/recommendations for international students: Required—TOEFL (minimum score 550 paper-based; 79 iBT), IELTS (minimum score 6.5). *Application deadline:* For fall admission, 12/1 priority date for domestic students, 6/25 for international students; for spring admission, 12/1 for domestic students, 11/12 for international students. Applications are processed on a rolling basis. Application fee: $45 ($75 for international students). Electronic applications accepted. *Expenses: Tuition, state resident:* full-time $2286; part-time $254 per credit hour. Tuition, nonresident: full-time $5544; part-time $616 per credit hour. *Required fees:* $440 per semester. Tuition and fees vary according to course load and campus/location. *Financial support:* In 2014–15, 61 research assistantships (averaging $9,562 per year), 7 teaching assistantships (averaging $11,088 per year) were awarded; career-related internships or fieldwork, Federal Work-Study, scholarships/grants, tuition waivers (partial), and unspecified assistantships also available. Support available to part-time students. Financial award application deadline: 3/15; financial award applicants required to submit FAFSA. *Unit head:* Dr. D. Christopher Wilson, Chair, 936-294-3052, Fax: 936-294-3798, E-mail: wilson@shsu.edu. *Application contact:* Dr. Jeffrey Anastasi, Assistant Professor/Coordinator of Master of Arts in Psychology Programs, 936-294-3049, Fax: 936-294-3798, E-mail: jeff.anastasi@shsu.edu.
Website: http://www.shsu.edu/~psy_www/

San Diego State University, Graduate and Research Affairs, College of Sciences, Department of Psychology, San Diego, CA 92182. Offers clinical psychology (MS, PhD); industrial and organizational psychology (MS); program evaluation (MS); psychology (MA). PhD offered jointly with University of California, San Diego. *Accreditation:* APA (one or more programs are accredited). Terminal master's awarded for partial completion of doctoral program. *Degree requirements:* For master's, thesis, oral exam; for doctorate, thesis/dissertation. *Entrance requirements:* For master's, GRE General Test, GRE Subject Test, 3 letters of recommendation; for doctorate, GRE General Test, GRE Subject Test, minimum GPA of 3.0, 3 letters of recommendation. Additional exam requirements/recommendations for international students: Required—TOEFL. Electronic applications accepted.

San Jose State University, Graduate Studies and Research, College of Social Sciences, Department of Psychology, San Jose, CA 95192-0001. Offers clinical psychology (MS); experimental psychology (MA); industrial/organizational psychology (MS); psychology (MA). *Degree requirements:* For master's, comprehensive exam, thesis (for some programs). *Entrance requirements:* For master's, GRE General Test, minimum GPA of 3.0. Electronic applications accepted. *Faculty research:* Drug and alcohol abuse, neurohormonal mechanisms in motion sickness, behavior modification, sleep research, genetics.

Saybrook University, School of Clinical Psychology, San Francisco, CA 94111-1920. Offers MA. Program offered jointly with Bastyr University. *Degree requirements:* For master's, thesis (for some programs), oral exams. *Entrance requirements:* For master's, bachelor's degree from an accredited university or college. *Faculty research:* Family systems theory, marriage and family therapy, systems consultation, family and culture of origin, personal authority.

The School of Professional Psychology at Forest Institute, Graduate Programs, Springfield, MO 65807. Offers applied behavior analysis (MS); clinical psychology (MA, Psy D); counseling psychology (MA); marriage and family therapy (MA, PGC). *Accreditation:* AAMFT/COAMFTE; APA (one or more programs are accredited). Part-time and evening/weekend programs available. Terminal master's awarded for partial completion of doctoral program. *Degree requirements:* For master's, thesis, practicum; for doctorate, comprehensive exam, thesis/dissertation, internship, practicum. *Entrance requirements:* For master's, GRE General Test, interview, minimum GPA of 3.0, 12 hours in psychology; for doctorate, GRE General Test (minimum combined Verbal and Quantitative score of 1000, Analytic Writing 4.0), interview, minimum GPA of 3.0, 18 hours in psychology. Additional exam requirements/recommendations for international students: Required—TOEFL (minimum score 550 paper-based). Electronic applications accepted. *Faculty research:* Forensics/corrections, marriage and family therapy, child and adolescent, integrated health care, neuropsychology.

Seattle Pacific University, PhD in Clinical Psychology Program, Seattle, WA 98119-1997. Offers PhD. *Accreditation:* APA. *Students:* 51 full-time (45 women), 20 part-time (16 women); includes 11 minority (3 Black or African American, non-Hispanic/Latino; 3 Asian, non-Hispanic/Latino; 3 Hispanic/Latino; 2 Two or more races, non-Hispanic/Latino), 1 international. Average age 27. 153 applicants, 7% accepted, 11 enrolled. In 2014, 12 doctorates awarded. *Degree requirements:* For doctorate, thesis/dissertation, clinical internship, practicum. *Entrance requirements:* For doctorate, GRE (preferred

minimum score 1100 verbal and quantitative, taken within the last five years), BA, personal statement. Additional exam requirements/recommendations for international students: Required—TOEFL (minimum score 600 paper-based). *Application deadline:* For fall admission, 12/15 for domestic and international students. Electronic applications accepted. *Expenses:* Expenses: Contact institution. *Financial support:* Fellowships and scholarships/grants available. Financial award applicants required to submit FAFSA. *Faculty research:* Social network support, attachment, integration of faith and family psychology, developmental psychology. *Unit head:* Dr. David G. Stewart, Chair, 206-281-2660, E-mail: davidste@spu.edu. *Application contact:* 206-281-2091.
Website: http://www.spu.edu/depts/spfc/clinicalpsych/index.asp

Siena Heights University, Graduate College, Adrian, MI 49221-1796. Offers clinical mental health counseling (MA); educational leadership (Specialist); leadership (MA), including health care leadership, organizational leadership; teacher education (MA), including early childhood education, early childhood education: Montessori, education leadership: principal, elementary education: reading K-12, leadership: higher education, secondary education: reading K-12, special education: cognitive impairment, special education: learning disabilities. Part-time and evening/weekend programs available. *Faculty:* 37. *Students:* 3 full-time (2 women), 237 part-time (158 women). In 2014, 32 master's awarded. *Degree requirements:* For master's, thesis, presentation. *Entrance requirements:* For master's, minimum GPA of 3.0, current resume, essay, all post-secondary transcripts, 3 letters of reference, conviction disclosure form; copy of teaching certificate (for some education programs); for Specialist, master's degree, minimum GPA of 3.0, current resume, essay, all post-secondary transcripts, 3 letters of reference, conviction disclosure form; copy of teaching certificate (for some education programs). *Application deadline:* Applications are processed on a rolling basis. Application fee: $50. Electronic applications accepted. *Expenses: Tuition:* Part-time $562 per credit hour. *Required fees:* $135 per term. *Financial support:* Career-related internships or fieldwork, Federal Work-Study, and unspecified assistantships available. Financial award application deadline: 9/1; financial award applicants required to submit FAFSA. *Unit head:* Dr. Linda S. Pettit, Dean, Graduate College, 517-264-7661, Fax: 517-264-7714, E-mail: lpettit@sienahts.edu.
Website: http://www.sienaheights.edu

Slippery Rock University of Pennsylvania, Graduate Studies (Recruitment), College of Education, Department of Counseling and Development, Slippery Rock, PA 16057-1383. Offers clinical mental health counseling (MA), including addiction, adult, older adult, school and youth; student affairs (MA), including higher education; student affairs in higher education (MA), including college counseling. *Accreditation:* ACA; NCATE. Part-time and evening/weekend programs available. *Faculty:* 9 full-time (5 women). *Students:* 84 full-time (69 women), 16 part-time (13 women); includes 13 minority (8 Black or African American, non-Hispanic/Latino; 1 American Indian or Alaska Native, non-Hispanic/Latino; 2 Hispanic/Latino; 2 Two or more races, non-Hispanic/Latino), 1 international. Average age 29. 128 applicants, 51% accepted, 41 enrolled. In 2014, 45 master's awarded. *Degree requirements:* For master's, comprehensive exam, thesis (for some programs). *Entrance requirements:* For master's, GRE General Test or MAT, official transcripts, minimum GPA of 2.75 or 3.0 (depending on program), personal statement, three letters of recommendation, interview. Additional exam requirements/recommendations for international students: Required—TOEFL (minimum score 550 paper-based; 80 iBT). *Application deadline:* For fall admission, 1/15 priority date for domestic and international students. Application fee: $25 ($30 for international students). Electronic applications accepted. *Expenses:* Tuition, state resident: full-time $8172; part-time $454 per credit. Tuition, nonresident: full-time $12,258; part-time $681 per credit. *Required fees:* $2326; $200 per credit. Tuition and fees vary according to degree level and program. *Financial support:* Career-related internships or fieldwork, Federal Work-Study, institutionally sponsored loans, scholarships/grants, tuition waivers (partial), and unspecified assistantships available. Support available to part-time students. Financial award application deadline: 5/1; financial award applicants required to submit FAFSA. *Unit head:* Dr. Stacy Jacob, Graduate Coordinator, 724-738-2758, Fax: 724-738-4859, E-mail: stacy.jacob@sru.edu. *Application contact:* Brandi Weber-Mortimer, Director of Graduate Admissions, 724-738-2051, Fax: 724-738-2146, E-mail: graduate.admissions@sru.edu.
Website: http://srudss.ingeniuxondemand.com/academics/colleges-and-departments/coe/departments/counseling-and-development

Sofia University, Residential Programs, Palo Alto, CA 94303. Offers clinical psychology (Psy D); counseling psychology (MA); transpersonal psychology (MA, PhD). Part-time and evening/weekend programs available. Terminal master's awarded for partial completion of doctoral program. *Degree requirements:* For doctorate, thesis/dissertation. *Entrance requirements:* For master's, bachelor's degree; for doctorate, bachelor's degree; master's degree (for some programs). Electronic applications accepted.

Sonoma State University, School of Social Sciences, Department of Counseling, Rohnert Park, CA 94928-3609. Offers counseling (MA); licensed professional clinical counseling (MA); marriage, family, and child counseling (MA); pupil personnel services (MA). *Accreditation:* ACA. Part-time programs available. *Degree requirements:* For master's, internship. *Entrance requirements:* For master's, minimum GPA of 3.0. Additional exam requirements/recommendations for international students: Required—TOEFL (minimum score 500 paper-based).

Southeastern Oklahoma State University, School of Behavioral Sciences, Durant, OK 74701-0609. Offers clinical mental health counseling (MS). Part-time and evening/weekend programs available. *Degree requirements:* For master's, comprehensive exam, thesis optional. *Entrance requirements:* For master's, GRE General Test, minimum GPA of 3.0 in last 60 hours or 2.75 overall. Additional exam requirements/recommendations for international students: Required—TOEFL (minimum score 550 paper-based; 79 iBT). Electronic applications accepted.

Southern Illinois University Carbondale, Graduate School, College of Liberal Arts, Department of Psychology, Carbondale, IL 62901-4701. Offers clinical psychology (PhD); counseling psychology (PhD); experimental psychology (MA, MS). *Accreditation:* APA (one or more programs are accredited). *Faculty:* 27 full-time (14 women), 1 part-time/adjunct (0 women). *Students:* 70 full-time (46 women), 35 part-time (20 women); includes 10 minority (8 Black or African American, non-Hispanic/Latino; 2 Asian, non-Hispanic/Latino), 12 international. 274 applicants, 11% accepted, 20 enrolled. In 2014, 10 master's, 10 doctorates awarded. *Degree requirements:* For master's, thesis; for doctorate, thesis/dissertation. *Entrance requirements:* For master's, GRE General Test, GRE Subject Test, minimum GPA of 2.7; for doctorate, GRE General Test, GRE Subject Test, minimum GPA of 3.25. Additional exam requirements/recommendations for international students: Required—TOEFL. *Application deadline:* For fall admission, 3/1 priority date for domestic students. Applications are processed on a rolling basis. Application fee: $50. *Expenses:* Tuition, state resident: full-time $10,176; part-time $1153 per credit. Tuition, nonresident: full-time $20,814; part-time $1744 per credit. *Required fees:* $7092; $394 per credit. $2364 per semester. *Financial support:* In 2014–15, 82 students received support, including 14 fellowships with full tuition reimbursements available, 23 research assistantships with full tuition reimbursements available, 22 teaching assistantships with full tuition reimbursements available; Federal Work-Study, institutionally sponsored loans, and tuition waivers (full) also available. *Faculty research:* Developmental neuropsychology; smoking, affect, and cognition; personality measurement; vocational psychology; program evaluation. *Unit head:* Dr. Meera Komarraju, Chair, 618-453-3529, E-mail: meerak@siu.edu. *Application contact:* Stacia Werner, Office Specialist, 618-453-3564, E-mail: gradpsych@siu.edu.
Website: http://psychology.siuc.edu/

Southern Illinois University Edwardsville, Graduate School, School of Education, Health, and Human Behavior, Department of Psychology, Program in Clinical Child and School Psychology, Edwardsville, IL 62026-0001. Offers MS. Part-time programs available. *Students:* 12 full-time (11 women), 8 part-time (6 women); includes 4 minority (2 Black or African American, non-Hispanic/Latino; 1 Hispanic/Latino; 1 Two or more races, non-Hispanic/Latino). 55 applicants, 16% accepted. In 2014, 10 master's awarded. *Degree requirements:* For master's, thesis (for some programs), research project. *Entrance requirements:* For master's, GRE. Additional exam requirements/recommendations for international students: Required—TOEFL (minimum score 550 paper-based, 79 iBT), IELTS (minimum score 6.5), Michigan Test of English Language Proficiency or PTE. *Application deadline:* For fall admission, 2/1 for domestic and international students. Application fee: $30. Electronic applications accepted. *Expenses:* Tuition, state resident: full-time $5026. Tuition, nonresident: full-time $12,566. *International tuition:* $25,136 full-time. *Required fees:* $1682. Tuition and fees vary according to course load, campus/location and program. *Financial support:* Institutionally sponsored loans, scholarships/grants, and unspecified assistantships available. Financial award application deadline: 3/1; financial award applicants required to submit FAFSA. *Unit head:* Dr. Jeremy Jewell, Director, 618-650-2202, E-mail: jejewel@siue.edu. *Application contact:* Melissa K. Mace, Assistant Director of Graduate and International Education, 618-650-2756, Fax: 618-650-3618, E-mail: mmace@siue.edu.
Website: http://www.siue.edu/education/psychology/

Southern Illinois University Edwardsville, Graduate School, School of Education, Health, and Human Behavior, Department of Psychology, Program in Clinical Psychology, Edwardsville, IL 62026-0001. Offers MA. Part-time and evening/weekend programs available. *Students:* 50 full-time (40 women), 17 part-time (14 women); includes 8 minority (3 Black or African American, non-Hispanic/Latino; 1 Hispanic/Latino; 4 Two or more races, non-Hispanic/Latino), 2 international. 130 applicants, 22% accepted. In 2014, 28 master's awarded. *Degree requirements:* For master's, comprehensive exam (for some programs), thesis (for some programs). *Entrance requirements:* For master's, GRE. Additional exam requirements/recommendations for international students: Required—TOEFL (minimum score 550 paper-based; 79 iBT), IELTS (minimum score 6.5). *Application deadline:* For fall admission, 1/15 for domestic and international students. Application fee: $30. Electronic applications accepted. *Expenses:* Tuition, state resident: full-time $5026. Tuition, nonresident: full-time $12,566. *International tuition:* $25,136 full-time. *Required fees:* $1682. Tuition and fees vary according to course load, campus/location and program. *Financial support:* Institutionally sponsored loans, scholarships/grants, and unspecified assistantships available. Financial award application deadline: 3/1; financial award applicants required to submit FAFSA. *Unit head:* Dr. Paul Rose, Chair, 618-650-2202, E-mail: prose@siue.edu. *Application contact:* Melissa K. Mace, Assistant Director of Admissions for Graduate and International Recruitment, 618-650-2756, Fax: 618-650-3618, E-mail: mmace@siue.edu.
Website: http://www.siue.edu/education/psychology/graduate/clinical-adult-psychology/index.shtml

Southern Methodist University, Dedman College of Humanities and Sciences, Department of Psychology, Program in Clinical Psychology, Dallas, TX 75275. Offers PhD. *Accreditation:* APA. *Degree requirements:* For doctorate, comprehensive exam, thesis/dissertation, research presentation and publication. *Entrance requirements:* For doctorate, GRE General Test, minimum GPA of 3.0, 3 letters of recommendation. Additional exam requirements/recommendations for international students: Required—TOEFL (minimum score 550 paper-based). Electronic applications accepted. *Faculty research:* Family violence, family assessment, anxiety disorders, personality disorders.

South University, Program in Clinical Mental Health Counseling, Cleveland, OH 44128. Offers MA.

Spalding University, Graduate Studies, Kosair College of Health and Natural Sciences, School of Professional Psychology, Louisville, KY 40203-2188. Offers clinical psychology (MA, Psy D). *Accreditation:* APA (one or more programs are accredited). Part-time programs available. *Faculty:* 8 full-time (4 women), 11 part-time/adjunct (6 women). *Students:* 122 full-time (99 women), 55 part-time (41 women); includes 20 minority (5 Black or African American, non-Hispanic/Latino; 5 Asian, non-Hispanic/Latino; 4 Hispanic/Latino; 1 Native Hawaiian or other Pacific Islander, non-Hispanic/Latino; 5 Two or more races, non-Hispanic/Latino), 2 international. Average age 29. 151 applicants, 33% accepted, 30 enrolled. In 2014, 25 master's, 23 doctorates awarded. Terminal master's awarded for partial completion of doctoral program. *Degree requirements:* For master's, comprehensive exam; for doctorate, thesis/dissertation. *Entrance requirements:* For master's and doctorate, GRE General Test, 18 hours of undergraduate course work in psychology, interview, letters of recommendation, writing sample, autobiographical statement. Additional exam requirements/recommendations for international students: Required—TOEFL (minimum score 535 paper-based). *Application deadline:* For fall admission, 1/15 priority date for domestic and international students. Application fee: $30. *Financial support:* In 2014–15, 56 research assistantships (averaging $2,920 per year) were awarded; career-related internships or fieldwork, scholarships/grants, and unspecified assistantships also available. Financial award application deadline: 3/30; financial award applicants required to submit FAFSA. *Faculty research:* Substance abuse, prayer research, end-of-life issues, complementary and alternative medicine, research methodology and statistical inference. *Unit head:* Dr. Steven Katsikas, Chair, 502-873-4459, E-mail: skatsikas@spalding.edu. *Application contact:* Elizabeth A. Simpson, Administrative Assistant, 502-585-7127, Fax: 502-585-7159, E-mail: esimpson@spalding.edu.

Springfield College, Graduate Programs, Programs in Psychology and Counseling, Springfield, MA 01109-3797. Offers athletic counseling (MS, CAGS); clinical mental health counseling (M Ed, CAGS); counseling psychology (Psy D); industrial and organizational psychology (M Ed, CAGS); school guidance counseling (M Ed, CAGS); student personnel administration in higher education (M Ed). Part-time programs available. *Degree requirements:* For master's, research project, portfolio; for doctorate, dissertation project, 1500 hours of counseling psychology practicum, full-year internship. *Entrance requirements:* Additional exam requirements/recommendations for international students: Required—TOEFL (minimum score 550 paper-based). *Application deadline:* For fall admission, 1/15 priority date for domestic students, 1/15 for international students; for winter admission, 11/1 for domestic and international students; for spring admission, 11/1 for domestic and international students. Applications are processed on a rolling basis. Application fee: $50. Electronic applications accepted. *Financial support:* Fellowships with partial tuition reimbursements, teaching assistantships with partial tuition reimbursements, career-related internships or fieldwork, Federal Work-Study, institutionally sponsored loans, and unspecified assistantships available. Financial award application deadline: 3/1; financial award applicants required to submit FAFSA. *Unit head:* Dr. Allison Cumming-

McCann, Chair, 413-748-3075, Fax: 413-748-3854, E-mail: acumming@springfieldcollege.edu. *Application contact:* Mary DeAngelo, Director of Enrollment Management, 413-748-3136, E-mail: mdeangel@spfldcol.edu. Website: http://www.springfieldcollege.edu/academic-programs/psychology-department/graduate-programs-in-psychology/index#.U1F-dKJWiSo

State University of New York at Plattsburgh, Division of Education, Health, and Human Services, Department of Counselor Education, Plattsburgh, NY 12901-2681. Offers clinical mental health counseling (MS, Advanced Certificate); school counselor (MS Ed, CAS); student affairs counseling (MS). *Accreditation:* ACA (one or more programs are accredited); Teacher Education Accreditation Council. Part-time programs available. *Students:* 44 full-time (36 women), 14 part-time (11 women); includes 7 minority (2 Black or African American, non-Hispanic/Latino; 1 American Indian or Alaska Native, non-Hispanic/Latino; 4 Hispanic/Latino), 5 international. Average age 27. *Entrance requirements:* For master's, GRE General Test or MAT, minimum GPA of 2.8. Additional exam requirements/recommendations for international students: Required—TOEFL. *Application deadline:* For fall admission, 2/15 priority date for domestic students; for spring admission, 10/15 priority date for domestic students. Applications are processed on a rolling basis. Application fee: $75. *Financial support:* Research assistantships, teaching assistantships, career-related internships or fieldwork, Federal Work-Study, and administrative assistantships, editorial assistantships available. Support available to part-time students. Financial award application deadline: 4/15; financial award applicants required to submit FAFSA. *Faculty research:* Campus violence, program accreditation, substance abuse, vocational assessment, group counseling, divorce. *Unit head:* Dr. Julia Davis, Coordinator, 518-564-4179, E-mail: jdavi004@plattsburgh.edu. *Application contact:* Betsy Kane, Director, Graduate Admissions, 518-564-4723, Fax: 518-564-4722, E-mail: bkane002@plattsburgh.edu.

Stony Brook University, State University of New York, Graduate School, College of Arts and Sciences, Department of Psychology, Program in Clinical Psychology, Stony Brook, NY 11794. Offers PhD. *Accreditation:* APA. *Students:* 31 full-time (26 women); includes 6 minority (1 Black or African American, non-Hispanic/Latino; 2 Asian, non-Hispanic/Latino; 3 Hispanic/Latino), 5 international. Average age 27. 282 applicants, 6% accepted, 8 enrolled. In 2014, 6 doctorates awarded. *Degree requirements:* For doctorate, thesis/dissertation. *Entrance requirements:* For doctorate, GRE General Test, GRE Subject Test. Additional exam requirements/recommendations for international students: Required—TOEFL. *Application deadline:* For fall admission, 1/15 for domestic students; for spring admission, 10/1 for domestic students. Application fee: $100. *Expenses:* Tuition, state resident: full-time $10,370; part-time $432 per credit. Tuition, nonresident: full-time $20,190; part-time $841 per credit. *Required fees:* $1431. *Unit head:* Dr. Arthur Samuel, Chair, 631-632-7792, Fax: 631-632-7876, E-mail: arthur.samuel@stonybrook.edu. *Application contact:* Marilynn Wollmuth, Coordinator, 631-632-7855, Fax: 631-632-7876, E-mail: marilyn.wollmuth@stonybrook.edu.

Suffolk University, College of Arts and Sciences, Department of Psychology, Boston, MA 02108-2770. Offers clinical psychology (PhD); college admission counseling (Certificate); mental health counseling (MS, CAGS); school counseling (MS, CAGS). *Accreditation:* APA. *Faculty:* 14 full-time (6 women), 6 part-time/adjunct (4 women). *Students:* 61 full-time (52 women), 39 part-time (33 women); includes 23 minority (6 Black or African American, non-Hispanic/Latino; 7 Asian, non-Hispanic/Latino; 8 Hispanic/Latino; 2 Two or more races, non-Hispanic/Latino), 6 international. Average age 27. 384 applicants, 18% accepted, 33 enrolled. In 2014, 33 master's, 21 doctorates, 6 other advanced degrees awarded. *Degree requirements:* For doctorate, thesis/dissertation, practicum. *Entrance requirements:* For doctorate, GRE General Test or MAT, 2 letters of recommendation, resume. Additional exam requirements/recommendations for international students: Required—TOEFL (minimum score 550 paper-based; 80 iBT). *Application deadline:* For fall admission, 12/15 for domestic and international students. Applications are processed on a rolling basis. Application fee: $50. Electronic applications accepted. *Expenses:* Expenses: Contact institution. *Financial support:* In 2014–15, 62 students received support, including 60 fellowships (averaging $16,231 per year); career-related internships or fieldwork, Federal Work-Study, and institutionally sponsored loans also available. Support available to part-time students. Financial award application deadline: 4/1; financial award applicants required to submit FAFSA. *Faculty research:* Assessing exposure in the context of a family-based cognitive behavioral treatment for pediatric OCD, a mindfulness approach to designing and testing the efficacy of a new sexual revictimization prevention program for college women, olfaction and decision-making in substance-dependent individuals, the role of experiential avoidance in Generalized Anxiety Disorder, ego development as a predictor of dogmatism and intolerance in the political right and left. *Unit head:* Dr. Gary Fireman, Chairperson, 617-305-6368, Fax: 617-367-2924, E-mail: gfireman@suffolk.edu. *Application contact:* Cory Meyers, Director of Graduate Admissions, 617-573-8302, Fax: 617-305-1733, E-mail: grad.admission@suffolk.edu. Website: http://www.suffolk.edu/college/departments/9912.php

Sul Ross State University, School of Arts and Sciences, Department of Behavioral and Social Sciences, Program in Psychology, Alpine, TX 79832. Offers clinical psychology (MA); general psychology (MA). *Entrance requirements:* For master's, GRE General Test, minimum GPA of 2.5 in last 60 hours of undergraduate work.

Syracuse University, College of Arts and Sciences, Program in Clinical Psychology, Syracuse, NY 13244. Offers PhD. *Accreditation:* APA. *Students:* 24 full-time (20 women), 1 part-time (0 women); includes 5 minority (1 Black or African American, non-Hispanic/Latino; 2 Asian, non-Hispanic/Latino; 2 Hispanic/Latino), 1 international. Average age 27. 183 applicants, 3% accepted, 5 enrolled. In 2014, 1 degree awarded. Terminal master's awarded for partial completion of doctoral program. *Degree requirements:* For doctorate, comprehensive exam, thesis/dissertation. *Entrance requirements:* For doctorate, GRE General Test, GRE Subject Test. Additional exam requirements/recommendations for international students: Required—TOEFL (minimum score 100 iBT). *Application deadline:* For fall admission, 1/1 priority date for domestic and international students. Application fee: $75. Electronic applications accepted. *Expenses: Tuition:* Part-time $1341 per credit. *Financial support:* Fellowships with full tuition reimbursements, research assistantships with full and partial tuition reimbursements, and teaching assistantships with full and partial tuition reimbursements available. Financial award application deadline: 1/1; financial award applicants required to submit FAFSA. *Unit head:* Dr. Kevin Antshel, Chair, 315-443-9450. *Application contact:* Alecia Zema, Admin. Ass't, 315-443-2760. Website: http://psychology.syr.edu/graduate/Clinical.html

Syracuse University, School of Education, Program in Clinical Mental Health Counseling, Syracuse, NY 13244. Offers MS. Part-time programs available. *Students:* 43 full-time (35 women), 9 part-time (7 women); includes 12 minority (5 Black or African American, non-Hispanic/Latino; 5 Hispanic/Latino; 2 Two or more races, non-Hispanic/Latino), 9 international. Average age 26. 50 applicants, 60% accepted, 17 enrolled. In 2014, 13 master's awarded. *Entrance requirements:* For master's, GRE General Test or MAT, interview. Additional exam requirements/recommendations for international students: Required—TOEFL (minimum score 100 iBT). *Application deadline:* For fall admission, 2/1 priority date for domestic students; for spring admission, 10/15 priority date for domestic and international students. Application fee: $75. Electronic applications accepted. *Expenses: Tuition:* Part-time $1341 per credit. *Financial support:* Fellowships with full tuition reimbursements available. Financial award application deadline: 1/1. *Unit head:* Dr. Nicole Hill, Chair, 315-443-2266, E-mail: nrhill@syr.edu. *Application contact:* Laurie Deyo, Graduate Recruiter, School of Education, 315-443-2505, E-mail: e-gradrcrt@syr.edu. Website: http://soeweb.syr.edu/academic/counseling_and_human_services/graduate/masters/clinical_mental_health_counseling/default.aspx

Teachers College, Columbia University, Graduate Faculty of Education, Department of Counseling and Clinical Psychology, Program in Clinical Psychology, New York, NY 10027-6696. Offers PhD. *Accreditation:* APA. *Faculty:* 9 full-time, 2 part-time/adjunct. *Students:* 153 full-time (117 women), 248 part-time (192 women); includes 108 minority (25 Black or African American, non-Hispanic/Latino; 1 American Indian or Alaska Native, non-Hispanic/Latino; 34 Asian, non-Hispanic/Latino; 38 Hispanic/Latino; 10 Two or more races, non-Hispanic/Latino), 78 international. Average age 27. 634 applicants, 67% accepted, 159 enrolled. In 2014, 6 doctorates awarded. *Degree requirements:* For doctorate, comprehensive exam, thesis/dissertation, twelve-month clinical internship, original piece of empirical research. *Entrance requirements:* For doctorate, GRE. *Application deadline:* For fall admission, 12/15 for domestic students. Application fee: $65. Electronic applications accepted. *Expenses: Tuition:* Full-time $33,552; part-time $1398 per credit. *Required fees:* $418 per semester. *Financial support:* Career-related internships or fieldwork, Federal Work-Study, institutionally sponsored loans, and tuition waivers (partial) available. Support available to part-time students. Financial award application deadline: 2/1. *Faculty research:* Psychotherapy education, trauma, stress, psychopathology, life span and aging issues. *Unit head:* Prof. Barry Farber, Program Coordinator, 212-678-3125, E-mail: bf39@columbia.edu. *Application contact:* David Estrella, Director of Admission, 212-678-3305, E-mail: dpe2103@columbia.edu. Website: http://www.tc.columbia.edu/ccp/clinical/

Texas A&M University, College of Liberal Arts, Department of Psychology, College Station, TX 77843. Offers behavioral and cellular neuroscience (PhD); clinical psychology (PhD); cognitive psychology (PhD); developmental psychology (PhD); industrial/organizational psychology (PhD); psychology (MS); social psychology (PhD). *Accreditation:* APA (one or more programs are accredited). *Faculty:* 35. *Students:* 82 full-time (45 women), 15 part-time (12 women); includes 30 minority (6 Black or African American, non-Hispanic/Latino; 6 Asian, non-Hispanic/Latino; 18 Hispanic/Latino), 11 international. Average age 28. 375 applicants, 5% accepted, 8 enrolled. In 2014, 8 master's, 16 doctorates awarded. *Degree requirements:* For doctorate, comprehensive exam (for some programs), thesis/dissertation. *Entrance requirements:* For doctorate, GRE General Test. Additional exam requirements/recommendations for international students: Required—TOEFL. *Application deadline:* For fall admission, 1/5 for domestic and international students. Application fee: $50 ($90 for international students). Electronic applications accepted. *Expenses:* Tuition, state resident: full-time $4078; part-time $226.55 per credit hour. Tuition, nonresident: full-time $10,594; part-time $577.55 per credit hour. *Required fees:* $2813; $237.70 per credit hour. $278.50 per semester. Tuition and fees vary according to degree level and student level. *Financial support:* In 2014–15, 84 students received support, including 25 fellowships with full and partial tuition reimbursements available (averaging $17,037 per year), 20 research assistantships with full and partial tuition reimbursements available (averaging $8,269 per year), 57 teaching assistantships with full and partial tuition reimbursements available (averaging $7,431 per year); career-related internships or fieldwork, institutionally sponsored loans, scholarships/grants, traineeships, health care benefits, tuition waivers (full and partial), and unspecified assistantships also available. Support available to part-time students. Financial award application deadline: 1/5; financial award applicants required to submit FAFSA. *Unit head:* Dr. Doug Woods, Head, 979-845-2540, E-mail: dowoods@tamu.edu. *Application contact:* Dr. Charles D. Samuelson, Director of Graduate Studies, 979-845-0880, Fax: 979-845-4727, E-mail: c-samuelson@tamu.edu. Website: http://psychology.tamu.edu

Texas A&M University–Central Texas, Graduate Studies and Research, Killeen, TX 76549. Offers accounting (MS); business administration (MBA); clinical mental health counseling (MS); criminal justice (MCJ); curriculum and instruction (M Ed); educational administration (M Ed); educational psychology - experimental psychology (MS); history (MA); human resource management (MS); information systems (MS); liberal studies (MS); management and leadership (MS); marriage and family therapy (MS); mathematics (MS); political science (MA); school counseling (M Ed); school psychology (Ed S).

Texas Tech University, Graduate School, College of Arts and Sciences, Department of Psychological Sciences, Lubbock, TX 79409-2051. Offers clinical psychology (PhD); counseling psychology (MA, PhD); general experimental psychology (MA, PhD); psychology (MA). *Accreditation:* APA (one or more programs are accredited). *Faculty:* 32 full-time (14 women), 1 part-time/adjunct (0 women). *Students:* 96 full-time (60 women), 18 part-time (16 women); includes 25 minority (4 Black or African American, non-Hispanic/Latino; 5 Asian, non-Hispanic/Latino; 14 Hispanic/Latino; 2 Two or more races, non-Hispanic/Latino), 6 international. Average age 27. 281 applicants, 17% accepted, 24 enrolled. In 2014, 12 master's, 16 doctorates awarded. *Degree requirements:* For doctorate, comprehensive exam, thesis/dissertation, 100 credit hours of organized courses, research credits, and practica. *Entrance requirements:* For master's, GRE General Test, GRE Subject Test, essays; for doctorate, GRE General Test, essays. Additional exam requirements/recommendations for international students: Required—TOEFL (minimum score 550 paper-based; 79 iBT). *Application deadline:* For fall admission, 6/1 priority date for domestic students, 1/15 priority date for international students; for spring admission, 9/1 priority date for domestic students, 6/15 priority date for international students. Applications are processed on a rolling basis. Application fee: $60. Electronic applications accepted. *Expenses:* Tuition, state resident: full-time $6310; part-time $262.92 per credit hour. Tuition, nonresident: full-time $14,998; part-time $624.92 per credit hour. *Required fees:* $2701; $36.50 per credit. $912.50 per semester. Tuition and fees vary according to course load. *Financial support:* In 2014–15, 102 students received support, including 101 fellowships (averaging $4,037 per year), 23 research assistantships (averaging $13,150 per year), 72 teaching assistantships (averaging $10,753 per year). Financial award application deadline: 4/15; financial award applicants required to submit FAFSA. *Faculty research:* Health psychology, addictive behaviors, depression and suicide risk, sexuality/sexual risk behaviors/HIV, neuroscience/neuroimaging. *Total annual research expenditures:* $345,735. *Unit head:* Dr. Lee M. Cohen, Professor and Chair, 806-834-2530, Fax: 806-742-0818, E-mail: lee.cohen@ttu.edu. *Application contact:* Kay Hill, Admissions Coordinator, 806-742-3711 Ext. 222, Fax: 806-742-0818, E-mail: kay.hill@ttu.edu. Website: http://www.depts.ttu.edu/psy/

Towson University, Program in Clinical Psychology, Towson, MD 21252-0001. Offers MA. Part-time and evening/weekend programs available. *Students:* 92 full-time (72 women), 12 part-time (8 women); includes 24 minority (13 Black or African American, non-Hispanic/Latino; 2 Asian, non-Hispanic/Latino; 3 Hispanic/Latino; 6 Two or more races, non-Hispanic/Latino), 1 international. *Degree requirements:* For master's, thesis (for some programs). *Entrance requirements:* For master's, GRE, minimum GPA of 3.0, letters of recommendation. *Application deadline:* For fall admission, 2/1 for domestic and international students. Application fee: $45. Electronic applications accepted. *Financial*

support: Application deadline: 4/1. *Unit head:* Dr. Elizabeth Katz, Graduate Program Director, 410-704-3221, E-mail: clinincalpsyc@towson.edu. *Application contact:* Alicia Arkell-Kleis, Information Contact, 410-704-6004, E-mail: grads@towson.edu.
Website: http://grad.towson.edu/program/master/psyc-clpy-ma/

Trinity Washington University, School of Education, Washington, DC 20017-1094. Offers clinical mental health counseling (MA); early childhood education (MAT); educating for change (M Ed); educational administration (MSA); elementary education (MAT); reading (M Ed); school counseling (MA); secondary education (MAT), including English, social studies; special education (MAT). *Accreditation:* NCATE. Part-time and evening/weekend programs available. *Degree requirements:* For master's, thesis (for some programs), capstone project(s). *Entrance requirements:* For master's, PRAXIS I, minimum GPA of 2.8. Additional exam requirements/recommendations for international students: Required—TOEFL (minimum score 550 paper-based). *Faculty research:* Technology, literacy, special education, organizations, inclusion models.

Troy University, Graduate School, College of Education, Program in Counseling and Psychology, Troy, AL 36082. Offers agency counseling (Ed S); clinical mental health (MS); community counseling (MS, Ed S); corrections counseling (MS); rehabilitation counseling (MS); school psychology (MS, Ed S); school psychometry (MS); social service counseling (MS); student affairs counseling (MS); substance abuse counseling (MS). *Accreditation:* ACA; CORE; NCATE. Part-time and evening/weekend programs available. *Faculty:* 41 full-time (18 women), 32 part-time/adjunct (18 women). *Students:* 358 full-time (286 women), 503 part-time (425 women); includes 572 minority (481 Black or African American, non-Hispanic/Latino; 3 American Indian or Alaska Native, non-Hispanic/Latino; 5 Asian, non-Hispanic/Latino; 62 Hispanic/Latino; 21 Two or more races, non-Hispanic/Latino). Average age 34. 248 applicants, 86% accepted, 139 enrolled. In 2014, 212 master's, 4 other advanced degrees awarded. *Degree requirements:* For master's, comprehensive exam, thesis. *Entrance requirements:* For master's, GRE (minimum score of 850 on old exam or 290 on new exam), GMAT (minimum score of 380), or MAT (minimum score of 385), bachelor's degree; minimum undergraduate GPA of 2.5 or 3.0 on last 30 semester hours, letter of recommendation. Additional exam requirements/recommendations for international students: Required—TOEFL (minimum score 523 paper-based; 70 iBT), IELTS (minimum score 6). *Application deadline:* Applications are processed on a rolling basis. Application fee: $50. Electronic applications accepted. *Expenses:* Tuition, state resident: full-time $6570; part-time $365 per credit hour. Tuition, nonresident: full-time $13,140; part-time $730 per credit hour. *Required fees:* $365 per credit hour. *Unit head:* Dr. Andrew Creamer, Chair, 334-670-3350, Fax: 334-670-3291, E-mail: acreamer@troy.edu. *Application contact:* Jessica A. Kimbro, Director of Graduate Admissions, 334-670-3178, E-mail: jacord@troy.edu.

Uniformed Services University of the Health Sciences, F. Edward Hebert School of Medicine, Graduate Programs in the Biomedical Sciences and Public Health, Department of Medical and Clinical Psychology, Bethesda, MD 20814. Offers clinical psychology (PhD); medical psychology (PhD). PhD in clinical psychology available to active duty military only. *Accreditation:* APA. Terminal master's awarded for partial completion of doctoral program. *Degree requirements:* For doctorate, comprehensive exam, thesis/dissertation, qualifying exam. *Entrance requirements:* For doctorate, GRE General Test, minimum GPA of 3.0, U.S. citizenship. Additional exam requirements/recommendations for international students: Required—TOEFL. Electronic applications accepted. *Faculty research:* Addictive and appetitive behavior, psychopharmacology, stress and eating, obesity, health.

Union College, Graduate Programs, Department of Psychology, Barbourville, KY 40906-1499. Offers clinical psychology (MA); counseling psychology (MA); school psychology (MA).

Union Institute & University, Graduate Programs in Psychology, Cincinnati, OH 45206-1925. Offers clinical psychology (Psy D). Psy D offered in Ohio and Vermont. Postbaccalaureate distance learning degree programs offered (minimal on-campus study). *Faculty:* 9 full-time (7 women), 8 part-time/adjunct (4 women). *Students:* 66 full-time (45 women), 21 part-time (16 women); includes 13 minority (5 Black or African American, non-Hispanic/Latino; 2 American Indian or Alaska Native, non-Hispanic/Latino; 1 Asian, non-Hispanic/Latino; 4 Hispanic/Latino; 1 Native Hawaiian or other Pacific Islander, non-Hispanic/Latino). Average age 38. Terminal master's awarded for partial completion of doctoral program. *Degree requirements:* For master's, thesis, internship; for doctorate, thesis/dissertation, internship, practicum. *Entrance requirements:* For master's and doctorate, transcripts, letters of recommendation, essay. *Application deadline:* Applications are processed on a rolling basis. Application fee: $50. Electronic applications accepted. *Expenses: Tuition:* Full-time $26,640; part-time $719 per credit hour. *Required fees:* $216; $54 per semester. Part-time tuition and fees vary according to course load, degree level and program. *Financial support:* Federal Work-Study available. Financial award applicants required to submit FAFSA. *Unit head:* Dr. Bill Lax, Dean, 802-254-0152, E-mail: bill.lax@myunion.edu. *Application contact:* Director of Admissions, 888-828-8575.

Universidad de Iberoamerica, Graduate School, San Jose, Costa Rica. Offers clinical neuropsychology (PhD); clinical psychology (M Psych); educational psychology (M Psych); forensic psychology (M Psych); hospital management (MHA); intensive care nursing (MN); medicine (MD).

Université Laval, Faculty of Social Sciences, School of Psychology, Programs in Psychology, Québec, QC G1K 7P4, Canada. Offers clinical psychology (PhD); community psychology (PhD); psychology (PhD, Psy D). *Degree requirements:* For doctorate, comprehensive exam, thesis/dissertation. *Entrance requirements:* For doctorate, comprehension of written English, knowledge of French, interview. Electronic applications accepted.

University at Albany, State University of New York, College of Arts and Sciences, Department of Psychology, Albany, NY 12222-0001. Offers behavioral neuroscience (PhD); clinical psychology (PhD); cognitive psychology (PhD); industrial/organizational psychology (MA, PhD); social-personality psychology (PhD). *Accreditation:* APA (one or more programs are accredited). *Degree requirements:* For doctorate, thesis/dissertation. *Entrance requirements:* For doctorate, GRE General Test, GRE Subject Test. Additional exam requirements/recommendations for international students: Required—TOEFL (minimum score 550 paper-based). Electronic applications accepted.

The University of Akron, Graduate School, College of Health Professions, School of Counseling, Akron, OH 44325. Offers classroom guidance for teachers (MA, MS); clinical mental health counseling (MA, MS); counseling psychology (PhD); counselor education and supervision (PhD); marriage and family therapy (MA, MS); school counseling (MA, MS). *Faculty:* 9 full-time (6 women), 28 part-time/adjunct (22 women). *Students:* 158 full-time (131 women), 150 part-time (123 women); includes 59 minority (40 Black or African American, non-Hispanic/Latino; 1 American Indian or Alaska Native, non-Hispanic/Latino; 3 Asian, non-Hispanic/Latino; 6 Hispanic/Latino; 9 Two or more races, non-Hispanic/Latino), 6 international. Average age 30. 207 applicants, 36% accepted, 56 enrolled. In 2014, 79 master's, 6 doctorates awarded. Terminal master's awarded for partial completion of doctoral program. *Degree requirements:* For master's, comprehensive exam; for doctorate, one foreign language, comprehensive exam, thesis/dissertation, written and oral exams. *Entrance requirements:* For master's, minimum GPA of 2.75, three letters of recommendation; for doctorate, GRE, interview, minimum GPA of 3.25, three letters of recommendation, resume. Additional exam requirements/recommendations for international students: Required—TOEFL (minimum score 550 paper-based; 79 iBT), IELTS (minimum score 6.5). *Application deadline:* For fall admission, 12/1 for domestic and international students; for spring admission, 10/1 for domestic and international students. Applications are processed on a rolling basis. Application fee: $45 ($70 for international students). Electronic applications accepted. *Expenses:* Tuition, state resident: full-time $7578; part-time $421 per credit hour. Tuition, nonresident: full-time $12,977; part-time $721 per credit hour. *Required fees:* $1388; $35 per credit hour. Tuition and fees vary according to course load. *Financial support:* In 2014–15, 33 teaching assistantships with full tuition reimbursements were awarded. *Faculty research:* Mindfulness, traumatology, suicidality, multiculturalism, couple and family therapy/counseling. *Unit head:* Dr. Karin Jordan, Chair, 330-972-5515, E-mail: kj25@uakron.edu.
Website: http://www.uakron.edu/education/academic-programs/counseling/index.dot

The University of Alabama, Graduate School, College of Arts and Sciences, Department of Psychology, Tuscaloosa, AL 35487. Offers clinical psychology (PhD); experimental psychology (PhD). *Accreditation:* APA. *Faculty:* 33 full-time (19 women), 2 part-time/adjunct (both women). *Students:* 88 full-time (64 women), 13 part-time (10 women); includes 14 minority (1 Black or African American, non-Hispanic/Latino; 4 Asian, non-Hispanic/Latino; 7 Hispanic/Latino; 2 Two or more races, non-Hispanic/Latino), 9 international. Average age 27. 318 applicants, 8% accepted, 19 enrolled. In 2014, 20 doctorates awarded. *Degree requirements:* For doctorate, thesis/dissertation, internship (for clinical psychology). *Entrance requirements:* For doctorate, GRE. Additional exam requirements/recommendations for international students: Required—TOEFL (minimum score 550 paper-based). *Application deadline:* For fall admission, 12/1 for domestic and international students. Application fee: $50 ($60 for international students). Electronic applications accepted. *Expenses:* Tuition, state resident: full-time $9826. Tuition, nonresident: full-time $24,950. *Financial support:* In 2014–15, 73 students received support, including 12 fellowships with full tuition reimbursements available (averaging $17,000 per year), 40 research assistantships with full and partial tuition reimbursements available (averaging $12,744 per year), 34 teaching assistantships with full and partial tuition reimbursements available (averaging $13,824 per year); career-related internships or fieldwork, institutionally sponsored loans, scholarships/grants, health care benefits, and unspecified assistantships also available. Financial award application deadline: 12/1. *Faculty research:* Cognitive development/disability, child clinical, psychology and law, health/aging, social psychology. *Total annual research expenditures:* $2.9 million. *Unit head:* Dr. Beverly E. Thorn, Chair, 205-348-1913, Fax: 205-348-8648, E-mail: bthorn@ua.edu. *Application contact:* Mary Beth Hubbard, Information Contact, 205-348-1919, Fax: 205-348-8648, E-mail: mbhubbard@as.ua.edu.
Website: http://www.psychology.ua.edu

The University of Alabama at Birmingham, College of Arts and Sciences, Program in Psychology, Birmingham, AL 35294. Offers behavioral neuroscience (PhD); lifespan developmental psychology (PhD); medical/clinical psychology (PhD); psychology (MA). *Accreditation:* APA (one or more programs are accredited). *Students:* 69 full-time (51 women), 2 part-time (both women); includes 14 minority (2 Black or African American, non-Hispanic/Latino; 2 Asian, non-Hispanic/Latino; 4 Hispanic/Latino; 6 Two or more races, non-Hispanic/Latino), 4 international. Average age 26. In 2014, 8 master's, 15 doctorates awarded. *Entrance requirements:* For master's and doctorate, GRE General Test, letters of recommendation. *Application deadline:* Applications are processed on a rolling basis. Electronic applications accepted. *Expenses:* Tuition, state resident: full-time $7090; part-time $370 per credit hour. Tuition, nonresident: full-time $16,072; part-time $869 per credit hour. Full-time tuition and fees vary according to course load and program. *Financial support:* Fellowships, research assistantships, and teaching assistantships available. *Faculty research:* Biological basis of behavior structure, function of the nervous system. *Unit head:* Dr. Karlene K. Ball, Chair, 205-934-2610, Fax: 205-975-2295, E-mail: psych-dept@uab.edu. *Application contact:* Susan Noblitt Banks, Director of Graduate School Operations, 205-934-8227, Fax: 205-934-8413, E-mail: gradschool@uab.edu.
Website: http://www.uab.edu/cas/psychology/graduate

University of Alaska Anchorage, College of Arts and Sciences, Department of Psychology, Anchorage, AK 99508. Offers clinical psychology (MS); clinical-community psychology with rural-indigenous emphasis (PhD). Part-time programs available. *Degree requirements:* For master's, thesis. *Entrance requirements:* For master's, GRE General Test, GRE Subject Test, interview, references; for doctorate, interview, bachelor's or master's degree in psychology. Additional exam requirements/recommendations for international students: Required—TOEFL (minimum score 550 paper-based). *Faculty research:* Substance abuse, childhood autism, biofeedback, psychological assessment, mental health in Native Alaskans.

University of Alaska Fairbanks, College of Liberal Arts, Department of Psychology, Fairbanks, AK 99775-6480. Offers clinical-community psychology (PhD), including rural cross-cultural emphasis. Program offered jointly with University of Alaska Anchorage. *Faculty:* 9 full-time (5 women). *Students:* 4 full-time (3 women), 16 part-time (10 women); includes 4 minority (1 Asian, non-Hispanic/Latino; 1 Hispanic/Latino; 2 Two or more races, non-Hispanic/Latino), 1 international. Average age 30. 8 applicants, 63% accepted, 5 enrolled. In 2014, 1 doctorate awarded. *Degree requirements:* For doctorate, comprehensive exam, thesis/dissertation, oral defense of dissertation. *Entrance requirements:* For doctorate, bachelor's degree from accredited institution with minimum cumulative undergraduate and major GPA of 3.0; criminal background check; interview; course work in abnormal psychology, statistics, and research methods. Additional exam requirements/recommendations for international students: Required—TOEFL (minimum score 550 paper-based; 80 iBT), IELTS (minimum score 6.5). *Application deadline:* For fall admission, 1/15 for domestic and international students. Application fee: $60. Electronic applications accepted. *Expenses:* Tuition, state resident: full-time $7614; part-time $423 per credit. Tuition, nonresident: full-time $15,552; part-time $864 per credit. Tuition and fees vary according to course level, course load and reciprocity agreements. *Financial support:* In 2014–15, 12 teaching assistantships with full tuition reimbursements (averaging $13,286 per year) were awarded; fellowships with full tuition reimbursements, research assistantships with full tuition reimbursements, career-related internships or fieldwork, Federal Work-Study, scholarships/grants, health care benefits, and unspecified assistantships also available. Support available to part-time students. Financial award application deadline: 7/1; financial award applicants required to submit FAFSA. *Faculty research:* Clinical and community psychology; rural, indigenous, and cultural psychology. *Unit head:* Dr. David Webster, Doctoral Program Director, 907-474-7007, Fax: 907-474-5781, E-mail: fypsych@uaf.edu. *Application contact:* Mary Kreta, Director of Admissions, 907-474-7500, Fax: 907-474-7097, E-mail: admissions@uaf.edu.
Website: http://www.uaf.edu/psych/

University of Bridgeport, School of Arts and Sciences, Department of Counseling, Bridgeport, CT 06604. Offers clinical mental health counseling (MS); college student personnel (MS); community counseling (MS); human resource development (MS); human service (MS). Part-time and evening/weekend programs available. *Degree*

requirements: For master's, thesis, project. *Entrance requirements:* Additional exam requirements/recommendations for international students: Recommended—TOEFL (minimum score 550 paper-based; 80 iBT), IELTS (minimum score 6.5). Electronic applications accepted. *Expenses:* Contact institution. *Faculty research:* Corporate elder care programs.

The University of British Columbia, Faculty of Arts and Faculty of Graduate Studies, Department of Psychology, Vancouver, BC V6T 1Z4, Canada. Offers behavioral neuroscience (MA, PhD); clinical psychology (MA, PhD); cognitive science (MA, PhD); developmental psychology (MA, PhD); health psychology (MA, PhD); quantitative methods (MA, PhD); social/personality psychology (MA, PhD). *Accreditation:* APA (one or more programs are accredited). Terminal master's awarded for partial completion of doctoral program. *Degree requirements:* For master's, thesis; for doctorate, comprehensive exam, thesis/dissertation. *Entrance requirements:* For master's and doctorate, GRE General Test. Additional exam requirements/recommendations for international students: Required—TOEFL (minimum score 550 paper-based; 80 iBT). Electronic applications accepted. *Faculty research:* Clinical, developmental, social/personality, cognition, behavioral neuroscience.

University of Calgary, Faculty of Graduate Studies, Faculty of Arts, Department of Psychology, Calgary, AB T2N 1N4, Canada. Offers clinical psychology (M Sc, PhD); psychology (M Sc, PhD). *Degree requirements:* For master's, thesis; for doctorate, thesis/dissertation. *Entrance requirements:* For master's, GRE General Test, bachelor's degree in psychology, minimum GPA of 3.4. Additional exam requirements/recommendations for international students: Required—TOEFL (minimum score 550 paper-based). Electronic applications accepted. *Faculty research:* Cognition and cognitive development, social psychology, theoretical psychology, perception, aging.

University of California, San Diego, Graduate Division, Group in Clinical Psychology, San Diego, CA 92120-4913. Offers PhD. Program offered jointly with San Diego State University. *Accreditation:* APA. *Students:* 67 part-time (62 women); includes 21 minority (4 Black or African American, non-Hispanic/Latino; 1 American Indian or Alaska Native, non-Hispanic/Latino; 9 Asian, non-Hispanic/Latino; 7 Hispanic/Latino), 2 international. In 2014, 11 doctorates awarded. *Degree requirements:* For doctorate, comprehensive exam, thesis/dissertation, 1-year full-time internship. *Entrance requirements:* For doctorate, GRE General Test, GRE Subject Test, minimum GPA of 3.25. Additional exam requirements/recommendations for international students: Required—TOEFL, IELTS. *Application deadline:* For fall admission, 12/5 for domestic students. Electronic applications accepted. *Expenses:* Tuition, state resident: full-time $11,220; part-time $5610 per quarter. Tuition, nonresident: full-time $26,322; part-time $13,161 per quarter. *Required fees:* $570 per quarter. Tuition and fees vary according to program. *Financial support:* Fellowships, research assistantships, teaching assistantships, scholarships/grants, and unspecified assistantships available. Financial award applicants required to submit FAFSA. *Faculty research:* Behavioral medicine, experimental psychopathology, neuropsychology. *Unit head:* Igor Grant, Chair, 858-534-4044, E-mail: igrant@ucsd.edu. *Application contact:* Hana Lee, Program Coordinator, 858-822-5791, E-mail: hul009@ucsd.edu.
Website: http://clinpsyc.sdsu.edu/

University of California, Santa Barbara, Graduate Division, Gevirtz Graduate School of Education, Santa Barbara, CA 93106-9490. Offers counseling, clinical and school psychology (MA, PhD, Credential), including clinical psychology (PhD), counseling psychology (MA, PhD), pupil personnel services (Credential), school psychology (PhD); education (MA, PhD); teacher education (M Ed, Credential), including multiple subject teaching (Credential), single subject teaching (Credential), special education (Credential), teaching (M Ed); MA/PhD. *Accreditation:* APA (one or more programs are accredited). Terminal master's awarded for partial completion of doctoral program. *Degree requirements:* For master's, comprehensive exam (for some programs), thesis (for some programs); for doctorate, comprehensive exam (for some programs), thesis/dissertation. *Entrance requirements:* For master's and doctorate, GRE; for Credential, GRE or MAT, CSET, CBEST. Additional exam requirements/recommendations for international students: Required—TOEFL (minimum score 550 paper-based; 80 iBT), IELTS (minimum score 7). Electronic applications accepted. *Faculty research:* Needs of diverse students, school accountability and leadership, school violence, language learning and literacy, science/math education.

University of Central Florida, College of Sciences, Department of Psychology, Program in Clinical Psychology, Orlando, FL 32816. Offers MA, MS, PhD. *Accreditation:* APA. Part-time and evening/weekend programs available. *Students:* 62 full-time (45 women), 2 part-time (both women); includes 13 minority (1 Black or African American, non-Hispanic/Latino; 4 Asian, non-Hispanic/Latino; 7 Hispanic/Latino; 1 Two or more races, non-Hispanic/Latino). Average age 26. 290 applicants, 15% accepted, 21 enrolled. In 2014, 22 master's, 5 doctorates awarded. *Degree requirements:* For master's, thesis or alternative, clinical internship; for doctorate, thesis/dissertation, candidacy exam, internship. *Entrance requirements:* For master's and doctorate, GRE General Test, minimum GPA of 3.0 in last 60 hours, resume. Additional exam requirements/recommendations for international students: Required—TOEFL. *Application deadline:* For fall admission, 2/15 for domestic students. Application fee: $30. Electronic applications accepted. *Expenses:* Tuition, state resident: part-time $288.16 per credit hour. Tuition, nonresident: part-time $1073.31 per credit hour. *Financial support:* In 2014–15, 38 students received support, including 12 fellowships with partial tuition reimbursements available (averaging $5,900 per year), 10 research assistantships with partial tuition reimbursements available (averaging $8,200 per year), 27 teaching assistantships with partial tuition reimbursements available (averaging $9,600 per year); career-related internships or fieldwork, Federal Work-Study, institutionally sponsored loans, tuition waivers (partial), and unspecified assistantships also available. Financial award application deadline: 3/1; financial award applicants required to submit FAFSA. *Faculty research:* Professional ethical decision-making, computer experience and anxiety, effects of expert testimony on decision-making in a rape trial, religiosity, relationship beliefs and marital adjustment. *Unit head:* Dr. Deborah Beidel, Program Director, 407-254-3908, E-mail: deborah.beidel@ucf.edu. *Application contact:* Barbara Rodriguez Lamas, Director, Admissions and Student Services, 407-823-2766, Fax: 407-823-6442, E-mail: gradadmissions@ucf.edu.
Website: http://psychology.cos.ucf.edu/graduate/

University of Cincinnati, Graduate School, McMicken College of Arts and Sciences, Department of Psychology, Cincinnati, OH 45221. Offers clinical psychology (PhD); experimental psychology (PhD). *Accreditation:* APA. *Degree requirements:* For doctorate, comprehensive exam, thesis/dissertation. *Entrance requirements:* For doctorate, GRE General Test. Additional exam requirements/recommendations for international students: Required—TOEFL. *Faculty research:* Neuropsychology, human factors, health.

University of Colorado Denver, College of Liberal Arts and Sciences, Department of Psychology, Denver, CO 80217. Offers clinical health (PhD); psychology (MA). Part-time and evening/weekend programs available. *Faculty:* 17 full-time (6 women), 2 part-time/adjunct (both women). *Students:* 17 full-time (14 women), 11 part-time (8 women); includes 6 minority (3 Asian, non-Hispanic/Latino; 1 Hispanic/Latino; 2 Two or more races, non-Hispanic/Latino). Average age 30. 92 applicants, 7% accepted, 6 enrolled. In 2014, 4 master's awarded. *Degree requirements:* For master's, 31-33 semester hours,

thesis or internship, minimum GPA of 3.0; for doctorate, comprehensive exam, thesis/dissertation, 69 credits of coursework, minimum of 12 clinical practicum hours, 30 dissertation hours, three credits of pre-doctoral internship. *Entrance requirements:* For master's, GRE General Test; GRE Subject Test (recommended), undergraduate courses in psychological statistics, abnormal psychology and introductory psychology; minimum GPA of 3.0; three letters of recommendation; personal statement; resume; for doctorate, GRE General Test; GRE Subject Test (recommended), minimum GPA of 3.5; undergraduate courses in introductory psychology, psychological statistics, research methods and abnormal psychology; letters of recommendation; personal statement; resume. Additional exam requirements/recommendations for international students: Required—TOEFL (minimum score 537 paper-based; 75 iBT); Recommended—IELTS (minimum score 6.5). *Application deadline:* For fall admission, 12/15 for domestic students, 12/1 for international students. Application fee: $50 ($75 for international students). Electronic applications accepted. *Financial support:* In 2014–15, 28 students received support. Fellowships, research assistantships, teaching assistantships, career-related internships or fieldwork, Federal Work-Study, institutionally sponsored loans, scholarships/grants, and traineeships available. Financial award application deadline: 4/1; financial award applicants required to submit FAFSA. *Faculty research:* Organizational behavior, body image perception, professional ethics, infant perception and cognition, charismatic leadership. *Unit head:* Dr. Kevin S. Masters, Clinical Health Psychology Program Director, 303-352-3961, Fax: 303-556-3520, E-mail: kevin.masters@ucdenver.edu. *Application contact:* Anne Beard, Program Assistant, 303-556-2192, Fax: 303-556-3520, E-mail: anne.beard@ucdenver.edu.
Website: http://www.ucdenver.edu/academics/colleges/CLAS/Departments/psychology/Pages/Psychology.aspx

University of Colorado Denver, School of Education and Human Development, Program in Counseling Psychology and Counselor Education, Denver, CO 80217. Offers counseling (MA), including clinical mental health counseling, couple and family counseling, multicultural counseling, school counseling; school counseling (MA). *Accreditation:* ACA; NCATE. Part-time and evening/weekend programs available. *Students:* 196 full-time (158 women), 30 part-time (24 women); includes 42 minority (10 Black or African American, non-Hispanic/Latino; 4 Asian, non-Hispanic/Latino; 24 Hispanic/Latino; 4 Two or more races, non-Hispanic/Latino). Average age 30. 182 applicants, 30% accepted, 31 enrolled. In 2014, 72 master's awarded. *Degree requirements:* For master's, comprehensive exam (for some programs), thesis or alternative, 63-66 hours. *Entrance requirements:* For master's, GRE or MAT (unless applicant already holds a graduate degree), letters of recommendation, interview, resume, transcripts from all colleges/universities attended. Additional exam requirements/recommendations for international students: Required—TOEFL (minimum score 525 paper-based; 71 iBT); Recommended—IELTS (minimum score 6.3). *Application deadline:* For fall admission, 1/15 for domestic students, 1/1 for international students; for spring admission, 9/15 for domestic students, 9/1 for international students. Application fee: $50 ($75 for international students). Electronic applications accepted. *Expenses:* Expenses: Contact institution. *Financial support:* In 2014–15, 9 students received support. Research assistantships, Federal Work-Study, institutionally sponsored loans, scholarships/grants, and traineeships available. Financial award application deadline: 4/1; financial award applicants required to submit FAFSA. *Faculty research:* Spiritual issues in counseling, multicultural and diversity issues in counseling, adolescent suicide, career development. *Unit head:* Farah Ibrahim, Counseling Professor, 303-315-6329, E-mail: farah.ibrahim@ucdenver.edu. *Application contact:* Student Services Coordinator, 303-315-6300, Fax: 303-315-6311, E-mail: education@ucdenver.edu.
Website: http://www.ucdenver.edu/academics/colleges/SchoolOfEducation/Academics/MASTERS/counseling/Pages/default.aspx

University of Connecticut, Graduate School, College of Liberal Arts and Sciences, Department of Psychology, Storrs, CT 06269. Offers behavioral neuroscience (PhD); biopsychology (PhD); clinical psychology (MA, PhD); cognition and instruction (PhD); developmental psychology (MA, PhD); ecological psychology (PhD); experimental psychology (PhD); general psychology (MA, PhD); health psychology (Graduate Certificate); industrial/organizational psychology (PhD); language and cognition (PhD); neuroscience (PhD); occupational health psychology (Graduate Certificate); social psychology (MA, PhD). *Accreditation:* APA. Terminal master's awarded for partial completion of doctoral program. *Degree requirements:* For master's, comprehensive exam; for doctorate, thesis/dissertation. *Entrance requirements:* For master's and doctorate, GRE General Test, GRE Subject Test. Additional exam requirements/recommendations for international students: Required—TOEFL (minimum score 550 paper-based). Electronic applications accepted.

University of Dayton, Department of Counselor Education and Human Services, Dayton, OH 45469. Offers clinical mental health counseling (MS Ed); college student personnel (MS Ed); higher education administration (MS Ed); human services (MS Ed); school counseling (MS Ed); school psychology (MS Ed, Ed S). *Accreditation:* ACA; NCATE. Part-time and evening/weekend programs available. *Faculty:* 11 full-time (7 women), 34 part-time/adjunct (24 women). *Students:* 199 full-time (161 women), 113 part-time (95 women); includes 58 minority (49 Black or African American, non-Hispanic/Latino; 1 Asian, non-Hispanic/Latino; 7 Hispanic/Latino; 1 Two or more races, non-Hispanic/Latino), 8 international. Average age 31. 295 applicants, 47% accepted, 103 enrolled. In 2014, 146 master's, 8 Ed Ss awarded. *Degree requirements:* For master's, comprehensive exam (for some programs), thesis (for some programs), exit exam. *Entrance requirements:* For master's, MAT or GRE (if GPA less than 2.75), interview, writing sample. Additional exam requirements/recommendations for international students: Required—TOEFL (minimum score 550 paper-based; 80 iBT). *Application deadline:* For fall admission, 4/10 for domestic students, 4/10 priority date for international students; for winter admission, 9/10 for domestic students, 7/1 for international students; for spring admission, 9/10 for domestic students, 9/10 priority date for international students. Application fee: $0 ($50 for international students). Electronic applications accepted. *Expenses:* Tuition: Full-time $10,176; part-time $848 per credit. *Required fees:* $25; $25 per course. Part-time tuition and fees vary according to course level, course load, degree level and program. *Financial support:* In 2014–15, 10 research assistantships with full tuition reimbursements (averaging $8,720 per year) were awarded; career-related internships or fieldwork, institutionally sponsored loans, health care benefits, and unspecified assistantships also available. Financial award application deadline: 3/1; financial award applicants required to submit FAFSA. *Faculty research:* Mindfulness, forgiveness in relationships, positive psychology in couples counseling, traumatic brain injury responses, college student development. *Unit head:* Dr. Molly Schaller, Chairperson, 937-229-3644, Fax: 937-229-1055, E-mail: mschaller1@udayton.edu. *Application contact:* Kathleen Brown, Administrative Assistant, 937-229-3644, Fax: 937-229-1055, E-mail: kbrown1@udayton.edu.
Website: https://www.udayton.edu/education/departments_and_programs/edc/

University of Dayton, Program in Clinical Psychology, Dayton, OH 45469. Offers MA. *Faculty:* 13 full-time (7 women), 2 part-time/adjunct (1 woman). *Students:* 15 full-time (11 women). Average age 24. 91 applicants, 11% accepted, 9 enrolled. In 2014, 6 master's awarded. *Degree requirements:* For master's, thesis, clinical practicum. *Entrance requirements:* For master's, GRE General Test, GRE Subject Test (recommended), minimum undergraduate GPA of 3.0, 3.3 during final 2 years of course

work. Additional exam requirements/recommendations for international students: Required—TOEFL (minimum score 550 paper-based; 80 iBT). *Application deadline:* For fall admission, 3/1 priority date for domestic and international students. Application fee: $0 ($50 for international students). Electronic applications accepted. *Expenses: Tuition:* Full-time $10,176; part-time $848 per credit. *Required fees:* $25; $25 per course. Part-time tuition and fees vary according to course level, course load, degree level and program. *Financial support:* In 2014–15, 5 research assistantships with full tuition reimbursements (averaging $11,120 per year) were awarded; institutionally sponsored loans, traineeships, health care benefits, and unspecified assistantships also available. Financial award application deadline: 3/1; financial award applicants required to submit FAFSA. *Faculty research:* Family relationship issues, conduct disorders, trauma/revictimization, homelessness and other community problems. *Unit head:* Dr. Catherine L. Zois, Director, 937-229-2164, Fax: 937-229-3900, E-mail: czois1@udayton.edu. *Application contact:* 937-229-4462, E-mail: graduateadmission@udayton.edu.
Website: https://www.udayton.edu/artssciences/academics/psychology/grad/clinical_psych/index.php

University of Delaware, College of Arts and Sciences, Department of Psychology, Newark, DE 19716. Offers behavioral neuroscience (PhD); clinical psychology (PhD); cognitive psychology (PhD); social psychology (PhD). *Accreditation:* APA. *Degree requirements:* For doctorate, thesis/dissertation. *Entrance requirements:* For doctorate, GRE General Test. Additional exam requirements/recommendations for international students: Required—TOEFL (minimum score 600 paper-based). Electronic applications accepted. *Faculty research:* Emotion development, neural and cognitive aspects of memory, neural control of feeding, intergroup relations, social cognition and communication.

University of Denver, Division of Arts, Humanities and Social Sciences, Department of Psychology, Denver, CO 80208. Offers affective/social psychology (PhD); clinical child psychology (PhD); cognitive psychology (PhD); developmental psychology (PhD). *Accreditation:* APA. *Faculty:* 25 full-time (11 women), 4 part-time/adjunct (2 women). *Students:* 21 full-time (18 women), 5 part-time (all women); includes 7 minority (2 Black or African American, non-Hispanic/Latino; 3 Asian, non-Hispanic/Latino; 1 Hispanic/Latino; 1 Two or more races, non-Hispanic/Latino), 3 international. Average age 28. 348 applicants, 5% accepted, 6 enrolled. In 2014, 9 doctorates awarded. Terminal master's awarded for partial completion of doctoral program. *Degree requirements:* For doctorate, variable foreign language requirement, comprehensive exam (for some programs), thesis/dissertation. *Entrance requirements:* For doctorate, GRE General Test, master's degree, transcripts, biographical statement, three letters of recommendation. Additional exam requirements/recommendations for international students: Required—TOEFL (minimum score 550 paper-based; 80 iBT). *Application deadline:* For fall admission, 12/1 priority date for domestic and international students. Application fee: $65. Electronic applications accepted. *Expenses:* Expenses: $1,199 per credit hour. *Financial support:* In 2014–15, 26 students received support, including 13 research assistantships with full and partial tuition reimbursements available (averaging $12,821 per year), 20 teaching assistantships with full and partial tuition reimbursements available (averaging $15,333 per year); Federal Work-Study, institutionally sponsored loans, scholarships/grants, and unspecified assistantships also available. Support available to part-time students. Financial award application deadline: 2/15; financial award applicants required to submit FAFSA. *Faculty research:* Developmental cognitive neuroscience, social and emotional processes, child and adolescent development, clinical child psychology, cognitive psychology. *Total annual research expenditures:* $3 million. *Unit head:* Dr. George Potts, Chair, 303-871-3717, Fax: 303-871-4747, E-mail: gpotts@du.edu. *Application contact:* Paula Houghtaling, Graduate Program Administrator, 303-871-3803, Fax: 303-871-4747, E-mail: phoughta@du.edu.
Website: http://www.du.edu/ahss/psychology/index.html

University of Denver, Graduate School of Professional Psychology, Denver, CO 80208. Offers forensic psychology (MA); international disaster psychology (MA); sport and performance psychology (MA). *Accreditation:* APA. *Faculty:* 18 full-time (9 women), 23 part-time/adjunct (9 women). *Students:* 205 full-time (148 women), 51 part-time (38 women); includes 57 minority (11 Black or African American, non-Hispanic/Latino; 1 American Indian or Alaska Native, non-Hispanic/Latino; 15 Asian, non-Hispanic/Latino; 21 Hispanic/Latino; 9 Two or more races, non-Hispanic/Latino), 12 international. Average age 27. 720 applicants, 31% accepted, 102 enrolled. In 2014, 90 master's, 32 doctorates awarded. *Degree requirements:* For master's, comprehensive exam (for some programs); for doctorate, comprehensive exam (for some programs), paper, clinical internship. *Entrance requirements:* For master's and doctorate, GRE General Test, transcripts, resume, two letters of recommendation, essay. Additional exam requirements/recommendations for international students: Required—TOEFL (minimum score 550 paper-based; 80 iBT). *Application deadline:* For fall admission, 12/1 priority date for domestic and international students. Application fee: $65. Electronic applications accepted. *Expenses:* Expenses: $1,199 per credit hour. *Financial support:* In 2014–15, 76 students received support, including 33 teaching assistantships with full and partial tuition reimbursements available (averaging $3,042 per year); career-related internships or fieldwork, Federal Work-Study, institutionally sponsored loans, scholarships/grants, unspecified assistantships, and clinical assistantships also available. Support available to part-time students. Financial award application deadline: 2/15; financial award applicants required to submit FAFSA. *Unit head:* Dr. Shelly Smith-Acuna, Dean, 303-871-3880, E-mail: shelly.smith-acuna@du.edu. *Application contact:* Admissions Counselor, 303-871-3736, Fax: 303-871-7656, E-mail: gsppinfo@du.edu.
Website: http://www.du.edu/gspp/

University of Detroit Mercy, College of Liberal Arts and Education, Department of Psychology, Program in Clinical Psychology, Detroit, MI 48221. Offers MA, PhD. *Accreditation:* APA. *Degree requirements:* For doctorate, departmental qualifying exam.

University of Florida, Graduate School, College of Public Health and Health Professions, Department of Clinical and Health Psychology, Gainesville, FL 32610-0165. Offers clinical and translational science (PhD); clnical and health psychology (PhD); psychology (MA, MS). *Accreditation:* APA (one or more programs are accredited). *Faculty:* 22 full-time (10 women), 12 part-time/adjunct (4 women). *Students:* 95 full-time (64 women), 14 part-time (13 women); includes 22 minority (10 Black or African American, non-Hispanic/Latino; 1 American Indian or Alaska Native, non-Hispanic/Latino; 3 Asian, non-Hispanic/Latino; 8 Hispanic/Latino), 2 international. 323 applicants, 5% accepted, 12 enrolled. In 2014, 13 master's, 13 doctorates awarded. *Degree requirements:* For doctorate, comprehensive exam, thesis/dissertation, pre-doctoral internship. *Entrance requirements:* For master's and doctorate, GRE General Test, minimum GPA of 3.0. Additional exam requirements/recommendations for international students: Required—TOEFL (minimum score 550 paper-based; 80 iBT), IELTS (minimum score 6). *Application deadline:* For fall admission, 12/1 for domestic and international students. Application fee: $30. Electronic applications accepted. *Financial support:* In 2014–15, 8 teaching assistantships were awarded; career-related internships or fieldwork, Federal Work-Study, institutionally sponsored loans, scholarships/grants, and unspecified assistantships also available. Financial award application deadline: 12/1; financial award applicants required to submit FAFSA. *Faculty research:* Clinical child and pediatric psychology, medical psychology, neuropsychology, health promotion and aging. *Unit head:* William W. Latimer, PhD, Professor and Chair, 352-273-6556, Fax: 352-273-6156, E-mail: wwlatimer@phhp.ufl.edu. *Application contact:* Office of Admissions, 352-392-1365, E-mail: webrequests@admissions.ufl.edu.
Website: http://www.phhp.ufl.edu/chp/

University of Guelph, Graduate Studies, College of Social and Applied Human Sciences, Department of Psychology, Guelph, ON N1G 2W1, Canada. Offers applied social psychology (MA, PhD); clinical psychology: applied development emphasis (PhD); clinical psychology: applied developmental emphasis (MA); industrial/organizational psychology (MA, PhD); neuroscience and applied cognitive science (MA, PhD). *Degree requirements:* For master's, thesis; for doctorate, comprehensive exam, thesis/dissertation. *Entrance requirements:* For master's, GRE General Test, GRE Subject Test, minimum B+ average during previous 2 years of course work; for doctorate, GRE General Test, GRE Subject Test, minimum A- average. Additional exam requirements/recommendations for international students: Required—TOEFL (minimum score 89 iBT). Electronic applications accepted. *Faculty research:* Organizational psychology, reading comprehension and mathematical ability, drug addiction and relapse, gender issues and culture, memory, clinical psychology.

University of Hartford, College of Arts and Sciences, Department of Psychology, Program in Clinical Practices, West Hartford, CT 06117-1599. Offers clinical practices (Psy D); psychology (MA). *Accreditation:* APA. *Degree requirements:* For master's, comprehensive exam, thesis optional. *Entrance requirements:* For master's, GRE General Test, GRE Subject Test, minimum GPA of 3.0, 3 letters of recommendation. Additional exam requirements/recommendations for international students: Required—TOEFL (minimum score 550 paper-based). Electronic applications accepted. *Faculty research:* Attachment issues, child abuse prevention, master's psychologist issues, neuropsychology.

University of Hawaii at Manoa, Graduate Division, College of Social Sciences, Department of Psychology, Honolulu, HI 96822. Offers clinical psychology (PhD); community and cultural psychology (PhD); community and culture (MA); psychology (MA, PhD, Graduate Certificate). *Accreditation:* APA (one or more programs are accredited). Part-time programs available. Terminal master's awarded for partial completion of doctoral program. *Degree requirements:* For master's, comprehensive exam, thesis; for doctorate, comprehensive exam, thesis/dissertation. *Entrance requirements:* For master's and doctorate, GRE General Test, GRE Subject Test. Additional exam requirements/recommendations for international students: Required—TOEFL (minimum score 600 paper-based; 100 iBT), IELTS (minimum score 7). *Faculty research:* Cross-cultural psychology, health psychology, marine mammals, child/adult psychopathology.

University of Houston, College of Liberal Arts and Social Sciences, Department of Psychology, Houston, TX 77204. Offers clinical psychology (PhD); developmental psychology (PhD); industrial/organizational psychology (PhD); psychology (MA); social psychology (PhD). *Accreditation:* APA (one or more programs are accredited). *Degree requirements:* For master's, comprehensive exam, thesis; for doctorate, comprehensive exam, thesis/dissertation. *Entrance requirements:* For master's, GRE General Test, career statement, 3 letters of recommendation; for doctorate, GRE General Test, 3 letters of recommendation. Additional exam requirements/recommendations for international students: Required—TOEFL (minimum score 550 paper-based; 79 iBT). Electronic applications accepted. *Faculty research:* Health psychology, depression, child/family process, organizational effectiveness, close relationships.

University of Houston–Clear Lake, School of Human Sciences and Humanities, Programs in Human Sciences, Houston, TX 77058-1002. Offers behavioral sciences (MA), including criminology, cross cultural studies, general psychology, sociology; clinical psychology (MA); criminology (MA); cross cultural studies (MA); family therapy (MA); fitness and human performance (MA); school psychology (MA). *Accreditation:* AAMFT/COAMFTE. Part-time and evening/weekend programs available. Postbaccalaureate distance learning degree programs offered (minimal on-campus study). *Degree requirements:* For master's, thesis or alternative. *Entrance requirements:* For master's, GRE General Test. Additional exam requirements/recommendations for international students: Required—TOEFL (minimum score 550 paper-based). Electronic applications accepted. *Faculty research:* Smoking cessation, adolescent sexuality, white collar crime, serial murder, human factors/human computer interaction.

University of Indianapolis, Graduate Programs, School of Psychological Sciences, Indianapolis, IN 46227-3697. Offers clinical psychology (Psy D); clinical psychology/mental health counseling (MA). *Accreditation:* APA. *Faculty:* 14 full-time (7 women), 7 part-time/adjunct (5 women). *Students:* 115 full-time (96 women), 58 part-time (51 women); includes 24 minority (4 Black or African American, non-Hispanic/Latino; 10 Asian, non-Hispanic/Latino; 8 Hispanic/Latino; 2 Two or more races, non-Hispanic/Latino), 5 international. Average age 26. In 2014, 43 master's, 20 doctorates awarded. *Degree requirements:* For master's, practicum; for doctorate, comprehensive exam, thesis/dissertation, 1200 hours of clinical practicum, 2000-hour internship. *Entrance requirements:* For master's, GRE, 3 letters of recommendation; for doctorate, GRE, minimum GPA of 3.0, 18 hours of course work in psychology, 3 letters of recommendation. Additional exam requirements/recommendations for international students: Required—TOEFL (minimum score 550 paper-based). *Application deadline:* For fall admission, 2/25 for domestic students. Application fee: $50. *Financial support:* Federal Work-Study available. *Unit head:* Dr. Anita Jones Thomas, Dean, 317-788-3353, Fax: 317-788-2120, E-mail: thomasaj@uindy.edu. *Application contact:* School of Psychological Sciences, 317-788-3353, E-mail: psych@uindy.edu.
Website: http://psych.uindy.edu/

The University of Kansas, Graduate Studies, College of Liberal Arts and Sciences, Department of Psychology, Program in Clinical Child Psychology, Lawrence, KS 66045. Offers MA, PhD. Offered jointly with Department of Applied Behavioral Science. *Accreditation:* APA. *Faculty:* 6. *Students:* 26 full-time (22 women), 1 part-time (0 women); includes 5 minority (1 Black or African American, non-Hispanic/Latino; 1 Asian, non-Hispanic/Latino; 2 Hispanic/Latino; 1 Two or more races, non-Hispanic/Latino). Average age 27. 153 applicants, 6% accepted, 5 enrolled. In 2014, 3 master's, 1 doctorate awarded. *Degree requirements:* For master's, thesis; for doctorate, comprehensive exam, thesis/dissertation, clinical internship. *Entrance requirements:* For master's, GRE General Test, GRE Subject Test; for doctorate, GRE General Test, GRE Subject Test, minimum GPA of 3.5. Additional exam requirements/recommendations for international students: Required—TOEFL. *Application deadline:* For fall admission, 12/1 for domestic and international students. Application fee: $55 ($65 for international students). Electronic applications accepted. *Financial support:* Fellowships with tuition reimbursements, research assistantships with full tuition reimbursements, teaching assistantships with full tuition reimbursements, career-related internships or fieldwork, scholarships/grants, traineeships, health care benefits, and unspecified assistantships available. Financial award application deadline: 12/1. *Faculty research:* Pediatric psychology, serious emotional disorders and psychopathology classification issues, responses to disasters and terrorism, anxiety, stress, and coping; child maltreatment; bullying; aggression. *Unit head:* Dr. Ric G. Steele, Director, 785-864-0550, E-mail: rsteele@ku.edu. *Application contact:* Tammie Zordel, Senior Administrative Associate, 785-864-4226, Fax: 785-864-5596, E-mail: tzordel@ku.edu.
Website: http://www.clchild.ku.edu

University of La Verne, College of Arts and Sciences, Department of Psychology, Program in Clinical Psychology, La Verne, CA 91750-4443. Offers Psy D. Part-time programs available. *Faculty:* 7 full-time (3 women), 4 part-time/adjunct (2 women). *Students:* 30 full-time (26 women), 61 part-time (49 women); includes 43 minority (7 Black or African American, non-Hispanic/Latino; 8 Asian, non-Hispanic/Latino; 27 Hispanic/Latino; 1 Two or more races, non-Hispanic/Latino). Average age 29. In 2014, 6 doctorates awarded. *Degree requirements:* For doctorate, thesis/dissertation, clinical practica, clinical internship, competency exams, personal psychotherapy. *Entrance requirements:* For doctorate, GRE, minimum GPA of 3.1 undergraduate, 3 recommendations; interview; curriculum vitae. Additional exam requirements/recommendations for international students: Required—TOEFL (minimum score 600 paper-based; 100 iBT). *Application deadline:* For fall admission, 1/15 for domestic and international students. Application fee: $75. *Expenses:* Expenses: Contact institution. *Financial support:* Career-related internships or fieldwork, institutionally sponsored loans, scholarships/grants, and unspecified assistantships available. Financial award application deadline: 3/2; financial award applicants required to submit FAFSA. *Unit head:* Dr. Jerry Kernes, Program Chairperson, 909-448-4414, E-mail: jkernes@laverne.edu. *Application contact:* Christy Ranells, Associate Director of Graduate Admissions, 909-448-4644, Fax: 909-9712295, E-mail: cranells@laverne.edu.
Website: http://www.laverne.edu/psychology/psyd-program/

University of Louisiana at Monroe, Graduate School, College of Health and Pharmaceutical Sciences, Programs in Counseling, Monroe, LA 71209-0001. Offers clinical mental health counseling (MS); school counseling (MS). *Accreditation:* ACA; NCATE. Part-time and evening/weekend programs available. Postbaccalaureate distance learning degree programs offered (minimal on-campus study). *Degree requirements:* For master's, comprehensive exam, thesis. *Entrance requirements:* For master's, GRE General Test, minimum GPA of 2.8 in last 60 hours. Additional exam requirements/recommendations for international students: Required—TOEFL (minimum score 500 paper-based; 61 iBT). Electronic applications accepted.

University of Louisville, Graduate School, College of Arts and Sciences, Department of Psychological and Brain Sciences, Louisville, KY 40292-0001. Offers clinical psychology (PhD); experimental psychology (PhD). *Accreditation:* APA. *Students:* 65 full-time (46 women); includes 10 minority (4 Black or African American, non-Hispanic/Latino; 1 Asian, non-Hispanic/Latino; 4 Hispanic/Latino; 1 Two or more races, non-Hispanic/Latino), 3 international. Average age 28. 179 applicants, 1% accepted, 1 enrolled. In 2014, 2 doctorates awarded. *Degree requirements:* For doctorate, thesis/dissertation, preliminary exam, research, internship. *Entrance requirements:* For doctorate, GRE General Test. Additional exam requirements/recommendations for international students: Required—TOEFL. *Application deadline:* For fall admission, 12/1 for domestic students, 5/1 priority date for international students; for spring admission, 11/1 for international students; for summer admission, 4/1 for international students. Applications are processed on a rolling basis. Application fee: $60. Electronic applications accepted. *Expenses:* Tuition, state resident: full-time $11,326; part-time $630 per credit hour. Tuition, nonresident: full-time $23,568; part-time $1311 per credit hour. *Required fees:* $196. Tuition and fees vary according to program and reciprocity agreements. *Financial support:* Fellowships, teaching assistantships, and career-related internships or fieldwork available. *Faculty research:* Health psychology, geropsychology, psychopathology, cognitive and development sciences, vision and hearing sciences. *Unit head:* Dr. Suzanne Meeks, Chair, 502-852-6068, Fax: 502-852-8904, E-mail: smeeks@louisville.edu. *Application contact:* Libby Leggett, Director, Graduate Admissions, 502-852-3101, Fax: 502-852-6536, E-mail: gradadm@louisville.edu.
Website: http://louisville.edu/psychology

The University of Manchester, School of Psychological Sciences, Manchester, United Kingdom. Offers audiology (M Phil, PhD); clinical psychology (M Phil, PhD, Psy D); psychology (M Phil, PhD).

University of Manitoba, Faculty of Graduate Studies, Faculty of Arts, Department of Psychology, Winnipeg, MB R3T 2N2, Canada. Offers clinical psychology (PhD); psychology (MA, PhD); school psychology (MA). *Degree requirements:* For master's, thesis; for doctorate, one foreign language, thesis/dissertation. *Entrance requirements:* For master's and doctorate, GRE General Test.

University of Mary, Liffrig Family School of Education and Behavioral Sciences, Department of Behavioral Sciences, Bismarck, ND 58504-9652. Offers addiction counseling (MSC); clinical mental health counseling (MSC); military families (MSC); school counseling (MSC); student affairs (MSC). Part-time programs available. Postbaccalaureate distance learning degree programs offered (minimal on-campus study). *Degree requirements:* For master's, thesis, internship. *Entrance requirements:* For master's, coursework/experience in psychology, statistics, minimum GPA of 3.0. Additional exam requirements/recommendations for international students: Required—TOEFL (minimum score 500 paper-based; 71 iBT). *Application deadline:* For fall admission, 8/1 priority date for domestic students. Application fee: $40. *Expenses: Tuition:* Full-time $4772; part-time $530.25 per credit hour. *Required fees:* $20 per credit hour. Tuition and fees vary according to degree level and program. *Financial support:* Application deadline: 8/1; applicants required to submit FAFSA. *Application contact:* Jeanette Shaeffer, Accelerated and Distance Education Administrative Assistant, 701-355-8128, Fax: 701-255-7687, E-mail: jgschae@umary.edu.

University of Mary Hardin-Baylor, Graduate Studies in Counseling, Belton, TX 76513. Offers clinical and mental health counseling (MA); marriage, family and child counseling (MA); non-clinical professional studies (MA). Part-time and evening/weekend programs available. *Faculty:* 7 full-time (4 women), 1 (woman) part-time/adjunct. *Students:* 52 full-time (44 women), 19 part-time (16 women); includes 28 minority (11 Black or African American, non-Hispanic/Latino; 3 American Indian or Alaska Native, non-Hispanic/Latino; 5 Asian, non-Hispanic/Latino; 8 Hispanic/Latino; 1 Two or more races, non-Hispanic/Latino), 5 international. Average age 30. 26 applicants, 85% accepted, 13 enrolled. In 2014, 28 master's awarded. *Degree requirements:* For master's, comprehensive exam. *Entrance requirements:* For master's, GRE General Test (waived if GPA greater than 3.0), minimum GPA of 3.0 cumulative or last 60 hours, three letters of recommendation, interview. Additional exam requirements/recommendations for international students: Required—TOEFL (minimum score 100 iBT), IELTS (minimum score 7). *Application deadline:* For fall admission, 6/1 for domestic students, 4/30 priority date for international students; for spring admission, 11/1 for domestic students, 9/30 priority date for international students. Applications are processed on a rolling basis. Application fee: $35 ($135 for international students). Electronic applications accepted. *Expenses: Tuition:* Full-time $14,400; part-time $800 per credit hour. *Required fees:* $1350; $75 per credit hour. $50 per term. Tuition and fees vary according to degree level. *Financial support:* Federal Work-Study, unspecified assistantships, and scholarships for some active duty military personnel available. Support available to part-time students. Financial award applicants required to submit FAFSA. *Unit head:* Dr. Marta Garrett, Associate Professor/Director, Graduate Counseling, 254-295-5018, E-mail: mgarrett@umhb.edu. *Application contact:* Melissa Ford, Director of Graduate Admissions, 254-295-4020, Fax: 254-295-5038, E-mail: mford@umhb.edu.
Website: http://graduate.umhb.edu/counseling/

University of Maryland, College Park, Academic Affairs, College of Behavioral and Social Sciences, Department of Psychology, College Park, MD 20742. Offers clinical psychology (PhD); developmental psychology (PhD); experimental psychology (PhD); industrial psychology (MA, MS, PhD); social psychology (PhD). *Accreditation:* APA (one or more programs are accredited). *Degree requirements:* For master's, thesis; for doctorate, variable foreign language requirement, comprehensive exam, thesis/dissertation. *Entrance requirements:* For master's and doctorate, GRE General Test, GRE Subject Test, minimum GPA of 3.5, research and/or work experience, 3 letters of recommendation. Electronic applications accepted. *Faculty research:* Social stereotyping and prejudice, anxiety disorders, auditory neuroethology, counseling and social psychology.

University of Massachusetts Amherst, Graduate School, College of Natural Sciences, Department of Psychological and Brain Sciences, Amherst, MA 01003. Offers clinical psychology (MS, PhD); cognitive psychology (MS, PhD); developmental science (MS, PhD); psychology of peace and violence (MS, PhD); social psychology (MS, PhD). *Accreditation:* APA (one or more programs are accredited). *Faculty:* 62 full-time (31 women). *Students:* 47 full-time (32 women), 14 part-time (11 women); includes 12 minority (2 Black or African American, non-Hispanic/Latino; 6 Asian, non-Hispanic/Latino; 3 Hispanic/Latino; 1 Two or more races, non-Hispanic/Latino), 9 international. Average age 27. 317 applicants, 7% accepted, 11 enrolled. In 2014, 12 master's, 10 doctorates awarded. Terminal master's awarded for partial completion of doctoral program. *Degree requirements:* For master's, thesis; for doctorate, comprehensive exam, thesis/dissertation. *Entrance requirements:* For master's and doctorate, GRE General Test, 3 letters of recommendation. Additional exam requirements/recommendations for international students: Required—TOEFL (minimum score 550 paper-based; 80 iBT), IELTS (minimum score 6.5). *Application deadline:* For fall admission, 12/1 for domestic and international students. Applications are processed on a rolling basis. Application fee: $75. Electronic applications accepted. *Expenses:* Tuition, state resident: full-time $1980; part-time $110 per credit. Tuition, nonresident: full-time $14,644; part-time $414 per credit. *Required fees:* $11,417. One-time fee: $357. *Financial support:* Fellowships with full and partial tuition reimbursements, research assistantships with full and partial tuition reimbursements, teaching assistantships with full and partial tuition reimbursements, career-related internships or fieldwork, Federal Work-Study, scholarships/grants, traineeships, health care benefits, tuition waivers (full and partial), and unspecified assistantships available. Support available to part-time students. Financial award application deadline: 12/1. *Unit head:* Dr. Michael Constantino, Graduate Program Director, 413-545-2503, Fax: 413-545-0996. *Application contact:* Lindsay DeSantis, Supervisor of Admissions, 413-545-0722, Fax: 413-577-0010, E-mail: gradadm@grad.umass.edu.
Website: http://www.psych.umass.edu/

University of Massachusetts Boston, College of Liberal Arts, Program in Clinical Psychology, Boston, MA 02125-3393. Offers PhD. *Accreditation:* APA. *Degree requirements:* For doctorate, thesis/dissertation, practicum, qualifying exam, internship. *Entrance requirements:* For doctorate, GRE General Test, GRE Subject Test, minimum GPA of 2.75. *Application deadline:* For fall admission, 1/2 for domestic students. *Expenses:* Tuition, state resident: full-time $2590; part-time $108 per credit. Tuition, nonresident: full-time $9758; part-time $406.50 per credit. Tuition and fees vary according to course load and program. *Financial support:* Research assistantships with full tuition reimbursements, teaching assistantships with full tuition reimbursements, career-related internships or fieldwork, Federal Work-Study, and unspecified assistantships available. Support available to part-time students. Financial award application deadline: 3/1; financial award applicants required to submit FAFSA. *Faculty research:* Community psychology, psychology, racism and mental health, gender and culture, post-traumatic stress disorder. *Unit head:* Dr. Joan Liem, Director, 617-287-6340, E-mail: joan.liem@umb.edu. *Application contact:* Peggy Roldan Patel, Graduate Admissions Coordinator, 617-287-6400, Fax: 617-287-6236, E-mail: bos.gadm@dpc.umassp.edu.

University of Miami, Graduate School, College of Arts and Sciences, Department of Psychology, Coral Gables, FL 33124. Offers adult clinical (PhD); behavioral neuroscience (PhD); child clinical (PhD); developmental psychology (PhD); health clinical (PhD); psychology (MS). *Accreditation:* APA (one or more programs are accredited). *Degree requirements:* For doctorate, comprehensive exam, thesis/dissertation. *Entrance requirements:* For doctorate, GRE General Test, minimum GPA of 3.5. Additional exam requirements/recommendations for international students: Required—TOEFL. Electronic applications accepted. *Faculty research:* Behavioral factors in cardiovascular disease and cancer adult psychopathology, developmental disabilities, social and emotional development, mechanisms of coping.

University of Michigan, Horace H. Rackham School of Graduate Studies, College of Literature, Science, and the Arts, Department of Psychology, Ann Arbor, MI 48109. Offers biopsychology (PhD); clinical science (PhD); cognition and cognitive neuroscience (PhD); developmental psychology (PhD); personality and social contexts (PhD); social psychology (PhD). *Accreditation:* APA. *Faculty:* 57 full-time (27 women), 31 part-time/adjunct (17 women). *Students:* 118 full-time (80 women); includes 58 minority (15 Black or African American, non-Hispanic/Latino; 1 American Indian or Alaska Native, non-Hispanic/Latino; 15 Asian, non-Hispanic/Latino; 25 Hispanic/Latino; 2 Two or more races, non-Hispanic/Latino), 12 international. Average age 27. 687 applicants, 7% accepted, 25 enrolled. In 2014, 36 doctorates awarded. *Degree requirements:* For doctorate, comprehensive exam, thesis/dissertation, oral defense of dissertation, preliminary exam. *Entrance requirements:* For doctorate, GRE General Test. Additional exam requirements/recommendations for international students: Required—TOEFL. *Application deadline:* For fall admission, 12/1 for domestic and international students. Application fee: $75 ($90 for international students). Electronic applications accepted. *Financial support:* In 2014–15, 82 students received support, including 45 fellowships with full tuition reimbursements available (averaging $21,600 per year), 16 research assistantships with full tuition reimbursements available (averaging $28,450 per year), 50 teaching assistantships with full tuition reimbursements available (averaging $26,200 per year); career-related internships or fieldwork also available. Financial award application deadline: 4/15. *Unit head:* Prof. Patricia Reuter-Lorenz, Department Chair, 734-764-7429. *Application contact:* Danielle Joanette, Psychology Student Academic Affairs, 731-764-2580, Fax: 734-615-7584, E-mail: psych.saa@umich.edu.
Website: http://www.lsa.umich.edu/psych/

University of Michigan–Dearborn, College of Arts, Sciences, and Letters, Master of Science in Psychology Program, Dearborn, MI 48128. Offers clinical health psychology (MS); health psychology (MS). Part-time programs available. *Faculty:* 11 full-time (5 women). *Students:* 27 full-time (24 women), 6 part-time (all women); includes 4 minority (2 Asian, non-Hispanic/Latino; 2 Two or more races, non-Hispanic/Latino), 4 international. 60 applicants, 55% accepted, 19 enrolled. In 2014, 18 master's awarded. *Degree requirements:* For master's, oral defense of thesis. *Entrance requirements:* For master's, GRE, 3 letters of recommendation. Additional exam requirements/recommendations for international students: Required—TOEFL (minimum score 560 paper-based; 84 iBT), IELTS (minimum score 6.5). *Application deadline:* For fall admission, 3/15 for domestic and international students. Application fee: $60. Electronic

applications accepted. *Expenses:* Expenses: $613 per credit hour in-state, $351 for ninth credit hour and beyond in-state; $1,115 per credit hour out-state, $724 for ninth credit hour and beyond out-state; $267 in fees per term part-time, $329 full-time. *Financial support:* In 2014–15, 4 students received support. Scholarships/grants available. *Faculty research:* Cardiovascular reactivity, chronic pain, addiction, gender and health, couples and health, coping. *Unit head:* Dr. Nancy Wrobel, Program Director, 313-593-5088, E-mail: nwrobel@umich.edu. *Application contact:* Carol Ligienza, Coordinator, CASL Graduate Programs, 313-593-1183, Fax: 313-583-6700, E-mail: caslgrad@umich.edu.
Website: http://umdearborn.edu/casl/psychology/

University of Minnesota, Twin Cities Campus, Graduate School, College of Liberal Arts, Department of Psychology, Program in Clinical Psychology, Minneapolis, MN 55455-0213. Offers PhD. *Accreditation:* APA. *Degree requirements:* For doctorate, comprehensive exam, thesis/dissertation, internship. *Entrance requirements:* For doctorate, GRE General Test, minimum GPA of 3.5; 12 credits of upper-level psychology courses, including statistics or psychological measurement; previous course work in abnormal psychology. Additional exam requirements/recommendations for international students: Required—TOEFL (minimum score 550 paper-based; 79 iBT).

University of Mississippi, Graduate School, College of Liberal Arts, Department of Psychology, University, MS 38677. Offers clinical psychology (PhD); experimental psychology (PhD); psychology (MA). *Accreditation:* APA (one or more programs are accredited). *Degree requirements:* For master's, thesis; for doctorate, thesis/dissertation. *Entrance requirements:* For master's, GRE General Test, minimum GPA of 3.0; for doctorate, GRE General Test. Additional exam requirements/recommendations for international students: Required—TOEFL. Electronic applications accepted.

University of Missouri–Kansas City, College of Arts and Sciences, Department of Psychology, Kansas City, MO 64110-2499. Offers clinical psychology (PhD); community psychology (PhD); health psychology (PhD); psychology (MA). PhD (interdisciplinary) offered through the School of Graduate Studies. *Accreditation:* APA. *Faculty:* 10 full-time (7 women), 2 part-time/adjunct (1 woman). *Students:* 21 full-time (14 women), 10 part-time (6 women); includes 5 minority (1 Asian, non-Hispanic/Latino; 4 Hispanic/Latino). Average age 32. 109 applicants, 6% accepted, 6 enrolled. In 2014, 4 master's, 7 doctorates awarded. Terminal master's awarded for partial completion of doctoral program. *Degree requirements:* For master's, thesis; for doctorate, comprehensive exam, thesis/dissertation, residency. *Entrance requirements:* For master's, GRE, minimum GPA of 3.5, letter of recommendation; for doctorate, GRE, minimum GPA of 3.25. Additional exam requirements/recommendations for international students: Required—TOEFL (minimum score 550 paper-based; 80 iBT). *Application deadline:* For fall admission, 1/15 for domestic and international students. Applications are processed on a rolling basis. Application fee: $45 ($50 for international students). Electronic applications accepted. *Financial support:* In 2014–15, 8 research assistantships (averaging $11,229 per year), 20 teaching assistantships (averaging $12,015 per year) were awarded; career-related internships or fieldwork, Federal Work-Study, and institutionally sponsored loans also available. Support available to part-time students. Financial award application deadline: 3/1; financial award applicants required to submit FAFSA. *Faculty research:* HIV/AIDS research group, psycho-oncology, sensory and cognitive neuroscience, cognitive psychophysiology, obesity and related metabolic disorders. *Unit head:* Dr. Jennifer Lundgren, Department Chair, 816-235-5384, Fax: 816-235-1062, E-mail: lundgrenj@umkc.edu. *Application contact:* Dr. Cathy Rawlings, Director, Graduate Programs, 816-235-1318, Fax: 816-235-1062, E-mail: psychology@umkc.edu.
Website: http://cas.umkc.edu/psyc

University of Missouri–St. Louis, College of Arts and Sciences, Department of Psychology, St. Louis, MO 63121. Offers behavioral neuroscience (MA, PhD); clinical psychology (PhD); clinical psychology respecialization (Certificate); industrial/organizational psychology (MA, PhD); trauma studies (Certificate). *Accreditation:* APA (one or more programs are accredited). Evening/weekend programs available. *Faculty:* 20 full-time (12 women), 5 part-time/adjunct (0 women). *Students:* 61 full-time (39 women), 17 part-time (15 women); includes 8 minority (3 Black or African American, non-Hispanic/Latino; 1 American Indian or Alaska Native, non-Hispanic/Latino; 1 Asian, non-Hispanic/Latino; 3 Hispanic/Latino). Average age 27. 232 applicants, 8% accepted, 14 enrolled. In 2014, 17 master's, 15 doctorates awarded. Terminal master's awarded for partial completion of doctoral program. *Degree requirements:* For master's, thesis; for doctorate, thesis/dissertation. *Entrance requirements:* For master's, GRE General Test, 3 letters of recommendation; for doctorate, GRE General Test, GRE Subject Test, 3 letters of recommendation. Additional exam requirements/recommendations for international students: Required—TOEFL (minimum score 550 paper-based; 79 iBT), IELTS (minimum score 6.5). *Application deadline:* For fall admission, 12/15 for domestic and international students. Application fee: $50 ($40 for international students). Electronic applications accepted. *Expenses:* Tuition, state resident: full-time $7364; part-time $409.10 per hour. Tuition, nonresident: full-time $18,153; part-time $1008.50 per hour. *Financial support:* In 2014–15, 8 research assistantships with full and partial tuition reimbursements (averaging $10,600 per year), 25 teaching assistantships with full and partial tuition reimbursements (averaging $9,422 per year) were awarded; fellowships with full tuition reimbursements also available. Financial award applicants required to submit FAFSA. *Faculty research:* Bereavement and loss, neuroscience, post-traumatic stress disorder, conflict and negotiation, social psychology. *Unit head:* Dr. Brian Vandenberg, Chair, 314-516-5391, Fax: 314-516-5392, E-mail: umslpsychology@msx.umsl.edu. *Application contact:* 314-516-5458, Fax: 314-516-6996, E-mail: gradadm@umsl.edu.
Website: http://www.umsl.edu/divisions/artscience/psychology/

University of Missouri–St. Louis, College of Education, Division of Counseling, St. Louis, MO 63121. Offers clinical mental health counseling (M Ed); elementary school counseling (M Ed); secondary school counseling (M Ed). *Accreditation:* ACA; NCATE. Part-time and evening/weekend programs available. *Faculty:* 8 full-time (4 women), 7 part-time/adjunct (6 women). *Students:* 59 full-time (49 women), 158 part-time (131 women); includes 50 minority (40 Black or African American, non-Hispanic/Latino; 1 Asian, non-Hispanic/Latino; 5 Hispanic/Latino; 4 Two or more races, non-Hispanic/Latino), 4 international. Average age 32. 112 applicants, 46% accepted, 34 enrolled. In 2014, 51 master's awarded. *Degree requirements:* For master's, comprehensive exam. *Entrance requirements:* For master's, 3 letters of recommendation. Additional exam requirements/recommendations for international students: Recommended—TOEFL (minimum score 550 paper-based; 79 iBT), IELTS (minimum score 6.5). *Application deadline:* For fall admission, 5/1 for domestic and international students; for spring admission, 10/1 for domestic and international students. Application fee: $50 ($40 for international students). Electronic applications accepted. *Expenses:* Tuition, state resident: full-time $7364; part-time $409.10 per hour. Tuition, nonresident: full-time $18,153; part-time $1008.50 per hour. *Financial support:* In 2014–15, 1 teaching assistantship with full and partial tuition reimbursement (averaging $10,588 per year) was awarded. Financial award application deadline: 4/1; financial award applicants required to submit FAFSA. *Faculty research:* Vocational interests, self-concept, decision-making factors, developmental differences. *Unit head:* Dr. Mark Pope, Chair, 314-516-5782. *Application contact:* 314-516-5458, Fax: 314-516-6996, E-mail: gradadm@umsl.edu.

The University of Montana, Graduate School, College of Humanities and Sciences, Department of Psychology, Missoula, MT 59812-0002. Offers clinical psychology (PhD); experimental psychology (PhD), including animal behavior psychology, developmental psychology; school psychology (MA, PhD, Ed S). *Accreditation:* APA (one or more programs are accredited). Terminal master's awarded for partial completion of doctoral program. *Degree requirements:* For master's, thesis; for doctorate, thesis/dissertation. *Entrance requirements:* For master's, doctorate, and Ed S, GRE General Test. Additional exam requirements/recommendations for international students: Required—TOEFL.

The University of Montana, Graduate School, Phyllis J. Washington College of Education and Human Sciences, Department of Counselor Education, Missoula, MT 59812-0002. Offers clinical mental health counseling (MA); counseling and supervision (Ed D); counselor education (Ed S); intercultural youth and family development (MA); school counseling (MA). *Accreditation:* ACA. *Degree requirements:* For doctorate, thesis/dissertation. *Entrance requirements:* For master's, doctorate, and Ed S, GRE General Test. Additional exam requirements/recommendations for international students: Required—TOEFL.

University of Nebraska–Lincoln, Graduate College, College of Arts and Sciences, Department of Psychology, Lincoln, NE 68588. Offers biopsychology (PhD); clinical psychology (PhD); cognitive psychology (PhD); developmental psychology (PhD); psychology (MA); social/personality psychology (PhD); JD/MA; JD/PhD. *Accreditation:* APA (one or more programs are accredited). *Degree requirements:* For master's, thesis optional; for doctorate, comprehensive exam, thesis/dissertation. *Entrance requirements:* For master's and doctorate, GRE General Test. Additional exam requirements/recommendations for international students: Required—TOEFL (minimum score 550 paper-based). Electronic applications accepted. *Faculty research:* Law and psychology, rural mental health, chronic mental illness, neuropsychology, child clinical psychology.

University of Nevada, Las Vegas, Graduate College, College of Education, Department of Educational and Clinical Studies, Las Vegas, NV 89154-3066. Offers addiction studies (Advanced Certificate); counselor education (MS), including clinical mental health; educational and clinical studies (M Ed); mental health counseling (Advanced Certificate); special education (PhD); PhD/JD. Part-time and evening/weekend programs available. *Faculty:* 18 full-time (10 women), 12 part-time/adjunct (10 women). *Students:* 164 full-time (140 women), 206 part-time (167 women); includes 142 minority (39 Black or African American, non-Hispanic/Latino; 17 Asian, non-Hispanic/Latino; 62 Hispanic/Latino; 1 Native Hawaiian or other Pacific Islander, non-Hispanic/Latino; 23 Two or more races, non-Hispanic/Latino), 26 international. Average age 34. 184 applicants, 83% accepted, 117 enrolled. In 2014, 121 master's, 6 doctorates awarded. *Degree requirements:* For master's, comprehensive exam (for some programs), thesis (for some programs); for Advanced Certificate, thesis (for some programs). *Entrance requirements:* Additional exam requirements/recommendations for international students: Required—TOEFL (minimum score 550 paper-based; 80 iBT), IELTS (minimum score 7). *Application deadline:* For fall admission, 3/1 for domestic students, 5/1 for international students; for spring admission, 9/1 for domestic students, 10/1 for international students; for summer admission, 3/15 for domestic students. Application fee: $60 ($95 for international students). Electronic applications accepted. *Financial support:* In 2014–15, 32 students received support, including 6 research assistantships with partial tuition reimbursements available (averaging $10,708 per year), 26 teaching assistantships with partial tuition reimbursements available (averaging $14,792 per year); institutionally sponsored loans, scholarships/grants, health care benefits, and unspecified assistantships also available. Financial award application deadline: 3/1. *Faculty research:* Multicultural issues in counseling, academic interventions for students with disabilities, establishment of pro-social skills in young children with severe disabilities, inclusive strategies for students with disabilities, language and literacy for English language learners. *Total annual research expenditures:* $343,782. *Unit head:* Dr. Thomas Pierce, Interim Chair/Associate Professor, 702-895-1104, Fax: 702-895-5550, E-mail: tom.pierce@unlv.edu. *Application contact:* Graduate College Admissions Evaluator, 702-895-3320, Fax: 702-895-4180, E-mail: gradcollege@unlv.edu.
Website: http://education.unlv.edu/ecs/

University of Nevada, Reno, Graduate School, College of Liberal Arts, Department of Psychology, Program in Clinical Psychology, Reno, NV 89557. Offers PhD. Terminal master's awarded for partial completion of doctoral program. *Degree requirements:* For doctorate, comprehensive exam, thesis/dissertation. *Entrance requirements:* For doctorate, GRE Subject Test (psychology), minimum GPA of 3.0. Additional exam requirements/recommendations for international students: Required—TOEFL (minimum score 500 paper-based; 61 iBT), IELTS (minimum score 6). Electronic applications accepted. *Faculty research:* Health behavior, domestic violence, verbal relations, anxiety.

University of New Brunswick Saint John, Department of Psychology, Saint John, NB E2L 4L5, Canada. Offers clinical psychology (PhD); experimental psychology (MA, PhD). Part-time programs available. *Faculty:* 9 full-time (4 women). *Students:* 16 full-time (9 women). In 2014, 3 master's awarded. *Degree requirements:* For master's, thesis. *Entrance requirements:* For master's, GRE General and Subject Tests, honors thesis; minimum GPA of 3.7. Additional exam requirements/recommendations for international students: Required—TOEFL (minimum score 550 paper-based), TWE. *Application deadline:* For fall admission, 1/15 priority date for domestic students. Application fee: $50. Electronic applications accepted. *Financial support:* In 2014–15, 6 fellowships, 5 research assistantships, 16 teaching assistantships were awarded; unspecified assistantships also available. Support available to part-time students. Financial award application deadline: 2/1. *Faculty research:* Forensic psychology, peer relationships and social skills, polygraph techniques, addictions, attachment and social adjustment, neuroscience, optical illusions, graphical perception, associative learning in animals, bio-psychology. *Unit head:* Dr. Lisa Best, Director of Graduate Studies, 506-648-5562, Fax: 506-648-5780, E-mail: lbest@unb.ca. *Application contact:* Laura Galbraith, Secretary, 506-648-5640, Fax: 506-648-5780, E-mail: galbral@unb.ca.
Website: http://go.unb.ca/gradprograms

University of New Mexico, Graduate School, College of Arts and Sciences, Program in Psychology, Albuquerque, NM 87131-2039. Offers behavioral neuroscience (PhD); clinical psychology (PhD); cognitive neuroimaging (PhD); developmental psychology (PhD); evolution (PhD); health psychology (PhD); quantitative methodology (PhD). *Faculty:* 25 full-time (9 women), 1 (woman) part-time/adjunct. *Students:* 66 full-time (44 women), 12 part-time (6 women); includes 23 minority (2 Black or African American, non-Hispanic/Latino; 2 American Indian or Alaska Native, non-Hispanic/Latino; 4 Asian, non-Hispanic/Latino; 13 Hispanic/Latino; 2 Two or more races, non-Hispanic/Latino), 1 international. Average age 33. 135 applicants, 10% accepted, 13 enrolled. In 2014, 10 doctorates awarded. *Degree requirements:* For doctorate, comprehensive exam, thesis/dissertation. *Entrance requirements:* For doctorate, GRE General Test, GRE Subject Test (psychology), minimum GPA of 3.0. Additional exam requirements/recommendations for international students: Required—TOEFL (minimum score 550

paper-based; 79 iBT), IELTS (minimum score 6.5). *Application deadline:* For fall admission, 12/15 priority date for domestic and international students. Applications are processed on a rolling basis. Application fee: $50. Electronic applications accepted. *Financial support:* In 2014–15, 62 students received support, including 8 fellowships (averaging $13,124 per year), 37 research assistantships with full and partial tuition reimbursements available (averaging $11,655 per year), 67 teaching assistantships with full and partial tuition reimbursements available (averaging $13,600 per year); career-related internships or fieldwork, Federal Work-Study, institutionally sponsored loans, scholarships/grants, health care benefits, tuition waivers (partial), and unspecified assistantships also available. Financial award application deadline: 3/1; financial award applicants required to submit FAFSA. *Faculty research:* Addiction, cognition, brain and behavior, developmental, evolutionary, functioning neuroimaging, health psychology, learning and memory, neuroscience. *Unit head:* Dr. Jane Ellen Smith, Department Chair, 505-277-4121, Fax: 505-277-1394. *Application contact:* Rikk Murphy, Graduate Program Coordinator, 505-277-5009, Fax: 505-277-1394, E-mail: advising@unm.edu.
Website: http://psych.unm.edu

The University of North Carolina at Chapel Hill, Graduate School, College of Arts and Sciences, Department of Psychology, Chapel Hill, NC 27599-3270. Offers behavioral neuroscience psychology (PhD); clinical psychology (PhD); cognitive psychology (PhD); developmental psychology (PhD); quantitative psychology (PhD); social psychology (PhD). *Accreditation:* APA. *Degree requirements:* For doctorate, comprehensive exam, thesis/dissertation. *Entrance requirements:* For doctorate, GRE General Test, minimum GPA of 3.0. Additional exam requirements/recommendations for international students: Required—TOEFL (minimum score 550 paper-based; 79 iBT), IELTS (minimum score 7). Electronic applications accepted. *Faculty research:* Expressed emotion, cognitive development, social cognitive neuroscience, human memory personality.

The University of North Carolina at Charlotte, College of Liberal Arts and Sciences, Department of Psychology, Charlotte, NC 28223-0001. Offers clinical/community psychology (MA); cognitive sciences (Graduate Certificate); health psychology (PhD); industrial/organizational psychology (MA). Part-time programs available. *Faculty:* 31 full-time (17 women), 1 part-time/adjunct (0 women). *Students:* 42 full-time (35 women), 31 part-time (26 women); includes 18 minority (5 Black or African American, non-Hispanic/Latino; 2 Asian, non-Hispanic/Latino; 9 Hispanic/Latino; 2 Two or more races, non-Hispanic/Latino), 1 international. Average age 28. 243 applicants, 16% accepted, 25 enrolled. In 2014, 9 master's, 5 doctorates, 1 other advanced degree awarded. Terminal master's awarded for partial completion of doctoral program. *Degree requirements:* For master's, thesis; for doctorate, thesis/dissertation. *Entrance requirements:* For master's, GRE General Test, GRE Subject Test, minimum GPA of 3.0 in undergraduate major, 2.8 overall, letters of recommendation; for doctorate, GRE General Test, minimum GPA of 3.5, letters of recommendation. Additional exam requirements/recommendations for international students: Required—TOEFL (minimum score 557 paper-based; 83 iBT). *Application deadline:* For fall admission, 5/1 for domestic and international students. Application fee: $75. Electronic applications accepted. *Expenses:* Tuition, state resident: full-time $4008. Tuition, nonresident: full-time $16,295. *Required fees:* $2755. Tuition and fees vary according to course load and program. *Financial support:* In 2014–15, 33 students received support, including 16 research assistantships (averaging $15,239 per year), 17 teaching assistantships (averaging $12,809 per year); career-related internships or fieldwork, Federal Work-Study, institutionally sponsored loans, and scholarships/grants also available. Support available to part-time students. Financial award application deadline: 4/1; financial award applicants required to submit FAFSA. *Faculty research:* Neuropsychology of information processing, perception and human performance, computer-based applications in research and instruction, interventions to facilitate team effectiveness, post-traumatic psychological growth. *Total annual research expenditures:* $327,551. *Unit head:* Dr. Fary Cachelin, Chair, 704-687-1319, Fax: 704-687-1317, E-mail: fcacheli@uncc.edu. *Application contact:* Kathy B. Giddings, Director of Graduate Admissions, 704-687-5503, Fax: 704-687-1668, E-mail: gradadm@uncc.edu.
Website: http://psych.uncc.edu/graduate-programs

The University of North Carolina at Greensboro, Graduate School, College of Arts and Sciences, Department of Psychology, Greensboro, NC 27412-5001. Offers clinical psychology (MA, PhD); cognitive psychology (MA, PhD); developmental psychology (MA, PhD); social psychology (MA, PhD). *Accreditation:* APA (one or more programs are accredited). Terminal master's awarded for partial completion of doctoral program. *Degree requirements:* For master's, comprehensive exam, thesis; for doctorate, one foreign language, thesis/dissertation, preliminary exam. *Entrance requirements:* For master's and doctorate, GRE General Test. Additional exam requirements/recommendations for international students: Required—TOEFL. Electronic applications accepted. *Faculty research:* Sensory and perceptual determinants; evoked potential: disorders, deafness, and development.

University of North Dakota, Graduate School, College of Arts and Sciences, Department of Psychology, Grand Forks, ND 58202. Offers clinical psychology (PhD); counseling psychology (PhD); experimental psychology (PhD); forensic psychology (MA, MS); psychology (MA). *Accreditation:* APA (one or more programs are accredited). *Degree requirements:* For master's, thesis, final exam; for doctorate, comprehensive exam, thesis/dissertation, internship, final exam. *Entrance requirements:* For master's, GRE General Test, GRE Subject Test, minimum GPA of 3.0; for doctorate, GRE General Test, GRE Subject Test, minimum GPA of 3.5. Additional exam requirements/recommendations for international students: Required—TOEFL (minimum score 550 paper-based; 79 iBT), IELTS (minimum score 6.5). Electronic applications accepted. *Faculty research:* Developmental psychology, clinical social psychology, educational psychology, personality disorders.

University of North Georgia, Department of Psychology and Sociology, Dahlonega, GA 30597. Offers clinical mental health counseling (MS). *Accreditation:* ACA. Part-time and evening/weekend programs available. *Degree requirements:* For master's, one foreign language, thesis optional. *Entrance requirements:* For master's, GRE General Test, minimum GPA of 2.5, 3 letters of recommendation, interview, personal statement, resume. Additional exam requirements/recommendations for international students: Required—TOEFL (minimum score 550 paper-based; 79 iBT), IELTS (minimum score 6.5). Electronic applications accepted. *Faculty research:* Prejudice and counseling relationships, grow curve analysis of group dynamics, career-related daydreams.

University of North Texas, Robert B. Toulouse School of Graduate Studies, Denton, TX 76203-5459. Offers accounting (MS); applied anthropology (MA, MS); applied behavior analysis (Certificate); applied geography (MA); applied technology and performance improvement (M Ed, MS); art education (MA); art history (MA); art museum education (Certificate); arts leadership (Certificate); audiology (Au D); behavior analysis (MS); behavioral science (PhD); biochemistry and molecular biology (MS); biology (MA, MS); biomedical engineering (MS); business analysis (MS); chemistry (MS); clinical health psychology (PhD); communication studies (MA, MS); computer engineering (MS); computer science (MS); counseling (M Ed, MS), including clinical mental health counseling (MS), college and university counseling, elementary school counseling, secondary school counseling; creative writing (MA); criminal justice (MS); curriculum and instruction (M Ed); decision sciences (MBA); design (MA, MFA), including fashion design (MFA), innovation studies, interior design (MFA); early childhood studies (MS); economics (MS); educational leadership (M Ed, Ed D); educational psychology (MS, PhD), including family studies (MS), gifted and talented (MS), human development (MS), learning and cognition (MS), research, measurement and evaluation (MS); electrical engineering (MS); emergency management (MPA); engineering technology (MS); English (MA); English as a second language (MA); environmental science (MS); finance (MBA, MS); financial management (MPA); French (MA); health services management (MBA); higher education (M Ed, Ed D); history (MA, MS); hospitality management (MS); human resources management (MPA); information science (MS); information systems (PhD); information technologies (MBA); interdisciplinary studies (MA, MS); international studies (MA); international sustainable tourism (MS); jazz studies (MM); journalism (MA, MJ, Graduate Certificate), including interactive and virtual digital communication (Graduate Certificate), narrative journalism (Graduate Certificate), public relations (Graduate Certificate); kinesiology (MS); linguistics (MA); local government management (MPA); logistics (PhD); logistics and supply chain management (MBA); long-term care, senior housing, and aging services (MA); management (PhD); marketing (MBA); mathematics (MA, MS); mechanical and energy engineering (MS, PhD); music (MA), including ethnomusicology, music theory, musicology, performance; music composition (PhD); music education (MM Ed, PhD); nonprofit management (MPA); operations and supply chain management (MBA); performance (MM, DMA); philosophy (MA); political science (MA); professional and technical communication (MA); radio, television and film (MA, MFA); rehabilitation counseling (Certificate); sociology (MA); Spanish (MA); special education (M Ed); speech-language pathology (MA); strategic management (MBA); studio art (MFA); teaching (M Ed); MBA/MS. Part-time and evening/weekend programs available. Postbaccalaureate distance learning degree programs offered. *Faculty:* 651 full-time (215 women), 233 part-time/adjunct (139 women). *Students:* 3,040 full-time (1,598 women), 3,401 part-time (2,097 women); includes 1,740 minority (533 Black or African American, non-Hispanic/Latino; 15 American Indian or Alaska Native, non-Hispanic/Latino; 286 Asian, non-Hispanic/Latino; 746 Hispanic/Latino; 3 Native Hawaiian or other Pacific Islander, non-Hispanic/Latino; 157 Two or more races, non-Hispanic/Latino), 1,145 international. Terminal master's awarded for partial completion of doctoral program. *Degree requirements:* For master's, variable foreign language requirement, comprehensive exam (for some programs), thesis (for some programs); for doctorate, variable foreign language requirement, comprehensive exam (for some programs), thesis/dissertation; for other advanced degree, variable foreign language requirement, comprehensive exam (for some programs). *Entrance requirements:* For master's and doctorate, GRE, GMAT. Additional exam requirements/recommendations for international students: Required—TOEFL (minimum score 550 paper-based; 79 iBT). *Application deadline:* For fall admission, 7/15 for domestic students, 3/15 for international students; for spring admission, 11/15 for domestic students, 9/15 for international students; for summer admission, 5/1 for domestic students. Applications are processed on a rolling basis. Application fee: $60. Electronic applications accepted. *Expenses:* Tuition, state resident: full-time $5450; part-time $3633 per year. Tuition, nonresident: full-time $11,966; part-time $7977 per year. *Required fees:* $1301; $398 per credit hour. $685 per semester. Tuition and fees vary according to program and reciprocity agreements. *Financial support:* Fellowships with partial tuition reimbursements, research assistantships with partial tuition reimbursements, teaching assistantships, career-related internships or fieldwork, Federal Work-Study, institutionally sponsored loans, scholarships/grants, health care benefits, and library assistantships available. Support available to part-time students. Financial award applicants required to submit FAFSA. *Unit head:* Mark Wardell, Dean, 940-565-2383, E-mail: mark.wardell@unt.edu. *Application contact:* Toulouse School of Graduate Studies, 940-565-2383, Fax: 940-565-2141, E-mail: gradsch@unt.edu.
Website: http://tsgs.unt.edu/

University of Oregon, Graduate School, College of Arts and Sciences, Department of Psychology, Program in Clinical Psychology, Eugene, OR 97403. Offers PhD. *Accreditation:* APA. *Degree requirements:* For doctorate, thesis/dissertation. *Entrance requirements:* For doctorate, GRE General Test. Additional exam requirements/recommendations for international students: Required—TOEFL.

University of Phoenix–Phoenix Campus, College of Social Sciences, Tempe, AZ 85282-2371. Offers counseling (MS), including clinical mental health counseling, community counseling, counseling, marriage, family and child therapy; psychology (MS). Evening/weekend programs available. Postbaccalaureate distance learning degree programs offered. *Entrance requirements:* Additional exam requirements/recommendations for international students: Required—TOEFL, TOEIC (Test of English as an International Communication), Berlitz Online English Proficiency Exam, PTE, or IELTS. Electronic applications accepted. *Expenses:* Contact institution.

University of Puerto Rico, Río Piedras Campus, College of Social Sciences, Department of Psychology, San Juan, PR 00931-3300. Offers clinical psychology (MA); industrial organizational psychology (MA); investigative academic psychology (MA); psychology (PhD); social-community psychology (MA). Part-time programs available. *Degree requirements:* For master's, comprehensive exam, thesis; for doctorate, comprehensive exam, thesis/dissertation, internship. *Entrance requirements:* For master's, GRE or PAEG, interview, minimum GPA of 3.0; for doctorate, GRE or PAEG, interview, master's degree, minimum GPA of 3.0. *Faculty research:* Intervention on depressed Latino youth, biosychosocial training.

University of Regina, Faculty of Graduate Studies and Research, Faculty of Arts, Department of Psychology, Regina, SK S4S 0A2, Canada. Offers clinical psychology (MA, PhD); experimental and applied psychology (MA, PhD). *Faculty:* 20 full-time (9 women), 7 part-time/adjunct (5 women). *Students:* 57 full-time (46 women). 81 applicants, 25% accepted. In 2014, 12 master's, 4 doctorates awarded. *Degree requirements:* For master's, thesis; for doctorate, comprehensive exam, thesis/dissertation. *Entrance requirements:* For master's, GRE General Test; for doctorate, GRE General Test and GRE Subject Test (optional for those with a master's degree from a Canadian university). Additional exam requirements/recommendations for international students: Required—TOEFL (minimum score 580 paper-based; 80 iBT), IELTS (minimum score 6.5), PTE (minimum score 59). *Application deadline:* For fall admission, 1/15 for domestic and international students. Application fee: $100. Electronic applications accepted. *Expenses: Tuition, area resident:* Full-time $4900 Canadian dollars; part-time $837.65 Canadian dollars per semester. *International tuition:* $7900 Canadian dollars full-time. *Required fees:* $396 Canadian dollars; $86.90 Canadian dollars per semester. *Financial support:* In 2014–15, 17 fellowships (averaging $6,588 per year), 1 research assistantship (averaging $5,500 per year), 27 teaching assistantships (averaging $2,471 per year) were awarded; career-related internships or fieldwork and scholarships/grants also available. Financial award application deadline: 6/15. *Faculty research:* Clinical, experimental, cognitive, and applied psychology; post-traumatic stress disorder, anxiety, and panic disorder; traumatic brain injury; chronic pain; perception and memory. *Unit head:* Dr. Richard MacLennan, Department Head, 306-585-4458, Fax: 306-585-5429, E-mail: richard.maclennan@uregina.ca.
Website: http://www.uregina.ca/arts/psychology

University of Rhode Island, Graduate School, College of Arts and Sciences, Department of Psychology, Kingston, RI 02881. Offers behavioral science (PhD); clinical psychology (MA, PhD); school psychology (MS, PhD). *Accreditation:* APA (one or more

programs are accredited). Part-time programs available. *Faculty:* 19 full-time (10 women), 1 part-time/adjunct (0 women). *Students:* 108 full-time (83 women), 32 part-time (25 women); includes 34 minority (21 Black or African American, non-Hispanic/Latino; 2 American Indian or Alaska Native, non-Hispanic/Latino; 3 Asian, non-Hispanic/Latino; 7 Hispanic/Latino; 1 Two or more races, non-Hispanic/Latino), 7 international. In 2014, 20 master's awarded. *Degree requirements:* For master's, comprehensive exam, thesis optional; for doctorate, thesis/dissertation. *Entrance requirements:* For master's and doctorate, GRE, 3 letters of recommendation. Additional exam requirements/recommendations for international students: Required—TOEFL (minimum score 550 paper-based). *Application deadline:* For fall admission, 12/1 for domestic and international students. Application fee: $65. Electronic applications accepted. *Expenses:* Tuition, state resident: full-time $11,532; part-time $641 per credit. Tuition, nonresident: full-time $23,606; part-time $1311 per credit. *Required fees:* $1442; $39 per credit. $35 per semester. One-time fee: $155. *Financial support:* In 2014–15, 10 research assistantships with full and partial tuition reimbursements (averaging $12,774 per year), 23 teaching assistantships with full and partial tuition reimbursements (averaging $12,892 per year) were awarded. Financial award application deadline: 12/1; financial award applicants required to submit FAFSA. *Total annual research expenditures:* $22,461. *Unit head:* Dr. Su Boatright-Horowitz, Interim Chair, 401-874-4231, Fax: 401-874-2157, E-mail: ugpsych@aol.com. *Application contact:* Graduate Admission, 401-874-2872, E-mail: gradadm@etal.uri.edu.
Website: http://www.uri.edu/artsci/psy/

University of Rochester, School of Arts and Sciences, Department of Clinical and Social Sciences in Psychology, Rochester, NY 14627. Offers clinical psychology (PhD); developmental psychology (PhD); social-personality psychology (PhD). *Accreditation:* APA. *Faculty:* 14 full-time (7 women). *Students:* 46 full-time (37 women), 1 (woman) part-time; includes 6 minority (2 Asian, non-Hispanic/Latino; 3 Hispanic/Latino; 1 Two or more races, non-Hispanic/Latino), 6 international. 326 applicants, 4% accepted, 6 enrolled. In 2014, 9 doctorates awarded. Terminal master's awarded for partial completion of doctoral program. *Degree requirements:* For doctorate, thesis/dissertation, qualifying exam. *Entrance requirements:* For doctorate, GRE General Test. Additional exam requirements/recommendations for international students: Required—TOEFL. *Application deadline:* For fall admission, 12/15 priority date for domestic students. Application fee: $60. *Expenses: Tuition:* Full-time $46,150; part-time $1442 per credit hour. *Required fees:* $504. *Financial support:* Fellowships, research assistantships, teaching assistantships, career-related internships or fieldwork, and tuition waivers (full and partial) available. Financial award application deadline: 2/1. *Faculty research:* Clinical psychology, social-personality psychology, developmental psychology, human motivation. *Unit head:* Loisa Bennetto, Chair, 585-275-8712. *Application contact:* April Engram, Academic Coordinator/Analyst, 585-275-8704.
Website: http://www.psych.rochester.edu/csp/

University of Saint Francis, Graduate School, Department of Psychology and Counseling, Fort Wayne, IN 46808-3994. Offers clinical mental health counseling (MS, Post Master's Certificate); pastoral counseling (MS, Post Master's Certificate); psychology (MS); rehabilitation counseling (MS, Post Master's Certificate); school counseling (MS Ed). Part-time and evening/weekend programs available. *Faculty:* 3 full-time (1 woman). *Students:* 29 full-time (22 women), 20 part-time (all women); includes 10 minority (7 Black or African American, non-Hispanic/Latino; 2 Hispanic/Latino; 1 Two or more races, non-Hispanic/Latino), 1 international. Average age 32. 21 applicants, 90% accepted, 16 enrolled. In 2014, 23 master's awarded. *Entrance requirements:* For master's, minimum undergraduate GPA of 3.0; undergraduate coursework in psychology. Additional exam requirements/recommendations for international students: Required—TOEFL or IELTS. *Application deadline:* For fall admission, 7/1 for domestic students; for spring admission, 11/1 for domestic students. Applications are processed on a rolling basis. Application fee: $0. Electronic applications accepted. *Expenses:* Expenses: $830 per credit hour. *Financial support:* In 2014–15, 5 students received support. Federal Work-Study, scholarships/grants, and unspecified assistantships available. Support available to part-time students. Financial award application deadline: 3/10; financial award applicants required to submit FAFSA. *Unit head:* Dr. John Brinkman, Associate Professor/Chair, Department of Psychology and Counseling, 260-399-7700 Ext. 8425, Fax: 260-399-8170, E-mail: jbrinkman@sf.edu. *Application contact:* Kyle Richardson, Enrollment Specialist, 260-399-7700 Ext. 6310, Fax: 260-399-8152, E-mail: krichardson@sf.edu.
Website: http://psychology.sf.edu/

University of Saint Joseph, Department of Counseling and Applied Behavioral Studies, West Hartford, CT 06117-2700. Offers clinical mental health counseling (MA); school counseling (MA). Part-time and evening/weekend programs available. *Degree requirements:* For master's, comprehensive exam, thesis optional. *Entrance requirements:* For master's, 2 letters of recommendation. Electronic applications accepted. Application fee is waived when completed online. *Expenses: Tuition:* Part-time $700 per credit. *Required fees:* $42 per credit. Tuition and fees vary according to degree level, campus/location and program.

The University of Scranton, College of Graduate and Continuing Education, Department of Counseling and Human Services, Program in Clinical Mental Health Counseling, Scranton, PA 18510. Offers MS. *Accreditation:* ACA. Part-time and evening/weekend programs available. *Students:* 55 full-time (51 women), 7 part-time (5 women); includes 5 minority (1 Black or African American, non-Hispanic/Latino; 3 Hispanic/Latino; 1 Two or more races, non-Hispanic/Latino), 1 international. Average age 28. 46 applicants, 54% accepted. In 2014, 9 master's awarded. *Degree requirements:* For master's, comprehensive exam, capstone experience. *Entrance requirements:* For master's, minimum GPA of 3.0. Additional exam requirements/recommendations for international students: Required—TOEFL (minimum score 500 paper-based), IELTS (minimum score 6). *Application deadline:* For fall admission, 3/1 for domestic students. Application fee: $0. *Financial support:* Teaching assistantships, career-related internships or fieldwork, and Federal Work-Study available. Support available to part-time students. Financial award application deadline: 3/1. *Unit head:* Dr. Benjamin Willis, Program Director, 570-941-4236, Fax: 570-941-6492, E-mail: benjamin.willis@scranton.edu. *Application contact:* Joseph M. Roback, Director of Admissions, 570-941-4385, Fax: 570-941-5928, E-mail: robackj2@scranton.edu.

University of South Africa, College of Human Sciences, Pretoria, South Africa. Offers adult education (M Ed); African languages (MA, PhD); African politics (MA, PhD); Afrikaans (MA, PhD); ancient history (MA, PhD); ancient Near Eastern studies (MA, PhD); anthropology (MA, PhD); applied linguistics (MA); Arabic (MA, PhD); archaeology (MA); art history (MA); Biblical archaeology (MA); Biblical studies (M Th, D Th, PhD); Christian spirituality (M Th, D Th); church history (M Th, D Th); classical studies (MA, PhD); clinical psychology (MA); communication (MA, PhD); comparative education (M Ed, Ed D); consulting psychology (D Admin, D Com, PhD); curriculum studies (M Ed, Ed D); development studies (M Admin, MA, D Admin, PhD); didactics (M Ed, Ed D); education (M Tech); education management (M Ed, Ed D); educational psychology (M Ed); English (MA); environmental education (M Ed); French (MA, PhD); German (MA, PhD); Greek (MA); guidance and counseling (M Ed); health studies (MA, PhD), including health sciences education (MA), health services management (MA), medical and surgical nursing science (critical care general) (MA), midwifery and neonatal nursing science (MA), trauma and emergency care (MA); history (MA, PhD); history of education (Ed D); inclusive education (M Ed, Ed D); information and communications technology policy and regulation (MA); information science (MA, MIS, PhD); international politics (MA, PhD); Islamic studies (MA, PhD); Italian (MA, PhD); Judaica (MA, PhD); linguistics (MA, PhD); mathematical education (M Ed); mathematics education (MA); missiology (M Th, D Th); modern Hebrew (MA, PhD); musicology (MA, MMus, D Mus, PhD); natural science education (M Ed); New Testament (M Th, D Th); Old Testament (D Th); pastoral therapy (M Th, D Th); philosophy (MA); philosophy of education (M Ed, Ed D); politics (MA, PhD); Portuguese (MA, PhD); practical theology (M Th, D Th); psychology (MA, MS, PhD); psychology of education (M Ed, Ed D); public health (MA); religious studies (MA, D Th, PhD); Romance languages (MA); Russian (MA, PhD); Semitic languages (MA, PhD); social behavior studies in HIV/AIDS (MA); social science (mental health) (MA); social science in development studies (MA); social science in psychology (MA); social science in social work (MA); social science in sociology (MA); social work (MSW, DSW, PhD); socio-education (M Ed, Ed D); sociolinguistics (MA); sociology (MA, PhD); Spanish (MA, PhD); systematic theology (M Th, D Th); TESOL (teaching English to speakers of other languages) (MA); theological ethics (M Th, D Th); theory of literature (MA, PhD); urban ministries (D Th); urban ministry (M Th).

University of South Alabama, Graduate School, Program in Clinical and Counseling Psychology, Mobile, AL 36688. Offers PhD. *Faculty:* 6 full-time (3 women). *Students:* 27 full-time (19 women), 4 part-time (3 women); includes 4 minority (1 Black or African American, non-Hispanic/Latino; 1 American Indian or Alaska Native, non-Hispanic/Latino; 1 Asian, non-Hispanic/Latino; 1 Hispanic/Latino). Average age 28. 53 applicants, 32% accepted, 12 enrolled. In 2014, 6 doctorates awarded. *Degree requirements:* For doctorate, thesis/dissertation, capstone internship. *Entrance requirements:* For doctorate, GRE, three letters of recommendation, statement of purpose, curriculum vitae. Additional exam requirements/recommendations for international students: Required—TOEFL (minimum score 525 paper-based; 71 iBT). *Application deadline:* For fall admission, 12/15 for domestic students; for spring admission, 5/1 for domestic students. Application fee: $35. Electronic applications accepted. *Expenses:* Tuition, state resident: full-time $9288; part-time $387 per credit hour. Tuition, nonresident: full-time $18,576; part-time $774 per credit hour. Part-time tuition and fees vary according to course load and program. *Financial support:* Fellowships, research assistantships, teaching assistantships, career-related internships or fieldwork, Federal Work-Study, institutionally sponsored loans, scholarships/grants, and unspecified assistantships available. Support available to part-time students. Financial award application deadline: 5/31; financial award applicants required to submit FAFSA. *Unit head:* Dr. B. Keith Harrison, Dean and Associate Vice President for Academic Affairs, 251-460-6310, E-mail: gradschool@southalabama.edu. *Application contact:* Dr. Elise Labbe, Director of Clinical Training, 251-460-6622, E-mail: elabbe@southalabama.edu.
Website: http://www.southalabama.edu/ccp/

University of South Carolina, The Graduate School, College of Arts and Sciences, Department of Psychology, Program in Clinical/Community Psychology, Columbia, SC 29208. Offers clinical/community psychology (PhD); general psychology (MA). *Accreditation:* APA. *Degree requirements:* For master's, comprehensive exam, thesis; for doctorate, comprehensive exam, thesis/dissertation. *Entrance requirements:* For doctorate, GRE General Test, minimum GPA of 3.2. Additional exam requirements/recommendations for international students: Required—TOEFL. Electronic applications accepted. *Faculty research:* Developmental psychopathology, health disparities, community-level interventions for psychological well being.

University of South Carolina Aiken, Program in Applied Clinical Psychology, Aiken, SC 29801. Offers MS. Part-time programs available. *Faculty:* 8 full-time (7 women). *Students:* 21 full-time (15 women), 12 part-time (9 women); includes 3 minority (1 Black or African American, non-Hispanic/Latino; 1 Asian, non-Hispanic/Latino; 1 Two or more races, non-Hispanic/Latino). Average age 24. 57 applicants, 32% accepted, 13 enrolled. In 2014, 13 master's awarded. *Degree requirements:* For master's, thesis. *Entrance requirements:* For master's, GRE General Test. Additional exam requirements/recommendations for international students: Required—TOEFL (minimum score 550 paper-based; 80 iBT). *Application deadline:* For fall admission, 4/1 priority date for domestic and international students. Applications are processed on a rolling basis. Application fee: $45. Electronic applications accepted. *Expenses:* Tuition, state resident: full-time $12,024; part-time $501 per credit hour. Tuition, nonresident: full-time $25,770; part-time $1073.75 per credit hour. *Required fees:* $9 per credit hour. $25 per semester. Full-time tuition and fees vary according to course load. *Financial support:* In 2014–15, 23 students received support, including 20 research assistantships with partial tuition reimbursements available (averaging $1,750 per year), 3 teaching assistantships with partial tuition reimbursements available (averaging $1,100 per year); career-related internships or fieldwork, Federal Work-Study, scholarships/grants, tuition waivers (partial), and unspecified assistantships also available. Financial award application deadline: 3/15; financial award applicants required to submit FAFSA. *Faculty research:* Learning and motivation, addictive behaviors, neuroscience, childhood disorders, social and personality psychology. *Unit head:* Dr. Jane Stafford, Director, 803-641-3358, Fax: 803-641-3720, E-mail: jstafford@usca.edu. *Application contact:* Dan Robb, Associate Vice Chancellor for Enrollment Management, 803-641-3487, Fax: 803-641-3727, E-mail: danr@usca.edu.
Website: http://web.usca.edu/psychology/programs-and-courses/master-of-science.dot?

The University of South Dakota, Graduate School, College of Arts and Sciences, Department of Psychology, Vermillion, SD 57069-2390. Offers clinical psychology (MA, PhD); human factors (MA, PhD). *Accreditation:* APA (one or more programs are accredited). *Degree requirements:* For master's, comprehensive exam, thesis; for doctorate, comprehensive exam, thesis/dissertation. *Entrance requirements:* For master's, GRE, minimum GPA of 2.7; for doctorate, GRE General Test, GRE Subject Test, minimum GPA of 2.7. Additional exam requirements/recommendations for international students: Required—TOEFL (minimum score 550 paper-based; 79 iBT). Electronic applications accepted. *Faculty research:* Human-computer interactions, perceptual-cognitive processing, medical psychology, depression, moral psychology.

University of Southern California, Graduate School, Dana and David Dornsife College of Letters, Arts and Sciences, Department of Psychology, Los Angeles, CA 90089. Offers brain and cognitive science (PhD); clinical science (PhD); developmental psychology (PhD); human behavior (MHB); quantitative methods (PhD); social psychology (PhD). *Accreditation:* APA. *Degree requirements:* For doctorate, comprehensive exam, thesis/dissertation, one-year internship (for clinical science students). *Entrance requirements:* For doctorate, GRE. Additional exam requirements/recommendations for international students: Recommended—TOEFL (minimum score 600 paper-based; 100 iBT). Electronic applications accepted. *Faculty research:* Affective neuroscience; children and families; vision, culture and ethnicity; intergroup relations; aggression and violence; language and reading development; substance abuse.

University of Southern Mississippi, Graduate School, College of Education and Psychology, Department of Psychology, Hattiesburg, MS 39406-0001. Offers clinical psychology (PhD); counseling psychology (MS, PhD); experimental psychology (PhD); school psychology (PhD). *Accreditation:* APA (one or more programs are accredited). Terminal master's awarded for partial completion of doctoral program. *Degree*

requirements: For master's, comprehensive exam, thesis; for doctorate, comprehensive exam, thesis/dissertation. *Entrance requirements:* For master's, GRE General Test, minimum GPA of 3.0; for doctorate, GRE General Test, interview, minimum GPA of 3.5. Additional exam requirements/recommendations for international students: Required—TOEFL, IELTS. *Faculty research:* Psychopathology, alcohol and drug abuse, child clinical psychology, parenting, suicide, career/vocational, marine mammal, cognition, psychological psychology, behavioral interventions, positive psychology, anger/aggression, diversity issues.

University of South Florida, College of Arts and Sciences, Department of Psychology, Tampa, FL 33620-9951. Offers clinical psychology (PhD); cognitive and neural sciences (PhD); industrial-organizational psychology (PhD). *Accreditation:* APA. *Faculty:* 33 full-time (15 women), 1 part-time/adjunct. *Students:* 96 full-time (68 women), 18 part-time (11 women); includes 25 minority (2 Black or African American, non-Hispanic/Latino; 9 Asian, non-Hispanic/Latino; 10 Hispanic/Latino; 4 Two or more races, non-Hispanic/Latino), 12 international. Average age 28. 513 applicants, 5% accepted, 19 enrolled. In 2014, 16 doctorates awarded. *Degree requirements:* For doctorate, comprehensive exam, thesis/dissertation, internship. *Entrance requirements:* For doctorate, GRE General Test (minimum recommended verbal and quantitative scores each above the 50th percentile), minimum upper-division GPA of 3.4, three letters of recommendation, personal goals statement. Additional exam requirements/recommendations for international students: Required—TOEFL (minimum score 550 paper-based; 79 iBT) or IELTS (minimum score 6.5). *Application deadline:* For fall admission, 12/1 for domestic and international students. Application fee: $30. Electronic applications accepted. *Expenses:* Expenses: Contact institution. *Financial support:* In 2014–15, 75 students received support, including 18 research assistantships with tuition reimbursements available (averaging $14,727 per year), 57 teaching assistantships with tuition reimbursements available (averaging $14,543 per year); tuition waivers (partial) and unspecified assistantships also available. Financial award applicants required to submit FAFSA. *Faculty research:* Clinical, cognitive, neuroscience, social, and industrial/organizational. *Total annual research expenditures:* $1.7 million. *Unit head:* Dr. Toru Shimizu, Chairperson, 813-974-0352, Fax: 813-974-4617, E-mail: shimizu@usf.edu. *Application contact:* Dr. Joseph Vandello, Associate Professor and Graduate Program Director, 813-974-0362, Fax: 813-974-4617, E-mail: vandello@usf.edu. Website: http://psychology.usf.edu/

The University of Tennessee, Graduate School, College of Arts and Sciences, Department of Psychology, Knoxville, TN 37996. Offers clinical psychology (PhD); experimental psychology (MA, PhD); psychology (MA). *Accreditation:* APA (one or more programs are accredited). Terminal master's awarded for partial completion of doctoral program. *Degree requirements:* For master's, thesis; for doctorate, thesis/dissertation. *Entrance requirements:* For master's and doctorate, GRE General Test, GRE Subject Test, minimum GPA of 2.7. Additional exam requirements/recommendations for international students: Required—TOEFL. Electronic applications accepted.

The University of Texas at Austin, Graduate School, College of Liberal Arts, Department of Psychology, Austin, TX 78712-1111. Offers behavioral neuroscience (PhD); clinical psychology (PhD); cognitive systems (PhD); developmental psychology (PhD); individual differences and evolutionary psychology (PhD); perceptual systems (PhD); social psychology (PhD). *Accreditation:* APA. *Degree requirements:* For doctorate, thesis/dissertation. *Entrance requirements:* For doctorate, GRE General Test. Electronic applications accepted. *Faculty research:* Behavioral neuroscience, sensory neuroscience, evolutionary psychology, cognitive processes in psychopathology, cognitive processes and their development.

The University of Texas at El Paso, Graduate School, College of Liberal Arts, Department of Psychology, El Paso, TX 79968-0001. Offers clinical psychology (MA); experimental psychology (MA); psychology (PhD). Part-time and evening/weekend programs available. *Degree requirements:* For master's, thesis; for doctorate, thesis/dissertation. *Entrance requirements:* For master's, GRE, letters of recommendation; for doctorate, GRE, statement of purpose, letters of recommendation. Additional exam requirements/recommendations for international students: Required—TOEFL; Recommended—IELTS. Electronic applications accepted.

The University of Texas at Tyler, College of Education and Psychology, Department of Psychology and Counseling, Tyler, TX 75799-0001. Offers clinical psychology (MS), including neuropsychology, school psychology; counseling psychology (MA), including general, marriage and family; interdisciplinary studies (MSIS); school counseling (MA). Part-time and evening/weekend programs available. *Degree requirements:* For master's, comprehensive exam, thesis optional. *Entrance requirements:* For master's, GRE General Test, minimum GPA of 3.0. Additional exam requirements/recommendations for international students: Required—TOEFL. Electronic applications accepted. *Faculty research:* Neuropsychology, child abuse, psychometric properties of psychological instruments, maternal behavior, clinical practice issues, victimization of women, post-traumatic stress disorder.

The University of Texas of the Permian Basin, Office of Graduate Studies, College of Arts and Sciences, Department of Psychology, Odessa, TX 79762-0001. Offers applied research psychology (MA); clinical psychology (MA). Part-time and evening/weekend programs available. *Degree requirements:* For master's, comprehensive exam, thesis, practicum. *Entrance requirements:* For master's, GRE General Test, 3 letters of recommendation. Additional exam requirements/recommendations for international students: Required—TOEFL (minimum score 550 paper-based).

The University of Texas–Pan American, College of Social and Behavioral Sciences, Department of Psychology and Anthropology, Edinburg, TX 78539. Offers anthropology (MAIS); psychology (MA), including clinical psychology, experimental psychology. Part-time and evening/weekend programs available. *Degree requirements:* For master's, comprehensive exam, thesis optional, internship. *Entrance requirements:* For master's, GRE, letters of recommendation. Additional exam requirements/recommendations for international students: Required—TOEFL. Electronic applications accepted. *Expenses:* Tuition, state resident: full-time $4187; part-time $232.60 per credit hour. Tuition, nonresident: full-time $10,857; part-time $603.16 per credit hour. *Required fees:* $782; $27.50 per credit hour. $143.35 per semester. *Faculty research:* Biofeedback, acculturation, health, stress/trauma, neuropsychological assessment, false memories, children's theory of mind.

The University of Texas Southwestern Medical Center, Southwestern Graduate School of Biomedical Sciences, Clinical Psychology Program, Dallas, TX 75390. Offers PhD. *Accreditation:* APA. *Degree requirements:* For doctorate, thesis/dissertation, clinical and qualifying exams. *Entrance requirements:* For doctorate, GRE General Test, minimum undergraduate GPA of 3.0. Electronic applications accepted. *Faculty research:* Health psychology, depression, cross-cultural research, neuropsychology, sequelae children's illness.

University of the Cumberlands, Program in Clinical Psychology, Williamsburg, KY 40769-1372. Offers PhD. Part-time and evening/weekend programs available. Postbaccalaureate distance learning degree programs offered (minimal on-campus study).

University of the District of Columbia, College of Arts and Sciences, Department of Psychology and Counseling, Program in Clinical Psychology, Washington, DC 20008-1175. Offers MS.

The University of Toledo, College of Graduate Studies, College of Languages, Literature and Social Sciences, Department of Psychology, Toledo, OH 43606-3390. Offers clinical psychology (MA, PhD); experimental psychology (MA, PhD). *Accreditation:* APA. *Degree requirements:* For master's, comprehensive exam, thesis; for doctorate, comprehensive exam, thesis/dissertation. *Entrance requirements:* For master's and doctorate, GRE General Test, GRE Subject Test, minimum cumulative point-hour ratio of 2.7 for all previous academic work, three letters of recommendation, statement of purpose, transcripts from all prior institutions attended. Additional exam requirements/recommendations for international students: Required—TOEFL (minimum score 550 paper-based; 80 iBT). Electronic applications accepted. *Faculty research:* Neural taste response.

The University of Tulsa, Graduate School, Kendall College of Arts and Sciences, Department of Psychology, Program in Clinical Psychology, Tulsa, OK 74104-3189. Offers MA, PhD, JD/MA. *Accreditation:* APA (one or more programs are accredited). Part-time programs available. *Faculty:* 8 full-time (3 women). *Students:* 30 full-time (23 women), 12 part-time (8 women); includes 9 minority (1 Black or African American, non-Hispanic/Latino; 2 American Indian or Alaska Native, non-Hispanic/Latino; 2 Asian, non-Hispanic/Latino; 4 Hispanic/Latino), 1 international. Average age 27. 145 applicants, 9% accepted, 7 enrolled. In 2014, 11 master's, 1 doctorate awarded. Terminal master's awarded for partial completion of doctoral program. *Degree requirements:* For master's, thesis (for some programs), 6 credit hours of practicum training; for doctorate, comprehensive exam, thesis/dissertation, 1-year pre-doctoral internship. *Entrance requirements:* For master's and doctorate, GRE General Test, interview, resume. Additional exam requirements/recommendations for international students: Required—TOEFL (minimum score 577 paper-based; 91 iBT), IELTS (minimum score 6.5). *Application deadline:* For fall admission, 12/1 for domestic and international students. Application fee: $55. Electronic applications accepted. *Expenses: Tuition:* Full-time $20,160; part-time $1120 per credit hour. *Required fees:* $6 per credit hour. Tuition and fees vary according to course level and course load. *Financial support:* In 2014–15, 39 students received support, including 7 fellowships with full and partial tuition reimbursements available (averaging $17,589 per year), 13 research assistantships with full and partial tuition reimbursements available (averaging $15,540 per year), 19 teaching assistantships with full and partial tuition reimbursements available (averaging $12,433 per year); career-related internships or fieldwork, Federal Work-Study, health care benefits, tuition waivers (full and partial), and unspecified assistantships also available. Support available to part-time students. Financial award application deadline: 2/1; financial award applicants required to submit FAFSA. *Faculty research:* Traumatic stress studies, randomized control trials of exposure treatments, pain modulation, neuropsychological assessment of health/mental health, psychological assessment, psychometrics, ethics, longitudinal assessment of child development, trauma and journalism, MMPI studies. *Total annual research expenditures:* $944,778. *Unit head:* Dr. Michael Basso, Director, 918-631-3151, Fax: 918-631-2836, E-mail: michael-basso@utulsa.edu. *Application contact:* Information Contact, 800-882-4723, E-mail: grad@utulsa.edu.

University of Utah, Graduate School, College of Education, Department of Educational Psychology, Salt Lake City, UT 84112. Offers clinical mental health counseling (M Ed); counseling psychology (PhD); elementary education (M Ed); instructional design and educational technology (M Ed); instructional design and technology (MS); learning and cognition (MS, PhD); reading and literacy (M Ed, PhD); school counseling (M Ed); school psychology (M Ed, PhD); statistics (M Stat). *Accreditation:* APA (one or more programs are accredited). *Faculty:* 24 full-time (12 women), 25 part-time/adjunct (17 women). *Students:* 207 full-time (153 women), 1 part-time (0 women); includes 31 minority (1 Black or African American, non-Hispanic/Latino; 1 American Indian or Alaska Native, non-Hispanic/Latino; 9 Asian, non-Hispanic/Latino; 15 Hispanic/Latino; 1 Native Hawaiian or other Pacific Islander, non-Hispanic/Latino; 4 Two or more races, non-Hispanic/Latino), 3 international. Average age 32. 225 applicants, 38% accepted, 71 enrolled. In 2014, 68 master's, 11 doctorates awarded. Terminal master's awarded for partial completion of doctoral program. *Degree requirements:* For master's, variable foreign language requirement, comprehensive exam (for some programs), thesis (for some programs), projects; for doctorate, variable foreign language requirement, comprehensive exam, thesis/dissertation, oral exam. *Entrance requirements:* For master's and doctorate, GRE General Test, minimum GPA of 3.0. Additional exam requirements/recommendations for international students: Required—TOEFL (minimum score 80 iBT). *Application deadline:* For fall admission, 12/15 for domestic and international students; for winter admission, 11/1 for domestic and international students; for spring admission, 3/15 for domestic and international students. Application fee: $55 ($65 for international students). Electronic applications accepted. *Expenses:* Expenses: Contact institution. *Financial support:* In 2014–15, 84 students received support, including 10 fellowships with full and partial tuition reimbursements available (averaging $18,000 per year), 15 research assistantships with full and partial tuition reimbursements available (averaging $13,500 per year), 59 teaching assistantships with full and partial tuition reimbursements available (averaging $13,500 per year); career-related internships or fieldwork, Federal Work-Study, institutionally sponsored loans, scholarships/grants, health care benefits, and unspecified assistantships also available. Financial award application deadline: 4/1; financial award applicants required to submit FAFSA. *Faculty research:* Autism, computer technology and instruction, cognitive behavior, aging, group counseling. *Unit head:* Dr. Anne E. Cook, Chair, 801-581-7148, Fax: 801-581-5566, E-mail: anne.cook@utah.edu. *Application contact:* JoLynn N. Yates, Academic Program Specialist, 801-581-7148, Fax: 801-581-5566, E-mail: jo.yates@utah.edu.
Website: http://www.ed.utah.edu/edps/

University of Utah, Graduate School, College of Social and Behavioral Science, Department of Psychology, Salt Lake City, UT 84112. Offers clinical psychology (PhD); psychology (PhD). *Accreditation:* APA. *Faculty:* 29 full-time (14 women), 8 part-time/adjunct (4 women). *Students:* 54 full-time (39 women), 5 part-time (2 women); includes 6 minority (1 Black or African American, non-Hispanic/Latino; 3 Asian, non-Hispanic/Latino; 2 Hispanic/Latino), 1 international. Average age 28. 359 applicants, 7% accepted, 18 enrolled. In 2014, 12 doctorates awarded. *Degree requirements:* For doctorate, thesis/dissertation. *Entrance requirements:* For doctorate, GRE General Test. Additional exam requirements/recommendations for international students: Required—TOEFL (minimum score 500 paper-based). *Application deadline:* For fall admission, 12/15 for domestic and international students. Application fee: $55 ($65 for international students). Electronic applications accepted. *Financial support:* In 2014–15, 56 students received support, including 2 fellowships with full tuition reimbursements available (averaging $15,000 per year), 17 research assistantships with full tuition reimbursements available (averaging $15,000 per year), 37 teaching assistantships with full tuition reimbursements available (averaging $15,000 per year); career-related internships or fieldwork and health care benefits also available. Financial award applicants required to submit FAFSA. *Faculty research:* Cognitive neuroscience, health, social cognition, psychopathology, cognitive and social development. *Total annual research expenditures:* $1.9 million. *Unit head:* Dr. Carol Sansone, Chair, 801-581-

8925, Fax: 801-581-5841, E-mail: carol.sansone@psych.utah.edu. *Application contact:* Nancy Seegmiller, Program Manager, 801-581-8925, Fax: 801-581-5841, E-mail: nancy.seegmiller@psych.utah.edu.
Website: http://www.psych.utah.edu/

University of Vermont, Graduate College, College of Arts and Sciences, Department of Psychology, Burlington, VT 05405. Offers clinical psychology (PhD); psychology (PhD). *Accreditation:* APA. *Degree requirements:* For doctorate, thesis/dissertation. *Entrance requirements:* For doctorate, GRE General Test, writing sample (for clinical psychology). Additional exam requirements/recommendations for international students: Required—TOEFL (minimum score 550 paper-based; 80 iBT). Electronic applications accepted.

University of Victoria, Faculty of Graduate Studies, Faculty of Social Sciences, Department of Psychology, Victoria, BC V8W 2Y2, Canada. Offers clinical psychology (PhD); clinical psychology (neuropsychology) (M Sc); cognition and brain science (M Sc, PhD); experimental neuropsychology (M Sc, PhD); individualized study (M Sc, PhD); life span development psychology (PhD); life span developmental psychology (M Sc); social psychology (M Sc, PhD). *Accreditation:* APA (one or more programs are accredited). *Degree requirements:* For master's, thesis; for doctorate, thesis/dissertation, candidacy exam. *Entrance requirements:* For master's and doctorate, GRE General Test. Additional exam requirements/recommendations for international students: Required—TOEFL (minimum score 600 paper-based). Electronic applications accepted. *Faculty research:* Life span development psychology and aging, behavioral neuroscience, cognitive psychology, behavioral psychology, environmental psychology.

University of Virginia, Curry School of Education, Department of Human Services, Program in Clinical and School Psychology, Charlottesville, VA 22903. Offers PhD. *Students:* 26 full-time (23 women); includes 10 minority (5 Black or African American, non-Hispanic/Latino; 3 Asian, non-Hispanic/Latino; 1 Hispanic/Latino; 1 Two or more races, non-Hispanic/Latino). Average age 28. 145 applicants, 5% accepted, 6 enrolled. In 2014, 3 doctorates awarded. *Expenses:* Tuition, state resident: full-time $14,164; part-time $349 per credit hour. Tuition, nonresident: full-time $23,722; part-time $1300 per credit hour. *Required fees:* $2514. *Unit head:* Dr. Ronald Reeve, Director, 434-924-0790, E-mail: rer5r@virginia.edu.
Website: http://curry.virginia.edu/academics/areas-of-study/clinical-school-psychology

University of Washington, Graduate School, College of Arts and Sciences, Department of Psychology, Seattle, WA 98195. Offers animal behavior (PhD); child psychology (PhD); clinical psychology (PhD); cognition and perception (PhD); developmental psychology (PhD); quantitative psychology (PhD); social psychology and personality (PhD). *Accreditation:* APA. *Degree requirements:* For doctorate, thesis/dissertation. *Entrance requirements:* For doctorate, GRE General Test, minimum GPA of 3.0. Electronic applications accepted. *Faculty research:* Addictive behaviors, artificial intelligence, child psychopathology, mechanisms and development of vision, physiology of ingestive behaviors.

University of Windsor, Faculty of Graduate Studies, Faculty of Arts and Social Sciences, Department of Psychology, Windsor, ON N9B 3P4, Canada. Offers adult clinical (MA, PhD); applied social psychology (MA, PhD); child clinical (MA, PhD); clinical neuropsychology (MA, PhD). *Accreditation:* APA (one or more programs are accredited). *Degree requirements:* For master's, thesis; for doctorate, comprehensive exam, thesis/dissertation. *Entrance requirements:* For master's, GRE General Test, GRE Subject Test in psychology, minimum B average; for doctorate, GRE General Test, GRE Subject Test in psychology, master's degree. Additional exam requirements/recommendations for international students: Required—TOEFL (minimum score 600 paper-based). Electronic applications accepted. *Faculty research:* Gambling, suicidology, emotional competence, psychotherapy and trauma.

University of Wisconsin–Madison, Graduate School, College of Letters and Science, Department of Psychology, Program in Clinical Psychology, Madison, WI 53706-1380. Offers PhD. *Accreditation:* APA. *Degree requirements:* For doctorate, comprehensive exam, thesis/dissertation. *Entrance requirements:* For doctorate, GRE General Test, minimum undergraduate GPA of 3.0. Additional exam requirements/recommendations for international students: Required—TOEFL. Electronic applications accepted. *Expenses:* Tuition, state resident: full-time $10,723; part-time $745 per credit. Tuition, nonresident: full-time $24,054; part-time $1578 per credit. *Required fees:* $374 per semester. Tuition and fees vary according to course load, program and reciprocity agreements.

University of Wisconsin–Milwaukee, Graduate School, College of Letters and Sciences, Department of Psychology, Milwaukee, WI 53201-0413. Offers clinical psychology (MS, PhD); psychology (MS, PhD). *Accreditation:* APA (one or more programs are accredited). *Degree requirements:* For master's, thesis; for doctorate, variable foreign language requirement, thesis/dissertation. *Entrance requirements:* For master's and doctorate, GRE General Test, GRE Subject Test. Additional exam requirements/recommendations for international students: Required—TOEFL (minimum score 550 paper-based; 79 iBT), IELTS (minimum score 6.5). Electronic applications accepted.

University of Wisconsin–Stout, Graduate School, College of Human Development, Program in Clinical Mental Health Counseling, Menomonie, WI 54751. Offers MS. *Accreditation:* ACA. Part-time programs available. *Degree requirements:* For master's, comprehensive exam or thesis. *Entrance requirements:* For master's, minimum GPA of 2.75. Additional exam requirements/recommendations for international students: Required—TOEFL (minimum score 500 paper-based; 61 iBT). *Application deadline:* For fall admission, 2/1 priority date for domestic and international students; for spring admission, 10/1 priority date for domestic and international students. Application fee: $45. Electronic applications accepted. *Financial support:* Research assistantships with partial tuition reimbursements, teaching assistantships with partial tuition reimbursements, Federal Work-Study, scholarships/grants, tuition waivers (partial), and unspecified assistantships available. Support available to part-time students. Financial award application deadline: 5/1; financial award applicants required to submit FAFSA. *Faculty research:* Body image, gender issues, eating disorders, cognitive behavioral therapy. *Unit head:* Dr. John Klem, Director, 715-232-3094, Fax: 715-232-2356, E-mail: klemj@uwstout.edu. *Application contact:* Anne E. Johnson, Graduate Student Evaluator (Admissions and Assistantship Coordinator), 715-232-1322, Fax: 715-232-2413, E-mail: johnsona@uwstout.edu.
Website: http://www.uwstout.edu/programs/msmhc/

Utah State University, School of Graduate Studies, Emma Eccles Jones College of Education and Human Services, Department of Psychology, Logan, UT 84322. Offers clinical/counseling/school psychology (PhD); research and evaluation methodology (PhD); school counseling (MS); school psychology (MS). *Accreditation:* APA (one or more programs are accredited). Part-time and evening/weekend programs available. Postbaccalaureate distance learning degree programs offered (no on-campus study). Terminal master's awarded for partial completion of doctoral program. *Degree requirements:* For master's, thesis (for some programs); for doctorate, thesis/dissertation. *Entrance requirements:* For master's, GRE General Test (school psychology), MAT (school counseling), minimum GPA of 3.5; for doctorate, GRE General Test, minimum GPA of 3.5. Additional exam requirements/recommendations for international students: Required—TOEFL. *Faculty research:* Hearing loss detection in infancy, ADHD, eating disorders, domestic violence, neuropsychology, bilingual/Spanish speaking students/parents.

Valparaiso University, Graduate School, Department of Psychology, Valparaiso, IN 46383. Offers clinical mental health counseling (MA); JD/MA. Part-time and evening/weekend programs available. *Faculty:* 10 part-time/adjunct (5 women). *Students:* 38 full-time (32 women), 6 part-time (all women); includes 5 minority (1 Black or African American, non-Hispanic/Latino; 2 Hispanic/Latino; 2 Two or more races, non-Hispanic/Latino). Average age 28. In 2014, 21 master's awarded. *Degree requirements:* For master's, thesis or alternative, internship. *Entrance requirements:* For master's, minimum GPA of 3.0; 15 credits in the social/behavioral sciences (psychology, sociology, human development, etc.) with minimum GPA of 3.0; course in introductory psychology; recent statistics course with minimum B average. Additional exam requirements/recommendations for international students: Required—TOEFL (minimum score 550 paper-based; 80 iBT), IELTS (minimum score 6). *Application deadline:* Applications are processed on a rolling basis. Application fee: $30 ($50 for international students). Electronic applications accepted. *Expenses: Tuition:* Full-time $10,710; part-time $595 per credit hour. *Required fees:* $378; $101 per term. Tuition and fees vary according to course load and program. *Financial support:* Career-related internships or fieldwork, traineeships, and unspecified assistantships available. Support available to part-time students. Financial award applicants required to submit FAFSA. *Faculty research:* Environmental psychology, human sexuality, developmental psychopathology, social psychology. *Unit head:* Dr. David Simpson, Director of Graduate Programs, 219-464-6941, Fax: 219-464-6878, E-mail: david.simpson@valpo.edu. *Application contact:* Jessica Choquette, Graduate Admissions Specialist, 219-464-5313, Fax: 219-464-5381, E-mail: jessica.choquette@valpo.edu.
Website: http://www.valpo.edu/psychology/graduate/index.php

Vanguard University of Southern California, Graduate Program in Clinical Psychology, Costa Mesa, CA 92626-9601. Offers MS. Part-time and evening/weekend programs available. *Degree requirements:* For master's, thesis or alternative, completion of personal therapy. *Entrance requirements:* For master's, minimum GPA of 3.0. Additional exam requirements/recommendations for international students: Required—TOEFL (minimum score 550 paper-based; 79 iBT). Electronic applications accepted. *Expenses:* Contact institution.

Virginia Commonwealth University, Graduate School, College of Humanities and Sciences, Department of Psychology, Program in Clinical Psychology, Richmond, VA 23284-9005. Offers behavioral medicine (PhD); clinical child psychology (PhD). *Accreditation:* APA. *Degree requirements:* For doctorate, thesis/dissertation. *Entrance requirements:* For doctorate, GRE General Test. Additional exam requirements/recommendations for international students: Required—TOEFL (minimum score 600 paper-based; 100 iBT); Recommended—IELTS (minimum score 6.5). Electronic applications accepted. *Faculty research:* Clinical child/adolescent and behavioral medicine.

Virginia State University, College of Graduate Studies, College of Natural and Health Sciences, Department of Psychology, Petersburg, VA 23806-0001. Offers behavioral and community health sciences (PhD); clinical health psychology (PhD); clinical psychology (MS); general psychology (MS). *Degree requirements:* For master's, one foreign language, thesis. *Entrance requirements:* For master's, GRE General Test.

Walden University, Graduate Programs, School of Psychology, Minneapolis, MN 55401. Offers clinical psychology (MS), including counseling, general program; forensic psychology (MS), including forensic psychology in the community, general program, mental health applications, program planning and evaluation in forensic settings, psychology and legal systems; organizational psychology and development (Postbaccalaureate Certificate); psychology (MS, PhD), including applied psychology (MS), clinical psychology (PhD), counseling psychology (PhD), crisis management and response (MS), educational psychology, forensic psychology (PhD), general psychology (MS), general psychology research (PhD), health psychology, leadership development and coaching (MS), psychology of culture (MS), psychology, public administration, and social change (MS), social psychology, terrorism and security (MS); psychology respecialization (Post-Doctoral Certificate); teaching online (Post-Master's Certificate). Part-time and evening/weekend programs available. Postbaccalaureate distance learning degree programs offered (no on-campus study). *Faculty:* 56 full-time (36 women), 351 part-time/adjunct (201 women). *Students:* 2,757 full-time (2,202 women), 1,466 part-time (1,148 women); includes 1,849 minority (1,299 Black or African American, non-Hispanic/Latino; 37 American Indian or Alaska Native, non-Hispanic/Latino; 74 Asian, non-Hispanic/Latino; 315 Hispanic/Latino; 8 Native Hawaiian or other Pacific Islander, non-Hispanic/Latino; 116 Two or more races, non-Hispanic/Latino), 28 international. Average age 41. 913 applicants, 97% accepted, 851 enrolled. In 2014, 602 master's, 204 doctorates, 19 other advanced degrees awarded. Terminal master's awarded for partial completion of doctoral program. *Degree requirements:* For master's, thesis optional; for doctorate, thesis/dissertation, residency. *Entrance requirements:* For master's, bachelor's degree or higher; minimum GPA of 2.5; official transcripts; goal statement (for some programs); access to computer and Internet; for doctorate, master's degree or higher; three years of related professional or academic experience (preferred); minimum GPA of 3.0; goal statement and current resume (for select programs); official transcripts; access to computer and Internet; for other advanced degree, relevant work experience; access to computer and Internet. Additional exam requirements/recommendations for international students: Required—TOEFL (minimum score 550 paper-based, 79 iBT), IELTS (minimum score 6.5), Michigan English Language Assessment Battery (minimum score 82), or PTE (minimum score 53). *Application deadline:* Applications are processed on a rolling basis. Application fee: $0. Electronic applications accepted. *Expenses: Tuition:* Full-time $11,925; part-time $500 per credit hour. *Required fees:* $647. *Financial support:* Fellowships, Federal Work-Study, scholarships/grants, unspecified assistantships, and family tuition reduction, active duty/veteran tuition reduction, group tuition reduction, interest-free payment plans, employee tuition reduction available. Support available to part-time students. Financial award applicants required to submit FAFSA. *Unit head:* Dr. Marilyn Powell, Associate Dean, 866-492-5366. *Application contact:* Meghan Thomas, Vice President of Enrollment Management, 866-492-5336, E-mail: info@waldenu.edu.
Website: http://www.waldenu.edu/programs/colleges-schools/psychology

Washburn University, College of Arts and Sciences, Department of Psychology, Topeka, KS 66621. Offers clinical psychology (MA). Part-time programs available. *Faculty:* 7 full-time (3 women). *Students:* 22 full-time (17 women), 4 part-time (3 women); includes 2 minority (both Hispanic/Latino). Average age 29. 21 applicants, 71% accepted, 11 enrolled. In 2014, 6 master's awarded. *Degree requirements:* For master's, comprehensive exam (for some programs), thesis or alternative. *Entrance requirements:* For master's, GRE General Test, 15 hours of undergraduate course work in psychology. Additional exam requirements/recommendations for international students: Required—TOEFL (minimum score 80 iBT). *Application deadline:* For fall admission, 3/15 for domestic and international students; for spring admission, 12/1 for domestic and international students. Electronic applications accepted. *Expenses:* Tuition, state resident: full-time $6120; part-time $340 per credit hour. Tuition, nonresident: full-time $12,456; part-time $692 per credit hour. *Required fees:* $86; $43 per semester. Tuition

and fees vary according to program. *Financial support:* Unspecified assistantships available. *Faculty research:* Metacognition, anxiety disorders, auditory perception, sports performance psychology, ADHD. *Unit head:* Dr. Cindy Turk, Chair, 785-670-1565, Fax: 785-670-1239, E-mail: cindy.turk@washburn.edu. *Application contact:* Kris Klima, Director of Admissions, 785-670-1030, Fax: 785-670-1113, E-mail: admissions@washburn.edu.
Website: http://www.washburn.edu/academics/college-schools/arts-sciences/departments/psychology

Washington State University, College of Liberal Arts, Department of Psychology, Pullman, WA 99164. Offers clinical psychology (PhD); experimental psychology (PhD). Program applications must be made through the Pullman campus. *Accreditation:* APA (one or more programs are accredited). *Students:* 58 full-time (40 women), 5 part-time (3 women); includes 10 minority (1 Black or African American, non-Hispanic/Latino; 1 American Indian or Alaska Native, non-Hispanic/Latino; 2 Asian, non-Hispanic/Latino; 3 Hispanic/Latino; 3 Two or more races, non-Hispanic/Latino), 2 international. Average age 28. 236 applicants, 8% accepted, 12 enrolled. In 2014, 7 master's, 6 doctorates awarded. *Degree requirements:* For doctorate, comprehensive exam, thesis/dissertation, oral exam, written exam. *Entrance requirements:* For doctorate, GRE General Test, three letters of reference; summary data form; at least 18 credits of study in psychology; at least one course in statistics and research methodology; official transcripts; minimum cumulative undergraduate GPA of 3.0 or master's degree in psychology. Additional exam requirements/recommendations for international students: Required—TOEFL, IELTS. *Application deadline:* For fall admission, 12/1 priority date for domestic and international students. Application fee: $75. Electronic applications accepted. *Expenses:* Tuition, state resident: full-time $11,768. Tuition, nonresident: full-time $25,200. *Required fees:* $960. Tuition and fees vary according to program. *Financial support:* In 2014–15, 31 students received support, including 5 research assistantships with full and partial tuition reimbursements available (averaging $13,870 per year), 46 teaching assistantships with full and partial tuition reimbursements available (averaging $13,890 per year); fellowships, career-related internships or fieldwork, Federal Work-Study, institutionally sponsored loans, and unspecified assistantships also available. Financial award application deadline: 2/15; financial award applicants required to submit FAFSA. *Faculty research:* Adult psychopathology and therapy, child psychopathology, neuropsychology, health psychology. *Unit head:* Dr. David K. Marcus, Director of Clinical Training, 509-335-7750, Fax: 509-335-5043, E-mail: david.marcus@wsu.edu. *Application contact:* Graduate School Admissions, 800-GRADWSU, Fax: 509-335-1949, E-mail: gradsch@wsu.edu.
Website: https://psychology.wsu.edu/

Washington University in St. Louis, Graduate School of Arts and Sciences, Department of Psychology, St. Louis, MO 63130-4899. Offers aging and development (PhD); behavior, brain, and cognition (PhD); clinical psychology (PhD); social and personality psychology (PhD). *Accreditation:* APA. Terminal master's awarded for partial completion of doctoral program. *Degree requirements:* For doctorate, thesis/dissertation. *Entrance requirements:* For doctorate, GRE General Test. Additional exam requirements/recommendations for international students: Required—TOEFL. Electronic applications accepted.

Waynesburg University, Graduate and Professional Studies, Canonsburg, PA 15370. Offers business (MBA), including energy management, finance, health systems, human resources, leadership, market development; counseling (MA), including addictions counseling, clinical mental health; education (M Ed, MAT), including autism (M Ed), curriculum and instruction (M Ed), educational leadership (M Ed), online teaching (M Ed); nursing (MSN), including administration, education, informatics; nursing practice (DNP); special education (M Ed); technology (M Ed); MSN/MBA. *Accreditation:* AACN. Part-time and evening/weekend programs available. *Degree requirements:* For doctorate, thesis/dissertation. *Entrance requirements:* Additional exam requirements/recommendations for international students: Required—TOEFL. Electronic applications accepted.

Wayne State University, College of Liberal Arts and Sciences, Department of Psychology, Detroit, MI 48202. Offers behavioral and cognitive neuroscience (PhD); clinical psychology (PhD); cognitive, developmental and social psychology (PhD); industrial and organizational psychology (MA); social psychology (PhD). Doctoral programs admit for fall only. *Accreditation:* APA (one or more programs are accredited). *Faculty:* 37 full-time (13 women), 8 part-time/adjunct (4 women). *Students:* 107 full-time (74 women), 28 part-time (16 women); includes 19 minority (8 Black or African American, non-Hispanic/Latino; 2 Asian, non-Hispanic/Latino; 5 Hispanic/Latino; 4 Two or more races, non-Hispanic/Latino), 10 international. Average age 28. 397 applicants, 11% accepted, 25 enrolled. In 2014, 24 master's, 18 doctorates awarded. Terminal master's awarded for partial completion of doctoral program. *Degree requirements:* For master's, thesis (for some programs); for doctorate, thesis/dissertation, training assignments. *Entrance requirements:* For master's, GRE General Test, minimum undergraduate upper-division cumulative GPA of 3.0, courses in introductory psychology and statistics, two letters of recommendation, professional statement; for doctorate, GRE General Test, bachelor's, master's, or other advanced degree; at least three letters of recommendation; statement of purpose. Additional exam requirements/recommendations for international students: Required—TOEFL (minimum score 550 paper-based; 79 iBT), TWE (minimum score 5.5), Michigan English Language Assessment Battery (minimum score 85); Recommended—IELTS (minimum score 6.5). *Application deadline:* For fall admission, 12/1 for domestic and international students; for winter admission, 10/15 for domestic students, 9/1 for international students; for spring admission, 3/15 for domestic students, 1/1 for international students. Application fee: $0. Electronic applications accepted. *Expenses:* Tuition, state resident: full-time $10,294; part-time $571.90 per credit hour. Tuition, nonresident: full-time $29,730; part-time $1238.75 per credit hour. *Required fees:* $1365; $43.50 per credit hour. $291.10 per semester. Tuition and fees vary according to course load and program. *Financial support:* In 2014–15, 91 students received support, including 8 fellowships with tuition reimbursements available (averaging $15,983 per year), 12 research assistantships with tuition reimbursements available (averaging $17,862 per year), 49 teaching assistantships with tuition reimbursements available (averaging $16,838 per year); scholarships/grants, health care benefits, and unspecified assistantships also available. Financial award application deadline: 3/31; financial award applicants required to submit FAFSA. *Faculty research:* Neuroscience, including functional cognitive imaging, neural physiology, behavioral pharmacology, and neurobehavioral teratology; cognitive and neurochemical processes associated with aging, drug addiction and neurological disorders to studies of the neural circuits that underlie learning, emotion, and weight regulation; the life-long developmental plasticity of the neurobiological processes of behavior; neuropsychology; child clinical psychology; health psychology; community psychology. *Total annual research expenditures:* $2.1 million. *Unit head:* Boris Baltes, PhD, Chair/Professor, 313-577-2800, Fax: 313-577-7636, E-mail: b.baltes@wayne.edu. *Application contact:* Alia Allen, Academic Services Officer, 313-577-2823, E-mail: aallen@wayne.edu.
Website: http://clas.wayne.edu/psychology/

West Chester University of Pennsylvania, College of Arts and Sciences, Department of Psychology, West Chester, PA 19383. Offers clinical mental health (Certificate);

clinical psychology (MA); general psychology (MA); industrial psychology (MA). Part-time and evening/weekend programs available. *Faculty:* 14 full-time (11 women), 6 part-time/adjunct (4 women). *Students:* 74 full-time (46 women), 23 part-time (13 women); includes 12 minority (7 Black or African American, non-Hispanic/Latino; 1 Asian, non-Hispanic/Latino; 2 Hispanic/Latino; 2 Two or more races, non-Hispanic/Latino), 5 international. Average age 27. 158 applicants, 56% accepted, 42 enrolled. In 2014, 37 master's, 2 other advanced degrees awarded. *Degree requirements:* For master's, comprehensive exam, thesis (for some programs). *Entrance requirements:* For master's, GRE General Test, minimum GPA of 3.0, psychology 3.25; three letters of reference. Additional exam requirements/recommendations for international students: Required—TOEFL (minimum score 550 paper-based; 80 iBT). *Application deadline:* For fall admission, 4/15 priority date for domestic students, 3/15 for international students; for spring admission, 10/15 priority date for domestic students, 9/1 for international students. Applications are processed on a rolling basis. Application fee: $45. Electronic applications accepted. *Expenses:* Tuition, state resident: full-time $8172; part-time $454 per credit. Tuition, nonresident: full-time $12,258; part-time $681 per credit. *Required fees:* $2231; $110.78 per credit. Tuition and fees vary according to campus/location and program. *Financial support:* Unspecified assistantships available. Support available to part-time students. Financial award application deadline: 2/15; financial award applicants required to submit FAFSA. *Faculty research:* Stress, coping, and resilience; preventative interventions; workplace stress; organizational leadership; eating disorders; schizophrenia; diversity; cognition; animal behavior. *Unit head:* Dr. Loretta Rieser-Danner, Chairperson, 610-436-3106, E-mail: lrieser-danner@wcupa.edu. *Application contact:* Dr. Vanessa Johnson, Graduate Coordinator, 610-436-2749, E-mail: vjohnson@wcupa.edu.
Website: http://www.wcupa.edu/_academics/sch_cas.psy/

Western Illinois University, School of Graduate Studies, College of Arts and Sciences, Department of Psychology, Macomb, IL 61455-1390. Offers clinical/community mental health (MS); general psychology (MS); psychology (MS, SSP); school psychology (SSP). Part-time programs available. *Students:* 28 full-time (19 women), 10 part-time (5 women); includes 1 minority (Hispanic/Latino), 5 international. Average age 26. 69 applicants, 46% accepted, 12 enrolled. In 2014, 18 master's, 6 other advanced degrees awarded. *Degree requirements:* For master's, comprehensive exam (for some programs), thesis or alternative. *Entrance requirements:* For master's and SSP, GRE General Test. Additional exam requirements/recommendations for international students: Required—TOEFL (minimum score 550 paper-based; 80 iBT). *Application deadline:* Applications are processed on a rolling basis. Application fee: $30. Electronic applications accepted. *Financial support:* In 2014–15, 41 students received support, including 14 research assistantships with full tuition reimbursements available (averaging $7,544 per year), 34 teaching assistantships with full tuition reimbursements available (averaging $8,688 per year). Financial award applicants required to submit FAFSA. *Unit head:* Dr. Karen Sears, Interim Chairperson, 309-298-1593. *Application contact:* Dr. Nancy Parsons, Associate Provost and Director of Graduate Studies, 309-298-1806, Fax: 309-298-2345, E-mail: grad-office@wiu.edu.
Website: http://wiu.edu/psychology

Western Kentucky University, Graduate Studies, College of Education and Behavioral Sciences, Department of Psychology, Bowling Green, KY 42101. Offers clinical psychology (MA); experimental psychology (MA); general psychology (MA); industrial/organizational psychology (MA); school psychology (Ed S). *Degree requirements:* For master's, comprehensive exam, thesis (for some programs); for Ed S, thesis, oral exam. *Entrance requirements:* For master's, GRE General Test; for Ed S, GRE General Test, minimum GPA of 3.5. Additional exam requirements/recommendations for international students: Required—TOEFL (minimum score 555 paper-based; 79 iBT). *Faculty research:* Neural regeneration, enhancing mobility in the elderly, improvement in visual processing in older adults, lifespan development.

Western Michigan University, Graduate College, College of Arts and Sciences, Department of Psychology, Kalamazoo, MI 49008. Offers behavior analysis (MA, PhD); clinical psychology (PhD); industrial/organizational behavior management (MA). *Accreditation:* APA (one or more programs are accredited). *Degree requirements:* For master's, variable foreign language requirement, thesis; for doctorate, 2 foreign languages, comprehensive exam, thesis/dissertation. *Application deadline:* For fall admission, 2/15 for domestic students. *Financial support:* Application deadline: 2/15. *Application contact:* Admissions and Orientation, 269-387-2000, Fax: 269-387-2096.

West Virginia University, Eberly College of Arts and Sciences, Department of Psychology, Morgantown, WV 26506. Offers behavior analysis (PhD); clinical psychology (MA, PhD); development psychology (PhD); psychology (MS). *Accreditation:* APA (one or more programs are accredited). Part-time programs available. Terminal master's awarded for partial completion of doctoral program. *Degree requirements:* For master's, thesis optional; for doctorate, comprehensive exam, thesis/dissertation. *Entrance requirements:* For master's and doctorate, GRE General Test, minimum GPA of 3.0. Additional exam requirements/recommendations for international students: Required—TOEFL. *Faculty research:* Adult and child clinical psychology, behavioral assessment and therapy, child and adolescent behavior, life span development, experimental and applied behavior analysis.

Wheaton College, Graduate School, Department of Psychology, Wheaton, IL 60187-5593. Offers clinical mental health counseling (MA); clinical psychology (MA, Psy D); counseling ministries (MA); marriage and family therapy (MA). *Accreditation:* APA (one or more programs are accredited). *Students:* 104 full-time (78 women), 22 part-time (14 women); includes 25 minority (13 Black or African American, non-Hispanic/Latino; 8 Asian, non-Hispanic/Latino; 2 Hispanic/Latino; 2 Two or more races, non-Hispanic/Latino), 8 international. Average age 27. 141 applicants, 74% accepted, 64 enrolled. In 2014, 47 master's, 16 doctorates awarded. Terminal master's awarded for partial completion of doctoral program. *Degree requirements:* For master's, thesis or alternative; for doctorate, thesis/dissertation, internship. *Entrance requirements:* For master's, GRE General Test, 18 hours of course work in psychology; for doctorate, GRE General Test. Additional exam requirements/recommendations for international students: Required—TOEFL (minimum score 550 paper-based; 80 iBT), IELTS (minimum score 6.5), TOEFL (minimum score 600 paper-based; 90 iBT) or IELTS (minimum score 7.5) for Psy D. *Application deadline:* For fall admission, 3/1 priority date for domestic students, 1/1 for international students. Applications are processed on a rolling basis. Application fee: $30. *Financial support:* In 2014–15, 3 research assistantships (averaging $4,800 per year) were awarded; career-related internships or fieldwork, Federal Work-Study, scholarships/grants, and unspecified assistantships also available. Financial award application deadline: 3/1; financial award applicants required to submit FAFSA. *Unit head:* Dr. Terri Watson, Associate Dean of Psychology, 630-752-5104. *Application contact:* Dusty Di Santo, Director of Graduate Admissions, 630-752-5195, Fax: 630-752-7047, E-mail: graduate.admissions@wheaton.edu.
Website: http://www.wheaton.edu/academics/departments/psychology

Wichita State University, Graduate School, Fairmount College of Liberal Arts and Sciences, Department of Psychology, Wichita, KS 67260. Offers clinical (PhD); community (PhD); human factors (PhD). *Accreditation:* APA. Part-time programs available. *Unit head:* Dr. Alex Chaparro, Chair, 316-978-3170, Fax: 316-978-3006, E-mail: alex.chaparro@wichita.edu. *Application contact:* Jordan Oleson, Admissions

Coordinator, 316-978-3095, Fax: 316-978-3253, E-mail: jordan.oleson@wichita.edu.
Website: http://www.wichita.edu/psychology

Widener University, School of Human Service Professions, Institute for Graduate Clinical Psychology, Program in Clinical Psychology, Chester, PA 19013-5792. Offers Psy D, Psy D/M Ed, Psy D/MA, Psy D/MBA, Psy D/MHA, Psy D/MPA. *Accreditation:* APA. *Degree requirements:* For doctorate, thesis/dissertation, final oral and written qualifying exams. *Entrance requirements:* For doctorate, GRE General Test or MAT. Electronic applications accepted. *Expenses:* Contact institution. *Faculty research:* Cognitive and personality diagnostic testing, depression, child and adolescent competencies, learning disabilities, family therapy.

Widener University, School of Human Service Professions, Institute for Graduate Clinical Psychology, Program in Clinical Psychology and Health and Medical Services Administration, Chester, PA 19013-5792. Offers Psy D/MBA, Psy D/MHA. *Accreditation:* APA (one or more programs are accredited); CAHME. Electronic applications accepted. *Faculty research:* Psychosocial competence, family systems, medical care systems and financing.

William Paterson University of New Jersey, College of Humanities and Social Sciences, Wayne, NJ 07470-8420. Offers applied sociology (MA); clinical and counseling psychology (MA); creative and professional writing (MFA); English (MA); history (MA); public policy and international affairs (MA). Part-time and evening/weekend programs available. *Faculty:* 32 full-time (16 women), 3 part-time/adjunct (1 woman). *Students:* 50 full-time (30 women), 114 part-time (88 women); includes 64 minority (7 Black or African American, non-Hispanic/Latino; 1 American Indian or Alaska Native, non-Hispanic/Latino; 4 Asian, non-Hispanic/Latino; 50 Hispanic/Latino; 2 Two or more races, non-Hispanic/Latino), 2 international. Average age 34. 115 applicants, 81% accepted, 65 enrolled. In 2014, 42 master's awarded. Terminal master's awarded for partial completion of doctoral program. *Degree requirements:* For master's, thesis (for some programs), internship (for some programs). *Entrance requirements:* For master's, GRE/MAT, minimum GPA of 3.0; 2 letters of recommendation; writing sample/personal statement. Additional exam requirements/recommendations for international students: Required—TOEFL (minimum score 550 paper-based; 79 iBT), IELTS (minimum score 6). *Application deadline:* For fall admission, 6/1 for domestic students, 3/1 for international students; for spring admission, 11/1 for domestic students, 10/1 for international students. Applications are processed on a rolling basis. Application fee: $50. Electronic applications accepted. *Expenses:* Tuition, state resident: full-time $12,413; part-time $564.21 per credit. Tuition, nonresident: full-time $20,487; part-time $931.21 per credit. *Required fees:* $2107; $95.79 per credit. $478.95 per semester. Tuition and fees vary according to course load and degree level. *Financial support:* Research assistantships with full tuition reimbursements, Federal Work-Study, scholarships/grants, and unspecified assistantships available. Support available to part-time students. Financial award application deadline: 4/1; financial award applicants required to submit FAFSA. *Faculty research:* Sexual violence, history of science in Muslim societies, bioethics, teaching writing for transfer, psychological impact of microagressions on minority communities. *Unit head:* Dr. Kara Rabbitt, Dean, 973-720-2731, Fax: 973-720-2955, E-mail: rabbittk@wpunj.edu. *Application contact:* Tinu Adeniran, Associate Director, Graduate Admissions, 973-720-2764, Fax: 973-720-2035, E-mail: adenirant@wpunj.edu.
Website: http://www.wpunj.edu/cohss

Wilmington University, College of Social and Behavioral Sciences, New Castle, DE 19720-6491. Offers administration of human services (MS); administration of justice (MS); clinical mental health counseling (MS); homeland security (MS). *Accreditation:* ACA. Part-time and evening/weekend programs available. *Faculty:* 7 full-time (4 women), 70 part-time/adjunct (28 women). *Students:* 175 full-time (141 women), 468 part-time (350 women); includes 296 minority (266 Black or African American, non-Hispanic/Latino; 5 American Indian or Alaska Native, non-Hispanic/Latino; 3 Asian, non-Hispanic/Latino; 18 Hispanic/Latino; 2 Native Hawaiian or other Pacific Islander, non-Hispanic/Latino; 2 Two or more races, non-Hispanic/Latino), 4 international. Average age 35. 251 applicants, 100% accepted, 157 enrolled. In 2014, 170 master's awarded. *Entrance requirements:* Additional exam requirements/recommendations for international students: Required—TOEFL (minimum score 500 paper-based). *Application deadline:* Applications are processed on a rolling basis. Application fee: $35. Electronic applications accepted. *Financial support:* Applicants required to submit FAFSA. *Unit head:* Dr. Christian A. Trowbridge, Dean, 302-295-1151, Fax: 302-328-5164. *Application contact:* Laura Morris, Director of Admissions, 877-967-5464, E-mail: inquire@wilmcoll.edu.
Website: http://www.wilmu.edu/behavioralscience/

Wisconsin School of Professional Psychology, Program in Clinical Psychology, Milwaukee, WI 53225-4960. Offers MA, Psy D. *Accreditation:* APA. Part-time and evening/weekend programs available. Terminal master's awarded for partial completion of doctoral program. *Degree requirements:* For master's, candidacy exam, 500 hours of supervised clinical practica; for doctorate, thesis/dissertation, 1 year clinical intern and practicum experience (2000 hrs), candidacy and clinical exams. *Entrance requirements:* For master's, GRE General Test, GRE Subject Test, bachelor's degree in psychology, writing sample; for doctorate, GRE General Test, GRE Subject Test, master's degree in clinical psychology or equivalent, writing sample. *Faculty research:* Violence prevention, psychology of women, forensic psychology, custody evaluation, aging, harm reduction in AODA.

Wright Institute, Doctoral Program in Clinical Psychology, Berkeley, CA 94704-1796. Offers Psy D. *Accreditation:* APA. *Degree requirements:* For doctorate, comprehensive exam, thesis/dissertation. *Entrance requirements:* For doctorate, GRE General Test, statistics, human development, theories of personality or abnormal psychology. Additional exam requirements/recommendations for international students: Required—TOEFL (minimum score 600 paper-based). Electronic applications accepted. *Faculty research:* Time-limited dynamic psychotherapy; mindfulness/ACT; psychotherapy integration; empathy, altruism and survivor guilt; culturally-informed practice.

Wright State University, School of Professional Psychology, Dayton, OH 45435. Offers clinical psychology (Psy D). *Accreditation:* APA. *Degree requirements:* For doctorate, thesis/dissertation. *Entrance requirements:* For doctorate, GRE General Test, GRE Subject Test. Additional exam requirements/recommendations for international students: Required—TOEFL. *Expenses:* Contact institution.

Xavier University, College of Social Sciences, Health and Education, Department of Psychology, Cincinnati, OH 45207. Offers clinical psychology (Psy D); industrial-organizational psychology (MA). *Accreditation:* APA (one or more programs are accredited). *Faculty:* 16 full-time (9 women), 7 part-time/adjunct (3 women). *Students:* 89 full-time (67 women), 38 part-time (24 women); includes 18 minority (4 Black or African American, non-Hispanic/Latino; 7 Asian, non-Hispanic/Latino; 4 Hispanic/Latino; 3 Two or more races, non-Hispanic/Latino), 1 international. Average age 26. 235 applicants, 26% accepted, 35 enrolled. In 2014, 29 master's, 15 doctorates awarded. *Degree requirements:* For master's, one foreign language, comprehensive exam, thesis, internship; for doctorate, one foreign language, comprehensive exam, thesis/dissertation, internship. *Entrance requirements:* For master's, GRE, official transcript; 3 letters of recommendation; for doctorate, GRE General Test; GRE Subject Test in psychology (if no undergraduate degree in psychology), bachelor's or master's degree; 18 semester hours of psychology coursework; minimum GPA of 3.0; work and research experience; official transcript; 3 letters of recommendation; statement of purpose. Additional exam requirements/recommendations for international students: Required—TOEFL (minimum score 550 paper-based; 79 iBT), IELTS (minimum score 6.5). *Application deadline:* For fall admission, 12/1 for domestic and international students. Application fee: $35. Electronic applications accepted. *Expenses:* Expenses: $600 per credit hour (for MA); $760 per credit hour (for Psy D). *Financial support:* In 2014–15, 62 students received support, including 26 research assistantships with partial tuition reimbursements available, 4 teaching assistantships with partial tuition reimbursements available; career-related internships or fieldwork, traineeships, and unspecified assistantships also available. Financial award application deadline: 3/1; financial award applicants required to submit FAFSA. *Faculty research:* Older adults, clinical child and adolescent issues, personnel selection and employee behavior, at-risk youth, sexual abuse. *Unit head:* Dr. Karl Stukenberg, Chair, 513-745-1041, Fax: 513-745-3327, E-mail: stukenb@xavier.edu. *Application contact:* Margaret Maybury, Director, Academic Programs, 513-745-1053, Fax: 513-745-3347, E-mail: maybury@xavier.edu.
Website: http://www.xavier.edu/psychology-grad/

Xavier University, College of Social Sciences, Health and Education, School of Education, Department of Counseling, Cincinnati, OH 45207. Offers clinical mental health counseling (MA); school counseling (MA). Part-time and evening/weekend programs available. *Faculty:* 5 full-time (2 women), 10 part-time/adjunct (6 women). *Students:* 65 full-time (54 women), 75 part-time (60 women); includes 25 minority (14 Black or African American, non-Hispanic/Latino; 2 Asian, non-Hispanic/Latino; 7 Hispanic/Latino; 1 Native Hawaiian or other Pacific Islander, non-Hispanic/Latino; 1 Two or more races, non-Hispanic/Latino), 2 international. Average age 32. 56 applicants, 63% accepted, 16 enrolled. In 2014, 59 master's awarded. *Degree requirements:* For master's, internship. *Entrance requirements:* For master's, GRE or MAT, minimum GPA of 3.0; 2 letters of recommendation; resume; official transcript; statement of purpose. Additional exam requirements/recommendations for international students: Required—TOEFL (minimum score 550 paper-based; 79 iBT). *Application deadline:* For fall admission, 3/1 priority date for domestic and international students; for winter admission, 4/1 for domestic and international students; for spring admission, 10/1 priority date for domestic and international students; for summer admission, 3/1 priority date for domestic and international students. Application fee: $35. Electronic applications accepted. Application fee is waived when completed online. *Expenses:* Expenses: $568 per credit hour. *Financial support:* In 2014–15, 96 students received support. Tuition waivers (partial) and unspecified assistantships available. *Faculty research:* Supervision, ethics, consultation, self-injury, bullying. *Unit head:* Dr. Brent Richardson, Chair, 513-745-4294, Fax: 513-745-2920, E-mail: richardb@xavier.edu. *Application contact:* Roger Bosse, Graduate Services Director, 513-745-3357, Fax: 513-745-1048, E-mail: bosse@xavier.edu.
Website: http://www.xavier.edu/counseling/

Yale University, Graduate School of Arts and Sciences, Department of Psychology, New Haven, CT 06520. Offers behavioral neuroscience (PhD); clinical psychology (PhD); cognitive psychology (PhD); developmental psychology (PhD); social/personality psychology (PhD). *Accreditation:* APA. *Degree requirements:* For doctorate, thesis/dissertation. *Entrance requirements:* For doctorate, GRE General Test.

Yeshiva University, Ferkauf Graduate School of Psychology, Program in Clinical Psychology, New York, NY 10033-3201. Offers Psy D. *Accreditation:* APA. Part-time programs available. *Degree requirements:* For doctorate, comprehensive exam, thesis/dissertation. *Entrance requirements:* For doctorate, GRE General Test. *Faculty research:* Psychotherapy, family therapy, psychoanalysis, cognitive behavior therapy.

Yeshiva University, Ferkauf Graduate School of Psychology, Program in School/Clinical-Child Psychology, New York, NY 10033-3201. Offers Psy D. *Accreditation:* APA. Part-time programs available. *Degree requirements:* For doctorate, comprehensive exam, thesis/dissertation. *Entrance requirements:* For doctorate, GRE General Test. *Faculty research:* Testing, early childhood intervention, child and adolescent psychotherapy, clinical child psychology.

Cognitive Sciences

Arizona State University at the Tempe campus, College of Liberal Arts and Sciences, Department of Psychology, Tempe, AZ 85287-1104. Offers applied behavior analysis (MS); behavioral neuroscience (PhD); clinical psychology (PhD); cognitive science (PhD); developmental psychology (PhD); quantitative psychology (PhD); social psychology (PhD). *Accreditation:* APA. *Degree requirements:* For doctorate, comprehensive exam, thesis/dissertation, interactive Program of Study (iPOS) submitted before completing 50 percent of required credit hours. *Entrance requirements:* For doctorate, GRE General Test, GRE Subject Test, minimum GPA of 3.0 or equivalent in last 2 years of work leading to bachelor's degree. Additional exam requirements/recommendations for international students: Required—TOEFL, IELTS, or PTE. Electronic applications accepted.

Arizona State University at the Tempe campus, Ira A. Fulton Schools of Engineering, The Polytechnic School, Department of Engineering, Mesa, AZ 85212. Offers simulation, modeling, and applied cognitive science (PhD). Part-time programs available. *Degree requirements:* For doctorate, comprehensive exam, thesis/dissertation, interactive Program of Study (iPOS) submitted before completing 50 percent of required credit hours. *Entrance requirements:* For doctorate, GRE, master's degree in psychology, engineering, cognitive science, or computer science; 3 letters of recommendation; statement of research interests. Additional exam requirements/recommendations for international students: Required—TOEFL, IELTS, or PTE. Electronic applications accepted. *Faculty research:* Software process and automated workflow, software architecture, dotal technologies, relational database systems, embedded systems.

Ball State University, Graduate School, College of Sciences and Humanities, Department of Psychological Science, Program in Cognitive and Social Processes, Muncie, IN 47306-1099. Offers MA. *Students:* 16 full-time (10 women). Average age 23. 12 applicants, 67% accepted, 8 enrolled. In 2014, 7 master's awarded. Application fee: $50. *Financial support:* In 2014–15, 11 students received support, including 2 research assistantships with partial tuition reimbursements available (averaging $9,000 per year), 13 teaching assistantships with partial tuition reimbursements available (averaging $9,568 per year); unspecified assistantships also available. *Unit head:* Dr. Kerri Pickel, Program Director, 765-285-1711, Fax: 765-285-8980, E-mail: kpickel@bsu.edu.

Binghamton University, State University of New York, Graduate School, School of Arts and Sciences, Department of Psychology, Specialization in Cognitive and Behavioral Science, Vestal, NY 13850. Offers PhD. *Students:* 12 full-time (7 women), 8 part-time (4 women); includes 2 minority (1 Asian, non-Hispanic/Latino; 1 Hispanic/Latino), 2 international. Average age 28. 30 applicants, 17% accepted, 2 enrolled. In 2014, 2 doctorates awarded. *Degree requirements:* For doctorate, thesis/dissertation. *Entrance requirements:* For doctorate, GRE General Test. Additional exam requirements/recommendations for international students: Required—TOEFL (minimum score 550 paper-based; 80 iBT). *Application deadline:* For fall admission, 1/15 priority date for domestic and international students. Applications are processed on a rolling basis. Application fee: $75. Electronic applications accepted. *Expenses:* Tuition, state resident: full-time $7776; part-time $432 per credit. Tuition, nonresident: full-time $15,138; part-time $841 per credit. *Required fees:* $1754; $213 per credit. Tuition and fees vary according to degree level and program. *Financial support:* In 2014–15, 16 students received support, including 3 research assistantships with full tuition reimbursements available (averaging $16,500 per year), 12 teaching assistantships with full tuition reimbursements available (averaging $16,500 per year); career-related internships or fieldwork, Federal Work-Study, institutionally sponsored loans, scholarships/grants, traineeships, health care benefits, tuition waivers (full and partial), and unspecified assistantships also available. Financial award application deadline: 2/15; financial award applicants required to submit FAFSA. *Unit head:* Dr. Ralph R. Miller, Graduate Coordinator, 607-777-2291, E-mail: rmiler@binghamton.edu. *Application contact:* Kishan Zuber, Recruiting and Admissions Coordinator, 607-777-2151, Fax: 607-777-2501, E-mail: kzuber@binghamton.edu.

Brandeis University, Graduate School of Arts and Sciences, Department of Psychology, Waltham, MA 02454-9110. Offers brain, body and behavior (PhD); cognitive neuroscience (PhD); general psychology (MA); social/developmental psychology (PhD). Part-time programs available. Terminal master's awarded for partial completion of doctoral program. *Degree requirements:* For master's, thesis; for doctorate, thesis/dissertation, research reports. *Entrance requirements:* For master's and doctorate, GRE General Test; GRE Subject Test (recommended), 3 letters of recommendation, statement of purpose, transcript(s), resume. Additional exam requirements/recommendations for international students: Required—TOEFL (minimum score 600 paper-based; 100 iBT), PTE (minimum score 68); Recommended—IELTS (minimum score 7). Electronic applications accepted. *Faculty research:* Cognitive neuroscience, social developmental psychology, motor control, visual perception, taste physiology and psychophysics, memory, learning, aging, child development, aggression, emotion, personality and cognition in adulthood and old age, social relations and health, stereotypes, nonverbal communication.

Brown University, Graduate School, Department of Cognitive, Linguistic and Psychological Sciences, Providence, RI 02912. Offers cognitive science (Sc M, PhD); linguistics (AM, PhD); psychology (PhD). *Degree requirements:* For master's, one foreign language, thesis or alternative; for doctorate, 2 foreign languages, thesis/dissertation.

Carleton University, Faculty of Graduate Studies, Faculty of Arts and Social Sciences, Program in Cognitive Science, Ottawa, ON K1S 5B6, Canada. Offers PhD. *Degree requirements:* For doctorate, thesis/dissertation. *Entrance requirements:* For doctorate, master's degree. *Faculty research:* Language, attention, artificial intelligence, symbol recognition, consciousness.

Carnegie Mellon University, Dietrich College of Humanities and Social Sciences, Department of Psychology, Area of Cognitive Neuroscience, Pittsburgh, PA 15213-3891. Offers PhD. *Degree requirements:* For doctorate, comprehensive exam, thesis/dissertation. *Entrance requirements:* For doctorate, GRE General Test. Additional exam requirements/recommendations for international students: Required—TOEFL.

Carnegie Mellon University, Dietrich College of Humanities and Social Sciences, Department of Psychology, Area of Cognitive Psychology, Pittsburgh, PA 15213-3891. Offers PhD. *Degree requirements:* For doctorate, comprehensive exam, thesis/dissertation. *Entrance requirements:* For doctorate, GRE General Test. Additional exam requirements/recommendations for international students: Required—TOEFL.

Case Western Reserve University, School of Graduate Studies, Department of Cognitive Science, Cleveland, OH 44106. Offers cognitive linguistics (MA). Part-time programs available. *Faculty:* 5 full-time (2 women), 3 part-time/adjunct (1 woman). *Students:* 7 full-time (4 women). Average age 27. 3 applicants, 100% accepted, 3 enrolled. In 2014, 2 master's awarded. *Degree requirements:* For master's, thesis. *Entrance requirements:* For master's, GRE, Statement of purpose, three letters of recommendation, writing sample. Additional exam requirements/recommendations for international students: Required—TOEFL (minimum score 577 paper-based; 90 iBT); Recommended—IELTS (minimum score 7). *Application deadline:* For fall admission, 5/1 priority date for domestic students. Application fee: $50. Electronic applications accepted. *Faculty research:* The workings of the human mind in design, art, and technology; the interaction of brain and culture in development and evolution; the origins of human higher-order cognition; the role of the body and social interaction in shaping human cognition; the operation of systems that human beings have invented to guide their thought and action individually and culturally. *Unit head:* Dr. Todd Oakley, Chair, 216-368-4753, E-mail: coglingadmission@case.edu. *Application contact:* Susan M. Benedict, Admissions Coordinator, 216-368-4400, Fax: 216-368-4250, E-mail: susan.benedict@case.edu.
Website: http://cognitivescience.case.edu/

Central European University, Graduate Studies, Department of Cognitive Science, Budapest, Hungary. Offers PhD. *Faculty:* 14 full-time (4 women), 2 part-time/adjunct (0 women). *Students:* 23 full-time (12 women). Average age 27. 36 applicants, 22% accepted, 6 enrolled. *Degree requirements:* For doctorate, one foreign language, comprehensive exam, thesis/dissertation. *Entrance requirements:* For doctorate, essay, interview. Additional exam requirements/recommendations for international students: Recommended—TOEFL (minimum score 570 paper-based), IELTS (minimum score 6.5). *Application deadline:* For fall admission, 1/24 priority date for domestic and international students. Application fee: $40. Electronic applications accepted. *Expenses:* Tuition: Full-time 12,000 euros. *Required fees:* 200 euros. One-time fee: 500 euros full-time. *Financial support:* In 2014–15, 6 students received support, including 23 fellowships (averaging $10,000 per year); career-related internships or fieldwork, scholarships/grants, and health care benefits also available. *Faculty research:* Cognitive anthropology, developmental psychology, language and cognition, mathematical modeling of cognition, economics and cognition, social cognition. *Unit*

head: Dr. Gergely Csibra, Head, 36 1 88 333 44. *Application contact:* Zsuzsanna Jaszberenyi, Admissions Officer, 361-324-3009, Fax: 367-327-3211, E-mail: admissions@ceu.hu.
Website: http://cognitivescience.ceu.hu/

Claremont Graduate University, Graduate Programs, School of Social Science, Policy and Evaluation, Department of Psychology, Claremont, CA 91711-6160. Offers advanced study in evaluation (Certificate); cognitive psychology (MA, PhD); developmental psychology (MA, PhD); evaluation and applied research methods (MA, PhD); health behavior research and evaluation (MA, PhD); human resource development and evaluation (MA); industrial/organizational psychology (MA, PhD); organizational behavior (MA, PhD); organizational psychology (MA, PhD); social psychology (MA, PhD); MBA/PhD. Part-time programs available. *Faculty:* 18 full-time (7 women), 1 part-time/adjunct (0 women). *Students:* 256 full-time (160 women), 70 part-time (50 women); includes 93 minority (17 Black or African American, non-Hispanic/Latino; 3 American Indian or Alaska Native, non-Hispanic/Latino; 26 Asian, non-Hispanic/Latino; 30 Hispanic/Latino; 17 Two or more races, non-Hispanic/Latino), 35 international. Average age 30. In 2014, 56 master's, 15 doctorates, 7 other advanced degrees awarded. Terminal master's awarded for partial completion of doctoral program. *Entrance requirements:* For master's and doctorate, GRE General Test. Additional exam requirements/recommendations for international students: Required—TOEFL (minimum score 550 paper-based; 80 iBT). *Application deadline:* For fall admission, 1/15 priority date for domestic and international students. Applications are processed on a rolling basis. Application fee: $80. Electronic applications accepted. *Expenses: Tuition:* Full-time $41,784; part-time $1741 per credit. *Required fees:* $600; $300 per semester. *Financial support:* Fellowships, research assistantships, teaching assistantships, Federal Work-Study, institutionally sponsored loans, scholarships/grants, and tuition waivers (full and partial) available. Support available to part-time students. Financial award application deadline: 2/15; financial award applicants required to submit FAFSA. *Faculty research:* Social intervention, diversity in organizations, eyewitness memory, aging and cognition, drug policy. *Unit head:* William Crano, Chair, 909-621-8084, E-mail: william.crano@cgu.edu. *Application contact:* Annekah Hall, Assistant Director of Admissions, 909-607-3371, E-mail: annekah.hall@cgu.edu.
Website: http://www.cgu.edu/pages/502.asp

Cornell University, Graduate School, Graduate Fields of Arts and Sciences, Field of Information Science, Ithaca, NY 14853-0001. Offers cognition (PhD); human computer interaction (PhD); information science (PhD); information systems (PhD); social aspects of information (PhD). *Degree requirements:* For doctorate, comprehensive exam, thesis/dissertation. *Entrance requirements:* For doctorate, GRE General Test, 3 letters of recommendation. Additional exam requirements/recommendations for international students: Required—TOEFL (minimum score 550 paper-based; 77 iBT). Electronic applications accepted. *Faculty research:* Digital libraries, game theory, data mining, human-computer interaction, computational linguistics.

Dartmouth College, Arts and Sciences Graduate Programs, Department of Psychological and Brain Sciences, Program in Cognitive Neuroscience, Hanover, NH 03755. Offers PhD. *Students:* 6 full-time (2 women); includes 1 minority (Two or more races, non-Hispanic/Latino), 3 international. Average age 28. 11 applicants. In 2014, 3 doctorates awarded. *Entrance requirements:* Additional exam requirements/recommendations for international students: Required—TOEFL. *Application deadline:* For fall admission, 12/15 for domestic students. Application fee: $50. *Unit head:* Dr. Jay Hull, Chair, 603-646-2098, Fax: 603-646-1419. *Application contact:* Nancy Tenney, Department Administration, 603-646-3181, E-mail: nancy.tenney@dartmouth.edu.

Duke University, Graduate School, Department of Psychology and Neuroscience, Durham, NC 27708. Offers biological psychology (PhD); clinical psychology (PhD); cognitive psychology (PhD); developmental psychology (PhD); experimental psychology (PhD); health psychology (PhD); human social development (PhD); JD/MA. *Accreditation:* APA (one or more programs are accredited). *Degree requirements:* For doctorate, thesis/dissertation. *Entrance requirements:* For doctorate, GRE General Test. Additional exam requirements/recommendations for international students: Required—TOEFL (minimum score 577 paper-based; 90 iBT) or IELTS (minimum score 7). Electronic applications accepted. *Expenses: Tuition:* Full-time $45,760; part-time $2765 per credit. *Required fees:* $978. Full-time tuition and fees vary according to program.

Emory University, Laney Graduate School, Department of Psychology, Atlanta, GA 30322-1100. Offers clinical psychology (PhD); cognition and development (PhD); neuroscience and animal behavior (PhD). *Accreditation:* APA. *Degree requirements:* For doctorate, comprehensive exam, thesis/dissertation. *Entrance requirements:* For doctorate, GRE General Test, minimum GPA of 3.25. Additional exam requirements/recommendations for international students: Required—TOEFL. Electronic applications accepted. *Faculty research:* Neuroscience and animal behavior; adult and child psychopathology, cognition development assessment.

Florida State University, The Graduate School, College of Arts and Sciences, Department of Psychology, Program in Cognitive Psychology, Tallahassee, FL 32306. Offers PhD. *Faculty:* 9 full-time (2 women). *Students:* 25 full-time (8 women); includes 3 minority (2 Asian, non-Hispanic/Latino; 1 Hispanic/Latino). Average age 28. 50 applicants, 10% accepted, 5 enrolled. In 2014, 1 doctorate awarded. Terminal master's awarded for partial completion of doctoral program. *Degree requirements:* For doctorate, comprehensive exam, thesis/dissertation. *Entrance requirements:* For doctorate, GRE General Test, minimum GPA of 3.0, research experience, letters of recommendation. Additional exam requirements/recommendations for international students: Required—TOEFL (minimum score 550 paper-based; 80 iBT). *Application deadline:* For fall admission, 12/16 for domestic and international students. Application fee: $30. Electronic applications accepted. *Expenses: Tuition,* state resident: part-time $403.51 per credit hour. Tuition, nonresident: part-time $1004.85 per credit hour. *Required fees:* $75.81 per credit hour. One-time fee: $20 part-time. Tuition and fees vary according to campus/location. *Financial support:* In 2014–15, 25 students received support, including 3 fellowships with full tuition reimbursements available (averaging $20,000 per year), 7 research assistantships with full tuition reimbursements available (averaging $20,000 per year), 15 teaching assistantships with full tuition reimbursements available (averaging $17,775 per year); Federal Work-Study, institutionally sponsored loans, scholarships/grants, traineeships, health care benefits, and unspecified assistantships also available. Financial award application deadline: 12/16. *Faculty research:* Memory, learning and reading disabilities; expert performance; aging. *Total annual research expenditures:* $605,750. *Unit head:* Dr. Walter Boot, Director, 850-645-8734, Fax: 850-644-7739, E-mail: boot@psy.fsu.edu. *Application contact:* Cherie P. Miller, Graduate Program Assistant, 850-644-2499, Fax: 850-644-7739, E-mail: grad-info@psy.fsu.edu.
Website: http://www.psy.fsu.edu/

George Mason University, College of Humanities and Social Sciences, Department of Psychology, Fairfax, VA 22030. Offers applied developmental psychology (Certificate); cognitive and behavioral neuroscience (MA); human factors/applied cognition (MA); industrial/organizational psychology (MA, PhD); school psychology (MA). *Accreditation:* APA. *Faculty:* 43 full-time (22 women), 13 part-time/adjunct (8 women). *Students:* 167 full-time (114 women), 48 part-time (34 women); includes 41 minority (7 Black or African American, non-Hispanic/Latino; 8 Asian, non-Hispanic/Latino; 21 Hispanic/Latino; 1 Native Hawaiian or other Pacific Islander, non-Hispanic/Latino; 4 Two or more races,

non-Hispanic/Latino), 10 international. Average age 27. 833 applicants, 14% accepted, 75 enrolled. In 2014, 49 master's, 17 doctorates, 10 other advanced degrees awarded. *Degree requirements:* For master's, comprehensive exam, thesis (for biopsychology); for doctorate, comprehensive exam, thesis/dissertation, 2nd year project. *Entrance requirements:* For master's, GRE, 2 official transcripts; goals statement; 15 undergraduate credits in concentration for which the applicant is applying; for doctorate, GRE, 3 letters of recommendation; resume; goals statement; minimum GPA of 3.0 overall for last 60 undergraduate credits, 3.25 in psychology courses; 15 undergraduate credits in concentration for which the applicant is applying; 2 official transcripts; for Certificate, GRE, 2 official transcripts; expanded goals statement; 3 letters of recommendation. Additional exam requirements/recommendations for international students: Required—TOEFL (minimum score 570 paper-based; 80 iBT), IELTS (minimum score 6.5), PTE. Application fee: $65 ($80 for international students). Electronic applications accepted. *Expenses:* Tuition, state resident: full-time $9794; part-time $408 per credit hour. Tuition, nonresident: full-time $26,978; part-time $1124 per credit hour. *Required fees:* $2820; $118 per credit hour. Tuition and fees vary according to course load and program. *Financial support:* In 2014–15, 130 students received support, including 6 fellowships (averaging $6,576 per year), 84 research assistantships with full and partial tuition reimbursements available (averaging $15,356 per year), 63 teaching assistantships with full and partial tuition reimbursements available (averaging $13,274 per year); career-related internships or fieldwork, Federal Work-Study, scholarships/grants, tuition waivers (partial), unspecified assistantships, and health care benefits (for full-time research or teaching assistantship recipients) also available. Support available to part-time students. Financial award application deadline: 3/1; financial award applicants required to submit FAFSA. *Faculty research:* Applied developmental psychology, biopsychology, clinical psychology, human factors/applied cognition psychology, industrial/organizational psychology, school psychology. *Total annual research expenditures:* $5.2 million. *Unit head:* Reeshad Dalal, Department Chair, 703-993-9487, Fax: 703-993-1359, E-mail: rdalal@gmu.edu. *Application contact:* Adam Winsler, Associate Chair of Graduate Studies, 703-993-1881, Fax: 703-993-1359, E-mail: awinsler@gmu.edu.
Website: http://psychology.gmu.edu

The George Washington University, Columbian College of Arts and Sciences, Department of Psychology, Washington, DC 20052. Offers applied social psychology (PhD); clinical psychology (PhD); cognitive neuroscience (PhD). *Accreditation:* APA. Part-time and evening/weekend programs available. *Faculty:* 24 full-time (14 women), 1 (woman) part-time/adjunct. *Students:* 46 full-time (33 women), 24 part-time (15 women); includes 19 minority (7 Black or African American, non-Hispanic/Latino; 3 Asian, non-Hispanic/Latino; 8 Hispanic/Latino; 1 Two or more races, non-Hispanic/Latino), 8 international. Average age 28. 513 applicants, 3% accepted, 14 enrolled. In 2014, 10 doctorates awarded. *Degree requirements:* For doctorate, thesis/dissertation or alternative, general exam. *Entrance requirements:* For doctorate, GRE General Test, minimum GPA of 3.0. Additional exam requirements/recommendations for international students: Required—TOEFL (minimum score 550 paper-based; 80 iBT). *Application deadline:* For fall admission, 1/15 for domestic and international students. Application fee: $75. *Financial support:* In 2014–15, 62 students received support. Fellowships with tuition reimbursements available, teaching assistantships with tuition reimbursements available, career-related internships or fieldwork, Federal Work-Study, and tuition waivers available. *Unit head:* Dr. Paul Poppen, Chair, 202-994-6324, E-mail: pjp@gwu.edu. *Application contact:* Information Contact, 202-994-6320, Fax: 202-994-1602, E-mail: psydept@gwu.edu.
Website: http://psychology.columbian.gwu.edu/

Georgia State University, College of Arts and Sciences, Department of Psychology, Atlanta, GA 30302-3083. Offers clinical (PhD); cognitive sciences (PhD); community (PhD); developmental (PhD); neuropsychology and behavioral neuroscience (PhD). *Accreditation:* APA. *Faculty:* 29 full-time (17 women). *Students:* 116 full-time (95 women), 2 part-time (both women); includes 30 minority (10 Black or African American, non-Hispanic/Latino; 9 Asian, non-Hispanic/Latino; 6 Hispanic/Latino; 5 Two or more races, non-Hispanic/Latino), 10 international. Average age 28. 577 applicants, 7% accepted, 27 enrolled. In 2014, 16 doctorates awarded. *Degree requirements:* For doctorate, comprehensive exam, thesis/dissertation, residency year (for clinical only). *Entrance requirements:* For doctorate, GRE. Additional exam requirements/recommendations for international students: Required—TOEFL (minimum score 550 paper-based; 80 iBT). *Application deadline:* For fall admission, 12/1 for domestic and international students. Application fee: $50. Electronic applications accepted. *Expenses:* Tuition, state resident: full-time $6516; part-time $362 per credit hour. Tuition, nonresident: full-time $22,014; part-time $1223 per credit hour. *Required fees:* $2128 per semester. Tuition and fees vary according to course load and program. *Financial support:* In 2014–15, fellowships with full tuition reimbursements (averaging $19,282 per year), research assistantships with full tuition reimbursements (averaging $5,173 per year), teaching assistantships with full tuition reimbursements (averaging $6,389 per year) were awarded; scholarships/grants, traineeships, health care benefits, and unspecified assistantships also available. *Faculty research:* Clinical psychology, developmental psychology, community psychology, neuropsychology and behavioral neuroscience, cognitive sciences. *Unit head:* Dr. Lisa Armistead, Chair, 404-413-6205, Fax: 404-413-6207, E-mail: lparmistead@gsu.edu. *Application contact:* Dr. Lindsey Cohen, Director of Graduate Studies, 404-413-6263, Fax: 404-413-6207, E-mail: llcohen@gsu.edu.
Website: http://psychology.gsu.edu/graduate/areas-of-study/

The Graduate Center, City University of New York, Graduate Studies, Program in Psychology, New York, NY 10016-4039. Offers basic applied neurocognition (PhD); biopsychology (PhD); clinical psychology (PhD); developmental psychology (PhD); environmental psychology (PhD); experimental psychology (PhD); industrial psychology (PhD); learning processes (PhD); neuropsychology (PhD); psychology (PhD); social personality (PhD). *Degree requirements:* For doctorate, one foreign language, thesis/dissertation. *Entrance requirements:* For doctorate, GRE General Test. Additional exam requirements/recommendations for international students: Required—TOEFL. Electronic applications accepted.

Grand Canyon University, College of Doctoral Studies, Phoenix, AZ 85017-1097. Offers business administration (DBA); general psychology (PhD), including cognition and instruction, industrial and organizational psychology; organizational leadership (Ed D, PhD), including behavioral health (PhD), education and effective schools (PhD), higher education (PhD), instructional leadership (PhD), organizational development (Ed D). *Degree requirements:* For doctorate, comprehensive exam, thesis/dissertation. *Entrance requirements:* For doctorate, minimum GPA of 3.4 on earned advanced degree from regionally-accredited institution; transcripts; goals statement.

Harvard University, Graduate School of Arts and Sciences, Department of Psychology, Cambridge, MA 02138. Offers psychology (PhD), including behavior and decision analysis, cognition, developmental psychology, experimental psychology, personality, psychobiology, psychopathology; social psychology (PhD). *Accreditation:* APA. *Degree requirements:* For doctorate, thesis/dissertation, general exams. *Entrance requirements:* For doctorate, GRE General Test. Additional exam requirements/recommendations for international students: Required—TOEFL.

Harvard University, Harvard Graduate School of Education, Master's Programs in Education, Cambridge, MA 02138. Offers arts in education (Ed M); education policy and management (Ed M); higher education (Ed M); human development and psychology (Ed M); international education policy (Ed M); language and literacy (Ed M); learning and teaching (Ed M); mind, brain, and education (Ed M); prevention science and practice (Ed M); school leadership (Ed M); special studies (Ed M); teacher education (Ed M); technology, innovation, and education (Ed M). Part-time programs available. *Faculty:* 66 full-time (35 women), 82 part-time/adjunct (41 women). *Students:* 595 full-time (441 women), 71 part-time (48 women); includes 170 minority (33 Black or African American, non-Hispanic/Latino; 2 American Indian or Alaska Native, non-Hispanic/Latino; 69 Asian, non-Hispanic/Latino; 46 Hispanic/Latino; 20 Two or more races, non-Hispanic/Latino), 117 international. Average age 28. 1,741 applicants, 51% accepted, 613 enrolled. In 2014, 589 master's awarded. *Entrance requirements:* For master's, GRE General Test, statement of purpose, 3 letters of recommendation, resume, official transcripts. Additional exam requirements/recommendations for international students: Required—TOEFL (minimum score 613 paper-based; 104 iBT), TWE (minimum score 5). *Application deadline:* For fall admission, 1/5 for domestic and international students. Application fee: $85. Electronic applications accepted. *Expenses:* Expenses: Contact institution. *Financial support:* In 2014–15, 365 students received support, including 10 fellowships with full and partial tuition reimbursements available (averaging $15,790 per year), 6 teaching assistantships (averaging $4,281 per year); research assistantships, career-related internships or fieldwork, Federal Work-Study, institutionally sponsored loans, scholarships/grants, health care benefits, tuition waivers (full and partial), and unspecified assistantships also available. Support available to part-time students. Financial award application deadline: 2/1; financial award applicants required to submit FAFSA. *Faculty research:* Learning and development, educational leadership and organizations, education policy analysis. *Total annual research expenditures:* $34.3 million. *Unit head:* Jennifer L. Petrallia, Assistant Dean, 617-495-8445. *Application contact:* Information Contact, 617-495-3414, Fax: 617-496-3577, E-mail: gseadmissions@harvard.edu.
Website: http://www.gse.harvard.edu/

Indiana University Bloomington, University Graduate School, College of Arts and Sciences, Cognitive Science Program, Bloomington, IN 47406-7512. Offers PhD. *Faculty:* 68 full-time (17 women). *Students:* 20 full-time (6 women); includes 2 minority (1 Black or African American, non-Hispanic/Latino; 1 Hispanic/Latino), 4 international. Average age 22. 53 applicants, 17% accepted, 3 enrolled. In 2014, 3 doctorates awarded. *Degree requirements:* For doctorate, comprehensive exam, thesis/dissertation, research project; Content Specialization; Core courses; colloquia course;. *Entrance requirements:* For doctorate, GRE, 3 letters of reference, departmental questions form. Additional exam requirements/recommendations for international students: Required—TOEFL (minimum score 600 paper-based; 94 iBT). *Application deadline:* For fall admission, 1/3 for domestic students, 12/1 for international students. Application fee: $55 ($65 for international students). Electronic applications accepted. *Financial support:* In 2014–15, 2 students received support, including 2 fellowships with full tuition reimbursements available (averaging $24,000 per year), 1 research assistantship with full tuition reimbursement available (averaging $9,500 per year), 4 teaching assistantships with full tuition reimbursements available (averaging $18,933 per year); scholarships/grants, traineeships, unspecified assistantships, and Chilean scholarship also available. Financial award application deadline: 4/15. *Faculty research:* Learning concepts, neural network models, language, animal cognition, dynamic and robotics systems approaches to behavior and cognition. *Unit head:* Colin Allen, Director, 812-855-8916, E-mail: colallen@indiana.edu. *Application contact:* Susan Palmer, Information Contact, 812-855-8916, E-mail: stowle@indiana.edu.
Website: http://www.cogs.indiana.edu/

Indiana University Bloomington, University Graduate School, College of Arts and Sciences, Department of Psychological and Brain Sciences, Bloomington, IN 47405. Offers clinical science (PhD); cognitive neuroscience (PhD); cognitive psychology (PhD); developmental psychology (PhD); methods of behavior (PhD); molecular systems neuroscience (PhD); social psychology (PhD). *Accreditation:* APA. *Faculty:* 54 full-time (15 women). *Students:* 95 full-time (56 women); includes 19 minority (4 Black or African American, non-Hispanic/Latino; 7 Asian, non-Hispanic/Latino; 7 Hispanic/Latino; 1 Two or more races, non-Hispanic/Latino), 16 international. Average age 24. 364 applicants, 10% accepted, 20 enrolled. In 2014, 9 doctorates awarded. *Degree requirements:* For doctorate, comprehensive exam, 90 credit hours, 2 advanced statistics/methods courses, 2 written research projects, the teaching of psychology course, teaching 1 semester of undergraduate methods course, qualifying examination, minor or a second major, first-year research seminar course, dissertation defense, written dissertation. *Entrance requirements:* For doctorate, GRE. Additional exam requirements/recommendations for international students: Required—TOEFL (minimum score 550 paper-based; 79 iBT). *Application deadline:* For fall admission, 12/1 for domestic and international students. Application fee: $55 ($65 for international students). Electronic applications accepted. *Financial support:* Fellowships with full tuition reimbursements, research assistantships with full tuition reimbursements, teaching assistantships with full tuition reimbursements, career-related internships or fieldwork, scholarships/grants, traineeships, health care benefits, and unspecified assistantships available. *Faculty research:* Clinical science, cognitive neuroscience, cognitive psychology, developmental psychology, mechanisms of behavior, molecular and systems neuroscience, social psychology. *Unit head:* Dr. William Hetrick, Chair, 812-855-2012, Fax: 812-855-4691, E-mail: whetrick@indiana.edu. *Application contact:* Dale Sengelaub, Graduate Admissions, 812-855-9149, Fax: 812-855-4691, E-mail: psychgrd@indiana.edu.
Website: http://www.psych.indiana.edu

Iowa State University of Science and Technology, Department of Psychology, Ames, IA 50011. Offers cognitive psychology (PhD); counseling psychology (PhD); social psychology (PhD). *Accreditation:* APA. *Entrance requirements:* For doctorate, GRE General Test, GRE Subject Test (psychology), 3 letters of recommendation. Additional exam requirements/recommendations for international students: Required—TOEFL (minimum score 560 paper-based; 79 iBT), IELTS (minimum score 6.5). Electronic applications accepted. *Faculty research:* Counseling psychology, cognitive psychology, social psychology, health psychology, psychology and public policy.

Johns Hopkins University, Zanvyl Krieger School of Arts and Sciences, Department of Cognitive Science, Baltimore, MD 21218-2699. Offers PhD. Terminal master's awarded for partial completion of doctoral program. *Degree requirements:* For doctorate, thesis/dissertation, 2 research papers. *Entrance requirements:* For doctorate, GRE General Test, 3 letters of recommendation, sample of work, statement of purpose, original transcripts from all previous post-secondary institutions. Additional exam requirements/recommendations for international students: Required—TOEFL (minimum score 600 paper-based; 100 iBT), IELTS (minimum score 7). Electronic applications accepted. *Faculty research:* Acquisition and development, cognitive neuropsychology and neuroscience, computational studies, psycholinguistics and cognitive psychology, theoretical linguistics.

Louisiana State University and Agricultural & Mechanical College, Graduate School, College of Humanities and Social Sciences, Department of Psychology, Baton

Rouge, LA 70803. Offers biological psychology (MA, PhD); clinical psychology (MA, PhD); cognitive psychology (MA, PhD); developmental psychology (MA, PhD); school psychology (MA, PhD). PhD programs offered jointly with Southeastern Louisiana University. *Accreditation:* APA (one or more programs are accredited). *Faculty:* 22 full-time (10 women). *Students:* 67 full-time (54 women), 30 part-time (21 women); includes 13 minority (4 Black or African American, non-Hispanic/Latino; 3 Asian, non-Hispanic/Latino; 3 Hispanic/Latino; 3 Two or more races, non-Hispanic/Latino), 3 international. Average age 27. 221 applicants, 10% accepted, 22 enrolled. In 2014, 13 master's, 18 doctorates awarded. Terminal master's awarded for partial completion of doctoral program. *Degree requirements:* For master's, thesis; for doctorate, thesis/dissertation, 1-year internship. *Entrance requirements:* For master's and doctorate, GRE General Test, minimum GPA of 3.0. Additional exam requirements/recommendations for international students: Required—TOEFL (minimum score 550 paper-based; 79 iBT), IELTS (minimum score 6.5), or PTE (minimum score 59). *Application deadline:* For fall admission, 1/1 priority date for domestic students, 5/15 for international students; for spring admission, 10/15 for domestic and international students; for summer admission, 5/15 for domestic students, 5/5 for international students. Applications are processed on a rolling basis. Application fee: $50 ($70 for international students). Electronic applications accepted. *Financial support:* In 2014–15, 90 students received support, including 2 fellowships (averaging $15,763 per year), 8 research assistantships with partial tuition reimbursements available (averaging $16,669 per year), 49 teaching assistantships with partial tuition reimbursements available (averaging $13,003 per year); career-related internships or fieldwork, Federal Work-Study, institutionally sponsored loans, scholarships/grants, health care benefits, and tuition waivers (full and partial) also available. Financial award applicants required to submit FAFSA. *Faculty research:* Clinical psychology, autism, anxiety, addition, neuropsychology, school psychology, cognitive psychology, experimental psychology. *Total annual research expenditures:* $986,140. *Unit head:* Dr. Robert Matthews, Chair, 225-578-8745, Fax: 225-578-4125, E-mail: psmath@lsu.edu. *Application contact:* Dr. Jason Hicks, Coordinator of Graduate Studies, 225-578-4109, Fax: 225-578-4125, E-mail: jhicks@lsu.edu.
Website: http://www.lsu.edu/psychology/graduate.html

Massachusetts Institute of Technology, School of Science, Department of Brain and Cognitive Sciences, Cambridge, MA 02139. Offers cognitive science (PhD); neuroscience (PhD). *Faculty:* 37 full-time (14 women), 1 (woman) part-time/adjunct. *Students:* 102 full-time (30 women); includes 21 minority (2 Black or African American, non-Hispanic/Latino; 4 Asian, non-Hispanic/Latino; 10 Hispanic/Latino; 5 Two or more races, non-Hispanic/Latino), 28 international. Average age 28. 472 applicants, 7% accepted, 14 enrolled. In 2014, 9 doctorates awarded. *Degree requirements:* For doctorate, comprehensive exam, thesis/dissertation. *Entrance requirements:* For doctorate, GRE General Test. Additional exam requirements/recommendations for international students: Required—TOEFL (minimum score 577 paper-based; 90 iBT), IELTS (minimum score 7). *Application deadline:* For fall admission, 12/1 for domestic and international students. Application fee: $75. Electronic applications accepted. *Expenses: Tuition:* Full-time $44,720; part-time $699 per unit. *Required fees:* $296. *Financial support:* In 2014–15, 101 students received support, including 67 fellowships (averaging $33,500 per year), 30 research assistantships (averaging $36,000 per year), 5 teaching assistantships (averaging $35,800 per year); Federal Work-Study, institutionally sponsored loans, scholarships/grants, traineeships, health care benefits, and unspecified assistantships also available. Financial award application deadline: 4/15; financial award applicants required to submit FAFSA. *Faculty research:* Vision, audition, and other perceptual systems: physiology and computation; learning, memory, and executive control: molecular and systems approaches; sensorimotor systems: physiology and computation; neural and cognitive development and plasticity; language and high-level cognition: learning, acquisition, and computation. *Total annual research expenditures:* $32.5 million. *Unit head:* Prof. James Dicarlo, Head, 617-253-5748, Fax: 617-258-9126, E-mail: bcs-info@mit.edu. *Application contact:* Academic Office, 617-253-7403, Fax: 617-253-9767, E-mail: bcs-admissions@mit.edu.
Website: http://bcs.mit.edu/

Michigan Technological University, Graduate School, College of Sciences and Arts, Department of Cognitive and Learning Sciences, Houghton, MI 49931. Offers applied cognitive science and human factors (PhD); applied science education (MS). Part-time programs available. Postbaccalaureate distance learning degree programs offered (minimal on-campus study). *Faculty:* 15 full-time (5 women), 6 part-time/adjunct (2 women). *Students:* 16 full-time (11 women), 29 part-time (18 women); includes 7 minority (1 Black or African American, non-Hispanic/Latino; 1 American Indian or Alaska Native, non-Hispanic/Latino; 1 Asian, non-Hispanic/Latino; 4 Two or more races, non-Hispanic/Latino), 7 international. Average age 35. 36 applicants, 19% accepted, 5 enrolled. In 2014, 3 master's awarded. Terminal master's awarded for partial completion of doctoral program. *Degree requirements:* For master's, comprehensive exam (for some programs), thesis (for some programs); for doctorate, comprehensive exam, thesis/dissertation, applied internship experience. *Entrance requirements:* For master's, GRE (applied cognitive science and human factors program only), statement of purpose, official transcripts, 3 letters of recommendation, resume/curriculum vitae; for doctorate, GRE, statement of purpose, official transcripts, 3 letters of recommendation, resume/curriculum vitae. Additional exam requirements/recommendations for international students: Required—TOEFL (recommended score 90 iBT) or IELTS. *Application deadline:* For fall admission, 2/15 priority date for domestic and international students. Applications are processed on a rolling basis. Electronic applications accepted. *Expenses:* Tuition, state resident: full-time $14,769; part-time $820.50 per credit. Tuition, nonresident: full-time $14,769; part-time $820.50 per credit. *Required fees:* $248; $248 per year. Tuition and fees vary according to course load and program. *Financial support:* In 2014–15, 23 students received support, including 7 research assistantships with full and partial tuition reimbursements available (averaging $13,824 per year), 3 teaching assistantships (averaging $13,824 per year); career-related internships or fieldwork, Federal Work-Study, scholarships/grants, health care benefits, unspecified assistantships, and adjunct instructor positions also available. Financial award applicants required to submit FAFSA. *Faculty research:* Cognitive engineering and decision-making, human-centered design, individual differences in human performance, STEM education. *Total annual research expenditures:* $280,705. *Unit head:* Dr. Susan L. Amato-Henderson, Chair, 906-487-2536, Fax: 906-487-2468, E-mail: slamato@mtu.edu. *Application contact:* Carol T. Wingerson, Senior Staff Assistant, 906-487-2327, Fax: 906-487-2463, E-mail: gradadms@mtu.edu.
Website: http://cls.mtu.edu/

Mississippi State University, College of Arts and Sciences, Department of Psychology, Mississippi State, MS 39762. Offers applied cognitive science (PhD); clinical psychology (MS); experimental psychology (MS). *Faculty:* 19 full-time (7 women), 1 part-time/adjunct (0 women). *Students:* 36 full-time (23 women); includes 5 minority (2 Black or African American, non-Hispanic/Latino; 2 Asian, non-Hispanic/Latino; 1 Two or more races, non-Hispanic/Latino), 4 international. Average age 26. 64 applicants, 36% accepted, 20 enrolled. In 2014, 7 master's, 1 doctorate awarded. Terminal master's awarded for partial completion of doctoral program. *Degree requirements:* For master's, comprehensive exam, thesis; for doctorate, thesis/dissertation, qualifying exam, comprehensive written and oral exam. *Entrance*

requirements: For master's, GRE General Test, minimum GPA of 2.75 on last two years of undergraduate courses; for doctorate, GRE General Test, proficiency in at least 1 computer language, minimum GPA of 3.0. Additional exam requirements/recommendations for international students: Required—TOEFL (minimum score 477 paper-based; 53 iBT); Recommended—IELTS (minimum score 4.5). *Application deadline:* For fall admission, 1/15 priority date for domestic students, 5/1 for international students; for spring admission, 11/1 priority date for domestic students, 9/1 for international students. Applications are processed on a rolling basis. Application fee: $60. Electronic applications accepted. *Expenses:* Tuition, state resident: full-time $7140; part-time $783 per credit hour. Tuition, nonresident: full-time $18,478; part-time $2043 per credit hour. *Financial support:* In 2014–15, 6 research assistantships with full tuition reimbursements (averaging $12,729 per year), 18 teaching assistantships with full tuition reimbursements (averaging $8,808 per year) were awarded; career-related internships or fieldwork, Federal Work-Study, institutionally sponsored loans, scholarships/grants, and unspecified assistantships also available. Financial award application deadline: 4/1; financial award applicants required to submit FAFSA. *Faculty research:* Personality type, alcoholism, blindness and low vision, mental retardation, language comprehension. *Total annual research expenditures:* $1.1 million. *Unit head:* Dr. Mitchell E. Berman, Department Head, 662-325-3202, Fax: 662-325-7212, E-mail: mberman@psychology.msstate.edu. *Application contact:* Dr. Deborah Eakin, Graduate Coordinator, 662-325-3202, Fax: 662-325-7212, E-mail: grad@psychology.msstate.edu.
Website: http://www.psychology.msstate.edu/

New Mexico State University, College of Arts and Sciences, Department of Psychology, Las Cruces, NM 88003-8001. Offers cognitive psychology (PhD); engineering psychology (PhD); experimental psychology (MA); social psychology (PhD). Part-time programs available. *Faculty:* 11 full-time (3 women). *Students:* 31 full-time (15 women), 5 part-time (2 women); includes 7 minority (2 Asian, non-Hispanic/Latino; 3 Hispanic/Latino; 2 Two or more races, non-Hispanic/Latino), 5 international. Average age 29. 56 applicants, 27% accepted, 10 enrolled. In 2014, 6 master's, 5 doctorates awarded. *Degree requirements:* For master's, thesis; for doctorate, comprehensive exam, thesis/dissertation, work-related experience (teaching or internship). *Entrance requirements:* For master's, GRE General Test, letters of recommendation, curriculum vitae, personal statement; for doctorate, GRE General Test, letters of recommendation, master's thesis, curriculum vitae, personal statement. Additional exam requirements/recommendations for international students: Required—TOEFL (minimum score 550 paper-based; 79 iBT), IELTS (minimum score 6.5). *Application deadline:* For fall admission, 2/1 priority date for domestic students, 2/1 for international students. Applications are processed on a rolling basis. Application fee: $40 ($50 for international students). Electronic applications accepted. *Expenses:* Tuition, state resident: full-time $3969; part-time $220.50 per credit hour. Tuition, nonresident: full-time $13,838; part-time $768.80 per credit hour. *Required fees:* $853; $47.40 per credit hour. *Financial support:* In 2014–15, 34 students received support, including 7 fellowships (averaging $3,970 per year), 4 research assistantships (averaging $14,330 per year), 20 teaching assistantships (averaging $9,979 per year); career-related internships or fieldwork, Federal Work-Study, scholarships/grants, traineeships, health care benefits, and unspecified assistantships also available. Support available to part-time students. Financial award application deadline: 3/1. *Faculty research:* Engineering, cognitive, and social psychology; human/computer interaction; cognitive science. *Total annual research expenditures:* $184,443. *Unit head:* Dr. Dominic A. Simon, Academic Department Head, 575-646-2502, Fax: 575-646-6212, E-mail: domsimon@nmsu.edu. *Application contact:* Dr. Laura J. Madson, Chair of Graduate Committee, 575-646-6207, Fax: 575-646-6212, E-mail: lmadson@nmsu.edu.
Website: http://psych.nmsu.edu

The New School, The New School for Social Research, Department of Psychology, New York, NY 10011. Offers clinical psychology (PhD); cognitive, social and developmental psychology (PhD); general psychology (MA). *Accreditation:* APA (one or more programs are accredited). Part-time programs available. Terminal master's awarded for partial completion of doctoral program. *Degree requirements:* For master's, comprehensive exam (for some programs), thesis (for some programs); for doctorate, thesis/dissertation, qualifying exam. *Entrance requirements:* For master's, GRE General Test; for doctorate, GRE General Test, MA. Additional exam requirements/recommendations for international students: Required—TOEFL (minimum score 600 paper-based; 100 iBT). Electronic applications accepted. *Faculty research:* Consciousness, memory, language, perceptions, psychopathology.

New York University, Graduate School of Arts and Science, Department of Psychology, New York, NY 10012-1019. Offers cognition and perception (PhD); community psychology (PhD); general psychology (MA); industrial/organizational psychology (MA); psychotherapy and psychoanalysis (Advanced Certificate); social/personality psychology (PhD). Part-time programs available. *Students:* 270 full-time (183 women), 162 part-time (115 women); includes 92 minority (14 Black or African American, non-Hispanic/Latino; 36 Asian, non-Hispanic/Latino; 33 Hispanic/Latino; 9 Two or more races, non-Hispanic/Latino), 114 international. Average age 31. 874 applicants, 46% accepted, 153 enrolled. In 2014, 102 master's, 9 doctorates, 10 other advanced degrees awarded. Terminal master's awarded for partial completion of doctoral program. *Degree requirements:* For master's, comprehensive exam, thesis or alternative; for doctorate, thesis/dissertation. *Entrance requirements:* For master's and doctorate, GRE General Test. Additional exam requirements/recommendations for international students: Required—TOEFL. *Application deadline:* For fall admission, 12/12 for domestic and international students. Application fee: $100. *Financial support:* Fellowships with tuition reimbursements, research assistantships with tuition reimbursements, teaching assistantships with tuition reimbursements, career-related internships or fieldwork, Federal Work-Study, institutionally sponsored loans, scholarships/grants, traineeships, health care benefits, and unspecified assistantships available. Financial award application deadline: 12/12; financial award applicants required to submit FAFSA. *Faculty research:* Vision, memory, social cognition, social and cognitive development, relationships. *Unit head:* Gabriele Oettingen, Director of Graduate Studies, PhD Program, 212-998-7900, Fax: 212-995-4018, E-mail: psychq@psych.nyu.edu. *Application contact:* Adrienne Gans, Director of Graduate Studies, MA Program, 212-998-7900, Fax: 212-995-4018, E-mail: psychq@psych.nyu.edu.
Website: http://www.psych.nyu.edu/

North Dakota State University, College of Graduate and Interdisciplinary Studies, College of Science and Mathematics, Department of Psychology, Fargo, ND 58108. Offers clinical psychology (MS); cognitive and visual neuroscience (PhD); health and social psychology (PhD); psychology (MS). *Degree requirements:* For master's, thesis; for doctorate, thesis/dissertation. *Entrance requirements:* For master's and doctorate, GRE General Test, GRE Subject Test. Additional exam requirements/recommendations for international students: Required—TOEFL (minimum score 525 paper-based; 71 iBT). Electronic applications accepted. *Faculty research:* Cognition science, neuropsychology, group behavior, applied behavior analysis, behavior therapy.

Northwestern University, The Graduate School, Judd A. and Marjorie Weinberg College of Arts and Sciences, Department of Psychology, Evanston, IL 60208. Offers brain, behavior and cognition (PhD); clinical psychology (PhD); cognitive psychology

(PhD); personality psychology (PhD); social psychology (PhD); JD/PhD. Admissions and degrees offered through The Graduate School. *Accreditation:* APA (one or more programs are accredited). Part-time programs available. *Degree requirements:* For doctorate, thesis/dissertation. *Entrance requirements:* For doctorate, GRE General Test, GRE Subject Test. Additional exam requirements/recommendations for international students: Required—TOEFL. Electronic applications accepted. *Faculty research:* Memory and higher order cognition, anxiety and depression, effectiveness of psychotherapy, social cognition, molecular basis of memory.

The Ohio State University, Graduate School, College of Arts and Sciences, Division of Social and Behavioral Sciences, Department of Psychology, Columbus, OH 43210. Offers behavioral neuroscience (PhD); clinical psychology (PhD); cognitive psychology (PhD); developmental psychology (PhD); intellectual and developmental disabilities psychology (PhD); quantitative psychology (PhD); social psychology (PhD). *Accreditation:* APA. *Faculty:* 55. *Students:* 158 full-time (91 women); includes 26 minority (6 Black or African American, non-Hispanic/Latino; 2 American Indian or Alaska Native, non-Hispanic/Latino; 7 Asian, non-Hispanic/Latino; 9 Hispanic/Latino; 2 Two or more races, non-Hispanic/Latino), 23 international. Average age 27. In 2014, 12 doctorates awarded. *Degree requirements:* For doctorate, thesis/dissertation. *Entrance requirements:* For doctorate, GRE General Test. Additional exam requirements/ recommendations for international students: Required—TOEFL (minimum score 600 paper-based; 100 iBT); Recommended—IELTS (minimum score 8). *Application deadline:* For fall admission, 12/1 for domestic and international students. Applications are processed on a rolling basis. Application fee: $60 ($70 for international students). Electronic applications accepted. *Financial support:* Fellowships with tuition reimbursements, research assistantships with tuition reimbursements, and teaching assistantships with tuition reimbursements available. *Unit head:* Dr. Richard Petty, Chair, 614-292-1640, E-mail: petty.1@osu.edu. *Application contact:* Graduate and Professional Admissions, 614-292-9444, Fax: 614-292-3895, E-mail: gpadmissions@osu.edu.
Website: http://www.psy.ohio-state.edu/

Purdue University, Graduate School, College of Health and Human Sciences, Department of Psychological Sciences, West Lafayette, IN 47907. Offers behavioral neuroscience (PhD); clinical psychology (PhD); cognitive psychology (PhD); industrial/ organizational psychology (PhD); mathematical and computational cognitive science (PhD). *Accreditation:* APA. Terminal master's awarded for partial completion of doctoral program. *Degree requirements:* For doctorate, thesis/dissertation. *Entrance requirements:* For doctorate, GRE General Test, minimum undergraduate GPA of 3.0 or equivalent. Additional exam requirements/recommendations for international students: Required—TOEFL (minimum score 550 paper-based; 77 iBT); Recommended—TWE. Electronic applications accepted. *Faculty research:* Career development of women in science, development of friendships during childhood and adolescence, social competence, human information processing.

Queen's University at Kingston, School of Graduate Studies, Faculty of Arts and Sciences, Department of Psychology, Kingston, ON K7L 3N6, Canada. Offers brain behavior and cognitive science (MA, PhD); clinical psychology (MA, PhD); developmental psychology (MA, PhD); social personality psychology (MA, PhD). *Degree requirements:* For master's, thesis; for doctorate, comprehensive exam, thesis/ dissertation. *Entrance requirements:* For master's and doctorate, GRE General Test. Additional exam requirements/recommendations for international students: Required— TOEFL. *Faculty research:* Human development, social, personality, behavioral neuroscience, forensic.

Rensselaer Polytechnic Institute, Graduate School, School of Humanities, Arts, and Social Sciences, Program in Cognitive Science, Troy, NY 12180-3590. Offers PhD. *Faculty:* 14 full-time (5 women). *Students:* 13 full-time (2 women), 4 part-time (1 woman); includes 4 minority (1 Black or African American, non-Hispanic/Latino; 2 Asian, non-Hispanic/Latino; 1 Hispanic/Latino), 1 international. Average age 33. 22 applicants, 18% accepted, 3 enrolled. In 2014, 4 doctorates awarded. *Degree requirements:* For doctorate, thesis/dissertation. *Entrance requirements:* For doctorate, GRE. Additional exam requirements/recommendations for international students: Required—TOEFL (minimum score 600 paper-based; 100 iBT), IELTS (minimum score 7), PTE (minimum score 68). *Application deadline:* For fall admission, 1/1 priority date for domestic and international students. Applications are processed on a rolling basis. Electronic applications accepted. *Expenses: Tuition:* Full-time $46,700; part-time $1945 per credit. Tuition and fees vary according to course load. *Financial support:* In 2014–15, 13 students received support, including research assistantships (averaging $18,500 per year), teaching assistantships (averaging $18,500 per year); fellowships also available. Financial award application deadline: 1/1. *Faculty research:* Artificial intelligence, cognitive engineering, computational cognitive modeling, computational linguistics, human factors, perception and action, social interaction, social simulation and multi-agent modeling, theoretical neuroscience, vision science. *Total annual research expenditures:* $84,676. *Unit head:* Dr. Wayne Gray, Graduate Program Director, 518-276-3315, E-mail: grayw@rpi.edu. *Application contact:* Office of Graduate Admissions, 518-276-6216, E-mail: gradadmissions@rpi.edu.
Website: http://www.cogsci.rpi.edu/

Rice University, Graduate Programs, School of Social Sciences, Department of Psychology, Houston, TX 77251-1892. Offers cognitive sciences (MA, PhD); industrial-organizational/social psychology (MA, PhD); psychology (MA, PhD). Terminal master's awarded for partial completion of doctoral program. *Degree requirements:* For master's, thesis; for doctorate, thesis/dissertation. *Entrance requirements:* For doctorate, GRE General Test, minimum GPA of 3.0. Additional exam requirements/recommendations for international students: Required—TOEFL. Electronic applications accepted. *Faculty research:* Cognitive, cognitive neuropsychology, human factors, human-computer interaction, industrial-organizational psychology.

Rutgers, The State University of New Jersey, Newark, Graduate School, Program in Psychology, Newark, NJ 07102. Offers cognitive neuroscience (PhD); cognitive science (PhD); perception (PhD); psychobiology (PhD); social cognition (PhD). *Degree requirements:* For doctorate, comprehensive exam, thesis/dissertation. *Entrance requirements:* For doctorate, GRE General Test, GRE Subject Test, minimum undergraduate B average. Electronic applications accepted. *Faculty research:* Visual perception (luminance, motion), neuroendocrine mechanisms in behavior (reproduction, pain), attachment theory, connectionist modeling of cognition.

Rutgers, The State University of New Jersey, New Brunswick, Graduate School-New Brunswick, Program in Psychology, Piscataway, NJ 08854-8097. Offers behavioral neuroscience (PhD); clinical psychology (PhD); cognitive psychology (PhD); interdisciplinary health psychology (PhD); social psychology (PhD). *Accreditation:* APA. *Degree requirements:* For doctorate, comprehensive exam, thesis/dissertation. *Entrance requirements:* For doctorate, GRE General Test, 3 letters of recommendation. Additional exam requirements/recommendations for international students: Required— TOEFL (minimum score 577 paper-based). Electronic applications accepted. *Faculty research:* Learning and memory, behavioral ecology, hormones and behavior, psychopharmacology, anxiety disorders.

Stony Brook University, State University of New York, Graduate School, College of Arts and Sciences, Department of Psychology, Program in Cognitive/Experimental Psychology, Stony Brook, NY 11794. Offers PhD. *Students:* 15 full-time (10 women); includes 2 minority (1 Asian, non-Hispanic/Latino; 1 Hispanic/Latino), 3 international. Average age 28. 39 applicants, 18% accepted, 3 enrolled. In 2014, 3 doctorates awarded. *Degree requirements:* For doctorate, thesis/dissertation. *Entrance requirements:* For doctorate, GRE General Test, GRE Subject Test. Additional exam requirements/recommendations for international students: Required—TOEFL. *Application deadline:* For fall admission, 1/15 for domestic students; for spring admission, 10/1 for domestic students. Application fee: $100. *Expenses: Tuition,* state resident: full-time $10,370; part-time $432 per credit. Tuition, nonresident: full-time $20,190; part-time $841 per credit. *Required fees:* $1431. *Financial support:* In 2014–15, 1 fellowship was awarded. *Unit head:* Dr. Arthur Samuel, Chair, 631-632-7792, Fax: 631-632-7876, E-mail: arthur.samuel@stonybrook.edu. *Application contact:* Marilynn Wollmuth, Graduate Director, 631-632-7855, Fax: 631-632-7876, E-mail: marilynn.wollmuth@stonybrook.edu.

Texas A&M University, College of Liberal Arts, Department of Psychology, College Station, TX 77843. Offers behavioral and cellular neuroscience (PhD); clinical psychology (PhD); cognitive psychology (PhD); developmental psychology (PhD); industrial/organizational psychology (PhD); psychology (MS); social psychology (PhD). *Accreditation:* APA (one or more programs are accredited). *Faculty:* 35. *Students:* 82 full-time (45 women), 15 part-time (12 women); includes 30 minority (6 Black or African American, non-Hispanic/Latino; 6 Asian, non-Hispanic/Latino; 18 Hispanic/Latino), 11 international. Average age 28. 375 applicants, 5% accepted, 8 enrolled. In 2014, 8 master's, 16 doctorates awarded. *Degree requirements:* For doctorate, comprehensive exam (for some programs), thesis/dissertation. *Entrance requirements:* For doctorate, GRE General Test. Additional exam requirements/recommendations for international students: Required—TOEFL. *Application deadline:* For fall admission, 1/5 for domestic and international students. Application fee: $50 ($90 for international students). Electronic applications accepted. *Expenses: Tuition,* state resident: full-time $4078; part-time $226.55 per credit hour. Tuition, nonresident: full-time $10,594; part-time $577.55 per credit hour. *Required fees:* $2813; $237.70 per credit hour. $278.50 per semester. Tuition and fees vary according to degree level and student level. *Financial support:* In 2014–15, 84 students received support, including 25 fellowships with full and partial tuition reimbursements available (averaging $17,037 per year), 20 research assistantships with full and partial tuition reimbursements available (averaging $8,269 per year), 57 teaching assistantships with full and partial tuition reimbursements available (averaging $7,431 per year); career-related internships or fieldwork, institutionally sponsored loans, scholarships/grants, traineeships, health care benefits, tuition waivers (full and partial), and unspecified assistantships also available. Support available to part-time students. Financial award application deadline: 1/5; financial award applicants required to submit FAFSA. *Unit head:* Dr. Doug Woods, Head, 979-845-2540, E-mail: dowoods@tamu.edu. *Application contact:* Dr. Charles D. Samuelson, Director of Graduate Studies, 979-845-0880, Fax: 979-845-4727, E-mail: c-samuelson@tamu.edu.
Website: http://psychology.tamu.edu.

Texas Christian University, College of Science and Engineering, Department of Psychology, Fort Worth, TX 76129. Offers developmental trauma (MS); experimental psychology (MA, MS, PhD), including behavioral neuroscience (MS), cognition (MS), learning (MS), social (MS). *Faculty:* 12 full-time (5 women), 2 part-time/adjunct (1 woman). *Students:* 28 full-time (14 women); includes 1 minority (Hispanic/Latino), 3 international. Average age 27. 37 applicants, 22% accepted, 8 enrolled. In 2014, 2 master's, 6 doctorates awarded. Terminal master's awarded for partial completion of doctoral program. *Degree requirements:* For master's, thesis; for doctorate, thesis/ dissertation. *Entrance requirements:* For master's and doctorate, GRE General Test. Additional exam requirements/recommendations for international students: Required— TOEFL. *Application deadline:* For fall admission, 2/1 for domestic and international students; for spring admission, 12/1 for domestic students. Application fee: $60 ($0 for international students). Electronic applications accepted. *Expenses: Tuition:* Full-time $22,860; part-time $1270 per credit hour. *Financial support:* In 2014–15, 23 students received support, including 23 teaching assistantships with full tuition reimbursements available (averaging $19,750 per year); scholarships/grants and tuition waivers also available. Financial award application deadline: 2/1; financial award applicants required to submit FAFSA. *Faculty research:* Neuroscience, human and animal learning, cognition, development, experimental social psychology. *Unit head:* Dr. Mauricio Papini, Chair, 817-257-7410, Fax: 817-257-7681, E-mail: m.papini@tcu.edu. *Application contact:* Cindy Hayes, Administrative Assistant, 817-257-7410, Fax: 817-257-7681, E-mail: c.hayes@tcu.edu.
Website: http://www.psy.tcu.edu/gradpro.html

Tufts University, Graduate School of Arts and Sciences, Department of Psychology, Medford, MA 02155. Offers cognitive science (PhD); psychology (MS, PhD). *Students:* 36 full-time (28 women), 4 part-time (3 women); includes 9 minority (2 Black or African American, non-Hispanic/Latino; 4 Asian, non-Hispanic/Latino; 1 Hispanic/Latino; 2 Two or more races, non-Hispanic/Latino), 7 international. Average age 28. 174 applicants, 9% accepted, 5 enrolled. In 2014, 5 master's, 6 doctorates awarded. Terminal master's awarded for partial completion of doctoral program. *Degree requirements:* For master's, thesis; for doctorate, one foreign language, thesis/dissertation. *Entrance requirements:* For master's and doctorate, GRE General Test, GRE Subject Test. Additional exam requirements/recommendations for international students: Required—TOEFL (minimum score 550 paper-based; 80 iBT), IELTS (minimum score 6.5). *Application deadline:* For fall admission, 12/15 for domestic and international students. Applications are processed on a rolling basis. Application fee: $75. Electronic applications accepted. *Expenses: Tuition:* Full-time $45,590; part-time $1161 per credit hour. *Required fees:* $782. Full-time tuition and fees vary according to degree level, program and student level. Part-time tuition and fees vary according to course load. *Financial support:* Fellowships, research assistantships with full tuition reimbursements, teaching assistantships with full tuition reimbursements, Federal Work-Study, scholarships/ grants, tuition waivers (partial), and unspecified assistantships available. Support available to part-time students. Financial award application deadline: 12/15. *Unit head:* Dr. Holly Taylor, Graduate Program Director. *Application contact:* Office of Graduate Admissions, 617-627-3395, E-mail: gradadmissions@tufts.edu.
Website: http://ase.tufts.edu/psychology

Tufts University, School of Engineering, Department of Computer Science, Medford, MA 02155. Offers bioengineering (ME, MS), including bioinformatics; cognitive science (PhD); computer science (MS, PhD). Part-time programs available. *Students:* 57 full-time (17 women), 19 part-time (4 women); includes 13 minority (1 Black or African American, non-Hispanic/Latino; 4 Asian, non-Hispanic/Latino; 2 Hispanic/Latino; 6 Two or more races, non-Hispanic/Latino), 25 international. Average age 29. 218 applicants, 24% accepted, 23 enrolled. In 2014, 18 master's, 4 doctorates awarded. Terminal master's awarded for partial completion of doctoral program. *Degree requirements:* For master's, thesis (for some programs); for doctorate, thesis/dissertation. *Entrance requirements:* For master's and doctorate, GRE General Test. Additional exam requirements/recommendations for international students: Required—TOEFL (minimum score 550 paper-based; 80 iBT), IELTS (minimum score 6.5). *Application deadline:* For

fall admission, 1/15 for domestic and international students; for spring admission, 9/15 for domestic and international students. Applications are processed on a rolling basis. Application fee: $75. Electronic applications accepted. *Expenses: Tuition:* Full-time $45,590; part-time $1161 per credit hour. *Required fees:* $782. Full-time tuition and fees vary according to degree level, program and student level. Part-time tuition and fees vary according to course load. *Financial support:* Fellowships with full tuition reimbursements, research assistantships with full and partial tuition reimbursements, teaching assistantships with full and partial tuition reimbursements, Federal Work-Study, scholarships/grants, tuition waivers (partial), and unspecified assistantships available. Financial award application deadline: 4/15; financial award applicants required to submit FAFSA. *Faculty research:* Computational biology, computational geometry, and computational systems biology; cognitive sciences, human-computer interaction, and human-robotic interaction; visualization and graphics, educational technologies; machine learning and data mining; programming languages and systems. *Unit head:* Dr. Samuel Guyer, Graduate Program Director. *Application contact:* Office of Graduate Admissions, 617-623-3395, E-mail: gradadmissions@cs.tufts.edu. Website: http://www.cs.tufts.edu/

University at Albany, State University of New York, College of Arts and Sciences, Department of Psychology, Albany, NY 12222-0001. Offers behavioral neuroscience (PhD); clinical psychology (PhD); cognitive psychology (PhD); industrial/organizational psychology (MA, PhD); social-personality psychology (PhD). *Accreditation:* APA (one or more programs are accredited). *Degree requirements:* For doctorate, thesis/dissertation. *Entrance requirements:* For doctorate, GRE General Test, GRE Subject Test. Additional exam requirements/recommendations for international students: Required—TOEFL (minimum score 550 paper-based). Electronic applications accepted.

The University of British Columbia, Faculty of Arts and Faculty of Graduate Studies, Department of Psychology, Vancouver, BC V6T 1Z4, Canada. Offers behavioral neuroscience (MA, PhD); clinical psychology (MA, PhD); cognitive science (MA, PhD); developmental psychology (MA, PhD); health psychology (MA, PhD); quantitative methods (MA, PhD); social/personality psychology (MA, PhD). *Accreditation:* APA (one or more programs are accredited). Terminal master's awarded for partial completion of doctoral program. *Degree requirements:* For master's, thesis; for doctorate, comprehensive exam, thesis/dissertation. *Entrance requirements:* For master's and doctorate, GRE General Test. Additional exam requirements/recommendations for international students: Required—TOEFL (minimum score 550 paper-based; 80 iBT). Electronic applications accepted. *Faculty research:* Clinical, developmental, social/personality, cognition, behavioral neuroscience.

University of California, Merced, Graduate Division, School of Social Sciences, Humanities and Arts, Merced, CA 95343. Offers cognitive and information sciences (MA, PhD); psychology (MA, PhD); social sciences (MA, PhD); world cultures (MA, PhD). *Faculty:* 89 full-time (40 women). *Students:* 114 full-time (79 women), 2 part-time (1 woman); includes 43 minority (3 Black or African American, non-Hispanic/Latino; 1 American Indian or Alaska Native, non-Hispanic/Latino; 10 Asian, non-Hispanic/Latino; 24 Hispanic/Latino; 1 Native Hawaiian or other Pacific Islander, non-Hispanic/Latino; 4 Two or more races, non-Hispanic/Latino), 13 international. Average age 32. 127 applicants, 34% accepted, 22 enrolled. In 2014, 3 master's, 11 doctorates awarded. *Degree requirements:* For master's, variable foreign language requirement, comprehensive exam, thesis; for doctorate, variable foreign language requirement, comprehensive exam, thesis/dissertation. *Entrance requirements:* For master's and doctorate, GRE. Additional exam requirements/recommendations for international students: Required—TOEFL (minimum score 550 paper-based; 68 iBT); Recommended—IELTS. *Application deadline:* For fall admission, 1/15 for domestic and international students. Application fee: $80 ($100 for international students). Electronic applications accepted. *Expenses:* Tuition, state resident: full-time $11,220; part-time $2805 per semester. *Required fees:* $1940; $970 per semester hour. *Financial support:* In 2014–15, 29 fellowships with full and partial tuition reimbursements (averaging $7,056 per year) were awarded; scholarships/grants also available. *Faculty research:* Psychology, political science, social inequality, interdisciplinary, humanities, cognitive sciences. *Unit head:* Dr. Mark Aldenderfer, Dean, 209-228-7843, Fax: 209-228-4007, E-mail: maldenderfer@ucmerced.edu. *Application contact:* Tsu Ya, Graduate Admissions and Academic Services Manager, 209-228-4521, Fax: 209-228-6906, E-mail: tya@ucmerced.edu.

University of California, San Diego, Graduate Division, Department of Cognitive Science, La Jolla, CA 92093. Offers PhD. *Students:* 42 full-time (14 women), 2 part-time (1 woman); includes 6 minority (3 Asian, non-Hispanic/Latino; 3 Hispanic/Latino), 9 international. 160 applicants, 13% accepted, 11 enrolled. In 2014, 4 doctorates awarded. *Degree requirements:* For doctorate, one foreign language, thesis/dissertation, 1-quarter teaching assistantship for each academic year in residence. *Entrance requirements:* For doctorate, GRE General Test, minimum GPA of 3.0. Additional exam requirements/recommendations for international students: Required—TOEFL (minimum score 550 paper-based; 80 iBT), IELTS (minimum score 7). *Application deadline:* For fall admission, 12/2 for domestic students. Application fee: $90 ($110 for international students). Electronic applications accepted. *Expenses:* Tuition, state resident: full-time $11,220; part-time $5610 per quarter. Tuition, nonresident: full-time $26,322; part-time $13,161 per quarter. *Required fees:* $570 per quarter. Tuition and fees vary according to program. *Financial support:* Fellowships, research assistantships, teaching assistantships, scholarships/grants, and unspecified assistantships available. Financial award applicants required to submit FAFSA. *Faculty research:* Normal development of spatial analytic processing, flexible problem solving, specific language impairment, empirical analysis of change in scientific culture, co-evolutionary analysis of drug resistance in HIV. *Unit head:* Marta Kutas, Chair, 858-534-7141, E-mail: mkutas@ucsd.edu. *Application contact:* Beverley Walton, Graduate Coordinator, 858-534-7141, E-mail: gradinfo@cogsci.ucsd.edu. Website: http://www.cogsci.ucsd.edu/graduate-study/idp/

University of California, Santa Barbara, Graduate Division, College of Engineering, Department of Computer Science, Santa Barbara, CA 93106-5110. Offers cognitive science (PhD); computational science and engineering (PhD); computer science (MS, PhD); technology and society (PhD). Terminal master's awarded for partial completion of doctoral program. *Degree requirements:* For master's, comprehensive exam (for some programs), thesis (for some programs), project (for some programs); for doctorate, thesis/dissertation. *Entrance requirements:* For master's and doctorate, GRE. Additional exam requirements/recommendations for international students: Required—TOEFL (minimum score 600 paper-based; 100 iBT), IELTS (minimum score 7). Electronic applications accepted. *Faculty research:* Bioinformatics, cloud computing, computer architecture, computational science and engineering, database and information systems, foundations and algorithms, intelligent and interactive systems, programming languages, quantum computing, software engineering and security.

University of California, Santa Barbara, Graduate Division, College of Letters and Sciences, Division of Humanities and Fine Arts, Department of Religious Studies, Santa Barbara, CA 93106-3130. Offers ancient Mediterranean studies (PhD); cognitive science (PhD); European medieval studies (PhD); feminist studies (PhD); global studies (PhD); religious studies (MA, PhD); translation studies (PhD); MA/PhD. Terminal master's awarded for partial completion of doctoral program. *Degree requirements:* For master's, one foreign language, comprehensive exam (for some programs), thesis (for some programs), colloquium; for doctorate, 2 foreign languages, thesis/dissertation, methodology, colloquium. *Entrance requirements:* For master's and doctorate, GRE General Test. Additional exam requirements/recommendations for international students: Required—TOEFL (minimum score 550 paper-based; 80 iBT), IELTS (minimum score 7). Electronic applications accepted. *Faculty research:* Area studies; religious traditions; theory and method in the study of religion; religion, culture, and politics; spirituality and religious experience.

University of California, Santa Barbara, Graduate Division, College of Letters and Sciences, Division of Mathematics, Life, and Physical Sciences, Department of Geography, Santa Barbara, CA 93106-4060. Offers cognitive science (PhD); geography (MA, PhD); global studies (PhD); quantitative methods in the social sciences (PhD); technology and society (PhD); transportation (PhD); MA/PhD. Terminal master's awarded for partial completion of doctoral program. *Degree requirements:* For master's, comprehensive exam (for some programs), thesis or alternative; for doctorate, comprehensive exam, thesis/dissertation, 1 quarter of teaching assistantship. *Entrance requirements:* For master's and doctorate, GRE (minimum combined verbal and quantitative scores of 1100 in old scoring system or 301 in new scoring system). Additional exam requirements/recommendations for international students: Required—TOEFL (minimum score 550 paper-based; 80 iBT), IELTS (minimum score 7). Electronic applications accepted. *Faculty research:* Earth system science; human environment relations; modeling, measurement, and computation.

University of California, Santa Barbara, Graduate Division, College of Letters and Sciences, Division of Mathematics, Life, and Physical Sciences, Department of Psychological and Brain Sciences, Santa Barbara, CA 93106-9660. Offers cognitive science (PhD); psychology (PhD); quantitative methods in the social sciences (PhD); technology and society (PhD). Terminal master's awarded for partial completion of doctoral program. *Degree requirements:* For doctorate, comprehensive exam, thesis/dissertation, teaching assistant training, progress report, papers, mini-convention presentation, 1 quarter of student teaching or teaching assistant class with section lab, continued participation in research and weekly area meetings. *Entrance requirements:* For doctorate, GRE General Test. Additional exam requirements/recommendations for international students: Required—TOEFL (minimum score 550 paper-based; 80 iBT) or IELTS (minimum score 7). Electronic applications accepted. *Faculty research:* Social psychology; developmental and evolutionary psychology; neuroscience and behavior; cognition, perception and cognitive neuroscience.

University of California, Santa Barbara, Graduate Division, College of Letters and Sciences, Division of Social Sciences, Department of Communication, Santa Barbara, CA 93106-4020. Offers cognitive science (PhD); communication (PhD); feminist studies (PhD); language, interaction and social organization (PhD); quantitative methods in the social sciences (PhD); society and technology (PhD); MA/PhD. Terminal master's awarded for partial completion of doctoral program. *Degree requirements:* For doctorate, comprehensive exam, thesis/dissertation. *Entrance requirements:* For doctorate, GRE. Additional exam requirements/recommendations for international students: Required—TOEFL (minimum score 80 iBT), IELTS (minimum score 7). Electronic applications accepted. *Faculty research:* Interpersonal, intercultural, organizational, health, media.

University of Connecticut, Graduate School, College of Liberal Arts and Sciences, Department of Psychology, Storrs, CT 06269. Offers behavioral neuroscience (PhD); biopsychology (PhD); clinical psychology (MA, PhD); cognition and instruction (PhD); developmental psychology (MA, PhD); ecological psychology (PhD); experimental psychology (PhD); general psychology (MA, PhD); health psychology (Graduate Certificate); industrial/organizational psychology (PhD); language and cognition (PhD); neuroscience (PhD); occupational health psychology (Graduate Certificate); social psychology (MA, PhD). *Accreditation:* APA. Terminal master's awarded for partial completion of doctoral program. *Degree requirements:* For master's, comprehensive exam; for doctorate, thesis/dissertation. *Entrance requirements:* For master's and doctorate, GRE General Test, GRE Subject Test. Additional exam requirements/recommendations for international students: Required—TOEFL (minimum score 550 paper-based). Electronic applications accepted.

University of Connecticut, Graduate School, Neag School of Education, Department of Educational Psychology, Program in Cognition and Instruction, Storrs, CT 06269. Offers MA, PhD, Post-Master's Certificate. *Degree requirements:* For master's, comprehensive exam; for doctorate, thesis/dissertation. *Entrance requirements:* For doctorate, GRE General Test. Additional exam requirements/recommendations for international students: Required—TOEFL (minimum score 550 paper-based). Electronic applications accepted.

University of Delaware, College of Arts and Sciences, Department of Linguistics and Cognitive Science, Newark, DE 19716. Offers linguistics (PhD); linguistics and cognitive science (MA). *Degree requirements:* For doctorate, one foreign language, comprehensive exam, thesis/dissertation, publishable research papers. *Entrance requirements:* For master's, GRE General Test; for doctorate, GRE General Test, writing sample. Additional exam requirements/recommendations for international students: Required—TOEFL (minimum score 600 paper-based). Electronic applications accepted. *Faculty research:* East Asian, Austronesian and Romance languages, phonology, phonetics, syntax, cognitive science, semantics, psycholinguistics, language acquisition, endangered languages.

University of Delaware, College of Arts and Sciences, Department of Psychology, Newark, DE 19716. Offers behavioral neuroscience (PhD); clinical psychology (PhD); cognitive psychology (PhD); social psychology (PhD). *Accreditation:* APA. *Degree requirements:* For doctorate, thesis/dissertation. *Entrance requirements:* For doctorate, GRE General Test. Additional exam requirements/recommendations for international students: Required—TOEFL (minimum score 600 paper-based). Electronic applications accepted. *Faculty research:* Emotion development, neural and cognitive aspects of memory, neural control of feeding, intergroup relations, social cognition and communication.

University of Denver, Division of Arts, Humanities and Social Sciences, Department of Psychology, Denver, CO 80208. Offers affective/social psychology (PhD); clinical child psychology (PhD); cognitive psychology (PhD); developmental psychology (PhD). *Accreditation:* APA. *Faculty:* 25 full-time (11 women), 4 part-time/adjunct (2 women). *Students:* 21 full-time (18 women), 5 part-time (all women); includes 7 minority (2 Black or African American, non-Hispanic/Latino; 3 Asian, non-Hispanic/Latino; 1 Hispanic/Latino; 1 Two or more races, non-Hispanic/Latino), 3 international. Average age 28. 348 applicants, 5% accepted, 6 enrolled. In 2014, 9 doctorates awarded. Terminal master's awarded for partial completion of doctoral program. *Degree requirements:* For doctorate, variable foreign language requirement, comprehensive exam (for some programs), thesis/dissertation. *Entrance requirements:* For doctorate, GRE General Test, master's degree, transcripts, biographical statement, three letters of recommendation. Additional exam requirements/recommendations for international students: Required—TOEFL (minimum score 550 paper-based; 80 iBT). *Application deadline:* For fall admission, 12/1 priority date for domestic and international students. Application fee: $65. Electronic applications accepted. *Expenses:* Expenses: $1,199 per credit hour. *Financial support:* In 2014–15, 26 students received support, including 13 research assistantships with full

and partial tuition reimbursements available (averaging $12,821 per year), 20 teaching assistantships with full and partial tuition reimbursements available (averaging $15,333 per year); Federal Work-Study, institutionally sponsored loans, scholarships/grants, and unspecified assistantships also available. Support available to part-time students. Financial award application deadline: 2/15; financial award applicants required to submit FAFSA. *Faculty research:* Developmental cognitive neuroscience, social and emotional processes, child and adolescent development, clinical child psychology, cognitive psychology. *Total annual research expenditures:* $3 million. *Unit head:* Dr. George Potts, Chair, 303-871-3717, Fax: 303-871-4747, E-mail: gpotts@du.edu. *Application contact:* Paula Houghtaling, Graduate Program Administrator, 303-871-3803, Fax: 303-871-4747, E-mail: phoughta@du.edu.
Website: http://www.du.edu/ahss/psychology/index.html

University of Guelph, Graduate Studies, College of Social and Applied Human Sciences, Department of Psychology, Guelph, ON N1G 2W1, Canada. Offers applied social psychology (MA, PhD); clinical psychology: applied development emphasis (PhD); clinical psychology: applied developmental emphasis (MA); industrial/organizational psychology (MA, PhD); neuroscience and applied cognitive science (MA, PhD). *Degree requirements:* For master's, thesis; for doctorate, comprehensive exam, thesis/dissertation. *Entrance requirements:* For master's, GRE General Test, GRE Subject Test, minimum B+ average during previous 2 years of course work; for doctorate, GRE General Test, GRE Subject Test, minimum A- average. Additional exam requirements/recommendations for international students: Required—TOEFL (minimum score 89 iBT). Electronic applications accepted. *Faculty research:* Organizational psychology, reading comprehension and mathematical ability, drug addiction and relapse, gender issues and culture, memory, clinical psychology.

The University of Kansas, Graduate Studies, College of Liberal Arts and Sciences, Department of Psychology, Lawrence, KS 66045. Offers clinical child psychology (MA, PhD); clinical health and rehabilitation (PhD); cognitive psychology (PhD); developmental psychology (PhD); quantitative psychology (PhD); social psychology (MA). *Accreditation:* APA (one or more programs are accredited). *Faculty:* 36 full-time, 3 part-time/adjunct. *Students:* 81 full-time (49 women), 1 (woman) part-time; includes 12 minority (4 Black or African American, non-Hispanic/Latino; 5 Asian, non-Hispanic/Latino; 1 Hispanic/Latino; 2 Two or more races, non-Hispanic/Latino), 13 international. Average age 29. 194 applicants, 10% accepted, 9 enrolled. In 2014, 17 master's, 13 doctorates awarded. *Degree requirements:* For doctorate, variable foreign language requirement, comprehensive exam, thesis/dissertation. *Entrance requirements:* For doctorate, GRE General Test, minimum GPA of 3.0; undergraduate degree with 15 hours of course work in psychology, curriculum vitae, writing sample (clinical program only). Additional exam requirements/recommendations for international students: Required—TOEFL. *Application deadline:* For fall admission, 12/1 for domestic and international students. Application fee: $55 ($65 for international students). Electronic applications accepted. *Financial support:* In 2014–15, 1 fellowship with full tuition reimbursement (averaging $12,750 per year), 4 research assistantships with partial tuition reimbursements (averaging $12,980 per year), 70 teaching assistantships with partial tuition reimbursements (averaging $12,750 per year) were awarded; career-related internships or fieldwork, Federal Work-Study, scholarships/grants, health care benefits, and unspecified assistantships also available. Financial award application deadline: 12/1; financial award applicants required to submit FAFSA. *Faculty research:* Origins, correlates and treatment of depression; health and emotion; concentration on topics related to prejudice, stereotyping, and intergroup relations; memory, cognitive development, language, perception, attention, aging; psychometric methods, item response theory, structural equation modeling. *Unit head:* Ruth Anne Atchley, Chair, 785-864-4131. *Application contact:* Cathy O'Keefe, Graduate Officer, 785-864-4195, Fax: 785-864-5596, E-mail: cokeefe@ku.edu.
Website: http://www.psych.ku.edu/

University of Louisiana at Lafayette, College of Sciences, Institute of Cognitive Science, Lafayette, LA 70504. Offers PhD. *Degree requirements:* For doctorate, comprehensive exam, thesis/dissertation. *Entrance requirements:* For doctorate, GRE General Test, minimum GPA of 3.25. Additional exam requirements/recommendations for international students: Required—TOEFL (minimum score 550 paper-based). Electronic applications accepted. *Faculty research:* Computational models of cognition, comparative cognition, cognitive development, computational cognitive neuroscience, memory.

University of Maryland, Baltimore County, The Graduate School, College of Natural and Mathematical Sciences, Department of Biological Sciences, Program in Neuroscience and Cognitive Sciences, Baltimore, MD 21250. Offers PhD. *Faculty:* 6 full-time (3 women). *Students:* 2 full-time (1 woman); includes 1 minority (Black or African American, non-Hispanic/Latino), 1 international. Average age 25. 12 applicants, 8% accepted. *Degree requirements:* For doctorate, thesis/dissertation. *Entrance requirements:* For doctorate, GRE General Test, minimum GPA of 3.0. Additional exam requirements/recommendations for international students: Required—TOEFL (minimum score 80 iBT). *Application deadline:* For fall admission, 1/1 priority date for domestic and international students. Application fee: $50. Electronic applications accepted. *Expenses:* Tuition, state resident: part-time $557. Tuition, nonresident: part-time $922. *Required fees:* $122 per semester. One-time fee: $200 part-time. *Financial support:* In 2014–15, 2 students received support, including 2 fellowships with full tuition reimbursements available (averaging $23,000 per year); health care benefits also available. *Unit head:* Dr. Stephen Miller, Graduate Program Director, 410-455-3669, Fax: 410-455-3875, E-mail: biograd@umbc.edu. *Application contact:* Dr. Stephen Miller, Director, 410-455-3381, Fax: 410-455-3875, E-mail: biograd@umbc.edu.
Website: http://biology.umbc.edu

University of Maryland, College Park, Academic Affairs, College of Behavioral and Social Sciences, Program in Neurosciences and Cognitive Sciences, College Park, MD 20742. Offers PhD. *Degree requirements:* For doctorate, comprehensive exam, thesis/dissertation. *Entrance requirements:* For doctorate, GRE General Test, 3 letters of recommendation. Additional exam requirements/recommendations for international students: Required—TOEFL. Electronic applications accepted. *Faculty research:* Molecular neurobiology, cognition, neural and behavioral systems language, memory, human development.

University of Massachusetts Amherst, Graduate School, College of Natural Sciences, Department of Psychological and Brain Sciences, Amherst, MA 01003. Offers clinical psychology (MS, PhD); cognitive psychology (MS, PhD); developmental science (MS, PhD); psychology of peace and violence (MS, PhD); social psychology (MS, PhD). *Accreditation:* APA (one or more programs are accredited). *Faculty:* 62 full-time (31 women). *Students:* 47 full-time (32 women), 14 part-time (11 women); includes 12 minority (2 Black or African American, non-Hispanic/Latino; 6 Asian, non-Hispanic/Latino; 3 Hispanic/Latino; 1 Two or more races, non-Hispanic/Latino), 9 international. Average age 27. 317 applicants, 7% accepted, 11 enrolled. In 2014, 12 master's, 10 doctorates awarded. Terminal master's awarded for partial completion of doctoral program. *Degree requirements:* For master's, thesis; for doctorate, comprehensive exam, thesis/dissertation. *Entrance requirements:* For master's and doctorate, GRE General Test, 3 letters of recommendation. Additional exam requirements/recommendations for international students: Required—TOEFL (minimum score 550 paper-based; 80 iBT), IELTS (minimum score 6.5). *Application deadline:* For fall admission, 12/1 for domestic and international students. Applications are processed on a rolling basis. Application fee: $75. Electronic applications accepted. *Expenses:* Tuition, state resident: full-time $1980; part-time $110 per credit. Tuition, nonresident: full-time $14,644; part-time $414 per credit. *Required fees:* $11,417. One-time fee: $357. *Financial support:* Fellowships with full and partial tuition reimbursements, research assistantships with full and partial tuition reimbursements, teaching assistantships with full and partial tuition reimbursements, career-related internships or fieldwork, Federal Work-Study, scholarships/grants, traineeships, health care benefits, tuition waivers (full and partial), and unspecified assistantships available. Support available to part-time students. Financial award application deadline: 12/1. *Unit head:* Dr. Michael Constantino, Graduate Program Director, 413-545-2503, Fax: 413-545-0996. *Application contact:* Lindsay DeSantis, Supervisor of Admissions, 413-545-0722, Fax: 413-577-0010, E-mail: gradadm@grad.umass.edu.
Website: http://www.psych.umass.edu/

University of Massachusetts Amherst, Graduate School, Interdisciplinary Programs, Program in Neuroscience and Behavior, Amherst, MA 01003. Offers animal behavior and learning (PhD); molecular and cellular neuroscience (PhD); neural and behavioral development (PhD); neuroendocrinology (PhD); neuroscience and behavior (MS); sensorimotor, cognitive, and computational neuroscience (PhD). *Students:* 29 full-time (19 women), 1 (woman) part-time; includes 6 minority (1 Black or African American, non-Hispanic/Latino; 1 Asian, non-Hispanic/Latino; 4 Hispanic/Latino), 4 international. Average age 27. 127 applicants, 11% accepted, 7 enrolled. In 2014, 2 master's, 4 doctorates awarded. Terminal master's awarded for partial completion of doctoral program. *Degree requirements:* For master's, thesis or alternative; for doctorate, comprehensive exam, thesis/dissertation. *Entrance requirements:* For master's, GRE General Test; for doctorate, GRE General Test; GRE Subect Test in psychology, biology, or mathematics (recommended). Additional exam requirements/recommendations for international students: Required—TOEFL (minimum score 550 paper-based; 80 iBT), IELTS (minimum score 6.5). *Application deadline:* For fall admission, 12/15 for domestic and international students. Applications are processed on a rolling basis. Application fee: $75. Electronic applications accepted. *Expenses:* Tuition, state resident: full-time $1980; part-time $110 per credit. Tuition, nonresident: full-time $14,644; part-time $414 per credit. *Required fees:* $11,417. One-time fee: $357. *Financial support:* Fellowships with full and partial tuition reimbursements, research assistantships with full and partial tuition reimbursements, teaching assistantships with full and partial tuition reimbursements, career-related internships or fieldwork, Federal Work-Study, scholarships/grants, traineeships, health care benefits, tuition waivers (full and partial), and unspecified assistantships available. Support available to part-time students. Financial award application deadline: 12/14; financial award applicants required to submit FAFSA. *Unit head:* Dr. Melinda Novak, Graduate Program Director, 413-545-2046, Fax: 413-545-3243, E-mail: nsb@bio.umass.edu. *Application contact:* Lindsay DeSantis, Supervisor of Admissions, 413-545-0722, Fax: 413-577-0010, E-mail: gradadm@grad.umass.edu.
Website: http://www.umass.edu/neuro/

University of Massachusetts Boston, College of Liberal Arts, Program in Developmental and Brain Sciences, Boston, MA 02125-3393. Offers MA. *Entrance requirements:* Additional exam requirements/recommendations for international students: Required—TOEFL; Recommended—IELTS. *Expenses:* Tuition, state resident: full-time $2590; part-time $108 per credit. Tuition, nonresident: full-time $9758; part-time $406.50 per credit. Tuition and fees vary according to course load and program. *Unit head:* Dr. Donna Kuizenga, Dean, College of Liberal Arts, 617-287-6500, E-mail: donna.kuizenga@umb.edu. *Application contact:* Peggy Roldan Patel, Graduate Admissions Coordinator, 617-287-6400, Fax: 617-287-6236, E-mail: bos.gadm@dpc.umassp.edu.
Website: http://www.umb.edu/academics/cla/psychology/grad/dbs

University of Michigan, Horace H. Rackham School of Graduate Studies, College of Literature, Science, and the Arts, Department of Psychology, Ann Arbor, MI 48109. Offers biopsychology (PhD); clinical science (PhD); cognition and cognitive neuroscience (PhD); developmental psychology (PhD); personality and social contexts (PhD); social psychology (PhD). *Accreditation:* APA. *Faculty:* 57 full-time (27 women), 31 part-time/adjunct (17 women). *Students:* 118 full-time (80 women); includes 58 minority (15 Black or African American, non-Hispanic/Latino; 1 American Indian or Alaska Native, non-Hispanic/Latino; 15 Asian, non-Hispanic/Latino; 25 Hispanic/Latino; 2 Two or more races, non-Hispanic/Latino), 12 international. Average age 27. 687 applicants, 7% accepted, 25 enrolled. In 2014, 36 doctorates awarded. *Degree requirements:* For doctorate, comprehensive exam, thesis/dissertation, oral defense of dissertation, preliminary exam. *Entrance requirements:* For doctorate, GRE General Test. Additional exam requirements/recommendations for international students: Required—TOEFL. *Application deadline:* For fall admission, 12/1 for domestic and international students. Application fee: $75 ($90 for international students). Electronic applications accepted. *Financial support:* In 2014–15, 82 students received support, including 45 fellowships with full tuition reimbursements available (averaging $21,600 per year), 16 research assistantships with full tuition reimbursements available (averaging $28,450 per year), 50 teaching assistantships with full tuition reimbursements available (averaging $26,200 per year); career-related internships or fieldwork also available. Financial award application deadline: 4/15. *Unit head:* Prof. Patricia Reuter-Lorenz, Department Chair, 734-764-7429. *Application contact:* Danielle Joanette, Psychology Student Academic Affairs, 731-764-2580, Fax: 734-615-7584, E-mail: psych.saa@umich.edu.
Website: http://www.lsa.umich.edu/psych/

University of Minnesota, Twin Cities Campus, Graduate School, College of Liberal Arts, Department of Psychology, Program in Cognitive and Biological Psychology, Minneapolis, MN 55455-0213. Offers PhD. *Degree requirements:* For doctorate, comprehensive exam, thesis/dissertation. *Entrance requirements:* For doctorate, GRE General Test, GRE Subject Test (recommended), 12 credits of upper-level psychology courses, including a course in statistics or psychological measurement. Additional exam requirements/recommendations for international students: Required—TOEFL (minimum score 550 paper-based; 79 iBT).

University of Nebraska–Lincoln, Graduate College, College of Arts and Sciences, Department of Psychology, Lincoln, NE 68588. Offers biopsychology (PhD); clinical psychology (PhD); cognitive psychology (PhD); developmental psychology (PhD); psychology (MA); social/personality psychology (PhD); JD/MA; JD/PhD. *Accreditation:* APA (one or more programs are accredited). *Degree requirements:* For master's, thesis optional; for doctorate, comprehensive exam, thesis/dissertation. *Entrance requirements:* For master's and doctorate, GRE General Test. Additional exam requirements/recommendations for international students: Required—TOEFL (minimum score 550 paper-based). Electronic applications accepted. *Faculty research:* Law and psychology, rural mental health, chronic mental illness, neuropsychology, child clinical psychology.

University of Nebraska–Lincoln, Graduate College, College of Education and Human Sciences, Department of Educational Psychology, Lincoln, NE 68588. Offers cognition, learning and development (MA); counseling psychology (MA); educational psychology

(MA, Ed S); psychological studies in education (PhD), including cognition, learning and development, counseling psychology, quantitative, qualitative, and psychometric methods, school psychology; quantitative, qualitative, and psychometric methods (MA); school psychology (MA, Ed S). *Accreditation:* APA (one or more programs are accredited); NCATE. *Degree requirements:* For master's, thesis optional. *Entrance requirements:* For master's, GRE General Test. Additional exam requirements/recommendations for international students: Required—TOEFL (minimum score 500 paper-based). Electronic applications accepted. *Faculty research:* Measurement and assessment, metacognition, academic skills, child development, multicultural education and counseling.

University of Nevada, Reno, Graduate School, College of Liberal Arts, Department of Psychology, Program in Cognitive Brain Science, Reno, NV 89557. Offers MA, PhD. Terminal master's awarded for partial completion of doctoral program. *Degree requirements:* For master's, thesis optional; for doctorate, comprehensive exam, thesis/dissertation. *Entrance requirements:* For master's, GRE General Test, minimum GPA of 2.75; for doctorate, GRE General Test, minimum GPA of 3.0. Additional exam requirements/recommendations for international students: Required—TOEFL (minimum score 500 paper-based; 61 iBT), IELTS (minimum score 6). Electronic applications accepted. *Faculty research:* Comparative psychology, cognition, perception.

University of New Mexico, Graduate School, College of Arts and Sciences, Program in Psychology, Albuquerque, NM 87131-2039. Offers behavioral neuroscience (PhD); clinical psychology (PhD); cognitive neuroimaging (PhD); developmental psychology (PhD); evolution (PhD); health psychology (PhD); quantitative methodology (PhD). *Faculty:* 25 full-time (9 women), 1 (woman) part-time/adjunct. *Students:* 66 full-time (44 women), 12 part-time (6 women); includes 23 minority (2 Black or African American, non-Hispanic/Latino; 2 American Indian or Alaska Native, non-Hispanic/Latino; 4 Asian, non-Hispanic/Latino; 13 Hispanic/Latino; 2 Two or more races, non-Hispanic/Latino), 1 international. Average age 33. 135 applicants, 10% accepted, 13 enrolled. In 2014, 10 doctorates awarded. *Degree requirements:* For doctorate, comprehensive exam, thesis/dissertation. *Entrance requirements:* For doctorate, GRE General Test, GRE Subject Test (psychology), minimum GPA of 3.0. Additional exam requirements/recommendations for international students: Required—TOEFL (minimum score 550 paper-based; 79 iBT), IELTS (minimum score 6.5). *Application deadline:* For fall admission, 12/15 priority date for domestic and international students. Applications are processed on a rolling basis. Application fee: $50. Electronic applications accepted. *Financial support:* In 2014–15, 62 students received support, including 8 fellowships (averaging $13,124 per year), 37 research assistantships with full and partial tuition reimbursements available (averaging $11,655 per year), 67 teaching assistantships with full and partial tuition reimbursements available (averaging $13,600 per year); career-related internships or fieldwork, Federal Work-Study, institutionally sponsored loans, scholarships/grants, health care benefits, tuition waivers (partial), and unspecified assistantships also available. Financial award application deadline: 3/1; financial award applicants required to submit FAFSA. *Faculty research:* Addiction, cognition, brain and behavior, developmental, evolutionary, functioning neuroimaging, health psychology, learning and memory, neuroscience. *Unit head:* Dr. Jane Ellen Smith, Department Chair, 505-277-4121, Fax: 505-277-1394. *Application contact:* Rikk Murphy, Graduate Program Coordinator, 505-277-5009, Fax: 505-277-1394, E-mail: advising@unm.edu.
Website: http://psych.unm.edu

The University of North Carolina at Chapel Hill, Graduate School, College of Arts and Sciences, Department of Psychology, Chapel Hill, NC 27599-3270. Offers behavioral neuroscience psychology (PhD); clinical psychology (PhD); cognitive psychology (PhD); developmental psychology (PhD); quantitative psychology (PhD); social psychology (PhD). *Accreditation:* APA. *Degree requirements:* For doctorate, comprehensive exam, thesis/dissertation. *Entrance requirements:* For doctorate, GRE General Test, minimum GPA of 3.0. Additional exam requirements/recommendations for international students: Required—TOEFL (minimum score 550 paper-based; 79 iBT), IELTS (minimum score 7). Electronic applications accepted. *Faculty research:* Expressed emotion, cognitive development, social cognitive neuroscience, human memory personality.

The University of North Carolina at Charlotte, College of Liberal Arts and Sciences, Department of Psychology, Charlotte, NC 28223-0001. Offers clinical/community psychology (MA); cognitive sciences (Graduate Certificate); health psychology (PhD); industrial/organizational psychology (MA). Part-time programs available. *Faculty:* 31 full-time (17 women), 1 part-time/adjunct (0 women). *Students:* 42 full-time (35 women), 31 part-time (26 women); includes 18 minority (5 Black or African American, non-Hispanic/Latino; 2 Asian, non-Hispanic/Latino; 9 Hispanic/Latino; 2 Two or more races, non-Hispanic/Latino), 1 international. Average age 28. 243 applicants, 16% accepted, 25 enrolled. In 2014, 9 master's, 5 doctorates, 1 other advanced degree awarded. Terminal master's awarded for partial completion of doctoral program. *Degree requirements:* For master's, thesis; for doctorate, thesis/dissertation. *Entrance requirements:* For master's, GRE General Test, GRE Subject Test, minimum GPA of 3.0 in undergraduate major, 2.8 overall, letters of recommendation; for doctorate, GRE General Test, minimum GPA of 3.5, letters of recommendation. Additional exam requirements/recommendations for international students: Required—TOEFL (minimum score 557 paper-based; 83 iBT). *Application deadline:* For fall admission, 5/1 for domestic and international students. Application fee: $75. Electronic applications accepted. *Expenses:* Tuition, state resident: full-time $4008. Tuition, nonresident: full-time $16,295. *Required fees:* $2755. Tuition and fees vary according to course load and program. *Financial support:* In 2014–15, 33 students received support, including 16 research assistantships (averaging $15,239 per year), 17 teaching assistantships (averaging $12,809 per year); career-related internships or fieldwork, Federal Work-Study, institutionally sponsored loans, and scholarships/grants also available. Support available to part-time students. Financial award application deadline: 4/1; financial award applicants required to submit FAFSA. *Faculty research:* Neuropsychology of information processing, perception and human performance, computer-based applications in research and instruction, interventions to facilitate team effectiveness, post-traumatic psychological growth. *Total annual research expenditures:* $327,551. *Unit head:* Dr. Fary Cachelin, Chair, 704-687-1319, Fax: 704-687-1317, E-mail: fcacheli@uncc.edu. *Application contact:* Kathy B. Giddings, Director of Graduate Admissions, 704-687-5503, Fax: 704-687-1668, E-mail: gradadm@uncc.edu.
Website: http://psych.uncc.edu/graduate-programs

The University of North Carolina at Greensboro, Graduate School, College of Arts and Sciences, Department of Psychology, Greensboro, NC 27412-5001. Offers clinical psychology (MA, PhD); cognitive psychology (MA, PhD); developmental psychology (MA, PhD); social psychology (MA, PhD). *Accreditation:* APA (one or more programs are accredited). Terminal master's awarded for partial completion of doctoral program. *Degree requirements:* For master's, comprehensive exam, thesis; for doctorate, one foreign language, thesis/dissertation, preliminary exam. *Entrance requirements:* For master's and doctorate, GRE General Test. Additional exam requirements/recommendations for international students: Required—TOEFL. Electronic applications accepted. *Faculty research:* Sensory and perceptual determinants; evoked potential: disorders, deafness, and development.

University of Notre Dame, Graduate School, College of Arts and Letters, Division of Social Science, Department of Psychology, Notre Dame, IN 46556. Offers cognitive psychology (PhD); counseling psychology (PhD); developmental psychology (PhD); quantitative psychology (PhD). *Accreditation:* APA. *Degree requirements:* For doctorate, comprehensive exam, thesis/dissertation, candidacy exam. *Entrance requirements:* For doctorate, GRE General Test, GRE Subject Test (strongly recommended). Additional exam requirements/recommendations for international students: Required—TOEFL (minimum score 600 paper-based; 80 iBT). Electronic applications accepted. *Faculty research:* Cognitive and socio-emotional development, statistical methods and quantitative models applicable to psychology, interpersonal relations, life span development and developmental delay, childhood depression, structural equation and dynamical systems.

University of Oregon, Graduate School, College of Arts and Sciences, Department of Psychology, Eugene, OR 97403. Offers clinical psychology (PhD); cognitive psychology (MA, MS, PhD); developmental psychology (MA, MS, PhD); physiological psychology (MA, MS, PhD); psychology (MA, MS, PhD); social/personality psychology (MA, MS, PhD). *Accreditation:* APA (one or more programs are accredited). Terminal master's awarded for partial completion of doctoral program. *Degree requirements:* For doctorate, thesis/dissertation. *Entrance requirements:* For master's, GRE General Test, minimum GPA of 3.0; for doctorate, GRE General Test. Additional exam requirements/recommendations for international students: Required—TOEFL.

University of Rochester, School of Arts and Sciences, Department of Brain and Cognitive Sciences, Rochester, NY 14627. Offers PhD. *Faculty:* 19 full-time (4 women). *Students:* 35 full-time (19 women); includes 5 minority (2 Asian, non-Hispanic/Latino; 2 Hispanic/Latino; 1 Two or more races, non-Hispanic/Latino), 10 international. 121 applicants, 16% accepted, 11 enrolled. In 2014, 10 doctorates awarded. Terminal master's awarded for partial completion of doctoral program. *Degree requirements:* For doctorate, thesis/dissertation, qualifying exam. *Entrance requirements:* For doctorate, GRE General Test. Additional exam requirements/recommendations for international students: Required—TOEFL. *Application deadline:* For fall admission, 1/1 priority date for domestic students. Application fee: $60. Electronic applications accepted. *Expenses: Tuition:* Full-time $46,150; part-time $1442 per credit hour. *Required fees:* $504. *Financial support:* Fellowships, research assistantships, teaching assistantships, and tuition waivers (full and partial) available. Financial award application deadline: 1/1. *Faculty research:* Perception and action; language processing and acquisition; learning, development and neural plasticity; cognitive neuroscience; computation, cognition and the brain. *Unit head:* Gregory DeAngelis, Chair, 585-275-8677. *Application contact:* Kathy Corser, Graduate Program Coordinator, 585-275-1844.
Website: http://www.bcs.rochester.edu/graduate/index.html

University of Southern California, Graduate School, Dana and David Dornsife College of Letters, Arts and Sciences, Department of Psychology, Los Angeles, CA 90089. Offers brain and cognitive science (PhD); clinical science (PhD); developmental psychology (PhD); human behavior (MHB); quantitative methods (PhD); social psychology (PhD). *Accreditation:* APA. *Degree requirements:* For doctorate, comprehensive exam, thesis/dissertation, one-year internship (for clinical science students). *Entrance requirements:* For doctorate, GRE. Additional exam requirements/recommendations for international students: Recommended—TOEFL (minimum score 600 paper-based; 100 iBT). Electronic applications accepted. *Faculty research:* Affective neuroscience; children and families; vision, culture and ethnicity; intergroup relations; aggression and violence; language and reading development; substance abuse.

University of South Florida, College of Arts and Sciences, Department of Psychology, Tampa, FL 33620-9951. Offers clinical psychology (PhD); cognitive and neural sciences (PhD); industrial-organizational psychology (PhD). *Accreditation:* APA. *Faculty:* 33 full-time (15 women), 1 part-time/adjunct. *Students:* 96 full-time (68 women), 18 part-time (11 women); includes 25 minority (2 Black or African American, non-Hispanic/Latino; 9 Asian, non-Hispanic/Latino; 10 Hispanic/Latino; 4 Two or more races, non-Hispanic/Latino), 12 international. Average age 28. 513 applicants, 5% accepted, 19 enrolled. In 2014, 16 doctorates awarded. *Degree requirements:* For doctorate, comprehensive exam, thesis/dissertation, internship. *Entrance requirements:* For doctorate, GRE General Test (minimum recommended verbal and quantitative scores each above the 50th percentile), minimum upper-division GPA of 3.4, three letters of recommendation, personal goals statement. Additional exam requirements/recommendations for international students: Required—TOEFL (minimum score 550 paper-based; 79 iBT) or IELTS (minimum score 6.5). *Application deadline:* For fall admission, 12/1 for domestic and international students. Application fee: $30. Electronic applications accepted. *Expenses:* Expenses: Contact institution. *Financial support:* In 2014–15, 75 students received support, including 18 research assistantships with tuition reimbursements available (averaging $14,727 per year), 57 teaching assistantships with tuition reimbursements available (averaging $14,543 per year); tuition waivers (partial) and unspecified assistantships also available. Financial award applicants required to submit FAFSA. *Faculty research:* Clinical, cognitive, neuroscience, social, and industrial/organizational. *Total annual research expenditures:* $1.7 million. *Unit head:* Dr. Toru Shimizu, Chairperson, 813-974-0352, Fax: 813-974-4617, E-mail: shimizu@usf.edu. *Application contact:* Dr. Joseph Vandello, Associate Professor and Graduate Program Director, 813-974-0362, Fax: 813-974-4617, E-mail: vandello@usf.edu.
Website: http://psychology.usf.edu/

The University of Texas at Dallas, School of Behavioral and Brain Sciences, Program in Cognition and Neuroscience, Richardson, TX 75080. Offers applied cognition and neuroscience (MS); cognition and neuroscience (PhD). Part-time and evening/weekend programs available. *Faculty:* 30 full-time (12 women), 2 part-time/adjunct (1 woman). *Students:* 158 full-time (93 women), 40 part-time (24 women); includes 57 minority (10 Black or African American, non-Hispanic/Latino; 1 American Indian or Alaska Native, non-Hispanic/Latino; 22 Asian, non-Hispanic/Latino; 19 Hispanic/Latino; 5 Two or more races, non-Hispanic/Latino), 38 international. Average age 28. 180 applicants, 45% accepted, 62 enrolled. In 2014, 52 master's, 9 doctorates awarded. *Degree requirements:* For master's, internship; for doctorate, thesis/dissertation. *Entrance requirements:* For master's and doctorate, GRE General Test, minimum GPA of 3.0 in upper-level coursework in field. Additional exam requirements/recommendations for international students: Required—TOEFL (minimum score 550 paper-based). *Application deadline:* For fall admission, 7/15 for domestic students, 5/1 priority date for international students; for spring admission, 11/15 for domestic students, 9/1 priority date for international students. Applications are processed on a rolling basis. Application fee: $50 ($100 for international students). Electronic applications accepted. *Expenses:* Tuition, state resident: full-time $11,940; part-time $663 per credit. Tuition, nonresident: full-time $22,282; part-time $1238 per credit. *Financial support:* In 2014–15, 115 students received support, including 1 fellowship (averaging $5,585 per year), 24 research assistantships with partial tuition reimbursements available (averaging $19,438 per year), 37 teaching assistantships with partial tuition reimbursements available (averaging $16,857 per year); career-related internships or fieldwork, Federal Work-Study, institutionally sponsored loans, scholarships/grants, and unspecified assistantships also available. Support available to part-time students. Financial award application deadline: 4/30; financial award applicants required to submit FAFSA. *Faculty research:* Neural plasticity, neuroimaging, face recognition, cognitive and neurobiological mechanisms of human memory, treatment interventions for semantic memory retrieval problems. *Unit head:* Dr. James C. Bartlett, Program Head, 972-883-

2079, Fax: 972-883-2491, E-mail: jbartlet@utdallas.edu. *Application contact:* Dr. Christa McIntyre Rodriguez, Program Head, 972-883-2235, Fax: 972-883-2491, E-mail: christa.mcintyre@utdallas.edu.
Website: http://bbs.utdallas.edu/cogneuro/

University of Washington, Graduate School, College of Arts and Sciences, Department of Psychology, Seattle, WA 98195. Offers animal behavior (PhD); child psychology (PhD); clinical psychology (PhD); cognition and perception (PhD); developmental psychology (PhD); quantitative psychology (PhD); social psychology and personality (PhD). *Accreditation:* APA. *Degree requirements:* For doctorate, thesis/dissertation. *Entrance requirements:* For doctorate, GRE General Test, minimum GPA of 3.0. Electronic applications accepted. *Faculty research:* Addictive behaviors, artificial intelligence, child psychopathology, mechanisms and development of vision, physiology of ingestive behaviors.

University of Wisconsin–Madison, Graduate School, College of Letters and Science, Department of Psychology, Program in Cognitive Neurosciences, Madison, WI 53706-1380. Offers PhD. *Degree requirements:* For doctorate, comprehensive exam, thesis/dissertation. *Entrance requirements:* For doctorate, GRE General Test, minimum undergraduate GPA of 3.0. Additional exam requirements/recommendations for international students: Required—TOEFL. Electronic applications accepted. *Expenses:* Tuition, state resident: full-time $10,723; part-time $745 per credit. Tuition, nonresident: full-time $24,054; part-time $1578 per credit. *Required fees:* $374 per semester. Tuition and fees vary according to course load, program and reciprocity agreements.

University of Wisconsin–Madison, Graduate School, College of Letters and Science, Department of Psychology, Program in Perception, Madison, WI 53706-1380. Offers PhD. *Degree requirements:* For doctorate, comprehensive exam, thesis/dissertation. *Entrance requirements:* For doctorate, GRE General Test, minimum GPA of 3.0. Electronic applications accepted. *Expenses:* Tuition, state resident: full-time $10,723; part-time $745 per credit. Tuition, nonresident: full-time $24,054; part-time $1578 per credit. *Required fees:* $374 per semester. Tuition and fees vary according to course load, program and reciprocity agreements.

Washington University in St. Louis, Graduate School of Arts and Sciences, Department of Psychology, St. Louis, MO 63130-4899. Offers aging and development (PhD); behavior, brain, and cognition (PhD); clinical psychology (PhD); social and personality psychology (PhD). *Accreditation:* APA. Terminal master's awarded for partial completion of doctoral program. *Degree requirements:* For doctorate, thesis/dissertation. *Entrance requirements:* For doctorate, GRE General Test. Additional exam requirements/recommendations for international students: Required—TOEFL. Electronic applications accepted.

Wayne State University, College of Liberal Arts and Sciences, Department of Psychology, Detroit, MI 48202. Offers behavioral and cognitive neuroscience (PhD); clinical psychology (PhD); cognitive, developmental and social psychology (PhD); industrial and organizational psychology (MA); social psychology (PhD). Doctoral programs admit for fall only. *Accreditation:* APA (one or more programs are accredited). *Faculty:* 37 full-time (13 women), 8 part-time/adjunct (4 women). *Students:* 107 full-time (74 women), 28 part-time (16 women); includes 19 minority (8 Black or African American, non-Hispanic/Latino; 2 Asian, non-Hispanic/Latino; 5 Hispanic/Latino; 4 Two or more races, non-Hispanic/Latino), 10 international. Average age 28. 397 applicants, 11% accepted, 25 enrolled. In 2014, 24 master's, 18 doctorates awarded. Terminal master's awarded for partial completion of doctoral program. *Degree requirements:* For master's, thesis (for some programs); for doctorate, thesis/dissertation, training assignments. *Entrance requirements:* For master's, GRE General Test, minimum undergraduate upper-division cumulative GPA of 3.0, courses in introductory psychology and statistics, two letters of recommendation, professional statement; for doctorate, GRE General Test, bachelor's, master's, or other advanced degree; at least three letters of recommendation; statement of purpose. Additional exam requirements/recommendations for international students: Required—TOEFL (minimum score 550 paper-based; 79 iBT), TWE (minimum score 5.5), Michigan English Language Assessment Battery (minimum score 85); Recommended—IELTS (minimum score 6.5). *Application deadline:* For fall admission, 12/1 for domestic and international students; for winter admission, 10/15 for domestic students, 9/1 for international students; for spring admission, 3/15 for domestic students, 1/1 for international students. Application fee: $0. Electronic applications accepted. *Expenses:* Tuition, state resident: full-time $10,294; part-time $571.90 per credit hour. Tuition, nonresident: full-time $29,730; part-time $1238.75 per credit hour. *Required fees:* $1365; $43.50 per credit hour. $291.10 per semester. Tuition and fees vary according to course load and program. *Financial support:* In 2014–15, 91 students received support, including 8 fellowships with tuition reimbursements available (averaging $15,983 per year), 12 research assistantships with tuition reimbursements available (averaging $17,862 per year), 49 teaching assistantships with tuition reimbursements available (averaging $16,838 per year); scholarships/grants, health care benefits, and unspecified assistantships also available. Financial award application deadline: 3/31; financial award applicants required to submit FAFSA. *Faculty research:* Neuroscience, including functional cognitive imaging, neural physiology, behavioral pharmacology, and neurobehavioral teratology; cognitive and neurochemical processes associated with aging, drug addiction and neurological disorders to studies of the neural circuits that underlie learning, emotion, and weight regulation; the life-long developmental plasticity of the neurobiological processes of behavior; neuropsychology; child clinical psychology; health psychology; community psychology. *Total annual research expenditures:* $2.1 million. *Unit head:* Boris Baltes, PhD, Chair/Professor, 313-577-2800, Fax: 313-577-7636, E-mail: b.baltes@wayne.edu. *Application contact:* Alia Allen, Academic Services Officer, 313-577-2823, E-mail: aallen@wayne.edu.
Website: http://clas.wayne.edu/psychology/

Wilfrid Laurier University, Faculty of Graduate and Postdoctoral Studies, Faculty of Science, Department of Psychology, Waterloo, ON N2L 3C5, Canada. Offers behavioral neuroscience (M Sc, PhD); cognitive neuroscience (M Sc, PhD); community psychology (MA, PhD); social and developmental psychology (MA, PhD). Part-time programs available. *Degree requirements:* For master's, thesis; for doctorate, thesis/dissertation. *Entrance requirements:* For master's, GRE General Test, honors BA or the equivalent in psychology, minimum B average in undergraduate course work; for doctorate, GRE General Test, master's degree, minimum A- average. Additional exam requirements/recommendations for international students: Required—TOEFL (minimum score 89 iBT). Electronic applications accepted. *Faculty research:* Brain and cognition, community psychology, social and developmental psychology.

Yale University, Graduate School of Arts and Sciences, Department of Psychology, New Haven, CT 06520. Offers behavioral neuroscience (PhD); clinical psychology (PhD); cognitive psychology (PhD); developmental psychology (PhD); social/personality psychology (PhD). *Accreditation:* APA. *Degree requirements:* For doctorate, thesis/dissertation. *Entrance requirements:* For doctorate, GRE General Test.

Counseling Psychology

Abilene Christian University, Graduate School, College of Arts and Sciences, Department of Psychology, Program in Counseling Psychology, Abilene, TX 79699-9100. Offers MS. Part-time programs available. *Students:* 11 full-time (9 women), 4 part-time (2 women); includes 4 minority (2 Black or African American, non-Hispanic/Latino; 2 Two or more races, non-Hispanic/Latino). 33 applicants, 30% accepted, 7 enrolled. In 2014, 1 master's awarded. *Degree requirements:* For master's, comprehensive exam, thesis, practicum. *Entrance requirements:* Additional exam requirements/recommendations for international students: Required—TOEFL (minimum score 550 paper-based; 90 iBT), IELTS (minimum score 6.5), PTE. *Application deadline:* For fall admission, 3/1 priority date for domestic students; for spring admission, 11/1 for domestic students. Applications are processed on a rolling basis. Application fee: $50. Electronic applications accepted. *Expenses: Tuition:* Full-time $18,228; part-time $1016 per credit hour. *Financial support:* In 2014–15, 11 students received support. Applicants required to submit FAFSA. *Unit head:* Dr. Robert McKelvain, Graduate Director, 325-674-2286, Fax: 325-674-6968, E-mail: mckelvainr@acu.edu. *Application contact:* Corey Patterson, Director of Graduate Admission and Recruiting, 325-674-6566, Fax: 325-674-6717, E-mail: gradinfo@acu.edu.

Adelphi University, Derner Institute of Advanced Psychological Studies, Program in Mental Health Counseling, Garden City, NY 11530-0701. Offers MA. *Students:* 35 full-time (32 women), 2 part-time (1 woman); includes 9 minority (1 Black or African American, non-Hispanic/Latino; 1 Asian, non-Hispanic/Latino; 6 Hispanic/Latino; 1 Two or more races, non-Hispanic/Latino), 4 international. Average age 26. In 2014, 11 master's awarded. *Degree requirements:* For master's, comprehensive exam. *Entrance requirements:* For master's, GRE General Test, GRE Subject Test, minimum cumulative GPA of 3.1; interview; course work in developmental psychology, research methods, and psycho-pathology; 2 letters of recommendation. Additional exam requirements/recommendations for international students: Required—TOEFL (minimum score 550 paper-based; 80 iBT). *Application deadline:* For fall admission, 4/1 priority date for domestic students, 5/1 priority date for international students. Application fee: $50. Electronic applications accepted. *Financial support:* Research assistantships with full and partial tuition reimbursements, career-related internships or fieldwork, Federal Work-Study, institutionally sponsored loans, and unspecified assistantships available. *Unit head:* Dr. Errol Rodriguez, Assistant Dean, 516-237-8572, E-mail: erodriguez@adelphi.edu. *Application contact:* Christine Murphy, Director of Admissions, 516-877-3050, Fax: 516-877-3039, E-mail: graduateadmissions@adelphi.edu.
Website: http://derner.adelphi.edu/psychology/graduate/ma-mental-health-counseling/

Adler Graduate School, Program in Adlerian Counseling and Psychotherapy, Richfield, MN 55423. Offers Adlerian studies (MA); art therapy (MA); clinical counseling (MA); co-occurring substance abuse and mental health disorders (MA); marriage and family therapy (MA); school counseling (MA). Part-time and evening/weekend programs available. *Faculty:* 7 full-time (6 women), 68 part-time/adjunct (49 women). *Students:* 368 part-time (283 women); includes 61 minority (41 Black or African American, non-Hispanic/Latino; 4 American Indian or Alaska Native, non-Hispanic/Latino; 8 Asian, non-Hispanic/Latino; 8 Hispanic/Latino). Average age 40. In 2014, 90 master's awarded. *Degree requirements:* For master's, thesis or alternative, 500-700 hour internship (depending on license choice). *Entrance requirements:* For master's, personal goal statement, three letters of reference, resume or work history, official transcripts. *Application deadline:* Applications are processed on a rolling basis. Application fee: $50. Electronic applications accepted. *Expenses: Tuition:* Full-time $6060; part-time $505 per credit. *Financial support:* Career-related internships or fieldwork and tuition waivers available. Support available to part-time students. Financial award applicants required to submit FAFSA. *Unit head:* Dr. Dan Haugen, President, 612-767-7048, Fax: 612-861-7559, E-mail: haugen@alfredadler.edu. *Application contact:* Evelyn B. Haas, Director of Admissions, 612-767-7044, Fax: 612-861-7559, E-mail: ev@alfredadler.edu.

★ **Adler University,** Programs in Psychology, Chicago, IL 60602. Offers advanced Adlerian psychotherapy (Certificate); art therapy (MA); clinical neuropsychology (Certificate); clinical psychology (Psy D); community psychology (MA); counseling and organizational psychology (MA); counseling psychology (MA); criminology (MA); emergency management leadership (MA); forensic psychology (MA); marriage and family counseling (MA); marriage and family therapy (Certificate); military psychology (MA); nonprofit management (MA); organizational psychology (MA); police psychology (MA); public policy and administration (MA); rehabilitation counseling (MA); sport and health psychology (MA); substance abuse counseling (Certificate); Psy D/Certificate; Psy D/MACAT; Psy D/MACP; Psy D/MAMFC; Psy D/MASAC. *Accreditation:* APA. Part-time and evening/weekend programs available. Postbaccalaureate distance learning degree programs offered (minimal on-campus study). Terminal master's awarded for partial completion of doctoral program. *Degree requirements:* For master's, thesis or alternative, oral exam, practicum; for doctorate, thesis/dissertation, clinical exam, internship, oral exam, practicum, written qualifying exam. *Entrance requirements:* For master's, 12 semester hours in psychology, minimum GPA of 3.0; for doctorate, 18 semester hours in psychology, minimum GPA of 3.25; for Certificate, appropriate master's or doctoral degree. Additional exam requirements/recommendations for international students: Required—TOEFL (minimum score 550 paper-based; 79 iBT). Electronic applications accepted.

See Display on page 969 and Close-Up on page 1207.

Alabama Agricultural and Mechanical University, School of Graduate Studies, School of Education, Department of Counseling and Special Education, Huntsville, AL 35811. Offers communicative disorders (M Ed, MS); psychology and counseling (MS, Ed S), including clinical psychology (MS), counseling and guidance, counseling psychology (MS), personnel management (MS), psychometry (MS), school psychology (MS); special education (M Ed, MS). *Accreditation:* CORE; NCATE. Part-time and evening/weekend programs available. *Degree requirements:* For master's, comprehensive exam. *Entrance requirements:* For master's, GRE General Test. Additional exam requirements/recommendations for international students: Required—TOEFL (minimum score 500 paper-based; 61 iBT). *Faculty research:* Increasing numbers of minorities in special education and speech-language pathology.

Alaska Pacific University, Graduate Programs, Department of Counseling, Psychological Studies, and Human Services, Program in Counseling Psychology, Anchorage, AK 99508-4672. Offers MSCP.

Alfred University, Graduate School, Counseling and School Psychology Program, Alfred, NY 14802-1205. Offers mental health counseling (MS Ed); school counseling (MS Ed, CAS); school psychology (MA, Psy D, CAS). *Accreditation:* APA. *Degree requirements:* For master's, internship; for doctorate, thesis/dissertation, internship. *Entrance requirements:* For master's and doctorate, GRE General Test. Additional exam requirements/recommendations for international students: Required—TOEFL (minimum score 590 paper-based; 90 iBT), IELTS (minimum score 6.5). Electronic applications accepted. *Faculty research:* Family processes, alternative assessment approaches, behavior disorders in children, parent involvement, school psychology training issues.

Alliant International University–México City, California School of Professional Psychology, Mexico City, Mexico. Offers counseling psychology (MA). *Entrance requirements:* For master's, minimum GPA of 3.0. Additional exam requirements/recommendations for international students: Required—TOEFL (minimum score 550 paper-based; 80 iBT).

Amberton University, Graduate School, Programs in Counseling, Garland, TX 75041-5595. Offers MA. *Entrance requirements:* For master's, minimum GPA of 3.0. *Application deadline:* Applications are processed on a rolling basis. *Unit head:* Dr. Don Hebbard, Academic Dean, 972-279-6511 Ext. 153, Fax: 972-279-9773, E-mail: dhebbard@amberton.edu. *Application contact:* Adviser, 972-279-6511 Ext. 180, Fax: 972-279-9773, E-mail: advisor@amberton.edu.

American International College, School of Graduate and Adult Education, Graduate Psychology Department, Counseling Psychology Program, Springfield, MA 01109-3189. Offers MA. Evening/weekend programs available. Postbaccalaureate distance learning degree programs offered (minimal on-campus study). *Faculty:* 2 part-time/adjunct (1 woman). *Students:* 21 full-time (19 women), 1 (woman) part-time; includes 8 minority (6 Black or African American, non-Hispanic/Latino; 1 Asian, non-Hispanic/Latino; 1 Two or more races, non-Hispanic/Latino). Average age 35. 10 applicants, 100% accepted, 7 enrolled. *Entrance requirements:* For master's, graduate of accredited four-year college with minimum GPA of 3.0. Additional exam requirements/recommendations for international students: Required—TOEFL (minimum score 550 paper-based). *Application deadline:* Applications are processed on a rolling basis. Application fee: $50. Electronic applications accepted. *Expenses:* Expenses: $450 per credit; registration fee $30 per term. *Financial support:* Application deadline: 4/1; applicants required to submit FAFSA. *Unit head:* Nicholas Young, Dean of Low-Residency Programs, 413-563-6544, E-mail: nyoung1191@aol.com. *Application contact:* Kerry Barnes, Director of Graduate Admissions, 413-205-3703, Fax: 413-205-3051, E-mail: kerry.barnes@aic.edu. Website: http://www.aic.edu/academics/graduate

Amridge University, Graduate and Professional Programs, Montgomery, AL 36117. Offers behavioral leadership and management (MA); Biblical studies (MA, PhD); family therapy (D Min); leadership and management (MS); marriage and family therapy (M Div, MA, PhD); ministerial leadership (M Div, MS); pastoral counseling (M Div, MS); professional counseling (M Div, MA, PhD); theology (M Div, D Min). Part-time and evening/weekend programs available. Postbaccalaureate distance learning degree programs offered (no on-campus study). *Faculty:* 20 full-time (2 women), 7 part-time/adjunct (6 women). *Students:* 110 full-time (58 women), 224 part-time (139 women); includes 139 minority (133 Black or African American, non-Hispanic/Latino; 3 Asian, non-Hispanic/Latino; 3 Hispanic/Latino). Average age 35. 69 applicants, 75% accepted. In 2014, 72 master's, 11 doctorates awarded. *Degree requirements:* For master's, one foreign language, comprehensive exam (for some programs), thesis (for some programs); for doctorate, comprehensive exam (for some programs), thesis/dissertation (for some programs). *Entrance requirements:* For master's, official transcript showing an earned 4-year BA or BS from regionally- or nationally-accredited institution; for doctorate, official transcript showing earned graduate degree from regionally- or nationally-accredited institution; writing sample (e.g. career monograph, published journal article, term paper from master's degree or doctoral dissertation); interview. Additional exam requirements/recommendations for international students: Required—TOEFL. *Application deadline:* For fall admission, 9/1 priority date for domestic students; for spring admission, 1/1 priority date for domestic students. Applications are processed on a rolling basis. Application fee: $50. Electronic applications accepted. *Financial support:* In 2014–15, 102 students received support. Federal Work-Study and scholarships/grants available. Support available to part-time students. Financial award applicants required to submit FAFSA. *Faculty research:* Technology and mental healthcare, resilience in black families, theology and congregational ministry. *Unit head:* Brooks Housley, Student Affairs Coordinator, 888-790-8080 Ext. 2, Fax: 334-387-3878, E-mail: brookshousley@amridgeuniversity.edu. *Application contact:* Kristen Holcomb, Admissions Officer, 888-790-8080 Ext. 1, Fax: 334-387-3878, E-mail: admissions@amridgeuniversity.edu.

Andrews University, School of Graduate Studies, School of Education, Department of Graduate Psychology and Counseling, Program in Community Counseling, Berrien Springs, MI 49104. Offers clinical mental health counseling (MA); community counseling (MA). *Students:* 24 full-time (17 women), 1 (woman) part-time; includes 9 minority (5 Black or African American, non-Hispanic/Latino; 1 American Indian or Alaska Native, non-Hispanic/Latino; 1 Asian, non-Hispanic/Latino; 2 Hispanic/Latino), 5 international. Average age 32. 27 applicants, 56% accepted, 10 enrolled. In 2014, 4 master's awarded. *Degree requirements:* For master's, thesis optional. *Entrance requirements:* For master's, GRE. Additional exam requirements/recommendations for international students: Required—TOEFL (minimum score 550 paper-based). Application fee: $40. Tuition and fees vary according to course level. *Unit head:* Dr. Nancy Carbonell, Coordinator, 269-471-3472. *Application contact:* Monica Wringer, Supervisor of Graduate Admission, 800-253-2874, Fax: 269-471-6321, E-mail: graduate@andrews.edu.

Andrews University, School of Graduate Studies, School of Education, Department of Graduate Psychology and Counseling, Program in Counseling Psychology, Berrien Springs, MI 49104. Offers PhD. *Students:* 21 full-time (18 women), 2 part-time (both women); includes 8 minority (6 Black or African American, non-Hispanic/Latino; 1 Hispanic/Latino; 1 Two or more races, non-Hispanic/Latino), 4 international. Average age 36. 10 applicants, 50% accepted, 2 enrolled. In 2014, 2 doctorates awarded. *Degree requirements:* For doctorate, thesis/dissertation. *Entrance requirements:* Additional exam requirements/recommendations for international students: Required—TOEFL (minimum score 550 paper-based). Application fee: $40. Tuition and fees vary according to course level. *Unit head:* Dr. Carole Woolford, Coordinator, 269-471-6074. *Application contact:* Monica Wringer, Supervisor of Graduate Admission, 800-253-2874, Fax: 269-471-6321, E-mail: graduate@andrews.edu.

Angelo State University, College of Graduate Studies, College of Arts and Sciences, Department of Psychology, Sociology and Social Work, San Angelo, TX 76909. Offers psychology (MS), including applied psychology, counseling psychology, industrial and organizational psychology. Part-time and evening/weekend programs available. *Degree requirements:* For master's, comprehensive exam, thesis optional. *Entrance requirements:* For master's, GRE General Test (for industrial and organizational

psychology only), essay, letters of recommendation (for industrial and organizational psychology only). Additional exam requirements/recommendations for international students: Required—TOEFL or IELTS. Electronic applications accepted.

Anna Maria College, Graduate Division, Program in Counseling Psychology, Paxton, MA 01612. Offers counseling psychology (MA). Part-time and evening/weekend programs available. *Degree requirements:* For master's, comprehensive exam, practicum. *Entrance requirements:* Additional exam requirements/recommendations for international students: Required—TOEFL (minimum score 500 paper-based). Electronic applications accepted.

Antioch University Midwest, Graduate Programs, Individualized Liberal and Professional Studies Program, Yellow Springs, OH 45387-1609. Offers liberal and professional studies (MA), including counseling, creative writing, education, liberal studies, management, modern literature, psychology, visual arts. Part-time and evening/weekend programs available. Postbaccalaureate distance learning degree programs offered (minimal on-campus study). *Degree requirements:* For master's, thesis or alternative. *Entrance requirements:* For master's, resume, goal statement, interview. Electronic applications accepted. *Expenses:* Contact institution.

Antioch University New England, Graduate School, Department of Applied Psychology, Program in Clinical Mental Health Counseling, Keene, NH 03431-3552. Offers clinical mental health counseling (MA); substance abuse counseling (MA). *Accreditation:* ACA. *Degree requirements:* For master's, internship, practicum. *Entrance requirements:* For master's, previous course work and work experience in psychology. Additional exam requirements/recommendations for international students: Required—TOEFL (minimum score 550 paper-based). Electronic applications accepted. *Expenses:* Contact institution. *Faculty research:* Multicultural issues in field supervision.

Appalachian State University, Cratis D. Williams Graduate School, Department of Human Development and Psychological Counseling, Boone, NC 28608. Offers clinical mental health counseling (MA); college student development (MA); marriage and family therapy (MA); school counseling (MA). *Accreditation:* AAMFT/COAMFTE; ACA; NCATE. Part-time programs available. *Degree requirements:* For master's, comprehensive exam (for some programs), thesis optional, internships. *Entrance requirements:* For master's, GRE General Test, 3 letters of recommendation. Additional exam requirements/recommendations for international students: Required—TOEFL (minimum score 570 paper-based; 79 iBT), IELTS (minimum score 6.5). Electronic applications accepted. *Faculty research:* Multicultural counseling, addictions counseling, play therapy, expressive arts, child and adolescent therapy, sexual abuse counseling.

Argosy University, Chicago, College of Psychology and Behavioral Sciences, Doctoral Program in Clinical Psychology, Chicago, IL 60601. Offers child and adolescent psychology (Psy D); client-centered and experiential psychotherapies (Psy D); diversity and multicultural psychology (Psy D); family psychology (Psy D); forensic psychology (Psy D); health psychology (Psy D); neuropsychology (Psy D); organizational consulting (Psy D); psychoanalytic psychology (Psy D); psychology and spirituality (Psy D). *Accreditation:* APA.

Argosy University, Chicago, College of Psychology and Behavioral Sciences, Program in Counseling Psychology, Chicago, IL 60601. Offers counselor education and supervision (Ed D). *Accreditation:* ACA. Postbaccalaureate distance learning degree programs offered (minimal on-campus study).

Argosy University, Denver, College of Psychology and Behavioral Sciences, Denver, CO 80231. Offers clinical mental health counseling (MA); clinical psychology (MA, Psy D); counseling psychology (Ed D); counselor education and supervision (Ed D); forensic psychology (MA); industrial organizational psychology (MA); marriage and family therapy (MA, DMFT).

Argosy University, Hawai`i, College of Psychology and Behavioral Sciences, Program in Counseling Psychology, Honolulu, HI 96813. Offers Ed D.

Argosy University, Inland Empire, College of Psychology and Behavioral Sciences, Ontario, CA 91761. Offers clinical psychology/marriage and family therapy (MA); counseling psychology (Ed D); counseling psychology/marriage and family therapy (MA); forensic psychology (MA); industrial organizational psychology (MA); sport-exercise psychology (MA).

Argosy University, Los Angeles, College of Psychology and Behavioral Sciences, Santa Monica, CA 90045. Offers clinical psychology/marriage and family therapy (MA); counseling psychology (Ed D); counseling psychology/marriage and family therapy (MA); forensic psychology (MA).

Argosy University, Nashville, College of Psychology and Behavioral Sciences, Nashville, TN 37214. Offers counselor education and supervision (Ed D); mental health counseling (MA).

Argosy University, Orange County, College of Psychology and Behavioral Sciences, Program in Counseling Psychology, Orange, CA 92868. Offers counseling psychology (Ed D); marriage and family therapy (MA).

Argosy University, Phoenix, College of Psychology and Behavioral Sciences, Program in Mental Health Counseling, Phoenix, AZ 85021. Offers MA.

Argosy University, Salt Lake City, College of Psychology and Behavioral Sciences, Draper, UT 84020. Offers counseling psychology (Ed D); counselor education and supervision (Ed D); forensic psychology (MA); marriage and family therapy (MA, DMFT); mental health counseling (MA).

Argosy University, San Diego, College of Psychology and Behavioral Sciences, San Diego, CA 92108. Offers clinical psychology/marriage and family therapy (MA); counseling psychology (Ed D); counseling psychology/marriage and family therapy (MA); forensic psychology (MA).

Argosy University, San Francisco Bay Area, College of Psychology and Behavioral Sciences, Program in Counseling Psychology, Alameda, CA 94501. Offers MA, Ed D.

Argosy University, Sarasota, College of Psychology and Behavioral Sciences, Sarasota, FL 34235. Offers community counseling (MA); counseling psychology (Ed D); counselor education and supervision (Ed D); forensic psychology (MA); marriage and family therapy (MA); mental health counseling (MA); pastoral community counseling (Ed D).

Argosy University, Schaumburg, College of Behavioral Sciences, Schaumburg, IL 60173-5403. Offers clinical mental health counseling (MA); forensic psychology (MA, Post-Graduate Certificate); industrial organizational psychology (MA); sport-exercise psychology (MA). *Accreditation:* ACA; APA.

Argosy University, Seattle, College of Psychology and Behavioral Sciences, Program in Counseling Psychology, Seattle, WA 98121. Offers MA, Ed D.

Argosy University, Tampa, College of Psychology and Behavioral Sciences, Tampa, FL 33607. Offers clinical psychology (MA, Psy D), including clinical psychology; counselor education and supervision (Ed D); industrial organizational psychology (MA); marriage and family therapy (MA); mental health counseling (MA).

Argosy University, Washington DC, College of Psychology and Behavioral Sciences, Arlington, VA 22209. Offers clinical psychology (MA, Psy D), including child and family

psychology (Psy D), diversity and multicultural psychology (Psy D), forensic psychology (Psy D), health and neuropsychology (Psy D); community counseling (MA); counseling psychology (Ed D), including counselor education and supervision; counselor education and supervision (Ed D); forensic psychology (MA). *Accreditation:* APA.

Arizona State University at the Tempe campus, School of Letters and Sciences, Program in Counseling Psychology, Tempe, AZ 85287-0811. Offers PhD. *Accreditation:* APA. *Degree requirements:* For doctorate, comprehensive exam, thesis/dissertation, internship/practica, interactive Program of Study (iPOS) submitted before completing 50 percent of required credit hours. *Entrance requirements:* For doctorate, GRE, minimum GPA of 3.0 or equivalent in last 2 years of work leading to bachelor's degree, 3 letters of recommendation, personal statement describing history and academic/professional goals, completed Biographical Information form, 7-page sample of expository writing. Additional exam requirements/recommendations for international students: Required—TOEFL, IELTS, or PTE. Electronic applications accepted.

Arkansas State University, Graduate School, College of Education and Behavioral Science, Department of Psychology and Counseling, State University, AR 72467. Offers clinical mental health counseling (Certificate); college student personnel services (MS); psychology and counseling (Ed S); rehabilitation counseling (MRC); school counseling (MSE); student affairs (Certificate). *Accreditation:* ACA (one or more programs are accredited); CORE (one or more programs are accredited); NCATE. Part-time programs available. *Faculty:* 15 full-time (9 women). *Students:* 57 full-time (36 women), 51 part-time (38 women); includes 21 minority (19 Black or African American, non-Hispanic/Latino; 1 Hispanic/Latino; 1 Two or more races, non-Hispanic/Latino), 1 international. Average age 30. 102 applicants, 54% accepted, 48 enrolled. In 2014, 22 master's, 22 other advanced degrees awarded. *Degree requirements:* For master's and other advanced degree, comprehensive exam, thesis or alternative. *Entrance requirements:* For master's, GRE General Test or MAT (for MSE), appropriate bachelor's degree, interview, letters of reference, official transcripts, immunization records, written statement, 2-3 page autobiography; for other advanced degree, GRE General Test, interview, master's degree, letters of reference, official transcript, personal statement, immunization records. Additional exam requirements/recommendations for international students: Required—TOEFL (minimum score 550 paper-based; 79 iBT), IELTS (minimum score 6), PTE (minimum score 56). *Application deadline:* Applications are processed on a rolling basis. Application fee: $30 ($40 for international students). Electronic applications accepted. *Expenses:* Tuition, state resident: full-time $4392; part-time $244 per credit hour. Tuition, nonresident: full-time $8784; part-time $488 per credit hour. *International tuition:* $9484 full-time. *Required fees:* $1134; $63 per credit hour. $25 per term. Tuition and fees vary according to course load and program. *Financial support:* In 2014–15, 8 students received support. Teaching assistantships, career-related internships or fieldwork, scholarships/grants, and unspecified assistantships available. Financial award application deadline: 7/1; financial award applicants required to submit FAFSA. *Unit head:* Dr. Kris Biondolillo, Interim Chair, 870-972-3064, Fax: 870-972-3962, E-mail: kdbiondo@astate.edu. *Application contact:* Vickey Ring, Graduate Admissions Coordinator, 870-972-3029, Fax: 870-972-3857, E-mail: vickeyring@astate.edu.
Website: http://www.astate.edu/college/education/departments/psychology-and-counseling/index.dot

Ashland Theological Seminary, Graduate Programs, Ashland, OH 44805. Offers biblical and theological studies (MAR); Biblical, historical and theological studies (MA), including Anabaptism and Pietism, Christian theology, church history, New Testament, Old Testament; Christian ministry (MAPT), including Black church studies (M Div, MAPT, D Min), chaplaincy (M Div, MAPT), Christian formation (M Div, MAPT), evangelism/church renewal and missions (M Div, MAPT), general ministry (M Div, MAPT), pastoral counseling and care (M Div, MAPT), specialized ministry, spiritual formation (M Div, MAPT, D Min); Christian studies (Diploma); clinical counseling (MACC); counseling (MAC); ministry (D Min), including Black church studies (M Div, MAPT, D Min), Canadian church studies, formational counseling, independent design, spiritual formation (M Div, MAPT, D Min), transformational leadership, Wesleyan practices; pastoral ministry (M Div), including Biblical studies - Old or New Testament, Black church studies (M Div, MAPT, D Min), chaplaincy (M Div, MAPT), Christian formation (M Div, MAPT), evangelism/church renewal and missions (M Div, MAPT), general Biblical studies, general ministry (M Div, MAPT), pastoral counseling and care (M Div, MAPT), spiritual formation (M Div, MAPT, D Min), theology or history. MAC program offered in Detroit, MI. *Accreditation:* ATS. Part-time programs available. *Degree requirements:* For master's, 2 foreign languages, comprehensive exam (for some programs), thesis (for some programs); for doctorate, thesis/dissertation. *Entrance requirements:* For master's, bachelor's degree from accredited institution with a minimum undergraduate GPA of 2.75; for doctorate, M Div, minimum undergraduate GPA of 3.0. Additional exam requirements/recommendations for international students: Required—TOEFL (minimum score 500 paper-based; 65 iBT). Electronic applications accepted. *Faculty research:* Semitic languages and linguistics, rhetorical and social-scientific criticism, Anabaptist studies, inner spiritual healing, African-American clergy in film and literature.

Assumption College, Counseling Psychology Program, Worcester, MA 01609-1296. Offers child and family interventions (MA); cognitive-behavioral therapies (MA); counseling psychology (CAGS); general psychology (MA). Part-time and evening/weekend programs available. *Faculty:* 5 full-time (2 women), 9 part-time/adjunct (2 women). *Students:* 48 full-time (37 women), 35 part-time (33 women); includes 10 minority (3 Black or African American, non-Hispanic/Latino; 3 Asian, non-Hispanic/Latino; 2 Hispanic/Latino; 2 Two or more races, non-Hispanic/Latino), 3 international. Average age 27. 78 applicants, 60% accepted, 15 enrolled. In 2014, 42 master's, 2 other advanced degrees awarded. *Degree requirements:* For master's, comprehensive exam, internship, practicum; for CAGS, comprehensive exam. *Entrance requirements:* For master's, 3 letters of recommendation, resume, essay, psychology prerequisite coursework; for CAGS, 3 letters of recommendation, resume, interview, essay, master's degree in counseling psychology or mental health counseling. Additional exam requirements/recommendations for international students: Required—TOEFL (minimum score 540 paper-based; 76 iBT), IELTS (minimum score 6). *Application deadline:* For fall admission, 3/6 for domestic and international students; for winter admission, 2/1 for domestic students; for spring admission, 10/3 for domestic and international students; for summer admission, 2/6 for domestic and international students. Application fee: $30. Electronic applications accepted. *Expenses: Tuition:* Full-time $10,620; part-time $590 per credit. *Required fees:* $20 per term. Full-time tuition and fees vary according to course load and program. *Financial support:* In 2014–15, 21 students received support, including 16 fellowships with full tuition reimbursements available; tuition waivers (full and partial), unspecified assistantships, and institutional discounts also available. Financial award application deadline: 3/7; financial award applicants required to submit FAFSA. *Faculty research:* Mood disorders, adjustment to life-threatening illness, perception of movement, socioemotional development of young children, discovery versus disclosure. *Unit head:* Dr. Leonard A. Doerfler, Director, 508-767-7549, Fax: 508-767-7263, E-mail: doerfler@assumption.edu. *Application contact:* Dr. Landy Johnson, Director of Operations for Graduate and Professional Studies, 508-767-7666, Fax: 508-767-7030, E-mail: graduate@assumption.edu.
Website: http://graduate.assumption.edu/counseling-psychology/masterofarts

Athabasca University, Graduate Centre for Applied Psychology, Athabasca, AB T9S 3A3, Canada. Offers art therapy (MC); career counseling (MC); counseling (Advanced Certificate); counseling psychology (MC); school counseling (MC).

Austin Peay State University, College of Graduate Studies, College of Behavioral and Health Sciences, Department of Psychology, Program in Mental Health Counseling, Clarksville, TN 37044. Offers MS. *Degree requirements:* For master's, comprehensive exam.

Avila University, Department of Psychology, Kansas City, MO 64145-1698. Offers counseling psychology (MS). Part-time and evening/weekend programs available. *Faculty:* 7 full-time (6 women), 14 part-time/adjunct (8 women). *Students:* 131 full-time (104 women), 24 part-time (20 women); includes 54 minority (38 Black or African American, non-Hispanic/Latino; 2 American Indian or Alaska Native, non-Hispanic/Latino; 1 Asian, non-Hispanic/Latino; 10 Hispanic/Latino; 3 Two or more races, non-Hispanic/Latino), 1 international. Average age 33. 75 applicants, 61% accepted, 34 enrolled. In 2014, 37 master's awarded. *Degree requirements:* For master's, thesis optional, capstone project. *Entrance requirements:* For master's, bachelor's degree, minimum GPA of 3.0 in all previous undergraduate and graduate coursework, 2 letters of recommendation, letter of intent, resume. Additional exam requirements/recommendations for international students: Required—TOEFL (minimum score 80 iBT). *Application deadline:* Applications are processed on a rolling basis. Application fee: $0. Electronic applications accepted. *Expenses: Tuition:* Full-time $8604; part-time $478 per credit hour. *Required fees:* $684; $38 per credit hour. Tuition and fees vary according to program. *Financial support:* In 2014–15, 15 students received support, including 6 research assistantships with full and partial tuition reimbursements available; career-related internships or fieldwork, scholarships/grants, and unspecified assistantships also available. Support available to part-time students. Financial award applicants required to submit FAFSA. *Faculty research:* Emotional regulation, embodied cognition, mindful wellness, trauma and restorative justice, psychophysiology of public speaking anxiety. *Unit head:* Aaron R. Coffey, Director of Graduate Psychology Enrollment Management, 816-501-0419, Fax: 816-501-2455, E-mail: aaron.coffey@avila.edu. *Application contact:* Metra Augustin, Graduate Admissions Advisor, 816-501-2968, Fax: 816-501-2455, E-mail: gradpsych@avila.edu.
Website: http://www.avila.edu/psychology/

Ball State University, Graduate School, Teachers College, Department of Counseling Psychology and Guidance Services, Program in Counseling Psychology, Muncie, IN 47306-1099. Offers MA, PhD. *Accreditation:* ACA; APA. *Students:* 97 full-time (68 women), 25 part-time (16 women); includes 9 minority (4 Black or African American, non-Hispanic/Latino; 2 Asian, non-Hispanic/Latino; 3 Hispanic/Latino), 9 international. Average age 26. 96 applicants, 47% accepted, 41 enrolled. In 2014, 30 master's, 12 doctorates awarded. *Degree requirements:* For doctorate, thesis/dissertation. *Entrance requirements:* For doctorate, GRE General Test, interview, minimum graduate GPA of 3.2, resume. Application fee: $50. *Financial support:* In 2014–15, 66 students received support, including 23 research assistantships with partial tuition reimbursements available (averaging $9,141 per year), 26 teaching assistantships with partial tuition reimbursements available (averaging $8,726 per year); unspecified assistantships also available. Financial award application deadline: 3/1. *Unit head:* Dr. Sharon Bowman, Head, 765-285-8040, E-mail: sbowman@bsu.edu. *Application contact:* Dr. Robert Morris, Associate Provost for Research and Dean of the Graduate School, 765-285-1300, E-mail: rmorris@bsu.edu.
Website: http://www.bsu.edu/teachers/counseling/cpsy/

Baruch College of the City University of New York, Weissman School of Arts and Sciences, Program in Mental Health Counseling, New York, NY 10010-5585. Offers MA. *Faculty:* 10 full-time (6 women), 2 part-time/adjunct (both women). *Students:* 36 full-time (33 women); includes 11 minority (5 Black or African American, non-Hispanic/Latino; 1 American Indian or Alaska Native, non-Hispanic/Latino; 2 Asian, non-Hispanic/Latino; 3 Hispanic/Latino), 1 international. Average age 28. 76 applicants, 38% accepted, 18 enrolled. In 2014, 18 master's awarded. *Entrance requirements:* For master's, bachelor's degree from accredited institution, minimum undergraduate GPA of 3.2, relevant professional or volunteer experience, minimum of 15 credits in psychology, personal statement, three letters of recommendation, official transcript. Additional exam requirements/recommendations for international students: Required—TOEFL. *Application deadline:* For fall admission, 3/1 for domestic and international students. Application fee: $135. Electronic applications accepted. *Financial support:* Career-related internships or fieldwork and Federal Work-Study available. *Faculty research:* Character analysis; shame and guilt; self-perceptions and moral affect; pedagogical development; self-efficacy and cognitive performance; sleep loss, fatigue and effort; environmental sustainability; cultural competence; behavioral obesity treatment; ADHD. *Unit head:* Dr. Nita Lutwak, Director, 646-312-1000. *Application contact:* Michael J. Lovaglio, Director of Graduate Programs, 646-312-3897, Fax: 646-312-3871, E-mail: wsas.graduate.studies@baruch.cuny.edu.
Website: http://www.baruch.cuny.edu/wsas/academics/graduate_studies/mhc/

Bastyr University, School of Natural Health Arts and Sciences, Kenmore, WA 98028-4966. Offers counseling psychology (MA); holistic landscape design (Certificate); midwifery (MS); nutrition (MS); nutrition and clinical health psychology (MS). *Accreditation:* AND. Part-time programs available. *Students:* 373 full-time (334 women), 39 part-time (37 women); includes 71 minority (11 Black or African American, non-Hispanic/Latino; 1 American Indian or Alaska Native, non-Hispanic/Latino; 24 Asian, non-Hispanic/Latino; 14 Hispanic/Latino; 21 Two or more races, non-Hispanic/Latino), 20 international. Average age 30. *Degree requirements:* For master's, thesis optional. *Entrance requirements:* For master's, 1-2 years' basic sciences course work (depending on program). Additional exam requirements/recommendations for international students: Required—TOEFL (minimum score 550 paper-based; 79 iBT). *Application deadline:* For fall admission, 3/15 priority date for domestic and international students. Applications are processed on a rolling basis. Application fee: $75. *Financial support:* In 2014–15, 47 students received support. Career-related internships or fieldwork, Federal Work-Study, and scholarships/grants available. Support available to part-time students. Financial award application deadline: 4/15; financial award applicants required to submit FAFSA. *Faculty research:* Whole-food nutrition for type 2 diabetes; meditation in end-of-life care; stress management; Qi Gong, Tai Chi and yoga for older adults; Echinacea and immunology. *Unit head:* Dr. Timothy Callahan, Vice President and Provost, 425-602-3110, Fax: 425-823-6222. *Application contact:* Admissions Office, 425-602-3330, Fax: 425-602-3090, E-mail: admissions@bastyr.edu.
Website: http://www.bastyr.edu/academics/schools-departments/school-natural-health-arts-sciences

Bay Path University, Program in Developmental Psychology, Longmeadow, MA 01106-2292. Offers developmental psychology (MS); mental health counseling (MS). Part-time and evening/weekend programs available. *Students:* 3 full-time (all women), 10 part-time (all women); includes 4 minority (3 Black or African American, non-Hispanic/Latino; 1 Asian, non-Hispanic/Latino). Average age 35. 13 applicants, 77% accepted, 9 enrolled. In 2014, 11 master's awarded. *Degree requirements:* For master's, nine core courses (27 credits) and three elective courses (9 credits); 160 hours of community-based field work. *Entrance requirements:* For master's, bachelor's degree in psychology or related field; minimum cumulative GPA of 3.0; working knowledge of

statistics, research methods, abnormal psychology, personality, and developmental psychology (strongly recommended). *Application deadline:* Applications are processed on a rolling basis. Application fee: $45. Electronic applications accepted. Application fee is waived when completed online. *Financial support:* In 2014–15, 3 students received support. Scholarships/grants available. Financial award applicants required to submit FAFSA. *Unit head:* Dr. Mark Benander, Program Director, 413-565-1332. *Application contact:* Diane Ranaldi, Dean of Graduate Admissions, 413-565-1332, Fax: 413-565-1250, E-mail: dranaldi@baypath.edu.
Website: http://graduate.baypath.edu/Graduate-Programs/Programs-On-Campus/MS-Programs/Developmental-Psychology

Bethel University, Graduate School, St. Paul, MN 55112-6999. Offers autism spectrum disorders (Certificate); business administration (MBA); communication (MA); counseling psychology (MA); educational leadership (Ed D); gerontology (MA); international baccalaureate education (Certificate); K-12 education (MA); literacy education (MA, Certificate); nurse educator (Certificate); nurse leader (Certificate); nurse-midwifery (MS); nursing (MS); physician assistant (MS); postsecondary teaching (Certificate); special education (MA); strategic leadership (MA); teaching (MA). Part-time and evening/weekend programs available. Postbaccalaureate distance learning degree programs offered (no on-campus study). *Faculty:* 13 full-time (7 women), 89 part-time/adjunct (43 women). *Students:* 739 full-time (484 women), 337 part-time (219 women); includes 175 minority (96 Black or African American, non-Hispanic/Latino; 2 American Indian or Alaska Native, non-Hispanic/Latino; 40 Asian, non-Hispanic/Latino; 20 Hispanic/Latino; 1 Native Hawaiian or other Pacific Islander, non-Hispanic/Latino; 16 Two or more races, non-Hispanic/Latino), 26 international. Average age 35. 1,354 applicants, 42% accepted, 421 enrolled. In 2014, 166 master's, 9 doctorates, 11 other advanced degrees awarded. *Degree requirements:* For master's, comprehensive exam (for some programs), thesis (for some programs); for doctorate, comprehensive exam, thesis/dissertation. *Entrance requirements:* Additional exam requirements/recommendations for international students: Required—TOEFL (minimum score 550 paper-based, 80 iBT) or IELTS. *Application deadline:* Applications are processed on a rolling basis. Application fee: $0. Electronic applications accepted. *Financial support:* Teaching assistantships, career-related internships or fieldwork, and scholarships/grants available. Support available to part-time students. Financial award applicants required to submit FAFSA. *Unit head:* Dick Crombie, Vice-President/Dean, 651-635-8000, Fax: 651-635-8004, E-mail: gs@bethel.edu. *Application contact:* Director of Admissions, 651-635-8000, Fax: 651-635-8004, E-mail: gs@bethel.edu.
Website: https://www.bethel.edu/graduate/

Boston College, Lynch Graduate School of Education, Program in Counseling, Chestnut Hill, MA 02467-3800. Offers counseling psychology (PhD); mental health counseling (MA); school counseling (MA); MA/MA. *Accreditation:* APA (one or more programs are accredited). Terminal master's awarded for partial completion of doctoral program. *Degree requirements:* For master's, comprehensive exam; for doctorate, comprehensive exam, thesis/dissertation. *Entrance requirements:* For master's and doctorate, GRE General Test. Additional exam requirements/recommendations for international students: Required—TOEFL (minimum score 550 paper-based; 100 iBT). Electronic applications accepted. *Faculty research:* Reducing non-academic barriers to learning; race, gender, culture and social class issues in mental health; domestic violence; career development; community intervention and prevention.

Boston Graduate School of Psychoanalysis, Master's Programs, Brookline, MA 02446-4602. Offers mental health counseling (MA); psychoanalysis (MA); psychoanalysis, society and culture (MA). Part-time programs available. Terminal master's awarded for partial completion of doctoral program. *Degree requirements:* For master's, thesis. *Entrance requirements:* For master's, interview, BA, personal statement, writing sample, 3 letters of recommendation. Additional exam requirements/recommendations for international students: Required—TOEFL (minimum score 550 paper-based; 79 iBT). *Faculty research:* Qualitative and narrative research methodologies, ethical conflicts and dual loyalties in health professionals, psychodynamics of social processes, treatment approaches for intractable patients, psychoanalytic research methodologies.

Boston University, School of Medicine, Division of Graduate Medical Sciences, Program in Mental Health Counseling and Behavioral Medicine, Boston, MA 02215. Offers MA. *Expenses:* Tuition: Full-time $45,686; part-time $1428 per credit hour. *Required fees:* $660; $60 per semester. Tuition and fees vary according to program. *Faculty research:* HIV/AIDS, trauma, behavioral medicine (obesity, breast cancer), neurosciences, autism, serious mental illness, sports psychology. *Unit head:* Dr. Stephen Brady, Director, 617-414-2320, Fax: 617-414-2323, E-mail: sbrady@bu.edu. *Application contact:* Bernice Mark, Administrative Assistant, 617-414-2328, E-mail: nicey@bu.edu.
Website: http://www.bumc.bu.edu/mhbm/

Bowie State University, Graduate Programs, Program in Counseling Psychology, Bowie, MD 20715-9465. Offers MA. Part-time and evening/weekend programs available. *Faculty:* 8 full-time (3 women), 8 part-time/adjunct (3 women). *Students:* 50 full-time (42 women), 96 part-time (70 women); includes 127 minority (121 Black or African American, non-Hispanic/Latino; 2 Asian, non-Hispanic/Latino; 4 Hispanic/Latino). Average age 34. 83 applicants, 88% accepted, 60 enrolled. In 2014, 39 master's awarded. *Degree requirements:* For master's, comprehensive exam, thesis optional, research paper, practicum. *Entrance requirements:* For master's, minimum GPA of 2.5, 3 recommendations. *Application deadline:* For fall admission, 4/1 priority date for domestic and international students; for spring admission, 11/1 priority date for domestic and international students. Applications are processed on a rolling basis. Application fee: $40. Electronic applications accepted. *Expenses:* Tuition, state resident: full-time $8928; part-time $372 per credit. Tuition, nonresident: full-time $16,176; part-time $674 per credit. *Required fees:* $2141. *Financial support:* Career-related internships or fieldwork and institutionally sponsored loans available. Support available to part-time students. Financial award application deadline: 4/1. *Unit head:* Dr. Cheryl Blackman, Chairperson, 301-860-3257, E-mail: cblackman@bowiestate.edu. *Application contact:* Angela Issac, Information Contact, 301-860-4000.

Bowie State University, Graduate Programs, Program in Mental Health Counseling, Bowie, MD 20715-9465. Offers MA. Part-time and evening/weekend programs available. *Students:* 26 full-time (23 women), 39 part-time (35 women); includes 55 minority (51 Black or African American, non-Hispanic/Latino; 3 Asian, non-Hispanic/Latino; 1 Hispanic/Latino), 9 international. Average age 22. 10 applicants, 90% accepted, 8 enrolled. *Degree requirements:* For master's, comprehensive exam. *Entrance requirements:* For master's, 3 letters of recommendation, minimum GPA of 3.0, 12 undergraduate credit hours in counseling or psychology. *Application deadline:* For fall admission, 4/1 priority date for domestic and international students; for spring admission, 11/1 priority date for domestic and international students. Applications are processed on a rolling basis. Application fee: $50. Electronic applications accepted. *Expenses:* Tuition, state resident: full-time $8928; part-time $372 per credit. Tuition, nonresident: full-time $16,176; part-time $674 per credit. *Required fees:* $2141. *Unit head:* Rhonda Jeter-Tuilley, Chairperson, 301-860-3233, E-mail: rjeter@bowiestate.edu. *Application contact:* Angela Issac, Information Contact, 301-860-4000.

Bowling Green State University, Graduate College, College of Education and Human Development, School of Education and Intervention Services, Intervention Services Division, Program in Counseling, Bowling Green, OH 43403. Offers mental health counseling (MA); school counseling (M Ed). *Accreditation:* ACA; NCATE. Part-time programs available. *Degree requirements:* For master's, thesis or alternative. *Entrance requirements:* For master's, GRE General Test. Additional exam requirements/recommendations for international students: Required—TOEFL. Electronic applications accepted. *Faculty research:* Perfectionism, multicultural counseling, suicide, ethics and legal issues related to counseling, play therapy.

Bradley University, Graduate School, College of Education and Health Sciences, Department of Leadership in Education, Human Services, and Counseling, Peoria, IL 61625-0002. Offers human development counseling (MA), including clinical mental health counseling, school counseling; leadership in educational administration (MA); non-profit leadership (MA). *Accreditation:* ACA; NCATE. Part-time and evening/weekend programs available. *Faculty:* 8 full-time (5 women), 5 part-time/adjunct (2 women). *Students:* 43 full-time (34 women), 35 part-time (30 women); includes 4 minority (1 Black or African American, non-Hispanic/Latino; 1 American Indian or Alaska Native, non-Hispanic/Latino; 2 Asian, non-Hispanic/Latino), 1 international. 42 applicants, 71% accepted, 21 enrolled. In 2014, 26 master's awarded. *Degree requirements:* For master's, comprehensive exam, thesis optional. *Entrance requirements:* For master's, GRE General Test or MAT, interview, 3 letters of recommendation. Additional exam requirements/recommendations for international students: Required—TOEFL (minimum score 550 paper-based; 79 iBT), IELTS (minimum score 6.5). *Application deadline:* For fall admission, 5/15 priority date for domestic and international students; for spring admission, 10/15 priority date for domestic and international students. Applications are processed on a rolling basis. Application fee: $40 ($50 for international students). Electronic applications accepted. *Expenses:* Tuition: Full-time $14,580; part-time $810 per credit. *Required fees:* $224. Full-time tuition and fees vary according to course load. *Financial support:* In 2014–15, 6 research assistantships with full and partial tuition reimbursements (averaging $19,640 per year) were awarded; career-related internships or fieldwork, scholarships/grants, tuition waivers (partial), and unspecified assistantships also available. Support available to part-time students. Financial award application deadline: 4/1. *Unit head:* Dr. Christopher Rybak, Chair, 309-677-3193, E-mail: cjr@bradley.edu. *Application contact:* Kayla Carroll, Director of International Admissions and Student Services, 309-677-2375, E-mail: klcarroll@fsmail.bradley.edu.

Brandman University, School of Arts and Sciences, Irvine, CA 92618. Offers psychology (MA), including counseling, marriage and family therapy.

Brigham Young University, Graduate Studies, David O. McKay School of Education, Department of Counseling Psychology and Special Education, Provo, UT 84602-1001. Offers counseling psychology (PhD); school psychology (Ed S); special education (MS). Part-time and evening/weekend programs available. *Faculty:* 12 full-time (3 women), 9 part-time/adjunct (4 women). *Students:* 60 full-time (40 women), 27 part-time (22 women); includes 15 minority (2 Black or African American, non-Hispanic/Latino; 3 American Indian or Alaska Native, non-Hispanic/Latino; 2 Asian, non-Hispanic/Latino; 7 Hispanic/Latino; 1 Native Hawaiian or other Pacific Islander, non-Hispanic/Latino), 5 international. Average age 29. 65 applicants, 25% accepted, 16 enrolled. In 2014, 5 master's, 3 doctorates, 6 other advanced degrees awarded. *Degree requirements:* For master's and Ed S, comprehensive exam, thesis; for doctorate, comprehensive exam, thesis/dissertation. *Entrance requirements:* For master's, GRE General Test or MAT, minimum cumulative GPA of 3.0 in undergraduate coursework; for doctorate and Ed S, GRE General Test, minimum cumulative GPA of 3.0 in undergraduate coursework. Additional exam requirements/recommendations for international students: Required—TOEFL (minimum score 580 paper-based; 85 iBT), IELTS (minimum score 7). *Application deadline:* For fall admission, 1/15 for domestic and international students. Application fee: $50. Electronic applications accepted. *Expenses:* Expenses: Contact institution. *Financial support:* In 2014–15, 46 students received support, including 42 research assistantships with partial tuition reimbursements available (averaging $8,160 per year), 2 teaching assistantships with partial tuition reimbursements available (averaging $5,320 per year); institutionally sponsored loans and tuition waivers (partial) also available. Financial award application deadline: 3/31. *Faculty research:* Positive behavioral support in schools, spirituality in psychotherapy, multicultural psychology, gender issues in education, crisis management in schools. *Unit head:* Dr. Timothy B. Smith, Professor and Development Chair, 801-422-3857, Fax: 801-422-0198. *Application contact:* Diane E. Hancock, Department Secretary, 801-422-3859, Fax: 801-422-0198, E-mail: diane_hancock@byu.edu.
Website: http://education.byu.edu/cpse/

Brooklyn College of the City University of New York, School of Natural and Behavioral Sciences, Department of Health and Nutrition Sciences, Brooklyn, NY 11210-2889. Offers community health (MA), including community health education, thanatology; grief counseling (CAS); nutrition (MS); public health (MPH), including general public health, health care policy and administration. Part-time and evening/weekend programs available. *Degree requirements:* For master's, thesis or alternative. *Entrance requirements:* For master's, GRE, essay, 2 letters of recommendation. Additional exam requirements/recommendations for international students: Required—TOEFL. Electronic applications accepted. *Faculty research:* Medical ethics, relocation stress, risk reduction, disease prevention, history of public health, computer applications.

Brooklyn College of the City University of New York, School of Natural and Behavioral Sciences, Department of Psychology, Brooklyn, NY 11210-2889. Offers experimental psychology (MA); industrial and organizational psychology (MA), including human relations, organizational behavior; mental health counseling (MA); psychology (PhD). Part-time programs available. *Degree requirements:* For master's, comprehensive exam, thesis (for some programs). *Entrance requirements:* For master's, minimum GPA of 3.0, 2 letters of recommendation, essay; for doctorate, GRE. Additional exam requirements/recommendations for international students: Required—TOEFL (minimum score 520 paper-based; 69 iBT). Electronic applications accepted.

Caldwell University, Graduate Studies, Department of Psychology, Caldwell, NJ 07006-6195. Offers art therapy (MA); counseling (MA), including art therapy, mental health, school counseling; director of school counseling (Post-Master's Certificate); professional counselor (Post-Master's Certificate); school counselor (Post-Master's Certificate). *Accreditation:* ACA. Part-time and evening/weekend programs available. *Faculty:* 6 full-time (4 women), 13 part-time/adjunct (8 women). *Students:* 64 full-time (62 women), 70 part-time (62 women); includes 31 minority (14 Black or African American, non-Hispanic/Latino; 2 Asian, non-Hispanic/Latino; 12 Hispanic/Latino; 3 Two or more races, non-Hispanic/Latino). Average age 34. 83 applicants, 35% accepted, 29 enrolled. In 2014, 64 master's awarded. *Degree requirements:* For master's, comprehensive exam. *Entrance requirements:* For master's, GRE or MAT, interview. *Application deadline:* For fall admission, 7/1 for domestic and international students; for spring admission, 12/1 for domestic and international students. Applications are processed on a rolling basis. Application fee: $40. Electronic applications accepted. *Expenses: Tuition:* Part-time $930 per credit. *Financial support:* Career-related internships or fieldwork available. Financial award applicants required to submit FAFSA.

Counseling Psychology

Faculty research: Counseling, school counseling, art therapy. *Unit head:* Dr. Stacey Solomon, Program Coordinator, 973-618-3387, E-mail: ssolomon@caldwell.edu. *Application contact:* Vilma Mueller, Director of Graduate Studies, 973-618-3544, E-mail: graduate@caldwell.edu.

California Baptist University, Program in Counseling Ministry and Counseling Psychology (Dual Master's), Riverside, CA 92504-3206. Offers MA/MS. Part-time and evening/weekend programs available. *Faculty:* 17 full-time (10 women), 18 part-time/adjunct (10 women). *Students:* 9 full-time (7 women), 1 (woman) part-time; includes 6 minority (2 Asian, non-Hispanic/Latino; 4 Hispanic/Latino). Average age 34. 8 applicants, 25% accepted, 1 enrolled. *Entrance requirements:* Additional exam requirements/recommendations for international students: Required—TOEFL (minimum score 80 iBT). *Application deadline:* For fall admission, 8/1 priority date for domestic students, 7/1 for international students; for spring admission, 12/1 priority date for domestic students, 11/1 for international students. Applications are processed on a rolling basis. Application fee: $45. Electronic applications accepted. *Financial support:* Applicants required to submit CSS PROFILE or FAFSA. *Faculty research:* Law enforcement psychology, neurotheology, organizational neuroscience, integration of theology and behavioral science, cognitive development/cross-cultural psychology. *Unit head:* Dr. Jacqueline Gustafson, Dean, School of Behavioral Sciences, 951-343-4487, E-mail: jcraig@calbaptist.edu. *Application contact:* Dr. Angela Deulen, Director of Counseling Psychology Program, 951-343-4204, Fax: 877-228-8877, E-mail: adeulen@calbaptist.edu.
Website: http://www.calbaptist.edu/mft

California Baptist University, Program in Counseling Psychology, Riverside, CA 92504-3206. Offers counseling psychology (MS); forensic psychology (MS); professional clinical counselor (MS). Part-time and evening/weekend programs available. Postbaccalaureate distance learning degree programs offered (minimal on-campus study). *Faculty:* 16 full-time (10 women), 16 part-time/adjunct (9 women). *Students:* 233 full-time (200 women), 82 part-time (63 women); includes 186 minority (44 Black or African American, non-Hispanic/Latino; 5 American Indian or Alaska Native, non-Hispanic/Latino; 8 Asian, non-Hispanic/Latino; 121 Hispanic/Latino; 1 Native Hawaiian or other Pacific Islander, non-Hispanic/Latino; 7 Two or more races, non-Hispanic/Latino), 4 international. Average age 31. 184 applicants, 61% accepted, 74 enrolled. In 2014, 98 master's awarded. *Degree requirements:* For master's, comprehensive exam, 24 hours (individual) or 50 hours (group) psychotherapy, practicum. *Entrance requirements:* For master's, minimum undergraduate GPA of 2.75; official transcripts; three recommendations; 500-word essay; interview; 3 prerequisite courses completed with minimum C grade. Additional exam requirements/recommendations for international students: Required—TOEFL (minimum score 80 iBT). *Application deadline:* For fall admission, 8/1 priority date for domestic students, 7/1 for international students; for spring admission, 12/1 priority date for domestic students, 11/1 for international students. Applications are processed on a rolling basis. Application fee: $45. Electronic applications accepted. *Expenses:* Expenses: Contact institution. *Financial support:* Institutionally sponsored loans available. Financial award applicants required to submit CSS PROFILE or FAFSA. *Faculty research:* Identify formation, faith integration, psychological assessment, child abuse and child welfare, clinical psychology and crisis intervention techniques. *Unit head:* Dr. Jacqueline Gustafson, Dean, School of Behavioral Sciences, 951-343-4487, E-mail: jcraig@calbaptist.edu. *Application contact:* Mischa Routon, Associate Dean of Graduate Programs, 951-343-4206, Fax: 951-343-4569, E-mail: mrouton@calbaptist.edu.
Website: http://www.calbaptist.edu/mft/

California Institute of Integral Studies, School of Professional Psychology and Health, San Francisco, CA 94103. Offers clinical psychology (Psy D); community mental health (MA); drama therapy (MA); expressive arts therapy (MA); integral counseling psychology (MA); integrative health studies (MA); psychological studies (MA); somatic psychology (MA). *Accreditation:* APA. Part-time and evening/weekend programs available. *Students:* 522 full-time (397 women), 105 part-time (83 women); includes 155 minority (27 Black or African American, non-Hispanic/Latino; 3 American Indian or Alaska Native, non-Hispanic/Latino; 31 Asian, non-Hispanic/Latino; 62 Hispanic/Latino; 3 Native Hawaiian or other Pacific Islander, non-Hispanic/Latino; 29 Two or more races, non-Hispanic/Latino), 49 international. Average age 34. 351 applicants, 86% accepted, 175 enrolled. In 2014, 168 master's, 24 doctorates awarded. *Degree requirements:* For doctorate, comprehensive exam, thesis/dissertation. *Entrance requirements:* For master's, minimum GPA of 3.0, letters of recommendation, writing sample; for doctorate, GRE, MA in psychology or social work with appropriate practical experience for advanced standing, or BA with a minimum GPA of 3.1; letters of recommendation; writing sample. Additional exam requirements/recommendations for international students: Required—TOEFL. *Application deadline:* For fall admission, 2/1 priority date for domestic and international students; for spring admission, 10/15 priority date for domestic and international students. Applications are processed on a rolling basis. Application fee: $65. Electronic applications accepted. *Expenses: Tuition:* Full-time $18,270; part-time $1015 per credit. *Required fees:* $85 per semester hour. *Financial support:* In 2014–15, 464 students received support, including 5 research assistantships with tuition reimbursements available (averaging $800 per year), 36 teaching assistantships with tuition reimbursements available (averaging $825 per year); career-related internships or fieldwork, Federal Work-Study, and scholarships/grants also available. Support available to part-time students. Financial award application deadline: 4/15; financial award applicants required to submit FAFSA. *Faculty research:* Transpersonal psychology, somatic psychology, expressive arts therapy, drama therapy, community mental health, ecopsychology, integrative health. *Application contact:* David Townes, Senior Admissions Counselor, 415-575-6152, Fax: 415-575-1268, E-mail: admissions@ciis.edu.

California State University, Bakersfield, Division of Graduate Studies, School of Social Sciences and Education, Program in Counseling Psychology, Bakersfield, CA 93311. Offers MS. *Degree requirements:* For master's, comprehensive exam.

California State University, Sacramento, Office of Graduate Studies, College of Social Sciences and Interdisciplinary Studies, Department of Psychology, Sacramento, CA 95819. Offers applied behavior analysis (MA); counseling psychology (MA); industrial/organizational psychology (MA). Part-time programs available. *Degree requirements:* For master's, thesis, writing proficiency exam. *Entrance requirements:* For master's, GRE, minimum GPA of 3.0 during previous 2 years. Additional exam requirements/recommendations for international students: Required—TOEFL. Electronic applications accepted.

California State University, San Bernardino, Graduate Studies, College of Social and Behavioral Sciences, Department of Psychology, Program in Clinical/Counseling Psychology, San Bernardino, CA 92407-2397. Offers clinical psychology (MS). *Students:* 20 part-time (18 women); includes 15 minority (4 Black or African American, non-Hispanic/Latino; 1 Asian, non-Hispanic/Latino; 10 Hispanic/Latino). Average age 26. 94 applicants, 12% accepted, 11 enrolled. In 2014, 13 master's awarded. *Entrance requirements:* Additional exam requirements/recommendations for international students: Required—TOEFL. *Application deadline:* For fall admission, 7/17 for domestic students. Application fee: $55. *Expenses:* Tuition, state resident: full-time $6738; part-time $1302 per term. Tuition, nonresident: full-time $17,898; part-time $248 per unit. *Required fees:* $365 per quarter. Tuition and fees vary according to degree level and program. *Financial support:* Application deadline: 3/1. *Unit head:* Dr. Robert Ricco, Chair, 909-537-5485, Fax: 909-537-7003, E-mail: rricco@csusb.edu. *Application contact:* Stacy Brooks, Graduate Secretary, 909-537-5570, Fax: 909-537-7003, E-mail: sbrooks@csusb.edu.

California State University, Stanislaus, College of Human and Health Sciences, Program in Psychology (MA/MS), Turlock, CA 95382. Offers behavior analysis (MS); counseling psychology (MS); psychology (MA). Part-time programs available. *Degree requirements:* For master's, thesis. *Entrance requirements:* For master's, GRE, minimum GPA of 3.0, 3 letters of reference, 16 psychology prerequisites, personal statement. Additional exam requirements/recommendations for international students: Required—TOEFL (minimum score 550 paper-based). Electronic applications accepted. *Faculty research:* Hedonic tone judgment, syntax and autism, early literacy assessment and native and non-native languages.

Cambridge College, School of Psychology and Counseling, Cambridge, MA 02138-5304. Offers addiction counseling (M Ed); alcohol and drug counseling (Certificate); counseling psychology (M Ed, CAGS); counseling psychology: forensic counseling (M Ed); marriage and family therapy (M Ed); mental health and addiction counseling (M Ed); mental health counseling (M Ed); mental health counseling for school guidance counselors (Post Master's Certificate); psychological studies (M Ed); school adjustment and mental health counseling (M Ed); school adjustment, mental health and addiction counseling (M Ed); school guidance counselor (M Ed); trauma studies (Certificate). Part-time and evening/weekend programs available. *Degree requirements:* For master's and other advanced degree, thesis, practicum/internship. *Entrance requirements:* For master's, resume, 2 professional references; for other advanced degree, official transcripts, documents for transfer credit evaluation, resume, written personal statement/essay, 2 professional references, health insurance, immunizations form. Additional exam requirements/recommendations for international students: Required—TOEFL (minimum score 550 paper-based; 79 iBT), Michigan English Language Assessment Battery (minimum score 85); Recommended—IELTS (minimum score 6). Electronic applications accepted. *Expenses:* Contact institution. *Faculty research:* Trauma, drug and alcohol counseling, cross-cultural issues, school counseling, trauma in schools.

Capella University, Harold Abel School of Social and Behavioral Science, Master's Programs in Counseling, Minneapolis, MN 55402. Offers child and adolescent development (MS); general addiction counseling (MS); general marriage and family counseling/therapy (MS); general mental health counseling (MS); general school counseling (MS).

Capella University, Harold Abel School of Social and Behavioral Science, Master's Programs in Psychology, Minneapolis, MN 55402. Offers applied behavior analysis (MS); clinical psychology (MS); counseling psychology (MS); educational psychology (MS); evaluation, research, and measurement (MS); general advanced studies in human behavior (MS); general psychology (MS); industrial/organizational psychology (MS); leadership coaching psychology (MS); school psychology (MS); sport psychology (MS).

Carlos Albizu University, Miami Campus, Graduate Programs, Miami, FL 33172-2209. Offers clinical psychology (Psy D); entrepreneurship (MBA); exceptional student education (MS); human services (PhD); industrial/organizational psychology (MS); marriage and family therapy (MS); mental health counseling (MS); nonprofit management (MBA); organizational management (MBA); psychology (MS); school counseling (MS); teaching English as a second language (MS). *Accreditation:* APA. Part-time and evening/weekend programs available. Postbaccalaureate distance learning degree programs offered (minimal on-campus study). *Faculty:* 25 full-time (20 women), 29 part-time/adjunct (15 women). *Students:* 431 full-time (343 women), 264 part-time (225 women); includes 586 minority (45 Black or African American, non-Hispanic/Latino; 1 American Indian or Alaska Native, non-Hispanic/Latino; 8 Asian, non-Hispanic/Latino; 530 Hispanic/Latino; 2 Two or more races, non-Hispanic/Latino), 14 international. Average age 33. 189 applicants, 69% accepted, 111 enrolled. In 2014, 177 master's, 28 doctorates awarded. Terminal master's awarded for partial completion of doctoral program. *Degree requirements:* For master's, one foreign language, comprehensive exam, integrative project (MBA), research project (exceptional student education, teaching English as a second language); for doctorate, one foreign language, comprehensive exam, internship, project. *Entrance requirements:* For master's, 3 letters of recommendation, interview, minimum GPA of 3.0, resume, statement of purpose, official transcripts; for doctorate, 3 letters of recommendation, minimum GPA of 3.0, resume, interview, statement of purpose, official transcripts. Additional exam requirements/recommendations for international students: Required—Michigan Test of English Language Proficiency. *Application deadline:* For fall admission, 4/1 priority date for domestic students, 5/1 priority date for international students; for spring admission, 11/1 priority date for domestic students, 9/1 priority date for international students. Applications are processed on a rolling basis. Application fee: $50. Electronic applications accepted. *Expenses:* Expenses: $570 per credit (for master's programs); $750 per credit (for doctoral programs). *Financial support:* In 2014–15, 72 students received support. Federal Work-Study, scholarships/grants, and tuition discounts available. Financial award application deadline: 6/1; financial award applicants required to submit FAFSA. *Faculty research:* Psychotherapy, forensic psychology, neuropsychology, marketing strategy, entrepreneurship, special education. *Unit head:* Dr. Irene M. Bravo, Interim Provost, 305-593-1223 Ext. 3120, Fax: 305-592-7930, E-mail: ibravo@albizu.edu. *Application contact:* Vanessa Almendarez, Administrative Assistant, 305-593-1223 Ext. 3137, Fax: 305-593-1854, E-mail: valmendarez@albizu.edu.

Carlow University, College of Leadership and Social Change, Program in Counseling Psychology, Pittsburgh, PA 15213-3165. Offers Psy D. *Students:* 26 full-time (21 women), 12 part-time (8 women); includes 3 minority (all Black or African American, non-Hispanic/Latino). Average age 33. 22 applicants, 50% accepted, 7 enrolled. In 2014, 3 doctorates awarded. *Degree requirements:* For doctorate, thesis/dissertation, internship. *Entrance requirements:* For doctorate, GRE, resume or curriculum vitae; personal essay; reflective essay; official transcripts from all previous undergraduate and graduate institutions; three letters of recommendation; master's degree in closely-related field. Additional exam requirements/recommendations for international students: Required—TOEFL (minimum score 550 paper-based). *Application deadline:* Applications are processed on a rolling basis. Application fee is waived when completed online. *Expenses: Tuition:* Full-time $9750; part-time $785 per credit. Part-time tuition and fees vary according to degree level and program. *Unit head:* Dr. Mary C. Burke, Chair, PsyD Program, 412-575-6408, Fax: 412-578-6357, E-mail: mcburke@carlow.edu. *Application contact:* Dr. Kathleen A. Chrisman, Associate Director, Graduate Admissions, 412-578-8812, Fax: 412-578-8822, E-mail: kachrisman@carlow.edu.
Website: http://www.carlow.edu/PsyD_Counseling_Psychology.aspx

Carlow University, College of Leadership and Social Change, Program in Professional Counseling, Pittsburgh, PA 15213-3165. Offers drug and alcohol counseling (MS); professional counseling (MS, Certificate); school counseling (MS); school counselor (Certificate). Part-time and evening/weekend programs available. *Students:* 177 full-time

(149 women), 35 part-time (31 women); includes 45 minority (29 Black or African American, non-Hispanic/Latino; 2 Asian, non-Hispanic/Latino; 7 Hispanic/Latino; 7 Two or more races, non-Hispanic/Latino). Average age 31. 90 applicants, 96% accepted, 42 enrolled. In 2014, 56 master's awarded. *Entrance requirements:* For master's, personal essay; resume or curriculum vitae; three recommendations; official transcripts; interview; minimum undergraduate GPA of 3.0; undergraduate courses in statistics, abnormal psychology, and personality theory; undergraduate work or work experience in the helping professions. Additional exam requirements/recommendations for international students: Required—TOEFL (minimum score 550 paper-based). Application fee is waived when completed online. *Expenses: Tuition:* Full-time $9750; part-time $785 per credit. Part-time tuition and fees vary according to degree level and program. *Unit head:* Dr. Joseph Roberts, Director, Master in Professional Counseling Program, 412-575-6331, E-mail: jmroberts@carlow.edu. *Application contact:* Dr. Kathleen A. Chrisman, Associate Director, Graduate Admissions, 412-578-8812, Fax: 412-578-8822, E-mail: kachrisman@carlow.edu.
Website: http://www.carlow.edu/Master_of_Science_in_Professional_Counseling.aspx

Centenary College, Program in Counseling Psychology, Hackettstown, NJ 07840-2100. Offers counseling (MA); counseling psychology (MA). Part-time and evening/weekend programs available. Postbaccalaureate distance learning degree programs offered (minimal on-campus study). *Degree requirements:* For master's, thesis, fieldwork.

Central Michigan University, Central Michigan University Global Campus, Program in Counseling, Mount Pleasant, MI 48859. Offers professional counseling (MA); school counseling (MA). *Accreditation:* Teacher Education Accreditation Council. Part-time and evening/weekend programs available. *Entrance requirements:* For master's, MAT, minimum GPA of 2.7. Additional exam requirements/recommendations for international students: Required—TOEFL. Electronic applications accepted. *Financial support:* Scholarships/grants available. Support available to part-time students. *Unit head:* Dr. Twinet Parmer, Chair, 989-774-3776, E-mail: parme1t@cmich.edu. *Application contact:* 877-268-4636, E-mail: cmuglobal@cmich.edu.

Central Michigan University, College of Graduate Studies, College of Humanities and Social and Behavioral Sciences, Department of Psychology, Mount Pleasant, MI 48859. Offers clinical psychology (PhD); experimental psychology (MS, PhD), including applied experimental psychology (PhD), experimental psychology (MS); industrial and organizational psychology (MA, PhD), including industrial and organizational psychology, occupational health psychology (PhD); neuroscience (MS, PhD); school psychology (PhD, S Psy S), including psychological services (S Psy S), school psychology (PhD). *Accreditation:* APA (one or more programs are accredited). Terminal master's awarded for partial completion of doctoral program. *Degree requirements:* For master's, thesis or alternative; for doctorate, thesis/dissertation; for S Psy S, thesis. *Entrance requirements:* For doctorate, GRE. Electronic applications accepted. *Faculty research:* Experimental psychology, clinical psychology, industrial/organizational psychology, school psychology, neuroscience.

Central Washington University, Graduate Studies and Research, College of the Sciences, Department of Psychology, Program in Mental Health Counseling, Ellensburg, WA 98926. Offers MS. *Accreditation:* ACA. *Degree requirements:* For master's, thesis or alternative, internship. *Entrance requirements:* For master's, GRE General Test, minimum GPA of 3.0. Additional exam requirements/recommendations for international students: Required—TOEFL (minimum score 550 paper-based; 79 iBT). Electronic applications accepted.

Chaminade University of Honolulu, Graduate Services, Program in Counseling Psychology, Honolulu, HI 96816-1578. Offers marriage and family counseling (MSCP); mental health counseling (MSCP); school counseling (MSCP). Part-time and evening/weekend programs available. *Degree requirements:* For master's, comprehensive exam, internship/practicum. *Entrance requirements:* For master's, minimum undergraduate GPA of 3.0, 3 letters of recommendation, interview. Additional exam requirements/recommendations for international students: Required—TOEFL (minimum score 550 paper-based). Electronic applications accepted. *Faculty research:* Taoist/Buddhist psychology, psychology of T'ai Chi Ch'uan, sleep disorders, drug/alcohol prevention with adolescent girls, anger/aggression with kids.

Chatham University, Program in Counseling Psychology, Pittsburgh, PA 15232-2826. Offers child, adolescent and family (MSCP); counseling psychology (Psy D); health and holistic (MSCP); infant mental health (MSCP); organization and supervision (MSCP); sport and exercise (MSCP). Part-time and evening/weekend programs available. *Faculty:* 12 full-time (9 women), 13 part-time/adjunct (9 women). *Students:* 102 full-time (85 women), 38 part-time (32 women); includes 17 minority (7 Black or African American, non-Hispanic/Latino; 2 Asian, non-Hispanic/Latino; 6 Hispanic/Latino; 2 Two or more races, non-Hispanic/Latino), 7 international. Average age 29. 145 applicants, 73% accepted, 59 enrolled. In 2014, 67 master's, 3 doctorates awarded. *Degree requirements:* For master's, thesis optional, supervised internship; for doctorate, thesis/dissertation, internship. *Entrance requirements:* For master's, minimum GPA of 3.0; 2 letters of recommendation; resume; prerequisite coursework in statistics, biology, and psychology; for doctorate, GRE. Additional exam requirements/recommendations for international students: Required—TOEFL (minimum score 600 paper-based; 100 iBT), IELTS (minimum score 7), TWE. *Application deadline:* For fall admission, 4/1 priority date for domestic and international students; for spring admission, 11/1 for domestic students, 10/1 for international students. Applications are processed on a rolling basis. Application fee: $45. Electronic applications accepted. Application fee is waived when completed online. *Expenses: Tuition:* Full-time $15,318; part-time $851 per credit hour. *Required fees:* $440; $24 per credit hour. Tuition and fees vary according to course load, program and reciprocity agreements. *Financial support:* Career-related internships or fieldwork available. Financial award applicants required to submit FAFSA. *Faculty research:* Trauma and recovery, hypnosis, psychospiritual dimensions of healing, psychotherapy of schizophrenia. *Unit head:* Dr. Mary Beth Mannarino, Director, 412-365-1196, Fax: 412-365-1505, E-mail: mmannarino@chatham.edu. *Application contact:* Katie Noel, Assistant Director of Graduate Admission, 412-365-2758, Fax: 412-365-1609, E-mail: gradadmissions@chatham.edu.
Website: http://www.chatham.edu/mscp

Chestnut Hill College, School of Graduate Studies, Division of Psychology, Program in Clinical and Counseling Psychology, Philadelphia, PA 19118-2693. Offers addictions treatment (MS, CAS); child and adolescent therapy (MS, CAS); marriage and family therapy (MS, CAS); trauma studies (MS, CAS); treatment of autism spectrum disorders (MS, CAS). Part-time and evening/weekend programs available. *Faculty:* 4 full-time (3 women), 34 part-time/adjunct (24 women). *Students:* 88 full-time (73 women), 136 part-time (113 women); includes 41 minority (27 Black or African American, non-Hispanic/Latino; 1 Asian, non-Hispanic/Latino; 12 Hispanic/Latino; 1 Two or more races, non-Hispanic/Latino), 2 international. Average age 33. 119 applicants, 98% accepted, 70 enrolled. In 2014, 1,021 master's, 7 other advanced degrees awarded. *Degree requirements:* For master's, thesis optional, practica. *Entrance requirements:* For master's, GRE General Test, writing sample, letters of recommendation. Additional exam requirements/recommendations for international students: Required—TOEFL (minimum score 500 paper-based), IELTS (mnimum score 6.0), or TWE (minimum score 22). *Application deadline:* For fall admission, 7/1 for domestic and international students;

for spring admission, 11/1 for domestic and international students; for summer admission, 4/1 for domestic and international students. Applications are processed on a rolling basis. Application fee: $55. Electronic applications accepted. *Expenses:* Expenses: Contact institution. *Financial support:* Unspecified assistantships available. *Faculty research:* Play therapy, eating disorders, addictions, group psychology and group therapy, health psychology. *Unit head:* Dr. Cheryll Rothery, Chair, Psychology Division, 215-248-7023, Fax: 215-248-3619, E-mail: rotheryc@chc.edu. *Application contact:* Amy Boorse, Assistant Director of Graduate Admissions, 215-248-7097, Fax: 215-248-7161, E-mail: gradadmissions@chc.edu.
Website: http://www.chc.edu/Graduate/Programs/Masters/Clinical_and_Counseling_Psychology/

The Chicago School of Professional Psychology at Grayslake, Program in Clinical Counseling Psychology, Chicago, IL 60610. Offers counseling (MA), including child and adolescent treatment, generalist, health psychology, Latino mental health, supervision and leadership in mental health, treatment of addiction disorders.

City College of the City University of New York, Graduate School, College of Liberal Arts and Science, Program in Mental Health Counseling, New York, NY 10031-9198. Offers MA.

City University of Seattle, Graduate Division, Division of Arts and Sciences, Seattle, WA 98121. Offers counseling psychology (MA). Part-time and evening/weekend programs available. Postbaccalaureate distance learning degree programs offered (no on-campus study). *Faculty:* 3 full-time (2 women), 11 part-time/adjunct (8 women). *Students:* 58 full-time (45 women), 7 part-time (all women); includes 10 minority (3 Black or African American, non-Hispanic/Latino; 1 American Indian or Alaska Native, non-Hispanic/Latino; 2 Asian, non-Hispanic/Latino; 3 Hispanic/Latino; 1 Native Hawaiian or other Pacific Islander, non-Hispanic/Latino), 1 international. Average age 38. 17 applicants, 100% accepted, 17 enrolled. In 2014, 16 master's awarded. *Degree requirements:* For master's, comprehensive exam (for some programs), thesis (for some programs). *Entrance requirements:* For master's, baccalaureate degree or equivalent from an accredited or otherwise recognized institution. Additional exam requirements/recommendations for international students: Recommended—TOEFL (minimum score 567 paper-based; 87 iBT), IELTS, TWE. *Application deadline:* For fall admission, 9/1 for international students; for winter admission, 12/1 for international students; for spring admission, 3/1 for international students. Applications are processed on a rolling basis. Application fee: $50. Electronic applications accepted. *Expenses:* Expenses: Contact institution. *Financial support:* In 2014–15, 2 students received support. Federal Work-Study and scholarships/grants available. Support available to part-time students. Financial award applicants required to submit FAFSA. *Unit head:* Craig Schieber, Dean, 206-239-4840, Fax: 425-709-5363, E-mail: cshieber@cityu.edu. *Application contact:* 888-422-4898, Fax: 425-709-5361, E-mail: info@cityu.edu.
Website: http://www.cityu.edu/programs/sas/index.aspx

Clemson University, Graduate School, Eugene T. Moore School of Education, Program in Counselor Education, Clemson, SC 29634. Offers clinical mental health counseling (M Ed); school counseling (K-12) (M Ed); student affairs (higher education) (M Ed). *Accreditation:* ACA; NCATE. Part-time and evening/weekend programs available. *Students:* 133 full-time (106 women), 18 part-time (16 women); includes 26 minority (15 Black or African American, non-Hispanic/Latino; 2 Asian, non-Hispanic/Latino; 9 Hispanic/Latino), 1 international. Average age 26. 227 applicants, 49% accepted, 58 enrolled. In 2014, 78 master's awarded. *Degree requirements:* For master's, comprehensive exam. *Entrance requirements:* For master's, GRE General Test. Additional exam requirements/recommendations for international students: Required—TOEFL; Recommended—IELTS. *Application deadline:* For fall admission, 2/1 priority date for domestic students; for spring admission, 10/1 for domestic students. Applications are processed on a rolling basis. Application fee: $70 ($80 for international students). Electronic applications accepted. *Expenses:* Expenses: Contact institution. *Financial support:* In 2014–15, 2 students received support, including 2 teaching assistantships with partial tuition reimbursements available (averaging $13,459 per year); institutionally sponsored loans, health care benefits, and unspecified assistantships also available. Financial award application deadline: 6/1; financial award applicants required to submit FAFSA. *Faculty research:* At-risk youth, ethnic identity development across the life span, postsecondary transitions and college readiness, distance and distributed learning environments, the student veteran experience in college, student development theory. *Unit head:* Dr. George J. Petersen, Dean, School of Education, 864-656-4444, Fax: 864-656-0311, E-mail: soedean@clemson.edu. *Application contact:* Dr. David Fleming, Graduate Coordinator, 864-656-1881, Fax: 864-656-0311, E-mail: dflemin@clemson.edu.

Cleveland State University, College of Graduate Studies, College of Education and Human Services, Department of Counseling, Administration, Supervision and Adult Learning (CASAL), Cleveland, OH 44115. Offers adult learning and development (M Ed); chemical dependency counseling (Certificate); clinical mental health counseling (M Ed); early childhood mental health counseling (Certificate); educational administration and supervision (M Ed); organizational leadership (M Ed); school administration (Ed S); school counseling (M Ed). *Accreditation:* ACA (one or more programs are accredited). Part-time and evening/weekend programs available. *Faculty:* 15 full-time (8 women), 19 part-time/adjunct (10 women). *Students:* 76 full-time (59 women), 214 part-time (174 women); includes 110 minority (93 Black or African American, non-Hispanic/Latino; 3 Asian, non-Hispanic/Latino; 13 Hispanic/Latino; 1 Two or more races, non-Hispanic/Latino), 9 international. Average age 34. 57 applicants, 93% accepted, 51 enrolled. In 2014, 99 master's, 4 Certificates awarded. *Degree requirements:* For master's, comprehensive exam (for some programs), thesis optional, internship. *Entrance requirements:* For master's, GRE General Test or MAT, letter of recommendation and minimum GPA of 2.75 (for counseling); 2 letters of recommendation and interviews (for organizational leadership). Additional exam requirements/recommendations for international students: Required—TOEFL (minimum score 525 paper-based), IELTS (minimum score 6). *Application deadline:* For fall admission, 6/21 for domestic students, 5/15 for international students; for spring admission, 8/31 for domestic students, 11/1 for international students. Application fee: $30. Electronic applications accepted. *Expenses:* Tuition, state resident: full-time $9566; part-time $531 per credit hour. Tuition, nonresident: full-time $17,980; part-time $999 per credit hour. *Required fees:* $25 per semester. Tuition and fees vary according to degree level and program. *Financial support:* In 2014–15, 19 students received support, including 10 research assistantships with full and partial tuition reimbursements available (averaging $11,882 per year), 5 teaching assistantships with full and partial tuition reimbursements available (averaging $11,882 per year); scholarships/grants and unspecified assistantships also available. Support available to part-time students. *Faculty research:* Education law, career development, bullying, psychopharmacology, counseling and spirituality. *Total annual research expenditures:* $225,821. *Unit head:* Dr. Ann L. Bauer, Chairperson, 216-687-4582, Fax: 216-687-5378, E-mail: a.l.bauer@csuohio.edu. *Application contact:* Deborah L. Brown, Interim Assistant Director, Graduate Admissions, 216-523-7572, Fax: 216-687-5400, E-mail: d.l.brown@csuohio.edu.
Website: http://www.csuohio.edu/cehs/departments/CASAL/casal_dept.html

Counseling Psychology

Cleveland State University, College of Graduate Studies, College of Education and Human Services, Program in Urban Education, Specialization in Counseling Psychology, Cleveland, OH 44115. Offers PhD. *Faculty:* 5 full-time (3 women), 1 part-time/adjunct (0 women). *Students:* 8 full-time (7 women), 11 part-time (7 women); includes 4 minority (1 Black or African American, non-Hispanic/Latino; 2 Hispanic/Latino; 1 Two or more races, non-Hispanic/Latino; 2 international. Average age 29. 36 applicants, 31% accepted, 3 enrolled. In 2014, 2 doctorates awarded. *Degree requirements:* For doctorate, comprehensive exam, thesis/dissertation, internship. *Entrance requirements:* For doctorate, GRE (Verbal, Quantitative, and Writing), minimum undergraduate GPA of 2.75, graduate 3.0; 3 letters of recommendation; personal statement; curriculum vitae; interview. Additional exam requirements/recommendations for international students: Required—TOEFL (minimum score 525 paper-based), IELTS (minimum score 6). *Application deadline:* For fall admission, 1/15 for domestic and international students. Application fee: $30. Electronic applications accepted. *Expenses:* Tuition, state resident: full-time $9566; part-time $531 per credit hour. Tuition, nonresident: full-time $17,980; part-time $999 per credit hour. *Required fees:* $25 per semester. Tuition and fees vary according to degree level and program. *Financial support:* In 2014–15, 14 students received support, including 11 research assistantships with partial tuition reimbursements available (averaging $5,900 per year), 3 teaching assistantships with partial tuition reimbursements available (averaging $5,900 per year); tuition waivers (partial) and unspecified assistantships also available. Financial award application deadline: 1/15. *Faculty research:* Vocational psychology, low SES urban youth, women's identity and work, work and family integration, professional issues in psychology, clinical supervision and training, research productivity of psychologists and psychology trainees, leadership training in professional organizations, college students' development and adjustment, diversity issues with a focus on gender and sexual minorities, social constructionism, childhood career development, multicultural issues in mental health. *Unit head:* Dr. Graham Stead, Director of Doctoral Studies, 216-687-4697, Fax: 216-687-5378, E-mail: g.b.stead@csuohio.edu. *Application contact:* Rita M. Grabowski, Administrative Assistant, 216-687-4697, Fax: 216-687-5378, E-mail: r.grabowski@csuohio.edu. Website: http://www.csuohio.edu/cehs/departments/DOC/cp_doc.html

The College at Brockport, State University of New York, School of Education and Human Services, Department of Counselor Education, Brockport, NY 14420-2997. Offers college counseling (MS Ed, CAS); mental health counseling (MS, CAS); school counseling (MS Ed, CAS); school counselor supervision (CAS). *Accreditation:* ACA (one or more programs are accredited). Part-time programs available. *Faculty:* 5 full-time (3 women), 4 part-time/adjunct (3 women). *Students:* 37 full-time (29 women), 57 part-time (49 women); includes 21 minority (14 Black or African American, non-Hispanic/Latino; 3 Hispanic/Latino; 4 Two or more races, non-Hispanic/Latino). 64 applicants, 39% accepted, 16 enrolled. In 2014, 21 master's, 4 other advanced degrees awarded. *Degree requirements:* For master's, thesis, internship. *Entrance requirements:* For master's, group interview, letters of recommendation, written objectives; for CAS, master's degree, New York state school counselor certificate. Additional exam requirements/recommendations for international students: Required—TOEFL (minimum score 550 paper-based; 79 iBT), IELTS (minimum score 6.5). *Application deadline:* For fall admission, 2/1 priority date for domestic and international students; for spring admission, 9/1 priority date for domestic and international students; for summer admission, 2/1 priority date for domestic and international students. Application fee: $80. Electronic applications accepted. *Financial support:* In 2014–15, 1 fellowship with full tuition reimbursement (averaging $7,500 per year), 1 teaching assistantship with full tuition reimbursement (averaging $6,000 per year) were awarded; Federal Work-Study, scholarships/grants, and unspecified assistantships also available. Support available to part-time students. Financial award application deadline: 3/15; financial award applicants required to submit FAFSA. *Faculty research:* Gender and diversity issues; counseling outcomes; spirituality; school, college and mental health counseling; obesity. *Unit head:* Dr. Thomas Hernandez, Chair, 585-395-2258, Fax: 585-395-2366, E-mail: thernandez@brockport.edu. *Application contact:* Danielle A. Welch, Graduate Admissions Counselor, 585-395-5465, Fax: 585-395-2515. Website: http://www.brockport.edu/edc/

The College of New Rochelle, Graduate School, Division of Human Services, Program in Guidance and Counseling, New Rochelle, NY 10805-2308. Offers MS, Advanced Certificate. Part-time programs available. *Degree requirements:* For master's, internship. *Entrance requirements:* For master's, interview. *Expenses: Tuition:* Part-time $894 per credit. *Required fees:* $325 per semester.

The College of New Rochelle, Graduate School, Division of Human Services, Program in Mental Health Counseling, New Rochelle, NY 10805-2308. Offers mental health counseling (MS); thanatology (Certificate). *Degree requirements:* For Certificate, internship. *Expenses: Tuition:* Part-time $894 per credit. *Required fees:* $325 per semester.

College of Saint Elizabeth, Department of Psychology, Morristown, NJ 07960-6989. Offers counseling psychology (MA); forensic psychology (MA); mental health counseling (Certificate); student affairs in higher education (Certificate). Part-time programs available. *Degree requirements:* For master's, thesis or alternative. *Entrance requirements:* For master's, minimum GPA of 3.0, BA in psychology (preferred), 12 credits of course work in psychology. Additional exam requirements/recommendations for international students: Required—TOEFL. Electronic applications accepted.

College of St. Joseph, Graduate Programs, Division of Psychology and Human Services, Program in Clinical Mental Health Counseling, Rutland, VT 05701-3899. Offers MS. Part-time programs available. *Degree requirements:* For master's, comprehensive exam. *Entrance requirements:* For master's, official college transcripts; 2 letters of reference. Additional exam requirements/recommendations for international students: Required—TOEFL (minimum score 550 paper-based). Electronic applications accepted.

The College of Saint Rose, Graduate Studies, School of Education, Program in Counseling, Albany, NY 12203-1419. Offers counseling (MS Ed), including mental health counseling, school counseling; mental health counseling (Certificate); school counseling (Certificate). Part-time and evening/weekend programs available. *Entrance requirements:* For master's, minimum undergraduate GPA of 3.0. Additional exam requirements/recommendations for international students: Required—TOEFL (minimum score 550 paper-based). Electronic applications accepted.

College of Staten Island of the City University of New York, Graduate Programs, Division of Humanities and Social Sciences, Clinical Mental Health Counseling Program, Staten Island, NY 10314-6600. Offers MA. *Faculty:* 5 full-time (all women), 6 part-time/adjunct (4 women). *Students:* 62 full-time (51 women). Average age 27. 83 applicants, 35% accepted, 19 enrolled. In 2014, 19 master's awarded. *Degree requirements:* For master's, comprehensive exam, practicum, three internship courses. *Entrance requirements:* For master's, BA/BS; minimum GPA of 3.0; 15-19 undergraduate credits in psychology; two letters of recommendation; statement of intent; 1-2 page statement of intent detailing interest in the field, background information, academic and related experience, field placements, and the reasons the student chose this field of study. Additional exam requirements/recommendations for international students: Required—TOEFL (minimum score 600 paper-based; 100 iBT), IELTS (minimum score 7).

Application deadline: For fall admission, 3/10 for domestic and international students. Application fee: $125. *Expenses:* Tuition, state resident: full-time $9650; part-time $405 per credit. Tuition, nonresident: full-time $17,880; part-time $745 per credit. *Required fees:* $141.10 per semester. Tuition and fees vary according to program. *Financial support:* In 2014–15, 37 students received support. Career-related internships or fieldwork, Federal Work-Study, and scholarships/grants available. Support available to part-time students. Financial award applicants required to submit FAFSA. *Unit head:* Dr. Frances Melendez, Graduate Program Coordinator, 718-982-3960, Fax: 718-982-4114, E-mail: frances.melendez@csi.cuny.edu. *Application contact:* Sasha Spence, Assistant Director for Graduate Admissions, 718-982-2019, Fax: 718-982-2500, E-mail: sasha.spence@csi.cuny.edu. Website: http://csivc.csi.cuny.edu/psy/files/MHC.html

Colorado Christian University, Program in Counseling, Lakewood, CO 80226. Offers MAC. *Accreditation:* ACA. Part-time and evening/weekend programs available. *Degree requirements:* For master's, thesis optional. *Entrance requirements:* For master's, GRE General Test, 3 letters of recommendation. Additional exam requirements/recommendations for international students: Required—TOEFL. Electronic applications accepted. *Expenses:* Contact institution.

Columbus State University, Graduate Studies, College of Education and Health Professions, Department of Counseling, Foundations, and Leadership, Columbus, GA 31907-5645. Offers community counseling (MS); curriculum and leadership (Ed D); educational leadership (M Ed, Ed S); higher education (M Ed); school counseling (M Ed, Ed S). *Accreditation:* ACA; NCATE. Part-time and evening/weekend programs available. Postbaccalaureate distance learning degree programs offered (minimal on-campus study). *Faculty:* 12 full-time (4 women), 14 part-time/adjunct (10 women). *Students:* 112 full-time (81 women), 220 part-time (152 women); includes 173 minority (153 Black or African American, non-Hispanic/Latino; 3 Asian, non-Hispanic/Latino; 14 Hispanic/Latino; 3 Two or more races, non-Hispanic/Latino). Average age 37. 208 applicants, 60% accepted, 85 enrolled. In 2014, 30 master's, 4 doctorates, 33 other advanced degrees awarded. *Degree requirements:* For master's, thesis, exit exam; for doctorate, comprehensive exam, thesis/dissertation; for Ed S, thesis or alternative. *Entrance requirements:* For master's, GRE General Test, minimum undergraduate GPA of 2.75; for doctorate, GRE General Test, minimum graduate GPA of 3.5, four years of professional service; for Ed S, GRE General Test, minimum undergraduate GPA of 2.75, graduate 3.0. Additional exam requirements/recommendations for international students: Required—TOEFL (minimum score 550 paper-based; 79 iBT). *Application deadline:* For fall admission, 6/30 for domestic and international students; for spring admission, 11/1 for domestic and international students; for summer admission, 3/1 for domestic and international students. Applications are processed on a rolling basis. Application fee: $50. Electronic applications accepted. *Financial support:* In 2014–15, 224 students received support, including 9 research assistantships with partial tuition reimbursements available (averaging $3,000 per year); career-related internships or fieldwork, Federal Work-Study, institutionally sponsored loans, scholarships/grants, tuition waivers (partial), and unspecified assistantships also available. Support available to part-time students. Financial award application deadline: 5/1; financial award applicants required to submit FAFSA. *Unit head:* Dr. Michael L. Baltimore, Department Chair, 706-569-3013, Fax: 706-569-3134, E-mail: baltimore_michael@columbusstate.edu. *Application contact:* Kristin Williams, Director of International and Graduate Recruitment, 706-507-8848, Fax: 706-568-5091, E-mail: williams_kristin@columbusstate.edu. Website: http://cfl.columbusstate.edu/

Concordia University Chicago, College of Graduate and Innovative Programs, Program in Community Counseling, River Forest, IL 60305-1499. Offers MA. *Accreditation:* ACA. *Degree requirements:* For master's, final project. *Entrance requirements:* For master's, minimum GPA of 2.9. Additional exam requirements/recommendations for international students: Required—TOEFL (minimum score 550 paper-based). Electronic applications accepted.

Concordia University Wisconsin, Graduate Programs, Department of Psychology, Program in Professional Counseling, Mequon, WI 53097-2402. Offers MPC. Postbaccalaureate distance learning degree programs offered (minimal on-campus study). *Degree requirements:* For master's, comprehensive exam, thesis or alternative. *Entrance requirements:* For master's, minimum GPA of 3.0. Additional exam requirements/recommendations for international students: Required—TOEFL.

Dallas Baptist University, Dorothy M. Bush College of Education, Counseling Program, Main Campus, Dallas, TX 75211-9299. Offers MA. Part-time and evening/weekend programs available. *Entrance requirements:* For master's, GRE General Test, minimum GPA of 3.0. Additional exam requirements/recommendations for international students: Required—TOEFL. Electronic applications accepted. *Expenses: Tuition:* Full-time $14,130; part-time $785 per credit hour. *Required fees:* $200 per semester. Tuition and fees vary according to course level and course load. *Faculty research:* Therapy effectiveness.

Dallas Baptist University, Dorothy M. Bush College of Education, Counseling Program, North Campus, Dallas, TX 75211-9299. Offers MA. Part-time and evening/weekend programs available. *Expenses: Tuition:* Full-time $14,130; part-time $785 per credit hour. *Required fees:* $200 per semester. Tuition and fees vary according to course level and course load.

Delaware Valley University, Program in Counseling Psychology, Doylestown, PA 18901-2697. Offers child and adolescent therapy (MA); social justice community counseling (MA).

DePaul University, College of Education, Chicago, IL 60614. Offers bilingual bicultural education (M Ed, MA); counseling (M Ed, MA), including clinical mental health counseling, college student development, school counseling; curriculum studies (M Ed, MA, Ed D); early childhood education (M Ed, MA, Ed D); educating adults (MA); educational leadership (M Ed, MA, Ed D), including administration and supervision (M Ed, MA), principal preparation (M Ed, MA); elementary education (MA); mathematics education (MA); mathematics for teaching (MS); middle school mathematics education (MS); reading specialist (M Ed, MA); secondary education (M Ed); social and cultural foundations in education (MA); special education (M Ed, MA); world languages education (M Ed, MA). Part-time and evening/weekend programs available. Postbaccalaureate distance learning degree programs offered (no on-campus study). *Degree requirements:* For doctorate, thesis/dissertation. Electronic applications accepted.

Dominican University of California, School of Education and Counseling Psychology, Counseling Psychology Department, San Rafael, CA 94901-2298. Offers general (MS); marriage and family therapy (MS). Part-time and evening/weekend programs available. *Faculty:* 5 full-time (4 women), 8 part-time/adjunct (6 women). *Students:* 43 full-time (36 women), 42 part-time (40 women); includes 14 minority (1 Black or African American, non-Hispanic/Latino; 10 Hispanic/Latino; 1 Native Hawaiian or other Pacific Islander, non-Hispanic/Latino; 2 Two or more races, non-Hispanic/Latino). Average age 38. 45 applicants, 56% accepted, 20 enrolled. *Degree requirements:* For master's, comprehensive exam (for some programs), thesis (for some programs). *Entrance requirements:* For master's, minimum GPA of 3.0 for last 60 units, autobiography,

response to scenario. Additional exam requirements/recommendations for international students: Required—TOEFL (minimum score 550 paper-based; 80 iBT), IELTS (minimum score 6.5). *Application deadline:* For fall admission, 4/1 priority date for domestic and international students; for spring admission, 11/15 priority date for domestic and international students. Applications are processed on a rolling basis. Electronic applications accepted. Application fee is waived when completed online. *Expenses:* Expenses: $1,025 per unit. *Financial support:* Career-related internships or fieldwork, scholarships/grants, and health care benefits available. Support available to part-time students. Financial award application deadline: 3/2; financial award applicants required to submit FAFSA. *Unit head:* Dr. Robin R. Gayle, Chair, 415-485-3263. *Application contact:* Shana Friedman, Assistant Director, Graduate Admissions, 415-485-3246, Fax: 415-485-3214, E-mail: shana.friedman@dominican.edu.
Website: http://www.dominican.edu/academics/education/counpsych

Duquesne University, School of Education, Department of Counseling, Psychology, and Special Education, Program in Counselor Education, Pittsburgh, PA 15282-0001. Offers clinical mental health counseling (MS Ed, Post-Master's Certificate); counselor education and supervision (Ed D); counselor licensure (Post-Master's Certificate); marriage and family counseling (MS Ed); school counseling (MS Ed). *Accreditation:* ACA (one or more programs are accredited). Part-time and evening/weekend programs available. *Faculty:* 9 full-time (4 women). *Students:* 165 full-time (122 women), 21 part-time (18 women); includes 38 minority (26 Black or African American, non-Hispanic/Latino; 1 American Indian or Alaska Native, non-Hispanic/Latino; 2 Asian, non-Hispanic/Latino; 4 Hispanic/Latino; 5 Two or more races, non-Hispanic/Latino), 6 international. Average age 30. 207 applicants, 43% accepted, 57 enrolled. In 2014, 42 master's, 4 doctorates awarded. *Degree requirements:* For master's, thesis optional; for doctorate, thesis/dissertation. *Entrance requirements:* For master's, letters of recommendation, essay, interview, bachelor's degree; for doctorate, GRE, letters of recommendation, essay, interview, master's degree; for Post-Master's Certificate, GRE, letters of recommendation, essay, interview, bachelor's/master's degree. Additional exam requirements/recommendations for international students: Required—TOEFL (minimum score 550 paper-based), IELTS (minimum score 7). *Application deadline:* For fall admission, 3/1 for domestic students; for spring admission, 9/1 for domestic students. Applications are processed on a rolling basis. Application fee: $0. Electronic applications accepted. *Expenses: Tuition:* Full-time $18,882; part-time $1049 per credit. *Required fees:* $1800; $100 per credit. Tuition and fees vary according to program. *Financial support:* Research assistantships, teaching assistantships, and Federal Work-Study available. Support available to part-time students. *Unit head:* Dr. Jered Kolbert, Professor/Director, 412-396-4471, Fax: 412-396-1340, E-mail: kolbertj@duq.edu. *Application contact:* Michael Dolinger, Director of Student and Academic Services, 412-396-6647, Fax: 412-396-5585, E-mail: dolingerm@duq.edu.
Website: http://www.duq.edu/academics/schools/education/graduate-programs-education/ms-ed-counselor-education

Eastern Nazarene College, Adult and Graduate Studies, Program in Marriage and Family Therapy, Quincy, MA 02170. Offers MS. Part-time and evening/weekend programs available. *Entrance requirements:* For master's, 3 letters of recommendation, resume. Additional exam requirements/recommendations for international students: Required—TOEFL (minimum score 550 paper-based).

Eastern University, Department of Counseling Psychology, St. Davids, PA 19087-3696. Offers applied behavior analysis (MA); counseling (MA); school counseling (MA, Certificate); school psychology (MS, Certificate). Part-time programs available. *Faculty:* 6 full-time (3 women), 8 part-time/adjunct (6 women). *Students:* 61 full-time (49 women), 102 part-time (85 women); includes 51 minority (44 Black or African American, non-Hispanic/Latino; 1 American Indian or Alaska Native, non-Hispanic/Latino; 4 Hispanic/Latino; 2 Two or more races, non-Hispanic/Latino), 2 international. Average age 30. 117 applicants, 77% accepted, 68 enrolled. In 2014, 68 master's awarded. *Degree requirements:* For master's, internship. *Entrance requirements:* For master's, minimum GPA of 2.8 (3.0 for school psychology). Additional exam requirements/recommendations for international students: Required—TOEFL (minimum score 550 paper-based; 79 iBT). *Application deadline:* For fall admission, 6/15 for domestic students, 5/30 for international students. Applications are processed on a rolling basis. Application fee: $35. Electronic applications accepted. Application fee is waived when completed online. *Expenses: Tuition:* Full-time $15,600; part-time $650 per credit. *Required fees:* $30; $27.50 per semester. One-time fee: $50. Tuition and fees vary according to course load, degree level and program. *Financial support:* In 2014–15, 21 students received support, including 6 research assistantships with partial tuition reimbursements available (averaging $8,115 per year); scholarships/grants and unspecified assistantships also available. Financial award application deadline: 3/15. *Unit head:* Dr. Susan Edgar-Smith, Co-Chair, 610-341-4379. *Application contact:* Katelyn Ambrose, Enrollment Counselor, 610-225-5564, Fax: 610-341-1585, E-mail: kambrose@eastern.edu.
Website: http://www.eastern.edu/academics/programs/counseling-psychology-department

Eastern Washington University, Graduate Studies, College of Social and Behavioral Sciences and Social Work, Program in Mental Health Counseling, Cheney, WA 99004-2431. Offers applied psychology (MS); mental health counseling (MS).

East Texas Baptist University, Master of Arts in Counseling Program, Marshall, TX 75670-1498. Offers MA. Part-time programs available. *Faculty:* 4 full-time (0 women), 1 part-time/adjunct (0 women). *Students:* 22 full-time (14 women), 7 part-time (4 women); includes 12 minority (9 Black or African American, non-Hispanic/Latino; 2 Hispanic/Latino; 1 Two or more races, non-Hispanic/Latino). Average age 32. 26 applicants, 50% accepted, 10 enrolled. In 2014, 7 master's awarded. *Entrance requirements:* Additional exam requirements/recommendations for international students: Recommended—TOEFL (minimum score 550 paper-based; 79 iBT). *Application deadline:* For fall admission, 8/20 for domestic and international students; for spring admission, 1/7 for domestic and international students. Applications are processed on a rolling basis. Application fee: $50. Electronic applications accepted. *Expenses:* Expenses: Contact institution. *Financial support:* Federal Work-Study available. Financial award applicants required to submit FAFSA. *Unit head:* Dr. Gerald Nissley, Director, 903-923-2095, Fax: 903-923-2001, E-mail: macounsel@etbu.edu. *Application contact:* Den Murley, Graduate Services and Recruiting Coordinator, 903-923-2079, Fax: 903-934-8115, E-mail: dmurley@etbu.edu.
Website: http://www.etbu.edu/sciences/master-arts-counseling/

Edinboro University of Pennsylvania, Department of Counseling, School Psychology and Special Education, Edinboro, PA 16444. Offers counseling (MA), including art therapy, clinical mental health counseling, college counseling, rehabilitation counseling, school counseling; educational psychology (M Ed); school psychology (Ed S); special education (M Ed), including autism, behavior management. Part-time and evening/weekend programs available. *Degree requirements:* For master's, thesis or alternative, competency exam; for Ed S, thesis or alternative. *Entrance requirements:* For master's and Ed S, GRE or MAT, minimum QPA of 2.5. Electronic applications accepted.

Emporia State University, Program in Clinical Counseling, Emporia, KS 66801-5415. Offers MS. *Accreditation:* ACA. Part-time programs available. *Faculty:* 10 full-time (6 women), 1 (woman) part-time/adjunct. *Students:* 15 full-time (12 women), 9 part-time (8 women); includes 4 minority (1 Black or African American, non-Hispanic/Latino; 1 Hispanic/Latino; 2 Two or more races, non-Hispanic/Latino), 2 international. 13 applicants, 85% accepted, 1 enrolled. In 2014, 11 master's awarded. *Degree requirements:* For master's, comprehensive exam, internship. *Entrance requirements:* For master's, GRE or MAT. Additional exam requirements/recommendations for international students: Required—TOEFL (minimum score 520 paper-based; 68 iBT). *Application deadline:* For fall admission, 8/15 for domestic students. Applications are processed on a rolling basis. Application fee: $30 ($75 for international students). Electronic applications accepted. *Expenses:* Tuition, state resident: part-time $227 per credit hour. Tuition, nonresident: part-time $706 per credit hour. *Required fees:* $75 per credit hour. Tuition and fees vary according to campus/location. *Financial support:* In 2014–15, 1 research assistantship with full tuition reimbursement (averaging $7,344 per year) was awarded; Federal Work-Study, institutionally sponsored loans, health care benefits, and unspecified assistantships also available. Financial award application deadline: 3/15; financial award applicants required to submit FAFSA. *Unit head:* Dr. James Costello, Chair, 620-341-5791, E-mail: jcostell@emporia.edu. *Application contact:* Mary Sewell, Admissions Coordinator, 800-950-GRAD, Fax: 620-341-5909, E-mail: msewell@emporia.edu.

Evangel University, Department of Behavioral Sciences, Springfield, MO 65802. Offers clinical mental health counseling (MS). Part-time programs available. *Faculty:* 4 full-time (3 women), 2 part-time/adjunct (0 women). *Students:* 33 full-time (22 women), 20 part-time (12 women); includes 7 minority (2 Black or African American, non-Hispanic/Latino; 4 Hispanic/Latino; 1 Two or more races, non-Hispanic/Latino). Average age 35. 15 applicants, 93% accepted, 12 enrolled. In 2014, 18 master's awarded. *Degree requirements:* For master's, comprehensive exam, thesis optional. *Entrance requirements:* For master's, GRE General Test or MAT, minimum undergraduate GPA of 3.0, undergraduate major or minor in psychology. Additional exam requirements/recommendations for international students: Required—TOEFL (minimum score 550 paper-based). *Application deadline:* For fall admission, 7/15 priority date for domestic students, 8/1 for international students; for spring admission, 11/15 priority date for domestic students, 12/1 for international students. Applications are processed on a rolling basis. Application fee: $25. Electronic applications accepted. *Financial support:* In 2014–15, 6 students received support. Career-related internships or fieldwork, scholarships/grants, and unspecified assistantships available. Support available to part-time students. Financial award application deadline: 4/1; financial award applicants required to submit FAFSA. *Unit head:* Christine Arnzen, Program Coordinator, 417-865-2815 Ext. 8618, E-mail: arnzenc@evangel.edu. *Application contact:* Matt Petry, Admissions Representative, Graduate Studies, 417-865-2815 Ext. 7229, Fax: 417-575-5484, E-mail: petrym@evangel.edu.
Website: https://www.evangel.edu/departments/behavioral-social-sciences/about-the-department/

Fairfield University, Graduate School of Education and Allied Professions, Fairfield, CT 06824. Offers applied behavior analysis (ATC); applied psychology (MA); clinical mental health counseling (MA, CAS); early childhood studies (ATC); educational technology (MA); elementary education (MA, CAS); family studies (MA); integration of spirituality and religion in counseling (ATC); marriage and family therapy (MA); school counseling (MA, CAS); school psychology (MA, CAS); school-based marriage and family therapy (ATC); secondary education (MA); special education (MA, CAS); substance abuse counseling (ATC); teaching (Certificate); teaching and foundations (MA, CAS); TESOL, world languages, and bilingual education (MA, CAS). *Accreditation:* NCATE. Part-time and evening/weekend programs available. *Faculty:* 23 full-time (19 women), 32 part-time/adjunct (25 women). *Students:* 148 full-time (131 women), 286 part-time (238 women); includes 81 minority (18 Black or African American, non-Hispanic/Latino; 1 American Indian or Alaska Native, non-Hispanic/Latino; 14 Asian, non-Hispanic/Latino; 39 Hispanic/Latino; 9 Two or more races, non-Hispanic/Latino), 13 international. Average age 34. 264 applicants, 54% accepted, 68 enrolled. In 2014, 142 master's awarded. *Degree requirements:* For master's, comprehensive exam. *Entrance requirements:* For master's, PRAXIS I (for certification programs), minimum GPA of 3.0, 2 recommendations, resume. Additional exam requirements/recommendations for international students: Required—TOEFL (minimum score 550 paper-based; 84 iBT) or IELTS (minimum score 7.5). *Application deadline:* For fall admission, 2/15 for international students; for spring admission, 10/1 for international students. Application fee: $60. Electronic applications accepted. *Expenses:* Expenses: $675 per credit hour. *Financial support:* In 2014–15, 55 students received support. Career-related internships or fieldwork and unspecified assistantships available. Financial award applicants required to submit FAFSA. *Faculty research:* Literacy, spirituality, special education, bilingual/multicultural education, mentoring and professional development. *Unit head:* Dr. Robert D. Hannafin, Dean, 203-254-4250, Fax: 203-254-4241, E-mail: rhannafin@fairfield.edu. *Application contact:* Marianne Gumpper, Director of Graduate and Continuing Studies Admission, 203-254-4184, Fax: 203-254-4073, E-mail: gradadmis@fairfield.edu.
Website: http://www.fairfield.edu/academics/schoolscollegescenters/graduateschoolofeducationalliedprofessions/graduateprograms/

Fairleigh Dickinson University, College at Florham, Maxwell Becton College of Arts and Sciences, Department of Psychology, Program in Clinical Mental Health Counseling, Madison, NJ 07940-1099. Offers MA. *Accreditation:* ACA.

Fairleigh Dickinson University, College at Florham, Maxwell Becton College of Arts and Sciences, Department of Psychology, Program in Counseling, Madison, NJ 07940-1099. Offers MA. *Accreditation:* ACA.

Felician College, Program in Counseling Psychology, Lodi, NJ 07644-2117. Offers MA.

Fitchburg State University, Division of Graduate and Continuing Education, Programs in Counseling, Fitchburg, MA 01420-2697. Offers elementary school guidance counseling (MS); mental health counseling (MS); secondary school guidance counseling (MS). *Accreditation:* NCATE. Part-time and evening/weekend programs available. *Entrance requirements:* Additional exam requirements/recommendations for international students: Required—TOEFL (minimum score 550 paper-based; 79 iBT). Electronic applications accepted.

Florida Atlantic University, College of Education, Department of Counselor Education, Boca Raton, FL 33431-0991. Offers counselor education (M Ed, PhD, Ed S); marriage and family therapy (Ed S); mental health counseling (M Ed, Ed S); rehabilitation counseling (M Ed); school counseling (M Ed, Ed S). *Accreditation:* ACA; NCATE. Part-time and evening/weekend programs available. *Degree requirements:* For Ed S, departmental qualifying exam. *Entrance requirements:* For master's, GRE General Test, minimum GPA of 3.0 during previous 2 years; for Ed S, GRE General Test, minimum graduate GPA of 3.25. Additional exam requirements/recommendations for international students: Required—TOEFL (minimum score 500 paper-based; 61 iBT), IELTS (minimum score 6). *Expenses:* Tuition, state resident: full-time $7396; part-time $369.82 per credit hour. Tuition, nonresident: full-time $19,392; part-time $1024.81 per credit hour. Tuition and fees vary according to course load. *Faculty research:* Brief therapy, psychological type, marriage and family counseling, international programs, integrated services.

Counseling Psychology

Florida International University, College of Arts and Sciences, Department of Psychology, Miami, FL 33199. Offers behavioral analysis (MS); clinical science (PhD); counseling psychology (MS); developmental science (MS, PhD); legal psychology (PhD); organizational psychology (MS, PhD). Program has fall admissions only. Part-time and evening/weekend programs available. Terminal master's awarded for partial completion of doctoral program. *Degree requirements:* For master's, thesis; for doctorate, comprehensive exam, thesis/dissertation. *Entrance requirements:* For master's, GRE General Test, minimum GPA of 3.0, resume, 3 letters of recommendation; for doctorate, GRE General Test, 3 letters of recommendation, resume, letter of intent, two writing samples, minimum GPA of 3.0. Additional exam requirements/recommendations for international students: Required—TOEFL (minimum score 550 paper-based; 80 iBT). Electronic applications accepted. *Faculty research:* Legal psychology, organizational and industrial psychology, child behavior psychology.

Florida International University, College of Education, Department of Leadership and Professional Studies, Miami, FL 33199. Offers adult education and human resource development (MS, Ed D); counseling (MS), including rehabilitation counseling, school counseling; counselor education (MS), including clinical mental health counseling; educational administration and supervision (Ed D); educational leadership (MS, Certificate, Ed S); higher education (Ed D); higher education administration (MS); recreation and sport management (MS), including recreation and sport management, recreational therapy; school psychology (Ed S); urban education (MS), including instruction in urban settings, learning technologies, multicultural/bilingual, multicultural/TESOL, urban education. Part-time and evening/weekend programs available. *Degree requirements:* For doctorate, thesis/dissertation. *Entrance requirements:* For master's, minimum GPA of 3.0; for doctorate and other advanced degree, GRE General Test. Additional exam requirements/recommendations for international students: Required—TOEFL (minimum score 550 paper-based; 80 iBT), IELTS (minimum score 6.3). Electronic applications accepted.

Florida State University, The Graduate School, College of Education, Department of Educational Psychology and Learning Systems, Program in Counseling and Human Systems, Tallahassee, FL 32306. Offers counseling psychology and school psychology (PhD); MS/Ed S. *Accreditation:* ACA (one or more programs are accredited). *Faculty:* 13 full-time (8 women), 1 part-time/adjunct (0 women). *Students:* 100 full-time (84 women), 21 part-time (16 women); includes 31 minority (9 Black or African American, non-Hispanic/Latino; 1 American Indian or Alaska Native, non-Hispanic/Latino; 3 Asian, non-Hispanic/Latino; 18 Hispanic/Latino), 2 international. Average age 28. 192 applicants, 41% accepted, 41 enrolled. In 2014, 10 doctorates awarded. Terminal master's awarded for partial completion of doctoral program. *Degree requirements:* For doctorate, comprehensive exam, thesis/dissertation. *Entrance requirements:* Additional exam requirements/recommendations for international students: Required—PTE (minimum score 55), TOEFL (minimum score 550 paper-based, 80 iBT), IELTS (minimum score 6.5) or Michigan English Language Assessment Battery (minimum score 77). *Application deadline:* For fall admission, 1/15 for domestic and international students. Applications are processed on a rolling basis. Application fee: $30. Electronic applications accepted. *Expenses:* Expenses: Contact institution. *Financial support:* Fellowships with full and partial tuition reimbursements, research assistantships with full and partial tuition reimbursements, teaching assistantships with full and partial tuition reimbursements, scholarships/grants, tuition waivers (full and partial), and unspecified assistantships available. Financial award applicants required to submit FAFSA. *Faculty research:* Practitioner-scholar models; cultural diversity in populations; social, emotional, and vocational capabilities and talent identification of learners; counseling; technology and learners. *Unit head:* Dr. Frances Prevatt, Program Leader, 850-644-9445, Fax: 850-644-8776, E-mail: fprevatt@fsu.edu. *Application contact:* Lori Hayes, Program Assistant, 850-644-8046, Fax: 850-644-8776, E-mail: lahayes@fsu.edu.
Website: http://www.coe.fsu.edu/Current-Students/Departments/Educational-Psychology-and-Learning-Systems-EPLS/Current-Students/Psychological-and-Counseling-Ser

Fordham University, Graduate School of Education, Division of Psychological and Educational Services, New York, NY 10023. Offers counseling and personnel services (MSE, Adv C); counseling psychology (PhD); educational psychology (MSE, PhD); school psychology (PhD); urban and urban bilingual school psychology (Adv C). *Accreditation:* APA (one or more programs are accredited); NCATE. *Degree requirements:* For doctorate, thesis/dissertation. *Entrance requirements:* For doctorate, GRE General Test.

Fort Valley State University, College of Graduate Studies and Extended Education, Department of Counseling Psychology, Program in Mental Health Counseling, Fort Valley, GA 31030. Offers MS. *Accreditation:* ACA. Part-time programs available. *Degree requirements:* For master's, comprehensive exam (for some programs), thesis optional. *Entrance requirements:* For master's, GRE General Test or MAT. Additional exam requirements/recommendations for international students: Recommended—TOEFL.

Franciscan University of Steubenville, Graduate Programs, Department of Clinical Mental Health Counseling, Steubenville, OH 43952-1763. Offers MA. Part-time programs available. *Faculty:* 3 full-time (1 woman), 6 part-time/adjunct (3 women). *Students:* 38 full-time (28 women), 14 part-time (13 women); includes 14 minority (2 Black or African American, non-Hispanic/Latino; 9 Hispanic/Latino; 3 Two or more races, non-Hispanic/Latino). Average age 31. 39 applicants, 69% accepted, 22 enrolled. In 2014, 22 master's awarded. *Degree requirements:* For master's, case presentation, integrative paper. *Entrance requirements:* For master's, GRE General Test or MAT for those with a GPA below 3.0, minimum undergraduate GPA of 2.5. Additional exam requirements/recommendations for international students: Required—TOEFL. *Application deadline:* For fall admission, 7/1 for domestic students, 4/30 for international students; for spring admission, 12/15 for domestic students, 9/30 for international students. Applications are processed on a rolling basis. Application fee: $20. Electronic applications accepted. Application fee is waived when completed online. *Expenses:* Tuition: Full-time $12,330; part-time $685 per credit. *Required fees:* $288; $16 per credit. One-time fee: $170 full-time. Tuition and fees vary according to course load and program. *Financial support:* Career-related internships or fieldwork, Federal Work-Study, and scholarships/grants available. Support available to part-time students. Financial award application deadline: 7/1; financial award applicants required to submit FAFSA. *Unit head:* Dr. Christin Jungers, Program Director, 740-284-7220. *Application contact:* Mark McGuire, Director of Graduate Enrollment, 800-783-6220, Fax: 740-284-5456, E-mail: mmcguire@franciscan.edu.
Website: http://www.franciscan.edu/cmhc/

Francis Marion University, Graduate Programs, Department of Psychology, Florence, SC 29502-0547. Offers applied psychology (MS), including clinical/counseling psychology, school psychology; school psychology (SSP). Part-time and evening/weekend programs available. *Faculty:* 6 full-time (2 women), 4 part-time/adjunct (all women). *Students:* 35 full-time (30 women), 11 part-time (all women); includes 9 minority (7 Black or African American, non-Hispanic/Latino; 2 Asian, non-Hispanic/Latino), 1 international. Average age 26. 43 applicants, 100% accepted, 16 enrolled. In 2014, 15 master's, 6 other advanced degrees awarded. *Degree requirements:* For master's, internship. *Entrance requirements:* For master's, GRE General Test, official transcripts, two letters of recommendation, written statement. *Application deadline:* For

fall admission, 2/15 for domestic and international students; for spring admission, 10/15 for domestic and international students. Applications are processed on a rolling basis. Application fee: $35. Electronic applications accepted. *Expenses:* Tuition, state resident: full-time $9472; part-time $473.60 per credit hour. Tuition, nonresident: full-time $18,944; part-time $947.20 per credit hour. *Required fees:* $14 per credit hour. $107 per semester. Tuition and fees vary according to course load and program. *Financial support:* In 2014–15, 4 teaching assistantships (averaging $7,750 per year) were awarded; career-related internships or fieldwork, scholarships/grants, and unspecified assistantships also available. Support available to part-time students. Financial award application deadline: 3/1; financial award applicants required to submit FAFSA. *Faculty research:* Parenting and family relationships, child development, applied behavioral analysis, post-traumatic stress disorder, clinical psychology in adults. *Unit head:* Dr. William Wattles, Chair, 843-661-1641, Fax: 843-661-1628. *Application contact:* Sharekka Bridges, Administrative Assistant, 843-661-1641, Fax: 843-661-1628.
Website: http://www.fmarion.edu/academics/psychology

Frostburg State University, Graduate School, College of Liberal Arts and Sciences, Department of Psychology, Program in Counseling Psychology, Frostburg, MD 21532-1099. Offers MS. Part-time and evening/weekend programs available. *Degree requirements:* For master's, internship. *Entrance requirements:* For master's, GRE General Test or MAT, interview, minimum GPA of 3.0, resume. Additional exam requirements/recommendations for international students: Required—TOEFL. Electronic applications accepted.

Gallaudet University, The Graduate School, Washington, DC 20002-3625. Offers ASL/English bilingual early childhood education: birth to 5 (Certificate); audiology (Au D); clinical psychology (PhD); critical studies in the education of deaf learners (PhD); deaf and hard of hearing infants, toddlers, and their families (Certificate); deaf education (Ed S); deaf education: advanced studies (MA); deaf education: special programs (MA); deaf history (Certificate); deaf studies (MA, Certificate); educating deaf students with disabilities (Certificate); education: teacher preparation (MA), including deaf education, early childhood education and deaf education, elementary education and deaf education, secondary education and deaf education; educational neuroscience (PhD); hearing, speech and language sciences (MS, PhD); international development (MA); interpretation (MA, PhD), including combined interpreting practice and research (MA), interpreting research (MA); linguistics (MA, PhD); mental health counseling (MA); peer mentoring (Certificate); public administration (MPA); school counseling (MA); school psychology (Psy S); sign language teaching (MA); social work (MSW); speech-language pathology (MS). Part-time programs available. *Students:* 325 full-time (251 women), 118 part-time (90 women); includes 91 minority (41 Black or African American, non-Hispanic/Latino; 1 American Indian or Alaska Native, non-Hispanic/Latino; 14 Asian, non-Hispanic/Latino; 25 Hispanic/Latino; 10 Two or more races, non-Hispanic/Latino), 28 international. Average age 30. 617 applicants, 42% accepted, 171 enrolled. In 2014, 145 master's, 21 doctorates, 8 other advanced degrees awarded. Terminal master's awarded for partial completion of doctoral program. *Degree requirements:* For master's, comprehensive exam (for some programs), thesis optional; for doctorate, comprehensive exam, thesis/dissertation. *Entrance requirements:* For master's and doctorate, GRE General Test or MAT, letters of recommendation, interviews, goals statement, American Sign Language proficiency interview, written English competency. Additional exam requirements/recommendations for international students: Required—TOEFL. *Application deadline:* For fall admission, 2/15 for domestic students. Applications are processed on a rolling basis. Application fee: $75. Electronic applications accepted. *Expenses: Tuition:* Full-time $15,956; part-time $886.45 per credit hour. *Required fees:* $3404; $263 per semester. *Financial support:* Fellowships, research assistantships, teaching assistantships, career-related internships or fieldwork, Federal Work-Study, scholarships/grants, tuition waivers (partial), and unspecified assistantships available. Support available to part-time students. Financial award applicants required to submit FAFSA. *Faculty research:* Signing math dictionaries, telecommunications access, cancer genetics, linguistics, visual language and visual learning, integrated quantum materials, deaf legal discourse, advance recruitment and retention in geosciences. *Unit head:* Dr. Gaurav Mathur, Interim Dean, Graduate School and Continuing Studies, 202-250-2380, Fax: 202-651-5027, E-mail: gaurav.mathur@gallaudet.edu. *Application contact:* Wednesday Luria, Coordinator of Prospective Graduate Student Services, 202-651-5400, Fax: 202-651-5295, E-mail: graduate.school@gallaudet.edu.
Website: http://www.gallaudet.edu/x26696.xml

Gannon University, School of Graduate Studies, College of Humanities, Education, and Social Sciences, School of Humanities, Program in Clinical Mental Health Counseling, Erie, PA 16541-0001. Offers MS. *Accreditation:* ACA. Part-time and evening/weekend programs available. *Degree requirements:* For master's, thesis, internship. *Entrance requirements:* For master's, GRE, minimum GPA of 2.8, PA child abuse clearances. Additional exam requirements/recommendations for international students: Required—TOEFL (minimum score 79 iBT). Electronic applications accepted. *Faculty research:* Student learning outcomes in CACREP clinical mental health counselor education, affective forecasting and counseling outcomes in clinical mental health counseling.

Gardner-Webb University, Graduate School, School of Psychology, Program in Mental Health Counseling, Boiling Springs, NC 28017. Offers MA. *Accreditation:* ACA. Part-time and evening/weekend programs available. *Students:* 18 full-time (16 women), 31 part-time (25 women); includes 9 minority (7 Black or African American, non-Hispanic/Latino; 2 Hispanic/Latino). Average age 32. 63 applicants, 30% accepted, 19 enrolled. In 2014, 8 master's awarded. *Degree requirements:* For master's, comprehensive exam. *Entrance requirements:* For master's, GRE General Test, MAT, minimum GPA of 2.7. *Application deadline:* For fall admission, 7/1 priority date for domestic students. Applications are processed on a rolling basis. Application fee: $40. Electronic applications accepted. *Expenses: Tuition:* Part-time $406 per credit hour. Tuition and fees vary according to program. *Financial support:* Unspecified assistantships available. *Unit head:* Dr. Frieda Brown, Coordinator, 704-406-4436, Fax: 704-406-4329, E-mail: fbrown@gardner-webb.edu. *Application contact:* Office of Graduate Admissions, 877-498-4723, Fax: 704-406-3895, E-mail: gradinfo@gardner-webb.edu.

Geneva College, Master of Arts in Counseling Program, Beaver Falls, PA 15010-3599. Offers clinical mental health counseling (MA); marriage and family counseling (MA); school counseling (MA). *Accreditation:* ACA. Part-time and evening/weekend programs available. *Faculty:* 6 full-time (2 women), 7 part-time/adjunct (3 women). *Students:* 53 full-time (42 women), 42 part-time (31 women); includes 8 minority (all Black or African American, non-Hispanic/Latino). Average age 34. 42 applicants, 74% accepted, 27 enrolled. In 2014, 29 master's awarded. *Degree requirements:* For master's, 50-60 credits (depending on program), practicum, internship. *Entrance requirements:* For master's, minimum GPA of 3.0 (preferred), 3 letters of recommendation, essay on career goals, resume of educational and professional experiences. Additional exam requirements/recommendations for international students: Required—TOEFL. *Application deadline:* For fall admission, 9/1 for domestic students; for spring admission, 1/10 for domestic students. Applications are processed on a rolling basis. Electronic applications accepted. *Expenses:* Expenses: Contact institution. *Financial support:* In 2014–15, 5 students received support. Research assistantships, teaching

assistantships, career-related internships or fieldwork, and unspecified assistantships available. Financial award application deadline: 8/1; financial award applicants required to submit FAFSA. *Faculty research:* Blended family counseling; premarital and newlywed couples; religion in clinical supervision; conceptual mapping in research, supervision, and clinical work; Factor Analytic Study of the ROSI (Recovery Oriented System Indicators). *Unit head:* Dr. Shannon Shiderly, Program Director, 724-847-6649, Fax: 724-847-6101, E-mail: slshider@geneva.edu. *Application contact:* Marina Frazier, Graduate Program Manager, 724-847-6697, E-mail: counseling@geneva.edu. Website: http://www.geneva.edu/page/grad_counseling

George Fox University, College of Education, Graduate Department of Counseling, Newberg, OR 97132-2697. Offers clinical mental health counseling (MA); marriage, couple and family counseling (MA, Certificate); mental health trauma (Certificate); school counseling (MA, Certificate); school psychology (Certificate, Ed S). Part-time programs available. *Degree requirements:* For master's, clinical project. *Entrance requirements:* For master's, MAT or GRE, bachelor's degree from regionally-accredited college or university, minimum cumulative GPA of 3.0, 1 professional and 1 academic reference, resume, on-campus interview, official transcripts. Additional exam requirements/recommendations for international students: Required—TOEFL (minimum score 577 paper-based; 90 iBT), IELTS (minimum score 7). Electronic applications accepted. *Expenses:* Contact institution.

Georgian Court University, School of Arts and Sciences, Lakewood, NJ 08701-2697. Offers applied behavior analysis (MA); Catholic school leadership (Certificate); clinical mental health counseling (MA); holistic health studies (MA, Certificate); homeland security (MS); parish administration (Certificate); pastoral ministry (Certificate); professional counseling (Certificate); religious education (Certificate); school psychology (MA, Certificate); theology (MA, Certificate). Part-time and evening/weekend programs available. *Faculty:* 19 full-time (9 women), 9 part-time/adjunct (4 women). *Students:* 87 full-time (74 women), 127 part-time (110 women); includes 47 minority (14 Black or African American, non-Hispanic/Latino; 2 Asian, non-Hispanic/Latino; 23 Hispanic/Latino; 8 Two or more races, non-Hispanic/Latino). Average age 34. In 2014, 68 master's, 11 other advanced degrees awarded. *Degree requirements:* For master's, comprehensive exam (for some programs), thesis (for some programs). *Entrance requirements:* For master's, GRE, MAT, or NTE/PRAXIS, 3 letters of recommendation. Additional exam requirements/recommendations for international students: Required— TOEFL (minimum score 550 paper-based). *Application deadline:* For fall admission, 8/1 priority date for domestic students, 4/1 for international students; for spring admission, 1/1 priority date for domestic students, 7/1 for international students. Applications are processed on a rolling basis. Application fee: $40. Electronic applications accepted. *Expenses: Tuition:* Full-time $19,752; part-time $823 per credit. *Required fees:* $948; $243 per semester hour. Tuition and fees vary according to campus/location and program. *Financial support:* Scholarships/grants, health care benefits, and unspecified assistantships available. Financial award application deadline: 4/15; financial award applicants required to submit FAFSA. *Unit head:* Dr. Rita Kipp, Dean, 732-987-2493, Fax: 732-987-2007, E-mail: rkipp@georgian.edu. *Application contact:* Patrick Givens, Interim Director of Enrollment Management, 732-987-2736, Fax: 732-987-2084, E-mail: graduateadmissions@georgian.edu. Website: http://www.georgian.edu/arts_sciences/index.htm

Georgia State University, College of Education, Department of Counseling and Psychological Services, Program in Mental Health Counseling, Atlanta, GA 30302-3083. Offers MS, Ed S. *Accreditation:* ACA (one or more programs are accredited); APA (one or more programs are accredited). *Degree requirements:* For master's, comprehensive exam. *Entrance requirements:* For master's, GRE, goal statement, resume, 3 letters of recommendation, transcripts. Additional exam requirements/recommendations for international students: Required—TOEFL. *Application deadline:* For fall admission, 2/1 for domestic and international students. Application fee: $50. Electronic applications accepted. *Expenses:* Tuition, state resident: full-time $6516; part-time $362 per credit hour. Tuition, nonresident: full-time $22,014; part-time $1223 per credit hour. *Required fees:* $2128 per semester. Tuition and fees vary according to course load and program. *Financial support:* Research assistantships with full and partial tuition reimbursements, teaching assistantships with full and partial tuition reimbursements, career-related internships or fieldwork, scholarships/grants, health care benefits, and unspecified assistantships available. Financial award application deadline: 4/1. *Faculty research:* Motivational interviewing, basic counseling skills, group counseling, addictions, spirituality. *Unit head:* Dr. Brian Dew, Chairperson, 404-413-8168, Fax: 404-413-8013, E-mail: bdew@gsu.edu. *Application contact:* CPS Admissions Office, 404-413-8200. Website: http://cps.education.gsu.edu/programs/mental-health-counseling/

Goddard College, Graduate Division, Master of Arts in Psychology and Counseling Program, Plainfield, VT 05667-9432. Offers sexual orientation (MA). Part-time programs available. Postbaccalaureate distance learning degree programs offered (minimal on-campus study). *Faculty:* 1 (woman) full-time, 8 part-time/adjunct (6 women). *Students:* 49 full-time, 11 part-time. Average age 35. 30 applicants, 100% accepted, 18 enrolled. In 2014, 24 master's awarded. *Degree requirements:* For master's, thesis or alternative, clinical internship. *Entrance requirements:* For master's, eight specific undergraduate prerequisite courses taken within previous five years (preparatory semester at Goddard can substitute), statement of purpose, 3 letters of recommendation, interview. *Application deadline:* Applications are processed on a rolling basis. Application fee: $40. Electronic applications accepted. *Expenses: Tuition:* Full-time $16,578. Tuition and fees vary according to course load and program. *Financial support:* Scholarships/grants, tuition waivers (partial), and grants to help support internships for Vermont students available. Financial award applicants required to submit FAFSA. *Unit head:* Dr. Tracy Garrett, Program Director, 802-454-8311, Fax: 802-454-7835, E-mail: tracy.garrett@goddard.edu. *Application contact:* David DeLucca, Senior Admissions Counselor, 800-906-8312 Ext. 248, Fax: 802-454-1029, E-mail: david.delucca@goddard.edu. Website: http://www.goddard.edu/academics/ma/master-arts-counseling/

Gonzaga University, School of Education, Program in Counseling Psychology, Spokane, WA 99258. Offers MAC, MAP. *Accreditation:* ACA. Part-time programs available. *Faculty:* 6 full-time (3 women), 7 part-time/adjunct (5 women). *Students:* 61 full-time (52 women), 54 part-time (47 women); includes 10 minority (1 Black or African American, non-Hispanic/Latino; 2 Asian, non-Hispanic/Latino; 6 Hispanic/Latino; 1 Two or more races, non-Hispanic/Latino), 38 international. Average age 30. 124 applicants, 60% accepted, 56 enrolled. In 2014, 52 master's awarded. *Degree requirements:* For master's, comprehensive exam. *Entrance requirements:* For master's, GRE General Test or MAT, minimum B average in undergraduate course work. Additional exam requirements/recommendations for international students: Required—TOEFL. *Application deadline:* For fall admission, 3/1 for domestic students. Application fee: $50. Electronic applications accepted. *Expenses:* Expenses: Contact institution. *Financial support:* In 2014–15, 8 students received support. Teaching assistantships available. Support available to part-time students. Financial award application deadline: 2/1; financial award applicants required to submit FAFSA. *Unit head:* Dr. Mark Young, Department Chair, 509-313-3658, E-mail: young@gonzaga.edu. *Application contact:* 509-313-3481, Fax: 509-313-3491, E-mail: soegrad@gonzaga.edu.

Governors State University, College of Education, Program in Counseling, University Park, IL 60484. Offers MA. *Accreditation:* ACA. Part-time and evening/weekend programs available. *Degree requirements:* For master's, practicum. *Entrance requirements:* For master's, minimum GPA of 2.5 in last 60 hours of course work or minimum GPA of 2.25 and GRE General Test.

Grace College, Department of Counseling and Interpersonal Relations, Winona Lake, IN 46590-1294. Offers clinical mental health counseling (MA). *Accreditation:* ACA. Part-time programs available. *Degree requirements:* For master's, comprehensive exam, portfolio, internships. *Entrance requirements:* For master's, GRE, references, background check, interview, minimum GPA of 3.0. Additional exam requirements/recommendations for international students: Required—TOEFL. Electronic applications accepted. Application fee is waived when completed online. *Faculty research:* Trauma and sexual abuse.

Grace University, College of Graduate Studies, Counseling Program, Omaha, NE 68108. Offers MA. *Entrance requirements:* For master's, minimum undergraduate GPA of 3.0.

Grand Canyon University, College of Nursing and Health Sciences, Phoenix, AZ 85017-1097. Offers addiction counseling (MS); health care administration (MS); health care informatics (MS); marriage and family therapy (MS); professional counseling (MS); public health (MS). Part-time and evening/weekend programs available. Postbaccalaureate distance learning degree programs offered (no on-campus study). *Entrance requirements:* For master's, undergraduate degree with minimum GPA of 2.8. Additional exam requirements/recommendations for international students: Required— TOEFL (minimum score 575 paper-based; 90 iBT), IELTS (minimum score 7).

Harding University, College of Bible and Ministry, Program in Marriage and Family Therapy, Searcy, AR 72149-0001. Offers marriage and family therapy (MS); mental health counseling (MS). Part-time programs available. *Faculty:* 7 full-time (1 woman). *Students:* 22 full-time (12 women); includes 4 minority (2 Black or African American, non-Hispanic/Latino; 1 American Indian or Alaska Native, non-Hispanic/Latino; 1 Hispanic/Latino), 1 international. Average age 30. 17 applicants, 76% accepted, 13 enrolled. In 2014, 12 master's awarded. *Degree requirements:* For master's, comprehensive exam, 15-month practicum. *Entrance requirements:* For master's, GRE General Test, minimum undergraduate GPA of 2.75, graduate 3.0. *Application deadline:* For fall admission, 4/1 priority date for domestic students. Applications are processed on a rolling basis. Application fee: $40. *Expenses: Tuition:* Full-time $12,096; part-time $672 per credit hour. *Required fees:* $432; $24 per credit hour. Tuition and fees vary according to course load and degree level. *Financial support:* In 2014–15, 5 students received support. Scholarships/grants available. *Faculty research:* Forgiveness, substance abuse, post-traumatic stress disorder. *Unit head:* Dr. Lewis L. Moore, Chairman, 501-279-4347, Fax: 501-279-4417, E-mail: lmoore@harding.edu. *Application contact:* Ruth Ann Dawson, Office Manager, 501-279-4347, Fax: 501-279-4417, E-mail: radawson@harding.edu. Website: http://www.harding.edu/MFT/

Hardin-Simmons University, Graduate School, Cynthia Ann Parker College of Liberal Arts, Department of Psychology, Program in Clinical Counseling and Marriage and Family Therapy, Abilene, TX 79698-0001. Offers MA. Part-time programs available. *Faculty:* 5 full-time (3 women). *Students:* 20 full-time (18 women), 2 part-time (1 woman); includes 2 minority (both Hispanic/Latino). Average age 24. In 2014, 7 master's awarded. *Degree requirements:* For master's, comprehensive exam, clinical experience, project. *Entrance requirements:* For master's, minimum undergraduate GPA of 3.0 in major, 2.7 overall; 21 semester hours of course work in psychology, 18 of those in upper-division classes; writing sample; letters of recommendation. Additional exam requirements/recommendations for international students: Required—TOEFL (minimum score 550 paper-based; 75 iBT). *Application deadline:* For fall admission, 8/15 priority date for domestic students, 4/1 for international students; for spring admission, 1/5 priority date for domestic students, 9/1 for international students. Applications are processed on a rolling basis. Application fee: $50. *Expenses: Tuition:* Full-time $12,060; part-time $670 per credit hour. *Required fees:* $325; $110 per semester. Tuition and fees vary according to program. *Financial support:* In 2014–15, 17 students received support, including 20 fellowships (averaging $677 per year); career-related internships or fieldwork and scholarships/grants also available. Support available to part-time students. Financial award application deadline: 6/30; financial award applicants required to submit FAFSA. *Faculty research:* Family stress management, spirituality in marriage, intimacy and sexuality in marriage, sex education in the church, role of faith in marital satisfaction. *Unit head:* Dr. Gail Roaten, Program Director, 325-670-1534, Fax: 325-670-1458, E-mail: gail.roaten@hsutx.edu. *Application contact:* Dr. Nancy Kucinski, Dean of Graduate Studies, 325-670-1298, Fax: 325-670-1564, E-mail: gradoff@hsutx.edu. Website: http://www.hsutx.edu/academics/cap/graduate/fampsych

Heidelberg University, Program in Counseling, Tiffin, OH 44883-2462. Offers community mental health counseling (MA); school counseling (MA). *Accreditation:* ACA. Part-time and evening/weekend programs available. *Degree requirements:* For master's, thesis or alternative, counseling practicum, internship. *Entrance requirements:* For master's, GRE General Test, 12 hours of course work in behavioral sciences, minimum GPA of 2.9, 3 letters of reference. Additional exam requirements/recommendations for international students: Required—TOEFL.

Henderson State University, Graduate Studies, Teachers College, Department of Counselor Education, Arkadelphia, AR 71999-0001. Offers clinical mental health counseling (MS); developmental therapy (MS, Graduate Certificate); elementary school counseling (MSE); secondary school counseling (MSE). *Accreditation:* ACA; NCATE. Part-time programs available. *Entrance requirements:* For master's, GRE General Test or MAT, letters of recommendation, minimum GPA of 2.7, teacher certification. Additional exam requirements/recommendations for international students: Required— TOEFL (minimum score 600 paper-based); Recommended—IELTS (minimum score 6.5).

Hodges University, Graduate Programs, Naples, FL 34119. Offers accounting (M Acc); business administration (MBA); clinical mental health counseling (MS); health services administration (MS); information systems management (MIS); legal studies (MS); management (MSM). Part-time and evening/weekend programs available. Postbaccalaureate distance learning degree programs offered (no on-campus study). *Faculty:* 17 full-time (10 women), 4 part-time/adjunct (2 women). *Students:* 71 full-time (56 women), 133 part-time (109 women); includes 86 minority (26 Black or African American, non-Hispanic/Latino; 8 Asian, non-Hispanic/Latino; 51 Hispanic/Latino; 1 Two or more races, non-Hispanic/Latino). Average age 35. 48 applicants, 100% accepted, 48 enrolled. In 2014, 63 master's awarded. *Degree requirements:* For master's, comprehensive exam (for some programs), thesis (for some programs). *Entrance requirements:* For master's, essay. Additional exam requirements/recommendations for international students: Recommended—TOEFL. *Application deadline:* Applications are processed on a rolling basis. Application fee: $50. Electronic applications accepted. *Financial support:* Federal Work-Study and scholarships/grants available. Financial award application deadline: 7/9; financial award applicants required to submit FAFSA. *Unit head:* Dr. David Borofsky, President, 239-513-1122, Fax: 239-598-6253, E-mail:

dborofsky@hodges.edu. *Application contact:* Brent Passey, Chief Admissions Officer, 239-513-1122, Fax: 239-598-6253, E-mail: bpassey@hodges.edu.

Hofstra University, School of Health Sciences and Human Services, Programs in Counseling, Hempstead, NY 11549. Offers counseling (MS Ed, PD); creative arts therapy (MA); interdisciplinary transition specialist (Advanced Certificate); marriage and family therapy (MA); mental health counseling (MA); rehabilitation administration (PD); rehabilitation counseling (MS Ed, Advanced Certificate); rehabilitation counseling in mental health (MS Ed, Advanced Certificate); school counselor bilingual extension (Advanced Certificate). Part-time and evening/weekend programs available. *Students:* 138 full-time (128 women), 54 part-time (51 women); includes 53 minority (24 Black or African American, non-Hispanic/Latino; 1 American Indian or Alaska Native, non-Hispanic/Latino; 9 Asian, non-Hispanic/Latino; 18 Hispanic/Latino; 1 Two or more races, non-Hispanic/Latino), 6 international. Average age 30. 117 applicants, 83% accepted, 57 enrolled. In 2014, 72 master's, 4 other advanced degrees awarded. *Degree requirements:* For master's, comprehensive exam (for some programs), thesis (for some programs), internship, practicum, student teaching, seminars, minimum GPA of 3.0. *Entrance requirements:* For master's, GRE, interview, letters of recommendation, portfolio, essay, professional experience, certification; for other advanced degree, GRE, interview, letters of recommendation, essay, professional experience, resume, master's degree. Additional exam requirements/recommendations for international students: Required—TOEFL (minimum score 550 paper-based; 80 iBT). *Application deadline:* Applications are processed on a rolling basis. Application fee: $70 ($75 for international students). Electronic applications accepted. *Expenses: Tuition:* Full-time $20,610; part-time $1145 per credit hour. *Required fees:* $970; $165 per term. Tuition and fees vary according to program. *Financial support:* In 2014–15, 109 students received support, including 29 fellowships with full and partial tuition reimbursements available (averaging $3,381 per year), 4 research assistantships with full and partial tuition reimbursements available (averaging $7,324 per year); career-related internships or fieldwork, Federal Work-Study, institutionally sponsored loans, scholarships/grants, health care benefits, and tuition waivers (full and partial) also available. Support available to part-time students. Financial award applicants required to submit FAFSA. *Faculty research:* Bereavement, loss, and trauma counseling; conflict transformation, the impact of hope on academic success; student persistence; GLBTQ issues. *Unit head:* Dr. Holly Seirup, Chairperson, 516-463-5752, Fax: 516-463-6184, E-mail: vpshjs@hofstra.edu. *Application contact:* Sunil Samuel, Assistant Vice President of Admissions, 516-463-4723, Fax: 516-463-4664, E-mail: graduateadmission@hofstra.edu.
Website: http://www.hofstra.edu/academics/colleges/healthscienceshumanservices/

Holy Family University, Graduate School, School of Arts and Sciences, Program in Counseling Psychology, Philadelphia, PA 19114. Offers MS. Part-time and evening/weekend programs available. *Degree requirements:* For master's, comprehensive exam, thesis optional. *Entrance requirements:* For master's, GRE or MAT (if GPA is below 3.0), baccalaureate degree from accredited college or university; minimum undergraduate cumulative GPA of 3.0; 2 letters of recommendation; personal statement; official transcripts; interview. Additional exam requirements/recommendations for international students: Required—TOEFL (minimum score 550 paper-based; 79 iBT), IELTS (minimum score 6), PTE (minimum score 54). Electronic applications accepted.

Holy Names University, Graduate Division, Department of Counseling Psychology, Oakland, CA 94619-1699. Offers counseling psychology (MA); forensic psychology (MA, Certificate); pastoral counseling (MA, Certificate). Part-time and evening/weekend programs available. *Faculty:* 15. *Students:* 43 full-time (42 women), 40 part-time (33 women); includes 60 minority (33 Black or African American, non-Hispanic/Latino; 4 Asian, non-Hispanic/Latino; 19 Hispanic/Latino; 3 Native Hawaiian or other Pacific Islander, non-Hispanic/Latino; 1 Two or more races, non-Hispanic/Latino). Average age 31. 42 applicants, 62% accepted, 15 enrolled. In 2014, 39 master's, 18 other advanced degrees awarded. *Degree requirements:* For master's, comprehensive paper, seminars. *Entrance requirements:* For master's, minimum undergraduate GPA of 2.6 overall, 3.0 in major. Additional exam requirements/recommendations for international students: Required—TOEFL (minimum score 550 paper-based; 79 iBT). *Application deadline:* For fall admission, 8/1 priority date for domestic students, 7/15 for international students; for spring admission, 12/1 priority date for domestic students, 12/1 for international students; for summer admission, 5/1 priority date for domestic students, 5/1 for international students. Applications are processed on a rolling basis. Application fee: $65. Electronic applications accepted. Application fee is waived when completed online. *Financial support:* Career-related internships or fieldwork, Federal Work-Study, scholarships/grants, and unspecified assistantships available. Support available to part-time students. Financial award application deadline: 3/2; financial award applicants required to submit FAFSA. *Faculty research:* Cognitive psychology, anger management, grief and grief counseling, post-modernism and psychotherapy, spirituality and psychology. *Unit head:* Dr. Helen Shoemaker, Program Director, 510-436-1543, E-mail: shoemaker@hnu.edu. *Application contact:* 800-430-1321, Fax: 510-436-1325, E-mail: graduateadmissions@hnu.edu.

Houston Baptist University, College of Education and Behavioral Sciences, Program in Christian Counseling, Houston, TX 77074-3298. Offers MACC. Part-time and evening/weekend programs available. *Faculty:* 5 full-time (4 women), 6 part-time/adjunct (all women). *Students:* 8 full-time (7 women), 21 part-time (18 women); includes 20 minority (8 Black or African American, non-Hispanic/Latino; 1 Asian, non-Hispanic/Latino; 11 Hispanic/Latino), 1 international. Average age 33. 48 applicants, 19% accepted, 7 enrolled. In 2014, 1 master's awarded. *Degree requirements:* For master's, comprehensive exam. *Entrance requirements:* For master's, GRE, official transcripts, two recommendation forms, resume, baccalaureate degree in psychology or equivalent, interview. Additional exam requirements/recommendations for international students: Required—TOEFL. *Application deadline:* For fall admission, 8/1 for domestic students, 6/1 for international students; for winter admission, 10/1 for domestic and international students; for spring admission, 12/1 for domestic students, 10/1 for international students; for summer admission, 5/1 for domestic students, 3/1 for international students. Applications are processed on a rolling basis. Application fee: $0. Electronic applications accepted. *Expenses:* Expenses: Contact institution. *Financial support:* In 2014–15, 2 students received support. Federal Work-Study and scholarships/grants available. Support available to part-time students. Financial award application deadline: 4/1; financial award applicants required to submit FAFSA. *Faculty research:* Psychology - church collaboration, trauma recovery. *Unit head:* Dr. Stephanie Ellis, Chair, 281-649-3608, Fax: 281-649-3361, E-mail: sellis@hbu.edu. *Application contact:* Grace Rosales, Administrative Assistant to the Dean, 281-649-3131, E-mail: grosales@hbu.edu.
Website: http://www.hbu.edu/macc

Houston Baptist University, College of Education and Behavioral Sciences, Program in Counseling, Houston, TX 77074-3298. Offers MAC. Part-time and evening/weekend programs available. *Faculty:* 5 full-time (4 women), 6 part-time/adjunct (all women). *Students:* 7 full-time (all women), 16 part-time (4 women); includes 15 minority (6 Black or African American, non-Hispanic/Latino; 1 American Indian or Alaska Native, non-Hispanic/Latino; 8 Hispanic/Latino). Average age 29. 140 applicants, 21% accepted, 23 enrolled. *Degree requirements:* For master's, comprehensive exam, practicum. *Entrance requirements:* For master's, GRE (waived if GPA is 3.0 or higher), two academic professional recommendations, bachelor's degree, transcript, resume, interview. Additional exam requirements/recommendations for international students: Required—TOEFL. *Application deadline:* For fall admission, 8/1 for domestic students, 6/1 for international students; for spring admission, 12/1 for domestic students, 10/1 for international students; for summer admission, 5/1 for domestic students, 3/1 for international students. Applications are processed on a rolling basis. Application fee: $0. Electronic applications accepted. *Expenses:* Expenses: $1,500 per 3 credit hours (49 hour program); fees: $875 per semester. *Financial support:* In 2014–15, 4 students received support. Career-related internships or fieldwork, Federal Work-Study, and scholarships/grants available. Support available to part-time students. Financial award application deadline: 4/1; financial award applicants required to submit FAFSA. *Faculty research:* Multicultural psychology, counseling: technology integration. *Unit head:* Dr. Stephanie Ellis, Director, 281-649-3241, E-mail: sellis@hbu.edu. *Application contact:* Grace Rosales, Administrative Assistant to the Dean, 281-649-3131, E-mail: grosales@hbu.edu.
Website: http://www.hbu.edu/mac

Howard University, School of Education, Department of Human Development and Psychoeducational Studies, Program in Counseling Psychology, Washington, DC 20059-0002. Offers PhD. *Accreditation:* APA. Part-time programs available. *Degree requirements:* For doctorate, one foreign language, comprehensive exam, thesis/dissertation, expository writing exam, internship. *Entrance requirements:* For doctorate, GRE General Test, minimum GPA of 3.4. Additional exam requirements/recommendations for international students: Required—TOEFL (minimum score 550 paper-based; 79 iBT). Electronic applications accepted. *Faculty research:* Cultural issues in counseling and psychotherapy, counseling theory construction, self-actualization black psychology.

Humboldt State University, Academic Programs, College of Professional Studies, Department of Psychology, Arcata, CA 95521-8299. Offers psychology (MA), including academic research, counseling, school psychology. *Students:* 52 full-time (42 women), 6 part-time (3 women); includes 22 minority (15 Hispanic/Latino; 7 Two or more races, non-Hispanic/Latino). Average age 27. 73 applicants, 47% accepted, 24 enrolled. In 2014, 15 master's awarded. *Degree requirements:* For master's, thesis. *Entrance requirements:* For master's, appropriate bachelor's degree, minimum GPA of 2.5. Additional exam requirements/recommendations for international students: Required—TOEFL (minimum score 500 paper-based). *Application deadline:* For fall admission, 2/1 for domestic students, 2/15 for international students. Applications are processed on a rolling basis. Application fee: $55. *Expenses:* Tuition, state resident: full-time $6738; part-time $3906 per year. Tuition, nonresident: full-time $13,434; part-time $6138 per year. *Required fees:* $1690; $1266 per year. Tuition and fees vary according to program. *Financial support:* Career-related internships or fieldwork available. Financial award application deadline: 3/1; financial award applicants required to submit FAFSA. *Faculty research:* School psychology, counseling, eating disorders, mood induction, depression. *Unit head:* Dr. Gregg Gold, Chair, 707-826-3740, Fax: 707-826-4993, E-mail: gjg14@humboldt.edu. *Application contact:* Dr. Chris Aberson, Coordinator, 707-826-3670, Fax: 707-826-4993, E-mail: cla18@humboldt.edu.
Website: http://www2.humboldt.edu/psychology/programs-child/graduate-programs-psychology

Husson University, Graduate Programs in Counseling and Human Relations, Bangor, ME 04401-2999. Offers clinical mental health counseling (MS); human relations (MS); pastoral counseling (MS); school counseling (MS). Part-time and evening/weekend programs available. *Faculty:* 3 full-time (2 women), 2 part-time/adjunct (both women). *Students:* 39 full-time (33 women), 25 part-time (20 women); includes 3 minority (2 Black or African American, non-Hispanic/Latino; 1 Two or more races, non-Hispanic/Latino), 2 international. Average age 34. 55 applicants, 69% accepted, 32 enrolled. In 2014, 19 master's awarded. *Degree requirements:* For master's, comprehensive exam (for some programs), thesis optional. *Entrance requirements:* For master's, GRE or MAT, BS with minimum GPA of 3.0, letters of recommendation, interview. Additional exam requirements/recommendations for international students: Required—TOEFL (minimum score 550 paper-based; 80 iBT). *Application deadline:* For fall admission, 2/1 for domestic students. Applications are processed on a rolling basis. Application fee: $50. Electronic applications accepted. *Expenses:* Expenses: Contact institution. *Financial support:* In 2014–15, 1 student received support. Federal Work-Study, scholarships/grants, and unspecified assistantships available. Financial award application deadline: 4/15; financial award applicants required to submit FAFSA. *Faculty research:* Challenges and rewards of counseling practice in rural, small town and neighborhood settings. *Unit head:* Dr. Deborah Drew, Director, Graduate Counseling Programs, 207-992-4912, Fax: 207-992-4952, E-mail: drewd@husson.edu. *Application contact:* Kristen Card, Director of Graduate Admissions, 207-404-5660, Fax: 207-941-7935, E-mail: cardk@husson.edu.
Website: http://www.husson.edu/human-relations

Idaho State University, Office of Graduate Studies, Kasiska College of Health Professions, Department of Counseling, Pocatello, ID 83209-8120. Offers counseling (M Coun, Ed S), including marriage and family counseling (M Coun), mental health counseling (M Coun), school counseling (M Coun), student affairs and college counseling (M Coun); counselor education and counseling (PhD). *Accreditation:* ACA (one or more programs are accredited). Part-time programs available. *Degree requirements:* For master's, comprehensive exam, thesis, 4 semesters resident graduate study, practicum/internship; for doctorate, comprehensive exam, thesis/dissertation, 3 semesters internship, 4 consecutive semesters doctoral-level study on campus; for Ed S, comprehensive exam, thesis, case studies, oral exam. *Entrance requirements:* For master's, GRE General Test, MAT, minimum GPA of 3.0, bachelors degree, interview, 3 letters of recommendation; for doctorate, GRE General Test, MAT, minimum graduate GPA of 3.0, resume, interview, counseling license, master's degree; for Ed S, GRE General Test, minimum graduate GPA of 3.0, master's degree in counseling, 3 letters of recommendation, 2 years work experience. Additional exam requirements/recommendations for international students: Required—TOEFL (minimum score 600 paper-based; 80 iBT). Electronic applications accepted. *Faculty research:* Group counseling, multicultural counseling, family counseling, child therapy, supervision.

Illinois State University, Graduate School, College of Arts and Sciences, Department of Psychology, Normal, IL 61790-2200. Offers psychology (MA, MS), including clinical psychology, counseling psychology, developmental psychology, educational psychology, experimental psychology, measurement-evaluation, organizational-industrial psychology; school psychology (PhD, SSP). *Accreditation:* APA. *Degree requirements:* For master's, thesis or alternative; for doctorate, variable foreign language requirement, thesis/dissertation, 2 terms of residency, internship, practicum. *Entrance requirements:* For master's, GRE General Test, GRE Subject Test, minimum GPA of 3.0 in last 60 hours of course work; for doctorate, GRE General Test. *Faculty research:* Comprehensive evaluation system for the central region professional development grant, Illinois school psychology internship consortium, for children's sake.

Immaculata University, College of Graduate Studies, Department of Psychology, Immaculata, PA 19345. Offers clinical mental health counseling (MA); clinical psychology (Psy D); forensic psychology (Graduate Certificate); integrative psychotherapy (Graduate Certificate); neuropsychology (Graduate Certificate);

psychodynamic psychotherapy (Graduate Certificate); psychological testing (Graduate Certificate); school counseling (MA, Graduate Certificate); school psychology (MA). *Accreditation:* APA. Part-time and evening/weekend programs available. Terminal master's awarded for partial completion of doctoral program. *Degree requirements:* For master's, comprehensive exam, thesis optional; for doctorate, comprehensive exam, thesis/dissertation. *Entrance requirements:* For master's, GRE General Test or MAT, minimum GPA of 3.0; for doctorate, GRE General Test or MAT, minimum GPA of 3.5. Additional exam requirements/recommendations for international students: Required—TOEFL, IELTS. Electronic applications accepted. *Faculty research:* Supervision ethics, psychology of teaching, gender.

Indiana State University, College of Graduate and Professional Studies, Bayh College of Education, Department of Communication Disorders, Counseling and School and Educational Psychology, Terre Haute, IN 47809. Offers counseling psychology (MS, PhD); counselor education (PhD); mental health counseling (MS); school counseling (M Ed); school psychology (PhD, Ed S); MA/MS. *Accreditation:* ACA; NCATE. Part-time and evening/weekend programs available. *Degree requirements:* For master's, thesis optional; for doctorate, thesis/dissertation, research tools proficiency tests. *Entrance requirements:* For master's, GRE General Test or MAT, minimum undergraduate GPA of 2.75; for doctorate, GRE General Test, master's degree, minimum undergraduate GPA of 3.5. Electronic applications accepted. *Faculty research:* Vocational development supervision.

Indiana University Northwest, College of Arts and Sciences, Gary, IN 46408-1197. Offers clinical counseling (MS), including drug and alcohol counseling; liberal studies (MLS). *Students:* 7 full-time (5 women), 23 part-time (18 women); includes 15 minority (13 Black or African American, non-Hispanic/Latino; 2 Hispanic/Latino). 10 applicants, 80% accepted, 5 enrolled. In 2014, 2 master's awarded. *Unit head:* Robert Mucci, Graduate Program Director, 219-980-6607, E-mail: rmucci@iun.edu.
Website: http://www.iun.edu/coas/

Indiana Wesleyan University, Graduate School, College of Arts and Sciences, Marion, IN 46953. Offers addictions counseling (MS); clinical mental health counseling (MS); community counseling (MS); marriage and family therapy (MS); school counseling (MS); student development counseling and administration (MS). *Accreditation:* ACA. Part-time programs available. *Degree requirements:* For master's, thesis or alternative. *Entrance requirements:* For master's, GRE General Test. Additional exam requirements/recommendations for international students: Required—TOEFL. Electronic applications accepted. *Expenses:* Contact institution. *Faculty research:* Community counseling, multicultural counseling, addictions.

Instituto Tecnologico de Santo Domingo, Graduate School, Area of Humanities and Social Sciences, Santo Domingo, Dominican Republic. Offers accounting (Certificate); adult education (Certificate); applied linguistics (MA); economics (MA); education (M Ed); educational psychology (MA, Certificate); gender and development (MA, Certificate); humanistic studies (MA); international marketing management (Certificate); international relations in the Caribbean basin (Certificate); intervention systems in family therapy (MA); linguistic and literary communication (Certificate); pedagogical support (MA); social science education (M Ed); sustainable human development (MA); terminal illness and death psychology (Certificate); youth and adult education (M Ed).

Inter American University of Puerto Rico, Aguadilla Campus, Graduate School, Aguadilla, PR 00605. Offers accounting (MBA); counseling psychology specializing in family (MS); criminal justice (MA); educative management and leadership (MA); elementary education (M Ed); finance (MBA); human resources (MBA); industrial management (MBA); management information systems (MBA); marketing (MBA). Part-time and evening/weekend programs available. *Degree requirements:* For master's, comprehensive exam. *Entrance requirements:* For master's, EXADEP, 2 letters of recommendation, minimum GPA of 2.5. Electronic applications accepted.

Inter American University of Puerto Rico, Metropolitan Campus, Graduate Programs, Program in Psychology, San Juan, PR 00919-1293. Offers counseling psychology (MA, PhD); industrial/organizational psychology (MA, PhD); labor relations (MA); school psychology (MA, PhD). *Degree requirements:* For master's, comprehensive exam. *Entrance requirements:* For master's, GRE or EXADEP, interview. Electronic applications accepted.

Inter American University of Puerto Rico, San Germán Campus, Graduate Studies Center, Program in Psychology, San Germán, PR 00683-5008. Offers counseling psychology (MA, PhD); school psychology (MA, PhD). Part-time and evening/weekend programs available. *Degree requirements:* For master's, comprehensive exam, thesis; for doctorate, comprehensive exam, thesis/dissertation. *Entrance requirements:* For master's, GRE General Test or EXADEP, minimum GPA of 3.0; for doctorate, GRE, EXADEP or MAT, minimum GPA of 3.0.

Iona College, School of Arts and Science, Department of Psychology, New Rochelle, NY 10801-1890. Offers general-experimental psychology (MA); human resources (Certificate); industrial-organizational psychology (MA); mental health counseling (MA); organizational behavior (Certificate); psychology (MA); school psychology (MA). Part-time programs available. *Faculty:* 8 full-time (3 women), 5 part-time/adjunct (3 women). *Students:* 41 full-time (30 women), 33 part-time (22 women); includes 29 minority (12 Black or African American, non-Hispanic/Latino; 2 Asian, non-Hispanic/Latino; 15 Hispanic/Latino), 1 international. Average age 24. 65 applicants, 85% accepted, 22 enrolled. In 2014, 38 master's awarded. *Degree requirements:* For master's, thesis (for some programs), literature review (for some programs). *Entrance requirements:* For master's, BA in psychology including 3 credits in psychology statistics and 3 credits in experimental research methods; or 9 credits in psychology including 3 credits in psychology statistics, 3 credits in psychology research methods and 3 credits of upper-level coursework. Additional exam requirements/recommendations for international students: Required—TOEFL (minimum score 550 paper-based), IELTS (minimum score 6.5). *Application deadline:* For fall admission, 8/15 for domestic students, 5/1 for international students; for spring admission, 1/15 for domestic students, 9/1 for international students. Applications are processed on a rolling basis. Application fee: $50. Electronic applications accepted. *Expenses:* Tuition: Part-time $985 per credit. *Required fees:* $245 per term. *Financial support:* In 2014–15, 6 students received support, including 1 research assistantship with partial tuition reimbursement available (averaging $8,000 per year); tuition waivers (partial) and unspecified assistantships also available. Support available to part-time students. Financial award application deadline: 4/15; financial award applicants required to submit FAFSA. *Faculty research:* Non-suicidal self-injury, trauma response, performance appraisal and evaluation, diversity infusion, assessment and treatment of sexual offenders. *Unit head:* Patricia Oswald, PhD, Chair, 914-633-7788, E-mail: poswald@iona.edu. *Application contact:* Amanda St. Bernard, Assistant Director, Graduate Admissions, 914-633-2440, Fax: 914-633-2277, E-mail: astbernard@iona.edu.
Website: http://www.iona.edu/Academics/School-of-Arts-Science/Departments/Psychology/Graduate-Programs.aspx

Iowa State University of Science and Technology, Department of Psychology, Ames, IA 50011. Offers cognitive psychology (PhD); counseling psychology (PhD); social psychology (PhD). *Accreditation:* APA. *Entrance requirements:* For doctorate, GRE General Test, GRE Subject Test (psychology), 3 letters of recommendation. Additional

exam requirements/recommendations for international students: Required—TOEFL (minimum score 560 paper-based; 79 iBT), IELTS (minimum score 6.5). Electronic applications accepted. *Faculty research:* Counseling psychology, cognitive psychology, social psychology, health psychology, psychology and public policy.

James Madison University, The Graduate School, College of Health and Behavioral Sciences, Department of Graduate Psychology, Clinical Mental Health Counseling Program, Harrisonburg, VA 22807. Offers MA, Ed S. *Accreditation:* ACA (one or more programs are accredited). Part-time and evening/weekend programs available. *Students:* 57 full-time (40 women), 13 part-time (10 women); includes 15 minority (11 Black or African American, non-Hispanic/Latino; 3 Hispanic/Latino; 1 Two or more races, non-Hispanic/Latino), 1 international. Average age 28. 256 applicants, 21% accepted, 18 enrolled. In 2014, 30 master's, 8 other advanced degrees awarded. *Degree requirements:* For Ed S, comprehensive exam, thesis. *Application deadline:* For fall admission, 2/1 for domestic students. Application fee: $55. Electronic applications accepted. *Expenses:* Tuition, state resident: full-time $7812; part-time $434 per credit hour. Tuition, nonresident: full-time $20,430; part-time $1135 per credit hour. *Financial support:* In 2014–15, 14 students received support. Career-related internships or fieldwork, Federal Work-Study, and 13 assistantships (averaging $7530), 1 service assistantship (averaging $7530) available. Financial award application deadline: 3/1; financial award applicants required to submit FAFSA. *Unit head:* Dr. Robin Anderson, Department Head, 540-568-3293, E-mail: ander2rd@jmu.edu. *Application contact:* Lynette D. Michael, Director of Graduate Admissions and Student Records, 540-568-6131 Ext. 6395, Fax: 540-568-7860, E-mail: michaeld@jmu.edu.
Website: http://psyc.jmu.edu/counseling/clinical/

James Madison University, The Graduate School, College of Health and Behavioral Sciences, Department of Graduate Psychology, Program in Counseling and Supervision, Harrisonburg, VA 22807. Offers PhD. *Students:* 4 part-time (3 women); includes 1 minority (Hispanic/Latino). Average age 28. 3 applicants. Electronic applications accepted. *Expenses:* Tuition, state resident: full-time $7812; part-time $434 per credit hour. Tuition, nonresident: full-time $20,430; part-time $1135 per credit hour. *Financial support:* In 2014–15, 2 students received support, including 2 fellowships. Financial award application deadline: 3/1; financial award applicants required to submit FAFSA. *Unit head:* Dr. Robin Anderson, Department Head, 540-568-3293, E-mail: ander2rd@jmu.edu. *Application contact:* Lynette D. Michael, Director of Graduate Admissions and Student Records, 540-568-6131 Ext. 6395, Fax: 540-568-7860, E-mail: michaeld@jmu.edu.
Website: http://psyc.jmu.edu/counseling/supervision/

John Brown University, Graduate Counseling Programs, Siloam Springs, AR 72761-2121. Offers clinical mental health counseling (MS); marriage and family therapy (MS); play therapy (Graduate Certificate); school counseling (MS). *Accreditation:* NCATE. Part-time and evening/weekend programs available. *Faculty:* 5 full-time (0 women), 19 part-time/adjunct (6 women). *Students:* 104 full-time (82 women), 100 part-time (75 women); includes 46 minority (15 Black or African American, non-Hispanic/Latino; 4 American Indian or Alaska Native, non-Hispanic/Latino; 3 Asian, non-Hispanic/Latino; 19 Hispanic/Latino; 5 Two or more races, non-Hispanic/Latino). Average age 33. 102 applicants, 84% accepted, 71 enrolled. *Degree requirements:* For master's, practica or internships. *Entrance requirements:* For master's, GRE (minimum score of 300), recommendation forms from three people, 200-word essay describing professional plans and reason for seeking acceptance. Additional exam requirements/recommendations for international students: Required—TOEFL (minimum score 550 paper-based; 70 iBT). *Application deadline:* Applications are processed on a rolling basis. Application fee: $35 ($100 for international students). Electronic applications accepted. *Expenses:* Expenses: $532 per credit hour. *Financial support:* Fellowships, institutionally sponsored loans, scholarships/grants, and unspecified assistantships available. Financial award applicants required to submit FAFSA. *Unit head:* Dr. John V. Carmack, Program Director, 479-524-8630, E-mail: jcarmack@jbu.edu. *Application contact:* Nikki Rader, Graduate Counseling Representative, 479-524-7425, E-mail: nikki@jbu.edu.
Website: http://www.jbu.edu/

John Carroll University, Graduate School, Program in Community Counseling, University Heights, OH 44118-4581. Offers clinical counseling (Certificate); community counseling (MA). *Accreditation:* ACA. Part-time and evening/weekend programs available. *Degree requirements:* For master's, comprehensive exam, internship, practicum. *Entrance requirements:* For master's, MAT or GRE, minimum GPA of 2.75, statement of volunteer experience, interview, 12-18 hours social science course work, survey. Additional exam requirements/recommendations for international students: Required—TOEFL. Electronic applications accepted. *Faculty research:* Child and adolescent development, HIV, hypnosis, wellness, women's issues.

John F. Kennedy University, Graduate School of Holistic Studies, Department of Counseling Psychology, Program in Counseling Psychology, Pleasant Hill, CA 94523-4817. Offers holistic studies (MA); somatic psychology (MA); transpersonal psychology (MA). Part-time and evening/weekend programs available. *Degree requirements:* For master's, thesis or alternative. *Entrance requirements:* For master's, interview. Additional exam requirements/recommendations for international students: Required—TOEFL.

John F. Kennedy University, Graduate School of Professional Psychology, Program in Counseling Psychology, Pleasant Hill, CA 94523-4817. Offers MA. Part-time and evening/weekend programs available. *Degree requirements:* For master's, thesis or alternative. *Entrance requirements:* For master's, interview. Additional exam requirements/recommendations for international students: Required—TOEFL.

Johns Hopkins University, School of Education, Certificate Programs in Education, Baltimore, MD 21218-2699. Offers advanced methods for differentiated instruction and inclusive education (Certificate); applied behavior analysis (Certificate); counseling (CAGS); data-based decision making and organizational improvement (Certificate); early intervention/preschool special education specialist (Certificate); education leadership for independent schools (Certificate); education of students with autism and other pervasive developmental disorders (Certificate); evidence-based teaching in the health professions (Certificate); gifted education (Certificate); K-8 mathematics lead-teacher (Certificate); K-8 STEM education lead-teacher (Certificate); leadership for school, family, and community collaboration (Certificate); leadership in technology integration (Certificate); mental health counseling (Certificate); mind, brain, and teaching (Certificate); school administration and supervision (Certificate); urban education (Certificate). Part-time and evening/weekend programs available. Postbaccalaureate distance learning degree programs offered (no on-campus study). *Entrance requirements:* For degree, bachelor's degree from regionally- or nationally-accredited institution (master's for some programs), minimum GPA of 3.0 in all previous programs of study, official transcripts from all post-secondary institutions attended, essay, curriculum vitae/resume, minimum of two letters of recommendation. Additional exam requirements/recommendations for international students: Required—TOEFL (minimum score 600 paper-based; 100 iBT) or IELTS (minimum score 7). Electronic applications accepted.

Counseling Psychology

Johns Hopkins University, School of Education, Master's Programs in Education, Baltimore, MD 21218-2699. Offers counseling (MS), including mental health counseling, school counseling; education (MS), including educational studies, gifted education, reading, school administration and supervision, technology for educators; elementary education (MAT); health professions (M Ed); intelligence analysis (MS); management (MS); secondary education (MAT); special education (MS), including early childhood special education, general special education studies, mild to moderate disabilities, severe disabilities. Part-time and evening/weekend programs available. Postbaccalaureate distance learning degree programs offered (no on-campus study). *Degree requirements:* For master's, comprehensive exam (for some programs), portfolio, capstone project and/or internship; PRAXIS II (for teacher preparation programs that lead to licensure). *Entrance requirements:* For master's, GRE (for full-time programs only); PRAXIS I or equivalent (for teacher preparation programs that lead to licensure), bachelor's degree from regionally- or nationally-accredited institution, minimum GPA of 3.0 in all previous programs of study, official transcripts from all post-secondary institutions attended, essay, curriculum vitae/resume, minimum of two letters of recommendation. Additional exam requirements/recommendations for international students: Required—TOEFL (minimum score 600 paper-based; 100 iBT) or IELTS (minimum score 7). Electronic applications accepted.

Kean University, College of Humanities and Social Sciences, Program in Psychology, Union, NJ 07083. Offers human behavior and organizational psychology (MA); psychological services (MA). Part-time programs available. *Faculty:* 16 full-time (13 women). *Students:* 28 full-time (25 women), 24 part-time (13 women); includes 23 minority (12 Black or African American, non-Hispanic/Latino; 3 Asian, non-Hispanic/Latino; 7 Hispanic/Latino; 1 Two or more races, non-Hispanic/Latino), 1 international. Average age 29. 35 applicants, 89% accepted, 15 enrolled. In 2014, 22 master's awarded. *Degree requirements:* For master's, comprehensive exam, research component, two semesters of advanced seminar. *Entrance requirements:* For master's, GRE General Test, minimum GPA of 3.0; official transcripts from all institutions attended; two letters of recommendation; professional resume/curriculum vitae; 12 credits in behavioral sciences on the undergraduate level. Additional exam requirements/recommendations for international students: Required—TOEFL (minimum score 79 iBT). *Application deadline:* For fall admission, 6/1 for domestic and international students; for spring admission, 12/1 for domestic and international students. Applications are processed on a rolling basis. Application fee: $75 ($150 for international students). Electronic applications accepted. *Expenses:* Tuition, state resident: full-time $12,461; part-time $607 per credit. Tuition, nonresident: full-time $16,889; part-time $744 per credit. *Required fees:* $3141; $143 per credit. Tuition and fees vary according to course load, degree level and program. *Financial support:* In 2014–15, 3 research assistantships with full tuition reimbursements (averaging $3,742 per year) were awarded; scholarships/grants and unspecified assistantships also available. Financial award applicants required to submit FAFSA. *Unit head:* Dr. Muriel Singer, Program Coordinator, 908-737-5886, E-mail: msinger@kean.edu. *Application contact:* Reenat Hasan, Admissions Counselor, 908-737-7134, Fax: 908-737-7135, E-mail: rhasan@exchange.kean.edu.
Website: http://grad.kean.edu/masters-programs/psychological-services

Kean University, Nathan Weiss Graduate College, Program in Counselor Education, Union, NJ 07083. Offers alcohol and drug abuse counseling (MA); clinical mental health counseling (MA); school counseling (MA). *Accreditation:* ACA; NCATE. Part-time programs available. *Faculty:* 8 full-time (6 women). *Students:* 120 full-time (92 women), 144 part-time (122 women); includes 111 minority (47 Black or African American, non-Hispanic/Latino; 4 Asian, non-Hispanic/Latino; 58 Hispanic/Latino; 2 Two or more races, non-Hispanic/Latino), 2 international. Average age 32. 195 applicants, 48% accepted, 59 enrolled. In 2014, 62 master's awarded. *Degree requirements:* For master's, practicum, internship, portfolio. *Entrance requirements:* For master's, minimum GPA of 3.0, 2 letters of recommendation, personal statement, resume. Additional exam requirements/recommendations for international students: Required—TOEFL (minimum score 550 paper-based; 79 iBT). *Application deadline:* For fall admission, 3/2 for domestic and international students; for spring admission, 10/31 for domestic and international students. Applications are processed on a rolling basis. Application fee: $75 ($150 for international students). Electronic applications accepted. *Expenses:* Tuition, state resident: full-time $12,461; part-time $607 per credit. Tuition, nonresident: full-time $16,889; part-time $744 per credit. *Required fees:* $3141; $143 per credit. Tuition and fees vary according to course load, degree level and program. *Financial support:* In 2014–15, 14 research assistantships with full tuition reimbursements (averaging $3,742 per year) were awarded; scholarships/grants and unspecified assistantships also available. Financial award applicants required to submit FAFSA. *Unit head:* Dr. J. Barry Mascari, Program Coordinator, 908-737-5954, E-mail: jmascari@kean.edu. *Application contact:* Steven Koch, Admissions Counselor, 908-737-7136, Fax: 908-737-7135, E-mail: skoch@kean.edu.
Website: http://grad.kean.edu/counseling

Kent State University, Graduate School of Education, Health, and Human Services, School of Lifespan Development and Educational Sciences, Program in Clinical Mental Health Counseling, Kent, OH 44242-0001. Offers M Ed. *Accreditation:* ACA; NCATE. *Faculty:* 9 full-time (5 women), 12 part-time/adjunct (8 women). *Students:* 81 full-time (71 women), 53 part-time (47 women); includes 14 minority (5 Black or African American, non-Hispanic/Latino; 2 American Indian or Alaska Native, non-Hispanic/Latino; 4 Hispanic/Latino; 3 Native Hawaiian or other Pacific Islander, non-Hispanic/Latino). 110 applicants, 45% accepted. In 2014, 48 master's awarded. *Entrance requirements:* For master's, minimum GPA of 2.75, 2 letters of reference, goals statement, moral character form, interview. Additional exam requirements/recommendations for international students: Required—TOEFL (minimum score 550 paper-based; 80 iBT). *Application deadline:* For fall admission, 6/1 for domestic students; for spring admission, 10/1 for domestic students. Application fee: $45 ($60 for international students). Electronic applications accepted. *Expenses:* Tuition, state resident: full-time $8730; part-time $485 per credit hour. Tuition, nonresident: full-time $14,886; part-time $827 per credit hour. Tuition and fees vary according to campus/location and program. *Financial support:* In 2014–15, 5 research assistantships with full tuition reimbursements (averaging $8,500 per year) were awarded; career-related internships or fieldwork, Federal Work-Study, institutionally sponsored loans, scholarships/grants, health care benefits, unspecified assistantships, and 2 administrative assistantships (averaging $8,500 per year) also available. Support available to part-time students. Financial award application deadline: 4/1; financial award applicants required to submit FAFSA. *Faculty research:* Group work, personality assessment, family/child therapy, substance abuse counseling, clinical supervision. *Unit head:* Dr. Jason McGlothlin, Coordinator, 330-672-0716, E-mail: jmcgloth@kent.edu. *Application contact:* Nancy Miller, Academic Program Director, Office of Graduate Student Services, 330-672-2576, Fax: 330-672-9162, E-mail: ogs@kent.edu.

Kutztown University of Pennsylvania, College of Education, Program in Counseling Psychology, Kutztown, PA 19530-0730. Offers agency counseling (MA); marital and family therapy (MA). Part-time and evening/weekend programs available. *Faculty:* 8 full-time (3 women). *Students:* 72 full-time (63 women), 49 part-time (42 women); includes 21 minority (8 Black or African American, non-Hispanic/Latino; 2 Asian, non-Hispanic/Latino; 11 Hispanic/Latino). Average age 30. 83 applicants, 51% accepted, 29 enrolled. In 2014, 26 master's awarded. *Degree requirements:* For master's, comprehensive exam, thesis optional. *Entrance requirements:* For master's, GRE General Test, interview. Additional exam requirements/recommendations for international students: Required—TOEFL (minimum score 550 paper-based; 79 iBT). *Application deadline:* For fall admission, 3/1 for domestic and international students; for spring admission, 10/1 for domestic and international students. Application fee: $35. Electronic applications accepted. *Expenses: Tuition, area resident:* Part-time $454 per credit. Tuition, state resident: part-time $454 per credit. Tuition, nonresident: part-time $681 per credit. *Required fees:* $85 per credit. *Financial support:* Career-related internships or fieldwork, Federal Work-Study, scholarships/grants, and unspecified assistantships available. Financial award application deadline: 3/1; financial award applicants required to submit FAFSA. *Faculty research:* Family addictions. *Unit head:* Dr. Margaret Herrick, Chairperson, 610-683-4225, Fax: 610-683-1585, E-mail: herrick@kutztown.edu. *Application contact:* Kelly Hish, Admissions Clerk, 610-683-4200, Fax: 610-683-1393, E-mail: graduate@kutztown.edu.

Lamar University, College of Graduate Studies, College of Education and Human Development, Department of Counseling and Special Populations, Beaumont, TX 77710. Offers clinical mental health counseling (M Ed); school counseling (M Ed); special education (M Ed), including special education. *Faculty:* 21 full-time (16 women), 19 part-time/adjunct (15 women). *Students:* 12 full-time (11 women), 1,402 part-time (1,280 women); includes 618 minority (311 Black or African American, non-Hispanic/Latino; 5 American Indian or Alaska Native, non-Hispanic/Latino; 7 Asian, non-Hispanic/Latino; 273 Hispanic/Latino; 22 Two or more races, non-Hispanic/Latino), 7 international. Average age 37. 804 applicants, 88% accepted, 201 enrolled. In 2014, 412 master's awarded. *Entrance requirements:* Additional exam requirements/recommendations for international students: Required—TOEFL (minimum score 550 paper-based; 79 iBT), IELTS (minimum score 6.5). *Application deadline:* For fall admission, 8/10 for domestic students, 7/1 for international students; for spring admission, 1/5 for domestic students, 12/1 for international students. Applications are processed on a rolling basis. Application fee: $25 ($50 for international students). *Expenses:* Tuition, state resident: full-time $5724; part-time $1908 per semester. Tuition, nonresident: full-time $12,240; part-time $4080 per semester. *Required fees:* $1940; $318 per credit hour. *Unit head:* Dr. Carl J. Sheperis, Chair, 409-880-8978, Fax: 409-880-2263. *Application contact:* Melissa Gallien, Director, Admissions and Academic Services, 409-880-8888, Fax: 409-880-7419, E-mail: gradmissions@lamar.edu.
Website: http://education.lamar.edu/counseling-and-special-populations

Lancaster Bible College, Graduate School, Lancaster, PA 17601-5036. Offers adult ministries (MA); Bible (MA); children and family ministry (MA); church planting (MA); consulting resource teacher (M Ed); elementary school counseling (M Ed); leadership (PhD); leadership studies (MA); marriage and family counseling (MA); mental health counseling (MA); pastoral studies (MA); secondary school counseling (M Ed); sports ministry (MA); student ministry (MA); town and country ministry (MA). Part-time and evening/weekend programs available. *Degree requirements:* For master's, comprehensive exam (for some programs), thesis (for some programs). *Entrance requirements:* For master's, bachelor's degree with a minimum of 30 credits of course work in Bible, minimum undergraduate GPA of 3.0, interview. Additional exam requirements/recommendations for international students: Required—TOEFL.

La Salle University, School of Arts and Sciences, Program in Counseling and Family Therapy, Philadelphia, PA 19141-1199. Offers industrial/organizational management and human resources (MA); marriage and family therapy (MA); pastoral counseling (MA); professional clinical counseling (MA). *Accreditation:* APA. Part-time and evening/weekend programs available. *Degree requirements:* For master's, comprehensive exam. *Entrance requirements:* For master's, GRE or MAT (waived for applicants that already possess a master's degree in any field or for applicants that have a cumulative GPA of 3.5 or higher), minimum of 15 hours in psychology, counseling, or marriage and family studies; minimum GPA of 3.0; three letters of recommendation; personal statement; work experience (paid or volunteer). Additional exam requirements/recommendations for international students: Required—TOEFL. Electronic applications accepted. Application fee is waived when completed online. *Expenses:* Contact institution. *Faculty research:* Cognitive therapy, attribution theory, work habits, single parent families, treatment of addictions.

Lee University, Graduate Studies in Counseling, Cleveland, TN 37320-3450. Offers holistic child development (MS); marriage and family therapy (MS); school counseling (MS). Part-time programs available. *Faculty:* 8 full-time (3 women), 4 part-time/adjunct (0 women). *Students:* 57 full-time (42 women), 25 part-time (19 women); includes 13 minority (8 Black or African American, non-Hispanic/Latino; 1 Asian, non-Hispanic/Latino; 4 Hispanic/Latino), 2 international. Average age 28. 45 applicants, 78% accepted, 30 enrolled. In 2014, 42 master's awarded. *Degree requirements:* For master's, variable foreign language requirement, comprehensive exam (for some programs), thesis (for some programs), internship. *Entrance requirements:* For master's, GRE General Test or MAT (waived if undergraduate GPA is greater than 3.0 or if applicant already has a graduate degree), minimum undergraduate GPA of 3.0, 3 letters of recommendation, interview, official transcripts, essay. Additional exam requirements/recommendations for international students: Required—TOEFL (minimum score 450 paper-based). *Application deadline:* For fall admission, 4/1 priority date for domestic and international students; for spring admission, 10/1 priority date for domestic and international students. Applications are processed on a rolling basis. Application fee: $25. *Expenses: Tuition:* Full-time $10,260; part-time $570 per credit hour. *Required fees:* $35 per semester. One-time fee: $25. Tuition and fees vary according to program. *Financial support:* In 2014–15, 26 students received support. Career-related internships or fieldwork, Federal Work-Study, institutionally sponsored loans, scholarships/grants, and unspecified assistantships available. Financial award application deadline: 3/1; financial award applicants required to submit FAFSA. *Unit head:* Dr. Trevor Milliron, Director, 423-614-8126, Fax: 423-614-8129, E-mail: tmilliron@leeuniversity.edu. *Application contact:* Vicki Glasscock, Graduate Admissions Director, 423-614-8059, E-mail: vglasscock@leeuniversity.edu.
Website: http://www.leeuniversity.edu/academics/graduate/counseling/

Lehigh University, College of Education, Program in Counseling Psychology, Bethlehem, PA 18015. Offers counseling and human services (M Ed); counseling psychology (PhD); international counseling (M Ed, Certificate); school counseling (M Ed). *Accreditation:* APA (one or more programs are accredited). Part-time programs available. Postbaccalaureate distance learning degree programs offered (minimal on-campus study). *Faculty:* 5 full-time (3 women), 7 part-time/adjunct (5 women). *Students:* 57 full-time (48 women), 41 part-time (34 women); includes 15 minority (6 Black or African American, non-Hispanic/Latino; 3 Asian, non-Hispanic/Latino; 5 Hispanic/Latino; 1 Two or more races, non-Hispanic/Latino), 17 international. Average age 30. 181 applicants, 27% accepted, 14 enrolled. In 2014, 27 master's, 2 doctorates awarded. *Degree requirements:* For doctorate, comprehensive exam, thesis/dissertation. *Entrance requirements:* For master's, minimum GPA of 3.0, 2 letters of recommendation, essay, transcript; for doctorate, GRE General Test, 2 letters of recommendation, transcript, essay; for Certificate, minimum GPA of 3.0. Additional exam requirements/recommendations for international students: Required—TOEFL (minimum score 600 paper-based; 93 iBT). *Application deadline:* For fall admission, 2/15

for domestic students, 11/15 for international students; for winter admission, 2/1 for international students. Application fee: $65. Electronic applications accepted. Application fee is waived when completed online. *Expenses:* Expenses: $565 per credit; $200 internship fee (for some programs); $100 technology fee (for some programs); $75 printing fee. *Financial support:* In 2014–15, 21 students received support, including 2 fellowships with full and partial tuition reimbursements available (averaging $16,000 per year), 6 research assistantships with partial tuition reimbursements available (averaging $9,000 per year); career-related internships or fieldwork, Federal Work-Study, institutionally sponsored loans, scholarships/grants, tuition waivers (full and partial), and unspecified assistantships also available. Financial award application deadline: 2/15; financial award applicants required to submit FAFSA. *Faculty research:* Maternal/infant attachment, multicultural training and counseling, career development and health interventions, intersection of identities. *Total annual research expenditures:* $616,399. *Unit head:* Dr. Arnold R. Spokane, Director, 610-758-3257, Fax: 610-758-3227, E-mail: ars1@lehigh.edu. *Application contact:* Donna M. Johnson, Manager, Graduate Programs Admissions, 610-758-3231, Fax: 610-758-6223, E-mail: dmj4@lehigh.edu. Website: http://coe.lehigh.edu/academics/disciplines/cp

Lenoir-Rhyne University, Graduate Programs, School of Counseling, Programs in Counseling, Hickory, NC 28601. Offers clinical mental health counseling (MA). Part-time and evening/weekend programs available. *Faculty:* 6 full-time (4 women). *Students:* 73 full-time (62 women), 91 part-time (73 women); includes 25 minority (18 Black or African American, non-Hispanic/Latino; 1 Asian, non-Hispanic/Latino; 4 Hispanic/Latino; 2 Two or more races, non-Hispanic/Latino). Average age 32. In 2014, 34 master's awarded. *Degree requirements:* For master's, comprehensive exam, thesis optional. *Entrance requirements:* For master's, GRE General Test or MAT, writing sample; minimum undergraduate GPA of 2.7, graduate 3.0. Additional exam requirements/recommendations for international students: Required—TOEFL (minimum score 600 paper-based). *Application deadline:* Applications are processed on a rolling basis. Application fee: $35. Electronic applications accepted. *Expenses: Tuition:* Full-time $9000; part-time $500 per credit hour. Tuition and fees vary according to program. *Financial support:* Career-related internships or fieldwork available. Financial award application deadline: 3/1; financial award applicants required to submit FAFSA. *Unit head:* Dr. Amy Wood, Coordinator, 828-328-7728, Fax: 828-328-7368, E-mail: amy.wood@lr.edu. *Application contact:* Mary Ann Gosnell, 828-328-7111, E-mail: admission@lr.edu. Website: http://www.lr.edu/academics/programs/clinical-mental-health-and-school-counseling

Lesley University, Graduate School of Arts and Social Sciences, Cambridge, MA 02138-2790. Offers clinical mental health counseling (MA), including holistic counseling, school and community counseling, trauma studies; counseling psychology (MA, CAGS), including professional counseling (MA), school counseling (MA); creative writing (MFA); expressive therapies (MA, PhD, CAGS), including art (MA), clinical mental health counseling (MA), dance (MA), expressive therapies (MA), music (MA); independent studies (CAGS); independent study (MA); intercultural relations (MA, CAGS); interdisciplinary studies (MA), including individualized studies, integrative holistic health, mindfulness studies, peace and conflict transformation, trauma sensitive assessment, intervention, and consultation, women's studies; urban environmental leadership (MA). Part-time programs available. Postbaccalaureate distance learning degree programs offered (no on-campus study). *Faculty:* 35 full-time (25 women), 115 part-time/adjunct (90 women). *Students:* 420 full-time (379 women), 514 part-time (414 women); includes 142 minority (50 Black or African American, non-Hispanic/Latino; 5 American Indian or Alaska Native, non-Hispanic/Latino; 16 Asian, non-Hispanic/Latino; 48 Hispanic/Latino; 23 Two or more races, non-Hispanic/Latino), 46 international. Average age 33. In 2014, 475 master's, 11 doctorates, 4 other advanced degrees awarded. *Degree requirements:* For master's, internship, practicum, thesis (for expressive therapies); for doctorate, thesis/dissertation, arts apprenticeship, field placement; for CAGS, thesis, internship (for counseling psychology, expressive therapies). *Entrance requirements:* For master's, MAT (counseling psychology), interview, writing samples, art portfolio; for doctorate, GRE or MAT, interview, master's degree; for CAGS, interview, master's degree. Additional exam requirements/recommendations for international students: Required—TOEFL (minimum score 550 paper-based; 80 iBT). *Application deadline:* Applications are processed on a rolling basis. Application fee: $50. Electronic applications accepted. *Financial support:* Fellowships, career-related internships or fieldwork, Federal Work-Study, scholarships/grants, tuition waivers, and unspecified assistantships available. Financial award applicants required to submit FAFSA. *Faculty research:* Psychotherapy and culture; psychotherapy and psychological trauma; women's issues in art, teaching and psychotherapy; community-based art, psycho-spiritual inquiry. *Unit head:* Dr. Catherine Koverola, Dean, 617-349-8317, Fax: 617-349-8366, E-mail: koverola@lesley.edu. *Application contact:* Martha Sheehan, Director, Graduate Admissions, 888-LESLEYU, Fax: 617-349-8313, E-mail: info@lesley.edu. Website: http://www.lesley.edu/graduate-school-of-arts-and-social-sciences/

LeTourneau University, Graduate Programs, Longview, TX 75607-7001. Offers business administration (MBA); counseling (MA); curriculum and instruction (M Ed); education administration (M Ed); engineering (ME, MS); engineering management (MEM); health care administration (MS); marriage and family therapy (MA); psychology (MA); strategic leadership (MSL); teacher leadership (M Ed); teaching and learning (M Ed). Part-time programs available. Postbaccalaureate distance learning degree programs offered (no on-campus study). *Faculty:* 14 full-time (4 women), 41 part-time/adjunct (18 women). *Students:* 58 full-time (37 women), 359 part-time (289 women); includes 140 minority (78 Black or African American, non-Hispanic/Latino; 2 American Indian or Alaska Native, non-Hispanic/Latino; 4 Asian, non-Hispanic/Latino; 40 Hispanic/Latino; 16 Two or more races, non-Hispanic/Latino), 11 international. Average age 38. 199 applicants, 73% accepted, 130 enrolled. In 2014, 139 master's awarded. *Degree requirements:* For master's, thesis (for some programs). *Entrance requirements:* For master's, GRE (for engineering and psychology programs). Additional exam requirements/recommendations for international students: Required—TOEFL. *Application deadline:* For fall admission, 8/22 for domestic students, 8/29 for international students; for winter admission, 10/10 for domestic students; for spring admission, 1/2 for domestic students, 1/10 for international students; for summer admission, 5/1 for domestic and international students. Applications are processed on a rolling basis. Electronic applications accepted. Application fee is waived when completed online. *Financial support:* In 2014–15, 11 students received support, including 16 research assistantships (averaging $11,621 per year); institutionally sponsored loans and unspecified assistantships also available. Financial award applicants required to submit FAFSA. *Application contact:* Chris Fontaine, Assistant Vice President for Global Campus Admissions, 903-233-4312, E-mail: chrisfontaine@letu.edu. Website: http://www.letu.edu

Lewis & Clark College, Graduate School of Education and Counseling, Department of Counseling Psychology, Program in Professional Mental Health Counseling, Portland, OR 97219-7899. Offers MA, MS. Part-time and evening/weekend programs available. *Degree requirements:* For master's, thesis (MS). *Entrance requirements:* For master's, GRE General Test, minimum undergraduate GPA of 2.75. Additional exam

requirements/recommendations for international students: Required—TOEFL (minimum score 575 paper-based). Electronic applications accepted.

Lewis University, College of Arts and Sciences, Program in Clinical Mental Health Counseling, Romeoville, IL 60446. Offers child and adolescent counseling (MA); mental health counseling (MA). Part-time and evening/weekend programs available. *Students:* 19 full-time (16 women), 45 part-time (43 women); includes 20 minority (7 Black or African American, non-Hispanic/Latino; 3 Asian, non-Hispanic/Latino; 9 Hispanic/Latino; 1 Two or more races, non-Hispanic/Latino), 1 international. Average age 28. In 2014, 27 master's awarded. *Degree requirements:* For master's, comprehensive exam, thesis optional, practicum, internship. *Entrance requirements:* For master's, 15 hours of psychology, including statistics or research; 2 letters of recommendation; minimum GPA of 3.0 in last 60 hours; interview. Additional exam requirements/recommendations for international students: Required—TOEFL (minimum score 550 paper-based; 80 iBT). *Application deadline:* For fall admission, 5/1 priority date for international students; for spring admission, 11/15 priority date for international students. Applications are processed on a rolling basis. Application fee: $40. Electronic applications accepted. *Financial support:* Federal Work-Study, scholarships/grants, tuition waivers, and unspecified assistantships available. Financial award application deadline: 5/1; financial award applicants required to submit FAFSA. *Faculty research:* Cognitive development, attitude formation, juvenile delinquency, gender issues, work-family conflict. *Unit head:* Dr. Katherine Helm-Lewis, Director, 815-838-0500 Ext. 5604, Fax: 815-836-5032, E-mail: helmka@lewisu.edu. *Application contact:* Nancy Hanley, Information Contact, 815-838-0500 Ext. 5604, E-mail: hanleyna@lewisu.edu. Website: http://www.lewisu.edu/academics/grad.htm/

Liberty University, School of Behavioral Sciences, Lynchburg, VA 24515. Offers advanced clinical skills (PhD); clinical mental health counseling (MA); counselor education and supervision (PhD); human services counseling (MA), including addictions and recovery, business, child and family law, Christian ministries, criminal justice, crisis response and trauma, executive leadership, health and wellness, life coaching, marriage and family, military resilience; marriage and family therapy (MA); military resilience (Certificate); professional counseling (MA). Part-time programs available. Postbaccalaureate distance learning degree programs offered (minimal on-campus study). *Students:* 3,009 full-time (2,433 women), 6,251 part-time (4,981 women); includes 2,959 minority (2,520 Black or African American, non-Hispanic/Latino; 49 American Indian or Alaska Native, non-Hispanic/Latino; 51 Asian, non-Hispanic/Latino; 97 Hispanic/Latino; 9 Native Hawaiian or other Pacific Islander, non-Hispanic/Latino; 233 Two or more races, non-Hispanic/Latino), 153 international. Average age 38. 6,645 applicants, 55% accepted, 2039 enrolled. In 2014, 2,410 master's, 11 doctorates, 2 other advanced degrees awarded. *Application deadline:* Applications are processed on a rolling basis. Application fee: $50. Electronic applications accepted. *Financial support:* Applicants required to submit FAFSA. *Unit head:* Dr. Ronald Hawkins, Founding Dean, School of Behavioral Sciences. *Application contact:* Jay Bridge, Director of Admissions, 800-424-9595, Fax: 800-628-7977, E-mail: gradadmissions@liberty.edu.

Lindenwood University, Graduate Programs, School of Education, St. Charles, MO 63301-1695. Offers education (MA); educational administration (MA, Ed D, Ed S); English to speakers of other languages (MA); instructional leadership (Ed D, Ed S); library media (MA); professional counseling (MA); school administration (Ed S); school counseling (MA); teaching (MA). Part-time and evening/weekend programs available. Postbaccalaureate distance learning degree programs offered (no on-campus study). *Faculty:* 46 full-time (30 women), 227 part-time/adjunct (150 women). *Students:* 355 full-time (263 women), 1,689 part-time (1,303 women); includes 569 minority (491 Black or African American, non-Hispanic/Latino; 9 American Indian or Alaska Native, non-Hispanic/Latino; 7 Asian, non-Hispanic/Latino; 27 Hispanic/Latino; 1 Native Hawaiian or other Pacific Islander, non-Hispanic/Latino; 34 Two or more races, non-Hispanic/Latino), 27 international. Average age 36. 536 applicants, 76% accepted, 332 enrolled. In 2014, 645 master's, 46 doctorates, 59 other advanced degrees awarded. *Degree requirements:* For master's, thesis (for some programs), minimum GPA of 3.0; for doctorate, thesis/dissertation, minimum GPA of 3.0; for Ed S, comprehensive exam, project, minimum GPA of 3.0. *Entrance requirements:* For master's, interview, minimum GPA of 3.0, writing sample, letter of recommendation; for doctorate, GRE, minimum graduate GPA of 3.4, resume, interview, writing sample, 4 letters of recommendation; for Ed S, master's degree in education, relevant work experience. Additional exam requirements/recommendations for international students: Required—TOEFL (minimum score 550 paper-based; 80 iBT). *Application deadline:* For fall admission, 8/24 priority date for domestic and international students; for spring admission, 1/25 priority date for domestic and international students. Applications are processed on a rolling basis. Application fee: $30 ($100 for international students). Electronic applications accepted. *Expenses: Tuition:* Full-time $15,230; part-time $440 per credit hour. Required fees: $205 per semester. Tuition and fees vary according to course level, course load and degree level. *Financial support:* In 2014–15, 236 students received support. Career-related internships or fieldwork, Federal Work-Study, institutionally sponsored loans, scholarships/grants, tuition waivers (partial), and unspecified assistantships available. Financial award application deadline: 6/30; financial award applicants required to submit FAFSA. *Unit head:* Dr. Cynthia Bice, Dean, 636-949-4618, Fax: 636-949-4197, E-mail: cbice@lindenwood.edu. *Application contact:* Tyler Kostich, Director of Evening and Graduate Admissions, 636-949-4138, Fax: 636-949-4109, E-mail: adultadmissions@lindenwood.edu.

Lindsey Wilson College, School of Professional Counseling, Columbia, KY 42728. Offers counseling and human development (M Ed); counselor education and supervision (PhD). *Accreditation:* ACA (one or more programs are accredited). Part-time and evening/weekend programs available. Postbaccalaureate distance learning degree programs offered (minimal on-campus study).

Lipscomb University, Department of Graduate Psychology and Counseling, Nashville, TN 37204-3951. Offers clinical mental health counseling (MS); counseling psychology (Certificate); marriage and family therapy (MMFT); psychology (MS). Part-time and evening/weekend programs available. *Faculty:* 11 full-time (3 women), 6 part-time/adjunct (2 women). *Students:* 90 full-time (70 women), 40 part-time (32 women); includes 36 minority (25 Black or African American, non-Hispanic/Latino; 1 American Indian or Alaska Native, non-Hispanic/Latino; 2 Asian, non-Hispanic/Latino; 6 Hispanic/Latino; 2 Two or more races, non-Hispanic/Latino), 1 international. Average age 29. In 2014, 66 master's awarded. *Degree requirements:* For master's, thesis (for some programs), practicum, internship, capstone. *Entrance requirements:* For master's, GRE, resume, 3 reference letters, transcripts, goals statement. Additional exam requirements/recommendations for international students: Required—TOEFL (minimum score 570 paper-based; 80 iBT). *Application deadline:* For fall admission, 7/1 for domestic students; for spring admission, 11/1 for domestic students. Applications are processed on a rolling basis. Application fee: $50 ($75 for international students). Electronic applications accepted. *Expenses:* Expenses: $898 per credit hour. *Financial support:* Scholarships/grants and unspecified assistantships available. Financial award applicants required to submit FAFSA. *Faculty research:* Cognitive psychology, neuroscience, health psychology, grief issues. *Unit head:* Dr. Shanna Ray, Director/Professor of Psychology, 615-966-5833, E-mail: shanna.ray@lipscomb.edu. *Application contact:* Kathi Johnson, Recruiting and Marketing Coordinator, 615-966-5237, E-mail:

kathi.johnson@lipscomb.edu.
Website: http://www.lipscomb.edu/psychology/graduate-programs

Lock Haven University of Pennsylvania, College of Business, Information Systems and Human Services, Lock Haven, PA 17745-2390. Offers clinical mental health counseling (MS); sport science (MS). Postbaccalaureate distance learning degree programs offered (no on-campus study). *Degree requirements:* For master's, thesis. *Entrance requirements:* For master's, minimum undergraduate GPA of 3.0. Additional exam requirements/recommendations for international students: Required—TOEFL. Electronic applications accepted.

Long Island University–Hudson at Westchester, Graduate School, Purchase, NY 10577. Offers mental health counseling (MS), including Casac; school psychology (MS Ed). Part-time and evening/weekend programs available. Postbaccalaureate distance learning degree programs offered. *Faculty:* 6 full-time (5 women). *Students:* 53 full-time (41 women), 103 part-time (89 women); includes 50 minority (18 Black or African American, non-Hispanic/Latino; 3 Asian, non-Hispanic/Latino; 29 Hispanic/Latino), 1 international. Average age 35. In 2014, 95 master's, 19 other advanced degrees awarded. *Entrance requirements:* Additional exam requirements/recommendations for international students: Required—TOEFL. *Application deadline:* Applications are processed on a rolling basis. Application fee: $50. Electronic applications accepted. *Expenses: Tuition:* Part-time $1132 per credit. *Required fees:* $434 per semester. *Unit head:* Dr. Sylvia Blake, Dean and Chief Operating Officer, 914-831-2704, Fax: 914-251-5959, E-mail: sylvia.blake@liu.edu. *Application contact:* Cindy Pagnotta, Director of Marketing and Enrollment, 914-831-2701, Fax: 914-251-5959, E-mail: cindy.pagnotta@liu.edu.

Long Island University–LIU Brooklyn, School of Education, Brooklyn, NY 11201-8423. Offers applied behavior analysis (Advanced Certificate); bilingual education in urban settings (Advanced Certificate); bilingual school counselor (Advanced Certificate); childhood/early childhood urban education (MS Ed); early childhood urban education (MS Ed, Advanced Certificate); educational leadership (Advanced Certificate); marriage and family therapy (Advanced Certificate); school counselor (MS Ed, Advanced Certificate); teaching English to speakers of other languages (TESOL) (MS Ed). *Accreditation:* Teacher Education Accreditation Council. Part-time and evening/weekend programs available. *Faculty:* 20 full-time (14 women), 47 part-time/adjunct (34 women). *Students:* 224 full-time (183 women), 604 part-time (472 women); includes 551 minority (302 Black or African American, non-Hispanic/Latino; 3 American Indian or Alaska Native, non-Hispanic/Latino; 42 Asian, non-Hispanic/Latino; 189 Hispanic/Latino; 15 Two or more races, non-Hispanic/Latino), 10 international. Average age 36. 353 applicants, 61% accepted, 129 enrolled. In 2014, 213 master's, 16 other advanced degrees awarded. *Degree requirements:* For master's, thesis optional, electronic portfolio. *Entrance requirements:* For master's, 2 letters of recommendation; GPA requirement varies by program; some programs require interview, personal statement, writing assessment; for Advanced Certificate, 2 letters of recommendation, GPA requirement varies by program; interview; personal statement. Additional exam requirements/recommendations for international students: Required—TOEFL (minimum score 500 paper-based). *Application deadline:* For fall admission, 5/1 for international students; for spring admission, 11/1 for international students. Applications are processed on a rolling basis. Electronic applications accepted. *Expenses: Tuition:* Part-time $1132 per credit. *Required fees:* $434 per semester. *Financial support:* Career-related internships or fieldwork, scholarships/grants, tuition waivers (partial), and unspecified assistantships available. Support available to part-time students. Financial award applicants required to submit FAFSA. *Faculty research:* The intersection between race and gender in diverse women's leadership and health outcomes, selective mutism, risk factors among juvenile sex offenders and their reintegration into the school system, infant development, theoretical orientation in clinical practice. *Unit head:* Dr. Amy Patraka Ginsberg, Acting Dean (2015-2016), 718-488-1055, E-mail: amy.ginsberg@liu.edu. *Application contact:* Chanelle Lester, Director of Graduate Admissions, 718-780-4321, Fax: 718-780-6110, E-mail: chanelle.lester@liu.edu.
Website: http://www.liu.edu/Brooklyn/Academics/School-of-Education

Long Island University–LIU Post, College of Education, Information and Technology, Brookville, NY 11548-1300. Offers adolescence education (MS); art education (MS); childhood education (MS); childhood education literacy B-6 (MS); childhood/special education (MS); clinical mental health counseling (AC); early childhood education (MS); early childhood education/childhood education (MS); education (MS Ed); educational leadership (AC); educational technology (MS); information systems (MS); information technology education (MS); informational studies (PhD); public library administration (AC); student with disabilities, 7-12 generalist (AC); teaching students with speech language disabilities (MA). *Accreditation:* Teacher Education Accreditation Council. Part-time and evening/weekend programs available. *Faculty:* 62 full-time (35 women), 131 part-time/adjunct (49 women). *Students:* 422 full-time (359 women), 732 part-time (564 women); includes 257 minority (109 Black or African American, non-Hispanic/Latino; 31 Asian, non-Hispanic/Latino; 104 Hispanic/Latino; 1 Native Hawaiian or other Pacific Islander, non-Hispanic/Latino; 12 Two or more races, non-Hispanic/Latino), 44 international. Average age 31. 1,130 applicants, 65% accepted, 368 enrolled. In 2014, 366 master's, 17 doctorates, 140 other advanced degrees awarded. Terminal master's awarded for partial completion of doctoral program. *Degree requirements:* For master's, comprehensive exam (for some programs), thesis (for some programs); for doctorate, comprehensive exam, thesis/dissertation; for AC, internship. *Entrance requirements:* For master's, GRE (for some programs if GPA less than 3.0). Additional exam requirements/recommendations for international students: Required—TOEFL (minimum score 550 paper-based; 79 iBT), IELTS (minimum score 6.5). *Application deadline:* Applications are processed on a rolling basis. Application fee: $50. Electronic applications accepted. *Expenses:* Expenses: $1,132 per credit, $1,153 for speech language pathology (for master's programs); $1,505 per credit (for doctoral programs); $867 in fees for 12+ credits per term, $434 for less than 12 credits. *Financial support:* Career-related internships or fieldwork and Federal Work-Study available. Support available to part-time students. Financial award application deadline: 5/15; financial award applicants required to submit CSS PROFILE or FAFSA. *Total annual research expenditures:* $97,964. *Unit head:* Dr. Barbara Garii, Dean, 516-299-2210, Fax: 516-299-4167, E-mail: barbara.garii@liu.edu. *Application contact:* Carol Zerah, Director of Graduate and International Admissions, 516-299-2900 Ext. 3952, Fax: 516-299-3952, E-mail: enroll@cwpost.liu.edu.

Louisiana State University in Shreveport, College of Business, Education, and Human Development, Program in Counseling Psychology, Shreveport, LA 71115-2399. Offers MS. *Students:* 29 full-time (25 women), 12 part-time (10 women); includes 10 minority (9 Black or African American, non-Hispanic/Latino; 1 Two or more races, non-Hispanic/Latino), 1 international. Average age 30. 35 applicants, 100% accepted, 13 enrolled. In 2014, 17 master's awarded. *Degree requirements:* For master's, comprehensive exam, internship (600 clock hours). *Entrance requirements:* For master's, GRE, references, interview. Additional exam requirements/recommendations for international students: Required—TOEFL (minimum score 550 paper-based; 61 iBT). *Application deadline:* For fall admission, 6/30 for domestic and international students; for spring admission, 11/30 for domestic and international students; for summer admission, 4/30 for domestic and international students. Applications are processed on a rolling basis. Application fee: $20 ($30 for international students). Electronic applications accepted. *Expenses:* Tuition, state resident: full-time $5234; part-time $290.80 per credit hour. Tuition, nonresident: full-time $16,774; part-time $879.61 per credit hour. *Required fees:* $52.28 per credit hour. *Financial support:* In 2014–15, 8 research assistantships (averaging $3,500 per year) were awarded. Financial award applicants required to submit FAFSA. *Unit head:* Dr. Meredith G. Nelson, Program Director, 318-797-5199, Fax: 318-798-4171, E-mail: mnelson@pilot.lsus.edu. *Application contact:* Kimberly Thornton, Director of Admissions, 318-795-2405, Fax: 318-797-5286, E-mail: kimberly.thornton@lsus.edu.

Louisiana Tech University, Graduate School, College of Education, Department of Psychology and Behavioral Sciences, Ruston, LA 71272. Offers counseling and guidance (MA); counseling psychology (PhD); industrial and organizational psychology (MA, PhD). *Accreditation:* APA (one or more programs are accredited). Part-time programs available. *Degree requirements:* For master's, thesis or alternative; for doctorate, thesis/dissertation. *Entrance requirements:* For master's and doctorate, GRE General Test. *Application deadline:* For fall admission, 7/29 for domestic students; for spring admission, 2/3 for domestic students. Application fee: $20 ($30 for international students). *Financial support:* Fellowships, research assistantships, teaching assistantships, and career-related internships or fieldwork available. Financial award application deadline: 2/1. *Unit head:* Dr. Donna Thomas, Chair, 318-257-5066, Fax: 318-257-2379, E-mail: dthomas@latech.edu. *Application contact:* Dr. Cathy Stockton, Associate Dean of Graduate Studies, 318-257-3229, Fax: 318-257-2379, E-mail: cstock@latech.edu.
Website: http://www.latech.edu/education/psychology/

Loyola University Chicago, School of Education, Program in Counseling Psychology, Chicago, IL 60660. Offers PhD. *Accreditation:* APA. *Faculty:* 5 full-time (3 women), 6 part-time/adjunct (3 women). *Students:* 21. Average age 26. 60 applicants, 13% accepted, 4 enrolled. In 2014, 2 doctorates awarded. *Degree requirements:* For doctorate, comprehensive exam, thesis/dissertation. *Entrance requirements:* For doctorate, GRE General Test, GRE Subject Test, interview; minimum graduate GPA of 3.5, undergraduate 3.0; letters of recommendation. Additional exam requirements/recommendations for international students: Required—TOEFL (minimum score 550 paper-based; 79 iBT). *Application deadline:* For fall admission, 12/1 for domestic and international students. Application fee: $50. Electronic applications accepted. Application fee is waived when completed online. *Expenses: Tuition:* Full-time $17,370; part-time $965 per credit. *Required fees:* $138 per semester. *Financial support:* In 2014–15, 7 research assistantships with full tuition reimbursements (averaging $14,000 per year), 21 teaching assistantships with full tuition reimbursements (averaging $4,000 per year) were awarded; career-related internships or fieldwork, institutionally sponsored loans, scholarships/grants, traineeships, health care benefits, and unspecified assistantships also available. Financial award application deadline: 2/1; financial award applicants required to submit FAFSA. *Faculty research:* Career choice and development, multicultural counseling, psychological measurement, prevention and intervention, family therapy. *Unit head:* Dr. Steven Brown, Director, 312-915-6311, E-mail: sbrown@luc.edu. *Application contact:* Marie Hatland, Information Contact, 312-915-6800, E-mail: schleduc@luc.edu.

Loyola University Maryland, Graduate Programs, Loyola College of Arts and Sciences, Department of Psychology, Program in Counseling Psychology, Baltimore, MD 21210-2699. Offers MS, CAS. Part-time and evening/weekend programs available. *Degree requirements:* For master's, comprehensive exam, thesis; for CAS, thesis. *Entrance requirements:* For master's, GRE General Test, GRE Subject Test (recommended), transcript, essay, 3 letters of recommendation. Additional exam requirements/recommendations for international students: Required—TOEFL (minimum score 550 paper-based). Electronic applications accepted.

Lynchburg College, Graduate Studies, M Ed Program in Clinical Mental Health Counseling, Lynchburg, VA 24501-3199. Offers M Ed. *Accreditation:* ACA. Part-time and evening/weekend programs available. *Faculty:* 4 full-time (2 women), 2 part-time/adjunct (1 woman). *Students:* 31 full-time (29 women), 13 part-time (11 women); includes 10 minority (7 Black or African American, non-Hispanic/Latino; 1 American Indian or Alaska Native, non-Hispanic/Latino; 1 Hispanic/Latino; 1 Two or more races, non-Hispanic/Latino), 1 international. Average age 29. In 2014, 14 master's awarded. *Degree requirements:* For master's, counseling internship. *Entrance requirements:* For master's, GRE, minimum GPA of 3.0 (preferred), official transcripts (bachelor's, others as relevant), three letters of recommendation, career goals statement. Additional exam requirements/recommendations for international students: Required—TOEFL (minimum score 550 paper-based; 79 iBT), IELTS (minimum score 6.5). *Application deadline:* For fall admission, 7/31 for domestic students, 6/1 for international students; for spring admission, 11/30 for domestic students, 10/15 for international students. Applications are processed on a rolling basis. Application fee: $30. Electronic applications accepted. Application fee is waived when completed online. *Financial support:* Fellowships, research assistantships, Federal Work-Study, scholarships/grants, health care benefits, and unspecified assistantships available. Support available to part-time students. Financial award application deadline: 7/31; financial award applicants required to submit FAFSA. *Unit head:* Dr. Michael Williams, Assistant Professor and Program Director, Counselor Education, 434-544-8150, Fax: 434-544-8150, E-mail: williams.ma1@lynchburg.edu. *Application contact:* Christine Priller, Executive Assistant, Graduate Studies, 434-544-8383, Fax: 434-544-8483, E-mail: gradstudies@lynchburg.edu.
Website: http://www.lynchburg.edu/graduate/master-of-education-in-counselor-education/clinical-mental-health-counseling/

Marist College, Graduate Programs, School of Social and Behavioral Sciences, Poughkeepsie, NY 12601-1387. Offers education (M Ed, MA); mental health counseling (MA); school psychology (MA, Adv C). Part-time and evening/weekend programs available. *Degree requirements:* For master's, thesis optional. *Entrance requirements:* For master's, GRE General Test, letters of recommendation, minimum undergraduate GPA of 3.0, interview. Additional exam requirements/recommendations for international students: Required—TOEFL (minimum score 550 paper-based; 80 iBT); Recommended—IELTS (minimum score 6.5). Electronic applications accepted. *Faculty research:* AIDS prevention, educational intervention, humanistic counseling research, aging and development, neuroimaging.

Marquette University, Graduate School, College of Education, Department of Counselor Education and Counseling Psychology, Milwaukee, WI 53201-1881. Offers clinical mental health counseling (MS); community counseling (MA); counseling psychology (PhD); school counseling (MA). Part-time programs available. Terminal master's awarded for partial completion of doctoral program. *Degree requirements:* For master's, comprehensive exam, thesis (for some programs); for doctorate, thesis/dissertation, qualifying exam. *Entrance requirements:* For master's, GRE General Test or MAT, official transcripts from all current and previous colleges/universities except Marquette, three letters of recommendation, statement of purpose; for doctorate, GRE General Test, MAT, sample of written work, official transcripts from all current and previous colleges/universities except Marquette, three letters of recommendation, statement of purpose, resume/curriculum vitae. Additional exam requirements/recommendations for international students: Required—TOEFL (minimum score 530

paper-based). *Faculty research:* Ethical and legal issues in education, anxiety disorders, multicultural counseling, child psychopathology, group counseling and dynamics.

Marylhurst University, Department of Art Therapy Counseling, Marylhurst, OR 97036-0261. Offers art therapy (PGC); art therapy counseling (MA); counseling (PGC). Part-time programs available. *Students:* 38 full-time (35 women), 2 part-time (both women); includes 4 minority (3 Hispanic/Latino; 1 Two or more races, non-Hispanic/Latino). In 2014, 9 master's awarded. *Degree requirements:* For master's, comprehensive exam, practica. *Entrance requirements:* For master's, MAT, transcripts from all previous institutions attended, minimum undergraduate GPA of 3.0, letters of recommendation, course work in psychology and art, art portfolio, resume, autobiography. Additional exam requirements/recommendations for international students: Required—TOEFL (minimum score 550 paper-based; 79 iBT), IELTS (minimum score 6.5), PTE (minimum score 53). *Application deadline:* For fall admission, 1/31 priority date for domestic and international students. Applications are processed on a rolling basis. Application fee: $50. Electronic applications accepted. *Expenses:* Expenses: Contact institution. *Financial support:* Scholarships/grants available. Support available to part-time students. Financial award applicants required to submit FAFSA. *Faculty research:* Scientific approaches to art therapy research, child and adolescent psychotherapy, multicultural counseling. *Unit head:* Christine Turner, Chair, 503-636-8141, Fax: 503-636-9526, E-mail: cturner@marylhurst.edu. *Application contact:* Maruska Lynch, Graduate Admissions Counselor, 800-634-9982 Ext. 6322, Fax: 503-699-6320, E-mail: admissions@marylhurst.edu.
Website: http://marylhurst.edu/academics/schools-colleges-departments/art-music-creative-art-therapies/art-therapy-counseling/ma-art-therapy.html

Marymount University, School of Education and Human Services, Program in Counseling, Arlington, VA 22207-4299. Offers clinical mental health counseling (MA); counseling (Certificate); pastoral and spiritual care (MA); pastoral counseling (MA); school counseling (MA). *Accreditation:* ACA (one or more programs are accredited). Part-time and evening/weekend programs available. *Faculty:* 8 full-time (4 women), 7 part-time/adjunct (6 women). *Students:* 87 full-time (74 women), 44 part-time (37 women); includes 40 minority (14 Black or African American, non-Hispanic/Latino; 1 American Indian or Alaska Native, non-Hispanic/Latino; 6 Asian, non-Hispanic/Latino; 16 Hispanic/Latino; 3 Two or more races, non-Hispanic/Latino), 6 international. Average age 29. 87 applicants, 77% accepted, 42 enrolled. In 2014, 51 master's awarded. *Entrance requirements:* For master's, GRE, 2 letters of recommendation, interview, resume, personal statement; for Certificate, master's degree in counseling. Additional exam requirements/recommendations for international students: Required—TOEFL (minimum score 600 paper-based; 96 iBT), IELTS (minimum score 6.5). *Application deadline:* For fall admission, 2/3 priority date for domestic students, 7/1 for international students; for spring admission, 10/5 for domestic students. Application fee: $40. Electronic applications accepted. *Expenses: Tuition:* Part-time $885 per credit. *Required fees:* $10 per credit. One-time fee: $220 part-time. Tuition and fees vary according to program. *Financial support:* In 2014–15, 13 students received support, including 2 research assistantships with full and partial tuition reimbursements available, 1 teaching assistantship with full and partial tuition reimbursement available; career-related internships or fieldwork, Federal Work-Study, scholarships/grants, and unspecified assistantships also available. Support available to part-time students. Financial award applicants required to submit FAFSA. *Unit head:* Dr. Lisa Jackson-Cherry, Director, 703-284-1633, Fax: 703-284-5708, E-mail: lisa.jackson-cherry@marymount.edu. *Application contact:* Francesca Reed, Director, Graduate Admissions, 703-284-5901, Fax: 703-527-3815, E-mail: grad.admissions@marymount.edu.
Website: http://www.marymount.edu/Academics/School-of-Education-Human-Services/Graduate-Programs/Counseling-(M-A-)

Marywood University, Academic Affairs, Reap College of Education and Human Development, Department of Psychology and Counseling, Program in Mental Health Counseling, Scranton, PA 18509-1598. Offers MA. *Accreditation:* ACA. *Students:* 41 full-time (35 women), 6 part-time (5 women); includes 4 minority (1 Asian, non-Hispanic/Latino; 3 Hispanic/Latino), 1 international. Average age 27. In 2014, 9 master's awarded. *Application deadline:* For fall admission, 4/1 for domestic students, 3/31 for international students; for spring admission, 11/1 for domestic students, 8/31 for international students. Applications are processed on a rolling basis. Application fee: $35. Electronic applications accepted. *Expenses: Tuition:* Part-time $775 per credit. *Required fees:* $688 per semester. Tuition and fees vary according to degree level and campus/location. *Financial support:* Application deadline: 6/30. *Unit head:* Dr. Shamshad Ahmed, Coordinator, 570-348-6211 Ext. 2319, E-mail: sahmed@marywood.edu. *Application contact:* Tammy Manka, Associate Director of Graduate Admissions, 570-348-6211 Ext. 2322, E-mail: tmanka@marywood.edu.
Website: http://www.marywood.edu/counseling/degree-programs/mental-health-counseling-ma/

Massachusetts School of Professional Psychology, Graduate Programs, Boston, MA 02132. Offers applied psychology in higher education student personnel administration (MA); clinical psychology (Psy D); counseling psychology (MA); counseling psychology and community mental health (MA); counseling psychology and global mental health (MA); executive coaching (Graduate Certificate); forensic and counseling psychology (MA); leadership psychology (Psy D); organizational psychology (MA); primary care psychology (MA); respecialization in clinical psychology (Certificate); school psychology (Psy D); MA/CAGS. *Accreditation:* APA. *Degree requirements:* For master's, comprehensive exam (for some programs); for doctorate, thesis/dissertation (for some programs). Electronic applications accepted.

McGill University, Faculty of Graduate and Postdoctoral Studies, Faculty of Education, Department of Educational and Counseling Psychology, Montréal, QC H3A 2T5, Canada. Offers counseling psychology (MA, PhD); educational psychology (M Ed, MA, PhD); school/applied child psychology and applied developmental psychology (M Ed, MA, PhD, Diploma), including school psychology. *Accreditation:* APA.

McKendree University, Graduate Programs, Master of Arts Program in Clinical Mental Health Counseling, Lebanon, IL 62254-1299. Offers MA. Part-time and evening/weekend programs available. *Degree requirements:* For master's, comprehensive exam, internship. *Entrance requirements:* For master's, official transcripts from each college or university attended, minimum undergraduate GPA of 3.0, three letters of recommendation, personal statement, completion of six undergraduate credit hours in a behavior science, curriculum vitae or resume. Electronic applications accepted.

McNeese State University, Doré School of Graduate Studies, Burton College of Education, Department of Psychology, Lake Charles, LA 70609. Offers addiction treatment (MA); applied behavior analysis (MA); counseling psychology (MA); general/experimental psychology (MA). Evening/weekend programs available. *Entrance requirements:* For master's, GRE.

Medaille College, Programs in Psychology, Buffalo, NY 14214-2695. Offers clinical psychology (Psy D); marriage and family therapy (MA); mental health counseling (MA); psychology (MA). Part-time and evening/weekend programs available. *Degree requirements:* For master's, comprehensive exam (for some programs), thesis (for some programs). *Entrance requirements:* For master's, GRE General Test (psychology), minimum GPA of 2.75 (psychology). Additional exam requirements/recommendations

for international students: Required—TOEFL (minimum score 550 paper-based). Electronic applications accepted. *Faculty research:* Schizophrenia, Parkinson's Disease, eyewitness testimony, methodology.

Mercy College, School of Social and Behavioral Sciences, Program in Counseling, Dobbs Ferry, NY 10522-1189. Offers counseling (MS); family counseling (Certificate). Part-time and evening/weekend programs available. Postbaccalaureate distance learning degree programs offered (no on-campus study). *Students:* 42 full-time (38 women), 123 part-time (110 women); includes 117 minority (48 Black or African American, non-Hispanic/Latino; 2 American Indian or Alaska Native, non-Hispanic/Latino; 2 Asian, non-Hispanic/Latino; 62 Hispanic/Latino; 3 Two or more races, non-Hispanic/Latino). Average age 34. 93 applicants, 70% accepted, 40 enrolled. In 2014, 64 master's, 2 other advanced degrees awarded. *Degree requirements:* For master's, comprehensive exam (for some programs). *Entrance requirements:* For master's, essay, two professional letters of recommendation, resume, undergraduate transcript with minimum GPA of 3.0. Additional exam requirements/recommendations for international students: Required—TOEFL (minimum score 600 paper-based; 100 iBT), IELTS (minimum score 8). *Application deadline:* For fall admission, 8/1 for international students. Applications are processed on a rolling basis. Application fee: $40. Electronic applications accepted. *Expenses: Tuition:* Full-time $14,952; part-time $814 per credit. *Required fees:* $600; $150 per semester. Tuition and fees vary according to course load, degree level and program. *Financial support:* Career-related internships or fieldwork, Federal Work-Study, scholarships/grants, and unspecified assistantships available. Support available to part-time students. Financial award applicants required to submit FAFSA. *Unit head:* Dr. Karol Dean, Dean, School of Social and Behavioral Sciences, 914-674-7517, E-mail: kdean@mercy.edu. *Application contact:* Allison Gurdineer, Senior Director of Admissions, 914-637-2946, Fax: 914-674-7382, E-mail: admissions@mercy.edu.
Website: https://www.mercy.edu/degrees-programs/ms-counseling

Mercy College, School of Social and Behavioral Sciences, Program in Mental Health Counseling, Dobbs Ferry, NY 10522-1189. Offers MS. Part-time and evening/weekend programs available. *Students:* 113 full-time (94 women), 124 part-time (105 women); includes 180 minority (112 Black or African American, non-Hispanic/Latino; 6 Asian, non-Hispanic/Latino; 54 Hispanic/Latino; 2 Native Hawaiian or other Pacific Islander, non-Hispanic/Latino; 6 Two or more races, non-Hispanic/Latino), 2 international. Average age 34. 111 applicants, 56% accepted, 29 enrolled. In 2014, 35 master's awarded. *Degree requirements:* For master's, comprehensive exam. *Entrance requirements:* For master's, essay, resume, interview, two letters of recommendation, undergraduate transcript. Additional exam requirements/recommendations for international students: Required—TOEFL (minimum score 600 paper-based; 100 iBT), IELTS (minimum score 8). *Application deadline:* For fall admission, 8/1 for international students. Applications are processed on a rolling basis. Application fee: $40. Electronic applications accepted. *Expenses: Tuition:* Full-time $14,952; part-time $814 per credit. *Required fees:* $600; $150 per semester. Tuition and fees vary according to course load, degree level and program. *Financial support:* Career-related internships or fieldwork, Federal Work-Study, scholarships/grants, and unspecified assistantships available. Support available to part-time students. Financial award applicants required to submit FAFSA. *Unit head:* Dr. Karol Dean, Interim Dean, School of Social and Behavioral Sciences, 914-674-7809. *Application contact:* Allison Gurdineer, Senior Director of Admissions, 877-637-2946, Fax: 914-674-7382, E-mail: admissions@mercy.edu.
Website: https://www.mercy.edu/degrees-programs/ms-mental-health-counseling

Messiah College, Program in Counseling, Mechanicsburg, PA 17055. Offers clinical mental health counseling (MAC); counseling (CAGS); marriage, couple, and family counseling (MAC); school counseling (MAC). *Accreditation:* ACA. Part-time programs available. Postbaccalaureate distance learning degree programs offered (no on-campus study). *Entrance requirements:* For master's, minimum undergraduate cumulative GPA of 3.0, 2 recommendations, resume or curriculum vitae, interview; for CAGS, bachelor's degree, minimum undergraduate cumulative GPA of 3.0, essay, two recommendations, resume or curriculum vitae, interview. Electronic applications accepted.

Mid-America Christian University, Program in Counseling, Oklahoma City, OK 73170-4504. Offers marital and family therapy (MS); pastoral/spiritual direction (MS); professional counselor (MS). *Entrance requirements:* For master's, MAT, bachelor's degree from a regionally accredited college or university, minimum overall cumulative GPA of 2.75 of bachelor course work. Additional exam requirements/recommendations for international students: Required—TOEFL (minimum score 550 paper-based).

MidAmerica Nazarene University, Graduate Studies in Counseling, Olathe, KS 66062-1899. Offers counseling (MAC); play therapy (PMC). *Accreditation:* ACA. Evening/weekend programs available. *Entrance requirements:* For master's, Minnesota Multiphasic Personality Inventory, minimum GPA of 3.0. *Expenses:* Contact institution.

Middle Tennessee State University, College of Graduate Studies, College of Education, Department of Educational Leadership, Program in Professional Counseling, Murfreesboro, TN 37132. Offers mental health counseling (M Ed); school counseling (M Ed). *Accreditation:* ACA; NCATE. Part-time and evening/weekend programs available. Postbaccalaureate distance learning degree programs offered. *Faculty:* 25 full-time (14 women), 16 part-time/adjunct (11 women). *Students:* 30 full-time (25 women), 43 part-time (36 women); includes 11 minority (7 Black or African American, non-Hispanic/Latino; 2 Hispanic/Latino; 2 Two or more races, non-Hispanic/Latino). 71 applicants, 79% accepted. In 2014, 23 master's awarded. *Degree requirements:* For master's, comprehensive exam, thesis. *Entrance requirements:* For master's, GRE or MAT. Additional exam requirements/recommendations for international students: Required—TOEFL (minimum score 525 paper-based; 71 iBT) or IELTS (minimum score 6). *Application deadline:* For fall admission, 6/1 for domestic and international students. Applications are processed on a rolling basis. Application fee: $30. Electronic applications accepted. *Financial support:* Application deadline: 4/1. *Unit head:* Dr. James Huffman, Chair, 615-898-2855, Fax: 615-898-2859, E-mail: jim.huffman@mtsu.edu. *Application contact:* Dr. Michael D. Allen, Vice Provost for Research/Dean, 615-898-2840, Fax: 615-904-8020, E-mail: michael.allen@mtsu.edu.

Midwestern State University, Billie Doris McAda Graduate School, Prothro-Yeager College of Humanities and Social Sciences, Department of Psychology, Wichita Falls, TX 76308. Offers clinical/counseling psychology (MA). Part-time and evening/weekend programs available. *Degree requirements:* For master's, one foreign language, comprehensive exam, thesis optional. *Entrance requirements:* For master's, GRE General Test, 3 recommendation forms. Additional exam requirements/recommendations for international students: Required—TOEFL (minimum score 550 paper-based). *Application deadline:* For fall admission, 7/1 priority date for domestic students, 4/1 for international students; for spring admission, 11/1 priority date for domestic students, 8/1 for international students. Applications are processed on a rolling basis. Application fee: $35 ($50 for international students). Electronic applications accepted. *Financial support:* Teaching assistantships with partial tuition reimbursements, career-related internships or fieldwork, Federal Work-Study, institutionally sponsored loans, scholarships/grants, tuition waivers (partial), and unspecified assistantships available. Support available to part-time students. Financial award application deadline: 3/1; financial award applicants required to submit FAFSA. *Faculty research:* Child assessment and treatment outcomes, Christianity as it relates to

psychology, treatment of behavioral/emotional problems in childhood, people struggling with HIV/AIDS, educational psychology. *Unit head:* Barbara Waddell, Secretary, 940-397-4340, Fax: 940-397-4682, E-mail: barbara.waddell@mwsu.edu. *Application contact:* Barbara Waddell, Secretary, 940-397-4340, Fax: 940-397-4682, E-mail: barbara.waddell@mwsu.edu.
Website: http://www.mwsu.edu/academics/libarts/psychology/index

Minnesota State University Mankato, College of Graduate Studies, College of Education, Department of Counseling and Student Personnel, Mankato, MN 56001. Offers college student affairs (MS); counselor education and supervision (Ed D); marriage and family counseling (Certificate); mental health counseling (MS); professional school counseling (MS). *Accreditation:* ACA (one or more programs are accredited); NCATE. *Students:* 53 full-time (47 women), 57 part-time (44 women). *Degree requirements:* For master's, comprehensive exam, thesis or alternative. *Entrance requirements:* For master's, GRE General Test or MAT (if GPA less than 3.0 for last 2 years), minimum GPA of 3.0 during previous 2 years, 3 letters of reference. Additional exam requirements/recommendations for international students: Required—TOEFL. *Application deadline:* For fall admission, 1/15 priority date for domestic students. Applications are processed on a rolling basis. Application fee: $40. Electronic applications accepted. *Financial support:* Research assistantships with full tuition reimbursements, teaching assistantships with full tuition reimbursements, career-related internships or fieldwork, Federal Work-Study, institutionally sponsored loans, and unspecified assistantships available. Support available to part-time students. Financial award application deadline: 3/15; financial award applicants required to submit FAFSA. *Unit head:* Dr. Jacqueline Lewis, Chairperson, 507-389-5655. *Application contact:* 507-389-2321, E-mail: grad@mnsu.edu.

Mississippi College, Graduate School, School of Education, Department of Psychology and Counseling, Clinton, MS 39058. Offers counseling (Ed S); marriage and family counseling (MS); mental health counseling (MS); school counseling (M Ed). Part-time programs available. *Degree requirements:* For master's and Ed S, comprehensive exam, thesis optional. *Entrance requirements:* For master's, GRE or NTE. Additional exam requirements/recommendations for international students: Recommended—TOEFL, IELTS. Electronic applications accepted.

Missouri State University, Graduate College, College of Education, Department of Counseling, Leadership, and Special Education, Program in Counseling, Springfield, MO 65897. Offers elementary school counseling (MS); mental health counseling (MS); secondary school counseling (MS). Part-time and evening/weekend programs available. *Students:* 64 full-time (54 women), 60 part-time (51 women); includes 7 minority (1 Black or African American, non-Hispanic/Latino; 1 American Indian or Alaska Native, non-Hispanic/Latino; 4 Hispanic/Latino; 1 Two or more races, non-Hispanic/Latino), 3 international. Average age 30. 35 applicants, 71% accepted, 19 enrolled. In 2014, 25 master's awarded. *Degree requirements:* For master's, comprehensive exam, thesis or alternative. *Entrance requirements:* For master's, GRE or MAT, minimum GPA of 2.75. Additional exam requirements/recommendations for international students: Required—TOEFL (minimum score 550 paper-based; 79 iBT). *Application deadline:* For fall admission, 2/1 priority date for domestic students, 1/1 priority date for international students; for spring admission, 10/1 priority date for domestic students, 9/1 priority date for international students. Application fee: $35 ($50 for international students). Electronic applications accepted. *Expenses:* Tuition, state resident: full-time $2250; part-time $250 per credit hour. Tuition, nonresident: full-time $4509; part-time $501 per credit hour. Tuition and fees vary according to course level, course load and program. *Financial support:* Federal Work-Study, institutionally sponsored loans, scholarships/grants, and unspecified assistantships available. Financial award application deadline: 3/31; financial award applicants required to submit FAFSA. *Unit head:* Dr. Jeffrey Cornelius-White, Program Coordinator, 417-836-6517, Fax: 417-836-4918, E-mail: jcornelius-white@missouristate.edu. *Application contact:* Misty Stewart, Coordinator of Admissions and Recruitment, 417-836-6079, Fax: 417-836-6200, E-mail: mistystewart@missouristate.edu.
Website: http://education.missouristate.edu/clse/

Monmouth University, The Graduate School, Department of Psychology, West Long Branch, NJ 07764-1898. Offers mental health counseling (MS); professional counseling (PMC); psychological counseling (MA), including addiction studies, psychological counseling. *Accreditation:* ACA. Part-time and evening/weekend programs available. *Faculty:* 8 full-time (4 women), 11 part-time/adjunct (8 women). *Students:* 146 full-time (126 women), 111 part-time (94 women); includes 50 minority (10 Black or African American, non-Hispanic/Latino; 2 American Indian or Alaska Native, non-Hispanic/Latino; 7 Asian, non-Hispanic/Latino; 27 Hispanic/Latino; 4 Two or more races, non-Hispanic/Latino), 1 international. Average age 27. 96 applicants, 96% accepted, 59 enrolled. In 2014, 75 master's awarded. *Degree requirements:* For master's, comprehensive exam (for some programs), thesis optional, fieldwork. *Entrance requirements:* For master's, GRE, minimum GPA of 3.0 overall, 12 credits in psychology or closely-related field, two Monmouth University psychological counseling recommendation forms, essay form; for PMC, degree or current enrollment in CACREP-accredited master's program in counseling with minimum cumulative GPA of 3.0. Additional exam requirements/recommendations for international students: Required—TOEFL (minimum score 550 paper-based; 79 iBT), IELTS (minimum score 5), Michigan English Language Assessment Battery (minimum score 77) or Certificate of Advanced English (minimum score B2). *Application deadline:* For fall admission, 7/15 priority date for domestic students, 6/1 for international students; for spring admission, 11/15 priority date for domestic students, 11/1 for international students. Applications are processed on a rolling basis. Application fee: $50. Electronic applications accepted. *Expenses: Tuition:* Full-time $18,072; part-time $1004 per credit. *Required fees:* $157 per semester. *Financial support:* In 2014–15, 211 students received support, including 195 fellowships (averaging $3,010 per year), 13 research assistantships (averaging $11,728 per year); career-related internships or fieldwork, scholarships/grants, and unspecified assistantships also available. Support available to part-time students. Financial award applicants required to submit FAFSA. *Faculty research:* Violent crime, single parenting, the African-American male, counseling older women, successful behavior for under-achieving youth. *Unit head:* Dr. Stephanie Hall, Program Director, 732-571-3570, Fax: 732-923-4661, E-mail: shall@monmouth.edu. *Application contact:* Andrea Thompson, Graduate Admission Counselor, 732-571-3452, Fax: 732-263-5123, E-mail: gradadm@monmouth.edu.
Website: http://www.monmouth.edu/psychological_counseling

Montana State University Billings, College of Allied Health Professions, Program in Clinical Rehabilitation and Mental Health Counseling, Billings, MT 59101. Offers MS. *Accreditation:* CORE. Part-time programs available. *Degree requirements:* For master's, thesis or professional paper and/or field experience. *Entrance requirements:* For master's, GRE General Test or MAT, minimum GPA of 3.0. *Application deadline:* For fall admission, 7/15 for international students; for spring admission, 12/1 for international students. Applications are processed on a rolling basis. Application fee: $40. *Financial support:* Teaching assistantships, career-related internships or fieldwork, Federal Work-Study, institutionally sponsored loans, scholarships/grants, tuition waivers (partial), and unspecified assistantships available. Support available to part-time students. Financial award application deadline: 5/1; financial award applicants required to submit FAFSA. *Unit head:* Dr. Terry Blackwell, Chair, 406-896-5834, E-mail: tblackwell@msubillings.edu. *Application contact:* David M. Sullivan, Graduate Studies Counselor, 406-657-2053, Fax: 406-657-2299, E-mail: dsullivan@msubillings.edu.

Moody Theological Seminary?Michigan, Graduate Programs, Plymouth, MI 48170. Offers Bible (Graduate Certificate); Christian education (MA); counseling psychology (MA); divinity (M Div); theological studies (MA). *Accreditation:* ATS. Part-time and evening/weekend programs available. *Degree requirements:* For master's, one foreign language, thesis. *Faculty research:* Judaism, cults, world religions.

Morehead State University, Graduate Programs, College of Science and Technology, Department of Psychology, Morehead, KY 40351. Offers clinical/counseling psychology (MS); general/experimental psychology (MS). Part-time and evening/weekend programs available. *Degree requirements:* For master's, comprehensive exam, thesis optional. *Entrance requirements:* For master's, GRE General Test, 18 undergraduate hours in psychology, minimum GPA of 3.0, 3 letters of recommendation. Additional exam requirements/recommendations for international students: Required—TOEFL (minimum score 500 paper-based). Electronic applications accepted. *Faculty research:* Mood induction effects, serotonin receptor activity, stress, perceptual processes.

Mount Mary University, Graduate Division, Program in Counseling, Milwaukee, WI 53222-4597. Offers clinical mental health counseling (MS, Certificate); school counseling (MS, Certificate). Part-time and evening/weekend programs available. *Faculty:* 5 full-time (all women), 14 part-time/adjunct (12 women). *Students:* 97 full-time (90 women), 31 part-time (28 women); includes 46 minority (29 Black or African American, non-Hispanic/Latino; 1 American Indian or Alaska Native, non-Hispanic/Latino; 1 Asian, non-Hispanic/Latino; 8 Hispanic/Latino; 1 Native Hawaiian or other Pacific Islander, non-Hispanic/Latino; 6 Two or more races, non-Hispanic/Latino), 1 international. Average age 32. 64 applicants, 59% accepted, 18 enrolled. In 2014, 43 master's, 2 other advanced degrees awarded. *Degree requirements:* For master's, comprehensive exam, thesis or alternative. *Entrance requirements:* For master's, minimum GPA of 3.0. Additional exam requirements/recommendations for international students: Required—TOEFL (minimum score 550 paper-based, 80 iBT) or IELTS (minimum score 6.5). *Application deadline:* For fall admission, 5/1 for domestic and international students; for spring admission, 10/1 for domestic and international students; for summer admission, 4/15 for domestic and international students. Applications are processed on a rolling basis. Application fee: $50 ($0 for international students). Electronic applications accepted. *Expenses:* Expenses: Contact institution. *Financial support:* Career-related internships or fieldwork, Federal Work-Study, and unspecified assistantships available. Support available to part-time students. Financial award application deadline: 5/1; financial award applicants required to submit FAFSA. *Faculty research:* Cognitive behavioral interventions for depression, eating disorders and compliance. *Unit head:* Dr. Carrie King, Graduate Program Director, 414-258-4810 Ext. 318, E-mail: kingc@mtmary.edu. *Application contact:* Dr. Douglas J. Mickelson, Dean for Graduate Education, 414-256-1252, Fax: 414-256-0167, E-mail: mickelsd@mtmary.edu.
Website: http://www.mtmary.edu/majors-programs/graduate/counseling/index.html

Mount Saint Mary's University, Graduate Division, Los Angeles, CA 90049-1599. Offers business administration (MBA); counseling psychology (MS); creative writing (MFA); education (MS, Certificate); film and television (MFA); health policy and management (MS); humanities (MA); nursing (MSN, Certificate); physical therapy (DPT); religious studies (MA). Part-time and evening/weekend programs available. *Faculty:* 15 full-time (11 women), 61 part-time/adjunct (33 women). *Students:* 462 full-time (345 women), 218 part-time (175 women); includes 417 minority (66 Black or African American, non-Hispanic/Latino; 3 American Indian or Alaska Native, non-Hispanic/Latino; 69 Asian, non-Hispanic/Latino; 254 Hispanic/Latino; 11 Native Hawaiian or other Pacific Islander, non-Hispanic/Latino; 14 Two or more races, non-Hispanic/Latino), 1 international. Average age 33. 1,086 applicants, 25% accepted, 241 enrolled. In 2014, 181 master's, 28 doctorates, 22 other advanced degrees awarded. *Entrance requirements:* Additional exam requirements/recommendations for international students: Required—TOEFL. *Application deadline:* For fall admission, 6/30 priority date for domestic and international students; for spring admission, 10/30 priority date for domestic and international students; for summer admission, 3/30 priority date for domestic and international students. Applications are processed on a rolling basis. Application fee: $50. Electronic applications accepted. *Expenses: Tuition:* Full-time $9756; part-time $813 per unit. One-time fee: $128. Tuition and fees vary according to degree level and program. *Financial support:* In 2014–15, 213 students received support. Career-related internships or fieldwork, Federal Work-Study, institutionally sponsored loans, and tuition waivers (full and partial) available. Support available to part-time students. Financial award application deadline: 3/15; financial award applicants required to submit FAFSA. *Unit head:* Dr. Linda Moody, Graduate Dean, 213-477-2800, E-mail: gradprograms@msmu.edu. *Application contact:* Tara Wessel, Senior Graduate Admission Counselor, 213-477-2800, E-mail: gradprograms@msmu.edu.
Website: http://www.msmu.edu/graduate-programs/admission/

Naropa University, Graduate Programs, Program in Transpersonal Counseling Psychology, Boulder, CO 80302-6697. Offers art therapy (MA); counseling psychology (MA); wilderness therapy (MA). *Faculty:* 10 full-time (6 women), 26 part-time/adjunct (19 women). *Students:* 169 full-time (131 women), 67 part-time (49 women); includes 32 minority (2 Black or African American, non-Hispanic/Latino; 1 American Indian or Alaska Native, non-Hispanic/Latino; 1 Asian, non-Hispanic/Latino; 13 Hispanic/Latino; 15 Two or more races, non-Hispanic/Latino), 7 international. Average age 31. 174 applicants, 67% accepted, 81 enrolled. In 2014, 70 master's awarded. *Degree requirements:* For master's, internships, counseling practicum. *Entrance requirements:* For master's, in-person interview, course work in psychology, 2 letters of recommendation, extended resume, minimum 100 hours of paid or volunteer work in a helping profession (mental health, healthcare, teaching, etc.). Additional exam requirements/recommendations for international students: Required—TOEFL (minimum score 600 paper-based; 80 iBT). *Application deadline:* For fall admission, 1/15 priority date for domestic and international students. Applications are processed on a rolling basis. Application fee: $60. Electronic applications accepted. *Expenses: Tuition:* Full-time $23,400; part-time $975 per credit. *Required fees:* $335 per semester. Tuition and fees vary according to course load. *Financial support:* In 2014–15, 70 students received support, including 14 research assistantships with partial tuition reimbursements available (averaging $6,319 per year); career-related internships or fieldwork, scholarships/grants, tuition waivers (partial), and unspecified assistantships also available. Support available to part-time students. Financial award application deadline: 3/1; financial award applicants required to submit FAFSA. *Unit head:* Dr. Deborah Bowman, Dean, Graduate School of Psychology, 303-546-3559, E-mail: bowman@naropa.edu. *Application contact:* Office of Admissions, 303-546-3572, Fax: 303-546-3583, E-mail: admissions@naropa.edu.
Website: http://www.naropa.edu/academics/gsp/grad/transpersonal-counseling-psychology-ma/index.php

National University, Academic Affairs, College of Letters and Sciences, La Jolla, CA 92037-1011. Offers applied linguistics (MA); biology (MS); counseling psychology (MA), including licensed professional clinical counseling, marriage and family therapy; creative writing (MFA); English (MA), including Gothic studies, rhetoric; film studies (MA); forensic and crime science (Certificate); forensic studies (MFS), including criminalistics,

investigation; history (MA); human behavior (MA); mathematics for educators (MS); performance psychology (MA); strategic communications (MA). Part-time and evening/weekend programs available. Postbaccalaureate distance learning degree programs offered (no on-campus study). *Faculty:* 69 full-time (34 women), 100 part-time/adjunct (55 women). *Students:* 727 full-time (532 women), 349 part-time (240 women); includes 505 minority (128 Black or African American, non-Hispanic/Latino; 5 American Indian or Alaska Native, non-Hispanic/Latino; 52 Asian, non-Hispanic/Latino; 260 Hispanic/Latino; 9 Native Hawaiian or other Pacific Islander, non-Hispanic/Latino; 51 Two or more races, non-Hispanic/Latino), 4 international. Average age 34. In 2014, 569 master's awarded. *Degree requirements:* For master's, thesis (for some programs). *Entrance requirements:* For master's, interview, minimum GPA of 2.5. Additional exam requirements/recommendations for international students: Required—TOEFL (minimum score 550 paper-based; 79 iBT), IELTS (minimum score 6). *Application deadline:* Applications are processed on a rolling basis. Application fee: $60 ($65 for international students). Electronic applications accepted. *Expenses: Tuition:* Full-time $14,184; part-time $1773 per course. *Financial support:* Career-related internships or fieldwork, institutionally sponsored loans, scholarships/grants, and tuition waivers (partial) available. Support available to part-time students. Financial award application deadline: 6/30; financial award applicants required to submit FAFSA. *Unit head:* College of Letters and Sciences, 800-628-8648, E-mail: cols@nu.edu. *Application contact:* Frank Rojas, Interim Vice President for Enrollment Services, 800-628-8648, E-mail: advisor@nu.edu.
Website: http://www.nu.edu/OurPrograms/CollegeOfLettersAndSciences.html

New England College, Program in Community Mental Health Counseling, Henniker, NH 03242-3293. Offers human services (MS); mental health counseling (MS). Part-time and evening/weekend programs available. *Degree requirements:* For master's, internship.

New Jersey City University, Graduate Studies and Continuing Education, Debra Cannon Partridge Wolfe College of Education, Department of Educational Leadership and Counseling, Program in Counseling, Jersey City, NJ 07305-1597. Offers MA. Part-time and evening/weekend programs available. *Faculty:* 5 full-time (all women), 1 (woman) part-time/adjunct. *Students:* 54 full-time (41 women), 149 part-time (120 women); includes 131 minority (69 Black or African American, non-Hispanic/Latino; 7 Asian, non-Hispanic/Latino; 55 Hispanic/Latino), 2 international. Average age 34. 48 applicants, 90% accepted, 38 enrolled. In 2014, 36 master's awarded. *Entrance requirements:* Additional exam requirements/recommendations for international students: Required—TOEFL (minimum score 79 iBT). *Expenses: Tuition, area resident:* Part-time $538 per credit. Tuition, state resident: part-time $538 per credit. Tuition, nonresident: part-time $948 per credit. *Unit head:* Dr. Jennifer Hartman, 201-200-3124, E-mail: jhartman@njcu.edu. *Application contact:* Jose Balda, E-mail: jbalda@njcu.edu.

New Mexico Highlands University, Graduate Studies, College of Arts and Sciences, Department of Social and Behavioral Sciences, Las Vegas, NM 87701. Offers psychology (MS), including clinical psychology/counseling, general psychology; public affairs (MA), including applied sociology; Southwest studies (MA), including anthropology. Part-time programs available. *Faculty:* 11 full-time (5 women), 3 part-time/adjunct (all women). *Students:* 24 full-time (16 women), 19 part-time (14 women); includes 27 minority (3 Black or African American, non-Hispanic/Latino; 1 American Indian or Alaska Native, non-Hispanic/Latino; 23 Hispanic/Latino), 2 international. Average age 33. 45 applicants, 33% accepted, 15 enrolled. In 2014, 7 master's awarded. *Degree requirements:* For master's, comprehensive exam, thesis or alternative. *Entrance requirements:* For master's, minimum undergraduate GPA of 3.0. Additional exam requirements/recommendations for international students: Required—TOEFL (minimum score 540 paper-based). *Application deadline:* For fall admission, 8/1 priority date for domestic students. Applications are processed on a rolling basis. Application fee: $15. *Financial support:* In 2014–15, 34 teaching assistantships were awarded; career-related internships or fieldwork, Federal Work-Study, institutionally sponsored loans, scholarships/grants, tuition waivers (full and partial), and unspecified assistantships also available. Support available to part-time students. Financial award application deadline: 3/1; financial award applicants required to submit FAFSA. *Faculty research:* Southwest Native American resettlement development, community-level interventions, neurochemistry of personality, comparative criminal justice, social theory and activism. *Unit head:* Dr. Tom Ward, Program Coordinator, 505-454-3196, E-mail: tsward@nmhu.edu. *Application contact:* Diane Trujillo, Administrative Assistant for Graduate Studies, 505-454-3266, Fax: 505-426-2117, E-mail: dtrujillo@nmhu.edu.

New Mexico State University, College of Education, Department of Counseling and Educational Psychology, Las Cruces, NM 88003-8001. Offers counseling and guidance (MA), including counseling and guidance, educational diagnostics; school psychology (Ed S). *Accreditation:* ACA; APA (one or more programs are accredited); NCATE. Part-time programs available. *Faculty:* 15 full-time (13 women), 2 part-time/adjunct (1 woman). *Students:* 70 full-time (53 women), 21 part-time (16 women); includes 52 minority (3 Black or African American, non-Hispanic/Latino; 1 American Indian or Alaska Native, non-Hispanic/Latino; 5 Asian, non-Hispanic/Latino; 41 Hispanic/Latino; 2 Two or more races, non-Hispanic/Latino), 3 international. Average age 30. 101 applicants, 24% accepted, 23 enrolled. In 2014, 16 master's, 11 doctorates, 8 other advanced degrees awarded. *Degree requirements:* For master's, comprehensive exam, thesis optional, internship; for doctorate, comprehensive exam, thesis/dissertation, internship; for Ed S, comprehensive exam, thesis or alternative, internship. *Entrance requirements:* For master's, doctorate, and Ed S, GRE General Test, minimum GPA of 3.0. Additional exam requirements/recommendations for international students: Required—IELTS (minimum score 6.5); Recommended—TOEFL (minimum score 550 paper-based; 79 iBT). *Application deadline:* For fall admission, 12/15 for domestic and international students; for winter admission, 1/15 for domestic and international students; for spring admission, 2/1 priority date for domestic students, 2/1 for international students. Application fee: $40 ($50 for international students). Electronic applications accepted. *Expenses:* Tuition, state resident: full-time $3969; part-time $220.50 per credit hour. Tuition, nonresident: full-time $13,838; part-time $768.80 per credit hour. *Required fees:* $853; $47.40 per credit hour. *Financial support:* In 2014–15, 69 students received support, including 6 fellowships (averaging $3,970 per year), 9 research assistantships (averaging $10,292 per year), 18 teaching assistantships (averaging $9,734 per year); career-related internships or fieldwork, Federal Work-Study, scholarships/grants, traineeships, health care benefits, and unspecified assistantships also available. Support available to part-time students. Financial award application deadline: 3/1. *Faculty research:* Multicultural counseling and training, school and counseling psychology, social justice, integrated primary care behavioral health training, mental health disparities. *Total annual research expenditures:* $143,793. *Unit head:* Dr. Elsa Corina Arroyos, Interim Department Head, 575-646-2121, Fax: 575-646-8035, E-mail: elsaaj@nmsu.edu. *Application contact:* 575-646-2121, Fax: 575-646-8035, E-mail: cep@nmsu.edu.
Website: http://cep.education.nmsu.edu

New York University, Steinhardt School of Culture, Education, and Human Development, Department of Applied Psychology, Program in Counseling, New York, NY 10003. Offers counseling and guidance (MA, Advanced Certificate), including bilingual school counseling K-12 (MA), school counseling K-12 (MA); counseling for mental health and wellness (MA); counseling psychology (PhD); LGBT health, education, and social services (Advanced Certificate); Advanced Certificate/MPH; MA/Advanced Certificate. *Accreditation:* APA (one or more programs are accredited). Part-time programs available. *Faculty:* 13 full-time (9 women). *Students:* 135 full-time (110 women), 41 part-time (34 women); includes 73 minority (23 Black or African American, non-Hispanic/Latino; 16 Asian, non-Hispanic/Latino; 32 Hispanic/Latino; 2 Two or more races, non-Hispanic/Latino), 11 international. Average age 29. 663 applicants, 33% accepted, 74 enrolled. In 2014, 87 master's, 7 doctorates awarded. *Degree requirements:* For master's, thesis (for some programs); for doctorate, thesis/dissertation. *Entrance requirements:* For doctorate, GRE General Test, interview. Additional exam requirements/recommendations for international students: Required—TOEFL (minimum score 100 iBT). *Application deadline:* For fall admission, 12/1 priority date for domestic and international students. Applications are processed on a rolling basis. Application fee: $75. Electronic applications accepted. *Financial support:* Fellowships with full and partial tuition reimbursements, research assistantships, teaching assistantships with partial tuition reimbursements, career-related internships or fieldwork, Federal Work-Study, institutionally sponsored loans, scholarships/grants, tuition waivers (partial), and unspecified assistantships available. Support available to part-time students. Financial award application deadline: 2/1; financial award applicants required to submit FAFSA. *Faculty research:* Sexual and gender identities, group dynamics, psychopathy and personality, multicultural assessment, working people's lives. *Unit head:* Dr. Randolph Mowry, Co-Director, 212-998-5222, Fax: 212-995-4358, E-mail: randolph.mowry@nyu.edu. *Application contact:* 212-998-5030, Fax: 212-995-4328, E-mail: steinhardt.gradadmissions@nyu.edu.
Website: http://steinhardt.nyu.edu/appsych/counseling

Nicholls State University, Graduate Studies, College of Education, Department of Psychology and Counselor Education, Thibodaux, LA 70310. Offers psychological counseling (MA); school psychology (SSP). *Accreditation:* NCATE. Part-time and evening/weekend programs available. *Degree requirements:* For master's, comprehensive exam; for SSP, comprehensive exam, internship. *Entrance requirements:* For master's, GRE General Test. Electronic applications accepted.

Northeastern State University, College of Education, Department of Psychology and Counseling, Tahlequah, OK 74464-2399. Offers counseling psychology (MS); school counseling (M Ed); substance abuse counseling (MS). Part-time and evening/weekend programs available. *Faculty:* 12 full-time (6 women), 4 part-time/adjunct (2 women). *Students:* 80 full-time (67 women), 70 part-time (61 women); includes 47 minority (8 Black or African American, non-Hispanic/Latino; 21 American Indian or Alaska Native, non-Hispanic/Latino; 1 Asian, non-Hispanic/Latino; 5 Hispanic/Latino; 12 Two or more races, non-Hispanic/Latino), 2 international. Average age 34. In 2014, 43 master's awarded. *Degree requirements:* For master's, thesis (for some programs), written and oral examinations. *Entrance requirements:* For master's, GRE, minimum GPA of 2.5. Application fee: $25. *Expenses:* Tuition, state resident: part-time $178.75 per credit hour. Tuition, nonresident: part-time $451.75 per credit hour. *Required fees:* $37.40 per credit hour. *Financial support:* Teaching assistantships, career-related internships or fieldwork, and Federal Work-Study available. Financial award application deadline: 3/1. *Unit head:* Dr. Kenny Paris, Department Chair of Psychology and Counseling, 918-444-3021, E-mail: parisk@nsuok.edu. *Application contact:* Margie Railey, Administrative Assistant, 918-456-5511 Ext. 2093, Fax: 918-458-2061, E-mail: railey@nsouk.edu.
Website: https://academics.nsuok.edu/education/EducationHome/COEDepartments/PsychologyCounseling.aspx

Northeastern University, Bouvé College of Health Sciences, Boston, MA 02115-5096. Offers audiology (Au D); biotechnology (MS); counseling psychology (MS, PhD, CAGS); counseling/school psychology (PhD); exercise physiology (MS), including exercise physiology, public health; health informatics (MS); nursing (MS, PhD, CAGS), including acute care (MS), administration (MS), anesthesia (MS), primary care (MS), psychiatric mental health (MS); pharmaceutical sciences (PhD); pharmaceutics and drug delivery systems (MS); pharmacology (MS); physical therapy (DPT); physician assistant (MS); school psychology (PhD, CAGS); school/counseling psychology (PhD); speech language pathology (MS); urban public health (MPH); MS/MBA. *Accreditation:* ACPE (one or more programs are accredited). Part-time and evening/weekend programs available. *Degree requirements:* For doctorate, thesis/dissertation (for some programs); for CAGS, comprehensive exam.

Northern Arizona University, Graduate College, College of Education, Department of Educational Psychology, Flagstaff, AZ 86011. Offers counseling (MA); educational psychology (PhD), including counseling psychology, school psychology; human relations (M Ed); school counseling (M Ed); school psychology (Ed S); student affairs (M Ed). Part-time programs available. Postbaccalaureate distance learning degree programs offered. Terminal master's awarded for partial completion of doctoral program. *Degree requirements:* For master's, internship (for some programs); for doctorate, comprehensive exam, thesis/dissertation, internship. *Entrance requirements:* Additional exam requirements/recommendations for international students: Required—TOEFL (minimum score 550 paper-based; 80 iBT), IELTS (minimum score 7). Electronic applications accepted.

Northern Kentucky University, Office of Graduate Programs, College of Education and Human Services, Clinical Mental Health Counseling Program, Highland Heights, KY 41099. Offers MS. *Accreditation:* ACA. Part-time and evening/weekend programs available. *Faculty:* 7 full-time (3 women), 2 part-time/adjunct (1 woman). *Students:* 30 full-time (28 women), 30 part-time (27 women); includes 5 minority (all Black or African American, non-Hispanic/Latino). Average age 29. 40 applicants, 60% accepted, 14 enrolled. In 2014, 19 master's awarded. *Degree requirements:* For master's, comprehensive exam. *Entrance requirements:* For master's, GRE or MAT. Additional exam requirements/recommendations for international students: Required—TOEFL (minimum score 550 paper-based; 79 iBT); Recommended—IELTS (minimum score 6.5). *Application deadline:* For fall admission, 2/1 priority date for domestic students, 6/1 priority date for international students; for spring admission, 11/1 for domestic students, 10/1 for international students; for summer admission, 2/1 priority date for domestic students, 6/1 priority date for international students. Application fee: $40. Electronic applications accepted. *Expenses: Tuition, area resident:* Part-time $518 per credit hour. Tuition, state resident: part-time $630 per credit hour. Tuition, nonresident: part-time $797 per credit hour. *Required fees:* $192 per semester. Tuition and fees vary according to course load, degree level, campus/location, program and reciprocity agreements. *Financial support:* In 2014–15, 7 students received support. Applicants required to submit FAFSA. *Faculty research:* Preferences for college counseling, accreditation, partner violence prevention, data-based school counseling, creativity in counseling. *Unit head:* Dr. Greg Hatchett, Program Director, 859-572-6195, Fax: 859-572-6592, E-mail: hatchettg@nku.edu. *Application contact:* Alison Swanson, Graduate Admissions Coordinator, 859-572-6971, E-mail: swansona1@nku.edu.
Website: http://coehs.nku.edu/gradprograms/counseling/clinicalmentalhealthcounseling.html

Northern State University, MS Ed Program in Counseling, Aberdeen, SD 57401-7198. Offers clinical mental health counseling (MS Ed); school counseling (MS Ed). *Accreditation:* NCATE. Part-time programs available. Postbaccalaureate distance learning degree programs offered (minimal on-campus study). *Faculty:* 3 full-time (2 women), 2 part-time/adjunct (0 women). *Students:* 32 full-time (20 women), 25 part-time

(20 women); includes 1 minority (Black or African American, non-Hispanic/Latino). Average age 25. 30 applicants, 90% accepted, 22 enrolled. In 2014, 22 master's awarded. *Degree requirements:* For master's, comprehensive exam, thesis optional. *Entrance requirements:* For master's, minimum GPA of 2.75. Additional exam requirements/recommendations for international students: Required—TOEFL (minimum score 550 paper-based; 78 iBT), IELTS (minimum score 6). *Application deadline:* For fall admission, 8/15 for domestic and international students; for spring admission, 12/15 for domestic and international students. Applications are processed on a rolling basis. Application fee: $35. Electronic applications accepted. *Expenses:* Tuition, state resident: full-time $1817; part-time $202 per credit hour. Tuition, nonresident: full-time $3846; part-time $428 per credit hour. *Required fees:* $1072; $120 per credit hour. One-time fee: $35. *Financial support:* In 2014–15, 1 student received support, including 5 teaching assistantships with partial tuition reimbursements available (averaging $6,478 per year); career-related internships or fieldwork, Federal Work-Study, institutionally sponsored loans, scholarships/grants, and unspecified assistantships also available. Support available to part-time students. Financial award application deadline: 3/1; financial award applicants required to submit FAFSA. *Unit head:* Dr. Constance Geier, Dean of Education, 605-626-2558, Fax: 605-626-7190, E-mail: connie.geier@northern.edu. *Application contact:* Tammy K. Griffith, Program Assistant, 605-626-2558, Fax: 605-626-7190, E-mail: tammy.griffith@northern.edu.

Northwest Christian University, School of Education and Counseling, Eugene, OR 97401-3745. Offers clinical mental health counseling (MA); curriculum and instructional technology (M Ed); education (M Ed); school counseling (MA). Part-time and evening/weekend programs available. *Entrance requirements:* For master's, MAT, interview, minimum GPA of 3.0. *Application deadline:* For fall admission, 3/15 for domestic students. Applications are processed on a rolling basis. Application fee: $50. Electronic applications accepted. *Expenses: Tuition:* Full-time $13,920; part-time $580 per credit hour. *Required fees:* $80 per semester. Tuition and fees vary according to course load and program. *Financial support:* Scholarships/grants available. *Unit head:* Jim Howard, Dean, 541-684-7262, Fax: 541-684-7310. *Application contact:* Michael Fuller, Vice President for Enrollment and Student Development, 541-684-7201, Fax: 541-684-7333.

Northwestern Oklahoma State University, School of Professional Studies, Program in Counseling Psychology, Alva, OK 73717-2799. Offers MCP. Part-time programs available. *Faculty:* 5 full-time (4 women), 3 part-time/adjunct (2 women). *Students:* 56 full-time (50 women), 6 part-time (5 women); includes 2 minority (both Hispanic/Latino), 1 international. Average age 31. 29 applicants, 93% accepted, 27 enrolled. In 2014, 19 master's awarded. *Degree requirements:* For master's, comprehensive exam. *Entrance requirements:* For master's, GRE General Test or MAT, minimum GPA of 2.75. *Application deadline:* Applications are processed on a rolling basis. Application fee: $15. *Financial support:* Fellowships and Federal Work-Study available. Support available to part-time students. Financial award application deadline: 5/1; financial award applicants required to submit FAFSA. *Unit head:* Dr. Mark Davis, Chair, Psychology Department, 580-327-8443. *Application contact:* Rebekah Wagenbach, Coordinator of Graduate Studies, 580-327-8410, E-mail: rmwagenbach@nwosu.edu.
Website: http://www.nwosu.edu/psychology

Northwest University, College of Social and Behavioral Sciences, Kirkland, WA 98033. Offers counseling psychology (MA, Psy D); international community development (MA). Evening/weekend programs available. *Faculty:* 5 full-time (2 women), 17 part-time/adjunct (5 women). *Students:* 223 full-time (185 women), 55 part-time (41 women); includes 74 minority (13 Black or African American, non-Hispanic/Latino; 3 American Indian or Alaska Native, non-Hispanic/Latino; 30 Asian, non-Hispanic/Latino; 15 Hispanic/Latino; 1 Native Hawaiian or other Pacific Islander, non-Hispanic/Latino; 12 Two or more races, non-Hispanic/Latino), 6 international. Average age 37. 122 applicants, 80% accepted, 62 enrolled. In 2014, 56 master's, 3 doctorates awarded. *Entrance requirements:* For master's, 3 character references. Additional exam requirements/recommendations for international students: Required—TOEFL (minimum score 580 paper-based). *Application deadline:* For fall admission, 12/1 priority date for domestic and international students; for spring admission, 4/1 priority date for domestic and international students. Applications are processed on a rolling basis. Application fee: $75. *Expenses:* Expenses: Contact institution. *Financial support:* In 2014–15, 13 students received support. Career-related internships or fieldwork, health care benefits, and international student scholarships available. Financial award application deadline: 6/30. *Unit head:* Dr. Matt Nelson, Dean, 425-889-5328, E-mail: matt.nelson@northwestu.edu. *Application contact:* Daniela Zuniga, Enrollment Counselor, College of Social and Behavioral Sciences, 425-889-5249, E-mail: daniela.zuniga@northwestu.edu.
Website: http://www.northwestu.edu/social_behavioral

Nova Southeastern University, Center for Psychological Studies, Fort Lauderdale, FL 33314-7796. Offers clinical psychology (PhD, Psy D); counseling (MS); general psychology (MS); mental health counseling (MS); school counseling (MS). *Accreditation:* APA (one or more programs are accredited). Postbaccalaureate distance learning degree programs offered. *Faculty:* 50 full-time (19 women), 119 part-time/adjunct (69 women). *Students:* 1,827 (1,560 women); includes 842 minority (289 Black or African American, non-Hispanic/Latino; 2 American Indian or Alaska Native, non-Hispanic/Latino; 45 Asian, non-Hispanic/Latino; 478 Hispanic/Latino; 28 Two or more races, non-Hispanic/Latino), 41 international. Average age 31. 1,186 applicants, 51% accepted, 398 enrolled. In 2014, 344 master's, 117 doctorates, 10 other advanced degrees awarded. Terminal master's awarded for partial completion of doctoral program. *Degree requirements:* For master's, comprehensive exam, 3 practica; for doctorate, thesis/dissertation, clinical internship, competency exam; for Psy S, comprehensive exam, internship. *Entrance requirements:* For doctorate, GRE General Test, GRE Subject Test (recommended), minimum undergraduate GPA of 3.0; for Psy S, GRE General Test. Additional exam requirements/recommendations for international students: Required—TOEFL (minimum score 550 paper-based). *Application deadline:* Applications are processed on a rolling basis. Application fee: $50. Electronic applications accepted. *Expenses:* Expenses: Contact institution. *Financial support:* In 2014–15, 15 research assistantships, 68 teaching assistantships (averaging $4,800 per year) were awarded; career-related internships or fieldwork, Federal Work-Study, institutionally sponsored loans, scholarships/grants, and unspecified assistantships also available. Support available to part-time students. Financial award application deadline: 4/1. *Faculty research:* Clinical and child clinical psychology, geriatrics, interpersonal violence. *Unit head:* Karen Grosby, EdD, Dean, 954-262-5701, Fax: 954-262-3859, E-mail: grosby@nova.edu. *Application contact:* Carlos Perez, Enrollment Management, 954-262-5790, Fax: 954-262-3893, E-mail: cpsinfo@cps.nova.edu.
Website: http://www.cps.nova.edu/

Nyack College, Alliance Graduate School of Counseling, Nyack, NY 10960. Offers marriage and family therapy (MA); mental health counseling (MA). Part-time and evening/weekend programs available. *Students:* 107 full-time (88 women), 172 part-time (145 women); includes 212 minority (106 Black or African American, non-Hispanic/Latino; 41 Asian, non-Hispanic/Latino; 62 Hispanic/Latino; 3 Two or more races, non-Hispanic/Latino), 6 international. Average age 38. In 2014, 69 master's awarded. *Degree requirements:* For master's, comprehensive exam, counselor-in-training therapy, internship, CPCE exam. *Entrance requirements:* For master's, Millon Clinical Multiaxial Inventory-3, Minnesota Multiphasic Personality Inventory-2, transcripts, statement of Christian life and experience, statement of support systems. Additional exam requirements/recommendations for international students: Required—TOEFL (minimum score 83 iBT). *Application deadline:* For fall admission, 8/1 for domestic students, 2/15 for international students; for spring admission, 12/15 for domestic students, 7/15 for international students. Applications are processed on a rolling basis. Application fee: $30. Electronic applications accepted. *Expenses:* Expenses: Contact institution. *Financial support:* Career-related internships or fieldwork and scholarships/grants available. Financial award applicants required to submit FAFSA. *Unit head:* Dr. Carol Robles, Director, 845-770-5730, Fax: 845-348-3923. *Application contact:* 800-541-6891, Fax: 845-348-3912, E-mail: admissions.grad@nyack.edu.
Website: http://www.nyack.edu/agsc

Oakland University, Graduate Study and Lifelong Learning, School of Education and Human Services, Department of Counseling, Rochester, MI 48309-4401. Offers MA, PhD, Certificate. *Accreditation:* ACA (one or more programs are accredited). Part-time and evening/weekend programs available. *Degree requirements:* For doctorate, thesis/dissertation. *Entrance requirements:* Additional exam requirements/recommendations for international students: Required—TOEFL (minimum score 550 paper-based). Electronic applications accepted.

Old Dominion University, Darden College of Education, Counseling Program, Norfolk, VA 23529. Offers clinical mental health counseling (MS Ed); college counseling (MS Ed). *Accreditation:* ACA. Part-time and evening/weekend programs available. Postbaccalaureate distance learning degree programs offered (minimal on-campus study). *Faculty:* 13 full-time (6 women), 8 part-time/adjunct (7 women). *Students:* 123 full-time (103 women), 67 part-time (50 women); includes 68 minority (46 Black or African American, non-Hispanic/Latino; 5 Asian, non-Hispanic/Latino; 9 Hispanic/Latino; 8 Two or more races, non-Hispanic/Latino), 4 international. Average age 30. 128 applicants, 56% accepted, 63 enrolled. In 2014, 54 master's, 9 doctorates, 2 other advanced degrees awarded. *Degree requirements:* For master's and Ed S, comprehensive exam; for doctorate, comprehensive exam, thesis/dissertation. *Entrance requirements:* For master's and Ed S, GRE General Test, resume, essay, transcripts; for doctorate, GRE General Test, resume, interview, essay, transcripts. Additional exam requirements/recommendations for international students: Required—TOEFL. *Application deadline:* For fall admission, 3/1 for domestic and international students; for winter admission, 1/10 for domestic students; for spring admission, 11/1 for domestic students, 10/1 for international students; for summer admission, 3/1 for domestic students, 2/1 for international students. Application fee: $50. Electronic applications accepted. *Expenses:* Tuition, state resident: full-time $10,488; part-time $437 per credit. Tuition, nonresident: full-time $26,136; part-time $1089 per credit. *Required fees:* $64 per semester. One-time fee: $50. *Financial support:* In 2014–15, 125 students received support, including 2 fellowships with full tuition reimbursements available (averaging $15,000 per year), 20 research assistantships with partial tuition reimbursements available (averaging $10,000 per year), 14 teaching assistantships with full tuition reimbursements available (averaging $15,000 per year); career-related internships or fieldwork, Federal Work-Study, institutionally sponsored loans, scholarships/grants, traineeships, tuition waivers (partial), and unspecified assistantships also available. Support available to part-time students. Financial award applicants required to submit FAFSA. *Faculty research:* Group counseling, counselor education, career counseling, spirituality and counseling, school counseling, GLBT counseling, legal and ethical issues. *Total annual research expenditures:* $75,000. *Unit head:* Dr. Tim Grothaus, Graduate Program Director, 757-683-3326, Fax: 757-683-5756, E-mail: tgrothau@odu.edu. *Application contact:* Kelly Olds, Graduate Assistant, 757-683-3326, Fax: 757-683-5756, E-mail: kolds@odu.edu.
Website: http://www.education.odu.edu/chs/academics/counseling

Ottawa University, Graduate Studies-Arizona, Program in Professional Counseling, Ottawa, KS 66067-3399. Offers Christian counseling (MA); expressive arts therapy (MA); marriage and family therapy (MA); treatment of trauma, abuse and deprivation (MA). Programs offered in Mesa, Phoenix, Tempe and West Valley, AZ. Part-time and evening/weekend programs available. Postbaccalaureate distance learning degree programs offered. *Degree requirements:* For master's, comprehensive exam, thesis or alternative, field experience, practicum. *Entrance requirements:* For master's, minimum undergraduate GPA of 3.0; course work in theories of personality, abnormal psychology, and human growth and development. Additional exam requirements/recommendations for international students: Required—TOEFL (minimum score 550 paper-based).

Our Lady of the Lake University of San Antonio, School of Professional Studies, Program in Psychology, San Antonio, TX 78207-4689. Offers counseling psychology (MS, Psy D); marriage and family therapy (MS); school psychology (MS). *Accreditation:* APA (one or more programs are accredited). Part-time and evening/weekend programs available. *Degree requirements:* For master's, comprehensive exam, thesis optional, practicum; for doctorate, thesis/dissertation, internship, qualifying exam. *Entrance requirements:* For master's and doctorate, GRE General Test or MAT, interview. Additional exam requirements/recommendations for international students: Required—TOEFL. Electronic applications accepted. *Faculty research:* Marriage and family therapy, supervision, cross-cultural counseling, violence.

Pace University, Dyson College of Arts and Sciences, Department of Psychology, Program in Mental Health Counseling, New York, NY 10038. Offers loss and grief counseling (MS); mental health (MS, PhD); substance abuse (MS). Offered at Pleasantville, NY location only. Part-time and evening/weekend programs available. *Students:* 92 full-time (77 women), 53 part-time (40 women); includes 53 minority (15 Black or African American, non-Hispanic/Latino; 1 American Indian or Alaska Native, non-Hispanic/Latino; 9 Asian, non-Hispanic/Latino; 20 Hispanic/Latino; 8 Two or more races, non-Hispanic/Latino), 4 international. Average age 29. 80 applicants, 81% accepted, 36 enrolled. In 2014, 58 master's awarded. *Degree requirements:* For master's, comprehensive exam, qualifying exams, internship. *Entrance requirements:* For master's, GRE, resume, personal statement, two letters of reference, official transcripts, interview. Additional exam requirements/recommendations for international students: Required—TOEFL (minimum score 100 iBT). *Application deadline:* For fall admission, 8/1 priority date for domestic students, 6/1 for international students; for spring admission, 12/1 priority date for domestic students, 10/1 for international students. Applications are processed on a rolling basis. Application fee: $70. Electronic applications accepted. *Expenses: Tuition:* Part-time $1120 per credit. *Required fees:* $266 per semester. Tuition and fees vary according to course load, degree level and program. *Financial support:* Research assistantships, teaching assistantships, career-related internships or fieldwork, Federal Work-Study, and tuition waivers (partial) available. Financial award applicants required to submit FAFSA. *Unit head:* Dr. Ross Robak, Psychology Department Chair/Director, Graduate Program in Counseling, 914-773-3786, E-mail: rrobak@pace.edu. *Application contact:* Susan Ford-Goldschein, Director of Graduate Admissions, 914-422-4283, Fax: 914-422-4287, E-mail: gradwp@pace.edu.
Website: http://www.pace.edu/academics/graduate-students/degrees/mental-health-counseling-ms

Pacifica Graduate Institute, Graduate Programs, Carpinteria, CA 93013. Offers clinical psychology (PhD); counseling psychology (MA); depth psychology (MA, PhD);

mythological studies (MA, PhD). Terminal master's awarded for partial completion of doctoral program. *Degree requirements:* For master's, thesis (for some programs), practicum; for doctorate, comprehensive exam, thesis/dissertation, internship. *Entrance requirements:* For master's, resume, 3 letters of recommendation, writing sample, interview; for doctorate, resumé, 4 letters of recommendation, writing sample, interview. Additional exam requirements/recommendations for international students: Required—TOEFL. *Faculty research:* Imaginal and archetypal theory; post-Colonial psychoanalytic and Jungian theory; myth literature as it applies to the theory and practice of psychology.

Palm Beach Atlantic University, School of Education and Behavioral Studies, West Palm Beach, FL 33416-4708. Offers counseling psychology (MS), including addictions/mental health, general counseling, marriage and family therapy, mental health counseling, school guidance counseling. Part-time and evening/weekend programs available. *Faculty:* 9 full-time (3 women), 14 part-time/adjunct (8 women). *Students:* 286 full-time (237 women), 30 part-time (25 women); includes 151 minority (60 Black or African American, non-Hispanic/Latino; 5 Asian, non-Hispanic/Latino; 73 Hispanic/Latino; 13 Two or more races, non-Hispanic/Latino), 5 international. Average age 34. 111 applicants, 78% accepted, 75 enrolled. In 2014, 98 master's awarded. *Entrance requirements:* For master's, GRE or MAT and MMPI-2, minimum GPA of 3.0. Additional exam requirements/recommendations for international students: Required—TOEFL (minimum score 550 paper-based; 79 iBT). *Application deadline:* For fall admission, 7/15 priority date for domestic students; for spring admission, 11/15 priority date for domestic students. Applications are processed on a rolling basis. Application fee: $50. Electronic applications accepted. *Expenses: Tuition:* Part-time $510 per credit hour. *Financial support:* In 2014–15, 16 students received support. Tuition waivers and Employee Education grants available. Financial award application deadline: 5/1; financial award applicants required to submit FAFSA. *Unit head:* Dr. Gene Sale, Program Director, 561-803-2352. *Application contact:* Graduate Admissions, 888-468-6722, E-mail: grad@pba.edu.
Website: http://www.pba.edu/graduate-counseling-program

Palo Alto University, MA in Counseling Program, Palo Alto, CA 94304. Offers MA. Part-time programs available. Postbaccalaureate distance learning degree programs offered (no on-campus study). *Faculty:* 3 full-time (1 woman), 31 part-time/adjunct (19 women). *Students:* 182 full-time (149 women), 82 part-time (66 women); includes 112 minority (14 Black or African American, non-Hispanic/Latino; 41 Asian, non-Hispanic/Latino; 47 Hispanic/Latino; 2 Native Hawaiian or other Pacific Islander, non-Hispanic/Latino; 8 Two or more races, non-Hispanic/Latino). Average age 34. 122 applicants, 95% accepted, 82 enrolled. In 2014, 31 master's awarded. *Degree requirements:* For master's, capstone project. *Entrance requirements:* For master's, undergraduate degree in psychology with minimum GPA of 3.3. Additional exam requirements/recommendations for international students: Required—TOEFL. *Application deadline:* For fall admission, 6/30 priority date for domestic and international students; for winter admission, 12/1 for domestic and international students; for spring admission, 3/1 for domestic and international students; for summer admission, 5/15 priority date for domestic and international students. Applications are processed on a rolling basis. Application fee: $40. Electronic applications accepted. *Expenses:* Expenses: Contact institution. *Financial support:* In 2014–15, 2 students received support. Federal Work-Study and scholarships/grants available. Financial award application deadline: 1/15; financial award applicants required to submit FAFSA. *Unit head:* Dr. William Snow, Director of Counseling, 831-246-2440, E-mail: wsnow@paloaltou.edu. *Application contact:* Deanna Berger, Assistant Director of Admissions, 650-417-2023, E-mail: dberger@paloaltou.edu.
Website: http://www.paloaltou.edu/graduate-programs/masters-programs/ma-counseling

★ **Philadelphia College of Osteopathic Medicine,** Graduate and Professional Programs, Department of Psychology, Philadephia, PA 19131. Offers applied behavior analysis (Certificate); clinical health psychology (Post-Doctoral Certificate); clinical neuropsychology (Post-Doctoral Certificate); clinical psychology (Psy D); mental health counseling (MS); organizational development and leadership (MS); psychology (Certificate); school psychology (MS, Psy D, Ed S). *Accreditation:* APA. *Faculty:* 19 full-time (11 women), 122 part-time/adjunct (58 women). *Students:* 395 (304 women); includes 80 minority (49 Black or African American, non-Hispanic/Latino; 13 Asian, non-Hispanic/Latino; 7 Hispanic/Latino; 11 Two or more races, non-Hispanic/Latino). 345 applicants, 47% accepted, 113 enrolled. In 2014, 72 master's, 42 doctorates, 17 other advanced degrees awarded. Terminal master's awarded for partial completion of doctoral program. *Degree requirements:* For master's, comprehensive exam (for some programs), thesis (for some programs); for doctorate, comprehensive exam, thesis/dissertation. *Entrance requirements:* For master's, GRE or MAT, minimum GPA of 3.0; bachelor's degree from regionally-accredited college or university; for doctorate, PRAXIS II (for Psy D in school psychology), minimum undergraduate GPA of 3.0; for other advanced degree, GRE (for Ed S). Additional exam requirements/recommendations for international students: Required—TOEFL (minimum score 79 iBT). *Application deadline:* For fall admission, 3/1 priority date for domestic students. Applications are processed on a rolling basis. Application fee: $50. Electronic applications accepted. *Financial support:* In 2014–15, 28 teaching assistantships were awarded; Federal Work-Study, institutionally sponsored loans, and scholarships/grants also available. Financial award application deadline: 3/15; financial award applicants required to submit FAFSA. *Faculty research:* Adult and childhood anxiety and ADHD; coping with chronic illness; primary care psychology/integrated health care; applied behavior analysis; psychological, educational, and neuropsychological assessment. *Total annual research expenditures:* $533,489. *Unit head:* Dr. Robert DiTomasso, Chairman, 215-871-6442, Fax: 215-871-6458, E-mail: robertd@pcom.edu. *Application contact:* Kari A. Shotwell, Director of Admissions, 215-871-6700, Fax: 215-871-6719, E-mail: karis@pcom.edu.

See Display on page 990 and Close-Up on page 1211.

Phoenix Seminary, Graduate Programs, Phoenix, AZ 85018. Offers Biblical and theological studies (Graduate Diploma); Biblical communication (M Div); Biblical leadership (MA); Christian counseling (Graduate Diploma); counseling and family (M Div); leadership development (M Div); ministry (D Min); professional counseling (MA). *Accreditation:* ATS (one or more programs are accredited). Part-time and evening/weekend programs available. *Degree requirements:* For master's, 2 foreign languages, comprehensive exam; for doctorate, 2 foreign languages, thesis/dissertation. *Entrance requirements:* For master's, undergraduate degree with minimum GPA of 2.5; for doctorate, M Div (94 hours) with minimum GPA of 3.0. Additional exam requirements/recommendations for international students: Required—TOEFL (minimum score 587 paper-based; 92 iBT), TWE (minimum score 4.5).

Prescott College, Graduate Programs, Program in Counseling and Psychology, Prescott, AZ 86301. Offers adventure-based psychotherapy (MA); counseling psychology (MA); ecopsychology (MA); ecotherapy (MA); equine-assisted mental health (MA); expressive arts therapy (MA); somatic psychology (MA); student-directed independent study (MA). Part-time programs available. Postbaccalaureate distance learning degree programs offered (minimal on-campus study). *Degree requirements:* For master's, thesis, fieldwork or internship, practicum. *Entrance requirements:* For master's, 2 letters of recommendation, resume. Additional exam requirements/recommendations for international students: Required—TOEFL (minimum score 500 paper-based). Electronic applications accepted.

Providence University College & Theological Seminary, Theological Seminary, Otterburne, MB R0A 1G0, Canada. Offers children's ministry (Certificate); Christian studies (MA, Certificate); counseling (MA); cross-cultural discipleship (Certificate); divinity (M Div); educational studies (MA), including counseling psychology, educational ministries, student development, teaching English to speakers of other languages, training teachers of English to speakers of other languages; global studies (MA); lay counseling (Diploma); ministry (D Min); teaching English to speakers of other languages (Certificate); theological studies (MA); training teacher of English to speakers of other languages (Certificate); youth ministry (Certificate). *Accreditation:* ATS. Part-time programs available. *Degree requirements:* For master's, variable foreign language requirement, thesis (for some programs); for doctorate, thesis/dissertation. *Entrance requirements:* Additional exam requirements/recommendations for international students: Recommended—TOEFL (minimum score 550 paper-based). *Faculty research:* Studies in Isaiah, theology of sin.

Purdue University Calumet, Graduate Studies Office, School of Education, Program in Counseling, Hammond, IN 46323-2094. Offers human services (MS Ed); mental health counseling (MS Ed); school counseling (MS Ed). *Entrance requirements:* Additional exam requirements/recommendations for international students: Required—TOEFL.

Radford University, College of Graduate and Professional Studies, College of Education and Human Development, Department of Counselor Education, Radford, VA 24142. Offers clinical mental health counseling (MS); school counseling (MS). *Accreditation:* ACA; NCATE. Part-time and evening/weekend programs available. *Faculty:* 6 full-time (4 women), 4 part-time/adjunct (3 women). *Students:* 60 full-time (47 women), 15 part-time (13 women); includes 10 minority (4 Black or African American, non-Hispanic/Latino; 1 Asian, non-Hispanic/Latino; 2 Hispanic/Latino; 3 Two or more races, non-Hispanic/Latino), 2 international. Average age 27. 71 applicants, 77% accepted, 28 enrolled. In 2014, 27 master's awarded. *Degree requirements:* For master's, comprehensive exam, thesis optional. *Entrance requirements:* For master's, GRE or MAT, minimum GPA of 2.75, 3 letters of reference, personal essay, resume, official transcripts. Additional exam requirements/recommendations for international students: Required—TOEFL (minimum score 550 paper-based; 79 iBT), IELTS (minimum score 6.5). *Application deadline:* For fall admission, 2/15 priority date for domestic students, 12/1 for international students; for spring admission, 7/1 for international students. Applications are processed on a rolling basis. Application fee: $50. Electronic applications accepted. *Expenses:* Tuition, state resident: full-time $7187; part-time $299 per credit hour. Tuition, nonresident: full-time $16,394; part-time $683 per credit hour. *Required fees:* $2974; $125 per credit hour. Tuition and fees vary according to course load and program. *Financial support:* In 2014–15, 16 students received support, including 13 research assistantships (averaging $8,481 per year), 3 teaching assistantships with partial tuition reimbursements available (averaging $11,000 per year); career-related internships or fieldwork, Federal Work-Study, institutionally sponsored loans, scholarships/grants, and unspecified assistantships also available. Financial award application deadline: 3/1; financial award applicants required to submit FAFSA. *Unit head:* Dr. Nadine Hartig, Chair, 540-831-5214, Fax: 540-831-6755, E-mail: vgoad4@radford.edu. *Application contact:* Rebecca Conner, Director, Graduate Enrollment, 540-831-6296, Fax: 540-831-6061, E-mail: gradcollege@radford.edu.
Website: http://www.radford.edu/content/cehd/home/counselor-education.html

Radford University, College of Graduate and Professional Studies, College of Humanities and Behavioral Sciences, Department of Psychology, Program in Counseling Psychology, Radford, VA 24142. Offers Psy D. *Faculty:* 8 full-time (3 women). *Students:* 10 full-time (9 women), 5 part-time (3 women). Average age 28. 20 applicants, 35% accepted, 6 enrolled. In 2014, 3 doctorates awarded. *Degree requirements:* For doctorate, comprehensive exam, thesis/dissertation. *Entrance requirements:* For doctorate, GRE General Test, master's degree; minimum graduate GPA of 3.5; letter of interest describing professional and/or research experience; curriculum vitae/resume; essay on cultural background and experiences; 3 letters of recommendation; official transcripts. Additional exam requirements/recommendations for international students: Required—TOEFL (minimum score 550 paper-based; 79 iBT), IELTS (minimum score 6.5). *Application deadline:* For fall admission, 12/15 priority date for domestic students, 12/1 for international students. Applications are processed on a rolling basis. Application fee: $50. Electronic applications accepted. *Expenses:* Tuition, state resident: full-time $7187; part-time $299 per credit hour. Tuition, nonresident: full-time $16,394; part-time $683 per credit hour. *Required fees:* $2974; $125 per credit hour. Tuition and fees vary according to course load and program. *Financial support:* In 2014–15, 10 students received support, including 10 fellowships with full tuition reimbursements available (averaging $13,800 per year); career-related internships or fieldwork, Federal Work-Study, institutionally sponsored loans, and scholarships/grants also available. Financial award application deadline: 3/1; financial award applicants required to submit FAFSA. *Faculty research:* Human sexuality and conflict in close relationships, rural mental health and psychology practice, self-compassion and body image, effectiveness of multicultural training, treatments for post-traumatic stress disorder. *Unit head:* Dr. Sarah Hastings, Program Director, 540-831-5361, Fax: 540-831-6113, E-mail: slhasting@radford.edu. *Application contact:* Rebecca Conner, Director, Graduate Enrollment, 540-831-6296, Fax: 540-831-6061, E-mail: gradcollege@radford.edu.
Website: http://www.radford.edu/content/chbs/home/psychology/programs/counseling.html

Regent University, Graduate School, School of Psychology and Counseling, Virginia Beach, VA 23464-9800. Offers clinical psychology (Psy D); counseling (MA), including clinical mental health counseling, marriage, couple, and family counseling, school counseling; counseling studies (CAGS); counselor education and supervision (PhD); human services counseling (MA); M Div/MA; M Ed/MA; MBA/MA. PhD program offered online only. *Accreditation:* ACA; APA (one or more programs are accredited). Part-time and evening/weekend programs available. Postbaccalaureate distance learning degree programs offered (minimal on-campus study). *Faculty:* 29 full-time (15 women), 45 part-time/adjunct (29 women). *Students:* 257 full-time (211 women), 288 part-time (225 women); includes 156 minority (121 Black or African American, non-Hispanic/Latino; 2 American Indian or Alaska Native, non-Hispanic/Latino; 10 Asian, non-Hispanic/Latino; 23 Hispanic/Latino), 29 international. Average age 35. 681 applicants, 38% accepted, 170 enrolled. In 2014, 127 master's, 34 doctorates awarded. *Degree requirements:* For master's, thesis or alternative, internship, practicum, written competency exam; for doctorate, thesis/dissertation or alternative. *Entrance requirements:* For master's, GRE General Test (including writing exam), minimum undergraduate GPA of 2.75, 3 recommendations, resume, transcripts, writing sample; for doctorate, GRE General Test (including writing exam), GRE Subject Test, minimum undergraduate GPA of 3.0, graduate 3.5; 10-15 minute VHS tape demonstrating counseling skills; writing sample; 3 recommendations; resume. Additional exam requirements/recommendations for international students: Required—TOEFL (minimum score 577 paper-based). *Application deadline:* For fall admission, 4/1 priority date for domestic students; for spring admission, 11/1 priority date for domestic students. Applications are processed on a rolling basis. Application fee: $50. Electronic applications accepted. *Expenses:*

Expenses: Contact institution. *Financial support:* Research assistantships with full and partial tuition reimbursements, teaching assistantships with full and partial tuition reimbursements, career-related internships or fieldwork, scholarships/grants, and tuition waivers (full and partial) available. Support available to part-time students. Financial award application deadline: 9/1; financial award applicants required to submit FAFSA. *Faculty research:* Marriage enrichment, AIDS counseling, troubled youth, faith and learning, trauma. *Unit head:* Dr. William Hathaway, Dean, 757-352-4294, Fax: 757-352-4282, E-mail: willhat@regent.edu. *Application contact:* Matthew Chadwick, Director of Enrollment Support Services, 800-373-5504, Fax: 757-352-4381, E-mail: admissions@regent.edu.
Website: http://www.regent.edu/psychology/

Regis University, Rueckert-Hartman College for Health Professions, Division of Counseling and Family Therapy, Denver, CO 80221-1099. Offers counseling (MA); counseling children and adolescents (Post-Graduate Certificate); counseling military families (Post-Graduate Certificate); marriage and family therapy (MA, Post-Graduate Certificate); transformative counseling (Post-Graduate Certificate). *Accreditation:* ACA. Part-time and evening/weekend programs available. *Faculty:* 14 full-time (9 women), 23 part-time/adjunct (17 women). *Students:* 252 full-time (212 women), 126 part-time (93 women); includes 77 minority (9 Black or African American, non-Hispanic/Latino; 2 American Indian or Alaska Native, non-Hispanic/Latino; 7 Asian, non-Hispanic/Latino; 43 Hispanic/Latino; 16 Two or more races, non-Hispanic/Latino), 1 international. Average age 36. 103 applicants, 77% accepted, 67 enrolled. In 2014, 66 master's awarded. *Degree requirements:* For master's, thesis, internships, practicum. *Entrance requirements:* For master's, official transcript reflecting baccalaureate degree awarded from regionally-accredited college or university, interview, 2 recommendations, resume, criminal background check. Additional exam requirements/recommendations for international students: Required—TOEFL (minimum score 550 paper-based; 82 iBT). *Application deadline:* For fall admission, 6/15 for domestic students, 5/15 for international students; for spring admission, 11/1 for domestic students, 10/1 for international students; for summer admission, 3/1 for domestic students, 2/1 for international students. Application fee: $75. Electronic applications accepted. *Expenses:* Expenses: Contact institution. *Financial support:* In 2014–15, 8 students received support. Federal Work-Study and scholarships/grants available. Financial award application deadline: 4/15; financial award applicants required to submit FAFSA. *Faculty research:* Group development, counselor education, counsel and therapy, influence of technology on psychology, dream finding groups, adult development, depression. *Unit head:* Dr. Linda Osterlund, Associate Dean, Counseling and Family Therapy, 719-264-7011, Fax: 719-264-7095, E-mail: losterlan@regis.edu. *Application contact:* Sarah Engel, Director of Admissions, 303-458-4900, Fax: 303-964-5534, E-mail: regisadm@regis.edu.
Website: http://www.regis.edu/RHCHP/Schools/Counseling-and-Family-Therapy.aspx

Rhode Island College, School of Graduate Studies, Feinstein School of Education and Human Development, Department of Counseling, Educational Leadership, and School Psychology, Providence, RI 02908-1991. Offers advanced counseling (CGS); agency counseling (MA); co-occurring disorders (MA, CGS); educational leadership (M Ed); mental health counseling (CAGS); school counseling (MA); school psychology (CAGS); teacher leadership (CGS). *Accreditation:* NCATE. Part-time and evening/weekend programs available. *Faculty:* 9 full-time (5 women), 7 part-time/adjunct (6 women). *Students:* 32 full-time (25 women), 111 part-time (87 women); includes 17 minority (3 Black or African American, non-Hispanic/Latino; 3 Asian, non-Hispanic/Latino; 9 Hispanic/Latino; 1 Native Hawaiian or other Pacific Islander, non-Hispanic/Latino; 1 Two or more races, non-Hispanic/Latino), 1 international. Average age 34. In 2014, 42 master's, 24 other advanced degrees awarded. *Degree requirements:* For master's and other advanced degree, comprehensive exam (for some programs), thesis (for some programs). *Entrance requirements:* For master's, GRE General Test or MAT, undergraduate transcripts; minimum undergraduate GPA of 3.0; for other advanced degree, GRE or MAT (for most programs), undergraduate transcripts; minimum undergraduate GPA of 3.0; 3 letters of recommendation; current resume. Additional exam requirements/recommendations for international students: Recommended—TOEFL (minimum score 550 paper-based; 79 iBT). *Application deadline:* For fall admission, 3/1 for domestic students; for spring admission, 11/1 for domestic students. Applications are processed on a rolling basis. Application fee: $50. *Expenses:* Tuition, state resident: full-time $8928; part-time $372 per credit hour. Tuition, nonresident: full-time $17,376; part-time $724 per credit hour. *Required fees:* $602; $22 per credit. $72 per term. *Financial support:* In 2014–15, 3 teaching assistantships with full tuition reimbursements (averaging $3,000 per year) were awarded; career-related internships or fieldwork, Federal Work-Study, scholarships/grants, health care benefits, and unspecified assistantships also available. Support available to part-time students. Financial award application deadline: 5/15; financial award applicants required to submit FAFSA. *Unit head:* Dr. Kalina Brabeck, Chair, 401-456-8023. *Application contact:* Graduate Studies, 401-456-8700.
Website: http://www.ric.edu/counselingEducationalLeadershipSchoolPsychology/index.php

Richmont Graduate University, School of Counseling, Atlanta, GA 30327. Offers marriage and family therapy (MA); professional counseling (MA).

Rivier University, School of Graduate Studies, Department of Education, Nashua, NH 03060. Offers curriculum and instruction (M Ed); early childhood education (M Ed); educational administration (M Ed); educational studies (M Ed); elementary education (M Ed); elementary education and general special education (M Ed); emotional and behavioral disorders (M Ed); general social education (M Ed); leadership and learning (Ed D, CAGS); learning disabilities (M Ed); learning disabilities and reading (M Ed); mental health counseling (MA); reading (M Ed); school counseling (M Ed). Part-time and evening/weekend programs available. *Degree requirements:* For master's, comprehensive exam (for some programs), internships. *Entrance requirements:* For master's, GRE General Test or MAT.

Rosemont College, Schools of Graduate and Professional Studies, Counseling Psychology Program, Rosemont, PA 19010-1699. Offers human services (MA); school counseling (MA). Part-time and evening/weekend programs available. *Faculty:* 13 part-time/adjunct (7 women). *Students:* 64 full-time (58 women), 78 part-time (68 women); includes 64 minority (52 Black or African American, non-Hispanic/Latino; 4 Asian, non-Hispanic/Latino; 4 Hispanic/Latino; 4 Two or more races, non-Hispanic/Latino), 1 international. Average age 32. 93 applicants, 52% accepted, 29 enrolled. In 2014, 41 master's awarded. *Degree requirements:* For master's, thesis or alternative, practicum. *Entrance requirements:* For master's, minimum undergraduate GPA of 3.0, 3 letters of recommendation. Additional exam requirements/recommendations for international students: Required—TOEFL. *Application deadline:* Applications are processed on a rolling basis. Application fee: $50. Electronic applications accepted. Application fee is waived when completed online. *Expenses:* Expenses: Contact institution. *Financial support:* Institutionally sponsored loans and unspecified assistantships available. Financial award applicants required to submit FAFSA. *Faculty research:* Addictions counseling. *Unit head:* Abbey Wexler, Director, 610-527-0200 Ext. 2375, Fax: 610-526-2964, E-mail: awexler@rosemont.edu. *Application contact:* Graduate Admissions Counselor, 610-527-0200 Ext. 2596, Fax: 610-520-4399, E-mail: gpsadmissions@rosemont.edu. Website: http://www.rosemont.edu/

Rutgers, The State University of New Jersey, New Brunswick, Graduate School of Education, Department of Educational Psychology, Programs in School Counseling and Counseling Psychology, Piscataway, NJ 08854-8097. Offers Ed M. Part-time and evening/weekend programs available. *Entrance requirements:* For master's, GRE General Test, 3 letters of recommendation. Additional exam requirements/recommendations for international students: Required—TOEFL (minimum score 550 paper-based; 83 iBT). Electronic applications accepted. *Faculty research:* Children and family in cross-cultural context, attachment theory, multicultural counseling, therapy relationship.

Sage Graduate School, School of Health Sciences, Department of Psychology, Program in Counseling and Community Psychology, Troy, NY 12180-4115. Offers MA. *Faculty:* 4 full-time (3 women), 2 part-time/adjunct (1 woman). *Students:* 47 full-time (38 women), 39 part-time (33 women); includes 19 minority (10 Black or African American, non-Hispanic/Latino; 1 American Indian or Alaska Native, non-Hispanic/Latino; 1 Asian, non-Hispanic/Latino; 4 Hispanic/Latino; 3 Two or more races, non-Hispanic/Latino). Average age 30. 87 applicants, 56% accepted, 20 enrolled. In 2014, 15 master's awarded. *Degree requirements:* For master's, externship, internship, thesis or research seminar. *Entrance requirements:* For master's, minimum undergraduate GPA of 3.0, interview. *Application deadline:* Applications are processed on a rolling basis. Application fee: $40. *Expenses: Tuition:* Full-time $12,240; part-time $680 per credit hour. *Unit head:* Dr. Patricia O'Connor, Associate Dean, School of Health Sciences, 518-244-2073, Fax: 518-244-4571, E-mail: oconnp@sage.edu. *Application contact:* Dr. Sybillyn Jennings, Professor and Chair, 518-244-2074, Fax: 518-244-4545, E-mail: jennis@sage.edu.
Website: http://www.sage.edu/academics/psychology/programs/counseling/

St. Bonaventure University, School of Graduate Studies, School of Education, Program in Counselor Education, St. Bonaventure, NY 14778-2284. Offers community mental health counseling (MS Ed); rehabilitation counseling (MS Ed); school counseling (MS Ed); school counselor (Adv C). Program offered in Olean and Buffalo Center (Hamburg, NY). *Accreditation:* ACA. Part-time and evening/weekend programs available. *Faculty:* 4 full-time (1 woman), 6 part-time/adjunct (3 women). *Students:* 55 full-time (42 women), 13 part-time (10 women); includes 3 minority (1 Hispanic/Latino; 2 Two or more races, non-Hispanic/Latino), 1 international. Average age 29. 31 applicants, 97% accepted, 23 enrolled. In 2014, 26 master's awarded. *Degree requirements:* For master's, comprehensive exam, thesis optional, internship, portfolio; for Adv C, internship. *Entrance requirements:* For master's, statement of intent/writing sample; transcripts from all colleges previously attended; two references; interview; minimum undergraduate GPA of 3.0; for Adv C, interview, writing sample, minimum undergraduate GPA of 3.0, two letters of recommendation, master's degree, transcripts from all colleges previously attended. Additional exam requirements/recommendations for international students: Required—TOEFL (minimum score 550 paper-based; 79 iBT). *Application deadline:* For fall admission, 8/15 priority date for domestic students, 2/1 priority date for international students; for spring admission, 11/15 priority date for domestic students, 7/1 priority date for international students. Applications are processed on a rolling basis. Application fee: $0. Electronic applications accepted. *Expenses:* Expenses: $8,532 for Advanced Certificate; $34,128 for school counseling; $42,660 for community mental health counseling. *Financial support:* In 2014–15, 5 research assistantships with full and partial tuition reimbursements were awarded; career-related internships or fieldwork, Federal Work-Study, scholarships/grants, health care benefits, tuition waivers (partial), and unspecified assistantships also available. Support available to part-time students. Financial award application deadline: 4/15; financial award applicants required to submit FAFSA. *Unit head:* Dr. S. Alan Silliker, Director, 716-375-2368, Fax: 716-375-2360, E-mail: silliker@sbu.edu. *Application contact:* Bruce Campbell, Director of Graduate Admissions, 716-375-2429, Fax: 716-375-4015, E-mail: gradsch@sbu.edu.
Website: http://www.sbu.edu/academics/schools/education

St. Edward's University, New College, Program in Counseling, Austin, TX 78704. Offers MA. Part-time and evening/weekend programs available. *Students:* 83 full-time (63 women), 166 part-time (25 women); includes 84 minority (15 Black or African American, non-Hispanic/Latino; 2 American Indian or Alaska Native, non-Hispanic/Latino; 6 Asian, non-Hispanic/Latino; 52 Hispanic/Latino; 9 Two or more races, non-Hispanic/Latino), 2 international. Average age 32. 148 applicants, 58% accepted, 48 enrolled. In 2014, 86 master's awarded. *Degree requirements:* For master's, completion of 54 hours of coursework with minimum cumulative GPA of 3.0. *Entrance requirements:* For master's, GRE General Test, minimum GPA of 3.0 in last 60 hours or 2.75 overall. Additional exam requirements/recommendations for international students: Required—TOEFL (minimum score 79 iBT) or IELTS (minimum score 6). *Application deadline:* For fall admission, 6/1 priority date for domestic and international students; for spring admission, 10/1 priority date for domestic and international students; for summer admission, 3/1 priority date for domestic and international students. Applications are processed on a rolling basis. Application fee: $50. Electronic applications accepted. *Expenses: Tuition:* Full-time $22,448; part-time $1246 per credit hour. *Required fees:* $50 per trimester. Full-time tuition and fees vary according to course load and program. *Unit head:* Dr. Elizabeth Katz, Director, 512-464-8833, Fax: 512-448-8492, E-mail: elizk@stedwards.edu. *Application contact:* Office of Admission, 512-448-8500, Fax: 512-464-8877, E-mail: seu.admit@stedwards.edu.
Website: http://www.stedwards.edu

St. John Fisher College, Wegmans School of Nursing, Program in Mental Health Counseling, Rochester, NY 14618-3597. Offers MS. *Accreditation:* ACA. Part-time programs available. *Faculty:* 6 full-time (3 women). *Students:* 61 full-time (52 women), 15 part-time (14 women); includes 13 minority (6 Black or African American, non-Hispanic/Latino; 1 Asian, non-Hispanic/Latino; 6 Hispanic/Latino). Average age 30. 62 applicants, 68% accepted, 33 enrolled. In 2014, 27 master's awarded. *Degree requirements:* For master's, practicum experience, internship. *Entrance requirements:* For master's, GRE (if GPA below 3.0), 2 letters of recommendation, personal statement, current resume, interview. Additional exam requirements/recommendations for international students: Required—TOEFL (minimum score 575 paper-based; 80 iBT). *Application deadline:* Applications are processed on a rolling basis. Application fee: $30. Electronic applications accepted. *Expenses: Tuition:* Part-time $825 per credit hour. *Required fees:* $10 per credit hour. Tuition and fees vary according to course load, degree level and program. *Financial support:* Scholarships/grants available. Financial award applicants required to submit FAFSA. *Faculty research:* Social class issues, clinical supervision, counselor education, play therapy. *Unit head:* Dr. Rachel Jordan, Director, 585-899-3858, E-mail: rjordan@sjfc.edu. *Application contact:* Jose Perales, Director of Graduate Admissions, 585-385-8067, E-mail: jperales@sjfc.edu.

St. John's University, The School of Education, Department of Human Services and Counseling, Program in Clinical Mental Health Counseling, Queens, NY 11439. Offers MS Ed, Adv C. Part-time and evening/weekend programs available. *Students:* 48 full-time (43 women), 27 part-time (20 women); includes 37 minority (10 Black or African American, non-Hispanic/Latino; 8 Asian, non-Hispanic/Latino; 17 Hispanic/Latino; 2 Two or more races, non-Hispanic/Latino), 1 international. Average age 28. 57 applicants,

84% accepted, 14 enrolled. In 2014, 23 master's awarded. *Degree requirements:* For master's, internship, state examination. *Entrance requirements:* For master's, bachelor's degree from an accredited college or university, minimum GPA of 3.0, 2 letters of recommendation, interview, 18 credits in behavioral and social science. Additional exam requirements/recommendations for international students: Required—TOEFL (minimum score 600 paper-based; 100 iBT), IELTS (minimum score 7). *Application deadline:* For fall admission, 4/1 for domestic students, 4/1 priority date for international students; for spring admission, 11/1 for domestic students, 11/1 priority date for international students. Applications are processed on a rolling basis. Application fee: $70. Electronic applications accepted. *Expenses: Tuition:* Full-time $20,610; part-time $1145 per credit. *Required fees:* $170 per semester. *Financial support:* Research assistantships and career-related internships or fieldwork available. Support available to part-time students. Financial award application deadline: 3/1; financial award applicants required to submit FAFSA. *Unit head:* Dr. E. Francine Guastello, Chair, 718-990-1475, E-mail: guastelf@stjohns.edu. *Application contact:* Dr. Kelly K. Ronayne, Associate Dean for Graduate Admissions, 718-990-2304, Fax: 718-990-2343, E-mail: graded@stjohns.edu.

Saint Martin's University, Office of Graduate Studies, Program in Counseling Psychology, Lacey, WA 98503. Offers MAC. Part-time and evening/weekend programs available. *Faculty:* 2 full-time (1 woman), 5 part-time/adjunct (all women). *Students:* 90 full-time (74 women), 38 part-time (34 women); includes 24 minority (3 Black or African American, non-Hispanic/Latino; 2 Asian, non-Hispanic/Latino; 6 Hispanic/Latino; 3 Native Hawaiian or other Pacific Islander, non-Hispanic/Latino; 10 Two or more races, non-Hispanic/Latino). Average age 35. 38 applicants, 61% accepted, 20 enrolled. In 2014, 17 master's awarded. *Degree requirements:* For master's, clinical experience, interview. *Entrance requirements:* For master's, clinical experience. Additional exam requirements/recommendations for international students: Required—TOEFL (minimum score 550 paper-based; 79 iBT); Recommended—IELTS (minimum score 6.5). *Application deadline:* For fall admission, 4/1 priority date for domestic and international students; for spring admission, 11/1 priority date for domestic and international students. Applications are processed on a rolling basis. Application fee: $50. Electronic applications accepted. *Expenses: Tuition:* Part-time $1045 per credit. *Financial support:* Career-related internships or fieldwork, Federal Work-Study, and institutionally sponsored loans available. Support available to part-time students. Financial award application deadline: 3/1; financial award applicants required to submit FAFSA. *Faculty research:* Alcohol studies, clinical effectiveness, social justice, parent adolescent interaction. *Unit head:* Dr. Godfrey J. Ellis, Director, 360-438-4560, E-mail: gellis@stmartin.edu. *Application contact:* Bailey Craft, Assistant Director for Graduate Recruitment, 360-412-6142, E-mail: gradstudies@stmartin.edu.

St. Mary's University, Graduate School, Department of Counseling and Human Services, Program in Clinical Mental Health Counseling, San Antonio, TX 78228-8507. Offers MA. Part-time programs available. *Students:* 24 full-time (20 women), 15 part-time (11 women); includes 21 minority (2 Black or African American, non-Hispanic/Latino; 1 American Indian or Alaska Native, non-Hispanic/Latino; 1 Asian, non-Hispanic/Latino; 16 Hispanic/Latino; 1 Native Hawaiian or other Pacific Islander, non-Hispanic/Latino; 6 international. Average age 30. 30 applicants, 43% accepted, 7 enrolled. In 2014, 16 master's awarded. *Degree requirements:* For master's, comprehensive exam, internship. *Entrance requirements:* For master's, GRE, Application, GRE scores, undergraduate transcripts, references. Additional exam requirements/recommendations for international students: Required—TOEFL (minimum score 550 paper-based; 80 iBT). *Application deadline:* Applications are processed on a rolling basis. Application fee: $0. Electronic applications accepted. *Expenses: Tuition:* Full-time $15,070; part-time $800 per credit hour. *Required fees:* $156 per semester. *Financial support:* In 2014–15, 3 students received support. Fellowships available. Financial award application deadline: 3/31; financial award applicants required to submit FAFSA. *Unit head:* Dr. Julie Strentzsch, Program Director, E-mail: jstrentzsch@stmarytx.edu.
Website: https://www.stmarytx.edu/academics/graduate/masters/counseling/clinical-mental-health-counseling/

Saint Mary's University of Minnesota, Schools of Graduate and Professional Programs, Graduate School of Health and Human Services, Counseling and Psychological Services Program, Winona, MN 55987-1399. Offers addiction studies (Certificate); counseling and psychological services (MA).

Saint Mary's University of Minnesota, Schools of Graduate and Professional Programs, Graduate School of Health and Human Services, Counseling Psychology Program, Winona, MN 55987-1399. Offers Psy D.

Saint Paul University, Faculty of Human Sciences, Program in Counseling and Spirituality, Ottawa, ON K1S 1C4, Canada. Offers individual or marital/couple counseling (MA); spiritual care (MA). Part-time programs available. *Degree requirements:* For master's, research project or thesis. *Entrance requirements:* For master's, honors BA in human sciences, minimum B average, 12 theology credits.

St. Thomas University, Biscayne College, Department of Social Sciences and Counseling, Program in Mental Health Counseling, Miami Gardens, FL 33054-6459. Offers MS. Part-time and evening/weekend programs available. *Degree requirements:* For master's, comprehensive exam. *Entrance requirements:* For master's, interview, minimum GPA of 3.0 or GRE. Additional exam requirements/recommendations for international students: Required—TOEFL (minimum score 550 paper-based; 79 iBT). Electronic applications accepted.

Salem State University, School of Graduate Studies, Program in Counseling and Psychological Services, Salem, MA 01970-5353. Offers MS, Graduate Certificate. Part-time and evening/weekend programs available. *Entrance requirements:* For master's, GRE or MAT. Additional exam requirements/recommendations for international students: Required—TOEFL (minimum score 550 paper-based; 80 iBT) or IELTS (minimum score 5.5).

Salem State University, School of Graduate Studies, Program of Advanced Professional Studies in Counseling, Salem, MA 01970-5353. Offers Graduate Certificate. Part-time and evening/weekend programs available. *Entrance requirements:* Additional exam requirements/recommendations for international students: Required—TOEFL (minimum score 550 paper-based; 80 iBT) or IELTS (minimum score 5.5).

Salve Regina University, Holistic Graduate Programs, Newport, RI 02840-4192. Offers expressive and creative arts (CAGS, CGS); holistic counseling (MA); holistic leadership (MA, CAGS, CGS); holistic leadership and change management (CAGS); holistic studies (CGS); substance abuse and treatment (CAGS); substance abuse foundations in holistic studies (CGS). Part-time and evening/weekend programs available. *Faculty:* 2 full-time (both women), 10 part-time/adjunct (7 women). *Students:* 18 full-time (16 women), 65 part-time (57 women); includes 7 minority (1 Black or African American, non-Hispanic/Latino; 1 American Indian or Alaska Native, non-Hispanic/Latino; 1 Asian, non-Hispanic/Latino; 3 Hispanic/Latino; 1 Two or more races, non-Hispanic/Latino). Average age 41. 27 applicants, 100% accepted, 26 enrolled. In 2014, 16 master's, 5 other advanced degrees awarded. *Degree requirements:* For master's, internship, project. *Entrance requirements:* For master's, GMAT, GRE General Test, or MAT. Additional exam requirements/recommendations for international students: Required—TOEFL (minimum score 600 paper-based; 100 iBT) or IELTS. *Application deadline:* For fall admission, 3/15 priority date for domestic and international students; for spring

admission, 9/15 priority date for domestic and international students. Applications are processed on a rolling basis. Application fee: $60. Electronic applications accepted. *Expenses: Tuition:* Full-time $8550; part-time $475 per credit. *Required fees:* $50 per term. Tuition and fees vary according to course level, course load and degree level. *Financial support:* Career-related internships or fieldwork and Federal Work-Study available. Support available to part-time students. Financial award application deadline: 3/1; financial award applicants required to submit FAFSA. *Unit head:* Dr. Nancy Gordon, Director, 401-341-3290, E-mail: nancy.gordon@salve.edu. *Application contact:* Nicole Ferreira, Associate Director of Graduate Admissions, 401-341-2462, Fax: 401-341-2973, E-mail: nicole.ferreira@salve.edu.
Website: http://www.salve.edu/graduate-studies/holistic-studies

Salve Regina University, Program in Rehabilitation Counseling, Newport, RI 02840-4192. Offers mental health (CAGS), including rehabilitation counseling; rehabilitation counseling (MA); substance abuse (CGS), including foundations in rehabilitation counseling. *Accreditation:* CORE. Part-time and evening/weekend programs available. *Faculty:* 1 (woman) full-time, 8 part-time/adjunct (3 women). *Students:* 6 full-time (5 women), 64 part-time (53 women); includes 17 minority (9 Black or African American, non-Hispanic/Latino; 3 American Indian or Alaska Native, non-Hispanic/Latino; 5 Hispanic/Latino). Average age 37. 23 applicants, 100% accepted, 22 enrolled. In 2014, 14 master's, 4 other advanced degrees awarded. *Entrance requirements:* For master's, GMAT, GRE General Test or MAT. Additional exam requirements/recommendations for international students: Required—TOEFL (minimum score 600 paper-based; 100 iBT) or IELTS. *Application deadline:* For fall admission, 3/15 priority date for domestic and international students; for spring admission, 9/15 priority date for domestic and international students. Applications are processed on a rolling basis. Application fee: $60. Electronic applications accepted. *Expenses: Tuition:* Full-time $8550; part-time $475 per credit. *Required fees:* $50 per term. Tuition and fees vary according to course level, course load and degree level. *Financial support:* Career-related internships or fieldwork and Federal Work-Study available. Support available to part-time students. Financial award application deadline: 3/1; financial award applicants required to submit FAFSA. *Unit head:* Dr. Judith Drew, Director, 401-341-3189, E-mail: judith.drew@salve.edu. *Application contact:* Nicole Ferreira, Associate Director of Graduate Admissions, 401-341-2462, Fax: 401-341-2973, E-mail: nicole.ferreira@salve.edu.
Website: http://www.salve.edu/graduate-studies/rehabilitation-counseling

San Francisco State University, Division of Graduate Studies, College of Health and Social Sciences, Department of Counseling, San Francisco, CA 94132-1722. Offers clinical rehabilitation and mental health counseling (MS); counseling (MS); marriage, family, and child counseling (MSC); school counseling (Credential). *Accreditation:* ACA (one or more programs are accredited). Part-time programs available. *Application deadline:* Applications are processed on a rolling basis. *Expenses:* Tuition, state resident: full-time $6738. Tuition, nonresident: full-time $17,898; part-time $372 per credit hour. *Required fees:* $498 per semester. *Unit head:* Dr. Graciela Orozco, Chair, 415-338-2005, E-mail: counsel@sfsu.edu. *Application contact:* Katsufumi Araki, Academic Office Coordinator, 415-338-2005, E-mail: counsel@sfsu.edu.
Website: http://counseling.sfsu.edu

Santa Clara University, School of Education and Counseling Psychology, Santa Clara, CA 95053. Offers alternative and correctional education (Certificate); counseling (MA); counseling psychology (MA); educational administration (MA); interdisciplinary education (MA); teaching (MA). Part-time and evening/weekend programs available. *Faculty:* 27 full-time (16 women), 51 part-time/adjunct (29 women). *Students:* 335 full-time (262 women), 393 part-time (312 women); includes 266 minority (21 Black or African American, non-Hispanic/Latino; 86 Asian, non-Hispanic/Latino; 135 Hispanic/Latino; 24 Two or more races, non-Hispanic/Latino), 35 international. Average age 31. 507 applicants, 67% accepted, 241 enrolled. In 2014, 185 master's, 8 other advanced degrees awarded. *Degree requirements:* For master's, comprehensive exam (for some programs), thesis (for some programs); for Certificate, comprehensive exam. *Entrance requirements:* For master's, GRE or MAT, transcript, letters of recommendation, essay. Additional exam requirements/recommendations for international students: Required—TOEFL. *Application deadline:* For fall admission, 6/15 for domestic and international students; for winter admission, 10/15 for domestic and international students; for spring admission, 1/31 for domestic and international students. Applications are processed on a rolling basis. Application fee: $50. Electronic applications accepted. *Expenses:* Expenses: Contact institution. *Financial support:* In 2014–15, 329 students received support. Federal Work-Study, institutionally sponsored loans, and scholarships/grants available. Support available to part-time students. Financial award application deadline: 5/15; financial award applicants required to submit FAFSA. *Faculty research:* Education: meeting the needs of Latino/Latina students, historical and theoretical analysis of language coexistence, early childhood education, teaching of evolution in K-12 science classrooms, transactional learning communities; counseling psychology: grief counseling; maintenance of hope in the face of negative life events; educational and health disparities, with particular focus on Latinos; mindfulness, meditation, and compassion; life transitions. *Total annual research expenditures:* $206,541. *Unit head:* Nicholas Ladany, Dean, 408-554-4455, Fax: 408-554-5038, E-mail: nladany@scu.edu. *Application contact:* Kelly Pjesky, Admissions Director, 408-554-7884, Fax: 408-554-4367, E-mail: kpjesky@scu.edu.
Website: http://www.scu.edu/ecppm/

Saybrook University, LIOS MA Residential Programs, Kirkland, WA 98033. Offers leadership and organization development (MA); psychology counseling (MA). *Degree requirements:* For master's, thesis (for some programs), oral exams. *Entrance requirements:* For master's, bachelor's degree from an accredited university or college. Additional exam requirements/recommendations for international students: Recommended—TOEFL, IELTS, TWE.

The School of Professional Psychology at Forest Institute, Graduate Programs, Springfield, MO 65807. Offers applied behavior analysis (MS); clinical psychology (MA, Psy D); counseling psychology (MA); marriage and family therapy (MA, PGC). *Accreditation:* AAMFT/COAMFTE; APA (one or more programs are accredited). Part-time and evening/weekend programs available. Terminal master's awarded for partial completion of doctoral program. *Degree requirements:* For master's, thesis, practicum; for doctorate, comprehensive exam, thesis/dissertation, internship, practicum. *Entrance requirements:* For master's, GRE General Test, interview, minimum GPA of 3.0, 12 hours in psychology; for doctorate, GRE General Test (minimum combined Verbal and Quantitative score of 1000, Analytic Writing 4.0), interview, minimum GPA of 3.0, 18 hours in psychology. Additional exam requirements/recommendations for international students: Required—TOEFL (minimum score 550 paper-based). Electronic applications accepted. *Faculty research:* Forensics/corrections, marriage and family therapy, child and adolescent, integrated health care, neuropsychology.

The Seattle School of Theology and Psychology, Graduate Programs, Seattle, WA 98121. Offers Christian studies (MA); counseling psychology (MA); divinity (M Div). Part-time programs available. *Entrance requirements:* For master's, MAT.

Seton Hall University, College of Education and Human Services, Department of Professional Psychology and Family Therapy, Program in Counseling Psychology, South Orange, NJ 07079-2697. Offers counseling psychology (PhD); school counseling

(MA). *Accreditation:* APA. *Degree requirements:* For doctorate, comprehensive exam, thesis/dissertation, internship. *Entrance requirements:* For master's and doctorate, GRE, interview. *Faculty research:* Vocational indecision, coping skills, cognitive behavioral interventions, vocational development.

Siena Heights University, Graduate College, Adrian, MI 49221-1796. Offers clinical mental health counseling (MA); educational leadership (Specialist); leadership (MA), including health care leadership, organizational leadership; teacher education (MA), including early childhood education, early childhood education: Montessori, education leadership: principal, elementary education: reading K-12, leadership: higher education, secondary education: reading K-12, special education: cognitive impairment, special education: learning disabilities. Part-time and evening/weekend programs available. *Faculty:* 37. *Students:* 3 full-time (2 women), 237 part-time (158 women). In 2014, 32 master's awarded. *Degree requirements:* For master's, thesis, presentation. *Entrance requirements:* For master's, minimum GPA of 3.0, current resume, essay, all post-secondary transcripts, 3 letters of reference, conviction disclosure form; copy of teaching certificate (for some education programs); for Specialist, master's degree, minimum GPA of 3.0, current resume, essay, all post-secondary transcripts, 3 letters of reference, conviction disclosure form; copy of teaching certificate (for some education programs). *Application deadline:* Applications are processed on a rolling basis. Application fee: $50. Electronic applications accepted. *Expenses: Tuition:* Part-time $562 per credit hour. *Required fees:* $135 per term. *Financial support:* Career-related internships or fieldwork, Federal Work-Study, and unspecified assistantships available. Financial award application deadline: 9/1; financial award applicants required to submit FAFSA. *Unit head:* Dr. Linda S. Pettit, Dean, Graduate College, 517-264-7661, Fax: 517-264-7714, E-mail: lpettit@sienahts.edu.
Website: http://www.sienaheights.edu

Simpson University, School of Graduate Studies, Redding, CA 96003-8606. Offers counseling psychology (MA); organizational leadership (MA). Evening/weekend programs available. Postbaccalaureate distance learning degree programs offered (minimal on-campus study). *Faculty:* 19 part-time/adjunct (12 women). *Students:* 48 full-time (39 women), 4 part-time (3 women); includes 12 minority (3 Asian, non-Hispanic/Latino; 6 Hispanic/Latino; 3 Two or more races, non-Hispanic/Latino). Average age 34. In 2014, 14 master's awarded. *Degree requirements:* For master's, thesis optional, portfolio capstone and integrative essay. *Entrance requirements:* Additional exam requirements/recommendations for international students: Required—TOEFL (minimum score 550 paper-based; 79 iBT). *Application deadline:* For fall admission, 3/1 for domestic and international students; for winter admission, 9/15 for domestic and international students; for summer admission, 6/1 for domestic and international students. Application fee: $35. Electronic applications accepted. Tuition and fees vary according to program. *Financial support:* Applicants required to submit FAFSA. *Faculty research:* Development of executive functioning in young children, cognitive neuropsychology, historical issues in the neurosciences, neurotheology. *Unit head:* Adeline Jackson, Dean, 530-226-4788, E-mail: ajackson@simpsonu.edu. *Application contact:* Vanessa Buendia, Admissions Assistant, 530-226-4547, E-mail: vanessab@simpsonu.edu.
Website: http://gs.simpsonu.edu/

Slippery Rock University of Pennsylvania, Graduate Studies (Recruitment), College of Education, Department of Counseling and Development, Slippery Rock, PA 16057-1383. Offers clinical mental health counseling (MA), including addiction, adult, older adult, school and youth; student affairs (MA), including higher education; student affairs in higher education (MA), including college counseling. *Accreditation:* ACA; NCATE. Part-time and evening/weekend programs available. *Faculty:* 9 full-time (5 women). *Students:* 84 full-time (69 women), 16 part-time (13 women); includes 13 minority (8 Black or African American, non-Hispanic/Latino; 1 American Indian or Alaska Native, non-Hispanic/Latino; 2 Hispanic/Latino; 2 Two or more races, non-Hispanic/Latino), 1 international. Average age 29. 128 applicants, 51% accepted, 41 enrolled. In 2014, 45 master's awarded. *Degree requirements:* For master's, comprehensive exam, thesis (for some programs). *Entrance requirements:* For master's, GRE General Test or MAT, official transcripts, minimum GPA of 2.75 or 3.0 (depending on program), personal statement, three letters of recommendation, interview. Additional exam requirements/recommendations for international students: Required—TOEFL (minimum score 550 paper-based; 80 iBT). *Application deadline:* For fall admission, 1/15 priority date for domestic and international students. Application fee: $25 ($30 for international students). Electronic applications accepted. *Expenses:* Tuition, state resident: full-time $8172; part-time $454 per credit. Tuition, nonresident: full-time $12,258; part-time $681 per credit. *Required fees:* $2326; $200 per credit. Tuition and fees vary according to degree level and program. *Financial support:* Career-related internships or fieldwork, Federal Work-Study, institutionally sponsored loans, scholarships/grants, tuition waivers (partial), and unspecified assistantships available. Support available to part-time students. Financial award application deadline: 5/1; financial award applicants required to submit FAFSA. *Unit head:* Dr. Stacy Jacob, Graduate Coordinator, 724-738-2758, Fax: 724-738-4859, E-mail: stacy.jacob@sru.edu. *Application contact:* Brandi Weber-Mortimer, Director of Graduate Admissions, 724-738-2051, Fax: 724-738-2146, E-mail: graduate.admissions@sru.edu.
Website: http://srudss.ingeniuxondemand.com/academics/colleges-and-departments/coe/departments/counseling-and-development

Sofia University, Hybrid: Face-to-Face/Online Programs, Palo Alto, CA 94303. Offers counseling psychology (MA); psychology (PhD), including transpersonal psychology; spiritual guidance (MA); transpersonal psychology (MA, Certificate); women's spirituality (MA, Certificate). Postbaccalaureate distance learning degree programs offered (minimal on-campus study). *Entrance requirements:* For master's, bachelor's degree; for doctorate, bachelor's degree; master's degree. Electronic applications accepted.

Sofia University, Residential Programs, Palo Alto, CA 94303. Offers clinical psychology (Psy D); counseling psychology (MA); transpersonal psychology (MA, PhD). Part-time and evening/weekend programs available. Terminal master's awarded for partial completion of doctoral program. *Degree requirements:* For doctorate, thesis/dissertation. *Entrance requirements:* For master's, bachelor's degree; for doctorate, bachelor's degree; master's degree (for some programs). Electronic applications accepted.

Sonoma State University, School of Social Sciences, Department of Counseling, Rohnert Park, CA 94928-3609. Offers counseling (MA); licensed professional clinical counseling (MA); marriage, family, and child counseling (MA); pupil personnel services (MA). *Accreditation:* ACA. Part-time programs available. *Degree requirements:* For master's, internship. *Entrance requirements:* For master's, minimum GPA of 3.0. Additional exam requirements/recommendations for international students: Required—TOEFL (minimum score 500 paper-based).

Southeastern Oklahoma State University, School of Behavioral Sciences, Durant, OK 74701-0609. Offers clinical mental health counseling (MS). Part-time and evening/weekend programs available. *Degree requirements:* For master's, comprehensive exam, thesis optional. *Entrance requirements:* For master's, GRE General Test, minimum GPA of 3.0 in last 60 hours or 2.75 overall. Additional exam requirements/recommendations for international students: Required—TOEFL (minimum score 550 paper-based; 79 iBT). Electronic applications accepted.

Southeastern University, Department of Behavioral and Social Sciences, Lakeland, FL 33801-6099. Offers human services (MA); professional counseling (MS); school counseling (MS). Evening/weekend programs available.

Southeast Missouri State University, School of Graduate Studies, Department of Educational Leadership and Counseling, Counseling Program, Cape Girardeau, MO 63701-4799. Offers career counseling (MA); counseling education (Ed S); mental health counseling (MA); school counseling (MA). *Accreditation:* ACA; NCATE. Part-time and evening/weekend programs available. *Faculty:* 4 full-time (3 women), 2 part-time/adjunct (both women). *Students:* 32 full-time (28 women), 46 part-time (38 women); includes 7 minority (6 Black or African American, non-Hispanic/Latino; 1 Native Hawaiian or other Pacific Islander, non-Hispanic/Latino), 2 international. Average age 32. 28 applicants, 93% accepted, 25 enrolled. In 2014, 50 master's, 4 other advanced degrees awarded. *Degree requirements:* For master's and Ed S, comprehensive exam, thesis. *Entrance requirements:* For master's, GRE General Test or MAT, personal essay, interview; for Ed S, GRE General Test or MAT, minimum graduate GPA of 3.7. Additional exam requirements/recommendations for international students: Required—TOEFL (minimum score 550 paper-based; 79 iBT), IELTS (minimum score 6), PTE (minimum score 53). *Application deadline:* For fall admission, 3/1 for domestic and international students; for spring admission, 11/21 for domestic students, 10/1 for international students; for summer admission, 3/1 for domestic students. Applications are processed on a rolling basis. Application fee: $30 ($40 for international students). Electronic applications accepted. *Expenses:* Tuition, state resident: full-time $5256; part-time $292 per credit hour. Tuition, nonresident: full-time $9288; part-time $516 per credit hour. *Financial support:* In 2014–15, 13 students received support. Career-related internships or fieldwork, Federal Work-Study, scholarships/grants, traineeships, tuition waivers (full), and unspecified assistantships available. Financial award application deadline: 6/30; financial award applicants required to submit FAFSA. *Faculty research:* School counseling, mental health, career and family counseling, social justice and spirituality in counseling. *Unit head:* Dr. Melissa Odegard-Koester, Program Coordinator, 573-651-2420, Fax: 573-986-6512, E-mail: modegard@semo.edu.
Website: http://www.semo.edu/eduleadcounsel/

Southern Adventist University, School of Education and Psychology, Collegedale, TN 37315-0370. Offers clinical mental health counseling (MS); inclusive education (MS Ed); instructional leadership (MS Ed); literacy education (MS Ed); outdoor teacher education (MS Ed); school counseling (MS). *Accreditation:* NCATE. Part-time and evening/weekend programs available. *Degree requirements:* For master's, comprehensive exam (for some programs), thesis optional, position paper (MS), portfolio (MS Ed in outdoor teacher education). *Entrance requirements:* For master's, interview (MS); 9 semester hours of upper-division course work in psychology or related field, including 1 course in psychology research or statistics; 9 semester hours of education (MS Ed). Additional exam requirements/recommendations for international students: Required—TOEFL (minimum score 600 paper-based; 100 iBT). Electronic applications accepted.

Southern California Seminary, Graduate and Professional Programs, El Cajon, CA 92019. Offers Biblical studies (MABS); counseling psychology (MACP); marriage and family therapy (MAMFT); psychology (Psy D); religious studies (MRS); theology (M Div). Part-time and evening/weekend programs available. Postbaccalaureate distance learning degree programs offered (minimal on-campus study). *Degree requirements:* For master's, thesis (for some programs); for doctorate, thesis/dissertation. *Entrance requirements:* For doctorate, master's degree in psychology. Additional exam requirements/recommendations for international students: Required—TOEFL (minimum score 550 paper-based). Electronic applications accepted.

Southern Illinois University Carbondale, Graduate School, College of Liberal Arts, Department of Psychology, Carbondale, IL 62901-4701. Offers clinical psychology (PhD); counseling psychology (PhD); experimental psychology (MA, MS). *Accreditation:* APA (one or more programs are accredited). *Faculty:* 27 full-time (14 women), 1 part-time/adjunct (0 women). *Students:* 70 full-time (46 women), 35 part-time (20 women); includes 10 minority (8 Black or African American, non-Hispanic/Latino; 2 Asian, non-Hispanic/Latino), 12 international. 274 applicants, 11% accepted, 20 enrolled. In 2014, 10 master's, 10 doctorates awarded. *Degree requirements:* For master's, thesis; for doctorate, thesis/dissertation. *Entrance requirements:* For master's, GRE General Test, GRE Subject Test, minimum GPA of 2.7; for doctorate, GRE General Test, GRE Subject Test, minimum GPA of 3.25. Additional exam requirements/recommendations for international students: Required—TOEFL. *Application deadline:* For fall admission, 3/1 priority date for domestic students. Applications are processed on a rolling basis. Application fee: $50. *Expenses:* Tuition, state resident: full-time $10,176; part-time $1153 per credit. Tuition, nonresident: full-time $20,814; part-time $1744 per credit. *Required fees:* $7092; $394 per credit. $2364 per semester. *Financial support:* In 2014–15, 82 students received support, including 14 fellowships with full tuition reimbursements available, 23 research assistantships with full tuition reimbursements available, 22 teaching assistantships with full tuition reimbursements available; Federal Work-Study, institutionally sponsored loans, and tuition waivers (full) also available. *Faculty research:* Developmental neuropsychology; smoking, affect, and cognition; personality measurement; vocational psychology; program evaluation. *Unit head:* Dr. Meera Komarraju, Chair, 618-453-3529, E-mail: meerak@siu.edu. *Application contact:* Stacia Werner, Office Specialist, 618-453-3564, E-mail: gradpsych@siu.edu.
Website: http://psychology.siuc.edu/

Southern Nazarene University, College of Professional and Graduate Studies, Department of Psychology and Counseling, Bethany, OK 73008. Offers counseling psychology (MA, MSCP); marital and family therapy (MA). *Degree requirements:* For master's, thesis optional. *Entrance requirements:* For master's, English proficiency exam, minimum GPA of 3.0 in last 60 hours/major, 2.7 overall.

Southern Oregon University, Graduate Studies, Department of Psychology, Ashland, OR 97520. Offers MHC. Part-time programs available. Postbaccalaureate distance learning degree programs offered (minimal on-campus study). *Faculty:* 13 full-time (7 women), 10 part-time/adjunct (6 women). *Students:* 38 full-time (27 women), 3 part-time (2 women); includes 3 minority (1 American Indian or Alaska Native, non-Hispanic/Latino; 1 Asian, non-Hispanic/Latino; 1 Hispanic/Latino), 2 international. Average age 34. 61 applicants, 49% accepted, 21 enrolled. In 2014, 19 master's awarded. *Degree requirements:* For master's, thesis, portfolio, oral defense. *Entrance requirements:* For master's, GRE General Test, minimum cumulative GPA of 3.0 in the last 90 quarter credits (60 semester credits) of undergraduate coursework. Additional exam requirements/recommendations for international students: Required—TOEFL (minimum score 540 paper-based; 76 iBT), IELTS (minimum score 6), ELPT (minimum score 964) or ELS (minimum score 112). *Application deadline:* For fall admission, 7/31 priority date for domestic and international students; for winter admission, 11/15 priority date for domestic and international students; for spring admission, 1/7 priority date for domestic and international students. Applications are processed on a rolling basis. Application fee: $50. Electronic applications accepted. *Expenses:* Tuition, state resident: full-time $10,225; part-time $1515 per quarter. Tuition, nonresident: full-time $12,782; part-time $1894 per quarter. *Required fees:* $1395; $261 per quarter. *Financial support:* In 2014–15, 2 students received support, including 2 research assistantships with partial tuition reimbursements available; career-related internships or fieldwork, institutionally sponsored loans, scholarships/grants, and unspecified assistantships also available.

Unit head: Dr. Josie Wilson, Graduate Program Coordinator, 541-552-6946, E-mail: jwilson@sou.edu. *Application contact:* Lori Courtney, Graduate Coordinator, 541-552-6947, E-mail: courtney@sou.edu. Website: http://www.sou.edu/psychology/mhc

South University, Graduate Programs, College of Arts and Sciences, Program in Clinical Mental Health Counseling, Savannah, GA 31406. Offers MA.

South University, Program in Clinical Mental Health Counseling, Montgomery, AL 36116-1120. Offers MA.

South University, Program in Clinical Mental Health Counseling, Columbia, SC 29203. Offers MA.

South University, Program in Clinical Mental Health Counseling, Royal Palm Beach, FL 33411. Offers MA.

South University, Program in Clinical Mental Health Counseling, Glen Allen, VA 23060. Offers MA.

South University, Program in Clinical Mental Health Counseling, Virginia Beach, VA 23452. Offers MA.

South University, Program in Clinical Mental Health Counseling, Novi, MI 48377. Offers MA.

South University, Program in Clinical Mental Health Counseling, High Point, NC 27265. Offers MA.

South University, Program in Clinical Mental Health Counseling, Cleveland, OH 44128. Offers MA.

South University, Program in Clinical Mental Health Counseling, Austin, TX 78729. Offers MA.

Southwestern Assemblies of God University, Thomas F. Harrison School of Graduate Studies, Program in Counseling Psychology, Waxahachie, TX 75165-5735. Offers counseling psychology (clinical) (MCP); human services counseling (MS). Part-time programs available. *Degree requirements:* For master's, comprehensive written and oral exams. *Entrance requirements:* For master's, GRE General Test, minimum GPA of 2.5. Electronic applications accepted.

Southwestern College, Program in Art Therapy/Counseling, Santa Fe, NM 87502-4788. Offers MA. Part-time and evening/weekend programs available. *Degree requirements:* For master's, internship. *Entrance requirements:* For master's, resume, slide portfolio, interview, 3 letters of reference. Additional exam requirements/recommendations for international students: Required—TOEFL.

Southwestern College, Program in Counseling, Santa Fe, NM 87502-4788. Offers MA. Part-time and evening/weekend programs available. *Degree requirements:* For master's, internship. *Entrance requirements:* For master's, resume, 3 letters of reference, interview. Additional exam requirements/recommendations for international students: Required—TOEFL.

Southwestern College, Program in Grief, Loss and Trauma Counseling, Santa Fe, NM 87502-4788. Offers MA, Certificate. Part-time and evening/weekend programs available. Postbaccalaureate distance learning degree programs offered (minimal on-campus study). *Entrance requirements:* For master's, interview, references, resume; for Certificate, 3 letters of reference, interview.

Spring Arbor University, School of Human Services, Spring Arbor, MI 49283-9799. Offers counseling (MAC); family studies (MAFS); nursing (MSN). Part-time and evening/weekend programs available. Postbaccalaureate distance learning degree programs offered (no on-campus study). *Entrance requirements:* For master's, bachelor's degree from regionally-accredited college or university, minimum GPA of 3.0 for at least the last two years of the bachelor's degree, at least two recommendations from professional/academic individuals. Additional exam requirements/recommendations for international students: Required—TOEFL (minimum score 600 paper-based). Electronic applications accepted.

Springfield College, Graduate Programs, Programs in Psychology and Counseling, Springfield, MA 01109-3797. Offers athletic counseling (MS, CAGS); clinical mental health counseling (M Ed, CAGS); counseling psychology (Psy D); industrial and organizational psychology (M Ed, CAGS); school guidance counseling (M Ed, CAGS); student personnel administration in higher education (M Ed). Part-time programs available. *Degree requirements:* For master's, research project, portfolio; for doctorate, dissertation project, 1500 hours of counseling psychology practicum, full-year internship. *Entrance requirements:* Additional exam requirements/recommendations for international students: Required—TOEFL (minimum score 550 paper-based). *Application deadline:* For fall admission, 1/15 priority date for domestic students, 1/15 for international students; for winter admission, 11/1 for domestic and international students; for spring admission, 11/1 for domestic and international students. Applications are processed on a rolling basis. Application fee: $50. Electronic applications accepted. *Financial support:* Fellowships with partial tuition reimbursements, teaching assistantships with partial tuition reimbursements, career-related internships or fieldwork, Federal Work-Study, institutionally sponsored loans, and unspecified assistantships available. Financial award application deadline: 3/1; financial award applicants required to submit FAFSA. *Unit head:* Dr. Allison Cumming-McCann, Chair, 413-748-3075, Fax: 413-748-3854, E-mail: acumming@springfieldcollege.edu. *Application contact:* Mary DeAngelo, Director of Enrollment Management, 413-748-3136, E-mail: mdeangel@spfldcol.edu. Website: http://www.springfieldcollege.edu/academic-programs/psychology-department/graduate-programs-in-psychology/index#.U1F-dKJWiSo

State University of New York at New Paltz, Graduate School, School of Liberal Arts and Sciences, Department of Psychology, New Paltz, NY 12561. Offers mental health counseling (MS, AC); psychology (MA); school counseling (MS). Part-time and evening/weekend programs available. *Faculty:* 7 full-time (5 women), 1 (woman) part-time/adjunct. *Students:* 39 full-time (31 women), 23 part-time (16 women); includes 12 minority (1 Black or African American, non-Hispanic/Latino; 3 Asian, non-Hispanic/Latino; 4 Hispanic/Latino; 4 Two or more races, non-Hispanic/Latino), 1 international. Average age 28. 75 applicants, 61% accepted, 23 enrolled. In 2014, 30 master's awarded. *Degree requirements:* For master's, comprehensive exam, thesis. *Entrance requirements:* For master's, GRE General Test, minimum GPA of 3.0. Additional exam requirements/recommendations for international students: Required—TOEFL (minimum score 550 paper-based; 80 iBT), IELTS (minimum score 6.5). *Application deadline:* For fall admission, 2/1 priority date for domestic and international students; for spring admission, 11/15 priority date for domestic and international students. Application fee: $50. Electronic applications accepted. *Financial support:* In 2014–15, 6 teaching assistantships with partial tuition reimbursements (averaging $5,000 per year) were awarded. Financial award application deadline: 8/1. *Faculty research:* Disaster mental health, women's objectification, mate selection, cultural psychology, achievement motivation. *Unit head:* Dr. Glenn Geher, Chair, 845-257-3091, E-mail: geherg@newpaltz.edu. *Application contact:* Dr. Melanie Hill, Coordinator, 845-257-3475, E-mail: hillm@newpaltz.edu. Website: http://www.newpaltz.edu/psychology/

State University of New York at Oswego, Graduate Studies, School of Education, Department of Counseling and Psychological Services, Oswego, NY 13126. Offers mental health counseling (MS); MS/CAS. *Degree requirements:* For master's, comprehensive exam, thesis optional. *Entrance requirements:* For master's, GRE General Test, interview, minimum GPA of 3.0. Additional exam requirements/recommendations for international students: Required—TOEFL (minimum score 560 paper-based). *Faculty research:* Lowenfeld mosaics as predictor validation of preschool screening.

State University of New York at Plattsburgh, Division of Education, Health, and Human Services, Department of Counselor Education, Plattsburgh, NY 12901-2681. Offers clinical mental health counseling (MS, Advanced Certificate); school counselor (MS Ed, CAS); student affairs counseling (MS). *Accreditation:* ACA (one or more programs are accredited); Teacher Education Accreditation Council. Part-time programs available. *Students:* 44 full-time (36 women), 14 part-time (11 women); includes 7 minority (2 Black or African American, non-Hispanic/Latino; 1 American Indian or Alaska Native, non-Hispanic/Latino; 4 Hispanic/Latino), 5 international. Average age 27. *Entrance requirements:* For master's, GRE General Test or MAT, minimum GPA of 2.8. Additional exam requirements/recommendations for international students: Required—TOEFL. *Application deadline:* For fall admission, 2/15 priority date for domestic students; for spring admission, 10/15 priority date for domestic students. Applications are processed on a rolling basis. Application fee: $75. *Financial support:* Research assistantships, teaching assistantships, career-related internships or fieldwork, Federal Work-Study, and administrative assistantships, editorial assistantships available. Support available to part-time students. Financial award application deadline: 4/15; financial award applicants required to submit FAFSA. *Faculty research:* Campus violence, program accreditation, substance abuse, vocational assessment, group counseling, divorce. *Unit head:* Dr. Julia Davis, Coordinator, 518-564-4179, E-mail: jdavi004@plattsburgh.edu. *Application contact:* Betsy Kane, Director, Graduate Admissions, 518-564-4723, Fax: 518-564-4722, E-mail: bkane002@plattsburgh.edu.

State University of New York College at Old Westbury, Program in Mental Health Counseling, Old Westbury, NY 11568-0210. Offers MS. *Faculty:* 3 full-time (0 women), 3 part-time/adjunct (all women). *Students:* 27 full-time (24 women); includes 7 minority (2 Black or African American, non-Hispanic/Latino; 5 Hispanic/Latino). 23 applicants, 78% accepted, 14 enrolled. In 2014, 8 master's awarded. *Entrance requirements:* For master's, essay, letters of recommendation. *Expenses:* Tuition, state resident: full-time $9370; part-time $390 per credit. Tuition, nonresident: full-time $16,680; part-time $695 per credit. *Required fees:* $20.85 per credit. $72 per quarter. *Application contact:* Philip D'Angelo, Graduate Admissions Office, 516-876-3073, E-mail: enroll@oldwestbury.edu.

Stephens College, Division of Graduate and Continuing Studies, Programs in Counseling, Columbia, MO 65215-0002. Offers counseling (M Ed, PGC), including marriage and family therapy (M Ed), professional counseling (M Ed), school counseling (M Ed). Part-time and evening/weekend programs available. *Faculty:* 1 (woman) full-time, 14 part-time/adjunct (11 women). *Students:* 99 full-time (82 women), 24 part-time (22 women); includes 15 minority (8 Black or African American, non-Hispanic/Latino; 1 Asian, non-Hispanic/Latino; 6 Two or more races, non-Hispanic/Latino). Average age 34. 32 applicants, 69% accepted, 14 enrolled. In 2014, 36 master's awarded. *Degree requirements:* For master's, thesis. *Entrance requirements:* For master's, minimum GPA of 3.0 in last 60 hours. Additional exam requirements/recommendations for international students: Required—TOEFL. *Application deadline:* For fall admission, 7/25 priority date for domestic and international students; for winter admission, 12/1 priority date for domestic and international students; for spring admission, 4/25 priority date for domestic and international students. Applications are processed on a rolling basis. Application fee: $50. Electronic applications accepted. *Expenses:* Tuition: Full-time $4656; part-time $388 per credit hour. *Required fees:* $540; $45 per credit hour. *Financial support:* In 2014–15, 4 fellowships with full tuition reimbursements (averaging $8,710 per year) were awarded; scholarships/grants and unspecified assistantships also available. Financial award application deadline: 12/5; financial award applicants required to submit FAFSA. *Unit head:* Gina Sanders, Program Chair, 800-388-7579. *Application contact:* Lindsey Boudinot, Director of Graduate, Online and Certificate Programs, 800-388-7579, E-mail: online@stephens.edu.

Suffolk University, College of Arts and Sciences, Department of Psychology, Boston, MA 02108-2770. Offers clinical psychology (PhD); college admission counseling (Certificate); mental health counseling (MS, CAGS); school counseling (MS, CAGS). *Accreditation:* APA. *Faculty:* 14 full-time (6 women), 6 part-time/adjunct (4 women). *Students:* 61 full-time (52 women), 39 part-time (33 women); includes 23 minority (6 Black or African American, non-Hispanic/Latino; 7 Asian, non-Hispanic/Latino; 8 Hispanic/Latino; 2 Two or more races, non-Hispanic/Latino), 6 international. Average age 27. 384 applicants, 18% accepted, 33 enrolled. In 2014, 33 master's, 21 doctorates, 6 other advanced degrees awarded. *Degree requirements:* For doctorate, thesis/dissertation, practicum. *Entrance requirements:* For doctorate, GRE General Test or MAT, 2 letters of recommendation, resume. Additional exam requirements/recommendations for international students: Required—TOEFL (minimum score 550 paper-based; 80 iBT). *Application deadline:* For fall admission, 12/15 for domestic and international students. Applications are processed on a rolling basis. Application fee: $50. Electronic applications accepted. *Expenses:* Expenses: Contact institution. *Financial support:* In 2014–15, 62 students received support, including 60 fellowships (averaging $16,231 per year); career-related internships or fieldwork, Federal Work-Study, and institutionally sponsored loans also available. Support available to part-time students. Financial award application deadline: 4/1; financial award applicants required to submit FAFSA. *Faculty research:* Assessing exposure in the context of a family-based cognitive behavioral treatment for pediatric OCD, a mindfulness approach to designing and testing the efficacy of a new sexual revictimization prevention program for college women, olfaction and decision-making in substance-dependent individuals, the role of experiential avoidance in Generalized Anxiety Disorder, ego development as a predictor of dogmatism and intolerance in the political right and left. *Unit head:* Dr. Gary Fireman, Chairperson, 617-305-6368, Fax: 617-367-2924, E-mail: gfireman@suffolk.edu. *Application contact:* Cory Meyers, Director of Graduate Admissions, 617-573-8302, Fax: 617-305-1733, E-mail: grad.admission@suffolk.edu. Website: http://www.suffolk.edu/college/departments/9912.php

Tarleton State University, College of Graduate Studies, College of Education, Department of Psychology and Counseling, Stephenville, TX 76402. Offers counseling and psychology (M Ed), including counseling, counseling psychology, educational psychology; educational administration (M Ed); secondary education (Certificate); special education (Certificate). Part-time and evening/weekend programs available. Postbaccalaureate distance learning degree programs offered (minimal on-campus study). *Degree requirements:* For master's, comprehensive exam, thesis optional. *Entrance requirements:* For master's, GRE General Test, minimum GPA of 3.0. Additional exam requirements/recommendations for international students: Required—TOEFL (minimum score 550 paper-based; 80 iBT). Electronic applications accepted.

Teachers College, Columbia University, Graduate Faculty of Education, Department of Counseling and Clinical Psychology, Program in Counseling Psychology, New York, NY 10027. Offers Ed M, Ed D, PhD. *Accreditation:* APA (one or more programs are accredited). Part-time programs available. *Faculty:* 10 full-time, 15 part-time/adjunct.

Students: 161 full-time (139 women), 67 part-time (60 women); includes 96 minority (25 Black or African American, non-Hispanic/Latino; 36 Asian, non-Hispanic/Latino; 27 Hispanic/Latino; 8 Two or more races, non-Hispanic/Latino), 36 international. Average age 26. 437 applicants, 46% accepted, 72 enrolled. In 2014, 163 master's, 6 doctorates awarded. *Degree requirements:* For master's, comprehensive exam, special project; for doctorate, comprehensive exam, thesis/dissertation, research competence project. *Entrance requirements:* For doctorate, GRE General Test. *Application deadline:* For fall admission, 12/15 for domestic students. Application fee: $65. Electronic applications accepted. *Expenses: Tuition:* Full-time $33,552; part-time $1398 per credit. *Required fees:* $418 per semester. *Financial support:* Fellowships, research assistantships, teaching assistantships, career-related internships or fieldwork, Federal Work-Study, institutionally sponsored loans, and tuition waivers (full and partial) available. Support available to part-time students. Financial award application deadline: 2/1. *Faculty research:* Career development, mentoring racial identity, adult development, gender issues. *Unit head:* Prof. George V. Gushue, Director of Training, 212-678-3170, E-mail: gvg3@columbia.edu. *Application contact:* Melba Remice, Assistant Director of Admission, 212-678-4035, Fax: 212-678-4171, E-mail: ms2545@columbia.edu.
Website: http://www.tc.columbia.edu/ccp/CounPsych/

Temple University, College of Education, Department of Psychological Studies in Education, Philadelphia, PA 19122-6096. Offers adult and organizational development (Ed M); counseling psychology (Ed M, PhD), including agency counseling (Ed M), counseling psychology (PhD), school counseling (Ed M); education (PhD); educational leadership (Ed M); educational leadership and policy studies (Ed M, Ed D), including educational leadership; educational psychology (Ed M); school psychology (Ed M, PhD, Ed S); special education (Ed M). *Accreditation:* APA (one or more programs are accredited). Part-time and evening/weekend programs available. *Faculty:* 26 full-time (17 women), 35 part-time/adjunct (21 women). *Students:* 181 full-time (134 women), 182 part-time (125 women); includes 95 minority (64 Black or African American, non-Hispanic/Latino; 1 American Indian or Alaska Native, non-Hispanic/Latino; 8 Asian, non-Hispanic/Latino; 17 Hispanic/Latino; 5 Two or more races, non-Hispanic/Latino), 10 international. 281 applicants, 67% accepted, 118 enrolled. In 2014, 77 master's, 24 doctorates, 5 other advanced degrees awarded. Terminal master's awarded for partial completion of doctoral program. *Degree requirements:* For master's, thesis or alternative; for doctorate, thesis/dissertation. *Entrance requirements:* Additional exam requirements/recommendations for international students: Required—TOEFL (minimum score 550 paper-based; 79 iBT). *Application deadline:* For fall admission, 12/15 for international students; for spring admission, 8/1 for international students. Application fee: $60. *Expenses:* Tuition, state resident: full-time $14,490; part-time $805 per credit hour. Tuition, nonresident: full-time $19,850; part-time $1103 per credit hour. *Required fees:* $690. Full-time tuition and fees vary according to class time, course load, degree level, campus/location and program. *Financial support:* Fellowships, research assistantships with full tuition reimbursements, and teaching assistantships with full tuition reimbursements available. Financial award application deadline: 1/15; financial award applicants required to submit FAFSA. *Application contact:* Linda Pryor, Enrollment Management, 215-204-8011, E-mail: educate@temple.edu.
Website: http://education.temple.edu/pols

Tennessee State University, The School of Graduate Studies and Research, College of Education, Department of Psychology, Nashville, TN 37209-1561. Offers counseling psychology (MS, PhD); professional school counseling (MS); psychology (MS, PhD); school psychology (MS, PhD). *Accreditation:* APA. *Degree requirements:* For doctorate, thesis/dissertation (for some programs). *Entrance requirements:* For master's, GRE General Test or MAT; for doctorate, GRE General Test or MAT, minimum GPA of 3.25, work experience. Electronic applications accepted.

Tennessee Technological University, College of Graduate Studies, College of Education, Department of Counseling and Psychology, Cookeville, TN 38505. Offers agency counseling (Ed S); case management and supervision (MA); educational psychology (MA, Ed S); mental health counseling (MA); school counseling (MA, Ed S); school psychology (MA, Ed S). *Accreditation:* NCATE (one or more programs are accredited). Part-time and evening/weekend programs available. *Faculty:* 24 full-time (6 women). *Students:* 45 full-time (28 women), 31 part-time (26 women); includes 11 minority (4 Black or African American, non-Hispanic/Latino; 1 Asian, non-Hispanic/Latino; 1 Hispanic/Latino; 5 Two or more races, non-Hispanic/Latino). Average age 27. 37 applicants, 76% accepted, 19 enrolled. In 2014, 24 master's, 5 other advanced degrees awarded. *Degree requirements:* For master's and Ed S, comprehensive exam, thesis or alternative. *Entrance requirements:* For master's, GRE; for Ed S, MAT or GRE. Additional exam requirements/recommendations for international students: Required—TOEFL (minimum score 527 paper-based; 71 iBT), IELTS (minimum score 5.5), PTE (minimum score 48), or TOEIC (Test of English as an International Communication). *Application deadline:* For fall admission, 8/1 for domestic students, 5/1 for international students; for spring admission, 12/1 for domestic students, 10/1 for international students. Applications are processed on a rolling basis. Application fee: $35 ($40 for international students). Electronic applications accepted. *Expenses:* Tuition, state resident: full-time $9783; part-time $492 per credit hour. Tuition, nonresident: full-time $24,071; part-time $1179 per credit hour. *Financial support:* In 2014–15, 1 fellowship (averaging $8,000 per year), 8 research assistantships (averaging $4,000 per year), 3 teaching assistantships (averaging $4,000 per year) were awarded; career-related internships or fieldwork also available. Financial award application deadline: 4/1. *Unit head:* Dr. Barry Stein, Interim Chairperson, 931-372-3457, Fax: 931-372-6319, E-mail: bstein@tntech.edu. *Application contact:* Shelia K. Kendrick, Coordinator of Graduate Studies, 931-372-3808, Fax: 931-372-3497, E-mail: skendrick@tntech.edu.

Texas A&M International University, Office of Graduate Studies and Research, College of Arts and Sciences, Department of Psychology and Communication, Laredo, TX 78041-1900. Offers counseling psychology (MACP); psychology (MS). *Degree requirements:* For master's, thesis (for some programs). *Entrance requirements:* For master's, GRE General Test. Additional exam requirements/recommendations for international students: Required—TOEFL (minimum score 550 paper-based; 79 iBT).

Texas A&M University, College of Education and Human Development, Department of Educational Psychology, College Station, TX 77843. Offers bilingual education (M Ed, MS); counseling psychology (PhD); educational psychology (M Ed, MS, PhD); educational technology (M Ed); school psychology (PhD); special education (M Ed, MS). *Accreditation:* APA (one or more programs are accredited). Part-time and evening/weekend programs available. Postbaccalaureate distance learning degree programs offered (no on-campus study). *Faculty:* 45. *Students:* 165 full-time (133 women), 203 part-time (174 women); includes 128 minority (23 Black or African American, non-Hispanic/Latino; 1 American Indian or Alaska Native, non-Hispanic/Latino; 13 Asian, non-Hispanic/Latino; 84 Hispanic/Latino; 1 Native Hawaiian or other Pacific Islander, non-Hispanic/Latino; 6 Two or more races, non-Hispanic/Latino), 48 international. Average age 31. 251 applicants, 57% accepted, 99 enrolled. In 2014, 44 master's, 27 doctorates awarded. *Degree requirements:* For master's, thesis optional; for doctorate, thesis/dissertation. *Entrance requirements:* For master's and doctorate, GRE General Test. Additional exam requirements/recommendations for international students: Required—TOEFL. *Application deadline:* For fall admission, 12/1 for domestic students; for spring admission, 10/15 for domestic students. Application fee: $50 ($90 for international students). Electronic applications accepted. *Expenses:* Tuition, state resident: full-time $4078; part-time $226.55 per credit hour. Tuition, nonresident: full-time $10,594; part-time $577.55 per credit hour. *Required fees:* $2813; $237.70 per credit hour. $278.50 per semester. Tuition and fees vary according to degree level and student level. *Financial support:* In 2014–15, 191 students received support, including 21 fellowships with full and partial tuition reimbursements available (averaging $11,014 per year), 79 research assistantships with full and partial tuition reimbursements available (averaging $6,918 per year), 17 teaching assistantships with full and partial tuition reimbursements available (averaging $4,427 per year); career-related internships or fieldwork, institutionally sponsored loans, scholarships/grants, traineeships, health care benefits, tuition waivers (full and partial), and unspecified assistantships also available. Support available to part-time students. Financial award applicants required to submit FAFSA. *Unit head:* Dr. Victor Willson, Department Head, 979-845-1394, E-mail: v-willson@tamu.edu. *Application contact:* Kristie Stramaski, Senior Academic Advisor, 979-845-1833, E-mail: epsyadvisor@tamu.edu.
Website: http://epsy.tamu.edu

Texas A&M University–Texarkana, Graduate Studies and Research, College of Health and Behavioral Sciences, Texarkana, TX 75505-5518. Offers counseling psychology (MS). Part-time and evening/weekend programs available. *Degree requirements:* For master's, comprehensive exam (for some programs), thesis or alternative. *Entrance requirements:* For master's, minimum GPA of 3.0 in last 60 hours of bachelor's degree. Additional exam requirements/recommendations for international students: Required—TOEFL. Electronic applications accepted.

Texas Tech University, Graduate School, College of Arts and Sciences, Department of Psychological Sciences, Lubbock, TX 79409-2051. Offers clinical psychology (PhD); counseling psychology (MA, PhD); general experimental psychology (MA, PhD); psychology (MA). *Accreditation:* APA (one or more programs are accredited). *Faculty:* 32 full-time (14 women), 1 part-time/adjunct (0 women). *Students:* 96 full-time (60 women), 18 part-time (16 women); includes 25 minority (4 Black or African American, non-Hispanic/Latino; 5 Asian, non-Hispanic/Latino; 14 Hispanic/Latino; 2 Two or more races, non-Hispanic/Latino), 6 international. Average age 27. 281 applicants, 17% accepted, 24 enrolled. In 2014, 12 master's, 16 doctorates awarded. *Degree requirements:* For doctorate, comprehensive exam, thesis/dissertation, 100 credit hours of organized courses, research credits, and practica. *Entrance requirements:* For master's, GRE General Test, GRE Subject Test, essays; for doctorate, GRE General Test, essays. Additional exam requirements/recommendations for international students: Required—TOEFL (minimum score 550 paper-based; 79 iBT). *Application deadline:* For fall admission, 6/1 priority date for domestic students, 1/15 priority date for international students; for spring admission, 9/1 priority date for domestic students, 6/15 priority date for international students. Applications are processed on a rolling basis. Application fee: $60. Electronic applications accepted. *Expenses:* Tuition, state resident: full-time $6310; part-time $262.92 per credit hour. Tuition, nonresident: full-time $14,998; part-time $624.92 per credit hour. *Required fees:* $2701; $36.50 per credit. $912.50 per semester. Tuition and fees vary according to course load. *Financial support:* In 2014–15, 102 students received support, including 101 fellowships (averaging $4,037 per year), 23 research assistantships (averaging $13,150 per year), 72 teaching assistantships (averaging $10,753 per year). Financial award application deadline: 4/15; financial award applicants required to submit FAFSA. *Faculty research:* Health psychology, addictive behaviors, depression and suicide risk, sexuality/sexual risk behaviors/HIV, neuroscience/neuroimaging. *Total annual research expenditures:* $345,735. *Unit head:* Dr. Lee M. Cohen, Professor and Chair, 806-834-2530, Fax: 806-742-0818, E-mail: lee.cohen@ttu.edu. *Application contact:* Kay Hill, Admissions Coordinator, 806-742-3711 Ext. 222, Fax: 806-742-0818, E-mail: kay.hill@ttu.edu.
Website: http://www.depts.ttu.edu/psy/

Texas Wesleyan University, Graduate Programs, Programs in Education, Fort Worth, TX 76105-1536. Offers education (M Ed, Ed D); marriage and family therapy (MSMFT); professional counseling (MA); school counseling (MS). Part-time and evening/weekend programs available. Postbaccalaureate distance learning degree programs offered (no on-campus study). *Faculty:* 25 full-time (15 women), 8 part-time/adjunct (6 women). *Students:* 31 full-time (24 women), 205 part-time (177 women); includes 125 minority (64 Black or African American, non-Hispanic/Latino; 1 American Indian or Alaska Native, non-Hispanic/Latino; 1 Asian, non-Hispanic/Latino; 54 Hispanic/Latino; 5 Two or more races, non-Hispanic/Latino), 4 international. Average age 35. 144 applicants, 62% accepted, 81 enrolled. In 2014, 64 master's, 10 doctorates awarded. *Degree requirements:* For master's, comprehensive exam (for some programs); for doctorate, thesis/dissertation. *Entrance requirements:* For master's and doctorate, GRE General Test. Additional exam requirements/recommendations for international students: Required—TOEFL, IELTS. *Application deadline:* For fall admission, 6/15 for domestic students; for spring admission, 10/15 for domestic students. Applications are processed on a rolling basis. Application fee: $55. Electronic applications accepted. *Financial support:* Career-related internships or fieldwork, Federal Work-Study, scholarships/grants, and tuition waivers (full and partial) available. Support available to part-time students. Financial award application deadline: 3/15; financial award applicants required to submit FAFSA. *Faculty research:* Teacher effectiveness, bilingual education, analytic teaching. *Unit head:* Dr. Carlos Martinez, Dean, School of Education, 817-531-4940, Fax: 817-531-4943. *Application contact:* Beth Hargrove, Director of Graduate Admissions, 817-531-4498, Fax: 817-531-4261, E-mail: bhargrove@txwes.edu.
Website: https://txwes.edu/academics/school-of-education/

Texas Woman's University, Graduate School, College of Arts and Sciences, Department of Psychology and Philosophy, Denton, TX 76201. Offers counseling psychology (MA, PhD); school psychology (PhD, SSP). *Accreditation:* APA (one or more programs are accredited). Terminal master's awarded for partial completion of doctoral program. *Degree requirements:* For master's, comprehensive exam (for some programs), thesis (for some programs); for doctorate, comprehensive exam, thesis/dissertation, internship, residency. *Entrance requirements:* For master's, GRE (preferred minimum score 153 [500 old version] Verbal, 144 [500 old version] Quantitative, 4 Analytical), BA/BS or 18 hours in psychology; minimum GPA of 3.0, 3.5 in psychology classes; 3 letters of reference; curriculum vitae; essays; for doctorate, GRE (preferred minimum score 153 [500 old version] Verbal, 144 [500 old version] Quantitative, 4 Analytical), 3 letters of reference, minimum GPA of 3.0 overall and 3.5 in psychology classes, MA in psychology or related discipline with thesis, curriculum vitae, essays. Additional exam requirements/recommendations for international students: Required—TOEFL (minimum score 550 paper-based; 79 iBT). Electronic applications accepted. *Faculty research:* Women's anger, school neuropsychological theory and assessment, body image dysfunction, traumatic stress, classical ethics, mental health and behavioral needs of adolescents in alternative education.

Touro College, Graduate School of Psychology, New York, NY 10006. Offers general psychology (MS); industrial/organizational psychology (MS); mental health counseling (MS); school counseling (MS); school psychology (MS). *Students:* 101 full-time (80 women), 81 part-time (66 women); includes 76 minority (41 Black or African American, non-Hispanic/Latino; 1 American Indian or Alaska Native, non-Hispanic/Latino; 8 Asian, non-Hispanic/Latino; 26 Hispanic/Latino), 2 international. *Unit head:* Dr. Richard

Waxman, Dean, 212-242-4668 Ext. 6077, E-mail: richard.waxman@touro.edu. Website: http://gsp.touro.edu/

Towson University, Program in Counseling Psychology, Towson, MD 21252-0001. Offers CAS. Part-time and evening/weekend programs available. *Students:* 6 part-time (all women); includes 2 minority (1 Black or African American, non-Hispanic/Latino; 1 Hispanic/Latino). *Application deadline:* Applications are processed on a rolling basis. Application fee: $45. Electronic applications accepted. *Financial support:* Application deadline: 4/1. *Unit head:* Dr. Christa Schmidt, Graduate Program Director, 410-704-3063, E-mail: counselingpsychology@townson.edu. *Application contact:* Alicia Arkell-Kleis, Information Contact, 410-704-6004, Fax: 410-704-4675, E-mail: grads@towson.edu. Website: http://grad.towson.edu/program/certificate/cspy-cas/index.asp

Trinity Christian College, Program in Counseling Psychology, Palos Heights, IL 60463-0929. Offers MA. Evening/weekend programs available. Postbaccalaureate distance learning degree programs offered (minimal on-campus study).

Trinity International University, Trinity Evangelical Divinity School, Deerfield, IL 60015-1284. Offers Biblical and Near Eastern archaeology and languages (MA); Christian studies (MA, Certificate); Christian thought (MA); church history (MA, Th M); congregational ministry: pastor-teacher (M Div); congregational ministry: team ministry (M Div); counseling ministries (MA); counseling psychology (MA); cross-cultural ministry (M Div); educational studies (PhD); evangelism (MA); history of Christianity in America (MA); intercultural studies (MA, PhD); leadership and ministry management (D Min); military chaplaincy (D Min); ministry (MA); mission and evangelism (Th M); missions and evangelism (D Min); New Testament (MA, Th M); Old Testament (Th M); Old Testament and Semitic languages (MA); pastoral care (M Div); pastoral care and counseling (D Min); pastoral counseling and psychology (Th M); pastoral theology (Th M); philosophy of religion (MA); preaching (D Min); religion (MA); research ministry (M Div); systematic theology (Th M); theological studies (PhD); urban ministry (MA). *Accreditation:* ATS (one or more programs are accredited). Part-time programs available. Postbaccalaureate distance learning degree programs offered (minimal on-campus study). *Degree requirements:* For master's, comprehensive exam, thesis, fieldwork; for doctorate, comprehensive exam (for some programs), thesis/dissertation; for Certificate, comprehensive exam, integrative papers. *Entrance requirements:* For master's, GRE, MAT, minimum cumulative undergraduate GPA of 3.0; for doctorate, GRE, minimum cumulative graduate GPA of 3.2; for Certificate, GRE, MAT, minimum undergraduate GPA of 2.5. Additional exam requirements/recommendations for international students: Required—TOEFL (minimum score 580 paper-based), TWE (minimum score 4). Electronic applications accepted.

Trinity International University, Trinity Graduate School, Deerfield, IL 60015-1284. Offers bioethics (MA); communication and culture (MA); counseling psychology (MA); instructional leadership (M Ed); teaching (MA). Part-time and evening/weekend programs available. Postbaccalaureate distance learning degree programs offered (minimal on-campus study). *Degree requirements:* For master's, comprehensive exam. *Entrance requirements:* For master's, GRE General Test or MAT, minimum undergraduate GPA of 3.0. Additional exam requirements/recommendations for international students: Required—TOEFL (minimum score 580 paper-based), TWE (minimum score 4). Electronic applications accepted.

Trinity International University, South Florida Campus, Graduate School, Davie, FL 33324. Offers MA.

Trinity Washington University, School of Education, Washington, DC 20017-1094. Offers clinical mental health counseling (MA); early childhood education (MAT); educating for change (M Ed); educational administration (MSA); elementary education (MAT); reading (M Ed); school counseling (MA); secondary education (MAT), including English, social studies; special education (MAT). *Accreditation:* NCATE. Part-time and evening/weekend programs available. *Degree requirements:* For master's, thesis (for some programs), capstone project(s). *Entrance requirements:* For master's, PRAXIS I, minimum GPA of 2.8. Additional exam requirements/recommendations for international students: Required—TOEFL (minimum score 550 paper-based). *Faculty research:* Technology, literacy, special education, organizations, inclusion models.

Trinity Western University, School of Graduate Studies, Program in Counseling Psychology, Langley, BC V2Y 1Y1, Canada. Offers MA. *Accreditation:* ACA. Part-time programs available. *Degree requirements:* For master's, comprehensive exam, thesis. *Entrance requirements:* For master's, GRE (if out of school for 5 years prior to applying), BA in honors psychology, minimum GPA of 3.0 for 3rd and 4th year of BA. Additional exam requirements/recommendations for international students: Required—TOEFL (minimum score 600 paper-based). *Faculty research:* Meaning, group counseling, trauma, counseling supervision.

Union College, Graduate Programs, Department of Psychology, Barbourville, KY 40906-1499. Offers clinical psychology (MA); counseling psychology (MA); school psychology (MA).

United States International University, School of Arts and Sciences, Nairobi, Kenya. Offers counseling psychology (MA), including chemical dependency, health psychology; international relations (MA), including development studies, diplomacy and foreign policy, peace and conflict studies. Part-time and evening/weekend programs available. *Degree requirements:* For master's, thesis, practicum. *Entrance requirements:* For master's, GRE General Test, 2 letters of recommendation, resume. Additional exam requirements/recommendations for international students: Required—TOEFL. *Faculty research:* Trauma in children, African intellectualism, psychological assessment tools.

Universidad del Turabo, Graduate Programs, School of Social Sciences and Humanities, Programs in Psychology, Program in Counseling Psychology, Gurabo, PR 00778-3030. Offers M Psych, Psy D, Certificate.

Universidad Metropolitana, School of Social Sciences, Humanities and Communications, Program in Counseling Psychology, San Juan, PR 00928-1150. Offers MA.

University at Albany, State University of New York, School of Education, Department of Educational and Counseling Psychology, Program in Counseling Psychology, Albany, NY 12222-0001. Offers counseling psychology (PhD); mental health counseling (MS). Evening/weekend programs available. *Entrance requirements:* For master's, GRE General Test. Additional exam requirements/recommendations for international students: Required—TOEFL (minimum score 550 paper-based). Electronic applications accepted.

University at Buffalo, the State University of New York, Graduate School, Graduate School of Education, Department of Counseling, School, and Educational Psychology, Buffalo, NY 14260. Offers counseling/school psychology (PhD); counselor education (PhD); education studies (Ed M); educational psychology (MA, PhD); mental health counseling (MS, Certificate); rehabilitation counseling (MS, Advanced Certificate); school counseling (Ed M, Certificate). *Accreditation:* CORE (one or more programs are accredited). Part-time programs available. Postbaccalaureate distance learning degree programs offered (no on-campus study). *Faculty:* 19 full-time (11 women), 55 part-time/adjunct (39 women). *Students:* 158 full-time (123 women), 147 part-time (119 women); includes 37 minority (28 Black or African American, non-Hispanic/Latino; 2 American Indian or Alaska Native, non-Hispanic/Latino; 4 Asian, non-Hispanic/Latino; 3 Hispanic/Latino), 15 international. Average age 32. 341 applicants, 57% accepted, 124 enrolled. In 2014, 59 master's, 14 doctorates, 35 other advanced degrees awarded. *Degree requirements:* For master's, comprehensive exam (for some programs), thesis (for some programs); for doctorate, comprehensive exam, thesis/dissertation. *Entrance requirements:* For master's, GRE General Test, interview, letters of reference; for doctorate, GRE General Test, interview, letters of reference, writing sample. Additional exam requirements/recommendations for international students: Required—TOEFL (minimum score 79 iBT). *Application deadline:* For fall admission, 2/1 priority date for domestic and international students. Application fee: $50. Electronic applications accepted. *Financial support:* In 2014–15, 12 fellowships (averaging $9,384 per year), 37 research assistantships with tuition reimbursements (averaging $9,961 per year) were awarded; teaching assistantships, career-related internships or fieldwork, Federal Work-Study, institutionally sponsored loans, scholarships/grants, tuition waivers, and unspecified assistantships also available. Financial award application deadline: 2/1; financial award applicants required to submit FAFSA. *Faculty research:* Multicultural counseling, class size effects, good work in counseling, eating disorders, outcome assessment, change agents and therapeutic factors in group counseling. *Total annual research expenditures:* $1 million. *Unit head:* Dr. Jeremy Finn, Chair, 716-645-1126, Fax: 716-645-6616, E-mail: finn@buffalo.edu. *Application contact:* Joanne Laska, Admissions Assistant, 716-645-2110, Fax: 716-645-7937, E-mail: jlaska@buffalo.edu. Website: http://gse.buffalo.edu/csep

The University of Akron, Graduate School, Buchtel College of Arts and Sciences, Department of Psychology, Program in Counseling Psychology, Akron, OH 44325. Offers MA, PhD. *Accreditation:* APA (one or more programs are accredited). *Students:* 25 full-time (18 women), 6 part-time (all women); includes 5 minority (2 Black or African American, non-Hispanic/Latino; 1 Asian, non-Hispanic/Latino; 2 Hispanic/Latino). Average age 27. 59 applicants, 3% accepted, 2 enrolled. In 2014, 3 master's, 4 doctorates awarded. *Degree requirements:* For doctorate, comprehensive exam, thesis/dissertation. *Entrance requirements:* For doctorate, GRE General Test, bachelor's degree in psychology or equivalent; current curriculum vitae; declaration of intent outlining goals and interests; three letters of recommendation. Additional exam requirements/recommendations for international students: Required—TOEFL (minimum score 550 paper-based; 79 iBT), IELTS (minimum score 6.5). *Application deadline:* For fall admission, 12/1 for domestic and international students. Application fee: $45 ($70 for international students). Electronic applications accepted. *Expenses:* Tuition, state resident: full-time $7578; part-time $421 per credit hour. Tuition, nonresident: full-time $12,977; part-time $721 per credit hour. *Required fees:* $1388; $35 per credit hour. Tuition and fees vary according to course load. *Faculty research:* Counseling process and outcome, suicide, diversity issues and counseling psychology (e.g., gender, race, ethnicity, sexual orientation) vocational psychology, assessment. *Unit head:* Dr. Paul Levy, Chair, 330-972-8639, E-mail: pelevy@uakron.edu. Website: http://www.uakron.edu/psychology/academics/cpcp/

The University of Akron, Graduate School, College of Health Professions, School of Counseling, Program in Counseling Psychology, Akron, OH 44325. Offers PhD. *Accreditation:* APA. *Students:* 14 full-time (9 women), 9 part-time (8 women); includes 6 minority (5 Black or African American, non-Hispanic/Latino; 1 Asian, non-Hispanic/Latino), 3 international. Average age 30. 45 applicants, 7% accepted, 3 enrolled. In 2014, 3 doctorates awarded. *Degree requirements:* For doctorate, one foreign language, comprehensive exam, thesis/dissertation, written and oral exams. *Entrance requirements:* For doctorate, GRE, interview; minimum GPA of 3.25; three letters of recommendation; declaration of intent outlining occupational goals, interests, and commitment to program; current curriculum vitae. Additional exam requirements/recommendations for international students: Required—TOEFL (minimum score 550 paper-based), IELTS (minimum score 6.5). *Application deadline:* For fall admission, 12/1 for domestic and international students. Application fee: $45 ($70 for international students). Electronic applications accepted. *Expenses:* Tuition, state resident: full-time $7578; part-time $421 per credit hour. Tuition, nonresident: full-time $12,977; part-time $721 per credit hour. *Required fees:* $1388; $35 per credit hour. Tuition and fees vary according to course load. *Unit head:* Dr. Karin Jordan, Chair, 330-972-5155, E-mail: kj25@uakron.edu. *Application contact:* Dr. John Queener, Co-Director, 330-972-6149, E-mail: jqueener@uakron.edu.

University of Alberta, Faculty of Graduate Studies and Research, Department of Educational Psychology, Edmonton, AB T6G 2E1, Canada. Offers counseling psychology (M Ed, PhD); educational psychology (M Ed, PhD); instructional technology (M Ed); school counseling (M Ed); school psychology (M Ed, PhD); special education (M Ed, PhD); special education-deafness studies (M Ed); teaching English as a second language (M Ed). Part-time programs available. *Degree requirements:* For master's, thesis optional; for doctorate, comprehensive exam, thesis/dissertation. *Entrance requirements:* For master's and doctorate, minimum GPA of 3.0. Additional exam requirements/recommendations for international students: Required—TOEFL. *Faculty research:* Human learning, development and assessment.

The University of Arizona, College of Education, Department of Disability and Psychoeducational Studies, Program in Counseling and Mental Health, Tucson, AZ 85721. Offers rehabilitation counseling (MA); school counseling (MA). *Entrance requirements:* Additional exam requirements/recommendations for international students: Required—TOEFL (minimum score 550 paper-based; 80 iBT). *Faculty research:* Further knowledge and understanding of abilities, disabilities, adaptations, interventions, and support systems; preparing professionals to educate and facilitate the development of individuals with disabilities and special abilities; providing leadership at the local, state, national, and international levels.

University of Baltimore, Graduate School, Yale Gordon College of Arts and Sciences, Program in Applied Psychology, Baltimore, MD 21201-5779. Offers counseling psychology (MS). Part-time and evening/weekend programs available. *Degree requirements:* For master's, thesis optional. *Entrance requirements:* For master's, GRE, minimum GPA of 3.0. Additional exam requirements/recommendations for international students: Required—TOEFL (minimum score 550 paper-based). Electronic applications accepted. *Expenses:* Contact institution. *Faculty research:* Participatory decision-making, counter-productive workplace behavior, organizational consulting, substance abuse treatment, cognitive functioning in head injured.

University of Bridgeport, School of Arts and Sciences, Department of Counseling, Bridgeport, CT 06604. Offers clinical mental health counseling (MS); college student personnel (MS); community counseling (MS); human resource development (MS); human service (MS). Part-time and evening/weekend programs available. *Degree requirements:* For master's, thesis, project. *Entrance requirements:* Additional exam requirements/recommendations for international students: Recommended—TOEFL (minimum score 550 paper-based; 80 iBT), IELTS (minimum score 6.5). Electronic applications accepted. *Expenses:* Contact institution. *Faculty research:* Corporate elder care programs.

The University of British Columbia, Faculty of Education, Department of Educational and Counseling Psychology, and Special Education, Vancouver, BC V6T 1Z1, Canada. Offers counseling psychology (M Ed, MA, PhD); development, learning and culture (PhD); guidance studies (Diploma); human development, learning and culture (M Ed,

MA); measurement and evaluation and research methodology (M Ed); measurement, evaluation and research methodology (MA); measurement, evaluation, and research methodology (PhD); school psychology (M Ed, MA, PhD); special education (M Ed, MA, PhD, Diploma). Part-time programs available. *Degree requirements:* For master's, thesis (for some programs); for doctorate, comprehensive exam, thesis/dissertation. *Entrance requirements:* For master's, GRE General Test (counseling psychology MA); for doctorate, GRE General Test. Additional exam requirements/recommendations for international students: Required—TOEFL. Electronic applications accepted. *Faculty research:* Women, family, social problems, career transition, stress and coping problems.

University of Calgary, Faculty of Graduate Studies, Werklund School of Education, Division of Applied Psychology, Calgary, AB T2N 1N4, Canada. Offers counseling psychology (M Sc, MC, PhD); school and applied child psychology (M Ed, M Sc, PhD). Part-time programs available. *Degree requirements:* For master's, thesis (for some programs), final oral exam; for doctorate, thesis/dissertation, candidacy exam, final oral exam. *Entrance requirements:* For master's, minimum GPA of 3.0, 3 letters of reference; for doctorate, minimum GPA of 3.5, 3 letters of reference. *Faculty research:* Counselor education, family life studies, learning and cognition.

University of California, Berkeley, UC Berkeley Extension, Certificate Programs in Behavioral and Health Sciences, Berkeley, CA 94720-1500. Offers alcohol and drug abuse studies (Certificate).

University of California, Santa Barbara, Graduate Division, Gevirtz Graduate School of Education, Santa Barbara, CA 93106-9490. Offers counseling, clinical and school psychology (MA, PhD, Credential), including clinical psychology (PhD), counseling psychology (MA, PhD), pupil personnel services (Credential), school psychology (PhD); education (MA, PhD); teacher education (M Ed, Credential), including multiple subject teaching (Credential), single subject teaching (Credential), special education (Credential), teaching (M Ed); MA/PhD. *Accreditation:* APA (one or more programs are accredited). Terminal master's awarded for partial completion of doctoral program. *Degree requirements:* For master's, comprehensive exam (for some programs), thesis (for some programs); for doctorate, comprehensive exam (for some programs), thesis/dissertation. *Entrance requirements:* For master's and doctorate, GRE; for Credential, GRE or MAT, CSET, CBEST. Additional exam requirements/recommendations for international students: Required—TOEFL (minimum score 550 paper-based; 80 iBT), IELTS (minimum score 7). Electronic applications accepted. *Faculty research:* Needs of diverse students, school accountability and leadership, school violence, language learning and literacy, science/math education.

University of Central Arkansas, Graduate School, College of Health and Behavioral Sciences, Department of Counseling and Psychology, Program in Counseling Psychology, Conway, AR 72035-0001. Offers MS. *Degree requirements:* For master's, comprehensive exam, thesis optional. *Entrance requirements:* For master's, GRE General Test, minimum GPA of 2.7. Additional exam requirements/recommendations for international students: Required—TOEFL (minimum score 550 paper-based). Electronic applications accepted.

University of Central Missouri, The Graduate School, Warrensburg, MO 64093. Offers accountancy (MA); accounting (MBA); applied mathematics (MS); aviation safety (MA); biology (MS); business administration (MBA); career and technical education leadership (MS); college student personnel administration (MS); communication (MA); computer science (MS); counseling (MS); criminal justice (MS); educational leadership (Ed D); educational technology (MS); elementary and early childhood education (MSE); English (MA); environmental studies (MA); finance (MBA); history (MA); human services/educational technology (Ed S); human services/learning resources (Ed S); human services/professional counseling (Ed S); industrial hygiene (MS); industrial management (MS); information systems (MBA); information technology (MS); kinesiology (MS); library science and information services (MS); literacy education (MSE); marketing (MBA); mathematics (MS); music (MA); occupational safety management (MS); psychology (MS); rural family nursing (MS); school administration (MSE); social gerontology (MS); sociology (MA); special education (MSE); speech language pathology (MS); superintendency (Ed S); teaching (MAT); teaching English as a second language (MA); technology (MS); technology management (PhD); theatre (MA). Part-time programs available. *Faculty:* 314 full-time (137 women), 24 part-time/adjunct (14 women). *Students:* 1,624 full-time (542 women), 1,773 part-time (1,055 women); includes 194 minority (104 Black or African American, non-Hispanic/Latino; 6 American Indian or Alaska Native, non-Hispanic/Latino; 23 Asian, non-Hispanic/Latino; 41 Hispanic/Latino; 3 Native Hawaiian or other Pacific Islander, non-Hispanic/Latino; 17 Two or more races, non-Hispanic/Latino), 1,592 international. Average age 31. 2,800 applicants, 63% accepted, 1223 enrolled. In 2014, 796 master's, 81 other advanced degrees awarded. *Degree requirements:* For master's and Ed S, comprehensive exam (for some programs), thesis (for some programs). *Entrance requirements:* Additional exam requirements/recommendations for international students: Required—TOEFL (minimum score 550 paper-based; 79 iBT). *Application deadline:* For fall admission, 6/1 for domestic students; for spring admission, 10/1 for domestic and international students. Applications are processed on a rolling basis. Application fee: $30 ($75 for international students). Electronic applications accepted. *Expenses:* Tuition, state resident: full-time $6630; part-time $276.25 per credit hour. Tuition, nonresident: full-time $13,260; part-time $552.50 per credit hour. *Required fees:* $29 per credit hour. Tuition and fees vary according to campus/location. *Financial support:* In 2014–15, 118 students received support, including 271 research assistantships with full and partial tuition reimbursements available (averaging $7,500 per year), 109 teaching assistantships with full and partial tuition reimbursements available (averaging $7,500 per year); career-related internships or fieldwork, Federal Work-Study, scholarships/grants, and administrative and laboratory assistantships also available. Support available to part-time students. Financial award application deadline: 3/1; financial award applicants required to submit FAFSA. *Unit head:* Tina Church-Hockett, Director of Graduate School and International Admissions, 660-543-4621, Fax: 660-543-4778, E-mail: church@ucmo.edu. *Application contact:* Brittany Lawrence, Graduate Student Services Coordinator, 660-543-4621, Fax: 660-543-4778, E-mail: gradinfo@ucmo.edu.
Website: http://www.ucmo.edu/graduate/

University of Central Oklahoma, The Jackson College of Graduate Studies, College of Education and Professional Studies, Department of Psychology, Edmond, OK 73034-5209. Offers counseling psychology (MA); experimental psychology (MA); forensic psychology (MA); general psychology (MA); school psychology (MA). *Degree requirements:* For master's, thesis (for some programs). *Entrance requirements:* For master's, GRE. Additional exam requirements/recommendations for international students: Required—TOEFL (minimum score 550 paper-based; 79 iBT), IELTS (minimum score 6.5). Electronic applications accepted. *Faculty research:* Psychopharmacology, computer psychometrics, health psychology research.

University of Colorado Denver, School of Education and Human Development, Program in Counseling Psychology and Counselor Education, Denver, CO 80217. Offers counseling (MA), including clinical mental health counseling, couple and family counseling, multicultural counseling, school counseling; school counseling (MA). *Accreditation:* ACA; NCATE. Part-time and evening/weekend programs available. *Students:* 196 full-time (158 women), 30 part-time (24 women); includes 42 minority (10 Black or African American, non-Hispanic/Latino; 4 Asian, non-Hispanic/Latino; 24 Hispanic/Latino; 4 Two or more races, non-Hispanic/Latino). Average age 30. 182 applicants, 30% accepted, 31 enrolled. In 2014, 72 master's awarded. *Degree requirements:* For master's, comprehensive exam (for some programs), thesis or alternative, 63-66 hours. *Entrance requirements:* For master's, GRE or MAT (unless applicant already holds a graduate degree), letters of recommendation, interview, resume, transcripts from all colleges/universities attended. Additional exam requirements/recommendations for international students: Required—TOEFL (minimum score 525 paper-based; 71 iBT); Recommended—IELTS (minimum score 6.3). *Application deadline:* For fall admission, 1/15 for domestic students, 1/1 for international students; for spring admission, 9/15 for domestic students, 9/1 for international students. Application fee: $50 ($75 for international students). Electronic applications accepted. *Expenses:* Expenses: Contact institution. *Financial support:* In 2014–15, 9 students received support. Research assistantships, Federal Work-Study, institutionally sponsored loans, scholarships/grants, and traineeships available. Financial award application deadline: 4/1; financial award applicants required to submit FAFSA. *Faculty research:* Spiritual issues in counseling, multicultural and diversity issues in counseling, adolescent suicide, career development. *Unit head:* Farah Ibrahim, Counseling Professor, 303-315-6329, E-mail: farah.ibrahim@ucdenver.edu. *Application contact:* Student Services Coordinator, 303-315-6300, Fax: 303-315-6311, E-mail: education@ucdenver.edu.
Website: http://www.ucdenver.edu/academics/colleges/SchoolOfEducation/Academics/MASTERS/counseling/Pages/default.aspx

University of Connecticut, Graduate School, Neag School of Education, Department of Educational Psychology, Program in Counseling Psychology, Storrs, CT 06269. Offers counseling psychology (PhD); school counseling (MA, Post-Master's Certificate). *Accreditation:* ACA. Terminal master's awarded for partial completion of doctoral program. *Degree requirements:* For master's, comprehensive exam, thesis or alternative; for doctorate, thesis/dissertation. *Entrance requirements:* For doctorate, GRE General Test. Additional exam requirements/recommendations for international students: Required—TOEFL (minimum score 550 paper-based). Electronic applications accepted.

University of Dayton, Department of Counselor Education and Human Services, Dayton, OH 45469. Offers clinical mental health counseling (MS Ed); college student personnel (MS Ed); higher education administration (MS Ed); human services (MS Ed); school counseling (MS Ed); school psychology (MS Ed, Ed S). *Accreditation:* ACA; NCATE. Part-time and evening/weekend programs available. *Faculty:* 11 full-time (7 women), 34 part-time/adjunct (24 women). *Students:* 199 full-time (161 women), 113 part-time (95 women); includes 58 minority (49 Black or African American, non-Hispanic/Latino; 1 Asian, non-Hispanic/Latino; 7 Hispanic/Latino; 1 Two or more races, non-Hispanic/Latino), 8 international. Average age 31. 295 applicants, 47% accepted, 103 enrolled. In 2014, 146 master's, 8 Ed Ss awarded. *Degree requirements:* For master's, comprehensive exam (for some programs), thesis (for some programs), exit exam. *Entrance requirements:* For master's, MAT or GRE (if GPA less than 2.75), interview, writing sample. Additional exam requirements/recommendations for international students: Required—TOEFL (minimum score 550 paper-based; 80 iBT). *Application deadline:* For fall admission, 4/10 for domestic students, 4/10 priority date for international students; for winter admission, 9/10 for domestic students, 7/1 for international students; for spring admission, 9/10 for domestic students, 9/10 priority date for international students. Application fee: $0 ($50 for international students). Electronic applications accepted. *Expenses:* *Tuition:* Full-time $10,176; part-time $848 per credit. *Required fees:* $25; $25 per course. Part-time tuition and fees vary according to course level, course load, degree level and program. *Financial support:* In 2014–15, 10 research assistantships with full tuition reimbursements (averaging $8,720 per year) were awarded; career-related internships or fieldwork, institutionally sponsored loans, health care benefits, and unspecified assistantships also available. Financial award application deadline: 3/1; financial award applicants required to submit FAFSA. *Faculty research:* Mindfulness, forgiveness in relationships, positive psychology in couples counseling, traumatic brain injury responses, college student development. *Unit head:* Dr. Molly Schaller, Chairperson, 937-229-3644, Fax: 937-229-1055, E-mail: mschaller1@udayton.edu. *Application contact:* Kathleen Brown, Administrative Assistant, 937-229-3644, Fax: 937-229-1055, E-mail: kbrown1@udayton.edu.
Website: https://www.udayton.edu/education/departments_and_programs/edc/

University of Denver, Morgridge College of Education, Denver, CO 80208. Offers child, family and school psychology (MA, Ed S); counseling psychology (PhD); curriculum and instruction (MA, PhD); curriculum instruction and teaching (Certificate); educational leadership and policy studies (MA, PhD); library and information science (MLIS). *Accreditation:* ALA; APA (one or more programs are accredited). Part-time and evening/weekend programs available. Postbaccalaureate distance learning degree programs offered (no on-campus study). *Faculty:* 41 full-time (27 women), 62 part-time/adjunct (43 women). *Students:* 506 full-time (387 women), 325 part-time (237 women); includes 191 minority (50 Black or African American, non-Hispanic/Latino; 9 American Indian or Alaska Native, non-Hispanic/Latino; 21 Asian, non-Hispanic/Latino; 91 Hispanic/Latino; 3 Native Hawaiian or other Pacific Islander, non-Hispanic/Latino; 17 Two or more races, non-Hispanic/Latino), 23 international. Average age 32. 975 applicants, 73% accepted, 410 enrolled. In 2014, 234 master's, 38 doctorates, 178 other advanced degrees awarded. Terminal master's awarded for partial completion of doctoral program. *Degree requirements:* For master's, comprehensive exam; for doctorate, 2 foreign languages, comprehensive exam, thesis/dissertation. *Entrance requirements:* For master's and doctorate, GRE General Test or GMAT. Additional exam requirements/recommendations for international students: Required—TOEFL (minimum score 550 paper-based; 80 iBT). *Application deadline:* Applications are processed on a rolling basis. Application fee: $65. Electronic applications accepted. *Expenses:* Expenses: $1,199 per credit hour. *Financial support:* In 2014–15, 674 students received support, including 43 research assistantships with full and partial tuition reimbursements available (averaging $9,090 per year), 80 teaching assistantships with full and partial tuition reimbursements available (averaging $6,084 per year); career-related internships or fieldwork, Federal Work-Study, institutionally sponsored loans, scholarships/grants, and unspecified assistantships also available. Support available to part-time students. Financial award application deadline: 2/15; financial award applicants required to submit FAFSA. *Faculty research:* Principal and teacher preparation, development and assessments, gifted education, service-learning, early childhood, mathematics education, access to higher education. *Unit head:* Dr. Karen Riley, Interim Dean, 303-871-3665, E-mail: karen.riley@du.edu. *Application contact:* Jodi Dye, Assistant Director of Admissions, 303-871-2510, E-mail: jodi.dye@du.edu.
Website: http://morgridge.du.edu/

University of Florida, Graduate School, College of Liberal Arts and Sciences, Department of Psychology, Gainesville, FL 32661-2250. Offers counseling psychology (PhD); psychology (MA, MS, PhD), including psychology (PhD), women's and gender studies (PhD); JD/PhD. *Faculty:* 29 full-time (11 women), 9 part-time/adjunct (4 women). *Students:* 108 full-time (80 women), 11 part-time (8 women); includes 24 minority (6 Black or African American, non-Hispanic/Latino; 1 American Indian or Alaska Native, non-Hispanic/Latino; 7 Asian, non-Hispanic/Latino; 10 Hispanic/Latino), 16 international. 279 applicants, 10% accepted, 13 enrolled. In 2014, 13 master's, 18 doctorates

awarded. *Degree requirements:* For master's, comprehensive exam, thesis or alternative; for doctorate, comprehensive exam, thesis/dissertation. *Entrance requirements:* For master's and doctorate, GRE General Test, minimum GPA of 3.0. Additional exam requirements/recommendations for international students: Required—TOEFL (minimum score 550 paper-based; 80 iBT), IELTS (minimum score 6). *Application deadline:* For fall admission, 12/1 priority date for domestic students, 12/1 for international students. Applications are processed on a rolling basis. Application fee: $30. Electronic applications accepted. *Financial support:* In 2014–15, 15 fellowships, 11 research assistantships, 72 teaching assistantships were awarded; career-related internships or fieldwork and unspecified assistantships also available. Financial award application deadline: 12/9; financial award applicants required to submit FAFSA. *Faculty research:* Behavior analysis, behavioral and cognitive neuroscience, counseling, developmental psychology, social psychology. Total annual research expenditures: $1.8 million. *Unit head:* Neil E. Rowland, PhD, Chair, 352-273-2127, Fax: 352-392-7985, E-mail: nrowland@ufl.edu. *Application contact:* Main Office Information Contact, 352-392-0601, Fax: 352-392-7985, E-mail: psych-info@ufl.edu.
Website: http://www.psych.ufl.edu/

University of Great Falls, Graduate Studies, Program in Counseling, Great Falls, MT 59405. Offers MSC. Part-time and evening/weekend programs available. *Degree requirements:* For master's, thesis optional, internship. *Entrance requirements:* For master's, GRE General Test, 3 letters of recommendation. Additional exam requirements/recommendations for international students: Required—TOEFL (minimum score 500 paper-based). Electronic applications accepted. *Faculty research:* Self concept and adolescent offenders, juvenile delinquency, community mental health counseling.

University of Hawaii at Hilo, Program in Counseling Psychology, Hilo, HI 96720-4091. Offers MA. *Entrance requirements:* Additional exam requirements/recommendations for international students: Required—TOEFL, IELTS. *Expenses:* Tuition, state resident: full-time $5004; part-time $417 per credit hour. Tuition, nonresident: full-time $11,472; part-time $956 per credit hour. *Required fees:* $388; $139.50 per credit hour. Tuition and fees vary according to course load and program.

University of Houston, College of Education, Department of Educational Psychology, Houston, TX 77204. Offers administration and supervision - higher education (M Ed); counseling (M Ed); counseling psychology (PhD); educational psychology (M Ed); school psychology (PhD); school psychology and individual differences (PhD); special education (M Ed). *Accreditation:* NCATE. Part-time and evening/weekend programs available. Postbaccalaureate distance learning degree programs offered (no on-campus study). *Degree requirements:* For master's, comprehensive exam or thesis; for doctorate, comprehensive exam, thesis/dissertation. *Entrance requirements:* For master's, GRE, transcripts, 3 letters of recommendation, curriculum vita, goal statement; for doctorate, GRE, transcripts, 3 letters of recommendation, curriculum vita, goal statement, writing sample, interview. Additional exam requirements/recommendations for international students: Required—TOEFL (minimum score 550 paper-based; 79 iBT), IELTS (minimum score 6.5). Electronic applications accepted. *Faculty research:* Evidence-based assessment and intervention, multicultural issues in psychology, social and cultural context of learning, systemic barriers to college, motivational aspects of self-regulated learning.

University of Houston–Victoria, School of Arts and Sciences, Program in Psychology, Victoria, TX 77901-4450. Offers counseling psychology (MA); forensic psychology (MA); school psychology (MA). Part-time and evening/weekend programs available. Postbaccalaureate distance learning degree programs offered (minimal on-campus study). *Degree requirements:* For master's, project or thesis. *Entrance requirements:* For master's, GRE General Test. Additional exam requirements/recommendations for international students: Required—TOEFL (minimum score 550 paper-based). Electronic applications accepted.

University of Indianapolis, Graduate Programs, School of Psychological Sciences, Indianapolis, IN 46227-3697. Offers clinical psychology (Psy D); clinical psychology/mental health counseling (MA). *Accreditation:* APA. *Faculty:* 14 full-time (7 women), 7 part-time/adjunct (5 women). *Students:* 115 full-time (96 women), 58 part-time (51 women); includes 24 minority (4 Black or African American, non-Hispanic/Latino; 10 Asian, non-Hispanic/Latino; 8 Hispanic/Latino; 2 Two or more races, non-Hispanic/Latino), 5 international. Average age 26. In 2014, 43 master's, 20 doctorates awarded. *Degree requirements:* For master's, practicum; for doctorate, comprehensive exam, thesis/dissertation, 1200 hours of clinical practicum, 2000-hour internship. *Entrance requirements:* For master's, GRE, 3 letters of recommendation; for doctorate, GRE, minimum GPA of 3.0, 18 hours of course work in psychology, 3 letters of recommendation. Additional exam requirements/recommendations for international students: Required—TOEFL (minimum score 550 paper-based). *Application deadline:* For fall admission, 2/25 for domestic students. Application fee: $50. *Financial support:* Federal Work-Study available. *Unit head:* Dr. Anita Jones Thomas, Dean, 317-788-3353, Fax: 317-788-2120, E-mail: thomasaj@uindy.edu. *Application contact:* School of Psychological Sciences, 317-788-3353, E-mail: psych@uindy.edu.
Website: http://psych.uindy.edu/

The University of Iowa, Graduate College, College of Education, Department of Psychological and Quantitative Foundations, Iowa City, IA 52242-1316. Offers counseling psychology (PhD); educational measurement and statistics (MA, PhD); educational psychology (MA, PhD); school psychology (PhD, Ed S). *Accreditation:* APA. *Degree requirements:* For master's, thesis optional, exam; for doctorate, comprehensive exam, thesis/dissertation; for Ed S, exam. *Entrance requirements:* For master's, doctorate, and Ed S, GRE General Test, minimum GPA of 3.0. Additional exam requirements/recommendations for international students: Required—TOEFL (minimum score 550 paper-based; 81 iBT). Electronic applications accepted.

The University of Iowa, Graduate College, College of Education, Department of Rehabilitation and Counselor Education, Iowa City, IA 52242-1316. Offers counselor education and supervision (PhD); couple and family therapy (PhD); rehabilitation and mental health counseling (MA); rehabilitation counselor education (PhD); school counseling (MA). *Accreditation:* ACA (one or more programs are accredited); CORE (one or more programs are accredited). *Degree requirements:* For master's, thesis optional, exam; for doctorate, comprehensive exam, thesis/dissertation. *Entrance requirements:* For master's and doctorate, GRE General Test, minimum GPA of 3.0. Additional exam requirements/recommendations for international students: Required—TOEFL (minimum score 550 paper-based; 81 iBT). Electronic applications accepted.

The University of Kansas, Graduate Studies, School of Education, Department of Psychology and Research in Education, Program in Counseling Psychology, Lawrence, KS 66045. Offers MS, PhD. *Accreditation:* APA (one or more programs are accredited). Part-time programs available. *Faculty:* 15 full-time, 5 part-time/adjunct. *Students:* 61 full-time (46 women), 5 part-time (1 woman); includes 11 minority (2 Black or African American, non-Hispanic/Latino; 1 Asian, non-Hispanic/Latino; 2 Hispanic/Latino; 6 Two or more races, non-Hispanic/Latino), 3 international. Average age 27. 147 applicants, 21% accepted, 19 enrolled. In 2014, 16 master's, 2 doctorates awarded. Terminal master's awarded for partial completion of doctoral program. *Degree requirements:* For master's, thesis or alternative; for doctorate, comprehensive exam, thesis/dissertation.

Entrance requirements: For master's and doctorate, GRE General Test, minimum GPA of 3.0. Additional exam requirements/recommendations for international students: Required—TOEFL. *Application deadline:* For fall admission, 12/15 for domestic and international students. Application fee: $55 ($65 for international students). Electronic applications accepted. *Financial support:* Fellowships, research assistantships with full and partial tuition reimbursements, teaching assistantships with full and partial tuition reimbursements, career-related internships or fieldwork, scholarships/grants, and unspecified assistantships available. Financial award application deadline: 1/15. *Faculty research:* Career development, assessment and intervention, multi-cultural counseling, counselor training, positive psychology. *Unit head:* Dr. Changming Duan, Director of Counseling Psychology, 785-864-2426, E-mail: duanc@ku.edu. *Application contact:* Penny Fritts, Graduate Admissions Contact, 785-864-9645, E-mail: fritts@ku.edu.
Website: http://pre.soe.ku.edu/academics/cpsy/masters

University of Kentucky, Graduate School, College of Education, Program in Educational and Counseling Psychology, Lexington, KY 40506-0032. Offers counseling psychology (MS, PhD, Ed S); educational psychology (MS, PhD); school psychology (PhD, Ed S). *Accreditation:* APA (one or more programs are accredited); NCATE. *Degree requirements:* For doctorate, comprehensive exam, thesis/dissertation; for Ed S, comprehensive exam. *Entrance requirements:* For doctorate, GRE General Test, minimum graduate GPA of 3.0; for Ed S, GRE General Test. Additional exam requirements/recommendations for international students: Required—TOEFL (minimum score 550 paper-based). Electronic applications accepted.

University of Lethbridge, School of Graduate Studies, Lethbridge, AB T1K 3M4, Canada. Offers addictions counseling (M Sc); agricultural biotechnology (M Sc); agricultural studies (M Sc, MA); anthropology (MA); archaeology (M Sc, MA); art (MA, MFA); biochemistry (M Sc); biological sciences (M Sc); biomolecular science (PhD); biosystems and biodiversity (PhD); Canadian studies (MA); chemistry (M Sc); computer science (M Sc); computer science and geographical information science (M Sc); counseling (MC); counseling psychology (M Ed); dramatic arts (MA); earth, space, and physical science (PhD); economics (MA); education (MA); educational leadership (M Ed); English (MA); environmental science (M Sc); evolution and behavior (PhD); exercise science (M Sc); French (MA); French/German (MA); French/Spanish (MA); general education (M Ed); geography (M Sc, MA); German (MA); health sciences (M Sc); individualized multidisciplinary (M Sc, MA); kinesiology (M Sc, MA); management (M Sc), including accounting, finance, general management, human resource management and labor relations, information systems, international management, marketing, policy and strategy; mathematics (M Sc); modern languages (MA); music (M Mus, MA); Native American studies (MA); neuroscience (M Sc, PhD); new media (MA, MFA); nursing (M Sc, MN); philosophy (MA); physics (M Sc); political science (MA); psychology (M Sc, MA); religious studies (MA); sociology (MA); theatre and dramatic arts (MFA); theoretical and computational science (PhD); urban and regional studies (MA); women and gender studies (MA). Part-time and evening/weekend programs available. *Faculty:* 358. *Students:* 445 full-time (243 women), 116 part-time (72 women). Average age 31. 351 applicants, 26% accepted, 87 enrolled. In 2014, 129 master's, 13 doctorates awarded. *Degree requirements:* For master's, thesis (for some programs); for doctorate, comprehensive exam, thesis/dissertation. *Entrance requirements:* For master's, GMAT (for M Sc in management), bachelor's degree in related field, minimum GPA of 3.0 during previous 20 graded semester courses, 2 years' teaching or related experience (M Ed); for doctorate, master's degree, minimum graduate GPA of 3.5. Additional exam requirements/recommendations for international students: Required—TOEFL. Application fee: $100 Canadian dollars. *Financial support:* Fellowships, research assistantships, teaching assistantships, scholarships/grants, health care benefits, and unspecified assistantships available. *Faculty research:* Movement and brain plasticity, gibberellin physiology, photosynthesis, carbon cycling, molecular properties of main-group ring components. *Application contact:* School of Graduate Studies, 403-329-5194, E-mail: sgsinquiries@uleth.ca.
Website: http://www.uleth.ca/graduatestudies

University of Louisiana at Monroe, Graduate School, College of Health and Pharmaceutical Sciences, Programs in Counseling, Monroe, LA 71209-0001. Offers clinical mental health counseling (MS); school counseling (MS). *Accreditation:* ACA; NCATE. Part-time and evening/weekend programs available. Postbaccalaureate distance learning degree programs offered (minimal on-campus study). *Degree requirements:* For master's, comprehensive exam, thesis. *Entrance requirements:* For master's, GRE General Test, minimum GPA of 2.8 in last 60 hours. Additional exam requirements/recommendations for international students: Required—TOEFL (minimum score 500 paper-based; 61 iBT). Electronic applications accepted.

The University of Manchester, School of Education, Manchester, United Kingdom. Offers counseling (D Couns); counseling psychology (D Couns); education (M Phil, Ed D, PhD); educational and child psychology (Ed D); educational psychology (Ed D).

University of Mary, Liffrig Family School of Education and Behavioral Sciences, Department of Behavioral Sciences, Bismarck, ND 58504-9652. Offers addiction counseling (MSC); clinical mental health counseling (MSC); military families (MSC); school counseling (MSC); student affairs (MSC). Part-time programs available. Postbaccalaureate distance learning degree programs offered (minimal on-campus study). *Degree requirements:* For master's, thesis, internship. *Entrance requirements:* For master's, coursework/experience in psychology, statistics, minimum GPA of 3.0. Additional exam requirements/recommendations for international students: Required—TOEFL (minimum score 500 paper-based; 71 iBT). *Application deadline:* For fall admission, 8/1 priority date for domestic students. Application fee: $40. *Expenses:* Tuition: Full-time $4772; part-time $530.25 per credit hour. *Required fees:* $20 per credit hour. Tuition and fees vary according to degree level and program. *Financial support:* Application deadline: 8/1; applicants required to submit FAFSA. *Application contact:* Jeanette Shaeffer, Accelerated and Distance Education Administrative Assistant, 701-355-8128, Fax: 701-255-7687, E-mail: jgschae@umary.edu.

University of Mary Hardin-Baylor, Graduate Studies in Counseling, Belton, TX 76513. Offers clinical and mental health counseling (MA); marriage, family and child counseling (MA); non-clinical professional studies (MA). Part-time and evening/weekend programs available. *Faculty:* 7 full-time (4 women), 1 (woman) part-time/adjunct. *Students:* 52 full-time (44 women), 19 part-time (16 women); includes 28 minority (11 Black or African American, non-Hispanic/Latino; 3 American Indian or Alaska Native, non-Hispanic/Latino; 5 Asian, non-Hispanic/Latino; 8 Hispanic/Latino; 1 Two or more races, non-Hispanic/Latino), 5 international. Average age 30. 26 applicants, 85% accepted, 13 enrolled. In 2014, 28 master's awarded. *Degree requirements:* For master's, comprehensive exam. *Entrance requirements:* For master's, GRE General Test (waived if GPA greater than 3.0), minimum GPA of 3.0 cumulative or last 60 hours, three letters of recommendation, interview. Additional exam requirements/recommendations for international students: Required—TOEFL (minimum score 100 iBT), IELTS (minimum score 7). *Application deadline:* For fall admission, 6/1 for domestic students, 4/30 priority date for international students; for spring admission, 11/1 for domestic students, 9/30 priority date for international students. Applications are processed on a rolling basis. Application fee: $35 ($135 for international students). Electronic applications accepted. *Expenses:* Tuition: Full-time $14,400; part-time $800 per credit hour. *Required fees:* $1350; $75 per credit hour. $50 per term. Tuition and fees vary according to degree

level. *Financial support:* Federal Work-Study, unspecified assistantships, and scholarships for some active duty military personnel available. Support available to part-time students. Financial award applicants required to submit FAFSA. *Unit head:* Dr. Marta Garrett, Associate Professor/Director, Graduate Counseling, 254-295-5018, E-mail: mgarrett@umhb.edu. *Application contact:* Melissa Ford, Director of Graduate Admissions, 254-295-4020, Fax: 254-295-5038, E-mail: mford@umhb.edu.
Website: http://graduate.umhb.edu/counseling/

University of Maryland, College Park, Academic Affairs, College of Education, Department of Counseling, Higher Education and Special Education, College Park, MD 20742. Offers college student personnel (M Ed, MA); college student personnel administration (PhD); community counseling (CAGS); community/career counseling (M Ed, MA); counseling and personnel services (M Ed, MA, PhD), including art therapy (M Ed), college student personnel (M Ed), counseling and personnel services (PhD), counseling psychology (M Ed), mental health counseling (M Ed), school counseling (M Ed); counseling psychology (PhD); counselor education (PhD); rehabilitation counseling (M Ed, MA, AGSC); school counseling (M Ed, MA); school psychology (M Ed, MA, PhD). *Accreditation:* ACA (one or more programs are accredited); APA (one or more programs are accredited); NCATE. Part-time and evening/weekend programs available. Postbaccalaureate distance learning degree programs offered (no on-campus study). *Degree requirements:* For master's, thesis (for some programs); for doctorate, thesis/dissertation. *Entrance requirements:* For master's, GRE General Test or MAT, minimum GPA of 3.0, 3 letters of recommendation; for doctorate, GRE General Test or MAT, minimum GPA of 3.5, 3 letters of recommendation. Additional exam requirements/recommendations for international students: Required—TOEFL. Electronic applications accepted. *Faculty research:* Educational psychology, counseling, health.

University of Massachusetts Boston, College of Education and Human Development, Program in Counseling and School Psychology, Boston, MA 02125-3393. Offers PhD. *Accreditation:* CORE. Part-time and evening/weekend programs available. *Application deadline:* For fall admission, 12/1 for domestic students. *Expenses:* Tuition, state resident: full-time $2590; part-time $108 per credit. Tuition, nonresident: full-time $9758; part-time $406.50 per credit. Tuition and fees vary according to course load and program. *Financial support:* Research assistantships with full tuition reimbursements, teaching assistantships with full tuition reimbursements, career-related internships or fieldwork, Federal Work-Study, and unspecified assistantships available. Support available to part-time students. Financial award application deadline: 3/1; financial award applicants required to submit FAFSA. *Faculty research:* Persuasion and power in the counseling process, self-efficacy for counselors and clients, career and biracial issues in family therapy. *Unit head:* Dr. Virginia Harvey, Director, 617-287-7617. *Application contact:* Peggy Roldan Patel, Graduate Admissions Coordinator, 617-287-6400, Fax: 617-287-6236, E-mail: bos.gadm@dpc.umassp.edu.

University of Massachusetts Boston, College of Education and Human Development, Program in Mental Health Counseling, Boston, MA 02125-3393. Offers MS. *Expenses:* Tuition, state resident: full-time $2590; part-time $108 per credit. Tuition, nonresident: full-time $9758; part-time $406.50 per credit. Tuition and fees vary according to course load and program. *Financial support:* Research assistantships available. *Unit head:* Dr. Rick Houser, Director, 617-287-7668, E-mail: rick.houser@umb.edu. *Application contact:* Peggy Roldan Patel, Graduate Admissions Coordinator, 617-287-6400, Fax: 617-287-6236, E-mail: bos.gadm@dpc.umassp.edu.

University of Memphis, Graduate School, College of Education, Department of Counseling, Educational Psychology and Research, Memphis, TN 38152. Offers counseling (MS, Ed D), including community counseling (MS), rehabilitation counseling (MS), school counseling (MS); counseling psychology (PhD); educational psychology and research (MS, PhD), including educational psychology, educational research. *Accreditation:* ACA (one or more programs are accredited); APA (one or more programs are accredited); CORE (one or more programs are accredited); NCATE. *Faculty:* 26 full-time (11 women), 6 part-time/adjunct (2 women). *Students:* 137 full-time (105 women), 97 part-time (74 women); includes 60 minority (44 Black or African American, non-Hispanic/Latino; 1 American Indian or Alaska Native, non-Hispanic/Latino; 7 Hispanic/Latino; 8 Two or more races, non-Hispanic/Latino), 9 international. Average age 32. 141 applicants, 44% accepted, 30 enrolled. In 2014, 50 master's, 13 doctorates awarded. *Degree requirements:* For master's, comprehensive exam, thesis or alternative; for doctorate, comprehensive exam, thesis/dissertation. *Entrance requirements:* For master's, GRE General Test or MAT, minimum GPA of 2.5; for doctorate, GRE General Test. *Application deadline:* For fall admission, 10/1 for domestic students; for spring admission, 4/1 for domestic students. Application fee: $35 ($60 for international students). *Financial support:* In 2014–15, 130 students received support. Fellowships with full tuition reimbursements available, research assistantships with full tuition reimbursements available, teaching assistantships with full tuition reimbursements available, career-related internships or fieldwork, Federal Work-Study, scholarships/grants, and unspecified assistantships available. Financial award application deadline: 2/15; financial award applicants required to submit FAFSA. *Faculty research:* Anger management, aging and disability, supervision, multicultural counseling. *Unit head:* Dr. Douglas C. Strohmer, Chair, 901-678-2841, Fax: 901-678-5114. *Application contact:* Dr. Ernest A. Rakow, Associate Dean of Administration and Graduate Programs, 901-678-2399, Fax: 901-678-4778.
Website: http://coe.memphis.edu/cepr/

University of Miami, Graduate School, School of Education and Human Development, Department of Educational and Psychological Studies, Program in Counseling Psychology, Coral Gables, FL 33124. Offers PhD. *Accreditation:* APA. *Degree requirements:* For doctorate, thesis/dissertation, qualifying exam. *Entrance requirements:* For doctorate, GRE General Test. Additional exam requirements/recommendations for international students: Required—TOEFL (minimum score 550 paper-based; 80 iBT); Recommended—IELTS (minimum score 6.5). Electronic applications accepted. *Faculty research:* Cocaine recidivism, family systems, behavior and health, nontraditional families, stress and coping.

University of Minnesota, Twin Cities Campus, Graduate School, College of Liberal Arts, Department of Psychology, Program in Counseling Psychology, Minneapolis, MN 55455-0213. Offers PhD. *Accreditation:* APA. *Degree requirements:* For doctorate, comprehensive exam, thesis/dissertation, internship. *Entrance requirements:* For doctorate, GRE General Test, GRE Subject Test (recommended), 12 credits of upper-level psychology courses, including a course in statistics or psychological measurement. Additional exam requirements/recommendations for international students: Required—TOEFL (minimum score 550 paper-based; 79 iBT).

University of Missouri, Office of Research and Graduate Studies, College of Education, Department of Educational, School, and Counseling Psychology, Columbia, MO 65211. Offers counseling psychology (M Ed, MA, PhD, Ed S); educational psychology (M Ed, MA, PhD, Ed S); learning and instruction (M Ed); school psychology (M Ed, MA, PhD, Ed S). *Accreditation:* APA (one or more programs are accredited). Part-time programs available. *Faculty:* 25 full-time (13 women), 4 part-time/adjunct (2 women). *Students:* 185 full-time (115 women), 204 part-time (103 women); includes 79 minority (41 Black or African American, non-Hispanic/Latino; 8 Asian, non-Hispanic/Latino; 21 Hispanic/Latino; 9 Two or more races, non-Hispanic/Latino), 34 international. Average age 31. 354 applicants, 38% accepted, 116 enrolled. In 2014, 59 master's, 16 doctorates, 13 other advanced degrees awarded. *Degree requirements:* For doctorate, thesis/dissertation. *Entrance requirements:* For master's, doctorate, and Ed S, GRE General Test, minimum GPA of 3.0. Additional exam requirements/recommendations for international students: Required—TOEFL (minimum score 580 paper-based; 92 iBT). *Application deadline:* For fall admission, 12/1 priority date for domestic and international students. Applications are processed on a rolling basis. Application fee: $55 ($75 for international students). Electronic applications accepted. *Financial support:* Fellowships, research assistantships, teaching assistantships, institutionally sponsored loans, traineeships, health care benefits, and unspecified assistantships available. Support available to part-time students. *Faculty research:* Out-of-school learning, social cognitive career theory, black psychology and the intersectionality of social identities, test session behavior. *Unit head:* Dr. Matthew Martens, Division Executive Director, 573-882-9434, E-mail: martensmp@missouri.edu. *Application contact:* Latoya Luther, Senior Secretary, 573-882-7732, E-mail: lutherl@missouri.edu.
Website: http://education.missouri.edu/ESCP/

University of Missouri–Kansas City, School of Education, Kansas City, MO 64110-2499. Offers administration (Ed D); counseling and guidance (MA, Ed S), including mental health counseling (Ed S), school counseling (Ed S); counseling psychology (PhD); curriculum and instruction (MA, Ed S), including language and literacy (Ed S); education (PhD), including higher education administration, PK-12 education administration; educational administration (MA, Ed S), including advanced principal (Ed S), beginning principal (Ed S), district-level administration (Ed S); reading education (MA); special education (MA). PhD in education offered through the School of Graduate Studies. *Accreditation:* NCATE. Part-time and evening/weekend programs available. *Faculty:* 35 full-time (26 women), 75 part-time/adjunct (63 women). *Students:* 207 full-time (152 women), 382 part-time (273 women); includes 145 minority (89 Black or African American, non-Hispanic/Latino; 3 American Indian or Alaska Native, non-Hispanic/Latino; 15 Asian, non-Hispanic/Latino; 28 Hispanic/Latino; 1 Native Hawaiian or other Pacific Islander, non-Hispanic/Latino; 9 Two or more races, non-Hispanic/Latino), 26 international. Average age 33. 709 applicants, 60% accepted, 204 enrolled. In 2014, 152 master's, 21 doctorates, 38 other advanced degrees awarded. *Degree requirements:* For doctorate, thesis/dissertation, internship, practicum. *Entrance requirements:* For master's, GRE, minimum GPA of 2.75, 2 letters of reference, written statement of purpose; for doctorate, GRE, minimum GPA of 3.0; for Ed S, minimum GPA of 3.0. Additional exam requirements/recommendations for international students: Required—TOEFL (minimum score 550 paper-based; 80 iBT). *Application deadline:* For fall admission, 4/1 priority date for domestic and international students; for spring admission, 11/1 priority date for domestic and international students. Applications are processed on a rolling basis. Application fee: $45 ($50 for international students). *Financial support:* In 2014–15, 14 research assistantships with partial tuition reimbursements (averaging $12,943 per year) were awarded; career-related internships or fieldwork, Federal Work-Study, institutionally sponsored loans, and tuition waivers (full and partial) also available. Support available to part-time students. Financial award application deadline: 3/1; financial award applicants required to submit FAFSA. *Faculty research:* Urban education, inquiry-based field study, theories of counseling and psychotherapy, school literacy, educational technology. *Unit head:* Chris Brown, Interim Dean, 816-235-2234, Fax: 816-235-5270, E-mail: education@umkc.edu. *Application contact:* Erica Hernandez-Scott, Student Recruiter, 816-235-1295, Fax: 816-235-5270, E-mail: hernandeze@umkc.edu.
Website: http://education.umkc.edu

University of Missouri–St. Louis, College of Education, Division of Counseling, St. Louis, MO 63121. Offers clinical mental health counseling (M Ed); elementary school counseling (M Ed); secondary school counseling (M Ed). *Accreditation:* ACA; NCATE. Part-time and evening/weekend programs available. *Faculty:* 8 full-time (4 women), 7 part-time/adjunct (6 women). *Students:* 59 full-time (49 women), 158 part-time (131 women); includes 50 minority (40 Black or African American, non-Hispanic/Latino; 1 Asian, non-Hispanic/Latino; 5 Hispanic/Latino; 4 Two or more races, non-Hispanic/Latino), 4 international. Average age 32. 112 applicants, 46% accepted, 34 enrolled. In 2014, 51 master's awarded. *Degree requirements:* For master's, comprehensive exam. *Entrance requirements:* For master's, 3 letters of recommendation. Additional exam requirements/recommendations for international students: Recommended—TOEFL (minimum score 550 paper-based; 79 iBT), IELTS (minimum score 6.5). *Application deadline:* For fall admission, 5/1 for domestic and international students; for spring admission, 10/1 for domestic and international students. Application fee: $50 ($40 for international students). Electronic applications accepted. *Expenses:* Tuition, state resident: full-time $7364; part-time $409.10 per hour. Tuition, nonresident: full-time $18,153; part-time $1008.50 per hour. *Financial support:* In 2014–15, 1 teaching assistantship with full and partial tuition reimbursement (averaging $10,588 per year) was awarded. Financial award application deadline: 4/1; financial award applicants required to submit FAFSA. *Faculty research:* Vocational interests, self-concept, decision-making factors, developmental differences. *Unit head:* Dr. Mark Pope, Chair, 314-516-5782. *Application contact:* 314-516-5458, Fax: 314-516-6996, E-mail: gradadm@umsl.edu.

The University of Montana, Graduate School, Phyllis J. Washington College of Education and Human Sciences, Department of Counselor Education, Missoula, MT 59812-0002. Offers clinical mental health counseling (MA); counseling and supervision (Ed D); counselor education (Ed S); intercultural youth and family development (MA); school counseling (MA). *Accreditation:* ACA. *Degree requirements:* For doctorate, thesis/dissertation. *Entrance requirements:* For master's, doctorate, and Ed S, GRE General Test. Additional exam requirements/recommendations for international students: Required—TOEFL.

University of Nebraska at Kearney, Graduate Studies and Research, College of Education, Department of Counseling and School Psychology, Kearney, NE 68849-0001. Offers clinical mental health counseling (MS Ed); school counseling (MS Ed), including elementary, secondary; school psychology (Ed S); student affairs (MS Ed). *Accreditation:* ACA; NCATE. Part-time and evening/weekend programs available. Postbaccalaureate distance learning degree programs offered (no on-campus study). *Faculty:* 7 full-time (3 women). *Students:* 62 full-time (56 women), 67 part-time (56 women); includes 15 minority (13 Hispanic/Latino; 2 Two or more races, non-Hispanic/Latino), 2 international. 41 applicants, 88% accepted, 31 enrolled. In 2014, 28 master's, 6 Ed Ss awarded. *Degree requirements:* For master's, comprehensive exam, thesis optional; for Ed S, thesis. *Entrance requirements:* For master's and Ed S, personal statement, recommendations, resume, interview. Additional exam requirements/recommendations for international students: Recommended—TOEFL (minimum score 550 paper-based; 79 iBT), IELTS (minimum score 6.5). *Application deadline:* For fall admission, 6/15 for domestic and international students; for spring admission, 10/15 for domestic and international students; for summer admission, 3/15 for domestic and international students. Application fee: $45. Electronic applications accepted. *Expenses:* Tuition, state resident: full-time $3897; part-time $216.50 per credit hour. Tuition, nonresident: full-time $8550; part-time $475 per credit hour. *Required fees:* $414; $23 per credit. $96.50 per semester. One-time fee: $45. Tuition and fees vary according to course load and program. *Financial support:* In 2014–15, 8 research assistantships with full tuition reimbursements (averaging $9,900 per year) were awarded; career-related internships or fieldwork, scholarships/grants, health care benefits, and unspecified

assistantships also available. Support available to part-time students. Financial award application deadline: 2/28; financial award applicants required to submit FAFSA. *Faculty research:* Multicultural counseling and diversity issues, team decision-making, adult development, women's issues, brief therapy. *Unit head:* Dr. Grace Mims, Chair, Counseling and School Psychology, 308-865-8508, E-mail: mimsga@unk.edu. *Application contact:* Linda Johnson, Director, Graduate Admissions and Programs, 800-717-7881, Fax: 308-865-8837, E-mail: gradstudies@unk.edu.
Website: http://www.unk.edu/academics/csp/

University of Nebraska–Lincoln, Graduate College, College of Education and Human Sciences, Department of Educational Psychology, Lincoln, NE 68588. Offers cognition, learning and development (MA); counseling psychology (MA); educational psychology (MA, Ed S); psychological studies in education (PhD), including cognition, learning and development, counseling psychology, quantitative, qualitative, and psychometric methods, school psychology; quantitative, qualitative, and psychometric methods (MA); school psychology (MA, Ed S). *Accreditation:* APA (one or more programs are accredited); NCATE. *Degree requirements:* For master's, thesis optional. *Entrance requirements:* For master's, GRE General Test. Additional exam requirements/recommendations for international students: Required—TOEFL (minimum score 500 paper-based). Electronic applications accepted. *Faculty research:* Measurement and assessment, metacognition, academic skills, child development, multicultural education and counseling.

University of Nevada, Las Vegas, Graduate College, College of Education, Department of Educational and Clinical Studies, Las Vegas, NV 89154-3066. Offers addiction studies (Advanced Certificate); counselor education (MS), including clinical mental health; educational and clinical studies (M Ed); mental health counseling (Advanced Certificate); special education (PhD); PhD/JD. Part-time and evening/weekend programs available. *Faculty:* 18 full-time (10 women), 12 part-time/adjunct (10 women). *Students:* 164 full-time (140 women), 206 part-time (167 women); includes 142 minority (39 Black or African American, non-Hispanic/Latino; 17 Asian, non-Hispanic/Latino; 62 Hispanic/Latino; 1 Native Hawaiian or other Pacific Islander, non-Hispanic/Latino; 23 Two or more races, non-Hispanic/Latino), 26 international. Average age 34. 184 applicants, 83% accepted, 117 enrolled. In 2014, 121 master's, 6 doctorates awarded. *Degree requirements:* For master's, comprehensive exam (for some programs), thesis (for some programs); for Advanced Certificate, thesis (for some programs). *Entrance requirements:* Additional exam requirements/recommendations for international students: Required—TOEFL (minimum score 550 paper-based; 80 iBT), IELTS (minimum score 7). *Application deadline:* For fall admission, 3/1 for domestic students, 5/1 for international students; for spring admission, 9/1 for domestic students, 10/1 for international students; for summer admission, 3/15 for domestic students. Application fee: $60 ($95 for international students). Electronic applications accepted. *Financial support:* In 2014–15, 32 students received support, including 6 research assistantships with partial tuition reimbursements available (averaging $10,708 per year), 26 teaching assistantships with partial tuition reimbursements available (averaging $14,792 per year); institutionally sponsored loans, scholarships/grants, health care benefits, and unspecified assistantships also available. Financial award application deadline: 3/1. *Faculty research:* Multicultural issues in counseling, academic interventions for students with disabilities, establishment of pro-social skills in young children with severe disabilities, inclusive strategies for students with disabilities, language and literacy for English language learners. *Total annual research expenditures:* $343,782. *Unit head:* Dr. Thomas Pierce, Interim Chair/Associate Professor, 702-895-1104, Fax: 702-895-5550, E-mail: tom.pierce@unlv.edu. *Application contact:* Graduate College Admissions Evaluator, 702-895-3320, Fax: 702-895-4180, E-mail: gradcollege@unlv.edu.
Website: http://education.unlv.edu/ecs/

The University of North Carolina at Greensboro, Graduate School, School of Education, Department of Counseling and Educational Development, Greensboro, NC 27412-5001. Offers advanced school counseling (PMC); counseling and counselor education (PhD); counseling and educational development (MS); couple and family counseling (PMC); school counseling (PMC); MS/Ed S. *Accreditation:* ACA (one or more programs are accredited); NCATE. *Degree requirements:* For master's, comprehensive exam, practicum, internship; for doctorate, comprehensive exam, thesis/dissertation. *Entrance requirements:* For master's, doctorate, and PMC, GRE General Test. Additional exam requirements/recommendations for international students: Required—TOEFL. Electronic applications accepted. *Faculty research:* Gerontology, invitational theory, career development, marriage and family therapy, drug and alcohol abuse prevention.

The University of North Carolina at Pembroke, Graduate Studies, School of Education, Programs in Counseling, Pembroke, NC 28372-1510. Offers clinical mental health counseling (MA Ed); professional school counseling (MA Ed). *Accreditation:* NCATE. Part-time and evening/weekend programs available. *Degree requirements:* For master's, comprehensive exam, thesis optional. *Entrance requirements:* For master's, GRE General Test or MAT, minimum GPA of 3.0 in major, 2.5 overall. Additional exam requirements/recommendations for international students: Required—TOEFL.

University of North Dakota, Graduate School, College of Education and Human Development, Department of Counseling, Grand Forks, ND 58202. Offers MA. *Degree requirements:* For master's, comprehensive exam, thesis or alternative. *Entrance requirements:* For master's, GRE General Test or MAT, minimum GPA of 3.0. Additional exam requirements/recommendations for international students: Required—TOEFL (minimum score 550 paper-based; 79 iBT), IELTS (minimum score 6.5). Electronic applications accepted. *Faculty research:* Group dynamics, addictive behavior, item response theory, geopsychology, women's health.

University of Northern Iowa, Graduate College, College of Social and Behavioral Sciences, School of Applied Human Sciences, MA Program in Counseling, Cedar Falls, IA 50614. Offers mental health counseling (MA); school counseling (MA). *Accreditation:* ACA. Part-time and evening/weekend programs available. *Students:* 50 full-time (43 women), 33 part-time (24 women); includes 8 minority (3 Black or African American, non-Hispanic/Latino; 1 American Indian or Alaska Native, non-Hispanic/Latino; 1 Asian, non-Hispanic/Latino; 3 Hispanic/Latino), 1 international. 95 applicants, 25% accepted, 24 enrolled. In 2014, 17 master's awarded. *Degree requirements:* For master's, comprehensive exam, thesis or alternative. *Entrance requirements:* For master's, minimum GPA of 3.0. Additional exam requirements/recommendations for international students: Required—TOEFL (minimum score 500 paper-based; 61 iBT). *Application deadline:* For fall admission, 8/1 priority date for domestic students. Applications are processed on a rolling basis. Application fee: $50 ($70 for international students). Electronic applications accepted. *Expenses:* Tuition, state resident: full-time $7912; part-time $880 per credit. Tuition, nonresident: full-time $17,906; part-time $880 per credit. *Required fees:* $1101; $325.50 per credit. $465.63 per semester. Tuition and fees vary according to course load and program. *Financial support:* Career-related internships or fieldwork, Federal Work-Study, and tuition waivers (full and partial) available. Support available to part-time students. Financial award application deadline: 2/1. *Unit head:* Dr. Robert Swazo, Coordinator, 319-273-2675, Fax: 319-273-5175, E-mail: roberto.swazo@uni.edu. *Application contact:* Laurie S. Russell, Record Analyst, 319-273-2623, Fax: 319-273-2885, E-mail: laurie.russell@uni.edu.
Website: http://www.uni.edu/csbs/sahs/counseling

University of North Florida, College of Arts and Sciences, Department of Psychology, Jacksonville, FL 32224. Offers counseling psychology (MAC); general psychology (MA). Part-time and evening/weekend programs available. *Faculty:* 21 full-time (11 women). *Students:* 29 full-time (18 women), 7 part-time (6 women); includes 8 minority (2 Black or African American, non-Hispanic/Latino; 5 Hispanic/Latino; 1 Two or more races, non-Hispanic/Latino), 1 international. Average age 25. 87 applicants, 30% accepted, 16 enrolled. In 2014, 7 master's awarded. *Degree requirements:* For master's, comprehensive exam, thesis optional, practicum. *Entrance requirements:* For master's, GRE General Test, 2 letters of recommendation, minimum GPA of 3.0 in last 60 hours of course work. Additional exam requirements/recommendations for international students: Required—TOEFL (minimum score 500 paper-based; 61 iBT). *Application deadline:* For fall admission, 6/1 priority date for domestic students, 4/1 for international students. Applications are processed on a rolling basis. Application fee: $30. Electronic applications accepted. *Expenses:* Tuition, state resident: full-time $9794; part-time $408.10 per credit hour. Tuition, nonresident: full-time $22,383; part-time $932.61 per credit hour. *Required fees:* $2047; $85.29 per credit hour. Tuition and fees vary according to course load and program. *Financial support:* In 2014–15, 10 students received support, including 5 teaching assistantships (averaging $4,182 per year); research assistantships, Federal Work-Study, scholarships/grants, and tuition waivers (partial) also available. Financial award application deadline: 4/1; financial award applicants required to submit FAFSA. *Faculty research:* Sensory perception, social cognition, sexual behavior, evolutionary psychology, psychology and law. *Total annual research expenditures:* $68,180. *Unit head:* Dr. Michael Toglia, Chair, 904-620-1624, E-mail: m.toglia@unf.edu. *Application contact:* Dr. Amanda Pascale, Director, The Graduate School, 904-620-1360, Fax: 904-620-1362, E-mail: graduateschool@unf.edu.
Website: http://www.unf.edu/coas/psychology/

University of North Georgia, Department of Psychology and Sociology, Dahlonega, GA 30597. Offers clinical mental health counseling (MS). *Accreditation:* ACA. Part-time and evening/weekend programs available. *Degree requirements:* For master's, one foreign language, thesis optional. *Entrance requirements:* For master's, GRE General Test, minimum GPA of 2.5, 3 letters of recommendation, interview, personal statement, resume. Additional exam requirements/recommendations for international students: Required—TOEFL (minimum score 550 paper-based; 79 iBT), IELTS (minimum score 6.5). Electronic applications accepted. *Faculty research:* Prejudice and counseling relationships, grow curve analysis of group dynamics, career-related daydreams.

University of North Texas, Robert B. Toulouse School of Graduate Studies, Denton, TX 76203-5459. Offers accounting (MS); applied anthropology (MA, MS); applied behavior analysis (Certificate); applied geography (MA); applied technology and performance improvement (M Ed, MS); art education (MA); art history (MA); art museum education (Certificate); arts leadership (Certificate); audiology (Au D); behavior analysis (MS); behavioral science (PhD); biochemistry and molecular biology (MS); biology (MA, MS); biomedical engineering (MS); business analysis (MS); chemistry (MS); clinical health psychology (PhD); communication studies (MA, MS); computer engineering (MS); computer science (MS); counseling (M Ed, MS), including clinical mental health counseling (MS), college and university counseling, elementary school counseling, secondary school counseling; creative writing (MA); criminal justice (MS); curriculum and instruction (M Ed); decision sciences (MBA); design (MA, MFA), including fashion design (MFA), innovation studies, interior design (MFA); early childhood studies (MS); economics (MS); educational leadership (M Ed, Ed D); educational psychology (MS, PhD), including family studies (MS), gifted and talented (MS), human development (MS), learning and cognition (MS), research, measurement and evaluation (MS); electrical engineering (MS); emergency management (MPA); engineering technology (MS); English (MA); English as a second language (MA); environmental science (MS); finance (MBA, MS); financial management (MPA); French (MA); health services management (MBA); higher education (M Ed, Ed D); history (MA, MS); hospitality management (MS); human resources management (MPA); information science (MS); information systems (PhD); information technologies (MBA); interdisciplinary studies (MA, MS); international studies (MA); international sustainable tourism (MS); jazz studies (MM); journalism (MA, MJ, Graduate Certificate), including interactive and virtual digital communication (Graduate Certificate), narrative journalism (Graduate Certificate), public relations (Graduate Certificate); kinesiology (MS); linguistics (MA); local government management (MPA); logistics (PhD); logistics and supply chain management (MBA); long-term care, senior housing, and aging services (MA); management (PhD); marketing (MBA); mathematics (MA, MS); mechanical and energy engineering (MS, PhD); music (MA), including ethnomusicology, music theory, musicology, performance; music composition (PhD); music education (MM Ed, PhD); nonprofit management (MPA); operations and supply chain management (MBA); performance (MM, DMA); philosophy (MA); political science (MA); professional and technical communication (MA); radio, television and film (MA, MFA); rehabilitation counseling (Certificate); sociology (MA); Spanish (MA); special education (M Ed); speech-language pathology (MA); strategic management (MBA); studio art (MFA); teaching (M Ed); MBA/MS. Part-time and evening/weekend programs available. Postbaccalaureate distance learning degree programs offered. *Faculty:* 651 full-time (215 women), 233 part-time/adjunct (139 women). *Students:* 3,040 full-time (1,598 women), 3,401 part-time (2,097 women); includes 1,740 minority (533 Black or African American, non-Hispanic/Latino; 15 American Indian or Alaska Native, non-Hispanic/Latino; 286 Asian, non-Hispanic/Latino; 746 Hispanic/Latino; 3 Native Hawaiian or other Pacific Islander, non-Hispanic/Latino; 157 Two or more races, non-Hispanic/Latino), 1,145 international. Terminal master's awarded for partial completion of doctoral program. *Degree requirements:* For master's, variable foreign language requirement, comprehensive exam (for some programs), thesis (for some programs); for doctorate, variable foreign language requirement, comprehensive exam (for some programs), thesis/dissertation; for other advanced degree, variable foreign language requirement, comprehensive exam (for some programs). *Entrance requirements:* For master's and doctorate, GRE, GMAT. Additional exam requirements/recommendations for international students: Required—TOEFL (minimum score 550 paper-based; 79 iBT). *Application deadline:* For fall admission, 7/15 for domestic students, 3/15 for international students; for spring admission, 11/15 for domestic students, 9/15 for international students; for summer admission, 5/1 for domestic students. Applications are processed on a rolling basis. Application fee: $60. Electronic applications accepted. *Expenses:* Tuition, state resident: full-time $5450; part-time $3633 per year. Tuition, nonresident: full-time $11,966; part-time $7977 per year. *Required fees:* $1301; $398 per credit hour. $685 per semester. Tuition and fees vary according to program and reciprocity agreements. *Financial support:* Fellowships with partial tuition reimbursements, research assistantships with partial tuition reimbursements, teaching assistantships, career-related internships or fieldwork, Federal Work-Study, institutionally sponsored loans, scholarships/grants, health care benefits, and library assistantships available. Support available to part-time students. Financial award applicants required to submit FAFSA. *Unit head:* Mark Wardell, Dean, 940-565-2383, E-mail: mark.wardell@unt.edu. *Application contact:* Toulouse School of Graduate Studies, 940-565-2383, Fax: 940-565-2141, E-mail: gradsch@unt.edu.
Website: http://tsgs.unt.edu/

Counseling Psychology

University of Notre Dame, Graduate School, College of Arts and Letters, Division of Social Science, Department of Psychology, Notre Dame, IN 46556. Offers cognitive psychology (PhD); counseling psychology (PhD); developmental psychology (PhD); quantitative psychology (PhD). *Accreditation:* APA. *Degree requirements:* For doctorate, comprehensive exam, thesis/dissertation, candidacy exam. *Entrance requirements:* For doctorate, GRE General Test, GRE Subject Test (strongly recommended). Additional exam requirements/recommendations for international students: Required—TOEFL (minimum score 600 paper-based; 80 iBT). Electronic applications accepted. *Faculty research:* Cognitive and socio-emotional development, statistical methods and quantitative models applicable to psychology, interpersonal relations, life span development and developmental delay, childhood depression, structural equation and dynamical systems.

University of Oklahoma, Jeannine Rainbolt College of Education, Department of Educational Psychology, Program in Counseling Psychology, Norman, OK 73019. Offers PhD. *Accreditation:* APA. Part-time programs available. *Students:* 14 full-time (10 women), 17 part-time (11 women); includes 12 minority (2 Black or African American, non-Hispanic/Latino; 3 American Indian or Alaska Native, non-Hispanic/Latino; 1 Asian, non-Hispanic/Latino; 3 Hispanic/Latino; 3 Two or more races, non-Hispanic/Latino). Average age 30. 22 applicants. In 2014, 9 doctorates awarded. *Degree requirements:* For doctorate, comprehensive exam, thesis/dissertation, internship. *Entrance requirements:* For doctorate, GRE. Additional exam requirements/recommendations for international students: Required—TOEFL (minimum score 79 iBT). *Application deadline:* For fall admission, 1/10 for domestic and international students; for spring admission, 11/1 for domestic students, 9/1 for international students. Application fee: $50 ($100 for international students). Electronic applications accepted. *Expenses:* Tuition, state resident: full-time $4394; part-time $183.10 per credit hour. Tuition, nonresident: full-time $16,970; part-time $707.10 per credit hour. *Required fees:* $2892; $109.95 per credit hour. $126.50 per semester. *Financial support:* In 2014–15, 18 students received support. Scholarships/grants, health care benefits, and unspecified assistantships available. Financial award application deadline: 6/1; financial award applicants required to submit FAFSA. *Faculty research:* Social justice in counseling, trauma; assessment, relationships. *Unit head:* Dr. Xun Ge, Professor and Chair, 405-325-5974, Fax: 405-325-6655, E-mail: xge@ou.edu. *Application contact:* Anna Steele, Graduate Programs Officer, 405-325-4525, Fax: 405-325-6655, E-mail: anna.steele@ou.edu. Website: http://www.ou.edu/content/education/edpy/counseling-psychology-degrees-and-programs.html

University of Oklahoma, Jeannine Rainbolt College of Education, Department of Educational Psychology, Program in Professional Counseling, Norman, OK 73019. Offers M Ed. *Students:* 43 full-time (34 women), 5 part-time (4 women); includes 19 minority (2 Black or African American, non-Hispanic/Latino; 5 American Indian or Alaska Native, non-Hispanic/Latino; 1 Asian, non-Hispanic/Latino; 6 Hispanic/Latino; 5 Two or more races, non-Hispanic/Latino), 1 international. Average age 26. 35 applicants, 49% accepted, 16 enrolled. In 2014, 15 master's awarded. Terminal master's awarded for partial completion of doctoral program. *Degree requirements:* For master's, comprehensive exam, internship. *Entrance requirements:* For master's, GRE. Additional exam requirements/recommendations for international students: Required—TOEFL (minimum score 79 iBT). *Application deadline:* For fall admission, 1/31 for domestic and international students; for spring admission, 11/1 for domestic students, 9/1 for international students. Application fee: $50 ($100 for international students). Electronic applications accepted. *Expenses:* Tuition, state resident: full-time $4394; part-time $183.10 per credit hour. Tuition, nonresident: full-time $16,970; part-time $707.10 per credit hour. *Required fees:* $2892; $109.95 per credit hour. $126.50 per semester. *Financial support:* In 2014–15, 30 students received support. Scholarships/grants, health care benefits, and unspecified assistantships available. Financial award application deadline: 6/1; financial award applicants required to submit FAFSA. *Faculty research:* Counseling techniques, multicultural counseling, group counseling, couples and family counseling. *Unit head:* Dr. Xun Ge, Professor and Chair, 405-325-5974, Fax: 405-325-6655, E-mail: xge@ou.edu. *Application contact:* Anna Steele, Graduate Programs Officer, 405-325-4525, Fax: 405-325-6655, E-mail: anna.steele@ou.edu. Website: http://www.ou.edu/education/edpy

University of Pennsylvania, Graduate School of Education, Division of Applied Psychology and Human Development, Program in Counseling and Mental Health Services, Philadelphia, PA 19104. Offers M Phil, MS Ed. *Students:* 85 full-time (75 women), 1 (woman) part-time; includes 36 minority (11 Black or African American, non-Hispanic/Latino; 14 Asian, non-Hispanic/Latino; 7 Hispanic/Latino; 4 Two or more races, non-Hispanic/Latino), 23 international. 191 applicants, 71% accepted, 94 enrolled. In 2014, 67 master's awarded. *Degree requirements:* For master's, exam. *Entrance requirements:* For master's, GRE General Test. *Application deadline:* For fall admission, 12/15 priority date for domestic students. Applications are processed on a rolling basis. Application fee: $70. Electronic applications accepted. *Expenses:* Expenses: Contact institution. *Financial support:* Applicants required to submit FAFSA. *Faculty research:* Counseling in school, college, or agency. *Unit head:* Dr. Andrew Porter, Dean, 215-898-7014. *Application contact:* 215-898-6415, Fax: 215-746-6884, E-mail: admissions@gse.upenn.edu. Website: http://www.gse.upenn.edu/aphd/cmhs/msed

University of Pennsylvania, Graduate School of Education, Division of Applied Psychology and Human Development, Program in School and Mental Health Counseling, Philadelphia, PA 19104. Offers MS Ed. *Students:* 62 full-time (50 women), 1 (woman) part-time; includes 32 minority (17 Black or African American, non-Hispanic/Latino; 5 Asian, non-Hispanic/Latino; 6 Hispanic/Latino; 4 Two or more races, non-Hispanic/Latino), 1 international. 53 applicants, 81% accepted, 30 enrolled. In 2014, 36 master's awarded. *Application deadline:* For fall admission, 12/15 priority date for domestic students. Applications are processed on a rolling basis. Application fee: $70. Electronic applications accepted. *Expenses:* Expenses: Contact institution. *Financial support:* Fellowships, institutionally sponsored loans, scholarships/grants, traineeships, health care benefits, and unspecified assistantships available. *Faculty research:* Therapeutic interventions at a preschool level, childhood stress, college psychology, school and community psychology. *Unit head:* Dr. Andrew Porter, Dean, 215-898-7014. *Application contact:* 215-898-6415, Fax: 215-746-6884, E-mail: admissions@gse.upenn.edu. Website: http://www.gse.upenn.edu/smhc/

University of Phoenix–Las Vegas Campus, College of Human Services, Las Vegas, NV 89135. Offers marriage, family, and child therapy (MSC); mental health counseling (MSC); school counseling (MSC). Postbaccalaureate distance learning degree programs offered. *Entrance requirements:* For master's, minimum undergraduate GPA of 2.5, 3 years of work experience. Additional exam requirements/recommendations for international students: Required—TOEFL (minimum score 550 paper-based; 79 iBT). Electronic applications accepted.

University of Phoenix–Phoenix Campus, College of Social Sciences, Tempe, AZ 85282-2371. Offers counseling (MS), including clinical mental health counseling, community counseling, counseling, marriage, family and child therapy; psychology (MS). Evening/weekend programs available. Postbaccalaureate distance learning degree programs offered. *Entrance requirements:* Additional exam requirements/

recommendations for international students: Required—TOEFL, TOEIC (Test of English as an International Communication), Berlitz Online English Proficiency Exam, PTE, or IELTS. Electronic applications accepted. *Expenses:* Contact institution.

University of Phoenix–Puerto Rico Campus, College of Human Services, Guaynabo, PR 00968. Offers marriage and family counseling (MSC); mental health counseling (MSC). Evening/weekend programs available. *Degree requirements:* For master's, thesis (for some programs). *Entrance requirements:* For master's, Counselor Preparation Comprehensive Examination, minimum undergraduate GPA of 2.5, 3 years work experience. Additional exam requirements/recommendations for international students: Required—TOEFL (minimum score 550 paper-based; 79 iBT). Electronic applications accepted.

University of Puget Sound, School of Education, Program in Counseling, Tacoma, WA 98416. Offers learning, teaching, and leadership (M Ed); mental health counseling (M Ed); school counseling (M Ed). Part-time programs available. *Faculty:* 8 full-time (5 women). *Students:* 1 (woman) full-time, 30 part-time (24 women); includes 6 minority (2 Black or African American, non-Hispanic/Latino; 2 Hispanic/Latino; 1 Native Hawaiian or other Pacific Islander, non-Hispanic/Latino; 1 Two or more races, non-Hispanic/Latino). Average age 26. 36 applicants, 53% accepted, 16 enrolled. In 2014, 11 master's awarded. *Degree requirements:* For master's, capstone course. *Entrance requirements:* For master's, GRE General Test, minimum baccalaureate GPA of 3.0, resume, interview. Additional exam requirements/recommendations for international students: Required—TOEFL (minimum score 550 paper-based; 90 iBT). *Application deadline:* For fall admission, 3/1 priority date for domestic and international students. Applications are processed on a rolling basis. Application fee: $60. Electronic applications accepted. *Expenses:* Expenses: Contact institution. *Financial support:* Teaching assistantships and career-related internships or fieldwork available. Financial award application deadline: 3/31; financial award applicants required to submit FAFSA. *Faculty research:* Cross-role professional preparation, suicide prevention. *Unit head:* Grace Kirchner, Director, 253-879-3785, Fax: 253-879-3926, E-mail: kirchner@pugetsound.edu. *Application contact:* Karen Stump, Certification Officer/Admission Coordinator of Graduate Programs, 253-879-3382, Fax: 253-879-3926, E-mail: kstump@pugetsound.edu. Website: http://www.pugetsound.edu/academics/departments-and-programs/graduate/school-of-education/med/

University of Rhode Island, Graduate School, College of Human Science and Services, Department of Human Development and Family Studies, Kingston, RI 02881. Offers college student personnel (MS); human development and family studies (MS); marriage and family therapy (MS). *Accreditation:* AAMFT/COAMFTE. Part-time programs available. *Faculty:* 15 full-time (10 women). *Students:* 45 full-time (36 women), 11 part-time (9 women); includes 8 minority (5 Black or African American, non-Hispanic/Latino; 1 Asian, non-Hispanic/Latino; 2 Hispanic/Latino), 2 international. In 2014, 21 master's awarded. *Degree requirements:* For master's, comprehensive exam (for some programs), thesis optional. *Entrance requirements:* For master's, GRE or MAT, 2 letters of recommendation; resume (for college student personnel specialization). Additional exam requirements/recommendations for international students: Required—TOEFL (minimum score 550 paper-based). *Application deadline:* For fall admission, 1/15 for domestic and international students. Application fee: $65. Electronic applications accepted. *Expenses:* Tuition, state resident: full-time $11,532; part-time $641 per credit. Tuition, nonresident: full-time $23,606; part-time $1311 per credit. *Required fees:* $1442; $39 per credit. $35 per semester. One-time fee: $155. *Financial support:* In 2014–15, 2 research assistantships (averaging $10,563 per year), 4 teaching assistantships (averaging $10,563 per year) were awarded. Financial award application deadline: 1/15; financial award applicants required to submit FAFSA. *Total annual research expenditures:* $256,058. *Unit head:* Dr. Karen McCurdy, Chair, 401-874-5960, Fax: 401-874-4020, E-mail: kmccurdy@uri.edu. *Application contact:* Graduate Admissions, 401-874-2872, E-mail: gradadm@etal.uri.edu. Website: http://www.uri.edu/hss/hdf/

University of Saint Francis, Graduate School, Department of Psychology and Counseling, Fort Wayne, IN 46808-3994. Offers clinical mental health counseling (MS, Post Master's Certificate); pastoral counseling (MS, Post Master's Certificate); psychology (MS); rehabilitation counseling (MS, Post Master's Certificate); school counseling (MS Ed). Part-time and evening/weekend programs available. *Faculty:* 3 full-time (1 woman). *Students:* 29 full-time (22 women), 20 part-time (all women); includes 10 minority (7 Black or African American, non-Hispanic/Latino; 2 Hispanic/Latino; 1 Two or more races, non-Hispanic/Latino), 1 international. Average age 32. 21 applicants, 90% accepted, 16 enrolled. In 2014, 23 master's awarded. *Entrance requirements:* For master's, minimum undergraduate GPA of 3.0; undergraduate coursework in psychology. Additional exam requirements/recommendations for international students: Required—TOEFL or IELTS. *Application deadline:* For fall admission, 7/1 for domestic students; for spring admission, 11/1 for domestic students. Applications are processed on a rolling basis. Application fee: $0. Electronic applications accepted. *Expenses:* Expenses: $830 per credit hour. *Financial support:* In 2014–15, 5 students received support. Federal Work-Study, scholarships/grants, and unspecified assistantships available. Support available to part-time students. Financial award application deadline: 3/10; financial award applicants required to submit FAFSA. *Unit head:* Dr. John Brinkman, Associate Professor/Chair, Department of Psychology and Counseling, 260-399-7700 Ext. 8425, Fax: 260-399-8170, E-mail: jbrinkman@sf.edu. *Application contact:* Kyle Richardson, Enrollment Specialist, 260-399-7700 Ext. 6310, Fax: 260-399-8152, E-mail: krichardson@sf.edu. Website: http://psychology.sf.edu/

University of Saint Joseph, Department of Counseling and Applied Behavioral Studies, West Hartford, CT 06117-2700. Offers clinical mental health counseling (MA); school counseling (MA). Part-time and evening/weekend programs available. *Degree requirements:* For master's, comprehensive exam, thesis optional. *Entrance requirements:* For master's, 2 letters of recommendation. Electronic applications accepted. Application fee is waived when completed online. *Expenses: Tuition:* Part-time $700 per credit. *Required fees:* $42 per credit. Tuition and fees vary according to degree level, campus/location and program.

University of Saint Mary, Graduate Programs, Program in Counseling Psychology, Leavenworth, KS 66048-5082. Offers MA. Part-time and evening/weekend programs available. *Entrance requirements:* For master's, bachelor's degree in psychology from accredited college, official transcripts, minimum GPA of 2.75, three professional recommendations, essay. Application fee: $25. *Unit head:* Dr. David Greene, Department Chair, 913-758-6105, Fax: 913-345-2802, E-mail: greened@stmary.edu. *Application contact:* Dr. Les Hemphill, Director, 913-319-3015, Fax: 913-345-2802, E-mail: hemphill48@stmary.edu. Website: http://www.stmary.edu/success/Grad-Program/Master-of-Arts-in-Counseling-Psychology.aspx

University of St. Thomas, Graduate Studies, Graduate School of Professional Psychology, St. Paul, MN 55105-1096. Offers counseling psychology (MA, Psy D); family therapy (Certificate). *Accreditation:* APA. Part-time and evening/weekend programs available. *Degree requirements:* For master's, comprehensive exam, practicum; for doctorate, comprehensive exam, thesis/dissertation, qualifying exam,

practicum, internship. *Entrance requirements:* For master's, GRE, minimum GPA of 2.75, letters of recommendation, personal statement; for doctorate, GRE, minimum GPA of 3.2, letters of recommendation, personal statement. Additional exam requirements/recommendations for international students: Required—TOEFL (minimum score 550 paper-based; 80 iBT). *Expenses:* Contact institution. *Faculty research:* Elderly, neuropsychology, anxiety, family, therapist expertise, business of practice, religion and psychology, early attachment, relationship of science and practice in psychotherapy.

University of San Diego, School of Leadership and Education Sciences, School, Family, and Mental Health Professions Programs, San Diego, CA 92110-2492. Offers clinical mental health counseling (MA). *Accreditation:* ACA. Part-time and evening/weekend programs available. *Faculty:* 10 full-time (4 women), 23 part-time/adjunct (16 women). *Students:* 147 full-time (126 women), 33 part-time (31 women); includes 91 minority (13 Black or African American, non-Hispanic/Latino; 1 American Indian or Alaska Native, non-Hispanic/Latino; 15 Asian, non-Hispanic/Latino; 46 Hispanic/Latino; 16 Two or more races, non-Hispanic/Latino), 5 international. Average age 26. 315 applicants, 41% accepted, 65 enrolled. In 2014, 80 master's awarded. *Degree requirements:* For master's, comprehensive exam, international experience. *Entrance requirements:* For master's, minimum GPA of 3.0, interview with faculty member. Additional exam requirements/recommendations for international students: Required—TOEFL (minimum score 580 paper-based; 83 iBT), TWE. *Application deadline:* For fall admission, 2/21 for domestic students, 2/22 for international students. Applications are processed on a rolling basis. Application fee: $45. Electronic applications accepted. *Financial support:* In 2014–15, 149 students received support. Career-related internships or fieldwork, Federal Work-Study, institutionally sponsored loans, unspecified assistantships, and stipends available. Support available to part-time students. Financial award application deadline: 4/1; financial award applicants required to submit FAFSA. *Faculty research:* Action research, collaboration between family therapists and medical professionals, family therapy training and supervision, multicultural counseling, school counseling. *Unit head:* Dr. Ann Garland, Director, 619-260-7879, E-mail: agarland@sandiego.edu. *Application contact:* Monica Mahon, Director of Admissions and Enrollment, 619-260-4524, Fax: 619-260-4158, E-mail: grads@sandiego.edu.
Website: http://www.sandiego.edu/soles/departments/school-family-mental-health-professions/

University of San Francisco, School of Education, Department of Counseling Psychology, San Francisco, CA 94117-1080. Offers counseling (MA), including educational counseling, life transitions counseling, marital and family therapy. *Faculty:* 7 full-time (3 women), 53 part-time/adjunct (37 women). *Students:* 305 full-time (246 women), 30 part-time (27 women); includes 157 minority (24 Black or African American, non-Hispanic/Latino; 36 Asian, non-Hispanic/Latino; 81 Hispanic/Latino; 3 Native Hawaiian or other Pacific Islander, non-Hispanic/Latino; 13 Two or more races, non-Hispanic/Latino), 5 international. Average age 29. 316 applicants, 75% accepted, 106 enrolled. In 2014, 152 master's awarded. *Application deadline:* For fall admission, 3/1 priority date for domestic students, 3/1 for international students; for spring admission, 10/15 priority date for domestic students, 10/15 for international students. Applications are processed on a rolling basis. Application fee: $55 ($65 for international students). Electronic applications accepted. *Expenses: Tuition:* Full-time $21,762; part-time $1209 per credit hour. Tuition and fees vary according to degree level, campus/location and program. *Financial support:* In 2014–15, 86 students received support. Fellowships, research assistantships, and teaching assistantships available. Financial award application deadline: 3/2; financial award applicants required to submit FAFSA. *Unit head:* Dr. Brian Gerrard, Chair, 415-422-6868. *Application contact:* Amy Fogliani, Associate Director of Graduate Outreach, 415-422-5467, E-mail: schoolofeducation@usfca.edu.

The University of Scranton, College of Graduate and Continuing Education, Department of Counseling and Human Services, Program in Clinical Mental Health Counseling, Scranton, PA 18510. Offers MS. *Accreditation:* ACA. Part-time and evening/weekend programs available. *Students:* 55 full-time (51 women), 7 part-time (5 women); includes 5 minority (1 Black or African American, non-Hispanic/Latino; 3 Hispanic/Latino; 1 Two or more races, non-Hispanic/Latino), 1 international. Average age 28. 46 applicants, 54% accepted. In 2014, 9 master's awarded. *Degree requirements:* For master's, comprehensive exam, capstone experience. *Entrance requirements:* For master's, minimum GPA of 3.0. Additional exam requirements/recommendations for international students: Required—TOEFL (minimum score 500 paper-based), IELTS (minimum score 6). *Application deadline:* For fall admission, 3/1 for domestic students. Application fee: $0. *Financial support:* Teaching assistantships, career-related internships or fieldwork, and Federal Work-Study available. Support available to part-time students. Financial award application deadline: 3/1. *Unit head:* Dr. Benjamin Willis, Program Director, 570-941-4236, Fax: 570-941-6492, E-mail: benjamin.willis@scranton.edu. *Application contact:* Joseph M. Roback, Director of Admissions, 570-941-4385, Fax: 570-941-5928, E-mail: robackj2@scranton.edu.

University of South Africa, College of Human Sciences, Pretoria, South Africa. Offers adult education (M Ed); African languages (MA, PhD); African politics (MA, PhD); Afrikaans (MA, PhD); ancient history (MA, PhD); ancient Near Eastern studies (MA, PhD); anthropology (MA, PhD); applied linguistics (MA, PhD); Arabic (MA, PhD); archaeology (MA); art history (MA); Biblical archaeology (MA); Biblical studies (M Th, D Th, PhD); Christian spirituality (M Th, D Th); church history (M Th, D Th); classical studies (MA, PhD); clinical psychology (MA); communication (MA, PhD); comparative education (M Ed, Ed D); consulting psychology (D Admin, D Com, PhD); curriculum studies (M Ed, Ed D); development studies (M Admin, MA, D Admin, PhD); didactics (M Ed, Ed D); education (M Tech); education management (M Ed, Ed D); educational psychology (M Ed); English (MA); environmental education (M Ed); French (MA, PhD); German (MA, PhD); Greek (MA); guidance and counseling (M Ed); health studies (MA, PhD), including health sciences education (MA), health services management (MA), medical and surgical nursing science (critical care general) (MA), midwifery and neonatal nursing science (MA), trauma and emergency care (MA); history (MA, PhD); history of education (Ed D); inclusive education (M Ed, Ed D); information and communications technology policy and regulation (MA); information science (MA, MIS, PhD); international politics (MA, PhD); Islamic studies (MA, PhD); Italian (MA, PhD); Judaica (MA, PhD); linguistics (MA, PhD); mathematical education (M Ed); mathematics education (MA); missiology (M Th, D Th); modern Hebrew (MA, PhD); musicology (MA, MMus, D Mus, PhD); natural science education (M Ed); New Testament (M Th, D Th); Old Testament (D Th); pastoral therapy (M Th, D Th); philosophy (MA); philosophy of education (M Ed, Ed D); politics (MA, PhD); Portuguese (MA, PhD); practical theology (M Th, D Th); psychology (MA, MS, PhD); psychology of education (M Ed, Ed D); public health (MA); religious studies (MA, D Th, PhD); Romance languages (MA); Russian (MA, PhD); Semitic languages (MA, PhD); social behavior studies in HIV/AIDS (MA); social science (mental health) (MA); social science in development studies (MA); social science in psychology (MA); social science in social work (MA); social science in sociology (MA); social work (MSW, DSW, PhD); socio-education (M Ed, Ed D); sociolinguistics (MA); sociology (MA, PhD); Spanish (MA, PhD); systematic theology (M Th, D Th); TESOL (teaching English to speakers of other languages) (MA); theological ethics (M Th, D Th); theory of literature (MA, PhD); urban ministries (D Th); urban ministry (M Th).

University of South Alabama, Graduate School, Program in Clinical and Counseling Psychology, Mobile, AL 36688. Offers PhD. *Faculty:* 6 full-time (3 women). *Students:* 27 full-time (19 women), 4 part-time (3 women); includes 4 minority (1 Black or African American, non-Hispanic/Latino; 1 American Indian or Alaska Native, non-Hispanic/Latino; 1 Asian, non-Hispanic/Latino; 1 Hispanic/Latino). Average age 28. 53 applicants, 32% accepted, 12 enrolled. In 2014, 6 doctorates awarded. *Degree requirements:* For doctorate, thesis/dissertation, capstone internship. *Entrance requirements:* For doctorate, GRE, three letters of recommendation, statement of purpose, curriculum vitae. Additional exam requirements/recommendations for international students: Required—TOEFL (minimum score 525 paper-based; 71 iBT). *Application deadline:* For fall admission, 12/15 for domestic students; for spring admission, 5/1 for domestic students. Application fee: $35. Electronic applications accepted. *Expenses:* Tuition, state resident: full-time $9288; part-time $387 per credit hour. Tuition, nonresident: full-time $18,576; part-time $774 per credit hour. Part-time tuition and fees vary according to course load and program. *Financial support:* Fellowships, research assistantships, teaching assistantships, career-related internships or fieldwork, Federal Work-Study, institutionally sponsored loans, scholarships/grants, and unspecified assistantships available. Support available to part-time students. Financial award application deadline: 5/31; financial award applicants required to submit FAFSA. *Unit head:* Dr. B. Keith Harrison, Dean and Associate Vice President for Academic Affairs, 251-460-6310, E-mail: gradschool@southalabama.edu. *Application contact:* Dr. Elise Labbe, Director of Clinical Training, 251-460-6622, E-mail: elabbe@southalabama.edu.
Website: http://www.southalabama.edu/ccp/

University of Southern Maine, College of Management and Human Service, School of Education and Human Development, Program in Counselor Education, Portland, ME 04104-9300. Offers clinical mental health counseling (MS); counseling (CAS); culturally responsive practices in education and human development (CGS); mental health rehabilitation technician/community (CGS); rehabilitation counseling (MS); school counseling (MS); substance abuse counseling (CGS). *Accreditation:* ACA (one or more programs are accredited); CORE; Teacher Education Accreditation Council. Part-time and evening/weekend programs available. *Faculty:* 6 full-time (4 women), 3 part-time/adjunct (2 women). *Students:* 60 full-time (44 women), 82 part-time (67 women); includes 8 minority (2 Black or African American, non-Hispanic/Latino; 1 American Indian or Alaska Native, non-Hispanic/Latino; 1 Asian, non-Hispanic/Latino; 2 Hispanic/Latino; 2 Two or more races, non-Hispanic/Latino). Average age 36. 76 applicants, 75% accepted, 44 enrolled. In 2014, 35 master's, 8 other advanced degrees awarded. *Degree requirements:* For master's, comprehensive exam, thesis or alternative; for other advanced degree, thesis or alternative. *Entrance requirements:* For master's, GRE General Test or MAT, interview; for other advanced degree, master's degree. Additional exam requirements/recommendations for international students: Required—TOEFL (minimum score 550 paper-based; 79 iBT). *Application deadline:* For fall admission, 11/15 for domestic students. Application fee: $65. Electronic applications accepted. *Expenses: Tuition, area resident:* Full-time $6840; part-time $380 per credit hour. Tuition, state resident: full-time $10,260; part-time $570 per credit hour. Tuition, nonresident: full-time $18,468; part-time $1026 per credit hour. *Required fees:* $830; $83 per credit hour. Tuition and fees vary according to course load and program. *Financial support:* Research assistantships, career-related internships or fieldwork, Federal Work-Study, institutionally sponsored loans, scholarships/grants, and unspecified assistantships available. Support available to part-time students. Financial award application deadline: 3/1; financial award applicants required to submit FAFSA. *Faculty research:* Counselor licensure, group dynamics, counseling theories, healthy adaptation, counselor educator well-being. *Unit head:* Adele Baruch, Program Coordinator, 207-780-5317, E-mail: abaruch@usm.maine.edu. *Application contact:* Mary Sloan, Assistant Dean of Graduate Studies and Director of Graduate Admissions, 207-780-4386, E-mail: gradstudies@usm.maine.edu.
Website: http://usm.maine.edu/counselor-education

University of Southern Mississippi, Graduate School, College of Education and Psychology, Department of Psychology, Hattiesburg, MS 39406-0001. Offers clinical psychology (PhD); counseling psychology (MS, PhD); experimental psychology (PhD); school psychology (PhD). *Accreditation:* APA (one or more programs are accredited). Terminal master's awarded for partial completion of doctoral program. *Degree requirements:* For master's, comprehensive exam, thesis; for doctorate, comprehensive exam, thesis/dissertation. *Entrance requirements:* For master's, GRE General Test, minimum GPA of 3.0; for doctorate, GRE General Test, interview, minimum GPA of 3.5. Additional exam requirements/recommendations for international students: Required—TOEFL, IELTS. *Faculty research:* Psychopathology, alcohol and drug abuse, child clinical psychology, parenting, suicide, career/vocational, marine mammal, cognition, psychological psychology, behavioral interventions, positive psychology, anger/aggression, diversity issues.

University of South Florida, Innovative Education, Tampa, FL 33620-9951. *Unit head:* Kathy Barnes, Interdisciplinary Programs Coordinator, 813-974-8031, Fax: 813-974-7061, E-mail: barnesk@usf.edu. *Application contact:* Karen Tylinski, Metro Initiatives, 813-974-9943, Fax: 813-974-7061, E-mail: ktylinsk@usf.edu.
Website: http://www.usf.edu/innovative-education/

The University of Tennessee, Graduate School, College of Education, Health and Human Sciences, Department of Educational Psychology and Counseling, Knoxville, TN 37996. Offers adult education (MS); applied educational psychology (MS); collaborative learning (Ed D); college student personnel (MS); mental health counseling (MS); rehabilitation counseling (MS); school counseling (MS). *Accreditation:* ACA (one or more programs are accredited); CORE (one or more programs are accredited); NCATE. Part-time and evening/weekend programs available. *Degree requirements:* For master's, thesis optional. *Entrance requirements:* For master's, GRE General Test, minimum GPA of 2.7. Additional exam requirements/recommendations for international students: Required—TOEFL. Electronic applications accepted.

The University of Texas at Austin, Graduate School, College of Education, Department of Educational Psychology, Austin, TX 78712-1111. Offers academic educational psychology (M Ed, MA); counseling psychology (PhD); counselor education (M Ed); human development, culture and learning sciences (PhD); program evaluation (MA); quantitative methods (M Ed, MA, PhD); school psychology (MA, PhD). *Accreditation:* APA (one or more programs are accredited). *Degree requirements:* For master's, thesis optional; for doctorate, thesis/dissertation. *Entrance requirements:* For master's and doctorate, GRE General Test, 3 letters of recommendation. Additional exam requirements/recommendations for international students: Required—TOEFL.

The University of Texas at Tyler, College of Education and Psychology, Department of Psychology and Counseling, Tyler, TX 75799-0001. Offers clinical psychology (MS), including neuropsychology, school psychology; counseling psychology (MA), including general, marriage and family; interdisciplinary studies (MSIS); school counseling (MA). Part-time and evening/weekend programs available. *Degree requirements:* For master's, comprehensive exam, thesis optional. *Entrance requirements:* For master's, GRE General Test, minimum GPA of 3.0. Additional exam requirements/recommendations for international students: Required—TOEFL. Electronic applications accepted. *Faculty research:* Neuropsychology, child abuse, psychometric properties of

psychological instruments, maternal behavior, clinical practice issues, victimization of women, post-traumatic stress disorder.

University of the Cumberlands, Program in Professional Counseling, Williamsburg, KY 40769-1372. Offers MA. Program also offered in San Francisco. Part-time and evening/weekend programs available. Postbaccalaureate distance learning degree programs offered (minimal on-campus study). Electronic applications accepted.

University of the District of Columbia, College of Arts and Sciences, Department of Psychology and Counseling, Program in Counseling, Washington, DC 20008-1175. Offers MS.

University of the Southwest, Graduate Programs, Hobbs, NM 88240-9129. Offers business administration (MBA); curriculum and instruction (MSE); curriculum and instruction: bilingual (MSE); curriculum and instruction: TESOL (MSE); early childhood education (MSE); educational administration (MSE); mental health counseling (MSE); school counseling (MSE); special education (MSE); sports management (MBA). Part-time and evening/weekend programs available. Postbaccalaureate distance learning degree programs offered (no on-campus study). *Degree requirements:* For master's, comprehensive exam, thesis (for some programs). *Entrance requirements:* Additional exam requirements/recommendations for international students: Recommended—TOEFL. Electronic applications accepted.

University of Utah, Graduate School, College of Education, Department of Educational Psychology, Salt Lake City, UT 84112. Offers clinical mental health counseling (M Ed); counseling psychology (PhD); elementary education (M Ed); instructional design and educational technology (M Ed); instructional design and technology (MS); learning and cognition (MS, PhD); reading and literacy (M Ed, PhD); school counseling (M Ed); school psychology (M Ed, PhD); statistics (M Stat). *Accreditation:* APA (one or more programs are accredited). *Faculty:* 24 full-time (12 women), 25 part-time/adjunct (17 women). *Students:* 207 full-time (153 women), 1 part-time (0 women); includes 31 minority (1 Black or African American, non-Hispanic/Latino; 1 American Indian or Alaska Native, non-Hispanic/Latino; 9 Asian, non-Hispanic/Latino; 15 Hispanic/Latino; 1 Native Hawaiian or other Pacific Islander, non-Hispanic/Latino; 4 Two or more races, non-Hispanic/Latino), 3 international. Average age 32. 225 applicants, 38% accepted, 71 enrolled. In 2014, 68 master's, 11 doctorates awarded. Terminal master's awarded for partial completion of doctoral program. *Degree requirements:* For master's, variable foreign language requirement, comprehensive exam (for some programs), thesis (for some programs), projects; for doctorate, variable foreign language requirement, comprehensive exam, thesis/dissertation, oral exam. *Entrance requirements:* For master's and doctorate, GRE General Test, minimum GPA of 3.0. Additional exam requirements/recommendations for international students: Required—TOEFL (minimum score 80 iBT). *Application deadline:* For fall admission, 12/15 for domestic and international students; for winter admission, 11/1 for domestic and international students; for spring admission, 3/15 for domestic and international students. Application fee: $55 ($65 for international students). Electronic applications accepted. *Expenses:* Expenses: Contact institution. *Financial support:* In 2014–15, 84 students received support, including 10 fellowships with full and partial tuition reimbursements available (averaging $18,000 per year), 15 research assistantships with full and partial tuition reimbursements available (averaging $13,500 per year), 59 teaching assistantships with full and partial tuition reimbursements available (averaging $13,500 per year); career-related internships or fieldwork, Federal Work-Study, institutionally sponsored loans, scholarships/grants, health care benefits, and unspecified assistantships also available. Financial award application deadline: 4/1; financial award applicants required to submit FAFSA. *Faculty research:* Autism, computer technology and instruction, cognitive behavior, aging, group counseling. *Unit head:* Dr. Anne E. Cook, Chair, 801-581-7148, Fax: 801-581-5566, E-mail: anne.cook@utah.edu. *Application contact:* JoLynn N. Yates, Academic Program Specialist, 801-581-7148, Fax: 801-581-5566, E-mail: jo.yates@utah.edu.
Website: http://www.ed.utah.edu/edps/

University of Vermont, Graduate College, College of Education and Social Services, Department of Leadership and Developmental Sciences, Counseling Program, Burlington, VT 05405. Offers MS. *Accreditation:* ACA; NCATE. *Entrance requirements:* For master's, GRE General Test, resume. Additional exam requirements/recommendations for international students: Required—TOEFL (minimum score 550 paper-based; 80 iBT). Electronic applications accepted. *Faculty research:* Women and tenure, counseling children and adolescents.

University of Victoria, Faculty of Graduate Studies, Faculty of Education, Department of Educational Psychology and Leadership Studies, Victoria, BC V8W 2Y2, Canada. Offers aboriginal communities counseling (M Ed); counseling (M Ed, MA); educational psychology (M Ed, MA, PhD), including counseling psychology (M Ed, MA), leadership studies (PhD), learning and development (MA, PhD), measurement and evaluation, special education (M Ed, MA); leadership studies (M Ed, MA). Part-time programs available. *Degree requirements:* For master's, thesis (for some programs), comprehensive exam (M Ed); for doctorate, comprehensive exam, thesis/dissertation, candidacy exam. *Entrance requirements:* For master's, 2 years of work experience in a relevant field; for doctorate, GRE, 2 years of work experience in a relevant field, minimum B average. Additional exam requirements/recommendations for international students: Required—TOEFL (minimum score 575 paper-based), IELTS (minimum score 7). *Faculty research:* Learning and development (child, adolescent and adult), special education and exceptional children.

The University of Western Ontario, Faculty of Graduate Studies, Social Sciences Division, Faculty of Education, Program in Counseling Psychology, London, ON N6A 5B8, Canada. Offers M Ed. Part-time programs available. *Entrance requirements:* For master's, minimum B average, 3 yr experience in helping profession. *Faculty research:* Women's issues in counseling, causes for sexual harassment in the workplace, counselor memory and confidence in clinical judgements.

University of West Florida, College of Arts and Sciences: Arts, Department of Psychology, Pensacola, FL 32514-5750. Offers counseling (MA); counseling-licensed mental health counselor (MA); general psychology (MA); industrial-organizational (MA). Part-time programs available. *Degree requirements:* For master's, thesis (for some programs). *Entrance requirements:* For master's, GRE, official transcripts; minimum GPA of 3.0; writing sample; three letters of reference; field experience or skill sets; oral interview (for counseling specialization). Additional exam requirements/recommendations for international students: Required—TOEFL (minimum score 550 paper-based). *Faculty research:* Prose recall, brain imaging, peak performance, biofeedback and pain control, comparable worth.

University of Wisconsin–Madison, Graduate School, School of Education, Department of Counseling Psychology, Program in Counseling Psychology, Madison, WI 53706-1380. Offers PhD. *Accreditation:* APA. *Degree requirements:* For doctorate, thesis/dissertation. *Expenses:* Tuition, state resident: full-time $10,723; part-time $745 per credit. Tuition, nonresident: full-time $24,054; part-time $1578 per credit. *Required fees:* $374 per semester. Tuition and fees vary according to course load, program and reciprocity agreements.

University of Wisconsin–Milwaukee, Graduate School, School of Education, Department of Educational Psychology, Milwaukee, WI 53201-0413. Offers counseling psychology (PhD); educational statistics and measurement (MS, PhD); learning and development (MS, PhD); school and community counseling (MS); school psychology (PhD). *Accreditation:* APA. Part-time programs available. *Degree requirements:* For master's, comprehensive exam, thesis; for doctorate, thesis/dissertation. *Entrance requirements:* For master's, minimum GPA of 3.0; for doctorate, GRE General Test, minimum GPA of 3.0. Additional exam requirements/recommendations for international students: Required—TOEFL (minimum score 550 paper-based; 79 iBT), IELTS (minimum score 6.5). Electronic applications accepted.

University of Wisconsin–Stout, Graduate School, School of Education, Program in School Counseling, Menomonie, WI 54751. Offers MS. *Accreditation:* ACA. Part-time programs available. *Degree requirements:* For master's, thesis. *Entrance requirements:* For master's, minimum GPA of 2.75. Additional exam requirements/recommendations for international students: Required—TOEFL (minimum score 500 paper-based; 61 iBT). *Application deadline:* For fall admission, 2/1 priority date for domestic and international students; for spring admission, 10/1 priority date for domestic and international students. Application fee: $45. Electronic applications accepted. *Financial support:* Research assistantships with partial tuition reimbursements, teaching assistantships with partial tuition reimbursements, Federal Work-Study, scholarships/grants, tuition waivers (partial), and unspecified assistantships available. Support available to part-time students. Financial award application deadline: 5/1; financial award applicants required to submit FAFSA. *Faculty research:* Adventure-based learning, body image, domestic violence, resilience, school climate. *Unit head:* Dr. Denise Brouillard, Director, 715-232-2599, Fax: 715-232-1244, E-mail: brouillardd@uwstout.edu. *Application contact:* Anne E. Johnson, Graduate Student Evaluator (Admissions and Assistantship Coordinator), 715-232-1322, Fax: 715-232-2413, E-mail: johnsona@uwstout.edu.
Website: http://www.uwstout.edu/programs/msgc/

Utah State University, School of Graduate Studies, Emma Eccles Jones College of Education and Human Services, Department of Psychology, Logan, UT 84322. Offers clinical/counseling/school psychology (PhD); research and evaluation methodology (PhD); school counseling (MS); school psychology (MS). *Accreditation:* APA (one or more programs are accredited). Part-time and evening/weekend programs available. Postbaccalaureate distance learning degree programs offered (no on-campus study). Terminal master's awarded for partial completion of doctoral program. *Degree requirements:* For master's, thesis (for some programs); for doctorate, thesis/dissertation. *Entrance requirements:* For master's, GRE General Test (school psychology), MAT (school counseling), minimum GPA of 3.5; for doctorate, GRE General Test, minimum GPA of 3.5. Additional exam requirements/recommendations for international students: Required—TOEFL. *Faculty research:* Hearing loss detection in infancy, ADHD, eating disorders, domestic violence, neuropsychology, bilingual/Spanish speaking students/parents.

Virginia Commonwealth University, Graduate School, College of Humanities and Sciences, Department of Psychology, Program in Counseling Psychology, Richmond, VA 23284-9005. Offers PhD. *Accreditation:* ACA; APA. *Degree requirements:* For doctorate, thesis/dissertation. *Entrance requirements:* For doctorate, GRE General Test, GRE Subject Test. Additional exam requirements/recommendations for international students: Required—TOEFL (minimum score 600 paper-based; 100 iBT); Recommended—IELTS (minimum score 6.5). Electronic applications accepted.

Virginia Commonwealth University, Graduate School, School of Allied Health Professions, Program in Patient Counseling, Richmond, VA 23284-9005. Offers MS, CPC. *Accreditation:* ACA. *Entrance requirements:* For master's, GRE General Test. Additional exam requirements/recommendations for international students: Required—TOEFL (minimum score 600 paper-based; 100 iBT). Electronic applications accepted.

Viterbo University, Master of Science in Mental Health Counseling Program, La Crosse, WI 54601-4797. Offers addiction counseling (MS); child and adolescent counseling (MS); complementary health and wellness counseling (MS). Part-time and evening/weekend programs available. *Faculty:* 3 full-time (1 woman), 6 part-time/adjunct (3 women). *Students:* 52 full-time (43 women), 10 part-time (8 women); includes 6 minority (2 Black or African American, non-Hispanic/Latino; 1 Asian, non-Hispanic/Latino; 3 Two or more races, non-Hispanic/Latino), 1 international. Average age 33. 41 applicants, 51% accepted, 20 enrolled. In 2014, 12 master's awarded. *Degree requirements:* For master's, comprehensive exam, thesis, 54 credits of core program courses; 6 elective credits; minimum GPA of 3.0; action research project; practicum/internship experience. *Entrance requirements:* For master's, MAT, BS in a human service or social science discipline; prerequisite coursework in general psychology, behavior disorders/abnormal psychology, and research methods/statistics; minimum undergraduate cumulative GPA of 3.0; background check; personal statement; undergraduate transcripts; interview. Additional exam requirements/recommendations for international students: Required—TOEFL (minimum score 525 paper-based). *Application deadline:* For fall admission, 3/15 priority date for domestic students, 7/31 priority date for international students. Applications are processed on a rolling basis. Application fee: $50. Electronic applications accepted. Application fee is waived when completed online. *Expenses:* Expenses: $475 per credit. *Financial support:* Applicants required to submit FAFSA. *Faculty research:* Supervision, recovery substance abuse, culture, counseling theory, health and wellness. *Unit head:* Dr. Debra A. Murray, Program Director, 608-796-3720, E-mail: damurray@viterbo.edu. *Application contact:* Dr. Debra A. Murray, Program Director, 608-796-3720, E-mail: damurray@viterbo.edu.
Website: http://www.viterbo.edu/master-science-mental-health-counseling

Walden University, Graduate Programs, School of Counseling, Minneapolis, MN 55401. Offers addiction counseling (MS), including addictions and public health, child and adolescent counseling, family studies and interventions, forensic counseling, general program (MS, PhD), trauma and crisis counseling; counselor education and supervision (PhD), including consultation, counseling and social change, forensic mental health counseling, general program (MS, PhD), trauma and crisis; marriage, couple, and family counseling (MS), including forensic counseling, general program (MS, PhD), trauma and crisis counseling; mental health counseling (MS), including forensic counseling, general program (MS, PhD), trauma and crisis counseling; school counseling (MS), including addiction counseling, crisis and trauma, general program (MS, PhD), military families and culture. Part-time and evening/weekend programs available. Postbaccalaureate distance learning degree programs offered (no on-campus study). *Faculty:* 77 full-time (62 women), 314 part-time/adjunct (215 women). *Students:* 1,835 full-time (1,558 women), 1,518 part-time (1,293 women); includes 1,521 minority (1,135 Black or African American, non-Hispanic/Latino; 13 American Indian or Alaska Native, non-Hispanic/Latino; 27 Asian, non-Hispanic/Latino; 234 Hispanic/Latino; 5 Native Hawaiian or other Pacific Islander, non-Hispanic/Latino; 107 Two or more races, non-Hispanic/Latino), 16 international. Average age 38. 684 applicants, 91% accepted, 610 enrolled. In 2014, 592 master's, 4 doctorates awarded. *Degree requirements:* For master's, residency, field experience, professional development plan, licensure plan; for doctorate, thesis/dissertation, residency, practicum, internship. *Entrance requirements:* For master's, bachelor's degree or higher; minimum GPA of 2.5; official transcripts; goal statement (for some programs); access to computer and Internet; for doctorate, master's degree or higher; three years of related professional or academic experience (preferred); minimum GPA of 3.0; goal statement and current resume (for select programs); official transcripts; access to computer and Internet. Additional exam

requirements/recommendations for international students: Required—TOEFL (minimum score 550 paper-based, 79 iBT), IELTS (minimum score 6.5), Michigan English Language Assessment Battery (minimum score 82), or PTE (minimum score 53). *Application deadline:* Applications are processed on a rolling basis. Application fee: $0. Electronic applications accepted. *Expenses: Tuition:* Full-time $11,925; part-time $500 per credit hour. *Required fees:* $647. *Financial support:* Federal Work-Study, scholarships/grants, unspecified assistantships, and family tuition reduction, active duty/veteran tuition reduction, group tuition reduction, interest-free payment plans, employee tuition reduction available. Support available to part-time students. Financial award applicants required to submit FAFSA. *Unit head:* Dr. Savitri Dixon-Saxon, Associate Dean, 866-492-5336. *Application contact:* Meghan M. Thomas, Vice President of Enrollment Management, 866-492-5336, E-mail: info@waldenu.edu.

Walden University, Graduate Programs, School of Psychology, Minneapolis, MN 55401. Offers clinical psychology (MS), including counseling, general program; forensic psychology (MS), including forensic psychology in the community, general program, mental health applications, program planning and evaluation in forensic settings, psychology and legal systems; organizational psychology and development (Postbaccalaureate Certificate); psychology (MS, PhD), including applied psychology (MS), clinical psychology (PhD), counseling psychology (PhD), crisis management and response (MS), educational psychology, forensic psychology (PhD), general psychology (MS), general psychology research (PhD), health psychology, leadership development and coaching (MS), psychology of culture (MS), psychology, public administration, and social change (MS), social psychology, terrorism and security (MS); psychology respecialization (Post-Doctoral Certificate); teaching online (Post-Master's Certificate). Part-time and evening/weekend programs available. Postbaccalaureate distance learning degree programs offered (no on-campus study). *Faculty:* 56 full-time (36 women), 351 part-time/adjunct (201 women). *Students:* 2,757 full-time (2,202 women), 1,466 part-time (1,148 women); includes 1,849 minority (1,299 Black or African American, non-Hispanic/Latino; 37 American Indian or Alaska Native, non-Hispanic/Latino; 74 Asian, non-Hispanic/Latino; 315 Hispanic/Latino; 8 Native Hawaiian or other Pacific Islander, non-Hispanic/Latino; 116 Two or more races, non-Hispanic/Latino), 28 international. Average age 41. 913 applicants, 97% accepted, 851 enrolled. In 2014, 602 master's, 204 doctorates, 19 other advanced degrees awarded. Terminal master's awarded for partial completion of doctoral program. *Degree requirements:* For master's, thesis optional; for doctorate, thesis/dissertation, residency. *Entrance requirements:* For master's, bachelor's degree or higher; minimum GPA of 2.5; official transcripts; goal statement (for some programs); access to computer and Internet; for doctorate, master's degree or higher; three years of related professional or academic experience (preferred); minimum GPA of 3.0; goal statement and current resume (for select programs); official transcripts; access to computer and Internet; for other advanced degree, relevant work experience; access to computer and Internet. Additional exam requirements/recommendations for international students: Required—TOEFL (minimum score 550 paper-based, 79 iBT), IELTS (minimum score 6.5), Michigan English Language Assessment Battery (minimum score 82), or PTE (minimum score 53). *Application deadline:* Applications are processed on a rolling basis. Application fee: $0. Electronic applications accepted. *Expenses: Tuition:* Full-time $11,925; part-time $500 per credit hour. *Required fees:* $647. *Financial support:* Fellowships, Federal Work-Study, scholarships/grants, unspecified assistantships, and family tuition reduction, active duty/veteran tuition reduction, group tuition reduction, interest-free payment plans, employee tuition reduction available. Support available to part-time students. Financial award applicants required to submit FAFSA. *Unit head:* Dr. Marilyn Powell, Associate Dean, 866-492-5366. *Application contact:* Meghan Thomas, Vice President of Enrollment Management, 866-492-5336, E-mail: info@waldenu.edu.
Website: http://www.waldenu.edu/programs/colleges-schools/psychology

Walden University, Graduate Programs, School of Social Work and Human Services, Minneapolis, MN 55401. Offers addictions (MSW); addictions and social work (DSW); children, families, and couples (MSW); clinical expertise (DSW); criminal justice (DSW); crisis and trauma (MSW); disaster, crisis, and intervention (DSW); forensic populations and settings (MSW); general program (MSW); human services (MS, PhD), including clinical social work (PhD), criminal justice, disaster, crisis and intervention, family studies and intervention strategies (PhD), family studies and interventions, general program, human services administration, public health, social policy analysis and planning; medical social work (MSW, DSW); military families and culture (MSW); policy practice (DSW); social work (PhD), including addictions and social work, clinical expertise, disaster, crisis and intervention (MS, PhD), family studies and interventions (MS, PhD), medical social work, policy practice, social work administration; social work administration (DSW). Part-time and evening/weekend programs available. Postbaccalaureate distance learning degree programs offered (no on-campus study). *Faculty:* 18 full-time (11 women), 236 part-time/adjunct (156 women). *Students:* 1,400 full-time (1,205 women), 884 part-time (759 women); includes 1,586 minority (1,373 Black or African American, non-Hispanic/Latino; 20 American Indian or Alaska Native, non-Hispanic/Latino; 16 Asian, non-Hispanic/Latino; 120 Hispanic/Latino; 57 Two or more races, non-Hispanic/Latino), 14 international. Average age 40. 892 applicants, 96% accepted, 826 enrolled. In 2014, 61 master's, 14 doctorates awarded. *Degree requirements:* For master's, residency (for some programs); for doctorate, thesis/dissertation, residency. *Entrance requirements:* For master's, bachelor's degree or higher; minimum GPA of 2.5; official transcripts; goal statement (for some programs); access to computer and Internet; for doctorate, master's degree or higher; three years of related professional or academic experience (preferred); minimum GPA of 3.0; goal statement and current resume (for select programs); official transcripts; access to computer and Internet. Additional exam requirements/recommendations for international students: Required—TOEFL (minimum score 550 paper-based, 79 iBT), IELTS (minimum score 6.5), Michigan English Language Assessment Battery (minimum score 82), or PTE (minimum score 53). *Application deadline:* Applications are processed on a rolling basis. Application fee: $0. Electronic applications accepted. *Expenses: Tuition:* Full-time $11,925; part-time $500 per credit hour. *Required fees:* $647. *Financial support:* Fellowships, Federal Work-Study, scholarships/grants, unspecified assistantships, and family tuition reduction, active duty/veteran tuition reduction, group tuition reduction, interest-free payment plans, employee tuition reduction available. Support available to part-time students. Financial award applicants required to submit FAFSA. *Unit head:* Dr. Savitri Dixon-Saxon, Associate Dean, 866-492-5336. *Application contact:* Meghan Thomas, Vice President of Enrollment Management, 866-492-5336, E-mail: info@waldenu.edu.
Website: http://www.waldenu.edu/colleges-schools/school-of-social-work-and-human-services/academic-programs

Walla Walla University, Graduate School, School of Education and Psychology, Specialization in Counseling Psychology, College Place, WA 99324-1198. Offers MA. Part-time programs available. *Degree requirements:* For master's, thesis (for some programs). *Entrance requirements:* For master's, GRE General Test, minimum GPA of 2.75, course work in education and psychology. Additional exam requirements/recommendations for international students: Required—TOEFL (minimum score 550 paper-based; 79 iBT). Electronic applications accepted. *Faculty research:* Instructional psychology, moral development.

Walsh University, Graduate Studies, Program in Counseling and Human Development, North Canton, OH 44720-3396. Offers school counseling (MA); student affairs in higher education (MA). *Accreditation:* ACA. Part-time and evening/weekend programs available. *Faculty:* 6 full-time (5 women), 7 part-time/adjunct (4 women). *Students:* 38 full-time (27 women), 47 part-time (41 women); includes 3 minority (2 Black or African American, non-Hispanic/Latino; 1 Hispanic/Latino), 2 international. Average age 28. 85 applicants, 46% accepted, 34 enrolled. In 2014, 21 master's awarded. *Degree requirements:* For master's, comprehensive exam, internship, practicum. *Entrance requirements:* For master's, GRE (minimum score of 145 verbal and 146 quantitative) or MAT (minimum score of 397), interview, minimum GPA of 3.0, writing sample, reference forms, notarized affidavit of good moral conduct. Additional exam requirements/recommendations for international students: Required—TOEFL (minimum score 500 paper-based; 61 iBT). *Application deadline:* For fall admission, 7/15 priority date for domestic students. Applications are processed on a rolling basis. Application fee: $25. Electronic applications accepted. *Expenses: Tuition:* Full-time $11,250; part-time $625 per semester hour. Full-time tuition and fees vary according to program. *Financial support:* In 2014–15, 73 students received support, including 1 fellowship (averaging $14,355 per year), 3 research assistantships with partial tuition reimbursements available (averaging $11,250 per year), 11 teaching assistantships with partial tuition reimbursements available (averaging $7,500 per year); scholarships/grants, tuition waivers (full and partial), and unspecified assistantships also available. Support available to part-time students. Financial award application deadline: 12/31. *Faculty research:* Supervision of clinical mental health counselors; supervision of school counselors; cross-cultural training in counselor education; adventure-based therapies with children; counseling for intimate partner violence and relational issues; refugee mental health and trauma, career counseling for refugees; integration of neuroscience and culture in clinical mental health counseling; diversity and multiculturalism, with a focus on the intersection of religion and higher education. *Unit head:* Dr. Ruthann Anderson, Program Director, 330-490-7338, Fax: 330-490-7323, E-mail: randerson@walsh.edu. *Application contact:* Audra Dice, Graduate and Transfer Admissions Counselor, 330-490-7181, Fax: 330-244-4925, E-mail: adice@walsh.edu.
Website: http://www.walsh.edu/counseling-graduate-program

Washington Adventist University, Program in Counseling Psychology, Takoma Park, MD 20912. Offers MA. Part-time programs available. *Entrance requirements:* Additional exam requirements/recommendations for international students: Required—TOEFL (minimum score 550 paper-based), IELTS (minimum score 5).

Washington Adventist University, Program in Professional Counseling Psychology, Takoma Park, MD 20912. Offers MA. Part-time programs available. *Entrance requirements:* Additional exam requirements/recommendations for international students: Required—TOEFL (minimum score 550 paper-based), IELTS (minimum score 5).

Washington State University, College of Education, Department of Educational Leadership, Sports Studies, and Educational/Counseling Psychology, Pullman, WA 99164-2136. Offers counseling psychology (PhD); educational leadership (Ed M, MA, Ed D, PhD); educational psychology (MA, PhD); sport management (MA). Programs also offered at the Spokane, Tri-Cities, Vancouver and Global (online) campuses. Part-time programs available. Postbaccalaureate distance learning degree programs offered (no on-campus study). *Faculty:* 28 full-time (15 women), 19 part-time/adjunct (13 women). *Students:* 90 full-time (49 women), 129 part-time (73 women); includes 51 minority (8 Black or African American, non-Hispanic/Latino; 10 Asian, non-Hispanic/Latino; 25 Hispanic/Latino; 8 Two or more races, non-Hispanic/Latino), 8 international. Average age 34. 249 applicants, 39% accepted, 60 enrolled. In 2014, 39 master's, 18 doctorates awarded. *Median time to degree:* Of those who began their doctoral program in fall 2006, 88% received their degree in 8 years or less. *Degree requirements:* For master's, comprehensive exam (for some programs), thesis (for some programs), oral or written exam; for doctorate, comprehensive exam, thesis/dissertation, oral and written exam, internship. *Entrance requirements:* For master's and doctorate, GRE General Test, minimum GPA of 3.0, 3 letters of recommendation, transcripts showing all college or university course work, statement of professional objectives, current curriculum vitae/resume. Additional exam requirements/recommendations for international students: Required—TOEFL (minimum score 550 paper-based; 80 iBT). *Application deadline:* For fall admission, 1/10 priority date for domestic and international students; for spring admission, 9/1 priority date for domestic and international students. Application fee: $75. Electronic applications accepted. *Expenses:* Tuition, state resident: full-time $11,768. Tuition, nonresident: full-time $25,200. *Required fees:* $960. Tuition and fees vary according to program. *Financial support:* In 2014–15, 16 research assistantships (averaging $13,942 per year), 14 teaching assistantships (averaging $13,613 per year) were awarded. Financial award application deadline: 4/1; financial award applicants required to submit FAFSA. *Faculty research:* Multicultural counseling and career development, educational and psychological measurement issues, business decision-making process and power relationships, leadership practices and processes as suffused with and constituted by emotion work. *Total annual research expenditures:* $211,763. *Unit head:* Dr. Kelly Ward, Chair, 509-335-9117, Fax: 509-335-5907, E-mail: kaward@wsu.edu. *Application contact:* Dr. Jason Sievers, Director of Graduate Education, 509-335-9195, E-mail: jasievers@wsu.edu.
Website: http://education.wsu.edu/educational-leadership-sports-studies-educational-counseling-psychology/index.html

Washington University in St. Louis, Brown School of Social Work, St. Louis, MO 63130-4899. Offers affordable housing and mixed-income community management (Certificate); American Indian and Alaska native (MSW); children, youth and families (MSW); health (MSW); individualized (MSW), including health; mental health (MSW); older adults and aging societies (MSW); public health (MPH), including epidemiology/biostatistics, global health, health policy analysis, urban design; social and economic development (MSW); social work (MSW, PhD), including management (MSW), policy (MSW), research (MSW), sexual health and education (MSW), social entrepreneurship (MSW), system dynamics (MSW); violence and injury prevention (Certificate); JD/MSW; M Arch/MSW; MPH/MBA; MSW/M Div; MSW/MAPS; MSW/MBA; MSW/MPH. MSW/M Div and MSW/MAPS offered in partnership with Eden Theological Seminary. *Accreditation:* CSWE (one or more programs are accredited). *Faculty:* 42 full-time (24 women), 81 part-time/adjunct (49 women). *Students:* 272 full-time (229 women); includes 138 minority (47 Black or African American, non-Hispanic/Latino; 11 American Indian or Alaska Native, non-Hispanic/Latino; 54 Asian, non-Hispanic/Latino; 19 Hispanic/Latino; 7 Two or more races, non-Hispanic/Latino), 47 international. Average age 26. 817 applicants, 62% accepted, 303 enrolled. In 2014, 239 master's, 5 doctorates awarded. *Degree requirements:* For master's, 60 credit hours (MSW), 52 credit hours (MPH); practicum; for doctorate, comprehensive exam, thesis/dissertation. *Entrance requirements:* For master's, For public health: GRE, GMAT, LSAT, or MCAT, minimum GPA of 3.0; for doctorate, GRE, MA or MSW. Additional exam requirements/recommendations for international students: Required—TOEFL (minimum score 100 iBT) or IELTS. *Application deadline:* For fall admission, 3/1 priority date for domestic and international students. Applications are processed on a rolling basis. Application fee: $40. Electronic applications accepted. *Expenses:* Expenses: The tuition rate for new full-time MSW students for the 2015-2016 academic year is $38,234 per year. The tuition rate for new full-time MPH students for the 2015-2016 academic year is $33,132 per

year. *Financial support:* In 2014–15, 301 students received support. Fellowships, research assistantships, Federal Work-Study, institutionally sponsored loans, scholarships/grants, health care benefits, tuition waivers (partial), and unspecified assistantships available. Support available to part-time students. Financial award application deadline: 3/1; financial award applicants required to submit FAFSA. *Faculty research:* Mental health services, social development, child welfare, at-risk teens, autism, environmental health, health policy, health communications, obesity, gender and sexuality, violence and injury prevention, chronic disease prevention, poverty, older adults/aging societies, civic engagement, school social work, program evaluation, health disparities. *Unit head:* Jamie L. Adkisson, Director of Recruitment & Admissions, 314-935-3524, Fax: 314-935-4859, E-mail: jadkisson@wustl.edu. *Application contact:* Cate M. Valentine, Admissions Counselor, 314-935-8879, Fax: 314-935-4859, E-mail: cvalentine@wustl.edu.
Website: http://brownschool.wustl.edu

Wayland Baptist University, Graduate Programs, Programs in Behavioral and Social Sciences, Plainview, TX 79072-6998. Offers counseling (MA); government administration (MPA); history (MA); homeland security (MPA); justice administration (MPA). Part-time and evening/weekend programs available. Postbaccalaureate distance learning degree programs offered. *Faculty:* 19 full-time (5 women), 18 part-time/adjunct (8 women). *Students:* 17 full-time (12 women), 428 part-time (264 women); includes 208 minority (66 Black or African American, non-Hispanic/Latino; 6 American Indian or Alaska Native, non-Hispanic/Latino; 14 Asian, non-Hispanic/Latino; 98 Hispanic/Latino; 4 Native Hawaiian or other Pacific Islander, non-Hispanic/Latino; 20 Two or more races, non-Hispanic/Latino). Average age 38. 152 applicants, 93% accepted, 67 enrolled. In 2014, 158 master's awarded. *Degree requirements:* For master's, comprehensive exam. *Entrance requirements:* For master's, GRE, MAT. Additional exam requirements/recommendations for international students: Required—TOEFL (minimum score 500 paper-based; 61 iBT). *Application deadline:* Applications are processed on a rolling basis. Application fee: $50. Electronic applications accepted. *Expenses: Tuition:* Full-time $8910; part-time $495 per credit hour. *Required fees:* $970; $495 per credit hour. $485 per semester. *Financial support:* Federal Work-Study, institutionally sponsored loans, and scholarships/grants available. Support available to part-time students. Financial award application deadline: 5/1; financial award applicants required to submit FAFSA. *Unit head:* Dr. Estelle Owens, Chairman, 806-291-1171, Fax: 806-291-1972, E-mail: owensest@wbu.edu. *Application contact:* Amanda Stanton, Graduate Studies, 806-291-3423, Fax: 806-291-1950, E-mail: stanton@wbu.edu.

Waynesburg University, Graduate and Professional Studies, Canonsburg, PA 15370. Offers business (MBA), including energy management, finance, health systems, human resources, leadership, market development; counseling (MA), including addictions counseling, clinical mental health; education (M Ed, MAT), including autism (M Ed), curriculum and instruction (M Ed), educational leadership (M Ed), online teaching (M Ed); nursing (MSN), including administration, education, informatics; nursing practice (DNP); special education (M Ed); technology (M Ed); MSN/MBA. *Accreditation:* AACN. Part-time and evening/weekend programs available. *Degree requirements:* For doctorate, thesis/dissertation. *Entrance requirements:* Additional exam requirements/recommendations for international students: Required—TOEFL. Electronic applications accepted.

Webster University, College of Arts and Sciences, Department of Behavioral and Social Sciences, Program in Counseling, St. Louis, MO 63119-3194. Offers MA. Part-time programs available. *Entrance requirements:* Additional exam requirements/recommendations for international students: Required—TOEFL.

Western Kentucky University, Graduate Studies, College of Education and Behavioral Sciences, Department of Counseling and Student Affairs, Bowling Green, KY 42101. Offers counseling (MA Ed), including marriage and family therapy, mental health counseling; school counseling (P-12) (MA Ed); student affairs in higher education (MA Ed). *Accreditation:* ACA; NCATE. Part-time and evening/weekend programs available. *Degree requirements:* For master's, comprehensive exam, thesis optional. *Entrance requirements:* For master's, GRE General Test. Additional exam requirements/recommendations for international students: Required—TOEFL (minimum score 555 paper-based; 79 iBT). *Faculty research:* Counselor education, research for residential workers.

Western Michigan University, Graduate College, College of Education and Human Development, Department of Counselor Education and Counseling Psychology, Kalamazoo, MI 49008. Offers counseling psychology (MA, PhD); counselor education (MA, PhD), including counselor education (MA). *Accreditation:* ACA (one or more programs are accredited); APA (one or more programs are accredited); CORE; NCATE. *Degree requirements:* For doctorate, thesis/dissertation. *Application deadline:* For fall admission, 1/15 for domestic students. *Financial support:* Application deadline: 2/15. *Application contact:* Admissions and Orientation, 269-387-2000, Fax: 269-387-2096.

Western Washington University, Graduate School, College of Humanities and Social Sciences, Department of Psychology, Program in Mental Health Counseling, Bellingham, WA 98225-5996. Offers MS. *Accreditation:* ACA. *Degree requirements:* For master's, thesis optional. *Entrance requirements:* For master's, GRE General Test, minimum GPA of 3.0 in last 60 semester hours or last 90 quarter hours. Additional exam requirements/recommendations for international students: Required—TOEFL (minimum score 567 paper-based). Electronic applications accepted.

Westfield State University, Division of Graduate and Continuing Education, Department of Psychology, Westfield, MA 01086. Offers applied behavior analysis (MA); mental health counseling (MA); school guidance (MA). Part-time and evening/weekend programs available. *Degree requirements:* For master's, comprehensive exam. *Entrance requirements:* For master's, GRE General Test, MAT, minimum undergraduate GPA of 2.7.

Westminster College, Master of Science in Mental Health Counseling Program, Salt Lake City, UT 84105-3697. Offers MSMHC. Part-time and evening/weekend programs available. *Faculty:* 4 full-time (all women), 3 part-time/adjunct (2 women). *Students:* 31 full-time (24 women), 13 part-time (9 women); includes 5 minority (1 Asian, non-Hispanic/Latino; 4 Hispanic/Latino). Average age 31. 46 applicants, 52% accepted, 14 enrolled. In 2014, 8 master's awarded. *Degree requirements:* For master's, comprehensive exam, thesis, internship. *Entrance requirements:* For master's, GRE (taken within the past 5 years), evidence of baccalaureate degree from regionally-accredited college or university or a recognized international college or university; official copies of transcripts sent by the registrar of each college or university attended; three letters of recommendation; proof of clear state and federal background checks at the time of admission. Additional exam requirements/recommendations for international students: Required—TOEFL (minimum score 600 paper-based; 100 iBT), IELTS (minimum score 7.5). *Application deadline:* For fall admission, 8/15 for domestic students, 3/15 for international students. Application fee: $50. Electronic applications accepted. *Expenses:* Expenses: Contact institution. *Financial support:* In 2014–15, 1 student received support. Career-related internships or fieldwork, scholarships/grants, unspecified assistantships, and tuition reimbursements, tuition remission available. Support available to part-time students. Financial award applicants required to submit FAFSA. *Faculty research:* Mental health issues, trauma, eating disorder, anxiety, depression, interpersonal relationships. *Unit head:* Colleen Sandor Bennett-Murphy, Director, 801-832-2422, E-mail: lbennett-murphy@westminstercollege.edu. *Application contact:* Dr. John Baworowsky, Vice President of Enrollment Management, 801-832-2200, Fax: 801-832-3101, E-mail: admission@westminstercollege.edu.
Website: http://www.westminstercollege.edu/mspc/

West Virginia University, College of Human Resources and Education, Department of Counseling, Rehabilitation Counseling, and Counseling Psychology, Program in Counseling Psychology, Morgantown, WV 26506. Offers PhD. *Accreditation:* ACA; APA. *Degree requirements:* For doctorate, comprehensive exam, thesis/dissertation, APA-approved 1 year internship. *Entrance requirements:* For doctorate, GRE General Test, interview. Additional exam requirements/recommendations for international students: Required—TOEFL (minimum score 550 paper-based; 65 iBT). Electronic applications accepted.

Wheaton College, Graduate School, Department of Psychology, Wheaton, IL 60187-5593. Offers clinical mental health counseling (MA); clinical psychology (MA, Psy D); counseling ministries (MA); marriage and family therapy (MA). *Accreditation:* APA (one or more programs are accredited). *Students:* 104 full-time (78 women), 22 part-time (14 women); includes 25 minority (13 Black or African American, non-Hispanic/Latino; 8 Asian, non-Hispanic/Latino; 2 Hispanic/Latino; 2 Two or more races, non-Hispanic/Latino), 8 international. Average age 27. 141 applicants, 74% accepted, 64 enrolled. In 2014, 47 master's, 16 doctorates awarded. Terminal master's awarded for partial completion of doctoral program. *Degree requirements:* For master's, thesis or alternative; for doctorate, thesis/dissertation, internship. *Entrance requirements:* For master's, GRE General Test, 18 hours of course work in psychology; for doctorate, GRE General Test. Additional exam requirements/recommendations for international students: Required—TOEFL (minimum score 550 paper-based; 80 iBT), IELTS (minimum score 6.5), TOEFL (minimum score 600 paper-based; 90 iBT) or IELTS (minimum score 7.5) for Psy D. *Application deadline:* For fall admission, 3/1 priority date for domestic students, 1/1 for international students. Applications are processed on a rolling basis. Application fee: $30. *Financial support:* In 2014–15, 3 research assistantships (averaging $4,800 per year) were awarded; career-related internships or fieldwork, Federal Work-Study, scholarships/grants, and unspecified assistantships also available. Financial award application deadline: 3/1; financial award applicants required to submit FAFSA. *Unit head:* Dr. Terri Watson, Associate Dean of Psychology, 630-752-5104. *Application contact:* Dusty Di Santo, Director of Graduate Admissions, 630-752-5195, Fax: 630-752-7047, E-mail: graduate.admissions@wheaton.edu.
Website: http://www.wheaton.edu/academics/departments/psychology

William Carey University, School of Psychology and Counseling, Hattiesburg, MS 39401-5499. Offers counseling psychology (MS). Part-time programs available. *Entrance requirements:* For master's, GRE, PRAXIS, MAT, minimum GPA of 2.5. Additional exam requirements/recommendations for international students: Required—TOEFL (minimum score 550 paper-based). *Expenses:* Contact institution. *Faculty research:* Addiction prevention, psychometric measurement, crisis counseling, gerontology.

William Paterson University of New Jersey, College of Humanities and Social Sciences, Wayne, NJ 07470-8420. Offers applied sociology (MA); clinical and counseling psychology (MA); creative and professional writing (MFA); English (MA); history (MA); public policy and international affairs (MA). Part-time and evening/weekend programs available. *Faculty:* 32 full-time (16 women), 3 part-time/adjunct (1 woman). *Students:* 50 full-time (30 women), 114 part-time (88 women); includes 64 minority (7 Black or African American, non-Hispanic/Latino; 1 American Indian or Alaska Native, non-Hispanic/Latino; 4 Asian, non-Hispanic/Latino; 50 Hispanic/Latino; 2 Two or more races, non-Hispanic/Latino), 2 international. Average age 34. 115 applicants, 81% accepted, 65 enrolled. In 2014, 42 master's awarded. Terminal master's awarded for partial completion of doctoral program. *Degree requirements:* For master's, thesis (for some programs), internship (for some programs). *Entrance requirements:* For master's, GRE/MAT, minimum GPA of 3.0; 2 letters of recommendation; writing sample/personal statement. Additional exam requirements/recommendations for international students: Required—TOEFL (minimum score 550 paper-based; 79 iBT), IELTS (minimum score 6). *Application deadline:* For fall admission, 6/1 for domestic students, 3/1 for international students; for spring admission, 11/1 for domestic students, 10/1 for international students. Applications are processed on a rolling basis. Application fee: $50. Electronic applications accepted. *Expenses:* Tuition, state resident: full-time $12,413; part-time $564.21 per credit. Tuition, nonresident: full-time $20,487; part-time $931.21 per credit. *Required fees:* $2107; $95.79 per credit. $478.95 per semester. Tuition and fees vary according to course load and degree level. *Financial support:* Research assistantships with full tuition reimbursements, Federal Work-Study, scholarships/grants, and unspecified assistantships available. Support available to part-time students. Financial award application deadline: 4/1; financial award applicants required to submit FAFSA. *Faculty research:* Sexual violence, history of science in Muslim societies, bioethics, teaching writing for transfer, psychological impact of microagressions on minority communities. *Unit head:* Dr. Kara Rabbitt, Dean, 973-720-2731, Fax: 973-720-2955, E-mail: rabbittk@wpunj.edu. *Application contact:* Tinu Adeniran, Associate Director, Graduate Admissions, 973-720-2764, Fax: 973-720-2035, E-mail: adenirant@wpunj.edu.
Website: http://www.wpunj.edu/cohss

Wilmington University, College of Social and Behavioral Sciences, New Castle, DE 19720-6491. Offers administration of human services (MS); administration of justice (MS); clinical mental health counseling (MS); homeland security (MS). *Accreditation:* ACA. Part-time and evening/weekend programs available. *Faculty:* 7 full-time (4 women), 70 part-time/adjunct (28 women). *Students:* 175 full-time (141 women), 468 part-time (350 women); includes 296 minority (266 Black or African American, non-Hispanic/Latino; 5 American Indian or Alaska Native, non-Hispanic/Latino; 3 Asian, non-Hispanic/Latino; 18 Hispanic/Latino; 2 Native Hawaiian or other Pacific Islander, non-Hispanic/Latino; 2 Two or more races, non-Hispanic/Latino), 4 international. Average age 35. 251 applicants, 100% accepted, 157 enrolled. In 2014, 170 master's awarded. *Entrance requirements:* Additional exam requirements/recommendations for international students: Required—TOEFL (minimum score 500 paper-based). *Application deadline:* Applications are processed on a rolling basis. Application fee: $35. Electronic applications accepted. *Financial support:* Applicants required to submit FAFSA. *Unit head:* Dr. Christian A. Trowbridge, Dean, 302-295-1151, Fax: 302-328-5164. *Application contact:* Laura Morris, Director of Admissions, 877-967-5464, E-mail: inquire@wilmcoll.edu.
Website: http://www.wilmu.edu/behavioralscience/

Winebrenner Theological Seminary, Graduate Programs, Findlay, OH 45840. Offers clinical counseling (MA); family ministry (MA); practical theology (MA); theological studies (MA); theological/ministerial studies (D Min); theology/ministerial studies (M Div). *Accreditation:* ATS (one or more programs are accredited). Part-time programs available. Postbaccalaureate distance learning degree programs offered (minimal on-campus study). *Faculty:* 5 full-time (1 woman), 9 part-time/adjunct (2 women). *Students:* 26 full-time (11 women), 38 part-time (21 women); includes 8 minority (6 Black or African American, non-Hispanic/Latino; 2 Asian, non-Hispanic/Latino), 4 international. Average age 44. 24 applicants, 100% accepted, 19 enrolled. In 2014, 4 master's, 3 doctorates

awarded. *Degree requirements:* For master's, variable foreign language requirement, thesis (for some programs), supervised ministry; for doctorate, thesis/dissertation, research project. *Entrance requirements:* For doctorate, 3 years of post-M Div full-time ministry. Additional exam requirements/recommendations for international students: Required—TOEFL (minimum score 550 paper-based; 80 iBT). *Application deadline:* For fall admission, 8/15 priority date for domestic students, 7/15 priority date for international students; for winter admission, 12/15 priority date for domestic students, 11/15 priority date for international students; for spring admission, 4/15 priority date for domestic students, 3/15 priority date for international students. Applications are processed on a rolling basis. Application fee: $30. Electronic applications accepted. *Expenses: Tuition:* Full-time $12,555; part-time $465 per credit. *Required fees:* $135 per term. Tuition and fees vary according to degree level. *Financial support:* In 2014–15, 34 students received support, including 3 research assistantships with partial tuition reimbursements available (averaging $1,335 per year), teaching assistantships with partial tuition reimbursements available (averaging $1,335 per year); institutionally sponsored loans, scholarships/grants, tuition waivers (partial), unspecified assistantships, and denominational discounts also available. Financial award applicants required to submit FAFSA. *Faculty research:* Discipleship/spiritual growth, limbic system and pastoral care/counseling, Kingdom of God as central theological motif, series of 10 electronic articles in Logos software for print publication, classic texts of the Old Testament. *Unit head:* Dr. Joel W. Cocklin, Academic Dean, 419-434-4250, Fax: 419-434-4267, E-mail: jcocklin@winebrenner.edu. *Application contact:* Jim Wilder, Coordinator of Admissions, Marketing, and Church Relations, 419-434-4220, Fax: 419-434-4267, E-mail: admissions@winebrenner.edu.
Website: http://www.winebrenner.edu

Wright Institute, Program in Counseling Psychology, Berkeley, CA 94704-1796. Offers MA. Part-time and evening/weekend programs available. *Degree requirements:* For master's, comprehensive exam. *Entrance requirements:* Additional exam requirements/recommendations for international students: Required—TOEFL. Electronic applications accepted. *Faculty research:* Neuroscience, attachment, PTSD, psychotherapy process and outcome.

Xavier University, College of Social Sciences, Health and Education, School of Education, Department of Counseling, Cincinnati, OH 45207. Offers clinical mental health counseling (MA); school counseling (MA). Part-time and evening/weekend programs available. *Faculty:* 5 full-time (2 women), 10 part-time/adjunct (6 women). *Students:* 65 full-time (54 women), 75 part-time (60 women); includes 25 minority (14 Black or African American, non-Hispanic/Latino; 2 Asian, non-Hispanic/Latino; 7 Hispanic/Latino; 1 Native Hawaiian or other Pacific Islander, non-Hispanic/Latino; 1 Two or more races, non-Hispanic/Latino), 2 international. Average age 32. 56 applicants, 63% accepted, 16 enrolled. In 2014, 59 master's awarded. *Degree requirements:* For master's, internship. *Entrance requirements:* For master's, GRE or MAT, minimum GPA of 3.0; 2 letters of recommendation; resume; official transcript; statement of purpose. Additional exam requirements/recommendations for international students: Required—TOEFL (minimum score 550 paper-based; 79 iBT). *Application deadline:* For fall admission, 3/1 priority date for domestic and international students; for winter admission, 4/1 for domestic and international students; for spring admission, 10/1 priority date for domestic and international students; for summer admission, 3/1 priority date for domestic and international students. Application fee: $35. Electronic applications accepted. Application fee is waived when completed online. *Expenses:* Expenses: $568 per credit hour. *Financial support:* In 2014–15, 96 students received support. Tuition waivers (partial) and unspecified assistantships available. *Faculty research:* Supervision, ethics, consultation, self-injury, bullying. *Unit head:* Dr. Brent Richardson, Chair, 513-745-4294, Fax: 513-745-2920, E-mail: richardb@xavier.edu. *Application contact:* Roger Bosse, Graduate Services Director, 513-745-3357, Fax: 513-745-1048, E-mail: bosse@xavier.edu.
Website: http://www.xavier.edu/counseling/

Yeshiva University, Ferkauf Graduate School of Psychology, Program in Mental Health Counseling Psychology, New York, NY 10033-3201. Offers MA. Part-time programs available. *Entrance requirements:* For master's, GRE General Test. *Faculty research:* Substance abuse treatment, group therapy.

Youngstown State University, Graduate School, Beeghly College of Education, Department of Counseling, Youngstown, OH 44555-0001. Offers community counseling (MS Ed); school counseling (MS Ed). *Accreditation:* ACA; NCATE. Part-time and evening/weekend programs available. *Degree requirements:* For master's, comprehensive exam. *Entrance requirements:* For master's, MAT, interview, minimum GPA of 2.7. Additional exam requirements/recommendations for international students: Required—TOEFL. *Faculty research:* Suicide, euthanasia, ethical issues, marriage and family.

Developmental Psychology

Andrews University, School of Graduate Studies, School of Education, Department of Graduate Psychology and Counseling, Program in Educational and Developmental Psychology, Berrien Springs, MI 49104. Offers educational and developmental psychology (MA); educational psychology (Ed D, PhD). *Students:* 15 full-time (12 women), 7 part-time (5 women); includes 6 minority (3 Black or African American, non-Hispanic/Latino; 2 Asian, non-Hispanic/Latino; 1 Hispanic/Latino), 8 international. Average age 38. 13 applicants, 38% accepted, 1 enrolled. In 2014, 5 master's awarded. *Degree requirements:* For master's, thesis optional. *Entrance requirements:* For master's, GRE. Additional exam requirements/recommendations for international students: Required—TOEFL (minimum score 550 paper-based). *Application deadline:* Applications are processed on a rolling basis. Application fee: $40. Tuition and fees vary according to course level. *Unit head:* Dr. Jimmy Kijai, Coordinator, 269-471-6240. *Application contact:* Monica Wringer, Supervisor of Graduate Admission, 800-253-2874, Fax: 269-471-6321, E-mail: graduate@andrews.edu.

Arizona State University at the Tempe campus, College of Liberal Arts and Sciences, Department of Psychology, Tempe, AZ 85287-1104. Offers applied behavior analysis (MS); behavioral neuroscience (PhD); clinical psychology (PhD); cognitive science (PhD); developmental psychology (PhD); quantitative psychology (PhD); social psychology (PhD). *Accreditation:* APA. *Degree requirements:* For doctorate, comprehensive exam, thesis/dissertation, interactive Program of Study (iPOS) submitted before completing 50 percent of required credit hours. *Entrance requirements:* For doctorate, GRE General Test, GRE Subject Test, minimum GPA of 3.0 or equivalent in last 2 years of work leading to bachelor's degree. Additional exam requirements/recommendations for international students: Required—TOEFL, IELTS, or PTE. Electronic applications accepted.

Bay Path University, Program in Developmental Psychology, Longmeadow, MA 01106-2292. Offers developmental psychology (MS); mental health counseling (MS). Part-time and evening/weekend programs available. *Students:* 3 full-time (all women), 10 part-time (all women); includes 4 minority (3 Black or African American, non-Hispanic/Latino; 1 Asian, non-Hispanic/Latino). Average age 35. 13 applicants, 77% accepted, 9 enrolled. In 2014, 11 master's awarded. *Degree requirements:* For master's, nine core courses (27 credits) and three elective courses (9 credits); 160 hours of community-based field work. *Entrance requirements:* For master's, bachelor's degree in psychology or related field; minimum cumulative GPA of 3.0; working knowledge of statistics, research methods, abnormal psychology, personality, and developmental psychology (strongly recommended). *Application deadline:* Applications are processed on a rolling basis. Application fee: $45. Electronic applications accepted. Application fee is waived when completed online. *Financial support:* In 2014–15, 3 students received support. Scholarships/grants available. Financial award applicants required to submit FAFSA. *Unit head:* Dr. Mark Benander, Program Director, 413-565-1332. *Application contact:* Diane Ranaldi, Dean of Graduate Admissions, 413-565-1332, Fax: 413-565-1250, E-mail: dranaldi@baypath.edu.
Website: http://graduate.baypath.edu/Graduate-Programs/Programs-On-Campus/MS-Programs/Developmental-Psychology

Boston College, Lynch Graduate School of Education, Program in Applied Developmental and Educational Psychology, Chestnut Hill, MA 02467-3800. Offers MA, PhD. Part-time and evening/weekend programs available. Terminal master's awarded for partial completion of doctoral program. *Degree requirements:* For master's, comprehensive exam; for doctorate, comprehensive exam, thesis/dissertation. *Entrance requirements:* For master's and doctorate, GRE General Test. Additional exam requirements/recommendations for international students: Required—TOEFL (minimum score 100 iBT). Electronic applications accepted. *Faculty research:* Cognitive learning and culture, effects of social policy reform on children and families, psychosocial trauma, human rights and international justice, positive youth development, children and adolescents living in poverty.

Boston Graduate School of Psychoanalysis, CAGS and Certificate Programs, Brookline, MA 02446-4602. Offers child and adolescent intervention (CAGS); psychoanalysis (Certificate); psychoanalytic psychotherapy (CAGS). Part-time programs available. *Degree requirements:* For other advanced degree, thesis. *Entrance requirements:* For degree, interview, BA, writing sample, 3 letters of reference, transcripts. Additional exam requirements/recommendations for international students: Required—TOEFL (minimum score 550 paper-based; 79 iBT). *Faculty research:* Treatment approaches for intractable patients, unconscious symbolic processes, female adolescent development, evaluation of school mental health interventions, development of symbolic processes in early childhood.

Bowling Green State University, Graduate College, College of Arts and Sciences, Department of Psychology, Bowling Green, OH 43403. Offers clinical psychology (MA, PhD); developmental psychology (MA, PhD); experimental psychology (MA, PhD); industrial/organizational psychology (MA, PhD); quantitative psychology (MA, PhD). *Accreditation:* APA (one or more programs are accredited). *Degree requirements:* For doctorate, thesis/dissertation. *Entrance requirements:* For doctorate, GRE General Test, GRE Subject Test. Additional exam requirements/recommendations for international students: Required—TOEFL. Electronic applications accepted. *Faculty research:* Personnel psychology, developmental-mathematical models, behavioral medication, brain process, child/adolescent social cognition.

Brandeis University, Graduate School of Arts and Sciences, Department of Psychology, Waltham, MA 02454-9110. Offers brain, body and behavior (PhD); cognitive neuroscience (PhD); general psychology (MA); social/developmental psychology (PhD). Part-time programs available. Terminal master's awarded for partial completion of doctoral program. *Degree requirements:* For master's, thesis; for doctorate, thesis/dissertation, research reports. *Entrance requirements:* For master's and doctorate, GRE General Test; GRE Subject Test (recommended), 3 letters of recommendation, statement of purpose, transcript(s), resume. Additional exam requirements/recommendations for international students: Required—TOEFL (minimum score 600 paper-based; 100 iBT), PTE (minimum score 68); Recommended—IELTS (minimum score 7). Electronic applications accepted. *Faculty research:* Cognitive neuroscience, social developmental psychology, motor control, visual perception, taste physiology and psychophysics, memory, learning, aging, child development, aggression, emotion, personality and cognition in adulthood and old age, social relations and health, stereotypes, nonverbal communication.

Capella University, Harold Abel School of Social and Behavioral Science, Master's Programs in Counseling, Minneapolis, MN 55402. Offers child and adolescent development (MS); general addiction counseling (MS); general marriage and family counseling/therapy (MS); general mental health counseling (MS); general school counseling (MS).

Carnegie Mellon University, Dietrich College of Humanities and Social Sciences, Department of Psychology, Area of Developmental Psychology, Pittsburgh, PA 15213-3891. Offers PhD. *Degree requirements:* For doctorate, comprehensive exam, thesis/dissertation. *Entrance requirements:* For doctorate, GRE General Test. Additional exam requirements/recommendations for international students: Required—TOEFL. *Faculty research:* Cognitive development, language acquisition.

Chatham University, Program in Counseling Psychology, Pittsburgh, PA 15232-2826. Offers child, adolescent and family (MSCP); counseling psychology (Psy D); health and holistic (MSCP); infant mental health (MSCP); organization and supervision (MSCP); sport and exercise (MSCP). Part-time and evening/weekend programs available. *Faculty:* 12 full-time (9 women), 13 part-time/adjunct (9 women). *Students:* 102 full-time (85 women), 38 part-time (32 women); includes 17 minority (7 Black or African American, non-Hispanic/Latino; 2 Asian, non-Hispanic/Latino; 6 Hispanic/Latino; 2 Two or more races, non-Hispanic/Latino), 7 international. Average age 29. 145 applicants, 73% accepted, 59 enrolled. In 2014, 67 master's, 3 doctorates awarded. *Degree requirements:* For master's, thesis optional, supervised internship; for doctorate, thesis/dissertation, internship. *Entrance requirements:* For master's, minimum GPA of 3.0; 2 letters of recommendation; resume; prerequisite coursework in statistics, biology, and psychology; for doctorate, GRE. Additional exam requirements/recommendations for international students: Required—TOEFL (minimum score 600 paper-based; 100 iBT), IELTS (minimum score 7), TWE. *Application deadline:* For fall admission, 4/1 priority date for domestic and international students; for spring admission, 11/1 for domestic

students, 10/1 for international students. Applications are processed on a rolling basis. Application fee: $45. Electronic applications accepted. Application fee is waived when completed online. *Expenses: Tuition:* Full-time $15,318; part-time $851 per credit hour. *Required fees:* $440; $24 per credit hour. Tuition and fees vary according to course load, program and reciprocity agreements. *Financial support:* Career-related internships or fieldwork available. Financial award applicants required to submit FAFSA. *Faculty research:* Trauma and recovery, hypnosis, psychospiritual dimensions of healing, psychotherapy of schizophrenia. *Unit head:* Dr. Mary Beth Mannarino, Director, 412-365-1196, Fax: 412-365-1505, E-mail: mmannarino@chatham.edu. *Application contact:* Katie Noel, Assistant Director of Graduate Admission, 412-365-2758, Fax: 412-365-1609, E-mail: gradadmissions@chatham.edu.
Website: http://www.chatham.edu/mscp

Claremont Graduate University, Graduate Programs, School of Social Science, Policy and Evaluation, Department of Psychology, Claremont, CA 91711-6160. Offers advanced study in evaluation (Certificate); cognitive psychology (MA, PhD); developmental psychology (MA, PhD); evaluation and applied research methods (MA, PhD); health behavior research and evaluation (MA, PhD); human resource development and evaluation (MA); industrial/organizational psychology (MA, PhD); organizational behavior (MA, PhD); organizational psychology (MA, PhD); social psychology (MA, PhD); MBA/PhD. Part-time programs available. *Faculty:* 18 full-time (7 women), 1 part-time/adjunct (0 women). *Students:* 256 full-time (160 women), 70 part-time (50 women); includes 93 minority (17 Black or African American, non-Hispanic/Latino; 3 American Indian or Alaska Native, non-Hispanic/Latino; 26 Asian, non-Hispanic/Latino; 30 Hispanic/Latino; 17 Two or more races, non-Hispanic/Latino), 35 international. Average age 30. In 2014, 56 master's, 15 doctorates, 7 other advanced degrees awarded. Terminal master's awarded for partial completion of doctoral program. *Entrance requirements:* For master's and doctorate, GRE General Test. Additional exam requirements/recommendations for international students: Required—TOEFL (minimum score 550 paper-based; 80 iBT). *Application deadline:* For fall admission, 1/15 priority date for domestic and international students. Applications are processed on a rolling basis. Application fee: $80. Electronic applications accepted. *Expenses: Tuition:* Full-time $41,784; part-time $1741 per credit. *Required fees:* $600; $300 per semester. *Financial support:* Fellowships, research assistantships, teaching assistantships, Federal Work-Study, institutionally sponsored loans, scholarships/grants, and tuition waivers (full and partial) available. Support available to part-time students. Financial award application deadline: 2/15; financial award applicants required to submit FAFSA. *Faculty research:* Social intervention, diversity in organizations, eyewitness memory, aging and cognition, drug policy. *Unit head:* William Crano, Chair, 909-621-8084, E-mail: william.crano@cgu.edu. *Application contact:* Annekah Hall, Assistant Director of Admissions, 909-607-3371, E-mail: annekah.hall@cgu.edu.
Website: http://www.cgu.edu/pages/502.asp

Clark University, Graduate School, Hiatt School of Psychology, Program in Developmental Psychology, Worcester, MA 01610-1477. Offers PhD. *Students:* 8 full-time (7 women), 1 part-time (0 women); includes 1 minority (Asian, non-Hispanic/Latino), 2 international. Average age 28. In 2014, 1 doctorate awarded. *Degree requirements:* For doctorate, thesis/dissertation. *Entrance requirements:* For doctorate, GRE General Test. Additional exam requirements/recommendations for international students: Required—TOEFL. *Application deadline:* For fall admission, 12/15 priority date for domestic students, 12/15 for international students. Applications are processed on a rolling basis. Application fee: $75. *Expenses: Tuition:* Full-time $40,380; part-time $1262 per credit hour. *Required fees:* $30. *Financial support:* In 2014–15, fellowships with full tuition reimbursements (averaging $16,015 per year), research assistantships with full tuition reimbursements (averaging $16,015 per year), teaching assistantships with full tuition reimbursements (averaging $16,015 per year) were awarded; tuition waivers (full) also available. *Faculty research:* Development of psychological processes in sociocultural context, conceptualizing and reasoning, symbolization, parental structure in families of adolescents, transition to kindergarten. *Unit head:* Dr. Lene Jensen, Chair, 508-793-7274, E-mail: ljensen@clarku.edu. *Application contact:* Kelly Boulay, Departmental Administrator, 508-793-7274, Fax: 508-793-7265, E-mail: psychology@clarku.edu.
Website: http://www.clarku.edu/departments/psychology/grad/developmental/index.cfm

Clayton State University, School of Graduate Studies, College of Arts and Sciences, Program in Psychology, Morrow, GA 30260-0285. Offers applied developmental psychology (MS); clinical psychology (MS). *Entrance requirements:* For master's, GRE, 2 official transcripts; 3 letters of recommendation; statement of purpose; on-campus interview; background check. Additional exam requirements/recommendations for international students: Required—TOEFL (minimum score 550 paper-based). Electronic applications accepted.

Cornell University, Graduate School, Graduate Fields of Human Ecology, Field of Human Development, Ithaca, NY 14853-0001. Offers developmental psychology (MA, PhD), including cognitive development, developmental psychopathology, ecology of human development, social and personality development; human development and family studies (MA, PhD), including ecology of human development, family studies and the life course. *Degree requirements:* For doctorate, comprehensive exam, thesis/dissertation, pre-doctoral research project, teaching experience. *Entrance requirements:* For doctorate, GRE General Test, 2 letters of recommendation. Additional exam requirements/recommendations for international students: Required—TOEFL (minimum score 550 paper-based; 77 iBT). Electronic applications accepted. *Faculty research:* Cognitive development, developmental psychopathology, ecology of human development, family studies and the life course, social and personality development.

Delaware Valley University, Program in Counseling Psychology, Doylestown, PA 18901-2697. Offers child and adolescent therapy (MA); social justice community counseling (MA).

Duke University, Graduate School, Department of Psychology and Neuroscience, Durham, NC 27708. Offers biological psychology (PhD); clinical psychology (PhD); cognitive psychology (PhD); developmental psychology (PhD); experimental psychology (PhD); health psychology (PhD); human social development (PhD); JD/MA. *Accreditation:* APA (one or more programs are accredited). *Degree requirements:* For doctorate, thesis/dissertation. *Entrance requirements:* For doctorate, GRE General Test. Additional exam requirements/recommendations for international students: Required—TOEFL (minimum score 577 paper-based; 90 iBT) or IELTS (minimum score 7). Electronic applications accepted. *Expenses: Tuition:* Full-time $45,760; part-time $2765 per credit. *Required fees:* $978. Full-time tuition and fees vary according to program.

Emory University, Laney Graduate School, Department of Psychology, Atlanta, GA 30322-1100. Offers clinical psychology (PhD); cognition and development (PhD); neuroscience and animal behavior (PhD). *Accreditation:* APA. *Degree requirements:* For doctorate, comprehensive exam, thesis/dissertation. *Entrance requirements:* For doctorate, GRE General Test, minimum GPA of 3.25. Additional exam requirements/recommendations for international students: Required—TOEFL. Electronic applications accepted. *Faculty research:* Neuroscience and animal behavior; adult and child psychopathology, cognition development assessment.

Erikson Institute, Academic Programs, Chicago, IL 60654. Offers administration (Certificate); bilingual/ESL (Certificate); child development (MS); early childhood education (MS); infant mental health (Certificate); infant studies (Certificate); MS/MSW. MS/MSW offered jointly with Loyola University Chicago. Part-time and evening/weekend programs available. *Degree requirements:* For master's, comprehensive exam, internship; for Certificate, internship. *Entrance requirements:* For master's and Certificate, minimum GPA of 2.75. Additional exam requirements/recommendations for international students: Required—TOEFL. *Faculty research:* Assessment strategies from early childhood through elementary years; language, literacy, and the arts in children's development; inclusive special education; parent-child relationships; cognitive development.

Florida International University, College of Arts and Sciences, Department of Psychology, Miami, FL 33199. Offers behavioral analysis (MS); clinical science (PhD); counseling psychology (MS); developmental science (MS, PhD); legal psychology (PhD); organizational psychology (MS, PhD). Program has fall admissions only. Part-time and evening/weekend programs available. Terminal master's awarded for partial completion of doctoral program. *Degree requirements:* For master's, thesis; for doctorate, comprehensive exam, thesis/dissertation. *Entrance requirements:* For master's, GRE General Test, minimum GPA of 3.0, resume, 3 letters of recommendation; for doctorate, GRE General Test, 3 letters of recommendation, resume, letter of intent, two writing samples, minimum GPA of 3.0. Additional exam requirements/recommendations for international students: Required—TOEFL (minimum score 550 paper-based; 80 iBT). Electronic applications accepted. *Faculty research:* Legal psychology, organizational and industrial psychology, child behavior psychology.

Florida State University, The Graduate School, College of Arts and Sciences, Department of Psychology, Program in Developmental Psychology, Tallahassee, FL 32306. Offers PhD. *Faculty:* 12 full-time (5 women). *Students:* 8 full-time (6 women); includes 3 minority (all Black or African American, non-Hispanic/Latino). Average age 26. 17 applicants, 12% accepted. Terminal master's awarded for partial completion of doctoral program. *Degree requirements:* For doctorate, comprehensive exam, thesis/dissertation. *Entrance requirements:* For doctorate, GRE General Test, minimum GPA of 3.0, research experience, letters of recommendation. Additional exam requirements/recommendations for international students: Required—TOEFL (minimum score 550 paper-based; 80 iBT). *Application deadline:* For fall admission, 12/15 for domestic and international students. Application fee: $30. Electronic applications accepted. *Expenses:* Tuition, state resident: part-time $403.51 per credit hour. Tuition, nonresident: part-time $1004.85 per credit hour. *Required fees:* $75.81 per credit hour. One-time fee: $20 part-time. Tuition and fees vary according to campus/location. *Financial support:* In 2014–15, 8 students received support, including 4 fellowships with full tuition reimbursements available (averaging $20,000 per year), 1 research assistantship with full tuition reimbursement available (averaging $20,000 per year), 3 teaching assistantships with full tuition reimbursements available (averaging $17,775 per year); Federal Work-Study, institutionally sponsored loans, scholarships/grants, health care benefits, and unspecified assistantships also available. Financial award application deadline: 12/15. *Faculty research:* Learning disabilities, phonological processing, psychology of reading, emergent literacy, aging. *Unit head:* Dr. Christopher Schatschneider, Director, 850-644-4323, Fax: 850-644-7739, E-mail: schatschneider@psy.fsu.edu. *Application contact:* Cherie P. Miller, Graduate Program Assistant, 850-644-2499, Fax: 850-644-7739, E-mail: grad-info@psy.fsu.edu.
Website: http://www.psy.fsu.edu

Fordham University, Graduate School of Arts and Sciences, Department of Psychology, Program in Applied Developmental Psychology, New York, NY 10458. Offers PhD. *Students:* 21 full-time (18 women), 9 part-time (6 women); includes 6 minority (2 Black or African American, non-Hispanic/Latino; 3 Asian, non-Hispanic/Latino; 1 Hispanic/Latino), 7 international. Average age 31. 29 applicants, 21% accepted, 5 enrolled. In 2014, 8 doctorates awarded. *Degree requirements:* For doctorate, comprehensive exam, thesis/dissertation. *Entrance requirements:* For doctorate, GRE General Test, GRE Subject Test. Additional exam requirements/recommendations for international students: Required—TOEFL (minimum score 600 paper-based). *Application deadline:* For fall admission, 12/14 for domestic students. Application fee: $70. Electronic applications accepted. *Financial support:* In 2014–15, 15 students received support, including 1 fellowship with tuition reimbursement available (averaging $24,890 per year), 1 research assistantship with tuition reimbursement available (averaging $22,240 per year), 10 teaching assistantships with tuition reimbursements available (averaging $20,223 per year); career-related internships or fieldwork, institutionally sponsored loans, tuition waivers (full and partial), and unspecified assistantships also available. Financial award application deadline: 12/14. *Faculty research:* Development of citizenship, impact of participation in community service, impact of poverty on children, development of moral reasoning and behavior. *Unit head:* Dr. Barry Rosenfeld, Director, 718-817-3794, Fax: 718-817-3785, E-mail: tyip@fordham.edu. *Application contact:* Bernadette Valentino-Morrison, Director of Graduate Admissions, 718-817-4419, Fax: 718-817-3566, E-mail: valentinomor@fordham.edu.

George Mason University, College of Humanities and Social Sciences, Department of Psychology, Fairfax, VA 22030. Offers applied developmental psychology (Certificate); cognitive and behavioral neuroscience (MA); human factors/applied cognition (MA); industrial/organizational psychology (MA, PhD); school psychology (MA). *Accreditation:* APA. *Faculty:* 43 full-time (22 women), 13 part-time/adjunct (8 women). *Students:* 167 full-time (114 women), 48 part-time (34 women); includes 41 minority (7 Black or African American, non-Hispanic/Latino; 8 Asian, non-Hispanic/Latino; 21 Hispanic/Latino; 1 Native Hawaiian or other Pacific Islander, non-Hispanic/Latino; 4 Two or more races, non-Hispanic/Latino), 10 international. Average age 27. 833 applicants, 14% accepted, 75 enrolled. In 2014, 49 master's, 17 doctorates, 10 other advanced degrees awarded. *Degree requirements:* For master's, comprehensive exam, thesis (for biopsychology); for doctorate, comprehensive exam, thesis/dissertation, 2nd year project. *Entrance requirements:* For master's, GRE, 2 official transcripts; goals statement; 15 undergraduate credits in concentration for which the applicant is applying; for doctorate, GRE, 3 letters of recommendation; resume; goals statement; minimum GPA of 3.0 overall for last 60 undergraduate credits, 3.25 in psychology courses; 15 undergraduate credits in concentration for which the applicant is applying; 2 official transcripts; for Certificate, GRE, 2 official transcripts; expanded goals statement; 3 letters of recommendation. Additional exam requirements/recommendations for international students: Required—TOEFL (minimum score 570 paper-based; 80 iBT), IELTS (minimum score 6.5), PTE. Application fee: $65 ($80 for international students). Electronic applications accepted. *Expenses:* Tuition, state resident: full-time $9794; part-time $408 per credit hour. Tuition, nonresident: full-time $26,978; part-time $1124 per credit hour. *Required fees:* $2820; $118 per credit hour. Tuition and fees vary according to course load and program. *Financial support:* In 2014–15, 130 students received support, including 6 fellowships (averaging $6,576 per year), 84 research assistantships with full and partial tuition reimbursements available (averaging $15,356 per year), 63 teaching assistantships with full and partial tuition reimbursements available (averaging $13,274 per year); career-related internships or fieldwork, Federal Work-Study, scholarships/grants, tuition waivers (partial), unspecified assistantships, and health care benefits (for full-time research or teaching assistantship recipients) also

available. Support available to part-time students. Financial award application deadline: 3/1; financial award applicants required to submit FAFSA. *Faculty research:* Applied developmental psychology, biopsychology, clinical psychology, human factors/applied cognition psychology, industrial/organizational psychology, school psychology. *Total annual research expenditures:* $5.2 million. *Unit head:* Reeshad Dalal, Department Chair, 703-993-9487, Fax: 703-993-1359, E-mail: rdalal@gmu.edu. *Application contact:* Adam Winsler, Associate Chair of Graduate Studies, 703-993-1881, Fax: 703-993-1359, E-mail: awinsler@gmu.edu.
Website: http://psychology.gmu.edu

Georgia State University, College of Arts and Sciences, Department of Psychology, Atlanta, GA 30302-3083. Offers clinical (PhD); cognitive sciences (PhD); community (PhD); developmental (PhD); neuropsychology and behavioral neuroscience (PhD). *Accreditation:* APA. *Faculty:* 29 full-time (17 women). *Students:* 116 full-time (95 women), 2 part-time (both women); includes 30 minority (10 Black or African American, non-Hispanic/Latino; 9 Asian, non-Hispanic/Latino; 6 Hispanic/Latino; 5 Two or more races, non-Hispanic/Latino), 10 international. Average age 28. 577 applicants, 7% accepted, 27 enrolled. In 2014, 16 doctorates awarded. *Degree requirements:* For doctorate, comprehensive exam, thesis/dissertation, residency year (for clinical only). *Entrance requirements:* For doctorate, GRE. Additional exam requirements/recommendations for international students: Required—TOEFL (minimum score 550 paper-based; 80 iBT). *Application deadline:* For fall admission, 12/1 for domestic and international students. Application fee: $50. Electronic applications accepted. *Expenses:* Tuition, state resident: full-time $6516; part-time $362 per credit hour. Tuition, nonresident: full-time $22,014; part-time $1223 per credit hour. *Required fees:* $2128 per semester. Tuition and fees vary according to course load and program. *Financial support:* In 2014–15, fellowships with full tuition reimbursements (averaging $19,282 per year), research assistantships with full tuition reimbursements (averaging $5,173 per year), teaching assistantships with full tuition reimbursements (averaging $6,389 per year) were awarded; scholarships/grants, traineeships, health care benefits, and unspecified assistantships also available. *Faculty research:* Clinical psychology, developmental psychology, community psychology, neuropsychology and behavioral neuroscience, cognitive sciences. *Unit head:* Dr. Lisa Armistead, Chair, 404-413-6205, Fax: 404-413-6207, E-mail: lparmistead@gsu.edu. *Application contact:* Dr. Lindsey Cohen, Director of Graduate Studies, 404-413-6263, Fax: 404-413-6207, E-mail: llcohen@gsu.edu.
Website: http://psychology.gsu.edu/graduate/areas-of-study/

The Graduate Center, City University of New York, Graduate Studies, Program in Psychology, New York, NY 10016-4039. Offers basic applied neurocognition (PhD); biopsychology (PhD); clinical psychology (PhD); developmental psychology (PhD); environmental psychology (PhD); experimental psychology (PhD); industrial psychology (PhD); learning processes (PhD); neuropsychology (PhD); psychology (PhD); social personality (PhD). *Degree requirements:* For doctorate, one foreign language, thesis/dissertation. *Entrance requirements:* For doctorate, GRE General Test. Additional exam requirements/recommendations for international students: Required—TOEFL. Electronic applications accepted.

Harvard University, Graduate School of Arts and Sciences, Department of Psychology, Cambridge, MA 02138. Offers psychology (PhD), including behavior and decision analysis, cognition, developmental psychology, experimental psychology, personality, psychobiology, psychopathology; social psychology (PhD). *Accreditation:* APA. *Degree requirements:* For doctorate, thesis/dissertation, general exams. *Entrance requirements:* For doctorate, GRE General Test. Additional exam requirements/recommendations for international students: Required—TOEFL.

Howard University, Graduate School, Department of Psychology, Washington, DC 20059-0002. Offers clinical psychology (PhD); developmental psychology (PhD); experimental psychology (PhD); neuropsychology (PhD); personality psychology (PhD); psychology (MS); social psychology (PhD). *Accreditation:* APA (one or more programs are accredited). Part-time programs available. *Degree requirements:* For master's, thesis; for doctorate, comprehensive exam, thesis/dissertation, qualifying exam. *Entrance requirements:* For master's, GRE General Test, minimum GPA of 2.5, bachelor's degree in psychology or related field; for doctorate, GRE General Test, minimum GPA of 3.0. *Faculty research:* Personality and psychophysiology, educational and social development of African-American children, child and adult psychopathology.

Illinois State University, Graduate School, College of Arts and Sciences, Department of Psychology, Normal, IL 61790-2200. Offers psychology (MA, MS), including clinical psychology, counseling psychology, developmental psychology, educational psychology, experimental psychology, measurement-evaluation, organizational-industrial psychology; school psychology (PhD, SSP). *Accreditation:* APA. *Degree requirements:* For master's, thesis or alternative; for doctorate, variable foreign language requirement, thesis/dissertation, 2 terms of residency, internship, practicum. *Entrance requirements:* For master's, GRE General Test, GRE Subject Test, minimum GPA of 3.0 in last 60 hours of course work; for doctorate, GRE General Test. *Faculty research:* Comprehensive evaluation system for the central region professional development grant, Illinois school psychology internship consortium, for children's sake.

Indiana University Bloomington, University Graduate School, College of Arts and Sciences, Department of Psychological and Brain Sciences, Bloomington, IN 47405. Offers clinical science (PhD); cognitive neuroscience (PhD); cognitive psychology (PhD); developmental psychology (PhD); methods of behavior (PhD); molecular systems neuroscience (PhD); social psychology (PhD). *Accreditation:* APA. *Faculty:* 54 full-time (15 women). *Students:* 95 full-time (56 women); includes 19 minority (4 Black or African American, non-Hispanic/Latino; 7 Asian, non-Hispanic/Latino; 7 Hispanic/Latino; 1 Two or more races, non-Hispanic/Latino), 16 international. Average age 24. 364 applicants, 10% accepted, 20 enrolled. In 2014, 9 doctorates awarded. *Degree requirements:* For doctorate, comprehensive exam, 90 credit hours, 2 advanced statistics/methods courses, 2 written research projects, the teaching of psychology course, teaching 1 semester of undergraduate methods course, qualifying examination, minor or a second major, first-year research seminar course, dissertation defense, written dissertation. *Entrance requirements:* For doctorate, GRE. Additional exam requirements/recommendations for international students: Required—TOEFL (minimum score 550 paper-based; 79 iBT). *Application deadline:* For fall admission, 12/1 for domestic and international students. Application fee: $55 ($65 for international students). Electronic applications accepted. *Financial support:* Fellowships with full tuition reimbursements, research assistantships with full tuition reimbursements, teaching assistantships with full tuition reimbursements, career-related internships or fieldwork, scholarships/grants, traineeships, health care benefits, and unspecified assistantships available. *Faculty research:* Clinical science, cognitive neuroscience, cognitive psychology, developmental psychology, mechanisms of behavior, molecular and systems neuroscience, social psychology. *Unit head:* Dr. William Hetrick, Chair, 812-855-2012, Fax: 812-855-4691, E-mail: whetrick@indiana.edu. *Application contact:* Dale Sengelaub, Graduate Admissions, 812-855-9149, Fax: 812-855-4691, E-mail: psychgrd@indiana.edu.
Website: http://www.psych.indiana.edu

La Salle University, School of Arts and Sciences, Program in Clinical Psychology, Philadelphia, PA 19141-1199. Offers child clinical psychology (Psy D); clinical health

psychology (Psy D); clinical psychology (MA); general practice psychology (Psy D). *Accreditation:* AAMFT/COAMFTE. Part-time and evening/weekend programs available. Terminal master's awarded for partial completion of doctoral program. *Degree requirements:* For doctorate, comprehensive exam, thesis/dissertation. *Entrance requirements:* For doctorate, GRE (minimum scores of 148 on both the Verbal Reasoning and Quantitative Reasoning sections strongly recommended); GRE Subject Test in psychology for those entering with bachelor's degree, baccalaureate degree from accredited institution with major in psychology or related discipline; minimum undergraduate GPA of 3.0, 3.2 graduate; three letters of recommendation; statement of interest and intent; curriculum vitae or resume; personal interview. Additional exam requirements/recommendations for international students: Required—TOEFL. Electronic applications accepted. Application fee is waived when completed online. *Expenses:* Contact institution.

Louisiana State University and Agricultural & Mechanical College, Graduate School, College of Humanities and Social Sciences, Department of Psychology, Baton Rouge, LA 70803. Offers biological psychology (MA, PhD); clinical psychology (MA, PhD); cognitive psychology (MA, PhD); developmental psychology (MA, PhD); school psychology (MA, PhD). PhD programs offered jointly with Southeastern Louisiana University. *Accreditation:* APA (one or more programs are accredited). *Faculty:* 22 full-time (10 women). *Students:* 67 full-time (54 women), 30 part-time (21 women); includes 13 minority (4 Black or African American, non-Hispanic/Latino; 3 Asian, non-Hispanic/Latino; 3 Hispanic/Latino; 3 Two or more races, non-Hispanic/Latino), 3 international. Average age 27. 221 applicants, 10% accepted, 22 enrolled. In 2014, 13 master's, 18 doctorates awarded. Terminal master's awarded for partial completion of doctoral program. *Degree requirements:* For master's, thesis; for doctorate, thesis/dissertation, 1-year internship. *Entrance requirements:* For master's and doctorate, GRE General Test, minimum GPA of 3.0. Additional exam requirements/recommendations for international students: Required—TOEFL (minimum score 550 paper-based; 79 iBT), IELTS (minimum score 6.5), or PTE (minimum score 59). *Application deadline:* For fall admission, 1/1 priority date for domestic students, 5/15 for international students; for spring admission, 10/15 for domestic and international students; for summer admission, 5/15 for domestic students, 5/5 for international students. Applications are processed on a rolling basis. Application fee: $50 ($70 for international students). Electronic applications accepted. *Financial support:* In 2014–15, 90 students received support, including 2 fellowships (averaging $15,763 per year), 8 research assistantships with partial tuition reimbursements available (averaging $16,669 per year), 49 teaching assistantships with partial tuition reimbursements available (averaging $13,003 per year); career-related internships or fieldwork, Federal Work-Study, institutionally sponsored loans, scholarships/grants, health care benefits, and tuition waivers (full and partial) also available. Financial award applicants required to submit FAFSA. *Faculty research:* Clinical psychology, autism, anxiety, addition, neuropsychology, school psychology, cognitive psychology, experimental psychology. *Total annual research expenditures:* $986,140. *Unit head:* Dr. Robert Matthews, Chair, 225-578-8745, Fax: 225-578-4125, E-mail: psmath@lsu.edu. *Application contact:* Dr. Jason Hicks, Coordinator of Graduate Studies, 225-578-4109, Fax: 225-578-4125, E-mail: jhicks@lsu.edu.
Website: http://www.lsu.edu/psychology/graduate.html

Loyola University Chicago, Graduate School, Department of Psychology, Program in Developmental Psychology, Chicago, IL 60660. Offers MA, PhD. *Faculty:* 5 full-time (4 women). *Students:* 21 full-time (19 women), 3 part-time (all women); includes 4 minority (2 Black or African American, non-Hispanic/Latino; 2 Hispanic/Latino), 2 international. Average age 31. 23 applicants, 17% accepted, 2 enrolled. In 2014, 1 master's, 6 doctorates awarded. *Degree requirements:* For doctorate, comprehensive exam, thesis/dissertation, internship or student teaching. *Entrance requirements:* For doctorate, GRE General Test, GRE Subject Test. Additional exam requirements/recommendations for international students: Required—TOEFL (minimum score 500 paper-based). *Application deadline:* For fall admission, 1/15 for domestic students. Application fee: $50. Electronic applications accepted. Application fee is waived when completed online. *Expenses: Tuition:* Full-time $17,370; part-time $965 per credit. *Required fees:* $138 per semester. *Financial support:* In 2014–15, 6 students received support, including fellowships with full tuition reimbursements available (averaging $14,000 per year), research assistantships with full tuition reimbursements available (averaging $14,000 per year), teaching assistantships with full tuition reimbursements available (averaging $14,000 per year); career-related internships or fieldwork, scholarships/grants, and unspecified assistantships also available. Financial award application deadline: 12/15; financial award applicants required to submit FAFSA. *Faculty research:* Parenting, bilingualism, memory development, aggression and violence, education and social policy. *Total annual research expenditures:* $10,000. *Unit head:* Dr. Scott Tindale, Director, 773-508-3014, Fax: 773-508-8713, E-mail: rtindal@luc.edu. *Application contact:* Ron Martin, Assistant Director of Enrollment Management, 312-915-8950, Fax: 312-915-8905, E-mail: gradapp@luc.edu.

McGill University, Faculty of Graduate and Postdoctoral Studies, Faculty of Education, Department of Educational and Counseling Psychology, Montréal, QC H3A 2T5, Canada. Offers counseling psychology (MA, PhD); educational psychology (M Ed, MA, PhD); school/applied child psychology and applied developmental psychology (M Ed, MA, PhD, Diploma), including school psychology. *Accreditation:* APA.

The New School, The New School for Social Research, Department of Psychology, New York, NY 10011. Offers clinical psychology (PhD); cognitive, social and developmental psychology (PhD); general psychology (MA). *Accreditation:* APA (one or more programs are accredited). Part-time programs available. Terminal master's awarded for partial completion of doctoral program. *Degree requirements:* For master's, comprehensive exam (for some programs), thesis (for some programs); for doctorate, thesis/dissertation, qualifying exam. *Entrance requirements:* For master's, GRE General Test; for doctorate, GRE General Test, MA. Additional exam requirements/recommendations for international students: Required—TOEFL (minimum score 600 paper-based; 100 iBT). Electronic applications accepted. *Faculty research:* Consciousness, memory, language, perceptions, psychopathology.

New York University, Steinhardt School of Culture, Education, and Human Development, Department of Applied Psychology, Programs in Educational and Developmental Psychology, New York, NY 10003. Offers developmental psychology (PhD); human development and social intervention (MA); psychology and social intervention (PhD). *Accreditation:* APA (one or more programs are accredited). Part-time programs available. *Faculty:* 24 full-time (16 women). *Students:* 54 full-time (44 women), 6 part-time (all women); includes 23 minority (7 Black or African American, non-Hispanic/Latino; 5 Asian, non-Hispanic/Latino; 10 Hispanic/Latino; 1 Two or more races, non-Hispanic/Latino), 10 international. Average age 27. 137 applicants, 26% accepted, 13 enrolled. In 2014, 16 master's, 4 doctorates awarded. *Degree requirements:* For master's, thesis (for some programs); for doctorate, thesis/dissertation. *Entrance requirements:* For doctorate, GRE General Test, interview. Additional exam requirements/recommendations for international students: Required—TOEFL. *Application deadline:* For fall admission, 12/1 priority date for domestic and international students. Applications are processed on a rolling basis. Application fee: $75. Electronic applications accepted. *Financial support:* Teaching assistantships with partial tuition

reimbursements, career-related internships or fieldwork, Federal Work-Study, institutionally sponsored loans, and tuition waivers (partial) available. Support available to part-time students. Financial award application deadline: 2/1; financial award applicants required to submit FAFSA. *Faculty research:* Schools and communities, self-regulation and academic achievement, intervention and social change, trauma and resilience, cognition. *Unit head:* Prof. Clancy Blair, Director, 212-998-5853, Fax: 212-995-4358, E-mail: clancy.blair@nyu.edu. *Application contact:* 212-998-5030, Fax: 212-995-4328, E-mail: steinhardt.gradadmissions@nyu.edu.
Website: http://steinhardt.nyu.edu/appsych

North Carolina State University, Graduate School, College of Humanities and Social Sciences, Department of Psychology, Raleigh, NC 27695. Offers developmental psychology (PhD); ergonomics and experimental psychology (PhD); industrial/organizational psychology (PhD); psychology in the public interest (PhD); school psychology (PhD). *Accreditation:* APA. *Degree requirements:* For doctorate, comprehensive exam, thesis/dissertation. *Entrance requirements:* For doctorate, GRE General Test, GRE Subject Test (industrial/organizational psychology), MAT (recommended), minimum GPA of 3.0 in major. Electronic applications accepted. *Faculty research:* Cognitive and social development (human factors, families, the workplace, community issues and health, aging).

North Dakota State University, College of Graduate and Interdisciplinary Studies, College of Human Development and Education, Department of Human Development and Family Science, Program in Developmental Science, Fargo, ND 58108. Offers PhD. Electronic applications accepted.

The Ohio State University, Graduate School, College of Arts and Sciences, Division of Social and Behavioral Sciences, Department of Psychology, Columbus, OH 43210. Offers behavioral neuroscience (PhD); clinical psychology (PhD); cognitive psychology (PhD); developmental psychology (PhD); intellectual and developmental disabilities psychology (PhD); quantitative psychology (PhD); social psychology (PhD). *Accreditation:* APA. *Faculty:* 55. *Students:* 158 full-time (91 women); includes 26 minority (6 Black or African American, non-Hispanic/Latino; 2 American Indian or Alaska Native, non-Hispanic/Latino; 7 Asian, non-Hispanic/Latino; 9 Hispanic/Latino; 2 Two or more races, non-Hispanic/Latino), 23 international. Average age 27. In 2014, 12 doctorates awarded. *Degree requirements:* For doctorate, thesis/dissertation. *Entrance requirements:* For doctorate, GRE General Test. Additional exam requirements/recommendations for international students: Required—TOEFL (minimum score 600 paper-based; 100 iBT); Recommended—IELTS (minimum score 8). *Application deadline:* For fall admission, 12/1 for domestic and international students. Applications are processed on a rolling basis. Application fee: $60 ($70 for international students). Electronic applications accepted. *Financial support:* Fellowships with tuition reimbursements, research assistantships with tuition reimbursements, and teaching assistantships with tuition reimbursements available. *Unit head:* Dr. Richard Petty, Chair, 614-292-1640, E-mail: petty.1@osu.edu. *Application contact:* Graduate and Professional Admissions, 614-292-9444, Fax: 614-292-3895, E-mail: gpadmissions@osu.edu.
Website: http://www.psy.ohio-state.edu/

Pontificia Universidad Catolica Madre y Maestra, Graduate School, Faculty of Social and Administrative Sciences, Santiago, Dominican Republic. Offers business administration (MBA), including business development, finance, international business, management skills (M Mgmt, MBA), marketing, operations, strategic cost management, strategy, tourist destination planning and management; law (LL M), including civil law, corporate business law, criminal law, international relations, real estate law; management (M Mgmt), including higher financial management, insurance program administration, management skills (M Mgmt, MBA); psychology (MA), including clinical child and adolescent psychology, forensic psychology; strategic human resources (EMBA).

Queen's University at Kingston, School of Graduate Studies, Faculty of Arts and Sciences, Department of Psychology, Kingston, ON K7L 3N6, Canada. Offers brain behavior and cognitive science (MA, PhD); clinical psychology (MA, PhD); developmental psychology (MA, PhD); social personality psychology (MA, PhD). *Degree requirements:* For master's, thesis; for doctorate, comprehensive exam, thesis/dissertation. *Entrance requirements:* For master's and doctorate, GRE General Test. Additional exam requirements/recommendations for international students: Required—TOEFL. *Faculty research:* Human development, social, personality, behavioral neuroscience, forensic.

Teachers College, Columbia University, Graduate Faculty of Education, Department of Human Development, Program in Developmental Psychology, New York, NY 10027-6696. Offers MA, Ed D, PhD. *Faculty:* 4 full-time, 4 part-time/adjunct. *Students:* 28 full-time (24 women), 49 part-time (48 women); includes 27 minority (8 Black or African American, non-Hispanic/Latino; 5 Asian, non-Hispanic/Latino; 10 Hispanic/Latino; 4 Two or more races, non-Hispanic/Latino), 25 international. Average age 28. 105 applicants, 77% accepted, 30 enrolled. In 2014, 40 master's, 2 doctorates awarded. *Degree requirements:* For master's, special research project; for doctorate, thesis/dissertation, integrative project. *Entrance requirements:* For doctorate, GRE General Test. *Application deadline:* For fall admission, 12/15 for domestic students. Application fee: $65. *Expenses: Tuition:* Full-time $33,552; part-time $1398 per credit. *Required fees:* $418 per semester. *Financial support:* Research assistantships, teaching assistantships, career-related internships or fieldwork, Federal Work-Study, institutionally sponsored loans, and tuition waivers (full and partial) available. Support available to part-time students. Financial award application deadline: 2/1; financial award applicants required to submit FAFSA. *Faculty research:* Language development in infants, psychology of mathematics education, intellectual development, testing and assessment, cognitive development. *Unit head:* Prof. Jeanne Brooks-Gunn, Program Coordinator, 212-678-3369, Fax: 212-678-4171, E-mail: jb224@columbia.edu. *Application contact:* David Estrella, Associate Director of Admission, 212-678-3710, Fax: 212-678-4171, E-mail: tcinfo@tc.edu.
Website: http://www.tc.columbia.edu/hud/DevPsych/

Texas A&M University, College of Liberal Arts, Department of Psychology, College Station, TX 77843. Offers behavioral and cellular neuroscience (PhD); clinical psychology (PhD); cognitive psychology (PhD); developmental psychology (PhD); industrial/organizational psychology (PhD); psychology (MS); social psychology (PhD). *Accreditation:* APA (one or more programs are accredited). *Faculty:* 35. *Students:* 82 full-time (45 women), 15 part-time (12 women); includes 30 minority (6 Black or African American, non-Hispanic/Latino; 6 Asian, non-Hispanic/Latino; 18 Hispanic/Latino), 11 international. Average age 28. 375 applicants, 5% accepted, 8 enrolled. In 2014, 8 master's, 16 doctorates awarded. *Degree requirements:* For doctorate, comprehensive exam (for some programs), thesis/dissertation. *Entrance requirements:* For doctorate, GRE General Test. Additional exam requirements/recommendations for international students: Required—TOEFL. *Application deadline:* For fall admission, 1/5 for domestic and international students. Application fee: $50 ($90 for international students). Electronic applications accepted. *Expenses:* Tuition, state resident: full-time $4078; part-time $226.55 per credit hour. Tuition, nonresident: full-time $10,594; part-time $577.55 per credit hour. *Required fees:* $2813; $237.70 per credit hour. $278.50 per semester. Tuition and fees vary according to degree level and student level. *Financial support:* In 2014–15, 84 students received support, including 25 fellowships with full and partial tuition reimbursements available (averaging $17,037 per year), 20 research assistantships with full and partial tuition reimbursements available (averaging $8,269 per year), 57 teaching assistantships with full and partial tuition reimbursements available (averaging $7,431 per year); career-related internships or fieldwork, institutionally sponsored loans, scholarships/grants, traineeships, health care benefits, tuition waivers (full and partial), and unspecified assistantships also available. Support available to part-time students. Financial award application deadline: 1/5; financial award applicants required to submit FAFSA. *Unit head:* Dr. Doug Woods, Head, 979-845-2540, E-mail: dowoods@tamu.edu. *Application contact:* Dr. Charles D. Samuelson, Director of Graduate Studies, 979-845-0880, Fax: 979-845-4727, E-mail: c-samuelson@tamu.edu.
Website: http://psychology.tamu.edu

Texas Christian University, College of Science and Engineering, Department of Psychology, Fort Worth, TX 76129. Offers developmental trauma (MS); experimental psychology (MA, MS, PhD), including behavioral neuroscience (MS), cognition (MS), learning (MS), social (MS). *Faculty:* 12 full-time (5 women), 2 part-time/adjunct (1 woman). *Students:* 28 full-time (14 women); includes 1 minority (Hispanic/Latino), 3 international. Average age 27. 37 applicants, 22% accepted, 8 enrolled. In 2014, 2 master's, 6 doctorates awarded. Terminal master's awarded for partial completion of doctoral program. *Degree requirements:* For master's, thesis; for doctorate, thesis/dissertation. *Entrance requirements:* For master's and doctorate, GRE General Test. Additional exam requirements/recommendations for international students: Required—TOEFL. *Application deadline:* For fall admission, 2/1 for domestic and international students; for spring admission, 12/1 for domestic students. Application fee: $60 ($0 for international students). Electronic applications accepted. *Expenses: Tuition:* Full-time $22,860; part-time $1270 per credit hour. *Financial support:* In 2014–15, 23 students received support, including 23 teaching assistantships with full tuition reimbursements available (averaging $19,750 per year); scholarships/grants and tuition waivers also available. Financial award application deadline: 2/1; financial award applicants required to submit FAFSA. *Faculty research:* Neuroscience, human and animal learning, cognition, development, experimental social psychology. *Unit head:* Dr. Mauricio Papini, Chair, 817-257-7410, Fax: 817-257-7681, E-mail: m.papini@tcu.edu. *Application contact:* Cindy Hayes, Administrative Assistant, 817-257-7410, Fax: 817-257-7681, E-mail: c.hayes@tcu.edu.
Website: http://www.psy.tcu.edu/gradpro.html

Université de Montréal, Faculty of Arts and Sciences, School of Psychoeducation, Montréal, QC H3C 3J7, Canada. Offers M Sc, PhD. Part-time programs available. *Degree requirements:* For master's, one foreign language, thesis. Electronic applications accepted. *Faculty research:* Child maladjustment, family, prevention, treatment, antisocial behavior.

The University of Alabama at Birmingham, College of Arts and Sciences, Program in Psychology, Birmingham, AL 35294. Offers behavioral neuroscience (PhD); lifespan developmental psychology (PhD); medical/clinical psychology (PhD); psychology (MA). *Accreditation:* APA (one or more programs are accredited). *Students:* 69 full-time (51 women), 2 part-time (both women); includes 14 minority (2 Black or African American, non-Hispanic/Latino; 2 Asian, non-Hispanic/Latino; 4 Hispanic/Latino; 6 Two or more races, non-Hispanic/Latino), 4 international. Average age 26. In 2014, 8 master's, 15 doctorates awarded. *Entrance requirements:* For master's and doctorate, GRE General Test, letters of recommendation. *Application deadline:* Applications are processed on a rolling basis. Electronic applications accepted. *Expenses:* Tuition, state resident: full-time $7090; part-time $370 per credit hour. Tuition, nonresident: full-time $16,072; part-time $869 per credit hour. Full-time tuition and fees vary according to course load and program. *Financial support:* Fellowships, research assistantships, and teaching assistantships available. *Faculty research:* Biological basis of behavior structure, function of the nervous system. *Unit head:* Dr. Karlene K. Ball, Chair, 205-934-2610, Fax: 205-975-2295, E-mail: psych-dept@uab.edu. *Application contact:* Susan Noblitt Banks, Director of Graduate School Operations, 205-934-8227, Fax: 205-934-8413, E-mail: gradschool@uab.edu.
Website: http://www.uab.edu/cas/psychology/graduate

The University of British Columbia, Faculty of Arts and Faculty of Graduate Studies, Department of Psychology, Vancouver, BC V6T 1Z4, Canada. Offers behavioral neuroscience (MA, PhD); clinical psychology (MA, PhD); cognitive science (MA, PhD); developmental psychology (MA, PhD); health psychology (MA, PhD); quantitative methods (MA, PhD); social/personality psychology (MA, PhD). *Accreditation:* APA (one or more programs are accredited). Terminal master's awarded for partial completion of doctoral program. *Degree requirements:* For master's, thesis; for doctorate, comprehensive exam, thesis/dissertation. *Entrance requirements:* For master's and doctorate, GRE General Test. Additional exam requirements/recommendations for international students: Required—TOEFL (minimum score 550 paper-based; 80 iBT). Electronic applications accepted. *Faculty research:* Clinical, developmental, social/personality, cognition, behavioral neuroscience.

University of Connecticut, Graduate School, College of Liberal Arts and Sciences, Department of Psychology, Storrs, CT 06269. Offers behavioral neuroscience (PhD); biopsychology (PhD); clinical psychology (MA, PhD); cognition and instruction (PhD); developmental psychology (MA, PhD); ecological psychology (PhD); experimental psychology (PhD); general psychology (MA, PhD); health psychology (Graduate Certificate); industrial/organizational psychology (PhD); language and cognition (PhD); neuroscience (PhD); occupational health psychology (Graduate Certificate); social psychology (MA, PhD). *Accreditation:* APA. Terminal master's awarded for partial completion of doctoral program. *Degree requirements:* For master's, comprehensive exam; for doctorate, thesis/dissertation. *Entrance requirements:* For master's and doctorate, GRE General Test, GRE Subject Test. Additional exam requirements/recommendations for international students: Required—TOEFL (minimum score 550 paper-based). Electronic applications accepted.

University of Denver, Division of Arts, Humanities and Social Sciences, Department of Psychology, Denver, CO 80208. Offers affective/social psychology (PhD); clinical child psychology (PhD); cognitive psychology (PhD); developmental psychology (PhD). *Accreditation:* APA. *Faculty:* 25 full-time (11 women), 4 part-time/adjunct (2 women). *Students:* 21 full-time (18 women), 5 part-time (all women); includes 7 minority (2 Black or African American, non-Hispanic/Latino; 3 Asian, non-Hispanic/Latino; 1 Hispanic/Latino; 1 Two or more races, non-Hispanic/Latino), 3 international. Average age 28. 348 applicants, 5% accepted, 6 enrolled. In 2014, 9 doctorates awarded. Terminal master's awarded for partial completion of doctoral program. *Degree requirements:* For doctorate, variable foreign language requirement, comprehensive exam (for some programs), thesis/dissertation. *Entrance requirements:* For doctorate, GRE General Test, master's degree, transcripts, biographical statement, three letters of recommendation. Additional exam requirements/recommendations for international students: Required—TOEFL (minimum score 550 paper-based; 80 iBT). *Application deadline:* For fall admission, 12/1 priority date for domestic and international students. Application fee: $65. Electronic applications accepted. *Expenses:* Expenses: $1,199 per credit hour. *Financial support:* In 2014–15, 26 students received support, including 13 research assistantships with full and partial tuition reimbursements available (averaging $12,821 per year), 20 teaching

assistantships with full and partial tuition reimbursements available (averaging $15,333 per year); Federal Work-Study, institutionally sponsored loans, scholarships/grants, and unspecified assistantships also available. Support available to part-time students. Financial award application deadline: 2/15; financial award applicants required to submit FAFSA. *Faculty research:* Developmental cognitive neuroscience, social and emotional processes, child and adolescent development, clinical child psychology, cognitive psychology. *Total annual research expenditures:* $3 million. *Unit head:* Dr. George Potts, Chair, 303-871-3717, Fax: 303-871-4747, E-mail: gpotts@du.edu. *Application contact:* Paula Houghtaling, Graduate Program Administrator, 303-871-3803, Fax: 303-871-4747, E-mail: phoughta@du.edu.
Website: http://www.du.edu/ahss/psychology/index.html

University of Houston, College of Liberal Arts and Social Sciences, Department of Psychology, Houston, TX 77204. Offers clinical psychology (PhD); developmental psychology (PhD); industrial/organizational psychology (PhD); psychology (MA); social psychology (PhD). *Accreditation:* APA (one or more programs are accredited). *Degree requirements:* For master's, comprehensive exam, thesis; for doctorate, comprehensive exam, thesis/dissertation. *Entrance requirements:* For master's, GRE General Test, career statement, 3 letters of recommendation; for doctorate, GRE General Test, 3 letters of recommendation. Additional exam requirements/recommendations for international students: Required—TOEFL (minimum score 550 paper-based; 79 iBT). Electronic applications accepted. *Faculty research:* Health psychology, depression, child/family process, organizational effectiveness, close relationships.

University of Illinois at Chicago, Graduate College, College of Education, Department of Educational Psychology, Chicago, IL 60607-7128. Offers early childhood education (M Ed); educational psychology (PhD); measurement, evaluation, statistics, and assessment (M Ed); youth development (M Ed). Part-time programs available. Postbaccalaureate distance learning degree programs offered (no on-campus study). *Faculty:* 12 full-time (10 women), 5 part-time/adjunct (3 women). *Students:* 64 full-time (52 women), 115 part-time (81 women); includes 67 minority (28 Black or African American, non-Hispanic/Latino; 14 Asian, non-Hispanic/Latino; 20 Hispanic/Latino; 5 Two or more races, non-Hispanic/Latino), 1,115 international. Average age 34. 129 applicants, 57% accepted, 55 enrolled. In 2014, 46 master's, 2 doctorates awarded. *Expenses:* Tuition, state resident: full-time $11,254; part-time $468 per credit hour. Tuition, nonresident: full-time $23,252; part-time $968 per credit hour. *Required fees:* $1217 per term. Part-time tuition and fees vary according to course load, degree level and program. *Faculty research:* Children's construction of morality, development of resilience in the face of enduring economical difficulties, cognition and cognitive development, test fairness. *Total annual research expenditures:* $670,000. *Unit head:* Prof. Kimlerly Lawless, Chairperson, 312-996-2359, E-mail: klawless@uic.edu. *Application contact:* Receptionist, 312-413-2550, E-mail: gradcoll@uic.edu.
Website: http://education.uic.edu/academics-admissions/departments/department-educational-psychology#overview

The University of Kansas, Graduate Studies, College of Liberal Arts and Sciences, Department of Psychology, Lawrence, KS 66045. Offers clinical child psychology (MA, PhD); clinical health and rehabilitation (PhD); cognitive psychology (PhD); developmental psychology (PhD); quantitative psychology (PhD); social psychology (MA). *Accreditation:* APA (one or more programs are accredited). *Faculty:* 36 full-time, 3 part-time/adjunct. *Students:* 81 full-time (49 women), 1 (woman) part-time; includes 12 minority (4 Black or African American, non-Hispanic/Latino; 5 Asian, non-Hispanic/Latino; 1 Hispanic/Latino; 2 Two or more races, non-Hispanic/Latino), 13 international. Average age 29. 194 applicants, 10% accepted, 9 enrolled. In 2014, 17 master's, 13 doctorates awarded. *Degree requirements:* For doctorate, variable foreign language requirement, comprehensive exam, thesis/dissertation. *Entrance requirements:* For doctorate, GRE General Test, minimum GPA of 3.0; undergraduate degree with 15 hours of course work in psychology, curriculum vitae, writing sample (clinical program only). Additional exam requirements/recommendations for international students: Required—TOEFL. *Application deadline:* For fall admission, 12/1 for domestic and international students. Application fee: $55 ($65 for international students). Electronic applications accepted. *Financial support:* In 2014–15, 1 fellowship with full tuition reimbursement (averaging $12,750 per year), 4 research assistantships with partial tuition reimbursements (averaging $12,980 per year), 70 teaching assistantships with partial tuition reimbursements (averaging $12,750 per year) were awarded; career-related internships or fieldwork, Federal Work-Study, scholarships/grants, health care benefits, and unspecified assistantships also available. Financial award application deadline: 12/1; financial award applicants required to submit FAFSA. *Faculty research:* Origins, correlates and treatment of depression; health and emotion; concentration on topics related to prejudice, stereotyping, and intergroup relations; memory, cognitive development, language, perception, attention, aging; psychometric methods, item response theory, structural equation modeling. *Unit head:* Ruth Anne Atchley, Chair, 785-864-4131. *Application contact:* Cathy O'Keefe, Graduate Officer, 785-864-4195, Fax: 785-864-5596, E-mail: cokeefe@ku.edu.
Website: http://www.psych.ku.edu/

The University of Kansas, Graduate Studies, College of Liberal Arts and Sciences, Program in Child Language, Lawrence, KS 66045. Offers PhD. *Students:* 2 full-time (1 woman); includes 1 minority (Asian, non-Hispanic/Latino). Average age 28. 3 applicants, 67% accepted, 1 enrolled. In 2014, 3 doctorates awarded. *Degree requirements:* For doctorate, comprehensive exam, thesis/dissertation, written preliminary exam; training in responsible scholarship and research skills. *Entrance requirements:* For doctorate, GRE, minimum GPA of 3.0, 3 letters of reference, curriculum vitae, personal statement. Additional exam requirements/recommendations for international students: Required—TOEFL. *Application deadline:* For fall admission, 1/15 priority date for domestic and international students; for spring admission, 11/1 for domestic and international students. Applications are processed on a rolling basis. Application fee: $55 ($65 for international students). Electronic applications accepted. *Financial support:* Fellowships with full tuition reimbursements, research assistantships with full tuition reimbursements, teaching assistantships with full tuition reimbursements, career-related internships or fieldwork, traineeships, and unspecified assistantships available. Financial award application deadline: 2/1. *Faculty research:* Language impairments in children, specific language impairment, genetics of language acquisition, brain processing of language, language of aging. *Unit head:* Mabel L. Rice, Director, 785-864-4570, E-mail: mabel@ku.edu. *Application contact:* Linda Mann, Graduate Admissions Contact, 785-864-4570, E-mail: lkaymann@ku.edu.
Website: http://www.clp.ku.edu/

The University of Manchester, School of Education, Manchester, United Kingdom. Offers counseling (D Couns); counseling psychology (D Couns); education (M Phil, Ed D, PhD); educational and child psychology (Ed D); educational psychology (Ed D).

University of Maryland, Baltimore County, The Graduate School, College of Arts, Humanities and Social Sciences, Department of Psychology, Program in Applied Developmental Psychology, Baltimore, MD 21250. Offers PhD. *Faculty:* 8 full-time (5 women), 11 part-time/adjunct (4 women). *Students:* 25 full-time (24 women); includes 8 minority (1 Black or African American, non-Hispanic/Latino; 6 Asian, non-Hispanic/Latino; 1 Hispanic/Latino). Average age 27. 30 applicants, 37% accepted, 4 enrolled. In 2014, 4 doctorates awarded. *Degree requirements:* For doctorate, comprehensive exam, thesis/dissertation. *Entrance requirements:* For doctorate, GRE General Test, minimum GPA of 3.0. Additional exam requirements/recommendations for international students: Required—TOEFL. *Application deadline:* For fall admission, 1/9 for domestic and international students. Application fee: $50. Electronic applications accepted. *Expenses:* Tuition, state resident: part-time $557. Tuition, nonresident: part-time $922. *Required fees:* $122 per semester. One-time fee: $200 part-time. *Financial support:* In 2014–15, 3 fellowships with full and partial tuition reimbursements (averaging $16,795 per year), 2 research assistantships with full and partial tuition reimbursements (averaging $19,890 per year), 11 teaching assistantships with full and partial tuition reimbursements (averaging $16,795 per year) were awarded; career-related internships or fieldwork, Federal Work-Study, health care benefits, and unspecified assistantships also available. Financial award application deadline: 3/1; financial award applicants required to submit FAFSA. *Faculty research:* Early intervention and development, schooling and development, cultural aspects of development, development in high risk children, social-emotional development. *Total annual research expenditures:* $154,339. *Unit head:* Dr. Susan Sonnenschein, Director, 410-455-2361, Fax: 410-455-1055, E-mail: sonnenschein@umbc.edu. *Application contact:* Nicole Mooney, Program Management Specialist, 410-455-2567, Fax: 410-455-1055, E-mail: psycdept@umbc.edu.
Website: http://www.umbc.edu/gradschool/programs/psych_appdev.html

University of Maryland, College Park, Academic Affairs, College of Behavioral and Social Sciences, Department of Psychology, College Park, MD 20742. Offers clinical psychology (PhD); developmental psychology (PhD); experimental psychology (PhD); industrial psychology (MA, MS, PhD); social psychology (PhD). *Accreditation:* APA (one or more programs are accredited). *Degree requirements:* For master's, thesis; for doctorate, variable foreign language requirement, comprehensive exam, thesis/dissertation. *Entrance requirements:* For master's and doctorate, GRE General Test, GRE Subject Test, minimum GPA of 3.5, research and/or work experience, 3 letters of recommendation. Electronic applications accepted. *Faculty research:* Social stereotyping and prejudice, anxiety disorders, auditory neuroethology, counseling and social psychology.

University of Massachusetts Amherst, Graduate School, College of Natural Sciences, Department of Psychological and Brain Sciences, Amherst, MA 01003. Offers clinical psychology (MS, PhD); cognitive psychology (MS, PhD); developmental science (MS, PhD); psychology of peace and violence (MS, PhD); social psychology (MS, PhD). *Accreditation:* APA (one or more programs are accredited). *Faculty:* 62 full-time (31 women). *Students:* 47 full-time (32 women), 14 part-time (11 women); includes 12 minority (2 Black or African American, non-Hispanic/Latino; 6 Asian, non-Hispanic/Latino; 3 Hispanic/Latino; 1 Two or more races, non-Hispanic/Latino), 9 international. Average age 27. 317 applicants, 7% accepted, 11 enrolled. In 2014, 12 master's, 10 doctorates awarded. Terminal master's awarded for partial completion of doctoral program. *Degree requirements:* For master's, thesis; for doctorate, comprehensive exam, thesis/dissertation. *Entrance requirements:* For master's and doctorate, GRE General Test, 3 letters of recommendation. Additional exam requirements/recommendations for international students: Required—TOEFL (minimum score 550 paper-based; 80 iBT), IELTS (minimum score 6.5). *Application deadline:* For fall admission, 12/1 for domestic and international students. Applications are processed on a rolling basis. Application fee: $75. Electronic applications accepted. *Expenses:* Tuition, state resident: full-time $1980; part-time $110 per credit. Tuition, nonresident: full-time $14,644; part-time $414 per credit. *Required fees:* $11,417. One-time fee: $357. *Financial support:* Fellowships with full and partial tuition reimbursements, research assistantships with full and partial tuition reimbursements, teaching assistantships with full and partial tuition reimbursements, career-related internships or fieldwork, Federal Work-Study, scholarships/grants, traineeships, health care benefits, tuition waivers (full and partial), and unspecified assistantships available. Support available to part-time students. Financial award application deadline: 12/1. *Unit head:* Dr. Michael Constantino, Graduate Program Director, 413-545-2503, Fax: 413-545-0996. *Application contact:* Lindsay DeSantis, Supervisor of Admissions, 413-545-0722, Fax: 413-577-0010, E-mail: gradadm@grad.umass.edu.
Website: http://www.psych.umass.edu/

University of Miami, Graduate School, College of Arts and Sciences, Department of Psychology, Coral Gables, FL 33124. Offers adult clinical (PhD); behavioral neuroscience (PhD); child clinical (PhD); developmental psychology (PhD); health clinical (PhD); psychology (MS). *Accreditation:* APA (one or more programs are accredited). *Degree requirements:* For doctorate, comprehensive exam, thesis/dissertation. *Entrance requirements:* For doctorate, GRE General Test, minimum GPA of 3.5. Additional exam requirements/recommendations for international students: Required—TOEFL. Electronic applications accepted. *Faculty research:* Behavioral factors in cardiovascular disease and cancer adult psychopathology, developmental disabilities, social and emotional development, mechanisms of coping.

University of Michigan, Horace H. Rackham School of Graduate Studies, College of Literature, Science, and the Arts, Department of Psychology, Ann Arbor, MI 48109. Offers biopsychology (PhD); clinical science (PhD); cognition and cognitive neuroscience (PhD); developmental psychology (PhD); personality and social contexts (PhD); social psychology (PhD). *Accreditation:* APA. *Faculty:* 57 full-time (27 women), 31 part-time/adjunct (17 women). *Students:* 118 full-time (80 women); includes 58 minority (15 Black or African American, non-Hispanic/Latino; 1 American Indian or Alaska Native, non-Hispanic/Latino; 15 Asian, non-Hispanic/Latino; 25 Hispanic/Latino; 2 Two or more races, non-Hispanic/Latino), 12 international. Average age 27. 687 applicants, 7% accepted, 25 enrolled. In 2014, 36 doctorates awarded. *Degree requirements:* For doctorate, comprehensive exam, thesis/dissertation, oral defense of dissertation, preliminary exam. *Entrance requirements:* For doctorate, GRE General Test. Additional exam requirements/recommendations for international students: Required—TOEFL. *Application deadline:* For fall admission, 12/1 for domestic and international students. Application fee: $75 ($90 for international students). Electronic applications accepted. *Financial support:* In 2014–15, 82 students received support, including 45 fellowships with full tuition reimbursements available (averaging $21,600 per year), 16 research assistantships with full tuition reimbursements available (averaging $28,450 per year), 50 teaching assistantships with full tuition reimbursements available (averaging $26,200 per year); career-related internships or fieldwork also available. Financial award application deadline: 4/15. *Unit head:* Prof. Patricia Reuter-Lorenz, Department Chair, 734-764-7429. *Application contact:* Danielle Joanette, Psychology Student Academic Affairs, 731-764-2580, Fax: 734-615-7584, E-mail: psych.saa@umich.edu.
Website: http://www.lsa.umich.edu/psych/

The University of Montana, Graduate School, College of Humanities and Sciences, Department of Psychology, Missoula, MT 59812-0002. Offers clinical psychology (PhD); experimental psychology (PhD), including animal behavior psychology, developmental psychology; school psychology (MA, PhD, Ed S). *Accreditation:* APA (one or more programs are accredited). Terminal master's awarded for partial completion of doctoral program. *Degree requirements:* For master's, thesis; for doctorate, thesis/dissertation. *Entrance requirements:* For master's, doctorate, and Ed S, GRE General Test.

Developmental Psychology

Additional exam requirements/recommendations for international students: Required—TOEFL.

University of Nebraska–Lincoln, Graduate College, College of Arts and Sciences, Department of Psychology, Lincoln, NE 68588. Offers biopsychology (PhD); clinical psychology (PhD); cognitive psychology (PhD); developmental psychology (PhD); psychology (MA); social/personality psychology (PhD); JD/MA; JD/PhD. *Accreditation:* APA (one or more programs are accredited). *Degree requirements:* For master's, thesis optional; for doctorate, comprehensive exam, thesis/dissertation. *Entrance requirements:* For master's and doctorate, GRE General Test. Additional exam requirements/recommendations for international students: Required—TOEFL (minimum score 550 paper-based). Electronic applications accepted. *Faculty research:* Law and psychology, rural mental health, chronic mental illness, neuropsychology, child clinical psychology.

University of Nebraska–Lincoln, Graduate College, College of Education and Human Sciences, Department of Educational Psychology, Lincoln, NE 68588. Offers cognition, learning and development (MA); counseling psychology (MA); educational psychology (MA, Ed S); psychological studies in education (PhD), including cognition, learning and development, counseling psychology, quantitative, qualitative, and psychometric methods, school psychology; quantitative, qualitative, and psychometric methods (MA); school psychology (MA, Ed S). *Accreditation:* APA (one or more programs are accredited); NCATE. *Degree requirements:* For master's, thesis optional. *Entrance requirements:* For master's, GRE General Test. Additional exam requirements/recommendations for international students: Required—TOEFL (minimum score 500 paper-based). Electronic applications accepted. *Faculty research:* Measurement and assessment, metacognition, academic skills, child development, multicultural education and counseling.

University of New Mexico, Graduate School, College of Arts and Sciences, Program in Psychology, Albuquerque, NM 87131-2039. Offers behavioral neuroscience (PhD); clinical psychology (PhD); cognitive neuroimaging (PhD); developmental psychology (PhD); evolution (PhD); health psychology (PhD); quantitative methodology (PhD). *Faculty:* 25 full-time (9 women), 1 (woman) part-time/adjunct. *Students:* 66 full-time (44 women), 12 part-time (6 women); includes 23 minority (2 Black or African American, non-Hispanic/Latino; 2 American Indian or Alaska Native, non-Hispanic/Latino; 4 Asian, non-Hispanic/Latino; 13 Hispanic/Latino; 2 Two or more races, non-Hispanic/Latino), 1 international. Average age 33. 135 applicants, 10% accepted, 13 enrolled. In 2014, 10 doctorates awarded. *Degree requirements:* For doctorate, comprehensive exam, thesis/dissertation. *Entrance requirements:* For doctorate, GRE General Test, GRE Subject Test (psychology), minimum GPA of 3.0. Additional exam requirements/recommendations for international students: Required—TOEFL (minimum score 550 paper-based; 79 iBT), IELTS (minimum score 6.5). *Application deadline:* For fall admission, 12/15 priority date for domestic and international students. Applications are processed on a rolling basis. Application fee: $50. Electronic applications accepted. *Financial support:* In 2014–15, 62 students received support, including 8 fellowships (averaging $13,124 per year), 37 research assistantships with full and partial tuition reimbursements available (averaging $11,655 per year), 67 teaching assistantships with full and partial tuition reimbursements available (averaging $13,600 per year); career-related internships or fieldwork, Federal Work-Study, institutionally sponsored loans, scholarships/grants, health care benefits, tuition waivers (partial), and unspecified assistantships also available. Financial award application deadline: 3/1; financial award applicants required to submit FAFSA. *Faculty research:* Addiction, cognition, brain and behavior, developmental, evolutionary, functioning neuroimaging, health psychology, learning and memory, neuroscience. *Unit head:* Dr. Jane Ellen Smith, Department Chair, 505-277-4121, Fax: 505-277-1394. *Application contact:* Rikk Murphy, Graduate Program Coordinator, 505-277-5009, Fax: 505-277-1394, E-mail: advising@unm.edu. Website: http://psych.unm.edu

The University of North Carolina at Chapel Hill, Graduate School, College of Arts and Sciences, Department of Psychology, Chapel Hill, NC 27599-3270. Offers behavioral neuroscience psychology (PhD); clinical psychology (PhD); cognitive psychology (PhD); developmental psychology (PhD); quantitative psychology (PhD); social psychology (PhD). *Accreditation:* APA. *Degree requirements:* For doctorate, comprehensive exam, thesis/dissertation. *Entrance requirements:* For doctorate, GRE General Test, minimum GPA of 3.0. Additional exam requirements/recommendations for international students: Required—TOEFL (minimum score 550 paper-based; 79 iBT), IELTS (minimum score 7). Electronic applications accepted. *Faculty research:* Expressed emotion, cognitive development, social cognitive neuroscience, human memory personality.

The University of North Carolina at Greensboro, Graduate School, College of Arts and Sciences, Department of Psychology, Greensboro, NC 27412-5001. Offers clinical psychology (MA, PhD); cognitive psychology (MA, PhD); developmental psychology (MA, PhD); social psychology (MA, PhD). *Accreditation:* APA (one or more programs are accredited). Terminal master's awarded for partial completion of doctoral program. *Degree requirements:* For master's, comprehensive exam, thesis; for doctorate, one foreign language, thesis/dissertation, preliminary exam. *Entrance requirements:* For master's and doctorate, GRE General Test. Additional exam requirements/recommendations for international students: Required—TOEFL. Electronic applications accepted. *Faculty research:* Sensory and perceptual determinants; evoked potential: disorders, deafness, and development.

University of Notre Dame, Graduate School, College of Arts and Letters, Division of Social Science, Department of Psychology, Notre Dame, IN 46556. Offers cognitive psychology (PhD); counseling psychology (PhD); developmental psychology (PhD); quantitative psychology (PhD). *Accreditation:* APA. *Degree requirements:* For doctorate, comprehensive exam, thesis/dissertation, candidacy exam. *Entrance requirements:* For doctorate, GRE General Test, GRE Subject Test (strongly recommended). Additional exam requirements/recommendations for international students: Required—TOEFL (minimum score 600 paper-based; 80 iBT). Electronic applications accepted. *Faculty research:* Cognitive and socio-emotional development, statistical methods and quantitative models applicable to psychology, interpersonal relations, life span development and developmental delay, childhood depression, structural equation and dynamical systems.

University of Oregon, Graduate School, College of Arts and Sciences, Department of Psychology, Eugene, OR 97403. Offers clinical psychology (PhD); cognitive psychology (MA, MS, PhD); developmental psychology (MA, MS, PhD); physiological psychology (MA, MS, PhD); psychology (MA, MS, PhD); social/personality psychology (MA, MS, PhD). *Accreditation:* APA (one or more programs are accredited). Terminal master's awarded for partial completion of doctoral program. *Degree requirements:* For doctorate, thesis/dissertation. *Entrance requirements:* For master's, GRE General Test, minimum GPA of 3.0; for doctorate, GRE General Test. Additional exam requirements/recommendations for international students: Required—TOEFL.

University of Pittsburgh, School of Education, Department of Psychology in Education, Program in Applied Developmental Psychology, Pittsburgh, PA 15260. Offers M Ed, MS, PhD. Part-time and evening/weekend programs available. *Faculty:* 17 full-time (10 women), 13 part-time/adjunct (10 women). *Students:* 48 full-time (45 women), 25 part-time (22 women); includes 20 minority (9 Black or African American, non-Hispanic/Latino; 4 Asian, non-Hispanic/Latino; 4 Hispanic/Latino; 3 Two or more races, non-Hispanic/Latino), 8 international. Average age 29. 100 applicants, 64% accepted, 38 enrolled. In 2014, 28 master's, 1 doctorate awarded. *Degree requirements:* For master's, thesis. *Entrance requirements:* For doctorate, GRE. Additional exam requirements/recommendations for international students: Required—TOEFL. *Application deadline:* For fall admission, 2/1 for domestic students, 2/1 priority date for international students; for spring admission, 7/1 priority date for international students. Applications are processed on a rolling basis. Application fee: $50. Electronic applications accepted. *Expenses:* Tuition, state resident: full-time $20,742; part-time $838 per credit. Tuition, nonresident: full-time $33,960; part-time $1389 per credit. *Required fees:* $800; $205 per term. Tuition and fees vary according to program. *Financial support:* In 2014–15, fellowships with full and partial tuition reimbursements (averaging $20,500 per year), research assistantships with full and partial tuition reimbursements (averaging $17,800 per year), teaching assistantships with full and partial tuition reimbursements (averaging $17,800 per year) were awarded; tuition waivers (partial) also available. Support available to part-time students. Financial award applicants required to submit FAFSA. *Unit head:* Dr. Carl N. Johnson, Chairman, 412-624-6942, Fax: 412-624-7231, E-mail: johnson@pitt.edu. *Application contact:* Maggie Sikora, Graduate Enrollment Manager, 412-648-2230, Fax: 412-648-1899, E-mail: soeinfo@pitt.edu.

University of Rochester, School of Arts and Sciences, Department of Clinical and Social Sciences in Psychology, Rochester, NY 14627. Offers clinical psychology (PhD); developmental psychology (PhD); social-personality psychology (PhD). *Accreditation:* APA. *Faculty:* 14 full-time (7 women). *Students:* 46 full-time (37 women), 1 (woman) part-time; includes 6 minority (2 Asian, non-Hispanic/Latino; 3 Hispanic/Latino; 1 Two or more races, non-Hispanic/Latino), 6 international. 326 applicants, 4% accepted, 6 enrolled. In 2014, 9 doctorates awarded. Terminal master's awarded for partial completion of doctoral program. *Degree requirements:* For doctorate, thesis/dissertation, qualifying exam. *Entrance requirements:* For doctorate, GRE General Test. Additional exam requirements/recommendations for international students: Required—TOEFL. *Application deadline:* For fall admission, 12/15 priority date for domestic students. Application fee: $60. *Expenses: Tuition:* Full-time $46,150; part-time $1442 per credit hour. *Required fees:* $504. *Financial support:* Fellowships, research assistantships, teaching assistantships, career-related internships or fieldwork, and tuition waivers (full and partial) available. Financial award application deadline: 2/1. *Faculty research:* Clinical psychology, social-personality psychology, developmental psychology, human motivation. *Unit head:* Loisa Bennetto, Chair, 585-275-8712. *Application contact:* April Engram, Academic Coordinator/Analyst, 585-275-8704. Website: http://www.psych.rochester.edu/csp/

University of Southern California, Graduate School, Dana and David Dornsife College of Letters, Arts and Sciences, Department of Psychology, Los Angeles, CA 90089. Offers brain and cognitive science (PhD); clinical science (PhD); developmental psychology (PhD); human behavior (MHB); quantitative methods (PhD); social psychology (PhD). *Accreditation:* APA. *Degree requirements:* For doctorate, comprehensive exam, thesis/dissertation, one-year internship (for clinical science students). *Entrance requirements:* For doctorate, GRE. Additional exam requirements/recommendations for international students: Recommended—TOEFL (minimum score 600 paper-based; 100 iBT). Electronic applications accepted. *Faculty research:* Affective neuroscience; children and families; vision, culture and ethnicity; intergroup relations; aggression and violence; language and reading development; substance abuse.

The University of Texas at Austin, Graduate School, College of Liberal Arts, Department of Psychology, Austin, TX 78712-1111. Offers behavioral neuroscience (PhD); clinical psychology (PhD); cognitive systems (PhD); developmental psychology (PhD); individual differences and evolutionary psychology (PhD); perceptual systems (PhD); social psychology (PhD). *Accreditation:* APA. *Degree requirements:* For doctorate, thesis/dissertation. *Entrance requirements:* For doctorate, GRE General Test. Electronic applications accepted. *Faculty research:* Behavioral neuroscience, sensory neuroscience, evolutionary psychology, cognitive processes in psychopathology, cognitive processes and their development.

University of Victoria, Faculty of Graduate Studies, Faculty of Social Sciences, Department of Psychology, Victoria, BC V8W 2Y2, Canada. Offers clinical psychology (PhD); clinical psychology (neuropsychology) (M Sc); cognition and brain science (M Sc, PhD); experimental neuropsychology (M Sc, PhD); individualized study (M Sc, PhD); life span development psychology (PhD); life span developmental psychology (M Sc); social psychology (M Sc, PhD). *Accreditation:* APA (one or more programs are accredited). *Degree requirements:* For master's, thesis; for doctorate, thesis/dissertation, candidacy exam. *Entrance requirements:* For master's and doctorate, GRE General Test. Additional exam requirements/recommendations for international students: Required—TOEFL (minimum score 600 paper-based). Electronic applications accepted. *Faculty research:* Life span development psychology and aging, behavioral neuroscience, cognitive psychology, behavioral psychology, environmental psychology.

University of Washington, Graduate School, College of Arts and Sciences, Department of Psychology, Seattle, WA 98195. Offers animal behavior (PhD); child psychology (PhD); clinical psychology (PhD); cognition and perception (PhD); developmental psychology (PhD); quantitative psychology (PhD); social psychology and personality (PhD). *Accreditation:* APA. *Degree requirements:* For doctorate, thesis/dissertation. *Entrance requirements:* For doctorate, GRE General Test, minimum GPA of 3.0. Electronic applications accepted. *Faculty research:* Addictive behaviors, artificial intelligence, child psychopathology, mechanisms and development of vision, physiology of ingestive behaviors.

University of Wisconsin–Madison, Graduate School, College of Letters and Science, Department of Psychology, Program in Developmental Psychology, Madison, WI 53706-1380. Offers PhD. *Degree requirements:* For doctorate, comprehensive exam, thesis/dissertation. *Entrance requirements:* For doctorate, GRE General Test, minimum undergraduate GPA of 3.0. Additional exam requirements/recommendations for international students: Required—TOEFL. Electronic applications accepted. *Expenses:* Tuition, state resident: full-time $10,723; part-time $745 per credit. Tuition, nonresident: full-time $24,054; part-time $1578 per credit. *Required fees:* $374 per semester. Tuition and fees vary according to course load, program and reciprocity agreements.

University of Wisconsin–Milwaukee, Graduate School, School of Education, Department of Educational Psychology, Milwaukee, WI 53201-0413. Offers counseling psychology (PhD); educational statistics and measurement (MS, PhD); learning and development (MS, PhD); school and community counseling (MS); school psychology (PhD). *Accreditation:* APA. Part-time programs available. *Degree requirements:* For master's, comprehensive exam, thesis; for doctorate, thesis/dissertation. *Entrance requirements:* For master's, minimum GPA of 3.0; for doctorate, GRE General Test, minimum GPA of 3.0. Additional exam requirements/recommendations for international students: Required—TOEFL (minimum score 550 paper-based; 79 iBT), IELTS (minimum score 6.5). Electronic applications accepted.

Virginia Commonwealth University, Graduate School, College of Humanities and Sciences, Department of Psychology, Program in General Psychology, Richmond, VA 23284-9005. Offers biopsychology (PhD); developmental psychology (PhD); social

psychology (PhD). *Degree requirements:* For doctorate, thesis/dissertation. *Entrance requirements:* For doctorate, GRE General Test. Additional exam requirements/recommendations for international students: Required—TOEFL (minimum score 600 paper-based; 100 iBT; Recommended—IELTS (minimum score 6.5). Electronic applications accepted. *Faculty research:* Biopsychology, developmental and social psychology.

Viterbo University, Master of Science in Mental Health Counseling Program, La Crosse, WI 54601-4797. Offers addiction counseling (MS); child and adolescent counseling (MS); complementary health and wellness counseling (MS). Part-time and evening/weekend programs available. *Faculty:* 3 full-time (1 woman), 6 part-time/adjunct (3 women). *Students:* 52 full-time (43 women), 10 part-time (8 women); includes 6 minority (2 Black or African American, non-Hispanic/Latino; 1 Asian, non-Hispanic/Latino; 3 Two or more races, non-Hispanic/Latino), 1 international. Average age 33. 41 applicants, 51% accepted, 20 enrolled. In 2014, 12 master's awarded. *Degree requirements:* For master's, comprehensive exam, thesis, 54 credits of core program courses; 6 elective credits; minimum GPA of 3.0; action research project; practicum/internship experience. *Entrance requirements:* For master's, MAT, BS in a human service or social science discipline; prerequisite coursework in general psychology, behavior disorders/abnormal psychology, and research methods/statistics; minimum undergraduate cumulative GPA of 3.0; background check; personal statement; undergraduate transcripts; interview. Additional exam requirements/recommendations for international students: Required—TOEFL (minimum score 525 paper-based). *Application deadline:* For fall admission, 3/15 priority date for domestic students, 7/31 priority date for international students. Applications are processed on a rolling basis. Application fee: $50. Electronic applications accepted. Application fee is waived when completed online. *Expenses:* Expenses: $475 per credit. *Financial support:* Applicants required to submit FAFSA. *Faculty research:* Supervision, recovery substance abuse, culture, counseling theory, health and wellness. *Unit head:* Dr. Debra A. Murray, Program Director, 608-796-3720, E-mail: damurray@viterbo.edu. *Application contact:* Dr. Debra A. Murray, Program Director, 608-796-3720, E-mail: damurray@viterbo.edu. Website: http://www.viterbo.edu/master-science-mental-health-counseling

Washington University in St. Louis, Graduate School of Arts and Sciences, Department of Psychology, St. Louis, MO 63130-4899. Offers aging and development (PhD); behavior, brain, and cognition (PhD); clinical psychology (PhD); social and personality psychology (PhD). *Accreditation:* APA. Terminal master's awarded for partial completion of doctoral program. *Degree requirements:* For doctorate, thesis/dissertation. *Entrance requirements:* For doctorate, GRE General Test. Additional exam requirements/recommendations for international students: Required—TOEFL. Electronic applications accepted.

Wayne State University, College of Liberal Arts and Sciences, Department of Psychology, Detroit, MI 48202. Offers behavioral and cognitive neuroscience (PhD); clinical psychology (PhD); cognitive, developmental and social psychology (PhD); industrial and organizational psychology (MA); social psychology (PhD). Doctoral programs admit for fall only. *Accreditation:* APA (one or more programs are accredited). *Faculty:* 37 full-time (13 women), 8 part-time/adjunct (4 women). *Students:* 107 full-time (74 women), 28 part-time (16 women); includes 19 minority (8 Black or African American, non-Hispanic/Latino; 2 Asian, non-Hispanic/Latino; 5 Hispanic/Latino; 4 Two or more races, non-Hispanic/Latino), 10 international. Average age 28. 397 applicants, 11% accepted, 25 enrolled. In 2014, 24 master's, 18 doctorates awarded. Terminal master's awarded for partial completion of doctoral program. *Degree requirements:* For master's, thesis (for some programs); for doctorate, thesis/dissertation, training assignments. *Entrance requirements:* For master's, GRE General Test, minimum undergraduate upper-division cumulative GPA of 3.0, courses in introductory psychology and statistics, two letters of recommendation, professional statement; for doctorate, GRE General Test, bachelor's, master's, or other advanced degree; at least

three letters of recommendation; statement of purpose. Additional exam requirements/recommendations for international students: Required—TOEFL (minimum score 550 paper-based; 79 iBT), TWE (minimum score 5.5), Michigan English Language Assessment Battery (minimum score 85); Recommended—IELTS (minimum score 6.5). *Application deadline:* For fall admission, 12/1 for domestic and international students; for winter admission, 10/15 for domestic students, 9/1 for international students; for spring admission, 3/15 for domestic students, 1/1 for international students. Application fee: $0. Electronic applications accepted. *Expenses:* Tuition, state resident: full-time $10,294; part-time $571.90 per credit hour. Tuition, nonresident: full-time $29,730; part-time $1238.75 per credit hour. *Required fees:* $1365; $43.50 per credit hour. $291.10 per semester. Tuition and fees vary according to course load and program. *Financial support:* In 2014–15, 91 students received support, including 8 fellowships with tuition reimbursements available (averaging $15,983 per year), 12 research assistantships with tuition reimbursements available (averaging $17,862 per year), 49 teaching assistantships with tuition reimbursements available (averaging $16,838 per year); scholarships/grants, health care benefits, and unspecified assistantships also available. Financial award application deadline: 3/31; financial award applicants required to submit FAFSA. *Faculty research:* Neuroscience, including functional cognitive imaging, neural physiology, behavioral pharmacology, and neurobehavioral teratology; cognitive and neurochemical processes associated with aging, drug addiction and neurological disorders to studies of the neural circuits that underlie learning, emotion, and weight regulation; the life-long developmental plasticity of the neurobiological processes of behavior; neuropsychology; child clinical psychology; health psychology; community psychology. *Total annual research expenditures:* $2.1 million. *Unit head:* Boris Baltes, PhD, Chair/Professor, 313-577-2800, Fax: 313-577-7636, E-mail: b.baltes@wayne.edu. *Application contact:* Alia Allen, Academic Services Officer, 313-577-2823, E-mail: aallen@wayne.edu.
Website: http://clas.wayne.edu/psychology/

West Virginia University, Eberly College of Arts and Sciences, Department of Psychology, Morgantown, WV 26506. Offers behavior analysis (PhD); clinical psychology (MA, PhD); development psychology (PhD); psychology (MS). *Accreditation:* APA (one or more programs are accredited). Part-time programs available. Terminal master's awarded for partial completion of doctoral program. *Degree requirements:* For master's, thesis optional; for doctorate, comprehensive exam, thesis/dissertation. *Entrance requirements:* For master's and doctorate, GRE General Test, minimum GPA of 3.0. Additional exam requirements/recommendations for international students: Required—TOEFL. *Faculty research:* Adult and child clinical psychology, behavioral assessment and therapy, child and adolescent behavior, life span development, experimental and applied behavior analysis.

Wilfrid Laurier University, Faculty of Graduate and Postdoctoral Studies, Faculty of Science, Department of Psychology, Waterloo, ON N2L 3C5, Canada. Offers behavioral neuroscience (M Sc, PhD); cognitive neuroscience (M Sc, PhD); community psychology (MA, PhD); social and developmental psychology (MA, PhD). Part-time programs available. *Degree requirements:* For master's, thesis; for doctorate, thesis/dissertation. *Entrance requirements:* For master's, GRE General Test, honors BA or the equivalent in psychology, minimum B average in undergraduate course work; for doctorate, GRE General Test, master's degree, minimum A- average. Additional exam requirements/recommendations for international students: Required—TOEFL (minimum score 89 iBT). Electronic applications accepted. *Faculty research:* Brain and cognition, community psychology, social and developmental psychology.

Yale University, Graduate School of Arts and Sciences, Department of Psychology, New Haven, CT 06520. Offers behavioral neuroscience (PhD); clinical psychology (PhD); cognitive psychology (PhD); developmental psychology (PhD); social/personality psychology (PhD). *Accreditation:* APA. *Degree requirements:* For doctorate, thesis/dissertation. *Entrance requirements:* For doctorate, GRE General Test.

Experimental Psychology

Appalachian State University, Cratis D. Williams Graduate School, Department of Psychology, Boone, NC 28608. Offers clinical health psychology (MA); general experimental psychology (MA); industrial and organizational psychology (MA); MA/SSP. Part-time programs available. *Degree requirements:* For master's, comprehensive exam, thesis optional, exit exam. *Entrance requirements:* For master's, GRE General Test, 3 letters of recommendation. Additional exam requirements/recommendations for international students: Required—TOEFL (minimum score 550 paper-based; 79 iBT) or IELTS (minimum score 6.5). Electronic applications accepted. *Faculty research:* Eating disorders, school-based consultations, organizational behavior management, brain mechanisms of sound localization, parenting styles.

Auburn University, Graduate School, College of Liberal Arts, Department of Psychology, Auburn University, AL 36849. Offers applied behavior analysis in developmental disabilities (MS); clinical psychology (PhD); experimental psychology (PhD); industrial/organizational psychology (PhD). *Accreditation:* APA (one or more programs are accredited). Part-time programs available. *Faculty:* 23 full-time (9 women), 2 part-time/adjunct (both women). *Students:* 49 full-time (34 women), 47 part-time (31 women); includes 13 minority (6 Black or African American, non-Hispanic/Latino; 3 Asian, non-Hispanic/Latino; 4 Hispanic/Latino), 5 international. Average age 27. 328 applicants, 10% accepted, 23 enrolled. In 2014, 22 master's, 5 doctorates awarded. *Degree requirements:* For doctorate, thesis/dissertation. *Entrance requirements:* For master's, GRE General Test, GRE Subject Test, minimum GPA of 3.25 in psychology, 3.0 overall; for doctorate, GRE General Test, GRE Subject Test. *Application deadline:* For fall admission, 7/7 for domestic students; for spring admission, 11/24 for domestic students. Applications are processed on a rolling basis. Application fee: $50 ($60 for international students). Electronic applications accepted. *Expenses:* Tuition, state resident: full-time $8586; part-time $477 per credit hour. Tuition, nonresident: full-time $25,758; part-time $1431 per credit hour. *Required fees:* $804 per semester. Tuition and fees vary according to degree level and program. *Financial support:* Research assistantships, teaching assistantships, and Federal Work-Study available. Support available to part-time students. Financial award application deadline: 3/15; financial award applicants required to submit FAFSA. *Faculty research:* Clinical psychology, learning, industrial psychology, organizational psychology. *Total annual research expenditures:* $200,000. *Unit head:* Dr. Peter Chen, Head, 334-844-4412. *Application contact:* Dr. George Flowers, Dean of the Graduate School, 334-844-2125.

Bowling Green State University, Graduate College, College of Arts and Sciences, Department of Psychology, Bowling Green, OH 43403. Offers clinical psychology (MA, PhD); developmental psychology (MA, PhD); experimental psychology (MA, PhD); industrial/organizational psychology (MA, PhD); quantitative psychology (MA, PhD).

Accreditation: APA (one or more programs are accredited). *Degree requirements:* For doctorate, thesis/dissertation. *Entrance requirements:* For doctorate, GRE General Test, GRE Subject Test. Additional exam requirements/recommendations for international students: Required—TOEFL. Electronic applications accepted. *Faculty research:* Personnel psychology, developmental-mathematical models, behavioral medication, brain process, child/adolescent social cognition.

Brooklyn College of the City University of New York, School of Natural and Behavioral Sciences, Department of Psychology, Brooklyn, NY 11210-2889. Offers experimental psychology (MA); industrial and organizational psychology (MA), including human relations, organizational behavior; mental health counseling (MA); psychology (PhD). Part-time programs available. *Degree requirements:* For master's, comprehensive exam, thesis (for some programs). *Entrance requirements:* For master's, minimum GPA of 3.0, 2 letters of recommendation, essay; for doctorate, GRE. Additional exam requirements/recommendations for international students: Required—TOEFL (minimum score 520 paper-based; 69 iBT). Electronic applications accepted.

California State University, Northridge, Graduate Studies, College of Social and Behavioral Sciences, Department of Psychology, Northridge, CA 91330. Offers clinical psychology (MA); general-experimental psychology (MA); human factors and applied experimental psychology (MA). *Students:* 46 full-time (32 women), 16 part-time (10 women); includes 27 minority (3 Black or African American, non-Hispanic/Latino; 2 Asian, non-Hispanic/Latino; 20 Hispanic/Latino; 2 Two or more races, non-Hispanic/Latino). Average age 26. *Degree requirements:* For master's, thesis. *Entrance requirements:* For master's, GRE General Test, GRE Subject Test, minimum GPA of 3.0, letters of recommendation. Additional exam requirements/recommendations for international students: Required—TOEFL. *Application deadline:* For fall admission, 11/30 for domestic students. Application fee: $55. *Expenses: Required fees:* $12,402. *Financial support:* Application deadline: 3/1. *Unit head:* Jill Razani, Chair, 818-677-3506.
Website: http://www.csun.edu/csbs/departments/psychology/index.html

California State University, San Bernardino, Graduate Studies, College of Social and Behavioral Sciences, Department of Psychology, Program in General/Experimental Psychology, San Bernardino, CA 92407-2397. Offers MA. *Students:* 17 full-time (11 women), 17 part-time (11 women); includes 18 minority (1 Black or African American, non-Hispanic/Latino; 1 Asian, non-Hispanic/Latino; 13 Hispanic/Latino; 3 Two or more races, non-Hispanic/Latino), 3 international. Average age 27. 33 applicants, 52% accepted, 10 enrolled. In 2014, 7 master's awarded. *Degree requirements:* For master's, thesis. *Entrance requirements:* Additional exam requirements/recommendations for international students: Required—TOEFL. *Application deadline:* For fall admission, 7/17

Experimental Psychology

for domestic students; for spring admission, 3/1 for domestic students. Application fee: $55. *Expenses:* Tuition, state resident: full-time $6738; part-time $1302 per term. Tuition, nonresident: full-time $17,898; part-time $248 per unit. *Required fees:* $365 per quarter. Tuition and fees vary according to degree level and program. *Financial support:* Unspecified assistantships available. *Unit head:* Dr. Robert Ricco, Director, 909-537-5485, Fax: 909-537-7003, E-mail: rricco@csusb.edu. *Application contact:* Dr. Jeffrey Thompson, Dean, 909-537-5058, E-mail: jthompso@csusb.edu.

Case Western Reserve University, School of Graduate Studies, Psychological Sciences Department, Program in Experimental Psychology, Cleveland, OH 44106. Offers PhD. *Faculty:* 12 full-time (7 women). *Students:* 10 full-time (7 women); includes 2 minority (1 Black or African American, non-Hispanic/Latino; 1 Asian, non-Hispanic/Latino). Average age 27. 165 applicants, 4% accepted, 3 enrolled. In 2014, 1 doctorate awarded. *Degree requirements:* For doctorate, thesis/dissertation, internship. *Entrance requirements:* For doctorate, GRE General Test, GRE Subject Test; personal statement, three letters of recommendation; CV. Additional exam requirements/recommendations for international students: Required—TOEFL (minimum score 577 paper-based; 90 iBT); Recommended—IELTS (minimum score 7). *Application deadline:* For fall admission, 1/15 priority date for domestic students. Application fee: $50. Electronic applications accepted. *Financial support:* Research assistantships and teaching assistantships available. Financial award application deadline: 1/15; financial award applicants required to submit FAFSA. *Faculty research:* Development and evaluation of cognitive behavioral treatments for anxiety and mood disorders, evaluating treatments for post-traumatic stress disorder (PTSD), depression and bipolar disorder in youth, family relations and emotional expressions. *Unit head:* Dr. Lee Thompson, Chair, 216-368-2685, Fax: 216-368-4891, E-mail: cwrupsych@gmail.com. *Application contact:* Dr. James C. Overholser, Director of Clinical Training, 216-368-2686, Fax: 216-368-4891, E-mail: cwrupsych@gmail.com.
Website: http://psychsciences.case.edu/graduate/

The Catholic University of America, School of Arts and Sciences, Department of Psychology, Washington, DC 20064. Offers applied experimental psychology (PhD); clinical psychology (PhD); general psychology (MA); human factors (MA); MA/JD. *Accreditation:* APA (one or more programs are accredited). Part-time programs available. *Faculty:* 13 full-time (6 women), 7 part-time/adjunct (2 women). *Students:* 37 full-time (26 women), 42 part-time (33 women); includes 17 minority (1 Black or African American, non-Hispanic/Latino; 3 Asian, non-Hispanic/Latino; 7 Hispanic/Latino; 6 Two or more races, non-Hispanic/Latino), 3 international. Average age 28. 263 applicants, 14% accepted, 19 enrolled. In 2014, 19 master's, 6 doctorates awarded. *Degree requirements:* For master's, comprehensive exam, thesis (for some programs); for doctorate, comprehensive exam, thesis/dissertation. *Entrance requirements:* For master's, GRE General Test, statement of purpose, official copies of academic transcripts, three letters of recommendation; for doctorate, GRE General Test, GRE Subject Test, statement of purpose, official copies of academic transcripts, three letters of recommendation. Additional exam requirements/recommendations for international students: Required—TOEFL (minimum score 580 paper-based). *Application deadline:* For fall admission, 7/15 priority date for domestic students, 7/1 for international students; for spring admission, 11/15 priority date for domestic students, 11/1 for international students. Applications are processed on a rolling basis. Application fee: $55. Electronic applications accepted. *Expenses: Tuition:* Full-time $40,200; part-time $1600 per credit hour. *Required fees:* $400; $195 per semester. One-time fee: $425. *Financial support:* Fellowships, research assistantships, teaching assistantships, Federal Work-Study, scholarships/grants, tuition waivers (full and partial), and unspecified assistantships available. Financial award application deadline: 2/1; financial award applicants required to submit FAFSA. *Faculty research:* Clinical psychology, applied cognitive science, psychopathology, cognitive neuroscience, psychotherapy. *Total annual research expenditures:* $1.2 million. *Unit head:* Dr. Marc M. Sebrechts, Chair, 202-319-5750, Fax: 202-319-6263, E-mail: sebrechts@cua.edu. *Application contact:* Director of Graduate Admissions, 202-319-5057, Fax: 202-319-6533, E-mail: cua-admissions@cua.edu.
Website: http://psychology.cua.edu/

Central Michigan University, College of Graduate Studies, College of Humanities and Social and Behavioral Sciences, Department of Psychology, Program in Experimental Psychology, Mount Pleasant, MI 48859. Offers applied experimental psychology (PhD); experimental psychology (MS). Part-time programs available. *Degree requirements:* For master's, thesis or alternative; for doctorate, thesis/dissertation. Electronic applications accepted. *Faculty research:* Behavioral neuroscience, human development, perception and cognition, social/personal problem solving, psychophysiology.

Central Washington University, Graduate Studies and Research, College of the Sciences, Department of Psychology, Program in Experimental Psychology, Ellensburg, WA 98926. Offers MS. *Degree requirements:* For master's, thesis or alternative. *Entrance requirements:* For master's, GRE General Test, minimum GPA of 3.0. Additional exam requirements/recommendations for international students: Required—TOEFL (minimum score 550 paper-based; 79 iBT). Electronic applications accepted.

City College of the City University of New York, Graduate School, College of Liberal Arts and Science, Division of Social Science, Department of Psychology, New York, NY 10031-9198. Offers clinical psychology (PhD); experimental cognition (PhD); general psychology (MA); mental health counseling (MA). PhD program offered jointly with Graduate School and University Center of the City University of New York. *Accreditation:* APA (one or more programs are accredited). Part-time programs available. *Degree requirements:* For master's, one foreign language, comprehensive exam, thesis. *Entrance requirements:* For master's, GRE. Additional exam requirements/recommendations for international students: Required—TOEFL (minimum score 550 paper-based; 79 iBT). Electronic applications accepted. *Faculty research:* Social/personality psychology, physiological psychology, cognition and development.

The College of William and Mary, Faculty of Arts and Sciences, Department of Psychology, Williamsburg, VA 23187-8795. Offers MA. *Faculty:* 21 full-time (8 women). *Students:* 17 full-time (12 women); includes 6 minority (3 Asian, non-Hispanic/Latino; 3 Hispanic/Latino), 3 international. Average age 23. 113 applicants, 7% accepted, 8 enrolled. In 2014, 11 master's awarded. *Degree requirements:* For master's, thesis. *Entrance requirements:* For master's, GRE. Additional exam requirements/recommendations for international students: Required—TOEFL, IELTS. *Application deadline:* For fall admission, 2/1 for domestic and international students. Application fee: $45. Electronic applications accepted. *Financial support:* In 2014–15, 17 students received support, including 1 research assistantship (averaging $13,500 per year), 16 teaching assistantships (averaging $13,500 per year). *Faculty research:* Personality, developmental, clinical and neuroscience, social psychology. *Total annual research expenditures:* $570,118. *Unit head:* Dr. Janice Zeman, Chair, 757-221-3870, E-mail: jlzema@wm.edu. *Application contact:* Tracy Coates, Administrator of Graduate Student Services, 757-221-3870, Fax: 757-221-3896, E-mail: tlcoates@wm.edu.
Website: http://www.wm.edu/as/psychology

Cornell University, Graduate School, Graduate Fields of Arts and Sciences, Field of Psychology, Ithaca, NY 14853-0001. Offers biopsychology (PhD); human experimental psychology (PhD); personality and social psychology (PhD). *Degree requirements:* For doctorate, comprehensive exam, thesis/dissertation, 2 semesters of teaching experience. *Entrance requirements:* For doctorate, GRE General Test, 3 letters of

recommendation. Additional exam requirements/recommendations for international students: Required—TOEFL (minimum score 550 paper-based; 77 iBT). Electronic applications accepted. *Faculty research:* Sensory and perceptual systems, social cognition, cognitive development, quantitative and computational modeling, behavioral neuroscience.

Dallas Baptist University, Gary Cook School of Leadership, Program in Christian Education, Dallas, TX 75211-9299. Offers adult ministry (MA); business ministry (MA); Christian studies (MA); collegiate ministry (MA); communication ministry (MA); counseling ministry (MA); family ministry (MA); general ministry (MA); leading the nonprofit organization (MA); missions ministry (MA); small group ministry (MA); student ministry (MA); worship ministry (MA); MA/MA. Part-time and evening/weekend programs available. *Entrance requirements:* For master's, minimum GPA of 3.0. Additional exam requirements/recommendations for international students: Required—TOEFL. Electronic applications accepted. *Expenses: Tuition:* Full-time $14,130; part-time $785 per credit hour. *Required fees:* $200 per semester. Tuition and fees vary according to course level and course load.

Duke University, Graduate School, Department of Psychology and Neuroscience, Durham, NC 27708. Offers biological psychology (PhD); clinical psychology (PhD); cognitive psychology (PhD); developmental psychology (PhD); experimental psychology (PhD); health psychology (PhD); human social development (PhD); JD/MA. *Accreditation:* APA (one or more programs are accredited). *Degree requirements:* For doctorate, thesis/dissertation. *Entrance requirements:* For doctorate, GRE General Test. Additional exam requirements/recommendations for international students: Required—TOEFL (minimum score 577 paper-based; 90 iBT) or IELTS (minimum score 7). Electronic applications accepted. *Expenses: Tuition:* Full-time $45,760; part-time $2765 per credit. *Required fees:* $978. Full-time tuition and fees vary according to program.

Eastern Washington University, Graduate Studies, College of Social and Behavioral Sciences and Social Work, Department of Psychology, Cheney, WA 99004-2431. Offers clinical psychology (MS); experimental psychology (MS); psychology (MS). *Degree requirements:* For master's, comprehensive exam, thesis or alternative. *Entrance requirements:* For master's, GRE General Test, minimum GPA of 3.0.

Fairleigh Dickinson University, Metropolitan Campus, University College: Arts, Sciences, and Professional Studies, School of Psychology, Program in General-Theoretical Psychology, Teaneck, NJ 07666-1914. Offers MA, Certificate.

Florida Atlantic University, Charles E. Schmidt College of Science, Department of Psychology, Boca Raton, FL 33431-0991. Offers experimental psychology (PhD); psychology (MA). Terminal master's awarded for partial completion of doctoral program. *Degree requirements:* For master's, one foreign language, thesis or alternative; for doctorate, one foreign language, comprehensive exam, thesis/dissertation. *Entrance requirements:* For master's and doctorate, GRE General Test, minimum GPA of 3.0 during previous 2 years. Additional exam requirements/recommendations for international students: Required—TOEFL (minimum score 500 paper-based; 61 iBT), IELTS (minimum score 6). Electronic applications accepted. *Expenses:* Tuition, state resident: full-time $7396; part-time $369.82 per credit hour. Tuition, nonresident: full-time $19,392; part-time $1024.81 per credit hour. Tuition and fees vary according to course load. *Faculty research:* Cognition, psychobiology, developmental psychology, social psychology, neuroscience.

The Graduate Center, City University of New York, Graduate Studies, Program in Psychology, New York, NY 10016-4039. Offers basic applied neurocognition (PhD); biopsychology (PhD); clinical psychology (PhD); developmental psychology (PhD); environmental psychology (PhD); experimental psychology (PhD); industrial psychology (PhD); learning processes (PhD); neuropsychology (PhD); psychology (PhD); social personality (PhD). *Degree requirements:* For doctorate, one foreign language, thesis/dissertation. *Entrance requirements:* For doctorate, GRE General Test. Additional exam requirements/recommendations for international students: Required—TOEFL. Electronic applications accepted.

Harvard University, Graduate School of Arts and Sciences, Department of Psychology, Cambridge, MA 02138. Offers psychology (PhD), including behavior and decision analysis, cognition, developmental psychology, experimental psychology, personality, psychobiology, psychopathology; social psychology (PhD). *Accreditation:* APA. *Degree requirements:* For doctorate, thesis/dissertation, general exams. *Entrance requirements:* For doctorate, GRE General Test. Additional exam requirements/recommendations for international students: Required—TOEFL.

Howard University, Graduate School, Department of Psychology, Washington, DC 20059-0002. Offers clinical psychology (PhD); developmental psychology (PhD); experimental psychology (PhD); neuropsychology (PhD); personality psychology (PhD); psychology (MS); social psychology (PhD). *Accreditation:* APA (one or more programs are accredited). Part-time programs available. *Degree requirements:* For master's, thesis; for doctorate, comprehensive exam, thesis/dissertation, qualifying exam. *Entrance requirements:* For master's, GRE General Test, minimum GPA of 2.5, bachelor's degree in psychology or related field; for doctorate, GRE General Test, minimum GPA of 3.0. *Faculty research:* Personality and psychophysiology, educational and social development of African-American children, child and adult psychopathology.

Idaho State University, Office of Graduate Studies, College of Arts and Letters, Department of Psychology, Program in Experimental Psychology, Pocatello, ID 83209. Offers PhD. *Entrance requirements:* For doctorate, GRE, BA/BS in psychology or the equivalent, minimum undergraduate GPA of 3.0 for the last two years.

Illinois State University, Graduate School, College of Arts and Sciences, Department of Psychology, Normal, IL 61790-2200. Offers psychology (MA, MS), including clinical psychology, counseling psychology, developmental psychology, educational psychology, experimental psychology, measurement-evaluation, organizational-industrial psychology; school psychology (PhD, SSP). *Accreditation:* APA. *Degree requirements:* For master's, thesis or alternative; for doctorate, variable foreign language requirement, thesis/dissertation, 2 terms of residency, internship, practicum. *Entrance requirements:* For master's, GRE General Test, GRE Subject Test, minimum GPA of 3.0 in last 60 hours of course work; for doctorate, GRE General Test. *Faculty research:* Comprehensive evaluation system for the central region professional development grant, Illinois school psychology internship consortium, for children's sake.

Iona College, School of Arts and Science, Department of Psychology, New Rochelle, NY 10801-1890. Offers general-experimental psychology (MA); human resources (Certificate); industrial-organizational psychology (MA); mental health counseling (MA); organizational behavior (Certificate); psychology (MA); school psychology (MA). Part-time programs available. *Faculty:* 8 full-time (3 women), 5 part-time/adjunct (3 women). *Students:* 41 full-time (30 women), 33 part-time (22 women); includes 29 minority (12 Black or African American, non-Hispanic/Latino; 2 Asian, non-Hispanic/Latino; 15 Hispanic/Latino), 1 international. Average age 24. 65 applicants, 85% accepted, 22 enrolled. In 2014, 38 master's awarded. *Degree requirements:* For master's, thesis (for some programs), literature review (for some programs). *Entrance requirements:* For master's, BA in psychology including 3 credits in psychology statistics and 3 credits in experimental research methods; or 9 credits in psychology including 3 credits in psychology statistics, 3 credits in psychology research methods and 3 credits of upper-

level coursework. Additional exam requirements/recommendations for international students: Required—TOEFL (minimum score 550 paper-based), IELTS (minimum score 6.5). *Application deadline:* For fall admission, 8/15 for domestic students, 5/1 for international students; for spring admission, 1/15 for domestic students, 9/1 for international students. Applications are processed on a rolling basis. Application fee: $50. Electronic applications accepted. *Expenses: Tuition:* Part-time $985 per credit. *Required fees:* $245 per term. *Financial support:* In 2014–15, 6 students received support, including 1 research assistantship with partial tuition reimbursement available (averaging $8,000 per year); tuition waivers (partial) and unspecified assistantships also available. Support available to part-time students. Financial award application deadline: 4/15; financial award applicants required to submit FAFSA. *Faculty research:* Non-suicidal self-injury, trauma response, performance appraisal and evaluation, diversity infusion, assessment and treatment of sexual offenders. *Unit head:* Patricia Oswald, PhD, Chair, 914-633-7788, E-mail: poswald@iona.edu. *Application contact:* Amanda St. Bernard, Assistant Director, Graduate Admissions, 914-633-2440, Fax: 914-633-2277, E-mail: astbernard@iona.edu.
Website: http://www.iona.edu/Academics/School-of-Arts-Science/Departments/Psychology/Graduate-Programs.aspx

Kent State University, College of Arts and Sciences, Department of Psychological Sciences, Kent, OH 44242-0001. Offers clinical psychology (MA, PhD); experimental psychology (MA, PhD). *Accreditation:* APA (one or more programs are accredited). Part-time programs available. *Faculty:* 28 full-time (15 women). *Students:* 90 full-time (64 women), 1 part-time (0 women); includes 8 minority (4 Black or African American, non-Hispanic/Latino; 2 Asian, non-Hispanic/Latino; 2 Hispanic/Latino), 5 international. Average age 27. 858 applicants, 5% accepted, 31 enrolled. In 2014, 10 master's, 21 doctorates awarded. Terminal master's awarded for partial completion of doctoral program. *Degree requirements:* For master's, thesis; for doctorate, thesis/dissertation. *Entrance requirements:* For master's, GRE General Test, minimum GPA of 3.0, transcript, resume, statement of purpose, 3 letters of recommendation; for doctorate, GRE General Test, minimum GPA of 3.0, transcript, resume, statement of purpose, writing sample, 3 letters of recommendation. Additional exam requirements/recommendations for international students: Required—TOEFL (minimum score: paper-based 525, iBT 71), Michigan English Language Assessment Battery (minimum score of 75), IELTS (minimum score of 6.0), PTE Academic (minimum score of 48), or completion of ELS level 112 Intensive Program. *Application deadline:* For fall admission, 12/15 for domestic students, 1/1 for international students. Application fee: $45 ($70 for international students). Electronic applications accepted. *Expenses:* Tuition, state resident: full-time $8730; part-time $485 per credit hour. Tuition, nonresident: full-time $14,886; part-time $827 per credit hour. Tuition and fees vary according to campus/location and program. *Financial support:* Research assistantships with full tuition reimbursements, teaching assistantships with full tuition reimbursements, career-related internships or fieldwork, Federal Work-Study, and unspecified assistantships available. Financial award application deadline: 1/1. *Unit head:* Dr. Maria Zaragoza, Professor and Chair, 330-672-2018, E-mail: mzaragoz@kent.edu. *Application contact:* Dr. John Updegraff, Associate Professor and Graduate Coordinator, 330-672-2166, Fax: 330-672-3786, E-mail: jupdegr1@kent.edu.
Website: http://www.kent.edu/psychology/graduate-programs

Lakehead University, Graduate Studies, Department of Psychology, Thunder Bay, ON P7B 5E1, Canada. Offers clinical psychology (PhD); experimental psychology (MA). Part-time and evening/weekend programs available. *Degree requirements:* For master's, thesis optional; for doctorate, thesis/dissertation, 2 comprehensive exams, internship. *Entrance requirements:* For master's, GRE, honors degree in psychology, advanced course work in statistics, minimum B average; for doctorate, GRE, minimum B average. Additional exam requirements/recommendations for international students: Required—TOEFL. *Faculty research:* Chaos theory, health psychology, counseling psychology, gerontology, women's studies.

Laurentian University, School of Graduate Studies and Research, Programme in Psychology, Sudbury, ON P3E 2C6, Canada. Offers applied psychology (MA); experimental psychology (MA).

McGill University, Faculty of Graduate and Postdoctoral Studies, Faculty of Science, Department of Psychology, Montréal, QC H3A 2T5, Canada. Offers clinical psychology (PhD); experimental psychology (M Sc, MA, PhD). *Accreditation:* APA (one or more programs are accredited).

McNeese State University, Doré School of Graduate Studies, Burton College of Education, Department of Psychology, Lake Charles, LA 70609. Offers addiction treatment (MA); applied behavior analysis (MA); counseling psychology (MA); general/experimental psychology (MA). Evening/weekend programs available. *Entrance requirements:* For master's, GRE.

Memorial University of Newfoundland, School of Graduate Studies, Department of Psychology, St. John's, NL A1C 5S7, Canada. Offers applied social psychology (MASP); experimental psychology (M Sc, PhD). Part-time programs available. *Degree requirements:* For master's, workterms (MASP), thesis (M Sc); for doctorate, comprehensive exam, thesis/dissertation, oral thesis defense. *Entrance requirements:* For master's, GRE, honors bachelor's degree of high second class standing or equivalent; for doctorate, GRE, master's or honors degree. Additional exam requirements/recommendations for international students: Recommended—TOEFL. Electronic applications accepted. *Faculty research:* Behavioral neuroscience, cognition, theory and research on abnormal behavior.

Middle Tennessee State University, College of Graduate Studies, College of Behavioral and Health Sciences, Department of Psychology, Murfreesboro, TN 37132. Offers clinical psychology (MA); experimental psychology (MA); industrial/organizational psychology (MA); psychology (MA, Ed S); quantitative psychology (MA); school psychology (MA). Part-time and evening/weekend programs available. Postbaccalaureate distance learning degree programs offered. *Faculty:* 37 full-time (14 women), 3 part-time/adjunct (2 women). *Students:* 66 full-time (54 women), 47 part-time (37 women); includes 15 minority (8 Black or African American, non-Hispanic/Latino; 1 American Indian or Alaska Native, non-Hispanic/Latino; 2 Asian, non-Hispanic/Latino; 3 Hispanic/Latino; 1 Two or more races, non-Hispanic/Latino), 1 international. 225 applicants, 84% accepted. In 2014, 37 master's awarded. *Degree requirements:* For master's, comprehensive exam, thesis. *Entrance requirements:* For master's, GRE. Additional exam requirements/recommendations for international students: Required—TOEFL (minimum score 525 paper-based; 71 iBT) or IELTS (minimum score 6). *Application deadline:* For fall admission, 6/1 for domestic and international students. Applications are processed on a rolling basis. Application fee: $30. Electronic applications accepted. *Financial support:* In 2014–15, 38 students received support. Tuition waivers available. Support available to part-time students. Financial award application deadline: 4/1; financial award applicants required to submit FAFSA. *Faculty research:* Health psychology, industrial/organizational psychology, experimental psychology. *Unit head:* Dr. Greg Schmidt, Chair, 615-898-2706, Fax: 615-898-5027, E-mail: greg.schmidt@mtsu.edu. *Application contact:* Dr. Michael D. Allen, Vice Provost for Research/Dean, 615-898-2840, Fax: 615-904-8020, E-mail: michael.allen@mtsu.edu.

Mississippi State University, College of Arts and Sciences, Department of Psychology, Mississippi State, MS 39762. Offers applied cognitive science (PhD); clinical psychology (MS); experimental psychology (MS). *Faculty:* 19 full-time (7 women), 1 part-time/adjunct (0 women). *Students:* 36 full-time (23 women); includes 5 minority (2 Black or African American, non-Hispanic/Latino; 2 Asian, non-Hispanic/Latino; 1 Two or more races, non-Hispanic/Latino), 4 international. Average age 26. 64 applicants, 36% accepted, 20 enrolled. In 2014, 7 master's, 1 doctorate awarded. Terminal master's awarded for partial completion of doctoral program. *Degree requirements:* For master's, comprehensive exam, thesis; for doctorate, thesis/dissertation, qualifying exam, comprehensive written and oral exam. *Entrance requirements:* For master's, GRE General Test, minimum GPA of 2.75 on last two years of undergraduate courses; for doctorate, GRE General Test, proficiency in at least 1 computer language, minimum GPA of 3.0. Additional exam requirements/recommendations for international students: Required—TOEFL (minimum score 477 paper-based; 53 iBT); Recommended—IELTS (minimum score 4.5). *Application deadline:* For fall admission, 1/15 priority date for domestic students, 5/1 for international students; for spring admission, 11/1 priority date for domestic students, 9/1 for international students. Applications are processed on a rolling basis. Application fee: $60. Electronic applications accepted. *Expenses:* Tuition, state resident: full-time $7140; part-time $783 per credit hour. Tuition, nonresident: full-time $18,478; part-time $2043 per credit hour. *Financial support:* In 2014–15, 6 research assistantships with full tuition reimbursements (averaging $12,729 per year), 18 teaching assistantships with full tuition reimbursements (averaging $8,808 per year) were awarded; career-related internships or fieldwork, Federal Work-Study, institutionally sponsored loans, scholarships/grants, and unspecified assistantships also available. Financial award application deadline: 4/1; financial award applicants required to submit FAFSA. *Faculty research:* Personality type, alcoholism, blindness and low vision, mental retardation, language comprehension. *Total annual research expenditures:* $1.1 million. *Unit head:* Dr. Mitchell E. Berman, Department Head, 662-325-3202, Fax: 662-325-7212, E-mail: mberman@psychology.msstate.edu. *Application contact:* Dr. Deborah Eakin, Graduate Coordinator, 662-325-3202, Fax: 662-325-7212, E-mail: grad@psychology.msstate.edu.
Website: http://www.psychology.msstate.edu/

Missouri State University, Graduate College, College of Health and Human Services, Department of Psychology, Springfield, MO 65897. Offers clinical psychology (MS); experimental (MS). *Faculty:* 25 full-time (11 women), 4 part-time/adjunct (0 women). *Students:* 55 full-time (41 women), 7 part-time (5 women); includes 10 minority (3 Black or African American, non-Hispanic/Latino; 3 Asian, non-Hispanic/Latino; 4 Hispanic/Latino), 3 international. Average age 25. 119 applicants, 24% accepted, 23 enrolled. In 2014, 22 master's awarded. *Degree requirements:* For master's, comprehensive exam, thesis. *Entrance requirements:* For master's, GRE General Test, GRE Subject Test, minimum GPA of 3.25 in major, 3.0 overall; 20 hours of course work in psychology. Additional exam requirements/recommendations for international students: Required—TOEFL (minimum score 550 paper-based; 79 iBT). *Application deadline:* For fall admission, 3/1 priority date for domestic and international students. Application fee: $35 ($50 for international students). Electronic applications accepted. *Expenses:* Tuition, state resident: full-time $2250; part-time $250 per credit hour. Tuition, nonresident: full-time $4509; part-time $501 per credit hour. Tuition and fees vary according to course level, course load and program. *Financial support:* In 2014–15, 5 research assistantships with full tuition reimbursements (averaging $8,450 per year), 6 teaching assistantships with full tuition reimbursements (averaging $8,450 per year) were awarded; career-related internships or fieldwork, Federal Work-Study, institutionally sponsored loans, scholarships/grants, and unspecified assistantships also available. Financial award application deadline: 3/31; financial award applicants required to submit FAFSA. *Faculty research:* Work-family conflict, child forensic psychology, sports psychology, body image assessment, visual learning. *Unit head:* Dr. Robert Jones, Interim Head, 417-836-5797, Fax: 417-836-8330, E-mail: psychology@missouristate.edu. *Application contact:* Misty Stewart, Coordinator of Graduate Recruitment, 417-836-6079, Fax: 417-836-6200, E-mail: mistystewart@missouristate.edu.
Website: http://psychology.missouristate.edu/

Morehead State University, Graduate Programs, College of Science and Technology, Department of Psychology, Morehead, KY 40351. Offers clinical/counseling psychology (MS); general/experimental psychology (MS). Part-time and evening/weekend programs available. *Degree requirements:* For master's, comprehensive exam, thesis optional. *Entrance requirements:* For master's, GRE General Test, 18 undergraduate hours in psychology, minimum GPA of 3.0, 3 letters of recommendation. Additional exam requirements/recommendations for international students: Required—TOEFL (minimum score 500 paper-based). Electronic applications accepted. *Faculty research:* Mood induction effects, serotonin receptor activity, stress, perceptual processes.

New Mexico State University, College of Arts and Sciences, Department of Psychology, Las Cruces, NM 88003-8001. Offers cognitive psychology (PhD); engineering psychology (PhD); experimental psychology (MA); social psychology (PhD). Part-time programs available. *Faculty:* 11 full-time (3 women). *Students:* 31 full-time (15 women), 5 part-time (2 women); includes 7 minority (2 Asian, non-Hispanic/Latino; 3 Hispanic/Latino; 2 Two or more races, non-Hispanic/Latino), 5 international. Average age 29. 56 applicants, 27% accepted, 10 enrolled. In 2014, 6 master's, 5 doctorates awarded. *Degree requirements:* For master's, thesis; for doctorate, comprehensive exam, thesis/dissertation, work-related experience (teaching or internship). *Entrance requirements:* For master's, GRE General Test, letters of recommendation, curriculum vitae, personal statement; for doctorate, GRE General Test, letters of recommendation, master's thesis, curriculum vitae, personal statement. Additional exam requirements/recommendations for international students: Required—TOEFL (minimum score 550 paper-based; 79 iBT), IELTS (minimum score 6.5). *Application deadline:* For fall admission, 2/1 priority date for domestic students, 2/1 for international students. Applications are processed on a rolling basis. Application fee: $40 ($50 for international students). Electronic applications accepted. *Expenses:* Tuition, state resident: full-time $3969; part-time $220.50 per credit hour. Tuition, nonresident: full-time $13,838; part-time $768.80 per credit hour. *Required fees:* $853; $47.40 per credit hour. *Financial support:* In 2014–15, 34 students received support, including 7 fellowships (averaging $3,970 per year), 4 research assistantships (averaging $14,330 per year), 20 teaching assistantships (averaging $9,979 per year); career-related internships or fieldwork, Federal Work-Study, scholarships/grants, traineeships, health care benefits, and unspecified assistantships also available. Support available to part-time students. Financial award application deadline: 3/1. *Faculty research:* Engineering, cognitive, and social psychology; human/computer interaction; cognitive science. *Total annual research expenditures:* $184,443. *Unit head:* Dr. Dominic A. Simon, Academic Department Head, 575-646-2502, Fax: 575-646-6212, E-mail: domsimon@nmsu.edu. *Application contact:* Dr. Laura J. Madson, Chair of Graduate Committee, 575-646-6207, Fax: 575-646-6212, E-mail: lmadson@nmsu.edu.
Website: http://psych.nmsu.edu

North Carolina State University, Graduate School, College of Humanities and Social Sciences, Department of Psychology, Raleigh, NC 27695. Offers developmental psychology (PhD); ergonomics and experimental psychology (PhD); industrial/organizational psychology (PhD); psychology in the public interest (PhD); school

psychology (PhD). *Accreditation:* APA. *Degree requirements:* For doctorate, comprehensive exam, thesis/dissertation. *Entrance requirements:* For doctorate, GRE General Test, GRE Subject Test (industrial/organizational psychology), MAT (recommended), minimum GPA of 3.0 in major. Electronic applications accepted. *Faculty research:* Cognitive and social development (human factors, families, the workplace, community issues and health, aging).

Northeastern University, College of Science, Department of Psychology, Boston, MA 02115-5096. Offers experimental psychology (PhD). *Degree requirements:* For doctorate, thesis/dissertation. *Entrance requirements:* For doctorate, GRE General Test. Additional exam requirements/recommendations for international students: Required—TOEFL (minimum score 100 iBT). Electronic applications accepted. *Faculty research:* Behavioral, neuroscience language and cognition, perception, personality and social.

Nova Southeastern University, Farquhar College of Arts and Sciences, Program in Experimental Psychology, Fort Lauderdale, FL 33314-7796. Offers MS. *Faculty:* 13 full-time (6 women). *Students:* 10 full-time (6 women); includes 2 minority (1 Black or African American, non-Hispanic/Latino; 1 Hispanic/Latino). Average age 25. 21 applicants, 52% accepted, 5 enrolled. In 2014, 7 master's awarded. *Degree requirements:* For master's, comprehensive exam, thesis. *Entrance requirements:* For master's, GRE General Test; GRE Subject Test in psychology (if bachelor's degree not in psychology), 3 letters of recommendation, official transcripts, 500-word essay. Additional exam requirements/recommendations for international students: Required—TOEFL (minimum score 550 paper-based; 79 iBT). *Application deadline:* For fall admission, 6/1 for domestic and international students. Application fee: $50. Electronic applications accepted. *Expenses:* Expenses: $590 per credit; $25 registration fee (per semester); Student Services Fees: $150 (per semester) for 1-3 credits, $300 (per semester) for 4 or more credits. *Financial support:* Application deadline: 6/30; applicants required to submit FAFSA. *Faculty research:* Stress and cognitive processes, memory, neuroscience, autism, behavior analysis, evolutionary psychology, interpersonal perception, biological effects of sleep and sleep deprivation, human psychophysiology. *Unit head:* Dr. Glenn Scheyd, Jr., Associate Professor/Assistant Director, Division of Social and Behavioral Sciences, 954-262-7991, E-mail: scheydjr@nova.edu. *Application contact:* Isabelle De Castro, Graduate Program Enrollment Coordinator, 954-262-8361, E-mail: id7@nova.edu.
Website: http://www.fcas.nova.edu/programs/graduate/experimental_psychology/index.cfm

Ohio University, Graduate College, College of Arts and Sciences, Department of Psychology, Program in Experimental Psychology, Athens, OH 45701-2979. Offers MA, PhD. *Degree requirements:* For doctorate, one foreign language, comprehensive exam, thesis/dissertation. *Entrance requirements:* For doctorate, GRE General Test, GRE Subject Test, minimum graduate GPA of 3.4. Additional exam requirements/recommendations for international students: Required—TOEFL. *Faculty research:* Cognitive psychology, quantitative psychology, social psychology, judgment and decision-making, health psychology.

Old Dominion University, College of Sciences, Doctoral Program in Psychology, Norfolk, VA 23529. Offers applied experimental psychology (PhD); human factors psychology (PhD). *Faculty:* 22 full-time (7 women). *Students:* 35 full-time (16 women), 17 part-time (13 women); includes 8 minority (3 Black or African American, non-Hispanic/Latino; 5 Hispanic/Latino), 3 international. Average age 27. 82 applicants, 30% accepted, 7 enrolled. In 2014, 5 doctorates awarded. *Degree requirements:* For doctorate, thesis/dissertation, candidacy exam. *Entrance requirements:* For doctorate, GRE General Test, GRE Subject Test, 3 recommendation letters. Additional exam requirements/recommendations for international students: Required—TOEFL. *Application deadline:* For winter admission, 1/5 for domestic and international students. Application fee: $50. Electronic applications accepted. *Expenses:* Tuition, state resident: full-time $10,488; part-time $437 per credit. Tuition, nonresident: full-time $26,136; part-time $1089 per credit. *Required fees:* $64 per semester. One-time fee: $50. *Financial support:* In 2014–15, 42 students received support, including 4 research assistantships with full tuition reimbursements available (averaging $17,500 per year), 38 teaching assistantships with full tuition reimbursements available (averaging $17,500 per year). Financial award application deadline: 1/15. *Faculty research:* Human factors, industrial psychology, organizational psychology, applied experimental (health, developmental, quantitative). *Total annual research expenditures:* $978,563. *Unit head:* Dr. Bryan E. Porter, Graduate Program Director, 757-683-4458, Fax: 757-683-5087, E-mail: bporter@odu.edu. *Application contact:* William Heffelfinger, Director of Graduate Admissions, 757-683-5554, Fax: 757-683-3255, E-mail: gradadmit@odu.edu.
Website: http://sci.odu.edu/psychology/

Radford University, College of Graduate and Professional Studies, College of Humanities and Behavioral Sciences, Department of Psychology, Program in Psychology, Radford, VA 24142. Offers clinical psychology (MA, MS); experimental psychology (MA); industrial/organizational psychology (MA, MS). Part-time programs available. *Faculty:* 14 full-time (7 women). *Students:* 47 full-time (29 women); includes 3 minority (2 Asian, non-Hispanic/Latino; 1 Hispanic/Latino). Average age 24. 117 applicants, 40% accepted, 25 enrolled. In 2014, 27 master's awarded. *Degree requirements:* For master's, comprehensive exam, thesis (for some programs). *Entrance requirements:* For master's, GRE, minimum GPA of 3.0; 3 letters of reference; essay, resume, official transcripts. Additional exam requirements/recommendations for international students: Required—TOEFL (minimum score 550 paper-based; 79 iBT), IELTS (minimum score 6.5). *Application deadline:* For fall admission, 2/15 priority date for domestic students, 12/1 for international students; for spring admission, 7/1 for international students. Applications are processed on a rolling basis. Application fee: $50. Electronic applications accepted. *Expenses:* Tuition, state resident: full-time $7187; part-time $299 per credit hour. Tuition, nonresident: full-time $16,394; part-time $683 per credit hour. *Required fees:* $2974; $125 per credit hour. Tuition and fees vary according to course load and program. *Financial support:* In 2014–15, 39 students received support, including 22 research assistantships (averaging $5,946 per year), 15 teaching assistantships with partial tuition reimbursements available (averaging $10,467 per year); career-related internships or fieldwork, institutionally sponsored loans, scholarships/grants, and unspecified assistantships also available. Financial award application deadline: 3/1; financial award applicants required to submit FAFSA. *Faculty research:* Social cognition and interpersonal relationships, relationship between one's self-concept and social interactions, creativity and innovation, organizational politics and ethical decision-making, victimization in childhood. *Unit head:* Dr. Hilary M. Lips, Chair, 540-831-5361, Fax: 540-831-6113, E-mail: hlips@radford.edu. *Application contact:* Rebecca Conner, Director, Graduate Enrollment, 540-831-6296, Fax: 540-831-6061, E-mail: gradcollege@radford.edu.
Website: http://www.radford.edu/content/chbs/home/psychology/programs.html

Rivier University, School of Graduate Studies, Department of Psychology, Nashua, NH 03060. Offers clinical psychology (MS); experimental psychology (MS).

Rochester Institute of Technology, Graduate Enrollment Services, College of Liberal Arts, Psychology Department, MS Program in Experimental Psychology, Rochester, NY 14623-5604. Offers MS. Part-time programs available. *Students:* 6 full-time (3 women), 1 part-time; includes 1 minority (Hispanic/Latino), 2 international. Average age 27. 25 applicants, 36% accepted, 2 enrolled. *Degree requirements:* For master's, thesis. *Entrance requirements:* For master's, GRE and TOEFL, IELTS, or PTE for non-native English speakers, recommended minimum GPA of 3.0. Additional exam requirements/recommendations for international students: Required—PTE (minimum score 58), TOEFL (minimum score 550 paper-based; 79 iBT) or IELTS (minimum score 6.5). *Application deadline:* For fall admission, 2/15 priority date for domestic and international students; for spring admission, 12/15 priority date for domestic and international students. Applications are processed on a rolling basis. Electronic applications accepted. *Expenses:* Expenses: $1,673 per credit hour. *Financial support:* In 2014–15, 7 students received support. Research assistantships with partial tuition reimbursements available, teaching assistantships with partial tuition reimbursements available, career-related internships or fieldwork, Federal Work-Study, institutionally sponsored loans, scholarships/grants, and unspecified assistantships available. Support available to part-time students. Financial award applicants required to submit FAFSA. *Faculty research:* Perception, cognitive neuroscience, human factors in complex systems, developmental psychopathology, hemispheric specialization. *Unit head:* Dr. Suzanne Bamonto, Graduate Program Director, 585-475-2765, E-mail: sbggsp@rit.edu. *Application contact:* Diane Ellison, Associate Vice President, Graduate Enrollment Services, 585-475-2229, Fax: 585-475-7164, E-mail: gradinfo@rit.edu.
Website: http://www.rit.edu/cla/psychology/graduate/ms-experimental-psych/overview

St. John's University, St. John's College of Liberal Arts and Sciences, Department of Psychology, Program in General Experimental Psychology, Queens, NY 11439. Offers MA. Part-time and evening/weekend programs available. *Students:* 24 full-time (17 women), 6 part-time (3 women); includes 16 minority (4 Black or African American, non-Hispanic/Latino; 4 Asian, non-Hispanic/Latino; 8 Hispanic/Latino), 2 international. Average age 25. 43 applicants, 65% accepted, 13 enrolled. In 2014, 8 master's awarded. *Degree requirements:* For master's, comprehensive exam, thesis optional. *Entrance requirements:* For master's, minimum GPA of 3.0, 2 writing samples, bachelor's degree, minimum of 24 undergraduate credits in psychology, personal statement, transcript. Additional exam requirements/recommendations for international students: Required—TOEFL (minimum score 600 paper-based; 100 iBT), IELTS (minimum score 7). *Application deadline:* For fall admission, 5/1 priority date for domestic and international students; for spring admission, 11/1 priority date for domestic and international students. Applications are processed on a rolling basis. Application fee: $70. Electronic applications accepted. *Expenses: Tuition:* Full-time $20,610; part-time $1145 per credit. *Required fees:* $170 per semester. *Financial support:* Research assistantships, career-related internships or fieldwork, scholarships/grants, and unspecified assistantships available. Support available to part-time students. Financial award application deadline: 3/1; financial award applicants required to submit FAFSA. *Faculty research:* Learning and memory neuropsychology, perception, social psychology, developmental psychology. *Unit head:* Dr. Kate Walton, Coordinator, 718-990-1478, E-mail: waltonk@stjohns.edu. *Application contact:* Robert Medrano, Director of Graduate Admission, 718-990-1601, Fax: 718-990-5686, E-mail: gradhelp@stjohns.edu.

Saint Louis University, Graduate Education, College of Arts and Sciences and Graduate Education, Department of Psychology, St. Louis, MO 63103-2097. Offers clinical psychology (MS-R, PhD); experimental psychology (MS-R, PhD); industrial-organizational psychology (PhD); psychology (PhD). *Accreditation:* APA (one or more programs are accredited). Part-time programs available. *Degree requirements:* For master's, comprehensive exam, thesis; for doctorate, thesis/dissertation, clinical internship (for clinical psychology PhD). *Entrance requirements:* For master's, GRE General Test, interview, letters of recommendation, resume; for doctorate, GRE General Test, interview, letters of recommendation, resumé, transcripts, goal statement. Additional exam requirements/recommendations for international students: Required—TOEFL (minimum score 550 paper-based). Electronic applications accepted. *Faculty research:* Violence and trauma; neural basis of learning and memory function; eating disorders; body image and health behavior; prejudice, stereotyping, and victimization; memory, cognitive aging and language processing.

San Jose State University, Graduate Studies and Research, College of Social Sciences, Department of Psychology, San Jose, CA 95192-0001. Offers clinical psychology (MS); experimental psychology (MA); industrial/organizational psychology (MS); psychology (MA). *Degree requirements:* For master's, comprehensive exam, thesis (for some programs). *Entrance requirements:* For master's, GRE General Test, minimum GPA of 3.0. Electronic applications accepted. *Faculty research:* Drug and alcohol abuse, neurohormonal mechanisms in motion sickness, behavior modification, sleep research, genetics.

Seton Hall University, College of Arts and Sciences, Department of Psychology, South Orange, NJ 07079-2697. Offers experimental psychology (non-thesis) (MS), including data visualization and analysis. Part-time and evening/weekend programs available. *Faculty:* 12 full-time (7 women). *Students:* 20 full-time (11 women); includes 4 minority (1 Black or African American, non-Hispanic/Latino; 2 Asian, non-Hispanic/Latino; 1 Hispanic/Latino), 1 international. Average age 25. 31 applicants, 81% accepted, 12 enrolled. In 2014, 11 master's awarded. *Degree requirements:* For master's, thesis optional. *Entrance requirements:* For master's, GRE, minimum of 18 credits in psychology with at least a 3.0 (or B) GPA. Additional exam requirements/recommendations for international students: Required—TOEFL. *Application deadline:* For fall admission, 7/1 priority date for domestic and international students. Applications are processed on a rolling basis. Application fee: $75. Electronic applications accepted. *Financial support:* Research assistantships, teaching assistantships with full tuition reimbursements, career-related internships or fieldwork, Federal Work-Study, scholarships/grants, and unspecified assistantships available. Financial award applicants required to submit FAFSA. *Faculty research:* Behavioral neuroscience, cognitive psychology, social psychology, perception/motor skills, memory, depression, anxiety. *Unit head:* Dr. Amy Hunter, Chair, 973-761-9485, E-mail: amy.hunter@shu.edu. *Application contact:* Dr. Kelly Goedert, Director of Graduate Studies, 973-275-2703, Fax: 973-275-5829, E-mail: kelly.goedert@shu.edu.
Website: http://www.shu.edu/academics/artsci/psychology/index.cfm

Southern Illinois University Carbondale, Graduate School, College of Liberal Arts, Department of Psychology, Carbondale, IL 62901-4701. Offers clinical psychology (PhD); counseling psychology (PhD); experimental psychology (MA, MS). *Accreditation:* APA (one or more programs are accredited). *Faculty:* 27 full-time (14 women), 1 part-time/adjunct (0 women). *Students:* 70 full-time (46 women), 35 part-time (20 women); includes 10 minority (8 Black or African American, non-Hispanic/Latino; 2 Asian, non-Hispanic/Latino), 12 international. 274 applicants, 11% accepted, 20 enrolled. In 2014, 10 master's, 10 doctorates awarded. *Degree requirements:* For master's, thesis; for doctorate, thesis/dissertation. *Entrance requirements:* For master's, GRE General Test, GRE Subject Test, minimum GPA of 2.7; for doctorate, GRE General Test, GRE Subject Test, minimum GPA of 3.25. Additional exam requirements/recommendations for international students: Required—TOEFL. *Application deadline:* For fall admission, 3/1 priority date for domestic students. Applications are processed on a rolling basis. Application fee: $50. *Expenses:* Tuition, state resident: full-time $10,176; part-time $1153 per credit. Tuition, nonresident: full-time $20,814; part-time $1744 per credit. *Required fees:* $7092; $394 per credit. $2364 per semester. *Financial support:* In 2014–15, 82 students received support, including 14 fellowships with full tuition reimbursements available, 23 research assistantships with full tuition reimbursements

available, 22 teaching assistantships with full tuition reimbursements available; Federal Work-Study, institutionally sponsored loans, and tuition waivers (full) also available. *Faculty research:* Developmental neuropsychology; smoking, affect, and cognition; personality measurement; vocational psychology; program evaluation. *Unit head:* Dr. Meera Komarraju, Chair, 618-453-3529, E-mail: meerak@siu.edu. *Application contact:* Stacia Werner, Office Specialist, 618-453-3564, E-mail: gradpsych@siu.edu. Website: http://psychology.siuc.edu/

Southern Methodist University, Bobby B. Lyle School of Engineering, Department of Environmental and Civil Engineering, Dallas, TX 75275-0340. Offers air pollution control and atmospheric sciences (PhD); civil engineering (MS); environmental engineering (MS); environmental science (MS); structural engineering (PhD); sustainability and development (MA); water and wastewater engineering (PhD). Part-time and evening/weekend programs available. Postbaccalaureate distance learning degree programs offered (no on-campus study). Terminal master's awarded for partial completion of doctoral program. *Degree requirements:* For master's, thesis optional; for doctorate, thesis/dissertation, oral and written qualifying exams. *Entrance requirements:* For master's, GRE General Test, minimum GPA of 3.0 in last 2 years; bachelor's degree in engineering, mathematics, or sciences; for doctorate, GRE, BS and MS in related field, minimum GPA of 3.3. Additional exam requirements/recommendations for international students: Required—TOEFL. Electronic applications accepted. *Faculty research:* Human and environmental health effects of endocrine disrupters, development of air pollution control systems for diesel engines, structural analysis and design, modeling and design of waste treatment systems.

Stony Brook University, State University of New York, Graduate School, College of Arts and Sciences, Department of Psychology, Program in Cognitive/Experimental Psychology, Stony Brook, NY 11794. Offers PhD. *Students:* 15 full-time (10 women); includes 2 minority (1 Asian, non-Hispanic/Latino; 1 Hispanic/Latino), 3 international. Average age 28. 39 applicants, 18% accepted, 3 enrolled. In 2014, 3 doctorates awarded. *Degree requirements:* For doctorate, thesis/dissertation. *Entrance requirements:* For doctorate, GRE General Test, GRE Subject Test. Additional exam requirements/recommendations for international students: Required—TOEFL. *Application deadline:* For fall admission, 1/15 for domestic students; for spring admission, 10/1 for domestic students. Application fee: $100. *Expenses:* Tuition, state resident: full-time $10,370; part-time $432 per credit. Tuition, nonresident: full-time $20,190; part-time $841 per credit. *Required fees:* $1431. *Financial support:* In 2014–15, 1 fellowship was awarded. *Unit head:* Dr. Arthur Samuel, Chair, 631-632-7792, Fax: 631-632-7876, E-mail: arthur.samuel@stonybrook.edu. *Application contact:* Marilynn Wollmuth, Graduate Director, 631-632-7855, Fax: 631-632-7876, E-mail: marilynn.wollmuth@stonybrook.edu.

Syracuse University, College of Arts and Sciences, Program in Experimental Psychology, Syracuse, NY 13244. Offers PhD. Part-time programs available. *Students:* 4 full-time (2 women), 1 part-time (0 women), 1 international. Average age 27. 19 applicants, 11% accepted, 1 enrolled. In 2014, 1 doctorate awarded. Terminal master's awarded for partial completion of doctoral program. *Degree requirements:* For doctorate, comprehensive exam, thesis/dissertation. *Entrance requirements:* For doctorate, GRE General Test. Additional exam requirements/recommendations for international students: Required—TOEFL (minimum score 100 iBT). *Application deadline:* For fall admission, 12/15 priority date for domestic and international students. Application fee: $75. Electronic applications accepted. *Expenses: Tuition:* Part-time $1341 per credit. *Financial support:* Fellowships with full tuition reimbursements, research assistantships with full and partial tuition reimbursements, and teaching assistantships with full and partial tuition reimbursements available. Financial award application deadline: 1/1. *Unit head:* Dr. Amy Criss, Program Director, 315-443-3667, E-mail: acriss@syr.edu. *Application contact:* Alecia Zema, Information Contact, 315-443-12760. Website: http://psychweb.syr.edu/

Texas A&M University–Central Texas, Graduate Studies and Research, Killeen, TX 76549. Offers accounting (MS); business administration (MBA); clinical mental health counseling (MS); criminal justice (MCJ); curriculum and instruction (M Ed); educational administration (M Ed); educational psychology - experimental psychology (MS); history (MA); human resource management (MS); information systems (MS); liberal studies (MS); management and leadership (MS); marriage and family therapy (MS); mathematics (MS); political science (MA); school counseling (M Ed); school psychology (Ed S).

Texas Christian University, College of Science and Engineering, Department of Psychology, Fort Worth, TX 76129. Offers developmental trauma (MS); experimental psychology (MA, MS, PhD), including behavioral neuroscience (MS), cognition (MS), learning (MS), social (MS). *Faculty:* 12 full-time (5 women), 2 part-time/adjunct (1 woman). *Students:* 28 full-time (14 women); includes 1 minority (Hispanic/Latino), 3 international. Average age 27. 37 applicants, 22% accepted, 8 enrolled. In 2014, 2 master's, 6 doctorates awarded. Terminal master's awarded for partial completion of doctoral program. *Degree requirements:* For master's, thesis; for doctorate, thesis/dissertation. *Entrance requirements:* For master's and doctorate, GRE General Test. Additional exam requirements/recommendations for international students: Required—TOEFL. *Application deadline:* For fall admission, 2/1 for domestic and international students; for spring admission, 12/1 for domestic students. Application fee: $60 ($0 for international students). Electronic applications accepted. *Expenses: Tuition:* Full-time $22,860; part-time $1270 per credit hour. *Financial support:* In 2014–15, 23 students received support, including 23 teaching assistantships with full tuition reimbursements available (averaging $19,750 per year); scholarships/grants and tuition waivers also available. Financial award application deadline: 2/1; financial award applicants required to submit FAFSA. *Faculty research:* Neuroscience, human and animal learning, cognition, development, experimental social psychology. *Unit head:* Dr. Mauricio Papini, Chair, 817-257-7410, Fax: 817-257-7681, E-mail: m.papini@tcu.edu. *Application contact:* Cindy Hayes, Administrative Assistant, 817-257-7410, Fax: 817-257-7681, E-mail: c.hayes@tcu.edu. Website: http://www.psy.tcu.edu/gradpro.html

Texas Tech University, Graduate School, College of Arts and Sciences, Department of Psychological Sciences, Lubbock, TX 79409-2051. Offers clinical psychology (PhD); counseling psychology (MA, PhD); general experimental psychology (MA, PhD); psychology (MA). *Accreditation:* APA (one or more programs are accredited). *Faculty:* 32 full-time (14 women), 1 part-time/adjunct (0 women). *Students:* 96 full-time (60 women), 18 part-time (16 women); includes 25 minority (4 Black or African American, non-Hispanic/Latino; 5 Asian, non-Hispanic/Latino; 14 Hispanic/Latino; 2 Two or more races, non-Hispanic/Latino), 6 international. Average age 27. 281 applicants, 17% accepted, 24 enrolled. In 2014, 12 master's, 16 doctorates awarded. *Degree requirements:* For doctorate, comprehensive exam, thesis/dissertation, 100 credit hours of organized courses, research credits, and practica. *Entrance requirements:* For master's, GRE General Test, GRE Subject Test, essays; for doctorate, GRE General Test, essays. Additional exam requirements/recommendations for international students: Required—TOEFL (minimum score 550 paper-based; 79 iBT). *Application deadline:* For fall admission, 6/1 priority date for domestic students, 1/15 priority date for international students; for spring admission, 9/1 priority date for domestic students, 6/15 priority date for international students. Applications are processed on a rolling basis.

Application fee: $60. Electronic applications accepted. *Expenses:* Tuition, state resident: full-time $6310; part-time $262.92 per credit hour. Tuition, nonresident: full-time $14,998; part-time $624.92 per credit hour. *Required fees:* $2701; $36.50 per credit. $912.50 per semester. Tuition and fees vary according to course load. *Financial support:* In 2014–15, 102 students received support, including 101 fellowships (averaging $4,037 per year), 23 research assistantships (averaging $13,150 per year), 72 teaching assistantships (averaging $10,753 per year). Financial award application deadline: 4/15; financial award applicants required to submit FAFSA. *Faculty research:* Health psychology, addictive behaviors, depression and suicide risk, sexuality/sexual risk behaviors/HIV, neuroscience/neuroimaging. *Total annual research expenditures:* $345,735. *Unit head:* Dr. Lee M. Cohen, Professor and Chair, 806-834-2530, Fax: 806-742-0818, E-mail: lee.cohen@ttu.edu. *Application contact:* Kay Hill, Admissions Coordinator, 806-742-3711 Ext. 222, Fax: 806-742-0818, E-mail: kay.hill@ttu.edu. Website: http://www.depts.ttu.edu/psy/

The University of Alabama, Graduate School, College of Arts and Sciences, Department of Psychology, Tuscaloosa, AL 35487. Offers clinical psychology (PhD); experimental psychology (PhD). *Accreditation:* APA. *Faculty:* 33 full-time (19 women), 2 part-time/adjunct (both women). *Students:* 88 full-time (64 women), 13 part-time (10 women); includes 14 minority (1 Black or African American, non-Hispanic/Latino; 4 Asian, non-Hispanic/Latino; 7 Hispanic/Latino; 2 Two or more races, non-Hispanic/Latino), 9 international. Average age 27. 318 applicants, 8% accepted, 19 enrolled. In 2014, 20 doctorates awarded. *Degree requirements:* For doctorate, thesis/dissertation, internship (for clinical psychology). *Entrance requirements:* For doctorate, GRE. Additional exam requirements/recommendations for international students: Required—TOEFL (minimum score 550 paper-based). *Application deadline:* For fall admission, 12/1 for domestic and international students. Application fee: $50 ($60 for international students). Electronic applications accepted. *Expenses:* Tuition, state resident: full-time $9826. Tuition, nonresident: full-time $24,950. *Financial support:* In 2014–15, 73 students received support, including 12 fellowships with full tuition reimbursements available (averaging $17,000 per year), 40 research assistantships with full and partial tuition reimbursements available (averaging $12,744 per year), 34 teaching assistantships with full and partial tuition reimbursements available (averaging $13,824 per year); career-related internships or fieldwork, institutionally sponsored loans, scholarships/grants, health care benefits, and unspecified assistantships also available. Financial award application deadline: 12/1. *Faculty research:* Cognitive development/disability, child clinical, psychology and law, health/aging, social psychology. *Total annual research expenditures:* $2.9 million. *Unit head:* Dr. Beverly E. Thorn, Chair, 205-348-1913, Fax: 205-348-8648, E-mail: bthorn@ua.edu. *Application contact:* Mary Beth Hubbard, Information Contact, 205-348-1919, Fax: 205-348-8648, E-mail: mbhubbard@as.ua.edu. Website: http://www.psychology.ua.edu

University of Central Florida, College of Sciences, Department of Psychology, Program in Applied Experimental and Human Factors Psychology, Orlando, FL 32816. Offers MA, PhD. *Students:* 40 full-time (26 women), 7 part-time (4 women); includes 10 minority (1 Black or African American, non-Hispanic/Latino; 3 Asian, non-Hispanic/Latino; 3 Hispanic/Latino; 3 Two or more races, non-Hispanic/Latino), 1 international. Average age 29. 48 applicants, 19% accepted, 7 enrolled. In 2014, 9 master's, 6 doctorates awarded. *Degree requirements:* For doctorate, thesis/dissertation, departmental candidacy exam. *Entrance requirements:* For doctorate, GRE General Test, minimum GPA of 3.2 in last 60 hours or master's qualifying exam. Additional exam requirements/recommendations for international students: Required—TOEFL. *Application deadline:* For fall admission, 2/1 for domestic students. Application fee: $30. Electronic applications accepted. *Expenses:* Tuition, state resident: part-time $288.16 per credit hour. Tuition, nonresident: part-time $1073.31 per credit hour. *Financial support:* In 2014–15, 36 students received support, including 18 fellowships with partial tuition reimbursements available (averaging $8,200 per year), 15 research assistantships with partial tuition reimbursements available (averaging $13,400 per year), 18 teaching assistantships with partial tuition reimbursements available (averaging $10,100 per year); career-related internships or fieldwork, Federal Work-Study, institutionally sponsored loans, tuition waivers (partial), and unspecified assistantships also available. Financial award application deadline: 3/1; financial award applicants required to submit FAFSA. *Faculty research:* Visual performance, team training, controls/displays, synthetic speech, alarms/warning. *Unit head:* Dr. Mustapha Mouloua, Program Director, 407-823-2910, E-mail: mustapha.mouloua@ucf.edu. *Application contact:* Barbara Rodriguez Lamas, Director, Admissions and Student Services, 407-823-2766, Fax: 407-823-6442, E-mail: gradadmissions@ucf.edu. Website: http://psychology.cos.ucf.edu/graduate/

University of Central Oklahoma, The Jackson College of Graduate Studies, College of Education and Professional Studies, Department of Psychology, Edmond, OK 73034-5209. Offers counseling psychology (MA); experimental psychology (MA); forensic psychology (MA); general psychology (MA); school psychology (MA). *Degree requirements:* For master's, thesis (for some programs). *Entrance requirements:* For master's, GRE. Additional exam requirements/recommendations for international students: Required—TOEFL (minimum score 550 paper-based; 79 iBT), IELTS (minimum score 6.5). Electronic applications accepted. *Faculty research:* Psychopharmacology, computer psychometrics, health psychology research.

University of Cincinnati, Graduate School, McMicken College of Arts and Sciences, Department of Psychology, Cincinnati, OH 45221. Offers clinical psychology (PhD); experimental psychology (PhD). *Accreditation:* APA. *Degree requirements:* For doctorate, comprehensive exam, thesis/dissertation. *Entrance requirements:* For doctorate, GRE General Test. Additional exam requirements/recommendations for international students: Required—TOEFL. *Faculty research:* Neuropsychology, human factors, health.

University of Connecticut, Graduate School, College of Liberal Arts and Sciences, Department of Psychology, Storrs, CT 06269. Offers behavioral neuroscience (PhD); biopsychology (PhD); clinical psychology (MA, PhD); cognition and instruction (PhD); developmental psychology (MA, PhD); ecological psychology (PhD); experimental psychology (PhD); general psychology (MA, PhD); health psychology (Graduate Certificate); industrial/organizational psychology (PhD); language and cognition (PhD); neuroscience (PhD); occupational health psychology (Graduate Certificate); social psychology (MA, PhD). *Accreditation:* APA. Terminal master's awarded for partial completion of doctoral program. *Degree requirements:* For master's, comprehensive exam; for doctorate, thesis/dissertation. *Entrance requirements:* For master's and doctorate, GRE General Test, GRE Subject Test. Additional exam requirements/recommendations for international students: Required—TOEFL (minimum score 550 paper-based). Electronic applications accepted.

University of Hartford, College of Arts and Sciences, Department of Psychology, Program in General Experimental Psychology, West Hartford, CT 06117-1599. Offers MA. Part-time programs available. *Degree requirements:* For master's, comprehensive exam, thesis or alternative. *Entrance requirements:* For master's, GRE General Test, GRE Subject Test, minimum GPA of 3.0, 3 letters of recommendation. Additional exam requirements/recommendations for international students: Required—TOEFL (minimum

score 550 paper-based). Electronic applications accepted. *Faculty research:* Decision making, social judgment and stereotyping, stress and health.

University of Louisville, Graduate School, College of Arts and Sciences, Department of Psychological and Brain Sciences, Louisville, KY 40292-0001. Offers clinical psychology (PhD); experimental psychology (PhD). *Accreditation:* APA. *Students:* 65 full-time (46 women); includes 10 minority (4 Black or African American, non-Hispanic/Latino; 1 Asian, non-Hispanic/Latino; 4 Hispanic/Latino; 1 Two or more races, non-Hispanic/Latino), 3 international. Average age 28. 179 applicants, 1% accepted, 1 enrolled. In 2014, 2 doctorates awarded. *Degree requirements:* For doctorate, thesis/dissertation, preliminary exam, research, internship. *Entrance requirements:* For doctorate, GRE General Test. Additional exam requirements/recommendations for international students: Required—TOEFL. *Application deadline:* For fall admission, 12/1 for domestic students, 5/1 priority date for international students; for spring admission, 11/1 for international students; for summer admission, 4/1 for international students. Applications are processed on a rolling basis. Application fee: $60. Electronic applications accepted. *Expenses:* Tuition, state resident: full-time $11,326; part-time $630 per credit hour. Tuition, nonresident: full-time $23,568; part-time $1311 per credit hour. *Required fees:* $196. Tuition and fees vary according to program and reciprocity agreements. *Financial support:* Fellowships, teaching assistantships, and career-related internships or fieldwork available. *Faculty research:* Health psychology, geropsychology, psychopathology, cognitive and development sciences, vision and hearing sciences. *Unit head:* Dr. Suzanne Meeks, Chair, 502-852-6068, Fax: 502-852-8904, E-mail: smeeks@louisville.edu. *Application contact:* Libby Leggett, Director, Graduate Admissions, 502-852-3101, Fax: 502-852-6536, E-mail: gradadm@louisville.edu. Website: http://louisville.edu/psychology

University of Maryland, College Park, Academic Affairs, College of Behavioral and Social Sciences, Department of Psychology, College Park, MD 20742. Offers clinical psychology (PhD); developmental psychology (PhD); experimental psychology (PhD); industrial psychology (MA, MS, PhD); social psychology (PhD). *Accreditation:* APA (one or more programs are accredited). *Degree requirements:* For master's, thesis; for doctorate, variable foreign language requirement, comprehensive exam, thesis/dissertation. *Entrance requirements:* For master's and doctorate, GRE General Test, GRE Subject Test, minimum GPA of 3.5, research and/or work experience, 3 letters of recommendation. Electronic applications accepted. *Faculty research:* Social stereotyping and prejudice, anxiety disorders, auditory neuroethology, counseling and social psychology.

University of Mississippi, Graduate School, College of Liberal Arts, Department of Psychology, University, MS 38677. Offers clinical psychology (PhD); experimental psychology (PhD); psychology (MA). *Accreditation:* APA (one or more programs are accredited). *Degree requirements:* For master's, thesis; for doctorate, thesis/dissertation. *Entrance requirements:* For master's, GRE General Test, minimum GPA of 3.0; for doctorate, GRE General Test. Additional exam requirements/recommendations for international students: Required—TOEFL. Electronic applications accepted.

The University of Montana, Graduate School, College of Humanities and Sciences, Department of Psychology, Missoula, MT 59812-0002. Offers clinical psychology (PhD); experimental psychology (PhD), including animal behavior psychology, developmental psychology; school psychology (MA, PhD, Ed S). *Accreditation:* APA (one or more programs are accredited). Terminal master's awarded for partial completion of doctoral program. *Degree requirements:* For master's, thesis; for doctorate, thesis/dissertation. *Entrance requirements:* For master's, doctorate, and Ed S, GRE General Test. Additional exam requirements/recommendations for international students: Required—TOEFL.

University of New Brunswick Saint John, Department of Psychology, Saint John, NB E2L 4L5, Canada. Offers clinical psychology (PhD); experimental psychology (MA, PhD). Part-time programs available. *Faculty:* 9 full-time (4 women). *Students:* 16 full-time (9 women). In 2014, 3 master's awarded. *Degree requirements:* For master's, thesis. *Entrance requirements:* For master's, GRE General and Subject Tests, honors thesis; minimum GPA of 3.7. Additional exam requirements/recommendations for international students: Required—TOEFL (minimum score 550 paper-based), TWE. *Application deadline:* For fall admission, 1/15 priority date for domestic students. Application fee: $50. Electronic applications accepted. *Financial support:* In 2014–15, 6 fellowships, 5 research assistantships, 16 teaching assistantships were awarded; unspecified assistantships also available. Support available to part-time students. Financial award application deadline: 2/1. *Faculty research:* Forensic psychology, peer relationships and social skills, polygraph techniques, addictions, attachment and social adjustment, neuroscience, optical illusions, graphical perception, associative learning in animals, bio-psychology. *Unit head:* Dr. Lisa Best, Director of Graduate Studies, 506-648-5562, Fax: 506-648-5780, E-mail: lbest@unb.ca. *Application contact:* Laura Galbraith, Secretary, 506-648-5640, Fax: 506-648-5780, E-mail: galbral@unb.ca. Website: http://go.unb.ca/gradprograms

University of North Dakota, Graduate School, College of Arts and Sciences, Department of Psychology, Grand Forks, ND 58202. Offers clinical psychology (PhD); counseling psychology (PhD); experimental psychology (PhD); forensic psychology (MA, MS); psychology (MA). *Accreditation:* APA (one or more programs are accredited). *Degree requirements:* For master's, thesis, final exam; for doctorate, comprehensive exam, thesis/dissertation, internship, final exam. *Entrance requirements:* For master's, GRE General Test, GRE Subject Test, minimum GPA of 3.0; for doctorate, GRE General Test, GRE Subject Test, minimum GPA of 3.5. Additional exam requirements/recommendations for international students: Required—TOEFL (minimum score 550 paper-based; 79 iBT), IELTS (minimum score 6.5). Electronic applications accepted. *Faculty research:* Developmental psychology, clinical social psychology, educational psychology, personality disorders.

University of Regina, Faculty of Graduate Studies and Research, Faculty of Arts, Department of Psychology, Regina, SK S4S 0A2, Canada. Offers clinical psychology (MA, PhD); experimental and applied psychology (MA, PhD). *Faculty:* 20 full-time (9 women), 7 part-time/adjunct (5 women). *Students:* 57 full-time (46 women). 81 applicants, 25% accepted. In 2014, 12 master's, 4 doctorates awarded. *Degree requirements:* For master's, thesis; for doctorate, comprehensive exam, thesis/dissertation. *Entrance requirements:* For master's, GRE General Test; for doctorate, GRE General Test and GRE Subject Test (optional for those with a master's degree from a Canadian university). Additional exam requirements/recommendations for international students: Required—TOEFL (minimum score 580 paper-based; 80 iBT), IELTS (minimum score 6.5), PTE (minimum score 59). *Application deadline:* For fall admission, 1/15 for domestic and international students. Application fee: $100. Electronic applications accepted. *Expenses:* Tuition, area resident: Full-time $4900 Canadian dollars; part-time $837.65 Canadian dollars per semester. *International tuition:* $7900 Canadian dollars full-time. *Required fees:* $396 Canadian dollars; $86.90 Canadian dollars per semester. *Financial support:* In 2014–15, 17 fellowships (averaging $6,588 per year), 1 research assistantship (averaging $5,500 per year), 27 teaching assistantships (averaging $2,471 per year) were awarded; career-related internships or fieldwork and scholarships/grants also available. Financial award application deadline: 6/15. *Faculty research:* Clinical, experimental, cognitive, and applied psychology; post-traumatic stress disorder, anxiety, and panic disorder; traumatic brain injury; chronic pain; perception and memory. *Unit head:* Dr. Richard MacLennan, Department Head, 306-585-4458, Fax: 306-585-5429, E-mail: richard.maclennan@uregina.ca. Website: http://www.uregina.ca/arts/psychology

University of South Carolina, The Graduate School, College of Arts and Sciences, Department of Psychology, Program in Experimental Psychology, Columbia, SC 29208. Offers MA, PhD. Terminal master's awarded for partial completion of doctoral program. *Degree requirements:* For master's, comprehensive exam, thesis; for doctorate, comprehensive exam, thesis/dissertation. *Entrance requirements:* For master's and doctorate, GRE General Test. Additional exam requirements/recommendations for international students: Required—TOEFL. Electronic applications accepted. *Faculty research:* Cognition, development, neuroscience.

University of Southern Mississippi, Graduate School, College of Education and Psychology, Department of Psychology, Hattiesburg, MS 39406-0001. Offers clinical psychology (PhD); counseling psychology (MS, PhD); experimental psychology (PhD); school psychology (PhD). *Accreditation:* APA (one or more programs are accredited). Terminal master's awarded for partial completion of doctoral program. *Degree requirements:* For master's, comprehensive exam, thesis; for doctorate, comprehensive exam, thesis/dissertation. *Entrance requirements:* For master's, GRE General Test, minimum GPA of 3.0; for doctorate, GRE General Test, interview, minimum GPA of 3.5. Additional exam requirements/recommendations for international students: Required—TOEFL, IELTS. *Faculty research:* Psychopathology, alcohol and drug abuse, child clinical psychology, parenting, suicide, career/vocational, marine mammal, cognition, psychological psychology, behavioral interventions, positive psychology, anger/aggression, diversity issues.

The University of Tennessee, Graduate School, College of Arts and Sciences, Department of Psychology, Knoxville, TN 37996. Offers clinical psychology (PhD); experimental psychology (MA, PhD); psychology (MA). *Accreditation:* APA (one or more programs are accredited). Terminal master's awarded for partial completion of doctoral program. *Degree requirements:* For master's, thesis; for doctorate, thesis/dissertation. *Entrance requirements:* For master's and doctorate, GRE General Test, GRE Subject Test, minimum GPA of 2.7. Additional exam requirements/recommendations for international students: Required—TOEFL. Electronic applications accepted.

The University of Tennessee at Chattanooga, Program in Psychology, Chattanooga, TN 37403. Offers industrial/organizational psychology (MS); research psychology (MS). Part-time and evening/weekend programs available. *Faculty:* 10 full-time (4 women), 1 part-time/adjunct (0 women). *Students:* 38 full-time (20 women), 4 part-time (2 women); includes 3 minority (1 American Indian or Alaska Native, non-Hispanic/Latino; 2 Hispanic/Latino), 1 international. Average age 25. 54 applicants, 57% accepted, 18 enrolled. In 2014, 22 master's awarded. *Degree requirements:* For master's, comprehensive exam (for some programs), thesis (for some programs), practicum (industrial/organizational psychology). *Entrance requirements:* For master's, GRE General Test, minimum GPA of 2.5 on all undergraduate coursework or 3.0 in senior year. Additional exam requirements/recommendations for international students: Required—TOEFL (minimum score 550 paper-based; 79 iBT), IELTS (minimum score 6). *Application deadline:* For fall admission, 6/13 priority date for domestic students, 6/1 for international students; for spring admission, 10/15 priority date for domestic students, 10/1 for international students. Applications are processed on a rolling basis. Application fee: $30 ($35 for international students). Electronic applications accepted. *Expenses:* Tuition, state resident: full-time $7708; part-time $428 per credit hour. Tuition, nonresident: full-time $23,826; part-time $1323 per credit hour. *Required fees:* $1708; $252 per credit hour. *Financial support:* In 2014–15, 19 research assistantships with tuition reimbursements (averaging $5,800 per year), 6 teaching assistantships with tuition reimbursements (averaging $5,982 per year) were awarded; career-related internships or fieldwork, scholarships/grants, and unspecified assistantships also available. Support available to part-time students. Financial award applicants required to submit FAFSA. *Faculty research:* Decision processes, philosophical psychology, memory, social cognition, employee selection. *Total annual research expenditures:* $180,611. *Unit head:* Dr. Brian O'Leary, Department Head, 423-425-4283, Fax: 423-425-4284, E-mail: brian-o'leary@utc.edu. *Application contact:* Dr. J. Randy Walker, Interim Dean of Graduate Studies, 423-425-4478, Fax: 423-425-5223, E-mail: randy-walker@utc.edu. Website: http://www.utc.edu/Academic/Psychology/

The University of Texas at Arlington, Graduate School, College of Science, Department of Psychology, Arlington, TX 76019. Offers experimental psychology (PhD); health psychology (PhD); industrial organizational psychology (MS); psychology (MS). Part-time programs available. Terminal master's awarded for partial completion of doctoral program. *Degree requirements:* For master's, comprehensive exam or thesis; for doctorate, thesis/dissertation (for some programs). *Entrance requirements:* For master's and doctorate, GRE General Test, minimum GPA of 3.0 in last 60 hours of course work. Additional exam requirements/recommendations for international students: Required—TOEFL (minimum score 550 paper-based).

The University of Texas at El Paso, Graduate School, College of Liberal Arts, Department of Psychology, El Paso, TX 79968-0001. Offers clinical psychology (MA); experimental psychology (MA); psychology (PhD). Part-time and evening/weekend programs available. *Degree requirements:* For master's, thesis; for doctorate, thesis/dissertation. *Entrance requirements:* For master's, GRE, letters of recommendation; for doctorate, GRE, statement of purpose, letters of recommendation. Additional exam requirements/recommendations for international students: Required—TOEFL; Recommended—IELTS. Electronic applications accepted.

The University of Texas of the Permian Basin, Office of Graduate Studies, College of Arts and Sciences, Department of Psychology, Odessa, TX 79762-0001. Offers applied research psychology (MA); clinical psychology (MA). Part-time and evening/weekend programs available. *Degree requirements:* For master's, comprehensive exam, thesis, practicum. *Entrance requirements:* For master's, GRE General Test, 3 letters of recommendation. Additional exam requirements/recommendations for international students: Required—TOEFL (minimum score 550 paper-based).

The University of Texas–Pan American, College of Social and Behavioral Sciences, Department of Psychology and Anthropology, Edinburg, TX 78539. Offers anthropology (MAIS); psychology (MA), including clinical psychology, experimental psychology. Part-time and evening/weekend programs available. *Degree requirements:* For master's, comprehensive exam, thesis optional, internship. *Entrance requirements:* For master's, GRE, letters of recommendation. Additional exam requirements/recommendations for international students: Required—TOEFL. Electronic applications accepted. *Expenses:* Tuition, state resident: full-time $4187; part-time $232.60 per credit hour. Tuition, nonresident: full-time $10,857; part-time $603.16 per credit hour. *Required fees:* $782; $27.50 per credit hour. $143.35 per semester. *Faculty research:* Biofeedback, acculturation, health, stress/trauma, neuropsychological assessment, false memories, children's theory of mind.

The University of Toledo, College of Graduate Studies, College of Languages, Literature and Social Sciences, Department of Psychology, Toledo, OH 43606-3390.

Offers clinical psychology (MA, PhD); experimental psychology (MA, PhD). *Accreditation:* APA. *Degree requirements:* For master's, comprehensive exam, thesis; for doctorate, comprehensive exam, thesis/dissertation. *Entrance requirements:* For master's and doctorate, GRE General Test, GRE Subject Test, minimum cumulative point-hour ratio of 2.7 for all previous academic work, three letters of recommendation, statement of purpose, transcripts from all prior institutions attended. Additional exam requirements/recommendations for international students: Required—TOEFL (minimum score 550 paper-based; 80 iBT). Electronic applications accepted. *Faculty research:* Neural taste response.

University of Victoria, Faculty of Graduate Studies, Faculty of Social Sciences, Department of Psychology, Victoria, BC V8W 2Y2, Canada. Offers clinical psychology (PhD); clinical psychology (neuropsychology) (M Sc); cognition and brain science (M Sc, PhD); experimental neuropsychology (M Sc, PhD); individualized study (M Sc, PhD); life span development psychology (PhD); life span developmental psychology (M Sc); social psychology (M Sc, PhD). *Accreditation:* APA (one or more programs are accredited). *Degree requirements:* For master's, thesis; for doctorate, thesis/dissertation, candidacy exam. *Entrance requirements:* For master's and doctorate, GRE General Test. Additional exam requirements/recommendations for international students: Required—TOEFL (minimum score 600 paper-based). Electronic applications accepted. *Faculty research:* Life span development psychology and aging, behavioral neuroscience, cognitive psychology, behavioral psychology, environmental psychology.

University of Wisconsin–Oshkosh, Graduate Studies, College of Letters and Science, Department of Psychology, Oshkosh, WI 54901. Offers experimental psychology (MS); industrial/organizational psychology (MS). *Degree requirements:* For master's, thesis. *Entrance requirements:* For master's, GRE, 10 semester hours of undergraduate course work in psychology. Additional exam requirements/recommendations for international students: Required—TOEFL (minimum score 550 paper-based; 79 iBT). Electronic applications accepted. *Faculty research:* Performance evaluation, training, biological bases of behavior, tactile perception, aging.

Washington State University, College of Liberal Arts, Department of Psychology, Pullman, WA 99164. Offers clinical psychology (PhD); experimental psychology (PhD). Program applications must be made through the Pullman campus. *Accreditation:* APA (one or more programs are accredited). *Students:* 58 full-time (40 women), 5 part-time (3 women); includes 10 minority (1 Black or African American, non-Hispanic/Latino; 1 American Indian or Alaska Native, non-Hispanic/Latino; 2 Asian, non-Hispanic/Latino; 3 Hispanic/Latino; 3 Two or more races, non-Hispanic/Latino), 2 international. Average age 28. 236 applicants, 8% accepted, 12 enrolled. In 2014, 7 master's, 6 doctorates awarded. *Degree requirements:* For doctorate, comprehensive exam, thesis/ dissertation, oral exam, written exam. *Entrance requirements:* For doctorate, GRE General Test, three letters of reference; summary data form; at least 18 credits of study in psychology; at least one course in statistics and research methodology; official transcripts; minimum cumulative undergraduate GPA of 3.0 or master's degree in psychology. Additional exam requirements/recommendations for international students: Required—TOEFL, IELTS. *Application deadline:* For fall admission, 12/1 priority date for domestic and international students. Application fee: $75. Electronic applications accepted. *Expenses:* Tuition, state resident: full-time $11,768. Tuition, nonresident: full-time $25,200. *Required fees:* $960. Tuition and fees vary according to program. *Financial support:* In 2014–15, 31 students received support, including 5 research assistantships with full and partial tuition reimbursements available (averaging $13,870 per year), 46 teaching assistantships with full and partial tuition reimbursements available (averaging $13,890 per year); fellowships, career-related internships or fieldwork, Federal Work-Study, institutionally sponsored loans, and unspecified assistantships also available. Financial award application deadline: 2/15; financial award applicants required to submit FAFSA. *Faculty research:* Adult psychopathology and therapy, child psychopathology, neuropsychology, health psychology. *Unit head:* Dr. David K. Marcus, Director of Clinical Training, 509-335-7750, Fax: 509-335-5043, E-mail: david.marcus@wsu.edu. *Application contact:* Graduate School Admissions, 800-GRADWSU, Fax: 509-335-1949, E-mail: gradsch@wsu.edu. Website: https://psychology.wsu.edu/

Western Kentucky University, Graduate Studies, College of Education and Behavioral Sciences, Department of Psychology, Bowling Green, KY 42101. Offers clinical psychology (MA); experimental psychology (MA); general psychology (MA); industrial/ organizational psychology (MA); school psychology (Ed S). *Degree requirements:* For master's, comprehensive exam, thesis (for some programs); for Ed S, thesis, oral exam. *Entrance requirements:* For master's, GRE General Test; for Ed S, GRE General Test, minimum GPA of 3.5. Additional exam requirements/recommendations for international students: Required—TOEFL (minimum score 555 paper-based; 79 iBT). *Faculty research:* Neural regeneration, enhancing mobility in the elderly, improvement in visual processing in older adults, lifespan development.

Western Washington University, Graduate School, College of Humanities and Social Sciences, Department of Psychology, Program in Experimental Psychology, Bellingham, WA 98225-5996. Offers MS. *Degree requirements:* For master's, thesis. *Entrance requirements:* For master's, GRE General Test, minimum GPA of 3.0 in last 60 semester hours or last 90 quarter hours. Additional exam requirements/ recommendations for international students: Required—TOEFL (minimum score 567 paper-based). Electronic applications accepted.

Forensic Psychology

★ **Adler University,** Programs in Psychology, Chicago, IL 60602. Offers advanced Adlerian psychotherapy (Certificate); art therapy (MA); clinical neuropsychology (Certificate); clinical psychology (Psy D); community psychology (MA); counseling and organizational psychology (MA); counseling psychology (MA); criminology (MA); emergency management leadership (MA); forensic psychology (MA); marriage and family counseling (MA); marriage and family therapy (Certificate); military psychology (MA); nonprofit management (MA); organizational psychology (MA); police psychology (MA); public policy and administration (MA); rehabilitation counseling (MA); sport and health psychology (MA); substance abuse counseling (Certificate); Psy D/Certificate; Psy D/MACAT; Psy D/MACP; Psy D/MAMFC; Psy D/MASAC. *Accreditation:* APA. Part-time and evening/weekend programs available. Postbaccalaureate distance learning degree programs offered (minimal on-campus study). Terminal master's awarded for partial completion of doctoral program. *Degree requirements:* For master's, thesis or alternative, oral exam, practicum; for doctorate, thesis/dissertation, clinical exam, internship, oral exam, practicum, written qualifying exam. *Entrance requirements:* For master's, 12 semester hours in psychology, minimum GPA of 3.0; for doctorate, 18 semester hours in psychology, minimum GPA of 3.25; for Certificate, appropriate master's or doctoral degree. Additional exam requirements/recommendations for international students: Required—TOEFL (minimum score 550 paper-based; 79 iBT). Electronic applications accepted.
See Display on page 969 and Close-Up on page 1207.

Alliant International University–Fresno, California School of Forensic Studies, PhD Program in Clinical Forensic Psychology, Fresno, CA 93727. Offers PhD. *Degree requirements:* For doctorate, comprehensive exam, thesis/dissertation, research internship. *Entrance requirements:* For doctorate, minimum GPA of 3.0, letters of recommendation, essay, interview. Additional exam requirements/recommendations for international students: Required—TOEFL (minimum score 550 paper-based), TWE (minimum score 5). *Faculty research:* Effects of stress in law enforcement officers, treatment for mentally ill offenders, psychotic disorders and violence, behavioral threat assessment/risk analysis, juvenile delinquency.

Alliant International University–Fresno, California School of Forensic Studies, PsyD Program in Clinical Forensic Psychology, Fresno, CA 93727. Offers victimology (Psy D). *Degree requirements:* For doctorate, comprehensive exam, thesis/dissertation, internship. *Entrance requirements:* For doctorate, minimum GPA of 3.0, recommendations, essay, interview. Additional exam requirements/recommendations for international students: Required—TOEFL (minimum score 550 paper-based), TWE (minimum score 5). Electronic applications accepted. *Faculty research:* Correctional psychology, psychopathology, police psychology, substance abuse and ADHD, investigative psychology.

Alliant International University–Irvine, California School of Forensic Studies, Irvine, CA 92606. Offers Psy D. *Degree requirements:* For doctorate, comprehensive exam, thesis/dissertation, internship. *Entrance requirements:* For doctorate, minimum GPA of 3.0, recommendations, essay. Additional exam requirements/recommendations for international students: Required—TOEFL (minimum score 80 iBT), TWE (minimum score 5). Electronic applications accepted. *Faculty research:* Detecting deception, psychological safety of undercover police officers, domestic violence, risk assessment, competency evaluations.

Alliant International University–Los Angeles, California School of Forensic Studies, Alhambra, CA 91803-1360. Offers forensic psychology (Psy D). *Degree requirements:* For doctorate, comprehensive exam, thesis/dissertation. *Entrance requirements:* For doctorate, interview; master's degree in psychology, forensic psychology, criminology, criminal justice, social work or law; minimum GPA of 3.0 in psychology and overall. Additional exam requirements/recommendations for international students: Required—TOEFL (minimum score 600 paper-based), TWE (minimum score 5). *Faculty research:* Court testimony, juvenile offenders, violence risk assessment, Miranda rights, police psychology.

Alliant International University–Sacramento, California School of Forensic Studies, Program in Clinical Forensic Psychology, Sacramento, CA 95833. Offers Psy D. *Degree requirements:* For doctorate, comprehensive exam, thesis/dissertation. *Entrance requirements:* For doctorate, minimum GPA of 3.0, recommendations, essay. Additional exam requirements/recommendations for international students: Required—TOEFL (minimum score 550 paper-based; 80 iBT), TWE (minimum score 5). Electronic applications accepted. *Faculty research:* Correctional mental health treatment, psychopathy, child maltreatment, interventions for delinquent youth, malingering.

Alliant International University–San Diego, California School of Forensic Studies, Psy D Program in Clinical Forensic Psychology, San Diego, CA 92131-1799. Offers Psy D. *Degree requirements:* For doctorate, comprehensive exam, internship. *Entrance requirements:* Additional exam requirements/recommendations for international students: Required—TOEFL (minimum score 550 paper-based; 80 iBT), TWE (minimum score 5).

Alliant International University–San Francisco, California School of Forensic Studies, San Francisco, CA 94133-1221. Offers applied criminology (MS), including victimology; clinical forensic psychology (PhD, Psy D). *Degree requirements:* For doctorate, comprehensive exam, thesis/dissertation, internship. *Entrance requirements:* For master's, minimum GPA of 3.0, recommendations, essay; for doctorate, minimum GPA of 3.0, recommendations, essay, interview. Additional exam requirements/recommendations for international students: Required—TOEFL (minimum score 550 paper-based; 80 iBT), TWE (minimum score 5). *Faculty research:* Post-traumatic stress disorder, correctional mental health.

American International College, School of Graduate and Adult Education, Graduate Psychology Department, Forensic Psychology Program, Springfield, MA 01109-3189. Offers MS. Part-time and evening/weekend programs available. *Faculty:* 1 full-time (0 women), 3 part-time/adjunct (2 women). *Students:* 6 full-time (all women), 23 part-time (20 women); includes 12 minority (7 Black or African American, non-Hispanic/Latino; 1 Asian, non-Hispanic/Latino; 4 Hispanic/Latino). Average age 27. 31 applicants, 74% accepted, 8 enrolled. In 2014, 13 master's awarded. Terminal master's awarded for partial completion of doctoral program. *Degree requirements:* For master's, comprehensive exam (for some programs), thesis or alternative. *Entrance requirements:* For master's, graduate of accredited four-year college with minimum GPA of 2.75. Additional exam requirements/recommendations for international students: Required—TOEFL, IELTS. *Application deadline:* For fall admission, 4/15 for domestic students, 4/15 priority date for international students. Applications are processed on a rolling basis. Application fee: $50. Electronic applications accepted. *Expenses:* Expenses: $795 per credit; registration fee $30 per term. *Financial support:* Career-related internships or fieldwork available. Financial award applicants required to submit FAFSA. *Unit head:* Dr. Lina Racicot, Director, 413-205-3909, Fax: 413-205-3943, E-mail: lina.racicot@aic.edu. *Application contact:* Kerry Barnes, Director of Graduate Admissions, 413-205-3703, Fax: 413-205-3051, E-mail: kerry.barnes@aic.edu.
Website: http://www.aic.edu/academics/graduate

Argosy University, Atlanta, College of Psychology and Behavioral Sciences, Atlanta, GA 30328. Offers clinical psychology (MA, Psy D, Postdoctoral Respecialization Certificate), including child and family psychology (Psy D), general adult clinical (Psy D), health psychology (Psy D), neuropsychology/geropsychology (Psy D); community counseling (MA), including marriage and family therapy; counselor education and supervision (Ed D); forensic psychology (MA); industrial organizational psychology (MA); marriage and family therapy (Certificate); sport-exercise psychology (MA). *Accreditation:* APA.

Forensic Psychology

Argosy University, Chicago, College of Psychology and Behavioral Sciences, Doctoral Program in Clinical Psychology, Chicago, IL 60601. Offers child and adolescent psychology (Psy D); client-centered and experiential psychotherapies (Psy D); diversity and multicultural psychology (Psy D); family psychology (Psy D); forensic psychology (Psy D); health psychology (Psy D); neuropsychology (Psy D); organizational consulting (Psy D); psychoanalytic psychology (Psy D); psychology and spirituality (Psy D). *Accreditation:* APA.

Argosy University, Dallas, College of Psychology and Behavioral Sciences, Program in Forensic Psychology, Farmers Branch, TX 75244. Offers MA.

Argosy University, Denver, College of Psychology and Behavioral Sciences, Denver, CO 80231. Offers clinical mental health counseling (MA); clinical psychology (MA, Psy D); counseling psychology (Ed D); counselor education and supervision (Ed D); forensic psychology (MA); industrial organizational psychology (MA); marriage and family therapy (MA, DMFT).

Argosy University, Hawai'i, College of Psychology and Behavioral Sciences, Program in Forensic Psychology, Honolulu, HI 96813. Offers MA.

Argosy University, Inland Empire, College of Psychology and Behavioral Sciences, Ontario, CA 91761. Offers clinical psychology/marriage and family therapy (MA); counseling psychology (Ed D); counseling psychology/marriage and family therapy (MA); forensic psychology (MA); industrial organizational psychology (MA); sport-exercise psychology (MA).

Argosy University, Los Angeles, College of Psychology and Behavioral Sciences, Santa Monica, CA 90045. Offers clinical psychology/marriage and family therapy (MA); counseling psychology (Ed D); counseling psychology/marriage and family therapy (MA); forensic psychology (MA).

Argosy University, Orange County, College of Psychology and Behavioral Sciences, Program in Forensic Psychology, Orange, CA 92868. Offers MA.

Argosy University, Phoenix, College of Psychology and Behavioral Sciences, Program in Forensic Psychology, Phoenix, AZ 85021. Offers MA.

Argosy University, Salt Lake City, College of Psychology and Behavioral Sciences, Draper, UT 84020. Offers counseling psychology (Ed D); counselor education and supervision (Ed D); forensic psychology (MA); marriage and family therapy (MA, DMFT); mental health counseling (MA).

Argosy University, San Diego, College of Psychology and Behavioral Sciences, San Diego, CA 92108. Offers clinical psychology/marriage and family therapy (MA); counseling psychology (Ed D); counseling psychology/marriage and family therapy (MA); forensic psychology (MA).

Argosy University, San Francisco Bay Area, College of Psychology and Behavioral Sciences, Program in Forensic Psychology, Alameda, CA 94501. Offers MA.

Argosy University, Sarasota, College of Psychology and Behavioral Sciences, Sarasota, FL 34235. Offers community counseling (MA); counseling psychology (Ed D); counselor education and supervision (Ed D); forensic psychology (MA); marriage and family therapy (MA); mental health counseling (MA); pastoral community counseling (Ed D).

Argosy University, Schaumburg, College of Behavioral Sciences, Schaumburg, IL 60173-5403. Offers clinical mental health counseling (MA); forensic psychology (MA, Post-Graduate Certificate); industrial organizational psychology (MA); sport-exercise psychology (MA). *Accreditation:* ACA; APA.

Argosy University, Twin Cities, College of Psychology and Behavioral Sciences, Eagan, MN 55121. Offers clinical psychology (MA, Psy D), including child and family psychology (Psy D), forensic psychology (Psy D), health and neuropsychology (Psy D), trauma (Psy D); forensic counseling (Post-Graduate Certificate); forensic psychology (MA); industrial organizational psychology (MA); marriage and family therapy (MA, DMFT), including forensic counseling (MA). *Accreditation:* AAMFT; AAMFT/COAMFTE; APA.

Argosy University, Washington DC, College of Psychology and Behavioral Sciences, Arlington, VA 22209. Offers clinical psychology (MA, Psy D), including child and family psychology (Psy D), diversity and multicultural psychology (Psy D), forensic psychology (Psy D), health and neuropsychology (Psy D); community counseling (MA); counseling psychology (Ed D), including counselor education and supervision; counselor education and supervision (Ed D); forensic psychology (MA). *Accreditation:* APA.

California Baptist University, Program in Counseling Psychology, Riverside, CA 92504-3206. Offers counseling psychology (MS); forensic psychology (MS); professional clinical counselor (MS). Part-time and evening/weekend programs available. Postbaccalaureate distance learning degree programs offered (minimal on-campus study). *Faculty:* 16 full-time (10 women), 16 part-time/adjunct (9 women). *Students:* 233 full-time (200 women), 82 part-time (63 women); includes 186 minority (44 Black or African American, non-Hispanic/Latino; 5 American Indian or Alaska Native, non-Hispanic/Latino; 8 Asian, non-Hispanic/Latino; 121 Hispanic/Latino; 1 Native Hawaiian or other Pacific Islander, non-Hispanic/Latino; 7 Two or more races, non-Hispanic/Latino), 4 international. Average age 31. 184 applicants, 61% accepted, 74 enrolled. In 2014, 98 master's awarded. *Degree requirements:* For master's, comprehensive exam, 24 hours (individual) or 50 hours (group) psychotherapy, practicum. *Entrance requirements:* For master's, minimum undergraduate GPA of 2.75; official transcripts; three recommendations; 500-word essay; interview; 3 prerequisite courses completed with minimum C grade. Additional exam requirements/recommendations for international students: Required—TOEFL (minimum score 80 iBT). *Application deadline:* For fall admission, 8/1 priority date for domestic students; 7/1 for international students; for spring admission, 12/1 priority date for domestic students, 11/1 for international students. Applications are processed on a rolling basis. Application fee: $45. Electronic applications accepted. *Expenses:* Expenses: Contact institution. *Financial support:* Institutionally sponsored loans available. Financial award applicants required to submit CSS PROFILE or FAFSA. *Faculty research:* Identify formation, faith integration, psychological assessment, child abuse and child welfare, clinical psychology and crisis intervention techniques. *Unit head:* Dr. Jacqueline Gustafson, Dean, School of Behavioral Sciences, 951-343-4487, E-mail: jcraig@calbaptist.edu. *Application contact:* Mischa Routon, Associate Dean of Graduate Programs, 951-343-4206, Fax: 951-343-4569, E-mail: mrouton@calbaptist.edu. Website: http://www.calbaptist.edu/mft/

California Baptist University, Program in Forensic Psychology, Riverside, CA 92504-3206. Offers MA. Part-time and evening/weekend programs available. *Faculty:* 9 full-time (5 women), 1 (woman) part-time/adjunct. *Students:* 52 full-time (42 women), 11 part-time (7 women); includes 34 minority (7 Black or African American, non-Hispanic/Latino; 2 American Indian or Alaska Native, non-Hispanic/Latino; 1 Asian, non-Hispanic/Latino; 24 Hispanic/Latino). Average age 28. 32 applicants, 59% accepted, 19 enrolled. In 2014, 18 master's awarded. *Degree requirements:* For master's, thesis, 9-month practicum. *Entrance requirements:* For master's, minimum undergraduate GPA of 2.75; three recommendations; 500-word essay; interview; four prerequisite courses completed with minimum C grade. Additional exam requirements/recommendations for international students: Required—TOEFL (minimum score 80 iBT). *Application deadline:*

For fall admission, 8/1 priority date for domestic students, 7/1 for international students; for spring admission, 12/1 priority date for domestic students, 11/1 for international students. Applications are processed on a rolling basis. Application fee: $45. Electronic applications accepted. *Expenses:* Expenses: Contact institution. *Financial support:* Institutionally sponsored loans available. Financial award applicants required to submit CSS PROFILE or FAFSA. *Faculty research:* Criminal profiling, police psychology, post-traumatic stress disorder in law enforcement, religiosity as a protective factor in the incarcerated, media influence on perception of police. *Unit head:* Dr. Jacqueline Gustafson, Dean, School of Behavioral Sciences, 951-343-4487, E-mail: jcraig@calbaptist.edu. *Application contact:* Dr. Anne-Marie Larsen, Director, Graduate Program in Forensic Psychology, 951-343-4761, E-mail: alarsen@calbaptist.edu. Website: http://www.calbaptist.edu/for_psych/

Cambridge College, School of Psychology and Counseling, Cambridge, MA 02138-5304. Offers addiction counseling (M Ed); alcohol and drug counseling (Certificate); counseling psychology (M Ed, CAGS); counseling psychology: forensic counseling (M Ed); marriage and family therapy (M Ed); mental health and addiction counseling (M Ed); mental health counseling (M Ed); mental health counseling for school guidance counselors (Post Master's Certificate); psychological studies (M Ed); school adjustment and mental health counseling (M Ed); school adjustment, mental health and addiction counseling (M Ed); school guidance counselor (M Ed); trauma studies (Certificate). Part-time and evening/weekend programs available. *Degree requirements:* For master's and other advanced degree, thesis, practicum/internship. *Entrance requirements:* For master's, resume, 2 professional references; for other advanced degree, official transcripts, documents for transfer credit evaluation, resume, written personal statement/essay, 2 professional references, health insurance, immunizations form. Additional exam requirements/recommendations for international students: Required—TOEFL (minimum score 550 paper-based; 79 iBT), Michigan English Language Assessment Battery (minimum score 85); Recommended—IELTS (minimum score 6). Electronic applications accepted. *Expenses:* Contact institution. *Faculty research:* Trauma, drug and alcohol counseling, cross-cultural issues, school counseling, trauma in schools.

Castleton State College, Division of Graduate Studies, Department of Psychology, Castleton, VT 05735. Offers forensic psychology (MA). *Degree requirements:* For master's, thesis. *Entrance requirements:* For master's, GRE General Test, minimum undergraduate GPA of 3.5, previous course work in research methodology and statistics. Additional exam requirements/recommendations for international students: Required—TOEFL. *Faculty research:* Psychology and law, juvenile delinquency, criminal psychology, correctional psychology, police psychology.

The Chicago School of Professional Psychology, Program in Clinical Forensic Psychology, Chicago, IL 60610. Offers Psy D. *Degree requirements:* For doctorate, thesis/dissertation. *Entrance requirements:* For doctorate, GRE. Additional exam requirements/recommendations for international students: Required—TOEFL, IELTS.

The Chicago School of Professional Psychology, Program in Forensic Psychology, Chicago, IL 60610. Offers MA. *Degree requirements:* For master's, thesis optional. *Entrance requirements:* For master's, GRE (highly recommended), 1 course each in research methods, statistics, and psychology. Additional exam requirements/recommendations for international students: Required—TOEFL (minimum score 550 paper-based; 79 iBT).

The Chicago School of Professional Psychology at Downtown Los Angeles, Program in Clinical Forensic Psychology, Los Angeles, CA 90017. Offers Psy D.

The Chicago School of Professional Psychology at Irvine, Program in Clinical Forensic Psychology, Irvine, CA 92612. Offers Psy D.

The Chicago School of Professional Psychology: Online, Program in Forensic Psychology, Chicago, IL 60654. Offers MA, Certificate.

College of Saint Elizabeth, Department of Psychology, Morristown, NJ 07960-6989. Offers counseling psychology (MA); forensic psychology (MA); mental health counseling (Certificate); student affairs in higher education (Certificate). Part-time programs available. *Degree requirements:* For master's, thesis or alternative. *Entrance requirements:* For master's, minimum GPA of 3.0, BA in psychology (preferred), 12 credits of course work in psychology. Additional exam requirements/recommendations for international students: Required—TOEFL. Electronic applications accepted.

Concordia University, St. Paul, College of Education and Science, St. Paul, MN 55104-5494. Offers criminal justice (MA); curriculum and instruction (MA Ed), including K-12 reading; differentiated instruction (MA Ed); early childhood education (MA Ed); educational leadership (MA Ed); educational technology (MA Ed); exercise science (MA); family life education (MA); forensic mental health (MA); K-12 principal licensure (Ed S); K-12 reading (Certificate); physical therapy (DPT); special education (MA Ed, Certificate), including autism spectrum disorder (MA Ed), emotional and behavioral disorders (MA Ed), learning disabilities (MA Ed); sports management (MA); superintendent (Ed S). *Accreditation:* NCATE. Part-time and evening/weekend programs available. Postbaccalaureate distance learning degree programs offered (minimal on-campus study). *Faculty:* 16 full-time (9 women), 122 part-time/adjunct (72 women). *Students:* 1,147 full-time (810 women), 118 part-time (84 women); includes 147 minority (71 Black or African American, non-Hispanic/Latino; 12 American Indian or Alaska Native, non-Hispanic/Latino; 28 Asian, non-Hispanic/Latino; 20 Hispanic/Latino; 1 Native Hawaiian or other Pacific Islander, non-Hispanic/Latino; 15 Two or more races, non-Hispanic/Latino), 47 international. Average age 34. 874 applicants, 64% accepted, 440 enrolled. In 2014, 348 master's, 85 other advanced degrees awarded. *Degree requirements:* For master's, thesis (for some programs); for doctorate, clinical internships; capstone projects; for other advanced degree, e-folio review of competencies. *Entrance requirements:* For master's, official transcripts from regionally-accredited institution stating the conferral of a bachelor's degree with minimum cumulative GPA of 3.0; personal statement; professional resume; practitioner in field through work or volunteerism; resume; for doctorate, GRE (taken within last five years), bachelor's degree with minimum cumulative GPA of 3.0; 100 physical therapy observation hours; 2 letters of recommendation; for other advanced degree, at least three years of teaching experience, master's degree, valid MN teaching license. Additional exam requirements/recommendations for international students: Recommended—TOEFL (minimum score 547 paper-based; 78 iBT), IELTS (minimum score 6). *Application deadline:* For fall admission, 8/1 for domestic and international students; for spring admission, 12/1 for domestic and international students; for summer admission, 5/1 for domestic and international students. Applications are processed on a rolling basis. Application fee: $50. Electronic applications accepted. *Expenses: Tuition:* Full-time $4416; part-time $368 per credit. Tuition and fees vary according to degree level and program. *Financial support:* Applicants required to submit FAFSA. *Unit head:* Dr. Donald Helmstetter, Dean, 651-641-8227, Fax: 651-641-8807, E-mail: helmstetter@csp.edu. *Application contact:* Kimberly Craig, Associate Vice President, Cohort Enrollment Management, 651-603-6223, Fax: 651-603-6320, E-mail: craig@csp.edu.

Drexel University, College of Arts and Sciences, Department of Psychology, Clinical Psychology Program, Philadelphia, PA 19104-2875. Offers clinical psychology (PhD); forensic psychology (PhD); health psychology (PhD); neuropsychology (PhD).

Accreditation: APA. Terminal master's awarded for partial completion of doctoral program. *Degree requirements:* For doctorate, thesis/dissertation, qualifying exam. *Entrance requirements:* For doctorate, GRE General Test, GRE Subject Test, minimum GPA of 3.0. Electronic applications accepted. *Expenses:* Contact institution. *Faculty research:* Cognitive behavioral therapy, stress and coping, eating disorders, substance abuse, developmental disabilities.

Fairleigh Dickinson University, Metropolitan Campus, University College: Arts, Sciences, and Professional Studies, School of Psychology, Program in Forensic Psychology, Teaneck, NJ 07666-1914. Offers MA.

Fielding Graduate University, Graduate Programs, School of Psychology, Santa Barbara, CA 93105-3814. Offers clinical psychology (PhD, Graduate Certificate), including forensic psychology (PhD), health psychology (PhD), neuropsychology (PhD), parent-infant mental health (PhD), violence prevention and control (PhD); clinical psychology respecialization (Post-Doctoral Certificate); media psychology (MA, PhD), including forensic psychology (PhD); neuropsychology (Post-Doctoral Certificate). *Accreditation:* APA. Postbaccalaureate distance learning degree programs offered (minimal on-campus study). *Faculty:* 33 full-time (21 women), 40 part-time/adjunct (20 women). *Students:* 502 full-time (366 women), 79 part-time (62 women); includes 186 minority (69 Black or African American, non-Hispanic/Latino; 8 American Indian or Alaska Native, non-Hispanic/Latino; 23 Asian, non-Hispanic/Latino; 62 Hispanic/Latino; 1 Native Hawaiian or other Pacific Islander, non-Hispanic/Latino; 23 Two or more races, non-Hispanic/Latino), 4 international. Average age 45. 215 applicants, 56% accepted, 78 enrolled. In 2014, 15 master's, 54 doctorates, 9 other advanced degrees awarded. Terminal master's awarded for partial completion of doctoral program. *Degree requirements:* For master's, thesis or alternative, capstone project; for doctorate, comprehensive exam, thesis/dissertation. *Entrance requirements:* For master's, BA from regionally-accredited institution or equivalent, minimum GPA of 2.5; for doctorate, BA or MA from regionally-accredited institution or equivalent, writing sample, minimum GPA of 3.0. *Application deadline:* For fall admission, 3/6 for domestic students, 2/6 for international students; for spring admission, 11/1 for domestic and international students; for summer admission, 3/1 for domestic students, 2/1 for international students. Application fee: $75. Electronic applications accepted. *Expenses: Tuition:* Full-time $25,650; part-time $2880 per course. Tuition and fees vary according to degree level and program. *Financial support:* In 2014–15, 88 students received support, including 14 teaching assistantships (averaging $1,200 per year); scholarships/grants, health care benefits, tuition waivers (partial), and unspecified assistantships also available. Support available to part-time students. *Unit head:* Dr. Gerald Porter, Provost and Senior Vice President, 805-898-2940, E-mail: gporter@fielding.edu. *Application contact:* Enrollment Coordinator, 800-340-1099 Ext. 4098, Fax: 805-687-9793, E-mail: psyadmissions@fielding.edu.
Website: http://www.fielding.edu/programs/psy/default.aspx

The George Washington University, Graduate School of Education and Human Development, Department of Counseling and Human Development, Program in Forensic Rehabilitation Counseling, Washington, DC 20052. Offers Graduate Certificate. *Students:* 7 part-time (5 women); includes 1 minority (Hispanic/Latino). Average age 50. 9 applicants, 100% accepted, 5 enrolled. In 2014, 5 Graduate Certificates awarded. *Unit head:* Dr. Scott Beveridge, Assistant Professor, 202-994-2473, E-mail: beveridg@gwu.edu. *Application contact:* Sarah Lang, Director of Graduate Admissions, 202-994-1447, Fax: 202-994-7207, E-mail: slang@gwu.edu.
Website: http://gsehd.gwu.edu/forensic-rehabilitation-counseling-certificate

Holy Names University, Graduate Division, Department of Counseling Psychology, Oakland, CA 94619-1699. Offers counseling psychology (MA); forensic psychology (MA, Certificate); pastoral counseling (MA, Certificate). Part-time and evening/weekend programs available. *Faculty:* 15. *Students:* 43 full-time (42 women), 40 part-time (33 women); includes 60 minority (33 Black or African American, non-Hispanic/Latino; 4 Asian, non-Hispanic/Latino; 19 Hispanic/Latino; 3 Native Hawaiian or other Pacific Islander, non-Hispanic/Latino; 1 Two or more races, non-Hispanic/Latino). Average age 31. 42 applicants, 62% accepted, 15 enrolled. In 2014, 39 master's, 18 other advanced degrees awarded. *Degree requirements:* For master's, comprehensive paper, seminars. *Entrance requirements:* For master's, minimum undergraduate GPA of 2.6 overall, 3.0 in major. Additional exam requirements/recommendations for international students: Required—TOEFL (minimum score 550 paper-based; 79 iBT). *Application deadline:* For fall admission, 8/1 priority date for domestic students, 7/15 for international students; for spring admission, 12/1 priority date for domestic students, 12/1 for international students; for summer admission, 5/1 priority date for domestic students, 5/1 for international students. Applications are processed on a rolling basis. Application fee: $65. Electronic applications accepted. Application fee is waived when completed online. *Financial support:* Career-related internships or fieldwork, Federal Work-Study, scholarships/grants, and unspecified assistantships available. Support available to part-time students. Financial award application deadline: 3/2; financial award applicants required to submit FAFSA. *Faculty research:* Cognitive psychology, anger management, grief and grief counseling, post-modernism and psychotherapy, spirituality and psychology. *Unit head:* Dr. Helen Shoemaker, Program Director, 510-436-1543, E-mail: shoemaker@hnu.edu. *Application contact:* 800-430-1321, Fax: 510-436-1325, E-mail: graduateadmissions@hnu.edu.

Immaculata University, College of Graduate Studies, Department of Psychology, Immaculata, PA 19345. Offers clinical mental health counseling (MA); clinical psychology (Psy D); forensic psychology (Graduate Certificate); integrative psychotherapy (Graduate Certificate); neuropsychology (Graduate Certificate); psychodynamic psychotherapy (Graduate Certificate); psychological testing (Graduate Certificate); school counseling (MA, Graduate Certificate); school psychology (MA). *Accreditation:* APA. Part-time and evening/weekend programs available. Terminal master's awarded for partial completion of doctoral program. *Degree requirements:* For master's, comprehensive exam, thesis optional; for doctorate, comprehensive exam, thesis/dissertation. *Entrance requirements:* For master's, GRE General Test or MAT, minimum GPA of 3.0; for doctorate, GRE General Test or MAT, minimum GPA of 3.5. Additional exam requirements/recommendations for international students: Required—TOEFL, IELTS. Electronic applications accepted. *Faculty research:* Supervision ethics, psychology of teaching, gender.

John Jay College of Criminal Justice of the City University of New York, Graduate Studies, Program in Forensic Psychology, New York, NY 10019-1093. Offers MA, PhD, MA/JD. MA/JD offered with New York Law School. Part-time and evening/weekend programs available. *Degree requirements:* For master's, thesis or alternative, externship. *Entrance requirements:* For master's, GRE General Test, minimum B average in major. Additional exam requirements/recommendations for international students: Required—TOEFL (minimum score 500 paper-based).

John Jay College of Criminal Justice of the City University of New York, Graduate Studies, Programs in Criminal Justice, New York, NY 10019-1093. Offers criminal justice (MA, PhD); criminology and deviance (PhD); forensic psychology (PhD); forensic science (PhD); international crime and justice (MA); law and philosophy (PhD); organizational behavior (PhD); public policy (PhD). Part-time and evening/weekend programs available. Terminal master's awarded for partial completion of doctoral program. *Degree requirements:* For master's, thesis or alternative; for doctorate, one foreign language, thesis/dissertation. *Entrance requirements:* For master's, GRE General Test, minimum B average; for doctorate, GRE General Test. Additional exam requirements/recommendations for international students: Required—TOEFL (minimum score 500 paper-based).

Marymount University, School of Education and Human Services, Program in Forensic and Legal Psychology, Arlington, VA 22207-4299. Offers MA. Part-time and evening/weekend programs available. *Faculty:* 6 full-time (4 women), 6 part-time/adjunct (3 women). *Students:* 134 full-time (119 women), 35 part-time (32 women); includes 34 minority (15 Black or African American, non-Hispanic/Latino; 6 Asian, non-Hispanic/Latino; 8 Hispanic/Latino; 5 Two or more races, non-Hispanic/Latino), 1 international. Average age 25. 199 applicants, 80% accepted, 85 enrolled. In 2014, 84 master's awarded. *Entrance requirements:* For master's, GRE, 2 letters of recommendation, resume, personal statement. Additional exam requirements/recommendations for international students: Required—TOEFL (minimum score 600 paper-based; 96 iBT), IELTS (minimum score 6.5). *Application deadline:* For fall admission, 2/16 for domestic students, 2/17 for international students. Application fee: $40. Electronic applications accepted. *Expenses: Tuition:* Part-time $885 per credit. *Required fees:* $10 per credit. One-time fee: $220 part-time. Tuition and fees vary according to program. *Financial support:* In 2014–15, 14 students received support, including 5 research assistantships with full and partial tuition reimbursements available, 3 teaching assistantships with full and partial tuition reimbursements available; career-related internships or fieldwork, Federal Work-Study, scholarships/grants, and unspecified assistantships also available. Support available to part-time students. Financial award applicants required to submit FAFSA. *Unit head:* Dr. Jason Doll, Chair, 703-526-6821, Fax: 703-284-5708, E-mail: jason.doll@marymount.edu. *Application contact:* Francesca Reed, Director, Graduate Admissions, 703-284-5901, Fax: 703-527-3815, E-mail: grad.admissions@marymount.edu.
Website: http://www.marymount.edu/Academics/School-of-Education-Human-Services/Graduate-Programs/Forensic-Legal-Psychology-(M-A-)

Massachusetts School of Professional Psychology, Graduate Programs, Boston, MA 02132. Offers applied psychology in higher education student personnel administration (MA); clinical psychology (Psy D); counseling psychology (MA); counseling psychology and community mental health (MA); counseling psychology and global mental health (MA); executive coaching (Graduate Certificate); forensic and counseling psychology (MA); leadership psychology (Psy D); organizational psychology (MA); primary care psychology (MA); respecialization in clinical psychology (Certificate); school psychology (Psy D); MA/CAGS. *Accreditation:* APA. *Degree requirements:* For master's, comprehensive exam (for some programs); for doctorate, thesis/dissertation (for some programs). Electronic applications accepted.

Montclair State University, The Graduate School, College of Humanities and Social Sciences, Family/Civil Forensic Psychology Certificate Program, Montclair, NJ 07043-1624. Offers Certificate. *Students:* 1 (woman) full-time, 1 part-time (0 women); includes 1 minority (Black or African American, non-Hispanic/Latino). Average age 36. 3 applicants, 100% accepted, 1 enrolled. *Expenses:* Tuition, state resident: full-time $9960; part-time $553.35 per credit. Tuition, nonresident: full-time $15,074; part-time $837.43 per credit. *Required fees:* $1595; $88.63 per credit. Tuition and fees vary according to degree level and program. *Unit head:* Dr. Jason Dickinson, Coordinator. *Application contact:* Amy Aiello, Executive Director of The Graduate School, 973-655-5147, Fax: 973-655-7869, E-mail: graduate.school@montclair.edu.

Montclair State University, The Graduate School, College of Humanities and Social Sciences, Forensic Psychology Certificate Program, Montclair, NJ 07043-1624. Offers Certificate. Part-time and evening/weekend programs available. *Students:* 6 full-time (5 women); includes 2 minority (1 Black or African American, non-Hispanic/Latino; 1 Hispanic/Latino). Average age 33. 18 applicants, 61% accepted, 6 enrolled. In 2014, 4 Certificates awarded. *Entrance requirements:* For degree, 2 letters of recommendation, essay. Additional exam requirements/recommendations for international students: Required—TOEFL (minimum score 83 iBT), IELTS (minimum score 6.5). *Application deadline:* Applications are processed on a rolling basis. Application fee: $60. Electronic applications accepted. *Expenses:* Tuition, state resident: full-time $9960; part-time $553.35 per credit. Tuition, nonresident: full-time $15,074; part-time $837.43 per credit. *Required fees:* $1595; $88.63 per credit. Tuition and fees vary according to degree level and program. *Financial support:* Federal Work-Study, scholarships/grants, and unspecified assistantships available. Support available to part-time students. Financial award application deadline: 3/1; financial award applicants required to submit FAFSA. *Faculty research:* Forensic interviewing, child abuse. *Unit head:* Dr. Peter Vietze, Chairperson, 973-655-5201. *Application contact:* Amy Aiello, Executive Director of The Graduate School, 973-655-5147, Fax: 973-655-7869, E-mail: graduate.school@montclair.edu.
Website: http://chss.montclair.edu/forensics/

Oklahoma State University Center for Health Sciences, Graduate Program in Forensic Sciences, Tulsa, OK 74107. Offers forensic biology/DNA (MS); forensic pathology/death scene investigations (MS); forensic psychology (MS). Part-time and evening/weekend programs available. Postbaccalaureate distance learning degree programs offered (no on-campus study). *Faculty:* 3 full-time (0 women), 17 part-time/adjunct (8 women). *Students:* 13 full-time (11 women), 19 part-time (15 women); includes 7 minority (3 American Indian or Alaska Native, non-Hispanic/Latino; 1 Asian, non-Hispanic/Latino; 3 Hispanic/Latino), 1 international. Average age 31. 35 applicants, 43% accepted, 10 enrolled. In 2014, 11 master's awarded. *Degree requirements:* For master's, comprehensive exam, thesis (for some programs), creative component (for non-thesis options). *Entrance requirements:* For master's, MAT (for options in forensic science administration and forensic document examination) or GRE General Test, professional experience (for options in forensic science administration and forensic document examination). Additional exam requirements/recommendations for international students: Required—TOEFL (minimum score 100 iBT) or IELTS (minimum score 7.0). *Application deadline:* For fall admission, 3/1 for domestic and international students; for spring admission, 10/1 for domestic and international students; for summer admission, 7/1 for domestic and international students. Applications are processed on a rolling basis. Application fee: $50 ($75 for international students). Electronic applications accepted. *Expenses:* Tuition, state resident: full-time $22,835. Tuition, nonresident: full-time $44,966. *Required fees:* $1259. *Financial support:* In 2014–15, 20 students received support, including 8 research assistantships (averaging $12,000 per year); career-related internships or fieldwork, Federal Work-Study, and tuition waivers (partial) also available. Support available to part-time students. Financial award application deadline: 4/1; financial award applicants required to submit FAFSA. *Faculty research:* Studies on the variability in chromosomal DNA; development/enhancement of accessory methods useful for forensic DNA typing; development of universal methods useful for discriminating pathogenic bacteria; forensic dentistry; forensic chemistry in the areas of controlled substances, explosives, and technology; therapeutic jurisprudence, issues involving inmates and their families, institutional stress suicide. *Total annual research expenditures:* $58,000. *Unit head:* Dr. Robert W. Allen, Director, 918-561-1108, Fax: 918-561-8414. *Application contact:* Cathy Newsome, Coordinator, 918-561-1108, Fax: 918-561-8414, E-mail: cathy.newsome@okstate.edu.
Website: http://www.healthsciences.okstate.edu/forensic/index.cfm

Forensic Psychology

Pontificia Universidad Catolica Madre y Maestra, Graduate School, Faculty of Social and Administrative Sciences, Santiago, Dominican Republic. Offers business administration (MBA), including business development, finance, international business, management skills (M Mgmt, MBA), marketing, operations, strategic cost management, strategy, tourist destination planning and management; law (LL M), including civil law, corporate business law, criminal law, international relations, real estate law; management (M Mgmt), including higher financial management, insurance program administration, management skills (M Mgmt, MBA); psychology (MA), including clinical child and adolescent psychology, forensic psychology; strategic human resources (EMBA).

Prairie View A&M University, College of Juvenile Justice and Psychology, Prairie View, TX 77446-0519. Offers clinical adolescent psychology (PhD); juvenile forensic psychology (MSJFP); juvenile justice (MSJJ, PhD). Part-time and evening/weekend programs available. *Faculty:* 8 full-time (4 women). *Students:* 27 full-time (24 women), 33 part-time (27 women); includes 49 minority (48 Black or African American, non-Hispanic/Latino; 1 Two or more races, non-Hispanic/Latino), 9 international. Average age 34. 43 applicants, 77% accepted, 22 enrolled. In 2014, 9 master's, 1 doctorate awarded. *Degree requirements:* For master's, comprehensive exam (for some programs), thesis (for some programs); for doctorate, comprehensive exam, thesis/dissertation. *Entrance requirements:* For master's, GRE, minimum GPA of 2.75; for doctorate, GRE, previous course work in clinical adolescent psychology, minimum GPA of 3.5. Additional exam requirements/recommendations for international students: Required—TOEFL (minimum score 550 paper-based; 79 iBT). *Application deadline:* For fall admission, 7/1 priority date for domestic students, 6/1 priority date for international students; for spring admission, 11/1 priority date for domestic students, 10/1 priority date for international students; for summer admission, 3/1 priority date for domestic students, 2/1 priority date for international students. Applications are processed on a rolling basis. Application fee: $50. *Expenses:* Expenses: $6,686 tuition and fees. *Financial support:* Career-related internships or fieldwork, Federal Work-Study, institutionally sponsored loans, tuition waivers (full and partial), and unspecified assistantships available. Support available to part-time students. Financial award application deadline: 3/1; financial award applicants required to submit FAFSA. *Faculty research:* Juvenile justice, juvenile forensic psychology, teen court, graduate education, capital punishment. *Unit head:* Dr. Tamara L. Brown, Dean, 936-261-5206, Fax: 936-261-5253, E-mail: tlbrown@pvamu.edu. *Application contact:* Pauline Walker, Executive Secretary, Graduate Program, 936-261-3521, Fax: 936-261-3529, E-mail: pmwalker@pvamu.edu.

Roger Williams University, Feinstein College of Arts and Sciences, Bristol, RI 02809. Offers clinical psychology (MA); forensic psychology (MA). Part-time and evening/weekend programs available. Postbaccalaureate distance learning degree programs offered (minimal on-campus study). *Faculty:* 7 full-time (3 women). *Students:* 35 full-time (28 women), 1 (woman) part-time; includes 5 minority (1 Black or African American, non-Hispanic/Latino; 1 Asian, non-Hispanic/Latino; 2 Hispanic/Latino; 1 Two or more races, non-Hispanic/Latino), 2 international. Average age 23. 118 applicants, 58% accepted, 20 enrolled. In 2014, 21 master's awarded. *Degree requirements:* For master's, thesis optional, internship. *Entrance requirements:* For master's, GRE, 3 letters of recommendation. Additional exam requirements/recommendations for international students: Required—TOEFL (minimum score 85 iBT), IELTS. *Application deadline:* Applications are processed on a rolling basis. Application fee: $50. Electronic applications accepted. *Expenses:* Expenses: $14,724. *Financial support:* In 2014–15, 5 research assistantships (averaging $5,000 per year) were awarded. Financial award application deadline: 6/15; financial award applicants required to submit FAFSA. *Unit head:* Robert Eisinger, Dean, 401-254-3149, E-mail: reisinger@rwu.edu. *Application contact:* Lori Vales, Director of Graduate Admissions, 401-254-6200, Fax: 401-254-3557, E-mail: gradadmit@rwu.edu.
Website: http://www.rwu.edu/academics/schools/fcas/

Sage Graduate School, School of Health Sciences, Department of Psychology, Troy, NY 12180-4115. Offers community psychology (MA), including child care and children's services, community counseling, community health education, community psychology, general psychology; counseling and community psychology (MA); forensic mental health (MS, Certificate). Part-time and evening/weekend programs available. *Faculty:* 4 full-time (3 women), 4 part-time/adjunct (3 women). *Students:* 48 full-time (39 women), 40 part-time (33 women); includes 19 minority (10 Black or African American, non-Hispanic/Latino; 1 American Indian or Alaska Native, non-Hispanic/Latino; 1 Asian, non-Hispanic/Latino; 4 Hispanic/Latino; 3 Two or more races, non-Hispanic/Latino). Average age 29. 94 applicants, 57% accepted, 21 enrolled. In 2014, 16 master's awarded. *Degree requirements:* For master's, thesis or alternative. *Entrance requirements:* For master's, GRE General Test. Additional exam requirements/recommendations for international students: Required—TOEFL (minimum score 550 paper-based). *Application deadline:* Applications are processed on a rolling basis. Application fee: $40. *Expenses:* Tuition: Full-time $12,240; part-time $680 per credit hour. *Financial support:* Fellowships, research assistantships, Federal Work-Study, scholarships/grants, and unspecified assistantships available. Support available to part-time students. Financial award application deadline: 3/1; financial award applicants required to submit FAFSA. *Faculty research:* Effectiveness of arts integration programs in elementary and secondary schools, literacy-based substance abuse program, outcome evaluation of program to increase college entry among urban youth. *Unit head:* Dr. Patricia O'Connor, Interim Dean, School of Health Sciences, 518-244-2073, Fax: 518-244-4571, E-mail: oconnp@sage.edu. *Application contact:* Dr. Sybillyn Jennings, Department Chair, 518-244-2074, Fax: 518-244-4545, E-mail: jennis@sage.edu.

Sage Graduate School, School of Health Sciences, Program in Forensic Mental Health, Troy, NY 12180-4115. Offers MS, Certificate. Part-time and evening/weekend programs available. *Faculty:* 4 full-time (3 women), 3 part-time/adjunct (1 woman). *Students:* 19 full-time (15 women), 16 part-time (15 women); includes 7 minority (4 Black or African American, non-Hispanic/Latino; 2 Hispanic/Latino; 1 Two or more races, non-Hispanic/Latino). Average age 28. 63 applicants, 40% accepted, 16 enrolled. In 2014, 12 master's, 1 other advanced degree awarded. *Entrance requirements:* Additional exam requirements/recommendations for international students: Required—TOEFL (minimum score 550 paper-based). *Application deadline:* Applications are processed on a rolling basis. Application fee: $40. *Expenses:* Tuition: Full-time $12,240; part-time $680 per credit hour. *Financial support:* Fellowships, research assistantships, Federal Work-Study, scholarships/grants, and unspecified assistantships available. Support available to part-time students. *Unit head:* Dr. Maureen McLeod, Director, Forensic Mental Health, 518-244-2245, E-mail: mcleom@sage.edu. *Application contact:* Wendy D. Diefendorf, Director of Graduate and Adult Admission, 518-244-2443, Fax: 518-244-6880, E-mail: diefew@sage.edu.

Tiffin University, Program in Criminal Justice, Tiffin, OH 44883-2161. Offers crime analysis (MSCJ); criminal behavior (MSCJ); forensic psychology (MSCJ); homeland security administration (MSCJ); justice administration (MSCJ). Part-time and evening/weekend programs available. Postbaccalaureate distance learning degree programs offered (no on-campus study). *Degree requirements:* For master's, thesis optional. *Entrance requirements:* For master's, minimum undergraduate GPA of 2.5, work experience. Additional exam requirements/recommendations for international students:

Required—TOEFL (minimum score 550 paper-based; 79 iBT). Electronic applications accepted. *Faculty research:* Terrorism, intelligence, homeland security, guns and crime.

Trine University, Program in Criminal Justice, Angola, IN 46703-1764. Offers emergency management (MS); forensic psychology (MS); law (MS); public administration (MS). Part-time and evening/weekend programs available. *Students:* 46 part-time (39 women). In 2014, 20 master's awarded. *Entrance requirements:* Additional exam requirements/recommendations for international students: Required—TOEFL. *Expenses: Tuition:* Full-time $12,000; part-time $670 per credit hour. Tuition and fees vary according to degree level, campus/location, program and student level. *Financial support:* Application deadline: 3/1; applicants required to submit FAFSA. *Unit head:* Barbara E. Molargik-Fitch, JD, Director, 260-203-2693, Fax: 260-203-2965, E-mail: molargik-fitchb@trine.edu. *Application contact:* Cherie Ditto, Director of SPS Enrollment Services, 260-702-3592, E-mail: dittoc@trine.edu.
Website: http://www.trine.edu/academics/majors-and-minors/graduate/criminal-justice/index.aspx

Universidad de Iberoamerica, Graduate School, San Jose, Costa Rica. Offers clinical neuropsychology (PhD); clinical psychology (M Psych); educational psychology (M Psych); forensic psychology (M Psych); hospital management (MHA); intensive care nursing (MN); medicine (MD).

University of Central Oklahoma, The Jackson College of Graduate Studies, College of Education and Professional Studies, Department of Psychology, Edmond, OK 73034-5209. Offers counseling psychology (MA); experimental psychology (MA); forensic psychology (MA); general psychology (MA); school psychology (MA). *Degree requirements:* For master's, thesis (for some programs). *Entrance requirements:* For master's, GRE. Additional exam requirements/recommendations for international students: Required—TOEFL (minimum score 550 paper-based; 79 iBT), IELTS (minimum score 6.5). Electronic applications accepted. *Faculty research:* Psychopharmacology, computer psychometrics, health psychology research.

University of Denver, Graduate School of Professional Psychology, Denver, CO 80208. Offers forensic psychology (MA); international disaster psychology (MA); sport and performance psychology (MA). *Accreditation:* APA. *Faculty:* 18 full-time (9 women), 23 part-time/adjunct (9 women). *Students:* 205 full-time (148 women), 51 part-time (38 women); includes 57 minority (11 Black or African American, non-Hispanic/Latino; 1 American Indian or Alaska Native, non-Hispanic/Latino; 15 Asian, non-Hispanic/Latino; 21 Hispanic/Latino; 9 Two or more races, non-Hispanic/Latino), 12 international. Average age 27. 720 applicants, 31% accepted, 102 enrolled. In 2014, 90 master's, 32 doctorates awarded. *Degree requirements:* For master's, comprehensive exam (for some programs); for doctorate, comprehensive exam (for some programs), paper, clinical internship. *Entrance requirements:* For master's and doctorate, GRE General Test, transcripts, resume, two letters of recommendation, essay. Additional exam requirements/recommendations for international students: Required—TOEFL (minimum score 550 paper-based; 80 iBT). *Application deadline:* For fall admission, 12/1 priority date for domestic and international students. Application fee: $65. Electronic applications accepted. *Expenses:* Expenses: $1,199 per credit hour. *Financial support:* In 2014–15, 76 students received support, including 33 teaching assistantships with full and partial tuition reimbursements available (averaging $3,042 per year); career-related internships or fieldwork, Federal Work-Study, institutionally sponsored loans, scholarships/grants, unspecified assistantships, and clinical assistantships also available. Support available to part-time students. Financial award application deadline: 2/15; financial award applicants required to submit FAFSA. *Unit head:* Dr. Shelly Smith-Acuna, Dean, 303-871-3880, E-mail: shelly.smith-acuna@du.edu. *Application contact:* Admissions Counselor, 303-871-3736, Fax: 303-871-7656, E-mail: gsppinfo@du.edu.
Website: http://www.du.edu/gspp/

University of Houston–Victoria, School of Arts and Sciences, Program in Psychology, Victoria, TX 77901-4450. Offers counseling psychology (MA); forensic psychology (MA); school psychology (MA). Part-time and evening/weekend programs available. Postbaccalaureate distance learning degree programs offered (minimal on-campus study). *Degree requirements:* For master's, project or thesis. *Entrance requirements:* For master's, GRE General Test. Additional exam requirements/recommendations for international students: Required—TOEFL (minimum score 550 paper-based). Electronic applications accepted.

University of Louisiana at Monroe, Graduate School, College of Business and Social Sciences, Department of Psychology, Monroe, LA 71209-0001. Offers forensic psychology (MS); general psychology (MS); psychometrics (MS). Part-time and evening/weekend programs available. Postbaccalaureate distance learning degree programs offered (no on-campus study). *Degree requirements:* For master's, comprehensive exam, thesis optional. *Entrance requirements:* For master's, GRE General Test, minimum GPA of 2.75. Additional exam requirements/recommendations for international students: Required—TOEFL (minimum score 500 paper-based; 61 iBT). Electronic applications accepted.

University of New Haven, Graduate School, College of Arts and Sciences, Program in Community Psychology, West Haven, CT 06516-1916. Offers applications of psychology (Certificate); community clinical services (MA); community psychology (MA); forensic psychology (MA); program development (MA). Part-time and evening/weekend programs available. *Degree requirements:* For master's, thesis or alternative, fieldwork. *Entrance requirements:* Additional exam requirements/recommendations for international students: Required—TOEFL (minimum score 80 iBT), IELTS, PTE (minimum score 53). Electronic applications accepted. Application fee is waived when completed online. *Expenses: Tuition:* Full-time $22,248; part-time $824 per credit hour. *Required fees:* $45 per trimester.

University of New Haven, Graduate School, Henry C. Lee College of Criminal Justice and Forensic Sciences, Program in Criminal Justice, West Haven, CT 06516-1916. Offers crime analysis (MS); criminal justice (MS, PhD); criminal justice management (MS, Certificate); forensic computer investigation (MS, Certificate); forensic psychology (MS); information protection and security (Certificate); victim advocacy and services management (Certificate); victimology (MS). Part-time and evening/weekend programs available. Postbaccalaureate distance learning degree programs offered (no on-campus study). *Degree requirements:* For master's, thesis or alternative. *Entrance requirements:* Additional exam requirements/recommendations for international students: Required—TOEFL (minimum score 80 iBT), IELTS, PTE (minimum score 53). Electronic applications accepted. Application fee is waived when completed online. *Expenses: Tuition:* Full-time $22,248; part-time $824 per credit hour. *Required fees:* $45 per trimester.

University of North Dakota, Graduate School, College of Arts and Sciences, Department of Psychology, Grand Forks, ND 58202. Offers clinical psychology (PhD); counseling psychology (PhD); experimental psychology (PhD); forensic psychology (MA, MS); psychology (MA). *Accreditation:* APA (one or more programs are accredited). *Degree requirements:* For master's, thesis, final exam; for doctorate, comprehensive exam, thesis/dissertation, internship, final exam. *Entrance requirements:* For master's, GRE General Test, GRE Subject Test, minimum GPA of 3.0; for doctorate, GRE General Test, GRE Subject Test, minimum GPA of 3.5. Additional exam requirements/recommendations for international students: Required—TOEFL (minimum score 550

paper-based; 79 iBT), IELTS (minimum score 6.5). Electronic applications accepted. *Faculty research:* Developmental psychology, clinical social psychology, educational psychology, personality disorders.

Walden University, Graduate Programs, School of Counseling, Minneapolis, MN 55401. Offers addiction counseling (MS), including addictions and public health, child and adolescent counseling, family studies and interventions, forensic counseling, general program (MS, PhD), trauma and crisis counseling; counselor education and supervision (PhD), including consultation, counseling and social change, forensic mental health counseling, general program (MS, PhD), trauma and crisis; marriage, couple, and family counseling (MS), including forensic counseling, general program (MS, PhD), trauma and crisis counseling; mental health counseling (MS), including forensic counseling, general program (MS, PhD), trauma and crisis counseling; school counseling (MS), including addiction counseling, crisis and trauma, general program (MS, PhD), military families and culture. Part-time and evening/weekend programs available. Postbaccalaureate distance learning degree programs offered (no on-campus study). *Faculty:* 77 full-time (62 women), 314 part-time/adjunct (215 women). *Students:* 1,835 full-time (1,558 women), 1,518 part-time (1,293 women); includes 1,521 minority (1,135 Black or African American, non-Hispanic/Latino; 13 American Indian or Alaska Native, non-Hispanic/Latino; 27 Asian, non-Hispanic/Latino; 234 Hispanic/Latino; 5 Native Hawaiian or other Pacific Islander, non-Hispanic/Latino; 107 Two or more races, non-Hispanic/Latino), 16 international. Average age 38. 684 applicants, 91% accepted, 610 enrolled. In 2014, 592 master's, 4 doctorates awarded. *Degree requirements:* For master's, residency, field experience, professional development plan, licensure plan; for doctorate, thesis/dissertation, residency, practicum, internship. *Entrance requirements:* For master's, bachelor's degree or higher; minimum GPA of 2.5; official transcripts; goal statement (for some programs); access to computer and Internet; for doctorate, master's degree or higher; three years of related professional or academic experience (preferred); minimum GPA of 3.0; goal statement and current resume (for select programs); official transcripts; access to computer and Internet. Additional exam requirements/recommendations for international students: Required—TOEFL (minimum score 550 paper-based, 79 iBT), IELTS (minimum score 6.5), Michigan English Language Assessment Battery (minimum score 82), or PTE (minimum score 53). *Application deadline:* Applications are processed on a rolling basis. Application fee: $0. Electronic applications accepted. *Expenses: Tuition:* Full-time $11,925; part-time $500 per credit hour. *Required fees:* $647. *Financial support:* Federal Work-Study, scholarships/grants, unspecified assistantships, and family tuition reduction, active duty/veteran tuition reduction, group tuition reduction, interest-free payment plans, employee tuition reduction available. Support available to part-time students. Financial award applicants required to submit FAFSA. *Unit head:* Dr. Savitri Dixon-Saxon, Associate Dean, 866-492-5336. *Application contact:* Meghan M. Thomas, Vice President of Enrollment Management, 866-492-5336, E-mail: info@waldenu.edu.

Walden University, Graduate Programs, School of Psychology, Minneapolis, MN 55401. Offers clinical psychology (MS), including counseling, general program; forensic psychology (MS), including forensic psychology in the community, general program, mental health applications, program planning and evaluation in forensic settings, psychology and legal systems; organizational psychology and development (Postbaccalaureate Certificate); psychology (MS, PhD), including applied psychology (MS), clinical psychology (PhD), counseling psychology (PhD), crisis management and response (MS), educational psychology, forensic psychology (PhD), general psychology (MS), general psychology research (PhD), health psychology, leadership development and coaching (MS), psychology of culture (MS), psychology, public administration, and social change (MS), social psychology, terrorism and security (MS); psychology respecialization (Post-Doctoral Certificate); teaching online (Post-Master's Certificate). Part-time and evening/weekend programs available. Postbaccalaureate distance learning degree programs offered (no on-campus study). *Faculty:* 56 full-time (36 women), 351 part-time/adjunct (201 women). *Students:* 2,757 full-time (2,202 women), 1,466 part-time (1,148 women); includes 1,849 minority (1,299 Black or African American, non-Hispanic/Latino; 37 American Indian or Alaska Native, non-Hispanic/Latino; 74 Asian, non-Hispanic/Latino; 315 Hispanic/Latino; 8 Native Hawaiian or other Pacific Islander, non-Hispanic/Latino; 116 Two or more races, non-Hispanic/Latino), 28 international. Average age 41. 913 applicants, 97% accepted, 851 enrolled. In 2014, 602 master's, 204 doctorates, 19 other advanced degrees awarded. Terminal master's awarded for partial completion of doctoral program. *Degree requirements:* For master's, thesis optional; for doctorate, thesis/dissertation, residency. *Entrance requirements:* For master's, bachelor's degree or higher; minimum GPA of 2.5; official transcripts; goal statement (for some programs); access to computer and Internet; for doctorate, master's degree or higher; three years of related professional or academic experience (preferred); minimum GPA of 3.0; goal statement and current resume (for select programs); official transcripts; access to computer and Internet; for other advanced degree, relevant work experience; access to computer and Internet. Additional exam requirements/recommendations for international students: Required—TOEFL (minimum score 550 paper-based, 79 iBT), IELTS (minimum score 6.5), Michigan English Language Assessment Battery (minimum score 82), or PTE (minimum score 53). *Application deadline:* Applications are processed on a rolling basis. Application fee: $0. Electronic applications accepted. *Expenses: Tuition:* Full-time $11,925; part-time $500 per credit hour. *Required fees:* $647. *Financial support:* Fellowships, Federal Work-Study, scholarships/grants, unspecified assistantships, and family tuition reduction, active duty/veteran tuition reduction, group tuition reduction, interest-free payment plans, employee tuition reduction available. Support available to part-time students. Financial award applicants required to submit FAFSA. *Unit head:* Dr. Marilyn Powell, Associate Dean, 866-492-5366. *Application contact:* Meghan Thomas, Vice President of Enrollment Management, 866-492-5336, E-mail: info@waldenu.edu. Website: http://www.waldenu.edu/programs/colleges-schools/psychology

Genetic Counseling

Arcadia University, Graduate Studies, Program in Genetic Counseling, Glenside, PA 19038-3295. Offers MSGC. *Degree requirements:* For master's, thesis. *Entrance requirements:* For master's, GRE. Additional exam requirements/recommendations for international students: Required—TOEFL. *Expenses:* Contact institution.

Boston University, School of Medicine, Division of Graduate Medical Sciences, Program in Genetic Counseling, Boston, MA 02215. Offers MS. *Application deadline:* For fall admission, 2/1 for domestic students. *Expenses: Tuition:* Full-time $45,686; part-time $1428 per credit hour. *Required fees:* $660; $60 per semester. Tuition and fees vary according to program. *Financial support:* In 2014–15, 15 students received support. Institutionally sponsored loans and unspecified assistantships available. Financial award application deadline: 1/1; financial award applicants required to submit FAFSA. *Unit head:* MaryAnn Whalen Campion, Director, 617-638-7170, E-mail: maryann@bu.edu. *Application contact:* Maureen Flynn, Assistant Director, 617-638-7083, E-mail: gc4dna@bu.edu.
Website: http://www.bumc.bu.edu/gms/m-s-genetic-counseling-program/

Brandeis University, Graduate School of Arts and Sciences, Program in Genetic Counseling, Waltham, MA 02454-9110. Offers MS. *Faculty:* 2 full-time (1 woman), 9 part-time/adjunct (8 women). *Students:* 20 full-time (18 women); includes 3 minority (2 Asian, non-Hispanic/Latino; 1 Hispanic/Latino), 3 international. 118 applicants, 9% accepted, 11 enrolled. In 2014, 11 master's awarded. *Degree requirements:* For master's, thesis, proseminar and journal club, research project, internship/fieldwork. *Entrance requirements:* For master's, GRE General Test, resume, 3 letters of recommendation, statement of purpose, transcript(s). Additional exam requirements/recommendations for international students: Required—TOEFL (minimum score 600 paper-based; 100 iBT), PTE (minimum score 68); Recommended—IELTS (minimum score 7). *Application deadline:* For fall admission, 1/15 for domestic and international students. Application fee: $75. Electronic applications accepted. *Expenses:* Expenses: Contact institution. *Financial support:* Federal Work-Study, scholarships/grants, and tuition waivers (partial) available. Financial award application deadline: 4/15; financial award applicants required to submit FAFSA. *Unit head:* Dr. Judith Tsipis, Director, 781-736-3179, Fax: 781-736-3107, E-mail: tsipis@brandeis.edu. *Application contact:* Missy Goldberg, Department Administrator, 781-736-3179, Fax: 781-736-3107, E-mail: goldberg@brandeis.edu.
Website: http://www.bio.brandeis.edu/grad/gc/index.html

California State University, Stanislaus, College of Natural Sciences, Program in Genetic Counseling (MS), Turlock, CA 95382. Offers MS. *Degree requirements:* For master's, thesis. *Entrance requirements:* For master's, GRE, minimum GPA of 3.0, 3 letters of reference, personal statement. Additional exam requirements/recommendations for international students: Required—TOEFL (minimum score 550 paper-based). Electronic applications accepted. *Expenses:* Contact institution.

Case Western Reserve University, School of Medicine and School of Graduate Studies, Graduate Programs in Medicine, Department of Genetics and Genome Sciences, Program in Genetic Counseling, Cleveland, OH 44106. Offers MS. *Faculty:* 20 full-time (6 women). *Students:* 12 full-time (all women), 2 international. Average age 24. 49 applicants, 12% accepted, 6 enrolled. In 2014, 6 master's awarded. *Degree requirements:* For master's, comprehensive exam, thesis. *Entrance requirements:* For master's, GRE General Test. Additional exam requirements/recommendations for international students: Required—TOEFL. *Application deadline:* For fall admission, 1/1 for domestic and international students. Application fee: $50. *Financial support:* In 2014–15, 12 fellowships (averaging $5,000 per year) were awarded. Financial award application deadline: 2/28. *Faculty research:* Genetic testing, ethical issues in genetics,

cancer genetics, reproductive genetics, prenatal diagnosis. *Unit head:* Dr. Anne L. Matthews, Director, 216-368-1821, Fax: 216-368-3432, E-mail: alm14@po.cwru.edu. *Application contact:* Clarice D. Young, department Assistant, 216-368-3431, Fax: 216-368-1257, E-mail: cdy5@case.edu.
Website: http://www.genetics.case.edu/?page_id-22

Emory University, School of Medicine, Programs in Allied Health Professions, Genetic Counseling Training Program, Atlanta, GA 30322. Offers MM Sc. *Degree requirements:* For master's, thesis, capstone project. *Entrance requirements:* For master's, GRE General Test, minimum GPA of 3.0; prerequisites: genetics, statistics, psychology, and biochemistry. Additional exam requirements/recommendations for international students: Required—TOEFL. *Faculty research:* Cancer genetics, lysosomal storage disease, carrier screening, public health genomics, genetic counseling, psychology, molecular genetics.

Icahn School of Medicine at Mount Sinai, Graduate School of Biomedical Sciences, New York, NY 10029-6504. Offers biomedical sciences (MS, PhD); clinical research education (MS, PhD); community medicine (MPH); genetic counseling (MS); neurosciences (PhD); MD/PhD. Terminal master's awarded for partial completion of doctoral program. *Degree requirements:* For master's, thesis; for doctorate, comprehensive exam, thesis/dissertation. *Entrance requirements:* For master's, GRE General Test; for doctorate, GRE General Test, GRE Subject Test, 3 years of college pre-med course work. Additional exam requirements/recommendations for international students: Required—TOEFL. Electronic applications accepted. *Faculty research:* Cancer, genetics and genomics, immunology, neuroscience, developmental and stem cell biology, translational research.

Johns Hopkins University, Bloomberg School of Public Health, Department of Health, Behavior and Society, Baltimore, MD 21218-2699. Offers genetic counseling (Sc M); health education and health communication (MSPH); social and behavioral sciences (Dr PH, PhD); social factors in health (MHS). *Degree requirements:* For master's, comprehensive exam (for some programs), thesis (for some programs); for doctorate, comprehensive exam, thesis/dissertation. *Entrance requirements:* For master's, GRE, curriculum vitae, 3 letters of recommendation; for doctorate, GRE, transcripts, curriculum vitae, 3 recommendation letters. Additional exam requirements/recommendations for international students: Required—TOEFL (minimum score 600 paper-based; 100 iBT). Electronic applications accepted. *Faculty research:* Social determinants of health and structural and community-level inventions to improve health, communication and health education, behavioral and social aspects of genetic counseling.

McGill University, Faculty of Graduate and Postdoctoral Studies, Faculty of Medicine, Department of Human Genetics, Montréal, QC H3A 2T5, Canada. Offers genetic counseling (M Sc); human genetics (M Sc, PhD).

Northwestern University, The Graduate School, Program in Genetic Counseling, Evanston, IL 60208. Offers MS. *Degree requirements:* For master's, thesis. *Entrance requirements:* For master's, GRE General Test, interview. Additional exam requirements/recommendations for international students: Required—TOEFL. *Faculty research:* Preimplantation genetic diagnosis, gene expression in preimplantation embryos, fetal cells in maternal blood: first trimester prenatal screening for Down's Syndrome, genetic counseling efficacy and counseling issues in prenatal diagnosis.

Sarah Lawrence College, Graduate Studies, Joan H. Marks Graduate Program in Human Genetics, Bronxville, NY 10708-5999. Offers MS. Part-time programs available. *Degree requirements:* For master's, thesis, fieldwork. *Entrance requirements:* For master's, previous course work in biology, chemistry, developmental biology, genetics,

probability and statistics. Additional exam requirements/recommendations for international students: Required—TOEFL (minimum score 600 paper-based). Electronic applications accepted. *Expenses:* Contact institution.

Stanford University, School of Medicine, Graduate Programs in Medicine, Department of Genetics, Stanford, CA 94305-9991. Offers genetic counseling (MS); genetics (MS, PhD). *Degree requirements:* For doctorate, thesis/dissertation, qualifying examination. *Entrance requirements:* For doctorate, GRE General Test, GRE Subject Test. Additional exam requirements/recommendations for international students: Required—TOEFL. Electronic applications accepted. *Expenses: Tuition:* Full-time $44,184; part-time $982 per credit hour. *Required fees:* $191. *Faculty research:* Molecular biology of DNA replication in human cells, analysis of existing and search for new DNA polymorphisms in humans, molecular genetics of prokaryotic and eukaryotic genetic elements, proteins in DNA replication.

Université de Montréal, Faculty of Medicine, Program in Genetic Counseling, Montréal, QC H3C 3J7, Canada. Offers DESS.

The University of Alabama at Birmingham, School of Health Professions, Program in Genetic Counseling, Birmingham, AL 35294. Offers MS. *Students:* 12 full-time (all women), 1 (woman) part-time; includes 1 minority (Asian, non-Hispanic/Latino), 1 international. Average age 30. In 2014, 5 master's awarded. *Entrance requirements:* For master's, GRE, minimum undergraduate GPA of 3.0, letters of recommendation, paid or volunteer experience, personal statement. Additional exam requirements/recommendations for international students: Required—TOEFL, TWE. *Application deadline:* For fall admission, 1/15 for domestic students. Application fee: $0 ($60 for international students). Electronic applications accepted. *Expenses:* Tuition, state resident: full-time $7090; part-time $370 per credit hour. Tuition, nonresident: full-time $16,072; part-time $869 per credit hour. Full-time tuition and fees vary according to course load and program. *Unit head:* Dr. Christina B. Hurst, Graduate Program Director, 205-934-7299, E-mail: cbhurst@uab.edu. *Application contact:* Susan Noblitt Banks, Director of Graduate School Operations, 205-934-8227, Fax: 205-934-8413, E-mail: gradschool@uab.edu.
Website: http://www.uab.edu/shp/cds/genetic-counseling

University of Arkansas for Medical Sciences, College of Health Professions, Little Rock, AR 72205-7199. Offers audiology (Au D); communication sciences and disorders (MS, PhD); genetic counseling (MS); nuclear medicine advanced associate (MIS); physician assistant studies (MPAS); radiologist assistant (MIS). PhD offered through consortium with University of Arkansas at Little Rock and University of Central Arkansas. Part-time programs available. Postbaccalaureate distance learning degree programs offered (minimal on-campus study). *Degree requirements:* For master's, thesis (for some programs); for doctorate, comprehensive exam (for some programs), thesis/dissertation (for some programs). *Entrance requirements:* For master's, GRE. Additional exam requirements/recommendations for international students: Required—TOEFL (minimum score 550 paper-based; 79 iBT). Electronic applications accepted. *Expenses:* Contact institution. *Faculty research:* Auditory-based intervention, soy diet, nutrition and cancer.

The University of British Columbia, Faculty of Medicine, Department of Medical Genetics, M Sc Program in Genetic Counselling, Vancouver, BC V6H 3N1, Canada. Offers M Sc. Electronic applications accepted.

University of California, Irvine, School of Medicine, Department of Pediatrics, Program in Genetic Counseling, Irvine, CA 92697. Offers MS. *Students:* 11 full-time (all women), 1 (woman) part-time; includes 5 minority (2 Asian, non-Hispanic/Latino; 2 Hispanic/Latino; 1 Two or more races, non-Hispanic/Latino). Average age 29. 120 applicants, 10% accepted, 6 enrolled. In 2014, 6 master's awarded. *Degree requirements:* For master's, thesis. *Entrance requirements:* For master's, GRE General Test, minimum GPA of 3.0. Additional exam requirements/recommendations for international students: Required—TOEFL (minimum score 550 paper-based). *Application deadline:* For fall admission, 1/15 priority date for domestic students, 1/15 for international students. Applications are processed on a rolling basis. Application fee: $90 ($110 for international students). Electronic applications accepted. *Financial support:* In 2014–15, 3 students received support. Research assistantships with full tuition reimbursements available, teaching assistantships, career-related internships or fieldwork, institutionally sponsored loans, traineeships, health care benefits, and unspecified assistantships available. Financial award application deadline: 3/1; financial award applicants required to submit FAFSA. *Faculty research:* Gene mapping and linkage analysis, delineation of new malformation and chromosomal syndromes, ethical and counseling issues in genetics. *Unit head:* Pamela Flodman, Director, 714-456-8470, E-mail: pflodman@uci.edu.
Website: http://www.pediatrics.uci.edu/masters-genetic-counseling.asp

University of Cincinnati, Graduate School, College of Allied Health Sciences, Program in Genetic Counseling, Cincinnati, OH 45221. Offers medical genetics (MS). Part-time programs available. *Degree requirements:* For master's, thesis. *Entrance requirements:* For master's, GRE General Test. Additional exam requirements/recommendations for international students: Required—TOEFL. Electronic applications accepted. *Faculty research:* Lysosomal disease, Tourette's syndrome, epidemiology of Down syndrome, genetic counseling, genetic disease treatment.

University of Colorado Denver, School of Medicine, Graduate Program in Genetic Counseling, Aurora, CO 80045. Offers biophysics and genetics (MS, PhD). *Students:* 12 full-time (all women); includes 2 minority (1 Asian, non-Hispanic/Latino; 1 Hispanic/Latino). Average age 26. 104 applicants, 6% accepted, 6 enrolled. In 2014, 6 master's awarded. *Degree requirements:* For master's, 44 core semester hours, project or thesis; for doctorate, comprehensive exam, thesis/dissertation, 30 hours each of didactic course work and research credits. *Entrance requirements:* For master's, GRE, minimum undergraduate GPA of 3.0; 4 letters of recommendation; prerequisite coursework in biology, general chemistry, general biochemistry, general genetics, general psychology; experience in counseling and laboratory settings and strong understanding of genetic counseling field (highly recommended); for doctorate, GRE, three letters of recommendation, laboratory research experience and solid undergraduate foundation in mathematics and biological sciences. Additional exam requirements/recommendations for international students: Required—TOEFL (minimum score 570 paper-based; 89 iBT). *Application deadline:* For fall admission, 1/1 for domestic students, 12/1 for international students. Application fee: $50 ($75 for international students). Electronic applications accepted. *Expenses:* Expenses: Contact institution. *Financial support:* In 2014–15, 9 students received support. Fellowships, research assistantships, teaching assistantships, career-related internships or fieldwork, Federal Work-Study, institutionally sponsored loans, scholarships/grants, traineeships, and unspecified assistantships available. Financial award application deadline: 4/1; financial award applicants required to submit FAFSA. *Faculty research:* Psychosocial aspects of genetic counseling, clinical cytogenetics and molecular genetics, human inborn errors of metabolism, congenital malformations and disorders of the newborn, cancer genetics and genetic counseling. *Unit head:* Carol Walton, Director, 303-724-2370, E-mail: carol.walton@ucdenver.edu. *Application contact:* Associate Dean for Admissions, 303-724-8025, E-mail: somadmin@ucdenver.edu.
Website: http://www.ucdenver.edu/academics/colleges/Graduate-School/academic-programs/genetic-counseling/Pages/default.aspx

University of Maryland, Baltimore, School of Medicine, Genetic Counseling Training Program, Baltimore, MD 21201. Offers MGC. *Students:* 13 full-time (12 women); includes 1 minority (Asian, non-Hispanic/Latino). Average age 24. 100 applicants, 7% accepted, 7 enrolled. In 2014, 6 master's awarded. *Unit head:* Shannan DeLany Dixon, Director, 410-706-4713, Fax: 410-706-1644, E-mail: sdelany@som.umaryland.edu.

University of Michigan, Horace H. Rackham School of Graduate Studies, Program in Biomedical Sciences (PIBS), Department of Human Genetics, Ann Arbor, MI 48109. Offers genetic counseling (MS); human genetics (MS, PhD). *Faculty:* 35 full-time (16 women). *Students:* 39 full-time (24 women); includes 7 minority (6 Asian, non-Hispanic/Latino; 1 Two or more races, non-Hispanic/Latino), 8 international. Average age 26. 216 applicants, 15% accepted, 16 enrolled. In 2014, 11 master's, 4 doctorates awarded. Terminal master's awarded for partial completion of doctoral program. *Degree requirements:* For master's, research project; for doctorate, thesis/dissertation, oral preliminary exam, oral defense of dissertation. *Entrance requirements:* For master's, GRE General Test, 3 letters of recommendation; advocacy experience (for the MS in genetic counseling); for doctorate, GRE General Test, 3 letters of recommendation. Additional exam requirements/recommendations for international students: Required—TOEFL (minimum score 84 iBT). *Application deadline:* For fall admission, 12/1 for domestic and international students; for winter admission, 1/15 for domestic and international students; for spring admission, 5/1 for domestic students, 3/15 for international students. Application fee: $75 ($90 for international students). Electronic applications accepted. *Expenses:* Expenses: PhD pre-candidate and MS in-state students: $20,446 per year, PhD pre-candidate and MS out-of-state students: 40,972 per year; PhD candidate students: $11,236 per year. *Financial support:* In 2014–15, 31 students received support, including 27 fellowships with full and partial tuition reimbursements available (averaging $28,500 per year), 6 research assistantships with full tuition reimbursements available (averaging $28,500 per year), 4 teaching assistantships with full and partial tuition reimbursements available (averaging $8,900 per year); Federal Work-Study, institutionally sponsored loans, scholarships/grants, traineeships, health care benefits, and unspecified assistantships also available. Financial award application deadline: 4/30; financial award applicants required to submit FAFSA. *Faculty research:* Molecular genetics, developmental genetics, disease mechanisms, translational clinical research, statistical and population genetics. *Total annual research expenditures:* $6.8 million. *Unit head:* Dr. Sally A. Camper, Chair, 734-763-0682, Fax: 734-763-3784, E-mail: scamper@umich.edu. *Application contact:* Michelle S. Melis, Director of Student Life, 734-615-6538, Fax: 734-647-7022, E-mail: msmtegan@umich.edu.
Website: http://www.hg.med.umich.edu/

University of Minnesota, Twin Cities Campus, Graduate School, Program in Molecular, Cellular, Developmental Biology and Genetics, Minneapolis, MN 55455-0213. Offers genetic counseling (MS); molecular, cellular, developmental biology and genetics (PhD). Terminal master's awarded for partial completion of doctoral program. *Degree requirements:* For master's, thesis optional; for doctorate, thesis/dissertation. *Entrance requirements:* For master's and doctorate, GRE General Test. Additional exam requirements/recommendations for international students: Required—TOEFL (minimum score 625 paper-based; 80 iBT). Electronic applications accepted. *Faculty research:* Membrane receptors and membrane transport, cell interactions, cytoskeleton and cell mobility, regulation of gene expression, plant cell and molecular biology.

The University of North Carolina at Greensboro, Graduate School, School of Health and Human Sciences, Program in Genetic Counseling, Greensboro, NC 27412-5001. Offers MS. Electronic applications accepted.

University of Oklahoma Health Sciences Center, College of Medicine and Graduate College, Department of Genetic Counseling, Oklahoma City, OK 73190. Offers MS. *Entrance requirements:* For master's, GRE General Test, 3 letters of recommendation.

University of Pittsburgh, Graduate School of Public Health, Department of Human Genetics, Pittsburgh, PA 15260. Offers genetic counseling (MS); human genetics (MS, PhD); public health genetics (MPH, Certificate); MD/PhD; MS/MPH. *Faculty:* 16 full-time (7 women), 54 part-time/adjunct (41 women). *Students:* 45 full-time (29 women), 28 part-time (23 women); includes 11 minority (4 Black or African American, non-Hispanic/Latino; 2 Asian, non-Hispanic/Latino; 2 Hispanic/Latino; 3 Two or more races, non-Hispanic/Latino), 15 international. Average age 27. 112 applicants, 51% accepted, 22 enrolled. In 2014, 18 master's, 8 doctorates awarded. Terminal master's awarded for partial completion of doctoral program. *Degree requirements:* For master's, thesis (for some programs); for doctorate, thesis/dissertation. *Entrance requirements:* For master's, GRE General Test, previous course work in biochemistry, calculus, and genetics; for doctorate, GRE General Test. Additional exam requirements/recommendations for international students: Required—TOEFL (minimum score 550 paper-based, 80 iBT) or IELTS (minimum score 6.5). *Application deadline:* For fall admission, 1/15 for domestic students, 4/1 for international students; for winter admission, 9/1 for international students; for spring admission, 10/15 for domestic students, 8/1 for international students; for summer admission, 12/1 for international students. Applications are processed on a rolling basis. Application fee: $120. Electronic applications accepted. *Expenses:* Tuition, state resident: full-time $20,742; part-time $838 per credit. Tuition, nonresident: full-time $33,960; part-time $1389 per credit. *Required fees:* $800; $205 per term. Tuition and fees vary according to program. *Financial support:* In 2014–15, 2 fellowships, 21 research assistantships (averaging $15,147 per year) were awarded. *Faculty research:* Genetic mechanisms related to the transition from normal to disease states, how genes and the environment interact to affect the distribution of health and disease in human populations. *Total annual research expenditures:* $3.9 million. *Unit head:* Dr. Dietrich Stephan, Chairman, 412-648-3353, E-mail: dstephan@pitt.edu. *Application contact:* Noel Harrie, Student Services Coordinator, 412-624-3066, Fax: 412-624-3020, E-mail: nce1@pitt.edu.
Website: http://www.hgen.pitt.edu

University of South Carolina, School of Medicine and The Graduate School, Graduate Programs in Medicine, Program in Genetic Counseling, Columbia, SC 29203. Offers MS. *Degree requirements:* For master's, comprehensive exam, internship, practicum. *Entrance requirements:* For master's, GRE General Test. Electronic applications accepted. *Expenses:* Contact institution. *Faculty research:* Genetic counseling, international, transition, prenatal diagnosis.

The University of Texas Health Science Center at Houston, Graduate School of Biomedical Sciences, Program in Genetic Counseling, Houston, TX 77225-0036. Offers MS. *Degree requirements:* For master's, thesis. *Entrance requirements:* For master's, GRE General Test. Additional exam requirements/recommendations for international students: Required—TOEFL. Electronic applications accepted. *Expenses:* Tuition, state resident: full-time $4158; part-time $231 per hour. Tuition, nonresident: full-time $12,744; part-time $708 per hour. *Required fees:* $771 per semester. *Faculty research:* Psychosocial aspects of genetic counseling, risk assessment, cancer genetic counseling, multicultural genetic counseling, prenatal counseling.

University of Toronto, Faculty of Medicine, Department of Molecular Genetics, Toronto, ON M5S 2J7, Canada. Offers genetic counseling (M Sc); molecular genetics

(M Sc, PhD). *Degree requirements:* For master's, thesis; for doctorate, thesis/dissertation. *Entrance requirements:* For master's, B Sc or equivalent; for doctorate, M Sc or equivalent, minimum B+ average. Additional exam requirements/recommendations for international students: Required—TOEFL, IELTS (minimum score 7), Michigan English Language Assessment Battery (minimum score 85), or COPE (minimum score 4). Electronic applications accepted. *Faculty research:* Structural biology, developmental genetics, molecular medicine, genetic counseling.

University of Wisconsin–Madison, Graduate School, College of Agricultural and Life Sciences and Graduate Programs in Medicine, Department of Genetics, Program in Genetic Counseling, Madison, WI 53706-1380. Offers MS. *Expenses:* Tuition, state resident: full-time $10,723; part-time $745 per credit. Tuition, nonresident: full-time $24,054; part-time $1578 per credit. *Required fees:* $374 per semester. Tuition and fees vary according to course load, program and reciprocity agreements.

Wayne State University, School of Medicine, Office of Biomedical Graduate Programs, Genetic Counseling Graduate Program, Detroit, MI 48202. Offers MS. *Students:* 12 full-time (11 women). Average age 25. 68 applicants, 9% accepted, 6 enrolled. In 2014, 7 master's awarded. *Degree requirements:* For master's, research project, clinical internship. *Entrance requirements:* For master's, GRE, interview, recommendations, personal statement, minimum GPA of 3.0 majoring in biological or chemical sciences, advocacy experience, understanding of the genetic counseling profession. Additional exam requirements/recommendations for international students: Required—TOEFL (minimum score 550 paper-based; 100 iBT); Recommended—IELTS (minimum score 6.5), TWE (minimum score 5.5). *Application deadline:* For fall admission, 2/1 for domestic and international students; for winter admission, 10/1 for domestic students, 9/1 for international students; for spring admission, 2/1 for domestic students, 1/1 for international students. Application fee: $0. Electronic applications accepted. *Expenses:* Expenses: Contact institution. *Financial support:* Scholarships/grants available. Financial award application deadline: 3/31; financial award applicants required to submit FAFSA. *Unit head:* Angela M. Trepanier, Program Director, 313-577-6298, E-mail: geneticcounseling@med.wayne.edu.

Health Psychology

Adler University, Programs in Psychology, Chicago, IL 60602. Offers advanced Adlerian psychotherapy (Certificate); art therapy (MA); clinical neuropsychology (Certificate); clinical psychology (Psy D); community psychology (MA); counseling and organizational psychology (MA); counseling psychology (MA); criminology (MA); emergency management leadership (MA); forensic psychology (MA); marriage and family counseling (MA); marriage and family therapy (Certificate); military psychology (MA); nonprofit management (MA); organizational psychology (MA); police psychology (MA); public policy and administration (MA); rehabilitation counseling (MA); sport and health psychology (MA); substance abuse counseling (Certificate); Psy D/Certificate; Psy D/MACAT; Psy D/MACP; Psy D/MAMFC; Psy D/MASAC. *Accreditation:* APA. Part-time and evening/weekend programs available. Postbaccalaureate distance learning degree programs offered (minimal on-campus study). Terminal master's awarded for partial completion of doctoral program. *Degree requirements:* For master's, thesis or alternative, oral exam, practicum; for doctorate, thesis/dissertation, clinical exam, internship, oral exam, practicum, written qualifying exam. *Entrance requirements:* For master's, 12 semester hours in psychology, minimum GPA of 3.0; for doctorate, 18 semester hours in psychology, minimum GPA of 3.25; for Certificate, appropriate master's or doctoral degree. Additional exam requirements/recommendations for international students: Required—TOEFL (minimum score 550 paper-based; 79 iBT). Electronic applications accepted.
See Display on page 969 and Close-Up on page 1207.

Alliant International University–Los Angeles, California School of Professional Psychology, Psy D Program in Clinical Psychology, Alhambra, CA 91803-1360. Offers clinical health psychology (Psy D); family/child and couple clinical psychology (Psy D); multi-interest option (Psy D); multicultural community-clinical psychology (Psy D). *Accreditation:* APA. *Degree requirements:* For doctorate, comprehensive exam, thesis/dissertation. *Entrance requirements:* For doctorate, interview, minimum GPA of 3.0 in both psychology and overall. Additional exam requirements/recommendations for international students: Required—TOEFL (minimum score 600 paper-based), TWE. Electronic applications accepted. *Faculty research:* Child and family psychology, multicultural and community psychology, acculturation, lesbian and gay issues, women's health.

Appalachian State University, Cratis D. Williams Graduate School, Department of Psychology, Boone, NC 28608. Offers clinical health psychology (MA); general experimental psychology (MA); industrial and organizational psychology (MA); MA/SSP. Part-time programs available. *Degree requirements:* For master's, comprehensive exam, thesis optional, exit exam. *Entrance requirements:* For master's, GRE General Test, 3 letters of recommendation. Additional exam requirements/recommendations for international students: Required—TOEFL (minimum score 550 paper-based; 79 iBT) or IELTS (minimum score 6.5). Electronic applications accepted. *Faculty research:* Eating disorders, school-based consultations, organizational behavior management, brain mechanisms of sound localization, parenting styles.

Argosy University, Atlanta, College of Psychology and Behavioral Sciences, Atlanta, GA 30328. Offers clinical psychology (MA, Psy D, Postdoctoral Respecialization Certificate), including child and family psychology (Psy D), general adult clinical (Psy D), health psychology (Psy D), neuropsychology/geropsychology (Psy D); community counseling (MA), including marriage and family therapy; counselor education and supervision (Ed D); forensic psychology (MA); industrial organizational psychology (MA); marriage and family therapy (Certificate); sport-exercise psychology (MA). *Accreditation:* APA.

Argosy University, Chicago, College of Psychology and Behavioral Sciences, Doctoral Program in Clinical Psychology, Chicago, IL 60601. Offers child and adolescent psychology (Psy D); client-centered and experiential psychotherapies (Psy D); diversity and multicultural psychology (Psy D); family psychology (Psy D); forensic psychology (Psy D); health psychology (Psy D); neuropsychology (Psy D); organizational consulting (Psy D); psychoanalytic psychology (Psy D); psychology and spirituality (Psy D). *Accreditation:* APA.

Argosy University, Twin Cities, College of Psychology and Behavioral Sciences, Eagan, MN 55121. Offers clinical psychology (MA, Psy D), including child and family psychology (Psy D), forensic psychology (Psy D), health and neuropsychology (Psy D), trauma (Psy D); forensic counseling (Post-Graduate Certificate); forensic psychology (MA); industrial organizational psychology (MA); marriage and family therapy (MA, DMFT), including forensic counseling (MA). *Accreditation:* AAMFT; AAMFT/COAMFTE; APA.

Argosy University, Washington DC, College of Psychology and Behavioral Sciences, Arlington, VA 22209. Offers clinical psychology (MA, Psy D), including child and family psychology (Psy D), diversity and multicultural psychology (Psy D), forensic psychology (Psy D), health and neuropsychology (Psy D); community counseling (MA); counseling psychology (Ed D), including counselor education and supervision; counselor education and supervision (Ed D); forensic psychology (MA). *Accreditation:* APA.

Bastyr University, School of Natural Health Arts and Sciences, Kenmore, WA 98028-4966. Offers counseling psychology (MA); holistic landscape design (Certificate); midwifery (MS); nutrition (MS); nutrition and clinical health psychology (MS). *Accreditation:* AND. Part-time programs available. *Students:* 373 full-time (334 women), 39 part-time (37 women); includes 71 minority (11 Black or African American, non-Hispanic/Latino; 1 American Indian or Alaska Native, non-Hispanic/Latino; 24 Asian, non-Hispanic/Latino; 14 Hispanic/Latino; 21 Two or more races, non-Hispanic/Latino), 20 international. Average age 30. *Degree requirements:* For master's, thesis optional. *Entrance requirements:* For master's, 1-2 years' basic sciences course work (depending on program). Additional exam requirements/recommendations for international students: Required—TOEFL (minimum score 550 paper-based; 79 iBT). *Application deadline:* For fall admission, 3/15 priority date for domestic and international students. Applications are processed on a rolling basis. Application fee: $75. *Financial support:* In 2014–15, 47 students received support. Career-related internships or fieldwork, Federal Work-Study, and scholarships/grants available. Support available to part-time students. Financial award application deadline: 4/15; financial award applicants required to submit FAFSA. *Faculty research:* Whole-food nutrition for type 2 diabetes; meditation in end-of-life care; stress management; Qi Gong, Tai Chi and yoga for older adults; Echinacea and immunology. *Unit head:* Dr. Timothy Callahan, Vice President and Provost, 425-602-3110, Fax: 425-823-6222. *Application contact:* Admissions Office, 425-602-3330, Fax: 425-602-3090, E-mail: admissions@bastyr.edu.
Website: http://www.bastyr.edu/academics/schools-departments/school-natural-health-arts-sciences

California Institute of Integral Studies, School of Professional Psychology and Health, San Francisco, CA 94103. Offers clinical psychology (Psy D); community mental health (MA); drama therapy (MA); expressive arts therapy (MA); integral counseling psychology (MA); integrative health studies (MA); psychological studies (MA); somatic psychology (MA). *Accreditation:* APA. Part-time and evening/weekend programs available. *Students:* 522 full-time (397 women), 105 part-time (83 women); includes 155 minority (27 Black or African American, non-Hispanic/Latino; 3 American Indian or Alaska Native, non-Hispanic/Latino; 31 Asian, non-Hispanic/Latino; 62 Hispanic/Latino; 3 Native Hawaiian or other Pacific Islander, non-Hispanic/Latino; 29 Two or more races, non-Hispanic/Latino), 49 international. Average age 34. 351 applicants, 86% accepted, 175 enrolled. In 2014, 168 master's, 24 doctorates awarded. *Degree requirements:* For doctorate, comprehensive exam, thesis/dissertation. *Entrance requirements:* For master's, minimum GPA of 3.0, letters of recommendation, writing sample; for doctorate, GRE, MA in psychology or social work with appropriate practical experience for advanced standing, or BA with a minimum GPA of 3.1; letters of recommendation; writing sample. Additional exam requirements/recommendations for international students: Required—TOEFL. *Application deadline:* For fall admission, 2/1 priority date for domestic and international students; for spring admission, 10/15 priority date for domestic and international students. Applications are processed on a rolling basis. Application fee: $65. Electronic applications accepted. *Expenses:* Tuition: Full-time $18,270; part-time $1015 per credit. *Required fees:* $85 per semester hour. *Financial support:* In 2014–15, 464 students received support, including 5 research assistantships with tuition reimbursements available (averaging $800 per year), 36 teaching assistantships with tuition reimbursements available (averaging $825 per year); career-related internships or fieldwork, Federal Work-Study, and scholarships/grants also available. Support available to part-time students. Financial award application deadline: 4/15; financial award applicants required to submit FAFSA. *Faculty research:* Transpersonal psychology, somatic psychology, expressive arts therapy, drama therapy, community mental health, ecopsychology, integrative health. *Application contact:* David Townes, Senior Admissions Counselor, 415-575-6152, Fax: 415-575-1268, E-mail: admissions@ciis.edu.

Central Connecticut State University, School of Graduate Studies, College of Liberal Arts and Social Sciences, Department of Psychology, New Britain, CT 06050-4010. Offers community psychology (MA); general psychology (MA); health psychology (MA). Part-time and evening/weekend programs available. *Faculty:* 15 full-time (9 women). *Students:* 16 full-time (13 women), 18 part-time (14 women); includes 8 minority (2 Black or African American, non-Hispanic/Latino; 2 Asian, non-Hispanic/Latino; 4 Hispanic/Latino), 2 international. Average age 28. 27 applicants, 41% accepted, 6 enrolled. In 2014, 13 master's awarded. *Degree requirements:* For master's, comprehensive exam, thesis or alternative. *Entrance requirements:* For master's, minimum undergraduate GPA of 2.75, 3.0 in psychology courses; letters of recommendation. Additional exam requirements/recommendations for international students: Required—TOEFL (minimum score 550 paper-based; 79 iBT). *Application deadline:* For fall admission, 5/1 for domestic and international students; for spring admission, 11/1 for domestic and international students. Applications are processed on a rolling basis. Application fee: $50. Electronic applications accepted. *Expenses:* Tuition, area resident: Full-time $5730; part-time $534 per credit. Tuition, state resident: full-time $8596; part-time $534 per credit. Tuition, nonresident: full-time $15,964; part-time $548 per credit. *Required fees:* $4211; $215 per credit. *Financial support:* In 2014–15, 8 students received support, including 5 research assistantships; career-related internships or fieldwork, Federal Work-Study, scholarships/grants, and unspecified assistantships also available. Support available to part-time students. Financial award application deadline: 3/1; financial award applicants required to submit FAFSA. *Faculty research:* Clinical psychology, general psychology, child development, cognitive development, drugs/behavior. *Unit head:* Dr. Carolyn Fallahi, Chair, 860-832-3100, E-mail: fallahic@ccsu.edu. *Application contact:* Patricia Gardner, Associate Director of Graduate Studies, 860-832-2350, Fax: 860-832-2362, E-mail: graduateadmissions@ccsu.edu.
Website: http://web.ccsu.edu/psychology/

Central Michigan University, College of Graduate Studies, College of Humanities and Social and Behavioral Sciences, Department of Psychology, Program in Industrial and

Organizational Psychology, Mount Pleasant, MI 48859. Offers industrial and organizational psychology (MA, PhD); occupational health psychology (PhD). *Degree requirements:* For master's, thesis; for doctorate, comprehensive exam, thesis/dissertation. *Entrance requirements:* For master's and doctorate, GRE. Electronic applications accepted. *Faculty research:* Job stress, retirement, leadership, and careers; personality in the workplace, personnel selection, and structural equation modeling in industrial/organizational psychology; personnel psychology, evolutionary psychology, and influences on HRM utilization; occupational health psychology and job stress; work attitudes, psychological ownership in work, and performance appraisal.

Chatham University, Program in Counseling Psychology, Pittsburgh, PA 15232-2826. Offers child, adolescent and family (MSCP); counseling psychology (Psy D); health and holistic (MSCP); infant mental health (MSCP); organization and supervision (MSCP); sport and exercise (MSCP). Part-time and evening/weekend programs available. *Faculty:* 12 full-time (9 women), 13 part-time/adjunct (9 women). *Students:* 102 full-time (85 women), 38 part-time (32 women); includes 17 minority (7 Black or African American, non-Hispanic/Latino; 2 Asian, non-Hispanic/Latino; 6 Hispanic/Latino; 2 Two or more races, non-Hispanic/Latino), 7 international. Average age 29. 145 applicants, 73% accepted, 59 enrolled. In 2014, 67 master's, 3 doctorates awarded. *Degree requirements:* For master's, thesis optional, supervised internship; for doctorate, thesis/dissertation, internship. *Entrance requirements:* For master's, minimum GPA of 3.0; 2 letters of recommendation; resume; prerequisite coursework in statistics, biology, and psychology; for doctorate, GRE. Additional exam requirements/recommendations for international students: Required—TOEFL (minimum score 600 paper-based; 100 iBT), IELTS (minimum score 7), TWE. *Application deadline:* For fall admission, 4/1 priority date for domestic and international students; for spring admission, 11/1 for domestic students, 10/1 for international students. Applications are processed on a rolling basis. Application fee: $45. Electronic applications accepted. Application fee is waived when completed online. *Expenses: Tuition:* Full-time $15,318; part-time $851 per credit hour. *Required fees:* $440; $24 per credit hour. Tuition and fees vary according to course load, program and reciprocity agreements. *Financial support:* Career-related internships or fieldwork available. Financial award applicants required to submit FAFSA. *Faculty research:* Trauma and recovery, hypnosis, psychospiritual dimensions of healing, psychotherapy of schizophrenia. *Unit head:* Dr. Mary Beth Mannarino, Director, 412-365-1196, Fax: 412-365-1505, E-mail: mmannarino@chatham.edu. *Application contact:* Katie Noel, Assistant Director of Graduate Admission, 412-365-2758, Fax: 412-365-1609, E-mail: gradadmissions@chatham.edu.
Website: http://www.chatham.edu/mscp

Claremont Graduate University, Graduate Programs, School of Social Science, Policy and Evaluation, Department of Psychology, Claremont, CA 91711-6160. Offers advanced study in evaluation (Certificate); cognitive psychology (MA, PhD); developmental psychology (MA, PhD); evaluation and applied research methods (MA, PhD); health behavior research and evaluation (MA, PhD); human resource development and evaluation (MA); industrial/organizational psychology (MA, PhD); organizational behavior (MA, PhD); organizational psychology (MA, PhD); social psychology (MA, PhD); MBA/PhD. Part-time programs available. *Faculty:* 18 full-time (7 women), 1 part-time/adjunct (0 women). *Students:* 256 full-time (160 women), 70 part-time (50 women); includes 93 minority (17 Black or African American, non-Hispanic/Latino; 3 American Indian or Alaska Native, non-Hispanic/Latino; 26 Asian, non-Hispanic/Latino; 30 Hispanic/Latino; 17 Two or more races, non-Hispanic/Latino), 35 international. Average age 30. In 2014, 56 master's, 15 doctorates, 7 other advanced degrees awarded. Terminal master's awarded for partial completion of doctoral program. *Entrance requirements:* For master's and doctorate, GRE General Test. Additional exam requirements/recommendations for international students: Required—TOEFL (minimum score 550 paper-based; 80 iBT). *Application deadline:* For fall admission, 1/15 priority date for domestic and international students. Applications are processed on a rolling basis. Application fee: $80. Electronic applications accepted. *Expenses: Tuition:* Full-time $41,784; part-time $1741 per credit. *Required fees:* $600; $300 per semester. *Financial support:* Fellowships, research assistantships, teaching assistantships, Federal Work-Study, institutionally sponsored loans, scholarships/grants, and tuition waivers (full and partial) available. Support available to part-time students. Financial award application deadline: 2/15; financial award applicants required to submit FAFSA. *Faculty research:* Social intervention, diversity in organizations, eyewitness memory, aging and cognition, drug policy. *Unit head:* William Crano, Chair, 909-621-8084, E-mail: william.crano@cgu.edu. *Application contact:* Annekah Hall, Assistant Director of Admissions, 909-607-3371, E-mail: annekah.hall@cgu.edu.
Website: http://www.cgu.edu/pages/502.asp

Connecticut College, Department of Psychology, New London, CT 06320-4196. Offers behavioral medicine/health psychology (MA); clinical psychology (MA); neuroscience/psychobiology (MA); social/personality psychology (MA). Part-time programs available. *Students:* 4 full-time (2 women), 3 part-time (2 women). Average age 30. 7 applicants, 29% accepted, 2 enrolled. *Degree requirements:* For master's, thesis. *Entrance requirements:* For master's, GRE General Test, statistics course. Additional exam requirements/recommendations for international students: Required—TOEFL (minimum score 600 paper-based). *Application deadline:* For fall admission, 2/1 for domestic and international students. Application fee: $60. *Expenses: Tuition:* Full-time $12,120. *Financial support:* Tuition remission available. Financial award application deadline: 2/1; financial award applicants required to submit CSS PROFILE or FAFSA. *Unit head:* Dr. Ruth Grahn, Chair, 860-439-2387, Fax: 860-439-5300, E-mail: ruth.grahn@conncoll.edu. *Application contact:* Nancy M. MacLeod, Academic Department Assistant, 860-439-2330, Fax: 860-439-5300, E-mail: nancy.macleod@conncoll.edu.

Drexel University, College of Arts and Sciences, Department of Psychology, Clinical Psychology Program, Philadelphia, PA 19104-2875. Offers clinical psychology (PhD); forensic psychology (PhD); health psychology (PhD); neuropsychology (PhD). *Accreditation:* APA. Terminal master's awarded for partial completion of doctoral program. *Degree requirements:* For doctorate, thesis/dissertation, qualifying exam. *Entrance requirements:* For doctorate, GRE General Test, GRE Subject Test, minimum GPA of 3.0. Electronic applications accepted. *Expenses:* Contact institution. *Faculty research:* Cognitive behavioral therapy, stress and coping, eating disorders, substance abuse, developmental disabilities.

Drexel University, College of Arts and Sciences, Department of Psychology, Program in Law-Psychology, Philadelphia, PA 19104-2875. Offers JD/PhD. Electronic applications accepted. *Expenses:* Contact institution. *Faculty research:* Mental health law issues, professional ethics, social science applications to law.

Duke University, Graduate School, Department of Psychology and Neuroscience, Durham, NC 27708. Offers biological psychology (PhD); clinical psychology (PhD); cognitive psychology (PhD); developmental psychology (PhD); experimental psychology (PhD); health psychology (PhD); human social development (PhD); JD/MA. *Accreditation:* APA (one or more programs are accredited). *Degree requirements:* For doctorate, thesis/dissertation. *Entrance requirements:* For doctorate, GRE General Test. Additional exam requirements/recommendations for international students: Required—TOEFL (minimum score 577 paper-based; 90 iBT) or IELTS (minimum score 7). Electronic applications accepted. *Expenses: Tuition:* Full-time $45,760; part-time $2765 per credit. *Required fees:* $978. Full-time tuition and fees vary according to program.

East Carolina University, Graduate School, Thomas Harriot College of Arts and Sciences, Department of Psychology, Program in Health Psychology, Greenville, NC 27858-4353. Offers clinical health psychology (PhD); occupational health psychology (PhD); pediatric school psychology (PhD). *Entrance requirements:* For doctorate, GRE. *Expenses:* Tuition, state resident: full-time $4223. Tuition, nonresident: full-time $16,540. *Required fees:* $2184.

Fielding Graduate University, Graduate Programs, School of Psychology, Santa Barbara, CA 93105-3814. Offers clinical psychology (PhD, Graduate Certificate), including forensic psychology (PhD), health psychology (PhD), neuropsychology (PhD), parent-infant mental health (PhD), violence prevention and control (PhD); clinical psychology respecialization (Post-Doctoral Certificate); media psychology (MA, PhD), including forensic psychology (PhD); neuropsychology (Post-Doctoral Certificate). *Accreditation:* APA. Postbaccalaureate distance learning degree programs offered (minimal on-campus study). *Faculty:* 33 full-time (21 women), 40 part-time/adjunct (20 women). *Students:* 502 full-time (366 women), 79 part-time (62 women); includes 186 minority (69 Black or African American, non-Hispanic/Latino; 8 American Indian or Alaska Native, non-Hispanic/Latino; 23 Asian, non-Hispanic/Latino; 62 Hispanic/Latino; 1 Native Hawaiian or other Pacific Islander, non-Hispanic/Latino; 23 Two or more races, non-Hispanic/Latino), 4 international. Average age 45. 215 applicants, 56% accepted, 78 enrolled. In 2014, 15 master's, 54 doctorates, 9 other advanced degrees awarded. Terminal master's awarded for partial completion of doctoral program. *Degree requirements:* For master's, thesis or alternative, capstone project; for doctorate, comprehensive exam, thesis/dissertation. *Entrance requirements:* For master's, BA from regionally-accredited institution or equivalent, minimum GPA of 2.5; for doctorate, BA or MA from regionally-accredited institution or equivalent, writing sample, minimum GPA of 3.0. *Application deadline:* For fall admission, 3/6 for domestic students, 2/6 for international students; for spring admission, 11/1 for domestic and international students; for summer admission, 3/1 for domestic students, 2/1 for international students. Application fee: $75. Electronic applications accepted. *Expenses: Tuition:* Full-time $25,650; part-time $2880 per course. Tuition and fees vary according to degree level and program. *Financial support:* In 2014–15, 88 students received support, including 14 teaching assistantships (averaging $1,200 per year); scholarships/grants, health care benefits, tuition waivers (partial), and unspecified assistantships also available. Support available to part-time students. *Unit head:* Dr. Gerald Porter, Provost and Senior Vice President, 805-898-2940, E-mail: gporter@fielding.edu. *Application contact:* Enrollment Coordinator, 800-340-1099 Ext. 4098, Fax: 805-687-9793, E-mail: psyadmissions@fielding.edu.
Website: http://www.fielding.edu/programs/psy/default.aspx

Georgian Court University, School of Arts and Sciences, Lakewood, NJ 08701-2697. Offers applied behavior analysis (MA); Catholic school leadership (Certificate); clinical mental health counseling (MA); holistic health studies (MA, Certificate); homeland security (MS); parish administration (Certificate); pastoral ministry (Certificate); professional counseling (Certificate); religious education (Certificate); school psychology (MA, Certificate); theology (MA, Certificate). Part-time and evening/weekend programs available. *Faculty:* 19 full-time (9 women), 9 part-time/adjunct (4 women). *Students:* 87 full-time (74 women), 127 part-time (110 women); includes 47 minority (14 Black or African American, non-Hispanic/Latino; 2 Asian, non-Hispanic/Latino; 23 Hispanic/Latino; 8 Two or more races, non-Hispanic/Latino). Average age 34. In 2014, 68 master's, 11 other advanced degrees awarded. *Degree requirements:* For master's, comprehensive exam (for some programs), thesis (for some programs). *Entrance requirements:* For master's, GRE, MAT, or NTE/PRAXIS, 3 letters of recommendation. Additional exam requirements/recommendations for international students: Required—TOEFL (minimum score 550 paper-based). *Application deadline:* For fall admission, 8/1 priority date for domestic students, 4/1 for international students; for spring admission, 1/1 priority date for domestic students, 7/1 for international students. Applications are processed on a rolling basis. Application fee: $40. Electronic applications accepted. *Expenses: Tuition:* Full-time $19,752; part-time $823 per credit. *Required fees:* $948; $243 per semester hour. Tuition and fees vary according to campus/location and program. *Financial support:* Scholarships/grants, health care benefits, and unspecified assistantships available. Financial award application deadline: 4/15; financial award applicants required to submit FAFSA. *Unit head:* Dr. Rita Kipp, Dean, 732-987-2493, Fax: 732-987-2007, E-mail: rkipp@georgian.edu. *Application contact:* Patrick Givens, Interim Director of Enrollment Management, 732-987-2736, Fax: 732-987-2084, E-mail: graduateadmissions@georgian.edu.
Website: http://www.georgian.edu/arts_sciences/index.htm

John F. Kennedy University, Graduate School of Holistic Studies, Department of Counseling Psychology, Program in Counseling Psychology, Pleasant Hill, CA 94523-4817. Offers holistic studies (MA); somatic psychology (MA); transpersonal psychology (MA). Part-time and evening/weekend programs available. *Degree requirements:* For master's, thesis or alternative. *Entrance requirements:* For master's, interview. Additional exam requirements/recommendations for international students: Required—TOEFL.

La Salle University, School of Arts and Sciences, Program in Clinical Psychology, Philadelphia, PA 19141-1199. Offers child clinical psychology (Psy D); clinical health psychology (Psy D); clinical psychology (MA); general practice psychology (Psy D). *Accreditation:* AAMFT/COAMFTE. Part-time and evening/weekend programs available. Terminal master's awarded for partial completion of doctoral program. *Degree requirements:* For doctorate, comprehensive exam, thesis/dissertation. *Entrance requirements:* For doctorate, GRE (minimum scores of 148 on both the Verbal Reasoning and Quantitative Reasoning sections strongly recommended); GRE Subject Test in psychology for those entering with bachelor's degree, baccalaureate degree from accredited institution with major in psychology or related discipline; minimum undergraduate GPA of 3.0, 3.2 graduate; three letters of recommendation; statement of interest and intent; curriculum vitae or resume; personal interview. Additional exam requirements/recommendations for international students: Required—TOEFL. Electronic applications accepted. Application fee is waived when completed online. *Expenses:* Contact institution.

Lesley University, Graduate School of Arts and Social Sciences, Cambridge, MA 02138-2790. Offers clinical mental health counseling (MA), including holistic counseling, school and community counseling, trauma studies; counseling psychology (MA, CAGS), including professional counseling (MA), school counseling (MA); creative writing (MFA); expressive therapies (MA, PhD, CAGS), including art (MA), clinical mental health counseling (MA), dance (MA), expressive therapies (MA), music (MA); independent studies (CAGS); independent study (MA); intercultural relations (MA, CAGS); interdisciplinary studies (MA), including individualized studies, integrative holistic health, mindfulness studies, peace and conflict transformation, trauma sensitive assessment, intervention, and consultation, women's studies; urban environmental leadership (MA). Part-time programs available. Postbaccalaureate distance learning degree programs offered (no on-campus study). *Faculty:* 35 full-time (25 women), 115 part-time/adjunct (90 women). *Students:* 420 full-time (379 women), 514 part-time (414 women); includes 142 minority (50 Black or African American, non-Hispanic/Latino; 5 American Indian or

Alaska Native, non-Hispanic/Latino; 16 Asian, non-Hispanic/Latino; 48 Hispanic/Latino; 23 Two or more races, non-Hispanic/Latino), 46 international. Average age 33. In 2014, 475 master's, 11 doctorates, 4 other advanced degrees awarded. *Degree requirements:* For master's, internship, practicum, thesis (for expressive therapies); for doctorate, thesis/dissertation, arts apprenticeship, field placement; for CAGS, thesis, internship (for counseling psychology, expressive therapies). *Entrance requirements:* For master's, MAT (counseling psychology), interview, writing samples, art portfolio; for doctorate, GRE or MAT, interview, master's degree; for CAGS, interview, master's degree. Additional exam requirements/recommendations for international students: Required—TOEFL (minimum score 550 paper-based; 80 iBT). *Application deadline:* Applications are processed on a rolling basis. Application fee: $50. Electronic applications accepted. *Financial support:* Fellowships, career-related internships or fieldwork, Federal Work-Study, scholarships/grants, tuition waivers, and unspecified assistantships available. Financial award applicants required to submit FAFSA. *Faculty research:* Psychotherapy and culture; psychotherapy and psychological trauma; women's issues in art, teaching and psychotherapy; community-based art, psycho-spiritual inquiry. *Unit head:* Dr. Catherine Koverola, Dean, 617-349-8317, Fax: 617-349-8366, E-mail: koverola@lesley.edu. *Application contact:* Martha Sheehan, Director, Graduate Admissions, 888-LESLEYU, Fax: 617-349-8313, E-mail: info@lesley.edu. Website: http://www.lesley.edu/graduate-school-of-arts-and-social-sciences/

North Dakota State University, College of Graduate and Interdisciplinary Studies, College of Science and Mathematics, Department of Psychology, Fargo, ND 58108. Offers clinical psychology (MS); cognitive and visual neuroscience (PhD); health and social psychology (PhD); psychology (MS). *Degree requirements:* For master's, thesis; for doctorate, thesis/dissertation. *Entrance requirements:* For master's and doctorate, GRE General Test, GRE Subject Test. Additional exam requirements/recommendations for international students: Required—TOEFL (minimum score 525 paper-based; 71 iBT). Electronic applications accepted. *Faculty research:* Cognition science, neuropsychology, group behavior, applied behavior analysis, behavior therapy.

Northern Kentucky University, Office of Graduate Programs, College of Arts and Sciences, Program in Industrial-Organizational Psychology, Highland Heights, KY 41099. Offers industrial psychology (Certificate); industrial-organizational psychology (MS); occupational health psychology (Certificate); organizational psychology (Certificate). Part-time and evening/weekend programs available. *Faculty:* 3 full-time (1 woman), 1 (woman) part-time/adjunct. *Students:* 3 full-time (all women), 41 part-time (30 women); includes 10 minority (6 Black or African American, non-Hispanic/Latino; 1 Asian, non-Hispanic/Latino; 2 Hispanic/Latino; 1 Two or more races, non-Hispanic/Latino), 1 international. Average age 27. In 2014, 11 master's, 1 other advanced degree awarded. *Degree requirements:* For master's, thesis optional, capstone. *Entrance requirements:* For master's, GRE General Test (minimum scores of 141 verbal, 144 quantitative, and 3.5 writing), bachelor's degree with minimum GPA of 3.0, nine semester hours of psychology coursework, at least one undergraduate course in statistics with minimum B grade, official transcripts, current resume or vita, statement of personal interest, three letters of recommendation; for Certificate, official transcripts, bachelor's degree, minimum undergraduate GPA of 3.0, no grade lower than B on all graduate coursework previously taken that may apply. Additional exam requirements/recommendations for international students: Required—TOEFL (minimum score 79 iBT); Recommended—IELTS (minimum score 6.5). *Application deadline:* For fall admission, 3/1 priority date for domestic students, 6/1 for international students; for spring admission, 12/1 priority date for domestic students, 10/1 for international students; for summer admission, 5/1 priority date for domestic students. Application fee: $40. Electronic applications accepted. *Expenses: Tuition, area resident:* Part-time $518 per credit hour. Tuition, state resident: part-time $630 per credit hour. Tuition, nonresident: part-time $797 per credit hour. *Required fees:* $192 per semester. Tuition and fees vary according to course load, degree level, campus/location, program and reciprocity agreements. *Financial support:* In 2014–15, 13 students received support. Unspecified assistantships available. Financial award applicants required to submit FAFSA. *Faculty research:* Workplace bullying and abuse, assessment and situational judgment tasks, human factors and work design, racial and social stereotyping in employment, social conflict. *Unit head:* Dr. Kathleen Fuegen, Director, 859-572-5787, E-mail: fuegenk1@nku.edu. *Application contact:* Alison Swanson, Graduate Admissions Coordinator, 859-572-6971, E-mail: swansona1@nku.edu. Website: http://psychology.nku.edu/programs/graduate/index.php

Oklahoma State University, College of Education, School of Applied Health and Educational Psychology, Stillwater, OK 74078. Offers applied behavioral studies (Ed D); applied health and educational psychology (MS, PhD, Ed S). *Accreditation:* APA (one or more programs are accredited). Part-time programs available. *Faculty:* 41 full-time (22 women), 15 part-time/adjunct (10 women). *Students:* 178 full-time (119 women), 130 part-time (94 women); includes 80 minority (14 Black or African American, non-Hispanic/Latino; 14 American Indian or Alaska Native, non-Hispanic/Latino; 4 Asian, non-Hispanic/Latino; 24 Hispanic/Latino; 24 Two or more races, non-Hispanic/Latino), 10 international. Average age 30. 237 applicants, 37% accepted, 66 enrolled. In 2014, 84 master's, 33 doctorates awarded. *Degree requirements:* For master's, thesis (for some programs); for doctorate, comprehensive exam, thesis/dissertation. *Entrance requirements:* For master's and doctorate, GRE or GMAT. Additional exam requirements/recommendations for international students: Required—TOEFL (minimum score 550 paper-based; 79 iBT). *Application deadline:* For fall admission, 3/1 priority date for international students; for spring admission, 8/1 priority date for international students. Applications are processed on a rolling basis. Application fee: $40 ($75 for international students). Electronic applications accepted. *Expenses:* Tuition, state resident: full-time $4488; part-time $187 per credit hour. Tuition, nonresident: full-time $18,360; part-time $765 per credit hour. *Required fees:* $2413; $100.55 per credit hour. Tuition and fees vary according to campus/location. *Financial support:* In 2014–15, 30 research assistantships (averaging $9,530 per year), 70 teaching assistantships (averaging $9,677 per year) were awarded; career-related internships or fieldwork, Federal Work-Study, scholarships/grants, health care benefits, tuition waivers (partial), and unspecified assistantships also available. Support available to part-time students. Financial award application deadline: 3/1; financial award applicants required to submit FAFSA. *Unit head:* Dr. Aric Warren, Head, 405-744-6040, Fax: 405-744-6779, E-mail: aric.warren@okstate.edu. Website: http://education.okstate.edu/sahep

Prescott College, Graduate Programs, Program in Counseling and Psychology, Prescott, AZ 86301. Offers adventure-based psychotherapy (MA); counseling psychology (MA); ecopsychology (MA); ecotherapy (MA); equine-assisted mental health (MA); expressive arts therapy (MA); somatic psychology (MA); student-directed independent study (MA). Part-time programs available. Postbaccalaureate distance learning degree programs offered (minimal on-campus study). *Degree requirements:* For master's, thesis, fieldwork or internship, practicum. *Entrance requirements:* For master's, 2 letters of recommendation, resume. Additional exam requirements/recommendations for international students: Required—TOEFL (minimum score 500 paper-based). Electronic applications accepted.

Rhode Island College, School of Graduate Studies, Faculty of Arts and Sciences, Department of Psychology, Providence, RI 02908-1991. Offers health psychology

(CGS); psychology (MA). Part-time and evening/weekend programs available. *Faculty:* 5 full-time (2 women). *Students:* 2 full-time (both women), 9 part-time (4 women); includes 3 minority (1 Asian, non-Hispanic/Latino; 2 Hispanic/Latino). Average age 31. In 2014, 5 master's awarded. *Degree requirements:* For master's, comprehensive exam. *Entrance requirements:* For master's, GRE, 3 letters of recommendation. Additional exam requirements/recommendations for international students: Recommended—TOEFL (minimum score 550 paper-based; 79 iBT). *Application deadline:* For fall admission, 3/1 for domestic students; for spring admission, 11/1 for domestic students. Applications are processed on a rolling basis. Application fee: $50. *Expenses:* Tuition, state resident: full-time $8928; part-time $372 per credit hour. Tuition, nonresident: full-time $17,376; part-time $724 per credit hour. *Required fees:* $602; $22 per credit. $72 per term. *Financial support:* Teaching assistantships with full tuition reimbursements, Federal Work-Study, scholarships/grants, health care benefits, and unspecified assistantships available. Support available to part-time students. Financial award application deadline: 5/15; financial award applicants required to submit FAFSA. *Unit head:* Dr. Randi Kim, Chair, 401-456-8015. *Application contact:* Graduate Studies, 401-456-8700. Website: http://www.ric.edu/psychology/index.php

Rutgers, The State University of New Jersey, New Brunswick, Graduate School-New Brunswick, Program in Psychology, Piscataway, NJ 08854-8097. Offers behavioral neuroscience (PhD); clinical psychology (PhD); cognitive psychology (PhD); interdisciplinary health psychology (PhD); social psychology (PhD). *Accreditation:* APA. *Degree requirements:* For doctorate, comprehensive exam, thesis/dissertation. *Entrance requirements:* For doctorate, GRE General Test, 3 letters of recommendation. Additional exam requirements/recommendations for international students: Required—TOEFL (minimum score 577 paper-based). Electronic applications accepted. *Faculty research:* Learning and memory, behavioral ecology, hormones and behavior, psychopharmacology, anxiety disorders.

San Diego State University, Graduate and Research Affairs, College of Health and Human Services, Graduate School of Public Health, San Diego, CA 92182. Offers environmental health (MPH); epidemiology (MPH, PhD), including biostatistics (MPH); global emergency preparedness and response (MS); global health (PhD); health behavior (PhD); health promotion (MPH); health services administration (MPH); toxicology (MS); MPH/MA; MSW/MPH. *Accreditation:* CAHME (one or more programs are accredited); CEPH (one or more programs are accredited). Part-time programs available. *Degree requirements:* For master's, comprehensive exam (for some programs), thesis (for some programs); for doctorate, thesis/dissertation. *Entrance requirements:* For master's, GMAT (MPH in health services administration), GRE General Test; for doctorate, GRE General Test. Additional exam requirements/recommendations for international students: Required—TOEFL. *Faculty research:* Evaluation of tobacco, AIDS prevalence and prevention, mammography, infant death project, Alzheimer's in elderly Chinese.

Saybrook University, School of Psychology and Interdisciplinary Inquiry, San Francisco, CA 94111-1920. Offers human science (MA, PhD), including consciousness and spirituality, humanistic and transpersonal psychology, integrative health studies, organizational systems, social transformation; organizational systems (MA, PhD), including consciousness and spirituality, humanistic and transpersonal psychology, integrative health studies, leadership of sustainable systems (MA), organizational systems, social transformation; psychology (MA, PhD), including consciousness and spirituality, creativity studies (MA), humanistic and transpersonal psychology, integrative health studies, Jungian studies, marriage and family therapy (MA), organizational systems, social transformation. Postbaccalaureate distance learning degree programs offered (minimal on-campus study). Terminal master's awarded for partial completion of doctoral program. *Degree requirements:* For master's, thesis or alternative; for doctorate, thesis/dissertation. *Entrance requirements:* Additional exam requirements/recommendations for international students: Required—TOEFL (minimum score 580 paper-based; 93 iBT). Electronic applications accepted. *Faculty research:* Humanistic theory, health studies, organizational systems, consciousness and spirituality, social transformation.

Southwestern College, Program in Integral Somatic Psychology, Santa Fe, NM 87502-4788. Offers Certificate.

Stony Brook University, State University of New York, Graduate School, College of Arts and Sciences, Department of Psychology, Program in Social and Health Psychology, Stony Brook, NY 11794. Offers PhD. *Students:* 15 full-time (all women); includes 3 minority (2 Asian, non-Hispanic/Latino; 1 Two or more races, non-Hispanic/Latino). Average age 28. 68 applicants, 6% accepted, 1 enrolled. In 2014, 2 doctorates awarded. *Degree requirements:* For doctorate, thesis/dissertation. *Entrance requirements:* For doctorate, GRE General Test, GRE Subject Test. Additional exam requirements/recommendations for international students: Required—TOEFL. *Application deadline:* For fall admission, 1/15 for domestic students; for spring admission, 10/1 for domestic students. Application fee: $100. *Expenses:* Tuition, state resident: full-time $10,370; part-time $432 per credit. Tuition, nonresident: full-time $20,190; part-time $841 per credit. *Required fees:* $1431. *Financial support:* In 2014–15, 1 fellowship was awarded. *Unit head:* Dr. Arthur Samuel, Chair, 631-632-7792, Fax: 631-632-7876, E-mail: arthur.samuel@stonybrook.edu. *Application contact:* Marilynn Wollmuth, Coordinator, 631-632-7855, Fax: 631-632-7876, E-mail: marilyn.wollmuth@stonybrook.edu.

United States International University, School of Arts and Sciences, Nairobi, Kenya. Offers counseling psychology (MA), including chemical dependency, health psychology; international relations (MA), including development studies, diplomacy and foreign policy, peace and conflict studies. Part-time and evening/weekend programs available. *Degree requirements:* For master's, thesis, practicum. *Entrance requirements:* For master's, GRE General Test, 2 letters of recommendation, resume. Additional exam requirements/recommendations for international students: Required—TOEFL. *Faculty research:* Trauma in children, African intellectualism, psychological assessment tools.

The University of Alabama at Birmingham, School of Public Health, Program in Public Health, Birmingham, AL 35294. Offers applied epidemiology and pharmacoepidemiology (MSPH); biostatistics (MPH); clinical and translational science (MSPH); environmental health (MPH); environmental health and toxicology (MSPH); epidemiology (MPH); general theory and practice (MPH); health behavior (MPH); health care organization (MPH); health policy quantitative policy analysis (MPH); industrial hygiene (MPH, MSPH); maternal and child health policy (Dr PH); maternal and child health policy and leadership (MPH); occupational health and safety (MPH); outcomes research (MSPH, Dr PH); public health (PhD); public health management (Dr PH); public health preparedness management (MPH). *Accreditation:* CEPH. Part-time programs available. Postbaccalaureate distance learning degree programs offered (minimal on-campus study). *Students:* 184 full-time (129 women), 81 part-time (57 women); includes 81 minority (49 Black or African American, non-Hispanic/Latino; 1 American Indian or Alaska Native, non-Hispanic/Latino; 19 Asian, non-Hispanic/Latino; 8 Hispanic/Latino; 4 Two or more races, non-Hispanic/Latino), 47 international. Average age 29. In 2014, 134 master's, 2 doctorates awarded. *Degree requirements:* For doctorate, comprehensive exam, thesis/dissertation. *Entrance requirements:* For master's and doctorate, GRE. Additional exam requirements/recommendations for international students: Recommended—TOEFL (minimum score 550 paper-based; 79

Health Psychology

iBT), IELTS (minimum score 6.5). Electronic applications accepted. *Expenses:* Tuition, state resident: full-time $7090; part-time $370 per credit hour. Tuition, nonresident: full-time $16,072; part-time $869 per credit hour. Full-time tuition and fees vary according to course load and program. *Financial support:* Fellowships, traineeships, and health care benefits available. *Unit head:* Dr. Max Michael, III, Dean, 205-975-7742, Fax: 205-975-5484, E-mail: maxm@uab.edu. *Application contact:* Sue Chappell, Coordinator, Student Admissions and Records, 205-934-2684, E-mail: schappell@ms.soph.uab.edu.
Website: http://www.soph.uab.edu

The University of British Columbia, Faculty of Arts and Faculty of Graduate Studies, Department of Psychology, Vancouver, BC V6T 1Z4, Canada. Offers behavioral neuroscience (MA, PhD); clinical psychology (MA, PhD); cognitive science (MA, PhD); developmental psychology (MA, PhD); health psychology (MA, PhD); quantitative methods (MA, PhD); social/personality psychology (MA, PhD). *Accreditation:* APA (one or more programs are accredited). Terminal master's awarded for partial completion of doctoral program. *Degree requirements:* For master's, thesis; for doctorate, comprehensive exam, thesis/dissertation. *Entrance requirements:* For master's and doctorate, GRE General Test. Additional exam requirements/recommendations for international students: Required—TOEFL (minimum score 550 paper-based; 80 iBT). Electronic applications accepted. *Faculty research:* Clinical, developmental, social/personality, cognition, behavioral neuroscience.

University of Colorado Denver, College of Liberal Arts and Sciences, Department of Psychology, Denver, CO 80217. Offers clinical health (PhD); psychology (MA). Part-time and evening/weekend programs available. *Faculty:* 17 full-time (6 women), 2 part-time/adjunct (both women). *Students:* 17 full-time (14 women), 11 part-time (8 women); includes 6 minority (3 Asian, non-Hispanic/Latino; 1 Hispanic/Latino; 2 Two or more races, non-Hispanic/Latino). Average age 30. 92 applicants, 7% accepted, 6 enrolled. In 2014, 4 master's awarded. *Degree requirements:* For master's, 31-33 semester hours, thesis or internship, minimum GPA of 3.0; for doctorate, comprehensive exam, thesis/dissertation, 69 credits of coursework, minimum of 12 clinical practicum hours, 30 dissertation hours, three credits of pre-doctoral internship. *Entrance requirements:* For master's, GRE General Test; GRE Subject Test (recommended), undergraduate courses in psychological statistics, abnormal psychology and introductory psychology; minimum GPA of 3.0; three letters of recommendation; personal statement; resume; for doctorate, GRE General Test; GRE Subject Test (recommended), minimum GPA of 3.5; undergraduate courses in introductory psychology, psychological statistics, research methods and abnormal psychology; letters of recommendation; personal statement; resume. Additional exam requirements/recommendations for international students: Required—TOEFL (minimum score 537 paper-based; 75 iBT); Recommended—IELTS (minimum score 6.5). *Application deadline:* For fall admission, 12/15 for domestic students, 12/1 for international students. Application fee: $50 ($75 for international students). Electronic applications accepted. *Financial support:* In 2014–15, 28 students received support. Fellowships, research assistantships, teaching assistantships, career-related internships or fieldwork, Federal Work-Study, institutionally sponsored loans, scholarships/grants, and traineeships available. Financial award application deadline: 4/1; financial award applicants required to submit FAFSA. *Faculty research:* Organizational behavior, body image perception, professional ethics, infant perception and cognition, charismatic leadership. *Unit head:* Dr. Kevin S. Masters, Clinical Health Psychology Program Director, 303-352-3961, Fax: 303-556-3520, E-mail: kevin.masters@ucdenver.edu. *Application contact:* Anne Beard, Program Assistant, 303-556-2192, Fax: 303-556-3520, E-mail: anne.beard@ucdenver.edu.
Website: http://www.ucdenver.edu/academics/colleges/CLAS/Departments/psychology/Pages/Psychology.aspx

University of Connecticut, Graduate School, College of Liberal Arts and Sciences, Department of Psychology, Storrs, CT 06269. Offers behavioral neuroscience (PhD); biopsychology (PhD); clinical psychology (MA, PhD); cognition and instruction (PhD); developmental psychology (MA, PhD); ecological psychology (PhD); experimental psychology (PhD); general psychology (MA, PhD); health psychology (Graduate Certificate); industrial/organizational psychology (PhD); language and cognition (PhD); neuroscience (PhD); occupational health psychology (Graduate Certificate); social psychology (MA, PhD). *Accreditation:* APA. Terminal master's awarded for partial completion of doctoral program. *Degree requirements:* For master's, comprehensive exam; for doctorate, thesis/dissertation. *Entrance requirements:* For master's and doctorate, GRE General Test, GRE Subject Test. Additional exam requirements/recommendations for international students: Required—TOEFL (minimum score 550 paper-based). Electronic applications accepted.

University of Florida, Graduate School, College of Public Health and Health Professions, Department of Clinical and Health Psychology, Gainesville, FL 32610-0165. Offers clinical and translational science (PhD); clnical and health psychology (PhD); psychology (MA, MS). *Accreditation:* APA (one or more programs are accredited). *Faculty:* 22 full-time (10 women), 12 part-time/adjunct (4 women). *Students:* 95 full-time (64 women), 14 part-time (13 women); includes 22 minority (10 Black or African American, non-Hispanic/Latino; 1 American Indian or Alaska Native, non-Hispanic/Latino; 3 Asian, non-Hispanic/Latino; 8 Hispanic/Latino), 2 international. 323 applicants, 5% accepted, 12 enrolled. In 2014, 13 master's, 13 doctorates awarded. *Degree requirements:* For doctorate, comprehensive exam, thesis/dissertation, pre-doctoral internship. *Entrance requirements:* For master's and doctorate, GRE General Test, minimum GPA of 3.0. Additional exam requirements/recommendations for international students: Required—TOEFL (minimum score 550 paper-based; 80 iBT), IELTS (minimum score 6). *Application deadline:* For fall admission, 12/1 for domestic and international students. Application fee: $30. Electronic applications accepted. *Financial support:* In 2014–15, 8 teaching assistantships were awarded; career-related internships or fieldwork, Federal Work-Study, institutionally sponsored loans, scholarships/grants, and unspecified assistantships also available. Financial award application deadline: 12/1; financial award applicants required to submit FAFSA. *Faculty research:* Clinical child and pediatric psychology, medical psychology, neuropsychology, health promotion and aging. *Unit head:* William W. Latimer, PhD, Professor and Chair, 352-273-6556, Fax: 352-273-6156, E-mail: wwlatimer@phhp.ufl.edu. *Application contact:* Office of Admissions, 352-392-1365, E-mail: webrequests@admissions.ufl.edu.
Website: http://www.phhp.ufl.edu/chp/

University of Michigan–Dearborn, College of Arts, Sciences, and Letters, Master of Science in Psychology Program, Dearborn, MI 48128. Offers clinical health psychology (MS); health psychology (MS). Part-time programs available. *Faculty:* 11 full-time (5 women). *Students:* 27 full-time (24 women), 6 part-time (all women); includes 4 minority (2 Asian, non-Hispanic/Latino; 2 Two or more races, non-Hispanic/Latino), 4 international. 60 applicants, 55% accepted, 19 enrolled. In 2014, 18 master's awarded. *Degree requirements:* For master's, oral defense of thesis. *Entrance requirements:* For master's, GRE, 3 letters of recommendation. Additional exam requirements/recommendations for international students: Required—TOEFL (minimum score 560 paper-based; 84 iBT), IELTS (minimum score 6.5). *Application deadline:* For fall admission, 3/15 for domestic and international students. Application fee: $60. Electronic applications accepted. *Expenses:* Expenses: $613 per credit hour in-state, $351 for ninth credit hour and beyond in-state; $1,115 per credit hour out-state, $724 for ninth credit hour and beyond out-state; $267 in fees per term part-time, $329 full-time. *Financial support:* In 2014–15, 4 students received support. Scholarships/grants available. *Faculty research:* Cardiovascular reactivity, chronic pain, addiction, gender and health, couples and health, coping. *Unit head:* Dr. Nancy Wrobel, Program Director, 313-593-5088, E-mail: nwrobel@umich.edu. *Application contact:* Carol Ligienza, Coordinator, CASL Graduate Programs, 313-593-1183, Fax: 313-583-6700, E-mail: caslgrad@umich.edu.
Website: http://umdearborn.edu/casl/psychology/

University of Missouri–Kansas City, College of Arts and Sciences, Department of Psychology, Kansas City, MO 64110-2499. Offers clinical psychology (PhD); community psychology (PhD); health psychology (PhD); psychology (MA). PhD (interdisciplinary) offered through the School of Graduate Studies. *Accreditation:* APA. *Faculty:* 10 full-time (7 women), 2 part-time/adjunct (1 woman). *Students:* 21 full-time (14 women), 10 part-time (6 women); includes 5 minority (1 Asian, non-Hispanic/Latino; 4 Hispanic/Latino). Average age 32. 109 applicants, 6% accepted, 6 enrolled. In 2014, 4 master's, 7 doctorates awarded. Terminal master's awarded for partial completion of doctoral program. *Degree requirements:* For master's, thesis; for doctorate, comprehensive exam, thesis/dissertation, residency. *Entrance requirements:* For master's, GRE, minimum GPA of 3.5, letter of recommendation; for doctorate, GRE, minimum GPA of 3.25. Additional exam requirements/recommendations for international students: Required—TOEFL (minimum score 550 paper-based; 80 iBT). *Application deadline:* For fall admission, 1/15 for domestic and international students. Applications are processed on a rolling basis. Application fee: $45 ($50 for international students). Electronic applications accepted. *Financial support:* In 2014–15, 8 research assistantships (averaging $11,229 per year), 20 teaching assistantships (averaging $12,015 per year) were awarded; career-related internships or fieldwork, Federal Work-Study, and institutionally sponsored loans also available. Support available to part-time students. Financial award application deadline: 3/1; financial award applicants required to submit FAFSA. *Faculty research:* HIV/AIDS research group, psycho-oncology, sensory and cognitive neuroscience, cognitive psychophysiology, obesity and related metabolic disorders. *Unit head:* Dr. Jennifer Lundgren, Department Chair, 816-235-5384, Fax: 816-235-1062, E-mail: lundgrenj@umkc.edu. *Application contact:* Dr. Cathy Rawlings, Director, Graduate Programs, 816-235-1318, Fax: 816-235-1062, E-mail: psychology@umkc.edu.
Website: http://cas.umkc.edu/psyc

University of New Mexico, Graduate School, College of Arts and Sciences, Program in Psychology, Albuquerque, NM 87131-2039. Offers behavioral neuroscience (PhD); clinical psychology (PhD); cognitive neuroimaging (PhD); developmental psychology (PhD); evolution (PhD); health psychology (PhD); quantitative methodology (PhD). *Faculty:* 25 full-time (9 women), 1 (woman) part-time/adjunct. *Students:* 66 full-time (44 women), 12 part-time (6 women); includes 23 minority (2 Black or African American, non-Hispanic/Latino; 2 American Indian or Alaska Native, non-Hispanic/Latino; 4 Asian, non-Hispanic/Latino; 13 Hispanic/Latino; 2 Two or more races, non-Hispanic/Latino), 1 international. Average age 33. 135 applicants, 10% accepted, 13 enrolled. In 2014, 10 doctorates awarded. *Degree requirements:* For doctorate, comprehensive exam, thesis/dissertation. *Entrance requirements:* For doctorate, GRE General Test, GRE Subject Test (psychology), minimum GPA of 3.0. Additional exam requirements/recommendations for international students: Required—TOEFL (minimum score 550 paper-based; 79 iBT), IELTS (minimum score 6.5). *Application deadline:* For fall admission, 12/15 priority date for domestic and international students. Applications are processed on a rolling basis. Application fee: $50. Electronic applications accepted. *Financial support:* In 2014–15, 62 students received support, including 8 fellowships (averaging $13,124 per year), 37 research assistantships with full and partial tuition reimbursements available (averaging $11,655 per year), 67 teaching assistantships with full and partial tuition reimbursements available (averaging $13,600 per year); career-related internships or fieldwork, Federal Work-Study, institutionally sponsored loans, scholarships/grants, health care benefits, tuition waivers (partial), and unspecified assistantships also available. Financial award application deadline: 3/1; financial award applicants required to submit FAFSA. *Faculty research:* Addiction, cognition, brain and behavior, developmental, evolutionary, functioning neuroimaging, health psychology, learning and memory, neuroscience. *Unit head:* Dr. Jane Ellen Smith, Department Chair, 505-277-4121, Fax: 505-277-1394. *Application contact:* Rikk Murphy, Graduate Program Coordinator, 505-277-5009, Fax: 505-277-1394, E-mail: advising@unm.edu.
Website: http://psych.unm.edu

The University of North Carolina at Chapel Hill, Graduate School, Gillings School of Global Public Health, Department of Health Behavior, Chapel Hill, NC 27599-7440. Offers MPH, PhD, MPH/MCRP, MSPH/PhD. *Accreditation:* CEPH (one or more programs are accredited). *Degree requirements:* For master's, comprehensive exam, thesis, major paper; for doctorate, comprehensive exam, thesis/dissertation. *Entrance requirements:* For master's, GRE General Test, minimum GPA of 3.0 (recommended); for doctorate, GRE General Test, minimum GPA of 3.0 (recommended), master's degree. Additional exam requirements/recommendations for international students: Required—TOEFL. Electronic applications accepted. *Faculty research:* Cancer prevention and control, aging health promotion and disease prevention, adolescent health, nutrition intervention.

The University of North Carolina at Charlotte, College of Liberal Arts and Sciences, Department of Psychology, Charlotte, NC 28223-0001. Offers clinical/community psychology (MA); cognitive sciences (Graduate Certificate); health psychology (PhD); industrial/organizational psychology (MA). Part-time programs available. *Faculty:* 31 full-time (17 women), 1 part-time/adjunct (0 women). *Students:* 42 full-time (35 women), 31 part-time (26 women); includes 18 minority (5 Black or African American, non-Hispanic/Latino; 2 Asian, non-Hispanic/Latino; 9 Hispanic/Latino; 2 Two or more races, non-Hispanic/Latino), 1 international. Average age 28. 243 applicants, 16% accepted, 25 enrolled. In 2014, 9 master's, 5 doctorates, 1 other advanced degree awarded. Terminal master's awarded for partial completion of doctoral program. *Degree requirements:* For master's, thesis; for doctorate, thesis/dissertation. *Entrance requirements:* For master's, GRE General Test, GRE Subject Test, minimum GPA of 3.0 in undergraduate major, 2.8 overall, letters of recommendation; for doctorate, GRE General Test, minimum GPA of 3.5, letters of recommendation. Additional exam requirements/recommendations for international students: Required—TOEFL (minimum score 557 paper-based; 83 iBT). *Application deadline:* For fall admission, 5/1 for domestic and international students. Application fee: $75. Electronic applications accepted. *Expenses:* Tuition, state resident: full-time $4008. Tuition, nonresident: full-time $16,295. *Required fees:* $2755. Tuition and fees vary according to course load and program. *Financial support:* In 2014–15, 33 students received support, including 16 research assistantships (averaging $15,239 per year), 17 teaching assistantships (averaging $12,809 per year); career-related internships or fieldwork, Federal Work-Study, institutionally sponsored loans, and scholarships/grants also available. Support available to part-time students. Financial award application deadline: 4/1; financial award applicants required to submit FAFSA. *Faculty research:* Neuropsychology of information processing, perception and human performance, computer-based applications in research and instruction, interventions to facilitate team effectiveness, post-traumatic psychological growth. *Total annual research expenditures:* $327,551. *Unit head:* Dr. Fary Cachelin, Chair, 704-687-1319, Fax: 704-687-1317, E-mail: fcacheli@uncc.edu. *Application contact:* Kathy B.

Giddings, Director of Graduate Admissions, 704-687-5503, Fax: 704-687-1668, E-mail: gradadm@uncc.edu. Website: http://psych.uncc.edu/graduate-programs

The University of Texas at Arlington, Graduate School, College of Science, Department of Psychology, Arlington, TX 76019. Offers experimental psychology (PhD); health psychology (PhD); industrial organizational psychology (MS); psychology (MS). Part-time programs available. Terminal master's awarded for partial completion of doctoral program. *Degree requirements:* For master's, comprehensive exam or thesis; for doctorate, thesis/dissertation (for some programs). *Entrance requirements:* For master's and doctorate, GRE General Test, minimum GPA of 3.0 in last 60 hours of course work. Additional exam requirements/recommendations for international students: Required—TOEFL (minimum score 550 paper-based).

University of the Sciences, College of Graduate Studies, Program in Health Psychology, Philadelphia, PA 19104-4495. Offers MS. *Entrance requirements:* For master's, bachelor's degree in related field, minimum GPA of 3.0 in major. Additional exam requirements/recommendations for international students: Required—TOEFL, TWE. *Expenses:* Contact institution. *Faculty research:* Stress and immune system, women's health and breast cancer, memory, health care policy.

Virginia Commonwealth University, Graduate School, College of Humanities and Sciences, Department of Psychology, Richmond, VA 23284-9005. Offers clinical psychology (PhD), including behavioral medicine, clinical child psychology; counseling psychology (PhD); general psychology (PhD), including biopsychology, developmental psychology, social psychology; health psychology (PhD). *Accreditation:* APA. *Degree requirements:* For doctorate, thesis/dissertation. *Entrance requirements:* For doctorate, GRE General Test. Additional exam requirements/recommendations for international students: Required—TOEFL (minimum score 600 paper-based; 100 iBT); Recommended—IELTS (minimum score 6.5). Electronic applications accepted. *Faculty research:* Biopsychology, clinical psychology, counseling psychology, developmental psychology, health psychology, social psychology.

Virginia State University, College of Graduate Studies, College of Natural and Health Sciences, Department of Psychology, Petersburg, VA 23806-0001. Offers behavioral and community health sciences (PhD); clinical health psychology (PhD); clinical psychology (MS); general psychology (MS). *Degree requirements:* For master's, one foreign language, thesis. *Entrance requirements:* For master's, GRE General Test.

Viterbo University, Master of Science in Mental Health Counseling Program, La Crosse, WI 54601-4797. Offers addiction counseling (MS); child and adolescent counseling (MS); complementary health and wellness counseling (MS). Part-time and evening/weekend programs available. *Faculty:* 3 full-time (1 woman), 6 part-time/adjunct (3 women). *Students:* 52 full-time (43 women), 10 part-time (8 women); includes 6 minority (2 Black or African American, non-Hispanic/Latino; 1 Asian, non-Hispanic/Latino; 3 Two or more races, non-Hispanic/Latino), 1 international. Average age 33. 41 applicants, 51% accepted, 20 enrolled. In 2014, 12 master's awarded. *Degree requirements:* For master's, comprehensive exam, thesis, 54 credits of core program courses; 6 elective credits; minimum GPA of 3.0; action research project; practicum/internship experience. *Entrance requirements:* For master's, MAT, BS in a human service or social science discipline; prerequisite coursework in general psychology, behavior disorders/abnormal psychology, and research methods/statistics; minimum undergraduate cumulative GPA of 3.0; background check; personal statement; undergraduate transcripts; interview. Additional exam requirements/recommendations for international students: Required—TOEFL (minimum score 525 paper-based). *Application deadline:* For fall admission, 3/15 priority date for domestic students, 7/31 priority date for international students. Applications are processed on a rolling basis. Application fee: $50. Electronic applications accepted. Application fee is waived when completed online. *Expenses:* Expenses: $475 per credit. *Financial support:* Applicants required to submit FAFSA. *Faculty research:* Supervision, recovery substance abuse, culture, counseling theory, health and wellness. *Unit head:* Dr. Debra A. Murray, Program Director, 608-796-3720, E-mail: damurray@viterbo.edu. *Application contact:* Dr. Debra A. Murray, Program Director, 608-796-3720, E-mail: damurray@viterbo.edu. Website: http://www.viterbo.edu/master-science-mental-health-counseling

Walden University, Graduate Programs, School of Psychology, Minneapolis, MN 55401. Offers clinical psychology (MS), including counseling, general program; forensic psychology (MS), including forensic psychology in the community, general program, mental health applications, program planning and evaluation in forensic settings, psychology and legal systems; organizational psychology and development (Postbaccalaureate Certificate); psychology (MS, PhD), including applied psychology (MS), clinical psychology (PhD), counseling psychology (PhD), crisis management and response (MS), educational psychology, forensic psychology (PhD), general psychology (MS), general psychology research (PhD), health psychology, leadership development and coaching (MS), psychology of culture (MS), psychology, public administration, and social change (MS), social psychology, terrorism and security (MS); psychology respecialization (Post-Doctoral Certificate); teaching online (Post-Master's Certificate). Part-time and evening/weekend programs available. Postbaccalaureate distance learning degree programs offered (no on-campus study). *Faculty:* 56 full-time (36 women), 351 part-time/adjunct (201 women). *Students:* 2,757 full-time (2,202 women), 1,466 part-time (1,148 women); includes 1,849 minority (1,299 Black or African American, non-Hispanic/Latino; 37 American Indian or Alaska Native, non-Hispanic/Latino; 74 Asian, non-Hispanic/Latino; 315 Hispanic/Latino; 8 Native Hawaiian or other Pacific Islander, non-Hispanic/Latino; 116 Two or more races, non-Hispanic/Latino), 28 international. Average age 41. 913 applicants, 97% accepted, 851 enrolled. In 2014, 602 master's, 204 doctorates, 19 other advanced degrees awarded. Terminal master's awarded for partial completion of doctoral program. *Degree requirements:* For master's, thesis optional; for doctorate, thesis/dissertation, residency. *Entrance requirements:* For master's, bachelor's degree or higher; minimum GPA of 2.5; official transcripts; goal statement (for some programs); access to computer and Internet; for doctorate, master's degree or higher; three years of related professional or academic experience (preferred); minimum GPA of 3.0; goal statement and current resume (for select programs); official transcripts; access to computer and Internet; for other advanced degree, relevant work experience; access to computer and Internet. Additional exam requirements/recommendations for international students: Required—TOEFL (minimum score 550 paper-based, 79 iBT), IELTS (minimum score 6.5), Michigan English Language Assessment Battery (minimum score 82), or PTE (minimum score 53). *Application deadline:* Applications are processed on a rolling basis. Application fee: $0. Electronic applications accepted. *Expenses:* Tuition: Full-time $11,925; part-time $500 per credit hour. *Required fees:* $647. *Financial support:* Fellowships, Federal Work-Study, scholarships/grants, unspecified assistantships, and family tuition reduction, active duty/veteran tuition reduction, group tuition reduction, interest-free payment plans, employee tuition reduction available. Support available to part-time students. Financial award applicants required to submit FAFSA. *Unit head:* Dr. Marilyn Powell, Associate Dean, 866-492-5366. *Application contact:* Meghan Thomas, Vice President of Enrollment Management, 866-492-5336, E-mail: info@waldenu.edu. Website: http://www.waldenu.edu/programs/colleges-schools/psychology

Yeshiva University, Ferkauf Graduate School of Psychology, Program in Clinical Health Psychology, New York, NY 10033-3201. Offers PhD. *Accreditation:* APA. Part-time programs available. *Degree requirements:* For doctorate, comprehensive exam, thesis/dissertation. *Entrance requirements:* For doctorate, GRE General Test. *Faculty research:* Dieting, substance abuse, adolescent depression and suicide, cancer research, MS research.

Human Development

Argosy University, Chicago, College of Psychology and Behavioral Sciences, Doctoral Program in Clinical Psychology, Chicago, IL 60601. Offers child and adolescent psychology (Psy D); client-centered and experiential psychotherapies (Psy D); diversity and multicultural psychology (Psy D); family psychology (Psy D); forensic psychology (Psy D); health psychology (Psy D); neuropsychology (Psy D); organizational consulting (Psy D); psychoanalytic psychology (Psy D); psychology and spirituality (Psy D). *Accreditation:* APA.

Arizona State University at the Tempe campus, College of Liberal Arts and Sciences, School of Social and Family Dynamics, Tempe, AZ 85287-3701. Offers family and human development (MS, PhD); infant-family practice (MAS); marriage and family therapy (MAS); sociology (MA, PhD). Terminal master's awarded for partial completion of doctoral program. *Degree requirements:* For master's, thesis or alternative, interactive Program of Study (iPOS) submitted before completing 50 percent of required credit hours; for doctorate, thesis/dissertation, interactive Program of Study (iPOS) submitted before completing 50 percent of required credit hours. *Entrance requirements:* For master's and doctorate, GRE, minimum GPA of 3.0 or equivalent in last 2 years of work leading to bachelor's degree. Additional exam requirements/recommendations for international students: Required—TOEFL, IELTS, or PTE. Electronic applications accepted. *Expenses:* Contact institution.

Auburn University, Graduate School, College of Human Sciences, Department of Human Development and Family Studies, Auburn University, AL 36849. Offers MS, PhD. *Accreditation:* AAMFT/COAMFTE (one or more programs are accredited). Part-time programs available. *Faculty:* 18 full-time (10 women), 2 part-time/adjunct (both women). *Students:* 26 full-time (24 women), 16 part-time (9 women); includes 9 minority (6 Black or African American, non-Hispanic/Latino; 2 Asian, non-Hispanic/Latino; 1 Hispanic/Latino), 2 international. Average age 27. 46 applicants, 26% accepted, 11 enrolled. In 2014, 15 master's, 6 doctorates awarded. *Degree requirements:* For master's, thesis, oral exam; for doctorate, thesis/dissertation. *Entrance requirements:* For master's, GRE General Test; for doctorate, GRE General Test, master's degree. *Application deadline:* For fall admission, 7/7 for domestic students; for spring admission, 11/24 for domestic students. Applications are processed on a rolling basis. Application fee: $50 ($60 for international students). *Expenses:* Tuition, state resident: full-time $8586; part-time $477 per credit hour. Tuition, nonresident: full-time $25,758; part-time $1431 per credit hour. *Required fees:* $804 per semester. Tuition and fees vary according to degree level and program. *Financial support:* Research assistantships, teaching assistantships, and Federal Work-Study available. Support available to part-time students. Financial award application deadline: 3/15; financial award applicants required to submit FAFSA. *Faculty research:* Family influences on personality and social development, parent-child relations, infancy, day care, parent education. *Unit head:* Dr. Joe F. Pittman, Jr., Head, 334-844-3242, E-mail: mbradbar@humsci.auburn.edu. *Application contact:* Dr. George Flowers, Dean of the Graduate School, 334-844-2125. Website: http://www.humsci.auburn.edu/hdfs/

Bowling Green State University, Graduate College, College of Education and Human Development, School of Family and Consumer Sciences, Bowling Green, OH 43403. Offers food and nutrition (MFCS); human development and family studies (MFCS). Part-time programs available. *Degree requirements:* For master's, thesis. *Entrance requirements:* For master's, GRE General Test, minimum GPA of 3.0. Additional exam requirements/recommendations for international students: Required—TOEFL. Electronic applications accepted. *Faculty research:* Public health, wellness, social issues and policies, ethnic foods, nutrition and aging.

Bradley University, Graduate School, College of Education and Health Sciences, Department of Leadership in Education, Human Services, and Counseling, Peoria, IL 61625-0002. Offers human development counseling (MA), including clinical mental health counseling, school counseling; leadership in educational administration (MA); non-profit leadership (MA). *Accreditation:* ACA; NCATE. Part-time and evening/weekend programs available. *Faculty:* 8 full-time (5 women), 5 part-time/adjunct (2 women). *Students:* 43 full-time (34 women), 35 part-time (30 women); includes 4 minority (1 Black or African American, non-Hispanic/Latino; 1 American Indian or Alaska Native, non-Hispanic/Latino; 2 Asian, non-Hispanic/Latino), 1 international. 42 applicants, 71% accepted, 21 enrolled. In 2014, 26 master's awarded. *Degree requirements:* For master's, comprehensive exam, thesis optional. *Entrance requirements:* For master's, GRE General Test or MAT, interview, 3 letters of recommendation. Additional exam requirements/recommendations for international students: Required—TOEFL (minimum score 550 paper-based; 79 iBT), IELTS (minimum score 6.5). *Application deadline:* For fall admission, 5/15 priority date for domestic and international students; for spring admission, 10/15 priority date for domestic and international students. Applications are processed on a rolling basis. Application fee: $40 ($50 for international students). Electronic applications accepted. *Expenses:* Tuition: Full-time $14,580; part-time $810 per credit. *Required fees:* $224. Full-time tuition and fees vary according to course load. *Financial support:* In 2014–15, 6 research assistantships with full and partial tuition reimbursements (averaging $19,640 per year) were awarded; career-related internships or fieldwork, scholarships/grants, tuition waivers (partial), and unspecified assistantships also available. Support available to part-time students. Financial award application deadline: 4/1. *Unit head:* Dr. Christopher Rybak, Chair, 309-677-3193, E-mail: cjr@bradley.edu. *Application contact:* Kayla Carroll, Director of International Admissions and Student Services, 309-677-2375, E-mail: klcarroll@fsmail.bradley.edu.

Human Development

Brigham Young University, Graduate Studies, College of Family, Home, and Social Sciences, Program in Marriage, Family and Human Development, Provo, UT 84602. Offers MS, PhD. *Accreditation:* AAMFT/COAMFTE. *Faculty:* 24 full-time (5 women). *Students:* 23 full-time (11 women); includes 1 minority (Two or more races, non-Hispanic/Latino), 4 international. Average age 30. 20 applicants, 35% accepted, 7 enrolled. In 2014, 1 master's, 2 doctorates awarded. *Degree requirements:* For master's, thesis; for doctorate, comprehensive exam, thesis/dissertation. *Entrance requirements:* For master's and doctorate, GRE General Test, minimum GPA of 3.0 in last 60 semester hours, letters of recommendation. Additional exam requirements/recommendations for international students: Required—TOEFL (minimum score 580 paper-based; 85 iBT), IELTS (minimum score 7). *Application deadline:* For fall admission, 1/10 for domestic and international students. Application fee: $50. Electronic applications accepted. *Expenses: Tuition:* Full-time $6310; part-time $371 per credit hour. Tuition and fees vary according to program and student's religious affiliation. *Financial support:* In 2014–15, 14 students received support, including 14 research assistantships with full and partial tuition reimbursements available (averaging $8,560 per year), 2 teaching assistantships with full and partial tuition reimbursements available (averaging $2,800 per year); scholarships/grants and unspecified assistantships also available. Financial award application deadline: 3/20. *Faculty research:* Family studies and family process, marriage, adolescence and emerging adulthood, adult development and aging, child development. *Unit head:* Dr. Dean M. Busby, Director, School of Life, 801-422-2069, Fax: 801-422-0230, E-mail: dean_busby@byu.edu. *Application contact:* Graduate Secretary, 801-422-2060, E-mail: mfhdgrad@byu.edu.
Website: http://mfhd.byu.edu

Brock University, Faculty of Graduate Studies, Faculty of Social Sciences, Program in Psychology, St. Catharines, ON L2S 3A1, Canada. Offers behavioral neuroscience (MA, PhD); life span development (MA, PhD); social personality (MA, PhD). Part-time programs available. *Degree requirements:* For master's, thesis; for doctorate, thesis/dissertation. *Entrance requirements:* For master's, GRE, honors degree; for doctorate, GRE, master's degree. Additional exam requirements/recommendations for international students: Required—TOEFL (minimum score 550 paper-based; 80 iBT), IELTS (minimum score 6.5), TWE (minimum score 4). Electronic applications accepted. *Faculty research:* Social personality, behavioral neuroscience, life-span development.

Central Michigan University, College of Graduate Studies, College of Education and Human Services, Department of Human Environmental Studies, Mount Pleasant, MI 48859. Offers apparel product development and merchandising technology (MS); gerontology (Graduate Certificate); human development and family studies (MA); nutrition and dietetics (MS). Part-time and evening/weekend programs available. *Degree requirements:* For master's, thesis or alternative. Electronic applications accepted. *Faculty research:* Human growth and development, family studies and human sexuality, human nutrition and dietetics, apparel and textile retailing, computer-aided design for apparel.

Claremont Graduate University, Graduate Programs, School of Educational Studies, Claremont, CA 91711-6160. Offers Africana education (Certificate); education and policy (MA, PhD); higher education/student affairs (MA, PhD); human development (MA, PhD); public school administration (MA, PhD); quantitative evaluation (MA, PhD); special education (MA, PhD); teacher education (MA); teaching and learning (MA, PhD); urban leadership (PhD); MBA/PhD. PhD program offered jointly with San Diego State University. Part-time programs available. *Faculty:* 16 full-time (9 women), 1 part-time/adjunct (0 women). *Students:* 221 full-time (157 women), 195 part-time (147 women); includes 201 minority (51 Black or African American, non-Hispanic/Latino; 2 American Indian or Alaska Native, non-Hispanic/Latino; 41 Asian, non-Hispanic/Latino; 94 Hispanic/Latino; 2 Native Hawaiian or other Pacific Islander, non-Hispanic/Latino; 11 Two or more races, non-Hispanic/Latino), 14 international. Average age 39. In 2014, 44 master's, 35 doctorates, 13 other advanced degrees awarded. Terminal master's awarded for partial completion of doctoral program. *Entrance requirements:* For master's and doctorate, GRE General Test. Additional exam requirements/recommendations for international students: Required—TOEFL (minimum score 550 paper-based; 80 iBT). *Application deadline:* For fall admission, 4/1 priority date for domestic and international students. Applications are processed on a rolling basis. Application fee: $80. Electronic applications accepted. *Expenses: Tuition:* Full-time $41,784; part-time $1741 per credit. *Required fees:* $600; $300 per semester. *Financial support:* Fellowships, research assistantships, Federal Work-Study, institutionally sponsored loans, and scholarships/grants available. Support available to part-time students. Financial award application deadline: 2/15; financial award applicants required to submit FAFSA. *Faculty research:* Education administration, K-12 and higher education, multicultural education, education policy, diversity in higher education, faculty issues. *Unit head:* Scott Thomas, Dean, 909-621-8075, Fax: 909-621-8734, E-mail: scott.thomas@cgu.edu. *Application contact:* Rachel Camacho, Assistant Director of Admission, 909-607-9418.
Website: http://www.cgu.edu/pages/267.asp

Clemson University, Graduate School, College of Health and Human Development, Program in Youth Development, Clemson, SC 29634. Offers MS. *Faculty:* 1 full-time (0 women). *Students:* 3 full-time (1 woman), 38 part-time (27 women); includes 11 minority (10 Black or African American, non-Hispanic/Latino; 1 Hispanic/Latino), 1 international. Average age 32. 16 applicants, 75% accepted, 10 enrolled. In 2014, 23 master's awarded. *Entrance requirements:* For master's, GRE General Test. Additional exam requirements/recommendations for international students: Required—TOEFL. *Application deadline:* Applications are processed on a rolling basis. Application fee: $70 ($80 for international students). Electronic applications accepted. *Expenses:* Expenses: Contact institution. *Financial support:* In 2014–15, 3 students received support. *Unit head:* Dr. Kathy Headley, Associate Dean for Research and Graduate Programs, 864-656-2181, Fax: 864-656-5488, E-mail: ksn1177@clemson.edu. *Application contact:* Dr. William Quinn, Graduate Program Coordinator, 864-656-1501, Fax: 864-656-5488, E-mail: wquinn@clemson.edu.
Website: http://www.clemson.edu/hehd/departments/youthdevelopment/

Colorado State University, Graduate School, College of Health and Human Sciences, Department of Human Development and Family Studies, Fort Collins, CO 80523-1570. Offers MS, PhD. *Accreditation:* AAMFT/COAMFTE. *Faculty:* 16 full-time (12 women). *Students:* 33 full-time (29 women), 8 part-time (all women); includes 6 minority (1 Black or African American, non-Hispanic/Latino; 2 Asian, non-Hispanic/Latino; 3 Hispanic/Latino), 1 international. Average age 28. 72 applicants, 22% accepted, 12 enrolled. In 2014, 7 master's, 2 doctorates awarded. Terminal master's awarded for partial completion of doctoral program. *Degree requirements:* For master's, thesis; for doctorate, comprehensive exam, thesis/dissertation, competency exams. *Entrance requirements:* For master's, GRE General Test, transcript, 3 letters of recommendation, minimum GPA of 3.0, BS/BA, background in family studies, course work in human development, family studies, and statistics; for doctorate, GRE General Test, transcript, 3 letters of recommendation, minimum GPA of 3.0, BS/BA, background in family studies, course work in human development, family studies, and statistics. Additional exam requirements/recommendations for international students: Required—TOEFL (minimum score 550 paper-based; 80 iBT), IELTS. *Application deadline:* For fall admission, 1/2 for domestic and international students. Application fee: $50. Electronic applications accepted. *Expenses:* Tuition, state resident: full-time $9348; part-time $519 per credit. Tuition, nonresident: full-time $22,916; part-time $1273 per credit. *Required fees:* $1584. *Financial support:* In 2014–15, 31 students received support, including 1 fellowship (averaging $37,767 per year), 14 research assistantships with full tuition reimbursements available (averaging $9,223 per year), 16 teaching assistantships with full tuition reimbursements available (averaging $7,338 per year); scholarships/grants and unspecified assistantships also available. Financial award application deadline: 1/2; financial award applicants required to submit FAFSA. *Faculty research:* Risk, resilience and developmental psychopathology treatment; intervention and prevention science; emotion regulation and relational processes; adult development and aging. *Total annual research expenditures:* $1.7 million. *Unit head:* Dr. Lise Youngblade, Department Head, 970-491-3581, Fax: 970-491-7975, E-mail: lise.youngblade@colostate.edu. *Application contact:* Aimee Walker, Graduate Program Advisor, 970-491-3971, Fax: 970-491-7975, E-mail: aimee.walker@colostate.edu.
Website: http://www.hdfs.chhs.colostate.edu/

Cornell University, Graduate School, Graduate Fields of Human Ecology, Field of Human Development, Ithaca, NY 14853-0001. Offers developmental psychology (MA, PhD), including cognitive development, developmental psychopathology, ecology of human development, social and personality development; human development and family studies (MA, PhD), including ecology of human development, family studies and the life course. *Degree requirements:* For doctorate, comprehensive exam, thesis/dissertation, pre-doctoral research project, teaching experience. *Entrance requirements:* For doctorate, GRE General Test, 2 letters of recommendation. Additional exam requirements/recommendations for international students: Required—TOEFL (minimum score 550 paper-based; 77 iBT). Electronic applications accepted. *Faculty research:* Cognitive development, developmental psychopathology, ecology of human development, family studies and the life course, social and personality development.

Duke University, Graduate School, Department of Psychology and Neuroscience, Durham, NC 27708. Offers biological psychology (PhD); clinical psychology (PhD); cognitive psychology (PhD); developmental psychology (PhD); experimental psychology (PhD); health psychology (PhD); human social development (PhD); JD/MA. *Accreditation:* APA (one or more programs are accredited). *Degree requirements:* For doctorate, thesis/dissertation. *Entrance requirements:* For doctorate, GRE General Test. Additional exam requirements/recommendations for international students: Required—TOEFL (minimum score 577 paper-based; 90 iBT) or IELTS (minimum score 7). Electronic applications accepted. *Expenses: Tuition:* Full-time $45,760; part-time $2765 per credit. *Required fees:* $978. Full-time tuition and fees vary according to program.

East Tennessee State University, School of Graduate Studies, College of Education, Department of Counseling and Human Services, Johnson City, TN 37614. Offers MA. *Accreditation:* ACA; NCATE. Part-time programs available. *Faculty:* 18 full-time (12 women). *Students:* 63 full-time (49 women), 5 part-time (4 women); includes 4 minority (1 Asian, non-Hispanic/Latino; 3 Two or more races, non-Hispanic/Latino), 4 international. Average age 27. 78 applicants, 42% accepted, 25 enrolled. In 2014, 31 master's awarded. Terminal master's awarded for partial completion of doctoral program. *Degree requirements:* For master's, comprehensive exam, thesis optional, internship, student teaching, culminating experience. *Entrance requirements:* For master's, GRE General Test, minimum GPA of 3.0, three letters of recommendation, interview. Additional exam requirements/recommendations for international students: Required—TOEFL (minimum score 550 paper-based; 79 iBT). *Application deadline:* For fall admission, 2/1 for domestic and international students. Application fee: $35 ($45 for international students). Electronic applications accepted. *Financial support:* In 2014–15, 54 students received support, including 45 research assistantships with full tuition reimbursements available (averaging $6,000 per year), 5 teaching assistantships with full tuition reimbursements available (averaging $6,000 per year); career-related internships or fieldwork, institutionally sponsored loans, scholarships/grants, traineeships, and unspecified assistantships also available. Financial award application deadline: 7/1; financial award applicants required to submit FAFSA. *Faculty research:* Intervention and assistance with at-risk and under-served youth and high conflict families; service and social justice; women and girls' issues in counseling; counseling competence with LGBTQ individuals; counselor education and supervision. *Unit head:* Dr. Janna Scarborough, Interim Chair, 423-439-7692, Fax: 423-439-7790, E-mail: scarboro@etsu.edu. *Application contact:* Fiona Goodyear, Graduate Specialist, 423-439-6148, Fax: 423-439-5624, E-mail: goodyear@etsu.edu.
Website: http://www.etsu.edu/coe/chs/default.aspx

Erikson Institute, Academic Programs, Chicago, IL 60654. Offers administration (Certificate); bilingual/ESL (Certificate); child development (MS); early childhood education (MS); infant mental health (Certificate); infant studies (Certificate); MS/MSW. MS/MSW offered jointly with Loyola University Chicago. Part-time and evening/weekend programs available. *Degree requirements:* For master's, comprehensive exam, internship; for Certificate, internship. *Entrance requirements:* For master's and Certificate, minimum GPA of 2.75. Additional exam requirements/recommendations for international students: Required—TOEFL. *Faculty research:* Assessment strategies from early childhood through elementary years; language, literacy, and the arts in children's development; inclusive special education; parent-child relationships; cognitive development.

Fielding Graduate University, Graduate Programs, School of Human and Organization Development, Santa Barbara, CA 93105-3814. Offers comprehensive evidence-based coaching (Graduate Certificate); evidence based coaching for education leadership (Graduate Certificate); evidence based coaching for organization leadership (Graduate Certificate); evidence based coaching for personal development (Graduate Certificate); human and organizational systems (PhD), including aging, culture and society, information society and knowledge organizations, transformative learning for social justice; human development (PhD), including aging, culture and society, information society and knowledge organizations, transformative learning for social justice; nonprofit leadership (Graduate Certificate); organization consulting (Graduate Certificate); organizational development and leadership (MA). Postbaccalaureate distance learning degree programs offered (minimal on-campus study). *Faculty:* 19 full-time (12 women), 41 part-time/adjunct (20 women). *Students:* 273 full-time (196 women), 136 part-time (108 women); includes 115 minority (54 Black or African American, non-Hispanic/Latino; 3 American Indian or Alaska Native, non-Hispanic/Latino; 18 Asian, non-Hispanic/Latino; 21 Hispanic/Latino; 19 Two or more races, non-Hispanic/Latino), 1 international. Average age 49. 86 applicants, 99% accepted, 57 enrolled. In 2014, 18 master's, 65 doctorates, 123 other advanced degrees awarded. Terminal master's awarded for partial completion of doctoral program. *Degree requirements:* For master's, thesis or alternative; for doctorate, comprehensive exam, thesis/dissertation. *Entrance requirements:* For master's and Graduate Certificate, BA from regionally-accredited institution or equivalent; for doctorate, BA or MA from regionally-accredited institution or equivalent. *Application deadline:* For fall admission, 7/1 for domestic and international students; for spring admission, 9/1 for domestic and international students; for summer admission, 3/1 for domestic and international students. Application fee: $75. Electronic applications accepted. *Expenses: Tuition:* Full-time $25,650; part-time $2880 per course. Tuition and fees vary according to degree level and program. *Financial support:* In 2014–15, 57 students received support. Scholarships/grants, health care benefits,

tuition waivers (partial), and unspecified assistantships available. Support available to part-time students. Financial award applicants required to submit FAFSA. *Unit head:* Dr. Gerald Porter, Provost and Senior Vice President, 805-898-2940, Fax: 805-687-9793, E-mail: gporter@fielding.edu. *Application contact:* Enrollment Coordinator, 800-340-1099 Ext. 4098, Fax: 805-687-9793, E-mail: hodadmissions@fielding.edu. Website: http://www.fielding.edu/programs/hod/default.aspx

Georgetown University, Graduate School of Arts and Sciences, Edmund A. Walsh School of Foreign Service, Program in Global Human Development, Washington, DC 20057. Offers MA.

The George Washington University, Graduate School of Education and Human Development, Department of Educational Leadership, Individualized Master's Program, Washington, DC 20052. Offers MA Ed. *Students:* 12 part-time (9 women); includes 2 minority (1 Black or African American, non-Hispanic/Latino; 1 Asian, non-Hispanic/Latino). Average age 45. 11 applicants, 64% accepted, 5 enrolled. In 2014, 25 master's awarded. *Degree requirements:* For master's, comprehensive exam. *Entrance requirements:* For master's, GRE General Test or MAT, minimum GPA of 2.75. *Application deadline:* For fall admission, 3/1 priority date for domestic students; for spring admission, 10/1 for domestic students. Applications are processed on a rolling basis. Application fee: $75. *Financial support:* Application deadline: 1/15; applicants required to submit FAFSA. *Unit head:* Dr. Mary Hatwood Futrell, Dean, 202-994-6161, Fax: 202-994-7207, E-mail: mfutrell@gwu.edu. *Application contact:* Sarah Lang, Director of Graduate Admissions, 202-994-1447, Fax: 202-994-7207, E-mail: slang@gwu.edu.

Harvard University, Harvard Graduate School of Education, Master's Programs in Education, Cambridge, MA 02138. Offers arts in education (Ed M); education policy and management (Ed M); higher education (Ed M); human development and psychology (Ed M); international education policy (Ed M); language and literacy (Ed M); learning and teaching (Ed M); mind, brain, and education (Ed M); prevention science and practice (Ed M); school leadership (Ed M); special studies (Ed M); teacher education (Ed M); technology, innovation, and education (Ed M). Part-time programs available. *Faculty:* 66 full-time (35 women), 82 part-time/adjunct (41 women). *Students:* 595 full-time (441 women), 71 part-time (48 women); includes 170 minority (33 Black or African American, non-Hispanic/Latino; 2 American Indian or Alaska Native, non-Hispanic/Latino; 69 Asian, non-Hispanic/Latino; 46 Hispanic/Latino; 20 Two or more races, non-Hispanic/Latino), 117 international. Average age 28. 1,741 applicants, 51% accepted, 613 enrolled. In 2014, 589 master's awarded. *Entrance requirements:* For master's, GRE General Test, statement of purpose, 3 letters of recommendation, resume, official transcripts. Additional exam requirements/recommendations for international students: Required—TOEFL (minimum score 613 paper-based; 104 iBT), TWE (minimum score 5). *Application deadline:* For fall admission, 1/5 for domestic and international students. Application fee: $85. Electronic applications accepted. *Expenses:* Expenses: Contact institution. *Financial support:* In 2014-15, 365 students received support, including 10 fellowships with full and partial tuition reimbursements available (averaging $15,790 per year), 6 teaching assistantships (averaging $4,281 per year); research assistantships, career-related internships or fieldwork, Federal Work-Study, institutionally sponsored loans, scholarships/grants, health care benefits, tuition waivers (full and partial), and unspecified assistantships also available. Support available to part-time students. Financial award application deadline: 2/1; financial award applicants required to submit FAFSA. *Faculty research:* Learning and development, educational leadership and organizations, education policy analysis. *Total annual research expenditures:* $34.3 million. *Unit head:* Jennifer L. Petrallia, Assistant Dean, 617-495-8445. *Application contact:* Information Contact, 617-495-3414, Fax: 617-496-3577, E-mail: gseadmissions@harvard.edu. Website: http://www.gse.harvard.edu/

Hofstra University, School of Education, Programs in Teacher Education, Hempstead, NY 11549. Offers bilingual education (MA), including biology (MA, MS Ed), geology; business education (MS Ed); early childhood and childhood education (MS Ed), including French; early childhood education (MA); education technology (Advanced Certificate); elementary education (MA), including math. science, technology (STEM); English education (MS Ed); fine arts education (MS Ed), including biology (MA, MS Ed); foreign language and TESOL (MS Ed); learning and teaching (Ed D), including applied linguistics, art education, arts and humanities, early childhood education, English education, human development, math education, math, science, and technology, multicultural education, physical education, science education, social studies education, special education; mathematics education (MA, MS Ed); secondary education (Advanced Certificate); social studies education (MA, MS Ed). Part-time and evening/weekend programs available. Postbaccalaureate distance learning degree programs offered (minimal on-campus study). *Students:* 141 full-time (111 women), 119 part-time (84 women); includes 58 minority (13 Black or African American, non-Hispanic/Latino; 14 Asian, non-Hispanic/Latino; 28 Hispanic/Latino; 1 Native Hawaiian or other Pacific Islander, non-Hispanic/Latino; 2 Two or more races, non-Hispanic/Latino), 18 international. Average age 30. 301 applicants, 87% accepted, 112 enrolled. In 2014, 133 master's, 5 doctorates, 28 other advanced degrees awarded. *Degree requirements:* For master's, comprehensive exam, thesis (for some programs), exit project, student teaching, fieldwork, electronic portfolio, curriculum project, minimum GPA of 3.0; for doctorate, thesis/dissertation; for Advanced Certificate, 3 foreign languages, comprehensive exam (for some programs), thesis project. *Entrance requirements:* For master's, 2 letters of recommendation, portfolio, teacher certification (MA), interview, essay; for doctorate, GMAT, GRE, LSAT, or MAT; for Advanced Certificate, 2 letters of recommendation, essay, interview and/or portfolio, teaching certificate. Additional exam requirements/recommendations for international students: Required—TOEFL (minimum score 550 paper-based; 80 iBT). *Application deadline:* Applications are processed on a rolling basis. Application fee: $70 ($75 for international students). Electronic applications accepted. *Expenses:* Tuition: Full-time $20,610; part-time $1145 per credit hour. *Required fees:* $970; $165 per term. Tuition and fees vary according to program. *Financial support:* In 2014-15, 153 students received support, including 60 fellowships with full and partial tuition reimbursements available (averaging $5,084 per year), 4 research assistantships with full and partial tuition reimbursements available (averaging $7,095 per year); Federal Work-Study, institutionally sponsored loans, scholarships/grants, health care benefits, and tuition waivers (full and partial) also available. Support available to part-time students. Financial award applicants required to submit FAFSA. *Faculty research:* Appropriate content in secondary school disciplines, lesson development across content, interdisciplinary curriculum, multicultural education. *Unit head:* Dr. Eustace Thompson, Chairperson, 516-463-5749, Fax: 516-463-6275, E-mail: edaegt@hofstra.edu. *Application contact:* Sunil Samuel, Assistant Vice President of Admissions, 516-463-4723, Fax: 516-463-4664, E-mail: graduateadmission@hofstra.edu. Website: http://www.hofstra.edu/education/

Hood College, Graduate School, Programs in Human Sciences, Frederick, MD 21701-8575. Offers human sciences (MA), including psychology; thanatology (MA, Certificate). Part-time and evening/weekend programs available. *Degree requirements:* For master's, comprehensive exam, capstone/research project. *Entrance requirements:* For master's, minimum GPA of 2.75. Additional exam requirements/recommendations for international students: Required—TOEFL (minimum score 575 paper-based; 89 iBT), IELTS (minimum score 6.5). Electronic applications accepted. Application fee is waived when completed online. *Faculty research:* Mind-body medicine and multicultural healing, the New Orleans jazz funeral, death practices in African-American culture, bereavement theories and gender differences, Piaget's theory of cognitive development as a formal mathematical model.

Iowa State University of Science and Technology, Department of Human Development and Family Studies, Ames, IA 50011. Offers human development and family studies (MFCS, MS, PhD). *Accreditation:* AAMFT/COAMFTE. *Degree requirements:* For master's, thesis; for doctorate, thesis/dissertation. *Entrance requirements:* For master's and doctorate, GRE General Test. Additional exam requirements/recommendations for international students: Required—TOEFL (minimum score 550 paper-based; 79 iBT), IELTS (minimum score 6.5). Electronic applications accepted. *Faculty research:* Child development, early childhood education, family resource management and housing, life span studies.

Kansas State University, Graduate School, College of Human Ecology, Program in Human Ecology, Manhattan, KS 66506. Offers apparel and textiles (PhD); family life education and consultation (PhD); food service and hospitality management (PhD); lifespan and human development (PhD); marriage and family therapy (PhD); personal financial planning (PhD). *Students:* 51 full-time (31 women), 44 part-time (24 women); includes 20 minority (8 Black or African American, non-Hispanic/Latino; 1 American Indian or Alaska Native, non-Hispanic/Latino; 3 Asian, non-Hispanic/Latino; 4 Hispanic/Latino; 1 Native Hawaiian or other Pacific Islander, non-Hispanic/Latino; 3 Two or more races, non-Hispanic/Latino), 17 international. Average age 39. 44 applicants, 39% accepted, 14 enrolled. In 2014, 17 doctorates awarded. *Degree requirements:* For doctorate, thesis/dissertation. *Application deadline:* For fall admission, 2/1 priority date for domestic and international students; for spring admission, 8/1 priority date for domestic and international students. Applications are processed on a rolling basis. Application fee: $50 ($75 for international students). Electronic applications accepted. *Financial support:* Application deadline: 3/1. *Total annual research expenditures:* $1.8 million. *Unit head:* Dr. John Buckwalter, Dean, 785-532-5500, Fax: 785-532-5504, E-mail: jbb3@ksu.edu. *Application contact:* Application Contact, 785-532-5500, Fax: 785-532-5504, E-mail: he@ksu.edu.

Kansas State University, Graduate School, College of Human Ecology, School of Family Studies and Human Services, Manhattan, KS 66506. Offers communication sciences and disorders (MS); conflict resolution (Graduate Certificate); early childhood education (MS); family and community service (MS); family studies (MS); life span human development (MS); marriage and family therapy (MS); personal financial planning (MS, Graduate Certificate); youth development (MS, Graduate Certificate). *Accreditation:* AAMFT/COAMFTE; ASHA. Part-time programs available. Postbaccalaureate distance learning degree programs offered (no on-campus study). *Faculty:* 39 full-time (26 women), 9 part-time/adjunct (7 women). *Students:* 69 full-time (57 women), 141 part-time (99 women); includes 48 minority (15 Black or African American, non-Hispanic/Latino; 3 American Indian or Alaska Native, non-Hispanic/Latino; 3 Asian, non-Hispanic/Latino; 21 Hispanic/Latino; 2 Native Hawaiian or other Pacific Islander, non-Hispanic/Latino; 4 Two or more races, non-Hispanic/Latino), 3 international. Average age 31. 203 applicants, 38% accepted, 57 enrolled. In 2014, 48 master's, 28 other advanced degrees awarded. *Degree requirements:* For master's, comprehensive exam (for some programs), thesis optional. *Entrance requirements:* For master's, GRE, minimum GPA of 3.0 in last 2 years of undergraduate study. Additional exam requirements/recommendations for international students: Required—TOEFL (minimum score 600 paper-based). *Application deadline:* For fall admission, 2/1 priority date for domestic students, 1/1 priority date for international students; for spring admission, 10/1 priority date for domestic students, 8/1 priority date for international students; for summer admission, 2/1 priority date for domestic students, 12/1 priority date for international students. Applications are processed on a rolling basis. Application fee: $50 ($75 for international students). Electronic applications accepted. *Financial support:* In 2014-15, 25 research assistantships (averaging $10,000 per year), 9 teaching assistantships with full tuition reimbursements (averaging $10,000 per year) were awarded; unspecified assistantships also available. Financial award application deadline: 3/1. *Faculty research:* Health and security of military families, personal and family risk assessment and evaluation, disorders of communication and swallowing, families and health, financial decision-making. *Total annual research expenditures:* $8.4 million. *Unit head:* Dr. Dottie Durband, Director, 785-532-5510, Fax: 785-532-5505, E-mail: dottie@ksu.edu. *Application contact:* Connie Fechter, Administrative Specialist, 785-532-5510, Fax: 785-532-5505, E-mail: fechter@ksu.edu. Website: http://www.he.k-state.edu/fshs/

Kent State University, Graduate School of Education, Health, and Human Services, School of Lifespan Development and Educational Sciences, Program in Counseling and Human Development Services, Kent, OH 44242-0001. Offers PhD. *Accreditation:* ACA; NCATE. *Faculty:* 9 full-time (5 women), 12 part-time/adjunct (8 women). *Students:* 61 full-time (41 women), 13 part-time (7 women); includes 11 minority (8 Black or African American, non-Hispanic/Latino; 2 Asian, non-Hispanic/Latino; 1 Two or more races, non-Hispanic/Latino), 3 international. 31 applicants, 39% accepted. In 2014, 7 doctorates awarded. *Degree requirements:* For doctorate, comprehensive exam, thesis/dissertation. *Entrance requirements:* For doctorate, GRE General Test, preliminary written exam, 2 letters of reference, resume, interview. Additional exam requirements/recommendations for international students: Required—TOEFL (minimum score 550 paper-based; 80 iBT). *Application deadline:* For fall admission, 2/1 for domestic students. Application fee: $45 ($60 for international students). Electronic applications accepted. *Expenses:* Tuition, state resident: full-time $8730; part-time $485 per credit hour. Tuition, nonresident: full-time $14,886; part-time $827 per credit hour. Tuition and fees vary according to campus/location and program. *Financial support:* In 2014-15, 7 research assistantships with full tuition reimbursements (averaging $12,000 per year), 5 teaching assistantships with full tuition reimbursements (averaging $12,000 per year) were awarded; career-related internships or fieldwork, Federal Work-Study, institutionally sponsored loans, scholarships/grants, health care benefits, unspecified assistantships, and 4 administrative assistantships (averaging $12,000 per year) also available. Support available to part-time students. Financial award application deadline: 4/1; financial award applicants required to submit FAFSA. *Faculty research:* Family/child therapy, clinical supervision, group work, experiential training methods. *Unit head:* Dr. Jane Cox, Coordinator, 330-672-0698, Fax: 330-672-5396, E-mail: jcox8@kent.edu. *Application contact:* Nancy Miller, Academic Program Director, Office of Graduate Student Services, 330-672-2576, Fax: 330-672-9162, E-mail: ogs@kent.edu.

Kent State University, Graduate School of Education, Health, and Human Services, School of Lifespan Development and Educational Sciences, Program in Human Development and Family Studies, Kent, OH 44242-0001. Offers MA. *Faculty:* 8 full-time (5 women), 15 part-time/adjunct (13 women). *Students:* 7 full-time (6 women), 9 part-time (all women); includes 4 minority (all Black or African American, non-Hispanic/Latino), 1 international. 12 applicants, 25% accepted. In 2014, 2 master's awarded. *Degree requirements:* For master's, thesis optional. *Entrance requirements:* For master's, minimum undergraduate GPA of 3.0, 3 letters of reference, goals statement. Additional exam requirements/recommendations for international students: Required—

TOEFL (minimum score 550 paper-based; 80 iBT). Application fee: $45 ($60 for international students). *Expenses:* Tuition, state resident: full-time $8730; part-time $485 per credit hour. Tuition, nonresident: full-time $14,886; part-time $827 per credit hour. Tuition and fees vary according to campus/location and program. *Financial support:* In 2014–15, 6 research assistantships (averaging $8,500 per year) were awarded. *Unit head:* Dr. Kelly Cighy, Coordinator, 330-672-2449, E-mail: kcichy@kent.edu. *Application contact:* Nancy Miller, Academic Program Director, Office of Graduate Student Services, 330-672-2576, Fax: 330-672-9162, E-mail: ogs@kent.edu.

Laurentian University, School of Graduate Studies and Research, Programme in Human Development, Sudbury, ON P3E 2C6, Canada. Offers M Sc, MA. Interdisciplinary program consisting of the Departments of Psychology, Sociology, and Human Movement. Part-time programs available. *Degree requirements:* For master's, thesis or alternative. *Entrance requirements:* For master's, honors degree with second class or better. *Faculty research:* Aging and well-being, physical, social and cognitive development of children, social cognition and social relationships including peers and family, education and schooling.

Lindsey Wilson College, School of Professional Counseling, Columbia, KY 42728. Offers counseling and human development (M Ed); counselor education and supervision (PhD). *Accreditation:* ACA (one or more programs are accredited). Part-time and evening/weekend programs available. Postbaccalaureate distance learning degree programs offered (minimal on-campus study).

Marywood University, Academic Affairs, Center for Interdisciplinary Studies, Scranton, PA 18509-1598. Offers human development (PhD), including educational administration, health promotion, higher education administration, instructional leadership, social work. Part-time programs available. *Students:* 31 full-time (21 women), 36 part-time (23 women); includes 3 minority (1 Black or African American, non-Hispanic/Latino; 2 Hispanic/Latino), 2 international. Average age 39. 30 applicants, 63% accepted, 15 enrolled. In 2014, 11 doctorates awarded. *Application deadline:* For fall admission, 1/30 for domestic and international students. Applications are processed on a rolling basis. Application fee: $35. Electronic applications accepted. *Expenses:* Expenses: $885 per credit. *Financial support:* Application deadline: 6/30; applicants required to submit FAFSA. *Unit head:* Dr. Deborah Hokien, Director, 570-348-6279, E-mail: hokien@marywood.edu. *Application contact:* Tammy Manka, Assistant Director of Graduate Admissions, 570-348-6211 Ext. 2322, E-mail: tmanka@marywood.edu.
Website: http://www.marywood.edu/academics/gradcatalog/

Mississippi State University, College of Agriculture and Life Sciences, School of Human Sciences, Mississippi State, MS 39762. Offers agricultural sciences (PhD), including agriculture and extension education; agriculture and extension education (MS); human development and family studies (MS, PhD). *Accreditation:* NCATE (one or more programs are accredited). Part-time programs available. *Faculty:* 23 full-time (13 women), 1 part-time/adjunct (0 women). *Students:* 26 full-time (20 women), 65 part-time (41 women); includes 19 minority (17 Black or African American, non-Hispanic/Latino; 1 Hispanic/Latino; 1 Two or more races, non-Hispanic/Latino), 3 international. Average age 36. 37 applicants, 68% accepted, 20 enrolled. In 2014, 11 master's, 4 doctorates awarded. *Degree requirements:* For master's, thesis optional, comprehensive oral or written exam. *Entrance requirements:* For master's, GRE, minimum GPA of 2.75 in last 4 semesters of course work; for doctorate, minimum GPA of 3.0 on prior graduate work. Additional exam requirements/recommendations for international students: Required—TOEFL (minimum score 477 paper-based; 53 iBT); Recommended—IELTS (minimum score 4.5). *Application deadline:* For fall admission, 7/1 for domestic students, 5/1 for international students; for spring admission, 11/1 for domestic students, 9/1 for international students. Applications are processed on a rolling basis. Application fee: $60. Electronic applications accepted. *Expenses:* Tuition, state resident: full-time $7140; part-time $783 per credit hour. Tuition, nonresident: full-time $18,478; part-time $2043 per credit hour. *Financial support:* In 2014–15, 13 research assistantships (averaging $12,363 per year), 2 teaching assistantships with full tuition reimbursements (averaging $13,088 per year) were awarded; Federal Work-Study, institutionally sponsored loans, and unspecified assistantships also available. Financial award application deadline: 4/1; financial award applicants required to submit FAFSA. *Faculty research:* Animal welfare, agroscience, information technology, learning styles, problem solving. *Unit head:* Dr. Michael Newman, Director and Professor, 662-325-2950, E-mail: mnewman@humansci.msstate.edu. *Application contact:* Dr. Tommy Phillips, Graduate Coordinator, 662-325-0655, E-mail: tphillips@humansci.msstate.edu.
Website: http://www.humansci.msstate.edu

Montana State University, The Graduate School, College of Education, Health, and Human Development, Department of Health and Human Development, Bozeman, MT 59717. Offers family and consumer sciences (MS). *Accreditation:* ACA. Part-time programs available. Postbaccalaureate distance learning degree programs offered (no on-campus study). *Degree requirements:* For master's, comprehensive exam. *Entrance requirements:* For master's, GRE (minimum scores: verbal 480; quantitative 480). Additional exam requirements/recommendations for international students: Required—TOEFL (minimum score 550 paper-based). Electronic applications accepted. *Faculty research:* Community food systems, ethic of care for teachers and coaches, influence of public policy on families and communities, cost effectiveness of early childhood education, exercise metabolism, winter sport performance enhancement, assessment of physical activity.

National Louis University, National College of Education, Chicago, IL 60603. Offers administration and supervision (M Ed, Ed D, CAS, Ed S); curriculum and instruction (M Ed, MS Ed, CAS); early childhood administration (M Ed, CAS); early childhood education (M Ed, MAT, MS Ed, CAS); education (Ed D); educational psychology/human learning and development (M Ed, MS Ed, CAS, Ed S); elementary education (MAT); interdisciplinary curriculum and instruction (M Ed); mathematics education (M Ed, MS Ed, CAS); reading and language (M Ed, MS Ed, CAS); school psychology (M Ed, Ed S); science education (M Ed, MS Ed, CAS); secondary education (MAT); special education (M Ed, MAT, CAS); technology in education (M Ed, CAS). *Accreditation:* NCATE. Part-time and evening/weekend programs available. *Degree requirements:* For doctorate, comprehensive exam, thesis/dissertation. *Entrance requirements:* For master's, MAT or GRE, minimum GPA of 3.0; for doctorate, GRE General Test, minimum GPA of 3.25, interview, resume, writing sample, 4 recommendations. Additional exam requirements/recommendations for international students: Required—TOEFL (minimum score 550 paper-based; 79 iBT).

New York University, Steinhardt School of Culture, Education, and Human Development, New York, NY 10003. Offers MA, MFA, MM, MPH, MS, DPS, DPT, Ed D, PhD, Advanced Certificate, Post Master's Certificate, Postbaccalaureate Certificate, Advanced Certificate/MPH, MA/Advanced Certificate, MA/MA, MA/MS, MLIS/MA. *Accreditation:* Teacher Education Accreditation Council. Part-time programs available. *Faculty:* 291 full-time (173 women), 740 part-time/adjunct (392 women). *Students:* 2,129 full-time (1,587 women), 1,136 part-time (869 women); includes 854 minority (212 Black or African American, non-Hispanic/Latino; 5 American Indian or Alaska Native, non-Hispanic/Latino; 271 Asian, non-Hispanic/Latino; 288 Hispanic/Latino; 3 Native Hawaiian or other Pacific Islander, non-Hispanic/Latino; 75 Two or more races, non-Hispanic/Latino), 726 international. Average age 31. 6,757 applicants, 42% accepted, 1245 enrolled. In 2014, 1,316 master's, 109 doctorates, 36 other advanced degrees awarded. *Degree requirements:* For master's, thesis (for some programs); for doctorate, comprehensive exam (for some programs), thesis/dissertation. *Entrance requirements:* For doctorate, GRE General Test, interview. Additional exam requirements/recommendations for international students: Required—TOEFL (minimum score 100 iBT). *Application deadline:* For fall admission, 12/1 priority date for domestic students, 12/1 for international students; for spring admission, 1/1 for domestic and international students. Applications are processed on a rolling basis. Application fee: $75. Electronic applications accepted. *Expenses:* Expenses: Contact institution. *Financial support:* Fellowships with full and partial tuition reimbursements, research assistantships with full and partial tuition reimbursements, teaching assistantships with full and partial tuition reimbursements, career-related internships or fieldwork, Federal Work-Study, institutionally sponsored loans, scholarships/grants, traineeships, tuition waivers (partial), and unspecified assistantships available. Support available to part-time students. Financial award application deadline: 2/1; financial award applicants required to submit FAFSA. *Faculty research:* Equity, urban adolescents, arts in education, globalization, multivariate analysis, psychometrics. *Total annual research expenditures:* $30.4 million. *Unit head:* Dr. Dominic Brewer, Dean, 212-998-5000. *Application contact:* John Myers, Director of Enrollment Management, 212-998-5030, Fax: 212-995-4328, E-mail: steinhardt.gradadmissions@nyu.edu.
Website: http://steinhardt.nyu.edu/

New York University, Steinhardt School of Culture, Education, and Human Development, Department of Applied Psychology, Programs in Educational and Developmental Psychology, New York, NY 10003. Offers developmental psychology (PhD); human development and social intervention (MA); psychology and social intervention (PhD). *Accreditation:* APA (one or more programs are accredited). Part-time programs available. *Faculty:* 24 full-time (16 women). *Students:* 54 full-time (44 women), 6 part-time (all women); includes 23 minority (7 Black or African American, non-Hispanic/Latino; 5 Asian, non-Hispanic/Latino; 10 Hispanic/Latino; 1 Two or more races, non-Hispanic/Latino), 10 international. Average age 27. 137 applicants, 26% accepted, 13 enrolled. In 2014, 16 master's, 4 doctorates awarded. *Degree requirements:* For master's, thesis (for some programs); for doctorate, thesis/dissertation. *Entrance requirements:* For doctorate, GRE General Test, interview. Additional exam requirements/recommendations for international students: Required—TOEFL. *Application deadline:* For fall admission, 12/1 priority date for domestic and international students. Applications are processed on a rolling basis. Application fee: $75. Electronic applications accepted. *Financial support:* Teaching assistantships with partial tuition reimbursements, career-related internships or fieldwork, Federal Work-Study, institutionally sponsored loans, and tuition waivers (partial) available. Support available to part-time students. Financial award application deadline: 2/1; financial award applicants required to submit FAFSA. *Faculty research:* Schools and communities, self-regulation and academic achievement, intervention and social change, trauma and resilience, cognition. *Unit head:* Prof. Clancy Blair, Director, 212-998-5853, Fax: 212-995-4358, E-mail: clancy.blair@nyu.edu. *Application contact:* 212-998-5030, Fax: 212-995-4328, E-mail: steinhardt.gradadmissions@nyu.edu.
Website: http://steinhardt.nyu.edu/appsych

North Dakota State University, College of Graduate and Interdisciplinary Studies, College of Human Development and Education, Department of Human Development and Family Science, Program in Human Development, Fargo, ND 58108. Offers MS, PhD. *Degree requirements:* For master's, comprehensive exam, thesis. *Entrance requirements:* Additional exam requirements/recommendations for international students: Required—TOEFL (minimum score 525 paper-based; 71 iBT). *Faculty research:* Gerontology, wellness, counselor education.

Northern Arizona University, Graduate College, College of Social and Behavioral Sciences, Institute for Human Development, Flagstaff, AZ 86011. Offers assistive technology (Certificate); disability policy and practice (Certificate); positive behavior support (Certificate). Part-time programs available. *Entrance requirements:* Additional exam requirements/recommendations for international students: Required—TOEFL (minimum score 550 paper-based; 80 iBT), IELTS (minimum score 7). Electronic applications accepted.

Northwestern University, The Graduate School, School of Education and Social Policy, Program in Human Development and Social Policy, Evanston, IL 60208. Offers PhD. Admissions and degrees offered through The Graduate School. *Degree requirements:* For doctorate, comprehensive exam, thesis/dissertation. *Entrance requirements:* For doctorate, GRE General Test. Additional exam requirements/recommendations for international students: Required—TOEFL (minimum score 600 paper-based; 100 iBT). Electronic applications accepted. *Faculty research:* Individual development and the personal narrative; the life course and culture; development, intervention and culture; the life course and policy; analysis of policy effects on lives.

The Ohio State University, Graduate School, College of Education and Human Ecology, Department of Human Sciences, Columbus, OH 43210. Offers consumer sciences (MS, PhD); human development and family science (PhD); human nutrition (MS, PhD); kinesiology (MA, PhD). Part-time programs available. *Faculty:* 55. *Students:* 116 full-time (73 women), 7 part-time (4 women); includes 20 minority (10 Black or African American, non-Hispanic/Latino; 1 American Indian or Alaska Native, non-Hispanic/Latino; 4 Asian, non-Hispanic/Latino; 4 Hispanic/Latino; 1 Two or more races, non-Hispanic/Latino), 31 international. Average age 28. In 2014, 17 master's, 16 doctorates awarded. *Degree requirements:* For master's, thesis optional; for doctorate, thesis/dissertation. *Entrance requirements:* For master's and doctorate, GRE. Additional exam requirements/recommendations for international students: Required—TOEFL (minimum score 550 paper-based; 79 iBT), Michigan English Language Assessment Battery (minimum score 82); Recommended—IELTS (minimum score 7). *Application deadline:* For fall admission, 12/1 priority date for domestic and international students; for winter admission, 12/1 for domestic students, 11/1 for international students; for spring admission, 3/1 for domestic students, 2/1 for international students. Applications are processed on a rolling basis. Application fee: $60 ($70 for international students). Electronic applications accepted. *Financial support:* Fellowships with tuition reimbursements, research assistantships with tuition reimbursements, teaching assistantships with tuition reimbursements, Federal Work-Study, and institutionally sponsored loans available. Support available to part-time students. *Unit head:* Dr. Carl M. Maresh, Chair, E-mail: maresh.15@osu.edu. *Application contact:* Graduate and Professional Admissions, 614-292-9444, Fax: 614-292-3895, E-mail: gpadmissions@osu.edu.
Website: http://ehe.osu.edu/human-sciences/

Oklahoma State University, College of Arts and Sciences, Department of Psychology, Stillwater, OK 74078. Offers clinical psychology (PhD); general psychology (MS); lifespan development psychology (PhD). *Accreditation:* APA (one or more programs are accredited). *Faculty:* 31 full-time (16 women), 3 part-time/adjunct (2 women). *Students:* 39 full-time (27 women), 18 part-time (12 women); includes 12 minority (1 Black or African American, non-Hispanic/Latino; 5 American Indian or Alaska Native, non-Hispanic/Latino; 1 Hispanic/Latino; 1 Native Hawaiian or other Pacific Islander, non-Hispanic/Latino; 4 Two or more races, non-Hispanic/Latino), 2 international. Average age 27. 218 applicants, 7% accepted, 9 enrolled. In 2014, 9 master's, 9 doctorates

awarded. *Degree requirements:* For master's, thesis or alternative; for doctorate, comprehensive exam, thesis/dissertation. *Entrance requirements:* For master's and doctorate, GRE General Test. Additional exam requirements/recommendations for international students: Required—TOEFL (minimum score 550 paper-based; 79 iBT). *Application deadline:* For fall admission, 3/1 priority date for international students; for spring admission, 8/1 priority date for international students. Applications are processed on a rolling basis. Application fee: $40 ($75 for international students). Electronic applications accepted. *Expenses:* Tuition, state resident: full-time $4488; part-time $187 per credit hour. Tuition, nonresident: full-time $18,360; part-time $765 per credit hour. *Required fees:* $2413; $100.55 per credit hour. Tuition and fees vary according to campus/location. *Financial support:* In 2014–15, 14 research assistantships (averaging $14,585 per year), 46 teaching assistantships (averaging $13,749 per year) were awarded; career-related internships or fieldwork, Federal Work-Study, scholarships/grants, health care benefits, tuition waivers (partial), and unspecified assistantships also available. Support available to part-time students. Financial award application deadline: 3/1; financial award applicants required to submit FAFSA. *Unit head:* Dr. Thad Leffingwell, Department Head, 405-744-7494, Fax: 405-744-8067, E-mail: thad.leffingwell@okstate.edu. *Application contact:* Patricia Alexander, Graduate Advisor, 405-744-7591, Fax: 405-744-8967, E-mail: patricia.alexander@okstate.edu. Website: http://psychology.okstate.edu

Oregon State University, College of Public Health and Human Sciences, Program in Human Development and Family Studies, Corvallis, OR 97331. Offers MS, PhD. Part-time programs available. *Faculty:* 15 full-time (12 women), 2 part-time/adjunct (1 woman). *Students:* 36 full-time (24 women); includes 12 minority (2 Black or African American, non-Hispanic/Latino; 2 American Indian or Alaska Native, non-Hispanic/Latino; 3 Asian, non-Hispanic/Latino; 4 Hispanic/Latino; 1 Two or more races, non-Hispanic/Latino), 5 international. Average age 32. 20 applicants, 45% accepted, 6 enrolled. In 2014, 2 master's, 3 doctorates awarded. *Entrance requirements:* For master's, GRE; for doctorate, GRE, master's degree (including thesis). Additional exam requirements/recommendations for international students: Required—TOEFL (minimum score 80 iBT), IELTS (minimum score 6.5). *Application deadline:* For fall admission, 4/15 for domestic students. Application fee: $60. *Expenses:* Tuition, state resident: full-time $11,907; part-time $189 per credit hour. Tuition, nonresident: full-time $19,953; part-time $441 per credit hour. *Required fees:* $1472; $449 per term. One-time fee: $350. Tuition and fees vary according to course load and program. *Financial support:* Fellowships, research assistantships, and teaching assistantships available. Financial award application deadline: 1/2. *Unit head:* Dr. Karen Hooker, Professor/Co-Director. *Application contact:* Kaycee Headley, Advisor, 541-737-4765, E-mail: kaycee.headley@oregonstate.edu. Website: http://health.oregonstate.edu/degrees/graduate/hdfs

Our Lady of the Lake University of San Antonio, School of Professional Studies, Program in Human Sciences, San Antonio, TX 78207-4689. Offers MA. Part-time and evening/weekend programs available. *Degree requirements:* For master's, comprehensive exam. *Entrance requirements:* For master's, GRE General Test or MAT, interview. Additional exam requirements/recommendations for international students: Required—TOEFL. Electronic applications accepted. *Faculty research:* Non-clinical professionals with knowledge and skills in human relations and interpersonal communications.

Pacific Oaks College, Graduate School, Program in Human Development, Pasadena, CA 91103. Offers MA. Part-time and evening/weekend programs available. Postbaccalaureate distance learning degree programs offered (minimal on-campus study). *Degree requirements:* For master's, thesis. *Entrance requirements:* Additional exam requirements/recommendations for international students: Required—TOEFL (minimum score 550 paper-based). *Faculty research:* Bicultural development, teaching adults, art education, literacy development, adolescent development.

Penn State University Park, Graduate School, College of Health and Human Development, Department of Human Development and Family Studies, University Park, PA 16802. Offers MS, PhD. *Unit head:* Dr. Ann C. Crouter, Dean, 814-865-1420, Fax: 814-865-3282, E-mail: ac1@psu.edu. *Application contact:* Lori A. Stania, Director, Graduate Student Services, 814-867-5278, Fax: 814-863-4627, E-mail: gswww@psu.edu. Website: http://www.hhdev.psu.edu/hdfs/

Purdue University, Graduate School, College of Health and Human Sciences, Department of Child Development and Family Studies, West Lafayette, IN 47907. Offers developmental studies (MS, PhD); family studies (MS, PhD); marriage and family therapy (MS, PhD). *Accreditation:* AAMFT/COAMFTE (one or more programs are accredited). Part-time programs available. Terminal master's awarded for partial completion of doctoral program. *Degree requirements:* For master's, thesis; for doctorate, thesis/dissertation. *Entrance requirements:* For master's and doctorate, GRE General Test (minimum score 1000 combined verbal and quantitative), minimum undergraduate GPA of 3.0 or equivalent. Additional exam requirements/recommendations for international students: Required—TOEFL (minimum score 600 paper-based; 90 iBT), TWE (minimum score 4). Electronic applications accepted. *Faculty research:* Inclusion of children with special needs, families as learning environments, relationships in child care, work-family relations, AIDS prevention.

St. Lawrence University, Department of Education, Program in Counseling and Human Development, Canton, NY 13617-1455. Offers mental health counseling (MS); school counseling (M Ed, CAS). Part-time and evening/weekend programs available. *Entrance requirements:* For master's, GRE General Test. *Faculty research:* Defense mechanisms and mediation.

Saint Louis University, Graduate Education, College of Education and Public Service and Graduate Education, Department of Counseling and Family Therapy, St. Louis, MO 63103-2097. Offers counseling and family therapy (PhD); human development counseling (MA); marriage and family therapy (Certificate); school counseling (MA, MA-R). *Accreditation:* AAMFT/COAMFTE; NCATE. Part-time programs available. *Degree requirements:* For master's, comprehensive exam, thesis (for some programs); for doctorate, comprehensive exam, thesis/dissertation, preliminary oral and written exams. *Entrance requirements:* For master's, GRE General Test, letters of recommendation, resume; for doctorate, GRE General Test, letters of recommendation, resumé, transcripts, goal statement. Additional exam requirements/recommendations for international students: Required—TOEFL (minimum score 550 paper-based). Electronic applications accepted. *Faculty research:* Medical family therapy/collaborative health care multicultural counseling, mental health needs of diverse, minority, or Immigrant/refugee populations, divorce, aging families.

Saint Mary's University of Minnesota, Schools of Graduate and Professional Programs, Graduate School of Business and Technology, Human Development Program, Winona, MN 55987-1399. Offers MA.

Texas Tech University, Graduate School, College of Human Sciences, Department of Human Development and Family Studies, Lubbock, TX 79409-1230. Offers MS, PhD. *Accreditation:* AAMFT/COAMFTE (one or more programs are accredited). Part-time programs available. *Faculty:* 23 full-time (20 women), 5 part-time/adjunct (all women). *Students:* 45 full-time (41 women), 52 part-time (41 women); includes 16 minority (2

Black or African American, non-Hispanic/Latino; 2 American Indian or Alaska Native, non-Hispanic/Latino; 11 Hispanic/Latino; 1 Two or more races, non-Hispanic/Latino), 14 international. Average age 34. 45 applicants, 58% accepted, 11 enrolled. In 2014, 9 master's, 2 doctorates awarded. *Degree requirements:* For master's, thesis; for doctorate, comprehensive exam, thesis/dissertation. *Entrance requirements:* For master's and doctorate, GRE General Test. Additional exam requirements/recommendations for international students: Required—TOEFL (minimum score 550 paper-based; 79 iBT). *Application deadline:* For fall admission, 6/1 priority date for domestic students, 1/15 priority date for international students; for spring admission, 9/1 priority date for domestic students, 6/15 priority date for international students. Applications are processed on a rolling basis. Application fee: $60. Electronic applications accepted. *Expenses:* Tuition, state resident: full-time $6310; part-time $262.92 per credit hour. Tuition, nonresident: full-time $14,998; part-time $624.92 per credit hour. *Required fees:* $2701; $36.50 per credit. $912.50 per semester. Tuition and fees vary according to course load. *Financial support:* In 2014–15, 54 students received support, including 53 fellowships (averaging $4,883 per year), 11 research assistantships (averaging $15,016 per year), 43 teaching assistantships (averaging $9,712 per year). Financial award application deadline: 4/15; financial award applicants required to submit FAFSA. *Faculty research:* Parenting, marital and premarital relationships, adolescent risky behaviors, life span, child development. *Total annual research expenditures:* $222,808. *Unit head:* Dr. Jean Pearson Scott, Chairperson, 806-834-6589, Fax: 806-742-0285, E-mail: jean.scott@ttu.edu. *Application contact:* Monya Castle, Graduate Secretary, 806-742-3000 Ext. 250, Fax: 806-742-0285, E-mail: monya.castle@ttu.edu. Website: http://www.depts.ttu.edu/hdfs

Tufts University, Graduate School of Arts and Sciences, Eliot-Pearson Department of Child Study and Human Development, Medford, MA 02155. Offers child study and human development (MA, PhD); early childhood education (MAT). Part-time programs available. *Faculty:* 13 full-time (10 women), 22 part-time/adjunct (18 women). *Students:* 68 full-time (62 women), 31 part-time (24 women); includes 21 minority (6 Black or African American, non-Hispanic/Latino; 7 Asian, non-Hispanic/Latino; 4 Hispanic/Latino; 4 Two or more races, non-Hispanic/Latino), 11 international. Average age 28. 122 applicants, 58% accepted, 29 enrolled. In 2014, 42 master's, 3 doctorates awarded. *Degree requirements:* For master's, thesis (for some programs); for doctorate, thesis/dissertation. *Entrance requirements:* For master's and doctorate, GRE General Test. Additional exam requirements/recommendations for international students: Required—TOEFL (minimum score 550 paper-based; 80 iBT), IELTS (minimum score 6.5). *Application deadline:* For fall admission, 12/1 priority date for domestic and international students. Applications are processed on a rolling basis. Application fee: $75. Electronic applications accepted. *Expenses:* Tuition: Full-time $45,590; part-time $1161 per credit hour. *Required fees:* $782. Full-time tuition and fees vary according to degree level, program and student level. Part-time tuition and fees vary according to course load. *Financial support:* Fellowships, research assistantships with full and partial tuition reimbursements, teaching assistantships with full and partial tuition reimbursements, Federal Work-Study, scholarships/grants, tuition waivers (partial), and unspecified assistantships available. Support available to part-time students. Financial award application deadline: 5/15; financial award applicants required to submit FAFSA. *Unit head:* Dr. David Henry Feldman, Graduate Program Director. *Application contact:* Office of Graduate Admissions, 617-627-3395, E-mail: gradadmissions@tufts.edu. Website: http://ase.tufts.edu/epcd

The University of Alabama, Graduate School, College of Human Environmental Sciences, Department of Human Development and Family Studies, Tuscaloosa, AL 35487. Offers MSHES. *Faculty:* 9 full-time (8 women), 1 (woman) part-time/adjunct. *Students:* 22 full-time (19 women), 4 part-time (all women); includes 5 minority (3 Black or African American, non-Hispanic/Latino; 1 American Indian or Alaska Native, non-Hispanic/Latino; 1 Asian, non-Hispanic/Latino), 1 international. Average age 26. 25 applicants, 64% accepted, 11 enrolled. In 2014, 9 master's awarded. *Degree requirements:* For master's, comprehensive exam (for some programs), thesis (for some programs). *Entrance requirements:* For master's, GRE General Test or MAT, minimum GPA of 3.0. Additional exam requirements/recommendations for international students: Required—TOEFL. *Application deadline:* For fall admission, 12/15 priority date for domestic and international students. Applications are processed on a rolling basis. Application fee: $50 ($60 for international students). Electronic applications accepted. *Expenses:* Tuition, state resident: full-time $9826. Tuition, nonresident: full-time $24,950. *Financial support:* In 2014–15, 8 students received support, including 3 research assistantships with full tuition reimbursements available (averaging $13,140 per year), 5 teaching assistantships (averaging $13,140 per year); career-related internships or fieldwork, Federal Work-Study, scholarships/grants, health care benefits, and unspecified assistantships also available. Financial award application deadline: 3/15. *Faculty research:* Parent/child relationships, preschool curricula and quality measures for child care programs, family strengths and adolescent behaviors, depression in mothers and infants, word association and word learning in young children, bullying behaviors in children, attachment parenting, medical play therapy, socialization of young children, impact of daily experiences on relationship quality, re-entry of service members into civilian roles. *Total annual research expenditures:* $5,470. *Unit head:* Dr. Carroll M. Tingle, Chair, 205-348-6158, Fax: 205-348-8153, E-mail: ctingle@ches.ua.edu. *Application contact:* Dr. Maria Hernandez-Reif, Professor, 205-348-5894, Fax: 205-348-8153, E-mail: mhernandez-reif@ches.ua.edu. Website: http://www.ches.ua.edu/

The University of Arizona, College of Education, Department of Disability and Psychoeducational Studies, Tucson, AZ 85721. Offers counseling and mental health (MA), including rehabilitation counseling, school counseling; family studies and human development (M Ed); rehabilitation (MA, PhD); school counseling (M Ed); school psychology (PhD, Ed S); special education (MA, Ed D, PhD), including cross-categorical special education (MA), deaf and hard of hearing (MA), learning disabilities (MA), severe and multiple disabilities (MA), special education (Ed D, PhD), visual impairment (MA). *Accreditation:* CORE. Part-time programs available. Terminal master's awarded for partial completion of doctoral program. *Degree requirements:* For master's, comprehensive exam, thesis optional; for doctorate, comprehensive exam, thesis/dissertation. *Entrance requirements:* For master's, statement of purpose; for doctorate, GRE General Test (minimum score 1100) or MAT, 3 letters of recommendation. Additional exam requirements/recommendations for international students: Required—TOEFL (minimum score 550 paper-based; 79 iBT).

The University of British Columbia, Faculty of Education, Department of Educational and Counseling Psychology, and Special Education, Vancouver, BC V6T 1Z1, Canada. Offers counseling psychology (M Ed, MA, PhD); development, learning and culture (PhD); guidance studies (Diploma); human development, learning and culture (M Ed, MA); measurement and evaluation and research methodology (M Ed); measurement, evaluation and research methodology (MA); measurement, evaluation, and research methodology (PhD); school psychology (M Ed, MA, PhD); special education (M Ed, MA, PhD, Diploma). Part-time programs available. *Degree requirements:* For master's, thesis (for some programs); for doctorate, comprehensive exam, thesis/dissertation. *Entrance requirements:* For master's, GRE General Test (counseling psychology MA); for doctorate, GRE General Test. Additional exam requirements/recommendations for

international students: Required—TOEFL. Electronic applications accepted. *Faculty research:* Women, family, social problems, career transition, stress and coping problems.

University of California, Berkeley, Graduate Division, School of Education, Programs in Education, Berkeley, CA 94720-1500. Offers development in mathematics and science (MA); education in mathematics, science, and technology (MA, PhD); human development and education (MA, PhD); special education (PhD); MA/Credential; PhD/Credential; PhD/MA. Terminal master's awarded for partial completion of doctoral program. *Degree requirements:* For master's, exam or thesis; for doctorate, thesis/dissertation, oral qualifying exam. *Entrance requirements:* For master's and doctorate, GRE General Test, minimum GPA of 3.0 during last 2 years of undergraduate course work. Electronic applications accepted. *Faculty research:* Human development, social and moral educational psychology, developmental teacher preparation.

University of California, Davis, Graduate Studies, Graduate Group in Human Development, Davis, CA 95616. Offers PhD. *Degree requirements:* For doctorate, thesis/dissertation. *Entrance requirements:* For doctorate, GRE General Test, GRE Subject Test, minimum GPA of 3.0. Additional exam requirements/recommendations for international students: Required—TOEFL (minimum score 550 paper-based). Electronic applications accepted. *Faculty research:* Life span socioemotional and cognitive development, individual differences, relationship between biological and behavioral development, cross-cultural and cross-generational development.

University of Central Oklahoma, The Jackson College of Graduate Studies, College of Education and Professional Studies, Department of Human Environmental Sciences, Edmond, OK 73034-5209. Offers family and child studies (MS), including family life education, infant/child specialist, marriage and family therapy; nutrition-food management (MS). Part-time programs available. *Degree requirements:* For master's, comprehensive exam (for some programs), thesis (for some programs). *Entrance requirements:* For master's, GRE, essay, physical, CPR and First Aid training. Additional exam requirements/recommendations for international students: Required—TOEFL (minimum score 550 paper-based; 79 iBT), IELTS (minimum score 6.5). Electronic applications accepted.

University of Chicago, Division of the Social Sciences, Department of Comparative Human Development, Chicago, IL 60637. Offers PhD. *Students:* 52 full-time (36 women); includes 12 minority (6 Black or African American, non-Hispanic/Latino; 1 American Indian or Alaska Native, non-Hispanic/Latino; 2 Asian, non-Hispanic/Latino; 2 Hispanic/Latino; 1 Two or more races, non-Hispanic/Latino), 8 international. 51 applicants, 12% accepted, 5 enrolled. In 2014, 5 doctorates awarded. *Degree requirements:* For doctorate, one foreign language, thesis/dissertation, trial research project. *Entrance requirements:* For doctorate, GRE General Test. Additional exam requirements/recommendations for international students: Required—TOEFL (minimum score 104 iBT), IELTS (minimum score 7). *Application deadline:* For fall admission, 12/15 for domestic and international students. Application fee: $90. Electronic applications accepted. *Expenses: Tuition:* Full-time $46,899. *Required fees:* $347. *Financial support:* In 2014–15, 5 students received support, including 5 fellowships with full tuition reimbursements available (averaging $23,000 per year); career-related internships or fieldwork, Federal Work-Study, institutionally sponsored loans, scholarships/grants, and health care benefits also available. Financial award application deadline: 12/15. *Unit head:* Prof. Don Kulick, Chair. *Application contact:* Office of the Dean of Students, 773-702-8415, E-mail: admissions@ssd.uchicago.edu.
Website: http://humdev.uchicago.edu

University of Colorado Denver, School of Education and Human Development, Programs in Educational and School Psychology, Denver, CO 80217. Offers educational psychology (MA), including educational assessment, educational psychology, human development, human learning, partner schools, research and evaluation; school psychology (Ed S). Part-time and evening/weekend programs available. *Students:* 187 full-time (159 women), 64 part-time (49 women); includes 40 minority (2 Black or African American, non-Hispanic/Latino; 1 Asian, non-Hispanic/Latino; 25 Hispanic/Latino; 12 Two or more races, non-Hispanic/Latino), 8 international. Average age 29. 200 applicants, 73% accepted, 112 enrolled. In 2014, 49 master's, 10 other advanced degrees awarded. *Degree requirements:* For master's, comprehensive exam, 9 hours of core courses, embedded within a minimum of 36 to 38 hours of relevant coursework, including an educational psychology practicum, independent study project or thesis (recommended); for Ed S, comprehensive exam, minimum of 75 semester hours (61 hours of coursework, 6 of 500-hour practicum in field, and 8 of 1200-hour internship); PRAXIS II. *Entrance requirements:* For master's, GRE if undergraduate GPA below 2.75, resume, three letters of recommendation, transcripts; for Ed S, GRE, resume, letters of recommendation, transcripts. Additional exam requirements/recommendations for international students: Required—TOEFL (minimum score 537 paper-based; 75 iBT); Recommended—IELTS (minimum score 6.5). *Application deadline:* For fall admission, 4/15 for domestic students, 4/1 for international students; for spring admission, 9/15 for domestic students, 9/1 for international students. Application fee: $50 ($75 for international students). Electronic applications accepted. *Expenses:* Expenses: Contact institution. *Financial support:* In 2014–15, 21 students received support. Research assistantships, Federal Work-Study, institutionally sponsored loans, scholarships/grants, and traineeships available. Financial award application deadline: 4/1; financial award applicants required to submit FAFSA. *Faculty research:* Crisis response and intervention, school violence prevention, immigrant experience, educational environments for English language learners, culturally competent assessment and intervention, child and youth suicide. *Unit head:* Phil Strain, Professor of Educational Psychology, 303-315-4935, E-mail: phil.strain@ucdenver.edu. *Application contact:* Jason Clark, Director of Recruitment and Retention, 303-315-0183, E-mail: jason.clark@ucdenver.edu.
Website: http://www.ucdenver.edu/academics/colleges/SchoolOfEducation/Academics/MASTERS/EPSY/Pages/default.aspx

University of Connecticut, Graduate School, College of Liberal Arts and Sciences, Department of Human Development and Family Studies, Storrs, CT 06269. Offers culture, health and human development (Graduate Certificate); human development and family studies (MA, PhD). *Accreditation:* AAMFT/COAMFTE (one or more programs are accredited). Terminal master's awarded for partial completion of doctoral program. *Degree requirements:* For master's, comprehensive exam; for doctorate, thesis/dissertation. *Entrance requirements:* For doctorate, GRE General Test. Additional exam requirements/recommendations for international students: Required—TOEFL (minimum score 550 paper-based). Electronic applications accepted.

University of Dayton, Department of Counselor Education and Human Services, Dayton, OH 45469. Offers clinical mental health counseling (MS Ed); college student personnel (MS Ed); higher education administration (MS Ed); human services (MS Ed); school counseling (MS Ed); school psychology (MS Ed, Ed S). *Accreditation:* ACA; NCATE. Part-time and evening/weekend programs available. *Faculty:* 11 full-time (7 women), 34 part-time/adjunct (24 women). *Students:* 199 full-time (161 women), 113 part-time (95 women); includes 58 minority (49 Black or African American, non-Hispanic/Latino; 1 Asian, non-Hispanic/Latino; 7 Hispanic/Latino; 1 Two or more races, non-Hispanic/Latino), 8 international. Average age 31. 295 applicants, 47% accepted, 103 enrolled. In 2014, 146 master's, 8 Ed Ss awarded. *Degree requirements:* For master's, comprehensive exam (for some programs), thesis (for some programs), exit exam. *Entrance requirements:* For master's, MAT or GRE (if GPA less than 2.75), interview, writing sample. Additional exam requirements/recommendations for international students: Required—TOEFL (minimum score 550 paper-based; 80 iBT). *Application deadline:* For fall admission, 4/10 for domestic students, 4/10 priority date for international students; for winter admission, 9/10 for domestic students, 7/1 for international students; for spring admission, 9/10 for domestic students, 9/10 priority date for international students. Application fee: $0 ($50 for international students). Electronic applications accepted. *Expenses: Tuition:* Full-time $10,176; part-time $848 per credit. *Required fees:* $25; $25 per course. Part-time tuition and fees vary according to course level, course load, degree level and program. *Financial support:* In 2014–15, 10 research assistantships with full tuition reimbursements (averaging $8,720 per year) were awarded; career-related internships or fieldwork, institutionally sponsored loans, health care benefits, and unspecified assistantships also available. Financial award application deadline: 3/1; financial award applicants required to submit FAFSA. *Faculty research:* Mindfulness, forgiveness in relationships, positive psychology in couples counseling, traumatic brain injury responses, college student development. *Unit head:* Dr. Molly Schaller, Chairperson, 937-229-3644, Fax: 937-229-1055, E-mail: mschaller1@udayton.edu. *Application contact:* Kathleen Brown, Administrative Assistant, 937-229-3644, Fax: 937-229-1055, E-mail: kbrown1@udayton.edu.
Website: https://www.udayton.edu/education/departments_and_programs/edc/

University of Delaware, College of Education and Human Development, Department of Human Development and Family Studies, Newark, DE 19716. Offers MS, PhD. Part-time programs available. Terminal master's awarded for partial completion of doctoral program. *Degree requirements:* For master's, thesis or alternative; for doctorate, comprehensive exam, thesis/dissertation. *Entrance requirements:* For master's and doctorate, GRE General Test, 3 letters of recommendation. Additional exam requirements/recommendations for international students: Required—TOEFL. Electronic applications accepted. *Faculty research:* Early childhood inclusive education, relationships, family risk and resilience, disability issues, program development and evaluation.

University of Guelph, Graduate Studies, College of Social and Applied Human Sciences, Department of Family Relations and Applied Nutrition, Guelph, ON N1G 2W1, Canada. Offers applied nutrition (MAN); family relations and human development (M Sc, PhD), including applied human nutrition, couple and family therapy (M Sc), family relations and human development. *Accreditation:* AAMFT/COAMFTE (one or more programs are accredited). Part-time programs available. *Degree requirements:* For master's, thesis (for some programs); for doctorate, comprehensive exam, thesis/dissertation. *Entrance requirements:* For master's, minimum B+ average; for doctorate, master's degree in family relations and human development or related field with a minimum B+ average or master's degree in applied human nutrition. Additional exam requirements/recommendations for international students: Required—TOEFL (minimum score 600 paper-based). Electronic applications accepted. *Faculty research:* Child and adolescent development, social gerontology, family roles and relations, couple and family therapy, applied human nutrition.

University of Illinois at Chicago, Graduate College, College of Applied Health Sciences, Department of Disability and Human Development, Chicago, IL 60607-7128. Offers disability and human development (MS). *Accreditation:* AOTA. Part-time programs available. *Faculty:* 10 full-time (7 women), 2 part-time/adjunct (1 woman). *Students:* 36 full-time (28 women), 21 part-time (18 women); includes 11 minority (1 Black or African American, non-Hispanic/Latino; 2 Asian, non-Hispanic/Latino; 5 Hispanic/Latino; 3 Two or more races, non-Hispanic/Latino), 11 international. Average age 34. 34 applicants, 65% accepted, 12 enrolled. In 2014, 6 master's, 2 doctorates awarded. *Degree requirements:* For master's, thesis optional; for doctorate, thesis/dissertation. *Entrance requirements:* For master's and doctorate, GRE General Test. Additional exam requirements/recommendations for international students: Required—TOEFL. *Application deadline:* For fall admission, 1/1 for domestic and international students; for spring admission, 10/1 for domestic students, 7/15 for international students. Applications are processed on a rolling basis. Application fee: $60. Electronic applications accepted. *Expenses:* Tuition, state resident: full-time $11,254; part-time $468 per credit hour. Tuition, nonresident: full-time $23,252; part-time $968 per credit hour. *Required fees:* $1217 per term. Part-time tuition and fees vary according to course load, degree level and program. *Financial support:* In 2014–15, 2 fellowships with full tuition reimbursements were awarded; research assistantships with full tuition reimbursements, teaching assistantships with full tuition reimbursements, career-related internships or fieldwork, Federal Work-Study, institutionally sponsored loans, traineeships, tuition waivers (full), and unspecified assistantships also available. Financial award application deadline: 3/1; financial award applicants required to submit FAFSA. *Faculty research:* Emerging trends in disability, demography and financial structure of disability services, aging and disability, empowerment of people with disabilities, health promotion in disabilities. *Total annual research expenditures:* $5.7 million. *Unit head:* Prof. Tamar Heller, Department Head, 312-996-1647, Fax: 312-413-1630, E-mail: theller@uic.edu. *Application contact:* Dr. Maitha Abogado, Support Staff, 312-413-1466, Fax: 312-413-1630, E-mail: maitha@uic.edu.
Website: http://www.ahs.uic.edu/dhd/

University of Illinois at Springfield, Graduate Programs, College of Education and Human Services, Program in Human Development Counseling, Springfield, IL 62703-5407. Offers MA. *Accreditation:* ACA. Part-time and evening/weekend programs available. *Faculty:* 6 full-time (3 women), 1 (woman) part-time/adjunct. *Students:* 49 full-time (43 women), 58 part-time (46 women); includes 18 minority (11 Black or African American, non-Hispanic/Latino; 2 Hispanic/Latino; 5 Two or more races, non-Hispanic/Latino). Average age 31. 57 applicants, 26% accepted, 15 enrolled. In 2014, 28 master's awarded. *Degree requirements:* For master's, project, thesis, or comprehensive exam. *Entrance requirements:* For master's, minimum undergraduate GPA of 3.0 in last 60 hours of coursework, personal references, interview. Additional exam requirements/recommendations for international students: Required—TOEFL (minimum score 500 paper-based; 61 iBT). Application fee: $60 ($75 for international students). Electronic applications accepted. *Expenses:* Tuition, state resident: full-time $7662; part-time $319.25 per credit hour. Tuition, nonresident: full-time $15,966; part-time $665.25 per credit hour. *Financial support:* In 2014–15, fellowships with full tuition reimbursements (averaging $9,900 per year), research assistantships with full tuition reimbursements (averaging $9,600 per year), teaching assistantships with full tuition reimbursements (averaging $9,600 per year) were awarded; career-related internships or fieldwork, Federal Work-Study, scholarships/grants, health care benefits, and unspecified assistantships also available. Support available to part-time students. Financial award application deadline: 11/15; financial award applicants required to submit FAFSA. *Unit head:* Dr. William Abler, Program Administrator, 217-206-7567, Fax: 217-206-6775, E-mail: abler.bill@uis.edu. *Application contact:* Dr. Lynn Pardie, Office of Graduate Studies, 800-252-8533, Fax: 217-206-7623, E-mail: lpard1@uis.edu.
Website: http://www.uis.edu/hdc

University of Illinois at Urbana–Champaign, Graduate College, College of Agricultural, Consumer and Environmental Sciences, Department of Human and Community Development, Champaign, IL 61820. Offers MS, PhD. *Students:* 26 (20

women). Application fee: $70 ($90 for international students). *Unit head:* Susan Koerner, Head, 217-333-3790, Fax: 217-244-7877, E-mail: skoerner@illinois.edu. *Application contact:* Maria Rund, Secretary to the Head, 217-244-9544, Fax: 217-244-7877, E-mail: mrund@illinois.edu.
Website: http://www.hcd.illinois.edu/

University of Maine, Graduate School, College of Education and Human Development, Department of Educational Leadership, Higher Education, and Human Development, Orono, ME 04469. Offers educational leadership (M Ed, Ed D, CAS); higher education (MA, PhD, CAS); human development (MS). Part-time programs available. *Students:* 51 full-time (35 women), 72 part-time (43 women); includes 5 minority (2 Black or African American, non-Hispanic/Latino; 1 American Indian or Alaska Native, non-Hispanic/Latino; 2 Hispanic/Latino), 3 international. Average age 37. 53 applicants, 74% accepted, 28 enrolled. In 2014, 23 master's, 3 doctorates, 12 other advanced degrees awarded. *Degree requirements:* For master's, thesis (for some programs); for doctorate, comprehensive exam, thesis/dissertation. *Entrance requirements:* For master's, GRE General Test, MAT; for doctorate, GRE. Additional exam requirements/recommendations for international students: Required—TOEFL. *Application deadline:* For fall admission, 2/1 priority date for domestic students. Applications are processed on a rolling basis. Application fee: $65. Electronic applications accepted. *Expenses:* Tuition, state resident: part-time $658 per credit hour. Tuition, nonresident: part-time $1550 per credit hour. *Financial support:* In 2014–15, 27 students received support, including 4 teaching assistantships (averaging $14,600 per year); career-related internships or fieldwork, Federal Work-Study, institutionally sponsored loans, tuition waivers (full and partial), and unspecified assistantships also available. Financial award application deadline: 3/1. *Faculty research:* Leadership formation, school organization, collective efficacy and collaborative climate of high schools, change process in high schools, principalship; equity policy; gender and education; doctoral student development, retention, and attrition; faculty development and socialization; sexuality education and curriculum development; family/domestic violence; friendship/kin relationships; early childhood education; support for families with members with disabilities. *Unit head:* Dr. Susan Gardner, Coordinator, 207-581-3122, Fax: 207-581-3120. *Application contact:* Scott G. Delcourt, Senior Associate Dean of the Graduate School, 207-581-3291, Fax: 207-581-3232, E-mail: graduate@maine.edu.
Website: http://www.umaine.edu/edhd/

University of Maryland, College Park, Academic Affairs, College of Education, Department of Human Development and Quantitative Methodology, College Park, MD 20742. Offers MA, Ed D, PhD. *Entrance requirements:* Additional exam requirements/recommendations for international students: Required—TOEFL.

University of Missouri, Office of Research and Graduate Studies, College of Human Environmental Sciences, Department of Human Development and Family Studies, Columbia, MO 65211. Offers MA, MS, PhD. *Faculty:* 12 full-time (6 women). *Students:* 41 full-time (32 women), 36 part-time (34 women); includes 18 minority (11 Black or African American, non-Hispanic/Latino; 4 Hispanic/Latino; 3 Two or more races, non-Hispanic/Latino), 7 international. Average age 29. 51 applicants, 61% accepted, 24 enrolled. In 2014, 14 master's, 6 doctorates awarded. *Entrance requirements:* For master's, GRE General Test, minimum GPA of 3.0. Additional exam requirements/recommendations for international students: Required—TOEFL (minimum score 550 paper-based; 80 iBT). *Application deadline:* For fall admission, 12/15 priority date for domestic and international students; for winter admission, 11/15 priority date for domestic and international students. Applications are processed on a rolling basis. Application fee: $55 ($75 for international students). Electronic applications accepted. *Financial support:* Fellowships, research assistantships, teaching assistantships, institutionally sponsored loans, scholarships/grants, health care benefits, and unspecified assistantships available. Support available to part-time students. *Faculty research:* Adolescent sexual risk taking, adolescent pregnancy prevention, marital structure and process, evaluation of research methodology, remarriage and stepfamilies, family obligations, family structure stereotyping, families and health, parent-child and teacher-child interaction, early head start evaluation, gender issues. *Unit head:* Dr. Lawrence Ganong, Department Co-Chair, 573-882-6852, E-mail: ganongl@missouri.edu. *Application contact:* Dr. Tyler Jamison, Director of Graduate Studies, 573-882-1301, E-mail: jamisontb@missouri.edu.
Website: http://hdfs.missouri.edu/

University of Nebraska–Lincoln, Graduate College, College of Education and Human Sciences, Department of Child, Youth and Family Studies, Lincoln, NE 68588. Offers child development/early childhood education (MS, PhD); child, youth and family studies (MS); family and consumer sciences education (MS, PhD); family financial planning (MS); family science (MS, PhD); gerontology (PhD); human sciences (PhD), including child, youth and family studies, gerontology, medical family therapy; marriage and family therapy (MS); medical family therapy (PhD); youth development (MS). *Accreditation:* AAMFT/COAMFTE (one or more programs are accredited). Postbaccalaureate distance learning degree programs offered. *Degree requirements:* For master's, thesis optional. *Entrance requirements:* For master's, GRE. Additional exam requirements/recommendations for international students: Required—TOEFL (minimum score 550 paper-based). Electronic applications accepted. *Faculty research:* Marriage and family therapy, child development/early childhood education, family financial management.

University of Nebraska–Lincoln, Graduate College, College of Education and Human Sciences, Department of Special Education and Communication Disorders, Lincoln, NE 68588. Offers audiology research (PhD); clinical audiology (Au D); educational studies (PhD); human sciences (PhD), including communication disorders; special education (M Ed, MA, Ed S), including special education (M Ed, MA), special education and communication disorders (Ed S); speech-language pathology and audiology (MS, Au D), including audiology and hearing science (Au D), speech-language pathology (Au D), speech-language pathology and audiology (MS). *Accreditation:* ASHA (one or more programs are accredited); NCATE. *Degree requirements:* For master's, thesis optional. *Entrance requirements:* For master's, GRE General Test. Additional exam requirements/recommendations for international students: Required—TOEFL. Electronic applications accepted. *Faculty research:* Curriculum-based assessment, paraprofessional and parent training, behavior management for special needs individuals, augmentative communication, speech/language disorders.

University of Nebraska–Lincoln, Graduate College, College of Education and Human Sciences, Department of Textiles, Clothing and Design, Lincoln, NE 68588. Offers human sciences (PhD), including textiles, clothing and design (MS, PhD); merchandising (MS); textile history/quilt studies (MA); textile science (MS); textile-apparel (MA); textiles, clothing and design (MA, MS), including textiles, clothing and design (MS, PhD). Part-time programs available. Postbaccalaureate distance learning degree programs offered (minimal on-campus study). *Degree requirements:* For master's, thesis optional. *Entrance requirements:* For master's, GRE General Test. Additional exam requirements/recommendations for international students: Required—TOEFL (minimum score 550 paper-based). Electronic applications accepted. *Faculty research:* Merchandising, textile science, fiber arts, textile history, quilt studies.

University of Nevada, Reno, Graduate School, College of Education, Department of Human Development and Family Studies, Reno, NV 89557. Offers MS. *Degree requirements:* For master's, thesis optional. *Entrance requirements:* For master's, GRE General Test, minimum GPA of 2.75. Additional exam requirements/recommendations for international students: Required—TOEFL (minimum score 500 paper-based; 61 iBT), IELTS (minimum score 6). Electronic applications accepted. *Faculty research:* Early childhood/adolescent development, family studies.

University of New Mexico, Graduate School, College of Education, Program in Family Studies, Albuquerque, NM 87131-2039. Offers family life education (MA); family relations (MA); family studies (PhD); human development in families (MA). Part-time and evening/weekend programs available. *Faculty:* 4 full-time (1 woman). *Students:* 13 full-time (11 women), 17 part-time (14 women); includes 22 minority (3 Black or African American, non-Hispanic/Latino; 3 American Indian or Alaska Native, non-Hispanic/Latino; 1 Asian, non-Hispanic/Latino; 15 Hispanic/Latino), 1 international. Average age 36. 9 applicants, 56% accepted, 5 enrolled. In 2014, 2 master's, 1 doctorate awarded. *Degree requirements:* For master's, comprehensive exam, thesis (for some programs); for doctorate, comprehensive exam, thesis/dissertation. *Entrance requirements:* For master's, written paper, 3 letters of recommendation, personal statement; for doctorate, GRE General Test, written paper, 3 letters of recommendation, personal statement, interview. Additional exam requirements/recommendations for international students: Required—TOEFL (minimum score 550 paper-based). *Application deadline:* For fall admission, 3/15 priority date for domestic and international students; for spring admission, 10/15 priority date for domestic and international students. Applications are processed on a rolling basis. Application fee: $50. Electronic applications accepted. *Financial support:* In 2014–15, 20 students received support, including 1 fellowship (averaging $7,200 per year), 3 teaching assistantships with full and partial tuition reimbursements available (averaging $3,698 per year); unspecified assistantships also available. Financial award application deadline: 3/1; financial award applicants required to submit FAFSA. *Faculty research:* Home, community and school relations; multicultural issues; parent-child interactions; grandparents as primary caretakers for grandchildren; fathering; early childhood evaluation; early childhood development; globalization and indigenous cultures. *Unit head:* Dr. Ziarat Hossain, Program Coordinator, 505-277-4162, Fax: 505-277-8361, E-mail: zhossain@unm.edu. *Application contact:* Cynthia Salas, Department Administrator, 505-277-4535, Fax: 505-277-8361, E-mail: divbse@unm.edu.
Website: http://coe.unm.edu/departments/ifce/family-studies.html

The University of North Carolina at Greensboro, Graduate School, School of Health and Human Sciences, Department of Human Development and Family Studies, Greensboro, NC 27412-5001. Offers M Ed, MS, PhD. *Degree requirements:* For master's, one foreign language; for doctorate, one foreign language, thesis/dissertation. *Entrance requirements:* For master's and doctorate, GRE General Test. Additional exam requirements/recommendations for international students: Required—TOEFL. Electronic applications accepted. *Expenses:* Contact institution. *Faculty research:* Adolescent mothers, multi-handicapped, older adults.

University of North Texas, Robert B. Toulouse School of Graduate Studies, Denton, TX 76203-5459. Offers accounting (MS); applied anthropology (MA, MS); applied behavior analysis (Certificate); applied geography (MA); applied technology and performance improvement (M Ed, MS); art education (MA); art history (MA); art museum education (Certificate); arts leadership (Certificate); audiology (Au D); behavior analysis (MS); behavioral science (PhD); biochemistry and molecular biology (MS); biology (MA, MS); biomedical engineering (MS); business analysis (MS); chemistry (MS); clinical health psychology (PhD); communication studies (MA, MS); computer engineering (MS); computer science (MS); counseling (M Ed, MS), including clinical mental health counseling (MS), college and university counseling, elementary school counseling, secondary school counseling; creative writing (MA); criminal justice (MS); curriculum and instruction (M Ed); decision sciences (MBA); design (MA, MFA), including fashion design (MFA), innovation studies, interior design (MFA); early childhood studies (MS); economics (MS); educational leadership (M Ed, Ed D); educational psychology (MS, PhD), including family studies (MS), gifted and talented (MS), human development (MS), learning and cognition (MS), research, measurement and evaluation (MS); electrical engineering (MS); emergency management (MPA); engineering technology (MS); English (MA); English as a second language (MA); environmental science (MS); finance (MBA, MS); financial management (MPA); French (MA); health services management (MBA); higher education (M Ed, Ed D); history (MA, MS); hospitality management (MS); human resources management (MPA); information science (MS); information systems (PhD); information technologies (MBA); interdisciplinary studies (MA, MS); international studies (MA); international sustainable tourism (MS); jazz studies (MM); journalism (MA, MJ, Graduate Certificate), including interactive and virtual digital communication (Graduate Certificate), narrative journalism (Graduate Certificate), public relations (Graduate Certificate); kinesiology (MS); linguistics (MA); local government management (MPA); logistics (PhD); logistics and supply chain management (MBA); long-term care, senior housing, and aging services (MA); management (PhD); marketing (MBA); mathematics (MA, MS); mechanical and energy engineering (MS, PhD); music (MA), including ethnomusicology, music theory, musicology, performance; music composition (PhD); music education (MM Ed, PhD); nonprofit management (MPA); operations and supply chain management (MBA); performance (MM, DMA); philosophy (MA); political science (MA); professional and technical communication (MA); radio, television and film (MA, MFA); rehabilitation counseling (Certificate); sociology (MA); Spanish (MA); special education (M Ed); speech-language pathology (MA); strategic management (MBA); studio art (MFA); teaching (M Ed); MBA/MS. Part-time and evening/weekend programs available. Postbaccalaureate distance learning degree programs offered. *Faculty:* 651 full-time (215 women), 233 part-time/adjunct (139 women). *Students:* 3,040 full-time (1,598 women), 3,401 part-time (2,097 women); includes 1,740 minority (533 Black or African American, non-Hispanic/Latino; 15 American Indian or Alaska Native, non-Hispanic/Latino; 286 Asian, non-Hispanic/Latino; 746 Hispanic/Latino; 3 Native Hawaiian or other Pacific Islander, non-Hispanic/Latino; 157 Two or more races, non-Hispanic/Latino), 1,145 international. Terminal master's awarded for partial completion of doctoral program. *Degree requirements:* For master's, variable foreign language requirement, comprehensive exam (for some programs), thesis (for some programs); for doctorate, variable foreign language requirement, comprehensive exam (for some programs), thesis/dissertation; for other advanced degree, variable foreign language requirement, comprehensive exam (for some programs). *Entrance requirements:* For master's and doctorate, GRE, GMAT. Additional exam requirements/recommendations for international students: Required—TOEFL (minimum score 550 paper-based; 79 iBT). *Application deadline:* For fall admission, 7/15 for domestic students, 3/15 for international students; for spring admission, 11/15 for domestic students, 9/15 for international students; for summer admission, 5/1 for domestic students. Applications are processed on a rolling basis. Application fee: $60. Electronic applications accepted. *Expenses:* Tuition, state resident: full-time $5450; part-time $3633 per year. Tuition, nonresident: full-time $11,966; part-time $7977 per year. *Required fees:* $1301; $398 per credit hour. $685 per semester. Tuition and fees vary according to program and reciprocity agreements. *Financial support:* Fellowships with partial tuition reimbursements, research assistantships with partial tuition reimbursements, teaching assistantships, career-related internships or fieldwork, Federal Work-Study, institutionally sponsored loans, scholarships/grants, health care benefits, and library assistantships available. Support available to part-time students. Financial award applicants required to submit FAFSA. *Unit head:* Mark Wardell, Dean,

940-565-2383, E-mail: mark.wardell@unt.edu. *Application contact:* Toulouse School of Graduate Studies, 940-565-2383, Fax: 940-565-2141, E-mail: gradsch@unt.edu.
Website: http://tsgs.unt.edu/

University of Pennsylvania, Graduate School of Education, Division of Applied Psychology and Human Development, Program in Interdisciplinary Studies in Human Development, Philadelphia, PA 19104. Offers MS Ed, PhD. Part-time programs available. *Students:* 40 full-time (34 women), 7 part-time (6 women); includes 7 minority (4 Black or African American, non-Hispanic/Latino; 2 Asian, non-Hispanic/Latino; 1 Hispanic/Latino), 33 international. 131 applicants, 47% accepted, 25 enrolled. In 2014, 16 master's, 2 doctorates awarded. Terminal master's awarded for partial completion of doctoral program. *Degree requirements:* For master's, exam; for doctorate, thesis/dissertation, exam. *Entrance requirements:* For master's, GRE General Test; for doctorate, GRE General Test, GRE Subject Test. *Application deadline:* For fall admission, 12/15 priority date for domestic students. Applications are processed on a rolling basis. Application fee: $70. Electronic applications accepted. *Expenses:* Expenses: Contact institution. *Financial support:* Fellowships, research assistantships, institutionally sponsored loans, scholarships/grants, traineeships, health care benefits, and unspecified assistantships available. *Faculty research:* Child development, risk and resilience among vulnerable youth in high-risk environments. *Unit head:* Dr. Andrew Porter, Dean, 215-898-7014. *Application contact:* 215-898-6415, Fax: 215-746-6884, E-mail: admissions@gse.upenn.edu.
Website: http://www.gse.upenn.edu/aphd/ishd/msed

University of Rochester, Margaret Warner Graduate School of Education and Human Development, Doctoral Programs in Education, Rochester, NY 14627. Offers counseling (Ed D); educational administration (Ed D); educational policy and theory (PhD); higher education (PhD); human development in educational context (PhD); teaching, curriculum, and change (PhD). *Expenses: Tuition:* Full-time $46,150; part-time $1442 per credit hour. *Required fees:* $504.

University of Rochester, Margaret Warner Graduate School of Education and Human Development, Master's Program in Human Development, Rochester, NY 14627. Offers MS. *Expenses: Tuition:* Full-time $46,150; part-time $1442 per credit hour. *Required fees:* $504.

University of St. Thomas, Graduate Studies, School of Education, Department of Organization Learning and Development, St. Paul, MN 55105-1096. Offers human resources and change leadership (MA); learning, performance and technology (MA); organization development (Ed D). Part-time and evening/weekend programs available. Postbaccalaureate distance learning degree programs offered (minimal on-campus study). *Degree requirements:* For master's, practicum; for doctorate, comprehensive exam, thesis/dissertation. *Entrance requirements:* For master's, minimum GPA of 3.0, 2 letters of reference, personal statement, 2-5 years of organization experience; for doctorate, minimum GPA of 3.5, interview, 5-7 years of organization development or leadership experience. Additional exam requirements/recommendations for international students: Required—TOEFL (minimum score 550 paper-based). Electronic applications accepted. *Expenses:* Contact institution. *Faculty research:* Workplace conflict, physician leaders, virtual teams, technology use in schools/workplace, developing masterful practitioners.

University of South Africa, College of Human Sciences, Pretoria, South Africa. Offers adult education (M Ed); African languages (MA, PhD); African politics (MA, PhD); Afrikaans (MA, PhD); ancient history (MA, PhD); ancient Near Eastern studies (MA, PhD); anthropology (MA, PhD); applied linguistics (MA); Arabic (MA, PhD); archaeology (MA); art history (MA); Biblical archaeology (MA); Biblical studies (M Th, D Th, PhD); Christian spirituality (M Th, D Th); church history (M Th, D Th); classical studies (MA, PhD); clinical psychology (MA); communication (MA, PhD); comparative education (M Ed, Ed D); consulting psychology (D Admin, D Com, PhD); curriculum studies (M Ed, Ed D); development studies (M Admin, MA, D Admin, PhD); didactics (M Ed, Ed D); education (M Tech); education management (M Ed, Ed D); educational psychology (M Ed); English (MA); environmental education (M Ed); French (MA, PhD); German (MA, PhD); Greek (MA); guidance and counseling (M Ed); health studies (MA, PhD), including health sciences education (MA), health services management (MA), medical and surgical nursing science (critical care general) (MA), midwifery and neonatal nursing science (MA), trauma and emergency care (MA); history (MA, PhD); history of education (Ed D); inclusive education (M Ed, Ed D); information and communications technology policy and regulation (MA); information science (MA, MIS, PhD); international politics (MA, PhD); Islamic studies (MA, PhD); Italian (MA, PhD); Judaica (MA, PhD); linguistics (MA, PhD); mathematical education (M Ed); mathematics education (MA); missiology (M Th, D Th); modern Hebrew (MA, PhD); musicology (MA, MMus, D Mus, PhD); natural science education (M Ed); New Testament (M Th, D Th); Old Testament (D Th); pastoral therapy (M Th, D Th); philosophy (MA); philosophy of education (M Ed, Ed D); politics (MA, PhD); Portuguese (MA, PhD); practical theology (M Th, D Th); psychology (MA, MS, PhD); psychology of education (M Ed, Ed D); public health (MA); religious studies (MA, D Th, PhD); Romance languages (MA); Russian (MA, PhD); Semitic languages (MA, PhD); social behavior studies in HIV/AIDS (MA); social science (mental health) (MA); social science in development studies (MA); social science in psychology (MA); social science in social work (MA); social science in sociology (MA); social work (MSW, DSW, PhD); socio-education (M Ed, Ed D); sociolinguistics (MA); sociology (MA, PhD); Spanish (MA, PhD); systematic theology (M Th, D Th); TESOL (teaching English to speakers of other languages) (MA); theological ethics (M Th, D Th); theory of literature (MA, PhD); urban ministries (D Th); urban ministry (M Th).

The University of South Dakota, Graduate School, School of Education, Division of Counseling and Psychology in Education, Vermillion, SD 57069-2390. Offers counseling (MA, PhD, Ed S); human development and educational psychology (MA, PhD, Ed S); school psychology (PhD, Ed S). *Accreditation:* ACA (one or more programs are accredited); NCATE. Part-time programs available. *Degree requirements:* For master's and Ed S, comprehensive exam, thesis or alternative; for doctorate, comprehensive exam, thesis/dissertation. *Entrance requirements:* For master's and doctorate, GRE General Test, minimum GPA of 3.0. Additional exam requirements/recommendations for international students: Required—TOEFL (minimum score 550 paper-based; 79 iBT). Electronic applications accepted.

The University of Texas at Austin, Graduate School, College of Education, Department of Educational Psychology, Austin, TX 78712-1111. Offers academic educational psychology (M Ed, MA); counseling psychology (PhD); counselor education (M Ed); human development, culture and learning sciences (PhD); program evaluation (MA); quantitative methods (M Ed, MA, PhD); school psychology (MA, PhD). *Accreditation:* APA (one or more programs are accredited). *Degree requirements:* For master's, thesis optional; for doctorate, thesis/dissertation. *Entrance requirements:* For master's and doctorate, GRE General Test, 3 letters of recommendation. Additional exam requirements/recommendations for international students: Required—TOEFL.

The University of Texas at Austin, Graduate School, College of Fine Arts, Sarah and Ernest Butler School of Music, Austin, TX 78712-1111. Offers band and wind conducting (M Music, DMA); brass/woodwind/percussion (MM, DMA); chamber music (MM); choral conducting (MM, DMA); collaborative piano (MM, DMA); composition (MM, DMA), including composition, jazz, jazz (DMA); ethnomusicology (MM, PhD); literature and pedagogy (MM); music and human learning (MM, PhD); music and human learning (DMA), including jazz (MM, DMA), piano pedagogy; musicology (MM, PhD); opera performance (MM, DMA); orchestral conducting (MM, DMA); organ (MM), including sacred music; organ performance (MM, DMA); performance (MM), including jazz (MM, DMA); performance (DMA), including jazz (MM, DMA); piano (DMA), including jazz (MM, DMA); piano literature and pedagogy (MM); piano performance (MM, DMA); string performance (MM, DMA); theory (MM, PhD); vocal performance (MM, DMA); voice (DMA), including opera; voice performance pedagogy (DMA); woodwind, brass, percussion performance (MM). *Accreditation:* NASM. Part-time programs available. *Degree requirements:* For master's, one foreign language, comprehensive exam, thesis (for some programs), recital (performance or composition majors); for doctorate, one foreign language, comprehensive exam, thesis/dissertation (for some programs), recital (for performance or composition majors). *Entrance requirements:* For master's and doctorate, GRE General Test (except for performance or composition majors), audition (performance majors). Electronic applications accepted.

University of Utah, Graduate School, College of Social and Behavioral Science, Department of Family and Consumer Studies, Salt Lake City, UT 84112-0080. Offers human development and social policy (MS). Part-time programs available. *Faculty:* 15 full-time (7 women), 2 part-time/adjunct (1 woman). *Students:* 11 full-time (10 women), 2 part-time (both women); includes 3 minority (all Asian, non-Hispanic/Latino). Average age 32. 12 applicants, 67% accepted, 7 enrolled. In 2014, 5 master's awarded. *Degree requirements:* For master's, comprehensive exam (for some programs), thesis (for some programs), thesis or project. *Entrance requirements:* For master's, GRE General Test, minimum undergraduate GPA of 3.0, courses in research methods and statistics. Additional exam requirements/recommendations for international students: Required—TOEFL (minimum score 550 paper-based). *Application deadline:* For fall admission, 2/1 priority date for domestic and international students. Applications are processed on a rolling basis. Application fee: $55 ($65 for international students). Electronic applications accepted. *Financial support:* In 2014–15, 4 students received support, including 4 teaching assistantships with full tuition reimbursements available (averaging $13,500 per year). Financial award application deadline: 2/1. *Faculty research:* Social, physical, educational and economic contexts of individuals, families and communities. *Unit head:* Prof. Robert Nathan Mayer, PhD, Chair, 801-581-7712, Fax: 801-581-5156, E-mail: robert.mayer@fcs.utah.edu. *Application contact:* Prof. Sonia Salari, PhD, Graduate Director, 801-581-5725, E-mail: sonia.salari@fcs.utah.edu.
Website: http://fcs.utah.edu/

University of Victoria, Faculty of Graduate Studies, Faculty of Education, Department of Educational Psychology and Leadership Studies, Victoria, BC V8W 2Y2, Canada. Offers aboriginal communities counseling (M Ed); counseling (M Ed, MA); educational psychology (M Ed, MA, PhD), including counseling psychology (M Ed, MA), leadership studies (PhD), learning and development (MA, PhD), measurement and evaluation, special education (M Ed, MA); leadership studies (M Ed, MA). Part-time programs available. *Degree requirements:* For master's, thesis (for some programs), comprehensive exam (M Ed); for doctorate, comprehensive exam, thesis/dissertation, candidacy exam. *Entrance requirements:* For master's, 2 years of work experience in a relevant field; for doctorate, GRE, 2 years of work experience in a relevant field, minimum B average. Additional exam requirements/recommendations for international students: Required—TOEFL (minimum score 575 paper-based), IELTS (minimum score 7). *Faculty research:* Learning and development (child, adolescent and adult), special education and exceptional children.

University of Victoria, Faculty of Graduate Studies, Faculty of Human and Social Development, Studies in Policy and Practice Program, Victoria, BC V8W 2Y2, Canada. Offers MA. Part-time programs available. *Degree requirements:* For master's, thesis. *Entrance requirements:* For master's, resume. Additional exam requirements/recommendations for international students: Required—TOEFL (minimum score 575 paper-based), IELTS (minimum score 7). Electronic applications accepted. *Faculty research:* Women's issues, public policy formation and implementation, health promotion and education, children, youth and families.

University of Washington, Graduate School, College of Education, Program in Educational Psychology, Seattle, WA 98195. Offers educational psychology (PhD); human development and cognition (M Ed); learning sciences (M Ed, PhD); measurement, statistics and research design (M Ed); school psychology (M Ed). *Accreditation:* APA. *Degree requirements:* For master's, thesis optional; for doctorate, thesis/dissertation. *Entrance requirements:* For master's and doctorate, GRE General Test, minimum GPA of 3.0. Additional exam requirements/recommendations for international students: Required—TOEFL.

University of Wisconsin–Madison, Graduate School, School of Human Ecology, Program in Human Development and Family Studies, Madison, WI 53706-1380. Offers MS, PhD. Part-time programs available. Terminal master's awarded for partial completion of doctoral program. *Degree requirements:* For master's, thesis; for doctorate, comprehensive exam, thesis/dissertation. *Entrance requirements:* For master's, GRE General Test, 3 letters of recommendation; for doctorate, GRE General Test, MS or MA, 3 letters of recommendation. Additional exam requirements/recommendations for international students: Required—TOEFL (minimum score 580 paper-based; 92 iBT). Electronic applications accepted. *Expenses:* Tuition, state resident: full-time $10,723; part-time $745 per credit. Tuition, nonresident: full-time $24,054; part-time $1578 per credit. *Required fees:* $374 per semester. Tuition and fees vary according to course load, program and reciprocity agreements. *Faculty research:* Human development, adolescence, adulthood, prevention, intervention.

University of Wisconsin–Stevens Point, College of Professional Studies, School of Health Promotion and Human Development, Stevens Point, WI 54481-3897. Offers human and community resources (MS); nutritional sciences (MS). Part-time programs available. *Degree requirements:* For master's, thesis or alternative. *Entrance requirements:* For master's, minimum GPA of 2.75.

Utah State University, School of Graduate Studies, Emma Eccles Jones College of Education and Human Services, Department of Family, Consumer, and Human Development, Logan, UT 84322. Offers family and human development (MFHD); family, consumer, and human development (MS, PhD), including adolescence/youth (MS), adult development/aging (MS), consumer science (MS), infancy/childhood (MS), marriage and family relations (MS), marriage and family therapy (MS). *Accreditation:* AAMFT/COAMFTE (one or more programs are accredited). Part-time and evening/weekend programs available. Postbaccalaureate distance learning degree programs offered (minimal on-campus study). *Degree requirements:* For master's, thesis; for doctorate, comprehensive exam, thesis/dissertation, competencies. *Entrance requirements:* For master's, GRE General Test or MAT, minimum GPA of 3.0, 3 letters of recommendation; for doctorate, GRE, minimum GPA of 3.0, 3 letters of recommendation. Additional exam requirements/recommendations for international students: Required—TOEFL. Electronic applications accepted. *Faculty research:* Marriage and family relations, adolescent problem behavior, family financial management, early literacy, mental health in the elderly, parent child attachment.

Vanderbilt University, Peabody College, Department of Human and Organizational Development, Nashville, TN 37240-1001. Offers community development and action

(M Ed); human development counseling (M Ed). *Accreditation:* ACA; NCATE. Part-time programs available. *Degree requirements:* For master's, comprehensive exam, thesis optional. *Entrance requirements:* For master's, GRE General Test, MAT. Additional exam requirements/recommendations for international students: Required—TOEFL (minimum score 550 paper-based; 80 iBT). Electronic applications accepted. *Expenses:* Tuition: Full-time $42,768; part-time $1782 per credit hour. *Required fees:* $422. One-time fee: $30 full-time. *Faculty research:* Community psychology and community development; counseling and mental health services, prevention and positive youth development; organizational and community change; youth physical and behavioral health in schools and communities.

Virginia Polytechnic Institute and State University, Graduate School, College of Liberal Arts and Human Sciences, Blacksburg, VA 24061. Offers career and technical education (MS Ed, Ed D, PhD, Ed S); communication (MA); counselor education (MA Ed, Ed D, PhD, Ed S); creative writing (MFA); curriculum and instruction (MA Ed, Ed D, PhD, Ed S); educational leadership and policy studies (MA Ed, Ed D, PhD, Ed S); educational research and evaluation (PhD); English (MA); foreign languages, cultures, and literatures (MA); higher education and student affairs (MA Ed); history (MA); human development (MS, PhD); material culture and public humanities (MA); philosophy (MA); political science (MA); rhetoric and writing (PhD); science and technology studies (MS, PhD); social, political, ethical, and cultural thought (PhD); sociology (MS, PhD); theater arts (MFA). *Faculty:* 421 full-time (216 women), 2 part-time/adjunct (both women). *Students:* 642 full-time (437 women), 537 part-time (344 women); includes 235 minority (132 Black or African American, non-Hispanic/Latino; 2 American Indian or Alaska Native, non-Hispanic/Latino; 27 Asian, non-Hispanic/Latino; 52 Hispanic/Latino; 1 Native Hawaiian or other Pacific Islander, non-Hispanic/Latino; 21 Two or more races, non-Hispanic/Latino), 81 international. Average age 34. 890 applicants, 46% accepted, 303 enrolled. In 2014, 342 master's, 96 doctorates, 33 other advanced degrees awarded. *Degree requirements:* For master's, comprehensive exam (for some programs), thesis (for some programs); for doctorate, comprehensive exam (for some programs), thesis/dissertation (for some programs). *Entrance requirements:* For master's and doctorate, GRE/GMAT (may vary by department). Additional exam requirements/recommendations for international students: Required—TOEFL (minimum score 550 paper-based). *Application deadline:* For fall admission, 8/1 for domestic students, 4/1 for international students; for spring admission, 1/1 for domestic students, 9/1 for international students. Applications are processed on a rolling basis. Application fee: $75. Electronic applications accepted. *Expenses:* Tuition, state resident: full-time $11,656; part-time $647.50 per credit hour. Tuition, nonresident: full-time $23,351; part-time $1297.25 per credit hour. *Required fees:* $2533; $465.75 per semester. Tuition and fees vary according to course load, campus/location and program. *Financial support:* In 2014–15, 19 research assistantships with full tuition reimbursements (averaging $22,141 per year), 231 teaching assistantships with full tuition reimbursements (averaging $19,470 per year) were awarded. Financial award application deadline: 3/1; financial award applicants required to submit FAFSA. *Total annual research expenditures:* $6.5 million. *Unit head:* Elizabeth Spiller, Dean, 540-231-6779, Fax: 540-231-7157, E-mail: espiller@vt.edu. *Application contact:* Melissa Elliott, Executive Assistant, 540-231-6779, Fax: 540-231-7157, E-mail: elliott1@vt.edu. Website: http://www.clahs.vt.edu/

Washington State University, College of Agricultural, Human, and Natural Resource Sciences, Department of Human Development, Pullman, WA 99164-4852. Offers prevention science (PhD). Program also offered at the Spokane campus. Part-time programs available. *Students:* 19 full-time (17 women), 6 part-time (all women); includes 5 minority (1 Black or African American, non-Hispanic/Latino; 1 Asian, non-Hispanic/Latino; 2 Hispanic/Latino; 1 Two or more races, non-Hispanic/Latino), 5 international. Average age 31. 20 applicants, 35% accepted, 6 enrolled. *Degree requirements:* For doctorate, comprehensive exam, thesis/dissertation. *Entrance requirements:* For doctorate, GRE General Test, bachelor's or master's degree in prevention science related field (e.g., communication, educational psychology, human development, nursing, psychology, sociology); written statement specifying qualifications, educational goals, and career objectives; official copies of all college transcripts; three letters of reference. Additional exam requirements/recommendations for international students: Required—TOEFL, IELTS. *Application deadline:* For fall admission, 1/10 priority date for domestic students, 1/1 for international students. Application fee: $75. Electronic applications accepted. *Expenses:* Tuition, state resident: full-time $11,768. Tuition, nonresident: full-time $25,200. *Required fees:* $960. Tuition and fees vary according to program. *Financial support:* In 2014–15, 23 students received support, including 7 research assistantships with full tuition reimbursements available (averaging $14,498 per year), 10 teaching assistantships with full tuition reimbursements available (averaging $13,460 per year); fellowships with full tuition reimbursements available, institutionally sponsored loans, scholarships/grants, health care benefits, and unspecified assistantships also available. Financial award application deadline: 2/15; financial award applicants required to submit FAFSA. *Faculty research:* Prevention science, program implementation and dissemination, drug and alcohol prevention, health communication, equine assisted interventions, obesity prevention, health promotion in emerging adulthood, family processes, disenfranchised youth, rural poverty, adolescent sexuality, cultural competency, community collaborations, parent-child relationships, healthy aging. *Total annual research expenditures:* $551,000. *Unit head:* Dr. Thomas G. Power, Chair/Director of Prevention Science Program, 509-355-8439, Fax: 509-335-2456, E-mail: tompower@wsu.edu. *Application contact:* Graduate School Admissions, 800-GRADWSU, Fax: 509-335-1949, E-mail: gradsch@wsu.edu. Website: http://hd.wsu.edu/

West Virginia University, Davis College of Agriculture, Forestry and Consumer Sciences, Division of Resource Management and Sustainable Development, Morgantown, WV 26506. Offers agricultural and extension education (MS, PhD), including agricultural and extension education, teaching vocational-agriculture (MS); agricultural and resource economics (MS); human and community development (PhD); natural resource economics (PhD); resource management (PhD); resource management and sustainable development (PhD). Part-time programs available. *Degree requirements:* For master's, thesis; for doctorate, comprehensive exam, thesis/dissertation. *Entrance requirements:* For master's, GRE General Test. Additional exam requirements/recommendations for international students: Required—TOEFL. *Faculty research:* Environmental economics, energy economics, agriculture.

Wheelock College, Graduate Programs, Division of Arts and Sciences, Boston, MA 02215-4176. Offers human development (MS). *Entrance requirements:* Additional exam requirements/recommendations for international students: Required—TOEFL. Electronic applications accepted.

Industrial and Organizational Psychology

★ **Adler University,** Programs in Psychology, Chicago, IL 60602. Offers advanced Adlerian psychotherapy (Certificate); art therapy (MA); clinical neuropsychology (Certificate); clinical psychology (Psy D); community psychology (MA); counseling and organizational psychology (MA); counseling psychology (MA); criminology (MA); emergency management leadership (MA); forensic psychology (MA); marriage and family counseling (MA); marriage and family therapy (Certificate); military psychology (MA); nonprofit management (MA); organizational psychology (MA); police psychology (MA); public policy and administration (MA); rehabilitation counseling (MA); sport and health psychology (MA); substance abuse counseling (Certificate); Psy D/Certificate; Psy D/MACAT; Psy D/MACP; Psy D/MAMFC; Psy D/MASAC. *Accreditation:* APA. Part-time and evening/weekend programs available. Postbaccalaureate distance learning degree programs offered (minimal on-campus study). Terminal master's awarded for partial completion of doctoral program. *Degree requirements:* For master's, thesis or alternative, oral exam, practicum; for doctorate, thesis/dissertation, clinical exam, internship, oral exam, practicum, written qualifying exam. *Entrance requirements:* For master's, 12 semester hours in psychology, minimum GPA of 3.0; for doctorate, 18 semester hours in psychology, minimum GPA of 3.25; for Certificate, appropriate master's or doctoral degree. Additional exam requirements/recommendations for international students: Required—TOEFL (minimum score 550 paper-based; 79 iBT). Electronic applications accepted.
See Display on page 969 and Close-Up on page 1207.

Alliant International University–Fresno, California School of Professional Psychology, Organizational Psychology Programs, Fresno, CA 93727. Offers organizational behavior (MA); organizational development (Psy D); MA/PhD; Psy D/MA. Part-time and evening/weekend programs available. *Degree requirements:* For doctorate, thesis/dissertation. *Entrance requirements:* For doctorate, interview, minimum GPA of 3.0. Additional exam requirements/recommendations for international students: Required—TOEFL (minimum score 550 paper-based; 80 iBT), TWE (minimum score 5). Electronic applications accepted. *Faculty research:* Team development, international organizational development, mergers and acquisitions, strategic change, information technology implementations.

Alliant International University–Los Angeles, California School of Professional Psychology, Organizational Psychology Division, Alhambra, CA 91803-1360. Offers MA, PhD. Part-time programs available. Terminal master's awarded for partial completion of doctoral program. *Degree requirements:* For doctorate, comprehensive exam, thesis/dissertation. *Entrance requirements:* For master's and doctorate, interview, minimum GPA of 3.0 in both psychology and overall. Additional exam requirements/recommendations for international students: Required—TOEFL (minimum score 600 paper-based), TWE (minimum score 5). Electronic applications accepted. *Faculty research:* Organizational transitions, productivity, workforce demographics, management technology, comparative and international research.

Alliant International University–San Diego, California School of Professional Psychology, Organizational Psychology Division, San Diego, CA 92131-1799. Offers clinical/industrial organizational psychology (PhD); consulting psychology (PhD);

industrial/organizational psychology (MA, MS, PhD); leadership (PhD). Part-time and evening/weekend programs available. Terminal master's awarded for partial completion of doctoral program. *Degree requirements:* For doctorate, comprehensive exam, thesis/dissertation, internship/practicum. *Entrance requirements:* For master's and doctorate, minimum GPA of 3.0, recommendations, essay, interview. Additional exam requirements/recommendations for international students: Required—TOEFL (minimum score 550 paper-based; 80 iBT), TWE (minimum score 5). Electronic applications accepted. *Faculty research:* Cultural diversity in the workplace, work motivation, personnel and performance management, organizational diagnosis.

Alliant International University–San Francisco, California School of Professional Psychology, Organizational Psychology Division, San Francisco, CA 94133-1221. Offers MA, PhD. Part-time and evening/weekend programs available. Terminal master's awarded for partial completion of doctoral program. *Degree requirements:* For doctorate, comprehensive exam, thesis/dissertation, field placement. *Entrance requirements:* For master's and doctorate, minimum GPA of 3.0, interview. Additional exam requirements/recommendations for international students: Required—TOEFL (minimum score 550 paper-based; 80 iBT), TWE (minimum score 5). Electronic applications accepted. *Faculty research:* Leadership, ethics and management, career development, organizational behavior, strategic change.

American InterContinental University Online, Program in Business Administration, Schaumburg, IL 60173. Offers accounting and finance (MBA); finance (MBA); healthcare management (MBA); human resource management (MBA); international business (MBA); management (MBA); marketing (MBA); operations management (MBA); organizational psychology and development (MBA); project management (MBA). *Accreditation:* ACBSP. Evening/weekend programs available. Postbaccalaureate distance learning degree programs offered (no on-campus study). *Entrance requirements:* Additional exam requirements/recommendations for international students: Required—TOEFL (minimum score 550 paper-based). Electronic applications accepted.

Angelo State University, College of Graduate Studies, College of Arts and Sciences, Department of Psychology, Sociology and Social Work, San Angelo, TX 76909. Offers psychology (MS), including applied psychology, counseling psychology, industrial and organizational psychology. Part-time and evening/weekend programs available. *Degree requirements:* For master's, comprehensive exam, thesis optional. *Entrance requirements:* For master's, GRE General Test (for industrial and organizational psychology only), essay, letters of recommendation (for industrial and organizational psychology only). Additional exam requirements/recommendations for international students: Required—TOEFL or IELTS. Electronic applications accepted.

Appalachian State University, Cratis D. Williams Graduate School, Department of Psychology, Boone, NC 28608. Offers clinical health psychology (MA); general experimental psychology (MA); industrial and organizational psychology (MA); MA/SSP. Part-time programs available. *Degree requirements:* For master's, comprehensive exam, thesis optional, exit exam. *Entrance requirements:* For master's, GRE General Test, 3 letters of recommendation. Additional exam requirements/recommendations for international students: Required—TOEFL (minimum score 550 paper-based; 79 iBT) or

IELTS (minimum score 6.5). Electronic applications accepted. *Faculty research:* Eating disorders, school-based consultations, organizational behavior management, brain mechanisms of sound localization, parenting styles.

Argosy University, Atlanta, College of Psychology and Behavioral Sciences, Atlanta, GA 30328. Offers clinical psychology (MA, Psy D, Postdoctoral Respecialization Certificate), including child and family psychology (Psy D), general adult clinical (Psy D), health psychology (Psy D), neuropsychology/geropsychology (Psy D); community counseling (MA), including marriage and family therapy; counselor education and supervision (Ed D); forensic psychology (MA); industrial organizational psychology (MA); marriage and family therapy (Certificate); sport-exercise psychology (MA). *Accreditation:* APA.

Argosy University, Chicago, College of Psychology and Behavioral Sciences, Chicago, IL 60601. Offers clinical psychology (MA, Psy D), including child and adolescent psychology (Psy D), client-centered and experiential psychotherapies (Psy D), diversity and multicultural psychology (Psy D), family psychology (Psy D), forensic psychology (Psy D), health psychology (Psy D), neuropsychology (Psy D), organizational consulting (Psy D), psychoanalytic psychology (Psy D), psychology and spirituality (Psy D); community counseling (MA); counseling psychology (Ed D), including counselor education and supervision; counselor education and supervision (Ed D); industrial organizational psychology (MA). *Accreditation:* APA (one or more programs are accredited). Postbaccalaureate distance learning degree programs offered (minimal on-campus study).

Argosy University, Dallas, College of Psychology and Behavioral Sciences, Program in Industrial Organizational Psychology, Farmers Branch, TX 75244. Offers MA.

Argosy University, Denver, College of Psychology and Behavioral Sciences, Denver, CO 80231. Offers clinical mental health counseling (MA); clinical psychology (MA, Psy D); counseling psychology (Ed D); counselor education and supervision (Ed D); forensic psychology (MA); industrial organizational psychology (MA); marriage and family therapy (MA, DMFT).

Argosy University, Inland Empire, College of Psychology and Behavioral Sciences, Ontario, CA 91761. Offers clinical psychology/marriage and family therapy (MA); counseling psychology (Ed D); counseling psychology/marriage and family therapy (MA); forensic psychology (MA); industrial organizational psychology (MA); sport-exercise psychology (MA).

Argosy University, Phoenix, College of Psychology and Behavioral Sciences, Program in Industrial Organizational Psychology, Phoenix, AZ 85021. Offers MA.

Argosy University, Schaumburg, College of Behavioral Sciences, Schaumburg, IL 60173-5403. Offers clinical mental health counseling (MA); forensic psychology (MA, Post-Graduate Certificate); industrial organizational psychology (MA); sport-exercise psychology (MA). *Accreditation:* ACA; APA.

Argosy University, Tampa, College of Psychology and Behavioral Sciences, Tampa, FL 33607. Offers clinical psychology (MA, Psy D), including clinical psychology; counselor education and supervision (Ed D); industrial organizational psychology (MA); marriage and family therapy (MA); mental health counseling (MA).

Argosy University, Twin Cities, College of Psychology and Behavioral Sciences, Eagan, MN 55121. Offers clinical psychology (MA, Psy D), including child and family psychology (Psy D), forensic psychology (Psy D), health and neuropsychology (Psy D), trauma (Psy D); forensic counseling (Post-Graduate Certificate); forensic psychology (MA); industrial organizational psychology (MA); marriage and family therapy (MA, DMFT), including forensic counseling (MA). *Accreditation:* AAMFT; AAMFT/COAMFTE; APA.

Auburn University, Graduate School, College of Liberal Arts, Department of Psychology, Auburn University, AL 36849. Offers applied behavior analysis in developmental disabilities (MS); clinical psychology (PhD); experimental psychology (PhD); industrial/organizational psychology (PhD). *Accreditation:* APA (one or more programs are accredited). Part-time programs available. *Faculty:* 23 full-time (9 women), 2 part-time/adjunct (both women). *Students:* 49 full-time (34 women), 47 part-time (31 women); includes 13 minority (6 Black or African American, non-Hispanic/Latino; 3 Asian, non-Hispanic/Latino; 4 Hispanic/Latino), 5 international. Average age 27. 328 applicants, 10% accepted, 23 enrolled. In 2014, 22 master's, 5 doctorates awarded. *Degree requirements:* For doctorate, thesis/dissertation. *Entrance requirements:* For master's, GRE General Test, GRE Subject Test, minimum GPA of 3.25 in psychology, 3.0 overall; for doctorate, GRE General Test, GRE Subject Test. *Application deadline:* For fall admission, 7/7 for domestic students; for spring admission, 11/24 for domestic students. Applications are processed on a rolling basis. Application fee: $50 ($60 for international students). Electronic applications accepted. *Expenses:* Tuition, state resident: full-time $8586; part-time $477 per credit hour. Tuition, nonresident: full-time $25,758; part-time $1431 per credit hour. *Required fees:* $804 per semester. Tuition and fees vary according to degree level and program. *Financial support:* Research assistantships, teaching assistantships, and Federal Work-Study available. Support available to part-time students. Financial award application deadline: 3/15; financial award applicants required to submit FAFSA. *Faculty research:* Clinical psychology, learning, industrial psychology, organizational psychology. *Total annual research expenditures:* $200,000. *Unit head:* Dr. Peter Chen, Head, 334-844-4412. *Application contact:* Dr. George Flowers, Dean of the Graduate School, 334-844-2125.

Austin Peay State University, College of Graduate Studies, College of Behavioral and Health Sciences, Department of Psychology, Program in Industrial-Organizational Psychology, Clarksville, TN 37044. Offers MA. Postbaccalaureate distance learning degree programs offered (no on-campus study). *Degree requirements:* For master's, comprehensive exam. *Entrance requirements:* For master's, GRE, official transcripts, three letters of recommendation. Additional exam requirements/recommendations for international students: Required—TOEFL (minimum score 500 paper-based).

Baruch College of the City University of New York, Weissman School of Arts and Sciences, Program in Industrial/Organizational Psychology, New York, NY 10010-5585. Offers MS. Part-time and evening/weekend programs available. *Faculty:* 4 full-time (0 women), 6 part-time/adjunct (4 women). *Students:* 47 full-time (33 women), 33 part-time (22 women); includes 15 minority (6 Black or African American, non-Hispanic/Latino; 1 American Indian or Alaska Native, non-Hispanic/Latino; 4 Asian, non-Hispanic/Latino; 3 Hispanic/Latino; 1 Two or more races, non-Hispanic/Latino), 8 international. Average age 26. 136 applicants, 42% accepted, 28 enrolled. In 2014, 36 master's awarded. Terminal master's awarded for partial completion of doctoral program. *Degree requirements:* For master's, thesis or alternative. *Entrance requirements:* For master's, GRE, 2 letters of recommendation, personal essay, resume. Additional exam requirements/recommendations for international students: Required—TOEFL. *Application deadline:* For fall admission, 4/1 for domestic and international students; for spring admission, 11/1 for domestic and international students. Application fee: $135. Electronic applications accepted. *Financial support:* Career-related internships or fieldwork and Federal Work-Study available. Financial award applicants required to submit FAFSA. *Faculty research:* Examining possible explanations for race-based differences on intelligence and cognitive ability tests; developing alternative formats and types of intelligence tests as well as the examining the role of previous experience, test taking skills, and test characteristics on performance on these types of tests; identified employee surveys; personnel staffing and equal employment opportunity issues; leadership development; ;organizational culture. *Unit head:* Dr. Harold Goldstein, Director, 646-312-3820. *Application contact:* Michael J. Lovaglio, Director of Graduate Programs, 646-312-4490, Fax: 646-312-4491,
E-mail: wsas.graduate.studies@baruch.cuny.edu.
Website: http://www.baruch.cuny.edu/wsas/academics/graduate_studies/Grad_MS_IOPsych.htm

Baruch College of the City University of New York, Zicklin School of Business, Program in Industrial and Organizational Psychology, New York, NY 10010-5585. Offers MBA, MS, PhD. PhD offered jointly with Graduate School and University Center of the City University of New York. Part-time and evening/weekend programs available. *Degree requirements:* For master's, thesis or alternative; for doctorate, comprehensive exam, thesis/dissertation. *Entrance requirements:* For master's, GMAT or GRE General Test, 2 letters of recommendation, resumé, 2 years of work experience; for doctorate, GMAT or GRE General Test. Additional exam requirements/recommendations for international students: Required—TOEFL (minimum score 590 paper-based), TWE. *Faculty research:* Job attitudes, power and leadership in organizations, measurement issues in organizational behavior, work motivation, fair employment practices.

Bayamón Central University, Graduate Programs, Program in Organizational Psychology, Bayamón, PR 00960-1725. Offers MA. Part-time and evening/weekend programs available. *Degree requirements:* For master's, comprehensive exam. *Entrance requirements:* For master's, EXADEP, bachelor's degree in psychology or related field.

Bowling Green State University, Graduate College, College of Arts and Sciences, Department of Psychology, Bowling Green, OH 43403. Offers clinical psychology (MA, PhD); developmental psychology (MA, PhD); experimental psychology (MA, PhD); industrial/organizational psychology (MA, PhD); quantitative psychology (MA, PhD). *Accreditation:* APA (one or more programs are accredited). *Degree requirements:* For doctorate, thesis/dissertation. *Entrance requirements:* For doctorate, GRE General Test, GRE Subject Test. Additional exam requirements/recommendations for international students: Required—TOEFL. Electronic applications accepted. *Faculty research:* Personnel psychology, developmental-mathematical models, behavioral medication, brain process, child/adolescent social cognition.

Brooklyn College of the City University of New York, School of Natural and Behavioral Sciences, Department of Psychology, Brooklyn, NY 11210-2889. Offers experimental psychology (MA); industrial and organizational psychology (MA), including human relations, organizational behavior; mental health counseling (MA); psychology (PhD). Part-time programs available. *Degree requirements:* For master's, comprehensive exam, thesis (for some programs). *Entrance requirements:* For master's, minimum GPA of 3.0, 2 letters of recommendation, essay; for doctorate, GRE. Additional exam requirements/recommendations for international students: Required—TOEFL (minimum score 520 paper-based; 69 iBT). Electronic applications accepted.

California State University, Long Beach, Graduate Studies, College of Liberal Arts, Department of Psychology, Long Beach, CA 90840. Offers human factors (MS); industrial/organizational psychology (MS); psychology (MA). Part-time and evening/weekend programs available. *Degree requirements:* For master's, comprehensive exam, thesis. *Entrance requirements:* For master's, GRE General Test, GRE Subject Test. Electronic applications accepted. *Faculty research:* Physiological psychology, social and personality psychology, community-clinical psychology, industrial-organizational psychology, developmental psychology.

California State University, Sacramento, Office of Graduate Studies, College of Social Sciences and Interdisciplinary Studies, Department of Psychology, Sacramento, CA 95819. Offers applied behavior analysis (MA); counseling psychology (MA); industrial/organizational psychology (MA). Part-time programs available. *Degree requirements:* For master's, thesis, writing proficiency exam. *Entrance requirements:* For master's, GRE, minimum GPA of 3.0 during previous 2 years. Additional exam requirements/recommendations for international students: Required—TOEFL. Electronic applications accepted.

California State University, San Bernardino, Graduate Studies, College of Social and Behavioral Sciences, Department of Psychology, Program in Industrial/Organizational Psychology, San Bernardino, CA 92407-2397. Offers organizational psychology (MS). *Students:* 22 full-time (17 women), 8 part-time (3 women); includes 13 minority (1 Black or African American, non-Hispanic/Latino; 2 Asian, non-Hispanic/Latino; 8 Hispanic/Latino; 2 Two or more races, non-Hispanic/Latino), 2 international. Average age 26. 74 applicants, 18% accepted, 12 enrolled. In 2014, 4 master's awarded. *Degree requirements:* For master's, thesis. *Entrance requirements:* Additional exam requirements/recommendations for international students: Required—TOEFL. *Application deadline:* For fall admission, 7/17 for domestic students. Application fee: $55. *Expenses:* Tuition, state resident: full-time $6738; part-time $1302 per term. Tuition, nonresident: full-time $17,898; part-time $248 per unit. *Required fees:* $365 per quarter. Tuition and fees vary according to degree level and program. *Unit head:* Dr. Robert Ricco, Chair, 909-537-5485, Fax: 909-537-7003, E-mail: rricco@csusb.edu. *Application contact:* Dr. Jeffrey Thompson, Dean, 909-537-5058, E-mail: jthompso@csusb.edu.

Capella University, Harold Abel School of Social and Behavioral Science, Doctoral Programs in Psychology, Minneapolis, MN 55402. Offers addiction psychology (PhD); clinical psychology (Psy D); educational psychology (PhD); general advanced studies in human behavior (PhD); general psychology (PhD); industrial/organizational psychology (PhD); school psychology (Psy D).

Capella University, Harold Abel School of Social and Behavioral Science, Master's Programs in Psychology, Minneapolis, MN 55402. Offers applied behavior analysis (MS); clinical psychology (MS); counseling psychology (MS); educational psychology (MS); evaluation, research, and measurement (MS); general advanced studies in human behavior (MS); general psychology (MS); industrial/organizational psychology (MS); leadership coaching psychology (MS); school psychology (MS); sport psychology (MS).

Carlos Albizu University, Graduate Programs, San Juan, PR 00901. Offers clinical psychology (MS, PhD, Psy D); general psychology (PhD); industrial/organizational psychology (MS, PhD); speech and language pathology (MS). *Accreditation:* APA (one or more programs are accredited). Part-time and evening/weekend programs available. Terminal master's awarded for partial completion of doctoral program. *Degree requirements:* For master's, one foreign language, comprehensive exam, thesis; for doctorate, one foreign language, comprehensive exam, thesis/dissertation, written qualifying exams. *Entrance requirements:* For master's, GRE General Test or EXADEP, interview; minimum GPA of 2.8 (industrial/organizational psychology); for doctorate, GRE General Test or EXADEP, interview; minimum GPA of 3.0 (PhD in industrial/organizational psychology and clinical psychology), 3.25 (Psy D). *Faculty research:* Psychotherapeutic techniques for Hispanics, psychology of the aged, school dropouts, stress, violence.

Carlos Albizu University, Miami Campus, Graduate Programs, Miami, FL 33172-2209. Offers clinical psychology (Psy D); entrepreneurship (MBA); exceptional student education (MS); human services (PhD); industrial/organizational psychology (MS); marriage and family therapy (MS); mental health counseling (MS); nonprofit management (MBA); organizational management (MBA); psychology (MS); school counseling (MS); teaching English as a second language (MS). *Accreditation:* APA. Part-time and evening/weekend programs available. Postbaccalaureate distance learning degree programs offered (minimal on-campus study). *Faculty:* 25 full-time (20 women), 29 part-time/adjunct (15 women). *Students:* 431 full-time (343 women), 264 part-time (225 women); includes 586 minority (45 Black or African American, non-Hispanic/Latino; 1 American Indian or Alaska Native, non-Hispanic/Latino; 8 Asian, non-Hispanic/Latino; 530 Hispanic/Latino; 2 Two or more races, non-Hispanic/Latino), 14 international. Average age 33. 189 applicants, 69% accepted, 111 enrolled. In 2014, 177 master's, 28 doctorates awarded. Terminal master's awarded for partial completion of doctoral program. *Degree requirements:* For master's, one foreign language, comprehensive exam, integrative project (MBA), research project (exceptional student education, teaching English as a second language); for doctorate, one foreign language, comprehensive exam, internship, project. *Entrance requirements:* For master's, 3 letters of recommendation, interview, minimum GPA of 3.0, resume, statement of purpose, official transcripts; for doctorate, 3 letters of recommendation, minimum GPA of 3.0, resume, interview, statement of purpose, official transcripts. Additional exam requirements/recommendations for international students: Required—Michigan Test of English Language Proficiency. *Application deadline:* For fall admission, 4/1 priority date for domestic students, 5/1 priority date for international students; for spring admission, 11/1 priority date for domestic students, 9/1 priority date for international students. Applications are processed on a rolling basis. Application fee: $50. Electronic applications accepted. *Expenses:* Expenses: $570 per credit (for master's programs); $750 per credit (for doctoral programs). *Financial support:* In 2014–15, 72 students received support. Federal Work-Study, scholarships/grants, and tuition discounts available. Financial award application deadline: 6/1; financial award applicants required to submit FAFSA. *Faculty research:* Psychotherapy, forensic psychology, neuropsychology, marketing strategy, entrepreneurship, special education. *Unit head:* Dr. Irene M. Bravo, Interim Provost, 305-593-1223 Ext. 3120, Fax: 305-592-7930, E-mail: ibravo@albizu.edu. *Application contact:* Vanessa Almendarez, Administrative Assistant, 305-593-1223 Ext. 3137, Fax: 305-593-1854, E-mail: valmendarez@albizu.edu.

Central Michigan University, College of Graduate Studies, College of Humanities and Social and Behavioral Sciences, Department of Psychology, Program in Industrial and Organizational Psychology, Mount Pleasant, MI 48859. Offers industrial and organizational psychology (MA, PhD); occupational health psychology (PhD). *Degree requirements:* For master's, thesis; for doctorate, comprehensive exam, thesis/dissertation. *Entrance requirements:* For master's and doctorate, GRE. Electronic applications accepted. *Faculty research:* Job stress, retirement, leadership, and careers; personality in the workplace, personnel selection, and structural equation modeling in industrial/organizational psychology; personnel psychology, evolutionary psychology, and influences on HRM utilization; occupational health psychology and job stress; work attitudes, psychological ownership in work, and performance appraisal.

Chatham University, Program in Counseling Psychology, Pittsburgh, PA 15232-2826. Offers child, adolescent and family (MSCP); counseling psychology (Psy D); health and holistic (MSCP); infant mental health (MSCP); organization and supervision (MSCP); sport and exercise (MSCP). Part-time and evening/weekend programs available. *Faculty:* 12 full-time (9 women), 13 part-time/adjunct (9 women). *Students:* 102 full-time (85 women), 38 part-time (32 women); includes 17 minority (7 Black or African American, non-Hispanic/Latino; 2 Asian, non-Hispanic/Latino; 6 Hispanic/Latino; 2 Two or more races, non-Hispanic/Latino), 7 international. Average age 29. 145 applicants, 73% accepted, 59 enrolled. In 2014, 67 master's, 3 doctorates awarded. *Degree requirements:* For master's, thesis optional, supervised internship; for doctorate, thesis/dissertation, internship. *Entrance requirements:* For master's, minimum GPA of 3.0; 2 letters of recommendation; resume; prerequisite coursework in statistics, biology, and psychology; for doctorate, GRE. Additional exam requirements/recommendations for international students: Required—TOEFL (minimum score 600 paper-based; 100 iBT), IELTS (minimum score 7), TWE. *Application deadline:* For fall admission, 4/1 priority date for domestic and international students; for spring admission, 11/1 for domestic students, 10/1 for international students. Applications are processed on a rolling basis. Application fee: $45. Electronic applications accepted. Application fee is waived when completed online. *Expenses: Tuition:* Full-time $15,318; part-time $851 per credit hour. *Required fees:* $440; $24 per credit hour. Tuition and fees vary according to course load, program and reciprocity agreements. *Financial support:* Career-related internships or fieldwork available. Financial award applicants required to submit FAFSA. *Faculty research:* Trauma and recovery, hypnosis, psychospiritual dimensions of healing, psychotherapy of schizophrenia. *Unit head:* Dr. Mary Beth Mannarino, Director, 412-365-1196, Fax: 412-365-1505, E-mail: mmannarino@chatham.edu. *Application contact:* Katie Noel, Assistant Director of Graduate Admission, 412-365-2758, Fax: 412-365-1609, E-mail: gradadmissions@chatham.edu.
Website: http://www.chatham.edu/mscp

The Chicago School of Professional Psychology, Program in Business Psychology, Chicago, IL 60610. Offers business psychology (PhD); industrial and organizational business psychology (Psy D); industrial and organizational psychology (MA); organizational leadership (MA, PhD). *Degree requirements:* For doctorate, thesis/dissertation optional. *Entrance requirements:* For doctorate, GRE. Additional exam requirements/recommendations for international students: Required—TOEFL.

The Chicago School of Professional Psychology, Program in Industrial and Organizational Psychology, Chicago, IL 60610. Offers business psychology (Psy D); industrial and organizational psychology (MA). Part-time and evening/weekend programs available. *Degree requirements:* For master's, internship; for doctorate, thesis/dissertation, internship. *Entrance requirements:* For master's, 1 course each in psychology, statistics, and research methods. Additional exam requirements/recommendations for international students: Required—TOEFL (minimum score 550 paper-based; 79 iBT).

The Chicago School of Professional Psychology at Downtown Los Angeles, Program in Industrial and Organizational Psychology, Los Angeles, CA 90017. Offers MA.

The Chicago School of Professional Psychology: Online, PhD Program in Organizational Leadership, Chicago, IL 60654. Offers PhD.

The Chicago School of Professional Psychology: Online, Program in Applied Industrial and Organizational Psychology, Chicago, IL 60654. Offers MA, Certificate.

Claremont Graduate University, Graduate Programs, School of Social Science, Policy and Evaluation, Department of Psychology, Claremont, CA 91711-6160. Offers advanced study in evaluation (Certificate); cognitive psychology (MA, PhD); developmental psychology (MA, PhD); evaluation and applied research methods (MA, PhD); health behavior research and evaluation (MA, PhD); human resource development and evaluation (MA); industrial/organizational psychology (MA, PhD);

organizational behavior (MA, PhD); organizational psychology (MA, PhD); social psychology (MA, PhD); MBA/PhD. Part-time programs available. *Faculty:* 18 full-time (7 women), 1 part-time/adjunct (0 women). *Students:* 256 full-time (160 women), 70 part-time (50 women); includes 93 minority (17 Black or African American, non-Hispanic/Latino; 3 American Indian or Alaska Native, non-Hispanic/Latino; 26 Asian, non-Hispanic/Latino; 30 Hispanic/Latino; 17 Two or more races, non-Hispanic/Latino), 35 international. Average age 30. In 2014, 56 master's, 15 doctorates, 7 other advanced degrees awarded. Terminal master's awarded for partial completion of doctoral program. *Entrance requirements:* For master's and doctorate, GRE General Test. Additional exam requirements/recommendations for international students: Required—TOEFL (minimum score 550 paper-based; 80 iBT). *Application deadline:* For fall admission, 1/15 priority date for domestic and international students. Applications are processed on a rolling basis. Application fee: $80. Electronic applications accepted. *Expenses: Tuition:* Full-time $41,784; part-time $1741 per credit. *Required fees:* $600; $300 per semester. *Financial support:* Fellowships, research assistantships, teaching assistantships, Federal Work-Study, institutionally sponsored loans, scholarships/grants, and tuition waivers (full and partial) available. Support available to part-time students. Financial award application deadline: 2/15; financial award applicants required to submit FAFSA. *Faculty research:* Social intervention, diversity in organizations, eyewitness memory, aging and cognition, drug policy. *Unit head:* William Crano, Chair, 909-621-8084, E-mail: william.crano@cgu.edu. *Application contact:* Annekah Hall, Assistant Director of Admissions, 909-607-3371, E-mail: annekah.hall@cgu.edu. Website: http://www.cgu.edu/pages/502.asp

Clemson University, Graduate School, College of Business and Behavioral Science, Department of Psychology, Program in Industrial/Organizational Psychology, Clemson, SC 29634. Offers PhD. *Students:* 22 full-time (17 women), 2 part-time (1 woman); includes 1 minority (Two or more races, non-Hispanic/Latino), 1 international. Average age 26. 128 applicants, 6% accepted, 6 enrolled. In 2014, 1 doctorate awarded. *Degree requirements:* For doctorate, thesis/dissertation. *Entrance requirements:* For doctorate, GRE General Test. Additional exam requirements/recommendations for international students: Required—TOEFL. *Application deadline:* For fall admission, 1/15 for domestic students. Application fee: $70 ($80 for international students). Electronic applications accepted. *Expenses:* Expenses: Contact institution. *Financial support:* In 2014–15, 20 students received support, including 3 research assistantships with partial tuition reimbursements available (averaging $21,493 per year), 5 teaching assistantships with partial tuition reimbursements available (averaging $25,333 per year); fellowships with full and partial tuition reimbursements available, career-related internships or fieldwork, institutionally sponsored loans, scholarships/grants, health care benefits, and unspecified assistantships also available. Support available to part-time students. Financial award applicants required to submit FAFSA. *Faculty research:* Personnel selection; occupational health; judgment and decision-making; organizational psychology; aging, retirement, and return to work. *Unit head:* Dr. Patrick Raymark, Chair, 864-656-4715, Fax: 864-656-0358, E-mail: praymar@clemson.edu. *Application contact:* Dr. Robert Sinclair, Graduate Program Coordinator, 864-656-3931, Fax: 864-656-0358.
Website: http://www.clemson.edu/psych/grad/phd-io/

East Carolina University, Graduate School, Thomas Harriot College of Arts and Sciences, Department of Psychology, Program in Industrial and Organizational Psychology, Greenville, NC 27858-4353. Offers MA. *Accreditation:* APA. *Degree requirements:* For master's, one foreign language, comprehensive exam, thesis. *Entrance requirements:* For master's, GRE General Test, GRE Subject Test. Additional exam requirements/recommendations for international students: Required—TOEFL. *Expenses:* Tuition, state resident: full-time $4223. Tuition, nonresident: full-time $16,540. *Required fees:* $2184.

Eastern Kentucky University, The Graduate School, College of Arts and Sciences, Department of Psychology, Richmond, KY 40475-3102. Offers clinical psychology (MS); industrial/organizational psychology (MS); school psychology (Psy S). Part-time programs available. *Entrance requirements:* For master's and Psy S, GRE General Test, minimum GPA of 2.5. *Faculty research:* Autism, social psychology, parenting, assessment of depression/anxiety, reading.

Elmhurst College, Graduate Programs, Program in Industrial/Organizational Psychology, Elmhurst, IL 60126-3296. Offers MA. Part-time and evening/weekend programs available. *Faculty:* 1 full-time (0 women), 3 part-time/adjunct (1 woman). *Students:* 3 full-time (1 woman), 30 part-time (22 women); includes 3 minority (2 Black or African American, non-Hispanic/Latino; 1 Asian, non-Hispanic/Latino), 1 international. Average age 26. 55 applicants, 44% accepted, 16 enrolled. In 2014, 19 master's awarded. *Degree requirements:* For master's, thesis optional. *Entrance requirements:* For master's, GRE General Test, 3 recommendations, resume, statement of purpose. Additional exam requirements/recommendations for international students: Required—TOEFL (minimum score 550 paper-based; 79 iBT). *Application deadline:* Applications are processed on a rolling basis. Application fee: $0. Electronic applications accepted. *Expenses: Tuition:* Part-time $750 per semester hour. *Financial support:* In 2014–15, 14 students received support. Scholarships/grants available. Support available to part-time students. Financial award application deadline: 6/1; financial award applicants required to submit FAFSA. *Application contact:* Timothy J. Panfil, Director of Enrollment Management, School for Professional Studies, 630-617-3300 Ext. 3256, Fax: 630-617-6471, E-mail: panfilt@elmhurst.edu.
Website: http://www.elmhurst.edu/iop

Emporia State University, Program in Psychology, Emporia, KS 66801-5415. Offers general psychology (MS); industrial/organizational psychology (MS). Part-time programs available. *Faculty:* 8 full-time (4 women). *Students:* 19 full-time (11 women), 9 part-time (5 women); includes 6 minority (1 Black or African American, non-Hispanic/Latino; 1 American Indian or Alaska Native, non-Hispanic/Latino; 2 Hispanic/Latino; 2 Two or more races, non-Hispanic/Latino), 3 international. 14 applicants, 100% accepted, 9 enrolled. In 2014, 8 master's awarded. *Degree requirements:* For master's, comprehensive exam or thesis, internship. *Entrance requirements:* For master's, GRE General Test or MAT, essay exam, appropriate bachelor's degree, letters of recommendation. Additional exam requirements/recommendations for international students: Required—TOEFL (minimum score 520 paper-based; 68 iBT). *Application deadline:* For fall admission, 6/1 priority date for domestic students; for spring admission, 10/1 for domestic students. Applications are processed on a rolling basis. Application fee: $30 ($75 for international students). Electronic applications accepted. *Expenses:* Tuition, state resident: part-time $227 per credit hour. Tuition, nonresident: part-time $706 per credit hour. *Required fees:* $75 per credit hour. Tuition and fees vary according to campus/location. *Financial support:* In 2014–15, 13 teaching assistantships with full tuition reimbursements (averaging $7,344 per year) were awarded; career-related internships or fieldwork, Federal Work-Study, institutionally sponsored loans, health care benefits, and unspecified assistantships also available. Financial award application deadline: 3/15; financial award applicants required to submit FAFSA. *Faculty research:* Driving under the influence (DUI) personality, lifestyles and imposter phenomenon. *Unit head:* Dr. Brian W. Schrader, Chair, 620-341-5317, E-mail: bschrade@emporia.edu. *Application contact:* Mary Sewell, Admissions Coordinator, 800-950-GRAD, Fax: 620-341-5909, E-mail: msewell@emporia.edu.

Industrial and Organizational Psychology

Fairleigh Dickinson University, College at Florham, Maxwell Becton College of Arts and Sciences, Department of Psychology, Program in Industrial/Organizational Psychology, Madison, NJ 07940-1099. Offers MA, MA/MBA. *Entrance requirements:* For master's, GRE General Test.

Florida International University, College of Arts and Sciences, Department of Psychology, Miami, FL 33199. Offers behavioral analysis (MS); clinical science (PhD); counseling psychology (MS); developmental science (MS, PhD); legal psychology (PhD); organizational psychology (MS, PhD). Program has fall admissions only. Part-time and evening/weekend programs available. Terminal master's awarded for partial completion of doctoral program. *Degree requirements:* For master's, thesis; for doctorate, comprehensive exam, thesis/dissertation. *Entrance requirements:* For master's, GRE General Test, minimum GPA of 3.0, resume, 3 letters of recommendation; for doctorate, GRE General Test, 3 letters of recommendation, resume, letter of intent, two writing samples, minimum GPA of 3.0. Additional exam requirements/recommendations for international students: Required—TOEFL (minimum score 550 paper-based; 80 iBT). Electronic applications accepted. *Faculty research:* Legal psychology, organizational and industrial psychology, child behavior psychology.

George Mason University, College of Humanities and Social Sciences, Department of Psychology, Fairfax, VA 22030. Offers applied developmental psychology (Certificate); cognitive and behavioral neuroscience (MA); human factors/applied cognition (MA); industrial/organizational psychology (MA, PhD); school psychology (MA). *Accreditation:* APA. *Faculty:* 43 full-time (22 women), 13 part-time/adjunct (8 women). *Students:* 167 full-time (114 women), 48 part-time (34 women); includes 41 minority (7 Black or African American, non-Hispanic/Latino; 8 Asian, non-Hispanic/Latino; 21 Hispanic/Latino; 1 Native Hawaiian or other Pacific Islander, non-Hispanic/Latino; 4 Two or more races, non-Hispanic/Latino), 10 international. Average age 27. 833 applicants, 14% accepted, 75 enrolled. In 2014, 49 master's, 17 doctorates, 10 other advanced degrees awarded. *Degree requirements:* For master's, comprehensive exam, thesis (for biopsychology); for doctorate, comprehensive exam, thesis/dissertation, 2nd year project. *Entrance requirements:* For master's, GRE, 2 official transcripts; goals statement; 15 undergraduate credits in concentration for which the applicant is applying; for doctorate, GRE, 3 letters of recommendation; resume; goals statement; minimum GPA of 3.0 overall for last 60 undergraduate credits, 3.25 in psychology courses; 15 undergraduate credits in concentration for which the applicant is applying; 2 official transcripts; for Certificate, GRE, 2 official transcripts; expanded goals statement; 3 letters of recommendation. Additional exam requirements/recommendations for international students: Required—TOEFL (minimum score 570 paper-based; 80 iBT), IELTS (minimum score 6.5), PTE. Application fee: $65 ($80 for international students). Electronic applications accepted. *Expenses:* Tuition, state resident: full-time $9794; part-time $408 per credit hour. Tuition, nonresident: full-time $26,978; part-time $1124 per credit hour. *Required fees:* $2820; $118 per credit hour. Tuition and fees vary according to course load and program. *Financial support:* In 2014–15, 130 students received support, including 6 fellowships (averaging $6,576 per year), 84 research assistantships with full and partial tuition reimbursements available (averaging $15,356 per year), 63 teaching assistantships with full and partial tuition reimbursements available (averaging $13,274 per year); career-related internships or fieldwork, Federal Work-Study, scholarships/grants, tuition waivers (partial), unspecified assistantships, and health care benefits (for full-time research or teaching assistantship recipients) also available. Support available to part-time students. Financial award application deadline: 3/1; financial award applicants required to submit FAFSA. *Faculty research:* Applied developmental psychology, biopsychology, clinical psychology, human factors/applied cognition psychology, industrial/organizational psychology, school psychology. *Total annual research expenditures:* $5.2 million. *Unit head:* Reeshad Dalal, Department Chair, 703-993-9487, Fax: 703-993-1359, E-mail: rdalal@gmu.edu. *Application contact:* Adam Winsler, Associate Chair of Graduate Studies, 703-993-1881, Fax: 703-993-1359, E-mail: awinsler@gmu.edu.
Website: http://psychology.gmu.edu

The Graduate Center, City University of New York, Graduate Studies, Program in Psychology, New York, NY 10016-4039. Offers basic applied neurocognition (PhD); biopsychology (PhD); clinical psychology (PhD); developmental psychology (PhD); environmental psychology (PhD); experimental psychology (PhD); industrial psychology (PhD); learning processes (PhD); neuropsychology (PhD); psychology (PhD); social personality (PhD). *Degree requirements:* For doctorate, one foreign language, thesis/dissertation. *Entrance requirements:* For doctorate, GRE General Test. Additional exam requirements/recommendations for international students: Required—TOEFL. Electronic applications accepted.

Grand Canyon University, College of Doctoral Studies, Phoenix, AZ 85017-1097. Offers business administration (DBA); general psychology (PhD), including cognition and instruction, industrial and organizational psychology; organizational leadership (Ed D, PhD), including behavioral health (PhD), education and effective schools (PhD), higher education (PhD), instructional leadership (PhD), organizational development (Ed D). *Degree requirements:* For doctorate, comprehensive exam, thesis/dissertation. *Entrance requirements:* For doctorate, minimum GPA of 3.4 on earned advanced degree from regionally-accredited institution; transcripts; goals statement.

Hofstra University, College of Liberal Arts and Sciences, Programs in Psychology, Hempstead, NY 11549. Offers applied organizational psychology (PhD); clinical psychology (PhD); industrial/organizational psychology (MA); school-community psychology (Psy D). Part-time and evening/weekend programs available. *Students:* 226 full-time (146 women), 14 part-time (9 women); includes 42 minority (7 Black or African American, non-Hispanic/Latino; 2 American Indian or Alaska Native, non-Hispanic/Latino; 11 Asian, non-Hispanic/Latino; 17 Hispanic/Latino; 1 Native Hawaiian or other Pacific Islander, non-Hispanic/Latino; 4 Two or more races, non-Hispanic/Latino), 20 international. Average age 27. 313 applicants, 40% accepted, 67 enrolled. In 2014, 40 master's, 30 doctorates awarded. *Degree requirements:* For master's, comprehensive exam, thesis (for some programs), internship, minimum GPA of 3.0; for doctorate, comprehensive exam, thesis/dissertation, 1st year qualifying examination, 2nd year research project, successful practicum/externship placements, written presentation and successful oral defense of dissertation, completion of full-time internship. *Entrance requirements:* For master's, GRE General Test, minimum GPA of 3.0, essay, interview; for doctorate, GRE General Test, GRE Subject Test (psychology), 3 letters of recommendation, interview, essay, curriculum vitae. Additional exam requirements/recommendations for international students: Required—TOEFL (minimum score 550 paper-based; 80 iBT). *Application deadline:* For fall admission, 12/15 for domestic and international students. Application fee: $70 ($75 for international students). Electronic applications accepted. *Expenses: Tuition:* Full-time $20,610; part-time $1145 per credit hour. *Required fees:* $970; $165 per term. Tuition and fees vary according to program. *Financial support:* In 2014–15, 139 students received support, including 118 fellowships with full and partial tuition reimbursements available (averaging $7,236 per year), 7 research assistantships with full and partial tuition reimbursements available (averaging $5,788 per year); Federal Work-Study, institutionally sponsored loans, scholarships/grants, health care benefits, tuition waivers (full and partial), and diversity and endowed scholarships also available. Support available to part-time students. Financial award applicants required to submit FAFSA. *Faculty research:* Cognitive behavioral therapy for anxiety disorders, autism spectrum disorders, parent child interaction training (PCIT), positive organizational behavior, personnel selection and decision-making. *Unit head:* Dr. Keith Shafritz, Chairperson, 516-463-4856, Fax: 516-463-6052, E-mail: psykms@hofstra.edu. *Application contact:* Sunil Samuel, Assistant Vice President of Admissions, 516-463-4723, Fax: 516-463-4664,
E-mail: graduateadmission@hofstra.edu.
Website: http://www.hofstra.edu/hclas

Illinois Institute of Technology, Graduate College, Lewis College of Human Sciences, Department of Psychology, Chicago, IL 60616. Offers clinical psychology (PhD); industrial and organizational psychology (PhD); personnel and human resource development (MS); rehabilitation and mental health counseling (MS); rehabilitation counseling education (PhD). *Accreditation:* APA (one or more programs are accredited); CORE. Part-time and evening/weekend programs available. *Faculty:* 22 full-time (11 women), 3 part-time/adjunct (2 women). *Students:* 187 full-time (139 women), 11 part-time (8 women); includes 28 minority (5 Black or African American, non-Hispanic/Latino; 1 American Indian or Alaska Native, non-Hispanic/Latino; 7 Asian, non-Hispanic/Latino; 12 Hispanic/Latino; 3 Two or more races, non-Hispanic/Latino), 19 international. Average age 30. 293 applicants, 32% accepted, 38 enrolled. In 2014, 27 master's, 4 doctorates awarded. Terminal master's awarded for partial completion of doctoral program. *Degree requirements:* For master's, thesis (for some programs); for doctorate, comprehensive exam, thesis/dissertation, 107 credit hours minimum, 1 yr full-time internship, comprehensive exam, dissertation and oral defense. *Entrance requirements:* For master's, GRE General Test (minimum score 298 Quantitative and Verbal, 3.0 Analytical Writing), minimum gpa 3.0/4.0; 3 letters of recommendation. Applicants for master's degree programs should have a bachelor's degree from an accredited institution and meet the minimum standards listed above. The exception is the masters in Rehabilitation and Mental Health Counseling; for doctorate, GRE General Test (minimum score 298 Quantitative and Verbal, 3.0 Analytical Writing), Prerequisite to admission to doctoral programs are a bachelor's or master's degree from an accredited institution, superior academic records in both undergraduate and graduate programs, and favorable academic recommendations. GRE results are required for all psychology doctoral programs. Additional exam requirements/recommendations for international students: Required—TOEFL (minimum score 550 paper-based; 80 iBT). *Application deadline:* For fall admission, 1/15 for domestic and international students. Application fee: $50. Electronic applications accepted. *Expenses: Tuition:* Full-time $22,500; part-time $1250 per credit hour. *Required fees:* $30 per course. $260 per semester. One-time fee: $235. Tuition and fees vary according to course load and program. *Financial support:* Fellowships with full and partial tuition reimbursements, research assistantships with full and partial tuition reimbursements, career-related internships or fieldwork, Federal Work-Study, institutionally sponsored loans, scholarships/grants, traineeships, health care benefits, tuition waivers (partial), and unspecified assistantships available. Support available to part-time students. Financial award application deadline: 1/15; financial award applicants required to submit FAFSA. *Faculty research:* Clinical psychology, rehabilitation and mental health counseling, industrial organizational psychology. *Unit head:* Ronald Landis, Chair, 312-567-6467, Fax: 312-567-3493, E-mail: rlandis@iit.edu. *Application contact:* Rishab Malhotra, Director, Graduate Admissions, 866-472-3448, Fax: 312-567-3138, E-mail: inquiry.grad@iit.edu.
Website: http://iit.edu/psych/

Illinois State University, Graduate School, College of Arts and Sciences, Department of Psychology, Normal, IL 61790-2200. Offers psychology (MA, MS), including clinical psychology, counseling psychology, developmental psychology, educational psychology, experimental psychology, measurement-evaluation, organizational-industrial psychology; school psychology (PhD, SSP). *Accreditation:* APA. *Degree requirements:* For master's, thesis or alternative; for doctorate, variable foreign language requirement, thesis/dissertation, 2 terms of residency, internship, practicum. *Entrance requirements:* For master's, GRE General Test, GRE Subject Test, minimum GPA of 3.0 in last 60 hours of course work; for doctorate, GRE General Test. *Faculty research:* Comprehensive evaluation system for the central region professional development grant, Illinois school psychology internship consortium, for children's sake.

Indiana University–Purdue University Indianapolis, School of Science, Department of Psychology, Indianapolis, IN 46202-3275. Offers clinical psychology (MS); industrial/organizational psychology (MS); psychobiology of addictions (PhD). *Accreditation:* APA (one or more programs are accredited). *Faculty:* 25 full-time (13 women), 2 part-time/adjunct (both women). *Students:* 51 full-time (34 women), 9 part-time (6 women); includes 10 minority (3 Black or African American, non-Hispanic/Latino; 5 Asian, non-Hispanic/Latino; 1 Hispanic/Latino; 1 Two or more races, non-Hispanic/Latino), 2 international. Average age 28. 189 applicants, 10% accepted, 19 enrolled. In 2014, 15 master's, 4 doctorates awarded. Terminal master's awarded for partial completion of doctoral program. *Degree requirements:* For master's, thesis; for doctorate, thesis/dissertation. *Entrance requirements:* For master's, GRE General Test, minimum undergraduate GPA of 3.0; for doctorate, GRE General Test, GRE Subject Test (clinical psychology), minimum undergraduate GPA of 3.2. Additional exam requirements/recommendations for international students: Required—TOEFL (minimum score 567 paper-based; 86 iBT), IELTS (minimum score 6.5). *Application deadline:* For fall admission, 12/1 priority date for domestic and international students. Application fee: $60. Electronic applications accepted. *Financial support:* In 2014–15, 3 fellowships with partial tuition reimbursements (averaging $22,500 per year) were awarded; research assistantships with partial tuition reimbursements, teaching assistantships with partial tuition reimbursements, career-related internships or fieldwork, Federal Work-Study, institutionally sponsored loans, traineeships, health care benefits, and unspecified assistantships also available. Financial award application deadline: 3/1; financial award applicants required to submit FAFSA. *Faculty research:* Severe mental illness, health psychology, neurological research, alcoholism and psychopathology, functional activities within organizations. *Unit head:* Dr. Peggy S. Stockdale, Chair, 317-278-3838, E-mail: pstockda@iupui.edu. *Application contact:* Heather Sissons, Office Manager and Graduate Coordinator, 317-274-6945, E-mail: hsissons@iupui.edu.
Website: http://www.psych.iupui.edu/

Inter American University of Puerto Rico, Metropolitan Campus, Graduate Programs, Program in Psychology, San Juan, PR 00919-1293. Offers counseling psychology (MA, PhD); industrial/organizational psychology (MA, PhD); labor relations (MA); school psychology (MA, PhD). *Degree requirements:* For master's, comprehensive exam. *Entrance requirements:* For master's, GRE or EXADEP, interview. Electronic applications accepted.

Iona College, School of Arts and Science, Department of Psychology, New Rochelle, NY 10801-1890. Offers general-experimental psychology (MA); human resources (Certificate); industrial-organizational psychology (MA); mental health counseling (MA); organizational behavior (Certificate); psychology (MA); school psychology (MA). Part-time programs available. *Faculty:* 8 full-time (3 women), 5 part-time/adjunct (3 women). *Students:* 41 full-time (30 women), 33 part-time (22 women); includes 29 minority (12 Black or African American, non-Hispanic/Latino; 2 Asian, non-Hispanic/Latino; 15 Hispanic/Latino), 1 international. Average age 24. 65 applicants, 85% accepted, 22 enrolled. In 2014, 38 master's awarded. *Degree requirements:* For master's, thesis (for some programs), literature review (for some programs). *Entrance requirements:* For

master's, BA in psychology including 3 credits in psychology statistics and 3 credits in experimental research methods; or 9 credits in psychology including 3 credits in psychology statistics,3 credits in psychology research methods and 3 credits of upper-level coursework. Additional exam requirements/recommendations for international students: Required—TOEFL (minimum score 550 paper-based), IELTS (minimum score 6.5). *Application deadline:* For fall admission, 8/15 for domestic students, 5/1 for international students; for spring admission, 1/15 for domestic students, 9/1 for international students. Applications are processed on a rolling basis. Application fee: $50. Electronic applications accepted. *Expenses: Tuition:* Part-time $985 per credit. *Required fees:* $245 per term. *Financial support:* In 2014–15, 6 students received support, including 1 research assistantship with partial tuition reimbursement available (averaging $8,000 per year); tuition waivers (partial) and unspecified assistantships also available. Support available to part-time students. Financial award application deadline: 4/15; financial award applicants required to submit FAFSA. *Faculty research:* Non-suicidal self-injury, trauma response, performance appraisal and evaluation, diversity infusion, assessment and treatment of sexual offenders. *Unit head:* Patricia Oswald, PhD, Chair, 914-633-7788, E-mail: poswald@iona.edu. *Application contact:* Amanda St. Bernard, Assistant Director, Graduate Admissions, 914-633-2440, Fax: 914-633-2277, E-mail: astbernard@iona.edu.
Website: http://www.iona.edu/Academics/School-of-Arts-Science/Departments/Psychology/Graduate-Programs.aspx

John F. Kennedy University, Graduate School of Professional Psychology, Program in Organizational Psychology, Pleasant Hill, CA 94523-4817. Offers MA, Certificate. Part-time and evening/weekend programs available. *Degree requirements:* For master's, thesis or alternative. *Entrance requirements:* For master's, interview. Additional exam requirements/recommendations for international students: Required—TOEFL.

Kean University, College of Humanities and Social Sciences, Program in Psychology, Union, NJ 07083. Offers human behavior and organizational psychology (MA); psychological services (MA). Part-time programs available. *Faculty:* 16 full-time (13 women). *Students:* 28 full-time (25 women), 24 part-time (13 women); includes 23 minority (12 Black or African American, non-Hispanic/Latino; 3 Asian, non-Hispanic/Latino; 7 Hispanic/Latino; 1 Two or more races, non-Hispanic/Latino), 1 international. Average age 29. 35 applicants, 89% accepted, 15 enrolled. In 2014, 22 master's awarded. *Degree requirements:* For master's, comprehensive exam, research component, two semesters of advanced seminar. *Entrance requirements:* For master's, GRE General Test, minimum GPA of 3.0; official transcripts from all institutions attended; two letters of recommendation; professional resume/curriculum vitae; 12 credits in behavioral sciences on the undergraduate level. Additional exam requirements/recommendations for international students: Required—TOEFL (minimum score 79 iBT). *Application deadline:* For fall admission, 6/1 for domestic and international students; for spring admission, 12/1 for domestic and international students. Applications are processed on a rolling basis. Application fee: $75 ($150 for international students). Electronic applications accepted. *Expenses:* Tuition, state resident: full-time $12,461; part-time $607 per credit. Tuition, nonresident: full-time $16,889; part-time $744 per credit. *Required fees:* $3141; $143 per credit. Tuition and fees vary according to course load, degree level and program. *Financial support:* In 2014–15, 3 research assistantships with full tuition reimbursements (averaging $3,742 per year) were awarded; scholarships/grants and unspecified assistantships also available. Financial award applicants required to submit FAFSA. *Unit head:* Dr. Muriel Singer, Program Coordinator, 908-737-5886, E-mail: msinger@kean.edu. *Application contact:* Reenat Hasan, Admissions Counselor, 908-737-7134, Fax: 908-737-7135, E-mail: rhasan@exchange.kean.edu.
Website: http://grad.kean.edu/masters-programs/psychological-services

Keiser University, MS in Organizational Psychology Program, Ft. Lauderdale, FL 33309. Offers MS. *Degree requirements:* For master's, thesis.

Keiser University, PhD in Industrial and Organizational Psychology Program, Ft. Lauderdale, FL 33309. Offers PhD.

Lamar University, College of Graduate Studies, College of Arts and Sciences, Department of Psychology, Beaumont, TX 77710. Offers clinical psychology (MS); industrial/organizational psychology (MS). Part-time programs available. *Faculty:* 7 full-time (4 women). *Students:* 14 full-time (10 women), 8 part-time (5 women); includes 6 minority (2 Black or African American, non-Hispanic/Latino; 3 Hispanic/Latino; 1 Two or more races, non-Hispanic/Latino), 1 international. Average age 25. 14 applicants, 71% accepted, 4 enrolled. In 2014, 7 master's awarded. *Degree requirements:* For master's, thesis, practicum. *Entrance requirements:* For master's, GRE General Test, minimum GPA of 2.75 in last 60 hours of undergraduate course work. Additional exam requirements/recommendations for international students: Required—TOEFL (minimum score 550 paper-based; 79 iBT), IELTS (minimum score 6.5). *Application deadline:* For fall admission, 8/10 for domestic students, 7/1 for international students; for spring admission, 1/5 for domestic students, 12/1 for international students. Application fee: $25 ($50 for international students). *Expenses:* Tuition, state resident: full-time $5724; part-time $1908 per semester. Tuition, nonresident: full-time $12,240; part-time $4080 per semester. *Required fees:* $1940; $318 per credit hour. *Financial support:* In 2014–15, 12 students received support, including 3 teaching assistantships (averaging $4,500 per year); fellowships, research assistantships, career-related internships or fieldwork, Federal Work-Study, scholarships/grants, and tuition waivers (partial) also available. Support available to part-time students. Financial award application deadline: 4/1. *Faculty research:* Groupthink, health psychology, school psychology, behavioral neuroscience. *Unit head:* Dr. Edythe E Kirk, Interim Chair, 409-880-8285, Fax: 409-880-1710. *Application contact:* Melissa Gallien, Director, Admissions and Academic Services, 409-880-8888, Fax: 409-880-7419, E-mail: gradmissions@lamar.edu.
Website: http://artssciences.lamar.edu/psychology

Louisiana Tech University, Graduate School, College of Education, Department of Psychology and Behavioral Sciences, Ruston, LA 71272. Offers counseling and guidance (MA); counseling psychology (PhD); industrial and organizational psychology (MA, PhD). *Accreditation:* APA (one or more programs are accredited). Part-time programs available. *Degree requirements:* For master's, thesis or alternative; for doctorate, thesis/dissertation. *Entrance requirements:* For master's and doctorate, GRE General Test. *Application deadline:* For fall admission, 7/29 for domestic students; for spring admission, 2/3 for domestic students. Application fee: $20 ($30 for international students). *Financial support:* Fellowships, research assistantships, teaching assistantships, and career-related internships or fieldwork available. Financial award application deadline: 2/1. *Unit head:* Dr. Donna Thomas, Chair, 318-257-5066, Fax: 318-257-2379, E-mail: dthomas@latech.edu. *Application contact:* Dr. Cathy Stockton, Associate Dean of Graduate Studies, 318-257-3229, Fax: 318-257-2379, E-mail: cstock@latech.edu.
Website: http://www.latech.edu/education/psychology/

Massachusetts School of Professional Psychology, Graduate Programs, Boston, MA 02132. Offers applied psychology in higher education student personnel administration (MA); clinical psychology (Psy D); counseling psychology (MA); counseling psychology and community mental health (MA); counseling psychology and global mental health (MA); executive coaching (Graduate Certificate); forensic and counseling psychology (MA); leadership psychology (Psy D); organizational psychology (MA); primary care psychology (MA); respecialization in clinical psychology (Certificate); school psychology (Psy D); MA/CAGS. *Accreditation:* APA. *Degree requirements:* For master's, comprehensive exam (for some programs); for doctorate, thesis/dissertation (for some programs). Electronic applications accepted.

Middle Tennessee State University, College of Graduate Studies, College of Behavioral and Health Sciences, Department of Psychology, Murfreesboro, TN 37132. Offers clinical psychology (MA); experimental psychology (MA); industrial/organizational psychology (MA); psychology (MA, Ed S); quantitative psychology (MA); school psychology (MA). Part-time and evening/weekend programs available. Postbaccalaureate distance learning degree programs offered. *Faculty:* 37 full-time (14 women), 3 part-time/adjunct (2 women). *Students:* 66 full-time (54 women), 47 part-time (37 women); includes 15 minority (8 Black or African American, non-Hispanic/Latino; 1 American Indian or Alaska Native, non-Hispanic/Latino; 2 Asian, non-Hispanic/Latino; 3 Hispanic/Latino; 1 Two or more races, non-Hispanic/Latino), 1 international. 225 applicants, 84% accepted. In 2014, 37 master's awarded. *Degree requirements:* For master's, comprehensive exam, thesis. *Entrance requirements:* For master's, GRE. Additional exam requirements/recommendations for international students: Required—TOEFL (minimum score 525 paper-based; 71 iBT) or IELTS (minimum score 6). *Application deadline:* For fall admission, 6/1 for domestic and international students. Applications are processed on a rolling basis. Application fee: $30. Electronic applications accepted. *Financial support:* In 2014–15, 38 students received support. Tuition waivers available. Support available to part-time students. Financial award application deadline: 4/1; financial award applicants required to submit FAFSA. *Faculty research:* Health psychology, industrial/organizational psychology, experimental psychology. *Unit head:* Dr. Greg Schmidt, Chair, 615-898-2706, Fax: 615-898-5027, E-mail: greg.schmidt@mtsu.edu. *Application contact:* Dr. Michael D. Allen, Vice Provost for Research/Dean, 615-898-2840, Fax: 615-904-8020, E-mail: michael.allen@mtsu.edu.

Minnesota State University Mankato, College of Graduate Studies, College of Social and Behavioral Sciences, Department of Psychology, Mankato, MN 56001. Offers clinical psychology (MA); industrial/organizational psychology (MA); school psychology (Psy D). Part-time programs available. *Students:* 47 full-time (38 women), 11 part-time (9 women). *Degree requirements:* For master's, one foreign language, comprehensive exam, thesis (for some programs). *Entrance requirements:* For master's, GRE General Test, GRE Subject Test (clinical psychology), minimum GPA of 3.0 during previous 2 years, 3 letters of reference. Additional exam requirements/recommendations for international students: Required—TOEFL. *Application deadline:* For fall admission, 1/1 priority date for domestic students. Applications are processed on a rolling basis. Application fee: $40. Electronic applications accepted. *Financial support:* Research assistantships, teaching assistantships with full tuition reimbursements, career-related internships or fieldwork, Federal Work-Study, institutionally sponsored loans, and unspecified assistantships available. Support available to part-time students. Financial award application deadline: 3/15; financial award applicants required to submit FAFSA. *Faculty research:* Professional competency in hospitals, mood disturbance, 360-degree feedback, employee selection, planning fallacy. *Unit head:* Dr. Jeff Buchanan, Chairperson, 507-389-2724. *Application contact:* 507-389-2321, E-mail: grad@mnsu.edu.
Website: http://www.mnsu.edu/psych/

Montclair State University, The Graduate School, College of Humanities and Social Sciences, Program in Industrial and Organizational Psychology, Montclair, NJ 07043-1624. Offers MA. Part-time and evening/weekend programs available. *Students:* 11 full-time (9 women), 6 part-time (4 women); includes 5 minority (1 Black or African American, non-Hispanic/Latino; 1 Asian, non-Hispanic/Latino; 2 Hispanic/Latino; 1 Two or more races, non-Hispanic/Latino), 1 international. Average age 26. 60 applicants, 33% accepted, 13 enrolled. In 2014, 14 master's awarded. *Degree requirements:* For master's, thesis. *Entrance requirements:* For master's, GRE General Test, 2 letters of recommendation, essay. Additional exam requirements/recommendations for international students: Required—TOEFL (minimum score 83 iBT), IELTS (minimum score 6.5). *Application deadline:* Applications are processed on a rolling basis. Application fee: $60. Electronic applications accepted. *Expenses:* Tuition, state resident: full-time $9960; part-time $553.35 per credit. Tuition, nonresident: full-time $15,074; part-time $837.43 per credit. *Required fees:* $1595; $88.63 per credit. Tuition and fees vary according to degree level and program. *Financial support:* Federal Work-Study, scholarships/grants, and unspecified assistantships available. Support available to part-time students. Financial award application deadline: 3/1; financial award applicants required to submit FAFSA. *Faculty research:* Study of behavior in the work place; job satisfaction, organizational commitment and how to select individuals for given positions in an organization. *Unit head:* Dr. Peter Vietze, Chairperson, 973-655-5201. *Application contact:* Amy Aiello, Director of Admissions and Operations, 973-655-5147, Fax: 973-655-7869, E-mail: graduate.school@montclair.edu.
Website: http://www.montclair.edu/catalog/view_requirements.php?CurriculumID=3202

New York University, Graduate School of Arts and Science, Department of Psychology, New York, NY 10012-1019. Offers cognition and perception (PhD); community psychology (PhD); general psychology (MA); industrial/organizational psychology (MA); psychotherapy and psychoanalysis (Advanced Certificate); social/personality psychology (PhD). Part-time programs available. *Students:* 270 full-time (183 women), 162 part-time (115 women); includes 92 minority (14 Black or African American, non-Hispanic/Latino; 36 Asian, non-Hispanic/Latino; 33 Hispanic/Latino; 9 Two or more races, non-Hispanic/Latino), 114 international. Average age 31. 874 applicants, 46% accepted, 153 enrolled. In 2014, 102 master's, 9 doctorates, 10 other advanced degrees awarded. Terminal master's awarded for partial completion of doctoral program. *Degree requirements:* For master's, comprehensive exam, thesis or alternative; for doctorate, thesis/dissertation. *Entrance requirements:* For master's and doctorate, GRE General Test. Additional exam requirements/recommendations for international students: Required—TOEFL. *Application deadline:* For fall admission, 12/12 for domestic and international students. Application fee: $100. *Financial support:* Fellowships with tuition reimbursements, research assistantships with tuition reimbursements, teaching assistantships with tuition reimbursements, career-related internships or fieldwork, Federal Work-Study, institutionally sponsored loans, scholarships/grants, traineeships, health care benefits, and unspecified assistantships available. Financial award application deadline: 12/12; financial award applicants required to submit FAFSA. *Faculty research:* Vision, memory, social cognition, social and cognitive development, relationships. *Unit head:* Gabriele Oettingen, Director of Graduate Studies, PhD Program, 212-998-7900, Fax: 212-995-4018, E-mail: psychq@psych.nyu.edu. *Application contact:* Adrienne Gans, Director of Graduate Studies, MA Program, 212-998-7900, Fax: 212-995-4018, E-mail: psychq@psych.nyu.edu.
Website: http://www.psych.nyu.edu/

North Carolina State University, Graduate School, College of Humanities and Social Sciences, Department of Psychology, Raleigh, NC 27695. Offers developmental psychology (PhD); ergonomics and experimental psychology (PhD); industrial/organizational psychology (PhD); psychology in the public interest (PhD); school psychology (PhD). *Accreditation:* APA. *Degree requirements:* For doctorate,

comprehensive exam, thesis/dissertation. *Entrance requirements:* For doctorate, GRE General Test, GRE Subject Test (industrial/organizational psychology), MAT (recommended), minimum GPA of 3.0 in major. Electronic applications accepted. *Faculty research:* Cognitive and social development (human factors, families, the workplace, community issues and health, aging).

Northern Kentucky University, Office of Graduate Programs, College of Arts and Sciences, Program in Industrial-Organizational Psychology, Highland Heights, KY 41099. Offers industrial psychology (Certificate); industrial-organizational psychology (MS); occupational health psychology (Certificate); organizational psychology (Certificate). Part-time and evening/weekend programs available. *Faculty:* 3 full-time (1 woman), 1 (woman) part-time/adjunct. *Students:* 3 full-time (all women), 41 part-time (30 women); includes 10 minority (6 Black or African American, non-Hispanic/Latino; 1 Asian, non-Hispanic/Latino; 2 Hispanic/Latino; 1 Two or more races, non-Hispanic/Latino), 1 international. Average age 27. In 2014, 11 master's, 1 other advanced degree awarded. *Degree requirements:* For master's, thesis optional, capstone. *Entrance requirements:* For master's, GRE General Test (minimum scores of 141 verbal, 144 quantitative, and 3.5 writing), bachelor's degree with minimum GPA of 3.0, nine semester hours of psychology coursework, at least one undergraduate course in statistics with minimum B grade, official transcripts, current resume or vita, statement of personal interest, three letters of recommendation; for Certificate, official transcripts, bachelor's degree, minimum undergraduate GPA of 3.0, no grade lower than B on all graduate coursework previously taken that may apply. Additional exam requirements/recommendations for international students: Required—TOEFL (minimum score 79 iBT); Recommended—IELTS (minimum score 6.5). *Application deadline:* For fall admission, 3/1 priority date for domestic students, 6/1 for international students; for spring admission, 12/1 priority date for domestic students, 10/1 for international students; for summer admission, 5/1 priority date for domestic students. Application fee: $40. Electronic applications accepted. *Expenses: Tuition,* area resident: Part-time $518 per credit hour. Tuition, state resident: part-time $630 per credit hour. Tuition, nonresident: part-time $797 per credit hour. *Required fees:* $192 per semester. Tuition and fees vary according to course load, degree level, campus/location, program and reciprocity agreements. *Financial support:* In 2014–15, 13 students received support. Unspecified assistantships available. Financial award applicants required to submit FAFSA. *Faculty research:* Workplace bullying and abuse, assessment and situational judgment tasks, human factors and work design, racial and social stereotyping in employment, social conflict. *Unit head:* Dr. Kathleen Fuegen, Director, 859-572-5787, E-mail: fuegenk1@nku.edu. *Application contact:* Alison Swanson, Graduate Admissions Coordinator, 859-572-6971, E-mail: swansona1@nku.edu.
Website: http://psychology.nku.edu/programs/graduate/index.php

Ohio University, Graduate College, College of Arts and Sciences, Department of Psychology, Program in Organizational Psychology, Athens, OH 45701-2979. Offers MA, PhD. *Degree requirements:* For doctorate, one foreign language, comprehensive exam, thesis/dissertation. *Entrance requirements:* For doctorate, GRE General Test, GRE Subject Test. Additional exam requirements/recommendations for international students: Required—TOEFL. *Faculty research:* Performance appraisal, job satisfaction, organizational entry, sexual harassment.

★ **Philadelphia College of Osteopathic Medicine,** Graduate and Professional Programs, Department of Psychology, Philadephia, PA 19131. Offers applied behavior analysis (Certificate); clinical health psychology (Post-Doctoral Certificate); clinical neuropsychology (Post-Doctoral Certificate); clinical psychology (Psy D); mental health counseling (MS); organizational development and leadership (MS); psychology (Certificate); school psychology (MS, Psy D, Ed S). *Accreditation:* APA. *Faculty:* 19 full-time (11 women), 122 part-time/adjunct (58 women). *Students:* 395 (304 women); includes 80 minority (49 Black or African American, non-Hispanic/Latino; 13 Asian, non-Hispanic/Latino; 7 Hispanic/Latino; 11 Two or more races, non-Hispanic/Latino). 345 applicants, 47% accepted, 113 enrolled. In 2014, 72 master's, 42 doctorates, 17 other advanced degrees awarded. Terminal master's awarded for partial completion of doctoral program. *Degree requirements:* For master's, comprehensive exam (for some programs), thesis (for some programs); for doctorate, comprehensive exam, thesis/dissertation. *Entrance requirements:* For master's, GRE or MAT, minimum GPA of 3.0; bachelor's degree from regionally-accredited college or university; for doctorate, PRAXIS II (for Psy D in school psychology), minimum undergraduate GPA of 3.0; for other advanced degree, GRE (for Ed S). Additional exam requirements/recommendations for international students: Required—TOEFL (minimum score 79 iBT). *Application deadline:* For fall admission, 3/1 priority date for domestic students. Applications are processed on a rolling basis. Application fee: $50. Electronic applications accepted. *Financial support:* In 2014–15, 28 teaching assistantships were awarded; Federal Work-Study, institutionally sponsored loans, and scholarships/grants also available. Financial award application deadline: 3/15; financial award applicants required to submit FAFSA. *Faculty research:* Adult and childhood anxiety and ADHD; coping with chronic illness; primary care psychology/integrated health care; applied behavior analysis; psychological, educational, and neuropsychological assessment. *Total annual research expenditures:* $533,489. *Unit head:* Dr. Robert DiTomasso, Chairman, 215-871-6442, Fax: 215-871-6458, E-mail: robertd@pcom.edu. *Application contact:* Kari A. Shotwell, Director of Admissions, 215-871-6700, Fax: 215-871-6719, E-mail: karis@pcom.edu.

See Display on page 990 and Close-Up on page 1211.

Pontifical Catholic University of Puerto Rico, College of Graduate Studies in Behavioral Science and Community Affairs, Program in Industrial Psychology (Doctorate), Ponce, PR 00717-0777. Offers PhD. Part-time and evening/weekend programs available. *Entrance requirements:* For doctorate, EXADEP, minimum GPA of 2.75.

Purdue University, Graduate School, College of Health and Human Sciences, Department of Psychological Sciences, West Lafayette, IN 47907. Offers behavioral neuroscience (PhD); clinical psychology (PhD); cognitive psychology (PhD); industrial/organizational psychology (PhD); mathematical and computational cognitive science (PhD). *Accreditation:* APA. Terminal master's awarded for partial completion of doctoral program. *Degree requirements:* For doctorate, thesis/dissertation. *Entrance requirements:* For doctorate, GRE General Test, minimum undergraduate GPA of 3.0 or equivalent. Additional exam requirements/recommendations for international students: Required—TOEFL (minimum score 550 paper-based; 77 iBT); Recommended—TWE. Electronic applications accepted. *Faculty research:* Career development of women in science, development of friendships during childhood and adolescence, social competence, human information processing.

Radford University, College of Graduate and Professional Studies, College of Humanities and Behavioral Sciences, Department of Psychology, Program in Psychology, Radford, VA 24142. Offers clinical psychology (MA, MS); experimental psychology (MA); industrial/organizational psychology (MA, MS). Part-time programs available. *Faculty:* 14 full-time (7 women). *Students:* 47 full-time (29 women); includes 3 minority (2 Asian, non-Hispanic/Latino; 1 Hispanic/Latino). Average age 24. 117 applicants, 40% accepted, 25 enrolled. In 2014, 27 master's awarded. *Degree requirements:* For master's, comprehensive exam, thesis (for some programs). *Entrance*

requirements: For master's, GRE, minimum GPA of 3.0; 3 letters of reference; essay, resume, official transcripts. Additional exam requirements/recommendations for international students: Required—TOEFL (minimum score 550 paper-based; 79 iBT), IELTS (minimum score 6.5). *Application deadline:* For fall admission, 2/15 priority date for domestic students, 12/1 for international students; for spring admission, 7/1 for international students. Applications are processed on a rolling basis. Application fee: $50. Electronic applications accepted. *Expenses:* Tuition, state resident: full-time $7187; part-time $299 per credit hour. Tuition, nonresident: full-time $16,394; part-time $683 per credit hour. *Required fees:* $2974; $125 per credit hour. Tuition and fees vary according to course load and program. *Financial support:* In 2014–15, 39 students received support, including 22 research assistantships (averaging $5,946 per year), 15 teaching assistantships with partial tuition reimbursements available (averaging $10,467 per year); career-related internships or fieldwork, institutionally sponsored loans, scholarships/grants, and unspecified assistantships also available. Financial award application deadline: 3/1; financial award applicants required to submit FAFSA. *Faculty research:* Social cognition and interpersonal relationships, relationship between one's self-concept and social interactions, creativity and innovation, organizational politics and ethical decision-making, victimization in childhood. *Unit head:* Dr. Hilary M. Lips, Chair, 540-831-5361, Fax: 540-831-6113, E-mail: hlips@radford.edu. *Application contact:* Rebecca Conner, Director, Graduate Enrollment, 540-831-6296, Fax: 540-831-6061, E-mail: gradcollege@radford.edu.
Website: http://www.radford.edu/content/chbs/home/psychology/programs.html

Rice University, Graduate Programs, School of Social Sciences, Department of Psychology, Houston, TX 77251-1892. Offers cognitive sciences (MA, PhD); industrial-organizational/social psychology (MA, PhD); psychology (MA, PhD). Terminal master's awarded for partial completion of doctoral program. *Degree requirements:* For master's, thesis; for doctorate, thesis/dissertation. *Entrance requirements:* For doctorate, GRE General Test, minimum GPA of 3.0. Additional exam requirements/recommendations for international students: Required—TOEFL. Electronic applications accepted. *Faculty research:* Cognitive, cognitive neuropsychology, human factors, human-computer interaction, industrial-organizational psychology.

Roosevelt University, Graduate Division, College of Arts and Sciences, Department of Psychology, Program in Industrial/Organizational Psychology, Chicago, IL 60605. Offers MA, PhD.

St. Cloud State University, School of Graduate Studies, College of Liberal Arts, Program in Industrial-Organizational Psychology, St. Cloud, MN 56301-4498. Offers MS. *Degree requirements:* For master's, thesis or portfolio. *Entrance requirements:* For master's, GRE General Test, minimum GPA of 2.75. Additional exam requirements/recommendations for international students: Required—TOEFL (minimum score 550 paper-based) or IELTS (minimum score 6.5). Electronic applications accepted.

Saint Joseph's University, College of Arts and Sciences, Organization Development and Leadership Programs, Philadelphia, PA 19131-1395. Offers adult learning and training (MS); organization dynamics and leadership (MS); organizational psychology and development (MS). Part-time and evening/weekend programs available. Postbaccalaureate distance learning degree programs offered (no on-campus study). *Faculty:* 2 full-time (both women), 17 part-time/adjunct (10 women). *Students:* 25 full-time (16 women), 197 part-time (136 women); includes 61 minority (49 Black or African American, non-Hispanic/Latino; 6 Asian, non-Hispanic/Latino; 3 Hispanic/Latino; 2 Native Hawaiian or other Pacific Islander, non-Hispanic/Latino; 1 Two or more races, non-Hispanic/Latino), 1 international. Average age 38. 96 applicants, 74% accepted, 48 enrolled. In 2014, 76 master's awarded. *Entrance requirements:* For master's, GRE (if GPA less than 2.7), minimum GPA of 2.7, 2 letters of recommendation, resume, personal statement. Additional exam requirements/recommendations for international students: Required—TOEFL (minimum score 550 paper-based; 80 iBT). *Application deadline:* For fall admission, 7/15 priority date for domestic students, 4/15 for international students; for winter admission, 1/15 for international students; for spring admission, 11/15 priority date for domestic students, 10/15 for international students. Applications are processed on a rolling basis. Application fee: $35. Electronic applications accepted. *Financial support:* In 2014–15, 25 students received support. Applicants required to submit FAFSA. *Unit head:* Dr. Felice Tilin, Director, 610-660-1575, E-mail: ftilin@sju.edu. *Application contact:* Elisabeth Woodward, Director of Marketing and Admissions, Graduate Arts and Sciences, 610-660-3131, Fax: 610-660-3230, E-mail: gradstudies@sju.edu.
Website: http://www.sju.edu/majors-programs/graduate-arts-sciences/masters/organization-development-and-leadership-ms

Saint Louis University, Graduate Education, College of Arts and Sciences and Graduate Education, Department of Psychology, St. Louis, MO 63103-2097. Offers clinical psychology (MS-R, PhD); experimental psychology (MS-R, PhD); industrial-organizational psychology (PhD); psychology (PhD). *Accreditation:* APA (one or more programs are accredited). Part-time programs available. *Degree requirements:* For master's, comprehensive exam, thesis; for doctorate, thesis/dissertation, clinical internship (for clinical psychology PhD). *Entrance requirements:* For master's, GRE General Test, interview, letters of recommendation, resume; for doctorate, GRE General Test, interview, letters of recommendation, resumé, transcripts, goal statement. Additional exam requirements/recommendations for international students: Required—TOEFL (minimum score 550 paper-based). Electronic applications accepted. *Faculty research:* Violence and trauma; neural basis of learning and memory function; eating disorders; body image and health behavior; prejudice, stereotyping, and victimization; memory, cognitive aging and language processing.

Saint Mary's University, Faculty of Science, Department of Psychology, Halifax, NS B3H 3C3, Canada. Offers applied psychology (M Sc, PhD), including industrial/organizational psychology (M Sc). Part-time programs available. *Degree requirements:* For master's, thesis, 500-hour internship; for doctorate, comprehensive exam, thesis/dissertation, research project. *Entrance requirements:* For master's and doctorate, GRE General Test. *Faculty research:* Assessment, health psychology, social psychology, cognition.

St. Mary's University, Graduate School, Program in Industrial/Organizational Psychology, San Antonio, TX 78228-8507. Offers MA, MS. Part-time programs available. *Faculty:* 3 full-time (1 woman), 4 part-time/adjunct (1 woman). *Students:* 7 full-time (5 women), 11 part-time (8 women); includes 15 minority (2 Black or African American, non-Hispanic/Latino; 13 Hispanic/Latino). Average age 26. 17 applicants, 59% accepted, 3 enrolled. In 2014, 6 master's awarded. *Degree requirements:* For master's, comprehensive exam, thesis optional. *Entrance requirements:* For master's, GRE General Test. Additional exam requirements/recommendations for international students: Required—TOEFL (minimum score 550 paper-based; 80 iBT). *Application deadline:* Applications are processed on a rolling basis. Application fee: $0. Electronic applications accepted. *Expenses:* Tuition: full-time $15,070; part-time $800 per credit hour. *Required fees:* $156 per semester. *Financial support:* Fellowships, research assistantships, career-related internships or fieldwork, Federal Work-Study, institutionally sponsored loans, scholarships/grants, health care benefits, and unspecified assistantships available. Financial award application deadline: 3/31; financial award applicants required to submit FAFSA. *Faculty research:* Attitude change and persuasion, majority and minority influence, social influence, social norms and

behavior prediction, social undermining in the workplace. *Unit head:* Dr. Gregory Pool, Graduate Program Director, Industrial Organizational Psychology, 210-436-3314, Fax: 210-431-4301, E-mail: gpool@stmarytx.edu.
Website: https://www.stmarytx.edu/academics/graduate/masters/psychology/industrial-organizational/

San Diego State University, Graduate and Research Affairs, College of Sciences, Department of Psychology, San Diego, CA 92182. Offers clinical psychology (MS, PhD); industrial and organizational psychology (MS); program evaluation (MS); psychology (MA). PhD offered jointly with University of California, San Diego. *Accreditation:* APA (one or more programs are accredited). Terminal master's awarded for partial completion of doctoral program. *Degree requirements:* For master's, thesis, oral exam; for doctorate, thesis/dissertation. *Entrance requirements:* For master's, GRE General Test, GRE Subject Test, 3 letters of recommendation; for doctorate, GRE General Test, GRE Subject Test, minimum GPA of 3.0, 3 letters of recommendation. Additional exam requirements/recommendations for international students: Required—TOEFL. Electronic applications accepted.

San Francisco State University, Division of Graduate Studies, College of Science and Engineering, Department of Psychology, San Francisco, CA 94132-1722. Offers industrial/organizational psychology (MS); school psychology (Credential); social psychology (MA). *Expenses:* Tuition, state resident: full-time $6738. Tuition, nonresident: full-time $17,898; part-time $372 per credit hour. *Required fees:* $498 per semester. *Financial support:* Teaching assistantships available. Financial award application deadline: 3/1. *Unit head:* Dr. Jeffrey Cookston, Chair, 415-338-2167, Fax: 415-338-2398, E-mail: cookston@sfsu.edu. *Application contact:* Dr. Ryan Howell, Graduate Program Coordinator, 415-405-2140, Fax: 415-338-2398, E-mail: rhowell@sfsu.edu.
Website: http://psychology.sfsu.edu/graduate/application.html

San Jose State University, Graduate Studies and Research, College of Social Sciences, Department of Psychology, San Jose, CA 95192-0001. Offers clinical psychology (MS); experimental psychology (MA); industrial/organizational psychology (MS); psychology (MA). *Degree requirements:* For master's, comprehensive exam, thesis (for some programs). *Entrance requirements:* For master's, GRE General Test, minimum GPA of 3.0. Electronic applications accepted. *Faculty research:* Drug and alcohol abuse, neurohormonal mechanisms in motion sickness, behavior modification, sleep research, genetics.

Seattle Pacific University, Industrial Organizational Psychology Program, Seattle, WA 98119-1997. Offers MA, PhD. *Students:* 51 full-time (30 women), 34 part-time (21 women); includes 19 minority (3 Black or African American, non-Hispanic/Latino; 9 Asian, non-Hispanic/Latino; 2 Hispanic/Latino; 5 Two or more races, non-Hispanic/Latino), 3 international. Average age 28. 64 applicants, 44% accepted, 28 enrolled. In 2014, 10 master's, 6 doctorates awarded. *Degree requirements:* For master's, research project; for doctorate, thesis/dissertation, field placement. *Entrance requirements:* For master's, GRE (administered within five years of application to program, with minimum combined score of 950/295 new scoring on verbal and quantitative sections preferred), personal statement; recommendations; language competency; statement of financial support; for doctorate, GRE (administered within five years of application to program, with minimum combined score of 1100/300 new scoring on verbal and quantitative sections preferred), personal statement; recommendations; language competency; statement of financial support. Additional exam requirements/recommendations for international students: Required—TOEFL (minimum score 550 paper-based). *Application deadline:* For fall admission, 12/15 for domestic and international students. Application fee: $50. Electronic applications accepted. *Financial support:* Applicants required to submit FAFSA. *Unit head:* Dr. Robert B. McKenna, Chair, 206-281-2629, E-mail: rmckenna@spu.edu. *Application contact:* The Graduate Center, 206-281-2091.
Website: http://www.spu.edu/depts/spfc/orgpsych/

Southern Illinois University Edwardsville, Graduate School, School of Education, Health, and Human Behavior, Department of Psychology, Program in Industrial-Organizational Psychology, Edwardsville, IL 62026. Offers MA. Part-time programs available. *Students:* 21 full-time (19 women), 6 part-time (5 women); includes 3 minority (2 Black or African American, non-Hispanic/Latino; 1 Hispanic/Latino), 2 international. 30 applicants, 33% accepted. In 2014, 6 master's awarded. *Degree requirements:* For master's, thesis. *Entrance requirements:* For master's, GRE. Additional exam requirements/recommendations for international students: Required—TOEFL (minimum score 550 paper-based, 79 iBT), IELTS (minimum score 6.5), Michigan Test of English Language Proficiency or PTE. *Application deadline:* For fall admission, 2/1 for domestic and international students. Application fee: $30. Electronic applications accepted. *Expenses:* Tuition, state resident: full-time $5026. Tuition, nonresident: full-time $12,566. *International tuition:* $25,136 full-time. *Required fees:* $1682. Tuition and fees vary according to course load, campus/location and program. *Financial support:* Institutionally sponsored loans, scholarships/grants, and unspecified assistantships available. Financial award application deadline: 3/1; financial award applicants required to submit FAFSA. *Unit head:* Dr. Cynthia Nordstrom, Director, 618-650-2202, E-mail: cnordst@siue.edu. *Application contact:* Melissa K. Mace, Assistant Director of Graduate and International Recruitment, 618-650-2756, Fax: 618-650-3618, E-mail: mmace@siue.edu.
Website: http://www.siue.edu/education/psychology/

Springfield College, Graduate Programs, Programs in Psychology and Counseling, Springfield, MA 01109-3797. Offers athletic counseling (MS, CAGS); clinical mental health counseling (M Ed, CAGS); counseling psychology (Psy D); industrial and organizational psychology (M Ed, CAGS); school guidance counseling (M Ed, CAGS); student personnel administration in higher education (M Ed). Part-time programs available. *Degree requirements:* For master's, research project, portfolio; for doctorate, dissertation project, 1500 hours of counseling psychology practicum, full-year internship. *Entrance requirements:* Additional exam requirements/recommendations for international students: Required—TOEFL (minimum score 550 paper-based). *Application deadline:* For fall admission, 1/15 priority date for domestic students, 1/15 for international students; for winter admission, 11/1 for domestic and international students; for spring admission, 11/1 for domestic and international students. Applications are processed on a rolling basis. Application fee: $50. Electronic applications accepted. *Financial support:* Fellowships with partial tuition reimbursements, teaching assistantships with partial tuition reimbursements, career-related internships or fieldwork, Federal Work-Study, institutionally sponsored loans, and unspecified assistantships available. Financial award application deadline: 3/1; financial award applicants required to submit FAFSA. *Unit head:* Dr. Allison Cumming-McCann, Chair, 413-748-3075, Fax: 413-748-3854, E-mail: acumming@springfieldcollege.edu. *Application contact:* Mary DeAngelo, Director of Enrollment Management, 413-748-3136, E-mail: mdeangel@spfldcol.edu.
Website: http://www.springfieldcollege.edu/academic-programs/psychology-department/graduate-programs-in-psychology/index#.U1F-dKJWiSo

Teachers College, Columbia University, Graduate Faculty of Education, Department of Organization and Leadership, Program in Social and Organizational Psychology, New York, NY 10027-6696. Offers MA. *Faculty:* 11 full-time, 4 part-time/adjunct. *Students:* 163 full-time (105 women), 112 part-time (79 women); includes 67 minority (19 Black or African American, non-Hispanic/Latino; 26 Asian, non-Hispanic/Latino; 18 Hispanic/Latino; 4 Two or more races, non-Hispanic/Latino), 60 international. Average age 29. 304 applicants, 67% accepted, 87 enrolled. In 2014, 126 master's awarded. Terminal master's awarded for partial completion of doctoral program. *Degree requirements:* For master's, comprehensive exam. *Entrance requirements:* For master's, GRE, MAT, or GMAT, minimum GPA of 3.0. *Application deadline:* For fall admission, 12/15 for domestic students. Application fee: $65. Electronic applications accepted. *Expenses:* Tuition: Full-time $33,552; part-time $1398 per credit. *Required fees:* $418 per semester. *Financial support:* Fellowships, research assistantships, career-related internships or fieldwork, Federal Work-Study, institutionally sponsored loans, and tuition waivers (full and partial) available. Support available to part-time students. Financial award application deadline: 2/1. *Faculty research:* Conflict resolution, human resource and organization development, management competence, organizational culture, leadership. *Unit head:* Prof. Debra Noumair, Program Coordinator, 212-678-3395, E-mail: dn28@columbia.edu. *Application contact:* Lynda Hallmark, Program Manager, 212-678-3273, Fax: 212-678-3273, E-mail: hallmark@tc.edu.

Temple University, College of Education, Department of Psychological Studies in Education, Philadelphia, PA 19122-6096. Offers adult and organizational development (Ed M); counseling psychology (Ed M, PhD), including agency counseling (Ed M), counseling psychology (PhD), school counseling (Ed M); education (PhD); educational leadership (Ed M); educational leadership and policy studies (Ed M, Ed D), including educational leadership; educational psychology (Ed M); school psychology (Ed M, PhD, Ed S); special education (Ed M). *Accreditation:* APA (one or more programs are accredited). Part-time and evening/weekend programs available. *Faculty:* 26 full-time (17 women), 35 part-time/adjunct (21 women). *Students:* 181 full-time (134 women), 182 part-time (125 women); includes 95 minority (64 Black or African American, non-Hispanic/Latino; 1 American Indian or Alaska Native, non-Hispanic/Latino; 8 Asian, non-Hispanic/Latino; 17 Hispanic/Latino; 5 Two or more races, non-Hispanic/Latino), 10 international. 281 applicants, 67% accepted, 118 enrolled. In 2014, 77 master's, 24 doctorates, 5 other advanced degrees awarded. Terminal master's awarded for partial completion of doctoral program. *Degree requirements:* For master's, thesis or alternative; for doctorate, thesis/dissertation. *Entrance requirements:* Additional exam requirements/recommendations for international students: Required—TOEFL (minimum score 550 paper-based; 79 iBT). *Application deadline:* For fall admission, 12/15 for international students; for spring admission, 8/1 for international students. Application fee: $60. *Expenses:* Tuition, state resident: full-time $14,490; part-time $805 per credit hour. Tuition, nonresident: full-time $19,850; part-time $1103 per credit hour. *Required fees:* $690. Full-time tuition and fees vary according to class time, course load, degree level, campus/location and program. *Financial support:* Fellowships, research assistantships with full tuition reimbursements, and teaching assistantships with full tuition reimbursements available. Financial award application deadline: 1/15; financial award applicants required to submit FAFSA. *Application contact:* Linda Pryor, Enrollment Management, 215-204-8011, E-mail: educate@temple.edu.
Website: http://education.temple.edu/pols

Texas A&M University, College of Liberal Arts, Department of Psychology, College Station, TX 77843. Offers behavioral and cellular neuroscience (PhD); clinical psychology (PhD); cognitive psychology (PhD); developmental psychology (PhD); industrial/organizational psychology (PhD); psychology (MS); social psychology (PhD). *Accreditation:* APA (one or more programs are accredited). *Faculty:* 35. *Students:* 82 full-time (45 women), 15 part-time (12 women); includes 30 minority (6 Black or African American, non-Hispanic/Latino; 6 Asian, non-Hispanic/Latino; 18 Hispanic/Latino), 11 international. Average age 28. 375 applicants, 5% accepted, 8 enrolled. In 2014, 8 master's, 16 doctorates awarded. *Degree requirements:* For doctorate, comprehensive exam (for some programs), thesis/dissertation. *Entrance requirements:* For doctorate, GRE General Test. Additional exam requirements/recommendations for international students: Required—TOEFL. *Application deadline:* For fall admission, 1/5 for domestic and international students. Application fee: $50 ($90 for international students). Electronic applications accepted. *Expenses:* Tuition, state resident: full-time $4078; part-time $226.55 per credit hour. Tuition, nonresident: full-time $10,594; part-time $577.55 per credit hour. *Required fees:* $2813; $237.70 per credit hour. $278.50 per semester. Tuition and fees vary according to degree level and student level. *Financial support:* In 2014–15, 84 students received support, including 25 fellowships with full and partial tuition reimbursements available (averaging $17,037 per year), 20 research assistantships with full and partial tuition reimbursements available (averaging $8,269 per year), 57 teaching assistantships with full and partial tuition reimbursements available (averaging $7,431 per year); career-related internships or fieldwork, institutionally sponsored loans, scholarships/grants, traineeships, health care benefits, tuition waivers (full and partial), and unspecified assistantships also available. Support available to part-time students. Financial award application deadline: 1/5; financial award applicants required to submit FAFSA. *Unit head:* Dr. Doug Woods, Head, 979-845-2540, E-mail: dowoods@tamu.edu. *Application contact:* Dr. Charles D. Samuelson, Director of Graduate Studies, 979-845-0880, Fax: 979-845-4727, E-mail: c-samuelson@tamu.edu.
Website: http://psychology.tamu.edu

Touro College, Graduate School of Psychology, New York, NY 10006. Offers general psychology (MS); industrial/organizational psychology (MS); mental health counseling (MS); school counseling (MS); school psychology (MS). *Students:* 101 full-time (80 women), 81 part-time (66 women); includes 76 minority (41 Black or African American, non-Hispanic/Latino; 1 American Indian or Alaska Native, non-Hispanic/Latino; 8 Asian, non-Hispanic/Latino; 26 Hispanic/Latino), 2 international. *Unit head:* Dr. Richard Waxman, Dean, 212-242-4668 Ext. 6077, E-mail: richard.waxman@touro.edu.
Website: http://gsp.touro.edu/

University at Albany, State University of New York, College of Arts and Sciences, Department of Psychology, Albany, NY 12222-0001. Offers behavioral neuroscience (PhD); clinical psychology (PhD); cognitive psychology (PhD); industrial/organizational psychology (MA, PhD); social-personality psychology (PhD). *Accreditation:* APA (one or more programs are accredited). *Degree requirements:* For doctorate, thesis/dissertation. *Entrance requirements:* For doctorate, GRE General Test, GRE Subject Test. Additional exam requirements/recommendations for international students: Required—TOEFL (minimum score 550 paper-based). Electronic applications accepted.

The University of Akron, Graduate School, Buchtel College of Arts and Sciences, Department of Psychology, Program in Industrial/Organizational Psychology, Akron, OH 44325. Offers MA, PhD. *Students:* 37 full-time (19 women), 10 part-time (6 women); includes 8 minority (1 Black or African American, non-Hispanic/Latino; 4 Asian, non-Hispanic/Latino; 2 Hispanic/Latino; 1 Two or more races, non-Hispanic/Latino), 2 international. Average age 25. 107 applicants, 1% accepted, 1 enrolled. In 2014, 10 master's, 8 doctorates awarded. Terminal master's awarded for partial completion of doctoral program. *Degree requirements:* For master's, thesis or specialty exam; for doctorate, one foreign language, comprehensive exam, thesis/dissertation. *Entrance requirements:* For master's, GRE General Test, minimum GPA of 2.75, three letters of recommendation, personal statement, curriculum vitae; for doctorate, GRE General Test, minimum graduate GPA of 3.25, three letters of recommendation, personal statement, curriculum vitae. Additional exam requirements/recommendations for

international students: Required—TOEFL (minimum score 550 paper-based; 79 iBT), IELTS (minimum score 6.5). *Application deadline:* For fall admission, 1/15 for domestic and international students. Application fee: $45 ($70 for international students). Electronic applications accepted. *Expenses:* Tuition, state resident: full-time $7578; part-time $421 per credit hour. Tuition, nonresident: full-time $12,977; part-time $721 per credit hour. *Required fees:* $1388; $35 per credit hour. Tuition and fees vary according to course load. *Faculty research:* Personnel selection, performance management, leadership, self-regulation, affect. *Unit head:* Dr. Paul Levy, Chair, 330-972-8369, E-mail: pelevy@uakron.edu.
Website: http://www.uakron.edu/psychology/academics/industrial-organizational-psychology/index.dot

The University of Alabama in Huntsville, School of Graduate Studies, College of Liberal Arts, Department of Psychology, Huntsville, AL 35899. Offers industrial/organizational psychology (MA); psychology (MA). Part-time and evening/weekend programs available. *Degree requirements:* For master's, comprehensive exam, thesis or alternative, oral and written exams. *Entrance requirements:* For master's, GRE General Test, 15 hours of course work in psychology, minimum GPA of 3.25, sample of written work. Additional exam requirements/recommendations for international students: Required—TOEFL (minimum score 500 paper-based; 80 iBT), IELTS (minimum score 6.5). Electronic applications accepted. *Faculty research:* Virtual teams and teamwork, eyewitness identification, aging and memory, psychology of natural disasters and emergency preparedness, pain and pain management research.

University of Central Florida, College of Sciences, Department of Psychology, Program in Industrial/Organizational Psychology, Orlando, FL 32816. Offers MS, PhD. Part-time and evening/weekend programs available. *Students:* 49 full-time (26 women), 6 part-time (3 women); includes 13 minority (4 Black or African American, non-Hispanic/Latino; 3 Asian, non-Hispanic/Latino; 6 Hispanic/Latino), 1 international. Average age 26. 109 applicants, 24% accepted, 14 enrolled. In 2014, 22 master's awarded. *Degree requirements:* For master's, comprehensive exam, thesis, practicum. *Entrance requirements:* For master's, GRE General Test, minimum GPA of 3.0 in last 60 hours, resume. Additional exam requirements/recommendations for international students: Required—TOEFL. *Application deadline:* For fall admission, 2/1 for domestic students. Application fee: $30. Electronic applications accepted. *Expenses:* Tuition, state resident: part-time $288.16 per credit hour. Tuition, nonresident: part-time $1073.31 per credit hour. *Financial support:* In 2014–15, 29 students received support, including 9 fellowships (averaging $6,000 per year), 10 research assistantships with partial tuition reimbursements available (averaging $13,000 per year), 17 teaching assistantships with partial tuition reimbursements available (averaging $9,800 per year); career-related internships or fieldwork, Federal Work-Study, institutionally sponsored loans, tuition waivers (partial), and unspecified assistantships also available. Financial award application deadline: 3/1; financial award applicants required to submit FAFSA. *Faculty research:* Sports psychology, electronic selection systems, team training, stress effects, psychometrics. *Unit head:* Dr. Kimberly Smith-Jentsch, Program Director, 407-823-3577, E-mail: kimberly.jentsch@ucf.edu. *Application contact:* Barbara Rodriguez Lamas, Director, Admissions and Student Services, 407-823-2766, Fax: 407-823-6442, E-mail: gradadmissions@ucf.edu.
Website: http://psychology.cos.ucf.edu/graduate/

University of Connecticut, Graduate School, College of Liberal Arts and Sciences, Department of Psychology, Storrs, CT 06269. Offers behavioral neuroscience (PhD); biopsychology (PhD); clinical psychology (MA, PhD); cognition and instruction (PhD); developmental psychology (MA, PhD); ecological psychology (PhD); experimental psychology (PhD); general psychology (MA, PhD); health psychology (Graduate Certificate); industrial/organizational psychology (PhD); language and cognition (PhD); neuroscience (PhD); occupational health psychology (Graduate Certificate); social psychology (MA, PhD). *Accreditation:* APA. Terminal master's awarded for partial completion of doctoral program. *Degree requirements:* For master's, comprehensive exam; for doctorate, thesis/dissertation. *Entrance requirements:* For master's and doctorate, GRE General Test, GRE Subject Test. Additional exam requirements/recommendations for international students: Required—TOEFL (minimum score 550 paper-based). Electronic applications accepted.

University of Detroit Mercy, College of Liberal Arts and Education, Department of Psychology, Program in Industrial/Organizational Psychology, Detroit, MI 48221. Offers MA. *Entrance requirements:* For master's, GRE General Test, minimum GPA of 3.0.

University of Guelph, Graduate Studies, College of Social and Applied Human Sciences, Department of Psychology, Guelph, ON N1G 2W1, Canada. Offers applied social psychology (MA, PhD); clinical psychology: applied development emphasis (PhD); clinical psychology: applied developmental emphasis (MA); industrial/organizational psychology (MA, PhD); neuroscience and applied cognitive science (MA, PhD). *Degree requirements:* For master's, thesis; for doctorate, comprehensive exam, thesis/dissertation. *Entrance requirements:* For master's, GRE General Test, GRE Subject Test, minimum B+ average during previous 2 years of course work; for doctorate, GRE General Test, GRE Subject Test, minimum A- average. Additional exam requirements/recommendations for international students: Required—TOEFL (minimum score 89 iBT). Electronic applications accepted. *Faculty research:* Organizational psychology, reading comprehension and mathematical ability, drug addiction and relapse, gender issues and culture, memory, clinical psychology.

University of Houston, College of Liberal Arts and Social Sciences, Department of Psychology, Houston, TX 77204. Offers clinical psychology (PhD); developmental psychology (PhD); industrial/organizational psychology (PhD); psychology (MA); social psychology (PhD). *Accreditation:* APA (one or more programs are accredited). *Degree requirements:* For master's, comprehensive exam, thesis; for doctorate, comprehensive exam, thesis/dissertation. *Entrance requirements:* For master's, GRE General Test, career statement, 3 letters of recommendation; for doctorate, GRE General Test, 3 letters of recommendation. Additional exam requirements/recommendations for international students: Required—TOEFL (minimum score 550 paper-based; 79 iBT). Electronic applications accepted. *Faculty research:* Health psychology, depression, child/family process, organizational effectiveness, close relationships.

University of Maryland, Baltimore County, The Graduate School, College of Arts, Humanities and Social Sciences, Department of Psychology, Program in Industrial Organizational Psychology, Rockville, MD 20850. Offers MPS. Part-time and evening/weekend programs available. *Faculty:* 1 full-time (0 women), 11 part-time/adjunct (5 women). *Students:* 32 full-time (28 women), 53 part-time (42 women); includes 38 minority (20 Black or African American, non-Hispanic/Latino; 6 Asian, non-Hispanic/Latino; 10 Hispanic/Latino; 2 Native Hawaiian or other Pacific Islander, non-Hispanic/Latino). Average age 28. 110 applicants, 51% accepted, 38 enrolled. In 2014, 16 master's awarded. *Entrance requirements:* Additional exam requirements/recommendations for international students: Required—TOEFL. *Application deadline:* For fall admission, 3/1 for domestic students, 1/1 for international students. Applications are processed on a rolling basis. Application fee: $50. Electronic applications accepted. *Expenses:* Tuition, state resident: part-time $557. Tuition, nonresident: part-time $922. *Required fees:* $122 per semester. One-time fee: $200 part-time. *Financial support:* In 2014–15, 3 teaching assistantships with full tuition reimbursements (averaging $14,000 per year) were awarded. *Faculty research:* Organizations, human factors, group dynamics, change management. *Unit head:* Dr. Theodore Rosen, Program Director, 301-738-6171, E-mail: throsen@umbc.edu. *Application contact:* Ashley Waters, Program Coordinator, 301-738-6081, E-mail: awaters@umbc.edu.
Website: http://www.umbc.edu/io

University of Maryland, College Park, Academic Affairs, College of Behavioral and Social Sciences, Department of Psychology, College Park, MD 20742. Offers clinical psychology (PhD); developmental psychology (PhD); experimental psychology (PhD); industrial psychology (MA, MS, PhD); social psychology (PhD). *Accreditation:* APA (one or more programs are accredited). *Degree requirements:* For master's, thesis; for doctorate, variable foreign language requirement, comprehensive exam, thesis/dissertation. *Entrance requirements:* For master's and doctorate, GRE General Test, GRE Subject Test, minimum GPA of 3.5, research and/or work experience, 3 letters of recommendation. Electronic applications accepted. *Faculty research:* Social stereotyping and prejudice, anxiety disorders, auditory neuroethology, counseling and social psychology.

University of Minnesota, Twin Cities Campus, Graduate School, College of Liberal Arts, Department of Psychology, Program in Industrial/Organizational Psychology, Minneapolis, MN 55455-0213. Offers PhD. *Degree requirements:* For doctorate, comprehensive exam, thesis/dissertation. *Entrance requirements:* For doctorate, GRE General Test, GRE Subject Test (recommended), 12 credits of upper-level psychology courses, including a course in statistics or psychological measurement. Additional exam requirements/recommendations for international students: Required—TOEFL (minimum score 550 paper-based; 79 iBT).

University of Missouri–St. Louis, College of Arts and Sciences, Department of Psychology, St. Louis, MO 63121. Offers behavioral neuroscience (MA, PhD); clinical psychology (PhD); clinical psychology respecialization (Certificate); industrial/organizational psychology (MA, PhD); trauma studies (Certificate). *Accreditation:* APA (one or more programs are accredited). Evening/weekend programs available. *Faculty:* 20 full-time (12 women), 5 part-time/adjunct (0 women). *Students:* 61 full-time (39 women), 17 part-time (15 women); includes 8 minority (3 Black or African American, non-Hispanic/Latino; 1 American Indian or Alaska Native, non-Hispanic/Latino; 1 Asian, non-Hispanic/Latino; 3 Hispanic/Latino). Average age 27. 232 applicants, 8% accepted, 14 enrolled. In 2014, 17 master's, 15 doctorates awarded. Terminal master's awarded for partial completion of doctoral program. *Degree requirements:* For master's, thesis; for doctorate, thesis/dissertation. *Entrance requirements:* For master's, GRE General Test, 3 letters of recommendation; for doctorate, GRE General Test, GRE Subject Test, 3 letters of recommendation. Additional exam requirements/recommendations for international students: Required—TOEFL (minimum score 550 paper-based; 79 iBT), IELTS (minimum score 6.5). *Application deadline:* For fall admission, 12/15 for domestic and international students. Application fee: $50 ($40 for international students). Electronic applications accepted. *Expenses:* Tuition, state resident: full-time $7364; part-time $409.10 per hour. Tuition, nonresident: full-time $18,153; part-time $1008.50 per hour. *Financial support:* In 2014–15, 8 research assistantships with full and partial tuition reimbursements (averaging $10,600 per year), 25 teaching assistantships with full and partial tuition reimbursements (averaging $9,422 per year) were awarded; fellowships with full tuition reimbursements also available. Financial award applicants required to submit FAFSA. *Faculty research:* Bereavement and loss, neuroscience, post-traumatic stress disorder, conflict and negotiation, social psychology. *Unit head:* Dr. Brian Vandenberg, Chair, 314-516-5391, Fax: 314-516-5392, E-mail: umslpsychology@msx.umsl.edu. *Application contact:* 314-516-5458, Fax: 314-516-6996, E-mail: gradadm@umsl.edu.
Website: http://www.umsl.edu/divisions/artscience/psychology/

University of Nebraska at Omaha, Graduate Studies, College of Arts and Sciences, Department of Psychology, Omaha, NE 68182. Offers industrial/organizational psychology (MS); psychology (MS, PhD); school psychology (MS, Ed S). Part-time programs available. *Faculty:* 19 full-time (8 women). *Students:* 66 full-time (52 women), 53 part-time (33 women); includes 10 minority (2 Black or African American, non-Hispanic/Latino; 2 Asian, non-Hispanic/Latino; 6 Hispanic/Latino). Average age 26. 178 applicants, 31% accepted, 51 enrolled. In 2014, 20 master's, 6 doctorates, 10 other advanced degrees awarded. *Degree requirements:* For master's, comprehensive exam, thesis (for some programs); for doctorate, comprehensive exam, thesis/dissertation. *Entrance requirements:* For master's and doctorate, GRE, minimum GPA of 3.0, official transcripts, 3 letters of recommendation, statement of purpose, writing sample, resume. Additional exam requirements/recommendations for international students: Required—TOEFL, IELTS, PTE. *Application deadline:* For fall admission, 1/5 for domestic and international students. Application fee: $45. Electronic applications accepted. *Financial support:* In 2014–15, 42 students received support, including 16 research assistantships with tuition reimbursements available, 26 teaching assistantships with tuition reimbursements available; fellowships with tuition reimbursements available, career-related internships or fieldwork, Federal Work-Study, institutionally sponsored loans, scholarships/grants, tuition waivers (partial), and unspecified assistantships also available. Support available to part-time students. Financial award application deadline: 3/1; financial award applicants required to submit FAFSA. *Unit head:* Dr. Brigette Ryalls, Chairperson, 402-554-2341, E-mail: graduate@unomaha.edu. *Application contact:* Dr. Joseph Brown, Graduate Program Chair, 402-554-2341, E-mail: graduate@unomaha.edu.

University of New Haven, Graduate School, College of Arts and Sciences, Program in Industrial and Organizational Psychology, West Haven, CT 06516-1916. Offers conflict management (MA); human resource management (MA); industrial organizational psychology (MA); organizational development (MA); psychology of conflict management (Certificate). Part-time and evening/weekend programs available. *Degree requirements:* For master's, thesis or alternative, internship or practicum. *Entrance requirements:* Additional exam requirements/recommendations for international students: Required—TOEFL (minimum score 80 iBT), IELTS, PTE (minimum score 53). Electronic applications accepted. Application fee is waived when completed online. *Expenses:* Contact institution.

The University of North Carolina at Charlotte, College of Liberal Arts and Sciences, Department of Psychology, Charlotte, NC 28223-0001. Offers clinical/community psychology (MA); cognitive sciences (Graduate Certificate); health psychology (PhD); industrial/organizational psychology (MA). Part-time programs available. *Faculty:* 31 full-time (17 women), 1 part-time/adjunct (0 women). *Students:* 42 full-time (35 women), 31 part-time (26 women); includes 18 minority (5 Black or African American, non-Hispanic/Latino; 2 Asian, non-Hispanic/Latino; 9 Hispanic/Latino; 2 Two or more races, non-Hispanic/Latino), 1 international. Average age 28. 243 applicants, 16% accepted, 25 enrolled. In 2014, 9 master's, 5 doctorates, 1 other advanced degree awarded. Terminal master's awarded for partial completion of doctoral program. *Degree requirements:* For master's, thesis; for doctorate, thesis/dissertation. *Entrance requirements:* For master's, GRE General Test, GRE Subject Test, minimum GPA of 3.0 in undergraduate major, 2.8 overall, letters of recommendation; for doctorate, GRE General Test, minimum GPA of 3.5, letters of recommendation. Additional exam requirements/recommendations for international students: Required—TOEFL (minimum score 557 paper-based; 83 iBT). *Application deadline:* For fall admission, 5/1 for domestic and international students. Application fee: $75. Electronic applications accepted. *Expenses:* Tuition, state

resident: full-time $4008. Tuition, nonresident: full-time $16,295. *Required fees:* $2755. Tuition and fees vary according to course load and program. *Financial support:* In 2014–15, 33 students received support, including 16 research assistantships (averaging $15,239 per year), 17 teaching assistantships (averaging $12,809 per year); career-related internships or fieldwork, Federal Work-Study, institutionally sponsored loans, and scholarships/grants also available. Support available to part-time students. Financial award application deadline: 4/1; financial award applicants required to submit FAFSA. *Faculty research:* Neuropsychology of information processing, perception and human performance, computer-based applications in research and instruction, interventions to facilitate team effectiveness, post-traumatic psychological growth. *Total annual research expenditures:* $327,551. *Unit head:* Dr. Fary Cachelin, Chair, 704-687-1319, Fax: 704-687-1317, E-mail: fcacheli@uncc.edu. *Application contact:* Kathy B. Giddings, Director of Graduate Admissions, 704-687-5503, Fax: 704-687-1668, E-mail: gradadm@uncc.edu.
Website: http://psych.uncc.edu/graduate-programs

The University of North Carolina at Charlotte, College of Liberal Arts and Sciences, Interdisciplinary Liberal Arts and Sciences Programs, Charlotte, NC 28223-0001. Offers gerontology (MA, Graduate Certificate); Latin American studies (MA); liberal studies (MA); organizational psychology (PhD); public policy (PhD); women's studies (Graduate Certificate). *Faculty:* 6 full-time (3 women), 5 part-time/adjunct (all women). *Students:* 58 full-time (31 women), 55 part-time (45 women); includes 24 minority (15 Black or African American, non-Hispanic/Latino; 1 Asian, non-Hispanic/Latino; 6 Hispanic/Latino; 1 Native Hawaiian or other Pacific Islander, non-Hispanic/Latino; 1 Two or more races, non-Hispanic/Latino), 12 international. Average age 33. 96 applicants, 46% accepted, 29 enrolled. In 2014, 11 master's, 8 doctorates, 15 other advanced degrees awarded. Terminal master's awarded for partial completion of doctoral program. *Degree requirements:* For master's, thesis or alternative, comprehensive exam or project; for doctorate, thesis/dissertation. *Entrance requirements:* For master's, GRE General Test or MAT, minimum GPA of 3.0 during previous 2 years, 2.75 overall; for doctorate, GRE, letters of recommendation. Additional exam requirements/recommendations for international students: Required—TOEFL (minimum score 557 paper-based; 83 iBT). *Application deadline:* For fall admission, 5/1 priority date for domestic students, 5/1 for international students; for spring admission, 10/1 priority date for domestic students, 10/1 for international students. Applications are processed on a rolling basis. Application fee: $75. Electronic applications accepted. *Expenses:* Tuition, state resident: full-time $4008. Tuition, nonresident: full-time $16,295. *Required fees:* $2755. Tuition and fees vary according to course load and program. *Financial support:* In 2014–15, 24 students received support, including 20 research assistantships (averaging $10,400 per year), 4 teaching assistantships (averaging $8,250 per year); career-related internships or fieldwork, institutionally sponsored loans, scholarships/grants, and unspecified assistantships also available. Support available to part-time students. Financial award application deadline: 4/1; financial award applicants required to submit FAFSA. *Total annual research expenditures:* $15,045. *Unit head:* Dr. Nancy A. Gutierrez, Dean, 704-687-0081, Fax: 704-687-4347, E-mail: ngutierr@uncc.edu. *Application contact:* Kathy B. Giddings, Director of Graduate Admissions, 704-687-5503, Fax: 704-687-3279, E-mail: gradadm@uncc.edu.
Website: http://www.lbst.uncc.edu/

University of Oklahoma, College of Arts and Sciences, Department of Psychology, Program in Psychology, Norman, OK 73019. Offers industrial and organizational psychology (MS, PhD); psychology (MS, PhD). *Students:* 54 full-time (30 women), 21 part-time (9 women); includes 11 minority (1 Black or African American, non-Hispanic/Latino; 1 American Indian or Alaska Native, non-Hispanic/Latino; 5 Asian, non-Hispanic/Latino; 1 Hispanic/Latino; 1 Native Hawaiian or other Pacific Islander, non-Hispanic/Latino; 2 Two or more races, non-Hispanic/Latino), 3 international. Average age 27. 124 applicants, 7% accepted, 8 enrolled. In 2014, 5 master's, 13 doctorates awarded. Terminal master's awarded for partial completion of doctoral program. *Degree requirements:* For master's, comprehensive exam, thesis; for doctorate, thesis/dissertation. *Entrance requirements:* For master's and doctorate, GRE, 3 letters of recommendation, personal statement, research experience. Additional exam requirements/recommendations for international students: Required—TOEFL (minimum score 79 iBT). *Application deadline:* For fall admission, 1/1 for domestic and international students; for spring admission, 11/1 for domestic students, 9/1 for international students. Application fee: $50 ($100 for international students). Electronic applications accepted. *Expenses:* Tuition, state resident: full-time $4394; part-time $183.10 per credit hour. Tuition, nonresident: full-time $16,970; part-time $707.10 per credit hour. *Required fees:* $2892; $109.95 per credit hour. $126.50 per semester. *Financial support:* In 2014–15, 52 students received support. Health care benefits, tuition waivers (full), and unspecified assistantships available. Financial award application deadline: 6/1; financial award applicants required to submit FAFSA. *Faculty research:* Leading for creativity, innovation, ethical behavior, health and well-being, decision-making and risk. *Unit head:* Dr. Jorge Mendoza, Chair, 405-325-4511, Fax: 405-325-4737, E-mail: jmendoza@ou.edu. *Application contact:* Kathryn Paine, Graduate Admissions Coordinator, 405-325-4512, Fax: 405-325-4737, E-mail: kpaine@ou.edu.
Website: http://www.ou.edu/psychology

University of Phoenix–Online Campus, College of Social Science, Phoenix, AZ 85034-7209. Offers mediation (Certificate); psychology (MS), including behavioral health, industrial-organizational, psychology. Evening/weekend programs available. Postbaccalaureate distance learning degree programs offered. *Entrance requirements:* Additional exam requirements/recommendations for international students: Required—TOEFL, TOEIC (Test of English as an International Communication), Berlitz Online English Proficiency Exam, PTE, or IELTS. Electronic applications accepted. *Expenses:* Contact institution.

University of Phoenix–Online Campus, School of Advanced Studies, Phoenix, AZ 85034-7209. Offers business administration (DBA); education (Ed S); educational leadership (Ed D), including curriculum and instruction, education technology, educational leadership; health administration (DHA); higher education administration (PhD); industrial/organizational psychology (PhD); nursing (PhD); organizational leadership (DM), including information systems and technology, organizational leadership. Evening/weekend programs available. Postbaccalaureate distance learning degree programs offered. *Degree requirements:* For doctorate, thesis/dissertation. *Entrance requirements:* Additional exam requirements/recommendations for international students: Required—TOEFL, TOEIC (Test of English as an International Communication), Berlitz Online English Proficiency Exam, PTE, or IELTS. Electronic applications accepted. *Expenses:* Contact institution.

University of Phoenix–Washington D.C. Campus, College of Social Sciences, Washington, DC 20001. Offers industrial/organizational psychology (PhD); psychology (MS).

University of Puerto Rico, Río Piedras Campus, College of Social Sciences, Department of Psychology, San Juan, PR 00931-3300. Offers clinical psychology (MA); industrial organizational psychology (MA); investigative academic psychology (MA); psychology (PhD); social-community psychology (MA). Part-time programs available. *Degree requirements:* For master's, comprehensive exam, thesis; for doctorate, comprehensive exam, thesis/dissertation, internship. *Entrance requirements:* For master's, GRE or PAEG, interview, minimum GPA of 3.0; for doctorate, GRE or PAEG, interview, master's degree, minimum GPA of 3.0. *Faculty research:* Intervention on depressed Latino youth, biosychosocial training.

University of South Africa, College of Economic and Management Sciences, Pretoria, South Africa. Offers accounting (D Admin, D Com); accounting science (DA); auditing (D Admin, D Com); business administration (M Tech); business economics (D Admin); business leadership (DBL); business management (D Admin, D Com); economic management analysis (M Tech); economics (D Admin, D Com, PhD); human resource development (M Tech); industrial psychology (D Admin, D Com, PhD); logistics (D Com); marketing (M Tech); public administration (D Admin, D Com, DPA, PhD); public management (M Tech); quantitative management (D Admin, D Com); real estate (M Tech); statistics (D Admin, PhD); tourism management (D Admin, D Com); transport economics (D Admin, D Com).

University of South Africa, College of Human Sciences, Pretoria, South Africa. Offers adult education (M Ed); African languages (MA, PhD); African politics (MA, PhD); Afrikaans (MA, PhD); ancient history (MA, PhD); ancient Near Eastern studies (MA, PhD); anthropology (MA, PhD); applied linguistics (MA); Arabic (MA, PhD); archaeology (MA); art history (MA); Biblical archaeology (MA); Biblical studies (M Th, D Th, PhD); Christian spirituality (M Th, D Th); church history (M Th, D Th); classical studies (MA, PhD); clinical psychology (MA); communication (MA, PhD); comparative education (M Ed, Ed D); consulting psychology (D Admin, D Com, PhD); curriculum studies (M Ed, Ed D); development studies (M Admin, MA, D Admin, PhD); didactics (M Ed, Ed D); education (M Tech); education management (M Ed, Ed D); educational psychology (M Ed); English (MA); environmental education (M Ed); French (MA, PhD); German (MA, PhD); Greek (MA); guidance and counseling (M Ed); health studies (MA, PhD), including health sciences education (MA), health services management (MA), medical and surgical nursing science (critical care general) (MA), midwifery and neonatal nursing science (MA), trauma and emergency care (MA); history (MA, PhD); history of education (Ed D); inclusive education (M Ed, Ed D); information and communications technology policy and regulation (MA); information science (MA, MIS, PhD); international politics (MA, PhD); Islamic studies (MA, PhD); Italian (MA, PhD); Judaica (MA, PhD); linguistics (MA, PhD); mathematical education (M Ed); mathematics education (MA); missiology (M Th, D Th); modern Hebrew (MA, PhD); musicology (MA, MMus, D Mus, PhD); natural science education (M Ed); New Testament (M Th, D Th); Old Testament (D Th); pastoral therapy (M Th, D Th); philosophy (MA); philosophy of education (M Ed, Ed D); politics (MA, PhD); Portuguese (MA, PhD); practical theology (M Th, D Th); psychology (MA, MS, PhD); psychology of education (M Ed, Ed D); public health (MA); religious studies (MA, D Th, PhD); Romance languages (MA); Russian (MA, PhD); Semitic languages (MA, PhD); social behavior studies in HIV/AIDS (MA); social science (mental health) (MA); social science in development studies (MA); social science in psychology (MA); social science in social work (MA); social science in sociology (MA); social work (MSW, DSW, PhD); socio-education (M Ed, Ed D); sociolinguistics (MA); sociology (MA, PhD); Spanish (MA, PhD); systematic theology (M Th, D Th); TESOL (teaching English to speakers of other languages) (MA); theological ethics (M Th, D Th); theory of literature (MA, PhD); urban ministries (D Th); urban ministry (M Th).

University of South Florida, College of Arts and Sciences, Department of Psychology, Tampa, FL 33620-9951. Offers clinical psychology (PhD); cognitive and neural sciences (PhD); industrial-organizational psychology (PhD). *Accreditation:* APA. *Faculty:* 33 full-time (15 women), 1 part-time/adjunct. *Students:* 96 full-time (68 women), 18 part-time (11 women); includes 25 minority (2 Black or African American, non-Hispanic/Latino; 9 Asian, non-Hispanic/Latino; 10 Hispanic/Latino; 4 Two or more races, non-Hispanic/Latino), 12 international. Average age 28. 513 applicants, 5% accepted, 19 enrolled. In 2014, 16 doctorates awarded. *Degree requirements:* For doctorate, comprehensive exam, thesis/dissertation, internship. *Entrance requirements:* For doctorate, GRE General Test (minimum recommended verbal and quantitative scores each above the 50th percentile), minimum upper-division GPA of 3.4, three letters of recommendation, personal goals statement. Additional exam requirements/recommendations for international students: Required—TOEFL (minimum score 550 paper-based; 79 iBT) or IELTS (minimum score 6.5). *Application deadline:* For fall admission, 12/1 for domestic and international students. Application fee: $30. Electronic applications accepted. *Expenses:* Expenses: Contact institution. *Financial support:* In 2014–15, 75 students received support, including 18 research assistantships with tuition reimbursements available (averaging $14,727 per year), 57 teaching assistantships with tuition reimbursements available (averaging $14,543 per year); tuition waivers (partial) and unspecified assistantships also available. Financial award applicants required to submit FAFSA. *Faculty research:* Clinical, cognitive, neuroscience, social, and industrial/organizational. *Total annual research expenditures:* $1.7 million. *Unit head:* Dr. Toru Shimizu, Chairperson, 813-974-0352, Fax: 813-974-4617, E-mail: shimizu@usf.edu. *Application contact:* Dr. Joseph Vandello, Associate Professor and Graduate Program Director, 813-974-0362, Fax: 813-974-4617, E-mail: vandello@usf.edu.
Website: http://psychology.usf.edu/

The University of Tennessee, Graduate School, College of Business Administration, Program in Industrial and Organizational Psychology, Knoxville, TN 37996. Offers PhD. *Degree requirements:* For doctorate, thesis/dissertation. *Entrance requirements:* For doctorate, GRE General Test, minimum GPA of 2.7. Additional exam requirements/recommendations for international students: Required—TOEFL. Electronic applications accepted.

The University of Tennessee at Chattanooga, Program in Psychology, Chattanooga, TN 37403. Offers industrial/organizational psychology (MS); research psychology (MS). Part-time and evening/weekend programs available. *Faculty:* 10 full-time (4 women), 1 part-time/adjunct (0 women). *Students:* 38 full-time (20 women), 4 part-time (2 women); includes 3 minority (1 American Indian or Alaska Native, non-Hispanic/Latino; 2 Hispanic/Latino), 1 international. Average age 25. 54 applicants, 57% accepted, 18 enrolled. In 2014, 22 master's awarded. *Degree requirements:* For master's, comprehensive exam (for some programs), thesis (for some programs), practicum (industrial/organizational psychology). *Entrance requirements:* For master's, GRE General Test, minimum GPA of 2.5 on all undergraduate coursework or 3.0 in senior year. Additional exam requirements/recommendations for international students: Required—TOEFL (minimum score 550 paper-based; 79 iBT), IELTS (minimum score 6). *Application deadline:* For fall admission, 6/13 priority date for domestic students, 6/1 for international students; for spring admission, 10/15 priority date for domestic students, 10/1 for international students. Applications are processed on a rolling basis. Application fee: $30 ($35 for international students). Electronic applications accepted. *Expenses:* Tuition, state resident: full-time $7708; part-time $428 per credit hour. Tuition, nonresident: full-time $23,826; part-time $1323 per credit hour. *Required fees:* $1708; $252 per credit hour. *Financial support:* In 2014–15, 19 research assistantships with tuition reimbursements (averaging $5,800 per year), 6 teaching assistantships with tuition reimbursements (averaging $5,982 per year) were awarded; career-related internships or fieldwork, scholarships/grants, and unspecified assistantships also available. Support available to part-time students. Financial award applicants required to submit FAFSA. *Faculty research:* Decision processes, philosophical psychology, memory, social cognition, employee selection. *Total annual research expenditures:*

$180,611. *Unit head:* Dr. Brian O'Leary, Department Head, 423-425-4283, Fax: 423-425-4284, E-mail: brian-o'leary@utc.edu. *Application contact:* Dr. J. Randy Walker, Interim Dean of Graduate Studies, 423-425-4478, Fax: 423-425-5223, E-mail: randy-walker@utc.edu.
Website: http://www.utc.edu/Academic/Psychology/

The University of Texas at Arlington, Graduate School, College of Science, Department of Psychology, Arlington, TX 76019. Offers experimental psychology (PhD); health psychology (PhD); industrial organizational psychology (MS); psychology (MS). Part-time programs available. Terminal master's awarded for partial completion of doctoral program. *Degree requirements:* For master's, comprehensive exam or thesis; for doctorate, thesis/dissertation (for some programs). *Entrance requirements:* For master's and doctorate, GRE General Test, minimum GPA of 3.0 in last 60 hours of course work. Additional exam requirements/recommendations for international students: Required—TOEFL (minimum score 550 paper-based).

University of the Incarnate Word, Extended Academic Programs, Programs in Psychology, San Antonio, TX 78209-6397. Offers educational psychology (MS); industrial and organizational psychology (MS). *Faculty:* 1 full-time (0 women), 17 part-time/adjunct (7 women). *Students:* 7 part-time (4 women); includes 1 minority (Hispanic/Latino). Average age 36. 9 applicants, 33% accepted, 1 enrolled. *Expenses: Tuition:* Part-time $815 per credit hour. *Required fees:* $86 per credit hour. *Unit head:* Dr. Cyndi Porter, Vice President, 877-603-1130, E-mail: porter@uiwtx.edu. *Application contact:* Julie Weber, Director of Marketing and Recruitment, 210-318-1876, Fax: 210-829-2756, E-mail: eapadmission@uiwtx.edu.

The University of Tulsa, Graduate School, Kendall College of Arts and Sciences, Department of Psychology, Program in Industrial/Organizational Psychology, Tulsa, OK 74104-3189. Offers MA, PhD, JD/MA. Part-time programs available. *Faculty:* 5 full-time (2 women). *Students:* 21 full-time (13 women), 4 part-time (3 women); includes 5 minority (1 American Indian or Alaska Native, non-Hispanic/Latino; 2 Asian, non-Hispanic/Latino; 2 Hispanic/Latino), 4 international. Average age 27. 68 applicants, 32% accepted, 12 enrolled. In 2014, 15 master's, 1 doctorate awarded. Terminal master's awarded for partial completion of doctoral program. *Degree requirements:* For master's, comprehensive exam, thesis (for some programs), 200-hour internship; for doctorate, comprehensive exam, thesis/dissertation. *Entrance requirements:* For master's and doctorate, GRE General Test. Additional exam requirements/recommendations for international students: Required—TOEFL (minimum score 577 paper-based; 91 iBT), IELTS (minimum score 6.5). *Application deadline:* For fall admission, 12/15 for domestic and international students. Application fee: $55. Electronic applications accepted. *Expenses: Tuition:* Full-time $20,160; part-time $1120 per credit hour. *Required fees:* $6 per credit hour. Tuition and fees vary according to course level and course load. *Financial support:* In 2014–15, 25 students received support, including 5 fellowships with full and partial tuition reimbursements available (averaging $5,797 per year), 5 research assistantships with full and partial tuition reimbursements available (averaging $13,617 per year), 20 teaching assistantships with full and partial tuition reimbursements available (averaging $11,084 per year); career-related internships or fieldwork, Federal Work-Study, scholarships/grants, health care benefits, tuition waivers (full and partial), and unspecified assistantships also available. Support available to part-time students. Financial award application deadline: 2/1; financial award applicants required to submit FAFSA. *Faculty research:* Personnel testing and selection, training, performance appraisal, organizational development, job attitudes and motivation, leadership. *Unit head:* Dr. Robert Tett, Director, 918-631-2737, Fax: 918-631-2833, E-mail: robert-tett@utulsa.edu. *Application contact:* Information Contact, 800-882-4723, E-mail: grad@utulsa.edu.

University of West Florida, College of Arts and Sciences: Arts, Department of Psychology, Pensacola, FL 32514-5750. Offers counseling (MA); counseling-licensed mental health counselor (MA); general psychology (MA); industrial-organizational (MA). Part-time programs available. *Degree requirements:* For master's, thesis (for some programs). *Entrance requirements:* For master's, GRE, official transcripts; minimum GPA of 3.0; writing sample; three letters of reference; field experience or skill sets; oral interview (for counseling specialization). Additional exam requirements/recommendations for international students: Required—TOEFL (minimum score 550 paper-based). *Faculty research:* Prose recall, brain imaging, peak performance, biofeedback and pain control, comparable worth.

University of Wisconsin–Oshkosh, Graduate Studies, College of Letters and Science, Department of Psychology, Oshkosh, WI 54901. Offers experimental psychology (MS); industrial/organizational psychology (MS). *Degree requirements:* For master's, thesis. *Entrance requirements:* For master's, GRE, 10 semester hours of undergraduate course work in psychology. Additional exam requirements/recommendations for international students: Required—TOEFL (minimum score 550 paper-based; 79 iBT). Electronic applications accepted. *Faculty research:* Performance evaluation, training, biological bases of behavior, tactile perception, aging.

Walden University, Graduate Programs, School of Psychology, Minneapolis, MN 55401. Offers clinical psychology (MS), including counseling, general program; forensic psychology (MS), including forensic psychology in the community, general program, mental health applications, program planning and evaluation in forensic settings, psychology and legal systems; organizational psychology and development (Postbaccalaureate Certificate); psychology (MS, PhD), including applied psychology (MS), clinical psychology (PhD), counseling psychology (PhD), crisis management and response (MS), educational psychology, forensic psychology (PhD), general psychology (MS), general psychology research (PhD), health psychology, leadership development and coaching (MS), psychology of culture (MS), psychology, public administration, and social change (MS), social psychology, terrorism and security (MS); psychology respecialization (Post-Doctoral Certificate); teaching online (Post-Master's Certificate). Part-time and evening/weekend programs available. Postbaccalaureate distance learning degree programs offered (no on-campus study). *Faculty:* 56 full-time (36 women), 351 part-time/adjunct (201 women). *Students:* 2,757 full-time (2,202 women), 1,466 part-time (1,148 women); includes 1,849 minority (1,299 Black or African American, non-Hispanic/Latino; 37 American Indian or Alaska Native, non-Hispanic/Latino; 74 Asian, non-Hispanic/Latino; 315 Hispanic/Latino; 8 Native Hawaiian or other Pacific Islander, non-Hispanic/Latino; 116 Two or more races, non-Hispanic/Latino), 28 international. Average age 41. 913 applicants, 97% accepted, 851 enrolled. In 2014, 602 master's, 204 doctorates, 19 other advanced degrees awarded. Terminal master's awarded for partial completion of doctoral program. *Degree requirements:* For master's, thesis optional; for doctorate, thesis/dissertation, residency. *Entrance requirements:* For master's, bachelor's degree or higher; minimum GPA of 2.5; official transcripts; goal statement (for some programs); access to computer and Internet; for doctorate, master's degree or higher; three years of related professional or academic experience (preferred); minimum GPA of 3.0; goal statement and current resume (for select programs); official transcripts; access to computer and Internet; for other advanced degree, relevant work experience; access to computer and Internet. Additional exam requirements/recommendations for international students: Required—TOEFL (minimum score 550 paper-based, 79 iBT), IELTS (minimum score 6.5), Michigan English Language Assessment Battery (minimum score 82), or PTE (minimum score 53). *Application deadline:* Applications are processed on a rolling basis. Application fee: $0. Electronic applications accepted. *Expenses: Tuition:* Full-time $11,925; part-time $500 per credit hour. *Required fees:* $647. *Financial support:* Fellowships, Federal Work-Study, scholarships/grants, unspecified assistantships, and family tuition reduction, active duty/veteran tuition reduction, group tuition reduction, interest-free payment plans, employee tuition reduction available. Support available to part-time students. Financial award applicants required to submit FAFSA. *Unit head:* Dr. Marilyn Powell, Associate Dean, 866-492-5366. *Application contact:* Meghan Thomas, Vice President of Enrollment Management, 866-492-5336, E-mail: info@waldenu.edu.
Website: http://www.waldenu.edu/programs/colleges-schools/psychology

Wayne State University, College of Liberal Arts and Sciences, Department of Psychology, Program in Industrial and Organizational Psychology, Detroit, MI 48202. Offers MA. *Accreditation:* APA. Part-time programs available. *Faculty:* 8 full-time (2 women), 3 part-time/adjunct (1 woman). *Students:* 2 full-time (both women), 23 part-time (12 women); includes 3 minority (1 Black or African American, non-Hispanic/Latino; 2 Two or more races, non-Hispanic/Latino), 1 international. Average age 26. 62 applicants, 26% accepted, 8 enrolled. In 2014, 9 master's awarded. *Entrance requirements:* For master's, GRE General Test, minimum undergraduate upper-division cumulative GPA of 3.0, courses in introductory psychology and statistics, two letters of recommendation, professional statement. Additional exam requirements/recommendations for international students: Required—TOEFL (minimum score 550 paper-based; 79 iBT), TWE (minimum score 5.5), Michigan English Language Assessment Battery (minimum score 85); Recommended—IELTS (minimum score 6.5). *Application deadline:* For fall admission, 6/1 for domestic students, 5/1 for international students; for winter admission, 10/1 for domestic students, 9/1 for international students; for spring admission, 2/1 for domestic students, 1/1 for international students. Applications are processed on a rolling basis. Application fee: $0. Electronic applications accepted. *Expenses:* Tuition, state resident: full-time $10,294; part-time $571.90 per credit hour. Tuition, nonresident: full-time $29,730; part-time $1238.75 per credit hour. *Required fees:* $1365; $43.50 per credit hour. $291.10 per semester. Tuition and fees vary according to course load and program. *Financial support:* In 2014–15, 3 students received support. Scholarships/grants available. Financial award application deadline: 3/31; financial award applicants required to submit FAFSA. *Unit head:* Boris Baltes, PhD, Chair, 313-577-2800, Fax: 313-577-7636, E-mail: b.baltes@wayne.edu. *Application contact:* Alia Allen, Academic Service Officer, 313-577-2823, E-mail: aallen@wayne.edu.
Website: http://clas.wayne.edu/psychology/ma-io

West Chester University of Pennsylvania, College of Arts and Sciences, Department of Psychology, West Chester, PA 19383. Offers clinical mental health (Certificate); clinical psychology (MA); general psychology (MA); industrial psychology (MA). Part-time and evening/weekend programs available. *Faculty:* 14 full-time (11 women), 6 part-time/adjunct (4 women). *Students:* 74 full-time (46 women), 23 part-time (13 women); includes 12 minority (7 Black or African American, non-Hispanic/Latino; 1 Asian, non-Hispanic/Latino; 2 Hispanic/Latino; 2 Two or more races, non-Hispanic/Latino), 5 international. Average age 27. 158 applicants, 56% accepted, 42 enrolled. In 2014, 37 master's, 2 other advanced degrees awarded. *Degree requirements:* For master's, comprehensive exam, thesis (for some programs). *Entrance requirements:* For master's, GRE General Test, minimum GPA of 3.0, psychology 3.25; three letters of reference. Additional exam requirements/recommendations for international students: Required—TOEFL (minimum score 550 paper-based; 80 iBT). *Application deadline:* For fall admission, 4/15 priority date for domestic students, 3/15 for international students; for spring admission, 10/15 priority date for domestic students, 9/1 for international students. Applications are processed on a rolling basis. Application fee: $45. Electronic applications accepted. *Expenses:* Tuition, state resident: full-time $8172; part-time $454 per credit. Tuition, nonresident: full-time $12,258; part-time $681 per credit. *Required fees:* $2231; $110.78 per credit. Tuition and fees vary according to campus/location and program. *Financial support:* Unspecified assistantships available. Support available to part-time students. Financial award application deadline: 2/15; financial award applicants required to submit FAFSA. *Faculty research:* Stress, coping, and resilience; preventative interventions; workplace stress; organizational leadership; eating disorders; schizophrenia; diversity; cognition; animal behavior. *Unit head:* Dr. Loretta Rieser-Danner, Chairperson, 610-436-3106, E-mail: lrieser-danner@wcupa.edu. *Application contact:* Dr. Vanessa Johnson, Graduate Coordinator, 610-436-2749, E-mail: vjohnson@wcupa.edu.
Website: http://www.wcupa.edu/_academics/sch_cas.psy/

Western Kentucky University, Graduate Studies, College of Education and Behavioral Sciences, Department of Psychology, Bowling Green, KY 42101. Offers clinical psychology (MA); experimental psychology (MA); general psychology (MA); industrial/organizational psychology (MA); school psychology (Ed S). *Degree requirements:* For master's, comprehensive exam, thesis (for some programs); for Ed S, thesis, oral exam. *Entrance requirements:* For master's, GRE General Test; for Ed S, GRE General Test, minimum GPA of 3.5. Additional exam requirements/recommendations for international students: Required—TOEFL (minimum score 555 paper-based; 79 iBT). *Faculty research:* Neural regeneration, enhancing mobility in the elderly, improvement in visual processing in older adults, lifespan development.

Western Michigan University, Graduate College, College of Arts and Sciences, Department of Psychology, Kalamazoo, MI 49008. Offers behavior analysis (MA, PhD); clinical psychology (PhD); industrial/organizational behavior management (MA). *Accreditation:* APA (one or more programs are accredited). *Degree requirements:* For master's, variable foreign language requirement, thesis; for doctorate, 2 foreign languages, comprehensive exam, thesis/dissertation. *Application deadline:* For fall admission, 2/15 for domestic students. *Financial support:* Application deadline: 2/15. *Application contact:* Admissions and Orientation, 269-387-2000, Fax: 269-387-2096.

Wright State University, School of Graduate Studies, College of Science and Mathematics, Department of Psychology, Program in Human Factors and Industrial/Organizational Psychology, Dayton, OH 45435. Offers MS, PhD. *Degree requirements:* For master's, thesis; for doctorate, thesis/dissertation.

Xavier University, College of Social Sciences, Health and Education, Department of Psychology, Cincinnati, OH 45207. Offers clinical psychology (Psy D); industrial-organizational psychology (MA). *Accreditation:* APA (one or more programs are accredited). *Faculty:* 16 full-time (9 women), 7 part-time/adjunct (3 women). *Students:* 89 full-time (67 women), 38 part-time (24 women); includes 18 minority (4 Black or African American, non-Hispanic/Latino; 7 Asian, non-Hispanic/Latino; 4 Hispanic/Latino; 3 Two or more races, non-Hispanic/Latino), 1 international. Average age 26. 235 applicants, 26% accepted, 35 enrolled. In 2014, 29 master's, 15 doctorates awarded. *Degree requirements:* For master's, one foreign language, comprehensive exam, thesis, internship; for doctorate, one foreign language, comprehensive exam, thesis/dissertation, internship. *Entrance requirements:* For master's, GRE, official transcript; 3 letters of recommendation; for doctorate, GRE General Test; GRE Subject Test in psychology (if no undergraduate degree in psychology), bachelor's or master's degree; 18 semester hours of psychology coursework; minimum GPA of 3.0; work and research experience; official transcript; 3 letters of recommendation; statement of purpose. Additional exam requirements/recommendations for international students: Required—TOEFL (minimum score 550 paper-based; 79 iBT), IELTS (minimum score 6.5).

Application deadline: For fall admission, 12/1 for domestic and international students. Application fee: $35. Electronic applications accepted. *Expenses:* Expenses: $600 per credit hour (for MA); $760 per credit hour (for Psy D). *Financial support:* In 2014–15, 62 students received support, including 26 research assistantships with partial tuition reimbursements available, 4 teaching assistantships with partial tuition reimbursements available; career-related internships or fieldwork, traineeships, and unspecified assistantships also available. Financial award application deadline: 3/1; financial award applicants required to submit FAFSA. *Faculty research:* Older adults, clinical child and adolescent issues, personnel selection and employee behavior, at-risk youth, sexual abuse. *Unit head:* Dr. Karl Stukenberg, Chair, 513-745-1041, Fax: 513-745-3327, E-mail: stukenb@xavier.edu. *Application contact:* Margaret Maybury, Director, Academic Programs, 513-745-1053, Fax: 513-745-3347, E-mail: maybury@xavier.edu. Website: http://www.xavier.edu/psychology-grad/

Marriage and Family Therapy

Abilene Christian University, Graduate School, College of Biblical Studies, Program in Marriage and Family Therapy, Abilene, TX 79699-9100. Offers MMFT. *Accreditation:* AAMFT/COAMFTE. *Faculty:* 3 full-time (1 woman), 6 part-time/adjunct (2 women). *Students:* 41 full-time (29 women); includes 8 minority (2 Black or African American, non-Hispanic/Latino; 5 Hispanic/Latino; 1 Two or more races, non-Hispanic/Latino). 44 applicants, 57% accepted, 19 enrolled. In 2014, 23 master's awarded. *Degree requirements:* For master's, comprehensive exam, internship. *Entrance requirements:* For master's, GRE General Test, interview, writing sample. Additional exam requirements/recommendations for international students: Required—TOEFL (minimum score 550 paper-based; 90 iBT), IELTS (minimum score 6.5), PTE. *Application deadline:* For fall admission, 2/15 priority date for domestic students. Applications are processed on a rolling basis. Application fee: $50. Electronic applications accepted. *Expenses:* Expenses: Contact institution. *Financial support:* In 2014–15, 42 students received support. Research assistantships and career-related internships or fieldwork available. Support available to part-time students. Financial award application deadline: 4/1; financial award applicants required to submit FAFSA. *Faculty research:* Overeating variables, family systems, intervention strategies. *Unit head:* Dr. Jaime Goff, Chairperson/Graduate Director, 325-674-3778, Fax: 325-674-3749, E-mail: jaime.goff@acu.edu. *Application contact:* Corey Patterson, Director of Graduate Admission and Recruiting, 325-674-6566, Fax: 325-674-6717, E-mail: gradinfo@acu.edu.
Website: http://www.acu.edu/mft

Adler Graduate School, Program in Adlerian Counseling and Psychotherapy, Richfield, MN 55423. Offers Adlerian studies (MA); art therapy (MA); clinical counseling (MA); co-occurring substance abuse and mental health disorders (MA); marriage and family therapy (MA); school counseling (MA). Part-time and evening/weekend programs available. *Faculty:* 7 full-time (6 women), 68 part-time/adjunct (49 women). *Students:* 368 part-time (283 women); includes 61 minority (41 Black or African American, non-Hispanic/Latino; 4 American Indian or Alaska Native, non-Hispanic/Latino; 8 Asian, non-Hispanic/Latino; 8 Hispanic/Latino). Average age 40. In 2014, 90 master's awarded. *Degree requirements:* For master's, thesis or alternative, 500-700 hour internship (depending on license choice). *Entrance requirements:* For master's, personal goal statement, three letters of reference, resume or work history, official transcripts. *Application deadline:* Applications are processed on a rolling basis. Application fee: $50. Electronic applications accepted. *Expenses:* Tuition: Full-time $6060; part-time $505 per credit. *Financial support:* Career-related internships or fieldwork and tuition waivers available. Support available to part-time students. Financial award applicants required to submit FAFSA. *Unit head:* Dr. Dan Haugen, President, 612-767-7048, Fax: 612-861-7559, E-mail: haugen@alfredadler.edu. *Application contact:* Evelyn B. Haas, Director of Admissions, 612-767-7044, Fax: 612-861-7559, E-mail: ev@alfredadler.edu.

★ **Adler University,** Programs in Psychology, Chicago, IL 60602. Offers advanced Adlerian psychotherapy (Certificate); art therapy (MA); clinical neuropsychology (Certificate); clinical psychology (Psy D); community psychology (MA); counseling and organizational psychology (MA); counseling psychology (MA); criminology (MA); emergency management leadership (MA); forensic psychology (MA); marriage and family counseling (MA); marriage and family therapy (Certificate); military psychology (MA); nonprofit management (MA); organizational psychology (MA); police psychology (MA); public policy and administration (MA); rehabilitation counseling (MA); sport and health psychology (MA); substance abuse counseling (Certificate); Psy D/Certificate; Psy D/MACAT; Psy D/MACP; Psy D/MAMFC; Psy D/MASAC. *Accreditation:* APA. Part-time and evening/weekend programs available. Postbaccalaureate distance learning degree programs offered (minimal on-campus study). Terminal master's awarded for partial completion of doctoral program. *Degree requirements:* For master's, thesis or alternative, oral exam, practicum; for doctorate, thesis/dissertation, clinical exam, internship, oral exam, practicum, written qualifying exam. *Entrance requirements:* For master's, 12 semester hours in psychology, minimum GPA of 3.0; for doctorate, 18 semester hours in psychology, minimum GPA of 3.25; for Certificate, appropriate master's or doctoral degree. Additional exam requirements/recommendations for international students: Required—TOEFL (minimum score 550 paper-based; 79 iBT). Electronic applications accepted.
See Display on page 969 and Close-Up on page 1207.

Alliant International University–Irvine, California School of Professional Psychology, Program in Couple and Family Therapy, Irvine, CA 92606. Offers MA, Psy D. *Accreditation:* AAMFT/COAMFTE. Part-time programs available. *Degree requirements:* For doctorate, thesis/dissertation. *Entrance requirements:* For master's, minimum GPA of 3.0, letters of recommendation, interview; for doctorate, letters of recommendation, minimum GPA of 3.0, interview. Additional exam requirements/recommendations for international students: Required—TOEFL (minimum score 550 paper-based; 80 iBT), TWE (minimum score 5). Electronic applications accepted. *Faculty research:* Chemical dependency, gender issues in couples relationships, multicultural competence in therapy, contextual family therapy, relationship quality and stability.

Alliant International University–Los Angeles, California School of Professional Psychology, Program in Couple and Family Therapy, Alhambra, CA 91803-1360. Offers chemical dependency (MA); gerontology (MA); Latin American family therapy (MA). *Accreditation:* AAMFT/COAMFTE. Part-time and evening/weekend programs available. Terminal master's awarded for partial completion of doctoral program. *Degree requirements:* For master's, comprehensive exam, 50 hours of professional development activities. *Entrance requirements:* Additional exam requirements/recommendations for international students: Required—TOEFL (minimum score 550 paper-based). Electronic applications accepted. *Faculty research:* Foster care, therapy with minority couples, parenting, marriage, trauma.

Alliant International University–Los Angeles, California School of Professional Psychology, Psy D Program in Clinical Psychology, Alhambra, CA 91803-1360. Offers clinical health psychology (Psy D); family/child and couple clinical psychology (Psy D); multi-interest option (Psy D); multicultural community-clinical psychology (Psy D).

Accreditation: APA. *Degree requirements:* For doctorate, comprehensive exam, thesis/dissertation. *Entrance requirements:* For doctorate, interview, minimum GPA of 3.0 in both psychology and overall. Additional exam requirements/recommendations for international students: Required—TOEFL (minimum score 600 paper-based), TWE. Electronic applications accepted. *Faculty research:* Child and family psychology, multicultural and community psychology, acculturation, lesbian and gay issues, women's health.

Alliant International University–Sacramento, California School of Professional Psychology, Program in Couple and Family Therapy, Sacramento, CA 95833. Offers MA, Psy D. *Accreditation:* AAMFT/COAMFTE. *Degree requirements:* For master's, practicum; for doctorate, thesis/dissertation, practicum. *Entrance requirements:* For master's and doctorate, minimum GPA of 3.0, letters of recommendation, interview. Additional exam requirements/recommendations for international students: Required—TOEFL (minimum score 600 paper-based), TWE (minimum score 5). Electronic applications accepted. *Faculty research:* Adolescent risky behaviors including substance abuse, family therapy process, cultural issues, therapy with the LGBT community, commonalities of healthy and distressed couples.

Alliant International University–San Diego, California School of Professional Psychology, Program in Couple and Family Therapy, San Diego, CA 92131-1799. Offers marital and family therapy (MA, Psy D). *Accreditation:* AAMFT/COAMFTE. Part-time programs available. *Degree requirements:* For doctorate, thesis/dissertation. *Entrance requirements:* For master's and doctorate, minimum GPA of 3.0, letters of recommendation, interview. Additional exam requirements/recommendations for international students: Required—TOEFL (minimum score 550 paper-based; 80 iBT), TWE (minimum score 5). Electronic applications accepted. *Faculty research:* Chemical dependency, women's issues, emotionally-focused therapy, couple relationships, work/family/parenting.

Amridge University, Graduate and Professional Programs, Montgomery, AL 36117. Offers behavioral leadership and management (MA); Biblical studies (MA, PhD); family therapy (D Min); leadership and management (MS); marriage and family therapy (M Div, MA, PhD); ministerial leadership (M Div, MS); pastoral counseling (M Div, MS); professional counseling (M Div, MA, PhD); theology (M Div, D Min). Part-time and evening/weekend programs available. Postbaccalaureate distance learning degree programs offered (no on-campus study). *Faculty:* 20 full-time (2 women), 7 part-time/adjunct (6 women). *Students:* 110 full-time (58 women), 224 part-time (139 women); includes 139 minority (133 Black or African American, non-Hispanic/Latino; 3 Asian, non-Hispanic/Latino; 3 Hispanic/Latino). Average age 35. 69 applicants, 75% accepted. In 2014, 72 master's, 11 doctorates awarded. *Degree requirements:* For master's, one foreign language, comprehensive exam (for some programs), thesis (for some programs); for doctorate, comprehensive exam (for some programs), thesis/dissertation (for some programs). *Entrance requirements:* For master's, official transcript showing an earned 4-year BA or BS from regionally- or nationally-accredited institution; for doctorate, official transcript showing earned graduate degree from regionally- or nationally-accredited institution; writing sample (e.g. career monograph, published journal article, term paper from master's degree or doctoral dissertation); interview. Additional exam requirements/recommendations for international students: Required—TOEFL. *Application deadline:* For fall admission, 9/1 priority date for domestic students; for spring admission, 1/1 priority date for domestic students. Applications are processed on a rolling basis. Application fee: $50. Electronic applications accepted. *Financial support:* In 2014–15, 102 students received support. Federal Work-Study and scholarships/grants available. Support available to part-time students. Financial award applicants required to submit FAFSA. *Faculty research:* Technology and mental healthcare, resilience in black families, theology and congregational ministry. *Unit head:* Brooks Housley, Student Affairs Coordinator, 888-790-8080 Ext. 2, Fax: 334-387-3878, E-mail: brookshousley@amridgeuniversity.edu. *Application contact:* Kristen Holcomb, Admissions Officer, 888-790-8080 Ext. 1, Fax: 334-387-3878, E-mail: admissions@amridgeuniversity.edu.

Antioch University New England, Graduate School, Department of Applied Psychology, Program in Marriage and Family Therapy, Keene, NH 03431-3552. Offers MA, PhD, Certificate. *Accreditation:* AAMFT/COAMFTE. *Degree requirements:* For master's, internship, practicum. *Entrance requirements:* For master's, previous course work and work experience in psychology; resume; 3 letters of recommendation. Additional exam requirements/recommendations for international students: Required—TOEFL (minimum score 550 paper-based). Electronic applications accepted. *Expenses:* Contact institution. *Faculty research:* Use of reflective team model in case teaching and in organizational consulting, executive mentoring and coaching.

Appalachian State University, Cratis D. Williams Graduate School, Department of Human Development and Psychological Counseling, Boone, NC 28608. Offers clinical mental health counseling (MA); college student development (MA); marriage and family therapy (MA); school counseling (MA). *Accreditation:* AAMFT/COAMFTE; ACA; NCATE. Part-time programs available. *Degree requirements:* For master's, comprehensive exam (for some programs), thesis optional, internships. *Entrance requirements:* For master's, GRE General Test, 3 letters of recommendation. Additional exam requirements/recommendations for international students: Required—TOEFL (minimum score 570 paper-based; 79 iBT), IELTS (minimum score 6.5). Electronic applications accepted. *Faculty research:* Multicultural counseling, addictions counseling, play therapy, expressive arts, child and adolescent therapy, sexual abuse counseling.

Argosy University, Atlanta, College of Psychology and Behavioral Sciences, Atlanta, GA 30328. Offers clinical psychology (MA, Psy D, Postdoctoral Respecialization Certificate), including child and family psychology (Psy D), general adult clinical (Psy D), health psychology (Psy D), neuropsychology/geropsychology (Psy D); community counseling (MA), including marriage and family therapy; counselor education and supervision (Ed D); forensic psychology (MA); industrial organizational psychology (MA); marriage and family therapy (Certificate); sport-exercise psychology (MA). *Accreditation:* APA.

Marriage and Family Therapy

Argosy University, Chicago, College of Psychology and Behavioral Sciences, Doctoral Program in Clinical Psychology, Chicago, IL 60601. Offers child and adolescent psychology (Psy D); client-centered and experiential psychotherapies (Psy D); diversity and multicultural psychology (Psy D); family psychology (Psy D); forensic psychology (Psy D); health psychology (Psy D); neuropsychology (Psy D); organizational consulting (Psy D); psychoanalytic psychology (Psy D); psychology and spirituality (Psy D). *Accreditation:* APA.

Argosy University, Denver, College of Psychology and Behavioral Sciences, Denver, CO 80231. Offers clinical mental health counseling (MA); clinical psychology (MA, Psy D); counseling psychology (Ed D); counselor education and supervision (Ed D); forensic psychology (MA); industrial organizational psychology (MA); marriage and family therapy (MA, DMFT).

Argosy University, Hawai`i, College of Psychology and Behavioral Sciences, Program in Marriage and Family Therapy, Honolulu, HI 96813. Offers MA.

Argosy University, Inland Empire, College of Psychology and Behavioral Sciences, Ontario, CA 91761. Offers clinical psychology/marriage and family therapy (MA); counseling psychology (Ed D); counseling psychology/marriage and family therapy (MA); forensic psychology (MA); industrial organizational psychology (MA); sport-exercise psychology (MA).

Argosy University, Los Angeles, College of Psychology and Behavioral Sciences, Santa Monica, CA 90045. Offers clinical psychology/marriage and family therapy (MA); counseling psychology (Ed D); counseling psychology/marriage and family therapy (MA); forensic psychology (MA).

Argosy University, Orange County, College of Psychology and Behavioral Sciences, Program in Clinical Psychology, Orange, CA 92868. Offers child and adolescent psychology (Psy D); forensic psychology (Psy D); marriage and family therapy (MA). *Accreditation:* APA.

Argosy University, Orange County, College of Psychology and Behavioral Sciences, Program in Counseling Psychology, Orange, CA 92868. Offers counseling psychology (Ed D); marriage and family therapy (MA).

Argosy University, Salt Lake City, College of Psychology and Behavioral Sciences, Draper, UT 84020. Offers counseling psychology (Ed D); counselor education and supervision (Ed D); forensic psychology (MA); marriage and family therapy (MA, DMFT); mental health counseling (MA).

Argosy University, San Diego, College of Psychology and Behavioral Sciences, San Diego, CA 92108. Offers clinical psychology/marriage and family therapy (MA); counseling psychology (Ed D); counseling psychology/marriage and family therapy (MA); forensic psychology (MA).

Argosy University, Sarasota, College of Psychology and Behavioral Sciences, Sarasota, FL 34235. Offers community counseling (MA); counseling psychology (Ed D); counselor education and supervision (Ed D); forensic psychology (MA); marriage and family therapy (MA); mental health counseling (MA); pastoral community counseling (Ed D).

Argosy University, Tampa, College of Psychology and Behavioral Sciences, Program in Clinical Psychology, Tampa, FL 33607. Offers clinical psychology (MA, Psy D), including child and adolescent psychology (Psy D), geropsychology (Psy D), marriage/couples and family therapy (Psy D), neuropsychology (Psy D). *Accreditation:* APA.

Argosy University, Twin Cities, College of Psychology and Behavioral Sciences, Eagan, MN 55121. Offers clinical psychology (MA, Psy D), including child and family psychology (Psy D), forensic psychology (Psy D), health and neuropsychology (Psy D), trauma (Psy D); forensic counseling (Post-Graduate Certificate); forensic psychology (MA); industrial organizational psychology (MA); marriage and family therapy (MA, DMFT), including forensic counseling (MA). *Accreditation:* AAMFT; AAMFT/COAMFTE; APA.

Argosy University, Washington DC, College of Psychology and Behavioral Sciences, Arlington, VA 22209. Offers clinical psychology (MA, Psy D), including child and family psychology (Psy D), diversity and multicultural psychology (Psy D), forensic psychology (Psy D), health and neuropsychology (Psy D); community counseling (MA); counseling psychology (Ed D), including counselor education and supervision; counselor education and supervision (Ed D); forensic psychology (MA). *Accreditation:* APA.

Arizona State University at the Tempe campus, College of Liberal Arts and Sciences, School of Social and Family Dynamics, Tempe, AZ 85287-3701. Offers family and human development (MS, PhD); infant-family practice (MAS); marriage and family therapy (MAS); sociology (MA, PhD). Terminal master's awarded for partial completion of doctoral program. *Degree requirements:* For master's, thesis or alternative, interactive Program of Study (iPOS) submitted before completing 50 percent of required credit hours; for doctorate, thesis/dissertation, interactive Program of Study (iPOS) submitted before completing 50 percent of required credit hours. *Entrance requirements:* For master's and doctorate, GRE, minimum GPA of 3.0 or equivalent in last 2 years of work leading to bachelor's degree. Additional exam requirements/recommendations for international students: Required—TOEFL, IELTS, or PTE. Electronic applications accepted. *Expenses:* Contact institution.

Azusa Pacific University, School of Behavioral and Applied Sciences, Department of Graduate Psychology, Azusa, CA 91702-7000. Offers clinical psychology (MA, Psy D), including family therapy (MA). *Accreditation:* APA (one or more programs are accredited). Part-time and evening/weekend programs available. *Degree requirements:* For master's, comprehensive exam, 250 hours of clinical experience, individual and group therapy. *Entrance requirements:* For master's, interview, minimum GPA of 3.0, Minnesota Multiphasic Personality Inventory. Additional exam requirements/recommendations for international students: Required—TOEFL (minimum score 600 paper-based).

Barry University, School of Education, Program in Marital, Couple and Family Counseling/Therapy, Miami Shores, FL 33161-6695. Offers MS, Ed S. Part-time and evening/weekend programs available. *Degree requirements:* For master's, comprehensive exam, scholarly paper; for Ed S, comprehensive exam. *Entrance requirements:* For master's, GRE General Test or MAT, minimum GPA of 3.0; for Ed S, GRE General Test, minimum GPA of 3.0. Electronic applications accepted.

Bayamón Central University, Graduate Programs, Program in Education, Bayamón, PR 00960-1725. Offers administration and supervision (MA Ed); commercial education (MA Ed); elementary education (K–3) (MA Ed); family counseling (Graduate Certificate); guidance and counseling (MA Ed); pre-elementary teacher (MA Ed); rehabilitation counseling (MA Ed); special education (MA Ed), including attention deficit disorder, education of the autistic, learning disabilities. Part-time and evening/weekend programs available. *Degree requirements:* For master's, comprehensive exam. *Entrance requirements:* For master's, EXADEP, bachelor's degree in education or related field.

Bethel Seminary, Graduate and Professional Programs, St. Paul, MN 55112-6998. Offers Anglican studies (Certificate); children's and family ministry (MA); Christian studies (Certificate); Christian thought (MA); Greek and Hebrew language (M Div); Greek language (M Div); Hebrew language (M Div); marriage and family therapy (MA, Certificate); ministry (D Min); ministry practice (MA, Certificate); theological studies (MA,

Certificate); transformational leadership (MA); young life youth ministry (Certificate). *Accreditation:* ACIPE; ATS (one or more programs are accredited). Part-time and evening/weekend programs available. Postbaccalaureate distance learning degree programs offered (minimal on-campus study). *Faculty:* 15 full-time (3 women), 55 part-time/adjunct (27 women). *Students:* 422 full-time (167 women), 231 part-time (71 women); includes 165 minority (62 Black or African American, non-Hispanic/Latino; 58 Asian, non-Hispanic/Latino; 29 Hispanic/Latino; 1 Native Hawaiian or other Pacific Islander, non-Hispanic/Latino; 15 Two or more races, non-Hispanic/Latino), 16 international. Average age 37. 272 applicants, 77% accepted, 165 enrolled. In 2014, 147 master's, 13 doctorates, 8 other advanced degrees awarded. *Degree requirements:* For master's, variable foreign language requirement, thesis (for some programs); for doctorate, thesis/dissertation. *Entrance requirements:* For master's, letters of reference, transcripts, personal statement; for doctorate, M Div, letters of reference, organizational support; for Certificate, letters of reference, family essay, personal statement, and family of origin paper (for marriage and family therapy). Additional exam requirements/recommendations for international students: Required—TOEFL (minimum score 550 paper-based; 87 iBT). *Application deadline:* For fall admission, 8/1 priority date for domestic students, 8/1 for international students; for winter admission, 12/1 priority date for domestic students; for spring admission, 1/1 priority date for domestic students. Applications are processed on a rolling basis. Application fee: $0. Electronic applications accepted. *Financial support:* In 2014–15, 558 students received support, including 17 teaching assistantships; career-related internships or fieldwork, Federal Work-Study, and scholarships/grants also available. Financial award applicants required to submit FAFSA. *Faculty research:* Nature of theology, ethics, Biblical commentaries, nature of God, science and theology. *Unit head:* Dr. David Clark, Vice-President and Dean, Bethel Seminary, 651-638-6659. *Application contact:* Jen Niska, Director of Admissions, 651-638-6288, Fax: 651-638-6002, E-mail: bsem-admit@bethel.edu.

Brandman University, School of Arts and Sciences, Irvine, CA 92618. Offers psychology (MA), including counseling, marriage and family therapy.

Briercrest Seminary, Graduate Programs, Program in Christian Ministries, Caronport, SK S0H 0S0, Canada. Offers leadership (MA); marriage and family counseling (MA); missions (MA); pastoral counseling (MA); worship (MA); youth and family ministry (MA). Part-time programs available. *Degree requirements:* For master's, comprehensive exam, thesis optional. *Entrance requirements:* Additional exam requirements/recommendations for international students: Required—TOEFL (minimum score 550 paper-based).

Brigham Young University, Graduate Studies, College of Family, Home, and Social Sciences, Marriage and Family Therapy Program, Provo, UT 84602. Offers MS, PhD. *Faculty:* 10 full-time (2 women), 3 part-time/adjunct (all women). *Students:* 40 full-time (25 women); includes 7 minority (3 Asian, non-Hispanic/Latino; 4 Hispanic/Latino). Average age 25. 70 applicants, 20% accepted, 14 enrolled. In 2014, 15 master's, 4 doctorates awarded. *Degree requirements:* For master's, comprehensive exam, thesis, 500 clinical hours; for doctorate, comprehensive exam, thesis/dissertation, 500 clinical hours, portfolio. *Entrance requirements:* For master's and doctorate, GRE General Test, GRE Writing Test, minimum GPA of 3.0 in last 60 hours of course work. Additional exam requirements/recommendations for international students: Required—TOEFL. *Application deadline:* For fall admission, 12/1 for domestic and international students. Application fee: $50. Electronic applications accepted. *Expenses: Tuition:* Full-time $6310; part-time $371 per credit hour. Tuition and fees vary according to program and student's religious affiliation. *Financial support:* In 2014–15, 39 students received support, including 38 research assistantships with full and partial tuition reimbursements available (averaging $31,239 per year); fellowships, teaching assistantships, career-related internships or fieldwork, scholarships/grants, and tuition waivers (partial) also available. *Faculty research:* Therapy processes and outcome, preparation for marriage, family relationships across the life cycle, adjustment to medical illnesses, health-care costs, health family processes. *Total annual research expenditures:* $11,000. *Unit head:* Dr. Roy A. Bean, Program Director, 801-422-5680, Fax: 801-422-0163, E-mail: roy_bean@byu.edu. *Application contact:* Dr. Lauren A. Barnes, Director of Clinical Training, 801-422-3889, Fax: 801-422-0163, E-mail: lauren_barnes@byu.edu. Website: http://mft.byu.edu

California Lutheran University, Graduate Studies, Department of Psychology, Thousand Oaks, CA 91360-2787. Offers clinical psychology (MS, Psy D); marital and family therapy (MS). Part-time programs available. *Faculty:* 12 full-time (6 women), 19 part-time/adjunct (14 women). *Students:* 156 full-time (133 women), 28 part-time (25 women); includes 85 minority (5 Black or African American, non-Hispanic/Latino; 1 American Indian or Alaska Native, non-Hispanic/Latino; 6 Asian, non-Hispanic/Latino; 67 Hispanic/Latino; 2 Native Hawaiian or other Pacific Islander, non-Hispanic/Latino; 4 Two or more races, non-Hispanic/Latino), 6 international. Average age 31. 201 applicants, 57% accepted, 56 enrolled. In 2014, 64 master's awarded. *Degree requirements:* For master's, thesis or comprehensive exams; for doctorate, internship. *Entrance requirements:* For master's, GRE General Test, interview, minimum GPA of 3.0; for doctorate, GRE General Test. *Application deadline:* For fall admission, 1/15 priority date for domestic and international students. Applications are processed on a rolling basis. Application fee: $50. *Unit head:* Dr. Richard Holigrock, Dean, 805-493-3675. *Application contact:* 805-493-3325, Fax: 805-493-3861, E-mail: clugrad@callutheran.edu.

California State University, Chico, Office of Graduate Studies, College of Behavioral and Social Sciences, Department of Psychology, Program in Marriage and Family Therapy, Chico, CA 95929-0722. Offers MS. *Students:* 45 full-time (39 women), 7 part-time (6 women); includes 7 minority (all Hispanic/Latino). Average age 28. 50 applicants, 60% accepted, 21 enrolled. In 2014, 21 master's awarded. *Degree requirements:* For master's, oral and thesis or analytical review and written exam. *Entrance requirements:* For master's, GRE General Test or MAT, 3 letters of recommendation, three departmental recommendation forms, statement of purpose. Additional exam requirements/recommendations for international students: Required—TOEFL (minimum score 550 paper-based; 80 iBT), IELTS (minimum score 6.5), PTE. *Application deadline:* For fall admission, 3/1 for domestic and international students. Application fee: $55. Electronic applications accepted. *Expenses:* Tuition, state resident: full-time $7002. Tuition, nonresident: full-time $18,162. *Required fees:* $1530. Tuition and fees vary according to program. *Financial support:* Research assistantships available. Financial award application deadline: 3/1; financial award applicants required to submit FAFSA. *Unit head:* Dr. Brian Oppy, Chair, 530-898-5147, Fax: 530-898-4740, E-mail: psy@csuchico.edu. *Application contact:* Judy L. Rice, Graduate Admissions Coordinator, 530-898-5416, Fax: 530-898-3342, E-mail: jlrice@csuchico.edu. Website: http://catalog.csuchico.edu/viewer/12/PSYC/PSYCNONEMS.html

California State University, Dominguez Hills, College of Health, Human Services and Nursing, Program in Marital and Family Therapy, Carson, CA 90747-0001. Offers MS. Part-time and evening/weekend programs available. *Faculty:* 2 full-time (1 woman), 6 part-time/adjunct (3 women). *Students:* 39 full-time (29 women), 64 part-time (53 women); includes 70 minority (17 Black or African American, non-Hispanic/Latino; 2 Asian, non-Hispanic/Latino; 44 Hispanic/Latino; 1 Native Hawaiian or other Pacific Islander, non-Hispanic/Latino; 6 Two or more races, non-Hispanic/Latino). Average age 39. 37 applicants, 59% accepted, 14 enrolled. In 2014, 17 master's awarded. *Degree*

requirements: For master's, comprehensive exam. *Entrance requirements:* For master's, minimum GPA of 3.0. Additional exam requirements/recommendations for international students: Required—TOEFL (minimum score 550 paper-based). *Application deadline:* For fall admission, 8/1 for domestic students; for spring admission, 12/15 for domestic students. Applications are processed on a rolling basis. Application fee: $55. Electronic applications accepted. *Expenses:* Tuition, state resident: full-time $6738; part-time $3960 per year. Tuition, nonresident: full-time $13,434; part-time $8370 per year. *Required fees:* $623; $623 per year. *Faculty research:* Sociology of the family, clinical psychology theory, employee assistance programs, race and sport, secondary trauma. *Unit head:* Dr. Michael Laurent, Chair/Program Coordinator, 310-243-2693, E-mail: mlaurent@csudh.edu. *Application contact:* Brandy McLelland, Director of Student Information Services/Registrar, 310-243-3645, E-mail: bmclelland@csudh.edu.
Website: http://www4.csudh.edu/human-development/martial-family-therapy/index

California State University, East Bay, Office of Academic Programs and Graduate Studies, College of Education and Allied Studies, Department of Educational Psychology, Counseling Program, Hayward, CA 94542-3000. Offers clinical child/school psychology (MS); marriage and family therapy (MS); school counseling (MS). *Accreditation:* NCATE. *Degree requirements:* For master's, comprehensive exam, project or thesis. *Entrance requirements:* For master's, GRE or MAT, interview, minimum GPA of 2.5 during previous 2 years of course work. Additional exam requirements/recommendations for international students: Required—TOEFL (minimum score 550 paper-based). *Application deadline:* For fall admission, 6/30 for domestic and international students. Application fee: $55. Electronic applications accepted. *Expenses:* Tuition, state resident: full-time $7830; part-time $1302 per credit hour. Tuition, nonresident: full-time $16,368. *Required fees:* $327 per quarter. Tuition and fees vary according to course load and program. *Financial support:* Career-related internships or fieldwork, Federal Work-Study, and institutionally sponsored loans available. Support available to part-time students. Financial award application deadline: 3/2; financial award applicants required to submit FAFSA. *Unit head:* Dr. Jack Davis, Chair, Educational Psychology, 510-885-3011, Fax: 510-885-4642, E-mail: jack.davis@csueastbay.edu. *Application contact:* Prof. Greg Jennings, Graduate Coordinator, 510-885-2296, Fax: 510-885-4642, E-mail: greg.jennings@csueastbay.edu.
Website: http://www20.csueastbay.edu/ceas/departments/epsy/

California State University, Fresno, Division of Graduate Studies, School of Education and Human Development, Department of Counseling and Special Education, Program in Marriage and Family Therapy, Fresno, CA 93740-8027. Offers MS. *Accreditation:* ACA. Part-time and evening/weekend programs available. *Degree requirements:* For master's, thesis or alternative. *Entrance requirements:* For master's, GRE General Test, MAT, minimum GPA of 3.0. Additional exam requirements/recommendations for international students: Required—TOEFL. Electronic applications accepted. *Faculty research:* Child abuse prevention, early childhood education.

California State University, Long Beach, Graduate Studies, College of Education, Department of Advanced Studies in Education and Counseling, Master of Science in Counseling Program, Long Beach, CA 90840. Offers marriage and family therapy (MS); school counseling (MS); student development in higher education (MS). *Accreditation:* NCATE. *Degree requirements:* For master's, comprehensive exam or thesis. Electronic applications accepted.

California State University, Northridge, Graduate Studies, College of Education, Department of Educational Psychology and Counseling, Northridge, CA 91330. Offers counseling (MS), including career counseling, college counseling and student services, marriage and family therapy, school counseling, school psychology; educational psychology (MA Ed), including development, learning, and instruction, early childhood education. *Accreditation:* ACA (one or more programs are accredited); NCATE. Part-time and evening/weekend programs available. *Students:* 296 full-time (244 women), 86 part-time (77 women); includes 180 minority (18 Black or African American, non-Hispanic/Latino; 28 Asian, non-Hispanic/Latino; 126 Hispanic/Latino; 8 Two or more races, non-Hispanic/Latino), 12 international. Average age 30. *Entrance requirements:* For master's, GRE General Test or minimum GPA of 3.0. Additional exam requirements/recommendations for international students: Required—TOEFL. *Application deadline:* For fall admission, 11/30 for domestic students. Application fee: $55. *Expenses: Required fees:* $12,402. *Financial support:* Scholarships/grants available. Support available to part-time students. Financial award application deadline: 3/1. *Unit head:* Dr. Shari Tarver-Behring, Chair, 818-677-2599. *Application contact:* 818-677-3755.
Website: http://www.csun.edu/education/epc/index.html

California State University, Sacramento, Office of Graduate Studies, College of Education, Department of Counseling, Sacramento, CA 95819. Offers career counseling (MS); marriage and family therapy (MS); school counseling (MS); vocational rehabilitation counseling (MS). *Accreditation:* ACA. *Degree requirements:* For master's, thesis or project; writing proficiency exam. *Entrance requirements:* For master's, minimum GPA of 2.5. Additional exam requirements/recommendations for international students: Required—TOEFL. Electronic applications accepted.

Cambridge College, School of Psychology and Counseling, Cambridge, MA 02138-5304. Offers addiction counseling (M Ed); alcohol and drug counseling (Certificate); counseling psychology (M Ed, CAGS); counseling psychology: forensic counseling (M Ed); marriage and family therapy (M Ed); mental health and addiction counseling (M Ed); mental health counseling (M Ed); mental health counseling for school guidance counselors (Post Master's Certificate); psychological studies (M Ed); school adjustment and mental health counseling (M Ed); school adjustment, mental health and addiction counseling (M Ed); school guidance counselor (M Ed); trauma studies (Certificate). Part-time and evening/weekend programs available. *Degree requirements:* For master's and other advanced degree, thesis, practicum/internship. *Entrance requirements:* For master's, resume, 2 professional references; for other advanced degree, official transcripts, documents for transfer credit evaluation, resume, written personal statement/essay, 2 professional references, health insurance, immunizations form. Additional exam requirements/recommendations for international students: Required—TOEFL (minimum score 550 paper-based; 79 iBT), Michigan English Language Assessment Battery (minimum score 85); Recommended—IELTS (minimum score 6). Electronic applications accepted. *Expenses:* Contact institution. *Faculty research:* Trauma, drug and alcohol counseling, cross-cultural issues, school counseling, trauma in schools.

Capella University, Harold Abel School of Social and Behavioral Science, Master's Programs in Counseling, Minneapolis, MN 55402. Offers child and adolescent development (MS); general addiction counseling (MS); general marriage and family counseling/therapy (MS); general mental health counseling (MS); general school counseling (MS).

Carlos Albizu University, Miami Campus, Graduate Programs, Miami, FL 33172-2209. Offers clinical psychology (Psy D); entrepreneurship (MBA); exceptional student education (MS); human services (PhD); industrial/organizational psychology (MS); marriage and family therapy (MS); mental health counseling (MS); nonprofit management (MBA); organizational management (MBA); psychology (MS); school counseling (MS); teaching English as a second language (MS). *Accreditation:* APA. Part-time and evening/weekend programs available. Postbaccalaureate distance learning degree programs offered (minimal on-campus study). *Faculty:* 25 full-time (20 women), 29 part-time/adjunct (15 women). *Students:* 431 full-time (343 women), 264 part-time (225 women); includes 586 minority (45 Black or African American, non-Hispanic/Latino; 1 American Indian or Alaska Native, non-Hispanic/Latino; 8 Asian, non-Hispanic/Latino; 530 Hispanic/Latino; 2 Two or more races, non-Hispanic/Latino), 14 international. Average age 33. 189 applicants, 69% accepted, 111 enrolled. In 2014, 177 master's, 28 doctorates awarded. Terminal master's awarded for partial completion of doctoral program. *Degree requirements:* For master's, one foreign language, comprehensive exam, integrative project (MBA), research project (exceptional student education, teaching English as a second language); for doctorate, one foreign language, comprehensive exam, internship, project. *Entrance requirements:* For master's, 3 letters of recommendation, interview, minimum GPA of 3.0, resume, statement of purpose, official transcripts; for doctorate, 3 letters of recommendation, minimum GPA of 3.0, resume, interview, statement of purpose, official transcripts. Additional exam requirements/recommendations for international students: Required—Michigan Test of English Language Proficiency. *Application deadline:* For fall admission, 4/1 priority date for domestic students, 5/1 priority date for international students; for spring admission, 11/1 priority date for domestic students, 9/1 priority date for international students. Applications are processed on a rolling basis. Application fee: $50. Electronic applications accepted. *Expenses:* Expenses: $570 per credit (for master's programs); $750 per credit (for doctoral programs). *Financial support:* In 2014–15, 72 students received support. Federal Work-Study, scholarships/grants, and tuition discounts available. Financial award application deadline: 6/1; financial award applicants required to submit FAFSA. *Faculty research:* Psychotherapy, forensic psychology, neuropsychology, marketing strategy, entrepreneurship, special education. *Unit head:* Dr. Irene M. Bravo, Interim Provost, 305-593-1223 Ext. 3120, Fax: 305-592-7930, E-mail: ibravo@albizu.edu. *Application contact:* Vanessa Almendarez, Administrative Assistant, 305-593-1223 Ext. 3137, Fax: 305-593-1854, E-mail: valmendarez@albizu.edu.

Central Connecticut State University, School of Graduate Studies, School of Education and Professional Studies, Department of Counselor Education and Family Therapy, New Britain, CT 06050-4010. Offers marriage and family therapy (MS); professional counseling (MS, AC, Certificate); school counseling (MS); student development in higher education (MS). *Accreditation:* AAMFT/COAMFTE; ACA. Part-time and evening/weekend programs available. *Faculty:* 11 full-time (7 women), 21 part-time/adjunct (17 women). *Students:* 142 full-time (122 women), 208 part-time (165 women); includes 94 minority (49 Black or African American, non-Hispanic/Latino; 4 Asian, non-Hispanic/Latino; 34 Hispanic/Latino; 7 Two or more races, non-Hispanic/Latino), 2 international. Average age 34. 215 applicants, 53% accepted, 91 enrolled. In 2014, 101 master's, 5 other advanced degrees awarded. *Degree requirements:* For master's, comprehensive exam, thesis or alternative; for other advanced degree, qualifying exam. *Entrance requirements:* For master's, minimum undergraduate GPA of 2.7, essay, interview, letters of recommendation. Additional exam requirements/recommendations for international students: Required—TOEFL (minimum score 550 paper-based; 79 iBT). *Application deadline:* For fall admission, 4/1 for domestic and international students; for spring admission, 11/1 for domestic and international students. Applications are processed on a rolling basis. Application fee: $50. Electronic applications accepted. *Expenses: Tuition, area resident:* Full-time $5730; part-time $534 per credit. Tuition, state resident: full-time $8596; part-time $534 per credit. Tuition, nonresident: full-time $15,964; part-time $548 per credit. *Required fees:* $4211; $215 per credit. *Financial support:* In 2014–15, 41 students received support, including 21 research assistantships; career-related internships or fieldwork, Federal Work-Study, scholarships/grants, and unspecified assistantships also available. Support available to part-time students. Financial award application deadline: 3/1; financial award applicants required to submit FAFSA. *Faculty research:* Elementary and secondary school counseling, marriage and family therapy, rehabilitation counseling, counseling in higher educational settings. *Unit head:* Dr. Connie Tait, Chair, 860-832-2154, E-mail: taitc@ccsu.edu. *Application contact:* Patricia Gardner, Associate Director of Graduate Studies, 860-832-2350, Fax: 860-832-2362, E-mail: graduateadmissions@ccsu.edu.
Website: http://web.ccsu.edu/seps/departments/counselingFamilyTherapy/default.asp

Chaminade University of Honolulu, Graduate Services, Program in Counseling Psychology, Honolulu, HI 96816-1578. Offers marriage and family counseling (MSCP); mental health counseling (MSCP); school counseling (MSCP). Part-time and evening/weekend programs available. *Degree requirements:* For master's, comprehensive exam, internship/practicum. *Entrance requirements:* For master's, minimum undergraduate GPA of 3.0, 3 letters of recommendation, interview. Additional exam requirements/recommendations for international students: Required—TOEFL (minimum score 550 paper-based). Electronic applications accepted. *Faculty research:* Taoist/Buddhist psychology, psychology of T'ai Chi Ch'uan, sleep disorders, drug/alcohol prevention with adolescent girls, anger/aggression with kids.

Chapman University, Crean College of Health and Behavioral Sciences, Marriage and Family Therapy Program, Orange, CA 92866. Offers MA. *Accreditation:* AAMFT/COAMFTE. Part-time and evening/weekend programs available. *Faculty:* 4 full-time (2 women), 8 part-time/adjunct (6 women). *Students:* 33 full-time (26 women), 37 part-time (33 women); includes 28 minority (1 Black or African American, non-Hispanic/Latino; 1 American Indian or Alaska Native, non-Hispanic/Latino; 5 Asian, non-Hispanic/Latino; 18 Hispanic/Latino; 1 Native Hawaiian or other Pacific Islander, non-Hispanic/Latino; 2 Two or more races, non-Hispanic/Latino), 2 international. Average age 27. In 2014, 27 master's awarded. *Degree requirements:* For master's, comprehensive exam, thesis optional. *Entrance requirements:* For master's, GRE, minimum undergraduate GPA of 2.5. Additional exam requirements/recommendations for international students: Required—TOEFL (minimum score 550 paper-based; 80 iBT). *Application deadline:* For fall admission, 3/1 for domestic students; for spring admission, 11/1 for domestic students. Application fee: $55. Electronic applications accepted. *Expenses:* Expenses: Contact institution. *Financial support:* Fellowships, Federal Work-Study, and scholarships/grants available. Financial award applicants required to submit FAFSA. *Unit head:* Dr. Brennan Peterson, Chair, 714-744-7915, E-mail: bpeterson@chapman.edu. *Application contact:* Catherine Greenberg, Admission Counselor, 714-997-6711, E-mail: cgreen@chapman.edu.

Chatham University, Program in Counseling Psychology, Pittsburgh, PA 15232-2826. Offers child, adolescent and family (MSCP); counseling psychology (Psy D); health and holistic (MSCP); infant mental health (MSCP); organization and supervision (MSCP); sport and exercise (MSCP). Part-time and evening/weekend programs available. *Faculty:* 12 full-time (9 women), 13 part-time/adjunct (9 women). *Students:* 102 full-time (85 women), 38 part-time (32 women); includes 17 minority (7 Black or African American, non-Hispanic/Latino; 2 Asian, non-Hispanic/Latino; 6 Hispanic/Latino; 2 Two or more races, non-Hispanic/Latino), 7 international. Average age 29. 145 applicants, 73% accepted, 59 enrolled. In 2014, 67 master's, 3 doctorates awarded. *Degree requirements:* For master's, thesis optional, supervised internship; for doctorate, thesis/dissertation, internship. *Entrance requirements:* For master's, minimum GPA of 3.0; 2 letters of recommendation; resume; prerequisite coursework in statistics, biology, and psychology; for doctorate, GRE. Additional exam requirements/recommendations for

international students: Required—TOEFL (minimum score 600 paper-based; 100 iBT), IELTS (minimum score 7), TWE. *Application deadline:* For fall admission, 4/1 priority date for domestic and international students; for spring admission, 11/1 for domestic students, 10/1 for international students. Applications are processed on a rolling basis. Application fee: $45. Electronic applications accepted. Application fee is waived when completed online. *Expenses: Tuition:* Full-time $15,318; part-time $851 per credit hour. *Required fees:* $440; $24 per credit hour. Tuition and fees vary according to course load, program and reciprocity agreements. *Financial support:* Career-related internships or fieldwork available. Financial award applicants required to submit FAFSA. *Faculty research:* Trauma and recovery, hypnosis, psychospiritual dimensions of healing, psychotherapy of schizophrenia. *Unit head:* Dr. Mary Beth Mannarino, Director, 412-365-1196, Fax: 412-365-1505, E-mail: mmannarino@chatham.edu. *Application contact:* Katie Noel, Assistant Director of Graduate Admission, 412-365-2758, Fax: 412-365-1609, E-mail: gradadmissions@chatham.edu.
Website: http://www.chatham.edu/mscp

Chestnut Hill College, School of Graduate Studies, Division of Psychology, Program in Clinical and Counseling Psychology, Philadelphia, PA 19118-2693. Offers addictions treatment (MS, CAS); child and adolescent therapy (MS, CAS); marriage and family therapy (MS, CAS); trauma studies (MS, CAS); treatment of autism spectrum disorders (MS, CAS). Part-time and evening/weekend programs available. *Faculty:* 4 full-time (3 women), 34 part-time/adjunct (24 women). *Students:* 88 full-time (73 women), 136 part-time (113 women); includes 41 minority (27 Black or African American, non-Hispanic/Latino; 1 Asian, non-Hispanic/Latino; 12 Hispanic/Latino; 1 Two or more races, non-Hispanic/Latino), 2 international. Average age 33. 119 applicants, 98% accepted, 70 enrolled. In 2014, 1,021 master's, 7 other advanced degrees awarded. *Degree requirements:* For master's, thesis optional, practica. *Entrance requirements:* For master's, GRE General Test, writing sample, letters of recommendation. Additional exam requirements/recommendations for international students: Required—TOEFL (minimum score 500 paper-based), IELTS (mnimum score 6.0), or TWE (minimum score 22). *Application deadline:* For fall admission, 7/1 for domestic and international students; for spring admission, 11/1 for domestic and international students; for summer admission, 4/1 for domestic and international students. Applications are processed on a rolling basis. Application fee: $55. Electronic applications accepted. *Expenses:* Expenses: Contact institution. *Financial support:* Unspecified assistantships available. *Faculty research:* Play therapy, eating disorders, addictions, group psychology and group therapy, health psychology. *Unit head:* Dr. Cheryll Rothery, Chair, Psychology Division, 215-248-7023, Fax: 215-248-3619, E-mail: rotheryc@chc.edu. *Application contact:* Amy Boorse, Assistant Director of Graduate Admissions, 215-248-7097, Fax: 215-248-7161, E-mail: gradadmissions@chc.edu.
Website: http://www.chc.edu/Graduate/Programs/Masters/Clinical_and_Counseling_Psychology/

Chestnut Hill College, School of Graduate Studies, Division of Psychology, Program in Clinical Psychology, Philadelphia, PA 19118-2693. Offers marriage and family therapy (Psy D); psychological assessment (Psy D). *Accreditation:* APA. Part-time and evening/weekend programs available. *Faculty:* 7 full-time (4 women), 1 (woman) part-time/adjunct. *Students:* 112 full-time (80 women); includes 28 minority (11 Black or African American, non-Hispanic/Latino; 6 Asian, non-Hispanic/Latino; 9 Hispanic/Latino; 2 Two or more races, non-Hispanic/Latino), 1 international. Average age 30. 172 applicants, 23% accepted, 15 enrolled. In 2014, 21 doctorates awarded. *Degree requirements:* For doctorate, comprehensive exam, thesis/dissertation, internship, practica, clinical competency exam. *Entrance requirements:* For doctorate, GRE General Test, letters of recommendation, writing sample, master's degree in clinical/counseling psychology or closely-related field. Additional exam requirements/recommendations for international students: Required—TOEFL (minimum score 500 paper-based), IELTS (mnimum score 6.0), or TWE (minimum score 22). *Application deadline:* For fall admission, 7/1 for domestic and international students; for spring admission, 11/1 for domestic and international students; for summer admission, 4/1 for domestic and international students. Applications are processed on a rolling basis. Application fee: $60. Electronic applications accepted. *Expenses:* Expenses: $985 per credit hour. *Financial support:* Unspecified assistantships available. *Faculty research:* Psychological testing and assessment, GLBT issues, autism and developmental disorders, stepfamilies, gender issues. *Unit head:* Dr. Cheryll Rothery, Chair, Division of Psychology, 215-248-7023, Fax: 215-248-3619, E-mail: rotheryc@chc.edu. *Application contact:* Eileen Webb, Director of Psy D Admissions, 215-248-7077, Fax: 215-248-3619, E-mail: profpsyc@chc.edu.
Website: http://www.chc.edu/Graduate/Programs/

The Chicago School of Professional Psychology at Downtown Los Angeles, Program in Clinical Psychology, Los Angeles, CA 90017. Offers applied behavior analysis (MA); clinical psychology (Psy D); marital and family therapy (MA).

The Chicago School of Professional Psychology at Irvine, Program in Marital and Family Therapy, Irvine, CA 92612. Offers clinical psychology (MA), including marital and family therapy; management practice (Psy D); psychodynamic psychotherapy (Psy D).

The Chicago School of Professional Psychology at Westwood, Program in Clinical Psychology, Los Angeles, CA 90024. Offers marital and family therapy (MA).

The Chicago School of Professional Psychology at Westwood, Program in Marital and Family Therapy, Los Angeles, CA 90024. Offers management practice (Psy D); psychodynamic psychotherapy (Psy D).

Christian Theological Seminary, Graduate and Professional Programs, Indianapolis, IN 46208-3301. Offers educational and arts ministries (MA); marriage and family therapy (MA); pastoral care and counseling (D Min); psychotherapy and faith (MA); theological studies (MTS); theology (M Div). *Accreditation:* AAMFT/COAMFTE (one or more programs are accredited); ACIPE; ATS. Part-time programs available. Terminal master's awarded for partial completion of doctoral program. *Degree requirements:* For master's, comprehensive exam (for some programs), thesis (for some programs), missionary and cross-cultural experience (for M Div); for doctorate, comprehensive exam, thesis/dissertation. *Entrance requirements:* For doctorate, M Div. Additional exam requirements/recommendations for international students: Recommended—TOEFL. Electronic applications accepted. *Faculty research:* Faith formation, peer learning post graduation.

The College of New Jersey, Graduate Studies, School of Education, Department of Counselor Education, Program in Marriage and Family Therapy, Ewing, NJ 08628. Offers Ed S. Part-time programs available. *Students:* 8 full-time (6 women), 16 part-time (11 women); includes 10 minority (7 Black or African American, non-Hispanic/Latino; 2 Asian, non-Hispanic/Latino; 1 Hispanic/Latino). 19 applicants, 74% accepted, 11 enrolled. *Entrance requirements:* For degree, previous master's degree or higher. Additional exam requirements/recommendations for international students: Required—TOEFL. *Application deadline:* For fall admission, 2/1 priority date for domestic students; for spring admission, 10/1 priority date for domestic students. Applications are processed on a rolling basis. Application fee: $75. *Financial support:* Tuition waivers (partial) and unspecified assistantships available. Financial award application deadline: 5/1; financial award applicants required to submit FAFSA. *Unit head:* Dr. Mark Woodford, Coordinator, 609-771-3018, Fax: 609-637-5116, E-mail: woodford@tcnj.edu. *Application contact:* Susan L. Hydro, Director of Graduate and Intersession Programs, 609-771-2300, Fax: 609-637-5105, E-mail: graduate@tcnj.edu.

The College of New Rochelle, Graduate School, Division of Human Services, Program in Marriage and Family Therapy, New Rochelle, NY 10805-2308. Offers MMFT. *Degree requirements:* For master's, practica. *Entrance requirements:* For master's, minimum GPA of 3.0 in baccalaureate or other graduate-level work (overall and major field); undergraduate major in psychology, social work, or related field; personal statement; two letters of recommendation; official transcripts from all colleges/universities attended; proof of immunizations. *Expenses: Tuition:* Part-time $894 per credit. *Required fees:* $325 per semester.

Converse College, School of Education and Graduate Studies, Program in Marriage and Family Therapy, Spartanburg, SC 29302-0006. Offers MMFT.

Denver Seminary, Graduate and Professional Programs, Littleton, CO 80120. Offers apologetics (Certificate); biblical studies (MA); Christian formation and soul care (MA, Certificate); Christian studies (MA, Certificate); church and parachurch leadership (D Min); counseling licensure (MA); counseling ministry (MA); intercultural ministry (Certificate); leadership (MA, Certificate); marriage and family counseling (D Min); pastoral ministry (D Min); philosophy of religion (MA); spiritual guidance (Certificate); theology (M Div, Certificate); worship (Certificate); youth and family ministry (MA). *Accreditation:* ACA; ACIPE; ATS (one or more programs are accredited). Part-time and evening/weekend programs available. Postbaccalaureate distance learning degree programs offered. *Degree requirements:* For master's, 2 foreign languages, thesis (for some programs); for doctorate, 2 foreign languages, thesis/dissertation. *Entrance requirements:* For doctorate, M Div, 3 years of ministry experience. Additional exam requirements/recommendations for international students: Required—TOEFL (minimum score 575 paper-based; 90 iBT). Electronic applications accepted.

Dominican University of California, School of Education and Counseling Psychology, Counseling Psychology Department, San Rafael, CA 94901-2298. Offers general (MS); marriage and family therapy (MS). Part-time and evening/weekend programs available. *Faculty:* 5 full-time (4 women), 8 part-time/adjunct (6 women). *Students:* 43 full-time (36 women), 42 part-time (40 women); includes 14 minority (1 Black or African American, non-Hispanic/Latino; 10 Hispanic/Latino; 1 Native Hawaiian or other Pacific Islander, non-Hispanic/Latino; 2 Two or more races, non-Hispanic/Latino). Average age 38. 45 applicants, 56% accepted, 20 enrolled. *Degree requirements:* For master's, comprehensive exam (for some programs), thesis (for some programs). *Entrance requirements:* For master's, minimum GPA of 3.0 for last 60 units, autobiography, response to scenario. Additional exam requirements/recommendations for international students: Required—TOEFL (minimum score 550 paper-based; 80 iBT), IELTS (minimum score 6.5). *Application deadline:* For fall admission, 4/1 priority date for domestic and international students; for spring admission, 11/15 priority date for domestic and international students. Applications are processed on a rolling basis. Electronic applications accepted. Application fee is waived when completed online. *Expenses:* Expenses: $1,025 per unit. *Financial support:* Career-related internships or fieldwork, scholarships/grants, and health care benefits available. Support available to part-time students. Financial award application deadline: 3/2; financial award applicants required to submit FAFSA. *Unit head:* Dr. Robin R. Gayle, Chair, 415-485-3263. *Application contact:* Shana Friedman, Assistant Director, Graduate Admissions, 415-485-3246, Fax: 415-485-3214, E-mail: shana.friedman@dominican.edu.
Website: http://www.dominican.edu/academics/education/counpsych

Drexel University, College of Nursing and Health Professions, Department of Couple and Family Therapy, Philadelphia, PA 19104-2875. Offers MFT, PhD. *Accreditation:* AAMFT/COAMFTE (one or more programs are accredited). Part-time programs available. Terminal master's awarded for partial completion of doctoral program. *Degree requirements:* For master's, comprehensive exam, thesis; for doctorate, thesis/dissertation, qualifying exam. *Entrance requirements:* For master's, GRE General Test or MAT, minimum GPA of 2.75; for doctorate, GRE General Test, minimum GPA of 3.0. Electronic applications accepted. *Faculty research:* Family assessment, gender issues, chronic illness, early intervention.

Duquesne University, School of Education, Department of Counseling, Psychology, and Special Education, Program in Counselor Education, Pittsburgh, PA 15282-0001. Offers clinical mental health counseling (MS Ed, Post-Master's Certificate); counselor education and supervision (Ed D); counselor licensure (Post-Master's Certificate); marriage and family counseling (MS Ed); school counseling (MS Ed). *Accreditation:* ACA (one or more programs are accredited). Part-time and evening/weekend programs available. *Faculty:* 9 full-time (4 women). *Students:* 165 full-time (122 women), 21 part-time (18 women); includes 38 minority (26 Black or African American, non-Hispanic/Latino; 1 American Indian or Alaska Native, non-Hispanic/Latino; 2 Asian, non-Hispanic/Latino; 4 Hispanic/Latino; 5 Two or more races, non-Hispanic/Latino), 6 international. Average age 30. 207 applicants, 43% accepted, 57 enrolled. In 2014, 42 master's, 4 doctorates awarded. *Degree requirements:* For master's, thesis optional; for doctorate, thesis/dissertation. *Entrance requirements:* For master's, letters of recommendation, essay, interview, bachelor's degree; for doctorate, GRE, letters of recommendation, essay, interview, master's degree; for Post-Master's Certificate, GRE, letters of recommendation, essay, interview, bachelor's/master's degree. Additional exam requirements/recommendations for international students: Required—TOEFL (minimum score 550 paper-based), IELTS (minimum score 7). *Application deadline:* For fall admission, 3/1 for domestic students; for spring admission, 9/1 for domestic students. Applications are processed on a rolling basis. Application fee: $0. Electronic applications accepted. *Expenses: Tuition:* Full-time $18,882; part-time $1049 per credit. *Required fees:* $1800; $100 per credit. Tuition and fees vary according to program. *Financial support:* Research assistantships, teaching assistantships, and Federal Work-Study available. Support available to part-time students. *Unit head:* Dr. Jered Kolbert, Professor/Director, 412-396-4471, Fax: 412-396-1340, E-mail: kolbertj@duq.edu. *Application contact:* Michael Dolinger, Director of Student and Academic Services, 412-396-6647, Fax: 412-396-5585, E-mail: dolingerm@duq.edu.
Website: http://www.duq.edu/academics/schools/education/graduate-programs-education/ms-ed-counselor-education

East Carolina University, Graduate School, College of Human Ecology, Department of Child Development and Family Relations, Greenville, NC 27858-4353. Offers birth through kindergarten education (MA Ed); child development and family relations (MS); family and consumer sciences (MA Ed); marriage and family therapy (MS); medical family therapy (PhD). *Accreditation:* AAMFT/COAMFTE. Part-time programs available. *Degree requirements:* For master's, comprehensive exam, thesis optional. *Expenses:* Tuition, state resident: full-time $4223. Tuition, nonresident: full-time $16,540. *Required fees:* $2184. *Faculty research:* Child care quality, mental health delivery systems for children, family violence.

Eastern Nazarene College, Adult and Graduate Studies, Program in Marriage and Family Therapy, Quincy, MA 02170. Offers MS. Part-time and evening/weekend programs available. *Entrance requirements:* For master's, 3 letters of recommendation, resume. Additional exam requirements/recommendations for international students: Required—TOEFL (minimum score 550 paper-based).

Eastern University, Palmer Theological Seminary, King of Prussia, PA 19096-3430. Offers Biblical studies and theology (MTS); Christian counseling (MTS); Christian faith and public policy (MTS); divinity (M Div); general studies (MTS); leadership of missional church renewal (D Min); ministry (D Min), including marriage and family; M Div/MA; M Div/MBA; M Div/MSW. *Accreditation:* ACIPE; ATS; MSA/CIHE. Part-time programs available. Postbaccalaureate distance learning degree programs offered (minimal on-campus study). *Faculty:* 14 full-time (7 women), 17 part-time/adjunct (7 women). *Students:* 65 full-time (25 women), 185 part-time (102 women); includes 151 minority (145 Black or African American, non-Hispanic/Latino; 2 Asian, non-Hispanic/Latino; 3 Hispanic/Latino; 1 Two or more races, non-Hispanic/Latino), 3 international. Average age 47. 117 applicants, 56% accepted, 61 enrolled. In 2014, 53 master's, 17 doctorates awarded. *Degree requirements:* For master's, variable foreign language requirement, thesis (for some programs); for doctorate, thesis/dissertation. *Entrance requirements:* For master's, bachelor's degree from accredited institution; for doctorate, M Div or MA. Additional exam requirements/recommendations for international students: Required—TOEFL (minimum score 550 paper-based; 79 iBT). *Application deadline:* For fall admission, 8/1 priority date for domestic students, 3/31 for international students; for spring admission, 1/15 for domestic students, 10/31 for international students. Applications are processed on a rolling basis. Application fee: $30. Electronic applications accepted. Application fee is waived when completed online. *Expenses: Tuition:* Full-time $15,600; part-time $650 per credit. *Required fees:* $30; $27.50 per semester. One-time fee: $50. Tuition and fees vary according to course load, degree level and program. *Financial support:* In 2014–15, 130 students received support, including 2 fellowships (averaging $4,000 per year), 15 teaching assistantships (averaging $1,200 per year); career-related internships or fieldwork, Federal Work-Study, and scholarships/grants also available. Financial award application deadline: 8/1; financial award applicants required to submit FAFSA. *Faculty research:* Approaches to the spiritual formation of religious leaders; Latin, anti-Colonial, and constructive theologies; pastoral and ethical responses to human trafficking; inter-religious and political dimensions of peacemaking and social justice in Israel and the Palestinian Territories. *Unit head:* Dr. Edwin Aponte, Dean of the Seminary, 484-384-2935, E-mail: semdean@eastern.edu. *Application contact:* Tiffany S. Murphy, Director of Admissions, 610-896-5000 Ext. 2986, Fax: 484-654-3680, E-mail: semadmis@eastern.edu.
Website: http://www.palmerseminary.edu/

Eastern University, Program in Marriage and Family, St. Davids, PA 19087-3696. Offers PhD. Evening/weekend programs available. Postbaccalaureate distance learning degree programs offered (minimal on-campus study). *Faculty:* 1 (woman) full-time, 3 part-time/adjunct (2 women). *Students:* 50 full-time (34 women); includes 37 minority (34 Black or African American, non-Hispanic/Latino; 3 Hispanic/Latino). Average age 45. 17 applicants, 76% accepted, 12 enrolled. *Degree requirements:* For doctorate, thesis/dissertation. *Entrance requirements:* Additional exam requirements/recommendations for international students: Required—TOEFL (minimum score 550 paper-based; 79 iBT). *Application deadline:* For spring admission, 1/15 for domestic students. Application fee: $75. Application fee is waived when completed online. *Expenses: Tuition:* Full-time $15,600; part-time $650 per credit. *Required fees:* $30; $27.50 per semester. One-time fee: $50. Tuition and fees vary according to course load, degree level and program. *Unit head:* Dr. Gwen White, Director, 610-341-1596. *Application contact:* Deb Berghuis, Enrollment Counselor, 484-654-2361, Fax: 215-848-2651, E-mail: dberghui@eastern.edu.
Website: http://www.eastern.edu/academics/programs/da-marriage-and-family/da-marriage-and-family

Edgewood College, Program in Marriage and Family Therapy, Madison, WI 53711-1997. Offers MS. *Accreditation:* AAMFT/COAMFTE. Part-time and evening/weekend programs available. *Students:* 21 full-time (19 women), 33 part-time (30 women); includes 6 minority (4 Black or African American, non-Hispanic/Latino; 1 Asian, non-Hispanic/Latino; 1 Hispanic/Latino), 1 international. Average age 31. In 2014, 27 master's awarded. *Degree requirements:* For master's, research project. *Entrance requirements:* For master's, minimum GPA of 2.75, 2 letters of reference, interviews. Additional exam requirements/recommendations for international students: Required—TOEFL. *Application deadline:* For fall admission, 2/15 for domestic students; for spring admission, 10/15 for domestic students. Application fee: $30. Electronic applications accepted. *Expenses: Tuition:* Part-time $836 per credit. *Unit head:* Dr. Peter Fabian, Chair, 608-663-2233, Fax: 608-663-3291, E-mail: fabian@edgewood.edu. *Application contact:* Joann Eastman, Admissions Counselor, 608-663-3250, Fax: 608-663-2214, E-mail: gps@edgewood.edu.
Website: http://www.edgewood.edu/academics/graduate/MFT/default.aspx

Evangelical Seminary, Graduate and Professional Programs, Myerstown, PA 17067-1212. Offers Biblical studies (MAR); congregational ministry (M Div); global and contextual studies (M Div, MAR); historical and theological studies (MAR); interdisciplinary studies (MAR); marriage and family counseling (M Div); marriage and family therapy (MA); New Testament (MAR); Old Testament (MAR); spiritual formation (MAR); teaching ministry (M Div); youth ministry (M Div). *Accreditation:* ATS (one or more programs are accredited). Part-time programs available. Postbaccalaureate distance learning degree programs offered (minimal on-campus study). *Degree requirements:* For master's, 2 foreign languages. *Entrance requirements:* For master's, minimum GPA of 2.5. Additional exam requirements/recommendations for international students: Required—TOEFL (minimum score 550 paper-based). *Faculty research:* Literary form and structure within the Hebrew and Greek scriptures, Wesley studies, esoteric biblical languages, the Mosaic law and the Christian, ethics.

Fairfield University, Graduate School of Education and Allied Professions, Fairfield, CT 06824. Offers applied behavior analysis (ATC); applied psychology (MA); clinical mental health counseling (MA, CAS); early childhood studies (ATC); educational technology (MA); elementary education (MA, CAS); family studies (MA); integration of spirituality and religion in counseling (ATC); marriage and family therapy (MA); school counseling (MA, CAS); school psychology (MA, CAS); school-based marriage and family therapy (ATC); secondary education (MA); special education (MA, CAS); substance abuse counseling (ATC); teaching (Certificate); teaching and foundations (MA, CAS); TESOL, world languages, and bilingual education (MA, CAS). *Accreditation:* NCATE. Part-time and evening/weekend programs available. *Faculty:* 23 full-time (19 women), 32 part-time/adjunct (25 women). *Students:* 148 full-time (131 women), 286 part-time (238 women); includes 81 minority (18 Black or African American, non-Hispanic/Latino; 1 American Indian or Alaska Native, non-Hispanic/Latino; 14 Asian, non-Hispanic/Latino; 39 Hispanic/Latino; 9 Two or more races, non-Hispanic/Latino), 13 international. Average age 34. 264 applicants, 54% accepted, 68 enrolled. In 2014, 142 master's awarded. *Degree requirements:* For master's, comprehensive exam. *Entrance requirements:* For master's, PRAXIS I (for certification programs), minimum GPA of 3.0, 2 recommendations, resume. Additional exam requirements/recommendations for international students: Required—TOEFL (minimum score 550 paper-based; 84 iBT) or IELTS (minimum score 7.5). *Application deadline:* For fall admission, 2/15 for international students; for spring admission, 10/1 for international students. Application fee: $60. Electronic applications accepted. *Expenses:* Expenses: $675 per credit hour. *Financial support:* In 2014–15, 55 students received support. Career-related internships or fieldwork and unspecified assistantships available. Financial award applicants required to submit FAFSA. *Faculty research:* Literacy, spirituality, special education, bilingual/multicultural education, mentoring and professional development. *Unit head:* Dr. Robert D. Hannafin, Dean, 203-254-4250, Fax: 203-254-4241, E-mail: rhannafin@fairfield.edu. *Application contact:* Marianne Gumpper, Director of Graduate and Continuing Studies Admission, 203-254-4184, Fax: 203-254-4073, E-mail: gradadmis@fairfield.edu.
Website: http://www.fairfield.edu/academics/schoolscollegescenters/graduateschoolofeducationalliedprofessions/graduateprograms/

Florida Atlantic University, College of Education, Department of Counselor Education, Boca Raton, FL 33431-0991. Offers counselor education (M Ed, PhD, Ed S); marriage and family therapy (Ed S); mental health counseling (M Ed, Ed S); rehabilitation counseling (M Ed); school counseling (M Ed, Ed S). *Accreditation:* ACA; NCATE. Part-time and evening/weekend programs available. *Degree requirements:* For Ed S, departmental qualifying exam. *Entrance requirements:* For master's, GRE General Test, minimum GPA of 3.0 during previous 2 years; for Ed S, GRE General Test, minimum graduate GPA of 3.25. Additional exam requirements/recommendations for international students: Required—TOEFL (minimum score 500 paper-based; 61 iBT), IELTS (minimum score 6). *Expenses:* Tuition, state resident: full-time $7396; part-time $369.82 per credit hour. Tuition, nonresident: full-time $19,392; part-time $1024.81 per credit hour. Tuition and fees vary according to course load. *Faculty research:* Brief therapy, psychological type, marriage and family counseling, international programs, integrated services.

Florida State University, The Graduate School, College of Human Sciences, Department of Family and Child Sciences, Tallahassee, FL 32306-1491. Offers family and child sciences (MS); family relations (PhD); marriage and family therapy (PhD). *Accreditation:* AAMFT/COAMFTE. Part-time programs available. *Faculty:* 14 full-time (10 women). *Students:* 28 full-time (20 women), 6 part-time (5 women); includes 12 minority (7 Black or African American, non-Hispanic/Latino; 4 Hispanic/Latino; 1 Two or more races, non-Hispanic/Latino), 3 international. 39 applicants, 56% accepted, 16 enrolled. In 2014, 5 master's, 11 doctorates awarded. Terminal master's awarded for partial completion of doctoral program. *Degree requirements:* For master's, comprehensive exam, thesis optional; for doctorate, thesis/dissertation, preliminary examination; clinical examination (for marriage and family therapy). *Entrance requirements:* For master's and doctorate, GRE General Test, writing assessment, minimum GPA of 3.0. Additional exam requirements/recommendations for international students: Required—TOEFL (minimum score 80 iBT). *Application deadline:* For fall admission, 1/5 for domestic and international students; for spring admission, 11/1 priority date for domestic students, 10/1 priority date for international students. Applications are processed on a rolling basis. Application fee: $30. Electronic applications accepted. *Expenses:* Tuition, state resident: part-time $403.51 per credit hour. Tuition, nonresident: part-time $1004.85 per credit hour. *Required fees:* $75.81 per credit hour. One-time fee: $20 part-time. Tuition and fees vary according to campus/location. *Financial support:* In 2014–15, 33 students received support, including 3 fellowships with partial tuition reimbursements available (averaging $1,094 per year), 6 research assistantships with partial tuition reimbursements available (averaging $6,942 per year), 34 teaching assistantships with full tuition reimbursements available (averaging $16,000 per year); career-related internships or fieldwork, Federal Work-Study, institutionally sponsored loans, scholarships/grants, health care benefits, and unspecified assistantships also available. Financial award application deadline: 1/5; financial award applicants required to submit FAFSA. *Faculty research:* Family therapy, parent-child relations, distressed families and foster care, marital processes, relational interventions, family structural complexity. *Unit head:* Dr. Lenore McWey, Interim Chair, 850-644-3217, Fax: 850-644-3439, E-mail: lmcwey@fsu.edu. *Application contact:* Donna Romano, Office Administrator, 850-644-3217, Fax: 850-644-3439, E-mail: dromano@fsu.edu.

Fresno Pacific University, Biblical Seminary, Program in Marriage, Family, and Child Counseling, Fresno, CA 93702-4709. Offers MA. *Degree requirements:* For master's, thesis or alternative. *Entrance requirements:* For master's, minimum GPA of 3.0. Additional exam requirements/recommendations for international students: Required—TOEFL (minimum score 550 paper-based). *Application deadline:* For fall admission, 8/1 for domestic students; for spring admission, 12/1 for domestic students. Application fee: $35. *Expenses:* Expenses: $470 per unit. *Financial support:* Career-related internships or fieldwork, institutionally sponsored loans, scholarships/grants, and tuition waivers (partial) available. Support available to part-time students. Financial award application deadline: 5/1; financial award applicants required to submit FAFSA. *Unit head:* Dr. Cynthia McGrady, Director, 559-453-2369. *Application contact:* Amanda Krum-Stovall, Director of Graduate Admissions, 559-453-2016, E-mail: amanda.krum-stovall@fresno.edu.
Website: http://www.fresno.edu/programs-majors/biblical-seminary/marriage-and-family-therapy

Friends University, Graduate School, Wichita, KS 67213. Offers business law (MBL); Christian ministry (MACM); family therapy (MSFT); global (MBA), including accounting, business law, change management, health care leadership, management information systems, supply chain management and logistics; health care leadership (MHCL); management information systems (MMIS); operations management (MSOM); professional (MBA), including accounting, business law, change management, health care leadership, management information systems, supply chain management and logistics; teaching (MAT). Part-time and evening/weekend programs available. Postbaccalaureate distance learning degree programs offered (no on-campus study). *Degree requirements:* For master's, research project. *Entrance requirements:* For master's, bachelor's degree from accredited institution, official transcripts, interview with program director, letter(s) of recommendation. Additional exam requirements/recommendations for international students: Required—TOEFL (minimum score 560 paper-based). Electronic applications accepted.

Fuller Theological Seminary, Graduate Programs, Pasadena, CA 91182. Offers Christian leadership (MACL); clinical psychology (PhD, Psy D); family studies (MA); global leadership (MA); global ministries (D Min); global ministries (Korean language) (D Min); intercultural studies (MA, Th M, PhD); intercultural studies (Korean language) (MA); marital and family therapy (MS); marriage and family enrichment (Certificate); ministry (M Div, D Min); missiology (D Miss); missiology (Korean language) (Th M); theology (MA, Th M, PhD), including evangelism (MA), family life education (MA), pastoral ministry (MA), recovery ministry (MA), worship music ministry (MA), worship, theology, and the arts (MA), youth, family, and culture (MA); theology and ministry (MA).

Geneva College, Master of Arts in Counseling Program, Beaver Falls, PA 15010-3599. Offers clinical mental health counseling (MA); marriage and family counseling (MA); school counseling (MA). *Accreditation:* ACA. Part-time and evening/weekend programs available. *Faculty:* 6 full-time (2 women), 7 part-time/adjunct (3 women). *Students:* 53 full-time (42 women), 42 part-time (31 women); includes 8 minority (all Black or African American, non-Hispanic/Latino). Average age 34. 42 applicants, 74% accepted, 27 enrolled. In 2014, 29 master's awarded. *Degree requirements:* For master's, 50-60 credits (depending on program), practicum, internship. *Entrance requirements:* For master's, minimum GPA of 3.0 (preferred), 3 letters of recommendation, essay on career goals, resume of educational and professional experiences. Additional exam requirements/recommendations for international students: Required—TOEFL.

Application deadline: For fall admission, 9/1 for domestic students; for spring admission, 1/10 for domestic students. Applications are processed on a rolling basis. Electronic applications accepted. *Expenses:* Expenses: Contact institution. *Financial support:* In 2014–15, 5 students received support. Research assistantships, teaching assistantships, career-related internships or fieldwork, and unspecified assistantships available. Financial award application deadline: 8/1; financial award applicants required to submit FAFSA. *Faculty research:* Blended family counseling; premarital and newlywed couples; religion in clinical supervision; conceptual mapping in research, supervision, and clinical work; Factor Analytic Study of the ROSI (Recovery Oriented System Indicators). *Unit head:* Dr. Shannon Shiderly, Program Director, 724-847-6649, Fax: 724-847-6101, E-mail: slshider@geneva.edu. *Application contact:* Marina Frazier, Graduate Program Manager, 724-847-6697, E-mail: counseling@geneva.edu.
Website: http://www.geneva.edu/page/grad_counseling

George Fox University, College of Education, Graduate Department of Counseling, Newberg, OR 97132-2697. Offers clinical mental health counseling (MA); marriage, couple and family counseling (MA, Certificate); mental health trauma (Certificate); school counseling (MA, Certificate); school psychology (Certificate, Ed S). Part-time programs available. *Degree requirements:* For master's, clinical project. *Entrance requirements:* For master's, MAT or GRE, bachelor's degree from regionally-accredited college or university, minimum cumulative GPA of 3.0, 1 professional and 1 academic reference, resume, on-campus interview, official transcripts. Additional exam requirements/recommendations for international students: Required—TOEFL (minimum score 577 paper-based; 90 iBT), IELTS (minimum score 7). Electronic applications accepted. *Expenses:* Contact institution.

Grand Canyon University, College of Nursing and Health Sciences, Phoenix, AZ 85017-1097. Offers addiction counseling (MS); health care administration (MS); health care informatics (MS); marriage and family therapy (MS); professional counseling (MS); public health (MS). Part-time and evening/weekend programs available. Postbaccalaureate distance learning degree programs offered (no on-campus study). *Entrance requirements:* For master's, undergraduate degree with minimum GPA of 2.8. Additional exam requirements/recommendations for international students: Required—TOEFL (minimum score 575 paper-based; 90 iBT), IELTS (minimum score 7).

Harding University, College of Bible and Ministry, Program in Marriage and Family Therapy, Searcy, AR 72149-0001. Offers marriage and family therapy (MS); mental health counseling (MS). Part-time programs available. *Faculty:* 7 full-time (1 woman). *Students:* 22 full-time (12 women); includes 4 minority (2 Black or African American, non-Hispanic/Latino; 1 American Indian or Alaska Native, non-Hispanic/Latino; 1 Hispanic/Latino), 1 international. Average age 30. 17 applicants, 76% accepted, 13 enrolled. In 2014, 12 master's awarded. *Degree requirements:* For master's, comprehensive exam, 15-month practicum. *Entrance requirements:* For master's, GRE General Test, minimum undergraduate GPA of 2.75, graduate 3.0. *Application deadline:* For fall admission, 4/1 priority date for domestic students. Applications are processed on a rolling basis. Application fee: $40. *Expenses: Tuition:* Full-time $12,096; part-time $672 per credit hour. *Required fees:* $432; $24 per credit hour. Tuition and fees vary according to course load and degree level. *Financial support:* In 2014–15, 5 students received support. Scholarships/grants available. *Faculty research:* Forgiveness, substance abuse, post-traumatic stress disorder. *Unit head:* Dr. Lewis L. Moore, Chairman, 501-279-4347, Fax: 501-279-4417, E-mail: lmoore@harding.edu. *Application contact:* Ruth Ann Dawson, Office Manager, 501-279-4347, Fax: 501-279-4417, E-mail: radawson@harding.edu.
Website: http://www.harding.edu/MFT/

Hardin-Simmons University, Graduate School, Cynthia Ann Parker College of Liberal Arts, Department of Psychology, Program in Clinical Counseling and Marriage and Family Therapy, Abilene, TX 79698-0001. Offers MA. Part-time programs available. *Faculty:* 5 full-time (3 women). *Students:* 20 full-time (18 women), 2 part-time (1 woman); includes 2 minority (both Hispanic/Latino). Average age 24. In 2014, 7 master's awarded. *Degree requirements:* For master's, comprehensive exam, clinical experience, project. *Entrance requirements:* For master's, minimum undergraduate GPA of 3.0 in major, 2.7 overall; 21 semester hours of course work in psychology, 18 of those in upper-division classes; writing sample; letters of recommendation. Additional exam requirements/recommendations for international students: Required—TOEFL (minimum score 550 paper-based; 75 iBT). *Application deadline:* For fall admission, 8/15 priority date for domestic students, 4/1 for international students; for spring admission, 1/5 priority date for domestic students, 9/1 for international students. Applications are processed on a rolling basis. Application fee: $50. *Expenses: Tuition:* Full-time $12,060; part-time $670 per credit hour. *Required fees:* $325; $110 per semester. Tuition and fees vary according to program. *Financial support:* In 2014–15, 17 students received support, including 20 fellowships (averaging $677 per year); career-related internships or fieldwork and scholarships/grants also available. Support available to part-time students. Financial award application deadline: 6/30; financial award applicants required to submit FAFSA. *Faculty research:* Family stress management, spirituality in marriage, intimacy and sexuality in marriage, sex education in the church, role of faith in marital satisfaction. *Unit head:* Dr. Gail Roaten, Program Director, 325-670-1534, Fax: 325-670-1458, E-mail: gail.roaten@hsutx.edu. *Application contact:* Dr. Nancy Kucinski, Dean of Graduate Studies, 325-670-1298, Fax: 325-670-1564, E-mail: gradoff@hsutx.edu.
Website: http://www.hsutx.edu/academics/cap/graduate/fampsych

Hofstra University, School of Health Sciences and Human Services, Programs in Counseling, Hempstead, NY 11549. Offers counseling (MS Ed, PD); creative arts therapy (MA); interdisciplinary transition specialist (Advanced Certificate); marriage and family therapy (MA); mental health counseling (MA); rehabilitation administration (PD); rehabilitation counseling (MS Ed, Advanced Certificate); rehabilitation counseling in mental health (MS Ed, Advanced Certificate); school counselor bilingual extension (Advanced Certificate). Part-time and evening/weekend programs available. *Students:* 138 full-time (128 women), 54 part-time (51 women); includes 53 minority (24 Black or African American, non-Hispanic/Latino; 1 American Indian or Alaska Native, non-Hispanic/Latino; 9 Asian, non-Hispanic/Latino; 18 Hispanic/Latino; 1 Two or more races, non-Hispanic/Latino), 6 international. Average age 30. 117 applicants, 83% accepted, 57 enrolled. In 2014, 72 master's, 4 other advanced degrees awarded. *Degree requirements:* For master's, comprehensive exam (for some programs), thesis (for some programs), internship, practicum, student teaching, seminars, minimum GPA of 3.0. *Entrance requirements:* For master's, GRE, interview, letters of recommendation, portfolio, essay, professional experience, certification; for other advanced degree, GRE, interview, letters of recommendation, essay, professional experience, resume, master's degree. Additional exam requirements/recommendations for international students: Required—TOEFL (minimum score 550 paper-based; 80 iBT). *Application deadline:* Applications are processed on a rolling basis. Application fee: $70 ($75 for international students). Electronic applications accepted. *Expenses: Tuition:* Full-time $20,610; part-time $1145 per credit hour. *Required fees:* $970; $165 per term. Tuition and fees vary according to program. *Financial support:* In 2014–15, 109 students received support, including 29 fellowships with full and partial tuition reimbursements available (averaging $3,381 per year), 4 research assistantships with full and partial tuition reimbursements available (averaging $7,324 per year); career-related internships or fieldwork, Federal Work-Study, institutionally sponsored loans, scholarships/grants, health care benefits, and tuition waivers (full and partial) also available. Support available to part-time students. Financial award applicants required to submit FAFSA. *Faculty research:* Bereavement, loss, and trauma counseling; conflict transformation, the impact of hope on academic success; student persistence; GLBTQ issues. *Unit head:* Dr. Holly Seirup, Chairperson, 516-463-5752, Fax: 516-463-6184, E-mail: vpshjs@hofstra.edu. *Application contact:* Sunil Samuel, Assistant Vice President of Admissions, 516-463-4723, Fax: 516-463-4664, E-mail: graduateadmission@hofstra.edu.
Website: http://www.hofstra.edu/academics/colleges/healthscienceshumanservices/

Hope International University, School of Graduate and Professional Studies, Program in Marriage and Family Therapy, Fullerton, CA 92831-3138. Offers MA, MFT. *Accreditation:* AAMFT/COAMFTE. *Degree requirements:* For master's, comprehensive exam, thesis (for some programs), final exam, practicum. *Entrance requirements:* For master's, minimum GPA of 3.0, interview, bachelor's degree, 2 references. Additional exam requirements/recommendations for international students: Required—TOEFL (minimum score 550 paper-based; 86 iBT); Recommended—IELTS (minimum score 6.5). Electronic applications accepted. *Expenses:* Contact institution.

Idaho State University, Office of Graduate Studies, Kasiska College of Health Professions, Department of Counseling, Pocatello, ID 83209-8120. Offers counseling (M Coun, Ed S), including marriage and family counseling (M Coun), mental health counseling (M Coun), school counseling (M Coun), student affairs and college counseling (M Coun); counselor education and counseling (PhD). *Accreditation:* ACA (one or more programs are accredited). Part-time programs available. *Degree requirements:* For master's, comprehensive exam, thesis, 4 semesters resident graduate study, practicum/internship; for doctorate, comprehensive exam, thesis/dissertation, 3 semesters internship, 4 consecutive semesters doctoral-level study on campus; for Ed S, comprehensive exam, thesis, case studies, oral exam. *Entrance requirements:* For master's, GRE General Test, MAT, minimum GPA of 3.0, bachelors degree, interview, 3 letters of recommendation; for doctorate, GRE General Test, MAT, minimum graduate GPA of 3.0, resume, interview, counseling license, master's degree; for Ed S, GRE General Test, minimum graduate GPA of 3.0, master's degree in counseling, 3 letters of recommendation, 2 years work experience. Additional exam requirements/recommendations for international students: Required—TOEFL (minimum score 600 paper-based; 80 iBT). Electronic applications accepted. *Faculty research:* Group counseling, multicultural counseling, family counseling, child therapy, supervision.

Indiana University–Purdue University Fort Wayne, College of Education and Public Policy, Department of Professional Studies, Fort Wayne, IN 46805-1499. Offers counselor education (MS Ed); couple and family counseling (MS Ed); educational leadership (MS Ed); school counseling (MS Ed); special education (MS Ed, Certificate). Part-time programs available. *Faculty:* 7 full-time (6 women). *Students:* 14 full-time (10 women), 106 part-time (75 women); includes 18 minority (11 Black or African American, non-Hispanic/Latino; 1 Asian, non-Hispanic/Latino; 4 Hispanic/Latino; 2 Two or more races, non-Hispanic/Latino), 2 international. Average age 32. 21 applicants, 100% accepted, 18 enrolled. In 2014, 43 master's awarded. *Degree requirements:* For master's, comprehensive exam, practicum, internship, portfolio. *Entrance requirements:* For master's, minimum GPA of 2.5, three professional letters of recommendation. Additional exam requirements/recommendations for international students: Required—TOEFL (minimum score 550 paper-based; 79 iBT). *Application deadline:* For fall admission, 4/1 priority date for domestic and international students. Applications are processed on a rolling basis. Application fee: $55. *Financial support:* In 2014–15, 1 teaching assistantship with partial tuition reimbursement (averaging $13,522 per year) was awarded; scholarships/grants also available. Support available to part-time students. Financial award application deadline: 3/1; financial award applicants required to submit FAFSA. *Faculty research:* Learning opportunities with deafness and the hearing impaired, adolescent emotion, student evaluation of teaching. *Unit head:* Dr. Jane Leatherman, Chair, 260-481-5742, Fax: 260-481-5408, E-mail: leatherj@ipfw.edu. *Application contact:* Vicky L. Schmidt, Graduate Recorder, 260-481-6450, Fax: 260-481-5408, E-mail: schmidt@ipfw.edu.
Website: http://new.ipfw.edu/education

Indiana Wesleyan University, Graduate School, College of Arts and Sciences, Marion, IN 46953. Offers addictions counseling (MS); clinical mental health counseling (MS); community counseling (MS); marriage and family therapy (MS); school counseling (MS); student development counseling and administration (MS). *Accreditation:* ACA. Part-time programs available. *Degree requirements:* For master's, thesis or alternative. *Entrance requirements:* For master's, GRE General Test. Additional exam requirements/recommendations for international students: Required—TOEFL. Electronic applications accepted. *Expenses:* Contact institution. *Faculty research:* Community counseling, multicultural counseling, addictions.

Instituto Tecnologico de Santo Domingo, Graduate School, Area of Humanities and Social Sciences, Santo Domingo, Dominican Republic. Offers accounting (Certificate); adult education (Certificate); applied linguistics (MA); economics (MA); education (M Ed); educational psychology (MA, Certificate); gender and development (MA, Certificate); humanistic studies (MA); international marketing management (Certificate); international relations in the Caribbean basin (Certificate); intervention systems in family therapy (MA); linguistic and literary communication (Certificate); pedagogical support (MA); social science education (M Ed); sustainable human development (MA); terminal illness and death psychology (Certificate); youth and adult education (M Ed).

Iona College, School of Arts and Science, Marriage and Family Therapy Program, New Rochelle, NY 10801-1890. Offers MS. *Accreditation:* AAMFT/COAMFTE. Part-time programs available. *Faculty:* 3 full-time (1 woman), 2 part-time/adjunct (1 woman). *Students:* 34 full-time (28 women), 6 part-time (5 women); includes 17 minority (9 Black or African American, non-Hispanic/Latino; 8 Hispanic/Latino), 2 international. Average age 33. 20 applicants, 95% accepted, 16 enrolled. In 2014, 3 master's awarded. *Degree requirements:* For master's, thesis, project. *Entrance requirements:* For master's, interview, minimum GPA of 3.0. *Application deadline:* For fall admission, 8/1 priority date for domestic students, 7/1 for international students. Applications are processed on a rolling basis. Application fee: $50. Electronic applications accepted. *Expenses:* Expenses: Contact institution. *Financial support:* In 2014–15, 3 students received support. Career-related internships or fieldwork, tuition waivers (partial), and unspecified assistantships available. Support available to part-time students. Financial award application deadline: 4/15; financial award applicants required to submit FAFSA. *Unit head:* Robert Burns, PhD, Program Director, 914-633-2418, E-mail: rburns@iona.edu. *Application contact:* Frank Boughner, Director, Graduate Admissions, 914-633-2420, Fax: 914-633-2277, E-mail: fboughner@iona.edu.
Website: http://www.iona.edu/Academics/School-of-Arts-Science/Departments/Marriage-and-Family-Therapy/Graduate-Programs.aspx

John Brown University, Graduate Counseling Programs, Siloam Springs, AR 72761-2121. Offers clinical mental health counseling (MS); marriage and family therapy (MS); play therapy (Graduate Certificate); school counseling (MS). *Accreditation:* NCATE. Part-time and evening/weekend programs available. *Faculty:* 5 full-time (0 women), 19 part-time/adjunct (6 women). *Students:* 104 full-time (82 women), 100 part-time (75 women); includes 46 minority (15 Black or African American, non-Hispanic/Latino; 4 American Indian or Alaska Native, non-Hispanic/Latino; 3 Asian, non-Hispanic/Latino;

19 Hispanic/Latino; 5 Two or more races, non-Hispanic/Latino). Average age 33. 102 applicants, 84% accepted, 71 enrolled. *Degree requirements:* For master's, practica or internships. *Entrance requirements:* For master's, GRE (minimum score of 300), recommendation forms from three people, 200-word essay describing professional plans and reason for seeking acceptance. Additional exam requirements/ recommendations for international students: Required—TOEFL (minimum score 550 paper-based; 70 iBT). *Application deadline:* Applications are processed on a rolling basis. Application fee: $35 ($100 for international students). Electronic applications accepted. *Expenses:* Expenses: $532 per credit hour. *Financial support:* Fellowships, institutionally sponsored loans, scholarships/grants, and unspecified assistantships available. Financial award applicants required to submit FAFSA. *Unit head:* Dr. John V. Carmack, Program Director, 479-524-8630, E-mail: jcarmack@jbu.edu. *Application contact:* Nikki Rader, Graduate Counseling Representative, 479-524-7425, E-mail: nikki@jbu.edu.
Website: http://www.jbu.edu/

Johnson University, Graduate and Professional Programs, Knoxville, TN 37998-1001. Offers educational technology (MA); intercultural studies (MA); leadership studies (PhD); marriage and family therapy/professional counseling (MA); New Testament (MA); school counseling (MA); teacher education (MA). Part-time and evening/weekend programs available. Postbaccalaureate distance learning degree programs offered (no on-campus study). *Faculty:* 18 full-time (3 women), 39 part-time/adjunct (12 women). *Students:* 112 full-time (46 women), 117 part-time (45 women); includes 22 minority (10 Black or African American, non-Hispanic/Latino; 1 American Indian or Alaska Native, non-Hispanic/Latino; 2 Asian, non-Hispanic/Latino; 5 Hispanic/Latino; 4 Two or more races, non-Hispanic/Latino), 20 international. Average age 30. In 2014, 39 master's awarded. *Degree requirements:* For master's, variable foreign language requirement, comprehensive exam, thesis (for some programs), internships; for doctorate, variable foreign language requirement, comprehensive exam, thesis/dissertation, internships. *Entrance requirements:* For master's, doctorate, and Graduate Certificate, interview, 3 references, transcripts, essay, minimum GPA of 3.0. Additional exam requirements/ recommendations for international students: Required—TOEFL. *Application deadline:* For fall admission, 7/1 for domestic students; for spring admission, 11/1 for domestic students. Application fee: $50. Electronic applications accepted. *Expenses:* Expenses: $16,800; $11,625 (online master's degree); $32,310 (online doctoral degree). *Financial support:* Scholarships/grants available. Financial award application deadline: 4/15; financial award applicants required to submit FAFSA. *Unit head:* Tim Wingfield, VP for Enrollment Services, 865-573-4517. *Application contact:* Stacy Abernathy, Director of Graduate and Non-traditional Admissions, 865-573-4517.

Kansas State University, Graduate School, College of Human Ecology, Program in Human Ecology, Manhattan, KS 66506. Offers apparel and textiles (PhD); family life education and consultation (PhD); food service and hospitality management (PhD); lifespan and human development (PhD); marriage and family therapy (PhD); personal financial planning (PhD). *Students:* 51 full-time (31 women), 44 part-time (24 women); includes 20 minority (8 Black or African American, non-Hispanic/Latino; 1 American Indian or Alaska Native, non-Hispanic/Latino; 3 Asian, non-Hispanic/Latino; 4 Hispanic/ Latino; 1 Native Hawaiian or other Pacific Islander, non-Hispanic/Latino; 3 Two or more races, non-Hispanic/Latino), 17 international. Average age 39. 44 applicants, 39% accepted, 14 enrolled. In 2014, 17 doctorates awarded. *Degree requirements:* For doctorate, thesis/dissertation. *Application deadline:* For fall admission, 2/1 priority date for domestic and international students; for spring admission, 8/1 priority date for domestic and international students. Applications are processed on a rolling basis. Application fee: $50 ($75 for international students). Electronic applications accepted. *Financial support:* Application deadline: 3/1. *Total annual research expenditures:* $1.8 million. *Unit head:* Dr. John Buckwalter, Dean, 785-532-5500, Fax: 785-532-5504, E-mail: jbb3@ksu.edu. *Application contact:* Application Contact, 785-532-5500, Fax: 785-532-5504, E-mail: he@ksu.edu.

Kansas State University, Graduate School, College of Human Ecology, School of Family Studies and Human Services, Manhattan, KS 66506. Offers communication sciences and disorders (MS); conflict resolution (Graduate Certificate); early childhood education (MS); family and community service (MS); family studies (MS); life span human development (MS); marriage and family therapy (MS); personal financial planning (MS, Graduate Certificate); youth development (MS, Graduate Certificate). *Accreditation:* AAMFT/COAMFTE; ASHA. Part-time programs available. Postbaccalaureate distance learning degree programs offered (no on-campus study). *Faculty:* 39 full-time (26 women), 9 part-time/adjunct (7 women). *Students:* 69 full-time (57 women), 141 part-time (99 women); includes 48 minority (15 Black or African American, non-Hispanic/Latino; 3 American Indian or Alaska Native, non-Hispanic/ Latino; 3 Asian, non-Hispanic/Latino; 21 Hispanic/Latino; 2 Native Hawaiian or other Pacific Islander, non-Hispanic/Latino; 4 Two or more races, non-Hispanic/Latino), 3 international. Average age 31. 203 applicants, 38% accepted, 57 enrolled. In 2014, 48 master's, 28 other advanced degrees awarded. *Degree requirements:* For master's, comprehensive exam (for some programs), thesis optional. *Entrance requirements:* For master's, GRE, minimum GPA of 3.0 in last 2 years of undergraduate study. Additional exam requirements/recommendations for international students: Required—TOEFL (minimum score 600 paper-based). *Application deadline:* For fall admission, 2/1 priority date for domestic students, 1/1 priority date for international students; for spring admission, 10/1 priority date for domestic students, 8/1 priority date for international students; for summer admission, 2/1 priority date for domestic students, 12/1 priority date for international students. Applications are processed on a rolling basis. Application fee: $50 ($75 for international students). Electronic applications accepted. *Financial support:* In 2014–15, 25 research assistantships (averaging $10,000 per year), 9 teaching assistantships with full tuition reimbursements (averaging $10,000 per year) were awarded; unspecified assistantships also available. Financial award application deadline: 3/1. *Faculty research:* Health and security of military families, personal and family risk assessment and evaluation, disorders of communication and swallowing, families and health, financial decision-making. *Total annual research expenditures:* $8.4 million. *Unit head:* Dr. Dottie Durband, Director, 785-532-5510, Fax: 785-532-5505, E-mail: dottie@ksu.edu. *Application contact:* Connie Fechter, Administrative Specialist, 785-532-5510, Fax: 785-532-5505, E-mail: fechter@ksu.edu.
Website: http://www.he.k-state.edu/fshs/

Kean University, College of Humanities and Social Sciences, Program in Marriage and Family Therapy, Union, NJ 07083. Offers MA, Diploma. Part-time programs available. *Faculty:* 16 full-time (13 women). *Students:* 21 full-time (19 women), 26 part-time (19 women); includes 23 minority (9 Black or African American, non-Hispanic/Latino; 1 Asian, non-Hispanic/Latino; 13 Hispanic/Latino), 3 international. Average age 29. 19 applicants, 100% accepted, 12 enrolled. In 2014, 9 master's, 9 other advanced degrees awarded. *Degree requirements:* For Diploma, comprehensive exam, thesis, practicum in individual, marital and family therapy; internship. *Entrance requirements:* For degree, GRE General Test, minimum GPA of 3.0; official transcripts from all institutions attended; three letters of recommendation written by faculty and/or person(s) in professionally-related area; professional resume/curriculum vitae; interview; personal statement. Additional exam requirements/recommendations for international students: Required—TOEFL (minimum score 550 paper-based; 79 iBT). *Application deadline:* For fall admission, 6/1 for domestic and international students; for spring admission, 12/1 for domestic and international students. Applications are processed on a rolling basis. Application fee: $75 ($150 for international students). Electronic applications accepted. *Expenses:* Tuition, state resident: full-time $12,461; part-time $607 per credit. Tuition, nonresident: full-time $16,889; part-time $744 per credit. *Required fees:* $3141; $143 per credit. Tuition and fees vary according to course load, degree level and program. *Financial support:* In 2014–15, 6 research assistantships with full tuition reimbursements (averaging $3,742 per year) were awarded; scholarships/grants and unspecified assistantships also available. Financial award applicants required to submit FAFSA. *Unit head:* Dr. Muriel Singer, Program Coordinator, 908-737-5886, E-mail: msinger@kean.edu. *Application contact:* Ann-Marie Kay, Assistant Director of Graduate Admissions, 908-737-7132, Fax: 908-737-7135, E-mail: akay@kean.edu.
Website: http://grad.kean.edu/professional-diploma-programs/marriage-family-therapy

Kutztown University of Pennsylvania, College of Education, Program in Counseling Psychology, Kutztown, PA 19530-0730. Offers agency counseling (MA); marital and family therapy (MA). Part-time and evening/weekend programs available. *Faculty:* 8 full-time (3 women). *Students:* 72 full-time (63 women), 49 part-time (42 women); includes 21 minority (8 Black or African American, non-Hispanic/Latino; 2 Asian, non-Hispanic/ Latino; 11 Hispanic/Latino). Average age 30. 83 applicants, 51% accepted, 29 enrolled. In 2014, 26 master's awarded. *Degree requirements:* For master's, comprehensive exam, thesis optional. *Entrance requirements:* For master's, GRE General Test, interview. Additional exam requirements/recommendations for international students: Required—TOEFL (minimum score 550 paper-based; 79 iBT). *Application deadline:* For fall admission, 3/1 for domestic and international students; for spring admission, 10/1 for domestic and international students. Application fee: $35. Electronic applications accepted. *Expenses: Tuition, area resident:* Part-time $454 per credit. Tuition, state resident: part-time $454 per credit. Tuition, nonresident: part-time $681 per credit. *Required fees:* $85 per credit. *Financial support:* Career-related internships or fieldwork, Federal Work-Study, scholarships/grants, and unspecified assistantships available. Financial award application deadline: 3/1; financial award applicants required to submit FAFSA. *Faculty research:* Family addictions. *Unit head:* Dr. Margaret Herrick, Chairperson, 610-683-4225, Fax: 610-683-1585, E-mail: herrick@kutztown.edu. *Application contact:* Kelly Hish, Admissions Clerk, 610-683-4200, Fax: 610-683-1393, E-mail: graduate@kutztown.edu.

Lancaster Bible College, Graduate School, Lancaster, PA 17601-5036. Offers adult ministries (MA); Bible (MA); children and family ministry (MA); church planting (MA); consulting resource teacher (M Ed); elementary school counseling (M Ed); leadership (PhD); leadership studies (MA); marriage and family counseling (MA); mental health counseling (MA); pastoral studies (MA); secondary school counseling (M Ed); sports ministry (MA); student ministry (MA); town and country ministry (MA). Part-time and evening/weekend programs available. *Degree requirements:* For master's, comprehensive exam (for some programs), thesis (for some programs). *Entrance requirements:* For master's, bachelor's degree with a minimum of 30 credits of course work in Bible, minimum undergraduate GPA of 3.0, interview. Additional exam requirements/recommendations for international students: Required—TOEFL.

La Salle University, School of Arts and Sciences, Program in Counseling and Family Therapy, Philadelphia, PA 19141-1199. Offers industrial/organizational management and human resources (MA); marriage and family therapy (MA); pastoral counseling (MA); professional clinical counseling (MA). *Accreditation:* APA. Part-time and evening/ weekend programs available. *Degree requirements:* For master's, comprehensive exam. *Entrance requirements:* For master's, GRE or MAT (waived for applicants that already possess a master's degree in any field or for applicants that have a cumulative GPA of 3.5 or higher), minimum of 15 hours in psychology, counseling, or marriage and family studies; minimum GPA of 3.0; three letters of recommendation; personal statement; work experience (paid or volunteer). Additional exam requirements/ recommendations for international students: Required—TOEFL. Electronic applications accepted. Application fee is waived when completed online. *Expenses:* Contact institution. *Faculty research:* Cognitive therapy, attribution theory, work habits, single parent families, treatment of addictions.

Lee University, Graduate Studies in Counseling, Cleveland, TN 37320-3450. Offers holistic child development (MS); marriage and family therapy (MS); school counseling (MS). Part-time programs available. *Faculty:* 8 full-time (3 women), 4 part-time/adjunct (0 women). *Students:* 57 full-time (42 women), 25 part-time (19 women); includes 13 minority (8 Black or African American, non-Hispanic/Latino; 1 Asian, non-Hispanic/ Latino; 4 Hispanic/Latino), 2 international. Average age 28. 45 applicants, 78% accepted, 30 enrolled. In 2014, 42 master's awarded. *Degree requirements:* For master's, variable foreign language requirement, comprehensive exam (for some programs), thesis (for some programs), internship. *Entrance requirements:* For master's, GRE General Test or MAT (waived if undergraduate GPA is greater than 3.0 or if applicant already has a graduate degree), minimum undergraduate GPA of 3.0, 3 letters of recommendation, interview, official transcripts, essay. Additional exam requirements/ recommendations for international students: Required—TOEFL (minimum score 450 paper-based). *Application deadline:* For fall admission, 4/1 priority date for domestic and international students; for spring admission, 10/1 priority date for domestic and international students. Applications are processed on a rolling basis. Application fee: $25. *Expenses: Tuition:* Full-time $10,260; part-time $570 per credit hour. *Required fees:* $35 per semester. One-time fee: $25. Tuition and fees vary according to program. *Financial support:* In 2014–15, 26 students received support. Career-related internships or fieldwork, Federal Work-Study, institutionally sponsored loans, scholarships/grants, and unspecified assistantships available. Financial award application deadline: 3/1; financial award applicants required to submit FAFSA. *Unit head:* Dr. Trevor Milliron, Director, 423-614-8126, Fax: 423-614-8129, E-mail: tmilliron@leeuniversity.edu. *Application contact:* Vicki Glasscock, Graduate Admissions Director, 423-614-8059, E-mail: vglasscock@leeuniversity.edu.
Website: http://www.leeuniversity.edu/academics/graduate/counseling/

LeTourneau University, Graduate Programs, Longview, TX 75607-7001. Offers business administration (MBA); counseling (MA); curriculum and instruction (M Ed); education administration (M Ed); engineering (ME, MS); engineering management (MEM); health care administration (MS); marriage and family therapy (MA); psychology (MA); strategic leadership (MSL); teacher leadership (M Ed); teaching and learning (M Ed). Part-time programs available. Postbaccalaureate distance learning degree programs offered (no on-campus study). *Faculty:* 14 full-time (4 women), 41 part-time/ adjunct (18 women). *Students:* 58 full-time (37 women), 359 part-time (289 women); includes 140 minority (78 Black or African American, non-Hispanic/Latino; 2 American Indian or Alaska Native, non-Hispanic/Latino; 4 Asian, non-Hispanic/Latino; 40 Hispanic/ Latino; 16 Two or more races, non-Hispanic/Latino), 11 international. Average age 38. 199 applicants, 73% accepted, 130 enrolled. In 2014, 139 master's awarded. *Degree requirements:* For master's, thesis (for some programs). *Entrance requirements:* For master's, GRE (for engineering and psychology programs). Additional exam requirements/recommendations for international students: Required—TOEFL. *Application deadline:* For fall admission, 8/22 for domestic students, 8/29 for international students; for winter admission, 10/10 for domestic students; for spring admission, 1/2 for domestic students, 1/10 for international students; for summer admission, 5/1 for domestic and international students. Applications are processed on a

rolling basis. Electronic applications accepted. Application fee is waived when completed online. *Financial support:* In 2014–15, 11 students received support, including 16 research assistantships (averaging $11,621 per year); institutionally sponsored loans and unspecified assistantships also available. Financial award applicants required to submit FAFSA. *Application contact:* Chris Fontaine, Assistant Vice President for Global Campus Admissions, 903-233-4312, E-mail: chrisfontaine@letu.edu.
Website: http://www.letu.edu

Lewis & Clark College, Graduate School of Education and Counseling, Department of Counseling Psychology, Program in Marriage, Couple and Family Therapy, Portland, OR 97219-7899. Offers MA, MS. Part-time and evening/weekend programs available. *Degree requirements:* For master's, thesis (MS). *Entrance requirements:* For master's, GRE General Test, minimum undergraduate GPA of 2.75. Additional exam requirements/recommendations for international students: Required—TOEFL (minimum score 575 paper-based). Electronic applications accepted.

Liberty University, Liberty Baptist Theological Seminary, Lynchburg, VA 24515. Offers Biblical studies (M Div, MAR, MTS, Th M); church history (M Div, MAR, MTS, Th M); discipleship (D Min); discipleship and church ministry (M Div, MAR, MCM); evangelism and church planting (M Div, MAR, MCM, D Min); global studies (M Div, MAR, MCM, MGS, Th M); homiletics (M Div, MAR, MCM, Th M, D Min); leadership (M Div, MAR, MCM, D Min); marketplace chaplaincy (M Div, MAR, MCM); ministry (D Min); pastoral counseling (M Div, MA, MAR, MCM, D Min), including addictions and recovery (MA), crisis response and trauma (MA), discipleship and church ministries (MA), leadership (MA), life coaching (MA), marketplace chaplaincy (MA), marriage and family (MA), military resilience (MA), pastoral counseling (MA); pastoral ministries (M Div, MAR, MCM); religious education (MRE); theology (M Div, MAR, MTS, Th M); theology and apologetics (PhD); worship (M Div, MAR, MCM, D Min). Part-time programs available. Postbaccalaureate distance learning degree programs offered (minimal on-campus study). *Students:* 2,865 full-time (781 women), 3,750 part-time (1,139 women); includes 1,742 minority (1,382 Black or African American, non-Hispanic/Latino; 22 American Indian or Alaska Native, non-Hispanic/Latino; 116 Asian, non-Hispanic/Latino; 105 Hispanic/Latino; 7 Native Hawaiian or other Pacific Islander, non-Hispanic/Latino; 110 Two or more races, non-Hispanic/Latino), 227 international. Average age 41. 5,446 applicants, 39% accepted, 1340 enrolled. In 2014, 1,969 master's, 126 doctorates, 75 other advanced degrees awarded. *Degree requirements:* For master's, 2 foreign languages, thesis (for some programs); for doctorate, 2 foreign languages, thesis/dissertation. *Entrance requirements:* For master's, minimum undergraduate GPA of 2.0; for doctorate, GRE General Test or MAT, minimum graduate GPA of 3.0. Additional exam requirements/recommendations for international students: Required—TOEFL (minimum score 600 paper-based; 100 iBT). *Application deadline:* For fall admission, 6/1 for domestic students; for spring admission, 11/1 for domestic students. Applications are processed on a rolling basis. Application fee: $50. Electronic applications accepted. *Expenses:* Expenses: Contact institution. *Financial support:* Teaching assistantships with tuition reimbursements, career-related internships or fieldwork, and Federal Work-Study available. Financial award applicants required to submit FAFSA. *Unit head:* Dr. David Hirschman, Acting Dean, 434-592-4140, Fax: 434-522-0415, E-mail: dwhirschman@liberty.edu. *Application contact:* Jay Bridge, Director of Graduate Admissions, 800-424-9595, Fax: 800-628-7977, E-mail: gradadmissions@liberty.edu.
Website: http://www.liberty.edu/seminary/

Liberty University, School of Behavioral Sciences, Lynchburg, VA 24515. Offers advanced clinical skills (PhD); clinical mental health counseling (MA); counselor education and supervision (PhD); human services counseling (MA), including addictions and recovery, business, child and family law, Christian ministries, criminal justice, crisis response and trauma, executive leadership, health and wellness, life coaching, marriage and family, military resilience; marriage and family therapy (MA); military resilience (Certificate); professional counseling (MA). Part-time programs available. Postbaccalaureate distance learning degree programs offered (minimal on-campus study). *Students:* 3,009 full-time (2,433 women), 6,251 part-time (4,981 women); includes 2,959 minority (2,520 Black or African American, non-Hispanic/Latino; 49 American Indian or Alaska Native, non-Hispanic/Latino; 51 Asian, non-Hispanic/Latino; 97 Hispanic/Latino; 9 Native Hawaiian or other Pacific Islander, non-Hispanic/Latino; 233 Two or more races, non-Hispanic/Latino), 153 international. Average age 38. 6,645 applicants, 55% accepted, 2039 enrolled. In 2014, 2,410 master's, 11 doctorates, 2 other advanced degrees awarded. *Application deadline:* Applications are processed on a rolling basis. Application fee: $50. Electronic applications accepted. *Financial support:* Applicants required to submit FAFSA. *Unit head:* Dr. Ronald Hawkins, Founding Dean, School of Behavioral Sciences. *Application contact:* Jay Bridge, Director of Admissions, 800-424-9595, Fax: 800-628-7977, E-mail: gradadmissions@liberty.edu.

Lincoln Christian University, Hargrove School of Adult and Graduate Studies, Lincoln, IL 62656-2167. Offers bible and theology (MA); intercultural studies (MA); marriage and family therapy (MA); organizational leadership (MA); spiritual formation (MA); TESOL (MA). MA in marriage and family therapy offered in Las Vegas, NV; MA in spiritual formation program offered in Bloomington-Normal, IL. Postbaccalaureate distance learning degree programs offered (no on-campus study). *Faculty:* 6 full-time (3 women), 20 part-time/adjunct (3 women). *Students:* 5 full-time (4 women), 137 part-time (53 women); includes 33 minority (19 Black or African American, non-Hispanic/Latino; 3 American Indian or Alaska Native, non-Hispanic/Latino; 1 Asian, non-Hispanic/Latino; 7 Hispanic/Latino; 3 Two or more races, non-Hispanic/Latino), 7 international. Average age 39. 114 applicants, 68% accepted, 62 enrolled. In 2014, 53 master's awarded. *Degree requirements:* For master's, 2.5 cumulative GPA in Undergraduate Degree studies. *Entrance requirements:* For master's, If undergrad cum GPA is lower than 2.5 (on a 4.0 scale) applicant may be required to complete the Miller Analogies Test at an authorized center. Additional exam requirements/recommendations for international students: Required—TOEFL (minimum score 550 paper-based); Recommended—IELTS (minimum score 6). *Application deadline:* For fall admission, 8/1 for domestic students, 3/1 for international students; for spring admission, 11/15 for domestic students, 11/1 for international students. Application fee: $25 ($50 for international students). Application fee is waived when completed online. *Expenses: Tuition:* Full-time $7524; part-time $418 per credit hour. One-time fee: $144. Tuition and fees vary according to campus/location and program. *Financial support:* Applicants required to submit FAFSA.

Lipscomb University, Department of Graduate Psychology and Counseling, Nashville, TN 37204-3951. Offers clinical mental health counseling (MS); counseling psychology (Certificate); marriage and family therapy (MMFT); psychology (MS). Part-time and evening/weekend programs available. *Faculty:* 11 full-time (3 women), 6 part-time/adjunct (2 women). *Students:* 90 full-time (70 women), 40 part-time (32 women); includes 36 minority (25 Black or African American, non-Hispanic/Latino; 1 American Indian or Alaska Native, non-Hispanic/Latino; 2 Asian, non-Hispanic/Latino; 6 Hispanic/Latino; 2 Two or more races, non-Hispanic/Latino), 1 international. Average age 29. In 2014, 66 master's awarded. *Degree requirements:* For master's, thesis (for some programs), practicum, internship, capstone. *Entrance requirements:* For master's, GRE, resume, 3 reference letters, transcripts, goals statement. Additional exam requirements/recommendations for international students: Required—TOEFL (minimum score 570 paper-based; 80 iBT). *Application deadline:* For fall admission, 7/1 for domestic students; for spring admission, 11/1 for domestic students. Applications are processed on a rolling basis. Application fee: $50 ($75 for international students). Electronic applications accepted. *Expenses:* Expenses: $898 per credit hour. *Financial support:* Scholarships/grants and unspecified assistantships available. Financial award applicants required to submit FAFSA. *Faculty research:* Cognitive psychology, neuroscience, health psychology, grief issues. *Unit head:* Dr. Shanna Ray, Director/Professor of Psychology, 615-966-5833, E-mail: shanna.ray@lipscomb.edu. *Application contact:* Kathi Johnson, Recruiting and Marketing Coordinator, 615-966-5237, E-mail: kathi.johnson@lipscomb.edu.
Website: http://www.lipscomb.edu/psychology/graduate-programs

Long Island University–LIU Brooklyn, School of Education, Brooklyn, NY 11201-8423. Offers applied behavior analysis (Advanced Certificate); bilingual education in urban settings (Advanced Certificate); bilingual school counselor (Advanced Certificate); childhood/early childhood urban education (MS Ed); early childhood urban education (MS Ed, Advanced Certificate); educational leadership (Advanced Certificate); marriage and family therapy (Advanced Certificate); school counselor (MS Ed, Advanced Certificate); teaching English to speakers of other languages (TESOL) (MS Ed). *Accreditation:* Teacher Education Accreditation Council. Part-time and evening/weekend programs available. *Faculty:* 20 full-time (14 women), 47 part-time/adjunct (34 women). *Students:* 224 full-time (183 women), 604 part-time (472 women); includes 551 minority (302 Black or African American, non-Hispanic/Latino; 3 American Indian or Alaska Native, non-Hispanic/Latino; 42 Asian, non-Hispanic/Latino; 189 Hispanic/Latino; 15 Two or more races, non-Hispanic/Latino), 10 international. Average age 36. 353 applicants, 61% accepted, 129 enrolled. In 2014, 213 master's, 16 other advanced degrees awarded. *Degree requirements:* For master's, thesis optional, electronic portfolio. *Entrance requirements:* For master's, 2 letters of recommendation; GPA requirement varies by program; some programs require interview, personal statement, writing assessment; for Advanced Certificate, 2 letters of recommendation, GPA requirement varies by program; interview; personal statement. Additional exam requirements/recommendations for international students: Required—TOEFL (minimum score 500 paper-based). *Application deadline:* For fall admission, 5/1 for international students; for spring admission, 11/1 for international students. Applications are processed on a rolling basis. Electronic applications accepted. *Expenses: Tuition:* Part-time $1132 per credit. *Required fees:* $434 per semester. *Financial support:* Career-related internships or fieldwork, scholarships/grants, tuition waivers (partial), and unspecified assistantships available. Support available to part-time students. Financial award applicants required to submit FAFSA. *Faculty research:* The intersection between race and gender in diverse women's leadership and health outcomes, selective mutism, risk factors among juvenile sex offenders and their reintegration into the school system, infant development, theoretical orientation in clinical practice. *Unit head:* Dr. Amy Patraka Ginsberg, Acting Dean (2015-2016), 718-488-1055, E-mail: amy.ginsberg@liu.edu. *Application contact:* Chanelle Lester, Director of Graduate Admissions, 718-780-4321, Fax: 718-780-6110, E-mail: chanelle.lester@liu.edu.
Website: http://www.liu.edu/Brooklyn/Academics/School-of-Education

Loyola Marymount University, College of Fine Arts, Department of Marital and Family Therapy, Program in Marital and Family Therapy, Los Angeles, CA 90045-. Offers MA. *Degree requirements:* For master's, thesis, 840-hour internship. *Entrance requirements:* For master's, MAT, art portfolio, interview, autobiographical essay. Additional exam requirements/recommendations for international students: Required—TOEFL (minimum score 600 paper-based; 100 iBT). Electronic applications accepted. *Expenses:* Contact institution.

Maryville University of Saint Louis, College of Health Professions, Program in Rehabilitation Counseling, St. Louis, MO 63141-7299. Offers marriage and family therapy (MARC); music therapy (MARC); substance abuse (MARC). *Accreditation:* CORE. Part-time and evening/weekend programs available. *Faculty:* 3 full-time (1 woman), 3 part-time/adjunct (all women). *Students:* 9 full-time (all women), 25 part-time (23 women); includes 5 minority (4 Black or African American, non-Hispanic/Latino; 1 Two or more races, non-Hispanic/Latino). Average age 32. In 2014, 24 master's awarded. *Degree requirements:* For master's, internship, seminar. *Entrance requirements:* For master's, minimum cumulative GPA of 3.0, 2 letters of recommendation, interview. Additional exam requirements/recommendations for international students: Required—TOEFL (minimum score 550 paper-based). *Application deadline:* For fall admission, 1/15 for domestic students; for spring admission, 10/1 for domestic students. Application fee: $40 ($60 for international students). Electronic applications accepted. Application fee is waived when completed online. *Expenses: Tuition:* Full-time $24,694; part-time $755 per credit hour. Part-time tuition and fees vary according to course load and degree level. *Financial support:* Career-related internships or fieldwork, Federal Work-Study, and campus employment available. Financial award application deadline: 3/1; financial award applicants required to submit FAFSA. *Unit head:* Dr. Michael Kiener, Director, 314-529-9443, Fax: 314-529-9495, E-mail: mkiener@maryville.edu. *Application contact:* Crystal Jacobsmeyer, Assistant Director, Graduate Enrollment Advising, 314-529-9654, Fax: 314-529-9927, E-mail: cjacobsmeyer@maryville.edu.
Website: http://www.maryville.edu/hp/rehabilitation-counseling/

Medaille College, Programs in Psychology, Buffalo, NY 14214-2695. Offers clinical psychology (Psy D); marriage and family therapy (MA); mental health counseling (MA); psychology (MA). Part-time and evening/weekend programs available. *Degree requirements:* For master's, comprehensive exam (for some programs), thesis (for some programs). *Entrance requirements:* For master's, GRE General Test (psychology), minimum GPA of 2.75 (psychology). Additional exam requirements/recommendations for international students: Required—TOEFL (minimum score 550 paper-based). Electronic applications accepted. *Faculty research:* Schizophrenia, Parkinson's Disease, eyewitness testimony, methodology.

Mercy College, School of Social and Behavioral Sciences, Program in Counseling, Dobbs Ferry, NY 10522-1189. Offers counseling (MS); family counseling (Certificate). Part-time and evening/weekend programs available. Postbaccalaureate distance learning degree programs offered (no on-campus study). *Students:* 42 full-time (38 women), 123 part-time (110 women); includes 117 minority (48 Black or African American, non-Hispanic/Latino; 2 American Indian or Alaska Native, non-Hispanic/Latino; 2 Asian, non-Hispanic/Latino; 62 Hispanic/Latino; 3 Two or more races, non-Hispanic/Latino). Average age 34. 93 applicants, 70% accepted, 40 enrolled. In 2014, 64 master's, 2 other advanced degrees awarded. *Degree requirements:* For master's, comprehensive exam (for some programs). *Entrance requirements:* For master's, essay, two professional letters of recommendation, resume, undergraduate transcript with minimum GPA of 3.0. Additional exam requirements/recommendations for international students: Required—TOEFL (minimum score 600 paper-based; 100 iBT), IELTS (minimum score 8). *Application deadline:* For fall admission, 8/1 for international students. Applications are processed on a rolling basis. Application fee: $40. Electronic applications accepted. *Expenses: Tuition:* Full-time $14,952; part-time $814 per credit. *Required fees:* $600; $150 per semester. Tuition and fees vary according to course load, degree level and program. *Financial support:* Career-related internships or fieldwork, Federal Work-Study, scholarships/grants, and unspecified assistantships available.

Support available to part-time students. Financial award applicants required to submit FAFSA. *Unit head:* Dr. Karol Dean, Dean, School of Social and Behavioral Sciences, 914-674-7517, E-mail: kdean@mercy.edu. *Application contact:* Allison Gurdineer, Senior Director of Admissions, 914-637-2946, Fax: 914-674-7382, E-mail: admissions@mercy.edu.
Website: https://www.mercy.edu/degrees-programs/ms-counseling

Mercy College, School of Social and Behavioral Sciences, Program in Marriage and Family Therapy, Dobbs Ferry, NY 10522-1189. Offers MS. Part-time and evening/weekend programs available. *Students:* 12 full-time (all women), 37 part-time (31 women); includes 30 minority (15 Black or African American, non-Hispanic/Latino; 2 Asian, non-Hispanic/Latino; 12 Hispanic/Latino; 1 Two or more races, non-Hispanic/Latino), 2 international. Average age 34. 37 applicants, 32% accepted, 10 enrolled. In 2014, 17 master's awarded. *Degree requirements:* For master's, thesis (for some programs), practicum, research project. *Entrance requirements:* For master's, essay, resume, interview, two letters of recommendation, undergraduate transcript. Additional exam requirements/recommendations for international students: Required—TOEFL (minimum score 600 paper-based; 100 iBT), IELTS (minimum score 8). *Application deadline:* For fall admission, 8/1 for international students. Applications are processed on a rolling basis. Application fee: $40. Electronic applications accepted. *Expenses: Tuition:* Full-time $14,952; part-time $814 per credit. *Required fees:* $600; $150 per semester. Tuition and fees vary according to course load, degree level and program. *Financial support:* Career-related internships or fieldwork, Federal Work-Study, scholarships/grants, and unspecified assistantships available. Support available to part-time students. Financial award applicants required to submit FAFSA. *Unit head:* Dr. Karol Dean, Interim Dean, School of Social and Behavioral Sciences, 914-674-7517, E-mail: kdean@mercy.edu. *Application contact:* Allison Gurdineer, Senior Director of Admissions, 877-637-2946, Fax: 914-674-7382, E-mail: admissions@mercy.edu.
Website: https://www.mercy.edu/degrees-programs/ms-marriage-and-family-therapy

Messiah College, Program in Counseling, Mechanicsburg, PA 17055. Offers clinical mental health counseling (MAC); counseling (CAGS); marriage, couple, and family counseling (MAC); school counseling (MAC). *Accreditation:* ACA. Part-time programs available. Postbaccalaureate distance learning degree programs offered (no on-campus study). *Entrance requirements:* For master's, minimum undergraduate cumulative GPA of 3.0, 2 recommendations, resume or curriculum vitae, interview; for CAGS, bachelor's degree, minimum undergraduate cumulative GPA of 3.0, essay, two recommendations, resume or curriculum vitae, interview. Electronic applications accepted.

Michigan State University, The Graduate School, College of Social Science, Department of Family and Child Ecology, East Lansing, MI 48824. Offers child development (MA); community services (MS); family and child ecology (PhD); family studies (MA); marriage and family therapy (MA); youth development (MA). *Accreditation:* AAMFT/COAMFTE (one or more programs are accredited). *Entrance requirements:* For master's, GRE General Test, minimum GPA of 3.0 in last 2 years of undergraduate course work, 3 letters of recommendation; for doctorate, GRE General Test, minimum GPA of 3.0, 3 letters of recommendation, background in behavioral sciences. Additional exam requirements/recommendations for international students: Required—TOEFL. Electronic applications accepted.

Mid-America Christian University, Program in Counseling, Oklahoma City, OK 73170-4504. Offers marital and family therapy (MS); pastoral/spiritual direction (MS); professional counselor (MS). *Entrance requirements:* For master's, MAT, bachelor's degree from a regionally accredited college or university, minimum overall cumulative GPA of 2.75 of bachelor course work. Additional exam requirements/recommendations for international students: Required—TOEFL (minimum score 550 paper-based).

Minnesota State University Mankato, College of Graduate Studies, College of Education, Department of Counseling and Student Personnel, Mankato, MN 56001. Offers college student affairs (MS); counselor education and supervision (Ed D); marriage and family counseling (Certificate); mental health counseling (MS); professional school counseling (MS). *Accreditation:* ACA (one or more programs are accredited); NCATE. *Students:* 53 full-time (47 women), 57 part-time (44 women). *Degree requirements:* For master's, comprehensive exam, thesis or alternative. *Entrance requirements:* For master's, GRE General Test or MAT (if GPA less than 3.0 for last 2 years), minimum GPA of 3.0 during previous 2 years, 3 letters of reference. Additional exam requirements/recommendations for international students: Required—TOEFL. *Application deadline:* For fall admission, 1/15 priority date for domestic students. Applications are processed on a rolling basis. Application fee: $40. Electronic applications accepted. *Financial support:* Research assistantships with full tuition reimbursements, teaching assistantships with full tuition reimbursements, career-related internships or fieldwork, Federal Work-Study, institutionally sponsored loans, and unspecified assistantships available. Support available to part-time students. Financial award application deadline: 3/15; financial award applicants required to submit FAFSA. *Unit head:* Dr. Jacqueline Lewis, Chairperson, 507-389-5655. *Application contact:* 507-389-2321, E-mail: grad@mnsu.edu.

Mississippi College, Graduate School, School of Education, Department of Psychology and Counseling, Clinton, MS 39058. Offers counseling (Ed S); marriage and family counseling (MS); mental health counseling (MS); school counseling (M Ed). Part-time programs available. *Degree requirements:* For master's and Ed S, comprehensive exam, thesis optional. *Entrance requirements:* For master's, GRE or NTE. Additional exam requirements/recommendations for international students: Recommended—TOEFL, IELTS. Electronic applications accepted.

Mount Mercy University, Program in Marriage and Family Therapy, Cedar Rapids, IA 52402-4797. Offers MA. Evening/weekend programs available.

National University, Academic Affairs, College of Letters and Sciences, La Jolla, CA 92037-1011. Offers applied linguistics (MA); biology (MS); counseling psychology (MA), including licensed professional clinical counseling, marriage and family therapy; creative writing (MFA); English (MA), including Gothic studies, rhetoric; film studies (MA); forensic and crime science (Certificate); forensic studies (MFS), including criminalistics, investigation; history (MA); human behavior (MA); mathematics for educators (MS); performance psychology (MA); strategic communications (MA). Part-time and evening/weekend programs available. Postbaccalaureate distance learning degree programs offered (no on-campus study). *Faculty:* 69 full-time (34 women), 100 part-time/adjunct (55 women). *Students:* 727 full-time (532 women), 349 part-time (240 women); includes 505 minority (128 Black or African American, non-Hispanic/Latino; 5 American Indian or Alaska Native, non-Hispanic/Latino; 52 Asian, non-Hispanic/Latino; 260 Hispanic/Latino; 9 Native Hawaiian or other Pacific Islander, non-Hispanic/Latino; 51 Two or more races, non-Hispanic/Latino), 4 international. Average age 34. In 2014, 569 master's awarded. *Degree requirements:* For master's, thesis (for some programs). *Entrance requirements:* For master's, interview, minimum GPA of 2.5. Additional exam requirements/recommendations for international students: Required—TOEFL (minimum score 550 paper-based; 79 iBT), IELTS (minimum score 6). *Application deadline:* Applications are processed on a rolling basis. Application fee: $60 ($65 for international students). Electronic applications accepted. *Expenses: Tuition:* Full-time $14,184; part-time $1773 per course. *Financial support:* Career-related internships or fieldwork, institutionally sponsored loans, scholarships/grants, and tuition waivers (partial) available. Support available to part-time students. Financial award application deadline: 6/30; financial award applicants required to submit FAFSA. *Unit head:* College of Letters and Sciences, 800-628-8648, E-mail: cols@nu.edu. *Application contact:* Frank Rojas, Interim Vice President for Enrollment Services, 800-628-8648, E-mail: advisor@nu.edu.
Website: http://www.nu.edu/OurPrograms/CollegeOfLettersAndSciences.html

New Mexico State University, College of Agricultural, Consumer and Environmental Sciences, Department of Family and Consumer Sciences, Las Cruces, NM 88003. Offers family and child science (MS); family and consumer science education (MS); food science and technology (MS); human nutrition and dietetic science (MS); marriage and family therapy (MS). Part-time programs available. *Faculty:* 12 full-time (10 women). *Students:* 26 full-time (17 women), 10 part-time (8 women); includes 23 minority (1 Black or African American, non-Hispanic/Latino; 1 Asian, non-Hispanic/Latino; 21 Hispanic/Latino), 2 international. Average age 30. 19 applicants, 58% accepted, 10 enrolled. In 2014, 19 master's awarded. *Degree requirements:* For master's, comprehensive exam (for some programs), thesis (for some programs), oral exam. *Entrance requirements:* For master's, GRE, 3 letters of reference, resume, letter of interest. Additional exam requirements/recommendations for international students: Required—TOEFL (minimum score 550 paper-based; 79 iBT), IELTS (minimum score 6.5). *Application deadline:* For fall admission, 3/1 priority date for domestic and international students; for spring admission, 11/30 for domestic and international students. Applications are processed on a rolling basis. Application fee: $40 ($50 for international students). Electronic applications accepted. *Expenses:* Tuition, state resident: full-time $3969; part-time $220.50 per credit hour. Tuition, nonresident: full-time $13,838; part-time $768.80 per credit hour. *Required fees:* $853; $47.40 per credit hour. *Financial support:* In 2014–15, 24 students received support, including 2 fellowships (averaging $3,970 per year), 7 teaching assistantships (averaging $12,196 per year); career-related internships or fieldwork, Federal Work-Study, scholarships/grants, traineeships, health care benefits, and unspecified assistantships also available. Support available to part-time students. Financial award application deadline: 3/1. *Faculty research:* Food product analysis, childhood obesity, couple relationship education, military families, Latino college students. *Total annual research expenditures:* $448,204. *Unit head:* Dr. Esther Lynn Devall, Head, 575-646-3936, Fax: 575-646-1889, E-mail: edevall@nmsu.edu. *Application contact:* Dr. Margaret Ann Bock, Graduate Program Contact, 575-646-1178, Fax: 575-646-1889, E-mail: abock@nmsu.edu.
Website: http://aces.nmsu.edu/academics/fcs

Northcentral University, Graduate Studies, Prescott Valley, AZ 86314. Offers business (MBA, DBA, PhD, Post-Master's Certificate, Postbaccalaureate Certificate); education (M Ed, Ed D, PhD, Ed S, Post-Master's Certificate, Postbaccalaureate Certificate); marriage and family therapy (MA, PhD, Post-Master's Certificate, Postbaccalaureate Certificate); psychology (MA, PhD, Post-Master's Certificate, Postbaccalaureate Certificate). Part-time and evening/weekend programs available. Postbaccalaureate distance learning degree programs offered (no on-campus study). *Faculty:* 128 full-time (79 women), 378 part-time/adjunct (178 women). *Students:* 3,058 full-time (1,942 women), 10,343 part-time (6,423 women); includes 5,141 minority (3,568 Black or African American, non-Hispanic/Latino; 122 American Indian or Alaska Native, non-Hispanic/Latino; 257 Asian, non-Hispanic/Latino; 684 Hispanic/Latino; 61 Native Hawaiian or other Pacific Islander, non-Hispanic/Latino; 449 Two or more races, non-Hispanic/Latino). Average age 46. In 2014, 331 master's, 166 doctorates, 25 other advanced degrees awarded. *Entrance requirements:* For master's, bachelor's degree from regionally- or nationally-accredited institution, current resume or curriculum vitae, statement of intent, interview, and background check (for marriage and family therapy); for doctorate, post-baccalaureate master's degree and/or doctoral degree from nationally- or regionally-accredited academic institution; for other advanced degree, bachelor's-level or higher degree from accredited institution or university (for Post-Baccalaureate Certificate); master's and/or doctoral degree from regionally- or nationally-accredited academic institution (for Post-Master's Certificate). Additional exam requirements/recommendations for international students: Required—TOEFL (minimum score 95 iBT), IELTS (minimum score 6) or PTE (minimum score 65). *Application deadline:* Applications are processed on a rolling basis. Application fee: $0. Electronic applications accepted. *Expenses: Tuition:* Full-time $15,330; part-time $2550 per course. *Required fees:* $2550 per course. *Financial support:* Scholarships/grants available. *Faculty research:* Business management, curriculum and instruction, educational leadership, health psychology, organizational behavior. *Unit head:* Dr. Jim Dorris, Interim Provost and Chief Academic Officer, 888-327-2877, Fax: 928-759-6381, E-mail: provost@ncu.edu. *Application contact:* Ken Boutelle, Vice President, Enrollment Services, 480-253-3535, E-mail: kboutelle@ncu.edu.

North Dakota State University, College of Graduate and Interdisciplinary Studies, College of Human Development and Education, Department of Human Development and Family Science, Fargo, ND 58108. Offers couple and family therapy (MS); developmental science (PhD); family financial planning (MS, Certificate); gerontology (MS, PhD, Certificate); human development (MS, PhD). *Accreditation:* AAMFT/COAMFTE. Part-time and evening/weekend programs available. Postbaccalaureate distance learning degree programs offered (no on-campus study). *Degree requirements:* For master's, thesis or alternative; for doctorate, thesis/dissertation. *Entrance requirements:* Additional exam requirements/recommendations for international students: Required—TOEFL (minimum score 525 paper-based; 71 iBT). *Faculty research:* Family therapy, resilience, parenting, adolescent development, mental health.

See Display on page 864 and Close-Up on page 887.

Northeastern Illinois University, College of Graduate Studies and Research, College of Education, Program in Family Counseling, Chicago, IL 60625-4699. Offers MA.

Northern Kentucky University, Office of Graduate Programs, College of Informatics, Program in Communication, Highland Heights, KY 41099. Offers communication (MA); communication teaching (Certificate); documentary studies (Certificate); public relations (Certificate); relationships (Certificate). Part-time and evening/weekend programs available. *Faculty:* 7 full-time (4 women), 1 part-time/adjunct (0 women). *Students:* 9 full-time (1 woman), 17 part-time (11 women); includes 3 minority (all Black or African American, non-Hispanic/Latino), 2 international. Average age 30. In 2014, 13 master's, 2 other advanced degrees awarded. Terminal master's awarded for partial completion of doctoral program. *Degree requirements:* For master's, comprehensive exams, thesis or applied capstone project. *Entrance requirements:* For master's, GRE, minimum GPA of 3.0, 3 letters of recommendation, letter of intent. Additional exam requirements/recommendations for international students: Required—TOEFL (minimum score 79 iBT); Recommended—IELTS (minimum score 6.5). *Application deadline:* For fall admission, 8/1 for domestic students, 6/1 for international students; for spring admission, 12/1 for domestic students, 10/1 for international students. Applications are processed on a rolling basis. Application fee: $40. Electronic applications accepted. *Expenses: Tuition, area resident:* Part-time $518 per credit hour. Tuition, state resident: part-time $630 per credit hour. Tuition, nonresident: part-time $797 per credit hour. *Required fees:* $192 per semester. Tuition and fees vary according to course load, degree level, campus/location, program and reciprocity agreements. *Financial support:* In 2014–15, 7 students received support. Unspecified assistantships available. Financial award applicants required to submit FAFSA. *Faculty research:* Mediating effect of health communication, organizational communication, quantitative and qualitative research

methods, family and interpersonal communication. *Unit head:* Dr. Andrea Lambert-South, Graduate Program Director, 859-572-6615, E-mail: lamberta3@nku.edu. *Application contact:* Alison Swanson, Graduate Admissions Coordinator, 859-572-6971, E-mail: swansona1@nku.edu. Website: http://informatics.nku.edu/content/informatics/departments/communication/programs/communication—m-a—.html

Northwestern University, The Graduate School, Program in Marital and Family Therapy, Evanston, IL 60208. Offers MS. *Accreditation:* AAMFT/COAMFTE. *Entrance requirements:* For master's, GRE General Test. *Faculty research:* Marital and family therapy training, gender, psychotherapy outcome, adolescents and pre-school children at risk, families.

Northwest Nazarene University, Graduate Studies, Program in Counselor Education, Nampa, ID 83686-5897. Offers clinical counseling (MS); marriage and family counseling (MS); school counseling (MS). Part-time programs available. *Faculty:* 6 full-time (4 women), 10 part-time/adjunct (6 women). *Students:* 94 full-time (67 women), 29 part-time (22 women); includes 10 minority (2 Black or African American, non-Hispanic/Latino; 6 Hispanic/Latino; 2 Two or more races, non-Hispanic/Latino), 1 international. Average age 35. 47 applicants, 66% accepted, 25 enrolled. *Degree requirements:* For master's, comprehensive exam. *Entrance requirements:* For master's, minimum GPA of 3.0, BA. Additional exam requirements/recommendations for international students: Required—TOEFL. *Application deadline:* For fall admission, 2/15 for domestic and international students; for spring admission, 9/15 for domestic and international students. Application fee: $50. Electronic applications accepted. *Unit head:* Dr. Michael Pitts, Chair, 208-467-8040, Fax: 208-467-8339. *Application contact:* Marilyn Holly, Graduate Admissions Counselor, 208-467-8688, E-mail: mholly@nnu.edu.

Notre Dame de Namur University, Division of Academic Affairs, College of Arts and Sciences, Department of Clinical Psychology and Gerontology, Program in Clinical Psychology: Marital and Family Therapy, Belmont, CA 94002-1908. Offers MS. Part-time programs available. *Degree requirements:* For master's, thesis. *Entrance requirements:* Additional exam requirements/recommendations for international students: Required—TOEFL (minimum score 550 paper-based; 79 iBT). Electronic applications accepted.

Notre Dame de Namur University, Division of Academic Affairs, College of Arts and Sciences, Program in Art Therapy Psychology, Belmont, CA 94002-1908. Offers art therapy (MA, PhD); marriage and family therapy (MA). Part-time programs available. *Degree requirements:* For master's, thesis, oral presentation, portfolio; for doctorate, thesis/dissertation. *Entrance requirements:* For master's, interview, minimum GPA of 2.5; for doctorate, master's degree from accredited university in art therapy or in a related field; minimum of two years of clinical work in the field; portfolio; three professional recommendations; one published article or scholarly academic writing on an art therapy subject in publication acceptable form; interview. Additional exam requirements/recommendations for international students: Required—TOEFL (minimum score 550 paper-based; 79 iBT). Electronic applications accepted.

Nova Southeastern University, Graduate School of Humanities and Social Sciences, Fort Lauderdale, FL 33314-7796. Offers advanced conflict resolution practice (Graduate Certificate); college student affairs (MS); conflict analysis and resolution (MS, PhD); cross-disciplinary studies (MA); family studies (Graduate Certificate); family systems health care (Graduate Certificate); family therapy (MS, PhD); marriage and family therapy (DMFT); peace studies (Graduate Certificate); qualitative research (Graduate Certificate); solution focused coaching (Graduate Certificate). *Accreditation:* AAMFT/COAMFTE (one or more programs are accredited). Part-time and evening/weekend programs available. Postbaccalaureate distance learning degree programs offered (minimal on-campus study). *Faculty:* 29 full-time (18 women), 27 part-time/adjunct (21 women). *Students:* 502 full-time (363 women), 269 part-time (189 women); includes 415 minority (241 Black or African American, non-Hispanic/Latino; 1 American Indian or Alaska Native, non-Hispanic/Latino; 16 Asian, non-Hispanic/Latino; 136 Hispanic/Latino; 21 Two or more races, non-Hispanic/Latino), 56 international. Average age 37. 424 applicants, 58% accepted, 161 enrolled. In 2014, 140 master's, 50 doctorates, 11 other advanced degrees awarded. *Degree requirements:* For master's, thesis optional, comprehensive exams, portfolios (for some programs), table-top exams (for some programs); for doctorate, comprehensive exam, thesis/dissertation, qualifying exams, portfolios (for some programs). *Entrance requirements:* For master's, interview, minimum GPA of 3.0, writing sample; for doctorate, interview, minimum GPA of 3.5, master's degree in related field, writing sample; for Graduate Certificate, minimum GPA of 3.0. Additional exam requirements/recommendations for international students: Required—TOEFL. *Application deadline:* For fall admission, 5/17 priority date for domestic and international students; for winter admission, 12/1 priority date for domestic and international students; for spring admission, 4/1 priority date for domestic and international students. Applications are processed on a rolling basis. Application fee: $50. Electronic applications accepted. *Financial support:* In 2014–15, 7 students received support, including 26 research assistantships (averaging $15,000 per year); career-related internships or fieldwork, Federal Work-Study, scholarships/grants, and unspecified assistantships also available. Financial award application deadline: 4/1; financial award applicants required to submit CSS PROFILE. *Faculty research:* Conflict resolution, family therapy, peace research, international conflict, multi-disciplinary studies, college student affairs, national security affairs, health care conflict resolution, family systems health care, advanced family systems, qualitative research, solution-focused coaching. *Unit head:* Dr. Honggang Yang, Dean, 954-262-3016, Fax: 954-262-3968, E-mail: yangh@nova.edu. *Application contact:* Marcia Arango, Student Recruitment Coordinator, 954-262-3006, Fax: 954-262-3968, E-mail: marango@nsu.nova.edu. Website: http://shss.nova.edu/

Nyack College, Alliance Graduate School of Counseling, Nyack, NY 10960. Offers marriage and family therapy (MA); mental health counseling (MA). Part-time and evening/weekend programs available. *Students:* 107 full-time (88 women), 172 part-time (145 women); includes 212 minority (106 Black or African American, non-Hispanic/Latino; 41 Asian, non-Hispanic/Latino; 62 Hispanic/Latino; 3 Two or more races, non-Hispanic/Latino), 6 international. Average age 38. In 2014, 69 master's awarded. *Degree requirements:* For master's, comprehensive exam, counselor-in-training therapy, internship, CPCE exam. *Entrance requirements:* For master's, Millon Clinical Multiaxial Inventory-3, Minnesota Multiphasic Personality Inventory-2, transcripts, statement of Christian life and experience, statement of support systems. Additional exam requirements/recommendations for international students: Required—TOEFL (minimum score 83 iBT). *Application deadline:* For fall admission, 8/1 for domestic students, 2/15 for international students; for spring admission, 12/15 for domestic students, 7/15 for international students. Applications are processed on a rolling basis. Application fee: $30. Electronic applications accepted. *Expenses:* Expenses: Contact institution. *Financial support:* Career-related internships or fieldwork and scholarships/grants available. Financial award applicants required to submit FAFSA. *Unit head:* Dr. Carol Robles, Director, 845-770-5730, Fax: 845-348-3923. *Application contact:* 800-541-6891, Fax: 845-348-3912, E-mail: admissions.grad@nyack.edu. Website: http://www.nyack.edu/agsc

Oklahoma Baptist University, Program in Marriage and Family Therapy, Shawnee, OK 74804. Offers MS. Part-time and evening/weekend programs available. *Degree requirements:* For master's, thesis optional, practicum. *Entrance requirements:* For master's, GRE General Test. Additional exam requirements/recommendations for international students: Required—TOEFL. Electronic applications accepted. *Faculty research:* Marriage and family therapy supervision, intimate partner violence in migrant populations, medical family therapy, violence and aggression, protective factors and adolescent delinquency.

Oklahoma State University, College of Human Sciences, Department of Human Development and Family Science, Stillwater, OK 74078. Offers human development and family science (MS, PhD), including family financial planning (MS), human environmental sciences; marriage and family therapy (MS). *Accreditation:* AAMFT/COAMFTE (one or more programs are accredited). Postbaccalaureate distance learning degree programs offered. *Faculty:* 27 full-time (18 women), 9 part-time/adjunct (8 women). *Students:* 25 full-time (19 women), 45 part-time (39 women); includes 18 minority (7 Black or African American, non-Hispanic/Latino; 2 Asian, non-Hispanic/Latino; 1 Hispanic/Latino; 8 Two or more races, non-Hispanic/Latino), 2 international. Average age 30. 72 applicants, 33% accepted, 14 enrolled. In 2014, 24 master's, 3 doctorates awarded. *Degree requirements:* For master's, thesis (for some programs); for doctorate, comprehensive exam, thesis/dissertation. *Entrance requirements:* For master's and doctorate, GRE or GMAT. Additional exam requirements/recommendations for international students: Required—TOEFL (minimum score 550 paper-based; 79 iBT). *Application deadline:* For fall admission, 3/1 priority date for international students; for spring admission, 8/1 priority date for international students. Applications are processed on a rolling basis. Application fee: $40 ($75 for international students). Electronic applications accepted. *Expenses:* Tuition, state resident: full-time $4488; part-time $187 per credit hour. Tuition, nonresident: full-time $18,360; part-time $765 per credit hour. *Required fees:* $2413; $100.55 per credit hour. Tuition and fees vary according to campus/location. *Financial support:* In 2014–15, 35 research assistantships (averaging $11,436 per year), 24 teaching assistantships (averaging $10,007 per year) were awarded; career-related internships or fieldwork, Federal Work-Study, scholarships/grants, health care benefits, tuition waivers (partial), and unspecified assistantships also available. Support available to part-time students. Financial award application deadline: 3/1; financial award applicants required to submit FAFSA. *Faculty research:* Family relations and child development, consequences of adolescent parenting, family stress and coping, impacts of sexual abuse on families, children's social cognition and self-competence, gerontology and health care. *Unit head:* Dr. Jennifer Hayes-Grudo, Department Head, 405-744-5360, Fax: 405-744-6344, E-mail: jennifer.hays.grudo@okstate.edu. *Application contact:* Dr. Brandt Gardner, Graduate Coordinator, 405-744-8360, Fax: 405-744-6344, E-mail: brandt.gardner@okstate.edu. Website: http://humansciences.okstate.edu/hdfs/

Oral Roberts University, School of Theology and Missions, Tulsa, OK 74171. Offers biblical literature (MA), including advanced languages, Judaic-Christian studies; Christian counseling (MA), including marriage and family therapy; divinity (M Div); missions (MA); practical theology (MA); theological/historical studies (MA); theology (D Min). *Accreditation:* ATS. Part-time programs available. Postbaccalaureate distance learning degree programs offered (minimal on-campus study). *Degree requirements:* For master's, thesis (for some programs), practicum/internship; for doctorate, thesis/dissertation, applied research project. *Entrance requirements:* For master's, GRE General Test or MAT, minimum GPA of 2.5; for doctorate, M Div, minimum GPA of 3.0, 3 years of full-time ministry experience. Additional exam requirements/recommendations for international students: Required—TOEFL (minimum score 550 paper-based; 79 iBT). Electronic applications accepted.

Ottawa University, Graduate Studies-Arizona, Program in Professional Counseling, Ottawa, KS 66067-3399. Offers Christian counseling (MA); expressive arts therapy (MA); marriage and family therapy (MA); treatment of trauma, abuse and deprivation (MA). Programs offered in Mesa, Phoenix, Tempe and West Valley, AZ. Part-time and evening/weekend programs available. Postbaccalaureate distance learning degree programs offered. *Degree requirements:* For master's, comprehensive exam, thesis or alternative, field experience, practicum. *Entrance requirements:* For master's, minimum undergraduate GPA of 3.0; course work in theories of personality, abnormal psychology, and human growth and development. Additional exam requirements/recommendations for international students: Required—TOEFL (minimum score 550 paper-based).

Our Lady of Holy Cross College, Program in Education and Counseling, New Orleans, LA 70131-7399. Offers administration and supervision (M Ed); curriculum and instruction (M Ed); marriage and family counseling (MA); school counseling (M Ed, MA). *Accreditation:* ACA; NCATE. Part-time and evening/weekend programs available. *Degree requirements:* For master's, thesis. *Entrance requirements:* For master's, GRE General Test, minimum GPA of 2.7.

Our Lady of the Lake University of San Antonio, School of Professional Studies, Program in Psychology, San Antonio, TX 78207-4689. Offers counseling psychology (MS, Psy D); marriage and family therapy (MS); school psychology (MS). *Accreditation:* APA (one or more programs are accredited). Part-time and evening/weekend programs available. *Degree requirements:* For master's, comprehensive exam, thesis optional, practicum; for doctorate, thesis/dissertation, internship, qualifying exam. *Entrance requirements:* For master's and doctorate, GRE General Test or MAT, interview. Additional exam requirements/recommendations for international students: Required—TOEFL. Electronic applications accepted. *Faculty research:* Marriage and family therapy, supervision, cross-cultural counseling, violence.

Pacific Lutheran University, Graduate Programs and Continuing Education, Division of Social Sciences, Program in Marriage and Family Therapy, Tacoma, WA 98447. Offers MA. *Accreditation:* AAMFT/COAMFTE. Part-time programs available. *Faculty:* 3 full-time (2 women), 9 part-time/adjunct (6 women). *Students:* 44 full-time (38 women), 7 part-time (all women); includes 14 minority (3 Black or African American, non-Hispanic/Latino; 4 Asian, non-Hispanic/Latino; 5 Hispanic/Latino; 1 Native Hawaiian or other Pacific Islander, non-Hispanic/Latino; 1 Two or more races, non-Hispanic/Latino), 2 international. Average age 29. 99 applicants, 32% accepted, 20 enrolled. In 2014, 19 master's awarded. *Degree requirements:* For master's, thesis optional, clinical competency. *Entrance requirements:* Additional exam requirements/recommendations for international students: Required—TOEFL (minimum score 550 paper-based; 88 iBT). *Application deadline:* For fall admission, 1/31 priority date for domestic and international students; for spring admission, 3/1 for domestic students. Application fee: $40. Electronic applications accepted. Application fee is waived when completed online. *Expenses:* Tuition: Full-time $19,600; part-time $980 per semester hour. Tuition and fees vary according to program. *Financial support:* In 2014–15, 8 students received support, including 12 fellowships (averaging $2,292 per year); career-related internships or fieldwork, Federal Work-Study, scholarships/grants, health care benefits, and unspecified assistantships also available. Support available to part-time students. Financial award application deadline: 3/1; financial award applicants required to submit FAFSA. *Unit head:* Dr. David Ward, Associate Professor and Program Director, 253-535-8284, Fax: 253-536-5139, E-mail: warddb@plu.edu. *Application contact:* Marie

Boisvert, Director of Graduate Admission, 253-535-8570, Fax: 253-536-5136, E-mail: gradadmission@plu.edu. Website: http://www.plu.edu/marriage-family-therapy/

Pacific Oaks College, Graduate School, Program in Marriage and Family Therapy, Pasadena, CA 91103. Offers marriage, family and child counseling (MA). Part-time and evening/weekend programs available. *Degree requirements:* For master's, thesis. *Entrance requirements:* For master's, interview. Additional exam requirements/recommendations for international students: Required—TOEFL (minimum score 550 paper-based). *Faculty research:* Family systems, cross-cultural development, therapeutic intervention and Latino families, battered women.

Palm Beach Atlantic University, School of Education and Behavioral Studies, West Palm Beach, FL 33416-4708. Offers counseling psychology (MS), including addictions/mental health, general counseling, marriage and family therapy, mental health counseling, school guidance counseling. Part-time and evening/weekend programs available. *Faculty:* 9 full-time (3 women), 14 part-time/adjunct (8 women). *Students:* 286 full-time (237 women), 30 part-time (25 women); includes 151 minority (60 Black or African American, non-Hispanic/Latino; 5 Asian, non-Hispanic/Latino; 73 Hispanic/Latino; 13 Two or more races, non-Hispanic/Latino), 5 international. Average age 34. 111 applicants, 78% accepted, 75 enrolled. In 2014, 98 master's awarded. *Entrance requirements:* For master's, GRE or MAT and MMPI-2, minimum GPA of 3.0. Additional exam requirements/recommendations for international students: Required—TOEFL (minimum score 550 paper-based; 79 iBT). *Application deadline:* For fall admission, 7/15 priority date for domestic students; for spring admission, 11/15 priority date for domestic students. Applications are processed on a rolling basis. Application fee: $50. Electronic applications accepted. *Expenses: Tuition:* Part-time $510 per credit hour. *Financial support:* In 2014–15, 16 students received support. Tuition waivers and Employee Education grants available. Financial award application deadline: 5/1; financial award applicants required to submit FAFSA. *Unit head:* Dr. Gene Sale, Program Director, 561-803-2352. *Application contact:* Graduate Admissions, 888-468-6722, E-mail: grad@pba.edu.
Website: http://www.pba.edu/graduate-counseling-program

Pepperdine University, Graduate School of Education and Psychology, Division of Psychology, MA Program in Clinical Psychology (Day Format), Malibu, CA 90263. Offers marriage and family therapy (MA). *Students:* 305 full-time (256 women), 292 part-time (246 women); includes 213 minority (57 Black or African American, non-Hispanic/Latino; 1 American Indian or Alaska Native, non-Hispanic/Latino; 36 Asian, non-Hispanic/Latino; 98 Hispanic/Latino; 5 Native Hawaiian or other Pacific Islander, non-Hispanic/Latino; 16 Two or more races, non-Hispanic/Latino), 17 international. In 2014, 187 master's awarded. *Entrance requirements:* For master's, GRE (taken within last five years) or MAT (taken within last two years), two professional recommendations, two- to five-page typed personal statement. Additional exam requirements/recommendations for international students: Required—TOEFL. *Application deadline:* For fall admission, 2/1 for domestic students. Application fee: $55. *Unit head:* Dr. Helen Williams, Dean, 310-568-5600, E-mail: helen.williams@pepperdine.edu. *Application contact:* Deanna Schwartz, Psychology Admissions Manager, 310-568-5777, E-mail: deanna.lazaro@pepperdine.edu.
Website: http://gsep.pepperdine.edu/masters-clinical-psychology-mft-day/

Phillips Graduate Institute, Programs in Marriage and Family Therapy and School Counseling, Encino, CA 91316-1509. Offers art therapy (MA); marriage and family therapy (MA); school counseling (MA). Evening/weekend programs available. *Degree requirements:* For master's, comprehensive exam, thesis. *Entrance requirements:* For master's, minimum GPA of 2.5. Electronic applications accepted. *Faculty research:* Integration of interpersonal psychological theory, systems approach, firsthand experiential learning.

Purdue University, Graduate School, College of Health and Human Sciences, Department of Child Development and Family Studies, West Lafayette, IN 47907. Offers developmental studies (MS, PhD); family studies (MS, PhD); marriage and family therapy (MS, PhD). *Accreditation:* AAMFT/COAMFTE (one or more programs are accredited). Part-time programs available. Terminal master's awarded for partial completion of doctoral program. *Degree requirements:* For master's, thesis; for doctorate, thesis/dissertation. *Entrance requirements:* For master's and doctorate, GRE General Test (minimum score 1000 combined verbal and quantitative), minimum undergraduate GPA of 3.0 or equivalent. Additional exam requirements/recommendations for international students: Required—TOEFL (minimum score 600 paper-based; 90 iBT), TWE (minimum score 4). Electronic applications accepted. *Faculty research:* Inclusion of children with special needs, families as learning environments, relationships in child care, work-family relations, AIDS prevention.

Purdue University Calumet, Graduate Studies Office, School of Liberal Arts and Social Sciences, Department of Behavioral Sciences, Hammond, IN 46323-2094. Offers child development and family studies (MS); marriage and family therapy (MS). *Accreditation:* AAMFT/COAMFTE. Part-time programs available. *Degree requirements:* For master's, thesis. *Entrance requirements:* For master's, GRE, interview. Additional exam requirements/recommendations for international students: Required—TOEFL. *Faculty research:* Substance abuse, sexual abuse, couple therapy, professional issues, adolescent therapy.

Reformed Theological Seminary–Jackson Campus, Graduate and Professional Programs, Jackson, MS 39209-3099. Offers Bible, theology, and missions (Certificate); Biblical exegesis (M Div); biblical studies (MA); Christian education (MA); counseling (M Div); marriage and family therapy (MA); ministry (D Min); missions (M Div, MA, D Min); theological studies (MA). *Accreditation:* AAMFT/COAMFTE (one or more programs are accredited); ATS (one or more programs are accredited). *Faculty:* 10 full-time (0 women), 1 (woman) part-time/adjunct. *Students:* 50 full-time (14 women), 86 part-time (19 women). *Degree requirements:* For master's, thesis (for some programs), fieldwork; for doctorate, 2 foreign languages, thesis/dissertation. *Entrance requirements:* For master's, minimum GPA of 2.6; for doctorate, minimum GPA of 3.0. Additional exam requirements/recommendations for international students: Required—TOEFL. *Application deadline:* Applications are processed on a rolling basis. Application fee: $35. *Financial support:* Research assistantships, career-related internships or fieldwork, scholarships/grants, and tuition waivers (full and partial) available. Financial award application deadline: 5/1. *Application contact:* Brian Gault, Director of Admissions, 601-923-1600, Fax: 601-923-1654.

Regent University, Graduate School, School of Psychology and Counseling, Virginia Beach, VA 23464-9800. Offers clinical psychology (Psy D); counseling (MA), including clinical mental health counseling, marriage, couple, and family counseling, school counseling; counseling studies (CAGS); counselor education and supervision (PhD); human services counseling (MA); M Div/MA; M Ed/MA; MBA/MA. PhD program offered online only. *Accreditation:* ACA; APA (one or more programs are accredited). Part-time and evening/weekend programs available. Postbaccalaureate distance learning degree programs offered (minimal on-campus study). *Faculty:* 29 full-time (15 women), 45 part-time/adjunct (29 women). *Students:* 257 full-time (211 women), 288 part-time (225 women); includes 156 minority (121 Black or African American, non-Hispanic/Latino; 2 American Indian or Alaska Native, non-Hispanic/Latino; 10 Asian, non-Hispanic/Latino; 23 Hispanic/Latino), 29 international. Average age 35. 681 applicants, 38% accepted, 170 enrolled. In 2014, 127 master's, 34 doctorates awarded. *Degree requirements:* For master's, thesis or alternative, internship, practicum, written competency exam; for doctorate, thesis/dissertation or alternative. *Entrance requirements:* For master's, GRE General Test (including writing exam), minimum undergraduate GPA of 2.75, 3 recommendations, resume, transcripts, writing sample; for doctorate, GRE General Test (including writing exam), GRE Subject Test, minimum undergraduate GPA of 3.0, graduate 3.5; 10-15 minute VHS tape demonstrating counseling skills; writing sample; 3 recommendations; resume. Additional exam requirements/recommendations for international students: Required—TOEFL (minimum score 577 paper-based). *Application deadline:* For fall admission, 4/1 priority date for domestic students; for spring admission, 11/1 priority date for domestic students. Applications are processed on a rolling basis. Application fee: $50. Electronic applications accepted. *Expenses:* Expenses: Contact institution. *Financial support:* Research assistantships with full and partial tuition reimbursements, teaching assistantships with full and partial tuition reimbursements, career-related internships or fieldwork, scholarships/grants, and tuition waivers (full and partial) available. Support available to part-time students. Financial award application deadline: 9/1; financial award applicants required to submit FAFSA. *Faculty research:* Marriage enrichment, AIDS counseling, troubled youth, faith and learning, trauma. *Unit head:* Dr. William Hathaway, Dean, 757-352-4294, Fax: 757-352-4282, E-mail: willhat@regent.edu. *Application contact:* Matthew Chadwick, Director of Enrollment Support Services, 800-373-5504, Fax: 757-352-4381, E-mail: admissions@regent.edu.
Website: http://www.regent.edu/psychology/

Regis University, Rueckert-Hartman College for Health Professions, Division of Counseling and Family Therapy, Denver, CO 80221-1099. Offers counseling (MA); counseling children and adolescents (Post-Graduate Certificate); counseling military families (Post-Graduate Certificate); marriage and family therapy (MA, Post-Graduate Certificate); transformative counseling (Post-Graduate Certificate). *Accreditation:* ACA. Part-time and evening/weekend programs available. *Faculty:* 14 full-time (9 women), 23 part-time/adjunct (17 women). *Students:* 252 full-time (212 women), 126 part-time (93 women); includes 77 minority (9 Black or African American, non-Hispanic/Latino; 2 American Indian or Alaska Native, non-Hispanic/Latino; 7 Asian, non-Hispanic/Latino; 43 Hispanic/Latino; 16 Two or more races, non-Hispanic/Latino), 1 international. Average age 36. 103 applicants, 77% accepted, 67 enrolled. In 2014, 66 master's awarded. *Degree requirements:* For master's, thesis, internships, practicum. *Entrance requirements:* For master's, official transcript reflecting baccalaureate degree awarded from regionally-accredited college or university, interview, 2 recommendations, resume, criminal background check. Additional exam requirements/recommendations for international students: Required—TOEFL (minimum score 550 paper-based; 82 iBT). *Application deadline:* For fall admission, 6/15 for domestic students, 5/15 for international students; for spring admission, 11/1 for domestic students, 10/1 for international students; for summer admission, 3/1 for domestic students, 2/1 for international students. Application fee: $75. Electronic applications accepted. *Expenses:* Expenses: Contact institution. *Financial support:* In 2014–15, 8 students received support. Federal Work-Study and scholarships/grants available. Financial award application deadline: 4/15; financial award applicants required to submit FAFSA. *Faculty research:* Group development, counselor education, counsel and therapy, influence of technology on psychology, dream finding groups, adult development, depression. *Unit head:* Dr. Linda Osterlund, Associate Dean, Counseling and Family Therapy, 719-264-7011, Fax: 719-264-7095, E-mail: losterlan@regis.edu. *Application contact:* Sarah Engel, Director of Admissions, 303-458-4900, Fax: 303-964-5534, E-mail: regisadm@regis.edu.
Website: http://www.regis.edu/RHCHP/Schools/Counseling-and-Family-Therapy.aspx

Richmont Graduate University, School of Counseling, Atlanta, GA 30327. Offers marriage and family therapy (MA); professional counseling (MA).

St. Cloud State University, School of Graduate Studies, School of Health and Human Services, Department of Counseling and Community Psychology, Program in Marriage and Family Therapy, St. Cloud, MN 56301-4498. Offers MS. *Accreditation:* AAMFT/COAMFTE. *Entrance requirements:* Additional exam requirements/recommendations for international students: Required—Michigan English Language Assessment Battery; Recommended—TOEFL (minimum score 550 paper-based), IELTS (minimum score 6.5). Electronic applications accepted.

Saint Louis University, Graduate Education, College of Education and Public Service and Graduate Education, Department of Counseling and Family Therapy, St. Louis, MO 63103-2097. Offers counseling and family therapy (PhD); human development counseling (MA); marriage and family therapy (Certificate); school counseling (MA, MA-R). *Accreditation:* AAMFT/COAMFTE; NCATE. Part-time programs available. *Degree requirements:* For master's, comprehensive exam, thesis (for some programs); for doctorate, comprehensive exam, thesis/dissertation, preliminary oral and written exams. *Entrance requirements:* For master's, GRE General Test, letters of recommendation, resume; for doctorate, GRE General Test, letters of recommendation, resumé, transcripts, goal statement. Additional exam requirements/recommendations for international students: Required—TOEFL (minimum score 550 paper-based). Electronic applications accepted. *Faculty research:* Medical family therapy/collaborative health care multicultural counseling, mental health needs of diverse, minority, or Immigrant/refugee populations, divorce, aging families.

Saint Mary's College of California, Kalmanovitz School of Education, Program in Counseling, Moraga, CA 94575. Offers general counseling (MA); marital and family therapy (MA); school counseling (MA). Part-time and evening/weekend programs available. *Degree requirements:* For master's, thesis or alternative. *Entrance requirements:* For master's, interview, minimum GPA of 3.0. *Faculty research:* Counselor training effectiveness, multicultural development, empathy, the interface of spirituality and psychotherapy, gender issues.

St. Mary's University, Graduate School, Department of Counseling and Human Services, Program in Marriage and Family Therapy, San Antonio, TX 78228-8507. Offers MA, PhD. Part-time programs available. *Faculty:* 3 full-time (1 woman), 8 part-time/adjunct (5 women). *Students:* 47 full-time (35 women), 24 part-time (22 women); includes 35 minority (4 Black or African American, non-Hispanic/Latino; 5 Asian, non-Hispanic/Latino; 26 Hispanic/Latino), 6 international. Average age 32. 84 applicants, 54% accepted, 27 enrolled. In 2014, 15 master's, 1 doctorate awarded. *Degree requirements:* For master's, comprehensive exam, thesis optional, internship; for doctorate, comprehensive exam, thesis/dissertation, internship. *Entrance requirements:* For master's, GRE, MAT; for doctorate, GRE, master's degree, work experience, letters of recommendation. Additional exam requirements/recommendations for international students: Required—TOEFL (minimum score 550 paper-based; 80 iBT). *Application deadline:* Applications are processed on a rolling basis. Application fee: $0. Electronic applications accepted. *Expenses: Tuition:* Full-time $15,070; part-time $800 per credit hour. *Required fees:* $156 per semester. *Financial support:* In 2014–15, 1 fellowship (averaging $10,000 per year), 3 research assistantships (averaging $13,000 per year) were awarded; career-related internships or fieldwork, Federal Work-Study, institutionally sponsored loans, scholarships/grants, health care benefits, and unspecified assistantships also available. Financial award application deadline: 3/31; financial award applicants required to submit FAFSA. *Faculty research:* Impact of

technology on family relationships; military family life-shared parenting among couples with a history of intimate partner violence; parenting in low-income populations; family stability, rituals, and dynamics. *Unit head:* Dr. Carolyn Tubbs, Director Marriage and Family Therapy Program, 210-436-3011.
Website: https://www.stmarytx.edu/academics/graduate/masters/marriage-family-therapy-program/

Saint Mary's University of Minnesota, Schools of Graduate and Professional Programs, Graduate School of Health and Human Services, Marriage and Family Therapy Program, Winona, MN 55987-1399. Offers MA, Certificate. *Accreditation:* AAMFT/COAMFTE.

Saint Paul University, Faculty of Human Sciences, Program in Counseling and Spirituality, Ottawa, ON K1S 1C4, Canada. Offers individual or marital/couple counseling (MA); spiritual care (MA). Part-time programs available. *Degree requirements:* For master's, research project or thesis. *Entrance requirements:* For master's, honors BA in human sciences, minimum B average, 12 theology credits.

St. Thomas University, Biscayne College, Department of Social Sciences and Counseling, Program in Marriage and Family Therapy, Miami Gardens, FL 33054-6459. Offers MS, Post-Master's Certificate. Part-time and evening/weekend programs available. *Degree requirements:* For master's, comprehensive exam. *Entrance requirements:* For master's, interview, minimum GPA of 3.0 or GRE. Additional exam requirements/recommendations for international students: Required—TOEFL. Electronic applications accepted.

San Francisco State University, Division of Graduate Studies, College of Health and Social Sciences, Department of Counseling, San Francisco, CA 94132-1722. Offers clinical rehabilitation and mental health counseling (MS); counseling (MS); marriage, family, and child counseling (MSC); school counseling (Credential). *Accreditation:* ACA (one or more programs are accredited). Part-time programs available. *Application deadline:* Applications are processed on a rolling basis. *Expenses:* Tuition, state resident: full-time $6738. Tuition, nonresident: full-time $17,898; part-time $372 per credit hour. *Required fees:* $498 per semester. *Unit head:* Dr. Graciela Orozco, Chair, 415-338-2005, E-mail: counsel@sfsu.edu. *Application contact:* Katsufumi Araki, Academic Office Coordinator, 415-338-2005, E-mail: counsel@sfsu.edu.
Website: http://counseling.sfsu.edu

Saybrook University, School of Psychology and Interdisciplinary Inquiry, San Francisco, CA 94111-1920. Offers human science (MA, PhD), including consciousness and spirituality, humanistic and transpersonal psychology, integrative health studies, organizational systems, social transformation; organizational systems (MA, PhD), including consciousness and spirituality, humanistic and transpersonal psychology, integrative health studies, leadership of sustainable systems (MA), organizational systems, social transformation; psychology (MA, PhD), including consciousness and spirituality, creativity studies (MA), humanistic and transpersonal psychology, integrative health studies, Jungian studies, marriage and family therapy (MA), organizational systems, social transformation. Postbaccalaureate distance learning degree programs offered (minimal on-campus study). Terminal master's awarded for partial completion of doctoral program. *Degree requirements:* For master's, thesis or alternative; for doctorate, thesis/dissertation. *Entrance requirements:* Additional exam requirements/recommendations for international students: Required—TOEFL (minimum score 580 paper-based; 93 iBT). Electronic applications accepted. *Faculty research:* Humanistic theory, health studies, organizational systems, consciousness and spirituality, social transformation.

The School of Professional Psychology at Forest Institute, Graduate Programs, Springfield, MO 65807. Offers applied behavior analysis (MS); clinical psychology (MA, Psy D); counseling psychology (MA); marriage and family therapy (MA, PGC). *Accreditation:* AAMFT/COAMFTE; APA (one or more programs are accredited). Part-time and evening/weekend programs available. Terminal master's awarded for partial completion of doctoral program. *Degree requirements:* For master's, thesis, practicum; for doctorate, comprehensive exam, thesis/dissertation, internship, practicum. *Entrance requirements:* For master's, GRE General Test, interview, minimum GPA of 3.0, 12 hours in psychology; for doctorate, GRE General Test (minimum combined Verbal and Quantitative score of 1000, Analytic Writing 4.0), interview, minimum GPA of 3.0, 18 hours in psychology. Additional exam requirements/recommendations for international students: Required—TOEFL (minimum score 550 paper-based). Electronic applications accepted. *Faculty research:* Forensics/corrections, marriage and family therapy, child and adolescent, integrated health care, neuropsychology.

Seattle Pacific University, MS in Marriage and Family Therapy Program, Seattle, WA 98119-1997. Offers marriage and family therapy (MS); medical family therapy (Certificate). *Accreditation:* AAMFT/COAMFTE. Part-time programs available. *Students:* 62 full-time (45 women), 17 part-time (16 women); includes 10 minority (1 American Indian or Alaska Native, non-Hispanic/Latino; 3 Asian, non-Hispanic/Latino; 3 Hispanic/Latino; 3 Two or more races, non-Hispanic/Latino), 1 international. Average age 29. 90 applicants, 47% accepted, 42 enrolled. In 2014, 28 master's awarded. *Degree requirements:* For master's, thesis optional, internship, clinical portfolio. *Entrance requirements:* For master's, GRE General Test or MAT, interview. Additional exam requirements/recommendations for international students: Required—TOEFL (minimum score 550 paper-based). *Application deadline:* For fall admission, 1/23 for domestic students, 2/1 for international students. Applications are processed on a rolling basis. Application fee: $50. Electronic applications accepted. *Expenses:* Expenses: Contact institution. *Financial support:* Fellowships and Federal Work-Study available. Financial award applicants required to submit FAFSA. *Faculty research:* Roles of therapists, models of collaboration, medical and mental health theories of marriage and family therapy. *Unit head:* Dr. Scott Edwards, Chair, 206-281-2681, E-mail: sedwards@spu.edu.
Website: http://www.spu.edu/depts/spfc/mft/

Seton Hall University, College of Education and Human Services, Department of Professional Psychology and Family Therapy, Program in Marriage and Family Therapy, South Orange, NJ 07079-2697. Offers MS, Ed S, Professional Diploma. *Accreditation:* AAMFT/COAMFTE. Part-time programs available. *Degree requirements:* For master's, thesis, case study, internship; for other advanced degree, thesis, internship, case study. *Entrance requirements:* For master's, GRE, interview, personal statement, 3 letters of recommendation; for other advanced degree, GRE, interview, personal statement, 3 letters of recommendation; master's degree in related field and experience as a counselor (for Ed S); clinical degree and supervised clinical experience with couples and families (for Diploma). Additional exam requirements/recommendations for international students: Required—TOEFL (minimum score 85 iBT). Electronic applications accepted. *Faculty research:* Family systems, families and substance abuse, families and the legal system, family diversity, marriage and family therapy.

Seton Hill University, Program in Marriage and Family Therapy, Greensburg, PA 15601. Offers MA. *Accreditation:* AAMFT/COAMFTE. Part-time and evening/weekend programs available. *Faculty:* 2 full-time (0 women), 7 part-time/adjunct (5 women). *Students:* 20 full-time (13 women), 6 part-time (4 women); includes 7 minority (4 Black or African American, non-Hispanic/Latino; 3 Two or more races, non-Hispanic/Latino). Average age 28. 47 applicants, 53% accepted, 12 enrolled. In 2014, 17 master's awarded. *Entrance requirements:* For master's, 3 letters of recommendation, interview, resume, letter of intent, transcripts. Additional exam requirements/recommendations for international students: Required—TOEFL (minimum score 650 paper-based; 114 iBT), IELTS (minimum score 7). *Application deadline:* For fall admission, 8/15 priority date for domestic students; for spring admission, 12/15 for domestic students. Applications are processed on a rolling basis. Application fee: $35. Electronic applications accepted. *Expenses: Tuition:* Full-time $7362; part-time $818 per credit. *Required fees:* $34 per credit. *Financial support:* In 2014–15, 22 students received support. Federal Work-Study, scholarships/grants, tuition waivers (partial), and unspecified assistantships available. Support available to part-time students. Financial award application deadline: 8/15; financial award applicants required to submit FAFSA. *Faculty research:* Working with men in therapy, issues of social justice, working in issues of postpartum with new mothers. *Unit head:* Dr. DeMarquis Clarke, Director, 724-552-0339, E-mail: clarke@setonhill.edu. *Application contact:* Lisa Glessner, Program Counselor, 724-830-4209, E-mail: lglessner@setonhill.edu.
Website: http://www.setonhill.edu/academics/graduate_programs/marriage_and_family_therapy

Shippensburg University of Pennsylvania, School of Graduate Studies, College of Education and Human Services, Department of Counseling, Shippensburg, PA 17257-2299. Offers college counseling (MS); college student personnel (MS); couple and family counseling (Certificate); school counseling (M Ed). *Accreditation:* ACA (one or more programs are accredited); NCATE. Part-time and evening/weekend programs available. *Faculty:* 8 full-time (3 women), 1 (woman) part-time/adjunct. *Students:* 98 full-time (77 women), 38 part-time (30 women); includes 17 minority (12 Black or African American, non-Hispanic/Latino; 1 American Indian or Alaska Native, non-Hispanic/Latino; 2 Hispanic/Latino; 2 Two or more races, non-Hispanic/Latino), 2 international. Average age 29. 117 applicants, 45% accepted, 35 enrolled. In 2014, 40 master's awarded. *Degree requirements:* For master's, fieldwork, research project, internship, candidacy. *Entrance requirements:* For master's, GRE or MAT (for clinical mental health, student personnel, and college counseling applicants if GPA is less than 2.75), minimum GPA of 2.75 (3.0 for M Ed), resume, 3 letters of recommendation, one year of relevant work experience, on-campus interview, autobiographical statement. Additional exam requirements/recommendations for international students: Required—TOEFL (minimum score 580 paper-based); Recommended—IELTS (minimum score 6). *Application deadline:* For fall admission, 4/30 for international students; for spring admission, 9/30 for international students. Applications are processed on a rolling basis. Application fee: $45. Electronic applications accepted. *Expenses: Tuition, area resident:* Part-time $454 per credit. Tuition, state resident: part-time $454 per credit. Tuition, nonresident: part-time $681 per credit. *Required fees:* $133 per credit. *Financial support:* In 2014–15, 55 research assistantships with full tuition reimbursements (averaging $5,000 per year) were awarded; career-related internships or fieldwork, scholarships/grants, unspecified assistantships, and resident hall director and student payroll positions also available. Support available to part-time students. Financial award application deadline: 3/1; financial award applicants required to submit FAFSA. *Unit head:* Dr. Kurt L. Kraus, Chairperson, 717-477-1603, Fax: 717-477-4016, E-mail: klkrau@ship.edu. *Application contact:* Jeremy R. Goshorn, Assistant Dean of Graduate Admissions, 717-477-1231, Fax: 717-477-4016, E-mail: jrgoshorn@ship.edu.
Website: http://www.ship.edu/counsel/

Sioux Falls Seminary, Graduate and Professional Programs, Master of Divinity Program, Sioux Falls, SD 57105-1599. Offers marriage and family therapy (M Div); pastoral care and counseling (M Div). Program also offered in Omaha, NE. *Accreditation:* ACIPE. Part-time programs available. Postbaccalaureate distance learning degree programs offered (no on-campus study).

Sioux Falls Seminary, Graduate and Professional Programs, Program in Marriage and Family Therapy, Sioux Falls, SD 57105-1599. Offers MA, Certificate.

Sonoma State University, School of Social Sciences, Department of Counseling, Rohnert Park, CA 94928-3609. Offers counseling (MA); licensed professional clinical counseling (MA); marriage, family, and child counseling (MA); pupil personnel services (MA). *Accreditation:* ACA. Part-time programs available. *Degree requirements:* For master's, internship. *Entrance requirements:* For master's, minimum GPA of 3.0. Additional exam requirements/recommendations for international students: Required—TOEFL (minimum score 500 paper-based).

Southern California Seminary, Graduate and Professional Programs, El Cajon, CA 92019. Offers Biblical studies (MABS); counseling psychology (MACP); marriage and family therapy (MAMFT); psychology (Psy D); religious studies (MRS); theology (M Div). Part-time and evening/weekend programs available. Postbaccalaureate distance learning degree programs offered (minimal on-campus study). *Degree requirements:* For master's, thesis (for some programs); for doctorate, thesis/dissertation. *Entrance requirements:* For doctorate, master's degree in psychology. Additional exam requirements/recommendations for international students: Required—TOEFL (minimum score 550 paper-based). Electronic applications accepted.

Southern Nazarene University, College of Professional and Graduate Studies, Department of Psychology and Counseling, Bethany, OK 73008. Offers counseling psychology (MA, MSCP); marital and family therapy (MA). *Degree requirements:* For master's, thesis optional. *Entrance requirements:* For master's, English proficiency exam, minimum GPA of 3.0 in last 60 hours/major, 2.7 overall.

Stephens College, Division of Graduate and Continuing Studies, Programs in Counseling, Columbia, MO 65215-0002. Offers counseling (M Ed, PGC), including marriage and family therapy (M Ed), professional counseling (M Ed), school counseling (M Ed). Part-time and evening/weekend programs available. *Faculty:* 1 (woman) full-time, 14 part-time/adjunct (11 women). *Students:* 99 full-time (82 women), 24 part-time (22 women); includes 15 minority (8 Black or African American, non-Hispanic/Latino; 1 Asian, non-Hispanic/Latino; 6 Two or more races, non-Hispanic/Latino). Average age 34. 32 applicants, 69% accepted, 14 enrolled. In 2014, 36 master's awarded. *Degree requirements:* For master's, thesis. *Entrance requirements:* For master's, minimum GPA of 3.0 in last 60 hours. Additional exam requirements/recommendations for international students: Required—TOEFL. *Application deadline:* For fall admission, 7/25 priority date for domestic and international students; for winter admission, 12/1 priority date for domestic and international students; for spring admission, 4/25 priority date for domestic and international students. Applications are processed on a rolling basis. Application fee: $50. Electronic applications accepted. *Expenses: Tuition:* Full-time $4656; part-time $388 per credit hour. *Required fees:* $540; $45 per credit hour. *Financial support:* In 2014–15, 4 fellowships with full tuition reimbursements (averaging $8,710 per year) were awarded; scholarships/grants and unspecified assistantships also available. Financial award application deadline: 12/5; financial award applicants required to submit FAFSA. *Unit head:* Gina Sanders, Program Chair, 800-388-7579. *Application contact:* Lindsey Boudinot, Director of Graduate, Online and Certificate Programs, 800-388-7579, E-mail: online@stephens.edu.

Stetson University, College of Arts and Sciences, Division of Education, Department of Counselor Education, DeLand, FL 32723. Offers marriage, couple and family counseling (MS); school counseling (MS). *Accreditation:* ACA. Evening/weekend programs available. *Faculty:* 5 full-time (all women), 3 part-time/adjunct (all women). *Students:* 90

full-time (82 women), 10 part-time (9 women); includes 24 minority (6 Black or African American, non-Hispanic/Latino; 1 American Indian or Alaska Native, non-Hispanic/Latino; 1 Asian, non-Hispanic/Latino; 15 Hispanic/Latino; 1 Two or more races, non-Hispanic/Latino). Average age 29. 62 applicants, 60% accepted, 29 enrolled. In 2014, 19 master's awarded. *Entrance requirements:* For master's, GRE or MAT. Additional exam requirements/recommendations for international students: Required—TOEFL (minimum score 90 iBT), IELTS (minimum score 7). *Application deadline:* For fall admission, 8/1 priority date for domestic students; for spring admission, 1/1 priority date for domestic students; for summer admission, 5/1 priority date for domestic students. Applications are processed on a rolling basis. Application fee: $50. Electronic applications accepted. *Expenses:* Expenses: $821 per credit hour (for MS). *Financial support:* In 2014–15, 17 students received support. *Faculty research:* Play therapy, trauma, wellness, infertility, counselor education training, gatekeeping and counselor education. *Unit head:* Dr. Brigid Noonan-Klima, Chair, 386-822-8992. *Application contact:* Jamie Vanderlip, Assistant Director of Graduate Admissions, 386-822-7100, Fax: 386-822-7112, E-mail: jlvander@stetson.edu.

Syracuse University, Falk College of Sport and Human Dynamics, Dual Master's Program in Social Work and Marriage and Family Therapy, Syracuse, NY 13244. Offers MSW/MA. *Students:* 21 full-time (17 women), 6 part-time (5 women); includes 11 minority (5 Black or African American, non-Hispanic/Latino; 4 Hispanic/Latino; 1 Native Hawaiian or other Pacific Islander, non-Hispanic/Latino; 1 Two or more races, non-Hispanic/Latino). Average age 31. 77 applicants, 83% accepted, 23 enrolled. *Entrance requirements:* Additional exam requirements/recommendations for international students: Required—TOEFL or IELTS. *Application deadline:* For fall admission, 3/15 priority date for domestic and international students; for summer admission, 1/15 priority date for domestic students, 1/15 for international students. *Expenses: Tuition:* Part-time $1341 per credit. *Unit head:* Prof. Carrie Smith, Associate Professor/Director, School of Social Work, 315-443-5562, Fax: 315-443-2562, E-mail: falk@syr.edu. *Application contact:* Felicia Otero, Director of College Admissions, 315-443-5555, Fax: 315-443-2562, E-mail: falk@syr.edu.

Syracuse University, Falk College of Sport and Human Dynamics, Program in Marriage and Family Therapy, Syracuse, NY 13244. Offers MA. *Accreditation:* AAMFT/COAMFTE. Part-time programs available. *Students:* 46 full-time (41 women), 11 part-time (10 women); includes 16 minority (8 Black or African American, non-Hispanic/Latino; 1 American Indian or Alaska Native, non-Hispanic/Latino; 1 Asian, non-Hispanic/Latino; 2 Hispanic/Latino; 4 Two or more races, non-Hispanic/Latino), 9 international. Average age 27. 54 applicants, 83% accepted, 22 enrolled. In 2014, 39 master's awarded. *Degree requirements:* For master's, thesis or alternative, internship. *Entrance requirements:* For master's, GRE General Test. Additional exam requirements/recommendations for international students: Required—TOEFL (minimum score 100 iBT). *Application deadline:* For fall admission, 3/15 priority date for domestic students, 2/15 priority date for international students; for spring admission, 11/15 priority date for domestic and international students; for summer admission, 3/15 priority date for domestic and international students. Application fee: $75. Electronic applications accepted. *Expenses: Tuition:* Part-time $1341 per credit. *Financial support:* Fellowships with full tuition reimbursements, research assistantships with full and partial tuition reimbursements, teaching assistantships with full and partial tuition reimbursements, and tuition waivers available. Financial award application deadline: 1/1; financial award applicants required to submit FAFSA. *Unit head:* Dr. Thomas DeLara, Chair, 315-443-9403, E-mail: falk@syr.edu. *Application contact:* Felicia Otero, Director of Graduate Admissions, 315-443-5555, E-mail: falk@syr.edu.
Website: http://falk.syr.edu/MarriageFamilyTherapy/Default.aspx

Texas A&M University–Central Texas, Graduate Studies and Research, Killeen, TX 76549. Offers accounting (MS); business administration (MBA); clinical mental health counseling (MS); criminal justice (MCJ); curriculum and instruction (M Ed); educational administration (M Ed); educational psychology - experimental psychology (MS); history (MA); human resource management (MS); information systems (MS); liberal studies (MS); management and leadership (MS); marriage and family therapy (MS); mathematics (MS); political science (MA); school counseling (M Ed); school psychology (Ed S).

Texas Tech University, Graduate School, College of Human Sciences, Department of Community, Family, and Addiction Services, Lubbock, TX 79409-1250. Offers marriage and family therapy (MS, PhD). *Faculty:* 15 full-time (8 women), 2 part-time/adjunct (1 woman). *Students:* 45 full-time (30 women), 11 part-time (7 women); includes 14 minority (4 Black or African American, non-Hispanic/Latino; 1 Asian, non-Hispanic/Latino; 6 Hispanic/Latino; 3 Two or more races, non-Hispanic/Latino), 5 international. Average age 28. 50 applicants, 28% accepted, 14 enrolled. In 2014, 11 master's, 5 doctorates awarded. *Degree requirements:* For master's, comprehensive exam, thesis optional; for doctorate, thesis/dissertation. *Entrance requirements:* For master's and doctorate, GRE. Additional exam requirements/recommendations for international students: Required—TOEFL (minimum score 550 paper-based; 79 iBT). *Application deadline:* For fall admission, 6/1 priority date for domestic students, 1/15 priority date for international students; for spring admission, 9/1 priority date for domestic students, 6/15 priority date for international students. Applications are processed on a rolling basis. Application fee: $60. Electronic applications accepted. *Expenses:* Tuition, state resident: full-time $6310; part-time $262.92 per credit hour. Tuition, nonresident: full-time $14,998; part-time $624.92 per credit hour. *Required fees:* $2701; $36.50 per credit. $912.50 per semester. Tuition and fees vary according to course load. *Financial support:* In 2014–15, 47 students received support, including 46 fellowships (averaging $4,417 per year), 7 research assistantships (averaging $16,976 per year), 19 teaching assistantships (averaging $14,368 per year); career-related internships or fieldwork, Federal Work-Study, scholarships/grants, health care benefits, and unspecified assistantships also available. Financial award application deadline: 2/1; financial award applicants required to submit FAFSA. *Faculty research:* Medical family therapy, systemic intervention for intimate partner violence, neuroscience of addiction and the brain, long-term recovery from addictive disorders, co-parenting and parent-child relationships in diverse settings. *Total annual research expenditures:* $402,239. *Unit head:* Dr. Sterling T. Shumway, Department Chair, 806-742-3060, Fax: 806-742-0053, E-mail: sterling.shumway@ttu.edu. *Application contact:* Lori Minner, Senior Business Assistant, 806-742-3060 Ext. 244, Fax: 806-742-0053, E-mail: lori.minner@ttu.edu.
Website: http://www.depts.ttu.edu/hs/cfas

Texas Wesleyan University, Graduate Programs, Programs in Education, Fort Worth, TX 76105-1536. Offers education (M Ed, Ed D); marriage and family therapy (MSMFT); professional counseling (MA); school counseling (MS). Part-time and evening/weekend programs available. Postbaccalaureate distance learning degree programs offered (no on-campus study). *Faculty:* 25 full-time (15 women), 8 part-time/adjunct (6 women). *Students:* 31 full-time (24 women), 205 part-time (177 women); includes 125 minority (64 Black or African American, non-Hispanic/Latino; 1 American Indian or Alaska Native, non-Hispanic/Latino; 1 Asian, non-Hispanic/Latino; 54 Hispanic/Latino; 5 Two or more races, non-Hispanic/Latino), 4 international. Average age 35. 144 applicants, 62% accepted, 81 enrolled. In 2014, 64 master's, 10 doctorates awarded. *Degree requirements:* For master's, comprehensive exam (for some programs); for doctorate, thesis/dissertation. *Entrance requirements:* For master's and doctorate, GRE General Test. Additional exam requirements/recommendations for international students: Required—TOEFL, IELTS. *Application deadline:* For fall admission, 6/15 for domestic students; for spring admission, 10/15 for domestic students. Applications are processed on a rolling basis. Application fee: $55. Electronic applications accepted. *Financial support:* Career-related internships or fieldwork, Federal Work-Study, scholarships/grants, and tuition waivers (full and partial) available. Support available to part-time students. Financial award application deadline: 3/15; financial award applicants required to submit FAFSA. *Faculty research:* Teacher effectiveness, bilingual education, analytic teaching. *Unit head:* Dr. Carlos Martinez, Dean, School of Education, 817-531-4940, Fax: 817-531-4943. *Application contact:* Beth Hargrove, Director of Graduate Admissions, 817-531-4498, Fax: 817-531-4261, E-mail: bhargrove@txwes.edu.
Website: https://txwes.edu/academics/school-of-education/

Texas Woman's University, Graduate School, College of Professional Education, Department of Family Sciences, Denton, TX 76201. Offers child development (MS); counseling and development (MS); early childhood development and education (PhD); early childhood education (M Ed, MA, MS); family studies (MS, PhD); family therapy (MS, PhD). *Accreditation:* ACA (one or more programs are accredited). Part-time and evening/weekend programs available. Terminal master's awarded for partial completion of doctoral program. *Degree requirements:* For master's, comprehensive exam (for some programs), thesis (for some programs); for doctorate, comprehensive exam, thesis/dissertation. *Entrance requirements:* Additional exam requirements/recommendations for international students: Required—TOEFL (minimum score 550 paper-based; 79 iBT). Electronic applications accepted. *Faculty research:* Parenting/parent education, military families, play therapy, family sexuality, diversity, healthy relationships/healthy marriages, childhood obesity, male communication.

Thomas Jefferson University, Jefferson School of Health Professions, Department of Couple and Family Therapy, Philadelphia, PA 19107. Offers MFT. *Students:* 38 full-time (31 women); includes 5 minority (2 Black or African American, non-Hispanic/Latino; 2 Asian, non-Hispanic/Latino; 1 Hispanic/Latino), 1 international. Average age 27. 38 applicants, 66% accepted, 18 enrolled. In 2014, 3 master's awarded. *Entrance requirements:* Additional exam requirements/recommendations for international students: Required—TOEFL. *Application deadline:* For fall admission, 7/15 for domestic students. Applications are processed on a rolling basis. Application fee: $75. Electronic applications accepted. *Expenses:* Expenses: $28,544. *Financial support:* In 2014–15, 30 students received support. Federal Work-Study, institutionally sponsored loans, scholarships/grants, and unspecified assistantships available. Support available to part-time students. Financial award application deadline: 4/1; financial award applicants required to submit FAFSA. *Unit head:* Dr. Kenneth Covelman, Dean, 215-955-6000. *Application contact:* Donald Sharples, Director of Graduate Admissions, 215-503-1040, Fax: 215-503-7241, E-mail: donald.sharples@jefferson.edu.
Website: http://www.jefferson.edu/health_professions/departments/couple-family-therapy

Universidad de las Americas, A.C., Program in Psychology, Mexico City, Mexico. Offers family therapy (MA).

The University of Akron, Graduate School, College of Health Professions, School of Counseling, Program in Marriage and Family Therapy, Akron, OH 44325. Offers MA, MS. *Accreditation:* AAMFT/COAMFTE; ACA. *Students:* 57 full-time (48 women), 55 part-time (46 women); includes 22 minority (13 Black or African American, non-Hispanic/Latino; 1 American Indian or Alaska Native, non-Hispanic/Latino; 2 Asian, non-Hispanic/Latino; 3 Hispanic/Latino; 3 Two or more races, non-Hispanic/Latino), 1 international. Average age 31. 54 applicants, 48% accepted, 21 enrolled. In 2014, 24 master's awarded. *Degree requirements:* For master's, comprehensive exam. *Entrance requirements:* For master's, minimum GPA of 2.75, three letters of recommendation, interview. Additional exam requirements/recommendations for international students: Required—TOEFL (minimum score 550 paper-based; 79 iBT), IELTS (minimum score 6.5). *Application deadline:* For fall admission, 3/15 for domestic and international students; for spring admission, 10/1 for domestic and international students. Application fee: $45 ($70 for international students). Electronic applications accepted. *Expenses:* Tuition, state resident: full-time $7578; part-time $421 per credit hour. Tuition, nonresident: full-time $12,977; part-time $721 per credit hour. *Required fees:* $1388; $35 per credit hour. Tuition and fees vary according to course load. *Unit head:* Dr. Karin Jordan, Department Chair, 330-972-5155, E-mail: kj25@uakron.edu.

University of Central Florida, College of Education and Human Performance, Department of Educational and Human Sciences, Program in Marriage, Couple, and Family Therapy, Orlando, FL 32816. Offers MA, Certificate. *Students:* 58 full-time (55 women), 14 part-time (9 women); includes 19 minority (6 Black or African American, non-Hispanic/Latino; 3 Asian, non-Hispanic/Latino; 9 Hispanic/Latino; 1 Two or more races, non-Hispanic/Latino), 1 international. Average age 28. 62 applicants, 52% accepted, 25 enrolled. In 2014, 18 master's, 20 other advanced degrees awarded. *Expenses:* Tuition, state resident: part-time $288.16 per credit hour. Tuition, nonresident: part-time $1073.31 per credit hour. *Financial support:* In 2014–15, 4 students received support, including 3 fellowships (averaging $1,600 per year), 5 research assistantships (averaging $6,700 per year). *Unit head:* Dr. Sejal Barden, Program Coordinator, 407-823-6106, E-mail: sejal.barden@ucf.edu. *Application contact:* Barbara Rodriguez Lamas, Director, Admissions and Student Support, 407-823-2766, Fax: 407-823-6442, E-mail: gradadmissions@ucf.edu.

University of Central Oklahoma, The Jackson College of Graduate Studies, College of Education and Professional Studies, Department of Human Environmental Sciences, Edmond, OK 73034-5209. Offers family and child studies (MS), including family life education, infant/child specialist, marriage and family therapy; nutrition-food management (MS). Part-time programs available. *Degree requirements:* For master's, comprehensive exam (for some programs), thesis (for some programs). *Entrance requirements:* For master's, GRE, essay, physical, CPR and First Aid training. Additional exam requirements/recommendations for international students: Required—TOEFL (minimum score 550 paper-based; 79 iBT), IELTS (minimum score 6.5). Electronic applications accepted.

University of Colorado Denver, School of Education and Human Development, Program in Counseling Psychology and Counselor Education, Denver, CO 80217. Offers counseling (MA), including clinical mental health counseling, couple and family counseling, multicultural counseling, school counseling; school counseling (MA). *Accreditation:* ACA; NCATE. Part-time and evening/weekend programs available. *Students:* 196 full-time (158 women), 30 part-time (24 women); includes 42 minority (10 Black or African American, non-Hispanic/Latino; 4 Asian, non-Hispanic/Latino; 24 Hispanic/Latino; 4 Two or more races, non-Hispanic/Latino). Average age 30. 182 applicants, 30% accepted, 31 enrolled. In 2014, 72 master's awarded. *Degree requirements:* For master's, comprehensive exam (for some programs), thesis or alternative, 63-66 hours. *Entrance requirements:* For master's, GRE or MAT (unless applicant already holds a graduate degree), letters of recommendation, interview, resume, transcripts from all colleges/universities attended. Additional exam requirements/recommendations for international students: Required—TOEFL (minimum score 525 paper-based; 71 iBT); Recommended—IELTS (minimum score 6.3). *Application deadline:* For fall admission, 1/15 for domestic students, 1/1 for international students; for spring admission, 9/15 for domestic students, 9/1 for international students.

Marriage and Family Therapy

Application fee: $50 ($75 for international students). Electronic applications accepted. *Expenses:* Expenses: Contact institution. *Financial support:* In 2014–15, 9 students received support. Research assistantships, Federal Work-Study, institutionally sponsored loans, scholarships/grants, and traineeships available. Financial award application deadline: 4/1; financial award applicants required to submit FAFSA. *Faculty research:* Spiritual issues in counseling, multicultural and diversity issues in counseling, adolescent suicide, career development. *Unit head:* Farah Ibrahim, Counseling Professor, 303-315-6329, E-mail: farah.ibrahim@ucdenver.edu. *Application contact:* Student Services Coordinator, 303-315-6300, Fax: 303-315-6311, E-mail: education@ucdenver.edu.
Website: http://www.ucdenver.edu/academics/colleges/SchoolOfEducation/Academics/MASTERS/counseling/Pages/default.aspx

University of Florida, Graduate School, College of Education, School of Human Development and Organizational Studies in Education, Gainesville, FL 32611. Offers counseling and counselor education (Ed D, PhD), including counseling and counselor education, marriage and family counseling, mental health counseling, school counseling and guidance; educational leadership (M Ed, MAE, Ed D, PhD, Ed S), including educational leadership (Ed D, PhD), educational policy (Ed D, PhD); higher education administration (Ed D, PhD), including education policy (Ed D), educational policy, higher education administration; marriage and family counseling (M Ed, MAE, Ed D, PhD, Ed S); mental health counseling (M Ed, MAE, Ed D, PhD, Ed S); research and evaluation methodology (M Ed, MAE, Ed D, PhD); school counseling and guidance (M Ed, MAE, Ed D, PhD, Ed S); student personnel in higher education (M Ed, MAE). *Accreditation:* ACA (one or more programs are accredited); NCATE. Part-time programs available. Postbaccalaureate distance learning degree programs offered. *Faculty:* 20 full-time (11 women), 4 part-time/adjunct (1 woman). *Students:* 297 full-time (238 women), 219 part-time (161 women); includes 147 minority (62 Black or African American, non-Hispanic/Latino; 4 American Indian or Alaska Native, non-Hispanic/Latino; 12 Asian, non-Hispanic/Latino; 69 Hispanic/Latino), 41 international. 259 applicants, 52% accepted, 80 enrolled. In 2014, 58 master's, 13 doctorates, 61 other advanced degrees awarded. Terminal master's awarded for partial completion of doctoral program. *Degree requirements:* For master's, thesis optional; for doctorate, comprehensive exam, thesis/dissertation. *Entrance requirements:* For master's and doctorate, GRE General Test, minimum GPA of 3.0 (undergraduate), 3.5 (graduate); for Ed S, GRE General Test. Additional exam requirements/recommendations for international students: Required—TOEFL (minimum score 550 paper-based; 80 iBT), IELTS (minimum score 6). *Application deadline:* Applications are processed on a rolling basis. Application fee: $30. Electronic applications accepted. *Financial support:* In 2014–15, 10 fellowships, 48 research assistantships, 45 teaching assistantships were awarded; career-related internships or fieldwork and unspecified assistantships also available. Financial award applicants required to submit FAFSA. *Unit head:* Glenn E. Good, PhD, Dean and Professor, 352-273-4135, Fax: 352-846-2697, E-mail: ggood@ufl.edu. *Application contact:* Thomasenia L. Adams, PhD, Professor and Associate Dean, 352-273-4119, Fax: 352-846-2697, E-mail: tla@coe.ufl.edu.
Website: http://education.ufl.edu/hdose/

University of Guelph, Graduate Studies, College of Social and Applied Human Sciences, Department of Family Relations and Applied Nutrition, Guelph, ON N1G 2W1, Canada. Offers applied nutrition (MAN); family relations and human development (M Sc, PhD), including applied human nutrition, couple and family therapy (M Sc), family relations and human development. *Accreditation:* AAMFT/COAMFTE (one or more programs are accredited). Part-time programs available. *Degree requirements:* For master's, thesis (for some programs); for doctorate, comprehensive exam, thesis/dissertation. *Entrance requirements:* For master's, minimum B+ average; for doctorate, master's degree in family relations and human development or related field with a minimum B+ average or master's degree in applied human nutrition. Additional exam requirements/recommendations for international students: Required—TOEFL (minimum score 600 paper-based). Electronic applications accepted. *Faculty research:* Child and adolescent development, social gerontology, family roles and relations, couple and family therapy, applied human nutrition.

University of Houston–Clear Lake, School of Human Sciences and Humanities, Programs in Human Sciences, Houston, TX 77058-1002. Offers behavioral sciences (MA), including criminology, cross cultural studies, general psychology, sociology; clinical psychology (MA); criminology (MA); cross cultural studies (MA); family therapy (MA); fitness and human performance (MA); school psychology (MA). *Accreditation:* AAMFT/COAMFTE. Part-time and evening/weekend programs available. Postbaccalaureate distance learning degree programs offered (minimal on-campus study). *Degree requirements:* For master's, thesis or alternative. *Entrance requirements:* For master's, GRE General Test. Additional exam requirements/recommendations for international students: Required—TOEFL (minimum score 550 paper-based). Electronic applications accepted. *Faculty research:* Smoking cessation, adolescent sexuality, white collar crime, serial murder, human factors/human computer interaction.

The University of Iowa, Graduate College, College of Education, Department of Rehabilitation and Counselor Education, Iowa City, IA 52242-1316. Offers counselor education and supervision (PhD); couple and family therapy (PhD); rehabilitation and mental health counseling (MA); rehabilitation counselor education (PhD); school counseling (MA). *Accreditation:* ACA (one or more programs are accredited); CORE (one or more programs are accredited). *Degree requirements:* For master's, thesis optional, exam; for doctorate, comprehensive exam, thesis/dissertation. *Entrance requirements:* For master's and doctorate, GRE General Test, minimum GPA of 3.0. Additional exam requirements/recommendations for international students: Required—TOEFL (minimum score 550 paper-based; 81 iBT). Electronic applications accepted.

University of La Verne, College of Arts and Sciences, Department of Psychology, Program in Marriage and Family Therapy, La Verne, CA 91750-4443. Offers MS. Part-time programs available. *Faculty:* 7 full-time (5 women), 7 part-time/adjunct (4 women). *Students:* 36 full-time (31 women), 28 part-time (25 women); includes 44 minority (4 Black or African American, non-Hispanic/Latino; 3 Asian, non-Hispanic/Latino; 35 Hispanic/Latino; 2 Two or more races, non-Hispanic/Latino), 1 international. Average age 29. In 2014, 48 master's awarded. *Degree requirements:* For master's, thesis, competency exam, fieldwork, culminating project. *Entrance requirements:* For master's, minimum undergraduate GPA of 3.0, statement of purpose, 3 letters of recommendation, interview, curriculum vitae. Additional exam requirements/recommendations for international students: Required—TOEFL (minimum score 600 paper-based; 100 iBT). *Application deadline:* Applications are processed on a rolling basis. Application fee: $50. *Expenses:* Expenses: Contact institution. *Financial support:* Career-related internships or fieldwork, institutionally sponsored loans, and scholarships/grants available. Financial award application deadline: 3/2; financial award applicants required to submit FAFSA. *Unit head:* Dr. Amy Demyan, Department Chair, 909-448-4181, E-mail: ademyan@laverne.edu. *Application contact:* Christy Ranells, Associate Director of Graduate Admissions, 909-4484644, Fax: 909-392-2744, E-mail: cranells@laverne.edu.
Website: http://sites.laverne.edu/psychology/mft_program/

University of Louisiana at Monroe, Graduate School, College of Health and Pharmaceutical Sciences, Program in Marriage and Family Therapy, Monroe, LA 71209-0001. Offers MA, PhD. *Accreditation:* AAMFT/COAMFTE (one or more programs are accredited); ACA. Part-time and evening/weekend programs available. *Degree requirements:* For master's, thesis optional; for doctorate, comprehensive exam, thesis/dissertation, clinical experience. *Entrance requirements:* For master's, GRE General Test, minimum GPA of 2.8; for doctorate, GRE General Test, minimum GPA of 3.5. Additional exam requirements/recommendations for international students: Required—TOEFL (minimum score 500 paper-based; 61 iBT). Electronic applications accepted. *Faculty research:* Family systems, substance abuse.

University of Louisville, Graduate School, Raymond A. Kent School of Social Work, Louisville, KY 40292-0001. Offers marriage and family therapy (PMC), including mental health; social work (MSSW, PhD), including alcohol and drug counseling (MSSW), gerontology (MSSW), marriage and family (PhD), school social work (MSSW). *Accreditation:* AAMFT/COAMFTE; CSWE (one or more programs are accredited). Part-time and evening/weekend programs available. *Students:* 369 full-time (312 women), 101 part-time (89 women); includes 138 minority (95 Black or African American, non-Hispanic/Latino; 3 American Indian or Alaska Native, non-Hispanic/Latino; 5 Asian, non-Hispanic/Latino; 21 Hispanic/Latino; 14 Two or more races, non-Hispanic/Latino), 7 international. Average age 31. 425 applicants, 67% accepted, 176 enrolled. In 2014, 117 master's, 2 doctorates awarded. *Degree requirements:* For doctorate, comprehensive exam, thesis/dissertation. *Entrance requirements:* For master's, GRE or minimum GPA of 2.75; for doctorate, GRE General Test, interview, writing sample. Additional exam requirements/recommendations for international students: Required—TOEFL (minimum score 550 paper-based; 79 iBT). *Application deadline:* For fall admission, 7/31 for domestic and international students. Applications are processed on a rolling basis. Application fee: $60. Electronic applications accepted. *Expenses:* Tuition, state resident: full-time $11,326; part-time $630 per credit hour. Tuition, nonresident: full-time $23,568; part-time $1311 per credit hour. *Required fees:* $196. Tuition and fees vary according to program and reciprocity agreements. *Financial support:* Research assistantships with full tuition reimbursements, teaching assistantships with full tuition reimbursements, Federal Work-Study, institutionally sponsored loans, scholarships/grants, health care benefits, and unspecified assistantships available. Support available to part-time students. Financial award application deadline: 5/15; financial award applicants required to submit FAFSA. *Faculty research:* Child welfare, substance abuse, gerontology, family functioning, health behavior. *Total annual research expenditures:* $1.6 million. *Unit head:* Dr. Terry Singer, Dean, 502-852-6402, Fax: 502-852-0422, E-mail: terry.singer@louisville.edu. *Application contact:* Libby Leggett, Director, Graduate Admissions, 502-852-3101, Fax: 502-852-6536, E-mail: gradadm@louisville.edu.
Website: http://www.louisville.edu/kent

University of Mary Hardin-Baylor, Graduate Studies in Counseling, Belton, TX 76513. Offers clinical and mental health counseling (MA); marriage, family and child counseling (MA); non-clinical professional studies (MA). Part-time and evening/weekend programs available. *Faculty:* 7 full-time (4 women), 1 (woman) part-time/adjunct. *Students:* 52 full-time (44 women), 19 part-time (16 women); includes 28 minority (11 Black or African American, non-Hispanic/Latino; 3 American Indian or Alaska Native, non-Hispanic/Latino; 5 Asian, non-Hispanic/Latino; 8 Hispanic/Latino; 1 Two or more races, non-Hispanic/Latino), 5 international. Average age 30. 26 applicants, 85% accepted, 13 enrolled. In 2014, 28 master's awarded. *Degree requirements:* For master's, comprehensive exam. *Entrance requirements:* For master's, GRE General Test (waived if GPA greater than 3.0), minimum GPA of 3.0 cumulative or last 60 hours, three letters of recommendation, interview. Additional exam requirements/recommendations for international students: Required—TOEFL (minimum score 100 iBT), IELTS (minimum score 7). *Application deadline:* For fall admission, 6/1 for domestic students, 4/30 priority date for international students; for spring admission, 11/1 for domestic students, 9/30 priority date for international students. Applications are processed on a rolling basis. Application fee: $35 ($135 for international students). Electronic applications accepted. *Expenses: Tuition:* Full-time $14,400; part-time $800 per credit hour. *Required fees:* $1350; $75 per credit hour. $50 per term. Tuition and fees vary according to degree level. *Financial support:* Federal Work-Study, unspecified assistantships, and scholarships for some active duty military personnel available. Support available to part-time students. Financial award applicants required to submit FAFSA. *Unit head:* Dr. Marta Garrett, Associate Professor/Director, Graduate Counseling, 254-295-5018, E-mail: mgarrett@umhb.edu. *Application contact:* Melissa Ford, Director of Graduate Admissions, 254-295-4020, Fax: 254-295-5038, E-mail: mford@umhb.edu.
Website: http://graduate.umhb.edu/counseling/

University of Maryland, College Park, Academic Affairs, School of Public Health, Department of Family Science, College Park, MD 20742. Offers family studies (PhD); marriage and family therapy (MS); maternal and child health (PhD). *Accreditation:* AAMFT/COAMFTE. Part-time and evening/weekend programs available. *Degree requirements:* For master's, thesis or alternative; for doctorate, comprehensive exam, thesis/dissertation, oral defense. *Entrance requirements:* For master's, GRE General Test, minimum GPA of 3.0, 3 letters of recommendation; for doctorate, GRE General Test, minimum GPA of 3.0, 3 letters of recommendation, research sample. Electronic applications accepted. *Faculty research:* Family life quality, interracial couples, child support, homeless families, family and child well-being.

University of Massachusetts Boston, College of Education and Human Development, Program in Family Therapy, Boston, MA 02125-3393. Offers MS. *Accreditation:* AAMFT/COAMFTE. *Expenses:* Tuition, state resident: full-time $2590; part-time $108 per credit. Tuition, nonresident: full-time $9758; part-time $406.50 per credit. Tuition and fees vary according to course load and program. *Financial support:* Research assistantships available. *Unit head:* Dr. Gonzalo Bacigalupe, Director, 617-287-7631, E-mail: gonzalo.bacigalupe@umb.edu. *Application contact:* Peggy Roldan Patel, Graduate Admissions Coordinator, 617-287-6400, Fax: 617-287-6236, E-mail: bos.gadm@dpc.umassp.edu.

University of Miami, Graduate School, School of Education and Human Development, Department of Educational and Psychological Studies, Program in Counseling, Coral Gables, FL 33124. Offers counseling and research (MS Ed); Latino mental health (Certificate); marriage and family therapy (MS Ed); mental health counseling (MS Ed). Part-time and evening/weekend programs available. *Degree requirements:* For master's, comprehensive exam, personal growth experience. *Entrance requirements:* For master's, GRE General Test. Additional exam requirements/recommendations for international students: Required—TOEFL (minimum score 550 paper-based; 80 iBT); Recommended—IELTS (minimum score 6.5). Electronic applications accepted. *Faculty research:* Cocaine recidivism, HIV, non-traditional families, health psychology, diversity.

University of Minnesota, Twin Cities Campus, Graduate School, College of Education and Human Development, Department of Family Social Science, Minneapolis, MN 55455-0213. Offers marriage and family therapy (MA, PhD). *Accreditation:* AAMFT/COAMFTE (one or more programs are accredited). *Faculty:* 20 full-time (14 women). *Students:* 59 full-time (47 women), 26 part-time (21 women); includes 15 minority (1 Black or African American, non-Hispanic/Latino; 1 American Indian or Alaska Native, non-Hispanic/Latino; 5 Asian, non-Hispanic/Latino; 6 Hispanic/Latino; 2 Two or more races, non-Hispanic/Latino), 10 international. Average age 34. 73 applicants, 59% accepted, 34 enrolled. In 2014, 5 master's, 4 doctorates awarded.

Degree requirements: For master's, thesis; for doctorate, thesis/dissertation. *Entrance requirements:* For master's and doctorate, GRE General Test, minimum undergraduate GPA of 3.0 (preferred). Additional exam requirements/recommendations for international students: Required—TOEFL. *Application deadline:* For fall admission, 12/15 for domestic students. Application fee: $75 ($95 for international students). *Financial support:* In 2014–15, 37 research assistantships (averaging $8,001 per year), 10 teaching assistantships (averaging $9,055 per year) were awarded; fellowships, career-related internships or fieldwork, Federal Work-Study, institutionally sponsored loans, and tuition waivers (partial) also available. Financial award application deadline: 6/30; financial award applicants required to submit FAFSA. *Faculty research:* Child adjustment in family context; families and culture; families and financial decisions; family formation and intergenerational studies; families, loss, and trauma; intimate family relationships. *Total annual research expenditures:* $2.3 million. *Unit head:* Dr. Lynne Borden, Head, 612-625-1900, Fax: 612-625-4227, E-mail: lmborden@umn.edu. *Application contact:* Dr. Jodi Dworkin, Director of Graduate Studies, 612-625-3732, Fax: 612-625-4227, E-mail: jdworkin@umn.edu.
Website: http://www.cehd.umn.edu/fsos/

University of Mobile, Graduate Programs, Program in Marriage and Family Counseling, Mobile, AL 36613. Offers MA. Part-time programs available. *Faculty:* 2 full-time (0 women). *Students:* 14 full-time (all women), 39 part-time (31 women); includes 26 minority (all Black or African American, non-Hispanic/Latino). Average age 37. 21 applicants, 86% accepted, 18 enrolled. *Degree requirements:* For master's, comprehensive exam, thesis optional. *Entrance requirements:* For master's, GRE. Additional exam requirements/recommendations for international students: Required—TOEFL (minimum score 550 paper-based; 80 iBT). *Application deadline:* For fall admission, 8/3 priority date for domestic and international students; for spring admission, 12/23 priority date for domestic and international students. Applications are processed on a rolling basis. Application fee: $40 ($50 for international students). Electronic applications accepted. *Financial support:* Application deadline: 8/1; applicants required to submit FAFSA. *Unit head:* Dr. Tom Bevill, Department Chair, Social and Behavioral Sciences, 251-442-2411, Fax: 251-442-2523, E-mail: tbevill@umobile.edu. *Application contact:* Danielle M. Riley, Administrative Assistant to the Dean of Graduate Programs, 251-442-2270, Fax: 251-442-2523, E-mail: driley@umobile.edu.
Website: http://www.umobile.edu

University of Montevallo, College of Education, Program in Counseling, Montevallo, AL 35115. Offers community counseling (M Ed); couple, marriage and family (M Ed); school counseling (M Ed). *Accreditation:* ACA; NCATE. Part-time and evening/weekend programs available. *Students:* 41 full-time (34 women), 42 part-time (37 women); includes 20 minority (16 Black or African American, non-Hispanic/Latino; 2 Hispanic/Latino; 2 Two or more races, non-Hispanic/Latino). In 2014, 11 master's awarded. *Entrance requirements:* For master's, GRE General Test or MAT, minimum undergraduate GPA of 2.75 in last 60 hours or 2.5 overall, interview. Additional exam requirements/recommendations for international students: Required—TOEFL (minimum score 550 paper-based). *Application deadline:* For fall admission, 7/15 for domestic students; for spring admission, 11/15 for domestic students. Application fee: $25. *Financial support:* Federal Work-Study, scholarships/grants, and unspecified assistantships available. *Unit head:* Dr. Charlotte Daughhetee, Chair, 205-665-6358, E-mail: daughc@montevallo.edu. *Application contact:* Kevin Thornthwaite, Director, Graduate Admissions and Records, 205-665-6350, E-mail: graduate@montevallo.edu. Website: http://www.montevallo.edu/education/college-of-education/traditional-masters-degrees/counseling/

University of Nebraska–Lincoln, Graduate College, College of Education and Human Sciences, Department of Child, Youth and Family Studies, Lincoln, NE 68588. Offers child development/early childhood education (MS, PhD); child, youth and family studies (MS); family and consumer sciences education (MS, PhD); family financial planning (MS); family science (MS, PhD); gerontology (PhD); human sciences (PhD), including child, youth and family studies, gerontology, medical family therapy; marriage and family therapy (MS); medical family therapy (PhD); youth development (MS). *Accreditation:* AAMFT/COAMFTE (one or more programs are accredited). Postbaccalaureate distance learning degree programs offered. *Degree requirements:* For master's, thesis optional. *Entrance requirements:* For master's, GRE. Additional exam requirements/recommendations for international students: Required—TOEFL (minimum score 550 paper-based). Electronic applications accepted. *Faculty research:* Marriage and family therapy, child development/early childhood education, family financial management.

University of Nevada, Las Vegas, Graduate College, Greenspun College of Urban Affairs, Department of Marriage and Family Therapy, Las Vegas, NV 89154-3045. Offers MS. *Accreditation:* AAMFT/COAMFTE; ACA. Part-time programs available. *Faculty:* 4 full-time (2 women), 4 part-time/adjunct (2 women). *Students:* 59 full-time (44 women), 22 part-time (17 women); includes 26 minority (8 Black or African American, non-Hispanic/Latino; 3 Asian, non-Hispanic/Latino; 11 Hispanic/Latino; 1 Native Hawaiian or other Pacific Islander, non-Hispanic/Latino; 3 Two or more races, non-Hispanic/Latino), 5 international. Average age 29. 74 applicants, 38% accepted, 23 enrolled. In 2014, 28 master's awarded. *Degree requirements:* For master's, comprehensive exam (for some programs), thesis (for some programs). *Entrance requirements:* For master's, GRE General Test. Additional exam requirements/recommendations for international students: Required—TOEFL (minimum score 550 paper-based; 80 iBT), IELTS (minimum score 7). *Application deadline:* For fall admission, 1/15 for domestic students, 5/1 for international students; for spring admission, 10/1 for international students. Application fee: $60 ($95 for international students). Electronic applications accepted. *Expenses:* Expenses: Contact institution. *Financial support:* In 2014–15, 26 students received support, including 9 research assistantships with partial tuition reimbursements available (averaging $10,287 per year), 17 teaching assistantships with partial tuition reimbursements available (averaging $10,924 per year); institutionally sponsored loans, scholarships/grants, health care benefits, and unspecified assistantships also available. Financial award application deadline: 3/1. *Faculty research:* Forgiveness, couple change processes, sex therapy, infidelity, technology in couples and families. *Total annual research expenditures:* $2,351. *Unit head:* Dr. Joanne Thompson, Chair/Professor, 702-895-1817, E-mail: joanne.thompson@unlv.edu. *Application contact:* Graduate College Admissions Evaluator, 702-895-3320, Fax: 702-895-4180, E-mail: gradcollege@unlv.edu.
Website: http://mft.unlv.edu/grad.html

University of New Hampshire, Graduate School, School of Health and Human Services, Department of Family Studies, Durham, NH 03824. Offers human development and family studies (MS); marriage and family therapy (MS). Program offered in fall only. *Accreditation:* AAMFT/COAMFTE. Part-time programs available. *Faculty:* 7 full-time (4 women). *Students:* 13 full-time (12 women), 6 part-time (5 women); includes 3 minority (1 Asian, non-Hispanic/Latino; 2 Hispanic/Latino). Average age 28. 7 applicants, 100% accepted, 6 enrolled. *Degree requirements:* For master's, thesis or alternative. *Entrance requirements:* For master's, GRE General Test. Additional exam requirements/recommendations for international students: Required—TOEFL (minimum score 550 paper-based; 80 iBT). *Application deadline:* For fall

admission, 5/15 priority date for domestic students, 4/1 for international students. Applications are processed on a rolling basis. Application fee: $65. Electronic applications accepted. *Expenses:* Tuition, state resident: full-time $13,500; part-time $750 per credit hour. Tuition, nonresident: full-time $26,460; part-time $1110 per credit hour. *Required fees:* $1788; $447 per semester. *Financial support:* In 2014–15, 11 students received support, including 4 teaching assistantships; fellowships, research assistantships, career-related internships or fieldwork, Federal Work-Study, scholarships/grants, and tuition waivers (full and partial) also available. Support available to part-time students. Financial award application deadline: 2/15. *Unit head:* Kerry Kazura, Chairperson, 603-862-2135. *Application contact:* Matty Leighton, Administrative Assistant, 603-862-5021, E-mail: family.studies@unh.edu.
Website: http://www.chhs.unh.edu/hdfs

The University of North Carolina at Greensboro, Graduate School, School of Education, Department of Counseling and Educational Development, Greensboro, NC 27412-5001. Offers advanced school counseling (PMC); counseling and counselor education (PhD); counseling and educational development (MS); couple and family counseling (PMC); school counseling (PMC); MS/Ed S. *Accreditation:* ACA (one or more programs are accredited); NCATE. *Degree requirements:* For master's, comprehensive exam, practicum, internship; for doctorate, comprehensive exam, thesis/dissertation. *Entrance requirements:* For master's, doctorate, and PMC, GRE General Test. Additional exam requirements/recommendations for international students: Required—TOEFL. Electronic applications accepted. *Faculty research:* Gerontology, invitational theory, career development, marriage and family therapy, drug and alcohol abuse prevention.

University of Phoenix–Bay Area Campus, College of Social Sciences, San Jose, CA 95134-1805. Offers marriage, family, and child therapy (MSC). Evening/weekend programs available. *Degree requirements:* For master's, thesis or alternative. *Entrance requirements:* For master's, Comprehensive Cognitive Assessment, minimum undergraduate GPA of 2.5, 3 years of work experience.

University of Phoenix–Central Valley Campus, College of Human Services, Fresno, CA 93720-1562. Offers marriage, family and child therapy (MSC).

University of Phoenix–Las Vegas Campus, College of Human Services, Las Vegas, NV 89135. Offers marriage, family, and child therapy (MSC); mental health counseling (MSC); school counseling (MSC). Postbaccalaureate distance learning degree programs offered. *Entrance requirements:* For master's, minimum undergraduate GPA of 2.5, 3 years of work experience. Additional exam requirements/recommendations for international students: Required—TOEFL (minimum score 550 paper-based; 79 iBT). Electronic applications accepted.

University of Phoenix–Phoenix Campus, College of Social Sciences, Tempe, AZ 85282-2371. Offers counseling (MS), including clinical mental health counseling, community counseling, counseling, marriage, family and child therapy; psychology (MS). Evening/weekend programs available. Postbaccalaureate distance learning degree programs offered. *Entrance requirements:* Additional exam requirements/recommendations for international students: Required—TOEFL, TOEIC (Test of English as an International Communication), Berlitz Online English Proficiency Exam, PTE, or IELTS. Electronic applications accepted. *Expenses:* Contact institution.

University of Phoenix–Puerto Rico Campus, College of Human Services, Guaynabo, PR 00968. Offers marriage and family counseling (MSC); mental health counseling (MSC). Evening/weekend programs available. *Degree requirements:* For master's, thesis (for some programs). *Entrance requirements:* For master's, Counselor Preparation Comprehensive Examination, minimum undergraduate GPA of 2.5, 3 years work experience. Additional exam requirements/recommendations for international students: Required—TOEFL (minimum score 550 paper-based; 79 iBT). Electronic applications accepted.

University of Phoenix–Southern California Campus, College of Social Sciences, Costa Mesa, CA 92626. Offers counseling (MS), including counseling, marriage, family and child therapy; psychology (MS), including behavioral health. Evening/weekend programs available. Postbaccalaureate distance learning degree programs offered. *Entrance requirements:* Additional exam requirements/recommendations for international students: Required—TOEFL, TOEIC (Test of English as an International Communication), Berlitz Online English Proficiency Exam, PTE, or IELTS. Electronic applications accepted. *Expenses:* Contact institution.

University of Rochester, School of Medicine and Dentistry, Graduate Programs in Medicine and Dentistry, Department of Psychiatry, Rochester, NY 14627. Offers marriage and family therapy (MS). *Accreditation:* AAMFT/COAMFTE. Part-time programs available. *Degree requirements:* For master's, projects. *Entrance requirements:* For master's, GRE General Test. *Expenses: Tuition:* Full-time $46,150; part-time $1442 per credit hour. *Required fees:* $504.

University of Saint Joseph, Program in Marriage and Family Therapy, West Hartford, CT 06117-2700. Offers MA. *Accreditation:* AAMFT/COAMFTE. Part-time and evening/weekend programs available. *Degree requirements:* For master's, comprehensive exam, thesis or alternative, practicum, internship. *Entrance requirements:* For master's, 2 letters of recommendation. Electronic applications accepted. Application fee is waived when completed online. *Expenses: Tuition:* Part-time $700 per credit. *Required fees:* $42 per credit. Tuition and fees vary according to degree level, campus/location and program.

University of St. Thomas, Graduate Studies, Graduate School of Professional Psychology, St. Paul, MN 55105-1096. Offers counseling psychology (MA, Psy D); family therapy (Certificate). *Accreditation:* APA. Part-time and evening/weekend programs available. *Degree requirements:* For master's, comprehensive exam, practicum; for doctorate, comprehensive exam, thesis/dissertation, qualifying exam, practicum, internship. *Entrance requirements:* For master's, GRE, minimum GPA of 2.75, letters of recommendation, personal statement; for doctorate, GRE, minimum GPA of 3.2, letters of recommendation, personal statement. Additional exam requirements/recommendations for international students: Required—TOEFL (minimum score 550 paper-based; 80 iBT). *Expenses:* Contact institution. *Faculty research:* Elderly, neuropsychology, anxiety, family, therapist expertise, business of practice, religion and psychology, early attachment, relationship of science and practice in psychotherapy.

University of San Francisco, School of Education, Department of Counseling Psychology, San Francisco, CA 94117-1080. Offers counseling (MA), including educational counseling, life transitions counseling, marital and family therapy. *Faculty:* 7 full-time (3 women), 53 part-time/adjunct (37 women). *Students:* 305 full-time (246 women), 30 part-time (27 women); includes 157 minority (24 Black or African American, non-Hispanic/Latino; 36 Asian, non-Hispanic/Latino; 81 Hispanic/Latino; 3 Native Hawaiian or other Pacific Islander, non-Hispanic/Latino; 13 Two or more races, non-Hispanic/Latino), 5 international. Average age 29. 316 applicants, 75% accepted, 106 enrolled. In 2014, 152 master's awarded. *Application deadline:* For fall admission, 3/1 priority date for domestic students, 3/1 for international students; for spring admission, 10/15 priority date for domestic students, 10/15 for international students. Applications are processed on a rolling basis. Application fee: $55 ($65 for international students). Electronic applications accepted. *Expenses: Tuition:* Full-time $21,762; part-time $1209

per credit hour. Tuition and fees vary according to degree level, campus/location and program. *Financial support:* In 2014–15, 86 students received support. Fellowships, research assistantships, and teaching assistantships available. Financial award application deadline: 3/2; financial award applicants required to submit FAFSA. *Unit head:* Dr. Brian Gerrard, Chair, 415-422-6868. *Application contact:* Amy Fogliani, Associate Director of Graduate Outreach, 415-422-5467, E-mail: schoolofeducation@usfca.edu.

University of Southern California, Graduate School, Rossier School of Education, Master's Programs in Education, Los Angeles, CA 90089-4038. Offers educational counseling (ME); marriage, family and child counseling (MMFT); postsecondary administration and student affairs [PASA] (ME); school counseling (ME); teaching (online) (MAT); teaching and teaching credential (MAT); teaching English to speakers of other languages (MAT). Part-time and evening/weekend programs available. Postbaccalaureate distance learning degree programs offered (no on-campus study). *Degree requirements:* For master's, thesis optional. *Entrance requirements:* For master's, GRE (for all programs except MAT). Additional exam requirements/ recommendations for international students: Required—TOEFL (minimum score 100 iBT). Electronic applications accepted. *Faculty research:* College access and equity, preparing teachers for culturally diverse populations, sociocultural basis of learning as mediated by instruction with focus on reading and literacy in English learners, social and political aspects of teaching and learning English, school counselor development and training.

University of Southern Mississippi, Graduate School, College of Education and Psychology, Department of Child and Family Studies, Hattiesburg, MS 39406-0001. Offers child and family studies (MS); marriage and family therapy (MS). *Accreditation:* AAMFT/COAMFTE. Part-time programs available. *Degree requirements:* For master's, comprehensive exam, thesis optional. *Entrance requirements:* For master's, GRE General Test, minimum GPA of 2.75 on last 60 hours. Additional exam requirements/ recommendations for international students: Required—TOEFL. Electronic applications accepted. *Faculty research:* School food service, teen pregnancy, diet and cholesterol metabolism.

University of South Florida, College of Behavioral and Community Sciences, Department of Rehabilitation and Mental Health Counseling, Tampa, FL 33620-9951. Offers addictions and substance abuse counseling (MA); marriage and family therapy (MA). *Accreditation:* CORE. Part-time and evening/weekend programs available. *Faculty:* 5 full-time (3 women), 1 part-time/adjunct (0 women). *Students:* 63 full-time (52 women), 54 part-time (50 women); includes 32 minority (9 Black or African American, non-Hispanic/Latino; 3 Asian, non-Hispanic/Latino; 18 Hispanic/Latino; 1 Native Hawaiian or other Pacific Islander, non-Hispanic/Latino; 1 Two or more races, non-Hispanic/Latino), 1 international. Average age 30. 52 applicants, 67% accepted, 25 enrolled. In 2014, 41 master's awarded. *Degree requirements:* For master's, comprehensive exam, thesis optional. *Entrance requirements:* For master's, GRE General Test, three letters of recommendation, personal statement of intent, on-campus interview, undergraduate statistics or research methods course. Additional exam requirements/recommendations for international students: Required—TOEFL (minimum score 550 paper-based; 79 iBT) or IELTS (minimum score 6.5). *Application deadline:* For fall admission, 2/15 for domestic students, 1/2 for international students; for spring admission, 10/15 for domestic students, 6/1 for international students. Application fee: $30. Electronic applications accepted. *Total annual research expenditures:* $233,747. *Unit head:* Dr. Tennyson Wright, Chair and Associate Professor, 813-974-2963, Fax: 813-974-8080, E-mail: tjwright@usf.edu. *Application contact:* Dr. Gary DuDell, Instructor and Director of Graduate Studies, 813-974-1257, Fax: 813-974-8080, E-mail: gdudell@usf.edu.
Website: http://rmhc.cbcs.usf.edu/

University of South Florida, Innovative Education, Tampa, FL 33620-9951. *Unit head:* Kathy Barnes, Interdisciplinary Programs Coordinator, 813-974-8031, Fax: 813-974-7061, E-mail: barnesk@usf.edu. *Application contact:* Karen Tylinski, Metro Initiatives, 813-974-9943, Fax: 813-974-7061, E-mail: ktylinsk@usf.edu.
Website: http://www.usf.edu/innovative-education/

The University of Texas at Tyler, College of Education and Psychology, Department of Psychology and Counseling, Tyler, TX 75799-0001. Offers clinical psychology (MS), including neuropsychology, school psychology; counseling psychology (MA), including general, marriage and family; interdisciplinary studies (MSIS); school counseling (MA). Part-time and evening/weekend programs available. *Degree requirements:* For master's, comprehensive exam, thesis optional. *Entrance requirements:* For master's, GRE General Test, minimum GPA of 3.0. Additional exam requirements/ recommendations for international students: Required—TOEFL. Electronic applications accepted. *Faculty research:* Neuropsychology, child abuse, psychometric properties of psychological instruments, maternal behavior, clinical practice issues, victimization of women, post-traumatic stress disorder.

The University of West Alabama, School of Graduate Studies, College of Education, Departments of Instructional Leadership and Support/Curriculum and Instruction, Program in Continuing Education, Livingston, AL 35470. Offers counseling and psychology (MSCE); family counseling (MSCE); general (MSCE); guidance and counseling (MSCE). *Accreditation:* NCATE. Part-time and evening/weekend programs available. Postbaccalaureate distance learning degree programs offered (no on-campus study). *Faculty:* 13 full-time (8 women), 34 part-time/adjunct (25 women). *Students:* 600 (520 women); includes 459 minority (443 Black or African American, non-Hispanic/ Latino; 4 American Indian or Alaska Native, non-Hispanic/Latino; 5 Asian, non-Hispanic/ Latino; 4 Hispanic/Latino; 3 Two or more races, non-Hispanic/Latino). Average age 35. 178 applicants, 95% accepted, 121 enrolled. In 2014, 170 master's awarded. *Degree requirements:* For master's, comprehensive exam, thesis optional. *Entrance requirements:* For master's, GRE General Test, MAT, minimum GPA of 2.75. Additional exam requirements/recommendations for international students: Required—TOEFL (minimum score 500 paper-based; 61 iBT). *Application deadline:* For fall admission, 8/12 for domestic students; for spring admission, 3/24 for domestic students. Applications are processed on a rolling basis. Application fee: $25. Electronic applications accepted. *Expenses:* Tuition, state resident: full-time $1902; part-time $317 per credit hour. Tuition, nonresident: full-time $3804; part-time $634 per credit hour. *Required fees:* $50 per semester. One-time fee: $65. Tuition and fees vary according to course load. *Financial support:* Teaching assistantships, career-related internships or fieldwork, Federal Work-Study, scholarships/grants, and unspecified assistantships available. Support available to part-time students. Financial award applicants required to submit FAFSA. *Unit head:* Dr. Reenay Rogers, Chair of Instructional Leadership and Support, 205-652-5423, Fax: 205-652-3706, E-mail: rrogers@uwa.edu. *Application contact:* Dr. Kathy Chandler, Dean of Graduate Studies, 205-652-3421, Fax: 205-652-3670, E-mail: kchandler@uwa.edu.

The University of Winnipeg, Faculty of Theology, Winnipeg, MB R3B 2E9, Canada. Offers marriage and family therapy (MMFT, Certificate); sacred theology (STM); theology (M Div). *Accreditation:* AAMFT/COAMFTE; ATS. Part-time programs available.

University of Wisconsin–Milwaukee, Graduate School, School of Social Welfare, Department of Social Work, Milwaukee, WI 53201-0413. Offers applied gerontology (Certificate); marriage and family therapy (Certificate); non-profit management (Certificate); social work (MSW, PhD). *Accreditation:* CSWE. Part-time programs available. *Degree requirements:* For master's, thesis or alternative. *Entrance requirements:* For doctorate, GRE, bachelor's degree. Additional exam requirements/ recommendations for international students: Required—TOEFL (minimum score 550 paper-based; 79 iBT), IELTS (minimum score 6.5). Electronic applications accepted.

University of Wisconsin–Stout, Graduate School, College of Human Development, Program in Marriage and Family Therapy, Menomonie, WI 54751. Offers MS. *Accreditation:* AAMFT/COAMFTE. Part-time programs available. *Degree requirements:* For master's, thesis or alternative. *Entrance requirements:* For master's, minimum GPA of 2.75. Additional exam requirements/recommendations for international students: Required—TOEFL (minimum score 500 paper-based; 61 iBT). *Application deadline:* For fall admission, 2/1 priority date for domestic and international students. Application fee: $45. Electronic applications accepted. *Financial support:* Research assistantships with partial tuition reimbursements, teaching assistantships with partial tuition reimbursements, Federal Work-Study, scholarships/grants, tuition waivers (partial), and unspecified assistantships available. Support available to part-time students. Financial award application deadline: 5/1; financial award applicants required to submit FAFSA. *Faculty research:* Abuse, addiction, resilience, diversity, narrative therapy. *Unit head:* Dr. Bruce Kuehl, Director, 715-232-2404, Fax: 715-232-2524, E-mail: kuehlb@uwstout.edu. *Application contact:* Anne E. Johnson, Graduate Student Evaluator (Admissions and Assistantship Coordinator), 715-232-1322, Fax: 715-232-2413, E-mail: johnsona@uwstout.edu.
Website: http://www.uwstout.edu/programs/msmft/

Utah State University, School of Graduate Studies, Emma Eccles Jones College of Education and Human Services, Department of Family, Consumer, and Human Development, Logan, UT 84322. Offers family and human development (MFHD); family, consumer, and human development (MS, PhD), including adolescence/youth (MS), adult development/aging (MS), consumer science (MS), infancy/childhood (MS), marriage and family relations (MS), marriage and family therapy (MS). *Accreditation:* AAMFT/COAMFTE (one or more programs are accredited). Part-time and evening/ weekend programs available. Postbaccalaureate distance learning degree programs offered (minimal on-campus study). *Degree requirements:* For master's, thesis; for doctorate, comprehensive exam, thesis/dissertation, competencies. *Entrance requirements:* For master's, GRE General Test or MAT, minimum GPA of 3.0, 3 letters of recommendation; for doctorate, GRE, minimum GPA of 3.0, 3 letters of recommendation. Additional exam requirements/recommendations for international students: Required—TOEFL. Electronic applications accepted. *Faculty research:* Marriage and family relations, adolescent problem behavior, family financial management, early literacy, mental health in the elderly, parent child attachment.

Walden University, Graduate Programs, School of Counseling, Minneapolis, MN 55401. Offers addiction counseling (MS), including addictions and public health, child and adolescent counseling, family studies and interventions, forensic counseling, general program (MS, PhD), trauma and crisis counseling; counselor education and supervision (PhD), including consultation, counseling and social change, forensic mental health counseling, general program (MS, PhD), trauma and crisis; marriage, couple, and family counseling (MS), including forensic counseling, general program (MS, PhD), trauma and crisis counseling; mental health counseling (MS), including forensic counseling, general program (MS, PhD), trauma and crisis counseling; school counseling (MS), including addiction counseling, crisis and trauma, general program (MS, PhD), military families and culture. Part-time and evening/weekend programs available. Postbaccalaureate distance learning degree programs offered (no on-campus study). *Faculty:* 77 full-time (62 women), 314 part-time/adjunct (215 women). *Students:* 1,835 full-time (1,558 women), 1,518 part-time (1,293 women); includes 1,521 minority (1,135 Black or African American, non-Hispanic/Latino; 13 American Indian or Alaska Native, non-Hispanic/Latino; 27 Asian, non-Hispanic/Latino; 234 Hispanic/Latino; 5 Native Hawaiian or other Pacific Islander, non-Hispanic/Latino; 107 Two or more races, non-Hispanic/Latino), 16 international. Average age 38. 684 applicants, 91% accepted, 610 enrolled. In 2014, 592 master's, 4 doctorates awarded. *Degree requirements:* For master's, residency, field experience, professional development plan, licensure plan; for doctorate, thesis/dissertation, residency, practicum, internship. *Entrance requirements:* For master's, bachelor's degree or higher, minimum GPA of 2.5; official transcripts; goal statement (for some programs); access to computer and Internet; for doctorate, master's degree or higher; three years of related professional or academic experience (preferred); minimum GPA of 3.0; goal statement and current resume (for select programs); official transcripts; access to computer and Internet. Additional exam requirements/recommendations for international students: Required—TOEFL (minimum score 550 paper-based, 79 iBT), IELTS (minimum score 6.5), Michigan English Language Assessment Battery (minimum score 82), or PTE (minimum score 53). *Application deadline:* Applications are processed on a rolling basis. Application fee: $0. Electronic applications accepted. *Expenses: Tuition:* Full-time $11,925; part-time $500 per credit hour. *Required fees:* $647. *Financial support:* Federal Work-Study, scholarships/grants, unspecified assistantships, and family tuition reduction, active duty/ veteran tuition reduction, group tuition reduction, interest-free payment plans, employee tuition reduction available. Support available to part-time students. Financial award applicants required to submit FAFSA. *Unit head:* Dr. Savitri Dixon-Saxon, Associate Dean, 866-492-5336. *Application contact:* Meghan M. Thomas, Vice President of Enrollment Management, 866-492-5336, E-mail: info@waldenu.edu.

Western Kentucky University, Graduate Studies, College of Education and Behavioral Sciences, Department of Counseling and Student Affairs, Bowling Green, KY 42101. Offers counseling (MA Ed), including marriage and family therapy, mental health counseling; school counseling (P-12) (MA Ed); student affairs in higher education (MA Ed). *Accreditation:* ACA; NCATE. Part-time and evening/weekend programs available. *Degree requirements:* For master's, comprehensive exam, thesis optional. *Entrance requirements:* For master's, GRE General Test. Additional exam requirements/ recommendations for international students: Required—TOEFL (minimum score 555 paper-based; 79 iBT). *Faculty research:* Counselor education, research for residential workers.

Western Seminary–Sacramento Campus, Program in Marital and Family Therapy, Sacramento, CA 95821. Offers MA. *Entrance requirements:* For master's, essays, undergraduate transcripts, 4 recommendations. Additional exam requirements/ recommendations for international students: Required—TOEFL.

Western Seminary–San Jose Campus, Graduate Programs, Los Gatos, CA 95032-4520. Offers Bible and theology (Graduate Diploma); Bible, camp and conference ministry (CGS); Biblical and theological studies (MA), including exegetical track, theological track; coaching (CGS); expositional ministry (M Div); marital and family therapy (MA); ministry (Graduate Diploma); ministry and leadership (MA), including camp and conference ministry, coaching, pastoral care to women, youth ministry; pastoral care to women (CGS, Graduate Diploma); pastoral ministry (M Div); theology (CGS); youth and family (CGS). Part-time and evening/weekend programs available. Postbaccalaureate distance learning degree programs offered (minimal on-campus study). *Entrance requirements:* For master's, minimum GPA of 3.0. Electronic applications accepted.

Wheaton College, Graduate School, Department of Psychology, Wheaton, IL 60187-5593. Offers clinical mental health counseling (MA); clinical psychology (MA, Psy D); counseling ministries (MA); marriage and family therapy (MA). *Accreditation:* APA (one or more programs are accredited). *Students:* 104 full-time (78 women), 22 part-time (14 women); includes 25 minority (13 Black or African American, non-Hispanic/Latino; 8 Asian, non-Hispanic/Latino; 2 Hispanic/Latino; 2 Two or more races, non-Hispanic/Latino), 8 international. Average age 27. 141 applicants, 74% accepted, 64 enrolled. In 2014, 47 master's, 16 doctorates awarded. Terminal master's awarded for partial completion of doctoral program. *Degree requirements:* For master's, thesis or alternative; for doctorate, thesis/dissertation, internship. *Entrance requirements:* For master's, GRE General Test, 18 hours of course work in psychology; for doctorate, GRE General Test. Additional exam requirements/recommendations for international

students: Required—TOEFL (minimum score 550 paper-based; 80 iBT), IELTS (minimum score 6.5), TOEFL (minimum score 600 paper-based; 90 iBT) or IELTS (minimum score 7.5) for Psy D. *Application deadline:* For fall admission, 3/1 priority date for domestic students, 1/1 for international students. Applications are processed on a rolling basis. Application fee: $30. *Financial support:* In 2014–15, 3 research assistantships (averaging $4,800 per year) were awarded; career-related internships or fieldwork, Federal Work-Study, scholarships/grants, and unspecified assistantships also available. Financial award application deadline: 3/1; financial award applicants required to submit FAFSA. *Unit head:* Dr. Terri Watson, Associate Dean of Psychology, 630-752-5104. *Application contact:* Dusty Di Santo, Director of Graduate Admissions, 630-752-5195, Fax: 630-752-7047, E-mail: graduate.admissions@wheaton.edu.
Website: http://www.wheaton.edu/academics/departments/psychology

Psychoanalysis and Psychotherapy

Adler Graduate School, Program in Adlerian Counseling and Psychotherapy, Richfield, MN 55423. Offers Adlerian studies (MA); art therapy (MA); clinical counseling (MA); co-occurring substance abuse and mental health disorders (MA); marriage and family therapy (MA); school counseling (MA). Part-time and evening/weekend programs available. *Faculty:* 7 full-time (6 women), 68 part-time/adjunct (49 women). *Students:* 368 part-time (283 women); includes 61 minority (41 Black or African American, non-Hispanic/Latino; 4 American Indian or Alaska Native, non-Hispanic/Latino; 8 Asian, non-Hispanic/Latino; 8 Hispanic/Latino). Average age 40. In 2014, 90 master's awarded. *Degree requirements:* For master's, thesis or alternative, 500-700 hour internship (depending on license choice). *Entrance requirements:* For master's, personal goal statement, three letters of reference, resume or work history, official transcripts. *Application deadline:* Applications are processed on a rolling basis. Application fee: $50. Electronic applications accepted. *Expenses: Tuition:* Full-time $6060; part-time $505 per credit. *Financial support:* Career-related internships or fieldwork and tuition waivers available. Support available to part-time students. Financial award applicants required to submit FAFSA. *Unit head:* Dr. Dan Haugen, President, 612-767-7048, Fax: 612-861-7559, E-mail: haugen@alfredadler.edu. *Application contact:* Evelyn B. Haas, Director of Admissions, 612-767-7044, Fax: 612-861-7559, E-mail: ev@alfredadler.edu.

★ **Adler University,** Programs in Psychology, Chicago, IL 60602. Offers advanced Adlerian psychotherapy (Certificate); art therapy (MA); clinical neuropsychology (Certificate); clinical psychology (Psy D); community psychology (MA); counseling and organizational psychology (MA); counseling psychology (MA); criminology (MA); emergency management leadership (MA); forensic psychology (MA); marriage and family counseling (MA); marriage and family therapy (Certificate); military psychology (MA); nonprofit management (MA); organizational psychology (MA); police psychology (MA); public policy and administration (MA); rehabilitation counseling (MA); sport and health psychology (MA); substance abuse counseling (Certificate); Psy D/Certificate; Psy D/MACAT; Psy D/MACP; Psy D/MAMFC; Psy D/MASAC. *Accreditation:* APA. Part-time and evening/weekend programs available. Postbaccalaureate distance learning degree programs offered (minimal on-campus study). Terminal master's awarded for partial completion of doctoral program. *Degree requirements:* For master's, thesis or alternative, oral exam, practicum; for doctorate, thesis/dissertation, clinical exam, internship, oral exam, practicum, written qualifying exam. *Entrance requirements:* For master's, 12 semester hours in psychology, minimum GPA of 3.0; for doctorate, 18 semester hours in psychology, minimum GPA of 3.25; for Certificate, appropriate master's or doctoral degree. Additional exam requirements/recommendations for international students: Required—TOEFL (minimum score 550 paper-based; 79 iBT). Electronic applications accepted.
See Display on page 969 and Close-Up on page 1207.

Argosy University, Chicago, College of Psychology and Behavioral Sciences, Doctoral Program in Clinical Psychology, Chicago, IL 60601. Offers child and adolescent psychology (Psy D); client-centered and experiential psychotherapies (Psy D); diversity and multicultural psychology (Psy D); family psychology (Psy D); forensic psychology (Psy D); health psychology (Psy D); neuropsychology (Psy D); organizational consulting (Psy D); psychoanalytic psychology (Psy D); psychology and spirituality (Psy D). *Accreditation:* APA.

Atlantic University, Program in Integrated Imagery - Regression Hypnosis, Virginia Beach, VA 23451-2061. Offers Graduate Certificate. *Entrance requirements:* For degree, bachelor's degree, minimum undergraduate GPA of 3.0, official transcripts, 1000-word essay. Application fee: $50. *Expenses:* Expenses: Contact institution. *Application contact:* Rachel Alvidrez, Educational Services Manager, 757-631-8101, Fax: 757-631-8096, E-mail: info@atlanticuniv.edu.
Website: http://www.atlanticuniv.edu/integratedimagery.html

Boston Graduate School of Psychoanalysis, BGSP-New Jersey, Brookline, MA 02446-4602. Offers psychoanalysis (MA); psychoanalytic counseling (MA). Programs offered in conjunction with Academic of Clinical and Applied Psychoanalysis in Livingston, NJ.

Boston Graduate School of Psychoanalysis, CAGS and Certificate Programs, Brookline, MA 02446-4602. Offers child and adolescent intervention (CAGS); psychoanalysis (Certificate); psychoanalytic psychotherapy (CAGS). Part-time programs available. *Degree requirements:* For other advanced degree, thesis. *Entrance requirements:* For degree, interview, BA, writing sample, 3 letters of reference, transcripts. Additional exam requirements/recommendations for international students: Required—TOEFL (minimum score 550 paper-based; 79 iBT). *Faculty research:* Treatment approaches for intractable patients, unconscious symbolic processes, female adolescent development, evaluation of school mental health interventions, development of symbolic processes in early childhood.

Boston Graduate School of Psychoanalysis, Doctoral Programs, Brookline, MA 02446-4602. Offers psychoanalysis (Psya D); psychoanalysis, society and culture (Psya D). Part-time programs available. *Degree requirements:* For doctorate, thesis/dissertation. *Entrance requirements:* For doctorate, interview, BA, personal statement, writing sample, 3 letters of recommendation. Additional exam requirements/recommendations for international students: Required—TOEFL (minimum score 550 paper-based; 79 iBT). *Faculty research:* Unconscious symbolic processes, female adolescent development, psychodynamics of social processes, dreams and other symbolic processes, cultural expressions of psychopathology.

Boston Graduate School of Psychoanalysis, Master's Programs, Brookline, MA 02446-4602. Offers mental health counseling (MA); psychoanalysis (MA); psychoanalysis, society and culture (MA). Part-time programs available. Terminal master's awarded for partial completion of doctoral program. *Degree requirements:* For

master's, thesis. *Entrance requirements:* For master's, interview, BA, personal statement, writing sample, 3 letters of recommendation. Additional exam requirements/recommendations for international students: Required—TOEFL (minimum score 550 paper-based; 79 iBT). *Faculty research:* Qualitative and narrative research methodologies, ethical conflicts and dual loyalties in health professionals, psychodynamics of social processes, treatment approaches for intractable patients, psychoanalytic research methodologies.

Boston Graduate School of Psychoanalysis, New York Graduate School of Psychoanalysis, New York, NY 10011. Offers MA. Part-time programs available. *Degree requirements:* For master's, thesis. *Entrance requirements:* For master's, interview, BA, writing sample, letters of recommendation. Additional exam requirements/recommendations for international students: Required—TOEFL.

Immaculata University, College of Graduate Studies, Department of Psychology, Immaculata, PA 19345. Offers clinical mental health counseling (MA); clinical psychology (Psy D); forensic psychology (Graduate Certificate); integrative psychotherapy (Graduate Certificate); neuropsychology (Graduate Certificate); psychodynamic psychotherapy (Graduate Certificate); psychological testing (Graduate Certificate); school counseling (MA, Graduate Certificate); school psychology (MA). *Accreditation:* APA. Part-time and evening/weekend programs available. Terminal master's awarded for partial completion of doctoral program. *Degree requirements:* For master's, comprehensive exam, thesis optional; for doctorate, comprehensive exam, thesis/dissertation. *Entrance requirements:* For master's, GRE General Test or MAT, minimum GPA of 3.0; for doctorate, GRE General Test or MAT, minimum GPA of 3.5. Additional exam requirements/recommendations for international students: Required—TOEFL, IELTS. Electronic applications accepted. *Faculty research:* Supervision ethics, psychology of teaching, gender.

Naropa University, Graduate Programs, Program in Contemplative Psychotherapy, Boulder, CO 80302-6697. Offers MA. *Faculty:* 2 full-time (0 women), 7 part-time/adjunct (4 women). *Students:* 78 full-time (48 women); includes 6 minority (4 Hispanic/Latino; 2 Two or more races, non-Hispanic/Latino), 7 international. Average age 32. 63 applicants, 68% accepted, 35 enrolled. In 2014, 29 master's awarded. *Degree requirements:* For master's, thesis, internship. *Entrance requirements:* For master's, in-person interview, resume, 2 letters of recommendation, statement of interest, transcripts. Additional exam requirements/recommendations for international students: Required—TOEFL (minimum score 600 paper-based; 80 iBT). *Application deadline:* For fall admission, 1/15 priority date for domestic and international students. Applications are processed on a rolling basis. Application fee: $60. Electronic applications accepted. *Expenses: Tuition:* Full-time $23,400; part-time $975 per credit. *Required fees:* $335 per semester. Tuition and fees vary according to course load. *Financial support:* In 2014–15, 25 students received support, including 5 research assistantships with partial tuition reimbursements available (averaging $5,600 per year); career-related internships or fieldwork, scholarships/grants, tuition waivers (partial), and unspecified assistantships also available. Support available to part-time students. Financial award application deadline: 3/1; financial award applicants required to submit FAFSA. *Unit head:* Dr. Deborah Bowman, Dean, Graduate School of Psychology, 303-546-3559, E-mail: bowman@naropa.edu. *Application contact:* Office of Admissions, 303-546-3572, Fax: 303-546-3583.
Website: http://www.naropa.edu/academics/gsp/grad/contemplative-counseling-psychotherapy-ma/index.php

Naropa University, Graduate Programs, Program in Somatic Counseling Psychology, Concentration in Body Psychotherapy, Boulder, CO 80302-6697. Offers MA. *Faculty:* 4 full-time (3 women), 7 part-time/adjunct (all women). *Students:* 23 full-time (19 women), 9 part-time (8 women); includes 6 minority (2 American Indian or Alaska Native, non-Hispanic/Latino; 4 Two or more races, non-Hispanic/Latino), 2 international. Average age 35. 26 applicants, 77% accepted, 11 enrolled. In 2014, 15 master's awarded. *Degree requirements:* For master's, comprehensive exam, thesis, internship, counseling experiential, clinical practicum. *Entrance requirements:* For master's, interview; course work in psychology and anatomy; resume; 2 letters of recommendation; transcripts; minimum 100 hours of volunteer fieldwork experience in a supervised setting in the mental health field or through work in a community facility or service organization; supplemental essay; formal training in somatic practice. Additional exam requirements/recommendations for international students: Required—TOEFL (minimum score 600 paper-based; 80 iBT). *Application deadline:* For fall admission, 1/15 priority date for domestic and international students. Applications are processed on a rolling basis. Application fee: $60. Electronic applications accepted. *Expenses: Tuition:* Full-time $23,400; part-time $975 per credit. *Required fees:* $335 per semester. Tuition and fees vary according to course load. *Financial support:* In 2014–15, 11 students received support. Career-related internships or fieldwork, scholarships/grants, tuition waivers (partial), and unspecified assistantships available. Support available to part-time students. Financial award application deadline: 3/1; financial award applicants required to submit FAFSA. *Unit head:* Dr. Deborah Bowman, Dean, Graduate School of Psychology, 303-546-3559, E-mail: bowman@naropa.edu. *Application contact:* Office of Admissions, 303-546-3572, Fax: 303-546-3583, E-mail: admissions@naropa.edu.
Website: http://www.naropa.edu/academics/gsp/grad/somatic-counseling-psychology-ma/body-psychotherapy/index.php

New York University, Graduate School of Arts and Science, Department of Psychology, New York, NY 10012-1019. Offers cognition and perception (PhD); community psychology (PhD); general psychology (MA); industrial/organizational psychology (MA); psychotherapy and psychoanalysis (Advanced Certificate); social/personality psychology (PhD). Part-time programs available. *Students:* 270 full-time (183 women), 162 part-time (115 women); includes 92 minority (14 Black or African

American, non-Hispanic/Latino; 36 Asian, non-Hispanic/Latino; 33 Hispanic/Latino; 9 Two or more races, non-Hispanic/Latino), 114 international. Average age 31. 874 applicants, 46% accepted, 153 enrolled. In 2014, 102 master's, 9 doctorates, 10 other advanced degrees awarded. Terminal master's awarded for partial completion of doctoral program. *Degree requirements:* For master's, comprehensive exam, thesis or alternative; for doctorate, thesis/dissertation. *Entrance requirements:* For master's and doctorate, GRE General Test. Additional exam requirements/recommendations for international students: Required—TOEFL. *Application deadline:* For fall admission, 12/12 for domestic and international students. Application fee: $100. *Financial support:* Fellowships with tuition reimbursements, research assistantships with tuition reimbursements, teaching assistantships with tuition reimbursements, career-related internships or fieldwork, Federal Work-Study, institutionally sponsored loans, scholarships/grants, traineeships, health care benefits, and unspecified assistantships available. Financial award application deadline: 12/12; financial award applicants required to submit FAFSA. *Faculty research:* Vision, memory, social cognition, social and cognitive development, relationships. *Unit head:* Gabriele Oettingen, Director of Graduate Studies, PhD Program, 212-998-7900, Fax: 212-995-4018, E-mail: psychq@psych.nyu.edu. *Application contact:* Adrienne Gans, Director of Graduate Studies, MA Program, 212-998-7900, Fax: 212-995-4018, E-mail: psychq@psych.nyu.edu.
Website: http://www.psych.nyu.edu/

Prescott College, Graduate Programs, Program in Counseling and Psychology, Prescott, AZ 86301. Offers adventure-based psychotherapy (MA); counseling psychology (MA); ecopsychology (MA); ecotherapy (MA); equine-assisted mental health (MA); expressive arts therapy (MA); somatic psychology (MA); student-directed independent study (MA). Part-time programs available. Postbaccalaureate distance learning degree programs offered (minimal on-campus study). *Degree requirements:* For master's, thesis, fieldwork or internship, practicum. *Entrance requirements:* For master's, 2 letters of recommendation, resume. Additional exam requirements/recommendations for international students: Required—TOEFL (minimum score 500 paper-based). Electronic applications accepted.

Regent University, Graduate School, School of Communication and the Arts, Virginia Beach, VA 23464-9800. Offers acting (MFA); communication (MA, PhD), including political communication (MA), strategic communication (MA); directing for cinema/television (MFA); film and TV (MA), including producing, production, script writing; journalism (MA); producing for cinema/television (MFA); script and screenwriting (MFA); theatre (MA). Part-time programs available. Postbaccalaureate distance learning degree programs offered (minimal on-campus study). *Faculty:* 20 full-time (3 women), 26 part-time/adjunct (7 women). *Students:* 89 full-time (49 women), 211 part-time (125 women); includes 92 minority (69 Black or African American, non-Hispanic/Latino; 2 American Indian or Alaska Native, non-Hispanic/Latino; 2 Asian, non-Hispanic/Latino; 19 Hispanic/Latino), 10 international. Average age 35. 199 applicants, 53% accepted, 77 enrolled. In 2014, 48 master's, 8 doctorates awarded. *Degree requirements:* For master's, thesis or alternative; for doctorate, thesis/dissertation. *Entrance requirements:* For master's, GRE General Test or MAT, minimum undergraduate GPA of 3.0, writing sample, computer literacy survey, recommendation, resume, interview, audition (for MFA programs); for doctorate, GRE General Test, minimum graduate GPA of 3.0, writing sample, computer literacy survey, recommendation, interview, transcripts. Additional exam requirements/recommendations for international students: Required—TOEFL (minimum score 577 paper-based). *Application deadline:* For fall admission, 3/1 priority date for domestic students; for spring admission, 10/1 priority date for domestic students. Applications are processed on a rolling basis. Application fee: $50. Electronic applications accepted. *Expenses:* Expenses: Contact institution. *Financial support:* Fellowships with full and partial tuition reimbursements, career-related internships or fieldwork, scholarships/grants, tuition waivers (full and partial), and unspecified assistantships available. Support available to part-time students. Financial award application deadline: 9/1; financial award applicants required to submit FAFSA. *Faculty research:* Southern gospel music, education and entertainment, celebrities and the media, journalism and ethics, C.S. Lewis. *Unit head:* Dr. Mitch Land, Dean, 757-352-4916, Fax: 757-352-4291, E-mail: mland@regent.edu. *Application contact:* Matthew Chadwick, Director of Enrollment Support Services, 800-373-5504, Fax: 757-352-4381, E-mail: admissions@regent.edu.
Website: http://www.regent.edu/acad/schcom/

Rehabilitation Counseling

★ **Adler University,** Programs in Psychology, Chicago, IL 60602. Offers advanced Adlerian psychotherapy (Certificate); art therapy (MA); clinical neuropsychology (Certificate); clinical psychology (Psy D); community psychology (MA); counseling and organizational psychology (MA); counseling psychology (MA); criminology (MA); emergency management leadership (MA); forensic psychology (MA); marriage and family counseling (MA); marriage and family therapy (Certificate); military psychology (MA); nonprofit management (MA); organizational psychology (MA); police psychology (MA); public policy and administration (MA); rehabilitation counseling (MA); sport and health psychology (MA); substance abuse counseling (Certificate); Psy D/Certificate; Psy D/MACAT; Psy D/MACP; Psy D/MAMFC; Psy D/MASAC. *Accreditation:* APA. Part-time and evening/weekend programs available. Postbaccalaureate distance learning degree programs offered (minimal on-campus study). Terminal master's awarded for partial completion of doctoral program. *Degree requirements:* For master's, thesis or alternative, oral exam, practicum; for doctorate, thesis/dissertation, clinical exam, internship, oral exam, practicum, written qualifying exam. *Entrance requirements:* For master's, 12 semester hours in psychology, minimum GPA of 3.0; for doctorate, 18 semester hours in psychology, minimum GPA of 3.25; for Certificate, appropriate master's or doctoral degree. Additional exam requirements/recommendations for international students: Required—TOEFL (minimum score 550 paper-based; 79 iBT). Electronic applications accepted.

See Display on page 969 and Close-Up on page 1207.

Alabama State University, College of Health Sciences, Department of Rehabilitation Counseling, Montgomery, AL 36101-0271. Offers MRC. *Accreditation:* CORE. *Faculty:* 3 full-time (2 women). *Students:* 29 full-time (25 women), 2 part-time (1 woman); includes 29 minority (all Black or African American, non-Hispanic/Latino). Average age 28. 35 applicants, 66% accepted, 21 enrolled. In 2014, 22 master's awarded. *Degree requirements:* For master's, comprehensive exam. *Application deadline:* For fall admission, 4/1 priority date for domestic students. Application fee: $25. *Financial support:* In 2014–15, 3 research assistantships (averaging $4,920 per year) were awarded. *Unit head:* Dothel W. Edwards, Chair, 334-229-8858, E-mail: dedwards@alasu.edu. *Application contact:* Dr. William Person, Dean of Graduate Studies, 334-229-4274, Fax: 334-229-4928, E-mail: wperson@alasu.edu.
Website: http://www.alasu.edu/academics/colleges—departments/health-sciences/rehabilitation-studies/master-of-rehabilitation-counseling/index.aspx

Arkansas State University, Graduate School, College of Education and Behavioral Science, Department of Psychology and Counseling, State University, AR 72467. Offers clinical mental health counseling (Certificate); college student personnel services (MS); psychology and counseling (Ed S); rehabilitation counseling (MRC); school counseling (MSE); student affairs (Certificate). *Accreditation:* ACA (one or more programs are accredited); CORE (one or more programs are accredited); NCATE. Part-time programs available. *Faculty:* 15 full-time (9 women). *Students:* 57 full-time (36 women), 51 part-time (38 women); includes 21 minority (19 Black or African American, non-Hispanic/Latino; 1 Hispanic/Latino; 1 Two or more races, non-Hispanic/Latino), 1 international. Average age 30. 102 applicants, 54% accepted, 48 enrolled. In 2014, 22 master's, 22 other advanced degrees awarded. *Degree requirements:* For master's and other advanced degree, comprehensive exam, thesis or alternative. *Entrance requirements:* For master's, GRE General Test or MAT (for MSE), appropriate bachelor's degree, interview, letters of reference, official transcripts, immunization records, written statement, 2-3 page autobiography; for other advanced degree, GRE General Test, interview, master's degree, letters of reference, official transcript, personal statement, immunization records. Additional exam requirements/recommendations for international students: Required—TOEFL (minimum score 550 paper-based; 79 iBT), IELTS (minimum score 6), PTE (minimum score 56). *Application deadline:* Applications are processed on a rolling basis. Application fee: $30 ($40 for international students). Electronic applications accepted. *Expenses:* Tuition, state resident: full-time $4392; part-time $244 per credit hour. Tuition, nonresident: full-time $8784; part-time $488 per credit hour. *International tuition:* $9484 full-time. *Required fees:* $1134; $63 per credit hour. $25 per term. Tuition and fees vary according to course load and program. *Financial support:* In 2014–15, 8 students received support. Teaching assistantships, career-related internships or fieldwork, scholarships/grants, and unspecified assistantships available. Financial award application deadline: 7/1; financial award applicants required to submit FAFSA. *Unit head:* Dr. Kris Biondolillo, Interim Chair, 870-972-3064, Fax: 870-972-3962, E-mail: kdbiondo@astate.edu. *Application contact:* Vickey Ring, Graduate Admissions Coordinator, 870-972-3029, Fax: 870-972-3857, E-mail: vickeyring@astate.edu.
Website: http://www.astate.edu/college/education/departments/psychology-and-counseling/index.dot

Assumption College, Rehabilitation Counseling Program, Worcester, MA 01609-1296. Offers MA, CAGS. *Accreditation:* CORE. Part-time and evening/weekend programs available. Postbaccalaureate distance learning degree programs offered (minimal on-campus study). *Faculty:* 1 full-time (0 women), 15 part-time/adjunct (5 women). *Students:* 41 full-time (34 women), 48 part-time (31 women); includes 14 minority (10 Black or African American, non-Hispanic/Latino; 1 Asian, non-Hispanic/Latino; 2 Hispanic/Latino; 1 Two or more races, non-Hispanic/Latino), 1 international. Average age 33. 58 applicants, 64% accepted, 29 enrolled. In 2014, 34 master's, 1 other advanced degree awarded. *Degree requirements:* For master's, comprehensive exam, internship, practicum. *Entrance requirements:* For master's and CAGS, 3 letters of recommendation, resume, interview, essay. Additional exam requirements/recommendations for international students: Required—TOEFL (minimum score 540 paper-based; 76 iBT), IELTS (minimum score 6). *Application deadline:* For fall admission, 4/1 for domestic and international students; for winter admission, 2/1 for domestic and international students; for spring admission, 4/1 for domestic and international students. Applications are processed on a rolling basis. Application fee: $30. Electronic applications accepted. *Expenses: Tuition:* Full-time $10,620; part-time $590 per credit. *Required fees:* $20 per term. Full-time tuition and fees vary according to course load and program. *Financial support:* In 2014–15, 7 students received support. Scholarships/grants, tuition waivers (full and partial), unspecified assistantships, and institutional discounts available. Financial award application deadline: 3/1; financial award applicants required to submit FAFSA. *Faculty research:* Job placement for severe disabilities, vocational counseling, conflict resolution, health issues in mental illness. *Unit head:* A. Lee Pearson, Director, 508-767-7063, Fax: 508-798-2872, E-mail: lpearson@assumption.edu. *Application contact:* Dr. Landy Johnson, Director of Operations for Graduate and Professional Studies, 508-767-7666, Fax: 508-767-7030, E-mail: graduate@assumption.edu.
Website: http://graduate.assumption.edu/rehabilitation-counseling/masterofarts

Auburn University, Graduate School, College of Education, Department of Special Education, Rehabilitation, Counseling and School Psychology, Auburn University, AL 36849. Offers collaborative teacher special education (M Ed, MS); early childhood special education (M Ed, MS); rehabilitation counseling (M Ed, MS, PhD). *Accreditation:* CORE; NCATE. Part-time programs available. *Faculty:* 18 full-time (14 women), 8 part-time/adjunct (7 women). *Students:* 142 full-time (118 women), 80 part-time (64 women); includes 57 minority (53 Black or African American, non-Hispanic/Latino; 1 American Indian or Alaska Native, non-Hispanic/Latino; 2 Asian, non-Hispanic/Latino; 1 Hispanic/Latino). Average age 30. 239 applicants, 42% accepted, 83 enrolled. In 2014, 59 master's, 10 doctorates awarded. *Degree requirements:* For master's, thesis (for some programs); for doctorate, thesis/dissertation. *Entrance requirements:* For master's, GRE General Test; for doctorate, GRE General Test, interview. *Application deadline:* For fall admission, 7/7 for domestic students; for spring admission, 11/24 for domestic students. Applications are processed on a rolling basis. Application fee: $50 ($60 for international students). Electronic applications accepted. *Expenses:* Tuition, state resident: full-time $8586; part-time $477 per credit hour. Tuition, nonresident: full-time $25,758; part-time $1431 per credit hour. *Required fees:* $804 per semester. Tuition and fees vary according to degree level and program. *Financial support:* Research assistantships, teaching assistantships, and Federal Work-Study available. Support available to part-time students. Financial award application deadline: 3/15; financial award applicants required to submit FAFSA. *Faculty research:* Emotional conflict/behavior disorders, gifted and talented, learning disabilities, mental retardation, multi-handicapped. *Unit head:* Dr. E. Davis Martin, Jr., Head, 334-844-7676. *Application contact:* Dr. George Flowers, Dean of the Graduate School, 334-844-2125.

Barry University, School of Education, Program in Rehabilitation Counseling, Miami Shores, FL 33161-6695. Offers MS, Ed S. Part-time and evening/weekend programs available. *Degree requirements:* For master's, comprehensive exam, scholarly paper; for Ed S, comprehensive exam. *Entrance requirements:* For master's, GRE General

Test or MAT, minimum GPA of 3.0; for Ed S, GRE General Test, minimum GPA of 3.0. Electronic applications accepted.

Bayamón Central University, Graduate Programs, Program in Education, Bayamón, PR 00960-1725. Offers administration and supervision (MA Ed); commercial education (MA Ed); elementary education (K–3) (MA Ed); family counseling (Graduate Certificate); guidance and counseling (MA Ed); pre-elementary teacher (MA Ed); rehabilitation counseling (MA Ed); special education (MA Ed), including attention deficit disorder, education of the autistic, learning disabilities. Part-time and evening/weekend programs available. *Degree requirements:* For master's, comprehensive exam. *Entrance requirements:* For master's, EXADEP, bachelor's degree in education or related field.

Bowling Green State University, Graduate College, College of Education and Human Development, School of Education and Intervention Services, Intervention Services Division, Program in Rehabilitation Counseling, Bowling Green, OH 43403. Offers MRC. *Accreditation:* CORE. Part-time programs available. *Degree requirements:* For master's, thesis or alternative. *Entrance requirements:* For master's, GRE General Test, interview. Additional exam requirements/recommendations for international students: Required—TOEFL. Electronic applications accepted. *Faculty research:* Depression, disability management, schizophrenia, job analysis, rehabilitation counseling curriculum.

California State University, Fresno, Division of Graduate Studies, School of Education and Human Development, Department of Counseling and Special Education, Rehabilitation Counseling Program, Fresno, CA 93740-8027. Offers MS. *Accreditation:* CORE. Part-time and evening/weekend programs available. *Degree requirements:* For master's, thesis optional. *Entrance requirements:* For master's, GRE General Test, MAT, minimum GPA of 2.75. Additional exam requirements/recommendations for international students: Required—TOEFL. Electronic applications accepted. *Faculty research:* Aging, career development, job retention, rehabilitation administration.

California State University, Los Angeles, Graduate Studies, Charter College of Education, Division of Special Education and Counseling, Los Angeles, CA 90032-8530. Offers counseling (MS), including applied behavior analysis, community college counseling, rehabilitation counseling, school counseling, school psychology; special education (MA, PhD). *Accreditation:* ACA. Part-time and evening/weekend programs available. *Entrance requirements:* For master's, minimum GPA of 2.75 in last 90 units of course work, teaching certificate. Additional exam requirements/recommendations for international students: Required—TOEFL (minimum score 500 paper-based). Electronic applications accepted. *Expenses:* Tuition, state resident: full-time $6738; part-time $3609 per year. Tuition, nonresident: full-time $15,666; part-time $8073 per year. Tuition and fees vary according to course load, degree level and program.

California State University, San Bernardino, Graduate Studies, College of Education, Program in Counseling and Guidance, San Bernardino, CA 92407-2397. Offers counseling and guidance (MS); rehabilitation counseling (MA). *Accreditation:* NCATE. Part-time and evening/weekend programs available. *Students:* 123 full-time (104 women), 13 part-time (9 women); includes 88 minority (4 Black or African American, non-Hispanic/Latino; 3 Asian, non-Hispanic/Latino; 81 Hispanic/Latino), 1 international. Average age 27. 92 applicants, 74% accepted, 60 enrolled. In 2014, 33 master's awarded. *Degree requirements:* For master's, comprehensive exam, thesis or alternative. *Entrance requirements:* Additional exam requirements/recommendations for international students: Required—TOEFL. *Application deadline:* For fall admission, 7/17 for domestic students. Application fee: $55. *Expenses:* Tuition, state resident: full-time $6738; part-time $1302 per term. Tuition, nonresident: full-time $17,898; part-time $248 per unit. *Required fees:* $365 per quarter. Tuition and fees vary according to degree level and program. *Unit head:* Dr. Judith Sylva, Chair, 909-537-5606, E-mail: jsylva@csusb.edu. *Application contact:* Dr. Jeffrey Thompson, Dean of Graduate Studies, 909-537-5058, E-mail: jthompso@csusb.edu.

California State University, San Bernardino, Graduate Studies, College of Education, Programs in Special Education and Rehabilitation Counseling, San Bernardino, CA 92407-2397. Offers MA. *Accreditation:* CORE; NCATE. Part-time and evening/weekend programs available. *Students:* 64 full-time (58 women), 105 part-time (81 women); includes 90 minority (15 Black or African American, non-Hispanic/Latino; 1 American Indian or Alaska Native, non-Hispanic/Latino; 2 Asian, non-Hispanic/Latino; 63 Hispanic/Latino; 9 Two or more races, non-Hispanic/Latino), 7 international. Average age 35. 106 applicants, 82% accepted, 62 enrolled. In 2014, 58 master's awarded. *Degree requirements:* For master's, thesis or alternative. *Entrance requirements:* Additional exam requirements/recommendations for international students: Required—TOEFL. *Application deadline:* For fall admission, 7/17 for domestic students. Application fee: $55. *Expenses:* Tuition, state resident: full-time $6738; part-time $1302 per term. Tuition, nonresident: full-time $17,898; part-time $248 per unit. *Required fees:* $365 per quarter. Tuition and fees vary according to degree level and program. *Financial support:* Career-related internships or fieldwork and Federal Work-Study available. Support available to part-time students. *Unit head:* Dr. Judith Sylva, Chair, 909-537-5606, E-mail: jsylva@csusb.edu. *Application contact:* Dr. Jeffrey Thompson, Dean of Graduate Studies, 909-537-5058, E-mail: jthompso@csusb.edu.

Central Connecticut State University, School of Graduate Studies, School of Education and Professional Studies, Department of Counselor Education and Family Therapy, New Britain, CT 06050-4010. Offers marriage and family therapy (MS); professional counseling (MS, AC, Certificate); school counseling (MS); student development in higher education (MS). *Accreditation:* AAMFT/COAMFTE; ACA. Part-time and evening/weekend programs available. *Faculty:* 11 full-time (7 women), 21 part-time/adjunct (17 women). *Students:* 142 full-time (122 women), 208 part-time (165 women); includes 94 minority (49 Black or African American, non-Hispanic/Latino; 4 Asian, non-Hispanic/Latino; 34 Hispanic/Latino; 7 Two or more races, non-Hispanic/Latino), 2 international. Average age 34. 215 applicants, 53% accepted, 91 enrolled. In 2014, 101 master's, 5 other advanced degrees awarded. *Degree requirements:* For master's, comprehensive exam, thesis or alternative; for other advanced degree, qualifying exam. *Entrance requirements:* For master's, minimum undergraduate GPA of 2.7, essay, interview, letters of recommendation. Additional exam requirements/recommendations for international students: Required—TOEFL (minimum score 550 paper-based; 79 iBT). *Application deadline:* For fall admission, 4/1 for domestic and international students; for spring admission, 11/1 for domestic and international students. Applications are processed on a rolling basis. Application fee: $50. Electronic applications accepted. *Expenses: Tuition, area resident:* Full-time $5730; part-time $534 per credit. Tuition, state resident: full-time $8596; part-time $534 per credit. Tuition, nonresident: full-time $15,964; part-time $548 per credit. *Required fees:* $4211; $215 per credit. *Financial support:* In 2014–15, 41 students received support, including 21 research assistantships; career-related internships or fieldwork, Federal Work-Study, scholarships/grants, and unspecified assistantships also available. Support available to part-time students. Financial award application deadline: 3/1; financial award applicants required to submit FAFSA. *Faculty research:* Elementary and secondary school counseling, marriage and family therapy, rehabilitation counseling, counseling in higher educational settings. *Unit head:* Dr. Connie Tait, Chair, 860-832-2154, E-mail: taitc@ccsu.edu. *Application contact:* Patricia Gardner, Associate Director of Graduate Studies, 860-832-2350, Fax: 860-832-2362, E-mail: graduateadmissions@ccsu.edu. Website: http://web.ccsu.edu/seps/departments/counselingFamilyTherapy/default.asp

Coppin State University, Division of Graduate Studies, Division of Arts and Sciences, Department of Applied Psychology and Rehabilitation Counseling, Program in Rehabilitation Counseling, Baltimore, MD 21216-3698. Offers M Ed. *Accreditation:* CORE. Part-time programs available. *Degree requirements:* For master's, comprehensive exam (for some programs), thesis optional, internship, clinical requirements. *Entrance requirements:* For master's, GRE General Test, interview, minimum GPA of 3.0.

East Carolina University, Graduate School, College of Allied Health Sciences, Department of Addictions and Rehabilitation Studies, Greenville, NC 27858-4353. Offers military and trauma counseling (Certificate); rehabilitation and career counseling (MS); rehabilitation counseling (Certificate); rehabilitation counseling and administration (PhD); substance abuse and clinical counseling (MS); substance abuse counseling (Certificate); vocational evaluation (Certificate). *Accreditation:* CORE. Part-time and evening/weekend programs available. *Degree requirements:* For master's, comprehensive exam, thesis or alternative, internship. *Entrance requirements:* For master's, GRE General Test or MAT. Additional exam requirements/recommendations for international students: Required—TOEFL. *Application deadline:* For fall admission, 3/1 priority date for domestic students; for spring admission, 10/1 priority date for domestic students. Applications are processed on a rolling basis. Application fee: $50. *Expenses:* Tuition, state resident: full-time $4223. Tuition, nonresident: full-time $16,540. *Required fees:* $2184. *Financial support:* Research assistantships with partial tuition reimbursements, teaching assistantships with partial tuition reimbursements, Federal Work-Study, and scholarships/grants available. Support available to part-time students. Financial award application deadline: 3/1. *Unit head:* Dr. Paul Toriello, Chair, 252-744-6292, E-mail: toriellop@ecu.edu. Website: http://www.ecu.edu/rehb/

East Central University, School of Graduate Studies, Department of Human Resources, Ada, OK 74820. Offers administration (MSHR); counseling (MSHR); criminal justice (MSHR); human services (MSHR); rehabilitation counseling (MSHR). *Accreditation:* CORE. Part-time and evening/weekend programs available. *Degree requirements:* For master's, thesis optional. *Entrance requirements:* For master's, GRE General Test, MAT, minimum GPA of 2.5. Electronic applications accepted.

Edinboro University of Pennsylvania, Department of Counseling, School Psychology and Special Education, Edinboro, PA 16444. Offers counseling (MA), including art therapy, clinical mental health counseling, college counseling, rehabilitation counseling, school counseling; educational psychology (M Ed); school psychology (Ed S); special education (M Ed), including autism, behavior management. Part-time and evening/weekend programs available. *Degree requirements:* For master's, thesis or alternative, competency exam; for Ed S, thesis or alternative. *Entrance requirements:* For master's and Ed S, GRE or MAT, minimum QPA of 2.5. Electronic applications accepted.

Emporia State University, Program in Rehabilitation Counseling, Emporia, KS 66801-5415. Offers MS. *Accreditation:* CORE. Part-time programs available. *Students:* 6 full-time (3 women), 14 part-time (all women); includes 6 minority (2 Black or African American, non-Hispanic/Latino; 1 Asian, non-Hispanic/Latino; 3 Hispanic/Latino). 3 applicants, 100% accepted, 3 enrolled. In 2014, 7 master's awarded. *Degree requirements:* For master's, comprehensive exam or thesis, practicum. *Entrance requirements:* For master's, GRE or MAT, essay exam, appropriate bachelor's degree, interview, letters of recommendation. *Application deadline:* For fall admission, 8/15 priority date for domestic students. Applications are processed on a rolling basis. Application fee: $30 ($75 for international students). Electronic applications accepted. *Expenses:* Tuition, state resident: part-time $227 per credit hour. Tuition, nonresident: part-time $706 per credit hour. *Required fees:* $75 per credit hour. Tuition and fees vary according to campus/location. *Financial support:* Career-related internships or fieldwork, Federal Work-Study, institutionally sponsored loans, health care benefits, and unspecified assistantships available. Financial award application deadline: 3/15; financial award applicants required to submit FAFSA. *Unit head:* Dr. James Costello, Chair/Graduate Co-Coordinator, 620-341-5791, E-mail: jcostell@emporia.edu. *Application contact:* Mary Sewell, Admissions Coordinator, 800-950-GRAD, Fax: 620-341-5909, E-mail: msewell@emporia.edu.

Florida Atlantic University, College of Education, Department of Counselor Education, Boca Raton, FL 33431-0991. Offers counselor education (M Ed, PhD, Ed S); marriage and family therapy (Ed S); mental health counseling (M Ed, Ed S); rehabilitation counseling (M Ed); school counseling (M Ed, Ed S). *Accreditation:* ACA; NCATE. Part-time and evening/weekend programs available. *Degree requirements:* For Ed S, departmental qualifying exam. *Entrance requirements:* For master's, GRE General Test, minimum GPA of 3.0 during previous 2 years; for Ed S, GRE General Test, minimum graduate GPA of 3.25. Additional exam requirements/recommendations for international students: Required—TOEFL (minimum score 500 paper-based; 61 iBT), IELTS (minimum score 6). *Expenses:* Tuition, state resident: full-time $7396; part-time $369.82 per credit hour. Tuition, nonresident: full-time $19,392; part-time $1024.81 per credit hour. Tuition and fees vary according to course load. *Faculty research:* Brief therapy, psychological type, marriage and family counseling, international programs, integrated services.

Florida International University, College of Education, Department of Leadership and Professional Studies, Miami, FL 33199. Offers adult education and human resource development (MS, Ed D); counseling (MS), including rehabilitation counseling, school counseling; counselor education (MS), including clinical mental health counseling; educational administration and supervision (Ed D); educational leadership (MS, Certificate, Ed S); higher education (Ed D); higher education administration (MS); recreation and sport management (MS), including recreation and sport management, recreational therapy; school psychology (Ed S); urban education (MS), including instruction in urban settings, learning technologies, multicultural/bilingual, multicultural/TESOL, urban education. Part-time and evening/weekend programs available. *Degree requirements:* For doctorate, thesis/dissertation. *Entrance requirements:* For master's, minimum GPA of 3.0; for doctorate and other advanced degree, GRE General Test. Additional exam requirements/recommendations for international students: Required—TOEFL (minimum score 550 paper-based; 80 iBT), IELTS (minimum score 6.3). Electronic applications accepted.

Fort Valley State University, College of Graduate Studies and Extended Education, Department of Counseling Psychology, Program in Rehabilitation Counseling, Fort Valley, GA 31030. Offers MS. *Accreditation:* CORE. Part-time programs available. *Degree requirements:* For master's, comprehensive exam (for some programs), thesis optional. *Entrance requirements:* For master's, GRE General Test or MAT. Additional exam requirements/recommendations for international students: Recommended—TOEFL.

The George Washington University, Graduate School of Education and Human Development, Department of Counseling and Human Development, Program in Rehabilitation Counseling, Washington, DC 20052. Offers autism spectrum disorder (MA Ed/HD); substance abuse and psychiatric disabilities (MA Ed/HD); traumatic brain injury (MA Ed/HD). *Accreditation:* CORE. Postbaccalaureate distance learning degree programs offered. *Students:* 10 full-time (8 women), 21 part-time (14 women); includes 10 minority (7 Black or African American, non-Hispanic/Latino; 2 Asian, non-Hispanic/

Latino; 1 Two or more races, non-Hispanic/Latino), 2 international. Average age 31. 27 applicants, 89% accepted, 10 enrolled. In 2014, 17 master's awarded. *Entrance requirements:* For master's, GRE or MAT, two letters of recommendation, 1- to 2-page statement of purpose, official transcripts from all instiutions attended, resume. Additional exam requirements/recommendations for international students: Required—TOEFL or IELTS. Electronic applications accepted. *Unit head:* Dr. Kenneth C. Hergenrather, Director, 202-994-1334, E-mail: hergenkc@gwu.edu. *Application contact:* Sarah Lang, Director of Graduate Admissions, 202-994-1447, Fax: 202-994-7207, E-mail: slang@gwu.edu.
Website: http://gsehd.gwu.edu/rehabilitation-counseling-masters

Georgia State University, College of Education, Department of Counseling and Psychological Services, Program in Rehabilitation Counseling, Atlanta, GA 30302-3083. Offers MS. *Accreditation:* CORE. Postbaccalaureate distance learning degree programs offered (no on-campus study). *Degree requirements:* For master's, comprehensive exam. *Entrance requirements:* For master's, GRE, goal statement, resume, 3 letters of recommendation, transcripts. Additional exam requirements/recommendations for international students: Required—TOEFL. *Application deadline:* For fall admission, 2/1 for domestic and international students. Application fee: $50. Electronic applications accepted. *Expenses:* Tuition, state resident: full-time $6516; part-time $362 per credit hour. Tuition, nonresident: full-time $22,014; part-time $1223 per credit hour. *Required fees:* $2128 per semester. Tuition and fees vary according to course load and program. *Financial support:* In 2014–15, research assistantships with full and partial tuition reimbursements (averaging $13,000 per year), teaching assistantships with partial tuition reimbursements (averaging $1,000 per year) were awarded; career-related internships or fieldwork, institutionally sponsored loans, scholarships/grants, health care benefits, tuition waivers, and unspecified assistantships also available. Financial award application deadline: 4/1. *Faculty research:* Career counseling; sexual and gender minority issues; trauma, stress and coping; disability services; disability employment. *Unit head:* Dr. Brian Dew, Department Chair, 404-413-8168, Fax: 404-413-8013, E-mail: bdew@gsu.edu. *Application contact:* CPS Admissions Office, 404-413-8200.
Website: http://cps.education.gsu.edu/programs/clinical-rehabilitation-counseling/

Hofstra University, School of Health Sciences and Human Services, Programs in Counseling, Hempstead, NY 11549. Offers counseling (MS Ed, PD); creative arts therapy (MA); interdisciplinary transition specialist (Advanced Certificate); marriage and family therapy (MA); mental health counseling (MA); rehabilitation administration (PD); rehabilitation counseling (MS Ed, Advanced Certificate); rehabilitation counseling in mental health (MS Ed, Advanced Certificate); school counselor bilingual extension (Advanced Certificate). Part-time and evening/weekend programs available. *Students:* 138 full-time (128 women), 54 part-time (51 women); includes 53 minority (24 Black or African American, non-Hispanic/Latino; 1 American Indian or Alaska Native, non-Hispanic/Latino; 9 Asian, non-Hispanic/Latino; 18 Hispanic/Latino; 1 Two or more races, non-Hispanic/Latino), 6 international. Average age 30. 117 applicants, 83% accepted, 57 enrolled. In 2014, 72 master's, 4 other advanced degrees awarded. *Degree requirements:* For master's, comprehensive exam (for some programs), thesis (for some programs), internship, practicum, student teaching, seminars, minimum GPA of 3.0. *Entrance requirements:* For master's, GRE, interview, letters of recommendation, portfolio, essay, professional experience, certification; for other advanced degree, GRE, interview, letters of recommendation, essay, professional experience, resume, master's degree. Additional exam requirements/recommendations for international students: Required—TOEFL (minimum score 550 paper-based; 80 iBT). *Application deadline:* Applications are processed on a rolling basis. Application fee: $70 ($75 for international students). Electronic applications accepted. *Expenses: Tuition:* Full-time $20,610; part-time $1145 per credit hour. *Required fees:* $970; $165 per term. Tuition and fees vary according to program. *Financial support:* In 2014–15, 109 students received support, including 29 fellowships with full and partial tuition reimbursements available (averaging $3,381 per year), 4 research assistantships with full and partial tuition reimbursements available (averaging $7,324 per year); career-related internships or fieldwork, Federal Work-Study, institutionally sponsored loans, scholarships/grants, health care benefits, and tuition waivers (full and partial) also available. Support available to part-time students. Financial award applicants required to submit FAFSA. *Faculty research:* Bereavement, loss, and trauma counseling; conflict transformation, the impact of hope on academic success; student persistence; GLBTQ issues. *Unit head:* Dr. Holly Seirup, Chairperson, 516-463-5752, Fax: 516-463-6184, E-mail: vpshjs@hofstra.edu. *Application contact:* Sunil Samuel, Assistant Vice President of Admissions, 516-463-4723, Fax: 516-463-4664, E-mail: graduateadmission@hofstra.edu.
Website: http://www.hofstra.edu/academics/colleges/healthscienceshumanservices/

Hunter College of the City University of New York, Graduate School, School of Education, Department of Educational Foundations and Counseling Programs, Program in Rehabilitation Counseling, New York, NY 10065-5085. Offers MS Ed. *Accreditation:* CORE. *Degree requirements:* For master's, thesis, seminar. *Entrance requirements:* For master's, interview, minimum GPA of 2.7, recommendations. Additional exam requirements/recommendations for international students: Required—TOEFL, TWE. *Application deadline:* For fall admission, 4/1 for domestic students, 2/1 for international students; for spring admission, 11/1 for domestic students, 9/1 for international students. Applications are processed on a rolling basis. *Financial support:* Federal Work-Study and tuition waivers (partial) available. Support available to part-time students. *Unit head:* Dr. Arnold Wolf, Program Coordinator, 212-772-4616, E-mail: awo@hunter.cuny.edu. *Application contact:* Milena Solo, Director for Graduate Admissions, 212-772-4482, E-mail: admissions@hunter.cuny.edu.
Website: http://www.hunter.cuny.edu/school-of-education/programs/graduate/counseling/

Illinois Institute of Technology, Graduate College, Lewis College of Human Sciences, Department of Psychology, Chicago, IL 60616. Offers clinical psychology (PhD); industrial and organizational psychology (PhD); personnel and human resource development (MS); rehabilitation and mental health counseling (MS); rehabilitation counseling education (PhD). *Accreditation:* APA (one or more programs are accredited); CORE. Part-time and evening/weekend programs available. *Faculty:* 22 full-time (11 women), 3 part-time/adjunct (2 women). *Students:* 187 full-time (139 women), 11 part-time (8 women); includes 28 minority (5 Black or African American, non-Hispanic/Latino; 1 American Indian or Alaska Native, non-Hispanic/Latino; 7 Asian, non-Hispanic/Latino; 12 Hispanic/Latino; 3 Two or more races, non-Hispanic/Latino), 19 international. Average age 30. 293 applicants, 32% accepted, 38 enrolled. In 2014, 27 master's, 4 doctorates awarded. Terminal master's awarded for partial completion of doctoral program. *Degree requirements:* For master's, thesis (for some programs); for doctorate, comprehensive exam, thesis/dissertation, 107 credit hours minimum, 1 yr full-time internship, comprehensive exam, dissertation and oral defense. *Entrance requirements:* For master's, GRE General Test (minimum score 298 Quantitative and Verbal, 3.0 Analytical Writing), minimum gpa 3.0/4.0; 3 letters of recommendation. Applicants for master's degree programs should have a bachelor's degree from an accredited institution and meet the minimum standards listed above. The exception is the masters in Rehabilitation and Mental Health Counseling; for doctorate, GRE General Test (minimum score 298 Quantitative and Verbal, 3.0 Analytical Writing), Prerequisite to admission to doctoral programs are a bachelor's or master's degree from an accredited institution, superior academic records in both undergraduate and graduate programs, and favorable academic recommendations. GRE results are required for all psychology doctoral programs. Additional exam requirements/recommendations for international students: Required—TOEFL (minimum score 550 paper-based; 80 iBT). *Application deadline:* For fall admission, 1/15 for domestic and international students. Application fee: $50. Electronic applications accepted. *Expenses: Tuition:* Full-time $22,500; part-time $1250 per credit hour. *Required fees:* $30 per course. $260 per semester. One-time fee: $235. Tuition and fees vary according to course load and program. *Financial support:* Fellowships with full and partial tuition reimbursements, research assistantships with full and partial tuition reimbursements, career-related internships or fieldwork, Federal Work-Study, institutionally sponsored loans, scholarships/grants, traineeships, health care benefits, tuition waivers (partial), and unspecified assistantships available. Support available to part-time students. Financial award application deadline: 1/15; financial award applicants required to submit FAFSA. *Faculty research:* Clinical psychology, rehabilitation and mental health counseling, industrial organizational psychology. *Unit head:* Ronald Landis, Chair, 312-567-6467, Fax: 312-567-3493, E-mail: rlandis@iit.edu. *Application contact:* Rishab Malhotra, Director, Graduate Admissions, 866-472-3448, Fax: 312-567-3138, E-mail: inquiry.grad@iit.edu.
Website: http://iit.edu/psych/

Jackson State University, Graduate School, College of Education and Human Development, Department of School, Community and Rehabilitation Counseling, Jackson, MS 39217. Offers community and agency counseling (MS); guidance and counseling (MS, MS Ed); rehabilitation counseling (MS Ed). *Accreditation:* ACA; CORE (one or more programs are accredited); NCATE. Part-time and evening/weekend programs available. *Degree requirements:* For master's, comprehensive exam, thesis. *Entrance requirements:* For master's, GRE General Test. Additional exam requirements/recommendations for international students: Required—TOEFL (minimum score 520 paper-based; 67 iBT).

Kent State University, Graduate School of Education, Health, and Human Services, School of Lifespan Development and Educational Sciences, Program in Rehabilitation Counseling, Kent, OH 44242-0001. Offers M Ed. *Accreditation:* CORE. *Faculty:* 2 full-time (1 woman), 2 part-time/adjunct (both women). *Students:* 13 full-time (11 women), 13 part-time (9 women); includes 4 minority (3 Black or African American, non-Hispanic/Latino; 1 American Indian or Alaska Native, non-Hispanic/Latino). 12 applicants, 42% accepted. In 2014, 9 master's awarded. *Entrance requirements:* For master's, 2 letters of reference, goals statement, minimum undergraduate GPA of 2.75, interview. Additional exam requirements/recommendations for international students: Required—TOEFL (minimum score 550 paper-based; 80 iBT). *Application deadline:* Applications are processed on a rolling basis. Application fee: $45 ($60 for international students). Electronic applications accepted. *Expenses:* Tuition, state resident: full-time $8730; part-time $485 per credit hour. Tuition, nonresident: full-time $14,886; part-time $827 per credit hour. Tuition and fees vary according to campus/location and program. *Financial support:* In 2014–15, 1 research assistantship with full tuition reimbursement (averaging $8,500 per year) was awarded; Federal Work-Study, scholarships/grants, and unspecified assistantships also available. Financial award application deadline: 4/1; financial award applicants required to submit FAFSA. *Unit head:* Dr. Phillip Rumrill, Coordinator, 330-672-0600, E-mail: prumrill@kent.edu. *Application contact:* Nancy Miller, Academic Program Director, Office of Graduate Student Services, 330-672-2576, Fax: 330-672-9162, E-mail: ogs@kent.edu.
Website: http://www.kent.edu/ehhs/ldes/rhab

Langston University, School of Education and Behavioral Sciences, Langston, OK 73050. Offers bilingual/multicultural (M Ed); elementary education (M Ed); English as a second language (M Ed); rehabilitation counseling (M Sc); urban education (M Ed). *Accreditation:* CORE; NCATE (one or more programs are accredited). Part-time programs available. *Degree requirements:* For master's, comprehensive exam, thesis optional. *Entrance requirements:* For master's, GRE, writing skills test, minimum GPA of 2.5, 3 letters of recommendation. Additional exam requirements/recommendations for international students: Required—TOEFL, TWE. *Faculty research:* Bilingual/multicultural education, financing post-secondary education.

Louisiana State University Health Sciences Center, School of Allied Health Professions, Department of Clinical Rehabilitation and Counseling, New Orleans, LA 70112-2262. Offers MHS. *Accreditation:* CORE. *Faculty:* 3 full-time (1 woman). *Students:* 22 full-time (18 women); includes 10 minority (6 Black or African American, non-Hispanic/Latino; 1 Hispanic/Latino; 3 Two or more races, non-Hispanic/Latino). Average age 25. 22 applicants, 68% accepted, 15 enrolled. In 2014, 12 master's awarded. *Degree requirements:* For master's, clinical internship. *Entrance requirements:* For master's, GRE General Test, minimum GPA of 2.5, 2 letters of recommendation. *Application deadline:* For fall admission, 4/15 priority date for domestic students. Applications are processed on a rolling basis. Application fee: $50. *Financial support:* In 2014–15, 20 students received support. Application deadline: 4/15. *Faculty research:* Job placement, clinical judgment, counseling process, consumer satisfaction, vocational assessment. *Total annual research expenditures:* $10,000. *Unit head:* Dr. Erin M. Dugan, Interim Head, 504-556-3403, Fax: 504-568-4324, E-mail: emart3@lsuhsc.edu. *Application contact:* Yudialys Delgado Cazanas, Student Affairs Director, 504-568-4253, Fax: 504-568-3185, E-mail: ydelga@lsuhsc.edu.
Website: http://alliedhealth.lsuhsc.edu/rc/default.aspx

Maryville University of Saint Louis, College of Health Professions, Program in Rehabilitation Counseling, St. Louis, MO 63141-7299. Offers marriage and family therapy (MARC); music therapy (MARC); substance abuse (MARC). *Accreditation:* CORE. Part-time and evening/weekend programs available. *Faculty:* 3 full-time (1 woman), 3 part-time/adjunct (all women). *Students:* 9 full-time (all women), 25 part-time (23 women); includes 5 minority (4 Black or African American, non-Hispanic/Latino; 1 Two or more races, non-Hispanic/Latino). Average age 32. In 2014, 24 master's awarded. *Degree requirements:* For master's, internship, seminar. *Entrance requirements:* For master's, minimum cumulative GPA of 3.0, 2 letters of recommendation, interview. Additional exam requirements/recommendations for international students: Required—TOEFL (minimum score 550 paper-based). *Application deadline:* For fall admission, 1/15 for domestic students; for spring admission, 10/1 for domestic students. Application fee: $40 ($60 for international students). Electronic applications accepted. Application fee is waived when completed online. *Expenses: Tuition:* Full-time $24,694; part-time $755 per credit hour. Part-time tuition and fees vary according to course load and degree level. *Financial support:* Career-related internships or fieldwork, Federal Work-Study, and campus employment available. Financial award application deadline: 3/1; financial award applicants required to submit FAFSA. *Unit head:* Dr. Michael Kiener, Director, 314-529-9443, Fax: 314-529-9495, E-mail: mkiener@maryville.edu. *Application contact:* Crystal Jacobsmeyer, Assistant Director, Graduate Enrollment Advising, 314-529-9654, Fax: 314-529-9927, E-mail: cjacobsmeyer@maryville.edu.
Website: http://www.maryville.edu/hp/rehabilitation-counseling/

Mercer University, Graduate Studies, Cecil B. Day Campus, College of Continuing and Professional Studies, Macon, GA 31207. Offers certified rehabilitation counseling (MS); clinical mental health (MS); counselor education and supervision (PhD); human services (MS); organizational leadership (MS); public safety leadership (MS); school counseling (MS). Part-time and evening/weekend programs available. Postbaccalaureate distance

learning degree programs offered (minimal on-campus study). *Faculty:* 15 full-time (6 women), 23 part-time/adjunct (15 women). *Students:* 132 full-time (110 women), 230 part-time (184 women); includes 198 minority (167 Black or African American, non-Hispanic/Latino; 1 American Indian or Alaska Native, non-Hispanic/Latino; 10 Asian, non-Hispanic/Latino; 14 Hispanic/Latino; 3 Native Hawaiian or other Pacific Islander, non-Hispanic/Latino; 3 Two or more races, non-Hispanic/Latino), 3 international. Average age 32. In 2014, 126 master's, 1 doctorate awarded. *Degree requirements:* For master's, comprehensive exam (for some programs), thesis (for some programs); for doctorate, thesis/dissertation. *Entrance requirements:* For master's and doctorate, GRE or MAT. Additional exam requirements/recommendations for international students: Recommended—TOEFL (minimum score 550 paper-based; 80 iBT), IELTS (minimum score 6.5). *Application deadline:* For fall admission, 7/1 priority date for domestic and international students; for spring admission, 11/1 priority date for domestic and international students; for summer admission, 4/1 priority date for domestic and international students. Application fee: $35. Electronic applications accepted. Tuition and fees vary according to class time, degree level, campus/location and program. *Unit head:* Dr. Priscilla R. Danheiser, Dean, 678-547-6028, E-mail: danheiser_p@mercer.edu. *Application contact:* Carmen C. Jones, Associate Director of Admissions, 678-547-6346, E-mail: jones_c@mercer.edu.
Website: http://penfield.mercer.edu/programs/graduate-professional/

Michigan State University, The Graduate School, College of Education, Department of Counseling, Educational Psychology and Special Education, East Lansing, MI 48824. Offers counseling (MA); educational psychology and educational technology (PhD); educational technology (MA); measurement and quantitative methods (PhD); rehabilitation counseling (MA); rehabilitation counselor education (PhD); school psychology (MA, PhD, Ed S); special education (MA, PhD). *Accreditation:* APA (one or more programs are accredited); CORE (one or more programs are accredited). Part-time programs available. *Entrance requirements:* Additional exam requirements/recommendations for international students: Required—TOEFL. Electronic applications accepted.

Minnesota State University Mankato, College of Graduate Studies, College of Allied Health and Nursing, Program in Rehabilitation Counseling, Mankato, MN 56001. Offers MS. *Accreditation:* CORE. *Students:* 7 full-time (all women), 3 part-time (2 women). *Degree requirements:* For master's, comprehensive exam. *Entrance requirements:* For master's, GRE General Test, minimum GPA of 3.0 during previous 2 years, references. *Application deadline:* For fall admission, 3/1 priority date for domestic students. Applications are processed on a rolling basis. Application fee: $40. *Financial support:* Research assistantships with full tuition reimbursements and teaching assistantships with full tuition reimbursements available. Financial award application deadline: 3/15; financial award applicants required to submit FAFSA. *Unit head:* Dr. Bruce Poburka, Graduate Coordinator, 507-389-5843. *Application contact:* 507-389-2321, E-mail: grad@mnsu.edu.
Website: http://ahn.mnsu.edu/rehabilitation/

Mississippi State University, College of Education, Department of Counseling and Educational Psychology, Mississippi State, MS 39762. Offers college/postsecondary student counseling and personnel services (PhD); counselor education (MS), including clinical mental health, college counseling, rehabilitation, school counseling, student affairs in higher education; counselor education/student counseling and guidance services (PhD); education (Ed S), including counselor education, school psychology (PhD, Ed S); educational psychology (MS, PhD), including general education psychology (MS), general educational psychology (PhD), psychometry (MS), school psychology (PhD, Ed S). *Accreditation:* ACA (one or more programs are accredited); APA; CORE (one or more programs are accredited); NCATE. Part-time programs available. Postbaccalaureate distance learning degree programs offered (minimal on-campus study). *Faculty:* 21 full-time (15 women), 2 part-time/adjunct (both women). *Students:* 124 full-time (95 women), 72 part-time (63 women); includes 59 minority (48 Black or African American, non-Hispanic/Latino; 2 American Indian or Alaska Native, non-Hispanic/Latino; 6 Asian, non-Hispanic/Latino; 2 Hispanic/Latino; 1 Two or more races, non-Hispanic/Latino), 1 international. Average age 32. 138 applicants, 57% accepted, 53 enrolled. In 2014, 55 master's, 10 doctorates, 10 other advanced degrees awarded. Terminal master's awarded for partial completion of doctoral program. *Degree requirements:* For master's, comprehensive exam, thesis optional; for doctorate, thesis/dissertation, comprehensive oral and written exam. *Entrance requirements:* For master's, GRE (taken within the last five years), BS with minimum GPA of 2.75 on last 60 hours; for doctorate, GRE, MS from CACREP- or CORE-accredited program in counseling; for Ed S, GRE, MS in counseling or related field, minimum GPA of 3.3 on all graduate work. Additional exam requirements/recommendations for international students: Required—TOEFL (minimum score 550 paper-based; 79 iBT); Recommended—IELTS (minimum score 6.5). *Application deadline:* For fall admission, 2/1 priority date for domestic and international students. Applications are processed on a rolling basis. Application fee: $60. Electronic applications accepted. *Expenses:* Tuition, state resident: full-time $7140; part-time $783 per credit hour. Tuition, nonresident: full-time $18,478; part-time $2043 per credit hour. *Financial support:* In 2014–15, 3 research assistantships (averaging $9,800 per year), 9 teaching assistantships with full tuition reimbursements (averaging $8,401 per year) were awarded; career-related internships or fieldwork, Federal Work-Study, institutionally sponsored loans, and unspecified assistantships also available. Financial award application deadline: 2/1; financial award applicants required to submit FAFSA. *Faculty research:* HIV/AIDS in college population, substance abuse in youth and college students, ADHD and conduct disorders in youth, assessment and identification of early childhood disabilities, assessment and vocational transition of the disabled. *Unit head:* Dr. David Morse, Professor and Interim Head, 662-325-3426, Fax: 662-325-3263, E-mail: dmorse@colled.msstate.edu. *Application contact:* Dr. Charles Palmer, Graduate Coordinator, Counselor Education, 662-325-7917, Fax: 662-325-3263, E-mail: cpalmer@colled.msstate.edu.
Website: http://www.cep.msstate.edu/

Montana State University Billings, College of Allied Health Professions, Program in Clinical Rehabilitation and Mental Health Counseling, Billings, MT 59101. Offers MS. *Accreditation:* CORE. Part-time programs available. *Degree requirements:* For master's, thesis or professional paper and/or field experience. *Entrance requirements:* For master's, GRE General Test or MAT, minimum GPA of 3.0. *Application deadline:* For fall admission, 7/15 for international students; for spring admission, 12/1 for international students. Applications are processed on a rolling basis. Application fee: $40. *Financial support:* Teaching assistantships, career-related internships or fieldwork, Federal Work-Study, institutionally sponsored loans, scholarships/grants, tuition waivers (partial), and unspecified assistantships available. Support available to part-time students. Financial award application deadline: 5/1; financial award applicants required to submit FAFSA. *Unit head:* Dr. Terry Blackwell, Chair, 406-896-5834, E-mail: tblackwell@msubillings.edu. *Application contact:* David M. Sullivan, Graduate Studies Counselor, 406-657-2053, Fax: 406-657-2299, E-mail: dsullivan@msubillings.edu.

Northeastern Illinois University, College of Graduate Studies and Research, College of Education, Program in Rehabilitation Counseling, Chicago, IL 60625-4699. Offers MA.

Ohio University, Graduate College, Gladys W. and David H. Patton College of Education and Human Services, Department of Counseling and Higher Education, Athens, OH 45701-2979. Offers college student personnel (M Ed); community/agency counseling (M Ed); counselor education (PhD); higher education (PhD); rehabilitation counseling (M Ed); school counseling (M Ed). *Accreditation:* ACA; CORE. Part-time and evening/weekend programs available. *Degree requirements:* For master's, comprehensive exam (for some programs), thesis or alternative; for doctorate, comprehensive exam, thesis/dissertation. *Entrance requirements:* For master's, GRE General Test or MAT (if GPA less than 2.9), 3 letters of reference; for doctorate, GRE General Test, work experience, minimum GPA of 3.4. Additional exam requirements/recommendations for international students: Required—TOEFL (minimum score 550 paper-based; 80 iBT) or IELTS (minimum score 6.5). Electronic applications accepted. *Faculty research:* Youth violence, gender studies, student affairs, chemical dependency, disabilities issues.

Pontifical Catholic University of Puerto Rico, College of Graduate Studies in Behavioral Science and Community Affairs, Program in Rehabilitation Counseling, Ponce, PR 00717-0777. Offers MA. *Accreditation:* CORE. Part-time programs available. *Degree requirements:* For master's, thesis. *Entrance requirements:* For master's, EXADEP, GRE General Test, 3 letters of recommendation, interview, minimum GPA of 2.75.

Rutgers, The State University of New Jersey, Newark, School of Health Related Professions, Department of Psychiatric Rehabilitation and Counseling Professions, Program in Psychiatric Rehabilitation, Newark, NJ 07102. Offers MS, PhD. *Accreditation:* CORE. Part-time and evening/weekend programs available. Postbaccalaureate distance learning degree programs offered (minimal on-campus study). *Degree requirements:* For doctorate, comprehensive exam, thesis/dissertation. *Entrance requirements:* For master's, all transcripts, interview, statement of interest, bachelor's degree, 2 reference letters; for doctorate, GRE General Test, all transcripts, bachelor's degree, personal statement, 3 reference letters. Additional exam requirements/recommendations for international students: Required—TOEFL (minimum score 500 paper-based; 79 iBT). Electronic applications accepted.

Rutgers, The State University of New Jersey, Newark, School of Health Related Professions, Department of Psychiatric Rehabilitation and Counseling Professions, Program in Rehabilitation Counseling, Newark, NJ 07102. Offers community counseling (MS). Programs offered at Scotch Plains and Stratford campuses. *Accreditation:* CORE. Part-time and evening/weekend programs available. *Degree requirements:* For master's, internship, practicum. *Entrance requirements:* For master's, bachelor's degree with transcript, interview, personal goals statement, 2 reference letters. Additional exam requirements/recommendations for international students: Required—TOEFL (minimum score 500 paper-based; 79 iBT). Electronic applications accepted.

St. Bonaventure University, School of Graduate Studies, School of Education, Program in Counselor Education, St. Bonaventure, NY 14778-2284. Offers community mental health counseling (MS Ed); rehabilitation counseling (MS Ed); school counseling (MS Ed); school counselor (Adv C). Program offered in Olean and Buffalo Center (Hamburg, NY). *Accreditation:* ACA. Part-time and evening/weekend programs available. *Faculty:* 4 full-time (1 woman), 6 part-time/adjunct (3 women). *Students:* 55 full-time (42 women), 13 part-time (10 women); includes 3 minority (1 Hispanic/Latino; 2 Two or more races, non-Hispanic/Latino), 1 international. Average age 29. 31 applicants, 97% accepted, 23 enrolled. In 2014, 26 master's awarded. *Degree requirements:* For master's, comprehensive exam, thesis optional, internship, portfolio; for Adv C, internship. *Entrance requirements:* For master's, statement of intent/writing sample; transcripts from all colleges previously attended; two references; interview; minimum undergraduate GPA of 3.0; for Adv C, interview, writing sample, minimum undergraduate GPA of 3.0, two letters of recommendation, master's degree, transcripts from all colleges previously attended. Additional exam requirements/recommendations for international students: Required—TOEFL (minimum score 550 paper-based; 79 iBT). *Application deadline:* For fall admission, 8/15 priority date for domestic students, 2/1 priority date for international students; for spring admission, 11/15 priority date for domestic students, 7/1 priority date for international students. Applications are processed on a rolling basis. Application fee: $0. Electronic applications accepted. *Expenses:* Expenses: $8,532 for Advanced Certificate; $34,128 for school counseling; $42,660 for community mental health counseling. *Financial support:* In 2014–15, 5 research assistantships with full and partial tuition reimbursements were awarded; career-related internships or fieldwork, Federal Work-Study, scholarships/grants, health care benefits, tuition waivers (partial), and unspecified assistantships also available. Support available to part-time students. Financial award application deadline: 4/15; financial award applicants required to submit FAFSA. *Unit head:* Dr. S. Alan Silliker, Director, 716-375-2368, Fax: 716-375-2360, E-mail: silliker@sbu.edu. *Application contact:* Bruce Campbell, Director of Graduate Admissions, 716-375-2429, Fax: 716-375-4015, E-mail: gradsch@sbu.edu.
Website: http://www.sbu.edu/academics/schools/education

St. Cloud State University, School of Graduate Studies, School of Education, Department of Educational Leadership and Higher Education, Program in Rehabilitation Counseling, St. Cloud, MN 56301-4498. Offers MS. *Accreditation:* CORE. *Degree requirements:* For master's, comprehensive exam (for some programs), thesis or alternative. *Entrance requirements:* For master's, GRE General Test, minimum GPA of 2.75. Additional exam requirements/recommendations for international students: Required—Michigan English Language Assessment Battery; Recommended—TOEFL (minimum score 550 paper-based), IELTS (minimum score 6.5). Electronic applications accepted.

Salve Regina University, Program in Rehabilitation Counseling, Newport, RI 02840-4192. Offers mental health (CAGS), including rehabilitation counseling; rehabilitation counseling (MA); substance abuse (CGS), including foundations in rehabilitation counseling. *Accreditation:* CORE. Part-time and evening/weekend programs available. *Faculty:* 1 (woman) full-time, 8 part-time/adjunct (3 women). *Students:* 6 full-time (5 women), 64 part-time (53 women); includes 17 minority (9 Black or African American, non-Hispanic/Latino; 3 American Indian or Alaska Native, non-Hispanic/Latino; 5 Hispanic/Latino). Average age 37. 23 applicants, 100% accepted, 22 enrolled. In 2014, 14 master's, 4 other advanced degrees awarded. *Entrance requirements:* For master's, GMAT, GRE General Test or MAT. Additional exam requirements/recommendations for international students: Required—TOEFL (minimum score 600 paper-based; 100 iBT) or IELTS. *Application deadline:* For fall admission, 3/15 priority date for domestic and international students; for spring admission, 9/15 priority date for domestic and international students. Applications are processed on a rolling basis. Application fee: $60. Electronic applications accepted. *Expenses: Tuition:* Full-time $8550; part-time $475 per credit. *Required fees:* $50 per term. Tuition and fees vary according to course level, course load and degree level. *Financial support:* Career-related internships or fieldwork and Federal Work-Study available. Support available to part-time students. Financial award application deadline: 3/1; financial award applicants required to submit FAFSA. *Unit head:* Dr. Judith Drew, Director, 401-341-3189, E-mail: judith.drew@salve.edu. *Application contact:* Nicole Ferreira, Associate Director of Graduate Admissions, 401-341-2462, Fax: 401-341-2973, E-mail:

nicole.ferreira@salve.edu.
Website: http://www.salve.edu/graduate-studies/rehabilitation-counseling

San Diego State University, Graduate and Research Affairs, College of Education, Department of Administration, Rehabilitation and Post-Secondary Education, San Diego, CA 92182. Offers educational leadership in post-secondary education (MA); rehabilitation counseling (MS), including deafness. Evening/weekend programs available. Postbaccalaureate distance learning degree programs offered. *Degree requirements:* For master's, comprehensive exam (for some programs), thesis (for some programs). *Entrance requirements:* For master's, GRE General Test, letters of reference. Additional exam requirements/recommendations for international students: Required—TOEFL. Electronic applications accepted. *Faculty research:* Rehabilitation in cultural diversity, distance learning technology.

San Francisco State University, Division of Graduate Studies, College of Health and Social Sciences, Department of Counseling, San Francisco, CA 94132-1722. Offers clinical rehabilitation and mental health counseling (MS); counseling (MS); marriage, family, and child counseling (MSC); school counseling (Credential). *Accreditation:* ACA (one or more programs are accredited). Part-time programs available. *Application deadline:* Applications are processed on a rolling basis. *Expenses:* Tuition, state resident: full-time $6738. Tuition, nonresident: full-time $17,898; part-time $372 per credit hour. *Required fees:* $498 per semester. *Unit head:* Dr. Graciela Orozco, Chair, 415-338-2005, E-mail: counsel@sfsu.edu. *Application contact:* Katsufumi Araki, Academic Office Coordinator, 415-338-2005, E-mail: counsel@sfsu.edu.
Website: http://counseling.sfsu.edu

Southern University and Agricultural and Mechanical College, Graduate School, College of Sciences, Department of Psychology, Program in Rehabilitation Counseling, Baton Rouge, LA 70813. Offers MS. *Accreditation:* CORE. *Degree requirements:* For master's, comprehensive exam, thesis optional. *Entrance requirements:* For master's, GMAT or GRE General Test. Additional exam requirements/recommendations for international students: Required—TOEFL. *Faculty research:* Cultural diversity, professional preparation and participation of minorities, needs and satisfaction of students with disabilities, prediction model for rehabilitation outcome, diabetes.

Springfield College, Graduate Programs, Programs in Rehabilitation Counseling and Services, Springfield, MA 01109-3797. Offers alcohol and substance abuse services (M Ed); psychiatric rehabilitation and substance abuse counseling (M Ed). *Accreditation:* CORE (one or more programs are accredited). Part-time programs available. *Degree requirements:* For master's, comprehensive exam. *Entrance requirements:* Additional exam requirements/recommendations for international students: Required—TOEFL (minimum score 550 paper-based); Recommended—IELTS (minimum score 6). *Application deadline:* For fall admission, 1/15 for domestic and international students; for winter admission, 11/1 for international students; for spring admission, 11/1 for domestic and international students. Applications are processed on a rolling basis. Application fee: $50. Electronic applications accepted. *Financial support:* Fellowships with partial tuition reimbursements, teaching assistantships with partial tuition reimbursements, career-related internships or fieldwork, Federal Work-Study, institutionally sponsored loans, and unspecified assistantships available. Financial award application deadline: 3/1; financial award applicants required to submit FAFSA. *Unit head:* Deborah Cook, Director, 413-748-3321, E-mail: dcook@springfieldcollege.edu. *Application contact:* Mary DeAngelo, Director of Enrollment Management, 413-748-3136, Fax: 413-748-3694, E-mail: mdeangel@spfldcol.edu.

Texas Tech University Health Sciences Center, School of Allied Health Sciences, Program in Rehabilitation Counseling, Lubbock, TX 79430. Offers MRC. *Accreditation:* CORE. Part-time programs available. *Faculty:* 4 full-time (2 women). *Students:* 50 full-time (40 women), 68 part-time (50 women); includes 50 minority (24 Black or African American, non-Hispanic/Latino; 1 American Indian or Alaska Native, non-Hispanic/Latino; 3 Asian, non-Hispanic/Latino; 21 Hispanic/Latino; 1 Two or more races, non-Hispanic/Latino). Average age 36. 72 applicants, 86% accepted, 62 enrolled. In 2014, 24 master's awarded. *Entrance requirements:* Additional exam requirements/recommendations for international students: Required—TOEFL, IELTS. *Application deadline:* For fall admission, 6/1 for domestic students; for spring admission, 10/1 for domestic students. Applications are processed on a rolling basis. Application fee: $40. Electronic applications accepted. *Financial support:* Applicants required to submit FAFSA. *Unit head:* Dr. Evans Spears, Program Director, 806-743-2262, Fax: 806-743-3244, E-mail: evans.spears@ttuhsc.edu. *Application contact:* Lindsay Johnson, Associate Dean for Admissions and Student Affairs, 806-743-3220, Fax: 806-743-2994, E-mail: lindsay.johnson@ttuhsc.edu.
Website: http://www.ttuhsc.edu/sah/mrc/

Thomas University, Department of Human Services, Thomasville, GA 31792-7499. Offers community counseling (MSCC); rehabilitation counseling (MRC). *Accreditation:* CORE. Part-time programs available. *Entrance requirements:* For master's, resume, 3 academic/professional references. Additional exam requirements/recommendations for international students: Required—TOEFL (minimum score 600 paper-based). Electronic applications accepted.

Troy University, Graduate School, College of Education, Program in Counseling and Psychology, Troy, AL 36082. Offers agency counseling (Ed S); clinical mental health (MS); community counseling (MS, Ed S); corrections counseling (MS); rehabilitation counseling (MS); school psychology (MS, Ed S); school psychometry (MS); social service counseling (MS); student affairs counseling (MS); substance abuse counseling (MS). *Accreditation:* ACA; CORE; NCATE. Part-time and evening/weekend programs available. *Faculty:* 41 full-time (18 women), 32 part-time/adjunct (18 women). *Students:* 358 full-time (286 women), 503 part-time (425 women); includes 572 minority (481 Black or African American, non-Hispanic/Latino; 3 American Indian or Alaska Native, non-Hispanic/Latino; 5 Asian, non-Hispanic/Latino; 62 Hispanic/Latino; 21 Two or more races, non-Hispanic/Latino). Average age 34. 248 applicants, 86% accepted, 139 enrolled. In 2014, 212 master's, 4 other advanced degrees awarded. *Degree requirements:* For master's, comprehensive exam, thesis. *Entrance requirements:* For master's, GRE (minimum score of 850 on old exam or 290 on new exam), GMAT (minimum score of 380), or MAT (minimum score of 385), bachelor's degree; minimum undergraduate GPA of 2.5 or 3.0 on last 30 semester hours, letter of recommendation. Additional exam requirements/recommendations for international students: Required—TOEFL (minimum score 523 paper-based; 70 iBT), IELTS (minimum score 6). *Application deadline:* Applications are processed on a rolling basis. Application fee: $50. Electronic applications accepted. *Expenses:* Tuition, state resident: full-time $6570; part-time $365 per credit hour. Tuition, nonresident: full-time $13,140; part-time $730 per credit hour. *Required fees:* $365 per credit hour. *Unit head:* Dr. Andrew Creamer, Chair, 334-670-3350, Fax: 334-670-3291, E-mail: acreamer@troy.edu. *Application contact:* Jessica A. Kimbro, Director of Graduate Admissions, 334-670-3178, E-mail: jacord@troy.edu.

University at Buffalo, the State University of New York, Graduate School, Graduate School of Education, Department of Counseling, School, and Educational Psychology, Buffalo, NY 14260. Offers counseling/school psychology (PhD); counselor education (PhD); education studies (Ed M); educational psychology (MA, PhD); mental health counseling (MS, Certificate); rehabilitation counseling (MS, Advanced Certificate); school counseling (Ed M, Certificate). *Accreditation:* CORE (one or more programs are accredited). Part-time programs available. Postbaccalaureate distance learning degree programs offered (no on-campus study). *Faculty:* 19 full-time (11 women), 55 part-time/adjunct (39 women). *Students:* 158 full-time (123 women), 147 part-time (119 women); includes 37 minority (28 Black or African American, non-Hispanic/Latino; 2 American Indian or Alaska Native, non-Hispanic/Latino; 4 Asian, non-Hispanic/Latino; 3 Hispanic/Latino), 15 international. Average age 32. 341 applicants, 57% accepted, 124 enrolled. In 2014, 59 master's, 14 doctorates, 35 other advanced degrees awarded. *Degree requirements:* For master's, comprehensive exam (for some programs), thesis (for some programs); for doctorate, comprehensive exam, thesis/dissertation. *Entrance requirements:* For master's, GRE General Test, interview, letters of reference; for doctorate, GRE General Test, interview, letters of reference, writing sample. Additional exam requirements/recommendations for international students: Required—TOEFL (minimum score 79 iBT). *Application deadline:* For fall admission, 2/1 priority date for domestic and international students. Application fee: $50. Electronic applications accepted. *Financial support:* In 2014–15, 12 fellowships (averaging $9,384 per year), 37 research assistantships with tuition reimbursements (averaging $9,961 per year) were awarded; teaching assistantships, career-related internships or fieldwork, Federal Work-Study, institutionally sponsored loans, scholarships/grants, tuition waivers, and unspecified assistantships also available. Financial award application deadline: 2/1; financial award applicants required to submit FAFSA. *Faculty research:* Multicultural counseling, class size effects, good work in counseling, eating disorders, outcome assessment, change agents and therapeutic factors in group counseling. *Total annual research expenditures:* $1 million. *Unit head:* Dr. Jeremy Finn, Chair, 716-645-1126, Fax: 716-645-6616, E-mail: finn@buffalo.edu. *Application contact:* Joanne Laska, Admissions Assistant, 716-645-2110, Fax: 716-645-7937, E-mail: jlaska@buffalo.edu.
Website: http://gse.buffalo.edu/csep

The University of Arizona, College of Education, Department of Disability and Psychoeducational Studies, Program in Counseling and Mental Health, Tucson, AZ 85721. Offers rehabilitation counseling (MA); school counseling (MA). *Entrance requirements:* Additional exam requirements/recommendations for international students: Required—TOEFL (minimum score 550 paper-based; 80 iBT). *Faculty research:* Further knowledge and understanding of abilities, disabilities, adaptations, interventions, and support systems; preparing professionals to educate and facilitate the development of individuals with disabilities and special abilities; providing leadership at the local, state, national, and international levels.

The University of Arizona, College of Education, Department of Disability and Psychoeducational Studies, Program in Rehabilitation, Tucson, AZ 85721. Offers MA, PhD. *Entrance requirements:* For master's, GMAT, 3 letters of recommendation, statement of purpose; for doctorate, GMAT, 3 letters of recommendation. Additional exam requirements/recommendations for international students: Required—TOEFL (minimum score 550 paper-based; 79 iBT). Electronic applications accepted.

University of Arkansas, Graduate School, College of Education and Health Professions, Department of Rehabilitation, Human Resources and Communication Disorders, Program in Rehabilitation, Fayetteville, AR 72701-1201. Offers MS, PhD. *Accreditation:* CORE (one or more programs are accredited). Part-time programs available. *Degree requirements:* For doctorate, thesis/dissertation. *Entrance requirements:* For doctorate, GRE General Test. Electronic applications accepted.

University of Arkansas at Little Rock, Graduate School, College of Education, Department of Counseling, Adult and Rehabilitation Education, Little Rock, AR 72204-1099. Offers adult education (M Ed); counselor education (M Ed); rehabilitation counseling (MA, Graduate Certificate); rehabilitation for the blind: orientation and mobility (MA). *Accreditation:* CORE; NCATE. Part-time programs available. *Entrance requirements:* For master's, interview, minimum GPA of 2.75. *Application deadline:* Applications are processed on a rolling basis. *Expenses:* Tuition, state resident: full-time $6000; part-time $300 per credit hour. Tuition, nonresident: full-time $13,800; part-time $690 per credit hour. *Required fees:* $1126; $603 per term. One-time fee: $40 full-time. *Financial support:* Research assistantships with tuition reimbursements, teaching assistantships with tuition reimbursements, career-related internships or fieldwork, Federal Work-Study, and institutionally sponsored loans available. Support available to part-time students. Financial award application deadline: 6/30. *Faculty research:* Low vision, orientation and mobility instruction. *Unit head:* Bill Jacobson, Chair, 501-569-3169, E-mail: whjacobson@ualr.edu.
Website: http://ualr.edu/care/

University of Idaho, College of Graduate Studies, College of Education, Department of Leadership and Counseling, Boise, ID 83702. Offers adult/organizational learning and leadership (MS, Ed S); educational leadership (M Ed, Ed S); rehabilitation counseling and human services (M Ed, MS); school counseling (M Ed, MS); special education (M Ed). *Faculty:* 14 full-time, 8 part-time/adjunct. *Students:* 58 full-time (39 women), 200 part-time (121 women). Average age 39. In 2014, 76 master's, 30 other advanced degrees awarded. *Entrance requirements:* Additional exam requirements/recommendations for international students: Required—TOEFL (minimum score 550 paper-based). *Application deadline:* Applications are processed on a rolling basis. Application fee: $60. Electronic applications accepted. *Expenses:* Tuition, state resident: full-time $4784; part-time $280.50 per credit hour. Tuition, nonresident: full-time $18,314; part-time $957.50 per credit hour. *Required fees:* $2000; $58.50 per credit hour. Tuition and fees vary according to program. *Financial support:* Applicants required to submit FAFSA. *Unit head:* Dr. Kathy Canfield-Davis, Chair, 208-364-4047, E-mail: mweitz@uidaho.edu. *Application contact:* Sean Thomas, Graduate Recruitment Coordinator, 208-885-4001, Fax: 208-885-4406, E-mail: graduateadmissions@uidaho.edu.
Website: http://www.uidaho.edu/ed/leadershipcounseling

The University of Iowa, Graduate College, College of Education, Department of Rehabilitation and Counselor Education, Iowa City, IA 52242-1316. Offers counselor education and supervision (PhD); couple and family therapy (PhD); rehabilitation and mental health counseling (MA); rehabilitation counselor education (PhD); school counseling (MA). *Accreditation:* ACA (one or more programs are accredited); CORE (one or more programs are accredited). *Degree requirements:* For master's, thesis optional, exam; for doctorate, comprehensive exam, thesis/dissertation. *Entrance requirements:* For master's and doctorate, GRE General Test, minimum GPA of 3.0. Additional exam requirements/recommendations for international students: Required—TOEFL (minimum score 550 paper-based; 81 iBT). Electronic applications accepted.

The University of Kansas, Graduate Studies, College of Liberal Arts and Sciences, Department of Psychology, Lawrence, KS 66045. Offers clinical child psychology (MA, PhD); clinical health and rehabilitation (PhD); cognitive psychology (PhD); developmental psychology (PhD); quantitative psychology (PhD); social psychology (MA). *Accreditation:* APA (one or more programs are accredited). *Faculty:* 36 full-time, 3 part-time/adjunct. *Students:* 81 full-time (49 women), 1 (woman) part-time; includes 12 minority (4 Black or African American, non-Hispanic/Latino; 5 Asian, non-Hispanic/Latino; 1 Hispanic/Latino; 2 Two or more races, non-Hispanic/Latino), 13 international. Average age 29. 194 applicants, 10% accepted, 9 enrolled. In 2014, 17 master's, 13 doctorates awarded. *Degree requirements:* For doctorate, variable foreign language requirement, comprehensive exam, thesis/dissertation. *Entrance requirements:* For

doctorate, GRE General Test, minimum GPA of 3.0; undergraduate degree with 15 hours of course work in psychology, curriculum vitae, writing sample (clinical program only). Additional exam requirements/recommendations for international students: Required—TOEFL. *Application deadline:* For fall admission, 12/1 for domestic and international students. Application fee: $55 ($65 for international students). Electronic applications accepted. *Financial support:* In 2014–15, 1 fellowship with full tuition reimbursement (averaging $12,750 per year), 4 research assistantships with partial tuition reimbursements (averaging $12,980 per year), 70 teaching assistantships with partial tuition reimbursements (averaging $12,750 per year) were awarded; career-related internships or fieldwork, Federal Work-Study, scholarships/grants, health care benefits, and unspecified assistantships also available. Financial award application deadline: 12/1; financial award applicants required to submit FAFSA. *Faculty research:* Origins, correlates and treatment of depression; health and emotion; concentration on topics related to prejudice, stereotyping, and intergroup relations; memory, cognitive development, language, perception, attention, aging; psychometric methods, item response theory, structural equation modeling. *Unit head:* Ruth Anne Atchley, Chair, 785-864-4131. *Application contact:* Cathy O'Keefe, Graduate Officer, 785-864-4195, Fax: 785-864-5596, E-mail: cokeefe@ku.edu.
Website: http://www.psych.ku.edu/

University of Kentucky, Graduate School, College of Education, Program in Special Education, Lexington, KY 40506-0032. Offers early childhood (MS Ed); rehabilitation counseling (MRC, PhD); special education (MS Ed, PhD). *Accreditation:* CORE; NCATE. Terminal master's awarded for partial completion of doctoral program. *Degree requirements:* For master's, comprehensive exam, thesis optional; for doctorate, comprehensive exam, thesis/dissertation. *Entrance requirements:* For master's, GRE General Test, minimum undergraduate GPA of 2.75; for doctorate, GRE General Test, minimum graduate GPA of 3.0. Additional exam requirements/recommendations for international students: Required—TOEFL (minimum score 550 paper-based). Electronic applications accepted. *Faculty research:* Applied behavior analysis applications in special education, single subject research design in classroom settings, transition research across life span, rural special education personnel.

University of Louisiana at Lafayette, College of Liberal Arts, Department of Psychology, Program in Rehabilitation Counseling, Lafayette, LA 70504. Offers MS. *Entrance requirements:* For master's, GRE General Test, minimum GPA of 3.0. Additional exam requirements/recommendations for international students: Required—TOEFL (minimum score 550 paper-based). Electronic applications accepted. *Faculty research:* Vocational assessment, psychology.

University of Maryland, College Park, Academic Affairs, College of Education, Department of Counseling, Higher Education and Special Education, College Park, MD 20742. Offers college student personnel (M Ed, MA); college student personnel administration (PhD); community counseling (CAGS); community/career counseling (M Ed, MA); counseling and personnel services (M Ed, MA, PhD), including art therapy (M Ed), college student personnel (M Ed), counseling and personnel services (PhD), counseling psychology (M Ed), mental health counseling (M Ed), school counseling (M Ed); counseling psychology (PhD); counselor education (PhD); rehabilitation counseling (M Ed, MA, AGSC); school counseling (M Ed, MA); school psychology (M Ed, MA, PhD). *Accreditation:* ACA (one or more programs are accredited); APA (one or more programs are accredited); NCATE. Part-time and evening/weekend programs available. Postbaccalaureate distance learning degree programs offered (no on-campus study). *Degree requirements:* For master's, thesis (for some programs); for doctorate, thesis/dissertation. *Entrance requirements:* For master's, GRE General Test or MAT, minimum GPA of 3.0, 3 letters of recommendation; for doctorate, GRE General Test or MAT, minimum GPA of 3.5, 3 letters of recommendation. Additional exam requirements/recommendations for international students: Required—TOEFL. Electronic applications accepted. *Faculty research:* Educational psychology, counseling, health.

University of Maryland Eastern Shore, Graduate Programs, Department of Rehabilitation Services, Princess Anne, MD 21853-1299. Offers rehabilitation counseling (MS). *Accreditation:* CORE. Part-time and evening/weekend programs available. *Degree requirements:* For master's, internship. *Entrance requirements:* For master's, interview. Additional exam requirements/recommendations for international students: Required—TOEFL (minimum score 80 iBT). Electronic applications accepted. *Faculty research:* Long-term rehabilitation training.

University of Massachusetts Boston, Graduate School of Global Inclusion and Social Development, Program in Rehabilitation Counseling, Boston, MA 02125-3393. Offers MS. *Expenses:* Tuition, state resident: full-time $2590; part-time $108 per credit. Tuition, nonresident: full-time $9758; part-time $406.50 per credit. Tuition and fees vary according to course load and program. *Unit head:* Dr. Kristy Alster, Associate Provost, 617-287-5700, Fax: 617-287-5699, E-mail: kristine.alster@umb.edu. *Application contact:* Peggy Roldan Patel, Graduate Admissions Coordinator, 617-287-6400, Fax: 617-287-6236, E-mail: bos.gadm@dpc.umassp.edu.

University of Memphis, Graduate School, College of Education, Department of Counseling, Educational Psychology and Research, Memphis, TN 38152. Offers counseling (MS, Ed D), including community counseling (MS), rehabilitation counseling (MS), school counseling (MS); counseling psychology (PhD); educational psychology and research (MS, PhD), including educational psychology, educational research. *Accreditation:* ACA (one or more programs are accredited); APA (one or more programs are accredited); CORE (one or more programs are accredited); NCATE. *Faculty:* 26 full-time (11 women), 6 part-time/adjunct (2 women). *Students:* 137 full-time (105 women), 97 part-time (74 women); includes 60 minority (44 Black or African American, non-Hispanic/Latino; 1 American Indian or Alaska Native, non-Hispanic/Latino; 7 Hispanic/Latino; 8 Two or more races, non-Hispanic/Latino), 9 international. Average age 32. 141 applicants, 44% accepted, 30 enrolled. In 2014, 50 master's, 13 doctorates awarded. *Degree requirements:* For master's, comprehensive exam, thesis or alternative; for doctorate, comprehensive exam, thesis/dissertation. *Entrance requirements:* For master's, GRE General Test or MAT, minimum GPA of 2.5; for doctorate, GRE General Test. *Application deadline:* For fall admission, 10/1 for domestic students; for spring admission, 4/1 for domestic students. Application fee: $35 ($60 for international students). *Financial support:* In 2014–15, 130 students received support. Fellowships with full tuition reimbursements available, research assistantships with full tuition reimbursements available, teaching assistantships with full tuition reimbursements available, career-related internships or fieldwork, Federal Work-Study, scholarships/grants, and unspecified assistantships available. Financial award application deadline: 2/15; financial award applicants required to submit FAFSA. *Faculty research:* Anger management, aging and disability, supervision, multicultural counseling. *Unit head:* Dr. Douglas C. Strohmer, Chair, 901-678-2841, Fax: 901-678-5114. *Application contact:* Dr. Ernest A. Rakow, Associate Dean of Administration and Graduate Programs, 901-678-2399, Fax: 901-678-4778.
Website: http://coe.memphis.edu/cepr/

The University of North Carolina at Chapel Hill, School of Medicine and Graduate School, Graduate Programs in Medicine, Chapel Hill, NC 27599. Offers allied health sciences (MPT, MS, Au D, DPT, PhD), including human movement science (MS, PhD), occupational science (MS, PhD), physical therapy (MPT, MS, DPT), rehabilitation counseling and psychology (MS), speech and hearing sciences (MS, Au D, PhD); biochemistry and biophysics (MS, PhD); bioinformatics and computational biology (PhD); biomedical engineering (MS, PhD); cell and developmental biology (PhD); cell and molecular physiology (PhD); genetics and molecular biology (PhD); microbiology and immunology (MS, PhD), including immunology, microbiology; neurobiology (PhD); pathology and laboratory medicine (PhD), including experimental pathology; pharmacology (PhD); MD/PhD. Postbaccalaureate distance learning degree programs offered. Terminal master's awarded for partial completion of doctoral program. *Degree requirements:* For master's, comprehensive exam; for doctorate, thesis/dissertation. Electronic applications accepted. *Expenses:* Contact institution.

The University of North Carolina at Chapel Hill, School of Medicine and Graduate School, Graduate Programs in Medicine, Department of Allied Health Sciences, Division of Rehabilitation Counseling and Psychology, Chapel Hill, NC 27599. Offers MS. *Accreditation:* CORE. *Degree requirements:* For master's, comprehensive exam, thesis or alternative, internship. *Entrance requirements:* For master's, GRE. Additional exam requirements/recommendations for international students: Required—TOEFL (minimum score 550 paper-based). *Faculty research:* Motor development, motor control; treatment of sports/orthopedic patient problems; movement in older adults; postural control across the lifespan; research in clinical practice; fetal, preterm, and infant movement; functional assessment across the lifespan.

University of Northern Colorado, Graduate School, College of Natural and Health Sciences, School of Human Sciences, Program in Rehabilitation, Greeley, CO 80639. Offers human rehabilitation (PhD); rehabilitation counseling (MA). *Accreditation:* CORE (one or more programs are accredited). Part-time programs available. *Degree requirements:* For master's, comprehensive exam, thesis or alternative; for doctorate, comprehensive exam, thesis/dissertation. *Entrance requirements:* For master's, GRE General Test or MAT, 2 letters of recommendation; for doctorate, GRE General Test, 2 letters of recommendation. Electronic applications accepted.

University of North Florida, Brooks College of Health, Department of Public Health, Jacksonville, FL 32224. Offers aging services (Certificate); community health (MPH); geriatric management (MSH); health administration (MHA); rehabilitation counseling (MS). *Accreditation:* CEPH. Part-time and evening/weekend programs available. *Faculty:* 19 full-time (13 women), 3 part-time/adjunct (2 women). *Students:* 142 full-time (102 women), 52 part-time (30 women); includes 55 minority (23 Black or African American, non-Hispanic/Latino; 10 Asian, non-Hispanic/Latino; 15 Hispanic/Latino; 7 Two or more races, non-Hispanic/Latino), 7 international. Average age 29. 275 applicants, 39% accepted, 72 enrolled. In 2014, 66 master's awarded. *Degree requirements:* For master's, thesis optional. *Entrance requirements:* For master's, GRE General Test (MSH, MS, MPH); GMAT or GRE General Test (MHA), minimum GPA of 3.0 in last 60 hours. Additional exam requirements/recommendations for international students: Required—TOEFL (minimum score 500 paper-based). *Application deadline:* For fall admission, 7/1 for domestic students, 5/1 for international students; for spring admission, 11/1 for domestic students, 10/1 for international students. Application fee: $30. Electronic applications accepted. *Expenses:* Tuition, state resident: full-time $9794; part-time $408.10 per credit hour. Tuition, nonresident: full-time $22,383; part-time $932.61 per credit hour. *Required fees:* $2047; $85.29 per credit hour. Tuition and fees vary according to course load and program. *Financial support:* In 2014–15, 34 students received support, including 2 teaching assistantships (averaging $2,000 per year); research assistantships, career-related internships or fieldwork, Federal Work-Study, scholarships/grants, and tuition waivers (partial) also available. Support available to part-time students. Financial award application deadline: 4/1; financial award applicants required to submit FAFSA. *Faculty research:* Dietary supplements; alcohol, tobacco, and other drug use prevention; turnover among health professionals; aging; psychosocial aspects of disabilities. *Total annual research expenditures:* $57,986. *Unit head:* Dr. Jeffrey Harrison, Chair, 904-620-1440, Fax: 904-620-2848, E-mail: jeffrey.harrison@unf.edu. *Application contact:* Dr. Heather Kenney, Director of Advising, 904-620-2810, Fax: 904-620-1030, E-mail: heather.kenney@unf.edu.
Website: http://www.unf.edu/brooks/public_health/

University of North Texas, Robert B. Toulouse School of Graduate Studies, Denton, TX 76203-5459. Offers accounting (MS); applied anthropology (MA, MS); applied behavior analysis (Certificate); applied geography (MA); applied technology and performance improvement (M Ed, MS); art education (MA); art history (MA); art museum education (Certificate); arts leadership (Certificate); audiology (Au D); behavior analysis (MS); behavioral science (PhD); biochemistry and molecular biology (MS); biology (MA, MS); biomedical engineering (MS); business analysis (MS); chemistry (MS); clinical health psychology (PhD); communication studies (MA, MS); computer engineering (MS); computer science (MS); counseling (M Ed, MS), including clinical mental health counseling (MS), college and university counseling, elementary school counseling, secondary school counseling; creative writing (MA); criminal justice (MS); curriculum and instruction (M Ed); decision sciences (MBA); design (MA, MFA), including fashion design (MFA), innovation studies, interior design (MFA); early childhood studies (MS); economics (MS); educational leadership (M Ed, Ed D); educational psychology (MS, PhD), including family studies (MS), gifted and talented (MS), human development (MS), learning and cognition (MS), research, measurement and evaluation (MS); electrical engineering (MS); emergency management (MPA); engineering technology (MS); English (MA); English as a second language (MA); environmental science (MS); finance (MBA, MS); financial management (MPA); French (MA); health services management (MBA); higher education (M Ed, Ed D); history (MA, MS); hospitality management (MS); human resources management (MPA); information science (MS); information systems (PhD); information technologies (MBA); interdisciplinary studies (MA, MS); international studies (MA); international sustainable tourism (MS); jazz studies (MM); journalism (MA, MJ, Graduate Certificate), including interactive and virtual digital communication (Graduate Certificate), narrative journalism (Graduate Certificate), public relations (Graduate Certificate); kinesiology (MS); linguistics (MA); local government management (MPA); logistics (PhD); logistics and supply chain management (MBA); long-term care, senior housing, and aging services (MA); management (PhD); marketing (MBA); mathematics (MA, MS); mechanical and energy engineering (MS, PhD); music (MA), including ethnomusicology, music theory, musicology, performance; music composition (PhD); music education (MM Ed, PhD); nonprofit management (MPA); operations and supply chain management (MBA); performance (MM, DMA); philosophy (MA); political science (MA); professional and technical communication (MA); radio, television and film (MA, MFA); rehabilitation counseling (Certificate); sociology (MA); Spanish (MA); special education (M Ed); speech-language pathology (MA); strategic management (MBA); studio art (MFA); teaching (M Ed); MBA/MS. Part-time and evening/weekend programs available. Postbaccalaureate distance learning degree programs offered. *Faculty:* 651 full-time (215 women), 233 part-time/adjunct (139 women). *Students:* 3,040 full-time (1,598 women), 3,401 part-time (2,097 women); includes 1,740 minority (533 Black or African American, non-Hispanic/Latino; 15 American Indian or Alaska Native, non-Hispanic/Latino; 286 Asian, non-Hispanic/Latino; 746 Hispanic/Latino; 3 Native Hawaiian or other Pacific Islander, non-Hispanic/Latino; 157 Two or more races, non-Hispanic/Latino), 1,145 international. Terminal master's awarded for partial completion of doctoral program. *Degree requirements:* For master's, variable foreign language requirement, comprehensive exam (for some programs), thesis (for some programs); for doctorate, variable foreign language requirement, comprehensive exam (for some programs), thesis/dissertation; for other advanced

degree, variable foreign language requirement, comprehensive exam (for some programs). *Entrance requirements:* For master's and doctorate, GRE, GMAT. Additional exam requirements/recommendations for international students: Required—TOEFL (minimum score 550 paper-based; 79 iBT). *Application deadline:* For fall admission, 7/15 for domestic students, 3/15 for international students; for spring admission, 11/15 for domestic students, 9/15 for international students; for summer admission, 5/1 for domestic students. Applications are processed on a rolling basis. Application fee: $60. Electronic applications accepted. *Expenses:* Tuition, state resident: full-time $5450; part-time $3633 per year. Tuition, nonresident: full-time $11,966; part-time $7977 per year. *Required fees:* $1301; $398 per credit hour. $685 per semester. Tuition and fees vary according to program and reciprocity agreements. *Financial support:* Fellowships with partial tuition reimbursements, research assistantships with partial tuition reimbursements, teaching assistantships, career-related internships or fieldwork, Federal Work-Study, institutionally sponsored loans, scholarships/grants, health care benefits, and library assistantships available. Support available to part-time students. Financial award applicants required to submit FAFSA. *Unit head:* Mark Wardell, Dean, 940-565-2383, E-mail: mark.wardell@unt.edu. *Application contact:* Toulouse School of Graduate Studies, 940-565-2383, Fax: 940-565-2141, E-mail: gradsch@unt.edu.
Website: http://tsgs.unt.edu/

University of Puerto Rico, Río Piedras Campus, College of Social Sciences, Graduate School of Rehabilitation Counseling, San Juan, PR 00931-3300. Offers MRC. *Accreditation:* CORE. Part-time programs available. *Degree requirements:* For master's, comprehensive exam, thesis, internship. *Entrance requirements:* For master's, GRE or PAEG, interview, minimum GPA of 3.0, letter of recommendation.

University of Saint Francis, Graduate School, Department of Psychology and Counseling, Fort Wayne, IN 46808-3994. Offers clinical mental health counseling (MS, Post Master's Certificate); pastoral counseling (MS, Post Master's Certificate); psychology (MS); rehabilitation counseling (MS, Post Master's Certificate); school counseling (MS Ed). Part-time and evening/weekend programs available. *Faculty:* 3 full-time (1 woman). *Students:* 29 full-time (22 women), 20 part-time (all women); includes 10 minority (7 Black or African American, non-Hispanic/Latino; 2 Hispanic/Latino; 1 Two or more races, non-Hispanic/Latino), 1 international. Average age 32. 21 applicants, 90% accepted, 16 enrolled. In 2014, 23 master's awarded. *Entrance requirements:* For master's, minimum undergraduate GPA of 3.0; undergraduate coursework in psychology. Additional exam requirements/recommendations for international students: Required—TOEFL or IELTS. *Application deadline:* For fall admission, 7/1 for domestic students; for spring admission, 11/1 for domestic students. Applications are processed on a rolling basis. Application fee: $0. Electronic applications accepted. *Expenses:* Expenses: $830 per credit hour. *Financial support:* In 2014–15, 5 students received support. Federal Work-Study, scholarships/grants, and unspecified assistantships available. Support available to part-time students. Financial award application deadline: 3/10; financial award applicants required to submit FAFSA. *Unit head:* Dr. John Brinkman, Associate Professor/Chair, Department of Psychology and Counseling, 260-399-7700 Ext. 8425, Fax: 260-399-8170, E-mail: jbrinkman@sf.edu. *Application contact:* Kyle Richardson, Enrollment Specialist, 260-399-7700 Ext. 6310, Fax: 260-399-8152, E-mail: krichardson@sf.edu.
Website: http://psychology.sf.edu/

The University of Scranton, College of Graduate and Continuing Education, Department of Counseling and Human Services, Program in Rehabilitation Counseling, Scranton, PA 18510. Offers MS. *Accreditation:* CORE. Part-time and evening/weekend programs available. *Students:* 20 full-time (17 women), 5 part-time (4 women); includes 3 minority (1 Hispanic/Latino; 2 Two or more races, non-Hispanic/Latino). Average age 29. 15 applicants, 67% accepted. In 2014, 12 master's awarded. *Degree requirements:* For master's, comprehensive exam, capstone experience. *Entrance requirements:* For master's, minimum GPA of 3.0. Additional exam requirements/recommendations for international students: Required—TOEFL (minimum score 500 paper-based), IELTS (minimum score 6). *Application deadline:* For fall admission, 3/1 for domestic students. Application fee: $0. *Financial support:* Teaching assistantships, career-related internships or fieldwork, and Federal Work-Study available. Support available to part-time students. Financial award application deadline: 3/1. *Unit head:* Dr. Lori Bruch, Program Director, 570-941-4308, Fax: 570-941-5882, E-mail: bruchl1@scranton.edu. *Application contact:* Joseph M. Roback, Director of Admissions, 570-941-4385, Fax: 570-941-5928, E-mail: robackj2@scranton.edu.

University of South Carolina, School of Medicine and The Graduate School, Graduate Programs in Medicine, Program in Rehabilitation Counseling, Columbia, SC 29208. Offers psychiatric rehabilitation (Certificate); rehabilitation counseling (MRC). *Accreditation:* CORE. Part-time and evening/weekend programs available. *Degree requirements:* For master's, comprehensive exam, internship, practicum. *Entrance requirements:* For master's and Certificate, GRE General Test or GMAT. Electronic applications accepted. *Expenses:* Contact institution. *Faculty research:* Quality of life, alcohol dependency, technology for disabled, psychiatric rehabilitation, women with disabilities.

University of Southern Maine, College of Management and Human Service, School of Education and Human Development, Program in Counselor Education, Portland, ME 04104-9300. Offers clinical mental health counseling (MS); counseling (CAS); culturally responsive practices in education and human development (CGS); mental health rehabilitation technician/community (CGS); rehabilitation counseling (MS); school counseling (MS); substance abuse counseling (CGS). *Accreditation:* ACA (one or more programs are accredited); CORE; Teacher Education Accreditation Council. Part-time and evening/weekend programs available. *Faculty:* 6 full-time (4 women), 3 part-time/adjunct (2 women). *Students:* 60 full-time (44 women), 82 part-time (67 women); includes 8 minority (2 Black or African American, non-Hispanic/Latino; 1 American Indian or Alaska Native, non-Hispanic/Latino; 1 Asian, non-Hispanic/Latino; 2 Hispanic/Latino; 2 Two or more races, non-Hispanic/Latino). Average age 36. 76 applicants, 75% accepted, 44 enrolled. In 2014, 35 master's, 8 other advanced degrees awarded. *Degree requirements:* For master's, comprehensive exam, thesis or alternative; for other advanced degree, thesis or alternative. *Entrance requirements:* For master's, GRE General Test or MAT, interview; for other advanced degree, master's degree. Additional exam requirements/recommendations for international students: Required—TOEFL (minimum score 550 paper-based; 79 iBT). *Application deadline:* For fall admission, 11/15 for domestic students. Application fee: $65. Electronic applications accepted. *Expenses: Tuition, area resident:* Full-time $6840; part-time $380 per credit hour. Tuition, state resident: full-time $10,260; part-time $570 per credit hour. Tuition, nonresident: full-time $18,468; part-time $1026 per credit hour. *Required fees:* $830; $83 per credit hour. Tuition and fees vary according to course load and program. *Financial support:* Research assistantships, career-related internships or fieldwork, Federal Work-Study, institutionally sponsored loans, scholarships/grants, and unspecified assistantships available. Support available to part-time students. Financial award application deadline: 3/1; financial award applicants required to submit FAFSA. *Faculty research:* Counselor licensure, group dynamics, counseling theories, healthy adaptation, counselor educator well-being. *Unit head:* Adele Baruch, Program Coordinator, 207-780-5317, E-mail: abaruch@usm.maine.edu. *Application contact:* Mary Sloan, Assistant Dean of Graduate Studies and Director of Graduate Admissions, 207-780-4386, E-mail: gradstudies@usm.maine.edu.
Website: http://usm.maine.edu/counselor-education

University of South Florida, College of Behavioral and Community Sciences, Department of Rehabilitation and Mental Health Counseling, Tampa, FL 33620-9951. Offers addictions and substance abuse counseling (MA); marriage and family therapy (MA). *Accreditation:* CORE. Part-time and evening/weekend programs available. *Faculty:* 5 full-time (3 women), 1 part-time/adjunct (0 women). *Students:* 63 full-time (52 women), 54 part-time (50 women); includes 32 minority (9 Black or African American, non-Hispanic/Latino; 3 Asian, non-Hispanic/Latino; 18 Hispanic/Latino; 1 Native Hawaiian or other Pacific Islander, non-Hispanic/Latino; 1 Two or more races, non-Hispanic/Latino), 1 international. Average age 30. 52 applicants, 67% accepted, 25 enrolled. In 2014, 41 master's awarded. *Degree requirements:* For master's, comprehensive exam, thesis optional. *Entrance requirements:* For master's, GRE General Test, three letters of recommendation, personal statement of intent, on-campus interview, undergraduate statistics or research methods course. Additional exam requirements/recommendations for international students: Required—TOEFL (minimum score 550 paper-based; 79 iBT) or IELTS (minimum score 6.5). *Application deadline:* For fall admission, 2/15 for domestic students, 1/2 for international students; for spring admission, 10/15 for domestic students, 6/1 for international students. Application fee: $30. Electronic applications accepted. *Total annual research expenditures:* $233,747. *Unit head:* Dr. Tennyson Wright, Chair and Associate Professor, 813-974-2963, Fax: 813-974-8080, E-mail: tjwright@usf.edu. *Application contact:* Dr. Gary DuDell, Instructor and Director of Graduate Studies, 813-974-1257, Fax: 813-974-8080, E-mail: gdudell@usf.edu.
Website: http://rmhc.cbcs.usf.edu/

University of South Florida, Innovative Education, Tampa, FL 33620-9951. *Unit head:* Kathy Barnes, Interdisciplinary Programs Coordinator, 813-974-8031, Fax: 813-974-7061, E-mail: barnesk@usf.edu. *Application contact:* Karen Tylinski, Metro Initiatives, 813-974-9943, Fax: 813-974-7061, E-mail: ktylinsk@usf.edu.
Website: http://www.usf.edu/innovative-education/

The University of Tennessee, Graduate School, College of Education, Health and Human Sciences, Department of Educational Psychology and Counseling, Knoxville, TN 37996. Offers adult education (MS); applied educational psychology (MS); collaborative learning (Ed D); college student personnel (MS); mental health counseling (MS); rehabilitation counseling (MS); school counseling (MS). *Accreditation:* ACA (one or more programs are accredited); CORE (one or more programs are accredited); NCATE. Part-time and evening/weekend programs available. *Degree requirements:* For master's, thesis optional. *Entrance requirements:* For master's, GRE General Test, minimum GPA of 2.7. Additional exam requirements/recommendations for international students: Required—TOEFL. Electronic applications accepted.

The University of Texas at Austin, Graduate School, College of Education, Department of Special Education, Austin, TX 78712-1111. Offers autism and developmental disabilities (Ed D, PhD); autism and developmental disability (M Ed, MA); early childhood special education (M Ed, MA, Ed D, PhD); learning disabilities (Ed D, PhD); learning disabilities/behavior disorders (M Ed, MA); multicultural special education (M Ed, MA, Ed D, PhD); rehabilitation counselor (M Ed); rehabilitation counselor education (Ed D, PhD); special education administration (Ed D, PhD). *Accreditation:* CORE. Part-time and evening/weekend programs available. Postbaccalaureate distance learning degree programs offered (no on-campus study). *Degree requirements:* For master's, thesis or alternative; for doctorate, thesis/dissertation. *Entrance requirements:* For master's and doctorate, GRE General Test. *Faculty research:* Anchored instruction, reading disabilities, multicultural/bilingual.

The University of Texas at El Paso, Graduate School, College of Health Sciences, Rehabilitation Counseling Program, El Paso, TX 79968-0001. Offers MRC. *Accreditation:* CORE. Part-time and evening/weekend programs available. *Degree requirements:* For master's, comprehensive exam, thesis optional. *Entrance requirements:* For master's, GRE, minimum GPA of 3.0, statement of professional goals, letters of recommendation. Additional exam requirements/recommendations for international students: Required—TOEFL; Recommended—IELTS. Electronic applications accepted. *Faculty research:* Psychosocial adjustment to disability, attribution regarding disability, self-regulation, professional issues in rehabilitation counseling, rehabilitation education.

The University of Texas–Pan American, College of Health Sciences and Human Services, Department of Rehabilitation, Edinburg, TX 78539. Offers MS, PhD. *Accreditation:* CORE. Part-time and evening/weekend programs available. *Degree requirements:* For master's, comprehensive exam, thesis optional. *Entrance requirements:* For master's, minimum GPA of 3.0. *Expenses:* Tuition, state resident: full-time $4187; part-time $232.60 per credit hour. Tuition, nonresident: full-time $10,857; part-time $603.16 per credit hour. *Required fees:* $782; $27.50 per credit hour. $143.35 per semester. *Faculty research:* Attitudes and disability, substance abuse, multicultural counseling, Hispanics and disability, Social Security beneficiary characteristics.

The University of Texas Southwestern Medical Center, Southwestern School of Health Professions, Rehabilitation Counseling Psychology Program, Dallas, TX 75390. Offers MRC. *Accreditation:* CORE. *Degree requirements:* For master's, thesis. *Entrance requirements:* For master's, GRE General Test, minimum GPA of 3.0. Electronic applications accepted. *Faculty research:* Psychophysiology of stress and emotion, psychosocial rehabilitation, assessment of learning disabilities.

University of Wisconsin–Madison, Graduate School, School of Education, Department of Rehabilitation Psychology and Special Education, Program in Rehabilitation Psychology, Madison, WI 53706-1380. Offers MA, MS, PhD. *Accreditation:* CORE (one or more programs are accredited). *Degree requirements:* For doctorate, thesis/dissertation. *Expenses:* Tuition, state resident: full-time $10,723; part-time $745 per credit. Tuition, nonresident: full-time $24,054; part-time $1578 per credit. *Required fees:* $374 per semester. Tuition and fees vary according to course load, program and reciprocity agreements.

University of Wisconsin–Stout, Graduate School, College of Human Development, Program in Vocational Rehabilitation, Menomonie, WI 54751. Offers MS. *Accreditation:* CORE. Part-time programs available. Postbaccalaureate distance learning degree programs offered (no on-campus study). *Degree requirements:* For master's, comprehensive exam or thesis. *Entrance requirements:* For master's, minimum GPA of 2.75. Additional exam requirements/recommendations for international students: Required—TOEFL (minimum score 500 paper-based; 61 iBT). *Application deadline:* For fall admission, 3/15 priority date for domestic and international students. Application fee: $45. Electronic applications accepted. *Financial support:* Research assistantships with partial tuition reimbursements, teaching assistantships with partial tuition reimbursements, Federal Work-Study, scholarships/grants, tuition waivers (partial), and unspecified assistantships available. Support available to part-time students. Financial award application deadline: 5/1; financial award applicants required to submit FAFSA. *Faculty research:* Aging/gerontology, athletics, neuropsychology, recreation, transition to work. *Unit head:* Dr. Michelle Hamilton, Director, 715-232-1895, Fax: 715-232-2356, E-mail: hamiltonmi@uwstout.edu. *Application contact:* Anne Johnson, Graduate Student

Evaluator (Admissions and Assistantship Coordinator), 715-232-1322, Fax: 715-232-2413.
Website: http://www.uwstout.edu/programs/msvr/

Utah State University, School of Graduate Studies, Emma Eccles Jones College of Education and Human Services, Department of Special Education and Rehabilitation, Program in Rehabilitation Counselor Education, Logan, UT 84322. Offers MRC. *Accreditation:* CORE. Part-time programs available. Postbaccalaureate distance learning degree programs offered (minimal on-campus study). *Degree requirements:* For master's, internship. *Entrance requirements:* For master's, GRE General Test, minimum GPA of 3.0. Additional exam requirements/recommendations for international students: Required—TOEFL (minimum score 550 paper-based). Electronic applications accepted. *Expenses:* Contact institution. *Faculty research:* Distance education, Hispanic rehabilitation, transition from school to work.

Virginia Commonwealth University, Graduate School, School of Allied Health Professions, Department of Rehabilitation Counseling, Richmond, VA 23284-9005. Offers MS, CPC. *Accreditation:* CORE (one or more programs are accredited). *Entrance requirements:* For master's, GRE General Test or MAT. Additional exam requirements/recommendations for international students: Required—TOEFL (minimum score 600 paper-based; 100 iBT). Electronic applications accepted. *Faculty research:* Substance abuse/addictions, lifelong disabilities, consumer empowerment, counseling models, adjustment to disability.

Wayne State University, College of Education, Division of Theoretical and Behavioral Foundations, Detroit, MI 48202. Offers counseling (M Ed, MA, Ed D, PhD, Ed S); education evaluation and research (M Ed, Ed D, PhD); educational psychology (M Ed, PhD), including learning and instruction sciences (PhD), school psychology (PhD); rehabilitation counseling and community inclusion (MA); school and community psychology (MA); school psychology (Certificate). *Accreditation:* ACA (one or more programs are accredited); CORE (one or more programs are accredited). Evening/weekend programs available. *Students:* 237 full-time (197 women), 234 part-time (209 women); includes 172 minority (135 Black or African American, non-Hispanic/Latino; 1 American Indian or Alaska Native, non-Hispanic/Latino; 12 Asian, non-Hispanic/Latino; 11 Hispanic/Latino; 1 Native Hawaiian or other Pacific Islander, non-Hispanic/Latino; 12 Two or more races, non-Hispanic/Latino), 24 international. Average age 33. 297 applicants, 37% accepted, 75 enrolled. In 2014, 82 master's, 17 doctorates, 12 other advanced degrees awarded. *Degree requirements:* For master's, thesis (for some programs); for doctorate, thesis/dissertation. *Entrance requirements:* For master's, GRE; for doctorate, GRE, interview, minimum GPA of 3.0, curriculum vitae, references; for other advanced degree, master's degree in counseling and counseling license (for Ed S); good standing in school and community psychology MA program (for Certificate). Additional exam requirements/recommendations for international students: Required—TOEFL (minimum score 550 paper-based; 79 iBT), Michigan English Language Assessment Battery (minimum score 85); Recommended—IELTS (minimum score 6.5), TWE (minimum score 5.5). *Application deadline:* For fall admission, 6/1 priority date for domestic students, 5/1 priority date for international students; for winter admission, 10/1 priority date for domestic students, 9/1 priority date for international students; for spring admission, 2/1 priority date for domestic students, 1/1 priority date for international students. Applications are processed on a rolling basis. Application fee: $0. Electronic applications accepted. *Expenses:* Tuition, state resident: full-time $10,294; part-time $571.90 per credit hour. Tuition, nonresident: full-time $29,730; part-time $1238.75 per credit hour. *Required fees:* $1365; $43.50 per credit hour. $291.10 per semester. Tuition and fees vary according to course load and program. *Financial support:* In 2014–15, 143 students received support, including 2 research assistantships with tuition reimbursements available (averaging $16,838 per year); fellowships with tuition reimbursements available, teaching assistantships with tuition reimbursements available, Federal Work-Study, scholarships/grants, health care benefits, and unspecified assistantships also available. Support available to part-time students. Financial award application deadline: 3/31; financial award applicants required to submit FAFSA. *Faculty research:* Adolescents at risk, supervision of counseling. *Unit head:* Dr. Joanne Holbert, Interim Assistant Dean, 313-577-1691, E-mail: jholbert@wayne.edu. *Application contact:* Janice Green, Assistant Dean, 313-577-1605, E-mail: jwgreen@wayne.edu.
Website: http://coe.wayne.edu/tbf/index.php

Western Michigan University, Graduate College, College of Health and Human Services, Department of Blindness and Low Vision Studies, Kalamazoo, MI 49008. Offers orientation and mobility (MA); orientation and mobility of children (MA); vision rehabilitation therapy (MA). *Accreditation:* CORE. *Application deadline:* For fall admission, 2/15 for domestic students. *Financial support:* Application deadline: 2/15. *Application contact:* Admissions and Orientation, 269-387-2000, Fax: 269-387-2096.

Western Oregon University, Graduate Programs, College of Education, Division of Special Education, Program in Rehabilitation Counseling, Monmouth, OR 97361-1394. Offers MS. *Accreditation:* CORE. *Degree requirements:* For master's, thesis optional, oral exam, portfolio. *Entrance requirements:* For master's, interview, minimum GPA of 3.0. Additional exam requirements/recommendations for international students: Required—TOEFL (minimum score 550 paper-based; 79 iBT), IELTS (minimum score 6.5). *Faculty research:* Deafness, rehabilitation counseling.

Western Washington University, Graduate School, Woodring College of Education, Program in Rehabilitation Counseling, Bellingham, WA 98225-5996. Offers MA. *Accreditation:* CORE. Part-time and evening/weekend programs available. Postbaccalaureate distance learning degree programs offered (minimal on-campus study). *Degree requirements:* For master's, research project. *Entrance requirements:* For master's, GRE General Test or MAT, minimum GPA of 3.0 in last 60 semester hours or last 90 quarter hours of course work. Additional exam requirements/recommendations for international students: Required—TOEFL (minimum score 567 paper-based). Electronic applications accepted. *Faculty research:* Employment issues for individuals with significant disabilities, research and statistics techniques, rehabilitation counselor education.

West Virginia University, College of Human Resources and Education, Department of Counseling, Rehabilitation Counseling, and Counseling Psychology, Program in Rehabilitation Counseling, Morgantown, WV 26506. Offers MS. *Accreditation:* CORE. Part-time programs available. Postbaccalaureate distance learning degree programs offered (minimal on-campus study). *Degree requirements:* For master's, content exams. *Entrance requirements:* For master's, GRE General Test, minimum GPA of 2.5, interview. Additional exam requirements/recommendations for international students: Required—TOEFL (minimum score 550 paper-based; 65 iBT). Electronic applications accepted. *Faculty research:* Work adjustment, job modification for the handicapped, computer resource networks, vocational evaluation.

Wilberforce University, Program in Rehabilitation Counseling, Wilberforce, OH 45384. Offers MS. *Entrance requirements:* For master's, bachelor's degree, 3 letters of recommendation, interview. Additional exam requirements/recommendations for international students: Required—TOEFL.

Winston-Salem State University, Program in Rehabilitation Counseling, Winston-Salem, NC 27110-0003. Offers MRC. Part-time programs available. Postbaccalaureate distance learning degree programs offered (minimal on-campus study). *Degree requirements:* For master's, thesis optional. *Entrance requirements:* For master's, GRE, 3 letters of recommendation. Electronic applications accepted. *Faculty research:* Drug addiction, recovery, HIV/AIDS interventions.

Wright State University, School of Graduate Studies, College of Education and Human Services, Department of Human Services, Program in Rehabilitation Counseling, Dayton, OH 45435. Offers chemical dependency (MRC); severe disabilities (MRC). *Accreditation:* CORE. *Degree requirements:* For master's, comprehensive exam. *Entrance requirements:* For master's, GRE General Test, MAT, interview. Additional exam requirements/recommendations for international students: Required—TOEFL.

School Psychology

Abilene Christian University, Graduate School, College of Arts and Sciences, Department of Psychology, Specialist in School Psychology Program, Abilene, TX 79699-9100. Offers Specialist. *Students:* 8 full-time (7 women), 8 part-time (7 women); includes 3 minority (1 Black or African American, non-Hispanic/Latino; 2 Hispanic/Latino). 15 applicants, 33% accepted, 3 enrolled. *Entrance requirements:* Additional exam requirements/recommendations for international students: Required—TOEFL (minimum score 550 paper-based; 90 iBT), IELTS (minimum score 6.5), PTE. *Application deadline:* For fall admission, 3/1 priority date for domestic students; for spring admission, 11/1 for domestic students. Applications are processed on a rolling basis. Application fee: $50. Electronic applications accepted. *Expenses: Tuition:* Full-time $18,228; part-time $1016 per credit hour. *Financial support:* In 2014–15, 6 students received support. Federal Work-Study available. Support available to part-time students. Financial award application deadline: 4/1; financial award applicants required to submit FAFSA. *Unit head:* Dr. Rachel Team, Graduate Advisor, 325-674-2285, Fax: 325-674-6968, E-mail: rmg97j@acu.edu. *Application contact:* Corey Patterson, Director of Graduate Admission and Recruiting, 325-674-6566, Fax: 325-674-6717, E-mail: gradinfo@acu.edu.

Adelphi University, Derner Institute of Advanced Psychological Studies, Program in School Psychology, Garden City, NY 11530-0701. Offers MA. Part-time programs available. *Students:* 42 full-time (38 women), 24 part-time (all women); includes 19 minority (6 Black or African American, non-Hispanic/Latino; 1 Asian, non-Hispanic/Latino; 11 Hispanic/Latino; 1 Two or more races, non-Hispanic/Latino). Average age 26. In 2014, 20 master's awarded. *Degree requirements:* For master's, comprehensive exam. *Entrance requirements:* For master's, minimum GPA of 3.0; 15 credits of course work in psychology including general psychology, developmental child or adolescent psychology, abnormal personality in school psychology, tests and measurements, statistics; 3 letters of recommendation. Additional exam requirements/recommendations for international students: Required—TOEFL (minimum score 550 paper-based; 80 iBT). *Application deadline:* For fall admission, 5/1 for domestic students, 4/1 for international students. Application fee: $50. Electronic applications accepted. *Financial support:* Research assistantships with full and partial tuition reimbursements, career-related internships or fieldwork, Federal Work-Study, institutionally sponsored loans, and unspecified assistantships available. *Unit head:* Dr. Ionas Sapountzis, Director, 516-877-4743, E-mail: isapountzis@adelphi.edu. *Application contact:* Christine Murphy, Director of Admissions, 516-877-3050, Fax: 516-877-3039, E-mail: graduateadmissions@adelphi.edu.
Website: http://derner.adelphi.edu/psychology/graduate/ma-in-school-psychology/

Alabama Agricultural and Mechanical University, School of Graduate Studies, School of Education, Department of Counseling and Special Education, Huntsville, AL 35811. Offers communicative disorders (M Ed, MS); psychology and counseling (MS, Ed S), including clinical psychology (MS), counseling and guidance, counseling psychology (MS), personnel management (MS), psychometry (MS), school psychology (MS); special education (M Ed, MS). *Accreditation:* CORE; NCATE. Part-time and evening/weekend programs available. *Degree requirements:* For master's, comprehensive exam. *Entrance requirements:* For master's, GRE General Test. Additional exam requirements/recommendations for international students: Required—TOEFL (minimum score 500 paper-based; 61 iBT). *Faculty research:* Increasing numbers of minorities in special education and speech-language pathology.

Alfred University, Graduate School, Counseling and School Psychology Program, Alfred, NY 14802-1205. Offers mental health counseling (MS Ed); school counseling (MS Ed, CAS); school psychology (MA, Psy D, CAS). *Accreditation:* APA. *Degree requirements:* For master's, internship; for doctorate, thesis/dissertation, internship. *Entrance requirements:* For master's and doctorate, GRE General Test. Additional exam requirements/recommendations for international students: Required—TOEFL (minimum score 590 paper-based; 90 iBT), IELTS (minimum score 6.5). Electronic applications accepted. *Faculty research:* Family processes, alternative assessment approaches, behavior disorders in children, parent involvement, school psychology training issues.

Alliant International University–Irvine, Shirley M. Hufstedler School of Education, Educational Psychology Programs, Irvine, CA 92606. Offers educational psychology (Psy D); pupil personnel services (Credential); school psychology (MA). Part-time programs available. *Degree requirements:* For doctorate, thesis/dissertation. *Entrance requirements:* For master's, minimum GPA of 2.5, letters of recommendation; for doctorate, interview, minimum GPA of 3.0, letters of recommendation. Additional exam requirements/recommendations for international students: Required—TOEFL (minimum score 550 paper-based; 80 iBT), TWE (minimum score 5). *Faculty research:* School-based mental health.

Alliant International University–Los Angeles, Shirley M. Hufstedler School of Education, Educational Psychology Programs, Alhambra, CA 91803-1360. Offers educational psychology (Psy D); pupil personnel services (Credential); school psychology (MA). Part-time programs available. *Degree requirements:* For doctorate,

comprehensive exam, thesis/dissertation. *Entrance requirements:* For master's, minimum GPA of 2.5, letters of recommendation; for doctorate, interview, minimum GPA of 3.0, letters of recommendation. Additional exam requirements/recommendations for international students: Required—TOEFL (minimum score 550 paper-based), TWE (minimum score 5). Electronic applications accepted. *Faculty research:* Early identification and intervention with high-risk preschoolers, pediatric neuropsychology, interpersonal violence, ADHD, learning theories.

Alliant International University–San Diego, Shirley M. Hufstedler School of Education, Educational Psychology Programs, San Diego, CA 92131-1799. Offers educational psychology (Psy D); pupil personnel services (Credential); school neuropsychology (Certificate); school psychology (MA); school-based mental health (Certificate). Part-time programs available. *Degree requirements:* For doctorate, comprehensive exam, thesis/dissertation, internship. *Entrance requirements:* For master's, minimum GPA of 2.5, letters of recommendation; for doctorate, minimum GPA of 3.0, letters of recommendation. Additional exam requirements/recommendations for international students: Required—TOEFL (minimum score 550 paper-based; 80 iBT), TWE (minimum score 5). Electronic applications accepted. *Faculty research:* School-based mental health, pupil personnel services, childhood mood, school-based assessment.

Alliant International University–San Francisco, Shirley M. Hufstedler School of Education, Educational Psychology Programs, San Francisco, CA 94133-1221. Offers educational psychology (Psy D); pupil personnel services (Credential); school psychology (MA). Part-time programs available. Terminal master's awarded for partial completion of doctoral program. *Degree requirements:* For doctorate, thesis/dissertation. *Entrance requirements:* For master's, minimum GPA of 3.0, letters of recommendation; for doctorate, interview, minimum GPA of 3.0, letters of recommendation. Additional exam requirements/recommendations for international students: Required—TOEFL (minimum score 550 paper-based), TWE (minimum score 5). Electronic applications accepted. *Faculty research:* Social skills, ADHD, cognitive functioning and learning, innovative teaching methods.

American Public University System, AMU/APU Graduate Programs, Charles Town, WV 25414. Offers accounting (MBA, MS); criminal justice (MA), including business administration, emergency and disaster management, general (MA, MS); educational leadership (M Ed); emergency and disaster management (MA); entrepreneurship (MBA); environmental policy and management (MS), including environmental planning, environmental sustainability, fish and wildlife management, general (MA, MS), global environmental management; finance (MBA); general (MBA); global business management (MBA); history (MA), including American history, ancient and classical history, European history, global history, public history; homeland security (MA), including business administration, counter-terrorism studies, criminal justice, cyber, emergency management and public health, intelligence studies, transportation security; homeland security resource allocation (MBA); humanities (MA); information technology (MS), including digital forensics, enterprise software development, information assurance and security, IT project management; information technology management (MBA); intelligence studies (MA), including criminal intelligence, cyber, general (MA, MS), homeland security, intelligence analysis, intelligence collection, intelligence management, intelligence operations, terrorism studies; international relations and conflict resolution (MA), including comparative and security issues, conflict resolution, international and transnational security issues, peacekeeping; legal studies (MA); management (MA), including defense management, general (MA, MS), human resource management, organizational leadership, public administration; marketing (MBA); military history (MA), including American military history, American Revolution, civil war, war since 1945, World War II; military studies (MA), including joint warfare, strategic leadership; national security studies (MA), including general (MA, MS), homeland security, regional security studies, security and intelligence analysis, terrorism studies; nonprofit management (MBA); political science (MA), including American politics and government, comparative government and development, general (MA, MS), international relations, public policy; psychology (MA); public administration (MPA), including disaster management, environmental policy, health policy, human resources, national security, organizational management, security management; public health (MPH); reverse logistics management (MA); school counseling (M Ed); security management (MA); space studies (MS), including aerospace science, general (MA, MS), planetary science; sports and health sciences (MS); teaching (M Ed), including curriculum and instruction for elementary teachers, elementary reading, English language learners, instructional leadership, online learning, special education; transportation and logistics management (MA), including general (MA, MS), maritime engineering management, reverse logistics management. Programs offered via distance learning only. Part-time and evening/weekend programs available. Postbaccalaureate distance learning degree programs offered (no on-campus study). *Faculty:* 426 full-time (236 women), 1,864 part-time/adjunct (880 women). *Students:* 475 full-time (215 women), 10,067 part-time (4,085 women); includes 3,462 minority (1,863 Black or African American, non-Hispanic/Latino; 74 American Indian or Alaska Native, non-Hispanic/Latino; 273 Asian, non-Hispanic/Latino; 831 Hispanic/Latino; 78 Native Hawaiian or other Pacific Islander, non-Hispanic/Latino; 343 Two or more races, non-Hispanic/Latino), 131 international. Average age 36. In 2014, 3,740 master's awarded. *Degree requirements:* For master's, comprehensive exam or practicum. *Entrance requirements:* For master's, official transcript showing earned bachelor's degree from institution accredited by recognized accrediting body. Additional exam requirements/recommendations for international students: Required—TOEFL (minimum score 550 paper-based), IELTS (minimum score 6.5). *Application deadline:* Applications are processed on a rolling basis. Application fee: $0. Electronic applications accepted. *Financial support:* Applicants required to submit FAFSA. *Faculty research:* Military history, criminal justice, management performance, national security. *Unit head:* Dr. Karan Powell, Executive Vice President and Provost, 877-468-6268, Fax: 304-724-3780. *Application contact:* Terry Grant, Vice President of Enrollment Management, 877-468-6268, Fax: 304-724-3780, E-mail: info@apus.edu.
Website: http://www.apus.edu

Andrews University, School of Graduate Studies, School of Education, Department of Graduate Psychology and Counseling, Program in School Counseling, Berrien Springs, MI 49104. Offers MA. *Students:* 7 full-time (6 women); includes 4 minority (2 Black or African American, non-Hispanic/Latino; 1 Asian, non-Hispanic/Latino; 1 Hispanic/Latino), 1 international. Average age 31. 9 applicants, 33% accepted, 1 enrolled. In 2014, 2 master's awarded. *Degree requirements:* For master's, thesis optional. *Entrance requirements:* For master's, GRE. Additional exam requirements/recommendations for international students: Required—TOEFL (minimum score 550 paper-based). Application fee: $40. Tuition and fees vary according to course level. *Unit head:* Dr. Rudolph N. Bailey, Coordinator, 269-471-3466. *Application contact:* Monica Wringer, Supervisor of Graduate Admission, 800-253-2874, Fax: 269-471-6321, E-mail: graduate@andrews.edu.

Andrews University, School of Graduate Studies, School of Education, Department of Graduate Psychology and Counseling, Program in School Psychology, Berrien Springs, MI 49104. Offers Ed S. Part-time programs available. *Students:* 11 full-time (6 women); includes 3 minority (1 Black or African American, non-Hispanic/Latino; 2 Hispanic/Latino), 2 international. Average age 34. 8 applicants, 63% accepted, 1 enrolled. In 2014, 7 Ed Ss awarded. *Entrance requirements:* Additional exam requirements/recommendations for international students: Required—TOEFL (minimum score 550 paper-based). *Application deadline:* Applications are processed on a rolling basis. Application fee: $40. Tuition and fees vary according to course level. *Unit head:* Dr. Elizabeth Lundy, Coordinator, 269-471-6251. *Application contact:* Monica Wringer, Supervisor of Graduate Admission, 800-253-2874, Fax: 269-471-6321, E-mail: graduate@andrews.edu.

Appalachian State University, Cratis D. Williams Graduate School, Department of Human Development and Psychological Counseling, Boone, NC 28608. Offers clinical mental health counseling (MA); college student development (MA); marriage and family therapy (MA); school counseling (MA). *Accreditation:* AAMFT/COAMFTE; ACA; NCATE. Part-time programs available. *Degree requirements:* For master's, comprehensive exam (for some programs), thesis optional, internships. *Entrance requirements:* For master's, GRE General Test, 3 letters of recommendation. Additional exam requirements/recommendations for international students: Required—TOEFL (minimum score 570 paper-based; 79 iBT), IELTS (minimum score 6.5). Electronic applications accepted. *Faculty research:* Multicultural counseling, addictions counseling, play therapy, expressive arts, child and adolescent therapy, sexual abuse counseling.

Arcadia University, Graduate Studies, Department of Psychology, Glenside, PA 19038-3295. Offers community counseling (MACP); school counseling (MACP). Part-time programs available. *Degree requirements:* For master's, practicum. *Entrance requirements:* For master's, GRE General Test or MAT. *Expenses:* Contact institution.

Argosy University, Dallas, College of Education, Farmers Branch, TX 75244. Offers educational administration (MA Ed); educational leadership (Ed D); higher and postsecondary education (MA Ed); instructional leadership (MA Ed); school psychology (MA).

Argosy University, Hawai`i, College of Education, Program in School Psychology, Honolulu, HI 96813. Offers MA.

Argosy University, Phoenix, College of Education, Program in School Psychology, Phoenix, AZ 85021. Offers MA, Psy D.

Argosy University, Sarasota, College of Education, Sarasota, FL 34235. Offers community college executive leadership (Ed D); educational leadership (MA Ed, Ed D, Ed S), including higher education administration (Ed D), K-12 education (Ed D); school counseling (MA, Ed S); school psychology (MA); teaching and learning (MA Ed, Ed D, Ed S), including education technology (Ed D), higher education (Ed D), K-12 education (Ed D).

Arkansas State University, Graduate School, College of Education and Behavioral Science, Department of Psychology and Counseling, State University, AR 72467. Offers clinical mental health counseling (Certificate); college student personnel services (MS); psychology and counseling (Ed S); rehabilitation counseling (MRC); school counseling (MSE); student affairs (Certificate). *Accreditation:* ACA (one or more programs are accredited); CORE (one or more programs are accredited); NCATE. Part-time programs available. *Faculty:* 15 full-time (9 women). *Students:* 57 full-time (36 women), 51 part-time (38 women); includes 21 minority (19 Black or African American, non-Hispanic/Latino; 1 Hispanic/Latino; 1 Two or more races, non-Hispanic/Latino), 1 international. Average age 30. 102 applicants, 54% accepted, 48 enrolled. In 2014, 22 master's, 22 other advanced degrees awarded. *Degree requirements:* For master's and other advanced degree, comprehensive exam, thesis or alternative. *Entrance requirements:* For master's, GRE General Test or MAT (for MSE), appropriate bachelor's degree, interview, letters of reference, official transcripts, immunization records, written statement, 2-3 page autobiography; for other advanced degree, GRE General Test, interview, master's degree, letters of reference, official transcript, personal statement, immunization records. Additional exam requirements/recommendations for international students: Required—TOEFL (minimum score 550 paper-based; 79 iBT), IELTS (minimum score 6), PTE (minimum score 56). *Application deadline:* Applications are processed on a rolling basis. Application fee: $30 ($40 for international students). Electronic applications accepted. *Expenses:* Tuition, state resident: full-time $4392; part-time $244 per credit hour. Tuition, nonresident: full-time $8784; part-time $488 per credit hour. *International tuition:* $9484 full-time. *Required fees:* $1134; $63 per credit hour. $25 per term. Tuition and fees vary according to course load and program. *Financial support:* In 2014–15, 8 students received support. Teaching assistantships, career-related internships or fieldwork, scholarships/grants, and unspecified assistantships available. Financial award application deadline: 7/1; financial award applicants required to submit FAFSA. *Unit head:* Dr. Kris Biondolillo, Interim Chair, 870-972-3064, Fax: 870-972-3962, E-mail: kdbiondo@astate.edu. *Application contact:* Vickey Ring, Graduate Admissions Coordinator, 870-972-3029, Fax: 870-972-3857, E-mail: vickeyring@astate.edu.
Website: http://www.astate.edu/college/education/departments/psychology-and-counseling/index.dot

Assumption College, School Counseling Program, Worcester, MA 01609-1296. Offers school counseling (MA, CAGS); social worker/adjustment counselor (CAGS). Part-time and evening/weekend programs available. *Faculty:* 4 full-time (2 women), 6 part-time/adjunct (3 women). *Students:* 40 full-time (36 women), 22 part-time (21 women); includes 7 minority (1 Asian, non-Hispanic/Latino; 3 Hispanic/Latino; 3 Two or more races, non-Hispanic/Latino). Average age 28. 32 applicants, 69% accepted, 6 enrolled. In 2014, 36 master's, 5 other advanced degrees awarded. *Degree requirements:* For master's, comprehensive exam, internship, practicum; for CAGS, comprehensive exam, practicum. *Entrance requirements:* For master's, 3 letters of recommendation, resume, interview, essay; for CAGS, 3 letters of recommendation, resume, essay, interview. Additional exam requirements/recommendations for international students: Required—TOEFL (minimum score 540 paper-based; 76 iBT), IELTS (minimum score 6). *Application deadline:* For fall admission, 2/2 for domestic and international students; for winter admission, 2/1 for domestic and international students; for summer admission, 2/2 for domestic and international students. Application fee: $30. Electronic applications accepted. *Expenses: Tuition:* Full-time $10,620; part-time $590 per credit. *Required fees:* $20 per term. Full-time tuition and fees vary according to course load and program. *Financial support:* In 2014–15, 11 students received support. Tuition waivers (full and partial), unspecified assistantships, and institutional discounts available. Financial award application deadline: 5/1; financial award applicants required to submit FAFSA. *Faculty research:* Low dose stress reduction interventions for elementary school teachers. *Unit head:* Dr. Mary Ann Mariani, Director, 508-767-7087, Fax: 508-767-7263, E-mail: mmariani@assumption.edu. *Application contact:* Dr. Landy Johnson, Director of Operations for Graduate and Professional Studies, 508-767-7666, Fax: 508-767-7030, E-mail: graduate@assumption.edu.
Website: http://graduate.assumption.edu/school-counseling/masterofarts

Azusa Pacific University, School of Education, Department of School Counseling and School Psychology, Program in Educational Psychology, Azusa, CA 91702-7000. Offers MA.

Ball State University, Graduate School, Teachers College, Department of Educational Psychology, Program in School Psychology, Muncie, IN 47306-1099. Offers MA, PhD, Ed S. *Accreditation:* APA (one or more programs are accredited); NCATE. *Students:* 39

full-time (26 women), 14 part-time (12 women); includes 2 minority (1 Hispanic/Latino; 1 Two or more races, non-Hispanic/Latino), 1 international. Average age 26. 51 applicants, 37% accepted, 13 enrolled. In 2014, 9 master's, 4 doctorates, 6 other advanced degrees awarded. *Degree requirements:* For doctorate, thesis/dissertation; for Ed S, thesis. *Entrance requirements:* For master's and Ed S, GRE General Test; for doctorate, GRE General Test, interview, minimum graduate GPA of 3.2. Application fee: $50. *Financial support:* In 2014–15, 10 students received support, including 22 research assistantships with partial tuition reimbursements available (averaging $11,543 per year), 5 teaching assistantships with partial tuition reimbursements available (averaging $10,480 per year); unspecified assistantships also available. Financial award application deadline: 3/1. *Unit head:* Lisa Huffman, Head, 785-285-8511, Fax: 785-285-3653, E-mail: lhuffman@bsu.edu. *Application contact:* Dr. Robert Morris, Associate Provost for Research and Dean of the Graduate School, 765-285-1300, E-mail: rmorris@bsu.edu.

Barry University, College of Arts and Sciences, Department of Psychology, Miami Shores, FL 33161-6695. Offers clinical psychology (MS); school psychology (MS, SSP). Part-time and evening/weekend programs available. *Degree requirements:* For master's, thesis, practicum. *Entrance requirements:* For master's, GRE General Test, minimum GPA of 3.0, course work in psychology. Electronic applications accepted. *Faculty research:* Closed head injury, memory and aging, infant/mother interaction, evolutionary aspects of behavior, gender roles.

Baylor University, Graduate School, School of Education, Department of Educational Psychology, Waco, TX 76798-7301. Offers applied behavior analysis (MS Ed); educational psychology (MA, PhD); exceptionalities (PhD); learning and development (PhD); measurement (PhD); school psychology (Ed S). *Accreditation:* NCATE. *Degree requirements:* For master's, thesis optional; for doctorate, comprehensive exam, thesis/dissertation; for Ed S, comprehensive exam, thesis or alternative. *Entrance requirements:* For master's, minimum GPA of 3.0; for doctorate, GRE General Test, master's degree; for Ed S, GRE General Test. Additional exam requirements/recommendations for international students: Required—TOEFL. Electronic applications accepted. *Faculty research:* Individual differences, quantitative methods, gifted and talented, special education, school psychology, autism, applied behavior analysis, learning, human development.

Boston College, Lynch Graduate School of Education, Program in Counseling, Chestnut Hill, MA 02467-3800. Offers counseling psychology (PhD); mental health counseling (MA); school counseling (MA); MA/MA. *Accreditation:* APA (one or more programs are accredited). Terminal master's awarded for partial completion of doctoral program. *Degree requirements:* For master's, comprehensive exam; for doctorate, comprehensive exam, thesis/dissertation. *Entrance requirements:* For master's and doctorate, GRE General Test. Additional exam requirements/recommendations for international students: Required—TOEFL (minimum score 550 paper-based; 100 iBT). Electronic applications accepted. *Faculty research:* Reducing non-academic barriers to learning; race, gender, culture and social class issues in mental health; domestic violence; career development; community intervention and prevention.

Bowling Green State University, Graduate College, College of Education and Human Development, School of Education and Intervention Services, Intervention Services Division, Program in School Psychology, Bowling Green, OH 43403. Offers M Ed, Sp Ed. *Accreditation:* NCATE. Part-time programs available. *Degree requirements:* For master's, thesis or alternative, internship. *Entrance requirements:* For master's, GRE General Test. Additional exam requirements/recommendations for international students: Required—TOEFL. Electronic applications accepted. *Faculty research:* Family therapists/multicultural issues, pre-school readiness skills, family relations, multifaceted evaluation, multidisciplinary decision-making.

Brigham Young University, Graduate Studies, David O. McKay School of Education, Department of Counseling Psychology and Special Education, Provo, UT 84602-1001. Offers counseling psychology (PhD); school psychology (Ed S); special education (MS). Part-time and evening/weekend programs available. *Faculty:* 12 full-time (3 women), 9 part-time/adjunct (4 women). *Students:* 60 full-time (40 women), 27 part-time (22 women); includes 15 minority (2 Black or African American, non-Hispanic/Latino; 3 American Indian or Alaska Native, non-Hispanic/Latino; 2 Asian, non-Hispanic/Latino; 7 Hispanic/Latino; 1 Native Hawaiian or other Pacific Islander, non-Hispanic/Latino), 5 international. Average age 29. 65 applicants, 25% accepted, 16 enrolled. In 2014, 5 master's, 3 doctorates, 6 other advanced degrees awarded. *Degree requirements:* For master's and Ed S, comprehensive exam, thesis; for doctorate, comprehensive exam, thesis/dissertation. *Entrance requirements:* For master's, GRE General Test or MAT, minimum cumulative GPA of 3.0 in undergraduate coursework; for doctorate and Ed S, GRE General Test, minimum cumulative GPA of 3.0 in undergraduate coursework. Additional exam requirements/recommendations for international students: Required—TOEFL (minimum score 580 paper-based; 85 iBT), IELTS (minimum score 7). *Application deadline:* For fall admission, 1/15 for domestic and international students. Application fee: $50. Electronic applications accepted. *Expenses:* Expenses: Contact institution. *Financial support:* In 2014–15, 46 students received support, including 42 research assistantships with partial tuition reimbursements available (averaging $8,160 per year), 2 teaching assistantships with partial tuition reimbursements available (averaging $5,320 per year); institutionally sponsored loans and tuition waivers (partial) also available. Financial award application deadline: 3/31. *Faculty research:* Positive behavioral support in schools, spirituality in psychotherapy, multicultural psychology, gender issues in education, crisis management in schools. *Unit head:* Dr. Timothy B. Smith, Professor and Development Chair, 801-422-3857, Fax: 801-422-0198. *Application contact:* Diane E. Hancock, Department Secretary, 801-422-3859, Fax: 801-422-0198, E-mail: diane_hancock@byu.edu.
Website: http://education.byu.edu/cpse/

Brooklyn College of the City University of New York, School of Education, Program in School Psychologist, Brooklyn, NY 11210-2889. Offers play therapy (AC); school psychologist (MS Ed). Part-time and evening/weekend programs available. *Degree requirements:* For master's, internship. *Entrance requirements:* For master's, interview, previous course work in education and psychology, teaching certificate, resume, 2 letters of recommendation. Additional exam requirements/recommendations for international students: Required—TOEFL (minimum score 500 paper-based; 61 iBT). Electronic applications accepted.

Caldwell University, Graduate Studies, Department of Psychology, Caldwell, NJ 07006-6195. Offers art therapy (MA); counseling (MA), including art therapy, mental health, school counseling; director of school counseling (Post-Master's Certificate); professional counselor (Post-Master's Certificate); school counselor (Post-Master's Certificate). *Accreditation:* ACA. Part-time and evening/weekend programs available. *Faculty:* 6 full-time (4 women), 13 part-time/adjunct (8 women). *Students:* 64 full-time (62 women), 70 part-time (62 women); includes 31 minority (14 Black or African American, non-Hispanic/Latino; 2 Asian, non-Hispanic/Latino; 12 Hispanic/Latino; 3 Two or more races, non-Hispanic/Latino). Average age 34. 83 applicants, 35% accepted, 29 enrolled. In 2014, 64 master's awarded. *Degree requirements:* For master's, comprehensive exam. *Entrance requirements:* For master's, GRE or MAT, interview. *Application deadline:* For fall admission, 7/1 for domestic and international students; for spring admission, 12/1 for domestic and international students. Applications are processed on a rolling basis. Application fee: $40. Electronic applications accepted. *Expenses: Tuition:* Part-time $930 per credit. *Financial support:* Career-related internships or fieldwork available. Financial award applicants required to submit FAFSA. *Faculty research:* Counseling, school counseling, art therapy. *Unit head:* Dr. Stacey Solomon, Program Coordinator, 973-618-3387, E-mail: ssolomon@caldwell.edu. *Application contact:* Vilma Mueller, Director of Graduate Studies, 973-618-3544, E-mail: graduate@caldwell.edu.

California Baptist University, Program in School Psychology, Riverside, CA 92504-3206. Offers MS. Part-time and evening/weekend programs available. *Faculty:* 2 full-time (both women), 2 part-time/adjunct (1 woman). *Students:* 14 full-time (13 women), 2 part-time (both women); includes 7 minority (2 Black or African American, non-Hispanic/Latino; 1 Asian, non-Hispanic/Latino; 4 Hispanic/Latino). Average age 32. 28 applicants, 71% accepted, 13 enrolled. *Degree requirements:* For master's, 450 hours of introductory fieldwork, 1200 hours of field experience/internship, PRAXIS. *Entrance requirements:* For master's, CBEST, minimum GPA of 3.0, completion of prerequisites with minimum C grade, three letters of recommendation, 500-word essay. Additional exam requirements/recommendations for international students: Required—TOEFL (minimum score 80 iBT). *Application deadline:* For fall admission, 7/1 priority date for domestic and international students; for spring admission, 12/1 priority date for domestic students, 11/1 priority date for international students. Applications are processed on a rolling basis. Electronic applications accepted. *Expenses:* Expenses: Contact institution. *Faculty research:* Cultural competence, learning handicapped, cognitive development, school neuropsychology, behavioral assessment. *Unit head:* Dr. John Shoup, Dean, School of Education, 951-343-4205, E-mail: jshoup@calbaptist.edu. *Application contact:* Dr. Jane McGuire, Program Coordinator, School Psychology, 951-343-4707, E-mail: jmcguire@calbaptiat.edu.
Website: http://www.calbaptist.edu/academics/schools-colleges/school-education/programs/graduate/master-science-school-psychology/

California State University, East Bay, Office of Academic Programs and Graduate Studies, College of Education and Allied Studies, Department of Educational Psychology, Counseling Program, Hayward, CA 94542-3000. Offers clinical child/school psychology (MS); marriage and family therapy (MS); school counseling (MS). *Accreditation:* NCATE. *Degree requirements:* For master's, comprehensive exam, project or thesis. *Entrance requirements:* For master's, GRE or MAT, interview, minimum GPA of 2.5 during previous 2 years of course work. Additional exam requirements/recommendations for international students: Required—TOEFL (minimum score 550 paper-based). *Application deadline:* For fall admission, 6/30 for domestic and international students. Application fee: $55. Electronic applications accepted. *Expenses:* Tuition, state resident: full-time $7830; part-time $1302 per credit hour. Tuition, nonresident: full-time $16,368. *Required fees:* $327 per quarter. Tuition and fees vary according to course load and program. *Financial support:* Career-related internships or fieldwork, Federal Work-Study, and institutionally sponsored loans available. Support available to part-time students. Financial award application deadline: 3/2; financial award applicants required to submit FAFSA. *Unit head:* Dr. Jack Davis, Chair, Educational Psychology, 510-885-3011, Fax: 510-885-4642, E-mail: jack.davis@csueastbay.edu. *Application contact:* Prof. Greg Jennings, Graduate Coordinator, 510-885-2296, Fax: 510-885-4642, E-mail: greg.jennings@csueastbay.edu.
Website: http://www20.csueastbay.edu/ceas/departments/epsy/

California State University, Los Angeles, Graduate Studies, Charter College of Education, Division of Special Education and Counseling, Los Angeles, CA 90032-8530. Offers counseling (MS), including applied behavior analysis, community college counseling, rehabilitation counseling, school counseling, school psychology; special education (MA, PhD). *Accreditation:* ACA. Part-time and evening/weekend programs available. *Entrance requirements:* For master's, minimum GPA of 2.75 in last 90 units of course work, teaching certificate. Additional exam requirements/recommendations for international students: Required—TOEFL (minimum score 500 paper-based). Electronic applications accepted. *Expenses:* Tuition, state resident: full-time $6738; part-time $3609 per year. Tuition, nonresident: full-time $15,666; part-time $8073 per year. Tuition and fees vary according to course load, degree level and program.

California State University, Northridge, Graduate Studies, College of Education, Department of Educational Psychology and Counseling, Northridge, CA 91330. Offers counseling (MS), including career counseling, college counseling and student services, marriage and family therapy, school counseling, school psychology; educational psychology (MA Ed), including development, learning, and instruction, early childhood education. *Accreditation:* ACA (one or more programs are accredited); NCATE. Part-time and evening/weekend programs available. *Students:* 296 full-time (244 women), 86 part-time (77 women); includes 180 minority (18 Black or African American, non-Hispanic/Latino; 28 Asian, non-Hispanic/Latino; 126 Hispanic/Latino; 8 Two or more races, non-Hispanic/Latino), 12 international. Average age 30. *Entrance requirements:* For master's, GRE General Test or minimum GPA of 3.0. Additional exam requirements/recommendations for international students: Required—TOEFL. *Application deadline:* For fall admission, 11/30 for domestic students. Application fee: $55. *Expenses: Required fees:* $12,402. *Financial support:* Scholarships/grants available. Support available to part-time students. Financial award application deadline: 3/1. *Unit head:* Dr. Shari Tarver-Behring, Chair, 818-677-2599. *Application contact:* 818-677-3755.
Website: http://www.csun.edu/education/epc/index.html

California State University, Sacramento, Office of Graduate Studies, College of Education, Department of Special Education and School Psychology, Sacramento, CA 95819. Offers school psychology (MA); special education (MA). *Accreditation:* CORE. Part-time programs available. *Entrance requirements:* For master's, minimum GPA of 2.5. Additional exam requirements/recommendations for international students: Required—TOEFL. Electronic applications accepted. *Faculty research:* Reading and learning disabilities; vocational rehabilitation counseling issues and implementation; school-based crisis intervention; posttraumatic stress disorder; attention-deficit/hyperactivity disorder; school-based suicide prevention, intervention, and postvention; autism spectrum disorders; special education technology, strategies and assessment.

California University of Pennsylvania, School of Graduate Studies and Research, College of Education and Human Services, Program in School Psychology, California, PA 15419-1394. Offers MS. *Accreditation:* NCATE. Part-time and evening/weekend programs available. *Degree requirements:* For master's, comprehensive exam, thesis optional, internship. *Entrance requirements:* For master's, MAT or GRE, minimum GPA of 3.0, work experience in psychology, letters of reference. Additional exam requirements/recommendations for international students: Required—TOEFL (minimum score 550 paper-based; 80 iBT). Electronic applications accepted. *Expenses:* Tuition, state resident: full-time $10,896; part-time $454 per credit. Tuition, nonresident: full-time $16,344; part-time $681 per credit. *Required fees:* $2425.

Cambridge College, School of Education, Cambridge, MA 02138-5304. Offers autism specialist (M Ed); autism/behavior analyst (M Ed); behavior analyst (Post-Master's Certificate); behavioral management (M Ed); early childhood teacher (M Ed); education specialist in curriculum and instruction (CAGS); educational leadership (Ed D); elementary teacher (M Ed); English as a second language (M Ed, Certificate); general science (M Ed); health education (Post-Master's Certificate); health/family and consumer sciences (M Ed); history (M Ed); individualized (M Ed); information

technology literacy (M Ed); instructional technology (M Ed); interdisciplinary studies (M Ed); library teacher (M Ed); literacy education (M Ed); mathematics (M Ed); mathematics specialist (Certificate); middle school mathematics and science (M Ed); school administration (M Ed, CAGS); school guidance counselor (M Ed); school nurse education (M Ed); school social worker/school adjustment counselor (M Ed); special education administrator (CAGS); special education/moderate disabilities (M Ed); teaching skills and methodologies (M Ed). Part-time and evening/weekend programs available. Postbaccalaureate distance learning degree programs offered (minimal on-campus study). *Degree requirements:* For master's, thesis, internship/practicum (licensure program only); for doctorate, thesis/dissertation; for other advanced degree, thesis. *Entrance requirements:* For master's, interview, resume, documentation of licensure, 2 professional references; for doctorate, official transcripts, interview, resume, documentation of licensure (if any), written personal statement/essay, portfolio of scholarly and professional work, qualifying assessment, 2 professional references, health insurance, immunizations form; for other advanced degree, official transcripts, interview, resume, documentation of licensure (if any), written personal statement/essay, 2 professional references, health insurance, immunizations form. Additional exam requirements/recommendations for international students: Required—TOEFL (minimum score 550 paper-based; 79 iBT), Michigan English Language Assessment Battery (minimum score 85); Recommended—IELTS (minimum score 6). Electronic applications accepted. *Expenses:* Contact institution. *Faculty research:* Adult education, accelerated learning, mathematics education, brain compatible learning, special education and law.

Cambridge College, School of Psychology and Counseling, Cambridge, MA 02138-5304. Offers addiction counseling (M Ed); alcohol and drug counseling (Certificate); counseling psychology (M Ed, CAGS); counseling psychology: forensic counseling (M Ed); marriage and family therapy (M Ed); mental health and addiction counseling (M Ed); mental health counseling (M Ed); mental health counseling for school guidance counselors (Post Master's Certificate); psychological studies (M Ed); school adjustment and mental health counseling (M Ed); school adjustment, mental health and addiction counseling (M Ed); school guidance counselor (M Ed); trauma studies (Certificate). Part-time and evening/weekend programs available. *Degree requirements:* For master's and other advanced degree, thesis, practicum/internship. *Entrance requirements:* For master's, resume, 2 professional references; for other advanced degree, official transcripts, documents for transfer credit evaluation, resume, written personal statement/essay, 2 professional references, health insurance, immunizations form. Additional exam requirements/recommendations for international students: Required—TOEFL (minimum score 550 paper-based; 79 iBT), Michigan English Language Assessment Battery (minimum score 85); Recommended—IELTS (minimum score 6). Electronic applications accepted. *Expenses:* Contact institution. *Faculty research:* Trauma, drug and alcohol counseling, cross-cultural issues, school counseling, trauma in schools.

Canisius College, Graduate Division, School of Education and Human Services, Programs in Counseling and Human Services, Buffalo, NY 14208-1098. Offers community mental health counseling (MS); counseling and human services (MS); school agency counseling (MS). *Accreditation:* ACA. Part-time and evening/weekend programs available. *Faculty:* 6 full-time (3 women), 7 part-time/adjunct (5 women). *Students:* 96 full-time (76 women), 30 part-time (24 women); includes 19 minority (7 Black or African American, non-Hispanic/Latino; 1 American Indian or Alaska Native, non-Hispanic/Latino; 2 Asian, non-Hispanic/Latino; 6 Hispanic/Latino; 3 Two or more races, non-Hispanic/Latino). Average age 28. 103 applicants, 86% accepted, 41 enrolled. In 2014, 64 master's awarded. *Degree requirements:* For master's, thesis, research project. *Entrance requirements:* For master's, GRE (if cumulative GPA less than 2.7), transcripts, two letters of recommendation, interview, BA. Additional exam requirements/recommendations for international students: Required—TOEFL (minimum score 550 paper-based, 80 iBT), IELTS (minimum score 6.5), or CAEL (minimum score 70). *Application deadline:* Applications are processed on a rolling basis. Application fee: $25. Electronic applications accepted. Application fee is waived when completed online. *Financial support:* Research assistantships, career-related internships or fieldwork, Federal Work-Study, scholarships/grants, tuition waivers (partial), and unspecified assistantships available. Support available to part-time students. Financial award application deadline: 4/30; financial award applicants required to submit FAFSA. *Faculty research:* Impact of trauma on adults, long term psych-social impact on police officers. *Unit head:* Dr. Christine Moll, Chair, 716-888-3287, E-mail: moll@canisius.edu. *Application contact:* Kathleen B. Davis, Vice President of Enrollment Management, 716-888-2500, Fax: 716-888-3195, E-mail: daviskb@canisius.edu.
Website: http://www.canisius.edu/masters-counseling/

Capella University, Harold Abel School of Social and Behavioral Science, Doctoral Programs in Psychology, Minneapolis, MN 55402. Offers addiction psychology (PhD); clinical psychology (Psy D); educational psychology (PhD); general advanced studies in human behavior (PhD); general psychology (PhD); industrial/organizational psychology (PhD); school psychology (Psy D).

Capella University, Harold Abel School of Social and Behavioral Science, Master's Programs in Psychology, Minneapolis, MN 55402. Offers applied behavior analysis (MS); clinical psychology (MS); counseling psychology (MS); educational psychology (MS); evaluation, research, and measurement (MS); general advanced studies in human behavior (MS); general psychology (MS); industrial/organizational psychology (MS); leadership coaching psychology (MS); school psychology (MS); sport psychology (MS).

Carlos Albizu University, Miami Campus, Graduate Programs, Miami, FL 33172-2209. Offers clinical psychology (Psy D); entrepreneurship (MBA); exceptional student education (MS); human services (PhD); industrial/organizational psychology (MS); marriage and family therapy (MS); mental health counseling (MS); nonprofit management (MBA); organizational management (MBA); psychology (MS); school counseling (MS); teaching English as a second language (MS). *Accreditation:* APA. Part-time and evening/weekend programs available. Postbaccalaureate distance learning degree programs offered (minimal on-campus study). *Faculty:* 25 full-time (20 women), 29 part-time/adjunct (15 women). *Students:* 431 full-time (343 women), 264 part-time (225 women); includes 586 minority (45 Black or African American, non-Hispanic/Latino; 1 American Indian or Alaska Native, non-Hispanic/Latino; 8 Asian, non-Hispanic/Latino; 530 Hispanic/Latino; 2 Two or more races, non-Hispanic/Latino), 14 international. Average age 33. 189 applicants, 69% accepted, 111 enrolled. In 2014, 177 master's, 28 doctorates awarded. Terminal master's awarded for partial completion of doctoral program. *Degree requirements:* For master's, one foreign language, comprehensive exam, integrative project (MBA), research project (exceptional student education, teaching English as a second language); for doctorate, one foreign language, comprehensive exam, internship, project. *Entrance requirements:* For master's, 3 letters of recommendation, interview, minimum GPA of 3.0, resume, statement of purpose, official transcripts; for doctorate, 3 letters of recommendation, minimum GPA of 3.0, resume, interview, statement of purpose, official transcripts. Additional exam requirements/recommendations for international students: Required—Michigan Test of English Language Proficiency. *Application deadline:* For fall admission, 4/1 priority date for domestic students, 5/1 priority date for international students; for spring admission, 11/1 priority date for domestic students, 9/1 priority date for international students. Applications are processed on a rolling basis. Application fee: $50. Electronic applications accepted. *Expenses:* Expenses: $570 per credit (for master's programs); $750 per credit (for doctoral programs). *Financial support:* In 2014–15, 72 students received support. Federal Work-Study, scholarships/grants, and tuition discounts available. Financial award application deadline: 6/1; financial award applicants required to submit FAFSA. *Faculty research:* Psychotherapy, forensic psychology, neuropsychology, marketing strategy, entrepreneurship, special education. *Unit head:* Dr. Irene M. Bravo, Interim Provost, 305-593-1223 Ext. 3120, Fax: 305-592-7930, E-mail: ibravo@albizu.edu. *Application contact:* Vanessa Almendarez, Administrative Assistant, 305-593-1223 Ext. 3137, Fax: 305-593-1854, E-mail: valmendarez@albizu.edu.

Central Connecticut State University, School of Graduate Studies, School of Education and Professional Studies, Department of Counselor Education and Family Therapy, New Britain, CT 06050-4010. Offers marriage and family therapy (MS); professional counseling (MS, AC, Certificate); school counseling (MS); student development in higher education (MS). *Accreditation:* AAMFT/COAMFTE; ACA. Part-time and evening/weekend programs available. *Faculty:* 11 full-time (7 women), 21 part-time/adjunct (17 women). *Students:* 142 full-time (122 women), 208 part-time (165 women); includes 94 minority (49 Black or African American, non-Hispanic/Latino; 4 Asian, non-Hispanic/Latino; 34 Hispanic/Latino; 7 Two or more races, non-Hispanic/Latino), 2 international. Average age 34. 215 applicants, 53% accepted, 91 enrolled. In 2014, 101 master's, 5 other advanced degrees awarded. *Degree requirements:* For master's, comprehensive exam, thesis or alternative; for other advanced degree, qualifying exam. *Entrance requirements:* For master's, minimum undergraduate GPA of 2.7, essay, interview, letters of recommendation. Additional exam requirements/recommendations for international students: Required—TOEFL (minimum score 550 paper-based; 79 iBT). *Application deadline:* For fall admission, 4/1 for domestic and international students; for spring admission, 11/1 for domestic and international students. Applications are processed on a rolling basis. Application fee: $50. Electronic applications accepted. *Expenses: Tuition, area resident:* Full-time $5730; part-time $534 per credit. Tuition, state resident: full-time $8596; part-time $534 per credit. Tuition, nonresident: full-time $15,964; part-time $548 per credit. *Required fees:* $4211; $215 per credit. *Financial support:* In 2014–15, 41 students received support, including 21 research assistantships; career-related internships or fieldwork, Federal Work-Study, scholarships/grants, and unspecified assistantships also available. Support available to part-time students. Financial award application deadline: 3/1; financial award applicants required to submit FAFSA. *Faculty research:* Elementary and secondary school counseling, marriage and family therapy, rehabilitation counseling, counseling in higher educational settings. *Unit head:* Dr. Connie Tait, Chair, 860-832-2154, E-mail: taitc@ccsu.edu. *Application contact:* Patricia Gardner, Associate Director of Graduate Studies, 860-832-2350, Fax: 860-832-2362, E-mail: graduateadmissions@ccsu.edu.
Website: http://web.ccsu.edu/seps/departments/counselingFamilyTherapy/default.asp

Central Michigan University, College of Graduate Studies, College of Humanities and Social and Behavioral Sciences, Department of Psychology, Program in School Psychology, Mount Pleasant, MI 48859. Offers PhD, S Psy S. *Accreditation:* APA. *Degree requirements:* For doctorate, thesis/dissertation; for S Psy S, thesis. *Entrance requirements:* For doctorate, GRE. Electronic applications accepted. *Faculty research:* Psychology and education foundations, psychology and education assessment, intervention strategies.

Central Washington University, Graduate Studies and Research, College of the Sciences, Department of Psychology, Program in School Psychology, Ellensburg, WA 98926. Offers M Ed. *Degree requirements:* For master's, thesis or alternative, internship. *Entrance requirements:* For master's, GRE General Test, minimum GPA of 3.0. Additional exam requirements/recommendations for international students: Required—TOEFL (minimum score 550 paper-based; 79 iBT). Electronic applications accepted.

Chaminade University of Honolulu, Graduate Services, Program in Counseling Psychology, Honolulu, HI 96816-1578. Offers marriage and family counseling (MSCP); mental health counseling (MSCP); school counseling (MSCP). Part-time and evening/weekend programs available. *Degree requirements:* For master's, comprehensive exam, internship/practicum. *Entrance requirements:* For master's, minimum undergraduate GPA of 3.0, 3 letters of recommendation, interview. Additional exam requirements/recommendations for international students: Required—TOEFL (minimum score 550 paper-based). Electronic applications accepted. *Faculty research:* Taoist/Buddhist psychology, psychology of T'ai Chi Ch'uan, sleep disorders, drug/alcohol prevention with adolescent girls, anger/aggression with kids.

Chapman University, College of Educational Studies, Orange, CA 92866. Offers communication sciences and disorders (MS); counseling (MA), including school counseling (MA, Credential); education (PhD), including cultural and curricular studies, disability studies, leadership studies, school psychology (PhD, Credential); educational psychology (MA); leadership development (MA); pupil personnel services (Credential), including school counseling (MA, Credential), school psychology (PhD, Credential); school psychology (Ed S); single subject (Credential); special education (MA, Credential), including mild/moderate (Credential), moderate/severe (Credential); speech language pathology (Credential); teaching (MA), including elementary education, secondary education. *Accreditation:* Teacher Education Accreditation Council. Part-time and evening/weekend programs available. *Faculty:* 31 full-time (18 women), 78 part-time/adjunct (61 women). *Students:* 257 full-time (206 women), 187 part-time (141 women); includes 186 minority (9 Black or African American, non-Hispanic/Latino; 54 Asian, non-Hispanic/Latino; 104 Hispanic/Latino; 1 Native Hawaiian or other Pacific Islander, non-Hispanic/Latino; 18 Two or more races, non-Hispanic/Latino), 10 international. Average age 29. 614 applicants, 35% accepted, 131 enrolled. In 2014, 128 master's, 10 doctorates awarded. *Entrance requirements:* Additional exam requirements/recommendations for international students: Required—TOEFL (minimum score 550 paper-based; 80 iBT). *Application deadline:* Applications are processed on a rolling basis. Application fee: $60. Electronic applications accepted. *Financial support:* Fellowships and scholarships/grants available. Financial award application deadline: 6/30; financial award applicants required to submit FAFSA. *Unit head:* Dr. Don Cardinal, Dean, 714-997-6781, E-mail: cardinal@chapman.edu. *Application contact:* Admissions Coordinator, 714-997-6714.
Website: http://www.chapman.edu/CES/

The Chicago School of Professional Psychology, Program in School Psychology, Chicago, IL 60610. Offers Ed D, Ed S. Part-time programs available. *Entrance requirements:* For degree, GRE (recommended), minimum GPA of 3.2 (recommended); completion of one course in statistics or research methods and one course in psychology. Additional exam requirements/recommendations for international students: Required—TOEFL (minimum score 550 paper-based; 79 iBT).

The Chicago School of Professional Psychology at Grayslake, Program in School Psychology, Grayslake, IL 60030. Offers Ed S.

The Citadel, The Military College of South Carolina, Citadel Graduate College, Department of Psychology, Program in School Psychology, Charleston, SC 29409.

Offers Ed S. *Accreditation:* NCATE. Part-time and evening/weekend programs available. *Degree requirements:* For Ed S, comprehensive exam, thesis, internship. *Entrance requirements:* For degree, GRE (minimum score of 297, 150 on the verbal reasoning and 141 on the quantitative reasoning section) or MAT (minimum score of 410), minimum undergraduate GPA of 3.0, 2 letters of reference. Additional exam requirements/recommendations for international students: Required—TOEFL (minimum score 550 paper-based). Electronic applications accepted. *Faculty research:* Bowen Systems Theory, self-appraisal, emotional leadership, couples counseling.

The College of New Rochelle, Graduate School, Division of Human Services, Program in School Psychology, New Rochelle, NY 10805-2308. Offers MS. *Degree requirements:* For master's, comprehensive exam, clinical fieldwork journal. *Entrance requirements:* For master's, interview, minimum GPA of 3.0, course work in psychology, sample of written work. *Expenses: Tuition:* Part-time $894 per credit. *Required fees:* $325 per semester.

College of St. Joseph, Graduate Programs, Division of Psychology and Human Services, Program in School Guidance Counseling, Rutland, VT 05701-3899. Offers MS. Part-time and evening/weekend programs available. *Degree requirements:* For master's, comprehensive exam, thesis optional. *Entrance requirements:* For master's, PRAXIS I, official college transcripts; 2 letters of reference. Additional exam requirements/recommendations for international students: Required—TOEFL (minimum score 550 paper-based). Electronic applications accepted.

The College of Saint Rose, Graduate Studies, School of Education, Department of Educational Psychology, Albany, NY 12203-1419. Offers applied technology education (MS Ed); educational psychology (MS Ed); instructional technology (Certificate); school psychology (MS Ed, Certificate). Part-time and evening/weekend programs available. *Entrance requirements:* For master's, minimum undergraduate GPA of 3.0. Additional exam requirements/recommendations for international students: Required—TOEFL (minimum score 550 paper-based). Electronic applications accepted.

The College of William and Mary, School of Education, Program in School Psychology, Williamsburg, VA 23187-8795. Offers M Ed, Ed S. *Accreditation:* NCATE. *Faculty:* 3 full-time (2 women), 5 part-time/adjunct (4 women). *Students:* 17 full-time (14 women), 10 part-time (9 women), 1 international. Average age 26. 72 applicants, 43% accepted, 17 enrolled. In 2014, 9 master's, 14 Ed Ss awarded. *Degree requirements:* For Ed S, internship. *Entrance requirements:* For master's, GRE, minimum GPA of 3.0; for Ed S, GRE, minimum GPA of 3.5. Additional exam requirements/recommendations for international students: Required—TOEFL, IELTS. *Application deadline:* For fall admission, 1/15 for domestic and international students. Application fee: $50. Electronic applications accepted. *Financial support:* In 2014–15, 14 students received support, including 14 research assistantships (averaging $11,000 per year); career-related internships or fieldwork, Federal Work-Study, institutionally sponsored loans, scholarships/grants, and unspecified assistantships also available. Financial award application deadline: 1/15; financial award applicants required to submit FAFSA. *Faculty research:* Home schooling, gifted preschoolers, inclusive schools, ability testing. *Unit head:* Dr. Carol Tieso, Associate Dean, 757-221-2461, E-mail: cltles@wm.edu. *Application contact:* Dorothy Smith Osborne, Assistant Dean for Academic Programs and Student Services, 757-221-2317, Fax: 757-221-2293, E-mail: dsosbo@wm.edu.
Website: http://education.wm.edu

DePaul University, College of Education, Chicago, IL 60614. Offers bilingual bicultural education (M Ed, MA); counseling (M Ed, MA), including clinical mental health counseling, college student development, school counseling; curriculum studies (M Ed, MA, Ed D); early childhood education (M Ed, MA, Ed D); educating adults (MA); educational leadership (M Ed, MA, Ed D), including administration and supervision (M Ed, MA), principal preparation (M Ed, MA); elementary education (MA); mathematics education (MA); mathematics for teaching (MS); middle school mathematics education (MS); reading specialist (M Ed, MA); secondary education (M Ed); social and cultural foundations in education (MA); special education (M Ed, MA); world languages education (M Ed, MA). Part-time and evening/weekend programs available. Postbaccalaureate distance learning degree programs offered (no on-campus study). *Degree requirements:* For doctorate, thesis/dissertation. Electronic applications accepted.

Duquesne University, School of Education, Department of Counseling, Psychology, and Special Education, Program in School Psychology, Pittsburgh, PA 15282-0001. Offers child psychology (MS Ed). Part-time and evening/weekend programs available. *Faculty:* 7 full-time (4 women). *Students:* 91 full-time (77 women), 2 part-time (both women); includes 12 minority (3 Black or African American, non-Hispanic/Latino; 1 Asian, non-Hispanic/Latino; 5 Hispanic/Latino; 3 Two or more races, non-Hispanic/Latino), 4 international. Average age 26. 133 applicants, 34% accepted, 26 enrolled. In 2014, 23 master's, 12 doctorates, 1 other advanced degree awarded. *Degree requirements:* For master's, thesis optional; for doctorate, thesis/dissertation. *Entrance requirements:* For master's, bachelor's degree; for doctorate, GRE, letters of reference, letter of intent, interview, master's degree; for CAGS, GRE, letters of reference, letter of intent, interview, bachelor's/master's degree. Additional exam requirements/recommendations for international students: Required—TOEFL (minimum score 550 paper-based), IELTS (minimum score 7). *Application deadline:* For fall admission, 3/1 for domestic students; for spring admission, 9/1 for domestic students. Applications are processed on a rolling basis. Application fee: $0. Electronic applications accepted. *Expenses: Tuition:* Full-time $18,882; part-time $1049 per credit. *Required fees:* $1800; $100 per credit. Tuition and fees vary according to program. *Financial support:* Research assistantships and Federal Work-Study available. Support available to part-time students. *Unit head:* Dr. Ara Schmitt, Associate Professor, 412-396-1057, Fax: 412-396-1340, E-mail: schmitta2106@duq.edu. *Application contact:* Michael Dolinger, Director of Student and Academic Services, 412-396-6647, Fax: 412-396-5585, E-mail: dolingerm@duq.edu.
Website: http://www.duq.edu/academics/schools/education/graduate-programs-education/school-psychology-graduate-programs

East Carolina University, Graduate School, Thomas Harriot College of Arts and Sciences, Department of Psychology, Program in School Psychology, Greenville, NC 27858-4353. Offers MA/CAS. *Accreditation:* NCATE. Part-time and evening/weekend programs available. *Expenses:* Tuition, state resident: full-time $4223. Tuition, nonresident: full-time $16,540. *Required fees:* $2184.

Eastern Illinois University, Graduate School, College of Sciences, Department of Psychology, Charleston, IL 61920. Offers clinical psychology (MA); school psychology (SSP). Part-time and evening/weekend programs available. *Faculty:* 13. *Students:* 37 full-time (23 women), 13 part-time (8 women); includes 4 minority (2 Black or African American, non-Hispanic/Latino; 1 Hispanic/Latino; 1 Two or more races, non-Hispanic/Latino), 3 international. Average age 24. 85 applicants, 21% accepted, 15 enrolled. In 2014, 5 master's, 5 other advanced degrees awarded. *Degree requirements:* For master's, comprehensive exam, thesis; for SSP, thesis. *Entrance requirements:* For master's and SSP, GMAT or GRE. Additional exam requirements/recommendations for international students: Required—TOEFL (minimum score 500 paper-based; 61 iBT), IELTS (minimum score 6). *Application deadline:* For fall admission, 5/15 for domestic and international students; for spring admission, 10/15 for domestic and international students. Applications are processed on a rolling basis. Application fee: $30. Electronic applications accepted. *Expenses:* Tuition, state resident: full-time $3113; part-time $283 per credit hour. Tuition, nonresident: full-time $7469; part-time $679 per credit hour. *Required fees:* $2287; $96 per credit hour. Tuition and fees vary according to course load. *Financial support:* In 2014–15, 41 students received support, including 4 research assistantships with full tuition reimbursements available (averaging $8,100 per year), 8 teaching assistantships with full tuition reimbursements available (averaging $8,010 per year); career-related internships or fieldwork, Federal Work-Study, and unspecified assistantships also available. Support available to part-time students. Financial award application deadline: 3/1; financial award applicants required to submit FAFSA. *Unit head:* Assege Haile Mariam, Interim Department Chair, 217-581-6615, Fax: 217-581-6764, E-mail: ahailemariam@eiu.edu. *Application contact:* Department of Psychology, 217-581-2127, Fax: 217-581-6764, E-mail: psych@eiu.edu.
Website: http://www.eiu.edu/psych/index.php

Eastern Kentucky University, The Graduate School, College of Arts and Sciences, Department of Psychology, Richmond, KY 40475-3102. Offers clinical psychology (MS); industrial/organizational psychology (MS); school psychology (Psy S). Part-time programs available. *Entrance requirements:* For master's and Psy S, GRE General Test, minimum GPA of 2.5. *Faculty research:* Autism, social psychology, parenting, assessment of depression/anxiety, reading.

Eastern University, Department of Counseling Psychology, St. Davids, PA 19087-3696. Offers applied behavior analysis (MA); counseling (MA); school counseling (MA, Certificate); school psychology (MS, Certificate). Part-time programs available. *Faculty:* 6 full-time (3 women), 8 part-time/adjunct (6 women). *Students:* 61 full-time (49 women), 102 part-time (85 women); includes 51 minority (44 Black or African American, non-Hispanic/Latino; 1 American Indian or Alaska Native, non-Hispanic/Latino; 4 Hispanic/Latino; 2 Two or more races, non-Hispanic/Latino), 2 international. Average age 30. 117 applicants, 77% accepted, 68 enrolled. In 2014, 68 master's awarded. *Degree requirements:* For master's, internship. *Entrance requirements:* For master's, minimum GPA of 2.8 (3.0 for school psychology). Additional exam requirements/recommendations for international students: Required—TOEFL (minimum score 550 paper-based; 79 iBT). *Application deadline:* For fall admission, 6/15 for domestic students, 5/30 for international students. Applications are processed on a rolling basis. Application fee: $35. Electronic applications accepted. Application fee is waived when completed online. *Expenses: Tuition:* Full-time $15,600; part-time $650 per credit. *Required fees:* $30; $27.50 per semester. One-time fee: $50. Tuition and fees vary according to course load, degree level and program. *Financial support:* In 2014–15, 21 students received support, including 6 research assistantships with partial tuition reimbursements available (averaging $8,115 per year); scholarships/grants and unspecified assistantships also available. Financial award application deadline: 3/15. *Unit head:* Dr. Susan Edgar-Smith, Co-Chair, 610-341-4379. *Application contact:* Katelyn Ambrose, Enrollment Counselor, 610-225-5564, Fax: 610-341-1585, E-mail: kambrose@eastern.edu.
Website: http://www.eastern.edu/academics/programs/counseling-psychology-department

Eastern Washington University, Graduate Studies, College of Social and Behavioral Sciences and Social Work, Program in School Psychology, Cheney, WA 99004-2431. Offers MS. *Degree requirements:* For master's, comprehensive exam, thesis or alternative. *Entrance requirements:* For master's, GRE General Test, minimum GPA of 3.0.

Edinboro University of Pennsylvania, Department of Counseling, School Psychology and Special Education, Edinboro, PA 16444. Offers counseling (MA), including art therapy, clinical mental health counseling, college counseling, rehabilitation counseling, school counseling; educational psychology (M Ed); school psychology (Ed S); special education (M Ed), including autism, behavior management. Part-time and evening/weekend programs available. *Degree requirements:* For master's, thesis or alternative, competency exam; for Ed S, thesis or alternative. *Entrance requirements:* For master's and Ed S, GRE or MAT, minimum QPA of 2.5. Electronic applications accepted.

Emporia State University, Program in School Psychology, Emporia, KS 66801-5415. Offers MS, Ed S. *Accreditation:* NCATE. Part-time programs available. *Students:* 14 full-time (10 women), 5 part-time (4 women); includes 3 minority (1 Black or African American, non-Hispanic/Latino; 1 Asian, non-Hispanic/Latino; 1 Two or more races, non-Hispanic/Latino), 1 international. 5 applicants, 60% accepted, 3 enrolled. In 2014, 9 master's, 4 other advanced degrees awarded. *Degree requirements:* For master's, comprehensive exam or thesis, internship; for Ed S, comprehensive exam, thesis or alternative, internship. *Entrance requirements:* For master's, GRE General Test or MAT, essay exam, appropriate bachelor's degree, teacher certification, letters of recommendation; for Ed S, GRE, essay exam, letters of recommendation, teacher certification. Additional exam requirements/recommendations for international students: Required—TOEFL (minimum score 520 paper-based; 68 iBT). *Application deadline:* For fall admission, 8/15 priority date for domestic students. Applications are processed on a rolling basis. Application fee: $30 ($75 for international students). Electronic applications accepted. *Expenses:* Tuition, state resident: part-time $227 per credit hour. Tuition, nonresident: part-time $706 per credit hour. *Required fees:* $75 per credit hour. Tuition and fees vary according to campus/location. *Financial support:* Career-related internships or fieldwork, Federal Work-Study, institutionally sponsored loans, health care benefits, and unspecified assistantships available. Financial award application deadline: 3/15; financial award applicants required to submit FAFSA. *Unit head:* Dr. Brian W. Schrader, Chair, 620-341-5317, E-mail: bschrade@emporia.edu. *Application contact:* Mary Sewell, Admissions Coordinator, 800-950-GRAD, Fax: 620-341-5909, E-mail: msewell@emporia.edu.

Evangel University, School Counseling Program, Springfield, MO 65802. Offers MS. Part-time and evening/weekend programs available. *Faculty:* 1 (woman) full-time, 6 part-time/adjunct (4 women). *Students:* 10 full-time (7 women), 35 part-time (29 women); includes 1 minority (Black or African American, non-Hispanic/Latino). Average age 32. 13 applicants, 85% accepted, 9 enrolled. In 2014, 25 master's awarded. *Degree requirements:* For master's, comprehensive exam (for some programs), thesis or alternative. *Entrance requirements:* For master's, MAT (preferred) or GRE. Additional exam requirements/recommendations for international students: Required—TOEFL (minimum score 550 paper-based). *Application deadline:* For fall admission, 7/15 priority date for domestic students, 7/1 for international students; for spring admission, 11/15 priority date for domestic students, 12/1 for international students. Applications are processed on a rolling basis. Application fee: $25. Electronic applications accepted. *Financial support:* In 2014–15, 9 students received support. Career-related internships or fieldwork, scholarships/grants, and unspecified assistantships available. Support available to part-time students. Financial award application deadline: 4/1; financial award applicants required to submit FAFSA. *Unit head:* Debbie Bicket, Program Coordinator, 417-865-2815 Ext. 8567, Fax: 417-575-5484, E-mail: bicketd@evangel.edu. *Application contact:* Matt Petry, Admissions Representative, Graduate Studies, 417-865-2815 Ext. 7229, Fax: 417-575-5484, E-mail: petrym@evangel.edu.
Website: http://www.evangel.edu/academics/graduate-studies/graduate-programs

School Psychology

Fairfield University, Graduate School of Education and Allied Professions, Fairfield, CT 06824. Offers applied behavior analysis (ATC); applied psychology (MA); clinical mental health counseling (MA, CAS); early childhood studies (ATC); educational technology (MA); elementary education (MA, CAS); family studies (MA); integration of spirituality and religion in counseling (ATC); marriage and family therapy (MA); school counseling (MA, CAS); school psychology (MA, CAS); school-based marriage and family therapy (ATC); secondary education (MA); special education (MA, CAS); substance abuse counseling (ATC); teaching (Certificate); teaching and foundations (MA, CAS); TESOL, world languages, and bilingual education (MA, CAS). *Accreditation:* NCATE. Part-time and evening/weekend programs available. *Faculty:* 23 full-time (19 women), 32 part-time/adjunct (25 women). *Students:* 148 full-time (131 women), 286 part-time (238 women); includes 81 minority (18 Black or African American, non-Hispanic/Latino; 1 American Indian or Alaska Native, non-Hispanic/Latino; 14 Asian, non-Hispanic/Latino; 39 Hispanic/Latino; 9 Two or more races, non-Hispanic/Latino), 13 international. Average age 34. 264 applicants, 54% accepted, 68 enrolled. In 2014, 142 master's awarded. *Degree requirements:* For master's, comprehensive exam. *Entrance requirements:* For master's, PRAXIS I (for certification programs), minimum GPA of 3.0, 2 recommendations, resume. Additional exam requirements/recommendations for international students: Required—TOEFL (minimum score 550 paper-based; 84 iBT) or IELTS (minimum score 7.5). *Application deadline:* For fall admission, 2/15 for international students; for spring admission, 10/1 for international students. Application fee: $60. Electronic applications accepted. *Expenses:* Expenses: $675 per credit hour. *Financial support:* In 2014–15, 55 students received support. Career-related internships or fieldwork and unspecified assistantships available. Financial award applicants required to submit FAFSA. *Faculty research:* Literacy, spirituality, special education, bilingual/multicultural education, mentoring and professional development. *Unit head:* Dr. Robert D. Hannafin, Dean, 203-254-4250, Fax: 203-254-4241, E-mail: rhannafin@fairfield.edu. *Application contact:* Marianne Gumpper, Director of Graduate and Continuing Studies Admission, 203-254-4184, Fax: 203-254-4073, E-mail: gradadmis@fairfield.edu.
Website: http://www.fairfield.edu/academics/schoolscollegescenters/graduateschoolofeducationalliedprofessions/graduateprograms/

Fairleigh Dickinson University, Metropolitan Campus, University College: Arts, Sciences, and Professional Studies, School of Psychology, Program in School Psychology, Teaneck, NJ 07666-1914. Offers MA, Psy D.

Florida International University, College of Education, Department of Leadership and Professional Studies, Miami, FL 33199. Offers adult education and human resource development (MS, Ed D); counseling (MS), including rehabilitation counseling, school counseling; counselor education (MS), including clinical mental health counseling; educational administration and supervision (Ed D); educational leadership (MS, Certificate, Ed S); higher education (Ed D); higher education administration (MS); recreation and sport management (MS), including recreation and sport management, recreational therapy; school psychology (Ed S); urban education (MS), including instruction in urban settings, learning technologies, multicultural/bilingual, multicultural/TESOL, urban education. Part-time and evening/weekend programs available. *Degree requirements:* For doctorate, thesis/dissertation. *Entrance requirements:* For master's, minimum GPA of 3.0; for doctorate and other advanced degree, GRE General Test. Additional exam requirements/recommendations for international students: Required—TOEFL (minimum score 550 paper-based; 80 iBT), IELTS (minimum score 6.3). Electronic applications accepted.

Florida State University, The Graduate School, College of Education, Department of Educational Psychology and Learning Systems, Program in Counseling and Human Systems, Tallahassee, FL 32306. Offers counseling psychology and school psychology (PhD); MS/Ed S. *Accreditation:* ACA (one or more programs are accredited). *Faculty:* 13 full-time (8 women), 1 part-time/adjunct (0 women). *Students:* 100 full-time (84 women), 21 part-time (16 women); includes 31 minority (9 Black or African American, non-Hispanic/Latino; 1 American Indian or Alaska Native, non-Hispanic/Latino; 3 Asian, non-Hispanic/Latino; 18 Hispanic/Latino), 2 international. Average age 28. 192 applicants, 41% accepted, 41 enrolled. In 2014, 10 doctorates awarded. Terminal master's awarded for partial completion of doctoral program. *Degree requirements:* For doctorate, comprehensive exam, thesis/dissertation. *Entrance requirements:* Additional exam requirements/recommendations for international students: Required—PTE (minimum score 55), TOEFL (minimum score 550 paper-based, 80 iBT), IELTS (minimum score 6.5) or Michigan English Language Assessment Battery (minimum score 77). *Application deadline:* For fall admission, 1/15 for domestic and international students. Applications are processed on a rolling basis. Application fee: $30. Electronic applications accepted. *Expenses:* Expenses: Contact institution. *Financial support:* Fellowships with full and partial tuition reimbursements, research assistantships with full and partial tuition reimbursements, teaching assistantships with full and partial tuition reimbursements, scholarships/grants, tuition waivers (full and partial), and unspecified assistantships available. Financial award applicants required to submit FAFSA. *Faculty research:* Practitioner-scholar models; cultural diversity in populations; social, emotional, and vocational capabilities and talent identification of learners; counseling; technology and learners. *Unit head:* Dr. Frances Prevatt, Program Leader, 850-644-9445, Fax: 850-644-8776, E-mail: fprevatt@fsu.edu. *Application contact:* Lori Hayes, Program Assistant, 850-644-8046, Fax: 850-644-8776, E-mail: lahayes@fsu.edu.
Website: http://www.coe.fsu.edu/Current-Students/Departments/Educational-Psychology-and-Learning-Systems-EPLS/Current-Students/Psychological-and-Counseling-Ser

Fordham University, Graduate School of Education, Division of Psychological and Educational Services, New York, NY 10023. Offers counseling and personnel services (MSE, Adv C); counseling psychology (PhD); educational psychology (MSE, PhD); school psychology (PhD); urban and urban bilingual school psychology (Adv C). *Accreditation:* APA (one or more programs are accredited); NCATE. *Degree requirements:* For doctorate, thesis/dissertation. *Entrance requirements:* For doctorate, GRE General Test.

Fort Hays State University, Graduate School, College of Arts and Sciences, Department of Psychology, Program in School Psychology, Hays, KS 67601-4099. Offers Ed S. *Accreditation:* NCATE. *Degree requirements:* For Ed S, comprehensive exam, thesis. *Entrance requirements:* Additional exam requirements/recommendations for international students: Required—TOEFL (minimum score 550 paper-based). Electronic applications accepted.

Francis Marion University, Graduate Programs, Department of Psychology, Florence, SC 29502-0547. Offers applied psychology (MS), including clinical/counseling psychology, school psychology; school psychology (SSP). Part-time and evening/weekend programs available. *Faculty:* 6 full-time (2 women), 4 part-time/adjunct (all women). *Students:* 35 full-time (30 women), 11 part-time (all women); includes 9 minority (7 Black or African American, non-Hispanic/Latino; 2 Asian, non-Hispanic/Latino), 1 international. Average age 26. 43 applicants, 100% accepted, 16 enrolled. In 2014, 15 master's, 6 other advanced degrees awarded. *Degree requirements:* For master's, internship. *Entrance requirements:* For master's, GRE General Test, official transcripts, two letters of recommendation, written statement. *Application deadline:* For fall admission, 2/15 for domestic and international students; for spring admission, 10/15

for domestic and international students. Applications are processed on a rolling basis. Application fee: $35. Electronic applications accepted. *Expenses:* Tuition, state resident: full-time $9472; part-time $473.60 per credit hour. Tuition, nonresident: full-time $18,944; part-time $947.20 per credit hour. *Required fees:* $14 per credit hour. $107 per semester. Tuition and fees vary according to course load and program. *Financial support:* In 2014–15, 4 teaching assistantships (averaging $7,750 per year) were awarded; career-related internships or fieldwork, scholarships/grants, and unspecified assistantships also available. Support available to part-time students. Financial award application deadline: 3/1; financial award applicants required to submit FAFSA. *Faculty research:* Parenting and family relationships, child development, applied behavioral analysis, post-traumatic stress disorder, clinical psychology in adults. *Unit head:* Dr. William Wattles, Chair, 843-661-1641, Fax: 843-661-1628. *Application contact:* Sharekka Bridges, Administrative Assistant, 843-661-1641, Fax: 843-661-1628.
Website: http://www.fmarion.edu/academics/psychology

Fresno Pacific University, Graduate Programs, School of Education, Division of Pupil Personnel Services, Program in School Psychology, Fresno, CA 93702-4709. Offers MA. Part-time and evening/weekend programs available. *Degree requirements:* For master's, thesis or alternative. *Entrance requirements:* Additional exam requirements/recommendations for international students: Required—TOEFL (minimum score 550 paper-based). *Application deadline:* For fall admission, 7/15 for domestic and international students; for spring admission, 11/15 for domestic and international students. Applications are processed on a rolling basis. Application fee: $90. *Expenses:* Expenses: $545 per unit. *Financial support:* Scholarships/grants and tuition waivers (full and partial) available. Support available to part-time students. Financial award applicants required to submit FAFSA. *Unit head:* Dr. Robert P. Murray, Program Director, 559-573-7830, E-mail: robert.murray@fresno.edu. *Application contact:* Amanda Krum-Stovall, Director of Graduate Admissions, 559-453-2016, E-mail: amanda.krum-stovall@fresno.edu.
Website: http://www.fresno.edu/programs-majors/graduate/school-psychology

Gallaudet University, The Graduate School, Washington, DC 20002-3625. Offers ASL/English bilingual early childhood education: birth to 5 (Certificate); audiology (Au D); clinical psychology (PhD); critical studies in the education of deaf learners (PhD); deaf and hard of hearing infants, toddlers, and their families (Certificate); deaf education (Ed S); deaf education: advanced studies (MA); deaf education: special programs (MA); deaf history (Certificate); deaf studies (MA, Certificate); educating deaf students with disabilities (Certificate); education: teacher preparation (MA), including deaf education, early childhood education and deaf education, elementary education and deaf education, secondary education and deaf education; educational neuroscience (PhD); hearing, speech and language sciences (MS, PhD); international development (MA); interpretation (MA, PhD), including combined interpreting practice and research (MA), interpreting research (MA); linguistics (MA, PhD); mental health counseling (MA); peer mentoring (Certificate); public administration (MPA); school counseling (MA); school psychology (Psy S); sign language teaching (MA); social work (MSW); speech-language pathology (MS). Part-time programs available. *Students:* 325 full-time (251 women), 118 part-time (90 women); includes 91 minority (41 Black or African American, non-Hispanic/Latino; 1 American Indian or Alaska Native, non-Hispanic/Latino; 14 Asian, non-Hispanic/Latino; 25 Hispanic/Latino; 10 Two or more races, non-Hispanic/Latino), 28 international. Average age 30. 617 applicants, 42% accepted, 171 enrolled. In 2014, 145 master's, 21 doctorates, 8 other advanced degrees awarded. Terminal master's awarded for partial completion of doctoral program. *Degree requirements:* For master's, comprehensive exam (for some programs), thesis optional; for doctorate, comprehensive exam, thesis/dissertation. *Entrance requirements:* For master's and doctorate, GRE General Test or MAT, letters of recommendation, interviews, goals statement, American Sign Language proficiency interview, written English competency. Additional exam requirements/recommendations for international students: Required—TOEFL. *Application deadline:* For fall admission, 2/15 for domestic students. Applications are processed on a rolling basis. Application fee: $75. Electronic applications accepted. *Expenses:* Tuition: Full-time $15,956; part-time $886.45 per credit hour. *Required fees:* $3404; $263 per semester. *Financial support:* Fellowships, research assistantships, teaching assistantships, career-related internships or fieldwork, Federal Work-Study, scholarships/grants, tuition waivers (partial), and unspecified assistantships available. Support available to part-time students. Financial award applicants required to submit FAFSA. *Faculty research:* Signing math dictionaries, telecommunications access, cancer genetics, linguistics, visual language and visual learning, integrated quantum materials, deaf legal discourse, advance recruitment and retention in geosciences. *Unit head:* Dr. Gaurav Mathur, Interim Dean, Graduate School and Continuing Studies, 202-250-2380, Fax: 202-651-5027, E-mail: gaurav.mathur@gallaudet.edu. *Application contact:* Wednesday Luria, Coordinator of Prospective Graduate Student Services, 202-651-5400, Fax: 202-651-5295, E-mail: graduate.school@gallaudet.edu.
Website: http://www.gallaudet.edu/x26696.xml

Gardner-Webb University, Graduate School, School of Psychology, Program in School Counseling, Boiling Springs, NC 28017. Offers MA. *Accreditation:* NCATE. Part-time and evening/weekend programs available. *Students:* 23 part-time (21 women); includes 5 minority (3 Black or African American, non-Hispanic/Latino; 1 Asian, non-Hispanic/Latino; 1 Hispanic/Latino). Average age 29. 39 applicants, 33% accepted, 10 enrolled. In 2014, 14 master's awarded. *Degree requirements:* For master's, comprehensive exam. *Entrance requirements:* For master's, GRE General Test, MAT, minimum GPA of 2.7. *Application deadline:* For fall admission, 7/1 priority date for domestic students. Applications are processed on a rolling basis. Application fee: $40. Electronic applications accepted. *Expenses:* Tuition: Part-time $406 per credit hour. Tuition and fees vary according to program. *Financial support:* Unspecified assistantships available. *Unit head:* Dr. David Carscaddon, Coordinator, 704-406-4437, Fax: 704-406-4329, E-mail: ppartin@gardner-webb.edu. *Application contact:* Office of Graduate Admissions, 877-498-4723, Fax: 704-406-3895, E-mail: gradinfo@gardner-webb.edu.

George Fox University, College of Education, Graduate Department of Counseling, Newberg, OR 97132-2697. Offers clinical mental health counseling (MA); marriage, couple and family counseling (MA, Certificate); mental health trauma (Certificate); school counseling (MA, Certificate); school psychology (Certificate, Ed S). Part-time programs available. *Degree requirements:* For master's, clinical project. *Entrance requirements:* For master's, MAT or GRE, bachelor's degree from regionally-accredited college or university, minimum cumulative GPA of 3.0, 1 professional and 1 academic reference, resume, on-campus interview, official transcripts. Additional exam requirements/recommendations for international students: Required—TOEFL (minimum score 577 paper-based; 90 iBT), IELTS (minimum score 7). Electronic applications accepted. *Expenses:* Contact institution.

George Mason University, College of Humanities and Social Sciences, Department of Psychology, Program in School Psychology, Fairfax, VA 22030. Offers MA, Certificate. *Accreditation:* NCATE. *Faculty:* 1 full-time (0 women), 3 part-time/adjunct (2 women). *Students:* 6 part-time (all women); includes 2 minority (both Hispanic/Latino). Average age 27. 9 applicants. In 2014, 10 other advanced degrees awarded. *Entrance requirements:* Additional exam requirements/recommendations for international students: Required—TOEFL (minimum score 570 paper-based; 80 iBT), IELTS

(minimum score 6.5), PTE. *Application deadline:* For fall admission, 1/15 for domestic students. *Expenses:* Tuition, state resident: full-time $9794; part-time $408 per credit hour. Tuition, nonresident: full-time $26,978; part-time $1124 per credit hour. *Required fees:* $2820; $118 per credit hour. Tuition and fees vary according to course load and program. *Financial support:* In 2014–15, 1 student received support. Federal Work-Study, unspecified assistantships, and health care benefits (for full-time research or teaching assistantship recipients) available. Support available to part-time students. Financial award application deadline: 3/1; financial award applicants required to submit FAFSA. *Unit head:* Nicole Beadles, Director, 703-993-5127, Fax: 703-993-1359, E-mail: nbeadles@gmu.edu. *Application contact:* Debbie Wesley, Graduate Program Coordinator, 703-993-1548, Fax: 703-993-1359, E-mail: dwesley@gmu.edu.
Website: http://chss.gmu.edu/programs/la-ma-psyc-sch

Georgian Court University, School of Arts and Sciences, Lakewood, NJ 08701-2697. Offers applied behavior analysis (MA); Catholic school leadership (Certificate); clinical mental health counseling (MA); holistic health studies (MA, Certificate); homeland security (MS); parish administration (Certificate); pastoral ministry (Certificate); professional counseling (Certificate); religious education (Certificate); school psychology (MA, Certificate); theology (MA, Certificate). Part-time and evening/weekend programs available. *Faculty:* 19 full-time (9 women), 9 part-time/adjunct (4 women). *Students:* 87 full-time (74 women), 127 part-time (110 women); includes 47 minority (14 Black or African American, non-Hispanic/Latino; 2 Asian, non-Hispanic/Latino; 23 Hispanic/Latino; 8 Two or more races, non-Hispanic/Latino). Average age 34. In 2014, 68 master's, 11 other advanced degrees awarded. *Degree requirements:* For master's, comprehensive exam (for some programs), thesis (for some programs). *Entrance requirements:* For master's, GRE, MAT, or NTE/PRAXIS, 3 letters of recommendation. Additional exam requirements/recommendations for international students: Required—TOEFL (minimum score 550 paper-based). *Application deadline:* For fall admission, 8/1 priority date for domestic students, 4/1 for international students; for spring admission, 1/1 priority date for domestic students, 7/1 for international students. Applications are processed on a rolling basis. Application fee: $40. Electronic applications accepted. *Expenses: Tuition:* Full-time $19,752; part-time $823 per credit. *Required fees:* $948; $243 per semester hour. Tuition and fees vary according to campus/location and program. *Financial support:* Scholarships/grants, health care benefits, and unspecified assistantships available. Financial award application deadline: 4/15; financial award applicants required to submit FAFSA. *Unit head:* Dr. Rita Kipp, Dean, 732-987-2493, Fax: 732-987-2007, E-mail: rkipp@georgian.edu. *Application contact:* Patrick Givens, Interim Director of Enrollment Management, 732-987-2736, Fax: 732-987-2084, E-mail: graduateadmissions@georgian.edu.
Website: http://www.georgian.edu/arts_sciences/index.htm

Georgia Southern University, Jack N. Averitt College of Graduate Studies, College of Education, Department of Leadership, Technology, and Human Development, Program in School Psychology, Statesboro, GA 30460. Offers M Ed, Ed S. *Accreditation:* NCATE. Part-time and evening/weekend programs available. *Students:* 19 full-time (17 women), 9 part-time (8 women); includes 14 minority (10 Black or African American, non-Hispanic/Latino; 4 Hispanic/Latino), 1 international. Average age 28. 20 applicants, 50% accepted, 6 enrolled. In 2014, 4 master's, 10 Ed Ss awarded. *Degree requirements:* For Ed S, comprehensive exam. *Entrance requirements:* For degree, GRE General Test or MAT, minimum graduate GPA of 3.25, letters of reference, interview. Additional exam requirements/recommendations for international students: Required—TOEFL (minimum score 550 paper-based; 80 iBT), IELTS (minimum score 6). *Application deadline:* For fall admission, 4/10 for domestic students, 3/1 priority date for international students; for spring admission, 11/10 for domestic students, 10/1 for international students. Applications are processed on a rolling basis. Application fee: $50. Electronic applications accepted. *Expenses:* Tuition, state resident: full-time $7236; part-time $277 per semester hour. Tuition, nonresident: full-time $27,118; part-time $1105 per semester hour. *Required fees:* $2092. *Financial support:* In 2014–15, 11 students received support, including research assistantships with partial tuition reimbursements available (averaging $7,200 per year), teaching assistantships with partial tuition reimbursements available (averaging $7,200 per year); career-related internships or fieldwork, Federal Work-Study, scholarships/grants, tuition waivers (partial), and unspecified assistantships also available. Support available to part-time students. Financial award application deadline: 4/15; financial award applicants required to submit FAFSA. *Faculty research:* K-12 online learning as it applies to school psychology, supervision, training in school psychology, cyber bullying. *Unit head:* Dr. Dawn Tysinger, Coordinator, 912-478-5792, Fax: 912-478-7104, E-mail: dtysinger@georgiasouthern.edu. *Application contact:* Lydia Cross, Coordinator for Graduate Student Recruitment, 912-478-8664, E-mail: lcross@georgiasouthern.edu.
Website: http://coe.georgiasouthern.edu/espy/

Georgia State University, College of Education, Department of Counseling and Psychological Services, Program in School Psychology, Atlanta, GA 30302-3083. Offers M Ed, PhD, Ed S. *Accreditation:* APA (one or more programs are accredited); NCATE. Terminal master's awarded for partial completion of doctoral program. *Degree requirements:* For master's and Ed S, comprehensive exam; for doctorate, comprehensive exam, thesis/dissertation. *Entrance requirements:* For master's and doctorate, GRE, writing sample, resume, 3 letters of recommendation, goal statement, transcripts. Additional exam requirements/recommendations for international students: Required—TOEFL. *Application deadline:* For fall admission, 12/1 for domestic and international students. Application fee: $50. Electronic applications accepted. *Expenses:* Tuition, state resident: full-time $6516; part-time $362 per credit hour. Tuition, nonresident: full-time $22,014; part-time $1223 per credit hour. *Required fees:* $2128 per semester. Tuition and fees vary according to course load and program. *Financial support:* Fellowships with full tuition reimbursements, research assistantships with full and partial tuition reimbursements, teaching assistantships with full and partial tuition reimbursements, career-related internships or fieldwork, institutionally sponsored loans, scholarships/grants, health care benefits, and unspecified assistantships available. Financial award application deadline: 4/1. *Faculty research:* School safety, school climate, and classroom management; alternative schools; children with disabilities; prevention of bullying, cyberbullying, and the commercial sexual exploitation of children; school psychology professional diversity. *Unit head:* Dr. Brian Dew, Chairperson, 404-413-8168, Fax: 404-413-8013, E-mail: bdew@gsu.edu. *Application contact:* Nancy Keita, Director, Office of Academic Assistance and Graduate Admissions, 404-413-8001, E-mail: nkeita@gsu.edu.
Website: http://education.gsu.edu/CPS/4514.html

Grand Valley State University, College of Education, Program in School Counseling, Allendale, MI 49401-9403. Offers M Ed. Part-time programs available. *Students:* 15 full-time (13 women), 33 part-time (24 women); includes 8 minority (4 Black or African American, non-Hispanic/Latino; 1 Asian, non-Hispanic/Latino; 3 Hispanic/Latino). Average age 31. 15 applicants, 93% accepted, 8 enrolled. In 2014, 14 master's awarded. *Degree requirements:* For master's, thesis or project. *Entrance requirements:* For master's, GRE General Test or minimum GPA of 3.0. Additional exam requirements/recommendations for international students: Required—TOEFL. *Application deadline:* Applications are processed on a rolling basis. Application fee: $30. Electronic applications accepted. *Expenses:* Tuition, state resident: full-time $10,602; part-time $589 per credit hour. Tuition, nonresident: full-time $14,022; part-time $779 per credit hour. Tuition and fees vary according to degree level and program. *Financial support:* In 2014–15, 5 students received support, including 4 fellowships (averaging $4,229 per year), 3 research assistantships with full and partial tuition reimbursements available (averaging $9,834 per year); career-related internships or fieldwork also available. *Faculty research:* Multicultural issues in counselor education, use of technology in counseling programs. *Unit head:* Dr. Shawn Bultsma, Program Director, 616-331-6648, E-mail: bultsmas@gvsu.edu. *Application contact:* Thomas Owens, Student Information and Services Center, 616-331-6650, Fax: 616-331-6217, E-mail: owenst@gvsu.edu.

Grand Valley State University, College of Liberal Arts and Sciences, Program in School Psychology, Allendale, MI 49401-9403. Offers MS, Psy S. *Faculty:* 3 full-time (all women). *Students:* 12 full-time (8 women), 4 part-time (2 women); includes 2 minority (both Hispanic/Latino). Average age 27. 16 applicants, 81% accepted, 12 enrolled. *Expenses:* Tuition, state resident: full-time $10,602; part-time $589 per credit hour. Tuition, nonresident: full-time $14,022; part-time $779 per credit hour. Tuition and fees vary according to degree level and program. *Financial support:* In 2014–15, 4 students received support, including 2 fellowships (averaging $962 per year), 2 research assistantships (averaging $5,256 per year). *Unit head:* Dr. Robert Hendersen, Director, 616-331-2195, E-mail: hendersr@gvsu.edu. *Application contact:* Amy Campbell, Associate Director for Graduate Recruitment, 616-331-2409, Fax: 616-331-2480, E-mail: campbeam@gvsu.edu.
Website: http://www.gvsu.edu/grad/schoolpsy/

Heidelberg University, Program in Counseling, Tiffin, OH 44883-2462. Offers community mental health counseling (MA); school counseling (MA). *Accreditation:* ACA. Part-time and evening/weekend programs available. *Degree requirements:* For master's, thesis or alternative, counseling practicum, internship. *Entrance requirements:* For master's, GRE General Test, 12 hours of course work in behavioral sciences, minimum GPA of 2.9, 3 letters of reference. Additional exam requirements/recommendations for international students: Required—TOEFL.

Hofstra University, College of Liberal Arts and Sciences, Programs in Psychology, Hempstead, NY 11549. Offers applied organizational psychology (PhD); clinical psychology (PhD); industrial/organizational psychology (MA); school-community psychology (Psy D). Part-time and evening/weekend programs available. *Students:* 226 full-time (146 women), 14 part-time (9 women); includes 42 minority (7 Black or African American, non-Hispanic/Latino; 2 American Indian or Alaska Native, non-Hispanic/Latino; 11 Asian, non-Hispanic/Latino; 17 Hispanic/Latino; 1 Native Hawaiian or other Pacific Islander, non-Hispanic/Latino; 4 Two or more races, non-Hispanic/Latino), 20 international. Average age 27. 313 applicants, 40% accepted, 67 enrolled. In 2014, 40 master's, 30 doctorates awarded. *Degree requirements:* For master's, comprehensive exam, thesis (for some programs), internship, minimum GPA of 3.0; for doctorate, comprehensive exam, thesis/dissertation, 1st year qualifying examination, 2nd year research project, successful practicum/externship placements, written presentation and successful oral defense of dissertation, completion of full-time internship. *Entrance requirements:* For master's, GRE General Test, minimum GPA of 3.0, essay, interview; for doctorate, GRE General Test, GRE Subject Test (psychology), 3 letters of recommendation, interview, essay, curriculum vitae. Additional exam requirements/recommendations for international students: Required—TOEFL (minimum score 550 paper-based; 80 iBT). *Application deadline:* For fall admission, 12/15 for domestic and international students. Application fee: $70 ($75 for international students). Electronic applications accepted. *Expenses: Tuition:* Full-time $20,610; part-time $1145 per credit hour. *Required fees:* $970; $165 per term. Tuition and fees vary according to program. *Financial support:* In 2014–15, 139 students received support, including 118 fellowships with full and partial tuition reimbursements available (averaging $7,236 per year), 7 research assistantships with full and partial tuition reimbursements available (averaging $5,788 per year); Federal Work-Study, institutionally sponsored loans, scholarships/grants, health care benefits, tuition waivers (full and partial), and diversity and endowed scholarships also available. Support available to part-time students. Financial award applicants required to submit FAFSA. *Faculty research:* Cognitive behavioral therapy for anxiety disorders, autism spectrum disorders, parent child interaction training (PCIT), positive organizational behavior, personnel selection and decision-making. *Unit head:* Dr. Keith Shafritz, Chairperson, 516-463-4856, Fax: 516-463-6052, E-mail: psykms@hofstra.edu. *Application contact:* Sunil Samuel, Assistant Vice President of Admissions, 516-463-4723, Fax: 516-463-4664, E-mail: graduateadmission@hofstra.edu.
Website: http://www.hofstra.edu/hclas

Howard University, School of Education, Department of Human Development and Psychoeducational Studies, Program in School Psychology, Washington, DC 20059-0002. Offers M Ed, PhD. *Accreditation:* NCATE. *Degree requirements:* For doctorate, one foreign language, comprehensive exam, thesis/dissertation, expository writing exam, internship. *Entrance requirements:* For doctorate, GRE General Test, minimum GPA of 3.4. Additional exam requirements/recommendations for international students: Required—TOEFL (minimum score 550 paper-based; 79 iBT). Electronic applications accepted. *Faculty research:* Psychopathology, maltreatment abuse and neglect, children exposed to political unrest, family conflict and community violence.

Humboldt State University, Academic Programs, College of Professional Studies, Department of Psychology, Arcata, CA 95521-8299. Offers psychology (MA), including academic research, counseling, school psychology. *Students:* 52 full-time (42 women), 6 part-time (3 women); includes 22 minority (15 Hispanic/Latino; 7 Two or more races, non-Hispanic/Latino). Average age 27. 73 applicants, 47% accepted, 24 enrolled. In 2014, 15 master's awarded. *Degree requirements:* For master's, thesis. *Entrance requirements:* For master's, appropriate bachelor's degree, minimum GPA of 2.5. Additional exam requirements/recommendations for international students: Required—TOEFL (minimum score 500 paper-based). *Application deadline:* For fall admission, 2/1 for domestic students, 2/15 for international students. Applications are processed on a rolling basis. Application fee: $55. *Expenses:* Tuition, state resident: full-time $6738; part-time $3906 per year. Tuition, nonresident: full-time $13,434; part-time $6138 per year. *Required fees:* $1690; $1266 per year. Tuition and fees vary according to program. *Financial support:* Career-related internships or fieldwork available. Financial award application deadline: 3/1; financial award applicants required to submit FAFSA. *Faculty research:* School psychology, counseling, eating disorders, mood induction, depression. *Unit head:* Dr. Gregg Gold, Chair, 707-826-3740, Fax: 707-826-4993, E-mail: gjg14@humboldt.edu. *Application contact:* Dr. Chris Aberson, Coordinator, 707-826-3670, Fax: 707-826-4993, E-mail: cla18@humboldt.edu.
Website: http://www2.humboldt.edu/psychology/programs-child/graduate-programs-psychology

Husson University, Graduate Programs in Counseling and Human Relations, Bangor, ME 04401-2999. Offers clinical mental health counseling (MS); human relations (MS); pastoral counseling (MS); school counseling (MS). Part-time and evening/weekend programs available. *Faculty:* 3 full-time (2 women), 2 part-time/adjunct (both women). *Students:* 39 full-time (33 women), 25 part-time (20 women); includes 3 minority (2 Black or African American, non-Hispanic/Latino; 1 Two or more races, non-Hispanic/Latino), 2 international. Average age 34. 55 applicants, 69% accepted, 32 enrolled. In 2014, 19 master's awarded. *Degree requirements:* For master's, comprehensive exam (for some programs), thesis optional. *Entrance requirements:* For master's, GRE or MAT, BS with

minimum GPA of 3.0, letters of recommendation, interview. Additional exam requirements/recommendations for international students: Required—TOEFL (minimum score 550 paper-based; 80 iBT). *Application deadline:* For fall admission, 2/1 for domestic students. Applications are processed on a rolling basis. Application fee: $50. Electronic applications accepted. *Expenses:* Expenses: Contact institution. *Financial support:* In 2014–15, 1 student received support. Federal Work-Study, scholarships/grants, and unspecified assistantships available. Financial award application deadline: 4/15; financial award applicants required to submit FAFSA. *Faculty research:* Challenges and rewards of counseling practice in rural, small town and neighborhood settings. *Unit head:* Dr. Deborah Drew, Director, Graduate Counseling Programs, 207-992-4912, Fax: 207-992-4952, E-mail: drewd@husson.edu. *Application contact:* Kristen Card, Director of Graduate Admissions, 207-404-5660, Fax: 207-941-7935, E-mail: cardk@husson.edu.
Website: http://www.husson.edu/human-relations

Idaho State University, Office of Graduate Studies, College of Education, Department of School Psychology, Literacy, and Special Education, Pocatello, ID 83209-8059. Offers deaf education (M Ed); human exceptionality (M Ed); literacy (M Ed); school psychology (Ed S); special education (Ed S). Part-time programs available. *Degree requirements:* For master's, comprehensive exam, thesis (for some programs), oral thesis defense or written comprehensive exam and oral exam; for Ed S, comprehensive exam, thesis (for some programs), oral exam, specialist paper or portfolio. *Entrance requirements:* For master's, GRE or MAT, minimum undergraduate GPA of 3.0, bachelor's degree, professional experience in an educational context; for Ed S, GRE or MAT, master's degree in related field. Additional exam requirements/recommendations for international students: Required—TOEFL (minimum score 550 paper-based; 80 iBT). Electronic applications accepted. *Faculty research:* Literacy, school psychology, special education.

Idaho State University, Office of Graduate Studies, Kasiska College of Health Professions, Department of Counseling, Pocatello, ID 83209-8120. Offers counseling (M Coun, Ed S), including marriage and family counseling (M Coun), mental health counseling (M Coun), school counseling (M Coun), student affairs and college counseling (M Coun); counselor education and counseling (PhD). *Accreditation:* ACA (one or more programs are accredited). Part-time programs available. *Degree requirements:* For master's, comprehensive exam, thesis, 4 semesters resident graduate study, practicum/internship; for doctorate, comprehensive exam, thesis/dissertation, 3 semesters internship, 4 consecutive semesters doctoral-level study on campus; for Ed S, comprehensive exam, thesis, case studies, oral exam. *Entrance requirements:* For master's, GRE General Test, MAT, minimum GPA of 3.0, bachelors degree, interview, 3 letters of recommendation; for doctorate, GRE General Test, MAT, minimum graduate GPA of 3.0, resume, interview, counseling license, master's degree; for Ed S, GRE General Test, minimum graduate GPA of 3.0, master's degree in counseling, 3 letters of recommendation, 2 years work experience. Additional exam requirements/recommendations for international students: Required—TOEFL (minimum score 600 paper-based; 80 iBT). Electronic applications accepted. *Faculty research:* Group counseling, multicultural counseling, family counseling, child therapy, supervision.

Illinois State University, Graduate School, College of Arts and Sciences, Department of Psychology, Program in School Psychology, Normal, IL 61790-2200. Offers PhD, SSP. *Accreditation:* APA (one or more programs are accredited); NCATE (one or more programs are accredited). *Degree requirements:* For doctorate, variable foreign language requirement, thesis/dissertation, 2 terms of residency, internship, practicum. *Entrance requirements:* For doctorate, GRE General Test.

Immaculata University, College of Graduate Studies, Department of Psychology, Immaculata, PA 19345. Offers clinical mental health counseling (MA); clinical psychology (Psy D); forensic psychology (Graduate Certificate); integrative psychotherapy (Graduate Certificate); neuropsychology (Graduate Certificate); psychodynamic psychotherapy (Graduate Certificate); psychological testing (Graduate Certificate); school counseling (MA, Graduate Certificate); school psychology (MA). *Accreditation:* APA. Part-time and evening/weekend programs available. Terminal master's awarded for partial completion of doctoral program. *Degree requirements:* For master's, comprehensive exam, thesis optional; for doctorate, comprehensive exam, thesis/dissertation. *Entrance requirements:* For master's, GRE General Test or MAT, minimum GPA of 3.0; for doctorate, GRE General Test or MAT, minimum GPA of 3.5. Additional exam requirements/recommendations for international students: Required—TOEFL, IELTS. Electronic applications accepted. *Faculty research:* Supervision ethics, psychology of teaching, gender.

Indiana State University, College of Graduate and Professional Studies, Bayh College of Education, Department of Communication Disorders, Counseling and School and Educational Psychology, Terre Haute, IN 47809. Offers counseling psychology (MS, PhD); counselor education (PhD); mental health counseling (MS); school counseling (M Ed); school psychology (PhD, Ed S); MA/MS. *Accreditation:* ACA; NCATE. Part-time and evening/weekend programs available. *Degree requirements:* For master's, thesis optional; for doctorate, thesis/dissertation, research tools proficiency tests. *Entrance requirements:* For master's, GRE General Test or MAT, minimum undergraduate GPA of 2.75; for doctorate, GRE General Test, master's degree, minimum undergraduate GPA of 3.5. Electronic applications accepted. *Faculty research:* Vocational development supervision.

Indiana University Bloomington, School of Education, Department of Counseling and Educational Psychology, Bloomington, IN 47405-1006. Offers counseling (MS, PhD, Ed S); counselor education (MS, Ed S); educational psychology (MS, PhD); inquiry methodology (PhD); learning and developmental sciences (MS, PhD); school psychology (PhD, Ed S). *Accreditation:* ACA (one or more programs are accredited); APA (one or more programs are accredited); NCATE. Terminal master's awarded for partial completion of doctoral program. *Degree requirements:* For master's, thesis optional; for doctorate, thesis/dissertation; for Ed S, comprehensive exam or project. *Entrance requirements:* For master's, doctorate, and Ed S, GRE General Test. Additional exam requirements/recommendations for international students: Required—TOEFL. *Application deadline:* Applications are processed on a rolling basis. Application fee: $55 ($65 for international students). Electronic applications accepted. *Financial support:* Fellowships with partial tuition reimbursements, research assistantships with partial tuition reimbursements, teaching assistantships with partial tuition reimbursements, career-related internships or fieldwork, Federal Work-Study, institutionally sponsored loans, scholarships/grants, and unspecified assistantships available. Support available to part-time students. Financial award application deadline: 1/1; financial award applicants required to submit FAFSA. *Faculty research:* Counseling psychology, inquiry methodology, school psychology, learning sciences, human development, educational psychology. *Unit head:* Dr. Joyce Alexander, Chairperson, 812-856-8300, Fax: 812-856-8333, E-mail: cep@indiana.edu. *Application contact:* Jessica Durnal, Student Services Specialist, 812-856-8300, Fax: 812-856-8333, E-mail: cep@indiana.edu.
Website: http://education.indiana.edu/cep/

Indiana University of Pennsylvania, School of Graduate Studies and Research, College of Education and Educational Technology, Department of Educational and School Psychology, Program in School Psychology, Indiana, PA 15705-1087. Offers D Ed, Certificate. *Accreditation:* NCATE. Part-time and evening/weekend programs available. *Faculty:* 8 full-time (2 women). *Students:* 49 part-time (43 women); includes 6 minority (5 Black or African American, non-Hispanic/Latino; 1 Asian, non-Hispanic/Latino). Average age 34. 15 applicants, 47% accepted, 3 enrolled. In 2014, 7 doctorates awarded. *Degree requirements:* For doctorate, comprehensive exam, thesis/dissertation. *Entrance requirements:* For doctorate, GRE General Test, PRAXIS II School Psychology Exam, 2 letters of recommendation. Additional exam requirements/recommendations for international students: Required—TOEFL (minimum score 540 paper-based). *Application deadline:* For fall admission, 2/1 priority date for domestic students. Applications are processed on a rolling basis. Application fee: $50. Electronic applications accepted. *Financial support:* In 2014–15, 5 fellowships with full tuition reimbursements (averaging $843 per year), 1 teaching assistantship with partial tuition reimbursement (averaging $11,652 per year) were awarded; research assistantships with full and partial tuition reimbursements, career-related internships or fieldwork, Federal Work-Study, scholarships/grants, and unspecified assistantships also available. Support available to part-time students. Financial award application deadline: 4/15; financial award applicants required to submit FAFSA. *Unit head:* Dr. Joseph Kovaleski, Graduate Coordinator, 724-357-2316, E-mail: jkov@iup.edu.
Website: http://www.iup.edu/upper.aspx?id-94498

Inter American University of Puerto Rico, Metropolitan Campus, Graduate Programs, Program in Psychology, San Juan, PR 00919-1293. Offers counseling psychology (MA, PhD); industrial/organizational psychology (MA, PhD); labor relations (MA); school psychology (MA, PhD). *Degree requirements:* For master's, comprehensive exam. *Entrance requirements:* For master's, GRE or EXADEP, interview. Electronic applications accepted.

Inter American University of Puerto Rico, San Germán Campus, Graduate Studies Center, Program in Psychology, San Germán, PR 00683-5008. Offers counseling psychology (MA, PhD); school psychology (MA, PhD). Part-time and evening/weekend programs available. *Degree requirements:* For master's, comprehensive exam, thesis; for doctorate, comprehensive exam, thesis/dissertation. *Entrance requirements:* For master's, GRE General Test or EXADEP, minimum GPA of 3.0; for doctorate, GRE, EXADEP or MAT, minimum GPA of 3.0.

Iona College, School of Arts and Science, Department of Psychology, New Rochelle, NY 10801-1890. Offers general-experimental psychology (MA); human resources (Certificate); industrial-organizational psychology (MA); mental health counseling (MA); organizational behavior (Certificate); psychology (MA); school psychology (MA). Part-time programs available. *Faculty:* 8 full-time (3 women), 5 part-time/adjunct (3 women). *Students:* 41 full-time (30 women), 33 part-time (22 women); includes 29 minority (12 Black or African American, non-Hispanic/Latino; 2 Asian, non-Hispanic/Latino; 15 Hispanic/Latino), 1 international. Average age 24. 65 applicants, 85% accepted, 22 enrolled. In 2014, 38 master's awarded. *Degree requirements:* For master's, thesis (for some programs), literature review (for some programs). *Entrance requirements:* For master's, BA in psychology including 3 credits in psychology statistics and 3 credits in experimental research methods; or 9 credits in psychology including 3 credits in psychology statistics,3 credits in psychology research methods and 3 credits of upper-level coursework. Additional exam requirements/recommendations for international students: Required—TOEFL (minimum score 550 paper-based), IELTS (minimum score 6.5). *Application deadline:* For fall admission, 8/15 for domestic students, 5/1 for international students; for spring admission, 1/15 for domestic students, 9/1 for international students. Applications are processed on a rolling basis. Application fee: $50. Electronic applications accepted. *Expenses: Tuition:* Part-time $985 per credit. *Required fees:* $245 per term. *Financial support:* In 2014–15, 6 students received support, including 1 research assistantship with partial tuition reimbursement available (averaging $8,000 per year); tuition waivers (partial) and unspecified assistantships also available. Support available to part-time students. Financial award application deadline: 4/15; financial award applicants required to submit FAFSA. *Faculty research:* Non-suicidal self-injury, trauma response, performance appraisal and evaluation, diversity infusion, assessment and treatment of sexual offenders. *Unit head:* Patricia Oswald, PhD, Chair, 914-633-7788, E-mail: poswald@iona.edu. *Application contact:* Amanda St. Bernard, Assistant Director, Graduate Admissions, 914-633-2440, Fax: 914-633-2277, E-mail: astbernard@iona.edu.
Website: http://www.iona.edu/Academics/School-of-Arts-Science/Departments/Psychology/Graduate-Programs.aspx

James Madison University, The Graduate School, College of Health and Behavioral Sciences, Department of Graduate Psychology, Combined-Integrated Program in Clinical and School Psychology, Harrisonburg, VA 22807. Offers Psy D. Part-time and evening/weekend programs available. *Students:* 23 full-time (15 women); includes 4 minority (3 Black or African American, non-Hispanic/Latino; 1 Two or more races, non-Hispanic/Latino), 2 international. Average age 28. 32 applicants, 19% accepted, 6 enrolled. In 2014, 9 doctorates awarded. *Degree requirements:* For doctorate, thesis/dissertation. *Application deadline:* For fall admission, 2/1 for domestic students. Application fee: $55. Electronic applications accepted. *Expenses:* Tuition, state resident: full-time $7812; part-time $434 per credit hour. Tuition, nonresident: full-time $20,430; part-time $1135 per credit hour. *Financial support:* In 2014–15, 18 students received support, including 1 fellowship; teaching assistantships, unspecified assistantships, and 17 doctoral assistantships (averaging $14,790) also available. Financial award application deadline: 3/1; financial award applicants required to submit FAFSA. *Unit head:* Dr. Gregg R. Henriques, Graduate Program Director, 540-568-7857, E-mail: henrigg@jmu.edu. *Application contact:* Lynette D. Michael, Director of Graduate Admissions and Student Records, 540-568-6131 Ext. 6395, Fax: 540-568-7860, E-mail: michaeld@jmu.edu.
Website: http://www.psyc.jmu.edu/cipsyd/

James Madison University, The Graduate School, College of Health and Behavioral Sciences, Department of Graduate Psychology, Program in School Psychology, Harrisonburg, VA 22807. Offers MA, Ed S. *Accreditation:* APA (one or more programs are accredited); NCATE (one or more programs are accredited). Part-time and evening/weekend programs available. *Students:* 17 full-time (12 women), 10 part-time (7 women); includes 6 minority (3 Black or African American, non-Hispanic/Latino; 1 Asian, non-Hispanic/Latino; 2 Hispanic/Latino). Average age 28. 68 applicants, 25% accepted, 17 enrolled. In 2014, 10 master's awarded. *Degree requirements:* For master's, comprehensive exam; for Ed S, thesis. *Application deadline:* For fall admission, 2/1 for domestic students. Application fee: $55. Electronic applications accepted. *Expenses:* Tuition, state resident: full-time $7812; part-time $434 per credit hour. Tuition, nonresident: full-time $20,430; part-time $1135 per credit hour. *Financial support:* In 2014–15, 17 students received support, including 2 fellowships, 1 teaching assistantship with full tuition reimbursement available (averaging $8,837 per year); career-related internships or fieldwork, Federal Work-Study, and 14 assistantships (averaging $7263) also available. Financial award application deadline: 3/1; financial award applicants required to submit FAFSA. *Unit head:* Dr. Tammy D. Gilligan, Graduate Program Director, 540-568-6564, E-mail: gilligtd@jmu.edu. *Application contact:* Lynette D. Michael, Director of Graduate Admissions and Student Records, 540-568-6131 Ext.

6395, Fax: 540-568-7860, E-mail: michaeld@jmu.edu.
Website: http://psyc.jmu.edu/school/

Kean University, Nathan Weiss Graduate College, Program in Combined School and Clinical Psychology, Union, NJ 07083. Offers Psy D. Part-time programs available. *Faculty:* 7 full-time (3 women). *Students:* 19 full-time (14 women), 9 part-time (8 women); includes 4 minority (2 Black or African American, non-Hispanic/Latino; 1 Asian, non-Hispanic/Latino; 1 Hispanic/Latino), 1 international. Average age 29. *Degree requirements:* For doctorate, comprehensive exam, thesis/dissertation, externship. *Entrance requirements:* For doctorate, GRE General Test, GRE Subject Test in psychology (taken within last 5 years), minimum undergraduate GPA of 3.3, graduate 3.5; 3 letters of recommendation; personal interview; prerequisite coursework in theories of personality, abnormal psychology, tests and measurements, statistics, and experimental psychology; personal statement. Additional exam requirements/recommendations for international students: Required—TOEFL (minimum score 550 paper-based; 79 iBT). *Application deadline:* For fall admission, 2/2 for domestic and international students. Applications are processed on a rolling basis. Application fee: $75 ($150 for international students). Electronic applications accepted. *Expenses:* Expenses: Contact institution. *Financial support:* In 2014–15, 5 research assistantships with full tuition reimbursements were awarded; scholarships/grants and unspecified assistantships also available. Financial award applicants required to submit FAFSA. *Unit head:* Dr. Jennifer Block-Lerner, Program Coordinator, 908-737-5864, E-mail: jlerner@kean.edu. *Application contact:* Reenat Hasan, Admissions Counselor, 908-737-7134, Fax: 908-737-7135, E-mail: hasanr@kean.edu.
Website: http://grad.kean.edu/doctoral-programs/combined-school-and-clinical-psychology

Kean University, Nathan Weiss Graduate College, Program in School Psychology, Union, NJ 07083. Offers MA, Diploma. Part-time programs available. *Faculty:* 7 full-time (3 women). *Students:* 24 full-time (23 women), 11 part-time (all women); includes 10 minority (all Hispanic/Latino). Average age 24. 30 applicants, 67% accepted, 17 enrolled. In 2014, 12 master's, 10 other advanced degrees awarded. *Degree requirements:* For Diploma, comprehensive exam, practicum, externship. *Entrance requirements:* For degree, GRE General Test, minimum GPA of 3.0, interview, 3 letters of recommendation, prerequisites in psychology, official transcripts from all institutions attended, resume. Additional exam requirements/recommendations for international students: Required—TOEFL (minimum score 550 paper-based; 79 iBT). *Application deadline:* For fall admission, 3/2 for domestic and international students. Application fee: $75 ($150 for international students). Electronic applications accepted. *Expenses:* Tuition, state resident: full-time $12,461; part-time $607 per credit. Tuition, nonresident: full-time $16,889; part-time $744 per credit. *Required fees:* $3141; $143 per credit. Tuition and fees vary according to course load, degree level and program. *Financial support:* In 2014–15, 5 research assistantships with full tuition reimbursements (averaging $3,742 per year) were awarded; scholarships/grants and unspecified assistantships also available. Financial award applicants required to submit FAFSA. *Unit head:* Dr. Andrew Wolanin, Program Coordinator, 908-737-5863, E-mail: awolanin@kean.edu. *Application contact:* Ann-Marie Kay, Assistant Director for Graduate Admissions, 908-737-7132, Fax: 908-737-7135, E-mail: akay@kean.edu.
Website: http://grad.kean.edu/professional-diploma-programs/school-psychology

Keene State College, School of Professional and Graduate Studies, Keene, NH 03435. Offers curriculum and instruction (M Ed); education leadership (PMC); educational leadership (M Ed); safety and occupational health applied science (MS); school counselor (M Ed, PMC); special education (M Ed). *Accreditation:* NCATE. Part-time and evening/weekend programs available. *Faculty:* 12 full-time (6 women), 13 part-time/adjunct (8 women). *Students:* 50 full-time (42 women), 46 part-time (30 women); includes 5 minority (2 Asian, non-Hispanic/Latino; 2 Hispanic/Latino; 1 Two or more races, non-Hispanic/Latino). Average age 29. 42 applicants, 79% accepted, 23 enrolled. In 2014, 55 degrees awarded. *Degree requirements:* For master's, thesis (for some programs). *Entrance requirements:* For master's, PRAXIS I, 3 references; official transcripts; minimum GPA of 2.5; interview; essay; teacher/educator certificate; work/internship experience. Additional exam requirements/recommendations for international students: Required—TOEFL (minimum score 550 paper-based; 61 iBT). *Application deadline:* For fall admission, 4/1 for domestic and international students; for spring admission, 11/1 for domestic and international students; for summer admission, 3/1 for domestic and international students. Applications are processed on a rolling basis. Application fee: $50. Electronic applications accepted. *Expenses:* Tuition, state resident: full-time $10,410; part-time $480 per credit. Tuition, nonresident: full-time $18,330; part-time $530 per credit. *Required fees:* $2454; $98 per credit. Tuition and fees vary according to course load. *Financial support:* In 2014–15, 27 students received support. Career-related internships or fieldwork, Federal Work-Study, institutionally sponsored loans, scholarships/grants, and unspecified assistantships available. Support available to part-time students. Financial award application deadline: 3/1; financial award applicants required to submit FAFSA. *Unit head:* Dr. Wayne Hartz, Interim Dean of Professional and Graduate Studies, 603-358-2220, E-mail: whartz@keene.edu. *Application contact:* Peggy Richmond, Director of Admissions, 603-358-2276, Fax: 603-358-2767, E-mail: admissions@keene.edu.
Website: http://www.keene.edu/academics/graduate/

Kent State University, Graduate School of Education, Health, and Human Services, School of Lifespan Development and Educational Sciences, Program in School Psychology, Kent, OH 44242-0001. Offers M Ed, PhD, Ed S. *Accreditation:* APA; NCATE. *Faculty:* 4 full-time (1 woman), 3 part-time/adjunct (2 women). *Students:* 56 full-time (49 women); includes 6 minority (3 Black or African American, non-Hispanic/Latino; 1 Asian, non-Hispanic/Latino; 1 Hispanic/Latino; 1 Native Hawaiian or other Pacific Islander, non-Hispanic/Latino). 61 applicants, 13% accepted. In 2014, 19 master's, 2 doctorates, 8 other advanced degrees awarded. *Degree requirements:* For doctorate, comprehensive exam, thesis/dissertation. *Entrance requirements:* For master's, doctorate, and Ed S, GRE General Test, 2 letters of reference, goals statement, moral character form, sample of written work, resume, interview. Additional exam requirements/recommendations for international students: Required—TOEFL (minimum score 550 paper-based; 80 iBT). *Application deadline:* For fall admission, 6/15 for domestic students; for spring admission, 10/15 for domestic students. Application fee: $45 ($60 for international students). Electronic applications accepted. *Expenses:* Tuition, state resident: full-time $8730; part-time $485 per credit hour. Tuition, nonresident: full-time $14,886; part-time $827 per credit hour. Tuition and fees vary according to campus/location and program. *Financial support:* In 2014–15, 3 research assistantships with full tuition reimbursements (averaging $9,667 per year), 1 teaching assistantship with full tuition reimbursement (averaging $12,000 per year) were awarded; Federal Work-Study, scholarships/grants, unspecified assistantships, and 9 administrative assistantships (averaging $8,889 per year) also available. Financial award application deadline: 4/1; financial award applicants required to submit FAFSA. *Faculty research:* Special education policy and practice, treatment fidelity, school-based consultation. *Unit head:* Dr. Frank Sansoti, Coordinator, 330-672-0059, E-mail: fsansost@kent.edu. *Application contact:* Nancy Miller, Academic Program Director, Office of Graduate Student Services, 330-672-2576, Fax: 330-672-9162, E-mail: ogs@kent.edu.
Website: http://www.kent.edu/ehhs/ldes/spsy

La Sierra University, School of Education, Department of School Psychology and Counseling, Riverside, CA 92515. Offers counseling (MA); educational psychology (Ed S); school psychology (Ed S). Part-time and evening/weekend programs available. *Degree requirements:* For master's, thesis optional; for Ed S, practicum (educational psychology). *Entrance requirements:* For master's, California Basic Educational Skills Test, NTE, minimum GPA of 3.0; for Ed S, minimum GPA of 3.3. *Faculty research:* Equivalent score scales, self perception.

Lehigh University, College of Education, Program in School Psychology, Bethlehem, PA 18015. Offers PhD, Ed S. *Accreditation:* APA (one or more programs are accredited). Part-time programs available. *Faculty:* 7 full-time (5 women), 1 part-time/adjunct (0 women). *Students:* 35 full-time (31 women), 9 part-time (5 women); includes 1 minority (Asian, non-Hispanic/Latino). Average age 25. 73 applicants, 30% accepted, 7 enrolled. In 2014, 7 doctorates awarded. *Degree requirements:* For doctorate, comprehensive exam, thesis/dissertation, internship, research qualifying exam; for Ed S, comprehensive exam, internship. *Entrance requirements:* For doctorate and Ed S, GRE General Test, minimum GPA of 3.0, 2 letters of recommendation (at least one academic), transcripts. Additional exam requirements/recommendations for international students: Required—TOEFL (minimum score 600 paper-based; 93 iBT). *Application deadline:* For fall admission, 1/1 for domestic and international students. Application fee: $65. Electronic applications accepted. *Expenses:* Expenses: $565 per credit. *Financial support:* Fellowships with full and partial tuition reimbursements, research assistantships with full and partial tuition reimbursements, career-related internships or fieldwork, Federal Work-Study, institutionally sponsored loans, tuition waivers (full and partial), and unspecified assistantships available. Financial award application deadline: 1/31; financial award applicants required to submit FAFSA. *Faculty research:* Applied behavior analysis, developmental disabilities, at-risk students, learning and behavior problems, pediatric psychology. *Total annual research expenditures:* $78,276. *Unit head:* Dr. Patricia R. Manz, Coordinator, 610-758-5656, Fax: 610-758-6223, E-mail: phm3@lehigh.edu. *Application contact:* Sharon Y. Warden, Coordinator, 610-758-3256, Fax: 610-758-6223, E-mail: sy00@lehigh.edu.
Website: http://coe.lehigh.edu/academics/disciplines/sp

Lenoir-Rhyne University, Graduate Programs, School of Counseling, Program in School Counseling, Hickory, NC 28601. Offers MA. Part-time and evening/weekend programs available. *Faculty:* 2 part-time/adjunct (1 woman). *Students:* 3 full-time (all women), 13 part-time (11 women); includes 1 minority (Hispanic/Latino). Average age 32. In 2014, 2 master's awarded. *Degree requirements:* For master's, comprehensive exam, thesis optional. *Entrance requirements:* For master's, GRE General Test, minimum undergraduate GPA of 2.7, graduate 3.0; writing sample. Additional exam requirements/recommendations for international students: Required—TOEFL (minimum score 600 paper-based). *Application deadline:* Applications are processed on a rolling basis. Application fee: $35. Electronic applications accepted. *Expenses: Tuition:* Full-time $9000; part-time $500 per credit hour. Tuition and fees vary according to program. *Financial support:* Application deadline: 3/1; applicants required to submit FAFSA. *Unit head:* Dr. Amy Wood, Coordinator, 828-328-7728, Fax: 828-328-7368, E-mail: amy.wood@lr.edu. *Application contact:* 828-328-7300, Fax: 828-328-7378, E-mail: admission@lr.edu.

Lesley University, Graduate School of Arts and Social Sciences, Cambridge, MA 02138-2790. Offers clinical mental health counseling (MA), including holistic counseling, school and community counseling, trauma studies; counseling psychology (MA, CAGS), including professional counseling (MA), school counseling (MA); creative writing (MFA); expressive therapies (MA, PhD, CAGS), including art (MA), clinical mental health counseling (MA), dance (MA), expressive therapies (MA), music (MA); independent studies (CAGS); independent study (MA); intercultural relations (MA, CAGS); interdisciplinary studies (MA), including individualized studies, integrative holistic health, mindfulness studies, peace and conflict transformation, trauma sensitive assessment, intervention, and consultation, women's studies; urban environmental leadership (MA). Part-time programs available. Postbaccalaureate distance learning degree programs offered (no on-campus study). *Faculty:* 35 full-time (25 women), 115 part-time/adjunct (90 women). *Students:* 420 full-time (379 women), 514 part-time (414 women); includes 142 minority (50 Black or African American, non-Hispanic/Latino; 5 American Indian or Alaska Native, non-Hispanic/Latino; 16 Asian, non-Hispanic/Latino; 48 Hispanic/Latino; 23 Two or more races, non-Hispanic/Latino), 46 international. Average age 33. In 2014, 475 master's, 11 doctorates, 4 other advanced degrees awarded. *Degree requirements:* For master's, internship, practicum, thesis (for expressive therapies); for doctorate, thesis/dissertation, arts apprenticeship, field placement; for CAGS, thesis, internship (for counseling psychology, expressive therapies). *Entrance requirements:* For master's, MAT (counseling psychology), interview, writing samples, art portfolio; for doctorate, GRE or MAT, interview, master's degree; for CAGS, interview, master's degree. Additional exam requirements/recommendations for international students: Required—TOEFL (minimum score 550 paper-based; 80 iBT). *Application deadline:* Applications are processed on a rolling basis. Application fee: $50. Electronic applications accepted. *Financial support:* Fellowships, career-related internships or fieldwork, Federal Work-Study, scholarships/grants, tuition waivers, and unspecified assistantships available. Financial award applicants required to submit FAFSA. *Faculty research:* Psychotherapy and culture; psychotherapy and psychological trauma; women's issues in art, teaching and psychotherapy; community-based art, psycho-spiritual inquiry. *Unit head:* Dr. Catherine Koverola, Dean, 617-349-8317, Fax: 617-349-8366, E-mail: koverola@lesley.edu. *Application contact:* Martha Sheehan, Director, Graduate Admissions, 888-LESLEYU, Fax: 617-349-8313, E-mail: info@lesley.edu.
Website: http://www.lesley.edu/graduate-school-of-arts-and-social-sciences/

Lewis & Clark College, Graduate School of Education and Counseling, Department of Counseling Psychology, Program in School Psychology, Portland, OR 97219-7899. Offers Ed S. Part-time and evening/weekend programs available. *Entrance requirements:* Additional exam requirements/recommendations for international students: Required—TOEFL (minimum score 575 paper-based). Electronic applications accepted.

Lewis & Clark College, Graduate School of Education and Counseling, Department of Educational Leadership, Program in School Counseling, Portland, OR 97219-7899. Offers M Ed. Part-time and evening/weekend programs available. *Entrance requirements:* For master's, minimum undergraduate GPA of 2.75. Additional exam requirements/recommendations for international students: Required—TOEFL (minimum score 575 paper-based). Electronic applications accepted.

Lindenwood University, Graduate Programs, School of Education, St. Charles, MO 63301-1695. Offers education (MA); educational administration (MA, Ed D, Ed S); English to speakers of other languages (MA); instructional leadership (Ed D, Ed S); library media (MA); professional counseling (MA); school administration (Ed S); school counseling (MA); teaching (MA). Part-time and evening/weekend programs available. Postbaccalaureate distance learning degree programs offered (no on-campus study). *Faculty:* 46 full-time (30 women), 227 part-time/adjunct (150 women). *Students:* 355 full-time (263 women), 1,689 part-time (1,303 women); includes 569 minority (491 Black or African American, non-Hispanic/Latino; 9 American Indian or Alaska Native, non-Hispanic/Latino; 7 Asian, non-Hispanic/Latino; 27 Hispanic/Latino; 1 Native Hawaiian or other Pacific Islander, non-Hispanic/Latino; 34 Two or more races, non-Hispanic/Latino),

27 international. Average age 36. 536 applicants, 76% accepted, 332 enrolled. In 2014, 645 master's, 46 doctorates, 59 other advanced degrees awarded. *Degree requirements:* For master's, thesis (for some programs), minimum GPA of 3.0; for doctorate, thesis/dissertation, minimum GPA of 3.0; for Ed S, comprehensive exam, project, minimum GPA of 3.0. *Entrance requirements:* For master's, interview, minimum GPA of 3.0, writing sample, letter of recommendation; for doctorate, GRE, minimum graduate GPA of 3.4, resume, interview, writing sample, 4 letters of recommendation; for Ed S, master's degree in education, relevant work experience. Additional exam requirements/recommendations for international students: Required—TOEFL (minimum score 550 paper-based; 80 iBT). *Application deadline:* For fall admission, 8/24 priority date for domestic and international students; for spring admission, 1/25 priority date for domestic and international students. Applications are processed on a rolling basis. Application fee: $30 ($100 for international students). Electronic applications accepted. *Expenses: Tuition:* Full-time $15,230; part-time $440 per credit hour. *Required fees:* $205 per semester. Tuition and fees vary according to course level, course load and degree level. *Financial support:* In 2014–15, 236 students received support. Career-related internships or fieldwork, Federal Work-Study, institutionally sponsored loans, scholarships/grants, tuition waivers (partial), and unspecified assistantships available. Financial award application deadline: 6/30; financial award applicants required to submit FAFSA. *Unit head:* Dr. Cynthia Bice, Dean, 636-949-4618, Fax: 636-949-4197, E-mail: cbice@lindenwood.edu. *Application contact:* Tyler Kostich, Director of Evening and Graduate Admissions, 636-949-4138, Fax: 636-949-4109, E-mail: adultadmissions@lindenwood.edu.

Long Island University–Hudson at Westchester, Graduate School, Purchase, NY 10577. Offers mental health counseling (MS), including Casac; school psychology (MS Ed). Part-time and evening/weekend programs available. Postbaccalaureate distance learning degree programs offered. *Faculty:* 6 full-time (5 women). *Students:* 53 full-time (41 women), 103 part-time (89 women); includes 50 minority (18 Black or African American, non-Hispanic/Latino; 3 Asian, non-Hispanic/Latino; 29 Hispanic/Latino), 1 international. Average age 35. In 2014, 95 master's, 19 other advanced degrees awarded. *Entrance requirements:* Additional exam requirements/recommendations for international students: Required—TOEFL. *Application deadline:* Applications are processed on a rolling basis. Application fee: $50. Electronic applications accepted. *Expenses: Tuition:* Part-time $1132 per credit. *Required fees:* $434 per semester. *Unit head:* Dr. Sylvia Blake, Dean and Chief Operating Officer, 914-831-2704, Fax: 914-251-5959, E-mail: sylvia.blake@liu.edu. *Application contact:* Cindy Pagnotta, Director of Marketing and Enrollment, 914-831-2701, Fax: 914-251-5959, E-mail: cindy.pagnotta@liu.edu.

Louisiana State University and Agricultural & Mechanical College, Graduate School, College of Humanities and Social Sciences, Department of Psychology, Baton Rouge, LA 70803. Offers biological psychology (MA, PhD); clinical psychology (MA, PhD); cognitive psychology (MA, PhD); developmental psychology (MA, PhD); school psychology (MA, PhD). PhD programs offered jointly with Southeastern Louisiana University. *Accreditation:* APA (one or more programs are accredited). *Faculty:* 22 full-time (10 women). *Students:* 67 full-time (54 women), 30 part-time (21 women); includes 13 minority (4 Black or African American, non-Hispanic/Latino; 3 Asian, non-Hispanic/Latino; 3 Hispanic/Latino; 3 Two or more races, non-Hispanic/Latino), 3 international. Average age 27. 221 applicants, 10% accepted, 22 enrolled. In 2014, 13 master's, 18 doctorates awarded. Terminal master's awarded for partial completion of doctoral program. *Degree requirements:* For master's, thesis; for doctorate, thesis/dissertation, 1-year internship. *Entrance requirements:* For master's and doctorate, GRE General Test, minimum GPA of 3.0. Additional exam requirements/recommendations for international students: Required—TOEFL (minimum score 550 paper-based; 79 IBT), IELTS (minimum score 6.5), or PTE (minimum score 59). *Application deadline:* For fall admission, 1/1 priority date for domestic students, 5/15 for international students; for spring admission, 10/15 for domestic and international students; for summer admission, 5/15 for domestic students, 5/5 for international students. Applications are processed on a rolling basis. Application fee: $50 ($70 for international students). Electronic applications accepted. *Financial support:* In 2014–15, 90 students received support, including 2 fellowships (averaging $15,763 per year), 8 research assistantships with partial tuition reimbursements available (averaging $16,669 per year), 49 teaching assistantships with partial tuition reimbursements available (averaging $13,003 per year); career-related internships or fieldwork, Federal Work-Study, institutionally sponsored loans, scholarships/grants, health care benefits, and tuition waivers (full and partial) also available. Financial award applicants required to submit FAFSA. *Faculty research:* Clinical psychology, autism, anxiety, addition, neuropsychology, school psychology, cognitive psychology, experimental psychology. *Total annual research expenditures:* $986,140. *Unit head:* Dr. Robert Matthews, Chair, 225-578-8745, Fax: 225-578-4125, E-mail: psmath@lsu.edu. *Application contact:* Dr. Jason Hicks, Coordinator of Graduate Studies, 225-578-4109, Fax: 225-578-4125, E-mail: jhicks@lsu.edu.
Website: http://www.lsu.edu/psychology/graduate.html

Louisiana State University in Shreveport, College of Business, Education, and Human Development, Program in School Psychology, Shreveport, LA 71115-2399. Offers SSP. *Students:* 13 full-time (all women), 3 part-time (all women); includes 5 minority (4 Black or African American, non-Hispanic/Latino; 1 Two or more races, non-Hispanic/Latino). Average age 25. 12 applicants, 100% accepted, 5 enrolled. In 2014, 4 SSPs awarded. *Entrance requirements:* For degree, GRE General Test, minimum GPA of 2.75, references, letter of intent, interview. Additional exam requirements/recommendations for international students: Required—TOEFL (minimum score 550 paper-based; 61 iBT). *Application deadline:* For fall admission, 6/30 for domestic and international students; for spring admission, 11/30 for domestic and international students; for summer admission, 4/30 for domestic and international students. Applications are processed on a rolling basis. Application fee: $20 ($30 for international students). Electronic applications accepted. *Expenses:* Tuition, state resident: full-time $5234; part-time $290.80 per credit hour. Tuition, nonresident: full-time $16,774; part-time $879.61 per credit hour. *Required fees:* $52.28 per credit hour. *Financial support:* Unspecified assistantships available. Financial award applicants required to submit FAFSA. *Unit head:* Dr. Kevin Jones, Program Director, 318-797-5050, Fax: 318-798-4171, E-mail: ssp@lsus.edu. *Application contact:* Kimberly Thornton, Director of Admissions, 318-795-2405, Fax: 318-797-5286, E-mail: kimberly.thornton@lsus.edu.

Loyola Marymount University, School of Education, Department of Educational Support Services, Program in School Psychology, Los Angeles, CA 90045. Offers MA. Part-time and evening/weekend programs available. *Degree requirements:* For master's, comprehensive exam. *Entrance requirements:* For master's, GRE, CBEST, 3 letters of recommendation. Additional exam requirements/recommendations for international students: Required—TOEFL (minimum score 600 paper-based; 100 iBT). Electronic applications accepted.

Loyola University Chicago, School of Education, Program in School Psychology, Chicago, IL 60660. Offers Ed D, PhD, Ed S. PhD offered through the Graduate School. Part-time and evening/weekend programs available. *Faculty:* 7 full-time (6 women), 4 part-time/adjunct (1 woman). *Students:* 87. Average age 28. 57 applicants, 82% accepted, 43 enrolled. In 2014, 2 doctorates, 20 other advanced degrees awarded. Terminal master's awarded for partial completion of doctoral program. *Degree requirements:* For doctorate, comprehensive exam, thesis/dissertation. *Entrance requirements:* For doctorate, GRE, interview, letters of recommendation, minimum GPA of 3.0. Additional exam requirements/recommendations for international students: Required—TOEFL (minimum score 550 paper-based; 79 iBT). *Application deadline:* For fall admission, 12/1 for domestic and international students. Application fee: $50. Electronic applications accepted. Application fee is waived when completed online. *Expenses: Tuition:* Full-time $17,370; part-time $965 per credit. *Required fees:* $138 per semester. *Financial support:* In 2014–15, 28 fellowships with partial tuition reimbursements, 13 research assistantships with full tuition reimbursements (averaging $14,000 per year), 20 teaching assistantships (averaging $4,000 per year) were awarded; career-related internships or fieldwork, institutionally sponsored loans, scholarships/grants, health care benefits, tuition waivers (full and partial), and unspecified assistantships also available. Support available to part-time students. Financial award application deadline: 2/15. *Faculty research:* Learning theory and teaching, school reform, instructional intervention, violence prevention, mental health programming in schools and communities. *Unit head:* Dr. Lynne Golomb, Director, 312-915-6218, E-mail: lgolomb@luc.edu. *Application contact:* Marie Hatland, Information Contact, 312-915-6800, E-mail: schleduc@luc.edu.

Lynchburg College, Graduate Studies, M Ed Program in School Counseling, Lynchburg, VA 24501-3199. Offers M Ed. *Accreditation:* ACA. Part-time and evening/weekend programs available. *Faculty:* 4 full-time (2 women), 2 part-time/adjunct (1 woman). *Students:* 9 full-time (7 women), 10 part-time (8 women); includes 6 minority (4 Black or African American, non-Hispanic/Latino; 1 Asian, non-Hispanic/Latino; 1 Hispanic/Latino). Average age 28. In 2014, 5 master's awarded. *Degree requirements:* For master's, counseling internship. *Entrance requirements:* For master's, GRE, minimum GPA of 3.0 (preferred), official transcripts (bachelor's, others as relevant), three letters of recommendation, career goals statement. Additional exam requirements/recommendations for international students: Required—TOEFL (minimum score 550 paper-based; 79 iBT), IELTS (minimum score 6.5). *Application deadline:* For fall admission, 7/31 for domestic students, 6/1 for international students; for spring admission, 11/30 for domestic students, 10/15 for international students. Applications are processed on a rolling basis. Application fee: $30. Electronic applications accepted. Application fee is waived when completed online. *Financial support:* Fellowships, research assistantships, Federal Work-Study, scholarships/grants, health care benefits, and unspecified assistantships available. Support available to part-time students. Financial award application deadline: 7/31; financial award applicants required to submit FAFSA. *Unit head:* Dr. Jeanne Booth, Associate Professor/Coordinator of M Ed in School Counseling, 434-544-8551, Fax: 434-544-8483, E-mail: booth@lynchburg.edu. *Application contact:* Christine Priller, Executive Assistant, Graduate Studies, 434-544-8383, Fax: 434-544-8483, E-mail: gradstudies@lynchburg.edu.
Website: http://www.lynchburg.edu/graduate/master-of-education-in-counselor-education/school-counseling/

Marist College, Graduate Programs, School of Social and Behavioral Sciences, Poughkeepsie, NY 12601-1387. Offers education (M Ed, MA); mental health counseling (MA); school psychology (MA, Adv C). Part-time and evening/weekend programs available. *Degree requirements:* For master's, thesis optional. *Entrance requirements:* For master's, GRE General Test, letters of recommendation, minimum undergraduate GPA of 3.0, interview. Additional exam requirements/recommendations for international students: Required—TOEFL (minimum score 550 paper-based; 80 iBT); Recommended—IELTS (minimum score 6.5). Electronic applications accepted. *Faculty research:* AIDS prevention, educational intervention, humanistic counseling research, aging and development, neuroimaging.

Marshall University, Academic Affairs Division, Graduate School of Education and Professional Development, Program in School Psychology, Huntington, WV 25755. Offers Ed S. *Accreditation:* NCATE. Part-time and evening/weekend programs available. *Students:* 24 full-time (21 women), 18 part-time (15 women); includes 4 minority (1 Black or African American, non-Hispanic/Latino; 2 Hispanic/Latino; 1 Two or more races, non-Hispanic/Latino). Average age 31. In 2014, 11 Ed Ss awarded. *Entrance requirements:* For degree, master's degree in psychology. Application fee: $40. *Financial support:* Career-related internships or fieldwork and tuition waivers (full) available. Support available to part-time students. Financial award applicants required to submit FAFSA. *Unit head:* Dr. Sandra Stroebel, Program Director, 304-746-2032, E-mail: stroebel@marshall.edu. *Application contact:* Information Contact, 304-746-1900, Fax: 304-746-1902, E-mail: services@marshall.edu.

Massachusetts School of Professional Psychology, Graduate Programs, Boston, MA 02132. Offers applied psychology in higher education student personnel administration (MA); clinical psychology (Psy D); counseling psychology (MA); counseling psychology and community mental health (MA); counseling psychology and global mental health (MA); executive coaching (Graduate Certificate); forensic and counseling psychology (MA); leadership psychology (Psy D); organizational psychology (MA); primary care psychology (MA); respecialization in clinical psychology (Certificate); school psychology (Psy D); MA/CAGS. *Accreditation:* APA. *Degree requirements:* For master's, comprehensive exam (for some programs); for doctorate, thesis/dissertation (for some programs). Electronic applications accepted.

McGill University, Faculty of Graduate and Postdoctoral Studies, Faculty of Education, Department of Educational and Counseling Psychology, Montréal, QC H3A 2T5, Canada. Offers counseling psychology (MA, PhD); educational psychology (M Ed, MA, PhD); school/applied child psychology and applied developmental psychology (M Ed, MA, PhD, Diploma), including school psychology. *Accreditation:* APA.

McNeese State University, Doré School of Graduate Studies, Burton College of Education, Office of Graduate Education Programs, Program in School Counseling, Lake Charles, LA 70609. Offers M Ed. *Accreditation:* NCATE. Evening/weekend programs available. *Entrance requirements:* For master's, GRE, 18 hours in professional education.

Mercer University, Graduate Studies, Cecil B. Day Campus, College of Continuing and Professional Studies, Macon, GA 31207. Offers certified rehabilitation counseling (MS); clinical mental health (MS); counselor education and supervision (PhD); human services (MS); organizational leadership (MS); public safety leadership (MS); school counseling (MS). Part-time and evening/weekend programs available. Postbaccalaureate distance learning degree programs offered (minimal on-campus study). *Faculty:* 15 full-time (6 women), 23 part-time/adjunct (15 women). *Students:* 132 full-time (110 women), 230 part-time (184 women); includes 198 minority (167 Black or African American, non-Hispanic/Latino; 1 American Indian or Alaska Native, non-Hispanic/Latino; 10 Asian, non-Hispanic/Latino; 14 Hispanic/Latino; 3 Native Hawaiian or other Pacific Islander, non-Hispanic/Latino; 3 Two or more races, non-Hispanic/Latino), 3 international. Average age 32. In 2014, 126 master's, 1 doctorate awarded. *Degree requirements:* For master's, comprehensive exam (for some programs), thesis (for some programs); for doctorate, thesis/dissertation. *Entrance requirements:* For master's and doctorate, GRE or MAT. Additional exam requirements/recommendations for international students: Recommended—TOEFL (minimum score 550 paper-based; 80 iBT), IELTS (minimum score 6.5). *Application deadline:* For fall admission, 7/1 priority date for domestic and international students; for spring admission, 11/1 priority date for domestic and

international students; for summer admission, 4/1 priority date for domestic and international students. Application fee: $35. Electronic applications accepted. Tuition and fees vary according to class time, degree level, campus/location and program. *Unit head:* Dr. Priscilla R. Danheiser, Dean, 678-547-6028, E-mail: danheiser_p@mercer.edu. *Application contact:* Carmen C. Jones, Associate Director of Admissions, 678-547-6346, E-mail: jones_c@mercer.edu.
Website: http://penfield.mercer.edu/programs/graduate-professional/

Mercy College, School of Social and Behavioral Sciences, Program in School Psychology, Dobbs Ferry, NY 10522-1189. Offers MS. Part-time and evening/weekend programs available. *Students:* 29 full-time (27 women), 7 part-time (5 women); includes 23 minority (5 Black or African American, non-Hispanic/Latino; 17 Hispanic/Latino; 1 Native Hawaiian or other Pacific Islander, non-Hispanic/Latino). Average age 34. 68 applicants, 28% accepted, 9 enrolled. In 2014, 12 master's awarded. *Degree requirements:* For master's, thesis (for some programs), practicum, fieldwork, internship, integrative project. *Entrance requirements:* For master's, interview, 3 letters of recommendation, undergraduate transcript. Additional exam requirements/recommendations for international students: Required—TOEFL (minimum score 600 paper-based; 100 iBT), IELTS (minimum score 8). *Application deadline:* For fall admission, 8/1 for international students. Applications are processed on a rolling basis. Application fee: $40. Electronic applications accepted. *Expenses: Tuition:* Full-time $14,952; part-time $814 per credit. *Required fees:* $600; $150 per semester. Tuition and fees vary according to course load, degree level and program. *Financial support:* Career-related internships or fieldwork, Federal Work-Study, scholarships/grants, and unspecified assistantships available. Support available to part-time students. Financial award applicants required to submit FAFSA. *Unit head:* Dr. Karol Dean, Interim Dean, School of Social and Behavioral Sciences, 914-674-7517, E-mail: kdean@mercy.edu. *Application contact:* Allison Gurdineer, Senior Director of Admissions, 877-637-2946, Fax: 914-674-7382, E-mail: admissions@mercy.edu.
Website: https://www.mercy.edu/degrees-programs/ms-school-psychology

Michigan State University, The Graduate School, College of Education, Department of Counseling, Educational Psychology and Special Education, East Lansing, MI 48824. Offers counseling (MA); educational psychology and educational technology (PhD); educational technology (MA); measurement and quantitative methods (PhD); rehabilitation counseling (MA); rehabilitation counselor education (PhD); school psychology (MA, PhD, Ed S); special education (MA, PhD). *Accreditation:* APA (one or more programs are accredited); CORE (one or more programs are accredited). Part-time programs available. *Entrance requirements:* Additional exam requirements/recommendations for international students: Required—TOEFL. Electronic applications accepted.

Middle Tennessee State University, College of Graduate Studies, College of Behavioral and Health Sciences, Department of Psychology, Murfreesboro, TN 37132. Offers clinical psychology (MA); experimental psychology (MA); industrial/organizational psychology (MA); psychology (MA, Ed S); quantitative psychology (MA); school psychology (MA). Part-time and evening/weekend programs available. Postbaccalaureate distance learning degree programs offered. *Faculty:* 37 full-time (14 women), 3 part-time/adjunct (2 women). *Students:* 66 full-time (54 women), 47 part-time (37 women); includes 15 minority (8 Black or African American, non-Hispanic/Latino; 1 American Indian or Alaska Native, non-Hispanic/Latino; 2 Asian, non-Hispanic/Latino; 3 Hispanic/Latino; 1 Two or more races, non-Hispanic/Latino), 1 international. 225 applicants, 84% accepted. In 2014, 37 master's awarded. *Degree requirements:* For master's, comprehensive exam, thesis. *Entrance requirements:* For master's, GRE. Additional exam requirements/recommendations for international students: Required—TOEFL (minimum score 525 paper-based; 71 iBT) or IELTS (minimum score 6). *Application deadline:* For fall admission, 6/1 for domestic and international students. Applications are processed on a rolling basis. Application fee: $30. Electronic applications accepted. *Financial support:* In 2014–15, 38 students received support. Tuition waivers available. Support available to part-time students. Financial award application deadline: 4/1; financial award applicants required to submit FAFSA. *Faculty research:* Health psychology, industrial/organizational psychology, experimental psychology. *Unit head:* Dr. Greg Schmidt, Chair, 615-898-2706, Fax: 615-898-5027, E-mail: greg.schmidt@mtsu.edu. *Application contact:* Dr. Michael D. Allen, Vice Provost for Research/Dean, 615-898-2840, Fax: 615-904-8020, E-mail: michael.allen@mtsu.edu.

Millersville University of Pennsylvania, College of Graduate and Professional Studies, School of Education, Department of Psychology, Program in School Counseling, Millersville, PA 17551-0302. Offers M Ed. *Accreditation:* NCATE. Part-time programs available. *Faculty:* 17 full-time (12 women), 10 part-time/adjunct (8 women). *Students:* 19 full-time (18 women), 22 part-time (14 women); includes 5 minority (3 Black or African American, non-Hispanic/Latino; 2 Hispanic/Latino). Average age 27. 12 applicants, 92% accepted, 9 enrolled. In 2014, 6 master's awarded. *Degree requirements:* For master's, comprehensive exam, thesis optional, practicum, internship. *Entrance requirements:* For master's, GRE, 3 letters of recommendation, interview (in-person), official transcripts, goal statement. Additional exam requirements/recommendations for international students: Required—TOEFL (minimum score 500 paper-based, 65 iBT) or IELTS (minimum score 6). *Application deadline:* For fall admission, 1/15 for domestic and international students; for winter admission, 6/1 for domestic and international students; for spring admission, 10/1 for domestic and international students. Application fee: $40. Electronic applications accepted. *Expenses:* Tuition, state resident: full-time $8172. Tuition, nonresident: full-time $12,258. *Required fees:* $2300. Tuition and fees vary according to course load and program. *Financial support:* In 2014–15, 10 students received support, including 10 research assistantships with full tuition reimbursements available (averaging $4,390 per year); institutionally sponsored loans and unspecified assistantships also available. Support available to part-time students. Financial award application deadline: 3/15; financial award applicants required to submit FAFSA. *Faculty research:* Solution-focused counseling, the psychological and social impact of urban gardening with children, comprehensive developmental school counseling programs, sustainability education and research, national model implementation. *Unit head:* Dr. Jason B. Baker, Director, 717-871-7301, Fax: 717-871-7946, E-mail: jason.baker@millersville.edu. *Application contact:* Dr. Victor S. DeSantis, Dean of College of Graduate and Professional Studies/Associate Provost for Civic and Community Engagement, 717-871-7619, Fax: 717-871-7954, E-mail: victor.desantis@millersville.edu.
Website: http://www.millersville.edu/psychology/graduate/school-counseling/index.php

Millersville University of Pennsylvania, College of Graduate and Professional Studies, School of Education, Department of Psychology, Program in School Psychology, Millersville, PA 17551-0302. Offers MS. Part-time programs available. *Faculty:* 17 full-time (12 women), 10 part-time/adjunct (8 women). *Students:* 24 full-time (18 women), 7 part-time (5 women); includes 1 minority (Hispanic/Latino). Average age 25. 30 applicants, 70% accepted, 12 enrolled. In 2014, 7 master's awarded. *Degree requirements:* For master's, comprehensive exam, thesis optional, practicum, internship. *Entrance requirements:* For master's, GRE, 3 letters of recommendation, interview, official transcripts, goal statements. Additional exam requirements/recommendations for international students: Required—TOEFL (minimum score 500 paper-based, 65 iBT) or IELTS (minimum score 6). *Application deadline:* For fall admission, 1/15 for domestic and international students; for winter admission, 6/1 for domestic and international students; for spring admission, 10/1 for domestic and international students. Application fee: $40. Electronic applications accepted. *Expenses:* Tuition, state resident: full-time $8172. Tuition, nonresident: full-time $12,258. *Required fees:* $2300. Tuition and fees vary according to course load and program. *Financial support:* In 2014–15, 12 students received support, including 12 research assistantships with full tuition reimbursements available (averaging $4,817 per year); institutionally sponsored loans and unspecified assistantships also available. Support available to part-time students. Financial award application deadline: 3/15; financial award applicants required to submit FAFSA. *Faculty research:* Modification of ELL reading and writing instruction based on CALP, parent participation in ELL education, behavioral assessment tools for culturally diverse children. *Unit head:* Dr. Amelia Lopez, Director, 717-871-7301, Fax: 717-871-7946, E-mail: amelia.lopez@millersville.edu. *Application contact:* Dr. Victor S. DeSantis, Dean of College of Graduate and Professional Studies/Associate Provost for Civic and Community Engagement, 717-871-7619, Fax: 717-871-7954, E-mail: victor.desantis@millersville.edu.
Website: http://www.millersville.edu/psychology/graduate/school-psychology/index.php

Minnesota State University Mankato, College of Graduate Studies, College of Social and Behavioral Sciences, Department of Psychology, Mankato, MN 56001. Offers clinical psychology (MA); industrial/organizational psychology (MA); school psychology (Psy D). Part-time programs available. *Students:* 47 full-time (38 women), 11 part-time (9 women). *Degree requirements:* For master's, one foreign language, comprehensive exam, thesis (for some programs). *Entrance requirements:* For master's, GRE General Test, GRE Subject Test (clinical psychology), minimum GPA of 3.0 during previous 2 years, 3 letters of reference. Additional exam requirements/recommendations for international students: Required—TOEFL. *Application deadline:* For fall admission, 1/1 priority date for domestic students. Applications are processed on a rolling basis. Application fee: $40. Electronic applications accepted. *Financial support:* Research assistantships, teaching assistantships with full tuition reimbursements, career-related internships or fieldwork, Federal Work-Study, institutionally sponsored loans, and unspecified assistantships available. Support available to part-time students. Financial award application deadline: 3/15; financial award applicants required to submit FAFSA. *Faculty research:* Professional competency in hospitals, mood disturbance, 360-degree feedback, employee selection, planning fallacy. *Unit head:* Dr. Jeff Buchanan, Chairperson, 507-389-2724. *Application contact:* 507-389-2321, E-mail: grad@mnsu.edu.
Website: http://www.mnsu.edu/psych/

Minot State University, Graduate School, Program in School Psychology, Minot, ND 58707-0002. Offers Ed Sp. *Students:* 16 full-time (15 women), 3 part-time (2 women); includes 2 minority (1 American Indian or Alaska Native, non-Hispanic/Latino; 1 Two or more races, non-Hispanic/Latino), 9 international. In 2014, 3 Ed Sps awarded. *Degree requirements:* For Ed Sp, comprehensive exam, thesis optional. *Entrance requirements:* For degree, GRE General Test, minimum GPA of 3.0. Additional exam requirements/recommendations for international students: Required—TOEFL (minimum score 79 iBT), IELTS (minimum score 6). *Application deadline:* For fall admission, 3/15 for domestic students. Applications are processed on a rolling basis. Application fee: $35. *Expenses:* Tuition, state resident: full-time $5865; part-time $325.82 per credit hour. Tuition, nonresident: full-time $5865; part-time $325.82 per credit hour. *Required fees:* $1284. Tuition and fees vary according to course load. *Financial support:* In 2014–15, 7 students received support, including 5 research assistantships with partial tuition reimbursements available (averaging $1,370 per year); scholarships/grants, tuition waivers (partial), and unspecified assistantships also available. Support available to part-time students. Financial award application deadline: 2/15; financial award applicants required to submit FAFSA. *Unit head:* Dr. Darren Dobrinski, Chairperson, 701-858-4257. *Application contact:* Penny Brandt, Graduate Admissions Specialist, 701-858-3413, Fax: 701-858-4286, E-mail: graduate@minotstateu.edu.
Website: http://www.minotstateu.edu/graduate

Mississippi State University, College of Education, Department of Counseling and Educational Psychology, Mississippi State, MS 39762. Offers college/postsecondary student counseling and personnel services (PhD); counselor education (MS), including clinical mental health, college counseling, rehabilitation, school counseling, student affairs in higher education; counselor education/student counseling and guidance services (PhD); education (Ed S), including counselor education, school psychology (PhD, Ed S); educational psychology (MS, PhD), including general education psychology (MS), general educational psychology (PhD), psychometry (MS), school psychology (PhD, Ed S). *Accreditation:* ACA (one or more programs are accredited); APA; CORE (one or more programs are accredited); NCATE. Part-time programs available. Postbaccalaureate distance learning degree programs offered (minimal on-campus study). *Faculty:* 21 full-time (15 women), 2 part-time/adjunct (both women). *Students:* 124 full-time (95 women), 72 part-time (63 women); includes 59 minority (48 Black or African American, non-Hispanic/Latino; 2 American Indian or Alaska Native, non-Hispanic/Latino; 6 Asian, non-Hispanic/Latino; 2 Hispanic/Latino; 1 Two or more races, non-Hispanic/Latino), 1 international. Average age 32. 138 applicants, 57% accepted, 53 enrolled. In 2014, 55 master's, 10 doctorates, 10 other advanced degrees awarded. Terminal master's awarded for partial completion of doctoral program. *Degree requirements:* For master's, comprehensive exam, thesis optional; for doctorate, thesis/dissertation, comprehensive oral and written exam. *Entrance requirements:* For master's, GRE (taken within the last five years), BS with minimum GPA of 2.75 on last 60 hours; for doctorate, GRE, MS from CACREP- or CORE-accredited program in counseling; for Ed S, GRE, MS in counseling or related field, minimum GPA of 3.3 on all graduate work. Additional exam requirements/recommendations for international students: Required—TOEFL (minimum score 550 paper-based; 79 iBT); Recommended—IELTS (minimum score 6.5). *Application deadline:* For fall admission, 2/1 priority date for domestic and international students. Applications are processed on a rolling basis. Application fee: $60. Electronic applications accepted. *Expenses:* Tuition, state resident: full-time $7140; part-time $783 per credit hour. Tuition, nonresident: full-time $18,478; part-time $2043 per credit hour. *Financial support:* In 2014–15, 3 research assistantships (averaging $9,800 per year), 9 teaching assistantships with full tuition reimbursements (averaging $8,401 per year) were awarded; career-related internships or fieldwork, Federal Work-Study, institutionally sponsored loans, and unspecified assistantships also available. Financial award application deadline: 2/1; financial award applicants required to submit FAFSA. *Faculty research:* HIV/AIDS in college population, substance abuse in youth and college students, ADHD and conduct disorders in youth, assessment and identification of early childhood disabilities, assessment and vocational transition of the disabled. *Unit head:* Dr. David Morse, Professor and Interim Head, 662-325-3426, Fax: 662-325-3263, E-mail: dmorse@colled.msstate.edu. *Application contact:* Dr. Charles Palmer, Graduate Coordinator, Counselor Education, 662-325-7917, Fax: 662-325-3263, E-mail: cpalmer@colled.msstate.edu.
Website: http://www.cep.msstate.edu/

Montana State University, The Graduate School, College of Education, Health, and Human Development, Department of Education, Bozeman, MT 59717. Offers adult and higher education (Ed D); curriculum and instruction (M Ed, Ed D), including professional

School Psychology

educator (M Ed), technology education (M Ed); education (M Ed), including adult and higher education, educational leadership, school counseling; educational leadership (Ed D, Ed S). *Accreditation:* Teacher Education Accreditation Council. Part-time programs available. Postbaccalaureate distance learning degree programs offered (minimal on-campus study). *Degree requirements:* For master's, comprehensive exam; for doctorate, comprehensive exam, thesis/dissertation. *Entrance requirements:* For master's, GRE, 3 letters of reference, essays, BA transcripts; for doctorate, GRE, MAT, 3 letters of reference, essay, BA and M Ed transcripts; for Ed S, PRAXIS. Additional exam requirements/recommendations for international students: Required—TOEFL (minimum score 550 paper-based). Electronic applications accepted. *Faculty research:* Critical literacy; standards-based education; school Improvement, organizational change, leadership in rural education, leadership in Indian education; student Learning; multicultural/culturally responsive education for social justice Native American indigenous education, community-centered education teacher preparation.

Mount Saint Vincent University, Graduate Programs, Faculty of Education, Program in School Psychology, Halifax, NS B3M 2J6, Canada. Offers MASP. *Degree requirements:* For master's, thesis, 500 hour practicum. *Entrance requirements:* For master's, bachelor's degree in psychology or equivalent, related work experience. Electronic applications accepted. *Faculty research:* Relationship between cognitive and emotional development, expression of emotions, cognitive-behavioral constituents of racism.

National Louis University, National College of Education, Chicago, IL 60603. Offers administration and supervision (M Ed, Ed D, CAS, Ed S); curriculum and instruction (M Ed, MS Ed, CAS); early childhood administration (M Ed, CAS); early childhood education (M Ed, MAT, MS Ed, CAS); education (Ed D); educational psychology/human learning and development (M Ed, MS Ed, CAS, Ed S); elementary education (MAT); interdisciplinary curriculum and instruction (M Ed); mathematics education (M Ed, MS Ed, CAS); reading and language (M Ed, MS Ed, CAS); school psychology (M Ed, Ed S); science education (M Ed, MS Ed, CAS); secondary education (MAT); special education (M Ed, MAT, CAS); technology in education (M Ed, CAS). *Accreditation:* NCATE. Part-time and evening/weekend programs available. *Degree requirements:* For doctorate, comprehensive exam, thesis/dissertation. *Entrance requirements:* For master's, MAT or GRE, minimum GPA of 3.0; for doctorate, GRE General Test, minimum GPA of 3.25, interview, resume, writing sample, 4 recommendations. Additional exam requirements/recommendations for international students: Required—TOEFL (minimum score 550 paper-based; 79 iBT).

National University, Academic Affairs, School of Education, La Jolla, CA 92037-1011. Offers applied behavior analysis (Certificate); applied school leadership (MS); autism (Certificate); best practices (Certificate); e-teaching and learning (Certificate); early childhood education (Certificate); education (MA), including best practices (M Ed, MA), e-teaching and learning (M Ed, MA), education technology, teacher leadership (M Ed, MA), teaching and learning in a global society (M Ed, MA), teaching mathematics (M Ed, MA); education with preliminary multiple or single subject (M Ed), including best practices (M Ed, MA), e-teaching and learning (M Ed, MA), educational technology (M Ed, MA), teacher leadership (M Ed, MA), teaching and learning in a global society (M Ed, MA), teaching mathematics (M Ed, MA); educational administration (MS); educational and instructional technology (MS); educational counseling (MS); educational technology (Certificate); higher education administration (MS); innovative school leadership (MS); instructional leadership (MS); juvenile justice special education (MS); reading (Certificate); school psychology (MS); special education (MS), including deaf and hard-of-hearing, mild/moderate disabilities, moderate/severe disabilities; teacher leadership (Certificate); teaching (MA), including applied behavioral analysis, autism, best practices (M Ed, MA), e-teaching and learning (M Ed, MA), early childhood education, educational technology (M Ed, MA), reading, special education, teacher leadership (M Ed, MA), teaching and learning in a global society (M Ed, MA), teaching mathematics (M Ed, MA); teaching mathematics (Certificate). Part-time and evening/weekend programs available. Postbaccalaureate distance learning degree programs offered (no on-campus study). *Faculty:* 83 full-time (50 women), 309 part-time/adjunct (188 women). *Students:* 2,563 full-time (1,811 women), 1,992 part-time (1,374 women); includes 2,016 minority (363 Black or African American, non-Hispanic/Latino; 22 American Indian or Alaska Native, non-Hispanic/Latino; 273 Asian, non-Hispanic/Latino; 1,188 Hispanic/Latino; 27 Native Hawaiian or other Pacific Islander, non-Hispanic/Latino; 143 Two or more races, non-Hispanic/Latino), 2 international. Average age 34. In 2014, 1,813 master's awarded. *Degree requirements:* For master's, thesis (for some programs). *Entrance requirements:* For master's, interview, minimum GPA of 2.5. Additional exam requirements/recommendations for international students: Required—TOEFL (minimum score 550 paper-based; 79 iBT), IELTS (minimum score 6). *Application deadline:* Applications are processed on a rolling basis. Application fee: $60 ($65 for international students). Electronic applications accepted. *Expenses: Tuition:* Full-time $14,184; part-time $1773 per course. *Financial support:* Career-related internships or fieldwork, institutionally sponsored loans, scholarships/grants, and tuition waivers (partial) available. Support available to part-time students. Financial award application deadline: 6/30. *Faculty research:* Teacher education, special education, educational effectiveness, teaching abroad, school counseling. *Unit head:* School of Education, 800-628-8648, E-mail: soe@nu.edu. *Application contact:* Frank Rojas, Vice President for Enrollment Services, 800-628-8648, E-mail: advisor@nu.edu. Website: http://www.nu.edu/OurPrograms/SchoolOfEducation.html

New Jersey City University, Graduate Studies and Continuing Education, William J. Maxwell College of Arts and Sciences, Program in Educational Psychology, Jersey City, NJ 07305-1597. Offers educational psychology (MA); school psychology (PD). Part-time and evening/weekend programs available. *Faculty:* 3 full-time (0 women). *Students:* 14 full-time (all women), 3 part-time (2 women); includes 10 minority (1 Black or African American, non-Hispanic/Latino; 1 Asian, non-Hispanic/Latino; 8 Hispanic/Latino). Average age 30. 12 applicants, 83% accepted, 6 enrolled. In 2014, 10 master's, 5 other advanced degrees awarded. *Degree requirements:* For PD, summer internship or externship. *Entrance requirements:* For degree, GRE General Test. Additional exam requirements/recommendations for international students: Required—TOEFL (minimum score 79 iBT). *Application deadline:* For fall admission, 8/1 priority date for domestic students; for spring admission, 12/1 for domestic students. Applications are processed on a rolling basis. Application fee: $0. *Expenses: Tuition, area resident:* Part-time $538 per credit. Tuition, state resident: part-time $538 per credit. Tuition, nonresident: part-time $948 per credit. *Financial support:* Unspecified assistantships available. *Unit head:* Dr. David Hallerman, 201-200-3309, E-mail: dhallerman@njcu.edu. *Application contact:* E-mail: jbalda@njcu.edu.

New Jersey City University, Graduate Studies and Continuing Education, William J. Maxwell College of Arts and Sciences, Program in School Psychology, Jersey City, NJ 07305-1597. Offers PD. Part-time and evening/weekend programs available. *Faculty:* 3 full-time (0 women). *Students:* 19 full-time (14 women), 18 part-time (15 women); includes 20 minority (3 Black or African American, non-Hispanic/Latino; 2 Asian, non-Hispanic/Latino; 15 Hispanic/Latino). Average age 29. 8 applicants, 100% accepted, 6 enrolled. In 2014, 11 PDs awarded. *Entrance requirements:* Additional exam requirements/recommendations for international students: Required—TOEFL (minimum score 79 iBT). *Expenses: Tuition, area resident:* Part-time $538 per credit. Tuition, state resident: part-time $538 per credit. Tuition, nonresident: part-time $948 per credit. *Unit head:* Dr. James Lennon, Director, 201-200-3309, E-mail: jlennon@njcu.edu. *Application contact:* E-mail: jbalda@njcu.edu.

New Mexico State University, College of Education, Department of Counseling and Educational Psychology, Las Cruces, NM 88003-8001. Offers counseling and guidance (MA), including counseling and guidance, educational diagnostics; school psychology (Ed S). *Accreditation:* ACA; APA (one or more programs are accredited); NCATE. Part-time programs available. *Faculty:* 15 full-time (13 women), 2 part-time/adjunct (1 woman). *Students:* 70 full-time (53 women), 21 part-time (16 women); includes 52 minority (3 Black or African American, non-Hispanic/Latino; 1 American Indian or Alaska Native, non-Hispanic/Latino; 5 Asian, non-Hispanic/Latino; 41 Hispanic/Latino; 2 Two or more races, non-Hispanic/Latino), 3 international. Average age 30. 101 applicants, 24% accepted, 23 enrolled. In 2014, 16 master's, 11 doctorates, 8 other advanced degrees awarded. *Degree requirements:* For master's, comprehensive exam, thesis optional, internship; for doctorate, comprehensive exam, thesis/dissertation, internship; for Ed S, comprehensive exam, thesis or alternative, internship. *Entrance requirements:* For master's, doctorate, and Ed S, GRE General Test, minimum GPA of 3.0. Additional exam requirements/recommendations for international students: Required—IELTS (minimum score 6.5); Recommended—TOEFL (minimum score 550 paper-based; 79 iBT). *Application deadline:* For fall admission, 12/15 for domestic and international students; for winter admission, 1/15 for domestic and international students; for spring admission, 2/1 priority date for domestic students, 2/1 for international students. Application fee: $40 ($50 for international students). Electronic applications accepted. *Expenses:* Tuition, state resident: full-time $3969; part-time $220.50 per credit hour. Tuition, nonresident: full-time $13,838; part-time $768.80 per credit hour. *Required fees:* $853; $47.40 per credit hour. *Financial support:* In 2014–15, 69 students received support, including 6 fellowships (averaging $3,970 per year), 9 research assistantships (averaging $10,292 per year), 18 teaching assistantships (averaging $9,734 per year); career-related internships or fieldwork, Federal Work-Study, scholarships/grants, traineeships, health care benefits, and unspecified assistantships also available. Support available to part-time students. Financial award application deadline: 3/1. *Faculty research:* Multicultural counseling and training, school and counseling psychology, social justice, integrated primary care behavioral health training, mental health disparities. *Total annual research expenditures:* $143,793. *Unit head:* Dr. Elsa Corina Arroyos, Interim Department Head, 575-646-2121, Fax: 575-646-8035, E-mail: elsaaj@nmsu.edu. *Application contact:* 575-646-2121, Fax: 575-646-8035, E-mail: cep@nmsu.edu. Website: http://cep.education.nmsu.edu

Niagara University, Graduate Division of Education, Concentration in School Psychology, Niagara University, NY 14109. Offers MS, Certificate. Part-time programs available. *Students:* 23 full-time (21 women), 4 part-time (all women); includes 3 minority (1 Black or African American, non-Hispanic/Latino; 1 Hispanic/Latino; 1 Two or more races, non-Hispanic/Latino), 3 international. Average age 25. In 2014, 9 master's, 9 other advanced degrees awarded. *Entrance requirements:* Additional exam requirements/recommendations for international students: Required—TOEFL (minimum score 550 paper-based, 79 iBT), IELTS (minimum score 6), or GMAT/GRE (minimum score 600). *Application deadline:* For fall admission, 8/1 for domestic students. Application fee: $30. Tuition and fees vary according to program. *Financial support:* Research assistantships with full and partial tuition reimbursements, teaching assistantships with full and partial tuition reimbursements, career-related internships or fieldwork, Federal Work-Study, scholarships/grants, and unspecified assistantships available. Financial award application deadline: 4/15; financial award applicants required to submit FAFSA. *Unit head:* Dr. Kristine Augustyniak, Chair, 716-286-8548, E-mail: kma@niagara.edu. *Application contact:* Evan Pierce, Associate Dean for Graduate Recruitment, 716-286-8769, Fax: 716-286-8170, E-mail: epierce@niagara.edu. Website: http://www.niagara.edu/school-psychology

Nicholls State University, Graduate Studies, College of Education, Department of Psychology and Counselor Education, Thibodaux, LA 70310. Offers psychological counseling (MA); school psychology (SSP). *Accreditation:* NCATE. Part-time and evening/weekend programs available. *Degree requirements:* For master's, comprehensive exam; for SSP, comprehensive exam, internship. *Entrance requirements:* For master's, GRE General Test. Electronic applications accepted.

North Carolina State University, Graduate School, College of Humanities and Social Sciences, Department of Psychology, Raleigh, NC 27695. Offers developmental psychology (PhD); ergonomics and experimental psychology (PhD); industrial/organizational psychology (PhD); psychology in the public interest (PhD); school psychology (PhD). *Accreditation:* APA. *Degree requirements:* For doctorate, comprehensive exam, thesis/dissertation. *Entrance requirements:* For doctorate, GRE General Test, GRE Subject Test (industrial/organizational psychology), MAT (recommended), minimum GPA of 3.0 in major. Electronic applications accepted. *Faculty research:* Cognitive and social development (human factors, families, the workplace, community issues and health, aging).

Northeastern University, Bouvé College of Health Sciences, Boston, MA 02115-5096. Offers audiology (Au D); biotechnology (MS); counseling psychology (MS, PhD, CAGS); counseling/school psychology (PhD); exercise physiology (MS), including exercise physiology, public health; health informatics (MS); nursing (MS, PhD, CAGS), including acute care (MS), administration (MS), anesthesia (MS), primary care (MS), psychiatric mental health (MS); pharmaceutical sciences (PhD); pharmaceutics and drug delivery systems (MS); pharmacology (MS); physical therapy (DPT); physician assistant (MS); school psychology (PhD, CAGS); school/counseling psychology (PhD); speech language pathology (MS); urban public health (MPH); MS/MBA. *Accreditation:* ACPE (one or more programs are accredited). Part-time and evening/weekend programs available. *Degree requirements:* For doctorate, thesis/dissertation (for some programs); for CAGS, comprehensive exam.

Northern Arizona University, Graduate College, College of Education, Department of Educational Psychology, Flagstaff, AZ 86011. Offers counseling (MA); educational psychology (PhD), including counseling psychology, school psychology; human relations (M Ed); school counseling (M Ed); school psychology (Ed S); student affairs (M Ed). Part-time programs available. Postbaccalaureate distance learning degree programs offered. Terminal master's awarded for partial completion of doctoral program. *Degree requirements:* For master's, internship (for some programs); for doctorate, comprehensive exam, thesis/dissertation, internship. *Entrance requirements:* Additional exam requirements/recommendations for international students: Required—TOEFL (minimum score 550 paper-based; 80 iBT), IELTS (minimum score 7). Electronic applications accepted.

Northwest Nazarene University, Graduate Studies, Program in Counselor Education, Nampa, ID 83686-5897. Offers clinical counseling (MS); marriage and family counseling (MS); school counseling (MS). Part-time programs available. *Faculty:* 6 full-time (4 women), 10 part-time/adjunct (6 women). *Students:* 94 full-time (67 women), 29 part-time (22 women); includes 10 minority (2 Black or African American, non-Hispanic/Latino; 6 Hispanic/Latino; 2 Two or more races, non-Hispanic/Latino), 1 international. Average age 35. 47 applicants, 66% accepted, 25 enrolled. *Degree requirements:* For master's, comprehensive exam. *Entrance requirements:* For master's, minimum GPA of

3.0, BA. Additional exam requirements/recommendations for international students: Required—TOEFL. *Application deadline:* For fall admission, 2/15 for domestic and international students; for spring admission, 9/15 for domestic and international students. Application fee: $50. Electronic applications accepted. *Unit head:* Dr. Michael Pitts, Chair, 208-467-8040, Fax: 208-467-8339. *Application contact:* Marilyn Holly, Graduate Admissions Counselor, 208-467-8688, E-mail: mholly@nnu.edu.

Nova Southeastern University, Center for Psychological Studies, Fort Lauderdale, FL 33314-7796. Offers clinical psychology (PhD, Psy D); counseling (MS); general psychology (MS); mental health counseling (MS); school counseling (MS). *Accreditation:* APA (one or more programs are accredited). Postbaccalaureate distance learning degree programs offered. *Faculty:* 50 full-time (19 women), 119 part-time/adjunct (69 women). *Students:* 1,827 (1,560 women); includes 842 minority (289 Black or African American, non-Hispanic/Latino; 2 American Indian or Alaska Native, non-Hispanic/Latino; 45 Asian, non-Hispanic/Latino; 478 Hispanic/Latino; 28 Two or more races, non-Hispanic/Latino), 41 international. Average age 31. 1,186 applicants, 51% accepted, 398 enrolled. In 2014, 344 master's, 117 doctorates, 10 other advanced degrees awarded. Terminal master's awarded for partial completion of doctoral program. *Degree requirements:* For master's, comprehensive exam, 3 practica; for doctorate, thesis/dissertation, clinical internship, competency exam; for Psy S, comprehensive exam, internship. *Entrance requirements:* For doctorate, GRE General Test, GRE Subject Test (recommended), minimum undergraduate GPA of 3.0; for Psy S, GRE General Test. Additional exam requirements/recommendations for international students: Required—TOEFL (minimum score 550 paper-based). *Application deadline:* Applications are processed on a rolling basis. Application fee: $50. Electronic applications accepted. *Expenses:* Expenses: Contact institution. *Financial support:* In 2014–15, 15 research assistantships, 68 teaching assistantships (averaging $4,800 per year) were awarded; career-related internships or fieldwork, Federal Work-Study, institutionally sponsored loans, scholarships/grants, and unspecified assistantships also available. Support available to part-time students. Financial award application deadline: 4/1. *Faculty research:* Clinical and child clinical psychology, geriatrics, interpersonal violence. *Unit head:* Karen Grosby, EdD, Dean, 954-262-5701, Fax: 954-262-3859, E-mail: grosby@nova.edu. *Application contact:* Carlos Perez, Enrollment Management, 954-262-5790, Fax: 954-262-3893, E-mail: cpsinfo@cps.nova.edu.
Website: http://www.cps.nova.edu/

Oregon State University–Cascades, Program in Counseling, Bend, OR 97701. Offers community counseling (MS); school counseling (MS).

Ottawa University, Graduate Studies-Arizona, Program in Education, Ottawa, KS 66067-3399. Offers community college counseling (MA); curriculum and instruction (MA); early childhood (MA); education intervention (MA); education leadership (MA); education technology (MA); Montessori early childhood education (MA); Montessori elementary education (MA); professional development (MA); school guidance counseling (MA); special education - cross categorical (MA). Programs offered in Mesa, Phoenix, Tempe and West Valley, AZ. *Accreditation:* NCATE. Part-time programs available. *Degree requirements:* For master's, thesis or alternative. *Entrance requirements:* For master's, minimum undergraduate GPA of 3.0, copy of current state certification or teaching license. Additional exam requirements/recommendations for international students: Required—TOEFL (minimum score 550 paper-based). Electronic applications accepted. *Expenses:* Contact institution.

Our Lady of the Lake University of San Antonio, School of Professional Studies, Program in Psychology, San Antonio, TX 78207-4689. Offers counseling psychology (MS, Psy D); marriage and family therapy (MS); school psychology (MS). *Accreditation:* APA (one or more programs are accredited). Part-time and evening/weekend programs available. *Degree requirements:* For master's, comprehensive exam, thesis optional, practicum; for doctorate, thesis/dissertation, internship, qualifying exam. *Entrance requirements:* For master's and doctorate, GRE General Test or MAT, interview. Additional exam requirements/recommendations for international students: Required—TOEFL. Electronic applications accepted. *Faculty research:* Marriage and family therapy, supervision, cross-cultural counseling, violence.

Pace University, Dyson College of Arts and Sciences, Department of Psychology, Program in School-Clinical Child Psychology, New York, NY 10038. Offers school psychology (MS Ed); school-clinical psychology (Psy D). *Accreditation:* APA (one or more programs are accredited). *Students:* 85 full-time (71 women), 42 part-time (34 women); includes 29 minority (6 Black or African American, non-Hispanic/Latino; 12 Asian, non-Hispanic/Latino; 8 Hispanic/Latino; 1 Native Hawaiian or other Pacific Islander, non-Hispanic/Latino; 2 Two or more races, non-Hispanic/Latino), 10 international. Average age 27. 232 applicants, 36% accepted, 39 enrolled. In 2014, 11 master's, 23 doctorates awarded. Terminal master's awarded for partial completion of doctoral program. *Degree requirements:* For master's, comprehensive exam, qualifying exams, internship; for doctorate, comprehensive exam, qualifying exams, externship, internship, project. *Entrance requirements:* For master's, GRE General Test, GRE Subject Test, interview, 3 letters of recommendation, resume, personal statement; for doctorate, GRE General Test, GRE Subject Test (psychology), interview, transcripts, 3 letters of recommendation. Additional exam requirements/recommendations for international students: Required—TOEFL (minimum score 100 iBT). *Application deadline:* For fall admission, 1/15 priority date for domestic students, 11/15 for international students. Applications are processed on a rolling basis. Application fee: $70. Electronic applications accepted. *Expenses: Tuition:* Part-time $1120 per credit. *Required fees:* $266 per semester. Tuition and fees vary according to course load, degree level and program. *Financial support:* Research assistantships, teaching assistantships, career-related internships or fieldwork, Federal Work-Study, and tuition waivers (partial) available. Support available to part-time students. Financial award applicants required to submit FAFSA. *Unit head:* Dr. Barbara Mowder, Director of Graduate Psychology Programs, 212-346-1556, E-mail: bmowder@pace.edu. *Application contact:* Susan Ford-Goldschein, Director of Graduate Admissions, 212-346-1660, Fax: 212-346-1585, E-mail: gradnyc@pace.edu.
Website: http://www.pace.edu/dyson/academic-departments-and-programs/psychology—nyc/graduate-programs

Penn State University Park, Graduate School, College of Education, Department of Educational Psychology, Counseling, and Special Education, University Park, PA 16802. Offers counselor education (M Ed, D Ed, PhD, Certificate); educational psychology (MS, PhD, Certificate); school psychology (M Ed, MS, PhD, Certificate); special education (M Ed, MS, PhD, Certificate). *Unit head:* Dr. David H. Monk, Dean, 814-865-2523, Fax: 814-865-0555, E-mail: dhm6@psu.edu. *Application contact:* Lori A. Stania, Director, Graduate Student Services, 814-867-5278, Fax: 814-863-4627, E-mail: gswww@psu.edu.
Website: http://www.ed.psu.edu/epcse

★ **Philadelphia College of Osteopathic Medicine,** Graduate and Professional Programs, Department of Psychology, Philadephia, PA 19131. Offers applied behavior analysis (Certificate); clinical health psychology (Post-Doctoral Certificate); clinical neuropsychology (Post-Doctoral Certificate); clinical psychology (Psy D); mental health counseling (MS); organizational development and leadership (MS); psychology (Certificate); school psychology (MS, Psy D, Ed S). *Accreditation:* APA. *Faculty:* 19 full-time (11 women), 122 part-time/adjunct (58 women). *Students:* 395 (304 women); includes 80 minority (49 Black or African American, non-Hispanic/Latino; 13 Asian, non-Hispanic/Latino; 7 Hispanic/Latino; 11 Two or more races, non-Hispanic/Latino). 345 applicants, 47% accepted, 113 enrolled. In 2014, 72 master's, 42 doctorates, 17 other advanced degrees awarded. Terminal master's awarded for partial completion of doctoral program. *Degree requirements:* For master's, comprehensive exam (for some programs), thesis (for some programs); for doctorate, comprehensive exam, thesis/dissertation. *Entrance requirements:* For master's, GRE or MAT, minimum GPA of 3.0; bachelor's degree from regionally-accredited college or university; for doctorate, PRAXIS II (for Psy D in school psychology), minimum undergraduate GPA of 3.0; for other advanced degree, GRE (for Ed S). Additional exam requirements/recommendations for international students: Required—TOEFL (minimum score 79 iBT). *Application deadline:* For fall admission, 3/1 priority date for domestic students. Applications are processed on a rolling basis. Application fee: $50. Electronic applications accepted. *Financial support:* In 2014–15, 28 teaching assistantships were awarded; Federal Work-Study, institutionally sponsored loans, and scholarships/grants also available. Financial award application deadline: 3/15; financial award applicants required to submit FAFSA. *Faculty research:* Adult and childhood anxiety and ADHD; coping with chronic illness; primary care psychology/integrated health care; applied behavior analysis; psychological, educational, and neuropsychological assessment. *Total annual research expenditures:* $533,489. *Unit head:* Dr. Robert DiTomasso, Chairman, 215-871-6442, Fax: 215-871-6458, E-mail: robertd@pcom.edu. *Application contact:* Kari A. Shotwell, Director of Admissions, 215-871-6700, Fax: 215-871-6719, E-mail: karis@pcom.edu.

See Display on page 990 and Close-Up on page 1211.

Pittsburg State University, Graduate School, College of Education, Department of Psychology and Counseling, Program in School Psychology, Pittsburg, KS 66762. Offers Ed S. *Accreditation:* NCATE. *Degree requirements:* For Ed S, thesis or alternative. *Entrance requirements:* For degree, GRE General Test, minimum GPA of 3.0.

Plymouth State University, College of Graduate Studies, Graduate Studies in Education, Certificate of Advanced Graduate Studies Programs, Plymouth, NH 03264-1595. Offers clinical mental health counseling (CAGS); educational leadership (CAGS); higher education (CAGS); school psychology (CAGS). Part-time and evening/weekend programs available.

Plymouth State University, College of Graduate Studies, Graduate Studies in Education, Programs in Counseling, Plymouth, NH 03264-1595. Offers human relations (M Ed); school counseling (M Ed); school psychology (M Ed). *Accreditation:* ACA; NCATE. Part-time and evening/weekend programs available. *Degree requirements:* For master's, PRAXIS I. *Entrance requirements:* For master's, MAT, minimum GPA of 3.0.

Purdue University Calumet, Graduate Studies Office, School of Education, Program in Counseling, Hammond, IN 46323-2094. Offers human services (MS Ed); mental health counseling (MS Ed); school counseling (MS Ed). *Entrance requirements:* Additional exam requirements/recommendations for international students: Required—TOEFL.

Queens College of the City University of New York, Division of Graduate Studies, Division of Education, Department of Educational and Community Programs, Program in School Psychology, Flushing, NY 11367-1597. Offers MS Ed, AC. MS Ed offered jointly with Graduate School and University Center of the City University of New York. Part-time programs available. *Degree requirements:* For master's, internship, research project; for AC, thesis optional, internship. *Entrance requirements:* For master's, minimum GPA of 3.0; for AC, master's degree or equivalent. Additional exam requirements/recommendations for international students: Required—TOEFL.

Quincy University, Master of Science in Education Counseling Program, Quincy, IL 62301-2699. Offers school counseling (MS Ed). Part-time and evening/weekend programs available. *Faculty:* 2 full-time (1 woman). *Students:* 8 full-time (5 women), 28 part-time (26 women). In 2014, 5 master's awarded. *Degree requirements:* For master's, comprehensive exam, practicum, internship. *Entrance requirements:* For master's, MAT or GRE. Additional exam requirements/recommendations for international students: Required—TOEFL (minimum score 550 paper-based; 79 iBT). *Application deadline:* Applications are processed on a rolling basis. Application fee: $25. Electronic applications accepted. *Expenses: Tuition:* Full-time $9600; part-time $400 per semester hour. Tuition and fees vary according to course load, campus/location and program. *Financial support:* Applicants required to submit FAFSA. *Unit head:* Dr. Kenneth Oliver, Director, 217-228-5432 Ext. 3113, E-mail: oliveke@quincy.edu. *Application contact:* Office of Admissions, 217-228-5210, Fax: 217-228-5479, E-mail: admissions@quincy.edu.
Website: http://www.quincy.edu/academics/graduate-programs/counseling

Radford University, College of Graduate and Professional Studies, College of Humanities and Behavioral Sciences, Department of Psychology, Program in School Psychology, Radford, VA 24142. Offers Ed S. *Accreditation:* NCATE. *Faculty:* 5 full-time (3 women), 1 (woman) part-time/adjunct. *Students:* 11 full-time (9 women), 6 part-time (all women); includes 2 minority (both Black or African American, non-Hispanic/Latino). Average age 23. 34 applicants, 88% accepted, 7 enrolled. In 2014, 9 Ed Ss awarded. *Degree requirements:* For Ed S, comprehensive exam. *Entrance requirements:* For degree, GRE, minimum GPA of 3.0; 2 letters of reference; essay, resume, official transcripts. Additional exam requirements/recommendations for international students: Required—TOEFL (minimum score 550 paper-based; 79 iBT), IELTS (minimum score 6.5). *Application deadline:* For fall admission, 2/15 priority date for domestic students, 12/1 for international students; for spring admission, 7/1 for international students. Applications are processed on a rolling basis. Application fee: $50. Electronic applications accepted. *Expenses:* Tuition, state resident: full-time $7187; part-time $299 per credit hour. Tuition, nonresident: full-time $16,394; part-time $683 per credit hour. *Required fees:* $2974; $125 per credit hour. Tuition and fees vary according to course load and program. *Financial support:* In 2014–15, 10 students received support, including 8 research assistantships (averaging $4,500 per year), 1 teaching assistantship with partial tuition reimbursement available (averaging $10,000 per year); career-related internships or fieldwork, Federal Work-Study, institutionally sponsored loans, scholarships/grants, and unspecified assistantships also available. Financial award application deadline: 3/1; financial award applicants required to submit FAFSA. *Faculty research:* Civility in the classroom, intellectual assessment and identification of learning difficulties, behaviorally-based academic interventions in students experiencing learning difficulties, pediatric neuropsychology. *Unit head:* Dr. Eric M. Mesmer, Coordinator, 540-831-6891, Fax: 540-831-6113, E-mail: emesmer@radford.edu. *Application contact:* Rebecca Conner, Director, Graduate Enrollment, 540-831-6296, Fax: 540-831-6061, E-mail: gradcollege@radford.edu.
Website: http://www.radford.edu/content/chbs/home/psychology/programs/school.html

Rhode Island College, School of Graduate Studies, Feinstein School of Education and Human Development, Department of Counseling, Educational Leadership, and School Psychology, Providence, RI 02908-1991. Offers advanced counseling (CGS); agency counseling (MA); co-occurring disorders (MA, CGS); educational leadership (M Ed); mental health counseling (CAGS); school counseling (MA); school psychology (CAGS); teacher leadership (CGS). *Accreditation:* NCATE. Part-time and evening/weekend programs available. *Faculty:* 9 full-time (5 women), 7 part-time/adjunct (6 women).

Students: 32 full-time (25 women), 111 part-time (87 women); includes 17 minority (3 Black or African American, non-Hispanic/Latino; 3 Asian, non-Hispanic/Latino; 9 Hispanic/Latino; 1 Native Hawaiian or other Pacific Islander, non-Hispanic/Latino; 1 Two or more races, non-Hispanic/Latino), 1 international. Average age 34. In 2014, 42 master's, 24 other advanced degrees awarded. *Degree requirements:* For master's and other advanced degree, comprehensive exam (for some programs), thesis (for some programs). *Entrance requirements:* For master's, GRE General Test or MAT, undergraduate transcripts; minimum undergraduate GPA of 3.0; for other advanced degree, GRE or MAT (for most programs), undergraduate transcripts; minimum undergraduate GPA of 3.0; 3 letters of recommendation; current resume. Additional exam requirements/recommendations for international students: Recommended—TOEFL (minimum score 550 paper-based; 79 iBT). *Application deadline:* For fall admission, 3/1 for domestic students; for spring admission, 11/1 for domestic students. Applications are processed on a rolling basis. Application fee: $50. *Expenses:* Tuition, state resident: full-time $8928; part-time $372 per credit hour. Tuition, nonresident: full-time $17,376; part-time $724 per credit hour. *Required fees:* $602; $22 per credit. $72 per term. *Financial support:* In 2014–15, 3 teaching assistantships with full tuition reimbursements (averaging $3,000 per year) were awarded; career-related internships or fieldwork, Federal Work-Study, scholarships/grants, health care benefits, and unspecified assistantships also available. Support available to part-time students. Financial award application deadline: 5/15; financial award applicants required to submit FAFSA. *Unit head:* Dr. Kalina Brabeck, Chair, 401-456-8023. *Application contact:* Graduate Studies, 401-456-8700.
Website: http://www.ric.edu/counselingEducationalLeadershipSchoolPsychology/index.php

Rider University, Department of Graduate Education, Leadership and Counseling, Program in School Psychology, Lawrenceville, NJ 08648-3001. Offers Certificate, Ed S. *Entrance requirements:* For degree, GRE or MAT, resume, 2 professional references, interview, 1 year of counseling experience. Additional exam requirements/recommendations for international students: Required—TOEFL (minimum score 550 paper-based). *Faculty research:* Prenatal factors on child development, child abuse developmental assessments.

Rochester Institute of Technology, Graduate Enrollment Services, College of Liberal Arts, Psychology Department, Advanced Certificate Program in School Psychology, Rochester, NY 14623-5604. Offers Advanced Certificate. Part-time programs available. *Students:* 7 applicants. In 2014, 1 Advanced Certificate awarded. *Entrance requirements:* For degree, TOEFL, IELTS, or PTE for non-native English speakers, recommended minimum GPA of 3.0. Additional exam requirements/recommendations for international students: Required—PTE (minimum score 58), TOEFL (minimum score 550 paper-based; 79 iBT) or IELTS (minimum score 6.5). *Application deadline:* For fall admission, 2/15 priority date for domestic and international students; for spring admission, 12/15 priority date for domestic students, 11/15 priority date for international students. Applications are processed on a rolling basis. Electronic applications accepted. *Expenses:* Expenses: $1,673 per credit hour. *Financial support:* Career-related internships or fieldwork, Federal Work-Study, institutionally sponsored loans, and scholarships/grants available. Support available to part-time students. Financial award applicants required to submit FAFSA. *Unit head:* Dr. Suzanne Bamonto, Graduate Program Director, 585-475-2765, E-mail: sbggsp@rit.edu. *Application contact:* Diane Ellison, Associate Vice President, Graduate Enrollment Services, 585-475-2229, Fax: 585-475-7164, E-mail: gradinfo@rit.edu.
Website: http://www.rit.edu/cla/psychology/advanced-certificates/school-psychology

Rochester Institute of Technology, Graduate Enrollment Services, College of Liberal Arts, Psychology Department, MS Program in School Psychology, Rochester, NY 14623-5604. Offers MS. Part-time programs available. *Students:* 25 full-time (22 women), 2 part-time (both women); includes 3 minority (2 Black or African American, non-Hispanic/Latino; 1 Hispanic/Latino), 3 international. Average age 25. 39 applicants, 49% accepted, 7 enrolled. In 2014, 6 master's awarded. *Degree requirements:* For master's, internship and portfolio required. *Entrance requirements:* For master's, GRE and TOEFL, IELTS, or PTE for non-native English speakers, recommended minimum GPA of 3.0. Additional exam requirements/recommendations for international students: Required—PTE (minimum score 58), TOEFL (minimum score 550 paper-based; 79 iBT) or IELTS (minimum score 6.5). *Application deadline:* For fall admission, 2/15 priority date for domestic and international students; for spring admission, 12/15 priority date for domestic and international students. Applications are processed on a rolling basis. Electronic applications accepted. *Expenses:* Expenses: $1,673 per credit hour. *Financial support:* In 2014–15, 6 students received support. Research assistantships with partial tuition reimbursements available, teaching assistantships with partial tuition reimbursements available, career-related internships or fieldwork, Federal Work-Study, institutionally sponsored loans, scholarships/grants, and unspecified assistantships available. Support available to part-time students. Financial award applicants required to submit FAFSA. *Unit head:* Dr. Suzanne Bamonto, Graduate Program Director, 585-475-2765, E-mail: sbggsp@rit.edu. *Application contact:* Diane Ellison, Associate Vice President, Graduate Enrollment Services, 585-475-2229, Fax: 585-475-7164, E-mail: gradinfo@rit.edu.
Website: http://www.rit.edu/cla/psychology/graduate/ms-school-psych/overview

Rowan University, Graduate School, College of Education, Department of Educational Services and Leadership, Ed S in School Psychology Program, Glassboro, NJ 08028-1701. Offers Ed S. *Faculty:* 2 full-time (both women), 2 part-time/adjunct (both women). *Students:* 21 full-time (16 women), 26 part-time (20 women); includes 7 minority (3 Black or African American, non-Hispanic/Latino; 1 American Indian or Alaska Native, non-Hispanic/Latino; 3 Hispanic/Latino). Average age 30. 15 applicants, 100% accepted, 10 enrolled. In 2014, 26 Ed Ss awarded. *Degree requirements:* For Ed S, practicum, internship. *Entrance requirements:* For degree, master's degree, official transcripts, current professional resume, statement of professional objectives, two letters of recommendation, interview. *Application deadline:* For fall admission, 6/1 for domestic students; for spring admission, 11/1 for domestic students; for summer admission, 2/15 for domestic students. Applications are processed on a rolling basis. Application fee: $65. Electronic applications accepted. *Expenses: Tuition, area resident:* Part-time $648 per credit. Tuition, state resident: part-time $648 per credit. Tuition, nonresident: part-time $648 per credit. *Required fees:* $145 per credit. Tuition and fees vary according to degree level, campus/location, program and student level. *Unit head:* Dr. Horacio Sosa, Vice President, Global Learning and Partnerships, 856-256-4747, Fax: 856-256-5638, E-mail: sosa@rowan.edu. *Application contact:* Admissions and Enrollment Services, 856-256-4747, Fax: 856-256-5637, E-mail: globaladmissions@rowan.edu.
Website: http://www.rowancgce.com/education/eds-specialist

Rowan University, Graduate School, College of Education, Department of Educational Services and Leadership, Program in School Psychology, Glassboro, NJ 08028-1701. Offers MA. *Accreditation:* NCATE. Part-time and evening/weekend programs available. *Faculty:* 5 full-time (4 women), 4 part-time/adjunct (2 women). *Students:* 24 full-time (20 women), 10 part-time (all women); includes 5 minority (3 Black or African American, non-Hispanic/Latino; 1 Asian, non-Hispanic/Latino; 1 Hispanic/Latino). Average age 25. 20 applicants, 95% accepted, 13 enrolled. In 2014, 46 master's awarded. *Degree requirements:* For master's, comprehensive exam, thesis. *Entrance requirements:* For master's, GRE General Test, GRE Subject Test, interview, minimum GPA of 3.0. Additional exam requirements/recommendations for international students: Required—TOEFL. *Application deadline:* For fall admission, 6/1 for domestic students; for winter admission, 12/1 priority date for domestic students; for spring admission, 11/1 priority date for domestic students; for summer admission, 2/15 for domestic students. Application fee: $65. *Expenses: Tuition, area resident:* Part-time $648 per credit. Tuition, state resident: part-time $648 per credit. Tuition, nonresident: part-time $648 per credit. *Required fees:* $145 per credit. Tuition and fees vary according to degree level, campus/location, program and student level. *Financial support:* Career-related internships or fieldwork, scholarships/grants, and unspecified assistantships available. Support available to part-time students. *Unit head:* Dr. Horacio Sosa, Vice President, Global Learning and Partnerships, 856-256-4747, Fax: 856-256-5638, E-mail: sosa@rowan.edu. *Application contact:* Admissions and Enrollment Services, 856-256-4747, Fax: 856-256-5637, E-mail: globaladmissions@rowan.edu.
Website: http://www.rowancgce.com/education/ma-school-psych

Rutgers, The State University of New Jersey, New Brunswick, Graduate School of Applied and Professional Psychology, Program in School Psychology, Piscataway, NJ 08854-8097. Offers Psy M, Psy D. *Accreditation:* APA (one or more programs are accredited). *Degree requirements:* For doctorate, comprehensive exam, thesis/dissertation, 1 year internship. *Entrance requirements:* For doctorate, GRE General Test, GRE Subject Test, bachelor's degree in psychology or equivalent. Additional exam requirements/recommendations for international students: Required—TOEFL. Electronic applications accepted. *Expenses:* Contact institution. *Faculty research:* Consultation, program evaluation, applied educational psychology, exceptional children, crisis intervention.

St. John's University, St. John's College of Liberal Arts and Sciences, Department of Psychology, Program in School Psychology, Queens, NY 11439. Offers MS, Psy D. Part-time programs available. *Students:* 109 full-time (90 women), 30 part-time (24 women); includes 37 minority (8 Black or African American, non-Hispanic/Latino; 8 Asian, non-Hispanic/Latino; 20 Hispanic/Latino; 1 Two or more races, non-Hispanic/Latino), 2 international. Average age 27. 118 applicants, 35% accepted, 43 enrolled. In 2014, 29 master's, 25 doctorates awarded. *Degree requirements:* For master's, comprehensive exam, thesis optional; for doctorate, comprehensive exam, thesis/dissertation, internship, practicum. *Entrance requirements:* For master's, GRE General Test, GRE Subject Test, minimum GPA of 3.0, 2 writing samples, 3 letters of recommendation, minimum of 24 undergraduate credits in psychology, personal statement, transcript, bachelor's degree; for doctorate, GRE General Test, GRE Subject Test, minimum GPA of 3.0, 2 writing samples, 3 letters of recommendation, minimum of 24 undergraduate credits in psychology, personal statement. Additional exam requirements/recommendations for international students: Required—TOEFL (minimum score 600 paper-based; 100 iBT), IELTS (minimum score 7). *Application deadline:* For fall admission, 1/15 priority date for domestic and international students. Applications are processed on a rolling basis. Application fee: $70. Electronic applications accepted. *Expenses:* Expenses: Contact institution. *Financial support:* Fellowships, research assistantships, career-related internships or fieldwork, scholarships/grants, and unspecified assistantships available. Support available to part-time students. Financial award application deadline: 3/1; financial award applicants required to submit FAFSA. *Faculty research:* Therapeutic alliance, intelligence testing, multicultural assessment, neuropsychological assessment, adolescent suicide. *Unit head:* Dr. Mark Terjesen, Director, 718-990-5860, E-mail: schoolpsych@stjohns.edu. *Application contact:* Robert Medrano, Director of Graduate Admission, 718-990-1601, Fax: 718-990-5686, E-mail: gradhelp@stjohns.edu.

Sam Houston State University, College of Humanities and Social Sciences, Department of Psychology and Philosophy, Huntsville, TX 77341. Offers psychology (MA, PhD, SSP), including clinical psychology (MA, PhD), psychology (MA), school psychology (SSP). *Accreditation:* APA. Part-time programs available. *Faculty:* 27 full-time (9 women), 2 part-time/adjunct (0 women). *Students:* 74 full-time (58 women), 38 part-time (33 women); includes 12 minority (2 Black or African American, non-Hispanic/Latino; 1 American Indian or Alaska Native, non-Hispanic/Latino; 1 Asian, non-Hispanic/Latino; 5 Hispanic/Latino; 3 Two or more races, non-Hispanic/Latino), 8 international. Average age 27. 155 applicants, 32% accepted, 33 enrolled. In 2014, 25 master's, 9 doctorates awarded. Terminal master's awarded for partial completion of doctoral program. *Degree requirements:* For master's, comprehensive exam, thesis optional; for doctorate, comprehensive exam, thesis/dissertation. *Entrance requirements:* For master's, GRE General Test, personal statement, letters of recommendation; for doctorate, GRE General Test, GRE Subject Test (advanced psychology), personal essay, letters of recommendation, resume. Additional exam requirements/recommendations for international students: Required—TOEFL (minimum score 550 paper-based; 79 iBT), IELTS (minimum score 6.5). *Application deadline:* For fall admission, 12/1 priority date for domestic students, 6/25 for international students; for spring admission, 12/1 for domestic students, 11/12 for international students. Applications are processed on a rolling basis. Application fee: $45 ($75 for international students). Electronic applications accepted. *Expenses:* Tuition, state resident: full-time $2286; part-time $254 per credit hour. Tuition, nonresident: full-time $5544; part-time $616 per credit hour. *Required fees:* $440 per semester. Tuition and fees vary according to course load and campus/location. *Financial support:* In 2014–15, 61 research assistantships (averaging $9,562 per year), 7 teaching assistantships (averaging $11,088 per year) were awarded; career-related internships or fieldwork, Federal Work-Study, scholarships/grants, tuition waivers (partial), and unspecified assistantships also available. Support available to part-time students. Financial award application deadline: 3/15; financial award applicants required to submit FAFSA. *Unit head:* Dr. D. Christopher Wilson, Chair, 936-294-3052, Fax: 936-294-3798, E-mail: wilson@shsu.edu. *Application contact:* Dr. Jeffrey Anastasi, Assistant Professor/Coordinator of Master of Arts in Psychology Programs, 936-294-3049, Fax: 936-294-3798, E-mail: jeff.anastasi@shsu.edu.
Website: http://www.shsu.edu/~psy_www/

San Diego State University, Graduate and Research Affairs, College of Education, Department of Counseling and School Psychology, San Diego, CA 92182. Offers MS. *Accreditation:* NCATE. Evening/weekend programs available. *Degree requirements:* For master's, comprehensive exam (for some programs), thesis (for some programs). *Entrance requirements:* For master's, GRE General Test, interview, letters of reference. Additional exam requirements/recommendations for international students: Required—TOEFL. Electronic applications accepted. *Faculty research:* Multicultural and cross-cultural counseling and training, AIDS counseling.

San Francisco State University, Division of Graduate Studies, College of Science and Engineering, Department of Psychology, San Francisco, CA 94132-1722. Offers industrial/organizational psychology (MS); school psychology (Credential); social psychology (MA). *Expenses:* Tuition, state resident: full-time $6738. Tuition, nonresident: full-time $17,898; part-time $372 per credit hour. *Required fees:* $498 per semester. *Financial support:* Teaching assistantships available. Financial award application deadline: 3/1. *Unit head:* Dr. Jeffrey Cookston, Chair, 415-338-2167, Fax: 415-338-2398, E-mail: cookston@sfsu.edu. *Application contact:* Dr. Ryan Howell,

Graduate Program Coordinator, 415-405-2140, Fax: 415-338-2398, E-mail: rhowell@sfsu.edu. Website: http://psychology.sfsu.edu/graduate/application.html

Seattle University, College of Education, Program in Counseling and School Psychology, Seattle, WA 98122-1090. Offers MA, Certificate, Ed S. *Accreditation:* ACA; NCATE. Part-time and evening/weekend programs available. *Faculty:* 11 full-time (6 women), 3 part-time/adjunct (2 women). *Students:* 58 full-time (48 women), 136 part-time (112 women); includes 66 minority (9 Black or African American, non-Hispanic/Latino; 2 American Indian or Alaska Native, non-Hispanic/Latino; 12 Asian, non-Hispanic/Latino; 25 Hispanic/Latino; 18 Two or more races, non-Hispanic/Latino), 2 international. Average age 30. 171 applicants, 41% accepted, 49 enrolled. In 2014, 34 master's, 15 other advanced degrees awarded. *Degree requirements:* For master's, comprehensive exam. *Entrance requirements:* For master's, interview; GRE, MAT, or minimum GPA of 3.0; related work experience. Additional exam requirements/recommendations for international students: Required—TOEFL. *Application deadline:* For fall admission, 7/1 for domestic students; for winter admission, 10/20 for domestic students; for spring admission, 1/20 for domestic students. Application fee: $55. *Financial support:* In 2014–15, 20 students received support. *Unit head:* Hutch Haney, Director, 206-296-5750, E-mail: schpsy@seattleu.edu. *Application contact:* Janet Shandley, Associate Dean of Graduate Admissions, 206-296-5900, Fax: 206-298-5656, E-mail: grad_admissions@seattleu.edu.

Seton Hall University, College of Education and Human Services, Department of Professional Psychology and Family Therapy, Program in School and Community Psychology, South Orange, NJ 07079-2697. Offers MA. *Degree requirements:* For master's, comprehensive exam, thesis, internship. *Entrance requirements:* For master's, GRE or MAT, interview. *Faculty research:* Family systems, ethical behavior, childhood depression.

Slippery Rock University of Pennsylvania, Graduate Studies (Recruitment), College of Education, Department of Counseling and Development, Slippery Rock, PA 16057-1383. Offers clinical mental health counseling (MA), including addiction, adult, older adult, school and youth; student affairs (MA), including higher education; student affairs in higher education (MA), including college counseling. *Accreditation:* ACA; NCATE. Part-time and evening/weekend programs available. *Faculty:* 9 full-time (5 women). *Students:* 84 full-time (69 women), 16 part-time (13 women); includes 13 minority (8 Black or African American, non-Hispanic/Latino; 1 American Indian or Alaska Native, non-Hispanic/Latino; 2 Hispanic/Latino; 2 Two or more races, non-Hispanic/Latino), 1 international. Average age 29. 128 applicants, 51% accepted, 41 enrolled. In 2014, 45 master's awarded. *Degree requirements:* For master's, comprehensive exam, thesis (for some programs). *Entrance requirements:* For master's, GRE General Test or MAT, official transcripts, minimum GPA of 2.75 or 3.0 (depending on program), personal statement, three letters of recommendation, interview. Additional exam requirements/recommendations for international students: Required—TOEFL (minimum score 550 paper-based; 80 iBT). *Application deadline:* For fall admission, 1/15 priority date for domestic and international students. Application fee: $25 ($30 for international students). Electronic applications accepted. *Expenses:* Tuition, state resident: full-time $8172; part-time $454 per credit. Tuition, nonresident: full-time $12,258; part-time $681 per credit. *Required fees:* $2326; $200 per credit. Tuition and fees vary according to degree level and program. *Financial support:* Career-related internships or fieldwork, Federal Work-Study, institutionally sponsored loans, scholarships/grants, tuition waivers (partial), and unspecified assistantships available. Support available to part-time students. Financial award application deadline: 5/1; financial award applicants required to submit FAFSA. *Unit head:* Dr. Stacy Jacob, Graduate Coordinator, 724-738-2758, Fax: 724-738-4859, E-mail: stacy.jacob@sru.edu. *Application contact:* Brandi Weber-Mortimer, Director of Graduate Admissions, 724-738-2051, Fax: 724-738-2146, E-mail: graduate.admissions@sru.edu.
Website: http://srudss.ingeniuxondemand.com/academics/colleges-and-departments/coe/departments/counseling-and-development

Southern Connecticut State University, School of Graduate Studies, School of Education, Department of Counseling and School Psychology, New Haven, CT 06515-1355. Offers community counseling (MS); counseling (Diploma); school counseling (MS); school psychology (MS, Diploma). *Accreditation:* ACA (one or more programs are accredited); NCATE. *Degree requirements:* For master's, comprehensive exam. *Entrance requirements:* For master's, interview, previous course work in behavioral sciences, minimum QPA of 2.7. Electronic applications accepted.

Southern Illinois University Edwardsville, Graduate School, School of Education, Health, and Human Behavior, Department of Psychology, Program in School Psychology, Edwardsville, IL 62026. Offers SD. *Accreditation:* NCATE. Part-time and evening/weekend programs available. *Students:* 9 part-time (7 women); includes 1 minority (Black or African American, non-Hispanic/Latino). In 2014, 8 SDs awarded. *Degree requirements:* For SD, thesis. *Entrance requirements:* For degree, GRE. Additional exam requirements/recommendations for international students: Required—TOEFL (minimum score 550 paper-based; 79 iBT), IELTS (minimum score 6.5). *Application deadline:* For spring admission, 2/1 for domestic and international students. Application fee: $30. Electronic applications accepted. *Expenses:* Tuition, state resident: full-time $5026. Tuition, nonresident: full-time $12,566. *International tuition:* $25,136 full-time. *Required fees:* $1682. Tuition and fees vary according to course load, campus/location and program. *Financial support:* Fellowships, research assistantships, teaching assistantships, institutionally sponsored loans, scholarships/grants, and unspecified assistantships available. Financial award application deadline: 3/1; financial award applicants required to submit FAFSA. *Unit head:* Dr. Jeremy Jewell, Director, 618-650-2202, E-mail: jejewel@siue.edu. *Application contact:* Melissa K. Mace, Assistant Director of Admissions for Graduate and International Recruitment, 618-650-2756, Fax: 618-650-3618, E-mail: mmace@siue.edu.
Website: http://www.siue.edu/education/psychology/

Southwestern Oklahoma State University, College of Professional and Graduate Studies, School of Behavioral Sciences and Education, Specialization in School Psychology, Weatherford, OK 73096-3098. Offers MS.

State University of New York at Plattsburgh, School of Arts and Sciences, Department of Psychology, Plattsburgh, NY 12901-2681. Offers school psychology (MA, CAS). Part-time programs available. *Students:* 13 full-time (all women), 7 part-time (5 women); includes 1 minority (Hispanic/Latino), 1 international. Average age 25. *Entrance requirements:* For master's, GRE General Test, minimum GPA of 3.0. Additional exam requirements/recommendations for international students: Required—TOEFL. *Application deadline:* For fall admission, 2/15 priority date for domestic students. Applications are processed on a rolling basis. Application fee: $75. *Financial support:* Federal Work-Study available. Support available to part-time students. Financial award application deadline: 4/15; financial award applicants required to submit FAFSA. *Faculty research:* Alzheimer's disease, adolescent behavior, intellectual assessment, learning disabilities, reading skill acquisition. *Unit head:* Dr. Laci Charette, Program Coordinator, 518-564-3385, E-mail: charetlm@plattsburgh.edu. *Application contact:* Betsy Kane, Director, Graduate Admissions, 518-564-4723, Fax: 518-564-4722, E-mail: bkane002@plattsburgh.edu.

Stephen F. Austin State University, Graduate School, College of Education, Department of Human Services, Nacogdoches, TX 75962. Offers counseling (MA); school psychology (MA); special education (M Ed); speech pathology (MS). *Accreditation:* ACA (one or more programs are accredited); ASHA (one or more programs are accredited); CORE; NCATE. *Degree requirements:* For master's, comprehensive exam, thesis (for some programs). *Entrance requirements:* For master's, GRE General Test, minimum GPA of 2.8. Additional exam requirements/recommendations for international students: Required—TOEFL.

Suffolk University, College of Arts and Sciences, Department of Psychology, Boston, MA 02108-2770. Offers clinical psychology (PhD); college admission counseling (Certificate); mental health counseling (MS, CAGS); school counseling (MS, CAGS). *Accreditation:* APA. *Faculty:* 14 full-time (6 women), 6 part-time/adjunct (4 women). *Students:* 61 full-time (52 women), 39 part-time (33 women); includes 23 minority (6 Black or African American, non-Hispanic/Latino; 7 Asian, non-Hispanic/Latino; 8 Hispanic/Latino; 2 Two or more races, non-Hispanic/Latino), 6 international. Average age 27. 384 applicants, 18% accepted, 33 enrolled. In 2014, 33 master's, 21 doctorates, 6 other advanced degrees awarded. *Degree requirements:* For doctorate, thesis/dissertation, practicum. *Entrance requirements:* For doctorate, GRE General Test or MAT, 2 letters of recommendation, resume. Additional exam requirements/recommendations for international students: Required—TOEFL (minimum score 550 paper-based; 80 iBT). *Application deadline:* For fall admission, 12/15 for domestic and international students. Applications are processed on a rolling basis. Application fee: $50. Electronic applications accepted. *Expenses:* Expenses: Contact institution. *Financial support:* In 2014–15, 62 students received support, including 60 fellowships (averaging $16,231 per year); career-related internships or fieldwork, Federal Work-Study, and institutionally sponsored loans also available. Support available to part-time students. Financial award application deadline: 4/1; financial award applicants required to submit FAFSA. *Faculty research:* Assessing exposure in the context of a family-based cognitive behavioral treatment for pediatric OCD, a mindfulness approach to designing and testing the efficacy of a new sexual revictimization prevention program for college women, olfaction and decision-making in substance-dependent individuals, the role of experiential avoidance in Generalized Anxiety Disorder, ego development as a predictor of dogmatism and intolerance in the political right and left. *Unit head:* Dr. Gary Fireman, Chairperson, 617-305-6368, Fax: 617-367-2924, E-mail: gfireman@suffolk.edu. *Application contact:* Cory Meyers, Director of Graduate Admissions, 617-573-8302, Fax: 617-305-1733, E-mail: grad.admission@suffolk.edu.
Website: http://www.suffolk.edu/college/departments/9912.php

Syracuse University, College of Arts and Sciences, Program in School Psychology, Syracuse, NY 13244. Offers PhD. *Accreditation:* APA. *Students:* 16 full-time (13 women), 1 (woman) part-time; includes 2 minority (1 Black or African American, non-Hispanic/Latino; 1 Asian, non-Hispanic/Latino), 2 international. Average age 26. 50 applicants, 20% accepted, 3 enrolled. In 2014, 3 doctorates awarded. *Degree requirements:* For doctorate, comprehensive exam, thesis/dissertation. *Entrance requirements:* For doctorate, GRE General Test, GRE Subject Test. Additional exam requirements/recommendations for international students: Required—TOEFL (minimum score 100 iBT). *Application deadline:* For fall admission, 12/15 priority date for domestic and international students. Application fee: $75. Electronic applications accepted. *Expenses: Tuition:* Part-time $1341 per credit. *Financial support:* Fellowships with full tuition reimbursements, research assistantships with full and partial tuition reimbursements, and teaching assistantships with full and partial tuition reimbursements available. Financial award application deadline: 1/1; financial award applicants required to submit FAFSA. *Unit head:* Dr. Tanya Eckert, Graduate Director, 315-443-2354, Fax: 315-443-4085, E-mail: taeckert@syr.edu. *Application contact:* Alecia Zema, Information Contact, 315-443-2760, E-mail: azema@syr.edu.
Website: http://psychology.syr.edu/

Syracuse University, School of Education, Program in School Counseling, Syracuse, NY 13244. Offers MS, CAS. Part-time programs available. *Students:* 11 full-time (8 women), 3 part-time (all women); includes 3 minority (2 Black or African American, non-Hispanic/Latino; 1 Hispanic/Latino). Average age 24. 14 applicants, 57% accepted, 5 enrolled. In 2014, 5 master's, 4 other advanced degrees awarded. *Degree requirements:* For master's and CAS, thesis or alternative. *Entrance requirements:* For master's, GRE General Test or MAT, group interview; for CAS, master's degree in counseling; minimum of 60 credits beyond the baccalaureate, of which 30 credits must be taken at Syracuse University. Additional exam requirements/recommendations for international students: Required—TOEFL (minimum score 100 iBT). *Application deadline:* For fall admission, 1/15 priority date for domestic and international students; for spring admission, 10/15 priority date for domestic and international students. Applications are processed on a rolling basis. Application fee: $75. Electronic applications accepted. *Expenses: Tuition:* Part-time $1341 per credit. *Financial support:* Fellowships with full tuition reimbursements, research assistantships with full and partial tuition reimbursements, and teaching assistantships with full and partial tuition reimbursements available. Financial award application deadline: 1/1; financial award applicants required to submit FAFSA. *Unit head:* Dr. Melissa Luke, Chair, 315-443-2266, Fax: 315-443-5732, E-mail: mmluke@syr.edu. *Application contact:* Laurie Deyo, Graduate Recruiter, School of Education, 315-443-2505, E-mail: e-gradrcrt@syr.edu.
Website: http://soeweb.syr.edu/

Tarleton State University, College of Graduate Studies, College of Education, Department of Psychology and Counseling, Stephenville, TX 76402. Offers counseling and psychology (M Ed), including counseling, counseling psychology, educational psychology; educational administration (M Ed); secondary education (Certificate); special education (Certificate). Part-time and evening/weekend programs available. Postbaccalaureate distance learning degree programs offered (minimal on-campus study). *Degree requirements:* For master's, comprehensive exam, thesis optional. *Entrance requirements:* For master's, GRE General Test, minimum GPA of 3.0. Additional exam requirements/recommendations for international students: Required—TOEFL (minimum score 550 paper-based; 80 iBT). Electronic applications accepted.

Teachers College, Columbia University, Graduate Faculty of Education, Department of Health and Behavioral Studies, Program in Applied Educational Psychology-School Psychology, New York, NY 10027. Offers Ed M, MA, Ed D, PhD. *Accreditation:* APA (one or more programs are accredited). *Faculty:* 5 full-time. *Students:* 37 full-time (32 women), 41 part-time (37 women); includes 12 minority (3 Black or African American, non-Hispanic/Latino; 2 Asian, non-Hispanic/Latino; 6 Hispanic/Latino; 1 Two or more races, non-Hispanic/Latino), 5 international. Average age 26. 123 applicants, 33% accepted, 21 enrolled. In 2014, 59 master's, 5 doctorates awarded. *Degree requirements:* For master's, project; for doctorate, comprehensive exam, thesis/dissertation. *Entrance requirements:* For master's, GRE General Test (for Ed M); for doctorate, GRE General Test. *Application deadline:* For fall admission, 12/15 for domestic students. Application fee: $65. *Expenses: Tuition:* Full-time $33,552; part-time $1398 per credit. *Required fees:* $418 per semester. *Financial support:* Fellowships, research assistantships, career-related internships or fieldwork, Federal Work-Study, institutionally sponsored loans, and tuition waivers (full and partial) available. Support available to part-time students. Financial award application deadline: 2/1; financial award applicants required to submit FAFSA. *Faculty research:* Psychoeducational

assessment, observation and concept acquisition in young children, reading, mathematical thinking, memory. *Unit head:* Prof. Marla Brassard, Chair, 212-678-3368, E-mail: brassard@tc.edu. *Application contact:* Peter Shon, Assistant Director of Admission, 212-678-3305, Fax: 212-678-4171, E-mail: shon@exchange.tc.columbia.edu.
Website: http://www.tc.edu/hbs/SchoolPsych/

Temple University, College of Education, Department of Psychological Studies in Education, Philadelphia, PA 19122-6096. Offers adult and organizational development (Ed M); counseling psychology (Ed M, PhD), including agency counseling (Ed M), counseling psychology (PhD), school counseling (Ed M); education (PhD); educational leadership (Ed M); educational leadership and policy studies (Ed M, Ed D), including educational leadership; educational psychology (Ed M); school psychology (Ed M, PhD, Ed S); special education (Ed M). *Accreditation:* APA (one or more programs are accredited). Part-time and evening/weekend programs available. *Faculty:* 26 full-time (17 women), 35 part-time/adjunct (21 women). *Students:* 181 full-time (134 women), 182 part-time (125 women); includes 95 minority (64 Black or African American, non-Hispanic/Latino; 1 American Indian or Alaska Native, non-Hispanic/Latino; 8 Asian, non-Hispanic/Latino; 17 Hispanic/Latino; 5 Two or more races, non-Hispanic/Latino), 10 international. 281 applicants, 67% accepted, 118 enrolled. In 2014, 77 master's, 24 doctorates, 5 other advanced degrees awarded. Terminal master's awarded for partial completion of doctoral program. *Degree requirements:* For master's, thesis or alternative; for doctorate, thesis/dissertation. *Entrance requirements:* Additional exam requirements/recommendations for international students: Required—TOEFL (minimum score 550 paper-based; 79 iBT). *Application deadline:* For fall admission, 12/15 for international students; for spring admission, 8/1 for international students. Application fee: $60. *Expenses:* Tuition, state resident: full-time $14,490; part-time $805 per credit hour. Tuition, nonresident: full-time $19,850; part-time $1103 per credit hour. *Required fees:* $690. Full-time tuition and fees vary according to class time, course load, degree level, campus/location and program. *Financial support:* Fellowships, research assistantships with full tuition reimbursements, and teaching assistantships with full tuition reimbursements available. Financial award application deadline: 1/15; financial award applicants required to submit FAFSA. *Application contact:* Linda Pryor, Enrollment Management, 215-204-8011, E-mail: educate@temple.edu.
Website: http://education.temple.edu/pols

Tennessee State University, The School of Graduate Studies and Research, College of Education, Department of Psychology, Nashville, TN 37209-1561. Offers counseling psychology (MS, PhD); professional school counseling (MS); psychology (MS, PhD); school psychology (MS, PhD). *Accreditation:* APA. *Degree requirements:* For doctorate, thesis/dissertation (for some programs). *Entrance requirements:* For master's, GRE General Test or MAT; for doctorate, GRE General Test or MAT, minimum GPA of 3.25, work experience. Electronic applications accepted.

Tennessee Technological University, College of Graduate Studies, College of Education, Department of Counseling and Psychology, Cookeville, TN 38505. Offers agency counseling (Ed S); case management and supervision (MA); educational psychology (MA, Ed S); mental health counseling (MA); school counseling (MA, Ed S); school psychology (MA, Ed S). *Accreditation:* NCATE (one or more programs are accredited). Part-time and evening/weekend programs available. *Faculty:* 24 full-time (6 women). *Students:* 45 full-time (28 women), 31 part-time (26 women); includes 11 minority (4 Black or African American, non-Hispanic/Latino; 1 Asian, non-Hispanic/Latino; 1 Hispanic/Latino; 5 Two or more races, non-Hispanic/Latino). Average age 27. 37 applicants, 76% accepted, 19 enrolled. In 2014, 24 master's, 5 other advanced degrees awarded. *Degree requirements:* For master's and Ed S, comprehensive exam, thesis or alternative. *Entrance requirements:* For master's, GRE; for Ed S, MAT or GRE. Additional exam requirements/recommendations for international students: Required—TOEFL (minimum score 527 paper-based; 71 iBT), IELTS (minimum score 5.5), PTE (minimum score 48), or TOEIC (Test of English as an International Communication). *Application deadline:* For fall admission, 8/1 for domestic students, 5/1 for international students; for spring admission, 12/1 for domestic students, 10/1 for international students. Applications are processed on a rolling basis. Application fee: $35 ($40 for international students). Electronic applications accepted. *Expenses:* Tuition, state resident: full-time $9783; part-time $492 per credit hour. Tuition, nonresident: full-time $24,071; part-time $1179 per credit hour. *Financial support:* In 2014–15, 1 fellowship (averaging $8,000 per year), 8 research assistantships (averaging $4,000 per year), 3 teaching assistantships (averaging $4,000 per year) were awarded; career-related internships or fieldwork also available. Financial award application deadline: 4/1. *Unit head:* Dr. Barry Stein, Interim Chairperson, 931-372-3457, Fax: 931-372-6319, E-mail: bstein@tntech.edu. *Application contact:* Shelia K. Kendrick, Coordinator of Graduate Studies, 931-372-3808, Fax: 931-372-3497, E-mail: skendrick@tntech.edu.

Texas A&M University, College of Education and Human Development, Department of Educational Psychology, College Station, TX 77843. Offers bilingual education (M Ed, MS); counseling psychology (PhD); educational psychology (M Ed, MS, PhD); educational technology (M Ed); school psychology (PhD); special education (M Ed, MS). *Accreditation:* APA (one or more programs are accredited). Part-time and evening/weekend programs available. Postbaccalaureate distance learning degree programs offered (no on-campus study). *Faculty:* 45. *Students:* 165 full-time (133 women), 203 part-time (174 women); includes 128 minority (23 Black or African American, non-Hispanic/Latino; 1 American Indian or Alaska Native, non-Hispanic/Latino; 13 Asian, non-Hispanic/Latino; 84 Hispanic/Latino; 1 Native Hawaiian or other Pacific Islander, non-Hispanic/Latino; 6 Two or more races, non-Hispanic/Latino), 48 international. Average age 31. 251 applicants, 57% accepted, 99 enrolled. In 2014, 44 master's, 27 doctorates awarded. *Degree requirements:* For master's, thesis optional; for doctorate, thesis/dissertation. *Entrance requirements:* For master's and doctorate, GRE General Test. Additional exam requirements/recommendations for international students: Required—TOEFL. *Application deadline:* For fall admission, 12/1 for domestic students; for spring admission, 10/15 for domestic students. Application fee: $50 ($90 for international students). Electronic applications accepted. *Expenses:* Tuition, state resident: full-time $4078; part-time $226.55 per credit hour. Tuition, nonresident: full-time $10,594; part-time $577.55 per credit hour. *Required fees:* $2813; $237.70 per credit hour. $278.50 per semester. Tuition and fees vary according to degree level and student level. *Financial support:* In 2014–15, 191 students received support, including 21 fellowships with full and partial tuition reimbursements available (averaging $11,014 per year), 79 research assistantships with full and partial tuition reimbursements available (averaging $6,918 per year), 17 teaching assistantships with full and partial tuition reimbursements available (averaging $4,427 per year); career-related internships or fieldwork, institutionally sponsored loans, scholarships/grants, traineeships, health care benefits, tuition waivers (full and partial), and unspecified assistantships also available. Support available to part-time students. Financial award applicants required to submit FAFSA. *Unit head:* Dr. Victor Willson, Department Head, 979-845-1394, E-mail: v-willson@tamu.edu. *Application contact:* Kristie Stramaski, Senior Academic Advisor, 979-845-1833, E-mail: epsyadvisor@tamu.edu.
Website: http://epsy.tamu.edu

Texas A&M University–Central Texas, Graduate Studies and Research, Killeen, TX 76549. Offers accounting (MS); business administration (MBA); clinical mental health

counseling (MS); criminal justice (MCJ); curriculum and instruction (M Ed); educational administration (M Ed); educational psychology - experimental psychology (MS); history (MA); human resource management (MS); information systems (MS); liberal studies (MS); management and leadership (MS); marriage and family therapy (MS); mathematics (MS); political science (MA); school counseling (M Ed); school psychology (Ed S).

Texas State University, The Graduate College, College of Education, Department of Counseling, Leadership, Adult Education, and School Psychology, Program in School Psychology, San Marcos, TX 78666. Offers SSP. Part-time programs available. *Faculty:* 4 full-time (2 women), 6 part-time/adjunct (2 women). *Students:* 40 full-time (31 women), 14 part-time (13 women); includes 19 minority (2 Black or African American, non-Hispanic/Latino; 2 Asian, non-Hispanic/Latino; 12 Hispanic/Latino; 3 Two or more races, non-Hispanic/Latino), 1 international. Average age 27. 52 applicants, 69% accepted, 13 enrolled. *Entrance requirements:* Additional exam requirements/recommendations for international students: Required—TOEFL (minimum score 550 paper-based; 78 iBT). *Application deadline:* For fall admission, 2/15 for domestic and international students; for spring admission, 10/15 for domestic students, 10/1 for international students. Applications are processed on a rolling basis. Application fee: $40 ($90 for international students). Electronic applications accepted. *Expenses:* Expenses: $8,834 (tuition and fees combined). *Financial support:* In 2014–15, 39 students received support, including 4 research assistantships (averaging $11,968 per year), 5 teaching assistantships (averaging $7,291 per year); career-related internships or fieldwork, Federal Work-Study, and institutionally sponsored loans also available. Support available to part-time students. Financial award application deadline: 4/1; financial award applicants required to submit FAFSA. *Unit head:* Dr. Jon Lasser, Graduate Advisor, 512-245-3413, Fax: 512-245-8872, E-mail: lasser@txstate.edu. *Application contact:* Dr. Andrea Golato, Dean of Graduate School, 512-245-2581, Fax: 512-245-8365, E-mail: gradcollege@txstate.edu.
Website: http://www.txstate.edu/clas/school-psychology-program/Program-Information.html

Texas Woman's University, Graduate School, College of Arts and Sciences, Department of Psychology and Philosophy, Denton, TX 76201. Offers counseling psychology (MA, PhD); school psychology (PhD, SSP). *Accreditation:* APA (one or more programs are accredited). Terminal master's awarded for partial completion of doctoral program. *Degree requirements:* For master's, comprehensive exam (for some programs), thesis (for some programs); for doctorate, comprehensive exam, thesis/dissertation, internship, residency. *Entrance requirements:* For master's, GRE (preferred minimum score 153 [500 old version] Verbal, 144 [500 old version] Quantitative, 4 Analytical), BA/BS or 18 hours in psychology; minimum GPA of 3.0, 3.5 in psychology classes; 3 letters of reference; curriculum vitae; essays; for doctorate, GRE (preferred minimum score 153 [500 old version] Verbal, 144 [500 old version] Quantitative, 4 Analytical), 3 letters of reference, minimum GPA of 3.0 overall and 3.5 in psychology classes, MA in psychology or related discipline with thesis, curriculum vitae, essays. Additional exam requirements/recommendations for international students: Required—TOEFL (minimum score 550 paper-based; 79 iBT). Electronic applications accepted. *Faculty research:* Women's anger, school neuropsychological theory and assessment, body image dysfunction, traumatic stress, classical ethics, mental health and behavioral needs of adolescents in alternative education.

Touro College, Graduate School of Psychology, New York, NY 10006. Offers general psychology (MS); industrial/organizational psychology (MS); mental health counseling (MS); school counseling (MS); school psychology (MS). *Students:* 101 full-time (80 women), 81 part-time (66 women); includes 76 minority (41 Black or African American, non-Hispanic/Latino; 1 American Indian or Alaska Native, non-Hispanic/Latino; 8 Asian, non-Hispanic/Latino; 26 Hispanic/Latino), 2 international. *Unit head:* Dr. Richard Waxman, Dean, 212-242-4668 Ext. 6077, E-mail: richard.waxman@touro.edu.
Website: http://gsp.touro.edu/

Towson University, Program in School Psychology, Towson, MD 21252-0001. Offers CAS. Part-time and evening/weekend programs available. *Students:* 14 full-time (10 women), 11 part-time (all women); includes 6 minority (2 Black or African American, non-Hispanic/Latino; 2 Asian, non-Hispanic/Latino; 2 Hispanic/Latino). *Entrance requirements:* For degree, GRE General Test, minimum GPA of 3.2, interview, 21 credits of course work in psychology, 3 letters of recommendation, letter of intent. *Application deadline:* For fall admission, 1/15 for domestic students. Application fee: $45. Electronic applications accepted. *Financial support:* Application deadline: 4/1. *Unit head:* Dr. Susan Bartels, Graduate Program Director, 410-704-3070, E-mail: sbartels@towson.edu. *Application contact:* Alicia Arkell-Kleis, Information Contact, 410-704-6004, E-mail: grads@towson.edu.
Website: http://grad.towson.edu/program/master/psyc-scpy-ma/

Trinity University, Department of Education, Master of Arts in School Psychology Program, San Antonio, TX 78212-7200. Offers MA. *Accreditation:* NCATE. *Students:* 20 full-time (19 women), 11 part-time (10 women); includes 16 minority (1 Black or African American, non-Hispanic/Latino; 2 Asian, non-Hispanic/Latino; 13 Hispanic/Latino). Average age 26. In 2014, 8 master's awarded. *Application deadline:* For fall admission, 2/1 for domestic and international students. Application fee: $50. *Financial support:* Application deadline: 4/1. *Unit head:* Dr. Terry Robertson, Director, 210-999-7595, E-mail: terry.robertson@trinity.edu. *Application contact:* 210-999-7501, E-mail: smireles@trinity.edu.
Website: http://new.trinity.edu/academics/departments/education/master-arts-school-psychology

Troy University, Graduate School, College of Education, Program in Counseling and Psychology, Troy, AL 36082. Offers agency counseling (Ed S); clinical mental health (MS); community counseling (MS, Ed S); corrections counseling (MS); rehabilitation counseling (MS); school psychology (MS, Ed S); school psychometry (MS); social service counseling (MS); student affairs counseling (MS); substance abuse counseling (MS). *Accreditation:* ACA; CORE; NCATE. Part-time and evening/weekend programs available. *Faculty:* 41 full-time (18 women), 32 part-time/adjunct (18 women). *Students:* 358 full-time (286 women), 503 part-time (425 women); includes 572 minority (481 Black or African American, non-Hispanic/Latino; 3 American Indian or Alaska Native, non-Hispanic/Latino; 5 Asian, non-Hispanic/Latino; 62 Hispanic/Latino; 21 Two or more races, non-Hispanic/Latino). Average age 34. 248 applicants, 86% accepted, 139 enrolled. In 2014, 212 master's, 4 other advanced degrees awarded. *Degree requirements:* For master's, comprehensive exam, thesis. *Entrance requirements:* For master's, GRE (minimum score of 850 on old exam or 290 on new exam), GMAT (minimum score of 380), or MAT (minimum score of 385), bachelor's degree; minimum undergraduate GPA of 2.5 or 3.0 on last 30 semester hours, letter of recommendation. Additional exam requirements/recommendations for international students: Required—TOEFL (minimum score 523 paper-based; 70 iBT), IELTS (minimum score 6). *Application deadline:* Applications are processed on a rolling basis. Application fee: $50. Electronic applications accepted. *Expenses:* Tuition, state resident: full-time $6570; part-time $365 per credit hour. Tuition, nonresident: full-time $13,140; part-time $730 per credit hour. *Required fees:* $365 per credit hour. *Unit head:* Dr. Andrew Creamer, Chair, 334-670-3350, Fax: 334-670-3291, E-mail: acreamer@troy.edu. *Application*

contact: Jessica A. Kimbro, Director of Graduate Admissions, 334-670-3178, E-mail: jacord@troy.edu.

Tufts University, Graduate School of Arts and Sciences, Department of Education, Program in School Psychology, Medford, MA 02155. Offers MA, Ed S. *Faculty:* 4 full-time (2 women), 6 part-time/adjunct (5 women). *Students:* 42 full-time (33 women), 4 part-time (2 women); includes 13 minority (2 Black or African American, non-Hispanic/Latino; 7 Asian, non-Hispanic/Latino; 2 Hispanic/Latino; 2 Two or more races, non-Hispanic/Latino), 1 international. Average age 25. 79 applicants, 34% accepted, 15 enrolled. In 2014, 15 master's, 25 other advanced degrees awarded. *Entrance requirements:* For master's, GRE General Test. Additional exam requirements/recommendations for international students: Required—TOEFL (minimum score 550 paper-based; 80 iBT), IELTS (minimum score 6.5). *Application deadline:* For fall admission, 1/2 for domestic and international students; for spring admission, 10/15 for domestic students. Applications are processed on a rolling basis. Application fee: $75. Electronic applications accepted. *Expenses: Tuition:* Full-time $45,590; part-time $1161 per credit hour. *Required fees:* $782. Full-time tuition and fees vary according to degree level, program and student level. Part-time tuition and fees vary according to course load. *Financial support:* Federal Work-Study, scholarships/grants, and tuition waivers (full and partial) available. Financial award application deadline: 1/2. *Unit head:* Dr. Steve Luz-Alterman, Graduate Program Director. *Application contact:* Office of Graduate Admissions, 617-627-3395, E-mail: gradadmissions@tufts.edu. Website: http://ase.tufts.edu/education/programs/schoolPsych/

Union College, Graduate Programs, Department of Psychology, Barbourville, KY 40906-1499. Offers clinical psychology (MA); counseling psychology (MA); school psychology (MA).

University at Albany, State University of New York, School of Education, Department of Educational and Counseling Psychology, Albany, NY 12222-0001. Offers counseling psychology (MS, PhD), including counseling psychology (PhD), mental health counseling (MS); educational psychology (PhD); educational psychology and methodology (MS); educational research (CAS); school psychology (Psy D, CAS); special education (MS, PhD). *Accreditation:* APA (one or more programs are accredited). Evening/weekend programs available. *Degree requirements:* For doctorate, thesis/dissertation. *Entrance requirements:* For doctorate, GRE General Test. Additional exam requirements/recommendations for international students: Required—TOEFL (minimum score 550 paper-based). Electronic applications accepted.

The University of Akron, Graduate School, College of Health Professions, School of Counseling, Akron, OH 44325. Offers classroom guidance for teachers (MA, MS); clinical mental health counseling (MA, MS); counseling psychology (PhD); counselor education and supervision (PhD); marriage and family therapy (MA, MS); school counseling (MA, MS). *Faculty:* 9 full-time (6 women), 28 part-time/adjunct (22 women). *Students:* 158 full-time (131 women), 150 part-time (123 women); includes 59 minority (40 Black or African American, non-Hispanic/Latino; 1 American Indian or Alaska Native, non-Hispanic/Latino; 3 Asian, non-Hispanic/Latino; 6 Hispanic/Latino; 9 Two or more races, non-Hispanic/Latino), 6 international. Average age 30. 207 applicants, 36% accepted, 56 enrolled. In 2014, 79 master's, 6 doctorates awarded. Terminal master's awarded for partial completion of doctoral program. *Degree requirements:* For master's, comprehensive exam; for doctorate, one foreign language, comprehensive exam, thesis/dissertation, written and oral exams. *Entrance requirements:* For master's, minimum GPA of 2.75, three letters of recommendation; for doctorate, GRE, interview, minimum GPA of 3.25, three letters of recommendation, resume. Additional exam requirements/recommendations for international students: Required—TOEFL (minimum score 550 paper-based; 79 iBT), IELTS (minimum score 6.5). *Application deadline:* For fall admission, 12/1 for domestic and international students; for spring admission, 10/1 for domestic and international students. Applications are processed on a rolling basis. Application fee: $45 ($70 for international students). Electronic applications accepted. *Expenses:* Tuition: state resident: full-time $7578; part-time $421 per credit hour. Tuition, nonresident: full-time $12,977; part-time $721 per credit hour. *Required fees:* $1388; $35 per credit hour. Tuition and fees vary according to course load. *Financial support:* In 2014–15, 33 teaching assistantships with full tuition reimbursements were awarded. *Faculty research:* Mindfulness, traumatology, suicidality, multiculturalism, couple and family therapy/counseling. *Unit head:* Dr. Karin Jordan, Chair, 330-972-5515, E-mail: kj25@uakron.edu. Website: http://www.uakron.edu/education/academic-programs/counseling/index.dot

University of Alberta, Faculty of Graduate Studies and Research, Department of Educational Psychology, Edmonton, AB T6G 2E1, Canada. Offers counseling psychology (M Ed, PhD); educational psychology (M Ed, PhD); instructional technology (M Ed); school counseling (M Ed); school psychology (M Ed, PhD); special education (M Ed, PhD); special education-deafness studies (M Ed); teaching English as a second language (M Ed). Part-time programs available. *Degree requirements:* For master's, thesis optional; for doctorate, comprehensive exam, thesis/dissertation. *Entrance requirements:* For master's and doctorate, minimum GPA of 3.0. Additional exam requirements/recommendations for international students: Required—TOEFL. *Faculty research:* Human learning, development and assessment.

The University of Arizona, College of Education, Department of Disability and Psychoeducational Studies, Program in School Psychology, Tucson, AZ 85721. Offers PhD, Ed S. Part-time programs available. *Entrance requirements:* For doctorate, GRE General Test; for Ed S, minimum GPA of 3.5, 3 letters of recommendation, curriculum vitae, writing sample. Additional exam requirements/recommendations for international students: Required—TOEFL (minimum score 550 paper-based; 79 iBT). Electronic applications accepted.

The University of British Columbia, Faculty of Education, Department of Educational and Counseling Psychology, and Special Education, Vancouver, BC V6T 1Z1, Canada. Offers counseling psychology (M Ed, MA, PhD); development, learning and culture (PhD); guidance studies (Diploma); human development, learning and culture (M Ed, MA); measurement and evaluation and research methodology (M Ed); measurement, evaluation and research methodology (MA); measurement, evaluation, and research methodology (PhD); school psychology (M Ed, MA, PhD); special education (M Ed, MA, PhD, Diploma). Part-time programs available. *Degree requirements:* For master's, thesis (for some programs); for doctorate, comprehensive exam, thesis/dissertation. *Entrance requirements:* For master's, GRE General Test (counseling psychology MA); for doctorate, GRE General Test. Additional exam requirements/recommendations for international students: Required—TOEFL. Electronic applications accepted. *Faculty research:* Women, family, social problems, career transition, stress and coping problems.

University of Calgary, Faculty of Graduate Studies, Werklund School of Education, Division of Applied Psychology, Calgary, AB T2N 1N4, Canada. Offers counseling psychology (M Sc, MC, PhD); school and applied child psychology (M Ed, M Sc, PhD). Part-time programs available. *Degree requirements:* For master's, thesis (for some programs), final oral exam; for doctorate, thesis/dissertation, candidacy exam, final oral exam. *Entrance requirements:* For master's, minimum GPA of 3.0, 3 letters of reference; for doctorate, minimum GPA of 3.5, 3 letters of reference. *Faculty research:* Counselor education, family life studies, learning and cognition.

University of California, Riverside, Graduate Division, Graduate School of Education, Riverside, CA 92521-0102. Offers autism (M Ed); diversity and equity (M Ed); education specialist (Credential); education, society, and culture (MA, PhD); educational psychology (MA, PhD); general education (M Ed); higher education administration and policy (M Ed, PhD); multiple subject (Credential); reading (M Ed); school psychology (PhD); single subject (Credential); special education (M Ed, MA, PhD); TESOL (M Ed). *Faculty:* 19 full-time (9 women), 20 part-time/adjunct (15 women). *Students:* 246 full-time (185 women); includes 142 minority (8 Black or African American, non-Hispanic/Latino; 38 Asian, non-Hispanic/Latino; 80 Hispanic/Latino; 16 Two or more races, non-Hispanic/Latino), 20 international. Average age 31. 303 applicants, 68% accepted, 164 enrolled. In 2014, 56 master's, 13 doctorates, 69 other advanced degrees awarded. Terminal master's awarded for partial completion of doctoral program. *Degree requirements:* For master's, thesis optional, comprehensive exams or thesis (MA), case study or analytical report (M Ed); for doctorate, thesis/dissertation, written and oral qualifying exams, college teaching practicum. *Entrance requirements:* For master's, GRE General Test (for MA); CBEST and CSET (for M Ed in general education only), UCR Extension TESOL certificate (for M Ed with TESOL emphasis only); for doctorate, GRE General Test, writing sample; for Credential, CBEST, CSET. Additional exam requirements/recommendations for international students: Required—TOEFL (minimum score 550 paper-based; 80 iBT), IELTS (minimum score 7). *Application deadline:* For fall admission, 9/1 for domestic students, 5/1 for international students; for winter admission, 11/15 for domestic students, 7/1 for international students; for spring admission, 3/1 for domestic students, 10/1 for international students. Applications are processed on a rolling basis. Application fee: $80 ($100 for international students). Electronic applications accepted. *Expenses:* Tuition, state resident: full-time $5399. Tuition, nonresident: full-time $10,433. *Financial support:* In 2014–15, 87 students received support, including 38 fellowships with full tuition reimbursements available, 20 research assistantships with full tuition reimbursements available (averaging $15,413 per year), 5 teaching assistantships with full tuition reimbursements available (averaging $18,538 per year); career-related internships or fieldwork, Federal Work-Study, institutionally sponsored loans, scholarships/grants, and unspecified assistantships also available. Financial award application deadline: 1/5. *Faculty research:* Responsiveness to intervention, faculty core, response to intervention of English language learners, advanced modeling techniques, study on social capital, trust, and motivation. *Total annual research expenditures:* $1.4 million. *Unit head:* Prof. Thomas Smith, Dean and Professor, 951-827-5802, Fax: 951-827-3942, E-mail: thomas.smith@ucr.edu. *Application contact:* Prof. Michael Orosco, Assistant Professor and Graduate Advisor of Admissions, 951-827-6362, Fax: 951-827-3291, E-mail: edgrad@ucr.edu. Website: http://www.education.ucr.edu/

University of California, Santa Barbara, Graduate Division, Gevirtz Graduate School of Education, Santa Barbara, CA 93106-9490. Offers counseling, clinical and school psychology (MA, PhD, Credential), including clinical psychology (PhD), counseling psychology (MA, PhD), pupil personnel services (Credential), school psychology (PhD); education (MA, PhD); teacher education (M Ed, Credential), including multiple subject teaching (Credential), single subject teaching (Credential), special education (Credential), teaching (M Ed); MA/PhD. *Accreditation:* APA (one or more programs are accredited). Terminal master's awarded for partial completion of doctoral program. *Degree requirements:* For master's, comprehensive exam (for some programs), thesis (for some programs); for doctorate, comprehensive exam (for some programs), thesis/dissertation. *Entrance requirements:* For master's and doctorate, GRE; for Credential, GRE or MAT, CSET, CBEST. Additional exam requirements/recommendations for international students: Required—TOEFL (minimum score 550 paper-based; 80 iBT), IELTS (minimum score 7). Electronic applications accepted. *Faculty research:* Needs of diverse students, school accountability and leadership, school violence, language learning and literacy, science/math education.

University of Central Arkansas, Graduate School, College of Health and Behavioral Sciences, Department of Counseling and Psychology, Program in School Psychology, Conway, AR 72035-0001. Offers MS, PhD, PMC. *Accreditation:* APA; NCATE. Terminal master's awarded for partial completion of doctoral program. *Degree requirements:* For master's, comprehensive exam, thesis optional; for doctorate, comprehensive exam, thesis/dissertation. *Entrance requirements:* For master's, GRE General Test, minimum GPA of 2.7; for doctorate, GRE General Test. Additional exam requirements/recommendations for international students: Required—TOEFL (minimum score 550 paper-based). Electronic applications accepted.

University of Central Florida, College of Education and Human Performance, Department of Educational and Human Sciences, Program in School Psychology, Orlando, FL 32816. Offers Ed S. Part-time and evening/weekend programs available. *Students:* 45 full-time (41 women); includes 14 minority (3 Black or African American, non-Hispanic/Latino; 2 Asian, non-Hispanic/Latino; 9 Hispanic/Latino), 1 international. Average age 25. 76 applicants, 22% accepted, 15 enrolled. In 2014, 16 Ed Ss awarded. *Degree requirements:* For Ed S, thesis or alternative, practicum, internship. *Entrance requirements:* For degree, GRE General Test, minimum GPA of 3.0, resume, interview. Additional exam requirements/recommendations for international students: Required—TOEFL. *Application deadline:* For fall admission, 3/1 for domestic students. Application fee: $30. Electronic applications accepted. *Expenses:* Tuition, state resident: part-time $288.16 per credit hour. Tuition, nonresident: part-time $1073.31 per credit hour. *Financial support:* In 2014–15, 8 students received support, including 1 fellowship with partial tuition reimbursement available (averaging $5,000 per year), 7 research assistantships with partial tuition reimbursements available (averaging $7,200 per year); career-related internships or fieldwork, Federal Work-Study, institutionally sponsored loans, tuition waivers (partial), and unspecified assistantships also available. Financial award application deadline: 3/1; financial award applicants required to submit FAFSA. *Unit head:* Dr. Oliver Edwards, Program Coordinator, 407-823-2740, E-mail: oliver.edwards@ucf.edu. *Application contact:* Barbara Rodriguez Lamas, Director, Admissions and Student Services, 407-823-2766, Fax: 407-823-6442, E-mail: gradadmissions@ucf.edu.

University of Central Oklahoma, The Jackson College of Graduate Studies, College of Education and Professional Studies, Department of Psychology, Edmond, OK 73034-5209. Offers counseling psychology (MA); experimental psychology (MA); forensic psychology (MA); general psychology (MA); school psychology (MA). *Degree requirements:* For master's, thesis (for some programs). *Entrance requirements:* For master's, GRE. Additional exam requirements/recommendations for international students: Required—TOEFL (minimum score 550 paper-based; 79 iBT), IELTS (minimum score 6.5). Electronic applications accepted. *Faculty research:* Psychopharmacology, computer psychometrics, health psychology research.

University of Cincinnati, Graduate School, College of Education, Criminal Justice, and Human Services, Division of Human Services, Program in School Psychology, Cincinnati, OH 45221. Offers PhD, Ed S. *Accreditation:* NCATE. Part-time programs available. *Degree requirements:* For doctorate, comprehensive exam, thesis/dissertation. *Entrance requirements:* For doctorate, GRE General Test, GRE Subject Test. Additional exam requirements/recommendations for international students: Required—TOEFL (minimum score 520 paper-based; 68 iBT), OEPT. Electronic

applications accepted. *Faculty research:* School psychology services delivery, direct assessment and intervention.

University of Colorado Denver, School of Education and Human Development, Program in Counseling Psychology and Counselor Education, Denver, CO 80217. Offers counseling (MA), including clinical mental health counseling, couple and family counseling, multicultural counseling, school counseling; school counseling (MA). *Accreditation:* ACA; NCATE. Part-time and evening/weekend programs available. *Students:* 196 full-time (158 women), 30 part-time (24 women); includes 42 minority (10 Black or African American, non-Hispanic/Latino; 4 Asian, non-Hispanic/Latino; 24 Hispanic/Latino; 4 Two or more races, non-Hispanic/Latino). Average age 30. 182 applicants, 30% accepted, 31 enrolled. In 2014, 72 master's awarded. *Degree requirements:* For master's, comprehensive exam (for some programs), thesis or alternative, 63-66 hours. *Entrance requirements:* For master's, GRE or MAT (unless applicant already holds a graduate degree), letters of recommendation, interview, resume, transcripts from all colleges/universities attended. Additional exam requirements/recommendations for international students: Required—TOEFL (minimum score 525 paper-based; 71 iBT); Recommended—IELTS (minimum score 6.3). *Application deadline:* For fall admission, 1/15 for domestic students, 1/1 for international students; for spring admission, 9/15 for domestic students, 9/1 for international students. Application fee: $50 ($75 for international students). Electronic applications accepted. *Expenses:* Expenses: Contact institution. *Financial support:* In 2014–15, 9 students received support. Research assistantships, Federal Work-Study, institutionally sponsored loans, scholarships/grants, and traineeships available. Financial award application deadline: 4/1; financial award applicants required to submit FAFSA. *Faculty research:* Spiritual issues in counseling, multicultural and diversity issues in counseling, adolescent suicide, career development. *Unit head:* Farah Ibrahim, Counseling Professor, 303-315-6329, E-mail: farah.ibrahim@ucdenver.edu. *Application contact:* Student Services Coordinator, 303-315-6300, Fax: 303-315-6311, E-mail: education@ucdenver.edu.
Website: http://www.ucdenver.edu/academics/colleges/SchoolOfEducation/Academics/MASTERS/counseling/Pages/default.aspx

University of Colorado Denver, School of Education and Human Development, Programs in Educational and School Psychology, Denver, CO 80217. Offers educational psychology (MA), including educational assessment, educational psychology, human development, human learning, partner schools, research and evaluation; school psychology (Ed S). Part-time and evening/weekend programs available. *Students:* 187 full-time (159 women), 64 part-time (49 women); includes 40 minority (2 Black or African American, non-Hispanic/Latino; 1 Asian, non-Hispanic/Latino; 25 Hispanic/Latino; 12 Two or more races, non-Hispanic/Latino), 8 international. Average age 29. 200 applicants, 73% accepted, 112 enrolled. In 2014, 49 master's, 10 other advanced degrees awarded. *Degree requirements:* For master's, comprehensive exam, 9 hours of core courses, embedded within a minimum of 36 to 38 hours of relevant coursework, including an educational psychology practicum, independent study project or thesis (recommended); for Ed S, comprehensive exam, minimum of 75 semester hours (61 hours of coursework, 6 of 500-hour practicum in field, and 8 of 1200-hour internship); PRAXIS II. *Entrance requirements:* For master's, GRE if undergraduate GPA below 2.75, resume, three letters of recommendation, transcripts; for Ed S, GRE, resume, letters of recommendation, transcripts. Additional exam requirements/recommendations for international students: Required—TOEFL (minimum score 537 paper-based; 75 iBT); Recommended—IELTS (minimum score 6.5). *Application deadline:* For fall admission, 4/15 for domestic students, 4/1 for international students; for spring admission, 9/15 for domestic students, 9/1 for international students. Application fee: $50 ($75 for international students). Electronic applications accepted. *Expenses:* Expenses: Contact institution. *Financial support:* In 2014–15, 21 students received support. Research assistantships, Federal Work-Study, institutionally sponsored loans, scholarships/grants, and traineeships available. Financial award application deadline: 4/1; financial award applicants required to submit FAFSA. *Faculty research:* Crisis response and intervention, school violence prevention, immigrant experience, educational environments for English language learners, culturally competent assessment and intervention, child and youth suicide. *Unit head:* Phil Strain, Professor of Educational Psychology, 303-315-4935, E-mail: phil.strain@ucdenver.edu. *Application contact:* Jason Clark, Director of Recruitment and Retention, 303-315-0183, E-mail: jason.clark@ucdenver.edu.
Website: http://www.ucdenver.edu/academics/colleges/SchoolOfEducation/Academics/MASTERS/EPSY/Pages/default.aspx

University of Connecticut, Graduate School, Neag School of Education, Department of Educational Psychology, Program in School Psychology, Storrs, CT 06269. Offers MA, PhD, Post-Master's Certificate. *Accreditation:* APA; NCATE. Terminal master's awarded for partial completion of doctoral program. *Degree requirements:* For master's, comprehensive exam, thesis or alternative; for doctorate, thesis/dissertation. *Entrance requirements:* For doctorate, GRE General Test. Additional exam requirements/recommendations for international students: Required—TOEFL (minimum score 550 paper-based). Electronic applications accepted.

University of Dayton, Department of Counselor Education and Human Services, Dayton, OH 45469. Offers clinical mental health counseling (MS Ed); college student personnel (MS Ed); higher education administration (MS Ed); human services (MS Ed); school counseling (MS Ed); school psychology (MS Ed, Ed S). *Accreditation:* ACA; NCATE. Part-time and evening/weekend programs available. *Faculty:* 11 full-time (7 women), 34 part-time/adjunct (24 women). *Students:* 199 full-time (161 women), 113 part-time (95 women); includes 58 minority (49 Black or African American, non-Hispanic/Latino; 1 Asian, non-Hispanic/Latino; 7 Hispanic/Latino; 1 Two or more races, non-Hispanic/Latino), 8 international. Average age 31. 295 applicants, 47% accepted, 103 enrolled. In 2014, 146 master's, 8 Ed Ss awarded. *Degree requirements:* For master's, comprehensive exam (for some programs), thesis (for some programs), exit exam. *Entrance requirements:* For master's, MAT or GRE (if GPA less than 2.75), interview, writing sample. Additional exam requirements/recommendations for international students: Required—TOEFL (minimum score 550 paper-based; 80 iBT). *Application deadline:* For fall admission, 4/10 for domestic students, 4/10 priority date for international students; for winter admission, 9/10 for domestic students, 7/1 for international students; for spring admission, 9/10 for domestic students, 9/10 priority date for international students. Application fee: $0 ($50 for international students). Electronic applications accepted. *Expenses: Tuition:* Full-time $10,176; part-time $848 per credit. *Required fees:* $25; $25 per course. Part-time tuition and fees vary according to course level, course load, degree level and program. *Financial support:* In 2014–15, 10 research assistantships with full tuition reimbursements (averaging $8,720 per year) were awarded; career-related internships or fieldwork, institutionally sponsored loans, health care benefits, and unspecified assistantships also available. Financial award application deadline: 3/1; financial award applicants required to submit FAFSA. *Faculty research:* Mindfulness, forgiveness in relationships, positive psychology in couples counseling, traumatic brain injury responses, college student development. *Unit head:* Dr. Molly Schaller, Chairperson, 937-229-3644, Fax: 937-229-1055, E-mail: mschaller1@udayton.edu. *Application contact:* Kathleen Brown, Administrative Assistant, 937-229-3644, Fax: 937-229-1055, E-mail: kbrown1@udayton.edu.
Website: https://www.udayton.edu/education/departments_and_programs/edc/

University of Delaware, College of Education and Human Development, School of Education, Newark, DE 19716. Offers education (PhD); educational leadership (Ed D); higher education (M Ed); instruction (MI); reading (M Ed); school leadership (M Ed); school psychology (MA, Ed S); teaching English as a second language (TESL) (MA). *Accreditation:* NCATE. Part-time and evening/weekend programs available. Terminal master's awarded for partial completion of doctoral program. *Degree requirements:* For master's, comprehensive exam (for some programs), thesis (for some programs); for doctorate, comprehensive exam (for some programs), thesis/dissertation. *Entrance requirements:* For master's and doctorate, GRE, 3 letters of recommendation. Additional exam requirements/recommendations for international students: Required—TOEFL (minimum score 600 paper-based). Electronic applications accepted. *Faculty research:* Teacher education; curriculum theory and development; community based education models, educational leadership.

University of Denver, Morgridge College of Education, Denver, CO 80208. Offers child, family and school psychology (MA, Ed S); counseling psychology (PhD); curriculum and instruction (MA, PhD); curriculum instruction and teaching (Certificate); educational leadership and policy studies (MA, PhD); library and information science (MLIS). *Accreditation:* ALA; APA (one or more programs are accredited). Part-time and evening/weekend programs available. Postbaccalaureate distance learning degree programs offered (no on-campus study). *Faculty:* 41 full-time (27 women), 62 part-time/adjunct (43 women). *Students:* 506 full-time (387 women), 325 part-time (237 women); includes 191 minority (50 Black or African American, non-Hispanic/Latino; 9 American Indian or Alaska Native, non-Hispanic/Latino; 21 Asian, non-Hispanic/Latino; 91 Hispanic/Latino; 3 Native Hawaiian or other Pacific Islander, non-Hispanic/Latino; 17 Two or more races, non-Hispanic/Latino), 23 international. Average age 32. 975 applicants, 73% accepted, 410 enrolled. In 2014, 234 master's, 38 doctorates, 178 other advanced degrees awarded. Terminal master's awarded for partial completion of doctoral program. *Degree requirements:* For master's, comprehensive exam; for doctorate, 2 foreign languages, comprehensive exam, thesis/dissertation. *Entrance requirements:* For master's and doctorate, GRE General Test or GMAT. Additional exam requirements/recommendations for international students: Required—TOEFL (minimum score 550 paper-based; 80 iBT). *Application deadline:* Applications are processed on a rolling basis. Application fee: $65. Electronic applications accepted. *Expenses:* Expenses: $1,199 per credit hour. *Financial support:* In 2014–15, 674 students received support, including 43 research assistantships with full and partial tuition reimbursements available (averaging $9,090 per year), 80 teaching assistantships with full and partial tuition reimbursements available (averaging $6,084 per year); career-related internships or fieldwork, Federal Work-Study, institutionally sponsored loans, scholarships/grants, and unspecified assistantships also available. Support available to part-time students. Financial award application deadline: 2/15; financial award applicants required to submit FAFSA. *Faculty research:* Principal and teacher preparation, development and assessments, gifted education, service-learning, early childhood, mathematics education, access to higher education. *Unit head:* Dr. Karen Riley, Interim Dean, 303-871-3665, E-mail: karen.riley@du.edu. *Application contact:* Jodi Dye, Assistant Director of Admissions, 303-871-2510, E-mail: jodi.dye@du.edu.
Website: http://morgridge.du.edu/

University of Detroit Mercy, College of Liberal Arts and Education, Department of Psychology, Program in School Psychology, Detroit, MI 48221. Offers Spec.

University of Florida, Graduate School, College of Education, School of Special Education, School Psychology and Early Childhood Studies, Gainesville, FL 32611. Offers early childhood education (M Ed, MAE); school psychology (M Ed, MAE, Ed D, PhD, Ed S); special education (M Ed, MAE, Ed D, PhD, Ed S). *Accreditation:* NCATE. Part-time and evening/weekend programs available. Postbaccalaureate distance learning degree programs offered (no on-campus study). *Faculty:* 22 full-time (17 women), 1 (woman) part-time/adjunct. *Students:* 121 full-time (113 women), 40 part-time (39 women); includes 52 minority (21 Black or African American, non-Hispanic/Latino; 7 Asian, non-Hispanic/Latino; 24 Hispanic/Latino), 9 international. 110 applicants, 42% accepted, 20 enrolled. In 2014, 59 master's, 16 doctorates, 13 other advanced degrees awarded. *Degree requirements:* For master's, comprehensive exam (for some programs), thesis (MAE); for doctorate, comprehensive exam, thesis/dissertation. *Entrance requirements:* For master's and doctorate, GRE General Test, minimum GPA of 3.0; for Ed S, GRE General Test. Additional exam requirements/recommendations for international students: Required—TOEFL (minimum score 550 paper-based; 80 iBT), IELTS (minimum score 6). *Application deadline:* For fall admission, 12/15 priority date for domestic students, 12/15 for international students. Applications are processed on a rolling basis. Application fee: $30. Electronic applications accepted. *Financial support:* In 2014–15, 8 fellowships, 34 research assistantships, 26 teaching assistantships were awarded; career-related internships or fieldwork and unspecified assistantships also available. Financial award application deadline: 11/15; financial award applicants required to submit FAFSA. *Faculty research:* Teacher quality/teacher education, early childhood, autism, academic and behavioral assessment and interventions. *Total annual research expenditures:* $38.2 million. *Unit head:* Jean Crockett, PhD, Chair and Associate Professor, 352-273-4292, Fax: 352-392-2655, E-mail: crocketj@coe.ufl.edu. *Application contact:* Nancy L. Waldron, PhD, Professor and Graduate Coordinator, 352-273-4284, Fax: 352-392-2655, E-mail: waldron@coe.ufl.edu.
Website: http://education.ufl.edu/sespecs/

University of Hartford, College of Arts and Sciences, Department of Psychology, Program in School Psychology, West Hartford, CT 06117-1599. Offers MS. *Accreditation:* NCATE. Part-time programs available. *Degree requirements:* For master's, comprehensive exam. *Entrance requirements:* For master's, GRE General Test, GRE Subject Test, minimum GPA of 3.0, 3 letters of recommendation. Additional exam requirements/recommendations for international students: Required—TOEFL (minimum score 550 paper-based). Electronic applications accepted. *Faculty research:* Family therapy, child developments, clinical supervision.

University of Houston–Clear Lake, School of Human Sciences and Humanities, Programs in Human Sciences, Houston, TX 77058-1002. Offers behavioral sciences (MA), including criminology, cross cultural studies, general psychology, sociology; clinical psychology (MA); criminology (MA); cross cultural studies (MA); family therapy (MA); fitness and human performance (MA); school psychology (MA). *Accreditation:* AAMFT/COAMFTE. Part-time and evening/weekend programs available. Postbaccalaureate distance learning degree programs offered (minimal on-campus study). *Degree requirements:* For master's, thesis or alternative. *Entrance requirements:* For master's, GRE General Test. Additional exam requirements/recommendations for international students: Required—TOEFL (minimum score 550 paper-based). Electronic applications accepted. *Faculty research:* Smoking cessation, adolescent sexuality, white collar crime, serial murder, human factors/human computer interaction.

University of Houston–Victoria, School of Arts and Sciences, Program in Psychology, Victoria, TX 77901-4450. Offers counseling psychology (MA); forensic psychology (MA); school psychology (MA). Part-time and evening/weekend programs available. Postbaccalaureate distance learning degree programs offered (minimal on-campus study). *Degree requirements:* For master's, project or thesis. *Entrance requirements:* For master's, GRE General Test. Additional exam requirements/recommendations for

international students: Required—TOEFL (minimum score 550 paper-based). Electronic applications accepted.

The University of Iowa, Graduate College, College of Education, Department of Psychological and Quantitative Foundations, Iowa City, IA 52242-1316. Offers counseling psychology (PhD); educational measurement and statistics (MA, PhD); educational psychology (MA, PhD); school psychology (PhD, Ed S). *Accreditation:* APA. *Degree requirements:* For master's, thesis optional, exam; for doctorate, comprehensive exam, thesis/dissertation; for Ed S, exam. *Entrance requirements:* For master's, doctorate, and Ed S, GRE General Test, minimum GPA of 3.0. Additional exam requirements/recommendations for international students: Required—TOEFL (minimum score 550 paper-based; 81 iBT). Electronic applications accepted.

The University of Kansas, Graduate Studies, School of Education, Department of Psychology and Research in Education, Program in School Psychology, Lawrence, KS 66045. Offers PhD, Ed S. *Accreditation:* APA (one or more programs are accredited); NCATE. *Faculty:* 15 full-time, 5 part-time/adjunct. *Students:* 38 full-time (28 women), 2 part-time (both women); includes 3 minority (all Hispanic/Latino), 3 international. Average age 26. 49 applicants, 51% accepted, 14 enrolled. In 2014, 2 doctorates, 10 other advanced degrees awarded. *Degree requirements:* For doctorate, comprehensive exam, thesis/dissertation; for Ed S, comprehensive exam. *Entrance requirements:* For doctorate, GRE General Test; for Ed S, GRE General Test, minimum GPA of 3.0. Additional exam requirements/recommendations for international students: Required—TOEFL. *Application deadline:* For fall admission, 12/15 for domestic and international students. Application fee: $55 ($65 for international students). Electronic applications accepted. *Financial support:* Fellowships, research assistantships with full and partial tuition reimbursements, and teaching assistantships with full and partial tuition reimbursements available. Financial award application deadline: 2/1. *Faculty research:* Classroom management, anxiety in children and youth, child behavior and learning problems, behavioral and personality assessment, home/school/community partnerships. *Unit head:* Dr. Steven Lee, Chair, 785-864-3931, Fax: 785-864-3820, E-mail: swlee@ku.edu. *Application contact:* Penny Fritts, Admissions Coordinator, 785-864-9645, E-mail: fritts@ku.edu.
Website: http://www.soe.ku.edu/PRE/

University of Kentucky, Graduate School, College of Education, Program in Educational and Counseling Psychology, Lexington, KY 40506-0032. Offers counseling psychology (MS, PhD, Ed S); educational psychology (MS, PhD); school psychology (PhD, Ed S). *Accreditation:* APA (one or more programs are accredited); NCATE. *Degree requirements:* For doctorate, comprehensive exam, thesis/dissertation; for Ed S, comprehensive exam. *Entrance requirements:* For doctorate, GRE General Test, minimum graduate GPA of 3.0; for Ed S, GRE General Test. Additional exam requirements/recommendations for international students: Required—TOEFL (minimum score 550 paper-based). Electronic applications accepted.

University of La Verne, College of Education and Organizational Leadership, Program in Educational Counseling, La Verne, CA 91750-4443. Offers educational counseling (MS); pupil personnel services (Credential); school psychology (MS). Part-time programs available. *Faculty:* 3 full-time (2 women), 3 part-time/adjunct (all women). *Students:* 15 full-time (14 women), 46 part-time (37 women); includes 45 minority (5 Black or African American, non-Hispanic/Latino; 1 Asian, non-Hispanic/Latino; 37 Hispanic/Latino; 2 Two or more races, non-Hispanic/Latino). Average age 31. In 2014, 77 master's awarded. *Degree requirements:* For master's, thesis optional. *Entrance requirements:* For master's, California Basic Educational Skills Test, minimum undergraduate GPA of 2.75, graduate 3.0; interview; 1 year's experience working with children; 3 letters of reference. Additional exam requirements/recommendations for international students: Required—TOEFL (minimum score 550 paper-based). *Application deadline:* Applications are processed on a rolling basis. Application fee: $50. *Expenses:* Expenses: Contact institution. *Financial support:* Institutionally sponsored loans and unspecified assistantships available. Financial award application deadline: 3/2; financial award applicants required to submit FAFSA. *Unit head:* Laurie Schroeder, Chairperson, 909-448-4653, E-mail: lschroeder3@laverne.edu. *Application contact:* Christy Ranells, Admissions Information Specialist, 909-448-4644, Fax: 909-9712295, E-mail: cranells@laverne.edu.
Website: http://www.laverne.edu/education/

University of Manitoba, Faculty of Graduate Studies, Faculty of Arts, Department of Psychology, Winnipeg, MB R3T 2N2, Canada. Offers clinical psychology (PhD); psychology (MA, PhD); school psychology (MA). *Degree requirements:* For master's, thesis; for doctorate, one foreign language, thesis/dissertation. *Entrance requirements:* For master's and doctorate, GRE General Test.

University of Mary, Liffrig Family School of Education and Behavioral Sciences, Department of Behavioral Sciences, Bismarck, ND 58504-9652. Offers addiction counseling (MSC); clinical mental health counseling (MSC); military families (MSC); school counseling (MSC); student affairs (MSC). Part-time programs available. Postbaccalaureate distance learning degree programs offered (minimal on-campus study). *Degree requirements:* For master's, thesis, internship. *Entrance requirements:* For master's, coursework/experience in psychology, statistics, minimum GPA of 3.0. Additional exam requirements/recommendations for international students: Required—TOEFL (minimum score 500 paper-based; 71 iBT). *Application deadline:* For fall admission, 8/1 priority date for domestic students. Application fee: $40. *Expenses: Tuition:* Full-time $4772; part-time $530.25 per credit hour. *Required fees:* $20 per credit hour. Tuition and fees vary according to degree level and program. *Financial support:* Application deadline: 8/1; applicants required to submit FAFSA. *Application contact:* Jeanette Shaeffer, Accelerated and Distance Education Administrative Assistant, 701-355-8128, Fax: 701-255-7687, E-mail: jgschae@umary.edu.

University of Maryland, College Park, Academic Affairs, College of Education, Department of Counseling, Higher Education and Special Education, College Park, MD 20742. Offers college student personnel (M Ed, MA); college student personnel administration (PhD); community counseling (CAGS); community/career counseling (M Ed, MA); counseling and personnel services (M Ed, MA, PhD), including art therapy (M Ed), college student personnel (M Ed), counseling and personnel services (PhD), counseling psychology (M Ed), mental health counseling (M Ed), school counseling (M Ed); counseling psychology (PhD); counselor education (PhD); rehabilitation counseling (M Ed, MA, AGSC); school counseling (M Ed, MA); school psychology (M Ed, MA, PhD). *Accreditation:* ACA (one or more programs are accredited); APA (one or more programs are accredited); NCATE. Part-time and evening/weekend programs available. Postbaccalaureate distance learning degree programs offered (no on-campus study). *Degree requirements:* For master's, thesis (for some programs); for doctorate, thesis/dissertation. *Entrance requirements:* For master's, GRE General Test or MAT, minimum GPA of 3.0, 3 letters of recommendation; for doctorate, GRE General Test or MAT, minimum GPA of 3.5, 3 letters of recommendation. Additional exam requirements/recommendations for international students: Required—TOEFL. Electronic applications accepted. *Faculty research:* Educational psychology, counseling, health.

University of Massachusetts Amherst, Graduate School, College of Education, Program in Education, Amherst, MA 01003. Offers bilingual/English as a second language/multicultural education (M Ed, Ed S); child study and early education (M Ed);

children, families and schools (Ed D, Ed S); early childhood and elementary teacher education (M Ed); educational leadership (M Ed); educational policy and leadership (Ed D); higher education (M Ed); international education (M Ed); language, literacy and culture (Ed D); learning, media and technology (M Ed, Ed S); mathematics, science, and learning technologies (Ed D); psychometric methods, educational statistics and research methods (Ed D); reading and writing (M Ed); school counselor education (M Ed, Ed S); school psychology (Ed S); science education (Ed S); secondary teacher education (M Ed); social justice education (M Ed, Ed D, Ed S); special education (M Ed, Ed D, Ed S); teacher education and school improvement (Ed D, Ed S). *Accreditation:* NCATE. Part-time programs available. Postbaccalaureate distance learning degree programs offered (minimal on-campus study). *Faculty:* 99 full-time (57 women). *Students:* 353 full-time (252 women), 252 part-time (179 women); includes 113 minority (39 Black or African American, non-Hispanic/Latino; 5 American Indian or Alaska Native, non-Hispanic/Latino; 16 Asian, non-Hispanic/Latino; 42 Hispanic/Latino; 11 Two or more races, non-Hispanic/Latino), 104 international. Average age 34. 597 applicants, 53% accepted, 173 enrolled. In 2014, 161 master's, 37 doctorates, 26 other advanced degrees awarded. Terminal master's awarded for partial completion of doctoral program. *Degree requirements:* For doctorate, comprehensive exam, thesis/dissertation. *Entrance requirements:* Additional exam requirements/recommendations for international students: Required—TOEFL (minimum score 550 paper-based; 80 iBT), IELTS (minimum score 6.5). *Application deadline:* For fall admission, 1/2 for domestic and international students. Applications are processed on a rolling basis. Application fee: $75. Electronic applications accepted. *Expenses:* Tuition, state resident: full-time $1980; part-time $110 per credit. Tuition, nonresident: full-time $14,644; part-time $414 per credit. *Required fees:* $11,417. One-time fee: $357. *Financial support:* Fellowships with full and partial tuition reimbursements, research assistantships with full and partial tuition reimbursements, teaching assistantships with full and partial tuition reimbursements, career-related internships or fieldwork, Federal Work-Study, scholarships/grants, traineeships, health care benefits, tuition waivers (full and partial), and unspecified assistantships available. Support available to part-time students. Financial award application deadline: 1/2; financial award applicants required to submit FAFSA. *Unit head:* Dr. Linda L. Griffin, Graduate Program Director, 413-545-6984, Fax: 413-545-1523. *Application contact:* Lindsay DeSantis, Supervisor of Admissions, 413-545-0722, Fax: 413-577-0010, E-mail: gradadm@grad.umass.edu.
Website: http://www.umass.edu/education/

University of Massachusetts Amherst, Graduate School, College of Education, Program in School Psychology, Amherst, MA 01003. Offers M Ed, PhD, Ed S. *Accreditation:* APA; NCATE. Part-time programs available. *Students:* 28 full-time (26 women), 7 part-time (5 women); includes 2 minority (1 Black or African American, non-Hispanic/Latino; 1 Hispanic/Latino). Average age 27. 74 applicants, 27% accepted, 11 enrolled. In 2014, 12 master's, 2 doctorates awarded. Terminal master's awarded for partial completion of doctoral program. *Degree requirements:* For doctorate, comprehensive exam, thesis/dissertation. *Entrance requirements:* For doctorate, 3 letters of recommendation. Additional exam requirements/recommendations for international students: Required—TOEFL (minimum score 550 paper-based; 80 iBT), IELTS (minimum score 6.5). *Application deadline:* For fall admission, 1/15 for domestic and international students. Applications are processed on a rolling basis. Application fee: $75. Electronic applications accepted. *Expenses:* Tuition, state resident: full-time $1980; part-time $110 per credit. Tuition, nonresident: full-time $14,644; part-time $414 per credit. *Required fees:* $11,417. One-time fee: $357. *Financial support:* Fellowships with full and partial tuition reimbursements, research assistantships with full and partial tuition reimbursements, teaching assistantships with full and partial tuition reimbursements, career-related internships or fieldwork, Federal Work-Study, scholarships/grants, traineeships, health care benefits, tuition waivers (full and partial), and unspecified assistantships available. Support available to part-time students. Financial award application deadline: 1/15; financial award applicants required to submit FAFSA. *Unit head:* Dr. Linda L. Griffin, Graduate Program Director, 413-545-6984, Fax: 413-545-1523. *Application contact:* Lindsay DeSantis, Supervisor of Admissions, 413-545-0722, Fax: 413-577-0010, E-mail: gradadm@grad.umass.edu.
Website: http://www.umass.edu/education/departments/sd/school-psychology

University of Massachusetts Boston, College of Education and Human Development, Program in Counseling and School Psychology, Boston, MA 02125-3393. Offers PhD. *Accreditation:* CORE. Part-time and evening/weekend programs available. *Application deadline:* For fall admission, 12/1 for domestic students. *Expenses:* Tuition, state resident: full-time $2590; part-time $108 per credit. Tuition, nonresident: full-time $9758; part-time $406.50 per credit. Tuition and fees vary according to course load and program. *Financial support:* Research assistantships with full tuition reimbursements, teaching assistantships with full tuition reimbursements, career-related internships or fieldwork, Federal Work-Study, and unspecified assistantships available. Support available to part-time students. Financial award application deadline: 3/1; financial award applicants required to submit FAFSA. *Faculty research:* Persuasion and power in the counseling process, self-efficacy for counselors and clients, career and biracial issues in family therapy. *Unit head:* Dr. Virginia Harvey, Director, 617-287-7617. *Application contact:* Peggy Roldan Patel, Graduate Admissions Coordinator, 617-287-6400, Fax: 617-287-6236, E-mail: bos.gadm@dpc.umassp.edu.

University of Massachusetts Boston, College of Education and Human Development, Program in School Psychology, Boston, MA 02125-3393. Offers M Ed. Part-time and evening/weekend programs available. *Degree requirements:* For master's, comprehensive exam, practicum, final project. *Entrance requirements:* For master's, GRE General Test or MAT, minimum GPA of 3.0. *Application deadline:* For fall admission, 3/1 for domestic students; for spring admission, 11/1 for domestic students. *Expenses:* Tuition, state resident: full-time $2590; part-time $108 per credit. Tuition, nonresident: full-time $9758; part-time $406.50 per credit. Tuition and fees vary according to course load and program. *Financial support:* Research assistantships with full tuition reimbursements, teaching assistantships with full tuition reimbursements, career-related internships or fieldwork, Federal Work-Study, and unspecified assistantships available. Support available to part-time students. Financial award application deadline: 3/1; financial award applicants required to submit FAFSA. *Faculty research:* School psychology services, assessment of children, cultural and gender differences on psychological adjustment to disabilities. *Unit head:* Dr. Virginia Harvey, Director, 617-287-7617. *Application contact:* Peggy Roldan Patel, Graduate Admissions Coordinator, 617-287-6400, Fax: 617-287-6236, E-mail: bos.gadm@dpc.umassp.edu.

University of Memphis, Graduate School, College of Arts and Sciences, Department of Psychology, Memphis, TN 38152-3230. Offers psychology (MS), including general psychology; school psychology (MA); MS/PhD. *Faculty:* 26 full-time (10 women), 4 part-time/adjunct (0 women). *Students:* 96 full-time (66 women), 20 part-time (12 women); includes 19 minority (11 Black or African American, non-Hispanic/Latino; 4 Asian, non-Hispanic/Latino; 1 Hispanic/Latino; 3 Two or more races, non-Hispanic/Latino), 10 international. Average age 28. 298 applicants, 14% accepted, 15 enrolled. In 2014, 18 master's, 13 doctorates awarded. *Degree requirements:* For master's, comprehensive exam (for some programs), thesis (for some programs), 37 credit hours (MA); 33 credit hours with thesis or 36 with exam (MS); for doctorate, comprehensive exam (for some programs), thesis/dissertation, 80 semester hours, major area paper; clinical: 1-year placement and 1-year internship; internship (for school psychology). *Entrance*

requirements: For master's, GRE; for doctorate, GRE (minimum combined score of 1100), minimum GPA of 2.75, 18 hours of undergraduate psychology courses, transcripts, personal statement, letters of recommendation; for Ed S, GRE (minimum combined score of 1100), minimum GPA of 2.75, 18 hours of undergraduate psychology courses, letters of recommendation. Additional exam requirements/recommendations for international students: Required—TOEFL (minimum score 550 paper-based; 79 iBT). *Application deadline:* For fall admission, 12/5 for domestic students. Applications are processed on a rolling basis. Application fee: $35 ($60 for international students). Electronic applications accepted. *Financial support:* In 2014–15, 66 students received support. Fellowships with full tuition reimbursements available, research assistantships with full tuition reimbursements available, teaching assistantships with full tuition reimbursements available, Federal Work-Study, scholarships/grants, tuition waivers (partial), and unspecified assistantships available. Financial award application deadline: 2/15; financial award applicants required to submit FAFSA. *Faculty research:* Clinical health; school, child and family psychology; psychotherapy; cognitive and behavioral neuroscience; industrial-organizational psychology. *Unit head:* Dr. Robert Cohen, Coordinator of Graduate Programs, 901-678-4679, Fax: 901-678-2579, E-mail: rcohen@memphis.edu. *Application contact:* Lynell Connable, Graduate Secretary, 901-678-4340, Fax: 901-678-2579, E-mail: dconnabl@memphis.edu.
Website: http://www.memphis.edu/psychology

University of Minnesota, Twin Cities Campus, Graduate School, College of Education and Human Development, Department of Educational Psychology, Program in School Psychology, Minneapolis, MN 55455-0213. Offers MA, PhD, Ed S. *Accreditation:* APA. *Students:* 30 full-time (23 women), 12 part-time (10 women); includes 4 minority (1 Black or African American, non-Hispanic/Latino; 1 Asian, non-Hispanic/Latino; 2 Hispanic/Latino). Average age 29. 23 applicants, 43% accepted, 5 enrolled. In 2014, 10 master's, 7 doctorates, 7 other advanced degrees awarded. Application fee: $75 ($95 for international students). *Unit head:* Dr. Geoffrey Maruyama, Chair, 612-625-5861, Fax: 612-624-8241, E-mail: geoff@umn.edu. *Application contact:* Dr. Ernest Davenport, Director of Graduate Studies, 612-624-1040, E-mail: lqr6576@umn.edu.
Website: http://www.cehd.umn.edu/EdPsych/schoolPsych

University of Minnesota, Twin Cities Campus, Graduate School, College of Education and Human Development, Institute of Child Development, Minneapolis, MN 55455-0213. Offers child psychology (MA, PhD); early childhood education (M Ed, MA, PhD); school psychology (MA, PhD). *Faculty:* 17 full-time (8 women). *Students:* 61 full-time (55 women), 15 part-time (14 women); includes 13 minority (4 Black or African American, non-Hispanic/Latino; 2 Asian, non-Hispanic/Latino; 6 Hispanic/Latino; 1 Two or more races, non-Hispanic/Latino), 5 international. Average age 28. 142 applicants, 32% accepted, 29 enrolled. In 2014, 77 master's, 8 doctorates awarded. Application fee: $75 ($95 for international students). *Financial support:* In 2014–15, 26 fellowships (averaging $20,013 per year), 13 research assistantships with full tuition reimbursements (averaging $10,984 per year), 17 teaching assistantships with full tuition reimbursements (averaging $8,929 per year) were awarded. *Faculty research:* Developmental affective and cognitive neuroscience; developmental psychopathology; intervention and prevention science; social and emotional development; cognitive, language, and perceptual development. *Total annual research expenditures:* $8 million. *Unit head:* Dr. Stephanie Carlson, Director, 612-625-6127, E-mail: smc@umn.edu. *Application contact:* Dr. Michael Maratsos, Director of Graduate Studies, 612-624-1027, E-mail: marat001@umn.edu.
Website: http://www.cehd.umn.edu/ICD

University of Minnesota, Twin Cities Campus, Graduate School, College of Liberal Arts, Department of Psychology, Minneapolis, MN 55455-0213. Offers biological psychopathology (PhD); clinical psychology (PhD); cognitive and biological psychology (PhD); counseling psychology (PhD); industrial/organizational psychology (PhD); personality, individual differences, and behavior genetics (PhD); quantitative/psychometric methods (PhD); school psychology (PhD); social psychology (PhD). *Accreditation:* APA. *Degree requirements:* For doctorate, comprehensive exam, thesis/dissertation. *Entrance requirements:* For doctorate, GRE General Test, GRE Subject Test (recommended), 12 credits of upper-level psychology courses, including a course in statistics or psychological measurement. Additional exam requirements/recommendations for international students: Required—TOEFL (minimum score 79 iBT).

University of Missouri, Office of Research and Graduate Studies, College of Education, Department of Educational, School, and Counseling Psychology, Columbia, MO 65211. Offers counseling psychology (M Ed, MA, PhD, Ed S); educational psychology (M Ed, MA, PhD, Ed S); learning and instruction (M Ed); school psychology (M Ed, MA, PhD, Ed S). *Accreditation:* APA (one or more programs are accredited). Part-time programs available. *Faculty:* 25 full-time (13 women), 4 part-time/adjunct (2 women). *Students:* 185 full-time (115 women), 204 part-time (103 women); includes 79 minority (41 Black or African American, non-Hispanic/Latino; 8 Asian, non-Hispanic/Latino; 21 Hispanic/Latino; 9 Two or more races, non-Hispanic/Latino), 34 international. Average age 31. 354 applicants, 38% accepted, 116 enrolled. In 2014, 59 master's, 16 doctorates, 13 other advanced degrees awarded. *Degree requirements:* For doctorate, thesis/dissertation. *Entrance requirements:* For master's, doctorate, and Ed S, GRE General Test, minimum GPA of 3.0. Additional exam requirements/recommendations for international students: Required—TOEFL (minimum score 580 paper-based; 92 iBT). *Application deadline:* For fall admission, 12/1 priority date for domestic and international students. Applications are processed on a rolling basis. Application fee: $55 ($75 for international students). Electronic applications accepted. *Financial support:* Fellowships, research assistantships, teaching assistantships, institutionally sponsored loans, traineeships, health care benefits, and unspecified assistantships available. Support available to part-time students. *Faculty research:* Out-of-school learning, social cognitive career theory, black psychology and the intersectionality of social identities, test session behavior. *Unit head:* Dr. Matthew Martens, Division Executive Director, 573-882-9434, E-mail: martensmp@missouri.edu. *Application contact:* Latoya Luther, Senior Secretary, 573-882-7732, E-mail: lutherl@missouri.edu.
Website: http://education.missouri.edu/ESCP/

University of Missouri–St. Louis, College of Education, Division of Educational Psychology, Research, and Evaluation, St. Louis, MO 63121. Offers educational psychology (M Ed), including character and citizenship education, educational research and program evaluation; program evaluation and assessment (Certificate); school psychology (Ed S). *Faculty:* 8 full-time (1 woman), 22 part-time/adjunct (10 women). *Students:* 22 full-time (18 women), 36 part-time (30 women); includes 12 minority (10 Black or African American, non-Hispanic/Latino; 1 Hispanic/Latino; 1 Two or more races, non-Hispanic/Latino), 1 international. Average age 29. 44 applicants, 52% accepted, 13 enrolled. In 2014, 18 master's awarded. *Degree requirements:* For other advanced degree, comprehensive exam, thesis or alternative, internship. *Entrance requirements:* For degree, GRE General Test, 2-4 letters of recommendation, personal interview. Additional exam requirements/recommendations for international students: Required—IELTS (minimum score 6.5); Recommended—TOEFL (minimum score 550 paper-based; 79 iBT). *Application deadline:* For fall admission, 2/15 priority date for domestic students, 2/15 for international students. Application fee: $50 ($40 for international students). Electronic applications accepted. *Expenses:* Tuition, state resident: full-time $7364; part-time $409.10 per hour. Tuition, nonresident: full-time $18,153; part-time $1008.50 per hour. *Financial support:* Application deadline: 4/1; applicants required to submit FAFSA. *Faculty research:* Child/adolescent psychology, quantitative and qualitative methodology, evaluation processes, measurement and assessment. *Unit head:* Dr. Donald Gouwens, Chairperson, 314-516-4773, Fax: 314-516-5784, E-mail: gouwensd@msx.umsl.edu. *Application contact:* 314-516-5458, Fax: 314-516-6996, E-mail: gradadm@umsl.edu.
Website: https://coe.umsl.edu/mycoe/index.cfm?event=p2_pe:viewProgram&program_id=MEd.EdPsych_RschEval

The University of Montana, Graduate School, College of Humanities and Sciences, Department of Psychology, Program in School Psychology, Missoula, MT 59812-0002. Offers MA, PhD, Ed S. *Degree requirements:* For master's, oral exam, professional paper; for Ed S, thesis. *Entrance requirements:* For master's, GRE General Test, GRE Subject Test, minimum GPA of 3.25 during previous 2 years; for Ed S, GRE General Test. Additional exam requirements/recommendations for international students: Required—TOEFL. *Faculty research:* Child development and creativity, psychological measurement.

University of Nebraska at Kearney, Graduate Studies and Research, College of Education, Department of Counseling and School Psychology, Kearney, NE 68849-0001. Offers clinical mental health counseling (MS Ed); school counseling (MS Ed), including elementary, secondary; school psychology (Ed S); student affairs (MS Ed). *Accreditation:* ACA; NCATE. Part-time and evening/weekend programs available. Postbaccalaureate distance learning degree programs offered (no on-campus study). *Faculty:* 7 full-time (3 women). *Students:* 62 full-time (56 women), 67 part-time (56 women); includes 15 minority (13 Hispanic/Latino; 2 Two or more races, non-Hispanic/Latino), 2 international. 41 applicants, 88% accepted, 31 enrolled. In 2014, 28 master's, 6 Ed Ss awarded. *Degree requirements:* For master's, comprehensive exam, thesis optional; for Ed S, thesis. *Entrance requirements:* For master's and Ed S, personal statement, recommendations, resume, interview. Additional exam requirements/recommendations for international students: Recommended—TOEFL (minimum score 550 paper-based; 79 iBT), IELTS (minimum score 6.5). *Application deadline:* For fall admission, 6/15 for domestic and international students; for spring admission, 10/15 for domestic and international students; for summer admission, 3/15 for domestic and international students. Application fee: $45. Electronic applications accepted. *Expenses:* Tuition, state resident: full-time $3897; part-time $216.50 per credit hour. Tuition, nonresident: full-time $8550; part-time $475 per credit hour. *Required fees:* $414; $23 per credit. $96.50 per semester. One-time fee: $45. Tuition and fees vary according to course load and program. *Financial support:* In 2014–15, 8 research assistantships with full tuition reimbursements (averaging $9,900 per year) were awarded; career-related internships or fieldwork, scholarships/grants, health care benefits, and unspecified assistantships also available. Support available to part-time students. Financial award application deadline: 2/28; financial award applicants required to submit FAFSA. *Faculty research:* Multicultural counseling and diversity issues, team decision-making, adult development, women's issues, brief therapy. *Unit head:* Dr. Grace Mims, Chair, Counseling and School Psychology, 308-865-8508, E-mail: mimsga@unk.edu. *Application contact:* Linda Johnson, Director, Graduate Admissions and Programs, 800-717-7881, Fax: 308-865-8837, E-mail: gradstudies@unk.edu.
Website: http://www.unk.edu/academics/csp/

University of Nebraska at Omaha, Graduate Studies, College of Arts and Sciences, Department of Psychology, Omaha, NE 68182. Offers industrial/organizational psychology (MS); psychology (MS, PhD); school psychology (MS, Ed S). Part-time programs available. *Faculty:* 19 full-time (8 women). *Students:* 66 full-time (52 women), 53 part-time (33 women); includes 10 minority (2 Black or African American, non-Hispanic/Latino; 2 Asian, non-Hispanic/Latino; 6 Hispanic/Latino). Average age 26. 178 applicants, 31% accepted, 51 enrolled. In 2014, 20 master's, 6 doctorates, 10 other advanced degrees awarded. *Degree requirements:* For master's, comprehensive exam, thesis (for some programs); for doctorate, comprehensive exam, thesis/dissertation. *Entrance requirements:* For master's and doctorate, GRE, minimum GPA of 3.0, official transcripts, 3 letters of recommendation, statement of purpose, writing sample, resume. Additional exam requirements/recommendations for international students: Required—TOEFL, IELTS, PTE. *Application deadline:* For fall admission, 1/5 for domestic and international students. Application fee: $45. Electronic applications accepted. *Financial support:* In 2014–15, 42 students received support, including 16 research assistantships with tuition reimbursements available, 26 teaching assistantships with tuition reimbursements available; fellowships with tuition reimbursements available, career-related internships or fieldwork, Federal Work-Study, institutionally sponsored loans, scholarships/grants, tuition waivers (partial), and unspecified assistantships also available. Support available to part-time students. Financial award application deadline: 3/1; financial award applicants required to submit FAFSA. *Unit head:* Dr. Brigette Ryalls, Chairperson, 402-554-2341, E-mail: graduate@unomaha.edu. *Application contact:* Dr. Joseph Brown, Graduate Program Chair, 402-554-2341, E-mail: graduate@unomaha.edu.

University of Nebraska–Lincoln, Graduate College, College of Education and Human Sciences, Department of Educational Psychology, Lincoln, NE 68588. Offers cognition, learning and development (MA); counseling psychology (MA); educational psychology (MA, Ed S); psychological studies in education (PhD), including cognition, learning and development, counseling psychology, quantitative, qualitative, and psychometric methods, school psychology; quantitative, qualitative, and psychometric methods (MA); school psychology (MA, Ed S). *Accreditation:* APA (one or more programs are accredited); NCATE. *Degree requirements:* For master's, thesis optional. *Entrance requirements:* For master's, GRE General Test. Additional exam requirements/recommendations for international students: Required—TOEFL (minimum score 500 paper-based). Electronic applications accepted. *Faculty research:* Measurement and assessment, metacognition, academic skills, child development, multicultural education and counseling.

University of North Alabama, College of Education, Department of Counselor Education, Florence, AL 35632-0001. Offers school counseling P-12 (MA Ed). *Accreditation:* ACA; NCATE. Part-time and evening/weekend programs available. *Faculty:* 4 full-time (all women). *Students:* 21 full-time (17 women), 28 part-time (22 women); includes 2 minority (both Two or more races, non-Hispanic/Latino). Average age 34. 25 applicants, 60% accepted, 14 enrolled. In 2014, 21 master's awarded. *Degree requirements:* For master's, comprehensive exam. *Entrance requirements:* For master's, GRE, MAT, or NTE, minimum GPA of 2.5, Alabama Class B Certificate or equivalent, teaching experience. Additional exam requirements/recommendations for international students: Required—TOEFL (minimum score 550 paper-based; 79 iBT), IELTS (minimum score 6). *Application deadline:* For fall admission, 7/1 priority date for domestic students, 7/1 for international students; for spring admission, 12/1 for domestic and international students. Applications are processed on a rolling basis. Application fee: $25 ($50 for international students). Electronic applications accepted. *Expenses:* Tuition, state resident: full-time $5166; part-time $1722 per semester. Tuition, nonresident: full-time $10,332; part-time $3444 per semester. *Required fees:* $393.50 per semester. *Financial support:* Federal Work-Study available. Support available to

part-time students. Financial award application deadline: 4/1; financial award applicants required to submit FAFSA. *Unit head:* Dr. Sandra Loew, Chair, 256-765-4763, Fax: 256-765-4159, E-mail: saloew@una.edu. *Application contact:* Hillary N. Coats, Graduate Admissions Coordinator, 256-765-4447, E-mail: graduate@una.edu.
Website: http://www.una.edu/education/departments/counselor-education.html

The University of North Carolina at Chapel Hill, Graduate School, School of Education, Program in School Psychology, Chapel Hill, NC 27599. Offers M Ed, MA, PhD. *Accreditation:* APA (one or more programs are accredited); NCATE. *Degree requirements:* For master's, comprehensive exam, thesis (for some programs); for doctorate, comprehensive exam, thesis/dissertation. *Entrance requirements:* For master's and doctorate, GRE General Test, minimum GPA of 3.0 during last 2 years of undergraduate course work. Additional exam requirements/recommendations for international students: Required—TOEFL (minimum score 550 paper-based). Electronic applications accepted.

The University of North Carolina at Greensboro, Graduate School, School of Education, Department of Counseling and Educational Development, Greensboro, NC 27412-5001. Offers advanced school counseling (PMC); counseling and counselor education (PhD); counseling and educational development (MS); couple and family counseling (PMC); school counseling (PMC); MS/Ed S. *Accreditation:* ACA (one or more programs are accredited); NCATE. *Degree requirements:* For master's, comprehensive exam, practicum, internship; for doctorate, comprehensive exam, thesis/dissertation. *Entrance requirements:* For master's, doctorate, and PMC, GRE General Test. Additional exam requirements/recommendations for international students: Required—TOEFL. Electronic applications accepted. *Faculty research:* Gerontology, invitational theory, career development, marriage and family therapy, drug and alcohol abuse prevention.

University of Northern Colorado, Graduate School, College of Education and Behavioral Sciences, Department of School Psychology, Greeley, CO 80639. Offers PhD, Ed S. *Accreditation:* APA (one or more programs are accredited); NCATE. Part-time and evening/weekend programs available. *Degree requirements:* For doctorate, comprehensive exam, thesis/dissertation; for Ed S, comprehensive exam. *Entrance requirements:* For doctorate, GRE General Test, curriculum vitae, 3 letters of recommendation. Electronic applications accepted.

University of Northern Iowa, Graduate College, College of Education, Department of Educational Psychology and Foundations, Ed S Program in School Psychology, Cedar Falls, IA 50614. Offers Ed S. *Students:* 13 full-time (12 women), 1 (woman) part-time. 13 applicants, 46% accepted, 4 enrolled. In 2014, 8 Ed Ss awarded. Application fee: $50 ($70 for international students). *Expenses:* Tuition, state resident: full-time $7912; part-time $880 per credit. Tuition, nonresident: full-time $17,906; part-time $880 per credit. *Required fees:* $1101; $325.50 per credit. $465.63 per semester. Tuition and fees vary according to course load and program. *Unit head:* Dr. Kerri L. Clopton, Coordinator, 319-273-7940, Fax: 319-273-7732, E-mail: kerri.clopton@uni.edu. *Application contact:* Laurie S. Russell, Record Analyst, 319-273-2623, Fax: 319-273-2885, E-mail: laurie.russell@uni.edu.
Website: http://www.uni.edu/coe/departments/educational-psychology-foundations/eds-school-psychology

University of Northern Iowa, Graduate College, College of Social and Behavioral Sciences, School of Applied Human Sciences, Cedar Falls, IA 50614. Offers counseling (MA), including mental health counseling, school counseling; mental health counseling (MA); school counseling (MA). Part-time programs available. *Students:* 50 full-time (43 women), 33 part-time (24 women); includes 8 minority (3 Black or African American, non-Hispanic/Latino; 1 American Indian or Alaska Native, non-Hispanic/Latino; 1 Asian, non-Hispanic/Latino; 3 Hispanic/Latino), 1 international. 95 applicants, 25% accepted, 24 enrolled. In 2014, 17 master's awarded. *Degree requirements:* For master's, comprehensive exam, thesis (for some programs). *Entrance requirements:* Additional exam requirements/recommendations for international students: Required—TOEFL (minimum score 550 paper-based; 79 iBT). *Application deadline:* For fall admission, 2/1 for domestic students, 4/1 priority date for international students; for winter admission, 10/1 priority date for international students. Application fee: $50 ($70 for international students). Electronic applications accepted. *Expenses:* Tuition, state resident: full-time $7912; part-time $880 per credit. Tuition, nonresident: full-time $17,906; part-time $880 per credit. *Required fees:* $1101; $325.50 per credit. $465.63 per semester. Tuition and fees vary according to course load and program. *Financial support:* Unspecified assistantships available. Financial award application deadline: 2/1; financial award applicants required to submit FAFSA. *Unit head:* Dr. Howard L. Barnes, Director, 319-273-2358, E-mail: howard.barnes@uni.edu. *Application contact:* Laurie S. Russell, Record Analyst, 319-273-2623, Fax: 319-273-2885, E-mail: laurie.russell@uni.edu.
Website: http://www.uni.edu/csbs/sahs/counseling

University of Phoenix–Colorado Campus, College of Education, Lone Tree, CO 80124-5453. Offers administration and supervision (MAEd); curriculum instruction (MAEd); elementary teacher education (MAEd); school counseling (MSC); secondary teacher education (MAEd). Evening/weekend programs available. *Degree requirements:* For master's, thesis (for some programs). *Entrance requirements:* For master's, minimum undergraduate GPA of 2.5, 3 years work experience. Additional exam requirements/recommendations for international students: Required—TOEFL (minimum score 550 paper-based; 79 iBT). Electronic applications accepted.

University of Phoenix–Colorado Springs Downtown Campus, College of Education, Colorado Springs, CO 80903. Offers administration and supervision (MA Ed); curriculum and instruction (MA Ed); elementary teacher education (MA Ed); principal licensure certification (Certificate); school counseling (MSC); secondary teacher education (MA Ed). Evening/weekend programs available. *Degree requirements:* For master's, thesis (for some programs). *Entrance requirements:* For master's, minimum undergraduate GPA of 2.5, 3 years of work experience. Additional exam requirements/recommendations for international students: Required—TOEFL (minimum score 550 paper-based; 79 iBT). Electronic applications accepted.

University of Phoenix–Las Vegas Campus, College of Education, Las Vegas, NV 89135. Offers administration and supervision (MA Ed); curriculum and instruction (MA Ed); school counseling (MSC); teacher education-elementary licensure (MA Ed). Evening/weekend programs available. *Degree requirements:* For master's, thesis (for some programs). *Entrance requirements:* For master's, minimum undergraduate GPA of 2.5, 3 years of work experience. Additional exam requirements/recommendations for international students: Required—TOEFL (minimum score 550 paper-based; 79 iBT). Electronic applications accepted.

University of Phoenix–Puerto Rico Campus, College of Education, Guaynabo, PR 00968. Offers administration and supervision (MA Ed); early childhood education (MA Ed); school counselor (MSC). Evening/weekend programs available. *Degree requirements:* For master's, thesis (for some programs). *Entrance requirements:* For master's, minimum undergraduate GPA of 2.5, 3 years work experience. Additional exam requirements/recommendations for international students: Required—TOEFL (minimum score 550 paper-based; 79 iBT). Electronic applications accepted.

University of Phoenix–Utah Campus, College of Education, Salt Lake City, UT 84123-4617. Offers administration and supervision (MA Ed); curriculum and instruction (MA Ed); elementary teacher education (MA Ed); school counseling (MSC); secondary teacher education (MA Ed); special education (MA Ed). Evening/weekend programs available. *Degree requirements:* For master's, thesis (for some programs). *Entrance requirements:* For master's, minimum undergraduate GPA of 2.5, 3 years work experience. Additional exam requirements/recommendations for international students: Required—TOEFL (minimum score 550 paper-based; 79 iBT). Electronic applications accepted.

University of Rhode Island, Graduate School, College of Arts and Sciences, Department of Psychology, Kingston, RI 02881. Offers behavioral science (PhD); clinical psychology (MA, PhD); school psychology (MS, PhD). *Accreditation:* APA (one or more programs are accredited). Part-time programs available. *Faculty:* 19 full-time (10 women), 1 part-time/adjunct (0 women). *Students:* 108 full-time (83 women), 32 part-time (25 women); includes 34 minority (21 Black or African American, non-Hispanic/Latino; 2 American Indian or Alaska Native, non-Hispanic/Latino; 3 Asian, non-Hispanic/Latino; 7 Hispanic/Latino; 1 Two or more races, non-Hispanic/Latino), 7 international. In 2014, 20 master's awarded. *Degree requirements:* For master's, comprehensive exam, thesis optional; for doctorate, thesis/dissertation. *Entrance requirements:* For master's and doctorate, GRE, 3 letters of recommendation. Additional exam requirements/recommendations for international students: Required—TOEFL (minimum score 550 paper-based). *Application deadline:* For fall admission, 12/1 for domestic and international students. Application fee: $65. Electronic applications accepted. *Expenses:* Tuition, state resident: full-time $11,532; part-time $641 per credit. Tuition, nonresident: full-time $23,606; part-time $1311 per credit. *Required fees:* $1442; $39 per credit. $35 per semester. One-time fee: $155. *Financial support:* In 2014–15, 10 research assistantships with full and partial tuition reimbursements (averaging $12,774 per year), 23 teaching assistantships with full and partial tuition reimbursements (averaging $12,892 per year) were awarded. Financial award application deadline: 12/1; financial award applicants required to submit FAFSA. *Total annual research expenditures:* $22,461. *Unit head:* Dr. Su Boatright-Horowitz, Interim Chair, 401-874-4231, Fax: 401-874-2157, E-mail: ugpsych@aol.com. *Application contact:* Graduate Admission, 401-874-2872, E-mail: gradadm@etal.uri.edu.
Website: http://www.uri.edu/artsci/psy/

University of South Carolina, The Graduate School, College of Arts and Sciences, Department of Psychology, Program in School Psychology, Columbia, SC 29208. Offers PhD. *Accreditation:* APA; NCATE. *Degree requirements:* For doctorate, thesis/dissertation. *Entrance requirements:* For doctorate, GRE General Test, minimum GPA of 3.0. Additional exam requirements/recommendations for international students: Required—TOEFL. Electronic applications accepted. *Faculty research:* Preschool services, families and diversity life satisfaction, ADHD intervention, attachment.

The University of South Dakota, Graduate School, School of Education, Division of Counseling and Psychology in Education, Vermillion, SD 57069-2390. Offers counseling (MA, PhD, Ed S); human development and educational psychology (MA, PhD, Ed S); school psychology (PhD, Ed S). *Accreditation:* ACA (one or more programs are accredited); NCATE. Part-time programs available. *Degree requirements:* For master's and Ed S, comprehensive exam, thesis or alternative; for doctorate, comprehensive exam, thesis/dissertation. *Entrance requirements:* For master's and doctorate, GRE General Test, minimum GPA of 3.0. Additional exam requirements/recommendations for international students: Required—TOEFL (minimum score 550 paper-based; 79 iBT). Electronic applications accepted.

University of Southern Maine, College of Management and Human Service, School of Education and Human Development, Program in School Psychology, Portland, ME 04104-9300. Offers MS, Psy D. Part-time and evening/weekend programs available. *Faculty:* 2 full-time (1 woman), 3 part-time/adjunct (1 woman). *Students:* 9 full-time (7 women), 10 part-time (7 women); includes 1 minority (Asian, non-Hispanic/Latino). Average age 34. 10 applicants, 50% accepted, 2 enrolled. In 2014, 1 master's, 4 doctorates awarded. *Degree requirements:* For doctorate, comprehensive exam, thesis/dissertation, dissertation defense. *Entrance requirements:* For doctorate, GRE General Test, interview. Additional exam requirements/recommendations for international students: Required—TOEFL (minimum score 550 paper-based; 79 iBT). *Application deadline:* For fall admission, 12/1 for domestic students. Application fee: $65. Electronic applications accepted. *Expenses: Tuition, area resident:* Full-time $6840; part-time $380 per credit hour. Tuition, state resident: full-time $10,260; part-time $570 per credit hour. Tuition, nonresident: full-time $18,468; part-time $1026 per credit hour. *Required fees:* $830; $83 per credit hour. Tuition and fees vary according to course load and program. *Financial support:* Research assistantships, career-related internships or fieldwork, Federal Work-Study, institutionally sponsored loans, scholarships/grants, and unspecified assistantships available. Support available to part-time students. Financial award application deadline: 3/1; financial award applicants required to submit FAFSA. *Faculty research:* Academic interventions, applied behavior analysis, assessment methods, response to intervention, school psychology practices, positive behavioral interventions and supports, multi-tier systems of support. *Unit head:* Dr. Rachel Brown, Program Chair, 207-228-8322, E-mail: rbrown@usm.main.edu. *Application contact:* Mary Sloan, Assistant Dean of Graduate Studies and Director of Graduate Admissions, 207-780-4812, Fax: 207-780-4969, E-mail: gradstudies@usm.maine.edu.
Website: http://usm.maine.edu/school-psychology

University of Southern Mississippi, Graduate School, College of Education and Psychology, Department of Psychology, Hattiesburg, MS 39406-0001. Offers clinical psychology (PhD); counseling psychology (MS, PhD); experimental psychology (PhD); school psychology (PhD). *Accreditation:* APA (one or more programs are accredited). Terminal master's awarded for partial completion of doctoral program. *Degree requirements:* For master's, comprehensive exam, thesis; for doctorate, comprehensive exam, thesis/dissertation. *Entrance requirements:* For master's, GRE General Test, minimum GPA of 3.0; for doctorate, GRE General Test, interview, minimum GPA of 3.5. Additional exam requirements/recommendations for international students: Required—TOEFL, IELTS. *Faculty research:* Psychopathology, alcohol and drug abuse, child clinical psychology, parenting, suicide, career/vocational, marine mammal, cognition, psychological psychology, behavioral interventions, positive psychology, anger/aggression, diversity issues.

University of South Florida, College of Education, Department of Psychological and Social Foundations, Tampa, FL 33620-9951. Offers college student affairs (M Ed); counselor education (MA, PhD, Ed S); interdisciplinary (PhD, Ed S); school psychology (PhD, Ed S). Part-time and evening/weekend programs available. *Degree requirements:* For master's, comprehensive exam, thesis (for some programs); for doctorate, comprehensive exam, thesis/dissertation, multiple research methods; philosophies of inquiry (for some programs). *Entrance requirements:* For master's, GRE General Test, minimum GPA of 3.5 in last 60 hours of course work; for doctorate, GRE General Test, MAT, minimum GPA of 3.5 in last 60 hours of course work; for Ed S, GRE General Test. Additional exam requirements/recommendations for international students: Required—TOEFL (minimum score 550 paper-based; 79 iBT). Electronic applications accepted. *Faculty research:* College student affairs, counselor education, educational psychology, school psychology, social foundations.

The University of Tennessee, Graduate School, College of Education, Health and Human Sciences, Program in Education, Knoxville, TN 37996. Offers art education

(MS); counseling education (PhD); cultural studies in education (PhD); curriculum (MS, Ed S); curriculum, educational research and evaluation (Ed D, PhD); early childhood education (PhD); early childhood special education (MS); education of deaf and hard of hearing (MS); educational administration and policy studies (Ed D, PhD); educational administration and supervision (Ed S); educational psychology (Ed D, PhD); elementary education (MS, Ed S); elementary teaching (MS); English education (MS, Ed S); exercise science (PhD); foreign language/ESL education (MS, Ed S); instructional technology (MS, Ed D, PhD, Ed S); literacy, language and ESL education (PhD); literacy, language education, and ESL education (Ed D); mathematics education (MS, Ed S); modified and comprehensive special education (MS); reading education (MS, Ed S); school counseling (Ed S); school psychology (PhD, Ed S); science education (MS, Ed S); secondary teaching (MS); social foundations (MS); social science education (MS, Ed S); socio-cultural foundations of sports and education (PhD); special education (Ed S); teacher education (Ed D, PhD). *Accreditation:* NCATE. Part-time and evening/weekend programs available. *Degree requirements:* For master's and Ed S, thesis optional; for doctorate, variable foreign language requirement, thesis/dissertation. *Entrance requirements:* For master's, minimum GPA of 2.7; for doctorate and Ed S, GRE General Test, minimum GPA of 2.7. Additional exam requirements/recommendations for international students: Required—TOEFL. Electronic applications accepted.

The University of Tennessee at Chattanooga, School of Education, Chattanooga, TN 37403. Offers counseling (M Ed), including community counseling, school counseling; education (M Ed, Post-Master's Certificate), including elementary education (M Ed), school leadership, secondary education (M Ed), special education (M Ed); educational specialist (Ed S), including educational technology, school psychology; learning and leadership (Ed D), including educational leadership. *Accreditation:* ACA; NCATE. Part-time and evening/weekend programs available. Postbaccalaureate distance learning degree programs offered (no on-campus study). *Faculty:* 24 full-time (17 women), 6 part-time/adjunct (4 women). *Students:* 107 full-time (86 women), 263 part-time (192 women); includes 71 minority (46 Black or African American, non-Hispanic/Latino; 2 American Indian or Alaska Native, non-Hispanic/Latino; 5 Asian, non-Hispanic/Latino; 11 Hispanic/Latino; 7 Two or more races, non-Hispanic/Latino), 2 international. Average age 34. 121 applicants, 83% accepted, 67 enrolled. In 2014, 125 master's, 10 doctorates, 3 other advanced degrees awarded. *Degree requirements:* For master's, comprehensive exam, thesis optional, culminating experience; for doctorate, comprehensive exam, thesis/dissertation; for other advanced degree, internship. *Entrance requirements:* For master's, GRE General Test, PPST 1, teaching certificate; for doctorate, GRE General Test, master's degree, two years of practical work experience in organizational environment; for other advanced degree, GRE General Test, letters of reference. Additional exam requirements/recommendations for international students: Required—TOEFL (minimum score 550 paper-based; 79 iBT), IELTS (minimum score 6). *Application deadline:* For fall admission, 6/13 for domestic students, 6/1 for international students; for spring admission, 10/15 for domestic students, 10/1 for international students. Applications are processed on a rolling basis. Application fee: $30 ($35 for international students). Electronic applications accepted. *Expenses:* Tuition, state resident: full-time $7708; part-time $428 per credit hour. Tuition, nonresident: full-time $23,826; part-time $1323 per credit hour. *Required fees:* $1708; $252 per credit hour. *Financial support:* In 2014–15, 20 research assistantships with tuition reimbursements (averaging $6,340 per year), 4 teaching assistantships with tuition reimbursements (averaging $7,234 per year) were awarded; career-related internships or fieldwork, institutionally sponsored loans, scholarships/grants, and unspecified assistantships also available. Support available to part-time students. Financial award applicants required to submit FAFSA. *Faculty research:* School counseling, community counseling, elementary and secondary education, school leadership and administration. *Total annual research expenditures:* $967,880. *Unit head:* Dr. Linda Johnston, Director, 423-425-4122, Fax: 423-425-5380, E-mail: linda-johnston@utc.edu. *Application contact:* Dr. J. Randy Walker, Interim Dean of Graduate Studies, 423-425-4478, Fax: 423-425-5223, E-mail: randy-walker@utc.edu.
Website: http://www.utc.edu/school-education/abouttheschool/gradprograms.php

The University of Texas at Austin, Graduate School, College of Education, Department of Educational Psychology, Austin, TX 78712-1111. Offers academic educational psychology (M Ed, MA); counseling psychology (PhD); counselor education (M Ed); human development, culture and learning sciences (PhD); program evaluation (MA); quantitative methods (M Ed, MA, PhD); school psychology (MA, PhD). *Accreditation:* APA (one or more programs are accredited). *Degree requirements:* For master's, thesis optional; for doctorate, thesis/dissertation. *Entrance requirements:* For master's and doctorate, GRE General Test, 3 letters of recommendation. Additional exam requirements/recommendations for international students: Required—TOEFL.

The University of Texas at San Antonio, College of Education and Human Development, Department of Educational Psychology, San Antonio, TX 78207. Offers applied behavioral analysis (Certificate); digital learning design (Certificate); language acquisition and bilingual psychoeducational assessment (Certificate); school psychology (MA). Part-time programs available. *Faculty:* 10 full-time (7 women), 1 (woman) part-time/adjunct. *Students:* 37 full-time (30 women), 38 part-time (33 women); includes 48 minority (5 Black or African American, non-Hispanic/Latino; 1 Asian, non-Hispanic/Latino; 41 Hispanic/Latino; 1 Native Hawaiian or other Pacific Islander, non-Hispanic/Latino), 1 international. Average age 27. 46 applicants, 89% accepted, 20 enrolled. In 2014, 17 master's awarded. *Degree requirements:* For master's, comprehensive exam, thesis (for some programs). *Entrance requirements:* For master's, GRE, bachelor's degree with 18 credit hours in field of study or in another appropriate field of study, two letters of recommendation, statement of purpose; for Certificate, 18 hours in psychology, sociology, education, or anything related (for applied behavioral analysis); minimum GPA of 2.7 in last 30 hours (for language acquisition and bilingual psychoeducational assessment). Additional exam requirements/recommendations for international students: Required—TOEFL (minimum score 550 paper-based; 79 iBT), IELTS (minimum score 6.5). *Application deadline:* For fall admission, 7/1 for domestic students, 4/1 for international students; for spring admission, 11/1 for domestic students, 9/1 for international students; for summer admission, 3/1 for international students. Applications are processed on a rolling basis. Application fee: $45 ($80 for international students). Electronic applications accepted. *Expenses:* Tuition, state resident: full-time $4671; part-time $260 per credit hour. Tuition, nonresident: full-time $18,022; part-time $1001 per credit hour. *Financial support:* In 2014–15, 9 research assistantships (averaging $2,829 per year) were awarded. Financial award application deadline: 3/5; financial award applicants required to submit FAFSA. *Faculty research:* Teacher consultation and culturally responsive school psychology practices, youth mentoring, cross-age peer mentoring, adolescent connectedness, pair counseling. *Unit head:* Dr. Jeremy Sullivan, Department Chair, 210-458-2408, Fax: 210-458-2019, E-mail: jeremy.sullivan@utsa.edu. *Application contact:* Dr. John Pruiett, Development Specialist, 210-458-2721, Fax: 210-458-2019, E-mail: johnny.pruiett@utsa.edu.
Website: http://education.utsa.edu/educational_psychology

The University of Texas at Tyler, College of Education and Psychology, Department of Psychology and Counseling, Tyler, TX 75799-0001. Offers clinical psychology (MS), including neuropsychology, school psychology; counseling psychology (MA), including general, marriage and family; interdisciplinary studies (MSIS); school counseling (MA). Part-time and evening/weekend programs available. *Degree requirements:* For master's, comprehensive exam, thesis optional. *Entrance requirements:* For master's, GRE General Test, minimum GPA of 3.0. Additional exam requirements/recommendations for international students: Required—TOEFL. Electronic applications accepted. *Faculty research:* Neuropsychology, child abuse, psychometric properties of psychological instruments, maternal behavior, clinical practice issues, victimization of women, post-traumatic stress disorder.

The University of Texas–Pan American, College of Education, Department of Educational Psychology, Edinburg, TX 78539. Offers educational diagnostician (M Ed); gifted education (M Ed); guidance and counseling (M Ed); school psychology (MA); special education (M Ed). Part-time and evening/weekend programs available. *Degree requirements:* For master's, comprehensive exam (for some programs), thesis (for some programs). *Entrance requirements:* For master's, GRE General Test, interview. *Expenses:* Tuition, state resident: full-time $4187; part-time $232.60 per credit hour. Tuition, nonresident: full-time $10,857; part-time $603.16 per credit hour. *Required fees:* $782; $27.50 per credit hour. $143.35 per semester. *Faculty research:* Reading instruction, assessment practice, behavior interventions consultation, mental retardation.

University of the Pacific, Gladys L. Benerd School of Education, Department of Educational and School Psychology, Stockton, CA 95211-0197. Offers educational psychology (MA, Ed D); school psychology (Ed S). *Accreditation:* NCATE. *Students:* 13 full-time (11 women), 7 part-time (all women); includes 9 minority (1 American Indian or Alaska Native, non-Hispanic/Latino; 2 Asian, non-Hispanic/Latino; 6 Hispanic/Latino). Average age 28. 6 applicants, 100% accepted, 2 enrolled. In 2014, 19 master's, 3 doctorates awarded. *Degree requirements:* For master's, thesis; for doctorate, thesis/dissertation. *Entrance requirements:* For master's and doctorate, GRE General Test, GRE Subject Test. Additional exam requirements/recommendations for international students: Required—TOEFL (minimum score 475 paper-based). *Application deadline:* For fall admission, 3/1 priority date for domestic students; for spring admission, 10/1 priority date for domestic students. Applications are processed on a rolling basis. Application fee: $75. *Financial support:* In 2014–15, 4 teaching assistantships were awarded. Financial award application deadline: 3/1; financial award applicants required to submit FAFSA. *Unit head:* Dr. Linda Webster, Chairperson, 209-946-2559, E-mail: lwebster@pacific.edu. *Application contact:* Office of Graduate Admissions, 209-946-2344.

The University of Toledo, College of Graduate Studies, College of Social Justice and Human Service, Department of School Psychology, Higher Education and Counselor Education, Toledo, OH 43606-3390. Offers counselor education (MA, PhD); higher education (ME, PhD, Certificate); school psychology (MA, Ed S). Part-time programs available. *Degree requirements:* For master's, comprehensive exam, thesis or alternative; for doctorate, comprehensive exam, thesis/dissertation; for other advanced degree, thesis optional. *Entrance requirements:* For master's, doctorate, and other advanced degree, minimum cumulative GPA of 2.7 for all previous academic work, letters of recommendation. Additional exam requirements/recommendations for international students: Required—TOEFL (minimum score 550 paper-based; 80 iBT). Electronic applications accepted.

University of Utah, Graduate School, College of Education, Department of Educational Psychology, Salt Lake City, UT 84112. Offers clinical mental health counseling (M Ed); counseling psychology (PhD); elementary education (M Ed); instructional design and educational technology (M Ed); instructional design and technology (MS); learning and cognition (MS, PhD); reading and literacy (M Ed, PhD); school counseling (M Ed); school psychology (M Ed, PhD); statistics (M Stat). *Accreditation:* APA (one or more programs are accredited). *Faculty:* 24 full-time (12 women), 25 part-time/adjunct (17 women). *Students:* 207 full-time (153 women), 1 part-time (0 women); includes 31 minority (1 Black or African American, non-Hispanic/Latino; 1 American Indian or Alaska Native, non-Hispanic/Latino; 9 Asian, non-Hispanic/Latino; 15 Hispanic/Latino; 1 Native Hawaiian or other Pacific Islander, non-Hispanic/Latino; 4 Two or more races, non-Hispanic/Latino), 3 international. Average age 32. 225 applicants, 38% accepted, 71 enrolled. In 2014, 68 master's, 11 doctorates awarded. Terminal master's awarded for partial completion of doctoral program. *Degree requirements:* For master's, variable foreign language requirement, comprehensive exam (for some programs), thesis (for some programs), projects; for doctorate, variable foreign language requirement, comprehensive exam, thesis/dissertation, oral exam. *Entrance requirements:* For master's and doctorate, GRE General Test, minimum GPA of 3.0. Additional exam requirements/recommendations for international students: Required—TOEFL (minimum score 80 iBT). *Application deadline:* For fall admission, 12/15 for domestic and international students; for winter admission, 11/1 for domestic and international students; for spring admission, 3/15 for domestic and international students. Application fee: $55 ($65 for international students). Electronic applications accepted. *Expenses:* Expenses: Contact institution. *Financial support:* In 2014–15, 84 students received support, including 10 fellowships with full and partial tuition reimbursements available (averaging $18,000 per year), 15 research assistantships with full and partial tuition reimbursements available (averaging $13,500 per year), 59 teaching assistantships with full and partial tuition reimbursements available (averaging $13,500 per year); career-related internships or fieldwork, Federal Work-Study, institutionally sponsored loans, scholarships/grants, health care benefits, and unspecified assistantships also available. Financial award application deadline: 4/1; financial award applicants required to submit FAFSA. *Faculty research:* Autism, computer technology and instruction, cognitive behavior, aging, group counseling. *Unit head:* Dr. Anne E. Cook, Chair, 801-581-7148, Fax: 801-581-5566, E-mail: anne.cook@utah.edu. *Application contact:* JoLynn N. Yates, Academic Program Specialist, 801-581-7148, Fax: 801-581-5566, E-mail: jo.yates@utah.edu.
Website: http://www.ed.utah.edu/edps/

University of Virginia, Curry School of Education, Department of Human Services, Program in Clinical and School Psychology, Charlottesville, VA 22903. Offers PhD. *Students:* 26 full-time (23 women); includes 10 minority (5 Black or African American, non-Hispanic/Latino; 3 Asian, non-Hispanic/Latino; 1 Hispanic/Latino; 1 Two or more races, non-Hispanic/Latino). Average age 28. 145 applicants, 5% accepted, 6 enrolled. In 2014, 3 doctorates awarded. *Expenses:* Tuition, state resident: full-time $14,164; part-time $349 per credit hour. Tuition, nonresident: full-time $23,722; part-time $1300 per credit hour. *Required fees:* $2514. *Unit head:* Dr. Ronald Reeve, Director, 434-924-0790, E-mail: rer5r@virginia.edu.
Website: http://curry.virginia.edu/academics/areas-of-study/clinical-school-psychology

University of Virginia, Curry School of Education, Program in Education, Charlottesville, VA 22903. Offers administration and supervision (PhD); applied developmental science (PhD); counselor education (PhD); curriculum and instruction (PhD); early childhood special education (MT); education evaluation (PhD); educational psychology (PhD); educational research (PhD); elementary education (MT); English education (MT, PhD); foreign language education (MT); higher education (PhD); instructional technology (PhD); kinesiology (MT, PhD); math education (PhD); reading education (PhD); research, statistics and evaluation (PhD); school psychology (PhD); science education (PhD); social studies education (MT, PhD); special education (PhD); world languages education (MT). *Students:* 472 full-time (371 women), 32 part-time (24

women); includes 94 minority (25 Black or African American, non-Hispanic/Latino; 1 American Indian or Alaska Native, non-Hispanic/Latino; 36 Asian, non-Hispanic/Latino; 16 Hispanic/Latino; 16 Two or more races, non-Hispanic/Latino), 22 international. Average age 26. 330 applicants, 48% accepted, 79 enrolled. In 2014, 139 master's, 33 doctorates awarded. *Degree requirements:* For master's, comprehensive exam (for some programs), field project; for doctorate, comprehensive exam, thesis/dissertation. *Entrance requirements:* For doctorate, GRE General Test. Additional exam requirements/recommendations for international students: Required—TOEFL (minimum score 600 paper-based; 90 iBT), IELTS (minimum score 7). *Application deadline:* Applications are processed on a rolling basis. Application fee: $60. Electronic applications accepted. *Expenses:* Tuition, state resident: full-time $14,164; part-time $349 per credit hour. Tuition, nonresident: full-time $23,722; part-time $1300 per credit hour. *Required fees:* $2514. *Financial support:* Fellowships, research assistantships, and teaching assistantships available. Financial award application deadline: 1/5; financial award applicants required to submit FAFSA. *Unit head:* Robert C. Pianta, Dean, 434-924-3334, E-mail: pianta@virginia.edu. *Application contact:* Office of Admissions and Student Services, 434-924-0742, E-mail: curry-admissions@virginia.edu.
Website: http://curry.virginia.edu/teacher-education

University of Washington, Graduate School, College of Education, Program in Educational Psychology, Seattle, WA 98195. Offers educational psychology (PhD); human development and cognition (M Ed); learning sciences (M Ed, PhD); measurement, statistics and research design (M Ed); school psychology (M Ed). *Accreditation:* APA. *Degree requirements:* For master's, thesis optional; for doctorate, thesis/dissertation. *Entrance requirements:* For master's and doctorate, GRE General Test, minimum GPA of 3.0. Additional exam requirements/recommendations for international students: Required—TOEFL.

The University of West Alabama, School of Graduate Studies, College of Education, Departments of Instructional Leadership and Support/Curriculum and Instruction, Program in School Counseling, Livingston, AL 35470. Offers M Ed, Ed S. *Accreditation:* NCATE. Part-time and evening/weekend programs available. Postbaccalaureate distance learning degree programs offered (no on-campus study). *Faculty:* 9 full-time (4 women), 17 part-time/adjunct (14 women). *Students:* 441 (400 women); includes 183 minority (167 Black or African American, non-Hispanic/Latino; 5 American Indian or Alaska Native, non-Hispanic/Latino; 2 Asian, non-Hispanic/Latino; 5 Hispanic/Latino; 4 Two or more races, non-Hispanic/Latino). Average age 36. 139 applicants, 91% accepted, 94 enrolled. In 2014, 129 master's, 48 Ed Ss awarded. *Degree requirements:* For master's, comprehensive exam, thesis optional. *Entrance requirements:* For master's, GRE General Test, MAT, minimum GPA of 2.75. Additional exam requirements/recommendations for international students: Required—TOEFL (minimum score 500 paper-based; 61 iBT). *Application deadline:* For fall admission, 8/12 for domestic students; for spring admission, 3/21 for domestic students. Applications are processed on a rolling basis. Application fee: $25. Electronic applications accepted. *Expenses:* Tuition, state resident: full-time $1902; part-time $317 per credit hour. Tuition, nonresident: full-time $3804; part-time $634 per credit hour. *Required fees:* $50 per semester. One-time fee: $65. Tuition and fees vary according to course load. *Financial support:* Teaching assistantships, career-related internships or fieldwork, Federal Work-Study, scholarships/grants, and unspecified assistantships available. Support available to part-time students. Financial award application deadline: 3/1; financial award applicants required to submit FAFSA. *Unit head:* Dr. Reenay Rogers, Chair of Instructional Leadership and Support, 205-652-5423, Fax: 205-652-3706, E-mail: rrogers@uwa.edu. *Application contact:* Dr. Kathy Chandler, Dean of Graduate Studies, 205-652-3421, Fax: 205-652-3706, E-mail: kchandler@uwa.edu.
Website: http://www.uwa.edu/medschoolcounseling.aspx

University of Wisconsin–Eau Claire, College of Arts and Sciences, Department of Psychology, Eau Claire, WI 54702-4004. Offers school psychology (MSE, Ed S). Part-time programs available. *Degree requirements:* For master's, comprehensive exam, thesis, National Certified School Psychologist Professional Exam, written exam, externship. *Entrance requirements:* For master's, GRE, minimum undergraduate GPA of 3.0; courses in exceptional children and youth, statistics, psychopathology, and theories of counseling. Additional exam requirements/recommendations for international students: Required—TOEFL (minimum score 79 iBT).

University of Wisconsin–La Crosse, Graduate Studies, College of Liberal Studies, Department of Psychology, La Crosse, WI 54601-3742. Offers school psychology (MS Ed, Ed S). *Faculty:* 4 full-time (2 women). *Students:* 23 full-time (19 women), 6 part-time (5 women); includes 1 minority (Hispanic/Latino). Average age 24. 51 applicants, 35% accepted, 12 enrolled. In 2014, 11 master's, 14 Ed Ss awarded. *Degree requirements:* For master's, thesis, seminar, or comprehensive exams. *Entrance requirements:* For master's and Ed S, GRE. Additional exam requirements/recommendations for international students: Required—TOEFL (minimum score 550 paper-based; 79 iBT). *Application deadline:* For fall admission, 1/31 for domestic and international students. Electronic applications accepted. *Financial support:* In 2014–15, 6 research assistantships were awarded; Federal Work-Study, scholarships/grants, and health care benefits also available. Support available to part-time students. *Unit head:* Dr. Betsy Morgan, Chair, 608-785-6885, E-mail: bmorgan@uwlax.edu. *Application contact:* Brandon Schaller, Senior Graduate Student Status Examiner, 608-785-8941, E-mail: admissions@uwlax.edu.
Website: http://www.uwlax.edu/school-psychology/

University of Wisconsin–Milwaukee, Graduate School, School of Education, Program in School Psychology, Milwaukee, WI 53201-0413. Offers PhD, Ed S. *Accreditation:* APA. Electronic applications accepted.

University of Wisconsin–River Falls, Outreach and Graduate Studies, College of Education and Professional Studies, Department of Counseling and School Psychology, River Falls, WI 54022. Offers counseling (MSE); school psychology (MSE, Ed S). Part-time programs available. *Entrance requirements:* For master's, minimum GPA of 2.75, resume, 3 letters of reference, vita. Additional exam requirements/recommendations for international students: Required—TOEFL (minimum score 500 paper-based; 65 iBT), IELTS (minimum score 5.5). Electronic applications accepted.

University of Wisconsin–Stout, Graduate School, School of Education, Program in School Psychology, Menomonie, WI 54751. Offers MS Ed, Ed S. Part-time programs available. *Degree requirements:* For master's and Ed S, thesis. *Entrance requirements:* For master's, minimum GPA of 3.0; for Ed S, minimum GPA of 3.25. Additional exam requirements/recommendations for international students: Required—TOEFL (minimum score 500 paper-based; 61 iBT). *Application deadline:* For fall admission, 1/15 priority date for domestic and international students. Application fee: $45. Electronic applications accepted. *Financial support:* Research assistantships with partial tuition reimbursements, teaching assistantships with partial tuition reimbursements, Federal Work-Study, scholarships/grants, tuition waivers (partial), and unspecified assistantships available. Support available to part-time students. Financial award application deadline: 5/1; financial award applicants required to submit FAFSA. *Faculty research:* Intelligence assessment, eating disorders, intervention models, resilience, school violence. *Unit head:* Dr. Carlos Dejud, Director, 715-232-2229, Fax: 715-232-1244, E-mail: dejudc@uwstout.edu. *Application contact:* Anne E. Johnson, Graduate Student Evaluator (Admissions and Assistantship Coordinator), 715-232-1322, Fax: 715-232-2413, E-mail: johnsona@uwstout.edu.
Website: http://www.uwstout.edu/programs/edssp/

University of Wisconsin–Superior, Graduate Division, Department of Counseling and Psychological Professions, Superior, WI 54880-4500. Offers community counseling (MSE); human relations (MSE); school counseling (MSE). Part-time and evening/weekend programs available. *Degree requirements:* For master's, position paper, practicum. *Entrance requirements:* For master's, GRE and/or MAT, minimum GPA of 2.75. Electronic applications accepted. *Faculty research:* Women and power, intrafamily dynamics.

University of Wisconsin–Whitewater, School of Graduate Studies, College of Education and Professional Studies, Department of Counselor Education, Whitewater, WI 53190-1790. Offers community counseling (MS Ed); higher education (MS Ed); school counseling (MS Ed). *Accreditation:* ACA; NCATE. Part-time and evening/weekend programs available. *Degree requirements:* For master's, thesis or alternative. *Entrance requirements:* For master's, resume, 2 letters of reference, goal statement, autobiography. Additional exam requirements/recommendations for international students: Required—TOEFL (minimum score 550 paper-based; 80 iBT), IELTS (minimum score 6). Electronic applications accepted. *Faculty research:* Alcohol and other drugs, counseling effectiveness, teacher mentoring.

University of Wisconsin–Whitewater, School of Graduate Studies, College of Letters and Sciences, Department of Psychology, Program in Education Specialist, Whitewater, WI 53190-1790. Offers MSE, Ed S. Part-time and evening/weekend programs available. Postbaccalaureate distance learning degree programs offered (no on-campus study). *Degree requirements:* For Ed S, specialist project. *Entrance requirements:* For degree, master's degree in school psychology from an accredited school. Additional exam requirements/recommendations for international students: Required—TOEFL (minimum score 550 paper-based; 80 iBT), IELTS (minimum score 6). Electronic applications accepted.

Utah State University, School of Graduate Studies, Emma Eccles Jones College of Education and Human Services, Department of Psychology, Logan, UT 84322. Offers clinical/counseling/school psychology (PhD); research and evaluation methodology (PhD); school counseling (MS); school psychology (MS). *Accreditation:* APA (one or more programs are accredited). Part-time and evening/weekend programs available. Postbaccalaureate distance learning degree programs offered (no on-campus study). Terminal master's awarded for partial completion of doctoral program. *Degree requirements:* For master's, thesis (for some programs); for doctorate, thesis/dissertation. *Entrance requirements:* For master's, GRE General Test (school psychology), MAT (school counseling), minimum GPA of 3.5; for doctorate, GRE General Test, minimum GPA of 3.5. Additional exam requirements/recommendations for international students: Required—TOEFL. *Faculty research:* Hearing loss detection in infancy, ADHD, eating disorders, domestic violence, neuropsychology, bilingual/Spanish speaking students/parents.

Valparaiso University, Graduate School, Department of Education, Program in School Psychology, Valparaiso, IN 46383. Offers M Ed/Ed S. Part-time and evening/weekend programs available. *Students:* 21 full-time (18 women), 11 part-time (7 women); includes 3 minority (1 Asian, non-Hispanic/Latino; 1 Hispanic/Latino; 1 Two or more races, non-Hispanic/Latino), 2 international. Average age 29. *Entrance requirements:* Additional exam requirements/recommendations for international students: Required—TOEFL (minimum score 550 paper-based; 80 iBT), IELTS (minimum score 6). *Application deadline:* For fall admission, 3/1 priority date for domestic students. Applications are processed on a rolling basis. Application fee: $30 ($50 for international students). Electronic applications accepted. *Expenses: Tuition:* Full-time $10,710; part-time $595 per credit hour. *Required fees:* $378; $101 per term. Tuition and fees vary according to course load and program. *Financial support:* Unspecified assistantships available. Support available to part-time students. Financial award applicants required to submit FAFSA. *Unit head:* Dr. Kevin Gary, Chair, Department of Education, 219-464-6154, Fax: 219-464-6720. *Application contact:* Jessica Choquette, Graduate Admissions Specialist, 219-464-5313, Fax: 219-464-5381, E-mail: jessica.choquette@valpo.edu.
Website: http://www.valpo.edu/education/programs/schoolpsychology/

Wayne State University, College of Education, Division of Theoretical and Behavioral Foundations, Detroit, MI 48202. Offers counseling (M Ed, MA, Ed D, PhD, Ed S); education evaluation and research (M Ed, Ed D, PhD); educational psychology (M Ed, PhD), including learning and instruction sciences (PhD), school psychology (PhD); rehabilitation counseling and community inclusion (MA); school and community psychology (MA); school psychology (Certificate). *Accreditation:* ACA (one or more programs are accredited); CORE (one or more programs are accredited). Evening/weekend programs available. *Students:* 237 full-time (197 women), 234 part-time (209 women); includes 172 minority (135 Black or African American, non-Hispanic/Latino; 1 American Indian or Alaska Native, non-Hispanic/Latino; 12 Asian, non-Hispanic/Latino; 11 Hispanic/Latino; 1 Native Hawaiian or other Pacific Islander, non-Hispanic/Latino; 12 Two or more races, non-Hispanic/Latino), 24 international. Average age 33. 297 applicants, 37% accepted, 75 enrolled. In 2014, 82 master's, 17 doctorates, 12 other advanced degrees awarded. *Degree requirements:* For master's, thesis (for some programs); for doctorate, thesis/dissertation. *Entrance requirements:* For master's, GRE; for doctorate, GRE, interview, minimum GPA of 3.0, curriculum vitae, references; for other advanced degree, master's degree in counseling and counseling license (for Ed S); good standing in school and community psychology MA program (for Certificate). Additional exam requirements/recommendations for international students: Required—TOEFL (minimum score 550 paper-based; 79 iBT), Michigan English Language Assessment Battery (minimum score 85); Recommended—IELTS (minimum score 6.5), TWE (minimum score 5.5). *Application deadline:* For fall admission, 6/1 priority date for domestic students, 5/1 priority date for international students; for winter admission, 10/1 priority date for domestic students, 9/1 priority date for international students; for spring admission, 2/1 priority date for domestic students, 1/1 priority date for international students. Applications are processed on a rolling basis. Application fee: $0. Electronic applications accepted. *Expenses:* Tuition, state resident: full-time $10,294; part-time $571.90 per credit hour. Tuition, nonresident: full-time $29,730; part-time $1238.75 per credit hour. *Required fees:* $1365; $43.50 per credit hour. $291.10 per semester. Tuition and fees vary according to course load and program. *Financial support:* In 2014–15, 143 students received support, including 2 research assistantships with tuition reimbursements available (averaging $16,838 per year); fellowships with tuition reimbursements available, teaching assistantships with tuition reimbursements available, Federal Work-Study, scholarships/grants, health care benefits, and unspecified assistantships also available. Support available to part-time students. Financial award application deadline: 3/31; financial award applicants required to submit FAFSA. *Faculty research:* Adolescents at risk, supervision of counseling. *Unit head:* Dr. Joanne Holbert, Interim Assistant Dean, 313-577-1691, E-mail: jholbert@wayne.edu. *Application contact:* Janice Green, Assistant Dean, 313-577-1605, E-mail: jwgreen@wayne.edu.
Website: http://coe.wayne.edu/tbf/index.php

Western Carolina University, Graduate School, College of Education and Allied Professions, Department of Psychology, Cullowhee, NC 28723. Offers general

psychology (MA); school psychology (MA). Part-time programs available. *Degree requirements:* For master's, comprehensive exam, thesis. *Entrance requirements:* For master's, GRE General Test, appropriate undergraduate degree, interview, 3 letters of recommendation. Additional exam requirements/recommendations for international students: Required—TOEFL (minimum score 550 paper-based; 79 iBT). *Faculty research:* Five-factor model of personality, evolutionary psychology, stress and worry, body image and physical attractiveness, moral decision-making, memory, learning styles.

Western Illinois University, School of Graduate Studies, College of Arts and Sciences, Department of Psychology, Macomb, IL 61455-1390. Offers clinical/community mental health (MS); general psychology (MS); psychology (MS, SSP); school psychology (SSP). Part-time programs available. *Students:* 28 full-time (19 women), 10 part-time (5 women); includes 1 minority (Hispanic/Latino), 5 international. Average age 26. 69 applicants, 46% accepted, 12 enrolled. In 2014, 18 master's, 6 other advanced degrees awarded. *Degree requirements:* For master's, comprehensive exam (for some programs), thesis or alternative. *Entrance requirements:* For master's and SSP, GRE General Test. Additional exam requirements/recommendations for international students: Required—TOEFL (minimum score 550 paper-based; 80 iBT). *Application deadline:* Applications are processed on a rolling basis. Application fee: $30. Electronic applications accepted. *Financial support:* In 2014–15, 41 students received support, including 14 research assistantships with full tuition reimbursements available (averaging $7,544 per year), 34 teaching assistantships with full tuition reimbursements available (averaging $8,688 per year). Financial award applicants required to submit FAFSA. *Unit head:* Dr. Karen Sears, Interim Chairperson, 309-298-1593. *Application contact:* Dr. Nancy Parsons, Associate Provost and Director of Graduate Studies, 309-298-1806, Fax: 309-298-2345, E-mail: grad-office@wiu.edu.
Website: http://wiu.edu/psychology

Western Kentucky University, Graduate Studies, College of Education and Behavioral Sciences, Department of Psychology, Bowling Green, KY 42101. Offers clinical psychology (MA); experimental psychology (MA); general psychology (MA); industrial/organizational psychology (MA); school psychology (Ed S). *Degree requirements:* For master's, comprehensive exam, thesis (for some programs); for Ed S, thesis, oral exam. *Entrance requirements:* For master's, GRE General Test; for Ed S, GRE General Test, minimum GPA of 3.5. Additional exam requirements/recommendations for international students: Required—TOEFL (minimum score 555 paper-based; 79 iBT). *Faculty research:* Neural regeneration, enhancing mobility in the elderly, improvement in visual processing in older adults, lifespan development.

Wichita State University, Graduate School, College of Education, Department of Counseling, Educational Leadership, Educational and School Psychology, Wichita, KS 67260. Offers counseling (M Ed); educational leadership (M Ed, Ed D); educational psychology (M Ed); school psychology (Ed S). *Accreditation:* NCATE. Part-time and evening/weekend programs available. *Unit head:* Dr. Jean Patterson, Chairperson, 316-978-3325, Fax: 316-978-3102, E-mail: jean.patterson@wichita.edu. *Application contact:* Jordan Oleson, Admissions Coordinator, 316-978-3095, Fax: 316-978-3253, E-mail: jordan.oleson@wichita.edu.
Website: http://www.wichita.edu/cesp

Worcester State University, Graduate Studies, Department of Education, Program in School Psychology, Worcester, MA 01602-2597. Offers CAGS. *Faculty:* 12 full-time (11 women), 21 part-time/adjunct (9 women). *Students:* 19 full-time (17 women), 5 part-time (all women); includes 1 minority (Hispanic/Latino). Average age 26. 23 applicants, 57% accepted, 11 enrolled. In 2014, 11 CAGSs awarded. *Entrance requirements:* For degree, MTEL Communication and Literacy Skills test (strongly recommended), undergraduate major or concentration in psychology. Additional exam requirements/recommendations for international students: Required—TOEFL (minimum score 550 paper-based; 79 iBT). *Application deadline:* For fall admission, 3/1 priority date for domestic and international students. Applications are processed on a rolling basis. Application fee: $50. Electronic applications accepted. *Expenses: Tuition, area resident:* Part-time $150 per credit. Tuition, state resident: part-time $150 per credit. Tuition, nonresident: part-time $150 per credit. *Financial support:* In 2014–15, 3 research assistantships (averaging $4,800 per year) were awarded; career-related internships or fieldwork, scholarships/grants, and unspecified assistantships also available. Financial award application deadline: 3/1; financial award applicants required to submit FAFSA. *Unit head:* Dr. Diane Tighe Cooke, Coordinator, 508-929-8673, Fax: 508-929-8164, E-mail: dcooke@worcester.edu. *Application contact:* Sara Grady, Acting Associate Dean of Graduate and Continuing Education, 508-929-8787, Fax: 508-929-8100, E-mail: sara.grady@worcester.edu.

Yeshiva University, Ferkauf Graduate School of Psychology, Program in School/Clinical-Child Psychology, New York, NY 10033-3201. Offers Psy D. *Accreditation:* APA. Part-time programs available. *Degree requirements:* For doctorate, comprehensive exam, thesis/dissertation. *Entrance requirements:* For doctorate, GRE General Test. *Faculty research:* Testing, early childhood intervention, child and adolescent psychotherapy, clinical child psychology.

Youngstown State University, Graduate School, Beeghly College of Education, Department of Counseling, Youngstown, OH 44555-0001. Offers community counseling (MS Ed); school counseling (MS Ed). *Accreditation:* ACA; NCATE. Part-time and evening/weekend programs available. *Degree requirements:* For master's, comprehensive exam. *Entrance requirements:* For master's, MAT, interview, minimum GPA of 2.7. Additional exam requirements/recommendations for international students: Required—TOEFL. *Faculty research:* Suicide, euthanasia, ethical issues, marriage and family.

Social Psychology

★ **Adler University,** Programs in Psychology, Chicago, IL 60602. Offers advanced Adlerian psychotherapy (Certificate); art therapy (MA); clinical neuropsychology (Certificate); clinical psychology (Psy D); community psychology (MA); counseling and organizational psychology (MA); counseling psychology (MA); criminology (MA); emergency management leadership (MA); forensic psychology (MA); marriage and family counseling (MA); marriage and family therapy (Certificate); military psychology (MA); nonprofit management (MA); organizational psychology (MA); police psychology (MA); public policy and administration (MA); rehabilitation counseling (MA); sport and health psychology (MA); substance abuse counseling (Certificate); Psy D/Certificate; Psy D/MACAT; Psy D/MACP; Psy D/MAMFC; Psy D/MASAC. *Accreditation:* APA. Part-time and evening/weekend programs available. Postbaccalaureate distance learning degree programs offered (minimal on-campus study). Terminal master's awarded for partial completion of doctoral program. *Degree requirements:* For master's, thesis or alternative, oral exam, practicum; for doctorate, thesis/dissertation, clinical exam, internship, oral exam, practicum, written qualifying exam. *Entrance requirements:* For master's, 12 semester hours in psychology, minimum GPA of 3.0; for doctorate, 18 semester hours in psychology, minimum GPA of 3.25; for Certificate, appropriate master's or doctoral degree. Additional exam requirements/recommendations for international students: Required—TOEFL (minimum score 550 paper-based; 79 iBT). Electronic applications accepted.

See Display on page 969 and Close-Up on page 1207.

Alliant International University–Los Angeles, California School of Professional Psychology, Psy D Program in Clinical Psychology, Alhambra, CA 91803-1360. Offers clinical health psychology (Psy D); family/child and couple clinical psychology (Psy D); multi-interest option (Psy D); multicultural community-clinical psychology (Psy D). *Accreditation:* APA. *Degree requirements:* For doctorate, comprehensive exam, thesis/dissertation. *Entrance requirements:* For doctorate, interview, minimum GPA of 3.0 in both psychology and overall. Additional exam requirements/recommendations for international students: Required—TOEFL (minimum score 600 paper-based), TWE. Electronic applications accepted. *Faculty research:* Child and family psychology, multicultural and community psychology, acculturation, lesbian and gay issues, women's health.

Alvernia University, Graduate Studies, Department of Psychology and Counseling, Reading, PA 19607-1799. Offers community counseling (MA). *Entrance requirements:* For master's, GRE or MAT.

Alverno College, School of Arts and Sciences, Milwaukee, WI 53234-3922. Offers community-based research and consultation (MSCP); professional counselor (MSCP). Part-time and evening/weekend programs available. *Faculty:* 5 full-time (all women), 7 part-time/adjunct (all women). *Students:* 90 full-time (85 women), 24 part-time (23 women); includes 47 minority (25 Black or African American, non-Hispanic/Latino; 2 American Indian or Alaska Native, non-Hispanic/Latino; 4 Asian, non-Hispanic/Latino; 12 Hispanic/Latino; 1 Native Hawaiian or other Pacific Islander, non-Hispanic/Latino; 3 Two or more races, non-Hispanic/Latino), 1 international. Average age 34. 33 applicants, 88% accepted, 23 enrolled. In 2014, 26 master's awarded. *Entrance requirements:* Additional exam requirements/recommendations for international students: Required—TOEFL. *Application deadline:* For fall admission, 7/15 priority date for domestic and international students; for spring admission, 12/15 priority date for domestic and international students. Applications are processed on a rolling basis. Application fee: $0. Electronic applications accepted. Tuition and fees vary according to program. *Financial support:* In 2014–15, 4 students received support. Federal Work-Study and scholarships/grants available. Support available to part-time students. Financial award application deadline: 4/15; financial award applicants required to submit FAFSA. *Unit head:* Dr. Sandra Graham, Program Director, Master of Science in Community Psychology, 414-382-6366, Fax: 414-382-6354, E-mail: sandra.graham@alverno.edu. *Application contact:* Tamikia Taylor, Graduate and Adult Admissions Counselor, 414-382-6045, Fax: 414-382-6354, E-mail: tamikia.taylor@alverno.edu.

Andrews University, School of Graduate Studies, School of Education, Department of Graduate Psychology and Counseling, Program in Community Counseling, Berrien Springs, MI 49104. Offers clinical mental health counseling (MA); community counseling (MA). *Students:* 24 full-time (17 women), 1 (woman) part-time; includes 9 minority (5 Black or African American, non-Hispanic/Latino; 1 American Indian or Alaska Native, non-Hispanic/Latino; 1 Asian, non-Hispanic/Latino; 2 Hispanic/Latino), 5 international. Average age 32. 27 applicants, 56% accepted, 10 enrolled. In 2014, 4 master's awarded. *Degree requirements:* For master's, thesis optional. *Entrance requirements:* For master's, GRE. Additional exam requirements/recommendations for international students: Required—TOEFL (minimum score 550 paper-based). Application fee: $40. Tuition and fees vary according to course level. *Unit head:* Dr. Nancy Carbonell, Coordinator, 269-471-3472. *Application contact:* Monica Wringer, Supervisor of Graduate Admission, 800-253-2874, Fax: 269-471-6321, E-mail: graduate@andrews.edu.

Arcadia University, Graduate Studies, Department of Psychology, Glenside, PA 19038-3295. Offers community counseling (MACP); school counseling (MACP). Part-time programs available. *Degree requirements:* For master's, practicum. *Entrance requirements:* For master's, GRE General Test or MAT. *Expenses:* Contact institution.

Argosy University, Atlanta, College of Psychology and Behavioral Sciences, Atlanta, GA 30328. Offers clinical psychology (MA, Psy D, Postdoctoral Respecialization Certificate), including child and family psychology (Psy D), general adult clinical (Psy D), health psychology (Psy D), neuropsychology/geropsychology (Psy D); community counseling (MA), including marriage and family therapy; counselor education and supervision (Ed D); forensic psychology (MA); industrial organizational psychology (MA); marriage and family therapy (Certificate); sport-exercise psychology (MA). *Accreditation:* APA.

Argosy University, Chicago, College of Psychology and Behavioral Sciences, Chicago, IL 60601. Offers clinical psychology (MA, Psy D), including child and adolescent psychology (Psy D), client-centered and experiential psychotherapies (Psy D), diversity and multicultural psychology (Psy D), family psychology (Psy D), forensic psychology (Psy D), health psychology (Psy D), neuropsychology (Psy D), organizational consulting (Psy D), psychoanalytic psychology (Psy D), psychology and spirituality (Psy D); community counseling (MA); counseling psychology (Ed D), including counselor education and supervision; counselor education and supervision (Ed D); industrial organizational psychology (MA). *Accreditation:* APA (one or more programs are accredited). Postbaccalaureate distance learning degree programs offered (minimal on-campus study).

Argosy University, Dallas, College of Psychology and Behavioral Sciences, Program in Community Counseling, Farmers Branch, TX 75244. Offers MA.

Argosy University, Sarasota, College of Psychology and Behavioral Sciences, Sarasota, FL 34235. Offers community counseling (MA); counseling psychology (Ed D); counselor education and supervision (Ed D); forensic psychology (MA); marriage and family therapy (MA); mental health counseling (MA); pastoral community counseling (Ed D).

Argosy University, Washington DC, College of Psychology and Behavioral Sciences, Arlington, VA 22209. Offers clinical psychology (MA, Psy D), including child and family

psychology (Psy D), diversity and multicultural psychology (Psy D), forensic psychology (Psy D), health and neuropsychology (Psy D); community counseling (MA); counseling psychology (Ed D), including counselor education and supervision; counselor education and supervision (Ed D); forensic psychology (MA). *Accreditation:* APA.

Arizona State University at the Tempe campus, College of Liberal Arts and Sciences, Department of Psychology, Tempe, AZ 85287-1104. Offers applied behavior analysis (MS); behavioral neuroscience (PhD); clinical psychology (PhD); cognitive science (PhD); developmental psychology (PhD); quantitative psychology (PhD); social psychology (PhD). *Accreditation:* APA. *Degree requirements:* For doctorate, comprehensive exam, thesis/dissertation, interactive Program of Study (iPOS) submitted before completing 50 percent of required credit hours. *Entrance requirements:* For doctorate, GRE General Test, GRE Subject Test, minimum GPA of 3.0 or equivalent in last 2 years of work leading to bachelor's degree. Additional exam requirements/recommendations for international students: Required—TOEFL, IELTS, or PTE. Electronic applications accepted.

Ball State University, Graduate School, Teachers College, Department of Counseling Psychology and Guidance Services, Program in Social Psychology, Muncie, IN 47306-1099. Offers MA. *Students:* 13 full-time (7 women), 1 (woman) part-time, 1 international. Average age 26. 26 applicants, 38% accepted, 7 enrolled. In 2014, 3 master's awarded. *Entrance requirements:* For master's, GRE General Test. Application fee: $50. *Financial support:* In 2014–15, 2 students received support, including 3 research assistantships with partial tuition reimbursements available (averaging $8,760 per year), 2 teaching assistantships with partial tuition reimbursements available (averaging $6,860 per year); unspecified assistantships also available. Financial award application deadline: 3/1. *Unit head:* Dr. Sharon Bowman, Head, 765-285-8040, Fax: 765-285-2067, E-mail: sbowman@bsu.edu. *Application contact:* Dr. Michael White, Professor of Psychology, 765-285-8040, E-mail: 00mjwhite@bsu.edu.

Bowling Green State University, Graduate College, College of Arts and Sciences, Department of Sociology, Bowling Green, OH 43403. Offers demography and population studies (MA); social psychology (MA); sociology (PhD). Part-time programs available. *Degree requirements:* For master's, thesis or alternative; for doctorate, comprehensive exam, thesis/dissertation. *Entrance requirements:* For master's and doctorate, GRE General Test. Additional exam requirements/recommendations for international students: Required—TOEFL. Electronic applications accepted. *Faculty research:* Applied demography, criminology and deviance, family studies, population studies, social psychology.

Brandeis University, Graduate School of Arts and Sciences, Department of Psychology, Waltham, MA 02454-9110. Offers brain, body and behavior (PhD); cognitive neuroscience (PhD); general psychology (MA); social/developmental psychology (PhD). Part-time programs available. Terminal master's awarded for partial completion of doctoral program. *Degree requirements:* For master's, thesis; for doctorate, thesis/dissertation, research reports. *Entrance requirements:* For master's and doctorate, GRE General Test; GRE Subject Test (recommended), 3 letters of recommendation, statement of purpose, transcript(s), resume. Additional exam requirements/recommendations for international students: Required—TOEFL (minimum score 600 paper-based; 100 iBT), PTE (minimum score 68); Recommended—IELTS (minimum score 7). Electronic applications accepted. *Faculty research:* Cognitive neuroscience, social developmental psychology, motor control, visual perception, taste physiology and psychophysics, memory, learning, aging, child development, aggression, emotion, personality and cognition in adulthood and old age, social relations and health, stereotypes, nonverbal communication.

Brock University, Faculty of Graduate Studies, Faculty of Social Sciences, Program in Psychology, St. Catharines, ON L2S 3A1, Canada. Offers behavioral neuroscience (MA, PhD); life span development (MA, PhD); social personality (MA, PhD). Part-time programs available. *Degree requirements:* For master's, thesis; for doctorate, thesis/dissertation. *Entrance requirements:* For master's, GRE, honors degree; for doctorate, GRE, master's degree. Additional exam requirements/recommendations for international students: Required—TOEFL (minimum score 550 paper-based; 80 iBT), IELTS (minimum score 6.5), TWE (minimum score 4). Electronic applications accepted. *Faculty research:* Social personality, behavioral neuroscience, life-span development.

Brooklyn College of the City University of New York, School of Natural and Behavioral Sciences, Department of Psychology, Brooklyn, NY 11210-2889. Offers experimental psychology (MA); industrial and organizational psychology (MA), including human relations, organizational behavior; mental health counseling (MA); psychology (PhD). Part-time programs available. *Degree requirements:* For master's, comprehensive exam, thesis (for some programs). *Entrance requirements:* For master's, minimum GPA of 3.0, 2 letters of recommendation, essay; for doctorate, GRE. Additional exam requirements/recommendations for international students: Required—TOEFL (minimum score 520 paper-based; 69 iBT). Electronic applications accepted.

California Institute of Integral Studies, School of Professional Psychology and Health, San Francisco, CA 94103. Offers clinical psychology (Psy D); community mental health (MA); drama therapy (MA); expressive arts therapy (MA); integral counseling psychology (MA); integrative health studies (MA); psychological studies (MA); somatic psychology (MA). *Accreditation:* APA. Part-time and evening/weekend programs available. *Students:* 522 full-time (397 women), 105 part-time (83 women); includes 155 minority (27 Black or African American, non-Hispanic/Latino; 3 American Indian or Alaska Native, non-Hispanic/Latino; 31 Asian, non-Hispanic/Latino; 62 Hispanic/Latino; 3 Native Hawaiian or other Pacific Islander, non-Hispanic/Latino; 29 Two or more races, non-Hispanic/Latino), 49 international. Average age 34. 351 applicants, 86% accepted, 175 enrolled. In 2014, 168 master's, 24 doctorates awarded. *Degree requirements:* For doctorate, comprehensive exam, thesis/dissertation. *Entrance requirements:* For master's, minimum GPA of 3.0, letters of recommendation, writing sample; for doctorate, GRE, MA in psychology or social work with appropriate practical experience for advanced standing, or BA with a minimum GPA of 3.1; letters of recommendation; writing sample. Additional exam requirements/recommendations for international students: Required—TOEFL. *Application deadline:* For fall admission, 2/1 priority date for domestic and international students; for spring admission, 10/15 priority date for domestic and international students. Applications are processed on a rolling basis. Application fee: $65. Electronic applications accepted. *Expenses: Tuition:* Full-time $18,270; part-time $1015 per credit. *Required fees:* $85 per semester hour. *Financial support:* In 2014–15, 464 students received support, including 5 research assistantships with tuition reimbursements available (averaging $800 per year), 36 teaching assistantships with tuition reimbursements available (averaging $825 per year); career-related internships or fieldwork, Federal Work-Study, and scholarships/grants also available. Support available to part-time students. Financial award application deadline: 4/15; financial award applicants required to submit FAFSA. *Faculty research:* Transpersonal psychology, somatic psychology, expressive arts therapy, drama therapy, community mental health, ecopsychology, integrative health. *Application contact:* David Townes, Senior Admissions Counselor, 415-575-6152, Fax: 415-575-1268, E-mail: admissions@ciis.edu.

California State University, East Bay, Office of Academic Programs and Graduate Studies, College of Letters, Arts, and Social Sciences, Department of Social Work, Hayward, CA 94542-3000. Offers children, youth, and family services (MSW); community mental health services (MSW). *Accreditation:* CSWE. *Degree requirements:* For master's, comprehensive exam. *Entrance requirements:* For master's, minimum GPA of 2.8; courses in statistics and either human biology, physiology, or anatomy; liberal arts or social science baccalaureate degree; 3 letters of recommendation; personal statement; consent to criminal background check; student professional liability insurance. Additional exam requirements/recommendations for international students: Required—TOEFL (minimum score 550 paper-based). *Application deadline:* For fall admission, 3/15 for domestic and international students. Applications are processed on a rolling basis. Application fee: $55. Electronic applications accepted. *Expenses:* Tuition, state resident: full-time $7830; part-time $1302 per credit hour. Tuition, nonresident: full-time $16,368. *Required fees:* $327 per quarter. Tuition and fees vary according to course load and program. *Financial support:* Fellowships, career-related internships or fieldwork, Federal Work-Study, institutionally sponsored loans, and scholarships/grants available. Support available to part-time students. Financial award application deadline: 3/2; financial award applicants required to submit FAFSA. *Unit head:* Dr. Evaon Wong-Kim, Chair, 510-885-2148, E-mail: evaon@csueastbay.edu. *Application contact:* Dr. Donna Wiley, Interim Associate Vice President for Academic Programs and Graduate Studies, 510-885-3716, Fax: 510-885-4777, E-mail: donna.wiley@csueastbay.edu.
Website: http://www20.csueastbay.edu/class/departments/socialwork/

California State University, Fullerton, Graduate Studies, College of Humanities and Social Sciences, Department of Psychology, Fullerton, CA 92834-9480. Offers clinical/community psychology (MS); psychology (MA). Part-time programs available. *Students:* 83 full-time (57 women), 16 part-time (7 women); includes 45 minority (1 Black or African American, non-Hispanic/Latino; 9 Asian, non-Hispanic/Latino; 31 Hispanic/Latino; 4 Two or more races, non-Hispanic/Latino), 9 international. Average age 25. 110 applicants, 35% accepted, 37 enrolled. In 2014, 28 master's awarded. *Degree requirements:* For master's, thesis. *Entrance requirements:* For master's, GRE General Test, GRE Subject Test, undergraduate major in psychology or related field. Application fee: $55. *Financial support:* Career-related internships or fieldwork, Federal Work-Study, institutionally sponsored loans, and scholarships/grants available. Support available to part-time students. Financial award application deadline: 3/1; financial award applicants required to submit FAFSA. *Unit head:* Dr. Jack Mearns, Chair, 657-278-3514. *Application contact:* Admissions/Applications, 657-278-2371.

Canisius College, Graduate Division, School of Education and Human Services, Programs in Counseling and Human Services, Buffalo, NY 14208-1098. Offers community mental health counseling (MS); counseling and human services (MS); school agency counseling (MS). *Accreditation:* ACA. Part-time and evening/weekend programs available. *Faculty:* 6 full-time (3 women), 7 part-time/adjunct (5 women). *Students:* 96 full-time (76 women), 30 part-time (24 women); includes 19 minority (7 Black or African American, non-Hispanic/Latino; 1 American Indian or Alaska Native, non-Hispanic/Latino; 2 Asian, non-Hispanic/Latino; 6 Hispanic/Latino; 3 Two or more races, non-Hispanic/Latino). Average age 28. 103 applicants, 86% accepted, 41 enrolled. In 2014, 64 master's awarded. *Degree requirements:* For master's, thesis, research project. *Entrance requirements:* For master's, GRE (if cumulative GPA less than 2.7), transcripts, two letters of recommendation, interview, BA. Additional exam requirements/recommendations for international students: Required—TOEFL (minimum score 550 paper-based, 80 iBT), IELTS (minimum score 6.5), or CAEL (minimum score 70). *Application deadline:* Applications are processed on a rolling basis. Application fee: $25. Electronic applications accepted. Application fee is waived when completed online. *Financial support:* Research assistantships, career-related internships or fieldwork, Federal Work-Study, scholarships/grants, tuition waivers (partial), and unspecified assistantships available. Support available to part-time students. Financial award application deadline: 4/30; financial award applicants required to submit FAFSA. *Faculty research:* Impact of trauma on adults, long term psych-social impact on police officers. *Unit head:* Dr. Christine Moll, Chair, 716-888-3287, E-mail: moll@canisius.edu. *Application contact:* Kathleen B. Davis, Vice President of Enrollment Management, 716-888-2500, Fax: 716-888-3195, E-mail: daviskb@canisius.edu.
Website: http://www.canisius.edu/masters-counseling/

Carnegie Mellon University, Dietrich College of Humanities and Social Sciences, Department of Psychology, Program in Social/Personality/Health Psychology, Pittsburgh, PA 15213-3891. Offers PhD. *Degree requirements:* For doctorate, comprehensive exam, thesis/dissertation. *Entrance requirements:* For doctorate, GRE General Test. Additional exam requirements/recommendations for international students: Required—TOEFL.

Central Connecticut State University, School of Graduate Studies, College of Liberal Arts and Social Sciences, Department of Psychology, New Britain, CT 06050-4010. Offers community psychology (MA); general psychology (MA); health psychology (MA). Part-time and evening/weekend programs available. *Faculty:* 15 full-time (9 women). *Students:* 16 full-time (13 women), 18 part-time (14 women); includes 8 minority (2 Black or African American, non-Hispanic/Latino; 2 Asian, non-Hispanic/Latino; 4 Hispanic/Latino), 2 international. Average age 28. 27 applicants, 41% accepted, 6 enrolled. In 2014, 13 master's awarded. *Degree requirements:* For master's, comprehensive exam, thesis or alternative. *Entrance requirements:* For master's, minimum undergraduate GPA of 2.75, 3.0 in psychology courses; letters of recommendation. Additional exam requirements/recommendations for international students: Required—TOEFL (minimum score 550 paper-based; 79 iBT). *Application deadline:* For fall admission, 5/1 for domestic and international students; for spring admission, 11/1 for domestic and international students. Applications are processed on a rolling basis. Application fee: $50. Electronic applications accepted. *Expenses: Tuition, area resident:* Full-time $5730; part-time $534 per credit. Tuition, state resident: full-time $8596; part-time $534 per credit. Tuition, nonresident: full-time $15,964; part-time $548 per credit. *Required fees:* $4211; $215 per credit. *Financial support:* In 2014–15, 8 students received support, including 5 research assistantships; career-related internships or fieldwork, Federal Work-Study, scholarships/grants, and unspecified assistantships also available. Support available to part-time students. Financial award application deadline: 3/1; financial award applicants required to submit FAFSA. *Faculty research:* Clinical psychology, general psychology, child development, cognitive development, drugs/behavior. *Unit head:* Dr. Carolyn Fallahi, Chair, 860-832-3100, E-mail: fallahic@ccsu.edu. *Application contact:* Patricia Gardner, Associate Director of Graduate Studies, 860-832-2350, Fax: 860-832-2362, E-mail: graduateadmissions@ccsu.edu.
Website: http://web.ccsu.edu/psychology/

Claremont Graduate University, Graduate Programs, School of Social Science, Policy and Evaluation, Department of Psychology, Claremont, CA 91711-6160. Offers advanced study in evaluation (Certificate); cognitive psychology (MA, PhD); developmental psychology (MA, PhD); evaluation and applied research methods (MA, PhD); health behavior research and evaluation (MA, PhD); human resource development and evaluation (MA); industrial/organizational psychology (MA, PhD); organizational behavior (MA, PhD); organizational psychology (MA, PhD); social psychology (MA, PhD); MBA/PhD. Part-time programs available. *Faculty:* 18 full-time (7 women), 1 part-time/adjunct (0 women). *Students:* 256 full-time (160 women), 70 part-

time (50 women); includes 93 minority (17 Black or African American, non-Hispanic/Latino; 3 American Indian or Alaska Native, non-Hispanic/Latino; 26 Asian, non-Hispanic/Latino; 30 Hispanic/Latino; 17 Two or more races, non-Hispanic/Latino), 35 international. Average age 30. In 2014, 56 master's, 15 doctorates, 7 other advanced degrees awarded. Terminal master's awarded for partial completion of doctoral program. *Entrance requirements:* For master's and doctorate, GRE General Test. Additional exam requirements/recommendations for international students: Required—TOEFL (minimum score 550 paper-based; 80 iBT). *Application deadline:* For fall admission, 1/15 priority date for domestic and international students. Applications are processed on a rolling basis. Application fee: $80. Electronic applications accepted. *Expenses: Tuition:* Full-time $41,784; part-time $1741 per credit. *Required fees:* $600; $300 per semester. *Financial support:* Fellowships, research assistantships, teaching assistantships, Federal Work-Study, institutionally sponsored loans, scholarships/grants, and tuition waivers (full and partial) available. Support available to part-time students. Financial award application deadline: 2/15; financial award applicants required to submit FAFSA. *Faculty research:* Social intervention, diversity in organizations, eyewitness memory, aging and cognition, drug policy. *Unit head:* William Crano, Chair, 909-621-8084, E-mail: william.crano@cgu.edu. *Application contact:* Annekah Hall, Assistant Director of Admissions, 909-607-3371, E-mail: annekah.hall@cgu.edu.
Website: http://www.cgu.edu/pages/502.asp

Clark University, Graduate School, Hiatt School of Psychology, Program in Social Psychology, Worcester, MA 01610-1477. Offers PhD. *Students:* 7 full-time (5 women); includes 1 minority (Asian, non-Hispanic/Latino), 3 international. Average age 29. In 2014, 3 doctorates awarded. *Degree requirements:* For doctorate, thesis/dissertation. *Entrance requirements:* For doctorate, GRE General Test. Additional exam requirements/recommendations for international students: Required—TOEFL. *Application deadline:* For fall admission, 12/15 priority date for domestic and international students. Applications are processed on a rolling basis. Application fee: $75. *Expenses: Tuition:* Full-time $40,380; part-time $1262 per credit hour. *Required fees:* $30. *Financial support:* In 2014–15, fellowships with full tuition reimbursements (averaging $16,015 per year), research assistantships with full tuition reimbursements (averaging $16,015 per year), teaching assistantships with full tuition reimbursements (averaging $16,015 per year) were awarded; tuition waivers (full) also available. *Faculty research:* Conceptualizing and reasoning, symbolization, psychotherapy, metaphor, emotions and personalities. *Unit head:* Dr. Johanna Ray Vollhardt, Director, 508-793-7274, E-mail: jvollhardt@clarku.edu. *Application contact:* Kelly Boulay, Graduate School Secretary, 508-793-7274, Fax: 508-793-7265, E-mail: psychology@clarku.edu.
Website: http://www.clarku.edu/departments/psychology/grad/social/index.cfm

Cleveland State University, College of Graduate Studies, College of Education and Human Services, Department of Counseling, Administration, Supervision and Adult Learning (CASAL), Cleveland, OH 44115. Offers adult learning and development (M Ed); chemical dependency counseling (Certificate); clinical mental health counseling (M Ed); early childhood mental health counseling (Certificate); educational administration and supervision (M Ed); organizational leadership (M Ed); school administration (Ed S); school counseling (M Ed). *Accreditation:* ACA (one or more programs are accredited). Part-time and evening/weekend programs available. *Faculty:* 15 full-time (8 women), 19 part-time/adjunct (10 women). *Students:* 76 full-time (59 women), 214 part-time (174 women); includes 110 minority (93 Black or African American, non-Hispanic/Latino; 3 Asian, non-Hispanic/Latino; 13 Hispanic/Latino; 1 Two or more races, non-Hispanic/Latino), 9 international. Average age 34. 57 applicants, 93% accepted, 51 enrolled. In 2014, 99 master's, 4 Certificates awarded. *Degree requirements:* For master's, comprehensive exam (for some programs), thesis optional, internship. *Entrance requirements:* For master's, GRE General Test or MAT, letter of recommendation and minimum GPA of 2.75 (for counseling); 2 letters of recommendation and interviews (for organizational leadership). Additional exam requirements/recommendations for international students: Required—TOEFL (minimum score 525 paper-based), IELTS (minimum score 6). *Application deadline:* For fall admission, 6/21 for domestic students, 5/15 for international students; for spring admission, 8/31 for domestic students, 11/1 for international students. Application fee: $30. Electronic applications accepted. *Expenses:* Tuition, state resident: full-time $9566; part-time $531 per credit hour. Tuition, nonresident: full-time $17,980; part-time $999 per credit hour. *Required fees:* $25 per semester. Tuition and fees vary according to degree level and program. *Financial support:* In 2014–15, 19 students received support, including 10 research assistantships with full and partial tuition reimbursements available (averaging $11,882 per year), 5 teaching assistantships with full and partial tuition reimbursements available (averaging $11,882 per year); scholarships/grants and unspecified assistantships also available. Support available to part-time students. *Faculty research:* Education law, career development, bullying, psychopharmacology, counseling and spirituality. *Total annual research expenditures:* $225,821. *Unit head:* Dr. Ann L. Bauer, Chairperson, 216-687-4582, Fax: 216-687-5378, E-mail: a.l.bauer@csuohio.edu. *Application contact:* Deborah L. Brown, Interim Assistant Director, Graduate Admissions, 216-523-7572, Fax: 216-687-5400, E-mail: d.l.brown@csuohio.edu.
Website: http://www.csuohio.edu/cehs/departments/CASAL/casal_dept.html

College of St. Joseph, Graduate Programs, Division of Psychology and Human Services, Program in Community Counseling, Rutland, VT 05701-3899. Offers MS. Part-time and evening/weekend programs available. *Degree requirements:* For master's, comprehensive exam, thesis optional. *Entrance requirements:* For master's, official college transcripts; 2 letters of reference. Additional exam requirements/recommendations for international students: Required—TOEFL (minimum score 550 paper-based). Electronic applications accepted.

Connecticut College, Department of Psychology, New London, CT 06320-4196. Offers behavioral medicine/health psychology (MA); clinical psychology (MA); neuroscience/psychobiology (MA); social/personality psychology (MA). Part-time programs available. *Students:* 4 full-time (2 women), 3 part-time (2 women). Average age 30. 7 applicants, 29% accepted, 2 enrolled. *Degree requirements:* For master's, thesis. *Entrance requirements:* For master's, GRE General Test, statistics course. Additional exam requirements/recommendations for international students: Required—TOEFL (minimum score 600 paper-based). *Application deadline:* For fall admission, 2/1 for domestic and international students. Application fee: $60. *Expenses: Tuition:* Full-time $12,120. *Financial support:* Tuition remission available. Financial award application deadline: 2/1; financial award applicants required to submit CSS PROFILE or FAFSA. *Unit head:* Dr. Ruth Grahn, Chair, 860-439-2387, Fax: 860-439-5300, E-mail: ruth.grahn@conncoll.edu. *Application contact:* Nancy M. MacLeod, Academic Department Assistant, 860-439-2330, Fax: 860-439-5300, E-mail: nancy.macleod@conncoll.edu.

Cornell University, Graduate School, Graduate Fields of Arts and Sciences, Field of Psychology, Ithaca, NY 14853-0001. Offers biopsychology (PhD); human experimental psychology (PhD); personality and social psychology (PhD). *Degree requirements:* For doctorate, comprehensive exam, thesis/dissertation, 2 semesters of teaching experience. *Entrance requirements:* For doctorate, GRE General Test, 3 letters of recommendation. Additional exam requirements/recommendations for international students: Required—TOEFL (minimum score 550 paper-based; 77 iBT). Electronic applications accepted. *Faculty research:* Sensory and perceptual systems, social cognition, cognitive development, quantitative and computational modeling, behavioral neuroscience.

Cornell University, Graduate School, Graduate Fields of Arts and Sciences, Field of Sociology, Ithaca, NY 14853-0001. Offers economy and society (MA, PhD); gender and life course (MA, PhD); methodology (MA, PhD); organizations (MA, PhD); policy analysis (MA, PhD); political sociology/social movements (MA, PhD); racial and ethnic relations (MA, PhD); social networks (MA, PhD); social psychology (MA, PhD); social stratification (MA, PhD). Terminal master's awarded for partial completion of doctoral program. *Degree requirements:* For master's, thesis; for doctorate, thesis/dissertation, 1 year of teaching experience. *Entrance requirements:* For master's and doctorate, GRE General Test, 2 letters of recommendation, writing sample. Additional exam requirements/recommendations for international students: Required—TOEFL (minimum score 550 paper-based; 77 iBT). Electronic applications accepted. *Faculty research:* Comparative societal analysis, work and family, simulations, social class and mobility, racial segregation and inequality.

Creighton University, Graduate School, College of Arts and Sciences, Department of Education, Omaha, NE 68178-0001. Offers counselor education (MS), including community counseling, elementary school guidance, secondary school guidance; educational leadership (MS, Ed D), including elementary school administration (MS), leadership (Ed D), secondary school administration (MS), teacher leadership (MS); special populations in education (MS); teaching (M Ed), including elementary teaching, secondary teaching. *Accreditation:* NCATE. Part-time and evening/weekend programs available. Postbaccalaureate distance learning degree programs offered (minimal on-campus study). *Faculty:* 12 full-time (6 women). *Students:* 9 full-time (3 women), 103 part-time (70 women); includes 2 minority (1 Black or African American, non-Hispanic/Latino; 1 Hispanic/Latino). Average age 34. 15 applicants, 93% accepted, 14 enrolled. In 2014, 47 master's awarded. *Degree requirements:* For master's, comprehensive exam (for some programs), portfolio. *Entrance requirements:* For master's, GRE General Test, PPST, 3 letters of recommendation; writing samples, resume. Additional exam requirements/recommendations for international students: Required—TOEFL (minimum score 550 paper-based; 80 iBT). *Application deadline:* For fall admission, 7/1 priority date for domestic students, 3/1 priority date for international students; for winter admission, 12/1 for domestic students, 7/1 for international students; for spring admission, 4/1 for domestic students, 10/1 for international students; for summer admission, 3/1 for domestic and international students. Applications are processed on a rolling basis. Application fee: $50. Electronic applications accepted. *Expenses: Tuition:* Full-time $14,040; part-time $780 per credit hour. *Required fees:* $153 per semester. Tuition and fees vary according to course load, campus/location, program, reciprocity agreements and student's religious affiliation. *Financial support:* Scholarships/grants and tuition waivers (partial) available. Support available to part-time students. Financial award applicants required to submit FAFSA. *Unit head:* Dr. Debra Ponec, Chair, 402-280-2557, E-mail: dlponec@creighton.edu. *Application contact:* Lindsay Johnson, Director of Graduate and Adult Recruitment, 402-280-2703, Fax: 402-280-2423, E-mail: gradschool@creighton.edu.

Delaware Valley University, Program in Counseling Psychology, Doylestown, PA 18901-2697. Offers child and adolescent therapy (MA); social justice community counseling (MA).

Florida Agricultural and Mechanical University, Division of Graduate Studies, Research, and Continuing Education, College of Social Sciences, Arts and Humanities, Department of Psychology, Program in Community Psychology, Tallahassee, FL 32307-3200. Offers MS. *Degree requirements:* For master's, thesis, internship. *Entrance requirements:* For master's, GRE General Test, minimum GPA of 3.0, letters of recommendation (3). Additional exam requirements/recommendations for international students: Required—TOEFL. *Faculty research:* African-American personality and mental health, racism in the socialization of black children.

Florida State University, The Graduate School, College of Arts and Sciences, Department of Psychology, Program in Social Psychology, Tallahassee, FL 32306. Offers PhD. *Faculty:* 5 full-time (2 women). *Students:* 16 full-time (10 women), 1 (woman) part-time; includes 2 minority (both Hispanic/Latino). Average age 24. 128 applicants, 4% accepted, 2 enrolled. In 2014, 5 doctorates awarded. Terminal master's awarded for partial completion of doctoral program. *Degree requirements:* For doctorate, comprehensive exam, thesis/dissertation. *Entrance requirements:* For doctorate, GRE General Test, minimum GPA of 3.0, research experience, letters of recommendation. Additional exam requirements/recommendations for international students: Required—TOEFL (minimum score 550 paper-based; 80 iBT). *Application deadline:* For fall admission, 12/16 for domestic and international students. Application fee: $30. *Expenses:* Tuition, state resident: part-time $403.51 per credit hour. Tuition, nonresident: part-time $1004.85 per credit hour. *Required fees:* $75.81 per credit hour. One-time fee: $20 part-time. Tuition and fees vary according to campus/location. *Financial support:* In 2014–15, 16 students received support, including 2 fellowships with full tuition reimbursements available (averaging $20,000 per year), 3 research assistantships with full tuition reimbursements available (averaging $20,000 per year), 11 teaching assistantships with full tuition reimbursements available (averaging $17,775 per year); Federal Work-Study, institutionally sponsored loans, scholarships/grants, traineeships, and unspecified assistantships also available. Financial award application deadline: 12/16. *Faculty research:* Self and identity, prejudice and intergroup relations, evolutionary psychology, emotion, health. *Total annual research expenditures:* $318,829. *Unit head:* Dr. Roy Baumeister, Director, 850-644-4200, Fax: 850-644-7739, E-mail: baumeister@psy.fsu.edu. *Application contact:* Cherie P. Miller, Graduate Program Assistant, 850-644-2499, Fax: 850-644-7739, E-mail: grad-info@psy.fsu.edu.
Website: http://www.psy.fsu.edu/

Future Generations Graduate School, Program in Applied Community Change, Conservation, and Peacebuilding, Franklin, WV 26807. Offers conservation (MA); peacebuilding (MA). *Degree requirements:* For master's, one foreign language, applied practicum research. *Entrance requirements:* For master's, bachelor's degree, community involvement. Additional exam requirements/recommendations for international students: Required—TOEFL. Electronic applications accepted. *Faculty research:* Sustainable communities, community engagement, peacebuilding, seed-scale community development.

The George Washington University, Columbian College of Arts and Sciences, Department of Psychology, Washington, DC 20052. Offers applied social psychology (PhD); clinical psychology (PhD); cognitive neuroscience (PhD). *Accreditation:* APA. Part-time and evening/weekend programs available. *Faculty:* 24 full-time (14 women), 1 (woman) part-time/adjunct. *Students:* 46 full-time (33 women), 24 part-time (15 women); includes 19 minority (7 Black or African American, non-Hispanic/Latino; 3 Asian, non-Hispanic/Latino; 8 Hispanic/Latino; 1 Two or more races, non-Hispanic/Latino), 8 international. Average age 28. 513 applicants, 3% accepted, 14 enrolled. In 2014, 10 doctorates awarded. *Degree requirements:* For doctorate, thesis/dissertation or alternative, general exam. *Entrance requirements:* For doctorate, GRE General Test, minimum GPA of 3.0. Additional exam requirements/recommendations for international students: Required—TOEFL (minimum score 550 paper-based; 80 iBT). *Application deadline:* For fall admission, 1/15 for domestic and international students. Application

fee: $75. *Financial support:* In 2014–15, 62 students received support. Fellowships with tuition reimbursements available, teaching assistantships with tuition reimbursements available, career-related internships or fieldwork, Federal Work-Study, and tuition waivers available. *Unit head:* Dr. Paul Poppen, Chair, 202-994-6324, E-mail: pjp@gwu.edu. *Application contact:* Information Contact, 202-994-6320, Fax: 202-994-1602, E-mail: psydept@gwu.edu.
Website: http://psychology.columbian.gwu.edu/

Georgia State University, College of Arts and Sciences, Department of Psychology, Atlanta, GA 30302-3083. Offers clinical (PhD); cognitive sciences (PhD); community (PhD); developmental (PhD); neuropsychology and behavioral neuroscience (PhD). *Accreditation:* APA. *Faculty:* 29 full-time (17 women). *Students:* 116 full-time (95 women), 2 part-time (both women); includes 30 minority (10 Black or African American, non-Hispanic/Latino; 9 Asian, non-Hispanic/Latino; 6 Hispanic/Latino; 5 Two or more races, non-Hispanic/Latino), 10 international. Average age 28. 577 applicants, 7% accepted, 27 enrolled. In 2014, 16 doctorates awarded. *Degree requirements:* For doctorate, comprehensive exam, thesis/dissertation, residency year (for clinical only). *Entrance requirements:* For doctorate, GRE. Additional exam requirements/recommendations for international students: Required—TOEFL (minimum score 550 paper-based; 80 iBT). *Application deadline:* For fall admission, 12/1 for domestic and international students. Application fee: $50. Electronic applications accepted. *Expenses:* Tuition, state resident: full-time $6516; part-time $362 per credit hour. Tuition, nonresident: full-time $22,014; part-time $1223 per credit hour. *Required fees:* $2128 per semester. Tuition and fees vary according to course load and program. *Financial support:* In 2014–15, fellowships with full tuition reimbursements (averaging $19,282 per year), research assistantships with full tuition reimbursements (averaging $5,173 per year), teaching assistantships with full tuition reimbursements (averaging $6,389 per year) were awarded; scholarships/grants, traineeships, health care benefits, and unspecified assistantships also available. *Faculty research:* Clinical psychology, developmental psychology, community psychology, neuropsychology and behavioral neuroscience, cognitive sciences. *Unit head:* Dr. Lisa Armistead, Chair, 404-413-6205, Fax: 404-413-6207, E-mail: lparmistead@gsu.edu. *Application contact:* Dr. Lindsey Cohen, Director of Graduate Studies, 404-413-6263, Fax: 404-413-6207, E-mail: llcohen@gsu.edu.
Website: http://psychology.gsu.edu/graduate/areas-of-study/

The Graduate Center, City University of New York, Graduate Studies, Program in Psychology, New York, NY 10016-4039. Offers basic applied neurocognition (PhD); biopsychology (PhD); clinical psychology (PhD); developmental psychology (PhD); environmental psychology (PhD); experimental psychology (PhD); industrial psychology (PhD); learning processes (PhD); neuropsychology (PhD); psychology (PhD); social personality (PhD). *Degree requirements:* For doctorate, one foreign language, thesis/dissertation. *Entrance requirements:* For doctorate, GRE General Test. Additional exam requirements/recommendations for international students: Required—TOEFL. Electronic applications accepted.

Harvard University, Graduate School of Arts and Sciences, Department of Psychology, Cambridge, MA 02138. Offers psychology (PhD), including behavior and decision analysis, cognition, developmental psychology, experimental psychology, personality, psychobiology, psychopathology; social psychology (PhD). *Accreditation:* APA. *Degree requirements:* For doctorate, thesis/dissertation, general exams. *Entrance requirements:* For doctorate, GRE General Test. Additional exam requirements/recommendations for international students: Required—TOEFL.

Heidelberg University, Program in Counseling, Tiffin, OH 44883-2462. Offers community mental health counseling (MA); school counseling (MA). *Accreditation:* ACA. Part-time and evening/weekend programs available. *Degree requirements:* For master's, thesis or alternative, counseling practicum, internship. *Entrance requirements:* For master's, GRE General Test, 12 hours of course work in behavioral sciences, minimum GPA of 2.9, 3 letters of reference. Additional exam requirements/recommendations for international students: Required—TOEFL.

Hofstra University, College of Liberal Arts and Sciences, Programs in Psychology, Hempstead, NY 11549. Offers applied organizational psychology (PhD); clinical psychology (PhD); industrial/organizational psychology (MA); school-community psychology (Psy D). Part-time and evening/weekend programs available. *Students:* 226 full-time (146 women), 14 part-time (9 women); includes 42 minority (7 Black or African American, non-Hispanic/Latino; 2 American Indian or Alaska Native, non-Hispanic/Latino; 11 Asian, non-Hispanic/Latino; 17 Hispanic/Latino; 1 Native Hawaiian or other Pacific Islander, non-Hispanic/Latino; 4 Two or more races, non-Hispanic/Latino), 20 international. Average age 27. 313 applicants, 40% accepted, 67 enrolled. In 2014, 40 master's, 30 doctorates awarded. *Degree requirements:* For master's, comprehensive exam, thesis (for some programs), internship, minimum GPA of 3.0; for doctorate, comprehensive exam, thesis/dissertation, 1st year qualifying examination, 2nd year research project, successful practicum/externship placements, written presentation and successful oral defense of dissertation, completion of full-time internship. *Entrance requirements:* For master's, GRE General Test, minimum GPA of 3.0, essay, interview; for doctorate, GRE General Test, GRE Subject Test (psychology), 3 letters of recommendation, interview, essay, curriculum vitae. Additional exam requirements/recommendations for international students: Required—TOEFL (minimum score 550 paper-based; 80 iBT). *Application deadline:* For fall admission, 12/15 for domestic and international students. Application fee: $70 ($75 for international students). Electronic applications accepted. *Expenses:* Tuition: Full-time $20,610; part-time $1145 per credit hour. *Required fees:* $970; $165 per term. Tuition and fees vary according to program. *Financial support:* In 2014–15, 139 students received support, including 118 fellowships with full and partial tuition reimbursements available (averaging $7,236 per year), 7 research assistantships with full and partial tuition reimbursements available (averaging $5,788 per year); Federal Work-Study, institutionally sponsored loans, scholarships/grants, health care benefits, tuition waivers (full and partial), and diversity and endowed scholarships also available. Support available to part-time students. Financial award applicants required to submit FAFSA. *Faculty research:* Cognitive behavioral therapy for anxiety disorders, autism spectrum disorders, parent child interaction training (PCIT), positive organizational behavior, personnel selection and decision-making. *Unit head:* Dr. Keith Shafritz, Chairperson, 516-463-4856, Fax: 516-463-6052, E-mail: psykms@hofstra.edu. *Application contact:* Sunil Samuel, Assistant Vice President of Admissions, 516-463-4723, Fax: 516-463-4664, E-mail: graduateadmission@hofstra.edu.
Website: http://www.hofstra.edu/hclas

Howard University, Graduate School, Department of Psychology, Washington, DC 20059-0002. Offers clinical psychology (PhD); developmental psychology (PhD); experimental psychology (PhD); neuropsychology (PhD); personality psychology (PhD); psychology (MS); social psychology (PhD). *Accreditation:* APA (one or more programs are accredited). Part-time programs available. *Degree requirements:* For master's, thesis; for doctorate, comprehensive exam, thesis/dissertation, qualifying exam. *Entrance requirements:* For master's, GRE General Test, minimum GPA of 2.5, bachelor's degree in psychology or related field; for doctorate, GRE General Test, minimum GPA of 3.0. *Faculty research:* Personality and psychophysiology, educational and social development of African-American children, child and adult psychopathology.

Husson University, Graduate Programs in Counseling and Human Relations, Bangor, ME 04401-2999. Offers clinical mental health counseling (MS); human relations (MS); pastoral counseling (MS); school counseling (MS). Part-time and evening/weekend programs available. *Faculty:* 3 full-time (2 women), 2 part-time/adjunct (both women). *Students:* 39 full-time (33 women), 25 part-time (20 women); includes 3 minority (2 Black or African American, non-Hispanic/Latino; 1 Two or more races, non-Hispanic/Latino), 2 international. Average age 34. 55 applicants, 69% accepted, 32 enrolled. In 2014, 19 master's awarded. *Degree requirements:* For master's, comprehensive exam (for some programs), thesis optional. *Entrance requirements:* For master's, GRE or MAT, BS with minimum GPA of 3.0, letters of recommendation, interview. Additional exam requirements/recommendations for international students: Required—TOEFL (minimum score 550 paper-based; 80 iBT). *Application deadline:* For fall admission, 2/1 for domestic students. Applications are processed on a rolling basis. Application fee: $50. Electronic applications accepted. *Expenses:* Expenses: Contact institution. *Financial support:* In 2014–15, 1 student received support. Federal Work-Study, scholarships/grants, and unspecified assistantships available. Financial award application deadline: 4/15; financial award applicants required to submit FAFSA. *Faculty research:* Challenges and rewards of counseling practice in rural, small town and neighborhood settings. *Unit head:* Dr. Deborah Drew, Director, Graduate Counseling Programs, 207-992-4912, Fax: 207-992-4952, E-mail: drewd@husson.edu. *Application contact:* Kristen Card, Director of Graduate Admissions, 207-404-5660, Fax: 207-941-7935, E-mail: cardk@husson.edu.
Website: http://www.husson.edu/human-relations

Indiana University Bloomington, University Graduate School, College of Arts and Sciences, Department of Psychological and Brain Sciences, Bloomington, IN 47405. Offers clinical science (PhD); cognitive neuroscience (PhD); cognitive psychology (PhD); developmental psychology (PhD); methods of behavior (PhD); molecular systems neuroscience (PhD); social psychology (PhD). *Accreditation:* APA. *Faculty:* 54 full-time (15 women). *Students:* 95 full-time (56 women); includes 19 minority (4 Black or African American, non-Hispanic/Latino; 7 Asian, non-Hispanic/Latino; 7 Hispanic/Latino; 1 Two or more races, non-Hispanic/Latino), 16 international. Average age 24. 364 applicants, 10% accepted, 20 enrolled. In 2014, 9 doctorates awarded. *Degree requirements:* For doctorate, comprehensive exam, 90 credit hours, 2 advanced statistics/methods courses, 2 written research projects, the teaching of psychology course, teaching 1 semester of undergraduate methods course, qualifying examination, minor or a second major, first-year research seminar course, dissertation defense, written dissertation. *Entrance requirements:* For doctorate, GRE. Additional exam requirements/recommendations for international students: Required—TOEFL (minimum score 550 paper-based; 79 iBT). *Application deadline:* For fall admission, 12/1 for domestic and international students. Application fee: $55 ($65 for international students). Electronic applications accepted. *Financial support:* Fellowships with full tuition reimbursements, research assistantships with full tuition reimbursements, teaching assistantships with full tuition reimbursements, career-related internships or fieldwork, scholarships/grants, traineeships, health care benefits, and unspecified assistantships available. *Faculty research:* Clinical science, cognitive neuroscience, cognitive psychology, developmental psychology, mechanisms of behavior, molecular and systems neuroscience, social psychology. *Unit head:* Dr. William Hetrick, Chair, 812-855-2012, Fax: 812-855-4691, E-mail: whetrick@indiana.edu. *Application contact:* Dale Sengelaub, Graduate Admissions, 812-855-9149, Fax: 812-855-4691, E-mail: psychgrd@indiana.edu.
Website: http://www.psych.indiana.edu

Indiana University of Pennsylvania, School of Graduate Studies and Research, College of Education and Educational Technology, Department of Counseling, Program in Community Counseling, Indiana, PA 15705-1087. Offers MA. Part-time programs available. *Faculty:* 12 full-time (10 women), 6 part-time/adjunct (4 women). *Students:* 3 full-time (all women), 11 part-time (10 women); includes 2 minority (both Black or African American, non-Hispanic/Latino). Average age 35. 27 applicants, 11% accepted, 2 enrolled. In 2014, 44 master's awarded. *Entrance requirements:* For master's, specific guidelines for goal statement, 2 letters of recommendation. Additional exam requirements/recommendations for international students: Required—TOEFL (minimum score 540 paper-based). *Application deadline:* For fall admission, 3/17 priority date for domestic students. Application fee: $50. Electronic applications accepted. *Financial support:* In 2014–15, 1 research assistantship with full tuition reimbursement (averaging $5,440 per year) was awarded. Financial award application deadline: 4/15; financial award applicants required to submit FAFSA. *Unit head:* Dr. Claire Dandeneau, Chairperson/Graduate Coordinator, 724-357-2306, E-mail: candean@iup.edu.
Website: http://www.iup.edu/grad/communitycounseling/default.aspx

Indiana Wesleyan University, Graduate School, College of Arts and Sciences, Marion, IN 46953. Offers addictions counseling (MS); clinical mental health counseling (MS); community counseling (MS); marriage and family therapy (MS); school counseling (MS); student development counseling and administration (MS). *Accreditation:* ACA. Part-time programs available. *Degree requirements:* For master's, thesis or alternative. *Entrance requirements:* For master's, GRE General Test. Additional exam requirements/recommendations for international students: Required—TOEFL. Electronic applications accepted. *Expenses:* Contact institution. *Faculty research:* Community counseling, multicultural counseling, addictions.

Iowa State University of Science and Technology, Department of Psychology, Ames, IA 50011. Offers cognitive psychology (PhD); counseling psychology (PhD); social psychology (PhD). *Accreditation:* APA. *Entrance requirements:* For doctorate, GRE General Test, GRE Subject Test (psychology), 3 letters of recommendation. Additional exam requirements/recommendations for international students: Required—TOEFL (minimum score 560 paper-based; 79 iBT), IELTS (minimum score 6.5). Electronic applications accepted. *Faculty research:* Counseling psychology, cognitive psychology, social psychology, health psychology, psychology and public policy.

Lesley University, Graduate School of Arts and Social Sciences, Cambridge, MA 02138-2790. Offers clinical mental health counseling (MA), including holistic counseling, school and community counseling, trauma studies; counseling psychology (MA, CAGS), including professional counseling (MA), school counseling (MA); creative writing (MFA); expressive therapies (MA, PhD, CAGS), including art (MA), clinical mental health counseling (MA), dance (MA), expressive therapies (MA), music (MA); independent studies (CAGS); independent study (MA); intercultural relations (MA, CAGS); interdisciplinary studies (MA), including individualized studies, integrative holistic health, mindfulness studies, peace and conflict transformation, trauma sensitive assessment, intervention, and consultation, women's studies; urban environmental leadership (MA). Part-time programs available. Postbaccalaureate distance learning degree programs offered (no on-campus study). *Faculty:* 35 full-time (25 women), 115 part-time/adjunct (90 women). *Students:* 420 full-time (379 women), 514 part-time (414 women); includes 142 minority (50 Black or African American, non-Hispanic/Latino; 5 American Indian or Alaska Native, non-Hispanic/Latino; 16 Asian, non-Hispanic/Latino; 48 Hispanic/Latino; 23 Two or more races, non-Hispanic/Latino), 46 international. Average age 33. In 2014, 475 master's, 11 doctorates, 4 other advanced degrees awarded. *Degree requirements:* For master's, internship, practicum, thesis (for expressive therapies); for doctorate, thesis/dissertation, arts apprenticeship, field placement; for CAGS, thesis, internship (for

counseling psychology, expressive therapies). *Entrance requirements:* For master's, MAT (counseling psychology), interview, writing samples, art portfolio; for doctorate, GRE or MAT, interview, master's degree; for CAGS, interview, master's degree. Additional exam requirements/recommendations for international students: Required—TOEFL (minimum score 550 paper-based; 80 iBT). *Application deadline:* Applications are processed on a rolling basis. Application fee: $50. Electronic applications accepted. *Financial support:* Fellowships, career-related internships or fieldwork, Federal Work-Study, scholarships/grants, tuition waivers, and unspecified assistantships available. Financial award applicants required to submit FAFSA. *Faculty research:* Psychotherapy and culture; psychotherapy and psychological trauma; women's issues in art, teaching and psychotherapy; community-based art, psycho-spiritual inquiry. *Unit head:* Dr. Catherine Koverola, Dean, 617-349-8317, Fax: 617-349-8366, E-mail: koverola@lesley.edu. *Application contact:* Martha Sheehan, Director, Graduate Admissions, 888-LESLEYU, Fax: 617-349-8313, E-mail: info@lesley.edu.
Website: http://www.lesley.edu/graduate-school-of-arts-and-social-sciences/

Loyola University Chicago, Graduate School, Department of Psychology, Program in Applied Social Psychology, Chicago, IL 60660. Offers MA, PhD. *Faculty:* 7 full-time (2 women), 1 (woman) part-time/adjunct. *Students:* 22 full-time (17 women), 1 (woman) part-time; includes 8 minority (3 Black or African American, non-Hispanic/Latino; 1 Asian, non-Hispanic/Latino; 1 Hispanic/Latino; 3 Two or more races, non-Hispanic/Latino), 3 international. Average age 29. 89 applicants, 19% accepted, 5 enrolled. In 2014, 3 master's, 4 doctorates awarded. Terminal master's awarded for partial completion of doctoral program. *Degree requirements:* For master's, thesis; for doctorate, comprehensive exam, thesis/dissertation, internship. *Entrance requirements:* For master's and doctorate, GRE General Test, sample of written work. Additional exam requirements/recommendations for international students: Required—TOEFL. *Application deadline:* For fall admission, 1/15 for domestic and international students. Application fee: $50. Electronic applications accepted. Application fee is waived when completed online. *Expenses: Tuition:* Full-time $17,370; part-time $965 per credit. *Required fees:* $138 per semester. *Financial support:* In 2014–15, 1 fellowship with tuition reimbursement (averaging $16,000 per year), 5 research assistantships with tuition reimbursements (averaging $16,000 per year), 1 teaching assistantship with tuition reimbursement (averaging $16,000 per year) were awarded; career-related internships or fieldwork, Federal Work-Study, and scholarships/grants also available. Financial award application deadline: 12/15; financial award applicants required to submit FAFSA. *Faculty research:* Program evaluation, attitudes and prejudice, psychological well-being, self esteem and relationships, groups and organizations. *Total annual research expenditures:* $150,000. *Unit head:* Dr. Scott Tindale, Director, 773-508-3014. *Application contact:* Ron Martin, Assistant Director of Enrollment Management, 312-915-8950, Fax: 312-915-8905, E-mail: gradapp@luc.edu.

Loyola University Chicago, School of Education, Program in Community Counseling, Chicago, IL 60660. Offers M Ed, MA, Ed S. MA offered through the Graduate School. Part-time programs available. *Faculty:* 6 full-time (4 women), 6 part-time/adjunct (2 women). *Students:* 35. Average age 25. 56 applicants, 71% accepted, 13 enrolled. In 2014, 13 master's, 5 other advanced degrees awarded. *Degree requirements:* For master's and Ed S, comprehensive exam. *Entrance requirements:* For master's, GRE General Test, minimum GPA of 3.0, letters of recommendation, resume. Additional exam requirements/recommendations for international students: Required—TOEFL (minimum score 550 paper-based; 79 iBT). *Application deadline:* For fall admission, 1/1 for domestic and international students. Application fee: $50. Electronic applications accepted. Application fee is waived when completed online. *Expenses: Tuition:* Full-time $17,370; part-time $965 per credit. *Required fees:* $138 per semester. *Financial support:* Career-related internships or fieldwork, institutionally sponsored loans, scholarships/grants, and unspecified assistantships available. Support available to part-time students. Financial award application deadline: 2/1; financial award applicants required to submit FAFSA. *Faculty research:* Career development, prevention, group counseling, family therapy, multicultural counseling. *Unit head:* Dr. Steven Brown, Director, 312-915-6311, E-mail: sbrown@luc.edu. *Application contact:* Marie Hatland, Information Contact, 312-915-6800, E-mail: schleduc@luc.edu.

Marquette University, Graduate School, College of Education, Department of Counselor Education and Counseling Psychology, Milwaukee, WI 53201-1881. Offers clinical mental health counseling (MS); community counseling (MA); counseling psychology (PhD); school counseling (MA). Part-time programs available. Terminal master's awarded for partial completion of doctoral program. *Degree requirements:* For master's, comprehensive exam, thesis (for some programs); for doctorate, thesis/dissertation, qualifying exam. *Entrance requirements:* For master's, GRE General Test or MAT, official transcripts from all current and previous colleges/universities except Marquette, three letters of recommendation, statement of purpose; for doctorate, GRE General Test, MAT, sample of written work, official transcripts from all current and previous colleges/universities except Marquette, three letters of recommendation, statement of purpose, resume/curriculum vitae. Additional exam requirements/recommendations for international students: Required—TOEFL (minimum score 530 paper-based). *Faculty research:* Ethical and legal issues in education, anxiety disorders, multicultural counseling, child psychopathology, group counseling and dynamics.

Martin University, Division of Psychology, Indianapolis, IN 46218-3867. Offers community psychology (MS). Part-time and evening/weekend programs available. *Degree requirements:* For master's, thesis. *Entrance requirements:* For master's, GRE General Test, GRE Subject Test.

Marymount California University, Program in Community Psychology, Rancho Palos Verdes, CA 90275-6299. Offers MS.

Memorial University of Newfoundland, School of Graduate Studies, Department of Psychology, St. John's, NL A1C 5S7, Canada. Offers applied social psychology (MASP); experimental psychology (M Sc, PhD). Part-time programs available. *Degree requirements:* For master's, workterms (MASP), thesis (M Sc); for doctorate, comprehensive exam, thesis/dissertation, oral thesis defense. *Entrance requirements:* For master's, GRE, honors bachelor's degree of high second class standing or equivalent; for doctorate, GRE, master's or honors degree. Additional exam requirements/recommendations for international students: Recommended—TOEFL. Electronic applications accepted. *Faculty research:* Behavioral neuroscience, cognition, theory and research on abnormal behavior.

Mount Aloysius College, Program in Community Counseling, Cresson, PA 16630-1999. Offers MS. Part-time programs available.

Naropa University, Graduate Programs, Program in Transpersonal Ecopsychology, Boulder, CO 80302-6697. Offers MA. Part-time and evening/weekend programs available. Postbaccalaureate distance learning degree programs offered (minimal on-campus study). *Faculty:* 1 (woman) full-time, 3 part-time/adjunct (2 women). *Students:* 21 part-time (16 women); includes 1 minority (Hispanic/Latino), 1 international. Average age 37. 17 applicants, 71% accepted, 10 enrolled. In 2014, 9 master's awarded. *Degree requirements:* For master's, thesis, service learning. *Entrance requirements:* For master's, interview (by phone or in-person), technology form, resume, 2 letters of recommendation, transcripts, letter of interest. Additional exam requirements/recommendations for international students: Required—TOEFL (minimum score 600 paper-based; 80 iBT). *Application deadline:* For fall admission, 1/15 priority date for domestic and international students. Applications are processed on a rolling basis. Application fee: $60. Electronic applications accepted. *Expenses: Tuition:* Full-time $23,400; part-time $975 per credit. *Required fees:* $335 per semester. Tuition and fees vary according to course load. *Financial support:* In 2014–15, 3 students received support. Career-related internships or fieldwork, scholarships/grants, and tuition waivers (partial) available. Support available to part-time students. Financial award application deadline: 3/1; financial award applicants required to submit FAFSA. *Unit head:* Dr. Deborah Bowman, Dean, Graduate School of Psychology, 303-546-3559, E-mail: bowman@naropa.edu. *Application contact:* Office of Admissions, 303-546-3572, Fax: 303-546-3583, E-mail: admissions@naropa.edu.
Website: http://www.naropa.edu/academics/gsp/grad/ecopsychology-ma/index.php

New Mexico State University, College of Arts and Sciences, Department of Psychology, Las Cruces, NM 88003-8001. Offers cognitive psychology (PhD); engineering psychology (PhD); experimental psychology (MA); social psychology (PhD). Part-time programs available. *Faculty:* 11 full-time (3 women). *Students:* 31 full-time (15 women), 5 part-time (2 women); includes 7 minority (2 Asian, non-Hispanic/Latino; 3 Hispanic/Latino; 2 Two or more races, non-Hispanic/Latino), 5 international. Average age 29. 56 applicants, 27% accepted, 10 enrolled. In 2014, 6 master's, 5 doctorates awarded. *Degree requirements:* For master's, thesis; for doctorate, comprehensive exam, thesis/dissertation, work-related experience (teaching or internship). *Entrance requirements:* For master's, GRE General Test, letters of recommendation, curriculum vitae, personal statement; for doctorate, GRE General Test, letters of recommendation, master's thesis, curriculum vitae, personal statement. Additional exam requirements/recommendations for international students: Required—TOEFL (minimum score 550 paper-based; 79 iBT), IELTS (minimum score 6.5). *Application deadline:* For fall admission, 2/1 priority date for domestic students, 2/1 for international students. Applications are processed on a rolling basis. Application fee: $40 ($50 for international students). Electronic applications accepted. *Expenses:* Tuition, state resident: full-time $3969; part-time $220.50 per credit hour. Tuition, nonresident: full-time $13,838; part-time $768.80 per credit hour. *Required fees:* $853; $47.40 per credit hour. *Financial support:* In 2014–15, 34 students received support, including 7 fellowships (averaging $3,970 per year), 4 research assistantships (averaging $14,330 per year), 20 teaching assistantships (averaging $9,979 per year); career-related internships or fieldwork, Federal Work-Study, scholarships/grants, traineeships, health care benefits, and unspecified assistantships also available. Support available to part-time students. Financial award application deadline: 3/1. *Faculty research:* Engineering, cognitive, and social psychology; human/computer interaction; cognitive science. *Total annual research expenditures:* $184,443. *Unit head:* Dr. Dominic A. Simon, Academic Department Head, 575-646-2502, Fax: 575-646-6212, E-mail: domsimon@nmsu.edu. *Application contact:* Dr. Laura J. Madson, Chair of Graduate Committee, 575-646-6207, Fax: 575-646-6212, E-mail: lmadson@nmsu.edu.
Website: http://psych.nmsu.edu

New York University, Graduate School of Arts and Science, Department of Psychology, New York, NY 10012-1019. Offers cognition and perception (PhD); community psychology (PhD); general psychology (MA); industrial/organizational psychology (MA); psychotherapy and psychoanalysis (Advanced Certificate); social/personality psychology (PhD). Part-time programs available. *Students:* 270 full-time (183 women), 162 part-time (115 women); includes 92 minority (14 Black or African American, non-Hispanic/Latino; 36 Asian, non-Hispanic/Latino; 33 Hispanic/Latino; 9 Two or more races, non-Hispanic/Latino), 114 international. Average age 31. 874 applicants, 46% accepted, 153 enrolled. In 2014, 102 master's, 9 doctorates, 10 other advanced degrees awarded. Terminal master's awarded for partial completion of doctoral program. *Degree requirements:* For master's, comprehensive exam, thesis or alternative; for doctorate, thesis/dissertation. *Entrance requirements:* For master's and doctorate, GRE General Test. Additional exam requirements/recommendations for international students: Required—TOEFL. *Application deadline:* For fall admission, 12/12 for domestic and international students. Application fee: $100. *Financial support:* Fellowships with tuition reimbursements, research assistantships with tuition reimbursements, teaching assistantships with tuition reimbursements, career-related internships or fieldwork, Federal Work-Study, institutionally sponsored loans, scholarships/grants, traineeships, health care benefits, and unspecified assistantships available. Financial award application deadline: 12/12; financial award applicants required to submit FAFSA. *Faculty research:* Vision, memory, social cognition, social and cognitive development, relationships. *Unit head:* Gabriele Oettingen, Director of Graduate Studies, PhD Program, 212-998-7900, Fax: 212-995-4018, E-mail: psychq@psych.nyu.edu. *Application contact:* Adrienne Gans, Director of Graduate Studies, MA Program, 212-998-7900, Fax: 212-995-4018, E-mail: psychq@psych.nyu.edu.
Website: http://www.psych.nyu.edu/

Norfolk State University, School of Graduate Studies, School of Liberal Arts, Department of Psychology, Program in Community/Clinical Psychology, Norfolk, VA 23504. Offers MA. *Degree requirements:* For master's, comprehensive exam, thesis or alternative. *Entrance requirements:* For master's, minimum GPA of 2.7.

North Carolina Central University, School of Education, Department of Counselor Education, Durham, NC 27707-3129. Offers career counseling (MA); community agency counseling (MA); school counseling (MA). *Accreditation:* ACA; NCATE. Part-time and evening/weekend programs available. *Degree requirements:* For master's, comprehensive exam, thesis or alternative. *Entrance requirements:* For master's, GRE, minimum GPA of 3.0 in major, 2.5 overall. Additional exam requirements/recommendations for international students: Required—TOEFL. *Faculty research:* Becoming a leader, skill building in academia.

North Carolina State University, Graduate School, College of Education, Department of Curriculum and Instruction, Program in Agency Counseling, Raleigh, NC 27695. Offers M Ed, MS. *Degree requirements:* For master's, thesis optional. *Entrance requirements:* For master's, GRE General Test or MAT, minimum GPA of 3.0 in major. Electronic applications accepted. *Faculty research:* Cross-cultural issues, non-cognitive variables, achievement gaps, identity development, counseling supervision.

North Dakota State University, College of Graduate and Interdisciplinary Studies, College of Science and Mathematics, Department of Psychology, Fargo, ND 58108. Offers clinical psychology (MS); cognitive and visual neuroscience (PhD); health and social psychology (PhD); psychology (MS). *Degree requirements:* For master's, thesis; for doctorate, thesis/dissertation. *Entrance requirements:* For master's and doctorate, GRE General Test, GRE Subject Test. Additional exam requirements/recommendations for international students: Required—TOEFL (minimum score 525 paper-based; 71 iBT). Electronic applications accepted. *Faculty research:* Cognition science, neuropsychology, group behavior, applied behavior analysis, behavior therapy.

Northeastern Illinois University, College of Graduate Studies and Research, College of Education, Program in Community Counseling, Chicago, IL 60625-4699. Offers MA.

Northwestern University, The Graduate School, Judd A. and Marjorie Weinberg College of Arts and Sciences, Department of Psychology, Evanston, IL 60208. Offers brain, behavior and cognition (PhD); clinical psychology (PhD); cognitive psychology

(PhD); personality psychology (PhD); social psychology (PhD); JD/PhD. Admissions and degrees offered through The Graduate School. *Accreditation:* APA (one or more programs are accredited). Part-time programs available. *Degree requirements:* For doctorate, thesis/dissertation. *Entrance requirements:* For doctorate, GRE General Test, GRE Subject Test. Additional exam requirements/recommendations for international students: Required—TOEFL. Electronic applications accepted. *Faculty research:* Memory and higher order cognition, anxiety and depression, effectiveness of psychotherapy, social cognition, molecular basis of memory.

The Ohio State University, Graduate School, College of Arts and Sciences, Division of Social and Behavioral Sciences, Department of Psychology, Columbus, OH 43210. Offers behavioral neuroscience (PhD); clinical psychology (PhD); cognitive psychology (PhD); developmental psychology (PhD); intellectual and developmental disabilities psychology (PhD); quantitative psychology (PhD); social psychology (PhD). *Accreditation:* APA. *Faculty:* 55. *Students:* 158 full-time (91 women); includes 26 minority (6 Black or African American, non-Hispanic/Latino; 2 American Indian or Alaska Native, non-Hispanic/Latino; 7 Asian, non-Hispanic/Latino; 9 Hispanic/Latino; 2 Two or more races, non-Hispanic/Latino), 23 international. Average age 27. In 2014, 12 doctorates awarded. *Degree requirements:* For doctorate, thesis/dissertation. *Entrance requirements:* For doctorate, GRE General Test. Additional exam requirements/recommendations for international students: Required—TOEFL (minimum score 600 paper-based; 100 iBT); Recommended—IELTS (minimum score 8). *Application deadline:* For fall admission, 12/1 for domestic and international students. Applications are processed on a rolling basis. Application fee: $60 ($70 for international students). Electronic applications accepted. *Financial support:* Fellowships with tuition reimbursements, research assistantships with tuition reimbursements, and teaching assistantships with tuition reimbursements available. *Unit head:* Dr. Richard Petty, Chair, 614-292-1640, E-mail: petty.1@osu.edu. *Application contact:* Graduate and Professional Admissions, 614-292-9444, Fax: 614-292-3895, E-mail: gpadmissions@osu.edu.
Website: http://www.psy.ohio-state.edu/

Oregon State University–Cascades, Program in Counseling, Bend, OR 97701. Offers community counseling (MS); school counseling (MS).

Penn State Harrisburg, Graduate School, School of Behavioral Sciences and Education, Middletown, PA 17057-4898. Offers applied behavior analysis (MA); applied clinical psychology (MA); applied psychological research (MA); community psychology and social change (MA); health education (M Ed); literacy education (M Ed); teaching and curriculum (M Ed); training and development (M Ed). Part-time and evening/weekend programs available. *Unit head:* Dr. Mukund S. Kulkarni, Chancellor, 717-948-6105, Fax 717-948-6452, E-mail: msk5@psu.edu. *Application contact:* Robert W. Coffman, Jr., Director of Enrollment Management, Admissions, 717-948-6250, Fax: 717-948-6325, E-mail: ric1@psu.edu.
Website: http://harrisburg.psu.edu/behavioral-sciences-and-education/

Philadelphia University, College of Science, Health and the Liberal Arts, Program in Community and Trauma Counseling, Philadelphia, PA 19144. Offers MS.

Pittsburg State University, Graduate School, College of Education, Department of Psychology and Counseling, Program in Counselor Education, Pittsburg, KS 66762. Offers community counseling (MS); school counseling (MS). *Accreditation:* ACA; NCATE. *Degree requirements:* For master's, thesis or alternative. *Entrance requirements:* For master's, GRE General Test, minimum GPA of 2.8.

Queen's University at Kingston, School of Graduate Studies, Faculty of Arts and Sciences, Department of Psychology, Kingston, ON K7L 3N6, Canada. Offers brain behavior and cognitive science (MA, PhD); clinical psychology (MA, PhD); developmental psychology (MA, PhD); social personality psychology (MA, PhD). *Degree requirements:* For master's, thesis; for doctorate, comprehensive exam, thesis/dissertation. *Entrance requirements:* For master's and doctorate, GRE General Test. Additional exam requirements/recommendations for international students: Required—TOEFL. *Faculty research:* Human development, social, personality, behavioral neuroscience, forensic.

Rutgers, The State University of New Jersey, Newark, Graduate School, Program in Psychology, Newark, NJ 07102. Offers cognitive neuroscience (PhD); cognitive science (PhD); perception (PhD); psychobiology (PhD); social cognition (PhD). *Degree requirements:* For doctorate, comprehensive exam, thesis/dissertation. *Entrance requirements:* For doctorate, GRE General Test, GRE Subject Test, minimum undergraduate B average. Electronic applications accepted. *Faculty research:* Visual perception (luminance, motion), neuroendocrine mechanisms in behavior (reproduction, pain), attachment theory, connectionist modeling of cognition.

Rutgers, The State University of New Jersey, New Brunswick, Graduate School-New Brunswick, Program in Psychology, Piscataway, NJ 08854-8097. Offers behavioral neuroscience (PhD); clinical psychology (PhD); cognitive psychology (PhD); interdisciplinary health psychology (PhD); social psychology (PhD). *Accreditation:* APA. *Degree requirements:* For doctorate, comprehensive exam, thesis/dissertation. *Entrance requirements:* For doctorate, GRE General Test, 3 letters of recommendation. Additional exam requirements/recommendations for international students: Required—TOEFL (minimum score 577 paper-based). Electronic applications accepted. *Faculty research:* Learning and memory, behavioral ecology, hormones and behavior, psychopharmacology, anxiety disorders.

Sage Graduate School, School of Health Sciences, Department of Psychology, Program in Counseling and Community Psychology, Troy, NY 12180-4115. Offers MA. *Faculty:* 4 full-time (3 women), 2 part-time/adjunct (1 woman). *Students:* 47 full-time (38 women), 39 part-time (33 women); includes 19 minority (10 Black or African American, non-Hispanic/Latino; 1 American Indian or Alaska Native, non-Hispanic/Latino; 1 Asian, non-Hispanic/Latino; 4 Hispanic/Latino; 3 Two or more races, non-Hispanic/Latino). Average age 30. 87 applicants, 56% accepted, 20 enrolled. In 2014, 15 master's awarded. *Degree requirements:* For master's, externship, internship, thesis or research seminar. *Entrance requirements:* For master's, minimum undergraduate GPA of 3.0, interview. *Application deadline:* Applications are processed on a rolling basis. Application fee: $40. *Expenses: Tuition:* Full-time $12,240; part-time $680 per credit hour. *Unit head:* Dr. Patricia O'Connor, Associate Dean, School of Health Sciences, 518-244-2073, Fax: 518-244-4571, E-mail: oconnp@sage.edu. *Application contact:* Dr. Sybillyn Jennings, Professor and Chair, 518-244-2074, Fax: 518-244-4545, E-mail: jennis@sage.edu.
Website: http://www.sage.edu/academics/psychology/programs/counseling

St. Bonaventure University, School of Graduate Studies, School of Education, Program in Counselor Education, St. Bonaventure, NY 14778-2284. Offers community mental health counseling (MS Ed); rehabilitation counseling (MS Ed); school counseling (MS Ed); school counselor (Adv C). Program offered in Olean and Buffalo Center (Hamburg, NY). *Accreditation:* ACA. Part-time and evening/weekend programs available. *Faculty:* 4 full-time (1 woman), 6 part-time/adjunct (3 women). *Students:* 55 full-time (42 women), 13 part-time (10 women); includes 3 minority (1 Hispanic/Latino; 2 Two or more races, non-Hispanic/Latino), 1 international. Average age 29. 31 applicants, 97% accepted, 23 enrolled. In 2014, 26 master's awarded. *Degree requirements:* For master's, comprehensive exam, thesis optional, internship, portfolio;

for Adv C, internship. *Entrance requirements:* For master's, statement of intent/writing sample; transcripts from all colleges previously attended; two references; interview; minimum undergraduate GPA of 3.0; for Adv C, interview, writing sample, minimum undergraduate GPA of 3.0, two letters of recommendation, master's degree, transcripts from all colleges previously attended. Additional exam requirements/recommendations for international students: Required—TOEFL (minimum score 550 paper-based; 79 iBT). *Application deadline:* For fall admission, 8/15 priority date for domestic students, 2/1 priority date for international students; for spring admission, 11/15 priority date for domestic students, 7/1 priority date for international students. Applications are processed on a rolling basis. Application fee: $0. Electronic applications accepted. *Expenses:* Expenses: $8,532 for Advanced Certificate; $34,128 for school counseling; $42,660 for community mental health counseling. *Financial support:* In 2014–15, 5 research assistantships with full and partial tuition reimbursements were awarded; career-related internships or fieldwork, Federal Work-Study, scholarships/grants, health care benefits, tuition waivers (partial), and unspecified assistantships also available. Support available to part-time students. Financial award application deadline: 4/15; financial award applicants required to submit FAFSA. *Unit head:* Dr. S. Alan Silliker, Director, 716-375-2368, Fax: 716-375-2360, E-mail: silliker@sbu.edu. *Application contact:* Bruce Campbell, Director of Graduate Admissions, 716-375-2429, Fax: 716-375-4015, E-mail: gradsch@sbu.edu.
Website: http://www.sbu.edu/academics/schools/education

St. Cloud State University, School of Graduate Studies, School of Health and Human Services, Department of Counseling and Community Psychology, Program in Community Counseling, St. Cloud, MN 56301-4498. Offers MS. *Degree requirements:* For master's, comprehensive exam (for some programs), thesis or alternative. *Entrance requirements:* For master's, GRE General Test, minimum GPA of 2.75. Additional exam requirements/recommendations for international students: Required—Michigan English Language Assessment Battery; Recommended—TOEFL (minimum score 550 paper-based), IELTS (minimum score 6.5). Electronic applications accepted.

Saint Martin's University, Office of Graduate Studies, Program in Counseling Psychology, Lacey, WA 98503. Offers MAC. Part-time and evening/weekend programs available. *Faculty:* 2 full-time (1 woman), 5 part-time/adjunct (all women). *Students:* 90 full-time (74 women), 38 part-time (34 women); includes 24 minority (3 Black or African American, non-Hispanic/Latino; 2 Asian, non-Hispanic/Latino; 6 Hispanic/Latino; 3 Native Hawaiian or other Pacific Islander, non-Hispanic/Latino; 10 Two or more races, non-Hispanic/Latino). Average age 35. 38 applicants, 61% accepted, 20 enrolled. In 2014, 17 master's awarded. *Degree requirements:* For master's, clinical experience, interview. *Entrance requirements:* For master's, clinical experience. Additional exam requirements/recommendations for international students: Required—TOEFL (minimum score 550 paper-based; 79 iBT); Recommended—IELTS (minimum score 6.5). *Application deadline:* For fall admission, 4/1 priority date for domestic and international students; for spring admission, 11/1 priority date for domestic and international students. Applications are processed on a rolling basis. Application fee: $50. Electronic applications accepted. *Expenses: Tuition:* Part-time $1045 per credit. *Financial support:* Career-related internships or fieldwork, Federal Work-Study, and institutionally sponsored loans available. Support available to part-time students. Financial award application deadline: 3/1; financial award applicants required to submit FAFSA. *Faculty research:* Alcohol studies, clinical effectiveness, social justice, parent adolescent interaction. *Unit head:* Dr. Godfrey J. Ellis, Director, 360-438-4560, E-mail: gellis@stmartin.edu. *Application contact:* Bailey Craft, Assistant Director for Graduate Recruitment, 360-412-6142, E-mail: gradstudies@stmartin.edu.

San Francisco State University, Division of Graduate Studies, College of Science and Engineering, Department of Psychology, San Francisco, CA 94132-1722. Offers industrial/organizational psychology (MS); school psychology (Credential); social psychology (MA). *Expenses:* Tuition, state resident: full-time $6738. Tuition, nonresident: full-time $17,898; part-time $372 per credit hour. *Required fees:* $498 per semester. *Financial support:* Teaching assistantships available. Financial award application deadline: 3/1. *Unit head:* Dr. Jeffrey Cookston, Chair, 415-338-2167, Fax: 415-338-2398, E-mail: cookston@sfsu.edu. *Application contact:* Dr. Ryan Howell, Graduate Program Coordinator, 415-405-2140, Fax: 415-338-2398, E-mail: rhowell@sfsu.edu.
Website: http://psychology.sfsu.edu/graduate/application.html

Southwestern College, Program in Transformational Ecopsychology, Santa Fe, NM 87502-4788. Offers Certificate. *Entrance requirements:* For degree, 3 letters of reference, interview.

Stony Brook University, State University of New York, Graduate School, College of Arts and Sciences, Department of Psychology, Program in Social and Health Psychology, Stony Brook, NY 11794. Offers PhD. *Students:* 15 full-time (all women); includes 3 minority (2 Asian, non-Hispanic/Latino; 1 Two or more races, non-Hispanic/Latino). Average age 28. 68 applicants, 6% accepted, 1 enrolled. In 2014, 2 doctorates awarded. *Degree requirements:* For doctorate, thesis/dissertation. *Entrance requirements:* For doctorate, GRE General Test, GRE Subject Test. Additional exam requirements/recommendations for international students: Required—TOEFL. *Application deadline:* For fall admission, 1/15 for domestic students; for spring admission, 10/1 for domestic students. Application fee: $100. *Expenses:* Tuition, state resident: full-time $10,370; part-time $432 per credit. Tuition, nonresident: full-time $20,190; part-time $841 per credit. *Required fees:* $1431. *Financial support:* In 2014–15, 1 fellowship was awarded. *Unit head:* Dr. Arthur Samuel, Chair, 631-632-7792, Fax: 631-632-7876, E-mail: arthur.samuel@stonybrook.edu. *Application contact:* Marilynn Wollmuth, Coordinator, 631-632-7855, Fax: 631-632-7876, E-mail: marilyn.wollmuth@stonybrook.edu.

Syracuse University, College of Arts and Sciences, Program in Social Psychology, Syracuse, NY 13244. Offers PhD. Part-time programs available. *Students:* 4 full-time (1 woman), 1 (woman) part-time, 1 international. Average age 28. 26 applicants. *Degree requirements:* For doctorate, thesis/dissertation. *Entrance requirements:* For doctorate, GRE General Test, GRE Subject Test (recommended). Additional exam requirements/recommendations for international students: Required—TOEFL (minimum score 100 iBT). *Application deadline:* For fall admission, 12/15 priority date for domestic and international students. Application fee: $75. Electronic applications accepted. *Expenses: Tuition:* Part-time $1341 per credit. *Financial support:* Fellowships with full tuition reimbursements, research assistantships with full and partial tuition reimbursements, and teaching assistantships with full and partial tuition reimbursements available. Financial award application deadline: 1/1. *Unit head:* Dr. Leonard Newman, Graduate Director, 315-443-4633, Fax: 315-443-4085, E-mail: lsnewman@syr.edu. *Application contact:* Alecia Zema, Information Contact, 315-443-2760, E-mail: azema@syr.edu.
Website: http://psychweb.syr.edu/

Teachers College, Columbia University, Graduate Faculty of Education, Department of Organization and Leadership, Program in Social and Organizational Psychology, New York, NY 10027-6696. Offers MA. *Faculty:* 11 full-time, 4 part-time/adjunct. *Students:* 163 full-time (105 women), 112 part-time (79 women); includes 67 minority (19 Black or African American, non-Hispanic/Latino; 26 Asian, non-Hispanic/Latino; 18 Hispanic/Latino; 4 Two or more races, non-Hispanic/Latino), 60 international. Average age 29. 304 applicants, 67% accepted, 87 enrolled. In 2014, 126 master's awarded. Terminal

master's awarded for partial completion of doctoral program. *Degree requirements:* For master's, comprehensive exam. *Entrance requirements:* For master's, GRE, MAT, or GMAT, minimum GPA of 3.0. *Application deadline:* For fall admission, 12/15 for domestic students. Application fee: $65. Electronic applications accepted. *Expenses: Tuition:* Full-time $33,552; part-time $1398 per credit. *Required fees:* $418 per semester. *Financial support:* Fellowships, research assistantships, career-related internships or fieldwork, Federal Work-Study, institutionally sponsored loans, and tuition waivers (full and partial) available. Support available to part-time students. Financial award application deadline: 2/1. *Faculty research:* Conflict resolution, human resource and organization development, management competence, organizational culture, leadership. *Unit head:* Prof. Debra Noumair, Program Coordinator, 212-678-3395, E-mail: dn28@columbia.edu. *Application contact:* Lynda Hallmark, Program Manager, 212-678-3273, Fax: 212-678-3273, E-mail: hallmark@tc.edu.

Temple University, College of Education, Department of Psychological Studies in Education, Philadelphia, PA 19122-6096. Offers adult and organizational development (Ed M); counseling psychology (Ed M, PhD), including agency counseling (Ed M), counseling psychology (PhD), school counseling (Ed M); education (PhD); educational leadership (Ed M); educational leadership and policy studies (Ed M, Ed D), including educational leadership; educational psychology (Ed M); school psychology (Ed M, PhD, Ed S); special education (Ed M). *Accreditation:* APA (one or more programs are accredited). Part-time and evening/weekend programs available. *Faculty:* 26 full-time (17 women), 35 part-time/adjunct (21 women). *Students:* 181 full-time (134 women), 182 part-time (125 women); includes 95 minority (64 Black or African American, non-Hispanic/Latino; 1 American Indian or Alaska Native, non-Hispanic/Latino; 8 Asian, non-Hispanic/Latino; 17 Hispanic/Latino; 5 Two or more races, non-Hispanic/Latino), 10 international. 281 applicants, 67% accepted, 118 enrolled. In 2014, 77 master's, 24 doctorates, 5 other advanced degrees awarded. Terminal master's awarded for partial completion of doctoral program. *Degree requirements:* For master's, thesis or alternative; for doctorate, thesis/dissertation. *Entrance requirements:* Additional exam requirements/recommendations for international students: Required—TOEFL (minimum score 550 paper-based; 79 iBT). *Application deadline:* For fall admission, 12/15 for international students; for spring admission, 8/1 for international students. Application fee: $60. *Expenses:* Tuition, state resident: full-time $14,490; part-time $805 per credit hour. Tuition, nonresident: full-time $19,850; part-time $1103 per credit hour. *Required fees:* $690. Full-time tuition and fees vary according to class time, course load, degree level, campus/location and program. *Financial support:* Fellowships, research assistantships with full tuition reimbursements, and teaching assistantships with full tuition reimbursements available. Financial award application deadline: 1/15; financial award applicants required to submit FAFSA. *Application contact:* Linda Pryor, Enrollment Management, 215-204-8011, E-mail: educate@temple.edu. Website: http://education.temple.edu/pols

Texas A&M University, College of Liberal Arts, Department of Psychology, College Station, TX 77843. Offers behavioral and cellular neuroscience (PhD); clinical psychology (PhD); cognitive psychology (PhD); developmental psychology (PhD); industrial/organizational psychology (PhD); psychology (MS); social psychology (PhD). *Accreditation:* APA (one or more programs are accredited). *Faculty:* 35. *Students:* 82 full-time (45 women), 15 part-time (12 women); includes 30 minority (6 Black or African American, non-Hispanic/Latino; 6 Asian, non-Hispanic/Latino; 18 Hispanic/Latino), 11 international. Average age 28. 375 applicants, 5% accepted, 8 enrolled. In 2014, 8 master's, 16 doctorates awarded. *Degree requirements:* For doctorate, comprehensive exam (for some programs), thesis/dissertation. *Entrance requirements:* For doctorate, GRE General Test. Additional exam requirements/recommendations for international students: Required—TOEFL. *Application deadline:* For fall admission, 1/5 for domestic and international students. Application fee: $50 ($90 for international students). Electronic applications accepted. *Expenses:* Tuition, state resident: full-time $4078; part-time $226.55 per credit hour. Tuition, nonresident: full-time $10,594; part-time $577.55 per credit hour. *Required fees:* $2813; $237.70 per credit hour. $278.50 per semester. Tuition and fees vary according to degree level and student level. *Financial support:* In 2014–15, 84 students received support, including 25 fellowships with full and partial tuition reimbursements available (averaging $17,037 per year), 20 research assistantships with full and partial tuition reimbursements available (averaging $8,269 per year), 57 teaching assistantships with full and partial tuition reimbursements available (averaging $7,431 per year); career-related internships or fieldwork, institutionally sponsored loans, scholarships/grants, traineeships, health care benefits, tuition waivers (full and partial), and unspecified assistantships also available. Support available to part-time students. Financial award application deadline: 1/5; financial award applicants required to submit FAFSA. *Unit head:* Dr. Doug Woods, Head, 979-845-2540, E-mail: dowoods@tamu.edu. *Application contact:* Dr. Charles D. Samuelson, Director of Graduate Studies, 979-845-0880, Fax: 979-845-4727, E-mail: c-samuelson@tamu.edu. Website: http://psychology.tamu.edu

Texas Christian University, College of Science and Engineering, Department of Psychology, Fort Worth, TX 76129. Offers developmental trauma (MS); experimental psychology (MA, MS, PhD), including behavioral neuroscience (MS), cognition (MS), learning (MS), social (MS). *Faculty:* 12 full-time (5 women), 2 part-time/adjunct (1 woman). *Students:* 28 full-time (14 women); includes 1 minority (Hispanic/Latino), 3 international. Average age 27. 37 applicants, 22% accepted, 8 enrolled. In 2014, 2 master's, 6 doctorates awarded. Terminal master's awarded for partial completion of doctoral program. *Degree requirements:* For master's, thesis; for doctorate, thesis/dissertation. *Entrance requirements:* For master's and doctorate, GRE General Test. Additional exam requirements/recommendations for international students: Required—TOEFL. *Application deadline:* For fall admission, 2/1 for domestic and international students; for spring admission, 12/1 for domestic students. Application fee: $60 ($0 for international students). Electronic applications accepted. *Expenses: Tuition:* Full-time $22,860; part-time $1270 per credit hour. *Financial support:* In 2014–15, 23 students received support, including 23 teaching assistantships with full tuition reimbursements available (averaging $19,750 per year); scholarships/grants and tuition waivers also available. Financial award application deadline: 2/1; financial award applicants required to submit FAFSA. *Faculty research:* Neuroscience, human and animal learning, cognition, development, experimental social psychology. *Unit head:* Dr. Mauricio Papini, Chair, 817-257-7410, Fax: 817-257-7681, E-mail: m.papini@tcu.edu. *Application contact:* Cindy Hayes, Administrative Assistant, 817-257-7410, Fax: 817-257-7681, E-mail: c.hayes@tcu.edu. Website: http://www.psy.tcu.edu/gradpro.html

Texas State University, The Graduate College, College of Education, Department of Counseling, Leadership, Adult Education, and School Psychology, Program in Professional Counseling, San Marcos, TX 78666. Offers community counseling (MA). *Accreditation:* ACA. Part-time programs available. *Faculty:* 12 full-time (9 women), 7 part-time/adjunct (all women). *Students:* 92 full-time (79 women), 113 part-time (92 women); includes 50 minority (2 Black or African American, non-Hispanic/Latino; 7 Asian, non-Hispanic/Latino; 30 Hispanic/Latino; 11 Two or more races, non-Hispanic/Latino), 2 international. Average age 31. 115 applicants, 30% accepted, 20 enrolled. In 2014, 48 master's awarded. *Degree requirements:* For master's, comprehensive exam, internship. *Entrance requirements:* For master's, GRE General Test (minimum preferred

score of 291 [150 verbal, 141 quantitative]), minimum GPA of 3.0 in last 60 hours. Additional exam requirements/recommendations for international students: Required—TOEFL (minimum score 550 paper-based; 78 iBT). *Application deadline:* For fall admission, 2/15 for domestic and international students; for spring admission, 10/1 for domestic and international students. Applications are processed on a rolling basis. Application fee: $40 ($90 for international students). Electronic applications accepted. *Financial support:* In 2014–15, 101 students received support, including 7 research assistantships (averaging $11,619 per year), 8 teaching assistantships (averaging $7,595 per year); Federal Work-Study and institutionally sponsored loans also available. Support available to part-time students. Financial award application deadline: 4/1; financial award applicants required to submit FAFSA. *Unit head:* Dr. Linda Homeyer, Graduate Advisor, 512-245-8677, Fax: 512-245-8872, E-mail: profcounadm@txstate.edu. *Application contact:* Dr. Andrea Golato, Dean of Graduate School, 512-245-2581, Fax: 512-245-8365, E-mail: gradcollege@txstate.edu. Website: http://www.txstate.edu/clas/Professional-Counseling/Program-Information.html

Thomas University, Department of Human Services, Thomasville, GA 31792-7499. Offers community counseling (MSCC); rehabilitation counseling (MRC). *Accreditation:* CORE. Part-time programs available. *Entrance requirements:* For master's, resume, 3 academic/professional references. Additional exam requirements/recommendations for international students: Required—TOEFL (minimum score 600 paper-based). Electronic applications accepted.

Troy University, Graduate School, College of Education, Program in Counseling and Psychology, Troy, AL 36082. Offers agency counseling (Ed S); clinical mental health (MS); community counseling (MS, Ed S); corrections counseling (MS); rehabilitation counseling (MS); school psychology (MS, Ed S); school psychometry (MS); social service counseling (MS); student affairs counseling (MS); substance abuse counseling (MS). *Accreditation:* ACA; CORE; NCATE. Part-time and evening/weekend programs available. *Faculty:* 41 full-time (18 women), 32 part-time/adjunct (18 women). *Students:* 358 full-time (286 women), 503 part-time (425 women); includes 572 minority (481 Black or African American, non-Hispanic/Latino; 3 American Indian or Alaska Native, non-Hispanic/Latino; 5 Asian, non-Hispanic/Latino; 62 Hispanic/Latino; 21 Two or more races, non-Hispanic/Latino). Average age 34. 248 applicants, 86% accepted, 139 enrolled. In 2014, 212 master's, 4 other advanced degrees awarded. *Degree requirements:* For master's, comprehensive exam, thesis. *Entrance requirements:* For master's, GRE (minimum score of 850 on old exam or 290 on new exam), GMAT (minimum score of 380), or MAT (minimum score of 385), bachelor's degree; minimum undergraduate GPA of 2.5 or 3.0 on last 30 semester hours, letter of recommendation. Additional exam requirements/recommendations for international students: Required—TOEFL (minimum score 523 paper-based; 70 iBT), IELTS (minimum score 6). *Application deadline:* Applications are processed on a rolling basis. Application fee: $50. Electronic applications accepted. *Expenses:* Tuition, state resident: full-time $6570; part-time $365 per credit hour. Tuition, nonresident: full-time $13,140; part-time $730 per credit hour. *Required fees:* $365 per credit hour. *Unit head:* Dr. Andrew Creamer, Chair, 334-670-3350, Fax: 334-670-3291, E-mail: acreamer@troy.edu. *Application contact:* Jessica A. Kimbro, Director of Graduate Admissions, 334-670-3178, E-mail: jacord@troy.edu.

Université du Québec à Rimouski, Graduate Programs, Program in Psychosocial Studies, Rimouski, QC G5L 3A1, Canada. Offers MA.

Université Laval, Faculty of Social Sciences, School of Psychology, Programs in Psychology, Québec, QC G1K 7P4, Canada. Offers clinical psychology (PhD); community psychology (PhD); psychology (PhD, Psy D). *Degree requirements:* For doctorate, comprehensive exam, thesis/dissertation. *Entrance requirements:* For doctorate, comprehension of written English, knowledge of French, interview. Electronic applications accepted.

University at Albany, State University of New York, College of Arts and Sciences, Department of Psychology, Albany, NY 12222-0001. Offers behavioral neuroscience (PhD); clinical psychology (PhD); cognitive psychology (PhD); industrial/organizational psychology (MA, PhD); social-personality psychology (PhD). *Accreditation:* APA (one or more programs are accredited). *Degree requirements:* For doctorate, thesis/dissertation. *Entrance requirements:* For doctorate, GRE General Test, GRE Subject Test. Additional exam requirements/recommendations for international students: Required—TOEFL (minimum score 550 paper-based). Electronic applications accepted.

University of Alaska Anchorage, College of Arts and Sciences, Department of Psychology, Anchorage, AK 99508. Offers clinical psychology (MS); clinical-community psychology with rural-indigenous emphasis (PhD). Part-time programs available. *Degree requirements:* For master's, thesis. *Entrance requirements:* For master's, GRE General Test, GRE Subject Test, interview, references; for doctorate, interview, bachelor's or master's degree in psychology. Additional exam requirements/recommendations for international students: Required—TOEFL (minimum score 550 paper-based). *Faculty research:* Substance abuse, childhood autism, biofeedback, psychological assessment, mental health in Native Alaskans.

University of Alaska Fairbanks, College of Liberal Arts, Department of Psychology, Fairbanks, AK 99775-6480. Offers clinical-community psychology (PhD), including rural cross-cultural emphasis. Program offered jointly with University of Alaska Anchorage. *Faculty:* 9 full-time (5 women). *Students:* 4 full-time (3 women), 16 part-time (10 women); includes 4 minority (1 Asian, non-Hispanic/Latino; 1 Hispanic/Latino; 2 Two or more races, non-Hispanic/Latino), 1 international. Average age 30. 8 applicants, 63% accepted, 5 enrolled. In 2014, 1 doctorate awarded. *Degree requirements:* For doctorate, comprehensive exam, thesis/dissertation, oral defense of dissertation. *Entrance requirements:* For doctorate, bachelor's degree from accredited institution with minimum cumulative undergraduate and major GPA of 3.0; criminal background check; interview; course work in abnormal psychology, statistics, and research methods. Additional exam requirements/recommendations for international students: Required—TOEFL (minimum score 550 paper-based; 80 iBT), IELTS (minimum score 6.5). *Application deadline:* For fall admission, 1/15 for domestic and international students. Application fee: $60. Electronic applications accepted. *Expenses:* Tuition, state resident: full-time $7614; part-time $423 per credit. Tuition, nonresident: full-time $15,552; part-time $864 per credit. Tuition and fees vary according to course level, course load and reciprocity agreements. *Financial support:* In 2014–15, 12 teaching assistantships with full tuition reimbursements (averaging $13,286 per year) were awarded; fellowships with full tuition reimbursements, research assistantships with full tuition reimbursements, career-related internships or fieldwork, Federal Work-Study, scholarships/grants, health care benefits, and unspecified assistantships also available. Support available to part-time students. Financial award application deadline: 7/1; financial award applicants required to submit FAFSA. *Faculty research:* Clinical and community psychology; rural, indigenous, and cultural psychology. *Unit head:* Dr. David Webster, Doctoral Program Director, 907-474-7007, Fax: 907-474-5781, E-mail: fypsych@uaf.edu. *Application contact:* Mary Kreta, Director of Admissions, 907-474-7500, Fax: 907-474-7097, E-mail: admissions@uaf.edu. Website: http://www.uaf.edu/psych/

University of Alaska Fairbanks, School of Education, Program in Counseling, Fairbanks, AK 99775-7520. Offers community counseling (M Ed). Postbaccalaureate

distance learning degree programs offered (minimal on-campus study). *Students:* 21 full-time (18 women), 46 part-time (38 women); includes 8 minority (3 Black or African American, non-Hispanic/Latino; 1 American Indian or Alaska Native, non-Hispanic/Latino; 2 Hispanic/Latino; 1 Native Hawaiian or other Pacific Islander, non-Hispanic/Latino; 1 Two or more races, non-Hispanic/Latino), 1 international. Average age 36. 48 applicants, 56% accepted, 24 enrolled. In 2014, 13 master's, 3 other advanced degrees awarded. *Degree requirements:* For master's, comprehensive exam, oral defense of project or thesis. *Entrance requirements:* For master's, bachelor's degree from accredited institution with minimum cumulative undergraduate and major GPA of 3.0; for Graduate Certificate, master's degree from accredited institution with minimum GPA of 3.0. Additional exam requirements/recommendations for international students: Required—TOEFL (minimum score 550 paper-based; 79 iBT), IELTS (minimum score 6.5). *Application deadline:* For fall admission, 3/1 for domestic and international students; for spring admission, 10/1 for domestic students, 9/1 for international students. Applications are processed on a rolling basis. Application fee: $60. Electronic applications accepted. *Expenses:* Tuition, state resident: full-time $7614; part-time $423 per credit. Tuition, nonresident: full-time $15,552; part-time $864 per credit. Tuition and fees vary according to course level, course load and reciprocity agreements. *Financial support:* In 2014–15, 3 teaching assistantships with full tuition reimbursements (averaging $5,348 per year) were awarded; fellowships with full tuition reimbursements, career-related internships or fieldwork, Federal Work-Study, scholarships/grants, health care benefits, and unspecified assistantships also available. Support available to part-time students. Financial award application deadline: 7/1; financial award applicants required to submit FAFSA. *Unit head:* Allan Morotti, Interim Dean, 907-474-7341, Fax: 907-474-5451, E-mail: uaf-soe-school@alaska.edu. *Application contact:* Mary Kreta, Director of Admissions, 907-474-7500, Fax: 907-474-7097, E-mail: admissions@uaf.edu.
Website: https://sites.google.com/a/alaska.edu/soe-graduate/

University of Bridgeport, School of Arts and Sciences, Department of Counseling, Bridgeport, CT 06604. Offers clinical mental health counseling (MS); college student personnel (MS); community counseling (MS); human resource development (MS); human service (MS). Part-time and evening/weekend programs available. *Degree requirements:* For master's, thesis, project. *Entrance requirements:* Additional exam requirements/recommendations for international students: Recommended—TOEFL (minimum score 550 paper-based; 80 iBT), IELTS (minimum score 6.5). Electronic applications accepted. *Expenses:* Contact institution. *Faculty research:* Corporate elder care programs.

The University of British Columbia, Faculty of Arts and Faculty of Graduate Studies, Department of Psychology, Vancouver, BC V6T 1Z4, Canada. Offers behavioral neuroscience (MA, PhD); clinical psychology (MA, PhD); cognitive science (MA, PhD); developmental psychology (MA, PhD); health psychology (MA, PhD); quantitative methods (MA, PhD); social/personality psychology (MA, PhD). *Accreditation:* APA (one or more programs are accredited). Terminal master's awarded for partial completion of doctoral program. *Degree requirements:* For master's, thesis; for doctorate, comprehensive exam, thesis/dissertation. *Entrance requirements:* For master's and doctorate, GRE General Test. Additional exam requirements/recommendations for international students: Required—TOEFL (minimum score 550 paper-based; 80 iBT). Electronic applications accepted. *Faculty research:* Clinical, developmental, social/personality, cognition, behavioral neuroscience.

University of Central Arkansas, Graduate School, College of Health and Behavioral Sciences, Department of Counseling and Psychology, Program in Community Counseling, Conway, AR 72035-0001. Offers MS. *Degree requirements:* For master's, comprehensive exam, thesis optional. *Entrance requirements:* For master's, GRE General Test, minimum GPA of 2.7. Additional exam requirements/recommendations for international students: Required—TOEFL (minimum score 550 paper-based). Electronic applications accepted.

University of Connecticut, Graduate School, College of Liberal Arts and Sciences, Department of Psychology, Storrs, CT 06269. Offers behavioral neuroscience (PhD); biopsychology (PhD); clinical psychology (MA, PhD); cognition and instruction (PhD); developmental psychology (MA, PhD); ecological psychology (PhD); experimental psychology (PhD); general psychology (MA, PhD); health psychology (Graduate Certificate); industrial/organizational psychology (PhD); language and cognition (PhD); neuroscience (PhD); occupational health psychology (Graduate Certificate); social psychology (MA, PhD). *Accreditation:* APA. Terminal master's awarded for partial completion of doctoral program. *Degree requirements:* For master's, comprehensive exam; for doctorate, thesis/dissertation. *Entrance requirements:* For master's and doctorate, GRE General Test, GRE Subject Test. Additional exam requirements/recommendations for international students: Required—TOEFL (minimum score 550 paper-based). Electronic applications accepted.

University of Delaware, College of Arts and Sciences, Department of Psychology, Newark, DE 19716. Offers behavioral neuroscience (PhD); clinical psychology (PhD); cognitive psychology (PhD); social psychology (PhD). *Accreditation:* APA. *Degree requirements:* For doctorate, thesis/dissertation. *Entrance requirements:* For doctorate, GRE General Test. Additional exam requirements/recommendations for international students: Required—TOEFL (minimum score 600 paper-based). Electronic applications accepted. *Faculty research:* Emotion development, neural and cognitive aspects of memory, neural control of feeding, intergroup relations, social cognition and communication.

University of Denver, Division of Arts, Humanities and Social Sciences, Department of Psychology, Denver, CO 80208. Offers affective/social psychology (PhD); clinical child psychology (PhD); cognitive psychology (PhD); developmental psychology (PhD). *Accreditation:* APA. *Faculty:* 25 full-time (11 women), 4 part-time/adjunct (2 women). *Students:* 21 full-time (18 women), 5 part-time (all women); includes 7 minority (2 Black or African American, non-Hispanic/Latino; 3 Asian, non-Hispanic/Latino; 1 Hispanic/Latino; 1 Two or more races, non-Hispanic/Latino), 3 international. Average age 28. 348 applicants, 5% accepted, 6 enrolled. In 2014, 9 doctorates awarded. Terminal master's awarded for partial completion of doctoral program. *Degree requirements:* For doctorate, variable foreign language requirement, comprehensive exam (for some programs), thesis/dissertation. *Entrance requirements:* For doctorate, GRE General Test, master's degree, transcripts, biographical statement, three letters of recommendation. Additional exam requirements/recommendations for international students: Required—TOEFL (minimum score 550 paper-based; 80 iBT). *Application deadline:* For fall admission, 12/1 priority date for domestic and international students. Application fee: $65. Electronic applications accepted. *Expenses:* Expenses: $1,199 per credit hour. *Financial support:* In 2014–15, 26 students received support, including 13 research assistantships with full and partial tuition reimbursements available (averaging $12,821 per year), 20 teaching assistantships with full and partial tuition reimbursements available (averaging $15,333 per year); Federal Work-Study, institutionally sponsored loans, scholarships/grants, and unspecified assistantships also available. Support available to part-time students. Financial award application deadline: 2/15; financial award applicants required to submit FAFSA. *Faculty research:* Developmental cognitive neuroscience, social and emotional processes, child and adolescent development, clinical child psychology, cognitive psychology. *Total annual research expenditures:* $3 million. *Unit head:* Dr. George

Potts, Chair, 303-871-3717, Fax: 303-871-4747, E-mail: gpotts@du.edu. *Application contact:* Paula Houghtaling, Graduate Program Administrator, 303-871-3803, Fax: 303-871-4747, E-mail: phoughta@du.edu.
Website: http://www.du.edu/ahss/psychology/index.html

University of Guelph, Graduate Studies, College of Social and Applied Human Sciences, Department of Psychology, Guelph, ON N1G 2W1, Canada. Offers applied social psychology (MA, PhD); clinical psychology: applied development emphasis (PhD); clinical psychology: applied developmental emphasis (MA); industrial/organizational psychology (MA, PhD); neuroscience and applied cognitive science (MA, PhD). *Degree requirements:* For master's, thesis; for doctorate, comprehensive exam, thesis/dissertation. *Entrance requirements:* For master's, GRE General Test, GRE Subject Test, minimum B+ average during previous 2 years of course work; for doctorate, GRE General Test, GRE Subject Test, minimum A- average. Additional exam requirements/recommendations for international students: Required—TOEFL (minimum score 89 iBT). Electronic applications accepted. *Faculty research:* Organizational psychology, reading comprehension and mathematical ability, drug addiction and relapse, gender issues and culture, memory, clinical psychology.

University of Hawaii at Manoa, Graduate Division, College of Social Sciences, Department of Psychology, Honolulu, HI 96822. Offers clinical psychology (PhD); community and cultural psychology (PhD); community and culture (MA); psychology (MA, PhD, Graduate Certificate). *Accreditation:* APA (one or more programs are accredited). Part-time programs available. Terminal master's awarded for partial completion of doctoral program. *Degree requirements:* For master's, comprehensive exam, thesis; for doctorate, comprehensive exam, thesis/dissertation. *Entrance requirements:* For master's and doctorate, GRE General Test, GRE Subject Test. Additional exam requirements/recommendations for international students: Required—TOEFL (minimum score 600 paper-based; 100 iBT), IELTS (minimum score 7). *Faculty research:* Cross-cultural psychology, health psychology, marine mammals, child/adult psychopathology.

University of Houston, College of Liberal Arts and Social Sciences, Department of Psychology, Houston, TX 77204. Offers clinical psychology (PhD); developmental psychology (PhD); industrial/organizational psychology (PhD); psychology (MA); social psychology (PhD). *Accreditation:* APA (one or more programs are accredited). *Degree requirements:* For master's, comprehensive exam, thesis; for doctorate, comprehensive exam, thesis/dissertation. *Entrance requirements:* For master's, GRE General Test, career statement, 3 letters of recommendation; for doctorate, GRE General Test, 3 letters of recommendation. Additional exam requirements/recommendations for international students: Required—TOEFL (minimum score 550 paper-based; 79 iBT). Electronic applications accepted. *Faculty research:* Health psychology, depression, child/family process, organizational effectiveness, close relationships.

The University of Kansas, Graduate Studies, College of Liberal Arts and Sciences, Department of Psychology, Lawrence, KS 66045. Offers clinical child psychology (MA, PhD); clinical health and rehabilitation (PhD); cognitive psychology (PhD); developmental psychology (PhD); quantitative psychology (PhD); social psychology (MA). *Accreditation:* APA (one or more programs are accredited). *Faculty:* 36 full-time, 3 part-time/adjunct. *Students:* 81 full-time (49 women), 1 (woman) part-time; includes 12 minority (4 Black or African American, non-Hispanic/Latino; 5 Asian, non-Hispanic/Latino; 1 Hispanic/Latino; 2 Two or more races, non-Hispanic/Latino), 13 international. Average age 29. 194 applicants, 10% accepted, 9 enrolled. In 2014, 17 master's, 13 doctorates awarded. *Degree requirements:* For doctorate, variable foreign language requirement, comprehensive exam, thesis/dissertation. *Entrance requirements:* For doctorate, GRE General Test, minimum GPA of 3.0; undergraduate degree with 15 hours of course work in psychology, curriculum vitae, writing sample (clinical program only). Additional exam requirements/recommendations for international students: Required—TOEFL. *Application deadline:* For fall admission, 12/1 for domestic and international students. Application fee: $55 ($65 for international students). Electronic applications accepted. *Financial support:* In 2014–15, 1 fellowship with full tuition reimbursement (averaging $12,750 per year), 4 research assistantships with partial tuition reimbursements (averaging $12,980 per year), 70 teaching assistantships with partial tuition reimbursements (averaging $12,750 per year) were awarded; career-related internships or fieldwork, Federal Work-Study, scholarships/grants, health care benefits, and unspecified assistantships also available. Financial award application deadline: 12/1; financial award applicants required to submit FAFSA. *Faculty research:* Origins, correlates and treatment of depression; health and emotion; concentration on topics related to prejudice, stereotyping, and intergroup relations; memory, cognitive development, language, perception, attention, aging; psychometric methods, item response theory, structural equation modeling. *Unit head:* Ruth Anne Atchley, Chair, 785-864-4131. *Application contact:* Cathy O'Keefe, Graduate Officer, 785-864-4195, Fax: 785-864-5596, E-mail: cokeefe@ku.edu.
Website: http://www.psych.ku.edu/

University of Maryland, College Park, Academic Affairs, College of Behavioral and Social Sciences, Department of Psychology, College Park, MD 20742. Offers clinical psychology (PhD); developmental psychology (PhD); experimental psychology (PhD); industrial psychology (MA, MS, PhD); social psychology (PhD). *Accreditation:* APA (one or more programs are accredited). *Degree requirements:* For master's, thesis; for doctorate, variable foreign language requirement, comprehensive exam, thesis/dissertation. *Entrance requirements:* For master's and doctorate, GRE General Test, GRE Subject Test, minimum GPA of 3.5, research and/or work experience, 3 letters of recommendation. Electronic applications accepted. *Faculty research:* Social stereotyping and prejudice, anxiety disorders, auditory neuroethology, counseling and social psychology.

University of Massachusetts Amherst, Graduate School, College of Natural Sciences, Department of Psychological and Brain Sciences, Amherst, MA 01003. Offers clinical psychology (MS, PhD); cognitive psychology (MS, PhD); developmental science (MS, PhD); psychology of peace and violence (MS, PhD); social psychology (MS, PhD). *Accreditation:* APA (one or more programs are accredited). *Faculty:* 62 full-time (31 women). *Students:* 47 full-time (32 women), 14 part-time (11 women); includes 12 minority (2 Black or African American, non-Hispanic/Latino; 6 Asian, non-Hispanic/Latino; 3 Hispanic/Latino; 1 Two or more races, non-Hispanic/Latino), 9 international. Average age 27. 317 applicants, 7% accepted, 11 enrolled. In 2014, 12 master's, 10 doctorates awarded. Terminal master's awarded for partial completion of doctoral program. *Degree requirements:* For master's, thesis; for doctorate, comprehensive exam, thesis/dissertation. *Entrance requirements:* For master's and doctorate, GRE General Test, 3 letters of recommendation. Additional exam requirements/recommendations for international students: Required—TOEFL (minimum score 550 paper-based; 80 iBT), IELTS (minimum score 6.5). *Application deadline:* For fall admission, 12/1 for domestic and international students. Applications are processed on a rolling basis. Application fee: $75. Electronic applications accepted. *Expenses:* Tuition, state resident: full-time $1980; part-time $110 per credit. Tuition, nonresident: full-time $14,644; part-time $414 per credit. *Required fees:* $11,417. One-time fee: $357. *Financial support:* Fellowships with full and partial tuition reimbursements, research assistantships with full and partial tuition reimbursements, teaching assistantships with full and partial tuition reimbursements, career-related internships or

fieldwork, Federal Work-Study, scholarships/grants, traineeships, health care benefits, tuition waivers (full and partial), and unspecified assistantships available. Support available to part-time students. Financial award application deadline: 12/1. *Unit head:* Dr. Michael Constantino, Graduate Program Director, 413-545-2503, Fax: 413-545-0996. *Application contact:* Lindsay DeSantis, Supervisor of Admissions, 413-545-0722, Fax: 413-577-0010, E-mail: gradadm@grad.umass.edu.
Website: http://www.psych.umass.edu/

University of Massachusetts Lowell, College of Fine Arts, Humanities and Social Sciences, Department of Psychology, Lowell, MA 01854. Offers community social psychology (MA). Part-time programs available. *Degree requirements:* For master's, thesis optional. *Entrance requirements:* For master's, GRE General Test or MAT. Electronic applications accepted. *Faculty research:* Domestic violence, youth sports, teen pregnancy, substance abuse, family and work roles.

University of Michigan, Horace H. Rackham School of Graduate Studies, College of Literature, Science, and the Arts, Department of Psychology, Ann Arbor, MI 48109. Offers biopsychology (PhD); clinical science (PhD); cognition and cognitive neuroscience (PhD); developmental psychology (PhD); personality and social contexts (PhD); social psychology (PhD). *Accreditation:* APA. *Faculty:* 57 full-time (27 women), 31 part-time/adjunct (17 women). *Students:* 118 full-time (80 women); includes 58 minority (15 Black or African American, non-Hispanic/Latino; 1 American Indian or Alaska Native, non-Hispanic/Latino; 15 Asian, non-Hispanic/Latino; 25 Hispanic/Latino; 2 Two or more races, non-Hispanic/Latino), 12 international. Average age 27. 687 applicants, 7% accepted, 25 enrolled. In 2014, 36 doctorates awarded. *Degree requirements:* For doctorate, comprehensive exam, thesis/dissertation, oral defense of dissertation, preliminary exam. *Entrance requirements:* For doctorate, GRE General Test. Additional exam requirements/recommendations for international students: Required—TOEFL. *Application deadline:* For fall admission, 12/1 for domestic and international students. Application fee: $75 ($90 for international students). Electronic applications accepted. *Financial support:* In 2014–15, 82 students received support, including 45 fellowships with full tuition reimbursements available (averaging $21,600 per year), 16 research assistantships with full tuition reimbursements available (averaging $28,450 per year), 50 teaching assistantships with full tuition reimbursements available (averaging $26,200 per year); career-related internships or fieldwork also available. Financial award application deadline: 4/15. *Unit head:* Prof. Patricia Reuter-Lorenz, Department Chair, 734-764-7429. *Application contact:* Danielle Joanette, Psychology Student Academic Affairs, 731-764-2580, Fax: 734-615-7584, E-mail: psych.saa@umich.edu.
Website: http://www.lsa.umich.edu/psych/

University of Minnesota, Twin Cities Campus, Graduate School, College of Liberal Arts, Department of Psychology, Program in Social Psychology, Minneapolis, MN 55455-0213. Offers PhD. *Degree requirements:* For doctorate, comprehensive exam, thesis/dissertation. *Entrance requirements:* For doctorate, GRE General Test, GRE Subject Test (recommended), 12 credits of upper-level psychology courses, including a course in statistics or psychological measurement. Additional exam requirements/recommendations for international students: Required—TOEFL (minimum score 550 paper-based; 79 iBT).

University of Missouri–Kansas City, College of Arts and Sciences, Department of Psychology, Kansas City, MO 64110-2499. Offers clinical psychology (PhD); community psychology (PhD); health psychology (PhD); psychology (MA). PhD (interdisciplinary) offered through the School of Graduate Studies. *Accreditation:* APA. *Faculty:* 10 full-time (7 women), 2 part-time/adjunct (1 woman). *Students:* 21 full-time (14 women), 10 part-time (6 women); includes 5 minority (1 Asian, non-Hispanic/Latino; 4 Hispanic/Latino). Average age 32. 109 applicants, 6% accepted, 6 enrolled. In 2014, 4 master's, 7 doctorates awarded. Terminal master's awarded for partial completion of doctoral program. *Degree requirements:* For master's, thesis; for doctorate, comprehensive exam, thesis/dissertation, residency. *Entrance requirements:* For master's, GRE, minimum GPA of 3.5, letter of recommendation; for doctorate, GRE, minimum GPA of 3.25. Additional exam requirements/recommendations for international students: Required—TOEFL (minimum score 550 paper-based; 80 iBT). *Application deadline:* For fall admission, 1/15 for domestic and international students. Applications are processed on a rolling basis. Application fee: $45 ($50 for international students). Electronic applications accepted. *Financial support:* In 2014–15, 8 research assistantships (averaging $11,229 per year), 20 teaching assistantships (averaging $12,015 per year) were awarded; career-related internships or fieldwork, Federal Work-Study, and institutionally sponsored loans also available. Support available to part-time students. Financial award application deadline: 3/1; financial award applicants required to submit FAFSA. *Faculty research:* HIV/AIDS research group, psycho-oncology, sensory and cognitive neuroscience, cognitive psychophysiology, obesity and related metabolic disorders. *Unit head:* Dr. Jennifer Lundgren, Department Chair, 816-235-5384, Fax: 816-235-1062, E-mail: lundgrenj@umkc.edu. *Application contact:* Dr. Cathy Rawlings, Director, Graduate Programs, 816-235-1318, Fax: 816-235-1062, E-mail: psychology@umkc.edu.
Website: http://cas.umkc.edu/psyc

University of Montevallo, College of Education, Program in Counseling, Montevallo, AL 35115. Offers community counseling (M Ed); couple, marriage and family (M Ed); school counseling (M Ed). *Accreditation:* ACA; NCATE. Part-time and evening/weekend programs available. *Students:* 41 full-time (34 women), 42 part-time (37 women); includes 20 minority (16 Black or African American, non-Hispanic/Latino; 2 Hispanic/Latino; 2 Two or more races, non-Hispanic/Latino). In 2014, 11 master's awarded. *Entrance requirements:* For master's, GRE General Test or MAT, minimum undergraduate GPA of 2.75 in last 60 hours or 2.5 overall, interview. Additional exam requirements/recommendations for international students: Required—TOEFL (minimum score 550 paper-based). *Application deadline:* For fall admission, 7/15 for domestic students; for spring admission, 11/15 for domestic students. Application fee: $25. *Financial support:* Federal Work-Study, scholarships/grants, and unspecified assistantships available. *Unit head:* Dr. Charlotte Daughhetee, Chair, 205-665-6358, E-mail: daughc@montevallo.edu. *Application contact:* Kevin Thornthwaite, Director, Graduate Admissions and Records, 205-665-6350, E-mail: graduate@montevallo.edu.
Website: http://www.montevallo.edu/education/college-of-education/traditional-masters-degrees/counseling/

University of Nebraska–Lincoln, Graduate College, College of Arts and Sciences, Department of Psychology, Lincoln, NE 68588. Offers biopsychology (PhD); clinical psychology (PhD); cognitive psychology (PhD); developmental psychology (PhD); psychology (MA); social/personality psychology (PhD); JD/MA; JD/PhD. *Accreditation:* APA (one or more programs are accredited). *Degree requirements:* For master's, thesis optional; for doctorate, comprehensive exam, thesis/dissertation. *Entrance requirements:* For master's and doctorate, GRE General Test. Additional exam requirements/recommendations for international students: Required—TOEFL (minimum score 550 paper-based). Electronic applications accepted. *Faculty research:* Law and psychology, rural mental health, chronic mental illness, neuropsychology, child clinical psychology.

University of Nevada, Reno, Graduate School, Interdisciplinary Program in Social Psychology, Reno, NV 89557. Offers PhD. *Degree requirements:* For doctorate, one foreign language, thesis/dissertation. *Entrance requirements:* For doctorate, GRE General Test, GRE Subject Test (psychology or sociology), minimum GPA of 3.0. Additional exam requirements/recommendations for international students: Required—TOEFL (minimum score 500 paper-based; 61 iBT), IELTS (minimum score 6). Electronic applications accepted. *Faculty research:* Social psychological theory, social psychology of law.

University of New Haven, Graduate School, College of Arts and Sciences, Program in Community Psychology, West Haven, CT 06516-1916. Offers applications of psychology (Certificate); community clinical services (MA); community psychology (MA); forensic psychology (MA); program development (MA). Part-time and evening/weekend programs available. *Degree requirements:* For master's, thesis or alternative, fieldwork. *Entrance requirements:* Additional exam requirements/recommendations for international students: Required—TOEFL (minimum score 80 iBT), IELTS, PTE (minimum score 53). Electronic applications accepted. Application fee is waived when completed online. *Expenses: Tuition:* Full-time $22,248; part-time $824 per credit hour. *Required fees:* $45 per trimester.

The University of North Carolina at Chapel Hill, Graduate School, College of Arts and Sciences, Department of Psychology, Chapel Hill, NC 27599-3270. Offers behavioral neuroscience psychology (PhD); clinical psychology (PhD); cognitive psychology (PhD); developmental psychology (PhD); quantitative psychology (PhD); social psychology (PhD). *Accreditation:* APA. *Degree requirements:* For doctorate, comprehensive exam, thesis/dissertation. *Entrance requirements:* For doctorate, GRE General Test, minimum GPA of 3.0. Additional exam requirements/recommendations for international students: Required—TOEFL (minimum score 550 paper-based; 79 iBT), IELTS (minimum score 7). Electronic applications accepted. *Faculty research:* Expressed emotion, cognitive development, social cognitive neuroscience, human memory personality.

The University of North Carolina at Charlotte, College of Liberal Arts and Sciences, Department of Psychology, Charlotte, NC 28223-0001. Offers clinical/community psychology (MA); cognitive sciences (Graduate Certificate); health psychology (PhD); industrial/organizational psychology (MA). Part-time programs available. *Faculty:* 31 full-time (17 women), 1 part-time/adjunct (0 women). *Students:* 42 full-time (35 women), 31 part-time (26 women); includes 18 minority (5 Black or African American, non-Hispanic/Latino; 2 Asian, non-Hispanic/Latino; 9 Hispanic/Latino; 2 Two or more races, non-Hispanic/Latino), 1 international. Average age 28. 243 applicants, 16% accepted, 25 enrolled. In 2014, 9 master's, 5 doctorates, 1 other advanced degree awarded. Terminal master's awarded for partial completion of doctoral program. *Degree requirements:* For master's, thesis; for doctorate, thesis/dissertation. *Entrance requirements:* For master's, GRE General Test, GRE Subject Test, minimum GPA of 3.0 in undergraduate major, 2.8 overall, letters of recommendation; for doctorate, GRE General Test, minimum GPA of 3.5, letters of recommendation. Additional exam requirements/recommendations for international students: Required—TOEFL (minimum score 557 paper-based; 83 iBT). *Application deadline:* For fall admission, 5/1 for domestic and international students. Application fee: $75. Electronic applications accepted. *Expenses:* Tuition, state resident: full-time $4008. Tuition, nonresident: full-time $16,295. *Required fees:* $2755. Tuition and fees vary according to course load and program. *Financial support:* In 2014–15, 33 students received support, including 16 research assistantships (averaging $15,239 per year), 17 teaching assistantships (averaging $12,809 per year); career-related internships or fieldwork, Federal Work-Study, institutionally sponsored loans, and scholarships/grants also available. Support available to part-time students. Financial award application deadline: 4/1; financial award applicants required to submit FAFSA. *Faculty research:* Neuropsychology of information processing, perception and human performance, computer-based applications in research and instruction, interventions to facilitate team effectiveness, post-traumatic psychological growth. *Total annual research expenditures:* $327,551. *Unit head:* Dr. Fary Cachelin, Chair, 704-687-1319, Fax: 704-687-1317, E-mail: fcacheli@uncc.edu. *Application contact:* Kathy B. Giddings, Director of Graduate Admissions, 704-687-5503, Fax: 704-687-1668, E-mail: gradadm@uncc.edu.
Website: http://psych.uncc.edu/graduate-programs

The University of North Carolina at Charlotte, College of Liberal Arts and Sciences, Department of Sociology, Charlotte, NC 28223-0001. Offers health research (MA); mathematical sociology and quantitative methods (MA); organizations, occupations, and work (MA); political sociology (MA); race and gender (MA); social psychology (MA); social theory (MA); sociology of education (MA); stratification (MA). Part-time and evening/weekend programs available. *Faculty:* 16 full-time (10 women). *Students:* 11 full-time (5 women), 2 part-time (0 women); includes 5 minority (4 Black or African American, non-Hispanic/Latino; 1 Hispanic/Latino), 1 international. Average age 29. 14 applicants, 71% accepted, 5 enrolled. In 2014, 6 master's awarded. *Degree requirements:* For master's, thesis or comprehensive exam. *Entrance requirements:* For master's, GRE or MAT, minimum GPA of 3.0 in last 2 years, 2.75 overall. Additional exam requirements/recommendations for international students: Required—TOEFL (minimum score 557 paper-based; 83 iBT). *Application deadline:* For fall admission, 4/15 for domestic and international students; for spring admission, 10/1 for domestic and international students. Application fee: $75. Electronic applications accepted. *Expenses:* Tuition, state resident: full-time $4008. Tuition, nonresident: full-time $16,295. *Required fees:* $2755. Tuition and fees vary according to course load and program. *Financial support:* In 2014–15, 10 students received support, including 5 research assistantships (averaging $10,400 per year), 5 teaching assistantships (averaging $9,200 per year); career-related internships or fieldwork, institutionally sponsored loans, scholarships/grants, and unspecified assistantships also available. Support available to part-time students. Financial award application deadline: 4/1; financial award applicants required to submit FAFSA. *Faculty research:* Impact of race on high school course selection; income inequality within the United States and cross-nationally; small group interaction, nonverbal behaviors, identity, emotions, gender, and expectations; mathematical models of social processes. *Total annual research expenditures:* $413,099. *Unit head:* Dr. Lisa Walker, Chair, 704-687-7825, Fax: 704-687-3091, E-mail: lisa.walker@uncc.edu. *Application contact:* Kathy B. Giddings, Director of Graduate Admissions, 704-687-5503, Fax: 704-687-1668, E-mail: gradadm@uncc.edu.
Website: http://sociology.uncc.edu/

The University of North Carolina at Greensboro, Graduate School, College of Arts and Sciences, Department of Psychology, Greensboro, NC 27412-5001. Offers clinical psychology (MA, PhD); cognitive psychology (MA, PhD); developmental psychology (MA, PhD); social psychology (MA, PhD). *Accreditation:* APA (one or more programs are accredited). Terminal master's awarded for partial completion of doctoral program. *Degree requirements:* For master's, comprehensive exam, thesis; for doctorate, one foreign language, thesis/dissertation, preliminary exam. *Entrance requirements:* For master's and doctorate, GRE General Test. Additional exam requirements/recommendations for international students: Required—TOEFL. Electronic applications accepted. *Faculty research:* Sensory and perceptual determinants; evoked potential: disorders, deafness, and development.

University of Oregon, Graduate School, College of Arts and Sciences, Department of Psychology, Eugene, OR 97403. Offers clinical psychology (PhD); cognitive psychology (MA, MS, PhD); developmental psychology (MA, MS, PhD); physiological psychology (MA, MS, PhD); psychology (MA, MS, PhD); social/personality psychology (MA, MS,

PhD). *Accreditation:* APA (one or more programs are accredited). Terminal master's awarded for partial completion of doctoral program. *Degree requirements:* For doctorate, thesis/dissertation. *Entrance requirements:* For master's, GRE General Test, minimum GPA of 3.0; for doctorate, GRE General Test. Additional exam requirements/recommendations for international students: Required—TOEFL.

University of Phoenix–Minneapolis/St. Paul Campus, College of Human Services, St. Louis Park, MN 55426. Offers community counseling (MSC).

University of Phoenix–Phoenix Campus, College of Social Sciences, Tempe, AZ 85282-2371. Offers counseling (MS), including clinical mental health counseling, community counseling, counseling, marriage, family and child therapy; psychology (MS). Evening/weekend programs available. Postbaccalaureate distance learning degree programs offered. *Entrance requirements:* Additional exam requirements/recommendations for international students: Required—TOEFL, TOEIC (Test of English as an International Communication), Berlitz Online English Proficiency Exam, PTE, or IELTS. Electronic applications accepted. *Expenses:* Contact institution.

University of Puerto Rico, Río Piedras Campus, College of Social Sciences, Department of Psychology, San Juan, PR 00931-3300. Offers clinical psychology (MA); industrial organizational psychology (MA); investigative academic psychology (MA); psychology (PhD); social-community psychology (MA). Part-time programs available. *Degree requirements:* For master's, comprehensive exam, thesis; for doctorate, comprehensive exam, thesis/dissertation, internship. *Entrance requirements:* For master's, GRE or PAEG, interview, minimum GPA of 3.0; for doctorate, GRE or PAEG, interview, master's degree, minimum GPA of 3.0. *Faculty research:* Intervention on depressed Latino youth, biosychosocial training.

University of Rochester, Margaret Warner Graduate School of Education and Human Development, Master's Program in Counseling, Rochester, NY 14627. Offers school and community counseling (MS); school counseling (MS). *Expenses: Tuition:* Full-time $46,150; part-time $1442 per credit hour. *Required fees:* $504.

University of Rochester, School of Arts and Sciences, Department of Clinical and Social Sciences in Psychology, Rochester, NY 14627. Offers clinical psychology (PhD); developmental psychology (PhD); social-personality psychology (PhD). *Accreditation:* APA. *Faculty:* 14 full-time (7 women). *Students:* 46 full-time (37 women), 1 (woman) part-time; includes 6 minority (2 Asian, non-Hispanic/Latino; 3 Hispanic/Latino; 1 Two or more races, non-Hispanic/Latino), 6 international. 326 applicants, 4% accepted, 6 enrolled. In 2014, 9 doctorates awarded. Terminal master's awarded for partial completion of doctoral program. *Degree requirements:* For doctorate, thesis/dissertation, qualifying exam. *Entrance requirements:* For doctorate, GRE General Test. Additional exam requirements/recommendations for international students: Required—TOEFL. *Application deadline:* For fall admission, 12/15 priority date for domestic students. Application fee: $60. *Expenses: Tuition:* Full-time $46,150; part-time $1442 per credit hour. *Required fees:* $504. *Financial support:* Fellowships, research assistantships, teaching assistantships, career-related internships or fieldwork, and tuition waivers (full and partial) available. Financial award application deadline: 2/1. *Faculty research:* Clinical psychology, social-personality psychology, developmental psychology, human motivation. *Unit head:* Loisa Bennetto, Chair, 585-275-8712. *Application contact:* April Engram, Academic Coordinator/Analyst, 585-275-8704. Website: http://www.psych.rochester.edu/csp/

University of South Carolina, The Graduate School, College of Arts and Sciences, Department of Psychology, Program in Clinical/Community Psychology, Columbia, SC 29208. Offers clinical/community psychology (PhD); general psychology (MA). *Accreditation:* APA. *Degree requirements:* For master's, comprehensive exam, thesis; for doctorate, comprehensive exam, thesis/dissertation. *Entrance requirements:* For doctorate, GRE General Test, minimum GPA of 3.2. Additional exam requirements/recommendations for international students: Required—TOEFL. Electronic applications accepted. *Faculty research:* Developmental psychopathology, health disparities, community-level interventions for psychological well being.

University of Southern California, Graduate School, Dana and David Dornsife College of Letters, Arts and Sciences, Department of Psychology, Los Angeles, CA 90089. Offers brain and cognitive science (PhD); clinical science (PhD); developmental psychology (PhD); human behavior (MHB); quantitative methods (PhD); social psychology (PhD). *Accreditation:* APA. *Degree requirements:* For doctorate, comprehensive exam, thesis/dissertation, one-year internship (for clinical science students). *Entrance requirements:* For doctorate, GRE. Additional exam requirements/recommendations for international students: Recommended—TOEFL (minimum score 600 paper-based; 100 iBT). Electronic applications accepted. *Faculty research:* Affective neuroscience; children and families; vision, culture and ethnicity; intergroup relations; aggression and violence; language and reading development; substance abuse.

The University of Tennessee at Chattanooga, School of Education, Chattanooga, TN 37403. Offers counseling (M Ed), including community counseling, school counseling; education (M Ed, Post-Master's Certificate), including elementary education (M Ed), school leadership, secondary education (M Ed), special education (M Ed); educational specialist (Ed S), including educational technology, school psychology; learning and leadership (Ed D), including educational leadership. *Accreditation:* ACA; NCATE. Part-time and evening/weekend programs available. Postbaccalaureate distance learning degree programs offered (no on-campus study). *Faculty:* 24 full-time (17 women), 6 part-time/adjunct (4 women). *Students:* 107 full-time (86 women), 263 part-time (192 women); includes 71 minority (46 Black or African American, non-Hispanic/Latino; 2 American Indian or Alaska Native, non-Hispanic/Latino; 5 Asian, non-Hispanic/Latino; 11 Hispanic/Latino; 7 Two or more races, non-Hispanic/Latino), 2 international. Average age 34. 121 applicants, 83% accepted, 67 enrolled. In 2014, 125 master's, 10 doctorates, 3 other advanced degrees awarded. *Degree requirements:* For master's, comprehensive exam, thesis optional, culminating experience; for doctorate, comprehensive exam, thesis/dissertation; for other advanced degree, internship. *Entrance requirements:* For master's, GRE General Test, PPST 1, teaching certificate; for doctorate, GRE General Test, master's degree, two years of practical work experience in organizational environment; for other advanced degree, GRE General Test, letters of reference. Additional exam requirements/recommendations for international students: Required—TOEFL (minimum score 550 paper-based; 79 iBT), IELTS (minimum score 6). *Application deadline:* For fall admission, 6/13 for domestic students, 6/1 for international students; for spring admission, 10/15 for domestic students, 10/1 for international students. Applications are processed on a rolling basis. Application fee: $30 ($35 for international students). Electronic applications accepted. *Expenses:* Tuition, state resident: full-time $7708; part-time $428 per credit hour. Tuition, nonresident: full-time $23,826; part-time $1323 per credit hour. *Required fees:* $1708; $252 per credit hour. *Financial support:* In 2014–15, 20 research assistantships with tuition reimbursements (averaging $6,340 per year), 4 teaching assistantships with tuition reimbursements (averaging $7,234 per year) were awarded; career-related internships or fieldwork, institutionally sponsored loans, scholarships/grants, and unspecified assistantships also available. Support available to part-time students. Financial award applicants required to submit FAFSA. *Faculty research:* School counseling, community counseling, elementary and secondary education, school leadership and administration. *Total annual research expenditures:* $967,880. *Unit*

head: Dr. Linda Johnston, Director, 423-425-4122, Fax: 423-425-5380, E-mail: linda-johnston@utc.edu. *Application contact:* Dr. J. Randy Walker, Interim Dean of Graduate Studies, 423-425-4478, Fax: 423-425-5223, E-mail: randy-walker@utc.edu. Website: http://www.utc.edu/school-education/abouttheschool/gradprograms.php

The University of Tennessee at Martin, Graduate Programs, College of Education, Health and Behavioral Sciences, Program in Counseling, Martin, TN 38238. Offers community counseling (MS Ed); school counseling (MS Ed). *Accreditation:* NCATE. Part-time programs available. *Students:* 20 full-time (17 women), 57 part-time (51 women); includes 14 minority (12 Black or African American, non-Hispanic/Latino; 2 Hispanic/Latino). 40 applicants, 40% accepted, 14 enrolled. In 2014, 10 master's awarded. *Degree requirements:* For master's, comprehensive exam. *Entrance requirements:* For master's, GRE General Test, minimum GPA of 2.5, resume, letters of reference. Additional exam requirements/recommendations for international students: Required—TOEFL (minimum score 525 paper-based; 71 iBT). *Application deadline:* For fall admission, 7/27 priority date for domestic and international students; for spring admission, 12/17 priority date for domestic and international students. Applications are processed on a rolling basis. Application fee: $30 ($130 for international students). Electronic applications accepted. *Financial support:* Scholarships/grants and unspecified assistantships available. Support available to part-time students. Financial award application deadline: 2/15; financial award applicants required to submit FAFSA. *Unit head:* Dr. Gail Stephens, Interim Dean, 731-881-7127, Fax: 731-881-7975, E-mail: gstephe6@utm.edu. *Application contact:* Jolene L. Cunningham, Student Services Specialist, 731-881-7012, Fax: 731-881-7499, E-mail: jcunningham@utm.edu.

University of Victoria, Faculty of Graduate Studies, Faculty of Education, Department of Educational Psychology and Leadership Studies, Victoria, BC V8W 2Y2, Canada. Offers aboriginal communities counseling (M Ed); counseling (M Ed, MA); educational psychology (M Ed, MA, PhD), including counseling psychology (M Ed, MA), leadership studies (PhD), learning and development (MA, PhD), measurement and evaluation, special education (M Ed, MA); leadership studies (M Ed, MA). Part-time programs available. *Degree requirements:* For master's, thesis (for some programs), comprehensive exam (M Ed); for doctorate, comprehensive exam, thesis/dissertation, candidacy exam. *Entrance requirements:* For master's, 2 years of work experience in a relevant field; for doctorate, GRE, 2 years of work experience in a relevant field, minimum B average. Additional exam requirements/recommendations for international students: Required—TOEFL (minimum score 575 paper-based), IELTS (minimum score 7). *Faculty research:* Learning and development (child, adolescent and adult), special education and exceptional children.

University of Victoria, Faculty of Graduate Studies, Faculty of Social Sciences, Department of Psychology, Victoria, BC V8W 2Y2, Canada. Offers clinical psychology (PhD); clinical psychology (neuropsychology) (M Sc); cognition and brain science (M Sc, PhD); experimental neuropsychology (M Sc, PhD); individualized study (M Sc, PhD); life span development psychology (PhD); life span developmental psychology (M Sc); social psychology (M Sc, PhD). *Accreditation:* APA (one or more programs are accredited). *Degree requirements:* For master's, thesis; for doctorate, thesis/dissertation, candidacy exam. *Entrance requirements:* For master's and doctorate, GRE General Test. Additional exam requirements/recommendations for international students: Required—TOEFL (minimum score 600 paper-based). Electronic applications accepted. *Faculty research:* Life span development psychology and aging, behavioral neuroscience, cognitive psychology, behavioral psychology, environmental psychology.

University of Washington, Graduate School, College of Arts and Sciences, Department of Psychology, Seattle, WA 98195. Offers animal behavior (PhD); child psychology (PhD); clinical psychology (PhD); cognition and perception (PhD); developmental psychology (PhD); quantitative psychology (PhD); social psychology and personality (PhD). *Accreditation:* APA. *Degree requirements:* For doctorate, thesis/dissertation. *Entrance requirements:* For doctorate, GRE General Test, minimum GPA of 3.0. Electronic applications accepted. *Faculty research:* Addictive behaviors, artificial intelligence, child psychopathology, mechanisms and development of vision, physiology of ingestive behaviors.

University of Windsor, Faculty of Graduate Studies, Faculty of Arts and Social Sciences, Department of Psychology, Windsor, ON N9B 3P4, Canada. Offers adult clinical (MA, PhD); applied social psychology (MA, PhD); child clinical (MA, PhD); clinical neuropsychology (MA, PhD). *Accreditation:* APA (one or more programs are accredited). *Degree requirements:* For master's, thesis; for doctorate, comprehensive exam, thesis/dissertation. *Entrance requirements:* For master's, GRE General Test, GRE Subject Test in psychology, minimum B average; for doctorate, GRE General Test, GRE Subject Test in psychology, master's degree. Additional exam requirements/recommendations for international students: Required—TOEFL (minimum score 600 paper-based). Electronic applications accepted. *Faculty research:* Gambling, suicidology, emotional competence, psychotherapy and trauma.

University of Wisconsin–Madison, Graduate School, College of Letters and Science, Department of Psychology, Program in Social and Personality Psychology, Madison, WI 53706-1380. Offers PhD. *Degree requirements:* For doctorate, comprehensive exam, thesis/dissertation. *Entrance requirements:* For doctorate, GRE General Test, minimum undergraduate GPA of 3.0. Additional exam requirements/recommendations for international students: Required—TOEFL. Electronic applications accepted. *Expenses:* Tuition, state resident: full-time $10,723; part-time $745 per credit. Tuition, nonresident: full-time $24,054; part-time $1578 per credit. *Required fees:* $374 per semester. Tuition and fees vary according to course load, program and reciprocity agreements.

University of Wisconsin–Milwaukee, Graduate School, School of Education, Department of Educational Psychology, Milwaukee, WI 53201-0413. Offers counseling psychology (PhD); educational statistics and measurement (MS, PhD); learning and development (MS, PhD); school and community counseling (MS); school psychology (PhD). *Accreditation:* APA. Part-time programs available. *Degree requirements:* For master's, comprehensive exam, thesis; for doctorate, thesis/dissertation. *Entrance requirements:* For master's, minimum GPA of 3.0; for doctorate, GRE General Test, minimum GPA of 3.0. Additional exam requirements/recommendations for international students: Required—TOEFL (minimum score 550 paper-based; 79 iBT), IELTS (minimum score 6.5). Electronic applications accepted.

University of Wisconsin–Superior, Graduate Division, Department of Counseling and Psychological Professions, Superior, WI 54880-4500. Offers community counseling (MSE); human relations (MSE); school counseling (MSE). Part-time and evening/weekend programs available. *Degree requirements:* For master's, position paper, practicum. *Entrance requirements:* For master's, GRE and/or MAT, minimum GPA of 2.75. Electronic applications accepted. *Faculty research:* Women and power, intrafamily dynamics.

University of Wisconsin–Whitewater, School of Graduate Studies, College of Education and Professional Studies, Department of Counselor Education, Whitewater, WI 53190-1790. Offers community counseling (MS Ed); higher education (MS Ed); school counseling (MS Ed). *Accreditation:* ACA; NCATE. Part-time and evening/weekend programs available. *Degree requirements:* For master's, thesis or alternative. *Entrance requirements:* For master's, resume, 2 letters of reference, goal statement, autobiography. Additional exam requirements/recommendations for international

students: Required—TOEFL (minimum score 550 paper-based; 80 iBT), IELTS (minimum score 6). Electronic applications accepted. *Faculty research:* Alcohol and other drugs, counseling effectiveness, teacher mentoring.

Virginia Commonwealth University, Graduate School, College of Humanities and Sciences, Department of Psychology, Program in General Psychology, Richmond, VA 23284-9005. Offers biopsychology (PhD); developmental psychology (PhD); social psychology (PhD). *Degree requirements:* For doctorate, thesis/dissertation. *Entrance requirements:* For doctorate, GRE General Test. Additional exam requirements/recommendations for international students: Required—TOEFL (minimum score 600 paper-based; 100 iBT); Recommended—IELTS (minimum score 6.5). Electronic applications accepted. *Faculty research:* Biopsychology, developmental and social psychology.

Walden University, Graduate Programs, School of Psychology, Minneapolis, MN 55401. Offers clinical psychology (MS), including counseling, general program; forensic psychology (MS), including forensic psychology in the community, general program, mental health applications, program planning and evaluation in forensic settings, psychology and legal systems; organizational psychology and development (Postbaccalaureate Certificate); psychology (MS, PhD), including applied psychology (MS), clinical psychology (PhD), counseling psychology (PhD), crisis management and response (MS), educational psychology, forensic psychology (PhD), general psychology (MS), general psychology research (PhD), health psychology, leadership development and coaching (MS), psychology of culture (MS), psychology, public administration, and social change (MS), social psychology, terrorism and security (MS); psychology respecialization (Post-Doctoral Certificate); teaching online (Post-Master's Certificate). Part-time and evening/weekend programs available. Postbaccalaureate distance learning degree programs offered (no on-campus study). *Faculty:* 56 full-time (36 women), 351 part-time/adjunct (201 women). *Students:* 2,757 full-time (2,202 women), 1,466 part-time (1,148 women); includes 1,849 minority (1,299 Black or African American, non-Hispanic/Latino; 37 American Indian or Alaska Native, non-Hispanic/Latino; 74 Asian, non-Hispanic/Latino; 315 Hispanic/Latino; 8 Native Hawaiian or other Pacific Islander, non-Hispanic/Latino; 116 Two or more races, non-Hispanic/Latino), 28 international. Average age 41. 913 applicants, 97% accepted, 851 enrolled. In 2014, 602 master's, 204 doctorates, 19 other advanced degrees awarded. Terminal master's awarded for partial completion of doctoral program. *Degree requirements:* For master's, thesis optional; for doctorate, thesis/dissertation, residency. *Entrance requirements:* For master's, bachelor's degree or higher; minimum GPA of 2.5; official transcripts; goal statement (for some programs); access to computer and Internet; for doctorate, master's degree or higher; three years of related professional or academic experience (preferred); minimum GPA of 3.0; goal statement and current resume (for select programs); official transcripts; access to computer and Internet; for other advanced degree, relevant work experience; access to computer and Internet. Additional exam requirements/recommendations for international students: Required—TOEFL (minimum score 550 paper-based, 79 iBT), IELTS (minimum score 6.5), Michigan English Language Assessment Battery (minimum score 82), or PTE (minimum score 53). *Application deadline:* Applications are processed on a rolling basis. Application fee: $0. Electronic applications accepted. *Expenses: Tuition:* Full-time $11,925; part-time $500 per credit hour. *Required fees:* $647. *Financial support:* Fellowships, Federal Work-Study, scholarships/grants, unspecified assistantships, and family tuition reduction, active duty/veteran tuition reduction, group tuition reduction, interest-free payment plans, employee tuition reduction available. Support available to part-time students. Financial award applicants required to submit FAFSA. *Unit head:* Dr. Marilyn Powell, Associate Dean, 866-492-5366. *Application contact:* Meghan Thomas, Vice President of Enrollment Management, 866-492-5336, E-mail: info@waldenu.edu.
Website: http://www.waldenu.edu/programs/colleges-schools/psychology

Washington University in St. Louis, Graduate School of Arts and Sciences, Department of Psychology, St. Louis, MO 63130-4899. Offers aging and development (PhD); behavior, brain, and cognition (PhD); clinical psychology (PhD); social and personality psychology (PhD). *Accreditation:* APA. Terminal master's awarded for partial completion of doctoral program. *Degree requirements:* For doctorate, thesis/dissertation. *Entrance requirements:* For doctorate, GRE General Test. Additional exam requirements/recommendations for international students: Required—TOEFL. Electronic applications accepted.

Wayne State University, College of Liberal Arts and Sciences, Department of Psychology, Detroit, MI 48202. Offers behavioral and cognitive neuroscience (PhD); clinical psychology (PhD); cognitive, developmental and social psychology (PhD); industrial and organizational psychology (MA); social psychology (PhD). Doctoral programs admit for fall only. *Accreditation:* APA (one or more programs are accredited). *Faculty:* 37 full-time (13 women), 8 part-time/adjunct (4 women). *Students:* 107 full-time (74 women), 28 part-time (16 women); includes 19 minority (8 Black or African American, non-Hispanic/Latino; 2 Asian, non-Hispanic/Latino; 5 Hispanic/Latino; 4 Two or more races, non-Hispanic/Latino), 10 international. Average age 28. 397 applicants, 11% accepted, 25 enrolled. In 2014, 24 master's, 18 doctorates awarded. Terminal master's awarded for partial completion of doctoral program. *Degree requirements:* For master's, thesis (for some programs); for doctorate, thesis/dissertation, training assignments. *Entrance requirements:* For master's, GRE General Test, minimum undergraduate upper-division cumulative GPA of 3.0, courses in introductory psychology and statistics, two letters of recommendation, professional statement; for doctorate, GRE General Test, bachelor's, master's, or other advanced degree; at least three letters of recommendation; statement of purpose. Additional exam requirements/recommendations for international students: Required—TOEFL (minimum score 550 paper-based; 79 iBT), TWE (minimum score 5.5), Michigan English Language Assessment Battery (minimum score 85); Recommended—IELTS (minimum score 6.5). *Application deadline:* For fall admission, 12/1 for domestic and international students; for winter admission, 10/15 for domestic students, 9/1 for international students; for spring admission, 3/15 for domestic students, 1/1 for international students. Application fee: $0. Electronic applications accepted. *Expenses:* Tuition, state resident: full-time $10,294; part-time $571.90 per credit hour. Tuition, nonresident: full-time $29,730; part-time $1238.75 per credit hour. *Required fees:* $1365; $43.50 per credit hour. $291.10 per semester. Tuition and fees vary according to course load and program. *Financial support:* In 2014–15, 91 students received support, including 8 fellowships with tuition reimbursements available (averaging $15,983 per year), 12 research assistantships with tuition reimbursements available (averaging $17,862 per year), 49 teaching assistantships with tuition reimbursements available (averaging $16,838 per year); scholarships/grants, health care benefits, and unspecified assistantships also available. Financial award application deadline: 3/31; financial award applicants required to submit FAFSA. *Faculty research:* Neuroscience, including functional cognitive imaging, neural physiology, behavioral pharmacology, and neurobehavioral teratology; cognitive and neurochemical processes associated with aging, drug addiction and neurological disorders to studies of the neural circuits that underlie learning, emotion, and weight regulation; the life-long developmental plasticity of the neurobiological processes of behavior; neuropsychology; child clinical psychology; health psychology; community psychology. *Total annual research expenditures:* $2.1 million. *Unit head:* Boris Baltes, PhD, Chair/Professor, 313-577-2800, Fax: 313-577-7636, E-mail: b.baltes@wayne.edu. *Application contact:* Alia Allen, Academic Services Officer, 313-577-2823, E-mail: aallen@wayne.edu.
Website: http://clas.wayne.edu/psychology/

Western Carolina University, Graduate School, College of Education and Allied Professions, Department of Human Services, Cullowhee, NC 28723. Offers counseling (M Ed, MA Ed, MS), including community counseling (M Ed, MS), school counseling (MA Ed); human resources (MS). *Accreditation:* ACA (one or more programs are accredited). Part-time and evening/weekend programs available. Postbaccalaureate distance learning degree programs offered. *Degree requirements:* For master's, comprehensive exam, thesis or alternative. *Entrance requirements:* For master's, GRE General Test, appropriate undergraduate degree with minimum GPA of 3.0, 3 recommendations, writing sample, resume. Additional exam requirements/recommendations for international students: Required—TOEFL (minimum score 550 paper-based; 79 iBT). *Faculty research:* Marital and family development, spirituality in counseling, home school law, sexuality education, employee recruitment/retention.

Western Connecticut State University, Division of Graduate Studies, School of Professional Studies, Department of Education and Educational Psychology, Program in Community Counseling, Danbury, CT 06810-6885. Offers MS. *Accreditation:* ACA. Part-time programs available. *Degree requirements:* For master's, practicum, internship, completion of program in 6 years. *Entrance requirements:* For master's, minimum GPA of 2.8, 3 letters of reference, interview, 9 hours of psychology. Additional exam requirements/recommendations for international students: Recommended—TOEFL (minimum score 550 paper-based; 79 iBT), IELTS (minimum score 6). *Faculty research:* Community counseling.

Western Illinois University, School of Graduate Studies, College of Arts and Sciences, Department of Psychology, Macomb, IL 61455-1390. Offers clinical/community mental health (MS); general psychology (MS); psychology (MS, SSP); school psychology (SSP). Part-time programs available. *Students:* 28 full-time (19 women), 10 part-time (5 women); includes 1 minority (Hispanic/Latino), 5 international. Average age 26. 69 applicants, 46% accepted, 12 enrolled. In 2014, 18 master's, 6 other advanced degrees awarded. *Degree requirements:* For master's, comprehensive exam (for some programs), thesis or alternative. *Entrance requirements:* For master's and SSP, GRE General Test. Additional exam requirements/recommendations for international students: Required—TOEFL (minimum score 550 paper-based; 80 iBT). *Application deadline:* Applications are processed on a rolling basis. Application fee: $30. Electronic applications accepted. *Financial support:* In 2014–15, 41 students received support, including 14 research assistantships with full tuition reimbursements available (averaging $7,544 per year), 34 teaching assistantships with full tuition reimbursements available (averaging $8,688 per year). Financial award applicants required to submit FAFSA. *Unit head:* Dr. Karen Sears, Interim Chairperson, 309-298-1593. *Application contact:* Dr. Nancy Parsons, Associate Provost and Director of Graduate Studies, 309-298-1806, Fax: 309-298-2345, E-mail: grad-office@wiu.edu.
Website: http://wiu.edu/psychology

Wichita State University, Graduate School, Fairmount College of Liberal Arts and Sciences, Department of Psychology, Wichita, KS 67260. Offers clinical (PhD); community (PhD); human factors (PhD). *Accreditation:* APA. Part-time programs available. *Unit head:* Dr. Alex Chaparro, Chair, 316-978-3170, Fax: 316-978-3006, E-mail: alex.chaparro@wichita.edu. *Application contact:* Jordan Oleson, Admissions Coordinator, 316-978-3095, Fax: 316-978-3253, E-mail: jordan.oleson@wichita.edu.
Website: http://www.wichita.edu/psychology

Wilfrid Laurier University, Faculty of Graduate and Postdoctoral Studies, Faculty of Science, Department of Psychology, Waterloo, ON N2L 3C5, Canada. Offers behavioral neuroscience (M Sc, PhD); cognitive neuroscience (M Sc, PhD); community psychology (MA, PhD); social and developmental psychology (MA, PhD). Part-time programs available. *Degree requirements:* For master's, thesis; for doctorate, thesis/dissertation. *Entrance requirements:* For master's, GRE General Test, honors BA or the equivalent in psychology, minimum B average in undergraduate course work; for doctorate, GRE General Test, master's degree, minimum A- average. Additional exam requirements/recommendations for international students: Required—TOEFL (minimum score 89 iBT). Electronic applications accepted. *Faculty research:* Brain and cognition, community psychology, social and developmental psychology.

Yale University, Graduate School of Arts and Sciences, Department of Psychology, New Haven, CT 06520. Offers behavioral neuroscience (PhD); clinical psychology (PhD); cognitive psychology (PhD); developmental psychology (PhD); social/personality psychology (PhD). *Accreditation:* APA. *Degree requirements:* For doctorate, thesis/dissertation. *Entrance requirements:* For doctorate, GRE General Test.

Sport Psychology

★ **Adler University,** Programs in Psychology, Chicago, IL 60602. Offers advanced Adlerian psychotherapy (Certificate); art therapy (MA); clinical neuropsychology (Certificate); clinical psychology (Psy D); community psychology (MA); counseling and organizational psychology (MA); counseling psychology (MA); criminology (MA); emergency management leadership (MA); forensic psychology (MA); marriage and family counseling (MA); marriage and family therapy (Certificate); military psychology (MA); nonprofit management (MA); organizational psychology (MA); police psychology (MA); public policy and administration (MA); rehabilitation counseling (MA); sport and health psychology (MA); substance abuse counseling (Certificate); Psy D/Certificate; Psy D/MACAT; Psy D/MACP; Psy D/MAMFC; Psy D/MASAC. *Accreditation:* APA. Part-time and evening/weekend programs available. Postbaccalaureate distance learning degree programs offered (minimal on-campus study). Terminal master's awarded for partial completion of doctoral program. *Degree requirements:* For master's, thesis or alternative, oral exam, practicum; for doctorate, thesis/dissertation, clinical exam, internship, oral exam, practicum, written qualifying exam. *Entrance requirements:* For master's, 12 semester hours in

psychology, minimum GPA of 3.0; for doctorate, 18 semester hours in psychology, minimum GPA of 3.25; for Certificate, appropriate master's or doctoral degree. Additional exam requirements/recommendations for international students: Required—TOEFL (minimum score 550 paper-based; 79 iBT). Electronic applications accepted.
See Display on page 969 and Close-Up on page 1207.

Argosy University, Atlanta, College of Psychology and Behavioral Sciences, Atlanta, GA 30328. Offers clinical psychology (MA, Psy D, Postdoctoral Respecialization Certificate), including child and family psychology (Psy D), general adult clinical (Psy D), health psychology (Psy D), neuropsychology/geropsychology (Psy D); community counseling (MA), including marriage and family therapy; counselor education and supervision (Ed D); forensic psychology (MA); industrial organizational psychology (MA); marriage and family therapy (Certificate); sport-exercise psychology (MA). *Accreditation:* APA.

Argosy University, Inland Empire, College of Psychology and Behavioral Sciences, Ontario, CA 91761. Offers clinical psychology/marriage and family therapy (MA); counseling psychology (Ed D); counseling psychology/marriage and family therapy (MA); forensic psychology (MA); industrial organizational psychology (MA); sport-exercise psychology (MA).

Argosy University, Orange County, College of Psychology and Behavioral Sciences, Program in Sport-Exercise Psychology, Orange, CA 92868. Offers MA.

Argosy University, Phoenix, College of Psychology and Behavioral Sciences, Program in Clinical Psychology, Phoenix, AZ 85021. Offers clinical psychology (MA); neuropsychology (Psy D); sports-exercise psychology (Psy D). *Accreditation:* APA (one or more programs are accredited).

Argosy University, Phoenix, College of Psychology and Behavioral Sciences, Program in Sport–Exercise Psychology, Phoenix, AZ 85021. Offers MA.

Argosy University, San Francisco Bay Area, College of Psychology and Behavioral Sciences, Alameda, CA 94501. Offers clinical psychology (MA, Psy D); counseling psychology (MA, Ed D); forensic psychology (MA); sport-exercise psychology (MA). *Accreditation:* APA (one or more programs are accredited).

Argosy University, Schaumburg, College of Behavioral Sciences, Schaumburg, IL 60173-5403. Offers clinical mental health counseling (MA); forensic psychology (MA, Post-Graduate Certificate); industrial organizational psychology (MA); sport-exercise psychology (MA). *Accreditation:* ACA; APA.

Barry University, School of Human Performance and Leisure Sciences, Programs in Movement Science, Specialization in Sport and Exercise Psychology, Miami Shores, FL 33161-6695. Offers MS. *Entrance requirements:* For master's, GRE.

California State University, Fresno, Division of Graduate Studies, College of Health and Human Services, Department of Kinesiology, Fresno, CA 93740-8027. Offers exercise science (MA); sport psychology (MA). Part-time and evening/weekend programs available. *Degree requirements:* For master's, thesis or alternative. *Entrance requirements:* For master's, GRE General Test, minimum GPA of 2.7. Additional exam requirements/recommendations for international students: Required—TOEFL. Electronic applications accepted. *Faculty research:* Refugee education, homeless, geriatrics, fitness.

California State University, Long Beach, Graduate Studies, College of Health and Human Services, Department of Kinesiology, Long Beach, CA 90840. Offers adapted physical education (MA); coaching and student athlete development (MA); exercise physiology and nutrition (MS); exercise science (MS); individualized studies (MA); kinesiology (MA); pedagogical studies (MA); sport and exercise psychology (MS); sport management (MA); sports medicine and injury studies (MS). Part-time programs available. *Degree requirements:* For master's, oral and written comprehensive exams or thesis. *Entrance requirements:* For master's, GRE General Test, minimum GPA of 2.75 during previous 2 years of course work. Electronic applications accepted. *Faculty research:* Pulmonary functioning, feedback and practice structure, strength training, history and politics of sports, special population research issues.

California University of Pennsylvania, School of Graduate Studies and Research, College of Education and Human Services, Program in Exercise Science and Health Promotion, California, PA 15419-1394. Offers performance enhancement and injury prevention (MS); rehabilitation science (MS); sport psychology (MS); wellness and fitness (MS). Part-time and evening/weekend programs available. Postbaccalaureate distance learning degree programs offered (no on-campus study). *Degree requirements:* For master's, comprehensive exam, thesis optional. *Entrance requirements:* For master's, minimum QPA of 3.0. Additional exam requirements/recommendations for international students: Required—TOEFL (minimum score 550 paper-based; 80 iBT). Electronic applications accepted. *Expenses:* Contact institution. *Faculty research:* Reducing obesity in children, sport performance, creating unique biomechanical assessment techniques, Web-based training for fitness professionals, Webcams.

Capella University, Harold Abel School of Social and Behavioral Science, Master's Programs in Psychology, Minneapolis, MN 55402. Offers applied behavior analysis (MS); clinical psychology (MS); counseling psychology (MS); educational psychology (MS); evaluation, research, and measurement (MS); general advanced studies in human behavior (MS); general psychology (MS); industrial/organizational psychology (MS); leadership coaching psychology (MS); school psychology (MS); sport psychology (MS).

Chatham University, Program in Counseling Psychology, Pittsburgh, PA 15232-2826. Offers child, adolescent and family (MSCP); counseling psychology (Psy D); health and holistic (MSCP); infant mental health (MSCP); organization and supervision (MSCP); sport and exercise (MSCP). Part-time and evening/weekend programs available. *Faculty:* 12 full-time (9 women), 13 part-time/adjunct (9 women). *Students:* 102 full-time (85 women), 38 part-time (32 women); includes 17 minority (7 Black or African American, non-Hispanic/Latino; 2 Asian, non-Hispanic/Latino; 6 Hispanic/Latino; 2 Two or more races, non-Hispanic/Latino; 7 international. Average age 29. 145 applicants, 73% accepted, 59 enrolled. In 2014, 67 master's, 3 doctorates awarded. *Degree requirements:* For master's, thesis optional, supervised internship; for doctorate, thesis/dissertation, internship. *Entrance requirements:* For master's, minimum GPA of 3.0; 2 letters of recommendation; resume; prerequisite coursework in statistics, biology, and psychology; for doctorate, GRE. Additional exam requirements/recommendations for international students: Required—TOEFL (minimum score 600 paper-based; 100 iBT), IELTS (minimum score 7), TWE. *Application deadline:* For fall admission, 4/1 priority date for domestic and international students; for spring admission, 11/1 for domestic students, 10/1 for international students. Applications are processed on a rolling basis. Application fee: $45. Electronic applications accepted. Application fee is waived when completed online. *Expenses: Tuition:* Full-time $15,318; part-time $851 per credit hour. *Required fees:* $440; $24 per credit hour. Tuition and fees vary according to course load, program and reciprocity agreements. *Financial support:* Career-related internships or fieldwork available. Financial award applicants required to submit FAFSA. *Faculty research:* Trauma and recovery, hypnosis, psychospiritual dimensions of healing, psychotherapy of schizophrenia. *Unit head:* Dr. Mary Beth Mannarino, Director, 412-365-1196, Fax: 412-365-1505, E-mail: mmannarino@chatham.edu. *Application contact:*

Katie Noel, Assistant Director of Graduate Admission, 412-365-2758, Fax: 412-365-1609, E-mail: gradadmissions@chatham.edu.
Website: http://www.chatham.edu/mscp

Cleveland State University, College of Graduate Studies, College of Education and Human Services, Department of Health and Human Performance, Cleveland, OH 44115. Offers community health education (M Ed); exercise science (M Ed); human performance (M Ed); physical education pedagogy (M Ed); public health (MPH); school health education (M Ed); sport and exercise psychology (M Ed); sports management (M Ed). Part-time programs available. *Faculty:* 7 full-time (4 women), 3 part-time/adjunct (2 women). *Students:* 41 full-time (27 women), 71 part-time (45 women); includes 29 minority (24 Black or African American, non-Hispanic/Latino; 1 Asian, non-Hispanic/Latino; 3 Hispanic/Latino; 1 Two or more races, non-Hispanic/Latino), 10 international. Average age 27. 103 applicants, 72% accepted, 43 enrolled. In 2014, 47 master's awarded. *Degree requirements:* For master's, comprehensive exam, thesis optional. *Entrance requirements:* For master's, GRE General Test or MAT (if undergraduate GPA less than 2.75), minimum undergraduate GPA of 2.75. Additional exam requirements/recommendations for international students: Required—TOEFL (minimum score 525 paper-based), IELTS (minimum score 6). *Application deadline:* For fall admission, 7/15 priority date for domestic students; for spring admission, 12/15 priority date for domestic students. Applications are processed on a rolling basis. Application fee: $30. Electronic applications accepted. *Expenses:* Tuition, state resident: full-time $9566; part-time $531 per credit hour. Tuition, nonresident: full-time $17,980; part-time $999 per credit hour. *Required fees:* $25 per semester. Tuition and fees vary according to degree level and program. *Financial support:* In 2014–15, 6 research assistantships with full and partial tuition reimbursements (averaging $3,480 per year), 1 teaching assistantship with full and partial tuition reimbursement (averaging $3,480 per year) were awarded; career-related internships or fieldwork, tuition waivers (full), and unspecified assistantships also available. Financial award application deadline: 3/15. *Faculty research:* Bone density, marketing fitness centers, motor development of disabled, online learning and survey research. *Unit head:* Dr. Sheila M. Patterson, Chairperson, 216-687-4870, Fax: 216-687-5410, E-mail: s.m.patterson@csuohio.edu. *Application contact:* Deborah L. Brown, Interim Assistant Director, Graduate Admissions, 216-523-7572, Fax: 216-687-5400, E-mail: d.l.brown@csuohio.edu.
Website: http://www.csuohio.edu/cehs/departments/HPERD/hperd_dept.html

Florida State University, The Graduate School, College of Education, Department of Educational Psychology and Learning Systems, Program in Educational Psychology, Tallahassee, FL 32306. Offers learning and cognition (MS, PhD, Ed S); measurement and statistics (MS, PhD, Ed S); sport psychology (MS, PhD). *Faculty:* 10 full-time (7 women). *Students:* 97 full-time (48 women), 28 part-time (20 women); includes 28 minority (12 Black or African American, non-Hispanic/Latino; 1 American Indian or Alaska Native, non-Hispanic/Latino; 3 Asian, non-Hispanic/Latino; 11 Hispanic/Latino; 1 Two or more races, non-Hispanic/Latino), 52 international. Average age 34. 174 applicants, 66% accepted, 41 enrolled. In 2014, 20 master's, 7 doctorates awarded. Terminal master's awarded for partial completion of doctoral program. *Degree requirements:* For master's, comprehensive exam, thesis optional; for doctorate, comprehensive exam, thesis/dissertation. *Entrance requirements:* For master's and doctorate, GRE General Test, minimum GPA of 3.0. Additional exam requirements/recommendations for international students: Required—PTE (minimum score 55), TOEFL (minimum score 550 paper-based, 80 iBT), IELTS (minimum score 6.5) or Michigan English Language Assessment Battery (minimum score 77). *Application deadline:* For fall admission, 7/1 for domestic and international students; for winter admission, 11/1 for domestic and international students; for spring admission, 11/1 for domestic and international students; for summer admission, 3/1 for domestic and international students. Applications are processed on a rolling basis. Application fee: $30. Electronic applications accepted. *Expenses:* Expenses: Contact institution. *Financial support:* Fellowships with full and partial tuition reimbursements, research assistantships with full and partial tuition reimbursements, teaching assistantships with full and partial tuition reimbursements, scholarships/grants, tuition waivers (full and partial), and unspecified assistantships available. Financial award application deadline: 1/15; financial award applicants required to submit FAFSA. *Faculty research:* Meta analysis; item response theory (IRT)/mixture IRT; cognitive behavioral therapy (CBT); modeling, especially large data sets; learning and cognition, skill acquisition, self-perception, processes of motivation. *Unit head:* Dr. Betsy Becker, Chair, 850-644-2371, Fax: 850-644-8776, E-mail: bbecker@fsu.edu. *Application contact:* Peggy Lollie, Program Assistant, 850-644-8786, Fax: 850-644-8776, E-mail: plollie@fsu.edu.
Website: http://coe.fsu.edu/Academic-Programs/Departments/Educational-Psychology-and-Learning-Systems-EPLS/Degree-Programs/Educational-Psychology

John F. Kennedy University, Graduate School of Professional Psychology, Program in Sport Psychology, Pleasant Hill, CA 94523-4817. Offers MA. Part-time and evening/weekend programs available. *Degree requirements:* For master's, thesis or alternative. *Entrance requirements:* For master's, interview. Additional exam requirements/recommendations for international students: Required—TOEFL.

Lock Haven University of Pennsylvania, College of Business, Information Systems and Human Services, Lock Haven, PA 17745-2390. Offers clinical mental health counseling (MS); sport science (MS). Postbaccalaureate distance learning degree programs offered (no on-campus study). *Degree requirements:* For master's, thesis. *Entrance requirements:* For master's, minimum undergraduate GPA of 3.0. Additional exam requirements/recommendations for international students: Required—TOEFL. Electronic applications accepted.

Memorial University of Newfoundland, School of Graduate Studies, School of Human Kinetics and Recreation, St. John's, NL A1C 5S7, Canada. Offers administration, curriculum and supervision (MPE); biomechanics/ergonomics (MS Kin); exercise and work physiology (MS Kin); sport psychology (MS Kin). Part-time programs available. *Degree requirements:* For master's, thesis optional, seminars, thesis presentations. *Entrance requirements:* For master's, bachelor's degree in a related field, minimum B average. Electronic applications accepted. *Faculty research:* Administration, sociology of sports, kinesiology, physiology/recreation.

National University, Academic Affairs, College of Letters and Sciences, La Jolla, CA 92037-1011. Offers applied linguistics (MA); biology (MS); counseling psychology (MA), including licensed professional clinical counseling, marriage and family therapy; creative writing (MFA); English (MA), including Gothic studies, rhetoric; film studies (MA); forensic and crime science (Certificate); forensic studies (MFS), including criminalistics, investigation; history (MA); human behavior (MA); mathematics for educators (MS); performance psychology (MA); strategic communications (MA). Part-time and evening/weekend programs available. Postbaccalaureate distance learning degree programs offered (no on-campus study). *Faculty:* 69 full-time (34 women), 100 part-time/adjunct (55 women). *Students:* 727 full-time (532 women), 349 part-time (240 women); includes 505 minority (128 Black or African American, non-Hispanic/Latino; 5 American Indian or Alaska Native, non-Hispanic/Latino; 52 Asian, non-Hispanic/Latino; 260 Hispanic/Latino; 9 Native Hawaiian or other Pacific Islander, non-Hispanic/Latino; 51 Two or more races, non-Hispanic/Latino), 4 international. Average age 34. In 2014, 569 master's awarded. *Degree requirements:* For master's, thesis (for some programs). *Entrance requirements:* For master's, interview, minimum GPA of 2.5. Additional exam requirements/

recommendations for international students: Required—TOEFL (minimum score 550 paper-based; 79 iBT), IELTS (minimum score 6). *Application deadline:* Applications are processed on a rolling basis. Application fee: $60 ($65 for international students). Electronic applications accepted. *Expenses:* Tuition: Full-time $14,184; part-time $1773 per course. *Financial support:* Career-related internships or fieldwork, institutionally sponsored loans, scholarships/grants, and tuition waivers (partial) available. Support available to part-time students. Financial award application deadline: 6/30; financial award applicants required to submit FAFSA. *Unit head:* College of Letters and Sciences, 800-628-8648, E-mail: cols@nu.edu. *Application contact:* Frank Rojas, Interim Vice President for Enrollment Services, 800-628-8648, E-mail: advisor@nu.edu. Website: http://www.nu.edu/OurPrograms/CollegeOfLettersAndSciences.html

Oregon State University, College of Public Health and Human Sciences, Program in Exercise and Sport Science, Corvallis, OR 97331. Offers exercise physiology (PhD); movement studies in disability (MS, PhD); neuromechanics (PhD); physical activity and public health (PhD); sport and exercise psychology (PhD). Part-time programs available. *Faculty:* 12 full-time (6 women), 1 (woman) part-time/adjunct. *Students:* 40 full-time (21 women), 5 part-time (2 women); includes 6 minority (1 Black or African American, non-Hispanic/Latino; 3 Asian, non-Hispanic/Latino; 1 Hispanic/Latino; 1 Two or more races, non-Hispanic/Latino), 4 international. Average age 29. 68 applicants, 25% accepted, 14 enrolled. In 2014, 18 master's, 4 doctorates awarded. Terminal master's awarded for partial completion of doctoral program. *Degree requirements:* For master's, thesis; for doctorate, thesis/dissertation. *Entrance requirements:* For master's and doctorate, GRE, minimum GPA of 3.0 in last 90 hours. Additional exam requirements/recommendations for international students: Required—TOEFL (minimum score 80 iBT), IELTS (minimum score 6.5). *Application deadline:* For fall admission, 2/15 for domestic students. Application fee: $60. *Expenses:* Tuition, state resident: full-time $11,907; part-time $189 per credit hour. Tuition, nonresident: full-time $19,953; part-time $441 per credit hour. *Required fees:* $1472; $449 per term. One-time fee: $350. Tuition and fees vary according to course load and program. *Financial support:* Research assistantships, teaching assistantships, career-related internships or fieldwork, Federal Work-Study, and institutionally sponsored loans available. Support available to part-time students. Financial award application deadline: 12/1. *Faculty research:* Motor control, sports medicine, exercise physiology, sport psychology, biomechanics. *Unit head:* Dr. Vicki Ebbeck, Associate Professor, 541-737-6800. *Application contact:* Debi Rothermund, Exercise and Sports Science Advisor, 541-737-3324, E-mail: debi.rothermund@oregonstate.edu. Website: http://health.oregonstate.edu/degrees/graduate/exercise-sport-science

Purdue University, Graduate School, College of Health and Human Sciences, Department of Health and Kinesiology, West Lafayette, IN 47907. Offers athletic training education administration (MS, PhD); biomechanics (MS, PhD); exercise physiology (MS, PhD); health education (MS, PhD); history/philosophy of sport (MS, PhD); motor control and development (MS, PhD); physical education pedagogy (PhD); physical education teacher education (MS); recreation and sport management (MS, PhD); sport and exercise psychology (MS, PhD). Part-time programs available. *Degree requirements:* For master's, thesis optional; for doctorate, comprehensive exam, thesis/dissertation, qualifying examination, preliminary examination. *Entrance requirements:* For master's, GRE General Test (minimum score 1000 combined verbal and quantitative), minimum undergraduate GPA of 3.0 or equivalent; for doctorate, GRE General Test (minimum score 1100 combined verbal and quantitative), minimum undergraduate GPA of 3.0 or equivalent; master's degree with minimum GPA of 3.25 (recommended). Additional exam requirements/recommendations for international students: Required—TOEFL (minimum score 77 iBT); Recommended—TWE. Electronic applications accepted. *Faculty research:* Wellness, motivation, teaching effectiveness, learning and development.

Queen's University at Kingston, School of Graduate Studies, School of Kinesiology and Health Studies, Kingston, ON K7L 3N6, Canada. Offers applied exercise science (PhD); biomechanics/ergonomics (M Sc); exercise physiology (M Sc); social psychology of sport and exercise rehabilitation (MA); sociology of sport (MA). Part-time programs available. *Degree requirements:* For master's, thesis (for some programs); for doctorate, comprehensive exam, thesis/dissertation. *Entrance requirements:* For master's and doctorate, minimum B+ average. Additional exam requirements/recommendations for international students: Required—TOEFL. Electronic applications accepted. *Faculty research:* Expert performance ergonomics, obesity research, pregnancy and exercise, gender and sport participation.

Seton Hall University, College of Education and Human Services, Department of Professional Psychology and Family Therapy, Program in Psychological Studies, South Orange, NJ 07079-2697. Offers individualized (MA); marriage and family therapy (MA); sports and exercise psychology (MA). Part-time and evening/weekend programs available. *Degree requirements:* For master's, comprehensive exam. *Entrance requirements:* For master's, GRE or MAT. *Faculty research:* Cognitive style, self-esteem anxiety in preadolescence, object relation, bonding.

Southern Connecticut State University, School of Graduate Studies, School of Education, Department of Exercise Science, New Haven, CT 06515-1355. Offers human performance (MS); physical education (MS); school health education (MS); sport psychology (MS). Part-time and evening/weekend programs available. *Degree requirements:* For master's, thesis or alternative. *Entrance requirements:* For master's, interview. Electronic applications accepted.

Southern Illinois University Edwardsville, Graduate School, School of Education, Health, and Human Behavior, Department of Kinesiology and Health Education, Program in Exercise and Sport Psychology, Edwardsville, IL 62026. Offers MS. Part-time and evening/weekend programs available. *Students:* 14 full-time (4 women), 17 part-time (6 women); includes 12 minority (8 Black or African American, non-Hispanic/Latino; 2 Hispanic/Latino; 2 Two or more races, non-Hispanic/Latino), 2 international. 2 applicants, 100% accepted. In 2014, 6 master's awarded. *Degree requirements:* For master's, comprehensive exam (for some programs), thesis (for some programs). *Entrance requirements:* Additional exam requirements/recommendations for international students: Required—TOEFL (minimum score 550 paper-based, 79 iBT), IELTS (minimum score 6.5), Michigan Test of English Language Proficiency or PTE. *Application deadline:* For fall admission, 7/18 for domestic students, 6/1 for international students; for spring admission, 12/12 for domestic students, 10/1 for international students; for summer admission, 4/24 for domestic students, 3/1 for international students. Applications are processed on a rolling basis. Application fee: $30. Electronic applications accepted. *Expenses:* Tuition, state resident: full-time $5026. Tuition, nonresident: full-time $12,566. *International tuition:* $25,136 full-time. *Required fees:* $1682. Tuition and fees vary according to course load, campus/location and program. *Financial support:* Career-related internships or fieldwork, institutionally sponsored loans, scholarships/grants, and unspecified assistantships available. Financial award application deadline: 3/1; financial award applicants required to submit FAFSA. *Unit head:* Dr. Erik Kirk, Program Director, 618-650-2718, E-mail: ekirk@siue.edu. *Application contact:* Melissa K. Mace, Assistant Director of Graduate and International Recruitment, 618-650-2756, Fax: 618-650-3618, E-mail: mmace@siue.edu. Website: http://www.siue.edu/education/khe

Springfield College, Graduate Programs, Programs in Exercise Science and Sport Studies, Springfield, MA 01109-3797. Offers athletic training (MS); exercise physiology (MS); health promotion and disease prevention (MS); sport and exercise psychology (MS). Part-time programs available. Terminal master's awarded for partial completion of doctoral program. *Degree requirements:* For master's, comprehensive exam, research project or thesis; for doctorate, comprehensive exam, thesis/dissertation. *Entrance requirements:* For master's and doctorate, GRE General Test. Additional exam requirements/recommendations for international students: Required—TOEFL (minimum score 550 paper-based); Recommended—IELTS (minimum score 6). *Application deadline:* For fall admission, 1/15 for domestic and international students; for winter admission, 11/1 for domestic and international students; for spring admission, 11/1 for domestic and international students. Application fee: $50. Electronic applications accepted. *Financial support:* Fellowships with partial tuition reimbursements, teaching assistantships with partial tuition reimbursements, career-related internships or fieldwork, Federal Work-Study, institutionally sponsored loans, and unspecified assistantships available. Financial award application deadline: 3/1; financial award applicants required to submit FAFSA. *Unit head:* Sue Guyer, Chair, 413-748-3404, E-mail: mguyer@springfieldcollege.edu. *Application contact:* Mary DeAngelo, Director of Enrollment Management, 413-748-3136, Fax: 413-748-3694, E-mail: mdeangel@spfldcol.edu.

Springfield College, Graduate Programs, Programs in Psychology and Counseling, Springfield, MA 01109-3797. Offers athletic counseling (MS, CAGS); clinical mental health counseling (M Ed, CAGS); counseling psychology (Psy D); industrial and organizational psychology (M Ed, CAGS); school guidance counseling (M Ed, CAGS); student personnel administration in higher education (M Ed). Part-time programs available. *Degree requirements:* For master's, research project, portfolio; for doctorate, dissertation project, 1500 hours of counseling psychology practicum, full-year internship. *Entrance requirements:* Additional exam requirements/recommendations for international students: Required—TOEFL (minimum score 550 paper-based). *Application deadline:* For fall admission, 1/15 priority date for domestic students, 1/15 for international students; for winter admission, 11/1 for domestic and international students; for spring admission, 11/1 for domestic and international students. Applications are processed on a rolling basis. Application fee: $50. Electronic applications accepted. *Financial support:* Fellowships with partial tuition reimbursements, teaching assistantships with partial tuition reimbursements, career-related internships or fieldwork, Federal Work-Study, institutionally sponsored loans, and unspecified assistantships available. Financial award application deadline: 3/1; financial award applicants required to submit FAFSA. *Unit head:* Dr. Allison Cumming-McCann, Chair, 413-748-3075, Fax: 413-748-3854, E-mail: acumming@springfieldcollege.edu. *Application contact:* Mary DeAngelo, Director of Enrollment Management, 413-748-3136, E-mail: mdeangel@spfldcol.edu. Website: http://www.springfieldcollege.edu/academic-programs/psychology-department/graduate-programs-in-psychology/index#.U1F-dKJWiSo

University of Denver, Graduate School of Professional Psychology, Denver, CO 80208. Offers forensic psychology (MA); international disaster psychology (MA); sport and performance psychology (MA). *Accreditation:* APA. *Faculty:* 18 full-time (9 women), 23 part-time/adjunct (9 women). *Students:* 205 full-time (148 women), 51 part-time (38 women); includes 57 minority (11 Black or African American, non-Hispanic/Latino; 1 American Indian or Alaska Native, non-Hispanic/Latino; 15 Asian, non-Hispanic/Latino; 21 Hispanic/Latino; 9 Two or more races, non-Hispanic/Latino), 12 international. Average age 27. 720 applicants, 31% accepted, 102 enrolled. In 2014, 90 master's, 32 doctorates awarded. *Degree requirements:* For master's, comprehensive exam (for some programs); for doctorate, comprehensive exam (for some programs), paper, clinical internship. *Entrance requirements:* For master's and doctorate, GRE General Test, transcripts, resume, two letters of recommendation, essay. Additional exam requirements/recommendations for international students: Required—TOEFL (minimum score 550 paper-based; 80 iBT). *Application deadline:* For fall admission, 12/1 priority date for domestic and international students. Application fee: $65. Electronic applications accepted. *Expenses:* Expenses: $1,199 per credit hour. *Financial support:* In 2014–15, 76 students received support, including 33 teaching assistantships with full and partial tuition reimbursements available (averaging $3,042 per year); career-related internships or fieldwork, Federal Work-Study, institutionally sponsored loans, scholarships/grants, unspecified assistantships, and clinical assistantships also available. Support available to part-time students. Financial award application deadline: 2/15; financial award applicants required to submit FAFSA. *Unit head:* Dr. Shelly Smith-Acuna, Dean, 303-871-3880, E-mail: shelly.smith-acuna@du.edu. *Application contact:* Admissions Counselor, 303-871-3736, Fax: 303-871-7656, E-mail: gsppinfo@du.edu. Website: http://www.du.edu/gspp/

University of Rhode Island, Graduate School, College of Human Science and Services, Department of Kinesiology, Kingston, RI 02881. Offers cultural studies of sport and physical culture (MS); exercise science (MS); psychosocial/behavioral aspects of physical activity (MS). *Accreditation:* NCATE. Part-time programs available. *Faculty:* 16 full-time (11 women). *Students:* 13 full-time (7 women), 3 part-time (0 women); includes 2 minority (1 Black or African American, non-Hispanic/Latino; 1 Hispanic/Latino). In 2014, 8 master's awarded. *Degree requirements:* For master's, thesis optional. *Entrance requirements:* For master's, GRE, 2 letters of recommendation. Additional exam requirements/recommendations for international students: Required—TOEFL (minimum score 550 paper-based). *Application deadline:* For fall admission, 7/15 for domestic students, 2/1 for international students; for spring admission, 11/15 for domestic students, 7/15 for international students. Application fee: $65. Electronic applications accepted. *Expenses:* Tuition, state resident: full-time $11,532; part-time $641 per credit. Tuition, nonresident: full-time $23,606; part-time $1311 per credit. *Required fees:* $1442; $39 per credit. $35 per semester. One-time fee: $155. *Financial support:* In 2014–15, 5 teaching assistantships with full and partial tuition reimbursements (averaging $11,317 per year) were awarded. Financial award application deadline: 7/15; financial award applicants required to submit FAFSA. *Faculty research:* Strength training and older adults, interventions to promote a healthy lifestyle as well as analysis of the psychosocial outcomes of those interventions, effects of exercise and nutrition on skeletal muscle of aging healthy adults with CVD and other metabolic related diseases, physical activity and fitness of deaf children and youth. *Total annual research expenditures:* $51,804. *Unit head:* Dr. Deborah Riebe, Chair, 401-874-5444, Fax: 401-874-4215, E-mail: debriebe@uri.edu. *Application contact:* Dr. Matthew Delmonico, Graduate Program Director, 401-874-5440, E-mail: delmonico@uri.edu. Website: http://web.uri.edu/kinesiology/

The University of Texas at Austin, Graduate School, College of Education, Department of Kinesiology and Health Education, Austin, TX 78712-1111. Offers behavioral health (PhD); exercise and sport psychology (M Ed, MA); exercise science (M Ed, MS, PhD); health education (M Ed, MS, Ed D, PhD). Part-time programs available. Terminal master's awarded for partial completion of doctoral program. *Degree requirements:* For master's, thesis (for some programs); for doctorate, thesis/dissertation. *Entrance requirements:* For master's and doctorate, GRE General Test. Additional exam requirements/recommendations for international students: Required—TOEFL. Electronic applications accepted. *Faculty research:* Health promotion, human

performance and exercise biochemistry, motor behavior and biomechanics, sport management, aging and pediatric development.

West Virginia University, School of Physical Education, Morgantown, WV 26506. Offers athletic coaching education (MS); athletic training (MS); physical education/teacher education (MS, PhD), including curriculum and instruction (PhD), motor behavior (PhD), physical education supervision (PhD); sport and exercise psychology (PhD); sport management (MS). *Degree requirements:* For doctorate, comprehensive

exam, thesis/dissertation, oral exam. *Entrance requirements:* For master's, GRE or MAT, minimum GPA of 3.0; for doctorate, GRE General Test or MAT, minimum GPA of 3.5. Additional exam requirements/recommendations for international students: Required—TOEFL (minimum score 550 paper-based). Electronic applications accepted. *Faculty research:* Sport psychosociology, teacher education, exercise psychology, counseling.

Thanatology

Brooklyn College of the City University of New York, School of Natural and Behavioral Sciences, Department of Health and Nutrition Sciences, Program in Community Health, Brooklyn, NY 11210-2889. Offers community health education (MA); thanatology (MA). *Accreditation:* CEPH. *Degree requirements:* For master's, thesis or alternative. *Entrance requirements:* For master's, 2 letters of recommendation, essay. Additional exam requirements/recommendations for international students: Required—TOEFL. Electronic applications accepted. *Faculty research:* Diet restriction, religious practices in bereavement, diabetes, stress management, palliative care.

The College of New Rochelle, Graduate School, Division of Human Services, Program in Mental Health Counseling, New Rochelle, NY 10805-2308. Offers mental health counseling (MS); thanatology (Certificate). *Degree requirements:* For Certificate, internship. *Expenses: Tuition:* Part-time $894 per credit. *Required fees:* $325 per semester.

Hood College, Graduate School, Programs in Human Sciences, Frederick, MD 21701-8575. Offers human sciences (MA), including psychology; thanatology (MA, Certificate).

Part-time and evening/weekend programs available. *Degree requirements:* For master's, comprehensive exam, capstone/research project. *Entrance requirements:* For master's, minimum GPA of 2.75. Additional exam requirements/recommendations for international students: Required—TOEFL (minimum score 575 paper-based; 89 iBT), IELTS (minimum score 6.5). Electronic applications accepted. Application fee is waived when completed online. *Faculty research:* Mind-body medicine and multicultural healing, the New Orleans jazz funeral, death practices in African-American culture, bereavement theories and gender differences, Piaget's theory of cognitive development as a formal mathematical model.

Southwestern College, Program in Grief, Loss and Trauma Counseling, Santa Fe, NM 87502-4788. Offers MA, Certificate. Part-time and evening/weekend programs available. Postbaccalaureate distance learning degree programs offered (minimal on-campus study). *Entrance requirements:* For master's, interview, references, resume; for Certificate, 3 letters of reference, interview.

Transpersonal and Humanistic Psychology

Atlantic University, Program in Transpersonal Studies, Virginia Beach, VA 23451-2061. Offers MA. Part-time and evening/weekend programs available. Postbaccalaureate distance learning degree programs offered (no on-campus study). *Degree requirements:* For master's, thesis. *Entrance requirements:* For master's, official transcripts, 1000-word essay, interview. Additional exam requirements/recommendations for international students: Required—TOEFL (minimum score 550 paper-based). *Application deadline:* For fall admission, 7/19 for domestic students; for spring admission, 11/16 for domestic students; for summer admission, 3/15 for domestic students. Applications are processed on a rolling basis. Application fee: $50. Electronic applications accepted. *Expenses:* Expenses: Contact institution. *Application contact:* Rachel Alvidrez, Educational Services Manager, 757-631-8101, Fax: 757-631-8096, E-mail: info@atlanticuniv.edu.
Website: http://www.atlanticuniv.edu/MA_HistoryAndPerspective.html

John F. Kennedy University, Graduate School of Holistic Studies, Department of Counseling Psychology, Program in Counseling Psychology, Pleasant Hill, CA 94523-4817. Offers holistic studies (MA); somatic psychology (MA); transpersonal psychology (MA). Part-time and evening/weekend programs available. *Degree requirements:* For master's, thesis or alternative. *Entrance requirements:* For master's, interview. Additional exam requirements/recommendations for international students: Required—TOEFL.

John F. Kennedy University, Graduate School of Holistic Studies, Department of Integral Studies, Program in Consciousness and Transformative Studies, Pleasant Hill, CA 94523-4817. Offers MA. Part-time and evening/weekend programs available. *Degree requirements:* For master's, thesis or alternative. *Entrance requirements:* For master's, interview. Additional exam requirements/recommendations for international students: Required—TOEFL.

Michigan School of Professional Psychology, MA and Psy D Programs in Clinical Psychology, Farmington Hills, MI 48334. Offers MA, Psy D. Part-time programs available. *Faculty:* 9 full-time (4 women), 18 part-time/adjunct (15 women). *Students:* 93 full-time (68 women), 57 part-time (45 women); includes 31 minority (22 Black or African American, non-Hispanic/Latino; 5 Asian, non-Hispanic/Latino; 2 Hispanic/Latino; 2 Two or more races, non-Hispanic/Latino), 1 international. Average age 25. 150 applicants, 53% accepted, 60 enrolled. In 2014, 50 master's, 13 doctorates awarded. *Degree requirements:* For master's, practicum; for doctorate, comprehensive exam, thesis/dissertation, internship, practicum. *Entrance requirements:* For master's, undergraduate degree from accredited institution with minimum GPA of 2.5; major in psychology, social work, or counseling; for doctorate, GRE General Test, undergraduate degree from accredited institution with minimum GPA of 2.5; graduate degree in psychology, social work, or counseling from accredited institution with minimum GPA of 3.25; graduate-level practicum. Additional exam requirements/recommendations for international students: Required—TOEFL (minimum score 550 paper-based; 79 iBT). *Application deadline:* Applications are processed on a rolling basis. Application fee: $75. Electronic applications accepted. *Expenses: Tuition:* Full-time $28,504; part-time $12,147 per year. *Required fees:* $435 per semester. One-time fee: $75. Tuition and fees vary according to course load, degree level, program and student level. *Financial support:* In 2014–15, 6 students received support, including 3 research assistantships (averaging $1,200 per year), 4 teaching assistantships (averaging $1,200 per year); career-related internships or fieldwork, institutionally sponsored loans, scholarships/grants, and unspecified assistantships also available. Support available to part-time students. Financial award application deadline: 6/30; financial award applicants required to submit FAFSA. *Faculty research:* Qualitative research, existential, phenomenological psychology, multicultural, humanistic. *Unit head:* Dr. Lee Bach, Program Director, 248-476-1122, Fax: 248-476-1125. *Application contact:* Tori Holmes, Coordinator of Admissions and Student Engagement, 248-476-1122 Ext. 117, Fax: 248-476-1125, E-mail: tholmes@mispp.edu. Website: http://www.mispp.edu

Naropa University, Graduate Programs, Program in Transpersonal Counseling Psychology, Boulder, CO 80302-6697. Offers art therapy (MA); counseling psychology (MA); wilderness therapy (MA). *Faculty:* 10 full-time (6 women), 26 part-time/adjunct (19 women). *Students:* 169 full-time (131 women), 67 part-time (49 women); includes 32 minority (2 Black or African American, non-Hispanic/Latino; 1 American Indian or Alaska

Native, non-Hispanic/Latino; 1 Asian, non-Hispanic/Latino; 13 Hispanic/Latino; 15 Two or more races, non-Hispanic/Latino), 7 international. Average age 31. 174 applicants, 67% accepted, 81 enrolled. In 2014, 70 master's awarded. *Degree requirements:* For master's, internships, counseling practicum. *Entrance requirements:* For master's, in-person interview, course work in psychology, 2 letters of recommendation, extended resume, minimum 100 hours of paid or volunteer work in a helping profession (mental health, healthcare, teaching, etc.). Additional exam requirements/recommendations for international students: Required—TOEFL (minimum score 600 paper-based; 80 iBT). *Application deadline:* For fall admission, 1/15 priority date for domestic and international students. Applications are processed on a rolling basis. Application fee: $60. Electronic applications accepted. *Expenses: Tuition:* Full-time $23,400; part-time $975 per credit. *Required fees:* $335 per semester. Tuition and fees vary according to course load. *Financial support:* In 2014–15, 70 students received support, including 14 research assistantships with partial tuition reimbursements available (averaging $6,319 per year); career-related internships or fieldwork, scholarships/grants, tuition waivers (partial), and unspecified assistantships also available. Support available to part-time students. Financial award application deadline: 3/1; financial award applicants required to submit FAFSA. *Unit head:* Dr. Deborah Bowman, Dean, Graduate School of Psychology, 303-546-3559, E-mail: bowman@naropa.edu. *Application contact:* Office of Admissions, 303-546-3572, Fax: 303-546-3583, E-mail: admissions@naropa.edu. Website: http://www.naropa.edu/academics/gsp/grad/transpersonal-counseling-psychology-ma/index.php

Naropa University, Graduate Programs, Program in Transpersonal Ecopsychology, Boulder, CO 80302-6697. Offers MA. Part-time and evening/weekend programs available. Postbaccalaureate distance learning degree programs offered (minimal on-campus study). *Faculty:* 1 (woman) full-time, 3 part-time/adjunct (2 women). *Students:* 21 part-time (16 women); includes 1 minority (Hispanic/Latino), 1 international. Average age 37. 17 applicants, 71% accepted, 10 enrolled. In 2014, 9 master's awarded. *Degree requirements:* For master's, thesis, service learning. *Entrance requirements:* For master's, interview (by phone or in-person), technology form, resume, 2 letters of recommendation, transcripts, letter of interest. Additional exam requirements/recommendations for international students: Required—TOEFL (minimum score 600 paper-based; 80 iBT). *Application deadline:* For fall admission, 1/15 priority date for domestic and international students. Applications are processed on a rolling basis. Application fee: $60. Electronic applications accepted. *Expenses: Tuition:* Full-time $23,400; part-time $975 per credit. *Required fees:* $335 per semester. Tuition and fees vary according to course load. *Financial support:* In 2014–15, 3 students received support. Career-related internships or fieldwork, scholarships/grants, and tuition waivers (partial) available. Support available to part-time students. Financial award application deadline: 3/1; financial award applicants required to submit FAFSA. *Unit head:* Dr. Deborah Bowman, Dean, Graduate School of Psychology, 303-546-3559, E-mail: bowman@naropa.edu. *Application contact:* Office of Admissions, 303-546-3572, Fax: 303-546-3583, E-mail: admissions@naropa.edu. Website: http://www.naropa.edu/academics/gsp/grad/ecopsychology-ma/index.php

Saybrook University, School of Psychology and Interdisciplinary Inquiry, San Francisco, CA 94111-1920. Offers human science (MA, PhD), including consciousness and spirituality, humanistic and transpersonal psychology, integrative health studies, organizational systems, social transformation; organizational systems (MA, PhD), including consciousness and spirituality, humanistic and transpersonal psychology, integrative health studies, leadership of sustainable systems (MA), organizational systems, social transformation; psychology (MA, PhD), including consciousness and spirituality, creativity studies (MA), humanistic and transpersonal psychology, integrative health studies, Jungian studies, marriage and family therapy (MA), organizational systems, social transformation. Postbaccalaureate distance learning degree programs offered (minimal on-campus study). Terminal master's awarded for partial completion of doctoral program. *Degree requirements:* For master's, thesis or alternative; for doctorate, thesis/dissertation. *Entrance requirements:* Additional exam requirements/recommendations for international students: Required—TOEFL (minimum score 580 paper-based; 93 iBT). Electronic applications accepted. *Faculty research:* Humanistic theory, health studies, organizational systems, consciousness and spirituality, social transformation.

Transpersonal and Humanistic Psychology

Seattle University, College of Arts and Sciences, Department of Psychology, Seattle, WA 98122-1090. Offers existential and phenomenological therapeutic psychology (MA Psych). *Faculty:* 7 full-time (2 women), 5 part-time/adjunct (4 women). *Students:* 40 full-time (29 women), 5 part-time (2 women); includes 7 minority (1 Black or African American, non-Hispanic/Latino; 1 Asian, non-Hispanic/Latino; 1 Hispanic/Latino; 4 Two or more races, non-Hispanic/Latino), 3 international. Average age 31. 62 applicants, 48% accepted, 20 enrolled. In 2014, 22 master's awarded. *Degree requirements:* For master's, thesis optional. *Entrance requirements:* For master's, interview, minimum GPA of 3.0, previous undergraduate course work in psychology, experience (paid or volunteer) in counseling or human services. *Application deadline:* For fall admission, 1/15 for domestic and international students. Application fee: $55. Electronic applications accepted. *Financial support:* In 2014–15, 9 students received support. Career-related internships or fieldwork and Federal Work-Study available. Support available to part-time students. Financial award applicants required to submit FAFSA. *Faculty research:* Interpersonal relations, psychotherapy, qualitative research, trauma, philosophy and psychology. *Unit head:* Dr. Kevin Krycka, Director of Graduate Programs, 206-296-5398, Fax: 206-296-2141, E-mail: krycka@seattleu.edu. *Application contact:* Janet Shandley, Associate Dean of Graduate Admissions, 206-296-5900, Fax: 206-298-5656, E-mail: grad_admissions@seattleu.edu.
Website: http://www.seattleu.edu/artsci/departments/psychology/

Sofia University, Hybrid: Face-to-Face/Online Programs, Palo Alto, CA 94303. Offers counseling psychology (MA); psychology (PhD), including transpersonal psychology; spiritual guidance (MA); transpersonal psychology (MA, Certificate); women's spirituality (MA, Certificate). Postbaccalaureate distance learning degree programs offered (minimal on-campus study). *Entrance requirements:* For master's, bachelor's degree; for doctorate, bachelor's degree; master's degree. Electronic applications accepted.

Sofia University, Residential Programs, Palo Alto, CA 94303. Offers clinical psychology (Psy D); counseling psychology (MA); transpersonal psychology (MA, PhD). Part-time and evening/weekend programs available. Terminal master's awarded for partial completion of doctoral program. *Degree requirements:* For doctorate, thesis/dissertation. *Entrance requirements:* For master's, bachelor's degree; for doctorate, bachelor's degree; master's degree (for some programs). Electronic applications accepted.

ADELPHI UNIVERSITY
Gordon F. Derner Institute of Advanced Psychological Studies

Programs of Study

The Gordon F. Derner Institute of Advanced Psychological Studies offers a Ph.D. in Clinical Psychology program and Master of Arts programs in General Psychology, School Psychology, and Mental Health Counseling. There are also several postgraduate programs available.

The Ph.D. in Clinical Psychology program consists of 120 credits and emphasizes a psychodynamic approach to human behavior, preparing graduates for community practice. The program encompasses research; theory; the psychological, biological, and social bases of behavior; and extensive clinical practice in psychodiagnostics and psychotherapy. Four years of full-time study, supervised research, a one-year full-time internship, and a dissertation are required. The clinical psychology program has been accredited by the American Psychological Association (APA) since 1957.

The 36-credit Master of Arts in General Psychology program enables students to advance their exploration of human personality, psychodynamics, developmental and social psychology, and psychoanalytic theory. It requires the completion of a 36-credit course of study, which can be completed in one year of full-time study or two years of part-time study. Courses can be taken in various areas of psychology such as industrial/organizational, forensic psychology, clinical studies, and substance abuse counseling.

The Master of Arts in School Psychology program is a 72-credit program that can be completed in three years of full-time study or four years of part-time study. The program enables students to practice in a school setting using integrated skills, such as providing comprehensive psychoeducational evaluations and school consultations. The school practice core culminates with a full-time internship in a public school working under the supervision of a certified school psychologist.

The Master of Arts in Mental Health Counseling program helps students acquire knowledge and the clinical skills to become competent mental health counselors. Students acquire competency in the diagnosis and treatment of mental disorders, the ability to facilitate client growth, development, and respect for the ethics and standards of practice endorsed by the mental health counseling profession. The 60-credit curriculum, including an internship, can be completed in two years. The program complies with all standards for state and national accrediting groups. After licensure, mental health counselors may work in a variety of settings, such as hospitals, clinics, and private practice.

The Certificate of Respecialization in clinical psychology equips doctoral-level psychologists to make a career shift into clinical psychology for community practice. The program focuses on academic work and intensive clinical training, and requires two years of full-time study, supervised clinical practice, and a one-year full-time internship. Graduates of this program earn a Certificate of Respecialization in clinical psychology, which is recognized by the American Psychological Association.

Postgraduate programs are available for students who have already earned a Ph.D. in clinical psychology or are licensed mental health professionals—psychiatrists, social workers, and psychiatric nurses—who wish to expand the focus of their practice. Adelphi's postgraduate programs include psychoanalytic psychotherapy; psychoanalysis and psychotherapy; child, adolescent, and family psychotherapy; group psychotherapy; couple therapy; psychoanalytic supervision; and psychodynamic school psychology.

Research Facilities

The University's primary research holdings are at Swirbul Library and include 618,779 volumes (including bound periodicals and government publications); 791,000 items in microformats; 35,000 audiovisual items;

and online access to more than 135,000 e-book titles, 87,000 electronic journals, and 251 research databases.

Clinical facilities on campus include the Center for Psychological Services and the Postgraduate Psychotherapy Center. Clinical facilities are also located in many neighboring hospitals, public schools, and agencies. Research facilities include the University library and computing center and a number of Institute research laboratories.

Value

Established in 1896, Adelphi University is a fully accredited, private university with nearly 8,000 undergraduate, graduate, postgraduate, and returning-adult students in the arts and sciences, business, allied health, clinical psychology, education, nursing, and social work. Academic experts have chosen Adelphi University as the gold standard for northeastern colleges. Noted for high academic standards and reasonable tuition costs, this private liberal arts university has also been recognized as a best buy in the *Fiske Guide to Colleges* for ten straight years.

Financial Aid

Adelphi University offers a wide variety of federal aid programs; state grants; scholarship and fellowship programs; on- and off-campus employment; teaching, research, and clinical assistantships; and paid field placements.

Cost of Study

The 2015–16 tuition for full-time study (12–17 credits) is $43,320 per year for doctoral study in the Derner Institute of Advanced Psychological Studies. Tuition for part-time study (1–11 credits) is $1,230 per credit hour for master's degree programs. University fees range from about $370 to $850 per semester.

Living and Housing Costs

Housing may be available on a limited, first-come, first-served basis.

Location

Adelphi University is located in Nassau County on Long Island, part of the New York City metropolitan area. Students can draw upon the city's cultural and social resources, as well as the University's own extensive program in the arts.

The University

Adelphi University is set within a beautifully landscaped campus of 75 acres in the attractive residential community of Garden City, Long Island.

Applying

Application requirements can be found online at http://derner.adelphi.edu/admissions/graduate/.

Correspondence and Information

Dr. Jacques P. Barber, Dean
Gordon F. Derner Institute of Advanced Psychological Studies
Adelphi University
One South Avenue
Garden City, New York 11530
Phone: 800-ADELPHI (toll-free)
Fax: 516-877-3093
E-mail: admissions@adelphi.edu
Website: http://derner.adelphi.edu

Adelphi University

FULL-TIME FACULTY AND THEIR RESEARCH

Robert Bornstein, Ph.D., University at Buffalo. Personality disorders and assessment, unconscious processes, interpersonal dependency.

Jean Lau Chin, Ed.D., Columbia Teachers College. School psychology, psychology of women, diversity in clinical practice.

Francine Conway, Ph.D., Adelphi University. Aging, emotions, and health studies.

Rebecca Curtis, Ph.D., Columbia University. Social/clinical interface, psychotherapy research, self-defeating behavior.

Laura DeRose, Ph.D., Columbia University. Developmental psychology, pubertal development, adjustment during early adolescence.

Jennifer Durham, Psy.D., Rutgers University. Social justice in mental health, closing the achievement gap, couple and family therapy.

Katherine Fiori, Ph.D., University of Michigan. Developmental psychology, adult development, aging.

Jairo N. Fuertes, Ph.D., University of Maryland. Clinical assessment and intervention, case conceptualization and treatment planning, clinical supervision, psychopathology, research design.

Jerold Gold, Ph.D., Adelphi University. Interpersonal psychoanalysis, personality theory, psychotheory integration.

Denise A. Hien, Ph.D., Columbia University. Women's mental health and addictions.

Mark Hilsenroth, Ph.D., University of Tennessee. Psychodiagnostics.

Lawrence Josephs, Ph.D., University of Tennessee. Psychoanalysis, psychotherapy, self-psychology.

Morton Kissen, Ph.D., New School. ABPP. Object relations theory, projective testing, diagnostic issues.

Karen Lombardi, Ph.D., New York University. Child clinical psychology, psychoanalytic-developmental psychology, fairy tales and myths.

Robert Mendelsohn, Ph.D., University of Massachusetts. Short-term psychotherapy, psychoanalytic theory.

J. Christopher Muran, Ph.D., Hofstra University. Therapeutic relationship and alliance.

Joseph W. Newirth, Ph.D., University of Massachusetts; Psychoanalysis, object relations theory, disorders of self.

Michael O'Loughlin, Ph.D., Columbia Teachers College. Child psychotherapy, multicultural issues in school psychology.

Susan Petry, Ph.D., Columbia University. Sensation and perception.

Ionas Sapountzis, Ph.D., New York University. Childhood development, integrating treatment modalities.

Carolyn Springer, Ph.D., New York University. Statistics.

Kate Szymanski, Ph.D., Northeastern University. Small groups, social loafing, intrinsic/extrinsic motivation.

Joel Weinberger, Ph.D., New School. Human motivation.

The accessible faculty members in the Gordon F. Derner Institute of Advanced Psychological Studies are leaders in their fields.

Programs in the Gordon F. Derner Institute of Advanced Psychological Studies include a Ph.D. in Clinical Psychology and Master of Arts degrees in General Psychology, School Psychology, and Mental Health Counseling.

ADLER UNIVERSITY
Graduate Programs

 ADLER UNIVERSITY
For a more just society

★ For more information, visit http://petersons.to/adlerupsychology

Programs of Study

Founded in 1952, Adler University is the oldest independent school of psychology in North America. The University is named after Alfred Adler (1870–1937), the first community psychologist, whose theories and teachings of psychology emphasize the uniqueness of every individual's relationship with society. Adler University is committed to continuing Adler's pioneering work by graduating socially responsible practitioners, engaging communities, and advancing social justice. Students come from all over the world to study in a collaborative atmosphere with accomplished clinical faculty. The University offers both campus-based and online classes to accommodate recent college graduates and working professionals.

The University takes pride in its commitment to educate and train socially responsible practitioners in counseling, psychology, and policy-based fields through innovative programs that combine course work and community-based training that enable graduates to address a broad range of social issues that impact the clients they serve.

Adler University offers the following degree programs at its Chicago Campus:

The **Doctor of Psychology (Psy.D.) in Clinical Psychology** program utilizes a practitioner-scholar–based training model with an emphasis on socially responsible practice. It prepares graduates to conduct clinical interviews and psychological testing, create treatment plans, consult and collaborate with physicians and other professionals, and provide multiple forms of therapy to alleviate mental illness, behavioral problems, and emotional distress. Adler has received national recognition for its focus on socially responsible clinical practice emphasizing the broader social and systemic factors of human dysfunction. Upon completing foundational course work, students have the opportunity to be placed in internships at prestigious clinics, hospitals, mental health centers, and government agencies. Adler also offers a variety of emphasis including child and adolescent psychology, military clinical psychology, clinical neuropsychology, primary care psychology, and traumatic stress psychology. The Doctor of Psychology in Clinical Psychology program is accredited by the Committee on Accreditation of the American Psychological Association (APA), 750 First Street NE, Washington, D.C. 20002-4242; phone: 202-336-5510; website: http://www.apa.org/ed/accreditation. It also meets requirements of the National Register of Health Care providers in psychology and state licensure guidelines.

The **Doctor of Couple and Family Therapy** program is distinctly designed for experienced clinicians as well as recent graduates of master's degree programs. Students are prepared for careers as advanced therapists specializing in couple, marriage, and family therapy. With an emphasis on clinical practice and theoretical frameworks, our program enables students to apply comprehensive theory, research, and techniques addressed in coursework to their practicums and clinical work. The Doctor of Couple and Family Therapy program consists of intensive course work, clinical experiences, a dissertation, and a one-year full-time internship. Students are placed in internships at clinics, hospitals, mental health centers, schools, and social service agencies.

The **Doctor of Philosophy (Ph.D.) in Counselor Education and Supervision** program provides advanced training and academic orientation for practicing counselors to become expert clinicians, counselor educators in teaching, supervisors, and trainers of the new generation of counselors, researchers, and scholars, as well as leaders and advocates in the field of counseling. The program is designed to develop students' expertise and excellence in teaching, research, leadership and advocacy, advanced counseling, and supervision. To support the mission of Adler University, through the integration of reflective, experiential, and participant learning and social engagement, students are expected to become professionals who are also critical thinkers and courageous leaders, multiculturally competent, aware of self and the needs of others.

The **Master of Arts in Couple and Family Therapy** program prepares entry-level counselors to specialize in working with couples and families. Students complete course work and practicums focused on the understanding and integration of individual lifestyle dynamics with couple, marital, and family systems. Graduates have a theoretical understanding of marital and family systems, including developmental issues and major variations, assessment skills in lifestyle and systemic diagnosis, and intervention skills based on major models of marital and family therapy, with the theory and methods of individual psychology as the foundation.

The **Master of Arts in Counseling: Art Therapy** program combines traditional counseling theories and techniques with an understanding of the psychological aspects of the creative process and clinical training. The program, approved by the American Art Therapy Association, requires course work as well as clinical practicum experience under at least partial supervision of a registered art therapist (ATR). It provides students with the academic and clinical experiences required to apply for registration as an art therapist as well as sit for the Licensed Professional Counselor (LPC) examination in the state of Illinois.

The **Master of Arts in Counseling: Specialization in Rehabilitation Counseling** program prepares students to become certified rehabilitation counselors (CRC). It was the first program in a professional school of psychology to receive CORE—The Council on Rehabilitation Education accreditation. Rehabilitation counselors work with individuals who have mental, emotional, or physical handicaps, helping them to lead self-sufficient lives. Counselors determine the training and support their clients need to deal with the effects of their

conditions. Counselors evaluate clients and arrange for rehabilitation programs that may include medical care, psychological counseling, occupational therapy, and job placement and are employed by publicly funded agencies, schools, and medical facilities.

The **Master of Arts in Counseling: Specialization in Forensic Psychology** program prepares graduates for a highly specialized career that integrates knowledge of human behavior with active participation in the criminal justice system. Specialized course work exposes students to the predominant theories and techniques of forensic evaluation, including determination of a defendant's competency to stand trial, sanity at the time of an offense, and qualification for the death penalty in the event of a capital crime conviction. Students also develop a comprehensive understanding of techniques associated with the forensic practitioner's involvement in criminal investigations: activities such as forensic hypnosis, offender and geographic profiling, and the ongoing review of police interview and witness identification procedures. Students are introduced to such specialized topics as the psychological effects of incarceration, jury selection, the evaluation of sexually dangerous persons, and the psychosocial development of the criminal personality type.

The **Master of Arts in Counseling: Specialization in Sport and Health Psychology** program prepares graduates to address individual and systemic issues that affect sport performance and health. These areas overlap in the types of interventions used to produce positive changes (goal-setting and self-monitoring to improve consistency of practice or to lose weight). Sport and health goals also share the influence of various social and community factors such as coaches, family members, culture, and access to facilities. This unique program provides training and understanding of assessment, intervention, and analysis of systems that enable graduates to work within communities, schools, and professional organizations to address the diverse needs of people with varying ages, health issues, and athletic accomplishments.

The **Master of Arts in Counseling: Specialization in Clinical Mental Health Counseling** program at Adler University is unlike any other because it provides traditional graduate training with a focus on graduating socially responsible practitioners. Through this program, students are prepared for careers as counselors in a variety of mental health fields in settings such as mental health clinics, substance abuse treatment centers, private practice, and social service agencies. Clinical mental health counselors work with individuals, couples, and families in private and public sectors. Incorporating intensive coursework with practicums that provide real-world experience in clinical settings, the flexible program allows students to choose the format that best works with their schedule.

The **Master of Arts in Public Policy and Administration** offers students an opportunity to gain multidisciplinary knowledge, skills, and attitudes that will enable them to engage in advocacy; understand government and public policy; and manage nonprofit, private, and governmental organizations. A focus on excellent communication skills will enable graduates to successfully lead organizations, advance an advocacy agenda, and problem-solve in complex situations. Students can choose from two concentrations: urban mental health and human rights advocacy.

Adler University offers the following online programs through its Global Campus:

The **Master of Arts in Criminology** program is an online program that prepares practitioners to examine the causes and consequences of criminal behavior, understand the intricacies and challenges of modern-day criminal justice systems, and apply theoretical skills to address those challenges. Graduates complete their studies ready to develop intervention and prevention strategies that are practical, effective, socially responsible, and sustainable.

The **Master of Arts in Industrial and Organizational (I/O) Psychology** program, offered entirely online, is designed to meet the guidelines for education and training provided by the Society of Industrial and Organizational Psychology (SIOP) with unique emphasis on socially responsible practice. Professionals in this field apply methods of psychology to issues of critical relevance to business and industry, including talent management, coaching, leadership development, program evaluation, training, organizational change, team building, and work-life balance. Many I/O psychology professionals also work as consultants addressing organizational challenges such as change management, workplace diversity, and employee development and engagement.

The **Master of Arts in Psychology: Specialization in Military Psychology** program is designed to provide military and nonmilitary individuals and clinicians with an understanding of the theoretical evidence, scientific research, and practical aspects of the field of military psychology. Students are taught how to apply principles of military psychology to the interpersonal, managerial, and organizational dimensions of the military and support civilian environments. This allows for the development of leadership, innovation, and creativity that is required to advance social justice. Graduates are prepared for a range of positions within behavioral and medical health systems (government and non-government), enhanced private practices, advocacy and policy organizations, and community-based consumer organizations serving military personnel, veterans, retirees, and their families.

The **Masters of Arts in Nonprofit Management** is designed for professionals at all levels of nonprofit experience, from beginners to experts. Comprehensive

coursework prepares students for employment in one of the fastest-growing sectors through emphasizing skills needed to build, lead, and maintain healthy organizations. Students develop skills in employee management, daily operations, relationship management, advocacy, and collaboration. Immersive hands-on community engagement projects prepare students to work in positions that influence education, philanthropy, human service, health care, public policy, and more.

The **Master of Arts in Emergency Management Leadership** program is an online program that focuses on the emergency management leader and the human side of disasters. Students are taught to address long-term psychological and mental health needs of victims and responders. The program prepares students to develop the knowledge and skills of practices in the emergency management field, with a unique focus on the human and social factors inherent in all disasters.

Research Facilities

The Harold and Birdie Mosak Library provides resources and services to foster the educational and intellectual inquiry of students and faculty members. The Library provides on-site and remote online access to research databases in psychology, the social sciences, education, and criminal justice. In addition, the library subscribes to a growing collection of online resources, including more than 23,000 full-text electronic journals, 8,000 electronic books, and full-text collections of newspapers.

Financial Aid

Most students rely on a combination of scholarships, student loans, and paid employment (inside or outside of the school) to finance their graduate degrees and living expenses. The Office of Financial Aid is committed to helping students identify opportunities, understand options, and make choices that are right for them. Adler offers numerous scholarships based on a variety of criteria including financial need, academic excellence, mission-based, and community involvement and service.

Cost of Study

Tuition on the Chicago campus for 2015–16 is $1,145 per credit hour for M.A. programs and $1,330 per credit hour for the doctoral program. Tuition on the Vancouver campus for 2015–16 is Can$850 per credit hour for M.A. programs and Can$1000 per credit hour for the doctoral program. Tuition for online programs is $855 per credit hour. Tuition costs for each year vary depending on whether the student enrolls full-time or part-time. Courses are offered during fall, spring, and summer semesters.

Living and Housing Costs

The University does not provide housing but assists students in securing off-campus housing. Students typically live in apartments in the Chicago or Vancouver area. Living expenses vary considerably according to standard of living, housing, and transportation.

Student Groups

Adler University's commitment to social responsibility draws both recent college graduates and working professionals from all over the world to study in a collaborative atmosphere with accomplished faculty members. Reflecting the University's cultural and professional diversity, Adler's Student Association and more than twenty student organizations represent a range of different countries and personal and professional interests through on-and off-campus learning activities.

The Faculty

With an average class size of fewer than 12 students, faculty mentorship plays a very important role in the learning process at Adler. Faculty members are licensed professionals who combine clinical practice with their instructional duties. Many hold or have held leadership positions in professional organizations, and most present workshops and seminars throughout the United States, Europe, Canada, and other countries. Adler University's faculty members have a broad range of interest and specializations offering students a variety of expertise in the field of psychology.

Location

Adler University is located in Chicago, Illinois and Vancouver, British Columbia. Both downtown campuses are easily accessible by public transportation and provide students with a culturally diverse learning environment as well as hundreds of opportunities for clinical training across the United States and Canada.

The School

Adler University has provided quality education through a scholar/practitioner model for 60 years. Its mission is to train socially responsible graduates who continue the visionary work of Alfred Adler throughout the world. Enrolling more than 1,000 students in graduate programs at its campuses in Chicago, Vancouver, and Global, Adler is uniquely based on Alfred Adler's groundbreaking concept of social interest: that health resides in community life and connections. This concept is the foundation of the University's curricula, training, and community work including partnerships with more than 700 agencies. Its Institutes and Centers advance social justice for underserved and disadvantaged communities through applied research, community outreach, and public awareness initiatives. These include the Institute on Social Exclusion, the Institute on Public Safety and Social Justice, the Adler Child Guidance Center, and the LGBT Mental Health and Inclusion Center.

Applying

Adler employs a rolling admission process. This means that completed applications are reviewed through the year. Because most programs fill quickly, students are encouraged to begin the application process as early as possible. While applications are accepted throughout the year, February 15 is the priority deadline for the Psy.D. program (all tracks). All application materials should be submitted by this date.

Correspondence and Information

Chicago Admissions Office:
Adler University
17 North Dearborn Street
Chicago, Illinois 60602
United States
Phone: 312-662-4100
Fax: 312-662-4099
E-mail: admissions@adler.edu
Website: http://www.adler.edu

Vancouver Admissions Office:
Adler University
1090 West Georgia Street, Suite 1200
Vancouver, BC V6E 3V7
Canada
Phone: 604-482-5510
          866-874-4614 (toll-free)
Fax: 604-874-4634
E-mail: vanadmissions@adler.edu
Website: http://www.adler.edu

Global Campus Admissions Office:
Adler University
17 North Dearborn Street
Chicago, Illinois 60602
United States
Phone: 312-662-4000
E-mail: admissions@online.adler.edu
Website: http://online.adler.edu

The Harold and Birdie Mosak Library provides resources and services to foster the educational and intellectual inquiry of students and faculty members.

Adler University—for a more just society.

JACKSON STATE UNIVERSITY
Clinical Psychology Doctoral Program

Programs of Study

Jackson State University's (JSU) clinical psychology doctoral program provides graduate students with a Ph.D. degree in clinical psychology. The program training goals are the following:

- To produce graduates who are skilled in the science, theory, and practice of psychology

- To increase students' awareness, knowledge, and skills in multicultural psychology

- To produce graduates who have the requisite knowledge and skills to conduct their work in accordance with ethical, legal, and professional standards in their practice and research

- To produce students who will engage in clinical and research experiences targeting the diverse psychological, health, and service needs of ethnic minority populations

The program is structured so that students graduate in five years. During the first year of the program, students take prerequisite courses designed to prepare them to meet various research- and clinical-related program requirements. During the second year, students complete requirements such as the second-year paper and three clinical practica in JSU's on-campus Applied Psychological Services Clinic. In the third year, students are enrolled in clinical externships, which are placements at off-campus sites such as hospitals, state facilities, etc. under the supervision of licensed psychologists. Students also complete the Graduate Area Comprehensive Examination and Clinical Competency Examination. During the fourth year, students initiate the dissertation research process and apply for predoctoral internship. During the fifth year, students spend one year completing a predoctoral internship. Students are expected to work on research projects throughout their matriculation in the program. Current and past graduates have conducted research on topics that include health disparities, children, assessment, HIV/AIDS prevention/care, obesity, and more.

Research Facilities

There are a number of research laboratories available for graduate students within the department and throughout the campus. The department has eleven research laboratories. The program also provides two areas specifically for graduate students. One area is the student computer room, which has six computer workstations with the latest software (i.e., SPSS, Microsoft Office, and Qualtrics) and locked storage space available for students. The other area is the student lounge. The Division of Library and Information Services includes five branches that offer electronic access to the latest APA journals. The University has inter-library loan agreements with other local libraries. Students also have access to numerous technological services provided by JSU's Mississippi e-Center, which is a cutting-edge, information technology center that demonstrates JSU's leadership in the digital world. It employs a wide array of technology-enhanced learning, research, and business tools to engage students and faculty in innovative real-world exercises.

Financial Aid

Students enrolled in the program are provided a monthly stipend. Additional types of funding include tuition waivers, teaching assistantships, and research assistantships, which are distributed by the Division of Graduate Studies. In addition, advanced students (i.e., third year and above) are referred to local clinical psychologists seeking to pay students to conduct assessments and work on research projects. The graduate faculty strongly encourages students to seek federal funding via research and dissertation grants. The program has past recipients of the APA Minority Fellowship Award, Brown University Fellowship, Air Force Health Scholarship, and F-31 grants from the NIMH.

Cost of Study

Out-of-state fee per credit hour is $553 (1.0–8.0 hours). The out-of-state fee for full-time students is $4,978. The in-state fee per hour is $381 (1.0–8.0 hours), and the in-state fee for 9.0–13.0 hours is $3,433. Other designated fees include: graduate admissions $25, photo ID $25, parking $40, and dissertation fee $100.

Living and Housing Costs

JSU does provide graduate housing. Cost for a single room is $1,161 and a double room is $580. Some students reside at JSU's One University Place, a new building that also houses retail stores, a sports bar, and restaurant, that is located directly across the street from the psychology department. Costs at One University Place range from $735 to $1,550 for one- and two-bedroom units.

Student Group

As of fall 2015, there are a total of 39 students enrolled in the program at various stages of completion. There are 11 men, 28 women, and 1 international student. Students gaining admission to the program typically have strengths in the area of clinical and research experience. Moreover, graduate faculty members look for students with good writing and analytical skills.

Student Outcomes

Program graduates have various positions at different facilities nationally, including VA hospitals, state psychiatric facilities, private practices, correctional facilities, and universities. Currently, there are 2 recent graduates with post-doctoral employment at Ivy League schools, Yale and Columbia. In Mississippi, past graduates are employed at a number of VAMCs, medical centers, psychiatric facilities, community mental health centers, and the armed forces.

Location

JSU is Jackson, Mississippi's urban university. It is located just 1 mile from downtown, which has numerous venues for entertainment including art museums, concerts, festivals, and theaters. Annual downtown events include the state fair, Saint Patrick's Day Parade, and blues festivals. Fine dining and popular eateries are only a few miles away.

The University and The Department

Designated as a high research activity university, JSU enhances the state, nation, and world through comprehensive economic development, health care, technological, and educational initiatives. The Department of Psychology is a unit of the School of Social and Behavioral Science in the College of Liberal Arts. It is home to over 450 undergraduates. The department is committed to enhancing knowledge of psychological principles and practices through scholarship, research, undergraduate service-learning, and graduate clinical training.

Applying

Application requirements include three letters of recommendation, CV, GRE scores, two official transcripts, program application, and immunization record. The application deadline is January 15th of each year. Minimum requirements include 24 hours of psychology coursework and a minimum 3.0 GPA. Application materials should be submitted to the Division of Graduate Studies. The interview process and selection occurs yearly during the month of March. Selected students must notify us with his/her decision to accept or reject the offer by April 15th.

Correspondence and Information

Bryman Williams, Ph.D., Director of Clinical Training
Jackson State University
1325 J. R. Lynch Street / Box 17550
Jackson, Mississippi 39217-0350
Phone: 601-979-2371
Fax: 601-979-3947
E-mail: bryman.e.williams@jsums.edu
Website: http://www.jsums.edu/psychology/graduate/

THE FACULTY AND THEIR RESEARCH

Pamela Banks, Professor and Department Chair; Ph.D., University of Southern Mississippi. Anxiety disorders, violence prevention, anger management, stigma reduction, multicultural competencies.

Jackson State University

Taunjah P. Bell, Assistant Professor; Ph.D., Southern Illinois University, Carbondale. Relationship between vagus nerve stimulation and anxiety, neurobiological mechanisms underlying emotional control, impairments in neuromechanisms.

Richard Chiles, Assistant Professor; Ph.D., Northwestern University. Conceptualizations of psychoanalytic process, personality development.

Theresa Kearns-Cooper, Visiting Professor; Psy.D., Forest Institute of Professional Psychology. Suicide assessment and intervention, cross cultural issues, diagnosis and treatment of serious mental disorders.

Keith Hudson, Assistant Professor; Ph.D., Mississippi State University. Treatment modalities, marriage and family issues, adolescent delinquency, multidimensional influences.

Dawn McLin, Associate Professor; Ph.D., Mississippi State University. Multiculturalism, cultural competency, program evaluation, eating disorders/obesity among minorities, seatbelt use.

Cheryl Moreland, Assistant Professor; Ph.D., Southern Mississippi University. Racial identity development, HIV and risky sexual behaviors, multicultural counseling, group therapy.

Debra S. Pate, Associate Professor; Ph.D., California, San Diego. Human cognition, neuropsychology, psycholinguistics, history of psychology, caregiver issues, teaching of psychology.

Jacqueline Reese-Smith, Assistant Professor; Ph.D., University of Kansas. Health promotions, motivational interviewing and counseling, psychosocial determinants of obesity, chronic diseases.

Juliette Schweitzer, Visiting Professor; Ph.D., Jackson State University. Diagnosis and treatment of psychopathology, biofeedback/heart-rate variability, Partners for Change Outcome Management System, mindfulness.

Kaye Sly, Associate Professor; Ph.D., Southern Illinois University, Carbondale. HIV/STD prevention, women's health disparities, substance abuse treatment and prevention, dual diagnosis.

Bryman Williams, Assistant Professor and Director of Clinical Training; Ph.D., Jackson State University. HIV/AIDS prevention and care, violence among children, adult psychopathology, program evaluation, health disparities.

The west entrance to Jackson State University.

The entrance to the Department of Psychology at JSU.

PHILADELPHIA COLLEGE OF OSTEOPATHIC MEDICINE

Graduate Programs in Clinical Psychology, Counseling and Clinical Health Psychology, and School Psychology

 For more information, visit http://petersons.to/philiadephiacollegepsychology

Programs of Study

The Philadelphia College of Osteopathic Medicine (PCOM) Department of Psychology offers nine graduate programs taught by an internationally renowned, highly credentialed faculty. All faculty members in PCOM's psychology department are teaching faculty members who work closely with students to help them achieve their professional goals. Students often have the opportunity to coauthor scholarly papers, books, and professional presentations with faculty members. The Department of Psychology at PCOM offers a cognitive-behavioral theoretical orientation and teaches students to apply empirically-supported approaches in delivering clinical services. PCOM has one of the only psychology departments in the country that provides a standardized patient program for student training. The standardized patient program presents authentic clinical learning and skills situations in which "patients" simulate mental health conditions. Students conduct sessions with the patients, which are videotaped and reviewed by the faculty members to help train and assess students' skills. Students in the psychology programs may also have the opportunity for clinical experience at any of the College's urban health-care centers.

The 89-credit Psy.D. in clinical psychology program is designed to be completed in five years, including course work, practicum, internship, and dissertation. Graduates of this program are prepared to assume responsibilities in a broad range of clinical settings. Post-doctoral certificates in clinical health psychology and clinical neuropsychology will each provide one year (16 and 19 credits respectively) of post-doctoral specialty training to doctoral-level psychologists. The 65-credit Psy.D. in school psychology program is designed for certified school psychologists and can be completed in three years. The fourteen-month, 33-credit M.S. in school psychology program has an applied behavior analysis emphasis and prepares paraprofessionals in community and school settings to provide mental health services to children, youth, and families. This program, taken in sequence with the Ed.S. degree program, leads to certification in school psychology and also provides the required coursework to continue to accrue supervised experience towards behavior analysis certification (BCBA). The three-year, 45-credit Ed.S. program provides students with the knowledge and skills to assume the role of a school psychologist in diverse settings. The two-year M.S. in mental health counseling program has 48-credit and 60-credit options and trains graduates to provide evaluation, counseling, and therapy services to clients in a variety of clinical settings. Students in this program may complete concentrations in addictions and offender counseling or professional counseling. A Certificate of Advanced Graduate Study is offered for students who have already earned a master's degree and wish to complete an additional 12–18 credits at the master's level. The 36-credit M.S. in organizational development and leadership (ODL) program uses a unique combination of organizational theory and individual self-discovery to provide an essential leadership perspective in creating organizational change. Designed for the working professional, all classes for the M.S., Ed.S., CAGS, and Psy.D. programs are held in the evening and on weekends on the Philadelphia campus.

Research Facilities

The academic facilities at PCOM include state-of-the-art amphitheaters, classroom facilities, and standardized patient labs; a wireless campus and computer laboratories with extensive software, including PsycLIT and SPSS; a comfortable, sophisticated library with online access to electronic textbooks, journals, databases, and Internet guides; and access to the digital library and statistical programs through the Internet.

Financial Aid

The Financial Aid Office at PCOM offers financial assistance to students through the Federal Direct Loan program, institutional grants, and various alternative private loan programs.

Cost of Study

In 2015–16, the direct tuition costs of attending PCOM (including tuition, fees, books, and supplies) for the first year are approximately $24,177 for mental health counseling M.S. students, based on enrollment of 27 credits; $23,633 for school psychology M.S. students, based on enrollment of 27 credits; $8,331 for ODL M.S. students, based on enrollment of 9 credits; $17,505 for Ed.S. students, based on enrollment of 21 credits; $36,755 for Psy.D. in clinical psychology students, based on enrollment of 31 credits; and $31,481 for Psy.D. in school psychology students, based on enrollment of 28 credits

Living and Housing Costs

Students live off-campus within the Philadelphia metropolitan and suburban areas, as there is no on-campus housing. Room and board costs vary by each student's individual preferences.

Student Group

The programs seek a diverse group of students who are committed to excellence. The Psy.D. in clinical psychology program recruits in-practice professionals who have earned master's degrees in psychology, social work, counseling, psychiatric nursing, or a related field and are working in human services. This population brings to their studies a high level of maturity, established skills, diverse backgrounds, and a strong motivation to succeed. The Psy.D. in school psychology program recruits working school psychologists who want to be leaders in psychoeducational and mental health services to children, youth, and families. Students entering the Ed.S. program typically have completed master's degrees in psychology or education and have been working with school-aged children in some capacity. Candidates for the M.S. programs typically are working professionals and have bachelor's degrees in varying fields, having completed specific prerequisite courses. For 2014, the entering clinical psychology Psy.D. class had 26 students (selected from a pool of 134), with 73 percent women, 31 percent members of minority groups, and an average age of 27. The Psy.D. in school psychology program had a class of 15 students (selected from a pool of 23), with 73 percent women, 20 percent members of minority groups, and an average age of 34. The M.S. program in mental health counseling totaled 31 students (selected from a pool of 100), with 93 percent women, 35 percent members of minority groups, and an average age of 25. The Ed.S. program in school psychology numbered 10 students (selected from a pool of 20), with 80 percent women, 10 percent members of minority groups, and an average age of 28. The M.S. program in school psychology had 20 new students, (selected from a pool of 50), with 95 percent women, no members of minority groups, and an average age of 26. The M.S. program in organizational development and leadership enrolled 11 new students (selected from a pool of 18), with 82 percent women, 45 percent members of minority groups, and an average age of 33.

Location

Philadelphia College of Osteopathic Medicine is one of the largest of thirty-one osteopathic colleges in the United States, with campuses in both Philadelphia and suburban Atlanta. Psychology programs are offered only on the Philadelphia campus, which is located in a suburban setting on City Avenue, minutes away from Fairmount Park, Philadelphia's historic district, art museums, theaters, restaurants, and professional sports complexes. PCOM's facilities include two large lecture halls, small classrooms, labs for teaching and research, a state-of-the-art library, and scenic landscaping, all in a suburban setting.

The College and The Programs

PCOM, chartered in 1899, enrolls approximately 2,600 students in its various programs across both campuses. The clinical and teaching facility in Philadelphia makes an ideal home for psychology graduate programs. The graduate psychology programs at PCOM are accredited by the Department of Education of the Commonwealth of Pennsylvania and the Middle States Association of Colleges and Schools. The Psy.D. in clinical psychology program is accredited by the American Psychological Association and fulfills the requirements of the National Register for Healthcare Providers in Psychology. Clinical Psy.D. in clinical psychology graduates qualify to take the Examination for Professional Practice of Psychology Licensure in Pennsylvania and New Jersey. The curriculum provides Psy.D. in school psychology students with the knowledge and skills to assume the role of a school psychologist, practice in a variety of settings, and be prepared for eligibility for National Certification and for Pennsylvania licensure. The school psychology M.S., Ed.S., and Psy.D. programs have been approved by the National Association of School Psychologists. The M.S. in School Psychology course sequence is approved by the Behavior Analyst Certification Board (BACB). The M.S. in school psychology and CAGS in applied behavioral analysis course sequences are approved by the Behavior Analyst Certification Board (BACB). The M.S. program in mental health counseling has been designed to fulfill the Licensed Professional Counselor curriculum requirements in Pennsylvania and New Jersey.

Applying

Mental health counseling M.S. applicants need to have a baccalaureate degree from a regionally accredited institution, with basic psychology course work (introduction to psychology, abnormal psychology or psychopathology, and statistics). Psy.D. in clinical psychology applicants must have completed a master's degree in psychology or a related field at a regionally accredited institution and also completed developmental psychology, theories of personality, abnormal psychology or psychopathology, and statistics. Those applying to the certificate of advanced graduate studies program must have completed a master's degree in psychology or related field. Candidates for the post-doctoral certificate programs must have completed a doctoral degree in clinical psychology at a regionally accredited institution. Applicants to the M.S. in school psychology need to have a baccalaureate degree in psychology, education, or a related field from a regionally accredited institution and must have completed 6 credits each of English and math plus 15 credits in psychology or a related field. Applicants to either M.S. program in school psychology or mental health counseling must have taken the GRE or MAT exam. Applicants to the ODL program must have completed a bachelor's degree from a regionally accredited institution. Applicants to the Ed.S. program must

Philadelphia College of Osteopathic Medicine

have a master's degree in school psychology or a related field and must submit test scores from the GRE Psychology Subtest #81. Applicants to the Psy.D. in school psychology program must have a master's and specialist degree in school psychology and must be a licensed school psychologist. Candidates must also submit scores from the Praxis II School Psychology Specialty exam. All applicants to Psychology Department programs must submit official college transcripts from all schools attended and as many as three letters of recommendation with accompanying recommendation forms, along with a $75 application fee. Most programs require a specified writing sample and autobiographical statement. All programs utilize a rolling admissions policy. Finalists for all programs interview with the Admissions Committee and are then notified in writing of the committee's decision.

Correspondence and Information

Office of Admissions
Philadelphia College of Osteopathic Medicine
4170 City Avenue
Philadelphia, Pennsylvania 19131-1694
Phone: 215-871-6700
        800-999-6998 (toll-free)
Fax: 215-871-6719
E-mail: Admissions@pcom.edu
Website: http://admissions.pcom.edu

THE FACULTY AND THEIR RESEARCH

Robert A. DiTomasso, Ph.D., ABPP, Professor; Chair, Department of Psychology; and Director, Institutional Outcomes Assessment. Dr. DiTomasso has extensive teaching experience and has published dozens of chapters, articles, reviews, and books. He specializes in behavioral medicine, the cognitive behavioral treatment of anxiety and stress-related medical disorders, research design, psychometrics, methodology, program evaluation, and primary-care consultation. He also specializes in patient nonadherence to medical advice and instrument development for cognitive distortions, anger, health risk behaviors, and patient satisfaction with medical services.

Stephanie Felgoise, Ph.D., ABPP, Professor; Vice Chair, Department of Psychology; and Director, Doctor of Psychology in Clinical Psychology. Dr. Felgoise's research focuses on quality of life in, and psychosocial aspects of, ALS (Lou Gherig's Disease) and Long QT Syndrome (LQTS, a life-threatening cardiac arrhythmia condition). Research on these topics has emphasized factors relating to quality of life; social problem-solving, coping, and adjustment; resilience factors (hope, optimism, spirituality); and comorbid psychological conditions (i.e., anxiety, depression). She has also coauthored numerous national conference presentations and publications in psycho-oncology, sexual health and dysfunction, and coping and adjustment with chronic medical illness.

Sarah Levin Allen, Ph.D., CBIS, Assistant Professor. Dr. Allen specializes in the area of evidence-based interventions for schools as well as in schoolwide concussion management and recovery programming. Her work focuses on translating medical and neuropsychological intervention to schools, specifically promoting and integrating brain-based learning approaches into the classroom. She has a primary interest and expertise in building executive functioning skills through interventions that combine neuropsychology with behavioral approaches.

Jeffrey Branch, Ed.D., Assistant Professor and Director, Organizational Development and Leadership. Dr. Branch has extensive experience in organizational consultation and has held various leadership positions. His research and teaching expertise includes the intentional design and engagement of mentoring and coaching practices as a multidimensional curricular and cocurricular teaching and learning strategy to promote practitioner development.

Stacey C. Cahn, Ph.D., Associate Professor. Dr. Cahn's area of expertise is broadly clinical health psychology, including eating disorders, as well as the areas of sleep, depression in heart disease, and aging.

William Clinton, M.A., Instructor. Mr. Clinton has extensive experience in organizational consultation and has held various leadership positions. His specialty is in training practitioners to become effective leaders who implement change in organizational settings.

Terri Erbacher, Ph.D., Clinical Assistant Professor. Dr. Erbacher is a certified school psychologist and licensed psychologist. Her specific population and program expertise includes nonpublic elementary and secondary schools, autistic support, learning support, early intervention, and supervision of school psychology interns.

Jessica Glass Kendorski, Ph.D., NCSP, BCBA-D, Associate Professor and Director, M.S. in School Psychology. Dr. Kendorski is a certified school psychologist and board-certified behavior analyst. Her clinical experiences and research interests include data-based assessment and interventions in the residential and school settings, specifically, response to intervention, curriculum-based measurement, positive behavior support, and applied behavior analysis. She has extensive experience in supporting the emotional, social, and behavioral needs of children diagnosed with developmental disabilities.

Scott Glassman, Psy.D., Clinical Assistant Professor and Associate Director, M.S. in mental health counseling. Dr. Glassman's major areas of interest and expertise include motivational interviewing, primary care psychology, the patient centered medical home, cognitive behavioral approaches, psychological consultation, serious mental illness, and statistical methods.

Barbara Golden, Psy.D., ABPP, Professor and Director, Clinical Services. Dr. Golden's experience includes clinical service, administration, supervision, consultation, and education. Her primary areas of interest and research are in behavioral medicine, including nonpharmacological pain management, stress management, and somatization disorder, as well as in psychology and primary-care medicine.

Elizabeth Gosch, Ph.D., ABPP, Professor and Director, M.S. in mental health counseling. One of Dr. Gosch's primary areas of expertise is psychotherapy with children and adolescents. Her major research interest concerns the processes and effectiveness of psychotherapy with differing populations. She has published and lectured internationally on the cognitive behavioral treatment of anxiety in children.

Donald Masey, Psy.D., Clinical Associate Professor. Dr. Masey's research interests include memory and aging, psychological assessment, hospital practice for psychologists, practice models and issues in professional psychology, medical psychology, adult learning disabilities, and adult ADHD.

George McCloskey, Ph.D., Professor and Director of Research (School Psychology). Dr. McCloskey has accumulated a broad range of work experiences in the field of psychology over the last twenty-five years, including research, clinical work, administration, teaching, and business. His research and interests include neuropsychological process and learning, psychological and educational assessment and intervention, reading achievement, ADHD, executive dysfunction, memory problems, and expression disability.

Susan Panichelli Mindel, Ph.D., Assistant Professor and Director of Research (Clinical Psychology). Dr. Mindel has extensive experience in the delivery of cognitive-behavioral empirically supported treatments in children and adolescents. Her research interests include issues in clinical child psychology, with an emphasis on the prevention and treatment of anxiety disorders as well as diagnostic differences and treatment of subtypes of ADHD.

Stephen Poteau, Ph.D., Assistant Professor. Dr. Poteau's research interests include the implicit measurement of cognitive processes/implicit cognition, terror management theory, and social cognition/psychology.

Bradley Rosenfield, Psy.D., Assistant Professor. Dr. Rosenfield's research interests include cognitive behavioral therapy for adult ADHD, human-animal interactions, depressive disorders, somatic disorders, anxiety disorders, single session treatment for panic attacks, the social psychology of terrorism, multicultural counseling, communication skills, and treating difficult patients.

Virginia Burks Salzer, Ph.D., Associate Professor. Dr. Salzer's research interests include social information processing in the development of children's aggressive behavior, linkages between family and children's peer systems, comorbidity of children's externalizing and internalizing disorders, and impact of parental psychopathology and the development of childhood disorders.

Diane Smallwood, Psy.D., NCSP, Professor and Director, Ed.S. and Professional Education in School Psychology. In addition to school-based work experience, for the past twenty years, Dr. Smallwood has been involved in leadership activities at both the state and national levels. Her professional interests include school crisis prevention, intervention, and response; social-emotional learning; classroom resiliency; bullying and violence in schools; and translating research to practice.

Celine I. Thompson, Ph.D., Assistant Professor. Dr. Thompson's research interests include intersectionality, classroom social justice, and program evaluation. She has research experience working with minority youth around social-emotional skills development, as well as research experience working on smoking cessation projects.

Yuma I. Tomes, Ph.D., Associate Professor and Director, Doctor of Psychology in School Psychology. Dr. Tomes has accumulated a diverse range of work experiences in the field of psychology and education over the last ten years. He brings a unique perspective of clinical, teaching, research, and administrative experience to his position at PCOM. Dr. Tomes has worked as a psychologist in urban school districts. His major areas of interest are cross-cultural psychology, multicultural assessment, cognitive/learning styles, cognition and learning theories, psychological/educational assessments, consultation, and developmental issues.

Katy Tresco, Ph.D, Assistant Professor and Director of Training (School Psychology). Dr. Tresco has worked extensively with children and adolescents with ADHD and their families and continues to pursue research and clinical interests pertaining to assessment and intervention for externalizing behavior problems. Dr. Tresco's professional interests also include behavioral and collaborative consultation techniques and outcomes; home-school collaboration; response to intervention; and the use of school-based data-driven decision making, program evaluation, and improving access to and implementation of evidenced-based services for schools and families from undeserved and culturally diverse populations.

Beverly White, Psy.D., Clinical Assistant Professor and Assistant Director of Clinical Services. Dr. White has worked extensively with traumatized children and adolescents. She has published and has research interests in the areas of psychological assessment, dreams in CBT-oriented treatment, and crisis/trauma, post-traumatic stress, and CBT interventions. Other research interests include right/left-hemisphere performance and malfunction and multicultural issues.

Bruce Zahn, Ed.D., ABPP, Professor and Director of Clinical Training (Clinical Psychology). Dr. Zahn has published on cognitive behavioral therapy, childhood sexual abuse, multimodal therapy programs for adolescents, and psychological functioning in survivors of traumatic brain injury. His areas of expertise include geropsychology, behavioral medicine, cognitive behavioral therapy, self-esteem, group therapy, and supervision. Dr. Zahn's mentoring and research interests are in the areas of psychological testing (including projective personality assessment), post-traumatic stress disorder, managed-care issues, and chronic mental illness.

PCOM provides a collaborative learning environment for students.

Section 25
Public, Regional, and Industrial Affairs

This section contains a directory of institutions offering graduate work in public, regional, and industrial affairs, followed by an in-depth entry submitted by an institution that chose to prepare a detailed program description. Additional information about programs listed in the directory but not augmented by an in-depth entry may be obtained by writing directly to the dean of a graduate school or chair of a department at the address given in the directory.

For programs offering related work, see also in this book *Architecture, Area and Cultural Studies, Criminology and Forensics, Economics, Humanities, Political Science and International Affairs,* and *Sociology, Anthropology, and Archaeology.* In the other guides in this series:

Graduate Programs in the Biological/Biomedical Sciences & Health-Related Medical Professions

See *Public Health*

Graduate Programs in the Physical Sciences, Mathematics, Agricultural Sciences, the Environment & Natural Resources

See *Environmental Sciences and Management*

Graduate Programs in Engineering & Applied Sciences

See *Management of Engineering and Technology*

Graduate Programs in Business, Education, Information Studies, Law & Social Work

See *Business Administration and Management* and *Law*

CONTENTS

Disability Studies

Brandeis University, The Heller School for Social Policy and Management, Program in Social Policy, Waltham, MA 02454-9110. Offers assets and inequalities (PhD); children, youth and families (PhD); global health and development (PhD); health and behavioral health (PhD). *Degree requirements:* For doctorate, comprehensive exam, thesis/dissertation, qualifying paper, 2-year residency. *Entrance requirements:* For doctorate, GRE General Test, 3 letters of recommendation, statement of purpose, writing sample, at least 3-5 years of professional experience. Additional exam requirements/recommendations for international students: Required—TOEFL (minimum score 600 paper-based; 100 iBT). Electronic applications accepted. *Faculty research:* Health; mental health; substance abuse; children, youth, and families; aging; international and community development; disabilities; work and inequality; hunger and poverty.

Brock University, Faculty of Graduate Studies, Faculty of Social Sciences, Program in Applied Disability Studies, St. Catharines, ON L2S 3A1, Canada. Offers MA, MADS, Diploma. Part-time programs available. *Degree requirements:* For master's, thesis (for some programs). *Entrance requirements:* For master's, honors degree. Additional exam requirements/recommendations for international students: Required—TOEFL (minimum score 550 paper-based; 80 iBT), IELTS (minimum score 6.5). Electronic applications accepted.

California Baptist University, Program in Disability Studies, Riverside, CA 92503. Offers disability ministry (MA); disability policy (MA). Part-time and evening/weekend programs available. Postbaccalaureate distance learning degree programs offered (no on-campus study). *Faculty:* 3 full-time (1 woman), 3 part-time/adjunct (1 woman). *Students:* 1 (woman) full-time, 24 part-time (20 women); includes 14 minority (6 Black or African American, non-Hispanic/Latino; 1 Asian, non-Hispanic/Latino; 6 Hispanic/Latino; 1 Two or more races, non-Hispanic/Latino). Average age 39. 25 applicants, 64% accepted, 9 enrolled. In 2014, 6 master's awarded. *Degree requirements:* For master's, research thesis or capstone project. *Entrance requirements:* For master's, minimum undergraduate GPA of 2.75; transcripts of bachelor's degree; background in disability studies through coursework, degree, or experience; three recommendations; 500-word essay; interview. Additional exam requirements/recommendations for international students: Required—TOEFL (minimum score 80 iBT). *Application deadline:* For fall admission, 8/1 priority date for domestic students, 7/1 for international students; for spring admission, 12/1 priority date for domestic students, 11/1 for international students. Applications are processed on a rolling basis. Application fee: $45. Electronic applications accepted. *Expenses:* Expenses: Contact institution. *Financial support:* Institutionally sponsored loans available. Financial award applicants required to submit CSS PROFILE or FAFSA. *Faculty research:* Community integration of adults with disability, models of disability, Biblical perspectives on disability, building social competence in adolescents with Asperger's syndrome. *Unit head:* Dr. David Poole, Vice President, Online and Professional Studies, 951-343-3901, E-mail: dpoole@calbaptist.edu. *Application contact:* Dr. Jeff McNair, Program Director, MA in Disability Studies, 951-343-4489, E-mail: jmcnair@calbaptist.edu.
Website: http://www.cbuonline.edu/programs/program/master-of-arts-in-disability-studies

Chapman University, College of Educational Studies, Orange, CA 92866. Offers communication sciences and disorders (MS); counseling (MA), including school counseling (MA, Credential); education (PhD), including cultural and curricular studies, disability studies, leadership studies, school psychology (PhD, Credential); educational psychology (MA); leadership development (MA); pupil personnel services (Credential), including school counseling (MA, Credential), school psychology (PhD, Credential); school psychology (Ed S); single subject (Credential); special education (MA, Credential), including mild/moderate (Credential), moderate/severe (Credential); speech language pathology (Credential); teaching (MA), including elementary education, secondary education. *Accreditation:* Teacher Education Accreditation Council. Part-time and evening/weekend programs available. *Faculty:* 31 full-time (18 women), 78 part-time/adjunct (61 women). *Students:* 257 full-time (206 women), 187 part-time (141 women); includes 186 minority (9 Black or African American, non-Hispanic/Latino; 54 Asian, non-Hispanic/Latino; 104 Hispanic/Latino; 1 Native Hawaiian or other Pacific Islander, non-Hispanic/Latino; 18 Two or more races, non-Hispanic/Latino), 10 international. Average age 29. 614 applicants, 35% accepted, 131 enrolled. In 2014, 128 master's, 10 doctorates awarded. *Entrance requirements:* Additional exam requirements/recommendations for international students: Required—TOEFL (minimum score 550 paper-based; 80 iBT). *Application deadline:* Applications are processed on a rolling basis. Application fee: $60. Electronic applications accepted. *Financial support:* Fellowships and scholarships/grants available. Financial award application deadline: 6/30; financial award applicants required to submit FAFSA. *Unit head:* Dr. Don Cardinal, Dean, 714-997-6781, E-mail: cardinal@chapman.edu. *Application contact:* Admissions Coordinator, 714-997-6714.
Website: http://www.chapman.edu/CES/

Montclair State University, The Graduate School, College of Education and Human Services, Developmental Models of Autism Intervention Certificate Program, Montclair, NJ 07043-1624. Offers Certificate. Part-time and evening/weekend programs available. *Students:* 4 full-time (all women), 12 part-time (9 women); includes 4 minority (1 Black or African American, non-Hispanic/Latino; 1 Asian, non-Hispanic/Latino; 2 Hispanic/Latino). Average age 35. 2 applicants, 100% accepted, 2 enrolled. In 2014, 7 Certificates awarded. *Entrance requirements:* Additional exam requirements/recommendations for international students: Required—TOEFL (minimum score 83 iBT), IELTS (minimum score 6.5). *Application deadline:* Applications are processed on a rolling basis. Application fee: $60. Electronic applications accepted. *Expenses:* Tuition, state resident: full-time $9960; part-time $553.35 per credit. Tuition, nonresident: full-time $15,074; part-time $837.43 per credit. Required fees: $1595; $88.63 per credit. Tuition and fees vary according to degree level and program. *Financial support:* Scholarships/grants and unspecified assistantships available. Support available to part-time students. Financial award application deadline: 3/1; financial award applicants required to submit FAFSA. *Unit head:* Dr. Tina Jacobowitz, Chairperson, 973-655-7191. *Application contact:* Amy Aiello, Executive Director of The Graduate School, 973-655-5147, Fax: 973-655-7869, E-mail: graduate.school@montclair.edu.
Website: http://www.montclair.edu/catalog/view_requirements.php?CurriculumID=3050

Montclair State University, The Graduate School, College of Education and Human Services, Program in Learning Disabilities, Montclair, NJ 07043-1624. Offers M Ed. Part-time and evening/weekend programs available. *Students:* 26 part-time (24 women); includes 2 minority (both Hispanic/Latino). Average age 30. 11 applicants, 64% accepted, 7 enrolled. In 2014, 8 master's awarded. *Degree requirements:* For master's, comprehensive exam, thesis or alternative. *Entrance requirements:* For master's, GRE General Test, interview, 2 letters of recommendation. Additional exam requirements/recommendations for international students: Required—TOEFL (minimum score 83 iBT), IELTS (minimum score 6.5). *Application deadline:* Applications are processed on a rolling basis. Application fee: $60. Electronic applications accepted. *Expenses:* Tuition, state resident: full-time $9960; part-time $553.35 per credit. Tuition, nonresident: full-time $15,074; part-time $837.43 per credit. Required fees: $1595; $88.63 per credit. Tuition and fees vary according to degree level and program. *Financial support:* Federal Work-Study, scholarships/grants, and unspecified assistantships available. Support available to part-time students. Financial award application deadline: 3/1; financial award applicants required to submit FAFSA. *Unit head:* Dr. David Schwarzer, Chairperson, 973-655-5187. *Application contact:* Amy Aiello, Executive Director of The Graduate School, 973-655-5147, Fax: 973-655-7869, E-mail: graduate.school@montclair.edu.
Website: http://www.montclair.edu/cehs/academics/departments/sse/academic-programs/med-learning-disability/

Syracuse University, School of Education, Program in Disability Studies, Syracuse, NY 13244. Offers CAS. Part-time programs available. *Students:* 1 (woman) part-time. Average age 57. 3 applicants, 100% accepted, 1 enrolled. In 2014, 8 CASs awarded. *Entrance requirements:* Additional exam requirements/recommendations for international students: Required—TOEFL (minimum score 100 iBT). *Application deadline:* For fall admission, 1/15 priority date for domestic and international students; for spring admission, 10/15 priority date for domestic and international students. Applications are processed on a rolling basis. Application fee: $75. Electronic applications accepted. *Expenses: Tuition:* Part-time $1341 per credit. *Financial support:* Application deadline: 1/1. *Unit head:* Dr. Alan Foley, Program Coordinator, 315-443-3343, E-mail: isabilitystudies@syr.edu. *Application contact:* Laurie Deyo, Graduate Recruiter, School of Education, 315-443-2505, E-mail: e-gradrcrt@syr.edu.
Website: http://soeweb.syr.edu/

University of Hawaii at Manoa, Graduate Division, College of Education, Program in Disability and Diversity Studies, Honolulu, HI 96822. Offers Graduate Certificate. Part-time programs available. *Entrance requirements:* Additional exam requirements/recommendations for international students: Required—TOEFL (minimum score 500 paper-based; 61 iBT), IELTS (minimum score 5).

University of Illinois at Chicago, Graduate College, College of Applied Health Sciences, Department of Disability and Human Development, Chicago, IL 60607-7128. Offers disability and human development (MS). *Accreditation:* AOTA. Part-time programs available. *Faculty:* 10 full-time (7 women), 2 part-time/adjunct (1 woman). *Students:* 36 full-time (28 women), 21 part-time (18 women); includes 11 minority (1 Black or African American, non-Hispanic/Latino; 2 Asian, non-Hispanic/Latino; 5 Hispanic/Latino; 3 Two or more races, non-Hispanic/Latino), 11 international. Average age 34. 34 applicants, 65% accepted, 12 enrolled. In 2014, 6 master's, 2 doctorates awarded. *Degree requirements:* For master's, thesis optional; for doctorate, thesis/dissertation. *Entrance requirements:* For master's and doctorate, GRE General Test. Additional exam requirements/recommendations for international students: Required—TOEFL. *Application deadline:* For fall admission, 1/1 for domestic and international students; for spring admission, 10/1 for domestic students, 7/15 for international students. Applications are processed on a rolling basis. Application fee: $60. Electronic applications accepted. *Expenses:* Tuition, state resident: full-time $11,254; part-time $468 per credit hour. Tuition, nonresident: full-time $23,252; part-time $968 per credit hour. Required fees: $1217 per term. Part-time tuition and fees vary according to course load, degree level and program. *Financial support:* In 2014–15, 2 fellowships with full tuition reimbursements were awarded; research assistantships with full tuition reimbursements, teaching assistantships with full tuition reimbursements, career-related internships or fieldwork, Federal Work-Study, institutionally sponsored loans, traineeships, tuition waivers (full), and unspecified assistantships also available. Financial award application deadline: 3/1; financial award applicants required to submit FAFSA. *Faculty research:* Emerging trends in disability, demography and financial structure of disability services, aging and disability, empowerment of people with disabilities, health promotion in disabilities. *Total annual research expenditures:* $5.7 million. *Unit head:* Prof. Tamar Heller, Department Head, 312-996-1647, Fax: 312-413-1630, E-mail: theller@uic.edu. *Application contact:* Dr. Maitha Abogado, Support Staff, 312-413-1466, Fax: 312-413-1630, E-mail: maitha@uic.edu.
Website: http://www.ahs.uic.edu/dhd/

University of Manitoba, Faculty of Graduate Studies, Interdisciplinary Programs, Program in Disability Studies, Winnipeg, MB R3T 2N2, Canada. Offers M Sc, MA.

University of Northern British Columbia, Office of Graduate Studies, Prince George, BC V2N 4Z9, Canada. Offers business administration (Diploma); community health science (M Sc); disability management (MA); education (M Ed); first nations studies (MA); gender studies (MA); history (MA); interdisciplinary studies (MA); international studies (MA); mathematical, computer and physical sciences (M Sc); natural resources and environmental studies (M Sc, MA, MNRES, PhD); political science (MA); psychology (M Sc, PhD); social work (MSW). Part-time and evening/weekend programs available. Postbaccalaureate distance learning degree programs offered (no on-campus study). *Degree requirements:* For master's, thesis; for doctorate, thesis/dissertation. *Entrance requirements:* For master's, GRE, minimum B average in undergraduate course work; for doctorate, candidacy exam, minimum A average in graduate course work.

University of Pittsburgh, School of Law, Certificate Program in Disability Legal Studies, Pittsburgh, PA 15260. Offers Certificate. Part-time programs available. *Faculty:* 36 full-time (13 women), 120 part-time/adjunct (33 women). *Entrance requirements:* For degree, official transcript, two letters of recommendation, essay. *Application deadline:* For fall admission, 12/1 priority date for domestic students. Applications are processed on a rolling basis. *Expenses:* Tuition, state resident: full-time $20,742; part-time $838 per credit. Tuition, nonresident: full-time $33,960; part-time $1389 per credit. Required fees: $800; $205 per term. Tuition and fees vary according to program. *Financial support:* Institutionally sponsored loans available. *Unit head:* Prof. Alan Meisel, Director, 412-648-7120, Fax: 412-648-2649, E-mail: dlcert@pitt.edu. *Application contact:* Beth Ann Pischke, Assistant Dean of Admissions and Financial Aid, 412-648-7120, Fax: 412-648-2649, E-mail: pischke@pitt.edu.
Website: http://law.pitt.edu/academics/non-lawyers/dls

Utah State University, School of Graduate Studies, Emma Eccles Jones College of Education and Human Services, Department of Special Education and Rehabilitation, Logan, UT 84322. Offers disability disciplines (PhD); rehabilitation counselor education (MRC); special education (M Ed, MS, Ed S). Part-time programs available. Postbaccalaureate distance learning degree programs offered (minimal on-campus

study). *Degree requirements:* For master's, thesis (for some programs), internships (for some programs); for doctorate, comprehensive exam, thesis/dissertation. *Entrance requirements:* For master's and doctorate, GRE General Test, minimum GPA of 3.0. Additional exam requirements/recommendations for international students: Required— TOEFL (minimum score 550 paper-based). Electronic applications accepted. *Faculty research:* Applied behavior analysis, effective instructional practices, early childhood teacher training research, distance education, multicultural rehabilitation.

York University, Faculty of Graduate Studies, Faculty of Health, Program in Critical Disability Studies, Toronto, ON M3J 1P3, Canada. Offers MA, PhD. *Degree requirements:* For master's, thesis or alternative. *Entrance requirements:* Additional exam requirements/recommendations for international students: Required—TOEFL (minimum score 600 paper-based). Electronic applications accepted.

Emergency Management

Adelphi University, University College, Graduate Certificate in Emergency Management Program, Garden City, NY 11530-0701. Offers Certificate. Part-time and evening/weekend programs available. *Students:* 7 full-time (2 women), 17 part-time (9 women); includes 7 minority (4 Black or African American, non-Hispanic/Latino; 1 Asian, non-Hispanic/Latino; 1 Native Hawaiian or other Pacific Islander, non-Hispanic/Latino; 1 Two or more races, non-Hispanic/Latino). Average age 36. In 2014, 2 Certificates awarded. *Application deadline:* For fall admission, 5/1 for international students; for spring admission, 12/1 for international students. Applications are processed on a rolling basis. Application fee: $50. Electronic applications accepted. *Faculty research:* Emergency nursing, disaster management, disaster preparedness. *Unit head:* Shawn O'Riley, Dean, 516-877-3412, E-mail: ucinfo@adelphi.edu. *Application contact:* Christine Murphy, Director of Admissions, 516-877-3050, Fax: 516-877-3039, E-mail: graduateadmissions@adelphi.edu.
Website: http://academics.adelphi.edu/universitycollege/emergency-management-certificate.php

Adler University, Programs in Psychology, Chicago, IL 60602. Offers advanced Adlerian psychotherapy (Certificate); art therapy (MA); clinical neuropsychology (Certificate); clinical psychology (Psy D); community psychology (MA); counseling and organizational psychology (MA); counseling psychology (MA); criminology (MA); emergency management leadership (MA); forensic psychology (MA); marriage and family counseling (MA); marriage and family therapy (Certificate); military psychology (MA); nonprofit management (MA); organizational psychology (MA); police psychology (MA); public policy and administration (MA); rehabilitation counseling (MA); sport and health psychology (MA); substance abuse counseling (Certificate); Psy D/Certificate; Psy D/MACAT; Psy D/MACP; Psy D/MAMFC; Psy D/MASAC. *Accreditation:* APA. Part-time and evening/weekend programs available. Postbaccalaureate distance learning degree programs offered (minimal on-campus study). Terminal master's awarded for partial completion of doctoral program. *Degree requirements:* For master's, thesis or alternative, oral exam, practicum; for doctorate, thesis/dissertation, clinical exam, internship, oral exam, practicum, written qualifying exam. *Entrance requirements:* For master's, 12 semester hours in psychology, minimum GPA of 3.0; for doctorate, 18 semester hours in psychology, minimum GPA of 3.25; for Certificate, appropriate master's or doctoral degree. Additional exam requirements/recommendations for international students: Required—TOEFL (minimum score 550 paper-based; 79 iBT). Electronic applications accepted.

See Display on page 969 and Close-Up on page 1207.

American Public University System, AMU/APU Graduate Programs, Charles Town, WV 25414. Offers accounting (MBA, MS); criminal justice (MA), including business administration, emergency and disaster management, general (MA, MS); educational leadership (M Ed); emergency and disaster management (MA); entrepreneurship (MBA); environmental policy and management (MS), including environmental planning, environmental sustainability, fish and wildlife management, general (MA, MS), global environmental management; finance (MBA); general (MBA); global business management (MBA); history (MA), including American history, ancient and classical history, European history, global history, public history; homeland security (MA), including business administration, counter-terrorism studies, criminal justice, cyber, emergency management and public health, intelligence studies, transportation security; homeland security resource allocation (MBA); humanities (MA); information technology (MS), including digital forensics, enterprise software development, information assurance and security, IT project management; information technology management (MBA); intelligence studies (MA), including criminal intelligence, cyber, general (MA, MS), homeland security, intelligence analysis, intelligence collection, intelligence management, intelligence operations, terrorism studies; international relations and conflict resolution (MA), including comparative and security issues, conflict resolution, international and transnational security issues, peacekeeping; legal studies (MA); management (MA), including defense management, general (MA, MS), human resource management, organizational leadership, public administration; marketing (MBA); military history (MA), including American military history, American Revolution, civil war, war since 1945, World War II; military studies (MA), including joint warfare, strategic leadership; national security studies (MA), including general (MA, MS), homeland security, regional security studies, security and intelligence analysis, terrorism studies; nonprofit management (MBA); political science (MA), including American politics and government, comparative government and development, general (MA, MS), international relations, public policy; psychology (MA); public administration (MPA), including disaster management, environmental policy, health policy, human resources, national security, organizational management, security management; public health (MPH); reverse logistics management (MA); school counseling (M Ed); security management (MA); space studies (MS), including aerospace science, general (MA, MS), planetary science; sports and health sciences (MS); teaching (M Ed), including curriculum and instruction for elementary teachers, elementary reading, English language learners, instructional leadership, online learning, special education; transportation and logistics management (MA), including general (MA, MS), maritime engineering management, reverse logistics management. Programs offered via distance learning only. Part-time and evening/weekend programs available. Postbaccalaureate distance learning degree programs offered (no on-campus study). *Faculty:* 426 full-time (236 women), 1,864 part-time/adjunct (880 women). *Students:* 475 full-time (215 women), 10,067 part-time (4,085 women); includes 3,462 minority (1,863 Black or African American, non-Hispanic/Latino; 74 American Indian or Alaska Native, non-Hispanic/Latino; 273 Asian, non-Hispanic/Latino; 831 Hispanic/Latino; 78 Native Hawaiian or other Pacific Islander, non-Hispanic/Latino; 343 Two or more races, non-Hispanic/Latino), 131 international. Average age 36. In 2014, 3,740 master's awarded. *Degree requirements:* For master's, comprehensive exam or practicum. *Entrance requirements:* For master's, official transcript showing earned bachelor's degree from institution accredited by recognized accrediting body. Additional exam requirements/recommendations for international students: Required—TOEFL (minimum score 550 paper-based), IELTS (minimum score 6.5). *Application deadline:* Applications are

processed on a rolling basis. Application fee: $0. Electronic applications accepted. *Financial support:* Applicants required to submit FAFSA. *Faculty research:* Military history, criminal justice, management performance, national security. *Unit head:* Dr. Karan Powell, Executive Vice President and Provost, 877-468-6268, Fax: 304-724-3780. *Application contact:* Terry Grant, Vice President of Enrollment Management, 877-468-6268, Fax: 304-724-3780, E-mail: info@apus.edu.
Website: http://www.apus.edu

Anna Maria College, Graduate Division, Program in Emergency Management, Paxton, MA 01612. Offers MS, Graduate Certificate. Part-time and evening/weekend programs available. *Degree requirements:* For master's, thesis. *Entrance requirements:* For master's, minimum GPA of 2.7. Additional exam requirements/recommendations for international students: Required—TOEFL (minimum score 500 paper-based). Electronic applications accepted.

Arizona State University at the Tempe campus, College of Public Programs, School of Public Affairs, Phoenix, AZ 85004-0687. Offers emergency management and homeland security (MA); program evaluation (MS); public administration (MPA, PhD), including nonprofit administration (MPA), urban management (MPA); public policy (MPP); MPA/MSW. *Accreditation:* NASPAA (one or more programs are accredited). Part-time and evening/weekend programs available. Terminal master's awarded for partial completion of doctoral program. *Degree requirements:* For master's, thesis or alternative, policy analysis or capstone project; interactive Program of Study (iPOS) submitted before completing 50 percent of required credit hours; for doctorate, comprehensive exam, thesis/dissertation, interactive Program of Study (iPOS) submitted before completing 50 percent of required credit hours. *Entrance requirements:* For master's, GRE, minimum GPA of 3.0 or equivalent in last 2 years of work leading to bachelor's degree; for doctorate, GRE, minimum GPA of 3.0 or equivalent in last 2 years of work leading to bachelor's degree, 3 letters of recommendation, resume, statement of goals, samples of research reports. Additional exam requirements/recommendations for international students: Required—TOEFL (minimum score 600 paper-based; 100 iBT), IELTS (minimum score 6.5). Electronic applications accepted. *Expenses:* Contact institution.

Arkansas State University, Graduate School, College of Nursing and Health Professions, Disaster Preparedness Program, State University, AR 72467. Offers disaster preparedness and emergency management (MS); healthcare emergency management (Graduate Certificate). Part-time programs available. *Faculty:* 5 full-time (2 women). *Students:* 19 part-time (11 women); includes 1 minority (Black or African American, non-Hispanic/Latino), 1 international. Average age 37. 22 applicants, 68% accepted, 10 enrolled. In 2014, 15 master's awarded. *Degree requirements:* For master's and Graduate Certificate, comprehensive exam, thesis or alternative. *Entrance requirements:* For master's, GRE General Test or MAT, appropriate bachelor's degree, TB skin test, TB mask fit test, CPR certification, liability insurance; for Graduate Certificate, bachelor's degree, TB skin test, TB mask fit Test, CPR certification, liability insurance. Additional exam requirements/recommendations for international students: Required—TOEFL (minimum score 550 paper-based; 79 iBT), IELTS (minimum score 6), PTE (minimum score 56). *Application deadline:* For fall admission, 7/1 for domestic and international students; for spring admission, 11/15 for domestic students, 11/14 for international students. Applications are processed on a rolling basis. Application fee: $30 ($40 for international students). Electronic applications accepted. *Expenses:* Tuition, state resident: full-time $4392; part-time $244 per credit hour. Tuition, nonresident: full-time $8784; part-time $488 per credit hour. *International tuition:* $9484 full-time. *Required fees:* $1134; $63 per credit hour. $25 per term. Tuition and fees vary according to course load and program. *Financial support:* In 2014–15, 1 student received support. Career-related internships or fieldwork, scholarships/grants, and unspecified assistantships available. Financial award application deadline: 7/1; financial award applicants required to submit FAFSA. *Unit head:* Dr. Deborah Persell, Program Director, 870-680-8286, Fax: 870-972-3554, E-mail: dpersell@astate.edu. *Application contact:* Vickey Ring, Graduate Admissions Coordinator, 870-972-3029, Fax: 870-972-3857, E-mail: vickeyring@astate.edu.
Website: http://www.astate.edu/college/conhp/departments/disaster-preparedness/

Arkansas Tech University, College of Engineering and Applied Sciences, Russellville, AR 72801. Offers emergency management (MS); engineering (M Engr); information technology (MS). Part-time programs available. Postbaccalaureate distance learning degree programs offered (no on-campus study). *Students:* 83 full-time (31 women), 48 part-time (16 women); includes 14 minority (5 Black or African American, non-Hispanic/Latino; 1 American Indian or Alaska Native, non-Hispanic/Latino; 1 Asian, non-Hispanic/Latino; 3 Hispanic/Latino; 4 Two or more races, non-Hispanic/Latino), 60 international. Average age 28. In 2014, 39 degrees awarded. *Degree requirements:* For master's, comprehensive exam (for some programs), thesis (for some programs), internship. *Entrance requirements:* For master's, GRE General Test. Additional exam requirements/recommendations for international students: Required—TOEFL (minimum score 550 paper-based; 79 iBT), IELTS (minimum score 6). *Application deadline:* For fall admission, 3/1 priority date for domestic students, 5/1 priority date for international students; for spring admission, 10/1 priority date for domestic and international students. Applications are processed on a rolling basis. Application fee: $25 ($75 for international students). Electronic applications accepted. *Expenses:* Tuition, state resident: full-time $6264; part-time $261 per credit hour. Tuition, nonresident: full-time $12,528; part-time $522 per credit hour. *Required fees:* $423 per semester. Tuition and fees vary according to course load. *Financial support:* In 2014–15, research assistantships with full tuition reimbursements (averaging $4,800 per year), teaching assistantships with full tuition reimbursements (averaging $4,800 per year) were awarded; career-related internships or fieldwork, Federal Work-Study, scholarships/grants, health care benefits, and unspecified assistantships also available. Support available to part-time students. Financial award application deadline: 4/15; financial award applicants required to submit FAFSA. *Unit head:* Dr. William Hoefler, Dean, 479-968-0353, E-mail: whoeflerjr@atu.edu. *Application contact:* Dr. Mary B. Gunter, Dean of Graduate College,

479-968-0398, Fax: 479-964-0542, E-mail: gradcollege@atu.edu.
Website: http://www.atu.edu/appliedsci/

Auburn University at Montgomery, College of Public Policy and Justice, Department of Justice and Public Safety, Montgomery, AL 36124-4023. Offers criminal studies (MSJPS); homeland security (MSJPS); homeland security and emergency management (MS); legal studies (MSJPS); organizational leadership (MSJPS); paralegal (Certificate). Part-time and evening/weekend programs available. *Faculty:* 6 full-time (3 women), 4 part-time/adjunct (0 women). *Students:* 12 full-time (7 women), 43 part-time (26 women); includes 19 minority (all Black or African American, non-Hispanic/Latino). Average age 32. 34 applicants, 79% accepted, 15 enrolled. In 2014, 20 master's awarded. *Degree requirements:* For master's, comprehensive exam, thesis optional. *Entrance requirements:* For master's, GRE General Test or MAT. *Application deadline:* Applications are processed on a rolling basis. Electronic applications accepted. *Expenses:* Tuition, state resident: full-time $6264; part-time $348 per credit hour. Tuition, nonresident: full-time $14,094; part-time $783 per credit hour. *Financial support:* Career-related internships or fieldwork and scholarships/grants available. Support available to part-time students. Financial award application deadline: 3/1; financial award applicants required to submit FAFSA. *Faculty research:* Law enforcement, corrections, juvenile justice. *Unit head:* Dr. Ralph Ioimo, Head, 334-244-3691, Fax: 334-244-3244, E-mail: rioimo@aum.edu. *Application contact:* Shinae Yoon, Administrative Associate, 334-244-3692, Fax: 334-244-3244, E-mail: syoon1@aum.edu.

Benedictine University, Graduate Programs, Program in Public Health, Lisle, IL 60532-0900. Offers administration of health care institutions (MPH); dietetics (MPH); disaster management (MPH); health education (MPH); health information systems (MPH); MBA/MPH; MPH/MS. Part-time and evening/weekend programs available. Postbaccalaureate distance learning degree programs offered. *Entrance requirements:* For master's, MAT, GRE, or GMAT. Additional exam requirements/recommendations for international students: Required—TOEFL (minimum score 550 paper-based).

Boston University, School of Medicine, Division of Graduate Medical Sciences, Program in Healthcare Emergency Management, Boston, MA 02215. Offers MS. *Expenses: Tuition:* Full-time $45,686; part-time $1428 per credit hour. *Required fees:* $660; $60 per semester. Tuition and fees vary according to program. *Financial support:* Applicants required to submit FAFSA. *Unit head:* Dr. Kevin Thomas, Director, 617-414-2316, Fax: 617-414-2332, E-mail: kipthoma@bu.edu. *Application contact:* Patricia Jones, Program Manager and Admissions Director, 617-414-2315, E-mail: psterlin@bu.edu.
Website: http://www.bumc.bu.edu/bmcm/

Brandman University, School of Nursing and Health Professions, Irvine, CA 92618. Offers health administration (MHA); health risk and crisis communication (MS).

California Maritime Academy, Graduate Studies, Vallejo, CA 94590. Offers transportation and engineering management (MS), including engineering management, humanitarian disaster management, transportation. Postbaccalaureate distance learning degree programs offered (no on-campus study). *Faculty:* 14 part-time/adjunct (2 women). *Students:* 50 full-time (7 women); includes 12 minority (3 Black or African American, non-Hispanic/Latino; 4 Asian, non-Hispanic/Latino; 4 Hispanic/Latino; 1 Native Hawaiian or other Pacific Islander, non-Hispanic/Latino), 3 international. 36 applicants, 97% accepted, 35 enrolled. In 2014, 14 master's awarded. *Degree requirements:* For master's, capstone course and project. *Entrance requirements:* For master's, equivalent of four-year U.S. bachelor's degree with minimum GPA of 2.5 during last two years (60 semester units or 90 quarter units) of coursework in degree program; five years of professional experience or GMAT/GRE. Additional exam requirements/recommendations for international students: Required—TOEFL (minimum score 550 paper-based). *Application deadline:* Applications are processed on a rolling basis. Application fee: $55. Electronic applications accepted. *Unit head:* Dr. Jim Burns, Dean, Graduate Studies. *Application contact:* Kathy Arnold, Program Coordinator, 707-654-1271, Fax: 707-654-1158, E-mail: karnold@csum.edu.
Website: http://www.csum.edu/web/industry/graduate-studies

California State University, Long Beach, Graduate Studies, College of Health and Human Services, Department of Criminal Justice, Long Beach, CA 90840. Offers criminal justice (MS); emergency services administration (MS). Part-time programs available. *Degree requirements:* For master's, comprehensive course or thesis. *Entrance requirements:* For master's, minimum GPA of 3.0. Electronic applications accepted.

Capella University, School of Public Service Leadership, Doctoral Programs in Healthcare, Minneapolis, MN 55402. Offers criminal justice (PhD); emergency management (PhD); epidemiology (Dr PH); general health administration (DHA); general public administration (DPA); health advocacy and leadership (Dr PH); health care administration (PhD); health care leadership (DHA); health policy advocacy (DHA); multidisciplinary human services (PhD); nonprofit management and leadership (PhD); public safety leadership (PhD); social and community services (PhD).

Capella University, School of Public Service Leadership, Master's Programs in Healthcare, Minneapolis, MN 55402. Offers criminal justice (MS); emergency management (MS); general public health (MPH); gerontology (MS); health administration (MHA); health care operations (MHA); health management policy (MPH); health policy (MHA); homeland security (MS); multidisciplinary human services (MS); public administration (MPA); public safety leadership (MS); social and community services (MS); social behavioral sciences (MPH); MS/MPA.

Columbia Southern University, College of Safety and Emergency Services, Orange Beach, AL 36561. Offers criminal justice administration (MS); emergency services management (MS); occupational safety and health (MS), including environmental management. Part-time and evening/weekend programs available. Postbaccalaureate distance learning degree programs offered (no on-campus study). *Entrance requirements:* For master's, bachelor's degree from accredited/approved institution. Additional exam requirements/recommendations for international students: Required—TOEFL. Electronic applications accepted.

Drexel University, College of Nursing and Health Professions, Emergency and Public Safety Services Program, Philadelphia, PA 19104-2875. Offers MS. Part-time and evening/weekend programs available. *Degree requirements:* For master's, comprehensive exam. *Entrance requirements:* For master's, GRE General Test, minimum GPA of 2.75.

Excelsior College, School of Public Service, Albany, NY 12203-5159. Offers homeland security and emergency management (MSCJ); public administration (MPA). Part-time and evening/weekend programs available. Postbaccalaureate distance learning degree programs offered (no on-campus study). *Faculty:* 2 part-time/adjunct (0 women). *Students:* 122 part-time (25 women); includes 49 minority (25 Black or African American, non-Hispanic/Latino; 1 Asian, non-Hispanic/Latino; 18 Hispanic/Latino; 1 Native Hawaiian or other Pacific Islander, non-Hispanic/Latino; 4 Two or more races, non-Hispanic/Latino). Average age 40. In 2014, 12 master's awarded. Application fee: $110. *Expenses: Tuition:* Part-time $620 per credit hour. *Financial support:* Scholarships/grants available. Support available to part-time students. *Unit head:* Dr. Robert Waters, Dean, School of Public Service. *Application contact:* Admissions Counselor, 518-464-8500, Fax: 518-464-8777, E-mail: admissions@excelsior.edu.
Website: http://www.excelsior.edu/schools/public-service

Florida Institute of Technology, Graduate Programs, Extended Studies Division, Melbourne, FL 32901-6975. Offers acquisition and contract management (MS); aerospace engineering (MS); business administration (MBA, DBA); computer information systems (MS); computer science (MS); electrical engineering (MS); engineering management (MS); human resources management (MS); logistics management (MS), including humanitarian and disaster relief logistics; management (MS), including acquisition and contract management, e-business, human resources management, information systems, logistics management, management, transportation management; material acquisition management (MS); mechanical engineering (MS); operations research (MS); project management (MS), including information systems, operations research; public administration (MPA); quality management (MS); software engineering (MS); space systems (MS); space systems management (MS); supply chain management (MS); systems management (MS), including information systems, operations research; technology management (MS). Part-time and evening/weekend programs available. Postbaccalaureate distance learning degree programs offered (no on-campus study). *Faculty:* 7 full-time (1 woman), 112 part-time/adjunct (29 women). *Students:* 98 full-time (45 women), 975 part-time (396 women); includes 440 minority (292 Black or African American, non-Hispanic/Latino; 13 American Indian or Alaska Native, non-Hispanic/Latino; 32 Asian, non-Hispanic/Latino; 79 Hispanic/Latino; 1 Native Hawaiian or other Pacific Islander, non-Hispanic/Latino; 23 Two or more races, non-Hispanic/Latino), 4 international. Average age 37. 807 applicants, 56% accepted, 258 enrolled. In 2014, 457 master's awarded. *Degree requirements:* For master's, comprehensive exam (for some programs), capstone course. *Entrance requirements:* For master's, GMAT or resume showing 8 years of supervised experience, minimum GPA of 3.0, 2 letters of recommendation, resume. Additional exam requirements/recommendations for international students: Required—TOEFL (minimum score 550 paper-based; 79 iBT). *Application deadline:* For fall admission, 4/1 for international students; for spring admission, 9/30 for international students. Applications are processed on a rolling basis. Electronic applications accepted. *Expenses:* Expenses: Contact institution. *Financial support:* Application deadline: 3/1; applicants required to submit FAFSA. *Unit head:* Dr. Theodore R. Richardson, III, Senior Associate Dean, 321-674-8123, Fax: 321-674-7597, E-mail: trichardson@fit.edu. *Application contact:* Carolyn Farrior, Director of Graduate Admissions, Online Learning and Off-Campus Programs, 321-674-7118, Fax: 321-674-8216, E-mail: cfarrior@fit.edu.
Website: http://es.fit.edu

Fordham University, Graduate School of Arts and Sciences, Program in International Humanitarian Action, New York, NY 10458. Offers MA. Program offered in collaboration with the Institute for International Humanitarian Affairs (IIHA). *Students:* 8 part-time (6 women), 6 international. Average age 37. 39 applicants, 82% accepted, 12 enrolled. *Entrance requirements:* For master's, official transcripts, 3 letters of recommendation, resume, statement of interest. Application fee: $70. Electronic applications accepted. *Unit head:* Dr. Brendan Cahill, Dean, 212-636-6294, Fax: 212-636-7060, E-mail: iiha@fordham.edu. *Application contact:* Bernadette Valentino-Morrison, Director of Graduate Admissions, 718-817-4419, Fax: 718-817-3566, E-mail: valentinomor@fordham.edu.
Website: http://www.fordham.edu/academics/programs_at_fordham_/international_humani/index.asp

George Mason University, School of Policy, Government, and International Affairs, Program in Public Administration, Fairfax, VA 22030. Offers administration of justice (Certificate); association management (Certificate); biodefense (MS, PhD); critical analysis and strategic response to terrorism (Certificate); emergency management and homeland security (Certificate); nonprofit management (Certificate); political science (MA, PhD); public administration (MPA); public management (Certificate). *Accreditation:* NASPAA (one or more programs are accredited). *Entrance requirements:* For degree, expanded goals statement; 3 letters of recommendation; official transcripts; resume. Additional exam requirements/recommendations for international students: Required—TOEFL, IELTS, PTE. Application fee: $65 ($80 for international students). Electronic applications accepted. *Expenses:* Expenses: Contact institution. *Financial support:* Fellowships, research assistantships with full and partial tuition reimbursements, teaching assistantships with full and partial tuition reimbursements, career-related internships or fieldwork, Federal Work-Study, scholarships/grants, and unspecified assistantships available. Support available to part-time students. Financial award application deadline: 3/1; financial award applicants required to submit FAFSA. *Application contact:* Peg Koback, Education Support Specialist, 703-993-3707, Fax: 703-993-1399, E-mail: mkoback@gmu.edu.
Website: http://pia.gmu.edu/

Georgetown University, Graduate School of Arts and Sciences, School of Continuing Studies, Washington, DC 20057. Offers American studies (MALS); Catholic studies (MALS); classical civilizations (MALS); emergency and disaster management (MPS); ethics and the professions (MALS); hospitality management (MPS); human resources management (MPS); humanities (MALS); individualized study (MALS); international affairs (MALS); Islam and Muslim-Christian relations (MALS); journalism (MPS); liberal studies (DLS); literature and society (MALS); medieval and early modern European studies (MALS); public relations and corporate communications (MPS); real estate (MPS); religious studies (MALS); social and public policy (MALS); sports industry management (MPS); systems engineering management (MPS); technology management (MPS); the theory and practice of American democracy (MALS); urban and regional planning (MPS); visual culture (MALS). MPS in systems engineering management offered jointly with Stevens Institute of Technology. *Entrance requirements:* Additional exam requirements/recommendations for international students: Required—TOEFL.

The George Washington University, School of Medicine and Health Sciences, Health Sciences Programs, Washington, DC 20052. Offers clinical practice management (MSHS); clinical research administration (MSHS); emergency services management (MSHS); end-of-life care (MSHS); immunohematology (MSHS); immunohematology and biotechnology (MSHS); physical therapy (DPT); physician assistant (MSHS). Postbaccalaureate distance learning degree programs offered (no on-campus study). *Students:* 265 full-time (200 women), 2 part-time (1 woman); includes 63 minority (9 Black or African American, non-Hispanic/Latino; 2 American Indian or Alaska Native, non-Hispanic/Latino; 30 Asian, non-Hispanic/Latino; 19 Hispanic/Latino; 2 Native Hawaiian or other Pacific Islander, non-Hispanic/Latino; 1 Two or more races, non-Hispanic/Latino), 1 international. Average age 28. 1,868 applicants, 13% accepted, 112 enrolled. *Entrance requirements:* Additional exam requirements/recommendations for international students: Required—TOEFL (minimum score 550 paper-based). *Application deadline:* Applications are processed on a rolling basis. Application fee: $75. *Expenses:* Expenses: Contact institution. *Unit head:* Jean E. Johnson, Senior Associate Dean, 202-994-3725, E-mail: jejohns@gwu.edu. *Application contact:* Joke Ogundiran, Director of Admission, 202-994-1668, Fax: 202-994-0870, E-mail: jokeogun@gwu.edu.

Georgia State University, Andrew Young School of Policy Studies, Department of Public Management and Policy, Atlanta, GA 30303. Offers criminal justice (MPA); disaster management (Certificate); disaster policy (MPA); environmental policy (PhD);

health policy (PhD); management and finance (MPA); nonprofit management (MPA, Certificate); nonprofit policy (MPA); planning and economic development (MPP, Certificate); policy analysis and evaluation (MPA), including planning and economic development; public and nonprofit management (PhD); public finance and budgeting (PhD), including science and technology policy, urban and regional economic development; public finance policy (MPA), including social policy; public health (MPA). *Accreditation:* NASPAA (one or more programs are accredited). Part-time programs available. *Faculty:* 14 full-time (7 women). *Students:* 136 full-time (80 women), 85 part-time (47 women); includes 81 minority (60 Black or African American, non-Hispanic/Latino; 7 Asian, non-Hispanic/Latino; 11 Hispanic/Latino; 3 Two or more races, non-Hispanic/Latino), 25 international. Average age 30. 269 applicants, 59% accepted, 64 enrolled. In 2014, 80 master's, 7 other advanced degrees awarded. Terminal master's awarded for partial completion of doctoral program. *Degree requirements:* For master's, thesis optional; for doctorate, comprehensive exam, thesis/dissertation. *Entrance requirements:* For master's and doctorate, GRE. Additional exam requirements/recommendations for international students: Required—TOEFL (minimum score 603 paper-based; 100 iBT) or IELTS (minimum score 7). *Application deadline:* For fall admission, 2/15 for domestic and international students; for spring admission, 10/1 for domestic and international students. Application fee: $50. Electronic applications accepted. *Expenses:* Tuition, state resident: full-time $6516; part-time $362 per credit hour. Tuition, nonresident: full-time $22,014; part-time $1223 per credit hour. *Required fees:* $2128 per semester. Tuition and fees vary according to course load and program. *Financial support:* In 2014–15, fellowships (averaging $8,194 per year), research assistantships (averaging $8,068 per year), teaching assistantships (averaging $3,600 per year) were awarded; institutionally sponsored loans, scholarships/grants, health care benefits, and unspecified assistantships also available. Financial award application deadline: 2/1. *Faculty research:* Public budgeting and finance, public management, nonprofit management, performance measurement and management, urban development. *Unit head:* Dr. Gregory Burr Lewis, Chair and Professor, 404-413-0114, Fax: 404-413-0104, E-mail: glewis@gsu.edu. *Application contact:* Charisma Parker, Admissions Coordinator, 404-413-0030, Fax: 404-413-0023, E-mail: cparker28@gsu.edu.
Website: http://aysps.gsu.edu/pmap/

Grand Canyon University, College of Business, Phoenix, AZ 85017-1097. Offers accounting (MBA); corporate business administration (MBA); disaster preparedness and crisis management (MBA); executive fire service leadership (MS); finance (MBA); general management (MBA); government and policy (MPA); health care management (MPA); health systems management (MBA); human resource management (MBA); innovation (MBA); leadership (MBA, MS); management of information system (MBA); marketing (MBA); project-based (MBA); six sigma (MBA); strategic human resource management (MBA). *Accreditation:* ACBSP. Part-time and evening/weekend programs available. Postbaccalaureate distance learning degree programs offered (no on-campus study). *Entrance requirements:* For master's, equivalent of two years full-time professional work experience. Additional exam requirements/recommendations for international students: Required—TOEFL (minimum score 575 paper-based; 90 iBT), IELTS (minimum score 7). Electronic applications accepted.

Indiana University of Pennsylvania, School of Graduate Studies and Research, College of Natural Sciences and Mathematics, Science for Disaster Response Program, Indiana, PA 15705-1087. Offers MS. *Faculty:* 12 full-time (7 women). In 2014, 1 master's awarded. *Entrance requirements:* Additional exam requirements/recommendations for international students: Required—TOEFL (minimum score 540 paper-based). *Application deadline:* Applications are processed on a rolling basis. Application fee: $50. Electronic applications accepted. *Unit head:* Dr. N. Bharathan, Department of Biology Chairperson, 724-357-2584, E-mail: bharathn@iup.edu.
Website: http://www.iup.edu/wmdrealiti/

Indiana University–Purdue University Indianapolis, School of Public and Environmental Affairs, Indianapolis, IN 46202. Offers criminal justice and public safety (MS); homeland security and emergency management (Graduate Certificate); library management (Graduate Certificate); nonprofit management (Graduate Certificate); public affairs (MPA); public management (Graduate Certificate); social entrepreneurship: nonprofit and public benefit organizations (Graduate Certificate); JD/MPA; MLS/NMC; MLS/PMC; MPA/MA. *Accreditation:* CAHME (one or more programs are accredited); NASPAA. Part-time and evening/weekend programs available. Postbaccalaureate distance learning degree programs offered (no on-campus study). *Entrance requirements:* For master's, GRE General Test, GMAT or LSAT, minimum GPA of 3.0 (preferred). Additional exam requirements/recommendations for international students: Required—TOEFL (minimum score 93 iBT), IELTS (minimum score 6.5). Electronic applications accepted. *Faculty research:* Nonprofit and public management, public policy, urban policy, sustainability policy, disaster preparedness and recovery, vehicular safety, homicide, offender rehabilitation and re-entry.

Jacksonville State University, College of Graduate Studies and Continuing Education, College of Arts and Sciences, Emergency Management Program, Jacksonville, AL 36265-1602. Offers emergency management (MS, D Sc). Part-time and evening/weekend programs available. *Faculty:* 7 full-time (2 women). *Students:* 5 full-time (1 woman), 102 part-time (37 women); includes 12 minority (10 Black or African American, non-Hispanic/Latino; 1 American Indian or Alaska Native, non-Hispanic/Latino; 1 Hispanic/Latino), 4 international. Average age 39. 78 applicants, 55% accepted, 33 enrolled. In 2014, 29 master's awarded. *Degree requirements:* For master's, comprehensive exam, thesis (for some programs). *Entrance requirements:* Additional exam requirements/recommendations for international students: Required—TOEFL (minimum score 500 paper-based; 61 iBT). *Application deadline:* Applications are processed on a rolling basis. Application fee: $35. Electronic applications accepted. *Financial support:* In 2014–15, 11 students received support. Available to part-time students. Application deadline: 4/1; applicants required to submit FAFSA. *Unit head:* Dr. Jeff Ryan, Head, 256-782-8334, E-mail: jryan@jsu.edu. *Application contact:* Dr. Jean Pugliese, Associate Dean, 256-782-8278, Fax: 256-782-5321, E-mail: pugliese@jsu.edu.
Website: http://www.jsu.edu/iep/

Liberty University, School of Behavioral Sciences, Lynchburg, VA 24515. Offers advanced clinical skills (PhD); clinical mental health counseling (MA); counselor education and supervision (PhD); human services counseling (MA), including addictions and recovery, business, child and family law, Christian ministries, criminal justice, crisis response and trauma, executive leadership, health and wellness, life coaching, marriage and family, military resilience; marriage and family therapy (MA); military resilience (Certificate); professional counseling (MA). Part-time programs available. Postbaccalaureate distance learning degree programs offered (minimal on-campus study). *Students:* 3,009 full-time (2,433 women), 6,251 part-time (4,981 women); includes 2,959 minority (2,520 Black or African American, non-Hispanic/Latino; 49 American Indian or Alaska Native, non-Hispanic/Latino; 51 Asian, non-Hispanic/Latino; 97 Hispanic/Latino; 9 Native Hawaiian or other Pacific Islander, non-Hispanic/Latino; 233 Two or more races, non-Hispanic/Latino), 153 international. Average age 38. 6,645 applicants, 55% accepted, 2039 enrolled. In 2014, 2,410 master's, 11 doctorates, 2 other advanced degrees awarded. *Application deadline:* Applications are processed on a rolling basis. Application fee: $50. Electronic applications accepted. *Financial support:* Applicants required to submit FAFSA. *Unit head:* Dr. Ronald Hawkins, Founding Dean, School of Behavioral Sciences. *Application contact:* Jay Bridge, Director of Admissions, 800-424-9595, Fax: 800-628-7977, E-mail: gradadmissions@liberty.edu.

Lynn University, College of Arts and Sciences, Boca Raton, FL 33431-5598. Offers applied psychology (MS); criminal justice administration (MS); emergency planning and administration (MS). Part-time and evening/weekend programs available. Postbaccalaureate distance learning degree programs offered (no on-campus study). *Faculty:* 4 full-time (2 women), 10 part-time/adjunct (8 women). *Students:* 77 full-time (58 women), 36 part-time (21 women); includes 23 minority (12 Black or African American, non-Hispanic/Latino; 2 Asian, non-Hispanic/Latino; 9 Hispanic/Latino), 11 international. Average age 32. 103 applicants, 96% accepted, 71 enrolled. In 2014, 27 master's awarded. *Degree requirements:* For master's, comprehensive exam (for some programs), thesis (for some programs). *Entrance requirements:* For master's, bachelor's degree from accredited institution, resume, letter of recommendation, essay of professional goals, official transcripts. Additional exam requirements/recommendations for international students: Required—TOEFL (minimum score 550 paper-based; 80 iBT), IELTS (minimum score 6.5). *Application deadline:* For fall admission, 8/17 for domestic students, 8/3 for international students; for spring admission, 12/15 for domestic students, 11/24 for international students; for summer admission, 4/17 for domestic students, 4/6 for international students. Applications are processed on a rolling basis. Application fee: $45. Electronic applications accepted. *Expenses: Tuition:* Full-time $16,200; part-time $675 per credit hour. Tuition and fees vary according to class time, course load, degree level and program. *Financial support:* In 2014–15, 33 students received support. Career-related internships or fieldwork, Federal Work-Study, scholarships/grants, tuition waivers (full and partial), and unspecified assistantships available. Support available to part-time students. Financial award application deadline: 3/1; financial award applicants required to submit FAFSA. *Faculty research:* Terrorism, criminological theory, corrections, emergency planning, counseling. *Unit head:* Dr. Katrina Carter-Tellison, Dean, 561-237-7412, E-mail: kcartertellison@lynn.edu. *Application contact:* Steven Pruitt, Director of Graduate Admission, 561-237-7834, Fax: 561-237-7100, E-mail: admissionpm@lynn.edu.
Website: http://www.lynn.edu/academics/colleges/arts-and-sciences/

Massachusetts Maritime Academy, Program in Emergency Management, Buzzards Bay, MA 02532-1803. Offers MS.

Millersville University of Pennsylvania, College of Graduate and Professional Studies, School of Science and Mathematics, Center for Disaster Research and Education, Millersville, PA 17551-0302. Offers emergency management (MS). Part-time and evening/weekend programs available. Postbaccalaureate distance learning degree programs offered (no on-campus study). *Faculty:* 7 full-time (2 women), 2 part-time/adjunct (0 women). *Students:* 4 full-time (1 woman), 60 part-time (21 women); includes 6 minority (3 Black or African American, non-Hispanic/Latino; 1 Asian, non-Hispanic/Latino; 2 Hispanic/Latino), 1 international. Average age 32. 31 applicants, 100% accepted, 23 enrolled. In 2014, 21 master's awarded. *Degree requirements:* For master's, field practicum. *Entrance requirements:* For master's, GRE or MAT (if GPA less than 2.75), 3 letters of recommendation, interview (by telephone), resume, official transcripts, goal statement. Additional exam requirements/recommendations for international students: Required—TOEFL (minimum score 500 paper-based, 65 iBT) or IELTS (minimum score 6). *Application deadline:* For fall admission, 1/15 priority date for domestic and international students; for winter admission, 6/1 priority date for domestic and international students; for spring admission, 10/1 priority date for domestic and international students. Applications are processed on a rolling basis. Application fee: $40. Electronic applications accepted. *Expenses:* Tuition, state resident: full-time $8172. Tuition, nonresident: full-time $12,258. *Required fees:* $2300. Tuition and fees vary according to course load and program. *Financial support:* In 2014–15, 6 students received support, including 6 research assistantships with full tuition reimbursements available (averaging $4,233 per year); institutionally sponsored loans and unspecified assistantships also available. Support available to part-time students. Financial award application deadline: 3/15; financial award applicants required to submit FAFSA. *Faculty research:* Emergency management. *Total annual research expenditures:* $33,900. *Unit head:* Dr. Sepideh Yalda, Director, 717-871-7549, Fax: 717-871-2429, E-mail: sepi.yalda@millersville.edu. *Application contact:* Dr. Victor S. DeSantis, Dean of College of Graduate and Professional Studies/Associate Provost for Civic and Community Engagement, 717-871-7619, Fax: 717-871-7954, E-mail: victor.desantis@millersville.edu.
Website: http://www.millersville.edu/cdre/index.php

National University, Academic Affairs, School of Engineering and Computing, La Jolla, CA 92037-1011. Offers computer science (MS), including advanced computing, database engineering, software engineering; cyber security and information assurance (MS), including computer forensics, ethical hacking and penetration testing, health information assurance, information assurance and security; data analytics (MS); engineering management (MS), including enterprise architecture, project management, systems engineering, technology management; environmental engineering (MS); homeland security and emergency management (MS); management information systems (MS); project management (Certificate); sustainability management (MS); wireless communications (MS). Part-time and evening/weekend programs available. Postbaccalaureate distance learning degree programs offered (no on-campus study). *Faculty:* 24 full-time (5 women), 21 part-time/adjunct (5 women). *Students:* 275 full-time (72 women), 86 part-time (24 women); includes 147 minority (41 Black or African American, non-Hispanic/Latino; 48 Asian, non-Hispanic/Latino; 37 Hispanic/Latino; 7 Native Hawaiian or other Pacific Islander, non-Hispanic/Latino; 14 Two or more races, non-Hispanic/Latino), 95 international. Average age 33. In 2014, 281 master's awarded. *Degree requirements:* For master's, thesis (for some programs). *Entrance requirements:* For master's, interview, minimum GPA of 2.5. Additional exam requirements/recommendations for international students: Required—TOEFL (minimum score 550 paper-based; 79 iBT), IELTS (minimum score 6). *Application deadline:* Applications are processed on a rolling basis. Application fee: $60 ($65 for international students). Electronic applications accepted. *Expenses: Tuition:* Full-time $14,184; part-time $1773 per course. *Financial support:* Career-related internships or fieldwork, institutionally sponsored loans, scholarships/grants, and tuition waivers (partial) available. Support available to part-time students. Financial award application deadline: 6/30; financial award applicants required to submit FAFSA. *Faculty research:* Educational technology, scholarships in science. *Unit head:* School of Engineering and Computing, 800-628-8648, E-mail: soec@nu.edu. *Application contact:* Frank Rojas, Vice President for Enrollment Services, 800-628-8648, E-mail: advisor@nu.edu.
Website: http://www.nu.edu/OurPrograms/SchoolOfEngineeringAndTechnology.html

New Jersey Institute of Technology, College of Computing Science, Newark, NJ 07102. Offers computer science (MS, PhD), including bioinformatics (MS), computer science, computing and business (MS), cyber security and privacy (MS), software engineering (MS); information systems (MS, PhD), including business and information systems (MS), emergency management and business continuity (MS), information systems; information technology administration and security (MS). Part-time and evening/weekend programs available. Terminal master's awarded for partial completion

of doctoral program. *Degree requirements:* For master's, thesis optional; for doctorate, thesis/dissertation. *Entrance requirements:* For master's, GRE General Test; for doctorate, GRE General Test, minimum graduate GPA of 3.5. Additional exam requirements/recommendations for international students: Required—TOEFL (minimum score 550 paper-based; 79 iBT). Electronic applications accepted. *Faculty research:* Computer systems, communications and networking, artificial intelligence, database engineering, systems analysis.

New York Medical College, School of Health Sciences and Practice, Department of Health Policy and Management, Program in Emergency Preparedness, Valhalla, NY 10595-1691. Offers Graduate Certificate. Program offered in conjunction with the Center for Disaster Medicine. Part-time and evening/weekend programs available. Postbaccalaureate distance learning degree programs offered (no on-campus study). *Faculty:* 2 full-time, 5 part-time/adjunct. *Students:* 15 full-time, 30 part-time. Average age 32. 22 applicants, 73% accepted, 14 enrolled. *Entrance requirements:* Additional exam requirements/recommendations for international students: Required—TOEFL (minimum score 96 iBT), IELTS (minimum score 7). *Application deadline:* For fall admission, 8/1 for domestic students, 5/15 for international students; for spring admission, 12/1 for domestic students, 10/15 for international students; for summer admission, 5/1 for domestic students. Applications are processed on a rolling basis. Electronic applications accepted. *Expenses: Tuition:* Full-time $43,639; part-time $975 per credit. *Required fees:* $500; $95 per term. One-time fee: $140 part-time. Tuition and fees vary according to course load and program. *Unit head:* Dr. Frank Mineo, Director Emergency Preparedness, 914-594-4251, E-mail: frank_mineo@nymc.edu. *Application contact:* Pamela Suett, Director of Recruitment, 914-594-4510, Fax: 914-594-4292, E-mail: shsp_admissions@nymc.edu.
Website: http://www.nymc.edu/shsp

North Dakota State University, College of Graduate and Interdisciplinary Studies, College of Arts, Humanities and Social Sciences, Department of Sociology, Anthropology, and Emergency Management, Fargo, ND 58108. Offers community development (MA, MS); emergency management (MS, PhD); social science (MA, MS); sociology (MS). Part-time programs available. *Degree requirements:* For master's, thesis; for doctorate, comprehensive exam, thesis/dissertation. *Entrance requirements:* For master's, GRE (for emergency management), course work in sociology, minimum GPA of 3.2; for doctorate, GRE, minimum GPA of 3.2. Additional exam requirements/recommendations for international students: Required—TOEFL. Electronic applications accepted. *Faculty research:* Medical sociology, demography, ethnology, archaeology.

Nova Southeastern University, College of Osteopathic Medicine, Fort Lauderdale, FL 33328. Offers biomedical informatics (MS, Graduate Certificate), including biomedical informatics (MS), clinical informatics (Graduate Certificate), public health informatics (Graduate Certificate); disaster and emergency preparedness (MS); osteopathic medicine (DO); public health (MPH). *Accreditation:* AOsA. *Faculty:* 107 full-time (55 women), 1,235 part-time/adjunct (297 women). *Students:* 1,027 full-time (436 women), 189 part-time (124 women); includes 560 minority (92 Black or African American, non-Hispanic/Latino; 260 Asian, non-Hispanic/Latino; 174 Hispanic/Latino; 1 Native Hawaiian or other Pacific Islander, non-Hispanic/Latino; 33 Two or more races, non-Hispanic/Latino), 45 international. Average age 28. 4,012 applicants, 12% accepted, 246 enrolled. In 2014, 75 master's, 237 doctorates, 4 other advanced degrees awarded. *Entrance requirements:* For master's, GRE, licensed healthcare professional or GRE; for doctorate, MCAT, biology, chemistry, organic chemistry, physics (all with labs), and English. *Application deadline:* For fall admission, 1/15 for domestic students. Applications are processed on a rolling basis. Application fee: $50. Electronic applications accepted. *Expenses:* Expenses: Contact institution. *Financial support:* In 2014–15, 39 students received support, including 24 fellowships (averaging $45,593 per year); research assistantships, teaching assistantships, Federal Work-Study, and scholarships/grants also available. Financial award application deadline: 6/1; financial award applicants required to submit FAFSA. *Faculty research:* Teaching strategies, simulated patient use, HIV/AIDS education, minority health issues, managed care education. *Unit head:* Elaine M. Wallace, DO, Dean, 954-262-1407, E-mail: ewallace@nova.edu. *Application contact:* Monica Sanchez, Admissions Counselor, College of Osteopathic Medicine, 954-262-1110, Fax: 954-262-2282, E-mail: mh1156@nova.edu.
Website: http://www.medicine.nova.edu/

Oklahoma State University, College of Arts and Sciences, Department of Political Science, Stillwater, OK 74078. Offers fire and emergency management administration (MS, PhD); political science (MA). *Faculty:* 21 full-time (7 women), 2 part-time/adjunct (0 women). *Students:* 11 full-time (5 women), 62 part-time (12 women); includes 14 minority (4 Black or African American, non-Hispanic/Latino; 7 Hispanic/Latino; 3 Two or more races, non-Hispanic/Latino), 4 international. Average age 39. 42 applicants, 40% accepted, 14 enrolled. In 2014, 20 master's awarded. *Degree requirements:* For master's, comprehensive exam, thesis or creative component; for doctorate, comprehensive exam, thesis/dissertation. *Entrance requirements:* For master's, GRE; for doctorate, GRE. Additional exam requirements/recommendations for international students: Required—TOEFL (minimum score 550 paper-based; 79 iBT). *Application deadline:* For fall admission, 3/1 priority date for international students; for spring admission, 8/1 priority date for international students. Applications are processed on a rolling basis. Application fee: $40 ($75 for international students). Electronic applications accepted. *Expenses:* Tuition, state resident: full-time $4488; part-time $187 per credit hour. Tuition, nonresident: full-time $18,360; part-time $765 per credit hour. *Required fees:* $2413; $100.55 per credit hour. Tuition and fees vary according to campus/location. *Financial support:* In 2014–15, 1 research assistantship (averaging $19,644 per year), 10 teaching assistantships (averaging $16,961 per year) were awarded; career-related internships or fieldwork, Federal Work-Study, scholarships/grants, health care benefits, tuition waivers (partial), and unspecified assistantships also available. Support available to part-time students. Financial award application deadline: 3/1; financial award applicants required to submit FAFSA. *Faculty research:* Fire and emergency management, environmental dispute resolution, voting and elections, women and politics, urban politics. *Unit head:* Dr. Anthony Brown, Interim Department Head, 405-744-0420, Fax: 405-744-6534, E-mail: anthony.brown@okstate.edu. *Application contact:* Dr. Rebekah Herrick, Interim Director of Graduate Studies, 405-744-8437, Fax: 405-744-6534, E-mail: rebekah.herrick@okstate.edu.
Website: http://polsci.okstate.edu

Park University, School of Graduate and Professional Studies, Kansas City, MO 54105. Offers adult education (M Ed); business and government leadership (Graduate Certificate); business, government, and global society (MPA); communication and leadership (MA); creative and life writing (Graduate Certificate); disaster and emergency management (MPA, Graduate Certificate); educational leadership (M Ed); finance (MBA, Graduate Certificate); general business (MBA); global business (Graduate Certificate); healthcare administration (MHA); healthcare services management and leadership (Graduate Certificate); international business (MBA); language and literacy (M Ed), including English for speakers of other languages, special reading teacher/literacy coach; leadership of international healthcare organizations (Graduate Certificate); management information systems (MBA, Graduate Certificate); music performance (ADP, Graduate Certificate), including cello (MM, ADP), piano (MM, ADP), viola (MM, ADP), violin (MM, ADP); nonprofit and community services management (MPA); nonprofit leadership (Graduate Certificate); performance (MM), including cello (MM, ADP), piano (MM, ADP), viola (MM, ADP), violin (MM, ADP); public management (MPA); social work (MSW); teacher leadership (M Ed), including curriculum and assessment, instructional leader. Part-time and evening/weekend programs available. Postbaccalaureate distance learning degree programs offered (no on-campus study). *Degree requirements:* For master's, comprehensive exam (for some programs), thesis (for some programs), internship (for some programs); exam (for some programs). *Entrance requirements:* For master's, GRE or GMAT (for some programs), teacher certification (for some M Ed programs), letters of recommendation, essay, resume (for some programs). Additional exam requirements/recommendations for international students: Required—TOEFL (minimum score 550 paper-based; 79 iBT), IELTS (minimum score 6). Electronic applications accepted.

Philadelphia University, College of Science, Health and the Liberal Arts, Program in Disaster Medicine and Management, Philadelphia, PA 19144. Offers MS. Postbaccalaureate distance learning degree programs offered (minimal on-campus study).

Regent University, Graduate School, Robertson School of Government, Virginia Beach, VA 23464. Offers government (MA), including American government, international relations, political theory; public administration (MPA), including emergency management and homeland security, general public administration, nonprofit administration and faith-based organizations, public leadership and management. Part-time and evening/weekend programs available. Postbaccalaureate distance learning degree programs offered (minimal on-campus study). *Faculty:* 10 full-time (1 woman), 9 part-time/adjunct (2 women). *Students:* 34 full-time (15 women), 56 part-time (26 women); includes 21 minority (15 Black or African American, non-Hispanic/Latino; 6 Hispanic/Latino), 4 international. Average age 34. 106 applicants, 45% accepted, 33 enrolled. In 2014, 57 master's awarded. *Degree requirements:* For master's, thesis optional, internship. *Entrance requirements:* For master's, GRE General Test or LSAT, minimum undergraduate GPA of 3.0, writing sample, resume, interview, references. Additional exam requirements/recommendations for international students: Required—TOEFL (minimum score 577 paper-based). *Application deadline:* For fall admission, 5/1 priority date for domestic students; for spring admission, 11/1 priority date for domestic students. Applications are processed on a rolling basis. Application fee: $50. Electronic applications accepted. *Expenses:* Expenses: Contact institution. *Financial support:* Career-related internships or fieldwork, scholarships/grants, tuition waivers (full and partial), and unspecified assistantships available. Support available to part-time students. Financial award application deadline: 9/1; financial award applicants required to submit FAFSA. *Faculty research:* Education reform, political character issues, social capital concerns, administrative ethics, Biblical law and public policy. *Unit head:* Dr. Eric Patterson, Dean, 757-352-4616, Fax: 757-352-4735, E-mail: epatterson@regent.edu. *Application contact:* Matthew Chadwick, Director of Enrollment Support Services, 800-373-5504, Fax: 757-352-4381, E-mail: admissions@regent.edu.
Website: http://www.regent.edu/government/

Royal Roads University, Graduate Studies, Peace and Conflict Studies Program, Victoria, BC V9B 5Y2, Canada. Offers conflict analysis (G Dip); conflict analysis and management (MA); disaster and emergency management (MA); human security and peacebuilding (MA). Postbaccalaureate distance learning degree programs offered (minimal on-campus study). *Degree requirements:* For master's, thesis. *Entrance requirements:* For master's, 5-7 years of related work experience. Additional exam requirements/recommendations for international students: Required—TOEFL (paper-based 570) or IELTS (7) recommended. Electronic applications accepted. *Faculty research:* Conflict analysis, ethno-political conflict reconciliation, international relations, displaced persons.

Rutgers, The State University of New Jersey, New Brunswick, School of Public Health, Piscataway, NJ 08854. Offers biostatistics (MPH, MS, Dr PH, PhD); clinical epidemiology (Certificate); environmental and occupational health (MPH, Dr PH, PhD, Certificate); epidemiology (MPH, Dr PH, PhD); general public health (Certificate); health education and behavioral science (MPH, Dr PH, PhD); health systems and policy (MPH, PhD); public health preparedness (Certificate); DO/MPH; JD/MPH; MD/MPH; MPH/MBA; MPH/MSPA; MS/MPH; Psy D/MPH. *Accreditation:* CEPH. Part-time and evening/weekend programs available. *Degree requirements:* For master's, thesis, internship; for doctorate, comprehensive exam, thesis/dissertation. *Entrance requirements:* For master's, GRE General Test; for doctorate, GRE General Test, MPH (Dr PH); MA, MPH, or MS (PhD). Additional exam requirements/recommendations for international students: Required—TOEFL. Electronic applications accepted.

San Diego State University, Graduate and Research Affairs, College of Health and Human Services, Graduate School of Public Health, San Diego, CA 92182. Offers environmental health (MPH); epidemiology (MPH, PhD), including biostatistics (MPH); global emergency preparedness and response (MS); global health (PhD); health behavior (PhD); health promotion (MPH); health services administration (MPH); toxicology (MS); MPH/MA; MSW/MPH. *Accreditation:* CAHME (one or more programs are accredited); CEPH (one or more programs are accredited). Part-time programs available. *Degree requirements:* For master's, comprehensive exam (for some programs), thesis (for some programs); for doctorate, thesis/dissertation. *Entrance requirements:* For master's, GMAT (MPH in health services administration), GRE General Test; for doctorate, GRE General Test. Additional exam requirements/recommendations for international students: Required—TOEFL. *Faculty research:* Evaluation of tobacco, AIDS prevalence and prevention, mammography, infant death project, Alzheimer's in elderly Chinese.

Trident University International, College of Health Sciences, Program in Health Sciences, Cypress, CA 90630. Offers clinical research administration (MS, Certificate); emergency and disaster management (MS, Certificate); environmental health science (Certificate); health care administration (PhD); health care management (MS), including health informatics; health education (MS, Certificate); health informatics (Certificate); health sciences (PhD); international health (MS); international health: educator or researcher option (PhD); international health: practitioner option (PhD); law and expert witness studies (MS, Certificate); public health (MS); quality assurance (Certificate). Part-time and evening/weekend programs available. Postbaccalaureate distance learning degree programs offered (no on-campus study). *Degree requirements:* For doctorate, comprehensive exam, thesis/dissertation, defense of dissertation. *Entrance requirements:* For master's, minimum GPA of 2.5 (students with GPA 3.0 or greater may transfer up to 30% of graduate level credits); for doctorate, minimum GPA of 3.4, curriculum vitae, course work in research methods or statistics. Additional exam requirements/recommendations for international students: Required—TOEFL. Electronic applications accepted.

Trine University, Program in Criminal Justice, Angola, IN 46703-1764. Offers emergency management (MS); forensic psychology (MS); law (MS); public administration (MS). Part-time and evening/weekend programs available. *Students:* 46 part-time (39 women). In 2014, 20 master's awarded. *Entrance requirements:* Additional exam requirements/recommendations for international students: Required—TOEFL. *Expenses: Tuition:* Full-time $12,000; part-time $670 per credit hour. Tuition and fees vary according to degree level, campus/location, program and student level. *Financial*

support: Application deadline: 3/1; applicants required to submit FAFSA. *Unit head:* Barbara E. Molargik-Fitch, JD, Director, 260-203-2693, Fax: 260-203-2965, E-mail: molargik-fitchb@trine.edu. *Application contact:* Cherie Ditto, Director of SPS Enrollment Services, 260-702-3592, E-mail: dittoc@trine.edu.
Website: http://www.trine.edu/academics/majors-and-minors/graduate/criminal-justice/index.aspx

Tulane University, School of Social Work, New Orleans, LA 70118-5669. Offers disaster resilience leadership (MS); social work (MSW, DSW); JD/MSW; MSW/MPH. *Accreditation:* CSWE (one or more programs are accredited). Part-time programs available. *Degree requirements:* For master's, thesis. *Entrance requirements:* Additional exam requirements/recommendations for international students: Required—TOEFL. Electronic applications accepted. *Expenses: Tuition:* Full-time $46,326; part-time $2574 per credit hour. *Required fees:* $1980; $44.50 per credit hour. $550 per term. Tuition and fees vary according to course load and program.

Université de Montréal, Faculty of Medicine, Programs in Environment and Prevention, Montréal, QC H3C 3J7, Canada. Offers environment, health and disaster management (DESS). Electronic applications accepted. *Faculty research:* Health, environment, pollutants, protection, waste.

University of Central Florida, College of Health and Public Affairs, School of Public Administration, Orlando, FL 32816. Offers emergency management and homeland security (Certificate); fundraising (Certificate); non-profit management (MNM, Certificate); urban and regional planning (MS). *Accreditation:* NASPAA. Part-time and evening/weekend programs available. *Faculty:* 18 full-time (9 women), 19 part-time/adjunct (9 women). *Students:* 109 full-time (80 women), 274 part-time (202 women); includes 148 minority (82 Black or African American, non-Hispanic/Latino; 8 Asian, non-Hispanic/Latino; 51 Hispanic/Latino; 7 Two or more races, non-Hispanic/Latino), 5 international. Average age 32. 264 applicants, 77% accepted, 148 enrolled. In 2014, 123 master's, 26 other advanced degrees awarded. *Degree requirements:* For master's, comprehensive exam, thesis or alternative, research report. *Entrance requirements:* For master's, GRE General Test. *Application deadline:* For fall admission, 7/1 for domestic students; for spring admission, 12/1 for domestic students. Application fee: $30. Electronic applications accepted. *Expenses:* Tuition, state resident: part-time $288.16 per credit hour. Tuition, nonresident: part-time $1073.31 per credit hour. *Financial support:* In 2014–15, 4 students received support, including 2 fellowships with partial tuition reimbursements available (averaging $5,300 per year), 1 research assistantship with partial tuition reimbursement available (averaging $10,600 per year), 1 teaching assistantship (averaging $7,100 per year); career-related internships or fieldwork, Federal Work-Study, institutionally sponsored loans, tuition waivers (partial), and unspecified assistantships also available. Financial award application deadline: 3/1; financial award applicants required to submit FAFSA. *Unit head:* Dr. Mary Ann Feldheim, Director, 407-823-3693, Fax: 407-823-5651, E-mail: mary.feldheim@ucf.edu. *Application contact:* Barbara Rodriguez Lamas, Director, Admissions and Student Services, 407-823-2766, Fax: 407-823-6442, E-mail: gradadmissions@ucf.edu.
Website: https://www.cohpa.ucf.edu/publicadmin/

University of Chicago, Graham School of Continuing Liberal and Professional Studies, Program in Threat and Response Management, Chicago, IL 60637. Offers M Sc. Part-time and evening/weekend programs available. *Students:* 39 part-time (16 women); includes 8 minority (4 Black or African American, non-Hispanic/Latino; 2 Asian, non-Hispanic/Latino; 2 Hispanic/Latino). 34 applicants, 88% accepted, 25 enrolled. *Entrance requirements:* Additional exam requirements/recommendations for international students: Required—TOEFL (minimum score 104 iBT), IELTS (minimum score 7). *Application deadline:* For fall admission, 6/30 for domestic and international students. Electronic applications accepted. *Expenses: Tuition:* Full-time $46,899. *Required fees:* $347. *Application contact:* 773-702-1722, E-mail: msctrm@uchicago.edu.
Website: https://grahamschool.uchicago.edu/credit/master-science-threat-response-management/index

University of Colorado Denver, School of Public Affairs, Program in Criminology and Criminal Justice, Denver, CO 80217. Offers criminal justice (MCJ), including criminal justice, domestic violence, emergency management and homeland security. Part-time and evening/weekend programs available. *Students:* 40 full-time (27 women), 22 part-time (10 women); includes 12 minority (1 Black or African American, non-Hispanic/Latino; 3 Asian, non-Hispanic/Latino; 8 Hispanic/Latino), 1 international. Average age 33. 28 applicants, 71% accepted, 12 enrolled. In 2014, 22 master's awarded. *Degree requirements:* For master's, thesis or alternative, 36-39 semester credit hours. *Entrance requirements:* For master's, GRE, GMAT, LSAT, recommendations, official transcripts, current resume, essay. Additional exam requirements/recommendations for international students: Required—TOEFL (minimum score 537 paper-based; 75 iBT); Recommended—IELTS (minimum score 6.5). *Application deadline:* For fall admission, 3/15 priority date for domestic students, 3/1 priority date for international students; for spring admission, 10/15 priority date for domestic students, 10/1 priority date for international students. Application fee: $50 ($75 for international students). Electronic applications accepted. *Expenses:* Expenses: Contact institution. *Financial support:* In 2014–15, 10 students received support. Fellowships, research assistantships, teaching assistantships, Federal Work-Study, institutionally sponsored loans, scholarships/grants, traineeships, and unspecified assistantships available. Financial award application deadline: 4/1; financial award applicants required to submit FAFSA. *Faculty research:* White collar crime, women and the criminal justice system, applied family violence issues, intimate partner violence and domestic violence interventions, juvenile delinquency. *Unit head:* Dr. Callie Rennison, MCJ Program Director, 303-315-2813, Fax: 303-315-2229, E-mail: callie.rennison@ucdenver.edu. *Application contact:* Brendan Hardy, Director of Student Recruitment, 303-315-2227, Fax: 303-315-2229, E-mail: brendan.hardy@ucdenver.edu.
Website: http://ucdenver.edu/academics/colleges/SPA/Academics/programs/CriminalJustice/Pages/index.aspx

University of Colorado Denver, School of Public Affairs, Program in Public Affairs and Administration, Denver, CO 80127. Offers public administration (MPA), including domestic violence, emergency management and homeland security, environmental policy, management and law, homeland security and defense, local government, nonprofit management, public administration; public affairs (PhD). *Accreditation:* NASPAA. Part-time and evening/weekend programs available. Postbaccalaureate distance learning degree programs offered (no on-campus study). *Students:* 275 full-time (176 women), 140 part-time (93 women); includes 70 minority (7 Black or African American, non-Hispanic/Latino; 4 American Indian or Alaska Native, non-Hispanic/Latino; 9 Asian, non-Hispanic/Latino; 44 Hispanic/Latino; 2 Native Hawaiian or other Pacific Islander, non-Hispanic/Latino; 4 Two or more races, non-Hispanic/Latino), 19 international. Average age 34. 243 applicants, 71% accepted, 97 enrolled. In 2014, 127 master's, 5 doctorates awarded. *Degree requirements:* For master's, thesis or alternative, 36-39 credit hours; for doctorate, comprehensive exam, thesis/dissertation, minimum of 66 semester hours, including at least 30 hours of dissertation. *Entrance requirements:* For master's, GRE, GMAT or LSAT, resume, essay, transcripts, recommendations; for doctorate, GRE, resume, essay, transcripts, recommendations. Additional exam requirements/recommendations for international students: Required—TOEFL (minimum score 550 paper-based; 80 iBT); Recommended—IELTS (minimum score 6.5). *Application deadline:* For fall admission, 2/1 priority date for domestic students, 1/15 priority date for international students; for spring admission, 10/15 priority date for domestic students, 10/1 priority date for international students. Application fee: $50 ($75 for international students). Electronic applications accepted. *Expenses:* Expenses: Contact institution. *Financial support:* In 2014–15, 60 students received support. Fellowships with partial tuition reimbursements available, research assistantships with partial tuition reimbursements available, teaching assistantships with partial tuition reimbursements available, Federal Work-Study, institutionally sponsored loans, scholarships/grants, traineeships, and unspecified assistantships available. Financial award application deadline: 4/1; financial award applicants required to submit FAFSA. *Faculty research:* Housing, education and the social and economic issues of vulnerable populations; nonprofit governance and management; education finance, effectiveness and reform; P-20 education initiatives; municipal government accountability. *Unit head:* Dr. Christine Martell, Director of MPA Program, 303-315-2716, Fax: 303-315-2229, E-mail: christine.martell@ucdenver.edu. *Application contact:* Dawn Savage, Student Services Coordinator, 303-315-2743, Fax: 303-315-2229, E-mail: dawn.savage@ucdenver.edu.
Website: http://www.ucdenver.edu/academics/colleges/SPA/Academics/programs/PublicAffairsAdmin/Pages/index.aspx

University of Delaware, College of Arts and Sciences, School of Public Policy and Administration, Program in Disaster Science and Management, Newark, DE 19716. Offers MS, PhD.

University of Denver, University College, Denver, CO 80208. Offers geographic information systems (Certificate); global affairs (Certificate), including translation studies, world history and culture; information and communications technology (MCIS), including geographic information systems, information systems security, project management (MCIS, Certificate), software design and programming, technology management, telecommunications technology, Web design and development; leadership and organizations (Certificate), including human capital in organizations, philanthropic leadership, project management (MCIS, Certificate), strategic innovation and change; organizational and professional communication (MPS), including alternative dispute resolution, organizational communication, organizational development and training, public relations and marketing; security management (MAS, Certificate), including emergency planning and response, information security (MAS), organizational security. Part-time and evening/weekend programs available. Postbaccalaureate distance learning degree programs offered (no on-campus study). *Faculty:* 8 full-time (4 women), 133 part-time/adjunct (46 women). *Students:* 54 full-time (21 women), 1,327 part-time (775 women); includes 272 minority (106 Black or African American, non-Hispanic/Latino; 6 American Indian or Alaska Native, non-Hispanic/Latino; 26 Asian, non-Hispanic/Latino; 108 Hispanic/Latino; 1 Native Hawaiian or other Pacific Islander, non-Hispanic/Latino; 25 Two or more races, non-Hispanic/Latino), 116 international. Average age 35. 768 applicants, 95% accepted, 620 enrolled. In 2014, 391 master's, 196 other advanced degrees awarded. *Degree requirements:* For master's, capstone project. *Entrance requirements:* For master's, transcripts, two letters of recommendation, personal statement, resume. Additional exam requirements/recommendations for international students: Required—TOEFL (minimum score 550 paper-based; 80 iBT). *Application deadline:* For fall admission, 6/21 priority date for domestic students, 5/1 priority date for international students; for winter admission, 9/14 priority date for domestic students, 9/19 priority date for international students; for spring admission, 1/11 for domestic students, 12/12 for international students; for summer admission, 3/29 priority date for domestic students, 3/6 priority date for international students. Applications are processed on a rolling basis. Application fee: $75. Electronic applications accepted. *Expenses:* Expenses: $959 per credit hour. *Financial support:* In 2014–15, 19 students received support. Applicants required to submit FAFSA. *Unit head:* Dr. Michael McGuire, Interim Dean, 303-871-3518, E-mail: mmcguire@du.edu. *Application contact:* Information Contact, 303-871-2291, E-mail: ucoladm@du.edu.
Website: http://www.universitycollege.du.edu/

University of Florida, Graduate School, College of Design, Construction and Planning, M.E. Rinker, Sr. School of Construction Management, Gainesville, FL 32611-5703. Offers construction management (MSCM); fire and emergency services (MFES); historic preservation (MSCM); international construction (MICM), including historic preservation; sustainable construction (MSCM); sustainable design (MSCM). Part-time programs available. Postbaccalaureate distance learning degree programs offered. *Faculty:* 13 full-time (0 women). *Students:* 46 full-time (16 women), 11 part-time (4 women); includes 11 minority (1 Black or African American, non-Hispanic/Latino; 1 American Indian or Alaska Native, non-Hispanic/Latino; 2 Asian, non-Hispanic/Latino; 7 Hispanic/Latino), 23 international. 66 applicants, 88% accepted, 20 enrolled. In 2014, 37 master's awarded. *Degree requirements:* For master's, thesis. *Entrance requirements:* For master's, GRE General Test, minimum GPA of 3.0. Additional exam requirements/recommendations for international students: Required—TOEFL (minimum score 550 paper-based; 80 iBT), IELTS (minimum score 6). *Application deadline:* Applications are processed on a rolling basis. Application fee: $30. Electronic applications accepted. *Financial support:* In 2014–15, 6 research assistantships, 5 teaching assistantships were awarded; fellowships, career-related internships or fieldwork, and unspecified assistantships also available. Financial award applicants required to submit FAFSA. *Faculty research:* Safety, affordable housing, construction management, environmental issues, sustainable construction. *Unit head:* Dr. Robert J. Ries, Interim Director, 352-273-1155, Fax: 352-392-9606, E-mail: rriesi@ufl.edu. *Application contact:* Dr. R. Edward Minchin, Director of Master's Programs, 352-273-1153, Fax: 352-392-7266, E-mail: minch@ufl.edu.
Website: http://www.bcn.ufl.edu/

University of Hawaii at Manoa, Graduate Division, College of Social Sciences, Department of Urban and Regional Planning, Program in Disaster Preparedness and Emergency Management, Honolulu, HI 96822. Offers Graduate Certificate. Part-time programs available. *Entrance requirements:* Additional exam requirements/recommendations for international students: Required—TOEFL (minimum score 500 paper-based; 61 iBT), IELTS (minimum score 5).

University of Illinois at Springfield, Graduate Programs, College of Public Affairs and Administration, Program in Public Health, Springfield, IL 62703-5407. Offers community health education (Graduate Certificate); emergency preparedness and homeland security (Graduate Certificate); epidemiology (Graduate Certificate); public health (MPH). Part-time and evening/weekend programs available. Postbaccalaureate distance learning degree programs offered (no on-campus study). *Faculty:* 5 full-time (4 women), 3 part-time/adjunct (1 woman). *Students:* 45 full-time (33 women), 55 part-time (36 women); includes 28 minority (21 Black or African American, non-Hispanic/Latino; 4 Asian, non-Hispanic/Latino; 2 Hispanic/Latino; 1 Two or more races, non-Hispanic/Latino), 17 international. Average age 32. 88 applicants, 40% accepted, 26 enrolled. In 2014, 19 master's, 7 other advanced degrees awarded. *Degree requirements:* For master's, comprehensive exam, internship. *Entrance requirements:* For master's, GRE, minimum undergraduate GPA of 3.0, 3 letters of recommendation, statement of personal goals. Additional exam requirements/recommendations for international students: Required—TOEFL (minimum score 500 paper-based; 61 iBT). *Application deadline:* Applications are processed on a rolling basis. Application fee: $60 ($75 for international

students). Electronic applications accepted. *Expenses:* Tuition, state resident: full-time $7662; part-time $319.25 per credit hour. Tuition, nonresident: full-time $15,966; part-time $665.25 per credit hour. *Financial support:* In 2014–15, fellowships with full tuition reimbursements (averaging $9,900 per year), research assistantships with full tuition reimbursements (averaging $9,600 per year), teaching assistantships with full tuition reimbursements (averaging $9,600 per year) were awarded; career-related internships or fieldwork, Federal Work-Study, scholarships/grants, health care benefits, and unspecified assistantships also available. Support available to part-time students. Financial award application deadline: 11/15; financial award applicants required to submit FAFSA. *Unit head:* Dr. Sharron Lafollette, Program Administrator, 217-206-7894, Fax: 217-206-7279, E-mail: slafo1@uis.edu. *Application contact:* Dr. Lynn Pardie, Office of Graduate Studies, 800-252-8533, Fax: 217-206-7623, E-mail: lpard1@uis.edu.
Website: http://www.uis.edu/publichealth/

University of Nebraska Medical Center, Program in Emergency Preparedness, Omaha, NE 68198-4326. Offers MS. Part-time programs available. Postbaccalaureate distance learning degree programs offered. *Students:* 4 full-time (3 women), 3 part-time (all women), 3 international. Average age 38. 8 applicants, 88% accepted, 7 enrolled. In 2014, 1 master's awarded. *Degree requirements:* For master's, thesis. *Entrance requirements:* For master's, GRE. Additional exam requirements/recommendations for international students: Required—TOEFL (minimum score 550 paper-based; 80 iBT). *Application deadline:* For fall admission, 6/1 for domestic students, 4/1 for international students; for spring admission, 10/1 for domestic students, 8/1 for international students. Application fee: $45. Electronic applications accepted. *Expenses:* Tuition, state resident: full-time $7695; part-time $285 per credit hour. Tuition, nonresident: full-time $22,005; part-time $815 per credit hour. Tuition and fees vary according to course load and program. *Financial support:* Scholarships/grants available. Support available to part-time students. Financial award applicants required to submit FAFSA. *Unit head:* Dr. Sharon Medcalf, Associate Director, Center for Emergency Preparedness, 402-552-2529, E-mail: smedcalf@unmc.edu. *Application contact:* Jessica Tschirren, Coordinator, 402-561-7586, Fax: 402-561-7599, E-mail: jtschirren@unmc.edu.
Website: http://www.unmc.edu/publichealth/programs/msemergencypreparedness.html

University of Nevada, Las Vegas, Graduate College, Greenspun College of Urban Affairs, School of Environmental and Public Affairs, Las Vegas, NV 89154-4030. Offers environmental science (MS, PhD); non-profit management (Certificate); public administration (MPA, MS), including crisis and emergency management (MS); public affairs (PhD); public management (Certificate); urban leadership (MA); workforce development and organizational leadership (PhD). Part-time programs available. *Faculty:* 13 full-time (5 women), 7 part-time/adjunct (2 women). *Students:* 81 full-time (44 women), 115 part-time (60 women); includes 71 minority (24 Black or African American, non-Hispanic/Latino; 2 American Indian or Alaska Native, non-Hispanic/Latino; 5 Asian, non-Hispanic/Latino; 30 Hispanic/Latino; 3 Native Hawaiian or other Pacific Islander, non-Hispanic/Latino; 7 Two or more races, non-Hispanic/Latino), 8 international. Average age 37. 78 applicants, 86% accepted, 48 enrolled. In 2014, 50 master's, 6 doctorates, 19 other advanced degrees awarded. *Degree requirements:* For master's, comprehensive exam (for some programs), thesis; for doctorate, comprehensive exam (for some programs), thesis/dissertation. *Entrance requirements:* Additional exam requirements/recommendations for international students: Required—TOEFL (minimum score 550 paper-based; 80 iBT), IELTS (minimum score 7). *Application deadline:* For fall admission, 2/15 for domestic students, 5/1 for international students; for spring admission, 11/15 for domestic students, 10/1 for international students. Application fee: $60 ($95 for international students). Electronic applications accepted. *Financial support:* In 2014–15, 31 students received support, including 1 fellowship (averaging $25,000 per year), 13 research assistantships with partial tuition reimbursements available (averaging $13,473 per year), 17 teaching assistantships with partial tuition reimbursements available (averaging $13,206 per year); institutionally sponsored loans, scholarships/grants, health care benefits, and unspecified assistantships also available. Financial award application deadline: 3/1. *Faculty research:* Community and organizational resilience; environmental decision-making and management; budgeting and human resource/workforce management; urban design, sustainability and governance; public and non-profit management. *Total annual research expenditures:* $333,798. *Unit head:* Dr. Christopher Stream, Chair/Associate Professor, 702-895-5120, Fax: 702-895-4436, E-mail: chris.stream@unlv.edu. *Application contact:* Graduate College Admissions Evaluator, 702-895-3320, Fax: 702-895-4180, E-mail: gradcollege@unlv.edu.
Website: http://sepa.unlv.edu/

University of New Haven, Graduate School, Henry C. Lee College of Criminal Justice and Forensic Sciences, Program in Fire Science, West Haven, CT 06516-1916. Offers emergency management (MS, Certificate); fire administration (MS); fire science (MS); fire science technology (Certificate); fire/arson investigation (MS, Certificate); forensic science/fire science (Certificate); public safety management (MS, Certificate). Part-time and evening/weekend programs available. *Degree requirements:* For master's, thesis or alternative, research project or internship. *Entrance requirements:* Additional exam requirements/recommendations for international students: Required—TOEFL (minimum score 80 iBT), IELTS, PTE (minimum score 53). Electronic applications accepted. Application fee is waived when completed online. *Expenses: Tuition:* Full-time $22,248; part-time $824 per credit hour. *Required fees:* $45 per trimester.

The University of North Carolina at Charlotte, College of Liberal Arts and Sciences, Department of Political Science and Public Administration, Charlotte, NC 28223-0001. Offers emergency management (Graduate Certificate); non-profit management (Graduate Certificate); public administration (MPA), including arts administration, emergency management, non-profit management, public finance; public finance (Graduate Certificate); urban management and policy (Graduate Certificate). *Accreditation:* NASPAA. Part-time and evening/weekend programs available. *Faculty:* 15 full-time (8 women), 4 part-time/adjunct (1 woman). *Students:* 16 full-time (10 women), 83 part-time (51 women); includes 32 minority (21 Black or African American, non-Hispanic/Latino; 1 Asian, non-Hispanic/Latino; 7 Hispanic/Latino; 3 Two or more races, non-Hispanic/Latino). Average age 30. 60 applicants, 65% accepted, 25 enrolled. In 2014, 23 master's, 11 other advanced degrees awarded. Terminal master's awarded for partial completion of doctoral program. *Degree requirements:* For master's, thesis or alternative. *Entrance requirements:* For master's, GRE General Test or MAT, minimum GPA of 3.0 in undergraduate major, 2.75 overall. Additional exam requirements/recommendations for international students: Required—TOEFL (minimum score 557 paper-based; 83 iBT). *Application deadline:* For fall admission, 5/1 priority date for domestic students, 5/1 for international students; for spring admission, 10/1 priority date for domestic students, 10/1 for international students. Applications are processed on a rolling basis. Application fee: $75. Electronic applications accepted. *Expenses:* Tuition, state resident: full-time $4008. Tuition, nonresident: full-time $16,295. *Required fees:* $2755. Tuition and fees vary according to course load and program. *Financial support:* In 2014–15, 7 students received support, including 7 research assistantships (averaging $6,857 per year); career-related internships or fieldwork, Federal Work-Study, institutionally sponsored loans, scholarships/grants, and unspecified assistantships also available. Support available to part-time students. Financial award application deadline: 4/1; financial award applicants required to submit FAFSA. *Faculty research:* Health

policy and politics, managed care, issues of ethnic and racial disparities in health, aging policies, Central Asia. *Total annual research expenditures:* $348,793. *Unit head:* Dr. Greg Weeks, Chair, 704-687-7574, Fax: 704-687-1400, E-mail: gbweeks@uncc.edu. *Application contact:* Kathy B. Giddings, Director of Graduate Admissions, 704-687-5503, Fax: 704-687-1668, E-mail: gradadm@uncc.edu.
Website: https://politicalscience.uncc.edu/graduate

University of North Texas, Robert B. Toulouse School of Graduate Studies, Denton, TX 76203-5459. Offers accounting (MS); applied anthropology (MA, MS); applied behavior analysis (Certificate); applied geography (MA); applied technology and performance improvement (M Ed, MS); art education (MA); art history (MA); art museum education (Certificate); arts leadership (Certificate); audiology (Au D); behavior analysis (MS); behavioral science (PhD); biochemistry and molecular biology (MS); biology (MA, MS); biomedical engineering (MS); business analysis (MS); chemistry (MS); clinical health psychology (PhD); communication studies (MA, MS); computer engineering (MS); computer science (MS); counseling (M Ed, MS), including clinical mental health counseling (MS), college and university counseling, elementary school counseling, secondary school counseling; creative writing (MA); criminal justice (MS); curriculum and instruction (M Ed); decision sciences (MBA); design (MA, MFA), including fashion design (MFA), innovation studies, interior design (MFA); early childhood studies (MS); economics (MS); educational leadership (M Ed, Ed D); educational psychology (MS, PhD), including family studies (MS), gifted and talented (MS), human development (MS), learning and cognition (MS), research, measurement and evaluation (MS); electrical engineering (MS); emergency management (MPA); engineering technology (MS); English (MA); English as a second language (MA); environmental science (MS); finance (MBA, MS); financial management (MPA); French (MA); health services management (MBA); higher education (M Ed, Ed D); history (MA, MS); hospitality management (MS); human resources management (MPA); information science (MS); information systems (PhD); information technologies (MBA); interdisciplinary studies (MA, MS); international studies (MA); international sustainable tourism (MS); jazz studies (MM); journalism (MA, MJ, Graduate Certificate), including interactive and virtual digital communication (Graduate Certificate), narrative journalism (Graduate Certificate), public relations (Graduate Certificate); kinesiology (MS); linguistics (MA); local government management (MPA); logistics (PhD); logistics and supply chain management (MBA); long-term care, senior housing, and aging services (MA); management (PhD); marketing (MBA); mathematics (MA, MS); mechanical and energy engineering (MS, PhD); music (MA), including ethnomusicology, music theory, musicology, performance; music composition (PhD); music education (MM Ed, PhD); nonprofit management (MPA); operations and supply chain management (MBA); performance (MM, DMA); philosophy (MA); political science (MA); professional and technical communication (MA); radio, television and film (MA, MFA); rehabilitation counseling (Certificate); sociology (MA); Spanish (MA); special education (M Ed); speech-language pathology (MA); strategic management (MBA); studio art (MFA); teaching (M Ed); MBA/MS. Part-time and evening/weekend programs available. Postbaccalaureate distance learning degree programs offered. *Faculty:* 651 full-time (215 women), 233 part-time/adjunct (139 women). *Students:* 3,040 full-time (1,598 women), 3,401 part-time (2,097 women); includes 1,740 minority (533 Black or African American, non-Hispanic/Latino; 15 American Indian or Alaska Native, non-Hispanic/Latino; 286 Asian, non-Hispanic/Latino; 746 Hispanic/Latino; 3 Native Hawaiian or other Pacific Islander, non-Hispanic/Latino; 157 Two or more races, non-Hispanic/Latino), 1,145 international. Terminal master's awarded for partial completion of doctoral program. *Degree requirements:* For master's, variable foreign language requirement, comprehensive exam (for some programs), thesis (for some programs); for doctorate, variable foreign language requirement, comprehensive exam (for some programs), thesis/dissertation; for other advanced degree, variable foreign language requirement, comprehensive exam (for some programs). *Entrance requirements:* For master's and doctorate, GRE, GMAT. Additional exam requirements/recommendations for international students: Required—TOEFL (minimum score 550 paper-based; 79 iBT). *Application deadline:* For fall admission, 7/15 for domestic students, 3/15 for international students; for spring admission, 11/15 for domestic students, 9/15 for international students; for summer admission, 5/1 for domestic students. Applications are processed on a rolling basis. Application fee: $60. Electronic applications accepted. *Expenses:* Tuition, state resident: full-time $5450; part-time $3633 per year. Tuition, nonresident: full-time $11,966; part-time $7977 per year. *Required fees:* $1301; $398 per credit hour. $685 per semester. Tuition and fees vary according to program and reciprocity agreements. *Financial support:* Fellowships with partial tuition reimbursements, research assistantships with partial tuition reimbursements, teaching assistantships, career-related internships or fieldwork, Federal Work-Study, institutionally sponsored loans, scholarships/grants, health care benefits, and library assistantships available. Support available to part-time students. Financial award applicants required to submit FAFSA. *Unit head:* Mark Wardell, Dean, 940-565-2383, E-mail: mark.wardell@unt.edu. *Application contact:* Toulouse School of Graduate Studies, 940-565-2383, Fax: 940-565-2141, E-mail: gradsch@unt.edu.
Website: http://tsgs.unt.edu/

University of South Florida, Innovative Education, Tampa, FL 33620-9951. *Unit head:* Kathy Barnes, Interdisciplinary Programs Coordinator, 813-974-8031, Fax: 813-974-7061, E-mail: barnesk@usf.edu. *Application contact:* Karen Tylinski, Metro Initiatives, 813-974-9943, Fax: 813-974-7061, E-mail: ktylinsk@usf.edu.
Website: http://www.usf.edu/innovative-education/

The University of Toledo, College of Graduate Studies, College of Medicine and Life Sciences, Department of Public Health and Preventative Medicine, Toledo, OH 43606-3390. Offers biostatistics and epidemiology (Certificate); contemporary gerontological practice (Certificate); environmental and occupational health and safety (MPH); epidemiology (Certificate); global public health (Certificate); health promotion and education (MPH); industrial hygiene (MSOH); medical and health science teaching and learning (Certificate); occupational health (Certificate); public health administration (MPH); public health and emergency response (Certificate); public health epidemiology (MPH); public health nutrition (MPH); MD/MPH. Part-time and evening/weekend programs available. *Degree requirements:* For master's, thesis or alternative. *Entrance requirements:* For master's, GRE, minimum undergraduate GPA of 3.0, three letters of recommendation, statement of purpose, transcripts from all prior institutions attended, resume; for Certificate, minimum undergraduate GPA of 3.0, three letters of recommendation, statement of purpose, transcripts from all prior institutions attended, resume. Additional exam requirements/recommendations for international students: Required—TOEFL (minimum score 550 paper-based; 80 iBT), IELTS (minimum score 6.5). Electronic applications accepted.

Virginia Commonwealth University, Graduate School, College of Humanities and Sciences, Wilder School of Government and Public Affairs, Program in Homeland Security and Emergency Preparedness, Richmond, VA 23284-9005. Offers MA, Graduate Certificate. Part-time programs available. Postbaccalaureate distance learning degree programs offered. *Entrance requirements:* For master's, GRE, GMAT, MAT or LSAT, minimum GPA of 2.7; for Graduate Certificate, minimum GPA of 2.7. Additional exam requirements/recommendations for international students: Required—TOEFL (minimum score 600 paper-based; 100 iBT); Recommended—IELTS (minimum score 6.5). Electronic applications accepted.

Walden University, Graduate Programs, School of Counseling, Minneapolis, MN 55401. Offers addiction counseling (MS), including addictions and public health, child and adolescent counseling, family studies and interventions, forensic counseling, general program (MS, PhD), trauma and crisis counseling; counselor education and supervision (PhD), including consultation, counseling and social change, forensic mental health counseling, general program (MS, PhD), trauma and crisis; marriage, couple, and family counseling (MS), including forensic counseling, general program (MS, PhD), trauma and crisis counseling; mental health counseling (MS), including forensic counseling, general program (MS, PhD), trauma and crisis counseling; school counseling (MS), including addiction counseling, crisis and trauma, general program (MS, PhD), military families and culture. Part-time and evening/weekend programs available. Postbaccalaureate distance learning degree programs offered (no on-campus study). *Faculty:* 77 full-time (62 women), 314 part-time/adjunct (215 women). *Students:* 1,835 full-time (1,558 women), 1,518 part-time (1,293 women); includes 1,521 minority (1,135 Black or African American, non-Hispanic/Latino; 13 American Indian or Alaska Native, non-Hispanic/Latino; 27 Asian, non-Hispanic/Latino; 234 Hispanic/Latino; 5 Native Hawaiian or other Pacific Islander, non-Hispanic/Latino; 107 Two or more races, non-Hispanic/Latino), 16 international. Average age 38. 684 applicants, 91% accepted, 610 enrolled. In 2014, 592 master's, 4 doctorates awarded. *Degree requirements:* For master's, residency, field experience, professional development plan, licensure plan; for doctorate, thesis/dissertation, residency, practicum, internship. *Entrance requirements:* For master's, bachelor's degree or higher; minimum GPA of 2.5; official transcripts; goal statement (for some programs); access to computer and Internet; for doctorate, master's degree or higher; three years of related professional or academic experience (preferred); minimum GPA of 3.0; goal statement and current resume (for select programs); official transcripts; access to computer and Internet. Additional exam requirements/recommendations for international students: Required—TOEFL (minimum score 550 paper-based, 79 iBT), IELTS (minimum score 6.5), Michigan English Language Assessment Battery (minimum score 82), or PTE (minimum score 53). *Application deadline:* Applications are processed on a rolling basis. Application fee: $0. Electronic applications accepted. *Expenses: Tuition:* Full-time $11,925; part-time $500 per credit hour. *Required fees:* $647. *Financial support:* Federal Work-Study, scholarships/grants, unspecified assistantships, and family tuition reduction, active duty/veteran tuition reduction, group tuition reduction, interest-free payment plans, employee tuition reduction available. Support available to part-time students. Financial award applicants required to submit FAFSA. *Unit head:* Dr. Savitri Dixon-Saxon, Associate Dean, 866-492-5336. *Application contact:* Meghan M. Thomas, Vice President of Enrollment Management, 866-492-5336, E-mail: info@waldenu.edu.

Walden University, Graduate Programs, School of Public Policy and Administration, Minneapolis, MN 55401. Offers criminal justice (MPA, MPP, MS, Graduate Certificate), including emergency management (MS, PhD), general program (MS, PhD), homeland security and policy coordination (MS, PhD), law and public policy (MS, PhD), policy analysis (MS, PhD), public management and leadership (MS, PhD), self-designed (MS), terrorism, mediation, and peace (MS, PhD); criminal justice leadership and executive management (MS), including emergency management (MS, PhD), general program (MS, PhD), homeland security and policy coordination (MS, PhD), law and public policy (MS, PhD), policy analysis (MS, PhD), public management and leadership (MS, PhD), self-designed, terrorism, mediation, and peace (MS, PhD); emergency management (MPA, MPP, MS), including criminal justice (MS, PhD), general program (MS, PhD), homeland security (MS), public management and leadership (MS, PhD), terrorism and emergency management (MS); general program (MPA, MPP); government management (Graduate Certificate); health policy (MPA, MPP); homeland security (Graduate Certificate); homeland security and policy coordination (MPA, MPP); international nongovernmental organizations (MPA, MPP); law and public policy (MPA, MPP); local government management for sustainable communities (MPA, MPP); nonprofit management (Graduate Certificate); nonprofit management and leadership (MPA, MPP, MS); online teaching in higher education (Post-Master's Certificate); policy analysis (MPA); public management and leadership (MPA, MPP, Graduate Certificate); public policy (Graduate Certificate); public policy and administration (PhD), including criminal justice (MS, PhD), emergency management (MS, PhD), general program (MS, PhD), health policy, homeland security and policy coordination (MS, PhD), international nongovernmental organizations, law and public policy (MS, PhD), local government management for sustainable communities, nonprofit management and leadership, policy analysis (MS, PhD), public management and leadership (MS, PhD), terrorism, mediation, and peace (MS, PhD); strategic planning and public policy (Graduate Certificate); terrorism, mediation, and peace (MPA, MPP). Part-time and evening/weekend programs available. Postbaccalaureate distance learning degree programs offered (no on-campus study). *Faculty:* 13 full-time (5 women), 151 part-time/adjunct (65 women). *Students:* 1,009 full-time (573 women), 1,632 part-time (954 women); includes 1,553 minority (1,307 Black or African American, non-Hispanic/Latino; 15 American Indian or Alaska Native, non-Hispanic/Latino; 38 Asian, non-Hispanic/Latino; 127 Hispanic/Latino; 66 Two or more races, non-Hispanic/Latino), 15 international. Average age 42. 665 applicants, 97% accepted, 616 enrolled. In 2014, 317 master's, 95 doctorates, 34 other advanced degrees awarded. *Degree requirements:* For doctorate, thesis/dissertation, residency. *Entrance requirements:* For master's, bachelor's degree or higher; minimum GPA of 2.5; official transcripts; goal statement (for some programs); access to computer and Internet; for doctorate, master's degree or higher; three years of related professional or academic experience (preferred); minimum GPA of 3.0; goal statement and current resume (for select programs); official transcripts; access to computer and Internet; for other advanced degree, relevant work experience; access to computer and Internet. Additional exam requirements/recommendations for international students: Required—TOEFL (minimum score 550 paper-based, 79 iBT), IELTS (minimum score 6.5), Michigan English Language Assessment Battery (minimum score 82), or PTE (minimum score 53). *Application deadline:* Applications are processed on a rolling basis. Application fee: $0. Electronic applications accepted. *Expenses: Tuition:*

Full-time $11,925; part-time $500 per credit hour. *Required fees:* $647. *Financial support:* Fellowships, Federal Work-Study, scholarships/grants, unspecified assistantships, and family tuition reduction, active duty/veteran tuition reduction, group tuition reduction, interest-free payment plans, employee tuition reduction available. Support available to part-time students. Financial award applicants required to submit FAFSA. *Unit head:* Dr. Shana Garrett, Associate Dean, 866-492-5336. *Application contact:* Meghan Thomas, Vice President of Enrollment Management, 866-492-5336, E-mail: info@waldenu.edu.
Website: http://www.waldenu.edu/programs/colleges-schools/public-policy-and-administration

Walden University, Graduate Programs, School of Social Work and Human Services, Minneapolis, MN 55401. Offers addictions (MSW); addictions and social work (DSW); children, families, and couples (MSW); clinical expertise (DSW); criminal justice (DSW); crisis and trauma (MSW); disaster, crisis, and intervention (DSW); forensic populations and settings (MSW); general program (MSW); human services (MS, PhD), including clinical social work (PhD), criminal justice, disaster, crisis and intervention, family studies and intervention strategies (PhD), family studies and interventions, general program, human services administration, public health, social policy analysis and planning; medical social work (MSW, DSW); military families and culture (MSW); policy practice (DSW); social work (PhD), including addictions and social work, clinical expertise, disaster, crisis and intervention (MS, PhD), family studies and interventions (MS, PhD), medical social work, policy practice, social work administration; social work administration (DSW). Part-time and evening/weekend programs available. Postbaccalaureate distance learning degree programs offered (no on-campus study). *Faculty:* 18 full-time (11 women), 236 part-time/adjunct (156 women). *Students:* 1,400 full-time (1,205 women), 884 part-time (759 women); includes 1,586 minority (1,373 Black or African American, non-Hispanic/Latino; 20 American Indian or Alaska Native, non-Hispanic/Latino; 16 Asian, non-Hispanic/Latino; 120 Hispanic/Latino; 57 Two or more races, non-Hispanic/Latino), 14 international. Average age 40. 892 applicants, 96% accepted, 826 enrolled. In 2014, 61 master's, 14 doctorates awarded. *Degree requirements:* For master's, residency (for some programs); for doctorate, thesis/dissertation, residency. *Entrance requirements:* For master's, bachelor's degree or higher; minimum GPA of 2.5; official transcripts; goal statement (for some programs); access to computer and Internet; for doctorate, master's degree or higher; three years of related professional or academic experience (preferred); minimum GPA of 3.0; goal statement and current resume (for select programs); official transcripts; access to computer and Internet. Additional exam requirements/recommendations for international students: Required—TOEFL (minimum score 550 paper-based, 79 iBT), IELTS (minimum score 6.5), Michigan English Language Assessment Battery (minimum score 82), or PTE (minimum score 53). *Application deadline:* Applications are processed on a rolling basis. Application fee: $0. Electronic applications accepted. *Expenses: Tuition:* Full-time $11,925; part-time $500 per credit hour. *Required fees:* $647. *Financial support:* Fellowships, Federal Work-Study, scholarships/grants, unspecified assistantships, and family tuition reduction, active duty/veteran tuition reduction, group tuition reduction, interest-free payment plans, employee tuition reduction available. Support available to part-time students. Financial award applicants required to submit FAFSA. *Unit head:* Dr. Savitri Dixon-Saxon, Associate Dean, 866-492-5336. *Application contact:* Meghan Thomas, Vice President of Enrollment Management, 866-492-5336, E-mail: info@waldenu.edu.
Website: http://www.waldenu.edu/colleges-schools/school-of-social-work-and-human-services/academic-programs

West Chester University of Pennsylvania, College of Health Sciences, Department of Health, West Chester, PA 19383. Offers community health (MPH); emergency preparedness (Certificate); environmental health (MPH); health care management (MPH, Certificate); integrative health (MPH, Certificate); nutrition (MPH); school health (M Ed). *Accreditation:* CEPH. Part-time and evening/weekend programs available. *Faculty:* 16 full-time (14 women), 5 part-time/adjunct (4 women). *Students:* 117 full-time (87 women), 100 part-time (75 women); includes 76 minority (57 Black or African American, non-Hispanic/Latino; 9 Asian, non-Hispanic/Latino; 5 Hispanic/Latino; 5 Two or more races, non-Hispanic/Latino), 20 international. 128 applicants, 87% accepted, 70 enrolled. In 2014, 80 master's, 18 other advanced degrees awarded. *Degree requirements:* For master's, thesis or alternative, minimum GPA of 3.0; research report (for M Ed); major project and practicum (for MPH); for Certificate, minimum GPA of 3.0. *Entrance requirements:* For master's, goal statement, two letters of recommendation, undergraduate introduction to statistics course. Additional exam requirements/recommendations for international students: Required—TOEFL (minimum score 550 paper-based; 80 iBT). *Application deadline:* For fall admission, 4/15 priority date for domestic students, 3/15 for international students; for spring admission, 10/15 priority date for domestic students, 9/1 for international students. Applications are processed on a rolling basis. Application fee: $45. Electronic applications accepted. *Expenses:* Tuition, state resident: full-time $8172; part-time $454 per credit. Tuition, nonresident: full-time $12,258; part-time $681 per credit. *Required fees:* $2231; $110.78 per credit. Tuition and fees vary according to campus/location and program. *Financial support:* Unspecified assistantships available. Support available to part-time students. Financial award application deadline: 2/15; financial award applicants required to submit FAFSA. *Faculty research:* Healthy school communities, community health issues and evidence-based programs, environment and health, nutrition and health, integrative health. *Unit head:* Dr. Bethann Cinelli, Chair, 610-436-2267, E-mail: bcinelli@wcupa.edu. *Application contact:* Dr. Lynn Carson, Graduate Coordinator, 610-436-2138, E-mail: lcarson@wcupa.edu.
Website: http://www.wcupa.edu/_ACADEMICS/HealthSciences/health/

York University, Faculty of Graduate Studies, Faculty of Liberal Arts and Professional Studies, Program in Disaster and Emergency Management, Toronto, ON M3J 1P3, Canada. Offers MA.

Homeland Security

American Public University System, AMU/APU Graduate Programs, Charles Town, WV 25414. Offers accounting (MBA, MS); criminal justice (MA), including business administration, emergency and disaster management, general (MA, MS); educational leadership (M Ed); emergency and disaster management (MA); entrepreneurship (MBA); environmental policy and management (MS), including environmental planning, environmental sustainability, fish and wildlife management, general (MA, MS), global environmental management; finance (MBA); general (MBA); global business management (MBA); history (MA), including American history, ancient and classical history, European history, global history, public history; homeland security (MA),

including business administration, counter-terrorism studies, criminal justice, cyber, emergency management and public health, intelligence studies, transportation security; homeland security resource allocation (MBA); humanities (MA); information technology (MS), including digital forensics, enterprise software development, information assurance and security, IT project management; information technology management (MBA); intelligence studies (MA), including criminal intelligence, cyber, general (MA, MS), homeland security, intelligence analysis, intelligence collection, intelligence management, intelligence operations, terrorism studies; international relations and conflict resolution (MA), including comparative and security issues, conflict resolution,

international and transnational security issues, peacekeeping; legal studies (MA); management (MA), including defense management, general (MA, MS), human resource management, organizational leadership, public administration; marketing (MBA); military history (MA), including American military history, American Revolution, civil war, war since 1945, World War II; military studies (MA), including joint warfare, strategic leadership; national security studies (MA), including general (MA, MS), homeland security, regional security studies, security and intelligence analysis, terrorism studies; nonprofit management (MBA); political science (MA), including American politics and government, comparative government and development, general (MA, MS), international relations, public policy; psychology (MA); public administration (MPA), including disaster management, environmental policy, health policy, human resources, national security, organizational management, security management; public health (MPH); reverse logistics management (MA); school counseling (M Ed); security management (MA); space studies (MS), including aerospace science, general (MA, MS), planetary science; sports and health sciences (MS); teaching (M Ed), including curriculum and instruction for elementary teachers, elementary reading, English language learners, instructional leadership, online learning, special education; transportation and logistics management (MA), including general (MA, MS), maritime engineering management, reverse logistics management. Programs offered via distance learning only. Part-time and evening/weekend programs available. Postbaccalaureate distance learning degree programs offered (no on-campus study). *Faculty:* 426 full-time (236 women), 1,864 part-time/adjunct (880 women). *Students:* 475 full-time (215 women), 10,067 part-time (4,085 women); includes 3,462 minority (1,863 Black or African American, non-Hispanic/Latino; 74 American Indian or Alaska Native, non-Hispanic/Latino; 273 Asian, non-Hispanic/Latino; 831 Hispanic/Latino; 78 Native Hawaiian or other Pacific Islander, non-Hispanic/Latino; 343 Two or more races, non-Hispanic/Latino), 131 international. Average age 36. In 2014, 3,740 master's awarded. *Degree requirements:* For master's, comprehensive exam or practicum. *Entrance requirements:* For master's, official transcript showing earned bachelor's degree from institution accredited by recognized accrediting body. Additional exam requirements/recommendations for international students: Required—TOEFL (minimum score 550 paper-based), IELTS (minimum score 6.5). *Application deadline:* Applications are processed on a rolling basis. Application fee: $0. Electronic applications accepted. *Financial support:* Applicants required to submit FAFSA. *Faculty research:* Military history, criminal justice, management performance, national security. *Unit head:* Dr. Karan Powell, Executive Vice President and Provost, 877-468-6268, Fax: 304-724-3780. *Application contact:* Terry Grant, Vice President of Enrollment Management, 877-468-6268, Fax: 304-724-3780, E-mail: info@apus.edu.
Website: http://www.apus.edu

Arizona State University at the Tempe campus, College of Public Programs, School of Public Affairs, Phoenix, AZ 85004-0687. Offers emergency management and homeland security (MA); program evaluation (MS); public administration (MPA, PhD), including nonprofit administration (MPA), urban management (MPA); public policy (MPP); MPA/MSW. *Accreditation:* NASPAA (one or more programs are accredited). Part-time and evening/weekend programs available. Terminal master's awarded for partial completion of doctoral program. *Degree requirements:* For master's, thesis or alternative, policy analysis or capstone project; interactive Program of Study (iPOS) submitted before completing 50 percent of required credit hours; for doctorate, comprehensive exam, thesis/dissertation, interactive Program of Study (iPOS) submitted before completing 50 percent of required credit hours. *Entrance requirements:* For master's, GRE, minimum GPA of 3.0 or equivalent in last 2 years of work leading to bachelor's degree; for doctorate, GRE, minimum GPA of 3.0 or equivalent in last 2 years of work leading to bachelor's degree, 3 letters of recommendation, resume, statement of goals, samples of research reports. Additional exam requirements/recommendations for international students: Required—TOEFL (minimum score 600 paper-based; 100 iBT), IELTS (minimum score 6.5). Electronic applications accepted. *Expenses:* Contact institution.

Auburn University at Montgomery, College of Public Policy and Justice, Department of Justice and Public Safety, Montgomery, AL 36124-4023. Offers criminal studies (MSJPS); homeland security (MSJPS); homeland security and emergency management (MS); legal studies (MSJPS); organizational leadership (MSJPS); paralegal (Certificate). Part-time and evening/weekend programs available. *Faculty:* 6 full-time (3 women), 4 part-time/adjunct (0 women). *Students:* 12 full-time (7 women), 43 part-time (26 women); includes 19 minority (all Black or African American, non-Hispanic/Latino). Average age 32. 34 applicants, 79% accepted, 15 enrolled. In 2014, 20 master's awarded. *Degree requirements:* For master's, comprehensive exam, thesis optional. *Entrance requirements:* For master's, GRE General Test or MAT. *Application deadline:* Applications are processed on a rolling basis. Electronic applications accepted. *Expenses:* Tuition, state resident: full-time $6264; part-time $348 per credit hour. Tuition, nonresident: full-time $14,094; part-time $783 per credit hour. *Financial support:* Career-related internships or fieldwork and scholarships/grants available. Support available to part-time students. Financial award application deadline: 3/1; financial award applicants required to submit FAFSA. *Faculty research:* Law enforcement, corrections, juvenile justice. *Unit head:* Dr. Ralph Ioimo, Head, 334-244-3691, Fax: 334-244-3244, E-mail: rioimo@aum.edu. *Application contact:* Shinae Yoon, Administrative Associate, 334-244-3692, Fax: 334-244-3244, E-mail: syoon1@aum.edu.

Capella University, School of Public Service Leadership, Master's Programs in Healthcare, Minneapolis, MN 55402. Offers criminal justice (MS); emergency management (MS); general public health (MPH); gerontology (MS); health administration (MHA); health care operations (MHA); health management policy (MPH); health policy (MHA); homeland security (MS); multidisciplinary human services (MS); public administration (MPA); public safety leadership (MS); social and community services (MS); social behavioral sciences (MPH); MS/MPA.

Chaminade University of Honolulu, Graduate Services, Program in Criminal Justice Administration, Honolulu, HI 96816-1578. Offers criminal justice administration (MSCJA); homeland security leadership development (MSCJA, Certificate). Part-time and evening/weekend programs available. Postbaccalaureate distance learning degree programs offered (no on-campus study). *Degree requirements:* For master's, comprehensive exam. *Entrance requirements:* For master's, minimum undergraduate GPA of 3.0, 3 letters of recommendation. Additional exam requirements/recommendations for international students: Required—TOEFL (minimum score 550 paper-based). Electronic applications accepted. *Faculty research:* Penology, juvenile delinquency, multicultural and ethnic diversity in criminology, law enforcement administration and training, homeland security.

Columbus State University, Graduate Studies, College of Letters and Sciences, Program in Public Safety Administration, Columbus, GA 31907-5645. Offers MS. Part-time programs available. *Faculty:* 1 full-time (0 women), 4 part-time/adjunct (0 women). *Students:* 32 full-time (6 women), 147 part-time (46 women); includes 50 minority (48 Black or African American, non-Hispanic/Latino; 1 Hispanic/Latino; 1 Two or more races, non-Hispanic/Latino). Average age 44. 44 applicants, 93% accepted, 35 enrolled. In 2014, 46 master's awarded. *Degree requirements:* For master's, comprehensive exam. *Entrance requirements:* For master's, baccalaureate degree, employment in a public safety profession. Additional exam requirements/recommendations for international students: Required—TOEFL (minimum score 550 paper-based; 79 iBT). *Application deadline:* For fall admission, 6/30 for domestic students, 4/1 for international students; for spring admission, 11/1 for domestic and international students; for summer admission, 3/1 for domestic students, 2/1 for international students. Applications are processed on a rolling basis. Application fee: $50. Electronic applications accepted. *Financial support:* In 2014–15, 26 students received support. Applicants required to submit FAFSA. *Unit head:* Dr. Dennis Rome, Dean, 706-568-2056, E-mail: rome_dennis@columbusstate.edu. *Application contact:* Kristin Williams, Director of International and Graduate Recruitment, 706-507-8848, Fax: 706-568-5091, E-mail: williams_kristin@columbusstate.edu.
Website: http://cols.columbusstate.edu

Drexel University, Goodwin College of Professional Studies, School of Technology and Professional Studies, Philadelphia, PA 19104-2875. Offers construction management (MS); creativity and innovation (MS); engineering technology (MS); food science (MS); hospitality management (MS); professional studies: creativity studies (MS); professional studies: e-learning leadership (MS); professional studies: homeland security management (MS); project management (MS); property management (MS); sport management (MS). Part-time and evening/weekend programs available. *Entrance requirements:* Additional exam requirements/recommendations for international students: Required—TOEFL, IELTS. Electronic applications accepted. Application fee is waived when completed online.

Endicott College, Van Loan School of Graduate and Professional Studies, Program in Homeland Security, Beverly, MA 01915-2096. Offers MS. Part-time programs available. *Faculty:* 2 full-time (0 women), 5 part-time/adjunct (0 women). *Students:* 31 full-time (14 women), 2 part-time (0 women); includes 3 minority (1 Black or African American, non-Hispanic/Latino; 1 Hispanic/Latino; 1 Two or more races, non-Hispanic/Latino). Average age 29. 24 applicants, 75% accepted, 15 enrolled. In 2014, 11 master's awarded. *Degree requirements:* For master's, thesis. *Entrance requirements:* For master's, undergraduate transcript, two recommendations, personal statement. Additional exam requirements/recommendations for international students: Required—TOEFL. *Application deadline:* Applications are processed on a rolling basis. Application fee: $50. Electronic applications accepted. *Unit head:* Michael D. Andreas, Director, 978-232-2740, Fax: 978-232-3000, E-mail: mandreas@endicott.edu. *Application contact:* Ian Menchini, Director, Graduate Enrollment and Advising, 978-232-5292, Fax: 978-232-3000, E-mail: imenchin@endicott.edu.
Website: http://www.endicott.edu/VanLoan/Graduate-Studies/Master-Science/Homeland-Security.aspx

Excelsior College, School of Public Service, Albany, NY 12203-5159. Offers homeland security and emergency management (MSCJ); public administration (MPA). Part-time and evening/weekend programs available. Postbaccalaureate distance learning degree programs offered (no on-campus study). *Faculty:* 2 part-time/adjunct (0 women). *Students:* 122 part-time (25 women); includes 49 minority (25 Black or African American, non-Hispanic/Latino; 1 Asian, non-Hispanic/Latino; 18 Hispanic/Latino; 1 Native Hawaiian or other Pacific Islander, non-Hispanic/Latino; 4 Two or more races, non-Hispanic/Latino). Average age 40. In 2014, 12 master's awarded. Application fee: $110. *Expenses: Tuition:* Part-time $620 per credit hour. *Financial support:* Scholarships/grants available. Support available to part-time students. *Unit head:* Dr. Robert Waters, Dean, School of Public Service. *Application contact:* Admissions Counselor, 518-464-8500, Fax: 518-464-8777, E-mail: admissions@excelsior.edu.
Website: http://www.excelsior.edu/schools/public-service

Fairleigh Dickinson University, Metropolitan Campus, Anthony J. Petrocelli College of Continuing Studies, School of Administrative Science, Program in Homeland Security, Teaneck, NJ 07666-1914. Offers MSHS.

George Mason University, School of Policy, Government, and International Affairs, Program in Public Administration, Fairfax, VA 22030. Offers administration of justice (Certificate); association management (Certificate); biodefense (MS, PhD); critical analysis and strategic response to terrorism (Certificate); emergency management and homeland security (Certificate); nonprofit management (Certificate); political science (MA, PhD); public administration (MPA); public management (Certificate). *Accreditation:* NASPAA (one or more programs are accredited). *Entrance requirements:* For degree, expanded goals statement; 3 letters of recommendation; official transcripts; resume. Additional exam requirements/recommendations for international students: Required—TOEFL, IELTS, PTE. Application fee: $65 ($80 for international students). Electronic applications accepted. *Expenses:* Expenses: Contact institution. *Financial support:* Fellowships, research assistantships with full and partial tuition reimbursements, teaching assistantships with full and partial tuition reimbursements, career-related internships or fieldwork, Federal Work-Study, scholarships/grants, and unspecified assistantships available. Support available to part-time students. Financial award application deadline: 3/1; financial award applicants required to submit FAFSA. *Application contact:* Peg Koback, Education Support Specialist, 703-993-3707, Fax: 703-993-1399, E-mail: mkoback@gmu.edu.
Website: http://pia.gmu.edu/

Georgian Court University, School of Arts and Sciences, Lakewood, NJ 08701-2697. Offers applied behavior analysis (MA); Catholic school leadership (Certificate); clinical mental health counseling (MA); holistic health studies (MA, Certificate); homeland security (MS); parish administration (Certificate); pastoral ministry (Certificate); professional counseling (Certificate); religious education (Certificate); school psychology (MA, Certificate); theology (MA, Certificate). Part-time and evening/weekend programs available. *Faculty:* 19 full-time (9 women), 9 part-time/adjunct (4 women). *Students:* 87 full-time (74 women), 127 part-time (110 women); includes 47 minority (14 Black or African American, non-Hispanic/Latino; 2 Asian, non-Hispanic/Latino; 23 Hispanic/Latino; 8 Two or more races, non-Hispanic/Latino). Average age 34. In 2014, 68 master's, 11 other advanced degrees awarded. *Degree requirements:* For master's, comprehensive exam (for some programs), thesis (for some programs). *Entrance requirements:* For master's, GRE, MAT, or NTE/PRAXIS, 3 letters of recommendation. Additional exam requirements/recommendations for international students: Required—TOEFL (minimum score 550 paper-based). *Application deadline:* For fall admission, 8/1 priority date for domestic students, 4/1 for international students; for spring admission, 1/1 priority date for domestic students, 7/1 for international students. Applications are processed on a rolling basis. Application fee: $40. Electronic applications accepted. *Expenses: Tuition:* Full-time $19,752; part-time $823 per credit. *Required fees:* $948; $243 per semester hour. Tuition and fees vary according to campus/location and program. *Financial support:* Scholarships/grants, health care benefits, and unspecified assistantships available. Financial award application deadline: 4/15; financial award applicants required to submit FAFSA. *Unit head:* Dr. Rita Kipp, Dean, 732-987-2493, Fax: 732-987-2007, E-mail: rkipp@georgian.edu. *Application contact:* Patrick Givens, Interim Director of Enrollment Management, 732-987-2736, Fax: 732-987-2084, E-mail: graduateadmissions@georgian.edu.
Website: http://www.georgian.edu/arts_sciences/index.htm

Henley-Putnam University, Master of Science Program in Intelligence Management, San Jose, CA 95131. Offers MS. Part-time programs available. Postbaccalaureate distance learning degree programs offered. *Faculty:* 19 part-time/adjunct (3 women). *Students:* 49 full-time (9 women), 81 part-time (15 women); includes 6 minority (3 Black

or African American, non-Hispanic/Latino; 1 Asian, non-Hispanic/Latino; 2 Hispanic/Latino). Average age 35. 10 applicants, 100% accepted. In 2014, 23 master's awarded. *Degree requirements:* For master's, thesis. *Entrance requirements:* For master's, bachelor's degree from an institution accredited by an agency recognized by the U.S. Department of Education and/or the Council for Higher Education Accreditation; background check. Additional exam requirements/recommendations for international students: Required—TOEFL (minimum score 650 paper-based; 79 iBT); Recommended—IELTS (minimum score 7). *Application deadline:* Applications are processed on a rolling basis. *Expenses:* Expenses: Contact institution. *Financial support:* Scholarships/grants and unspecified assistantships available. *Unit head:* Barbara Burke, Associate Dean, 408-453-9900, E-mail: bburke@henley-putnam.edu. *Application contact:* Nancy Reggio, Director of Admissions, 888-852-8746, E-mail: nreggio@henley-putnam.edu.
Website: http://www.henley-putnam.edu/programs/masters/intelligence-management.aspx

Henley-Putnam University, Master of Science Program in Strategic Security and Protection Management, San Jose, CA 95131. Offers extremist organizations (MS). Part-time programs available. Postbaccalaureate distance learning degree programs offered (no on-campus study). *Faculty:* 17 part-time/adjunct (2 women). *Students:* 21 full-time (0 women), 41 part-time (8 women); includes 5 minority (3 Black or African American, non-Hispanic/Latino; 1 American Indian or Alaska Native, non-Hispanic/Latino; 1 Hispanic/Latino). Average age 36. 6 applicants, 100% accepted, 6 enrolled. In 2014, 23 master's awarded. *Degree requirements:* For master's, comprehensive exam, thesis. *Entrance requirements:* For master's, bachelor's degree from institution accredited by an agency recognized by the U.S. Department of Education and/or the Council for Higher Education Accreditation, background check. Additional exam requirements/recommendations for international students: Required—TOEFL (minimum score 650 paper-based; 79 iBT); Recommended—IELTS. *Application deadline:* Applications are processed on a rolling basis. *Expenses:* Expenses: Contact institution. *Financial support:* Scholarships/grants and unspecified assistantships available. *Unit head:* Dr. Scott Catino, Associate Dean, 408-453-9900, E-mail: scatino@henley-putnam.edu. *Application contact:* Nancy Reggio, Director of Admissions, 888-852-8746, E-mail: nreggio@henley-putnam.edu.

Henley-Putnam University, Master of Science Program in Terrorism and Counterterrorism Studies, San Jose, CA 95131. Offers intelligence operations (MS); protective intelligence (MS). Part-time programs available. Postbaccalaureate distance learning degree programs offered (no on-campus study). *Faculty:* 22 part-time/adjunct (5 women). *Students:* 55 full-time (12 women), 72 part-time (18 women); includes 11 minority (5 Black or African American, non-Hispanic/Latino; 4 Asian, non-Hispanic/Latino; 2 Hispanic/Latino). Average age 35. 17 applicants, 100% accepted, 17 enrolled. In 2014, 23 master's awarded. *Degree requirements:* For master's, thesis. *Entrance requirements:* For master's, bachelor's degree from institution accredited by an agency recognized by the U.S. Department of Education and/or the Council for Higher Education Accreditation, background check. Additional exam requirements/recommendations for international students: Required—TOEFL (minimum score 650 paper-based; 79 iBT); Recommended—IELTS (minimum score 7). *Application deadline:* Applications are processed on a rolling basis. *Expenses:* Expenses: Contact institution. *Financial support:* Scholarships/grants and unspecified assistantships available. *Unit head:* Diane Maye, Associate Dean, 408-453-9900, E-mail: dmaye@henley-putnam.edu. *Application contact:* Nancy Reggio, Director of Admissions, 888-852-8746 Ext. 9928, E-mail: nreggio@henley-putnam.edu.
Website: http://www.henley-putnam.edu/programs/masters/terrorism-and-counterterrorism-studies.aspx

Indiana University–Purdue University Indianapolis, School of Public and Environmental Affairs, Indianapolis, IN 46202. Offers criminal justice and public safety (MS); homeland security and emergency management (Graduate Certificate); library management (Graduate Certificate); nonprofit management (Graduate Certificate); public affairs (MPA); public management (Graduate Certificate); social entrepreneurship: nonprofit and public benefit organizations (Graduate Certificate); JD/MPA; MLS/NMC; MLS/PMC; MPA/MA. *Accreditation:* CAHME (one or more programs are accredited); NASPAA. Part-time and evening/weekend programs available. Postbaccalaureate distance learning degree programs offered (no on-campus study). *Entrance requirements:* For master's, GRE General Test, GMAT or LSAT, minimum GPA of 3.0 (preferred). Additional exam requirements/recommendations for international students: Required—TOEFL (minimum score 93 iBT), IELTS (minimum score 6.5). Electronic applications accepted. *Faculty research:* Nonprofit and public management, public policy, urban policy, sustainability policy, disaster preparedness and recovery, vehicular safety, homicide, offender rehabilitation and re-entry.

Johns Hopkins University, Zanvyl Krieger School of Arts and Sciences, Advanced Academic Programs, Program in Government, Washington, DC 20036. Offers global security studies (MA); government (MA); national securities study (Certificate); nonprofit management (Certificate); public management (MA); research administration (MS); MA/MBA. Part-time and evening/weekend programs available. Postbaccalaureate distance learning degree programs offered (minimal on-campus study). *Degree requirements:* For master's, thesis. *Entrance requirements:* For master's, minimum GPA of 3.0. Additional exam requirements/recommendations for international students: Required—TOEFL (minimum score 100 iBT). Electronic applications accepted.

Keiser University, MA in Criminal Justice-Homeland Security Program, Ft. Lauderdale, FL 33309. Offers MA.

Long Island University–Riverhead, Homeland Security and Terrorism Institute, Riverhead, NY 11901. Offers MS, Advanced Certificate. Part-time and evening/weekend programs available. Postbaccalaureate distance learning degree programs offered (no on-campus study). *Faculty:* 3 full-time (0 women), 4 part-time/adjunct (1 woman). *Students:* 6 full-time (4 women), 59 part-time (18 women); includes 23 minority (7 Black or African American, non-Hispanic/Latino; 2 Asian, non-Hispanic/Latino; 13 Hispanic/Latino; 1 Two or more races, non-Hispanic/Latino). Average age 33. 20 applicants, 95% accepted, 12 enrolled. In 2014, 20 master's, 23 other advanced degrees awarded. *Degree requirements:* For master's, thesis. *Entrance requirements:* For master's, minimum GPA of 3.0, 2 letters of reference. Additional exam requirements/recommendations for international students: Required—TOEFL (minimum score 79 iBT), IELTS (minimum score 6). *Application deadline:* Applications are processed on a rolling basis. Application fee: $50. Electronic applications accepted. Application fee is waived when completed online. *Expenses: Tuition:* Part-time $1132 per credit hour. *Required fees:* $434 per semester. *Financial support:* Career-related internships or fieldwork and scholarships/grants available. Support available to part-time students. Financial award applicants required to submit FAFSA. *Unit head:* Dr. Harvey Kushner, Director of Homeland Security and Terrorism Institute, 516-299-2986, Fax: 516-299-2587, E-mail: harvey.kushner@liu.edu. *Application contact:* Christina Seifert, Director of Admissions LIU Riverhead and LIU Brentwood, 631-287-8505, Fax: 631-287-8253, E-mail: christina.seifert@liu.edu.
Website: http://liu.edu/Riverhead

Missouri State University, Graduate College, College of Humanities and Public Affairs, Department of Criminology and Criminal Justice, Springfield, MO 65897. Offers

criminology (MS); homeland security and defense (Certificate). Part-time programs available. *Faculty:* 7 full-time (2 women). *Students:* 20 full-time (12 women), 33 part-time (20 women); includes 9 minority (3 Black or African American, non-Hispanic/Latino; 1 American Indian or Alaska Native, non-Hispanic/Latino; 2 Hispanic/Latino; 3 Two or more races, non-Hispanic/Latino). Average age 31. 19 applicants, 95% accepted, 16 enrolled. In 2014, 1 master's awarded. *Degree requirements:* For master's, comprehensive exam, thesis or alternative. *Entrance requirements:* For master's, bachelor's degree in criminology, criminal justice, or sociology; minimum undergraduate GPA of 3.0. Additional exam requirements/recommendations for international students: Required—TOEFL (minimum score 550 paper-based; 79 iBT). *Application deadline:* For fall admission, 7/20 for domestic students, 5/1 for international students; for spring admission, 12/20 for domestic students, 9/1 for international students. Applications are processed on a rolling basis. Application fee: $35 ($50 for international students). Electronic applications accepted. *Expenses:* Tuition, state resident: full-time $2250; part-time $250 per credit hour. Tuition, nonresident: full-time $4509; part-time $501 per credit hour. Tuition and fees vary according to course level, course load and program. *Financial support:* Federal Work-Study, institutionally sponsored loans, and unspecified assistantships available. Financial award application deadline: 3/1; financial award applicants required to submit FAFSA. *Faculty research:* Homeland security initiatives, juvenile policy and programs, law enforcement and drug abuse. *Unit head:* Dr. Brett Garland, Program Director, 417-836-6954, E-mail: brettgarland@missouristate.edu. *Application contact:* Misty Stewart, Coordinator of Graduate Recruitment, 417-836-6079, Fax: 417-836-6200, E-mail: mistystewart@missouristate.edu.
Website: http://criminology.missouristate.edu/

Missouri State University, Graduate College, Interdisciplinary Program in Administrative Studies, Springfield, MO 65897. Offers applied communication (MS); criminal justice (MS); environmental management (MS); homeland security (MS); sports management (MS). Part-time and evening/weekend programs available. Postbaccalaureate distance learning degree programs offered (no on-campus study). *Students:* 17 full-time (9 women), 64 part-time (29 women); includes 10 minority (4 Black or African American, non-Hispanic/Latino; 1 Asian, non-Hispanic/Latino; 2 Hispanic/Latino; 3 Two or more races, non-Hispanic/Latino), 3 international. Average age 33. 48 applicants, 73% accepted, 21 enrolled. In 2014, 16 master's awarded. *Degree requirements:* For master's, comprehensive exam, thesis or alternative. *Entrance requirements:* For master's, GRE, GMAT if GPA less than 3.0. Additional exam requirements/recommendations for international students: Required—TOEFL (minimum score 550 paper-based; 79 iBT). *Application deadline:* For fall admission, 7/20 priority date for domestic students; for spring admission, 12/20 priority date for domestic students. Applications are processed on a rolling basis. Application fee: $35 ($50 for international students). Electronic applications accepted. *Expenses:* Tuition, state resident: full-time $2250; part-time $250 per credit hour. Tuition, nonresident: full-time $4509; part-time $501 per credit hour. Tuition and fees vary according to course level, course load and program. *Financial support:* Career-related internships or fieldwork, Federal Work-Study, institutionally sponsored loans, scholarships/grants, and unspecified assistantships available. Support available to part-time students. Financial award application deadline: 3/31; financial award applicants required to submit FAFSA. *Unit head:* Dr. Gerald Masterson, Program Coordinator, 417-836-5251, Fax: 417-836-6888, E-mail: msas@missouristate.edu. *Application contact:* Misty Stewart, Coordinator of Graduate Recruitment, 417-836-6079, Fax: 417-836-6200, E-mail: mistystewart@missouristate.edu.
Website: http://msas.missouristate.edu

Monmouth University, The Graduate School, Department of Criminal Justice, West Long Branch, NJ 07764-1898. Offers criminal justice (MA, Certificate); homeland security (MS, Certificate). Part-time and evening/weekend programs available. Postbaccalaureate distance learning degree programs offered (minimal on-campus study). *Faculty:* 4 full-time (0 women), 5 part-time/adjunct (1 woman). *Students:* 22 full-time (12 women), 33 part-time (16 women); includes 11 minority (4 Black or African American, non-Hispanic/Latino; 1 Asian, non-Hispanic/Latino; 5 Hispanic/Latino; 1 Two or more races, non-Hispanic/Latino). Average age 27. 32 applicants, 97% accepted, 21 enrolled. In 2014, 18 master's awarded. *Degree requirements:* For master's, comprehensive exam (for some programs), thesis (for some programs). *Entrance requirements:* For master's, baccalaureate degree with minimum GPA of 3.0 in major, 2.5 overall; two letters of recommendation; personal essay. Additional exam requirements/recommendations for international students: Required—TOEFL (minimum score 550 paper-based; 79 iBT), IELTS (minimum score 6), TOEFL (minimum score 550 paper-based; 79 iBT), IELTS (minimum score 6), Michigan English Language Assessment Battery (minimum score 77) or Certificate ofAdvanced English (minimum score B2). *Application deadline:* For fall admission, 7/15 priority date for domestic students, 6/1 for international students; for spring admission, 11/15 priority date for domestic students, 11/1 for international students. Applications are processed on a rolling basis. Application fee: $50. Electronic applications accepted. *Expenses: Tuition:* Full-time $18,072; part-time $1004 per credit. *Required fees:* $157 per semester. *Financial support:* In 2014–15, 50 students received support, including 43 fellowships (averaging $2,881 per year), 4 research assistantships (averaging $5,198 per year); career-related internships or fieldwork, scholarships/grants, and unspecified assistantships also available. Support available to part-time students. Financial award applicants required to submit FAFSA. *Faculty research:* Violent crimes, criminal pathology, terrorism, computer crime, comparative criminal justice systems, homeland security. *Unit head:* John Comiskey, Program Director, Homeland Security, 732-571-3448, Fax: 732-263-5148, E-mail: jcomiske@monmouth.edu. *Application contact:* Andrea Thompson, Graduate Admission Counselor, 732-571-3452, Fax: 732-263-5123, E-mail: gradadm@monmouth.edu.
Website: http://www.monmouth.edu/academics/criminal_justice/default.asp

National Defense University, College of International Security Affairs, Washington, DC 20319-5066. Offers strategic security studies (MA), including conflict management, counterterrorism, homeland defense/ security, international security studies. Part-time and evening/weekend programs available. *Degree requirements:* For master's, thesis. *Entrance requirements:* Additional exam requirements/recommendations for international students: Required—TOEFL.

The National Graduate School of Quality Management, Graduate Programs, Falmouth, MA 02541. Offers homeland security (MS); quality systems management (MS, DBA).

National University, Academic Affairs, School of Engineering and Computing, La Jolla, CA 92037-1011. Offers computer science (MS), including advanced computing, database engineering, software engineering; cyber security and information assurance (MS), including computer forensics, ethical hacking and penetration testing, health information assurance, information assurance and security; data analytics (MS); engineering management (MS), including enterprise architecture, project management, systems engineering, technology management; environmental engineering (MS); homeland security and emergency management (MS); management information systems (MS); project management (Certificate); sustainability management (MS); wireless communications (MS). Part-time and evening/weekend programs available. Postbaccalaureate distance learning degree programs offered (no on-campus study).

Homeland Security

Faculty: 24 full-time (5 women), 21 part-time/adjunct (5 women). *Students:* 275 full-time (72 women), 86 part-time (24 women); includes 147 minority (41 Black or African American, non-Hispanic/Latino; 48 Asian, non-Hispanic/Latino; 37 Hispanic/Latino; 7 Native Hawaiian or other Pacific Islander, non-Hispanic/Latino; 14 Two or more races, non-Hispanic/Latino), 95 international. Average age 33. In 2014, 281 master's awarded. *Degree requirements:* For master's, thesis (for some programs). *Entrance requirements:* For master's, interview, minimum GPA of 2.5. Additional exam requirements/recommendations for international students: Required—TOEFL (minimum score 550 paper-based; 79 iBT), IELTS (minimum score 6). *Application deadline:* Applications are processed on a rolling basis. Application fee: $60 ($65 for international students). Electronic applications accepted. *Expenses: Tuition:* Full-time $14,184; part-time $1773 per course. *Financial support:* Career-related internships or fieldwork, institutionally sponsored loans, scholarships/grants, and tuition waivers (partial) available. Support available to part-time students. Financial award application deadline: 6/30; financial award applicants required to submit FAFSA. *Faculty research:* Educational technology, scholarships in science. *Unit head:* School of Engineering and Computing, 800-628-8648, E-mail: soec@nu.edu. *Application contact:* Frank Rojas, Vice President for Enrollment Services, 800-628-8648, E-mail: advisor@nu.edu. Website: http://www.nu.edu/OurPrograms/SchoolOfEngineeringAndTechnology.html

Naval Postgraduate School, Departments and Academic Groups, Department of National Security Affairs, Monterey, CA 93943. Offers national security affairs (MA); security studies (MA), including civil-military relations, combating terrorism: policy and strategy, defense decision-making and planning, Europe and Eurasia, Far East, Southeast Asia, the Pacific, homeland security and defense, Middle East, South Asia, Sub-Saharan Africa, stabilization and reconstruction, western hemisphere. Program only open to commissioned officers of the United States and friendly nations and selected United States federal civilian employees. Part-time programs available. *Degree requirements:* For master's, thesis (for some programs). *Faculty research:* Privatizing welfare in the Middle East; social construction of Russia's resurgence; institutions, ethnicity and political mobilization in South Africa; Hezbollah; China's strategic interests in Cambodia.

Northeastern University, College of Professional Studies, Boston, MA 02115-5096. Offers applied nutrition (MS); commerce and economic development (MS); corporate and organizational communication (MS); digital media (MPS); geographic information technology (MPS); global studies and international affairs (MS); homeland security (MA); human services (MS); informatics (MPS); leadership (MS); nonprofit management (MS); project management (MS); regulatory affairs for drugs, biologics, and medical devices (MS); regulatory affairs of food and food industries (MS); respiratory care leadership (MS); technical communication (MS). Postbaccalaureate distance learning degree programs offered (no on-campus study).

Northeastern University, College of Social Sciences and Humanities, Boston, MA 02115. Offers criminology and criminal justice (MSCJ); criminology and justice policy (PhD); economics (MA, PhD); English (MA, PhD); law and public policy (MS, PhD); political science (MA, PhD); public administration (MPA); public history (MA); security and resilience studies (MS); sociology (MA, PhD); urban and regional policy (MS); world history (MA, PhD). *Degree requirements:* For doctorate, variable foreign language requirement, comprehensive exam, thesis/dissertation. *Entrance requirements:* For master's and doctorate, GRE. Additional exam requirements/recommendations for international students: Required—TOEFL, IELTS. Electronic applications accepted.

Northwestern State University of Louisiana, Graduate Studies and Research, Department of Criminal Justice, History and Social Sciences, Program in Homeland Security, Natchitoches, LA 71497. Offers MS. *Degree requirements:* For master's, comprehensive exam, thesis or alternative. *Entrance requirements:* For master's, GRE General Test. Additional exam requirements/recommendations for international students: Required—TOEFL. Electronic applications accepted.

Notre Dame College, Graduate Programs, South Euclid, OH 44121-4293. Offers mild/moderate needs (M Ed); reading (M Ed); security policy studies (MA, Graduate Certificate); technology (M Ed). Part-time and evening/weekend programs available. *Degree requirements:* For master's, thesis. *Entrance requirements:* For master's, GRE General Test, MAT, minimum undergraduate GPA of 2.75, valid teaching certificate, bachelor's degree in an education-related field from accredited college or university, official transcripts of most recent college work. *Faculty research:* Cognitive psychology, teaching critical thinking in the classroom.

Pace University, Dyson College of Arts and Sciences, Department of Public Administration, New York, NY 10038. Offers environmental management (MPA); government management (MPA); health care administration (MPA); management for public safety and homeland security (MA); nonprofit management (MPA); JD/MPA. Offered at White Plains, NY location only. Part-time and evening/weekend programs available. *Faculty:* 6 full-time (3 women), 8 part-time/adjunct (2 women). *Students:* 76 full-time (54 women), 62 part-time (37 women); includes 67 minority (33 Black or African American, non-Hispanic/Latino; 6 Asian, non-Hispanic/Latino; 25 Hispanic/Latino; 3 Two or more races, non-Hispanic/Latino), 28 international. Average age 29. 113 applicants, 88% accepted, 54 enrolled. In 2014, 64 master's awarded. *Degree requirements:* For master's, capstone project. *Entrance requirements:* For master's, GRE General Test, 2 letters of recommendation, resume, personal statement, official transcripts. Additional exam requirements/recommendations for international students: Required—TOEFL (minimum score 100 iBT). *Application deadline:* For fall admission, 8/1 priority date for domestic students, 6/1 for international students; for spring admission, 12/1 priority date for domestic students, 10/1 for international students. Applications are processed on a rolling basis. Application fee: $70. Electronic applications accepted. *Expenses: Tuition:* Part-time $1120 per credit. *Required fees:* $266 per semester. Tuition and fees vary according to course load, degree level and program. *Financial support:* Research assistantships, career-related internships or fieldwork, Federal Work-Study, and tuition waivers (partial) available. Support available to part-time students. Financial award applicants required to submit FAFSA. *Unit head:* Dr. Farrokh Hormozi, Chairperson, 914-422-4285, E-mail: fhormozi@pace.edu. *Application contact:* Susan Ford-Goldschein, Director of Admissions, 914-422-4283, Fax: 914-422-4287, E-mail: gradwp@pace.edu. Website: http://www.pace.edu/dyson/academic-departments-and-programs/public-admin

Penn State University Park, Graduate School, Intercollege Graduate Programs, Intercollege Graduate Program in Homeland Security, University Park, PA 16802. Offers MPS. Program offered via the PSU World Campus. *Unit head:* Dr. Regina Vasilatos-Younken, Interim Dean, 814-865-2516, Fax: 814-863-4627, E-mail: rxv@psu.edu. *Application contact:* Lori A. Stania, Director, Graduate Student Services, 814-867-5278, Fax: 814-863-4627, E-mail: gswww@psu.edu.

Regent University, Graduate School, Robertson School of Government, Virginia Beach, VA 23464. Offers government (MA), including American government, international relations, political theory; public administration (MPA), including emergency management and homeland security, general public administration, nonprofit administration and faith-based organizations, public leadership and management. Part-time and evening/weekend programs available. Postbaccalaureate distance learning degree programs offered (minimal on-campus study). *Faculty:* 10 full-time (1 woman), 9 part-time/adjunct (2 women). *Students:* 34 full-time (15 women), 56 part-time (26 women); includes 21 minority (15 Black or African American, non-Hispanic/Latino; 6 Hispanic/Latino), 4 international. Average age 34. 106 applicants, 45% accepted, 33 enrolled. In 2014, 57 master's awarded. *Degree requirements:* For master's, thesis optional, internship. *Entrance requirements:* For master's, GRE General Test or LSAT, minimum undergraduate GPA of 3.0, writing sample, resume, interview, references. Additional exam requirements/recommendations for international students: Required—TOEFL (minimum score 577 paper-based). *Application deadline:* For fall admission, 5/1 priority date for domestic students; for spring admission, 11/1 priority date for domestic students. Applications are processed on a rolling basis. Application fee: $50. Electronic applications accepted. *Expenses:* Expenses: Contact institution. *Financial support:* Career-related internships or fieldwork, scholarships/grants, tuition waivers (full and partial), and unspecified assistantships available. Support available to part-time students. Financial award application deadline: 9/1; financial award applicants required to submit FAFSA. *Faculty research:* Education reform, political character issues, social capital concerns, administrative ethics, Biblical law and public policy. *Unit head:* Dr. Eric Patterson, Dean, 757-352-4616, Fax: 757-352-4735, E-mail: epatterson@regent.edu. *Application contact:* Matthew Chadwick, Director of Enrollment Support Services, 800-373-5504, Fax: 757-352-4381, E-mail: admissions@regent.edu. Website: http://www.regent.edu/government/

Saint Joseph's University, College of Arts and Sciences, Programs in Public Safety and Management, Philadelphia, PA 19131-1395. Offers homeland security (MS); public safety management (MS). Part-time and evening/weekend programs available. Postbaccalaureate distance learning degree programs offered. *Faculty:* 1 full-time (0 women), 7 part-time/adjunct (0 women). *Students:* 27 part-time (2 women); includes 2 minority (1 Black or African American, non-Hispanic/Latino; 1 Two or more races, non-Hispanic/Latino). Average age 37. 11 applicants, 100% accepted, 7 enrolled. In 2014, 14 master's awarded. *Entrance requirements:* For master's, GRE (if GPA less than 3.0), 2 letters of recommendation, resume, personal statement, official transcripts. Additional exam requirements/recommendations for international students: Required—TOEFL (minimum score 550 paper-based; 80 iBT). *Application deadline:* For fall admission, 7/15 priority date for domestic students, 4/15 for international students; for winter admission, 1/15 for international students; for spring admission, 11/15 priority date for domestic students, 10/15 for international students. Applications are processed on a rolling basis. Application fee: $35. Electronic applications accepted. *Financial support:* Applicants required to submit FAFSA. *Unit head:* Sylvia DeSantis. *Application contact:* Elisabeth Woodward, Director of Marketing and Admissions, Graduate Arts and Sciences, 610-660-3131, Fax: 610-660-3230, E-mail: gradstudies@sju.edu. Website: http://www.sju.edu/majors-programs/graduate-arts-sciences/masters/public-safety-management

St. Mary's University, Graduate School, Graduate Department of International Relations, San Antonio, TX 78228-8507. Offers international conflict resolution (MA); security policy (MA); JD/MA. Part-time and evening/weekend programs available. Postbaccalaureate distance learning degree programs offered (no on-campus study). *Faculty:* 4 full-time (2 women), 1 part-time/adjunct (0 women). *Students:* 15 full-time (9 women), 64 part-time (21 women); includes 31 minority (5 Black or African American, non-Hispanic/Latino; 1 American Indian or Alaska Native, non-Hispanic/Latino; 6 Asian, non-Hispanic/Latino; 18 Hispanic/Latino; 1 Native Hawaiian or other Pacific Islander, non-Hispanic/Latino), 7 international. Average age 32. 54 applicants, 65% accepted, 25 enrolled. In 2014, 34 master's, 7 other advanced degrees awarded. *Degree requirements:* For master's, one foreign language, comprehensive exam, thesis optional, Demonstration of a working knowledge of a foreign language. *Entrance requirements:* For master's, GRE General Test, GPA x Verbal GRE Score = 450. Minimum writing score is 4.0. Additional exam requirements/recommendations for international students: Required—TOEFL (minimum score 550 paper-based; 80 iBT), IELTS (minimum score 6). *Application deadline:* Applications are processed on a rolling basis. Application fee: $0. Electronic applications accepted. *Expenses: Tuition:* Full-time $15,070; part-time $800 per credit hour. *Required fees:* $156 per semester. *Financial support:* In 2014–15, 4 research assistantships (averaging $7,000 per year) were awarded; Federal Work-Study, scholarships/grants, tuition waivers (full), unspecified assistantships, and grant for active-duty and retired military, DOD employees, and their spouses also available. Financial award application deadline: 3/31; financial award applicants required to submit FAFSA. *Faculty research:* World religions and global affairs; human security and conflict transformation; military, security, peacekeeping; development studies, sustainability and the environment; migration and immigration policy. *Unit head:* Dr. Aaron Tyler, Chair Graduate International Relations, 210-436-3111, Fax: 210-431-4336, E-mail: atyler@stmarytx.edu. Website: https://www.stmarytx.edu/academics/graduate/masters/internationalrelations/

Salve Regina University, Program in Administration of Justice and Homeland Security, Newport, RI 02840-4192. Offers administration of justice and homeland security (MS); cybersecurity and intelligence (CGS); leadership in justice (CGS). Part-time and evening/weekend programs available. Postbaccalaureate distance learning degree programs offered (no on-campus study). *Faculty:* 2 full-time (0 women), 6 part-time/adjunct (1 woman). *Students:* 18 full-time (10 women), 58 part-time (15 women); includes 6 minority (1 Black or African American, non-Hispanic/Latino; 4 Hispanic/Latino; 1 Two or more races, non-Hispanic/Latino). Average age 31. 15 applicants, 100% accepted, 15 enrolled. In 2014, 23 master's awarded. *Entrance requirements:* For master's, GMAT, GRE General Test, or MAT. Additional exam requirements/recommendations for international students: Required—TOEFL (minimum score 600 paper-based; 100 iBT). *Application deadline:* For fall admission, 3/5 priority date for domestic students, 3/15 priority date for international students; for spring admission, 9/15 priority date for domestic students, 9/5 priority date for international students. Applications are processed on a rolling basis. Application fee: $60. Electronic applications accepted. *Expenses: Tuition:* Full-time $8550; part-time $475 per credit. *Required fees:* $50 per term. Tuition and fees vary according to course level, course load and degree level. *Financial support:* Career-related internships or fieldwork and Federal Work-Study available. Support available to part-time students. Financial award application deadline: 3/1; financial award applicants required to submit FAFSA. *Unit head:* David Smith, Director, 401-341-3210, E-mail: david.smith@salve.edu. *Application contact:* Nicole Ferreira, Associate Director of Graduate Admissions, 401-341-2462, Fax: 401-341-2973, E-mail: nicole.ferreira@salve.edu. Website: http://www.salve.edu/graduate-studies/administration-of-justice-and-homeland-security

Sam Houston State University, College of Criminal Justice, Department of Security Studies, Huntsville, TX 77341. Offers homeland security studies (MS). Part-time programs available. Postbaccalaureate distance learning degree programs offered (no on-campus study). *Faculty:* 5 full-time (1 woman), 1 part-time/adjunct (0 women). *Students:* 28 full-time (5 women), 7 part-time (3 women); includes 6 minority (3 Black or African American, non-Hispanic/Latino; 1 Asian, non-Hispanic/Latino; 2 Hispanic/Latino), 1 international. Average age 26. 21 applicants, 100% accepted, 21 enrolled. In 2014, 17 master's awarded. *Degree requirements:* For master's, thesis optional. *Entrance requirements:* For master's, undergraduate degree, official transcripts, three letters of recommendation, current resume, personal essay. Additional exam

requirements/recommendations for international students: Required—TOEFL (minimum score 550 paper-based; 79 iBT); Recommended—IELTS (minimum score 6.5). *Application deadline:* For fall admission, 2/1 for domestic and international students; for spring admission, 9/1 for domestic and international students. Applications are processed on a rolling basis. Application fee: $45 ($75 for international students). Electronic applications accepted. *Expenses:* Tuition, state resident: full-time $2286; part-time $254 per credit hour. Tuition, nonresident: full-time $5544; part-time $616 per credit hour. *Required fees:* $440 per semester. Tuition and fees vary according to course load and campus/location. *Financial support:* In 2014–15, 11 research assistantships (averaging $5,073 per year) were awarded; career-related internships or fieldwork, Federal Work-Study, scholarships/grants, tuition waivers, and unspecified assistantships also available. Support available to part-time students. Financial award application deadline: 3/15. *Unit head:* Dr. Jurg Gerber, Chair. *Application contact:* Doris Powell-Pratt, Graduate Advising Coordinator, 936-294-3637, Fax: 936-294-4055, E-mail: icc_dcp@shsu.edu.
Website: http://www.shsu.edu/academics/criminal-justice/departments/security-studies/

Southern Illinois University Carbondale, Graduate School, College of Applied Science, Program in Fire Service and Homeland Security, Carbondale, IL 62901-4701. Offers MS. Part-time and evening/weekend programs available. Postbaccalaureate distance learning degree programs offered. *Faculty:* 1 full-time (0 women). *Students:* 13 full-time (0 women), 1 part-time (0 women). Average age 25. 6 applicants, 67% accepted, 3 enrolled. In 2014, 11 master's awarded. *Entrance requirements:* Additional exam requirements/recommendations for international students: Required—TOEFL. *Application deadline:* Applications are processed on a rolling basis. Application fee: $50. Electronic applications accepted. *Expenses:* Tuition, state resident: full-time $10,176; part-time $1153 per credit. Tuition, nonresident: full-time $20,814; part-time $1744 per credit. *Required fees:* $7092; $394 per credit. $2364 per semester. *Unit head:* Gary Kistner, Coordinator, 618-453-7277, E-mail: siufire@siu.edu.

Texas A&M University, Bush School of Government and Public Service, College Station, TX 77843. Offers homeland security (Certificate); international affairs (MIA, Certificate); national security affairs (Certificate); non-profit management (Certificate); public service and administration (MPSA). *Accreditation:* NASPAA. *Faculty:* 60. *Students:* 313 full-time (146 women), 12 part-time (2 women); includes 61 minority (13 Black or African American, non-Hispanic/Latino; 7 Asian, non-Hispanic/Latino; 32 Hispanic/Latino; 1 Native Hawaiian or other Pacific Islander, non-Hispanic/Latino; 8 Two or more races, non-Hispanic/Latino), 44 international. Average age 28. 298 applicants, 71% accepted, 143 enrolled. In 2014, 137 master's awarded. *Degree requirements:* For master's, summer internship. *Entrance requirements:* For master's, GRE (preferred) or GMAT. Additional exam requirements/recommendations for international students: Required—TOEFL (minimum score 550 paper-based; 80 iBT), IELTS (minimum score 6). *Application deadline:* For fall admission, 1/20 for domestic and international students. Application fee: $50 ($90 for international students). Electronic applications accepted. *Expenses:* Tuition, state resident: full-time $4078; part-time $226.55 per credit hour. Tuition, nonresident: full-time $10,594; part-time $577.55 per credit hour. *Required fees:* $2813; $237.70 per credit hour. $278.50 per semester. Tuition and fees vary according to degree level and student level. *Financial support:* In 2014–15, 407 students received support, including 26 fellowships with full and partial tuition reimbursements available (averaging $15,902 per year), 44 research assistantships with full and partial tuition reimbursements available (averaging $7,163 per year); career-related internships or fieldwork, institutionally sponsored loans, scholarships/grants, traineeships, health care benefits, tuition waivers (full and partial), and unspecified assistantships also available. Support available to part-time students. Financial award application deadline: 2/1; financial award applicants required to submit FAFSA. *Faculty research:* Public policy, Presidential studies, public leadership, economic policy, social policy. *Unit head:* Dr. Ryan Crocker, Dean, 979-862-8007, E-mail: rcrocker@tamu.edu. *Application contact:* Kathryn Meyer, Director of Recruitment and Admissions, 979-458-4767, Fax: 979-845-4155, E-mail: bushschooladmissions@tamu.edu.
Website: http://bush.tamu.edu/

Thomas Edison State College, Heavin School of Arts and Sciences, Program in Homeland Security, Trenton, NJ 08608-1176. Offers Graduate Certificate. Part-time programs available. Postbaccalaureate distance learning degree programs offered (no on-campus study). *Entrance requirements:* Additional exam requirements/recommendations for international students: Required—TOEFL (minimum score 550 paper-based; 79 iBT). Electronic applications accepted.

Tiffin University, Program in Criminal Justice, Tiffin, OH 44883-2161. Offers crime analysis (MSCJ); criminal behavior (MSCJ); forensic psychology (MSCJ); homeland security administration (MSCJ); justice administration (MSCJ). Part-time and evening/weekend programs available. Postbaccalaureate distance learning degree programs offered (no on-campus study). *Degree requirements:* For master's, thesis optional. *Entrance requirements:* For master's, minimum undergraduate GPA of 2.5, work experience. Additional exam requirements/recommendations for international students: Required—TOEFL (minimum score 550 paper-based; 79 iBT). Electronic applications accepted. *Faculty research:* Terrorism, intelligence, homeland security, guns and crime.

Towson University, Program in Integrated Homeland Security Management, Towson, MD 21252-0001. Offers integrated homeland security management (MS); security assessment and management (Postbaccalaureate Certificate). Part-time and evening/weekend programs available. *Students:* 12 full-time (5 women), 32 part-time (13 women); includes 14 minority (11 Black or African American, non-Hispanic/Latino; 1 Hispanic/Latino; 2 Two or more races, non-Hispanic/Latino). *Entrance requirements:* For master's and Postbaccalaureate Certificate, BA in related field, 3 years of related work experience, resume, 2 letters of reference, minimum GPA of 3.0. *Application deadline:* Applications are processed on a rolling basis. Application fee: $45. Electronic applications accepted. *Financial support:* Application deadline: 4/1. *Unit head:* Dr. Nikki Austin, Graduate Program Director, 410-704-4208, E-mail: eaustin@towson.edu. *Application contact:* Alicia Arkell-Kleis, Information Contact, 410-704-6004, E-mail: grads@towson.edu.
Website: http://grad.towson.edu/program/master/ihsm-ms/index.asp

University at Albany, State University of New York, Nelson A. Rockefeller College of Public Affairs and Policy, Department of Public Administration and Policy, Albany, NY 12222-0001. Offers financial management and public economics (MPA); financial market regulation (MPA); health policy (MPA); healthcare management (MPA); homeland security (MPA); human resources management (MPA); information strategy and management (MPA); local government management (MPA); nonprofit management (MPA); nonprofit management and leadership (Certificate); organizational behavior and theory (MPA, PhD); planning and policy analysis (CAS); policy analytic methods (MPA); politics and administration (PhD); public finance (PhD); public management (PhD); public policy (PhD); public sector management (Certificate); women and public policy (Certificate); JD/MPA. JD/MPA offered jointly with Albany Law School. *Accreditation:* NASPAA (one or more programs are accredited). *Degree requirements:* For doctorate, one foreign language, thesis/dissertation. *Entrance requirements:* For doctorate, GRE General Test. Additional exam requirements/recommendations for international students: Required—TOEFL (minimum score 550 paper-based). Electronic applications accepted.

University of Central Florida, College of Health and Public Affairs, School of Public Administration, Orlando, FL 32816. Offers emergency management and homeland security (Certificate); fundraising (Certificate); non-profit management (MNM, Certificate); urban and regional planning (MS). *Accreditation:* NASPAA. Part-time and evening/weekend programs available. *Faculty:* 18 full-time (9 women), 19 part-time/adjunct (9 women). *Students:* 109 full-time (80 women), 274 part-time (202 women); includes 148 minority (82 Black or African American, non-Hispanic/Latino; 8 Asian, non-Hispanic/Latino; 51 Hispanic/Latino; 7 Two or more races, non-Hispanic/Latino), 5 international. Average age 32. 264 applicants, 77% accepted, 148 enrolled. In 2014, 123 master's, 26 other advanced degrees awarded. *Degree requirements:* For master's, comprehensive exam, thesis or alternative, research report. *Entrance requirements:* For master's, GRE General Test. *Application deadline:* For fall admission, 7/1 for domestic students; for spring admission, 12/1 for domestic students. Application fee: $30. Electronic applications accepted. *Expenses:* Tuition, state resident: part-time $288.16 per credit hour. Tuition, nonresident: part-time $1073.31 per credit hour. *Financial support:* In 2014–15, 4 students received support, including 2 fellowships with partial tuition reimbursements available (averaging $5,300 per year), 1 research assistantship with partial tuition reimbursement available (averaging $10,600 per year), 1 teaching assistantship (averaging $7,100 per year); career-related internships or fieldwork, Federal Work-Study, institutionally sponsored loans, tuition waivers (partial), and unspecified assistantships also available. Financial award application deadline: 3/1; financial award applicants required to submit FAFSA. *Unit head:* Dr. Mary Ann Feldheim, Director, 407-823-3693, Fax: 407-823-5651, E-mail: mary.feldheim@ucf.edu. *Application contact:* Barbara Rodriguez Lamas, Director, Admissions and Student Services, 407-823-2766, Fax: 407-823-6442, E-mail: gradadmissions@ucf.edu.
Website: https://www.cohpa.ucf.edu/publicadmin/

University of Colorado Denver, School of Public Affairs, Program in Public Affairs and Administration, Denver, CO 80127. Offers public administration (MPA), including domestic violence, emergency management and homeland security, environmental policy, management and law, homeland security and defense, local government, nonprofit management, public administration; public affairs (PhD). *Accreditation:* NASPAA. Part-time and evening/weekend programs available. Postbaccalaureate distance learning degree programs offered (no on-campus study). *Students:* 275 full-time (176 women), 140 part-time (93 women); includes 70 minority (7 Black or African American, non-Hispanic/Latino; 4 American Indian or Alaska Native, non-Hispanic/Latino; 9 Asian, non-Hispanic/Latino; 44 Hispanic/Latino; 2 Native Hawaiian or other Pacific Islander, non-Hispanic/Latino; 4 Two or more races, non-Hispanic/Latino), 19 international. Average age 34. 243 applicants, 71% accepted, 97 enrolled. In 2014, 127 master's, 5 doctorates awarded. *Degree requirements:* For master's, thesis or alternative, 36-39 credit hours; for doctorate, comprehensive exam, thesis/dissertation, minimum of 66 semester hours, including at least 30 hours of dissertation. *Entrance requirements:* For master's, GRE, GMAT or LSAT, resume, essay, transcripts, recommendations; for doctorate, GRE, resume, essay, transcripts, recommendations. Additional exam requirements/recommendations for international students: Required—TOEFL (minimum score 550 paper-based; 80 iBT); Recommended—IELTS (minimum score 6.5). *Application deadline:* For fall admission, 2/1 priority date for domestic students, 1/15 priority date for international students; for spring admission, 10/15 priority date for domestic students, 10/1 priority date for international students. Application fee: $50 ($75 for international students). Electronic applications accepted. *Expenses:* Expenses: Contact institution. *Financial support:* In 2014–15, 60 students received support. Fellowships with partial tuition reimbursements available, research assistantships with partial tuition reimbursements available, teaching assistantships with partial tuition reimbursements available, Federal Work-Study, institutionally sponsored loans, scholarships/grants, traineeships, and unspecified assistantships available. Financial award application deadline: 4/1; financial award applicants required to submit FAFSA. *Faculty research:* Housing, education and the social and economic issues of vulnerable populations; nonprofit governance and management; education finance, effectiveness and reform; P-20 education initiatives; municipal government accountability. *Unit head:* Dr. Christine Martell, Director of MPA Program, 303-315-2716, Fax: 303-315-2229, E-mail: christine.martell@ucdenver.edu. *Application contact:* Dawn Savage, Student Services Coordinator, 303-315-2743, Fax: 303-315-2229, E-mail: dawn.savage@ucdenver.edu.
Website: http://www.ucdenver.edu/academics/colleges/SPA/Academics/programs/PublicAffairsAdmin/Pages/index.aspx

University of Connecticut, Graduate School, eCampus, Program in Homeland Security Leadership, Storrs, CT 06269. Offers MPS.

University of Illinois at Springfield, Graduate Programs, College of Public Affairs and Administration, Program in Public Health, Springfield, IL 62703-5407. Offers community health education (Graduate Certificate); emergency preparedness and homeland security (Graduate Certificate); epidemiology (Graduate Certificate); public health (MPH). Part-time and evening/weekend programs available. Postbaccalaureate distance learning degree programs offered (no on-campus study). *Faculty:* 5 full-time (4 women), 3 part-time/adjunct (1 woman). *Students:* 45 full-time (33 women), 55 part-time (36 women); includes 28 minority (21 Black or African American, non-Hispanic/Latino; 4 Asian, non-Hispanic/Latino; 2 Hispanic/Latino; 1 Two or more races, non-Hispanic/Latino), 17 international. Average age 32. 88 applicants, 40% accepted, 26 enrolled. In 2014, 19 master's, 7 other advanced degrees awarded. *Degree requirements:* For master's, comprehensive exam, internship. *Entrance requirements:* For master's, GRE, minimum undergraduate GPA of 3.0, 3 letters of recommendation, statement of personal goals. Additional exam requirements/recommendations for international students: Required—TOEFL (minimum score 500 paper-based; 61 iBT). *Application deadline:* Applications are processed on a rolling basis. Application fee: $60 ($75 for international students). Electronic applications accepted. *Expenses:* Tuition, state resident: full-time $7662; part-time $319.25 per credit hour. Tuition, nonresident: full-time $15,966; part-time $665.25 per credit hour. *Financial support:* In 2014–15, fellowships with full tuition reimbursements (averaging $9,900 per year), research assistantships with full tuition reimbursements (averaging $9,600 per year), teaching assistantships with full tuition reimbursements (averaging $9,600 per year) were awarded; career-related internships or fieldwork, Federal Work-Study, scholarships/grants, health care benefits, and unspecified assistantships also available. Support available to part-time students. Financial award application deadline: 11/15; financial award applicants required to submit FAFSA. *Unit head:* Dr. Sharron Lafollette, Program Administrator, 217-206-7894, Fax: 217-206-7279, E-mail: slafo1@uis.edu. *Application contact:* Dr. Lynn Pardie, Office of Graduate Studies, 800-252-8533, Fax: 217-206-7623, E-mail: lpard1@uis.edu.
Website: http://www.uis.edu/publichealth/

University of Management and Technology, Program in Criminal Justice, Arlington, VA 22209. Offers homeland security (MS). Part-time and evening/weekend programs available. Postbaccalaureate distance learning degree programs offered (no on-campus study). *Entrance requirements:* Additional exam requirements/recommendations for international students: Required—TOEFL (minimum score 530 paper-based; 71 iBT).

University of Management and Technology, Program in Homeland Security, Arlington, VA 22209. Offers MS. *Degree requirements:* For master's, capstone.

Homeland Security

University of Massachusetts Lowell, College of Fine Arts, Humanities and Social Sciences, School of Criminology and Justice Studies, Lowell, MA 01854. Offers criminal justice (MA); criminology and criminal justice (PhD); security studies (MA, MS). Part-time and evening/weekend programs available. *Degree requirements:* For master's, thesis optional. *Entrance requirements:* For master's, GRE General Test or MAT. Electronic applications accepted. *Faculty research:* Family violence, criminal justice management, corrections, policing, delinquency.

University of New Haven, Graduate School, Henry C. Lee College of Criminal Justice and Forensic Sciences, National Security Program, West Haven, CT 06516-1916. Offers information protection and security (MS, Certificate); national security (MS, Certificate); national security administration (Certificate). Part-time and evening/weekend programs available. *Degree requirements:* For master's, thesis or alternative, research project or internship. *Entrance requirements:* Additional exam requirements/recommendations for international students: Required—TOEFL (minimum score 70 iBT), IELTS, or PTE (minimum score of 53). Electronic applications accepted. Application fee is waived when completed online. *Expenses: Tuition:* Full-time $22,248; part-time $824 per credit hour. *Required fees:* $45 per trimester.

University of Oklahoma Health Sciences Center, Graduate College, College of Public Health, Program in Preparedness and Terrorism, Oklahoma City, OK 73190. Offers MPH.

University of Phoenix–Online Campus, College of Justice and Security, Phoenix, AZ 85034-7209. Offers administration of justice and security (MS), including administration of justice and security, global and homeland security, law enforcement organizations; public administration (MPA). Evening/weekend programs available. Postbaccalaureate distance learning degree programs offered. *Entrance requirements:* Additional exam requirements/recommendations for international students: Required—TOEFL, TOEIC (Test of English as an International Communication), Berlitz Online English Proficiency Exam, PTE, or IELTS. Electronic applications accepted. *Expenses:* Contact institution.

University of Phoenix–Phoenix Campus, College of Criminal Justice and Security, Tempe, AZ 85282-2371. Offers administration of justice and security (MS); global and homeland security (MS); law enforcement organizations (MS); public administration (MPA). Evening/weekend programs available. Postbaccalaureate distance learning degree programs offered. *Entrance requirements:* Additional exam requirements/recommendations for international students: Required—TOEFL, TOEIC (Test of English as an International Communication), Berlitz Online English Proficiency Exam, PTE, or IELTS. Electronic applications accepted. *Expenses:* Contact institution.

University of Phoenix–Southern California Campus, College of Criminal Justice and Security, Costa Mesa, CA 92626. Offers administration of justice and security (MS), including administration of justice and security, global and homeland security, law enforcement organizations; public administration (MPA). Evening/weekend programs available. Postbaccalaureate distance learning degree programs offered. *Entrance requirements:* Additional exam requirements/recommendations for international students: Required—TOEFL, TOEIC (Test of English as an International Communication), Berlitz Online English Proficiency Exam, PTE, or IELTS. Electronic applications accepted. *Expenses:* Contact institution.

University of Southern California, Graduate School, School of Policy, Planning, and Development, Public Policy Programs, Los Angeles, CA 90089. Offers homeland security and public policy (Graduate Certificate); public policy (MPP, Graduate Certificate); M Pl/MPP; MPP/JD. Part-time programs available. Terminal master's awarded for partial completion of doctoral program. *Degree requirements:* For master's, practicum. *Entrance requirements:* For master's, GRE. Additional exam requirements/recommendations for international students: Required—TOEFL (minimum score 600 paper-based; 100 iBT). Electronic applications accepted. *Faculty research:* Urban political economy, community and economic development, environmental policy, transportation policy, housing policy.

Upper Iowa University, Online Master's Programs, Fayette, IA 52142-1857. Offers accounting (MBA); corporate financial management (MBA); global business (MBA); health and human services (MPA); higher education administration (MHEA); homeland security (MPA); human resources management (MBA); justice administration (MPA); organizational development (MBA); public personnel management (MPA); quality management (MBA). MBA also available at Madison, WI campus. Part-time programs available. Postbaccalaureate distance learning degree programs offered (no on-campus study). *Degree requirements:* For master's, research project. *Entrance requirements:* For master's, GMAT, GRE, or minimum GPA of 2.7 during last 60 hours. Additional exam requirements/recommendations for international students: Required—TOEFL (minimum score 570 paper-based). Electronic applications accepted. *Faculty research:* Total quality management, CQI, teams, organization culture and climate, management.

Virginia Commonwealth University, Graduate School, College of Humanities and Sciences, Wilder School of Government and Public Affairs, Program in Homeland Security and Emergency Preparedness, Richmond, VA 23284-9005. Offers MA, Graduate Certificate. Part-time programs available. Postbaccalaureate distance learning degree programs offered. *Entrance requirements:* For master's, GRE, GMAT, MAT or LSAT, minimum GPA of 2.7; for Graduate Certificate, minimum GPA of 2.7. Additional exam requirements/recommendations for international students: Required—TOEFL (minimum score 600 paper-based; 100 iBT); Recommended—IELTS (minimum score 6.5). Electronic applications accepted.

Walden University, Graduate Programs, School of Psychology, Minneapolis, MN 55401. Offers clinical psychology (MS), including counseling, general program; forensic psychology (MS), including forensic psychology in the community, general program, mental health applications, program planning and evaluation in forensic settings, psychology and legal systems; organizational psychology and development (Postbaccalaureate Certificate); psychology (MS, PhD), including applied psychology (MS), clinical psychology (PhD), counseling psychology (PhD), crisis management and response (MS), educational psychology, forensic psychology (PhD), general psychology (MS), general psychology research (PhD), health psychology, leadership development and coaching (MS), psychology of culture (MS), psychology, public administration, and social change (MS), social psychology, terrorism and security (MS); psychology respecialization (Post-Doctoral Certificate); teaching online (Post-Master's Certificate). Part-time and evening/weekend programs available. Postbaccalaureate distance learning degree programs offered (no on-campus study). *Faculty:* 56 full-time (36 women), 351 part-time/adjunct (201 women). *Students:* 2,757 full-time (2,202 women), 1,466 part-time (1,148 women); includes 1,849 minority (1,299 Black or African American, non-Hispanic/Latino; 37 American Indian or Alaska Native, non-Hispanic/Latino; 74 Asian, non-Hispanic/Latino; 315 Hispanic/Latino; 8 Native Hawaiian or other Pacific Islander, non-Hispanic/Latino; 116 Two or more races, non-Hispanic/Latino), 28 international. Average age 41. 913 applicants, 97% accepted, 851 enrolled. In 2014, 602 master's, 204 doctorates, 19 other advanced degrees awarded. Terminal master's awarded for partial completion of doctoral program. *Degree requirements:* For master's, thesis optional; for doctorate, thesis/dissertation, residency. *Entrance requirements:* For master's, bachelor's degree or higher; minimum GPA of 2.5; official transcripts; goal statement (for some programs); access to computer and Internet; for doctorate, master's degree or higher; three years of related professional or academic experience (preferred); minimum GPA of 3.0; goal statement and current resume (for select programs); official transcripts; access to computer and Internet; for other advanced degree, relevant work experience; access to computer and Internet. Additional exam requirements/recommendations for international students: Required—TOEFL (minimum score 550 paper-based, 79 iBT), IELTS (minimum score 6.5), Michigan English Language Assessment Battery (minimum score 82), or PTE (minimum score 53). *Application deadline:* Applications are processed on a rolling basis. Application fee: $0. Electronic applications accepted. *Expenses: Tuition:* Full-time $11,925; part-time $500 per credit hour. *Required fees:* $647. *Financial support:* Fellowships, Federal Work-Study, scholarships/grants, unspecified assistantships, and family tuition reduction, active duty/veteran tuition reduction, group tuition reduction, interest-free payment plans, employee tuition reduction available. Support available to part-time students. Financial award applicants required to submit FAFSA. *Unit head:* Dr. Marilyn Powell, Associate Dean, 866-492-5366. *Application contact:* Meghan Thomas, Vice President of Enrollment Management, 866-492-5336, E-mail: info@waldenu.edu.
Website: http://www.waldenu.edu/programs/colleges-schools/psychology

Walden University, Graduate Programs, School of Public Policy and Administration, Minneapolis, MN 55401. Offers criminal justice (MPA, MPP, MS, Graduate Certificate), including emergency management (MS, PhD), general program (MS, PhD), homeland security and policy coordination (MS, PhD), law and public policy (MS, PhD), policy analysis (MS, PhD), public management and leadership (MS, PhD), self-designed (MS), terrorism, mediation, and peace (MS, PhD); criminal justice leadership and executive management (MS), including emergency management (MS, PhD), general program (MS, PhD), homeland security and policy coordination (MS, PhD), law and public policy (MS, PhD), policy analysis (MS, PhD), public management and leadership (MS, PhD), self-designed, terrorism, mediation, and peace (MS, PhD); emergency management (MPA, MPP, MS), including criminal justice (MS, PhD), general program (MS, PhD), homeland security (MS), public management and leadership (MS, PhD), terrorism and emergency management (MS); general program (MPA, MPP); government management (Graduate Certificate); health policy (MPA, MPP); homeland security (Graduate Certificate); homeland security and policy coordination (MPA, MPP); international nongovernmental organizations (MPA, MPP); law and public policy (MPA, MPP); local government management for sustainable communities (MPA, MPP); nonprofit management (Graduate Certificate); nonprofit management and leadership (MPA, MPP, MS); online teaching in higher education (Post-Master's Certificate); policy analysis (MPA); public management and leadership (MPA, MPP, Graduate Certificate); public policy (Graduate Certificate); public policy and administration (PhD), including criminal justice (MS, PhD), emergency management (MS, PhD), general program (MS, PhD), health policy, homeland security and policy coordination (MS, PhD), international nongovernmental organizations, law and public policy (MS, PhD), local government management for sustainable communities, nonprofit management and leadership, policy analysis (MS, PhD), public management and leadership (MS, PhD), terrorism, mediation, and peace (MS, PhD); strategic planning and public policy (Graduate Certificate); terrorism, mediation, and peace (MPA, MPP). Part-time and evening/weekend programs available. Postbaccalaureate distance learning degree programs offered (no on-campus study). *Faculty:* 13 full-time (5 women), 151 part-time/adjunct (65 women). *Students:* 1,009 full-time (573 women), 1,632 part-time (954 women); includes 1,553 minority (1,307 Black or African American, non-Hispanic/Latino; 15 American Indian or Alaska Native, non-Hispanic/Latino; 38 Asian, non-Hispanic/Latino; 127 Hispanic/Latino; 66 Two or more races, non-Hispanic/Latino), 15 international. Average age 42. 665 applicants, 97% accepted, 616 enrolled. In 2014, 317 master's, 95 doctorates, 34 other advanced degrees awarded. *Degree requirements:* For doctorate, thesis/dissertation, residency. *Entrance requirements:* For master's, bachelor's degree or higher; minimum GPA of 2.5; official transcripts; goal statement (for some programs); access to computer and Internet; for doctorate, master's degree or higher; three years of related professional or academic experience (preferred); minimum GPA of 3.0; goal statement and current resume (for select programs); official transcripts; access to computer and Internet; for other advanced degree, relevant work experience; access to computer and Internet. Additional exam requirements/recommendations for international students: Required—TOEFL (minimum score 550 paper-based, 79 iBT), IELTS (minimum score 6.5), Michigan English Language Assessment Battery (minimum score 82), or PTE (minimum score 53). *Application deadline:* Applications are processed on a rolling basis. Application fee: $0. Electronic applications accepted. *Expenses: Tuition:* Full-time $11,925; part-time $500 per credit hour. *Required fees:* $647. *Financial support:* Fellowships, Federal Work-Study, scholarships/grants, unspecified assistantships, and family tuition reduction, active duty/veteran tuition reduction, group tuition reduction, interest-free payment plans, employee tuition reduction available. Support available to part-time students. Financial award applicants required to submit FAFSA. *Unit head:* Dr. Shana Garrett, Associate Dean, 866-492-5336. *Application contact:* Meghan Thomas, Vice President of Enrollment Management, 866-492-5336, E-mail: info@waldenu.edu.
Website: http://www.waldenu.edu/programs/colleges-schools/public-policy-and-administration

Wayland Baptist University, Graduate Programs, Programs in Behavioral and Social Sciences, Plainview, TX 79072-6998. Offers counseling (MA); government administration (MPA); history (MA); homeland security (MPA); justice administration (MPA). Part-time and evening/weekend programs available. Postbaccalaureate distance learning degree programs offered. *Faculty:* 19 full-time (5 women), 18 part-time/adjunct (8 women). *Students:* 17 full-time (12 women), 428 part-time (264 women); includes 208 minority (66 Black or African American, non-Hispanic/Latino; 6 American Indian or Alaska Native, non-Hispanic/Latino; 14 Asian, non-Hispanic/Latino; 98 Hispanic/Latino; 4 Native Hawaiian or other Pacific Islander, non-Hispanic/Latino; 20 Two or more races, non-Hispanic/Latino). Average age 38. 152 applicants, 93% accepted, 67 enrolled. In 2014, 158 master's awarded. *Degree requirements:* For master's, comprehensive exam. *Entrance requirements:* For master's, GRE, MAT. Additional exam requirements/recommendations for international students: Required—TOEFL (minimum score 500 paper-based; 61 iBT). *Application deadline:* Applications are processed on a rolling basis. Application fee: $50. Electronic applications accepted. *Expenses: Tuition:* Full-time $8910; part-time $495 per credit hour. *Required fees:* $970; $495 per credit hour. $485 per semester. *Financial support:* Federal Work-Study, institutionally sponsored loans, and scholarships/grants available. Support available to part-time students. Financial award application deadline: 5/1; financial award applicants required to submit FAFSA. *Unit head:* Dr. Estelle Owens, Chairman, 806-291-1171, Fax: 806-291-1972, E-mail: owensest@wbu.edu. *Application contact:* Amanda Stanton, Graduate Studies, 806-291-3423, Fax: 806-291-1950, E-mail: stanton@wbu.edu.

Western Kentucky University, Graduate Studies, Ogden College of Science and Engineering, Department of Physics and Astronomy, Bowling Green, KY 42101. Offers homeland security sciences (MS); physics (MA Ed).

Western Michigan University Cooley Law School, Graduate Programs, Lansing, MI 48901-3038. Offers administrative law (public law) (JD); business transactions (JD); Canadian law practice (JD); Constitutional law and civil rights (public law) (JD); corporate law and finance (LL M); environmental law (public law) (JD); general practice (JD), including solo and small firm; homeland and national security law (LL M); insurance law (LL M); intellectual property (JD); intellectual property law (LL M);

international law (JD); litigation (JD); self-directed (LL M, JD); tax law (LL M); taxation (JD); U.S. legal studies for foreign attorneys (LL M); JD/LL M; JD/MBA; JD/MPA; JD/MSW. *Accreditation:* ABA. Part-time and evening/weekend programs available. Postbaccalaureate distance learning degree programs offered (no on-campus study). *Faculty:* 75 full-time (36 women), 127 part-time/adjunct (43 women). *Students:* 343 full-time (178 women), 1,537 part-time (826 women). *Degree requirements:* For master's, thesis optional; for doctorate, minimum of 3 credits of clinical experience. *Entrance requirements:* For master's, JD or LL B; for doctorate, LSAT. Additional exam requirements/recommendations for international students: Required—TOEFL (for US legal studies for foreign attorneys LL M program). *Application deadline:* For fall admission, 9/1 for domestic and international students; for winter admission, 1/1 for domestic and international students; for spring admission, 5/1 for domestic and international students. Applications are processed on a rolling basis. Application fee: $0. Electronic applications accepted. *Expenses:* *Tuition:* Full-time $44,950; part-time $1550 per credit hour. *Required fees:* $40; $40 per year. Tuition and fees vary according to degree level and student level. *Financial support:* Career-related internships or fieldwork, Federal Work-Study, scholarships/grants, traineeships, and unspecified assistantships available. Support available to part-time students. Financial award applicants required to submit FAFSA. *Faculty research:* Wrongful convictions, civil rights, environmental law, litigation techniques, data mining, intellectual property, practical and skills-based legal education. *Unit head:* Don LeDuc, President and Dean, 517-371-5140 Ext. 2009, Fax: 517-334-5152. *Application contact:* Mohammed S. Sohail, Acting Director of Admissions, 517-371-5140 Ext. 2233, Fax: 517-334-5718, E-mail: sohailm@cooley.edu.
Website: http://www.cooley.edu/gradprograms/index.html

Wilmington University, College of Business, New Castle, DE 19720-6491. Offers accounting (MBA, MS); business administration (MBA, DBA); environmental stewardship (MBA); finance (MBA); health care administration (MBA, MSM); homeland security (MBA, MSM); human resource management (MSM); management information systems (MBA, MSN); marketing (MSM); marketing management (MBA); military leadership (MSM); organizational leadership (MBA, MSM); public administration (MSM). Part-time and evening/weekend programs available. *Faculty:* 20 full-time (6 women), 117 part-time/adjunct (48 women). *Students:* 585 full-time (298 women), 1,156 part-time (733 women); includes 665 minority (567 Black or African American, non-Hispanic/Latino; 11 American Indian or Alaska Native, non-Hispanic/Latino; 55 Asian, non-Hispanic/Latino; 26 Hispanic/Latino; 2 Native Hawaiian or other Pacific Islander, non-Hispanic/Latino; 4 Two or more races, non-Hispanic/Latino), 133 international. Average age 35. 1,323 applicants, 99% accepted, 643 enrolled. In 2014, 438 master's, 15 doctorates awarded. *Entrance requirements:* Additional exam requirements/recommendations for international students: Required—TOEFL (minimum score 500 paper-based). *Application deadline:* Applications are processed on a rolling basis. Application fee: $35. Electronic applications accepted. *Financial support:* Applicants required to submit FAFSA. *Unit head:* Dr. Donald W. Durandetta, Dean, 302-356-6780, E-mail: donald.w.durandetta@wilmu.edu. *Application contact:* Laura Morris, Director of Admissions, 877-967-5456, E-mail: infocenter@wilmu.edu.
Website: http://www.wilmu.edu/business/

Wilmington University, College of Social and Behavioral Sciences, New Castle, DE 19720-6491. Offers administration of human services (MS); administration of justice (MS); clinical mental health counseling (MS); homeland security (MS). *Accreditation:* ACA. Part-time and evening/weekend programs available. *Faculty:* 7 full-time (4 women), 70 part-time/adjunct (28 women). *Students:* 175 full-time (141 women), 468 part-time (350 women); includes 296 minority (266 Black or African American, non-Hispanic/Latino; 5 American Indian or Alaska Native, non-Hispanic/Latino; 3 Asian, non-Hispanic/Latino; 18 Hispanic/Latino; 2 Native Hawaiian or other Pacific Islander, non-Hispanic/Latino; 2 Two or more races, non-Hispanic/Latino), 4 international. Average age 35. 251 applicants, 100% accepted, 157 enrolled. In 2014, 170 master's awarded. *Entrance requirements:* Additional exam requirements/recommendations for international students: Required—TOEFL (minimum score 500 paper-based). *Application deadline:* Applications are processed on a rolling basis. Application fee: $35. Electronic applications accepted. *Financial support:* Applicants required to submit FAFSA. *Unit head:* Dr. Christian A. Trowbridge, Dean, 302-295-1151, Fax: 302-328-5164. *Application contact:* Laura Morris, Director of Admissions, 877-967-5464, E-mail: inquire@wilmcoll.edu.
Website: http://www.wilmu.edu/behavioralscience/

Industrial and Labor Relations

Baruch College of the City University of New York, Zicklin School of Business, Zicklin Executive Programs, Baruch Executive Master of Science in Industrial and Labor Relations Program, New York, NY 10010-5585. Offers MS. Part-time and evening/weekend programs available. *Entrance requirements:* For master's, professional experience in HR or labor relations. Additional exam requirements/recommendations for international students: Required—TOEFL. *Expenses:* Contact institution.

Carnegie Mellon University, Dietrich College of Humanities and Social Sciences, Department of History, Pittsburgh, PA 15213-3891. Offers African and African-American diaspora (PhD); culture and power (PhD); labor, politics and social movements (PhD); technology, environment, science and health (PhD); women, gender and the family (PhD). Part-time programs available. *Degree requirements:* For doctorate, oral and written comprehensive exams, dissertation defense. *Entrance requirements:* For doctorate, GRE General Test. Additional exam requirements/recommendations for international students: Required—TOEFL. Electronic applications accepted. *Faculty research:* Anthropology and history, African-American history, technology/environment, cultural history analysis.

Cleveland State University, Cleveland-Marshall College of Law, Cleveland, OH 44115. Offers business law (JD); civil litigation and dispute resolution (JD); criminal law (JD); employment labor law (JD); health care compliance (Certificate); health law (Certificate); international and comparative law (JD); law (LL M, MLS); JD/MAES; JD/MBA; JD/MPA; JD/MSES; JD/MUPDD. *Accreditation:* ABA. Part-time and evening/weekend programs available. *Faculty:* 37 full-time (16 women), 40 part-time/adjunct (11 women). *Students:* 307 full-time (129 women), 158 part-time (79 women); includes 86 minority (40 Black or African American, non-Hispanic/Latino; 3 American Indian or Alaska Native, non-Hispanic/Latino; 14 Asian, non-Hispanic/Latino; 21 Hispanic/Latino; 8 Two or more races, non-Hispanic/Latino), 9 international. Average age 28. 1,655 applicants, 38% accepted, 173 enrolled. In 2014, 151 doctorates, 3 Certificates awarded. *Degree requirements:* For master's, thesis for graduates of U.S. law schools (for LL M); 30 credits, 6 in required courses (for MLS); for doctorate, 90 credits (41 in required courses). *Entrance requirements:* For master's, JD or LL B (for LL M); bachelor's degree (for MLS); for doctorate, LSAT, bachelor's degree. Additional exam requirements/recommendations for international students: Required—TOEFL (minimum score 600 paper-based, 100 iBT) or IELTS (minimum score 7) for LL M. *Application deadline:* For fall admission, 5/1 for domestic and international students. Applications are processed on a rolling basis. Application fee: $0. Electronic applications accepted. *Expenses:* Expenses: Contact institution. *Financial support:* In 2014–15, 198 students received support, including 19 fellowships (averaging $2,500 per year), 27 research assistantships, 7 teaching assistantships with partial tuition reimbursements available (averaging $8,615 per year); career-related internships or fieldwork, Federal Work-Study, scholarships/grants, tuition waivers (full and partial), and unspecified assistantships also available. Support available to part-time students. Financial award application deadline: 5/1; financial award applicants required to submit FAFSA. *Faculty research:* Health law, international law, Constitutional law, criminal law, business law. *Unit head:* Craig M. Boise, Dean, 216-687-2300, Fax: 216-687-6881, E-mail: c.boise@csuohio.edu. *Application contact:* Christopher Lucak, Assistant Dean for Admissions, 216-687-4692, Fax: 216-687-6881, E-mail: c.lucak@csuohio.edu.
Website: http://www.law.csuohio.edu/

Cleveland State University, College of Graduate Studies, Monte Ahuja College of Business, Department of Management, Cleveland, OH 44115. Offers labor relations and human resources (MLRHR). Part-time and evening/weekend programs available. *Faculty:* 13 full-time (5 women), 8 part-time/adjunct (0 women). *Students:* 17 full-time (16 women), 27 part-time (23 women); includes 8 minority (5 Black or African American, non-Hispanic/Latino; 2 Asian, non-Hispanic/Latino; 1 Two or more races, non-Hispanic/Latino), 8 international. Average age 30. 98 applicants, 44% accepted, 5 enrolled. In 2014, 35 master's awarded. *Entrance requirements:* For master's, GMAT or GRE, minimum GPA of 3.0. Additional exam requirements/recommendations for international students: Required—TOEFL (minimum score 525 paper-based). *Application deadline:* For fall admission, 7/15 for domestic students; for spring admission, 12/15 for domestic students. Applications are processed on a rolling basis. Application fee: $30. Electronic applications accepted. *Expenses:* Tuition, state resident: full-time $9566; part-time $531 per credit hour. Tuition, nonresident: full-time $17,980; part-time $999 per credit hour. *Required fees:* $25 per semester. Tuition and fees vary according to degree level and program. *Financial support:* In 2014–15, 3 students received support, including 3 research assistantships with full and partial tuition reimbursements available (averaging $6,960 per year); tuition waivers (full) and unspecified assistantships also available. Financial award application deadline: 5/1; financial award applicants required to submit FAFSA. *Faculty research:* Human resource management, strategic management, organizational behavior, health care management. *Unit head:* Dr. Timothy G. DeGroot, Chairperson, 216-687-4747, Fax: 216-687-4708, E-mail: t.degroot@csuohio.edu. *Application contact:* Lisa Sample, Administrative Secretary, 216-687-4726, E-mail: l.m.sample@csuohio.edu.
Website: https://www.csuohio.edu/business/management/management

Cornell University, Graduate School, Graduate Fields of Industrial and Labor Relations, Ithaca, NY 14853. Offers collective bargaining, labor law and labor history (MILR, MPS, MS, PhD); economic and social statistics (MILR); human resource studies (MILR, MPS, MS, PhD); industrial and labor relations problems (MILR, MPS, MS, PhD); international and comparative labor (MILR, MPS, MS, PhD); labor economics (MILR, MPS, MS, PhD); organizational behavior (MILR, MPS, MS, PhD). *Degree requirements:* For master's, thesis (MS); for doctorate, comprehensive exam, thesis/dissertation, teaching experience. *Entrance requirements:* For master's and doctorate, GMAT or GRE General Test, 2 academic recommendations. Additional exam requirements/recommendations for international students: Required—TOEFL (minimum score 550 paper-based; 77 iBT). Electronic applications accepted. *Expenses:* Contact institution.

Georgetown University, Graduate School of Arts and Sciences, Department of Economics, Washington, DC 20057. Offers econometrics (PhD); economic development (PhD); economic theory (PhD); industrial organization (PhD); international macro and finance (PhD); international trade (PhD); labor economics (PhD); macroeconomics (PhD); public economics and political economy (PhD); MA/PhD; MS/MA. *Degree requirements:* For doctorate, comprehensive exam, thesis/dissertation. *Entrance requirements:* For doctorate, GRE General Test. Additional exam requirements/recommendations for international students: Required—TOEFL. *Faculty research:* International economics, economic development.

Georgia State University, Andrew Young School of Policy Studies, Department of Economics, Atlanta, GA 30302-3992. Offers economics (MA); environmental economics (PhD); experimental economics (PhD); labor economics (PhD); policy (MA); public finance (PhD); urban and regional economics (PhD). MA offered through the College of Arts and Sciences. Part-time programs available. *Faculty:* 27 full-time (5 women). *Students:* 111 full-time (42 women), 15 part-time (4 women); includes 20 minority (8 Black or African American, non-Hispanic/Latino; 3 Asian, non-Hispanic/Latino; 8 Hispanic/Latino; 1 Two or more races, non-Hispanic/Latino), 67 international. Average age 29. 182 applicants, 41% accepted, 33 enrolled. In 2014, 47 master's, 7 doctorates awarded. Terminal master's awarded for partial completion of doctoral program. *Degree requirements:* For master's, thesis optional; for doctorate, comprehensive exam, thesis/dissertation. *Entrance requirements:* For master's, GRE; for doctorate, GRE. Additional exam requirements/recommendations for international students: Required—TOEFL (minimum score 603 paper-based; 100 iBT) or IELTS (minimum score 7). *Application deadline:* For fall admission, 2/15 for domestic and international students; for spring admission, 10/1 for domestic and international students. Application fee: $50. Electronic applications accepted. *Expenses:* Tuition, state resident: full-time $6516; part-time $362 per credit hour. Tuition, nonresident: full-time $22,014; part-time $1223 per credit hour. *Required fees:* $2128 per semester. Tuition and fees vary according to course load and program. *Financial support:* In 2014–15, fellowships with full tuition reimbursements (averaging $11,333 per year), research assistantships with full tuition reimbursements (averaging $9,788 per year), teaching assistantships with full tuition reimbursements (averaging $3,000 per year) were awarded; career-related internships or fieldwork also available. Financial award application deadline: 2/15. *Faculty research:* Public, experimental, urban/environmental, labor, and health economics. *Unit head:* Dr. Sally Wallace, Department Chair, 404-413-0046, Fax: 404-413-0145, E-mail: swallace@gsu.edu. *Application contact:* Charisma Parker, Admissions Coordinator, 404-413-0030, Fax: 404-413-0023, E-mail: cparker28@gsu.edu.
Website: http://economics.gsu.edu/

Industrial and Labor Relations

Indiana University of Pennsylvania, School of Graduate Studies and Research, College of Health and Human Services, Department of Employment and Labor Relations, Program in Employment and Labor Relations, Indiana, PA 15705-1087. Offers MA. Part-time and evening/weekend programs available. *Faculty:* 4 full-time (1 woman). *Students:* 34 full-time (17 women), 26 part-time (16 women); includes 9 minority (5 Black or African American, non-Hispanic/Latino; 1 Hispanic/Latino; 3 Two or more races, non-Hispanic/Latino), 7 international. Average age 28. 63 applicants, 67% accepted, 33 enrolled. In 2014, 48 master's awarded. *Entrance requirements:* Additional exam requirements/recommendations for international students: Required— TOEFL (minimum score 550 paper-based). *Application deadline:* Applications are processed on a rolling basis. Application fee: $50. Electronic applications accepted. *Financial support:* In 2014–15, 1 fellowship with full tuition reimbursement (averaging $1,000 per year), 21 research assistantships with full and partial tuition reimbursements (averaging $3,589 per year) were awarded; career-related internships or fieldwork, Federal Work-Study, scholarships/grants, and unspecified assistantships also available. Financial award application deadline: 4/15; financial award applicants required to submit FAFSA. *Unit head:* Dr. David M. Piper, Coordinator, 724-357-4471, E-mail: david.piper@iup.edu.
Website: http://www.iup.edu/elr/programs/ma/

Inter American University of Puerto Rico, Metropolitan Campus, Graduate Programs, Program in Labor Relations, San Juan, PR 00919-1293. Offers MA. *Degree requirements:* For master's, comprehensive exam. *Entrance requirements:* For master's, GRE or EXADEP, interview. Electronic applications accepted.

Inter American University of Puerto Rico, Metropolitan Campus, Graduate Programs, Program in Psychology, San Juan, PR 00919-1293. Offers counseling psychology (MA, PhD); industrial/organizational psychology (MA, PhD); labor relations (MA); school psychology (MA, PhD). *Degree requirements:* For master's, comprehensive exam. *Entrance requirements:* For master's, GRE or EXADEP, interview. Electronic applications accepted.

Loyola University Chicago, Graduate School of Business, Institute of Human Resources and Employee Relations, Chicago, IL 60611. Offers MSHR, MBA/MSHR. Part-time and evening/weekend programs available. *Faculty:* 5 full-time (1 woman), 4 part-time/adjunct (2 women). *Students:* 8 full-time (7 women), 19 part-time (15 women); includes 8 minority (4 Black or African American, non-Hispanic/Latino; 1 Asian, non-Hispanic/Latino; 2 Hispanic/Latino; 1 Two or more races, non-Hispanic/Latino), 10 international. Average age 29. 70 applicants, 49% accepted, 7 enrolled. In 2014, 22 master's awarded. *Entrance requirements:* For master's, GMAT or GRE, a completed application form, official transcripts, two letters of recommendation, statement of purpose, resume. Additional exam requirements/recommendations for international students: Required—TOEFL (minimum score 90 iBT) or IELTS (minimum score 6.5). *Application deadline:* For fall admission, 7/15 for domestic and international students; for winter admission, 10/1 for domestic and international students; for spring admission, 1/15 for domestic and international students; for summer admission, 4/1 for domestic and international students. Applications are processed on a rolling basis. Application fee: $50. Electronic applications accepted. Application fee is waived when completed online. *Expenses:* Expenses: $4275 per course. *Financial support:* Scholarships/grants and unspecified assistantships available. *Faculty research:* Human resource management, labor relations, global human resource management, organizational development, compensation. *Unit head:* Dr. Al Gini, Chair, 312-915-6093, E-mail: agini@luc.edu. *Application contact:* Lauren Griffin, Enrollment Advisor, Quinlan School of Business Graduate Programs, 312-915-6124, Fax: 312-915-7207, E-mail: lgriffin3@luc.edu.
Website: http://www.luc.edu/quinlan/mba/masters-degree-in-human-resources/index.shtml

McMaster University, School of Graduate Studies, Faculty of Social Sciences, Program in Labour Studies, Hamilton, ON L8S 4M2, Canada. Offers work and society (MA).

Memorial University of Newfoundland, School of Graduate Studies, Interdisciplinary Program in Employment Relations, St. John's, NL A1C 5S7, Canada. Offers MER. Part-time programs available. *Degree requirements:* For master's, major supervised paper. *Entrance requirements:* For master's, undergraduate degree in related field, minimum B average. Electronic applications accepted.

Michigan State University, The Graduate School, College of Social Science, School of Labor and Industrial Relations, East Lansing, MI 48824. Offers human resources and labor relations (MLRHR); industrial relations and human resources (PhD). *Entrance requirements:* Additional exam requirements/recommendations for international students: Required—TOEFL.

New York Institute of Technology, School of Management, Department of Human Resource Management Studies, Old Westbury, NY 11568-8000. Offers human resource management (Advanced Certificate); human resource management and labor relations (MS). Part-time and evening/weekend programs available. *Degree requirements:* For master's, comprehensive exam, thesis optional. *Entrance requirements:* For master's, GRE, minimum QPA of 2.85, interview, 2 letters of recommendation. Additional exam requirements/recommendations for international students: Required—TOEFL (minimum score 550 paper-based; 79 iBT), IELTS (minimum score 6). Electronic applications accepted. *Faculty research:* Compensation and benefits, organizational management, industrial relations, disabilities.

The Ohio State University, Graduate School, Max M. Fisher College of Business, Program in Human Resource Management, Columbus, OH 43210. Offers human resource management (MHRM, PhD); labor and human resources (PhD). Part-time programs available. *Faculty:* 25. *Students:* 86 full-time (61 women), 21 part-time (14 women); includes 14 minority (6 Black or African American, non-Hispanic/Latino; 1 Asian, non-Hispanic/Latino; 5 Hispanic/Latino; 2 Two or more races, non-Hispanic/Latino), 28 international. Average age 26. In 2014, 50 master's, 1 doctorate awarded. *Degree requirements:* For doctorate, thesis/dissertation. *Entrance requirements:* For master's and doctorate, GRE General Test or GMAT. Additional exam requirements/recommendations for international students: Required—Michigan English Language Assessment Battery (minimum score 86); Recommended—TOEFL (minimum score 600 paper-based; 100 iBT), IELTS (minimum score 7). *Application deadline:* For fall admission, 11/15 priority date for domestic and international students; for spring admission, 10/1 for domestic students. Applications are processed on a rolling basis. Application fee: $60 ($70 for international students). Electronic applications accepted. *Financial support:* Fellowships with tuition reimbursements, research assistantships with tuition reimbursements, and teaching assistantships with tuition reimbursements available. *Unit head:* Ben Tepper, Chair, 614-688-2129, E-mail: tepper.15@osu.edu. *Application contact:* Graduate and Professional Admissions, 614-292-9444, Fax: 614-292-3895, E-mail: gpadmissions@osu.edu.
Website: http://fisher.osu.edu/departments/management-and-hr/

Penn State University Park, Graduate School, College of the Liberal Arts, School of Labor and Employment Relations, University Park, PA 16802. Offers human resources and employment relations (MS). *Unit head:* Dr. Susan Welch, Dean, 814-865-7691, Fax: 814-863-2085, E-mail: swelch@psu.edu. *Application contact:* Lori A. Stania, Director,

Graduate Student Services, 814-867-5278, Fax: 814-863-4627, E-mail: gswww@psu.edu. Website: http://lser.la.psu.edu/

Queen's University at Kingston, School of Graduate Studies, School of Industrial Relations, Kingston, ON K7L 3N6, Canada. Offers MIR. Part-time programs available. *Degree requirements:* For master's, research essay, skill seminars and modules. *Entrance requirements:* For master's, course work in micro-economics, macro-economics, and quantitative statistics. Additional exam requirements/recommendations for international students: Required—TOEFL (minimum score 600 paper-based). *Faculty research:* Collective bargaining and labor law, personnel and human relations, labor market analysis and policy, change management, teams.

Rutgers, The State University of New Jersey, New Brunswick, School of Management and Labor Relations, Program in Industrial Relations and Human Resources, Piscataway, NJ 08854-8097. Offers PhD. Part-time programs available. *Degree requirements:* For doctorate, comprehensive exam, thesis/dissertation. *Entrance requirements:* For doctorate, GRE or GMAT, 3 letters of recommendation. Additional exam requirements/recommendations for international students: Required—TOEFL (minimum score 575 paper-based; 91 iBT). Electronic applications accepted. *Faculty research:* Strategic human resources, labor relations, organizational change, worker representation.

Rutgers, The State University of New Jersey, New Brunswick, School of Management and Labor Relations, Program in Labor and Employment Relations, Piscataway, NJ 08854-8097. Offers MLER. Part-time programs available. Postbaccalaureate distance learning degree programs offered. *Degree requirements:* For master's, thesis optional. *Entrance requirements:* For master's, GRE General Test. Additional exam requirements/recommendations for international students: Required—TOEFL. Electronic applications accepted. *Expenses:* Contact institution. *Faculty research:* Labor history, women and work, labor education, comparative labor movements, labor involvement and corporate decision making.

Southern New Hampshire University, School of Business, Manchester, NH 03106-1045. Offers accounting (MBA, MS, Graduate Certificate); accounting finance (MS); accounting/auditing (MS); accounting/forensic accounting (MS); accounting/taxation (MS); athletic administration (MBA, Graduate Certificate); business administration (IMBA, MBA, Certificate, Graduate Certificate), including accounting (Certificate), business administration (MBA), business information systems (Graduate Certificate), human resource management (Certificate); corporate social responsibility (MBA); entrepreneurship (MBA); finance (MBA, MS, Graduate Certificate); finance/corporate finance (MS); finance/investments and securities (MS); forensic accounting (MBA); healthcare informatics (MBA); healthcare management (MBA); human resource management (Graduate Certificate); information technology (MS, Graduate Certificate); information technology management (MBA); international business (Graduate Certificate); international business and information technology (Graduate Certificate); international finance (Graduate Certificate); international sport management (Graduate Certificate); justice studies (MBA); leadership of nonprofit organizations (Graduate Certificate); marketing (MBA, MS, Graduate Certificate); operations and project management (MS); operations and supply chain management (MBA, Graduate Certificate); organizational leadership (MS); project management (MBA, Graduate Certificate); Six Sigma (MBA); Six Sigma quality (Graduate Certificate); social media marketing (MBA); sport management (MBA, MS, Graduate Certificate); sustainability and environmental compliance (MBA); workplace conflict management (MBA); MBA/Certificate. *Accreditation:* ACBSP. Part-time and evening/weekend programs available. Postbaccalaureate distance learning degree programs offered (no on-campus study). Terminal master's awarded for partial completion of doctoral program. *Degree requirements:* For master's, one foreign language, comprehensive exam (for some programs), thesis or alternative. *Entrance requirements:* For master's, minimum GPA of 2.5. Additional exam requirements/recommendations for international students: Required—TOEFL (minimum score 500 paper-based). Electronic applications accepted.

State University of New York Empire State College, School for Graduate Studies, Program in Labor and Policy Studies, Saratoga Springs, NY 12866-4391. Offers MA. Part-time and evening/weekend programs available. Postbaccalaureate distance learning degree programs offered (minimal on-campus study). *Degree requirements:* For master's, thesis, exam, final project. *Entrance requirements:* Additional exam requirements/recommendations for international students: Required—TOEFL (minimum score 600 paper-based). Electronic applications accepted. *Faculty research:* Work and technology, collective bargaining, labor law, human resources management, trade union governance.

Université de Montréal, Faculty of Arts and Sciences, School of Industrial Relations, Montréal, QC H3C 3J7, Canada. Offers M Sc, PhD, DESS. Part-time programs available. *Degree requirements:* For master's, thesis; for doctorate, thesis/dissertation, general exam. *Entrance requirements:* For master's, BS in industrial relations. Electronic applications accepted. *Faculty research:* Labor law, health and safety at work, stress, job satisfaction, labor economics.

Université du Québec à Trois-Rivières, Graduate Programs, Program in Labor Relations, Trois-Rivières, QC G9A 5H7, Canada. Offers DESS.

Université du Québec en Outaouais, Graduate Programs, Department of Industrial Relations, Gatineau, QC J8X 3X7, Canada. Offers M Sc, MA, PhD, Diploma. Part-time programs available. *Students:* 19 full-time, 46 part-time. *Degree requirements:* For master's, thesis (for some programs), internship (for some programs); for doctorate, thesis/dissertation. *Entrance requirements:* For master's, appropriate bachelor's degree, proficiency in French; for doctorate, appropriate master's degree, proficiency in French. *Application deadline:* For fall admission, 6/1 for domestic students, 4/15 for international students; for winter admission, 11/1 for domestic students, 9/15 for international students. Application fee: $30 Canadian dollars. *Financial support:* Fellowships, research assistantships, and teaching assistantships available. *Unit head:* Ali Bejaoui, Director, 819-773-1780, Fax: 819-773-1788, E-mail: ali.bejaoui@uqo.ca. *Application contact:* Registrar's Office, 819-773-1850, Fax: 819-773-1835, E-mail: registraire@uqo.ca.

Université Laval, Faculty of Social Sciences, Department of Industrial Relations, Programs in Industrial Relations, Québec, QC G1K 7P4, Canada. Offers MA, PhD. Terminal master's awarded for partial completion of doctoral program. *Degree requirements:* For master's, thesis (for some programs); for doctorate, comprehensive exam, thesis/dissertation. *Entrance requirements:* For master's and doctorate, knowledge of French, comprehension of written English. Electronic applications accepted.

University of Alberta, Faculty of Graduate Studies and Research, Doctoral Program in Business, Edmonton, AB T6G 2E1, Canada. Offers accounting (PhD); finance (PhD); human resources/industrial relations (PhD); management science (PhD); marketing (PhD); organizational analysis (PhD); MBA/PhD. *Accreditation:* AACSB. Part-time programs available. *Degree requirements:* For doctorate, comprehensive exam, thesis/dissertation. *Entrance requirements:* For doctorate, GMAT. Additional exam requirements/recommendations for international students: Required—TOEFL (minimum score 550 paper-based). Electronic applications accepted. *Faculty research:*

Accounting, capital markets and corporate finance, organizational change and human resource management, marketing, strategic management.

University of California, Berkeley, Graduate Division, Haas School of Business, PhD in Business Administration Program, Berkeley, CA 94720-1500. Offers accounting (PhD); business and public policy (PhD); finance (PhD); management of organizations (PhD); marketing (PhD); real estate (PhD). *Accreditation:* AACSB. *Students:* 76 full-time (29 women); includes 11 minority (4 Asian, non-Hispanic/Latino; 6 Hispanic/Latino; 1 Two or more races, non-Hispanic/Latino), 38 international. Average age 27. 489 applicants. In 2014, 14 doctorates awarded. *Degree requirements:* For doctorate, comprehensive exam, thesis/dissertation, written preliminary exams, oral qualifying exam. *Entrance requirements:* For doctorate, GMAT or GRE, minimum GPA of 3.0 in undergraduate and graduate coursework. Additional exam requirements/recommendations for international students: Required—TOEFL (minimum score 570 paper-based; 70 iBT), IELTS (minimum score 7). *Application deadline:* For fall admission, 12/10 for domestic and international students. Application fee: $90 ($110 for international students). Electronic applications accepted. *Financial support:* In 2014–15, 74 students received support, including 62 fellowships with full and partial tuition reimbursements available (averaging $30,000 per year), research assistantships with full and partial tuition reimbursements available (averaging $12,000 per year), teaching assistantships with full and partial tuition reimbursements available (averaging $13,000 per year); scholarships/grants, health care benefits, tuition waivers (full), unspecified assistantships, and transit passes, travel grants also available. Financial award application deadline: 12/10; financial award applicants required to submit FAFSA. *Faculty research:* Accounting, business and public policy, entrepreneurship, finance, management of organizations, marketing, operations and information technology management, real estate. *Unit head:* Dr. Martin Lettau, Director, 510-643-6349, Fax: 510-643-4255, E-mail: melhacker@haas.berkeley.edu. *Application contact:* Melissa Hacker, Director, Student Affairs, 510-642-3944, Fax: 510-643-4255, E-mail: melhacker@haas.berkeley.edu.
Website: http://www.haas.berkeley.edu/Phd/

University of California, Santa Barbara, Graduate Division, College of Letters and Sciences, Division of Social Sciences, Department of Economics, Santa Barbara, CA 93106-9210. Offers econometrics (PhD); economics (MA, PhD); environmental and natural resources (PhD); experimental and behavioral economics (PhD); labor economics (PhD); macroeconomic theory and policy (PhD); mathematical economics (PhD); public finance (PhD); MA/PhD. Terminal master's awarded for partial completion of doctoral program. *Degree requirements:* For master's, comprehensive exam; for doctorate, comprehensive exam, thesis/dissertation. *Entrance requirements:* For master's and doctorate, GRE General Test, 3 letters of recommendation, statement of purpose, personal achievements/contributions statement, resume/curriculum vitae, transcripts for post-secondary institutions attended. Additional exam requirements/recommendations for international students: Required—TOEFL (minimum score 550 paper-based; 80 iBT), IELTS (minimum score 7). Electronic applications accepted. *Faculty research:* Labor economics, econometrics, macroeconomic theory and policy, environmental and natural resources economics, experimental and behavioral economics.

University of Cincinnati, Graduate School, McMicken College of Arts and Sciences, Center for Organizational Leadership, Program in Labor and Employment Relations, Cincinnati, OH 45221. Offers MALER. Part-time and evening/weekend programs available. *Degree requirements:* For master's, thesis or alternative, final experience project. *Entrance requirements:* For master's, minimum undergraduate GPA of 3.0. Additional exam requirements/recommendations for international students: Required—TOEFL (minimum score 560 paper-based). Electronic applications accepted. *Faculty research:* Human resource management, diversity, leadership.

University of Cincinnati, Graduate School, McMicken College of Arts and Sciences, Department of Economics, Cincinnati, OH 45221. Offers applied economics (MA); labor and employment relations (MALER). Part-time and evening/weekend programs available. Electronic applications accepted.

University of Illinois at Urbana–Champaign, Graduate College, School of Labor and Employment Relations, Champaign, IL 61820. Offers human resources and industrial relations (MHRIR, PhD); MHRIR/JD; MHRIR/MBA. *Students:* 208 (145 women). Terminal master's awarded for partial completion of doctoral program. Application fee: $70 ($90 for international students). *Unit head:* Dr. Fritz Drasgow, Interim Dean, 217-333-1482, Fax: 217-244-9290, E-mail: fdrasgow@illinois.edu. *Application contact:* Elizabeth Barker, Assistant Dean, 217-333-2381, Fax: 217-244-9290, E-mail: ebarker@illinois.edu.
Website: http://www.ler.illinois.edu

University of Massachusetts Amherst, Graduate School, College of Social and Behavioral Sciences, The Labor Center, Amherst, MA 01003. Offers labor studies (MS); union leadership and administration (MS). Part-time programs available. Postbaccalaureate distance learning degree programs offered (minimal on-campus study). *Faculty:* 3 full-time (2 women). *Students:* 13 full-time (7 women), 48 part-time (23 women); includes 11 minority (2 Black or African American, non-Hispanic/Latino; 1 Asian, non-Hispanic/Latino; 5 Hispanic/Latino; 3 Two or more races, non-Hispanic/Latino), 6 international. Average age 40. 16 applicants, 88% accepted, 4 enrolled. In 2014, 21 master's awarded. *Degree requirements:* For master's, thesis or alternative. *Entrance requirements:* Additional exam requirements/recommendations for international students: Required—TOEFL (minimum score 550 paper-based; 80 iBT), IELTS (minimum score 6.5). *Application deadline:* For fall admission, 2/1 for domestic and international students; for spring admission, 10/1 for domestic and international students. Applications are processed on a rolling basis. Application fee: $75. Electronic applications accepted. *Expenses:* Tuition, state resident: full-time $1980; part-time $110 per credit. Tuition, nonresident: full-time $14,644; part-time $414 per credit. *Required fees:* $11,417. One-time fee: $357. *Financial support:* Fellowships with full and partial tuition reimbursements, research assistantships with full and partial tuition reimbursements, teaching assistantships with full and partial tuition reimbursements, career-related internships or fieldwork, Federal Work-Study, scholarships/grants, traineeships, health care benefits, tuition waivers (full and partial), and unspecified assistantships available. Support available to part-time students. Financial award application deadline: 2/1; financial award applicants required to submit FAFSA. *Unit head:* Dr. Eve Weinbaum, Graduate Program Director, 413-545-4875, Fax: 413-545-0110. *Application contact:* Lindsay DeSantis, Supervisor of Admissions, 413-545-0722, Fax: 413-577-0010, E-mail: gradadm@grad.umass.edu.
Website: http://www.umass.edu/lrrc/

University of Miami, Graduate School, School of Law, Coral Gables, FL 33124-8087. Offers business and financial law (Certificate); employment, labor and immigration law (JD, Certificate); estate planning (LL M); international arbitration (LL M); international law (LL M, Certificate), including general international law (LL M), inter-American law (LL M), U.S. and transnational law for foreign lawyers (LL M); law (JD); litigation specialization (Certificate); ocean and coastal law (LL M); real property development (real estate) (LL M); tax law (LL M); taxation of cross-border investment (LL M); JD/LL M; JD/LL M/MBA; JD/MA; JD/MBA; JD/MD; JD/MM; JD/MPH; JD/MPS; JD/MS Ed; JD/PhD. *Accreditation:* ABA. *Faculty:* 82 full-time (42 women), 108 part-time/adjunct (36 women). *Students:* 1,176 full-time (521 women); includes 402 minority (79 Black or African American, non-Hispanic/Latino; 7 American Indian or Alaska Native, non-Hispanic/Latino; 31 Asian, non-Hispanic/Latino; 266 Hispanic/Latino; 1 Native Hawaiian or other Pacific Islander, non-Hispanic/Latino; 18 Two or more races, non-Hispanic/Latino), 38 international. Average age 24. 3,300 applicants, 53% accepted, 308 enrolled. In 2014, 430 doctorates awarded. *Entrance requirements:* For doctorate, LSAT, 2 letters of recommendation. Additional exam requirements/recommendations for international students: Required—TOEFL (minimum score 580 paper-based; 92 iBT). *Application deadline:* For fall admission, 1/6 priority date for domestic and international students. Applications are processed on a rolling basis. Application fee: $60. Electronic applications accepted. *Expenses:* Expenses: Contact institution. *Financial support:* Fellowships, research assistantships, career-related internships or fieldwork, Federal Work-Study, institutionally sponsored loans, scholarships/grants, and unspecified assistantships available. Financial award application deadline: 3/1; financial award applicants required to submit FAFSA. *Faculty research:* National security law, international finance, Internet law/law of electronic commerce, law of the seas, art law/cultural heritage law. *Unit head:* Michael Goodnight, Associate Dean of Admissions and Enrollment Management, 305-284-2527, Fax: 305-284-3084, E-mail: mgoodnig@law.miami.edu. *Application contact:* Therese Lambert, Director of Student Recruitment, 305-284-6746, Fax: 305-284-3084, E-mail: tlambert@law.miami.edu.
Website: http://www.law.miami.edu/

University of Minnesota, Twin Cities Campus, Carlson School of Management, Master of Arts Program in Human Resources and Industrial Relations, Minneapolis, MN 55455-0213. Offers MA. *Accreditation:* AACSB. Part-time and evening/weekend programs available. *Faculty:* 16 full-time (9 women), 12 part-time/adjunct (5 women). *Students:* 121 full-time (78 women), 46 part-time (33 women); includes 22 minority (6 Black or African American, non-Hispanic/Latino; 2 American Indian or Alaska Native, non-Hispanic/Latino; 10 Asian, non-Hispanic/Latino; 4 Hispanic/Latino), 51 international. Average age 26. 298 applicants, 44% accepted, 72 enrolled. In 2014, 81 master's awarded. *Degree requirements:* For master's, thesis or alternative, 48 course credits. *Entrance requirements:* For master's, GMAT or GRE General Test, undergraduate degree from accredited institution, course in microeconomics. Additional exam requirements/recommendations for international students: Required—TOEFL (minimum score 550 paper-based; 79 iBT), IELTS (minimum score 6.5). *Application deadline:* For fall admission, 6/15 for domestic and international students; for spring admission, 10/15 for domestic and international students. Applications are processed on a rolling basis. Application fee: $75 ($95 for international students). *Expenses:* Expenses: $20,780 for residents per year, $32,680 for non-residents. *Financial support:* In 2014–15, 63 students received support, including 51 fellowships (averaging $7,500 per year), 2 research assistantships with partial tuition reimbursements available (averaging $14,500 per year), 10 teaching assistantships with partial tuition reimbursements available (averaging $9,000 per year); career-related internships or fieldwork, Federal Work-Study, institutionally sponsored loans, scholarships/grants, health care benefits, tuition waivers (full and partial), and unspecified assistantships also available. Financial award application deadline: 2/1; financial award applicants required to submit FAFSA. *Faculty research:* Staffing, training, and development; compensation and benefits; organization theory; collective bargaining. *Total annual research expenditures:* $27,000. *Unit head:* Stacy Doepner-Hove, Director, 612-625-8732, Fax: 612-624-8360, E-mail: doepn002@umn.edu. *Application contact:* Patti Blair, Admissions Coordinator, 612-624-5704, Fax: 612-624-8360, E-mail: hrirgrad@umn.edu.
Website: http://www.csom.umn.edu/chrls/

University of New Haven, Graduate School, College of Business, Program in Labor Relations, West Haven, CT 06516-1916. Offers private sector (MS); public sector (MS). Part-time and evening/weekend programs available. *Degree requirements:* For master's, thesis optional. *Entrance requirements:* Additional exam requirements/recommendations for international students: Required—TOEFL (minimum score 80 iBT), IELTS, PTE (minimum score 53). Electronic applications accepted. Application fee is waived when completed online. *Expenses:* Contact institution.

University of New Haven, Graduate School, College of Business, Program in Public Administration, West Haven, CT 06516-1916. Offers city management (MPA); community-clinical services (MPA); health care management (MPA); long-term health care (MPA); personnel and labor relations (MPA); public administration (MPA, Certificate); public management (Certificate); MBA/MPA. Part-time and evening/weekend programs available. *Degree requirements:* For master's, thesis or alternative. *Entrance requirements:* Additional exam requirements/recommendations for international students: Required—TOEFL (minimum score 80 iBT), IELTS, PTE (minimum score 53). Electronic applications accepted. Application fee is waived when completed online. *Expenses:* Contact institution.

University of Rhode Island, Graduate School, Labor Research Center, Kingston, RI 02881. Offers labor relations and human resources (MS); MS/JD. Part-time and evening/weekend programs available. *Faculty:* 1 full-time (0 women), 2 part-time/adjunct (1 woman). *Students:* 8 full-time (7 women), 21 part-time (14 women); includes 5 minority (3 Black or African American, non-Hispanic/Latino; 1 Hispanic/Latino; 1 Two or more races, non-Hispanic/Latino), 1 international. In 2014, 5 master's awarded. *Entrance requirements:* For master's, GRE, MAT, GMAT, or LSAT, 2 letters of recommendation. Additional exam requirements/recommendations for international students: Required—TOEFL (minimum score 550 paper-based). *Application deadline:* For fall admission, 7/15 for domestic students, 2/1 for international students; for spring admission, 11/15 for domestic students, 7/15 for international students. Application fee: $65. Electronic applications accepted. *Expenses:* Tuition, state resident: full-time $11,532; part-time $641 per credit. Tuition, nonresident: full-time $23,606; part-time $1311 per credit. *Required fees:* $1442; $39 per credit. $35 per semester. One-time fee: $155. *Financial support:* In 2014–15, 2 teaching assistantships (averaging $15,844 per year) were awarded; institutionally sponsored loans also available. Financial award application deadline: 2/1; financial award applicants required to submit FAFSA. *Unit head:* Dr. Richard Scholl, Director, 401-874-4347, Fax: 401-874-2954, E-mail: rscholl@uri.edu. *Application contact:* Graduate Admission, 401-874-2872, E-mail: gradadm@etal.uri.edu.
Website: http://www.uri.edu/research/lrc/

University of Toronto, School of Graduate Studies, Faculty of Arts and Science, Centre for Industrial Relations and Human Resources, Toronto, ON M5S 2J7, Canada. Offers MIRHR, PhD. Part-time programs available. *Degree requirements:* For doctorate, thesis/dissertation. *Entrance requirements:* For master's, GRE or GMAT (for applicants who completed degree outside of Canada), minimum B+ in final 2 years of bachelor's degree completion, 2 letters of reference, resume; for doctorate, GRE or GMAT, MIR or equivalent, minimum B+ average, 3 letters of reference, resume. Additional exam requirements/recommendations for international students: Required—TOEFL (minimum score 600 paper-based; 100 iBT), IELTS, TWE (minimum score 5), Michigan English Language Assessment Battery, or COPE. Electronic applications accepted. *Expenses:* Contact institution.

University of Wisconsin–Milwaukee, Graduate School, College of Letters and Sciences, Interdepartmental Program in Human Resources and Labor Relations, Milwaukee, WI 53201-0413. Offers human resources and labor relations (MHRLR);

international human resources and labor relations (Certificate); mediation and negotiation (Certificate). Part-time programs available. *Entrance requirements:* For master's, GMAT or GRE General Test. Additional exam requirements/recommendations for international students: Required—TOEFL (minimum score 550 paper-based; 79 iBT), IELTS (minimum score 6.5). Electronic applications accepted.

Wayne State University, College of Liberal Arts and Sciences, Program in Employment and Labor Relations, Detroit, MI 48202. Offers MA. *Students:* 5 full-time (3 women), 32 part-time (19 women); includes 17 minority (13 Black or African American, non-Hispanic/Latino; 1 Asian, non-Hispanic/Latino; 2 Hispanic/Latino; 1 Two or more races, non-Hispanic/Latino), 1 international. Average age 37. 26 applicants, 65% accepted, 8 enrolled. In 2014, 10 master's awarded. *Entrance requirements:* For master's, GRE or GMAT, three letters of recommendation written by former college or university professors and/or current employers, baccalaureate degree from accredited institution. Additional exam requirements/recommendations for international students: Required—TOEFL (minimum score 550 paper-based; 79 iBT), IELTS (minimum score 6.5), Michigan English Language Assessment Battery (minimum score 85). *Application deadline:* For fall admission, 6/1 priority date for domestic students, 5/1 priority date for international students; for winter admission, 10/1 priority date for domestic students, 9/1 priority date for international students; for spring admission, 2/1 priority date for domestic students, 1/1 priority date for international students. Applications are processed on a rolling basis. Application fee: $0. Electronic applications accepted. *Expenses:* Tuition, state resident: full-time $10,294; part-time $571.90 per credit hour. Tuition, nonresident: full-time $29,730; part-time $1238.75 per credit hour. *Required fees:* $1365; $43.50 per credit hour. $291.10 per semester. Tuition and fees vary according to course load and program. *Financial support:* In 2014–15, 3 students received support. Scholarships/grants available. Financial award application deadline: 3/31; financial award applicants required to submit FAFSA. *Total annual research expenditures:* $105,820. *Unit head:* Dr. Marick Masters, Director, 313-577-5358, E-mail: marickm@wayne.edu. *Application contact:* Linda Johnson, Academic Services Officer, 313-577-0175, E-mail: ab1232@wayne.edu.
Website: http://clas.wayne.edu/labor/Master-of-Arts-in-Employment-and-Labor-Relations

Wayne State University, Law School, Detroit, MI 48202. Offers corporate and finance law (LL M); labor and employment law (LL M); law (JD); taxation (LL M); United States law (LL M); JD/MA; JD/MADR; JD/MBA; JD/MS. *Accreditation:* ABA. Part-time and evening/weekend programs available. *Faculty:* 37 full-time (16 women), 15 part-time/adjunct (2 women). *Students:* 377 full-time (160 women), 64 part-time (29 women); includes 60 minority (29 Black or African American, non-Hispanic/Latino; 4 American Indian or Alaska Native, non-Hispanic/Latino; 12 Asian, non-Hispanic/Latino; 8 Hispanic/Latino; 7 Two or more races, non-Hispanic/Latino), 17 international. Average age 27. 702 applicants, 48% accepted, 121 enrolled. In 2014, 3 master's, 174 doctorates awarded. *Degree requirements:* For master's, essay. *Entrance requirements:* For master's, JD from ABA-accredited institution and member institution of the AALS; for doctorate, LSAT, LDAS report, bachelor's degree from accredited institution, personal statement, transcripts from all U.S. undergraduate schools attended and an analysis and summary of the transcripts; letter of recommendation (up to two are accepted). Additional exam requirements/recommendations for international students: Required—TOEFL (minimum score 600 paper-based), Michigan English Language Assessment Battery (minimum score 85); Recommended—IELTS (minimum score 6.5). *Application deadline:* For fall admission, 5/15 for domestic and international students. Application fee: $0. Electronic applications accepted. *Expenses:* Expenses: Contact institution. *Financial support:* In 2014–15, 285 students received support. Scholarships/grants available. Support available to part-time students. Financial award application deadline: 3/31; financial award applicants required to submit FAFSA. *Faculty research:* Public interest law, tax law, international law, environmental law, health law. *Unit head:* Jocelyn Benson, Dean, 313-577-3933. *Application contact:* Joshua R. Davis, Director of Admissions, 313-577-3937, Fax: 313-577-8129, E-mail: lawinquire@wayne.edu. Website: http://law.wayne.edu/

West Virginia University, College of Business and Economics, Program in Industrial Relations, Morgantown, WV 26506. Offers MSIR. *Accreditation:* AACSB. *Entrance requirements:* For master's, GRE or GMAT, minimum GPA of 3.0. Additional exam requirements/recommendations for international students: Required—TOEFL. Electronic applications accepted. *Faculty research:* Labor relations, mediation, leadership, benefits.

Philanthropic Studies

Indiana University–Purdue University Indianapolis, Lilly Family School of Philanthropy, Indianapolis, IN 46202. Offers MA, XMA, PhD. *Faculty:* 52 full-time, 10 part-time/adjunct. *Students:* 63 full-time (41 women), 48 part-time (40 women); includes 24 minority (14 Black or African American, non-Hispanic/Latino; 7 Asian, non-Hispanic/Latino; 1 Hispanic/Latino; 2 Two or more races, non-Hispanic/Latino), 13 international. Average age 37. 72 applicants, 67% accepted, 29 enrolled. In 2014, 30 master's, 2 doctorates awarded. *Degree requirements:* For master's, thesis optional; for doctorate, thesis/dissertation. *Entrance requirements:* For master's, GRE General Test (minimum score 500 quantitative, 500 verbal, 4.5 analytical writing), minimum undergraduate GPA of 3.0; for doctorate, GRE General Test (minimum score: 500 quantitative, 500 verbal, 4.5 analytical writing), minimum GPA of 3.0, master's degree. *Application deadline:* For fall admission, 1/15 for domestic students, 1/1 for international students. Application fee: $55 ($65 for international students). *Financial support:* In 2014–15, fellowships with partial tuition reimbursements (averaging $13,000 per year), research assistantships with partial tuition reimbursements (averaging $9,500 per year), teaching assistantships with partial tuition reimbursements (averaging $12,000 per year) were awarded; career-related internships or fieldwork, Federal Work-Study, institutionally sponsored loans, and scholarships/grants also available. Financial award application deadline: 3/1; financial award applicants required to submit FAFSA. *Unit head:* Dr. Gregory Witkowski, Director of Graduate Studies, 317-278-8970, E-mail: gwitkows@iupui.edu. Website: http://www.philanthropy.iupui.edu

Saint Mary's University of Minnesota, Schools of Graduate and Professional Programs, Graduate School of Business and Technology, Philanthropy and Development Program, Winona, MN 55987-1399. Offers MA.

Public Administration

Adelphi University, University College, Graduate Certificate in Emergency Management Program, Garden City, NY 11530-0701. Offers Certificate. Part-time and evening/weekend programs available. *Students:* 7 full-time (2 women), 17 part-time (9 women); includes 7 minority (4 Black or African American, non-Hispanic/Latino; 1 Asian, non-Hispanic/Latino; 1 Native Hawaiian or other Pacific Islander, non-Hispanic/Latino; 1 Two or more races, non-Hispanic/Latino). Average age 36. In 2014, 2 Certificates awarded. *Application deadline:* For fall admission, 5/1 for international students; for spring admission, 12/1 for international students. Applications are processed on a rolling basis. Application fee: $50. Electronic applications accepted. *Faculty research:* Emergency nursing, disaster management, disaster preparedness. *Unit head:* Shawn O'Riley, Dean, 516-877-3412, E-mail: ucinfo@adelphi.edu. *Application contact:* Christine Murphy, Director of Admissions, 516-877-3050, Fax: 516-877-3039, E-mail: graduateadmissions@adelphi.edu.
Website: http://academics.adelphi.edu/universitycollege/emergency-management-certificate.php

Adler University, Programs in Psychology, Chicago, IL 60602. Offers advanced Adlerian psychotherapy (Certificate); art therapy (MA); clinical neuropsychology (Certificate); clinical psychology (Psy D); community psychology (MA); counseling and organizational psychology (MA); counseling psychology (MA); criminology (MA); emergency management leadership (MA); forensic psychology (MA); marriage and family counseling (MA); marriage and family therapy (Certificate); military psychology (MA); nonprofit management (MA); organizational psychology (MA); police psychology (MA); public policy and administration (MA); rehabilitation counseling (MA); sport and health psychology (MA); substance abuse counseling (Certificate); Psy D/Certificate; Psy D/MACAT; Psy D/MACP; Psy D/MAMFC; Psy D/MASAC. *Accreditation:* APA. Part-time and evening/weekend programs available. Postbaccalaureate distance learning degree programs offered (minimal on-campus study). Terminal master's awarded for partial completion of doctoral program. *Degree requirements:* For master's, thesis or alternative, oral exam, practicum; for doctorate, thesis/dissertation, clinical exam, internship, oral exam, practicum, written qualifying exam. *Entrance requirements:* For master's, 12 semester hours in psychology, minimum GPA of 3.0; for doctorate, 18 semester hours in psychology, minimum GPA of 3.25; for Certificate, appropriate master's or doctoral degree. Additional exam requirements/recommendations for international students: Required—TOEFL (minimum score 550 paper-based; 79 iBT). Electronic applications accepted.
See Display on page 969 and Close-Up on page 1207.

Albany State University, College of Arts and Humanities, Albany, GA 31705-2717. Offers English education (M Ed); public administration (MPA), including community and economic development administration, criminal justice administration, general administration, health administration and policy, human resources management, public policy, water resources management; social work (MSW). Part-time programs available. *Degree requirements:* For master's, comprehensive exam, professional portfolio (for MPA), internship, capstone report. *Entrance requirements:* For master's, GRE, MAT, minimum GPA of 3.0, official transcript, pre-medical record/certificate of immunization, letters of reference. Electronic applications accepted. *Faculty research:* HIV prevention for minority students.

Albany State University, College of Sciences and Health Professions, Albany, GA 31705-2717. Offers criminal justice (MS), including corrections, forensic science, law enforcement, public administration; mathematics education (M Ed); nursing (MSN), including RN to MSN family nurse practitioner, RN to MSN nurse educator; science education (M Ed). Part-time and evening/weekend programs available. Postbaccalaureate distance learning degree programs offered. *Degree requirements:* For master's, comprehensive exam, thesis. *Entrance requirements:* For master's, GRE or MAT, official transcript, letters of recommendations, pre-medical/certificate of immunizations. Electronic applications accepted.

American Public University System, AMU/APU Graduate Programs, Charles Town, WV 25414. Offers accounting (MBA, MS); criminal justice (MA), including business administration, emergency and disaster management, general (MA, MS); educational leadership (M Ed); emergency and disaster management (MA); entrepreneurship (MBA); environmental policy and management (MS), including environmental planning, environmental sustainability, fish and wildlife management, general (MA, MS), global environmental management; finance (MBA); general (MBA); global business management (MBA); history (MA), including American history, ancient and classical history, European history, global history, public history; homeland security (MA), including business administration, counter-terrorism studies, criminal justice, cyber, emergency management and public health, intelligence studies, transportation security; homeland security resource allocation (MBA); humanities (MA); information technology (MS), including digital forensics, enterprise software development, information assurance and security, IT project management; information technology management (MBA); intelligence studies (MA), including criminal intelligence, cyber, general (MA, MS), homeland security, intelligence analysis, intelligence collection, intelligence management, intelligence operations, terrorism studies; international relations and conflict resolution (MA), including comparative and security issues, conflict resolution, international and transnational security issues, peacekeeping; legal studies (MA); management (MA), including defense management, general (MA, MS), human resource management, organizational leadership, public administration; marketing (MBA); military

history (MA), including American military history, American Revolution, civil war, war since 1945, World War II; military studies (MA), including joint warfare, strategic leadership; national security studies (MA), including general (MA, MS), homeland security, regional security studies, security and intelligence analysis, terrorism studies; nonprofit management (MBA); political science (MA), including American politics and government, comparative government and development, general (MA, MS), international relations, public policy; psychology (MA); public administration (MPA), including disaster management, environmental policy, health policy, human resources, national security, organizational management, security management; public health (MPH); reverse logistics management (MA); school counseling (M Ed); security management (MA); space studies (MS), including aerospace science, general (MA, MS), planetary science; sports and health sciences (MS); teaching (M Ed), including curriculum and instruction for elementary teachers, elementary reading, English language learners, instructional leadership, online learning, special education; transportation and logistics management (MA), including general (MA, MS), maritime engineering management, reverse logistics management. Programs offered via distance learning only. Part-time and evening/weekend programs available. Postbaccalaureate distance learning degree programs offered (no on-campus study). *Faculty:* 426 full-time (236 women), 1,864 part-time/adjunct (880 women). *Students:* 475 full-time (215 women), 10,067 part-time (4,085 women); includes 3,462 minority (1,863 Black or African American, non-Hispanic/Latino; 74 American Indian or Alaska Native, non-Hispanic/Latino; 273 Asian, non-Hispanic/Latino; 831 Hispanic/Latino; 78 Native Hawaiian or other Pacific Islander, non-Hispanic/Latino; 343 Two or more races, non-Hispanic/Latino), 131 international. Average age 36. In 2014, 3,740 master's awarded. *Degree requirements:* For master's, comprehensive exam or practicum. *Entrance requirements:* For master's, official transcript showing earned bachelor's degree from institution accredited by recognized accrediting body. Additional exam requirements/recommendations for international students: Required—TOEFL (minimum score 550 paper-based), IELTS (minimum score 6.5). *Application deadline:* Applications are processed on a rolling basis. Application fee: $0. Electronic applications accepted. *Financial support:* Applicants required to submit FAFSA. *Faculty research:* Military history, criminal justice, management performance, national security. *Unit head:* Dr. Karan Powell, Executive Vice President and Provost, 877-468-6268, Fax: 304-724-3780. *Application contact:* Terry Grant, Vice President of Enrollment Management, 877-468-6268, Fax: 304-724-3780, E-mail: info@apus.edu.
Website: http://www.apus.edu

The American University in Cairo, School of Global Affairs and Public Policy, Department of Public Policy and Administration, Cairo, Egypt. Offers global affairs (MGA); public administration (MPA, Diploma); public policy (MPP, Diploma). Tuition and fees vary according to course load and program.

American University of Beirut, Graduate Programs, Faculty of Arts and Sciences, Beirut, Lebanon. Offers anthropology (MA); Arab and Middle Eastern history (PhD); Arabic language and literature (MA, PhD); archaeology (MA); biology (MS); cell and molecular biology (PhD); chemistry (MS); clinical psychology (MA); computational sciences (MS); computer science (MS); economics (MA); English language (MA); English literature (MA); environmental policy planning (MS); financial economics (MAFE); geology (MS); history (MA); mathematics (MA, MS); media studies (MA); Middle Eastern studies (MA); physics (MS); political studies (MA); psychology (MA); public administration (MA); sociology (MA); statistics (MA, MS); theoretical physics (PhD); transnational American studies (MA). Part-time programs available. *Faculty:* 107 full-time (32 women), 6 part-time/adjunct (2 women). *Students:* 230 full-time (161 women), 209 part-time (146 women). Average age 26. 261 applicants, 70% accepted, 83 enrolled. In 2014, 68 master's, 2 doctorates awarded. *Degree requirements:* For master's, one foreign language, comprehensive exam, thesis (for some programs); for doctorate, one foreign language, comprehensive exam, thesis/dissertation. *Entrance requirements:* For master's, GRE (for some MA/MS programs), letter of recommendation; for doctorate, GRE, letters of recommendation. Additional exam requirements/recommendations for international students: Required—TOEFL (minimum score 600 paper-based; 97 iBT), IELTS (minimum score 7). *Application deadline:* For fall admission, 4/1 for domestic and international students; for spring admission, 11/1 for domestic and international students. Application fee: $50. Electronic applications accepted. *Expenses: Tuition:* Full-time $15,462; part-time $859 per credit. *Required fees:* $692. Tuition and fees vary according to course load and program. *Financial support:* Research assistantships, career-related internships or fieldwork, institutionally sponsored loans, scholarships/grants, health care benefits, and unspecified assistantships available. Financial award application deadline: 2/4; financial award applicants required to submit FAFSA. *Faculty research:* Determinants of language proficiency among Arab learners of English as a foreign language; opinion mining, information retrieval, runtime verification, high performance computing; solar and fuel cells, self-organizing systems, heterocyclic chemistry, air and water chemistry; complex analysis, harmonic analysis, number theory; social and political psychology, clinical psychology; thin films physics and technology; theory of soft matter; religious and ethnic conflict; sports and politics. *Total annual research expenditures:* $966,000. *Unit head:* Dr. Patrick McGreevy, Dean, 961-1374374 Ext. 3800, Fax: 961-1744461, E-mail: pm07@aub.edu.lb. *Application contact:* Dr. Salim Kanaan, Director, Admissions Office, 961-1350000 Ext. 2590, Fax: 961-1750775, E-mail: sk00@aub.edu.lb.
Website: http://www.aub.edu.lb/fas/

Anna Maria College, Graduate Division, Program in Public Administration, Paxton, MA 01612. Offers MPA.

Appalachian State University, Cratis D. Williams Graduate School, Department of Government and Justice Studies, Boone, NC 28608. Offers criminal justice (MS); political science (MA), including American government, environmental politics and policy analysis, international relations; public administration (MPA), including public management, town, city and county management. Part-time programs available. Postbaccalaureate distance learning degree programs offered (no on-campus study). *Degree requirements:* For master's, variable foreign language requirement, comprehensive exam, thesis optional. *Entrance requirements:* For master's, GRE General Test, 3 letters of recommendation. Additional exam requirements/recommendations for international students: Required—TOEFL (minimum score 570 paper-based; 79 iBT), IELTS (minimum score 6.5). Electronic applications accepted. *Faculty research:* Campaign finance, emerging democracies, bureaucratic politics, judicial behavior, administration of justice.

Argosy University, Chicago, College of Business, Chicago, IL 60601. Offers accounting (DBA); customized professional concentration (MBA, DBA); finance (MBA); fraud examination (MBA); global business sustainability (DBA); healthcare administration (MBA); information systems (DBA); information systems management (MBA); international business (MBA, DBA); management (MBA, MSM, DBA); marketing (MBA, DBA); organizational leadership (Ed D); public administration (MBA); sustainable management (MBA). Postbaccalaureate distance learning degree programs offered (minimal on-campus study).

Argosy University, Dallas, College of Business, Farmers Branch, TX 75244. Offers accounting (DBA, AGC); corporate compliance (MBA, Graduate Certificate); customized professional concentration (MBA); finance (MBA, Graduate Certificate); fraud examination (MBA, Graduate Certificate); global business sustainability (DBA, AGC); healthcare administration (Graduate Certificate); healthcare management (MBA); information systems (MBA, DBA, AGC); information systems management (Graduate Certificate); international business (MBA, DBA, AGC, Graduate Certificate); management (MBA, DBA, AGC, Graduate Certificate); marketing (MBA, DBA, AGC, Graduate Certificate); public administration (MBA, Graduate Certificate); sustainable management (MBA, Graduate Certificate).

Argosy University, Denver, College of Business, Denver, CO 80231. Offers accounting (DBA); corporate compliance (MBA); customized professional concentration (MBA, DBA); finance (MBA); fraud examination (MBA); global business sustainability (DBA); healthcare administration (MBA); information systems (DBA); information systems management (MBA); international business (MBA, DBA); management (MBA, MSM, DBA); marketing (MBA, DBA); organizational leadership (Ed D); public administration (MBA); sustainable management (MBA).

Argosy University, Inland Empire, College of Business, Ontario, CA 91761. Offers accounting (DBA); corporate compliance (MBA); customized professional concentration (MBA, DBA); finance (MBA); fraud examination (MBA); global business sustainability (DBA); healthcare administration (MBA); information systems (DBA); information systems management (MBA); international business (MBA, DBA); management (MBA, MSM, DBA); marketing (MBA, DBA); organizational leadership (Ed D); public administration (MBA); sustainable management (MBA).

Argosy University, Los Angeles, College of Business, Santa Monica, CA 90045. Offers accounting (DBA); corporate compliance (MBA); customized professional concentration (MBA, DBA); finance (MBA); fraud examination (MBA); global business sustainability (DBA); healthcare administration (MBA); information systems (DBA); information systems management (MBA); international business (MBA, DBA); management (MBA, MSM, DBA); marketing (MBA, DBA); organizational leadership (Ed D); public administration (MBA); sustainable management (MBA).

Argosy University, Orange County, College of Business, Orange, CA 92868. Offers accounting (DBA, Adv C); corporate compliance (MBA); customized professional concentration (MBA, DBA); finance (MBA, Certificate); fraud examination (MBA); global business sustainability (DBA); healthcare administration (MBA, Certificate); information systems (DBA, Adv C, Certificate); information systems management (MBA); international business (MBA, DBA, Adv C, Certificate); management (MBA, MSM, DBA, Adv C); marketing (MBA, DBA, Adv C, Certificate); organizational leadership (Ed D); public administration (MBA, Certificate); sustainable management (MBA).

Argosy University, Phoenix, College of Business, Phoenix, AZ 85021. Offers accounting (DBA); corporate compliance (MBA); customized professional concentration (MBA, DBA); finance (MBA); fraud examination (MBA); global business sustainability (DBA); healthcare administration (MBA); information systems (DBA); information systems management (MBA); international business (MBA, DBA); management (MBA, DBA); marketing (MBA, DBA); public administration (MBA); sustainable management (MBA).

Argosy University, Salt Lake City, College of Business, Draper, UT 84020. Offers accounting (DBA); corporate compliance (MBA); customized professional concentration (MBA, DBA); finance (MBA); fraud examination (MBA); global business sustainability (DBA); healthcare administration (MBA); information systems (DBA); information systems management (MBA); international business (MBA, DBA); management (MBA, DBA); marketing (MBA, DBA); public administration (MBA); sustainable management (MBA).

Argosy University, San Diego, College of Business, San Diego, CA 92108. Offers accounting (DBA); corporate compliance (MBA); customized professional concentration (MBA, DBA); finance (MBA); fraud examination (MBA); global business sustainability (DBA); information systems (DBA); information systems management (MBA); international business (MBA, DBA); management (MBA, MSM, DBA); marketing (MBA, DBA); organizational leadership (Ed D); public administration (MBA).

Argosy University, San Francisco Bay Area, College of Business, Alameda, CA 94501. Offers accounting (DBA); corporate compliance (MBA); customized professional concentration (MBA, DBA); finance (MBA); fraud examination (MBA); global business sustainability (DBA); healthcare administration (MBA); information systems (DBA); information systems management (MBA); international business (MBA, DBA); management (MBA, MSM, DBA); marketing (MBA, DBA); organizational leadership (Ed D); public administration (MBA); sustainable management (MBA).

Argosy University, Sarasota, College of Business, Sarasota, FL 34235. Offers accounting (DBA, Adv C); corporate compliance (MBA, DBA, Certificate); customized professional concentration (MBA, DBA); finance (MBA, Certificate); fraud examination (MBA, Certificate); global business sustainability (DBA, Adv C); healthcare administration (MBA, Certificate); information systems (DBA, Adv C, Certificate); information systems management (MBA); international business (MBA, DBA, Adv C, Certificate); management (MBA, MSM, DBA, Adv C, Certificate); marketing (MBA, DBA, Adv C, Certificate); organizational leadership (Ed D); public administration (MBA, Certificate); sustainable management (MBA, Certificate).

Argosy University, Schaumburg, Graduate School of Business and Management, Schaumburg, IL 60173-5403. Offers accounting (DBA, Adv C); customized professional concentration (MBA, DBA); finance (MBA, Certificate); fraud examination (MBA); healthcare administration (MBA, Certificate); human resource management (MS); information systems (Adv C, Certificate); information systems management (MBA); international business (MBA, DBA, Adv C, Certificate); management (MBA, MSM, DBA, Adv C, Certificate); marketing (MBA, DBA, Adv C, Certificate); organizational leadership (MS, Ed D); public administration (MBA); sustainable management (MBA).

Argosy University, Seattle, College of Business, Seattle, WA 98121. Offers accounting (DBA); corporate compliance (MBA); customized professional concentration (MBA, DBA); finance (MBA); fraud examination (MBA); global business sustainability (DBA); healthcare administration (MBA); information systems (DBA); information systems management (MBA); international business (MBA, DBA); management (MBA, MSM, DBA); marketing (MBA, DBA); organizational leadership (Ed D); public administration (MBA); sustainable management (MBA).

Argosy University, Tampa, College of Business, Tampa, FL 33607. Offers accounting (DBA); corporate compliance (MBA); customized professional concentration (MBA, DBA); finance (MBA); fraud examination (MBA); global business sustainability (DBA); healthcare administration (MBA); information systems (DBA); information systems management (MBA); international business (MBA, DBA); management (MBA, MSM, DBA); marketing (MBA, DBA); organizational leadership (Ed D); public administration (MBA); sustainable management (MBA).

Argosy University, Twin Cities, College of Business, Eagan, MN 55121. Offers accounting (DBA); customized professional concentration (MBA, DBA); finance (MBA); fraud examination (MBA); global business sustainability (DBA); healthcare administration (MBA); information systems (DBA); information systems management (MBA); international business (MBA, DBA); management (MBA, MSM, DBA); marketing (MBA, DBA); organizational leadership (Ed D); public administration (MBA); sustainable management (MBA).

Public Administration

Argosy University, Washington DC, College of Business, Arlington, VA 22209. Offers accounting (DBA); customized professional concentration (MBA, DBA); finance (MBA); fraud examination (MBA); global business sustainability (DBA); healthcare administration (MBA); information systems (DBA); information systems management (MBA); international business (MBA, DBA, Certificate); management (MBA, MSM, DBA); marketing (MBA, DBA, Certificate); organizational leadership (Ed D); public administration (MBA); sustainable management (MBA).

Arizona State University at the Tempe campus, College of Public Programs, School of Public Affairs, Phoenix, AZ 85004-0687. Offers emergency management and homeland security (MA); program evaluation (MS); public administration (MPA, PhD), including nonprofit administration (MPA), urban management (MPA); public policy (MPP); MPA/MSW. *Accreditation:* NASPAA (one or more programs are accredited). Part-time and evening/weekend programs available. Terminal master's awarded for partial completion of doctoral program. *Degree requirements:* For master's, thesis or alternative, policy analysis or capstone project; interactive Program of Study (iPOS) submitted before completing 50 percent of required credit hours; for doctorate, comprehensive exam, thesis/dissertation, interactive Program of Study (iPOS) submitted before completing 50 percent of required credit hours. *Entrance requirements:* For master's, GRE, minimum GPA of 3.0 or equivalent in last 2 years of work leading to bachelor's degree; for doctorate, GRE, minimum GPA of 3.0 or equivalent in last 2 years of work leading to bachelor's degree, 3 letters of recommendation, resume, statement of goals, samples of research reports. Additional exam requirements/recommendations for international students: Required—TOEFL (minimum score 600 paper-based; 100 iBT), IELTS (minimum score 6.5). Electronic applications accepted. *Expenses:* Contact institution.

Arkansas State University, Graduate School, College of Humanities and Social Sciences, Department of Political Science, State University, AR 72467. Offers political science (MA); political science education (SCCT); public administration (MPA). *Accreditation:* NASPAA (one or more programs are accredited). Part-time programs available. *Faculty:* 7 full-time (2 women). *Students:* 25 full-time (8 women), 153 part-time (86 women); includes 69 minority (50 Black or African American, non-Hispanic/Latino; 3 American Indian or Alaska Native, non-Hispanic/Latino; 3 Asian, non-Hispanic/Latino; 9 Hispanic/Latino; 4 Two or more races, non-Hispanic/Latino), 15 international. Average age 34. 184 applicants, 57% accepted, 69 enrolled. In 2014, 41 master's awarded. *Degree requirements:* For master's, comprehensive exam, thesis or alternative; for SCCT, comprehensive exam. *Entrance requirements:* For master's, GRE General Test or MAT, GMAT, appropriate bachelor's degree, letters of recommendation, official transcripts, immunization records, statement of purpose; for SCCT, GRE General Test or MAT, GMAT, interview, master's degree, official transcript, letters of recommendation, immunization records. Additional exam requirements/recommendations for international students: Required—TOEFL (minimum score 550 paper-based; 79 iBT), IELTS (minimum score 6), PTE (minimum score 56). *Application deadline:* For fall admission, 7/1 for domestic and international students; for spring admission, 11/15 for domestic students, 11/14 for international students. Applications are processed on a rolling basis. Application fee: $30 ($40 for international students). Electronic applications accepted. *Expenses:* Tuition, state resident: full-time $4392; part-time $244 per credit hour. Tuition, nonresident: full-time $8784; part-time $488 per credit hour. *International tuition:* $9484 full-time. *Required fees:* $1134; $63 per credit hour. $25 per term. Tuition and fees vary according to course load and program. *Financial support:* In 2014–15, 17 students received support. Teaching assistantships, career-related internships or fieldwork, scholarships/grants, and unspecified assistantships available. Financial award application deadline: 7/1; financial award applicants required to submit FAFSA. *Unit head:* Dr. William McLean, Chair, 870-972-3048, Fax: 870-972-2720, E-mail: wmclean@astate.edu. *Application contact:* Vickey Ring, Graduate Admissions Coordinator, 870-972-3029, Fax: 870-972-3857, E-mail: vickeyring@astate.edu.
Website: http://www.astate.edu/college/humanities-and-social-sciences/departments/political-science/

Auburn University, Graduate School, College of Liberal Arts, Department of Political Science, Program in Public Administration, Auburn University, AL 36849. Offers MPA, PhD, Graduate Certificate, MPA/MCP. PhD offered jointly with Auburn University Montgomery. *Accreditation:* NASPAA (one or more programs are accredited). Part-time programs available. *Faculty:* 20 full-time (8 women), 7 part-time/adjunct (3 women). *Students:* 41 full-time (16 women), 49 part-time (22 women); includes 21 minority (all Black or African American, non-Hispanic/Latino), 9 international. Average age 35. 58 applicants, 48% accepted, 12 enrolled. In 2014, 21 master's, 4 doctorates awarded. *Degree requirements:* For master's, internship or research project; for doctorate, thesis/dissertation. *Entrance requirements:* For master's, GRE General Test, sample of written work; for doctorate, GRE General Test. *Application deadline:* For fall admission, 7/7 for domestic students; for spring admission, 11/24 for domestic students. Applications are processed on a rolling basis. Application fee: $50 ($60 for international students). Electronic applications accepted. *Expenses:* Tuition, state resident: full-time $8586; part-time $477 per credit hour. Tuition, nonresident: full-time $25,758; part-time $1431 per credit hour. *Required fees:* $804 per semester. Tuition and fees vary according to degree level and program. *Financial support:* Fellowships, research assistantships, teaching assistantships, career-related internships or fieldwork, and Federal Work-Study available. Support available to part-time students. Financial award application deadline: 3/15; financial award applicants required to submit FAFSA. *Faculty research:* Privatization studies, policy evolution, water resources, election administration. *Unit head:* Dr. Kathleen Hale, Head, 334-844-6155. *Application contact:* Dr. George Flowers, Dean of the Graduate School, 334-844-2125.
Website: http://www.cla.auburn.edu/polisci/

Auburn University at Montgomery, College of Public Policy and Justice, Department of Political Science and Public Administration, Montgomery, AL 36124-4023. Offers international relations (MIR); nonprofit management and leadership (Certificate); political science (MPS); public administration (MPA); public administration and public policy (PhD); public health care administration and policy (Certificate). PhD offered jointly with Auburn University. *Accreditation:* NASPAA (one or more programs are accredited). Part-time and evening/weekend programs available. *Faculty:* 5 full-time (1 woman), 1 part-time/adjunct (0 women). *Students:* 9 full-time (7 women), 40 part-time (26 women); includes 16 minority (13 Black or African American, non-Hispanic/Latino; 1 American Indian or Alaska Native, non-Hispanic/Latino; 1 Hispanic/Latino; 1 Two or more races, non-Hispanic/Latino), 2 international. Average age 29. 20 applicants, 90% accepted, 12 enrolled. In 2014, 13 master's awarded. *Degree requirements:* For master's, comprehensive exam; for doctorate, thesis/dissertation. *Entrance requirements:* For master's, GRE General Test or MAT; for doctorate, GRE General Test. *Application deadline:* Applications are processed on a rolling basis. Electronic applications accepted. *Expenses:* Tuition, state resident: full-time $6264; part-time $348 per credit hour. Tuition, nonresident: full-time $14,094; part-time $783 per credit hour. *Financial support:* In 2014–15, 1 teaching assistantship was awarded; research assistantships, career-related internships or fieldwork, and scholarships/grants also available. Support available to part-time students. Financial award application deadline: 3/1; financial award applicants required to submit FAFSA. *Unit head:* Dr. Andrew Cortell, Department Head, 334-244-3622, E-mail: acortell@aum.edu.
Website: http://www.cla.auburn.edu/polisci/graduate-programs/phd-in-public-administration-and-public-policy/

Azusa Pacific University, School of Business and Management, Azusa, CA 91702-7000. Offers business administration (MBA); diversity for strategic advantage (MA); entrepreneurship (MBA); finance (MBA); human and organizational development (MA); human resources and organizational development (MBA); human resources management (MA); international business (MBA); marketing (MBA); non-profit management (MA); organizational development and change (MA); performance improvement (MA); public administration (MA); strategic management (MBA). Part-time and evening/weekend programs available. *Degree requirements:* For master's, thesis (for some programs), final project. *Entrance requirements:* For master's, GMAT, minimum GPA of 3.0. Additional exam requirements/recommendations for international students: Required—TOEFL (minimum score 600 paper-based). *Expenses:* Contact institution. *Faculty research:* Gender issues, financial risk, leadership and ethics, marketing strategy.

Ball State University, Graduate School, College of Sciences and Humanities, Department of Political Science, Program in Public Administration, Muncie, IN 47306-1099. Offers criminal justice (MPA); public administration (MPA), including criminal justice. *Students:* 10 full-time (5 women), 2 part-time (1 woman); includes 1 minority (American Indian or Alaska Native, non-Hispanic/Latino), 3 international. Average age 25. 8 applicants, 63% accepted, 2 enrolled. In 2014, 5 master's awarded. *Entrance requirements:* For master's, GRE General Test. Application fee: $50. *Financial support:* In 2014–15, 3 students received support, including 5 research assistantships with partial tuition reimbursements available (averaging $10,117 per year), 1 teaching assistantship with partial tuition reimbursement available (averaging $8,675 per year); unspecified assistantships also available. Financial award application deadline: 3/1. *Faculty research:* Employment training programs, personnel and labor relations, planning. *Unit head:* Dr. Joseph Losco, Director, 765-285-8780, Fax: 765-285-5345, E-mail: jlosco@bsu.edu. *Application contact:* Dr. Gary Crawley, Associate Provost for Research and Dean of the Graduate School, 765-285-8785, E-mail: gcrawley@bsu.edu.
Website: http://www.bsu.edu/poli-sci/

Barry University, School of Adult and Continuing Education, Program in Public Administration, Miami Shores, FL 33161-6695. Offers MPA. Part-time and evening/weekend programs available. *Entrance requirements:* For master's, GMAT, GRE or MAT, recommendations. Electronic applications accepted.

Baruch College of the City University of New York, School of Public Affairs, Program in Public Administration, New York, NY 10010-5585. Offers general public administration (MPA); health care policy (MPA); nonprofit administration (MPA); policy analysis and evaluation (MPA); public management (MPA); MS/MPA. *Accreditation:* NASPAA. Part-time and evening/weekend programs available. *Degree requirements:* For master's, thesis, capstone. *Entrance requirements:* For master's, GRE General Test. Additional exam requirements/recommendations for international students: Required—TOEFL. Electronic applications accepted. *Expenses:* Contact institution. *Faculty research:* Urbanization, population and poverty in the developing world, housing and community development, labor unions and housing, government-nongovernment relations, immigration policy, social network analysis, cross-sectoral governance, comparative healthcare systems, program evaluation, social welfare policy, health outcomes, educational policy and leadership, transnationalism, infant health, welfare reform, racial/ethnic disparities in health, urban politics, homelessness, race and ethnic relations.

Baylor University, Graduate School, College of Arts and Sciences, Department of Political Science, Waco, TX 76798. Offers international studies (MA); political science (MA, PhD); public policy and administration (MPPA); JD/MPPA. Terminal master's awarded for partial completion of doctoral program. *Degree requirements:* For master's, variable foreign language requirement, comprehensive exam (for some programs), thesis (for some programs); for doctorate, variable foreign language requirement, comprehensive exam, thesis/dissertation. *Entrance requirements:* For master's and doctorate, GRE General Test. Additional exam requirements/recommendations for international students: Required—TOEFL. Electronic applications accepted.

Belhaven University, School of Business, Jackson, MS 39202-1789. Offers business administration (MBA); health administration (MBA); human resources (MBA, MSL); leadership (MBA); public administration (MPA); sports administration (MBA). MBA program also offered in Houston, TX, Memphis, TN and Orlando, FL. Part-time and evening/weekend programs available. Postbaccalaureate distance learning degree programs offered. *Faculty:* 18 full-time (6 women), 59 part-time/adjunct (23 women). *Students:* 111 full-time (91 women), 170 part-time (136 women); includes 227 minority (218 Black or African American, non-Hispanic/Latino; 2 American Indian or Alaska Native, non-Hispanic/Latino; 3 Hispanic/Latino; 2 Native Hawaiian or other Pacific Islander, non-Hispanic/Latino; 2 Two or more races, non-Hispanic/Latino). Average age 35. In 2014, 190 master's awarded. *Degree requirements:* For master's, comprehensive exam (for some programs), thesis (for some programs). *Entrance requirements:* For master's, GMAT, GRE General Test or MAT, minimum GPA of 2.8. *Application deadline:* Applications are processed on a rolling basis. Application fee: $25. Electronic applications accepted. *Expenses: Tuition:* Full-time $14,715; part-time $545 per credit. *Financial support:* Applicants required to submit FAFSA. *Unit head:* Dr. Ralph Mason, Dean, 601-968-8949, Fax: 601-968-8951, E-mail: cmason@belhaven.edu. *Application contact:* Dr. Audrey Kelleher, Vice President of Adult and Graduate Marketing and Development, 407-804-1424, Fax: 407-620-5210, E-mail: akelleher@belhaven.edu.
Website: http://www.belhaven.edu/campuses/index.htm

Bellevue University, Graduate School, College of Professional Studies, Bellevue, NE 68005-3098. Offers instructional design and development (MS); justice administration and criminal management (MS); leadership (MA); organizational performance (MS); public administration (MPA); security management (MS).

Binghamton University, State University of New York, Graduate School, College of Community and Public Affairs, Department of Public Administration, Vestal, NY 13850. Offers MPA. *Faculty:* 7 full-time (4 women), 2 part-time/adjunct (1 woman). *Students:* 39 full-time (27 women), 42 part-time (30 women); includes 10 minority (6 Black or African American, non-Hispanic/Latino; 1 Asian, non-Hispanic/Latino; 3 Hispanic/Latino), 10 international. Average age 32. 161 applicants, 60% accepted, 26 enrolled. In 2014, 28 master's awarded. *Degree requirements:* For master's, thesis. *Entrance requirements:* Additional exam requirements/recommendations for international students: Required—TOEFL (minimum score 90 iBT). Application fee: $75. *Expenses:* Tuition, state resident: full-time $7776; part-time $432 per credit. Tuition, nonresident: full-time $15,138; part-time $841 per credit. *Required fees:* $1754; $213 per credit. Tuition and fees vary according to degree level and program. *Financial support:* In 2014–15, 16 students received support. Career-related internships or fieldwork, Federal Work-Study, institutionally sponsored loans, scholarships/grants, health care benefits, and unspecified assistantships available. Financial award application deadline: 2/15; financial award applicants required to submit FAFSA. *Unit head:* Dr. David Campbell, Chairperson, 607-777-9181, E-mail: dcamp@binghamton.edu. *Application contact:* Kishan Zuber, Recruiting and Admissions Coordinator, 607-777-2151, Fax: 607-777-2501, E-mail: kzuber@binghamton.edu.

Boise State University, College of Social Sciences and Public Affairs, Department of Public Policy and Administration, Boise, ID 83725-0399. Offers environmental and natural resources policy and administration (MPA); general public administration (MPA); public policy and administration (Graduate Certificate); state and local government policy and administration (MPA). *Accreditation:* NASPAA. Part-time programs available. *Faculty:* 12 full-time, 16 part-time/adjunct. *Students:* 22 full-time (11 women), 72 part-time (45 women); includes 5 minority (1 Asian, non-Hispanic/Latino; 4 Hispanic/Latino). 52 applicants, 90% accepted, 22 enrolled. In 2014, 27 master's, 6 other advanced degrees awarded. *Degree requirements:* For master's, comprehensive exam, directed research project, internship. *Entrance requirements:* For master's, GRE General Test, minimum GPA of 3.0. Additional exam requirements/recommendations for international students: Required—TOEFL. *Application deadline:* For fall admission, 3/1 priority date for domestic students; for spring admission, 10/1 priority date for domestic students. Applications are processed on a rolling basis. Application fee: $55. Electronic applications accepted. *Expenses:* Tuition, state resident: part-time $331 per credit hour. Tuition, nonresident: part-time $531 per credit hour. *Financial support:* In 2014–15, 2 students received support. Federal Work-Study, institutionally sponsored loans, and unspecified assistantships available. Support available to part-time students. Financial award application deadline: 3/1. *Unit head:* Dr. Gregory Hill, Graduate Program Director, 208-426-2917, E-mail: greghill@boisestate.edu. *Application contact:* Linda Platt, Supervisor, Graduate Admission and Degree Services, 208-426-1074, Fax: 208-426-2789, E-mail: lplatt@boisestate.edu.
Website: http://sspa.boisestate.edu/publicpolicy/

Bowie State University, Graduate Programs, Program in Public Administration, Bowie, MD 20715-9465. Offers MPA. *Accreditation:* NASPAA. Part-time and evening/weekend programs available. *Students:* 50 full-time (35 women), 59 part-time (39 women); includes 101 minority (85 Black or African American, non-Hispanic/Latino; 2 Asian, non-Hispanic/Latino; 4 Hispanic/Latino; 10 Two or more races, non-Hispanic/Latino), 6 international. Average age 30. 43 applicants, 100% accepted, 28 enrolled. In 2014, 36 master's awarded. *Degree requirements:* For master's, comprehensive exam. *Entrance requirements:* For master's, minimum undergraduate GPA of 2.5. *Application deadline:* For fall admission, 4/1 priority date for domestic and international students; for spring admission, 11/1 priority date for domestic and international students. Applications are processed on a rolling basis. Electronic applications accepted. *Expenses:* Tuition, state resident: full-time $8928; part-time $372 per credit. Tuition, nonresident: full-time $16,176; part-time $674 per credit. *Required fees:* $2141. *Unit head:* James Caillier, Program Coordinator, 801-860-3637, E-mail: jcaillier@bowiestate.edu. *Application contact:* Angela Issac, Information Contact, 301-860-4000.

Bowling Green State University, Graduate College, College of Arts and Sciences, Department of Political Science, Program in Public Administration, Bowling Green, OH 43403. Offers MPA. *Degree requirements:* For master's, comprehensive exam or thesis, experiential paper for all non-thesis students. *Entrance requirements:* For master's, GRE General Test. Additional exam requirements/recommendations for international students: Required—TOEFL. Electronic applications accepted. *Faculty research:* Public sector labor relations, administrative law, sexual harassment and violence in the public workplace.

Brandman University, School of Business and Professional Studies, Irvine, CA 92618. Offers business administration (MBA); human resources (MS); organizational leadership (MA); public administration (MPA).

Bridgewater State University, College of Graduate Studies, School of Arts and Sciences, Department of Political Science, Program in Public Administration, Bridgewater, MA 02325-0001. Offers MPA. *Accreditation:* NASPAA. *Entrance requirements:* For master's, GRE General Test.

Brigham Young University, Graduate Studies, Marriott School of Management, Executive Master of Public Administration Program, Provo, UT 84602. Offers EMPA, JD/MPA. *Accreditation:* NASPAA (one or more programs are accredited). Part-time and evening/weekend programs available. *Students:* 133 part-time (47 women); includes 18 minority (2 Black or African American, non-Hispanic/Latino; 1 American Indian or Alaska Native, non-Hispanic/Latino; 2 Asian, non-Hispanic/Latino; 5 Hispanic/Latino; 8 Native Hawaiian or other Pacific Islander, non-Hispanic/Latino), 3 international. Average age 39. 68 applicants, 78% accepted, 49 enrolled. In 2014, 45 master's awarded. *Entrance requirements:* Additional exam requirements/recommendations for international students: Required—TOEFL (minimum score 580 paper-based; 85 iBT). *Application deadline:* For fall admission, 5/1 for domestic and international students. Application fee: $50. Electronic applications accepted. *Expenses:* Expenses: Contact institution. *Financial support:* Teaching assistantships available. Financial award application deadline: 6/15; financial award applicants required to submit FAFSA. *Unit head:* Dr. Jeffrey Thompson, Director, 801-422-4221, Fax: 801-422-0311, E-mail: mpa@byu.edu. *Application contact:* Catherine L. Cooper, Associate Director, 801-422-4221, Fax: 801-422-0311, E-mail: mpa@byu.edu.
Website: http://empa.byu.edu

Brigham Young University, Graduate Studies, Marriott School of Management, Master of Public Administration Program, Provo, UT 84602. Offers finance (MPA); human resources (MPA); local government (MPA); nonprofit management (MPA); JD/MPA. *Students:* 100 full-time (51 women); includes 15 minority (1 Black or African American, non-Hispanic/Latino; 4 Asian, non-Hispanic/Latino; 7 Hispanic/Latino; 3 Native Hawaiian or other Pacific Islander, non-Hispanic/Latino), 12 international. Average age 27. 86 applicants, 69% accepted, 46 enrolled. In 2014, 49 master's awarded. *Entrance requirements:* For master's, GRE or GMAT, minimum GPA of 3.0, MPA Excel prep course. Additional exam requirements/recommendations for international students: Required—TOEFL (minimum score 580 paper-based; 85 iBT). *Application deadline:* For fall admission, 2/1 for domestic and international students. Application fee: $50. Electronic applications accepted. *Expenses: Tuition:* Full-time $6310; part-time $371 per credit hour. Tuition and fees vary according to program and student's religious affiliation. *Financial support:* In 2014–15, 94 students received support. Career-related internships or fieldwork, institutionally sponsored loans, and scholarships/grants available. Financial award application deadline: 4/15; financial award applicants required to submit FAFSA. *Faculty research:* Taxes, budgeting, nonprofit, ethics, decision modeling, work balance, organizational behavior. *Unit head:* Dr. Jeffery Thompson, Director, 801-422-4221, Fax: 801-422-0311, E-mail: mpa@byu.edu. *Application contact:* Catherine Cooper, Associate Director, 801-422-4221, Fax: 801-422-0311, E-mail: mpa@byu.edu.
Website: http://mpa.byu.edu

California Baptist University, Program in Public Administration, Riverside, CA 92504-3206. Offers public administration (MPA); strategic innovation (MPA). Part-time and evening/weekend programs available. Postbaccalaureate distance learning degree programs offered (minimal on-campus study). *Faculty:* 5 full-time (3 women), 2 part-time/adjunct (0 women). *Students:* 71 full-time (33 women), 27 part-time (21 women); includes 61 minority (13 Black or African American, non-Hispanic/Latino; 7 Asian, non-Hispanic/Latino; 40 Hispanic/Latino; 1 Native Hawaiian or other Pacific Islander, non-Hispanic/Latino), 1 international. Average age 35. 90 applicants, 66% accepted, 36 enrolled. In 2014, 105 master's awarded. *Degree requirements:* For master's, comprehensive exam or thesis. *Entrance requirements:* For master's, minimum GPA of 2.75; bachelor's degree in applicable field or any field with five years of managerial

experience; three recommendations; resume; 500-word essay. Additional exam requirements/recommendations for international students: Required—TOEFL (minimum score 80 iBT). *Application deadline:* For fall admission, 8/1 priority date for domestic students, 7/1 for international students; for spring admission, 12/1 priority date for domestic students, 11/1 for international students. Applications are processed on a rolling basis. Application fee: $45. Electronic applications accepted. *Expenses:* Expenses: Contact institution. *Financial support:* Applicants required to submit CSS PROFILE or FAFSA. *Faculty research:* Policy networks, water policy, democratic theory, international relations, political theory and philosophy. *Unit head:* Dr. David Poole, Vice President, Online and Professional Studies, 951-343-3902, E-mail: dpoole@calbaptist.edu. *Application contact:* Dr. Elaine Ahumada, Director, MPA Program, 951-343-3929, Fax: 951-343-4661, E-mail: eahumada@calbaptist.edu.
Website: http://www.cbuonline.edu/programs/program/master-of-public-administration

California Lutheran University, Graduate Studies, Program in Public Policy and Administration, Thousand Oaks, CA 91360-2787. Offers MPPA. *Faculty:* 3 full-time (1 woman), 7 part-time/adjunct (3 women). *Students:* 51 full-time (28 women), 28 part-time (16 women); includes 22 minority (4 Black or African American, non-Hispanic/Latino; 4 Asian, non-Hispanic/Latino; 14 Hispanic/Latino), 29 international. Average age 32. 43 applicants, 58% accepted, 13 enrolled. In 2014, 69 master's awarded. *Degree requirements:* For master's, comprehensive exam, thesis or project, internship. *Entrance requirements:* For master's, GMAT or GRE General Test, interview, minimum GPA of 3.0. *Application deadline:* Applications are processed on a rolling basis. Application fee: $50. *Expenses:* Expenses: Contact institution. *Unit head:* Dr. Jamshid Damooei, Director, 805-493-3360. *Application contact:* 805-493-3325, Fax: 805-493-3861, E-mail: clugrad@callutheran.edu.

California State Polytechnic University, Pomona, Program in Public Administration, Pomona, CA 91768-2557. Offers MPA. *Accreditation:* NASPAA. Part-time programs available. *Students:* 6 full-time (2 women), 37 part-time (21 women); includes 25 minority (3 Black or African American, non-Hispanic/Latino; 6 Asian, non-Hispanic/Latino; 15 Hispanic/Latino; 1 Two or more races, non-Hispanic/Latino), 2 international. Average age 31. 40 applicants, 70% accepted, 15 enrolled. In 2014, 14 master's awarded. *Degree requirements:* For master's, thesis or alternative. *Entrance requirements:* For master's, GRE General Test. *Application deadline:* For fall admission, 5/1 priority date for domestic students; for winter admission, 10/15 priority date for domestic students; for spring admission, 1/20 priority date for domestic students. Applications are processed on a rolling basis. Application fee: $55. Electronic applications accepted. *Expenses:* Tuition, state resident: full-time $6738. Tuition, nonresident: full-time $12,300. *Required fees:* $1400. *Unit head:* Dr. Sandra M. Emerson, MPA Director/Interim Chair, 909-869-3879, Fax: 909-869-6995, E-mail: smemerson@cpp.edu.
Website: http://www.cpp.edu/~mpa/

California State University, Bakersfield, Division of Graduate Studies, School of Business and Public Administration, Program in Public Administration, Bakersfield, CA 93311. Offers MPA. *Accreditation:* NASPAA. *Degree requirements:* For master's, thesis or alternative. *Entrance requirements:* For master's, minimum GPA of 3.0, official transcripts, personal statement. Additional exam requirements/recommendations for international students: Required—TOEFL (minimum score 550 paper-based; 79 iBT), IELTS (minimum score 7). Electronic applications accepted.

California State University, Chico, Office of Graduate Studies, College of Behavioral and Social Sciences, Political Science Department, Program in Public Administration, Chico, CA 95929-0722. Offers health administration (MPA); local government management (MPA). *Accreditation:* NASPAA. Part-time programs available. *Students:* 29 full-time (20 women), 21 part-time (14 women); includes 2 minority (both Asian, non-Hispanic/Latino), 19 international. Average age 32. 24 applicants, 63% accepted, 9 enrolled. In 2014, 22 master's awarded. *Degree requirements:* For master's, thesis or culminating practicum. *Entrance requirements:* For master's, 2 letters of recommendation. Additional exam requirements/recommendations for international students: Required—TOEFL (minimum score 550 paper-based; 80 iBT), IELTS (minimum score 6.5). *Application deadline:* For fall admission, 3/1 priority date for domestic students, 3/1 for international students; for spring admission, 9/15 priority date for domestic students, 9/15 for international students. Applications are processed on a rolling basis. Application fee: $55. Electronic applications accepted. *Expenses:* Tuition, state resident: full-time $7002. Tuition, nonresident: full-time $18,162. *Required fees:* $1530. Tuition and fees vary according to program. *Financial support:* Fellowships and career-related internships or fieldwork available. *Unit head:* Dr. Ryan Patten, Chair, 530-898-6506, Fax: 530-898-5301, E-mail: rpatten@csuchico.edu. *Application contact:* Judy L. Rice, School of Graduate, International, and Interdisciplinary Studies, 530-898-6880, Fax: 530-898-6889, E-mail: jlrice@csuchico.edu.
Website: http://catalog.csuchico.edu/viewer/12/POLS/PADMNONEMP.html

California State University, Dominguez Hills, College of Business Administration and Public Policy, Program in Public Administration, Carson, CA 90747-0001. Offers MPA. *Accreditation:* NASPAA. Part-time and evening/weekend programs available. Postbaccalaureate distance learning degree programs offered (no on-campus study). *Faculty:* 6 full-time (4 women), 5 part-time/adjunct (2 women). *Students:* 46 full-time (28 women), 212 part-time (151 women); includes 114 minority (67 Black or African American, non-Hispanic/Latino; 2 American Indian or Alaska Native, non-Hispanic/Latino; 28 Asian, non-Hispanic/Latino; 8 Hispanic/Latino; 1 Native Hawaiian or other Pacific Islander, non-Hispanic/Latino; 8 Two or more races, non-Hispanic/Latino), 4 international. Average age 35. 198 applicants, 75% accepted, 109 enrolled. In 2014, 20 master's awarded. *Degree requirements:* For master's, thesis or alternative, capstone project. *Entrance requirements:* For master's, GRE, minimum GPA of 2.75. Additional exam requirements/recommendations for international students: Required—TOEFL (minimum score 550 paper-based; 79 iBT). *Application deadline:* For fall admission, 4/1 for domestic and international students; for spring admission, 11/1 for domestic students, 10/1 for international students. Application fee: $55. *Expenses:* Tuition, state resident: full-time $6738; part-time $3960 per year. Tuition, nonresident: full-time $13,434; part-time $8370 per year. *Required fees:* $623; $623 per year. *Faculty research:* Applied public management. *Unit head:* Betty Vu, Director of MBA and MPA Programs, 310-243-3165, E-mail: bvu@csudh.edu. *Application contact:* April Uhlig, MPA Online Program Coordinator, 310-243-3465, E-mail: auhlig@csudh.edu.
Website: http://www4.csudh.edu/mpa/student-services/index

California State University, East Bay, Office of Academic Programs and Graduate Studies, College of Letters, Arts, and Social Sciences, Department of Public Affairs and Administration, Program in Public Administration, Hayward, CA 94542-3000. Offers health care administration (MPA); public management and policy analysis (MPA). Part-time and evening/weekend programs available. *Degree requirements:* For master's, comprehensive exam (for some programs), comprehensive exam or thesis. *Entrance requirements:* For master's, minimum GPA of 2.5; statement of purpose; 2 letters of recommendation; professional resume/curriculum vitae. Additional exam requirements/recommendations for international students: Required—TOEFL (minimum score 550 paper-based; 79 iBT). *Application deadline:* For fall admission, 6/18 for domestic and international students. Application fee: $55. Electronic applications accepted. *Expenses:* Tuition, state resident: full-time $7830; part-time $1302 per credit hour. Tuition,

nonresident: full-time $16,368. *Required fees:* $327 per quarter. Tuition and fees vary according to course load and program. *Financial support:* Fellowships, teaching assistantships, career-related internships or fieldwork, Federal Work-Study, institutionally sponsored loans, and scholarships/grants available. Support available to part-time students. Financial award application deadline: 3/2; financial award applicants required to submit FAFSA. *Unit head:* Dr. Toni Fogarty, Chair, 510-885-2268, E-mail: toni.fogarty@csueastbay.edu. *Application contact:* Prof. Michael Moon, Public Administration Graduate Advisor, 510-885-2545, Fax: 510-885-3726, E-mail: michael.moon@csueastbay.edu.

California State University, Fresno, Division of Graduate Studies, College of Social Sciences, Department of Political Science, Program in Public Administration, Fresno, CA 93740-8027. Offers MPA. *Accreditation:* NASPAA. Part-time and evening/weekend programs available. *Degree requirements:* For master's, thesis or alternative. *Entrance requirements:* For master's, GRE General Test or GMAT, minimum GPA of 3.0. Additional exam requirements/recommendations for international students: Required—TOEFL. Electronic applications accepted.

California State University, Fullerton, Graduate Studies, College of Humanities and Social Sciences, Division of Politics, Administration, and Justice, Fullerton, CA 92834-9480. Offers political science (MA); public administration (MPA). *Accreditation:* NASPAA (one or more programs are accredited). Part-time programs available. *Students:* 20 full-time (8 women), 85 part-time (40 women); includes 62 minority (3 Black or African American, non-Hispanic/Latino; 18 Asian, non-Hispanic/Latino; 38 Hispanic/Latino; 1 Native Hawaiian or other Pacific Islander, non-Hispanic/Latino; 2 Two or more races, non-Hispanic/Latino), 6 international. Average age 30. 97 applicants, 59% accepted, 32 enrolled. In 2014, 34 master's awarded. *Degree requirements:* For master's, comprehensive exam, project or thesis. *Entrance requirements:* For master's, minimum GPA of 2.5 in last 60 units of course work, 12 units of course work in social sciences. Application fee: $55. *Financial support:* Career-related internships or fieldwork, Federal Work-Study, institutionally sponsored loans, and scholarships/grants available. Support available to part-time students. Financial award application deadline: 3/1; financial award applicants required to submit FAFSA. *Faculty research:* Emergency management plans. *Unit head:* Dr. Stephen Stambough, Chair, 657-278-2933. *Application contact:* Admissions/Applications, 657-278-2371.

California State University, Long Beach, Graduate Studies, College of Health and Human Services, Graduate Center for Public Policy and Administration, Long Beach, CA 90840. Offers MPA. *Accreditation:* NASPAA. Part-time and evening/weekend programs available. *Degree requirements:* For master's, comprehensive exam. *Entrance requirements:* For master's, minimum GPA of 2.75. Electronic applications accepted. *Faculty research:* Transportation access, air quality controls, coastal issues, intergovernmental relations.

California State University, Los Angeles, Graduate Studies, College of Natural and Social Sciences, Department of Political Science, Los Angeles, CA 90032-8530. Offers political science (MA); public administration (MS). Part-time and evening/weekend programs available. *Degree requirements:* For master's, comprehensive exam or thesis. *Entrance requirements:* Additional exam requirements/recommendations for international students: Required—TOEFL (minimum score 500 paper-based). Electronic applications accepted. *Expenses:* Tuition, state resident: full-time $6738; part-time $3609 per year. Tuition, nonresident: full-time $15,666; part-time $8073 per year. Tuition and fees vary according to course load, degree level and program. *Faculty research:* Government; public policy and law; international, political, and economic relations; comparative politics.

California State University, Northridge, Graduate Studies, The Tseng College of Extended Learning, Northridge, CA 91330. Offers business administration (Graduate Certificate); health administration (MPA); health education (MPH); knowledge management (MKM); music industry administration (MA); nonprofit-sector management (Graduate Certificate); public administration (MPA); public sector management and leadership (MPA); social work (MSW); taxation (MS); tourism, hospitality and recreation management (MS). *Students:* 5 part-time (2 women); includes 2 minority (1 Black or African American, non-Hispanic/Latino; 1 American Indian or Alaska Native, non-Hispanic/Latino). Average age 50. *Entrance requirements:* For master's, GRE (if cumulative undergraduate GPA less than 3.0). *Expenses: Required fees:* $12,402. *Unit head:* Joyce Feucht-Haviar, Dean, 866-873-6439.

California State University, Sacramento, Office of Graduate Studies, College of Social Sciences and Interdisciplinary Studies, Program in Public Policy and Administration, Sacramento, CA 95819. Offers MPPA. Part-time programs available. *Degree requirements:* For master's, thesis or alternative, writing proficiency exam. *Entrance requirements:* Additional exam requirements/recommendations for international students: Required—TOEFL. Electronic applications accepted. *Faculty research:* Education policy, urban policy, collaborative governance, judicial administration, and California state/local governance.

California State University, San Bernardino, Graduate Studies, College of Business and Public Administration, Program in Public Administration, San Bernardino, CA 92407-2397. Offers MPA. *Accreditation:* NASPAA. Part-time and evening/weekend programs available. *Students:* 29 full-time (12 women), 189 part-time (132 women); includes 128 minority (34 Black or African American, non-Hispanic/Latino; 1 American Indian or Alaska Native, non-Hispanic/Latino; 10 Asian, non-Hispanic/Latino; 77 Hispanic/Latino; 6 Two or more races, non-Hispanic/Latino), 19 international. Average age 30. 135 applicants, 63% accepted, 55 enrolled. In 2014, 62 master's awarded. *Degree requirements:* For master's, comprehensive exam. *Entrance requirements:* Additional exam requirements/recommendations for international students: Required—TOEFL. *Application deadline:* For fall admission, 7/17 for domestic students. Application fee: $55. *Expenses:* Tuition, state resident: full-time $6738; part-time $1302 per term. Tuition, nonresident: full-time $17,898; part-time $248 per unit. *Required fees:* $365 per quarter. Tuition and fees vary according to degree level and program. *Financial support:* Institutionally sponsored loans available. Financial award application deadline: 3/1. *Unit head:* Dr. Jonathan Anderson, Chair, 909-537-5759, E-mail: jfanders@csusb.edu. *Application contact:* Dr. Jeffrey Thompson, Dean of Graduate Studies, 909-537-5058, E-mail: jthompso@csusb.edu.

California State University, Stanislaus, College of Humanities and Social Sciences, Program in Public Administration (MPA), Turlock, CA 95382. Offers MPA. *Accreditation:* NASPAA. Part-time and evening/weekend programs available. *Degree requirements:* For master's, comprehensive exam, thesis or alternative. *Entrance requirements:* For master's, minimum GPA of 2.7, 3 letters of reference, personal statement. Additional exam requirements/recommendations for international students: Required—TOEFL (minimum score 550 paper-based), ELPT (minimum score 954). Electronic applications accepted. *Faculty research:* Blogging in the Middle East, incumbency and electoral competitiveness, legislative acceptance of gubernatorial budget proposals.

Capella University, School of Public Service Leadership, Doctoral Programs in Healthcare, Minneapolis, MN 55402. Offers criminal justice (PhD); emergency management (PhD); epidemiology (Dr PH); general health administration (DHA); general public administration (DPA); health advocacy and leadership (Dr PH); health care administration (PhD); health care leadership (DHA); health policy advocacy (DHA); multidisciplinary human services (PhD); nonprofit management and leadership (PhD); public safety leadership (PhD); social and community services (PhD).

Capella University, School of Public Service Leadership, Master's Programs in Healthcare, Minneapolis, MN 55402. Offers criminal justice (MS); emergency management (MS); general public health (MPH); gerontology (MS); health administration (MHA); health care operations (MHA); health management policy (MPH); health policy (MHA); homeland security (MS); multidisciplinary human services (MS); public administration (MPA); public safety leadership (MS); social and community services (MS); social behavioral sciences (MPH); MS/MPA.

Carleton University, Faculty of Graduate Studies, Faculty of Public Affairs and Management, School of Public Policy and Administration, Ottawa, ON K1S 5B6, Canada. Offers public administration (MA, DPA); public policy (PhD). Part-time programs available. *Degree requirements:* For master's, thesis optional; for doctorate, one foreign language, comprehensive exam, thesis/dissertation. *Entrance requirements:* For master's, GRE, honors degree; for doctorate, master's degree. Additional exam requirements/recommendations for international students: Required—TOEFL. *Faculty research:* Canadian public administration and policy, development administration, public policy analysis, public management.

Carnegie Mellon University, H. John Heinz III College, School of Public Policy and Management, Master of Public Management Program, Pittsburgh, PA 15213-3891. Offers MPM. Part-time and evening/weekend programs available. *Degree requirements:* For master's, internship. *Entrance requirements:* For master's, undergraduate degree; five years of full-time, relevant work experience.

Central Michigan University, Central Michigan University Global Campus, Program in Administration, Mount Pleasant, MI 48859. Offers acquisitions administration (MSA, Certificate); engineering management administration (MSA, Certificate); general administration (MSA, Certificate); health services administration (MSA, Certificate); human resources administration (MSA, Certificate); information resource management (MSA); information resource management administration (Certificate); international administration (MSA, Certificate); leadership (MSA, Certificate); philanthropy and fundraising administration (MSA, Certificate); public administration (MSA, Certificate); recreation and park administration (MSA); research administration (MSA, Certificate). Part-time and evening/weekend programs available. Postbaccalaureate distance learning degree programs offered (no on-campus study). *Students:* Average age 38. *Entrance requirements:* For master's, minimum GPA of 2.7 in major. *Application deadline:* Applications are processed on a rolling basis. Application fee: $50. Electronic applications accepted. *Financial support:* Scholarships/grants available. Support available to part-time students. Financial award applicants required to submit FAFSA. *Unit head:* Dr. Patricia Chase, Director, 989-774-6525, E-mail: chase1pb@cmich.edu. *Application contact:* 877-268-4636, E-mail: cmuglobal@cmich.edu.

Central Michigan University, Central Michigan University Global Campus, Program in Public Administration, Mount Pleasant, MI 48859. Offers general (MPA); public management (MPA); state and local government (MPA). *Accreditation:* NASPAA. Part-time and evening/weekend programs available. *Entrance requirements:* For master's, minimum GPA of 2.8. Additional exam requirements/recommendations for international students: Required—TOEFL. Electronic applications accepted. *Financial support:* Scholarships/grants available. Support available to part-time students. *Unit head:* Dr. Lawrence Sych, Program Director, 989-774-3316, E-mail: sych1l@cmich.edu. *Application contact:* 877-268-4636, E-mail: cmuglobal@cmich.edu.

Central Michigan University, College of Graduate Studies, College of Humanities and Social and Behavioral Sciences, Department of Political Science, Program in Public Administration, Mount Pleasant, MI 48859. Offers professional development in public administration (Graduate Certificate); public administration (MPA); public management (MPA); state and local government (MPA). Part-time programs available. *Degree requirements:* For master's, thesis or alternative. Electronic applications accepted.

Central Michigan University, College of Graduate Studies, Interdisciplinary Administration Programs, Mount Pleasant, MI 48859. Offers acquisitions administration (MSA, Graduate Certificate); general administration (MSA, Graduate Certificate); health services administration (MSA, Graduate Certificate); human resource administration (Graduate Certificate); human resources administration (MSA); information resource management (MSA, Graduate Certificate); international administration (MSA, Graduate Certificate); leadership (MSA, Graduate Certificate); public administration (MSA, Graduate Certificate); research administration (Graduate Certificate); sport administration (MSA). *Accreditation:* AACSB. Part-time and evening/weekend programs available. Postbaccalaureate distance learning degree programs offered (no on-campus study). *Degree requirements:* For master's, thesis or alternative. *Entrance requirements:* For master's, bachelor's degree with minimum GPA of 2.7. Electronic applications accepted. *Faculty research:* Interdisciplinary studies in acquisitions administration, health services administration, sport administration, recreation and park administration, and international administration.

Cheyney University of Pennsylvania, Graduate Programs, Program in Public Administration, Cheyney, PA 19319. Offers MPA.

City College of the City University of New York, Graduate School, College of Liberal Arts and Science, Division of Social Science, New York, NY 10031-9198. Offers economics (MA); international relations (MA); psychology (MA, PhD), including clinical psychology (PhD), experimental cognition (PhD), general psychology (MA), mental health counseling (MA); public service management (MPA); sociology (MA). Part-time programs available. *Entrance requirements:* For master's, GRE. Additional exam requirements/recommendations for international students: Required—TOEFL (minimum score 500 paper-based; 61 iBT). Electronic applications accepted.

Clark Atlanta University, School of Arts and Sciences, Department of Public Administration, Atlanta, GA 30314. Offers MPA. *Accreditation:* NASPAA. Part-time programs available. *Faculty:* 4 full-time (2 women). *Students:* 28 full-time (13 women), 18 part-time (13 women); includes 33 minority (all Black or African American, non-Hispanic/Latino), 8 international. Average age 28. 25 applicants, 84% accepted, 13 enrolled. In 2014, 9 master's awarded. *Degree requirements:* For master's, one foreign language, thesis or alternative. *Entrance requirements:* For master's, GRE General Test, minimum GPA of 2.5. Additional exam requirements/recommendations for international students: Required—TOEFL (minimum score 500 paper-based; 61 iBT). *Application deadline:* For fall admission, 4/1 for domestic and international students; for spring admission, 11/1 for domestic and international students. Applications are processed on a rolling basis. Application fee: $40 ($55 for international students). *Expenses: Tuition:* Full-time $14,904; part-time $828 per credit hour. *Required fees:* $746; $373 per semester. *Financial support:* Scholarships/grants and unspecified assistantships available. Financial award application deadline: 4/30; financial award applicants required to submit FAFSA. *Faculty research:* Nutrition education, Africa. *Unit head:* Dr. Henry Elonge, Chairperson, 404-880-6653, E-mail: helonge@cau.edu. *Application contact:* Michelle Clark-Davis, Graduate Program Admissions, 404-880-6605, E-mail: cauadmissions@cau.edu.

Clark University, Graduate School, College of Professional and Continuing Education, Program in Public Administration, Worcester, MA 01610-1477. Offers MPA, Certificate.

Part-time and evening/weekend programs available. *Students:* 29 full-time (18 women), 21 part-time (14 women); includes 5 minority (4 Black or African American, non-Hispanic/Latino; 1 Hispanic/Latino), 16 international. Average age 28. 96 applicants, 77% accepted, 28 enrolled. In 2014, 56 master's awarded. *Degree requirements:* For master's, thesis optional. *Entrance requirements:* Additional exam requirements/recommendations for international students: Required—TOEFL. *Application deadline:* Applications are processed on a rolling basis. Application fee: $75. Electronic applications accepted. *Expenses: Tuition:* Full-time $40,380; part-time $1262 per credit hour. *Required fees:* $30. *Financial support:* Career-related internships or fieldwork available. Support available to part-time students. *Unit head:* Dr. William Fisher, Dean, 508-793-7676. *Application contact:* Ethan Bernstein, Director of Graduate Admissions, 508-793-7373, E-mail: gradadmissions@clarku.edu.
Website: http://copace.clarku.edu/graduate-programs/masters-public-administration/index.cfm

Clemson University, Graduate School, Program in Public Administration, Clemson, SC 29634. Offers MPA. Part-time and evening/weekend programs available. Postbaccalaureate distance learning degree programs offered. *Students:* 7 full-time (all women), 34 part-time (14 women); includes 11 minority (10 Black or African American, non-Hispanic/Latino; 1 Hispanic/Latino). Average age 33. 15 applicants, 53% accepted, 8 enrolled. In 2014, 13 master's awarded. *Degree requirements:* For master's, comprehensive exam (for some programs), thesis or alternative, capstone project or comprehensive exams. *Entrance requirements:* For master's, GRE, 2 letters of recommendation. Additional exam requirements/recommendations for international students: Required—TOEFL. *Application deadline:* For fall admission, 6/1 for domestic students; for spring admission, 11/1 for domestic students; for summer admission, 3/15 for domestic students. Applications are processed on a rolling basis. Application fee: $70 ($80 for international students). Electronic applications accepted. *Expenses:* Expenses: Contact institution. *Financial support:* Institutionally sponsored loans available. Financial award applicants required to submit FAFSA. *Faculty research:* International partnerships to strengthen democracy and economic development, evaluation of public projects, strategic planning in public administration. *Unit head:* Dr. Lori Ann Dickes, Coordinator, 864-656-7831, E-mail: lorid@clemson.edu. *Application contact:* Carolyn Benson, Information Contact, 864-656-4463, E-mail: cbenson@clemson.edu.
Website: http://www.grad.clemson.edu/mpa/

Cleveland State University, College of Graduate Studies, Maxine Goodman Levin College of Urban Affairs, Program in Public Administration, Cleveland, OH 44115. Offers city management (MPA); economic development (MPA); healthcare administration (MPA); local and urban management (Certificate); non-profit management (MPA, Certificate); public financial management (MPA); public management (MPA); urban economic development (Certificate); JD/MPA. *Accreditation:* NASPAA. Part-time and evening/weekend programs available. *Faculty:* 23 full-time (11 women), 23 part-time/adjunct (6 women). *Students:* 16 full-time (11 women), 64 part-time (40 women); includes 23 minority (19 Black or African American, non-Hispanic/Latino; 3 Hispanic/Latino; 1 Two or more races, non-Hispanic/Latino), 3 international. Average age 36. 67 applicants, 51% accepted, 13 enrolled. In 2014, 41 master's awarded. *Degree requirements:* For master's, thesis or alternative, capstone course. *Entrance requirements:* For master's, GRE General Test (minimum scores in 40th percentile verbal and quantitative, 4.0 writing), minimum GPA of 3.0. Additional exam requirements/recommendations for international students: Required—TOEFL (minimum score 525 paper-based; 65 iBT), IELTS, or ITEP. *Application deadline:* For fall admission, 7/15 priority date for domestic students; 5/15 for international students; for spring admission, 11/1 for international students. Applications are processed on a rolling basis. Application fee: $30. Electronic applications accepted. *Expenses:* Expenses: $9,615 full-time, in-state tuition and fees. *Financial support:* In 2014–15, 16 students received support, including 4 research assistantships with full and partial tuition reimbursements available (averaging $7,200 per year), 3 teaching assistantships with full and partial tuition reimbursements available (averaging $2,400 per year); career-related internships or fieldwork, scholarships/grants, traineeships, and unspecified assistantships also available. Support available to part-time students. Financial award application deadline: 3/1; financial award applicants required to submit FAFSA. *Faculty research:* City management, nonprofit management, health care administration, public management, economic development. *Unit head:* Dr. Nicholas Zingale, Director, 216-802-3398, Fax: 216-687-9342, E-mail: n.zingale@csuohio.edu. *Application contact:* David Arrighi, Graduate Academic Advisor, 216-523-7522, Fax: 216-687-5398, E-mail: urbanprograms@csuohio.edu.
Website: http://urban.csuohio.edu/academics/graduate/mpa/

Cleveland State University, College of Graduate Studies, Maxine Goodman Levin College of Urban Affairs, Program in Urban Studies and Public Affairs, Cleveland, OH 44115. Offers communication (PhD); public administration (PhD); urban policy and development (PhD). Part-time and evening/weekend programs available. *Faculty:* 23 full-time (11 women), 23 part-time/adjunct (6 women). *Students:* 10 full-time (6 women), 26 part-time (13 women); includes 5 minority (4 Black or African American, non-Hispanic/Latino; 1 Asian, non-Hispanic/Latino), 10 international. Average age 40. 32 applicants, 34% accepted, 2 enrolled. In 2014, 3 doctorates awarded. *Degree requirements:* For doctorate, comprehensive exam, thesis/dissertation. *Entrance requirements:* For doctorate, GRE General Test (minimum score: verbal and quantitative 50th percentile, analytical writing 4.0), minimum GPA of 3.5. Additional exam requirements/recommendations for international students: Required—TOEFL (minimum score 525 paper-based; 65 iBT), IELTS, or ITEP. *Application deadline:* For fall admission, 1/31 for domestic and international students. Application fee: $30. Electronic applications accepted. *Expenses:* Expenses: $9,615 full-time, in-state tuition and fees. *Financial support:* In 2014–15, 15 students received support, including 7 research assistantships with full and partial tuition reimbursements available (averaging $9,200 per year), 3 teaching assistantships with full and partial tuition reimbursements available (averaging $8,600 per year); scholarships/grants and unspecified assistantships also available. Support available to part-time students. Financial award application deadline: 3/1; financial award applicants required to submit FAFSA. *Faculty research:* Urban and public policy, public affairs. *Unit head:* Dr. Wendy Kellogg, Director, 216-687-5265, E-mail: w.kellogg@csuohio.edu. *Application contact:* David Arrighi, Graduate Academic Advisor, 216-523-7522, Fax: 216-687-5398, E-mail: urbanprograms@csuohio.edu.
Website: http://urban.csuohio.edu/academics/graduate/phd/

The College at Brockport, State University of New York, School of Education and Human Services, Department of Public Administration, Brockport, NY 14420-2997. Offers arts administration (AGC); nonprofit management (AGC); public administration (MPA), including health care management, nonprofit management, public management. *Accreditation:* NASPAA. Part-time and evening/weekend programs available. *Faculty:* 4 full-time (3 women), 4 part-time/adjunct (2 women). *Students:* 42 full-time (24 women), 56 part-time (39 women); includes 22 minority (12 Black or African American, non-Hispanic/Latino; 2 Asian, non-Hispanic/Latino; 3 Hispanic/Latino; 5 Two or more races, non-Hispanic/Latino). 89 applicants, 79% accepted, 50 enrolled. In 2014, 34 master's, 7 other advanced degrees awarded. *Degree requirements:* For master's, thesis or alternative. *Entrance requirements:* For master's, GRE or minimum GPA of 3.0, letters of recommendation, statement of objectives, current resume. Additional exam

requirements/recommendations for international students: Required—TOEFL (minimum score 550 paper-based; 79 iBT), IELTS (minimum score 6.5). *Application deadline:* For fall admission, 8/15 priority date for domestic and international students; for spring admission, 1/15 priority date for domestic and international students; for summer admission, 4/15 priority date for domestic and international students. Application fee: $50. Electronic applications accepted. *Financial support:* In 2014–15, 1 fellowship with full tuition reimbursement (averaging $7,500 per year), 1 teaching assistantship with full tuition reimbursement (averaging $6,000 per year) were awarded; Federal Work-Study, scholarships/grants, and unspecified assistantships also available. Support available to part-time students. Financial award application deadline: 3/15; financial award applicants required to submit FAFSA. *Faculty research:* E-government, performance management, nonprofits and policy implementation, Medicaid and disabilities. *Unit head:* Dr. Celia Watt, Graduate Director, 585-395-5538, Fax: 585-395-2172, E-mail: cwatt@brockport.edu. *Application contact:* Danielle A. Welch, Graduate Admissions Counselor, 585-395-2525, Fax: 585-395-2515.
Website: http://www.brockport.edu/pubadmin

College of Charleston, Graduate School, School of Humanities and Social Sciences, Program in Public Administration, Charleston, SC 29424-0001. Offers MPA. Program offered jointly with University of South Carolina. *Accreditation:* NASPAA. Part-time and evening/weekend programs available. *Degree requirements:* For master's, thesis optional, internship, capstone seminar. *Entrance requirements:* For master's, GRE General Test, previous course work in statistics, 3 letters of recommendation, minimum GPA of 3.0. Additional exam requirements/recommendations for international students: Required—TOEFL (minimum score 81 iBT). Electronic applications accepted. *Faculty research:* Local government, environmental policy, budgeting, ethics.

The College of New Rochelle, Graduate School, Division of Human Services, Program in Public Administration, New Rochelle, NY 10805-2308. Offers long term care administration (MPA); public administration (MPA). *Degree requirements:* For master's, comprehensive exam, internship. *Entrance requirements:* For master's, minimum GPA of 3.0, personal statement, two letters of recommendation, official transcripts of all colleges/universities attended, proof of immunizations. *Expenses: Tuition:* Part-time $894 per credit. *Required fees:* $325 per semester.

College of Saint Elizabeth, Program in Justice Studies, Morristown, NJ 07960-6989. Offers justice administration and public service (MA). Part-time programs available. *Degree requirements:* For master's, thesis or alternative. *Entrance requirements:* For master's, minimum GPA of 3.0, writing sample, interview. Additional exam requirements/recommendations for international students: Required—TOEFL. Electronic applications accepted.

Columbia University, School of International and Public Affairs, Program in Public Policy and Administration, New York, NY 10027. Offers MPA, JD/MPA, MPA/MS, MPH/MPA. *Accreditation:* NASPAA. *Entrance requirements:* For master's, GRE General Test. Additional exam requirements/recommendations for international students: Required—TOEFL (minimum score 600 paper-based; 100 iBT). Electronic applications accepted.

Columbus State University, Graduate Studies, College of Letters and Sciences, Department of Political Science, Columbus, GA 31907-5645. Offers public administration (MPA). Part-time and evening/weekend programs available. *Faculty:* 7 full-time (2 women), 3 part-time/adjunct (1 woman). *Students:* 48 full-time (28 women), 116 part-time (67 women); includes 87 minority (74 Black or African American, non-Hispanic/Latino; 2 American Indian or Alaska Native, non-Hispanic/Latino; 10 Hispanic/Latino; 1 Two or more races, non-Hispanic/Latino), 1 international. Average age 33. 142 applicants, 49% accepted, 50 enrolled. In 2014, 34 master's awarded. *Degree requirements:* For master's, comprehensive exam. *Entrance requirements:* For master's, GRE General Test, minimum GPA of 2.75, three letters of recommendation. Additional exam requirements/recommendations for international students: Required—TOEFL (minimum score 550 paper-based; 79 iBT). *Application deadline:* For fall admission, 6/30 for domestic students; 5/1 for international students; for spring admission, 11/1 for domestic and international students; for summer admission, 3/1 for domestic and international students. Applications are processed on a rolling basis. Application fee: $40. Electronic applications accepted. *Financial support:* In 2014–15, 91 students received support, including 8 research assistantships with partial tuition reimbursements available (averaging $3,000 per year); career-related internships or fieldwork, Federal Work-Study, institutionally sponsored loans, scholarships/grants, tuition waivers (partial), and unspecified assistantships also available. Support available to part-time students. Financial award application deadline: 5/1; financial award applicants required to submit FAFSA. *Unit head:* Dr. Frederick Gordon, Director, 706-565-7875, E-mail: gordon_frederick@colstate.edu. *Application contact:* Kristin Williams, Director of International and Graduate Recruitment, 706-507-8848, Fax: 706-568-5091, E-mail: williams_kristin@columbusstate.edu.
Website: http://politicalscience.columbusstate.edu/ •

Concordia University, School of Graduate Studies, Faculty of Arts and Science, Department of Political Science, Montréal, QC H3G 1M8, Canada. Offers political science (PhD); public policy and public administration (MA), including geography. *Degree requirements:* For master's, one foreign language, comprehensive exam, thesis optional, internship. *Entrance requirements:* For master's, honors degree or equivalent. Additional exam requirements/recommendations for international students: Required—TOEFL. *Faculty research:* International public policy and administration, Quebec public administration, public policy and social/political theory, geography and public policy, public administration and decision making.

Concordia University Wisconsin, Graduate Programs, School of Business and Legal Studies, MBA Program, Mequon, WI 53097-2402. Offers finance (MBA); health care administration (MBA); human resource management (MBA); international business (MBA); international business-bilingual English/Chinese (MBA); management (MBA); management information systems (MBA); managerial communications (MBA); marketing (MBA); public administration (MBA); risk management (MBA). Postbaccalaureate distance learning degree programs offered (minimal on-campus study). *Degree requirements:* For master's, comprehensive exam, thesis or alternative. *Entrance requirements:* Additional exam requirements/recommendations for international students: Required—TOEFL. *Expenses:* Contact institution.

Copenhagen Business School, Graduate Programs, Copenhagen, Denmark. Offers business administration (Exec MBA, MBA, PhD); business administration and information systems (M Sc); business, language and culture (M Sc); economics and business administration (M Sc); health management (MHM); international business and politics (M Sc); public administration (MPA); shipping and logistics (Exec MBA); technology, market and organization (MBA).

Cumberland University, Program in Public Service Administration, Lebanon, TN 37087. Offers MS. Part-time and evening/weekend programs available. *Degree requirements:* For master's, comprehensive exam. *Entrance requirements:* For master's, MAT, 3 letters of recommendation. Additional exam requirements/recommendations for international students: Required—TOEFL (minimum score 500 paper-based).

Dalhousie University, Faculty of Management, School of Public Administration, Halifax, NS B3H 3J5, Canada. Offers management (MPA); public administration (MPA,

GDPA); LL B/MPA; MLIS/MPA. Part-time programs available. *Entrance requirements:* For master's, GMAT. Additional exam requirements/recommendations for international students: Required—TOEFL, IELTS, CANTEST, CAEL, or Michigan English Language Assessment Battery. Electronic applications accepted. *Expenses:* Contact institution. *Faculty research:* Municipal management, policy and program management, environmental policy, economic and social policy, business and government.

DePaul University, College of Liberal Arts and Social Sciences, Chicago, IL 60614. Offers Arabic (MA); Chinese (MA); English (MA); French (MA); German (MA); history (MA); interdisciplinary studies (MA, MS); international public service (MS); international studies (MA); Italian (MA); Japanese (MA); leadership and policy studies (MS); liberal studies (MA); new media studies (MA); nonprofit management (MNM); public administration (MPA); public health (MPH); public service management (MS); social work (MSW); sociology (MA); Spanish (MA); sustainable urban development (MA); women and gender studies (MA); writing and publishing (MA); writing, rhetoric, and discourse (MA); MA/PhD. Part-time and evening/weekend programs available. Postbaccalaureate distance learning degree programs offered (no on-campus study). Terminal master's awarded for partial completion of doctoral program. *Degree requirements:* For master's, variable foreign language requirement, comprehensive exam (for some programs), thesis (for some programs). Electronic applications accepted.

DeVry University, Graduate Programs, Downers Grove, IL 60515. Offers accounting and financial management (MAFM); business administration (MBA); education (MS); educational technology (MS); electrical engineering (MS); human resources management (MHRM); information systems management (MISM); network and communications management (MNCM); project management (MPM); public administration (MPA).

Drake University, College of Business and Public Administration, Des Moines, IA 50311-4516. Offers M Acc, MBA, MFM, MPA, JD/MBA, JD/MPA, Pharm D/MBA, Pharm D/MPA. *Accreditation:* AACSB. Part-time and evening/weekend programs available. *Faculty:* 13 full-time (5 women). *Students:* 44 full-time (20 women), 246 part-time (129 women); includes 32 minority (10 Black or African American, non-Hispanic/Latino; 6 Asian, non-Hispanic/Latino; 12 Hispanic/Latino; 4 Two or more races, non-Hispanic/Latino), 21 international. Average age 31. 93 applicants, 83% accepted, 70 enrolled. In 2014, 202 master's awarded. *Degree requirements:* For master's, comprehensive exam (for some programs), thesis (for some programs), internships. *Entrance requirements:* For master's, GMAT, letters of recommendation, resume. Additional exam requirements/recommendations for international students: Required—TOEFL (minimum score 550 paper-based). *Application deadline:* For fall admission, 8/15 priority date for domestic students; for winter admission, 12/20 priority date for domestic students; for spring admission, 12/1 priority date for domestic students. Applications are processed on a rolling basis. Application fee: $25. Electronic applications accepted. *Expenses:* Expenses: Contact institution. *Financial support:* Fellowships with tuition reimbursements, teaching assistantships, career-related internships or fieldwork, and institutionally sponsored loans available. Support available to part-time students. Financial award application deadline: 3/1; financial award applicants required to submit FAFSA. *Faculty research:* Venture capital, online commerce, professional ethics, process improvement, project management. *Unit head:* Dr. Charles Edwards, Dean, 515-271-2871, Fax: 515-271-4518, E-mail: charles.edwards@drake.edu. *Application contact:* Danette Kenne, Director of Graduate Programs, 515-271-2188, Fax: 515-271-4518, E-mail: cbpa.gradprograms@drake.edu.
Website: http://www.drake.edu/cbpa/

Duquesne University, Graduate School of Liberal Arts, Graduate Center for Social and Public Policy, Pittsburgh, PA 15282-0001. Offers conflict resolution and peace studies (Certificate); social and public policy (MA, Certificate). Part-time and evening/weekend programs available. *Faculty:* 6 full-time (2 women), 1 (woman) part-time/adjunct. *Students:* 25 full-time (16 women), 2 part-time (1 woman); includes 4 minority (1 Black or African American, non-Hispanic/Latino; 1 Asian, non-Hispanic/Latino; 2 Two or more races, non-Hispanic/Latino), 2 international. Average age 29. 32 applicants, 63% accepted, 10 enrolled. In 2014, 16 master's awarded. *Degree requirements:* For master's, thesis. *Entrance requirements:* For master's, GRE General Test. Additional exam requirements/recommendations for international students: Required—TOEFL. *Application deadline:* For fall admission, 4/30 priority date for domestic and international students; for spring admission, 11/1 priority date for domestic and international students. Applications are processed on a rolling basis. Electronic applications accepted. *Expenses: Tuition:* Full-time $18,882; part-time $1049 per credit. *Required fees:* $1800; $100 per credit. Tuition and fees vary according to program. *Financial support:* In 2014–15, 20 students received support, including 13 teaching assistantships with full and partial tuition reimbursements available (averaging $10,000 per year); career-related internships or fieldwork, institutionally sponsored loans, scholarships/grants, tuition waivers (full and partial), and unspecified assistantships also available. Support available to part-time students. Financial award application deadline: 5/1. *Faculty research:* Program evaluation, environmental policy, criminal justice policy, health care policy. *Total annual research expenditures:* $30,000. *Unit head:* Dr. Michael Irwin, Director, 412-396-6488, E-mail: irwinm@duq.edu. *Application contact:* Linda Rendulic, Assistant to the Dean, 412-396-6400, E-mail: rendulic@duq.edu.
Website: http://www.duq.edu/academics/schools/liberal-arts/graduate-school/programs/social-and-public-policy

East Carolina University, Graduate School, College of Human Ecology, Department of Criminal Justice, Greenville, NC 27858-4353. Offers criminal justice (MS); criminal justice education (Certificate); public management and leadership (Certificate); security studies (Certificate). Part-time and evening/weekend programs available. Postbaccalaureate distance learning degree programs offered (no on-campus study). *Degree requirements:* For master's, thesis, internship. *Entrance requirements:* For master's, GRE or MAT, bachelor's degree in criminal justice or related field. Additional exam requirements/recommendations for international students: Required—TOEFL. *Expenses:* Tuition, state resident: full-time $4223. Tuition, nonresident: full-time $16,540. *Required fees:* $2184. *Faculty research:* Corrections, policing, international criminal justice, terrorism.

East Carolina University, Graduate School, Thomas Harriot College of Arts and Sciences, Department of Political Science, Greenville, NC 27858-4353. Offers community health administration (Certificate); public administration (MPA); security studies (Certificate). *Accreditation:* NASPAA. Part-time and evening/weekend programs available. *Degree requirements:* For master's, one foreign language, comprehensive exam. *Entrance requirements:* For master's, GRE General Test. Additional exam requirements/recommendations for international students: Required—TOEFL. *Expenses:* Tuition, state resident: full-time $4223. Tuition, nonresident: full-time $16,540. *Required fees:* $2184.

Eastern Kentucky University, The Graduate School, College of Arts and Sciences, Department of Government, Program in General Public Administration, Richmond, KY 40475-3102. Offers community development (MPA); community health administration (MPA); general public administration (MPA). *Accreditation:* NASPAA. Part-time and evening/weekend programs available. *Entrance requirements:* For master's, GRE General Test, minimum GPA of 2.5.

Eastern Michigan University, Graduate School, College of Arts and Sciences, Department of Political Science, Programs in Public Administration, Ypsilanti, MI 48197. Offers management of public healthcare services (Graduate Certificate); public administration (MPA); public budget management (Graduate Certificate); public land planning (Graduate Certificate); public management (Graduate Certificate); public policy analysis (Graduate Certificate). *Accreditation:* NASPAA. *Students:* 5 full-time (2 women), 57 part-time (24 women); includes 18 minority (13 Black or African American, non-Hispanic/Latino; 2 Asian, non-Hispanic/Latino; 3 Hispanic/Latino), 1 international. Average age 36. 50 applicants, 66% accepted, 17 enrolled. In 2014, 25 master's, 9 other advanced degrees awarded. Application fee: $45. *Unit head:* Dr. Gregory Plagens, Program Director, 734-487-2522, Fax: 734-487-3340, E-mail: gregory.plagens@emich.edu. *Application contact:* Dr. Barbara Patrick, Program Advisor, 734-487-1453, Fax: 734-487-3340, E-mail: bpatric1@emich.edu.

Eastern Washington University, Graduate Studies, College of Business and Public Administration, Program in Public Administration, Cheney, WA 99004-2431. Offers MPA, MBA/MPA, MPA/MSW, MPA/MURP. Part-time and evening/weekend programs available. *Degree requirements:* For master's, comprehensive exam, thesis optional. *Entrance requirements:* For master's, minimum GPA of 3.0.

East Tennessee State University, School of Graduate Studies, College of Arts and Sciences, Department of Political Science, International Affairs and Public Administration, Johnson City, TN 37614. Offers economic development (Postbaccalaureate Certificate); not-for-profit administration (MPA); planning and development (MPA); public financial management (MPA); urban planning (Postbaccalaureate Certificate). Part-time programs available. *Faculty:* 7 full-time (2 women), 1 part-time/adjunct (0 women). *Students:* 19 full-time (5 women), 9 part-time (4 women); includes 3 minority (2 Black or African American, non-Hispanic/Latino; 1 Hispanic/Latino), 6 international. Average age 29. 48 applicants, 33% accepted, 10 enrolled. In 2014, 7 master's, 1 other advanced degree awarded. *Degree requirements:* For master's, internship. *Entrance requirements:* For master's, GRE General Test, three letters of recommendation; for Postbaccalaureate Certificate, GRE General Test. Additional exam requirements/recommendations for international students: Required—TOEFL (minimum score 550 paper-based; 79 iBT). *Application deadline:* For fall admission, 6/1 for domestic students, 4/29 for international students; for spring admission, 11/1 for domestic students, 9/30 for international students. Application fee: $35 ($45 for international students). Electronic applications accepted. *Financial support:* In 2014–15, 16 students received support, including 16 research assistantships with full tuition reimbursements available (averaging $6,000 per year), 4 teaching assistantships with full tuition reimbursements available (averaging $6,000 per year); career-related internships or fieldwork, institutionally sponsored loans, scholarships/grants, and unspecified assistantships also available. Financial award application deadline: 7/1; financial award applicants required to submit FAFSA. *Faculty research:* Labor issues, presidency, public law in American politics, East Asian politics, European politics, Middle Eastern politics, development in comparative politics, international political economy, international relations, world politics in international affairs. *Unit head:* Dr. Andrew Battista, Chair, 423-439-4217, Fax: 423-439-4348, E-mail: battista@etsu.edu. *Application contact:* Angela Edwards, Graduate Specialist, 423-439-4703, Fax: 423-439-5624, E-mail: edwardag@etsu.edu.
Website: http://www.etsu.edu/cas/polisci/

The Evergreen State College, Graduate Programs, Program in Public Administration, Olympia, WA 98505. Offers MPA. Part-time and evening/weekend programs available. *Faculty:* 5 full-time (2 women), 11 part-time/adjunct (4 women). *Students:* 132 full-time (89 women), 38 part-time (27 women); includes 68 minority (13 Black or African American, non-Hispanic/Latino; 19 American Indian or Alaska Native, non-Hispanic/Latino; 6 Asian, non-Hispanic/Latino; 13 Hispanic/Latino; 17 Two or more races, non-Hispanic/Latino). Average age 37. 143 applicants, 77% accepted, 92 enrolled. In 2014, 58 master's awarded. *Degree requirements:* For master's, 6-credit capstone course or 8-credit thesis. *Entrance requirements:* For master's, minimum GPA of 3.0 in last 90 quarter hours toward BA/BS; 4 quarter credits in statistics within past 5 years; evidence of writing, analytical, and general communication skills at appropriate level for graduate study. Additional exam requirements/recommendations for international students: Required—TOEFL (minimum score 600 paper-based; 100 iBT). *Application deadline:* For fall admission, 2/2 priority date for domestic and international students. Applications are processed on a rolling basis. Application fee: $50. Electronic applications accepted. *Expenses:* Expenses: $9,318 in-state; $21,477 out-of-state. *Financial support:* In 2014–15, 93 students received support, including 19 fellowships with partial tuition reimbursements available (averaging $892 per year); career-related internships or fieldwork, Federal Work-Study, institutionally sponsored loans, scholarships/grants, and tuition waivers (partial) also available. Support available to part-time students. Financial award application deadline: 3/1; financial award applicants required to submit FAFSA. *Faculty research:* Public, international and nonprofit administration; public finance; organizational theory/behavior/change/dynamic; leadership and decision-making processes; federal/state/tribal constitutions; housing/natural resource/environmental policy; political science; forestry, regional planning; third world/indigenous studies; tribal sovereignty and self-government; Constitutional legal history and public policy US/Canada/New Zealand; democratic governance; social research methods; urban studies. *Unit head:* Dr. Cheryl Simrell King, MPA Program Director, 360-867-5541, E-mail: kingcs@evergreen.edu. *Application contact:* Randee Gibbons, Associate MPA Program Director, 360-867-6554, E-mail: gibbonsr@evergreen.edu.
Website: http://www.evergreen.edu/mpa/

Excelsior College, School of Public Service, Albany, NY 12203-5159. Offers homeland security and emergency management (MSCJ); public administration (MPA). Part-time and evening/weekend programs available. Postbaccalaureate distance learning degree programs offered (no on-campus study). *Faculty:* 2 part-time/adjunct (0 women). *Students:* 122 part-time (25 women); includes 49 minority (25 Black or African American, non-Hispanic/Latino; 1 Asian, non-Hispanic/Latino; 18 Hispanic/Latino; 1 Native Hawaiian or other Pacific Islander, non-Hispanic/Latino; 4 Two or more races, non-Hispanic/Latino). Average age 40. In 2014, 12 master's awarded. Application fee: $110. *Expenses: Tuition:* Part-time $620 per credit hour. *Financial support:* Scholarships/grants available. Support available to part-time students. *Unit head:* Dr. Robert Waters, Dean, School of Public Service. *Application contact:* Admissions Counselor, 518-464-8500, Fax: 518-464-8777, E-mail: admissions@excelsior.edu.
Website: http://www.excelsior.edu/schools/public-service

Fairfield University, College of Arts and Sciences, Fairfield, CT 06824. Offers American studies (MA); communication (MA); creative writing (MFA); mathematics (MS); public administration (MPA). Part-time and evening/weekend programs available. Postbaccalaureate distance learning degree programs offered (minimal on-campus study). *Faculty:* 35 full-time (20 women), 5 part-time/adjunct (1 woman). *Students:* 54 full-time (35 women), 65 part-time (37 women); includes 18 minority (4 Black or African American, non-Hispanic/Latino; 4 Asian, non-Hispanic/Latino; 6 Hispanic/Latino; 1 Native Hawaiian or other Pacific Islander, non-Hispanic/Latino; 3 Two or more races, non-Hispanic/Latino), 6 international. Average age 35. 77 applicants, 69% accepted, 27 enrolled. In 2014, 51 master's awarded. *Degree requirements:* For master's, capstone research course. *Entrance requirements:* For master's, minimum GPA of 3.0, 2 letters of

recommendation, resume. Additional exam requirements/recommendations for international students: Required—TOEFL (minimum score 550 paper-based; 80 iBT) or IELTS (minimum score 6.5). *Application deadline:* For fall admission, 5/14 for international students; for spring admission, 10/15 for international students. Applications are processed on a rolling basis. Application fee: $60. Electronic applications accepted. *Expenses: Tuition:* Part-time $695 per credit hour. Full-time tuition and fees vary according to degree level and program. *Financial support:* In 2014–15, 41 students received support. Scholarships/grants and unspecified assistantships available. Financial award applicants required to submit FAFSA. *Faculty research:* Ethical theory, media industries, community-based teaching and learning, non commutative algebra and partial differential equations, cancer research in biology and physics. *Unit head:* Dr. James Simon, Dean, 203-254-4000 Ext. 2221, Fax: 203-254-4119, E-mail: jsimon@fairfield.edu. *Application contact:* Marianne Gumpper, Director of Graduate and Continuing Studies Admission, 203-254-4184, Fax: 203-254-4073, E-mail: gradadmis@fairfield.edu.
Website: http://www.fairfield.edu/academics/schoolscollegescenters/collegeofartssciences/graduateprograms/

Fairleigh Dickinson University, College at Florham, Anthony J. Petrocelli College of Continuing Studies, Public Administration Institute, Program in Public Administration, Madison, NJ 07940-1099. Offers MPA.

Fairleigh Dickinson University, Metropolitan Campus, Anthony J. Petrocelli College of Continuing Studies, Public Administration Institute, Program in Public Administration, Teaneck, NJ 07666-1914. Offers MPA, Certificate.

Florida Agricultural and Mechanical University, Division of Graduate Studies, Research, and Continuing Education, College of Social Sciences, Arts and Humanities, Department of History and Political Science, Program in Applied Social Science, Tallahassee, FL 32307-3200. Offers criminal justice (MASS); history (MASS); political science (MASS); public administration (MASS). Part-time programs available. *Degree requirements:* For master's, thesis optional. *Entrance requirements:* For master's, GRE General Test, minimum GPA of 3.0. *Faculty research:* Southern history, black history, election trends, Presidential history.

Florida Atlantic University, College of Design and Social Inquiry, School of Public Administration, Boca Raton, FL 33431-0991. Offers MNM, MPA, PhD. *Accreditation:* NASPAA (one or more programs are accredited). Part-time and evening/weekend programs available. *Degree requirements:* For master's, thesis optional; for doctorate, comprehensive exam, thesis/dissertation. *Entrance requirements:* For master's, GRE General Test, minimum GPA of 3.0; for doctorate, GRE General Test, faculty reference, scholarly writing samples, letters of recommendation. Additional exam requirements/recommendations for international students: Required—TOEFL (minimum score 500 paper-based; 61 iBT), IELTS (minimum score 6). *Expenses: Tuition,* state resident: full-time $7396; part-time $369.82 per credit hour. Tuition, nonresident: full-time $19,392; part-time $1024.81 per credit hour. Tuition and fees vary according to course load. *Faculty research:* Public finance and budgeting, public management, evaluation, criminal justice, postmodern public administration.

Florida Gulf Coast University, College of Arts and Sciences, Program in Public Administration, Fort Myers, FL 33965-6565. Offers environmental policy (MPA); management (MPA). *Accreditation:* NASPAA. Part-time programs available. *Faculty:* 230 full-time (93 women), 158 part-time/adjunct (72 women). *Students:* 15 full-time (10 women), 53 part-time (37 women); includes 17 minority (5 Black or African American, non-Hispanic/Latino; 11 Hispanic/Latino; 1 Two or more races, non-Hispanic/Latino), 1 international. Average age 35. 33 applicants, 73% accepted, 18 enrolled. In 2014, 14 master's awarded. *Entrance requirements:* For master's, GRE General Test, MAT, minimum GPA of 3.0. Additional exam requirements/recommendations for international students: Required—TOEFL (minimum score 550 paper-based). *Application deadline:* For fall admission, 7/1 priority date for domestic students; for spring admission, 10/15 for domestic students. Applications are processed on a rolling basis. Application fee: $30. Electronic applications accepted. *Expenses: Tuition,* state resident: full-time $6974. Tuition, nonresident: full-time $28,170. *Required fees:* $1987. Tuition and fees vary according to course load. *Financial support:* In 2014–15, 13 students received support, including 5 research assistantships; career-related internships or fieldwork and tuition waivers (full and partial) also available. Support available to part-time students. Financial award application deadline: 6/30; financial award applicants required to submit FAFSA. *Faculty research:* Personnel, public policy, public finance, housing policy. *Unit head:* Dr. Roger Green, Chair, 239-590-7838, E-mail: rgreen@fgcu.edu. *Application contact:* Dr. Margaret Banyan, Assistant Professor/Director of MPA Program, 239-590-7850, Fax: 239-590-7846, E-mail: mbanyan@fgcu.edu.

Florida Institute of Technology, Graduate Programs, Extended Studies Division, Melbourne, FL 32901-6975. Offers acquisition and contract management (MS); aerospace engineering (MS); business administration (MBA, DBA); computer information systems (MS); computer science (MS); electrical engineering (MS); engineering management (MS); human resources management (MS); logistics management (MS), including humanitarian and disaster relief logistics; management (MS), including acquisition and contract management, e-business, human resources management, information systems, logistics management, management, transportation management; material acquisition management (MS); mechanical engineering (MS); operations research (MS); project management (MS), including information systems, operations research; public administration (MPA); quality management (MS); software engineering (MS); space systems (MS); space systems management (MS); supply chain management (MS); systems management (MS), including information systems, operations research; technology management (MS). Part-time and evening/weekend programs available. Postbaccalaureate distance learning degree programs offered (no on-campus study). *Faculty:* 7 full-time (1 woman), 112 part-time/adjunct (29 women). *Students:* 98 full-time (45 women), 975 part-time (396 women); includes 440 minority (292 Black or African American, non-Hispanic/Latino; 13 American Indian or Alaska Native, non-Hispanic/Latino; 32 Asian, non-Hispanic/Latino; 79 Hispanic/Latino; 1 Native Hawaiian or other Pacific Islander, non-Hispanic/Latino; 23 Two or more races, non-Hispanic/Latino), 4 international. Average age 37. 807 applicants, 56% accepted, 258 enrolled. In 2014, 457 master's awarded. *Degree requirements:* For master's, comprehensive exam (for some programs), capstone course. *Entrance requirements:* For master's, GMAT or resume showing 8 years of supervised experience, minimum GPA of 3.0, 2 letters of recommendation, resume. Additional exam requirements/ recommendations for international students: Required—TOEFL (minimum score 550 paper-based; 79 iBT). *Application deadline:* For fall admission, 4/1 for international students; for spring admission, 9/30 for international students. Applications are processed on a rolling basis. Electronic applications accepted. *Expenses:* Expenses: Contact institution. *Financial support:* Application deadline: 3/1; applicants required to submit FAFSA. *Unit head:* Dr. Theodore R. Richardson, III, Senior Associate Dean, 321-674-8123, Fax: 321-674-7597, E-mail: trichardson@fit.edu. *Application contact:* Carolyn Farrior, Director of Graduate Admissions, Online Learning and Off-Campus Programs, 321-674-7118, Fax: 321-674-8216, E-mail: cfarrior@fit.edu.
Website: http://es.fit.edu

Florida International University, College of Arts and Sciences, Department of Public Administration, Miami, FL 33199. Offers public administration (MPA); public affairs

(PhD); JD/MPA; MS/MPA. *Accreditation:* NASPAA (one or more programs are accredited). Part-time and evening/weekend programs available. *Degree requirements:* For doctorate, comprehensive exam, thesis/dissertation. *Entrance requirements:* For master's, minimum undergraduate GPA of 3.0 in upper-level coursework, 1 letter of recommendation, letter of intent; for doctorate, GRE, minimum undergraduate GPA of 3.0 in upper-level coursework, 3 letters of recommendation, samples of scholarly written work, interview (when student lives within 50 miles of campus). Additional exam requirements/recommendations for international students: Required—TOEFL (minimum score 550 paper-based; 80 iBT). Electronic applications accepted.

Florida State University, The Graduate School, College of Social Sciences and Public Policy, Reubin O'D. Askew School of Public Administration and Policy, Tallahassee, FL 32306-2250. Offers MPA, PhD, Certificate, JD/MPA, MPA/MSC, MPA/MSP, MPA/MSW. *Accreditation:* NASPAA (one or more programs are accredited). Part-time and evening/weekend programs available. *Faculty:* 10 full-time (2 women), 8 part-time/adjunct (3 women). *Students:* 69 full-time (29 women), 123 part-time (70 women); includes 49 minority (29 Black or African American, non-Hispanic/Latino; 14 Hispanic/Latino; 6 Two or more races, non-Hispanic/Latino), 56 international. Average age 25. 166 applicants, 63% accepted, 46 enrolled. In 2014, 69 master's, 7 doctorates awarded. *Degree requirements:* For master's, action report; for doctorate, comprehensive exam, thesis/dissertation. *Entrance requirements:* For master's, GRE General Test, GMAT, MAT, LSAT, minimum undergraduate upper-division GPA of 3.0; for doctorate, GRE General Test (minimum score of 1100 or equivalent); GMAT; MAT; LSAT, minimum undergraduate GPA of 3.0, graduate 3.5. Additional exam requirements/ recommendations for international students: Required—PTE (minimum score 55), TOEFL (minimum score 550 paper-based, 80 iBT), IELTS (minimum score 6.5) or Michigan English Language Assessment Battery (minimum score 77). *Application deadline:* For fall admission, 7/1 for domestic students, 5/1 for international students; for spring admission, 11/1 for domestic students, 9/1 for international students; for summer admission, 3/1 for domestic students, 1/1 for international students. Applications are processed on a rolling basis. Application fee: $30. Electronic applications accepted. *Expenses: Tuition,* state resident: part-time $403.51 per credit hour. Tuition, nonresident: part-time $1004.85 per credit hour. *Required fees:* $75.81 per credit hour. One-time fee: $20 part-time. Tuition and fees vary according to campus/location. *Financial support:* In 2014–15, 29 students received support, including 6 fellowships with full tuition reimbursements available (averaging $18,000 per year), 14 research assistantships with full tuition reimbursements available (averaging $15,000 per year), 5 teaching assistantships with full tuition reimbursements available (averaging $15,000 per year); career-related internships or fieldwork, Federal Work-Study, institutionally sponsored loans, scholarships/grants, tuition waivers (full), and unspecified assistantships also available. Support available to part-time students. Financial award application deadline: 2/1; financial award applicants required to submit FAFSA. *Faculty research:* Financial management, public policy and development, strategic management, state and local government, public and nonprofit management, international and nongovernmental organizations. *Unit head:* Dr. William Earle Klay, Director, 850-644-3525, Fax: 850-644-7617, E-mail: eklay@fsu.edu. *Application contact:* Velda Williams, Academic Program Specialist, 850-644-3060, Fax: 850-644-7617, E-mail: vwilliams3@fsu.edu.
Website: http://askew.fsu.edu/

Framingham State University, Continuing Education, Program in Public Administration, Framingham, MA 01701-9101. Offers MA. Part-time and evening/weekend programs available.

Gallaudet University, The Graduate School, Washington, DC 20002-3625. Offers ASL/English bilingual early childhood education: birth to 5 (Certificate); audiology (Au D); clinical psychology (PhD); critical studies in the education of deaf learners (PhD); deaf and hard of hearing infants, toddlers, and their families (Certificate); deaf education (Ed S); deaf education: advanced studies (MA); deaf education: special programs (MA); deaf history (Certificate); deaf studies (MA, Certificate); educating deaf students with disabilities (Certificate); education: teacher preparation (MA), including deaf education, early childhood education and deaf education, elementary education and deaf education, secondary education and deaf education; educational neuroscience (PhD); hearing, speech and language sciences (MS, PhD); international development (MA); interpretation (MA, PhD), including combined interpreting practice and research (MA), interpreting research (MA); linguistics (MA, PhD); mental health counseling (MA); peer mentoring (Certificate); public administration (MPA); school counseling (MA); school psychology (Psy S); sign language teaching (MA); social work (MSW); speech-language pathology (MS). Part-time programs available. *Students:* 325 full-time (251 women), 118 part-time (90 women); includes 91 minority (41 Black or African American, non-Hispanic/Latino; 1 American Indian or Alaska Native, non-Hispanic/Latino; 14 Asian, non-Hispanic/Latino; 25 Hispanic/Latino; 10 Two or more races, non-Hispanic/Latino), 28 international. Average age 30. 617 applicants, 42% accepted, 171 enrolled. In 2014, 145 master's, 21 doctorates, 8 other advanced degrees awarded. Terminal master's awarded for partial completion of doctoral program. *Degree requirements:* For master's, comprehensive exam (for some programs), thesis optional; for doctorate, comprehensive exam, thesis/dissertation. *Entrance requirements:* For master's and doctorate, GRE General Test or MAT, letters of recommendation, interviews, goals statement, American Sign Language proficiency interview, written English competency. Additional exam requirements/recommendations for international students: Required—TOEFL. *Application deadline:* For fall admission, 2/15 for domestic students. Applications are processed on a rolling basis. Application fee: $75. Electronic applications accepted. *Expenses: Tuition:* Full-time $15,956; part-time $886.45 per credit hour. *Required fees:* $3404; $263 per semester. *Financial support:* Fellowships, research assistantships, teaching assistantships, career-related internships or fieldwork, Federal Work-Study, scholarships/grants, tuition waivers (partial), and unspecified assistantships available. Support available to part-time students. Financial award applicants required to submit FAFSA. *Faculty research:* Signing math dictionaries, telecommunications access, cancer genetics, linguistics, visual language and visual learning, integrated quantum materials, deaf legal discourse, advance recruitment and retention in geosciences. *Unit head:* Dr. Gaurav Mathur, Interim Dean, Graduate School and Continuing Studies, 202-250-2380, Fax: 202-651-5027, E-mail: gaurav.mathur@gallaudet.edu. *Application contact:* Wednesday Luria, Coordinator of Prospective Graduate Student Services, 202-651-5400, Fax: 202-651-5295, E-mail: graduate.school@gallaudet.edu.
Website: http://www.gallaudet.edu/x26696.xml

Gannon University, School of Graduate Studies, College of Engineering and Business, Dahlkemper School of Business, Program in Public Administration, Erie, PA 16541-0001. Offers MPA. Part-time and evening/weekend programs available. Postbaccalaureate distance learning degree programs offered (no on-campus study). *Degree requirements:* For master's, thesis or alternative, research project. *Entrance requirements:* For master's, GRE or GMAT. Additional exam requirements/ recommendations for international students: Required—TOEFL (minimum score 79 iBT). Electronic applications accepted.

George Mason University, School of Policy, Government, and International Affairs, Program in Public Administration, Fairfax, VA 22030. Offers administration of justice

(Certificate); association management (Certificate); biodefense (MS, PhD); critical analysis and strategic response to terrorism (Certificate); emergency management and homeland security (Certificate); nonprofit management (Certificate); political science (MA, PhD); public administration (MPA); public management (Certificate). *Accreditation:* NASPAA (one or more programs are accredited). *Entrance requirements:* For degree, expanded goals statement; 3 letters of recommendation; official transcripts; resume. Additional exam requirements/recommendations for international students: Required—TOEFL, IELTS, PTE. Application fee: $65 ($80 for international students). Electronic applications accepted. *Expenses:* Expenses: Contact institution. *Financial support:* Fellowships, research assistantships with full and partial tuition reimbursements, teaching assistantships with full and partial tuition reimbursements, career-related internships or fieldwork, Federal Work-Study, scholarships/grants, and unspecified assistantships available. Support available to part-time students. Financial award application deadline: 3/1; financial award applicants required to submit FAFSA. *Application contact:* Peg Koback, Education Support Specialist, 703-993-3707, Fax: 703-993-1399, E-mail: mkoback@gmu.edu.
Website: http://pia.gmu.edu/

The George Washington University, Columbian College of Arts and Sciences, Trachtenberg School of Public Policy and Public Administration, Washington, DC 20052. Offers public administration (MPA); public policy (MPP); public policy and administration (PhD); JD/MPP; MPA/JD; PhD/MPP. Part-time and evening/weekend programs available. *Faculty:* 39 full-time (14 women), 19 part-time/adjunct (10 women). *Students:* 273 full-time (182 women), 129 part-time (94 women); includes 58 minority (26 Black or African American, non-Hispanic/Latino; 1 American Indian or Alaska Native, non-Hispanic/Latino; 22 Asian, non-Hispanic/Latino; 8 Hispanic/Latino; 1 Native Hawaiian or other Pacific Islander, non-Hispanic/Latino). Average age 26. 812 applicants, 61% accepted, 140 enrolled. In 2014, 134 master's, 10 doctorates awarded. *Degree requirements:* For master's, capstone project; for doctorate, comprehensive exam, thesis/dissertation. *Entrance requirements:* For master's and doctorate, GRE General Test, minimum GPA of 3.0. Additional exam requirements/recommendations for international students: Required—TOEFL (minimum score 600 paper-based; 100 iBT). *Application deadline:* For fall admission, 1/5 priority date for domestic and international students. Application fee: $75. Electronic applications accepted. *Financial support:* In 2014–15, 92 students received support. Fellowships, research assistantships, teaching assistantships, Federal Work-Study, scholarships/grants, health care benefits, and unspecified assistantships available. Financial award application deadline: 1/5. *Faculty research:* Education policy, budget and finance, health policy, regulatory policy, program evaluation. *Unit head:* Dr. Kathyrn E. Newcomer, Director, 202-994-3959, Fax: 202-994-3959, E-mail: newcomer@gwu.edu. *Application contact:* Denee Bottoms, Assistant Director of Graduate Studies, 202-994-6295, Fax: 202-994-6792, E-mail: tspppa@gwu.edu.
Website: http://www.tspppa.gwu.edu/

Georgia College & State University, Graduate School, College of Arts and Sciences, Department of Government and Sociology, Program in Public Administration, Milledgeville, GA 31061. Offers MPA. *Accreditation:* NASPAA. Part-time and evening/weekend programs available. *Students:* 11 full-time (8 women), 34 part-time (21 women); includes 18 minority (15 Black or African American, non-Hispanic/Latino; 1 Asian, non-Hispanic/Latino; 1 Hispanic/Latino; 1 Two or more races, non-Hispanic/Latino), 1 international. Average age 32. 19 applicants, 84% accepted, 8 enrolled. In 2014, 19 master's awarded. *Degree requirements:* For master's, capstone project or thesis, minimum GPA of 3.0. *Entrance requirements:* For master's, GRE General Test or MAT, transcript of all undergraduate and graduate work. Additional exam requirements/recommendations for international students: Recommended—TOEFL (minimum score 550 paper-based; 79 iBT), IELTS. *Application deadline:* For fall admission, 7/1 for domestic students, 4/1 for international students; for spring admission, 11/1 for domestic students, 9/1 for international students; for summer admission, 4/1 for domestic students. Application fee: $40. Electronic applications accepted. *Expenses: Tuition, area resident:* Part-time $283 per credit hour. Tuition, nonresident: part-time $1027 per credit hour. *Required fees:* $995 per semester. Full-time tuition and fees vary according to course load, degree level, campus/location and program. *Financial support:* In 2014–15, 3 research assistantships were awarded; career-related internships or fieldwork and unspecified assistantships also available. Support available to part-time students. Financial award application deadline: 3/1; financial award applicants required to submit FAFSA. *Unit head:* Dr. Costas Spirou, Chair, Government and Sociology, 478-445-4562, E-mail: costas.spirou@gcsu.edu. *Application contact:* Dr. Min Kim, MPA Coordinator, 478-445-7393, E-mail: mpa@gcsu.edu.

Georgia Southern University, Jack N. Averitt College of Graduate Studies, College of Liberal Arts and Social Sciences, Department of Non-Profit and Public Studies, Program in Public Administration, Statesboro, GA 30460. Offers MPA. *Accreditation:* NASPAA. Part-time and evening/weekend programs available. *Students:* 25 full-time (14 women), 17 part-time (11 women); includes 16 minority (7 Black or African American, non-Hispanic/Latino; 8 Hispanic/Latino; 1 Two or more races, non-Hispanic/Latino), 5 international. Average age 29. 18 applicants, 83% accepted, 12 enrolled. In 2014, 9 master's awarded. *Degree requirements:* For master's, comprehensive exam, internship, terminal exam. *Entrance requirements:* For master's, GRE General Test, minimum GPA of 2.5, resume, undergraduate major appropriate to field, letters of reference. Additional exam requirements/recommendations for international students: Required—TOEFL (minimum score 550 paper-based; 80 iBT). *Application deadline:* For fall admission, 3/1 priority date for domestic and international students; for spring admission, 10/1 priority date for domestic students, 10/1 for international students. Applications are processed on a rolling basis. Application fee: $50. Electronic applications accepted. *Expenses:* Tuition, state resident: full-time $7236; part-time $277 per semester hour. Tuition, nonresident: full-time $27,118; part-time $1105 per semester hour. *Required fees:* $2092. *Financial support:* In 2014–15, 16 students received support, including research assistantships with partial tuition reimbursements available (averaging $7,200 per year), teaching assistantships with partial tuition reimbursements available (averaging $7,200 per year); career-related internships or fieldwork, Federal Work-Study, scholarships/grants, tuition waivers (partial), and unspecified assistantships also available. Support available to part-time students. Financial award application deadline: 4/15; financial award applicants required to submit FAFSA. *Faculty research:* Comparative public administration, equal employment policies, gangs, environmental policy, AIDS policy. *Unit head:* Dr. Trenton Davis, Director, 912-478-5430, Fax: 912-478-8029, E-mail: tjdavis@georgiasouthern.edu.
Website: http://centers.georgiasouthern.edu/ipns/mpa/

Georgia State University, Andrew Young School of Policy Studies, Department of Criminal Justice and Criminology, Atlanta, GA 30302-4018. Offers criminal justice (MS, PhD); public administration (MS). Part-time programs available. *Faculty:* 13 full-time (4 women). *Students:* 37 full-time (26 women), 5 part-time (3 women); includes 15 minority (9 Black or African American, non-Hispanic/Latino; 1 American Indian or Alaska Native, non-Hispanic/Latino; 2 Asian, non-Hispanic/Latino; 2 Hispanic/Latino; 1 Two or more races, non-Hispanic/Latino), 3 international. Average age 30. 41 applicants, 49% accepted, 10 enrolled. In 2014, 11 master's, 1 doctorate awarded. Terminal master's awarded for partial completion of doctoral program. *Degree requirements:* For master's, thesis optional; for doctorate, comprehensive exam, thesis/dissertation. *Entrance requirements:* For master's, GRE; for doctorate, GRE. Additional exam requirements/recommendations for international students: Required—TOEFL (minimum score 603 paper-based; 100 iBT) or IELTS (minimum score 7). *Application deadline:* For fall admission, 2/15 for domestic and international students; for spring admission, 10/1 for domestic and international students. Application fee: $50. Electronic applications accepted. *Expenses:* Tuition, state resident: full-time $6516; part-time $362 per credit hour. Tuition, nonresident: full-time $22,014; part-time $1223 per credit hour. *Required fees:* $2128 per semester. Tuition and fees vary according to course load and program. *Financial support:* In 2014–15, fellowships with full tuition reimbursements (averaging $22,000 per year), research assistantships with full tuition reimbursements (averaging $14,000 per year), teaching assistantships with full tuition reimbursements (averaging $14,000 per year) were awarded; career-related internships or fieldwork, Federal Work-Study, scholarships/grants, traineeships, health care benefits, and unspecified assistantships also available. Financial award application deadline: 2/15. *Faculty research:* Urban violence, drugs, victimization, criminal justice, criminology. *Unit head:* Dr. Brian K. Payne, Professor of Criminal Justice and Criminology/Department Chair, 404-413-1020, Fax: 404-413-1030, E-mail: bpayne@gsu.edu. *Application contact:* Charisma Parker, Admissions Coordinator, 404-413-0030, Fax: 404-413-0023, E-mail: cparker28@gsu.edu.
Website: http://aysps.gsu.edu/cj/

Golden Gate University, Ageno School of Business, San Francisco, CA 94105-2968. Offers accounting (MBA); business administration (EMBA, MBA, PMBA, DBA); finance (MBA, MS, Certificate); financial planning (MS, Certificate); healthcare information systems (Certificate); human resource management (MBA, MS); human resources management (Certificate); information systems (MS); information technology (MBA); information technology management (Certificate); integrated marketing and communications (MS, Certificate); international business (MBA); management (MBA); marketing (MBA, MS, Certificate); operations supply chain management (Certificate); psychology (MA, Certificate); public administration (EMPA); public relations (MS, Certificate); technical market analysis (Certificate); JD/MBA. Part-time and evening/weekend programs available. *Degree requirements:* For doctorate, thesis/dissertation, qualifying examination. *Entrance requirements:* For master's, GMAT (MBA), minimum GPA of 2.5 (MS). Additional exam requirements/recommendations for international students: Required—TOEFL (minimum score 550 paper-based; 79 iBT). Electronic applications accepted. *Expenses:* Contact institution.

Governors State University, College of Business and Public Administration, Program in Public Administration, University Park, IL 60484. Offers MPA. *Accreditation:* NASPAA. Part-time and evening/weekend programs available. *Degree requirements:* For master's, comprehensive exam, thesis or alternative, internship or previous work in field. *Entrance requirements:* For master's, minimum GPA of 2.5. *Faculty research:* State and local politics.

Grambling State University, School of Graduate Studies and Research, College of Arts and Sciences, Department of Political Science and Public Administration, Grambling, LA 71270. Offers health services administration (MPA); human resource management (MPA); public management (MPA); state and local government (MPA). *Accreditation:* NASPAA. Part-time programs available. *Degree requirements:* For master's, comprehensive exam (for some programs), thesis optional. *Entrance requirements:* For master's, GRE, minimum GPA of 2.75 on last degree. Additional exam requirements/recommendations for international students: Required—TOEFL (minimum score 500 paper-based; 62 iBT). Electronic applications accepted.

Grand Canyon University, College of Business, Phoenix, AZ 85017-1097. Offers accounting (MBA); corporate business administration (MBA); disaster preparedness and crisis management (MBA); executive fire service leadership (MS); finance (MBA); general management (MBA); government and policy (MPA); health care management (MPA); health systems management (MBA); human resource management (MBA); innovation (MBA); leadership (MBA, MS); management of information system (MBA); marketing (MBA); project-based (MBA); six sigma (MBA); strategic human resource management (MBA). *Accreditation:* ACBSP. Part-time and evening/weekend programs available. Postbaccalaureate distance learning degree programs offered (no on-campus study). *Entrance requirements:* For master's, equivalent of two years full-time professional work experience. Additional exam requirements/recommendations for international students: Required—TOEFL (minimum score 575 paper-based; 90 iBT), IELTS (minimum score 7). Electronic applications accepted.

Grand Valley State University, College of Community and Public Service, School of Public and Nonprofit Administration, Allendale, MI 49401-9403. Offers MHA, MPA, MPNL. *Accreditation:* NASPAA. Part-time and evening/weekend programs available. *Faculty:* 13 full-time (6 women), 7 part-time/adjunct (3 women). *Students:* 60 full-time (40 women), 123 part-time (87 women); includes 33 minority (12 Black or African American, non-Hispanic/Latino; 3 Asian, non-Hispanic/Latino; 11 Hispanic/Latino; 7 Two or more races, non-Hispanic/Latino), 8 international. Average age 32. 87 applicants, 92% accepted, 40 enrolled. In 2014, 77 master's awarded. *Application deadline:* For fall admission, 5/1 priority date for domestic students; for winter admission, 11/1 priority date for domestic students. Applications are processed on a rolling basis. Application fee: $30. Electronic applications accepted. *Expenses:* Tuition, state resident: full-time $10,602; part-time $589 per credit hour. Tuition, nonresident: full-time $14,022; part-time $779 per credit hour. Tuition and fees vary according to degree level and program. *Financial support:* In 2014–15, 27 students received support, including 12 fellowships (averaging $4,631 per year), 17 research assistantships with tuition reimbursements available (averaging $9,140 per year); career-related internships or fieldwork, Federal Work-Study, scholarships/grants, and unspecified assistantships also available. Financial award application deadline: 5/1. *Faculty research:* Comparative urban systems, ethics and public management, local economic development, public and nonprofit boards and governance. *Unit head:* Dr. Richard Jelier, Director, 616-331-6575, Fax: 616-331-7120, E-mail: jelierr@gvsu.edu. *Application contact:* Tracey James-Heer, Associate Director for Graduate Recruitment, 616-331-2025, Fax: 616-486-6476, E-mail: james-ht@gvsu.edu.
Website: http://www.gvsu.edu/spnha/

Hamline University, School of Business, St. Paul, MN 55104-1284. Offers business administration (MBA); nonprofit management (MA); public administration (MA, DPA); JD/MA; JD/MBA; MBA/MA. Part-time and evening/weekend programs available. Postbaccalaureate distance learning degree programs offered (minimal on-campus study). *Faculty:* 4 full-time (1 woman), 21 part-time/adjunct (4 women). *Students:* 78 full-time (36 women), 387 part-time (197 women); includes 43 minority (22 Black or African American, non-Hispanic/Latino; 1 American Indian or Alaska Native, non-Hispanic/Latino; 15 Asian, non-Hispanic/Latino; 4 Hispanic/Latino; 1 Two or more races, non-Hispanic/Latino), 20 international. Average age 34. 140 applicants, 79% accepted, 91 enrolled. In 2014, 168 master's, 5 doctorates awarded. *Degree requirements:* For master's, thesis (for some programs); for doctorate, comprehensive exam, thesis/dissertation. *Entrance requirements:* For master's, personal statement, official transcripts, curriculum vitae, letters of recommendation, writing sample; for doctorate, personal statement, curriculum vitae, official transcripts, letters of recommendation, writing sample. Additional exam requirements/recommendations for international students: Required—TOEFL (minimum score 550 paper-based; 80 iBT). *Application*

deadline: Applications are processed on a rolling basis. Application fee: $0 ($100 for international students). Electronic applications accepted. *Expenses: Tuition:* Full-time $10,530; part-time $405 per credit. *Required fees:* $3 per credit. One-time fee: $190. Tuition and fees vary according to course load, degree level and program. *Financial support:* Career-related internships or fieldwork, Federal Work-Study, scholarships/grants, and unspecified assistantships available. Support available to part-time students. Financial award applicants required to submit FAFSA. *Faculty research:* Liberal arts-based business programs, experiential learning, organizational process/politics, gender differences, social equity. *Unit head:* Dr. Anne McCarthy, Dean, 651-523-2284, Fax: 651-523-3098, E-mail: amccarthy02@hamline.edu. *Application contact:* Shawn Skoog, Director of Graduate Recruitment and Admission, 651-523-2900, Fax: 651-523-3058, E-mail: sskoog03@hamline.edu.
Website: http://www.hamline.edu/business

Harrisburg University of Science and Technology, Program in Project Management, Harrisburg, PA 17101. Offers construction services (MS); governmental services (MS); information technology (MS). Part-time and evening/weekend programs available. *Entrance requirements:* For master's, BS, BBA. Additional exam requirements/recommendations for international students: Required—TOEFL (minimum score 520 paper-based; 80 iBT). Electronic applications accepted.

Harvard University, John F. Kennedy School of Government, Master in Public Administration/International Development Program, Cambridge, MA 02138. Offers MPAID. *Students:* 137 full-time (65 women); includes 15 minority (1 Black or African American, non-Hispanic/Latino; 8 Asian, non-Hispanic/Latino; 3 Hispanic/Latino; 3 Two or more races, non-Hispanic/Latino), 109 international. Average age 29. 278 applicants, 36% accepted, 65 enrolled. In 2014, 58 master's awarded. *Entrance requirements:* For master's, GMAT or GRE General Test (for joint Business School applicants), one course each in microeconomics and macroeconomics; two college-level calculus courses (one must contain multivariable calculus); bachelor's degree; 2-3 years of professional experience in development (strongly encouraged). Additional exam requirements/recommendations for international students: Required—TOEFL (minimum score 600 paper-based; 100 iBT). *Application deadline:* For fall admission, 12/1 for domestic students. Application fee: $100. Electronic applications accepted. *Financial support:* Fellowships, research assistantships, teaching assistantships, career-related internships or fieldwork, Federal Work-Study, institutionally sponsored loans, scholarships/grants, health care benefits, and unspecified assistantships available. Financial award application deadline: 2/6; financial award applicants required to submit CSS PROFILE or FAFSA. *Unit head:* Carol Finney, Director, 617-495-7799, E-mail: carol_finney@harvard.edu. *Application contact:* 617-495-2133, E-mail: mpaid_program@hks.harvard.edu.
Website: http://www.hks.harvard.edu/degrees/masters/mpa-id

Harvard University, John F. Kennedy School of Government, Mid-Career Program in Public Administration, Cambridge, MA 02138. Offers MPA. *Students:* 216 full-time (89 women), 5 part-time (1 woman); includes 42 minority (10 Black or African American, non-Hispanic/Latino; 8 Asian, non-Hispanic/Latino; 13 Hispanic/Latino; 11 Two or more races, non-Hispanic/Latino), 113 international. Average age 38. 760 applicants, 46% accepted, 217 enrolled. In 2014, 174 master's awarded. *Entrance requirements:* For master's, GMAT or GRE General Test, minimum 7 years of professional experience. Additional exam requirements/recommendations for international students: Required—TOEFL (minimum score 600 paper-based; 100 iBT), TWE. *Application deadline:* For fall admission, 12/1 for domestic students. Applications are processed on a rolling basis. Application fee: $100. Electronic applications accepted. *Expenses:* Expenses: Contact institution. *Financial support:* Fellowships, Federal Work-Study, institutionally sponsored loans, scholarships/grants, health care benefits, and unspecified assistantships available. Financial award application deadline: 3/26; financial award applicants required to submit CSS PROFILE or FAFSA. *Unit head:* Amy Davies, Director, 617-496-1100, E-mail: amy_davies@harvard.edu. *Application contact:* 617-495-1155, E-mail: admissions@hks.harvard.edu.
Website: http://www.hks.harvard.edu/

Harvard University, John F. Kennedy School of Government, Program in Public Administration, Cambridge, MA 02138. Offers MPA. *Students:* 147 full-time (53 women), 3 part-time (2 women); includes 31 minority (4 Black or African American, non-Hispanic/Latino; 14 Asian, non-Hispanic/Latino; 4 Hispanic/Latino; 9 Two or more races, non-Hispanic/Latino), 80 international. Average age 30. 172 applicants, 55% accepted, 72 enrolled. In 2014, 99 master's awarded. *Entrance requirements:* For master's, GMAT or GRE General Test, minimum of 3 years of work experience. Additional exam requirements/recommendations for international students: Required—TOEFL (minimum score 600 paper-based; 100 iBT), TWE. *Application deadline:* For fall admission, 12/1 for domestic students. Application fee: $100. Electronic applications accepted. *Financial support:* Fellowships, research assistantships, teaching assistantships, career-related internships or fieldwork, Federal Work-Study, institutionally sponsored loans, scholarships/grants, health care benefits, and unspecified assistantships available. Financial award application deadline: 2/6; financial award applicants required to submit CSS PROFILE or FAFSA. *Unit head:* Amy Davies, Director, 617-496-1100, E-mail: amy_davies@harvard.edu. *Application contact:* 617-495-1155.
Website: http://www.hks.harvard.edu/

Hilbert College, Program in Public Administration, Hamburg, NY 14075-1597. Offers MPA. Evening/weekend programs available. *Faculty:* 3 full-time (1 woman), 12 part-time/adjunct (3 women). *Students:* 19 full-time (11 women), 6 part-time (4 women); includes 6 minority (4 Black or African American, non-Hispanic/Latino; 2 Two or more races, non-Hispanic/Latino), 1 international. Average age 35. 19 applicants, 42% accepted, 7 enrolled. In 2014, 12 master's awarded. *Degree requirements:* For master's, final capstone project. *Entrance requirements:* For master's, admissions statement/essay, official transcripts from all prior colleges, two letters of recommendation, current resume, relevant work experience, baccalaureate degree from accredited college or university with minimum cumulative GPA of 3.0, personal interview. Additional exam requirements/recommendations for international students: Recommended—TOEFL. *Application deadline:* Applications are processed on a rolling basis. Application fee: $20. Electronic applications accepted. Application fee is waived when completed online. *Expenses:* Expenses: Contact institution. *Financial support:* In 2014–15, 6 students received support. Scholarships/grants available. Financial award application deadline: 7/1; financial award applicants required to submit FAFSA. *Unit head:* Dr. Walter Iwanenko, Dean of Graduate Studies/Professor of Public Administration, 716-649-7900 Ext. 331, E-mail: wiwanenko@hilbert.edu. *Application contact:* Kim Chiarmonte, Director, Center for Adult and Graduate Studies, 716-926-8948, Fax: 716-649-0702, E-mail: kchiarmonte@hilbert.edu.
Website: http://www.hilbert.edu/grad/mpa

Hood College, Graduate School, Department of Economics and Business Administration, Frederick, MD 21701-8575. Offers accounting (MBA); administration and management (MBA); finance (MBA); human resource management (MBA); information systems (MBA); marketing (MBA); public management (MBA). *Accreditation:* ACBSP. Part-time and evening/weekend programs available. *Degree requirements:* For master's, capstone/final research project. *Entrance requirements:* For master's, minimum GPA of 2.75, resume, letters of recommendation. Additional exam

requirements/recommendations for international students: Required—TOEFL (minimum score 575 paper-based; 89 iBT), IELTS (minimum score 6.5). Electronic applications accepted. Application fee is waived when completed online. *Faculty research:* Corporate strategy and sustainable competitive advantages, business ethics, entrepreneurship, investments management, economic development.

Howard University, Graduate School, Department of Political Science, Program in Public Administration, Washington, DC 20059-0002. Offers MAPA. Part-time programs available. *Degree requirements:* For master's, comprehensive exam. *Entrance requirements:* For master's, GRE General Test, minimum GPA of 3.0.

Idaho State University, Office of Graduate Studies, College of Arts and Letters, Department of Political Science, Program in Public Administration, Pocatello, ID 83209-8073. Offers MPA. Part-time programs available. *Degree requirements:* For master's, comprehensive exam, thesis optional, public service internship. *Entrance requirements:* For master's, GRE General Test, course work in humanities and social sciences, 3 letters of recommendation. Additional exam requirements/recommendations for international students: Required—TOEFL (minimum score 550 paper-based; 80 iBT). Electronic applications accepted. *Faculty research:* Constitutional law, policy theory, public administration, international affairs.

Illinois Institute of Technology, Stuart School of Business, Program in Public Administration, Chicago, IL 60661. Offers MPA, JD/MPA, MBA/MPA. Part-time and evening/weekend programs available. *Faculty:* 36 full-time (10 women), 12 part-time/adjunct (2 women). *Students:* 42 full-time (27 women), 24 part-time (15 women); includes 6 minority (3 Black or African American, non-Hispanic/Latino; 3 Hispanic/Latino), 38 international. Average age 29. 81 applicants, 65% accepted, 22 enrolled. In 2014, 90 master's awarded. *Entrance requirements:* For master's, minimum cumulative undergraduate GPA: 3.0/4.0. Additional exam requirements/recommendations for international students: Required—TOEFL (minimum score 575 paper-based; 90 iBT); Recommended—IELTS (minimum score 7). *Application deadline:* For fall admission, 8/1 for domestic students, 5/1 for international students; for spring admission, 12/15 for domestic students, 10/15 for international students. Applications are processed on a rolling basis. Application fee: $75. Electronic applications accepted. *Expenses: Tuition:* Full-time $22,500; part-time $1250 per credit hour. *Required fees:* $30 per course. $260 per semester. One-time fee: $235. Tuition and fees vary according to course load and program. *Financial support:* Fellowships with partial tuition reimbursements, Federal Work-Study, institutionally sponsored loans, scholarships/grants, and health care benefits available. Support available to part-time students. Financial award applicants required to submit FAFSA. *Faculty research:* Comparative public administration and policy, migration and ethnic politics, social dimension and impact of science and technology, urban politics, urban ethnography. *Unit head:* Dr. Roland Calia, Program Director, 312-906-6505, E-mail: rcalia@stuart.iit.edu. *Application contact:* Rishab Malhotra, Director, Graduate Admission, 866-472-3448, Fax: 312-567-3138, E-mail: inquiry.grad@iit.edu.

Indiana State University, College of Graduate and Professional Studies, College of Arts and Sciences, Department of Political Science, Terre Haute, IN 47809. Offers political science (MA, MS); public administration (MPA). *Degree requirements:* For master's, thesis (for some programs). *Entrance requirements:* For master's, GRE or minimum undergraduate GPA of 2.75, 18 semester hours of course work in political science. Additional exam requirements/recommendations for international students: Required—TOEFL (minimum score 550 paper-based). Electronic applications accepted.

Indiana University Bloomington, School of Public and Environmental Affairs, Public Affairs Programs, Bloomington, IN 47405. Offers economic development (MPA); energy (MPA); environmental policy (PhD); environmental policy and natural resource management (MPA); information systems (MPA); international development (MPA); local government management (MPA); nonprofit management (MPA, Certificate); policy analysis (MPA); public budgeting and financial management (Certificate); public finance (PhD); public financial administration (MPA); public management (MPA, PhD, Certificate); public policy analysis (PhD); social entrepreneurship (Certificate); specialized public affairs (MPA); sustainability and sustainable development (MPA); JD/MPA; MPA/MA; MPA/MIS; MPA/MLS; MSES/MPA. *Accreditation:* NASPAA (one or more programs are accredited). Part-time programs available. *Degree requirements:* For master's, capstone, internship; for doctorate, comprehensive exam, thesis/dissertation. *Entrance requirements:* For master's, GRE General Test or GMAT, official transcripts, 3 letters of recommendation, resume, personal statement; for doctorate, GRE General Test, official transcripts, 3 letters of recommendation, statement of purpose. Additional exam requirements/recommendations for international students: Required—TOEFL (minimum score 600 paper-based; 96 iBT); Recommended—IELTS (minimum score 7). Electronic applications accepted. *Faculty research:* International development, environmental policy and resource management, policy analysis, public finance, public management, urban management, nonprofit management, energy policy, social policy, public finance.

Indiana University Kokomo, Department of Public Administration and Health Management, Kokomo, IN 46904-9003. Offers MPM, Graduate Certificate. *Students:* 13 full-time (12 women), 12 part-time (8 women); includes 4 minority (3 Black or African American, non-Hispanic/Latino; 1 Two or more races, non-Hispanic/Latino), 1 international. 10 applicants, 100% accepted, 9 enrolled. In 2014, 12 master's, 2 other advanced degrees awarded. *Unit head:* Alan Krabbenhoft, Dean, 765-455-9275, E-mail: agkrabbe@iuk.edu. *Application contact:* Admissions Office, 765-455-9357.
Website: http://www.iuk.edu/public-administration-and-health-management/index.php

Indiana University Northwest, School of Public and Environmental Affairs, Gary, IN 46408-1197. Offers criminal justice (MPA); environmental affairs (Graduate Certificate); health services (MPA); nonprofit management (Certificate); public management (MPA). *Accreditation:* NASPAA (one or more programs are accredited). Part-time programs available. *Faculty:* 5 full-time (3 women). *Students:* 12 full-time (7 women), 39 part-time (23 women); includes 37 minority (26 Black or African American, non-Hispanic/Latino; 1 Asian, non-Hispanic/Latino; 9 Hispanic/Latino; 1 Two or more races, non-Hispanic/Latino). Average age 38. 30 applicants, 93% accepted, 25 enrolled. In 2014, 29 master's, 15 other advanced degrees awarded. *Entrance requirements:* For master's, GRE General Test or GMAT, letters of recommendation. *Application deadline:* For fall admission, 8/15 priority date for domestic students. Applications are processed on a rolling basis. *Financial support:* Career-related internships or fieldwork, Federal Work-Study, and tuition waivers (partial) available. Support available to part-time students. Financial award application deadline: 3/1. *Faculty research:* Employment in income security policies, evidence in criminal justice, equal employment law, social welfare policy and welfare reform, public finance in developing countries. *Unit head:* Dr. Barbara Peat, Department Chair, 219-981-5645, E-mail: bpeat@iun.edu. *Application contact:* Susan Zinner, 219-980-6836, E-mail: speanw@iun.edu.
Website: http://www.iun.edu/spea/index.htm

Indiana University–Purdue University Indianapolis, School of Public and Environmental Affairs, Indianapolis, IN 46202. Offers criminal justice and public safety (MS); homeland security and emergency management (Graduate Certificate); library management (Graduate Certificate); nonprofit management (Graduate Certificate); public affairs (MPA); public management (Graduate Certificate); social

entrepreneurship: nonprofit and public benefit organizations (Graduate Certificate); JD/MPA; MLS/NMC; MLS/PMC; MPA/MA. *Accreditation:* CAHME (one or more programs are accredited); NASPAA. Part-time and evening/weekend programs available. Postbaccalaureate distance learning degree programs offered (no on-campus study). *Entrance requirements:* For master's, GRE General Test, GMAT or LSAT, minimum GPA of 3.0 (preferred). Additional exam requirements/recommendations for international students: Required—TOEFL (minimum score 93 iBT), IELTS (minimum score 6.5). Electronic applications accepted. *Faculty research:* Nonprofit and public management, public policy, urban policy, sustainability policy, disaster preparedness and recovery, vehicular safety, homicide, offender rehabilitation and re-entry.

Institute of Public Administration, Programs in Public Administration, Dublin, Ireland. Offers healthcare management (MA); local government management (MA); public management (MA, Diploma).

Instituto Tecnológico y de Estudios Superiores de Monterrey, Campus Ciudad Juárez, Program in Applied Public Management, Ciudad Juárez, Mexico. Offers MPM.

Iowa State University of Science and Technology, Department of Political Science, Ames, IA 50011. Offers political science (MA); public administration (MPA); JD/MA. JD/MA offered jointly with Drake University. *Degree requirements:* For master's, thesis (for some programs). *Entrance requirements:* For master's, GRE General Test, GMAT or LSAT. Additional exam requirements/recommendations for international students: Required—TOEFL (minimum score 570 paper-based; 80 iBT), IELTS (minimum score 6.5). Electronic applications accepted.

Jackson State University, Graduate School, College of Public Service, Department of Public Policy and Administration, Jackson, MS 39217. Offers MPPA, PhD. *Accreditation:* NASPAA (one or more programs are accredited). Evening/weekend programs available. *Degree requirements:* For master's, comprehensive exam, thesis optional; for doctorate, comprehensive exam, thesis/dissertation. *Entrance requirements:* For master's, GRE General Test; for doctorate, GRE, GMAT, MAT. Additional exam requirements/recommendations for international students: Required—TOEFL (minimum score 520 paper-based; 67 iBT).

James Madison University, The Graduate School, College of Arts and Letters, Department of Political Science, Program in Public Administration, Harrisonburg, VA 22807. Offers public administration (MPA), including international stabilization and recovery, management in international non-governmental organizations, nonprofit management, public and nonprofit management, public management. Public and Nonprofit Management program offered in Roanoke. *Accreditation:* NASPAA. Part-time programs available. *Students:* 18 full-time (10 women), 19 part-time (10 women); includes 6 minority (2 Black or African American, non-Hispanic/Latino; 2 Hispanic/Latino; 2 Two or more races, non-Hispanic/Latino), 1 international. Average age 28. 27 applicants, 89% accepted, 12 enrolled. In 2014, 25 master's awarded. *Degree requirements:* For master's, comprehensive exam. *Application deadline:* For fall admission, 5/1 for domestic students; for spring admission, 9/1 for domestic students. *Application fee:* $55. Electronic applications accepted. *Expenses:* Tuition, state resident: full-time $7812; part-time $434 per credit hour. Tuition, nonresident: full-time $20,430; part-time $1135 per credit hour. *Financial support:* In 2014–15, 21 students received support. Federal Work-Study and 21 assistantships (averaging $7086) available. Financial award application deadline: 3/1; financial award applicants required to submit FAFSA. *Unit head:* Dr. Charles Blake, Department Head, 540-568-6149, E-mail: blakech@jmu.edu. *Application contact:* Lynette D. Michael, Director of Graduate Admissions and Student Records, 540-568-6131 Ext. 6131, Fax: 540-568-7860, E-mail: michaeld@jmu.edu.
Website: http://www.jmu.edu/mpa

John Jay College of Criminal Justice of the City University of New York, Graduate Studies, Program in Public Administration, New York, NY 10019-1093. Offers MPA. *Accreditation:* NASPAA. Part-time and evening/weekend programs available. *Degree requirements:* For master's, thesis or alternative. *Entrance requirements:* For master's, minimum B average. Additional exam requirements/recommendations for international students: Required—TOEFL (minimum score 500 paper-based).

Johns Hopkins University, Zanvyl Krieger School of Arts and Sciences, Advanced Academic Programs, Program in Government, Washington, DC 20036. Offers global security studies (MA); government (MA); national securities study (Certificate); nonprofit management (Certificate); public management (MA); research administration (MS); MA/MBA. Part-time and evening/weekend programs available. Postbaccalaureate distance learning degree programs offered (minimal on-campus study). *Degree requirements:* For master's, thesis. *Entrance requirements:* For master's, minimum GPA of 3.0. Additional exam requirements/recommendations for international students: Required—TOEFL (minimum score 100 iBT). Electronic applications accepted.

Kansas State University, Graduate School, College of Arts and Sciences, Department of Political Science, Manhattan, KS 66506. Offers political science (MA), including international service, political science; public administration (MPA). Part-time programs available. *Faculty:* 16 full-time (4 women), 1 (woman) part-time/adjunct. *Students:* 24 full-time (15 women), 14 part-time (6 women); includes 7 minority (3 Black or African American, non-Hispanic/Latino; 1 Asian, non-Hispanic/Latino; 3 Hispanic/Latino), 4 international. Average age 29. 25 applicants, 68% accepted, 11 enrolled. In 2014, 20 master's awarded. *Degree requirements:* For master's, thesis or alternative. *Entrance requirements:* For master's, GRE (recommended), minimum GPA of 3.0. Additional exam requirements/recommendations for international students: Required—TOEFL (minimum score 550 paper-based). *Application deadline:* For fall admission, 2/1 priority date for domestic and international students; for spring admission, 8/1 priority date for domestic and international students. Applications are processed on a rolling basis. *Application fee:* $50 ($75 for international students). Electronic applications accepted. *Financial support:* In 2014–15, 10 teaching assistantships with tuition reimbursements (averaging $9,286 per year) were awarded; fellowships, research assistantships, career-related internships or fieldwork, Federal Work-Study, institutionally sponsored loans, and scholarships/grants also available. Support available to part-time students. Financial award application deadline: 3/1; financial award applicants required to submit FAFSA. *Faculty research:* Armed conflict, civil military relations, comparative public administration and policy, electoral competition, legislative studies. *Unit head:* Dr. Jeff Pickering, Head, 785-532-0454, Fax: 785-532-2339, E-mail: jjp@ksu.edu. *Application contact:* Dr. James Franke, Director, 785-532-0451, Fax: 785-532-2339, E-mail: jfranke@ksu.edu.
Website: http://www.k-state.edu/polsci/

Kean University, College of Business and Public Management, Program in Public Administration, Union, NJ 07083. Offers environmental management (MPA); health services administration (MPA); non-profit management (MPA); public administration (MPA). *Accreditation:* NASPAA. Part-time programs available. *Faculty:* 14 full-time (4 women). *Students:* 65 full-time (38 women), 80 part-time (48 women); includes 95 minority (67 Black or African American, non-Hispanic/Latino; 5 Asian, non-Hispanic/Latino; 21 Hispanic/Latino; 2 Two or more races, non-Hispanic/Latino), 3 international. Average age 32. 53 applicants, 85% accepted, 32 enrolled. In 2014, 54 master's awarded. *Degree requirements:* For master's, thesis, internship, research seminar. *Entrance requirements:* For master's, minimum cumulative GPA of 3.0, official

transcripts from all institutions attended, two letters of recommendation, personal statement, writing sample, professional resume/curriculum vitae. Additional exam requirements/recommendations for international students: Required—TOEFL (minimum score 550 paper-based; 79 iBT). *Application deadline:* For fall admission, 6/1 for domestic and international students; for spring admission, 12/1 for domestic and international students. Applications are processed on a rolling basis. *Application fee:* $75 ($150 for international students). Electronic applications accepted. *Expenses:* Tuition, state resident: full-time $12,461; part-time $607 per credit. Tuition, nonresident: full-time $16,889; part-time $744 per credit. *Required fees:* $3141; $143 per credit. Tuition and fees vary according to course load, degree level and program. *Financial support:* In 2014–15, 10 research assistantships with full tuition reimbursements (averaging $3,742 per year) were awarded; scholarships/grants and unspecified assistantships also available. Financial award applicants required to submit FAFSA. *Unit head:* Dr. Patricia Moore, Program Coordinator, 908-737-4314, E-mail: pmoore@kean.edu. *Application contact:* Reenat Hasan, Admissions Counselor, 908-737-7134, Fax: 908-737-7135, E-mail: hasanr@kean.edu.
Website: http://grad.kean.edu/masters-programs/public-administration

Kennesaw State University, College of Humanities and Social Sciences, Program in Public Administration, Kennesaw, GA 30144. Offers MPA. *Accreditation:* NASPAA. Part-time and evening/weekend programs available. *Students:* 31 full-time (21 women), 52 part-time (32 women); includes 40 minority (36 Black or African American, non-Hispanic/Latino; 1 Asian, non-Hispanic/Latino; 3 Hispanic/Latino), 11 international. Average age 30. 44 applicants, 75% accepted, 26 enrolled. In 2014, 41 master's awarded. *Degree requirements:* For master's, thesis optional. *Entrance requirements:* For master's, GRE General Test, minimum GPA of 2.75. Additional exam requirements/recommendations for international students: Required—TOEFL (minimum score 550 paper-based; 80 iBT), IELTS (minimum score 6.5). *Application deadline:* For fall admission, 6/1 for domestic and international students; for winter admission, 12/1 for domestic and international students; for spring admission, 11/1 for domestic and international students; for summer admission, 4/1 for domestic and international students. Applications are processed on a rolling basis. *Application fee:* $60. Electronic applications accepted. *Expenses:* Tuition, state resident: part-time $275 per semester hour. Tuition, nonresident: part-time $990 per semester hour. *Financial support:* In 2014–15, 2 research assistantships with full tuition reimbursements (averaging $8,000 per year) were awarded; Federal Work-Study and unspecified assistantships also available. Support available to part-time students. Financial award application deadline: 4/1; financial award applicants required to submit FAFSA. *Unit head:* Dr. David Shock, Director, 470-578-6227, E-mail: dsock@kennesaw.edu. *Application contact:* Maureen Wilson, Admissions Counselor, 470-578-7869, Fax: 470-578-9172, E-mail: ksugrad@kennesaw.edu.
Website: http://www.kennesaw.edu/

Kent State University, College of Arts and Sciences, Department of Political Science, Kent, OH 44242-0001. Offers public administration (MPA). Part-time and evening/weekend programs available. Postbaccalaureate distance learning degree programs offered. *Faculty:* 20 full-time (5 women). *Students:* 45 full-time (19 women), 43 part-time (23 women); includes 8 minority (1 Black or African American, non-Hispanic/Latino; 1 Asian, non-Hispanic/Latino; 2 Hispanic/Latino; 4 Two or more races, non-Hispanic/Latino), 11 international. Average age 33. 107 applicants, 50% accepted, 38 enrolled. In 2014, 16 master's, 4 doctorates awarded. *Degree requirements:* For master's, thesis optional; for doctorate, 2 foreign languages, thesis/dissertation. *Entrance requirements:* For master's, GRE General Test, minimum GPA of 3.0, transcript, resume, statement of purpose, 3 letters of recommendation; for doctorate, GRE General Test, minimum GPA of 3.0, transcript, statement of purpose/intent, writing sample, 3 letters of recommendation. Additional exam requirements/recommendations for international students: Required—TOEFL (minimum score: paper-based 525, iBT 71), Michigan English Language Assessment Battery (minimum score of 75), IELTS (minimum score of 6.0), PTE Academic (minimum score of 48), or completion of ELS level 112 Intensive Program. *Application deadline:* For fall admission, 7/31 for domestic students; for spring admission, 11/15 for domestic students; for summer admission, 3/31 for domestic students. *Application fee:* $45 ($70 for international students). Electronic applications accepted. *Expenses:* Tuition, state resident: full-time $8730; part-time $485 per credit hour. Tuition, nonresident: full-time $14,886; part-time $827 per credit hour. Tuition and fees vary according to campus/location and program. *Financial support:* Research assistantships with full tuition reimbursements, teaching assistantships with full tuition reimbursements, career-related internships or fieldwork, Federal Work-Study, and unspecified assistantships available. Financial award application deadline: 2/1. *Unit head:* Dr. Andrew Barnes, Associate Professor and Chair, 330-672-2060, E-mail: abarnes3@kent.edu. *Application contact:* Dr. Michael Ensley, Graduate Coordinator, 330-672-2060, E-mail: polisci@kent.edu.
Website: http://www.kent.edu/stark/political-science

Kentucky State University, College of Professional Studies, Frankfort, KY 40601. Offers nursing (DNP); public administration (MPA), including human resource management, international development, management information systems, nonprofit management; special education (MA). Part-time and evening/weekend programs available. Postbaccalaureate distance learning degree programs offered (minimal on-campus study). *Faculty:* 10 full-time (5 women). *Students:* 20 full-time (16 women), 50 part-time (33 women); includes 45 minority (44 Black or African American, non-Hispanic/Latino; 1 Two or more races, non-Hispanic/Latino). Average age 34. 50 applicants, 82% accepted, 24 enrolled. In 2014, 24 master's awarded. *Degree requirements:* For master's, comprehensive exam, thesis optional; for doctorate, comprehensive exam. *Entrance requirements:* For master's, GMAT, GRE; for doctorate, RN license. Additional exam requirements/recommendations for international students: Required—TOEFL (minimum score 525 paper-based). *Application deadline:* Applications are processed on a rolling basis. *Application fee:* $30 ($100 for international students). Electronic applications accepted. *Expenses:* Tuition, state resident: full-time $7164; part-time $398 per credit hour. Tuition, nonresident: full-time $10,782; part-time $599 per credit hour. Tuition and fees vary according to course load. *Financial support:* In 2014–15, 4 students received support. Scholarships/grants and tuition waivers (partial) available. Financial award application deadline: 4/15; financial award applicants required to submit FAFSA. *Unit head:* Dr. Lorna Shaw-Berbick, Dean, 502-597-6443. *Application contact:* Dr. James Obielodan, Director of Graduate Studies, 502-597-4723, E-mail: james.obielodan@kysu.edu.
Website: http://kysu.edu/academics/college-of-professional-studies/

Kutztown University of Pennsylvania, College of Liberal Arts and Sciences, Program in Public Administration, Kutztown, PA 19530-0730. Offers MPA. Part-time and evening/weekend programs available. *Faculty:* 4 full-time (1 woman). *Students:* 8 full-time (6 women), 18 part-time (11 women); includes 2 minority (both Black or African American, non-Hispanic/Latino), 1 international. Average age 31. 10 applicants, 60% accepted, 4 enrolled. In 2014, 15 master's awarded. *Degree requirements:* For master's, comprehensive exam, thesis optional. *Entrance requirements:* For master's, GRE General Test. Additional exam requirements/recommendations for international students: Required—TOEFL (minimum score 550 paper-based; 79 iBT). *Application deadline:* For fall admission, 8/1 priority date for domestic and international students; for spring admission, 12/1 priority date for domestic and international students. Applications are processed on a rolling basis. *Application fee:* $35. Electronic applications accepted.

Expenses: Tuition, area resident: Part-time $454 per credit. Tuition, state resident: part-time $454 per credit. Tuition, nonresident: part-time $681 per credit. *Required fees:* $85 per credit. *Financial support:* Career-related internships or fieldwork, Federal Work-Study, scholarships/grants, and unspecified assistantships available. Financial award application deadline: 3/1; financial award applicants required to submit FAFSA. *Faculty research:* Structure of code enforcement offices in smaller developing communities. *Unit head:* Dr. Steve Lem, Chairperson, 610-683-4471, Fax: 610-683-4603, E-mail: lem@kutztown.edu. *Application contact:* Kelly Hish, Admissions Clerk, 610-683-4200, Fax: 610-683-1393, E-mail: graduate@kutztown.edu.

Lamar University, College of Graduate Studies, College of Arts and Sciences, Department of Political Science, Beaumont, TX 77710. Offers public administration (MPA). Part-time programs available. *Faculty:* 4 full-time (2 women). *Students:* 12 full-time (5 women), 9 part-time (6 women); includes 12 minority (8 Black or African American, non-Hispanic/Latino; 3 Hispanic/Latino; 1 Two or more races, non-Hispanic/Latino), 4 international. Average age 32. 7 applicants, 86% accepted, 3 enrolled. In 2014, 19 master's awarded. *Entrance requirements:* For master's, GRE General Test. Additional exam requirements/recommendations for international students: Required—TOEFL (minimum score 550 paper-based; 79 iBT), IELTS (minimum score 6.5). *Application deadline:* For fall admission, 8/10 for domestic students, 7/1 for international students; for spring admission, 1/5 for domestic students, 12/1 for international students. Applications are processed on a rolling basis. Application fee: $25 ($50 for international students). *Expenses:* Tuition, state resident: full-time $5724; part-time $1908 per semester. Tuition, nonresident: full-time $12,240; part-time $4080 per semester. *Required fees:* $1940; $318 per credit hour. *Financial support:* Fellowships, research assistantships, teaching assistantships, career-related internships or fieldwork, Federal Work-Study, and institutionally sponsored loans available. Financial award application deadline: 4/1. *Faculty research:* Political activities of administrators, administrative response to Hurricane Rita, budgeting, environmental politics, urban planning. *Unit head:* Dr. Terri Davis, Chair, 409-880-8285, Fax: 409-880-8710. *Application contact:* Melissa Gallien, Director, Admissions and Academic Services, 409-880-8888, Fax: 409-880-7419, E-mail: gradmissions@lamar.edu.
Website: http://artssciences.lamar.edu/political-science

Liberty University, Helms School of Government, Lynchburg, VA 24515. Offers criminal justice (MS); public policy (MA), including campaigns and elections, international affairs, Middle East affairs, public administration, public policy. Part-time programs available. Postbaccalaureate distance learning degree programs offered (no on-campus study). *Students:* 248 full-time (119 women), 522 part-time (209 women); includes 194 minority (157 Black or African American, non-Hispanic/Latino; 8 American Indian or Alaska Native, non-Hispanic/Latino; 7 Asian, non-Hispanic/Latino; 5 Hispanic/Latino; 1 Native Hawaiian or other Pacific Islander, non-Hispanic/Latino; 16 Two or more races, non-Hispanic/Latino), 14 international. Average age 34. 837 applicants, 55% accepted, 226 enrolled. In 2014, 65 degrees awarded. *Entrance requirements:* For master's, minimum undergraduate GPA of 3.0. Additional exam requirements/recommendations for international students: Required—TOEFL (minimum score 600 paper-based; 100 iBT). *Application deadline:* Applications are processed on a rolling basis. Application fee: $50. Electronic applications accepted. *Unit head:* Shawn D. Akers, Dean, 434-592-4986. *Application contact:* Jay Bridge, Director of Admissions, 800-424-9595, Fax: 800-628-7977, E-mail: gradadmissions@liberty.edu.

Liberty University, School of Business, Lynchburg, VA 24515. Offers accounting (MBA, MS, DBA); business administration (MBA); criminal justice (MBA); cyber security (MS); executive leadership (MA); healthcare (MBA); human resources (DBA); information systems (MS), including information assurance, technology management; international business (MBA, DBA); leadership (MBA, DBA); marketing (MBA, MS, DBA), including digital marketing and advertising (MS), project management (MS), public relations (MS), sports marketing and media (MS); project management (MBA, DBA); public administration (MBA); public relations (MBA). Part-time programs available. Postbaccalaureate distance learning degree programs offered (minimal on-campus study). *Students:* 1,520 full-time (813 women), 4,179 part-time (1,982 women); includes 1,402 minority (1,110 Black or African American, non-Hispanic/Latino; 30 American Indian or Alaska Native, non-Hispanic/Latino; 82 Asian, non-Hispanic/Latino; 59 Hispanic/Latino; 7 Native Hawaiian or other Pacific Islander, non-Hispanic/Latino; 114 Two or more races, non-Hispanic/Latino), 119 international. Average age 35. 5,645 applicants, 49% accepted, 1445 enrolled. In 2014, 1,474 master's, 63 other advanced degrees awarded. *Entrance requirements:* For master's, minimum undergraduate GPA of 3.0, 15 hours of upper-level business courses. Additional exam requirements/recommendations for international students: Required—TOEFL (minimum score 600 paper-based; 100 iBT). *Application deadline:* Applications are processed on a rolling basis. Application fee: $50. Electronic applications accepted. *Expenses:* Expenses: Contact institution. *Unit head:* Dr. Scott Hicks, Dean, 434-592-4808, Fax: 434-582-2366, E-mail: smhicks@liberty.edu. *Application contact:* Jay Bridge, Director of Graduate Admissions, 800-424-9595, Fax: 800-628-7977, E-mail: gradadmissions@liberty.edu.
Website: http://www.liberty.edu/academics/business/index.cfm?PID-149

Lincoln University, Graduate Studies, Jefferson City, MO 65101. Offers business administration (MBA), including accounting, entrepreneurship, management, public administration and policy; educational leadership (Ed S), including elementary leadership, secondary leadership, superintendency; guidance and counseling (M Ed), including community/agency counseling, elementary school, secondary school; history (MA); school administration and supervision (M Ed), including elementary school administration, secondary school administration, special education administration; school teaching (M Ed), including elementary school teaching, secondary school teaching; sociology (MA); sociology/criminal justice (MA). Part-time and evening/weekend programs available. Postbaccalaureate distance learning degree programs offered (minimal on-campus study). *Students:* 57 full-time (35 women), 83 part-time (50 women); includes 64 minority (47 Black or African American, non-Hispanic/Latino; 1 American Indian or Alaska Native, non-Hispanic/Latino; 14 Asian, non-Hispanic/Latino; 1 Hispanic/Latino; 1 Two or more races, non-Hispanic/Latino), 9 international. Average age 33. 60 applicants, 68% accepted, 31 enrolled. In 2014, 52 master's, 2 other advanced degrees awarded. *Degree requirements:* For master's and Ed S, comprehensive exam, thesis optional. *Entrance requirements:* For master's and Ed S, GRE, MAT or GMAT, minimum GPA of 2.75 in major, 2.5 overall; 3 letters of recommendation; minimum C average in English composition; personal statement of purpose. Additional exam requirements/recommendations for international students: Required—TOEFL (minimum score 500 paper-based; 61 iBT). *Application deadline:* For fall admission, 8/1 priority date for domestic and international students; for spring admission, 12/1 priority date for domestic and international students; for summer admission, 5/1 priority date for domestic and international students. Applications are processed on a rolling basis. Application fee: $30. *Expenses:* Tuition, state resident: full-time $6840; part-time $285 per credit hour. Tuition, nonresident: full-time $12,720; part-time $530 per credit hour. *Required fees:* $737; $737 per year. *Financial support:* In 2014–15, 1 fellowship with tuition reimbursement, 11 research assistantships with tuition reimbursements were awarded; Federal Work-Study and scholarships/grants also available. Support available to part-time students. Financial award application deadline: 3/1; financial award applicants required to submit FAFSA. *Unit head:* Dr. Linda S. Bickel, Dean, 573-681-5247, Fax: 573-681-5106, E-mail: gradschool@lincolnu.edu. *Application contact:* Irasema Steck, Administrative Assistant, 573-681-5247, Fax: 573-681-5106, E-mail: gradschool@lincolnu.edu.
Website: http://www.lincolnu.edu/web/graduate-studies/graduate-studies

Lindenwood University, Graduate Programs, School of Business and Entrepreneurship, St. Charles, MO 63301-1695. Offers accountancy (M Acc); accounting (MBA); business administration (MBA); entrepreneurial studies (MBA); finance (MBA, MS); human resource management (MBA); international business (MBA); management (MBA); marketing (MBA, MS); public management (MBA); sport management (MA); supply chain management (MBA). *Accreditation:* ACBSP. Part-time and evening/weekend programs available. Postbaccalaureate distance learning degree programs offered (no on-campus study). *Faculty:* 18 full-time (9 women), 41 part-time/adjunct (9 women). *Students:* 88 full-time (46 women), 338 part-time (158 women); includes 78 minority (50 Black or African American, non-Hispanic/Latino; 3 American Indian or Alaska Native, non-Hispanic/Latino; 3 Asian, non-Hispanic/Latino; 13 Hispanic/Latino; 9 Two or more races, non-Hispanic/Latino), 113 international. Average age 28. 242 applicants, 52% accepted, 147 enrolled. In 2014, 212 master's awarded. *Degree requirements:* For master's, comprehensive exam (for some programs), thesis (for some programs), minimum GPA of 3.0. *Entrance requirements:* For master's, interview, minimum GPA of 3.0, letter of recommendation. Additional exam requirements/recommendations for international students: Required—TOEFL (minimum score 550 paper-based; 80 iBT). *Application deadline:* For fall admission, 9/7 priority date for domestic and international students; for winter admission, 1/4 priority date for domestic and international students; for spring admission, 3/7 priority date for domestic and international students; for summer admission, 5/23 priority date for domestic and international students. Applications are processed on a rolling basis. Application fee: $30 ($100 for international students). Electronic applications accepted. *Expenses: Tuition:* Full-time $15,230; part-time $440 per credit hour. *Required fees:* $205 per semester. Tuition and fees vary according to course level, course load and degree level. *Financial support:* In 2014–15, 163 students received support. Career-related internships or fieldwork, Federal Work-Study, institutionally sponsored loans, scholarships/grants, tuition waivers (partial), and unspecified assistantships available. Financial award application deadline: 6/30; financial award applicants required to submit FAFSA. *Unit head:* Roger Ellis, Dean, 636-949-4839, E-mail: rellis@lindenwood.edu. *Application contact:* Tyler Kostich, Director of Evening and Graduate Admissions, 636-949-4138, Fax: 636-949-4109, E-mail: adultadmissions@lindenwood.edu.
Website: http://www.lindenwood.edu

Lindenwood University, Graduate Programs, School of Human Services, St. Charles, MO 63301-1695. Offers nonprofit administration (MA); public administration (MPA). Part-time programs available. Postbaccalaureate distance learning degree programs offered (no on-campus study). *Faculty:* 3 full-time (1 woman), 4 part-time/adjunct (3 women). *Students:* 7 full-time (5 women), 77 part-time (61 women); includes 51 minority (43 Black or African American, non-Hispanic/Latino; 1 American Indian or Alaska Native, non-Hispanic/Latino; 2 Hispanic/Latino; 5 Two or more races, non-Hispanic/Latino), 1 international. Average age 32. 56 applicants, 57% accepted, 23 enrolled. In 2014, 12 master's awarded. *Degree requirements:* For master's, minimum cumulative GPA of 3.0, directed internship, capstone project. *Entrance requirements:* Additional exam requirements/recommendations for international students: Required—TOEFL (minimum score 550 paper-based; 80 iBT). *Application deadline:* For fall admission, 8/24 priority date for domestic and international students; for spring admission, 1/25 priority date for domestic and international students. Applications are processed on a rolling basis. Application fee: $30 ($100 for international students). Electronic applications accepted. *Expenses: Tuition:* Full-time $15,230; part-time $440 per credit hour. *Required fees:* $205 per semester. Tuition and fees vary according to course level, course load and degree level. *Financial support:* In 2014–15, 48 students received support. Career-related internships or fieldwork, institutionally sponsored loans, scholarships/grants, tuition waivers, and unspecified assistantships available. Financial award application deadline: 6/30; financial award applicants required to submit FAFSA. *Unit head:* Dr. Carla Mueller, Dean, 636-949-4731, E-mail: cmueller@lindenwood.edu. *Application contact:* Tyler Kostich, Dean of Evening Admissions and Extension Campuses, 636-949-4138, Fax: 636-949-4109, E-mail: adultadmissions@lindenwood.edu.
Website: http://www.lindenwood.edu/humanServices/

Long Island University–LIU Brooklyn, School of Business, Public Administration and Information Sciences, Brooklyn, NY 11201-8423. Offers accounting (MBA); accounting (MS); computer science (MS); entrepreneurship (MBA); finance (MBA); health administration (MPA); human resources management (MS); international business (MBA); management (MBA); management information systems (MBA); marketing (MBA); public administration (MPA); taxation (MS). Part-time and evening/weekend programs available. *Faculty:* 16 full-time (7 women), 29 part-time/adjunct (6 women). *Students:* 230 full-time (155 women), 239 part-time (166 women); includes 321 minority (210 Black or African American, non-Hispanic/Latino; 2 American Indian or Alaska Native, non-Hispanic/Latino; 46 Asian, non-Hispanic/Latino; 56 Hispanic/Latino; 2 Native Hawaiian or other Pacific Islander, non-Hispanic/Latino; 5 Two or more races, non-Hispanic/Latino), 69 international. Average age 37. 481 applicants, 79% accepted, 153 enrolled. In 2014, 158 master's awarded. *Degree requirements:* For master's, thesis optional. *Entrance requirements:* For master's, GMAT or GRE General Test (Excluding MPA), 2 letters of recommendation, personal statement & resume. Additional exam requirements/recommendations for international students: Required—TOEFL (minimum score 550 paper-based; 79 iBT). *Application deadline:* For fall admission, 5/1 for international students; for spring admission, 11/1 for international students. Applications are processed on a rolling basis. Application fee: $30. Electronic applications accepted. *Expenses: Tuition:* Part-time $1132 per credit. *Required fees:* $434 per semester. *Financial support:* Scholarships/grants and unspecified assistantships available. Support available to part-time students. Financial award application deadline: 2/15; financial award applicants required to submit FAFSA. *Unit head:* Dr. Edward Rogoff, Dean, 718-488-1130. *Application contact:* Richard Sunday, Dean of Admissions, 718-488-1011, Fax: 718-780-6110, E-mail: bkln-admissions@liu.edu.
Website: http://www.liu.edu/

Long Island University–LIU Post, College of Liberal Arts and Sciences, Brookville, NY 11548-1300. Offers public administration (MPA). Part-time and evening/weekend programs available. Postbaccalaureate distance learning degree programs offered (minimal on-campus study). *Faculty:* 79 full-time (35 women), 40 part-time/adjunct (16 women). *Students:* 229 full-time (157 women), 212 part-time (143 women); includes 116 minority (49 Black or African American, non-Hispanic/Latino; 25 Asian, non-Hispanic/Latino; 35 Hispanic/Latino; 7 Two or more races, non-Hispanic/Latino), 38 international. Average age 31. 631 applicants, 54% accepted, 155 enrolled. In 2014, 70 master's, 15 doctorates, 19 other advanced degrees awarded. *Degree requirements:* For master's, comprehensive exam (for some programs), thesis (for some programs); for doctorate, comprehensive exam, thesis/dissertation, externship, internship. *Entrance requirements:* For doctorate, GRE General Test. Additional exam requirements/recommendations for international students: Required—TOEFL (minimum score 550 paper-based; 79 iBT), IELTS (minimum score 6.5). *Application deadline:* Applications are processed on a rolling basis. Application fee: $50. Electronic applications accepted. *Expenses:* Expenses: $22,110 tuition and fees (for full-time master's), $52,000 per year for the first 3 years (for full-time doctoral). *Financial support:* In 2014–15, 54 fellowships

(averaging $11,000 per year), 6 research assistantships with full and partial tuition reimbursements, 19 teaching assistantships with full and partial tuition reimbursements were awarded; Federal Work-Study, institutionally sponsored loans, and scholarships/grants also available. Support available to part-time students. Financial award application deadline: 5/15; financial award applicants required to submit CSS PROFILE or FAFSA. *Faculty research:* Biology, criminal justice, earth and environmental science, English, health care and public administration, history, mathematics, political science, psychology, Spanish. *Unit head:* Dr. Nicholas J. Ramer, Acting Dean, 516-299-2233, Fax: 516-299-4140, E-mail: nicholas.ramer@liu.edu. *Application contact:* Carol Zerah, Director of Graduate Admissions, 516-299-2900 Ext. 3952, Fax: 516-299-2137, E-mail: enroll@cwpost.liu.edu.
Website: http://liu.edu/CWPost/Academics/Schools/CLAS

Louisiana State University and Agricultural & Mechanical College, Graduate School, E. J. Ourso College of Business, Public Administration Institute, Baton Rouge, LA 70803. Offers MPA, JD/MPA. *Accreditation:* NASPAA. Part-time programs available. *Faculty:* 5 full-time (1 woman). *Students:* 44 full-time (24 women), 45 part-time (28 women); includes 27 minority (24 Black or African American, non-Hispanic/Latino; 3 Hispanic/Latino). Average age 30. 30 applicants, 87% accepted, 19 enrolled. In 2014, 41 master's awarded. *Degree requirements:* For master's, comprehensive exam. *Entrance requirements:* For master's, GRE General Test, minimum GPA of 3.0. Additional exam requirements/recommendations for international students: Required—TOEFL (minimum score 550 paper-based; 79 IBT), IELTS (minimum score 6.5), or PTE (minimum score 59). *Application deadline:* For fall admission, 1/1 priority date for domestic students, 5/15 for international students; for spring admission, 10/15 for domestic and international students. Applications are processed on a rolling basis. Application fee: $50 ($70 for international students). Electronic applications accepted. *Financial support:* In 2014–15, 72 students received support, including 6 research assistantships with full and partial tuition reimbursements available (averaging $11,500 per year), 6 teaching assistantships with partial tuition reimbursements available (averaging $13,457 per year); Federal Work-Study, scholarships/grants, health care benefits, and unspecified assistantships also available. Support available to part-time students. Financial award applicants required to submit FAFSA. *Faculty research:* Policy analysis, health care policy, financial and budget analysis. *Total annual research expenditures:* $86,566. *Unit head:* Dr. James A. Richardson, Director, 225-578-6745, Fax: 225-578-9078, E-mail: parich@lsu.edu.
Website: http://www.business.lsu.edu/pai

Louisiana State University and Agricultural & Mechanical College, Graduate School, Manship School of Mass Communication, Baton Rouge, LA 70803. Offers MMC, PhD, JD/MMC. *Accreditation:* ACEJMC. Part-time programs available. Postbaccalaureate distance learning degree programs offered (minimal on-campus study). *Faculty:* 24 full-time (12 women). *Students:* 62 full-time (42 women), 14 part-time (11 women); includes 20 minority (15 Black or African American, non-Hispanic/Latino; 1 Asian, non-Hispanic/Latino; 3 Hispanic/Latino; 1 Two or more races, non-Hispanic/Latino), 16 international. Average age 27. 62 applicants, 48% accepted, 22 enrolled. In 2014, 20 master's, 3 doctorates awarded. *Degree requirements:* For master's, thesis; for doctorate, thesis/dissertation. *Entrance requirements:* For master's, GRE General Test, minimum GPA of 3.0. Additional exam requirements/recommendations for international students: Required—TOEFL (minimum score 550 paper-based; 79 IBT), IELTS (minimum score 6.5), or PTE (minimum score 59). *Application deadline:* For fall admission, 1/1 priority date for domestic students, 5/15 for international students; for spring admission, 10/15 for domestic and international students; for summer admission, 5/15 for domestic and international students. Applications are processed on a rolling basis. Application fee: $50 ($70 for international students). Electronic applications accepted. *Financial support:* In 2014–15, 61 students received support, including 1 fellowship (averaging $33,839 per year), 31 research assistantships with full and partial tuition reimbursements available (averaging $15,839 per year), 14 teaching assistantships with full and partial tuition reimbursements available (averaging $15,557 per year); career-related internships or fieldwork, Federal Work-Study, institutionally sponsored loans, scholarships/grants, health care benefits, tuition waivers (full and partial), and unspecified assistantships also available. Support available to part-time students. Financial award application deadline: 3/1; financial award applicants required to submit FAFSA. *Faculty research:* Media effects, political communication, new media technologies, persuasive communication, journalism processes and practice. *Total annual research expenditures:* $82,923. *Unit head:* Dr. Jerry Ceppos, Dean, 225-578-3488, Fax: 225-578-2125, E-mail: jceppos@lsu.edu. *Application contact:* Dr. Amy L. Reynolds, Associate Dean of Graduate Studies and Research, 225-578-9294, Fax: 225-578-2125, E-mail: areynolds@lsu.edu.
Website: http://www.manship.lsu.edu/

Marist College, Graduate Programs, School of Management, Program in Public Administration, Poughkeepsie, NY 12601-1387. Offers MPA. Part-time and evening/weekend programs available. Postbaccalaureate distance learning degree programs offered (no on-campus study). *Entrance requirements:* For master's, GRE General Test, resume. Additional exam requirements/recommendations for international students: Required—TOEFL (minimum score 550 paper-based; 80 iBT); Recommended—IELTS (minimum score 6.5). Electronic applications accepted. *Faculty research:* Public policy analysis, health administration.

Marquette University, Graduate School, College of Professional Studies, Milwaukee, WI 53201-1881. Offers criminal justice administration (MLS, Certificate); dispute resolution (MDR, MLS); health care administration (MLS); leadership studies (Certificate); non-profit sector administration (MLS); public service (MAPS, MLS); sports leadership (MLS). Part-time and evening/weekend programs available. Postbaccalaureate distance learning degree programs offered (no on-campus study). *Degree requirements:* For master's, comprehensive exam (for some programs). *Entrance requirements:* For master's, GRE General Test (preferred), GMAT, or LSAT, official transcripts from all current and previous colleges/universities except Marquette, three letters of recommendation, statement of purpose. Additional exam requirements/recommendations for international students: Required—TOEFL. Electronic applications accepted.

Marshall University, Academic Affairs Division, College of Liberal Arts, Department of Political Science, Huntington, WV 25755. Offers MA, MPA. *Students:* 13 full-time (5 women), 6 part-time (5 women); includes 2 minority (both Hispanic/Latino), 1 international. Average age 28. In 2014, 5 master's awarded. *Degree requirements:* For master's, thesis optional. *Entrance requirements:* For master's, GRE General Test. Application fee: $40. *Unit head:* Dr. George Davis, Chair, 304-696-2766, Fax: 304-696-3245, E-mail: davg@marshall.edu. *Application contact:* Graduate Admissions, 304-746-1900, Fax: 304-746-1902, E-mail: services@marshall.edu.
Website: http://www.marshall.edu/polsci/

Marywood University, Academic Affairs, College of Health and Human Services, School of Social Work and Administrative Services, Program in Public Administration, Scranton, PA 18509-1598. Offers MPA. Part-time programs available. *Students:* 9 full-time (5 women), 3 part-time (all women); includes 2 minority (1 Black or African American, non-Hispanic/Latino; 1 Hispanic/Latino), 2 international. Average age 32. In 2014, 3 master's awarded. *Application deadline:* For fall admission, 4/1 for domestic students, 3/31 for international students; for spring admission, 11/1 for domestic students, 8/31 for international students. Applications are processed on a rolling basis. Application fee: $35. Electronic applications accepted. *Expenses: Tuition:* Part-time $775 per credit. *Required fees:* $688 per semester. Tuition and fees vary according to degree level and campus/location. *Financial support:* Application deadline: 6/30; applicants required to submit FAFSA. *Unit head:* Dr. Lloyd L. Lyter, Director, School of Social Work and Administrative Studies, 570-348-6282 Ext. 2388, E-mail: lyter@marywood.edu. *Application contact:* Tammy Manka, Assistant Director of Graduate Admissions, 570-348-6211 Ext. 2322, E-mail: tmanka@marywood.edu.
Website: http://www.marywood.edu/academics/gradcatalog/

McMaster University, School of Graduate Studies, Faculty of Social Sciences, Department of Political Science, Hamilton, ON L8S 4M2, Canada. Offers international relations (PhD); political science (MA); public and the global economy (MA); public policy (PhD); public policy and administration (MA). MA program in public policy and administration offered jointly with University of Guelph. Part-time programs available. *Degree requirements:* For master's, thesis or alternative. *Entrance requirements:* For master's, minimum B+ average. Additional exam requirements/recommendations for international students: Required—TOEFL (minimum score 580 paper-based). *Faculty research:* Organizational theory, internationalization of public policy, water resource policies, political interest intermediation, comparative politics.

Metropolitan College of New York, Program in Public Administration, New York, NY 10013. Offers MPA. Evening/weekend programs available. *Degree requirements:* For master's, thesis. *Entrance requirements:* For master's, appropriate work experience, interview, minimum GPA of 2.7, internship or job in administrative setting. Additional exam requirements/recommendations for international students: Required—TOEFL (minimum score 600 paper-based). Electronic applications accepted. *Expenses:* Contact institution. *Faculty research:* Transnational politics and culture, women and social policy, confidentiality in the human services, concepts of marginality, ethics in social policy.

Metropolitan State University, College of Management, St. Paul, MN 55106-5000. Offers business administration (MBA, DBA); database administration (Graduate Certificate); healthcare information technology management (Graduate Certificate); information assurance security (Graduate Certificate); management information systems (MMIS); MIS generalist (Graduate Certificate); MIS systems analysis and design (Graduate Certificate); project management (Graduate Certificate); public and nonprofit administration (MPNA). Part-time and evening/weekend programs available. *Degree requirements:* For master's, thesis optional, computer language (MMIS). *Entrance requirements:* For master's, GMAT (for MBA), resume. Additional exam requirements/recommendations for international students: Required—TOEFL (minimum score 550 paper-based). Electronic applications accepted. *Faculty research:* Yugoslav economic system, workers' cooperatives, participative management and job enrichment, global business systems.

Mid-America Christian University, Program in Public Administration, Oklahoma City, OK 73170-4504. Offers MA. *Entrance requirements:* For master's, bachelor's degree from a regionally accredited college or university, minimum overall cumulative GPA of 2.75 of bachelor course work. Additional exam requirements/recommendations for international students: Required—TOEFL (minimum score 550 paper-based).

Middlebury Institute of International Studies, Graduate School of International Policy and Management, Program in Public Administration, Monterey, CA 93940-2691. Offers MPA. *Degree requirements:* For master's, one foreign language. *Entrance requirements:* For master's, minimum GPA of 3.0, proficiency in a foreign language. Additional exam requirements/recommendations for international students: Required—TOEFL (minimum score 550 paper-based; 80 iBT). *Application deadline:* For fall admission, 3/15 priority date for domestic and international students; for spring admission, 10/1 priority date for domestic and international students. Applications are processed on a rolling basis. Application fee: $50. Electronic applications accepted. *Expenses: Tuition:* Full-time $36,020; part-time $1715 per credit. *Required fees:* $53 per semester. *Financial support:* Career-related internships or fieldwork, Federal Work-Study, institutionally sponsored loans, and scholarships/grants available. Support available to part-time students. Financial award application deadline: 3/15; financial award applicants required to submit FAFSA. *Unit head:* Beryl Levinger, Chair, 831-233-3340, Fax: 831-647-4199, E-mail: blevinger@miis.edu. *Application contact:* 831-647-4123, Fax: 831-647-6405, E-mail: admit@miis.edu.
Website: http://www.miis.edu/academics/programs/development-practice-policy/mpa

Minnesota State University Mankato, College of Graduate Studies, College of Social and Behavioral Sciences, Department of Government, Program in Public Administration, Mankato, MN 56001. Offers MPA. *Students:* 11 full-time (4 women), 30 part-time (9 women). *Degree requirements:* For master's, one foreign language, comprehensive exam, thesis or alternative. *Entrance requirements:* For master's, minimum GPA of 3.0 during previous 2 years. Additional exam requirements/recommendations for international students: Required—TOEFL. *Application deadline:* For fall admission, 3/1 priority date for domestic students. Applications are processed on a rolling basis. Application fee: $40. Electronic applications accepted. *Financial support:* Research assistantships with full tuition reimbursements, teaching assistantships with full tuition reimbursements, and unspecified assistantships available. Financial award application deadline: 3/15; financial award applicants required to submit FAFSA. *Unit head:* Dr. Scott Granberg-Rademacker, Graduate Coordinator, 507-389-6939. *Application contact:* 507-389-2321, E-mail: grad@mnsu.edu.

Mississippi State University, College of Arts and Sciences, Department of Political Science and Public Administration, Mississippi State, MS 39762. Offers political science (MA); public policy and administration (MPPA, PhD). *Accreditation:* NASPAA (one or more programs are accredited). Evening/weekend programs available. Postbaccalaureate distance learning degree programs offered (no on-campus study). *Faculty:* 11 full-time (2 women), 1 part-time/adjunct (0 women). *Students:* 38 full-time (20 women), 41 part-time (24 women); includes 31 minority (26 Black or African American, non-Hispanic/Latino; 1 American Indian or Alaska Native, non-Hispanic/Latino; 3 Hispanic/Latino; 1 Two or more races, non-Hispanic/Latino), 3 international. Average age 30. 32 applicants, 63% accepted, 14 enrolled. In 2014, 28 master's, 5 doctorates awarded. *Degree requirements:* For master's, thesis optional, comprehensive oral or written exam; for doctorate, thesis/dissertation, comprehensive oral and written exam. *Entrance requirements:* For master's, GRE, minimum GPA of 3.0 on the last two years of undergraduate courses or graduate work; for doctorate, GRE General Test, minimum graduate GPA of 3.35. Additional exam requirements/recommendations for international students: Required—TOEFL (minimum score 600 paper-based; 100 iBT); Recommended—IELTS (minimum score 7.5). *Application deadline:* For fall admission, 8/1 priority date for domestic students, 5/1 for international students; for spring admission, 12/1 priority date for domestic students, 9/1 for international students. Applications are processed on a rolling basis. Application fee: $60. Electronic applications accepted. *Expenses:* Tuition, state resident: full-time $7140; part-time $783 per credit hour. Tuition, nonresident: full-time $18,478; part-time $2043 per credit hour. *Financial support:* In 2014–15, 1 research assistantship with full tuition reimbursement (averaging $9,250 per year), 9 teaching assistantships with full tuition reimbursements (averaging $8,993 per year) were awarded; Federal Work-Study,

institutionally sponsored loans, scholarships/grants, and unspecified assistantships also available. Financial award application deadline: 4/1; financial award applicants required to submit FAFSA. *Faculty research:* American politics, international relations, state and local government, comparative government, public administration. *Total annual research expenditures:* $807,000. *Unit head:* Dr. K. C. Morrison, Department Head, 662-325-2711, Fax: 662-325-2716, E-mail: kcmorrison@ps.msstate.edu. *Application contact:* Dr. Christine Rush, Graduate Coordinator, 662-325-2711, Fax: 662-325-2716, E-mail: clr449@msstate.edu.
Website: http://www.pspa.msstate.edu/

Missouri State University, Graduate College, College of Humanities and Public Affairs, Department of Political Science, Program in Public Administration, Springfield, MO 65897. Offers MPA. *Accreditation:* NASPAA. Part-time programs available. *Students:* 17 full-time (6 women), 11 part-time (8 women); includes 2 minority (both Black or African American, non-Hispanic/Latino), 9 international. Average age 31. 12 applicants, 58% accepted, 5 enrolled. In 2014, 1 master's awarded. *Degree requirements:* For master's, comprehensive exam, thesis or alternative, internship. *Entrance requirements:* For master's, GRE, minimum GPA of 3.0. Additional exam requirements/recommendations for international students: Required—TOEFL (minimum score 550 paper-based; 79 iBT). *Application deadline:* For fall admission, 7/20 priority date for domestic students, 5/1 for international students; for spring admission, 12/20 priority date for domestic students, 9/1 for international students. Applications are processed on a rolling basis. Application fee: $35 ($50 for international students). Electronic applications accepted. *Expenses:* Tuition, state resident: full-time $2250; part-time $250 per credit hour. Tuition, nonresident: full-time $4509; part-time $501 per credit hour. Tuition and fees vary according to course level, course load and program. *Financial support:* Career-related internships or fieldwork, Federal Work-Study, institutionally sponsored loans, scholarships/grants, and unspecified assistantships available. Support available to part-time students. Financial award application deadline: 3/31; financial award applicants required to submit FAFSA. *Faculty research:* Public management, environmental policy, health care policy, law and religion. *Unit head:* Dr. Patrick Scott, Program Director, 417-836-5028, Fax: 417-836-6655, E-mail: pscott@missouristate.edu. *Application contact:* Misty Stewart, Coordinator of Graduate Recruitment, 417-836-6079, Fax: 417-836-6200, E-mail: mistystewart@missouristate.edu.
Website: http://polsci.missouristate.edu/mpa/

Missouri State University, Graduate College, Interdisciplinary Program in Administrative Studies, Springfield, MO 65897. Offers applied communication (MS); criminal justice (MS); environmental management (MS); homeland security (MS); sports management (MS). Part-time and evening/weekend programs available. Postbaccalaureate distance learning degree programs offered (no on-campus study). *Students:* 17 full-time (9 women), 64 part-time (29 women); includes 10 minority (4 Black or African American, non-Hispanic/Latino; 1 Asian, non-Hispanic/Latino; 2 Hispanic/Latino; 3 Two or more races, non-Hispanic/Latino), 3 international. Average age 33. 48 applicants, 73% accepted, 21 enrolled. In 2014, 16 master's awarded. *Degree requirements:* For master's, comprehensive exam, thesis or alternative. *Entrance requirements:* For master's, GRE, GMAT if GPA less than 3.0. Additional exam requirements/recommendations for international students: Required—TOEFL (minimum score 550 paper-based; 79 iBT). *Application deadline:* For fall admission, 7/20 priority date for domestic students; for spring admission, 12/20 priority date for domestic students. Applications are processed on a rolling basis. Application fee: $35 ($50 for international students). Electronic applications accepted. *Expenses:* Tuition, state resident: full-time $2250; part-time $250 per credit hour. Tuition, nonresident: full-time $4509; part-time $501 per credit hour. Tuition and fees vary according to course level, course load and program. *Financial support:* Career-related internships or fieldwork, Federal Work-Study, institutionally sponsored loans, scholarships/grants, and unspecified assistantships available. Support available to part-time students. Financial award application deadline: 3/31; financial award applicants required to submit FAFSA. *Unit head:* Dr. Gerald Masterson, Program Coordinator, 417-836-5251, Fax: 417-836-6888, E-mail: msas@missouristate.edu. *Application contact:* Misty Stewart, Coordinator of Graduate Recruitment, 417-836-6079, Fax: 417-836-6200, E-mail: mistystewart@missouristate.edu.
Website: http://msas.missouristate.edu

Montana State University, The Graduate School, College of Letters and Science, Department of Political Science, Bozeman, MT 59717. Offers public administration (MPA). Program offered jointly with The University of Montana. Part-time programs available. *Degree requirements:* For master's, comprehensive exam, thesis (for some programs). *Entrance requirements:* For master's, GRE General Test. Additional exam requirements/recommendations for international students: Required—TOEFL (minimum score 550 paper-based). Electronic applications accepted. *Faculty research:* National resource policy, political economy of agriculture, qualitative methods, organizational theory.

Montana State University Billings, College of Arts and Sciences, Program in Public Administration, Billings, MT 59101. Offers MPA. *Application deadline:* For fall admission, 7/15 for domestic students; for spring admission, 12/1 for domestic students. Application fee: $40. *Unit head:* Joy Honea, Chair, 406-657-2996, E-mail: jhonea@msbillings.edu. *Application contact:* David M. Sullivan, Graduate Studies Counselor, 406-657-2053, Fax: 406-657-2299, E-mail: dsullivan@msubillings.edu.

Morehead State University, Graduate Programs, Institute for Regional Analysis and Public Policy, Morehead, KY 40351. Offers public administration (MPA). *Accreditation:* NASPAA. *Entrance requirements:* For master's, GRE. Additional exam requirements/recommendations for international students: Required—TOEFL (minimum score 500 paper-based). Electronic applications accepted.

National University, Academic Affairs, School of Professional Studies, La Jolla, CA 92037-1011. Offers criminal justice (MCJ); digital cinema (MFA); digital journalism (MA); juvenile justice (MS); professional screen writing (MFA); public administration (MPA), including human resource management, organizational leadership, public finance. Part-time and evening/weekend programs available. Postbaccalaureate distance learning degree programs offered (no on-campus study). *Faculty:* 19 full-time (8 women), 28 part-time/adjunct (7 women). *Students:* 277 full-time (141 women), 140 part-time (80 women); includes 248 minority (102 Black or African American, non-Hispanic/Latino; 23 Asian, non-Hispanic/Latino; 102 Hispanic/Latino; 5 Native Hawaiian or other Pacific Islander, non-Hispanic/Latino; 16 Two or more races, non-Hispanic/Latino), 8 international. Average age 37. *Degree requirements:* For master's, thesis (for some programs). *Entrance requirements:* For master's, interview, minimum GPA of 2.5. Additional exam requirements/recommendations for international students: Required—TOEFL (minimum score 550 paper-based; 79 iBT), IELTS (minimum score 6). *Application deadline:* Applications are processed on a rolling basis. Application fee: $60 ($65 for international students). Electronic applications accepted. *Expenses:* Tuition: Full-time $14,184; part-time $1773 per course. *Financial support:* Career-related internships or fieldwork, institutionally sponsored loans, scholarships/grants, and tuition waivers (partial) available. Support available to part-time students. Financial award application deadline: 6/30; financial award applicants required to submit FAFSA. *Unit head:* School of Professional Studies, 800-628-8648, E-mail: sops@nu.edu. *Application contact:* Frank Rojas, Vice President for Enrollment Services, 800-628-8648, E-mail:

advisor@nu.edu.
Website: http://www.nu.edu/OurPrograms/School-of-Professional-Studies.html

New Charter University, College of Public Policy and Administration, Program in Public Administration, San Francisco, CA 94105. Offers MPA. Part-time and evening/weekend programs available. Postbaccalaureate distance learning degree programs offered (no on-campus study). *Entrance requirements:* For master's, course work in calculus, statistics. Additional exam requirements/recommendations for international students: Required—TOEFL (minimum score 550 paper-based). Electronic applications accepted.

New York University, Robert F. Wagner Graduate School of Public Service, Executive Master of Public Administration Program, New York, NY 10010. Offers global public policy and management (EMPA); MSW/EMPA. EMPA in global public policy and management offered jointly with University College London. *Accreditation:* AACSB. Part-time programs available. *Faculty:* 1 full-time (0 women), 4 part-time/adjunct (2 women). *Students:* 11 full-time (7 women), 70 part-time (49 women); includes 20 minority (8 Black or African American, non-Hispanic/Latino; 5 Asian, non-Hispanic/Latino; 6 Hispanic/Latino; 1 Two or more races, non-Hispanic/Latino), 7 international. Average age 38. 94 applicants, 74% accepted, 46 enrolled. In 2014, 45 master's awarded. *Entrance requirements:* Additional exam requirements/recommendations for international students: Required—TOEFL (minimum score 100 iBT), IELTS (minimum score 7.5), TWE. *Application deadline:* For fall admission, 5/1 for domestic and international students. Application fee: $85. Electronic applications accepted. *Expenses:* Expenses: Contact institution. *Financial support:* In 2014–15, 5 students received support, including 10 fellowships with partial tuition reimbursements available (averaging $22,046 per year); scholarships/grants and health care benefits also available. Support available to part-time students. Financial award application deadline: 5/1; financial award applicants required to submit FAFSA. *Unit head:* David Elcott, Director, 212-992-9894, Fax: 212-995-4164, E-mail: david.elcott@nyu.edu. *Application contact:* Jay Esposito, Associate Director of Admissions, 212-998-7414, Fax: 212-995-4611, E-mail: wagner.admissions@nyu.edu.
Website: http://wagner.nyu.edu/executivempa/

New York University, Robert F. Wagner Graduate School of Public Service, Program in Public Administration, New York, NY 10010. Offers public administration (PhD); public and nonprofit management and policy (MPA, Advanced Certificate), including financial management and public finance (MPA), management (MPA); management for public and nonprofit organizations (Advanced Certificate), public policy analysis; JD/MPA; MBA/MPA; MPA/MA. *Accreditation:* NASPAA (one or more programs are accredited). Part-time programs available. *Faculty:* 26 full-time (12 women), 45 part-time/adjunct (27 women). *Students:* 381 full-time (275 women), 237 part-time (156 women); includes 191 minority (51 Black or African American, non-Hispanic/Latino; 2 American Indian or Alaska Native, non-Hispanic/Latino; 59 Asian, non-Hispanic/Latino; 67 Hispanic/Latino; 1 Native Hawaiian or other Pacific Islander, non-Hispanic/Latino; 11 Two or more races, non-Hispanic/Latino), 138 international. Average age 27. 951 applicants, 63% accepted, 238 enrolled. In 2014, 233 master's, 6 doctorates, 1 other advanced degree awarded. *Degree requirements:* For master's, thesis or alternative, capstone end event; for doctorate, one foreign language, comprehensive exam, thesis/dissertation, preliminary qualifying examination. *Entrance requirements:* Additional exam requirements/recommendations for international students: Required—TOEFL (minimum score 100 iBT), IELTS (minimum score 7.5), TWE. *Application deadline:* For fall admission, 1/5 for domestic and international students; for spring admission, 10/1 for domestic and international students. Application fee: $85. Electronic applications accepted. *Expenses:* Expenses: Contact institution. *Financial support:* In 2014–15, 152 students received support, including 137 fellowships with full and partial tuition reimbursements available (averaging $16,683 per year), 2 research assistantships with full tuition reimbursements available (averaging $56,524 per year); career-related internships or fieldwork, Federal Work-Study, scholarships/grants, health care benefits, and unspecified assistantships also available. Support available to part-time students. Financial award application deadline: 1/5; financial award applicants required to submit FAFSA. *Unit head:* Prof. Katherine O'Regan, Associate Professor of Public Policy, 212-998-7498, E-mail: katherine.oregan@nyu.edu. *Application contact:* Sandra Oliveira, Admissions Officer, 212-998-7414, Fax: 212-995-4611, E-mail: wagner.admissions@nyu.edu.
Website: http://wagner.nyu.edu/

North Carolina Central University, College of Behavioral and Social Sciences, Department of Public Administration, Durham, NC 27707-3129. Offers MPA. *Accreditation:* NASPAA. Part-time and evening/weekend programs available. *Degree requirements:* For master's, one foreign language, comprehensive exam, thesis or alternative. *Entrance requirements:* For master's, GRE, minimum GPA of 3.0 in major, 2.5 overall. Additional exam requirements/recommendations for international students: Required—TOEFL. *Faculty research:* Racial diversity and community policing, economic development, issues in urban transportation.

North Carolina State University, Graduate School, College of Humanities and Social Sciences, School of Public and International Affairs, Program in Public Administration, Raleigh, NC 27695. Offers MPA, PhD. *Accreditation:* NASPAA. *Degree requirements:* For master's, thesis optional; for doctorate, thesis/dissertation. *Entrance requirements:* For master's, GRE General Test, minimum GPA of 3.0 during previous 2 years; for doctorate, GRE General Test. Electronic applications accepted. *Faculty research:* Public budgeting, human resources, public information technology, nonprofit management, environmental policy.

Northeastern University, College of Social Sciences and Humanities, Boston, MA 02115. Offers criminology and criminal justice (MSCJ); criminology and justice policy (PhD); economics (MA, PhD); English (MA, PhD); law and public policy (MS, PhD); political science (MA, PhD); public administration (MPA); public history (MA); security and resilience studies (MS); sociology (MA, PhD); urban and regional policy (MS); world history (MA, PhD). *Degree requirements:* For doctorate, variable foreign language requirement, comprehensive exam, thesis/dissertation. *Entrance requirements:* For master's and doctorate, GRE. Additional exam requirements/recommendations for international students: Required—TOEFL, IELTS. Electronic applications accepted.

Northern Arizona University, Graduate College, College of Social and Behavioral Sciences, Department of Politics and International Affairs, Flagstaff, AZ 86011. Offers political science (MA, PhD); public administration (MPA); public management (Certificate). Part-time programs available. *Degree requirements:* For master's, comprehensive exam (for some programs), thesis optional; for doctorate, one foreign language, comprehensive exam, thesis/dissertation. *Entrance requirements:* For master's, GRE (minimum 70th percentile ranking in each testing area preferred); for doctorate, GRE (minimum score in 70th percentile in each testing area preferred). Additional exam requirements/recommendations for international students: Required—TOEFL (minimum score 550 paper-based; 80 iBT), IELTS (minimum score 7). Electronic applications accepted.

Northern Illinois University, Graduate School, College of Liberal Arts and Sciences, Department of Political Science, Division of Public Administration, De Kalb, IL 60115-2854. Offers MPA. *Accreditation:* NASPAA. Part-time and evening/weekend programs available. *Faculty:* 5 full-time (1 woman), 3 part-time/adjunct (1 woman). *Students:* 42 full-time (15 women), 27 part-time (14 women); includes 13 minority (6 Black or African

American, non-Hispanic/Latino; 1 Asian, non-Hispanic/Latino; 3 Hispanic/Latino; 3 Two or more races, non-Hispanic/Latino), 3 international. Average age 32. 46 applicants, 54% accepted, 18 enrolled. In 2014, 31 master's awarded. *Degree requirements:* For master's, comprehensive exam, internship, research paper. *Entrance requirements:* For master's, GRE General Test, minimum GPA of 2.75, 9 hours in social science. Additional exam requirements/recommendations for international students: Required—TOEFL (minimum score 550 paper-based). *Application deadline:* For fall admission, 3/1 priority date for domestic students, 5/1 for international students; for spring admission, 10/1 priority date for domestic students, 10/1 for international students. Applications are processed on a rolling basis. Application fee: $40. Electronic applications accepted. *Financial support:* In 2014–15, 23 research assistantships with full tuition reimbursements, 1 teaching assistantship were awarded; fellowships with full tuition reimbursements, career-related internships or fieldwork, Federal Work-Study, scholarships/grants, tuition waivers (full), and unspecified assistantships also available. Support available to part-time students. Financial award applicants required to submit FAFSA. *Faculty research:* Urban service and management, manpower public policy, performance appraisal, bureaucratic politics. *Unit head:* Dr. Kurt Thurmaier, Chair, 815-753-0311, Fax: 815-753-2539, E-mail: kthur@niu.edu. *Application contact:* Graduate School Office, 815-753-0395, E-mail: gradsch@niu.edu.
Website: http://www.niu.edu/pub_ad/

Northern Kentucky University, Office of Graduate Programs, College of Arts and Sciences, Program in Public Administration, Highland Heights, KY 41099. Offers nonprofit management (Certificate); public administration (MPA). *Accreditation:* NASPAA. Part-time programs available. *Faculty:* 7 full-time (2 women), 2 part-time/adjunct (both women). *Students:* 7 full-time (1 woman), 62 part-time (38 women); includes 12 minority (9 Black or African American, non-Hispanic/Latino; 1 Asian, non-Hispanic/Latino; 2 Hispanic/Latino). Average age 34. 49 applicants, 55% accepted, 15 enrolled. In 2014, 17 master's awarded. *Degree requirements:* For master's, 39 semester hours, including completion of the capstone course. *Entrance requirements:* For master's, GRE, minimum GPA of 2.5, letters of references, portfolios; for Certificate, minimum GPA of 2.0. Additional exam requirements/recommendations for international students: Required—TOEFL (minimum score 79 iBT); Recommended—IELTS (minimum score 6.5). *Application deadline:* For fall admission, 7/1 priority date for domestic students, 6/1 for international students; for spring admission, 12/1 priority date for domestic students, 10/1 for international students; for summer admission, 5/1 for domestic students, 4/1 for international students. Applications are processed on a rolling basis. Application fee: $40. Electronic applications accepted. *Expenses: Tuition, area resident:* Part-time $518 per credit hour. Tuition, state resident: part-time $630 per credit hour. Tuition, nonresident: part-time $797 per credit hour. *Required fees:* $192 per semester. Tuition and fees vary according to course load, degree level, campus/location, program and reciprocity agreements. *Financial support:* In 2014–15, 12 students received support. Unspecified assistantships available. Financial award applicants required to submit FAFSA. *Faculty research:* Nonprofit management, human resource management, urban planning, service-learning, homeland security. *Unit head:* Dr. Shamima Ahmed, Program Chair of Political Science, Criminal Justice and Organizational Leadership, 859-572-6402, Fax: 859-572-6184, E-mail: ahmed@nku.edu. *Application contact:* Alison Swanson, Graduate Admissions Coordinator, 859-572-6971, E-mail: swansona1@nku.edu.
Website: http://psc-cj.nku.edu/programs/public/masters/index.php

Northern Michigan University, Office of Graduate Education and Research, College of Health Sciences and Professional Studies, School of Education, Leadership and Public Service, Marquette, MI 49855-5301. Offers administration and supervision (MAE); elementary education (MAE); higher education in student affairs (MA); instruction (MAE); learning disabilities (MAE); public administration (MPA), including criminal justice administration, human resource administration, public administration, public management, state and local government; reading education (MAE), including reading, reading specialist; science education (MS); secondary education (MAE). *Accreditation:* Teacher Education Accreditation Council. Part-time programs available. Postbaccalaureate distance learning degree programs offered (no on-campus study). *Faculty:* 11 full-time (6 women). *Students:* 38 full-time (23 women), 211 part-time (157 women); includes 11 minority (1 Black or African American, non-Hispanic/Latino; 8 American Indian or Alaska Native, non-Hispanic/Latino; 1 Hispanic/Latino; 1 Two or more races, non-Hispanic/Latino). Average age 32. 121 applicants, 88% accepted, 87 enrolled. In 2014, 48 master's awarded. *Degree requirements:* For master's, thesis (for some programs). *Entrance requirements:* For master's, minimum GPA of 3.0. Additional exam requirements/recommendations for international students: Required—TOEFL (minimum score 550 paper-based; 79 iBT), IELTS (minimum score 6.5). *Application deadline:* For fall admission, 7/1 priority date for domestic students; for winter admission, 11/15 for domestic students; for spring admission, 3/17 for domestic students. Applications are processed on a rolling basis. Application fee: $50. Electronic applications accepted. *Expenses:* Tuition, state resident: full-time $7716; part-time $441 per credit hour. Tuition, nonresident: full-time $10,812; part-time $634.50 per credit hour. *Required fees:* $31.88 per semester. Tuition and fees vary according to course load, degree level and program. *Financial support:* Research assistantships with full tuition reimbursements, career-related internships or fieldwork, Federal Work-Study, institutionally sponsored loans, and unspecified assistantships available. Support available to part-time students. Financial award application deadline: 3/1; financial award applicants required to submit FAFSA. *Unit head:* Dr. Joseph Lubig, Associate Dean, School of Education, Leadership, and Public Service, 906-227-2780, Fax: 906-227-2764, E-mail: jlubig@nmu.edu. *Application contact:* Nancy E. Carter, Certification Counselor and Graduate Programs Coordinator, 906-227-1625, Fax: 906-227-2764, E-mail: ncarter@nmu.edu.
Website: http://www.nmu.edu/education/

Northwestern University, School of Professional Studies, Program in Public Policy and Administration, Evanston, IL 60208. Offers global policy (MA); health services policy (MA); public administration (MA); public policy (MA). Postbaccalaureate distance learning degree programs offered.

Norwich University, College of Graduate and Continuing Studies, Master of Public Administration Program, Northfield, VT 05663. Offers fiscal management (MPA); international development and influence (MPA); policy analysis and analytics (MPA). Evening/weekend programs available. Postbaccalaureate distance learning degree programs offered (minimal on-campus study). *Faculty:* 13 part-time/adjunct (8 women). *Students:* 70 full-time (23 women); includes 9 minority (4 Black or African American, non-Hispanic/Latino; 1 American Indian or Alaska Native, non-Hispanic/Latino; 1 Native Hawaiian or other Pacific Islander, non-Hispanic/Latino; 3 Two or more races, non-Hispanic/Latino). Average age 38. 48 applicants, 100% accepted, 35 enrolled. In 2014, 79 master's awarded. *Entrance requirements:* For master's, minimum undergraduate GPA of 2.75. Additional exam requirements/recommendations for international students: Required—TOEFL (minimum score 550 paper-based; 80 iBT), IELTS (minimum score 6.5). *Application deadline:* For fall admission, 8/8 for domestic and international students; for winter admission, 11/7 for domestic and international students; for spring admission, 2/16 for domestic and international students; for summer admission, 5/18 for domestic and international students. Applications are processed on a rolling basis. Electronic applications accepted. *Expenses:* Expenses: Contact institution. *Financial support:* In 2014–15, 34 students received support. Scholarships/grants available. Financial award applicants required to submit FAFSA. *Faculty research:* Pre-employment investigations for public safety professionals, sustainability programs and policy implementation, innovative voting procedures. *Unit head:* Dr. Rosemarie Pelletier, Program Director, 802-485-2767, Fax: 802-485-2533, E-mail: rpellet2@norwich.edu. *Application contact:* Lars Nielsen, Associate Program Director, 802-485-2853, Fax: 802-485-2533, E-mail: lnielsen@norwich.edu.
Website: http://online.norwich.edu/degree-programs/masters/master-public-administration/overview

Notre Dame de Namur University, Division of Academic Affairs, School of Business and Management, Program in Public Administration, Belmont, CA 94002-1908. Offers human resource management (MPA); public administration (MPA); public affairs administration (MPA); social enterprise (MPA). Part-time and evening/weekend programs available. Postbaccalaureate distance learning degree programs offered (no on-campus study). *Entrance requirements:* For master's, interview, minimum GPA of 2.5. Additional exam requirements/recommendations for international students: Required—TOEFL (minimum score 550 paper-based; 79 iBT). Electronic applications accepted.

Nova Southeastern University, H. Wayne Huizenga School of Business and Entrepreneurship, Fort Lauderdale, FL 33314-7796. Offers leadership (MS); public administration (MPA); taxation (M Tax); JD/MBA; Pharm D/MBA. Part-time and evening/weekend programs available. Postbaccalaureate distance learning degree programs offered (minimal on-campus study). *Faculty:* 56 full-time (23 women), 79 part-time/adjunct (21 women). *Students:* 148 full-time (86 women), 2,831 part-time (1,794 women); includes 2,035 minority (964 Black or African American, non-Hispanic/Latino; 2 American Indian or Alaska Native, non-Hispanic/Latino; 90 Asian, non-Hispanic/Latino; 919 Hispanic/Latino; 2 Native Hawaiian or other Pacific Islander, non-Hispanic/Latino; 58 Two or more races, non-Hispanic/Latino), 193 international. Average age 33. 1,080 applicants, 66% accepted, 532 enrolled. In 2014, 1,172 master's awarded. *Degree requirements:* For master's, thesis optional. *Entrance requirements:* Additional exam requirements/recommendations for international students: Required—TOEFL (minimum score 550 paper-based; 79 iBT), IELTS (minimum score 6), PTE (minimum score 54). *Application deadline:* Applications are processed on a rolling basis. Application fee: $50. Electronic applications accepted. *Financial support:* In 2014–15, 2 students received support. Federal Work-Study and scholarships/grants available. Support available to part-time students. Financial award applicants required to submit FAFSA. *Faculty research:* Reputation management, call centers, international social capital, corporate earnings guidance, corporate governance. *Unit head:* Dr. J. Preston Jones, Dean, 954-262-5127, E-mail: fieldsm@nova.edu. *Application contact:* Zeida Rodriguez, Associate Director of Enrollment Services, 954-262-5163, Fax: 954-262-3822, E-mail: zeida@nova.edu.
Website: http://www.huizenga.nova.edu

Oakland University, Graduate Study and Lifelong Learning, College of Arts and Sciences, Department of Political Science, Rochester, MI 48309-4401. Offers public administration (MPA). *Accreditation:* NASPAA. Part-time and evening/weekend programs available. *Entrance requirements:* For master's, minimum GPA of 3.0. Additional exam requirements/recommendations for international students: Required—TOEFL (minimum score 550 paper-based). Electronic applications accepted.

Ohio Dominican University, Graduate Programs, Division of Business, Program in Business Administration, Columbus, OH 43219-2099. Offers accounting (MBA); finance (MBA); leadership (MBA); public administration (MBA). Part-time and evening/weekend programs available. Postbaccalaureate distance learning degree programs offered (no on-campus study). *Students:* 165 full-time (78 women), 39 part-time (22 women). *Entrance requirements:* For master's, minimum GPA of 3.0, 2 letters of recommendation. Additional exam requirements/recommendations for international students: Required—TOEFL (minimum score 550 paper-based), IELTS (minimum score 6.5). *Application deadline:* For fall admission, 7/15 priority date for domestic and international students; for spring admission, 12/15 priority date for domestic and international students; for summer admission, 5/15 priority date for domestic and international students. Applications are processed on a rolling basis. Application fee: $25. Electronic applications accepted. *Expenses: Tuition:* Full-time $6792; part-time $566 per credit hour. *Required fees:* $200 per semester. Tuition and fees vary according to program and student's religious affiliation. *Financial support:* Applicants required to submit FAFSA. *Unit head:* Dr. Anna Parkman, Director of Graduate Business Programs, 614-251-4569, E-mail: emanu@ohiodominican.edu. *Application contact:* John W. Naughton, Director for Graduate Admissions, 614-251-4615, Fax: 614-251-6654, E-mail: grad@ohiodominican.edu.
Website: http://www.ohiodominican.edu/academics/graduate/mba

The Ohio State University, Graduate School, John Glenn College of Public Affairs, Columbus, OH 43210. Offers public administration (MA, MPA); public policy and management (PhD). *Accreditation:* NASPAA (one or more programs are accredited). Part-time programs available. *Faculty:* 20. *Students:* 155 full-time (85 women), 45 part-time (35 women); includes 29 minority (11 Black or African American, non-Hispanic/Latino; 8 Asian, non-Hispanic/Latino; 6 Hispanic/Latino; 1 Native Hawaiian or other Pacific Islander, non-Hispanic/Latino; 3 Two or more races, non-Hispanic/Latino), 18 international. Average age 30. In 2014, 86 master's, 2 doctorates awarded. *Degree requirements:* For doctorate, thesis/dissertation. *Entrance requirements:* For master's, GRE General Test (for MPA), minimum GPA of 3.0 (for MA); for doctorate, GRE General Test. Additional exam requirements/recommendations for international students: Required—TOEFL (minimum score 600 paper-based; 100 iBT); Recommended—IELTS (minimum score 7.5). *Application deadline:* For fall admission, 12/1 priority date for domestic students, 11/1 priority date for international students; for winter admission, 12/1 for domestic students, 11/1 for international students; for spring admission, 11/15 for domestic and international students; for summer admission, 4/1 for domestic and international students. Applications are processed on a rolling basis. Application fee: $60 ($70 for international students). Electronic applications accepted. *Financial support:* Fellowships, research assistantships, teaching assistantships, Federal Work-Study, institutionally sponsored loans, and unspecified assistantships available. Support available to part-time students. *Unit head:* Dr. Trevor Brown, Dean, 614-292-4533, Fax: 614-292-4868, E-mail: brown.2296@osu.edu. *Application contact:* Graduate and Professional Admissions, 614-292-6031, Fax: 614-292-3656, E-mail: gpadmissions@osu.edu. Website: http://glennschool.osu.edu/

Ohio University, Graduate College, Voinovich School of Leadership and Public Affairs, Athens, OH 45701-2979. Offers environmental studies (MS); public administration (MPA). Electronic applications accepted.

Old Dominion University, Strome College of Business, Doctoral Program in Public Administration and Urban Policy, Norfolk, VA 23529. Offers PhD. Part-time and evening/weekend programs available. *Faculty:* 9 full-time (3 women). *Students:* 11 full-time (8 women), 22 part-time (12 women); includes 9 minority (4 Black or African American, non-Hispanic/Latino; 4 Hispanic/Latino; 1 Native Hawaiian or other Pacific Islander, non-Hispanic/Latino), 6 international. Average age 40. 13 applicants, 31% accepted, 4 enrolled. In 2014, 1 doctorate awarded. *Degree requirements:* For doctorate, comprehensive exam, thesis/dissertation. *Entrance requirements:* For doctorate, GMAT,

GRE General Test, master's degree, minimum graduate GPA of 3.25. Additional exam requirements/recommendations for international students: Required—TOEFL (minimum score 550 paper-based; 79 iBT). *Application deadline:* For fall admission, 3/15 priority date for domestic and international students. Application fee: $50. Electronic applications accepted. *Expenses:* Expenses: Contact institution. *Financial support:* In 2014–15, 14 students received support, including 4 fellowships with full tuition reimbursements available (averaging $7,500 per year), 8 research assistantships with full tuition reimbursements available (averaging $6,000 per year), 2 teaching assistantships with full tuition reimbursements available (averaging $7,500 per year); unspecified assistantships also available. Financial award application deadline: 3/15; financial award applicants required to submit FAFSA. *Faculty research:* Educational needs and program development, policy analysis and administration, excellence norms for cooperative education programs. *Total annual research expenditures:* $60,000. *Unit head:* Dr. John Morris, Graduate Program Director, 757-683-6555, Fax: 757-683-4886, E-mail: jmorris@odu.edu. *Application contact:* Megan S. Jones, Graduate Program Manager, 757-683-3961, Fax: 757-683-4886, E-mail: mmjones@odu.edu.
Website: http://www.odu.edu/business/departments/sps/academics/paup

Old Dominion University, Strome College of Business, MBA Program, Norfolk, VA 23529. Offers business and economic forecasting (MBA); financial analysis and valuation (MBA); health sciences administration (MBA); information technology and enterprise integration (MBA); international business (MBA); maritime and port management (MBA); public administration (MBA). *Accreditation:* AACSB. Part-time and evening/weekend programs available. Postbaccalaureate distance learning degree programs offered (no on-campus study). *Faculty:* 83 full-time (19 women), 5 part-time/adjunct (2 women). *Students:* 37 full-time (24 women), 86 part-time (40 women); includes 22 minority (9 Black or African American, non-Hispanic/Latino; 5 Asian, non-Hispanic/Latino; 2 Hispanic/Latino; 6 Two or more races, non-Hispanic/Latino), 13 international. Average age 29. 200 applicants, 37% accepted, 54 enrolled. In 2014, 61 degrees awarded. *Entrance requirements:* For master's, GMAT, GRE, letter of reference, resume, essay. Additional exam requirements/recommendations for international students: Required—TOEFL (minimum score 550 paper-based; 80 iBT). *Application deadline:* For fall admission, 6/1 priority date for domestic students, 4/15 priority date for international students; for spring admission, 11/1 priority date for domestic students, 10/1 priority date for international students; for summer admission, 3/1 priority date for domestic students, 2/1 priority date for international students. Applications are processed on a rolling basis. Application fee: $50. Electronic applications accepted. *Expenses:* Expenses: Contact institution. *Financial support:* In 2014–15, 47 students received support, including 94 research assistantships with partial tuition reimbursements available (averaging $8,900 per year); career-related internships or fieldwork, scholarships/grants, and unspecified assistantships also available. Support available to part-time students. Financial award application deadline: 2/15; financial award applicants required to submit FAFSA. *Faculty research:* International business, buyer behavior, financial markets, strategy, operations research, maritime and transportation economics. *Unit head:* Dr. Kiran Karaude, Graduate Program Director, 757-683-3585, Fax: 757-683-5750, E-mail: mbainfo@odu.edu. *Application contact:* Sandi Phillips, MBA Program Assistant, 757-683-3585, Fax: 757-683-5750, E-mail: mbainfo@odu.edu.
Website: http://www.odu.edu/mba/

Old Dominion University, Strome College of Business, Program in Public Administration, Norfolk, VA 23529. Offers MPA. *Accreditation:* NASPAA. Part-time and evening/weekend programs available. *Faculty:* 9 full-time (3 women), 10 part-time/adjunct (7 women). *Students:* 35 full-time (19 women), 96 part-time (43 women); includes 52 minority (40 Black or African American, non-Hispanic/Latino; 1 Asian, non-Hispanic/Latino; 2 Hispanic/Latino; 9 Two or more races, non-Hispanic/Latino), 3 international. Average age 34. 61 applicants, 85% accepted, 37 enrolled. In 2014, 54 master's awarded. *Degree requirements:* For master's, thesis optional, capstone seminar. *Entrance requirements:* For master's, GRE or work experience. Additional exam requirements/recommendations for international students: Required—TOEFL (minimum score 550 paper-based; 79 iBT). *Application deadline:* For fall admission, 7/15 for domestic and international students; for spring admission, 11/15 for domestic and international students. Applications are processed on a rolling basis. Application fee: $50. Electronic applications accepted. *Expenses:* Expenses: Contact institution. *Financial support:* In 2014–15, 5 students received support, including 5 research assistantships with partial tuition reimbursements available (averaging $6,400 per year); unspecified assistantships also available. Financial award application deadline: 2/15; financial award applicants required to submit FAFSA. *Faculty research:* Environmental administration, personnel policy analysis, urban administration, non-profit management, transportation policy. *Unit head:* Dr. David W. Chapman, Graduate Program Director, 757-683-7053, Fax: 757-683-5639, E-mail: dchapman@odu.edu. *Application contact:* Megan S. Jones, Graduate Program Manager, 757-683-3961, Fax: 757-683-4886, E-mail: mmjones@odu.edu.
Website: http://www.odu.edu/business/departments/sps/academics/mpa

Pace University, Dyson College of Arts and Sciences, Department of Public Administration, New York, NY 10038. Offers environmental management (MPA); government management (MPA); health care administration (MPA); management for public safety and homeland security (MA); nonprofit management (MPA); JD/MPA. Offered at White Plains, NY location only. Part-time and evening/weekend programs available. *Faculty:* 6 full-time (3 women), 8 part-time/adjunct (2 women). *Students:* 76 full-time (54 women), 62 part-time (37 women); includes 67 minority (33 Black or African American, non-Hispanic/Latino; 6 Asian, non-Hispanic/Latino; 25 Hispanic/Latino; 3 Two or more races, non-Hispanic/Latino), 28 international. Average age 29. 113 applicants, 88% accepted, 54 enrolled. In 2014, 64 master's awarded. *Degree requirements:* For master's, capstone project. *Entrance requirements:* For master's, GRE General Test, 2 letters of recommendation, resume, personal statement, official transcripts. Additional exam requirements/recommendations for international students: Required—TOEFL (minimum score 100 iBT). *Application deadline:* For fall admission, 8/1 priority date for domestic students, 6/1 for international students; for spring admission, 12/1 priority date for domestic students, 10/1 for international students. Applications are processed on a rolling basis. Application fee: $70. Electronic applications accepted. *Expenses:* Tuition: Part-time $1120 per credit. *Required fees:* $266 per semester. Tuition and fees vary according to course load, degree level and program. *Financial support:* Research assistantships, career-related internships or fieldwork, Federal Work-Study, and tuition waivers (partial) available. Support available to part-time students. Financial award applicants required to submit FAFSA. *Unit head:* Dr. Farrokh Hormozi, Chairperson, 914-422-4285, E-mail: fhormozi@pace.edu. *Application contact:* Susan Ford-Goldschein, Director of Admissions, 914-422-4283, Fax: 914-422-4287, E-mail: gradwp@pace.edu.
Website: http://www.pace.edu/dyson/academic-departments-and-programs/public-admin

Park University, School of Graduate and Professional Studies, Kansas City, MO 54105. Offers adult education (M Ed); business and government leadership (Graduate Certificate); business, government, and global society (MPA); communication and leadership (MA); creative and life writing (Graduate Certificate); disaster and emergency management (MPA, Graduate Certificate); educational leadership (M Ed); finance

(MBA, Graduate Certificate); general business (MBA); global business (Graduate Certificate); healthcare administration (MHA); healthcare services management and leadership (Graduate Certificate); international business (MBA); language and literacy (M Ed), including English for speakers of other languages, special reading teacher/literacy coach; leadership of international healthcare organizations (Graduate Certificate); management information systems (MBA, Graduate Certificate); music performance (ADP, Graduate Certificate), including cello (MM, ADP), piano (MM, ADP), viola (MM, ADP), violin (MM, ADP); nonprofit and community services management (MPA); nonprofit leadership (Graduate Certificate); performance (MM), including cello (MM, ADP), piano (MM, ADP), viola (MM, ADP), violin (MM, ADP); public management (MPA); social work (MSW); teacher leadership (M Ed), including curriculum and assessment, instructional leader. Part-time and evening/weekend programs available. Postbaccalaureate distance learning degree programs offered (no on-campus study). *Degree requirements:* For master's, comprehensive exam (for some programs), thesis (for some programs), internship (for some programs); exam (for some programs). *Entrance requirements:* For master's, GRE or GMAT (for some programs), teacher certification (for some M Ed programs), letters of recommendation, essay, resume (for some programs). Additional exam requirements/recommendations for international students: Required—TOEFL (minimum score 550 paper-based; 79 iBT), IELTS (minimum score 6). Electronic applications accepted.

Penn State Harrisburg, Graduate School, School of Public Affairs, Middletown, PA 17057-4898. Offers criminal justice (MA); health administration (MHA); long term care (Certificate); non-profit administration (Certificate); policy analysis and evaluation (Certificate); public administration (MPA, PhD); public budgeting and financial management (Certificate); public sector human resource management (Certificate). *Accreditation:* NASPAA. *Unit head:* Dr. Mukund S. Kulkarni, Chancellor, 717-948-6105, Fax: 717-948-6452, E-mail: msk5@psu.edu. *Application contact:* Robert W. Coffman, Jr., Director of Enrollment Management, Admissions, 717-948-6250, Fax: 717-948-6325, E-mail: ric1@psu.edu.
Website: http://harrisburg.psu.edu/public-affairs

Pepperdine University, School of Public Policy, Malibu, CA 90263. Offers American politics (MPP); economics (MPP); international relations (MPP); public policy (MPP); state and local policy (MPP). *Faculty:* 6 full-time (2 women), 7 part-time/adjunct (1 woman). *Students:* 74 full-time (42 women), 10 part-time (5 women); includes 22 minority (11 Black or African American, non-Hispanic/Latino; 3 American Indian or Alaska Native, non-Hispanic/Latino; 3 Asian, non-Hispanic/Latino; 2 Hispanic/Latino; 1 Native Hawaiian or other Pacific Islander, non-Hispanic/Latino; 2 Two or more races, non-Hispanic/Latino), 21 international. 157 applicants, 65% accepted, 32 enrolled. In 2014, 52 master's awarded. *Entrance requirements:* For master's, GRE or GMAT, 2 letters of recommendation, resume, two essays. Additional exam requirements/recommendations for international students: Required—TOEFL. *Application deadline:* For fall admission, 6/15 for domestic students. Applications are processed on a rolling basis. Application fee: $50. Electronic applications accepted. *Financial support:* Institutionally sponsored loans and scholarships/grants available. Financial award application deadline: 5/1; financial award applicants required to submit FAFSA. *Unit head:* Dr. James R. Wilburn, Dean, School of Public Policy, 310-506-7490, Fax: 310-506-7494, E-mail: james.wilburn@pepperdine.edu. *Application contact:* Melinda E. van Hemert, Director of Recruitment and Career Services, 310-506-7492, Fax: 310-506-7494, E-mail: melinda.vanhemert@pepperdine.edu.
Website: http://publicpolicy.pepperdine.edu/

Pontifical Catholic University of Puerto Rico, College of Graduate Studies in Behavioral Science and Community Affairs, Program in Public Administration, Ponce, PR 00717-0777. Offers MSS. Part-time and evening/weekend programs available. *Degree requirements:* For master's, thesis. *Entrance requirements:* For master's, EXADEP, 3 letters of recommendation, interview, minimum GPA of 2.75.

Portland State University, Graduate Studies, College of Urban and Public Affairs, Hatfield School of Government, Division of Public Administration, Portland, OR 97207-0751. Offers public administration (MPA); public affairs and policy (PhD). *Accreditation:* NASPAA (one or more programs are accredited). Part-time and evening/weekend programs available. *Faculty:* 15 full-time (9 women), 8 part-time/adjunct (2 women). *Students:* 112 full-time (78 women), 137 part-time (96 women); includes 45 minority (5 Black or African American, non-Hispanic/Latino; 7 American Indian or Alaska Native, non-Hispanic/Latino; 11 Asian, non-Hispanic/Latino; 12 Hispanic/Latino; 10 Two or more races, non-Hispanic/Latino), 15 international. Average age 34. 175 applicants, 59% accepted, 76 enrolled. In 2014, 75 master's, 8 doctorates awarded. *Degree requirements:* For master's, internship (MPA), practicum (MPH); for doctorate, comprehensive exam, thesis/dissertation. *Entrance requirements:* For master's, GRE (minimum scores: verbal 150, quantitative 149, and analytic writing 4.5), minimum GPA of 3.0, 3 recommendation letters, resume, 500-word statement of intent; for doctorate, GRE, 3 recommendation letters, resume, 500-word personal essay. Additional exam requirements/recommendations for international students: Required—TOEFL (minimum score 550 paper-based; 80 iBT), IELTS (minimum score 7). *Application deadline:* For fall admission, 4/1 for domestic students, 3/1 for international students; for winter admission, 9/1 for domestic students, 8/1 for international students; for spring admission, 11/1 for domestic and international students. Application fee: $50. *Expenses:* Tuition, state resident: part-time $222 per credit. Tuition, nonresident: part-time $527 per credit. *Required fees:* $22 per contact hour. $100 per quarter. Tuition and fees vary according to program. *Financial support:* In 2014–15, 7 research assistantships with full tuition reimbursements (averaging $6,249 per year), 3 teaching assistantships with full tuition reimbursements (averaging $6,846 per year) were awarded; career-related internships or fieldwork, Federal Work-Study, scholarships/grants, tuition waivers (partial), and unspecified assistantships also available. Support available to part-time students. Financial award application deadline: 3/1; financial award applicants required to submit FAFSA. *Faculty research:* Public budgeting, program evaluation, nonprofit management, natural resources policy and administration. *Total annual research expenditures:* $897,649. *Unit head:* Dr. Douglas Morgan, Chair, 503-725-8216, Fax: 503-725-8250, E-mail: morgandf@pdx.edu. *Application contact:* Megan Heljeson, Office Coordinator, 503-725-3921, Fax: 503-725-8250, E-mail: meloos@pdx.edu.
Website: http://www.pdx.edu/hatfieldschool/division-of-public-administration

Post University, Program in Public Administration, Waterbury, CT 06723-2540. Offers MPA. Postbaccalaureate distance learning degree programs offered (no on-campus study).

Regent University, Graduate School, Robertson School of Government, Virginia Beach, VA 23464. Offers government (MA), including American government, international relations, political theory; public administration (MPA), including emergency management and homeland security, general public administration, nonprofit administration and faith-based organizations, public leadership and management. Part-time and evening/weekend programs available. Postbaccalaureate distance learning degree programs offered (minimal on-campus study). *Faculty:* 10 full-time (1 woman), 9 part-time/adjunct (2 women). *Students:* 34 full-time (15 women), 56 part-time (26 women); includes 21 minority (15 Black or African American, non-Hispanic/Latino; 6 Hispanic/Latino), 4 international. Average age 34. 106 applicants, 45% accepted, 33 enrolled. In 2014, 57 master's awarded. *Degree requirements:* For master's, thesis

optional, internship. *Entrance requirements:* For master's, GRE General Test or LSAT, minimum undergraduate GPA of 3.0, writing sample, resume, interview, references. Additional exam requirements/recommendations for international students: Required—TOEFL (minimum score 577 paper-based). *Application deadline:* For fall admission, 5/1 priority date for domestic students; for spring admission, 11/1 priority date for domestic students. Applications are processed on a rolling basis. Application fee: $50. Electronic applications accepted. *Expenses:* Expenses: Contact institution. *Financial support:* Career-related internships or fieldwork, scholarships/grants, tuition waivers (full and partial), and unspecified assistantships available. Support available to part-time students. Financial award application deadline: 9/1; financial award applicants required to submit FAFSA. *Faculty research:* Education reform, political character issues, social capital concerns, administrative ethics, Biblical law and public policy. *Unit head:* Dr. Eric Patterson, Dean, 757-352-4616, Fax: 757-352-4735, E-mail: epatterson@regent.edu. *Application contact:* Matthew Chadwick, Director of Enrollment Support Services, 800-373-5504, Fax: 757-352-4381, E-mail: admissions@regent.edu.
Website: http://www.regent.edu/government/

Rhode Island College, School of Graduate Studies, Faculty of Arts and Sciences, Department of Political Science, Providence, RI 02908-1991. Offers public administration (MPA). Part-time and evening/weekend programs available. *Faculty:* 4 full-time (1 woman). *Entrance requirements:* For master's, GRE, GMAT, or MAT. Additional exam requirements/recommendations for international students: Recommended—TOEFL (minimum score 550 paper-based; 79 iBT). *Application deadline:* For fall admission, 3/1 for domestic students; for spring admission, 11/1 for domestic students. Applications are processed on a rolling basis. *Expenses:* Tuition, state resident: full-time $8928; part-time $372 per credit hour. Tuition, nonresident: full-time $17,376; part-time $724 per credit hour. *Required fees:* $602; $22 per credit. $72 per term. *Financial support:* Career-related internships or fieldwork, Federal Work-Study, scholarships/grants, health care benefits, and unspecified assistantships available. Support available to part-time students. Financial award application deadline: 5/15; financial award applicants required to submit FAFSA. *Unit head:* Dr. Thomas Schmeling, Chair, 401-456-8056. *Application contact:* Graduate Studies, 401-456-8700.
Website: http://www.ric.edu/politicalscience/index.php

Roger Williams University, School of Justice Studies, Bristol, RI 02809. Offers criminal justice (MS); cybersecurity (MS); leadership (MS), including health care administration (MPA, MS), public management (MPA, MS); public administration (MPA), including health care administration (MPA, MS), public management (MPA, MS); MS/JD. Part-time and evening/weekend programs available. Postbaccalaureate distance learning degree programs offered. *Faculty:* 4 full-time (2 women), 5 part-time/adjunct (0 women). *Students:* 13 full-time (7 women), 88 part-time (41 women); includes 10 minority (4 Black or African American, non-Hispanic/Latino; 2 Asian, non-Hispanic/Latino; 4 Hispanic/Latino), 5 international. Average age 36. 69 applicants, 61% accepted, 24 enrolled. In 2014, 30 master's awarded. *Degree requirements:* For master's, comprehensive exam, thesis optional. *Entrance requirements:* For master's, 2 letters of recommendation. Additional exam requirements/recommendations for international students: Recommended—TOEFL (minimum score 85 iBT), IELTS. *Application deadline:* Applications are processed on a rolling basis. Application fee: $50. Electronic applications accepted. *Expenses:* Expenses: $14,724. *Financial support:* Application deadline: 6/15; applicants required to submit FAFSA. *Unit head:* Dr. Stephanie Manzi, Dean, 401-254-3021, Fax: 401-254-3431, E-mail: smanzi@rwu.edu. *Application contact:* Lori Vales, Graduate Admissions Coordinator, 401-254-6200, Fax: 401-254-3557, E-mail: gradadmit@rwu.edu.
Website: http://www.rwu.edu/academics/departments/criminaljustice.htm#graduate

Roosevelt University, Graduate Division, College of Arts and Sciences, Department of Political Science and Public Administration, Program in Public Administration, Chicago, IL 60605. Offers MPA. Part-time and evening/weekend programs available. *Degree requirements:* For master's, thesis optional. *Entrance requirements:* For master's, minimum undergraduate GPA of 3.0. *Faculty research:* Health policy issues, environmental policy, local government administration.

Rutgers, The State University of New Jersey, Camden, Graduate School of Arts and Sciences, Department of Public Policy and Administration, Camden, NJ 08102. Offers education policy and leadership (MPA); international public service and development (MPA); public management (MPA); JD/MPA; MPA/MA. *Accreditation:* NASPAA. Part-time and evening/weekend programs available. *Degree requirements:* For master's, directed study, research workshop, 42 credits. *Entrance requirements:* For master's, GRE General Test, GMAT or LSAT, 3 letters of recommendation; resume. Additional exam requirements/recommendations for international students: Required—TOEFL (minimum score 550 paper-based), IELTS. Electronic applications accepted. *Faculty research:* Nonprofit management, county and municipal administration, health and human services, government communication, administrative law, educational finance.

Rutgers, The State University of New Jersey, Newark, Graduate School, Program in Public Administration, Newark, NJ 07102. Offers health care administration (MPA); human resources administration (MPA); public administration (PhD); public management (MPA); public policy analysis (MPA); urban systems and issues (MPA). *Accreditation:* NASPAA (one or more programs are accredited). Part-time and evening/weekend programs available. *Degree requirements:* For master's, comprehensive exam, thesis or alternative; for doctorate, thesis/dissertation. *Entrance requirements:* For master's, GRE, minimum undergraduate B average; for doctorate, GRE, MPA, minimum B average. Electronic applications accepted. *Faculty research:* Government finance, municipal and state government, public productivity.

Sage Graduate School, School of Management, Program in Organization Management, Troy, NY 12180-4115. Offers organization management (MS); public administration (MS). Part-time and evening/weekend programs available. *Faculty:* 2 full-time (both women), 9 part-time/adjunct (2 women). *Students:* 4 full-time (1 woman), 20 part-time (12 women); includes 2 minority (1 Black or African American, non-Hispanic/Latino; 1 Hispanic/Latino), 1 international. Average age 33. 21 applicants, 57% accepted, 3 enrolled. In 2014, 21 master's awarded. *Degree requirements:* For master's, capstone seminar. *Entrance requirements:* For master's, minimum GPA of 2.75. Additional exam requirements/recommendations for international students: Required—TOEFL (minimum score 550 paper-based). *Application deadline:* Applications are processed on a rolling basis. Application fee: $40. *Expenses: Tuition:* Full-time $12,240; part-time $680 per credit hour. *Financial support:* Fellowships, research assistantships, Federal Work-Study, scholarships/grants, tuition waivers (partial), and unspecified assistantships available. Support available to part-time students. Financial award application deadline: 3/1; financial award applicants required to submit FAFSA. *Unit head:* Dr. Kimberly Fredericks, Associate Dean, School of Management, 518-292-1782, Fax: 518-292-1964, E-mail: fredek1@sage.edu. *Application contact:* Wendy D. Diefendorf, Director of Graduate and Adult Admission, 518-244-2443, Fax: 518-244-6880, E-mail: diefew@sage.edu.
Website: http://www.sage.edu/academics/management/programs/organization_management/

Saginaw Valley State University, College of Arts and Behavioral Sciences, Program in Administrative Science, University Center, MI 48710. Offers MA. Part-time and evening/weekend programs available. *Students:* 16 full-time (10 women), 39 part-time (26 women); includes 13 minority (10 Black or African American, non-Hispanic/Latino; 2 Hispanic/Latino; 1 Two or more races, non-Hispanic/Latino), 1 international. Average age 30. 28 applicants, 64% accepted, 14 enrolled. In 2014, 32 master's awarded. *Degree requirements:* For master's, thesis optional. *Entrance requirements:* For master's, minimum GPA of 2.75. Additional exam requirements/recommendations for international students: Required—TOEFL (minimum score 580 paper-based). *Application deadline:* For fall admission, 7/15 for international students; for winter admission, 11/15 for international students; for spring admission, 4/15 for international students. Applications are processed on a rolling basis. Application fee: $30 ($90 for international students). Electronic applications accepted. *Expenses:* Tuition, state resident: full-time $8957; part-time $497.60 per credit hour. Tuition, nonresident: full-time $17,081; part-time $948.95 per credit hour. *Required fees:* $263; $14.60 per credit hour. Tuition and fees vary according to degree level. *Financial support:* Federal Work-Study and scholarships/grants available. Support available to part-time students. Financial award application deadline: 4/1; financial award applicants required to submit FAFSA. *Unit head:* Dr. Joseph Jaksa, Program Coordinator, 989-964-2178, E-mail: jjjaksa@svsu.edu. *Application contact:* Jenna Briggs, Director, Graduate and International Admissions, 989-964-6096, Fax: 989-964-2788, E-mail: gradadm@svsu.edu.

St. John's University, St. John's College of Liberal Arts and Sciences, Department of Government and Politics, Program in Government and Politics, Queens, NY 11439. Offers government and politics (MA); public administration (Adv C); JD/MA. Part-time and evening/weekend programs available. *Students:* 34 full-time (13 women), 33 part-time (18 women); includes 26 minority (11 Black or African American, non-Hispanic/Latino; 1 Asian, non-Hispanic/Latino; 11 Hispanic/Latino; 3 Two or more races, non-Hispanic/Latino), 2 international. Average age 27. 76 applicants, 78% accepted, 26 enrolled. In 2014, 49 master's, 8 other advanced degrees awarded. *Degree requirements:* For master's, comprehensive exam, thesis optional. *Entrance requirements:* For master's, minimum GPA of 3.0, 18 credits at undergraduate level in government and politics. Additional exam requirements/recommendations for international students: Required—TOEFL (minimum score 600 paper-based; 100 iBT), IELTS (minimum score 7). *Application deadline:* For fall admission, 5/1 priority date for domestic and international students; for spring admission, 11/1 priority date for domestic and international students. Applications are processed on a rolling basis. Application fee: $70. Electronic applications accepted. *Expenses: Tuition:* Full-time $20,610; part-time $1145 per credit. *Required fees:* $170 per semester. *Financial support:* Research assistantships and scholarships/grants available. Support available to part-time students. Financial award application deadline: 3/1; financial award applicants required to submit FAFSA. *Unit head:* Dr. Diane Heith, Chair, 718-990-6329, E-mail: heithd@stjohns.edu. *Application contact:* Robert Medrano, Director of Graduate Admissions, 718-990-1601, Fax: 718-990-5686, E-mail: gradhelp@stjohns.edu.

Saint Louis University, Graduate Education, College of Education and Public Service, Department of Public Policy Studies, St. Louis, MO 63103-2097. Offers geographic information systems (Certificate); organizational development (Certificate); public administration (MAPA); public policy analysis (PhD); urban affairs (MAUA); urban planning and real estate development (MUPRED). *Accreditation:* NASPAA. Part-time programs available. *Degree requirements:* For master's, comprehensive exam (for some programs), thesis (for some programs); for doctorate, comprehensive exam, thesis/dissertation, preliminary exams. *Entrance requirements:* For master's, GMAT, GRE General Test, or LSAT, letters of recommendation, resume; for doctorate, GMAT, GRE General Test, or LSAT, letters of recommendation, resumé, interview, transcripts, goal statement. Additional exam requirements/recommendations for international students: Required—TOEFL (minimum score 525 paper-based). Electronic applications accepted. *Faculty research:* Urban politics, brown fields, e-government, and administration, evaluation research, community development, electronic government and governance.

St. Mary's University, Graduate School, Program in Public Administration, San Antonio, TX 78228-8507. Offers public administration (MPA); public communication, public policy and public leadership (Certificate); JD/MPA. Part-time programs available. Postbaccalaureate distance learning degree programs offered (no on-campus study). *Faculty:* 3 full-time (0 women), 4 part-time/adjunct (1 woman). *Students:* 14 full-time (7 women), 14 part-time (8 women); includes 16 minority (all Hispanic/Latino), 6 international. Average age 29. 28 applicants, 39% accepted, 7 enrolled. In 2014, 22 master's awarded. *Degree requirements:* For master's, comprehensive exam, internship. *Entrance requirements:* For master's, GRE General Test, Writing sample or GPA X Average GRE [(Verbal + Quantitative + Analytical) / 3] = 1380. Additional exam requirements/recommendations for international students: Required—TOEFL (minimum score 550 paper-based; 80 iBT). *Application deadline:* Applications are processed on a rolling basis. Application fee: $0. Electronic applications accepted. *Expenses: Tuition:* Full-time $15,070; part-time $800 per credit hour. *Required fees:* $156 per semester. *Financial support:* Career-related internships or fieldwork, Federal Work-Study, and institutionally sponsored loans available. Financial award application deadline: 3/31; financial award applicants required to submit FAFSA. *Faculty research:* Municipal service delivery, election systems, urban management and planning. *Unit head:* Dr. Henry Flores, Director, Graduate Public Administration, 210-436-3110, E-mail: hflores@stmarytx.edu.
Website: https://www.stmarytx.edu/academics/graduate/masters/mpa/

Saint Peter's University, Program in Public Administration, Jersey City, NJ 07306-5997. Offers MPA. *Degree requirements:* For master's, capstone project.

St. Thomas University, School of Business, Department of Management, Miami Gardens, FL 33054-6459. Offers accounting (MBA); general management (MSM, Certificate); health management (MBA, MSM, Certificate); human resource management (MBA, MSM, Certificate); international business (MBA, MIB, MSM, Certificate); justice administration (MSM, Certificate); management accounting (MSM, Certificate); public management (MSM, Certificate); sports administration (MS). Part-time and evening/weekend programs available. *Degree requirements:* For master's, comprehensive exam. *Entrance requirements:* For master's, interview, minimum GPA of 3.0 or GMAT. Additional exam requirements/recommendations for international students: Required—TOEFL (minimum score 550 paper-based; 79 iBT). Electronic applications accepted.

Sam Houston State University, College of Humanities and Social Sciences, Department of Political Science, Huntsville, TX 77341. Offers political science (MA); public administration (MPA). Part-time programs available. Postbaccalaureate distance learning degree programs offered (minimal on-campus study). *Faculty:* 16 full-time (6 women), 1 (woman) part-time/adjunct. *Students:* 9 full-time (4 women), 47 part-time (19 women); includes 19 minority (7 Black or African American, non-Hispanic/Latino; 1 Asian, non-Hispanic/Latino; 9 Hispanic/Latino; 2 Two or more races, non-Hispanic/Latino), 4 international. Average age 36. 29 applicants, 79% accepted, 19 enrolled. In 2014, 18 master's awarded. *Degree requirements:* For master's, comprehensive exam, thesis optional, internship. *Entrance requirements:* For master's, GRE General Test, GMAT, writing sample of scholarly work, letters of recommendation, statement of purpose, resume. Additional exam requirements/recommendations for international students: Required—TOEFL (minimum score 550 paper-based; 79 iBT), IELTS (minimum score 6.5). *Application deadline:* For fall admission, 8/1 for domestic students,

6/25 for international students; for spring admission, 12/1 for domestic students, 11/12 for international students; for summer admission, 5/15 for domestic students, 4/9 for international students. Applications are processed on a rolling basis. Application fee: $45 ($75 for international students). Electronic applications accepted. *Expenses:* Tuition, state resident: full-time $2286; part-time $254 per credit hour. Tuition, nonresident: full-time $5544; part-time $616 per credit hour. *Required fees:* $440 per semester. Tuition and fees vary according to course load and campus/location. *Financial support:* In 2014–15, 7 research assistantships (averaging $7,111 per year) were awarded; career-related internships or fieldwork, Federal Work-Study, scholarships/grants, tuition waivers (partial), and unspecified assistantships also available. Support available to part-time students. Financial award application deadline: 3/15; financial award applicants required to submit FAFSA. *Unit head:* Dr. Tamara Waggener, Chair, 936-294-1466, Fax: 936-294-4172, E-mail: pol_taw@shsu.edu. *Application contact:* Dr. Heather Evans, Advisor, 936-294-3378, Fax: 936-294-4172, E-mail: hke002@shsu.edu. Website: http://www.shsu.edu/academics/political-science/graduate.html

San Diego State University, Graduate and Research Affairs, College of Professional Studies and Fine Arts, School of Public Affairs, Program in Public Administration, San Diego, CA 92182. Offers MPA. *Accreditation:* NASPAA. Part-time programs available. *Entrance requirements:* For master's, GRE General Test, 2 letters of reference. Additional exam requirements/recommendations for international students: Required—TOEFL. Electronic applications accepted.

San Francisco State University, Division of Graduate Studies, College of Health and Social Sciences, Public Administration Program, San Francisco, CA 94132-1722. Offers criminal justice administration (MPA); environmental administration and policy (MPA); nonprofit administration (MPA); public management (MPA); public policy (MPA); urban administration (MPA). *Accreditation:* NASPAA. *Expenses:* Tuition, state resident: full-time $6738. Tuition, nonresident: full-time $17,898; part-time $372 per credit hour. *Required fees:* $498 per semester. *Unit head:* Dr. Elizabeth Brown, Director of the School of Public Affairs and Civic Engagement, 415-817-4455, Fax: 415-817-4464, E-mail: mpa@sfsu.edu. *Application contact:* Dr. Sheldon Gen, Graduate Coordinator, 415-817-4458, Fax: 415-817-4464, E-mail: sgen@sfsu.edu.
Website: http://mpa.sfsu.edu/

San Jose State University, Graduate Studies and Research, College of Social Sciences, Department of Political Science, San Jose, CA 95192-0001. Offers public administration (MPA). *Accreditation:* NASPAA. Part-time and evening/weekend programs available. *Degree requirements:* For master's, comprehensive exam, thesis or alternative. *Entrance requirements:* For master's, GRE Subject Test. Additional exam requirements/recommendations for international students: Required—TOEFL (minimum score 575 paper-based). Electronic applications accepted. *Faculty research:* Modern political philosophy, international relations in the Middle East, public policy, American public policy, political parties and political reform.

Savannah State University, Master of Public Administration Program, Savannah, GA 31404. Offers city management (MPA); human resources (MPA). *Accreditation:* NASPAA. Part-time programs available. *Faculty:* 4 full-time (1 woman). *Students:* 3 full-time (1 woman), 6 part-time (4 women); all minorities (all Black or African American, non-Hispanic/Latino). Average age 32. 9 applicants, 33% accepted, 2 enrolled. In 2014, 10 master's awarded. *Degree requirements:* For master's, comprehensive exam, thesis, public service internship, capstone seminar. *Entrance requirements:* For master's, GRE General Test, GMAT, or MAT, minimum cumulative GPA of 2.5, 3 letters of recommendation, essay, official transcripts, resume, essay of 500-1000 words detailing reasons for pursuing degree. Additional exam requirements/recommendations for international students: Required—TOEFL. *Application deadline:* For fall admission, 6/15 for domestic students, 6/1 for international students; for spring admission, 10/1 for domestic and international students; for summer admission, 3/1 for domestic and international students. Applications are processed on a rolling basis. Application fee: $25. Electronic applications accepted. *Expenses:* Expenses: Contact institution. *Financial support:* Career-related internships or fieldwork, Federal Work-Study, institutionally sponsored loans, scholarships/grants, health care benefits, and unspecified assistantships available. Financial award application deadline: 7/15; financial award applicants required to submit FAFSA. *Faculty research:* Community development, human resources, leadership, conflict resolution, city management, non-profit management. *Unit head:* Dr. David Bell, MPA Program Coordinator, 912-358-3211, E-mail: mpa@savannahstate.edu. *Application contact:* Dr. Nat Hardy, Director of Graduate Studies, 912-358-4195, E-mail: grad@savannahstate.edu.
Website: http://www.savannahstate.edu/prospective-student/degrees-grad-pa.shtml

Seattle University, College of Arts and Sciences, Institute of Public Service, Seattle, WA 98122-1090. Offers MNPL, MPA. *Accreditation:* NASPAA. Part-time and evening/weekend programs available. *Faculty:* 8 full-time (4 women), 10 part-time/adjunct (7 women). *Students:* 14 full-time (9 women), 170 part-time (118 women); includes 56 minority (11 Black or African American, non-Hispanic/Latino; 3 American Indian or Alaska Native, non-Hispanic/Latino; 16 Asian, non-Hispanic/Latino; 14 Hispanic/Latino; 12 Two or more races, non-Hispanic/Latino), 1 international. Average age 31. 100 applicants, 55% accepted, 44 enrolled. In 2014, 77 master's awarded. *Degree requirements:* For master's, thesis. *Entrance requirements:* For master's, minimum GPA of 3.0, letters of recommendation, current resume (reflecting two years of relevant professional experience in a nonprofit organization preferred). Additional exam requirements/recommendations for international students: Required—TOEFL, IELTS. *Application deadline:* For fall admission, 7/20 priority date for domestic students, 7/20 for international students; for winter admission, 10/20 priority date for domestic students, 10/20 for international students; for spring admission, 2/20 priority date for domestic students, 2/20 for international students. Applications are processed on a rolling basis. Application fee: $55. Electronic applications accepted. *Financial support:* In 2014–15, 32 students received support. Career-related internships or fieldwork, Federal Work-Study, and unspecified assistantships available. Support available to part-time students. Financial award applicants required to submit FAFSA. *Faculty research:* Leadership development, decision-making, and advocacy; government and nonprofit management, processes, and program analysis; organizational theory and structure; policy formation and analysis, financial analysis and planning. *Unit head:* Dr. John Collins, Interim Director, Institute of Public Service, 206-296-5442, Fax: 206-296-5997, E-mail: collinsj@seattleu.edu. *Application contact:* Janet Shandley, Associate Dean of Graduate Admissions, 206-296-5900, Fax: 206-298-5656, E-mail: grad_admissions@seattleu.edu.
Website: http://www.seattleu.edu/artsci/departments/ips/

Seton Hall University, College of Arts and Sciences, Department of Public and Healthcare Administration, South Orange, NJ 07079-2697. Offers nonprofit organization management (Graduate Certificate); public administration (MPA), including health policy and management, nonprofit organization management, public service: leadership, governance, and policy. *Accreditation:* NASPAA. Part-time and evening/weekend programs available. *Faculty:* 7 full-time (4 women), 6 part-time/adjunct (2 women). *Students:* 21 full-time (9 women), 30 part-time (14 women); includes 15 minority (8 Black or African American, non-Hispanic/Latino; 5 Asian, non-Hispanic/Latino; 2 Hispanic/Latino), 1 international. Average age 32. 51 applicants, 63% accepted, 21 enrolled. In 2014, 28 master's awarded. *Degree requirements:* For master's, thesis or alternative,

internship or practicum. *Entrance requirements:* Additional exam requirements/recommendations for international students: Required—TOEFL. *Application deadline:* For fall admission, 7/1 priority date for domestic and international students; for spring admission, 11/1 priority date for domestic and international students. Applications are processed on a rolling basis. Application fee: $75. Electronic applications accepted. *Financial support:* Research assistantships, career-related internships or fieldwork, Federal Work-Study, scholarships/grants, and unspecified assistantships available. Financial award applicants required to submit FAFSA. *Unit head:* Dr. Roseanne Mirabella, Chair, 973-761-9384, E-mail: roseanne.mirabella@shu.edu. *Application contact:* Dr. Matthew Hale, Director of Graduate Studies, 973-761-9510, Fax: 973-275-2463, E-mail: matthew.hale@shu.edu.
Website: http://www.shu.edu/academics/artsci/political-science-public-affairs/

Shippensburg University of Pennsylvania, School of Graduate Studies, College of Arts and Sciences, Department of Political Science, Shippensburg, PA 17257-2299. Offers MPA. Part-time and evening/weekend programs available. *Faculty:* 5 full-time (2 women). *Students:* 8 full-time (6 women), 13 part-time (6 women); includes 7 minority (4 Black or African American, non-Hispanic/Latino; 1 Asian, non-Hispanic/Latino; 1 Hispanic/Latino; 1 Two or more races, non-Hispanic/Latino), 1 international. Average age 30. 12 applicants, 50% accepted, 4 enrolled. In 2014, 15 master's awarded. *Degree requirements:* For master's, thesis or internship. *Entrance requirements:* For master's, GRE or MAT (if GPA less than 2.75), resume, 2-3 page writing sample, 6 credits of course work in political science or public administration. Additional exam requirements/recommendations for international students: Required—TOEFL (minimum score 580 paper-based); Recommended—IELTS (minimum score 6). *Application deadline:* For fall admission, 4/30 for international students; for spring admission, 9/30 for international students. Applications are processed on a rolling basis. Application fee: $45. Electronic applications accepted. *Expenses: Tuition,* area resident: Part-time $454 per credit. Tuition, state resident: part-time $454 per credit. Tuition, nonresident: part-time $681 per credit. *Required fees:* $133 per credit. *Financial support:* In 2014–15, 5 research assistantships with full tuition reimbursements (averaging $5,000 per year) were awarded; career-related internships or fieldwork, scholarships/grants, unspecified assistantships, and resident hall director and student payroll positions also available. Support available to part-time students. Financial award application deadline: 3/1; financial award applicants required to submit FAFSA. *Unit head:* Dr. Niel N. Brasher, Program Coordinator, 717-477-1372, Fax: 717-477-4030, E-mail: cnbras@ship.edu. *Application contact:* Jeremy R. Goshorn, Assistant Dean of Graduate Admissions, 717-477-1231, Fax: 717-477-4016, E-mail: jrgoshorn@ship.edu.
Website: http://www.ship.edu/political_science

Sonoma State University, School of Social Sciences, Department of Political Science, Rohnert Park, CA 94928. Offers administration of nonprofit agencies (Certificate); public administration (MPA). Part-time and evening/weekend programs available. *Degree requirements:* For master's, thesis or alternative. *Entrance requirements:* For master's, GRE General Test, minimum GPA of 3.0. Additional exam requirements/recommendations for international students: Required—TOEFL (minimum score 500 paper-based).

Southeast Missouri State University, School of Graduate Studies, Department of Political Science, Philosophy and Religion, Cape Girardeau, MO 63701-4799. Offers public administration (MPA). Part-time and evening/weekend programs available. *Faculty:* 4 full-time (1 woman). *Students:* 17 full-time (11 women), 18 part-time (8 women); includes 2 minority (both Black or African American, non-Hispanic/Latino), 12 international. Average age 27. 22 applicants, 82% accepted, 16 enrolled. In 2014, 8 master's awarded. *Degree requirements:* For master's, comprehensive exam (for some programs), thesis or alternative, internship paper. *Entrance requirements:* For master's, statement of interest. Additional exam requirements/recommendations for international students: Required—TOEFL (minimum score 550 paper-based; 79 iBT), IELTS (minimum score 6), PTE (minimum score 53). *Application deadline:* For fall admission, 8/1 for domestic students, 6/1 for international students; for spring admission, 11/21 for domestic students, 10/1 for international students; for summer admission, 5/15 for domestic students. Applications are processed on a rolling basis. Application fee: $30 ($40 for international students). Electronic applications accepted. *Expenses:* Tuition, state resident: full-time $5256; part-time $292 per credit hour. Tuition, nonresident: full-time $9288; part-time $516 per credit hour. *Financial support:* In 2014–15, 19 students received support. Career-related internships or fieldwork, Federal Work-Study, scholarships/grants, traineeships, tuition waivers (full), and unspecified assistantships available. Financial award application deadline: 6/30; financial award applicants required to submit FAFSA. *Faculty research:* Rural public administration, public policy analysis, budgeting, emergency management. *Unit head:* Dr. Hamner Hill, Chairperson, Department of Political Science, Philosophy, and Religion, 573-651-2816, Fax: 573-651-2695, E-mail: hhill@semo.edu. *Application contact:* Dr. Rick Althaus, Graduate Coordinator, Department of Political Science, Philosophy, and Religion, 573-651-2700, Fax: 573-651-2695, E-mail: ralthaus@semo.edu.
Website: http://www.semo.edu/polisci/

Southern Arkansas University–Magnolia, School of Graduate Studies, Magnolia, AR 71753. Offers agriculture (MS); business administration (MBA); computer and information sciences (MS); education (M Ed), including counseling and development, curriculum and instruction, educational administration and supervision, elementary education, reading, secondary education, TESOL; kinesiology (M Ed); library media and information specialist (M Ed); mental health and clinical counseling (MS); public administration (MPA); school counseling (M Ed); teaching (MAT). *Accreditation:* NCATE. Part-time and evening/weekend programs available. Postbaccalaureate distance learning degree programs offered. *Faculty:* 32 full-time (16 women), 18 part-time/adjunct (12 women). *Students:* 121 full-time (65 women), 356 part-time (234 women); includes 101 minority (76 Black or African American, non-Hispanic/Latino; 14 American Indian or Alaska Native, non-Hispanic/Latino; 5 Asian, non-Hispanic/Latino; 2 Hispanic/Latino; 4 Two or more races, non-Hispanic/Latino), 65 international. Average age 33. 204 applicants, 78% accepted, 160 enrolled. In 2014, 149 master's awarded. *Degree requirements:* For master's, comprehensive exam (for some programs), thesis optional. *Entrance requirements:* For master's, GRE, MAT or GMAT, minimum GPA of 2.5. Additional exam requirements/recommendations for international students: Required—TOEFL, IELTS. *Application deadline:* For fall admission, 7/20 for domestic students, 7/10 for international students; for winter admission, 12/1 for domestic and international students; for spring admission, 12/1 for domestic and international students; for summer admission, 4/1 for domestic and international students. Applications are processed on a rolling basis. Application fee: $25 ($50 for international students). Electronic applications accepted. *Expenses:* Tuition, state resident: full-time $4716; part-time $262 per credit. Tuition, nonresident: full-time $7020; part-time $390 per credit. *Required fees:* $831; $277 per course. Tuition and fees vary according to class time, course level, course load, degree level, campus/location, program, student level and student's religious affiliation. *Financial support:* Career-related internships or fieldwork, Federal Work-Study, scholarships/grants, tuition waivers (full), and unspecified assistantships available. Financial award applicants required to submit FAFSA. *Faculty research:* Alternative certification for teachers, supervision of instruction, instructional leadership, counseling. *Unit head:* Dr. Kim Bloss, Dean, School of Graduate Studies, 870-235-4150, Fax: 870-235-5227, E-mail: kkbloss@saumag.edu.

Application contact: Shrijana Malakar, Admissions Specialist, 870-235-4150, Fax: 870-235-5227, E-mail: smalakar@saumag.edu.
Website: http://www.saumag.edu/graduate

Southern Illinois University Carbondale, Graduate School, College of Liberal Arts, Department of Political Science, Public Administration Program, Carbondale, IL 62901-4701. Offers MPA, JD/MPA. *Accreditation:* NASPAA. Part-time programs available. *Faculty:* 4 full-time (0 women). *Students:* 29 full-time (10 women), 37 part-time (14 women); includes 15 minority (12 Black or African American, non-Hispanic/Latino; 2 American Indian or Alaska Native, non-Hispanic/Latino; 1 Hispanic/Latino), 4 international. Average age 31. 34 applicants, 65% accepted, 13 enrolled. In 2014, 15 master's awarded. *Degree requirements:* For master's, thesis or alternative. *Entrance requirements:* For master's, minimum GPA of 2.7. Additional exam requirements/recommendations for international students: Required—TOEFL. *Application deadline:* Applications are processed on a rolling basis. Application fee: $50. *Expenses:* Tuition, state resident: full-time $10,176; part-time $1153 per credit. Tuition, nonresident: full-time $20,814; part-time $1744 per credit. *Required fees:* $7092; $394 per credit. $2364 per semester. *Financial support:* In 2014–15, 26 students received support, including 2 fellowships with full tuition reimbursements available, 10 teaching assistantships with full tuition reimbursements available; research assistantships with full tuition reimbursements available, career-related internships or fieldwork, Federal Work-Study, institutionally sponsored loans, and tuition waivers (full) also available. Support available to part-time students. Financial award application deadline: 2/1. *Faculty research:* Natural resources and environmental management, intergovernmental relations, state mandates, rural administration, economic development policy, nonprofit management. *Unit head:* Dr. Randolph Burnside, Director, 618-453-3172, E-mail: burnside@siu.edu. *Application contact:* Christy Stewart, Office Specialist, 618-453-3177, E-mail: cstewart@siu.edu.

Southern Illinois University Edwardsville, Graduate School, College of Arts and Sciences, Department of Public Administration and Policy Analysis, Edwardsville, IL 62026. Offers public administration (MPA). *Accreditation:* NASPAA. Part-time and evening/weekend programs available. *Faculty:* 7 full-time (2 women). *Students:* 68 full-time (43 women), 54 part-time (33 women); includes 46 minority (30 Black or African American, non-Hispanic/Latino; 1 American Indian or Alaska Native, non-Hispanic/Latino; 2 Asian, non-Hispanic/Latino; 7 Hispanic/Latino; 1 Native Hawaiian or other Pacific Islander, non-Hispanic/Latino; 5 Two or more races, non-Hispanic/Latino), 6 international. 67 applicants, 84% accepted. In 2014, 58 master's awarded. *Degree requirements:* For master's, comprehensive exam. *Entrance requirements:* Additional exam requirements/recommendations for international students: Required—TOEFL (minimum score 550 paper-based; 79 iBT), IELTS (minimum score 6.5). *Application deadline:* For fall admission, 7/24 for domestic students, 7/15 for international students; for spring admission, 12/11 for domestic students, 11/15 for international students; for summer admission, 4/29 for domestic students, 4/15 for international students. Applications are processed on a rolling basis. Application fee: $30. Electronic applications accepted. *Expenses:* Tuition, state resident: full-time $5026. Tuition, nonresident: full-time $12,566. *International tuition:* $25,136 full-time. *Required fees:* $1682. Tuition and fees vary according to course load, campus/location and program. *Financial support:* In 2014–15, 27 students received support, including 1 fellowship with full tuition reimbursement available (averaging $8,370 per year), 21 research assistantships with full tuition reimbursements available, 5 teaching assistantships with full tuition reimbursements available; career-related internships or fieldwork, institutionally sponsored loans, scholarships/grants, and unspecified assistantships also available. Financial award application deadline: 3/1; financial award applicants required to submit FAFSA. *Unit head:* Dr. Drew Dolan, Director, 618-650-3753, E-mail: ddolan@siue.edu. *Application contact:* Melissa K Mace, Assistant Director of Admissions for Graduate and International Recruitment, 618-650-2756, Fax: 618-650-3618, E-mail: mmace@siue.edu.
Website: http://www.siue.edu/artsandsciences/papa/

Southern University and Agricultural and Mechanical College, Graduate School, Nelson Mandela School of Public Policy and Urban Affairs, Department of Public Administration, Baton Rouge, LA 70813. Offers MPA. *Accreditation:* NASPAA. Part-time and evening/weekend programs available. *Degree requirements:* For master's, thesis. *Entrance requirements:* For master's, GRE General Test. Additional exam requirements/recommendations for international students: Required—TOEFL (minimum score 525 paper-based). *Faculty research:* Fiscal policy, public finance policy and practitioner interests; minority politics, healthcare and political economy.

Southern Utah University, Program in Public Administration, Cedar City, UT 84720-2498. Offers MPA. Part-time and evening/weekend programs available. Postbaccalaureate distance learning degree programs offered. *Students:* 34 full-time (23 women), 53 part-time (27 women); includes 7 minority (3 Black or African American, non-Hispanic/Latino; 2 Asian, non-Hispanic/Latino; 2 Hispanic/Latino), 4 international. Average age 33. 47 applicants, 79% accepted, 31 enrolled. In 2014, 29 master's awarded. *Entrance requirements:* For master's, GMAT, GRE, MAT, or LSAT. Additional exam requirements/recommendations for international students: Required—TOEFL (minimum score 550 paper-based, 79 iBT) or IELTS (minimum score 6). *Application deadline:* For fall admission, 7/15 for domestic and international students; for spring admission, 11/15 for domestic and international students; for summer admission, 4/15 for domestic and international students. Applications are processed on a rolling basis. Application fee: $60 ($65 for international students). Electronic applications accepted. Tuition and fees vary according to program. *Financial support:* Tuition waivers (full and partial) and unspecified assistantships available. Financial award application deadline: 5/31. *Unit head:* Dr. Patricia Keehley, MPA Program Director, 435-865-8153, Fax: 435-586-1925, E-mail: keehley@suu.edu.
Website: http://www.suu.edu/hss/polscj/mpa/

South University, Graduate Programs, College of Business, Program in Public Administration, Savannah, GA 31406. Offers MPA.

South University, Program in Public Administration, Montgomery, AL 36116-1120. Offers MPA.

South University, Program in Public Administration, Royal Palm Beach, FL 33411. Offers MPA.

Stephen F. Austin State University, Graduate School, College of Liberal Arts, Department of Political Science and Geography, Nacogdoches, TX 75962. Offers public administration (MPA). *Degree requirements:* For master's, thesis optional. *Entrance requirements:* For master's, GRE General Test. Additional exam requirements/recommendations for international students: Required—TOEFL.

Strayer University, Graduate Studies, Washington, DC 20005-2603. Offers accounting (MS); acquisition (MBA); business administration (MBA); communications technology (MS); educational management (M Ed); finance (MBA); health services administration (MHSA); hospitality and tourism management (MBA); human resource management (MBA); information systems (MS), including computer security management, decision support system management, enterprise resource management, network management, software engineering management, systems development management; management (MBA); management information systems (MS); marketing (MBA); professional accounting (MS), including accounting information systems, controllership, taxation; public administration (MPA); supply chain management (MBA); technology in education (M Ed). Programs also offered at campus locations in Birmingham, AL; Chamblee, GA; Cobb County, GA; Morrow, GA; White Marsh, MD; Charleston, SC; Columbia, SC; Greensboro, NC; Greenville, SC; Lexington, KY; Louisville, KY; Nashville, TN; North Raleigh, NC; Washington, DC. Part-time and evening/weekend programs available. Postbaccalaureate distance learning degree programs offered (minimal on-campus study). *Degree requirements:* For master's, thesis. *Entrance requirements:* For master's, GMAT, GRE General Test, bachelor's degree from an accredited college or university, minimum undergraduate GPA of 2.75. Electronic applications accepted.

Suffolk University, Sawyer Business School, Department of Public Administration, Boston, MA 02108-2770. Offers nonprofit management (MPA); public administration (CASPA); state and local government (MPA); JD/MPA; MPA/MS. *Accreditation:* NASPAA (one or more programs are accredited). Part-time and evening/weekend programs available. *Faculty:* 7 full-time (3 women), 1 (woman) part-time/adjunct. *Students:* 30 full-time (15 women), 82 part-time (47 women); includes 28 minority (16 Black or African American, non-Hispanic/Latino; 1 American Indian or Alaska Native, non-Hispanic/Latino; 3 Asian, non-Hispanic/Latino; 5 Hispanic/Latino; 3 Two or more races, non-Hispanic/Latino), 4 international. Average age 33. 158 applicants, 53% accepted, 45 enrolled. In 2014, 58 master's awarded. *Entrance requirements:* Additional exam requirements/recommendations for international students: Required—TOEFL (minimum score 550 paper-based; 80 iBT). *Application deadline:* For fall admission, 6/15 priority date for domestic students, 6/15 for international students; for spring admission, 11/1 priority date for domestic students, 11/1 for international students. Applications are processed on a rolling basis. Application fee: $50. Electronic applications accepted. *Expenses:* Expenses: Contact institution. *Financial support:* In 2014–15, 57 students received support, including 57 fellowships (averaging $9,051 per year); career-related internships or fieldwork and Federal Work-Study also available. Support available to part-time students. Financial award application deadline: 4/1; financial award applicants required to submit FAFSA. *Faculty research:* Local government, health care, federal policy, mental health, HIV/AIDS. *Unit head:* Brendan Burke, Director/Department Chair, 617-305-1992, Fax: 617-227-4618, E-mail: bburke@suffolk.edu. *Application contact:* Cory Meyers, Director of Graduate Admissions, 617-573-8302, Fax: 617-305-1733, E-mail: grad.admission@suffolk.edu.
Website: http://www.suffolk.edu/mpa

Syracuse University, Maxwell School of Citizenship and Public Affairs, Executive Master of Public Administration Program, Syracuse, NY 13244. Offers MPA. Part-time programs available. *Students:* 28 full-time (12 women), 21 part-time (13 women); includes 2 minority (both Black or African American, non-Hispanic/Latino), 26 international. Average age 40. 51 applicants, 55% accepted, 23 enrolled. In 2014, 69 master's awarded. *Entrance requirements:* For master's, 7 years of mid-career experience. Additional exam requirements/recommendations for international students: Required—TOEFL (minimum score 100 iBT). *Application deadline:* For fall admission, 2/1 priority date for domestic and international students; for spring admission, 8/15 priority date for domestic and international students. Applications are processed on a rolling basis. Application fee: $75. Electronic applications accepted. *Expenses: Tuition:* Part-time $1341 per credit. *Financial support:* Application deadline: 2/1. *Unit head:* Prof. Steve Lux, Director, 315-443-4000. *Application contact:* Margaret Lane, Assistant Director, 315-443-8708, E-mail: melane@syr.edu.
Website: http://www.maxwell.syr.edu/

Syracuse University, Maxwell School of Citizenship and Public Affairs, Joint Program in International Relations/Public Administration, Syracuse, NY 13244. Offers MPA/MA. *Students:* 26 full-time (15 women), 1 part-time (0 women); includes 8 minority (2 Black or African American, non-Hispanic/Latino; 3 Asian, non-Hispanic/Latino; 2 Hispanic/Latino; 1 Two or more races, non-Hispanic/Latino), 3 international. Average age 27. 71 applicants, 72% accepted, 20 enrolled. *Entrance requirements:* Additional exam requirements/recommendations for international students: Required—TOEFL (minimum score 100 iBT). *Application deadline:* For fall admission, 2/1 for domestic and international students; for summer admission, 2/1 priority date for domestic and international students. Application fee: $75. Electronic applications accepted. *Expenses: Tuition:* Part-time $1341 per credit. *Financial support:* Fellowships with full tuition reimbursements, research assistantships with full and partial tuition reimbursements, and teaching assistantships with full and partial tuition reimbursements available. Financial award application deadline: 1/1; financial award applicants required to submit FAFSA. *Unit head:* Donald Planty, Chair and Ambassador, 315-443-2306. *Application contact:* Christine Omolino, 315-443-4000, E-mail: comolino@syr.eduu.
Website: http://www.maxwell.syr.edu/

Syracuse University, Maxwell School of Citizenship and Public Affairs, Program in Public Administration, Syracuse, NY 13244. Offers MPA, PhD, CAS, JD/MPA, MPA/MA. *Accreditation:* NASPAA (one or more programs are accredited). Part-time programs available. *Students:* 130 full-time (78 women), 10 part-time (8 women); includes 23 minority (3 Black or African American, non-Hispanic/Latino; 1 American Indian or Alaska Native, non-Hispanic/Latino; 4 Asian, non-Hispanic/Latino; 13 Hispanic/Latino; 2 Two or more races, non-Hispanic/Latino), 42 international. Average age 28. 511 applicants, 59% accepted, 100 enrolled. In 2014, 124 master's, 4 doctorates, 19 other advanced degrees awarded. *Degree requirements:* For doctorate, comprehensive exam, thesis/dissertation. *Entrance requirements:* For master's, GRE General Test (MPA), 7 years of work experience (EMPA); for doctorate, GRE General Test. Additional exam requirements/recommendations for international students: Required—TOEFL (minimum score 100 iBT). *Application deadline:* For fall admission, 2/1 priority date for domestic and international students. Application fee: $75. Electronic applications accepted. *Expenses: Tuition:* Part-time $1341 per credit. *Financial support:* Fellowships with full tuition reimbursements, research assistantships with full and partial tuition reimbursements, teaching assistantships with full and partial tuition reimbursements, scholarships/grants, and unspecified assistantships available. Financial award application deadline: 1/1; financial award applicants required to submit FAFSA. *Unit head:* Dr. Ross Rubenstein, Chair, 315-443-4000, Fax: 315-443-5330. *Application contact:* Christine Omolino, Associate Director, 315-443-3712, Fax: 315-443-5330, E-mail: comolino@syr.edu.
Website: http://www.maxwell.syr.edu/

Tennessee State University, The School of Graduate Studies and Research, College of Public Service and Urban Affairs, Nashville, TN 37209-1561. Offers human resource management (MPS); public administration (MPA, PhD); social work (MSW); strategic leadership (MPS); training and development (MPS). *Accreditation:* NASPAA (one or more programs are accredited). Part-time and evening/weekend programs available. *Degree requirements:* For master's, comprehensive exam, thesis optional; for doctorate, comprehensive exam, thesis/dissertation. *Entrance requirements:* For master's, GRE General Test, minimum GPA of 2.5, writing sample; for doctorate, GRE General Test, minimum GPA of 3.25, writing sample. *Faculty research:* Total quality management and process improvement, national health care policy and administration, starting non-profit ventures, public service ethics, state education financing across the U.S. public.

Texas A&M International University, Office of Graduate Studies and Research, College of Arts and Sciences, Department of Public Affairs and Social Research,

Laredo, TX 78041-1900. Offers criminal justice (MS); history and political thought (MA); political science (MA); public administration (MPA). *Degree requirements:* For master's, comprehensive exam (for some programs), thesis (for some programs). *Entrance requirements:* For master's, GRE General Test. Additional exam requirements/recommendations for international students: Required—TOEFL (minimum score 550 paper-based; 79 iBT).

Texas A&M University, Bush School of Government and Public Service, College Station, TX 77843. Offers homeland security (Certificate); international affairs (MIA, Certificate); national security affairs (Certificate); non-profit management (Certificate); public service and administration (MPSA). *Accreditation:* NASPAA. *Faculty:* 60. *Students:* 313 full-time (146 women), 12 part-time (2 women); includes 61 minority (13 Black or African American, non-Hispanic/Latino; 7 Asian, non-Hispanic/Latino; 32 Hispanic/Latino; 1 Native Hawaiian or other Pacific Islander, non-Hispanic/Latino; 8 Two or more races, non-Hispanic/Latino), 44 international. Average age 28. 298 applicants, 71% accepted, 143 enrolled. In 2014, 137 master's awarded. *Degree requirements:* For master's, summer internship. *Entrance requirements:* For master's, GRE (preferred) or GMAT. Additional exam requirements/recommendations for international students: Required—TOEFL (minimum score 550 paper-based; 80 iBT), IELTS (minimum score 6). *Application deadline:* For fall admission, 1/20 for domestic and international students. Application fee: $50 ($90 for international students). Electronic applications accepted. *Expenses:* Tuition, state resident: full-time $4078; part-time $226.55 per credit hour. Tuition, nonresident: full-time $10,594; part-time $577.55 per credit hour. *Required fees:* $2813; $237.70 per credit hour. $278.50 per semester. Tuition and fees vary according to degree level and student level. *Financial support:* In 2014–15, 407 students received support, including 26 fellowships with full and partial tuition reimbursements available (averaging $15,902 per year), 44 research assistantships with full and partial tuition reimbursements available (averaging $7,163 per year); career-related internships or fieldwork, institutionally sponsored loans, scholarships/grants, traineeships, health care benefits, tuition waivers (full and partial), and unspecified assistantships also available. Support available to part-time students. Financial award application deadline: 2/1; financial award applicants required to submit FAFSA. *Faculty research:* Public policy, Presidential studies, public leadership, economic policy, social policy. *Unit head:* Dr. Ryan Crocker, Dean, 979-862-8007, E-mail: rcrocker@tamu.edu. *Application contact:* Kathryn Meyer, Director of Recruitment and Admissions, 979-458-4767, Fax: 979-845-4155, E-mail: bushschooladmissions@tamu.edu.
Website: http://bush.tamu.edu/

Texas A&M University–Corpus Christi, College of Graduate Studies, College of Liberal Arts, Corpus Christi, TX 78412-5503. Offers communication (MA); English (MA); history (MA); psychology (MA); public administration (MPA); studio art (MA, MFA). Part-time and evening/weekend programs available. *Students:* 85 full-time (56 women), 100 part-time (68 women); includes 85 minority (3 Black or African American, non-Hispanic/Latino; 2 American Indian or Alaska Native, non-Hispanic/Latino; 4 Asian, non-Hispanic/Latino; 74 Hispanic/Latino; 2 Two or more races, non-Hispanic/Latino), 12 international. Average age 31. 206 applicants, 60% accepted, 83 enrolled. In 2014, 64 master's awarded. *Degree requirements:* For master's, comprehensive exam, thesis (for some programs). *Entrance requirements:* For master's, GRE General Test. Additional exam requirements/recommendations for international students: Required—TOEFL. *Application deadline:* For fall admission, 7/15 priority date for domestic students, 5/1 priority date for international students; for spring admission, 11/15 priority date for domestic students, 9/1 priority date for international students. Applications are processed on a rolling basis. Application fee: $50 ($70 for international students). Electronic applications accepted. *Financial support:* Research assistantships, teaching assistantships, career-related internships or fieldwork, Federal Work-Study, institutionally sponsored loans, scholarships/grants, health care benefits, and unspecified assistantships available. Support available to part-time students. Financial award application deadline: 3/15; financial award applicants required to submit FAFSA. *Unit head:* Dr. Mark Hartlaub, Interim Dean, 361-825-2659, Fax: 361-825-5844, E-mail: mark.hartlaub@tamucc.edu. *Application contact:* Graduate Admissions Coordinator, 361-825-2177, Fax: 361-825-2755, E-mail: gradweb@tamucc.edu.
Website: http://cla.tamucc.edu/

Texas Southern University, School of Public Affairs, Program in Public Administration, Houston, TX 77004-4584. Offers MPA. *Accreditation:* NASPAA. *Degree requirements:* For master's, comprehensive exam, thesis optional. *Entrance requirements:* For master's, GRE General Test, minimum GPA of 2.5. Additional exam requirements/recommendations for international students: Required—TOEFL. Electronic applications accepted.

Texas State University, The Graduate College, College of Liberal Arts, Department of Political Science, Program in Public Administration, San Marcos, TX 78666. Offers international relations (MPA); public finance administration (MPA); urban and environmental planning (MPA). *Accreditation:* NASPAA. Part-time and evening/weekend programs available. *Faculty:* 6 full-time (3 women), 1 (woman) part-time/adjunct. *Students:* 29 full-time (16 women), 67 part-time (30 women); includes 45 minority (7 Black or African American, non-Hispanic/Latino; 3 Asian, non-Hispanic/Latino; 31 Hispanic/Latino; 4 Two or more races, non-Hispanic/Latino), 2 international. Average age 33. 42 applicants, 83% accepted, 16 enrolled. In 2014, 39 master's awarded. *Degree requirements:* For master's, comprehensive exam, applied research project. *Entrance requirements:* For master's, The Public Administration program requires an official Graduate Record Exam (GRE) score to be submitted prior to admission consideration with with a preferred score of 297., baccalaureate degree from regionally-accredited university with minimum GPA of 3.0 on last 60 undergraduate semester hours. Additional exam requirements/recommendations for international students: Required—TOEFL (minimum score 550 paper-based; 78 iBT), TWE. *Application deadline:* For fall admission, 6/15 priority date for domestic students, 6/1 priority date for international students; for spring admission, 10/15 priority date for domestic students, 10/1 priority date for international students; for summer admission, 4/15 for domestic students, 3/15 for international students. Applications are processed on a rolling basis. Application fee: $40 ($90 for international students). Electronic applications accepted. *Expenses:* Expenses: $8,834 (tuition and fees combined). *Financial support:* In 2014–15, 42 students received support, including 3 research assistantships (averaging $10,708 per year), 1 teaching assistantship (averaging $12,464 per year); career-related internships or fieldwork, Federal Work-Study, institutionally sponsored loans, scholarships/grants, and unspecified assistantships also available. Support available to part-time students. Financial award application deadline: 4/1; financial award applicants required to submit FAFSA. *Unit head:* Dr. Thomas Longoria, Graduate Advisor, 512-245-7582, Fax: 512-245-7815, E-mail: tl28@txstate.edu. *Application contact:* Dr. Andrea Golato, Dean of Graduate School, 512-245-2581, Fax: 512-245-8365, E-mail: gradcollege@txstate.edu.
Website: http://www.polisci.txstate.edu/public_administration/

Texas Tech University, Graduate School, College of Arts and Sciences, Department of Political Science, Lubbock, TX 79409-1015. Offers political science (MA, PhD); public administration (MPA); JD/MPA; MPA/MA; MPA/MS. *Accreditation:* NASPAA (one or more programs are accredited). *Faculty:* 26 full-time (5 women), 3 part-time/adjunct (1 woman). *Students:* 48 full-time (15 women), 24 part-time (11 women); includes 16 minority (5 Black or African American, non-Hispanic/Latino; 1 Asian, non-Hispanic/Latino; 10 Hispanic/Latino), 7 international. Average age 29. 49 applicants, 53% accepted, 17 enrolled. In 2014, 21 master's, 2 doctorates awarded. *Degree requirements:* For master's, thesis or alternative; for doctorate, thesis/dissertation. *Entrance requirements:* For master's and doctorate, GRE General Test, 3 letters of reference. Additional exam requirements/recommendations for international students: Required—TOEFL (minimum score 550 paper-based; 79 iBT). *Application deadline:* For fall admission, 6/1 priority date for domestic students, 1/15 priority date for international students; for spring admission, 9/1 priority date for domestic students, 6/15 priority date for international students. Applications are processed on a rolling basis. Application fee: $60. Electronic applications accepted. *Expenses:* Tuition, state resident: full-time $6310; part-time $262.92 per credit hour. Tuition, nonresident: full-time $14,998; part-time $624.92 per credit hour. *Required fees:* $2701; $36.50 per credit. $912.50 per semester. Tuition and fees vary according to course load. *Financial support:* In 2014–15, 46 students received support, including 40 fellowships (averaging $1,708 per year), 1 research assistantship (averaging $25,800 per year), 31 teaching assistantships (averaging $12,226 per year). Financial award application deadline: 4/15; financial award applicants required to submit FAFSA. *Faculty research:* State politics, American institutions and behavior, Asian politics, international and comparative political relations and economics, public administration and organizations. *Total annual research expenditures:* $77,245. *Unit head:* Dr. Dennis Patterson, Chair, 806-742-3121, Fax: 806-742-0850, E-mail: dennis.patterson@ttu.edu. *Application contact:* Dr. Frank Thames, Associate Chair, 806-742-4049, Fax: 806-742-0850, E-mail: frank.thames@ttu.edu.
Website: http://www.depts.ttu.edu/politicalscience/

Thomas Edison State College, John S. Watson School of Public Service and Continuing Studies, Trenton, NJ 08608-1176. Offers public service leadership (MPSL). Part-time programs available. Postbaccalaureate distance learning degree programs offered (no on-campus study). *Entrance requirements:* Additional exam requirements/recommendations for international students: Required—TOEFL (minimum score 550 paper-based; 79 iBT). Electronic applications accepted.

Trident University International, College of Business Administration, Program in Business Administration, Cypress, CA 90630. Offers business administration (PhD); conflict and negotiation management (MBA); criminal justice administration (MBA); entrepreneurship (MBA); finance (MBA); general management (MBA); government accounting (MBA); human resource management (MBA); information security and digital assurance management (MBA); information technology management (MBA); international business (MBA); logistics management (MBA); marketing (MBA); project management (MBA); public management (MBA); quality management (MBA); strategic leadership (MBA). Part-time and evening/weekend programs available. Postbaccalaureate distance learning degree programs offered (no on-campus study). *Degree requirements:* For doctorate, comprehensive exam, thesis/dissertation, defense of dissertation. *Entrance requirements:* For master's, minimum GPA of 2.5 (students with GPA 3.0 or greater may transfer up to 30% of graduate level credits); for doctorate, minimum GPA of 3.4, curriculum vitae, course work in research methods or statistics. Additional exam requirements/recommendations for international students: Required—TOEFL. Electronic applications accepted.

Trine University, Program in Criminal Justice, Angola, IN 46703-1764. Offers emergency management (MS); forensic psychology (MS); law (MS); public administration (MS). Part-time and evening/weekend programs available. *Students:* 46 part-time (39 women). In 2014, 20 master's awarded. *Entrance requirements:* Additional exam requirements/recommendations for international students: Required—TOEFL. *Expenses:* Tuition: Full-time $12,000; part-time $670 per credit hour. Tuition and fees vary according to degree level, campus/location, program and student level. *Financial support:* Application deadline: 3/1; applicants required to submit FAFSA. *Unit head:* Barbara E. Molargik-Fitch, JD, Director, 260-203-2693, Fax: 260-203-2965, E-mail: molargik-fitchb@trine.edu. *Application contact:* Cherie Ditto, Director of SPS Enrollment Services, 260-702-3592, E-mail: dittoc@trine.edu.
Website: http://www.trine.edu/academics/majors-and-minors/graduate/criminal-justice/index.aspx

Troy University, Graduate School, College of Arts and Sciences, Program in Public Administration, Troy, AL 36082. Offers government contracting (MPA); health care administration (MPA); justice administration (MPA); national security affairs (MPA); nonprofit management (MPA); public human resources management (MPA); public management (MPA). *Accreditation:* NASPAA. Part-time and evening/weekend programs available. Postbaccalaureate distance learning degree programs offered (no on-campus study). *Faculty:* 14 full-time (9 women), 8 part-time/adjunct (4 women). *Students:* 56 full-time (37 women), 255 part-time (154 women); includes 181 minority (157 Black or African American, non-Hispanic/Latino; 4 Asian, non-Hispanic/Latino; 14 Hispanic/Latino; 6 Two or more races, non-Hispanic/Latino). Average age 32. 182 applicants, 67% accepted, 64 enrolled. In 2014, 108 master's awarded. *Degree requirements:* For master's, capstone course with minimum B grade, minimum GPA of 3.0, admission to candidacy. *Entrance requirements:* For master's, GRE (minimum score of 920 on old exam or 294 on new exam), MAT (minimum score of 400) or GMAT (minimum score of 490), bachelor's degree; minimum undergraduate GPA of 2.5 or 3.0 on last 30 semester hours, letter of recommendation; essay, resume. Additional exam requirements/recommendations for international students: Required—TOEFL (minimum score 523 paper-based; 70 iBT), IELTS (minimum score 6). *Application deadline:* Applications are processed on a rolling basis. Application fee: $50. Electronic applications accepted. *Expenses:* Tuition, state resident: full-time $6570; part-time $365 per credit hour. Tuition, nonresident: full-time $13,140; part-time $730 per credit hour. *Required fees:* $365 per credit hour. *Financial support:* Available to part-time students. Applicants required to submit FAFSA. *Unit head:* Dr. Pamela Trump Dunning, Director, 334-808-6507, Fax: 334-670-5647, E-mail: pdunningl@troy.edu. *Application contact:* Jessica A. Kimbro, Director of Graduate Admissions, 334-670-3178, E-mail: jacord@troy.edu.

Troy University, Graduate School, College of Business, Program in Management, Troy, AL 36082. Offers applied management (MSM); healthcare management (MSM); human resources management (MSM); information systems (MSM); international hospitality management (MSM); international management (MSM); leadership and organizational effectiveness (MSM); public management (MS, MSM). *Accreditation:* ACBSP. Part-time and evening/weekend programs available. *Faculty:* 8 full-time (6 women). *Students:* 21 full-time (13 women), 131 part-time (75 women); includes 92 minority (79 Black or African American, non-Hispanic/Latino; 2 American Indian or Alaska Native, non-Hispanic/Latino; 4 Hispanic/Latino; 7 Two or more races, non-Hispanic/Latino). Average age 36. 96 applicants, 97% accepted, 5 enrolled. In 2014, 53 master's awarded. *Degree requirements:* For master's, Graduate Educational Testing Service Major Field Test, capstone exam, minimum GPA of 3.0. *Entrance requirements:* For master's, GRE (minimum score of 900 on old exam or 294 on new exam) or GMAT (minimum score of 500), bachelor's degree; minimum undergraduate GPA of 2.5 or 3.0 on last 30 semester hours, letter of recommendation. Additional exam requirements/recommendations for international students: Required—TOEFL (minimum score 523 paper-based; 70 iBT), IELTS (minimum score 6). *Application deadline:* Applications are processed on a rolling basis. Application fee: $50. Electronic applications accepted. *Expenses:* Expenses: Contact institution. *Unit head:* Dr. Bob Wheatley, Director,

Graduate Business Programs, 334-670-3143, Fax: 334-670-3599, E-mail: rwheat@troy.edu. *Application contact:* Jessica A. Kimbro, Director of Graduate Admissions, 334-670-3178, E-mail: kimbro@troy.edu.

Tufts University, Graduate School of Arts and Sciences, Graduate Certificate Programs, Program Evaluation Program, Medford, MA 02155. Offers Certificate. Part-time and evening/weekend programs available. Electronic applications accepted. *Expenses:* Contact institution.

Université de Moncton, Faculty of Arts and Social Sciences, Department of Public Administration, Moncton, NB E1A 3E9, Canada. Offers MPA, LL B/MPA. Part-time and evening/weekend programs available. *Degree requirements:* For master's, one foreign language. *Entrance requirements:* For master's, minimum GPA of 3.0. *Faculty research:* Public sector reform, privatization, economic modeling, public policy.

Université de Sherbrooke, Faculty of Administration, Program in Public Management, Sherbrooke, QC J1K 2R1, Canada. Offers M Adm. *Degree requirements:* For master's, one foreign language, thesis. *Entrance requirements:* For master's, bachelor's degree in related field, minimum GPA of 3.0 (on 4.3 scale). Electronic applications accepted.

Université du Québec à Montréal, Graduate Programs, Program in Urban Analysis and Management, Montréal, QC H3C 3P8, Canada. Offers MA. Program offered jointly with Université du Québec, École nationale d'administration publique and Université du Québec, Institut National de la Recherche Scientifique. Part-time programs available. *Entrance requirements:* For master's, appropriate bachelor's degree or equivalent and proficiency in French.

Université du Québec, École nationale d'administration publique, Graduate Program in Public Administration, Diploma Program in Public Administration, Quebec, QC G1K 9E5, Canada. Offers Diploma.

Université du Québec, École nationale d'administration publique, Graduate Program in Public Administration, Doctorate Program in Public Administration, Quebec, QC G1K 9E5, Canada. Offers PhD.

University at Albany, State University of New York, Nelson A. Rockefeller College of Public Affairs and Policy, Department of Public Administration and Policy, Albany, NY 12222-0001. Offers financial management and public economics (MPA); financial market regulation (MPA); health policy (MPA); healthcare management (MPA); homeland security (MPA); human resources management (MPA); information strategy and management (MPA); local government management (MPA); nonprofit management (MPA); nonprofit management and leadership (Certificate); organizational behavior and theory (MPA, PhD); planning and policy analysis (CAS); policy analytic methods (MPA); politics and administration (PhD); public finance (PhD); public management (PhD); public policy (PhD); public sector management (Certificate); women and public policy (Certificate); JD/MPA. JD/MPA offered jointly with Albany Law School. *Accreditation:* NASPAA (one or more programs are accredited). *Degree requirements:* For doctorate, one foreign language, thesis/dissertation. *Entrance requirements:* For doctorate, GRE General Test. Additional exam requirements/recommendations for international students: Required—TOEFL (minimum score 550 paper-based). Electronic applications accepted.

The University of Akron, Graduate School, Buchtel College of Arts and Sciences, Department of Public Administration and Urban Studies, Program in Public Administration, Akron, OH 44325. Offers MPA, JD/MPA. *Students:* 35 full-time (16 women), 27 part-time (20 women); includes 17 minority (13 Black or African American, non-Hispanic/Latino; 2 American Indian or Alaska Native, non-Hispanic/Latino; 1 Asian, non-Hispanic/Latino; 1 Two or more races, non-Hispanic/Latino), 12 international. Average age 33. 48 applicants, 75% accepted, 15 enrolled. In 2014, 30 master's awarded. *Degree requirements:* For master's, thesis optional. *Entrance requirements:* For master's, GRE, GMAT, LSAT, MAT (if undergraduate cumulative GPA less than 3.0), minimum GPA of 3.0, resume, one-page personal essay, three letters of recommendation. Additional exam requirements/recommendations for international students: Required—TOEFL (minimum score 550 paper-based; 79 iBT). *Application deadline:* For fall admission, 7/1 priority date for domestic and international students; for spring admission, 11/15 priority date for domestic and international students; for summer admission, 4/1 priority date for domestic and international students. Applications are processed on a rolling basis. Application fee: $45 ($70 for international students). Electronic applications accepted. *Expenses:* Tuition, state resident: full-time $7578; part-time $421 per credit hour. Tuition, nonresident: full-time $12,977; part-time $721 per credit hour. *Required fees:* $1388; $35 per credit hour. Tuition and fees vary according to course load. *Unit head:* Dr. John Green, Interim Chair, 330-972-5182, E-mail: green@uakron.edu. *Application contact:* Graduate Director.

The University of Alabama, Graduate School, College of Arts and Sciences, Department of Political Science, Tuscaloosa, AL 35487. Offers political science (MA, PhD); public administration (MPA). Part-time programs available. *Faculty:* 16 full-time (5 women). *Students:* 58 full-time (15 women), 10 part-time (3 women); includes 15 minority (11 Black or African American, non-Hispanic/Latino; 2 Asian, non-Hispanic/Latino; 1 Hispanic/Latino; 1 Two or more races, non-Hispanic/Latino), 3 international. Average age 29. 59 applicants, 71% accepted, 21 enrolled. In 2014, 10 master's, 5 doctorates awarded. Terminal master's awarded for partial completion of doctoral program. *Degree requirements:* For master's, comprehensive exam, thesis optional; for doctorate, comprehensive exam, thesis/dissertation. *Entrance requirements:* For master's and doctorate, GRE, minimum undergraduate GPA of 3.0. Additional exam requirements/recommendations for international students: Required—TOEFL. *Application deadline:* For fall admission, 6/30 for domestic and international students; for spring admission, 10/15 for domestic and international students. Applications are processed on a rolling basis. Application fee: $50 ($60 for international students). Electronic applications accepted. *Expenses:* Tuition, state resident: full-time $9826. Tuition, nonresident: full-time $24,950. *Financial support:* In 2014–15, 15 students received support, including 3 fellowships with full tuition reimbursements available (averaging $15,000 per year), teaching assistantships with full tuition reimbursements available (averaging $12,500 per year); career-related internships or fieldwork and Federal Work-Study also available. Financial award application deadline: 2/15. *Faculty research:* American politics, comparative politics, international relations, public policy and administration, political theory. *Total annual research expenditures:* $43,562. *Unit head:* Dr. Richard C. Fording, Chair and Professor, 205-348-5981, Fax: 205-348-5298, E-mail: rcfording@as.ua.edu. *Application contact:* Dr. Douglas Gibler, Graduate Advisor, 205-348-5528, Fax: 205-348-5298, E-mail: dmgibler@bama.ua.edu.
Website: http://www.as.ua.edu/psc/

The University of Alabama at Birmingham, College of Arts and Sciences, Program in Public Administration, Birmingham, AL 35294. Offers MPA. *Accreditation:* NASPAA. Part-time and evening/weekend programs available. *Students:* 36 full-time (24 women), 68 part-time (49 women); includes 44 minority (34 Black or African American, non-Hispanic/Latino; 2 Asian, non-Hispanic/Latino; 4 Hispanic/Latino; 4 Two or more races, non-Hispanic/Latino), 1 international. Average age 32. In 2014, 50 master's awarded. *Degree requirements:* For master's, thesis or alternative. *Entrance requirements:* For master's, GRE General Test (preferred), references. Additional exam requirements/recommendations for international students: Required—TOEFL (minimum score 500 paper-based; 70 iBT). *Application deadline:* For fall admission, 7/1 for domestic students; for spring admission, 11/1 for domestic students. Applications are processed on a rolling basis. Application fee: $45 ($60 for international students). Electronic applications accepted. *Expenses:* Tuition, state resident: full-time $7090; part-time $370 per credit hour. Tuition, nonresident: full-time $16,072; part-time $869 per credit hour. Full-time tuition and fees vary according to course load and program. *Financial support:* Scholarships/grants available. *Unit head:* Dr. Akhlaque Haque, Program Director, 205-934-4653, E-mail: mpa@uab.edu. *Application contact:* Susan Noblitt Banks, Director of Graduate School Operations, 205-934-8227, Fax: 205-934-8413, E-mail: gradschool@uab.edu.
Website: http://www.uab.edu/cas/government/graduate-program

University of Alaska Anchorage, College of Business and Public Policy, Program in Public Administration, Anchorage, AK 99508. Offers MPA. Part-time programs available. *Degree requirements:* For master's, comprehensive exam, thesis or alternative, capstone project. *Entrance requirements:* For master's, GRE General Test. Additional exam requirements/recommendations for international students: Required—TOEFL (minimum score 550 paper-based). *Faculty research:* Policy analysis, policy and administration issues in the North, hypothetical government policies, public management in health care.

University of Alaska Southeast, Graduate Programs, Program in Public Administration, Juneau, AK 99801. Offers MPA. Part-time and evening/weekend programs available. Postbaccalaureate distance learning degree programs offered (no on-campus study). *Degree requirements:* For master's, capstone course or thesis. *Entrance requirements:* For master's, minimum GPA of 3.0, curriculum vitae, letters of reference. Additional exam requirements/recommendations for international students: Recommended—TOEFL. Electronic applications accepted. *Faculty research:* Democratic governance, public administrative theory, local government.

The University of Arizona, College of Social and Behavioral Sciences, Program in Public Administration, Tucson, AZ 85721. Offers public administration (MPA); public administration and policy (PhD). *Accreditation:* NASPAA. *Degree requirements:* For master's, internship of 400 hours; for doctorate, comprehensive exam, thesis/dissertation. *Entrance requirements:* For doctorate, GMAT or GRE, minimum graduate GPA of 3.5, letter of interest, 3 letters of recommendation, resume. Additional exam requirements/recommendations for international students: Required—TOEFL (minimum score 650 paper-based; 115 iBT). Electronic applications accepted. *Expenses:* Contact institution.

University of Arkansas, Graduate School, J. William Fulbright College of Arts and Sciences, Department of Political Science, Program in Public Administration, Fayetteville, AR 72701-1201. Offers MPA. *Degree requirements:* For master's, comprehensive exam, thesis or alternative. *Entrance requirements:* For master's, GRE General Test. Electronic applications accepted.

University of Arkansas at Little Rock, Graduate School, College of Social Sciences and Communication, Program in Public Administration, Little Rock, AR 72204-1099. Offers MPA. *Accreditation:* NASPAA. Part-time and evening/weekend programs available. *Degree requirements:* For master's, comprehensive exam. *Entrance requirements:* For master's, GRE General Test or MAT, minimum GPA of 2.7. *Application deadline:* For fall admission, 7/15 for domestic students; for spring admission, 11/15 for domestic students. Applications are processed on a rolling basis. *Expenses:* Tuition, state resident: full-time $6000; part-time $300 per credit hour. Tuition, nonresident: full-time $13,800; part-time $690 per credit hour. *Required fees:* $1126; $603 per term. One-time fee: $40 full-time. *Financial support:* Research assistantships with tuition reimbursements, career-related internships or fieldwork, Federal Work-Study, institutionally sponsored loans, and unspecified assistantships available. Support available to part-time students. Financial award application deadline: 4/15. *Faculty research:* State and local administration, nonprofit management. *Unit head:* Hunter Bacot, Director, Institute of Government, 501-569-3564, E-mail: ahbacot@ualr.edu. *Application contact:* Jerry Stevenson, Coordinator, 501-569-3037, E-mail: jgstevenson@ualr.edu.
Website: http://ualr.edu/iog/mpa/

University of Baltimore, Graduate School, College of Public Affairs, Doctoral Program in Public Administration, Baltimore, MD 21201-5779. Offers DPA. Part-time and evening/weekend programs available. *Degree requirements:* For doctorate, thesis/dissertation. *Entrance requirements:* For doctorate, GRE. Additional exam requirements/recommendations for international students: Required—TOEFL.

University of Baltimore, Graduate School, College of Public Affairs, Master's Program in Public Administration, Baltimore, MD 21201-5779. Offers MPA, JD/MPA. *Accreditation:* NASPAA. Part-time and evening/weekend programs available. Postbaccalaureate distance learning degree programs offered (minimal on-campus study). *Entrance requirements:* For master's, interview, minimum GPA of 3.0. Additional exam requirements/recommendations for international students: Required—TOEFL (minimum score 550 paper-based). Electronic applications accepted. *Expenses:* Contact institution. *Faculty research:* Welfare policy, public administration ethics, bureaucratic politics, public sector budgeting, program evaluation.

University of Central Florida, College of Health and Public Affairs, School of Public Administration, Orlando, FL 32816. Offers emergency management and homeland security (Certificate); fundraising (Certificate); non-profit management (MNM, Certificate); urban and regional planning (MS). *Accreditation:* NASPAA. Part-time and evening/weekend programs available. *Faculty:* 18 full-time (9 women), 19 part-time/adjunct (9 women). *Students:* 109 full-time (80 women), 274 part-time (202 women); includes 148 minority (82 Black or African American, non-Hispanic/Latino; 8 Asian, non-Hispanic/Latino; 51 Hispanic/Latino; 7 Two or more races, non-Hispanic/Latino), 5 international. Average age 32. 264 applicants, 77% accepted, 148 enrolled. In 2014, 123 master's, 26 other advanced degrees awarded. *Degree requirements:* For master's, comprehensive exam, thesis or alternative, research report. *Entrance requirements:* For master's, GRE General Test. *Application deadline:* For fall admission, 7/1 for domestic students; for spring admission, 12/1 for domestic students. Application fee: $30. Electronic applications accepted. *Expenses:* Tuition, state resident: part-time $288.16 per credit hour. Tuition, nonresident: part-time $1073.31 per credit hour. *Financial support:* In 2014–15, 4 students received support, including 2 fellowships with partial tuition reimbursements available (averaging $5,300 per year), 1 research assistantship with partial tuition reimbursement available (averaging $10,600 per year), 1 teaching assistantship (averaging $7,100 per year); career-related internships or fieldwork, Federal Work-Study, institutionally sponsored loans, tuition waivers (partial), and unspecified assistantships also available. Financial award application deadline: 3/1; financial award applicants required to submit FAFSA. *Unit head:* Dr. Mary Ann Feldheim, Director, 407-823-3693, Fax: 407-823-5651, E-mail: mary.feldheim@ucf.edu. *Application contact:* Barbara Rodriguez Lamas, Director, Admissions and Student Services, 407-823-2766, Fax: 407-823-6442, E-mail: gradadmissions@ucf.edu.
Website: https://www.cohpa.ucf.edu/publicadmin/

University of Central Oklahoma, The Jackson College of Graduate Studies, College of Liberal Arts, Department of Political Science, Edmond, OK 73034-5209. Offers international affairs (MA); political science (MA); public administration (MPA). Part-time programs available. *Degree requirements:* For master's, comprehensive exam (for some

programs), thesis (for some programs). *Entrance requirements:* For master's, GRE, 18 undergraduate hours in political science. Additional exam requirements/recommendations for international students: Required—TOEFL (minimum score 550 paper-based; 79 iBT), IELTS (minimum score 6.5). Electronic applications accepted.

University of Colorado Colorado Springs, School of Public Affairs, Colorado Springs, CO 80933-7150. Offers criminal justice (MCJ); public administration (MPA). *Accreditation:* NASPAA. Part-time and evening/weekend programs available. Postbaccalaureate distance learning degree programs offered (minimal on-campus study). *Faculty:* 12 full-time (6 women), 17 part-time/adjunct (8 women). *Students:* 23 full-time (11 women), 104 part-time (49 women); includes 37 minority (13 Black or African American, non-Hispanic/Latino; 1 American Indian or Alaska Native, non-Hispanic/Latino; 6 Asian, non-Hispanic/Latino; 15 Hispanic/Latino; 1 Native Hawaiian or other Pacific Islander, non-Hispanic/Latino; 1 Two or more races, non-Hispanic/Latino), 7 international. Average age 35. 49 applicants, 90% accepted, 32 enrolled. In 2014, 34 master's awarded. *Degree requirements:* For master's, internship, capstone project, or thesis. *Entrance requirements:* For master's, GRE General Test, GMAT, LSAT, minimum GPA of 3.0. Additional exam requirements/recommendations for international students: Recommended—TOEFL (minimum score 550 paper-based; 80 iBT). *Application deadline:* For fall admission, 6/1 for domestic and international students; for spring admission, 11/1 for domestic and international students. Applications are processed on a rolling basis. Application fee: $60 ($100 for international students). *Expenses:* Expenses: Contact institution. *Financial support:* In 2014–15, 28 students received support, including 1 teaching assistantship (averaging $6,000 per year); fellowships, career-related internships or fieldwork, Federal Work-Study, and scholarships/grants also available. Support available to part-time students. Financial award application deadline: 3/1; financial award applicants required to submit FAFSA. *Faculty research:* Intimate partner violence, risk and protective factors for violent victimization, intersections of race, class, gender and crime, effective interventions for adult and juvenile offenders, sex trafficking, sentencing disparities for disadvantaged populations, child maltreatment, biosocial and developmental explanations of crime, public personnel management, organizational behavior and development, strategic leadership, national security, program evaluation, social policy, group dynamics. *Total annual research expenditures:* $120,922. *Unit head:* Dr. Terry Schwartz, Interim Dean, 719-255-4047, E-mail: tschwart@uccs.edu. *Application contact:* Crista Hill, Outreach Student Services Specialist, 719-255-4993, Fax: 719-255-4183, E-mail: chill12@uccs.edu.
Website: http://www.uccs.edu/spa/

University of Colorado Denver, School of Public Affairs, Program in Public Affairs and Administration, Denver, CO 80127. Offers public administration (MPA), including domestic violence, emergency management and homeland security, environmental policy, management and law, homeland security and defense, local government, nonprofit management, public administration; public affairs (PhD). *Accreditation:* NASPAA. Part-time and evening/weekend programs available. Postbaccalaureate distance learning degree programs offered (no on-campus study). *Students:* 275 full-time (176 women), 140 part-time (93 women); includes 70 minority (7 Black or African American, non-Hispanic/Latino; 4 American Indian or Alaska Native, non-Hispanic/Latino; 9 Asian, non-Hispanic/Latino; 44 Hispanic/Latino; 2 Native Hawaiian or other Pacific Islander, non-Hispanic/Latino; 4 Two or more races, non-Hispanic/Latino), 19 international. Average age 34. 243 applicants, 71% accepted, 97 enrolled. In 2014, 127 master's, 5 doctorates awarded. *Degree requirements:* For master's, thesis or alternative, 36-39 credit hours; for doctorate, comprehensive exam, thesis/dissertation, minimum of 66 semester hours, including at least 30 hours of dissertation. *Entrance requirements:* For master's, GRE, GMAT or LSAT, resume, essay, transcripts, recommendations; for doctorate, GRE, resume, essay, transcripts, recommendations. Additional exam requirements/recommendations for international students: Required—TOEFL (minimum score 550 paper-based; 80 iBT); Recommended—IELTS (minimum score 6.5). *Application deadline:* For fall admission, 2/1 priority date for domestic students, 1/15 priority date for international students; for spring admission, 10/15 priority date for domestic students, 10/1 priority date for international students. Application fee: $50 ($75 for international students). Electronic applications accepted. *Expenses:* Expenses: Contact institution. *Financial support:* In 2014–15, 60 students received support. Fellowships with partial tuition reimbursements available, research assistantships with partial tuition reimbursements available, teaching assistantships with partial tuition reimbursements available, Federal Work-Study, institutionally sponsored loans, scholarships/grants, traineeships, and unspecified assistantships available. Financial award application deadline: 4/1; financial award applicants required to submit FAFSA. *Faculty research:* Housing, education and the social and economic issues of vulnerable populations; nonprofit governance and management; education finance, effectiveness and reform; P-20 education initiatives; municipal government accountability. *Unit head:* Dr. Christine Martell, Director of MPA Program, 303-315-2716, Fax: 303-315-2229, E-mail: christine.martell@ucdenver.edu. *Application contact:* Dawn Savage, Student Services Coordinator, 303-315-2743, Fax: 303-315-2229, E-mail: dawn.savage@ucdenver.edu.
Website: http://www.ucdenver.edu/academics/colleges/SPA/Academics/programs/PublicAffairsAdmin/Pages/index.aspx

University of Connecticut, Graduate School, College of Liberal Arts and Sciences, Department of Public Policy, Field of Public Administration, Storrs, CT 06269. Offers nonprofit management (Graduate Certificate); public administration (MPA); public financial management (Graduate Certificate); JD/MPA; MPA/MSW. *Accreditation:* NASPAA. *Degree requirements:* For master's, comprehensive exam, internship. *Entrance requirements:* For master's, GRE General Test. Additional exam requirements/recommendations for international students: Required—TOEFL (minimum score 550 paper-based). Electronic applications accepted.

University of Dayton, Program in Public Administration, Dayton, OH 45469. Offers MPA. *Accreditation:* NASPAA. Part-time and evening/weekend programs available. *Faculty:* 6 full-time (2 women), 5 part-time/adjunct (3 women). *Students:* 16 full-time (9 women), 6 part-time (5 women); includes 6 minority (3 Black or African American, non-Hispanic/Latino; 1 Asian, non-Hispanic/Latino; 1 Hispanic/Latino; 1 Two or more races, non-Hispanic/Latino), 3 international. Average age 32. 63 applicants, 52% accepted, 20 enrolled. In 2014, 8 master's awarded. *Degree requirements:* For master's, internship or public service project. *Entrance requirements:* For master's, GRE General Test. Additional exam requirements/recommendations for international students: Required—TOEFL (minimum score 550 paper-based; 85 iBT). *Application deadline:* For fall admission, 4/1 priority date for domestic and international students; for winter admission, 7/1 for international students; for spring admission, 11/1 priority date for international students. Applications are processed on a rolling basis. Application fee: $0 ($50 for international students). Electronic applications accepted. *Expenses:* Tuition: Full-time $10,176; part-time $848 per credit. *Required fees:* $25; $25 per course. Part-time tuition and fees vary according to course level, course load, degree level and program. *Financial support:* In 2014–15, 3 research assistantships with full tuition reimbursements (averaging $11,360 per year) were awarded; career-related internships or fieldwork, institutionally sponsored loans, health care benefits, and unspecified assistantships also available. Financial award application deadline: 3/1; financial award applicants required to submit FAFSA. *Faculty research:* Ethics, leadership, state government, environmental policy, welfare reforms, state legislatures. *Unit head:* Dr. Michelle Pautz, Graduate Program Director, 937-229-3651, Fax: 937-229-1400, E-mail: mpautz1@udayton.edu. *Application contact:* 937-229-4462, E-mail: graduateadmission@udayton.edu.
Website: https://www.udayton.edu/artssciences/academics/politicalscience/grad/index.php

★ **University of Delaware,** College of Arts and Sciences, School of Public Policy and Administration, Program in Public Administration, Newark, DE 19716. Offers MPA. *Accreditation:* NASPAA. Part-time and evening/weekend programs available. *Degree requirements:* For master's, internship or thesis. *Entrance requirements:* For master's, GRE General Test. Additional exam requirements/recommendations for international students: Required—TOEFL. Electronic applications accepted. *Faculty research:* State and local management, community development and nonprofit leadership, drug and alcohol epidemiology, fiscal and financial policy, transportation impacts and management.

See Display on next page and Close-Up on page 1311.

University of Evansville, Center for Adult Education, Evansville, IN 47722. Offers public service administration (MS). Part-time and evening/weekend programs available. *Faculty:* 8 part-time/adjunct (2 women). *Students:* 32 full-time (20 women); includes 4 minority (all Black or African American, non-Hispanic/Latino), 1 international. Average age 36. 13 applicants, 100% accepted, 10 enrolled. In 2014, 17 master's awarded. *Entrance requirements:* For master's, GRE or MAT, minimum undergraduate GPA of 3.0, resume, minimum of 3 years' work experience, 2 letters of reference. Additional exam requirements/recommendations for international students: Required—TOEFL (minimum score 79 iBT), IELTS (minimum score 6.5). *Application deadline:* For fall admission, 7/15 for domestic students; for spring admission, 11/30 for domestic students. Application fee: $35. *Expenses:* Expenses: $9,138. *Financial support:* In 2014–15, 7 students received support. Unspecified assistantships available. Financial award application deadline: 6/1; financial award applicants required to submit FAFSA. *Unit head:* Kristie Byrns, Director, 812-488-2981, Fax: 812-488-2432, E-mail: cae@evansville.edu. *Application contact:* Kristie Byrns, Director, 812-488-2981, Fax: 812-488-2432, E-mail: cae@evansville.edu.
Website: http://www.evansville.edu/adulteducation/

The University of Findlay, Office of Graduate Admissions, Findlay, OH 45840-3653. Offers athletic training (MAT); business (MBA), including health care management, hospitality management, organizational leadership, public management; education (MA Ed), including administration, children's literature, early childhood, human resource development, reading, science, special education, technology; environmental, safety and health management (MSEM); health informatics (MS); occupational therapy (MOT); pharmacy (Pharm D); physical therapy (DPT); physician assistant (MPA); rhetoric and writing (MA); teaching English to speakers of other languages (TESOL) and bilingual education (MA). Part-time and evening/weekend programs available. Postbaccalaureate distance learning degree programs offered (no on-campus study). *Faculty:* 213 full-time (102 women), 62 part-time/adjunct (37 women). *Students:* 690 full-time (385 women), 515 part-time (316 women); includes 101 minority (43 Black or African American, non-Hispanic/Latino; 1 American Indian or Alaska Native, non-Hispanic/Latino; 19 Asian, non-Hispanic/Latino; 27 Hispanic/Latino; 11 Two or more races, non-Hispanic/Latino), 214 international. Average age 28. 765 applicants, 66% accepted, 289 enrolled. In 2014, 225 master's, 104 doctorates awarded. *Degree requirements:* For master's, thesis, cumulative project, capstone project. *Entrance requirements:* For master's, GRE/GMAT, bachelor's degree from accredited institution, minimum undergraduate GPA of 2.5 in last 64 hours of course work; for doctorate, GRE, minimum cumulative GPA of 3.0. Additional exam requirements/recommendations for international students: Required—TOEFL (minimum score 80 iBT). *Application deadline:* Applications are processed on a rolling basis. Application fee: $25. Electronic applications accepted. Tuition and fees vary according to degree level and program. *Financial support:* In 2014–15, 11 research assistantships with full and partial tuition reimbursements (averaging $4,000 per year), 10 teaching assistantships with full and partial tuition reimbursements (averaging $3,600 per year) were awarded; career-related internships or fieldwork, Federal Work-Study, health care benefits, and unspecified assistantships also available. Financial award application deadline: 4/1; financial award applicants required to submit FAFSA. *Unit head:* Christopher M. Harris, Director of Admissions, 419-434-4347, E-mail: harrisc1@findlay.edu. *Application contact:* Austyn Erickson, Graduate Admissions Counselor, 419-434-4693, Fax: 419-434-4898, E-mail: ericksona@findlay.edu.
Website: http://www.findlay.edu/admissions/graduate/Pages/default.aspx

University of Georgia, School of Public and International Affairs, Department of Public Administration and Policy, Athens, GA 30602. Offers public administration (MPA, PhD). *Accreditation:* NASPAA (one or more programs are accredited). *Degree requirements:* For master's, internship; for doctorate, thesis/dissertation. *Entrance requirements:* For master's and doctorate, GRE General Test. Electronic applications accepted.

University of Guam, Office of Graduate Studies, School of Business and Public Administration, Public Administration Program, Mangilao, GU 96923. Offers MPA. *Entrance requirements:* For master's, GRE General Test. Additional exam requirements/recommendations for international students: Required—TOEFL.

University of Guelph, Graduate Studies, College of Social and Applied Human Sciences, Department of Political Science, Guelph, ON N1G 2W1, Canada. Offers comparative politics (MA); international development (MA); political science (MA); public policy and public administration (MA); the Americas (Canada emphasis) (MA). MA in public policy and public administration offered in collaboration with Department of Political Science of McMaster University. *Degree requirements:* For master's, thesis or paper. *Entrance requirements:* For master's, minimum B average during previous 2 years of course work, 4 year Honours Degree in Political Science. Additional exam requirements/recommendations for international students: Required—TOEFL. Electronic applications accepted. *Faculty research:* Political ethics, constitutional power.

University of Hawaii at Manoa, Graduate Division, College of Social Sciences, Department of Public Administration, Honolulu, HI 96822. Offers MPA, Graduate Certificate. Part-time programs available. *Degree requirements:* For master's, thesis optional, practicum. *Entrance requirements:* Additional exam requirements/recommendations for international students: Required—TOEFL (minimum score 540 paper-based; 76 iBT), IELTS (minimum score 5). *Faculty research:* Public sector finance and the budget process, collaboration between sectors, organizational problem solving and communication processes, system reform in government organizations, public policy analysis.

University of Houston, College of Liberal Arts and Social Sciences, Department of Political Science, Houston, TX 77204. Offers political science (MA, PhD); public administration (MA). Part-time programs available. Terminal master's awarded for partial completion of doctoral program. *Degree requirements:* For master's, thesis optional; for doctorate, thesis/dissertation. *Entrance requirements:* For master's and doctorate, GRE. Additional exam requirements/recommendations for international students: Required—TOEFL (minimum score 550 paper-based; 79 iBT). *Faculty research:* American politics, political theory, judicial process, public policy, comparative politics.

Public Administration

University of Idaho, College of Graduate Studies, College of Letters, Arts and Social Sciences, The Martin School, Political Science Department, Moscow, ID 83844-3165. Offers political science (MA, PhD); public administration (MPA). *Faculty:* 6 full-time, 1 part-time/adjunct. *Students:* 7 full-time, 8 part-time. Average age 35. In 2014, 9 master's, 1 doctorate awarded. *Degree requirements:* For doctorate, thesis/dissertation. *Entrance requirements:* For master's, minimum GPA of 2.8; for doctorate, minimum undergraduate GPA of 2.8, 3.0 graduate. *Application deadline:* For fall admission, 8/1 for domestic students; for spring admission, 12/15 for domestic students. Applications are processed on a rolling basis. Application fee: $60. *Expenses:* Tuition, state resident: full-time $4784; part-time $280.50 per credit hour. Tuition, nonresident: full-time $18,314; part-time $957.50 per credit hour. *Required fees:* $2000; $58.50 per credit hour. Tuition and fees vary according to program. *Financial support:* Research assistantships and teaching assistantships available. Financial award applicants required to submit FAFSA. *Unit head:* Dr. Brian Ellison, Director, 208-885-6328. *Application contact:* Sean Scoggin, Graduate Recruitment Coordinator, 208-885-4001, Fax: 208-885-4406, E-mail: graduateadmissions@uidaho.edu.
Website: http://www.uidaho.edu/class/politicalscience

University of Illinois at Chicago, Graduate College, College of Urban Planning and Public Affairs, Department of Public Administration, Chicago, IL 60607-7128. Offers MPA, PhD. *Accreditation:* NASPAA (one or more programs are accredited). Part-time and evening/weekend programs available. *Faculty:* 10 full-time (4 women), 8 part-time/adjunct (3 women). *Students:* 84 full-time (35 women), 99 part-time (49 women); includes 42 minority (17 Black or African American, non-Hispanic/Latino; 7 Asian, non-Hispanic/Latino; 17 Hispanic/Latino; 1 Two or more races, non-Hispanic/Latino), 72 international. Average age 29. 195 applicants, 70% accepted, 62 enrolled. In 2014, 50 master's, 2 doctorates awarded. Terminal master's awarded for partial completion of doctoral program. *Degree requirements:* For master's, internship/project. *Entrance requirements:* For master's, GRE General Test, minimum GPA of 3.0. Additional exam requirements/recommendations for international students: Required—TOEFL. *Application deadline:* For fall admission, 1/1 for domestic and international students; for spring admission, 11/1 for domestic students, 7/15 for international students. Applications are processed on a rolling basis. Application fee: $60. Electronic applications accepted. *Expenses:* Expenses: $18,046 in-state; $30,044 out-of-state. *Financial support:* Fellowships with full tuition reimbursements, research assistantships with full tuition reimbursements, teaching assistantships with full tuition reimbursements, career-related internships or fieldwork, Federal Work-Study, scholarships/grants, traineeships, tuition waivers (full), and unspecified assistantships available. Financial award application deadline: 3/1; financial award applicants required to submit FAFSA. *Faculty research:* E-government, science and technology policy, financial management, urban policy, nonprofit management, public management. *Total annual research expenditures:* $121,000. *Unit head:* Prof. Jared Carr, Professor and Department Head, 312-413-7853, Fax: 312-996-8804, E-mail: jbcarr@uic.edu. *Application contact:* Receptionist, 312-413-2550, E-mail: gradcoll@uic.edu.
Website: http://cuppa-pa.uic.edu/

University of Illinois at Springfield, Graduate Programs, College of Public Affairs and Administration, Program in Public Administration, Springfield, IL 62703-5407. Offers management of nonprofit organizations (Graduate Certificate); public administration (MPA, DPA). *Accreditation:* NASPAA. Part-time and evening/weekend programs available. Postbaccalaureate distance learning degree programs offered (no on-campus study). *Faculty:* 12 full-time (5 women), 3 part-time/adjunct (2 women). *Students:* 43 full-time (21 women), 200 part-time (102 women); includes 71 minority (47 Black or African American, non-Hispanic/Latino; 6 Asian, non-Hispanic/Latino; 12 Hispanic/Latino; 6 Two or more races, non-Hispanic/Latino), 9 international. Average age 33. 178 applicants, 39% accepted, 53 enrolled. In 2014, 75 master's, 1 doctorate, 14 other advanced degrees awarded. *Degree requirements:* For master's, thesis or seminar; for doctorate, comprehensive exam, thesis/dissertation. *Entrance requirements:* For master's, minimum undergraduate GPA of 2.5; completion of prerequisites that include undergraduate coursework in political science in U.S. government, microeconomics or a market economics survey course, and competence in one computer spreadsheet application package; resume; career goals statement; for doctorate, GRE, minimum

graduate GPA of 3.25; writing sample; 3 letters of reference; interview. Additional exam requirements/recommendations for international students: Required—TOEFL (minimum score 550 paper-based). Application fee: $60 ($75 for international students). Electronic applications accepted. *Expenses:* Tuition, state resident: full-time $7662; part-time $319.25 per credit hour. Tuition, nonresident: full-time $15,966; part-time $665.25 per credit hour. *Financial support:* In 2014–15, fellowships with full tuition reimbursements (averaging $9,900 per year), research assistantships with full tuition reimbursements (averaging $9,600 per year), teaching assistantships with full tuition reimbursements (averaging $9,600 per year) were awarded; career-related internships or fieldwork, Federal Work-Study, scholarships/grants, health care benefits, and unspecified assistantships also available. Support available to part-time students. Financial award application deadline: 11/15; financial award applicants required to submit FAFSA. *Unit head:* Dr. Will Miller, Program Administrator, 217-206-8361, E-mail: wmill3@uis.edu. *Application contact:* Dr. Lynn Pardie, Office of Graduate Studies, 800-252-8533, Fax: 217-206-7623, E-mail: lpard1@uis.edu.
Website: http://www.uis.edu/publicadministration/

The University of Kansas, Graduate Studies, College of Liberal Arts and Sciences, School of Public Affairs and Administration, Lawrence, KS 66045-3129. Offers MPA, PhD, JD/MPA, MUP/MPA. *Accreditation:* NASPAA. Part-time and evening/weekend programs available. *Faculty:* 13 full-time, 10 part-time/adjunct. *Students:* 44 full-time (16 women), 76 part-time (45 women); includes 22 minority (11 Black or African American, non-Hispanic/Latino; 3 American Indian or Alaska Native, non-Hispanic/Latino; 5 Hispanic/Latino; 3 Two or more races, non-Hispanic/Latino), 3 international. Average age 36. 68 applicants, 54% accepted, 26 enrolled. In 2014, 36 master's, 3 doctorates awarded. Terminal master's awarded for partial completion of doctoral program. *Degree requirements:* For master's, comprehensive exam; for doctorate, comprehensive exam, thesis/dissertation. *Entrance requirements:* For master's and doctorate, GRE General Test. Additional exam requirements/recommendations for international students: Required—TOEFL. *Application deadline:* For fall admission, 11/1 priority date for domestic students, 2/1 priority date for international students; for spring admission, 5/1 for domestic students, 10/1 for international students. Application fee: $55 ($65 for international students). Electronic applications accepted. *Financial support:* Fellowships, research assistantships with full and partial tuition reimbursements, teaching assistantships with full and partial tuition reimbursements, career-related internships or fieldwork, institutionally sponsored loans, scholarships/grants, and unspecified assistantships available. Financial award application deadline: 2/1. *Faculty research:* Collaboration, law and society, social equity, performance management, sustainability. *Unit head:* Reggie Robinson, Director, 785-864-3527, E-mail: rlrobinson@ku.edu. *Application contact:* Angie Soden, Graduate Admissions Contact, 785-864-3527, E-mail: a641s910@ku.edu.
Website: http://www.kupa.ku.edu/

University of Kentucky, Graduate School, Martin School of Public Policy and Administration, Lexington, KY 40506-0032. Offers public administration (MPA); public policy (MPP); public policy and administration (PhD). *Accreditation:* NASPAA (one or more programs are accredited). *Degree requirements:* For master's, comprehensive exam; for doctorate, comprehensive exam, thesis/dissertation. *Entrance requirements:* For master's, GMAT or GRE General Test, minimum undergraduate GPA of 2.75; for doctorate, GMAT or GRE General Test, minimum graduate GPA of 3.0. Additional exam requirements/recommendations for international students: Required—TOEFL (minimum score 550 paper-based). Electronic applications accepted. *Faculty research:* Public financial management, education finance and policy, health finance and policy, welfare policy, program evaluation.

University of La Verne, College of Business and Public Management, Doctoral Program in Public Administration, La Verne, CA 91750-4443. Offers DPA. Part-time programs available. *Faculty:* 13 full-time (6 women), 4 part-time/adjunct (2 women). *Students:* 1 full-time (0 women), 68 part-time (34 women); includes 42 minority (15 Black or African American, non-Hispanic/Latino; 2 Asian, non-Hispanic/Latino; 23 Hispanic/Latino; 1 Native Hawaiian or other Pacific Islander, non-Hispanic/Latino; 1 Two or more races, non-Hispanic/Latino), 5 international. Average age 42. In 2014, 13 doctorates

awarded. *Degree requirements:* For doctorate, thesis/dissertation. *Entrance requirements:* For doctorate, MAT, GMAT or GRE, minimum undergraduate GPA of 3.25, interview, 3 letters of recommendation, statement of purpose. Additional exam requirements/recommendations for international students: Required—TOEFL (minimum score 550 paper-based). Application fee: $75. *Expenses:* Expenses: Contact institution. *Financial support:* Institutionally sponsored loans available. Financial award application deadline: 3/2; financial award applicants required to submit FAFSA. *Unit head:* Dr. Suzanne Beaumaster, Chairperson, 909-593-3511 Ext. 4817, E-mail: sbeaumaster@laverne.edu. *Application contact:* Matthew Rinehart, Assistant Director of Graduate Admissions, 909-4484948, Fax: 909-9712295, E-mail: mrinehart@laverne.edu.
Website: http://laverne.edu/business-and-public-administration/public-administration/

University of La Verne, College of Business and Public Management, Master's Program in Public Administration, La Verne, CA 91750-4443. Offers non-profit (MPA); policy (MPA); urban management and affairs (MPA). *Accreditation:* NASPAA. Part-time programs available. *Faculty:* 13 full-time (6 women), 4 part-time/adjunct (2 women). *Students:* 32 full-time (23 women), 36 part-time (21 women); includes 48 minority (6 Black or African American, non-Hispanic/Latino; 3 Asian, non-Hispanic/Latino; 39 Hispanic/Latino), 4 international. Average age 34. In 2014, 30 master's awarded. *Entrance requirements:* For master's, minimum undergraduate GPA of 3.0, statement of purpose, 2 letters of recommendation, resume. Additional exam requirements/recommendations for international students: Required—TOEFL (minimum score 550 paper-based). *Application deadline:* Applications are processed on a rolling basis. Application fee: $50. *Expenses:* Expenses: Contact institution. *Financial support:* Fellowships and research assistantships available. Financial award application deadline: 3/2; financial award applicants required to submit FAFSA. *Unit head:* Dr. Jack Meek, Chairperson, 909-448-4941, E-mail: jmeek@laverne.edu. *Application contact:* Matthew Rinehart, Associate Director of Graduate Admissions, 909-4484948, Fax: 909-9712295, E-mail: mrinehart@laverne.edu.
Website: http://laverne.edu/business-and-public-administration/public-administration/

University of Louisville, Graduate School, College of Arts and Sciences, Department of Urban and Public Affairs, Louisville, KY 40208. Offers public administration (MPA), including human resources management, non-profit management, public policy and administration; urban and public affairs (PhD), including urban planning and development, urban policy and administration; urban planning (MUP), including administration of planning organizations, housing and community development, land use and environmental planning, spatial analysis. Part-time and evening/weekend programs available. *Students:* 76 full-time (35 women), 22 part-time (14 women); includes 16 minority (10 Black or African American, non-Hispanic/Latino; 1 Asian, non-Hispanic/Latino; 3 Hispanic/Latino; 2 Two or more races, non-Hispanic/Latino), 6 international. Average age 30. 89 applicants, 71% accepted, 33 enrolled. In 2014, 13 master's, 4 doctorates awarded. Terminal master's awarded for partial completion of doctoral program. *Degree requirements:* For master's, internship; for doctorate, comprehensive exam, thesis/dissertation. *Entrance requirements:* For master's, GRE General Test, minimum GPA of 3.0; for doctorate, GRE General Test, master's degree in appropriate field. Additional exam requirements/recommendations for international students: Required—TOEFL (minimum score 550 paper-based; 79 iBT). *Application deadline:* For fall admission, 7/15 for domestic students, 5/1 priority date for international students; for spring admission, 11/15 for domestic students, 11/1 priority date for international students; for summer admission, 4/1 priority date for international students. Applications are processed on a rolling basis. Application fee: $60. Electronic applications accepted. *Expenses:* Tuition, state resident: full-time $11,326; part-time $630 per credit hour. Tuition, nonresident: full-time $23,568; part-time $1311 per credit hour. *Required fees:* $196. Tuition and fees vary according to program and reciprocity agreements. *Financial support:* Fellowships, research assistantships, and health care benefits available. Financial award application deadline: 3/1. *Faculty research:* Housing and community development, performance-based budgeting, environmental policy and natural hazards, sustainability, real estate development, comparative urban development. *Unit head:* Dr. David Simpson, Chair, 502-852-8019, Fax: 502-852-4558, E-mail: dave.simpson@louisville.edu. *Application contact:* Libby Leggett, Director, Graduate Admissions, 502-852-3101, Fax: 502-852-4558, E-mail: gradadm@louisville.edu.
Website: http://supa.louisville.edu

University of Management and Technology, Program in Public Administration, Arlington, VA 22209. Offers MPA, Advanced Certificate.

University of Manitoba, Faculty of Graduate Studies, Faculty of Arts, Department of Political Studies, Program in Public Administration, Winnipeg, MB R3T 2N2, Canada. Offers MPA. Program offered jointly with The University of Winnipeg. *Degree requirements:* For master's, thesis or alternative.

University of Maryland, College Park, Academic Affairs, Joint Program in Business and Management/Public Policy, College Park, MD 20742. Offers MBA/MPM. *Accreditation:* AACSB. Electronic applications accepted.

University of Maryland, College Park, Academic Affairs, School of Public Policy, Joint Program in Public Policy/Law, College Park, MD 20742. Offers JD/MPM. Electronic applications accepted.

University of Maryland, College Park, Academic Affairs, School of Public Policy, Public Management Program, College Park, MD 20742. Offers MPM. *Accreditation:* NASPAA. *Degree requirements:* For master's, internship. *Entrance requirements:* For master's, GRE General Test, minimum GPA of 3.0. Additional exam requirements/recommendations for international students: Required—TOEFL. Electronic applications accepted. *Faculty research:* International security, economic policy, financial management, social policy.

University of Massachusetts Amherst, Graduate School, College of Social and Behavioral Sciences, Center for Public Policy and Administration, Amherst, MA 01003. Offers MPP, MPPA, MPH/MPPA, MPPA/M Ed, MPPA/MBA, MRP/MPPA. Part-time programs available. *Students:* 23 full-time (13 women), 13 part-time (9 women); includes 9 minority (2 Black or African American, non-Hispanic/Latino; 3 Asian, non-Hispanic/Latino; 3 Hispanic/Latino; 1 Two or more races, non-Hispanic/Latino), 7 international. Average age 30. 99 applicants, 56% accepted, 23 enrolled. In 2014, 27 master's awarded. *Degree requirements:* For master's, thesis or alternative. *Entrance requirements:* For master's, GRE General Test. Additional exam requirements/recommendations for international students: Required—TOEFL (minimum score 550 paper-based; 80 iBT), IELTS (minimum score 6.5). *Application deadline:* For fall admission, 2/1 for domestic and international students. Applications are processed on a rolling basis. Application fee: $75. Electronic applications accepted. *Expenses:* Tuition, state resident: full-time $1980; part-time $110 per credit. Tuition, nonresident: full-time $14,644; part-time $414 per credit. *Required fees:* $11,417. One-time fee: $357. *Financial support:* Fellowships with full and partial tuition reimbursements, research assistantships with full and partial tuition reimbursements, teaching assistantships, career-related internships or fieldwork, Federal Work-Study, scholarships/grants, traineeships, health care benefits, tuition waivers (full and partial), and unspecified assistantships available. Support available to part-time students. Financial award application deadline: 2/1; financial award applicants required to submit FAFSA. *Unit*

head: Dr. Lee Badgett, Graduate Program Director, 413-545-3956, Fax: 413-545-1108, E-mail: info@pubpol.umass.edu. *Application contact:* Lindsay DeSantis, Supervisor of Admissions, 413-545-0722, Fax: 413-577-0010, E-mail: gradadm@grad.umass.edu.
Website: http://www.masspolicy.org

University of Massachusetts Amherst, Graduate School, Interdisciplinary Programs, Dual Degree Program in Education and Public Policy and Administration, Amherst, MA 01003. Offers MPPA/M Ed. *Students:* 1 (woman) full-time. Average age 24. 2 applicants, 100% accepted, 1 enrolled. *Entrance requirements:* Additional exam requirements/recommendations for international students: Required—TOEFL (minimum score 550 paper-based; 80 iBT), IELTS (minimum score 6.5). *Application deadline:* For fall admission, 2/1 for domestic and international students. Applications are processed on a rolling basis. Application fee: $75. Electronic applications accepted. *Expenses:* Tuition, state resident: full-time $1980; part-time $110 per credit. Tuition, nonresident: full-time $14,644; part-time $414 per credit. *Required fees:* $11,417. One-time fee: $357. *Financial support:* Career-related internships or fieldwork, Federal Work-Study, scholarships/grants, traineeships, health care benefits, tuition waivers, and unspecified assistantships available. Support available to part-time students. Financial award application deadline: 2/1. *Unit head:* Dr. Lee Badgett, Professor, 413-545-3162, E-mail: szoller@pubpol.umass.edu. *Application contact:* Lindsay DeSantis, Supervisor of Admissions, 413-545-0722, Fax: 413-577-0010, E-mail: gradadm@grad.umass.edu.
Website: http://www.masspolicy.org/academics/mppa/public-policy-higher-education

University of Massachusetts Amherst, Graduate School, Interdisciplinary Programs, Dual Degree Program in Management and Public Policy and Administration, Amherst, MA 01003. Offers MPPA/MBA. *Accreditation:* AACSB. Part-time programs available. *Students:* 7 full-time (6 women); includes 2 minority (1 Asian, non-Hispanic/Latino; 1 Hispanic/Latino). Average age 30. 13 applicants, 85% accepted, 6 enrolled. *Entrance requirements:* Additional exam requirements/recommendations for international students: Required—TOEFL (minimum score 600 paper-based; 100 iBT), IELTS (minimum score 7). *Application deadline:* For fall admission, 2/1 for domestic and international students. Applications are processed on a rolling basis. Application fee: $75. Electronic applications accepted. *Expenses:* Tuition, state resident: full-time $1980; part-time $110 per credit. Tuition, nonresident: full-time $14,644; part-time $414 per credit. *Required fees:* $11,417. One-time fee: $357. *Financial support:* Career-related internships or fieldwork, Federal Work-Study, scholarships/grants, traineeships, health care benefits, tuition waivers (full), and unspecified assistantships available. Support available to part-time students. Financial award application deadline: 2/1. *Unit head:* Dr. Lee Badgett, Graduate Program Director, 413-545-3956, Fax: 413-545-1108, E-mail: szoller@pubpol.umass.edu. *Application contact:* Lindsay DeSantis, Supervisor of Admissions, 413-545-0722, Fax: 413-577-0010, E-mail: gradadm@grad.umass.edu.
Website: http://www.masspolicy.org/acad_mppa_mba.html

University of Massachusetts Amherst, Graduate School, Interdisciplinary Programs, Dual Degree Program in Public Policy and Administration and Public Health, Amherst, MA 01003. Offers MPH/MPPA. *Students:* 2 full-time (both women). Average age 42. *Entrance requirements:* Additional exam requirements/recommendations for international students: Required—TOEFL (minimum score 550 paper-based; 80 iBT), IELTS (minimum score 6.5). *Application deadline:* For fall admission, 2/1 for domestic and international students. Applications are processed on a rolling basis. Application fee: $75. Electronic applications accepted. *Expenses:* Tuition, state resident: full-time $1980; part-time $110 per credit. Tuition, nonresident: full-time $14,644; part-time $414 per credit. *Required fees:* $11,417. One-time fee: $357. *Financial support:* Career-related internships or fieldwork, Federal Work-Study, scholarships/grants, traineeships, health care benefits, tuition waivers, and unspecified assistantships available. Support available to part-time students. Financial award application deadline: 2/1. *Unit head:* Dr. Lee Badgett, Director, 413-545-2714, E-mail: szoller@pubpol.umass.edu. *Application contact:* Lindsay DeSantis, Supervisor of Admissions, 413-545-0722, Fax: 413-577-0010, E-mail: gradadm@grad.umass.edu.
Website: http://www.masspolicy.org/academics/mppa/public-policy-public-health

University of Massachusetts Amherst, Graduate School, Interdisciplinary Programs, Dual Degree Program in Regional Planning and Public Policy and Administration, Amherst, MA 01003. Offers MPPA/MRP. *Students:* 2 full-time (1 woman), 1 (woman) part-time. Average age 25. *Entrance requirements:* Additional exam requirements/recommendations for international students: Required—TOEFL (minimum score 550 paper-based; 80 iBT), IELTS (minimum score 6.5). *Application deadline:* For fall admission, 2/1 priority date for domestic students, 2/1 for international students. Applications are processed on a rolling basis. Electronic applications accepted. *Expenses:* Tuition, state resident: full-time $1980; part-time $110 per credit. Tuition, nonresident: full-time $14,644; part-time $414 per credit. *Required fees:* $11,417. One-time fee: $357. *Financial support:* Application deadline: 2/1. *Unit head:* Dr. Mark Hamin, Graduate Program Director, 413-545-2714, E-mail: szoller@pubpol.umass.edu. *Application contact:* Lindsay DeSantis, Supervisor of Admissions, 413-545-0722, Fax: 413-577-0010, E-mail: gradadm@grad.umass.edu.
Website: http://www.masspolicy.org/acad_mppa_planning.html

University of Massachusetts Dartmouth, Graduate School, College of Arts and Sciences, Department of Public Policy, North Dartmouth, MA 02747-2300. Offers public management (Graduate Certificate). Part-time programs available. Postbaccalaureate distance learning degree programs offered (no on-campus study). *Faculty:* 5 full-time (1 woman), 1 part-time/adjunct (0 women). *Students:* 18 full-time (8 women), 60 part-time (36 women); includes 20 minority (6 Black or African American, non-Hispanic/Latino; 1 Asian, non-Hispanic/Latino; 7 Hispanic/Latino; 6 Two or more races, non-Hispanic/Latino). Average age 34. 63 applicants, 92% accepted, 38 enrolled. In 2014, 12 master's, 14 other advanced degrees awarded. *Degree requirements:* For master's, portfolio of professional work. *Entrance requirements:* For master's, GRE or GMAT (waived with successful completion of environmental/educational policy graduate certificates at UMass Dartmouth), statement of purpose (minimum of 300 words), resume, 2 letters of recommendation, official transcripts; for Graduate Certificate, statement of purpose (minimum of 300 words), resume, 2 letters of recommendation, official transcripts. Additional exam requirements/recommendations for international students: Required—TOEFL (minimum score 600 paper-based). *Application deadline:* For fall admission, 3/1 priority date for domestic students, 2/1 priority date for international students; for spring admission, 12/15 priority date for domestic students, 11/15 priority date for international students. Applications are processed on a rolling basis. Application fee: $60. Electronic applications accepted. *Expenses:* Tuition, state resident: full-time $2071; part-time $86.29 per credit. Tuition, nonresident: full-time $8099; part-time $337.46 per credit. *Required fees:* $16,520; $712.33 per credit. Tuition and fees vary according to course load and reciprocity agreements. *Financial support:* In 2014–15, 1 research assistantship with full tuition reimbursement (averaging $12,900 per year) was awarded; career-related internships or fieldwork, Federal Work-Study, and unspecified assistantships also available. Support available to part-time students. Financial award application deadline: 3/1; financial award applicants required to submit FAFSA. *Faculty research:* Demographic analysis, legal and regulatory framework, human rights policy, globalization policies, women's public policy issues, educational leadership, environmental law. *Total annual research expenditures:* $829,000. *Unit head:* Chad McGuire, Graduate Program Director, 508-999-8520, Fax: 508-999-8374,

E-mail: cmcguire@umassd.edu. *Application contact:* Steven Briggs, Director of Marketing and Recruitment for Graduate Studies, 508-999-8604, Fax: 508-999-8183, E-mail: graduate@umassd.edu.
Website: http://www.umassd.edu/cas/departmentsanddegreeprograms/publicpolicy/

University of Memphis, Graduate School, College of Arts and Sciences, Division of Public and Nonprofit Administration, Memphis, TN 38152. Offers MPA. *Accreditation:* NASPAA. Part-time and evening/weekend programs available. Postbaccalaureate distance learning degree programs offered (minimal on-campus study). *Faculty:* 5 full-time (3 women), 1 (woman) part-time/adjunct. *Students:* 22 full-time (17 women), 34 part-time (29 women); includes 37 minority (36 Black or African American, non-Hispanic/Latino; 1 Two or more races, non-Hispanic/Latino), 2 international. Average age 37. 28 applicants, 82% accepted, 3 enrolled. In 2014, 23 master's awarded. *Degree requirements:* For master's, comprehensive exam, thesis or alternative, internship. *Entrance requirements:* For master's, GRE General Test, GMAT, or MAT, minimum GPA of 3.0. Additional exam requirements/recommendations for international students: Required—TOEFL. *Application deadline:* For fall admission, 7/1 for domestic students, 5/15 for international students; for spring admission, 12/1 for domestic students, 9/15 for international students. Applications are processed on a rolling basis. Application fee: $35 ($60 for international students). *Financial support:* In 2014–15, 37 students received support. Fellowships, research assistantships with full tuition reimbursements available, career-related internships or fieldwork, Federal Work-Study, scholarships/grants, and unspecified assistantships available. Support available to part-time students. Financial award application deadline: 2/15; financial award applicants required to submit FAFSA. *Faculty research:* Nonprofit organization governance, local government management, community collaboration, urban problems, accountability. *Unit head:* Dr. Michael Howell-Moroney, Director, 901-678-3360, Fax: 901-678-2981, E-mail: mhwllmrn@memphis.edu. *Application contact:* Dr. Charles Menifield, Graduate Admissions Coordinator, 901-678-3360, Fax: 901-678-2981, E-mail: cmenifld@memphis.edu.
Website: http://www.memphis.edu/padm/

University of Michigan–Dearborn, College of Arts, Sciences, and Letters, Master of Public Administration Program, Dearborn, MI 48128. Offers MPA. Part-time and evening/weekend programs available. *Faculty:* 4 full-time (1 woman), 9 part-time/adjunct (2 women). *Students:* 14 full-time (11 women), 50 part-time (37 women); includes 24 minority (16 Black or African American, non-Hispanic/Latino; 1 American Indian or Alaska Native, non-Hispanic/Latino; 6 Hispanic/Latino; 1 Two or more races, non-Hispanic/Latino), 2 international. 30 applicants, 60% accepted, 14 enrolled. In 2014, 37 master's awarded. *Degree requirements:* For master's, assessment seminar. *Entrance requirements:* For master's, GRE or minimum undergraduate GPA of 3.0, 3 letters of recommendation. Additional exam requirements/recommendations for international students: Required—TOEFL (minimum score 560 paper-based; 84 iBT), IELTS (minimum score 6.5). *Application deadline:* For fall admission, 8/1 priority date for domestic students, 5/1 priority date for international students; for winter admission, 12/1 priority date for domestic students, 9/1 priority date for international students; for spring admission, 4/1 priority date for domestic students, 1/1 priority date for international students. Applications are processed on a rolling basis. Application fee: $60. *Expenses:* Expenses: $541 per credit hour in-state, $351 for ninth credit hour and beyond; $1,115 per credit hour out-state, $724 for ninth credit hour and beyond; $267 in fees per term part-time, $329 full-time. *Financial support:* Career-related internships or fieldwork and Federal Work-Study available. Support available to part-time students. Financial award applicants required to submit FAFSA. *Faculty research:* Federal, state, and local agency management; independent sector management; educational administration. *Unit head:* Dr. Paul Draus, Director, 313-583-6628, E-mail: draus@umich.edu. *Application contact:* Carol Ligienza, Coordinator, CASL Graduate Programs, 313-593-1183, Fax: 313-583-6700, E-mail: caslgrad@umich.edu.
Website: http://umdearborn.edu/casl/mpad/

University of Michigan–Flint, Graduate Programs, Program in Public Administration, Flint, MI 48502-1950. Offers administration of non-profit agencies (MPA); criminal justice administration (MPA); educational administration (MPA); healthcare administration (MPA). Part-time programs available. *Faculty:* 1 full-time (0 women), 8 part-time/adjunct (3 women). *Students:* 15 full-time (9 women), 118 part-time (81 women); includes 35 minority (26 Black or African American, non-Hispanic/Latino; 1 American Indian or Alaska Native, non-Hispanic/Latino; 7 Hispanic/Latino; 1 Two or more races, non-Hispanic/Latino), 5 international. Average age 33. 69 applicants, 75% accepted, 38 enrolled. In 2014, 43 master's awarded. *Degree requirements:* For master's, thesis or alternative, internship. *Entrance requirements:* For master's, minimum GPA of 3.0; 1 course each in American government, microeconomics and statistics. Additional exam requirements/recommendations for international students: Required—TOEFL (minimum score 84 iBT), IELTS (minimum score 6.5). *Application deadline:* For fall admission, 8/1 for domestic students, 5/1 for international students; for winter admission, 11/15 for domestic students, 9/1 for international students; for spring admission, 3/15 for domestic students, 1/1 for international students; for summer admission, 5/15 for domestic students. Applications are processed on a rolling basis. Application fee: $55. Electronic applications accepted. Application fee is waived when completed online. *Expenses:* Expenses: Contact institution. *Financial support:* Career-related internships or fieldwork, Federal Work-Study, and scholarships/grants available. Support available to part-time students. Financial award application deadline: 3/1; financial award applicants required to submit FAFSA. *Unit head:* Dr. Kathryn Schellenberg, Director, 810-762-3340, E-mail: kathsch@umflint.edu. *Application contact:* Bradley T. Maki, Director of Graduate Admissions, 810-762-3171, Fax: 810-766-6789, E-mail: bmaki@umflint.edu.
Website: http://www.umflint.edu/graduateprograms/public-administration-mpa

University of Missouri, Office of Research and Graduate Studies, Harry S Truman School of Public Affairs, Columbia, MO 65211. Offers grantsmanship (Graduate Certificate); nonprofit management (Graduate Certificate); organizational change (Graduate Certificate); public affairs (MPA, PhD); public management (Graduate Certificate); science and public policy (Graduate Certificate). *Accreditation:* NASPAA. *Faculty:* 12 full-time (5 women). *Students:* 83 full-time (51 women), 86 part-time (33 women); includes 22 minority (16 Black or African American, non-Hispanic/Latino; 1 American Indian or Alaska Native, non-Hispanic/Latino; 3 Asian, non-Hispanic/Latino; 2 Hispanic/Latino), 35 international. Average age 33. 152 applicants, 53% accepted, 51 enrolled. In 2014, 53 master's, 1 doctorate, 19 other advanced degrees awarded. *Entrance requirements:* For master's, GRE General Test, minimum GPA of 3.0. Additional exam requirements/recommendations for international students: Required—TOEFL (minimum score 550 paper-based; 79 iBT). *Application deadline:* For fall admission, 2/1 priority date for domestic and international students. Applications are processed on a rolling basis. Application fee: $55 ($75 for international students). Electronic applications accepted. *Financial support:* Fellowships, research assistantships, teaching assistantships, institutionally sponsored loans, scholarships/grants, traineeships, health care benefits, and unspecified assistantships available. Support available to part-time students. *Faculty research:* Public service ethics, history and theory, organizational symbolism and culture; program evaluation and social policy, with special emphasis on child development, education and health policies; organization theory and applied psychoanalytic theory; foreign policy and international political economy; health care delivery for persons with disabilities and health policy; survival strategies employed by low-income households; rural economic development, fiscal and economic impact analysis. *Unit head:* Dr. Bart Wechsler, Director, 573-882-3304, E-mail: wechslerb@missouri.edu. *Application contact:* Nicole Harris, Assistant Program Director for Student Services, 573-882-3471, E-mail: harrisnr@missouri.edu.
Website: http://truman.missouri.edu/

University of Missouri–Kansas City, Henry W. Bloch School of Management, Kansas City, MO 64110-2499. Offers accounting (MS); business administration (MBA); entrepreneurial real estate (MERE); entrepreneurship and innovation (PhD); finance (MS); public affairs (MPA, PhD); JD/MBA; LL M/MPA. PhD (interdisciplinary) offered through the School of Graduate Studies. *Accreditation:* AACSB; NASPAA. Part-time and evening/weekend programs available. *Faculty:* 55 full-time (16 women), 39 part-time/adjunct (9 women). *Students:* 266 full-time (115 women), 359 part-time (163 women); includes 99 minority (35 Black or African American, non-Hispanic/Latino; 3 American Indian or Alaska Native, non-Hispanic/Latino; 32 Asian, non-Hispanic/Latino; 18 Hispanic/Latino; 1 Native Hawaiian or other Pacific Islander, non-Hispanic/Latino; 10 Two or more races, non-Hispanic/Latino), 101 international. Average age 30. 399 applicants, 55% accepted, 220 enrolled. In 2014, 292 master's, 1 doctorate awarded. Terminal master's awarded for partial completion of doctoral program. *Entrance requirements:* For master's, GMAT, GRE, 2 essays, 2 references, support of employer; for doctorate, GRE, minimum GPA of 3.0. Additional exam requirements/recommendations for international students: Required—TOEFL (minimum score 550 paper-based; 80 iBT). *Application deadline:* For fall admission, 5/1 priority date for domestic and international students; for spring admission, 10/1 priority date for domestic and international students. Applications are processed on a rolling basis. Application fee: $45 ($50 for international students). Electronic applications accepted. *Financial support:* In 2014–15, 38 research assistantships with partial tuition reimbursements (averaging $10,037 per year), 9 teaching assistantships with partial tuition reimbursements (averaging $12,927 per year) were awarded; career-related internships or fieldwork, Federal Work-Study, institutionally sponsored loans, scholarships/grants, tuition waivers (full and partial), and unspecified assistantships also available. Support available to part-time students. Financial award application deadline: 3/1; financial award applicants required to submit FAFSA. *Faculty research:* Entrepreneurship, finance, non-profit, risk management. *Unit head:* Dr. David Donnelly, Dean, 816-235-1333, Fax: 816-235-2206, E-mail: donnellyd@umkc.edu. *Application contact:* 816-235-1111, E-mail: admit@umkc.edu.
Website: http://www.bloch.umkc.edu

University of Missouri–St. Louis, College of Arts and Sciences, Department of Political Science, St. Louis, MO 63121. Offers American politics (MA); comparative politics (MA); international politics (MA); political process and behavior (MA); political science (PhD); public administration and public policy (MA); urban and regional politics (MA). Part-time and evening/weekend programs available. *Faculty:* 17 full-time (4 women), 6 part-time/adjunct (2 women). *Students:* 22 full-time (7 women), 35 part-time (20 women); includes 6 minority (5 Black or African American, non-Hispanic/Latino; 1 American Indian or Alaska Native, non-Hispanic/Latino), 5 international. Average age 35. 27 applicants, 63% accepted, 12 enrolled. In 2014, 6 master's, 3 doctorates awarded. Terminal master's awarded for partial completion of doctoral program. *Degree requirements:* For master's, thesis optional; for doctorate, thesis/dissertation. *Entrance requirements:* For master's, GRE General Test, 2 letters of recommendation; for doctorate, GRE General Test, 3 letters of recommendation. Additional exam requirements/recommendations for international students: Required—TOEFL (minimum score 550 paper-based; 79 iBT), IELTS (minimum score 6.5). *Application deadline:* For fall admission, 2/15 priority date for domestic and international students; for spring admission, 10/15 priority date for domestic and international students. Applications are processed on a rolling basis. Application fee: $50 ($40 for international students). Electronic applications accepted. *Expenses:* Tuition, state resident: full-time $7364; part-time $409.10 per hour. Tuition, nonresident: full-time $18,153; part-time $1008.50 per hour. *Financial support:* In 2014–15, 3 research assistantships with full and partial tuition reimbursements (averaging $10,800 per year), 10 teaching assistantships with full and partial tuition reimbursements (averaging $10,800 per year) were awarded; fellowships and career-related internships or fieldwork also available. Support available to part-time students. Financial award application deadline: 3/15; financial award applicants required to submit FAFSA. *Faculty research:* Public policy, urban politics and administration, American government. *Unit head:* Dr. David Kimball, Director of Graduate Studies, 314-516-5521, Fax: 314-516-5268, E-mail: umslpolisci@umsl.edu. *Application contact:* 314-516-5458, Fax: 314-516-6996, E-mail: gradadm@umsl.edu.
Website: http://www.umsl.edu/~polisci/

University of Missouri–St. Louis, Graduate School, Program in Public Policy Administration, St. Louis, MO 63121. Offers local government management (MPPA, Certificate); managing human resources and organization (MPPA); nonprofit organization management (MPPA); nonprofit organization management and leadership (Certificate); policy research and analysis (MPPA). *Accreditation:* NASPAA. Part-time and evening/weekend programs available. *Faculty:* 8 part-time/adjunct (5 women). *Students:* 16 full-time (9 women), 61 part-time (35 women); includes 23 minority (20 Black or African American, non-Hispanic/Latino; 1 Asian, non-Hispanic/Latino; 1 Hispanic/Latino; 1 Two or more races, non-Hispanic/Latino), 2 international. Average age 33. 34 applicants, 74% accepted, 16 enrolled. In 2014, 22 master's, 21 Certificates awarded. *Degree requirements:* For master's, exit project. *Entrance requirements:* For master's, 3 letters of recommendation. Additional exam requirements/recommendations for international students: Recommended—TOEFL (minimum score 550 paper-based), IELTS (minimum score 6.5). *Application deadline:* For fall admission, 7/1 priority date for domestic and international students; for spring admission, 12/1 priority date for domestic and international students. Applications are processed on a rolling basis. Application fee: $50 ($40 for international students). Electronic applications accepted. *Expenses:* Tuition, state resident: full-time $7364; part-time $409.10 per hour. Tuition, nonresident: full-time $18,153; part-time $1008.50 per hour. *Financial support:* In 2014–15, 2 research assistantships with full and partial tuition reimbursements (averaging $12,000 per year) were awarded; career-related internships or fieldwork also available. Financial award application deadline: 4/1; financial award applicants required to submit FAFSA. *Faculty research:* Urban policy, public finance, evaluation. *Unit head:* Dr. Deborah Balser, Director, 314-516-5145, Fax: 314-516-5210, E-mail: balserd@msx.umsl.edu. *Application contact:* 314-516-5458, Fax: 314-516-6996, E-mail: gradadm@umsl.edu.
Website: http://www.umsl.edu/divisions/graduate/mppa/

The University of Montana, Graduate School, College of Humanities and Sciences, Department of Political Science, Program in Public Administration, Missoula, MT 59812-0002. Offers MPA, JD/MPA. MPA offered jointly with Montana State University. *Degree requirements:* For master's, professional paper. *Entrance requirements:* For master's, GRE General Test.

University of Nebraska at Omaha, Graduate Studies, College of Public Affairs and Community Service, School of Public Administration, Omaha, NE 68182. Offers public administration (MPA, PhD); public management (Certificate); urban studies (MS). *Accreditation:* NASPAA (one or more programs are accredited). Part-time and evening/weekend programs available. Postbaccalaureate distance learning degree programs offered (no on-campus study). *Faculty:* 21 full-time (8 women). *Students:* 36 full-time (19

women), 167 part-time (83 women); includes 33 minority (16 Black or African American, non-Hispanic/Latino; 1 American Indian or Alaska Native, non-Hispanic/Latino; 3 Asian, non-Hispanic/Latino; 6 Hispanic/Latino; 7 Two or more races, non-Hispanic/Latino), 14 international. Average age 33. 118 applicants, 51% accepted, 51 enrolled. In 2014, 54 master's, 4 doctorates, 4 other advanced degrees awarded. *Degree requirements:* For master's, comprehensive exam (for some programs), thesis (for some programs); for doctorate, comprehensive exam, thesis/dissertation. *Entrance requirements:* For master's, GRE General Test, minimum GPA of 3.0, 2 letters of recommendation, statement of purpose, resume, official transcripts; for doctorate, GRE General Test, master's degree, minimum GPA of 3.2, 3 letters of recommendation, statement of purpose, resume, official transcripts; for Certificate, 3 years of work experience in the public sector, official transcripts, resume, statement of purpose, minimum undergraduate GPA of 3.0. Additional exam requirements/recommendations for international students: Required—TOEFL (minimum score 550 paper-based; 80 iBT), IELTS (minimum score 5.5), PTE (minimum score 44). *Application deadline:* For fall admission, 6/1 for domestic and international students; for spring admission, 10/1 for domestic and international students. Applications are processed on a rolling basis. Application fee: $45. Electronic applications accepted. *Financial support:* In 2014–15, 23 students received support, including 17 research assistantships with tuition reimbursements available, 6 teaching assistantships with tuition reimbursements available; career-related internships or fieldwork, Federal Work-Study, institutionally sponsored loans, scholarships/grants, tuition waivers (partial), and unspecified assistantships also available. Support available to part-time students. Financial award application deadline: 3/1; financial award applicants required to submit FAFSA. *Unit head:* Dr. Ethel Williams, Director, 402-554-2341, E-mail: graduate@unomaha.edu. *Application contact:* Dr. Meagan Van Gelder, Graduate Program Chair, 402-554-2341, E-mail: graduate@unomaha.edu.

University of Nevada, Las Vegas, Graduate College, Greenspun College of Urban Affairs, School of Environmental and Public Affairs, Las Vegas, NV 89154-4030. Offers environmental science (MS, PhD); non-profit management (Certificate); public administration (MPA, MS), including crisis and emergency management (MS); public affairs (PhD); public management (Certificate); urban leadership (MA); workforce development and organizational leadership (PhD). Part-time programs available. *Faculty:* 13 full-time (5 women), 7 part-time/adjunct (2 women). *Students:* 81 full-time (44 women), 115 part-time (60 women); includes 71 minority (24 Black or African American, non-Hispanic/Latino; 2 American Indian or Alaska Native, non-Hispanic/Latino; 5 Asian, non-Hispanic/Latino; 30 Hispanic/Latino; 3 Native Hawaiian or other Pacific Islander, non-Hispanic/Latino; 7 Two or more races, non-Hispanic/Latino), 8 international. Average age 37. 78 applicants, 86% accepted, 48 enrolled. In 2014, 50 master's, 6 doctorates, 19 other advanced degrees awarded. *Degree requirements:* For master's, comprehensive exam (for some programs), thesis; for doctorate, comprehensive exam (for some programs), thesis/dissertation. *Entrance requirements:* Additional exam requirements/recommendations for international students: Required—TOEFL (minimum score 550 paper-based; 80 iBT), IELTS (minimum score 7). *Application deadline:* For fall admission, 2/15 for domestic students, 5/1 for international students; for spring admission, 11/15 for domestic students, 10/1 for international students. Application fee: $60 ($95 for international students). Electronic applications accepted. *Financial support:* In 2014–15, 31 students received support, including 1 fellowship (averaging $25,000 per year), 13 research assistantships with partial tuition reimbursements available (averaging $13,473 per year), 17 teaching assistantships with partial tuition reimbursements available (averaging $13,206 per year); institutionally sponsored loans, scholarships/grants, health care benefits, and unspecified assistantships also available. Financial award application deadline: 3/1. *Faculty research:* Community and organizational resilience; environmental decision-making and management; budgeting and human resource/workforce management; urban design, sustainability and governance; public and non-profit management. *Total annual research expenditures:* $333,798. *Unit head:* Dr. Christopher Stream, Chair/Associate Professor, 702-895-5120, Fax: 702-895-4436, E-mail: chris.stream@unlv.edu. *Application contact:* Graduate College Admissions Evaluator, 702-895-3320, Fax: 702-895-4180, E-mail: gradcollege@unlv.edu.
Website: http://sepa.unlv.edu/

University of Nevada, Reno, Graduate School, College of Liberal Arts, Department of Political Science, Program in Public Administration and Policy, Reno, NV 89557. Offers public administration (MPA). *Degree requirements:* For master's, comprehensive exam, oral exam/thesis or professional paper. *Entrance requirements:* For master's, GRE General Test, GMAT, or LSAT, minimum GPA of 2.75. Additional exam requirements/recommendations for international students: Required—TOEFL (minimum score 500 paper-based; 61 iBT), IELTS (minimum score 6). Electronic applications accepted. *Faculty research:* Administrative processes and problems, public policy issues.

University of New Brunswick Fredericton, School of Graduate Studies, Faculty of Business Administration, Fredericton, NB E3B 5A3, Canada. Offers business administration (MBA); engineering management (MBA); entrepreneurship (MBA); sports and recreation management (MBA); MBA/LL B. Part-time programs available. *Faculty:* 22 full-time (3 women), 4 part-time/adjunct (1 woman). *Students:* 33 full-time (13 women), 38 part-time (12 women), 1 international. In 2014, 54 master's awarded. *Degree requirements:* For master's, thesis optional. *Entrance requirements:* For master's, GMAT (minimum score 550), minimum GPA of 3.0; 3-5 years of work experience; 3 letters of reference with at least one academic reference. Additional exam requirements/recommendations for international students: Required—TOEFL (minimum score 580 paper-based; 92 iBT) or IELTS (minimum score 7). *Application deadline:* For fall admission, 10/31 priority date for domestic and international students; for spring admission, 3/31 priority date for domestic and international students. Application fee: $50 Canadian dollars. Electronic applications accepted. *Financial support:* In 2014–15, 6 fellowships, 3 research assistantships (averaging $4,500 per year), 22 teaching assistantships (averaging $2,250 per year) were awarded. *Faculty research:* Entrepreneurship, finance, law, sport and recreation management, engineering management. *Unit head:* Dr. Donglei Du, Director of Graduate Studies, 506-458-7353, Fax: 506-453-3561, E-mail: ddu@unb.ca. *Application contact:* Marilyn Davis, Acting Graduate Secretary, 506-453-4766, Fax: 506-453-3561, E-mail: mbacontact@unb.ca.
Website: http://go.unb.ca/gradprograms

University of New Hampshire, Graduate School, College of Liberal Arts, Department of Political Science, Program in Public Administration, Durham, NH 03824. Offers MPA. Part-time programs available. *Students:* 7 full-time (2 women), 25 part-time (10 women); includes 3 minority (2 Black or African American, non-Hispanic/Latino; 1 Hispanic/Latino). Average age 34. 22 applicants, 73% accepted, 10 enrolled. In 2014, 19 master's awarded. *Entrance requirements:* For master's, GMAT or GRE General Test. Additional exam requirements/recommendations for international students: Required—TOEFL (minimum score 550 paper-based; 80 iBT). *Application deadline:* For fall admission, 6/1 priority date for domestic students, 4/1 for international students; for spring admission, 12/1 for domestic students. Applications are processed on a rolling basis. Application fee: $65. Electronic applications accepted. *Expenses:* Tuition, state resident: full-time $13,500; part-time $750 per credit hour. Tuition, nonresident: full-time $26,460; part-time $1110 per credit hour. *Required fees:* $1788; $447 per semester. *Financial support:* In 2014–15, 1 student received support, including 1 fellowship; research assistantships, teaching assistantships, career-related internships or fieldwork, Federal Work-Study, scholarships/grants, and tuition waivers (full and partial) also available. Support available to part-time students. Financial award application deadline: 2/15. *Unit head:* Stacy VanDeever, Chairperson, 603-862-0167. *Application contact:* Tama Andrews, Administrative Assistant, 603-862-2321, E-mail: mpa.ma.political.science.grad@unh.edu.
Website: http://cola.unh.edu/political-science/program/public-administration-mpa

University of New Hampshire, Graduate School Manchester Campus, Manchester, NH 03101. Offers business administration (MBA); counseling (M Ed); education (M Ed, MAT); educational administration and supervision (M Ed, Ed S); information technology (MS); management of technology (MS); public administration (MPA); public health (MPH, Certificate); social work (MSW); software systems engineering (Certificate). Part-time and evening/weekend programs available. *Students:* 1 (woman) full-time, 14 part-time (0 women); includes 1 minority (Hispanic/Latino), 4 international. Average age 34. 11 applicants, 64% accepted, 5 enrolled. *Degree requirements:* For master's, thesis or alternative. *Entrance requirements:* Additional exam requirements/recommendations for international students: Required—TOEFL (minimum score 550 paper-based; 80 iBT). *Application deadline:* For fall admission, 6/1 for domestic students, 4/1 for international students; for spring admission, 12/1 for domestic students. Applications are processed on a rolling basis. Application fee: $65. Electronic applications accepted. *Expenses:* Tuition, state resident: full-time $13,500; part-time $750 per credit hour. Tuition, nonresident: full-time $26,460; part-time $1110 per credit hour. *Required fees:* $1788; $447 per semester. *Financial support:* Fellowships, research assistantships, teaching assistantships, Federal Work-Study, scholarships/grants, health care benefits, and unspecified assistantships available. Support available to part-time students. Financial award application deadline: 3/1; financial award applicants required to submit FAFSA. *Unit head:* Candice Morey, Director, 603-641-4313, E-mail: unhm.gradcenter@unh.edu. *Application contact:* Graduate Admissions Office, 603-862-3000, Fax: 603-862-0275, E-mail: grad.school@unh.edu.
Website: http://www.gradschool.unh.edu/manchester/

University of New Haven, Graduate School, College of Business, Program in Public Administration, West Haven, CT 06516-1916. Offers city management (MPA); community-clinical services (MPA); health care management (MPA); long-term health care (MPA); personnel and labor relations (MPA); public administration (MPA, Certificate); public management (Certificate); MBA/MPA. Part-time and evening/weekend programs available. *Degree requirements:* For master's, thesis or alternative. *Entrance requirements:* Additional exam requirements/recommendations for international students: Required—TOEFL (minimum score 80 iBT), IELTS, PTE (minimum score 53). Electronic applications accepted. Application fee is waived when completed online. *Expenses:* Contact institution.

University of New Haven, Graduate School, Henry C. Lee College of Criminal Justice and Forensic Sciences, National Security Program, West Haven, CT 06516-1916. Offers information protection and security (MS, Certificate); national security (MS, Certificate); national security administration (Certificate). Part-time and evening/weekend programs available. *Degree requirements:* For master's, thesis or alternative, research project or internship. *Entrance requirements:* Additional exam requirements/recommendations for international students: Required—TOEFL (minimum score 70 iBT), IELTS, or PTE (minimum score of 53). Electronic applications accepted. Application fee is waived when completed online. *Expenses: Tuition:* Full-time $22,248; part-time $824 per credit hour. *Required fees:* $45 per trimester.

University of New Haven, Graduate School, Henry C. Lee College of Criminal Justice and Forensic Sciences, Program in Fire Science, West Haven, CT 06516-1916. Offers emergency management (MS, Certificate); fire administration (MS); fire science (MS); fire science technology (Certificate); fire/arson investigation (MS, Certificate); forensic science/fire science (Certificate); public safety management (MS, Certificate). Part-time and evening/weekend programs available. *Degree requirements:* For master's, thesis or alternative, research project or internship. *Entrance requirements:* Additional exam requirements/recommendations for international students: Required—TOEFL (minimum score 80 iBT), IELTS, PTE (minimum score 53). Electronic applications accepted. Application fee is waived when completed online. *Expenses: Tuition:* Full-time $22,248; part-time $824 per credit hour. *Required fees:* $45 per trimester.

University of New Mexico, Graduate School, School of Public Administration, Program in Public Administration, Albuquerque, NM 87131-2039. Offers MPA. *Faculty:* 7 full-time (1 woman), 4 part-time/adjunct (0 women). *Students:* 56 full-time (31 women), 123 part-time (77 women); includes 114 minority (5 Black or African American, non-Hispanic/Latino; 28 American Indian or Alaska Native, non-Hispanic/Latino; 6 Asian, non-Hispanic/Latino; 72 Hispanic/Latino; 3 Two or more races, non-Hispanic/Latino), 9 international. Average age 36. 55 applicants, 65% accepted, 27 enrolled. In 2014, 94 master's awarded. *Entrance requirements:* For master's, baccalaureate degree from accredited college or university with minimum undergraduate GPA of 3.0 for last 60 hours or overall major; letter of intent; three letters of recommendation; resume; official transcripts. *Application deadline:* For fall admission, 4/1 for domestic students, 3/1 for international students; for spring admission, 10/1 for domestic students, 8/1 for international students. Application fee: $50. Electronic applications accepted. *Unit head:* Dr. Uday Desai, Director, 505-277-1092, Fax: 505-277-2529, E-mail: ucdesai@unm.edu. *Application contact:* Gene V. Henley, Associate Director and Graduate Academic Advisor, 505-277-9196, Fax: 505-277-2529, E-mail: spadvise@unm.edu.
Website: http://spa.unm.edu/mpa-graduate-program/

University of New Orleans, Graduate School, College of Liberal Arts, Department of Political Science, Program in Public Administration, New Orleans, LA 70148. Offers MPA. *Accreditation:* NASPAA. *Degree requirements:* For master's, thesis. *Entrance requirements:* For master's, GRE General Test. Additional exam requirements/recommendations for international students: Required—TOEFL (minimum score 550 paper-based; 79 iBT), IELTS (minimum score 6.5). Electronic applications accepted.

The University of North Carolina at Chapel Hill, Graduate School, School of Government, Chapel Hill, NC 27599. Offers MPA, JD/MPA, MPA/MRP, MPA/MSW. *Accreditation:* NASPAA. *Degree requirements:* For master's, comprehensive exam. *Entrance requirements:* For master's, GRE General Test, minimum GPA of 3.0. Additional exam requirements/recommendations for international students: Required—TOEFL. Electronic applications accepted. *Faculty research:* Local government management, nonprofit management.

The University of North Carolina at Charlotte, College of Liberal Arts and Sciences, Department of Political Science and Public Administration, Charlotte, NC 28223-0001. Offers emergency management (Graduate Certificate); non-profit management (Graduate Certificate); public administration (MPA), including arts administration, emergency management, non-profit management, public finance; public finance (Graduate Certificate); urban management and policy (Graduate Certificate). *Accreditation:* NASPAA. Part-time and evening/weekend programs available. *Faculty:* 15 full-time (8 women), 4 part-time/adjunct (1 woman). *Students:* 16 full-time (10 women), 83 part-time (51 women); includes 32 minority (21 Black or African American, non-Hispanic/Latino; 1 Asian, non-Hispanic/Latino; 7 Hispanic/Latino; 3 Two or more

races, non-Hispanic/Latino). Average age 30. 60 applicants, 65% accepted, 25 enrolled. In 2014, 23 master's, 11 other advanced degrees awarded. Terminal master's awarded for partial completion of doctoral program. *Degree requirements:* For master's, thesis or alternative. *Entrance requirements:* For master's, GRE General Test or MAT, minimum GPA of 3.0 in undergraduate major, 2.75 overall. Additional exam requirements/recommendations for international students: Required—TOEFL (minimum score 557 paper-based; 83 iBT). *Application deadline:* For fall admission, 5/1 priority date for domestic students, 5/1 for international students; for spring admission, 10/1 priority date for domestic students, 10/1 for international students. Applications are processed on a rolling basis. Application fee: $75. Electronic applications accepted. *Expenses:* Tuition, state resident: full-time $4008. Tuition, nonresident: full-time $16,295. *Required fees:* $2755. Tuition and fees vary according to course load and program. *Financial support:* In 2014–15, 7 students received support, including 7 research assistantships (averaging $6,857 per year); career-related internships or fieldwork, Federal Work-Study, institutionally sponsored loans, scholarships/grants, and unspecified assistantships also available. Support available to part-time students. Financial award application deadline: 4/1; financial award applicants required to submit FAFSA. *Faculty research:* Health policy and politics, managed care, issues of ethnic and racial disparities in health, aging policies, Central Asia. *Total annual research expenditures:* $348,793. *Unit head:* Dr. Greg Weeks, Chair, 704-687-7574, Fax: 704-687-1400, E-mail: gbweeks@uncc.edu. *Application contact:* Kathy B. Giddings, Director of Graduate Admissions, 704-687-5503, Fax: 704-687-1668, E-mail: gradadm@uncc.edu. Website: https://politicalscience.uncc.edu/graduate

The University of North Carolina at Pembroke, Graduate Studies, Public Administration Program, Pembroke, NC 28372-1510. Offers MPA. Part-time and evening/weekend programs available. Postbaccalaureate distance learning degree programs offered. *Degree requirements:* For master's, comprehensive exam, thesis optional. *Entrance requirements:* For master's, GRE General Test or MAT, minimum GPA of 3.0 in major, 2.5 overall; interview. Additional exam requirements/recommendations for international students: Required—TOEFL.

The University of North Carolina Wilmington, College of Arts and Sciences, Department of Public and International Affairs, Wilmington, NC 28403-3297. Offers coastal and ocean policy (MS); conflict management (Graduate Certificate); conflict management and resolution (MA); public administration (MPA). *Accreditation:* NASPAA. Part-time programs available. *Faculty:* 14 full-time (4 women). *Students:* 54 full-time (32 women), 67 part-time (44 women); includes 17 minority (11 Black or African American, non-Hispanic/Latino; 1 American Indian or Alaska Native, non-Hispanic/Latino; 1 Asian, non-Hispanic/Latino; 4 Hispanic/Latino), 1 international. 55 applicants, 100% accepted, 39 enrolled. In 2014, 26 master's awarded. *Degree requirements:* For master's, comprehensive exam, thesis or alternative, practicum. *Entrance requirements:* For master's, GRE, GMAT. Additional exam requirements/recommendations for international students: Required—TOEFL (minimum score 79 iBT), IELTS. *Application deadline:* For fall admission, 4/15 for domestic students; for spring admission, 11/5 for domestic students. Application fee: $60. *Expenses:* Tuition, state resident: full-time $3240. Tuition, nonresident: full-time $9208. *Required fees:* $1967. *Financial support:* Application deadline: 3/15; applicants required to submit FAFSA. *Unit head:* Dr. Earl Sheridan, Chair, 910-962-3222, Fax: 910-962-3286, E-mail: sheridan@uncw.edu. *Application contact:* Dr. Mark Imperial, MPA Program Director and Internship Coordinator/Program Director, Master of Coastal and Ocean Policy, 910-962-7928, Fax: 910-962-3286, E-mail: imperialm@uncw.edu. Website: http://www.uncw.edu/pia/graduate/index.html

University of North Dakota, Graduate School, College of Business and Public Administration, Department of Public Administration, Grand Forks, ND 58202. Offers MPA. *Accreditation:* NASPAA. Part-time programs available. Postbaccalaureate distance learning degree programs offered (minimal on-campus study). *Degree requirements:* For master's, comprehensive exam, thesis or alternative, final exam. *Entrance requirements:* For master's, GRE General Test, GMAT or LSAT, minimum GPA of 3.0. Additional exam requirements/recommendations for international students: Required—TOEFL (minimum score 550 paper-based; 79 iBT), IELTS (minimum score 6.5). Electronic applications accepted.

University of North Florida, College of Arts and Sciences, Department of Political Science and Public Administration, Jacksonville, FL 32224. Offers nonprofit management (Graduate Certificate); public administration (MPA). *Accreditation:* NASPAA. Part-time programs available. *Faculty:* 14 full-time (5 women), 1 part-time/adjunct (0 women). *Students:* 14 full-time (11 women), 40 part-time (21 women); includes 20 minority (11 Black or African American, non-Hispanic/Latino; 8 Hispanic/Latino; 1 Two or more races, non-Hispanic/Latino), 3 international. Average age 32. 35 applicants, 51% accepted, 7 enrolled. In 2014, 35 master's awarded. *Degree requirements:* For master's, thesis or alternative, internship. *Entrance requirements:* For master's, GRE General Test, minimum GPA of 3.0 in last 60 hours, 2 letters of recommendation, interview. Additional exam requirements/recommendations for international students: Required—TOEFL (minimum score 500 paper-based; 61 iBT). *Application deadline:* For fall admission, 7/1 priority date for domestic students, 5/1 for international students; for spring admission, 11/1 priority date for domestic students, 10/1 for international students. Application fee: $30. Electronic applications accepted. *Expenses:* Tuition, state resident: full-time $9794; part-time $408.10 per credit hour. Tuition, nonresident: full-time $22,383; part-time $932.61 per credit hour. *Required fees:* $2047; $85.29 per credit hour. Tuition and fees vary according to course load and program. *Financial support:* In 2014–15, 9 students received support. Research assistantships, teaching assistantships, career-related internships or fieldwork, Federal Work-Study, scholarships/grants, tuition waivers (partial), and unspecified assistantships available. Financial award application deadline: 4/1; financial award applicants required to submit FAFSA. *Faculty research:* America's usage of the Internet, use of information communication technologies by educators and children. *Total annual research expenditures:* $147. *Unit head:* Dr. Matthew T. Corrigan, Chair, 904-620-2977, Fax: 904-620-2979, E-mail: mcorriga@unf.edu. *Application contact:* Dr. Amanda Pascale, Director, The Graduate School, 904-620-1360, Fax: 907-620-1362, E-mail: graduateschool@unf.edu. Website: http://www.unf.edu/coas/pspa/

University of North Georgia, Department of Political Science and Criminal Justice, Dahlonega, GA 30597. Offers criminal justice (MS); international affairs (MAIA); public administration (MPA). Part-time and evening/weekend programs available. Postbaccalaureate distance learning degree programs offered (no on-campus study). *Degree requirements:* For master's, thesis optional, internship. *Entrance requirements:* For master's, GRE or GMAT, minimum undergraduate GPA of 2.5, 3 letters of recommendation. Additional exam requirements/recommendations for international students: Required—TOEFL (minimum score 550 paper-based; 79 iBT), IELTS (minimum score 6.5). Electronic applications accepted.

University of North Texas, Robert B. Toulouse School of Graduate Studies, Denton, TX 76203-5459. Offers accounting (MS); applied anthropology (MA, MS); applied behavior analysis (Certificate); applied geography (MA); applied technology and performance improvement (M Ed, MS); art education (MA); art history (MA); art museum education (Certificate); arts leadership (Certificate); audiology (Au D); behavior analysis

(MS); behavioral science (PhD); biochemistry and molecular biology (MS); biology (MA, MS); biomedical engineering (MS); business analysis (MS); chemistry (MS); clinical health psychology (PhD); communication studies (MA, MS); computer engineering (MS); computer science (MS); counseling (M Ed, MS), including clinical mental health counseling (MS), college and university counseling, elementary school counseling, secondary school counseling; creative writing (MA); criminal justice (MS); curriculum and instruction (M Ed); decision sciences (MBA); design (MA, MFA), including fashion design (MFA), innovation studies, interior design (MFA); early childhood studies (MS); economics (MS); educational leadership (M Ed, Ed D); educational psychology (MS, PhD), including family studies (MS), gifted and talented (MS), human development (MS), learning and cognition (MS), research, measurement and evaluation (MS); electrical engineering (MS); emergency management (MPA); engineering technology (MS); English (MA); English as a second language (MA); environmental science (MS); finance (MBA, MS); financial management (MPA); French (MA); health services management (MBA); higher education (M Ed, Ed D); history (MA, MS); hospitality management (MS); human resources management (MPA); information science (MS); information systems (PhD); information technologies (MBA); interdisciplinary studies (MA, MS); international studies (MA); international sustainable tourism (MS); jazz studies (MM); journalism (MA, MJ, Graduate Certificate), including interactive and virtual digital communication (Graduate Certificate), narrative journalism (Graduate Certificate), public relations (Graduate Certificate); kinesiology (MS); linguistics (MA); local government management (MPA); logistics (PhD); logistics and supply chain management (MBA); long-term care, senior housing, and aging services (MA); management (PhD); marketing (MBA); mathematics (MA, MS); mechanical and energy engineering (MS, PhD); music (MA), including ethnomusicology, music theory, musicology, performance; music composition (PhD); music education (MM Ed, PhD); nonprofit management (MPA); operations and supply chain management (MBA); performance (MM, DMA); philosophy (MA); political science (MA); professional and technical communication (MA); radio, television and film (MA, MFA); rehabilitation counseling (Certificate); sociology (MA); Spanish (MA); special education (M Ed); speech-language pathology (MA); strategic management (MBA); studio art (MFA); teaching (M Ed); MBA/MS. Part-time and evening/weekend programs available. Postbaccalaureate distance learning degree programs offered. *Faculty:* 651 full-time (215 women), 233 part-time/adjunct (139 women). *Students:* 3,040 full-time (1,598 women), 3,401 part-time (2,097 women); includes 1,740 minority (533 Black or African American, non-Hispanic/Latino; 15 American Indian or Alaska Native, non-Hispanic/Latino; 286 Asian, non-Hispanic/Latino; 746 Hispanic/Latino; 3 Native Hawaiian or other Pacific Islander, non-Hispanic/Latino; 157 Two or more races, non-Hispanic/Latino), 1,145 international. Terminal master's awarded for partial completion of doctoral program. *Degree requirements:* For master's, variable foreign language requirement, comprehensive exam (for some programs), thesis (for some programs); for doctorate, variable foreign language requirement, comprehensive exam (for some programs), thesis/dissertation; for other advanced degree, variable foreign language requirement, comprehensive exam (for some programs). *Entrance requirements:* For master's and doctorate, GRE, GMAT. Additional exam requirements/recommendations for international students: Required—TOEFL (minimum score 550 paper-based; 79 iBT). *Application deadline:* For fall admission, 7/15 for domestic students, 3/15 for international students; for spring admission, 11/15 for domestic students, 9/15 for international students; for summer admission, 5/1 for domestic students. Applications are processed on a rolling basis. Application fee: $60. Electronic applications accepted. *Expenses:* Tuition, state resident: full-time $5450; part-time $3633 per year. Tuition, nonresident: full-time $11,966; part-time $7977 per year. *Required fees:* $1301; $398 per credit hour. $685 per semester. Tuition and fees vary according to program and reciprocity agreements. *Financial support:* Fellowships with partial tuition reimbursements, research assistantships with partial tuition reimbursements, teaching assistantships, career-related internships or fieldwork, Federal Work-Study, institutionally sponsored loans, scholarships/grants, health care benefits, and library assistantships available. Support available to part-time students. Financial award applicants required to submit FAFSA. *Unit head:* Mark Wardell, Dean, 940-565-2383, E-mail: mark.wardell@unt.edu. *Application contact:* Toulouse School of Graduate Studies, 940-565-2383, Fax: 940-565-2141, E-mail: gradsch@unt.edu. Website: http://tsgs.unt.edu/

University of Oklahoma, College of Arts and Sciences, Department of Political Science, Program in Public Administration, Norman, OK 73019. Offers non-profit management (MPA); public administration (MPA); public policy (MPA). Part-time and evening/weekend programs available. *Students:* 23 full-time (13 women), 23 part-time (11 women); includes 14 minority (3 Black or African American, non-Hispanic/Latino; 3 American Indian or Alaska Native, non-Hispanic/Latino; 1 Asian, non-Hispanic/Latino; 2 Hispanic/Latino; 5 Two or more races, non-Hispanic/Latino). Average age 30. 25 applicants, 72% accepted, 12 enrolled. In 2014, 28 master's awarded. Terminal master's awarded for partial completion of doctoral program. *Degree requirements:* For master's, comprehensive exam, thesis or alternative, 36 hours. *Entrance requirements:* For master's, GRE, statement of purpose, two letters of recommendation. Additional exam requirements/recommendations for international students: Required—TOEFL (minimum score 100 iBT). *Application deadline:* For fall admission, 2/15 for domestic students, 4/1 for international students; for spring admission, 10/1 for domestic students, 9/1 for international students; for summer admission, 2/1 for international students. Applications are processed on a rolling basis. Application fee: $50 ($100 for international students). Electronic applications accepted. *Expenses:* Tuition, state resident: full-time $4394; part-time $183.10 per credit hour. Tuition, nonresident: full-time $16,970; part-time $707.10 per credit hour. *Required fees:* $2892; $109.95 per credit hour. $126.50 per semester. *Financial support:* In 2014–15, 27 students received support. Career-related internships or fieldwork, scholarships/grants, health care benefits, and unspecified assistantships available. Support available to part-time students. Financial award application deadline: 6/1; financial award applicants required to submit FAFSA. *Faculty research:* Public management, nonprofit administration, public policy, policy analysis, program evaluation. *Unit head:* Dr. Alisa Fryar, Director of Graduate Programs in Public Administration, 405-325-1845, Fax: 405-325-0718, E-mail: ahicklin@ou.edu. *Application contact:* Jeff Alexander, Graduate Programs Coordinator, 405-325-1845, Fax: 405-325-0718, E-mail: jjalexander@ou.edu. Website: http://psc.ou.edu/mpa

University of Ottawa, Faculty of Graduate and Postdoctoral Studies, Interdisciplinary Programs, Ottawa, ON K1N 6N5, Canada. Offers e-business (Certificate); e-commerce (Certificate); finance (Certificate); health services and policies research (Diploma); population health (PhD); population health risk assessment and management (Certificate); public management and governance (Certificate); systems science (Certificate).

University of Pennsylvania, School of Arts and Sciences, Fels Institute of Government, Philadelphia, PA 19104. Offers economic development and growth (Certificate); government administration (MGA); nonprofit administration (Certificate); organization dynamics (MS); politics (Certificate); public administration (MPA); public finance (Certificate). Part-time and evening/weekend programs available. *Students:* 62 full-time (32 women), 75 part-time (45 women); includes 31 minority (17 Black or African American, non-Hispanic/Latino; 6 Asian, non-Hispanic/Latino; 4 Hispanic/Latino; 4 Two or more races, non-Hispanic/Latino), 20 international. 445 applicants, 24% accepted, 47

enrolled. In 2014, 56 master's, 31 other advanced degrees awarded. *Entrance requirements:* For master's, GRE, GMAT, or LSAT. Additional exam requirements/recommendations for international students: Required—TOEFL, IELTS. *Application deadline:* For fall admission, 1/15 for domestic students. Applications are processed on a rolling basis. Application fee: $70. *Financial support:* Fellowships, institutionally sponsored loans, and scholarships/grants available. Financial award application deadline: 1/15; financial award applicants required to submit FAFSA. *Unit head:* John J. Mulhern, Executive Director, 215-898-2600, E-mail: david_thornburgh@sas.upenn.edu. *Application contact:* 215-746-6684, Fax: 215-898-6238, E-mail: felsinstitute@sas.upenn.edu.
Website: http://www.fels.upenn.edu/

University of Phoenix–Atlanta Campus, School of Business, Sandy Springs, GA 30350-4153. Offers accounting (MBA); business administration (MBA); global management (MBA); human resources management (MBA, MM); management (MM); marketing (MBA); public administration (MM). Evening/weekend programs available. Postbaccalaureate distance learning degree programs offered. *Degree requirements:* For master's, thesis (for some programs). *Entrance requirements:* For master's, minimum undergraduate GPA of 3.0, 3 years of work experience. Additional exam requirements/recommendations for international students: Required—TOEFL (minimum score 550 paper-based; 79 iBT).

University of Phoenix–Augusta Campus, School of Business, Augusta, GA 30909-4583. Offers accounting (MBA); business administration (MBA); business and management (MBA, MM); global management (MBA); human resources management (MBA, MM); management (MM); marketing (MBA); public administration (MBA, MM). Postbaccalaureate distance learning degree programs offered.

University of Phoenix–Austin Campus, School of Business, Austin, TX 78759. Offers accounting (MBA); business administration (MBA); business and management (MBA); e-business (MBA); global management (MBA); human resources management (MBA, MM); management (MM); marketing (MBA); public administration (MBA). Postbaccalaureate distance learning degree programs offered.

University of Phoenix–Bay Area Campus, School of Business, San Jose, CA 95134-1805. Offers accountancy (MS); accounting (MBA); business administration (MBA, DBA); energy management (MBA); global management (MBA); health care management (MBA); human resource management (MBA); human resources management (MM); management (MM); marketing (MBA); organizational leadership (DM); project management (MBA); public administration (MPA); technology management (MBA). Evening/weekend programs available. Postbaccalaureate distance learning degree programs offered (no on-campus study). *Degree requirements:* For master's, thesis (for some programs). *Entrance requirements:* For master's, minimum undergraduate GPA of 3.0, 3 years of work experience. Additional exam requirements/recommendations for international students: Required—TOEFL (minimum score 550 paper-based; 79 iBT). Electronic applications accepted.

University of Phoenix–Birmingham Campus, College of Graduate Business and Management, Birmingham, AL 35242. Offers accounting (MBA); business administration (MBA); global management (MBA); human resources management (MBA, MM); management (MM); marketing (MBA); public administration (MM).

University of Phoenix–Central Valley Campus, School of Business, Fresno, CA 93720-1562. Offers accounting (MBA); business administration (MBA); global management (MBA); human resources management (MBA, MM); management (MM); marketing (MBA); public administration (MBA, MM).

University of Phoenix–Cleveland Campus, School of Business, Beachwood, OH 44122. Offers accounting (MBA); business administration (MBA); global management (MBA); human resources management (MBA, MM); management (MM); marketing (MBA); public administration (MBA, MM). Evening/weekend programs available. Postbaccalaureate distance learning degree programs offered (no on-campus study). *Degree requirements:* For master's, thesis (for some programs). *Entrance requirements:* For master's, minimum undergraduate GPA of 3.0, 3 years of work experience. Additional exam requirements/recommendations for international students: Required—TOEFL (minimum score 550 paper-based; 79 iBT). Electronic applications accepted.

University of Phoenix–Colorado Campus, School of Business, Lone Tree, CO 80124-5453. Offers accountancy (MSA); accounting (MBA); business administration (MBA); e-business (MBA); global management (MBA); human resources management (MBA, MM); management (MM); marketing (MBA); public administration (MBA, MM). Evening/weekend programs available. Postbaccalaureate distance learning degree programs offered. *Degree requirements:* For master's, thesis (for some programs). *Entrance requirements:* For master's, minimum undergraduate GPA of 3.0, 3 years work experience. Additional exam requirements/recommendations for international students: Required—TOEFL (minimum score 550 paper-based; 79 iBT). Electronic applications accepted.

University of Phoenix–Colorado Springs Downtown Campus, School of Business, Colorado Springs, CO 80903. Offers accounting (MBA); business administration (MBA); global management (MBA); human resources management (MBA, MM); management (MM); marketing (MBA); public administration (MM). Evening/weekend programs available. *Degree requirements:* For master's, thesis (for some programs). *Entrance requirements:* For master's, minimum undergraduate GPA of 3.0, 3 years of work experience. Additional exam requirements/recommendations for international students: Required—TOEFL (minimum score 550 paper-based; 79 iBT). Electronic applications accepted.

University of Phoenix–Columbus Georgia Campus, School of Business, Columbus, GA 31909. Offers accounting (MBA); business administration (MBA); global management (MBA); human resources management (MBA, MM); management (MM); marketing (MBA); public administration (MBA). Evening/weekend programs available. *Degree requirements:* For master's, thesis (for some programs). *Entrance requirements:* For master's, minimum undergraduate GPA of 3.0, 3 years of work experience. Additional exam requirements/recommendations for international students: Required—TOEFL (minimum score 550 paper-based; 79 iBT). Electronic applications accepted.

University of Phoenix–Dallas Campus, School of Business, Dallas, TX 75251. Offers accounting (MBA); business administration (MBA); global management (MBA); human resources management (MBA, MM); management (MM); marketing (MBA); public administration (MBA, MM). Evening/weekend programs available. Postbaccalaureate distance learning degree programs offered. *Degree requirements:* For master's, thesis (for some programs). *Entrance requirements:* For master's, 3 years of work experience, minimum undergraduate GPA of 3.0. Additional exam requirements/recommendations for international students: Required—TOEFL (minimum score 550 paper-based; 79 iBT). Electronic applications accepted.

University of Phoenix–Des Moines Campus, School of Business, Des Moines, IA 50309. Offers accounting (MBA); business administration (MBA); global management (MBA); human resources management (MBA, MM); management (MM); marketing (MBA); public administration (MBA, MM). Postbaccalaureate distance learning degree programs offered.

University of Phoenix–Hawaii Campus, School of Business, Honolulu, HI 96813-4317. Offers accounting (MBA); business administration (MBA); global management (MBA); human resources management (MBA, MM); management (MM); marketing (MBA); public administration (MBA, MM). Evening/weekend programs available. *Degree requirements:* For master's, thesis (for some programs). *Entrance requirements:* For master's, minimum undergraduate GPA of 3.0, 3 years of work experience. Additional exam requirements/recommendations for international students: Required—TOEFL (minimum score 550 paper-based; 79 iBT). Electronic applications accepted.

University of Phoenix–Houston Campus, School of Business, Houston, TX 77079-2004. Offers accounting (MBA); business administration (MBA); global management (MBA); human resources management (MBA, MM); management (MM); marketing (MBA); public administration (MBA, MM). Evening/weekend programs available. Postbaccalaureate distance learning degree programs offered. *Degree requirements:* For master's, thesis (for some programs). *Entrance requirements:* For master's, 3 years of work experience, minimum undergraduate GPA of 3.0. Additional exam requirements/recommendations for international students: Required—TOEFL (minimum score 550 paper-based; 79 iBT). Electronic applications accepted.

University of Phoenix–Idaho Campus, School of Business, Meridian, ID 83642-5114. Offers accounting (MBA); administration (MBA); global management (MBA); human resources management (MBA, MM); management (MM); marketing (MBA); public administration (MM). Evening/weekend programs available. Postbaccalaureate distance learning degree programs offered. *Degree requirements:* For master's, thesis (for some programs). *Entrance requirements:* For master's, 3 years of work experience, minimum undergraduate GPA of 3.0. Additional exam requirements/recommendations for international students: Required—TOEFL (minimum score 550 paper-based). Electronic applications accepted.

University of Phoenix–Indianapolis Campus, School of Business, Indianapolis, IN 46250-932. Offers accounting (MBA); business administration (MBA); global management (MBA); human resources management (MBA, MM); management (MM); marketing (MBA); public administration (MM). Evening/weekend programs available. *Degree requirements:* For master's, thesis (for some programs). *Entrance requirements:* For master's, minimum undergraduate GPA of 3.0, 3 years of work experience. Additional exam requirements/recommendations for international students: Required—TOEFL (minimum score 550 paper-based). Electronic applications accepted.

University of Phoenix–Jersey City Campus, School of Business, Jersey City, NJ 07310. Offers accounting (MBA); business administration (MBA); global management (MBA); human resources management (MBA, MM); management (MM); marketing (MBA); public administration (MBA, MM).

University of Phoenix–Kansas City Campus, School of Business, Kansas City, MO 64131. Offers accounting (MBA); business administration (MBA); global management (MBA); human resources management (MBA, MM); management (MM); marketing (MBA); public administration (MBA). Evening/weekend programs available. *Degree requirements:* For master's, thesis (for some programs). *Entrance requirements:* For master's, minimum undergraduate GPA of 3.0, 3 years of work experience. Additional exam requirements/recommendations for international students: Required—TOEFL (minimum score 550 paper-based). Electronic applications accepted.

University of Phoenix–Las Vegas Campus, School of Business, Las Vegas, NV 89135. Offers accounting (MBA); business administration (MBA); global management (MBA); human resources management (MBA, MM); management (MM); marketing (MBA); public administration (MM). Evening/weekend programs available. Postbaccalaureate distance learning degree programs offered (no on-campus study). *Degree requirements:* For master's, thesis (for some programs). *Entrance requirements:* For master's, minimum undergraduate GPA of 3.0, 3 years of work experience. Additional exam requirements/recommendations for international students: Required—TOEFL (minimum score 550 paper-based; 79 iBT). Electronic applications accepted.

University of Phoenix–Memphis Campus, School of Business, Cordova, TN 38018. Offers accounting (MBA); business and management (MBA); e-business (MBA); global management (MBA); human resources management (MBA, MM); management (MM); marketing (MBA); public administration (MBA, MM).

University of Phoenix–Minneapolis/St. Paul Campus, School of Business, St. Louis Park, MN 55426. Offers accounting (MBA); business administration (MBA); global management (MBA); human resources management (MBA); management (MM); marketing (MBA); public administration (MBA).

University of Phoenix–North Florida Campus, School of Business, Jacksonville, FL 32216-0959. Offers accounting (MBA); business administration (MBA); global management (MBA); human resources management (MBA, MM); management (MM); marketing (MBA); public administration (MBA, MM). Evening/weekend programs available. *Degree requirements:* For master's, thesis (for some programs). *Entrance requirements:* For master's, minimum undergraduate GPA of 3.0, 3 years work experience. Additional exam requirements/recommendations for international students: Required—TOEFL (minimum score 550 paper-based; 79 iBT). Electronic applications accepted.

University of Phoenix–Online Campus, College of Justice and Security, Phoenix, AZ 85034-7209. Offers administration of justice and security (MS), including administration of justice and security, global and homeland security, law enforcement organizations; public administration (MPA). Evening/weekend programs available. Postbaccalaureate distance learning degree programs offered. *Entrance requirements:* Additional exam requirements/recommendations for international students: Required—TOEFL, TOEIC (Test of English as an International Communication), Berlitz Online English Proficiency Exam, PTE, or IELTS. Electronic applications accepted. *Expenses:* Contact institution.

University of Phoenix–Online Campus, School of Business, Phoenix, AZ 85034-7209. Offers accountancy (MS); accounting (MBA, Certificate); business administration (MBA); energy management (MBA); global management (MBA); health care management (MBA); human resource management (MBA, Certificate); human resources management (MM); management (MM); marketing (MBA, Certificate); project management (MBA, Certificate); public administration (MBA, MM); technology management (MBA). Evening/weekend programs available. Postbaccalaureate distance learning degree programs offered. *Entrance requirements:* Additional exam requirements/recommendations for international students: Required—TOEFL, TOEIC (Test of English as an International Communication), Berlitz Online English Proficiency Exam, PTE, or IELTS. Electronic applications accepted. *Expenses:* Contact institution.

University of Phoenix–Oregon Campus, School of Business, Tigard, OR 97223. Offers accounting (MBA); business administration (MBA); global management (MBA); human resource management (MM); human resources management (MBA); management (MM); marketing (MBA); public administration (MM). Evening/weekend programs available. *Degree requirements:* For master's, thesis (for some programs). *Entrance requirements:* For master's, minimum undergraduate GPA of 3.0, 3 years of work experience. Additional exam requirements/recommendations for international students: Required—TOEFL (minimum score 550 paper-based; 79 iBT). Electronic applications accepted.

University of Phoenix–Philadelphia Campus, School of Business, Wayne, PA 19087-2121. Offers accounting (MBA); business administration (MBA); global management (MBA); human resources management (MBA, MM); management (MM); marketing (MBA); public administration (MM). Evening/weekend programs available. *Degree requirements:* For master's, thesis (for some programs). *Entrance requirements:* For master's, minimum undergraduate GPA of 3.0, 3 years work experience. Additional exam requirements/recommendations for international students: Required—TOEFL (minimum score 550 paper-based; 79 iBT). Electronic applications accepted.

University of Phoenix–Phoenix Campus, College of Criminal Justice and Security, Tempe, AZ 85282-2371. Offers administration of justice and security (MS); global and homeland security (MS); law enforcement organizations (MS); public administration (MPA). Evening/weekend programs available. Postbaccalaureate distance learning degree programs offered. *Entrance requirements:* Additional exam requirements/recommendations for international students: Required—TOEFL, TOEIC (Test of English as an International Communication), Berlitz Online English Proficiency Exam, PTE, or IELTS. Electronic applications accepted. *Expenses:* Contact institution.

University of Phoenix–Richmond-Virginia Beach Campus, School of Business, Glen Allen, VA 23060. Offers accounting (MBA); business administration (MBA); global management (MBA); human resources management (MBA, MM); management (MM); marketing (MBA); public administration (MBA, MM). Evening/weekend programs available. *Degree requirements:* For master's, thesis (for some programs). *Entrance requirements:* For master's, minimum undergraduate GPA of 3.0, 3 years work experience. Additional exam requirements/recommendations for international students: Required—TOEFL (minimum score 550 paper-based; 79 iBT). Electronic applications accepted.

University of Phoenix–Sacramento Valley Campus, School of Business, Sacramento, CA 95833-3632. Offers accounting (MBA); business administration (MBA); global management (MBA); human resources management (MBA, MM); management (MM); marketing (MBA); public administration (MBA, MM). Evening/weekend programs available. *Degree requirements:* For master's, thesis (for some programs). *Entrance requirements:* For master's, minimum undergraduate GPA of 3.0, 3 years work experience. Additional exam requirements/recommendations for international students: Required—TOEFL (minimum score 550 paper-based; 79 iBT). Electronic applications accepted.

University of Phoenix–St. Louis Campus, School of Business, St. Louis, MO 63043. Offers accounting (MBA); business administration (MBA); global management (MBA); human resources management (MBA, MM); management (MM); marketing (MBA); public administration (MM). Evening/weekend programs available. *Degree requirements:* For master's, thesis (for some programs). *Entrance requirements:* For master's, 3 years of work experience, minimum undergraduate GPA of 3.0. Additional exam requirements/recommendations for international students: Required—TOEFL (minimum score 550 paper-based; 79 iBT). Electronic applications accepted.

University of Phoenix–San Antonio Campus, School of Business, San Antonio, TX 78230. Offers accounting (MBA); business administration (MBA); e-business (MBA); global management (MBA); human resources management (MBA, MM); management (MM); marketing (MBA); public administration (MBA, MM).

University of Phoenix–San Diego Campus, School of Business, San Diego, CA 92123. Offers accounting (MBA); business administration (MBA); global management (MBA); human resources management (MBA, MM); management (MM); marketing (MBA); public administration (MBA). Evening/weekend programs available. *Degree requirements:* For master's, thesis (for some programs). *Entrance requirements:* For master's, 3 years of work experience, minimum undergraduate GPA of 3.0. Additional exam requirements/recommendations for international students: Required—TOEFL (minimum score 550 paper-based; 79 iBT). Electronic applications accepted.

University of Phoenix–Savannah Campus, School of Business, Savannah, GA 31405-7400. Offers accounting (MBA); business administration (MBA); global management (MBA); human resources management (MBA, MM); management (MM); marketing (MBA); public administration (MBA, MM).

University of Phoenix–Southern California Campus, College of Criminal Justice and Security, Costa Mesa, CA 92626. Offers administration of justice and security (MS), including administration of justice and security, global and homeland security, law enforcement organizations; public administration (MPA). Evening/weekend programs available. Postbaccalaureate distance learning degree programs offered. *Entrance requirements:* Additional exam requirements/recommendations for international students: Required—TOEFL, TOEIC (Test of English as an International Communication), Berlitz Online English Proficiency Exam, PTE, or IELTS. Electronic applications accepted. *Expenses:* Contact institution.

University of Phoenix–South Florida Campus, School of Business, Miramar, FL 33030. Offers accounting (MBA); business administration (MBA); global management (MBA); human resource management (MBA); human resources management (MM); management (MM); marketing (MBA); public administration (MBA, MM). Evening/weekend programs available. *Degree requirements:* For master's, thesis (for some programs). *Entrance requirements:* For master's, minimum undergraduate GPA of 3.0, 3 years work experience. Additional exam requirements/recommendations for international students: Required—TOEFL (minimum score 550 paper-based; 79 iBT). Electronic applications accepted.

University of Phoenix–Washington D.C. Campus, School of Business, Washington, DC 20001. Offers accountancy (MS); business administration (MBA, DBA); human resources management (MM); management (MM); organizational leadership (DM); public administration (MPA).

University of Pittsburgh, Graduate School of Public and International Affairs, Doctoral Program in Public and International Affairs, Pittsburgh, PA 15260. Offers international affairs (PhD). *Accreditation:* NASPAA. *Faculty:* 34 full-time (12 women), 11 part-time/adjunct (3 women). *Students:* 32 full-time (15 women); includes 1 minority (Asian, non-Hispanic/Latino), 12 international. Average age 36. 72 applicants, 21% accepted, 7 enrolled. In 2014, 3 doctorates awarded. *Degree requirements:* For doctorate, comprehensive exam, thesis/dissertation, mid-term evaluation, preliminary exam, annual review. *Entrance requirements:* For doctorate, GRE or GMAT, 2 letters of recommendation, resume, undergraduate transcripts, personal statement, writing sample. Additional exam requirements/recommendations for international students: Required—TOEFL (minimum score 600 paper-based; 100 iBT); Recommended—IELTS (minimum score 7), TWE (minimum score 4). *Application deadline:* For fall admission, 1/15 for domestic and international students. Application fee: $50. Electronic applications accepted. *Expenses:* Tuition, state resident: full-time $20,742; part-time $838 per credit. Tuition, nonresident: full-time $33,960; part-time $1389 per credit. *Required fees:* $800; $205 per term. Tuition and fees vary according to program. *Financial support:* In 2014–15, 15 students received support, including 15 research assistantships (averaging $13,980 per year). Financial award application deadline: 1/15; financial award applicants required to submit FAFSA. *Faculty research:* International political economy, international development, public policy and management, international security. *Total annual research expenditures:* $640,844. *Unit head:* Dr. Nuno Themudo, Program Director, 412-648-7632, Fax: 412-648-7641, E-mail: themudo@pitt.edu. *Application contact:* Julie Korade, Doctoral Program Administrator/Graduate Enrollment Counselor, 412-648-7640, Fax: 412-648-7641, E-mail: korade@pitt.edu.
Website: http://www.gspia.pitt.edu/

University of Pittsburgh, Graduate School of Public and International Affairs, Master of Public Administration Program, Pittsburgh, PA 15260. Offers energy and environment (MPA); governance and international public management (MPA); policy research and analysis (MPA); public and nonprofit management (MPA); urban affairs and planning (MPA); JD/MPA; MPA/MID; MPA/MPIA; MPH/MPA; MSIS/MPA; MSW/MPA. Part-time and evening/weekend programs available. *Faculty:* 32 full-time (12 women), 13 part-time/adjunct (5 women). *Students:* 99 full-time (69 women), 15 part-time (10 women); includes 8 minority (5 Black or African American, non-Hispanic/Latino; 1 Asian, non-Hispanic/Latino; 1 Hispanic/Latino; 1 Two or more races, non-Hispanic/Latino), 52 international. Average age 26. 273 applicants, 70% accepted, 51 enrolled. In 2014, 50 master's awarded. *Degree requirements:* For master's, thesis optional, internship, capstone seminar. *Entrance requirements:* For master's, GRE General Test or GMAT, 2 letters of recommendation, resume; undergraduate transcripts, personal statement. Additional exam requirements/recommendations for international students: Required—TOEFL (minimum score 550 paper-based; 80 iBT); Recommended—IELTS (minimum score 7), TWE (minimum score 4). *Application deadline:* For fall admission, 2/1 for domestic students, 1/15 for international students; for spring admission, 11/1 for domestic students, 8/1 for international students. Application fee: $50. Electronic applications accepted. *Expenses:* Tuition, state resident: full-time $20,742; part-time $838 per credit. Tuition, nonresident: full-time $33,960; part-time $1389 per credit. *Required fees:* $800; $205 per term. Tuition and fees vary according to program. *Financial support:* In 2014–15, 17 students received support, including 3 fellowships (averaging $13,980 per year); scholarships/grants, unspecified assistantships, and student employment also available. Financial award application deadline: 2/1. *Faculty research:* Urban management, regional development, disaster response management, public program evaluation, comparative regional governance, nonprofit management, health policy, environmental policy, strategic management, human resources management. *Total annual research expenditures:* $640,844. *Unit head:* Dr. David Y. Miller, Director, 412-648-7606, Fax: 412-648-2605, E-mail: dymiller@pitt.edu. *Application contact:* Elizabeth A. Hruby, Graduate Enrollment Counselor, 412-648-7640, Fax: 412-648-7641, E-mail: eah44@pitt.edu.
Website: http://www.gspia.pitt.edu/

University of Puerto Rico, Río Piedras Campus, College of Social Sciences, School of Public Administration, San Juan, PR 00931-3300. Offers MPA. Part-time programs available. *Degree requirements:* For master's, comprehensive exam, thesis. *Entrance requirements:* For master's, GRE or PAEG, interview, minimum GPA of 3.0, letter of recommendation.

University of Regina, Faculty of Graduate Studies and Research, Johnson-Shoyama Graduate School of Public Policy, Regina, SK S4S 0A2, Canada. Offers economic analysis for public policy (Master's Certificate); health administration (MHA); health systems management (Master's Certificate); public management (MPA, Master's Certificate); public policy (MPA, MPP, PhD); public policy analysis (Master's Certificate). Part-time programs available. *Faculty:* 8 full-time (4 women), 12 part-time/adjunct (3 women). *Students:* 60 full-time (33 women), 109 part-time (66 women). 133 applicants, 35% accepted. In 2014, 26 master's, 1 doctorate, 13 other advanced degrees awarded. *Degree requirements:* For master's, thesis (for some programs); for doctorate, thesis/dissertation. *Entrance requirements:* For doctorate, master's degree, intended research program in an area of public policy. Additional exam requirements/recommendations for international students: Required—TOEFL (minimum score 580 paper-based; 80 iBT), IELTS (minimum score 6.5), PTE (minimum score 59). *Application deadline:* For fall admission, 2/1 for domestic and international students. Application fee: $100. Electronic applications accepted. *Expenses:* Expenses: $4,304.85 per semester of full time study (for MHA), $2,588.85 (for MPA), $1,450.35 (for MPP); $1,450.35 (for PhD). *Financial support:* In 2014–15, 11 fellowships (averaging $6,000 per year), 15 teaching assistantships (averaging $2,435 per year) were awarded; research assistantships, career-related internships or fieldwork, and scholarships/grants also available. Financial award application deadline: 6/15. *Faculty research:* Governance and administration, public finance, public policy analysis, non-governmental organizations and alternative service delivery, micro-economics for policy analysis. *Unit head:* Dr. Kathleen McNutt, Executive Director, Main Campus, 306-585-4759, Fax: 306-585-5461, E-mail: kathy.mcnutt@uregina.ca. *Application contact:* Constance Heshka-Argue, Manager, Main Campus, 306-585-5462, Fax: 306-585-5461, E-mail: connie.heska-argue@uregina.ca.
Website: http://www.schoolofpublicpolicy.sk.ca/

University of Rhode Island, Graduate School, College of Arts and Sciences, Department of Political Science, Kingston, RI 02881. Offers political science (MA), including American politics, comparative government, international relations, public policy; public policy and administration (MPA); MLIS/MPA. Part-time programs available. *Faculty:* 11 full-time (4 women). *Students:* 20 full-time (11 women), 28 part-time (21 women); includes 9 minority (4 Black or African American, non-Hispanic/Latino; 3 Asian, non-Hispanic/Latino; 2 Hispanic/Latino), 2 international. In 2014, 20 master's awarded. *Degree requirements:* For master's, comprehensive exam (for some programs), thesis optional. *Entrance requirements:* For master's, GRE, GMAT or MAT, 2 letters of recommendation. Additional exam requirements/recommendations for international students: Required—TOEFL (minimum score 550 paper-based). *Application deadline:* For fall admission, 2/1 for international students; for spring admission, 7/15 for international students. Application fee: $65. Electronic applications accepted. *Expenses:* Tuition, state resident: full-time $11,532; part-time $641 per credit. Tuition, nonresident: full-time $23,606; part-time $1311 per credit. *Required fees:* $1442; $39 per credit. $35 per semester. One-time fee: $155. *Financial support:* In 2014–15, 3 teaching assistantships with full and partial tuition reimbursements (averaging $12,675 per year) were awarded. Financial award application deadline: 7/15; financial award applicants required to submit FAFSA. *Unit head:* Dr. Brian Krueger, Department Chair, 401-874-4058, Fax: 401-874-4072, E-mail: bkrueger@uri.edu. *Application contact:* Dr. Robert Weygand, Director, 401-874-2124, Fax: 401-874-4072, E-mail: bobw@uri.edu.
Website: http://www.uri.edu/artsci/psc/

University of San Francisco, School of Management, Master of Public Administration Program, Concentration in Public Administration, San Francisco, CA 94117-1080. Offers MPA. Part-time and evening/weekend programs available. *Faculty:* 7 full-time (0 women), 10 part-time/adjunct (7 women). *Students:* Average age 33. 95 applicants, 78% accepted, 48 enrolled. In 2014, 51 master's awarded. *Entrance requirements:* For master's, minimum GPA of 3.0. Application fee: $55 ($65 for international students). *Expenses: Tuition:* Full-time $21,762; part-time $1209 per credit hour. Tuition and fees vary according to degree level, campus/location and program. *Financial support:* In 2014–15, 1 student received support. Application deadline: 3/2; applicants required to submit FAFSA. *Unit head:* Dr. Maurice Penner, Director, 415-422-2142. *Application contact:* 415-422-6000, E-mail: graduate@usfca.edu.

University of South Africa, College of Economic and Management Sciences, Pretoria, South Africa. Offers accounting (D Admin, D Com); accounting science (DA); auditing

(D Admin, D Com); business administration (M Tech); business economics (D Admin); business leadership (DBL); business management (D Admin, D Com); economic management analysis (M Tech); economics (D Admin, D Com, PhD); human resource development (M Tech); industrial psychology (D Admin, D Com, PhD); logistics (D Com); marketing (M Tech); public administration (D Admin, D Com, DPA, PhD); public management (M Tech); quantitative management (D Admin, D Com); real estate (M Tech); statistics (D Admin, PhD); tourism management (D Admin, D Com); transport economics (D Admin, D Com).

University of South Alabama, College of Arts and Sciences, Department of Political Science and Criminal Justice, Mobile, AL 36688. Offers public administration (MPA). Part-time and evening/weekend programs available. *Faculty:* 3 full-time (1 woman), 1 part-time/adjunct (0 women). *Students:* 23 full-time (14 women), 3 part-time (2 women); includes 8 minority (6 Black or African American, non-Hispanic/Latino; 1 Asian, non-Hispanic/Latino; 1 Two or more races, non-Hispanic/Latino). Average age 32. 20 applicants, 50% accepted, 8 enrolled. In 2014, 14 master's awarded. *Degree requirements:* For master's, comprehensive exam, thesis optional. *Entrance requirements:* For master's, GRE, minimum GPA of 3.0. Additional exam requirements/recommendations for international students: Required—TOEFL. *Application deadline:* For fall admission, 7/15 priority date for domestic students, 6/15 priority date for international students; for spring admission, 12/1 priority date for domestic students, 11/1 priority date for international students; for summer admission, 5/1 priority date for domestic students, 4/1 priority date for international students. Applications are processed on a rolling basis. Application fee: $35. Electronic applications accepted. *Expenses:* Tuition, state resident: full-time $9288; part-time $387 per credit hour. Tuition, nonresident: full-time $18,576; part-time $774 per credit hour. Part-time tuition and fees vary according to course load and program. *Financial support:* Fellowships, research assistantships, teaching assistantships, career-related internships or fieldwork, Federal Work-Study, institutionally sponsored loans, scholarships/grants, and unspecified assistantships available. Support available to part-time students. Financial award application deadline: 4/15; financial award applicants required to submit FAFSA. *Unit head:* Dr. Nader Entessar, Chair, Political Science/Criminal Justice, 251-460-6280, E-mail: nentessar@southalabama.edu. *Application contact:* Dr. Samuel Fisher, Director of Graduate Studies, Political Science/Criminal Justice, 251-460-7204, Fax: 251-460-7928, E-mail: sfisher@southalabama.edu.
Website: http://www.southalabama.edu/colleges/artsandsci/poliscie/

University of South Carolina, The Graduate School, College of Arts and Sciences, Department of Political Science, Program in Public Administration, Columbia, SC 29208. Offers MPA, JD/MPA, MSW/MPA. MPA offered jointly with Clemson University, The Graduate School of the College of Charleston. *Accreditation:* NASPAA. Part-time and evening/weekend programs available. *Degree requirements:* For master's, capstone seminar. *Entrance requirements:* For master's, GRE General Test, minimum GPA of 3.0. Additional exam requirements/recommendations for international students: Required—TOEFL. Electronic applications accepted. *Faculty research:* Public policy, organizational theory, personnel administration, budgeting, finance.

The University of South Dakota, Graduate School, College of Arts and Sciences, Department of Political Science, Vermillion, SD 57069-2390. Offers American political institutions (PhD); American politics and public policy (MA); political science (EMPA, MA); public administration (MPA, PhD); public policy (PhD); JD/MA. *Accreditation:* NASPAA (one or more programs are accredited). Part-time programs available. Postbaccalaureate distance learning degree programs offered. *Degree requirements:* For master's, comprehensive exam, thesis (for some programs). *Entrance requirements:* For master's, GRE or LSAT (MPA), GRE General Test (MA), minimum GPA of 2.7. Additional exam requirements/recommendations for international students: Required—TOEFL (minimum score 550 paper-based; 79 iBT). Electronic applications accepted.

University of Southern California, Graduate School, School of Policy, Planning, and Development, Master of Public Administration Program, Los Angeles, CA 90089. Offers nonprofit management and policy (Graduate Certificate); political management (Graduate Certificate); public administration (MPA); public management (Graduate Certificate); MPA/JD; MPA/M Pl; MPA/MA; MPA/MAJCS; MPA/MS; MPA/MSW. *Accreditation:* NASPAA (one or more programs are accredited). Part-time and evening/weekend programs available. Postbaccalaureate distance learning degree programs offered (minimal on-campus study). Terminal master's awarded for partial completion of doctoral program. *Degree requirements:* For master's, capstone, internship. *Entrance requirements:* For master's, GRE, GMAT. Additional exam requirements/recommendations for international students: Required—TOEFL (minimum score 600 paper-based; 100 iBT). Electronic applications accepted. *Faculty research:* Collaborative governance and decision-making, nonprofit management, environmental management, institutional analysis, local government, civic engagement.

University of Southern Indiana, Graduate Studies, College of Liberal Arts, Program in Public Administration, Evansville, IN 47712-3590. Offers MPA. Part-time and evening/weekend programs available. *Faculty:* 4 full-time (1 woman), 2 part-time/adjunct (1 woman). *Students:* 8 full-time (5 women), 33 part-time (24 women); includes 6 minority (5 Black or African American, non-Hispanic/Latino; 1 Two or more races, non-Hispanic/Latino), 1 international. Average age 31. In 2014, 7 master's awarded. *Entrance requirements:* For master's, GMAT or GRE, 2 letters of reference, analytical writing sample, minimum GPA of 2.7. Additional exam requirements/recommendations for international students: Required—TOEFL (minimum score 550 paper-based; 79 iBT), IELTS (minimum score 6). *Application deadline:* For fall admission, 8/15 priority date for domestic students, 3/1 priority date for international students. Applications are processed on a rolling basis. Application fee: $40. Electronic applications accepted. *Financial support:* In 2014–15, 9 students received support. Federal Work-Study, scholarships/grants, tuition waivers (full and partial), and unspecified assistantships available. Financial award application deadline: 3/1; financial award applicants required to submit FAFSA. *Unit head:* Dr. Matthew Hanka, Director, 812-461-5204, E-mail: mjhanka@usi.edu. *Application contact:* Dr. Mayola Rowser, Director, Graduate Studies, 812-465-7016, E-mail: mrowser@usi.edu.
Website: http://www.usi.edu/liberalarts/master-of-public-administration

University of South Florida, Innovative Education, Tampa, FL 33620-9951. *Unit head:* Kathy Barnes, Interdisciplinary Programs Coordinator, 813-974-8031, Fax: 813-974-7061, E-mail: barnesk@usf.edu. *Application contact:* Karen Tylinski, Metro Initiatives, 813-974-9943, Fax: 813-974-7061, E-mail: ktylinsk@usf.edu.
Website: http://www.usf.edu/innovative-education/

The University of Tennessee, Graduate School, College of Arts and Sciences, Department of Political Science, Program in Public Administration, Knoxville, TN 37996. Offers MPA, JD/MPA. *Accreditation:* NASPAA. Part-time programs available. *Degree requirements:* For master's, thesis or alternative. *Entrance requirements:* For master's, GRE General Test, minimum GPA of 2.7. Additional exam requirements/recommendations for international students: Required—TOEFL. Electronic applications accepted.

The University of Tennessee at Chattanooga, Department of Political Science, Chattanooga, TN 37403. Offers local government management (MPA); non profit management (MPA); public administration (MPA); public administration and non-profit management (Postbaccalaureate Certificate). Part-time and evening/weekend programs available. *Faculty:* 3 full-time (0 women). *Students:* 13 full-time (6 women), 18 part-time (12 women); includes 4 minority (3 Black or African American, non-Hispanic/Latino; 1 Hispanic/Latino). Average age 29. 16 applicants, 88% accepted, 11 enrolled. In 2014, 12 master's awarded. *Degree requirements:* For master's, comprehensive exam, thesis or alternative, internship. *Entrance requirements:* For master's, GRE General Test. Additional exam requirements/recommendations for international students: Required—TOEFL (minimum score 550 paper-based; 79 iBT), IELTS (minimum score 6). *Application deadline:* For fall admission, 6/13 priority date for domestic students, 6/1 for international students; for spring admission, 10/15 priority date for domestic students, 10/1 for international students. Applications are processed on a rolling basis. Application fee: $30 ($35 for international students). Electronic applications accepted. *Expenses:* Tuition, state resident: full-time $7708; part-time $428 per credit hour. Tuition, nonresident: full-time $23,826; part-time $1323 per credit hour. *Required fees:* $1708; $252 per credit hour. *Financial support:* In 2014–15, 3 research assistantships with tuition reimbursements (averaging $6,860 per year) were awarded; career-related internships or fieldwork, scholarships/grants, and unspecified assistantships also available. Support available to part-time students. *Faculty research:* Organizational cultures and renewal, management theory, public policy, policy analysis, nonprofit organization. *Unit head:* Dr. Michelle D. Deardorf, Department Head, 423-425-4231, Fax: 423-425-2373, E-mail: michelle-deardorff@utc.edu. *Application contact:* Dr. J. Randy Walker, Interim Dean of Graduate Studies, 423-425-4478, Fax: 423-425-5223, E-mail: randy-walker@utc.edu.
Website: http://www.utc.edu/Academic/PoliticalScience/

The University of Texas at Arlington, Graduate School, School of Urban and Public Affairs, Program in Public Administration, Arlington, TN 76019. Offers MPA. *Accreditation:* NASPAA. Part-time and evening/weekend programs available. Postbaccalaureate distance learning degree programs offered (no on-campus study). *Degree requirements:* For master's, comprehensive exam, thesis or alternative. *Entrance requirements:* For master's, GRE General Test, three letters of recommendation, essay (approximately 250 words), minimum GPA of 3.0. Additional exam requirements/recommendations for international students: Required—TOEFL (minimum score 550 paper-based). Electronic applications accepted. *Faculty research:* Environment, statistics, public administration, social welfare, economic development, economics, budgeting, planning.

The University of Texas at Austin, Graduate School, Lyndon B. Johnson School of Public Affairs, Austin, TX 78712-1111. Offers global policy studies (MGPS); public affairs (MP Aff); public leadership (EMPL); public policy (PhD); JD/MP Aff; MBA/MP Aff; MP Aff/MA; MP Aff/MSE. *Accreditation:* NASPAA (one or more programs are accredited). Part-time programs available. *Degree requirements:* For master's, thesis, summer internship; for doctorate, thesis/dissertation. *Entrance requirements:* For master's, GRE General Test (for MP Aff and MGPS), minimum GPA of 3.0 in upper-division classes, seven years of experience in the public sector, and interview (for EMPL); for doctorate, GRE General Test, master's degree in policy-related field. Additional exam requirements/recommendations for international students: Required—TOEFL. Electronic applications accepted. *Faculty research:* Human resource development, health and social policy, philanthropy and community service, ethical leadership, urban and international policy, science and technology policy.

The University of Texas at San Antonio, College of Public Policy, Department of Public Administration, San Antonio, TX 78207. Offers MPA. *Accreditation:* NASPAA. Part-time and evening/weekend programs available. *Faculty:* 10 full-time (5 women), 4 part-time/adjunct (1 woman). *Students:* 45 full-time (23 women), 120 part-time (71 women); includes 118 minority (19 Black or African American, non-Hispanic/Latino; 1 American Indian or Alaska Native, non-Hispanic/Latino; 5 Asian, non-Hispanic/Latino; 86 Hispanic/Latino; 1 Native Hawaiian or other Pacific Islander, non-Hispanic/Latino; 6 Two or more races, non-Hispanic/Latino), 3 international. Average age 33. 85 applicants, 80% accepted, 43 enrolled. In 2014, 43 master's awarded. *Degree requirements:* For master's, comprehensive exam, final exit paper. *Entrance requirements:* For master's, bachelor's degree with 18 credit hours in field of study or in another appropriate field of study, two letters of recommendation, statement of purpose. Additional exam requirements/recommendations for international students: Required—TOEFL (minimum score 550 paper-based; 79 iBT), IELTS (minimum score 6.5). *Application deadline:* For fall admission, 7/1 for domestic students, 4/1 for international students; for spring admission, 11/1 for domestic students, 9/1 for international students; for summer admission, 5/1 for domestic students, 3/1 for international students. Application fee: $45 ($80 for international students). Electronic applications accepted. *Expenses:* Tuition, state resident: full-time $4671; part-time $260 per credit hour. Tuition, nonresident: full-time $18,022; part-time $1001 per credit hour. *Financial support:* Scholarships/grants and unspecified assistantships available. Financial award application deadline: 2/15. *Faculty research:* Public administration, public policy, nonprofit management, urban and regional planning, urban and regional management. *Unit head:* Dr. Christopher G. Reddick, Department Chair, 210-458-2501, Fax: 210-458-2536, E-mail: chris.reddick@utsa.edu. *Application contact:* Dr. Jennifer K. Alexander, Graduate Advisor of Record, 210-458-2532, Fax: 210-458-2536, E-mail: jennifer.alexander@utsa.edu.
Website: http://copp.utsa.edu/public-administration/

The University of Texas at Tyler, College of Arts and Sciences, Department of Social Sciences, Tyler, TX 75799-0001. Offers criminal justice (MS); public administration (MPA); sociology (MS). Part-time and evening/weekend programs available. *Degree requirements:* For master's, comprehensive exam, thesis optional. *Entrance requirements:* For master's, GRE General Test, minimum GPA of 3.0. Additional exam requirements/recommendations for international students: Required—TOEFL. *Faculty research:* Urban segregation, minority business, violent crime, gender discrimination.

The University of Texas–Pan American, College of Social and Behavioral Sciences, Program in Public Administration, Edinburg, TX 78539. Offers MPA. Part-time and evening/weekend programs available. *Degree requirements:* For master's, comprehensive exam (for some programs), thesis optional. *Entrance requirements:* For master's, GRE General Test. Additional exam requirements/recommendations for international students: Required—TOEFL. Electronic applications accepted. *Expenses:* Tuition, state resident: full-time $4187; part-time $232.60 per credit hour. Tuition, nonresident: full-time $10,857; part-time $603.16 per credit hour. *Required fees:* $782; $27.50 per credit hour. $143.35 per semester. *Faculty research:* Immigration policy reform, agriculture food policy, social service delivery systems, community development, social welfare policy reform, urban/city management.

University of the District of Columbia, School of Business and Public Administration, Program in Public Administration, Washington, DC 20008-1175. Offers MPA. Part-time and evening/weekend programs available. *Degree requirements:* For master's, comprehensive exam, thesis optional. *Entrance requirements:* For master's, GMAT or GRE General Test, writing proficiency exam. *Faculty research:* Government management, public personnel management, urban management, management information systems, public financial management.

University of the Virgin Islands, Graduate Programs, Division of Humanities and Social Sciences, Saint Thomas, VI 00802-9990. Offers MPA. Part-time and evening/

weekend programs available. *Degree requirements:* For master's, comprehensive exam, thesis or alternative. *Entrance requirements:* For master's, GMAT, GRE, minimum GPA of 2.5. Additional exam requirements/recommendations for international students: Required—TOEFL (minimum score 550 paper-based). *Faculty research:* Ethical issues of arbitration, spiritual leadership, accountability.

The University of Toledo, College of Graduate Studies, College of Languages, Literature and Social Sciences, Department of Political Science and Public Administration, Toledo, OH 43606-3390. Offers health care policy and administration (Certificate); management of non-profit organizations (Certificate); municipal administration (Certificate); political science (MA); public administration (MPA); JD/MPA. *Accreditation:* NASPAA. Part-time programs available. *Degree requirements:* For master's, comprehensive exam (for some programs), thesis. *Entrance requirements:* For master's, GRE General Test, minimum cumulative point-hour ratio of 2.7 (3.0 for MPA) for all previous academic work, three letters of recommendation, statement of purpose, transcripts from all prior institutions attended; for Certificate, minimum cumulative point-hour ratio of 2.7 for all previous academic work, three letters of recommendation, statement of purpose, transcripts from all prior institutions attended. Additional exam requirements/recommendations for international students: Required—TOEFL (minimum score 550 paper-based; 80 iBT). Electronic applications accepted. *Faculty research:* Economic development, health care, Third World, criminal justice, Eastern Europe.

University of Utah, Graduate School, College of Social and Behavioral Science, Department of Political Science, Program in Political Science, Salt Lake City, UT 84112. Offers American politics (MA, MS, PhD); comparative politics (MA, MS, PhD); international relations (MA, MS, PhD); political theory (MA, MS, PhD); public administration (MA, MS, PhD). *Faculty:* 32 full-time (7 women), 10 part-time/adjunct (3 women). *Students:* 67 full-time (25 women); includes 11 minority (1 Black or African American, non-Hispanic/Latino; 1 American Indian or Alaska Native, non-Hispanic/Latino; 4 Asian, non-Hispanic/Latino; 5 Two or more races, non-Hispanic/Latino), 9 international. Average age 34. 35 applicants, 71% accepted, 12 enrolled. In 2014, 6 master's, 6 doctorates awarded. Terminal master's awarded for partial completion of doctoral program. *Degree requirements:* For master's, variable foreign language requirement, thesis or research paper; for doctorate, comprehensive exam, thesis/dissertation. *Entrance requirements:* For master's and doctorate, GRE General Test, minimum GPA of 3.2. Additional exam requirements/recommendations for international students: Required—TOEFL (minimum score 580 paper-based; 61 iBT), IELTS (minimum score 6). *Application deadline:* For fall admission, 1/15 priority date for domestic and international students; for spring admission, 10/1 for domestic and international students. Application fee: $55 ($65 for international students). Electronic applications accepted. *Financial support:* In 2014–15, 4 students received support, including 2 fellowships with full tuition reimbursements available (averaging $15,250 per year), 14 teaching assistantships with full tuition reimbursements available (averaging $13,750 per year); career-related internships or fieldwork, scholarships/grants, health care benefits, and unspecified assistantships also available. Financial award application deadline: 1/15; financial award applicants required to submit FAFSA. *Faculty research:* International politics, comparative politics, political theory, American politics, public administration. *Total annual research expenditures:* $24,651. *Unit head:* Brent Steele, Chair, 801-587-7754, Fax: 801-585-6492, E-mail: brent.steele@utah.edu. *Application contact:* Mary Ann Underwood, Graduate Coordinator/Advisor, 801-581-8608, Fax: 801-585-6492, E-mail: maryann.underwood@poli-sci.utah.edu.
Website: http://www.poli-sci.utah.edu/

University of Utah, Graduate School, College of Social and Behavioral Science, Department of Political Science, Program in Public Administration, Salt Lake City, UT 84112. Offers Exec MPA, MPA, JD/MPA, MHA/MPA, MPA/Ed D, MPA/MPH, MPA/MSW, MPA/PhD. *Accreditation:* NASPAA (one or more programs are accredited). Part-time and evening/weekend programs available. *Students:* 40 full-time (18 women), 94 part-time (50 women); includes 21 minority (2 Black or African American, non-Hispanic/Latino; 3 Asian, non-Hispanic/Latino; 8 Hispanic/Latino; 5 Native Hawaiian or other Pacific Islander, non-Hispanic/Latino; 3 Two or more races, non-Hispanic/Latino), 4 international. Average age 35. 90 applicants, 89% accepted, 6 enrolled. In 2014, 57 master's awarded. *Degree requirements:* For master's, internship, research paper. *Entrance requirements:* For master's, GMAT, GRE General Test, LSAT, MAT, minimum GPA of 3.2. Additional exam requirements/recommendations for international students: Required—TOEFL (minimum score 580 paper-based; 92 iBT), IELTS (minimum score 7). *Application deadline:* For fall admission, 2/1 priority date for domestic and international students. Application fee: $55 ($65 for international students). *Expenses:* Expenses: Contact institution. *Financial support:* In 2014–15, 25 students received support, including 3 research assistantships with full tuition reimbursements available; career-related internships or fieldwork also available. Financial award application deadline: 4/15; financial award applicants required to submit FAFSA. *Faculty research:* Non-profit organizations, health policy, environmental policy and natural resources, law and ethics, human resource management, local government, education, conflict resolution, organization theory and behavior, crisis management, policy analysis and program evaluation. *Unit head:* Lina Svedin, MPA Director, 801-581-7031, E-mail: lina.svedin@poli-sci.utah.edu. *Application contact:* Sandy Hiskey, Program Coordinator, 801-581-7390, Fax: 801-585-6492, E-mail: sandy.hiskey@mpa.utah.edu.
Website: http://www.mpa.utah.edu

University of Vermont, Graduate College, College of Agriculture and Life Sciences, Department of Community Development and Applied Economics, Program in Public Administration, Burlington, VT 05405. Offers MPA. *Accreditation:* NASPAA. *Entrance requirements:* For master's, GRE General Test. Additional exam requirements/recommendations for international students: Required—TOEFL (minimum score 550 paper-based; 80 iBT). Electronic applications accepted.

University of Victoria, Faculty of Graduate Studies, Faculty of Human and Social Development, School of Public Administration, Victoria, BC V8W 2Y2, Canada. Offers dispute resolution (MADR); public administration (MPA, PhD); MPA/LL B. Part-time and evening/weekend programs available. Postbaccalaureate distance learning degree programs offered. *Degree requirements:* For master's, thesis (for some programs), report; for doctorate, thesis/dissertation, candidacy exam. *Entrance requirements:* For master's, GMAT or GRE General Test, professional resume; for doctorate, GMAT or GRE General Test. Additional exam requirements/recommendations for international students: Required—TOEFL (minimum score 610 paper-based). Electronic applications accepted. *Faculty research:* Policy analysis, local government, performance management, energy markets, labor markets.

University of Washington, Graduate School, Evans School of Public Affairs, Seattle, WA 98195. Offers public administration (MPA); public policy and management (PhD); JD/MPA; MPA/MAIS; MPA/MPH; MPA/MS; MPA/MUP. *Accreditation:* NASPAA. Part-time and evening/weekend programs available. *Degree requirements:* For master's, thesis, internship or cooperative experience. *Entrance requirements:* For master's and doctorate, GRE General Test, minimum GPA of 3.0. Additional exam requirements/recommendations for international students: Required—TOEFL (minimum score 580 paper-based; 92 iBT). Electronic applications accepted. *Faculty research:* Environmental policy, education and social policy, nonprofit management, international affairs, urban and regional development.

University of West Florida, College of Arts and Sciences: Arts, Department of Government, Pensacola, FL 32514-5750. Offers political science (MA), including public administration, security and diplomacy. Part-time and evening/weekend programs available. *Degree requirements:* For master's, thesis or alternative. *Entrance requirements:* For master's, GRE, official transcripts; minimum GPA of 3.0; 500-word writing sample in form of letter of intent; resume. Additional exam requirements/recommendations for international students: Required—TOEFL (minimum score 550 paper-based). *Faculty research:* Political campaigns, elections, law enforcement, growth management.

University of West Florida, College of Professional Studies, Department of Research and Advanced Studies, Pensacola, FL 32514-5750. Offers administration (MSA), including acquisition and contract administration, biomedical/pharmaceutical, criminal justice administration, database administration, education leadership, healthcare administration, human performance technology, leadership, nursing administration, public administration, software engineering and administration; college student personnel administration (M Ed), including college personnel administration, guidance and counseling; curriculum and instruction (M Ed, Ed S); educational leadership (M Ed); middle and secondary level education and ESOL (M Ed). Part-time and evening/weekend programs available. *Entrance requirements:* For master's, GRE or MAT, official transcripts; minimum undergraduate GPA of 3.0; letter of intent; three letters of recommendation; resume. Additional exam requirements/recommendations for international students: Required—TOEFL (minimum score 550 paper-based).

University of West Florida, College of Professional Studies, Program in Administration, Pensacola, FL 32514-5750. Offers acquisition and contract administration (MSA); database administration (MSA); health care administration (MSA); human performance technology (MSA); leadership (MSA); public administration (MSA); software engineering administration (MSA). Part-time and evening/weekend programs available. Postbaccalaureate distance learning degree programs offered (no on-campus study). *Entrance requirements:* For master's, GRE General Test, letter of intent, names of references. Additional exam requirements/recommendations for international students: Required—TOEFL (minimum score 550 paper-based).

University of West Georgia, College of Social Sciences, Department of Political Science, Carrollton, GA 30118. Offers public administration (MPA); public management (Certificate). *Accreditation:* NASPAA (one or more programs are accredited). Part-time programs available. *Faculty:* 11 full-time (2 women). *Students:* 22 full-time (11 women), 24 part-time (9 women); includes 19 minority (18 Black or African American, non-Hispanic/Latino; 1 Asian, non-Hispanic/Latino), 1 international. Average age 28. 19 applicants, 74% accepted, 10 enrolled. In 2014, 6 master's, 3 other advanced degrees awarded. *Degree requirements:* For master's, exit paper. *Entrance requirements:* For master's, GRE General Test, minimum GPA of 2.3; for Certificate, minimum GPA of 2.5. Additional exam requirements/recommendations for international students: Required—TOEFL (minimum score 523 paper-based; 69 iBT); Recommended—IELTS (minimum score 6). *Application deadline:* For fall admission, 7/31 for domestic students, 6/1 for international students; for spring admission, 11/30 for domestic students, 10/15 for international students. Applications are processed on a rolling basis. Application fee: $40. Electronic applications accepted. *Financial support:* In 2014–15, 4 students received support, including 6 research assistantships with full and partial tuition reimbursements available (averaging $5,500 per year); career-related internships or fieldwork and unspecified assistantships also available. Support available to part-time students. Financial award application deadline: 4/1; financial award applicants required to submit FAFSA. *Faculty research:* State and local government, environmental health, administrative studies, planning, gun control. *Unit head:* Dr. J. Salvador Peralta, Chair, 678-839-4993, Fax: 678-839-5009, E-mail: jperalta@westa.edu. *Application contact:* Trish Wells, Graduate Studies Associate, 678-839-5170, Fax: 678-839-5171, E-mail: pwells@westga.edu.
Website: http://www.westga.edu/polisci

The University of Winnipeg, Graduate Studies, Program in Public Administration, Winnipeg, MB R3B 2E9, Canada. Offers MPA. Program offered jointly with University of Manitoba. Part-time programs available. *Degree requirements:* For master's, comprehensive exam, thesis optional. *Entrance requirements:* For master's, minimum GPA of 3.0 in last 60 credit hours. *Faculty research:* Policy evaluation, federalism, administrative innovation, administrative ethics, economic development/administration.

University of Wisconsin–Milwaukee, Graduate School, College of Letters and Sciences, Interdepartmental Program in Public Administration, Milwaukee, WI 53201-0413. Offers MPA, MPA/MUP. Part-time programs available. *Degree requirements:* For master's, thesis or alternative. *Entrance requirements:* For master's, GRE General Test, minimum GPA of 3.0. Additional exam requirements/recommendations for international students: Required—TOEFL (minimum score 550 paper-based; 79 iBT), IELTS (minimum score 6.5). Electronic applications accepted.

University of Wisconsin–Oshkosh, Graduate Studies, College of Letters and Science, Department of Public Administration, Oshkosh, WI 54901. Offers general agency (MPA); health care (MPA). Part-time and evening/weekend programs available. *Degree requirements:* For master's, thesis or alternative. *Entrance requirements:* For master's, public service-related experience, resume, sample of written work. Additional exam requirements/recommendations for international students: Required—TOEFL (minimum score 550 paper-based; 79 iBT). Electronic applications accepted. *Faculty research:* Drug policy, local government state revenues and expenditures, health care regulation.

University of Wyoming, College of Arts and Sciences, Department of Political Science, Program in Public Administration, Laramie, WY 82071. Offers MPA. Part-time programs available. Postbaccalaureate distance learning degree programs offered (minimal on-campus study). *Degree requirements:* For master's, comprehensive exam (for some programs), thesis (for some programs). *Entrance requirements:* For master's, GRE General Test, minimum GPA of 3.0. Additional exam requirements/recommendations for international students: Required—TOEFL (minimum score 525 paper-based). Electronic applications accepted. *Faculty research:* Public policy, public ethics, administrative theory, natural resource policy.

Upper Iowa University, Online Master's Programs, Fayette, IA 52142-1857. Offers accounting (MBA); corporate financial management (MBA); global business (MBA); health and human services (MPA); higher education administration (MHEA); homeland security (MPA); human resources management (MBA); justice administration (MPA); organizational development (MBA); public personnel management (MPA); quality management (MBA). MBA also available at Madison, WI campus. Part-time programs available. Postbaccalaureate distance learning degree programs offered (no on-campus study). *Degree requirements:* For master's, research project. *Entrance requirements:* For master's, GMAT, GRE, or minimum GPA of 2.7 during last 60 hours. Additional exam requirements/recommendations for international students: Required—TOEFL (minimum score 570 paper-based). Electronic applications accepted. *Faculty research:* Total quality management, CQI, teams, organization culture and climate, management.

Villanova University, Graduate School of Liberal Arts and Sciences, Department of Public Administration, Villanova, PA 19085-1699. Offers MPA. *Accreditation:* NASPAA. Part-time and evening/weekend programs available. Postbaccalaureate distance learning degree programs offered (no on-campus study). *Faculty:* 23. *Students:* 190 full-

time (101 women), 81 part-time (39 women); includes 87 minority (53 Black or African American, non-Hispanic/Latino; 1 American Indian or Alaska Native, non-Hispanic/Latino; 6 Asian, non-Hispanic/Latino; 20 Hispanic/Latino; 1 Native Hawaiian or other Pacific Islander, non-Hispanic/Latino; 6 Two or more races, non-Hispanic/Latino), 2 international. Average age 36. 61 applicants, 98% accepted, 57 enrolled. In 2014, 41 master's awarded. *Degree requirements:* For master's, comprehensive exam. *Entrance requirements:* For master's, GRE General Test, minimum GPA of 3.0, statement of goals, 3 letters of recommendation. Additional exam requirements/recommendations for international students: Required—TOEFL. *Application deadline:* For fall admission, 5/1 for international students; for spring admission, 10/15 for international students. Applications are processed on a rolling basis. Application fee: $50. Electronic applications accepted. *Financial support:* Career-related internships or fieldwork, scholarships/grants, and unspecified assistantships available. Financial award application deadline: 3/15; financial award applicants required to submit FAFSA. *Unit head:* Dr. Christine Palus, Director, 610-519-3934.
Website: http://www1.villanova.edu/villanova/artsci/publicadmin.html

Virginia Commonwealth University, Graduate School, College of Humanities and Sciences, Wilder School of Government and Public Affairs, Department of Political Science and Public Administration, Richmond, VA 23284-9005. Offers nonprofit management (CPM); public administration (MPA); public management (CPM). *Accreditation:* NASPAA (one or more programs are accredited). Part-time programs available. *Entrance requirements:* For master's, GRE, GMAT or LSAT. Additional exam requirements/recommendations for international students: Required—TOEFL (minimum score 600 paper-based; 100 iBT); Recommended—IELTS (minimum score 6.5). Electronic applications accepted. *Faculty research:* Environmental policy, executive leadership, human resource management, local government management, nonprofit management, public financial management, public policy analysis and evaluation.

Virginia Polytechnic Institute and State University, Graduate School, College of Architecture and Urban Studies, Blacksburg, VA 24061. Offers architecture (MS Arch); architecture and design research (PhD); building/construction science and management (MS); creative technologies (MFA); environmental design and planning (PhD); landscape architecture (MLA); planning, governance, and globalization (PhD); public administration (MPA); public administration/public affairs (PhD, Certificate); public and international affairs (MPIA); urban and regional planning (MURP); MS/MA. *Accreditation:* ASLA (one or more programs are accredited). *Faculty:* 133 full-time (54 women), 2 part-time/adjunct (1 woman). *Students:* 316 full-time (166 women), 237 part-time (108 women); includes 104 minority (46 Black or African American, non-Hispanic/Latino; 1 American Indian or Alaska Native, non-Hispanic/Latino; 20 Asian, non-Hispanic/Latino; 21 Hispanic/Latino; 16 Two or more races, non-Hispanic/Latino), 108 international. Average age 32. 609 applicants, 50% accepted, 108 enrolled. In 2014, 155 master's, 29 doctorates awarded. *Degree requirements:* For master's, comprehensive exam (for some programs), thesis (for some programs); for doctorate, comprehensive exam (for some programs), thesis/dissertation (for some programs). *Entrance requirements:* For master's and doctorate, GRE/GMAT (may vary by department). Additional exam requirements/recommendations for international students: Required—TOEFL (minimum score 550 paper-based). *Application deadline:* For fall admission, 8/1 for domestic students, 4/1 for international students; for spring admission, 1/1 for domestic students, 9/1 for international students. Applications are processed on a rolling basis. Application fee: $75. Electronic applications accepted. *Expenses:* Tuition, state resident: full-time $11,656; part-time $647.50 per credit hour. Tuition, nonresident: full-time $23,351; part-time $1297.25 per credit hour. *Required fees:* $2533; $465.75 per semester. Tuition and fees vary according to course load, campus/location and program. *Financial support:* In 2014–15, 13 research assistantships with full tuition reimbursements (averaging $20,302 per year), 44 teaching assistantships with full tuition reimbursements (averaging $19,484 per year) were awarded. Financial award application deadline: 3/1; financial award applicants required to submit FAFSA. *Total annual research expenditures:* $3.2 million. *Unit head:* Dr. A. J. Davis, Dean, 540-231-6416, Fax: 540-231-6332, E-mail: davisa@vt.edu. *Application contact:* Christine Mattsson-Coon, Executive Assistant, 540-231-6416, Fax: 540-231-6332, E-mail: cmattsso@vt.edu.
Website: http://www.caus.vt.edu/

Walden University, Graduate Programs, School of Public Policy and Administration, Minneapolis, MN 55401. Offers criminal justice (MPA, MPP, MS, Graduate Certificate), including emergency management (MS, PhD), general program (MS, PhD), homeland security and policy coordination (MS, PhD), law and public policy (MS, PhD), policy analysis (MS, PhD), public management and leadership (MS, PhD), self-designed (MS), terrorism, mediation, and peace (MS, PhD); criminal justice leadership and executive management (MS), including emergency management (MS, PhD), general program (MS, PhD), homeland security and policy coordination (MS, PhD), law and public policy (MS, PhD), policy analysis (MS, PhD), public management and leadership (MS, PhD), self-designed, terrorism, mediation, and peace (MS, PhD); emergency management (MPA, MPP, MS), including criminal justice (MS, PhD), general program (MS, PhD), homeland security (MS), public management and leadership (MS, PhD), terrorism and emergency management (MS); general program (MPA, MPP); government management (Graduate Certificate); health policy (MPA, MPP); homeland security (Graduate Certificate); homeland security and policy coordination (MPA, MPP); international nongovernmental organizations (MPA, MPP); law and public policy (MPA, MPP); local government management for sustainable communities (MPA, MPP); nonprofit management (Graduate Certificate); nonprofit management and leadership (MPA, MPP, MS); online teaching in higher education (Post-Master's Certificate); policy analysis (MPA); public management and leadership (MPA, MPP, Graduate Certificate); public policy (Graduate Certificate); public policy and administration (PhD), including criminal justice (MS, PhD), emergency management (MS, PhD), general program (MS, PhD), health policy, homeland security and policy coordination (MS, PhD), international nongovernmental organizations, law and public policy (MS, PhD), local government management for sustainable communities, nonprofit management and leadership, policy analysis (MS, PhD), public management and leadership (MS, PhD), terrorism, mediation, and peace (MS, PhD); strategic planning and public policy (Graduate Certificate); terrorism, mediation, and peace (MPA, MPP). Part-time and evening/weekend programs available. Postbaccalaureate distance learning degree programs offered (no on-campus study). *Faculty:* 13 full-time (5 women), 151 part-time/adjunct (65 women). *Students:* 1,009 full-time (573 women), 1,632 part-time (954 women); includes 1,553 minority (1,307 Black or African American, non-Hispanic/Latino; 15 American Indian or Alaska Native, non-Hispanic/Latino; 38 Asian, non-Hispanic/Latino; 127 Hispanic/Latino; 66 Two or more races, non-Hispanic/Latino), 15 international. Average age 42. 665 applicants, 97% accepted, 616 enrolled. In 2014, 317 master's, 95 doctorates, 34 other advanced degrees awarded. *Degree requirements:* For doctorate, thesis/dissertation, residency. *Entrance requirements:* For master's, bachelor's degree or higher; minimum GPA of 2.5; official transcripts; goal statement (for some programs); access to computer and Internet; for doctorate, master's degree or higher; three years of related professional or academic experience (preferred); minimum GPA of 3.0; goal statement and current resume (for select programs); official transcripts; access to computer and Internet; for other advanced degree, relevant work experience; access to computer and Internet. Additional exam requirements/recommendations for international students: Required—TOEFL (minimum score 550 paper-based, 79 iBT), IELTS (minimum score 6.5), Michigan English Language Assessment Battery (minimum score 82), or PTE (minimum score 53). *Application deadline:* Applications are processed on a rolling basis. Application fee: $0. Electronic applications accepted. *Expenses:* *Tuition:* Full-time $11,925; part-time $500 per credit hour. *Required fees:* $647. *Financial support:* Fellowships, Federal Work-Study, scholarships/grants, unspecified assistantships, and family tuition reduction, active duty/veteran tuition reduction, group tuition reduction, interest-free payment plans, employee tuition reduction available. Support available to part-time students. Financial award applicants required to submit FAFSA. *Unit head:* Dr. Shana Garrett, Associate Dean, 866-492-5336. *Application contact:* Meghan Thomas, Vice President of Enrollment Management, 866-492-5336, E-mail: info@waldenu.edu.
Website: http://www.waldenu.edu/programs/colleges-schools/public-policy-and-administration

Washington Adventist University, Program in Public Administration, Takoma Park, MD 20912. Offers MPA. Part-time programs available. *Entrance requirements:* Additional exam requirements/recommendations for international students: Required—TOEFL (minimum score 550 paper-based), IELTS (minimum score 5).

Wayne State University, College of Liberal Arts and Sciences, Department of Political Science, Program in Public Administration, Detroit, MI 48202. Offers MPA. *Accreditation:* NASPAA. Part-time and evening/weekend programs available. *Students:* 12 full-time (8 women), 51 part-time (37 women); includes 21 minority (14 Black or African American, non-Hispanic/Latino; 2 Asian, non-Hispanic/Latino; 2 Hispanic/Latino; 3 Two or more races, non-Hispanic/Latino), 3 international. Average age 32. 90 applicants, 34% accepted, 17 enrolled. In 2014, 25 master's awarded. *Degree requirements;* For master's, comprehensive exam. *Entrance requirements:* For master's, GRE General Test, minimum undergraduate upper-division GPA of 3.0 or master's degree, personal statement. Additional exam requirements/recommendations for international students: Required—TOEFL (minimum score 550 paper-based; 79 iBT), TWE (minimum score 5.5), Michigan English Language Assessment Battery (minimum score 85); Recommended—IELTS (minimum score 6.5). *Application deadline:* For fall admission, 6/1 priority date for domestic students, 5/1 priority date for international students; for winter admission, 10/1 priority date for domestic students, 9/1 priority date for international students; for spring admission, 2/1 priority date for domestic students, 1/1 priority date for international students. Applications are processed on a rolling basis. Application fee: $0. Electronic applications accepted. *Expenses:* Tuition, state resident: full-time $10,294; part-time $571.90 per credit hour. Tuition, nonresident: full-time $29,730; part-time $1238.75 per credit hour. *Required fees:* $1365; $43.50 per credit hour. $291.10 per semester. Tuition and fees vary according to course load and program. *Financial support:* In 2014–15, 11 students received support. Fellowships, teaching assistantships, scholarships/grants, health care benefits, and unspecified assistantships available. Financial award application deadline: 3/31; financial award applicants required to submit FAFSA. *Faculty research:* Urban politics, urban education, state administration. *Unit head:* Dr. Daniel Geller, Department Chair, 313-577-6328, E-mail: dgeller@wayne.edu. *Application contact:* Dr. Brady Baybeck, Associate Professor/Director, 313-577-2630, E-mail: mpa@wayne.edu.
Website: http://clas.wayne.edu/mpa

Webster University, George Herbert Walker School of Business and Technology, Department of Management, St. Louis, MO 63119-3194. Offers business and organizational security management (MA); health administration (MHA); health care management (MA); health services management (MA); human resources development (MA); human resources management (MA); information technology management (MS); management and leadership (MA); marketing (MA); nonprofit leadership (MA); procurement and acquisitions management (MA); public administration (MPA); space systems operations management (MS). Part-time and evening/weekend programs available. Postbaccalaureate distance learning degree programs offered (no on-campus study). *Degree requirements:* For master's, thesis (for some programs). *Entrance requirements:* Additional exam requirements/recommendations for international students: Required—TOEFL.

West Chester University of Pennsylvania, College of Business and Public Affairs, Department of Public Policy and Administration, West Chester, PA 19383. Offers general public administration (MPA); human resource management (MPA, Certificate); non profit administration (Certificate); nonprofit administration (MPA); public administration (Certificate). Part-time and evening/weekend programs available. Postbaccalaureate distance learning degree programs offered (no on-campus study). *Faculty:* 5 full-time (3 women), 1 (woman) part-time/adjunct. *Students:* 61 full-time (29 women), 72 part-time (39 women); includes 48 minority (40 Black or African American, non-Hispanic/Latino; 2 Asian, non-Hispanic/Latino; 6 Hispanic/Latino), 4 international. Average age 29. 64 applicants, 98% accepted, 38 enrolled. In 2014, 53 master's, 5 other advanced degrees awarded. *Degree requirements:* For master's, capstone project. *Entrance requirements:* For master's and Certificate, statement of professional goals, resume, two letters of reference, academic transcripts. Additional exam requirements/recommendations for international students: Required—TOEFL (minimum score 550 paper-based; 80 iBT). *Application deadline:* For fall admission, 4/15 priority date for domestic students, 3/15 for international students; for spring admission, 10/15 priority date for domestic students, 9/1 for international students. Applications are processed on a rolling basis. Application fee: $45. Electronic applications accepted. *Expenses:* Tuition, state resident: full-time $8172; part-time $454 per credit. Tuition, nonresident: full-time $12,258; part-time $681 per credit. *Required fees:* $2231; $110.78 per credit. Tuition and fees vary according to campus/location and program. *Financial support:* Unspecified assistantships available. Support available to part-time students. Financial award application deadline: 2/15; financial award applicants required to submit FAFSA. *Faculty research:* Public policy, economic development, research methodology, urban politics, public administration. *Unit head:* Dr. Jeffery Osgood, Department Chair/Director of MPA Program, 610-436-2286, E-mail: josgood@wcupa.edu. *Application contact:* Office of Graduate Studies and Extended Education, 610-436-2943, Fax: 610-436-2763, E-mail: gradstudy@wcupa.edu.
Website: http://catalog.wcupa.edu/graduate/business-public-affairs/public-policy-administration/

Western International University, Graduate Programs in Business, Master of Public Administration Program, Phoenix, AZ 85021-2718. Offers MPA. Part-time and evening/weekend programs available. Postbaccalaureate distance learning degree programs offered (no on-campus study). *Entrance requirements:* For master's, minimum GPA of 2.75. Additional exam requirements/recommendations for international students: Required—TOEFL (minimum score 550 paper-based; 79 iBT), TWE (minimum score 5), or IELTS (minimum score 6.5). Electronic applications accepted.

Western Kentucky University, Graduate Studies, Potter College of Arts and Letters, Department of Political Science, Bowling Green, KY 42101. Offers MPA. *Accreditation:* NASPAA. Part-time and evening/weekend programs available. *Degree requirements:* For master's, comprehensive exam, final exam. *Entrance requirements:* For master's, GRE General Test, minimum GPA of 2.75. Additional exam requirements/recommendations for international students: Required—TOEFL (minimum score 555

paper-based; 79 iBT). *Faculty research:* Role of non-profits, comparative policy analysis, social welfare policy, rural administration, ethics and bureaucracy.

Western Michigan University, Graduate College, College of Arts and Sciences, Department of Political Science, Kalamazoo, MI 49008. Offers international development administration (MIDA), including Peace Corps; political science (MA, PhD). *Degree requirements:* For master's, thesis optional; for doctorate, thesis/dissertation. *Application deadline:* For fall admission, 2/15 for domestic students. *Financial support:* Application deadline: 2/15; applicants required to submit FAFSA. *Application contact:* Admissions and Orientation, 269-387-2000, Fax: 269-387-2096.

Western Michigan University, Graduate College, College of Arts and Sciences, School of Public Affairs and Administration, Kalamazoo, MI 49008. Offers health care administration (MPA, Graduate Certificate); nonprofit leadership and administration (Graduate Certificate); public administration (PhD). *Accreditation:* NASPAA (one or more programs are accredited). *Degree requirements:* For doctorate, thesis/dissertation. *Application deadline:* For fall admission, 2/15 for domestic students. *Financial support:* Application deadline: 2/15. *Application contact:* Admissions and Orientation, 269-387-2000, Fax: 269-387-2096.

West Virginia University, Eberly College of Arts and Sciences, School of Applied Social Sciences, Division of Public Administration, Morgantown, WV 26506. Offers legal studies (MLS); public administration (MPA); JD/MPA; MSW/MPA. *Accreditation:* NASPAA. Part-time programs available. *Degree requirements:* For master's, internship. *Entrance requirements:* For master's, GRE General Test, minimum GPA of 2.75. Additional exam requirements/recommendations for international students: Required—TOEFL. Electronic applications accepted. *Faculty research:* Public management and organization, conflict resolution, work satisfaction, health administration, social policy and welfare.

Wichita State University, Graduate School, Fairmount College of Liberal Arts and Sciences, Hugo Wall School of Public Affairs, Wichita, KS 67260. Offers public administration (MPA). *Accreditation:* NASPAA. Part-time programs available. *Unit head:* Dr. Nancy McCarthy Snyder, Director, 316-978-7240, Fax: 316-978-6533, E-mail: nancy.mccarthy-snyder@wichita.edu. *Application contact:* Jordan Oleson, Admissions Coordinator, 316-978-3095, E-mail: jordan.oleson@wichita.edu.
Website: http://www.sjcny.edu

Widener University, College of Arts and Sciences, Program in Public Administration, Chester, PA 19013-5792. Offers MPA, Psy D/MPA. Part-time and evening/weekend programs available. *Degree requirements:* For master's, thesis or comprehensive exam. *Entrance requirements:* For master's, minimum undergraduate GPA of 3.0. Electronic applications accepted. *Expenses:* Contact institution. *Faculty research:* Intergovernmental relations, nonprofit organizations, public policy, political economy, bureaucratic politics.

Wilmington University, College of Business, New Castle, DE 19720-6491. Offers accounting (MBA, MS); business administration (MBA, DBA); environmental stewardship (MBA); finance (MBA); health care administration (MBA, MSM); homeland security (MBA, MSM); human resource management (MSM); management information systems (MBA, MSN); marketing (MSM); marketing management (MBA); military leadership (MSM); organizational leadership (MBA, MSM); public administration (MSM). Part-time and evening/weekend programs available. *Faculty:* 20 full-time (6 women), 117 part-time/adjunct (48 women). *Students:* 585 full-time (298 women), 1,156 part-time (733 women); includes 665 minority (567 Black or African American, non-Hispanic/Latino; 11 American Indian or Alaska Native, non-Hispanic/Latino; 55 Asian, non-Hispanic/Latino; 26 Hispanic/Latino; 2 Native Hawaiian or other Pacific Islander, non-Hispanic/Latino; 4 Two or more races, non-Hispanic/Latino), 133 international. Average age 35. 1,323 applicants, 99% accepted, 643 enrolled. In 2014, 438 master's, 15 doctorates awarded. *Entrance requirements:* Additional exam requirements/recommendations for international students: Required—TOEFL (minimum score 500 paper-based). *Application deadline:* Applications are processed on a rolling basis. Application fee: $35. Electronic applications accepted. *Financial support:* Applicants required to submit FAFSA. *Unit head:* Dr. Donald W. Durandetta, Dean, 302-356-6780, E-mail: donald.w.durandetta@wilmu.edu. *Application contact:* Laura Morris, Director of Admissions, 877-967-5456, E-mail: infocenter@wilmu.edu.
Website: http://www.wilmu.edu/business/

Wright State University, School of Graduate Studies, College of Liberal Arts, Department of Urban Affairs and Geography, Dayton, OH 45435. Offers public administration (MPA). *Accreditation:* NASPAA. *Degree requirements:* For master's, thesis optional. *Entrance requirements:* For master's, interview, minimum GPA of 2.7. Additional exam requirements/recommendations for international students: Required—TOEFL. *Faculty research:* Strategic planning, economic development, housing and public management.

York University, Faculty of Graduate Studies, Faculty of Liberal Arts and Professional Studies, Program in Public Policy, Administration and Law, Toronto, ON M3J 1P3, Canada. Offers MPPAL.

Public Affairs

American University, School of Communication, Program in Journalism and Public Affairs, Washington, DC 20016-8001. Offers interactive journalism (MA). *Accreditation:* ACEJMC; NASPAA. *Faculty:* 13 full-time (5 women), 4 part-time/adjunct (all women). *Students:* 28 full-time (22 women). 137 applicants, 55% accepted, 30 enrolled. In 2014, 28 master's awarded. *Degree requirements:* For master's, comprehensive exam, thesis or alternative. *Entrance requirements:* Additional exam requirements/recommendations for international students: Required—TOEFL (minimum score 600 paper-based; 100 iBT), IELTS (minimum score 7). *Application deadline:* For fall admission, 2/1 priority date for domestic students, 4/1 priority date for international students. Applications are processed on a rolling basis. Application fee: $55. Electronic applications accepted. *Financial support:* In 2014–15, 3 fellowships with full and partial tuition reimbursements (averaging $27,000 per year), 14 research assistantships with partial tuition reimbursements (averaging $7,000 per year), 3 teaching assistantships with partial tuition reimbursements (averaging $7,000 per year) were awarded; career-related internships or fieldwork, Federal Work-Study, institutionally sponsored loans, scholarships/grants, tuition waivers (partial), and unspecified assistantships also available. Financial award application deadline: 2/1; financial award applicants required to submit FAFSA. *Faculty research:* Government and media effects of journalistic practices and policies, race and gender and the media, investigative reporting, computer-assisted reporting. *Unit head:* Prof. John Watson, Division Director, 202-885-2083, Fax: 202-885-2099, E-mail: jwatson@american.edu. *Application contact:* Sharmeen Ahsan-Bracciale, Graduate Admissions Office, 202-885-2040, Fax: 202-885-2019, E-mail: sharmeen@american.edu.
Website: http://www.american.edu/soc/journalism/index.cfm

Arizona State University at the Tempe campus, College of Public Programs, School of Public Affairs, Phoenix, AZ 85004-0687. Offers emergency management and homeland security (MA); program evaluation (MS); public administration (MPA, PhD), including nonprofit administration (MPA), urban management (MPA); public policy (MPP); MPA/MSW. *Accreditation:* NASPAA (one or more programs are accredited). Part-time and evening/weekend programs available. Terminal master's awarded for partial completion of doctoral program. *Degree requirements:* For master's, thesis or alternative, policy analysis or capstone project; interactive Program of Study (iPOS) submitted before completing 50 percent of required credit hours; for doctorate, comprehensive exam, thesis/dissertation, interactive Program of Study (iPOS) submitted before completing 50 percent of required credit hours. *Entrance requirements:* For master's, GRE, minimum GPA of 3.0 or equivalent in last 2 years of work leading to bachelor's degree; for doctorate, GRE, minimum GPA of 3.0 or equivalent in last 2 years of work leading to bachelor's degree, 3 letters of recommendation, resume, statement of goals, samples of research reports. Additional exam requirements/recommendations for international students: Required—TOEFL (minimum score 600 paper-based; 100 iBT), IELTS (minimum score 6.5). Electronic applications accepted. *Expenses:* Contact institution.

Clemson University, Graduate School, Program in International Family and Community Studies, Clemson, SC 29634. Offers PhD. *Faculty:* 5 full-time (3 women), 5 part-time/adjunct (3 women). *Students:* 12 full-time (11 women), 22 part-time (18 women); includes 5 minority (1 Black or African American, non-Hispanic/Latino; 3 Asian, non-Hispanic/Latino; 1 Hispanic/Latino), 15 international. Average age 36. In 2014, 1 doctorate awarded. *Degree requirements:* For doctorate, thesis/dissertation. *Entrance requirements:* For doctorate, GRE General Test. Additional exam requirements/recommendations for international students: Required—TOEFL. *Application deadline:* Applications are processed on a rolling basis. Application fee: $70 ($80 for international students). Electronic applications accepted. *Expenses:* Expenses: Contact institution. *Financial support:* In 2014–15, 9 students received support, including 9 research assistantships with partial tuition reimbursements available (averaging $21,444 per year); fellowships with full and partial tuition reimbursements available, teaching assistantships, career-related internships or fieldwork, institutionally sponsored loans, scholarships/grants, health care benefits, and unspecified assistantships also available. Support available to part-time students. *Total annual research expenditures:* $728,285. *Unit head:* Dr. Mark Small, Director, 864-656-6286, E-mail: msmall@clemson.edu. *Application contact:* Information Contact, 864-656-3195, E-mail: gradapp@clemson.edu.
Website: http://www.grad.clemson.edu/programs/Family-Community-Studies/

Cleveland State University, College of Graduate Studies, Maxine Goodman Levin College of Urban Affairs, Program in Urban Studies and Public Affairs, Cleveland, OH 44115. Offers communication (PhD); public administration (PhD); urban policy and development (PhD). Part-time and evening/weekend programs available. *Faculty:* 23 full-time (11 women), 23 part-time/adjunct (6 women). *Students:* 10 full-time (6 women), 26 part-time (13 women); includes 5 minority (4 Black or African American, non-Hispanic/Latino; 1 Asian, non-Hispanic/Latino), 10 international. Average age 40. 32 applicants, 34% accepted, 2 enrolled. In 2014, 3 doctorates awarded. *Degree requirements:* For doctorate, comprehensive exam, thesis/dissertation. *Entrance requirements:* For doctorate, GRE General Test (minimum score: verbal and quantitative 50th percentile, analytical writing 4.0), minimum GPA of 3.5. Additional exam requirements/recommendations for international students: Required—TOEFL (minimum score 525 paper-based; 65 iBT), IELTS, or ITEP. *Application deadline:* For fall admission, 1/31 for domestic and international students. Application fee: $30. Electronic applications accepted. *Expenses:* Expenses: $9,615 full-time, in-state tuition and fees. *Financial support:* In 2014–15, 15 students received support, including 7 research assistantships with full and partial tuition reimbursements available (averaging $9,200 per year), 3 teaching assistantships with full and partial tuition reimbursements available (averaging $8,600 per year); scholarships/grants and unspecified assistantships also available. Support available to part-time students. Financial award application deadline: 3/1; financial award applicants required to submit FAFSA. *Faculty research:* Urban and public policy, public affairs. *Unit head:* Dr. Wendy Kellogg, Director, 216-687-5265, E-mail: w.kellogg@csuohio.edu. *Application contact:* David Arrighi, Graduate Academic Advisor, 216-523-7522, Fax: 216-687-5398, E-mail: urbanprograms@csuohio.edu.
Website: http://urban.csuohio.edu/academics/graduate/phd/

Concordia University, School of Graduate Studies, Faculty of Arts and Science, School of Community and Public Affairs, Montréal, QC H3G 1M8, Canada. Offers community economic development (Diploma).

Cornell University, Graduate School, Graduate Fields of Human Ecology, Field of Public Affairs, Ithaca, NY 14853-0001. Offers MPA. *Degree requirements:* For master's, thesis, research project, paper. *Entrance requirements:* For master's, GRE General Test, 2 letters of recommendation. Additional exam requirements/recommendations for international students: Required—TOEFL (minimum score 550 paper-based; 77 iBT). Electronic applications accepted.

Florida International University, College of Arts and Sciences, Department of Public Administration, Miami, FL 33199. Offers public administration (MPA); public affairs (PhD); JD/MPA; MS/MPA. *Accreditation:* NASPAA (one or more programs are accredited). Part-time and evening/weekend programs available. *Degree requirements:* For doctorate, comprehensive exam, thesis/dissertation. *Entrance requirements:* For master's, minimum undergraduate GPA of 3.0 in upper-level coursework, 1 letter of recommendation, letter of intent; for doctorate, GRE, minimum undergraduate GPA of 3.0 in upper-level coursework, 3 letters of recommendation, samples of scholarly written work, interview (when student lives within 50 miles of campus). Additional exam requirements/recommendations for international students: Required—TOEFL (minimum score 550 paper-based; 80 iBT). Electronic applications accepted.

George Mason University, College of Humanities and Social Sciences, Department of Philosophy, Fairfax, VA 22030. Offers ethics and public affairs (MA). *Faculty:* 11 full-time (3 women), 8 part-time/adjunct (1 woman). *Students:* 1 (woman) full-time, 12 part-time (1 woman); includes 2 minority (1 Black or African American, non-Hispanic/Latino; 1

Two or more races, non-Hispanic/Latino). Average age 39. 14 applicants, 57% accepted, 3 enrolled. In 2014, 2 master's awarded. *Degree requirements:* For master's, thesis optional. *Entrance requirements:* For master's, 3 letters of recommendation; official transcript; expanded goals statement; writing sample; resume. Additional exam requirements/recommendations for international students: Required—TOEFL (minimum score 570 paper-based; 80 iBT), IELTS (minimum score 6.5), PTE. *Application deadline:* For fall admission, 3/1 priority date for domestic students; for spring admission, 11/1 priority date for domestic students. Application fee: $65 ($80 for international students). Electronic applications accepted. *Expenses:* Tuition, state resident: full-time $9794; part-time $408 per credit hour. Tuition, nonresident: full-time $26,978; part-time $1124 per credit hour. *Required fees:* $2820; $118 per credit hour. Tuition and fees vary according to course load and program. *Financial support:* In 2014–15, 2 students received support, including 2 teaching assistantships (averaging $7,000 per year); career-related internships or fieldwork, Federal Work-Study, scholarships/grants, unspecified assistantships, and health care benefits (for full-time research or teaching assistantship recipients) also available. Financial award application deadline: 3/1; financial award applicants required to submit FAFSA. *Faculty research:* Cultural studies, political theory philosophy, social and political philosophy, feminist theory, analytical and Continental philosophy, philosophy of science. *Total annual research expenditures:* $6,841. *Unit head:* Ted Kinnaman, Chair/Associate Professor, 703-993-4328, Fax: 703-993-1297, E-mail: tkinnama@gmu.edu. *Application contact:* Rose Cherubin, Graduate Coordinator, 703-993-1332, Fax: 703-993-1297, E-mail: rcherubi@gmu.edu.
Website: http://philosophy.gmu.edu/

The George Washington University, Columbian College of Arts and Sciences, School of Media and Public Affairs, Washington, DC 20052. Offers MA, Graduate Certificate. *Accreditation:* NASPAA. *Faculty:* 25 full-time (10 women). *Students:* 26 full-time (16 women), 11 part-time (8 women); includes 8 minority (1 Asian, non-Hispanic/Latino; 7 Hispanic/Latino), 7 international. Average age 26. 85 applicants, 56% accepted, 21 enrolled. In 2014, 22 master's, 16 other advanced degrees awarded. *Degree requirements:* For master's, thesis optional. *Entrance requirements:* For master's, GRE General Test. Additional exam requirements/recommendations for international students: Required—TOEFL (minimum score 550 paper-based; 80 iBT). *Application deadline:* For fall admission, 4/1 priority date for domestic students, 1/15 priority date for international students; for spring admission, 10/1 priority date for domestic students, 9/1 priority date for international students. Applications are processed on a rolling basis. Application fee: $75. Electronic applications accepted. *Financial support:* In 2014–15, fellowships with tuition reimbursements (averaging $10,000 per year), teaching assistantships with tuition reimbursements (averaging $5,000 per year) were awarded. Financial award application deadline: 1/15. *Unit head:* Frank Sesno, Director, 202-994-9553, E-mail: sesno@gwu.edu. *Application contact:* Information Contact, 202-994-6227, Fax: 202-994-5806, E-mail: smpa@gwu.edu.
Website: http://www.gwu.edu/~smpa/

Indiana University Bloomington, School of Public and Environmental Affairs, Public Affairs Programs, Bloomington, IN 47405. Offers economic development (MPA); energy (MPA); environmental policy (PhD); environmental policy and natural resource management (MPA); information systems (MPA); international development (MPA); local government management (MPA); nonprofit management (MPA, Certificate); policy analysis (MPA); public budgeting and financial management (Certificate); public finance (PhD); public financial administration (MPA); public management (MPA, PhD, Certificate); public policy analysis (PhD); social entrepreneurship (Certificate); specialized public affairs (MPA); sustainability and sustainable development (MPA); JD/MPA; MPA/MA; MPA/MIS; MPA/MLS; MSES/MPA. *Accreditation:* NASPAA (one or more programs are accredited). Part-time programs available. *Degree requirements:* For master's, capstone, internship; for doctorate, comprehensive exam, thesis/dissertation. *Entrance requirements:* For master's, GRE General Test or GMAT, official transcripts, 3 letters of recommendation, resume, personal statement; for doctorate, GRE General Test, official transcripts, 3 letters of recommendation, statement of purpose. Additional exam requirements/recommendations for international students: Required—TOEFL (minimum score 600 paper-based; 96 iBT); Recommended—IELTS (minimum score 7). Electronic applications accepted. *Faculty research:* International development, environmental policy and resource management, policy analysis, public finance, public management, urban management, nonprofit management, energy policy, social policy, public finance.

Indiana University Northwest, School of Public and Environmental Affairs, Gary, IN 46408-1197. Offers criminal justice (MPA); environmental affairs (Graduate Certificate); health services (MPA); nonprofit management (Certificate); public management (MPA). *Accreditation:* NASPAA (one or more programs are accredited). Part-time programs available. *Faculty:* 5 full-time (3 women). *Students:* 12 full-time (7 women), 39 part-time (23 women); includes 37 minority (26 Black or African American, non-Hispanic/Latino; 1 Asian, non-Hispanic/Latino; 9 Hispanic/Latino; 1 Two or more races, non-Hispanic/Latino). Average age 38. 30 applicants, 93% accepted, 25 enrolled. In 2014, 29 master's, 15 other advanced degrees awarded. *Entrance requirements:* For master's, GRE General Test or GMAT, letters of recommendation. *Application deadline:* For fall admission, 8/15 priority date for domestic students. Applications are processed on a rolling basis. *Financial support:* Career-related internships or fieldwork, Federal Work-Study, and tuition waivers (partial) available. Support available to part-time students. Financial award application deadline: 3/1. *Faculty research:* Employment in income security policies, evidence in criminal justice, equal employment law, social welfare policy and welfare reform, public finance in developing countries. *Unit head:* Dr. Barbara Peat, Department Chair, 219-981-5645, E-mail: bpeat@iun.edu. *Application contact:* Susan Zinner, 219-980-6836, E-mail: speanw@iun.edu.
Website: http://www.iun.edu/spea/index.htm

Indiana University of Pennsylvania, School of Graduate Studies and Research, College of Humanities and Social Sciences, Department of Political Science, Program in Public Affairs, Indiana, PA 15705-1087. Offers MA. Part-time programs available. *Faculty:* 7 full-time (4 women). *Students:* 16 full-time (7 women), 4 part-time (1 woman); includes 2 minority (1 Black or African American, non-Hispanic/Latino; 1 Two or more races, non-Hispanic/Latino), 4 international. Average age 27. 17 applicants, 65% accepted, 7 enrolled. In 2014, 10 master's awarded. *Degree requirements:* For master's, thesis optional. *Entrance requirements:* For master's, 2 letters of recommendation. Additional exam requirements/recommendations for international students: Required—TOEFL (minimum score 550 paper-based). *Application deadline:* Applications are processed on a rolling basis. Application fee: $50. Electronic applications accepted. *Financial support:* In 2014–15, 2 fellowships with full tuition reimbursements (averaging $1,000 per year), 11 research assistantships with full and partial tuition reimbursements (averaging $2,479 per year) were awarded; career-related internships or fieldwork, Federal Work-Study, scholarships/grants, and unspecified assistantships also available. Support available to part-time students. Financial award application deadline: 4/15; financial award applicants required to submit FAFSA. *Unit head:* Dr. Sarah Wheeler, Graduate Coordinator, 724-357-2290, E-mail: wheeler@iup.edu.
Website: http://www.iup.edu/grad/publicaffairs/default.aspx

Indiana University–Purdue University Indianapolis, School of Public and Environmental Affairs, Indianapolis, IN 46202. Offers criminal justice and public safety (MS); homeland security and emergency management (Graduate Certificate); library management (Graduate Certificate); nonprofit management (Graduate Certificate); public affairs (MPA); public management (Graduate Certificate); social entrepreneurship: nonprofit and public benefit organizations (Graduate Certificate); JD/MPA; MLS/NMC; MLS/PMC; MPA/MA. *Accreditation:* CAHME (one or more programs are accredited); NASPAA. Part-time and evening/weekend programs available. Postbaccalaureate distance learning degree programs offered (no on-campus study). *Entrance requirements:* For master's, GRE General Test, GMAT or LSAT, minimum GPA of 3.0 (preferred). Additional exam requirements/recommendations for international students: Required—TOEFL (minimum score 93 iBT), IELTS (minimum score 6.5). Electronic applications accepted. *Faculty research:* Nonprofit and public management, public policy, urban policy, sustainability policy, disaster preparedness and recovery, vehicular safety, homicide, offender rehabilitation and re-entry.

Indiana University South Bend, College of Liberal Arts and Sciences, South Bend, IN 46634-7111. Offers applied mathematics and computer science (MS); English (MA); liberal studies (MLS); public affairs (MPA). Part-time and evening/weekend programs available. *Faculty:* 79 full-time (33 women). *Students:* 41 full-time (26 women), 89 part-time (59 women); includes 24 minority (12 Black or African American, non-Hispanic/Latino; 1 Asian, non-Hispanic/Latino; 3 Hispanic/Latino; 1 Native Hawaiian or other Pacific Islander, non-Hispanic/Latino; 7 Two or more races, non-Hispanic/Latino), 15 international. Average age 37. 58 applicants, 72% accepted, 33 enrolled. In 2014, 33 master's awarded. *Degree requirements:* For master's, thesis (for some programs). *Entrance requirements:* For master's, minimum GPA of 3.0. Additional exam requirements/recommendations for international students: Required—TOEFL. *Application deadline:* For fall admission, 7/31 priority date for domestic students, 7/1 priority date for international students; for spring admission, 3/31 priority date for domestic students, 11/1 priority date for international students. Applications are processed on a rolling basis. *Financial support:* In 2014–15, 5 teaching assistantships were awarded; Federal Work-Study also available. Support available to part-time students. *Faculty research:* Artificial intelligence, bioinformatics, English language and literature, creative writing, computer networks. *Total annual research expenditures:* $127,000. *Unit head:* Dr. Elizabeth E. Dunn, Dean, 574-520-4290, E-mail: elizdunn@iusb.edu. *Application contact:* Admissions Counselor, 574-520-4839, Fax: 574-520-4834, E-mail: graduate@iusb.edu.
Website: https://www.iusb.edu/clas/academics/index.php

The Institute of World Politics, Graduate Programs in National Security, Intelligence, and International Affairs, Washington, DC 20036. Offers American foreign policy (Certificate); comparative political culture (Certificate); counterintelligence (Certificate); democracy building (Certificate); intelligence (Certificate); international politics (Certificate); national security affairs (Certificate); public diplomacy and political warfare (Certificate); statecraft and national security affairs (MA); statecraft and world politics (MA); strategic intelligence studies (MA). Part-time and evening/weekend programs available. *Degree requirements:* For master's, comprehensive exam, thesis optional. *Entrance requirements:* For master's, GRE General Test. Additional exam requirements/recommendations for international students: Required—TOEFL. Electronic applications accepted. *Faculty research:* Intelligence, national security, statecraft.

Jackson State University, Graduate School, College of Public Service, Jackson, MS 39217. Offers MPPA, MS, PhD. *Degree requirements:* For master's, comprehensive exam. *Entrance requirements:* For master's, GRE General Test. Additional exam requirements/recommendations for international students: Required—TOEFL.

McMaster University, School of Graduate Studies, Faculty of Social Sciences, Department of Political Science, Hamilton, ON L8S 4M2, Canada. Offers international relations (PhD); political science (MA); public and the global economy (MA); public policy (PhD); public policy and administration (MA). MA program in public policy and administration offered jointly with University of Guelph. Part-time programs available. *Degree requirements:* For master's, thesis or alternative. *Entrance requirements:* For master's, minimum B+ average. Additional exam requirements/recommendations for international students: Required—TOEFL (minimum score 580 paper-based). *Faculty research:* Organizational theory, internationalization of public policy, water resource policies, political interest intermediation, comparative politics.

Murray State University, College of Humanities and Fine Arts, Department of Government, Laws and International Affairs, Program in Public Administration, Murray, KY 42071. Offers public affairs (MPA). Part-time programs available. Postbaccalaureate distance learning degree programs offered (minimal on-campus study). *Degree requirements:* For master's, capstone course. *Entrance requirements:* For master's, GRE General Test. Additional exam requirements/recommendations for international students: Required—TOEFL.

New Mexico Highlands University, Graduate Studies, College of Arts and Sciences, Department of History, Political Science, and Languages and Culture, Las Vegas, NM 87701. Offers public affairs (MA), including historical and cross-cultural perspectives, history/political science, political and governmental processes. *Faculty:* 9 full-time (3 women), 1 part-time/adjunct (0 women). *Students:* 13 full-time (6 women), 12 part-time (1 woman); includes 15 minority (all Hispanic/Latino), 5 international. Average age 34. 12 applicants, 100% accepted, 4 enrolled. In 2014, 1 master's awarded. *Degree requirements:* For master's, comprehensive exam, thesis or alternative. *Entrance requirements:* Additional exam requirements/recommendations for international students: Required—TOEFL (minimum score 540 paper-based). *Application deadline:* For fall admission, 8/1 priority date for domestic students. Applications are processed on a rolling basis. Application fee: $15. *Financial support:* In 2014–15, 11 teaching assistantships were awarded; research assistantships, career-related internships or fieldwork, Federal Work-Study, institutionally sponsored loans, scholarships/grants, traineeships, tuition waivers (full and partial), and unspecified assistantships also available. Support available to part-time students. Financial award application deadline: 3/1. *Unit head:* Dr. Steven Williams, Associate Professor, 505-454-3435. *Application contact:* Diane Trujillo, Administrative Assistant, Graduate Studies, 505-454-3266, Fax: 505-426-2117, E-mail: dtrujillo@nmhu.edu.
Website: http://www.nmhu.edu/current-students/graduate/arts-and-sciences/history-political-science-languages-and-culture/

New Mexico Highlands University, Graduate Studies, College of Arts and Sciences, Department of Social and Behavioral Sciences, Las Vegas, NM 87701. Offers psychology (MS), including clinical psychology/counseling, general psychology; public affairs (MA), including applied sociology; Southwest studies (MA), including anthropology. Part-time programs available. *Faculty:* 11 full-time (5 women), 3 part-time/adjunct (all women). *Students:* 24 full-time (16 women), 19 part-time (14 women); includes 27 minority (3 Black or African American, non-Hispanic/Latino; 1 American Indian or Alaska Native, non-Hispanic/Latino; 23 Hispanic/Latino), 2 international. Average age 33. 45 applicants, 33% accepted, 15 enrolled. In 2014, 7 master's awarded. *Degree requirements:* For master's, comprehensive exam, thesis or alternative. *Entrance requirements:* For master's, minimum undergraduate GPA of 3.0. Additional exam requirements/recommendations for international students: Required—TOEFL (minimum score 540 paper-based). *Application deadline:* For fall admission, 8/1 priority date for domestic students. Applications are processed on a rolling basis. Application fee: $15. *Financial support:* In 2014–15, 34 teaching assistantships were

awarded; career-related internships or fieldwork, Federal Work-Study, institutionally sponsored loans, scholarships/grants, tuition waivers (full and partial), and unspecified assistantships also available. Support available to part-time students. Financial award application deadline: 3/1; financial award applicants required to submit FAFSA. *Faculty research:* Southwest Native American resettlement development, community-level interventions, neurochemistry of personality, comparative criminal justice, social theory and activism. *Unit head:* Dr. Tom Ward, Program Coordinator, 505-454-3196, E-mail: tsward@nmhu.edu. *Application contact:* Diane Trujillo, Administrative Assistant for Graduate Studies, 505-454-3266, Fax: 505-426-2117, E-mail: dtrujillo@nmhu.edu.

Notre Dame de Namur University, Division of Academic Affairs, School of Business and Management, Program in Public Administration, Belmont, CA 94002-1908. Offers human resource management (MPA); public administration (MPA); public affairs administration (MPA); social enterprise (MPA). Part-time and evening/weekend programs available. Postbaccalaureate distance learning degree programs offered (no on-campus study). *Entrance requirements:* For master's, interview, minimum GPA of 2.5. Additional exam requirements/recommendations for international students: Required—TOEFL (minimum score 550 paper-based; 79 iBT). Electronic applications accepted.

The Ohio State University, Graduate School, John Glenn College of Public Affairs, Columbus, OH 43210. Offers public administration (MA, MPA); public policy and management (PhD). *Accreditation:* NASPAA (one or more programs are accredited). Part-time programs available. *Faculty:* 20. *Students:* 155 full-time (85 women), 45 part-time (35 women); includes 29 minority (11 Black or African American, non-Hispanic/Latino; 8 Asian, non-Hispanic/Latino; 6 Hispanic/Latino; 1 Native Hawaiian or other Pacific Islander, non-Hispanic/Latino; 3 Two or more races, non-Hispanic/Latino), 18 international. Average age 30. In 2014, 86 master's, 2 doctorates awarded. *Degree requirements:* For doctorate, thesis/dissertation. *Entrance requirements:* For master's, GRE General Test (for MPA), minimum GPA of 3.0 (for MA); for doctorate, GRE General Test. Additional exam requirements/recommendations for international students: Required—TOEFL (minimum score 600 paper-based; 100 iBT); Recommended—IELTS (minimum score 7.5). *Application deadline:* For fall admission, 12/1 priority date for domestic students, 11/1 priority date for international students; for winter admission, 12/1 for domestic students, 11/1 for international students; for spring admission, 11/15 for domestic and international students; for summer admission, 4/1 for domestic and international students. Applications are processed on a rolling basis. Application fee: $60 ($70 for international students). Electronic applications accepted. *Financial support:* Fellowships, research assistantships, teaching assistantships, Federal Work-Study, institutionally sponsored loans, and unspecified assistantships available. Support available to part-time students. *Unit head:* Dr. Trevor Brown, Dean, 614-292-4533, Fax: 614-292-4868, E-mail: brown.2296@osu.edu. *Application contact:* Graduate and Professional Admissions, 614-292-6031, Fax: 614-292-3656, E-mail: gpadmissions@osu.edu.
Website: http://glennschool.osu.edu/

Park University, School of Graduate and Professional Studies, Kansas City, MO 54105. Offers adult education (M Ed); business and government leadership (Graduate Certificate); business, government, and global society (MPA); communication and leadership (MA); creative and life writing (Graduate Certificate); disaster and emergency management (MPA, Graduate Certificate); educational leadership (M Ed); finance (MBA, Graduate Certificate); general business (MBA); global business (Graduate Certificate); healthcare administration (MHA); healthcare services management and leadership (Graduate Certificate); international business (MBA); language and literacy (M Ed), including English for speakers of other languages, special reading teacher/literacy coach; leadership of international healthcare organizations (Graduate Certificate); management information systems (MBA, Graduate Certificate); music performance (ADP, Graduate Certificate), including cello (MM, ADP), piano (MM, ADP), viola (MM, ADP), violin (MM, ADP); nonprofit and community services management (MPA); nonprofit leadership (Graduate Certificate); performance (MM), including cello (MM, ADP), piano (MM, ADP), viola (MM, ADP), violin (MM, ADP); public management (MPA); social work (MSW); teacher leadership (M Ed), including curriculum and assessment, instructional leader. Part-time and evening/weekend programs available. Postbaccalaureate distance learning degree programs offered (no on-campus study). *Degree requirements:* For master's, comprehensive exam (for some programs), thesis (for some programs), internship (for some programs); exam (for some programs). *Entrance requirements:* For master's, GRE or GMAT (for some programs), teacher certification (for some M Ed programs), letters of recommendation, essay, resume (for some programs). Additional exam requirements/recommendations for international students: Required—TOEFL (minimum score 550 paper-based; 79 iBT), IELTS (minimum score 6). Electronic applications accepted.

Penn State Harrisburg, Graduate School, School of Public Affairs, Middletown, PA 17057-4898. Offers criminal justice (MA); health administration (MHA); long term care (Certificate); non-profit administration (Certificate); policy analysis and evaluation (Certificate); public administration (MPA, PhD); public budgeting and financial management (Certificate); public sector human resource management (Certificate). *Accreditation:* NASPAA. *Unit head:* Dr. Mukund S. Kulkarni, Chancellor, 717-948-6105, Fax: 717-948-6452, E-mail: msk5@psu.edu. *Application contact:* Robert W. Coffman, Jr., Director of Enrollment Management, Admissions, 717-948-6250, Fax: 717-948-6325, E-mail: ric1@psu.edu.
Website: http://harrisburg.psu.edu/public-affairs

Portland State University, Graduate Studies, College of Urban and Public Affairs, Hatfield School of Government, Division of Public Administration, Portland, OR 97207-0751. Offers public administration (MPA); public affairs and policy (PhD). *Accreditation:* NASPAA (one or more programs are accredited). Part-time and evening/weekend programs available. *Faculty:* 15 full-time (9 women), 8 part-time/adjunct (2 women). *Students:* 112 full-time (78 women), 137 part-time (96 women); includes 45 minority (5 Black or African American, non-Hispanic/Latino; 7 American Indian or Alaska Native, non-Hispanic/Latino; 11 Asian, non-Hispanic/Latino; 12 Hispanic/Latino; 10 Two or more races, non-Hispanic/Latino), 15 international. Average age 34. 175 applicants, 59% accepted, 76 enrolled. In 2014, 75 master's, 8 doctorates awarded. *Degree requirements:* For master's, internship (MPA), practicum (MPH); for doctorate, comprehensive exam, thesis/dissertation. *Entrance requirements:* For master's, GRE (minimum scores: verbal 150, quantitative 149, and analytic writing 4.5), minimum GPA of 3.0, 3 recommendation letters, resume, 500-word statement of intent; for doctorate, GRE, 3 recommendation letters, resume, 500-word personal essay. Additional exam requirements/recommendations for international students: Required—TOEFL (minimum score 550 paper-based; 80 iBT), IELTS (minimum score 7). *Application deadline:* For fall admission, 4/1 for domestic students, 3/1 for international students; for winter admission, 9/1 for domestic students, 8/1 for international students; for spring admission, 11/1 for domestic and international students. Application fee: $50. *Expenses:* Tuition, state resident: part-time $222 per credit. Tuition, nonresident: part-time $527 per credit. *Required fees:* $22 per contact hour. $100 per quarter. Tuition and fees vary according to program. *Financial support:* In 2014–15, 7 research assistantships with full tuition reimbursements (averaging $6,249 per year), 3 teaching assistantships with full tuition reimbursements (averaging $6,846 per year) were awarded; career-related internships or fieldwork, Federal Work-Study, scholarships/grants, tuition waivers (partial), and unspecified assistantships also available. Support available to part-time students. Financial award application deadline: 3/1; financial award applicants required to submit FAFSA. *Faculty research:* Public budgeting, program evaluation, nonprofit management, natural resources policy and administration. *Total annual research expenditures:* $897,649. *Unit head:* Dr. Douglas Morgan, Chair, 503-725-8216, Fax: 503-725-8250, E-mail: morgandf@pdx.edu. *Application contact:* Megan Heljeson, Office Coordinator, 503-725-3921, Fax: 503-725-8250, E-mail: meloos@pdx.edu.
Website: http://www.pdx.edu/hatfieldschool/division-of-public-administration

Princeton University, Graduate School, Program in Population Studies, Princeton, NJ 08544-1019. Offers demography (PhD, Certificate); economics and demography (PhD); public affairs and demography (PhD); sociology and demography (PhD). *Degree requirements:* For doctorate, thesis/dissertation. *Entrance requirements:* For doctorate, GRE General Test. Additional exam requirements/recommendations for international students: Required—TOEFL (minimum score 600 paper-based). Electronic applications accepted. *Faculty research:* Models, fertility, infant and child mortality, migration.

Princeton University, Graduate School, Woodrow Wilson School of Public and International Affairs, Princeton, NJ 08544-1019. Offers public affairs (MPA, PhD); public policy (MPP); JD/MPA. JD/MPA offered jointly with Columbia University, New York University, Stanford University. Terminal master's awarded for partial completion of doctoral program. *Degree requirements:* For master's, internship; for doctorate, one foreign language, thesis/dissertation. *Entrance requirements:* For master's, GRE General Test, original policy memo; for doctorate, GRE General Test. Additional exam requirements/recommendations for international students: Required—TOEFL (minimum score 600 paper-based). Electronic applications accepted.

Texas A&M University, Bush School of Government and Public Service, College Station, TX 77843. Offers homeland security (Certificate); international affairs (MIA, Certificate); national security affairs (Certificate); non-profit management (Certificate); public service and administration (MPSA). *Accreditation:* NASPAA. *Faculty:* 60. *Students:* 313 full-time (146 women), 12 part-time (2 women); includes 61 minority (13 Black or African American, non-Hispanic/Latino; 7 Asian, non-Hispanic/Latino; 32 Hispanic/Latino; 1 Native Hawaiian or other Pacific Islander, non-Hispanic/Latino; 8 Two or more races, non-Hispanic/Latino), 44 international. Average age 28. 298 applicants, 71% accepted, 143 enrolled. In 2014, 137 master's awarded. *Degree requirements:* For master's, summer internship. *Entrance requirements:* For master's, GRE (preferred) or GMAT. Additional exam requirements/recommendations for international students: Required—TOEFL (minimum score 550 paper-based; 80 iBT), IELTS (minimum score 6). *Application deadline:* For fall admission, 1/20 for domestic and international students. Application fee: $50 ($90 for international students). Electronic applications accepted. *Expenses:* Tuition, state resident: full-time $4078; part-time $226.55 per credit hour. Tuition, nonresident: full-time $10,594; part-time $577.55 per credit hour. *Required fees:* $2813; $237.70 per credit hour. $278.50 per semester. Tuition and fees vary according to degree level and student level. *Financial support:* In 2014–15, 407 students received support, including 26 fellowships with full and partial tuition reimbursements available (averaging $15,902 per year), 44 research assistantships with full and partial tuition reimbursements available (averaging $7,163 per year); career-related internships or fieldwork, institutionally sponsored loans, scholarships/grants, traineeships, health care benefits, tuition waivers (full and partial), and unspecified assistantships also available. Support available to part-time students. Financial award application deadline: 2/1; financial award applicants required to submit FAFSA. *Faculty research:* Public policy, Presidential studies, public leadership, economic policy, social policy. *Unit head:* Dr. Ryan Crocker, Dean, 979-862-8007, E-mail: rcrocker@tamu.edu. *Application contact:* Kathryn Meyer, Director of Recruitment and Admissions, 979-458-4767, Fax: 979-845-4155, E-mail: bushschooladmissions@tamu.edu.
Website: http://bush.tamu.edu/

The University of Alabama in Huntsville, School of Graduate Studies, College of Liberal Arts, Program in Public Affairs, Huntsville, AL 35899. Offers MA. Part-time and evening/weekend programs available. *Degree requirements:* For master's, comprehensive exam, thesis or alternative, oral and written exams. *Entrance requirements:* For master's, GRE General Test, minimum GPA of 3.0. Additional exam requirements/recommendations for international students: Required—TOEFL (minimum score 500 paper-based; 80 iBT), IELTS (minimum score 6.5). Electronic applications accepted. *Faculty research:* Public policy and the law, middle eastern engagements, globalization, American politics, politics in south and central America.

University of Arkansas at Little Rock, Graduate School, Clinton School of Public Service, Little Rock, AR 72204-1099. Offers MPS, Graduate Certificate. *Expenses:* Tuition, state resident: full-time $6000; part-time $300 per credit hour. Tuition, nonresident: full-time $13,800; part-time $690 per credit hour. *Required fees:* $1126; $603 per term. One-time fee: $40 full-time. *Unit head:* Dana J. Steele, Assistant Dean of the Graduate School, 501-569-3206, Fax: 501-569-3039, E-mail: djsteele@ualr.edu. *Application contact:* Robert J. Torvestad, Student Services, 501-683-5216, E-mail: rjtorvestad@clintonschool.edu.

University of Baltimore, Graduate School, College of Public Affairs, Baltimore, MD 21201-5779. Offers MPA, MS, DPA, JD/MPA, JD/MS.

University of Central Florida, College of Health and Public Affairs, Program in Public Affairs, Orlando, FL 32816. Offers public affairs (PhD); research administration (MRA, Certificate). Part-time and evening/weekend programs available. *Students:* 47 full-time (24 women), 66 part-time (44 women); includes 35 minority (15 Black or African American, non-Hispanic/Latino; 1 American Indian or Alaska Native, non-Hispanic/Latino; 8 Asian, non-Hispanic/Latino; 9 Hispanic/Latino; 2 Two or more races, non-Hispanic/Latino), 12 international. Average age 38. 67 applicants, 52% accepted, 18 enrolled. In 2014, 19 master's, 8 doctorates awarded. *Degree requirements:* For doctorate, thesis/dissertation, candidacy and qualifying exams. *Entrance requirements:* For doctorate, GRE General Test or minimum GPA of 3.0 during final 60 hours. Additional exam requirements/recommendations for international students: Required—TOEFL. *Application deadline:* For fall admission, 2/7 priority date for domestic students. Application fee: $30. Electronic applications accepted. *Expenses:* Tuition, state resident: part-time $288.16 per credit hour. Tuition, nonresident: part-time $1073.31 per credit hour. *Financial support:* In 2014–15, 31 students received support, including 16 fellowships with partial tuition reimbursements available (averaging $6,600 per year), 10 research assistantships with partial tuition reimbursements available (averaging $7,300 per year), 13 teaching assistantships with partial tuition reimbursements available (averaging $6,800 per year); career-related internships or fieldwork, Federal Work-Study, institutionally sponsored loans, tuition waivers (partial), and unspecified assistantships also available. Financial award application deadline: 3/1; financial award applicants required to submit FAFSA. *Unit head:* Dr. Lynette Feder, Director, 407-823-3650, Fax: 407-823-0822, E-mail: lynette.feder@ucf.edu. *Application contact:* Barbara Rodriguez Lamas, Director, Admissions and Student Services, 407-823-2766, Fax: 407-823-6442, E-mail: gradadmissions@ucf.edu.
Website: http://www.ucf.edu/academics/public-affairs-phd/

University of Colorado Colorado Springs, School of Public Affairs, Colorado Springs, CO 80933-7150. Offers criminal justice (MCJ); public administration (MPA).

Accreditation: NASPAA. Part-time and evening/weekend programs available. Postbaccalaureate distance learning degree programs offered (minimal on-campus study). *Faculty:* 12 full-time (6 women), 17 part-time/adjunct (8 women). *Students:* 23 full-time (11 women), 104 part-time (49 women); includes 37 minority (13 Black or African American, non-Hispanic/Latino; 1 American Indian or Alaska Native, non-Hispanic/Latino; 6 Asian, non-Hispanic/Latino; 15 Hispanic/Latino; 1 Native Hawaiian or other Pacific Islander, non-Hispanic/Latino; 1 Two or more races, non-Hispanic/Latino), 7 international. Average age 35. 49 applicants, 90% accepted, 32 enrolled. In 2014, 34 master's awarded. *Degree requirements:* For master's, internship, capstone project, or thesis. *Entrance requirements:* For master's, GRE General Test, GMAT, LSAT, minimum GPA of 3.0. Additional exam requirements/recommendations for international students: Recommended—TOEFL (minimum score 550 paper-based; 80 iBT). *Application deadline:* For fall admission, 6/1 for domestic and international students; for spring admission, 11/1 for domestic and international students. Applications are processed on a rolling basis. Application fee: $60 ($100 for international students). *Expenses:* Expenses: Contact institution. *Financial support:* In 2014–15, 28 students received support, including 1 teaching assistantship (averaging $6,000 per year); fellowships, career-related internships or fieldwork, Federal Work-Study, and scholarships/grants also available. Support available to part-time students. Financial award application deadline: 3/1; financial award applicants required to submit FAFSA. *Faculty research:* Intimate partner violence, risk and protective factors for violent victimization, intersections of race, class, gender and crime, effective interventions for adult and juvenile offenders, sex trafficking, sentencing disparities for disadvantaged populations, child maltreatment, biosocial and developmental explanations of crime, public personnel management, organizational behavior and development, strategic leadership, national security, program evaluation, social policy, group dynamics. *Total annual research expenditures:* $120,922. *Unit head:* Dr. Terry Schwartz, Interim Dean, 719-255-4047, E-mail: tschwart@uccs.edu. *Application contact:* Crista Hill, Outreach Student Services Specialist, 719-255-4993, Fax: 719-255-4183, E-mail: chill12@uccs.edu.
Website: http://www.uccs.edu/spa/

University of Colorado Denver, School of Public Affairs, Program in Public Affairs and Administration, Denver, CO 80127. Offers public administration (MPA), including domestic violence, emergency management and homeland security, environmental policy, management and law, homeland security and defense, local government, nonprofit management, public administration; public affairs (PhD). *Accreditation:* NASPAA. Part-time and evening/weekend programs available. Postbaccalaureate distance learning degree programs offered (no on-campus study). *Students:* 275 full-time (176 women), 140 part-time (93 women); includes 70 minority (7 Black or African American, non-Hispanic/Latino; 4 American Indian or Alaska Native, non-Hispanic/Latino; 9 Asian, non-Hispanic/Latino; 44 Hispanic/Latino; 2 Native Hawaiian or other Pacific Islander, non-Hispanic/Latino; 4 Two or more races, non-Hispanic/Latino), 19 international. Average age 34. 243 applicants, 71% accepted, 97 enrolled. In 2014, 127 master's, 5 doctorates awarded. *Degree requirements:* For master's, thesis or alternative, 36-39 credit hours; for doctorate, comprehensive exam, thesis/dissertation, minimum of 66 semester hours, including at least 30 hours of dissertation. *Entrance requirements:* For master's, GRE, GMAT or LSAT, resume, essay, transcripts, recommendations; for doctorate, GRE, resume, essay, transcripts, recommendations. Additional exam requirements/recommendations for international students: Required—TOEFL (minimum score 550 paper-based; 80 iBT); Recommended—IELTS (minimum score 6.5). *Application deadline:* For fall admission, 2/1 priority date for domestic students, 1/15 priority date for international students; for spring admission, 10/15 priority date for domestic students, 10/1 priority date for international students. Application fee: $50 ($75 for international students). Electronic applications accepted. *Expenses:* Expenses: Contact institution. *Financial support:* In 2014–15, 60 students received support. Fellowships with partial tuition reimbursements available, research assistantships with partial tuition reimbursements available, teaching assistantships with partial tuition reimbursements available, Federal Work-Study, institutionally sponsored loans, scholarships/grants, traineeships, and unspecified assistantships available. Financial award application deadline: 4/1; financial award applicants required to submit FAFSA. *Faculty research:* Housing, education and the social and economic issues of vulnerable populations; nonprofit governance and management; education finance, effectiveness and reform; P-20 education initiatives; municipal government accountability. *Unit head:* Dr. Christine Martell, Director of MPA Program, 303-315-2716, Fax: 303-315-2229, E-mail: christine.martell@ucdenver.edu. *Application contact:* Dawn Savage, Student Services Coordinator, 303-315-2743, Fax: 303-315-2229, E-mail: dawn.savage@ucdenver.edu.
Website: http://www.ucdenver.edu/academics/colleges/SPA/Academics/programs/PublicAffairsAdmin/Pages/index.aspx

University of Florida, Graduate School, College of Liberal Arts and Sciences, Department of Political Science, Gainesville, FL 32611. Offers educational policy (PhD); international development policy and administration (MA, Certificate); international relations (MA, MAT); political campaigning (MA, Certificate); political science (MA, PhD); public affairs (MA, Certificate); tropical conservation and development (MA, PhD); JD/MA. *Faculty:* 25 full-time (9 women), 4 part-time/adjunct (1 woman). *Students:* 115 full-time (45 women), 19 part-time (7 women); includes 26 minority (12 Black or African American, non-Hispanic/Latino; 6 Asian, non-Hispanic/Latino; 8 Hispanic/Latino), 34 international. 136 applicants, 44% accepted, 22 enrolled. In 2014, 28 master's, 8 doctorates awarded. Terminal master's awarded for partial completion of doctoral program. *Degree requirements:* For master's, variable foreign language requirement, comprehensive exam (for some programs), thesis or alternative, internship (for some programs); for doctorate, variable foreign language requirement, comprehensive exam, thesis/dissertation. *Entrance requirements:* For master's and doctorate, GRE General Test 308 combined verbal/math, minimum GPA of 3.5. Additional exam requirements/recommendations for international students: Required—TOEFL (minimum score 550 paper-based; 80 iBT), IELTS (minimum score 6). *Application deadline:* For fall admission, 1/15 priority date for domestic students, 1/15 for international students. Applications are processed on a rolling basis. Application fee: $30. Electronic applications accepted. *Financial support:* In 2014–15, 13 fellowships, 13 research assistantships, 50 teaching assistantships were awarded; career-related internships or fieldwork, Federal Work-Study, institutionally sponsored loans, and unspecified assistantships also available. Financial award application deadline: 1/15; financial award applicants required to submit FAFSA. *Faculty research:* American electoral politics and political institutions, comparative democratization and development, theories of international relation, and political theory. *Total annual research expenditures:* $208,864. *Unit head:* Ido Oren, PhD, Professor and Chair, 352-273-2393, Fax: 352-392-8127, E-mail: oren@ufl.edu. *Application contact:* Leslie Anderson, PhD, Graduate Coordinator, 352-273-3725, Fax: 352-392-8127, E-mail: landerso@ufl.edu.
Website: http://polisci.ufl.edu/

University of Louisville, Graduate School, College of Arts and Sciences, Department of Urban and Public Affairs, Louisville, KY 40208. Offers public administration (MPA), including human resources management, non-profit management, public policy and administration; urban and public affairs (PhD), including urban planning and development, urban policy and administration; urban planning (MUP), including administration of planning organizations, housing and community development, land use and environmental planning, spatial analysis. Part-time and evening/weekend programs available. *Students:* 76 full-time (35 women), 22 part-time (14 women); includes 16 minority (10 Black or African American, non-Hispanic/Latino; 1 Asian, non-Hispanic/Latino; 3 Hispanic/Latino; 2 Two or more races, non-Hispanic/Latino), 6 international. Average age 30. 89 applicants, 71% accepted, 33 enrolled. In 2014, 13 master's, 4 doctorates awarded. Terminal master's awarded for partial completion of doctoral program. *Degree requirements:* For master's, internship; for doctorate, comprehensive exam, thesis/dissertation. *Entrance requirements:* For master's, GRE General Test, minimum GPA of 3.0; for doctorate, GRE General Test, master's degree in appropriate field. Additional exam requirements/recommendations for international students: Required—TOEFL (minimum score 550 paper-based; 79 iBT). *Application deadline:* For fall admission, 7/15 for domestic students, 5/1 priority date for international students; for spring admission, 11/15 for domestic students, 11/1 priority date for international students; for summer admission, 4/1 priority date for international students. Applications are processed on a rolling basis. Application fee: $60. Electronic applications accepted. *Expenses:* Tuition, state resident: full-time $11,326; part-time $630 per credit hour. Tuition, nonresident: full-time $23,568; part-time $1311 per credit hour. *Required fees:* $196. Tuition and fees vary according to program and reciprocity agreements. *Financial support:* Fellowships, research assistantships, and health care benefits available. Financial award application deadline: 3/1. *Faculty research:* Housing and community development, performance-based budgeting, environmental policy and natural hazards, sustainability, real estate development, comparative urban development. *Unit head:* Dr. David Simpson, Chair, 502-852-8019, Fax: 502-852-4558, E-mail: dave.simpson@louisville.edu. *Application contact:* Libby Leggett, Director, Graduate Admissions, 502-852-3101, Fax: 502-852-4558, E-mail: gradadm@louisville.edu.
Website: http://supa.louisville.edu

University of Massachusetts Boston, John W. McCormack Graduate School of Policy and Global Studies, Program in Public Affairs, Boston, MA 02125-3393. Offers MS. Part-time and evening/weekend programs available. *Degree requirements:* For master's, final project. *Entrance requirements:* For master's, GRE General Test or MAT, minimum GPA of 2.75. *Application deadline:* For fall admission, 3/1 for domestic students. *Expenses:* Tuition, state resident: full-time $2590; part-time $108 per credit. Tuition, nonresident: full-time $9758; part-time $406.50 per credit. Tuition and fees vary according to course load and program. *Financial support:* Research assistantships with full tuition reimbursements, teaching assistantships with full tuition reimbursements, career-related internships or fieldwork, Federal Work-Study, and unspecified assistantships available. Support available to part-time students. Financial award application deadline: 3/1; financial award applicants required to submit FAFSA. *Faculty research:* Leadership and policy implementation, public management, disability; human services and sound policy. *Unit head:* Dr. Constance Chan, Director, 617-287-6938, E-mail: connie.chan@umb.edu. *Application contact:* Peggy Roldan Patel, Graduate Admissions Coordinator, 617-287-6400, Fax: 617-287-6236, E-mail: bos.gadm@dpc.umassp.edu.

University of Minnesota, Twin Cities Campus, Graduate School, Hubert H. Humphrey School of Public Affairs, Program in Public Affairs, Minneapolis, MN 55455. Offers MPA. *Accreditation:* NASPAA. Part-time and evening/weekend programs available. *Students:* 28 part-time (15 women); includes 2 minority (1 Black or African American, non-Hispanic/Latino; 1 American Indian or Alaska Native, non-Hispanic/Latino), 4 international. Average age 42. 63 applicants, 56% accepted, 28 enrolled. In 2014, 43 master's awarded. *Entrance requirements:* For master's, 10 years of work experience, minimum undergraduate GPA of 3.0. Additional exam requirements/recommendations for international students: Required—TOEFL (minimum score 600 paper-based; 100 iBT), IELTS (minimum score 7). *Application deadline:* For fall admission, 4/1 priority date for domestic students, 4/1 for international students; for spring admission, 10/15 for domestic and international students. Applications are processed on a rolling basis. Application fee: $75 ($95 for international students). Electronic applications accepted. *Expenses:* Expenses: $1239 per credit state resident; $1924.50 per credit nonresident. *Financial support:* In 2014–15, 6 students received support, including fellowships with full and partial tuition reimbursements available (averaging $10,300 per year); career-related internships or fieldwork, Federal Work-Study, scholarships/grants, health care benefits, tuition waivers (full and partial), and unspecified assistantships also available. Support available to part-time students. Financial award application deadline: 4/1. *Faculty research:* Public and non-profit leadership and management, social policy, urban and regional planning, economic and community development, foreign policy and international affairs. *Unit head:* Laura Bloomberg, Associate Dean, 612-625-0608, Fax: 612-626-0002, E-mail: bloom004@umn.edu. *Application contact:* Amy Luitjens, Director of Admissions, 612-626-7229, Fax: 612-626-0002, E-mail: luitjens@umn.edu.
Website: http://www.hhh.umn.edu/degrees/mpa/

University of Missouri, Office of Research and Graduate Studies, Harry S Truman School of Public Affairs, Columbia, MO 65211. Offers grantsmanship (Graduate Certificate); nonprofit management (Graduate Certificate); organizational change (Graduate Certificate); public affairs (MPA, PhD); public management (Graduate Certificate); science and public policy (Graduate Certificate). *Accreditation:* NASPAA. *Faculty:* 12 full-time (5 women). *Students:* 83 full-time (51 women), 86 part-time (33 women); includes 22 minority (16 Black or African American, non-Hispanic/Latino; 1 American Indian or Alaska Native, non-Hispanic/Latino; 3 Asian, non-Hispanic/Latino; 2 Hispanic/Latino), 35 international. Average age 33. 152 applicants, 53% accepted, 51 enrolled. In 2014, 53 master's, 1 doctorate, 19 other advanced degrees awarded. *Entrance requirements:* For master's, GRE General Test, minimum GPA of 3.0. Additional exam requirements/recommendations for international students: Required—TOEFL (minimum score 550 paper-based; 79 iBT). *Application deadline:* For fall admission, 2/1 priority date for domestic and international students. Applications are processed on a rolling basis. Application fee: $55 ($75 for international students). Electronic applications accepted. *Financial support:* Fellowships, research assistantships, teaching assistantships, institutionally sponsored loans, scholarships/grants, traineeships, health care benefits, and unspecified assistantships available. Support available to part-time students. *Faculty research:* Public service ethics, history and theory, organizational symbolism and culture; program evaluation and social policy, with special emphasis on child development, education and health policies; organization theory and applied psychoanalytic theory; foreign policy and international political economy; health care delivery for persons with disabilities and health policy; survival strategies employed by low-income households; rural economic development, fiscal and economic impact analysis. *Unit head:* Dr. Bart Wechsler, Director, 573-882-3304, E-mail: wechslerb@missouri.edu. *Application contact:* Nicole Harris, Assistant Program Director for Student Services, 573-882-3471, E-mail: harrisnr@missouri.edu.
Website: http://truman.missouri.edu/

University of Missouri–Kansas City, Henry W. Bloch School of Management, Kansas City, MO 64110-2499. Offers accounting (MS); business administration (MBA); entrepreneurial real estate (MERE); entrepreneurship and innovation (PhD); finance (MS); public affairs (MPA, PhD); JD/MBA; LL M/MPA. PhD (interdisciplinary) offered through the School of Graduate Studies. *Accreditation:* AACSB; NASPAA. Part-time and evening/weekend programs available. *Faculty:* 55 full-time (16 women), 39 part-time/adjunct (9 women). *Students:* 266 full-time (115 women), 359 part-time (163 women);

includes 99 minority (35 Black or African American, non-Hispanic/Latino; 3 American Indian or Alaska Native, non-Hispanic/Latino; 32 Asian, non-Hispanic/Latino; 18 Hispanic/Latino; 1 Native Hawaiian or other Pacific Islander, non-Hispanic/Latino; 10 Two or more races, non-Hispanic/Latino), 101 international. Average age 30. 399 applicants, 55% accepted, 220 enrolled. In 2014, 292 master's, 1 doctorate awarded. Terminal master's awarded for partial completion of doctoral program. *Entrance requirements:* For master's, GMAT, GRE, 2 essays, 2 references, support of employer; for doctorate, GRE, minimum GPA of 3.0. Additional exam requirements/recommendations for international students: Required—TOEFL (minimum score 550 paper-based; 80 iBT). *Application deadline:* For fall admission, 5/1 priority date for domestic and international students; for spring admission, 10/1 priority date for domestic and international students. Applications are processed on a rolling basis. Application fee: $45 ($50 for international students). Electronic applications accepted. *Financial support:* In 2014–15, 38 research assistantships with partial tuition reimbursements (averaging $10,037 per year), 9 teaching assistantships with partial tuition reimbursements (averaging $12,927 per year) were awarded; career-related internships or fieldwork, Federal Work-Study, institutionally sponsored loans, scholarships/grants, tuition waivers (full and partial), and unspecified assistantships also available. Support available to part-time students. Financial award application deadline: 3/1; financial award applicants required to submit FAFSA. *Faculty research:* Entrepreneurship, finance, non-profit, risk management. *Unit head:* Dr. David Donnelly, Dean, 816-235-1333, Fax: 816-235-2206, E-mail: donnellyd@umkc.edu. *Application contact:* 816-235-1111, E-mail: admit@umkc.edu.
Website: http://www.bloch.umkc.edu

University of Nevada, Las Vegas, Graduate College, Greenspun College of Urban Affairs, School of Environmental and Public Affairs, Las Vegas, NV 89154-4030. Offers environmental science (MS, PhD); non-profit management (Certificate); public administration (MPA, MS), including crisis and emergency management (MS); public affairs (PhD); public management (Certificate); urban leadership (MA); workforce development and organizational leadership (PhD). Part-time programs available. *Faculty:* 13 full-time (5 women), 7 part-time/adjunct (2 women). *Students:* 81 full-time (44 women), 115 part-time (60 women); includes 71 minority (24 Black or African American, non-Hispanic/Latino; 2 American Indian or Alaska Native, non-Hispanic/Latino; 5 Asian, non-Hispanic/Latino; 30 Hispanic/Latino; 3 Native Hawaiian or other Pacific Islander, non-Hispanic/Latino; 7 Two or more races, non-Hispanic/Latino), 8 international. Average age 37. 78 applicants, 86% accepted, 48 enrolled. In 2014, 50 master's, 6 doctorates, 19 other advanced degrees awarded. *Degree requirements:* For master's, comprehensive exam (for some programs), thesis; for doctorate, comprehensive exam (for some programs), thesis/dissertation. *Entrance requirements:* Additional exam requirements/recommendations for international students: Required—TOEFL (minimum score 550 paper-based; 80 iBT), IELTS (minimum score 7). *Application deadline:* For fall admission, 2/15 for domestic students, 5/1 for international students; for spring admission, 11/15 for domestic students, 10/1 for international students. Application fee: $60 ($95 for international students). Electronic applications accepted. *Financial support:* In 2014–15, 31 students received support, including 1 fellowship (averaging $25,000 per year), 13 research assistantships with partial tuition reimbursements available (averaging $13,473 per year), 17 teaching assistantships with partial tuition reimbursements available (averaging $13,206 per year); institutionally sponsored loans, scholarships/grants, health care benefits, and unspecified assistantships also available. Financial award application deadline: 3/1. *Faculty research:* Community and organizational resilience; environmental decision-making and management; budgeting and human resource/workforce management; urban design, sustainability and governance; public and non-profit management. *Total annual research expenditures:* $333,798. *Unit head:* Dr. Christopher Stream, Chair/Associate Professor, 702-895-5120, Fax: 702-895-4436, E-mail: chris.stream@unlv.edu. *Application contact:* Graduate College Admissions Evaluator, 702-895-3320, Fax: 702-895-4180, E-mail: gradcollege@unlv.edu.
Website: http://sepa.unlv.edu/

The University of North Carolina at Greensboro, Graduate School, College of Arts and Sciences, Department of Political Science, Greensboro, NC 27412-5001. Offers nonprofit management (Certificate); public affairs (MPA); urban and economic development (Certificate). *Accreditation:* NASPAA. *Degree requirements:* For master's, comprehensive exam. *Entrance requirements:* For master's, GRE General Test. Additional exam requirements/recommendations for international students: Required—TOEFL. Electronic applications accepted. *Faculty research:* U.S. Constitution, Canadian parliament, public management, ethical challenge of public service.

University of San Francisco, College of Arts and Sciences, Public Affairs and Practical Politics Program, San Francisco, CA 94117-1080. Offers MPA. *Accreditation:* NASPAA. *Faculty:* 2 full-time (1 woman), 7 part-time/adjunct (2 women). *Students:* 40 full-time (26 women); includes 22 minority (8 Black or African American, non-Hispanic/Latino; 3 Asian, non-Hispanic/Latino; 9 Hispanic/Latino; 2 Two or more races, non-Hispanic/Latino), 4 international. Average age 27. 70 applicants, 79% accepted, 23 enrolled. In 2014, 30 master's awarded. *Degree requirements:* For master's, internship, capstone project. *Application deadline:* For fall admission, 3/1 for domestic students. *Expenses:* *Tuition:* Full-time $21,762; part-time $1209 per credit hour. Tuition and fees vary according to degree level, campus/location and program. *Financial support:* In 2014–15, 14 students received support. Scholarships/grants available. *Unit head:* Angela Fleekop, Administrative Director, 415-422-5662. *Application contact:* Mark Landerghini, Information Contact, 415-422-5101, Fax: 415-422-2217, E-mail: asgraduate@usfca.edu.
Website: http://usfca.edu/mopa/

University of Saskatchewan, College of Graduate Studies and Research, School of Public Policy, Saskatoon, SK S7N 5A2, Canada. Offers MIT, MPA, MPP, PhD.

University of South Florida, Innovative Education, Tampa, FL 33620-9951. *Unit head:* Kathy Barnes, Interdisciplinary Programs Coordinator, 813-974-8031, Fax: 813-974-7061, E-mail: barnesk@usf.edu. *Application contact:* Karen Tylinski, Metro Initiatives, 813-974-9943, Fax: 813-974-7061, E-mail: ktylinsk@usf.edu.
Website: http://www.usf.edu/innovative-education/

The University of Texas at Arlington, Graduate School, School of Urban and Public Affairs, Program in Urban Planning and Public Policy, Arlington, TX 76019. Offers PhD. Part-time and evening/weekend programs available. *Degree requirements:* For doctorate, comprehensive exam, thesis/dissertation. *Entrance requirements:* For doctorate, GRE General Test, 3 letters of recommendation, 250-word essay. Electronic applications accepted. *Faculty research:* Environment urban policy personnel, research theoretical foundations, urban problems.

The University of Texas at Austin, Graduate School, Lyndon B. Johnson School of Public Affairs, Austin, TX 78712-1111. Offers global policy studies (MGPS); public affairs (MP Aff); public leadership (EMPL); public policy (PhD); JD/MP Aff; MBA/MP Aff; MP Aff/MA; MP Aff/MSE. *Accreditation:* NASPAA (one or more programs are accredited). Part-time programs available. *Degree requirements:* For master's, thesis, summer internship; for doctorate, thesis/dissertation. *Entrance requirements:* For master's, GRE General Test (for MP Aff and MGPS), minimum GPA of 3.0 in upper-division classes, seven years of experience in the public sector, and interview (for EMPL); for doctorate, GRE General Test, master's degree in policy-related field. Additional exam requirements/recommendations for international students: Required—TOEFL. Electronic applications accepted. *Faculty research:* Human resource development, health and social policy, philanthropy and community service, ethical leadership, urban and international policy, science and technology policy.

The University of Texas at Dallas, School of Economic, Political and Policy Sciences, Program in Public Affairs and Sociology, Richardson, TX 75080. Offers applied sociology (MS); public affairs (MPA, PhD). *Accreditation:* NASPAA. Part-time and evening/weekend programs available. *Faculty:* 13 full-time (5 women), 3 part-time/adjunct (0 women). *Students:* 39 full-time (25 women), 64 part-time (40 women); includes 36 minority (15 Black or African American, non-Hispanic/Latino; 3 Asian, non-Hispanic/Latino; 15 Hispanic/Latino; 3 Two or more races, non-Hispanic/Latino), 15 international. Average age 37. 98 applicants, 45% accepted, 20 enrolled. In 2014, 23 master's, 14 doctorates awarded. *Degree requirements:* For master's, internship; for doctorate, thesis/dissertation. *Entrance requirements:* For master's and doctorate, GRE (minimum combined score of 1000 on verbal and quantitative), minimum GPA of 3.0 in upper-level course work in field. Additional exam requirements/recommendations for international students: Required—TOEFL (minimum score 550 paper-based). *Application deadline:* For fall admission, 7/15 for domestic students, 5/1 priority date for international students; for spring admission, 11/15 for domestic students, 9/1 priority date for international students. Applications are processed on a rolling basis. Application fee: $50 ($100 for international students). Electronic applications accepted. *Expenses:* Tuition, state resident: full-time $11,940; part-time $663 per credit. Tuition, nonresident: full-time $22,282; part-time $1238 per credit. *Financial support:* In 2014–15, 46 students received support, including 9 teaching assistantships with partial tuition reimbursements available (averaging $12,222 per year); research assistantships with partial tuition reimbursements available, career-related internships or fieldwork, Federal Work-Study, institutionally sponsored loans, and scholarships/grants also available. Support available to part-time students. Financial award application deadline: 4/30; financial award applicants required to submit FAFSA. *Faculty research:* Corporate citizenship and urban problem solving, policy analysis, presidential decision-making, hazardous material safety, emergency management. *Unit head:* Dr. Sheryl Skaggs, Program Head, 972-883-4460, Fax: 972-883-2735, E-mail: slskaggs@utdallas.edu. *Application contact:* Dr. Katie Doctor, Graduate Program Administrator, 972-883-4936, Fax: 972-883-2735, E-mail: kdoctor@utdallas.edu.
Website: http://www.utdallas.edu/epps/public-affairs/

University of Washington, Graduate School, Evans School of Public Affairs, Seattle, WA 98195. Offers public administration (MPA); public policy and management (PhD); JD/MPA; MPA/MAIS; MPA/MPH; MPA/MS; MPA/MUP. *Accreditation:* NASPAA. Part-time and evening/weekend programs available. *Degree requirements:* For master's, thesis, internship or cooperative experience. *Entrance requirements:* For master's and doctorate, GRE General Test, minimum GPA of 3.0. Additional exam requirements/recommendations for international students: Required—TOEFL (minimum score 580 paper-based; 92 iBT). Electronic applications accepted. *Faculty research:* Environmental policy, education and social policy, nonprofit management, international affairs, urban and regional development.

University of Waterloo, Graduate Studies, Faculty of Arts, Department of Anthropology, Waterloo, ON N2L 3G1, Canada. Offers anthropology (MA); public issues (MA). *Entrance requirements:* Additional exam requirements/recommendations for international students: Required—TOEFL. Electronic applications accepted. *Faculty research:* Applied socio-cultural anthropology and archaeology.

University of Wisconsin–Madison, Graduate School, College of Letters and Science, Robert M. La Follette School of Public Affairs, Public Policy and Administration Program, Madison, WI 53706-1380. Offers MIPA, MPA. Part-time programs available. Electronic applications accepted. *Expenses:* Tuition, state resident: full-time $10,723; part-time $745 per credit. Tuition, nonresident: full-time $24,054; part-time $1578 per credit. *Required fees:* $374 per semester. Tuition and fees vary according to course load, program and reciprocity agreements.

Virginia Commonwealth University, Graduate School, College of Humanities and Sciences, Wilder School of Government and Public Affairs, Richmond, VA 23284-9005. Offers MA, MPA, MS, MURP, PhD, CASR, CCJA, CPM, CURP, Certificate, Graduate Certificate, JD/MURP, MSW/Certificate.

Virginia Polytechnic Institute and State University, Graduate School, College of Architecture and Urban Studies, Blacksburg, VA 24061. Offers architecture (MS Arch); architecture and design research (PhD); building/construction science and management (MS); creative technologies (MFA); environmental design and planning (PhD); landscape architecture (MLA); planning, governance, and globalization (PhD); public administration (MPA); public administration/public affairs (PhD, Certificate); public and international affairs (MPIA); urban and regional planning (MURP); MS/MA. *Accreditation:* ASLA (one or more programs are accredited). *Faculty:* 133 full-time (54 women), 2 part-time/adjunct (1 woman). *Students:* 316 full-time (166 women), 237 part-time (108 women); includes 104 minority (46 Black or African American, non-Hispanic/Latino; 1 American Indian or Alaska Native, non-Hispanic/Latino; 20 Asian, non-Hispanic/Latino; 21 Hispanic/Latino; 16 Two or more races, non-Hispanic/Latino), 108 international. Average age 32. 609 applicants, 50% accepted, 108 enrolled. In 2014, 155 master's, 29 doctorates awarded. *Degree requirements:* For master's, comprehensive exam (for some programs), thesis (for some programs); for doctorate, comprehensive exam (for some programs), thesis/dissertation (for some programs). *Entrance requirements:* For master's and doctorate, GRE/GMAT (may vary by department). Additional exam requirements/recommendations for international students: Required—TOEFL (minimum score 550 paper-based). *Application deadline:* For fall admission, 8/1 for domestic students, 4/1 for international students; for spring admission, 1/1 for domestic students, 9/1 for international students. Applications are processed on a rolling basis. Application fee: $75. Electronic applications accepted. *Expenses:* Tuition, state resident: full-time $11,656; part-time $647.50 per credit hour. Tuition, nonresident: full-time $23,351; part-time $1297.25 per credit hour. *Required fees:* $2533; $465.75 per semester. Tuition and fees vary according to course load, campus/location and program. *Financial support:* In 2014–15, 13 research assistantships with full tuition reimbursements (averaging $20,302 per year), 44 teaching assistantships with full tuition reimbursements (averaging $19,484 per year) were awarded. Financial award application deadline: 3/1; financial award applicants required to submit FAFSA. *Total annual research expenditures:* $3.2 million. *Unit head:* Dr. A. J. Davis, Dean, 540-231-6416, Fax: 540-231-6332, E-mail: davisa@vt.edu. *Application contact:* Christine Mattsson-Coon, Executive Assistant, 540-231-6416, Fax: 540-231-6332, E-mail: cmattsso@vt.edu.
Website: http://www.caus.vt.edu/

Washington State University, College of Liberal Arts, School of Politics, Philosophy and Public Affairs, Pullman, WA 99164-4880. Offers bioethics (Graduate Certificate); political science (MA, PhD); public affairs (MPA). MPA, MA, and PhD programs also offered at the Vancouver campus; Graduate Certificate offered through Global (online) campus. Postbaccalaureate distance learning degree programs offered (no on-campus study). *Students:* 33 full-time (13 women), 15 part-time (9 women); includes 9 minority (1 Black or African American, non-Hispanic/Latino; 1 American Indian or Alaska Native,

non-Hispanic/Latino; 1 Asian, non-Hispanic/Latino; 5 Hispanic/Latino; 1 Two or more races, non-Hispanic/Latino), 4 international. Average age 30. 52 applicants, 54% accepted, 16 enrolled. In 2014, 12 master's, 2 doctorates, 6 other advanced degrees awarded. Terminal master's awarded for partial completion of doctoral program. *Degree requirements:* For master's, comprehensive exam (for some programs), thesis, oral exam; for doctorate, comprehensive exam, thesis/dissertation, oral exam, written exam. *Entrance requirements:* For master's, GRE General Test, minimum GPA of 3.0; for doctorate, GRE General Test, minimum GPA of 3.5. Additional exam requirements/recommendations for international students: Required—TOEFL. *Application deadline:* For fall admission, 2/1 for domestic and international students; for spring admission, 11/1 for domestic students, 7/1 for international students. Application fee: $75. Electronic applications accepted. *Expenses:* Tuition, state resident: full-time $11,768. Tuition, nonresident: full-time $25,200. *Required fees:* $960. Tuition and fees vary according to program. *Financial support:* In 2014–15, 34 students received support, including 2 research assistantships with full and partial tuition reimbursements available (averaging $14,411 per year), 21 teaching assistantships with full and partial tuition reimbursements available (averaging $14,120 per year). Financial award application deadline: 2/1; financial award applicants required to submit FAFSA. *Faculty research:* Political psychology and image theory, grass roots environmental policy, federal juvenile policy. *Unit head:* Dr. Thomas Preston, Professor/Director, 509-335-5225, Fax: 509-335-7990, E-mail: tpreston@wsu.edu. *Application contact:* Bonnie Kemper, Graduate and Student Records Coordinator, 509-335-2545, Fax: 509-335-1949, E-mail: bkemper@wsu.edu. Website: http://libarts.wsu.edu/pppa/

West Chester University of Pennsylvania, College of Business and Public Affairs, West Chester, PA 19383. Offers MA, MBA, MPA, MS, MSA, MSW, Certificate. Part-time and evening/weekend programs available. Postbaccalaureate distance learning degree programs offered (minimal on-campus study). *Faculty:* 39 full-time (21 women), 23 part-time/adjunct (22 women). *Students:* 260 full-time (177 women), 326 part-time (178 women); includes 199 minority (153 Black or African American, non-Hispanic/Latino; 1 American Indian or Alaska Native, non-Hispanic/Latino; 13 Asian, non-Hispanic/Latino; 26 Hispanic/Latino; 6 Two or more races, non-Hispanic/Latino), 9 international. Average age 30. 452 applicants, 83% accepted, 234 enrolled. In 2014, 157 master's, 31 other advanced degrees awarded. *Degree requirements:* For master's, comprehensive exam (for some programs), thesis (for some programs). *Entrance requirements:* Additional

exam requirements/recommendations for international students: Required—TOEFL (minimum score 550 paper-based; 80 iBT). *Application deadline:* For fall admission, 4/15 priority date for domestic students, 3/15 for international students; for spring admission, 10/15 priority date for domestic students, 9/1 for international students. Applications are processed on a rolling basis. Application fee: $45. Electronic applications accepted. *Expenses:* Expenses: Contact institution. *Financial support:* Career-related internships or fieldwork and unspecified assistantships available. Support available to part-time students. Financial award application deadline: 2/15; financial award applicants required to submit FAFSA. *Unit head:* Dr. Michelle L. Patrick, Dean, 610-436-2930, Fax: 610-436-3170, E-mail: mpatrick@wcupa.edu. *Application contact:* Office of Graduate Studies and Extended Education, 610-436-2943, Fax: 610-436-2763, E-mail: gradstudy@wcupa.edu.
Website: http://www.wcumba.org

Western Carolina University, Graduate School, College of Arts and Sciences, Department of Political Science and Public Affairs, Cullowhee, NC 28723. Offers MPA. Part-time and evening/weekend programs available. *Degree requirements:* For master's, comprehensive exam. *Entrance requirements:* For master's, GRE General Test, appropriate undergraduate degree, 3 letters of recommendation. Additional exam requirements/recommendations for international students: Required—TOEFL (minimum score 550 paper-based; 79 iBT). *Faculty research:* Press-government relations, comparative governments, gender in politics, Latin American political systems, foreign policy, trust in government, zoning.

Western Michigan University, Graduate College, College of Arts and Sciences, School of Public Affairs and Administration, Kalamazoo, MI 49008. Offers health care administration (MPA, Graduate Certificate); nonprofit leadership and administration (Graduate Certificate); public administration (PhD). *Accreditation:* NASPAA (one or more programs are accredited). *Degree requirements:* For doctorate, thesis/dissertation. *Application deadline:* For fall admission, 2/15 for domestic students. *Financial support:* Application deadline: 2/15. *Application contact:* Admissions and Orientation, 269-387-2000, Fax: 269-387-2096.

York University, Faculty of Graduate Studies, Glendon Campus, Program in Public and International Affairs, Toronto, ON M3J 1P3, Canada. Offers MA.

Public Policy

Adler University, Programs in Psychology, Chicago, IL 60602. Offers advanced Adlerian psychotherapy (Certificate); art therapy (MA); clinical neuropsychology (Certificate); clinical psychology (Psy D); community psychology (MA); counseling and organizational psychology (MA); counseling psychology (MA); criminology (MA); emergency management leadership (MA); forensic psychology (MA); marriage and family counseling (MA); marriage and family therapy (Certificate); military psychology (MA); nonprofit management (MA); organizational psychology (MA); police psychology (MA); public policy and administration (MA); rehabilitation counseling (MA); sport and health psychology (MA); substance abuse counseling (Certificate); Psy D/Certificate; Psy D/MACAT; Psy D/MACP; Psy D/MAMFC; Psy D/MASAC. *Accreditation:* APA. Part-time and evening/weekend programs available. Postbaccalaureate distance learning degree programs offered (minimal on-campus study). Terminal master's awarded for partial completion of doctoral program. *Degree requirements:* For master's, thesis or alternative, oral exam, practicum; for doctorate, thesis/dissertation, clinical exam, internship, oral exam, practicum, written qualifying exam. *Entrance requirements:* For master's, 12 semester hours in psychology, minimum GPA of 3.0; for doctorate, 18 semester hours in psychology, minimum GPA of 3.25; for Certificate, appropriate master's or doctoral degree. Additional exam requirements/recommendations for international students: Required—TOEFL (minimum score 550 paper-based; 79 iBT). Electronic applications accepted.

See Display on page 969 and Close-Up on page 1207.

Albany State University, College of Arts and Humanities, Albany, GA 31705-2717. Offers English education (M Ed); public administration (MPA), including community and economic development administration, criminal justice administration, general administration, health administration and policy, human resources management, public policy, water resources management; social work (MSW). Part-time programs available. *Degree requirements:* For master's, comprehensive exam, professional portfolio (for MPA), internship, capstone report. *Entrance requirements:* For master's, GRE, MAT, minimum GPA of 3.0, official transcript, pre-medical record/certificate of immunization, letters of reference. Electronic applications accepted. *Faculty research:* HIV prevention for minority students.

American Public University System, AMU/APU Graduate Programs, Charles Town, WV 25414. Offers accounting (MBA, MS); criminal justice (MA), including business administration, emergency and disaster management, general (MA, MS); educational leadership (M Ed); emergency and disaster management (MA); entrepreneurship (MBA); environmental policy and management (MS), including environmental planning, environmental sustainability, fish and wildlife management, general (MA, MS), global environmental management; finance (MBA); general (MBA); global business management (MBA); history (MA), including American history, ancient and classical history, European history, global history, public history; homeland security (MA), including business administration, counter-terrorism studies, criminal justice, cyber, emergency management and public health, intelligence studies, transportation security; homeland security resource allocation (MBA); humanities (MA); information technology (MS), including digital forensics, enterprise software development, information assurance and security, IT project management; information technology management (MBA); intelligence studies (MA), including criminal intelligence, cyber, general (MA, MS), homeland security, intelligence analysis, intelligence collection, intelligence management, intelligence operations, terrorism studies; international relations and conflict resolution (MA), including comparative and security issues, conflict resolution, international and transnational security issues, peacekeeping; legal studies (MA); management (MA), including defense management, general (MA, MS), human resource management, organizational leadership, public administration; marketing (MBA); military history (MA), including American military history, American Revolution, civil war, war since 1945, World War II; military studies (MA), including joint warfare, strategic leadership; national security studies (MA), including general (MA, MS), homeland security, regional security studies, security and intelligence analysis, terrorism studies; nonprofit management (MBA); political science (MA), including American politics and government, comparative government and development, general (MA, MS), international relations, public policy; psychology (MA); public administration (MPA),

including disaster management, environmental policy, health policy, human resources, national security, organizational management, security management; public health (MPH); reverse logistics management (MA); school counseling (M Ed); security management (MA); space studies (MS), including aerospace science, general (MA, MS), planetary science; sports and health sciences (MS); teaching (M Ed), including curriculum and instruction for elementary teachers, elementary reading, English language learners, instructional leadership, online learning, special education; transportation and logistics management (MA), including general (MA, MS), maritime engineering management, reverse logistics management. Programs offered via distance learning only. Part-time and evening/weekend programs available. Postbaccalaureate distance learning degree programs offered (no on-campus study). *Faculty:* 426 full-time (236 women), 1,864 part-time/adjunct (880 women). *Students:* 475 full-time (215 women), 10,067 part-time (4,085 women); includes 3,462 minority (1,863 Black or African American, non-Hispanic/Latino; 74 American Indian or Alaska Native, non-Hispanic/Latino; 273 Asian, non-Hispanic/Latino; 831 Hispanic/Latino; 78 Native Hawaiian or other Pacific Islander, non-Hispanic/Latino; 343 Two or more races, non-Hispanic/Latino), 131 international. Average age 36. In 2014, 3,740 master's awarded. *Degree requirements:* For master's, comprehensive exam or practicum. *Entrance requirements:* For master's, official transcript showing earned bachelor's degree from institution accredited by recognized accrediting body. Additional exam requirements/recommendations for international students: Required—TOEFL (minimum score 550 paper-based), IELTS (minimum score 6.5). *Application deadline:* Applications are processed on a rolling basis. Application fee: $0. Electronic applications accepted. *Financial support:* Applicants required to submit FAFSA. *Faculty research:* Military history, criminal justice, management performance, national security. *Unit head:* Dr. Karan Powell, Executive Vice President and Provost, 877-468-6268, Fax: 304-724-3780. *Application contact:* Terry Grant, Vice President of Enrollment Management, 877-468-6268, Fax: 304-724-3780, E-mail: info@apus.edu.
Website: http://www.apus.edu

The American University in Cairo, School of Global Affairs and Public Policy, Department of Public Policy and Administration, Cairo, Egypt. Offers global affairs (MGA); public administration (MPA, Diploma); public policy (MPP, Diploma). Tuition and fees vary according to course load and program.

The American University of Paris, Graduate Programs, Paris, France. Offers cross-cultural and sustainable business management (MA); cultural translation (MA); global communications (MA); global communications and civil society (MA); international affairs (MA); international affairs, conflict resolution and civil society development (MA); Middle East and Islamic studies (MA); Middle East and Islamic studies and international affairs (MA); public policy and international affairs (MA); public policy and international law (MA). *Degree requirements:* For master's, thesis (for some programs). *Entrance requirements:* For master's, minimum undergraduate GPA of 3.0. Additional exam requirements/recommendations for international students: Recommended—TOEFL, IELTS. Electronic applications accepted.

Arizona State University at the Tempe campus, College of Public Programs, School of Public Affairs, Phoenix, AZ 85004-0687. Offers emergency management and homeland security (MA); program evaluation (MS); public administration (MPA, PhD), including nonprofit administration (MPA), urban management (MPA); public policy (MPP); MPA/MSW. *Accreditation:* NASPAA (one or more programs are accredited). Part-time and evening/weekend programs available. Terminal master's awarded for partial completion of doctoral program. *Degree requirements:* For master's, thesis or alternative, policy analysis or capstone project; interactive Program of Study (iPOS) submitted before completing 50 percent of required credit hours; for doctorate, comprehensive exam, thesis/dissertation, interactive Program of Study (iPOS) submitted before completing 50 percent of required credit hours. *Entrance requirements:* For master's, GRE, minimum GPA of 3.0 or equivalent in last 2 years of work leading to bachelor's degree; for doctorate, GRE, minimum GPA of 3.0 or equivalent in last 2 years of work leading to bachelor's degree, 3 letters of recommendation, resume, statement of goals, samples of research reports. Additional exam requirements/recommendations for international students: Required—TOEFL (minimum score 600 paper-based; 100 iBT),

IELTS (minimum score 6.5). Electronic applications accepted. *Expenses:* Contact institution.

Arizona State University at the Tempe campus, Sandra Day O'Connor College of Law, Tempe, AZ 85287-7906. Offers biotechnology and genomics (LL M); global legal studies (LL M); law (MLS, JD); law (customized) (LL M); tribal policy, law and government (LL M); JD/MBA; JD/MD; JD/PhD. JD/MD offered jointly with Mayo Medical School. *Accreditation:* ABA. *Faculty:* 59 full-time (24 women), 67 part-time/adjunct (16 women). *Students:* 616 full-time (249 women), 45 part-time (18 women); includes 181 minority (28 Black or African American, non-Hispanic/Latino; 21 American Indian or Alaska Native, non-Hispanic/Latino; 23 Asian, non-Hispanic/Latino; 76 Hispanic/Latino; 3 Native Hawaiian or other Pacific Islander, non-Hispanic/Latino; 30 Two or more races, non-Hispanic/Latino), 20 international. Average age 28. 1,410 applicants, 44% accepted, 143 enrolled. In 2014, 9 master's, 198 doctorates awarded. *Degree requirements:* For doctorate, papers. *Entrance requirements:* For master's, bachelor's degree and JD (for LL M); for doctorate, LSAT, bachelor's degree. Additional exam requirements/recommendations for international students: Required—TOEFL (minimum score 550 paper-based; 80 iBT). *Application deadline:* For fall admission, 2/1 priority date for domestic and international students. Applications are processed on a rolling basis. Application fee: $65. Electronic applications accepted. *Expenses:* Expenses: Contact institution. *Financial support:* Research assistantships, teaching assistantships, career-related internships or fieldwork, Federal Work-Study, institutionally sponsored loans, scholarships/grants, tuition waivers (full and partial), and unspecified assistantships available. Financial award application deadline: 3/15; financial award applicants required to submit FAFSA. *Faculty research:* Emerging technologies and the law, Indian law, law and philosophy, international law, intellectual property. *Total annual research expenditures:* $1.3 million. *Unit head:* Douglas Sylvester, Dean/Professor, 480-965-6188, Fax: 480-965-6521, E-mail: douglas.sylvester@asu.edu. *Application contact:* Chitra Damania, Director of Operations, 480-965-1474, Fax: 480-727-7930, E-mail: law.admissions@asu.edu.
Website: http://www.law.asu.edu/

Arizona State University at the Tempe campus, School of Letters and Sciences, Program in Applied Ethics, Tempe, AZ 85287-4503. Offers biomedical and health ethics (MA); ethics and emerging technologies (MA); public administration, policy and ethics (MA); science, technology and ethics (MA). Part-time and evening/weekend programs available. *Degree requirements:* For master's, thesis or alternative, applied project, interactive Program of Study (iPOS) submitted before completing 50 percent of required credit hours. *Entrance requirements:* For master's, GRE (for ethics and emerging technologies concentration), minimum GPA of 3.0 or equivalent in last 2 years of work leading to bachelor's degree, 2 letters of recommendation, resume, personal statement of interest and qualifications. Additional exam requirements/recommendations for international students: Required—TOEFL (minimum score 550 paper-based; 80 iBT). Electronic applications accepted.

Auburn University at Montgomery, College of Public Policy and Justice, Department of Political Science and Public Administration, Montgomery, AL 36124-4023. Offers international relations (MIR); nonprofit management and leadership (Certificate); political science (MPS); public administration (MPA); public administration and public policy (PhD); public health care administration and policy (Certificate). PhD offered jointly with Auburn University. *Accreditation:* NASPAA (one or more programs are accredited). Part-time and evening/weekend programs available. *Faculty:* 5 full-time (1 woman), 1 part-time/adjunct (0 women). *Students:* 9 full-time (7 women), 40 part-time (26 women); includes 16 minority (13 Black or African American, non-Hispanic/Latino; 1 American Indian or Alaska Native, non-Hispanic/Latino; 1 Hispanic/Latino; 1 Two or more races, non-Hispanic/Latino), 2 international. Average age 29. 20 applicants, 90% accepted, 12 enrolled. In 2014, 13 master's awarded. *Degree requirements:* For master's, comprehensive exam; for doctorate, thesis/dissertation. *Entrance requirements:* For master's, GRE General Test or MAT; for doctorate, GRE General Test. *Application deadline:* Applications are processed on a rolling basis. Electronic applications accepted. *Expenses:* Tuition, state resident: full-time $6264; part-time $348 per credit hour. Tuition, nonresident: full-time $14,094; part-time $783 per credit hour. *Financial support:* In 2014–15, 1 teaching assistantship was awarded; research assistantships, career-related internships or fieldwork, and scholarships/grants also available. Support available to part-time students. Financial award application deadline: 3/1; financial award applicants required to submit FAFSA. *Unit head:* Dr. Andrew Cortell, Department Head, 334-244-3622, E-mail: acortell@aum.edu.
Website: http://www.cla.auburn.edu/polisci/graduate-programs/phd-in-public-administration-and-public-policy/

Baruch College of the City University of New York, School of Public Affairs, Program in Public Administration, New York, NY 10010-5585. Offers general public administration (MPA); health care policy (MPA); nonprofit administration (MPA); policy analysis and evaluation (MPA); public management (MPA); MS/MPA. *Accreditation:* NASPAA. Part-time and evening/weekend programs available. *Degree requirements:* For master's, thesis, capstone. *Entrance requirements:* For master's, GRE General Test. Additional exam requirements/recommendations for international students: Required—TOEFL. Electronic applications accepted. *Expenses:* Contact institution. *Faculty research:* Urbanization, population and poverty in the developing world, housing and community development, labor unions and housing, government-nongovernment relations, immigration policy, social network analysis, cross-sectoral governance, comparative healthcare systems, program evaluation, social welfare policy, health outcomes, educational policy and leadership, transnationalism, infant health, welfare reform, racial/ethnic disparities in health, urban politics, homelessness, race and ethnic relations.

Baylor University, Graduate School, College of Arts and Sciences, Department of Political Science, Waco, TX 76798. Offers international studies (MA); political science (MA, PhD); public policy and administration (MPPA); JD/MPPA. Terminal master's awarded for partial completion of doctoral program. *Degree requirements:* For master's, variable foreign language requirement, comprehensive exam (for some programs), thesis (for some programs); for doctorate, variable foreign language requirement, comprehensive exam, thesis/dissertation. *Entrance requirements:* For master's and doctorate, GRE General Test. Additional exam requirements/recommendations for international students: Required—TOEFL. Electronic applications accepted.

Boise State University, College of Social Sciences and Public Affairs, Department of Public Policy and Administration, Boise, ID 83725-0399. Offers environmental and natural resources policy and administration (MPA); general public administration (MPA); public policy and administration (Graduate Certificate); state and local government policy and administration (MPA). *Accreditation:* NASPAA. Part-time programs available. *Faculty:* 12 full-time, 16 part-time/adjunct. *Students:* 22 full-time (11 women), 72 part-time (45 women); includes 5 minority (1 Asian, non-Hispanic/Latino; 4 Hispanic/Latino). 52 applicants, 90% accepted, 22 enrolled. In 2014, 27 master's, 6 other advanced degrees awarded. *Degree requirements:* For master's, comprehensive exam, directed research project, internship. *Entrance requirements:* For master's, GRE General Test, minimum GPA of 3.0. Additional exam requirements/recommendations for international students: Required—TOEFL. *Application deadline:* For fall admission, 3/1 priority date for domestic students; for spring admission, 10/1 priority date for domestic students.

Applications are processed on a rolling basis. Application fee: $55. Electronic applications accepted. *Expenses:* Tuition, state resident: part-time $331 per credit hour. Tuition, nonresident: part-time $531 per credit hour. *Financial support:* In 2014–15, 2 students received support. Federal Work-Study, institutionally sponsored loans, and unspecified assistantships available. Support available to part-time students. Financial award application deadline: 3/1. *Unit head:* Dr. Gregory Hill, Graduate Program Director, 208-426-2917, E-mail: greghill@boisestate.edu. *Application contact:* Linda Platt, Supervisor, Graduate Admission and Degree Services, 208-426-1074, Fax: 208-426-2789, E-mail: lplatt@boisestate.edu.
Website: http://sspa.boisestate.edu/publicpolicy/

Brandeis University, Graduate School of Arts and Sciences, Joint Master's Programs in Women's and Gender Studies, Waltham, MA 02454-9110. Offers anthropology and women's and gender studies (MA); English and women's and gender studies (MA); history and women's and gender studies (MA); Near Eastern and Judaic studies and women's and gender studies (MA); psychology and women's and gender studies (MA); public policy and women's and gender studies (MA); social policy and women's and gender studies (MA); sociology and women's and gender studies (MA); sustainable international development and women's/gender studies (MA). *Degree requirements:* For master's, thesis. *Entrance requirements:* For master's, GRE, sample of written work, resume, statement of purpose, transcript(s), letters of recommendation. Additional exam requirements/recommendations for international students: Required—TOEFL (minimum score 600 paper-based; 100 iBT), PTE (minimum score 68); Recommended—IELTS (minimum score 7). Electronic applications accepted. *Faculty research:* Anthropology, English, history, music, Near Eastern and Judaic studies, public policy, psychology, sociology, and sustainable international development.

Brandeis University, The Heller School for Social Policy and Management, Program in Public Policy, Waltham, MA 02454-9110. Offers aging (MPP); behavioral health (MPP); children, youth and families (MPP); general social policy (MPP); health (MPP); poverty alleviation and development (MPP); MPP/MA. *Degree requirements:* For master's, thesis. *Entrance requirements:* For master's, GRE, 3 letters of recommendation, statement of purpose, 3 to 5 years of professional experience. Additional exam requirements/recommendations for international students: Required—TOEFL (minimum score 600 paper-based; 100 iBT). Electronic applications accepted. *Faculty research:* Health and behavioral health, children and families, disabilities, aging policy, substance abuse, work, inequality and social change, women/gender, poverty alleviation.

Brock University, Faculty of Graduate Studies, Faculty of Social Sciences, Program in Political Science, St. Catharines, ON L2S 3A1, Canada. Offers Canadian politics (MA); comparative politics (MA); international relations (MA); political theory or philosophy (MA); public policy (MA). Part-time programs available. *Degree requirements:* For master's, thesis optional. *Entrance requirements:* For master's, honors degree. Additional exam requirements/recommendations for international students: Required—TOEFL (minimum score 550 paper-based; 80 iBT), IELTS (minimum score 6.5), TWE (minimum score 4). Electronic applications accepted. *Faculty research:* Public administration reform, economic and social justice, politics of societies, Canadian politics, international relations.

Brooklyn College of the City University of New York, School of Humanities and Social Sciences, Department of Political Science, Brooklyn, NY 11210-2889. Offers international affairs (MA); political science (MA); urban policy and administration (MA). Part-time and evening/weekend programs available. *Degree requirements:* For master's, comprehensive exam (for some programs), thesis or alternative, foreign language exam (for international affairs program). *Entrance requirements:* For master's, 2 letters of recommendation, personal statement. Additional exam requirements/recommendations for international students: Required—TOEFL (minimum score 500 paper-based; 61 iBT). *Faculty research:* Ethics and politics, politics of criminal justice, Western Europe, international law and politics, labor politics.

Brown University, Graduate School, A. Alfred Taubman Center for Public Policy and American Institutions, Providence, RI 02912. Offers MPA, MPP, MD/MPP. *Entrance requirements:* For master's, GRE, 3 letters of recommendation. Additional exam requirements/recommendations for international students: Required—TOEFL.

California Lutheran University, Graduate Studies, Program in Public Policy and Administration, Thousand Oaks, CA 91360-2787. Offers MPPA. *Faculty:* 3 full-time (1 woman), 7 part-time/adjunct (3 women). *Students:* 51 full-time (28 women), 28 part-time (16 women); includes 22 minority (4 Black or African American, non-Hispanic/Latino; 4 Asian, non-Hispanic/Latino; 14 Hispanic/Latino), 29 international. Average age 32. 43 applicants, 58% accepted, 13 enrolled. In 2014, 69 master's awarded. *Degree requirements:* For master's, comprehensive exam, thesis or project, internship. *Entrance requirements:* For master's, GMAT or GRE General Test, interview, minimum GPA of 3.0. *Application deadline:* Applications are processed on a rolling basis. Application fee: $50. *Expenses:* Expenses: Contact institution. *Unit head:* Dr. Jamshid Damooei, Director, 805-493-3360. *Application contact:* 805-493-3325, Fax: 805-493-3861, E-mail: clugrad@callutheran.edu.

California State University, East Bay, Office of Academic Programs and Graduate Studies, College of Letters, Arts, and Social Sciences, Department of Public Affairs and Administration, Program in Public Administration, Hayward, CA 94542-3000. Offers health care administration (MPA); public management and policy analysis (MPA). Part-time and evening/weekend programs available. *Degree requirements:* For master's, comprehensive exam (for some programs), comprehensive exam or thesis. *Entrance requirements:* For master's, minimum GPA of 2.5; statement of purpose; 2 letters of recommendation; professional resume/curriculum vitae. Additional exam requirements/recommendations for international students: Required—TOEFL (minimum score 550 paper-based; 79 iBT). *Application deadline:* For fall admission, 6/18 for domestic and international students. Application fee: $55. Electronic applications accepted. *Expenses:* Tuition, state resident: full-time $7830; part-time $1302 per credit hour. Tuition, nonresident: full-time $16,368. *Required fees:* $327 per quarter. Tuition and fees vary according to course load and program. *Financial support:* Fellowships, teaching assistantships, career-related internships or fieldwork, Federal Work-Study, institutionally sponsored loans, and scholarships/grants available. Support available to part-time students. Financial award application deadline: 3/2; financial award applicants required to submit FAFSA. *Unit head:* Dr. Toni Fogarty, Chair, 510-885-2268, E-mail: toni.fogarty@csueastbay.edu. *Application contact:* Prof. Michael Moon, Public Administration Graduate Advisor, 510-885-2545, Fax: 510-885-3726, E-mail: michael.moon@csueastbay.edu.

California State University, Long Beach, Graduate Studies, College of Health and Human Services, Graduate Center for Public Policy and Administration, Long Beach, CA 90840. Offers MPA. *Accreditation:* NASPAA. Part-time and evening/weekend programs available. *Degree requirements:* For master's, comprehensive exam. *Entrance requirements:* For master's, minimum GPA of 2.75. Electronic applications accepted. *Faculty research:* Transportation access, air quality controls, coastal issues, intergovernmental relations.

California State University, Sacramento, Office of Graduate Studies, College of Social Sciences and Interdisciplinary Studies, Program in Public Policy and Administration, Sacramento, CA 95819. Offers MPPA. Part-time programs available.

Degree requirements: For master's, thesis or alternative, writing proficiency exam. *Entrance requirements:* Additional exam requirements/recommendations for international students: Required—TOEFL. Electronic applications accepted. *Faculty research:* Education policy, urban policy, collaborative governance, judicial administration, and California state/local governance.

Carleton University, Faculty of Graduate Studies, Faculty of Public Affairs and Management, School of Public Policy and Administration, Ottawa, ON K1S 5B6, Canada. Offers public administration (MA, DPA); public policy (PhD). Part-time programs available. *Degree requirements:* For master's, thesis optional; for doctorate, one foreign language, comprehensive exam, thesis/dissertation. *Entrance requirements:* For master's, GRE, honors degree; for doctorate, master's degree. Additional exam requirements/recommendations for international students: Required—TOEFL. *Faculty research:* Canadian public administration and policy, development administration, public policy analysis, public management.

Carnegie Mellon University, Dietrich College of Humanities and Social Sciences, Department of Statistics, Pittsburgh, PA 15213-3891. Offers machine learning and statistics (PhD); mathematical finance (PhD); statistics (MS, PhD), including applied statistics (PhD), computational statistics (PhD), theoretical statistics (PhD); statistics and public policy (PhD). Terminal master's awarded for partial completion of doctoral program. *Degree requirements:* For doctorate, comprehensive exam, thesis/dissertation. *Entrance requirements:* For master's and doctorate, GRE General Test. Additional exam requirements/recommendations for international students: Required—TOEFL. *Faculty research:* Stochastic processes, Bayesian statistics, statistical computing, decision theory, psychiatric statistics.

Carnegie Mellon University, Heinz College Australia, Master of Science in Public Policy and Management Program (Adelaide, South Australia), Adelaide, PA 5000, Australia. Offers MS. *Entrance requirements:* For master's, GRE or GMAT, college-level course in advanced algebra/pre-calculus; college-level courses in economics and statistics (recommended). Additional exam requirements/recommendations for international students: Required—TOEFL or IELTS.

Carnegie Mellon University, H. John Heinz III College, School of Public Policy and Management, Master of Science in Public Policy and Management Program, Pittsburgh, PA 15213-3891. Offers MS. Program also offered with second-year study in Washington, DC. *Degree requirements:* For master's, internship. *Entrance requirements:* For master's, GRE or GMAT, college-level course in advanced algebra/pre-calculus; college-level courses in economics and statistics (recommended). Additional exam requirements/recommendations for international students: Required—TOEFL or IELTS. Electronic applications accepted.

Carnegie Mellon University, H. John Heinz III College, School of Public Policy and Management, PhD in Public Policy and Management Program, Pittsburgh, PA 15213-3891. Offers PhD. *Entrance requirements:* For doctorate, GRE or GMAT. Additional exam requirements/recommendations for international students: Required—TOEFL or IELTS.

Central European University, Graduate Studies, Public Policy Programs, Budapest, Hungary. Offers MA, PhD. *Faculty:* 23 full-time (7 women), 14 part-time/adjunct (5 women). *Students:* 129 full-time (75 women). Average age 28. 920 applicants, 23% accepted, 69 enrolled. In 2014, 29 master's, 1 doctorate awarded. *Degree requirements:* For master's, one foreign language, thesis; for doctorate, one foreign language, comprehensive exam, thesis/dissertation. *Entrance requirements:* For master's and doctorate, interview. Additional exam requirements/recommendations for international students: Required—TOEFL (minimum score 570 paper-based); Recommended—IELTS (minimum score 6.5). *Application deadline:* For fall admission, 1/24 for domestic and international students. Application fee: $40. Electronic applications accepted. *Expenses:* Tuition: Full-time 12,000 euros. *Required fees:* 200 euros. One-time fee: 500 euros full-time. *Financial support:* In 2014–15, 97 students received support, including 97 fellowships (averaging $6,100 per year), career-related internships or fieldwork, scholarships/grants, health care benefits, and tuition waivers (full and partial) also available. *Faculty research:* European Union politics and policy, regional integration; global governance; the regulatory state and executive governance; public management and public administration; core public services and the welfare state; political economy, international political economy; economic and fiscal policy; political parties and public policy. *Unit head:* Dr. Wolfang Reinicke, Head, 361-327-3110, E-mail: spp@ceu.hu. *Application contact:* Zsuzsanna Jaszberenyi, Admissions Officer, 361-324-3009, Fax: 367-327-3211, E-mail: admissions@ceu.hu.
Website: http://publicpolicy.ceu.hu/

Claremont Graduate University, Graduate Programs, School of Social Science, Policy and Evaluation, Department of Economics, Claremont, CA 91711-6160. Offers business and financial economics (MA, PhD); economic development (Certificate); international and development economics (PhD); international economics policy and development (MA); international money and finance (PhD); neuroeconomics and behavioral economics (PhD); political economy and public policy (MA); public choice and public economics (PhD); MBA/PhD. Part-time programs available. *Faculty:* 9 full-time (2 women), 1 part-time/adjunct (0 women). *Students:* 107 full-time (33 women), 35 part-time (15 women); includes 22 minority (3 Black or African American, non-Hispanic/Latino; 11 Asian, non-Hispanic/Latino; 6 Hispanic/Latino; 2 Two or more races, non-Hispanic/Latino), 73 international. Average age 32. In 2014, 15 master's, 11 doctorates awarded. *Entrance requirements:* For master's and doctorate, GRE General Test or GMAT. Additional exam requirements/recommendations for international students: Required—TOEFL (minimum score 550 paper-based; 80 iBT). *Application deadline:* For fall admission, 2/1 priority date for domestic and international students. Applications are processed on a rolling basis. Application fee: $80. Electronic applications accepted. *Expenses:* Tuition: Full-time $41,784; part-time $1741 per credit. *Required fees:* $600; $300 per semester. *Financial support:* Fellowships, research assistantships, teaching assistantships, Federal Work-Study, institutionally sponsored loans, and scholarships/grants available. Support available to part-time students. Financial award application deadline: 2/15; financial award applicants required to submit FAFSA. *Faculty research:* International and financial economics, law and economics, regulation, public choice economics. *Unit head:* Heather Campbell, Chair, 909-621-8689, E-mail: heather.campbell@cgu.edu. *Application contact:* Annekah Hall, Assistant Director of Admissions, 909-607-3371, E-mail: annekah.hall@cgu.edu.
Website: http://www.cgu.edu/pages/466.asp

Claremont Graduate University, Graduate Programs, School of Social Science, Policy and Evaluation, Department of Politics and Policy, Claremont, CA 91711-6160. Offers American politics (MA, PhD); comparative politics (PhD); international political economy (MA); international studies (MA); political philosophy (PhD); political science (PhD); politics, economics and business (MA); public policy (MA, PhD); world politics (PhD); MBA/PhD. Part-time programs available. *Faculty:* 7 full-time (5 women), 2 part-time/adjunct (0 women). *Students:* 112 full-time (38 women), 39 part-time (9 women); includes 37 minority (7 Black or African American, non-Hispanic/Latino; 1 American Indian or Alaska Native, non-Hispanic/Latino; 12 Asian, non-Hispanic/Latino; 14 Hispanic/Latino; 1 Native Hawaiian or other Pacific Islander, non-Hispanic/Latino; 2 Two or more races, non-Hispanic/Latino), 30 international. Average age 34. In 2014, 22

master's, 12 doctorates awarded. Terminal master's awarded for partial completion of doctoral program. *Entrance requirements:* For master's and doctorate, GRE General Test. Additional exam requirements/recommendations for international students: Required—TOEFL (minimum score 550 paper-based; 80 iBT). *Application deadline:* For fall admission, 2/1 priority date for domestic and international students. Applications are processed on a rolling basis. Application fee: $80. Electronic applications accepted. *Expenses:* Tuition: Full-time $41,784; part-time $1741 per credit. *Required fees:* $600; $300 per semester. *Financial support:* Fellowships, research assistantships, teaching assistantships, Federal Work-Study, institutionally sponsored loans, and scholarships/grants available. Support available to part-time students. Financial award application deadline: 2/15; financial award applicants required to submit FAFSA. *Faculty research:* Environmental policy, international debt, global democratization, Third World development, public sector discrimination. *Unit head:* Heather Campbell, Chair, 909-621-8689, E-mail: heather.campbell@cgu.edu. *Application contact:* Annekah Hall, Assistant Director of Admissions, 909-607-3371, E-mail: annekah.hall@cgu.edu.
Website: http://www.cgu.edu/pages/458.asp

Claremont Graduate University, Graduate Programs, School of Social Science, Policy and Evaluation, Program in Public Policy and Evaluation, Claremont, CA 91711-6160. Offers MA. *Students:* 2 full-time (0 women), 2 part-time (0 women), 1 international. Average age 27. In 2014, 1 master's awarded. *Entrance requirements:* For master's, GRE General Test. Additional exam requirements/recommendations for international students: Required—TOEFL (minimum score 550 paper-based; 80 iBT). *Application deadline:* For fall admission, 2/1 priority date for domestic and international students. Application fee: $80. Electronic applications accepted. *Expenses:* Tuition: Full-time $41,784; part-time $1741 per credit. *Required fees:* $600; $300 per semester. *Financial support:* Fellowships, Federal Work-Study, institutionally sponsored loans, and scholarships/grants available. Support available to part-time students. Financial award application deadline: 2/15; financial award applicants required to submit FAFSA. *Unit head:* Stewart Donaldson, Dean, 909-607-8235, E-mail: stewart.donaldson@cgu.edu. *Application contact:* Annekah Hall, Assistant Director of Admissions, 909-607-3371, E-mail: annekah.hall@cgu.edu.
Website: http://www.cgu.edu/pages/4256.asp

Clemson University, Graduate School, Program in Policy Studies, Clemson, SC 29634. Offers PhD, Certificate. *Faculty:* 25 full-time (5 women), 8 part-time/adjunct (1 woman). *Students:* 9 full-time (2 women), 8 part-time (4 women), 5 international. Average age 38. 6 applicants, 67% accepted, 3 enrolled. *Degree requirements:* For doctorate, thesis/dissertation. *Entrance requirements:* For doctorate, GRE General Test. Additional exam requirements/recommendations for international students: Required—TOEFL. *Application deadline:* Applications are processed on a rolling basis. Application fee: $70 ($80 for international students). Electronic applications accepted. *Financial support:* In 2014–15, 5 students received support, including 5 research assistantships with partial tuition reimbursements available (averaging $15,200 per year); fellowships with full and partial tuition reimbursements available, teaching assistantships with partial tuition reimbursements available, career-related internships or fieldwork, institutionally sponsored loans, scholarships/grants, health care benefits, and unspecified assistantships also available. Support available to part-time students. *Unit head:* Dr. Bruce W. Ransom, II, Coordinator, 864-656-0214, E-mail: bruce@strom.clemson.edu. *Application contact:* Dr. Tristam Aldridge, Interim Associate Dean, 864-656-2561, Fax: 864-656-5344, E-mail: saldrid@clemson.edu.
Website: http://www.strom.clemson.edu/policystudies/

Cleveland State University, College of Graduate Studies, Maxine Goodman Levin College of Urban Affairs, Program in Urban Studies, Cleveland, OH 44115. Offers community and neighborhood development (MS); economic development (MS); law and public policy (MS); public finance (MS); urban economic development (Certificate); urban policy analysis (MS); urban real estate development (MS); urban real estate development and finance (Certificate). Part-time and evening/weekend programs available. *Faculty:* 23 full-time (11 women), 23 part-time/adjunct (6 women). *Students:* 5 full-time (1 woman), 8 part-time (2 women); includes 1 minority (Black or African American, non-Hispanic/Latino). Average age 34. 21 applicants, 29% accepted, 4 enrolled. In 2014, 4 master's awarded. *Degree requirements:* For master's, thesis or alternative, exit project. *Entrance requirements:* For master's, GRE General Test (minimum score: verbal and quantitative combined 40th percentile, analytical writing 4.0), minimum GPA of 3.0. Additional exam requirements/recommendations for international students: Required—TOEFL (minimum score 525 paper-based; 65 iBT), IELTS, or ITEP. *Application deadline:* For fall admission, 1/15 priority date for domestic students, 1/15 for international students. Applications are processed on a rolling basis. Application fee: $30. Electronic applications accepted. *Expenses:* Expenses: $9,615 full-time, in-state tuition and fees. *Financial support:* In 2014–15, 4 students received support, including 3 research assistantships with full and partial tuition reimbursements available (averaging $7,200 per year), 2 teaching assistantships with full and partial tuition reimbursements available (averaging $4,800 per year); career-related internships or fieldwork, scholarships/grants, traineeships, and unspecified assistantships also available. Support available to part-time students. Financial award application deadline: 3/1; financial award applicants required to submit FAFSA. *Faculty research:* Environmental issues, economic development, urban and public policy, public management. *Unit head:* Dr. Brian Mikelbank, Director, 216-875-9980, Fax: 216-687-9342, E-mail: b.mikelbank@csuohio.edu. *Application contact:* David Arrighi, Graduate Academic Advisor, 216-523-7522, Fax: 216-687-5398, E-mail: urbanprograms@csuohio.edu.
Website: http://urban.csuohio.edu/academics/graduate/msus/

The College of William and Mary, Faculty of Arts and Sciences, Thomas Jefferson Program in Public Policy, Williamsburg, VA 23187-8795. Offers MPP, JD/MPP, MBA/MPP, MS/MPP. *Faculty:* 15 full-time (6 women), 3 part-time/adjunct (0 women). *Students:* 33 full-time (15 women); includes 7 minority (1 Black or African American, non-Hispanic/Latino; 1 Asian, non-Hispanic/Latino; 3 Hispanic/Latino; 2 Two or more races, non-Hispanic/Latino), 2 international. Average age 26. 60 applicants, 57% accepted, 18 enrolled. In 2014, 19 master's awarded. *Entrance requirements:* For master's, GRE General Test. Additional exam requirements/recommendations for international students: Required—TOEFL (minimum score 600 paper-based; 100 iBT), IELTS (minimum score 7.5). *Application deadline:* For fall admission, 2/15 priority date for domestic and international students. Application fee: $45. Electronic applications accepted. *Financial support:* In 2014–15, 34 students received support, including 20 research assistantships with partial tuition reimbursements available (averaging $7,000 per year), 15 teaching assistantships with partial tuition reimbursements available (averaging $8,000 per year); career-related internships or fieldwork and unspecified assistantships also available. Financial award application deadline: 2/15; financial award applicants required to submit FAFSA. *Faculty research:* Social policy, international development, health care policy, environmental policy, state and local policy, education policy, regulatory policy. *Total annual research expenditures:* $136,331. *Unit head:* Dr. Sarah Stafford, Director, 757-221-1317, Fax: 757-221-2390, E-mail: slstaf@wm.edu. *Application contact:* Sophie Correll, Administrative Assistant, 757-221-2368, Fax: 757-221-2390, E-mail: sbcorr@wm.edu.
Website: http://www.wm.edu/publicpolicy

Public Policy

Columbia University, School of International and Public Affairs, Program in Public Policy and Administration, New York, NY 10027. Offers MPA, JD/MPA, MPA/MS, MPH/MPA. *Accreditation:* NASPAA. *Entrance requirements:* For master's, GRE General Test. Additional exam requirements/recommendations for international students: Required—TOEFL (minimum score 600 paper-based; 100 iBT). Electronic applications accepted.

Concordia University, School of Graduate Studies, Faculty of Arts and Science, Department of Political Science, Montréal, QC H3G 1M8, Canada. Offers political science (PhD); public policy and public administration (MA), including geography. *Degree requirements:* For master's, one foreign language, comprehensive exam, thesis optional, internship. *Entrance requirements:* For master's, honors degree or equivalent. Additional exam requirements/recommendations for international students: Required—TOEFL. *Faculty research:* International public policy and administration, Quebec public administration, public policy and social/political theory, geography and public policy, public administration and decision making.

Cornell University, Graduate School, Graduate Fields of Arts and Sciences, Field of Government, Ithaca, NY 14853-0001. Offers American politics (PhD); comparative politics (PhD); international relations (PhD); political methodology (PhD); political thought (PhD); public policy (PhD). *Degree requirements:* For doctorate, comprehensive exam, thesis/dissertation. *Entrance requirements:* For doctorate, GRE General Test, sample of written work, 3 letters of recommendation. Additional exam requirements/recommendations for international students: Required—TOEFL (minimum score 550 paper-based; 77 iBT). Electronic applications accepted. *Faculty research:* Political theory, American politics, comparative politics, international relations, methodology.

Cornell University, Graduate School, Graduate Fields of Human Ecology, Field of Policy Analysis and Management, Ithaca, NY 14853-0001. Offers consumer policy (PhD); family and social welfare policy (PhD); health administration (MHA); health management and policy (PhD); public policy (PhD). *Degree requirements:* For master's, thesis; for doctorate, thesis/dissertation. *Entrance requirements:* For master's, GRE General Test or GMAT, 2 letters of recommendation; for doctorate, GRE General Test, 2 letters of recommendation. Additional exam requirements/recommendations for international students: Required—TOEFL (minimum score 550 paper-based; 77 iBT). Electronic applications accepted. *Faculty research:* Health policy, family policy, social welfare policy, program evaluation, consumer policy.

DePaul University, College of Liberal Arts and Social Sciences, Chicago, IL 60614. Offers Arabic (MA); Chinese (MA); English (MA); French (MA); German (MA); history (MA); interdisciplinary studies (MA, MS); international public service (MS); international studies (MA); Italian (MA); Japanese (MA); leadership and policy studies (MS); liberal studies (MA); new media studies (MA); nonprofit management (MNM); public administration (MPA); public health (MPH); public service management (MS); social work (MSW); sociology (MA); Spanish (MA); sustainable urban development (MA); women and gender studies (MA); writing and publishing (MA); writing, rhetoric, and discourse (MA); MA/PhD. Part-time and evening/weekend programs available. Postbaccalaureate distance learning degree programs offered (no on-campus study). Terminal master's awarded for partial completion of doctoral program. *Degree requirements:* For master's, variable foreign language requirement, comprehensive exam (for some programs), thesis (for some programs). Electronic applications accepted.

Duke University, Graduate School, PhD Program in Public Policy, Durham, NC 27708. Offers PhD. *Entrance requirements:* For doctorate, GRE General Test. Additional exam requirements/recommendations for international students: Required—TOEFL (minimum score 577 paper-based; 90 iBT) or IELTS. Electronic applications accepted. *Expenses:* Tuition: Full-time $45,760; part-time $2765 per credit. *Required fees:* $978. Full-time tuition and fees vary according to program.

Duke University, Sanford School of Public Policy, MPP Program, Durham, NC 27708-0243. Offers MPP, MBA/MPP, MD/MPP, MEM/MPP, MPP/JD, MPP/M Div. *Faculty:* 120 full-time (75 women). *Students:* 120 full-time (75 women); includes 22 minority (5 Black or African American, non-Hispanic/Latino; 1 American Indian or Alaska Native, non-Hispanic/Latino; 10 Asian, non-Hispanic/Latino; 6 Hispanic/Latino), 22 international. Average age 26. 367 applicants, 66 enrolled. In 2014, 78 master's awarded. *Entrance requirements:* For master's, GRE. Additional exam requirements/recommendations for international students: Required—TOEFL (minimum score 100 iBT), IELTS. *Application deadline:* For fall admission, 1/5 priority date for domestic and international students. Application fee: $80. Electronic applications accepted. *Expenses:* Expenses: Contact institution. *Financial support:* In 2014–15, 120 students received support, including teaching assistantships (averaging $4,000 per year); fellowships, research assistantships, career-related internships or fieldwork, Federal Work-Study, scholarships/grants, and unspecified assistantships also available. Financial award application deadline: 12/31; financial award applicants required to submit FAFSA. *Unit head:* Mac McCorkle, Director of Graduate Studies, 919-613-9206, Fax: 919-684-9940. *Application contact:* Jessica Pan, Director of Admissions, 919-613-9244, Fax: 919-684-9940, E-mail: mppadmit@duke.edu.
Website: http://www.sanford.duke edu

Duquesne University, Graduate School of Liberal Arts, Graduate Center for Social and Public Policy, Pittsburgh, PA 15282-0001. Offers conflict resolution and peace studies (Certificate); social and public policy (MA, Certificate). Part-time and evening/weekend programs available. *Faculty:* 6 full-time (2 women), 1 (woman) part-time/adjunct. *Students:* 25 full-time (16 women), 2 part-time (1 woman); includes 4 minority (1 Black or African American, non-Hispanic/Latino; 1 Asian, non-Hispanic/Latino; 2 Two or more races, non-Hispanic/Latino), 2 international. Average age 29. 32 applicants, 63% accepted, 10 enrolled. In 2014, 16 master's awarded. *Degree requirements:* For master's, thesis. *Entrance requirements:* For master's, GRE General Test. Additional exam requirements/recommendations for international students: Required—TOEFL. *Application deadline:* For fall admission, 4/30 priority date for domestic and international students; for spring admission, 11/1 priority date for domestic and international students. Applications are processed on a rolling basis. Electronic applications accepted. *Expenses:* Tuition: Full-time $18,882; part-time $1049 per credit. *Required fees:* $1800; $100 per credit. Tuition and fees vary according to program. *Financial support:* In 2014–15, 20 students received support, including 13 teaching assistantships with full and partial tuition reimbursements available (averaging $10,000 per year); career-related internships or fieldwork, institutionally sponsored loans, scholarships/grants, tuition waivers (full and partial), and unspecified assistantships also available. Support available to part-time students. Financial award application deadline: 5/1. *Faculty research:* Program evaluation, environmental policy, criminal justice policy, health care policy. Total annual research expenditures: $30,000. *Unit head:* Dr. Michael Irwin, Director, 412-396-6488, E-mail: irwinm@duq.edu. *Application contact:* Linda Rendulic, Assistant to the Dean, 412-396-6400, E-mail: rendulic@duq.edu.
Website: http://www.duq.edu/academics/schools/liberal-arts/graduate-school/programs/social-and-public-policy

Eastern Michigan University, Graduate School, College of Arts and Sciences, Department of Political Science, Programs in Public Administration, Ypsilanti, MI 48197. Offers management of public healthcare services (Graduate Certificate); public administration (MPA); public budget management (Graduate Certificate); public land

planning (Graduate Certificate); public management (Graduate Certificate); public policy analysis (Graduate Certificate). *Accreditation:* NASPAA. *Students:* 5 full-time (2 women), 57 part-time (24 women); includes 18 minority (13 Black or African American, non-Hispanic/Latino; 2 Asian, non-Hispanic/Latino; 3 Hispanic/Latino), 1 international. Average age 36. 50 applicants, 66% accepted, 17 enrolled. In 2014, 25 master's, 9 other advanced degrees awarded. Application fee: $45. *Unit head:* Dr. Gregory Plagens, Program Director, 734-487-2522, Fax: 734-487-3340, E-mail: gregory.plagens@emich.edu. *Application contact:* Dr. Barbara Patrick, Program Advisor, 734-487-1453, Fax: 734-487-3340, E-mail: bpatric1@emich.edu.

Eastern University, Palmer Theological Seminary, King of Prussia, PA 19096-3430. Offers Biblical studies and theology (MTS); Christian counseling (MTS); Christian faith and public policy (MTS); divinity (M Div); general studies (MTS); leadership of missional church renewal (D Min); ministry (D Min), including marriage and family; M Div/MA; M Div/MBA; M Div/MSW. *Accreditation:* ACIPE; ATS; MSA/CIHE. Part-time programs available. Postbaccalaureate distance learning degree programs offered (minimal on-campus study). *Faculty:* 14 full-time (7 women), 17 part-time/adjunct (7 women). *Students:* 65 full-time (25 women), 185 part-time (102 women); includes 151 minority (145 Black or African American, non-Hispanic/Latino; 2 Asian, non-Hispanic/Latino; 3 Hispanic/Latino; 1 Two or more races, non-Hispanic/Latino), 3 international. Average age 47. 117 applicants, 56% accepted, 61 enrolled. In 2014, 53 master's, 17 doctorates awarded. *Degree requirements:* For master's, variable foreign language requirement, thesis (for some programs); for doctorate, thesis/dissertation. *Entrance requirements:* For master's, bachelor's degree from accredited institution; for doctorate, M Div or MA. Additional exam requirements/recommendations for international students: Required—TOEFL (minimum score 550 paper-based; 79 iBT). *Application deadline:* For fall admission, 8/1 priority date for domestic students, 3/31 for international students; for spring admission, 1/15 for domestic students, 10/31 for international students. Applications are processed on a rolling basis. Application fee: $30. Electronic applications accepted. Application fee is waived when completed online. *Expenses:* Tuition: Full-time $15,600; part-time $650 per credit. *Required fees:* $30; $27.50 per semester. One-time fee: $50. Tuition and fees vary according to course load, degree level and program. *Financial support:* In 2014–15, 130 students received support, including 2 fellowships (averaging $4,000 per year), 15 teaching assistantships (averaging $1,200 per year); career-related internships or fieldwork, Federal Work-Study, and scholarships/grants also available. Financial award application deadline: 8/1; financial award applicants required to submit FAFSA. *Faculty research:* Approaches to the spiritual formation of religious leaders; Latin, anti-Colonial, and constructive theologies; pastoral and ethical responses to human trafficking; inter-religious and political dimensions of peacemaking and social justice in Israel and the Palestinian Territories. *Unit head:* Dr. Edwin Aponte, Dean of the Seminary, 484-384-2935, E-mail: semdean@eastern.edu. *Application contact:* Tiffany S. Murphy, Director of Admissions, 610-896-5000 Ext. 2986, Fax: 484-654-3680, E-mail: semadmis@eastern.edu.
Website: http://www.palmerseminary.edu/

Florida State University, The Graduate School, College of Social Sciences and Public Policy, Reubin O'D. Askew School of Public Administration and Policy, Tallahassee, FL 32306-2250. Offers MPA, PhD, Certificate, JD/MPA, MPA/MSC, MPA/MSP, MPA/MSW. *Accreditation:* NASPAA (one or more programs are accredited). Part-time and evening/weekend programs available. *Faculty:* 10 full-time (2 women), 8 part-time/adjunct (3 women). *Students:* 69 full-time (29 women), 123 part-time (70 women); includes 49 minority (29 Black or African American, non-Hispanic/Latino; 14 Hispanic/Latino; 6 Two or more races, non-Hispanic/Latino), 56 international. Average age 25. 166 applicants, 63% accepted, 46 enrolled. In 2014, 69 master's, 7 doctorates awarded. *Degree requirements:* For master's, action report; for doctorate, comprehensive exam, thesis/dissertation. *Entrance requirements:* For master's, GRE General Test, GMAT, MAT, LSAT, minimum undergraduate upper-division GPA of 3.0; for doctorate, GRE General Test (minimum score of 1100 or equivalent); GMAT; MAT; LSAT, minimum undergraduate GPA of 3.0, graduate 3.5. Additional exam requirements/recommendations for international students: Required—PTE (minimum score 55), TOEFL (minimum score 550 paper-based, 80 iBT), IELTS (minimum score 6.5) or Michigan English Language Assessment Battery (minimum score 77). *Application deadline:* For fall admission, 7/1 for domestic students, 5/1 for international students; for spring admission, 11/1 for domestic students, 9/1 for international students; for summer admission, 3/1 for domestic students, 1/1 for international students. Applications are processed on a rolling basis. Application fee: $30. Electronic applications accepted. *Expenses:* Tuition, state resident: part-time $403.51 per credit hour. Tuition, nonresident: part-time $1004.85 per credit hour. *Required fees:* $75.81 per credit hour. One-time fee: $20 part-time. Tuition and fees vary according to campus/location. *Financial support:* In 2014–15, 29 students received support, including 6 fellowships with full tuition reimbursements available (averaging $18,000 per year), 14 research assistantships with full tuition reimbursements available (averaging $15,000 per year), 5 teaching assistantships with full tuition reimbursements available (averaging $15,000 per year); career-related internships or fieldwork, Federal Work-Study, institutionally sponsored loans, scholarships/grants, tuition waivers (full), and unspecified assistantships also available. Support available to part-time students. Financial award application deadline: 2/1; financial award applicants required to submit FAFSA. *Faculty research:* Financial management, public policy and development, strategic management, state and local government, public and nonprofit management, international and nongovernmental organizations. *Unit head:* Dr. William Earle Klay, Director, 850-644-3525, Fax: 850-644-7617, E-mail: eklay@fsu.edu. *Application contact:* Velda Williams, Academic Program Specialist, 850-644-3060, Fax: 850-644-7617, E-mail: vwilliams3@fsu.edu.
Website: http://askew.fsu.edu/

Frederick S. Pardee RAND Graduate School, Program in Policy Analysis, Santa Monica, CA 90407-2138. Offers M Phil, PhD. *Faculty:* 227 part-time/adjunct (85 women). *Students:* 102 full-time (49 women); includes 16 minority (3 Black or African American, non-Hispanic/Latino; 8 Asian, non-Hispanic/Latino; 5 Hispanic/Latino), 39 international. Average age 31. 139 applicants, 26% accepted, 21 enrolled. In 2014, 12 master's, 20 doctorates awarded. *Degree requirements:* For doctorate, comprehensive exam, thesis/dissertation. *Entrance requirements:* For doctorate, GMAT or GRE General Test, resume or curriculum vitae, essay, three letters of recommendation. Additional exam requirements/recommendations for international students: Required—TOEFL. *Application deadline:* For fall admission, 1/8 for domestic and international students. Application fee: $50. Electronic applications accepted. *Expenses:* Tuition: Full-time $26,500. Full-time tuition and fees vary according to student level. *Financial support:* In 2014–15, 26 students received support, including 67 fellowships with full and partial tuition reimbursements available (averaging $21,167 per year), 94 research assistantships (averaging $44,669 per year), 26 teaching assistantships (averaging $2,000 per year); career-related internships or fieldwork, scholarships/grants, and health care benefits also available. *Faculty research:* Education, defense policy, health, labor and population, justice. *Unit head:* Dr. Susan L. Marquis, Dean, 310-393-0411 Ext. 7075, Fax: 310-451-6978. *Application contact:* Mary Parker, Registrar/Admissions Manager, 310-393-0411 Ext. 7690, Fax: 310-451-6978, E-mail: mfparker@prgs.edu.
Website: http://www.prgs.edu

George Mason University, School of Policy, Government, and International Affairs, Program in Public Policy, Arlington, VA 22201. Offers MPP, PhD. *Faculty:* 32 full-time (13 women), 16 part-time/adjunct (4 women). *Students:* 161 full-time (75 women), 295 part-time (137 women); includes 145 minority (57 Black or African American, non-Hispanic/Latino; 2 American Indian or Alaska Native, non-Hispanic/Latino; 32 Asian, non-Hispanic/Latino; 36 Hispanic/Latino; 3 Native Hawaiian or other Pacific Islander, non-Hispanic/Latino; 15 Two or more races, non-Hispanic/Latino), 40 international. Average age 32. 308 applicants, 66% accepted, 87 enrolled. In 2014, 164 master's, 22 doctorates awarded. *Degree requirements:* For master's, thesis or alternative, professional experience; for doctorate, comprehensive exam, thesis/dissertation, field studies. *Entrance requirements:* For master's, GRE/GMAT (for students seeking merit-based scholarships), bachelor's degree with minimum GPA of 3.0, current resume, 2 letters of recommendation, expanded goals statement, 2 copies of official transcripts; for doctorate, GMAT or GRE General Test, master's degree with minimum GPA of 3.0; current resume; expanded goals statement; 2 official copies of transcripts; writing sample. Additional exam requirements/recommendations for international students: Required—TOEFL (minimum score 575 paper-based; 80 iBT), IELTS (minimum score 6.5), PTE. *Application deadline:* For fall admission, 6/1 priority date for domestic students, 5/1 priority date for international students; for spring admission, 12/1 priority date for domestic students, 11/1 priority date for international students. Applications are processed on a rolling basis. Application fee: $65 ($80 for international students). Electronic applications accepted. *Expenses:* Expenses: Contact institution. *Financial support:* In 2014–15, 38 students received support, including 6 fellowships (averaging $6,758 per year), 34 research assistantships with full and partial tuition reimbursements available (averaging $20,676 per year), 1 teaching assistantship with full and partial tuition reimbursement available (averaging $6,222 per year); career-related internships or fieldwork, Federal Work-Study, scholarships/grants, unspecified assistantships, and health care benefits (for full-time research or teaching assistantship recipients) also available. Support available to part-time students. Financial award application deadline: 3/1; financial award applicants required to submit FAFSA. *Unit head:* James Pfiffner, Director, Doctoral Program in Public Policy, 703-703-1417, Fax: 703-993-2284, E-mail: pfiffner@gmu.edu. *Application contact:* Travis Major, Director of Graduate Admissions, 703-993-3183, Fax: 703-993-4876, E-mail: tmajor@gmu.edu.
Website: http://spgia.gmu.edu/programs/graduate-degrees/master-of-public-policy-mpp/

Georgetown University, Graduate School of Arts and Sciences, Department of Government, Washington, DC 20057. Offers American government (MA); conflict resolution (MA); democracy and governance (MA); development, management and policy (MA); government (PhD); MA/PhD. Terminal master's awarded for partial completion of doctoral program. *Degree requirements:* For master's, one foreign language, comprehensive exam; for doctorate, one foreign language, comprehensive exam, thesis/dissertation. *Entrance requirements:* For master's, GRE General Test, minimum B average; for doctorate, GRE General Test, MA. Additional exam requirements/recommendations for international students: Required—TOEFL. *Faculty research:* Western Europe, Latin America, the Middle East, political theory, international relations and law, methodology, American politics and institutions.

Georgetown University, Graduate School of Arts and Sciences, McCourt School of Public Policy, Washington, DC 20057. Offers policy management (MPM); public policy (MPP); MBA/MPP; MPP/JD; MPP/MA; MPP/MS; MPP/PhD. *Entrance requirements:* For master's, GRE General Test, minimum B average. Additional exam requirements/recommendations for international students: Required—TOEFL. *Faculty research:* Social policy, government, private sector.

Georgetown University, Graduate School of Arts and Sciences, School of Continuing Studies, Washington, DC 20057. Offers American studies (MALS); Catholic studies (MALS); classical civilizations (MALS); emergency and disaster management (MPS); ethics and the professions (MALS); hospitality management (MPS); human resources management (MPS); humanities (MALS); individualized study (MALS); international affairs (MALS); Islam and Muslim-Christian relations (MALS); journalism (MPS); liberal studies (DLS); literature and society (MALS); medieval and early modern European studies (MALS); public relations and corporate communications (MPS); real estate (MPS); religious studies (MALS); social and public policy (MALS); sports industry management (MPS); systems engineering management (MPS); technology management (MPS); the theory and practice of American democracy (MALS); urban and regional planning (MPS); visual culture (MALS). MPS in systems engineering management offered jointly with Stevens Institute of Technology. *Entrance requirements:* Additional exam requirements/recommendations for international students: Required—TOEFL.

The George Washington University, Columbian College of Arts and Sciences, Department of Philosophy, Washington, DC 20052. Offers philosophy and social policy (MA). *Degree requirements:* For master's, comprehensive exam, thesis or alternative. *Entrance requirements:* For master's, GRE General Test, interview, minimum GPA of 3.0. Additional exam requirements/recommendations for international students: Required—TOEFL (minimum score 600 paper-based; 100 iBT). *Application deadline:* For fall admission, 4/1 priority date for domestic and international students; for spring admission, 10/1 priority date for domestic students, 9/1 priority date for international students. Applications are processed on a rolling basis. Application fee: $60. Electronic applications accepted. *Financial support:* In 2014–15, 2 students received support. Fellowships with tuition reimbursements available, Federal Work-Study, and institutionally sponsored loans available. Financial award application deadline: 1/15. *Unit head:* Dr. William B. Griffith, Academic Director, 202-994-8684, E-mail: wbg@gwu.edu. *Application contact:* Information Contact, 202-994-6265, Fax: 202-994-8683, E-mail: philosop@gwu.edu.
Website: http://departments.columbian.gwu.edu/philosophy

The George Washington University, Columbian College of Arts and Sciences, Trachtenberg School of Public Policy and Public Administration, Washington, DC 20052. Offers public administration (MPA); public policy (MPP); public policy and administration (PhD); JD/MPP; MPA/JD; PhD/MPP. Part-time and evening/weekend programs available. *Faculty:* 39 full-time (14 women), 19 part-time/adjunct (10 women). *Students:* 273 full-time (182 women), 129 part-time (94 women); includes 58 minority (26 Black or African American, non-Hispanic/Latino; 1 American Indian or Alaska Native, non-Hispanic/Latino; 22 Asian, non-Hispanic/Latino; 8 Hispanic/Latino; 1 Native Hawaiian or other Pacific Islander, non-Hispanic/Latino). Average age 26. 812 applicants, 61% accepted, 140 enrolled. In 2014, 134 master's, 10 doctorates awarded. *Degree requirements:* For master's, capstone project; for doctorate, comprehensive exam, thesis/dissertation. *Entrance requirements:* For master's and doctorate, GRE General Test, minimum GPA of 3.0. Additional exam requirements/recommendations for international students: Required—TOEFL (minimum score 600 paper-based; 100 iBT). *Application deadline:* For fall admission, 1/5 priority date for domestic and international students. Application fee: $75. Electronic applications accepted. *Financial support:* In 2014–15, 92 students received support. Fellowships, research assistantships, teaching assistantships, Federal Work-Study, scholarships/grants, health care benefits, and unspecified assistantships available. Financial award application deadline: 1/5. *Faculty research:* Education policy, budget and finance, health policy, regulatory policy, program evaluation. *Unit head:* Dr. Kathyrn E. Newcomer, Director, 202-994-3959, Fax: 202-994-3959, E-mail: newcomer@gwu.edu. *Application contact:* Denee Bottoms, Assistant Director of Graduate Studies, 202-994-6295, Fax: 202-994-6792, E-mail: tspppa@gwu.edu.
Website: http://www.tspppa.gwu.edu/

The George Washington University, School of Business, Department of Strategic Management and Public Policy, Washington, DC 20052. Offers MBA, PhD. *Accreditation:* NASPAA. Part-time and evening/weekend programs available. *Faculty:* 16 full-time (4 women). *Students:* 181 full-time (73 women), 4 part-time (3 women); includes 28 minority (7 Black or African American, non-Hispanic/Latino; 12 Asian, non-Hispanic/Latino; 4 Hispanic/Latino; 2 Native Hawaiian or other Pacific Islander, non-Hispanic/Latino; 3 Two or more races, non-Hispanic/Latino), 86 international. Average age 29. 584 applicants, 45% accepted, 92 enrolled. In 2014, 112 master's awarded. *Degree requirements:* For doctorate, thesis/dissertation. *Entrance requirements:* For master's, GMAT; for doctorate, GMAT or GRE. Additional exam requirements/recommendations for international students: Required—TOEFL. *Application deadline:* For fall admission, 4/1 priority date for domestic students; for spring admission, 10/1 for domestic students. Applications are processed on a rolling basis. Application fee: $75. *Financial support:* In 2014–15, 1 student received support. Fellowships, teaching assistantships, career-related internships or fieldwork, Federal Work-Study, and institutionally sponsored loans available. Financial award application deadline: 4/1. *Unit head:* Dr. Jennifer Griffin, Chair, 202-994-7872, E-mail: jgriffin@gwu.edu. *Application contact:* Christopher Storer, Executive Director, Graduate Admissions, 202-994-1212, E-mail: gwmba@gwu.edu.
Website: http://business.gwu.edu/smpp/

Georgia Institute of Technology, Graduate Studies, Ivan Allen College of Liberal Arts, School of Public Policy, Atlanta, GA 30332-0001. Offers MS, PhD. Part-time programs available. *Students:* 58 full-time (36 women), 8 part-time (4 women); includes 14 minority (5 Black or African American, non-Hispanic/Latino; 6 Asian, non-Hispanic/Latino; 2 Hispanic/Latino; 1 Two or more races, non-Hispanic/Latino), 22 international. Average age 29. 104 applicants, 25% accepted, 7 enrolled. In 2014, 20 master's, 9 doctorates awarded. Terminal master's awarded for partial completion of doctoral program. *Degree requirements:* For master's, professional paper, public policy workshop or thesis; internship; minimum overall GPA of 3.0; for doctorate, comprehensive exam, thesis/dissertation, minimum overall GPA of 3.0, one year of full-time residency. *Entrance requirements:* For master's and doctorate, GRE, three letters of recommendation, transcripts from each college/university attended, admissions essays. Additional exam requirements/recommendations for international students: Required—TOEFL (minimum score 600 paper-based; 100 iBT). *Application deadline:* For fall admission, 12/1 priority date for domestic and international students; for spring admission, 3/1 for domestic students. Applications are processed on a rolling basis. Application fee: $75. Electronic applications accepted. *Expenses:* Tuition, state resident: full-time $12,344; part-time $515 per credit hour. Tuition, nonresident: full-time $27,600; part-time $1150 per credit hour. *Required fees:* $1196 per term. Part-time tuition and fees vary according to course load. *Financial support:* Fellowships, research assistantships, teaching assistantships, career-related internships or fieldwork, Federal Work-Study, institutionally sponsored loans, tuition waivers (partial), and unspecified assistantships available. Support available to part-time students. Financial award application deadline: 5/1. *Faculty research:* National/regional science and technology policy, environmental policy, urban policy and planning, telecommunications policy. *Total annual research expenditures:* $1.4 million. *Unit head:* Kim Isett, Director, 404-385-2586, E-mail: kim.isett@pubpolicy.gatech.edu. *Application contact:* Jade Charnigo, Graduate Coordinator, 404-894-0417, E-mail: jade.charnigo@pubpolicy.gatech.edu.
Website: http://www.spp.gatech.edu

Georgia State University, Andrew Young School of Policy Studies, Department of Public Management and Policy, Atlanta, GA 30303. Offers criminal justice (MPA); disaster management (Certificate); disaster policy (MPA); environmental policy (PhD); health policy (PhD); management and finance (MPA); nonprofit management (MPA, Certificate); nonprofit policy (MPA); planning and economic development (MPP, Certificate); policy analysis and evaluation (MPA), including planning and economic development; public and nonprofit management (PhD); public finance and budgeting (PhD), including science and technology policy, urban and regional economic development; public finance policy (MPA), including social policy; public health (MPA). *Accreditation:* NASPAA (one or more programs are accredited). Part-time programs available. *Faculty:* 14 full-time (7 women). *Students:* 136 full-time (80 women), 85 part-time (47 women); includes 81 minority (60 Black or African American, non-Hispanic/Latino; 7 Asian, non-Hispanic/Latino; 11 Hispanic/Latino; 3 Two or more races, non-Hispanic/Latino), 25 international. Average age 30. 269 applicants, 59% accepted, 64 enrolled. In 2014, 80 master's, 7 other advanced degrees awarded. Terminal master's awarded for partial completion of doctoral program. *Degree requirements:* For master's, thesis optional; for doctorate, comprehensive exam, thesis/dissertation. *Entrance requirements:* For master's and doctorate, GRE. Additional exam requirements/recommendations for international students: Required—TOEFL (minimum score 603 paper-based; 100 iBT) or IELTS (minimum score 7). *Application deadline:* For fall admission, 2/15 for domestic and international students; for spring admission, 10/1 for domestic and international students. Application fee: $50. Electronic applications accepted. *Expenses:* Tuition, state resident: full-time $6516; part-time $362 per credit hour. Tuition, nonresident: full-time $22,014; part-time $1223 per credit hour. *Required fees:* $2128 per semester. Tuition and fees vary according to course load and program. *Financial support:* In 2014–15, fellowships (averaging $8,194 per year), research assistantships (averaging $8,068 per year), teaching assistantships (averaging $3,600 per year) were awarded; institutionally sponsored loans, scholarships/grants, health care benefits, and unspecified assistantships also available. Financial award application deadline: 2/1. *Faculty research:* Public budgeting and finance, public management, nonprofit management, performance measurement and management, urban development. *Unit head:* Dr. Gregory Burr Lewis, Chair and Professor, 404-413-0114, Fax: 404-413-0104, E-mail: glewis@gsu.edu. *Application contact:* Charisma Parker, Admissions Coordinator, 404-413-0030, Fax: 404-413-0023, E-mail: cparker28@gsu.edu.
Website: http://aysps.gsu.edu/pmap/

The Graduate Center, City University of New York, Graduate Studies, Interdisciplinary Studies, New York, NY 10016-4039. Offers language in social context (PhD); medieval studies (PhD); public policy (MA, PhD); urban studies (MA, PhD); women's studies (MA, PhD). Terminal master's awarded for partial completion of doctoral program. *Degree requirements:* For master's, thesis; for doctorate, comprehensive exam, thesis/dissertation. *Entrance requirements:* For master's and doctorate, GRE General Test.

Harvard University, Graduate School of Arts and Sciences and John F. Kennedy School of Government, Committee on Public Policy, Cambridge, MA 02138. Offers PhD. *Degree requirements:* For doctorate, thesis/dissertation, exams. *Entrance requirements:* For doctorate, GRE General Test or GMAT, Harvard MPP degree. Additional exam requirements/recommendations for international students: Required—TOEFL.

Harvard University, Graduate School of Arts and Sciences, Program in Social Policy, Cambridge, MA 02138. Offers PhD.

Public Policy

Harvard University, John F. Kennedy School of Government, Doctoral Programs in Government, Cambridge, MA 02138. Offers political economy and government (PhD); public policy (PhD). *Students:* 20 full-time (11 women); includes 3 minority (all Two or more races, non-Hispanic/Latino), 6 international. Average age 27. 243 applicants, 7% accepted, 11 enrolled. *Degree requirements:* For doctorate, comprehensive exam, thesis/dissertation. *Entrance requirements:* For doctorate, GRE General Test, course work in macroeconomics, multi-variable calculus. Additional exam requirements/recommendations for international students: Required—TOEFL (minimum score 600 paper-based; 100 iBT), TWE. *Application deadline:* For fall admission, 12/2 for domestic students. Application fee: $100. Electronic applications accepted. *Financial support:* Fellowships, research assistantships, teaching assistantships, Federal Work-Study, institutionally sponsored loans, scholarships/grants, health care benefits, and unspecified assistantships available. *Unit head:* Nicole Tateosian, Director, 617-495-1190, E-mail: nicole_tateosian@harvard.edu. *Application contact:* 617-495-1155, Fax: 617-496-1165, E-mail: ksg_admissions@harvard.edu.
Website: http://www.hks.harvard.edu/

Harvard University, John F. Kennedy School of Government, Program in Public Policy, Cambridge, MA 02138. Offers public policy (MPP); JD/MPP; MBA/MPP; MD/MPP. *Students:* 393 full-time (190 women), 20 part-time (7 women); includes 115 minority (16 Black or African American, non-Hispanic/Latino; 1 American Indian or Alaska Native, non-Hispanic/Latino; 39 Asian, non-Hispanic/Latino; 30 Hispanic/Latino; 1 Native Hawaiian or other Pacific Islander, non-Hispanic/Latino; 28 Two or more races, non-Hispanic/Latino), 101 international. Average age 27. 1,759 applicants, 22% accepted, 212 enrolled. In 2014, 182 master's awarded. *Entrance requirements:* For master's, GMAT or GRE General Test. Additional exam requirements/recommendations for international students: Required—TOEFL (minimum score 600 paper-based; 100 iBT), TWE. *Application deadline:* For fall admission, 12/1 for domestic students. Application fee: $100. Electronic applications accepted. *Financial support:* Fellowships, research assistantships, teaching assistantships, career-related internships or fieldwork, Federal Work-Study, institutionally sponsored loans, scholarships/grants, health care benefits, and unspecified assistantships available. Financial award application deadline: 2/6; financial award applicants required to submit CSS PROFILE or FAFSA. *Unit head:* Eleni Cortis, Director, 617-496-8382, E-mail: eleni_cortis@hks.harvard.edu. *Application contact:* 617-495-1155.
Website: http://www.hks.harvard.edu/

Indiana University Bloomington, School of Public and Environmental Affairs, Public Affairs Programs, Bloomington, IN 47405. Offers economic development (MPA); energy (MPA); environmental policy (PhD); environmental policy and natural resource management (MPA); information systems (MPA); international development (MPA); local government management (MPA); nonprofit management (MPA, Certificate); policy analysis (MPA); public budgeting and financial management (Certificate); public finance (PhD); public financial administration (MPA); public management (MPA, PhD, Certificate); public policy analysis (PhD); social entrepreneurship (Certificate); specialized public affairs (MPA); sustainability and sustainable development (MPA); JD/MPA; MPA/MA; MPA/MIS; MPA/MLS; MSES/MPA. *Accreditation:* NASPAA (one or more programs are accredited). Part-time programs available. *Degree requirements:* For master's, capstone, internship; for doctorate, comprehensive exam, thesis/dissertation. *Entrance requirements:* For master's, GRE General Test or GMAT, official transcripts, 3 letters of recommendation, resume, personal statement; for doctorate, GRE General Test, official transcripts, 3 letters of recommendation, statement of purpose. Additional exam requirements/recommendations for international students: Required—TOEFL (minimum score 600 paper-based; 96 iBT); Recommended—IELTS (minimum score 7). Electronic applications accepted. *Faculty research:* International development, environmental policy and resource management, policy analysis, public finance, public management, urban management, nonprofit management, energy policy, social policy, public finance.

Indiana University–Purdue University Fort Wayne, College of Education and Public Policy, Department of Public Policy, Fort Wayne, IN 46805-1499. Offers public management (MPM, Certificate). *Accreditation:* NASPAA (one or more programs are accredited). Part-time programs available. *Faculty:* 4 full-time (1 woman). *Students:* 6 full-time (3 women), 22 part-time (13 women); includes 10 minority (1 Black or African American, non-Hispanic/Latino; 3 Asian, non-Hispanic/Latino; 5 Hispanic/Latino; 1 Two or more races, non-Hispanic/Latino), 1 international. Average age 31. 16 applicants, 94% accepted, 9 enrolled. In 2014, 14 master's, 4 Certificates awarded. *Degree requirements:* For master's, internship. *Entrance requirements:* For master's, GRE General Test or GMAT, minimum GPA of 3.0, 3 letters of reference. Additional exam requirements/recommendations for international students: Required—TOEFL (minimum score 550 paper-based; 79 iBT). *Application deadline:* Applications are processed on a rolling basis. Application fee: $55. *Financial support:* In 2014–15, 1 teaching assistantship with partial tuition reimbursement (averaging $13,522 per year) was awarded; career-related internships or fieldwork and scholarships/grants also available. Support available to part-time students. Financial award application deadline: 3/1; financial award applicants required to submit FAFSA. *Faculty research:* Opioid safety, homeless and stigma. *Total annual research expenditures:* $8,419. *Unit head:* Dr. Brian Fife, Chair/Director, 260-481-6349, Fax: 260-481-6346, E-mail: fifeb@ipfw.edu.
Website: http://www.ipfw.edu/publicpolicy

The Institute of World Politics, Graduate Programs in National Security, Intelligence, and International Affairs, Washington, DC 20036. Offers American foreign policy (Certificate); comparative political culture (Certificate); counterintelligence (Certificate); democracy building (Certificate); intelligence (Certificate); international politics (Certificate); national security affairs (Certificate); public diplomacy and political warfare (Certificate); statecraft and national security affairs (MA); statecraft and world politics (MA); strategic intelligence studies (MA). Part-time and evening/weekend programs available. *Degree requirements:* For master's, comprehensive exam, thesis optional. *Entrance requirements:* For master's, GRE General Test. Additional exam requirements/recommendations for international students: Required—TOEFL. Electronic applications accepted. *Faculty research:* Intelligence, national security, statecraft.

Jackson State University, Graduate School, College of Public Service, Department of Public Policy and Administration, Jackson, MS 39217. Offers MPPA, PhD. *Accreditation:* NASPAA (one or more programs are accredited). Evening/weekend programs available. *Degree requirements:* For master's, comprehensive exam, thesis optional; for doctorate, comprehensive exam, thesis/dissertation. *Entrance requirements:* For master's, GRE General Test; for doctorate, GRE, GMAT, MAT. Additional exam requirements/recommendations for international students: Required—TOEFL (minimum score 520 paper-based; 67 iBT).

John Jay College of Criminal Justice of the City University of New York, Graduate Studies, Programs in Criminal Justice, New York, NY 10019-1093. Offers criminal justice (MA, PhD); criminology and deviance (PhD); forensic psychology (PhD); forensic science (PhD); international crime and justice (MA); law and philosophy (PhD); organizational behavior (PhD); public policy (PhD). Part-time and evening/weekend programs available. Terminal master's awarded for partial completion of doctoral program. *Degree requirements:* For master's, thesis or alternative; for doctorate, one foreign language, thesis/dissertation. *Entrance requirements:* For master's, GRE

General Test, minimum B average; for doctorate, GRE General Test. Additional exam requirements/recommendations for international students: Required—TOEFL (minimum score 500 paper-based).

Johns Hopkins University, Bloomberg School of Public Health, Department of Health Policy and Management, Baltimore, MD 21205-1996. Offers bioethics and policy (PhD); health and public policy (PhD); health care management and leadership (Dr PH); health economics (MHS); health economics and policy (PhD); health finance and management (MHA); health policy (MSPH); health services research and policy (PhD); public policy (MPP). *Accreditation:* CAHME (one or more programs are accredited). Part-time programs available. *Degree requirements:* For master's, thesis (for some programs), internship (for some programs); for doctorate, comprehensive exam, thesis/dissertation, 1-year full-time residency (for some programs), oral and written exams. *Entrance requirements:* For master's, GRE General Test or GMAT, 3 letters of recommendation, curriculum vitae/resume; for doctorate, GRE General Test or GMAT, 3 letters of recommendation, curriculum vitae, transcripts. Additional exam requirements/recommendations for international students: Recommended—TOEFL (minimum score 600 paper-based; 100 iBT), IELTS. Electronic applications accepted. *Faculty research:* Quality of care and health outcomes, health care finance and technology, health disparities and vulnerable populations, injury prevention, health policy and health care policy.

Liberty University, Helms School of Government, Lynchburg, VA 24515. Offers criminal justice (MS); public policy (MA), including campaigns and elections, international affairs, Middle East affairs, public administration, public policy. Part-time programs available. Postbaccalaureate distance learning degree programs offered (no on-campus study). *Students:* 248 full-time (119 women), 522 part-time (209 women); includes 194 minority (157 Black or African American, non-Hispanic/Latino; 8 American Indian or Alaska Native, non-Hispanic/Latino; 7 Asian, non-Hispanic/Latino; 5 Hispanic/Latino; 1 Native Hawaiian or other Pacific Islander, non-Hispanic/Latino; 16 Two or more races, non-Hispanic/Latino), 14 international. Average age 34. 837 applicants, 55% accepted, 226 enrolled. In 2014, 65 degrees awarded. *Entrance requirements:* For master's, minimum undergraduate GPA of 3.0. Additional exam requirements/recommendations for international students: Required—TOEFL (minimum score 600 paper-based; 100 iBT). *Application deadline:* Applications are processed on a rolling basis. Application fee: $50. Electronic applications accepted. *Unit head:* Shawn D. Akers, Dean, 434-592-4986. *Application contact:* Jay Bridge, Director of Admissions, 800-424-9595, Fax: 800-628-7977, E-mail: gradadmissions@liberty.edu.

Lincoln University, Graduate Studies, Jefferson City, MO 65101. Offers business administration (MBA), including accounting, entrepreneurship, management, public administration and policy; educational leadership (Ed S), including elementary leadership, secondary leadership, superintendency; guidance and counseling (M Ed), including community/agency counseling, elementary school, secondary school; history (MA); school administration and supervision (M Ed), including elementary school administration, secondary school administration, special education administration; school teaching (M Ed), including elementary school teaching, secondary school teaching; sociology (MA); sociology/criminal justice (MA). Part-time and evening/weekend programs available. Postbaccalaureate distance learning degree programs offered (minimal on-campus study). *Students:* 57 full-time (35 women), 83 part-time (50 women); includes 64 minority (47 Black or African American, non-Hispanic/Latino; 1 American Indian or Alaska Native, non-Hispanic/Latino; 14 Asian, non-Hispanic/Latino; 1 Hispanic/Latino; 1 Two or more races, non-Hispanic/Latino), 9 international. Average age 33. 60 applicants, 68% accepted, 31 enrolled. In 2014, 52 master's, 2 other advanced degrees awarded. *Degree requirements:* For master's and Ed S, comprehensive exam, thesis optional. *Entrance requirements:* For master's and Ed S, GRE, MAT or GMAT, minimum GPA of 2.75 in major, 2.5 overall; 3 letters of recommendation; minimum C average in English composition; personal statement of purpose. Additional exam requirements/recommendations for international students: Required—TOEFL (minimum score 500 paper-based; 61 iBT). *Application deadline:* For fall admission, 8/1 priority date for domestic and international students; for spring admission, 12/1 priority date for domestic and international students; for summer admission, 5/1 priority date for domestic and international students. Applications are processed on a rolling basis. Application fee: $30. *Expenses:* Tuition, state resident: full-time $6840; part-time $285 per credit hour. Tuition, nonresident: full-time $12,720; part-time $530 per credit hour. *Required fees:* $737; $737 per year. *Financial support:* In 2014–15, 1 fellowship with tuition reimbursement, 11 research assistantships with tuition reimbursements were awarded; Federal Work-Study and scholarships/grants also available. Support available to part-time students. Financial award application deadline: 3/1; financial award applicants required to submit FAFSA. *Unit head:* Dr. Linda S. Bickel, Dean, 573-681-5247, Fax: 573-681-5106, E-mail: gradschool@lincolnu.edu. *Application contact:* Irasema Steck, Administrative Assistant, 573-681-5247, Fax: 573-681-5106, E-mail: gradschool@lincolnu.edu.
Website: http://www.lincolnu.edu/web/graduate-studies/graduate-studies

Longwood University, College of Graduate and Professional Studies, Department of Sociology, Anthropology, and Criminal Justice Studies, Farmville, VA 23909. Offers criminal justice and social policy (MS). Part-time and evening/weekend programs available. *Faculty:* 11 full-time (5 women), 2 part-time/adjunct (0 women). *Students:* 5 full-time (3 women), 2 part-time (1 woman); includes 1 minority (Hispanic/Latino). 7 applicants, 71% accepted, 1 enrolled. In 2014, 3 master's awarded. *Degree requirements:* For master's, comprehensive exam (for some programs), thesis (for some programs). *Entrance requirements:* For master's, minimum GPA of 2.75, bachelor's degree from regionally-accredited institution, 2 recommendations, 500-word personal essay, official transcripts. Additional exam requirements/recommendations for international students: Required—TOEFL (minimum score 570 paper-based), IELTS (minimum score 6.5). *Application deadline:* For fall admission, 5/1 priority date for domestic students; for spring admission, 10/1 priority date for domestic students; for summer admission, 2/1 priority date for domestic students. Applications are processed on a rolling basis. Application fee: $50. Electronic applications accepted. *Expenses:* Tuition, state resident: part-time $430 per credit hour. Tuition, nonresident: part-time $1001 per credit hour. Tuition and fees vary according to campus/location and program. *Financial support:* Career-related internships or fieldwork and Federal Work-Study available. Financial award applicants required to submit FAFSA. *Unit head:* Dr. William C. Burger, Graduate Program Coordinator - Sociology/Criminal Justice & Social Policy, 434-395-2247, E-mail: burgerwc@longwood.edu. *Application contact:* College of Graduate and Professional Studies, 434-395-2380, Fax: 434-395-2750, E-mail: graduate@longwood.edu. Website: http://www.longwood.edu/sacjs/

Loyola University Chicago, Graduate School, Program in Public Policy, Chicago, IL 60660. Offers MPP. Part-time and evening/weekend programs available. *Faculty:* 2 full-time (both women), 3 part-time/adjunct (1 woman). *Students:* 13 full-time (5 women), 8 part-time (4 women); includes 8 minority (1 Asian, non-Hispanic/Latino; 6 Hispanic/Latino; 1 Two or more races, non-Hispanic/Latino), 1 international. Average age 27. 33 applicants, 85% accepted, 10 enrolled. In 2014, 7 master's awarded. *Degree requirements:* For master's, internship or capstone experience. *Entrance requirements:* For master's, GRE. Additional exam requirements/recommendations for international students: Required—TOEFL. *Application deadline:* For fall admission, 6/30 for domestic

students. Applications are processed on a rolling basis. Application fee: $0. Electronic applications accepted. *Expenses: Tuition:* Full-time $17,370; part-time $965 per credit. *Required fees:* $138 per semester. *Financial support:* In 2014–15, 5 students received support, including 5 fellowships (averaging $5,000 per year); Fulbright scholarships also available. Financial award application deadline: 2/15; financial award applicants required to submit FAFSA. *Faculty research:* Urban public policy. *Unit head:* Dr. Annette Steinacker, Director, 773-508-3396. *Application contact:* Ron Martin, Assistant Director of Enrollment Management, 312-915-8950, Fax: 312-915-8905, E-mail: gradapp@luc.edu.

McMaster University, School of Graduate Studies, Faculty of Social Sciences, Department of Political Science, Hamilton, ON L8S 4M2, Canada. Offers international relations (PhD); political science (MA); public and the global economy (MA); public policy (PhD); public policy and administration (MA). MA program in public policy and administration offered jointly with University of Guelph. Part-time programs available. *Degree requirements:* For master's, thesis or alternative. *Entrance requirements:* For master's, minimum B+ average. Additional exam requirements/recommendations for international students: Required—TOEFL (minimum score 580 paper-based). *Faculty research:* Organizational theory, internationalization of public policy, water resource policies, political interest intermediation, comparative politics.

Mills College, Graduate Studies, Joint MBA/MPP Program, Oakland, CA 94613-1000. Offers MBA/MPP. *Faculty:* 3 full-time (2 women), 4 part-time/adjunct (3 women). *Students:* 10 full-time (8 women), 1 (woman) part-time. Average age 34. 16 applicants, 31% accepted, 3 enrolled. *Application deadline:* For winter admission, 2/1 priority date for domestic students, 12/15 priority date for international students. Application fee: $50. Electronic applications accepted. *Expenses: Tuition:* Full-time $31,620; part-time $7905 per course. *Required fees:* $1118. *Financial support:* In 2014–15, 5 students received support. *Application deadline:* 2/1; applicants required to submit FAFSA. *Faculty research:* Diversity and inclusion, applied econometrics, non-profit management, business communication and effective public speaking, social media, Internet marketing, organizational and cultural chance, economics of the family, urbanization and land conservation, gender and science, comparative race and ethnic relations. *Unit head:* Carol Chetkovich, Professor of Public Policy, 510-430-3370, Fax: 510-430-2159, E-mail: cchetkov@mills.edu. *Application contact:* Shrim Bathey, Director of Graduate Admission, 510-430-3309, Fax: 510-430-2159, E-mail: grad-admission@mills.edu. Website: http://www.mills.edu/academics/graduate/ppol/program/joint_MPPMBA.php

Mills College, Graduate Studies, Program in Public Policy, Oakland, CA 94613-1000. Offers MPP. *Faculty:* 2 full-time (1 woman), 3 part-time/adjunct (2 women). *Students:* 14 full-time (all women), 1 part-time (0 women). Average age 35. 44 applicants, 84% accepted, 23 enrolled. In 2014, 11 master's awarded. *Degree requirements:* For master's, thesis. *Entrance requirements:* For master's, GRE, SAT, or ACT, statement of purpose, resume. Additional exam requirements/recommendations for international students: Required—TOEFL (minimum score 550 paper-based; 80 iBT) or IELTS (minimum score 6). *Application deadline:* For fall admission, 1/15 for domestic students, 12/15 for international students. Applications are processed on a rolling basis. Application fee: $50. *Expenses: Tuition:* Full-time $31,620; part-time $7905 per course. *Required fees:* $1118. *Financial support:* In 2014–15, 22 students received support, including 32 fellowships with full and partial tuition reimbursements available (averaging $7,856 per year), 10 teaching assistantships with full and partial tuition reimbursements available (averaging $1,596 per year); scholarships/grants also available. Financial award application deadline: 2/1; financial award applicants required to submit FAFSA. *Faculty research:* Organizational culture and change, economics of the family, urbanization and land conservation, gender and science, comparative race and ethnic relations. *Unit head:* Carol Chetkovich, Program Director, 510-430-3370, E-mail: cchetkov@mills.edu. *Application contact:* Shrim Bathey, Director of Graduate Admission, 510-430-3309, Fax: 510-430-2159, E-mail: grad-admission@mills.edu. Website: http://www.mills.edu/publicpolicy

Mississippi State University, College of Arts and Sciences, Department of Political Science and Public Administration, Mississippi State, MS 39762. Offers political science (MA); public policy and administration (MPPA, PhD). *Accreditation:* NASPAA (one or more programs are accredited). Evening/weekend programs available. Postbaccalaureate distance learning degree programs offered (no on-campus study). *Faculty:* 11 full-time (2 women), 1 part-time/adjunct (0 women). *Students:* 38 full-time (20 women), 41 part-time (24 women); includes 31 minority (26 Black or African American, non-Hispanic/Latino; 1 American Indian or Alaska Native, non-Hispanic/Latino; 3 Hispanic/Latino; 1 Two or more races, non-Hispanic/Latino), 3 international. Average age 30. 32 applicants, 63% accepted, 14 enrolled. In 2014, 28 master's, 5 doctorates awarded. *Degree requirements:* For master's, thesis optional, comprehensive oral or written exam; for doctorate, thesis/dissertation, comprehensive oral and written exam. *Entrance requirements:* For master's, GRE, minimum GPA of 3.0 on the last two years of undergraduate courses or graduate work; for doctorate, GRE General Test, minimum graduate GPA of 3.35. Additional exam requirements/recommendations for international students: Required—TOEFL (minimum score 600 paper-based; 100 iBT); Recommended—IELTS (minimum score 7.5). *Application deadline:* For fall admission, 8/1 priority date for domestic students, 5/1 for international students; for spring admission, 12/1 priority date for domestic students, 9/1 for international students. Applications are processed on a rolling basis. Application fee: $60. Electronic applications accepted. *Expenses:* Tuition, state resident: full-time $7140; part-time $783 per credit hour. Tuition, nonresident: full-time $18,478; part-time $2043 per credit hour. *Financial support:* In 2014–15, 1 research assistantship with full tuition reimbursement (averaging $9,250 per year), 9 teaching assistantships with full tuition reimbursements (averaging $8,993 per year) were awarded; Federal Work-Study, institutionally sponsored loans, scholarships/grants, and unspecified assistantships also available. Financial award application deadline: 4/1; financial award applicants required to submit FAFSA. *Faculty research:* American politics, international relations, state and local government, comparative government, public administration. *Total annual research expenditures:* $807,000. *Unit head:* Dr. K. C. Morrison, Department Head, 662-325-2711, Fax: 662-325-2716, E-mail: kcmorrison@ps.msstate.edu. *Application contact:* Dr. Christine Rush, Graduate Coordinator, 662-325-2711, Fax: 662-325-2716, E-mail: clr449@msstate.edu. Website: http://www.pspa.msstate.edu/

Monmouth University, The Graduate School, Department of Public Policy, West Long Branch, NJ 07764-1898. Offers MA. Part-time and evening/weekend programs available. *Faculty:* 5 full-time (2 women), 1 part-time/adjunct (0 women). *Students:* 15 full-time (9 women), 22 part-time (14 women); includes 8 minority (3 Black or African American, non-Hispanic/Latino; 2 Asian, non-Hispanic/Latino; 3 Hispanic/Latino), 5 international. Average age 27. 18 applicants, 94% accepted, 11 enrolled. In 2014, 12 master's awarded. *Degree requirements:* For master's, comprehensive exam (for some programs), thesis (for some programs). *Entrance requirements:* For master's, minimum overall GPA of 2.75, personal statement (500 words maximum) on goals and interests in field, two letters of recommendation. Additional exam requirements/recommendations for international students: Required—TOEFL (minimum score 550 paper-based, 79 iBT), IELTS (minimum score 6), Michigan English Language Assessment Battery (minimum score 77) or Certificate ofAdvanced English(minimum score B2). *Application deadline:*

For fall admission, 7/15 for domestic students, 6/1 for international students; for spring admission, 11/15 for domestic students, 11/1 for international students. Application fee: $50. *Expenses: Tuition:* Full-time $18,072; part-time $1004 per credit. *Required fees:* $157 per semester. *Financial support:* In 2014–15, 37 students received support, including 37 fellowships (averaging $4,867 per year), 5 research assistantships (averaging $9,009 per year); career-related internships or fieldwork, scholarships/grants, and unspecified assistantships also available. Support available to part-time students. Financial award applicants required to submit FAFSA. *Faculty research:* Political theory, international relations and comparative politics, globalization, politics of language, family sociology, race-class-gender studies, the U.S. Senate and impact of domestic politics on U.S. foreign policy. *Unit head:* Dr. Stephen Chapman, Program Director, 732-571-3444, Fax: 732-263-5162, E-mail: schapman@monmouth.edu. *Application contact:* Andrea Thompson, Graduate Admission Counselor, 732-571-3452, Fax: 732-263-5123, E-mail: gradadm@monmouth.edu. Website: http://www.monmouth.edu/publicpolicy

Morehead State University, Graduate Programs, College of Business and Public Affairs, School of Public Affairs, Morehead, KY 40351. Offers public policy (MPA). *Accreditation:* NASPAA. Part-time and evening/weekend programs available. *Degree requirements:* For master's, comprehensive exam, thesis. *Entrance requirements:* For master's, GRE, thesis (two-page paper to be used as writing sample on personal, education or career goals). Additional exam requirements/recommendations for international students: Required—TOEFL (minimum score 500 paper-based). Electronic applications accepted.

National Louis University, College of Arts and Sciences, Chicago, IL 60603. Offers adult education (Ed D); counseling and human services (MS); language and academic development (M Ed, Certificate); psychology (MA, PhD, Certificate); public policy (MA); written communication (MS, Certificate). Part-time and evening/weekend programs available. Postbaccalaureate distance learning degree programs offered (minimal on-campus study). *Degree requirements:* For master's and Certificate, comprehensive exam (for some programs), thesis (for some programs); for doctorate, thesis/dissertation. *Entrance requirements:* For master's, MAT or GRE, 3 professional or academic references, interview, minimum GPA of 3.0; for doctorate, GRE General Test, MAT, or Watson-Glaser Critical Thinking Appraisal, three professional or academic references, statement of academic and professional goals, 3 years of experience in field, interview, master's degree, resume, writing sample; for Certificate, GRE, MAT, or Watson-Glaser Critical Thinking Appraisal, three professional or academic references, statement of academic and professional goals, interview, minimum GPA of 3.0. Additional exam requirements/recommendations for international students: Required—Department of Language Studies Assessment or TOEFL (minimum score 550 paper-based; 79 iBT). Electronic applications accepted.

New England College, Program in Public Policy, Henniker, NH 03242-3293. Offers MA. Part-time and evening/weekend programs available. Postbaccalaureate distance learning degree programs offered (no on-campus study). *Degree requirements:* For master's, thesis. *Entrance requirements:* Additional exam requirements/recommendations for international students: Recommended—TOEFL (minimum score 600 paper-based). Electronic applications accepted.

The New School, The New School for Public Engagement, Program in Public and Urban Policy, New York, NY 10011. Offers PhD. Part-time and evening/weekend programs available. *Degree requirements:* For doctorate, thesis/dissertation, qualifying exams. *Entrance requirements:* For doctorate, GRE General Test, MA in political science, urban policy or public policy. Additional exam requirements/recommendations for international students: Required—TOEFL (minimum score 600 paper-based; 100 iBT). Electronic applications accepted.

New York University, Robert F. Wagner Graduate School of Public Service, Executive Master of Public Administration Program, New York, NY 10010. Offers global public policy and management (EMPA); MSW/EMPA. EMPA in global public policy and management offered jointly with University College London. *Accreditation:* AACSB. Part-time programs available. *Faculty:* 1 full-time (0 women), 4 part-time/adjunct (2 women). *Students:* 11 full-time (7 women), 70 part-time (49 women); includes 20 minority (8 Black or African American, non-Hispanic/Latino; 5 Asian, non-Hispanic/Latino; 6 Hispanic/Latino; 1 Two or more races, non-Hispanic/Latino), 7 international. Average age 38. 94 applicants, 74% accepted, 46 enrolled. In 2014, 45 master's awarded. *Entrance requirements:* Additional exam requirements/recommendations for international students: Required—TOEFL (minimum score 100 iBT), IELTS (minimum score 7.5), TWE. *Application deadline:* For fall admission, 5/1 for domestic and international students. Application fee: $85. Electronic applications accepted. *Expenses:* Expenses: Contact institution. *Financial support:* In 2014–15, 5 students received support, including 10 fellowships with partial tuition reimbursements available (averaging $22,046 per year); scholarships/grants and health care benefits also available. Support available to part-time students. Financial award application deadline: 5/1; financial award applicants required to submit FAFSA. *Unit head:* David Elcott, Director, 212-992-9894, Fax: 212-995-4164, E-mail: david.elcott@nyu.edu. *Application contact:* Jay Esposito, Associate Director of Admissions, 212-998-7414, Fax: 212-995-4611, E-mail: wagner.admissions@nyu.edu. Website: http://wagner.nyu.edu/executivempa/

Northeastern University, College of Social Sciences and Humanities, Boston, MA 02115. Offers criminology and criminal justice (MSCJ); criminology and justice policy (PhD); economics (MA, PhD); English (MA, PhD); law and public policy (MS, PhD); political science (MA, PhD); public administration (MPA); public history (MA); security and resilience studies (MS); sociology (MA, PhD); urban and regional policy (MS); world history (MA, PhD). *Degree requirements:* For doctorate, variable foreign language requirement, comprehensive exam, thesis/dissertation. *Entrance requirements:* For master's and doctorate, GRE. Additional exam requirements/recommendations for international students: Required—TOEFL, IELTS. Electronic applications accepted.

Northwestern University, The Graduate School, School of Education and Social Policy, Program in Human Development and Social Policy, Evanston, IL 60208. Offers PhD. Admissions and degrees offered through The Graduate School. *Degree requirements:* For doctorate, comprehensive exam, thesis/dissertation. *Entrance requirements:* For doctorate, GRE General Test. Additional exam requirements/recommendations for international students: Required—TOEFL (minimum score 600 paper-based; 100 iBT). Electronic applications accepted. *Faculty research:* Individual development and the personal narrative; the life course and culture; development, intervention and culture; the life course and policy; analysis of policy effects on lives.

Northwestern University, School of Professional Studies, Program in Public Policy and Administration, Evanston, IL 60208. Offers global policy (MA); health services policy (MA); public administration (MA); public policy (MA). Postbaccalaureate distance learning degree programs offered.

Norwich University, College of Graduate and Continuing Studies, Master of Public Administration Program, Northfield, VT 05663. Offers fiscal management (MPA); international development and influence (MPA); policy analysis and analytics (MPA). Evening/weekend programs available. Postbaccalaureate distance learning degree programs offered (minimal on-campus study). *Faculty:* 13 part-time/adjunct (8 women).

Students: 70 full-time (23 women); includes 9 minority (4 Black or African American, non-Hispanic/Latino; 1 American Indian or Alaska Native, non-Hispanic/Latino; 1 Native Hawaiian or other Pacific Islander, non-Hispanic/Latino; 3 Two or more races, non-Hispanic/Latino). Average age 38. 48 applicants, 100% accepted, 35 enrolled. In 2014, 79 master's awarded. *Entrance requirements:* For master's, minimum undergraduate GPA of 2.75. Additional exam requirements/recommendations for international students: Required—TOEFL (minimum score 550 paper-based; 80 iBT), IELTS (minimum score 6.5). *Application deadline:* For fall admission, 8/8 for domestic and international students; for winter admission, 11/7 for domestic and international students; for spring admission, 2/16 for domestic and international students; for summer admission, 5/18 for domestic and international students. Applications are processed on a rolling basis. Electronic applications accepted. *Expenses:* Expenses: Contact institution. *Financial support:* In 2014–15, 34 students received support. Scholarships/grants available. Financial award applicants required to submit FAFSA. *Faculty research:* Pre-employment investigations for public safety professionals, sustainability programs and policy implementation, innovative voting procedures. *Unit head:* Dr. Rosemarie Pelletier, Program Director, 802-485-2767, Fax: 802-485-2533, E-mail: rpellet2@norwich.edu. *Application contact:* Lars Nielsen, Associate Program Director, 802-485-2853, Fax: 802-485-2533, E-mail: lnielsen@norwich.edu.
Website: http://online.norwich.edu/degree-programs/masters/master-public-administration/overview

The Ohio State University, Graduate School, John Glenn College of Public Affairs, Columbus, OH 43210. Offers public administration (MA, MPA); public policy and management (PhD). *Accreditation:* NASPAA (one or more programs are accredited). Part-time programs available. *Faculty:* 20. *Students:* 155 full-time (85 women), 45 part-time (35 women); includes 29 minority (11 Black or African American, non-Hispanic/Latino; 8 Asian, non-Hispanic/Latino; 6 Hispanic/Latino; 1 Native Hawaiian or other Pacific Islander, non-Hispanic/Latino; 3 Two or more races, non-Hispanic/Latino), 18 international. Average age 30. In 2014, 86 master's, 2 doctorates awarded. *Degree requirements:* For doctorate, thesis/dissertation. *Entrance requirements:* For master's, GRE General Test (for MPA), minimum GPA of 3.0 (for MA); for doctorate, GRE General Test. Additional exam requirements/recommendations for international students: Required—TOEFL (minimum score 600 paper-based; 100 iBT); Recommended—IELTS (minimum score 7.5). *Application deadline:* For fall admission, 12/1 priority date for domestic students, 11/1 priority date for international students; for winter admission, 12/1 for domestic students, 11/1 for international students; for spring admission, 11/15 for domestic and international students; for summer admission, 4/1 for domestic and international students. Applications are processed on a rolling basis. Application fee: $60 ($70 for international students). Electronic applications accepted. *Financial support:* Fellowships, research assistantships, teaching assistantships, Federal Work-Study, institutionally sponsored loans, and unspecified assistantships available. Support available to part-time students. *Unit head:* Dr. Trevor Brown, Dean, 614-292-4533, Fax: 614-292-4868, E-mail: brown.2296@osu.edu. *Application contact:* Graduate and Professional Admissions, 614-292-6031, Fax: 614-292-3656, E-mail: gpadmissions@osu.edu.
Website: http://glennschool.osu.edu/

Oregon State University, College of Liberal Arts, Program in Public Policy, Corvallis, OR 97331. Offers MPP, PhD. Part-time programs available. *Faculty:* 30 full-time (13 women), 3 part-time/adjunct (1 woman). *Students:* 73 full-time (45 women), 7 part-time (3 women); includes 10 minority (1 Asian, non-Hispanic/Latino; 7 Hispanic/Latino; 2 Two or more races, non-Hispanic/Latino), 27 international. Average age 30. 81 applicants, 49% accepted, 30 enrolled. In 2014, 26 master's awarded. *Entrance requirements:* For master's and doctorate, GRE. Additional exam requirements/recommendations for international students: Required—TOEFL, IELTS (minimum score 6.5). *Application deadline:* For fall admission, 8/1 for domestic students, 4/1 for international students; for winter admission, 12/1 for domestic students, 7/1 for international students; for spring admission, 2/1 for domestic students, 10/1 for international students; for summer admission, 5/1 for domestic students, 1/1 for international students. Application fee: $60. *Expenses:* Tuition, state resident: full-time $11,907; part-time $189 per credit hour. Tuition, nonresident: full-time $19,953; part-time $441 per credit hour. *Required fees:* $1472; $449 per term. One-time fee: $350. Tuition and fees vary according to course load and program. *Financial support:* Application deadline: 1/15. *Unit head:* Dr. Denise Lach, Director. *Application contact:* Dr. Brent Steel, Professor and Director, Public Policy Graduate Program, 541-737-6133, E-mail: schoolofpublicpolicy@oregonstate.edu.
Website: http://oregonstate.edu/cla/spp/

Penn State Harrisburg, Graduate School, School of Public Affairs, Middletown, PA 17057-4898. Offers criminal justice (MA); health administration (MHA); long term care (Certificate); non-profit administration (Certificate); policy analysis and evaluation (Certificate); public administration (MPA, PhD); public budgeting and financial management (Certificate); public sector human resource management (Certificate). *Accreditation:* NASPAA. *Unit head:* Dr. Mukund S. Kulkarni, Chancellor, 717-948-6105, Fax: 717-948-6452, E-mail: msk5@psu.edu. *Application contact:* Robert W. Coffman, Jr., Director of Enrollment Management, Admissions, 717-948-6250, Fax: 717-948-6325, E-mail: ric1@psu.edu.
Website: http://harrisburg.psu.edu/public-affairs

Pepperdine University, School of Public Policy, Malibu, CA 90263. Offers American politics (MPP); economics (MPP); international relations (MPP); public policy (MPP); state and local policy (MPP). *Faculty:* 6 full-time (2 women), 7 part-time/adjunct (1 woman). *Students:* 74 full-time (42 women), 10 part-time (5 women); includes 22 minority (11 Black or African American, non-Hispanic/Latino; 3 American Indian or Alaska Native, non-Hispanic/Latino; 3 Asian, non-Hispanic/Latino; 2 Hispanic/Latino; 1 Native Hawaiian or other Pacific Islander, non-Hispanic/Latino; 2 Two or more races, non-Hispanic/Latino), 21 international. 157 applicants, 65% accepted, 32 enrolled. In 2014, 52 master's awarded. *Entrance requirements:* For master's, GRE or GMAT, 2 letters of recommendation, resume, two essays. Additional exam requirements/recommendations for international students: Required—TOEFL. *Application deadline:* For fall admission, 6/15 for domestic students. Applications are processed on a rolling basis. Application fee: $50. Electronic applications accepted. *Financial support:* Institutionally sponsored loans and scholarships/grants available. Financial award application deadline: 5/1; financial award applicants required to submit FAFSA. *Unit head:* Dr. James R. Wilburn, Dean, School of Public Policy, 310-506-7490, Fax: 310-506-7494, E-mail: james.wilburn@pepperdine.edu. *Application contact:* Melinda E. van Hemert, Director of Recruitment and Career Services, 310-506-7492, Fax: 310-506-7494, E-mail: melinda.vanhemert@pepperdine.edu.
Website: http://publicpolicy.pepperdine.edu/

Portland State University, Graduate Studies, College of Urban and Public Affairs, Hatfield School of Government, Division of Public Administration, Portland, OR 97207-0751. Offers public administration (MPA); public affairs and policy (PhD). *Accreditation:* NASPAA (one or more programs are accredited). Part-time and evening/weekend programs available. *Faculty:* 15 full-time (9 women), 8 part-time/adjunct (2 women). *Students:* 112 full-time (78 women), 137 part-time (96 women); includes 45 minority (5 Black or African American, non-Hispanic/Latino; 7 American Indian or Alaska Native, non-Hispanic/Latino; 11 Asian, non-Hispanic/Latino; 12 Hispanic/Latino; 10 Two or more races, non-Hispanic/Latino), 15 international. Average age 34. 175 applicants, 59% accepted, 76 enrolled. In 2014, 75 master's, 8 doctorates awarded. *Degree requirements:* For master's, internship (MPA), practicum (MPH); for doctorate, comprehensive exam, thesis/dissertation. *Entrance requirements:* For master's, GRE (minimum scores: verbal 150, quantitative 149, and analytic writing 4.5), minimum GPA of 3.0, 3 recommendation letters, resume, 500-word statement of intent; for doctorate, GRE, 3 recommendation letters, resume, 500-word personal essay. Additional exam requirements/recommendations for international students: Required—TOEFL (minimum score 550 paper-based; 80 iBT), IELTS (minimum score 7). *Application deadline:* For fall admission, 4/1 for domestic students, 3/1 for international students; for winter admission, 9/1 for domestic students, 8/1 for international students; for spring admission, 11/1 for domestic and international students. Application fee: $50. *Expenses:* Tuition, state resident: part-time $222 per credit. Tuition, nonresident: part-time $527 per credit. *Required fees:* $22 per contact hour. $100 per quarter. Tuition and fees vary according to program. *Financial support:* In 2014–15, 7 research assistantships with full tuition reimbursements (averaging $6,249 per year), 3 teaching assistantships with full tuition reimbursements (averaging $6,846 per year) were awarded; career-related internships or fieldwork, Federal Work-Study, scholarships/grants, tuition waivers (partial), and unspecified assistantships also available. Support available to part-time students. Financial award application deadline: 3/1; financial award applicants required to submit FAFSA. *Faculty research:* Public budgeting, program evaluation, nonprofit management, natural resources policy and administration. *Total annual research expenditures:* $897,649. *Unit head:* Dr. Douglas Morgan, Chair, 503-725-8216, Fax: 503-725-8250, E-mail: morgandf@pdx.edu. *Application contact:* Megan Heljeson, Office Coordinator, 503-725-3921, Fax: 503-725-8250, E-mail: meloos@pdx.edu.
Website: http://www.pdx.edu/hatfieldschool/division-of-public-administration

Princeton University, Graduate School, Woodrow Wilson School of Public and International Affairs, Princeton, NJ 08544-1019. Offers public affairs (MPA, PhD); public policy (MPP); JD/MPA. JD/MPA offered jointly with Columbia University, New York University, Stanford University. Terminal master's awarded for partial completion of doctoral program. *Degree requirements:* For master's, internship; for doctorate, one foreign language, thesis/dissertation. *Entrance requirements:* For master's, GRE General Test, original policy memo; for doctorate, GRE General Test. Additional exam requirements/recommendations for international students: Required—TOEFL (minimum score 600 paper-based). Electronic applications accepted.

Queen's University at Kingston, School of Graduate Studies, School of Policy Studies, Kingston, ON K7L 3N6, Canada. Offers MIR, MPA. Part-time programs available. *Entrance requirements:* For master's, minimum B+ average. Additional exam requirements/recommendations for international students: Required—TOEFL. *Faculty research:* Public management, social policy, defense management, health policy, the third sector.

Rochester Institute of Technology, Graduate Enrollment Services, College of Liberal Arts, Department of Public Policy, MS Program in Science, Technology and Public Policy, Rochester, NY 14623-5604. Offers MS. Part-time programs available. *Students:* 4 full-time (1 woman), 2 part-time (1 woman), 1 international. Average age 28. 4 applicants, 50% accepted. In 2014, 2 master's awarded. *Degree requirements:* For master's, thesis. *Entrance requirements:* For master's, GRE and TOEFL, IELTS, or PTE for non-native English speakers, Recommended minimum GPA of 3.0. Additional exam requirements/recommendations for international students: Required—TOEFL (minimum score 570 paper-based; 88 iBT), PTE (minimum score 58), TOEFL (minimum score 550 paper-based; 79 iBT) or IELTS (minimum score 6.5). *Application deadline:* For fall admission, 2/15 priority date for domestic and international students; for spring admission, 12/15 priority date for domestic and international students. Applications are processed on a rolling basis. Electronic applications accepted. *Expenses:* Expenses: $1,673 per credit hour. *Financial support:* In 2014–15, 4 students received support. Research assistantships with partial tuition reimbursements available, teaching assistantships with partial tuition reimbursements available, career-related internships or fieldwork, Federal Work-Study, institutionally sponsored loans, scholarships/grants, and unspecified assistantships available. Support available to part-time students. *Faculty research:* Environmental policy, information and communications policy, energy policy, biotechnology policy. *Unit head:* Franz Foltz, Graduate Program Director, 585-475-5368, E-mail: fafgsh@rit.edu. *Application contact:* Diane Ellison, Associate Vice President, Graduate Enrollment Services, 585-475-2229, Fax: 585-475-7164, E-mail: gradinfo@rit.edu.
Website: http://www.rit.edu/cla/publicpolicy/academics/science-technology-and-public-policy-ms

Rutgers, The State University of New Jersey, Camden, Graduate School of Arts and Sciences, Department of Public Policy and Administration, Camden, NJ 08102. Offers education policy and leadership (MPA); international public service and development (MPA); public management (MPA); JD/MPA; MPA/MA. *Accreditation:* NASPAA. Part-time and evening/weekend programs available. *Degree requirements:* For master's, directed study, research workshop, 42 credits. *Entrance requirements:* For master's, GRE General Test, GMAT or LSAT, 3 letters of recommendation; resume. Additional exam requirements/recommendations for international students: Required—TOEFL (minimum score 550 paper-based), IELTS. Electronic applications accepted. *Faculty research:* Nonprofit management, county and municipal administration, health and human services, government communication, administrative law, educational finance.

Rutgers, The State University of New Jersey, Newark, Graduate School, Program in Public Administration, Newark, NJ 07102. Offers health care administration (MPA); human resources administration (MPA); public administration (PhD); public management (MPA); public policy analysis (MPA); urban systems and issues (MPA). *Accreditation:* NASPAA (one or more programs are accredited). Part-time and evening/weekend programs available. *Degree requirements:* For master's, comprehensive exam, thesis or alternative; for doctorate, thesis/dissertation. *Entrance requirements:* For master's, GRE, minimum undergraduate B average; for doctorate, GRE, MPA, minimum B average. Electronic applications accepted. *Faculty research:* Government finance, municipal and state government, public productivity.

Rutgers, The State University of New Jersey, Newark, School of Public Health, Newark, NJ 07107-1709. Offers clinical epidemiology (Certificate); dental public health (MPH); general public health (Certificate); public policy and oral health services administration (Certificate); quantitative methods (MPH); urban health (MPH); DMD/MPH; MD/MPH; MS/MPH. *Accreditation:* CEPH. Part-time and evening/weekend programs available. *Degree requirements:* For master's, thesis, internship. *Entrance requirements:* For master's, GRE General Test. Additional exam requirements/recommendations for international students: Required—TOEFL. Electronic applications accepted.

Rutgers, The State University of New Jersey, New Brunswick, Edward J. Bloustein School of Planning and Public Policy, Doctoral Program in Planning and Public Policy, New Brunswick, NJ 08901. Offers PhD. *Accreditation:* NASPAA. Part-time programs available. *Degree requirements:* For doctorate, comprehensive exam, thesis/dissertation. *Entrance requirements:* For doctorate, GRE, master's degree. Additional exam requirements/recommendations for international students: Required—TOEFL (minimum score 575 paper-based; 88 iBT). Electronic applications accepted. *Faculty*

research: Housing and community development, land use and transportation, politics and policy analysis, urban and regional economics, international development.

Rutgers, The State University of New Jersey, New Brunswick, Edward J. Bloustein School of Planning and Public Policy, Program in Public Policy, New Brunswick, NJ 08901. Offers MPAP, MPP, JD/MPAP, MBA/MPP, MCRP/MPP. JD/MPAP offered jointly with Rutgers, The State University of New Jersey, Camden. *Accreditation:* NASPAA. Part-time and evening/weekend programs available. *Entrance requirements:* For master's, GRE General Test. Additional exam requirements/recommendations for international students: Required—TOEFL (minimum score 575 paper-based; 88 iBT). Electronic applications accepted. *Faculty research:* Environment, social and health policy, public opinion, economics, education policy, community development.

Saint Louis University, Graduate Education, College of Education and Public Service, Department of Public Policy Studies, St. Louis, MO 63103-2097. Offers geographic information systems (Certificate); organizational development (Certificate); public administration (MAPA); public policy analysis (PhD); urban affairs (MAUA); urban planning and real estate development (MUPRED). *Accreditation:* NASPAA. Part-time programs available. *Degree requirements:* For master's, comprehensive exam (for some programs), thesis (for some programs); for doctorate, comprehensive exam, thesis/ dissertation, preliminary exams. *Entrance requirements:* For master's, GMAT, GRE General Test, or LSAT, letters of recommendation, resume; for doctorate, GMAT, GRE General Test, or LSAT, letters of recommendation, resumé, interview, transcripts, goal statement. Additional exam requirements/recommendations for international students: Required—TOEFL (minimum score 525 paper-based). Electronic applications accepted. *Faculty research:* Urban politics, brown fields, e-government, and administration, evaluation research, community development, electronic government and governance.

St. Mary's University, Graduate School, Department of English and Communication Studies, Program in Communication Studies, San Antonio, TX 78228-8507. Offers communication studies (MA); public communication, public policy and public leadership (Certificate); JD/MA. Part-time programs available. Postbaccalaureate distance learning degree programs offered (minimal on-campus study). *Faculty:* 7 full-time (3 women), 3 part-time/adjunct (2 women). *Students:* 4 full-time (all women), 13 part-time (9 women); includes 12 minority (2 Black or African American, non-Hispanic/Latino; 9 Hispanic/ Latino; 1 Native Hawaiian or other Pacific Islander, non-Hispanic/Latino), 2 international. Average age 27. 17 applicants, 29% accepted, 4 enrolled. In 2014, 1 master's awarded. *Degree requirements:* For master's, comprehensive exam. *Entrance requirements:* For master's, GRE General Test, MAT, GPA X Average GRE Score [(Verbal + Quantitative)] / Analytical writing minimum of 4.0 = 1350; Up to 10 percent of students in the program may be accepted with less than the minimum index if they demonstrate to the Graduate Communication Committee that they can perform at the graduate level. Additional exam requirements/recommendations for international students: Required—TOEFL (minimum score 550 paper-based; 80 iBT). *Application deadline:* For fall admission, 8/1 priority date for domestic students. Applications are processed on a rolling basis. Application fee: $0. Electronic applications accepted. *Expenses:* Tuition: Full-time $15,070; part-time $800 per credit hour. *Required fees:* $156 per semester. *Financial support:* In 2014–15, 1 research assistantship (averaging $7,000 per year) was awarded; career-related internships or fieldwork, Federal Work-Study, institutionally sponsored loans, scholarships/grants, and health care benefits also available. Financial award application deadline: 3/31; financial award applicants required to submit FAFSA. *Faculty research:* Media and power; rise of the political right; income inequality and social justice; development communication; interpersonal and rhetorical communication; social movements; gender, critical theory; cultural and postcolonial theory. *Unit head:* Dr. Kathleen Maloney, Associate Professor of English and Communication Studies, 210-431-2005, E-mail: kmaloney@stmarytx.edu.
Website: https://www.stmarytx.edu/academics/graduate/masters/communication/

San Francisco State University, Division of Graduate Studies, College of Health and Social Sciences, Public Administration Program, San Francisco, CA 94132-1722. Offers criminal justice administration (MPA); environmental administration and policy (MPA); nonprofit administration (MPA); public management (MPA); public policy (MPA); urban administration (MPA). *Accreditation:* NASPAA. *Expenses:* Tuition, state resident: full-time $6738. Tuition, nonresident: full-time $17,898; part-time $372 per credit hour. *Required fees:* $498 per semester. *Unit head:* Dr. Elizabeth Brown, Director of the School of Public Affairs and Civic Engagement, 415-817-4455, Fax: 415-817-4464, E-mail: mpa@sfsu.edu. *Application contact:* Dr. Sheldon Gen, Graduate Coordinator, 415-817-4458, Fax: 415-817-4464, E-mail: sgen@sfsu.edu.
Website: http://mpa.sfsu.edu/

Seton Hall University, College of Arts and Sciences, Department of Public and Healthcare Administration, South Orange, NJ 07079-2697. Offers nonprofit organization management (Graduate Certificate); public administration (MPA), including health policy and management, nonprofit organization management, public service: leadership, governance, and policy. *Accreditation:* NASPAA. Part-time and evening/weekend programs available. *Faculty:* 7 full-time (4 women), 6 part-time/adjunct (2 women). *Students:* 21 full-time (9 women), 30 part-time (14 women); includes 15 minority (8 Black or African American, non-Hispanic/Latino; 5 Asian, non-Hispanic/Latino; 2 Hispanic/ Latino), 1 international. Average age 32. 51 applicants, 63% accepted, 21 enrolled. In 2014, 28 master's awarded. *Degree requirements:* For master's, thesis or alternative, internship or practicum. *Entrance requirements:* Additional exam requirements/ recommendations for international students: Required—TOEFL. *Application deadline:* For fall admission, 7/1 priority date for domestic and international students; for spring admission, 11/1 priority date for domestic and international students. Applications are processed on a rolling basis. Application fee: $75. Electronic applications accepted. *Financial support:* Research assistantships, career-related internships or fieldwork, Federal Work-Study, scholarships/grants, and unspecified assistantships available. Financial award applicants required to submit FAFSA. *Unit head:* Dr. Roseanne Mirabella, Chair, 973-761-9384, E-mail: roseanne.mirabella@shu.edu. *Application contact:* Dr. Matthew Hale, Director of Graduate Studies, 973-761-9510, Fax: 973-275-2463, E-mail: matthew.hale@shu.edu.
Website: http://www.shu.edu/academics/artsci/political-science-public-affairs/

Simmons College, College of Arts and Sciences, Boston, MA 02115. Offers behavior analysis (MS, PhD, Ed S); educational leadership (MS Ed); elementary, middle or high school teacher (MAT); general and special education (MAT); public policy (MPP); special education (MS Ed, Ed S), including assistive technology, language and literacy, moderate and severe disabilities; teaching English as a second language (MA, CAGS); MA/MA; MA/MS. Part-time programs available. *Faculty:* 16 full-time (12 women), 1 (woman) part-time/adjunct. *Students:* 51 full-time (40 women), 85 part-time (73 women); includes 18 minority (6 Black or African American, non-Hispanic/Latino; 1 Asian, non-Hispanic/Latino; 9 Hispanic/Latino; 2 Two or more races, non-Hispanic/Latino), 2 international. 56 applicants, 84% accepted, 17 enrolled. In 2014, 306 master's, 11 doctorates awarded. Terminal master's awarded for partial completion of doctoral program. *Degree requirements:* For master's, thesis (for some programs). *Entrance requirements:* For master's, GRE. Additional exam requirements/recommendations for international students: Required—TOEFL (minimum score 600 paper-based; 100 iBT). *Application deadline:* For fall admission, 8/1 for domestic and international students; for spring admission, 12/15 for domestic and international students; for summer admission,

5/1 for domestic and international students. Applications are processed on a rolling basis. Application fee: $35. Electronic applications accepted. *Expenses:* Expenses: Contact institution. *Financial support:* Fellowships with partial tuition reimbursements, teaching assistantships with partial tuition reimbursements, and scholarships/grants available. Financial award applicants required to submit FAFSA. *Unit head:* Dr. Renee White, Dean, 617-521-2079. *Application contact:* Patricia Flaherty, Director, Graduate Studies Admission, 617-521-3902, Fax: 617-521-3058, E-mail: gsa@simmons.edu.
Website: http://www.simmons.edu/gradstudies/

Simon Fraser University, Office of Graduate Studies, Faculty of Arts and Social Sciences, School of Public Policy, Vancouver, BC V6B 5K3, Canada. Offers MPP. *Degree requirements:* For master's, thesis or alternative, internship. *Entrance requirements:* For master's, GRE (for applicants with non-Canadian degrees), minimum GPA of 3.0 (on scale of 4.33), or 3.33 based on last 60 credits of undergraduate courses. Additional exam requirements/recommendations for international students: Recommended—TOEFL (minimum score 580 paper-based; 93 iBT), IELTS (minimum score 7), TWE (minimum score 5). Electronic applications accepted. *Expenses:* Contact institution. *Faculty research:* Health policy, labor market and immigration, gender and discrimination, taxation policy, environmental policy.

Southern University and Agricultural and Mechanical College, Graduate School, Nelson Mandela School of Public Policy and Urban Affairs, Program in Public Policy, Baton Rouge, LA 70813. Offers PhD. *Degree requirements:* For doctorate, comprehensive exam, thesis/dissertation. *Entrance requirements:* For doctorate, GRE General Test. Additional exam requirements/recommendations for international students: Required—TOEFL (minimum score 525 paper-based).

State University of New York Empire State College, School for Graduate Studies, Program in Social Policy, Saratoga Springs, NY 12866-4391. Offers MA. Part-time and evening/weekend programs available. Postbaccalaureate distance learning degree programs offered (minimal on-campus study). *Degree requirements:* For master's, thesis, exam, final project. *Entrance requirements:* Additional exam requirements/ recommendations for international students: Required—TOEFL (minimum score 600 paper-based). Electronic applications accepted. *Faculty research:* Study of culture, society and mass communications, urban culture and policy, social decision-making processes.

Stony Brook University, State University of New York, Graduate School, College of Arts and Sciences, Department of Political Science, Program in Public Policy and Urban Development, Stony Brook, NY 11794. Offers MA. *Students:* 33 full-time (15 women), 11 part-time (6 women); includes 10 minority (2 Black or African American, non-Hispanic/ Latino; 4 Asian, non-Hispanic/Latino; 4 Hispanic/Latino), 13 international. 51 applicants, 84% accepted, 25 enrolled. In 2014, 34 master's awarded. *Entrance requirements:* Additional exam requirements/recommendations for international students: Required— TOEFL. *Application deadline:* For fall admission, 7/1 for domestic students, 5/15 for international students. Application fee: $100. *Expenses:* Tuition, state resident: full-time $10,370; part-time $432 per credit. Tuition, nonresident: full-time $20,190; part-time $841 per credit. *Required fees:* $1431. *Unit head:* Dr. Peter Salins, Program Director, 631-632-7667, E-mail: peter.salins@stonybrook.edu. *Application contact:* Carri Ann Horner, Graduate Program Coordinator, 631-632-7667, Fax: 631-632-4116, E-mail: carri.horner@stonybrook.edu.

Suffolk University, College of Arts and Sciences, Department of Philosophy, Boston, MA 02108-2770. Offers administration of higher education (M Ed, CAGS); ethics and public policy (MS). Part-time and evening/weekend programs available. *Faculty:* 5 full-time (1 woman), 1 part-time/adjunct (0 women). *Students:* 25 full-time (20 women), 34 part-time (25 women); includes 12 minority (1 Black or African American, non-Hispanic/ Latino; 1 Asian, non-Hispanic/Latino; 9 Hispanic/Latino; 1 Two or more races, non-Hispanic/Latino), 3 international. Average age 28. 72 applicants, 63% accepted, 19 enrolled. In 2014, 30 master's awarded. *Degree requirements:* For master's, internship or thesis; practicum (for M Ed). *Entrance requirements:* For master's, GRE General Test, MAT, GMAT, statement of professional goals, official transcripts, 2 letters of recommendation, resume. Additional exam requirements/recommendations for international students: Required—TOEFL (minimum score 550 paper-based; 80 iBT). *Application deadline:* For fall and spring admission, 6/15 priority date for domestic and international students. Applications are processed on a rolling basis. Application fee: $50. Electronic applications accepted. *Expenses:* Expenses: Contact institution. *Financial support:* In 2014–15, 35 students received support, including 35 fellowships (averaging $8,008 per year); career-related internships or fieldwork, Federal Work-Study, institutionally sponsored loans, and unspecified assistantships also available. Support available to part-time students. Financial award application deadline: 4/1; financial award applicants required to submit FAFSA. *Faculty research:* Predicting competent Head Start preschoolers, cultural differences, school counseling technology, sibling attachment in divorce cases, consequences of ethical breaches by human resource professionals. *Unit head:* Dr. Greg Fried, Chair of Philosophy Department, 617-573-8109, E-mail: gfried@suffolk.edu. *Application contact:* Cory Meyers, Director of Graduate Admissions, 617-573-8302, Fax: 617-305-1733, E-mail: grad.admission@suffolk.edu.
Website: http://www.suffolk.edu/college/departments/9942.php

Trinity College, Graduate Programs, Program in Public Policy Studies, Hartford, CT 06106-3100. Offers MA. Part-time and evening/weekend programs available. *Degree requirements:* For master's, thesis optional, departmental qualifying exam. *Entrance requirements:* For master's, minimum GPA of 3.0.

Tufts University, Graduate School of Arts and Sciences, Department of Urban and Environmental Policy and Planning, Medford, MA 02155. Offers community development (MA); environmental policy (MA); health and human welfare (MA); housing policy (MA); international environment/development policy (MA); public policy (MPP); MA/MS; MALD/MA. *Accreditation:* ACSP (one or more programs are accredited). Part-time programs available. *Faculty:* 13 full-time (5 women), 15 part-time/adjunct (8 women). *Students:* 62 full-time (43 women), 36 part-time (26 women); includes 24 minority (10 Black or African American, non-Hispanic/Latino; 7 Asian, non-Hispanic/ Latino; 6 Hispanic/Latino; 1 Two or more races, non-Hispanic/Latino), 10 international. Average age 30. 119 applicants, 81% accepted, 32 enrolled. In 2014, 64 master's awarded. *Degree requirements:* For master's, thesis, internship. *Entrance requirements:* For master's, GRE General Test. Additional exam requirements/recommendations for international students: Required—TOEFL (minimum score 550 paper-based; 80 iBT), IELTS (minimum score 6.5). *Application deadline:* For fall admission, 1/15 for domestic and international students. Applications are processed on a rolling basis. Application fee: $75. Electronic applications accepted. *Expenses:* Expenses: Contact institution. *Financial support:* Teaching assistantships with partial tuition reimbursements, career-related internships or fieldwork, Federal Work-Study, scholarships/grants, tuition waivers (partial), and unspecified assistantships available. Support available to part-time students. Financial award application deadline: 1/15; financial award applicants required to submit FAFSA. *Unit head:* Dr. Weiping Wu, Graduate Program Director. *Application contact:* Office of Graduate Admissions, 617-627-3395, E-mail: gradadmissions@tufts.edu.
Website: http://ase.tufts.edu/uep/

Public Policy

Union Institute & University, Individualized Master of Arts Program, Cincinnati, OH 45206-1925. Offers creativity studies (MA); health and wellness (MA); history and culture (MA); leadership, public policy, and social issues (MA); literature and writing (MA). Part-time programs available. *Faculty:* 4 full-time (2 women), 3 part-time/adjunct (2 women). *Students:* 14 full-time (11 women), 107 part-time (75 women); includes 36 minority (29 Black or African American, non-Hispanic/Latino; 3 American Indian or Alaska Native, non-Hispanic/Latino; 3 Hispanic/Latino; 1 Two or more races, non-Hispanic/Latino). Average age 40. *Degree requirements:* For master's, thesis. *Entrance requirements:* For master's, transcript, essay, 3 letters of recommendation, resume. *Application deadline:* For spring admission, 3/13 for domestic students. Applications are processed on a rolling basis. Application fee: $50. Electronic applications accepted. *Expenses: Tuition:* Full-time $26,640; part-time $719 per credit hour. *Required fees:* $216; $54 per semester. Part-time tuition and fees vary according to course load, degree level and program. *Financial support:* Career-related internships or fieldwork and tuition waivers available. Financial award applicants required to submit FAFSA. *Unit head:* Andrea Scarpino, Program Director, 802-828-8777. *Application contact:* Director of Admissions, 800-861-6400.
Website: https://www.myunion.edu/academics/masters-programs/master-of-arts/

Union Institute & University, PhD Program in Interdisciplinary Studies, Cincinnati, OH 45206-1925. Offers ethical and creative leadership (PhD), including Martin Luther King studies; humanities and culture (PhD), including Martin Luther King studies; public policy and social change (PhD), including Martin Luther King studies. Program requires participation in brief on-campus residencies twice each year (January and July). Postbaccalaureate distance learning degree programs offered (minimal on-campus study). *Faculty:* 6 full-time (4 women), 9 part-time/adjunct (7 women). *Students:* 92 full-time (51 women), 15 part-time (10 women); includes 37 minority (25 Black or African American, non-Hispanic/Latino; 4 American Indian or Alaska Native, non-Hispanic/Latino; 2 Asian, non-Hispanic/Latino; 3 Hispanic/Latino; 3 Native Hawaiian or other Pacific Islander, non-Hispanic/Latino), 1 international. Average age 46. *Degree requirements:* For doctorate, comprehensive exam, thesis/dissertation. *Entrance requirements:* For doctorate, master's degree, three letters of recommendation, statement of purpose. *Application deadline:* Applications are processed on a rolling basis. Application fee: $50. *Expenses: Tuition:* Full-time $26,640; part-time $719 per credit hour. *Required fees:* $216; $54 per semester. Part-time tuition and fees vary according to course load, degree level and program. *Financial support:* Federal Work-Study, scholarships/grants, and tuition waivers (partial) available. Financial award application deadline: 5/1; financial award applicants required to submit FAFSA. *Faculty research:* Social responsibility, ethical leadership, Martin Luther King studies. *Unit head:* Dr. Arlene Sacks, Dean, 513-861-6400, E-mail: arlene.sacks@myunion.edu. *Application contact:* Admissions Counselor, 800-486-3116.
Website: https://www.myunion.edu/academics/doctoral-programs/phd/

Universidad Autonoma de Guadalajara, Graduate Programs, Guadalajara, Mexico. Offers administrative law and justice (LL M); advertising and corporate communications (MA); architecture (M Arch); business (MBA); computational science (MCC); education (Ed M, Ed D); English-Spanish translation (MA); entrepreneurship and management (MBA); integrated management of digital animation (MA); international business (MIB); international corporate law (LL M); internet technologies (MS); manufacturing systems (MMS); occupational health (MS); philosophy (MA, PhD); power electronics (MS); quality systems (MQS); renewable energy (MS); social evaluation of projects (MBA); strategic market research (MBA); tax law (MA); teaching mathematics (MA).

Universidad del Este, Graduate School, Carolina, PR 00984. Offers accounting (MBA); adult education (M Ed); agribusiness (MBA); criminal justice and criminology (MA); curriculum and instruction - early education (M Ed); curriculum and instruction - elementary (M Ed); curriculum and instruction - English (M Ed); curriculum and instruction - Spanish (M Ed); human resources (MBA); information security management (MBA); information technology and Web business development (MBA); management (MBA); public policy (MPA); social work (MA), including clinical social work; special education (M Ed); strategic leadership (MBA).

Université de Montréal, Faculty of Arts and Sciences, Program in Societies, Public Policies and Health, Montréal, QC H3C 3J7, Canada. Offers DESS.

University at Albany, State University of New York, Nelson A. Rockefeller College of Public Affairs and Policy, Department of Public Administration and Policy, Albany, NY 12222-0001. Offers financial management and public economics (MPA); financial market regulation (MPA); health policy (MPA); healthcare management (MPA); homeland security (MPA); human resources management (MPA); information strategy and management (MPA); local government management (MPA); nonprofit management (MPA); nonprofit management and leadership (Certificate); organizational behavior and theory (MPA, PhD); planning and policy analysis (CAS); policy analytic methods (MPA); politics and administration (PhD); public finance (PhD); public management (PhD); public policy (PhD); public sector management (Certificate); women and public policy (Certificate); JD/MPA. JD/MPA offered jointly with Albany Law School. *Accreditation:* NASPAA (one or more programs are accredited). *Degree requirements:* For doctorate, one foreign language, thesis/dissertation. *Entrance requirements:* For doctorate, GRE General Test. Additional exam requirements/recommendations for international students: Required—TOEFL (minimum score 550 paper-based). Electronic applications accepted.

The University of Arizona, College of Social and Behavioral Sciences, Program in Public Administration, Tucson, AZ 85721. Offers public administration (MPA); public administration and policy (PhD). *Accreditation:* NASPAA. *Degree requirements:* For master's, internship of 400 hours; for doctorate, comprehensive exam, thesis/dissertation. *Entrance requirements:* For doctorate, GMAT or GRE, minimum graduate GPA of 3.5, letter of interest, 3 letters of recommendation, resume. Additional exam requirements/recommendations for international students: Required—TOEFL (minimum score 650 paper-based; 115 iBT). Electronic applications accepted. *Expenses:* Contact institution.

University of Arkansas, Graduate School, Interdisciplinary Program in Public Policy, Fayetteville, AR 72701-1201. Offers PhD. *Degree requirements:* For doctorate, thesis/dissertation. Electronic applications accepted.

University of California, Berkeley, Graduate Division, Graduate School of Public Policy, Berkeley, CA 94720-1500. Offers MPP, PhD, JD/MPP, MPP/MA, MPP/MPH, MPP/MS. *Degree requirements:* For doctorate, thesis/dissertation, qualifying exam. *Entrance requirements:* For master's and doctorate, GRE General Test, minimum GPA of 3.0, 3 letters of recommendation.

University of California, Berkeley, Graduate Division, Haas School of Business, PhD in Business Administration Program, Berkeley, CA 94720-1500. Offers accounting (PhD); business and public policy (PhD); finance (PhD); management of organizations (PhD); marketing (PhD); real estate (PhD). *Accreditation:* AACSB. *Students:* 76 full-time (29 women); includes 11 minority (4 Asian, non-Hispanic/Latino; 6 Hispanic/Latino; 1 Two or more races, non-Hispanic/Latino), 38 international. Average age 27. 489 applicants. In 2014, 14 doctorates awarded. *Degree requirements:* For doctorate, comprehensive exam, thesis/dissertation, written preliminary exams, oral qualifying exam. *Entrance requirements:* For doctorate, GMAT or GRE, minimum GPA of 3.0 in undergraduate and graduate coursework. Additional exam requirements/recommendations for international students: Required—TOEFL (minimum score 570 paper-based; 70 iBT), IELTS (minimum score 7). *Application deadline:* For fall admission, 12/10 for domestic and international students. Application fee: $90 ($110 for international students). Electronic applications accepted. *Financial support:* In 2014–15, 74 students received support, including 62 fellowships with full and partial tuition reimbursements available (averaging $30,000 per year), research assistantships with full and partial tuition reimbursements available (averaging $12,000 per year), teaching assistantships with full and partial tuition reimbursements available (averaging $13,000 per year); scholarships/grants, health care benefits, tuition waivers (full), unspecified assistantships, and transit passes, travel grants also available. Financial award application deadline: 12/10; financial award applicants required to submit FAFSA. *Faculty research:* Accounting, business and public policy, entrepreneurship, finance, management of organizations, marketing, operations and information technology management, real estate. *Unit head:* Dr. Martin Lettau, Director, 510-643-6349, Fax: 510-643-4255, E-mail: melhacker@haas.berkeley.edu. *Application contact:* Melissa Hacker, Director, Student Affairs, 510-642-3944, Fax: 510-643-4255, E-mail: melhacker@haas.berkeley.edu.
Website: http://www.haas.berkeley.edu/Phd/

University of California, Los Angeles, Graduate Division, School of Public Affairs, Program in Public Policy, Los Angeles, CA 90095. Offers MPP. *Entrance requirements:* For master's, GRE General Test, minimum GPA of 3.0. Additional exam requirements/recommendations for international students: Required—TOEFL. Electronic applications accepted.

University of California, San Diego, Graduate Division, School of Global Policy and Strategy, Program in Public Policy, La Jolla, CA 92093. Offers MPP. *Faculty:* 33 full-time (9 women), 20 part-time/adjunct (4 women). *Students:* 460 applicants, 120 enrolled. *Entrance requirements:* For master's, GMAT or GRE General Test. Additional exam requirements/recommendations for international students: Required—TOEFL (minimum score 90 iBT), IELTS (minimum score 7). *Application deadline:* For fall admission, 1/15 for domestic and international students. Applications are processed on a rolling basis. Application fee: $50. Electronic applications accepted. *Expenses:* Tuition, state resident: full-time $11,220; part-time $5610 per quarter. Tuition, nonresident: full-time $26,322; part-time $13,161 per quarter. *Required fees:* $570 per quarter. Tuition and fees vary according to program. *Unit head:* Sonja Steinbrech, Director of Enrollment, 858-534-7162, E-mail: ssteinbrech@ucsd.edu. *Application contact:* Admissions Representative, 858-534-5914, Fax: 858-534-1135, E-mail: gps-apply@uscd.edu.
Website: http://gps.ucsd.edu/academics/mpp.html

University of Chicago, Harris School of Public Policy, Master of Arts in Public Policy Program, Chicago, IL 60637. Offers public policy studies (AM); research methods (AM). *Students:* 10 full-time (2 women); includes 1 minority (Black or African American, non-Hispanic/Latino), 5 international. 29 applicants, 66% accepted, 9 enrolled. *Entrance requirements:* For master's, GRE General Test, graduate degree. Additional exam requirements/recommendations for international students: Required—TOEFL (minimum score 600 paper-based; 104 iBT), IELTS (minimum score 7). *Application deadline:* For fall admission, 1/10 for domestic and international students. Application fee: $75. Electronic applications accepted. *Expenses: Tuition:* Full-time $46,899. *Required fees:* $347. *Financial support:* Fellowships, Federal Work-Study, institutionally sponsored loans, and scholarships/grants available. Financial award application deadline: 1/10; financial award applicants required to submit FAFSA. *Unit head:* Daniel Diermeier, Dean. *Application contact:* Allison Bevan, Director of Admissions, 773-702-8401, E-mail: harrisadmissions@uchicago.edu.
Website: http://harris.uchicago.edu/degrees/masters-degree/one-year-am

University of Chicago, Harris School of Public Policy, Master of Public Policy Program, Chicago, IL 60637. Offers MPP. *Students:* 274 full-time (138 women), 11 part-time (6 women); includes 49 minority (14 Black or African American, non-Hispanic/Latino; 19 Asian, non-Hispanic/Latino; 14 Hispanic/Latino; 2 Two or more races, non-Hispanic/Latino), 132 international. 737 applicants, 57% accepted, 129 enrolled. *Entrance requirements:* For master's, GRE General Test. Additional exam requirements/recommendations for international students: Required—TOEFL (minimum score 600 paper-based; 104 iBT), IELTS (minimum score 7). *Application deadline:* For fall admission, 1/10 priority date for domestic and international students. Application fee: $75. Electronic applications accepted. *Expenses: Tuition:* Full-time $46,899. *Required fees:* $347. *Financial support:* Federal Work-Study, institutionally sponsored loans, and scholarships/grants available. Financial award application deadline: 1/10; financial award applicants required to submit FAFSA. *Unit head:* Daniel Deirmeier, Dean, 773-702-8400. *Application contact:* Allison Bevan, Director of Admissions, 773-702-8401, E-mail: harrisadmissions@uchicago.edu.
Website: http://harris.uchicago.edu/degrees/masters-degree/MPP

University of Chicago, Harris School of Public Policy, PhD Program in Public Policy, Chicago, IL 60637. Offers PhD. *Students:* 36 full-time (16 women); includes 4 minority (2 Asian, non-Hispanic/Latino; 1 Hispanic/Latino; 1 Two or more races, non-Hispanic/Latino), 22 international. 212 applicants, 12% accepted, 4 enrolled. *Degree requirements:* For doctorate, comprehensive exam, thesis/dissertation, four qualifying examinations. *Entrance requirements:* For doctorate, GRE General Test. Additional exam requirements/recommendations for international students: Required—TOEFL (minimum score 600 paper-based; 104 iBT), IELTS (minimum score 7). *Application deadline:* For fall admission, 12/3 for domestic and international students. Application fee: $75. Electronic applications accepted. *Expenses: Tuition:* Full-time $46,899. *Required fees:* $347. *Financial support:* Fellowships, teaching assistantships, institutionally sponsored loans, and scholarships/grants available. Financial award application deadline: 12/3; financial award applicants required to submit FAFSA. *Faculty research:* Health policy, municipal finance, cultural policy, urban policy, data science. *Unit head:* Dan Black, Director, 773-702-0623, E-mail: danblack@uchicago.edu. *Application contact:* Allison Bevan, Director of Admissions, 773-702-8401, E-mail: harrisadmissions@uchicago.edu.
Website: http://harris.uchicago.edu/degrees/phd

University of Colorado Boulder, Graduate School, College of Arts and Sciences, Department of Political Science, Boulder, CO 80309. Offers international affairs (MA); political science (MA, PhD); public policy (MA). *Faculty:* 26 full-time (8 women). *Students:* 53 full-time (20 women), 5 part-time (0 women); includes 6 minority (3 American Indian or Alaska Native, non-Hispanic/Latino; 1 Asian, non-Hispanic/Latino; 2 Hispanic/Latino), 5 international. Average age 30. 120 applicants, 26% accepted, 10 enrolled. In 2014, 11 master's, 4 doctorates awarded. Terminal master's awarded for partial completion of doctoral program. *Degree requirements:* For master's, comprehensive exam, thesis; for doctorate, one foreign language, thesis/dissertation. *Entrance requirements:* For master's, GRE General Test, minimum undergraduate GPA of 3.0; for doctorate, GRE General Test, minimum GPA of 3.5 (undergraduate), 3.0 (graduate). *Application deadline:* For fall admission, 12/15 for domestic and international students. Application fee: $50 ($60 for international students). Electronic applications accepted. *Financial support:* In 2014–15, 142 students received support, including 21 fellowships (averaging $2,782 per year), 1 research assistantship with full and partial tuition reimbursement available (averaging $39,356 per year), 49 teaching

assistantships with full and partial tuition reimbursements available (averaging $38,468 per year); institutionally sponsored loans, scholarships/grants, health care benefits, and unspecified assistantships also available. Financial award application deadline: 12/31; financial award applicants required to submit FAFSA. *Faculty research:* Political science, democracy, comparative government, political economics/economy, international relations. *Total annual research expenditures:* $752,632.
Website: http://polsci.colorado.edu/

University of Delaware, Center for Energy and Environmental Policy, Newark, DE 19716. Offers energy and environmental policy (MA, MEEP, PhD); urban affairs and public policy (PhD), including technology, environment, and society. *Degree requirements:* For master's, analytical paper or thesis; for doctorate, comprehensive exam, thesis/dissertation. *Entrance requirements:* For master's, GRE General Test, minimum GPA of 3.0; for doctorate, GRE General Test, minimum GPA of 3.5. Additional exam requirements/recommendations for international students: Required—TOEFL. Electronic applications accepted. *Faculty research:* Sustainable development, renewable energy, climate change, environmental policy, environmental justice, disaster policy.

University of Delaware, College of Arts and Sciences, School of Public Policy and Administration, Program in Urban Affairs and Public Policy, Newark, DE 19716. Offers governance planning and management (PhD); historic preservation (MA); social and urban policy (PhD); technology, environment and society (PhD); urban affairs and public policy (MA). Part-time programs available. Terminal master's awarded for partial completion of doctoral program. *Degree requirements:* For master's, analytical paper or thesis; for doctorate, thesis/dissertation. *Entrance requirements:* For master's, GRE General Test, minimum GPA of 3.0; for doctorate, GRE General Test, minimum GPA of 3.5. Additional exam requirements/recommendations for international students: Required—TOEFL. Electronic applications accepted. *Faculty research:* Political economy; social policy analysis; technology and society; historic preservation; urban policy.

University of Denver, Division of Arts, Humanities and Social Sciences, Institute for Public Policy, Denver, CO 80208. Offers MPP. *Faculty:* 4 full-time (0 women). *Students:* 20 full-time (13 women), 2 part-time (0 women); includes 4 minority (1 Black or African American, non-Hispanic/Latino; 3 Hispanic/Latino), 1 international. Average age 28. 32 applicants, 84% accepted, 8 enrolled. In 2014, 11 master's awarded. *Degree requirements:* For master's, thesis or alternative, policy memorandum capstone. *Entrance requirements:* For master's, GRE General Test, bachelor's degree, transcripts, personal statement, three letters of recommendation, interview. Additional exam requirements/recommendations for international students: Required—TOEFL (minimum score 587 paper-based; 95 iBT). *Application deadline:* For fall admission, 6/15 priority date for domestic and international students; for winter admission, 11/15 priority date for domestic and international students. Applications are processed on a rolling basis. Application fee: $65. Electronic applications accepted. *Expenses:* Expenses: $1,199 per credit hour. *Financial support:* In 2014–15, 21 students received support, including 3 teaching assistantships with full and partial tuition reimbursements available (averaging $4,583 per year); Federal Work-Study, scholarships/grants, and unspecified assistantships also available. Financial award application deadline: 2/15; financial award applicants required to submit FAFSA. *Faculty research:* Healthcare, urban planning, politics of mobility and migration, securities and regulatory policy, aging. *Unit head:* Richard Caldwell, Co-Director, 303-871-2468, Fax: 303-871-3066, E-mail: richard.caldwell@du.edu. *Application contact:* Erin Dietrich, Manager, Admissions and Communications, 303-871-3252, Fax: 303-871-3066, E-mail: erin.dietrich@du.edu.
Website: http://www.du.edu/ahss/centers/ipps/

University of Georgia, School of Public and International Affairs, Department of Public Administration and Policy, Athens, GA 30602. Offers public administration (MPA, PhD). *Accreditation:* NASPAA (one or more programs are accredited). *Degree requirements:* For master's, internship; for doctorate, thesis/dissertation. *Entrance requirements:* For master's and doctorate, GRE General Test. Electronic applications accepted.

University of Guelph, Graduate Studies, College of Social and Applied Human Sciences, Department of Political Science, Guelph, ON N1G 2W1, Canada. Offers comparative politics (MA); international development (MA); political science (MA); public policy and public administration (MA); the Americas (Canada emphasis) (MA). MA in public policy and public administration offered in collaboration with Department of Political Science of McMaster University. *Degree requirements:* For master's, thesis or paper. *Entrance requirements:* For master's, minimum B average during previous 2 years of course work, 4 year Honours Degree in Political Science. Additional exam requirements/recommendations for international students: Required—TOEFL. Electronic applications accepted. *Faculty research:* Political ethics, constitutional power.

University of Hawaii at Manoa, Graduate Division, College of Social Sciences, Public Policy Center, Honolulu, HI 96822. Offers Graduate Certificate. Part-time programs available. *Entrance requirements:* Additional exam requirements/recommendations for international students: Required—TOEFL (minimum score 500 paper-based; 61 iBT), IELTS (minimum score 5).

University of Kentucky, Graduate School, Martin School of Public Policy and Administration, Lexington, KY 40506-0032. Offers public administration (MPA); public policy (MPP); public policy and administration (PhD). *Accreditation:* NASPAA (one or more programs are accredited). *Degree requirements:* For master's, comprehensive exam; for doctorate, comprehensive exam, thesis/dissertation. *Entrance requirements:* For master's, GMAT or GRE General Test, minimum undergraduate GPA of 2.75; for doctorate, GMAT or GRE General Test, minimum graduate GPA of 3.0. Additional exam requirements/recommendations for international students: Required—TOEFL (minimum score 550 paper-based). Electronic applications accepted. *Faculty research:* Public financial management, education finance and policy, health finance and policy, welfare policy, program evaluation.

University of Louisville, Graduate School, College of Arts and Sciences, Department of Urban and Public Affairs, Louisville, KY 40208. Offers public administration (MPA), including human resources management, non-profit management, public policy and administration; urban and public affairs (PhD), including urban planning and development, urban policy and administration; urban planning (MUP), including administration of planning organizations, housing and community development, land use and environmental planning, spatial analysis. Part-time and evening/weekend programs available. *Students:* 76 full-time (35 women), 22 part-time (14 women); includes 16 minority (10 Black or African American, non-Hispanic/Latino; 1 Asian, non-Hispanic/Latino; 3 Hispanic/Latino; 2 Two or more races, non-Hispanic/Latino), 6 international. Average age 30. 89 applicants, 71% accepted, 33 enrolled. In 2014, 13 master's, 4 doctorates awarded. Terminal master's awarded for partial completion of doctoral program. *Degree requirements:* For master's, internship; for doctorate, comprehensive exam, thesis/dissertation. *Entrance requirements:* For master's, GRE General Test, minimum GPA of 3.0; for doctorate, GRE General Test, master's degree in appropriate field. Additional exam requirements/recommendations for international students: Required—TOEFL (minimum score 550 paper-based; 79 iBT). *Application deadline:* For fall admission, 7/15 for domestic students, 5/1 priority date for international students; for spring admission, 11/15 for domestic students, 11/1 priority date for international students; for summer admission, 4/1 priority date for international students. Applications are processed on a rolling basis. Application fee: $60. Electronic applications accepted. *Expenses:* Tuition, state resident: full-time $11,326; part-time $630 per credit hour. Tuition, nonresident: full-time $23,568; part-time $1311 per credit hour. *Required fees:* $196. Tuition and fees vary according to program and reciprocity agreements. *Financial support:* Fellowships, research assistantships, and health care benefits available. Financial award application deadline: 3/1. *Faculty research:* Housing and community development, performance-based budgeting, environmental policy and natural hazards, sustainability, real estate development, comparative urban development. *Unit head:* Dr. David Simpson, Chair, 502-852-8019, Fax: 502-852-4558, E-mail: dave.simpson@louisville.edu. *Application contact:* Libby Leggett, Director, Graduate Admissions, 502-852-3101, Fax: 502-852-4558, E-mail: gradadm@louisville.edu.
Website: http://supa.louisville.edu

University of Maryland, Baltimore County, The Graduate School, College of Arts, Humanities and Social Sciences, Department of Economics, Program in Economic Policy Analysis, Baltimore, MD 21250. Offers MA. Part-time programs available. *Faculty:* 25 full-time (9 women), 3 part-time/adjunct (1 woman). *Students:* 6 full-time (3 women), 11 part-time (4 women); includes 2 minority (both Black or African American, non-Hispanic/Latino), 7 international. Average age 26. 14 applicants, 36% accepted, 1 enrolled. In 2014, 9 master's awarded. *Degree requirements:* For master's, comprehensive exam, capstone research project. *Entrance requirements:* For master's, GRE General Test, undergraduate coursework in economic theory, econometrics, calculus. Additional exam requirements/recommendations for international students: Required—TOEFL. *Application deadline:* For fall admission, 7/1 priority date for domestic students, 3/1 priority date for international students; for spring admission, 1/1 priority date for domestic students, 9/15 priority date for international students. Applications are processed on a rolling basis. Application fee: $45. Electronic applications accepted. *Expenses:* Tuition, state resident: part-time $557. Tuition, nonresident: part-time $922. *Required fees:* $122 per semester. One-time fee: $200 part-time. *Financial support:* In 2014–15, 6 students received support, including 5 research assistantships with full and partial tuition reimbursements available (averaging $12,560 per year), 1 teaching assistantship with partial tuition reimbursement available (averaging $6,500 per year); Federal Work-Study, health care benefits, tuition waivers (full and partial), and unspecified assistantships also available. Support available to part-time students. Financial award application deadline: 4/15; financial award applicants required to submit FAFSA. *Faculty research:* International trade policy analysis, health and hospital policy evaluation, environmental policy analysis, economics of education, economic growth and development. *Total annual research expenditures:* $28,539. *Unit head:* Dr. David F. Mitch, Chair, 410-455-2157, Fax: 410-455-1054, E-mail: mitch@umbc.edu. *Application contact:* Dr. Tim H. Gindling, Graduate Program Director, 410-455-3629, Fax: 410-455-1054, E-mail: econ-masters@umbc.edu.
Website: http://www.umbc.edu/economics/grad_intro.html

University of Maryland, Baltimore County, The Graduate School, College of Arts, Humanities and Social Sciences, Department of Public Policy, Program in Public Policy, Baltimore, MD 21250. Offers economics (PhD); educational policy (MPP); evaluation and analytical methods (MPP); health policy (MPP); policy history (PhD); public management (MPP, PhD); urban policy (MPP, PhD). Part-time and evening/weekend programs available. *Faculty:* 9 full-time (3 women), 1 part-time/adjunct (0 women). *Students:* 50 full-time (29 women), 68 part-time (39 women); includes 28 minority (15 Black or African American, non-Hispanic/Latino; 8 Asian, non-Hispanic/Latino; 3 Hispanic/Latino; 1 Native Hawaiian or other Pacific Islander, non-Hispanic/Latino; 1 Two or more races, non-Hispanic/Latino), 9 international. Average age 35. 71 applicants, 58% accepted, 25 enrolled. In 2014, 23 master's, 13 doctorates awarded. Terminal master's awarded for partial completion of doctoral program. *Degree requirements:* For master's, thesis optional, public analysis paper; for doctorate, comprehensive exam, thesis/dissertation, comprehensive and field qualifying exams. *Entrance requirements:* For master's and doctorate, GRE General Test, 3 academic letters of reference, transcripts, resume, research paper. Additional exam requirements/recommendations for international students: Required—TOEFL (minimum score 550 paper-based; 80 iBT). *Application deadline:* For fall admission, 1/15 priority date for domestic students, 1/1 priority date for international students; for spring admission, 11/1 priority date for domestic students, 5/1 priority date for international students. Applications are processed on a rolling basis. Application fee: $50. Electronic applications accepted. *Expenses:* Expenses: $679 per credit resident; $1,114 non-resident. *Financial support:* In 2014–15, 26 students received support, including 1 fellowship with full tuition reimbursement available (averaging $12,000 per year), 25 research assistantships with full tuition reimbursements available (averaging $20,000 per year); career-related internships or fieldwork, Federal Work-Study, scholarships/grants, health care benefits, and unspecified assistantships also available. Support available to part-time students. Financial award application deadline: 1/15; financial award applicants required to submit FAFSA. *Faculty research:* Health policy, education policy, urban policy, public management, evaluation and analytical methods. *Unit head:* Dr. Donald F. Norris, Director, 410-455-1455, E-mail: norris@umbc.edu. *Application contact:* Sally F. Helms, Administrator of Academic Affairs, 410-455-3202, Fax: 410-455-1172, E-mail: gradpubpol@umbc.edu.
Website: http://www.umbc.edu/pubpol

University of Maryland, College Park, Academic Affairs, A. James Clark School of Engineering and School of Public Policy, Program in Engineering and Public Policy, College Park, MD 20742. Offers MS.

University of Maryland, College Park, Academic Affairs, School of Public Policy, Policy Studies Program, College Park, MD 20742. Offers PhD. *Degree requirements:* For doctorate, comprehensive exam, thesis/dissertation, written and oral exams. *Entrance requirements:* For doctorate, GRE General Test, writing sample. Electronic applications accepted.

University of Maryland, College Park, Academic Affairs, School of Public Policy, Programs in Public Policy, College Park, MD 20742. Offers MPP. *Accreditation:* NASPAA. *Entrance requirements:* Additional exam requirements/recommendations for international students: Required—TOEFL. Electronic applications accepted.

University of Massachusetts Amherst, Graduate School, College of Social and Behavioral Sciences, Center for Public Policy and Administration, Amherst, MA 01003. Offers MPP, MPPA, MPH/MPPA, MPPA/M Ed, MPPA/MBA, MRP/MPPA. Part-time programs available. *Students:* 23 full-time (13 women), 13 part-time (9 women); includes 9 minority (2 Black or African American, non-Hispanic/Latino; 3 Asian, non-Hispanic/Latino; 3 Hispanic/Latino; 1 Two or more races, non-Hispanic/Latino), 7 international. Average age 30. 99 applicants, 56% accepted, 23 enrolled. In 2014, 27 master's awarded. *Degree requirements:* For master's, thesis or alternative. *Entrance requirements:* For master's, GRE General Test. Additional exam requirements/recommendations for international students: Required—TOEFL (minimum score 550 paper-based; 80 iBT), IELTS (minimum score 6.5). *Application deadline:* For fall admission, 2/1 for domestic and international students. Applications are processed on a rolling basis. Application fee: $75. Electronic applications accepted. *Expenses:* Tuition, state resident: full-time $1980; part-time $110 per credit. Tuition, nonresident: full-time $14,644; part-time $414 per credit. *Required fees:* $11,417. One-time fee: $357.

Financial support: Fellowships with full and partial tuition reimbursements, research assistantships with full and partial tuition reimbursements, teaching assistantships, career-related internships or fieldwork, Federal Work-Study, scholarships/grants, traineeships, health care benefits, tuition waivers (full and partial), and unspecified assistantships available. Support available to part-time students. Financial award application deadline: 2/1; financial award applicants required to submit FAFSA. *Unit head:* Dr. Lee Badgett, Graduate Program Director, 413-545-3956, Fax: 413-545-1108, E-mail: info@pubpol.umass.edu. *Application contact:* Lindsay DeSantis, Supervisor of Admissions, 413-545-0722, Fax: 413-577-0010, E-mail: gradadm@grad.umass.edu.
Website: http://www.masspolicy.org/

University of Massachusetts Amherst, Graduate School, Interdisciplinary Programs, Dual Degree Program in Education and Public Policy and Administration, Amherst, MA 01003. Offers MPPA/M Ed. *Students:* 1 (woman) full-time. Average age 24. 2 applicants, 100% accepted, 1 enrolled. *Entrance requirements:* Additional exam requirements/recommendations for international students: Required—TOEFL (minimum score 550 paper-based; 80 iBT), IELTS (minimum score 6.5). *Application deadline:* For fall admission, 2/1 for domestic and international students. Applications are processed on a rolling basis. Application fee: $75. Electronic applications accepted. *Expenses:* Tuition, state resident: full-time $1980; part-time $110 per credit. Tuition, nonresident: full-time $14,644; part-time $414 per credit. *Required fees:* $11,417. One-time fee: $357. *Financial support:* Career-related internships or fieldwork, Federal Work-Study, scholarships/grants, traineeships, health care benefits, tuition waivers, and unspecified assistantships available. Support available to part-time students. Financial award application deadline: 2/1. *Unit head:* Dr. Lee Badgett, Professor, 413-545-3162, E-mail: szoller@pubpol.umass.edu. *Application contact:* Lindsay DeSantis, Supervisor of Admissions, 413-545-0722, Fax: 413-577-0010, E-mail: gradadm@grad.umass.edu.
Website: http://www.masspolicy.org/academics/mppa/public-policy-higher-education

University of Massachusetts Amherst, Graduate School, Interdisciplinary Programs, Dual Degree Program in Management and Public Policy and Administration, Amherst, MA 01003. Offers MPPA/MBA. *Accreditation:* AACSB. Part-time programs available. *Students:* 7 full-time (6 women); includes 2 minority (1 Asian, non-Hispanic/Latino; 1 Hispanic/Latino). Average age 30. 13 applicants, 85% accepted, 6 enrolled. *Entrance requirements:* Additional exam requirements/recommendations for international students: Required—TOEFL (minimum score 600 paper-based; 100 iBT), IELTS (minimum score 7). *Application deadline:* For fall admission, 2/1 for domestic and international students. Applications are processed on a rolling basis. Application fee: $75. Electronic applications accepted. *Expenses:* Tuition, state resident: full-time $1980; part-time $110 per credit. Tuition, nonresident: full-time $14,644; part-time $414 per credit. *Required fees:* $11,417. One-time fee: $357. *Financial support:* Career-related internships or fieldwork, Federal Work-Study, scholarships/grants, traineeships, health care benefits, tuition waivers (full), and unspecified assistantships available. Support available to part-time students. Financial award application deadline: 2/1. *Unit head:* Dr. Lee Badgett, Graduate Program Director, 413-545-3956, Fax: 413-545-1108, E-mail: szoller@pubpol.umass.edu. *Application contact:* Lindsay DeSantis, Supervisor of Admissions, 413-545-0722, Fax: 413-577-0010, E-mail: gradadm@grad.umass.edu.
Website: http://www.masspolicy.org/acad_mppa_mba.html

University of Massachusetts Amherst, Graduate School, Interdisciplinary Programs, Dual Degree Program in Public Policy and Administration and Public Health, Amherst, MA 01003. Offers MPH/MPPA. *Students:* 2 full-time (both women). Average age 42. *Entrance requirements:* Additional exam requirements/recommendations for international students: Required—TOEFL (minimum score 550 paper-based; 80 iBT), IELTS (minimum score 6.5). *Application deadline:* For fall admission, 2/1 for domestic and international students. Applications are processed on a rolling basis. Application fee: $75. Electronic applications accepted. *Expenses:* Tuition, state resident: full-time $1980; part-time $110 per credit. Tuition, nonresident: full-time $14,644; part-time $414 per credit. *Required fees:* $11,417. One-time fee: $357. *Financial support:* Career-related internships or fieldwork, Federal Work-Study, scholarships/grants, traineeships, health care benefits, tuition waivers, and unspecified assistantships available. Support available to part-time students. Financial award application deadline: 2/1. *Unit head:* Dr. Lee Badgett, Director, 413-545-2714, E-mail: szoller@pubpol.umass.edu. *Application contact:* Lindsay DeSantis, Supervisor of Admissions, 413-545-0722, Fax: 413-577-0010, E-mail: gradadm@grad.umass.edu.
Website: http://www.masspolicy.org/academics/mppa/public-policy-public-health

University of Massachusetts Amherst, Graduate School, Interdisciplinary Programs, Dual Degree Program in Regional Planning and Public Policy and Administration, Amherst, MA 01003. Offers MPPA/MRP. *Students:* 2 full-time (1 woman), 1 (woman) part-time. Average age 25. *Entrance requirements:* Additional exam requirements/recommendations for international students: Required—TOEFL (minimum score 550 paper-based; 80 iBT), IELTS (minimum score 6.5). *Application deadline:* For fall admission, 2/1 priority date for domestic students, 2/1 for international students. Applications are processed on a rolling basis. Electronic applications accepted. *Expenses:* Tuition, state resident: full-time $1980; part-time $110 per credit. Tuition, nonresident: full-time $14,644; part-time $414 per credit. *Required fees:* $11,417. One-time fee: $357. *Financial support:* Application deadline: 2/1. *Unit head:* Dr. Mark Hamin, Graduate Program Director, 413-545-2714, E-mail: szoller@pubpol.umass.edu. *Application contact:* Lindsay DeSantis, Supervisor of Admissions, 413-545-0722, Fax: 413-577-0010, E-mail: gradadm@grad.umass.edu.
Website: http://www.masspolicy.org/acad_mppa_planning.html

University of Massachusetts Boston, John W. McCormack Graduate School of Policy and Global Studies, Program in Public Policy, Boston, MA 02125-3393. Offers MS, PhD. Evening/weekend programs available. *Degree requirements:* For doctorate, comprehensive exam, thesis/dissertation, practicum, oral exam. *Entrance requirements:* For doctorate, GRE General Test. *Application deadline:* For fall admission, 1/15 for domestic students. *Expenses:* Tuition, state resident: full-time $2590; part-time $108 per credit. Tuition, nonresident: full-time $9758; part-time $406.50 per credit. Tuition and fees vary according to course load and program. *Financial support:* Research assistantships with full tuition reimbursements, teaching assistantships with full tuition reimbursements, career-related internships or fieldwork, Federal Work-Study, and unspecified assistantships available. Support available to part-time students. Financial award application deadline: 3/1; financial award applicants required to submit FAFSA. *Faculty research:* Political economy, public managerial control, healthcare policy, planning and public policy theory, economic development. *Unit head:* Dr. Constance Chan, Director, 617-287-6938, E-mail: connie.chan@umb.edu. *Application contact:* Peggy Roldan Patel, Graduate Admissions Coordinator, 617-287-6400, Fax: 617-287-6236, E-mail: bos.gadm@dpc.umassp.edu.

University of Massachusetts Dartmouth, Graduate School, College of Arts and Sciences, Department of Public Policy, North Dartmouth, MA 02747-2300. Offers public management (Graduate Certificate). Part-time programs available. Postbaccalaureate distance learning degree programs offered (no on-campus study). *Faculty:* 5 full-time (1 woman), 1 part-time/adjunct (0 women). *Students:* 18 full-time (8 women), 60 part-time (36 women); includes 20 minority (6 Black or African American, non-Hispanic/Latino; 1 Asian, non-Hispanic/Latino; 7 Hispanic/Latino; 6 Two or more races, non-Hispanic/Latino). Average age 34. 63 applicants, 92% accepted, 38 enrolled. In 2014, 12 master's, 14 other advanced degrees awarded. *Degree requirements:* For master's, portfolio of professional work. *Entrance requirements:* For master's, GRE or GMAT (waived with successful completion of environmental/educational policy graduate certificates at UMass Dartmouth), statement of purpose (minimum of 300 words), resume, 2 letters of recommendation, official transcripts; for Graduate Certificate, statement of purpose (minimum of 300 words), resume, 2 letters of recommendation, official transcripts. Additional exam requirements/recommendations for international students: Required—TOEFL (minimum score 600 paper-based). *Application deadline:* For fall admission, 3/1 priority date for domestic students, 2/1 priority date for international students; for spring admission, 12/15 priority date for domestic students, 11/15 priority date for international students. Applications are processed on a rolling basis. Application fee: $60. Electronic applications accepted. *Expenses:* Tuition, state resident: full-time $2071; part-time $86.29 per credit. Tuition, nonresident: full-time $8099; part-time $337.46 per credit. *Required fees:* $16,520; $712.33 per credit. Tuition and fees vary according to course load and reciprocity agreements. *Financial support:* In 2014–15, 1 research assistantship with full tuition reimbursement (averaging $12,900 per year) was awarded; career-related internships or fieldwork, Federal Work-Study, and unspecified assistantships also available. Support available to part-time students. Financial award application deadline: 3/1; financial award applicants required to submit FAFSA. *Faculty research:* Demographic analysis, legal and regulatory framework, human rights policy, globalization policies, women's public policy issues, educational leadership, environmental law. *Total annual research expenditures:* $829,000. *Unit head:* Chad McGuire, Graduate Program Director, 508-999-8520, Fax: 508-999-8374, E-mail: cmcguire@umassd.edu. *Application contact:* Steven Briggs, Director of Marketing and Recruitment for Graduate Studies, 508-999-8604, Fax: 508-999-8183, E-mail: graduate@umassd.edu.
Website: http://www.umassd.edu/cas/departmentsanddegreeprograms/publicpolicy/

University of Memphis, Graduate School, College of Arts and Sciences, Division of Public and Nonprofit Administration, Memphis, TN 38152. Offers MPA. *Accreditation:* NASPAA. Part-time and evening/weekend programs available. Postbaccalaureate distance learning degree programs offered (minimal on-campus study). *Faculty:* 5 full-time (3 women), 1 (woman) part-time/adjunct. *Students:* 22 full-time (17 women), 34 part-time (29 women); includes 37 minority (36 Black or African American, non-Hispanic/Latino; 1 Two or more races, non-Hispanic/Latino), 2 international. Average age 37. 28 applicants, 82% accepted, 3 enrolled. In 2014, 23 master's awarded. *Degree requirements:* For master's, comprehensive exam, thesis or alternative, internship. *Entrance requirements:* For master's, GRE General Test, GMAT, or MAT, minimum GPA of 3.0. Additional exam requirements/recommendations for international students: Required—TOEFL. *Application deadline:* For fall admission, 7/1 for domestic students, 5/15 for international students; for spring admission, 12/1 for domestic students, 9/15 for international students. Applications are processed on a rolling basis. Application fee: $35 ($60 for international students). *Financial support:* In 2014–15, 37 students received support. Fellowships, research assistantships with full tuition reimbursements available, career-related internships or fieldwork, Federal Work-Study, scholarships/grants, and unspecified assistantships available. Support available to part-time students. Financial award application deadline: 2/15; financial award applicants required to submit FAFSA. *Faculty research:* Nonprofit organization governance, local government management, community collaboration, urban problems, accountability. *Unit head:* Dr. Michael Howell-Moroney, Director, 901-678-3360, Fax: 901-678-2981, E-mail: mhwllmrn@memphis.edu. *Application contact:* Dr. Charles Menifield, Graduate Admissions Coordinator, 901-678-3360, Fax: 901-678-2981, E-mail: cmenifld@memphis.edu.
Website: http://www.memphis.edu/padm/

University of Michigan, Gerald R. Ford School of Public Policy, Ann Arbor, MI 48109. Offers MPA, MPP, PhD, JD/MPP, MBA/MPP, MD/MPP, MHSA/MPP, MPH/MPP, MPP/AM, MPP/MA, MPP/MIS, MPP/MS, MPP/MUP, MSW/MPP. Part-time programs available. *Degree requirements:* For doctorate, comprehensive exam, thesis/dissertation. *Entrance requirements:* For master's and doctorate, GRE. Additional exam requirements/recommendations for international students: Required—TOEFL (minimum score 600 paper-based; 100 iBT). Electronic applications accepted. *Faculty research:* U.S. social policy; international economic policy; quantitative policy analysis; environmental policy; health policy.

University of Michigan, Horace H. Rackham School of Graduate Studies, College of Literature, Science, and the Arts, Department of Economics, Ann Arbor, MI 48109. Offers applied economics (AM); economics (AM, PhD); public policy and economics (PhD); social work and economics (PhD); JD/PhD; MPP/AM. Terminal master's awarded for partial completion of doctoral program. *Degree requirements:* For doctorate, comprehensive exam, thesis/dissertation, oral defense of dissertation; preliminary exams in microeconomics, macroeconomics, and 2 fields. *Entrance requirements:* For master's and doctorate, GRE General Test. Additional exam requirements/recommendations for international students: Required—TOEFL (minimum score 600 paper-based; 100 iBT). Electronic applications accepted. *Faculty research:* Econometric analysis, finance, industrial organization, international trade, public finance, economic development, economic history, health, labor, natural resources, population studies, macro theory, micro theory.

University of Michigan, Horace H. Rackham School of Graduate Studies, College of Literature, Science, and the Arts, Department of Political Science, Ann Arbor, MI 48109. Offers political science (PhD); political science and public policy (PhD); social work and political science (PhD). *Faculty:* 47 full-time (17 women), 10 part-time/adjunct (4 women). *Students:* 126 full-time (63 women); includes 26 minority (9 Black or African American, non-Hispanic/Latino; 7 Asian, non-Hispanic/Latino; 7 Hispanic/Latino; 3 Two or more races, non-Hispanic/Latino), 28 international. 322 applicants, 13% accepted, 18 enrolled. In 2014, 17 doctorates awarded. Terminal master's awarded for partial completion of doctoral program. *Degree requirements:* For doctorate, comprehensive exam, thesis/dissertation, oral defense of dissertation, preliminary exam. *Entrance requirements:* For doctorate, GRE General Test. Additional exam requirements/recommendations for international students: Required—TOEFL. *Application deadline:* For fall admission, 12/15 for domestic and international students. Application fee: $75 ($90 for international students). Electronic applications accepted. *Financial support:* In 2014–15, 23 fellowships with full tuition reimbursements (averaging $18,600 per year), 5 research assistantships with full tuition reimbursements (averaging $18,600 per year), 35 teaching assistantships with full tuition reimbursements (averaging $18,600 per year) were awarded; health care benefits, tuition waivers, and unspecified assistantships also available. Financial award application deadline: 12/15. *Faculty research:* Political theory, American politics, world politics, comparative politics, methodology, public law. *Unit head:* Nancy Burns, Chair, 734-764-6313, Fax: 734-764-3522. *Application contact:* Kathryn Cardenas, Graduate Program Coordinator, 734-764-6313, Fax: 734-764-3522, E-mail: kmcard@umich.edu.
Website: http://www.lsa.umich.edu/polisci

University of Michigan, Horace H. Rackham School of Graduate Studies, College of Literature, Science, and the Arts, Department of Sociology, Ann Arbor, MI 48109. Offers public policy and sociology (PhD); social work and sociology (PhD); sociology (PhD). *Faculty:* 39 full-time (18 women), 9 part-time/adjunct (2 women). *Students:* 93 full-time

(59 women); includes 26 minority (6 Black or African American, non-Hispanic/Latino; 5 Asian, non-Hispanic/Latino; 6 Hispanic/Latino; 9 Two or more races, non-Hispanic/Latino), 11 international. Average age 33. 255 applicants, 13% accepted, 14 enrolled. In 2014, 15 doctorates awarded. *Degree requirements:* For doctorate, comprehensive exam, thesis/dissertation, oral defense of dissertation, preliminary exam. *Entrance requirements:* For doctorate, GRE General Test, letters of recommendation, writing sample, academic statement of purpose, personal statement, transcript. Additional exam requirements/recommendations for international students: Required—TOEFL (minimum score 560 paper-based; 84 iBT). *Application deadline:* For fall admission, 12/15 for domestic and international students. Application fee: $75 ($90 for international students). Electronic applications accepted. *Financial support:* In 2014–15, 85 students received support. Health care benefits available. *Faculty research:* Power, history and social change; gender and sexuality; race and ethnicity; economic sociology; social demography. *Total annual research expenditures:* $269,377. *Unit head:* Alford A. Young, Jr., Chair, 734-764-5554, Fax: 734-763-6887, E-mail: ayoun@umich.edu. *Application contact:* Thea Bude, Graduate Program Coordinator, 734-647-4428, Fax: 734-763-6887, E-mail: sociology.graduate.program@umich.edu.
Website: http://www.lsa.umich.edu/soc/

University of Michigan–Dearborn, College of Arts, Sciences, and Letters, Master of Public Policy Program, Dearborn, MI 48128. Offers MPP. Part-time and evening/weekend programs available. *Faculty:* 8 full-time (4 women). *Students:* 5 full-time (2 women), 6 part-time (3 women); includes 1 minority (Asian, non-Hispanic/Latino), 2 international. 7 applicants, 86% accepted, 3 enrolled. In 2014, 8 master's awarded. *Degree requirements:* For master's, thesis (for some programs). *Entrance requirements:* For master's, GRE, 3 letters of recommendation. Additional exam requirements/recommendations for international students: Required—TOEFL (minimum score 560 paper-based; 84 iBT), IELTS (minimum score 6.5). *Application deadline:* For fall admission, 8/1 priority date for domestic students, 5/1 priority date for international students; for winter admission, 12/1 priority date for domestic students, 9/1 priority date for international students; for spring admission, 4/1 priority date for domestic students, 1/1 priority date for international students. Application fee: $60. *Expenses:* Expenses: $613 per credit hour in-state, $351 for ninth credit hour and beyond in-state; $1,115 per credit hour out-state, $724 for ninth credit hour and beyond out-state; $267 in fees per term part-time, $329 full-time. *Financial support:* Career-related internships or fieldwork and scholarships/grants available. Support available to part-time students. Financial award applicants required to submit FAFSA. *Faculty research:* Peace and conflict studies, courts and public policy, public policy and the media, neighborhood revitalization. *Unit head:* Dr. Paul Draus, Director, 313-583-6628, Fax: 313-583-6700, E-mail: draus@umich.edu. *Application contact:* Carol Ligienza, Coordinator, CASL Graduate Programs, 313-593-1183, Fax: 313-583-6700, E-mail: caslgrad@umich.edu.
Website: http://www.umd.umich.edu/mpp/

University of Minnesota, Twin Cities Campus, Graduate School, Hubert H. Humphrey School of Public Affairs, Program in Public Policy, Minneapolis, MN 55455. Offers MPP, JD/MPP, MBA/MPP, MPP/MPH, MSW/MPP. Part-time programs available. *Students:* 81 full-time; includes 8 minority (5 Black or African American, non-Hispanic/Latino; 2 Asian, non-Hispanic/Latino; 1 Hispanic/Latino), 13 international. Average age 25. 276 applicants, 67% accepted, 81 enrolled. In 2014, 87 master's awarded. *Degree requirements:* For master's, thesis or alternative, internship or equivalent work experience. *Entrance requirements:* For master's, GRE General Test, minimum undergraduate GPA of 3.0. Additional exam requirements/recommendations for international students: Required—TOEFL (minimum score 600 paper-based; 100 iBT), IELTS (minimum score 7). *Application deadline:* For fall admission, 4/1 for domestic and international students. Applications are processed on a rolling basis. Application fee: $75 ($95 for international students). Electronic applications accepted. *Financial support:* In 2014–15, 68 students received support, including fellowships with full and partial tuition reimbursements available (averaging $9,000 per year), research assistantships with full and partial tuition reimbursements available (averaging $26,000 per year), teaching assistantships with full and partial tuition reimbursements available (averaging $18,000 per year); career-related internships or fieldwork, Federal Work-Study, scholarships/grants, health care benefits, tuition waivers (full and partial), and unspecified assistantships also available. Financial award application deadline: 1/15. *Faculty research:* Social policy, public and non-profit management and leadership, community and economic development, foreign policy and international affairs, women and public policy. *Unit head:* Laura Bloomberg, Associate Dean, 612-625-0608, Fax: 612-626-0002, E-mail: bloom004@umn.edu. *Application contact:* Amy Luitjens, Director of Admissions, 612-626-7229, Fax: 612-626-0002, E-mail: luitjens@umn.edu.
Website: http://www.hhh.umn.edu/degrees/mpp/

University of Missouri, Office of Research and Graduate Studies, Harry S Truman School of Public Affairs, Columbia, MO 65211. Offers grantsmanship (Graduate Certificate); nonprofit management (Graduate Certificate); organizational change (Graduate Certificate); public affairs (MPA, PhD); public management (Graduate Certificate); science and public policy (Graduate Certificate). *Accreditation:* NASPAA. *Faculty:* 12 full-time (5 women). *Students:* 83 full-time (51 women), 86 part-time (33 women); includes 22 minority (16 Black or African American, non-Hispanic/Latino; 1 American Indian or Alaska Native, non-Hispanic/Latino; 3 Asian, non-Hispanic/Latino; 2 Hispanic/Latino), 35 international. Average age 33. 152 applicants, 53% accepted, 51 enrolled. In 2014, 53 master's, 1 doctorate, 19 other advanced degrees awarded. *Entrance requirements:* For master's, GRE General Test, minimum GPA of 3.0. Additional exam requirements/recommendations for international students: Required—TOEFL (minimum score 550 paper-based; 79 iBT). *Application deadline:* For fall admission, 2/1 priority date for domestic and international students. Applications are processed on a rolling basis. Application fee: $55 ($75 for international students). Electronic applications accepted. *Financial support:* Fellowships, research assistantships, teaching assistantships, institutionally sponsored loans, scholarships/grants, traineeships, health care benefits, and unspecified assistantships available. Support available to part-time students. *Faculty research:* Public service ethics, history and theory, organizational symbolism and culture; program evaluation and social policy, with special emphasis on child development, education and health policies; organization theory and applied psychoanalytic theory; foreign policy and international political economy; health care delivery for persons with disabilities and health policy; survival strategies employed by low-income households; rural economic development, fiscal and economic impact analysis. *Unit head:* Dr. Bart Wechsler, Director, 573-882-3304, E-mail: wechslerb@missouri.edu. *Application contact:* Nicole Harris, Assistant Program Director for Student Services, 573-882-3471, E-mail: harrisnr@missouri.edu.
Website: http://truman.missouri.edu/

University of Missouri–St. Louis, College of Arts and Sciences, Department of Political Science, St. Louis, MO 63121. Offers American politics (MA); comparative politics (MA); international politics (MA); political process and behavior (MA); political science (PhD); public administration and public policy (MA); urban and regional politics (MA). Part-time and evening/weekend programs available. *Faculty:* 17 full-time (4 women), 6 part-time/adjunct (2 women). *Students:* 22 full-time (7 women), 35 part-time (20 women); includes 6 minority (5 Black or African American, non-Hispanic/Latino; 1 American Indian or Alaska Native, non-Hispanic/Latino), 5 international. Average age 35. 27 applicants, 63% accepted, 12 enrolled. In 2014, 6 master's, 3 doctorates awarded. Terminal master's awarded for partial completion of doctoral program. *Degree requirements:* For master's, thesis optional; for doctorate, thesis/dissertation. *Entrance requirements:* For master's, GRE General Test, 2 letters of recommendation; for doctorate, GRE General Test, 3 letters of recommendation. Additional exam requirements/recommendations for international students: Required—TOEFL (minimum score 550 paper-based; 79 iBT), IELTS (minimum score 6.5). *Application deadline:* For fall admission, 2/15 priority date for domestic and international students; for spring admission, 10/15 priority date for domestic and international students. Applications are processed on a rolling basis. Application fee: $50 ($40 for international students). Electronic applications accepted. *Expenses:* Tuition, state resident: full-time $7364; part-time $409.10 per hour. Tuition, nonresident: full-time $18,153; part-time $1008.50 per hour. *Financial support:* In 2014–15, 3 research assistantships with full and partial tuition reimbursements (averaging $10,800 per year), 10 teaching assistantships with full and partial tuition reimbursements (averaging $10,800 per year) were awarded; fellowships and career-related internships or fieldwork also available. Support available to part-time students. Financial award application deadline: 3/15; financial award applicants required to submit FAFSA. *Faculty research:* Public policy, urban politics and administration, American government. *Unit head:* Dr. David Kimball, Director of Graduate Studies, 314-516-5521, Fax: 314-516-5268, E-mail: umslpolisci@umsl.edu. *Application contact:* 314-516-5458, Fax: 314-516-6996, E-mail: gradadm@umsl.edu.
Website: http://www.umsl.edu/~polisci/

University of Missouri–St. Louis, Graduate School, Program in Public Policy Administration, St. Louis, MO 63121. Offers local government management (MPPA, Certificate); managing human resources and organization (MPPA); nonprofit organization management (MPPA); nonprofit organization management and leadership (Certificate); policy research and analysis (MPPA). *Accreditation:* NASPAA. Part-time and evening/weekend programs available. *Faculty:* 8 part-time/adjunct (5 women). *Students:* 16 full-time (9 women), 61 part-time (35 women); includes 23 minority (20 Black or African American, non-Hispanic/Latino; 1 Asian, non-Hispanic/Latino; 1 Hispanic/Latino; 1 Two or more races, non-Hispanic/Latino), 2 international. Average age 33. 34 applicants, 74% accepted, 16 enrolled. In 2014, 22 master's, 21 Certificates awarded. *Degree requirements:* For master's, exit project. *Entrance requirements:* For master's, 3 letters of recommendation. Additional exam requirements/recommendations for international students: Recommended—TOEFL (minimum score 550 paper-based), IELTS (minimum score 6.5). *Application deadline:* For fall admission, 7/1 priority date for domestic and international students; for spring admission, 12/1 priority date for domestic and international students. Applications are processed on a rolling basis. Application fee: $50 ($40 for international students). Electronic applications accepted. *Expenses:* Tuition, state resident: full-time $7364; part-time $409.10 per hour. Tuition, nonresident: full-time $18,153; part-time $1008.50 per hour. *Financial support:* In 2014–15, 2 research assistantships with full and partial tuition reimbursements (averaging $12,000 per year) were awarded; career-related internships or fieldwork also available. Financial award application deadline: 4/1; financial award applicants required to submit FAFSA. *Faculty research:* Urban policy, public finance, evaluation. *Unit head:* Dr. Deborah Balser, Director, 314-516-5145, Fax: 314-516-5210, E-mail: balserd@msx.umsl.edu. *Application contact:* 314-516-5458, Fax: 314-516-6996, E-mail: gradadm@umsl.edu.
Website: http://www.umsl.edu/divisions/graduate/mppa/

University of Nebraska–Lincoln, Graduate College, College of Arts and Sciences, Department of Political Science, Lincoln, NE 68588. Offers political science (MA, PhD); public policy analysis (Graduate Certificate). *Degree requirements:* For master's, thesis optional; for doctorate, variable foreign language requirement, comprehensive exam, thesis/dissertation. *Entrance requirements:* For master's and doctorate, GRE General Test, writing sample. Additional exam requirements/recommendations for international students: Required—TOEFL (minimum score 600 paper-based). Electronic applications accepted. *Faculty research:* Public policy; comparative politics; international relations; political theory, behavior, and methodology; American politics.

University of New Brunswick Fredericton, School of Graduate Studies, Policy Studies Program, Fredericton, NB E3B 5A3, Canada. Offers citizen engagement/dispute resolution (M Phil); community development (M Phil); international development (M Phil); leadership (M Phil); sustainability/environmental issues (M Phil); worldviews (M Phil). Part-time programs available. *Faculty:* 17 full-time (9 women), 1 part-time/adjunct (0 women). *Students:* 14 full-time (7 women), 4 part-time (3 women). In 2014, 3 master's awarded. *Degree requirements:* For master's, thesis, report. *Entrance requirements:* For master's, minimum GPA of 3.5. Additional exam requirements/recommendations for international students: Required—TWE (minimum score 5.5), TOEFL (minimum score 600 paper-based; 100 iBT) or IELTS (minimum score 7). *Application deadline:* Applications are processed on a rolling basis. Application fee: $50 Canadian dollars. Electronic applications accepted. *Financial support:* In 2014–15, 3 fellowships, research assistantships (averaging $5,600 per year), teaching assistantships (averaging $4,400 per year) were awarded. *Faculty research:* International development, worldviews, citizenship/dispute resolution, sustainability/environmental issues, leadership, community development. *Unit head:* Dr. Linda Eyre, Dean of Graduate Studies, 506-447-3044, Fax: 506-453-4817, E-mail: gradidst@unb.ca. *Application contact:* Janet Amirault, Graduate Secretary, 506-458-7558, Fax: 506-453-4817, E-mail: jamiraul@unb.ca.
Website: http://www.unb.ca/gradstudies/programs/mphil/index.html

The University of North Carolina at Chapel Hill, Graduate School, College of Arts and Sciences, Department of Public Policy, Chapel Hill, NC 27599. Offers PhD. *Degree requirements:* For doctorate, thesis/dissertation. *Entrance requirements:* For doctorate, GRE General Test. Electronic applications accepted. *Faculty research:* Environmental policy; energy policy; economic development and science and technology policy; social policy; welfare, education and low-income communities.

The University of North Carolina at Charlotte, College of Liberal Arts and Sciences, Department of Political Science and Public Administration, Charlotte, NC 28223-0001. Offers emergency management (Graduate Certificate); non-profit management (Graduate Certificate); public administration (MPA), including arts administration, emergency management, non-profit management, public finance; public finance (Graduate Certificate); urban management and policy (Graduate Certificate). *Accreditation:* NASPAA. Part-time and evening/weekend programs available. *Faculty:* 15 full-time (8 women), 4 part-time/adjunct (1 woman). *Students:* 16 full-time (10 women), 83 part-time (51 women); includes 32 minority (21 Black or African American, non-Hispanic/Latino; 1 Asian, non-Hispanic/Latino; 7 Hispanic/Latino; 3 Two or more races, non-Hispanic/Latino). Average age 30. 60 applicants, 65% accepted, 25 enrolled. In 2014, 23 master's, 11 other advanced degrees awarded. Terminal master's awarded for partial completion of doctoral program. *Degree requirements:* For master's, thesis or alternative. *Entrance requirements:* For master's, GRE General Test or MAT, minimum GPA of 3.0 in undergraduate major, 2.75 overall. Additional exam requirements/recommendations for international students: Required—TOEFL (minimum score 557 paper-based; 83 iBT). *Application deadline:* For fall admission, 5/1 priority date for domestic students, 5/1 for international students; for spring admission, 10/1 priority date for domestic students, 10/1 for international students. Applications are processed on a rolling basis. Application fee: $75. Electronic applications accepted. *Expenses:* Tuition, state resident: full-time $4008. Tuition, nonresident: full-time $16,295. *Required fees:*

$2755. Tuition and fees vary according to course load and program. *Financial support:* In 2014–15, 7 students received support, including 7 research assistantships (averaging $6,857 per year); career-related internships or fieldwork, Federal Work-Study, institutionally sponsored loans, scholarships/grants, and unspecified assistantships also available. Support available to part-time students. Financial award application deadline: 4/1; financial award applicants required to submit FAFSA. *Faculty research:* Health policy and politics, managed care, issues of ethnic and racial disparities in health, aging policies, Central Asia. *Total annual research expenditures:* $348,793. *Unit head:* Dr. Greg Weeks, Chair, 704-687-7574, Fax: 704-687-1400, E-mail: gbweeks@uncc.edu. *Application contact:* Kathy B. Giddings, Director of Graduate Admissions, 704-687-5503, Fax: 704-687-1668, E-mail: gradadm@uncc.edu.
Website: https://politicalscience.uncc.edu/graduate

The University of North Carolina at Charlotte, College of Liberal Arts and Sciences, Interdisciplinary Liberal Arts and Sciences Programs, Charlotte, NC 28223-0001. Offers gerontology (MA, Graduate Certificate); Latin American studies (MA); liberal studies (MA); organizational psychology (PhD); public policy (PhD); women's studies (Graduate Certificate). *Faculty:* 6 full-time (3 women), 5 part-time/adjunct (all women). *Students:* 58 full-time (31 women), 55 part-time (45 women); includes 24 minority (15 Black or African American, non-Hispanic/Latino; 1 Asian, non-Hispanic/Latino; 6 Hispanic/Latino; 1 Native Hawaiian or other Pacific Islander, non-Hispanic/Latino; 1 Two or more races, non-Hispanic/Latino), 12 international. Average age 33. 96 applicants, 46% accepted, 29 enrolled. In 2014, 11 master's, 8 doctorates, 15 other advanced degrees awarded. Terminal master's awarded for partial completion of doctoral program. *Degree requirements:* For master's, thesis or alternative, comprehensive exam or project; for doctorate, thesis/dissertation. *Entrance requirements:* For master's, GRE General Test or MAT, minimum GPA of 3.0 during previous 2 years, 2.75 overall; for doctorate, GRE, letters of recommendation. Additional exam requirements/recommendations for international students: Required—TOEFL (minimum score 557 paper-based; 83 iBT). *Application deadline:* For fall admission, 5/1 priority date for domestic students, 5/1 for international students; for spring admission, 10/1 priority date for domestic students, 10/1 for international students. Applications are processed on a rolling basis. Application fee: $75. Electronic applications accepted. *Expenses:* Tuition, state resident: full-time $4008. Tuition, nonresident: full-time $16,295. *Required fees:* $2755. Tuition and fees vary according to course load and program. *Financial support:* In 2014–15, 24 students received support, including 20 research assistantships (averaging $10,400 per year), 4 teaching assistantships (averaging $8,250 per year); career-related internships or fieldwork, institutionally sponsored loans, scholarships/grants, and unspecified assistantships also available. Support available to part-time students. Financial award application deadline: 4/1; financial award applicants required to submit FAFSA. *Total annual research expenditures:* $15,045. *Unit head:* Dr. Nancy A. Gutierrez, Dean, 704-687-0081, Fax: 704-687-4347, E-mail: ngutierr@uncc.edu. *Application contact:* Kathy B. Giddings, Director of Graduate Admissions, 704-687-5503, Fax: 704-687-3279, E-mail: gradadm@uncc.edu.
Website: http://www.lbst.uncc.edu/

University of Northern Iowa, Graduate College, College of Social and Behavioral Sciences, MPP Program in Public Policy, Cedar Falls, IA 50614. Offers MPP. Part-time programs available. *Students:* 8 full-time (5 women), 2 part-time (1 woman); includes 1 minority (Hispanic/Latino), 3 international. 8 applicants. In 2014, 11 master's awarded. *Degree requirements:* For master's, comprehensive exam (for some programs). *Entrance requirements:* For master's, minimum GPA of 3.0. Additional exam requirements/recommendations for international students: Required—TOEFL (minimum score 500 paper-based; 61 iBT). *Application deadline:* For fall admission, 3/1 priority date for domestic students. Applications are processed on a rolling basis. Application fee: $50 ($70 for international students). Electronic applications accepted. *Expenses:* Tuition, state resident: full-time $7912; part-time $880 per credit. Tuition, nonresident: full-time $17,906; part-time $880 per credit. *Required fees:* $1101; $325.50 per credit. $465.63 per semester. Tuition and fees vary according to course load and program. *Financial support:* Career-related internships or fieldwork, Federal Work-Study, institutionally sponsored loans, tuition waivers (full), and unspecified assistantships available. Financial award application deadline: 2/1. *Unit head:* Dr. Carol A. Weisenberger, Interim Director, 319-273-2910, Fax: 319-273-7126, E-mail: carol.weisenberger@uni.edu. *Application contact:* Laurie S. Russell, Record Analyst, 319-273-2623, Fax: 319-273-2885, E-mail: laurie.russell@uni.edu.

University of Oklahoma, College of Arts and Sciences, Department of Political Science, Program in Public Administration, Norman, OK 73019. Offers non-profit management (MPA); public administration (MPA); public policy (MPA). Part-time and evening/weekend programs available. *Students:* 23 full-time (13 women), 23 part-time (11 women); includes 14 minority (3 Black or African American, non-Hispanic/Latino; 3 American Indian or Alaska Native, non-Hispanic/Latino; 1 Asian, non-Hispanic/Latino; 2 Hispanic/Latino; 5 Two or more races, non-Hispanic/Latino). Average age 30. 25 applicants, 72% accepted, 12 enrolled. In 2014, 28 master's awarded. Terminal master's awarded for partial completion of doctoral program. *Degree requirements:* For master's, comprehensive exam, thesis or alternative, 36 hours. *Entrance requirements:* For master's, GRE, statement of purpose, two letters of recommendation. Additional exam requirements/recommendations for international students: Required—TOEFL (minimum score 100 iBT). *Application deadline:* For fall admission, 2/15 for domestic students, 4/1 for international students; for spring admission, 10/1 for domestic students, 9/1 for international students; for summer admission, 2/1 for international students. Applications are processed on a rolling basis. Application fee: $50 ($100 for international students). Electronic applications accepted. *Expenses:* Tuition, state resident: full-time $4394; part-time $183.10 per credit hour. Tuition, nonresident: full-time $16,970; part-time $707.10 per credit hour. *Required fees:* $2892; $109.95 per credit hour. $126.50 per semester. *Financial support:* In 2014–15, 27 students received support. Career-related internships or fieldwork, scholarships/grants, health care benefits, and unspecified assistantships available. Support available to part-time students. Financial award application deadline: 6/1; financial award applicants required to submit FAFSA. *Faculty research:* Public management, nonprofit administration, public policy, policy analysis, program evaluation. *Unit head:* Dr. Alisa Fryar, Director of Graduate Programs in Public Administration, 405-325-1845, Fax: 405-325-0718, E-mail: ahicklin@ou.edu. *Application contact:* Jeff Alexander, Graduate Programs Coordinator, 405-325-1845, Fax: 405-325-0718, E-mail: jjalexander@ou.edu.
Website: http://psc.ou.edu/mpa

University of Oregon, Graduate School, School of Architecture and Allied Arts, Department of Planning, Public Policy, and Management, Program in Public Policy and Management, Eugene, OR 97403. Offers MA; MPA, MS. *Accreditation:* NASPAA. Part-time and evening/weekend programs available. *Degree requirements:* For master's, thesis. *Entrance requirements:* For master's, minimum GPA of 3.0. Additional exam requirements/recommendations for international students: Required—TOEFL. *Faculty research:* Community economic development, families in poverty, health services.

University of Pennsylvania, Wharton School, Department of Business and Public Policy, Philadelphia, PA 19104. Offers MBA, PhD. *Degree requirements:* For doctorate, thesis/dissertation. *Entrance requirements:* For doctorate, GRE General Test. *Faculty*

research: International policy, business and government, regulation, urban development and policy, transportation.

University of Pittsburgh, Graduate School of Public and International Affairs, Doctoral Program in Public and International Affairs, Pittsburgh, PA 15260. Offers international affairs (PhD). *Accreditation:* NASPAA. *Faculty:* 34 full-time (12 women), 11 part-time/adjunct (3 women). *Students:* 32 full-time (15 women); includes 1 minority (Asian, non-Hispanic/Latino), 12 international. Average age 36. 72 applicants, 21% accepted, 7 enrolled. In 2014, 3 doctorates awarded. *Degree requirements:* For doctorate, comprehensive exam, thesis/dissertation, mid-term evaluation, preliminary exam, annual review. *Entrance requirements:* For doctorate, GRE or GMAT, 2 letters of recommendation, resume, undergraduate transcripts, personal statement, writing sample. Additional exam requirements/recommendations for international students: Required—TOEFL (minimum score 600 paper-based; 100 iBT); Recommended—IELTS (minimum score 7), TWE (minimum score 4). *Application deadline:* For fall admission, 1/15 for domestic and international students. Application fee: $50. Electronic applications accepted. *Expenses:* Tuition, state resident: full-time $20,742; part-time $838 per credit. Tuition, nonresident: full-time $33,960; part-time $1389 per credit. *Required fees:* $800; $205 per term. Tuition and fees vary according to program. *Financial support:* In 2014–15, 15 students received support, including 15 research assistantships (averaging $13,980 per year). Financial award application deadline: 1/15; financial award applicants required to submit FAFSA. *Faculty research:* International political economy, international development, public policy and management, international security. *Total annual research expenditures:* $640,844. *Unit head:* Dr. Nuno Themudo, Program Director, 412-648-7632, Fax: 412-648-7641, E-mail: themudo@pitt.edu. *Application contact:* Julie Korade, Doctoral Program Administrator/Graduate Enrollment Counselor, 412-648-7640, Fax: 412-648-7641, E-mail: korade@pitt.edu.
Website: http://www.gspia.pitt.edu/

University of Pittsburgh, Graduate School of Public and International Affairs, Master of Public Administration Program, Pittsburgh, PA 15260. Offers energy and environment (MPA); governance and international public management (MPA); policy research and analysis (MPA); public and nonprofit management (MPA); urban affairs and planning (MPA); JD/MPA; MPA/MID; MPA/MPIA; MPH/MPA; MSIS/MPA; MSW/MPA. Part-time and evening/weekend programs available. *Faculty:* 32 full-time (12 women), 13 part-time/adjunct (5 women). *Students:* 99 full-time (69 women), 15 part-time (10 women); includes 8 minority (5 Black or African American, non-Hispanic/Latino; 1 Asian, non-Hispanic/Latino; 1 Hispanic/Latino; 1 Two or more races, non-Hispanic/Latino), 52 international. Average age 26. 273 applicants, 70% accepted, 51 enrolled. In 2014, 50 master's awarded. *Degree requirements:* For master's, thesis optional, internship, capstone seminar. *Entrance requirements:* For master's, GRE General Test or GMAT, 2 letters of recommendation, resume; undergraduate transcripts, personal statement. Additional exam requirements/recommendations for international students: Required—TOEFL (minimum score 550 paper-based; 80 iBT); Recommended—IELTS (minimum score 7), TWE (minimum score 4). *Application deadline:* For fall admission, 2/1 for domestic students, 1/15 for international students; for spring admission, 11/1 for domestic students, 8/1 for international students. Application fee: $50. Electronic applications accepted. *Expenses:* Tuition, state resident: full-time $20,742; part-time $838 per credit. Tuition, nonresident: full-time $33,960; part-time $1389 per credit. *Required fees:* $800; $205 per term. Tuition and fees vary according to program. *Financial support:* In 2014–15, 17 students received support, including 3 fellowships (averaging $13,980 per year); scholarships/grants, unspecified assistantships, and student employment also available. Financial award application deadline: 2/1. *Faculty research:* Urban management, regional development, disaster response management, public program evaluation, comparative regional governance, nonprofit management, health policy, environmental policy, strategic management, human resources management. *Total annual research expenditures:* $640,844. *Unit head:* Dr. David Y. Miller, Director, 412-648-7606, Fax: 412-648-2605, E-mail: dymiller@pitt.edu. *Application contact:* Elizabeth A. Hruby, Graduate Enrollment Counselor, 412-648-7640, Fax: 412-648-7641, E-mail: eah44@pitt.edu.
Website: http://www.gspia.pitt.edu/

University of Pittsburgh, Graduate School of Public and International Affairs, Master of Public Policy and Management Program for Mid-Career Professionals, Pittsburgh, PA 15260. Offers MPPM. Part-time and evening/weekend programs available. *Faculty:* 34 full-time (12 women), 11 part-time/adjunct (3 women). *Students:* 13 full-time (4 women), 35 part-time (20 women); includes 9 minority (7 Black or African American, non-Hispanic/Latino; 1 Hispanic/Latino; 1 Two or more races, non-Hispanic/Latino), 8 international. Average age 41. 43 applicants, 81% accepted, 24 enrolled. In 2014, 20 master's awarded. *Degree requirements:* For master's, thesis optional, capstone seminar. *Entrance requirements:* For master's, 2 letters of recommendation, resume, personal statement, 5 years of full-time supervisory or budgetary experience. Additional exam requirements/recommendations for international students: Required—TOEFL (minimum score 550 paper-based; 80 iBT); Recommended—IELTS (minimum score 7), TWE (minimum score 4). *Application deadline:* For fall admission, 6/1 priority date for domestic students, 1/15 for international students; for spring admission, 11/1 priority date for domestic students, 8/1 for international students; for summer admission, 3/1 priority date for domestic students. Applications are processed on a rolling basis. Application fee: $50. Electronic applications accepted. *Expenses:* Tuition, state resident: full-time $20,742; part-time $838 per credit. Tuition, nonresident: full-time $33,960; part-time $1389 per credit. *Required fees:* $800; $205 per term. Tuition and fees vary according to program. *Financial support:* In 2014–15, 10 students received support. Scholarships/grants available. Support available to part-time students. Financial award application deadline: 2/1. *Faculty research:* Nonprofit management, urban and regional affairs, policy analysis and evaluation, security and intelligence studies, international political economy, nongovernmental organizations, civil society, development planning, environmental sustainability, human security, energy policy. *Total annual research expenditures:* $640,844. *Unit head:* Dr. George Dougherty, Jr., Director, Executive Education, 412-648-7603, Fax: 412-648-2605, E-mail: gwdjr@pitt.edu. *Application contact:* Michael T. Rizzi, Director of Student Services, 412-648-7640, Fax: 412-648-7641, E-mail: rizzim@pitt.edu.
Website: http://www.gspia.pitt.edu/

University of Puerto Rico, Río Piedras Campus, Graduate School of Planning, San Juan, PR 00931-3300. Offers economic planning systems (MP); environmental planning (MP); social policy and planning (MP); urban and territorial planning (MP). *Accreditation:* ACSP. Part-time programs available. *Degree requirements:* For master's, comprehensive exam, thesis, planning project defense. *Entrance requirements:* For master's, PAEG, GRE, minimum GPA of 3.0, 2 letters of recommendation. *Faculty research:* Municipalities, historic Atlas, Puerto Rico, economic future.

University of Regina, Faculty of Graduate Studies and Research, Johnson-Shoyama Graduate School of Public Policy, Regina, SK S4S 0A2, Canada. Offers economic analysis for public policy (Master's Certificate); health administration (MHA); health systems management (Master's Certificate); public management (MPA, Master's Certificate); public policy (MPA, MPP, PhD); public policy analysis (Master's Certificate). Part-time programs available. *Faculty:* 8 full-time (4 women), 12 part-time/adjunct (3 women). *Students:* 60 full-time (33 women), 109 part-time (66 women). 133 applicants,

35% accepted. In 2014, 26 master's, 1 doctorate, 13 other advanced degrees awarded. *Degree requirements:* For master's, thesis (for some programs); for doctorate, thesis/dissertation. *Entrance requirements:* For doctorate, master's degree, intended research program in an area of public policy. Additional exam requirements/recommendations for international students: Required—TOEFL (minimum score 580 paper-based; 80 iBT), IELTS (minimum score 6.5), PTE (minimum score 59). *Application deadline:* For fall admission, 2/1 for domestic and international students. Application fee: $100. Electronic applications accepted. *Expenses:* Expenses: $4,304.85 per semester of full time study (for MHA), $2,588.85 (for MPA), $1,450.35 (for MPP); $1,450.35 (for PhD). *Financial support:* In 2014–15, 11 fellowships (averaging $6,000 per year), 15 teaching assistantships (averaging $2,435 per year) were awarded; research assistantships, career-related internships or fieldwork, and scholarships/grants also available. Financial award application deadline: 6/15. *Faculty research:* Governance and administration, public finance, public policy analysis, non-governmental organizations and alternative service delivery, micro-economics for policy analysis. *Unit head:* Dr. Kathleen McNutt, Executive Director, Main Campus, 306-585-4759, Fax: 306-585-5461, E-mail: kathy.mcnutt@uregina.ca. *Application contact:* Constance Heshka-Argue, Manager, Main Campus, 306-585-5462, Fax: 306-585-5461, E-mail: connie.heska-argue@uregina.ca.
Website: http://www.schoolofpublicpolicy.sk.ca/

University of Rhode Island, Graduate School, College of Arts and Sciences, Department of Political Science, Kingston, RI 02881. Offers political science (MA), including American politics, comparative government, international relations, public policy; public policy and administration (MPA); MLIS/MPA. Part-time programs available. *Faculty:* 11 full-time (4 women). *Students:* 20 full-time (11 women), 28 part-time (21 women); includes 9 minority (4 Black or African American, non-Hispanic/Latino; 3 Asian, non-Hispanic/Latino; 2 Hispanic/Latino), 2 international. In 2014, 20 master's awarded. *Degree requirements:* For master's, comprehensive exam (for some programs), thesis optional. *Entrance requirements:* For master's, GRE, GMAT or MAT, 2 letters of recommendation. Additional exam requirements/recommendations for international students: Required—TOEFL (minimum score 550 paper-based). *Application deadline:* For fall admission, 2/1 for international students; for spring admission, 7/15 for international students. Application fee: $65. Electronic applications accepted. *Expenses:* Tuition, state resident: full-time $11,532; part-time $641 per credit. Tuition, nonresident: full-time $23,606; part-time $1311 per credit. *Required fees:* $1442; $39 per credit. $35 per semester. One-time fee: $155. *Financial support:* In 2014–15, 3 teaching assistantships with full and partial tuition reimbursements (averaging $12,675 per year) were awarded. Financial award application deadline: 7/15; financial award applicants required to submit FAFSA. *Unit head:* Dr. Brian Krueger, Department Chair, 401-874-4058, Fax: 401-874-4072, E-mail: bkrueger@uri.edu. *Application contact:* Dr. Robert Weygand, Director, 401-874-2124, Fax: 401-874-4072, E-mail: bobw@uri.edu.
Website: http://www.uri.edu/artsci/psc/

University of Rochester, Simon Business School, Part-Time MBA Program, Rochester, NY 14627. Offers accounting and information systems (MBA); business environment and public policy (MBA); business systems consulting (MBA); competitive and organizational strategy (MBA); computers and information systems (MBA); corporate accounting (MBA); electronic commerce (MBA); entrepreneurship (MBA); finance (MBA); health sciences management (MBA); international management (MBA); manufacturing management (MBA); marketing (MBA); operations management - services (MBA); public accounting (MBA). Part-time and evening/weekend programs available. *Entrance requirements:* For master's, GRE or GMAT, resume, recommendation letters, essays, transcipts. Electronic applications accepted. *Expenses:* *Tuition:* Full-time $46,150; part-time $1442 per credit hour. *Required fees:* $504.

University of Saskatchewan, College of Graduate Studies and Research, School of Public Policy, Saskatoon, SK S7N 5A2, Canada. Offers MIT, MPA, MPP, PhD.

The University of South Dakota, Graduate School, College of Arts and Sciences, Department of Political Science, Vermillion, SD 57069-2390. Offers American political institutions (PhD); American politics and public policy (MA); political science (EMPA, MA); public administration (MPA, PhD); public policy (PhD); JD/MA. *Accreditation:* NASPAA (one or more programs are accredited). Part-time programs available. Postbaccalaureate distance learning degree programs offered. *Degree requirements:* For master's, comprehensive exam, thesis (for some programs). *Entrance requirements:* For master's, GRE or LSAT (MPA), GRE General Test (MA), minimum GPA of 2.7. Additional exam requirements/recommendations for international students: Required—TOEFL (minimum score 550 paper-based; 79 iBT). Electronic applications accepted.

University of Southern California, Graduate School, School of Policy, Planning, and Development, Doctor of Philosophy in Public Policy and Management Program, Los Angeles, CA 90089. Offers PhD. *Degree requirements:* For doctorate, thesis/dissertation. *Entrance requirements:* For doctorate, GRE. Additional exam requirements/recommendations for international students: Required—TOEFL (minimum score 600 paper-based; 100 iBT). Electronic applications accepted. *Faculty research:* Governance: effective institutions, leadership, management, community and economic development, institutional analysis, civic engagement.

University of Southern California, Graduate School, School of Policy, Planning, and Development, Public Policy Programs, Los Angeles, CA 90089. Offers homeland security and public policy (Graduate Certificate); public policy (MPP, Graduate Certificate); M Pl/MPP; MPP/JD. Part-time programs available. Terminal master's awarded for partial completion of doctoral program. *Degree requirements:* For master's, practicum. *Entrance requirements:* For master's, GRE. Additional exam requirements/recommendations for international students: Required—TOEFL (minimum score 600 paper-based; 100 iBT). Electronic applications accepted. *Faculty research:* Urban political economy, community and economic development, environmental policy, transportation policy, housing policy.

University of Southern Maine, College of Management and Human Service, Muskie School of Public Service, Program in Public Policy and Management, Portland, ME 04104-9300. Offers MPPM, JD/MPPM. Part-time and evening/weekend programs available. Postbaccalaureate distance learning degree programs offered (minimal on-campus study). *Faculty:* 4 full-time (3 women). *Students:* 19 full-time (11 women), 56 part-time (24 women); includes 9 minority (3 American Indian or Alaska Native, non-Hispanic/Latino; 3 Asian, non-Hispanic/Latino; 1 Hispanic/Latino; 2 Two or more races, non-Hispanic/Latino), 1 international. Average age 32. 18 applicants, 100% accepted, 16 enrolled. In 2014, 20 master's awarded. *Degree requirements:* For master's, thesis, capstone project, field experience. *Entrance requirements:* For master's, GRE General Test or LSAT. Additional exam requirements/recommendations for international students: Required—TOEFL. *Application deadline:* For fall admission, 2/1 priority date for domestic and international students; for spring admission, 12/1 for domestic and international students. Applications are processed on a rolling basis. Application fee: $65. Electronic applications accepted. *Expenses: Tuition, area resident:* Full-time $6840; part-time $380 per credit hour. Tuition, state resident: full-time $10,260; part-time $570 per credit hour. Tuition, nonresident: full-time $18,468; part-time $1026 per credit hour. *Required fees:* $830; $83 per credit hour. Tuition and fees vary according to course load and program. *Financial support:* Fellowships, research assistantships, teaching assistantships, career-related internships or fieldwork, Federal Work-Study, scholarships/grants, tuition waivers (partial), and unspecified assistantships available. Financial award application deadline: 4/1; financial award applicants required to submit FAFSA. *Faculty research:* State and local public finance, education finance, applied social science methodology, nonprofit and higher education organizational management, public service ethics, comparative public policy. *Unit head:* Dr. Josephine LaPlante, Chair, 207-780-4863, E-mail: jlaplante@usm.maine.edu. *Application contact:* Mary Sloan, Assistant Dean of Graduate Studies and Director of Graduate Admissions, 207-780-4812, E-mail: gradstudies@usm.maine.edu.

University of South Florida, College of Arts and Sciences, Department of Government and International Affairs, Tampa, FL 33620-9951. Offers government (PhD); Latin American, Caribbean and Latino studies (MA); political science (MA), including comparative government and politics, international relations, public policy. Part-time and evening/weekend programs available. *Faculty:* 10 full-time (1 woman). *Students:* 56 full-time (29 women), 47 part-time (23 women); includes 18 minority (6 Black or African American, non-Hispanic/Latino; 1 Asian, non-Hispanic/Latino; 9 Hispanic/Latino; 2 Two or more races, non-Hispanic/Latino), 9 international. Average age 33. 73 applicants, 51% accepted, 25 enrolled. In 2014, 45 master's, 2 doctorates awarded. *Degree requirements:* For master's, comprehensive exam, thesis; for doctorate, comprehensive exam, thesis/dissertation. *Entrance requirements:* For master's, GRE General Test, minimum GPA of 3.0 in upper-division undergraduate course work; letters of recommendation (2 for MPA, 3 for MPS); 500-word personal statement and undergraduate background in political science or related fields (for MPS); one-page career statement (for MPA); for doctorate, GRE General Test, 500-word personal statement, three letters of recommendation, transcripts of MA/BA coursework, writing sample. Additional exam requirements/recommendations for international students: Required—TOEFL (minimum score 550 paper-based; 79 iBT) or IELTS (minimum score 6.5). *Application deadline:* For fall admission, 2/15 for domestic students, 1/2 for international students; for spring admission, 10/15 for domestic students, 6/1 for international students. Applications are processed on a rolling basis. Application fee: $30. Electronic applications accepted. *Financial support:* In 2014–15, 18 students received support, including 18 teaching assistantships with tuition reimbursements available (averaging $12,390 per year); unspecified assistantships also available. Financial award application deadline: 4/1. *Faculty research:* Citizenship and identity, social movements, global governance, American politics, public policy. *Unit head:* Dr. Steven Tauber, Associate Professor and Interim Chair, 813-974-2278, Fax: 813-974-0832, E-mail: stauber@usf.edu. *Application contact:* Dr. Bernd Reiter, Associate Professor and Director of Graduate Studies, 813-974-3583, Fax: 813-974-0832, E-mail: breiter@usf.edu.
Website: http://gia.usf.edu/

The University of Texas at Austin, Graduate School, Lyndon B. Johnson School of Public Affairs, Austin, TX 78712-1111. Offers global policy studies (MGPS); public affairs (MP Aff); public leadership (EMPL); public policy (PhD); JD/MP Aff; MBA/MP Aff; MP Aff/MA; MP Aff/MSE. *Accreditation:* NASPAA (one or more programs are accredited). Part-time programs available. *Degree requirements:* For master's, thesis, summer internship; for doctorate, thesis/dissertation. *Entrance requirements:* For master's, GRE General Test (for MP Aff and MGPS), minimum GPA of 3.0 in upper-division classes, seven years of experience in the public sector, and interview (for EMPL); for doctorate, GRE General Test, master's degree in policy-related field. Additional exam requirements/recommendations for international students: Required—TOEFL. Electronic applications accepted. *Faculty research:* Human resource development, health and social policy, philanthropy and community service, ethical leadership, urban and international policy, science and technology policy.

The University of Texas at Dallas, School of Economic, Political and Policy Sciences, Program in Public Policy and Political Economy, Richardson, TX 75080. Offers international political economy (MS); public policy (MPP); public policy and political economy (PhD). Part-time and evening/weekend programs available. *Faculty:* 14 full-time (1 woman), 1 part-time/adjunct (0 women). *Students:* 41 full-time (13 women), 35 part-time (16 women); includes 22 minority (6 Black or African American, non-Hispanic/Latino; 1 American Indian or Alaska Native, non-Hispanic/Latino; 8 Asian, non-Hispanic/Latino; 7 Hispanic/Latino), 21 international. Average age 36. 52 applicants, 60% accepted, 12 enrolled. In 2014, 18 master's, 3 doctorates awarded. *Degree requirements:* For doctorate, thesis/dissertation. *Entrance requirements:* For master's and doctorate, GRE General Test, minimum GPA of 3.0 in upper-level course work in field. Additional exam requirements/recommendations for international students: Required—TOEFL (minimum score 550 paper-based). *Application deadline:* For fall admission, 7/15 for domestic students, 5/1 priority date for international students; for spring admission, 11/15 for domestic students, 9/1 priority date for international students. Applications are processed on a rolling basis. Application fee: $50 ($100 for international students). Electronic applications accepted. *Expenses:* Tuition, state resident: full-time $11,940; part-time $663 per credit. Tuition, nonresident: full-time $22,282; part-time $1238 per credit. *Financial support:* In 2014–15, 49 students received support, including 4 research assistantships with partial tuition reimbursements available (averaging $12,070 per year), 15 teaching assistantships with partial tuition reimbursements available (averaging $11,790 per year); career-related internships or fieldwork, Federal Work-Study, institutionally sponsored loans, scholarships/grants, and unspecified assistantships also available. Support available to part-time students. Financial award application deadline: 4/30; financial award applicants required to submit FAFSA. *Faculty research:* Ethnicity, community and local public good provision; community mental health policy; Texas Schools Project; biological and chemical arms control; cross-disciplinary applications of quantitative methodology. *Unit head:* Dr. Jennifer Holmes, Program Head, 972-883-6843, Fax: 972-883-6297, E-mail: jholmes@utdallas.edu. *Application contact:* Betsy Albritton, Graduate Program Administrator, 972-883-6406, Fax: 972-883-6297, E-mail: pppe@utdallas.edu.
Website: http://www.utdallas.edu/epps/public-policy-and-political-economy/

University of the Pacific, McGeorge School of Law, Sacramento, CA 95817. Offers advocacy (JD); international water resources law (JSD); public policy and law (LL M); JD/MBA; JD/MPPA. *Accreditation:* ABA. Part-time and evening/weekend programs available. *Students:* 430 full-time (232 women), 169 part-time (84 women); includes 203 minority (19 Black or African American, non-Hispanic/Latino; 7 American Indian or Alaska Native, non-Hispanic/Latino; 93 Asian, non-Hispanic/Latino; 83 Hispanic/Latino; 1 Two or more races, non-Hispanic/Latino), 24 international. Average age 28. 1,144 applicants, 72% accepted, 156 enrolled. In 2014, 11 master's, 187 doctorates awarded. *Degree requirements:* For master's, thesis (for some programs); for doctorate, thesis/dissertation (for some programs). *Entrance requirements:* For master's, JD; for doctorate, LSAT (for JD), LL M (for JSD). Additional exam requirements/recommendations for international students: Required—TOEFL (minimum score 600 paper-based; 100 iBT). *Application deadline:* For fall admission, 3/15 priority date for domestic students. Applications are processed on a rolling basis. Application fee: $50. Electronic applications accepted. *Expenses:* Expenses: Contact institution. *Financial support:* Fellowships, research assistantships, teaching assistantships, career-related internships or fieldwork, Federal Work-Study, institutionally sponsored loans, and scholarships/grants available. Support available to part-time students. Financial award applicants required to submit FAFSA. *Faculty research:* International legal studies, public policy and law, advocacy, intellectual property law, taxation, criminal law. *Unit*

head: Francis Jay Mootz, III, Dean, 916-739-7151, E-mail: jmootz@pacific.edu. *Application contact:* 916-739-7105, Fax: 916-739-7301, E-mail: mcgeorge@pacific.edu.
Website: http://www.mcgeorge.edu/

University of Utah, Graduate School, College of Social and Behavioral Science, Department of Political Science, Program in Public Policy, Salt Lake City, UT 84112. Offers MPP, MPP/JD, MPP/MPH. Part-time and evening/weekend programs available. *Students:* 22 full-time (7 women), 9 part-time (4 women); includes 4 minority (1 Asian, non-Hispanic/Latino; 3 Hispanic/Latino), 1 international. Average age 31. 15 applicants, 93% accepted, 8 enrolled. In 2014, 10 master's awarded. *Degree requirements:* For master's, project. *Entrance requirements:* For master's, GRE, LSAT, GMAT, or MAT. Additional exam requirements/recommendations for international students: Required—TOEFL (minimum score 583 paper-based; 93 iBT). *Application deadline:* For fall admission, 2/15 for domestic and international students. Application fee: $55 ($65 for international students). Electronic applications accepted. *Expenses:* Expenses: Contact institution. *Financial support:* In 2014–15, 9 students received support, including 1 fellowship (averaging $6,500 per year), 4 research assistantships (averaging $13,000 per year). *Unit head:* Lina Svedin, Director, 801-581-7031, E-mail: lina.svedin@poli-sci.utah.edu. *Application contact:* Elizabeth Henke, Program Manager, 801-585-7834, E-mail: elizabeth.henke@cppa.utah.edu.
Website: http://www.mpp.utah.edu

University of Virginia, Frank Batten Sr. School of Leadership and Public Policy, Charlottesville, VA 22903. Offers MPP, JD/MPP, MBA/MPP, MPP/MPH, MPP/MUEP, MPP/PhD. *Faculty:* 12 full-time (6 women), 4 part-time/adjunct (1 woman). *Students:* 95 full-time (46 women); includes 17 minority (6 Black or African American, non-Hispanic/Latino; 6 Asian, non-Hispanic/Latino; 2 Hispanic/Latino; 3 Two or more races, non-Hispanic/Latino), 8 international. Average age 24. 152 applicants, 56% accepted, 24 enrolled. In 2014, 52 master's awarded. *Entrance requirements:* Additional exam requirements/recommendations for international students: Required—TOEFL, IELTS. *Application deadline:* For fall admission, 2/20 for domestic and international students. Applications are processed on a rolling basis. Electronic applications accepted. *Expenses:* Tuition, state resident: full-time $14,164; part-time $349 per credit hour. Tuition, nonresident: full-time $23,722; part-time $1300 per credit hour. *Required fees:* $2514. *Unit head:* Allan C. Stam, Dean, 434-924-0812, Fax: 434-243-2318, E-mail: stam@virginia.edu. *Application contact:* Kellie Sauls, Director of Admissions and Financial Aid, 434-243-3731, Fax: 434-243-2318, E-mail: fbsadmissions@eservices.virginia.edu.
Website: http://batten.virginia.edu/

University of Washington, Graduate School, Evans School of Public Affairs, Seattle, WA 98195. Offers public administration (MPA); public policy and management (PhD); JD/MPA; MPA/MAIS; MPA/MPH; MPA/MS; MPA/MUP. *Accreditation:* NASPAA. Part-time and evening/weekend programs available. *Degree requirements:* For master's, thesis, internship or cooperative experience. *Entrance requirements:* For master's and doctorate, GRE General Test, minimum GPA of 3.0. Additional exam requirements/recommendations for international students: Required—TOEFL (minimum score 580 paper-based; 92 iBT). Electronic applications accepted. *Faculty research:* Environmental policy, education and social policy, nonprofit management, international affairs, urban and regional development.

University of Washington, Bothell, Master of Arts in Policy Studies Program, Bothell, WA 98011-8246. Offers MA. Evening/weekend programs available. *Degree requirements:* For master's, thesis. *Entrance requirements:* For master's, GRE, statistics and micro-economics courses. Additional exam requirements/recommendations for international students: Required—TOEFL. Electronic applications accepted. *Faculty research:* Policy studies, cultural studies, cultural and environmental politics, disability studies, public policy.

Vanderbilt University, Graduate School, Program in Community Research and Action, Nashville, TN 37240-1001. Offers MS, PhD. *Faculty:* 13 full-time (6 women), 3 part-time/adjunct (2 women). *Students:* 24 full-time (17 women); includes 8 minority (3 Black or African American, non-Hispanic/Latino; 2 Asian, non-Hispanic/Latino; 1 Hispanic/Latino; 2 Two or more races, non-Hispanic/Latino), 2 international. Average age 31. 72 applicants, 13% accepted, 7 enrolled. In 2014, 1 master's, 2 doctorates awarded. *Degree requirements:* For master's, thesis; for doctorate, thesis/dissertation, internship, fundable grant proposal. *Entrance requirements:* For doctorate, GRE General Test. Additional exam requirements/recommendations for international students: Required—TOEFL (minimum score 570 paper-based; 88 iBT). *Application deadline:* For fall admission, 12/31 for domestic and international students. Electronic applications accepted. *Expenses: Tuition:* Full-time $42,768; part-time $1782 per credit hour. *Required fees:* $422. One-time fee: $30 full-time. *Financial support:* Fellowships with tuition reimbursements, research assistantships with full tuition reimbursements, teaching assistantships with full tuition reimbursements, Federal Work-Study, institutionally sponsored loans, scholarships/grants, traineeships, and health care benefits available. Financial award application deadline: 1/15; financial award applicants required to submit CSS PROFILE or FAFSA. *Faculty research:* Applied psychological research, community theory, mental health, public policy, race dynamics. *Unit head:* Dr. Paul Dokecki, Director of Graduate Studies, 615-322-8418, Fax: 615-322-1141, E-mail: paul.r.dokecki@vanderbilt.edu. *Application contact:* Sherrie Lane, Administrative Assistant, 615-322-8484, Fax: 615-322-1141, E-mail: sherrie.a.lane@vanderbilt.edu.
Website: http://peabody.vanderbilt.edu/departments/hod/graduate-programs/phd_in_community_research_and_action/community_research_and_action_program.php

Virginia Commonwealth University, Graduate School, College of Humanities and Sciences, Wilder School of Government and Public Affairs, Center for Public Policy, Richmond, VA 23284-9005. Offers public policy and administration (PhD). *Degree requirements:* For doctorate, thesis/dissertation. *Entrance requirements:* For doctorate, GMAT, GRE General Test, LSAT, or MAT. Additional exam requirements/recommendations for international students: Required—TOEFL (minimum score 600 paper-based; 100 iBT); Recommended—IELTS (minimum score 6.5). Electronic applications accepted.

Virginia Polytechnic Institute and State University, Graduate School, College of Science, Blacksburg, VA 24061. Offers biological sciences (MS, PhD); biomedical technology development and management (MS); chemistry (MS, PhD); economics (MA, PhD); geosciences (MS, PhD); mathematics (MS, PhD); physics (MS, PhD); psychology (MS, PhD); statistics (MS, PhD). *Faculty:* 274 full-time (75 women), 3 part-time/adjunct (all women). *Students:* 544 full-time (212 women), 29 part-time (12 women); includes 54 minority (14 Black or African American, non-Hispanic/Latino; 9 Asian, non-Hispanic/Latino; 16 Hispanic/Latino; 15 Two or more races, non-Hispanic/Latino), 243 international. Average age 27. 1,105 applicants, 22% accepted, 104 enrolled. In 2014, 83 master's, 67 doctorates awarded. *Median time to degree:* Of those who began their doctoral program in fall 2006, 54% received their degree in 8 years or less. *Degree requirements:* For master's, comprehensive exam (for some programs), thesis (for some programs); for doctorate, comprehensive exam (for some programs), thesis/dissertation (for some programs). *Entrance requirements:* For master's and doctorate, GRE/GMAT (may vary by department). Additional exam requirements/recommendations for international students: Required—TOEFL (minimum score 550 paper-based). *Application deadline:* For fall admission, 8/1 for domestic students, 4/1 for international students; for spring admission, 1/1 for domestic students, 9/1 for international students. Applications are processed on a rolling basis. Application fee: $75. Electronic applications accepted. *Expenses:* Tuition, state resident: full-time $11,656; part-time $647.50 per credit hour. Tuition, nonresident: full-time $23,351; part-time $1297.25 per credit hour. *Required fees:* $2533; $465.75 per semester. Tuition and fees vary according to course load, campus/location and program. *Financial support:* In 2014–15, 1 fellowship with full tuition reimbursement (averaging $5,938 per year), 143 research assistantships with full tuition reimbursements (averaging $22,569 per year), 355 teaching assistantships with full tuition reimbursements (averaging $21,476 per year) were awarded. Financial award application deadline: 3/1; financial award applicants required to submit FAFSA. *Total annual research expenditures:* $24.3 million. *Unit head:* Dr. Lay Nam Chang, Dean, 540-231-5422, Fax: 540-231-3380, E-mail: laynam@vt.edu. *Application contact:* Diane Stearns, Assistant to the Dean, 540-231-7515, Fax: 540-231-3380, E-mail: dstearns@vt.edu.
Website: http://www.science.vt.edu/

Walden University, Graduate Programs, Richard W. Riley College of Education and Leadership, Minneapolis, MN 55401. *Accreditation:* NCATE. Part-time and evening/weekend programs available. Postbaccalaureate distance learning degree programs offered (no on-campus study). *Faculty:* 66 full-time (48 women), 921 part-time/adjunct (643 women). *Students:* 7,964 full-time (6,643 women), 1,885 part-time (1,539 women); includes 4,331 minority (3,474 Black or African American, non-Hispanic/Latino; 47 American Indian or Alaska Native, non-Hispanic/Latino; 115 Asian, non-Hispanic/Latino; 508 Hispanic/Latino; 22 Native Hawaiian or other Pacific Islander, non-Hispanic/Latino; 165 Two or more races, non-Hispanic/Latino), 55 international. Average age 40. 2,478 applicants, 99% accepted, 2373 enrolled. In 2014, 1,891 master's, 395 doctorates, 503 other advanced degrees awarded. *Degree requirements:* For doctorate, thesis/dissertation (for some programs), residency; for other advanced degree, residency (for some programs). *Entrance requirements:* For master's, bachelor's degree or higher; minimum GPA of 2.5; official transcripts; goal statement (for some programs); access to computer and Internet; for doctorate, master's degree or higher; three years of related professional or academic experience (preferred); minimum GPA of 3.0; goal statement and current resume (for select programs); official transcripts; access to computer and Internet; for other advanced degree, relevant work experience; access to computer and Internet. Additional exam requirements/recommendations for international students: Required—TOEFL (minimum score 550 paper-based, 79 iBT), IELTS (minimum score 6.5), Michigan English Language Assessment Battery (minimum score 82), or PTE (minimum score 53). *Application deadline:* Applications are processed on a rolling basis. Application fee: $0. Electronic applications accepted. *Expenses: Tuition:* Full-time $11,925; part-time $500 per credit hour. *Required fees:* $647. *Financial support:* Fellowships, Federal Work-Study, scholarships/grants, unspecified assistantships, and family tuition reduction, active duty/veteran tuition reduction, group tuition reduction, interest-free payment plans, employee tuition reduction available. Support available to part-time students. Financial award applicants required to submit FAFSA. *Unit head:* Dr. Kate Steffens, Dean, 866-492-5336. *Application contact:* Meghan M. Thomas, Vice President of Enrollment Management, 866-492-5336, E-mail: info@waldenu.edu.
Website: http://www.waldenu.edu/colleges-schools/riley-college-of-education/

Walden University, Graduate Programs, School of Public Policy and Administration, Minneapolis, MN 55401. Offers criminal justice (MPA, MPP, MS, Graduate Certificate), including emergency management (MS, PhD), general program (MS, PhD), homeland security and policy coordination (MS, PhD), law and public policy (MS, PhD), policy analysis (MS, PhD), public management and leadership (MS, PhD), self-designed (MS), terrorism, mediation, and peace (MS, PhD); criminal justice leadership and executive management (MS), including emergency management (MS, PhD), general program (MS, PhD), homeland security and policy coordination (MS, PhD), law and public policy (MS, PhD), policy analysis (MS, PhD), public management and leadership (MS, PhD), self-designed, terrorism, mediation, and peace (MS, PhD); emergency management (MPA, MPP, MS), including criminal justice (MS, PhD), general program (MS, PhD), homeland security (MS), public management and leadership (MS, PhD), terrorism and emergency management (MS); general program (MPA, MPP); government management (Graduate Certificate); health policy (MPA, MPP); homeland security (Graduate Certificate); homeland security and policy coordination (MPA, MPP); international nongovernmental organizations (MPA, MPP); law and public policy (MPA, MPP); local government management for sustainable communities (MPA, MPP); nonprofit management (Graduate Certificate); nonprofit management and leadership (MPA, MPP, MS); online teaching in higher education (Post-Master's Certificate); policy analysis (MPA); public management and leadership (MPA, MPP, Graduate Certificate); public policy (Graduate Certificate); public policy and administration (PhD), including criminal justice (MS, PhD), emergency management (MS, PhD), general program (MS, PhD), health policy, homeland security and policy coordination (MS, PhD), international nongovernmental organizations, law and public policy (MS, PhD), local government management for sustainable communities, nonprofit management and leadership, policy analysis (MS, PhD), public management and leadership (MS, PhD), terrorism, mediation, and peace (MS, PhD); strategic planning and public policy (Graduate Certificate); terrorism, mediation, and peace (MPA, MPP). Part-time and evening/weekend programs available. Postbaccalaureate distance learning degree programs offered (no on-campus study). *Faculty:* 13 full-time (5 women), 151 part-time/adjunct (65 women). *Students:* 1,009 full-time (573 women), 1,632 part-time (954 women); includes 1,553 minority (1,307 Black or African American, non-Hispanic/Latino; 15 American Indian or Alaska Native, non-Hispanic/Latino; 38 Asian, non-Hispanic/Latino; 127 Hispanic/Latino; 66 Two or more races, non-Hispanic/Latino), 15 international. Average age 42. 665 applicants, 97% accepted, 616 enrolled. In 2014, 317 master's, 95 doctorates, 34 other advanced degrees awarded. *Degree requirements:* For doctorate, thesis/dissertation, residency. *Entrance requirements:* For master's, bachelor's degree or higher; minimum GPA of 2.5; official transcripts; goal statement (for some programs); access to computer and Internet; for doctorate, master's degree or higher; three years of related professional or academic experience (preferred); minimum GPA of 3.0; goal statement and current resume (for select programs); official transcripts; access to computer and Internet; for other advanced degree, relevant work experience; access to computer and Internet. Additional exam requirements/recommendations for international students: Required—TOEFL (minimum score 550 paper-based, 79 iBT), IELTS (minimum score 6.5), Michigan English Language Assessment Battery (minimum score 82), or PTE (minimum score 53). *Application deadline:* Applications are processed on a rolling basis. Application fee: $0. Electronic applications accepted. *Expenses: Tuition:* Full-time $11,925; part-time $500 per credit hour. *Required fees:* $647. *Financial support:* Fellowships, Federal Work-Study, scholarships/grants, unspecified assistantships, and family tuition reduction, active duty/veteran tuition reduction, group tuition reduction, interest-free payment plans, employee tuition reduction available. Support available to part-time students. Financial award applicants required to submit FAFSA. *Unit head:* Dr. Shana Garrett, Associate Dean, 866-492-5336. *Application contact:* Meghan Thomas, Vice President of Enrollment Management, 866-492-5336, E-mail: info@waldenu.edu.
Website: http://www.waldenu.edu/programs/colleges-schools/public-policy-and-administration

Walden University, Graduate Programs, School of Social Work and Human Services, Minneapolis, MN 55401. Offers addictions (MSW); addictions and social work (DSW); children, families, and couples (MSW); clinical expertise (DSW); criminal justice (DSW); crisis and trauma (MSW); disaster, crisis, and intervention (DSW); forensic populations and settings (MSW); general program (MSW); human services (MS, PhD), including clinical social work (PhD), criminal justice, disaster, crisis and intervention, family studies and intervention strategies (PhD), family studies and interventions, general program, human services administration, public health, social policy analysis and planning; medical social work (MSW, DSW); military families and culture (MSW); policy practice (DSW); social work (PhD), including addictions and social work, clinical expertise, disaster, crisis and intervention (MS, PhD), family studies and interventions (MS, PhD), medical social work, policy practice, social work administration; social work administration (DSW). Part-time and evening/weekend programs available. Postbaccalaureate distance learning degree programs offered (no on-campus study). *Faculty:* 18 full-time (11 women), 236 part-time/adjunct (156 women). *Students:* 1,400 full-time (1,205 women), 884 part-time (759 women); includes 1,586 minority (1,373 Black or African American, non-Hispanic/Latino; 20 American Indian or Alaska Native, non-Hispanic/Latino; 16 Asian, non-Hispanic/Latino; 120 Hispanic/Latino; 57 Two or more races, non-Hispanic/Latino), 14 international. Average age 40. 892 applicants, 96% accepted, 826 enrolled. In 2014, 61 master's, 14 doctorates awarded. *Degree requirements:* For master's, residency (for some programs); for doctorate, thesis/dissertation, residency. *Entrance requirements:* For master's, bachelor's degree or higher; minimum GPA of 2.5; official transcripts; goal statement (for some programs); access to computer and Internet; for doctorate, master's degree or higher; three years of related professional or academic experience (preferred); minimum GPA of 3.0; goal statement and current resume (for select programs); official transcripts; access to computer and Internet. Additional exam requirements/recommendations for international students: Required—TOEFL (minimum score 550 paper-based, 79 iBT), IELTS (minimum score 6.5), Michigan English Language Assessment Battery (minimum score 82), or PTE (minimum score 53). *Application deadline:* Applications are processed on a rolling basis. Application fee: $0. Electronic applications accepted. *Expenses: Tuition:* Full-time $11,925; part-time $500 per credit hour. *Required fees:* $647. *Financial support:* Fellowships, Federal Work-Study, scholarships/grants, unspecified assistantships, and family tuition reduction, active duty/veteran tuition reduction, group tuition reduction, interest-free payment plans, employee tuition reduction available. Support available to part-time students. Financial award applicants required to submit FAFSA. *Unit head:* Dr. Savitri Dixon-Saxon, Associate Dean, 866-492-5336. *Application contact:* Meghan Thomas, Vice President of Enrollment Management, 866-492-5336, E-mail: info@waldenu.edu.
Website: http://www.waldenu.edu/colleges-schools/school-of-social-work-and-human-services/academic-programs

Washington University in St. Louis, Graduate School of Arts and Sciences, Program in Political Economy and Public Policy, St. Louis, MO 63130-4899. Offers MA. *Degree requirements:* For master's, thesis or alternative. *Entrance requirements:* For master's, GRE General Test. Electronic applications accepted.

Wayne State University, College of Liberal Arts and Sciences, Department of Political Science, Detroit, MI 48202. Offers political science (MA, PhD); public administration (MPA), including economic development policy and management, health and human services policy and management, human and fiscal resource management, nonprofit policy and management, organizational behavior and management, urban and metropolitan policy and management; JD/MA. *Accreditation:* NASPAA. *Students:* 56 full-time (25 women), 78 part-time (49 women); includes 41 minority (28 Black or African American, non-Hispanic/Latino; 4 Asian, non-Hispanic/Latino; 5 Hispanic/Latino; 4 Two or more races, non-Hispanic/Latino), 12 international. Average age 34. 153 applicants, 41% accepted, 34 enrolled. In 2014, 30 master's, 5 doctorates awarded. *Degree requirements:* For master's, comprehensive exam; for doctorate, thesis/dissertation. *Entrance requirements:* For master's, GRE General Test, substantial undergraduate preparation in the social sciences (recommended); for doctorate, GRE General Test, 3 letters of recommendation; autobiography; interview. Additional exam requirements/recommendations for international students: Required—TOEFL (minimum score 550 paper-based; 79 iBT), TWE (minimum score 5.5), Michigan English Language Assessment Battery (minimum score 85); Recommended—IELTS (minimum score 6.5). *Application deadline:* For fall admission, 5/1 priority date for domestic and international students; for winter admission, 10/1 priority date for domestic students, 9/1 priority date for international students; for spring admission, 2/1 priority date for domestic students, 1/1 priority date for international students. Applications are processed on a rolling basis. Application fee: $0. Electronic applications accepted. *Expenses:* Tuition, state resident: full-time $10,294; part-time $571.90 per credit hour. Tuition, nonresident: full-time $29,730; part-time $1238.75 per credit hour. *Required fees:* $1365; $43.50 per credit hour. $291.10 per semester. Tuition and fees vary according to course load and program. *Financial support:* In 2014–15, 41 students received support, including 4 fellowships with tuition reimbursements available (averaging $14,146 per year), 13 teaching assistantships with tuition reimbursements available (averaging $16,838 per year); research assistantships with tuition reimbursements available, scholarships/grants, health care benefits, and unspecified assistantships also available. Financial award application deadline: 3/31; financial award applicants required to submit FAFSA. *Faculty research:* American politics and public policy, comparative politics and international relations, political theory, public administration, urban politics. *Unit head:* Dr. Daniel Geller, Chair, 313-577-6328, Fax: 313-993-3435, E-mail: dgeller@wayne.edu. *Application contact:* Dr. Sharon Lean, Graduate Director, E-mail: gradpolisci@wayne.edu.
Website: http://clas.wayne.edu/politicalscience/

West Virginia University, Eberly College of Arts and Sciences, Department of Political Science, Morgantown, WV 26506. Offers American public policy and politics (MA); international and comparative public policy and politics (MA); political science (PhD); public policy analysis (PhD). Terminal master's awarded for partial completion of doctoral program. *Degree requirements:* For master's, thesis optional; for doctorate, comprehensive exam, thesis/dissertation. *Entrance requirements:* For master's, GRE General Test, minimum GPA of 2.75; for doctorate, GRE General Test, minimum GPA of 3.0. Additional exam requirements/recommendations for international students: Required—TOEFL. *Faculty research:* Public policy, research methods, foreign policy analysis, judicial politics, environmental and energy policy.

Wilfrid Laurier University, Faculty of Graduate and Postdoctoral Studies, School of International Policy and Governance, International Public Policy Program, Waterloo, ON N2L 3C5, Canada. Offers global governance (MIPP); human security (MIPP); international economic relations (MIPP); international environmental policy (MIPP). Offered jointly with University of Waterloo. *Entrance requirements:* For master's, honours BA with minimum B average. Additional exam requirements/recommendations for international students: Required—TOEFL (minimum score 89 iBT). Electronic applications accepted. *Faculty research:* International environmental policy, international economic relations, human security, global governance.

William Paterson University of New Jersey, College of Humanities and Social Sciences, Wayne, NJ 07470-8420. Offers applied sociology (MA); clinical and counseling psychology (MA); creative and professional writing (MFA); English (MA); history (MA); public policy and international affairs (MA). Part-time and evening/weekend programs available. *Faculty:* 32 full-time (16 women), 3 part-time/adjunct (1 woman). *Students:* 50 full-time (30 women), 114 part-time (88 women); includes 64 minority (7 Black or African American, non-Hispanic/Latino; 1 American Indian or Alaska Native, non-Hispanic/Latino; 4 Asian, non-Hispanic/Latino; 50 Hispanic/Latino; 2 Two or more races, non-Hispanic/Latino), 2 international. Average age 34. 115 applicants, 81% accepted, 65 enrolled. In 2014, 42 master's awarded. Terminal master's awarded for partial completion of doctoral program. *Degree requirements:* For master's, thesis (for some programs), internship (for some programs). *Entrance requirements:* For master's, GRE/MAT, minimum GPA of 3.0; 2 letters of recommendation; writing sample/personal statement. Additional exam requirements/recommendations for international students: Required—TOEFL (minimum score 550 paper-based; 79 iBT), IELTS (minimum score 6). *Application deadline:* For fall admission, 6/1 for domestic students, 3/1 for international students; for spring admission, 11/1 for domestic students, 10/1 for international students. Applications are processed on a rolling basis. Application fee: $50. Electronic applications accepted. *Expenses:* Tuition, state resident: full-time $12,413; part-time $564.21 per credit. Tuition, nonresident: full-time $20,487; part-time $931.21 per credit. *Required fees:* $2107; $95.79 per credit. $478.95 per semester. Tuition and fees vary according to course load and degree level. *Financial support:* Research assistantships with full tuition reimbursements, Federal Work-Study, scholarships/grants, and unspecified assistantships available. Support available to part-time students. Financial award application deadline: 4/1; financial award applicants required to submit FAFSA. *Faculty research:* Sexual violence, history of science in Muslim societies, bioethics, teaching writing for transfer, psychological impact of microagressions on minority communities. *Unit head:* Dr. Kara Rabbitt, Dean, 973-720-2731, Fax: 973-720-2955, E-mail: rabbittk@wpunj.edu. *Application contact:* Tinu Adeniran, Associate Director, Graduate Admissions, 973-720-2764, Fax: 973-720-2035, E-mail: adenirant@wpunj.edu.
Website: http://www.wpunj.edu/cohss

York University, Faculty of Graduate Studies, Faculty of Liberal Arts and Professional Studies, Program in Public Policy, Administration and Law, Toronto, ON M3J 1P3, Canada. Offers MPPAL.

Rural Planning and Studies

Brandon University, Department of Rural Development, Brandon, MB R7A 6A9, Canada. Offers MRD, Diploma. *Degree requirements:* For master's, thesis. *Entrance requirements:* For master's, minimum GPA of 3.0, 2 letters of reference. Additional exam requirements/recommendations for international students: Required—TOEFL (minimum score 580 paper-based). Electronic applications accepted. *Faculty research:* Regional development, healthy communities, economic impact analysis, rural tourism, resource management.

California State University, Chico, Office of Graduate Studies, College of Behavioral and Social Sciences, Department of Geography and Planning, Chico, CA 95929-0722. Offers geography (MA), including environmental policy and planning, geography. Part-time programs available. *Faculty:* 1 (woman) full-time. *Students:* 1 (woman) part-time. Average age 44. In 2014, 5 master's awarded. *Degree requirements:* For master's, thesis or project. *Entrance requirements:* For master's, GRE, two letters of recommendation, statement of purpose, writing sample. Additional exam requirements/recommendations for international students: Required—TOEFL (minimum score 550 paper-based; 80 iBT), IELTS (minimum score 6.5), PTE (minimum score 59). *Application deadline:* For fall admission, 3/1 priority date for domestic students, 3/1 for international students; for spring admission, 9/15 priority date for domestic students, 9/15 for international students. Application fee: $55. Electronic applications accepted. *Expenses:* Tuition, state resident: full-time $7002. Tuition, nonresident: full-time $18,162. *Required fees:* $1530. Tuition and fees vary according to program. *Financial support:* Fellowships, teaching assistantships, career-related internships or fieldwork, institutionally sponsored loans, scholarships/grants, and unspecified assistantships available. Financial award application deadline: 3/1; financial award applicants required to submit FAFSA. *Unit head:* Dr. Jacquelyn Chase, Chair, 530-898-5285, Fax: 530-898-6781, E-mail: geop@csuchico.edu. *Application contact:* Judy L. Rice, Graduate Admissions Coordinator, 530-898-5416, Fax: 530-898-3342, E-mail: jlrice@csuchico.edu.
Website: http://www.csuchico.edu/geop/

Dalhousie University, Faculty of Architecture and Planning, School of Planning, Halifax, NS B3J 2X4, Canada. Offers M Eng, M Plan, MPS. *Degree requirements:* For master's, thesis. *Entrance requirements:* Additional exam requirements/recommendations for international students: Required—TOEFL, IELTS, CANTEST, CAEL, or Michigan English Language Assessment Battery. Electronic applications accepted.

East Carolina University, Graduate School, Thomas Harriot College of Arts and Sciences, Department of Geography, Planning, and Environment, Greenville, NC 27858-4353. Offers economic development (Certificate); geographic information science and technology (Certificate); geography (MA), including geography, planning, rural development. Part-time and evening/weekend programs available. *Degree requirements:* For master's, one foreign language, comprehensive exam, thesis optional. *Entrance requirements:* For master's, GRE General Test. Additional exam requirements/recommendations for international students: Required—TOEFL. *Expenses:* Tuition, state resident: full-time $4223. Tuition, nonresident: full-time $16,540. *Required fees:* $2184.

Iowa State University of Science and Technology, Department of History, Ames, IA 50011. Offers agricultural history and rural studies (PhD); history (MA); history of technology and science (MA, PhD). *Degree requirements:* For master's, thesis or alternative; for doctorate, thesis/dissertation. *Entrance requirements:* For master's and

doctorate, GRE General Test. Additional exam requirements/recommendations for international students: Required—TOEFL (minimum score 600 paper-based; 79 iBT), IELTS (minimum score 7). Electronic applications accepted.

Iowa State University of Science and Technology, Program in Agricultural History and Rural Studies, Ames, IA 50011. Offers PhD. *Entrance requirements:* Additional exam requirements/recommendations for international students: Required—TOEFL (minimum score 600 paper-based; 79 iBT), IELTS (minimum score 7). Electronic applications accepted.

Université Laval, Faculty of Agricultural and Food Sciences, Program in Integrated Rural Development, Québec, QC G1K 7P4, Canada. Offers Diploma. *Entrance requirements:* For degree, good knowledge of French. Electronic applications accepted.

University of Alaska Fairbanks, College of Rural and Community Development, Department of Alaska Native Studies and Rural Development, Fairbanks, AK 99775. Offers rural development (MA). Part-time programs available. Postbaccalaureate distance learning degree programs offered (minimal on-campus study). *Faculty:* 8 full-time (7 women). *Students:* 5 full-time (3 women), 22 part-time (21 women); includes 14 minority (12 American Indian or Alaska Native, non-Hispanic/Latino; 1 Asian, non-Hispanic/Latino; 1 Two or more races, non-Hispanic/Latino). Average age 38. 15 applicants, 53% accepted, 7 enrolled. In 2014, 11 master's awarded. *Degree requirements:* For master's, comprehensive exam, oral defense of project or thesis. *Entrance requirements:* For master's, bachelor's degree from accredited institution with minimum cumulative undergraduate and major GPA of 3.0. Additional exam requirements/recommendations for international students: Required—TOEFL (minimum score 550 paper-based; 79 iBT). *Application deadline:* For fall admission, 6/1 for domestic students, 3/1 for international students; for spring admission, 10/15 for domestic students, 9/1 for international students. Applications are processed on a rolling basis. Application fee: $60. Electronic applications accepted. *Expenses:* Tuition, state resident: full-time $7614; part-time $423 per credit. Tuition, nonresident: full-time $15,552; part-time $864 per credit. Tuition and fees vary according to course level, course load and reciprocity agreements. *Financial support:* In 2014–15, 1 research assistantship with full tuition reimbursement (averaging $14,162 per year), 1 teaching assistantship with full tuition reimbursement (averaging $11,955 per year) were awarded; fellowships with full tuition reimbursements, Federal Work-Study, scholarships/grants, and health care benefits also available. Support available to part-time students. Financial award application deadline: 2/15; financial award applicants required to submit FAFSA. *Faculty research:* International indigenous leadership development, interrelationships between rural communities and global economy. *Unit head:* Phillip Charette, Director, 907-474-6528, Fax: 907-474-6325, E-mail: fydanrd@uaf.edu. *Application contact:* Mary Kreta, Director of Admissions, 907-474-7500, Fax: 907-474-7097, E-mail: admissions@uaf.edu.
Website: http://www.uaf.edu/danrd/

University of Guelph, Graduate Studies, Ontario Agricultural College, School of Environmental Design and Rural Development, Interdisciplinary Program in Rural Studies, Guelph, ON N1G 2W1, Canada. Offers PhD. Offered in cooperation with the Department of Food, Agricultural and Resource Economics, and the Department of Geography. Part-time programs available. *Degree requirements:* For doctorate, thesis/dissertation, qualifying exam. *Entrance requirements:* Additional exam requirements/recommendations for international students: Required—TOEFL (minimum score 600 paper-based), IELTS (minimum score 7). Electronic applications accepted. *Faculty research:* Sustainable rural communities, human resource development, rural planning and development.

University of Guelph, Graduate Studies, Ontario Agricultural College, School of Environmental Design and Rural Development, Program in Capacity Development and Extension, Guelph, ON N1G 2W1, Canada. Offers M Sc. Part-time programs available. *Degree requirements:* For master's, thesis optional. *Entrance requirements:* For master's, minimum B- average in previous 2 years of course work. Additional exam requirements/recommendations for international students: Required—TOEFL (minimum score 550 paper-based; 89 iBT), IELTS (minimum score 6.5). Electronic applications accepted. *Faculty research:* Adult learning in non-formal settings, communication technology for remote areas, rural quality of life.

University of Guelph, Graduate Studies, Ontario Agricultural College, School of Environmental Design and Rural Development, Program in Rural Planning and Development, Guelph, ON N1G 2W1, Canada. Offers international rural planning and development (M Sc); rural planning and development in Canada (M Sc). M Sc offered in cooperation with Departments of Food, Agricultural and Resource Economics; Geography; Land Resource Science; and others by arrangement. Part-time programs available. *Degree requirements:* For master's, thesis or alternative. *Entrance requirements:* For master's, minimum B- average during previous 2 years of course work. Additional exam requirements/recommendations for international students: Required—TOEFL (minimum score 550 paper-based), IELTS (minimum score 6.5). Electronic applications accepted. *Faculty research:* Canadian and international rural planning, resource and economic development, tourism.

The University of Montana, Graduate School, College of Humanities and Sciences, Department of Geography, Missoula, MT 59812-0002. Offers community and environmental planning (MA); geography (MA, MS). *Entrance requirements:* For master's, GRE General Test. Additional exam requirements/recommendations for international students: Required—TOEFL.

University of Wyoming, College of Arts and Sciences, Department of Geography, Program in Rural Planning and Natural Resources, Laramie, WY 82071. Offers community and regional planning and natural resources (MP). *Degree requirements:* For master's, thesis or alternative. *Entrance requirements:* For master's, GRE General Test, minimum GPA of 3.0. Additional exam requirements/recommendations for international students: Required—TOEFL. *Faculty research:* Rural and small town planning, public land management.

Sustainable Development

Acadia University, Faculty of Professional Studies, School of Recreation Management and Community Development, Wolfville, NS B4P 2R6, Canada. Offers MR. *Degree requirements:* For master's, thesis. *Entrance requirements:* Additional exam requirements/recommendations for international students: Required—TOEFL (minimum score 630 paper-based; 93 iBT), IELTS (minimum score 6.5).

American University, School of International Service, Washington, DC 20016-8071. Offers comparative and regional studies (Certificate); cross-cultural communication (Certificate); development management (MS); ethics, peace, and global affairs (MA); European studies (Certificate); global environmental policy (MA, Certificate); global information technology (Certificate); international affairs (MA), including comparative and international disability policy, comparative and regional studies, international economic relations, international politics, natural resources and sustainable development, U.S. foreign policy; international communication (MA, Certificate); international development (MA, Certificate); international economic policy (Certificate); international economic relations (Certificate); international media (MA); international peace and conflict resolution (MA, Certificate); international politics (Certificate); international relations (PhD); international service (MIS); peacebuilding (Certificate); social enterprise (MA); the Americas (Certificate); United States foreign policy (Certificate); JD/MA. Part-time and evening/weekend programs available. Postbaccalaureate distance learning degree programs offered (no on-campus study). *Faculty:* 112 full-time (43 women), 59 part-time/adjunct (27 women). *Students:* 545 full-time (335 women), 443 part-time (271 women); includes 231 minority (82 Black or African American, non-Hispanic/Latino; 8 American Indian or Alaska Native, non-Hispanic/Latino; 51 Asian, non-Hispanic/Latino; 81 Hispanic/Latino; 2 Native Hawaiian or other Pacific Islander, non-Hispanic/Latino; 7 Two or more races, non-Hispanic/Latino), 120 international. Average age 28. 1,991 applicants, 70% accepted, 365 enrolled. In 2014, 426 master's, 9 doctorates, 6 other advanced degrees awarded. Terminal master's awarded for partial completion of doctoral program. *Degree requirements:* For master's, one foreign language, comprehensive exam, thesis or alternative; for doctorate, one foreign language, comprehensive exam, thesis/dissertation. *Entrance requirements:* For master's, GRE, transcripts, resume, 2 letters of recommendation, statement of purpose; for doctorate, GRE, transcripts, resume, 3 letters of recommendation, statement of purpose. Additional exam requirements/recommendations for international students: Required—TOEFL (minimum score 600 paper-based; 100 iBT). *Application deadline:* For fall admission, 1/15 for domestic students; for spring admission, 10/1 for domestic students, 9/15 for international students. Application fee: $50. Electronic applications accepted. *Financial support:* Application deadline: 1/15. *Unit head:* Dr. James Goldgeier, Dean, 202-885-1603, Fax: 202-885-2494, E-mail: goldgeier@american.edu. *Application contact:* Jia Jiang, Associate Director, Graduate Education Enrollment, 202-885-1689, Fax: 202-885-1109, E-mail: jiang@american.edu.
Website: http://www.american.edu/sis/

Antioch University Los Angeles, Graduate Programs, Program in Urban Sustainability, Culver City, CA 90230. Offers MA.

Antioch University New England, Graduate School, Department of Education, Experienced Educators Program, Keene, NH 03431-3552. Offers foundations of education (M Ed), including applied behavioral analysis, autism spectrum disorders, educating for sustainability, next-generation learning using technology, problem-based learning using critical skills, teacher leadership; principal certification (PMC). *Degree requirements:* For master's, thesis, practicum. *Entrance requirements:* For master's, previous course work and work experience in education. Additional exam requirements/recommendations for international students: Required—TOEFL (minimum score 550 paper-based). Electronic applications accepted. *Expenses:* Contact institution. *Faculty research:* Classroom action research, school restructuring, problem-based learning, brain-based learning.

Antioch University New England, Graduate School, Department of Environmental Studies, Program in Advocacy for Social Justice and Sustainability, Keene, NH 03431-3552. Offers MS. *Degree requirements:* For master's, practicum, seminar. *Entrance requirements:* For master's, samples of written work, portfolio, letters of recommendation, interview. Additional exam requirements/recommendations for international students: Required—TOEFL (minimum score 550 paper-based). Electronic applications accepted.

Appalachian State University, Cratis D. Williams Graduate School, Center for Appalachian Studies, Boone, NC 28608. Offers culture (MA); roots and music (MA); sustainable development (MA). Part-time programs available. *Degree requirements:* For master's, one foreign language, comprehensive exam, thesis optional. *Entrance requirements:* For master's, GRE General Test, 3 letters of recommendation. Additional exam requirements/recommendations for international students: Required—TOEFL (minimum score 570 paper-based; 79 iBT), IELTS (minimum score 6.5). Electronic applications accepted. *Faculty research:* Appalachian culture, sustainable development, Appalachian music.

Arizona State University at the Tempe campus, School of Sustainability, Tempe, AZ 85287-5502. Offers sustainability (MA, MS, PhD); sustainable technology and management (Graduate Certificate). Part-time and evening/weekend programs available. Terminal master's awarded for partial completion of doctoral program. *Degree requirements:* For master's, thesis, interactive Program of Study (iPOS) submitted before completing 50 percent of required credit hours; for doctorate, comprehensive exam, thesis/dissertation, interactive Program of Study (iPOS) submitted before completing 50 percent of required credit hours. *Entrance requirements:* For master's, GRE; for doctorate, GRE, minimum GPA of 3.0 or equivalent in last 2 years of work leading to bachelor's degree. Additional exam requirements/recommendations for international students: Required—TOEFL, IELTS, or PTE. Electronic applications accepted.

Boston Architectural College, Graduate Programs, Boston, MA 02115-2795. Offers architecture (M Arch); historic preservation (MDS); interior design (MID); landscape architecture (MLA); sustainable design (MDS). *Accreditation:* CIDA. *Degree requirements:* For master's, thesis. *Entrance requirements:* For master's, portfolio (recommended). Electronic applications accepted.

Brandeis University, The Heller School for Social Policy and Management, Program in Nonprofit Management, Waltham, MA 02454-9110. Offers child, youth, and family management (MBA); health care management (MBA); social impact management (MBA); social policy and management (MBA); sustainable development (MBA); MBA/MA; MBA/MD. MBA/MD program offered in conjunction with Tufts University School of Medicine. *Accreditation:* AACSB. Part-time programs available. *Degree requirements:* For master's, team consulting project. *Entrance requirements:* For master's, GMAT (preferred) or GRE, 2 letters of recommendation, problem statement analysis, 3-5 years of professional experience. Additional exam requirements/recommendations for international students: Required—TOEFL (minimum score 600 paper-based; 100 iBT).

Electronic applications accepted. *Expenses:* Contact institution. *Faculty research:* Health care; children and families; elder and disabled services; social impact management; organizations in the non-profit, for-profit, or public sector.

Brandeis University, The Heller School for Social Policy and Management, Program in Sustainable International Development, Waltham, MA 02454-9110. Offers international development (MA); MA/JD; MA/MA; MBA/MA. MA/JD program offered in conjunction with Northeastern University School of Law. *Degree requirements:* For master's, 2nd year fieldwork or internship; capstone paper and presentation. *Entrance requirements:* For master's, 3 letters of recommendation, curriculum vitae or resume, 3 years of development experience (international experience preferred). Additional exam requirements/recommendations for international students: Required—TOEFL (minimum score 600 paper-based; 100 iBT). Electronic applications accepted. *Faculty research:* Water resource management, human rights, biosphere management, rural development, public policy and governance, gender, conservation, civil society, poverty eradication, project planning and implementation, evaluation, organizational management.

California State University, Stanislaus, College of Natural Sciences, Program in Ecology and Sustainability (MS), Turlock, CA 95382. Offers ecological conservation (MS); ecological economics (MS). Part-time programs available. *Degree requirements:* For master's, thesis. *Entrance requirements:* For master's, GRE, minimum GPA of 3.0, 3 letters of recommendation, personal statement. Additional exam requirements/ recommendations for international students: Required—TOEFL (minimum score 550 paper-based). Electronic applications accepted.

Carnegie Mellon University, Carnegie Institute of Technology, Department of Civil and Environmental Engineering, Pittsburgh, PA 15213. Offers advanced infrastructure systems (MS, PhD); advanced infrastructure systems technology development and application (MS); air quality engineering and science (MS); civil and environmental engineering (MS, PhD); civil and environmental engineering/engineering and public policy (PhD); civil engineering (MS, PhD); computational mechanics (MS, PhD); computational modeling and monitoring for resilient structural and material systems (MS); energy infrastructure systems (MS); environmental engineering (MS, PhD); environmental management and science (MS, PhD); IT-based sustainable global infrastructure and construction management (MS); sustainability and green design (MS); water quality engineering and science (MS). Part-time programs available. *Faculty:* 21 full-time (5 women), 12 part-time/adjunct (3 women). *Students:* 229 full-time (99 women), 31 part-time (11 women); includes 18 minority (4 Black or African American, non-Hispanic/Latino; 13 Asian, non-Hispanic/Latino; 1 Hispanic/Latino), 193 international. Average age 26. 590 applicants, 68% accepted, 124 enrolled. In 2014, 85 master's, 11 doctorates awarded. Terminal master's awarded for partial completion of doctoral program. *Degree requirements:* For master's, thesis optional; for doctorate, comprehensive exam, thesis/dissertation, two-part qualifying exam, public defense of dissertation. *Entrance requirements:* For master's, GRE General Test, BS in engineering, science or mathematics; for doctorate, GRE General Test, BS or MS in engineering, science or mathematics. Additional exam requirements/recommendations for international students: Required—TOEFL (minimum score 84 iBT) or IELTS. *Application deadline:* For fall admission, 1/5 priority date for domestic and international students; for spring admission, 9/15 priority date for domestic and international students. Application fee: $65. Electronic applications accepted. *Financial support:* In 2014–15, 169 students received support. Fellowships with full and partial tuition reimbursements available, research assistantships with full and partial tuition reimbursements available, scholarships/grants, tuition waivers (full and partial), unspecified assistantships, and service assistantships available. Financial award application deadline: 1/5. *Faculty research:* Advanced infrastructure systems; environmental engineering, sustainability, and science; mechanics, materials, and computing. *Total annual research expenditures:* $4.9 million. *Unit head:* Dr. David A. Dzombak, Head, 412-268-2941, Fax: 412-268-7813, E-mail: dzombak@cmu.edu. *Application contact:* Melissa L. Brown, Director of Graduate Admissions & Recruiting, 412-268-8762, Fax: 412-268-7813, E-mail: mlb2@andrew.cmu.edu.
Website: http://www.cmu.edu/cee/

City College of the City University of New York, Graduate School, Program in Sustainability in the Urban Environment, New York, NY 10031-9198. Offers MS. *Degree requirements:* For master's, capstone project.

Clarkson University, Graduate School, Institute for a Sustainable Environment, Potsdam, NY 13699. Offers MS, PhD. Part-time programs available. *Faculty:* 10 full-time (4 women), 2 part-time/adjunct (both women). *Students:* 25 full-time (12 women), 4 part-time (1 woman), 14 international. Average age 28. 33 applicants, 58% accepted, 7 enrolled. In 2014, 11 master's, 3 doctorates awarded. Terminal master's awarded for partial completion of doctoral program. *Degree requirements:* For master's, thesis; for doctorate, comprehensive exam, thesis/dissertation, departmental qualifying exam. *Entrance requirements:* For master's and doctorate, GRE, transcripts of all college coursework, resume, personal statement, three letters of recommendation. Additional exam requirements/recommendations for international students: Required—TOEFL (minimum score 550 paper-based; 80 iBT), IELTS (minimum score 6.5). *Application deadline:* For fall admission, 1/30 priority date for domestic and international students; for spring admission, 9/1 priority date for domestic and international students. Applications are processed on a rolling basis. Application fee: $25 ($35 for international students). Electronic applications accepted. *Expenses: Tuition:* Full-time $16,680; part-time $1390 per credit. *Required fees:* $295 per semester. *Financial support:* In 2014–15, 26 students received support, including fellowships with full tuition reimbursements available (averaging $24,029 per year), 12 research assistantships with full tuition reimbursements available (averaging $24,029 per year), 4 teaching assistantships with full tuition reimbursements available (averaging $24,029 per year); scholarships/grants, tuition waivers (partial), and unspecified assistantships also available. *Faculty research:* Scrubbing technology, Great Lakes fish, CO in biofuel, pellet boilers, nanomaterial penetration of protective gloves. *Total annual research expenditures:* $769,274. *Unit head:* Dr. Philip Hopke, Director, 315-268-3856, Fax: 315-268-4291, E-mail: hopkepk@clarkson.edu. *Application contact:* Mary Jane Smalling, Administrative Assistant, 315-268-2318, Fax: 315-268-4291, E-mail: isegrad@clarkson.edu.
Website: http://www.clarkson.edu/ise/

Clark University, Graduate School, Department of International Development, Community, and Environment, Worcester, MA 01610-1477. Offers community development and planning (MA); environmental science and policy (MS); geographic information science for development and environment (MS); international development and social change (MA); MA/MBA; MBA/MS. *Faculty:* 16 full-time (8 women), 8 part-time/adjunct (2 women). *Students:* 161 full-time (97 women), 21 part-time (7 women); includes 31 minority (13 Black or African American, non-Hispanic/Latino; 1 American Indian or Alaska Native, non-Hispanic/Latino; 8 Asian, non-Hispanic/Latino; 7 Hispanic/ Latino; 2 Two or more races, non-Hispanic/Latino), 47 international. Average age 27. 364 applicants, 86% accepted, 113 enrolled. In 2014, 115 master's awarded. *Degree requirements:* For master's, thesis. *Entrance requirements:* For master's, 3 references, resume or curriculum vitae. Additional exam requirements/recommendations for international students: Required—TOEFL (minimum score 575 paper-based; 90 iBT) or IELTS (minimum score 6.5). *Application deadline:* For fall admission, 1/15 for domestic students. Application fee: $75. *Expenses: Tuition:* Full-time $40,380; part-time $1262 per credit hour. *Required fees:* $30. *Financial support:* Fellowships with partial tuition reimbursements, research assistantships with partial tuition reimbursements, teaching assistantships with partial tuition reimbursements, institutionally sponsored loans, and scholarships/grants available. *Faculty research:* Community action research, gender analysis, environmental risk assessment, land-use planning, geographic information systems, HIV and AIDS, global health and social justice, environmental health, climate change and sustainability. *Total annual research expenditures:* $140,000. *Unit head:* Dr. Ellen Foley, Interim Director, 508-793-7201, Fax: 508-793-8820, E-mail: dbell@clarku.edu. *Application contact:* Erika Paradis, Student and Academic Services Director, 508-793-7201, Fax: 508-793-8820, E-mail: eparadis@clarku.edu.
Website: http://www.clarku.edu/departments/idce/default.cfm

Cleveland State University, College of Graduate Studies, Maxine Goodman Levin College of Urban Affairs, Program in Urban Planning, Design, and Development, Cleveland, OH 44115. Offers economic development (MUPDD); environmental sustainability (MUPDD); geographic information systems (MUPDD, Certificate); historic preservation (MUPDD); housing and neighborhood development (MUPDD); urban economic development (Certificate); urban real estate development and finance (MUPDD, Certificate); JD/MUPDD. *Accreditation:* ACSP. Part-time and evening/ weekend programs available. *Faculty:* 23 full-time (11 women), 23 part-time/adjunct (6 women). *Students:* 11 full-time (5 women), 25 part-time (10 women); includes 8 minority (2 Black or African American, non-Hispanic/Latino; 1 Asian, non-Hispanic/Latino; 2 Hispanic/Latino; 3 Two or more races, non-Hispanic/Latino), 3 international. Average age 38. 48 applicants, 56% accepted, 5 enrolled. In 2014, 16 master's awarded. *Degree requirements:* For master's, thesis or alternative, planning studio. *Entrance requirements:* For master's, GRE General Test (minimum score: 50th percentile combined verbal and quantitative, 4.0 analytical writing), minimum GPA of 3.0. Additional exam requirements/recommendations for international students: Required—TOEFL (minimum score 525 paper-based; 65 iBT), IELTS, or ITEP. *Application deadline:* For fall admission, 7/15 priority date for domestic students, 5/15 for international students; for spring admission, 11/1 for international students. Applications are processed on a rolling basis. Application fee: $30. Electronic applications accepted. *Expenses:* Expenses: $9,615 full-time, in-state tuition and fees. *Financial support:* In 2014–15, 10 students received support, including 7 research assistantships with full and partial tuition reimbursements available (averaging $5,600 per year), 2 teaching assistantships with full and partial tuition reimbursements available (averaging $2,000 per year); career-related internships or fieldwork, Federal Work-Study, scholarships/ grants, tuition waivers, and unspecified assistantships also available. Support available to part-time students. Financial award application deadline: 3/1; financial award applicants required to submit FAFSA. *Faculty research:* Housing and neighborhood development, urban housing policy, environmental sustainability, economic development, GIS and planning decision support. *Unit head:* Dr. Dennis Keating, Director, 216-687-2298, Fax: 216-687-2013, E-mail: w.keating@csuohio.edu. *Application contact:* David Arrighi, Graduate Academic Advisor, 216-523-7522, Fax: 216-687-5398, E-mail: urbanprograms@csuohio.edu.
Website: http://urban.csuohio.edu/academics/graduate/mupdd/

Columbia University, Graduate School of Arts and Sciences, New York, NY 10027. Offers African-American studies (MA); American studies (MA); anthropology (MA, PhD); art history and archaeology (MA, PhD); astronomy (PhD); biological sciences (PhD); biotechnology (MA); chemical physics (PhD); chemistry (PhD); classical studies (MA, PhD); classics (MA, PhD); climate and society (MA); earth and environmental sciences (PhD); East Asia: regional studies (MA); East Asian languages and cultures (MA, PhD); ecology, evolution and environmental biology (MA), including conservation biology; ecology, evolution, and environmental biology (PhD), including ecology and evolutionary biology, evolutionary primatology; economics (PhD); English and comparative literature (MA, PhD); French and Romance philology (MA, PhD); Germanic languages (MA, PhD); global French studies (MA); Hispanic cultural studies (MA); history (PhD); history and literature (MA); human rights studies (MA); Islamic studies (MA); Italian (MA, PhD); Japanese pedagogy (MA); Jewish studies (MA); Latin America and the Caribbean: regional studies (MA); Latin American and Iberian cultures (PhD); mathematics (MA, PhD), including finance (MA); medieval and Renaissance studies (MA); Middle Eastern, South Asian, and African studies (MA, PhD); modern art: critical and curatorial studies (MA); modern European studies (MA); museum anthropology (MA); music (DMA, PhD); oral history (MA); philosophical foundations of physics (MA); philosophy (MA, PhD); physics (PhD); political science (MA, PhD); psychology (PhD); quantitative methods in the social sciences (MA); religion (MA, PhD); Russia, Eurasia and East Europe: regional studies (MA); Russian translation (MA); Slavic cultures (MA); Slavic languages (MA, PhD); sociology (MA, PhD); South Asian studies (MA); statistics (MA, PhD); theatre (PhD); JD/PhD; MA/MS; MD/PhD; MPA/MA. Dual-degree programs require admission to both Graduate School of Arts and Sciences and another Columbia school. Part-time and evening/weekend programs available. Terminal master's awarded for partial completion of doctoral program. *Degree requirements:* For master's, thesis (for some programs); for doctorate, comprehensive exam, thesis/dissertation. *Entrance requirements:* For master's and doctorate, GRE General Test, GRE Subject Test (for some programs). Electronic applications accepted. *Faculty research:* Humanities, natural sciences, social sciences.

Columbia University, School of International and Public Affairs, Program in Development Practice, New York, NY 10027. Offers MPA. Offered through The Earth Institute.

The Conway School, Graduate Program in Sustainable Landscape Planning and Design, Conway, MA 01341-0179. Offers landscape design (MA). *Degree requirements:* For master's, projects. *Faculty research:* Restoration of native plant communities; integration of humanities, environment, and design.

Cornell University, Graduate School, Graduate Fields of Agriculture and Life Sciences and Graduate Fields of Engineering, Field of Biological and Environmental Engineering, Ithaca, NY 14853-0001. Offers bioenergy and integrated energy systems (M Eng, MPS, MS, PhD); biological engineering (M Eng, MPS, MS, PhD); bioprocess engineering (M Eng, MPS, MS, PhD); ecohydrology (M Eng, MPS, MS, PhD); environmental engineering (M Eng, MPS, MS, PhD); environmental management (MPS); food engineering (M Eng, MPS, MS, PhD); industrial biotechnology (M Eng, MPS, MS, PhD); nanobiotechnology (M Eng, MPS, MS, PhD); sustainable systems (M Eng, MPS, MS, PhD); synthetic biology (MS); syntheticbiology (M Eng, MPS, PhD). Terminal master's awarded for partial completion of doctoral program. *Degree requirements:* For master's, thesis (MS); for doctorate, comprehensive exam, thesis/dissertation. *Entrance requirements:* For master's, letters of recommendation (3 for MS, 2 for M Eng and MPS); for doctorate, GRE General Test, 3 letters of recommendation. Additional exam requirements/recommendations for international students: Required—TOEFL (minimum score 550 paper-based; 77 iBT). Electronic applications accepted. *Faculty research:* Biological and food engineering, environmental, soil and water engineering, international agricultural engineering, structures and controlled environments, machine systems and energy.

DePaul University, College of Liberal Arts and Social Sciences, Chicago, IL 60614. Offers Arabic (MA); Chinese (MA); English (MA); French (MA); German (MA); history

(MA); interdisciplinary studies (MA, MS); international public service (MS); international studies (MA); Italian (MA); Japanese (MA); leadership and policy studies (MS); liberal studies (MA); new media studies (MA); nonprofit management (MNM); public administration (MPA); public health (MPH); public service management (MS); social work (MSW); sociology (MA); Spanish (MA); sustainable urban development (MA); women and gender studies (MA); writing and publishing (MA); writing, rhetoric, and discourse (MA); MA/PhD. Part-time and evening/weekend programs available. Postbaccalaureate distance learning degree programs offered (no on-campus study). Terminal master's awarded for partial completion of doctoral program. *Degree requirements:* For master's, variable foreign language requirement, comprehensive exam (for some programs), thesis (for some programs). Electronic applications accepted.

Eastern Illinois University, Graduate School, Lumpkin College of Business and Applied Sciences, School of Technology, Program in Sustainable Energy, Charleston, IL 61920. Offers MS, MS/MBA, MS/MS. Part-time and evening/weekend programs available. *Faculty:* 28. *Students:* 14 full-time (4 women), 2 part-time (both women), 13 international. Average age 27. 31 applicants, 65% accepted, 11 enrolled. In 2014, 4 master's awarded. *Degree requirements:* For master's, comprehensive exam. *Entrance requirements:* For master's, GMAT or GRE. Additional exam requirements/recommendations for international students: Required—TOEFL (minimum score 500 paper-based; 61 iBT), IELTS (minimum score 6). *Application deadline:* For fall admission, 5/15 for domestic and international students; for spring admission, 10/15 for domestic and international students. Applications are processed on a rolling basis. Application fee: $30. Electronic applications accepted. *Expenses:* Tuition, state resident: full-time $3113; part-time $283 per credit hour. Tuition, nonresident: full-time $7469; part-time $679 per credit hour. *Required fees:* $2287; $96 per credit hour. Tuition and fees vary according to course load. *Financial support:* In 2014–15, 18 students received support, including 5 research assistantships with full tuition reimbursements available (averaging $7,830 per year); career-related internships or fieldwork, Federal Work-Study, and unspecified assistantships also available. Support available to part-time students. Financial award application deadline: 3/1; financial award applicants required to submit FAFSA. *Unit head:* Peter Ping Liu, Graduate Coordinator, 217-581-6267, Fax: 217-581-6607, E-mail: pliu@eiu.edu.
Website: http://www.eiu.edu/sustainable/

Emory University, Laney Graduate School, Program in Development Practice, Atlanta, GA 30322-1100. Offers MDP. *Entrance requirements:* Additional exam requirements/recommendations for international students: Recommended—TOEFL.

Fashion Institute of Technology, School of Graduate Studies, Program in Sustainable Interior Environments, New York, NY 10001-5992. Offers MA.
See Display on page 84 and Close-Up on page 101.

Florida Atlantic University, College of Design and Social Inquiry, School of Urban and Regional Planning, Boca Raton, FL 33431-0991. Offers economic development and tourism (Certificate); environmental planning (Certificate); sustainable community planning (Certificate); urban and regional planning (MURP); visual planning technology (Certificate). *Accreditation:* ACSP. Part-time and evening/weekend programs available. *Entrance requirements:* For master's, GRE General Test, minimum GPA of 3.0. Additional exam requirements/recommendations for international students: Required—TOEFL (minimum score 500 paper-based; 61 iBT), IELTS (minimum score 6). *Expenses:* Tuition, state resident: full-time $7396; part-time $369.82 per credit hour. Tuition, nonresident: full-time $19,392; part-time $1024.81 per credit hour. Tuition and fees vary according to course load. *Faculty research:* Growth management, urban design, computer applications/geographical information systems, environmental planning.

Future Generations Graduate School, Program in Applied Community Change, Conservation, and Peacebuilding, Franklin, WV 26807. Offers conservation (MA); peacebuilding (MA). *Degree requirements:* For master's, one foreign language, applied practicum research. *Entrance requirements:* For master's, bachelor's degree, community involvement. Additional exam requirements/recommendations for international students: Required—TOEFL. Electronic applications accepted. *Faculty research:* Sustainable communities, community engagement, peacebuilding, seed-scale community development.

Hawai`i Pacific University, College of Humanities and Social Sciences, Program in Global Leadership and Sustainable Development, Honolulu, HI 96813. Offers MA. Part-time and evening/weekend programs available. *Faculty:* 6 full-time (2 women), 1 part-time/adjunct (0 women). *Students:* 32 full-time (22 women), 9 part-time (6 women); includes 17 minority (2 Black or African American, non-Hispanic/Latino; 8 Asian, non-Hispanic/Latino; 3 Hispanic/Latino; 4 Two or more races, non-Hispanic/Latino). Average age 31. 34 applicants, 59% accepted, 10 enrolled. In 2014, 21 master's awarded. *Degree requirements:* For master's, thesis. *Entrance requirements:* Additional exam requirements/recommendations for international students: Recommended—TOEFL (minimum score 550 paper-based; 80 iBT), TWE (minimum score 5). *Application deadline:* For fall admission, 2/15 priority date for domestic students; for spring admission, 10/15 priority date for domestic students. Applications are processed on a rolling basis. Application fee: $50. Electronic applications accepted. *Expenses: Tuition:* Full-time $15,570; part-time $865 per credit. *Required fees:* $13. One-time fee: $50. Tuition and fees vary according to course load and program. *Financial support:* In 2014–15, 7 students received support. Career-related internships or fieldwork, Federal Work-Study, scholarships/grants, tuition waivers, and unspecified assistantships available. Financial award application deadline: 3/1; financial award applicants required to submit FAFSA. *Unit head:* Dr. Carlos Juarez, Department Chair, 808-566-2493, Fax: 808-544-1424, E-mail: cjuarez@hpu.edu. *Application contact:* Danny Lam, Assistant Director of Graduate Admissions, 808-543-8034, Fax: 808-544-0280, E-mail: grad@hpu.edu.
Website: http://www.hpu.edu/CHSS/SocialSciences/GLSD/

HEC Montreal, School of Business Administration, Graduate Diploma Programs in Administration, Program in Management and Sustainable Development, Montréal, QC H3T 2A7, Canada. Offers Graduate Diploma. All courses are given in French. *Students:* 9 full-time (6 women), 42 part-time (24 women). 35 applicants, 71% accepted, 17 enrolled. In 2014, 33 Graduate Diplomas awarded. *Degree requirements:* For Graduate Diploma, one foreign language. *Entrance requirements:* For degree, bachelor's degree (not in administration). *Application deadline:* For fall admission, 4/15 for domestic and international students; for winter admission, 9/15 for domestic and international students. Application fee: $83. Electronic applications accepted. *Financial support:* Research assistantships, teaching assistantships, and scholarships/grants available. Financial award application deadline: 9/2. *Unit head:* Silvia Ponce, Director, 514-340-6393, Fax: 514-340-6915, E-mail: silvia.ponce@hec.ca. *Application contact:* Jo Anne Audet, Administrative Director, 514-340-1315, Fax: 514-340-6411, E-mail: joanne.audet@hec.ca.
Website: http://www.hec.ca/programmes_formations/des/dess/dess_gestion_developpement_durable/index.html

Hofstra University, College of Liberal Arts and Sciences, Program in Sustainability Studies, Hempstead, NY 11549. Offers MA. *Accreditation:* APA; NCATE. Part-time and evening/weekend programs available. *Entrance requirements:* For master's, minimum GPA of 3.0, essay, 3 letters of recommendation. Additional exam requirements/recommendations for international students: Required—TOEFL (minimum score 550 paper-based; 80 iBT). *Application deadline:* Applications are processed on a rolling basis. Application fee: $70 ($75 for international students). Electronic applications accepted. *Expenses: Tuition:* Full-time $20,610; part-time $1145 per credit hour. *Required fees:* $970; $165 per term. Tuition and fees vary according to program. *Financial support:* Fellowships with full and partial tuition reimbursements, research assistantships with full and partial tuition reimbursements, career-related internships or fieldwork, Federal Work-Study, institutionally sponsored loans, scholarships/grants, tuition waivers (full and partial), and unspecified assistantships available. Support available to part-time students. Financial award applicants required to submit FAFSA. *Faculty research:* Urban sustainability, suburban sustainability, sustainable energy policy, greenhouse gas accounting, karst land use. *Unit head:* Dr. Robert Brinkmann, Program Director, 516-463-7348, Fax: 516-463-5120, E-mail: gsgrzb@hofstra.edu. *Application contact:* Sunil Samuel, Assistant Vice President of Admissions, 516-463-4723, Fax: 516-463-4664, E-mail: graduateadmission@hofstra.edu.
Website: http://www.hofstra.edu/hclas

Instituto Centroamericano de Administración de Empresas, Graduate Programs, La Garita, Costa Rica. Offers agribusiness management (MIAM); business administration (EMBA); finance (MBA); real estate management (MGREM); sustainable development (MBA); technology (MBA). *Degree requirements:* For master's, comprehensive exam, essay. *Entrance requirements:* For master's, GMAT or GRE General Test, fluency in Spanish, interview, letters of recommendation, minimum 1 year of work experience. Additional exam requirements/recommendations for international students: Recommended—TOEFL. Electronic applications accepted. *Faculty research:* Competitiveness, production.

Instituto Tecnologico de Santo Domingo, Graduate School, Area of Humanities and Social Sciences, Santo Domingo, Dominican Republic. Offers accounting (Certificate); adult education (Certificate); applied linguistics (MA); economics (MA); education (M Ed); educational psychology (MA, Certificate); gender and development (MA, Certificate); humanistic studies (MA); international marketing management (Certificate); international relations in the Caribbean basin (Certificate); intervention systems in family therapy (MA); linguistic and literary communication (Certificate); pedagogical support (MA); social science education (M Ed); sustainable human development (MA); terminal illness and death psychology (Certificate); youth and adult education (M Ed).

Iowa State University of Science and Technology, Program in Sustainable Agriculture, Ames, IA 50011. Offers MS, PhD. *Entrance requirements:* For master's and doctorate, GRE General Test. Additional exam requirements/recommendations for international students: Required—TOEFL (minimum score 570 paper-based; 80 iBT), IELTS (minimum score 6.5). Electronic applications accepted.

Judson University, Graduate Programs, Master of Architecture Program, Elgin, IL 60123-1498. Offers architecture (M Arch); sustainable design (M Arch); traditional architecture and urbanism (M Arch). Part-time programs available. *Degree requirements:* For master's, thesis optional, 1600-hour practicum/preceptorship completed prior to enrollment. *Entrance requirements:* For master's, GRE, Judson BA in architecture or equivalent; minimum cumulative undergraduate GPA of 2.75, 3.0 in architecture; comprehensive portfolio; letter of intent. Additional exam requirements/recommendations for international students: Required—TOEFL (minimum score 550 paper-based), IELTS (minimum score 6.5). *Application deadline:* For fall admission, 2/15 priority date for domestic and international students; for winter admission, 11/15 for domestic students; for spring admission, 11/15 for domestic and international students. Applications are processed on a rolling basis. Application fee: $100. Electronic applications accepted. *Expenses:* Expenses: Contact institution. *Financial support:* Teaching assistantships with partial tuition reimbursements, career-related internships or fieldwork, Federal Work-Study, and unspecified assistantships available. Financial award application deadline: 7/1; financial award applicants required to submit FAFSA. *Faculty research:* Sustainable design, urbanism, daylighting, acoustics, digital media and fabrication. *Unit head:* Keelan Kaiser, Chair, 847-628-1011, E-mail: kkaiser@judsonu.edu. *Application contact:* Nathan McNeely, Director of Admissions, 847-628-2510, E-mail: nmcneely@judsonu.edu.
Website: http://www.judsonu.edu/ArchMaster/

Lenoir-Rhyne University, Graduate Programs, School of Natural Sciences, Program in Sustainability Studies, Hickory, NC 28601. Offers MS. Part-time and evening/weekend programs available. Postbaccalaureate distance learning degree programs offered (no on-campus study). *Faculty:* 1 full-time. *Students:* 2 full-time (1 woman), 12 part-time (8 women), 1 international. Average age 34. *Entrance requirements:* For master's, GRE General Test or MAT, essay; minimum GPA of 2.7 undergraduate, 3.0 graduate. Additional exam requirements/recommendations for international students: Required—TOEFL (minimum score 600 paper-based). Application fee: $35. Electronic applications accepted. *Expenses: Tuition:* Full-time $9000; part-time $500 per credit hour. Tuition and fees vary according to program. *Unit head:* Dr. Amy Wood, Coordinator, 828-328-7728, Fax: 828-328-7368, E-mail: amy.wood@lr.edu. *Application contact:* Mary Ann Gosnell, Associate Director of Enrollment Management Graduate Studies and Adult Learners, 828-328-7300, E-mail: admission@lr.edu.
Website: http://www.lr.edu/academics/programs/sustainability-studies

Lesley University, Graduate School of Arts and Social Sciences, Cambridge, MA 02138-2790. Offers clinical mental health counseling (MA), including holistic counseling, school and community counseling, trauma studies; counseling psychology (MA, CAGS), including professional counseling (MA), school counseling (MA); creative writing (MFA); expressive therapies (MA, PhD, CAGS), including art (MA), clinical mental health counseling (MA), dance (MA), expressive therapies (MA), music (MA); independent studies (CAGS); independent study (MA); intercultural relations (MA, CAGS); interdisciplinary studies (MA), including individualized studies, integrative holistic health, mindfulness studies, peace and conflict transformation, trauma sensitive assessment, intervention, and consultation, women's studies; urban environmental leadership (MA). Part-time programs available. Postbaccalaureate distance learning degree programs offered (no on-campus study). *Faculty:* 35 full-time (25 women), 115 part-time/adjunct (90 women). *Students:* 420 full-time (379 women), 514 part-time (414 women); includes 142 minority (50 Black or African American, non-Hispanic/Latino; 5 American Indian or Alaska Native, non-Hispanic/Latino; 16 Asian, non-Hispanic/Latino; 48 Hispanic/Latino; 23 Two or more races, non-Hispanic/Latino), 46 international. Average age 33. In 2014, 475 master's, 11 doctorates, 4 other advanced degrees awarded. *Degree requirements:* For master's, internship, practicum, thesis (for expressive therapies); for doctorate, thesis/dissertation, arts apprenticeship, field placement; for CAGS, thesis, internship (for counseling psychology, expressive therapies). *Entrance requirements:* For master's, MAT (counseling psychology), interview, writing samples, art portfolio; for doctorate, GRE or MAT, interview, master's degree; for CAGS, interview, master's degree. Additional exam requirements/recommendations for international students: Required—TOEFL (minimum score 550 paper-based; 80 iBT). *Application deadline:* Applications are processed on a rolling basis. Application fee: $50. Electronic applications accepted. *Financial support:* Fellowships, career-related internships or fieldwork, Federal Work-Study, scholarships/grants, tuition waivers, and unspecified assistantships available.

Financial award applicants required to submit FAFSA. *Faculty research:* Psychotherapy and culture; psychotherapy and psychological trauma; women's issues in art, teaching and psychotherapy; community-based art, psycho-spiritual inquiry. *Unit head:* Dr. Catherine Koverola, Dean, 617-349-8317, Fax: 617-349-8366, E-mail: koverola@lesley.edu. *Application contact:* Martha Sheehan, Director, Graduate Admissions, 888-LESLEYU, Fax: 617-349-8313, E-mail: info@lesley.edu. Website: http://www.lesley.edu/graduate-school-of-arts-and-social-sciences/

Lipscomb University, Institute for Sustainable Practice, Nashville, TN 37204-3951. Offers MS, Certificate, MBA/MS. Part-time and evening/weekend programs available. Postbaccalaureate distance learning degree programs offered (minimal on-campus study). *Faculty:* 1 full-time (0 women), 3 part-time/adjunct (0 women). *Students:* 7 full-time (3 women), 3 part-time (all women); includes 1 minority (Native Hawaiian or other Pacific Islander, non-Hispanic/Latino). Average age 32. 19 applicants, 26% accepted, 5 enrolled. In 2014, 9 master's, 2 other advanced degrees awarded. *Degree requirements:* For master's, capstone project. *Entrance requirements:* For master's, GRE or GMAT, 2 references, interview. Additional exam requirements/recommendations for international students: Required—TOEFL (minimum score 570 paper-based; 80 iBT). *Application deadline:* For fall admission, 7/15 for domestic students; for spring admission, 12/15 for domestic students. Applications are processed on a rolling basis. Application fee: $50 ($75 for international students). Electronic applications accepted. *Expenses:* Expenses: $1,230 per credit hour. *Financial support:* Unspecified assistantships available. Financial award applicants required to submit FAFSA. *Faculty research:* Water and energy sustainability practices, sociology of conversation and natural resource management, new sustainability practices in forestry. *Unit head:* G. Dodd Galbreath, Executive Director, 615-966-1771, E-mail: dodd.galbreath@lipscomb.edu. *Application contact:* Emily Stutzman Jones, Academic Director, 615-966-5076, E-mail: emily.jones@lipscomb.edu.
Website: http://lipscomb.edu/sustainability

Minneapolis College of Art and Design, Certificate Programs, Minneapolis, MN 55404-4347. Offers design (Certificate); fine arts (Certificate); graphic design (Certificate); media (Certificate); sustainable design (Certificate). Part-time programs available. Postbaccalaureate distance learning degree programs offered. *Degree requirements:* For Certificate, final project. *Entrance requirements:* For degree, resume, portfolio, letter of recommendation. Additional exam requirements/recommendations for international students: Required—TOEFL (minimum score 550 paper-based; 79 iBT). Electronic applications accepted. *Faculty research:* Visual arts.

Mississippi State University, College of Forest Resources, Department of Sustainable Bioproducts, Mississippi State, MS 39762. Offers forest products (MS); forest resources (PhD), including forest products. *Faculty:* 10 full-time (2 women), 1 part-time/adjunct (0 women). *Students:* 24 full-time (13 women), 4 part-time (1 woman); includes 1 minority (Asian, non-Hispanic/Latino), 16 international. Average age 29. 21 applicants, 71% accepted, 10 enrolled. In 2014, 3 master's, 3 doctorates awarded. *Degree requirements:* For master's, thesis optional; for doctorate, comprehensive exam, thesis/dissertation. *Entrance requirements:* For master's, GRE (if undergraduate GPA of last two years less than 3.0); for doctorate, GRE if undergraduate GPA of last two years is below 3.0. Additional exam requirements/recommendations for international students: Required—TOEFL (minimum score 550 paper-based; 79 iBT); Recommended—IELTS (minimum score 6.5). *Application deadline:* For fall admission, 7/1 for domestic students, 5/1 for international students; for spring admission, 11/1 for domestic students, 9/1 for international students. Applications are processed on a rolling basis. Application fee: $60. Electronic applications accepted. *Expenses:* Tuition, state resident: full-time $7140; part-time $783 per credit hour. Tuition, nonresident: full-time $18,478; part-time $2043 per credit hour. *Financial support:* In 2014–15, 19 research assistantships with full tuition reimbursements (averaging $15,611 per year) were awarded; Federal Work-Study, institutionally sponsored loans, and unspecified assistantships also available. Financial award application deadline: 4/1; financial award applicants required to submit FAFSA. *Faculty research:* Wood property enhancement and durability, environmental science and chemistry, wood-based composites, primary wood production, furniture manufacturing and management. *Unit head:* Dr. Rubin Shmulsky, Department Head, 662-325-2243, Fax: 662-325-8126, E-mail: rshmulsky@cfr.msstate.edu.
Website: http://www.cfr.msstate.edu/forestp/index.asp

Montclair State University, The Graduate School, College of Science and Mathematics, Program in Sustainability Science, Montclair, NJ 07043-1624. Offers MS. *Students:* 5 full-time (2 women), 2 part-time (1 woman); includes 3 minority (1 Black or African American, non-Hispanic/Latino; 2 Asian, non-Hispanic/Latino). Average age 28. 4 applicants, 75% accepted, 2 enrolled. In 2014, 2 master's awarded. *Expenses:* Tuition, state resident: full-time $9960; part-time $553.35 per credit. Tuition, nonresident: full-time $15,074; part-time $837.43 per credit. *Required fees:* $1595; $88.63 per credit. Tuition and fees vary according to degree level and program. *Unit head:* Dr. Robert Taylor. *Application contact:* Amy Aiello, Director of Graduate Admissions and Operations, 973-655-5147, Fax: 973-655-7869, E-mail: graduate.school@montclair.edu.

New York School of Interior Design, Program in Sustainable Interior Environments, New York, NY 10021-5110. Offers MPS. *Entrance requirements:* For master's, first-professional degree in interior design, architecture, or closely-related field; portfolio. Additional exam requirements/recommendations for international students: Required—TOEFL (minimum score 550 paper-based; 79 iBT). Electronic applications accepted.

New York University, Graduate School of Arts and Science, Program in Historical and Sustainable Architecture, New York, NY 10012-1019. Offers MA. *Students:* 12 full-time (8 women); includes 2 minority (both Hispanic/Latino). Average age 25. 17 applicants, 100% accepted, 12 enrolled. In 2014, 14 master's awarded. *Entrance requirements:* For master's, GRE, writing sample. *Application deadline:* For fall admission, 3/1 for domestic and international students. Application fee: $100. *Financial support:* Application deadline: 3/1. *Unit head:* Mosette Broderick, Director of Graduate Studies, 212-998-8180, Fax: 212-995-4152, E-mail: histsust@nyu.edu. *Application contact:* Jon Ritter, Assistant Director, 212-998-8180, Fax: 212-995-4152, E-mail: histsust@nyu.edu. Website: http://arthistory.as.nyu.edu/

New York University, School of Continuing and Professional Studies, Schack Institute of Real Estate, Program in Real Estate Development, New York, NY 10012-1019. Offers global real estate (MS); sustainable development (MS); the business of development (MS). Part-time and evening/weekend programs available. *Faculty:* 5 full-time (3 women). *Students:* 52 full-time (21 women), 104 part-time (22 women); includes 30 minority (9 Black or African American, non-Hispanic/Latino; 11 Asian, non-Hispanic/Latino; 8 Hispanic/Latino; 2 Two or more races, non-Hispanic/Latino), 36 international. Average age 29. 147 applicants, 67% accepted, 44 enrolled. In 2014, 56 master's awarded. *Degree requirements:* For master's, thesis, capstone project. *Entrance requirements:* For master's, GRE or GMAT (only upon request), bachelor's degree, resume with relevant professional work, internship or volunteer experience, two letters of recommendation, statement of purpose. Additional exam requirements/recommendations for international students: Required—TOEFL (minimum score 600 paper-based; 100 iBT), IELTS (minimum score 7). *Application deadline:* For fall admission, 2/1 priority date for domestic and international students; for spring admission, 10/15 priority date for domestic students, 8/15 priority date for international

students. Applications are processed on a rolling basis. Application fee: $50. Electronic applications accepted. *Financial support:* In 2014–15, 49 students received support, including 44 fellowships (averaging $1,562 per year); career-related internships or fieldwork, Federal Work-Study, and scholarships/grants also available. Support available to part-time students. Financial award application deadline: 4/1; financial award applicants required to submit FAFSA. *Faculty research:* Valuation, real estate capital markets, regional economics, real estate investment trusts. *Unit head:* Rosemary Scanlon, Divisional Dean. *Application contact:* Office of Admissions, 212-998-7100, E-mail: sps.gradadmissions@nyu.edu.
Website: http://www.sps.nyu.edu/academics/departments/schack/academic-offerings/graduate/ms-in-real-estate-development.html

Northern Arizona University, Graduate College, College of Social and Behavioral Sciences, Program in Sustainable Communities, Flagstaff, AZ 86011. Offers MA. Part-time programs available. *Degree requirements:* For master's, thesis. *Entrance requirements:* For master's, minimum GPA of 3.0. Additional exam requirements/recommendations for international students: Required—TOEFL (minimum score 550 paper-based; 80 iBT), IELTS (minimum score 7). Electronic applications accepted.

Pace University, Pace Law School, White Plains, NY 10603. Offers comparative legal studies (LL M); environmental law (LL M, SJD), including climate change (LL M), land use and sustainability (LL M); law (JD); JD/LL M; JD/MA; JD/MBA; JD/MEM; JD/MPA; JD/MS. JD/MA offered jointly with Sarah Lawrence College; JD/MEM offered jointly with Yale University School of Forestry and Environmental Studies. *Accreditation:* ABA. Part-time programs available. *Degree requirements:* For master's, writing sample; for doctorate, thesis/dissertation (for some programs), extensive thesis proposal (for SJD). *Entrance requirements:* For doctorate, LSAT (for JD). Additional exam requirements/recommendations for international students: Required—TOEFL (minimum score 600 paper-based); Recommended—TWE. Electronic applications accepted. *Expenses:* Contact institution. *Faculty research:* Reform of energy regulations, international law, land use law, prosecutorial misconduct, corporation law, international sale of goods.

Penn State University Park, Graduate School, Intercollege Graduate Programs, Intercollege Program in Renewable Energy and Sustainability Systems, University Park, PA 16802. Offers MPS. *Unit head:* Dr. Regina Vasilatos-Younken, Interim Dean, 814-865-2516, Fax: 814-863-4627, E-mail: rxv@psu.edu. *Application contact:* Lori A. Stania, Director, Graduate Student Services, 814-867-5278, Fax: 814-863-4627, E-mail: gswww@psu.edu.

Philadelphia University, College of Architecture and the Built Environment, Program in Sustainable Design, Philadelphia, PA 19144. Offers MS. Part-time programs available. Postbaccalaureate distance learning degree programs offered (no on-campus study).

Pratt Institute, School of Architecture, Sustainable Environmental Systems Program, Brooklyn, NY 11205-3899. Offers MS. Part-time programs available. *Faculty:* 5 part-time/adjunct (3 women). *Students:* 16 full-time (12 women), 3 part-time (2 women); includes 6 minority (2 Black or African American, non-Hispanic/Latino; 1 Asian, non-Hispanic/Latino; 3 Hispanic/Latino), 5 international. Average age 31. 30 applicants, 83% accepted, 6 enrolled. In 2014, 15 master's awarded. *Degree requirements:* For master's, thesis. *Entrance requirements:* For master's, portfolio or writing sample, letters of recommendation. Additional exam requirements/recommendations for international students: Required—TOEFL (minimum score 550 paper-based; 79 iBT). *Application deadline:* For fall admission, 1/5 for domestic and international students; for spring admission, 10/1 for domestic and international students. Application fee: $50 ($90 for international students). Electronic applications accepted. *Financial support:* Career-related internships or fieldwork, Federal Work-Study, institutionally sponsored loans, scholarships/grants, and unspecified assistantships available. Support available to part-time students. Financial award application deadline: 2/1; financial award applicants required to submit FAFSA. *Unit head:* Jaime Stein, Chairperson, 718-399-4323, E-mail: jstein9@pratt.edu. *Application contact:* Young Hah, Director of Graduate Admissions, 718-636-3683, Fax: 718-399-4242, E-mail: yhah@pratt.edu.
Website: https://www.pratt.edu/academics/architecture/sustainable-environmental-systems/

See Display on page 112 and Close-Up on page 139.

Ramapo College of New Jersey, Master of Arts in Sustainability Studies Program, Mahwah, NJ 07430. Offers MA. Part-time and evening/weekend programs available. *Degree requirements:* For master's, thesis, capstone projects. *Entrance requirements:* For master's, official transcript; personal statement; 2 letters of recommendation; resume (recommended). Additional exam requirements/recommendations for international students: Required—TOEFL (minimum score 550 paper-based; 79 iBT); Recommended—IELTS. Electronic applications accepted. *Faculty research:* Urban ecology, tropical forest ecology, governance and organizational development, political economy, political science, law and society, political ecology, ecological planning, permaculture, psycho-social impact assessment of environmental disaster and change.

Rochester Institute of Technology, Graduate Enrollment Services, Golisano Institute for Sustainability, Architecture and Sustainability Department, MS Program in Sustainable Systems, Rochester, NY 14623-5608. Offers MS. Part-time programs available. *Students:* 17 full-time (5 women), 4 part-time; includes 2 minority (1 Asian, non-Hispanic/Latino; 1 Two or more races, non-Hispanic/Latino), 8 international. Average age 27. 49 applicants, 69% accepted, 11 enrolled. In 2014, 5 master's awarded. *Degree requirements:* For master's, thesis or alternative, thesis or project. *Entrance requirements:* For master's, GRE and TOEFL, IELTS, or PTE for non-native English speakers, Recommended minimum GPA of 3.0. Additional exam requirements/recommendations for international students: Required—PTE (minimum score 58), TOEFL (minimum score 550 paper-based; 79 iBT) or IELTS (minimum score 6.5). *Application deadline:* For fall admission, 2/15 priority date for domestic and international students; for spring admission, 12/15 priority date for domestic and international students. Applications are processed on a rolling basis. Application fee: $60. Electronic applications accepted. *Expenses:* Expenses: $1,673 per credit hour. *Financial support:* In 2014–15, 17 students received support. Research assistantships with partial tuition reimbursements available, teaching assistantships with partial tuition reimbursements available, career-related internships or fieldwork, Federal Work-Study, institutionally sponsored loans, scholarships/grants, and unspecified assistantships available. Support available to part-time students. Financial award applicants required to submit FAFSA. *Faculty research:* Product design, systems analysis, sustainable design, remanufacturing, life cycle engineering, manufacturing strategies. *Unit head:* Prof. Gabrielle Gaustad, Associate Academic Director, 585-475-7363, E-mail: info@sustainability.rit.edu. *Application contact:* Diane Ellison, Associate Vice President, Graduate Enrollment Services, 585-475-2229, Fax: 585-475-7164, E-mail: gradinfo@rit.edu.
Website: http://www.rit.edu/gis/academics/ms-sustainability/

Rochester Institute of Technology, Graduate Enrollment Services, Golisano Institute for Sustainability, Architecture and Sustainability Department, PhD Program in Sustainability, Rochester, NY 14623-5608. Offers PhD. *Students:* 15 full-time (7 women), 2 part-time (both women); includes 2 minority (1 Hispanic/Latino; 1 Two or more races, non-Hispanic/Latino), 6 international. Average age 30. 65 applicants, 6% accepted, 4 enrolled. *Degree requirements:* For doctorate, comprehensive exam, thesis/

dissertation. *Entrance requirements:* For doctorate, GRE, and TOEFL, IELTS, or PTE for non-native English speakers, Recommended minimum GPA of 3.0. Additional exam requirements/recommendations for international students: Required—PTE (minimum score 58), TOEFL (minimum score 550 paper-based; 79 iBT) or IELTS (minimum score 6.5). *Application deadline:* For fall admission, 1/15 priority date for domestic and international students. Applications are processed on a rolling basis. Application fee: $60. Electronic applications accepted. *Expenses:* Expenses: $1,673 per credit hour. *Financial support:* In 2014–15, 20 students received support. Research assistantships with full and partial tuition reimbursements available, teaching assistantships with full and partial tuition reimbursements available, career-related internships or fieldwork, Federal Work-Study, institutionally sponsored loans, scholarships/grants, and unspecified assistantships available. Support available to part-time students. Financial award applicants required to submit FAFSA. *Faculty research:* Alternative energy development, sustainable production, sustainable mobility, eco-IT. *Unit head:* Prof. Gabrielle Gaustad, Associate Academic Director, 585-475-7363, E-mail: info@sustainability.rit.edu. *Application contact:* Diane Ellison, Associate Vice President, Graduate Enrollment Services, 585-475-2229, Fax: 585-475-7164, E-mail: gradinfo@rit.edu.
Website: http://www.rit.edu/gis/academics/ph.d-sustainability/

Rochester Institute of Technology, Graduate Enrollment Services, Kate Gleason College of Engineering, Industrial and Systems Engineering Department, ME Program in Sustainable Engineering, Rochester, NY 14623-5603. Offers ME. *Students:* 4 full-time. Average age 23. 5 applicants, 80% accepted, 2 enrolled. In 2014, 2 master's awarded. *Degree requirements:* For master's, capstone project. *Entrance requirements:* For master's, TOEFL, IELTS, or PTE for non-native English speakers, Recommended minimum GPA of 3.0. Additional exam requirements/recommendations for international students: Required—PTE (minimum score 58), TOEFL (minimum score 550 paper-based; 79 iBT) or IELTS (minimum score 6.5). *Application deadline:* For fall admission, 2/15 priority date for domestic and international students; for spring admission, 12/15 priority date for domestic and international students. Applications are processed on a rolling basis. Electronic applications accepted. *Expenses:* Expenses: $1,673 per credit hour. *Financial support:* In 2014–15, 5 students received support. Research assistantships with partial tuition reimbursements available, teaching assistantships with partial tuition reimbursements available, career-related internships or fieldwork, Federal Work-Study, institutionally sponsored loans, scholarships/grants, and unspecified assistantships available. Support available to part-time students. Financial award applicants required to submit FAFSA. *Faculty research:* Advanced manufacturing, engineering education, ergonomics and human factors, healthcare delivery systems, operations research and simulation, systems engineering, production and logistics, sustainable engineering, energy. *Unit head:* Dr. Brian Thorn, Associate Professor, 585-475-6166, E-mail: bkteie@rit.edu. *Application contact:* Diane Ellison, Associate Vice President, Graduate Enrollment Services, 585-475-2229, Fax: 585-475-7164, E-mail: gradinfo@rit.edu.
Website: http://www.rit.edu/kgcoe/ise/program/master-engineering-degrees/master-engineering-sustainable-engineering

Rochester Institute of Technology, Graduate Enrollment Services, Kate Gleason College of Engineering, Industrial and Systems Engineering Department, MS Program in Sustainable Engineering, Rochester, NY 14623-5603. Offers MS. Part-time programs available. *Students:* 8 full-time (6 women), 4 part-time (2 women), 4 international. Average age 24. 23 applicants, 30% accepted, 5 enrolled. In 2014, 1 master's awarded. *Degree requirements:* For master's, thesis. *Entrance requirements:* For master's, GRE and TOEFL, IELTS, or PTE for non-native English speakers, Recommended minimum GPA of 3.0. Additional exam requirements/recommendations for international students: Required—PTE (minimum score 58), TOEFL (minimum score 550 paper-based; 79 iBT) or IELTS (minimum score 6.5). *Application deadline:* For fall admission, 2/15 priority date for domestic and international students; for spring admission, 12/15 priority date for domestic and international students. Applications are processed on a rolling basis. Electronic applications accepted. *Expenses:* Expenses: $1,673 per credit hour. *Financial support:* In 2014–15, 7 students received support. Research assistantships with partial tuition reimbursements available, teaching assistantships with partial tuition reimbursements available, career-related internships or fieldwork, Federal Work-Study, institutionally sponsored loans, scholarships/grants, and unspecified assistantships available. Support available to part-time students. Financial award applicants required to submit FAFSA. *Faculty research:* Advanced manufacturing, engineering education, ergonomics and human factors, healthcare delivery systems, operations research and simulation, systems engineering; production and logistics, sustainable engineering, energy. *Unit head:* Dr. Brian Thorn, Associate Professor, 585-475-6166, E-mail: bkteie@rit.edu. *Application contact:* Diane Ellison, Associate Vice President, Graduate Enrollment Services, 585-475-2229, Fax: 585-475-7164, E-mail: gradinfo@rit.edu.
Website: http://www.rit.edu/kgcoe/ise/program/master-science-degrees/master-science-sustainable-engineering

St. Edward's University, School of Behavioral and Social Sciences, Austin, TX 78704. Offers environmental management and sustainability (PSM). *Students:* 33 full-time (18 women); includes 12 minority (2 Black or African American, non-Hispanic/Latino; 1 Asian, non-Hispanic/Latino; 8 Hispanic/Latino; 1 Two or more races, non-Hispanic/Latino), 1 international. Average age 25. 132 applicants, 41% accepted, 18 enrolled. *Degree requirements:* For master's, 34 hours with minimum cumulative GPA of 3.0. *Entrance requirements:* For master's, GRE or GMAT, 2 letters of recommendation, resume or curriculum vitae, minimum GPA of 3.0 in last 60 hours of course work. Additional exam requirements/recommendations for international students: Required—TOEFL (minimum score 79 iBT) or IELTS (minimum score 6). *Application deadline:* For fall admission, 2/15 priority date for domestic and international students. Applications are processed on a rolling basis. Application fee: $50. Electronic applications accepted. *Expenses:* Expenses: $22,428 (summer not included), $100 technology fee. *Unit head:* Dr. Peter Beck, Director, 512-428-1249, Fax: 512-448-8492, E-mail: billq@stedwards.edu. *Application contact:* Office of Admission, 512-448-8500, Fax: 512-464-8877, E-mail: seu.admit@stedwards.edu.
Website: http://www.stedwards.edu

Savannah College of Art and Design, Graduate School, Program in Design for Sustainability, Savannah, GA 31402-3146. Offers MA. Part-time programs available. *Students:* 4 full-time (all women), 2 part-time (1 woman), 1 international. Average age 27. 11 applicants, 27% accepted, 1 enrolled. In 2014, 3 master's awarded. *Degree requirements:* For master's, thesis, final project. *Entrance requirements:* For master's, portfolio. Additional exam requirements/recommendations for international students: Required—TOEFL (minimum score 550 paper-based, 85 iBT), IELTS (minimum score 6.5), or ACTFL. *Application deadline:* For fall admission, 4/1 for domestic and international students. Applications are processed on a rolling basis. Application fee: $40. Electronic applications accepted. *Expenses: Tuition:* Full-time $34,605; part-time $3845 per course. One-time fee: $500. Tuition and fees vary according to course load. *Financial support:* Fellowships, career-related internships or fieldwork, Federal Work-Study, and scholarships/grants available. Financial award application deadline: 4/1; financial award applicants required to submit FAFSA. *Unit head:* Owen Foster, Chair. *Application contact:* Jenny Jaquillard, Executive Director of Admissions, Recruitment and Events, 912-525-5100, Fax: 912-525-5985, E-mail: admission@scad.edu.
Website: http://www.scad.edu/academics/programs/design-sustainability

Saybrook University, School of Psychology and Interdisciplinary Inquiry, San Francisco, CA 94111-1920. Offers human science (MA, PhD), including consciousness and spirituality, humanistic and transpersonal psychology, integrative health studies, organizational systems, social transformation; organizational systems (MA, PhD), including consciousness and spirituality, humanistic and transpersonal psychology, integrative health studies, leadership of sustainable systems (MA), organizational systems, social transformation; psychology (MA, PhD), including consciousness and spirituality, creativity studies (MA), humanistic and transpersonal psychology, integrative health studies, Jungian studies, marriage and family therapy (MA), organizational systems, social transformation. Postbaccalaureate distance learning degree programs offered (minimal on-campus study). Terminal master's awarded for partial completion of doctoral program. *Degree requirements:* For master's, thesis or alternative; for doctorate, thesis/dissertation. *Entrance requirements:* Additional exam requirements/recommendations for international students: Required—TOEFL (minimum score 580 paper-based; 93 iBT). Electronic applications accepted. *Faculty research:* Humanistic theory, health studies, organizational systems, consciousness and spirituality, social transformation.

SIT Graduate Institute, Graduate Programs, Master's Programs in Intercultural Service, Leadership, and Management, Brattleboro, VT 05302-0676. Offers conflict transformation (MA); intercultural service, leadership, and management (MA); international education (MA); sustainable development (MA). Postbaccalaureate distance learning degree programs offered (minimal on-campus study). *Students:* 28 full-time (20 women); includes 3 minority (1 American Indian or Alaska Native, non-Hispanic/Latino; 1 Asian, non-Hispanic/Latino; 1 Hispanic/Latino), 4 international. Average age 27. 730 applicants, 95% accepted, 164 enrolled. In 2014, 179 master's awarded. *Degree requirements:* For master's, one foreign language, thesis. *Entrance requirements:* For master's, 3 letters of reference. Additional exam requirements/recommendations for international students: Required—TOEFL, IELTS. *Application deadline:* Applications are processed on a rolling basis. Application fee: $50. *Financial support:* Career-related internships or fieldwork, Federal Work-Study, institutionally sponsored loans, and scholarships/grants available. Financial award application deadline: 3/7; financial award applicants required to submit FAFSA. *Faculty research:* Intercultural communication, conflict resolution, international education, world issues, international affairs. *Unit head:* Dr. Daniel Yalowitz, SIT Graduate Institute Dean, 802-336-1616, Fax: 802-258-3500. *Application contact:* Information Contact, 800-336-1616, Fax: 802-258-3500, E-mail: admissions@sit.edu.
Website: http://www.sit.edu/graduate

Southern Methodist University, Bobby B. Lyle School of Engineering, Department of Environmental and Civil Engineering, Dallas, TX 75275-0340. Offers air pollution control and atmospheric sciences (PhD); civil engineering (MS); environmental engineering (MS); environmental science (MS); structural engineering (PhD); sustainability and development (MA); water and wastewater engineering (PhD). Part-time and evening/weekend programs available. Postbaccalaureate distance learning degree programs offered (no on-campus study). Terminal master's awarded for partial completion of doctoral program. *Degree requirements:* For master's, thesis optional; for doctorate, thesis/dissertation, oral and written qualifying exams. *Entrance requirements:* For master's, GRE General Test, minimum GPA of 3.0 in last 2 years; bachelor's degree in engineering, mathematics, or sciences; for doctorate, GRE, BS and MS in related field, minimum GPA of 3.3. Additional exam requirements/recommendations for international students: Required—TOEFL. Electronic applications accepted. *Faculty research:* Human and environmental health effects of endocrine disrupters, development of air pollution control systems for diesel engines, structural analysis and design, modeling and design of waste treatment systems.

Stanford University, School of Engineering, Department of Civil and Environmental Engineering, Stanford, CA 94305-9991. Offers atmosphere and energy (MS, PhD); construction (MS), including construction engineering and management, design-construction integration, sustainable design and construction; environmental engineering and science (MS, PhD, Eng); environmental fluid mechanics and hydrology (PhD); geomechanics (MS); structural engineering (MS). Terminal master's awarded for partial completion of doctoral program. *Degree requirements:* For doctorate, thesis/dissertation, qualifying exam; for Eng, thesis. *Entrance requirements:* For master's, doctorate, and Eng, GRE General Test. Additional exam requirements/recommendations for international students: Required—TOEFL. Electronic applications accepted. *Expenses: Tuition:* Full-time $44,184; part-time $982 per credit hour. *Required fees:* $191.

State University of New York College of Environmental Science and Forestry, Department of Paper and Bioprocess Engineering, Syracuse, NY 13210-2779. Offers biomaterials engineering (MS, PhD); bioprocess engineering (MPS, MS, PhD); bioprocessing (Advanced Certificate); paper science and engineering (MPS, MS, PhD); sustainable engineering management (MPS). *Degree requirements:* For master's, thesis; for doctorate, comprehensive exam, thesis/dissertation; for Advanced Certificate, 15 credit hours. *Entrance requirements:* For master's and doctorate, GRE General Test, minimum GPA of 3.0; for Advanced Certificate, BS, calculus plus science major. Additional exam requirements/recommendations for international students: Required—TOEFL (minimum score 550 paper-based; 80 iBT), IELTS (minimum score 6). *Faculty research:* Sustainable products and processes, biorefinery, pulping and papermaking, nanocellulose, bioconversions, process control and modeling.

State University of New York College of Environmental Science and Forestry, Department of Sustainable Construction Management and Engineering, Syracuse, NY 13210-2779. Offers construction management (MPS, MS, PhD); sustainable construction (MPS, MS, PhD); wood science (MPS, MS, PhD). *Degree requirements:* For master's, thesis (for some programs); for doctorate, comprehensive exam, thesis/dissertation. *Entrance requirements:* For master's and doctorate, GRE General Test, minimum GPA of 3.0. Additional exam requirements/recommendations for international students: Required—TOEFL (minimum score 550 paper-based; 80 iBT), IELTS (minimum score 6).

Temple University, School of Environmental Design, Department of Community and Regional Planning, Ambler, PA 19002. Offers community and regional planning (MS); sustainable community planning (MS); transportation planning (MS). *Accreditation:* ACSP. Part-time and evening/weekend programs available. *Faculty:* 5 full-time (2 women), 6 part-time/adjunct (2 women). *Students:* 16 full-time (3 women), 17 part-time (7 women); includes 4 minority (1 Black or African American, non-Hispanic/Latino; 2 Hispanic/Latino; 1 Two or more races, non-Hispanic/Latino). 16 applicants, 94% accepted, 10 enrolled. In 2014, 9 master's awarded. *Entrance requirements:* For master's, GRE or GMAT, 2 letters of recommendation, minimum undergraduate GPA of 3.0, statement of goals. Additional exam requirements/recommendations for international students: Required—TOEFL (minimum score 550 paper-based; 79 iBT). *Application deadline:* For fall admission, 7/1 for domestic students, 12/15 for international students; for spring admission, 11/1 for domestic students, 8/1 for international students. Applications are processed on a rolling basis. Application fee: $60. *Expenses:* Tuition, state resident: full-time $14,490; part-time $805 per credit hour.

Tuition, nonresident: full-time $19,850; part-time $1103 per credit hour. *Required fees:* $690. Full-time tuition and fees vary according to class time, course load, degree level, campus/location and program. *Financial support:* In 2014–15, 5 students received support. Fellowships with full tuition reimbursements available, research assistantships with full tuition reimbursements available, Federal Work-Study, scholarships/grants, health care benefits, and unspecified assistantships available. Financial award application deadline: 1/15; financial award applicants required to submit FAFSA. *Faculty research:* Regional environmental planning, collaboration, management community development through sustainable food systems, storm water management and floodplain mapping, land use policy innovations, community planning for aging. *Unit head:* Dr. Deborah Howe, Chair, 267-468-8300, Fax: 267-468-8315, E-mail: deborah.howe@temple.edu.
Website: http://www.temple.edu/ambler/crp/

Texas A&M University–Kingsville, College of Graduate Studies, College of Engineering, Program in Sustainable Energy Systems Engineering, Kingsville, TX 78363. Offers PhD. *Degree requirements:* For doctorate, variable foreign language requirement, comprehensive exam, thesis/dissertation (for some programs). *Entrance requirements:* For doctorate, GRE, MAT, GMAT, bachelor's or master's degree in engineering or science, curriculum vitae, official transcripts, statement of purpose, three letters of recommendation. Additional exam requirements/recommendations for international students: Required—TOEFL (minimum score 550 paper-based; 79 iBT). *Application deadline:* For fall admission, 8/15 for domestic students, 6/1 for international students; for spring admission, 12/15 for domestic students, 10/1 for international students; for summer admission, 5/15 for domestic students, 4/1 for international students. Applications are processed on a rolling basis. Application fee: $35 ($50 for international students). Electronic applications accepted. *Financial support:* Career-related internships or fieldwork, Federal Work-Study, institutionally sponsored loans, scholarships/grants, health care benefits, tuition waivers (full and partial), and unspecified assistantships available. Support available to part-time students. Financial award application deadline: 5/1; financial award applicants required to submit FAFSA. *Unit head:* Dr. Stephan Nix, Dean, 361-593-4857, E-mail: stephan.nix@tamuk.edu. *Application contact:* Dr. Mohamed Abdelrahman, Dean, College of Graduate Studies, 361-593-2809, E-mail: mohamed.abdelrahman@tamuk.edu.

Texas State University, The Graduate College, College of Applied Arts, Interdisciplinary Studies Program in Sustainability, San Marcos, TX 78666. Offers MAIS, MSIS. Part-time programs available. *Students:* 3 full-time (1 woman), 4 part-time (3 women); includes 1 minority (Two or more races, non-Hispanic/Latino). Average age 37. 12 applicants, 83% accepted, 2 enrolled. In 2014, 6 master's awarded. *Degree requirements:* For master's, comprehensive exam, thesis optional. *Entrance requirements:* For master's, GRE (preferred), bachelor's degree from accredited institution, minimum GPA of 2.75 on the last 60 hours of undergraduate work, statement of personal goals, letter of intent to mentor from faculty member who will serve as research advisor and chair the master's committee. Additional exam requirements/recommendations for international students: Required—TOEFL (minimum score 550 paper-based; 78 iBT). *Application deadline:* For fall admission, 6/15 priority date for domestic students, 6/1 for international students; for spring admission, 10/15 priority date for domestic students, 10/1 for international students. Applications are processed on a rolling basis. Application fee: $40 ($90 for international students). *Expenses:* Expenses: $8,834 (tuition and fees combined). *Financial support:* In 2014–15, 5 students received support, including 1 research assistantship (averaging $10,152 per year); teaching assistantships, Federal Work-Study, and scholarships/grants also available. Support available to part-time students. Financial award application deadline: 4/1; financial award applicants required to submit FAFSA. *Faculty research:* Climate change, sustainable clothing. *Total annual research expenditures:* $42,800. *Unit head:* Dr. Gwendolyn Hustvedt, Graduate Advisor, 512-245-4689, E-mail: sustainablemasters@txstate.edu. *Application contact:* Dr. Andrea Golato, Dean of Graduate School, 512-245-2581, Fax: 512-245-8365, E-mail: gradcollege@txstate.edu.
Website: http://psych.txstate.edu

Texas Tech University, Graduate School, College of Arts and Sciences, Department of Biological Sciences, Lubbock, TX 79409-3131. Offers biology (MS, PhD); environmental sustainability and natural resources management (PSM); microbiology (MS); zoology (MS, PhD). Part-time programs available. *Faculty:* 41 full-time (11 women), 2 part-time/adjunct (both women). *Students:* 82 full-time (43 women), 6 part-time (4 women); includes 6 minority (1 Black or African American, non-Hispanic/Latino; 1 Asian, non-Hispanic/Latino; 3 Hispanic/Latino; 1 Two or more races, non-Hispanic/Latino), 41 international. Average age 29. 84 applicants, 27% accepted, 16 enrolled. In 2014, 13 master's, 17 doctorates awarded. *Degree requirements:* For master's, thesis or alternative; for doctorate, thesis/dissertation. *Entrance requirements:* For master's and doctorate, GRE General Test. Additional exam requirements/recommendations for international students: Required—TOEFL (minimum score 550 paper-based; 79 iBT). *Application deadline:* For fall admission, 6/1 priority date for domestic students, 1/15 priority date for international students; for spring admission, 9/1 priority date for domestic students, 6/15 priority date for international students. Applications are processed on a rolling basis. Application fee: $60. Electronic applications accepted. *Expenses:* Tuition, state resident: full-time $6310; part-time $262.92 per credit hour. Tuition, nonresident: full-time $14,998; part-time $624.92 per credit hour. *Required fees:* $2701; $36.50 per credit. $912.50 per semester. Tuition and fees vary according to course load. *Financial support:* In 2014–15, 90 students received support, including 73 fellowships (averaging $1,659 per year), 11 research assistantships (averaging $19,258 per year), 72 teaching assistantships (averaging $15,254 per year). Financial award application deadline: 4/15; financial award applicants required to submit FAFSA. *Faculty research:* Biodiversity, genomics and evolution, climate change in arid ecosystems, plant biology and biotechnology, animal communication and behavior, zoonotic and emerging diseases. *Total annual research expenditures:* $1.3 million. *Unit head:* Dr. Llewellyn D. Densmore, Chair, 806-742-2715, Fax: 806-742-2963, E-mail: lou.densmore@ttu.edu. *Application contact:* Dr. Randall M. Jeter, Graduate Adviser, 806-742-2710 Ext. 270, Fax: 806-742-2963, E-mail: randall.jeter@ttu.edu.
Website: http://www.biol.ttu.edu/default.aspx

Texas Tech University, Graduate School, Interdisciplinary Programs, Lubbock, TX 79409-1030. Offers arid land studies (MS); biotechnology (MS); heritage management (MS); interdisciplinary studies (MA, MS); museum science (MA); wind science and engineering (PhD); JD/MS. Part-time programs available. *Faculty:* 4 full-time (3 women). *Students:* 112 full-time (70 women), 122 part-time (70 women); includes 71 minority (20 Black or African American, non-Hispanic/Latino; 1 American Indian or Alaska Native, non-Hispanic/Latino; 4 Asian, non-Hispanic/Latino; 40 Hispanic/Latino; 6 Two or more races, non-Hispanic/Latino), 43 international. Average age 30. 172 applicants, 65% accepted, 70 enrolled. In 2014, 56 master's, 4 doctorates awarded. Terminal master's awarded for partial completion of doctoral program. *Degree requirements:* For master's, comprehensive exam (for some programs), thesis (for some programs); for doctorate, comprehensive exam, thesis/dissertation (for some programs). *Entrance requirements:* Additional exam requirements/recommendations for international students: Required—TOEFL (minimum score 550 paper-based; 79 iBT). *Application deadline:* For fall admission, 6/1 priority date for domestic students, 1/15 priority date for international students; for spring admission, 9/1 priority date for domestic students, 6/15 priority date for international students. Applications are processed on a rolling basis. Application fee: $60. Electronic applications accepted. *Expenses:* Tuition, state resident: full-time $6310; part-time $262.92 per credit hour. Tuition, nonresident: full-time $14,998; part-time $624.92 per credit hour. *Required fees:* $2701; $36.50 per credit. $912.50 per semester. Tuition and fees vary according to course load. *Financial support:* In 2014–15, 201 students received support, including 196 fellowships (averaging $2,655 per year), 5 research assistantships (averaging $12,144 per year), 2 teaching assistantships (averaging $7,785 per year); scholarships/grants and unspecified assistantships also available. Financial award application deadline: 4/15; financial award applicants required to submit FAFSA. *Total annual research expenditures:* $241,842. *Unit head:* Dr. Mark Sheridan, Vice Provost for Graduate and Postdoctoral Affairs/Dean of the Graduate School, 806-742-2787, Fax: 806-742-1746, E-mail: mark.sheridan@ttu.edu. *Application contact:* Shannon Samson, Coordinator of Graduate School Recruitment, 806-834-5201, Fax: 806-742-1746, E-mail: gradschool@ttu.edu.
Website: http://www.depts.ttu.edu/gradschool/about/INDS/index.php

University of Alaska Fairbanks, School of Natural Resources and Extension, Fairbanks, AK 99775-7140. Offers natural resources and sustainability (PhD); natural resources management (MS). Part-time programs available. *Faculty:* 19 full-time (5 women), 2 part-time/adjunct (both women). *Students:* 26 full-time (17 women), 23 part-time (16 women); includes 2 minority (both Two or more races, non-Hispanic/Latino), 6 international. Average age 35. 34 applicants, 44% accepted, 11 enrolled. In 2014, 7 master's, 2 doctorates awarded. *Degree requirements:* For master's, comprehensive exam, thesis (for some programs), oral defense of project or thesis; for doctorate, comprehensive exam, thesis/dissertation, defense of the dissertation. *Entrance requirements:* For master's, GRE General Test, bachelor's degree from accredited institution with minimum cumulative undergraduate and major GPA of 3.0; for doctorate, minimum cumulative GPA of 3.0. Additional exam requirements/recommendations for international students: Required—TOEFL (minimum score 550 paper-based; 89 iBT), IELTS (minimum score 6.5). *Application deadline:* For fall admission, 6/1 for domestic students, 3/1 for international students; for spring admission, 10/15 for domestic students, 9/1 for international students. Applications are processed on a rolling basis. Application fee: $60. Electronic applications accepted. *Expenses:* Tuition, state resident: full-time $7614; part-time $423 per credit. Tuition, nonresident: full-time $15,552; part-time $864 per credit. Tuition and fees vary according to course level, course load and reciprocity agreements. *Financial support:* In 2014–15, 13 research assistantships with full tuition reimbursements (averaging $11,089 per year), 4 teaching assistantships with full tuition reimbursements (averaging $10,741 per year) were awarded; fellowships with full tuition reimbursements, career-related internships or fieldwork, Federal Work-Study, scholarships/grants, health care benefits, and unspecified assistantships also available. Support available to part-time students. Financial award application deadline: 2/15; financial award applicants required to submit FAFSA. *Faculty research:* Conservation biology, soil/water conservation, land use policy and planning in the arctic and subarctic, forest ecosystem management, subarctic agricultural production. *Total annual research expenditures:* $2.8 million. *Unit head:* Stephen Sparrow, Interim Dean, 907-474-9450, Fax: 907-474-6268, E-mail: fysnras@uaf.edu. *Application contact:* Mary Kreta, Director of Admissions, 907-474-7500, Fax: 907-474-7097, E-mail: admissions@uaf.edu.
Website: http://www.uaf.edu/snre/

University of Calgary, Faculty of Graduate Studies, Faculty of Environmental Design, Calgary, AB T2N 1N4, Canada. Offers architecture (M Arch); environmental design (M Env Des, PhD); planning (M Plan). *Degree requirements:* For master's, thesis; for doctorate, thesis/dissertation. *Entrance requirements:* For master's, minimum GPA of 3.0; for doctorate, minimum GPA of 3.5. Additional exam requirements/recommendations for international students: Required—TOEFL (minimum score 550 paper-based). *Faculty research:* Sustainable development in architecture, planning and product design, energy and environment, impact assessment, ecotourism.

University of California, Berkeley, UC Berkeley Extension, Certificate Programs in Sustainability Studies, Berkeley, CA 94720-1500. Offers leadership in sustainability and environmental management (Professional Certificate); solar energy and green building (Professional Certificate); sustainable design (Professional Certificate).

University of California, Santa Barbara, Graduate Division, College of Letters and Sciences, Division of Social Sciences, Department of Global and International Studies, Santa Barbara, CA 93106-7065. Offers global culture, ideology, and religion (MA); global government, civil society, and human rights (MA); global studies (PhD); political economy, sustainable development, and the environment (MA). *Degree requirements:* For master's, one foreign language, thesis, 2 years of a second language. *Entrance requirements:* For master's, GRE, 2 years of a second language with minimum B grade in the final term, 3 letters of recommendation, resume/curriculum vitae, personal statement, writing sample. Additional exam requirements/recommendations for international students: Required—TOEFL (minimum score 600 paper-based; 94 iBT), IELTS (minimum score 7). Electronic applications accepted. *Faculty research:* Global culture, ideology, and religion; global governance, civil society, and human rights; political economy, sustainable development and the environment.

University of Colorado Denver, College of Architecture and Planning, Program in Design and Planning, Denver, CO 80217. Offers history of architecture, landscape and urbanism (PhD); sustainable and healthy environments (PhD). Part-time programs available. *Students:* 9 full-time (3 women), 11 part-time (9 women); includes 1 minority (Hispanic/Latino), 7 international. Average age 38. 32 applicants, 6% accepted, 1 enrolled. In 2014, 4 doctorates awarded. *Degree requirements:* For doctorate, comprehensive exam, thesis/dissertation. *Entrance requirements:* For doctorate, GRE (minimum score of 158 for both verbal and quantitative; writing 4.0), minimum undergraduate GPA of 3.0, graduate 3.5; writing sample; three letters of recommendation; statement of personal and professional goals. Additional exam requirements/recommendations for international students: Required—TOEFL (minimum score 80 iBT); Recommended—IELTS (minimum score 6.8). *Application deadline:* For fall admission, 2/2 for domestic students, 1/2 for international students; for spring admission, 10/1 for domestic students. Application fee: $50 ($75 for international students). Electronic applications accepted. *Expenses:* Expenses: Contact institution. *Financial support:* In 2014–15, 2 students received support. Fellowships, research assistantships, teaching assistantships, Federal Work-Study, institutionally sponsored loans, scholarships/grants, traineeships, and unspecified assistantships available. Financial award application deadline: 4/1; financial award applicants required to submit FAFSA. *Faculty research:* Land use and environmental planning and design; design and planning processes and practices; history, theory, and criticism of the built environment. *Unit head:* Dr. Osman Attmann, Director, 303-315-0032, Fax: 303-556-3687, E-mail: o.attmann@ucdenver.edu. *Application contact:* Rachael Kuroiwa, Manager of Admissions and Outreach, 303-315-2325, E-mail: rachael.kuroiwa@ucdenver.edu.
Website: http://www.ucdenver.edu/academics/colleges/ArchitecturePlanning/Academics/DegreePrograms/PhD/Pages/PhD.aspx

University of Colorado Denver, College of Engineering and Applied Science, Department of Civil Engineering, Denver, CO 80217. Offers civil engineering (EASPh D); civil engineering systems (PhD); environmental and sustainability engineering (MS, PhD); geographic information systems (MS); geotechnical engineering

(MS, PhD); hydrology and hydraulics (MS, PhD); structural engineering (MS, PhD); transportation engineering (MS, PhD). Part-time and evening/weekend programs available. *Faculty:* 15 full-time (4 women), 11 part-time/adjunct (2 women). *Students:* 64 full-time (15 women), 43 part-time (8 women); includes 15 minority (3 Black or African American, non-Hispanic/Latino; 3 Asian, non-Hispanic/Latino; 6 Hispanic/Latino; 3 Two or more races, non-Hispanic/Latino), 34 international. Average age 32. 136 applicants, 54% accepted, 28 enrolled. In 2014, 35 master's, 9 doctorates awarded. *Degree requirements:* For master's, comprehensive exam, 30 credit hours, project or thesis; for doctorate, comprehensive exam, thesis/dissertation, 60 credit hours (30 of which are dissertation research). *Entrance requirements:* For master's, GRE, statement of purpose, transcripts, three references; for doctorate, GRE, statement of purpose, transcripts, references, letter of support from faculty stating willingness to serve as dissertation advisor and outlining plan for financial support. Additional exam requirements/recommendations for international students: Required—TOEFL (minimum score 537 paper-based; 75 iBT); Recommended—IELTS (minimum score 6.5). *Application deadline:* For fall admission, 5/1 for domestic students, 4/1 for international students; for spring admission, 10/1 for domestic students, 9/1 for international students; for summer admission, 2/15 for domestic students, 1/15 for international students. Application fee: $50 ($75 for international students). Electronic applications accepted. *Expenses:* Expenses: Contact institution. *Financial support:* In 2014–15, 26 students received support. Fellowships, research assistantships, teaching assistantships, career-related internships or fieldwork, Federal Work-Study, institutionally sponsored loans, scholarships/grants, traineeships, and unspecified assistantships available. Financial award application deadline: 4/1; financial award applicants required to submit FAFSA. *Faculty research:* Earthquake source physics, environmental biotechnology, hydrologic and hydraulic engineering, sustainability assessments, transportation energy use and greenhouse gas emissions. *Unit head:* Dr. Kevin Rens, Chair, 303-556-8017, E-mail: kevin.rens@ucdenver.edu. *Application contact:* Tammy Southern, Program Assistant, 303-556-6712, E-mail: tamara.southern@ucdenver.edu.
Website: http://www.ucdenver.edu/academics/colleges/Engineering/Programs/Civil-Engineering/Pages/CivilEngineering.aspx

University of Colorado Denver, College of Liberal Arts and Sciences, Department of Anthropology, Denver, CO 80217. Offers archaeological studies (MA); biological anthropology (MA); medical anthropology (MA); sustainable development and political ecology (MA). Part-time and evening/weekend programs available. *Faculty:* 10 full-time (4 women), 2 part-time/adjunct (1 woman). *Students:* 28 full-time (22 women), 11 part-time (9 women); includes 9 minority (2 Black or African American, non-Hispanic/Latino; 1 Asian, non-Hispanic/Latino; 5 Hispanic/Latino; 1 Two or more races, non-Hispanic/Latino). Average age 30. 50 applicants, 50% accepted, 11 enrolled. In 2014, 17 master's awarded. *Degree requirements:* For master's, comprehensive exam, thesis or alternative, 30-36 credit hours. *Entrance requirements:* For master's, GRE General Test, minimum GPA of 3.0 for all undergraduate studies, transcripts from all undergraduate/graduate institutions attended, prior training in anthropology, three letters of recommendation, statement of purpose. Additional exam requirements/recommendations for international students: Required—TOEFL (minimum score 537 paper-based; 75 iBT); Recommended—IELTS (minimum score 6.5). *Application deadline:* For fall admission, 2/15 for domestic students, 1/15 for international students. Application fee: $50 ($75 for international students). Electronic applications accepted. *Financial support:* Fellowships, research assistantships, teaching assistantships, Federal Work-Study, institutionally sponsored loans, scholarships/grants, and traineeships available. Financial award application deadline: 4/1; financial award applicants required to submit FAFSA. *Faculty research:* Applied medical anthropology, primate social behavior, environmental anthropology, Southwestern and Mexican archaeology, human ecology. *Unit head:* Dr. Christopher Beekman, Chair of the Department of Anthropology, 303-556-6040, E-mail: christopher.beekman@ucdenver.edu. *Application contact:* Charles Musiba, Acting Graduate Director, 303-556-6082, Fax: 303-556-8501, E-mail: charles.musiba@ucdenver.edu.
Website: http://www.ucdenver.edu/academics/colleges/CLAS/Departments/anthropology/Programs/Masters/Pages/Masters.aspx

University of Connecticut, Graduate School, eCampus, Program in Humanitarian Services Administration, Storrs, CT 06269. Offers MPS. Postbaccalaureate distance learning degree programs offered. *Entrance requirements:* For master's, minimum GPA of 3.0 or greater than 3.0 for the last 2 years of study; 3 letters of reference. Additional exam requirements/recommendations for international students: Required—TOEFL (minimum score 540 paper-based).

University of Florida, Graduate School, College of Liberal Arts and Sciences, Center for Latin American Studies, Gainesville, FL 32611. Offers Latin American studies (MA, Certificate); sustainable development practice (MDP); tropical conservation and development (MA); JD/MA. Part-time programs available. *Faculty:* 3 part-time/adjunct (all women). *Students:* 16 full-time (13 women), 4 part-time (3 women); includes 8 minority (1 Black or African American, non-Hispanic/Latino; 7 Hispanic/Latino). 57 applicants, 63% accepted, 18 enrolled. In 2014, 4 master's awarded. *Degree requirements:* For master's, thesis. *Entrance requirements:* For master's, GRE General Test, minimum GPA of 3.0. Additional exam requirements/recommendations for international students: Required—TOEFL (minimum score 550 paper-based; 80 iBT), IELTS (minimum score 6). *Application deadline:* For fall admission, 6/1 priority date for domestic students. Applications are processed on a rolling basis. Application fee: $30. Electronic applications accepted. *Financial support:* In 2014–15, 15 fellowships, 19 research assistantships, 3 teaching assistantships were awarded; career-related internships or fieldwork, Federal Work-Study, institutionally sponsored loans, and unspecified assistantships also available. Financial award application deadline: 3/1; financial award applicants required to submit FAFSA. *Faculty research:* Tropical conservation and development; ethnicity in the Americas, Brazil, and Cuba; North American Free Trade Agreement (NAFTA). *Unit head:* Philip Williams, PhD, Director, 352-273-4702, Fax: 352-392-7682, E-mail: pjw@latam.ufl.edu. *Application contact:* Richmond F. Brown, PhD, Associate Director, 352-273-4708, Fax: 352-392-7682, E-mail: rfbrown@ufl.edu.
Website: http://www.latam.ufl.edu/

University of Georgia, School of Ecology, Athens, GA 30602. Offers conservation ecology and sustainable development (MS); ecology (MS, PhD). *Degree requirements:* For master's, thesis; for doctorate, one foreign language, thesis/dissertation. *Entrance requirements:* For master's and doctorate, GRE General Test. Electronic applications accepted.

University of Maryland, College Park, Academic Affairs, College of Computer, Mathematical and Natural Sciences, Department of Biology, Program in Sustainable Development and Conservation Biology, College Park, MD 20742. Offers MS. Part-time and evening/weekend programs available. *Degree requirements:* For master's, internship, scholarly paper. *Entrance requirements:* For master's, GRE General Test, minimum GPA of 3.0, 3 letters of recommendation. Electronic applications accepted. *Faculty research:* Biodiversity, global change, conservation.

University of Massachusetts Amherst, Graduate School, College of Natural Sciences, Department of Environmental Conservation, Program in Sustainability Science, Amherst, MA 01003. Offers MS. Part-time programs available. *Students:* 19 full-time (12 women), 5 part-time (2 women); includes 1 minority (Black or African American, non-Hispanic/Latino), 3 international. Average age 26. 46 applicants, 61% accepted, 19 enrolled. In 2014, 13 master's awarded. *Degree requirements:* For master's, internship. *Entrance requirements:* Additional exam requirements/recommendations for international students: Required—TOEFL (minimum score 550 paper-based; 80 iBT), IELTS (minimum score 6.5). *Application deadline:* For fall admission, 2/1 for domestic and international students; for spring admission, 10/1 for domestic and international students. Applications are processed on a rolling basis. Application fee: $75. Electronic applications accepted. *Expenses:* Tuition, state resident: full-time $1980; part-time $110 per credit. Tuition, nonresident: full-time $14,644; part-time $414 per credit. *Required fees:* $11,417. One-time fee: $357. *Financial support:* Fellowships with full and partial tuition reimbursements, research assistantships with full and partial tuition reimbursements, teaching assistantships with full and partial tuition reimbursements, career-related internships or fieldwork, Federal Work-Study, scholarships/grants, traineeships, health care benefits, tuition waivers (full and partial), and unspecified assistantships available. Support available to part-time students. Financial award application deadline: 2/1. *Unit head:* Dr. Craig Nicolson, Graduate Program Director, 413-545-2257, E-mail: craign@eco.umass.edu. *Application contact:* Lindsay DeSantis, Supervisor of Admissions, 413-545-0721, Fax: 413-577-0100, E-mail: gradadm@grad.umass.edu.
Website: http://eco.umass.edu/degree-programs/sustainability-science/

University of Massachusetts Lowell, Francis College of Engineering, Department of Civil and Environmental Engineering, Lowell, MA 01854. Offers civil and environmental engineering (MS Eng, Certificate); environmental engineering (D Eng); environmental studies (MSES, PhD, Certificate), including environmental engineering (MSES), environmental studies (PhD, Certificate); sustainable infrastructure for developing nations (Certificate). Part-time programs available. *Degree requirements:* For master's, thesis optional. *Entrance requirements:* For master's, GRE General Test. *Faculty research:* Bridge design, traffic control, groundwater remediation, pile capacity.

University of Michigan, School of Natural Resources and Environment, Program in Natural Resources and Environment, Ann Arbor, MI 48109-1041. Offers aquatic sciences: research and management (MS); behavior, education and communication (MS); conservation biology (MS); conservation ecology (MS); environmental informatics (MS); environmental justice (MS); environmental policy and planning (MS); natural resources and environment (PhD); sustainable systems (MS); terrestrial ecosystems (MS); MS/JD; MS/MBA; MUP/MS. Terminal master's awarded for partial completion of doctoral program. *Degree requirements:* For master's, practicum or group project; for doctorate, comprehensive exam, thesis/dissertation, oral defense of dissertation, preliminary exam. *Entrance requirements:* For master's, GRE General Test; for doctorate, GRE General Test, master's degree. Additional exam requirements/recommendations for international students: Required—TOEFL (minimum score 560 paper-based; 84 iBT). Electronic applications accepted. *Faculty research:* Stream ecology and fish biology, plant-insect interactions, environmental education, resource control and reproductive success, remote sensing, conservation ecology, sustainable systems.

University of New Brunswick Fredericton, School of Graduate Studies, Policy Studies Program, Fredericton, NB E3B 5A3, Canada. Offers citizen engagement/dispute resolution (M Phil); community development (M Phil); international development (M Phil); leadership (M Phil); sustainability/environmental issues (M Phil); worldviews (M Phil). Part-time programs available. *Faculty:* 17 full-time (9 women), 1 part-time/adjunct (0 women). *Students:* 14 full-time (7 women), 4 part-time (3 women). In 2014, 3 master's awarded. *Degree requirements:* For master's, thesis, report. *Entrance requirements:* For master's, minimum GPA of 3.5. Additional exam requirements/recommendations for international students: Required—TWE (minimum score 5.5), TOEFL (minimum score 600 paper-based; 100 iBT) or IELTS (minimum score 7). *Application deadline:* Applications are processed on a rolling basis. Application fee: $50 Canadian dollars. Electronic applications accepted. *Financial support:* In 2014–15, 3 fellowships, research assistantships (averaging $5,600 per year), teaching assistantships (averaging $4,400 per year) were awarded. *Faculty research:* International development, worldviews, citizenship/dispute resolution, sustainability/environmental issues, leadership, community development. *Unit head:* Dr. Linda Eyre, Dean of Graduate Studies, 506-447-3044, Fax: 506-453-4817, E-mail: gradidst@unb.ca. *Application contact:* Janet Amirault, Graduate Secretary, 506-458-7558, Fax: 506-453-4817, E-mail: jamiraul@unb.ca.
Website: http://www.unb.ca/gradstudies/programs/mphil/index.html

University of Oklahoma, College of Architecture, Division of Interior Design, Norman, OK 73019. Offers architectural lighting (MID); design process management (MID); interior design (MID); sustainable living (MID). Part-time and evening/weekend programs available. *Students:* 2 full-time (both women), 1 international. Average age 26. 3 applicants, 67% accepted. In 2014, 3 master's awarded. *Degree requirements:* For master's, comprehensive exam, project or thesis. *Entrance requirements:* For master's, undergraduate degree in interior design or related field, portfolio of design work, letter of intent, three letters of recommendation. Additional exam requirements/recommendations for international students: Required—TOEFL (minimum score 79 iBT). *Application deadline:* For fall admission, 6/1 for domestic and international students; for spring admission, 10/15 for domestic and international students. Application fee: $50 ($100 for international students). Electronic applications accepted. *Expenses:* Tuition, state resident: full-time $4394; part-time $183.10 per credit hour. Tuition, nonresident: full-time $16,970; part-time $707.10 per credit hour. *Required fees:* $2892; $109.95 per credit hour. $126.50 per semester. *Financial support:* In 2014–15, 1 student received support, including 1 research assistantship (averaging $10,372 per year), 2 teaching assistantships with partial tuition reimbursements available (averaging $10,372 per year); career-related internships or fieldwork, scholarships/grants, and unspecified assistantships also available. Financial award application deadline: 6/1; financial award applicants required to submit FAFSA. *Faculty research:* Environmental and human behavior, indoor environmental quality, pedagogical exploration, building information modeling for cognitive spatial problem solving, community health and environmental design. *Unit head:* Mia Kile, Academic Director, 405-325-1051, Fax: 405-325-7558, E-mail: mkile@ou.edu. *Application contact:* Hans-Peter Wachter, Graduate Liaison and Associate Professor, 405-325-8780, Fax: 405-325-7558, E-mail: hepw@ou.edu. Website: http://www.ou.edu/content/architecture/interior_design.html

University of Oklahoma, College of Atmospheric and Geographic Sciences, Department of Geography and Environmental Sustainability, Norman, OK 73019. Offers environmental sustainability (MS); geography (MA, PhD). Part-time programs available. *Faculty:* 21 full-time (5 women), 2 part-time/adjunct (1 woman). *Students:* 18 full-time (8 women), 19 part-time (8 women); includes 4 minority (2 American Indian or Alaska Native, non-Hispanic/Latino; 1 Asian, non-Hispanic/Latino; 1 Hispanic/Latino), 9 international. Average age 32. 11 applicants, 27% accepted, 1 enrolled. In 2014, 3 master's, 3 doctorates awarded. Terminal master's awarded for partial completion of doctoral program. *Degree requirements:* For master's, comprehensive exam (for some programs), thesis (for some programs); for doctorate, one foreign language, comprehensive exam (for some programs), thesis/dissertation (for some programs), 4

required courses plus 4 elective courses. *Entrance requirements:* For master's, GRE, BA/BS in relevant area from accredited institution, minimum GPA of 3.0; for doctorate, MA/MS in relevant area from accredited institution, minimum GPA of 3.0. Additional exam requirements/recommendations for international students: Required—TOEFL (minimum score 79 iBT). *Application deadline:* For fall admission, 1/15 for domestic and international students; for spring admission, 11/1 for domestic and international students. Application fee: $50 ($100 for international students). Electronic applications accepted. *Expenses:* Tuition, state resident: full-time $4394; part-time $183.10 per credit hour. Tuition, nonresident: full-time $16,970; part-time $707.10 per credit hour. *Required fees:* $2892; $109.95 per credit hour. $126.50 per semester. *Financial support:* In 2014–15, 30 students received support, including 1 fellowship with full tuition reimbursement available (averaging $5,000 per year), 5 research assistantships with partial tuition reimbursements available (averaging $14,948 per year), 13 teaching assistantships with partial tuition reimbursements available (averaging $15,359 per year); career-related internships or fieldwork, Federal Work-Study, institutionally sponsored loans, scholarships/grants, traineeships, health care benefits, and unspecified assistantships also available. Financial award application deadline: 6/1; financial award applicants required to submit FAFSA. *Faculty research:* Land use land cover change, indigenous geography, physical and human geography, GIS and remote sensing, environmental sustainability and renewable energy, human-environment interactions, climate, climate change, climate variability, climate and water resources. *Total annual research expenditures:* $1 million. *Unit head:* Dr. Aondover Tarhule, Associate Professor and Chair, 405-325-0540, Fax: 405-325-6090, E-mail: atarhule@ou.edu. *Application contact:* Dr. Scott Greene, Professor and Graduate Liaison, 405-325-4319, Fax: 405-325-6090, E-mail: jgreene@ou.edu.
Website: http://geography.ou.edu

University of Southern California, Graduate School, School of Policy, Planning, and Development, Master of Planning Program, Los Angeles, CA 90089. Offers sustainable cities (Graduate Certificate); transportation systems (Graduate Certificate); urban planning (M Pl); M Arch/M Pl; M Pl/MA; M Pl/MPP; M Pl/MRED; M Pl/MS; M Pl/MSW; MBA/M Pl; ML Arch/M Pl; MPA/M Pl. *Accreditation:* ACSP. Part-time programs available. *Degree requirements:* For master's, comprehensive exam, internship. *Entrance requirements:* For master's, GRE, GMAT. Additional exam requirements/recommendations for international students: Required—TOEFL (minimum score 600 paper-based; 100 iBT). Electronic applications accepted. *Faculty research:* Transportation and infrastructure, comparative international development, healthy communities, social economic development, sustainable community planning.

University of Southern California, Graduate School, Viterbi School of Engineering, Sonny Astani Department of Civil Engineering, Los Angeles, CA 90089. Offers applied mechanics (MS); civil engineering (MS, PhD); computer-aided engineering (ME, Graduate Certificate); construction management (MCM); engineering technology commercialization (Graduate Certificate); environmental engineering (MS, PhD); environmental quality management (ME); structural design (ME); sustainable cities (Graduate Certificate); transportation systems (MS, Graduate Certificate); water and waste management (MS). Part-time and evening/weekend programs available. Terminal master's awarded for partial completion of doctoral program. *Degree requirements:* For master's, thesis optional; for doctorate, thesis/dissertation. *Entrance requirements:* For master's and doctorate, GRE General Test. Additional exam requirements/recommendations for international students: Recommended—TOEFL. Electronic applications accepted. *Faculty research:* Geotechnical engineering, transportation engineering, structural engineering, construction management, environmental engineering, water resources.

University of South Florida, College of Global Sustainability, Tampa, FL 33620-9951. Offers entrepreneurship (MA); sustainable energy (MA); sustainable tourism (MA); water (MA); MA/MS. *Faculty:* 5 full-time (0 women). *Students:* 30 full-time (16 women), 43 part-time (28 women); includes 23 minority (4 Black or African American, non-Hispanic/Latino; 3 Asian, non-Hispanic/Latino; 14 Hispanic/Latino; 2 Two or more races, non-Hispanic/Latino), 15 international. Average age 30. 88 applicants, 68% accepted, 44 enrolled. In 2014, 3 master's awarded. *Degree requirements:* For master's, comprehensive exam (for some programs), thesis or alternative, internship. *Entrance requirements:* For master's, minimum GPA of 3.0 in undergraduate coursework; at least two letters of recommendation (one must be academic); 200-250-word essay on student's background, professional goals, and reasons for seeking degree. Additional exam requirements/recommendations for international students: Required—TOEFL (minimum score 550 paper-based; 79 iBT). *Faculty research:* Global sustainability, integrated resource management, systems thinking, green communities, entrepreneurship, ecotourism. *Total annual research expenditures:* $125,823. *Unit head:* Dr. Rafael Perez, Interim Dean, 813-974-9694, E-mail: perez@usf.edu.
Website: http://psgs.usf.edu/

University of South Florida, Innovative Education, Tampa, FL 33620-9951. *Unit head:* Kathy Barnes, Interdisciplinary Programs Coordinator, 813-974-8031, Fax: 813-974-7061, E-mail: barnesk@usf.edu. *Application contact:* Karen Tylinski, Metro Initiatives, 813-974-9943, Fax: 813-974-7061, E-mail: ktylinsk@usf.edu.
Website: http://www.usf.edu/innovative-education/

The University of Texas at Arlington, Graduate School, School of Urban and Public Affairs, Program in Interdisciplinary Studies, Arlington, TX 76019. Offers sustainability (MA). Part-time and evening/weekend programs available. *Entrance requirements:* For master's, GRE or GMAT, resume, essay, two letters of recommendation. Additional exam requirements/recommendations for international students: Required—TOEFL (minimum score 550 paper-based). Electronic applications accepted.

The University of Texas at Austin, Graduate School, School of Architecture, Program in Sustainable Design, Austin, TX 78712-1111. Offers M Arch I, M Arch II, MSSD.

University of Washington, Graduate School, College of the Environment, School of Forest Resources, Seattle, WA 98195. Offers bioresource science and engineering (MS, PhD); environmental horticulture (MEH); forest ecology (MS, PhD); forest management (MFR); forest soils (MS, PhD); restoration ecology (MS, PhD); restoration ecology and environmental horticulture (MS, PhD); social sciences (MS, PhD); sustainable resource management (MS, PhD); wildlife science (MS, PhD); MFR/MAIS; MPA/MS. *Accreditation:* SAF. Part-time programs available. *Faculty:* 40 full-time (10 women), 14 part-time/adjunct (3 women). *Students:* 146 full-time (69 women); includes 20 minority (2 Black or African American, non-Hispanic/Latino; 6 American Indian or Alaska Native, non-Hispanic/Latino; 7 Asian, non-Hispanic/Latino; 3 Hispanic/Latino; 2 Native Hawaiian or other Pacific Islander, non-Hispanic/Latino), 23 international. Average age 31. 212 applicants, 31% accepted, 40 enrolled. In 2014, 31 master's, 10 doctorates awarded. *Degree requirements:* For master's, thesis; for doctorate, comprehensive exam, thesis/dissertation. *Entrance requirements:* For master's and doctorate, GRE, minimum GPA of 3.0. Additional exam requirements/recommendations for international students: Required—TOEFL. *Application deadline:* For fall admission, 12/31 priority date for domestic students; for winter admission, 9/1 for domestic students; for spring admission, 11/1 for domestic students. Application fee: $85. Electronic applications accepted. *Financial support:* In 2014–15, 140 students received support, including 12 fellowships with full tuition reimbursements available (averaging $18,000 per year), 27 research assistantships with full tuition reimbursements available (averaging $18,000 per year), 6 teaching assistantships with full tuition reimbursements available (averaging $18,000 per year); Federal Work-Study, institutionally sponsored loans, scholarships/grants, health care benefits, tuition waivers (full), and unspecified assistantships also available. Financial award application deadline: 12/31. *Faculty research:* Ecosystem analysis, silviculture and forest protection, paper science and engineering, environmental horticulture and urban forestry, natural resource policy and economics, restoration ecology and environment horticulture, conservation, human dimensions, wildlife, bioresource science and engineering. *Unit head:* Michelle Trudeau, Director of Student Services, 206-616-1533, E-mail: michtru@uw.edu. *Application contact:* David Campbell, Graduate Student Advisor, 206-543-7081, Fax: 206-685-0790, E-mail: davidc23@uw.edu.
Website: http://www.sefs.uw.edu

University of Washington, Graduate School, School of Law, Seattle, WA 98195-3020. Offers Asian law (LL M, PhD); intellectual property law and policy (LL M); law (JD); law of sustainable international development (LL M); taxation (LL M); JD/LL M; JD/MA; JD/MAIS; JD/MBA; JD/MPA; JD/MS; JD/PhD. *Accreditation:* ABA. *Degree requirements:* For master's, thesis; for doctorate, thesis/dissertation (for some programs). *Entrance requirements:* For master's, language proficiency (LL M in Asian law); for doctorate, LSAT (for JD). Additional exam requirements/recommendations for international students: Required—TOEFL. *Expenses:* Contact institution. *Faculty research:* Asian, international and comparative law, intellectual property law, health law, environmental law, taxation.

The University of Western Ontario, Faculty of Graduate Studies, Physical Sciences Division, Department of Earth Sciences, London, ON N6A 5B8, Canada. Offers environment and sustainability (MES); geology (M Sc, PhD); geology and environmental science (M Sc, PhD); geophysics (M Sc, PhD); geophysics and environmental science (M Sc, PhD). *Degree requirements:* For master's, thesis; for doctorate, thesis/dissertation, qualifying exam. *Entrance requirements:* For master's, honors in B Sc; for doctorate, M Sc. Additional exam requirements/recommendations for international students: Required—TOEFL. *Faculty research:* Geophysics, geochemistry, paleontology, sedimentology/stratigraphy, glaciology/quaternary.

University of Wisconsin–Madison, Graduate School, Gaylord Nelson Institute for Environmental Studies, Environmental Conservation Program, Madison, WI 53706-1380. Offers MS. *Degree requirements:* For master's, thesis or alternative, spring/summer leadership (internship) experience. *Entrance requirements:* Additional exam requirements/recommendations for international students: Required—TOEFL (minimum score 550 paper-based; 80 iBT). Electronic applications accepted. *Expenses:* Tuition, state resident: full-time $10,723; part-time $745 per credit. Tuition, nonresident: full-time $24,054; part-time $1578 per credit. *Required fees:* $374 per semester. Tuition and fees vary according to course load, program and reciprocity agreements. *Faculty research:* Ornithology, forestry, sociology, rural sociology, plant ecology, biodiversity, sustainability, sustainable development, conservation biology.

Walden University, Graduate Programs, School of Public Policy and Administration, Minneapolis, MN 55401. Offers criminal justice (MPA, MPP, MS, Graduate Certificate), including emergency management (MS, PhD), general program (MS, PhD), homeland security and policy coordination (MS, PhD), law and public policy (MS, PhD), policy analysis (MS, PhD), public management and leadership (MS, PhD), self-designed (MS), terrorism, mediation, and peace (MS, PhD); criminal justice leadership and executive management (MS), including emergency management (MS, PhD), general program (MS, PhD), homeland security and policy coordination (MS, PhD), law and public policy (MS, PhD), policy analysis (MS, PhD), public management and leadership (MS, PhD), self-designed, terrorism, mediation, and peace (MS, PhD); emergency management (MPA, MPP, MS), including criminal justice (MS, PhD), general program (MS, PhD), homeland security (MS), public management and leadership (MS, PhD), terrorism and emergency management (MS); general program (MPA, MPP); government management (Graduate Certificate); health policy (MPA, MPP); homeland security (Graduate Certificate); homeland security and policy coordination (MPA, MPP); international nongovernmental organizations (MPA, MPP); law and public policy (MPA, MPP); local government management for sustainable communities (MPA, MPP); nonprofit management (Graduate Certificate); nonprofit management and leadership (MPA, MPP, MS); online teaching in higher education (Post-Master's Certificate); policy analysis (MPA); public management and leadership (MPA, MPP, Graduate Certificate); public policy (Graduate Certificate); public policy and administration (PhD), including criminal justice (MS, PhD), emergency management (MS, PhD), general program (MS, PhD), health policy, homeland security and policy coordination (MS, PhD), international nongovernmental organizations, law and public policy (MS, PhD), local government management for sustainable communities, nonprofit management and leadership, policy analysis (MS, PhD), public management and leadership (MS, PhD), terrorism, mediation, and peace (MS, PhD); strategic planning and public policy (Graduate Certificate); terrorism, mediation, and peace (MPA, MPP). Part-time and evening/weekend programs available. Postbaccalaureate distance learning degree programs offered (no on-campus study). *Faculty:* 13 full-time (5 women), 151 part-time/adjunct (65 women). *Students:* 1,009 full-time (573 women), 1,632 part-time (954 women); includes 1,553 minority (1,307 Black or African American, non-Hispanic/Latino; 15 American Indian or Alaska Native, non-Hispanic/Latino; 38 Asian, non-Hispanic/Latino; 127 Hispanic/Latino; 66 Two or more races, non-Hispanic/Latino), 15 international. Average age 42. 665 applicants, 97% accepted, 616 enrolled. In 2014, 317 master's, 95 doctorates, 34 other advanced degrees awarded. *Degree requirements:* For doctorate, thesis/dissertation, residency. *Entrance requirements:* For master's, bachelor's degree or higher; minimum GPA of 2.5; official transcripts; goal statement (for some programs); access to computer and Internet; for doctorate, master's degree or higher; three years of related professional or academic experience (preferred); minimum GPA of 3.0; goal statement and current resume (for select programs); official transcripts; access to computer and Internet; for other advanced degree, relevant work experience; access to computer and Internet. Additional exam requirements/recommendations for international students: Required—TOEFL (minimum score 550 paper-based, 79 iBT), IELTS (minimum score 6.5), Michigan English Language Assessment Battery (minimum score 82), or PTE (minimum score 53). *Application deadline:* Applications are processed on a rolling basis. Application fee: $0. Electronic applications accepted. *Expenses: Tuition:* Full-time $11,925; part-time $500 per credit hour. *Required fees:* $647. *Financial support:* Fellowships, Federal Work-Study, scholarships/grants, unspecified assistantships, and family tuition reduction, active duty/veteran tuition reduction, group tuition reduction, interest-free payment plans, employee tuition reduction available. Support available to part-time students. Financial award applicants required to submit FAFSA. *Unit head:* Dr. Shana Garrett, Associate Dean, 866-492-5336. *Application contact:* Meghan Thomas, Vice President of Enrollment Management, 866-492-5336, E-mail: info@waldenu.edu.
Website: http://www.waldenu.edu/programs/colleges-schools/public-policy-and-administration

Wayne State University, College of Engineering, Program in Sustainable Engineering, Detroit, MI 48202. Offers Graduate Certificate. *Entrance requirements:* For degree, currently enrolled in a College of Engineering graduate program or BS in engineering; minimum GPA of 3.0. Additional exam requirements/recommendations for international

students: Required—TOEFL (minimum score 550 paper-based; 79 iBT), TWE (minimum score 5.5), Michigan English Language Assessment Battery (minimum score 85); Recommended—IELTS (minimum score 6.5). *Application deadline:* For fall admission, 6/1 priority date for domestic students, 5/1 priority date for international students; for winter admission, 10/1 priority date for domestic students, 9/1 priority date for international students; for spring admission, 2/1 priority date for domestic students, 1/1 priority date for international students. Applications are processed on a rolling basis. Application fee: $0. Electronic applications accepted. *Expenses:* Expenses: Contact institution. *Financial support:* Application deadline: 3/31; applicants required to submit FAFSA. *Unit head:* Dr. Carol Miller, Professor, 313-577-3789, Fax: 313-577-3881, E-mail: cmiller@eng.wayne.edu.
Website: http://engineering.wayne.edu/che/certificate/sustainable-eng.php

West Chester University of Pennsylvania, College of Education, Department of Professional and Secondary Education, West Chester, PA 19383. Offers education for sustainability (Certificate); educational technology (Certificate); entrepreneurial education (Certificate); secondary education (M Ed). Part-time programs available. *Faculty:* 8 full-time (3 women). *Students:* 25 part-time (17 women); includes 3 minority (1 Black or African American, non-Hispanic/Latino; 2 Hispanic/Latino). Average age 29. 16 applicants, 81% accepted, 8 enrolled. In 2014, 9 master's, 4 Certificates awarded. *Degree requirements:* For master's, comprehensive exam, thesis (for some programs), 36 credits. *Entrance requirements:* For master's, GRE or MAT, teaching certification (strongly recommended); for Certificate, minimum GPA of 3.0. Additional exam requirements/recommendations for international students: Required—TOEFL (minimum score 550 paper-based; 80 iBT). *Application deadline:* For fall admission, 4/15 priority date for domestic students, 3/15 for international students; for spring admission, 10/15 priority date for domestic students, 9/1 for international students. Applications are processed on a rolling basis. Application fee: $45. Electronic applications accepted. *Expenses:* Tuition, state resident: full-time $8172; part-time $454 per credit. Tuition, nonresident: full-time $12,258; part-time $681 per credit. *Required fees:* $2231; $110.78 per credit. Tuition and fees vary according to campus/location and program. *Financial support:* Unspecified assistantships available. Support available to part-time students. Financial award application deadline: 2/15; financial award applicants required to submit FAFSA. *Faculty research:* Technology integration: preparing our teachers for the twenty-first century, critical pedagogy. *Unit head:* Dr. John Elmore, Chair, 610-436-6934, Fax: 610-436-3102, E-mail: jelmore@wcupa.edu. *Application contact:* Dr. Rob Haworth, Graduate Coordinator, 610-436-2246, Fax: 610-436-3102, E-mail: rhaworth@wcupa.edu.
Website: http://catalog.wcupa.edu/graduate/education/professional-secondary-education/

Western Illinois University, School of Graduate Studies, College of Arts and Sciences, Department of Geography, Macomb, IL 61455-1390. Offers community development and planning (Certificate); geography (MA); GIS analysis (Certificate). Part-time programs available. *Students:* 12 full-time (5 women), 2 part-time (1 woman); includes 3 minority (2 Black or African American, non-Hispanic/Latino; 1 Hispanic/Latino). Average age 27. 14 applicants, 86% accepted, 6 enrolled. In 2014, 2 master's, 2 other advanced degrees awarded. *Degree requirements:* For master's, thesis or alternative. *Entrance requirements:* Additional exam requirements/recommendations for international students: Required—TOEFL (minimum score 550 paper-based; 80 iBT). *Application deadline:* Applications are processed on a rolling basis. Application fee: $30. Electronic applications accepted. *Financial support:* In 2014–15, 8 students received support, including 2 research assistantships with full tuition reimbursements available (averaging $7,544 per year), 6 teaching assistantships with full tuition reimbursements available (averaging $8,688 per year). Financial award applicants required to submit FAFSA. *Unit head:* Dr. Sam Thompson, Chairperson, 309-298-1648. *Application contact:* Dr. Nancy Parsons, Associate Provost and Director of Graduate School, 309-298-1806, Fax: 309-298-2345, E-mail: grad-office@wiu.edu.
Website: http://wiu.edu/geography

West Virginia University, Davis College of Agriculture, Forestry and Consumer Sciences, Division of Resource Management and Sustainable Development, Program in Resource Management and Sustainable Development, Morgantown, WV 26506. Offers PhD. Part-time programs available. *Degree requirements:* For doctorate, thesis/dissertation. *Entrance requirements:* For doctorate, GRE General Test. Additional exam requirements/recommendations for international students: Required—TOEFL.

Xavier University, College of Arts and Sciences, Department of Interdisciplinary Studies, Cincinnati, OH 45207. Offers urban sustainability and resilience (MA). *Faculty:* 1 (woman) full-time. *Students:* 5 full-time (1 woman); includes 1 minority (Hispanic/Latino), 2 international. Average age 34. 7 applicants, 71% accepted, 4 enrolled. *Degree requirements:* For master's, thesis (for some programs), internship. *Entrance requirements:* For master's, MAT or GRE, official transcript, resume, 500-word statement of purpose, two letters of reference. Additional exam requirements/recommendations for international students: Required—TOEFL (minimum score 550 paper-based; 79 iBT). *Application deadline:* For fall admission, 3/1 for domestic students; for spring admission, 10/1 for domestic students. Application fee: $35. Electronic applications accepted. Application fee is waived when completed online. *Expenses:* Expenses: $600 per credit hour. *Financial support:* In 2014–15, 2 students received support. Applicants required to submit FAFSA. *Unit head:* Dr. Janice B. Walker, Dean, College of Arts and Sciences, 513-745-3101, Fax: 513-745-1099, E-mail: walker@xavier.edu. *Application contact:* Roger Bosse, Graduate Services Director, 513-745-3357, Fax: 513-745-1048, E-mail: bosse@xavier.edu.
Website: http://www.xavier.edu/urbansustainability/

Urban and Regional Planning

Alabama Agricultural and Mechanical University, School of Graduate Studies, College of Agricultural, Life and Natural Sciences, Department of Community and Regional Planning, Huntsville, AL 35811. Offers urban and regional planning (MURP). *Accreditation:* ACSP. Part-time and evening/weekend programs available. *Degree requirements:* For master's, comprehensive exam. *Entrance requirements:* For master's, GRE General Test. Additional exam requirements/recommendations for international students: Required—TOEFL (minimum score 500 paper-based; 61 iBT). Electronic applications accepted. *Faculty research:* Urban and rural research, needs assessment and community trends through analysis of social indicators, fiscal impact studies, rural transportation, health care.

American University of Beirut, Graduate Programs, Faculty of Agricultural and Food Sciences, Beirut, Lebanon. Offers agricultural economics (MS); animal sciences (MS); ecosystem management (MSES); food technology (MS); irrigation (MS); nutrition (MS); plant protection (MS); plant science (MS); poultry science (MS); rural community development (MS). Part-time programs available. *Faculty:* 17 full-time (4 women), 4 part-time/adjunct (1 woman). *Students:* 15 full-time (13 women), 58 part-time (40 women). Average age 26. 60 applicants, 55% accepted, 12 enrolled. In 2014, 33 master's awarded. *Degree requirements:* For master's, one foreign language, comprehensive exam, thesis (for some programs). *Entrance requirements:* Additional exam requirements/recommendations for international students: Required—TOEFL (minimum score 600 paper-based; 100 iBT), IELTS (minimum score 7.5). *Application deadline:* For fall admission, 2/10 for domestic and international students; for spring admission, 11/3 for domestic and international students. Application fee: $50. Electronic applications accepted. *Expenses:* Tuition: Full-time $15,462; part-time $859 per credit. *Required fees:* $692. Tuition and fees vary according to course load and program. *Financial support:* In 2014–15, 1 research assistantship with partial tuition reimbursement (averaging $1,800 per year), 34 teaching assistantships with full and partial tuition reimbursements (averaging $1,220 per year) were awarded; scholarships/grants, health care benefits, and unspecified assistantships also available. Financial award application deadline: 2/2. *Faculty research:* Nutrition and non-communicable diseases in Lebanon, nutritional assessment in Arab youth, establishing food trails across Lebanon, feasibility of groundwater recharge in improving rural livelihoods, landscape atlas for Lebanon. *Total annual research expenditures:* $618,504. *Unit head:* Prof. Nahla Hwalla, Dean, 961-1343002 Ext. 4400, Fax: 961-1744460, E-mail: nahla@aub.edu.lb. *Application contact:* Dr. Rabih Talhouk, Director, Graduate Council, 961-1350000 Ext. 4386, Fax: 961-1374374, E-mail: graduate.council@aub.edu.lb.
Website: http://www.aub.edu.lb/fafs/fafs_home/Pages/index.aspx

American University of Beirut, Graduate Programs, Faculty of Engineering and Architecture, Beirut, Lebanon. Offers applied energy (ME); civil engineering (PhD); electrical and computer engineering (PhD); engineering management (MEM); environmental and water resources (ME); environmental technology (MSES); mechanical engineering (ME, PhD); urban design (MUD); urban planning and policy (MUPP). Part-time programs available. *Faculty:* 93 full-time (18 women), 3 part-time/adjunct (1 woman). *Students:* 268 full-time (111 women), 58 part-time (27 women). Average age 26. 225 applicants, 68% accepted, 79 enrolled. In 2014, 114 master's, 9 doctorates awarded. Terminal master's awarded for partial completion of doctoral program. *Degree requirements:* For master's, one foreign language, comprehensive exam, thesis (for some programs); for doctorate, one foreign language, comprehensive exam, thesis/dissertation, publications. *Entrance requirements:* For master's, letters of recommendation; for doctorate, GRE, letters of recommendation, master's degree, transcripts, curriculum vitae, interview. Additional exam requirements/recommendations for international students: Required—TOEFL (minimum score 600 paper-based; 100 iBT), IELTS (minimum score 7.5). *Application deadline:* For fall admission, 2/5 priority date for domestic and international students; for spring admission, 11/1 priority date for domestic students, 11/1 for international students. Application fee: $50. Electronic applications accepted. *Expenses:* Tuition: Full-time $15,462; part-time $859 per credit. *Required fees:* $692. Tuition and fees vary according to course load and program. *Financial support:* In 2014–15, 190 students received support, including 2 fellowships with full tuition reimbursements available (averaging $24,800 per year), 64 research assistantships with full tuition reimbursements available (averaging $24,800 per year), 124 teaching assistantships with full tuition reimbursements available (averaging $9,800 per year); career-related internships or fieldwork, institutionally sponsored loans, scholarships/grants, health care benefits, and unspecified assistantships also available. *Total annual research expenditures:* $1.5 million. *Unit head:* Prof. Makram T. Suidan, Dean, 961-1350000 Ext. 3400, Fax: 961-1744462, E-mail: msuidan@aub.edu.lb. *Application contact:* Dr. Salim Kanaan, Director, Admissions Office, 961-1350000 Ext. 2594, Fax: 961-1750775, E-mail: sk00@aub.edu.lb.
Website: http://staff.aub.edu.lb/~webfea

American University of Sharjah, Graduate Programs, Sharjah, United Arab Emirates. Offers accounting (MS); business (EMBA, MBA); chemical engineering (MS Ch E); civil engineering (MSCE); computer engineering (MS); electrical engineering (MSEE); engineering systems management (MS); mathematics (MS); mechanical engineering (MSME); mechatronics engineering (MS); teaching English to speakers of other languages (MA); translation and interpreting (MA); urban planning (MUP). Part-time and evening/weekend programs available. *Degree requirements:* For master's, thesis (for some programs). *Entrance requirements:* For master's, GMAT (for MBA). Additional exam requirements/recommendations for international students: Required—TOEFL (minimum score 550 paper-based; 80 iBT), TWE (minimum score 5); Recommended—IELTS (minimum score 6.5). Electronic applications accepted. *Faculty research:* Water pollution, management and waste water treatment, energy and sustainability, air pollution, Islamic finance, family business and small and medium enterprises.

Arizona State University at the Tempe campus, College of Liberal Arts and Sciences, School of Geographical Sciences and Urban Planning, Tempe, AZ 85287-5302. Offers geographic information systems (MAS); geographical information science (Graduate Certificate); geography (MA, PhD); transportation systems (Graduate Certificate); urban and environmental planning (MUEP); urban planning (PhD). Terminal master's awarded for partial completion of doctoral program. *Degree requirements:* For master's, thesis, interactive Program of Study (iPOS) submitted before completing 50 percent of required credit hours; for doctorate, comprehensive exam, thesis/dissertation, interactive Program of Study (iPOS) submitted before completing 50 percent of required credit hours. *Entrance requirements:* For master's and doctorate, GRE, minimum GPA of 3.0 or equivalent in last 2 years of work leading to bachelor's degree. Additional exam requirements/recommendations for international students: Required—TOEFL, IELTS, or PTE. Electronic applications accepted. *Expenses:* Contact institution.

Arizona State University at the Tempe campus, College of Public Programs, School of Community Resources and Development, Phoenix, AZ 85004-0685. Offers community resources and development (MS, PhD); nonprofit leadership and management (Graduate Certificate); nonprofit studies (MNpS); sustainable tourism (MAS). *Accreditation:* ACSP. Part-time and evening/weekend programs available. Terminal master's awarded for partial completion of doctoral program. *Degree requirements:* For master's, thesis or alternative, interactive Program of Study (iPOS) submitted before completing 50 percent of required credit hours; for doctorate, comprehensive exam, thesis/dissertation, interactive Program of Study (iPOS) submitted before completing 50 percent of required credit hours. *Entrance requirements:*

For master's and doctorate, GRE, minimum GPA of 3.0 or equivalent in last 2 years of work leading to bachelor's degree. Additional exam requirements/recommendations for international students: Required—TOEFL, IELTS, or PTE. Electronic applications accepted. *Expenses:* Contact institution.

Arizona State University at the Tempe campus, College of Public Programs, School of Public Affairs, Phoenix, AZ 85004-0687. Offers emergency management and homeland security (MA); program evaluation (MS); public administration (MPA, PhD), including nonprofit administration (MPA), urban management (MPA); public policy (MPP); MPA/MSW. *Accreditation:* NASPAA (one or more programs are accredited). Part-time and evening/weekend programs available. Terminal master's awarded for partial completion of doctoral program. *Degree requirements:* For master's, thesis or alternative, policy analysis or capstone project; interactive Program of Study (iPOS) submitted before completing 50 percent of required credit hours; for doctorate, comprehensive exam, thesis/dissertation, interactive Program of Study (iPOS) submitted before completing 50 percent of required credit hours. *Entrance requirements:* For master's, GRE, minimum GPA of 3.0 or equivalent in last 2 years of work leading to bachelor's degree; for doctorate, GRE, minimum GPA of 3.0 or equivalent in last 2 years of work leading to bachelor's degree, 3 letters of recommendation, resume, statement of goals, samples of research reports. Additional exam requirements/recommendations for international students: Required—TOEFL (minimum score 600 paper-based; 100 iBT), IELTS (minimum score 6.5). Electronic applications accepted. *Expenses:* Contact institution.

Auburn University, Graduate School, College of Architecture, Design, and Construction, Program in Community Planning, Auburn University, AL 36849. Offers MCP, MPA/MCP. *Accreditation:* ACSP. Part-time programs available. *Faculty:* 27 full-time (10 women), 9 part-time/adjunct (1 woman). *Students:* 23 full-time (11 women), 1 (woman) part-time; includes 6 minority (5 Black or African American, non-Hispanic/Latino; 1 Asian, non-Hispanic/Latino), 4 international. Average age 27. 39 applicants, 92% accepted, 8 enrolled. In 2014, 18 master's awarded. *Degree requirements:* For master's, oral exam, project. *Entrance requirements:* For master's, GRE General Test. *Application deadline:* For fall admission, 7/7 for domestic students; for spring admission, 11/24 for domestic students. Applications are processed on a rolling basis. Application fee: $50 ($60 for international students). Electronic applications accepted. *Expenses:* Tuition, state resident: full-time $8586; part-time $477 per credit hour. Tuition, nonresident: full-time $25,758; part-time $1431 per credit hour. *Required fees:* $804 per semester. Tuition and fees vary according to degree level and program. *Financial support:* Federal Work-Study available. Support available to part-time students. Financial award application deadline: 3/15; financial award applicants required to submit FAFSA. *Unit head:* Dr. David Hinson, Head, 334-844-4516. *Application contact:* Dr. George Flowers, Dean of the Graduate School, 334-844-2125.
Website: http://cadc.auburn.edu/studentservices/Pages/APLA/APLA_MCP_Degree.aspx

Ball State University, Graduate School, College of Architecture and Planning, Department of Urban Planning, Muncie, IN 47306-1099. Offers MURP. *Accreditation:* ACSP. *Faculty:* 10 full-time (2 women). *Students:* 27 full-time (10 women), 5 part-time (2 women); includes 1 minority (Black or African American, non-Hispanic/Latino), 9 international. Average age 25. 24 applicants, 96% accepted, 8 enrolled. In 2014, 14 master's awarded. *Degree requirements:* For master's, thesis. *Entrance requirements:* For master's, writing sample. Application fee: $50. *Financial support:* In 2014–15, 21 students received support, including 2 research assistantships with partial tuition reimbursements available (averaging $4,505 per year); unspecified assistantships also available. Financial award application deadline: 3/1. *Faculty research:* Computer-assisted land-use analysis. *Unit head:* Dr. Michael Burayidi, Chairperson, 765-285-1963, Fax: 765-285-2648, E-mail: mburayidi@bsu.edu.
Website: http://www.bsu.edu/cap/planning/planning.html/

See Display on page 108 and Close-Up on page 135.

Boise State University, College of Social Sciences and Public Affairs, Department of Community and Regional Planning, Boise, ID 83725-0399. Offers MCRP, Graduate Certificate. Application fee: $55. *Expenses:* Tuition, state resident: part-time $331 per credit hour. Tuition, nonresident: part-time $531 per credit hour. *Unit head:* Dr. Jaap Vos, Director, 208-426-4370.
Website: http://sspa.boisestate.edu/planning/

Boston University, Metropolitan College, Program in City Planning, Boston, MA 02215. Offers MCP. Part-time and evening/weekend programs available. *Faculty:* 2 full-time (1 woman), 6 part-time/adjunct (2 women). *Students:* 14 full-time (9 women), 19 part-time (4 women); includes 7 minority (4 Black or African American, non-Hispanic/Latino; 2 Asian, non-Hispanic/Latino; 1 Two or more races, non-Hispanic/Latino), 11 international. Average age 26. 45 applicants, 87% accepted, 9 enrolled. In 2014, 14 master's awarded. *Degree requirements:* For master's, thesis optional. *Entrance requirements:* Additional exam requirements/recommendations for international students: Required—TOEFL (minimum score 84 iBT). *Application deadline:* For fall admission, 7/15 priority date for domestic and international students; for spring admission, 12/15 priority date for domestic students, 11/15 priority date for international students. Applications are processed on a rolling basis. Application fee: $80. Electronic applications accepted. *Expenses:* Expenses: $800 per credit part-time; student services fees: $60 per semester; technology fee of $60 per credit (for online courses). *Financial support:* In 2014–15, 4 research assistantships (averaging $4,200 per year) were awarded; career-related internships or fieldwork and unspecified assistantships also available. Support available to part-time students. Financial award application deadline: 6/15; financial award applicants required to submit FAFSA. *Faculty research:* Housing, community development and land use planning, environmental management and planning, international comparative development planning. *Unit head:* Dr. Daniel P. LeClair, Chair, 617-353-3025, Fax: 617-358-3595, E-mail: dleclair@bu.edu. *Application contact:* Dr. Madhu Dutta-Koehler, Assistant Professor and Faculty Coordinator, 617-358-3264, Fax: 617-358-3595, E-mail: duttam@bu.edu.
Website: http://www.bu.edu/cityplanning/

California Polytechnic State University, San Luis Obispo, College of Architecture and Environmental Design, Department of City and Regional Planning, San Luis Obispo, CA 93407. Offers MCRP, MCRP/MS. *Accreditation:* ACSP. Part-time programs available. *Faculty:* 7 full-time (2 women), 1 part-time/adjunct (0 women). *Students:* 38 full-time (18 women), 2 part-time (1 woman); includes 14 minority (1 Black or African American, non-Hispanic/Latino; 2 Asian, non-Hispanic/Latino; 10 Hispanic/Latino; 1 Two or more races, non-Hispanic/Latino), 1 international. Average age 26. 69 applicants, 67% accepted, 22 enrolled. In 2014, 24 master's awarded. *Degree requirements:* For master's, thesis. *Application deadline:* For fall admission, 2/1 for domestic and international students; for winter admission, 11/1 for domestic students, 6/30 for international students. Applications are processed on a rolling basis. Application fee: $55. Electronic applications accepted. *Expenses:* Tuition, state resident: full-time $6738; part-time $3906 per year. Tuition, nonresident: full-time $15,666; part-time $8370 per year. *Required fees:* $3447; $1001 per quarter. One-time fee: $3447 full-time; $3003 part-time. *Financial support:* Fellowships, research assistantships, career-related internships or fieldwork, Federal Work-Study, institutionally sponsored loans, and unspecified assistantships available. Support available to part-time students. Financial award application deadline: 3/2; financial award applicants required to submit FAFSA. *Faculty research:* Community sustainability, climate action planning, natural hazards, small town and rural planning, subdivision site design. *Unit head:* Cornelius Nuworsoo, Graduate Coordinator, 805-756-2573, Fax: 805-756-1340, E-mail: cnuworso@calpoly.edu. *Application contact:* Dr. James Maraviglia, Associate Vice Provost for Marketing and Enrollment Development, 805-756-2311, Fax: 805-756-5400, E-mail: admissions@calpoly.edu.
Website: http://www.planning.calpoly.edu/

California State Polytechnic University, Pomona, Program in Urban and Regional Planning, Pomona, CA 91768-2557. Offers MURP. *Accreditation:* ACSP. Part-time programs available. *Students:* 26 full-time (13 women), 16 part-time (9 women); includes 27 minority (4 Black or African American, non-Hispanic/Latino; 8 Asian, non-Hispanic/Latino; 14 Hispanic/Latino; 1 Two or more races, non-Hispanic/Latino), 3 international. Average age 28. 70 applicants, 74% accepted, 19 enrolled. In 2014, 20 master's awarded. *Degree requirements:* For master's, thesis or alternative. *Entrance requirements:* For master's, GRE General Test. *Application deadline:* For fall admission, 5/1 priority date for domestic students; for winter admission, 10/15 priority date for domestic students; for spring admission, 1/20 priority date for domestic students. Applications are processed on a rolling basis. Application fee: $55. Electronic applications accepted. *Expenses:* Tuition, state resident: full-time $6738. Tuition, nonresident: full-time $12,300. *Required fees:* $1400. *Financial support:* Career-related internships or fieldwork, Federal Work-Study, and institutionally sponsored loans available. Support available to part-time students. Financial award application deadline: 3/2; financial award applicants required to submit FAFSA. *Unit head:* Dr. Do-Hyung Kim, Graduate Coordinator, 909-869-4645, Fax: 909-869-4688, E-mail: dohyungkim@cpp.edu.
Website: http://www.cpp.edu/~urp/programs/masters.shtml

California State University, Chico, Office of Graduate Studies, College of Behavioral and Social Sciences, Department of Geography and Planning, Chico, CA 95929-0722. Offers geography (MA), including environmental policy and planning, geography. Part-time programs available. *Faculty:* 1 (woman) full-time. *Students:* 1 (woman) part-time. Average age 44. In 2014, 5 master's awarded. *Degree requirements:* For master's, thesis or project. *Entrance requirements:* For master's, GRE, two letters of recommendation, statement of purpose, writing sample. Additional exam requirements/recommendations for international students: Required—TOEFL (minimum score 550 paper-based; 80 iBT), IELTS (minimum score 6.5), PTE (minimum score 59). *Application deadline:* For fall admission, 3/1 priority date for domestic students, 3/1 for international students; for spring admission, 9/15 priority date for domestic students, 9/15 for international students. Application fee: $55. Electronic applications accepted. *Expenses:* Tuition, state resident: full-time $7002. Tuition, nonresident: full-time $18,162. *Required fees:* $1530. Tuition and fees vary according to program. *Financial support:* Fellowships, teaching assistantships, career-related internships or fieldwork, institutionally sponsored loans, scholarships/grants, and unspecified assistantships available. Financial award application deadline: 3/1; financial award applicants required to submit FAFSA. *Unit head:* Dr. Jacquelyn Chase, Chair, 530-898-5285, Fax: 530-898-6781, E-mail: geop@csuchico.edu. *Application contact:* Judy L. Rice, Graduate Admissions Coordinator, 530-898-5416, Fax: 530-898-3342, E-mail: jlrice@csuchico.edu.
Website: http://www.csuchico.edu/geop/

The Catholic University of America, School of Architecture and Planning, Washington, DC 20064. Offers MS Arch St. Part-time programs available. *Faculty:* 22 full-time (9 women), 31 part-time/adjunct (9 women). *Students:* 90 full-time (38 women), 31 part-time (14 women); includes 33 minority (10 Black or African American, non-Hispanic/Latino; 5 Asian, non-Hispanic/Latino; 10 Hispanic/Latino; 8 Two or more races, non-Hispanic/Latino), 16 international. Average age 28. 93 applicants, 97% accepted, 45 enrolled. In 2014, 42 master's awarded. *Degree requirements:* For master's, thesis. *Entrance requirements:* For master's, GRE (minimum score: 1000), minimum GPA of 2.8, portfolio, statement of purpose, official copies of academic transcripts, three letters of recommendation. Additional exam requirements/recommendations for international students: Required—TOEFL (minimum score 580 paper-based). *Application deadline:* For fall admission, 1/15 priority date for domestic students, 1/15 for international students; for spring admission, 10/15 priority date for domestic students, 10/15 for international students. Applications are processed on a rolling basis. Application fee: $55. Electronic applications accepted. *Expenses:* Expenses: Contact institution. *Financial support:* Fellowships, research assistantships, teaching assistantships, Federal Work-Study, scholarships/grants, tuition waivers (full and partial), and unspecified assistantships available. Financial award application deadline: 2/1; financial award applicants required to submit FAFSA. *Faculty research:* Architectural history, cultural studies/sacred space, design technologies, digital media, real estate development, urban design. *Total annual research expenditures:* $98,238. *Unit head:* Randall Ott, Dean, 202-319-5784, Fax: 202-319-2023, E-mail: ott@cua.edu. *Application contact:* Director of Graduate Admissions, 202-319-5057, Fax: 202-319-6533, E-mail: cua-admissions@cua.edu.
Website: http://architecture.cua.edu/

Clark University, Graduate School, Department of International Development, Community, and Environment, Program in Community Development and Planning, Worcester, MA 01610-1477. Offers MA, MA/MBA. *Students:* 34 full-time (24 women), 4 part-time (3 women); includes 10 minority (4 Black or African American, non-Hispanic/Latino; 1 Asian, non-Hispanic/Latino; 5 Hispanic/Latino). Average age 25. 79 applicants, 81% accepted, 28 enrolled. In 2014, 29 master's awarded. *Degree requirements:* For master's, thesis. *Entrance requirements:* For master's, 3 references, resume or curriculum vitae. Additional exam requirements/recommendations for international students: Required—TOEFL (minimum score 575 paper-based; 90 iBT) or IELTS (minimum score 6.5). *Application deadline:* For fall admission, 1/15 for domestic students. Application fee: $75. *Expenses: Tuition:* Full-time $40,380; part-time $1262 per credit hour. *Required fees:* $30. *Financial support:* Fellowships with partial tuition reimbursements, research assistantships with partial tuition reimbursements, teaching assistantships with partial tuition reimbursements, institutionally sponsored loans, and scholarships/grants available. *Faculty research:* Urban revitalization, youth and gang violence, amenities, systemic education reform, housing for disabled residents, economic development in neighborhood planning. *Unit head:* Dr. Ellen Foley, Interim Director, 508-793-7201, Fax: 508-793-8820. *Application contact:* Erika Paradis, Student and Academic Services Director, 508-793-7201, Fax: 508-793-8820, E-mail: eparadis@clarku.edu.
Website: http://www.clarku.edu/departments/idce/programs/cdp/default.html

Clemson University, Graduate School, College of Architecture, Arts, and Humanities, Department of Planning, Development and Preservation, Program in City and Regional Planning, Clemson, SC 29634. Offers MCRP. *Students:* 23 full-time (10 women), 1 part-time (0 women); includes 4 minority (1 Black or African American, non-Hispanic/Latino; 1 Asian, non-Hispanic/Latino; 1 Hispanic/Latino; 1 Two or more races, non-Hispanic/Latino), 6 international. Average age 26. 85 applicants, 76% accepted, 21 enrolled. In 2014, 12 master's awarded. *Degree requirements:* For master's, departmental paper or

thesis. *Entrance requirements:* For master's, GRE General Test. Additional exam requirements/recommendations for international students: Required—TOEFL. *Application deadline:* For fall admission, 2/15 priority date for domestic and international students. Applications are processed on a rolling basis. Application fee: $70 ($80 for international students). Electronic applications accepted. *Financial support:* In 2014–15, 8 students received support, including 8 teaching assistantships with partial tuition reimbursements available (averaging $6,600 per year); fellowships with full and partial tuition reimbursements available, research assistantships with partial tuition reimbursements available, career-related internships or fieldwork, Federal Work-Study, institutionally sponsored loans, scholarships/grants, health care benefits, and unspecified assistantships also available. Financial award application deadline: 4/15; financial award applicants required to submit FAFSA. *Faculty research:* Coastal planning, transportation, land use and urban design, economic development, geographic information systems. *Unit head:* Dr. James H. Spencer, Chair, Department of Planning, Development and Preservation, 864-656-1527, E-mail: jhspenc@clemson.edu. *Application contact:* Dr. Cliff Ellis, Director, 864-656-2477, Fax: 864-656-7519, E-mail: cliffoe@clemson.edu.
Website: http://www.clemson.edu/caah/pdp/city-and-regional-planning/

Cleveland State University, College of Graduate Studies, Maxine Goodman Levin College of Urban Affairs, Program in Public Administration, Cleveland, OH 44115. Offers city management (MPA); economic development (MPA); healthcare administration (MPA); local and urban management (Certificate); non-profit management (MPA, Certificate); public financial management (MPA); public management (MPA); urban economic development (Certificate); JD/MPA. *Accreditation:* NASPAA. Part-time and evening/weekend programs available. *Faculty:* 23 full-time (11 women), 23 part-time/adjunct (6 women). *Students:* 16 full-time (11 women), 64 part-time (40 women); includes 23 minority (19 Black or African American, non-Hispanic/Latino; 3 Hispanic/Latino; 1 Two or more races, non-Hispanic/Latino), 3 international. Average age 36. 67 applicants, 51% accepted, 13 enrolled. In 2014, 41 master's awarded. *Degree requirements:* For master's, thesis or alternative, capstone course. *Entrance requirements:* For master's, GRE General Test (minimum scores in 40th percentile verbal and quantitative, 4.0 writing), minimum GPA of 3.0. Additional exam requirements/recommendations for international students: Required—TOEFL (minimum score 525 paper-based; 65 iBT), IELTS, or ITEP. *Application deadline:* For fall admission, 7/15 priority date for domestic students, 5/15 for international students; for spring admission, 11/1 for international students. Applications are processed on a rolling basis. Application fee: $30. Electronic applications accepted. *Expenses:* Expenses: $9,615 full-time, in-state tuition and fees. *Financial support:* In 2014–15, 16 students received support, including 4 research assistantships with full and partial tuition reimbursements available (averaging $7,200 per year), 3 teaching assistantships with full and partial tuition reimbursements available (averaging $2,400 per year); career-related internships or fieldwork, scholarships/grants, traineeships, and unspecified assistantships also available. Support available to part-time students. Financial award application deadline: 3/1; financial award applicants required to submit FAFSA. *Faculty research:* City management, nonprofit management, health care administration, public management, economic development. *Unit head:* Dr. Nicholas Zingale, Director, 216-802-3398, Fax: 216-687-9342, E-mail: n.zingale@csuohio.edu. *Application contact:* David Arrighi, Graduate Academic Advisor, 216-523-7522, Fax: 216-687-5398, E-mail: urbanprograms@csuohio.edu.
Website: http://urban.csuohio.edu/academics/graduate/mpa/

Cleveland State University, College of Graduate Studies, Maxine Goodman Levin College of Urban Affairs, Program in Urban Planning, Design, and Development, Cleveland, OH 44115. Offers economic development (MUPDD); environmental sustainability (MUPDD); geographic information systems (MUPDD, Certificate); historic preservation (MUPDD); housing and neighborhood development (MUPDD); urban economic development (Certificate); urban real estate development and finance (MUPDD, Certificate); JD/MUPDD. *Accreditation:* ACSP. Part-time and evening/weekend programs available. *Faculty:* 23 full-time (11 women), 23 part-time/adjunct (6 women). *Students:* 11 full-time (5 women), 25 part-time (10 women); includes 8 minority (2 Black or African American, non-Hispanic/Latino; 1 Asian, non-Hispanic/Latino; 2 Hispanic/Latino; 3 Two or more races, non-Hispanic/Latino), 3 international. Average age 38. 48 applicants, 56% accepted, 5 enrolled. In 2014, 16 master's awarded. *Degree requirements:* For master's, thesis or alternative, planning studio. *Entrance requirements:* For master's, GRE General Test (minimum score: 50th percentile combined verbal and quantitative, 4.0 analytical writing), minimum GPA of 3.0. Additional exam requirements/recommendations for international students: Required—TOEFL (minimum score 525 paper-based; 65 iBT), IELTS, or ITEP. *Application deadline:* For fall admission, 7/15 priority date for domestic students, 5/15 for international students; for spring admission, 11/1 for international students. Applications are processed on a rolling basis. Application fee: $30. Electronic applications accepted. *Expenses:* Expenses: $9,615 full-time, in-state tuition and fees. *Financial support:* In 2014–15, 10 students received support, including 7 research assistantships with full and partial tuition reimbursements available (averaging $5,600 per year), 2 teaching assistantships with full and partial tuition reimbursements available (averaging $2,000 per year); career-related internships or fieldwork, Federal Work-Study, scholarships/grants, tuition waivers, and unspecified assistantships also available. Support available to part-time students. Financial award application deadline: 3/1; financial award applicants required to submit FAFSA. *Faculty research:* Housing and neighborhood development, urban housing policy, environmental sustainability, economic development, GIS and planning decision support. *Unit head:* Dr. Dennis Keating, Director, 216-687-2298, Fax: 216-687-2013, E-mail: w.keating@csuohio.edu. *Application contact:* David Arrighi, Graduate Academic Advisor, 216-523-7522, Fax: 216-687-5398, E-mail: urbanprograms@csuohio.edu.
Website: http://urban.csuohio.edu/academics/graduate/mupdd/

Cleveland State University, College of Graduate Studies, Maxine Goodman Levin College of Urban Affairs, Program in Urban Studies, Cleveland, OH 44115. Offers community and neighborhood development (MS); economic development (MS); law and public policy (MS); public finance (MS); urban economic development (Certificate); urban policy analysis (MS); urban real estate development (MS); urban real estate development and finance (Certificate). Part-time and evening/weekend programs available. *Faculty:* 23 full-time (11 women), 23 part-time/adjunct (6 women). *Students:* 5 full-time (1 woman), 8 part-time (2 women); includes 1 minority (Black or African American, non-Hispanic/Latino). Average age 34. 21 applicants, 29% accepted, 4 enrolled. In 2014, 4 master's awarded. *Degree requirements:* For master's, thesis or alternative, exit project. *Entrance requirements:* For master's, GRE General Test (minimum score: verbal and quantitative combined 40th percentile, analytical writing 4.0), minimum GPA of 3.0. Additional exam requirements/recommendations for international students: Required—TOEFL (minimum score 525 paper-based; 65 iBT), IELTS, or ITEP. *Application deadline:* For fall admission, 1/15 priority date for domestic students, 1/15 for international students. Applications are processed on a rolling basis. Application fee: $30. Electronic applications accepted. *Expenses:* Expenses: $9,615 full-time, in-state tuition and fees. *Financial support:* In 2014–15, 4 students received support, including 3 research assistantships with full and partial tuition reimbursements available (averaging $7,200 per year), 2 teaching assistantships with full and partial

tuition reimbursements available (averaging $4,800 per year); career-related internships or fieldwork, scholarships/grants, traineeships, and unspecified assistantships also available. Support available to part-time students. Financial award application deadline: 3/1; financial award applicants required to submit FAFSA. *Faculty research:* Environmental issues, economic development, urban and public policy, public management. *Unit head:* Dr. Brian Mikelbank, Director, 216-875-9980, Fax: 216-687-9342, E-mail: b.mikelbank@csuohio.edu. *Application contact:* David Arrighi, Graduate Academic Advisor, 216-523-7522, Fax: 216-687-5398, E-mail: urbanprograms@csuohio.edu.
Website: http://urban.csuohio.edu/academics/graduate/msus/

College of Charleston, Graduate School, School of Humanities and Social Sciences, Program in Urban and Regional Planning, Charleston, SC 29424-0001. Offers Certificate. Part-time and evening/weekend programs available. *Entrance requirements:* Additional exam requirements/recommendations for international students: Required—TOEFL (minimum score 81 iBT). Electronic applications accepted.

Columbia University, Graduate School of Architecture, Planning, and Preservation, Program in Urban Planning, New York, NY 10027. Offers MS, PhD, JD/MS, M Arch/MS, MBA/MS, MIA/MS, MPH/MS, MS/MS. PhD offered through the Graduate School of Arts and Sciences. *Accreditation:* ACSP (one or more programs are accredited). *Degree requirements:* For master's, thesis. *Entrance requirements:* For master's, GRE General Test.

Concordia University, School of Graduate Studies, Faculty of Arts and Science, School of Community and Public Affairs, Montréal, QC H3G 1M8, Canada. Offers community economic development (Diploma).

Cornell University, Graduate School, Graduate Fields of Architecture, Art and Planning, Field of City and Regional Planning, Ithaca, NY 14853-0001. Offers city and regional planning (MRP, PhD); environmental planning and design (MRP, PhD); historic preservation planning (MA); international development planning (MRP, PhD); planning theory and systems analysis (MRP, PhD); regional economics and development planning (MRP, PhD); regional science (MRP, PhD); social and health systems planning (MRP, PhD); urban and regional theory (MRP, PhD); urban planning history (MRP, PhD). *Accreditation:* ACSP (one or more programs are accredited). *Degree requirements:* For master's, thesis (MA); for doctorate, comprehensive exam, thesis/dissertation. *Entrance requirements:* For master's and doctorate, GRE General Test, 2 letters of recommendation. Additional exam requirements/recommendations for international students: Required—TOEFL (minimum score 600 paper-based; 77 iBT). Electronic applications accepted. *Faculty research:* Land use planning, economic development, international development, historic preservation, community development.

Cornell University, Graduate School, Graduate Fields of Architecture, Art and Planning, Field of Regional Science, Ithaca, NY 14853-0001. Offers environmental studies (MA, MS, PhD); international spatial problems (MA, MS, PhD); location theory (MA, MS, PhD); multiregional economic analysis (MA, MS, PhD); peace science (MA, MS, PhD); planning methods (MA, MS, PhD); urban and regional economics (MA, MS, PhD). Terminal master's awarded for partial completion of doctoral program. *Degree requirements:* For master's, thesis; for doctorate, comprehensive exam, thesis/dissertation. *Entrance requirements:* For master's and doctorate, GRE General Test, 2 letters of recommendation. Additional exam requirements/recommendations for international students: Required—TOEFL (minimum score 600 paper-based; 77 iBT). Electronic applications accepted. *Faculty research:* Urban and regional growth, spatial economics, formation of spatial patterns by socioeconomic systems, non-linear dynamics and complex systems, environmental-economic systems.

Dalhousie University, Faculty of Architecture and Planning, School of Planning, Halifax, NS B3J 2X4, Canada. Offers M Eng, M Plan, MPS. *Degree requirements:* For master's, thesis. *Entrance requirements:* Additional exam requirements/recommendations for international students: Required—TOEFL, IELTS, CANTEST, CAEL, or Michigan English Language Assessment Battery. Electronic applications accepted.

Delta State University, Graduate Programs, College of Arts and Sciences, Division of Social Sciences and History, Program in Community Development, Cleveland, MS 38733-0001. Offers MS. Part-time programs available. *Students:* 8 full-time (6 women), 9 part-time (5 women); includes 11 minority (all Black or African American, non-Hispanic/Latino). Average age 33. 9 applicants, 100% accepted, 3 enrolled. In 2014, 3 master's awarded. *Degree requirements:* For master's, thesis or alternative. *Application deadline:* For fall admission, 8/1 priority date for domestic students; for spring admission, 12/1 priority date for domestic students. Applications are processed on a rolling basis. Application fee: $30. *Expenses:* Tuition, state resident: full-time $6012; part-time $334 per credit hour. Tuition, nonresident: full-time $6012; part-time $334 per credit hour. Part-time tuition and fees vary according to course load. *Financial support:* Research assistantships, career-related internships or fieldwork, Federal Work-Study, and institutionally sponsored loans available. Support available to part-time students. Financial award application deadline: 6/1. *Unit head:* Dr. Paulette Miekle, Chair, 662-846-4065, Fax: 662-846-4016, E-mail: pmeikleyaw@deltastate.edu. *Application contact:* Dr. Beverly Moon, Dean of Graduate Studies, 662-846-4873, Fax: 662-846-4313, E-mail: grad-info@deltastate.edu.
Website: http://www.deltastate.edu/pages/3335.asp

East Carolina University, Graduate School, Thomas Harriot College of Arts and Sciences, Department of Geography, Planning, and Environment, Greenville, NC 27858-4353. Offers economic development (Certificate); geographic information science and technology (Certificate); geography (MA), including geography, planning, rural development. Part-time and evening/weekend programs available. *Degree requirements:* For master's, one foreign language, comprehensive exam, thesis optional. *Entrance requirements:* For master's, GRE General Test. Additional exam requirements/recommendations for international students: Required—TOEFL. *Expenses:* Tuition, state resident: full-time $4223. Tuition, nonresident: full-time $16,540. *Required fees:* $2184.

Eastern Kentucky University, The Graduate School, College of Arts and Sciences, Department of Government, Program in General Public Administration, Richmond, KY 40475-3102. Offers community development (MPA); community health administration (MPA); general public administration (MPA). *Accreditation:* NASPAA. Part-time and evening/weekend programs available. *Entrance requirements:* For master's, GRE General Test, minimum GPA of 2.5.

Eastern Michigan University, Graduate School, College of Arts and Sciences, Department of Geography and Geology, Program in Urban and Regional Planning, Ypsilanti, MI 48197. Offers MS. *Accreditation:* ACSP. *Students:* 3 full-time (2 women), 9 part-time (4 women); includes 3 minority (2 Black or African American, non-Hispanic/Latino; 1 Hispanic/Latino), 2 international. Average age 30. 20 applicants, 70% accepted, 5 enrolled. In 2014, 9 master's awarded. Application fee: $45. *Application contact:* Dr. Heather Khan, Program Advisor, 734-487-0218, Fax: 734-487-6979, E-mail: hkhan3@emich.edu.

Eastern Michigan University, Graduate School, College of Arts and Sciences, Department of Political Science, Programs in Public Administration, Ypsilanti, MI 48197.

Offers management of public healthcare services (Graduate Certificate); public administration (MPA); public budget management (Graduate Certificate); public land planning (Graduate Certificate); public management (Graduate Certificate); public policy analysis (Graduate Certificate). *Accreditation:* NASPAA. *Students:* 5 full-time (2 women), 57 part-time (24 women); includes 18 minority (13 Black or African American, non-Hispanic/Latino; 2 Asian, non-Hispanic/Latino; 3 Hispanic/Latino), 1 international. Average age 36. 50 applicants, 66% accepted, 17 enrolled. In 2014, 25 master's, 9 other advanced degrees awarded. Application fee: $45. *Unit head:* Dr. Gregory Plagens, Program Director, 734-487-2522, Fax: 734-487-3340, E-mail: gregory.plagens@emich.edu. *Application contact:* Dr. Barbara Patrick, Program Advisor, 734-487-1453, Fax: 734-487-3340, E-mail: bpatric1@emich.edu.

Eastern University, Department of Urban Studies, St. Davids, PA 19087-3696. Offers urban studies (MA), including arts in transformation, community development, youth leadership. Part-time and evening/weekend programs available. Postbaccalaureate distance learning degree programs offered (minimal on-campus study). *Faculty:* 3 full-time (1 woman), 4 part-time/adjunct (1 woman). *Students:* 13 full-time (11 women), 48 part-time (44 women); includes 38 minority (33 Black or African American, non-Hispanic/Latino; 1 Asian, non-Hispanic/Latino; 3 Hispanic/Latino; 1 Two or more races, non-Hispanic/Latino). Average age 30. 38 applicants, 97% accepted, 19 enrolled. In 2014, 19 master's awarded. *Entrance requirements:* For master's, minimum GPA of 2.5. Additional exam requirements/recommendations for international students: Required—TOEFL (minimum score 550 paper-based; 79 iBT). *Application deadline:* For fall admission, 8/14 for domestic students; for spring admission, 12/20 for domestic students. Applications are processed on a rolling basis. Application fee: $35. Application fee is waived when completed online. *Expenses: Tuition:* Full-time $15,600; part-time $650 per credit. *Required fees:* $30; $27.50 per semester. One-time fee: $50. Tuition and fees vary according to course load, degree level and program. *Financial support:* In 2014–15, 34 students received support. Scholarships/grants available. Financial award application deadline: 3/15; financial award applicants required to submit FAFSA. *Unit head:* Dr. Kimberlee Johnson, Chair, 215-769-3128. *Application contact:* Whitney Monn, Program Recruiter, 215-769-3121, Fax: 215-848-2651, E-mail: wmonn@eastern.edu. Website: http://www.eastern.edu/academics/programs/urban-studies-department/urban-studies-concentrations

Eastern University, School of Leadership and Development, St. Davids, PA 19087-3696. Offers economic development (MBA), including international development, urban development (MA, MBA); international development (MA), including global development, urban development (MA, MBA); nonprofit management (MS); organizational leadership (MA); M Div/MBA. Part-time and evening/weekend programs available. Postbaccalaureate distance learning degree programs offered (minimal on-campus study). *Faculty:* 6 full-time (3 women), 19 part-time/adjunct (8 women). *Students:* 112 full-time (62 women), 49 part-time (27 women); includes 36 minority (19 Black or African American, non-Hispanic/Latino; 2 American Indian or Alaska Native, non-Hispanic/Latino; 5 Asian, non-Hispanic/Latino; 7 Hispanic/Latino; 1 Native Hawaiian or other Pacific Islander, non-Hispanic/Latino; 2 Two or more races, non-Hispanic/Latino), 15 international. Average age 33. 62 applicants, 90% accepted, 46 enrolled. In 2014, 106 master's awarded. *Degree requirements:* For master's, thesis (for some programs). *Entrance requirements:* For master's, GMAT (for MBA), minimum GPA of 2.5. Additional exam requirements/recommendations for international students: Required—TOEFL (minimum score 550 paper-based; 79 iBT). *Application deadline:* For fall admission, 8/14 for domestic students. Applications are processed on a rolling basis. Application fee: $35. Application fee is waived when completed online. *Expenses:* Expenses: Contact institution. *Financial support:* In 2014–15, 131 students received support, including 3 fellowships with partial tuition reimbursements available (averaging $2,500 per year), 7 research assistantships with partial tuition reimbursements available (averaging $1,500 per year); scholarships/grants and unspecified assistantships also available. Financial award application deadline: 3/15; financial award applicants required to submit FAFSA. *Faculty research:* Micro-level economic development, China welfare and economic development, macroethics, micro- and macro-level economic development in transitional economics, organizational effectiveness. *Unit head:* Beth Birmingham, Chair, 610-341-4380. *Application contact:* Lindsey Perry, Enrollment Counselor, 484-581-1311, Fax: 484-581-1276, E-mail: lperry@eastern.edu. Website: http://www.eastern.edu/academics/programs/school-leadership-and-development

Eastern Washington University, Graduate Studies, College of Business and Public Administration, Program in Urban and Regional Planning, Cheney, WA 99004-2431. Offers MURP, MPA/MURP. *Accreditation:* ACSP. *Degree requirements:* For master's, comprehensive exam, thesis or alternative. *Entrance requirements:* For master's, minimum GPA of 3.0.

East Tennessee State University, School of Graduate Studies, College of Arts and Sciences, Department of Political Science, International Affairs and Public Administration, Johnson City, TN 37614. Offers economic development (Postbaccalaureate Certificate); not-for-profit administration (MPA); planning and development (MPA); public financial management (MPA); urban planning (Postbaccalaureate Certificate). Part-time programs available. *Faculty:* 7 full-time (2 women), 1 part-time/adjunct (0 women). *Students:* 19 full-time (5 women), 9 part-time (4 women); includes 3 minority (2 Black or African American, non-Hispanic/Latino; 1 Hispanic/Latino), 6 international. Average age 29. 48 applicants, 33% accepted, 10 enrolled. In 2014, 7 master's, 1 other advanced degree awarded. *Degree requirements:* For master's, internship. *Entrance requirements:* For master's, GRE General Test, three letters of recommendation; for Postbaccalaureate Certificate, GRE General Test. Additional exam requirements/recommendations for international students: Required—TOEFL (minimum score 550 paper-based; 79 iBT). *Application deadline:* For fall admission, 6/1 for domestic students, 4/29 for international students; for spring admission, 11/1 for domestic students, 9/30 for international students. Application fee: $35 ($45 for international students). Electronic applications accepted. *Financial support:* In 2014–15, 16 students received support, including 16 research assistantships with full tuition reimbursements available (averaging $6,000 per year), 4 teaching assistantships with full tuition reimbursements available (averaging $6,000 per year); career-related internships or fieldwork, institutionally sponsored loans, scholarships/grants, and unspecified assistantships also available. Financial award application deadline: 7/1; financial award applicants required to submit FAFSA. *Faculty research:* Labor issues, presidency, public law in American politics, East Asian politics, European politics, Middle Eastern politics, development in comparative politics, international political economy, international relations, world politics in international affairs. *Unit head:* Dr. Andrew Battista, Chair, 423-439-4217, Fax: 423-439-4348, E-mail: battista@etsu.edu. *Application contact:* Angela Edwards, Graduate Specialist, 423-439-4703, Fax: 423-439-5624, E-mail: edwardag@etsu.edu. Website: http://www.etsu.edu/cas/polisci/

Florida Atlantic University, College of Design and Social Inquiry, School of Urban and Regional Planning, Boca Raton, FL 33431-0991. Offers economic development and tourism (Certificate); environmental planning (Certificate); sustainable community planning (Certificate); urban and regional planning (MURP); visual planning technology (Certificate). *Accreditation:* ACSP. Part-time and evening/weekend programs available.

Entrance requirements: For master's, GRE General Test, minimum GPA of 3.0. Additional exam requirements/recommendations for international students: Required—TOEFL (minimum score 500 paper-based; 61 iBT), IELTS (minimum score 6). *Expenses:* Tuition, state resident: full-time $7396; part-time $369.82 per credit hour. Tuition, nonresident: full-time $19,392; part-time $1024.81 per credit hour. Tuition and fees vary according to course load. *Faculty research:* Growth management, urban design, computer applications/geographical information systems, environmental planning.

Florida State University, The Graduate School, College of Social Sciences and Public Policy, Department of Urban and Regional Planning, Tallahassee, FL 32306. Offers MSP, PhD, JD/MSP, MA/MSP, MPA/MSP, MPH/MSP, MSD/MSP. *Accreditation:* ACSP (one or more programs are accredited). Part-time programs available. *Faculty:* 11 full-time (4 women), 7 part-time/adjunct (3 women). *Students:* 85 full-time (45 women), 20 part-time (10 women); includes 46 minority (14 Black or African American, non-Hispanic/Latino; 7 Asian, non-Hispanic/Latino; 20 Hispanic/Latino; 5 Two or more races, non-Hispanic/Latino), 8 international. Average age 28. 83 applicants, 87% accepted, 45 enrolled. In 2014, 42 master's, 2 doctorates awarded. *Degree requirements:* For master's, capstone project, internship; for doctorate, thesis/dissertation. *Entrance requirements:* For master's and doctorate, GRE General Test, minimum GPA of 3.0. Additional exam requirements/recommendations for international students: Required—TOEFL (minimum score 600 paper-based; 100 iBT); Recommended—IELTS (minimum score 7). *Application deadline:* For fall admission, 2/15 priority date for domestic students, 11/15 priority date for international students; for spring admission, 11/1 for domestic students, 9/1 for international students. Applications are processed on a rolling basis. Application fee: $30. Electronic applications accepted. *Expenses:* Tuition, state resident: part-time $403.51 per credit hour. Tuition, nonresident: part-time $1004.85 per credit hour. *Required fees:* $75.81 per credit hour. One-time fee: $20 part-time. Tuition and fees vary according to campus/location. *Financial support:* In 2014–15, 41 students received support, including 5 fellowships with full tuition reimbursements available (averaging $17,200 per year), 26 research assistantships with full tuition reimbursements available (averaging $7,500 per year), 10 teaching assistantships with full tuition reimbursements available (averaging $15,000 per year); career-related internships or fieldwork, Federal Work-Study, institutionally sponsored loans, and tuition waivers (partial) also available. Financial award application deadline: 2/15; financial award applicants required to submit FAFSA. *Faculty research:* Land use planning, environmental planning, developing countries, transportation, sustainable and healthy communities, housing and community development. *Total annual research expenditures:* $550,000. *Unit head:* Dr. Jeffrey R. Brown, Associate Professor and Chairperson, 850-644-4510, Fax: 850-645-4841, E-mail: jrbrown3@fsu.edu. *Application contact:* Susan A. Taylor, Admissions Coordinator, 850-644-4510, Fax: 850-644-4841, E-mail: durp@coss.fsu.edu. Website: http://www.coss.fsu.edu/durp/

Future Generations Graduate School, Program in Applied Community Change, Conservation, and Peacebuilding, Franklin, WV 26807. Offers conservation (MA); peacebuilding (MA). *Degree requirements:* For master's, one foreign language, applied practicum research. *Entrance requirements:* For master's, bachelor's degree, community involvement. Additional exam requirements/recommendations for international students: Required—TOEFL. Electronic applications accepted. *Faculty research:* Sustainable communities, community engagement, peacebuilding, seed-scale community development.

Georgetown University, Graduate School of Arts and Sciences, School of Continuing Studies, Washington, DC 20057. Offers American studies (MALS); Catholic studies (MALS); classical civilizations (MALS); emergency and disaster management (MPS); ethics and the professions (MALS); hospitality management (MPS); human resources management (MPS); humanities (MALS); individualized study (MALS); international affairs (MALS); Islam and Muslim-Christian relations (MALS); journalism (MPS); liberal studies (DLS); literature and society (MALS); medieval and early modern European studies (MALS); public relations and corporate communications (MPS); real estate (MPS); religious studies (MALS); social and public policy (MALS); sports industry management (MPS); systems engineering management (MPS); technology management (MPS); the theory and practice of American democracy (MALS); urban and regional planning (MPS); visual culture (MALS). MPS in systems engineering management offered jointly with Stevens Institute of Technology. *Entrance requirements:* Additional exam requirements/recommendations for international students: Required—TOEFL.

Georgia Institute of Technology, Graduate Studies, College of Architecture, School of City and Regional Planning, Atlanta, GA 30332-0001. Offers city and regional planning (PhD); economic development (MCRP); environmental planning and management (MCRP); geographic information systems (MCRP); land and community development (MCRP); land use planning (MCRP); transportation (MCRP); urban design (MCRP); MCP/MSCE. *Accreditation:* ACSP. *Degree requirements:* For master's, thesis, internship. *Entrance requirements:* For master's, GRE General Test, minimum GPA of 2.7. Additional exam requirements/recommendations for international students: Required—TOEFL. Electronic applications accepted. *Expenses:* Tuition, state resident: full-time $12,344; part-time $515 per credit hour. Tuition, nonresident: full-time $27,600; part-time $1150 per credit hour. *Required fees:* $1196 per term. Part-time tuition and fees vary according to course load.

Georgia State University, Andrew Young School of Policy Studies, Department of Public Management and Policy, Atlanta, GA 30303. Offers criminal justice (MPA); disaster management (Certificate); disaster policy (MPA); environmental policy (PhD); health policy (PhD); management and finance (MPA); nonprofit management (MPA, Certificate); nonprofit policy (MPA); planning and economic development (MPP, Certificate); policy analysis and evaluation (MPA), including planning and economic development; public and nonprofit management (PhD); public finance and budgeting (PhD), including science and technology policy, urban and regional economic development; public finance policy (MPA), including social policy; public health (MPA). *Accreditation:* NASPAA (one or more programs are accredited). Part-time programs available. *Faculty:* 14 full-time (7 women). *Students:* 136 full-time (80 women), 85 part-time (47 women); includes 81 minority (60 Black or African American, non-Hispanic/Latino; 7 Asian, non-Hispanic/Latino; 11 Hispanic/Latino; 3 Two or more races, non-Hispanic/Latino), 25 international. Average age 30. 269 applicants, 59% accepted, 64 enrolled. In 2014, 80 master's, 7 other advanced degrees awarded. Terminal master's awarded for partial completion of doctoral program. *Degree requirements:* For master's, thesis optional; for doctorate, comprehensive exam, thesis/dissertation. *Entrance requirements:* For master's and doctorate, GRE. Additional exam requirements/recommendations for international students: Required—TOEFL (minimum score 603 paper-based; 100 iBT) or IELTS (minimum score 7). *Application deadline:* For fall admission, 2/15 for domestic and international students; for spring admission, 10/1 for domestic and international students. Application fee: $50. Electronic applications accepted. *Expenses:* Tuition, state resident: full-time $6516; part-time $362 per credit hour. Tuition, nonresident: full-time $22,014; part-time $1223 per credit hour. *Required fees:* $2128 per semester. Tuition and fees vary according to course load and program. *Financial support:* In 2014–15, fellowships (averaging $8,194 per year), research

assistantships (averaging $8,068 per year), teaching assistantships (averaging $3,600 per year) were awarded; institutionally sponsored loans, scholarships/grants, health care benefits, and unspecified assistantships also available. Financial award application deadline: 2/1. *Faculty research:* Public budgeting and finance, public management, nonprofit management, performance measurement and management, urban development. *Unit head:* Dr. Gregory Burr Lewis, Chair and Professor, 404-413-0114, Fax: 404-413-0104, E-mail: glewis@gsu.edu. *Application contact:* Charisma Parker, Admissions Coordinator, 404-413-0030, Fax: 404-413-0023, E-mail: cparker28@gsu.edu.
Website: http://aysps.gsu.edu/pmap/

Harvard University, Graduate School of Arts and Sciences, Committee on Architecture, Landscape Architecture, and Urban Planning, Cambridge, MA 02138. Offers architecture (PhD); landscape architecture (PhD); urban planning (PhD). *Degree requirements:* For doctorate, one foreign language, thesis/dissertation, oral exam. *Entrance requirements:* For doctorate, GRE General Test. Additional exam requirements/recommendations for international students: Required—TOEFL.

Harvard University, Graduate School of Design, Department of Urban Planning and Design, Cambridge, MA 02138. Offers urban planning (MUP); urban planning and design (MAUD, MLAUD). *Accreditation:* ACSP (one or more programs are accredited). *Entrance requirements:* For master's, GRE General Test. Additional exam requirements/recommendations for international students: Required—TOEFL (minimum score 600 paper-based; 104 iBT). Electronic applications accepted.

Hunter College of the City University of New York, Graduate School, School of Arts and Sciences, Department of Urban Affairs and Planning, Program in Urban Planning, New York, NY 10065-5085. Offers MUP, JD/MUP. JD/MUP offered jointly with Brooklyn Law School. *Accreditation:* ACSP. Part-time programs available. *Faculty:* 5 full-time (3 women), 4 part-time/adjunct (2 women). *Students:* 45 full-time (21 women), 61 part-time (31 women); includes 28 minority (11 Black or African American, non-Hispanic/Latino; 8 Asian, non-Hispanic/Latino; 9 Hispanic/Latino), 3 international. Average age 30. 128 applicants, 73% accepted, 32 enrolled. In 2014, 46 master's awarded. *Degree requirements:* For master's, planning studio and internship. *Entrance requirements:* For master's, minimum 12 credits of course work in social sciences, 2 letters of recommendation. Additional exam requirements/recommendations for international students: Required—TOEFL. *Application deadline:* For fall admission, 4/1 for domestic students, 2/1 for international students; for spring admission, 11/1 for domestic students, 9/1 for international students. *Financial support:* In 2014–15, 4 fellowships with full tuition reimbursements (averaging $9,000 per year), 10 teaching assistantships (averaging $1,200 per year) were awarded; research assistantships, career-related internships or fieldwork, Federal Work-Study, and tuition waivers (partial) also available. Support available to part-time students. *Faculty research:* Community and economic development, transportation planning and policy, geographic information systems, housing, land use. *Unit head:* Dr. John Chin, Program Director, 212-772-5603, E-mail: john.chin@hunter.cuny.edu. *Application contact:* Milena Solo, Director for Graduate Admissions, 212-772-4480, E-mail: admissions@hunter.cuny.edu.
Website: http://maxweber.hunter.cuny.edu/urban/

Indiana University of Pennsylvania, School of Graduate Studies and Research, College of Humanities and Social Sciences, Department of Geography and Regional Planning, Regional Planning Track, Indiana, PA 15705-1087. Offers MS. Part-time programs available. *Faculty:* 10 full-time (1 woman), 1 (woman) part-time/adjunct. *Students:* 6 full-time (1 woman); includes 1 minority (Hispanic/Latino). Average age 31. 3 applicants, 67% accepted, 2 enrolled. In 2014, 1 master's awarded. *Degree requirements:* For master's, thesis optional. *Entrance requirements:* Additional exam requirements/recommendations for international students: Required—TOEFL (minimum score 550 paper-based). *Application deadline:* Applications are processed on a rolling basis. Application fee: $50. Electronic applications accepted. *Financial support:* In 2014–15, 2 research assistantships with full and partial tuition reimbursements (averaging $2,978 per year) were awarded; fellowships with full tuition reimbursements, career-related internships or fieldwork, Federal Work-Study, scholarships/grants, and unspecified assistantships also available. Financial award application deadline: 4/15; financial award applicants required to submit FAFSA. *Unit head:* Dr. Richard Hoch, Graduate Coordinator, 724-357-5990, E-mail: richard.hoch@iup.edu.
Website: http://www.iup.edu/upper.aspx?id-90827

Iowa State University of Science and Technology, Department of Community and Regional Planning, Ames, IA 50011. Offers community and regional planning (MCRP); transportation (MS); M Arch/MCRP; MBA/MCRP; MCRP/MLA; MCRP/MPA. *Accreditation:* ACSP (one or more programs are accredited). *Degree requirements:* For master's, thesis or alternative. *Entrance requirements:* For master's, GRE General Test. Additional exam requirements/recommendations for international students: Required—TOEFL (minimum score 550 paper-based; 79 iBT), IELTS (minimum score 6.5). Electronic applications accepted. *Faculty research:* Economic development, housing, land use, geographic information systems planning in developing nations, regional and community revitalization, transportation planning in developing countries.

Jackson State University, Graduate School, College of Public Service, Department of Urban and Regional Planning, Jackson, MS 39217. Offers MS, PhD. *Accreditation:* ACSP. *Degree requirements:* For master's, comprehensive exam. *Entrance requirements:* For master's, GRE General Test. Additional exam requirements/recommendations for international students: Required—TOEFL (minimum score 520 paper-based; 67 iBT).

Kansas State University, Graduate School, College of Architecture, Planning and Design, Department of Interior Architecture and Product Design, Manhattan, KS 66506. Offers MIAPD. *Accreditation:* ACSP. Part-time and evening/weekend programs available. Postbaccalaureate distance learning degree programs offered. *Faculty:* 13 full-time (5 women). *Students:* 35 full-time (24 women), 1 (woman) part-time; includes 5 minority (2 Black or African American, non-Hispanic/Latino; 1 Asian, non-Hispanic/Latino; 2 Two or more races, non-Hispanic/Latino), 1 international. Average age 22. 13 applicants, 100% accepted, 13 enrolled. In 2014, 31 master's awarded. *Degree requirements:* For master's, thesis, oral exam, culminating project. *Entrance requirements:* For master's, minimum GPA of 3.0, portfolio. Additional exam requirements/recommendations for international students: Required—TOEFL (minimum score 600 paper-based; 95 iBT) or IELTS (minimum score 7). *Application deadline:* For fall admission, 2/1 priority date for domestic students, 1/1 for international students; for spring admission, 8/1 for domestic and international students. Applications are processed on a rolling basis. Application fee: $90 ($100 for international students). Electronic applications accepted. *Financial support:* In 2014–15, 8 teaching assistantships with full tuition reimbursements (averaging $7,500 per year) were awarded; career-related internships or fieldwork, Federal Work-Study, institutionally sponsored loans, and scholarships/grants also available. Support available to part-time students. Financial award application deadline: 3/1; financial award applicants required to submit FAFSA. *Faculty research:* Planning interior spaces for exhibition; residential and commercial spaces; design of objects such as furniture, lighting, equipment, finishing treatments and accessories. *Total annual research expenditures:* $1,523. *Unit head:* Katherine Ankerson, Head, 785-532-5992, Fax: 785-532-6722, E-mail: ankerson@ksu.edu. *Application contact:* Neal Hubbell, Director, 785-532-5992, Fax: 785-532-6722, E-mail: nhubbel@ksu.edu.
Website: http://apdesign.k-state.edu/iapd/

Kansas State University, Graduate School, College of Architecture, Planning and Design, Department of Landscape Architecture and Regional and Community Planning, Manhattan, KS 66506. Offers community development (MS); landscape architecture (MLA); regional and community planning (MRCP). *Accreditation:* ASLA. Part-time programs available. *Faculty:* 17 full-time (6 women), 1 (woman) part-time/adjunct. *Students:* 50 full-time (25 women), 25 part-time (13 women); includes 11 minority (4 Black or African American, non-Hispanic/Latino; 7 Hispanic/Latino), 3 international. Average age 24. 53 applicants, 43% accepted, 21 enrolled. In 2014, 38 master's awarded. *Degree requirements:* For master's, thesis, residency, oral exam. *Entrance requirements:* For master's, portfolio. Additional exam requirements/recommendations for international students: Required—TOEFL (minimum score 600 paper-based). *Application deadline:* For fall admission, 2/1 priority date for domestic and international students; for spring admission, 8/1 priority date for domestic and international students. Applications are processed on a rolling basis. Application fee: $80. Electronic applications accepted. *Financial support:* In 2014–15, 2 research assistantships (averaging $9,500 per year), 10 teaching assistantships with full tuition reimbursements (averaging $7,366 per year) were awarded; fellowships, career-related internships or fieldwork, Federal Work-Study, institutionally sponsored loans, and scholarships/grants also available. Support available to part-time students. Financial award application deadline: 3/15; financial award applicants required to submit FAFSA. *Faculty research:* Community planning and design, design and planning theory, geospatial technology infrastructure, watershed restoration, landscape ecology. *Total annual research expenditures:* $110,033. *Unit head:* Prof. Stephanie Rolley, Head, 785-532-5961, Fax: 785-532-6722, E-mail: srolley@ksu.edu. *Application contact:* Rachel Robillard, Application Contact, 785-532-5961, Fax: 785-532-6722, E-mail: rjack@ksu.edu.
Website: http://apdesign.k-state.edu/larcp/

Lesley University, Graduate School of Arts and Social Sciences, Cambridge, MA 02138-2790. Offers clinical mental health counseling (MA), including holistic counseling, school and community counseling, trauma studies; counseling psychology (MA, CAGS), including professional counseling (MA), school counseling (MA); creative writing (MFA); expressive therapies (MA, PhD, CAGS), including art (MA), clinical mental health counseling (MA), dance (MA), expressive therapies (MA), music (MA); independent studies (CAGS); independent study (MA); intercultural relations (MA, CAGS); interdisciplinary studies (MA), including individualized studies, integrative holistic health, mindfulness studies, peace and conflict transformation, trauma sensitive assessment, intervention, and consultation, women's studies; urban environmental leadership (MA). Part-time programs available. Postbaccalaureate distance learning degree programs offered (no on-campus study). *Faculty:* 35 full-time (25 women), 115 part-time/adjunct (90 women). *Students:* 420 full-time (379 women), 514 part-time (414 women); includes 142 minority (50 Black or African American, non-Hispanic/Latino; 5 American Indian or Alaska Native, non-Hispanic/Latino; 16 Asian, non-Hispanic/Latino; 48 Hispanic/Latino; 23 Two or more races, non-Hispanic/Latino), 46 international. Average age 33. In 2014, 475 master's, 11 doctorates, 4 other advanced degrees awarded. *Degree requirements:* For master's, internship, practicum, thesis (for expressive therapies); for doctorate, thesis/dissertation, arts apprenticeship, field placement; for CAGS, thesis, internship (for counseling psychology, expressive therapies). *Entrance requirements:* For master's, MAT (counseling psychology), interview, writing samples, art portfolio; for doctorate, GRE or MAT, interview, master's degree; for CAGS, interview, master's degree. Additional exam requirements/recommendations for international students: Required—TOEFL (minimum score 550 paper-based; 80 iBT). *Application deadline:* Applications are processed on a rolling basis. Application fee: $50. Electronic applications accepted. *Financial support:* Fellowships, career-related internships or fieldwork, Federal Work-Study, scholarships/grants, tuition waivers, and unspecified assistantships available. Financial award applicants required to submit FAFSA. *Faculty research:* Psychotherapy and culture; psychotherapy and psychological trauma; women's issues in art, teaching and psychotherapy; community-based art, psycho-spiritual inquiry. *Unit head:* Dr. Catherine Koverola, Dean, 617-349-8317, Fax: 617-349-8366, E-mail: koverola@lesley.edu. *Application contact:* Martha Sheehan, Director, Graduate Admissions, 888-LESLEYU, Fax: 617-349-8313, E-mail: info@lesley.edu.
Website: http://www.lesley.edu/graduate-school-of-arts-and-social-sciences/

Loyola University Chicago, Institute of Pastoral Studies, Master of Arts in Social Justice and Community Development Program, Chicago, IL 60611. Offers MA, MSW/MA. *Degree requirements:* For master's, internship. *Entrance requirements:* Additional exam requirements/recommendations for international students: Required—TOEFL. *Expenses: Tuition:* Full-time $17,370; part-time $965 per credit. *Required fees:* $138 per semester. *Unit head:* Dr. Melissa Browning, Graduate Program Director, 312-915-7453, Fax: 312-915-7410, E-mail: mbrowning@luc.edu. *Application contact:* Rachel D. Gibbons, Assistant Director, 312-915-7450, Fax: 312-915-7410, E-mail: rgibbon@luc.edu.

Massachusetts Institute of Technology, School of Architecture and Planning, Department of Urban Studies and Planning, Cambridge, MA 02139-4307. Offers city planning (MCP); urban and regional planning (PhD); urban and regional studies (PhD); urban studies and planning (SM). *Accreditation:* ACSP (one or more programs are accredited). *Faculty:* 24 full-time (6 women). *Students:* 183 full-time (108 women), 1 part-time (0 women); includes 52 minority (8 Black or African American, non-Hispanic/Latino; 20 Asian, non-Hispanic/Latino; 16 Hispanic/Latino; 8 Two or more races, non-Hispanic/Latino), 47 international. Average age 29. 487 applicants, 22% accepted, 71 enrolled. In 2014, 70 master's, 7 doctorates awarded. Terminal master's awarded for partial completion of doctoral program. *Degree requirements:* For master's, thesis, MCP program requires a practicum course; for doctorate, comprehensive exam, thesis/dissertation. *Entrance requirements:* For master's and doctorate, GRE General Test. Additional exam requirements/recommendations for international students: Required—TOEFL (minimum score 600 paper-based; 100 iBT), IELTS (minimum score 7). *Application deadline:* For fall admission, 1/3 for domestic and international students. Application fee: $75. Electronic applications accepted. *Expenses: Tuition:* Full-time $44,720; part-time $699 per unit. *Required fees:* $296. *Financial support:* In 2014–15, 163 students received support, including 77 fellowships (averaging $23,500 per year), 68 research assistantships (averaging $22,600 per year), 18 teaching assistantships (averaging $34,600 per year); Federal Work-Study, institutionally sponsored loans, scholarships/grants, health care benefits, and unspecified assistantships also available. Financial award application deadline: 4/15; financial award applicants required to submit FAFSA. *Faculty research:* City and regional sustainable design and development; housing, community, and economic development; environmental and landscape planning; international development, infrastructure systems and energy policy; geographic information and communication technologies. *Total annual research expenditures:* $4.4 million. *Unit head:* Prof. Eran Ben-Joseph, Head, 617-253-1907, Fax: 617-253-2654, E-mail: duspinfo@mit.edu. *Application contact:* Graduate Admissions, 617-253-4543, Fax: 617-253-2654, E-mail: duspapply@mit.edu.
Website: http://dusp.mit.edu/

McGill University, Faculty of Graduate and Postdoctoral Studies, Faculty of Engineering, School of Urban Planning, Montréal, QC H3A 2T5, Canada. Offers

environmental planning (MUP); housing (MUP); transportation (MUP); urban design (MUP); urban planning, policy and design (PhD).

Michigan State University, The Graduate School, College of Agriculture and Natural Resources and College of Social Science, School of Planning, Design and Construction, East Lansing, MI 48824. Offers construction management (MS, PhD); environmental design (MA); interior design and facilities management (MA); international planning studies (MIPS); urban and regional planning (MURP). *Degree requirements:* For master's, thesis or alternative. *Entrance requirements:* Additional exam requirements/recommendations for international students: Required—TOEFL. Electronic applications accepted.

Minnesota State University Mankato, College of Graduate Studies, College of Social and Behavioral Sciences, Department of Urban and Regional Studies, Mankato, MN 56001. Offers local government management (Certificate); urban and regional studies (MA); urban planning (MA, Certificate). *Students:* 18 full-time (5 women), 15 part-time (6 women). *Degree requirements:* For master's, one foreign language, comprehensive exam, thesis or alternative. *Entrance requirements:* For master's, minimum GPA of 3.0 during previous 2 years, 2 letters of recommendation. Additional exam requirements/recommendations for international students: Required—TOEFL. *Application deadline:* For fall admission, 7/1 priority date for domestic students; for spring admission, 11/1 for domestic students. Applications are processed on a rolling basis. Application fee: $40. Electronic applications accepted. *Financial support:* Fellowships with partial tuition reimbursements, research assistantships with full tuition reimbursements, teaching assistantships with full tuition reimbursements, career-related internships or fieldwork, Federal Work-Study, institutionally sponsored loans, and unspecified assistantships available. Support available to part-time students. Financial award application deadline: 3/15; financial award applicants required to submit FAFSA. *Unit head:* Dr. Mirium Porter, Graduate Coordinator, 507-389-1714. *Application contact:* 507-389-2321, E-mail: grad@mnsu.edu.
Website: http://sbs.mnsu.edu/ursi/graduate/

Missouri State University, Graduate College, College of Natural and Applied Sciences, Department of Geography, Geology, and Planning, Springfield, MO 65897. Offers geography, geology and planning (MNAS); secondary education (MS Ed), including earth science, physical geography. *Accreditation:* ACSP. Part-time and evening/weekend programs available. *Faculty:* 18 full-time (4 women), 1 part-time/adjunct (0 women). *Students:* 12 full-time (5 women), 12 part-time (8 women); includes 1 minority (Asian, non-Hispanic/Latino), 3 international. Average age 30. 16 applicants, 100% accepted, 9 enrolled. In 2014, 11 master's awarded. *Degree requirements:* For master's, comprehensive exam, thesis (for some programs). *Entrance requirements:* For master's, GRE General Test (MS, MNAS), minimum undergraduate GPA of 3.0 (MS, MNAS), 9-12 teacher certification (MS Ed). Additional exam requirements/recommendations for international students: Required—TOEFL (minimum score 550 paper-based; 79 iBT). *Application deadline:* For fall admission, 7/20 priority date for domestic students, 5/1 for international students; for spring admission, 12/20 priority date for domestic students, 9/1 for international students. Applications are processed on a rolling basis. Application fee: $35 ($50 for international students). Electronic applications accepted. *Expenses:* Tuition, state resident: full-time $2250; part-time $250 per credit hour. Tuition, nonresident: full-time $4509; part-time $501 per credit hour. Tuition and fees vary according to course level, course load and program. *Financial support:* In 2014–15, 3 research assistantships with full tuition reimbursements (averaging $11,574 per year), 12 teaching assistantships with full tuition reimbursements (averaging $9,365 per year) were awarded; career-related internships or fieldwork, Federal Work-Study, institutionally sponsored loans, scholarships/grants, and unspecified assistantships also available. Financial award application deadline: 3/31; financial award applicants required to submit FAFSA. *Faculty research:* Stratigraphy and ancient meteorite impacts, environmental geochemistry of karst, hyperspectral image processing, water quality, small town planning. *Unit head:* Dr. Thomas Plymate, Head, 417-836-5800, Fax: 417-836-6934, E-mail: tomplymate@missouristate.edu. *Application contact:* Misty Stewart, Coordinator of Graduate Recruitment, 417-836-6079, Fax: 417-836-6200, E-mail: mistystewart@missouristate.edu.
Website: http://geosciences.missouristate.edu/

Morgan State University, School of Graduate Studies, Institute of Architecture and Planning, Program in City and Regional Planning, Baltimore, MD 21251. Offers MCRP. *Accreditation:* ACSP. *Degree requirements:* For master's, thesis. *Entrance requirements:* Additional exam requirements/recommendations for international students: Required—TOEFL (minimum score 550 paper-based). *Faculty research:* Nonprofit organizations, community development, urban design, transportation, international planning.

New York University, Polytechnic School of Engineering, Department of Civil and Urban Engineering, Major in Urban Systems Engineering and Management, New York, NY 10012-1019. Offers MS. *Students:* 2 full-time (1 woman), 4 part-time (1 woman); includes 3 minority (1 Black or African American, non-Hispanic/Latino; 1 Asian, non-Hispanic/Latino; 1 Hispanic/Latino). Average age 29. 11 applicants, 45% accepted, 3 enrolled. In 2014, 3 master's awarded. *Application deadline:* For fall admission, 2/15 priority date for domestic and international students; for spring admission, 11/1 priority date for domestic and international students. Application fee: $75. *Unit head:* Dr. Illan Juran, Head, 718-260-3717, E-mail: ijuran@nyu.edu. *Application contact:* Raymond Lutzky, Director of Graduate Enrollment Management, 718-637-5984, Fax: 718-260-3624, E-mail: rlutzky@poly.edu.

New York University, Robert F. Wagner Graduate School of Public Service, Program in Urban Planning, New York, NY 10012-1019. Offers MUP, JD/MUP. *Accreditation:* ACSP (one or more programs are accredited). Part-time programs available. *Faculty:* 5 full-time (3 women), 20 part-time/adjunct (9 women). *Students:* 61 full-time (41 women), 24 part-time (12 women); includes 24 minority (7 Black or African American, non-Hispanic/Latino; 8 Asian, non-Hispanic/Latino; 4 Hispanic/Latino; 5 Two or more races, non-Hispanic/Latino), 16 international. Average age 27. 173 applicants, 71% accepted, 34 enrolled. In 2014, 53 master's awarded. *Degree requirements:* For master's, thesis or alternative, end event capstone program. *Entrance requirements:* Additional exam requirements/recommendations for international students: Required—TOEFL (minimum score 100 iBT), IELTS (minimum score 7.5), TWE. *Application deadline:* For fall admission, 1/5 for domestic and international students; for spring admission, 10/1 for domestic and international students. Application fee: $85. Electronic applications accepted. *Financial support:* In 2014–15, 26 students received support, including 10 fellowships with full and partial tuition reimbursements available (averaging $22,727 per year), 2 research assistantships with full tuition reimbursements available (averaging $56,524 per year); career-related internships or fieldwork, Federal Work-Study, scholarships/grants, health care benefits, and unspecified assistantships also available. Support available to part-time students. Financial award application deadline: 1/6; financial award applicants required to submit FAFSA. *Unit head:* Prof. Ingrid Gould Ellen, Director, 212-998-7533, Fax: 212-995-4164, E-mail: ingrid.ellen@nyu.edu. *Application contact:* Sandra Oliveira, Admissions Officer, 212-998-7414, Fax: 212-995-4611, E-mail: wagner.admissions@nyu.edu.
Website: http://wagner.nyu.edu/urbanplanning

North Dakota State University, College of Graduate and Interdisciplinary Studies, College of Arts, Humanities and Social Sciences, Department of Sociology, Anthropology, and Emergency Management, Program in Community Development, Fargo, ND 58108. Offers MA, MS. Electronic applications accepted.

Northern Arizona University, Graduate College, College of Social and Behavioral Sciences, Department of Geography, Planning, and Recreation, Flagstaff, AZ 86011. Offers applied geospatial sciences (MS); community planning (Certificate); geographic information systems (Certificate). Postbaccalaureate distance learning degree programs offered. *Degree requirements:* For master's, thesis optional. *Entrance requirements:* For master's, GRE General Test. Additional exam requirements/recommendations for international students: Required—TOEFL (minimum score 550 paper-based; 80 iBT), IELTS (minimum score 7). Electronic applications accepted.

Northwest Nazarene University, Graduate Studies, Program in Social Work, Nampa, ID 83686-5897. Offers addiction studies (MSW); clinical mental health practice (MSW); management, community planning and social administration (MSW); medical social work (MSW). *Accreditation:* CSWE. Part-time programs available. Postbaccalaureate distance learning degree programs offered (no on-campus study). *Faculty:* 10 full-time (6 women), 5 part-time/adjunct (4 women). *Students:* 129 full-time (97 women), 33 part-time (29 women); includes 23 minority (3 Black or African American, non-Hispanic/Latino; 1 American Indian or Alaska Native, non-Hispanic/Latino; 12 Hispanic/Latino; 7 Two or more races, non-Hispanic/Latino). Average age 27. 152 applicants, 54% accepted, 73 enrolled. In 2014, 54 master's awarded. *Degree requirements:* For master's, comprehensive exam. *Application deadline:* Applications are processed on a rolling basis. Application fee: $50. Electronic applications accepted. *Unit head:* Dr. Lawanna Lancaster, Director, 208-467-8679, E-mail: msw@nnu.edu. *Application contact:* Jodie Engel, Program Assistant, 208-467-8679, Fax: 208-467-8879, E-mail: jrodriguez-engel@nnu.edu.

Northwest University, College of Social and Behavioral Sciences, Kirkland, WA 98033. Offers counseling psychology (MA, Psy D); international community development (MA). Evening/weekend programs available. *Faculty:* 5 full-time (2 women), 17 part-time/adjunct (5 women). *Students:* 223 full-time (185 women), 55 part-time (41 women); includes 74 minority (13 Black or African American, non-Hispanic/Latino; 3 American Indian or Alaska Native, non-Hispanic/Latino; 30 Asian, non-Hispanic/Latino; 15 Hispanic/Latino; 1 Native Hawaiian or other Pacific Islander, non-Hispanic/Latino; 12 Two or more races, non-Hispanic/Latino), 6 international. Average age 37. 122 applicants, 80% accepted, 62 enrolled. In 2014, 56 master's, 3 doctorates awarded. *Entrance requirements:* For master's, 3 character references. Additional exam requirements/recommendations for international students: Required—TOEFL (minimum score 580 paper-based). *Application deadline:* For fall admission, 12/1 priority date for domestic and international students; for spring admission, 4/1 priority date for domestic and international students. Applications are processed on a rolling basis. Application fee: $75. *Expenses:* Expenses: Contact institution. *Financial support:* In 2014–15, 13 students received support. Career-related internships or fieldwork, health care benefits, and international student scholarships available. Financial award application deadline: 6/30. *Unit head:* Dr. Matt Nelson, Dean, 425-889-5328, E-mail: matt.nelson@northwestu.edu. *Application contact:* Daniela Zuniga, Enrollment Counselor, College of Social and Behavioral Sciences, 425-889-5249, E-mail: daniela.zuniga@northwestu.edu.
Website: http://www.northwestu.edu/social_behavioral

The Ohio State University, Graduate School, College of Engineering, Austin E. Knowlton School of Architecture, Columbus, OH 43210. Offers architecture (M Arch); city and regional planning (MCRP, PhD); landscape architecture (M Land Arch). *Accreditation:* ACSP; ASLA. *Faculty:* 33. *Students:* 187 full-time (83 women), 6 part-time (1 woman); includes 22 minority (5 Black or African American, non-Hispanic/Latino; 1 American Indian or Alaska Native, non-Hispanic/Latino; 5 Asian, non-Hispanic/Latino; 10 Hispanic/Latino; 1 Two or more races, non-Hispanic/Latino), 41 international. Average age 26. In 2014, 51 master's, 2 doctorates awarded. *Degree requirements:* For doctorate, thesis/dissertation. *Entrance requirements:* For master's, GRE or GMAT (city and regional planning), portfolio (for architecture and landscape architecture); for doctorate, GRE or GMAT (city and regional planning), example of research or written work. Additional exam requirements/recommendations for international students: Required—TOEFL (minimum score 600 paper-based; 100 iBT), Michigan English Language Assessment Battery (minimum score 86); Recommended—IELTS (minimum score 8). *Application deadline:* For fall admission, 1/1 priority date for domestic students, 12/1 priority date for international students; for winter admission, 12/1 for domestic students, 11/1 for international students; for spring admission, 12/1 for domestic students, 11/1 for international students; for summer admission, 4/1 for domestic students, 5/30 for international students. Applications are processed on a rolling basis. Application fee: $60 ($70 for international students). Electronic applications accepted. *Financial support:* Fellowships with tuition reimbursements, research assistantships with tuition reimbursements, Federal Work-Study, institutionally sponsored loans, and unspecified assistantships available. Support available to part-time students. *Unit head:* Michael B. Cadwell, Director and Walter H. Kidd Professor, 614-292-3174, E-mail: cadwell.1@osu.edu. *Application contact:* Graduate and Professional Admissions, 614-292-9444, Fax: 614-292-3895, E-mail: gpadmissions@osu.edu.
Website: http://knowlton.osu.edu/

Philadelphia University, College of Architecture and the Built Environment, Program in Geodesign, Philadelphia, PA 19144. Offers MS. Part-time programs available.

Portland State University, Graduate Studies, College of Urban and Public Affairs, Nohad A. Toulan School of Urban Studies and Planning, Program in Urban and Regional Planning, Portland, OR 97207-0751. Offers MURP. *Accreditation:* ACSP. Part-time programs available. *Students:* 77 full-time (42 women), 6 part-time (5 women); includes 12 minority (4 Asian, non-Hispanic/Latino; 6 Hispanic/Latino; 2 Two or more races, non-Hispanic/Latino), 4 international. Average age 29. In 2014, 37 master's awarded. *Degree requirements:* For master's, workshop. *Entrance requirements:* For master's, GRE (recommended), minimum GPA of 3.0, transcripts, statement of purpose, 3 letters of recommendation, resume. Additional exam requirements/recommendations for international students: Required—TOEFL (minimum score 550 paper-based; 80 iBT). *Application deadline:* For fall admission, 1/15 for domestic and international students. Application fee: $50. *Expenses:* Tuition, state resident: part-time $222 per credit. Tuition, nonresident: part-time $527 per credit. *Required fees:* $22 per contact hour. $100 per quarter. Tuition and fees vary according to program. *Financial support:* Research assistantships, teaching assistantships, career-related internships or fieldwork, Federal Work-Study, and unspecified assistantships available. Support available to part-time students. Financial award application deadline: 3/1; financial award applicants required to submit FAFSA. *Faculty research:* Policy planning and administration, community development, land-use and environment, transportation, urban and regional analysis. *Unit head:* Dr. Connie Ozawa, Director, 503-725-5126, E-mail: ozawac@pdx.edu. *Application contact:* Tracy Braden, Office Coordinator, 503-725-5477, Fax: 503-725-8770, E-mail: tbraden@pdx.edu.
Website: http://www.pdx.edu/usp/

Pratt Institute, School of Architecture, Program in City and Regional Planning, Brooklyn, NY 11205-3899. Offers MSCRP. *Accreditation:* ACSP. Part-time programs

available. *Faculty:* 5 full-time (2 women), 31 part-time/adjunct (9 women). *Students:* 79 full-time (40 women), 4 part-time (2 women); includes 24 minority (13 Black or African American, non-Hispanic/Latino; 6 Asian, non-Hispanic/Latino; 5 Hispanic/Latino), 8 international. Average age 28. 109 applicants, 81% accepted, 26 enrolled. In 2014, 35 master's awarded. *Degree requirements:* For master's, thesis. *Entrance requirements:* For master's, writing sample, bachelor's degree, transcripts, letters of recommendation, portfolio. Additional exam requirements/recommendations for international students: Required—TOEFL (minimum score 550 paper-based; 79 iBT). *Application deadline:* For fall admission, 1/5 for domestic and international students; for spring admission, 10/1 for domestic and international students. Applications are processed on a rolling basis. Application fee: $50 ($90 for international students). Electronic applications accepted. *Financial support:* Career-related internships or fieldwork, Federal Work-Study, institutionally sponsored loans, scholarships/grants, health care benefits, and unspecified assistantships available. Support available to part-time students. Financial award application deadline: 2/1; financial award applicants required to submit FAFSA. *Faculty research:* Advocacy planning, community development, comprehensive physical planning, transportation planning, real estate development. *Unit head:* John Shapiro, Chairperson, 718-399-4391, E-mail: jshapir6@pratt.edu. *Application contact:* Young Hah, Director of Graduate Admissions, 718-636-3683, Fax: 718-399-4242, E-mail: yhah@pratt.edu.
Website: https://www.pratt.edu/academics/architecture/city-and-regional-planning/

See Display on page 112 and Close-Up on page 139.

Queen's University at Kingston, School of Graduate Studies, School of Urban and Regional Planning, Kingston, ON K7L 3N6, Canada. Offers M Pl. Part-time programs available. *Degree requirements:* For master's, thesis optional. *Entrance requirements:* Additional exam requirements/recommendations for international students: Required—TOEFL (minimum score 580 paper-based). *Faculty research:* Housing, real estate development, human services, environmental services, land use planning.

Rutgers, The State University of New Jersey, New Brunswick, Edward J. Bloustein School of Planning and Public Policy, Doctoral Program in Planning and Public Policy, New Brunswick, NJ 08901. Offers PhD. *Accreditation:* NASPAA. Part-time programs available. *Degree requirements:* For doctorate, comprehensive exam, thesis/dissertation. *Entrance requirements:* For doctorate, GRE, master's degree. Additional exam requirements/recommendations for international students: Required—TOEFL (minimum score 575 paper-based; 88 iBT). Electronic applications accepted. *Faculty research:* Housing and community development, land use and transportation, politics and policy analysis, urban and regional economics, international development.

Rutgers, The State University of New Jersey, New Brunswick, Edward J. Bloustein School of Planning and Public Policy, Program in Urban Planning and Policy Development, New Brunswick, NJ 08901. Offers MCRP, MCRS, JD/MCRP, MBA/MCRP. *Accreditation:* ACSP (one or more programs are accredited). Part-time and evening/weekend programs available. *Entrance requirements:* For master's, GRE General Test. Additional exam requirements/recommendations for international students: Required—TOEFL (minimum score 575 paper-based; 88 iBT). Electronic applications accepted. *Faculty research:* Land use, transportation, housing, environmental planning, urban redevelopment, international development.

St. Catharine College, School of Graduate Studies, St. Catharine, KY 40061-9499. Offers leadership (MA), including community and regional studies, health promotion. *Degree requirements:* For master's, thesis or alternative. *Entrance requirements:* For master's, GRE, official transcripts. Additional exam requirements/recommendations for international students: Required—TOEFL, IELTS, or Michigan English Language Assessment Battery. Electronic applications accepted.

San Diego State University, Graduate and Research Affairs, College of Professional Studies and Fine Arts, School of Public Affairs, Program in City Planning, San Diego, CA 92182. Offers MCP. Part-time programs available. *Entrance requirements:* For master's, GRE General Test. Additional exam requirements/recommendations for international students: Required—TOEFL. Electronic applications accepted. *Faculty research:* Community development, housing, sustainable development, visioning.

San Jose State University, Graduate Studies and Research, College of Social Sciences, Department of Urban and Regional Planning, San Jose, CA 95192-0001. Offers MUP, Certificate. *Accreditation:* ACSP. Part-time programs available. *Degree requirements:* For master's, comprehensive exam, thesis or alternative. *Entrance requirements:* For master's, GRE, minimum GPA of 3.0. Electronic applications accepted. *Faculty research:* Retirement communities, planning and problems, women in suburbia, influence on urban development, Taiwanese urban development issues.

Savannah State University, Master of Public Administration Program, Savannah, GA 31404. Offers city management (MPA); human resources (MPA). *Accreditation:* NASPAA. Part-time programs available. *Faculty:* 4 full-time (1 woman). *Students:* 3 full-time (1 woman), 6 part-time (4 women); all minorities (all Black or African American, non-Hispanic/Latino). Average age 32. 9 applicants, 33% accepted, 2 enrolled. In 2014, 10 master's awarded. *Degree requirements:* For master's, comprehensive exam, thesis, public service internship, capstone seminar. *Entrance requirements:* For master's, GRE General Test, GMAT, or MAT, minimum cumulative GPA of 2.5, 3 letters of recommendation, essay, official transcripts, resume, essay of 500-1000 words detailing reasons for pursuing degree. Additional exam requirements/recommendations for international students: Required—TOEFL. *Application deadline:* For fall admission, 6/15 for domestic students, 6/1 for international students; for spring admission, 10/1 for domestic and international students; for summer admission, 3/1 for domestic and international students. Applications are processed on a rolling basis. Application fee: $25. Electronic applications accepted. *Expenses:* Expenses: Contact institution. *Financial support:* Career-related internships or fieldwork, Federal Work-Study, institutionally sponsored loans, scholarships/grants, health care benefits, and unspecified assistantships available. Financial award application deadline: 7/15; financial award applicants required to submit FAFSA. *Faculty research:* Community development, human resources, leadership, conflict resolution, city management, non-profit management. *Unit head:* Dr. David Bell, MPA Program Coordinator, 912-358-3211, E-mail: mpa@savannahstate.edu. *Application contact:* Dr. Nat Hardy, Director of Graduate Studies, 912-358-4195, E-mail: grad@savannahstate.edu.
Website: http://www.savannahstate.edu/prospective-student/degrees-grad-pa.shtml

State University of New York College of Environmental Science and Forestry, Department of Landscape Architecture, Syracuse, NY 13210-2779. Offers community design and planning (MLA, MS); cultural landscape studies and conservation (MLA, MS); landscape and urban ecology (MLA, MS). *Accreditation:* ASLA (one or more programs are accredited). *Degree requirements:* For master's, comprehensive exam (for some programs), thesis (for some programs). *Entrance requirements:* For master's, GRE General Test, minimum GPA of 3.0. Additional exam requirements/recommendations for international students: Required—TOEFL (minimum score 550 paper-based; 80 iBT), IELTS (minimum score 6), or STEP Aiken (grade 1). *Faculty research:* Site analysis and design, city and regional planning, community environments.

State University of New York College of Environmental Science and Forestry, Program in Environmental Science, Syracuse, NY 13210-2779. Offers biophysical and ecological economics (MPS); coupled natural and human systems (MPS); ecosystem restoration (MPS); environmental and community land planning (MPS, MS); environmental and natural resources policy (PhD); environmental communication and participatory processes (PhD); environmental monitoring and modeling (MPS); environmental policy and democratic processes (MPS, MS); water and wetland resource studies (MPS, MS). Part-time programs available. *Degree requirements:* For master's, thesis (for some programs); for doctorate, comprehensive exam, thesis/dissertation. *Entrance requirements:* For master's and doctorate, GRE General Test, minimum GPA of 3.0. Additional exam requirements/recommendations for international students: Required—TOEFL (minimum score 550 paper-based; 80 iBT), IELTS (minimum score 6). *Faculty research:* Environmental education/communications, water resources, land resources, waste management.

Syracuse University, Maxwell School of Citizenship and Public Affairs, Program in Public Infrastructure Management and Leadership, Syracuse, NY 13244. Offers CAS. Part-time programs available. *Students:* 1 applicant, 100% accepted. *Entrance requirements:* Additional exam requirements/recommendations for international students: Required—TOEFL. *Application deadline:* For fall admission, 2/1 priority date for domestic students; for spring admission, 8/15 priority date for domestic and international students. Application fee: $75. *Expenses: Tuition:* Part-time $1341 per credit. *Unit head:* Center for Technology and Information Policy, 315-443-1800. *Application contact:* Denise Mallor-Breen, Grad Contact, 315-443-3159, E-mail: dmbreen@maxwell@syr.edu.
Website: http://www.maxwell.syr.edu/

Temple University, School of Environmental Design, Department of Community and Regional Planning, Ambler, PA 19002. Offers community and regional planning (MS); sustainable community planning (MS); transportation planning (MS). *Accreditation:* ACSP. Part-time and evening/weekend programs available. *Faculty:* 5 full-time (2 women), 6 part-time/adjunct (2 women). *Students:* 16 full-time (3 women), 17 part-time (7 women); includes 4 minority (1 Black or African American, non-Hispanic/Latino; 2 Hispanic/Latino; 1 Two or more races, non-Hispanic/Latino). 16 applicants, 94% accepted, 10 enrolled. In 2014, 9 master's awarded. *Entrance requirements:* For master's, GRE or GMAT, 2 letters of recommendation, minimum undergraduate GPA of 3.0, statement of goals. Additional exam requirements/recommendations for international students: Required—TOEFL (minimum score 550 paper-based; 79 iBT). *Application deadline:* For fall admission, 7/1 for domestic students, 12/15 for international students; for spring admission, 11/1 for domestic students, 8/1 for international students. Applications are processed on a rolling basis. Application fee: $60. *Expenses:* Tuition, state resident: full-time $14,490; part-time $805 per credit hour. Tuition, nonresident: full-time $19,850; part-time $1103 per credit hour. *Required fees:* $690. Full-time tuition and fees vary according to class time, course load, degree level, campus/location and program. *Financial support:* In 2014–15, 5 students received support. Fellowships with full tuition reimbursements available, research assistantships with full tuition reimbursements available, Federal Work-Study, scholarships/grants, health care benefits, and unspecified assistantships available. Financial award application deadline: 1/15; financial award applicants required to submit FAFSA. *Faculty research:* Regional environmental planning, collaboration, management community development through sustainable food systems, storm water management and floodplain mapping, land use policy innovations, community planning for aging. *Unit head:* Dr. Deborah Howe, Chair, 267-468-8300, Fax: 267-468-8315, E-mail: deborah.howe@temple.edu.
Website: http://www.temple.edu/ambler/crp/

Texas A&M University, College of Architecture, Department of Landscape Architecture and Urban Planning, College Station, TX 77843. Offers land and property development (MLPD); landscape architecture (MLA); urban and regional planning (MUP); urban and regional science (PhD). *Accreditation:* ACSP (one or more programs are accredited); ASLA (one or more programs are accredited). *Faculty:* 28. *Students:* 157 full-time (80 women), 20 part-time (10 women); includes 26 minority (9 Black or African American, non-Hispanic/Latino; 4 Asian, non-Hispanic/Latino; 13 Hispanic/Latino), 105 international. Average age 29. 247 applicants, 63% accepted, 70 enrolled. In 2014, 54 master's, 7 doctorates awarded. Terminal master's awarded for partial completion of doctoral program. *Degree requirements:* For master's, thesis optional, professional internship; for doctorate, comprehensive exam, thesis/dissertation, seminar. *Entrance requirements:* For master's, GMAT or GRE General Test, portfolio (MLA), minimum GPA of 3.0; for doctorate, GMAT or GRE General Test. Additional exam requirements/recommendations for international students: Required—TOEFL. *Application deadline:* For fall admission, 12/1 priority date for domestic and international students; for spring admission, 8/1 for domestic students. Applications are processed on a rolling basis. Application fee: $50 ($90 for international students). Electronic applications accepted. *Expenses:* Tuition, state resident: full-time $4078; part-time $226.55 per credit hour. Tuition, nonresident: full-time $10,594; part-time $577.55 per credit hour. *Required fees:* $2813; $237.70 per credit hour. $278.50 per semester. Tuition and fees vary according to degree level and student level. *Financial support:* In 2014–15, 135 students received support, including 3 fellowships with full and partial tuition reimbursements available (averaging $20,750 per year), 41 research assistantships with full and partial tuition reimbursements available (averaging $5,280 per year), 11 teaching assistantships with full and partial tuition reimbursements available (averaging $6,281 per year); career-related internships or fieldwork, institutionally sponsored loans, scholarships/grants, traineeships, health care benefits, tuition waivers (full and partial), and unspecified assistantships also available. Support available to part-time students. Financial award application deadline: 4/1; financial award applicants required to submit FAFSA. *Faculty research:* Erosion control/water quality, geographic information systems/spatial information technology, transport hazards, international sustainable development. *Unit head:* Dr. Forster Ndubisi, Head, 979-845-1019, Fax: 979-862-1784. *Application contact:* Thena Morris, Administrative Assistant, 979-845-6582, Fax: 979-845-4491, E-mail: t-morris@tamu.edu.
Website: http://laup.arch.tamu.edu/

Texas Southern University, School of Public Affairs, Program in Urban Planning and Environmental Policy, Houston, TX 77004-4584. Offers MS, PhD. *Accreditation:* ACSP. Part-time and evening/weekend programs available. *Degree requirements:* For master's, comprehensive exam, thesis optional. *Entrance requirements:* For master's, GRE General Test, minimum GPA of 2.5. Additional exam requirements/recommendations for international students: Required—TOEFL. Electronic applications accepted.

Texas State University, The Graduate College, College of Liberal Arts, Department of Political Science, Program in Public Administration, San Marcos, TX 78666. Offers international relations (MPA); public finance administration (MPA); urban and environmental planning (MPA). *Accreditation:* NASPAA. Part-time and evening/weekend programs available. *Faculty:* 6 full-time (3 women), 1 (woman) part-time/adjunct. *Students:* 29 full-time (16 women), 67 part-time (30 women); includes 45 minority (7 Black or African American, non-Hispanic/Latino; 3 Asian, non-Hispanic/Latino; 31 Hispanic/Latino; 4 Two or more races, non-Hispanic/Latino), 2 international. Average age 33. 42 applicants, 83% accepted, 16 enrolled. In 2014, 39 master's awarded. *Degree requirements:* For master's, comprehensive exam, applied research project.

Entrance requirements: For master's, The Public Administration program requires an official Graduate Record Exam (GRE) score to be submitted prior to admission consideration with with a preferred score of 297., baccalaureate degree from regionally-accredited university with minimum GPA of 3.0 on last 60 undergraduate semester hours. Additional exam requirements/recommendations for international students: Required—TOEFL (minimum score 550 paper-based; 78 iBT), TWE. *Application deadline:* For fall admission, 6/15 priority date for domestic students, 6/1 priority date for international students; for spring admission, 10/15 priority date for domestic students, 10/1 priority date for international students; for summer admission, 4/15 for domestic students, 3/15 for international students. Applications are processed on a rolling basis. Application fee: $40 ($90 for international students). Electronic applications accepted. *Expenses:* Expenses: $8,834 (tuition and fees combined). *Financial support:* In 2014–15, 42 students received support, including 3 research assistantships (averaging $10,708 per year), 1 teaching assistantship (averaging $12,464 per year); career-related internships or fieldwork, Federal Work-Study, institutionally sponsored loans, scholarships/grants, and unspecified assistantships also available. Support available to part-time students. Financial award application deadline: 4/1; financial award applicants required to submit FAFSA. *Unit head:* Dr. Thomas Longoria, Graduate Advisor, 512-245-7582, Fax: 512-245-7815, E-mail: tl28@txstate.edu. *Application contact:* Dr. Andrea Golato, Dean of Graduate School, 512-245-2581, Fax: 512-245-8365, E-mail: gradcollege@txstate.edu.
Website: http://www.polisci.txstate.edu/public_administration/

Tufts University, Graduate School of Arts and Sciences, Department of Urban and Environmental Policy and Planning, Medford, MA 02155. Offers community development (MA); environmental policy (MA); health and human welfare (MA); housing policy (MA); international environment/development policy (MA); public policy (MPP); MA/MS; MALD/MA. *Accreditation:* ACSP (one or more programs are accredited). Part-time programs available. *Faculty:* 13 full-time (5 women), 15 part-time/adjunct (8 women). *Students:* 62 full-time (43 women), 36 part-time (26 women); includes 24 minority (10 Black or African American, non-Hispanic/Latino; 7 Asian, non-Hispanic/Latino; 6 Hispanic/Latino; 1 Two or more races, non-Hispanic/Latino), 10 international. Average age 30. 119 applicants, 81% accepted, 32 enrolled. In 2014, 64 master's awarded. *Degree requirements:* For master's, thesis, internship. *Entrance requirements:* For master's, GRE General Test. Additional exam requirements/recommendations for international students: Required—TOEFL (minimum score 550 paper-based; 80 iBT), IELTS (minimum score 6.5). *Application deadline:* For fall admission, 1/15 for domestic and international students. Applications are processed on a rolling basis. Application fee: $75. Electronic applications accepted. *Expenses:* Expenses: Contact institution. *Financial support:* Teaching assistantships with partial tuition reimbursements, career-related internships or fieldwork, Federal Work-Study, scholarships/grants, tuition waivers (partial), and unspecified assistantships available. Support available to part-time students. Financial award application deadline: 1/15; financial award applicants required to submit FAFSA. *Unit head:* Dr. Weiping Wu, Graduate Program Director. *Application contact:* Office of Graduate Admissions, 617-627-3395, E-mail: gradadmissions@tufts.edu.
Website: http://ase.tufts.edu/uep/

Université de Montréal, Faculty of Environmental Design and Planning, Montréal, QC H3C 3J7, Canada. Offers environmental design and planning (M Sc A, PhD); environmental planning and design projects (DESS); game design (DESS); urban management for developing countries (DESS); urban planning (M Urb). DESS programs offered jointly with HEC Montreal and École Polytechnique de Montréal. *Accreditation:* ACSP. *Degree requirements:* For doctorate, thesis/dissertation, general exam. Electronic applications accepted. *Expenses:* Contact institution. *Faculty research:* Wayfinding, environmental evaluation, housing studies, urban design, urban and regional planning.

Université du Québec à Rimouski, Graduate Programs, Program in Regional Development, Rimouski, QC G5L 3A1, Canada. Offers MA, PhD, Diploma. PhD offered jointly with Université du Québec à Chicoutimi; Diploma with Université du Québec, École nationale d'administration publique. Part-time programs available. *Degree requirements:* For master's, thesis. *Entrance requirements:* For master's, appropriate bachelor's degree, proficiency in French.

Université du Québec en Outaouais, Graduate Programs, Program in Regional Development, Gatineau, QC J8X 3X7, Canada. Offers MA. Part-time programs available. *Students:* 15 full-time, 55 part-time. *Degree requirements:* For master's, thesis (for some programs). *Application deadline:* For fall admission, 6/1 priority date for domestic students, 4/15 for international students; for winter admission, 11/1 priority date for domestic students, 9/15 for international students. Application fee: $30. *Unit head:* Charmain Levy, Director, 819-595-3900 Ext. 2295, Fax: 819-595-2226, E-mail: charmain.levy@uqo.ca. *Application contact:* Registrar's Office, 819-773-1850, Fax: 819-773-1835, E-mail: registraire@uqo.ca.

Université Laval, Faculty of Architecture, Planning and Visual Arts, Department of Regional Planning, Programs in Planning and Regional Development, Québec, QC G1K 7P4, Canada. Offers MATDR, PhD. Terminal master's awarded for partial completion of doctoral program. *Degree requirements:* For master's, thesis (for some programs); for doctorate, comprehensive exam, thesis/dissertation. *Entrance requirements:* For master's and doctorate, knowledge of French and English. Electronic applications accepted.

University at Albany, State University of New York, College of Arts and Sciences, Department of Geography and Planning, Program in Regional Planning, Albany, NY 12222-0001. Offers MRP. *Accreditation:* ACSP. Part-time programs available. *Degree requirements:* For master's, thesis optional. *Entrance requirements:* Additional exam requirements/recommendations for international students: Required—TOEFL (minimum score 550 paper-based). Electronic applications accepted. *Faculty research:* Urban planning, Third World development, political and social aspects of planning, urban housing and employment, environmental planning.

University at Buffalo, the State University of New York, Graduate School, School of Architecture and Planning, Department of Urban and Regional Planning, Buffalo, NY 14214. Offers historic preservation (Certificate); urban and regional planning (PhD); JD/MUP; M Arch/MUP. *Accreditation:* ACSP. Part-time programs available. *Faculty:* 14 full-time (4 women), 13 part-time/adjunct (2 women). *Students:* 97 full-time (45 women), 8 part-time (3 women); includes 12 minority (7 Black or African American, non-Hispanic/Latino; 2 Asian, non-Hispanic/Latino; 3 Two or more races, non-Hispanic/Latino), 39 international. Average age 25. 183 applicants, 62% accepted, 45 enrolled. In 2014, 34 master's awarded. *Degree requirements:* For master's, thesis or alternative, project; for doctorate, thesis/dissertation. *Entrance requirements:* For master's, minimum GPA of 3.0, resume, 3 letters of recommendation, 500-word personal statement, transcripts; for doctorate, GRE, transcripts, 3 letters of recommendation, minimum GPA of 3.0, resume, research statement, writing sample. Additional exam requirements/recommendations for international students: Required—TOEFL (minimum score 550 paper-based; 79 iBT), IELTS (minimum score 6.5). *Application deadline:* For fall admission, 3/1 priority date for domestic and international students; for spring admission, 10/31 priority date for domestic students, 10/1 priority date for international students. Applications are processed on a rolling basis. Application fee: $75. Electronic applications accepted. *Expenses:* Expenses: $6,242.50 per semester resident tuition and fees, $11,125.50 non-resident. *Financial support:* In 2014–15, 2 fellowships with full tuition reimbursements (averaging $21,878 per year), 20 research assistantships with full and partial tuition reimbursements (averaging $6,604 per year), 13 teaching assistantships with partial tuition reimbursements (averaging $4,834 per year) were awarded; career-related internships or fieldwork, Federal Work-Study, institutionally sponsored loans, scholarships/grants, health care benefits, tuition waivers (partial), and unspecified assistantships also available. Support available to part-time students. Financial award application deadline: 3/1; financial award applicants required to submit FAFSA. *Faculty research:* Economic and international development, environmental and land use planning, GIS and spatial modeling, urban design and physical planning, neighborhood planning and community development. *Total annual research expenditures:* $1.1 million. *Unit head:* Dr. Ernest Sternberg, Professor, 716-829-3671 Ext. 109, Fax: 716-829-3256, E-mail: ezs@buffalo.edu. *Application contact:* Norma Everett, Assistant to the Chair, 716-829-3283, Fax: 716-829-3256, E-mail: norma.everett@buffalo.edu.
Website: http://www.ap.buffalo.edu/planning/

The University of Alabama, Graduate School, College of Arts and Sciences, Department of Geography, Tuscaloosa, AL 35487. Offers earth system science (MS); geographic information science (MS); planning (MS). Part-time programs available. *Faculty:* 14 full-time (1 woman), 1 (woman) part-time/adjunct. *Students:* 26 full-time (10 women), 5 part-time (2 women); includes 1 minority (Two or more races, non-Hispanic/Latino), 4 international. Average age 27. 19 applicants, 68% accepted, 10 enrolled. In 2014, 12 master's awarded. *Degree requirements:* For master's, comprehensive exam (for some programs), thesis (for some programs). *Entrance requirements:* For master's, GRE, minimum GPA of 3.0. Additional exam requirements/recommendations for international students: Required—TOEFL (minimum score 550 paper-based; 79 iBT). *Application deadline:* For fall admission, 2/15 priority date for domestic and international students; for spring admission, 10/1 priority date for domestic and international students. Applications are processed on a rolling basis. Application fee: $50 ($60 for international students). Electronic applications accepted. *Expenses:* Tuition, state resident: full-time $9826. Tuition, nonresident: full-time $24,950. *Financial support:* In 2014–15, 16 students received support, including fellowships with full tuition reimbursements available (averaging $15,000 per year), 4 research assistantships with full tuition reimbursements available (averaging $13,311 per year), 18 teaching assistantships with full tuition reimbursements available (averaging $13,311 per year); career-related internships or fieldwork, health care benefits, and unspecified assistantships also available. Financial award application deadline: 2/15. *Faculty research:* Earth system science; geographic information science; urban, regional and environmental planning; ecology. *Total annual research expenditures:* $393,294. *Unit head:* Dr. Douglas Sherman, Chair, 205-348-5047, Fax: 205-348-2278, E-mail: douglas.j.sherman@ua.edu. *Application contact:* Dr. Justin Hart, Assistant Professor, 205-348-5047, Fax: 205-348-2278, E-mail: hart013@ua.edu.
Website: http://geography.ua.edu

The University of Arizona, College of Architecture, Planning, and Landscape Architecture, Planning Program, Tucson, AZ 85721. Offers MS. *Accreditation:* ACSP. *Entrance requirements:* For master's, GRE, 3 letters of recommendation, letter of intent. Additional exam requirements/recommendations for international students: Required—TOEFL (minimum score 573 paper-based; 80 iBT). Electronic applications accepted.

The University of British Columbia, School of Community and Regional Planning, Vancouver, BC V6T 1Z1, Canada. Offers M Sc P, MAP, PhD. *Accreditation:* ACSP (one or more programs are accredited). *Degree requirements:* For master's, thesis; for doctorate, thesis/dissertation, oral exam. *Entrance requirements:* For master's, GRE (recommended); for doctorate, MCRP or equivalent. Additional exam requirements/recommendations for international students: Required—TOEFL (minimum score 600 paper-based). Electronic applications accepted. *Faculty research:* Natural resources management, international development, urban spatial, urban policy and community development planning.

University of California, Berkeley, Graduate Division, College of Environmental Design, Department of City and Regional Planning, Berkeley, CA 94720-1500. Offers MCP, PhD, JD/MCP, M Arch/MCP, MCP/MPH, MCP/MS, MLA/MCP. JD/MCP offered jointly with University of California, Hastings College of the Law and School of Law. *Accreditation:* ACSP. *Degree requirements:* For master's, professional project or thesis; for doctorate, thesis/dissertation, qualifying exam. *Entrance requirements:* For master's and doctorate, GRE General Test, minimum GPA of 3.0, 3 letters of recommendation. Additional exam requirements/recommendations for international students: Required—TOEFL. *Faculty research:* Housing and project development, physical planning and design, community and economic development, geographic information systems, transportation.

University of California, Davis, Graduate Studies, Graduate Group in Community Development, Davis, CA 95616. Offers MS. *Degree requirements:* For master's, comprehensive exam (for some programs), thesis (for some programs). *Entrance requirements:* For master's, GRE General Test, minimum GPA of 3.0. Additional exam requirements/recommendations for international students: Required—TOEFL (minimum score 550 paper-based). Electronic applications accepted. *Faculty research:* Globalization; community economic change; urban and regional development; community planning design and sustainability; race, ethnic, and gender roles; community organization and political mobilization.

University of California, Irvine, School of Social Ecology, Department of Planning, Policy and Design, Irvine, CA 92697. Offers planning, policy and design (PhD); urban and regional planning (MURP). *Accreditation:* ACSP (one or more programs are accredited). *Students:* 130 full-time (75 women); includes 53 minority (2 Black or African American, non-Hispanic/Latino; 1 American Indian or Alaska Native, non-Hispanic/Latino; 23 Asian, non-Hispanic/Latino; 19 Hispanic/Latino; 8 Two or more races, non-Hispanic/Latino), 36 international. Average age 29. 383 applicants, 54% accepted, 66 enrolled. In 2014, 54 master's, 8 doctorates awarded. *Degree requirements:* For doctorate, thesis/dissertation, research project. *Entrance requirements:* For master's and doctorate, GRE General Test, minimum GPA of 3.0. Additional exam requirements/recommendations for international students: Required—TOEFL (minimum score 550 paper-based). *Application deadline:* For fall admission, 1/15 priority date for domestic and international students. Application fee: $90 ($110 for international students). Electronic applications accepted. *Financial support:* Fellowships with tuition reimbursements, research assistantships with full tuition reimbursements, teaching assistantships with tuition reimbursements, institutionally sponsored loans, traineeships, health care benefits, and unspecified assistantships available. Financial award application deadline: 1/15; financial award applicants required to submit FAFSA. *Faculty research:* Community and social policy, economic development, land-use and growth management, transportation planning, environmental policy. *Unit head:* David L. Feldman, Chair, 949-824-4384, Fax: 949-824-3056, E-mail: feldmand@uci.edu. *Application contact:* Janet Gallagher, Graduate Coordinator, 949-824-9849, Fax: 949-824-8566, E-mail: janetg@uci.edu.
Website: http://www.seweb.uci.edu/ppd/

University of California, Los Angeles, Graduate Division, School of Public Affairs, Department of Urban Planning, Los Angeles, CA 90095. Offers MA, PhD, JD/MA, MA/

MA, MBA/MA. *Accreditation:* ACSP (one or more programs are accredited). *Degree requirements:* For master's, comprehensive exam or thesis; for doctorate, thesis/dissertation, oral and written qualifying exams. *Entrance requirements:* For master's, GRE General Test (recommended); for doctorate, GRE General Test, master's degree in urban planning or related field. Additional exam requirements/recommendations for international students: Required—TOEFL. Electronic applications accepted. *Faculty research:* Industrial hazards, political economy of South and Southeast Asia, historic preservation, flexible production in U.S. and Western Europe, land-use controls.

University of Central Arkansas, Graduate School, College of Liberal Arts, Department of Geography, Conway, AR 72035-0001. Offers community and economic development (MS); geographic information systems (MGIS, Certificate). Part-time programs available. Postbaccalaureate distance learning degree programs offered (minimal on-campus study). *Entrance requirements:* Additional exam requirements/recommendations for international students: Required—TOEFL (minimum score 550 paper-based). Electronic applications accepted.

University of Central Florida, College of Health and Public Affairs, School of Public Administration, Orlando, FL 32816. Offers emergency management and homeland security (Certificate); fundraising (Certificate); non-profit management (MNM, Certificate); urban and regional planning (MS). *Accreditation:* NASPAA. Part-time and evening/weekend programs available. *Faculty:* 18 full-time (9 women), 19 part-time/adjunct (9 women). *Students:* 109 full-time (80 women), 274 part-time (202 women); includes 148 minority (82 Black or African American, non-Hispanic/Latino; 8 Asian, non-Hispanic/Latino; 51 Hispanic/Latino; 7 Two or more races, non-Hispanic/Latino), 5 international. Average age 32. 264 applicants, 77% accepted, 148 enrolled. In 2014, 123 master's, 26 other advanced degrees awarded. *Degree requirements:* For master's, comprehensive exam, thesis or alternative, research report. *Entrance requirements:* For master's, GRE General Test. *Application deadline:* For fall admission, 7/1 for domestic students; for spring admission, 12/1 for domestic students. Application fee: $30. Electronic applications accepted. *Expenses:* Tuition, state resident: part-time $288.16 per credit hour. Tuition, nonresident: part-time $1073.31 per credit hour. *Financial support:* In 2014–15, 4 students received support, including 2 fellowships with partial tuition reimbursements available (averaging $5,300 per year), 1 research assistantship with partial tuition reimbursement available (averaging $10,600 per year), 1 teaching assistantship (averaging $7,100 per year); career-related internships or fieldwork, Federal Work-Study, institutionally sponsored loans, tuition waivers (partial), and unspecified assistantships also available. Financial award application deadline: 3/1; financial award applicants required to submit FAFSA. *Unit head:* Dr. Mary Ann Feldheim, Director, 407-823-3693, Fax: 407-823-5651, E-mail: mary.feldheim@ucf.edu. *Application contact:* Barbara Rodriguez Lamas, Director, Admissions and Student Services, 407-823-2766, Fax: 407-823-6442, E-mail: gradadmissions@ucf.edu.
Website: https://www.cohpa.ucf.edu/publicadmin/

University of Cincinnati, Graduate School, College of Design, Architecture, Art, and Planning, School of Planning, Program in Community Planning, Cincinnati, OH 45221. Offers MCP, JD/MCP. *Accreditation:* ACSP. *Degree requirements:* For master's, thesis. *Entrance requirements:* For master's, GRE General Test. Additional exam requirements/recommendations for international students: Required—TOEFL.

University of Colorado Denver, College of Architecture and Planning, Program in Design and Planning, Denver, CO 80217. Offers history of architecture, landscape and urbanism (PhD); sustainable and healthy environments (PhD). Part-time programs available. *Students:* 9 full-time (3 women), 11 part-time (9 women); includes 1 minority (Hispanic/Latino), 7 international. Average age 38. 32 applicants, 6% accepted, 1 enrolled. In 2014, 4 doctorates awarded. *Degree requirements:* For doctorate, comprehensive exam, thesis/dissertation. *Entrance requirements:* For doctorate, GRE (minimum score of 158 for both verbal and quantitative; writing 4.0), minimum undergraduate GPA of 3.0, graduate 3.5; writing sample; three letters of recommendation; statement of personal and professional goals. Additional exam requirements/recommendations for international students: Required—TOEFL (minimum score 80 iBT); Recommended—IELTS (minimum score 6.8). *Application deadline:* For fall admission, 2/2 for domestic students, 1/2 for international students; for spring admission, 10/1 for domestic students. Application fee: $50 ($75 for international students). Electronic applications accepted. *Expenses:* Expenses: Contact institution. *Financial support:* In 2014–15, 2 students received support. Fellowships, research assistantships, teaching assistantships, Federal Work-Study, institutionally sponsored loans, scholarships/grants, traineeships, and unspecified assistantships available. Financial award application deadline: 4/1; financial award applicants required to submit FAFSA. *Faculty research:* Land use and environmental planning and design; design and planning processes and practices; history, theory, and criticism of the built environment. *Unit head:* Dr. Osman Attmann, Director, 303-315-0032, Fax: 303-556-3687, E-mail: o.attmann@ucdenver.edu. *Application contact:* Rachael Kuroiwa, Manager of Admissions and Outreach, 303-315-2325, E-mail: rachael.kuroiwa@ucdenver.edu.
Website: http://www.ucdenver.edu/academics/colleges/ArchitecturePlanning/Academics/DegreePrograms/PhD/Pages/PhD.aspx

University of Colorado Denver, College of Architecture and Planning, Program in Urban and Regional Planning, Denver, CO 80217. Offers economic and community development planning (MURP); land use and environmental planning (MURP); urban place making (MURP). *Accreditation:* ACSP. Part-time programs available. *Students:* 84 full-time (39 women), 9 part-time (4 women); includes 14 minority (1 Black or African American, non-Hispanic/Latino; 1 American Indian or Alaska Native, non-Hispanic/Latino; 1 Asian, non-Hispanic/Latino; 7 Hispanic/Latino; 4 Two or more races, non-Hispanic/Latino), 5 international. Average age 30. 149 applicants, 64% accepted, 44 enrolled. In 2014, 57 master's awarded. *Degree requirements:* For master's, thesis, minimum of 51 semester hours. *Entrance requirements:* For master's, GRE (for students with an undergraduate GPA below 3.0), sample of writing or work project; statement of interest; resume; three letters of recommendation. Additional exam requirements/recommendations for international students: Required—TOEFL (minimum score 75 iBT). *Application deadline:* For fall admission, 2/1 priority date for domestic students, 1/1 priority date for international students; for spring admission, 10/1 for domestic students. Application fee: $50 ($75 for international students). Electronic applications accepted. *Expenses:* Expenses: Contact institution. *Financial support:* In 2014–15, 18 students received support. Fellowships, research assistantships, teaching assistantships, Federal Work-Study, institutionally sponsored loans, scholarships/grants, and traineeships available. Financial award application deadline: 4/1; financial award applicants required to submit FAFSA. *Faculty research:* Physical planning, environmental planning, economic development planning. *Unit head:* Jeremy Nemeth, Associate Professor/Chair/Director, 303-315-0069, E-mail: jeremy.nemeth@ucdenver.edu. *Application contact:* Rachael Kuroiwa, Manager of Admissions and Outreach, 303-315-2325, E-mail: rachael.kuroiwa@ucdenver.edu.
Website: http://www.ucdenver.edu/academics/colleges/ArchitecturePlanning/Academics/DegreePrograms/MURP/Pages/MURP.aspx

University of Florida, Graduate School, College of Design, Construction and Planning, Department of Urban and Regional Planning, Gainesville, FL 32611-5706. Offers geographic information systems (MAURP); historic preservation (MAURP); sustainable design (MAURP); tropical conservation and development (MAURP); urban and regional planning (MAURP, MURP); wetland sciences (MAURP); JD/MAURP. *Accreditation:* ACSP (one or more programs are accredited). Postbaccalaureate distance learning degree programs offered. *Faculty:* 11 full-time (6 women), 2 part-time/adjunct (0 women). *Students:* 52 full-time (27 women), 60 part-time (34 women); includes 23 minority (5 Black or African American, non-Hispanic/Latino; 1 American Indian or Alaska Native, non-Hispanic/Latino; 2 Asian, non-Hispanic/Latino; 15 Hispanic/Latino), 28 international. 122 applicants, 66% accepted, 29 enrolled. In 2014, 9 master's awarded. *Entrance requirements:* For master's, GRE General Test, minimum GPA of 3.0. Additional exam requirements/recommendations for international students: Required—TOEFL (minimum score 550 paper-based; 80 iBT), IELTS (minimum score 6). *Application deadline:* For fall admission, 6/1 priority date for domestic students; for spring admission, 10/1 priority date for domestic students. Applications are processed on a rolling basis. Application fee: $30. Electronic applications accepted. *Financial support:* In 2014–15, 5 research assistantships, 2 teaching assistantships were awarded; fellowships, career-related internships or fieldwork, Federal Work-Study, and unspecified assistantships also available. Support available to part-time students. Financial award applicants required to submit FAFSA. *Faculty research:* Planning and information systems, urban and environmental design, community and economic development, transportation and growth management. *Unit head:* Joseli Macedo, PhD, Associate Professor and Interim Chair, 352-392-0997 Ext. 461, Fax: 352-392-3308, E-mail: joseli@ufl.edu. *Application contact:* Paul D. Zwick, PhD, Professor, Director of the GeoPlan Center, and Graduate Coordinator, 352-392-0997 Ext. 427, Fax: 352-392-3308, E-mail: pdzwick@ufl.edu.
Website: http://dcp.ufl.edu/urp

University of Florida, Graduate School, College of Design, Construction and Planning, Doctoral Program in Design, Construction and Planning, Gainesville, FL 32611. Offers construction management (PhD); design, construction and planning (PhD); geographic information systems (PhD); historic preservation (PhD); interior design (PhD); landscape architecture (PhD); urban and regional planning (PhD). *Students:* 79 full-time (32 women), 21 part-time (7 women); includes 12 minority (4 Black or African American, non-Hispanic/Latino; 1 American Indian or Alaska Native, non-Hispanic/Latino; 4 Asian, non-Hispanic/Latino; 3 Hispanic/Latino), 51 international. 92 applicants, 25% accepted, 14 enrolled. In 2014, 18 doctorates awarded. *Degree requirements:* For doctorate, thesis/dissertation. *Entrance requirements:* For doctorate, GRE General Test, minimum GPA of 3.0. Additional exam requirements/recommendations for international students: Required—TOEFL (minimum score 550 paper-based; 80 iBT), IELTS (minimum score 6). *Application deadline:* For fall admission, 2/1 for domestic and international students. Applications are processed on a rolling basis. Application fee: $30. Electronic applications accepted. *Financial support:* In 2014–15, 3 fellowships, 26 research assistantships, 30 teaching assistantships were awarded; unspecified assistantships also available. Financial award applicants required to submit FAFSA. *Faculty research:* Architecture, building construction, urban and regional planning. *Unit head:* Zhong-Ren Peng, PhD, Professor/Director, 352-392-0997 Ext. 429, Fax: 352-392-3308, E-mail: zpeng@ufl.edu. *Application contact:* Zhong-Ren Peng, PhD, Professor/Director, 352-392-0997 Ext. 429, Fax: 352-392-3308, E-mail: zpeng@ufl.edu.
Website: http://www.dcp.ufl.edu/docprogram/

University of Hawaii at Manoa, Graduate Division, College of Social Sciences, Department of Urban and Regional Planning, Honolulu, HI 96822. Offers community planning and social policy (MURP); disaster preparedness and emergency management (Graduate Certificate); environmental planning and management (MURP); land use and infrastructure planning (MURP); urban and regional planning (PhD, Graduate Certificate); urban and regional planning in Asia and Pacific (MURP). *Accreditation:* ACSP. Part-time programs available. *Entrance requirements:* For master's, GRE General Test, minimum GPA of 3.0; for doctorate, GRE General Test. Additional exam requirements/recommendations for international students: Required—TOEFL (minimum score 500 paper-based; 61 iBT), IELTS (minimum score 5).

University of Idaho, College of Graduate Studies, College of Art and Architecture, Program in Bioregional Planning and Community Design, Moscow, ID 83844-2481. Offers MS. *Faculty:* 5 full-time, 1 part-time/adjunct. *Students:* 10 full-time, 5 part-time. Average age 33. In 2014, 6 master's awarded. *Entrance requirements:* Additional exam requirements/recommendations for international students: Required—TOEFL. *Application deadline:* Applications are processed on a rolling basis. Application fee: $60. Electronic applications accepted. *Expenses:* Tuition, state resident: full-time $4784; part-time $280.50 per credit hour. Tuition, nonresident: full-time $18,314; part-time $957.50 per credit hour. *Required fees:* $2000; $58.50 per credit hour. Tuition and fees vary according to program. *Financial support:* Applicants required to submit FAFSA. *Faculty research:* Environment and behavior interaction, geographic trade, design development, economic development, natural resource policy. *Unit head:* Dr. Mark Hoversten, Dean, 208-885-7448, E-mail: bioregionalplanning@uidaho.edu. *Application contact:* Sean Scoggin, Graduate Recruitment Coordinator, 208-885-4001, Fax: 208-805-4406, E-mail: graduateadmissions@uidaho.edu.
Website: http://www.uidaho.edu/caa/biop

University of Illinois at Chicago, Graduate College, College of Urban Planning and Public Affairs, Program in Urban Planning and Policy, Chicago, IL 60607-7128. Offers MUPP, PhD. *Accreditation:* ACSP (one or more programs are accredited). Part-time programs available. *Faculty:* 18 full-time (5 women), 11 part-time/adjunct (4 women). *Students:* 136 full-time (68 women), 44 part-time (28 women); includes 43 minority (13 Black or African American, non-Hispanic/Latino; 1 American Indian or Alaska Native, non-Hispanic/Latino; 6 Asian, non-Hispanic/Latino; 18 Hispanic/Latino; 5 Two or more races, non-Hispanic/Latino), 28 international. Average age 28. 256 applicants, 71% accepted, 61 enrolled. In 2014, 90 master's awarded. *Degree requirements:* For master's, thesis or alternative, internship; for doctorate, thesis/dissertation. *Entrance requirements:* For master's and doctorate, GRE General Test, minimum GPA of 2.75, writing sample. Additional exam requirements/recommendations for international students: Required—TOEFL. *Application deadline:* For fall admission, 1/1 for domestic and international students. Applications are processed on a rolling basis. Application fee: $60. Electronic applications accepted. *Expenses:* Expenses: $19,316 in-state; $31,314 out-of-state. *Financial support:* In 2014–15, 1 fellowship with full tuition reimbursement was awarded; research assistantships with full tuition reimbursements, teaching assistantships with full tuition reimbursements, career-related internships or fieldwork, Federal Work-Study, scholarships/grants, traineeships, tuition waivers (full), and unspecified assistantships also available. Financial award application deadline: 3/1; financial award applicants required to submit FAFSA. *Faculty research:* Urban and regional economic and workforce development issues, current policy issues and social trends, racial justice and related issues of poverty, quality of life of people living in Chicago and other great cities of the world. *Total annual research expenditures:* $75,000. *Unit head:* Prof. Curtis Winkle, Head, 312-996-2155, Fax: 312-413-2314, E-mail: cwinkle@uic.edu. *Application contact:* Martin Jaffe, Director of Graduate Studies, 312-996-2178, E-mail: mjaffe@uic.edu.
Website: http://www.uic.edu/cuppa/upp/

University of Illinois at Urbana–Champaign, Graduate College, College of Fine and Applied Arts, Department of Urban and Regional Planning, Champaign, IL 61820. Offers regional planning (PhD); urban planning (MUP); JD/MUP; M Arch/MUP; MLA/MUP.

Accreditation: ACSP (one or more programs are accredited). *Students:* 71 (36 women). Application fee: $70 ($90 for international students). *Financial support:* Tuition waivers available. *Unit head:* Robert Olshansky, Head, 217-244-7681, Fax: 217-244-1717, E-mail: robo@illinois.edu. *Application contact:* Bumsoo Lee, Assistant Professor, 217-333-3601, Fax: 217-244-1717, E-mail: bumsoo@illinois.edu.
Website: http://www.urban.illinois.edu/

The University of Iowa, Graduate College, Program in Urban and Regional Planning, Iowa City, IA 52242-1316. Offers MA, MS, JD/MA, MHA/MA, MHA/MS, MS/MA, MS/MS, MSW/MA, MSW/MS. *Accreditation:* ACSP. *Degree requirements:* For master's, thesis optional, portfolio. *Entrance requirements:* For master's, GRE General Test, minimum GPA of 3.0. Additional exam requirements/recommendations for international students: Required—TOEFL (minimum score 600 paper-based; 100 iBT). Electronic applications accepted.

The University of Kansas, Graduate Studies, School of Architecture, Design, and Planning, Department of Urban Planning, Lawrence, KS 66045. Offers MUP, JD/MUP, M Arch/MUP, MUP/MA, MUP/MPA. *Accreditation:* ACSP. Part-time programs available. *Faculty:* 5 full-time. *Students:* 38 full-time (14 women), 5 part-time (3 women); includes 4 minority (1 Asian, non-Hispanic/Latino; 3 Hispanic/Latino), 11 international. Average age 26. 57 applicants, 65% accepted, 16 enrolled. In 2014, 11 master's awarded. *Degree requirements:* For master's, comprehensive exam, thesis or alternative. *Entrance requirements:* For master's, GRE, three letters of reference, resume. Additional exam requirements/recommendations for international students: Required—TOEFL (minimum score 570 paper-based). *Application deadline:* For fall admission, 7/1 for domestic students, 6/1 for international students; for spring admission, 12/1 for domestic students, 11/1 for international students. Applications are processed on a rolling basis. Application fee: $55 ($65 for international students). Electronic applications accepted. *Financial support:* In 2014–15, 4 fellowships (averaging $3,440 per year) were awarded; research assistantships with partial tuition reimbursements and career-related internships or fieldwork also available. Financial award application deadline: 2/1. *Faculty research:* Environmental land use, housing and economic development, community development and transportation, urban mass transportation, urban sprawl. *Unit head:* Stacey M. Swearingen White, Chair, 785-864-3530, E-mail: sswhite@ku.edu. *Application contact:* Pat Owens, Senior Administrative Associate, 785-864-4184, E-mail: patowens@ku.edu.
Website: http://urbanplanning.ku.edu/

University of Louisville, Graduate School, College of Arts and Sciences, Department of Urban and Public Affairs, Louisville, KY 40208. Offers public administration (MPA), including human resources management, non-profit management, public policy and administration; urban and public affairs (PhD), including urban planning and development, urban policy and administration; urban planning (MUP), including administration of planning organizations, housing and community development, land use and environmental planning, spatial analysis. Part-time and evening/weekend programs available. *Students:* 76 full-time (35 women), 22 part-time (14 women); includes 16 minority (10 Black or African American, non-Hispanic/Latino; 1 Asian, non-Hispanic/Latino; 3 Hispanic/Latino; 2 Two or more races, non-Hispanic/Latino), 6 international. Average age 30. 89 applicants, 71% accepted, 33 enrolled. In 2014, 13 master's, 4 doctorates awarded. Terminal master's awarded for partial completion of doctoral program. *Degree requirements:* For master's, internship; for doctorate, comprehensive exam, thesis/dissertation. *Entrance requirements:* For master's, GRE General Test, minimum GPA of 3.0; for doctorate, GRE General Test, master's degree in appropriate field. Additional exam requirements/recommendations for international students: Required—TOEFL (minimum score 550 paper-based; 79 iBT). *Application deadline:* For fall admission, 7/15 for domestic students, 5/1 priority date for international students; for spring admission, 11/15 for domestic students, 11/1 priority date for international students; for summer admission, 4/1 priority date for international students. Applications are processed on a rolling basis. Application fee: $60. Electronic applications accepted. *Expenses:* Tuition, state resident: full-time $11,326; part-time $630 per credit hour. Tuition, nonresident: full-time $23,568; part-time $1311 per credit hour. *Required fees:* $196. Tuition and fees vary according to program and reciprocity agreements. *Financial support:* Fellowships, research assistantships, and health care benefits available. Financial award application deadline: 3/1. *Faculty research:* Housing and community development, performance-based budgeting, environmental policy and natural hazards, sustainability, real estate development, comparative urban development. *Unit head:* Dr. David Simpson, Chair, 502-852-8019, Fax: 502-852-4558, E-mail: dave.simpson@louisville.edu. *Application contact:* Libby Leggett, Director, Graduate Admissions, 502-852-3101, Fax: 502-852-4558, E-mail: gradadm@louisville.edu.
Website: http://supa.louisville.edu

University of Manitoba, Faculty of Graduate Studies, Faculty of Architecture, Department of City Planning, Winnipeg, MB R3T 2N2, Canada. Offers MCP. *Accreditation:* ACSP. *Degree requirements:* For master's, thesis.

University of Maryland, College Park, Academic Affairs, School of Architecture, Planning and Preservation, Program in Urban Studies and Planning, College Park, MD 20742. Offers urban and regional planning/design (PhD); urban studies and planning (MCP). *Accreditation:* ACSP. Part-time and evening/weekend programs available. *Entrance requirements:* For master's and doctorate, GRE General Test, minimum GPA of 3.0, 3 letters of recommendation. Additional exam requirements/recommendations for international students: Required—TOEFL. Electronic applications accepted. *Faculty research:* Policy analysis, urban planning, program planning and management, economic development planning.

University of Massachusetts Amherst, Graduate School, College of Social and Behavioral Sciences, Department of Landscape Architecture and Regional Planning, Dual Program in Landscape Architecture and Regional Planning, Amherst, MA 01003. Offers MLA/MRP. *Accreditation:* ACSP; ASLA. Part-time programs available. *Students:* 3 full-time (2 women), 1 part-time (0 women). Average age 30. 4 applicants, 100% accepted, 2 enrolled. *Entrance requirements:* Additional exam requirements/recommendations for international students: Required—TOEFL (minimum score 550 paper-based; 80 iBT), IELTS (minimum score 6.5). *Application deadline:* For fall admission, 2/1 for domestic and international students. Applications are processed on a rolling basis. Application fee: $75. Electronic applications accepted. *Expenses:* Tuition, state resident: full-time $1980; part-time $110 per credit. Tuition, nonresident: full-time $14,644; part-time $414 per credit. *Required fees:* $11,417. One-time fee: $357. *Financial support:* Fellowships with full and partial tuition reimbursements, research assistantships with full and partial tuition reimbursements, teaching assistantships with full and partial tuition reimbursements, career-related internships or fieldwork, Federal Work-Study, scholarships/grants, traineeships, health care benefits, tuition waivers (full and partial), and unspecified assistantships available. Support available to part-time students. Financial award application deadline: 2/1; financial award applicants required to submit FAFSA. *Unit head:* Dr. Robert L. Ryan, Graduate Program Director, 413-545-2266, Fax: 413-545-1772. *Application contact:* Lindsay DeSantis, Supervisor of Admissions, 413-545-0721, Fax: 413-577-0010, E-mail: gradadm@grad.umass.edu.
Website: http://www.umass.edu/larp/academics/dual-degrees/mlamrp

University of Massachusetts Amherst, Graduate School, College of Social and Behavioral Sciences, Department of Landscape Architecture and Regional Planning, Program in Regional Planning, Amherst, MA 01003. Offers MRP, PhD, M Arch/MRP, MRP/MPPA. *Accreditation:* ACSP (one or more programs are accredited). Part-time programs available. *Students:* 37 full-time (20 women), 9 part-time (3 women); includes 5 minority (1 Black or African American, non-Hispanic/Latino; 1 Asian, non-Hispanic/Latino; 2 Hispanic/Latino; 1 Two or more races, non-Hispanic/Latino), 8 international. Average age 31. 68 applicants, 43% accepted, 15 enrolled. In 2014, 14 master's, 3 doctorates awarded. Terminal master's awarded for partial completion of doctoral program. *Degree requirements:* For master's, thesis or alternative; for doctorate, comprehensive exam, thesis/dissertation. *Entrance requirements:* For master's and doctorate, GRE General Test. Additional exam requirements/recommendations for international students: Required—TOEFL (minimum score 550 paper-based; 80 iBT), IELTS (minimum score 6.5). *Application deadline:* For fall admission, 2/1 for domestic and international students. Applications are processed on a rolling basis. Application fee: $75. Electronic applications accepted. *Expenses:* Tuition, state resident: full-time $1980; part-time $110 per credit. Tuition, nonresident: full-time $14,644; part-time $414 per credit. *Required fees:* $11,417. One-time fee: $357. *Financial support:* Fellowships with full and partial tuition reimbursements, research assistantships with full and partial tuition reimbursements, teaching assistantships with full and partial tuition reimbursements, career-related internships or fieldwork, Federal Work-Study, scholarships/grants, traineeships, health care benefits, tuition waivers (full and partial), and unspecified assistantships available. Support available to part-time students. Financial award application deadline: 2/1; financial award applicants required to submit FAFSA. *Unit head:* Dr. Mark Hamin, Graduate Program Director, 413-545-2266, Fax: 413-545-1772. *Application contact:* Lindsay DeSantis, Supervisor of Admissions, 413-545-0722, Fax: 413-577-0010, E-mail: gradadm@grad.umass.edu.
Website: http://www.umass.edu/larp/

University of Massachusetts Amherst, Graduate School, Interdisciplinary Programs, Dual Degree Program in Regional Planning and Public Policy and Administration, Amherst, MA 01003. Offers MPPA/MRP. *Students:* 2 full-time (1 woman), 1 (woman) part-time. Average age 25. *Entrance requirements:* Additional exam requirements/recommendations for international students: Required—TOEFL (minimum score 550 paper-based; 80 iBT), IELTS (minimum score 6.5). *Application deadline:* For fall admission, 2/1 priority date for domestic students, 2/1 for international students. Applications are processed on a rolling basis. Electronic applications accepted. *Expenses:* Tuition, state resident: full-time $1980; part-time $110 per credit. Tuition, nonresident: full-time $14,644; part-time $414 per credit. *Required fees:* $11,417. One-time fee: $357. *Financial support:* Application deadline: 2/1. *Unit head:* Dr. Mark Hamin, Graduate Program Director, 413-545-2714, E-mail: szoller@pubpol.umass.edu. *Application contact:* Lindsay DeSantis, Supervisor of Admissions, 413-545-0722, Fax: 413-577-0010, E-mail: gradadm@grad.umass.edu.
Website: http://www.masspolicy.org/acad_mppa_planning.html

University of Massachusetts Lowell, College of Fine Arts, Humanities and Social Sciences, Program in Regional Economic and Social Development, Lowell, MA 01854. Offers MA, Graduate Certificate. Part-time programs available. *Entrance requirements:* For master's, GRE. Electronic applications accepted.

University of Memphis, Graduate School, College of Arts and Sciences, Division of City and Regional Planning, Memphis, TN 38152. Offers MCRP. *Accreditation:* ACSP. *Faculty:* 3 full-time (1 woman), 1 part-time/adjunct (0 women). *Students:* 23 full-time (9 women), 5 part-time (2 women); includes 7 minority (3 Black or African American, non-Hispanic/Latino; 1 Asian, non-Hispanic/Latino; 3 Two or more races, non-Hispanic/Latino), 1 international. Average age 29. 20 applicants, 85% accepted, 9 enrolled. In 2014, 7 master's awarded. *Degree requirements:* For master's, comprehensive exam, thesis. *Entrance requirements:* For master's, GRE General Test. *Application deadline:* For fall admission, 7/1 for domestic students; for spring admission, 12/1 for domestic students. Applications are processed on a rolling basis. Application fee: $35 ($60 for international students). *Financial support:* In 2014–15, 14 students received support. Research assistantships with full tuition reimbursements available, career-related internships or fieldwork, Federal Work-Study, scholarships/grants, and unspecified assistantships available. Financial award application deadline: 2/15; financial award applicants required to submit FAFSA. *Faculty research:* Growth planning, site design, economic development, housing, smart growth. *Unit head:* Kenneth Reardon, Director and Coordinator of Graduate Studies in Planning, 901-678-2161, Fax: 901-678-4162, E-mail: kreardon@memphis.edu. *Application contact:* Dr. Linda Bennett, Associate Dean for Graduate Studies and Research, 901-678-2253, Fax: 901-678-4831, E-mail: lbennett@memphis.edu.
Website: http://www.memphis.edu/planning/

University of Michigan, Taubman College of Architecture and Urban Planning, Urban Planning Master's Program, Ann Arbor, MI 48109. Offers MUP, MSW/MUP. *Accreditation:* ACSP (one or more programs are accredited). Part-time programs available. *Degree requirements:* For master's, thesis or alternative. *Application deadline:* For fall admission, 1/15 for domestic and international students; for winter admission, 11/15 for domestic students, 10/15 for international students. Electronic applications accepted. *Financial support:* Application deadline: 1/5. *Faculty research:* Housing community and economic development, transportation planning, physical planning and urban design, planning in developing countries, land use and environmental planning.

University of Michigan, Taubman College of Architecture and Urban Planning, Urban Planning PhD Program, Ann Arbor, MI 48109. Offers PhD. *Degree requirements:* For doctorate, comprehensive exam, thesis/dissertation. *Application deadline:* For fall admission, 1/15 for domestic and international students. Electronic applications accepted. *Financial support:* Application deadline: 1/15.

University of Minnesota, Twin Cities Campus, Graduate School, Hubert H. Humphrey School of Public Affairs, Program in Urban and Regional Planning, Minneapolis, MN 55455. Offers MURP, JD/MURP, MURP/MPH, MURP/MS, MURP/MSW. *Accreditation:* ACSP (one or more programs are accredited). Part-time programs available. *Students:* 38 full-time; includes 7 minority (2 Black or African American, non-Hispanic/Latino; 2 American Indian or Alaska Native, non-Hispanic/Latino; 1 Asian, non-Hispanic/Latino; 2 Hispanic/Latino), 5 international. Average age 25. 105 applicants, 64% accepted, 38 enrolled. In 2014, 35 master's awarded. *Degree requirements:* For master's, thesis or alternative, internship or equivalent work experience. *Entrance requirements:* For master's, GRE General Test, minimum undergraduate GPA of 3.0. Additional exam requirements/recommendations for international students: Required—TOEFL (minimum score 600 paper-based; 100 iBT), IELTS (minimum score 7). *Application deadline:* For fall admission, 4/1 for domestic and international students. Applications are processed on a rolling basis. Application fee: $75 ($95 for international students). Electronic applications accepted. *Expenses:* Expenses: State resident full-time: $17603 per year, nonresident full-time: $25,417 per year (6-15 credits per semester). *Financial support:* In 2014–15, 34 students received support, including fellowships with full and partial tuition reimbursements available (averaging $8,000 per year), research assistantships with full and partial tuition reimbursements available (averaging $25,000 per year); career-related internships or fieldwork, Federal Work-Study, scholarships/grants, health care benefits, tuition waivers (full and partial), and unspecified assistantships also available. Financial award application deadline: 1/15. *Faculty research:* Policy planning, resource allocation planning, regulatory planning, program planning, project planning. *Unit head:* Laura Bloomberg, Associate Dean, 612-

625-0608, Fax: 612-626-0002, E-mail: bloom004@umn.edu. *Application contact:* Amy Luitjens, Director of Admissions, 612-626-7229, Fax: 612-626-0002, E-mail: luitjens@umn.edu.
Website: http://www.hhh.umn.edu/degrees/murp/

University of Nebraska–Lincoln, Graduate College, College of Agricultural Sciences and Natural Resources, Department of Agricultural Economics, Lincoln, NE 68588. Offers agribusiness (MBA); agricultural economics (MS, PhD); community development (M Ag). *Degree requirements:* For master's, thesis optional; for doctorate, comprehensive exam, thesis/dissertation. *Entrance requirements:* For master's and doctorate, GRE General Test. Additional exam requirements/recommendations for international students: Required—TOEFL (minimum score 550 paper-based). Electronic applications accepted. *Faculty research:* Marketing and agribusiness, production economics, resource law, international trade and development, rural policy and revitalization.

University of Nebraska–Lincoln, Graduate College, College of Architecture, Department of Community and Regional Planning, Lincoln, NE 68588. Offers MCRP, JD/MCRP, M Arch/MCRP, MCRP/MSCE. *Accreditation:* ACSP. *Degree requirements:* For master's, thesis optional. *Entrance requirements:* For master's, GRE General Test. Additional exam requirements/recommendations for international students: Required—TOEFL (minimum score 550 paper-based). Electronic applications accepted. *Faculty research:* Economic development, community development and improvement, social planning, land use planning, physical planning, environmental planning.

University of New Brunswick Fredericton, School of Graduate Studies, Policy Studies Program, Fredericton, NB E3B 5A3, Canada. Offers citizen engagement/dispute resolution (M Phil); community development (M Phil); international development (M Phil); leadership (M Phil); sustainability/environmental issues (M Phil); worldviews (M Phil). Part-time programs available. *Faculty:* 17 full-time (9 women), 1 part-time/adjunct (0 women). *Students:* 14 full-time (7 women), 4 part-time (3 women). In 2014, 3 master's awarded. *Degree requirements:* For master's, thesis, report. *Entrance requirements:* For master's, minimum GPA of 3.5. Additional exam requirements/recommendations for international students: Required—TWE (minimum score 5.5), TOEFL (minimum score 600 paper-based; 100 iBT) or IELTS (minimum score 7). *Application deadline:* Applications are processed on a rolling basis. Application fee: $50 Canadian dollars. Electronic applications accepted. *Financial support:* In 2014–15, 3 fellowships, research assistantships (averaging $5,600 per year), teaching assistantships (averaging $4,400 per year) were awarded. *Faculty research:* International development, worldviews, citizenship/dispute resolution, sustainability/environmental issues, leadership, community development. *Unit head:* Dr. Linda Eyre, Dean of Graduate Studies, 506-447-3044, Fax: 506-453-4817, E-mail: gradidst@unb.ca. *Application contact:* Janet Amirault, Graduate Secretary, 506-458-7558, Fax: 506-453-4817, E-mail: jamiraul@unb.ca.
Website: http://www.unb.ca/gradstudies/programs/mphil/index.html

University of New Hampshire, Graduate School, Interdisciplinary Programs, Program in Community Development Policy and Practice, Durham, NH 03824. Offers MA. *Students:* 8 part-time (4 women); includes 1 minority (Black or African American, non-Hispanic/Latino), 2 international. Average age 31. 3 applicants, 33% accepted. *Degree requirements:* For master's, project. *Entrance requirements:* Additional exam requirements/recommendations for international students: Required—TOEFL (minimum score 550 paper-based; 80 iBT). *Application deadline:* For fall admission, 2/15 for domestic students. Applications are processed on a rolling basis. Application fee: $65. Electronic applications accepted. *Expenses:* Tuition, state resident: full-time $13,500; part-time $750 per credit hour. Tuition, nonresident: full-time $26,460; part-time $1110 per credit hour. *Required fees:* $1788; $447 per semester. *Financial support:* In 2014–15, 6 students received support. Fellowships, research assistantships, teaching assistantships, and scholarships/grants available. *Unit head:* Michael Swack, Chairperson, 603-862-3201, Fax: 603-862-0275, E-mail: harry.richards@unh.edu. *Application contact:* Robin Husslage, Administrative Assistant, 603-862-1871, E-mail: college.teaching@unh.edu.
Website: http://carsey.unh.edu/macdpp

University of New Haven, Graduate School, College of Business, Program in Public Administration, West Haven, CT 06516-1916. Offers city management (MPA); community-clinical services (MPA); health care management (MPA); long-term health care (MPA); personnel and labor relations (MPA); public administration (MPA, Certificate); public management (Certificate); MBA/MPA. Part-time and evening/weekend programs available. *Degree requirements:* For master's, thesis or alternative. *Entrance requirements:* Additional exam requirements/recommendations for international students: Required—TOEFL (minimum score 80 iBT), IELTS, PTE (minimum score 53). Electronic applications accepted. Application fee is waived when completed online. *Expenses:* Contact institution.

University of New Mexico, Graduate School, School of Architecture and Planning, Program in Community and Regional Planning, Albuquerque, NM 87131-2039. Offers MCRP, MCRP/MA, MPA/MCRP. *Accreditation:* ACSP. Part-time programs available. *Faculty:* 8 full-time (4 women), 8 part-time/adjunct (2 women). *Students:* 42 full-time (26 women), 34 part-time (13 women); includes 36 minority (2 Black or African American, non-Hispanic/Latino; 10 American Indian or Alaska Native, non-Hispanic/Latino; 21 Hispanic/Latino; 3 Two or more races, non-Hispanic/Latino), 2 international. Average age 33. 41 applicants, 71% accepted, 22 enrolled. In 2014, 21 master's awarded. *Degree requirements:* For master's, thesis. *Entrance requirements:* For master's, minimum GPA of 3.0 in last two years of graduate study, 3 letters of recommendation, letter of intent, resume, copies of all official transcripts. Additional exam requirements/recommendations for international students: Required—TOEFL (minimum score 550 paper-based; 79 iBT). *Application deadline:* For fall admission, 1/30 priority date for domestic students, 1/30 for international students. Application fee: $50. Electronic applications accepted. *Financial support:* In 2014–15, 64 students received support, including 8 fellowships (averaging $6,238 per year), 4 research assistantships with partial tuition reimbursements available (averaging $10,419 per year), 2 teaching assistantships with partial tuition reimbursements available (averaging $8,837 per year); career-related internships or fieldwork, Federal Work-Study, institutionally sponsored loans, scholarships/grants, health care benefits, tuition waivers (full), and unspecified assistantships also available. Support available to part-time students. Financial award application deadline: 3/1; financial award applicants required to submit FAFSA. *Faculty research:* Community development, urban and ecological design, land economics, community-based planning, environmental dispute resolution, environmental justice, indigenous planning, watershed management. *Unit head:* Dr. Teresa L. Cordova, Program Director, 505-277-3922, Fax: 505-277-0076, E-mail: tcordova@unm.edu. *Application contact:* Elizabeth M. Rowe, Senior Academic Advisor, 505-277-1303, Fax: 505-277-0076, E-mail: erowe@unm.edu. Website: http://www.unm.edu/~crp

University of New Orleans, Graduate School, College of Liberal Arts, School of Urban Planning and Regional Studies, Program in Urban and Regional Planning, New Orleans, LA 70148. Offers MURP. *Accreditation:* ACSP. *Degree requirements:* For master's, thesis. *Entrance requirements:* For master's, GRE General Test. Additional exam requirements/recommendations for international students: Required—TOEFL (minimum score 550 paper-based; 79 iBT), IELTS (minimum score 6.5). Electronic applications accepted. *Faculty research:* Urban economic development, environmental planning and analysis, social and cultural change.

University of North Alabama, Office of Professional and Interdisciplinary Studies, Florence, AL 35632-0001. Offers community development (MPS); information technology (MPS); security and safety leadership (MPS). Part-time and evening/weekend programs available. *Students:* 11 full-time (2 women), 34 part-time (23 women); includes 10 minority (all Black or African American, non-Hispanic/Latino), 5 international. Average age 36. 25 applicants, 76% accepted, 15 enrolled. In 2014, 2 master's awarded. *Degree requirements:* For master's, comprehensive exam (for some programs), thesis optional. *Entrance requirements:* For master's, ETS PPI, baccalaureate degree from accredited institution; minimum cumulative GPA of 2.75 or 3.0 in last 60 hours of undergraduate study; personal statement. Additional exam requirements/recommendations for international students: Required—TOEFL (minimum score 550 paper-based; 79 iBT), IELTS (minimum score 6). *Application deadline:* For fall admission, 7/1 for domestic and international students; for spring admission, 12/1 for domestic and international students. Applications are processed on a rolling basis. Application fee: $25 ($50 for international students). Electronic applications accepted. *Expenses:* Tuition, state resident: full-time $5166; part-time $1722 per semester. Tuition, nonresident: full-time $10,332; part-time $3444 per semester. *Required fees:* $393.50 per semester. *Financial support:* Applicants required to submit FAFSA. *Unit head:* Dr. Craig T. Robertson, Director, 256-765-5003, E-mail: ctrobertson@una.edu. *Application contact:* Hillary N. Coats, Graduate Admissions Coordinator, 256-765-4447, E-mail: graduate@una.edu.
Website: http://www.una.edu/masters-professional-studies/index.html

The University of North Carolina at Chapel Hill, Graduate School, College of Arts and Sciences, Department of City and Regional Planning, Chapel Hill, NC 27599-3140. Offers city and regional planning (MCRP); planning (PhD); public policy analysis (PhD); JD/MCRP; MBA/MCRP; MPA/MCRP. *Accreditation:* ACSP (one or more programs are accredited). *Degree requirements:* For master's, project; for doctorate, comprehensive exam, thesis/dissertation. *Entrance requirements:* For master's and doctorate, GRE General Test. Additional exam requirements/recommendations for international students: Required—TOEFL (minimum score 550 paper-based). Electronic applications accepted. *Faculty research:* Developing areas, transportation, affordable housing, growth management, coastal zone management.

The University of North Carolina at Charlotte, College of Liberal Arts and Sciences, Department of Political Science and Public Administration, Charlotte, NC 28223-0001. Offers emergency management (Graduate Certificate); non-profit management (Graduate Certificate); public administration (MPA), including arts administration, emergency management, non-profit management, public finance; public finance (Graduate Certificate); urban management and policy (Graduate Certificate). *Accreditation:* NASPAA. Part-time and evening/weekend programs available. *Faculty:* 15 full-time (8 women), 4 part-time/adjunct (1 woman). *Students:* 16 full-time (10 women), 83 part-time (51 women); includes 32 minority (21 Black or African American, non-Hispanic/Latino; 1 Asian, non-Hispanic/Latino; 7 Hispanic/Latino; 3 Two or more races, non-Hispanic/Latino). Average age 30. 60 applicants, 65% accepted, 25 enrolled. In 2014, 23 master's, 11 other advanced degrees awarded. Terminal master's awarded for partial completion of doctoral program. *Degree requirements:* For master's, thesis or alternative. *Entrance requirements:* For master's, GRE General Test or MAT, minimum GPA of 3.0 in undergraduate major, 2.75 overall. Additional exam requirements/recommendations for international students: Required—TOEFL (minimum score 557 paper-based; 83 iBT). *Application deadline:* For fall admission, 5/1 priority date for domestic students, 5/1 for international students; for spring admission, 10/1 priority date for domestic students, 10/1 for international students. Applications are processed on a rolling basis. Application fee: $75. Electronic applications accepted. *Expenses:* Tuition, state resident: full-time $4008. Tuition, nonresident: full-time $16,295. *Required fees:* $2755. Tuition and fees vary according to course load and program. *Financial support:* In 2014–15, 7 students received support, including 7 research assistantships (averaging $6,857 per year); career-related internships or fieldwork, Federal Work-Study, institutionally sponsored loans, scholarships/grants, and unspecified assistantships also available. Support available to part-time students. Financial award application deadline: 4/1; financial award applicants required to submit FAFSA. *Faculty research:* Health policy and politics, managed care, issues of ethnic and racial disparities in health, aging policies, Central Asia. *Total annual research expenditures:* $348,793. *Unit head:* Dr. Greg Weeks, Chair, 704-687-7574, Fax: 704-687-1400, E-mail: gbweeks@uncc.edu. *Application contact:* Kathy B. Giddings, Director of Graduate Admissions, 704-687-5503, Fax: 704-687-1668, E-mail: gradadm@uncc.edu.
Website: https://politicalscience.uncc.edu/graduate

University of Oklahoma, College of Architecture, Division of Regional and City Planning, Norman, OK 73019. Offers MRCP, MRCP/MLA. Part-time programs available. *Students:* 17 full-time (8 women), 8 part-time (5 women); includes 5 minority (2 Black or African American, non-Hispanic/Latino; 2 Hispanic/Latino; 1 Two or more races, non-Hispanic/Latino), 6 international. Average age 31. 22 applicants, 73% accepted, 7 enrolled. In 2014, 7 master's awarded. *Degree requirements:* For master's, comprehensive exam, thesis optional. *Entrance requirements:* Additional exam requirements/recommendations for international students: Required—TOEFL (minimum score 79 iBT). *Application deadline:* For fall admission, 4/1 for domestic and international students; for spring admission, 9/1 for domestic and international students. Applications are processed on a rolling basis. Application fee: $50 ($100 for international students). Electronic applications accepted. *Expenses:* Tuition, state resident: full-time $4394; part-time $183.10 per credit hour. Tuition, nonresident: full-time $16,970; part-time $707.10 per credit hour. *Required fees:* $2892; $109.95 per credit hour. $126.50 per semester. *Financial support:* In 2014–15, 18 students received support. Career-related internships or fieldwork, scholarships/grants, tuition waivers (full and partial), and unspecified assistantships available. Financial award application deadline: 6/1; financial award applicants required to submit FAFSA. *Faculty research:* Climate change, tribal planning, placemaking, active living, participatory planning methods. *Unit head:* Dr. Dawn Jourdan, Associate Professor and Director, 405-325-3502, Fax: 405-325-7558, E-mail: dawnjourdan@ou.edu. *Application contact:* K. Meghan Wieters, Graduate Liaison, 405-325-2444, Fax: 405-325-7558, E-mail: kmeghanwieters@ou.edu.
Website: http://rcpl.ou.edu

University of Oregon, Graduate School, School of Architecture and Allied Arts, Department of Planning, Public Policy, and Management, Program in Community and Regional Planning, Eugene, OR 97403. Offers MCRP. *Accreditation:* ACSP. Part-time programs available. *Degree requirements:* For master's, thesis or alternative. *Entrance requirements:* For master's, minimum GPA of 3.0. Additional exam requirements/recommendations for international students: Required—TOEFL. *Faculty research:* Community economic development, tourism, families in poverty.

University of Pennsylvania, School of Design, Department of City and Regional Planning, Philadelphia, PA 19104. Offers city and regional planning (PhD); city planning (MCP); GIS and spatial analysis (Certificate); land preservation (Certificate); urban design (Certificate); urban redevelopment (Certificate); urban spatial analytics (MUSA). *Accreditation:* ACSP (one or more programs are accredited). *Faculty:* 15 full-time (6 women), 6 part-time/adjunct (0 women). *Students:* 158 full-time (87 women), 9 part-time

(8 women); includes 32 minority (3 Black or African American, non-Hispanic/Latino; 15 Asian, non-Hispanic/Latino; 6 Hispanic/Latino; 1 Native Hawaiian or other Pacific Islander, non-Hispanic/Latino; 7 Two or more races, non-Hispanic/Latino), 62 international. 475 applicants, 46% accepted, 75 enrolled. In 2014, 89 master's, 3 other advanced degrees awarded. *Degree requirements:* For doctorate, thesis/dissertation, 20 approved courses, 4 seminars, 2 methods courses, writing and presentation/scholarly preparation, qualifying examination, final defense. *Entrance requirements:* For master's, GRE General Test; for doctorate, GRE General Test, writing sample. Additional exam requirements/recommendations for international students: Required—TOEFL, IELTS. *Application deadline:* For fall admission, 1/14 priority date for domestic and international students. Application fee: $80. Electronic applications accepted. *Financial support:* Fellowships, research assistantships, teaching assistantships, institutionally sponsored loans, scholarships/grants, and health care benefits available. Financial award application deadline: 2/15; financial award applicants required to submit FAFSA. *Faculty research:* Growth management, transportation planning, urban simulation modeling, housing, development planning. *Unit head:* Marilyn Jordan Taylor, Dean, 215-898-6520, E-mail: mjtaylor@design.upenn.edu. *Application contact:* Office of Admissions and Financial Aid, 215-898-6520, E-mail: admissions@design.upenn.edu.
Website: http://www.design.upenn.edu/city-regional-planning/graduate/work

University of Pittsburgh, Graduate School of Public and International Affairs, Master of International Development Program, Pittsburgh, PA 15260. Offers human security (MID); nongovernmental organizations and civil society (MID); urban affairs and planning (MID); MID/JD; MID/MBA; MID/MPH; MID/MPIA; MID/MSIS; MID/MSW; MPA/MID. Part-time and evening/weekend programs available. *Faculty:* 34 full-time (12 women), 11 part-time/adjunct (3 women). *Students:* 60 full-time (43 women), 3 part-time (1 woman); includes 16 minority (3 Black or African American, non-Hispanic/Latino; 10 Asian, non-Hispanic/Latino; 2 Hispanic/Latino; 1 Two or more races, non-Hispanic/Latino), 7 international. Average age 26. 94 applicants, 86% accepted, 26 enrolled. In 2014, 27 master's awarded. *Degree requirements:* For master's, thesis optional, internship, capstone seminar. *Entrance requirements:* For master's, GRE General Test or GMAT, 2 letters of recommendation; undergraduate transcripts; resume; personal statement. Additional exam requirements/recommendations for international students: Required—TOEFL (minimum score 550 paper-based; 80 iBT); Recommended—IELTS (minimum score 7), TWE (minimum score 4). *Application deadline:* For fall admission, 2/1 for domestic students, 1/15 for international students; for spring admission, 11/1 for domestic students, 8/1 for international students. Application fee: $50. Electronic applications accepted. *Expenses:* Tuition, state resident: full-time $20,742; part-time $838 per credit. Tuition, nonresident: full-time $33,960; part-time $1389 per credit. *Required fees:* $800; $205 per term. Tuition and fees vary according to program. *Financial support:* In 2014–15, 26 students received support, including 1 fellowship (averaging $18,000 per year); scholarships/grants, unspecified assistantships, and student employment also available. Financial award application deadline: 2/1. *Faculty research:* Nongovernmental organizations, religion and civil society, international development, development economics and policy, human rights and development, humanitarian intervention, ethnic conflict and civil war, post-conflict peace-building, corruption and transnational governance, civil society and public affairs, political constraints on rural development. *Total annual research expenditures:* $640,844. *Unit head:* Dr. Paul J. Nelson, Director, 412-648-7645, Fax: 412-648-2605, E-mail: pjnelson@pitt.edu. *Application contact:* Elizabeth A. Hruby, Graduate Enrollment Counselor, 412-648-7640, Fax: 412-648-7641, E-mail: eah44@pitt.edu.
Website: http://www.gspia.pitt.edu/

University of Pittsburgh, Graduate School of Public and International Affairs, Master of Public Administration Program, Pittsburgh, PA 15260. Offers energy and environment (MPA); governance and international public management (MPA); policy research and analysis (MPA); public and nonprofit management (MPA); urban affairs and planning (MPA); JD/MPA; MPA/MID; MPA/MPIA; MPH/MPA; MSIS/MPA; MSW/MPA. Part-time and evening/weekend programs available. *Faculty:* 32 full-time (12 women), 13 part-time/adjunct (5 women). *Students:* 99 full-time (69 women), 15 part-time (10 women); includes 8 minority (5 Black or African American, non-Hispanic/Latino; 1 Asian, non-Hispanic/Latino; 1 Hispanic/Latino; 1 Two or more races, non-Hispanic/Latino), 52 international. Average age 26. 273 applicants, 70% accepted, 51 enrolled. In 2014, 50 master's awarded. *Degree requirements:* For master's, thesis optional, internship, capstone seminar. *Entrance requirements:* For master's, GRE General Test or GMAT, 2 letters of recommendation, resume; undergraduate transcripts, personal statement. Additional exam requirements/recommendations for international students: Required—TOEFL (minimum score 550 paper-based; 80 iBT); Recommended—IELTS (minimum score 7), TWE (minimum score 4). *Application deadline:* For fall admission, 2/1 for domestic students, 1/15 for international students; for spring admission, 11/1 for domestic students, 8/1 for international students. Application fee: $50. Electronic applications accepted. *Expenses:* Tuition, state resident: full-time $20,742; part-time $838 per credit. Tuition, nonresident: full-time $33,960; part-time $1389 per credit. *Required fees:* $800; $205 per term. Tuition and fees vary according to program. *Financial support:* In 2014–15, 17 students received support, including 3 fellowships (averaging $13,980 per year); scholarships/grants, unspecified assistantships, and student employment also available. Financial award application deadline: 2/1. *Faculty research:* Urban management, regional development, disaster response management, public program evaluation, comparative regional governance, nonprofit management, health policy, environmental policy, strategic management, human resources management. *Total annual research expenditures:* $640,844. *Unit head:* Dr. David Y. Miller, Director, 412-648-7606, Fax: 412-648-2605, E-mail: dymiller@pitt.edu. *Application contact:* Elizabeth A. Hruby, Graduate Enrollment Counselor, 412-648-7640, Fax: 412-648-7641, E-mail: eah44@pitt.edu.
Website: http://www.gspia.pitt.edu/

University of Puerto Rico, Río Piedras Campus, Graduate School of Planning, San Juan, PR 00931-3300. Offers economic planning systems (MP); environmental planning (MP); social policy and planning (MP); urban and territorial planning (MP). *Accreditation:* ACSP. Part-time programs available. *Degree requirements:* For master's, comprehensive exam, thesis, planning project defense. *Entrance requirements:* For master's, PAEG, GRE, minimum GPA of 3.0, 2 letters of recommendation. *Faculty research:* Municipalities, historic Atlas, Puerto Rico, economic future.

University of Southern California, Graduate School, School of Policy, Planning, and Development, Doctor of Philosophy in Urban Planning and Development Program, Los Angeles, CA 90089. Offers PhD. *Degree requirements:* For doctorate, thesis/dissertation. *Entrance requirements:* For doctorate, GRE. Additional exam requirements/recommendations for international students: Required—TOEFL (minimum score 600 paper-based; 100 iBT). Electronic applications accepted. *Faculty research:* Transportation and infrastructure, healthy urban and place development, social economic development, sustainable community planning.

University of Southern California, Graduate School, School of Policy, Planning, and Development, Doctor of Policy, Planning, and Development Program, Los Angeles, CA 90089. Offers DPPD. *Accreditation:* ACSP. Part-time programs available. *Degree requirements:* For doctorate, project. *Entrance requirements:* Additional exam requirements/recommendations for international students: Required—TOEFL (minimum score 600 paper-based; 100 iBT). Electronic applications accepted. *Faculty research:* Governance: effective institutions, leadership, management, healthy urban and place development, sustainability, community, public policy and planning, societal problem solving and analysis.

University of Southern California, Graduate School, School of Policy, Planning, and Development, Master of Planning Program, Los Angeles, CA 90089. Offers sustainable cities (Graduate Certificate); transportation systems (Graduate Certificate); urban planning (M Pl); M Arch/M Pl; M Pl/MA; M Pl/MPP; M Pl/MRED; M Pl/MS; M Pl/MSW; MBA/M Pl; ML Arch/M Pl; MPA/M Pl. *Accreditation:* ACSP. Part-time programs available. *Degree requirements:* For master's, comprehensive exam, internship. *Entrance requirements:* For master's, GRE, GMAT. Additional exam requirements/recommendations for international students: Required—TOEFL (minimum score 600 paper-based; 100 iBT). Electronic applications accepted. *Faculty research:* Transportation and infrastructure, comparative international development, healthy communities, social economic development, sustainable community planning.

University of Southern Maine, College of Management and Human Service, Muskie School of Public Service, Program in Community Planning and Development, Portland, ME 04104-9300. Offers MCPD, CGS, JD/MCPD. *Accreditation:* ACSP. Part-time and evening/weekend programs available. *Faculty:* 2 full-time (0 women), 1 part-time/adjunct (0 women). *Students:* 14 full-time (7 women), 7 part-time (4 women); includes 1 minority (Asian, non-Hispanic/Latino). Average age 33. 15 applicants, 80% accepted, 6 enrolled. In 2014, 11 master's awarded. *Degree requirements:* For master's, thesis, capstone project, field experience. *Entrance requirements:* For master's, GRE General Test or LSAT. Additional exam requirements/recommendations for international students: Required—TOEFL. *Application deadline:* For fall admission, 2/1 priority date for domestic and international students; for spring admission, 12/1 for domestic and international students. Applications are processed on a rolling basis. Application fee: $65. Electronic applications accepted. *Expenses: Tuition, area resident:* Full-time $6840; part-time $380 per credit hour. Tuition, state resident: full-time $10,260; part-time $570 per credit hour. Tuition, nonresident: full-time $18,468; part-time $1026 per credit hour. *Required fees:* $830; $83 per credit hour. Tuition and fees vary according to course load and program. *Financial support:* Fellowships, research assistantships, career-related internships or fieldwork, Federal Work-Study, scholarships/grants, tuition waivers (partial), and unspecified assistantships available. Financial award application deadline: 4/1; financial award applicants required to submit FAFSA. *Faculty research:* Urban and regional growth and change, sustainability, responses to climate and environmental risks, food systems planning and policy, transportation, energy, landscape modeling and simulation. *Unit head:* Dr. Charles Colgan, Chair, 207-780-4008, E-mail: csc@usm.maine.edu. *Application contact:* Mary Sloan, Assistant Dean of Graduate Studies and Director of Graduate Admissions, 207-780-4812, E-mail: gradstudies@usm.maine.edu.

University of South Florida, College of Arts and Sciences, Department of Geography, Tampa, FL 33620-9951. Offers environmental geography (MA); environmental science and policy (MS); geographic information science and spatial analysis (MA); geography and environmental science and policy (PhD); human geography (MA); urban and regional planning (MURP). Part-time and evening/weekend programs available. *Students:* 15 full-time (9 women), 12 part-time (4 women); includes 11 minority (4 Black or African American, non-Hispanic/Latino; 5 Hispanic/Latino; 2 Two or more races, non-Hispanic/Latino), 2 international. Average age 32. 39 applicants, 62% accepted, 9 enrolled. In 2014, 10 master's awarded. *Degree requirements:* For master's, comprehensive exam, thesis (for some programs); for doctorate, comprehensive exam, thesis/dissertation. *Entrance requirements:* For master's, GRE General Test (within the last 5 years), minimum GPA of 3.0 for last 60 credits of undergraduate degree, letter of intent, two letters of recommendation (three for MS); for doctorate, GRE General Test (within the last 5 years), minimum GPA of 3.2 for all academic work prior to admission, letter of intent, two letters of recommendation. Additional exam requirements/recommendations for international students: Required—TOEFL (minimum score 550 paper-based; 79 iBT) or IELTS (minimum score 6.5) for MA and MURP; TOEFL (minimum score 600 paper-based) for MS and PhD. *Application deadline:* For fall admission, 2/15 for domestic students, 1/2 for international students; for spring admission, 10/15 for domestic students, 6/1 for international students. Application fee: $30. *Financial support:* In 2014–15, 28 students received support, including 3 research assistantships (averaging $12,345 per year), 25 teaching assistantships with tuition reimbursements available (averaging $12,807 per year); unspecified assistantships also available. Financial award application deadline: 3/1. *Faculty research:* Geography: human geography, environmental geography, geographic information science and spatial analysis, urban geography, social theory; environmental science, policy, and planning: water resources, wildlife ecology, Karst and wetland environments, natural hazards, soil contamination, meteorology and climatology, environmental sustainability and policy, urban and regional planning. *Total annual research expenditures:* $89,465. *Unit head:* Dr. Jayajit Chakraborty, Professor and Chair, Geography Division, 813-974-8188, Fax: 813-974-5911, E-mail: jchakrab@usf.edu. *Application contact:* Dr. Jennifer Collins, Associate Professor and Graduate Program Coordinator, 813-974-4242, Fax: 813-974-5911, E-mail: collinsjm@usf.edu.
Website: http://gep.usf.edu/

University of South Florida, Innovative Education, Tampa, FL 33620-9951. *Unit head:* Kathy Barnes, Interdisciplinary Programs Coordinator, 813-974-8031, Fax: 813-974-7061, E-mail: barnesk@usf.edu. *Application contact:* Karen Tylinski, Metro Initiatives, 813-974-9943, Fax: 813-974-7061, E-mail: ktylinsk@usf.edu.
Website: http://www.usf.edu/innovative-education/

The University of Texas at Arlington, Graduate School, School of Urban and Public Affairs, Program in City and Regional Planning, Arlington, TX 76019. Offers MCRP. *Accreditation:* ACSP. Part-time and evening/weekend programs available. *Degree requirements:* For master's, comprehensive exam (for some programs), thesis or alternative. *Entrance requirements:* For master's, GRE General Test, three letters of recommendation, essay (approximately 250 words), minimum GPA of 3.0. Additional exam requirements/recommendations for international students: Required—TOEFL (minimum score 550 paper-based). Electronic applications accepted. *Faculty research:* Urban structure, GIS environmental resolutions, qualitative methods, planning history/theory.

The University of Texas at Arlington, Graduate School, School of Urban and Public Affairs, Program in Public and Urban Administration, Arlington, TX 76019. Offers MA. Part-time and evening/weekend programs available. *Degree requirements:* For master's, thesis or alternative. *Entrance requirements:* For master's, GRE General Test, 3 letters of recommendation, 250-word essay. Additional exam requirements/recommendations for international students: Required—TOEFL (minimum score 550 paper-based). *Faculty research:* Personnel, non-profit organizational change, welfare policy, urban research.

The University of Texas at Arlington, Graduate School, School of Urban and Public Affairs, Program in Urban Planning and Public Policy, Arlington, TX 76019. Offers PhD. Part-time and evening/weekend programs available. *Degree requirements:* For doctorate, comprehensive exam, thesis/dissertation. *Entrance requirements:* For doctorate, GRE General Test, 3 letters of recommendation, 250-word essay. Electronic

applications accepted. *Faculty research:* Environment urban policy personnel, research theoretical foundations, urban problems.

The University of Texas at Austin, Graduate School, School of Architecture, Program in Community and Regional Planning, Austin, TX 78712-1111. Offers MSCRP, PhD, JD/MSCRP, MSCRP/MA. *Accreditation:* ACSP. *Degree requirements:* For master's, thesis; for doctorate, thesis/dissertation. *Entrance requirements:* For master's and doctorate, GRE General Test. Electronic applications accepted.

The University of Texas at San Antonio, College of Architecture, Program in Urban and Regional Planning, San Antonio, TX 78249-0617. Offers MS. Part-time programs available. *Students:* 22 full-time (14 women), 18 part-time (9 women); includes 20 minority (2 Black or African American, non-Hispanic/Latino; 17 Hispanic/Latino; 1 Two or more races, non-Hispanic/Latino), 3 international. Average age 31. 10 applicants, 70% accepted, 6 enrolled. In 2014, 6 master's awarded. *Entrance requirements:* For master's, GRE, transcripts, two letters of recommendation, letter of intent. Additional exam requirements/recommendations for international students: Required—TOEFL (minimum score 550 paper-based; 79 iBT), IELTS (minimum score 6.5). Application fee: $45 ($80 for international students). *Expenses:* Tuition, state resident: full-time $4671; part-time $260 per credit hour. Tuition, nonresident: full-time $18,022; part-time $1001 per credit hour. *Unit head:* Dr. Richard Tangum, Program Coordinator, Department of Architecture, 210-458-2559, Fax: 210-458-3016, E-mail: richard.tangum@utsa.edu. *Application contact:* Dr. Hazem Rashed-Ali, Associate Dean, College of Architecture, 210-458-3088, Fax: 210-458-3088, E-mail: hazem.rashedali@utsa.edu.
Website: http://architecture.utsa.edu/academic-programs/urban-and-regional-planning/

The University of Toledo, College of Graduate Studies, College of Languages, Literature and Social Sciences, Department of Geography and Planning, Toledo, OH 43606-3390. Offers geographic information science and applied geographics (Certificate); geography and planning (MA); spatially-integrated social science (PhD). Part-time programs available. *Degree requirements:* For master's, comprehensive exam, thesis; for doctorate, thesis/dissertation. *Entrance requirements:* For master's and doctorate, GRE General Test, minimum cumulative point-hour ratio of 2.7 for all previous academic work, three letters of recommendation; for Certificate, minimum cumulative point-hour ratio of 2.7 for all previous academic work, three letters of recommendation. Additional exam requirements/recommendations for international students: Required—TOEFL (minimum score 550 paper-based; 80 iBT). Electronic applications accepted.

University of Toronto, School of Graduate Studies, Faculty of Arts and Science, Department of Geography, Program in Planning, Toronto, ON M5S 2J7, Canada. Offers M Sc Pl, MUDS, PhD. Part-time programs available. *Degree requirements:* For master's, summer internship. *Entrance requirements:* For master's, bachelor's degree in planning, geography, social science or a closely related professional field, minimum B+ average in final year, 3 letters of reference; for doctorate, minimum A- or equivalent standing in previous master's program. Additional exam requirements/recommendations for international students: Required—TOEFL (minimum score 580 paper-based; 93 iBT), TWE (minimum score 5). Electronic applications accepted. *Expenses:* Contact institution.

University of Utah, Graduate School, College of Architecture and Planning, Department of City and Metropolitan Planning, Salt Lake City, UT 84112. Offers city and metropolitan planning (MCMP); metropolitan planning, policy and design (PhD). Part-time programs available. *Faculty:* 6 full-time (2 women), 8 part-time/adjunct (3 women). *Students:* 46 full-time (18 women), 13 part-time (3 women); includes 5 minority (2 Black or African American, non-Hispanic/Latino; 2 Hispanic/Latino; 1 Two or more races, non-Hispanic/Latino), 11 international. Average age 33. 62 applicants, 69% accepted, 21 enrolled. In 2014, 17 master's awarded. *Degree requirements:* For master's, thesis or alternative, comprehensive project; for doctorate, thesis/dissertation. *Entrance requirements:* For master's, GRE, minimum undergraduate GPA of 3.0; for doctorate, GRE, minimum GPA of 3.5. Additional exam requirements/recommendations for international students: Required—TOEFL (minimum score 500 paper-based; 61 iBT); Recommended—IELTS (minimum score 6). *Application deadline:* For fall admission, 1/15 priority date for domestic and international students; for spring admission, 11/1 for domestic and international students. Applications are processed on a rolling basis. Application fee: $55 ($65 for international students). Electronic applications accepted. *Expenses:* Expenses: Contact institution. *Financial support:* In 2014–15, 25 students received support, including 1 fellowship with full tuition reimbursement available (averaging $25,000 per year), 3 research assistantships with full and partial tuition reimbursements available (averaging $16,000 per year), 21 teaching assistantships with full and partial tuition reimbursements available (averaging $10,006 per year); career-related internships or fieldwork, Federal Work-Study, scholarships/grants, health care benefits, and unspecified assistantships also available. Financial award application deadline: 1/15; financial award applicants required to submit FAFSA. *Faculty research:* Transportation, land use, smart growth, public health, climate change, urban design, sustainable communities, community-based decision-making process, urban morphology, theory and practice in scenario-planning techniques, community-engaged teaching methodologies, interactions between federal environmental policies and state/local community development patterns, values in architecture and planning practices. *Total annual research expenditures:* $847,693. *Unit head:* Keith Bartholomew, Chair, 801-585-9354, E-mail: bartholomew@arch.utah.edu. *Application contact:* Saolo Betham, Recruitment & Admissions Advisor, 801-581-2361, Fax: 801-581-8217, E-mail: recruitment@arch.utah.edu.
Website: http://www.plan.utah.edu/

University of Virginia, School of Architecture, Department of Urban and Environmental Planning, Charlottesville, VA 22903. Offers MUEP, JD/MUEP, MPP/MUEP. *Accreditation:* ACSP (one or more programs are accredited). *Faculty:* 7 full-time (4 women). *Students:* 52 full-time (28 women); includes 6 minority (4 Black or African American, non-Hispanic/Latino; 2 Hispanic/Latino), 12 international. Average age 24. 115 applicants, 65% accepted, 31 enrolled. In 2014, 24 master's awarded. *Entrance requirements:* For master's, GRE General Test, previous course work in statistics, 3 letters of recommendation. Additional exam requirements/recommendations for international students: Required—TOEFL (minimum score 600 paper-based; 90 iBT). *Application deadline:* For fall admission, 1/15 for domestic students, 1/16 for international students. Applications are processed on a rolling basis. Application fee: $60. Electronic applications accepted. *Expenses:* Tuition, state resident: full-time $14,164; part-time $349 per credit hour. Tuition, nonresident: full-time $23,722; part-time $1300 per credit hour. *Required fees:* $2514. *Financial support:* Applicants required to submit FAFSA. *Faculty research:* Urban development, land use, environment, policy analysis, historic preservation. *Unit head:* Timothy Beatley, Chair, 434-924-6457, Fax: 434-982-2678, E-mail: tb6d@virginia.edu. *Application contact:* Kristine Nelson, Director of Admissions and Financial Aid, 434-924-6442, Fax: 434-982-2678, E-mail: arch-admissions@virginia.edu.
Website: http://www.arch.virginia.edu/academics/disciplines/planning

University of Washington, Graduate School, College of Built Environments, Department of Urban Design and Planning, Seattle, WA 98195. Offers urban design and planning (PhD); urban planning (MUP). *Accreditation:* ACSP (one or more programs are accredited). *Degree requirements:* For master's, thesis or alternative; for doctorate, thesis/dissertation. *Entrance requirements:* For master's and doctorate, GRE General Test, minimum GPA of 3.0. Additional exam requirements/recommendations for international students: Required—TOEFL. *Faculty research:* Land-use and growth management, urban form and travel behavior, geographic information systems/remote sensing, historic preservation, urban ecology and environmental planning.

University of Waterloo, Graduate Studies, Faculty of Environment, Program in Local Economic Development, Waterloo, ON N2L 3G1, Canada. Offers MAES. Part-time programs available. *Degree requirements:* For master's, internship, research paper. Electronic applications accepted.

University of Waterloo, Graduate Studies, Faculty of Environment, School of Planning, Waterloo, ON N2L 3G1, Canada. Offers MA, MAES, MES, PhD. Part-time programs available. *Degree requirements:* For master's, thesis (for some programs); for doctorate, comprehensive exam, thesis/dissertation. *Entrance requirements:* For master's, honors degree, minimum B+ average; for doctorate, master's degree, minimum A- average, resume. Additional exam requirements/recommendations for international students: Required—TOEFL, TWE. Electronic applications accepted. *Faculty research:* Environmental planning, planning for resource development, urban planning and information systems, social planning, urban design.

University of Wisconsin–Madison, Graduate School, College of Letters and Science and College of Agricultural and Life Sciences, Department of Urban and Regional Planning, Madison, WI 53706-1380. Offers MS, PhD. *Accreditation:* ACSP (one or more programs are accredited). Part-time programs available. *Degree requirements:* For master's, thesis optional, internship; for doctorate, thesis/dissertation, 3 preliminary exams. *Entrance requirements:* For master's, GRE, minimum GPA of 3.0, previous course work in statistics; for doctorate, 1 year of experience, master's degree in related field. Electronic applications accepted. *Expenses:* Tuition, state resident: full-time $10,723; part-time $745 per credit. Tuition, nonresident: full-time $24,054; part-time $1578 per credit. *Required fees:* $374 per semester. Tuition and fees vary according to course load, program and reciprocity agreements. *Faculty research:* Land use, environmental planning, community development, economic development planning.

University of Wisconsin–Milwaukee, Graduate School, School of Architecture and Urban Planning, Department of Urban Planning, Milwaukee, WI 53201-0413. Offers geographic information systems (Certificate); real estate development (Certificate); urban planning (MUP); M Arch/MUP; MPA/MUP; MUP/MS. *Accreditation:* ACSP. Part-time programs available. *Degree requirements:* For master's, comprehensive exam, thesis or alternative. *Entrance requirements:* For master's, GRE General Test. Additional exam requirements/recommendations for international students: Required—TOEFL (minimum score 550 paper-based; 79 iBT), IELTS (minimum score 6.5). Electronic applications accepted.

Utah State University, School of Graduate Studies, College of Humanities, Arts and Social Sciences, Department of Landscape Architecture and Environmental Planning, Logan, UT 84322. Offers bioregional planning (MS); landscape architecture (MLA). *Accreditation:* ASLA (one or more programs are accredited). *Degree requirements:* For master's, thesis. *Entrance requirements:* For master's, GRE General Test, minimum GPA of 3.0. Additional exam requirements/recommendations for international students: Required—TOEFL. *Faculty research:* Visual resource management, planning for wildlife, agricultural land preservation, watershed planning, community planning and design.

Utah State University, School of Graduate Studies, College of Natural Resources, Department of Environment and Society, Logan, UT 84322. Offers bioregional planning (MS); geography (MA, MS); human dimensions of ecosystem science and management (MS, PhD); recreation resource management (MS, PhD). *Degree requirements:* For master's, comprehensive exam, thesis (for some programs). *Entrance requirements:* For master's and doctorate, GRE General Test, minimum GPA of 3.0. Additional exam requirements/recommendations for international students: Required—TOEFL. Electronic applications accepted. *Faculty research:* Geographic information systems/geographic and environmental education, bioregional planning, natural resource and environmental policy, outdoor recreation and tourism, natural resource and environmental management.

Vanderbilt University, Peabody College, Department of Human and Organizational Development, Nashville, TN 37240-1001. Offers community development and action (M Ed); human development counseling (M Ed). *Accreditation:* ACA; NCATE. Part-time programs available. *Degree requirements:* For master's, comprehensive exam, thesis optional. *Entrance requirements:* For master's, GRE General Test, MAT. Additional exam requirements/recommendations for international students: Required—TOEFL (minimum score 550 paper-based; 80 iBT). Electronic applications accepted. *Expenses:* *Tuition:* Full-time $42,768; part-time $1782 per credit hour. *Required fees:* $422. One-time fee: $30 full-time. *Faculty research:* Community psychology and community development; counseling and mental health services, prevention and positive youth development; organizational and community change; youth physical and behavioral health in schools and communities.

Virginia Commonwealth University, Graduate School, College of Humanities and Sciences, Wilder School of Government and Public Affairs, Department of Urban Studies and Planning, Program in Urban and Regional Planning, Richmond, VA 23284-9005. Offers urban and regional planning (MURP); urban revitalization (Certificate); JD/MURP. *Degree requirements:* For master's, thesis optional, internship. *Entrance requirements:* For master's, GRE General Test, GMAT, or LSAT, minimum GPA of 2.7. Additional exam requirements/recommendations for international students: Required—TOEFL (minimum score 600 paper-based; 100 iBT); Recommended—IELTS (minimum score 6.5). Electronic applications accepted.

Virginia Polytechnic Institute and State University, Graduate School, College of Architecture and Urban Studies, Blacksburg, VA 24061. Offers architecture (MS Arch); architecture and design research (PhD); building/construction science and management (MS); creative technologies (MFA); environmental design and planning (PhD); landscape architecture (MLA); planning, governance, and globalization (PhD); public administration (MPA); public administration/public affairs (PhD, Certificate); public and international affairs (MPIA); urban and regional planning (MURP); MS/MA. *Accreditation:* ASLA (one or more programs are accredited). *Faculty:* 133 full-time (54 women), 2 part-time/adjunct (1 woman). *Students:* 316 full-time (166 women), 237 part-time (108 women); includes 104 minority (46 Black or African American, non-Hispanic/Latino; 1 American Indian or Alaska Native, non-Hispanic/Latino; 20 Asian, non-Hispanic/Latino; 21 Hispanic/Latino; 16 Two or more races, non-Hispanic/Latino), 108 international. Average age 32. 609 applicants, 50% accepted, 108 enrolled. In 2014, 155 master's, 29 doctorates awarded. *Degree requirements:* For master's, comprehensive exam (for some programs), thesis (for some programs); for doctorate, comprehensive exam (for some programs), thesis/dissertation (for some programs). *Entrance requirements:* For master's and doctorate, GRE/GMAT (may vary by department). Additional exam requirements/recommendations for international students: Required—TOEFL (minimum score 550 paper-based). *Application deadline:* For fall admission, 8/1 for domestic students, 4/1 for international students; for spring admission, 1/1 for domestic students, 9/1 for international students. Applications are processed on a rolling basis. Application fee: $75. Electronic applications accepted. *Expenses:* Tuition, state

resident: full-time $11,656; part-time $647.50 per credit hour. Tuition, nonresident: full-time $23,351; part-time $1297.25 per credit hour. *Required fees:* $2533; $465.75 per semester. Tuition and fees vary according to course load, campus/location and program. *Financial support:* In 2014–15, 13 research assistantships with full tuition reimbursements (averaging $20,302 per year), 44 teaching assistantships with full tuition reimbursements (averaging $19,484 per year) were awarded. Financial award application deadline: 3/1; financial award applicants required to submit FAFSA. *Total annual research expenditures:* $3.2 million. *Unit head:* Dr. A. J. Davis, Dean, 540-231-6416, Fax: 540-231-6332, E-mail: davisa@vt.edu. *Application contact:* Christine Mattsson-Coon, Executive Assistant, 540-231-6416, Fax: 540-231-6332, E-mail: cmattsso@vt.edu.
Website: http://www.caus.vt.edu/

Wayne State University, College of Liberal Arts and Sciences, Department of Urban Studies and Planning, Detroit, MI 48202. Offers economic development (Graduate Certificate); urban studies and planning (MUP). *Accreditation:* ACSP. Evening/weekend programs available. *Students:* 16 full-time (6 women), 43 part-time (22 women); includes 23 minority (19 Black or African American, non-Hispanic/Latino; 1 Asian, non-Hispanic/Latino; 2 Hispanic/Latino; 1 Two or more races, non-Hispanic/Latino), 6 international. Average age 29. 74 applicants, 38% accepted, 19 enrolled. In 2014, 21 master's awarded. *Degree requirements:* For master's, thesis or essay. *Entrance requirements:* For degree, graduate degree or actively pursuing a graduate degree at WSU; personal statement of interest. Additional exam requirements/recommendations for international students: Required—TOEFL (minimum score 550 paper-based; 79 iBT), TWE (minimum score 5.5), Michigan English Language Assessment Battery (minimum score 85); Recommended—IELTS (minimum score 6.5). *Application deadline:* For fall admission, 6/1 priority date for domestic students, 5/1 priority date for international students; for winter admission, 10/1 priority date for domestic students, 9/1 priority date for international students; for spring admission, 2/1 priority date for domestic students, 1/1 priority date for international students. Applications are processed on a rolling basis. Application fee: $0. Electronic applications accepted. *Expenses:* Tuition, state resident: full-time $10,294; part-time $571.90 per credit hour. Tuition, nonresident: full-time $29,730; part-time $1238.75 per credit hour. *Required fees:* $1365; $43.50 per credit hour. $291.10 per semester. Tuition and fees vary according to course load and program. *Financial support:* In 2014–15, 11 students received support, including 1 research assistantship (averaging $16,508 per year); scholarships/grants and unspecified assistantships also available. Financial award application deadline: 3/31; financial award applicants required to submit FAFSA. *Unit head:* Dr. Kami Pothukuchi, Interim Chair, 313-577-4296, E-mail: k.pothukuchi@wayne.edu. *Application contact:* Dr. Robin Boyle, 313-577-2701, E-mail: dusp@wayne.edu.
Website: http://clas.wayne.edu/dusp/

West Chester University of Pennsylvania, College of Business and Public Affairs, Department of Geography and Planning, West Chester, PA 19383. Offers geographic information systems (Certificate); geography (MA); urban and regional planning (MPA, Certificate). Part-time and evening/weekend programs available. Postbaccalaureate distance learning degree programs offered (no on-campus study). *Faculty:* 6 full-time (3 women). *Students:* 16 full-time (3 women), 9 part-time (5 women); includes 1 minority (Black or African American, non-Hispanic/Latino), 1 international. Average age 29. 18 applicants, 100% accepted, 10 enrolled. In 2014, 12 master's, 21 other advanced degrees awarded. *Degree requirements:* For master's, thesis optional, 33 credits or 11 courses: 5-6 required, 5-6 electives, thesis or independent research course; for Certificate, 18 credits or 6 courses. *Entrance requirements:* For master's and Certificate, minimum GPA of 2.8, resume, two letters of recommendation. Additional exam requirements/recommendations for international students: Required—TOEFL (minimum score 550 paper-based; 80 iBT). *Application deadline:* For fall admission, 4/15 priority date for domestic students, 3/15 for international students; for spring admission, 10/15 priority date for domestic students, 9/1 for international students. Applications are processed on a rolling basis. Application fee: $45. Electronic applications accepted. *Expenses:* Tuition, state resident: full-time $8172; part-time $454 per credit. Tuition, nonresident: full-time $12,258; part-time $681 per credit. *Required fees:* $2231; $110.78 per credit. Tuition and fees vary according to campus/location and program. *Financial support:* Unspecified assistantships available. Support available to part-time students. Financial award application deadline: 2/15; financial award applicants required to submit FAFSA. *Faculty research:* Sustainability and environmental conservation, land use/suburban planning, geographic information systems, transportation planning, housing. *Unit head:* Dr. Dottie Ives Dewey, Chair/Graduate Coordinator for GIS Certificate Program, 610-436-2746, Fax: 610-436-2889, E-mail: divesdewey@wcupa.edu. *Application contact:* Dr. Matin Katirai, Graduate Coordinator, 610-436-2392, Fax: 610-436-2889, E-mail: mkatirai@wcupa.edu.
Website: http://www.wcupa.edu/_academics/sch_sba.geo/default.asp

West Virginia University, Davis College of Agriculture, Forestry and Consumer Sciences, Division of Resource Management and Sustainable Development, Morgantown, WV 26506. Offers agricultural and extension education (MS, PhD), including agricultural and extension education, teaching vocational-agriculture (MS); agricultural and resource economics (MS); human and community development (PhD); natural resource economics (PhD); resource management (PhD); resource management and sustainable development (PhD). Part-time programs available. *Degree requirements:* For master's, thesis; for doctorate, comprehensive exam, thesis/dissertation. *Entrance requirements:* For master's, GRE General Test. Additional exam requirements/recommendations for international students: Required—TOEFL. *Faculty research:* Environmental economics, energy economics, agriculture.

West Virginia University, Eberly College of Arts and Sciences, Department of Geology and Geography, Program in Geography, Morgantown, WV 26506. Offers energy and environmental resources (MA); geographic information systems (PhD); geography-regional development (PhD); GIS/cartographic analysis (MA); regional development (MA). Part-time programs available. *Degree requirements:* For master's, thesis, oral and written exams; for doctorate, comprehensive exam, thesis/dissertation, oral and written exams. *Entrance requirements:* For master's and doctorate, GRE General Test, minimum GPA of 3.0. Additional exam requirements/recommendations for international students: Required—TOEFL. Electronic applications accepted. *Faculty research:* Space, place and development, geographic information science, environmental geography.

Urban Studies

Arizona State University at the Tempe campus, College of Liberal Arts and Sciences, School of Human Evolution and Social Change, Tempe, AZ 85287-2402. Offers anthropology (MA, PhD), including anthropology (PhD), archaeology (PhD), bioarchaeology (PhD), evolutionary (PhD), museum studies (MA), sociocultural (PhD); applied mathematics for the life and social sciences (PhD); environmental social science (PhD), including environmental social science, urbanism; global health (MA, PhD), including complex adaptive systems science (PhD), evolutionary global health sciences (PhD), health and culture (PhD), urbanism (PhD); immigration studies (Graduate Certificate). Terminal master's awarded for partial completion of doctoral program. *Degree requirements:* For master's, thesis or alternative, interactive Program of Study (iPOS) submitted before completing 50 percent of required credit hours; for doctorate, comprehensive exam, thesis/dissertation, interactive Program of Study (iPOS) submitted before completing 50 percent of required credit hours. *Entrance requirements:* For master's and doctorate, GRE, minimum GPA of 3.0 or equivalent in last 2 years of work leading to bachelor's degree. Additional exam requirements/recommendations for international students: Required—TOEFL, IELTS, or PTE. Electronic applications accepted.

Azusa Pacific University, Haggard Graduate School of Theology, Program in Pastoral Studies, Concentration in Urban Studies, Azusa, CA 91702-7000. Offers MAPS.

Boston University, Metropolitan College, Program in Urban Affairs, Boston, MA 02215. Offers MUA. Part-time and evening/weekend programs available. *Faculty:* 2 full-time (1 woman), 6 part-time/adjunct (2 women). *Students:* 1 full-time (0 women), 10 part-time (3 women); includes 4 minority (3 Black or African American, non-Hispanic/Latino; 1 Hispanic/Latino), 3 international. Average age 35. 9 applicants, 89% accepted, 5 enrolled. In 2014, 14 master's awarded. *Degree requirements:* For master's, thesis optional. *Entrance requirements:* Additional exam requirements/recommendations for international students: Required—TOEFL. *Application deadline:* For fall admission, 7/15 priority date for domestic and international students; for spring admission, 12/15 for domestic students, 11/15 priority date for international students. Applications are processed on a rolling basis. Application fee: $80. Electronic applications accepted. *Expenses:* Expenses: $800 per credit part-time; student services fees: $60 per semester; technology fee of $60 per credit (for online courses). *Financial support:* In 2014–15, 4 research assistantships (averaging $4,200 per year) were awarded; career-related internships or fieldwork, Federal Work-Study, and unspecified assistantships also available. Support available to part-time students. Financial award application deadline: 6/15; financial award applicants required to submit FAFSA. *Faculty research:* Housing, community development and land use planning, environmental management and planning, international comparative development planning, sustainability. *Unit head:* Dr. Daniel P. LeClair, Chair, 617-353-3025, Fax: 617-358-3595, E-mail: dleclair@bu.edu. *Application contact:* Dr. Madhu Dutta-Koehler, 617-358-2364, E-mail: duttam@bu.edu.

Brooklyn College of the City University of New York, School of Humanities and Social Sciences, Department of Political Science, Brooklyn, NY 11210-2889. Offers international affairs (MA); political science (MA); urban policy and administration (MA). Part-time and evening/weekend programs available. *Degree requirements:* For master's, comprehensive exam (for some programs), thesis or alternative, foreign language exam (for international affairs program). *Entrance requirements:* For master's, 2 letters of recommendation, personal statement. Additional exam requirements/recommendations for international students: Required—TOEFL (minimum score 500 paper-based; 61 iBT). *Faculty research:* Ethics and politics, politics of criminal justice, Western Europe, international law and politics, labor politics.

Cleveland State University, College of Graduate Studies, Maxine Goodman Levin College of Urban Affairs, Program in Urban Studies, Cleveland, OH 44115. Offers community and neighborhood development (MS); economic development (MS); law and public policy (MS); public finance (MS); urban economic development (Certificate); urban policy analysis (MS); urban real estate development (MS); urban real estate development and finance (Certificate). Part-time and evening/weekend programs available. *Faculty:* 23 full-time (11 women), 23 part-time/adjunct (6 women). *Students:* 5 full-time (1 woman), 8 part-time (2 women); includes 1 minority (Black or African American, non-Hispanic/Latino). Average age 34. 21 applicants, 29% accepted, 4 enrolled. In 2014, 4 master's awarded. *Degree requirements:* For master's, thesis or alternative, exit project. *Entrance requirements:* For master's, GRE General Test (minimum score: verbal and quantitative combined 40th percentile, analytical writing 4.0), minimum GPA of 3.0. Additional exam requirements/recommendations for international students: Required—TOEFL (minimum score 525 paper-based; 65 iBT), IELTS, or ITEP. *Application deadline:* For fall admission, 1/15 priority date for domestic students, 1/15 for international students. Applications are processed on a rolling basis. Application fee: $30. Electronic applications accepted. *Expenses:* Expenses: $9,615 full-time, in-state tuition and fees. *Financial support:* In 2014–15, 4 students received support, including 3 research assistantships with full and partial tuition reimbursements available (averaging $7,200 per year), 2 teaching assistantships with full and partial tuition reimbursements available (averaging $4,800 per year); career-related internships or fieldwork, scholarships/grants, traineeships, and unspecified assistantships also available. Support available to part-time students. Financial award application deadline: 3/1; financial award applicants required to submit FAFSA. *Faculty research:* Environmental issues, economic development, urban and public policy, public management. *Unit head:* Dr. Brian Mikelbank, Director, 216-875-9980, Fax: 216-687-9342, E-mail: b.mikelbank@csuohio.edu. *Application contact:* David Arrighi, Graduate Academic Advisor, 216-523-7522, Fax: 216-687-5398, E-mail: urbanprograms@csuohio.edu.
Website: http://urban.csuohio.edu/academics/graduate/msus/

Cleveland State University, College of Graduate Studies, Maxine Goodman Levin College of Urban Affairs, Program in Urban Studies and Public Affairs, Cleveland, OH 44115. Offers communication (PhD); public administration (PhD); urban policy and development (PhD). Part-time and evening/weekend programs available. *Faculty:* 23 full-time (11 women), 23 part-time/adjunct (6 women). *Students:* 10 full-time (6 women), 26 part-time (13 women); includes 5 minority (4 Black or African American, non-Hispanic/Latino; 1 Asian, non-Hispanic/Latino), 10 international. Average age 40. 32 applicants, 34% accepted, 2 enrolled. In 2014, 3 doctorates awarded. *Degree requirements:* For doctorate, comprehensive exam, thesis/dissertation. *Entrance requirements:* For doctorate, GRE General Test (minimum score: verbal and quantitative 50th percentile, analytical writing 4.0), minimum GPA of 3.5. Additional exam requirements/recommendations for international students: Required—TOEFL (minimum score 525 paper-based; 65 iBT), IELTS, or ITEP. *Application deadline:* For fall

admission, 1/31 for domestic and international students. Application fee: $30. Electronic applications accepted. *Expenses:* Expenses: $9,615 full-time, in-state tuition and fees. *Financial support:* In 2014–15, 15 students received support, including 7 research assistantships with full and partial tuition reimbursements available (averaging $9,200 per year), 3 teaching assistantships with full and partial tuition reimbursements available (averaging $8,600 per year); scholarships/grants and unspecified assistantships also available. Support available to part-time students. Financial award application deadline: 3/1; financial award applicants required to submit FAFSA. *Faculty research:* Urban and public policy, public affairs. *Unit head:* Dr. Wendy Kellogg, Director, 216-687-5265, E-mail: w.kellogg@csuohio.edu. *Application contact:* David Arrighi, Graduate Academic Advisor, 216-523-7522, Fax: 216-687-5398, E-mail: urbanprograms@csuohio.edu. Website: http://urban.csuohio.edu/academics/graduate/phd/

Concordia University, School of Graduate Studies, Faculty of Arts and Science, Department of Geography, Planning and Environment, Montréal, QC H3G 1M8, Canada. Offers environmental impact assessment (Diploma); geography, urban and environmental studies (M Sc).

Eastern Michigan University, Graduate School, College of Education, Department of Teacher Education, Program in Urban/Diversity Education, Ypsilanti, MI 48197. Offers MA. *Students:* 6 part-time (all women); includes 3 minority (1 Black or African American, non-Hispanic/Latino; 2 Asian, non-Hispanic/Latino). Average age 27. 2 applicants, 100% accepted, 1 enrolled. In 2014, 4 master's awarded. Application fee: $45. *Application contact:* Dr. Patricia Williams-Boyd, Advisor, 734-487-3260, Fax: 734-487-2101, E-mail: pwilliams1@emich.edu.

Eastern University, Department of Urban Studies, St. Davids, PA 19087-3696. Offers urban studies (MA), including arts in transformation, community development, youth leadership. Part-time and evening/weekend programs available. Postbaccalaureate distance learning degree programs offered (minimal on-campus study). *Faculty:* 3 full-time (1 woman), 4 part-time/adjunct (1 woman). *Students:* 13 full-time (11 women), 48 part-time (44 women); includes 38 minority (33 Black or African American, non-Hispanic/Latino; 1 Asian, non-Hispanic/Latino; 3 Hispanic/Latino; 1 Two or more races, non-Hispanic/Latino). Average age 30. 38 applicants, 97% accepted, 19 enrolled. In 2014, 19 master's awarded. *Entrance requirements:* For master's, minimum GPA of 2.5. Additional exam requirements/recommendations for international students: Required—TOEFL (minimum score 550 paper-based; 79 iBT). *Application deadline:* For fall admission, 8/14 for domestic students; for spring admission, 12/20 for domestic students. Applications are processed on a rolling basis. Application fee: $35. Application fee is waived when completed online. *Expenses: Tuition:* Full-time $15,600; part-time $650 per credit. *Required fees:* $30; $27.50 per semester. One-time fee: $50. Tuition and fees vary according to course load, degree level and program. *Financial support:* In 2014–15, 34 students received support. Scholarships/grants available. Financial award application deadline: 3/15; financial award applicants required to submit FAFSA. *Unit head:* Dr. Kimberlee Johnson, Chair, 215-769-3128. *Application contact:* Whitney Monn, Program Recruiter, 215-769-3121, Fax: 215-848-2651, E-mail: wmonn@eastern.edu. Website: http://www.eastern.edu/academics/programs/urban-studies-department/urban-studies-concentrations

Fordham University, Graduate School of Arts and Sciences, Program in Urban Studies, New York, NY 10458. Offers MA. *Students:* 2 full-time (1 woman), 6 part-time (4 women). Average age 28. 21 applicants, 86% accepted, 14 enrolled. In 2014, 5 master's awarded. *Degree requirements:* For master's, internship or field work, research project. Application fee: $70. *Financial support:* Tuition waivers (partial) available. *Unit head:* Dr. Rosemary Wakeman, Director, 212-636-7359, E-mail: rwakeman@fordham.edu. *Application contact:* Bernadette Valentino-Morrison, Director of Graduate Admissions, 718-817-4419, Fax: 718-817-3566, E-mail: valentinomor@fordham.edu.

The Graduate Center, City University of New York, Graduate Studies, Interdisciplinary Studies, New York, NY 10016-4039. Offers language in social context (PhD); medieval studies (PhD); public policy (MA, PhD); urban studies (MA, PhD); women's studies (MA, PhD). Terminal master's awarded for partial completion of doctoral program. *Degree requirements:* For master's, thesis; for doctorate, comprehensive exam, thesis/dissertation. *Entrance requirements:* For master's and doctorate, GRE General Test.

Hunter College of the City University of New York, Graduate School, School of Arts and Sciences, Department of Urban Affairs and Planning, Program in Urban Affairs, New York, NY 10065-5085. Offers MS. Part-time programs available. *Faculty:* 5 full-time (3 women), 4 part-time/adjunct (2 women). *Students:* 7 full-time (2 women), 52 part-time (29 women); includes 28 minority (18 Black or African American, non-Hispanic/Latino; 2 Asian, non-Hispanic/Latino; 8 Hispanic/Latino), 2 international. Average age 32. 39 applicants, 67% accepted, 16 enrolled. In 2014, 28 master's awarded. *Degree requirements:* For master's, thesis or alternative, 2 formal reports, internship. *Entrance requirements:* For master's, minimum 12 credits of course work in social sciences. Additional exam requirements/recommendations for international students: Required—TOEFL. *Application deadline:* For fall admission, 4/1 priority date for domestic students, 2/1 for international students; for spring admission, 11/1 priority date for domestic students, 9/1 for international students. Applications are processed on a rolling basis. *Financial support:* Fellowships, research assistantships, teaching assistantships, career-related internships or fieldwork, Federal Work-Study, scholarships/grants, and unspecified assistantships available. *Faculty research:* Women, tourism, youth, immigration, employment. *Unit head:* Dr. Owen D. Gutfreund, Director, 212-396-6248, E-mail: owen.gutfreund@hunter.cuny.edu. *Application contact:* Milena Solo, Director for Graduate Admissions, 212-772-4480, E-mail: admissions@hunter.cuny.edu. Website: http://maxweber.hunter.cuny.edu/urban/index.php

Le Moyne College, Department of Education, Syracuse, NY 13214. Offers adolescent education (MS Ed, MST); adolescent education/special education (MS Ed, MST); adolescent English (MST), including grades 7-12; adolescent English/special education (MST), including grades 7-12; adolescent foreign language (MST), including grades 7-12; adolescent history (MST), including grades 7-12; childhood education (MS Ed); childhood education/special education (MS Ed); elementary education (MS Ed); general education (MS Ed); inclusive childhood education (MST); literacy education (MS Ed), including birth to grade 6, grades 5-12; school building leader (MS Ed); school building leadership (CAS); school district business leader (MS Ed, CAS); school district leader (MS Ed); school district leadership (CAS); secondary education (MS Ed); special education (MS Ed); teaching English to speakers of other languages (MS Ed); urban studies (MS Ed). *Accreditation:* Teacher Education Accreditation Council. Part-time and evening/weekend programs available. *Faculty:* 7 full-time (4 women), 54 part-time/adjunct (34 women). *Students:* 18 full-time (14 women), 180 part-time (133 women); includes 16 minority (8 Black or African American, non-Hispanic/Latino; 1 American Indian or Alaska Native, non-Hispanic/Latino; 2 Asian, non-Hispanic/Latino; 5 Hispanic/Latino), 2 international. Average age 28. 127 applicants, 99% accepted, 110 enrolled. In 2014, 196 master's, 30 CASs awarded. *Degree requirements:* For master's, thesis. *Entrance requirements:* For master's, bachelor's degree, 2 letters of recommendation, transcripts. Additional exam requirements/recommendations for international students: Required—TOEFL (minimum score 550 paper-based; 79 iBT); Recommended—IELTS (minimum score 6.5). *Application deadline:* For fall admission, 4/1 priority date for domestic and international students; for spring admission, 10/1 priority date for domestic

and international students; for summer admission, 3/1 priority date for domestic and international students. Applications are processed on a rolling basis. Application fee: $50. *Expenses:* Expenses: $663 per credit. *Financial support:* In 2014–15, 14 students received support. Career-related internships or fieldwork and health care benefits available. Support available to part-time students. Financial award applicants required to submit FAFSA. *Faculty research:* Minority teachers, special education, multiculturalism, literacy, technology, media literacy learning, autism, school district organization, service-learning, higher level problem solving, teacher leadership. *Unit head:* Dr. Stephen C. Fleury, Chair, Department of Education, 315-445-4376, Fax: 315-445-4744, E-mail: fleurysc@lemoyne.edu. *Application contact:* Kristen P. Trapasso, Senior Director of Enrollment Management, 315-445-5444, Fax: 315-445-6092, E-mail: trapaskp@lemoyne.edu.
Website: http://www.lemoyne.edu/education

Loyola University Chicago, Graduate School, Program in Urban Affairs, Chicago, IL 60660. Offers MA. Part-time and evening/weekend programs available. *Faculty:* 2 full-time (both women), 3 part-time/adjunct (1 woman). *Students:* 5 full-time (4 women); includes 2 minority (both Hispanic/Latino). Average age 25. 8 applicants, 88% accepted, 3 enrolled. In 2014, 1 master's awarded. *Degree requirements:* For master's, internship or capstone experience. *Entrance requirements:* For master's, GRE. Additional exam requirements/recommendations for international students: Required—TOEFL. *Application deadline:* For fall admission, 6/30 for domestic students. Applications are processed on a rolling basis. Application fee: $0. Electronic applications accepted. *Expenses: Tuition:* Full-time $17,370; part-time $965 per credit. *Required fees:* $138 per semester. *Financial support:* Tuition waivers and Fulbright scholarships available. Financial award application deadline: 2/15; financial award applicants required to submit FAFSA. *Faculty research:* Urban public policy. *Unit head:* Dr. Annette Steinacker, Director, 773-508-3396. *Application contact:* Ron Martin, Assistant Director of Enrollment Management, 312-915-8950, Fax: 312-915-8905, E-mail: gradapp@luc.edu.

Massachusetts Institute of Technology, School of Architecture and Planning, Department of Urban Studies and Planning, Cambridge, MA 02139-4307. Offers city planning (MCP); urban and regional planning (PhD); urban and regional studies (PhD); urban studies and planning (SM). *Accreditation:* ACSP (one or more programs are accredited). *Faculty:* 24 full-time (6 women). *Students:* 183 full-time (108 women), 1 part-time (0 women); includes 52 minority (8 Black or African American, non-Hispanic/Latino; 20 Asian, non-Hispanic/Latino; 16 Hispanic/Latino; 8 Two or more races, non-Hispanic/Latino), 47 international. Average age 29. 487 applicants, 22% accepted, 71 enrolled. In 2014, 70 master's, 7 doctorates awarded. Terminal master's awarded for partial completion of doctoral program. *Degree requirements:* For master's, thesis, MCP program requires a practicum course; for doctorate, comprehensive exam, thesis/dissertation. *Entrance requirements:* For master's and doctorate, GRE General Test. Additional exam requirements/recommendations for international students: Required—TOEFL (minimum score 600 paper-based; 100 iBT), IELTS (minimum score 7). *Application deadline:* For fall admission, 1/3 for domestic and international students. Application fee: $75. Electronic applications accepted. *Expenses: Tuition:* Full-time $44,720; part-time $699 per unit. *Required fees:* $296. *Financial support:* In 2014–15, 163 students received support, including 77 fellowships (averaging $23,500 per year), 68 research assistantships (averaging $22,600 per year), 18 teaching assistantships (averaging $34,600 per year); Federal Work-Study, institutionally sponsored loans, scholarships/grants, health care benefits, and unspecified assistantships also available. Financial award application deadline: 4/15; financial award applicants required to submit FAFSA. *Faculty research:* City and regional sustainable design and development; housing, community, and economic development; environmental and landscape planning; international development, infrastructure systems and energy policy; geographic information and communication technologies. *Total annual research expenditures:* $4.4 million. *Unit head:* Prof. Eran Ben-Joseph, Head, 617-253-1907, Fax: 617-253-2654, E-mail: duspinfo@mit.edu. *Application contact:* Graduate Admissions, 617-253-4543, Fax: 617-253-2654, E-mail: duspapply@mit.edu.
Website: http://dusp.mit.edu/

Minnesota State University Mankato, College of Graduate Studies, College of Social and Behavioral Sciences, Department of Urban and Regional Studies, Mankato, MN 56001. Offers local government management (Certificate); urban and regional studies (MA); urban planning (MA, Certificate). *Students:* 18 full-time (5 women), 15 part-time (6 women). *Degree requirements:* For master's, one foreign language, comprehensive exam, thesis or alternative. *Entrance requirements:* For master's, minimum GPA of 3.0 during previous 2 years, 2 letters of recommendation. Additional exam requirements/recommendations for international students: Required—TOEFL. *Application deadline:* For fall admission, 7/1 priority date for domestic students; for spring admission, 11/1 for domestic students. Applications are processed on a rolling basis. Application fee: $40. Electronic applications accepted. *Financial support:* Fellowships with partial tuition reimbursements, research assistantships with full tuition reimbursements, teaching assistantships with full tuition reimbursements, career-related internships or fieldwork, Federal Work-Study, institutionally sponsored loans, and unspecified assistantships available. Support available to part-time students. Financial award application deadline: 3/15; financial award applicants required to submit FAFSA. *Unit head:* Dr. Mirium Porter, Graduate Coordinator, 507-389-1714. *Application contact:* 507-389-2321, E-mail: grad@mnsu.edu.
Website: http://sbs.mnsu.edu/ursi/graduate/

Moody Bible Institute, Graduate School, Chicago, IL 60610-3284. Offers biblical studies (MABS, Graduate Certificate); intercultural studies (MAIS, Graduate Certificate); ministry (M Div, M Min); spiritual formation and discipleship (MASF, Graduate Certificate); urban studies (MA, Graduate Certificate). *Accreditation:* ATS. Part-time programs available. *Degree requirements:* For master's, 2 foreign languages, fieldwork (MABS); colloquium, field research project (MA Min). *Entrance requirements:* For master's, 30 hours in Bible/theology, 2 years of ministry experience (MA Min).

New Jersey City University, Graduate Studies and Continuing Education, Debra Cannon Partridge Wolfe College of Education, Department of Educational Leadership and Counseling, Jersey City, NJ 07305-1597. Offers counseling (MA); educational administration and supervision (MA); urban education (MA). Part-time and evening/weekend programs available. *Faculty:* 4 full-time (all women), 10 part-time/adjunct (6 women). *Students:* 31 full-time (27 women), 174 part-time (132 women); includes 102 minority (15 Black or African American, non-Hispanic/Latino; 6 Asian, non-Hispanic/Latino; 81 Hispanic/Latino), 3 international. Average age 37. 46 applicants, 91% accepted, 39 enrolled. In 2014, 85 master's awarded. *Entrance requirements:* Additional exam requirements/recommendations for international students: Required—TOEFL (minimum score 79 iBT). *Application deadline:* For fall admission, 8/1 priority date for domestic students; for spring admission, 12/1 for domestic students. Applications are processed on a rolling basis. Application fee: $0. *Expenses: Tuition, area resident:* Part-time $538 per credit. *Tuition, state resident:* part-time $538 per credit. *Tuition, nonresident:* part-time $948 per credit. *Financial support:* Fellowships, teaching assistantships, career-related internships or fieldwork, and unspecified assistantships available. *Unit head:* Dr. Jennifer Hartman, 201-200-3012, E-mail: jhartman@njcu.edu. *Application contact:* Jose Balda, E-mail: jbalda@njcu.edu.
Website: http://www.njcu.edu/edld/

New Jersey Institute of Technology, College of Architecture, Newark, NJ 07102. Offers architecture (M Arch, MS Arch); infrastructure planning (MIP); urban systems (PhD); M Arch/MIP; M Arch/MS. Part-time and evening/weekend programs available. Terminal master's awarded for partial completion of doctoral program. *Degree requirements:* For master's, thesis (for some programs). *Entrance requirements:* For master's, GRE General Test, minimum GPA of 3.0. Additional exam requirements/recommendations for international students: Required—TOEFL (minimum score 550 paper-based; 79 iBT). Electronic applications accepted. *Faculty research:* Building sciences, community and urban design history and theory, computer-aided architecture.

The New School, The New School for Public Engagement, Program in Urban Policy Analysis and Management, New York, NY 10011. Offers MS. *Accreditation:* NASPAA. Part-time programs available. *Degree requirements:* For master's, thesis. *Entrance requirements:* For master's, interview. Additional exam requirements/recommendations for international students: Required—TOEFL (minimum score 600 paper-based; 100 iBT). Electronic applications accepted. *Faculty research:* Community and economic development, national urban policy, social welfare policy, management of low-income housing, race and gender issues.

New York University, Polytechnic School of Engineering, Department of Civil and Urban Engineering, Major in Urban Systems Engineering and Management, New York, NY 10012-1019. Offers MS. *Students:* 2 full-time (1 woman), 4 part-time (1 woman); includes 3 minority (1 Black or African American, non-Hispanic/Latino; 1 Asian, non-Hispanic/Latino; 1 Hispanic/Latino). Average age 29. 11 applicants, 45% accepted, 3 enrolled. In 2014, 3 master's awarded. *Application deadline:* For fall admission, 2/15 priority date for domestic and international students; for spring admission, 11/1 priority date for domestic and international students. Application fee: $75. *Unit head:* Dr. Illan Juran, Head, 718-260-3717, E-mail: ijuran@nyu.edu. *Application contact:* Raymond Lutzky, Director of Graduate Enrollment Management, 718-637-5984, Fax: 718-260-3624, E-mail: rlutzky@poly.edu.

Norfolk State University, School of Graduate Studies, School of Liberal Arts, Department of Sociology, Program in Urban Affairs, Norfolk, VA 23504. Offers MA. Part-time programs available. *Degree requirements:* For master's, thesis. *Entrance requirements:* For master's, minimum GPA of 2.5.

North Dakota State University, College of Graduate and Interdisciplinary Studies, Interdisciplinary Program in Transportation and Logistics, Fargo, ND 58108. Offers managerial logistics (MML); transportation and logistics (PhD); transportation and urban systems (MS). *Entrance requirements:* For doctorate, 1 year of calculus, statistics and probability, minimum GPA of 3.0. Additional exam requirements/recommendations for international students: Required—TOEFL (minimum score 550 paper-based; 79 iBT). *Faculty research:* Supply chain optimization, spatial analysis of transportation networks, advanced traffic analysis, transportation demand, railroad/intermodal freight.

Northeastern University, Bouvé College of Health Sciences, Boston, MA 02115-5096. Offers audiology (Au D); biotechnology (MS); counseling psychology (MS, PhD, CAGS); counseling/school psychology (PhD); exercise physiology (MS), including exercise physiology, public health; health informatics (MS); nursing (MS, PhD, CAGS), including acute care (MS), administration (MS), anesthesia (MS), primary care (MS), psychiatric mental health (MS); pharmaceutical sciences (PhD); pharmaceutics and drug delivery systems (MS); pharmacology (MS); physical therapy (DPT); physician assistant (MS); school psychology (PhD, CAGS); school/counseling psychology (PhD); speech language pathology (MS); urban public health (MPH); MS/MBA. *Accreditation:* ACPE (one or more programs are accredited). Part-time and evening/weekend programs available. *Degree requirements:* For doctorate, thesis/dissertation (for some programs); for CAGS, comprehensive exam.

Northeastern University, College of Social Sciences and Humanities, Boston, MA 02115. Offers criminology and criminal justice (MSCJ); criminology and justice policy (PhD); economics (MA, PhD); English (MA, PhD); law and public policy (MS, PhD); political science (MA, PhD); public administration (MPA); public history (MA); security and resilience studies (MS); sociology (MA, PhD); urban and regional policy (MS); world history (MA, PhD). *Degree requirements:* For doctorate, variable foreign language requirement, comprehensive exam, thesis/dissertation. *Entrance requirements:* For master's and doctorate, GRE. Additional exam requirements/recommendations for international students: Required—TOEFL, IELTS. Electronic applications accepted.

Old Dominion University, Strome College of Business, Doctoral Program in Public Administration and Urban Policy, Norfolk, VA 23529. Offers PhD. Part-time and evening/weekend programs available. *Faculty:* 9 full-time (3 women). *Students:* 11 full-time (8 women), 22 part-time (12 women); includes 9 minority (4 Black or African American, non-Hispanic/Latino; 4 Hispanic/Latino; 1 Native Hawaiian or other Pacific Islander, non-Hispanic/Latino), 6 international. Average age 40. 13 applicants, 31% accepted, 4 enrolled. In 2014, 1 doctorate awarded. *Degree requirements:* For doctorate, comprehensive exam, thesis/dissertation. *Entrance requirements:* For doctorate, GMAT, GRE General Test, master's degree, minimum graduate GPA of 3.25. Additional exam requirements/recommendations for international students: Required—TOEFL (minimum score 550 paper-based; 79 iBT). *Application deadline:* For fall admission, 3/15 priority date for domestic and international students. Application fee: $50. Electronic applications accepted. *Expenses:* Expenses: Contact institution. *Financial support:* In 2014–15, 14 students received support, including 4 fellowships with full tuition reimbursements available (averaging $7,500 per year), 8 research assistantships with full tuition reimbursements available (averaging $6,000 per year), 2 teaching assistantships with full tuition reimbursements available (averaging $7,500 per year); unspecified assistantships also available. Financial award application deadline: 3/15; financial award applicants required to submit FAFSA. *Faculty research:* Educational needs and program development, policy analysis and administration, excellence norms for cooperative education programs. *Total annual research expenditures:* $60,000. *Unit head:* Dr. John Morris, Graduate Program Director, 757-683-6555, Fax: 757-683-4886, E-mail: jmorris@odu.edu. *Application contact:* Megan S. Jones, Graduate Program Manager, 757-683-3961, Fax: 757-683-4886, E-mail: mmjones@odu.edu. Website: http://www.odu.edu/business/departments/sps/academics/paup

Portland State University, Graduate Studies, College of Urban and Public Affairs, Nohad A. Toulan School of Urban Studies and Planning, Program in Urban Studies, Portland, OR 97207-0751. Offers MUS, PhD. *Students:* 42 full-time (18 women), 29 part-time (18 women); includes 10 minority (3 Black or African American, non-Hispanic/Latino; 4 Asian, non-Hispanic/Latino; 3 Hispanic/Latino), 29 international. Average age 29. In 2014, 7 master's, 5 doctorates awarded. *Degree requirements:* For doctorate, comprehensive exam, thesis/dissertation, residency. *Entrance requirements:* For master's and doctorate, GRE General Test, minimum GPA of 3.0, 3 letters of recommendation, resume, statement of purpose, transcripts. Additional exam requirements/recommendations for international students: Required—TOEFL (minimum score 550 paper-based; 80 iBT). *Application deadline:* For fall admission, 1/15 for domestic and international students; for winter admission, 9/1 for domestic and international students. Application fee: $50. Electronic applications accepted. *Expenses:* Tuition, state resident: part-time $222 per credit. Tuition, nonresident: part-time $527 per credit. *Required fees:* $22 per contact hour. $100 per quarter. Tuition and fees vary according to program. *Financial support:* Research assistantships available. Financial

award application deadline: 3/1. *Unit head:* James Strathman, Director, 503-725-4069, Fax: 503-725-8770, E-mail: strathmanj@pdx.edu. *Application contact:* Bryony Mangan, Administrative Program Assistant, 503-725-4068, Fax: 503-725-8770, E-mail: bmangan@pdx.edu.

Queens College of the City University of New York, Division of Graduate Studies, Social Science Division, Department of Urban Studies, Flushing, NY 11367-1597. Offers MA. Part-time and evening/weekend programs available. *Degree requirements:* For master's, thesis. *Entrance requirements:* For master's, minimum GPA of 3.0. Additional exam requirements/recommendations for international students: Required—TOEFL.

Rutgers, The State University of New Jersey, Newark, Graduate School, Program in Public Administration, Newark, NJ 07102. Offers health care administration (MPA); human resources administration (MPA); public administration (PhD); public management (MPA); public policy analysis (MPA); urban systems and issues (MPA). *Accreditation:* NASPAA (one or more programs are accredited). Part-time and evening/weekend programs available. *Degree requirements:* For master's, comprehensive exam, thesis or alternative; for doctorate, thesis/dissertation. *Entrance requirements:* For master's, GRE, minimum undergraduate B average; for doctorate, GRE, MPA, minimum B average. Electronic applications accepted. *Faculty research:* Government finance, municipal and state government, public productivity.

Rutgers, The State University of New Jersey, Newark, Graduate School, Program in Urban Systems, Newark, NJ 07102. Offers PhD. Program offered jointly with New Jersey Institute of Technology.

Saint Louis University, Graduate Education, College of Education and Public Service, Department of Public Policy Studies, St. Louis, MO 63103-2097. Offers geographic information systems (Certificate); organizational development (Certificate); public administration (MAPA); public policy analysis (PhD); urban affairs (MAUA); urban planning and real estate development (MUPRED). *Accreditation:* NASPAA. Part-time programs available. *Degree requirements:* For master's, comprehensive exam (for some programs), thesis (for some programs); for doctorate, comprehensive exam, thesis/dissertation, preliminary exams. *Entrance requirements:* For master's, GMAT, GRE General Test, or LSAT, letters of recommendation, resume; for doctorate, GMAT, GRE General Test, or LSAT, letters of recommendation, resumé, interview, transcripts, goal statement. Additional exam requirements/recommendations for international students: Required—TOEFL (minimum score 525 paper-based). Electronic applications accepted. *Faculty research:* Urban politics, brown fields, e-government, and administration, evaluation research, community development, electronic government and governance.

Savannah State University, Master of Science in Urban Studies and Planning Program, Savannah, GA 31404. Offers MSUS. Part-time programs available. *Faculty:* 3 full-time (1 woman). *Students:* 4 full-time (3 women), 2 part-time (both women); includes 5 minority (all Black or African American, non-Hispanic/Latino). Average age 40. 7 applicants, 57% accepted, 3 enrolled. In 2014, 3 master's awarded. *Degree requirements:* For master's, thesis or capstone project. *Entrance requirements:* For master's, GRE or MAT, minimum cumulative GPA of 2.6, 3 letters of recommendation, statement of interest, official transcripts, curriculum vitae. Additional exam requirements/recommendations for international students: Required—TOEFL. *Application deadline:* For fall admission, 6/15 priority date for domestic students, 6/1 for international students; for spring admission, 10/1 priority date for domestic students, 10/1 for international students; for summer admission, 3/1 for domestic and international students. Applications are processed on a rolling basis. Application fee: $25. Electronic applications accepted. *Expenses:* Expenses: Contact institution. *Financial support:* Career-related internships or fieldwork, Federal Work-Study, institutionally sponsored loans, scholarships/grants, health care benefits, and unspecified assistantships available. Support available to part-time students. Financial award application deadline: 7/15; financial award applicants required to submit FAFSA. *Unit head:* Dr. Benn Bongang, Chair/Professor, 912-358-3210, E-mail: bongang@savannahstate.edu. *Application contact:* Dr. Deden Rukmana, Program Coordinator, 912-358-3218, E-mail: msusp@savannahstate.edu. Website: http://www.savannahstate.edu/class/programs-grad-urbanstudies.shtml

Simon Fraser University, Office of Graduate Studies, Faculty of Arts and Social Sciences, Urban Studies Program, Vancouver, BC V6B 5K3, Canada. Offers M Urb, Graduate Diploma. Part-time programs available. *Degree requirements:* For master's, project. *Entrance requirements:* For master's, minimum GPA of 3.0 (on scale of 4.33), or 3.33 based on last 60 credits of undergraduate courses; for Graduate Diploma, minimum GPA of 2.5 (on scale of 4.33), or 2.67 based on the last 60 credits of undergraduate courses. Additional exam requirements/recommendations for international students: Recommended—TOEFL (minimum score 580 paper-based; 93 iBT), IELTS (minimum score 7), TWE (minimum score 5). Electronic applications accepted. *Faculty research:* Urban history; public policy and culture; environmental, transportation, and energy policy; urban governance and administration; urban sustainability.

Temple University, College of Liberal Arts, Department of Geography and Urban Studies, Philadelphia, PA 19122-6096. Offers geography and urban studies (MA); urban studies (PhD). *Faculty:* 9 full-time (3 women), 1 (woman) part-time/adjunct. *Students:* 23 full-time (12 women), 4 part-time (2 women); includes 7 minority (5 Black or African American, non-Hispanic/Latino; 1 Hispanic/Latino; 1 Two or more races, non-Hispanic/Latino), 3 international. 48 applicants, 38% accepted, 10 enrolled. In 2014, 6 master's, 2 doctorates awarded. *Degree requirements:* For master's, comprehensive exam, thesis or alternative. *Entrance requirements:* For master's, GRE General Test, minimum GPA of 3.0, 3 letters of recommendation; for doctorate, GRE, minimum GPA of 3.0, 3 letters of recommendation. Additional exam requirements/recommendations for international students: Required—TOEFL (minimum score 575 paper-based; 88 iBT). *Application deadline:* For fall admission, 1/15 for domestic students, 12/15 for international students; for spring admission, 10/15 for domestic students, 8/1 for international students. Applications are processed on a rolling basis. Application fee: $60. Electronic applications accepted. *Expenses:* Tuition, state resident: full-time $14,490; part-time $805 per credit hour. Tuition, nonresident: full-time $19,850; part-time $1103 per credit hour. *Required fees:* $690. Full-time tuition and fees vary according to class time, course load, degree level, campus/location and program. *Financial support:* Fellowships, teaching assistantships, career-related internships or fieldwork, Federal Work-Study, and tuition waivers (partial) available. Financial award application deadline: 1/15; financial award applicants required to submit FAFSA. *Faculty research:* Social justice, sustainability, globalization, geographic methods, urban processes. *Unit head:* Dr. C. Hamil Pearsall, Graduate Director, 215-204-3074, Fax: 215-204-7833, E-mail: hamil.pearsall@temple.edu. *Application contact:* Tycina Cousin, Coordinator, 215-204-7692, Fax: 215-204-7833, E-mail: tcousin@temple.edu. Website: http://www.cla.temple.edu/gus/

Tufts University, Graduate School of Arts and Sciences, Department of Urban and Environmental Policy and Planning, Medford, MA 02155. Offers community development (MA); environmental policy (MA); health and human welfare (MA); housing policy (MA); international environment/development policy (MA); public policy (MPP); MA/MS; MALD/MA. *Accreditation:* ACSP (one or more programs are accredited). Part-time programs available. *Faculty:* 13 full-time (5 women), 15 part-time/adjunct (8

women). *Students:* 62 full-time (43 women), 36 part-time (26 women); includes 24 minority (10 Black or African American, non-Hispanic/Latino; 7 Asian, non-Hispanic/Latino; 6 Hispanic/Latino; 1 Two or more races, non-Hispanic/Latino), 10 international. Average age 30. 119 applicants, 81% accepted, 32 enrolled. In 2014, 64 master's awarded. *Degree requirements:* For master's, thesis, internship. *Entrance requirements:* For master's, GRE General Test. Additional exam requirements/recommendations for international students: Required—TOEFL (minimum score 550 paper-based; 80 iBT), IELTS (minimum score 6.5). *Application deadline:* For fall admission, 1/15 for domestic and international students. Applications are processed on a rolling basis. Application fee: $75. Electronic applications accepted. *Expenses:* Expenses: Contact institution. *Financial support:* Teaching assistantships with partial tuition reimbursements, career-related internships or fieldwork, Federal Work-Study, scholarships/grants, tuition waivers (partial), and unspecified assistantships available. Support available to part-time students. Financial award application deadline: 1/15; financial award applicants required to submit FAFSA. *Unit head:* Dr. Weiping Wu, Graduate Program Director. *Application contact:* Office of Graduate Admissions, 617-627-3395, E-mail: gradadmissions@tufts.edu.
Website: http://ase.tufts.edu/uep/

Université du Québec à Montréal, Graduate Programs, Program in Urban Analysis and Management, Montréal, QC H3C 3P8, Canada. Offers MA. Program offered jointly with Université du Québec, École nationale d'administration publique and Université du Québec, Institut National de la Recherche Scientifique. Part-time programs available. *Entrance requirements:* For master's, appropriate bachelor's degree or equivalent and proficiency in French.

Université du Québec à Montréal, Graduate Programs, Program in Urban Studies, Montréal, QC H3C 3P8, Canada. Offers MA, PhD. Part-time programs available. *Degree requirements:* For doctorate, thesis/dissertation. *Entrance requirements:* For doctorate, appropriate master's degree or equivalent, proficiency in French.

Université du Québec, École nationale d'administration publique, Graduate Program in Public Administration, Program in Urban Analysis and Management, Quebec, QC G1K 9E5, Canada. Offers MAGU. Part-time programs available. *Entrance requirements:* For master's, appropriate bachelor's degree, proficiency in French.

Université du Québec, Institut National de la Recherche Scientifique, Graduate Programs, Research Center–Urbanization Culture Society, Montreal, QC H2X 1E3, Canada. Offers demography (M Sc, PhD); research practices and public action (MA, DESS); urban studies (M Sc, PhD). Part-time programs available. *Faculty:* 32 full-time. *Students:* 81 full-time (47 women), 20 part-time (15 women), 11 international. Average age 31. 31 applicants, 84% accepted, 22 enrolled. In 2014, 7 master's, 4 doctorates awarded. *Degree requirements:* For master's, thesis (for some programs); for doctorate, thesis/dissertation. *Entrance requirements:* For master's, appropriate bachelor's degree, proficiency in French; for doctorate, appropriate master's degree, proficiency in French; for DESS, proficiency in French. *Application deadline:* For fall admission, 3/30 for domestic and international students; for winter admission, 11/1 for domestic and international students; for spring admission, 3/1 for domestic and international students. Application fee: $45. Electronic applications accepted. *Financial support:* In 2014–15, fellowships (averaging $16,500 per year) were awarded; research assistantships also available. *Faculty research:* Mobility and migration, cultural policies, knowledge mobilization, spatial analysis of data, social demography. *Unit head:* Claire Poitras, Director, 514-499-4002, E-mail: claire.poitras@ucs.inrs.ca. *Application contact:* Sylvie Richard, Registrar, 418-654-2518, Fax: 418-654-3858, E-mail: sylvie.richard@adm.inrs.ca.
Website: http://www.ucs.inrs.ca

University at Albany, State University of New York, College of Arts and Sciences, Department of Sociology, Albany, NY 12222-0001. Offers demography (Certificate); sociology (MA, PhD); urban policy (Certificate). Terminal master's awarded for partial completion of doctoral program. *Degree requirements:* For master's, thesis; for doctorate, thesis/dissertation, 2 specialization exams, research tool. *Entrance requirements:* For master's and doctorate, GRE General Test. Additional exam requirements/recommendations for international students: Required—TOEFL. Electronic applications accepted. *Faculty research:* Gender and equality, crime and deviance, aging, work and organizations, social demography.

University of California, Irvine, School of Social Ecology, Department of Planning, Policy and Design, Irvine, CA 92697. Offers planning, policy and design (PhD); urban and regional planning (MURP). *Accreditation:* ACSP (one or more programs are accredited). *Students:* 130 full-time (75 women); includes 53 minority (2 Black or African American, non-Hispanic/Latino; 1 American Indian or Alaska Native, non-Hispanic/Latino; 23 Asian, non-Hispanic/Latino; 19 Hispanic/Latino; 8 Two or more races, non-Hispanic/Latino), 36 international. Average age 29. 383 applicants, 54% accepted, 66 enrolled. In 2014, 54 master's, 8 doctorates awarded. *Degree requirements:* For doctorate, thesis/dissertation, research project. *Entrance requirements:* For master's and doctorate, GRE General Test, minimum GPA of 3.0. Additional exam requirements/recommendations for international students: Required—TOEFL (minimum score 550 paper-based). *Application deadline:* For fall admission, 1/15 priority date for domestic and international students. Application fee: $90 ($110 for international students). Electronic applications accepted. *Financial support:* Fellowships with tuition reimbursements, research assistantships with full tuition reimbursements, teaching assistantships with tuition reimbursements, institutionally sponsored loans, traineeships, health care benefits, and unspecified assistantships available. Financial award application deadline: 1/15; financial award applicants required to submit FAFSA. *Faculty research:* Community and social policy, economic development, land-use and growth management, transportation planning, environmental policy. *Unit head:* David L. Feldman, Chair, 949-824-4384, Fax: 949-824-3056, E-mail: feldmand@uci.edu. *Application contact:* Janet Gallagher, Graduate Coordinator, 949-824-9849, Fax: 949-824-8566, E-mail: janetg@uci.edu.
Website: http://www.seweb.uci.edu/ppd/

University of Delaware, Center for Energy and Environmental Policy, Newark, DE 19716. Offers energy and environmental policy (MA, MEEP, PhD); urban affairs and public policy (PhD), including technology, environment, and society. *Degree requirements:* For master's, analytical paper or thesis; for doctorate, comprehensive exam, thesis/dissertation. *Entrance requirements:* For master's, GRE General Test, minimum GPA of 3.0; for doctorate, GRE General Test, minimum GPA of 3.5. Additional exam requirements/recommendations for international students: Required—TOEFL. Electronic applications accepted. *Faculty research:* Sustainable development, renewable energy, climate change, environmental policy, environmental justice, disaster policy.

University of Delaware, College of Arts and Sciences, School of Public Policy and Administration, Program in Urban Affairs and Public Policy, Newark, DE 19716. Offers governance planning and management (PhD); historic preservation (MA); social and urban policy (PhD); technology, environment and society (PhD); urban affairs and public policy (MA). Part-time programs available. Terminal master's awarded for partial completion of doctoral program. *Degree requirements:* For master's, analytical paper or thesis; for doctorate, thesis/dissertation. *Entrance requirements:* For master's, GRE General Test, minimum GPA of 3.0; for doctorate, GRE General Test, minimum GPA of 3.5. Additional exam requirements/recommendations for international students: Required—TOEFL. Electronic applications accepted. *Faculty research:* Political economy; social policy analysis; technology and society; historic preservation; urban policy.

University of Lethbridge, School of Graduate Studies, Lethbridge, AB T1K 3M4, Canada. Offers addictions counseling (M Sc); agricultural biotechnology (M Sc); agricultural studies (M Sc, MA); anthropology (MA); archaeology (M Sc, MA); art (MA, MFA); biochemistry (M Sc); biological sciences (M Sc); biomolecular science (PhD); biosystems and biodiversity (PhD); Canadian studies (MA); chemistry (M Sc); computer science (M Sc); computer science and geographical information science (M Sc); counseling (MC); counseling psychology (M Ed); dramatic arts (MA); earth, space, and physical science (PhD); economics (MA); education (MA); educational leadership (M Ed); English (MA); environmental science (M Sc); evolution and behavior (PhD); exercise science (M Sc); French (MA); French/German (MA); French/Spanish (MA); general education (M Ed); geography (M Sc, MA); German (MA); health sciences (M Sc); individualized multidisciplinary (M Sc, MA); kinesiology (M Sc, MA); management (M Sc), including accounting, finance, general management, human resource management and labor relations, information systems, international management, marketing, policy and strategy; mathematics (M Sc); modern languages (MA); music (M Mus, MA); Native American studies (MA); neuroscience (M Sc, PhD); new media (MA, MFA); nursing (M Sc, MN); philosophy (MA); physics (M Sc); political science (MA); psychology (M Sc, MA); religious studies (MA); sociology (MA); theatre and dramatic arts (MFA); theoretical and computational science (PhD); urban and regional studies (MA); women and gender studies (MA). Part-time and evening/weekend programs available. *Faculty:* 358. *Students:* 445 full-time (243 women), 116 part-time (72 women). Average age 31. 351 applicants, 26% accepted, 87 enrolled. In 2014, 129 master's, 13 doctorates awarded. *Degree requirements:* For master's, thesis (for some programs); for doctorate, comprehensive exam, thesis/dissertation. *Entrance requirements:* For master's, GMAT (for M Sc in management), bachelor's degree in related field, minimum GPA of 3.0 during previous 20 graded semester courses, 2 years' teaching or related experience (M Ed); for doctorate, master's degree, minimum graduate GPA of 3.5. Additional exam requirements/recommendations for international students: Required—TOEFL. Application fee: $100 Canadian dollars. *Financial support:* Fellowships, research assistantships, teaching assistantships, scholarships/grants, health care benefits, and unspecified assistantships available. *Faculty research:* Movement and brain plasticity, gibberellin physiology, photosynthesis, carbon cycling, molecular properties of main-group ring components. *Application contact:* School of Graduate Studies, 403-329-5194, E-mail: sgsinquiries@uleth.ca.
Website: http://www.uleth.ca/graduatestudies/

University of Louisville, Graduate School, College of Arts and Sciences, Department of Urban and Public Affairs, Louisville, KY 40208. Offers public administration (MPA), including human resources management, non-profit management, public policy and administration; urban and public affairs (PhD), including urban planning and development, urban policy and administration; urban planning (MUP), including administration of planning organizations, housing and community development, land use and environmental planning, spatial analysis. Part-time and evening/weekend programs available. *Students:* 76 full-time (35 women), 22 part-time (14 women); includes 16 minority (10 Black or African American, non-Hispanic/Latino; 1 Asian, non-Hispanic/Latino; 3 Hispanic/Latino; 2 Two or more races, non-Hispanic/Latino), 6 international. Average age 30. 89 applicants, 71% accepted, 33 enrolled. In 2014, 13 master's, 4 doctorates awarded. Terminal master's awarded for partial completion of doctoral program. *Degree requirements:* For master's, internship; for doctorate, comprehensive exam, thesis/dissertation. *Entrance requirements:* For master's, GRE General Test, minimum GPA of 3.0; for doctorate, GRE General Test, master's degree in appropriate field. Additional exam requirements/recommendations for international students: Required—TOEFL (minimum score 550 paper-based; 79 iBT). *Application deadline:* For fall admission, 7/15 for domestic students, 5/1 priority date for international students; for spring admission, 11/15 for domestic students, 11/1 priority date for international students; for summer admission, 4/1 priority date for international students. Applications are processed on a rolling basis. Application fee: $60. Electronic applications accepted. *Expenses:* Tuition, state resident: full-time $11,326; part-time $630 per credit hour. Tuition, nonresident: full-time $23,568; part-time $1311 per credit hour. *Required fees:* $196. Tuition and fees vary according to program and reciprocity agreements. *Financial support:* Fellowships, research assistantships, and health care benefits available. Financial award application deadline: 3/1. *Faculty research:* Housing and community development, performance-based budgeting, environmental policy and natural hazards, sustainability, real estate development, comparative urban development. *Unit head:* Dr. David Simpson, Chair, 502-852-8019, Fax: 502-852-4558, E-mail: dave.simpson@louisville.edu. *Application contact:* Libby Leggett, Director, Graduate Admissions, 502-852-3101, Fax: 502-852-4558, E-mail: gradadm@louisville.edu.
Website: http://supa.louisville.edu

University of Maryland, Baltimore County, The Graduate School, College of Arts, Humanities and Social Sciences, Department of Public Policy, Program in Public Policy, Baltimore, MD 21250. Offers economics (PhD); educational policy (MPP); evaluation and analytical methods (MPP); health policy (MPP); policy history (PhD); public management (MPP, PhD); urban policy (MPP, PhD). Part-time and evening/weekend programs available. *Faculty:* 9 full-time (3 women), 1 part-time/adjunct (0 women). *Students:* 50 full-time (29 women), 68 part-time (39 women); includes 28 minority (15 Black or African American, non-Hispanic/Latino; 8 Asian, non-Hispanic/Latino; 3 Hispanic/Latino; 1 Native Hawaiian or other Pacific Islander, non-Hispanic/Latino; 1 Two or more races, non-Hispanic/Latino), 9 international. Average age 35. 71 applicants, 58% accepted, 25 enrolled. In 2014, 23 master's, 13 doctorates awarded. Terminal master's awarded for partial completion of doctoral program. *Degree requirements:* For master's, thesis optional, public analysis paper; for doctorate, comprehensive exam, thesis/dissertation, comprehensive and field qualifying exams. *Entrance requirements:* For master's and doctorate, GRE General Test, 3 academic letters of reference, transcripts, resume, research paper. Additional exam requirements/recommendations for international students: Required—TOEFL (minimum score 550 paper-based; 80 iBT). *Application deadline:* For fall admission, 1/15 priority date for domestic students, 1/1 priority date for international students; for spring admission, 11/1 priority date for domestic students, 5/1 priority date for international students. Applications are processed on a rolling basis. Application fee: $50. Electronic applications accepted. *Expenses:* Expenses: $679 per credit resident; $1,114 non-resident. *Financial support:* In 2014–15, 26 students received support, including 1 fellowship with full tuition reimbursement available (averaging $12,000 per year), 25 research assistantships with full tuition reimbursements available (averaging $20,000 per year); career-related internships or fieldwork, Federal Work-Study, scholarships/grants, health care benefits, and unspecified assistantships also available. Support available to part-time students. Financial award application deadline: 1/15; financial award applicants required to submit FAFSA. *Faculty research:* Health policy, education policy, urban policy, public management, evaluation and analytical methods. *Unit head:* Dr. Donald F. Norris, Director, 410-455-1455, E-mail: norris@umbc.edu. *Application contact:* Sally F. Helms, Administrator of Academic Affairs, 410-455-3202, Fax: 410-455-1172, E-mail:

gradpubpol@umbc.edu.
Website: http://www.umbc.edu/pubpol

University of New Orleans, Graduate School, College of Liberal Arts, School of Urban Planning and Regional Studies, Program in Urban Studies, New Orleans, LA 70148. Offers MS, PhD. *Degree requirements:* For master's, thesis; for doctorate, thesis/dissertation. *Entrance requirements:* For master's, GRE General Test. Additional exam requirements/recommendations for international students: Required—TOEFL (minimum score 550 paper-based; 79 iBT), IELTS (minimum score 6.5). Electronic applications accepted. *Faculty research:* Urban economic development, environmental planning and analysis, social and cultural change.

University of Oklahoma, College of Architecture, Division of Architecture, Norman, OK 73019. Offers architectural urban studies (MS), including architectural urban studies, environmental technology, human resources; architecture (M Arch). *Faculty:* 41 full-time (15 women), 2 part-time/adjunct (both women). *Students:* 16 full-time (5 women), 15 part-time (9 women); includes 11 minority (2 Asian, non-Hispanic/Latino; 4 Hispanic/Latino; 5 Two or more races, non-Hispanic/Latino), 5 international. Average age 31. 25 applicants, 84% accepted, 10 enrolled. In 2014, 6 master's awarded. *Degree requirements:* For master's, thesis or alternative, portfolio, project. *Entrance requirements:* For master's, GRE General Test, portfolio. Additional exam requirements/recommendations for international students: Required—TOEFL (minimum score 79 iBT). *Application deadline:* For fall admission, 4/1 for domestic and international students. Application fee: $50 ($100 for international students). Electronic applications accepted. *Expenses:* Tuition, state resident: full-time $4394; part-time $183.10 per credit hour. Tuition, nonresident: full-time $16,970; part-time $707.10 per credit hour. *Required fees:* $2892; $109.95 per credit hour. $126.50 per semester. *Financial support:* In 2014–15, 16 students received support, including 2 research assistantships with partial tuition reimbursements available (averaging $10,372 per year), 2 teaching assistantships with partial tuition reimbursements available (averaging $10,372 per year); scholarships/grants and unspecified assistantships also available. Financial award application deadline: 6/1; financial award applicants required to submit FAFSA. *Faculty research:* Rammed earth bricks, energy sustainability, acoustics, Italian architecture, architectural design. *Total annual research expenditures:* $132,781. *Unit head:* Dr. Hans Butzer, Director, 405-325-2444, Fax: 405-325-7558, E-mail: butzer@ou.edu. *Application contact:* Joel Dietrich, Professor Emeritus, 405-325-2444, Fax: 405-325-7558, E-mail: dietrich@ou.edu.
Website: http://arch.ou.edu

University of San Francisco, College of Arts and Sciences, Urban Affairs Program, San Francisco, CA 94117. Offers MA. *Faculty:* 3 full-time (1 woman), 4 part-time/adjunct (1 woman). *Students:* 21 full-time (13 women); includes 7 minority (2 Black or African American, non-Hispanic/Latino; 4 Hispanic/Latino; 1 Two or more races, non-Hispanic/Latino), 3 international. Average age 28. 31 applicants, 81% accepted, 11 enrolled. *Application deadline:* For fall admission, 5/1 for domestic students. *Expenses:* Tuition: Full-time $21,762; part-time $1209 per credit hour. Tuition and fees vary according to degree level, campus/location and program. *Financial support:* In 2014–15, 16 students received support. *Unit head:* Angela Fleekop, Administrative Director, 415-422-5662. *Application contact:* Angela Fleekop, Director of Administration, 415-422-5662, E-mail: urbanaffairs@usfca.edu.
Website: http://www.usfca.edu/artsci/maua/

The University of Texas at Arlington, Graduate School, School of Urban and Public Affairs, Program in Urban Affairs, Arlington, TX 76019. Offers MA. *Degree requirements:* For master's, project or thesis. Electronic applications accepted.

University of Wisconsin–Milwaukee, Graduate School, College of Letters and Sciences, Department of History, Milwaukee, WI 53201-0413. Offers global history (PhD); history (MA); modern studies (PhD); urban history (PhD). Part-time programs available. *Degree requirements:* For master's, comprehensive exam, thesis or alternative; for doctorate, thesis/dissertation. *Entrance requirements:* For master's and doctorate, GRE General Test. Additional exam requirements/recommendations for international students: Required—TOEFL (minimum score 550 paper-based; 79 iBT), IELTS (minimum score 6.5). Electronic applications accepted.

University of Wisconsin–Milwaukee, Graduate School, College of Letters and Sciences, Interdepartmental Program in Urban Studies, Milwaukee, WI 53201-0413. Offers MS, PhD, MLIS/MS. *Degree requirements:* For master's, thesis or alternative; for doctorate, thesis/dissertation. *Entrance requirements:* For doctorate, GRE General Test. Additional exam requirements/recommendations for international students: Required—TOEFL (minimum score 550 paper-based; 79 iBT), IELTS (minimum score 6.5). Electronic applications accepted.

Virginia Polytechnic Institute and State University, Graduate School, College of Architecture and Urban Studies, Blacksburg, VA 24061. Offers architecture (MS Arch); architecture and design research (PhD); building/construction science and management (MS); creative technologies (MFA); environmental design and planning (PhD); landscape architecture (MLA); planning, governance, and globalization (PhD); public administration (MPA); public administration/public affairs (PhD, Certificate); public and international affairs (MPIA); urban and regional planning (MURP); MS/MA. *Accreditation:* ASLA (one or more programs are accredited). *Faculty:* 133 full-time (54 women), 2 part-time/adjunct (1 woman). *Students:* 316 full-time (166 women), 237 part-time (108 women); includes 104 minority (46 Black or African American, non-Hispanic/Latino; 1 American Indian or Alaska Native, non-Hispanic/Latino; 20 Asian, non-Hispanic/Latino; 21 Hispanic/Latino; 16 Two or more races, non-Hispanic/Latino), 108 international. Average age 32. 609 applicants, 50% accepted, 108 enrolled. In 2014, 155 master's, 29 doctorates awarded. *Degree requirements:* For master's, comprehensive exam (for some programs), thesis (for some programs); for doctorate, comprehensive exam (for some programs), thesis/dissertation (for some programs). *Entrance requirements:* For master's and doctorate, GRE/GMAT (may vary by department). Additional exam requirements/recommendations for international students: Required—TOEFL (minimum score 550 paper-based). *Application deadline:* For fall admission, 8/1 for domestic students, 4/1 for international students; for spring admission, 1/1 for domestic students, 9/1 for international students. Applications are processed on a rolling basis. Application fee: $75. Electronic applications accepted. *Expenses:* Tuition, state resident: full-time $11,656; part-time $647.50 per credit hour. Tuition, nonresident: full-time $23,351; part-time $1297.25 per credit hour. *Required fees:* $2533; $465.75 per semester. Tuition and fees vary according to course load, campus/location and program. *Financial support:* In 2014–15, 13 research assistantships with full tuition reimbursements (averaging $20,302 per year), 44 teaching assistantships with full tuition reimbursements (averaging $19,484 per year) were awarded. Financial award application deadline: 3/1; financial award applicants required to submit FAFSA. *Total annual research expenditures:* $3.2 million. *Unit head:* Dr. A. J. Davis, Dean, 540-231-6416, Fax: 540-231-6332, E-mail: davisa@vt.edu. *Application contact:* Christine Mattsson-Coon, Executive Assistant, 540-231-6416, Fax: 540-231-6332, E-mail: cmattsso@vt.edu.
Website: http://www.caus.vt.edu/

Wayne State University, College of Liberal Arts and Sciences, Department of Political Science, Detroit, MI 48202. Offers political science (MA, PhD); public administration (MPA), including economic development policy and management, health and human services policy and management, human and fiscal resource management, nonprofit policy and management, organizational behavior and management, urban and metropolitan policy and management; JD/MA. *Accreditation:* NASPAA. *Students:* 56 full-time (25 women), 78 part-time (49 women); includes 41 minority (28 Black or African American, non-Hispanic/Latino; 4 Asian, non-Hispanic/Latino; 5 Hispanic/Latino; 4 Two or more races, non-Hispanic/Latino), 12 international. Average age 34. 153 applicants, 41% accepted, 34 enrolled. In 2014, 30 master's, 5 doctorates awarded. *Degree requirements:* For master's, comprehensive exam; for doctorate, thesis/dissertation. *Entrance requirements:* For master's, GRE General Test, substantial undergraduate preparation in the social sciences (recommended); for doctorate, GRE General Test, 3 letters of recommendation; autobiography; interview. Additional exam requirements/recommendations for international students: Required—TOEFL (minimum score 550 paper-based; 79 iBT), TWE (minimum score 5.5), Michigan English Language Assessment Battery (minimum score 85); Recommended—IELTS (minimum score 6.5). *Application deadline:* For fall admission, 5/1 priority date for domestic and international students; for winter admission, 10/1 priority date for domestic students, 9/1 priority date for international students; for spring admission, 2/1 priority date for domestic students, 1/1 priority date for international students. Applications are processed on a rolling basis. Application fee: $0. Electronic applications accepted. *Expenses:* Tuition, state resident: full-time $10,294; part-time $571.90 per credit hour. Tuition, nonresident: full-time $29,730; part-time $1238.75 per credit hour. *Required fees:* $1365; $43.50 per credit hour. $291.10 per semester. Tuition and fees vary according to course load and program. *Financial support:* In 2014–15, 41 students received support, including 4 fellowships with tuition reimbursements available (averaging $14,146 per year), 13 teaching assistantships with tuition reimbursements available (averaging $16,838 per year); research assistantships with tuition reimbursements available, scholarships/grants, health care benefits, and unspecified assistantships also available. Financial award application deadline: 3/31; financial award applicants required to submit FAFSA. *Faculty research:* American politics and public policy, comparative politics and international relations, political theory, public administration, urban politics. *Unit head:* Dr. Daniel Geller, Chair, 313-577-6328, Fax: 313-993-3435, E-mail: dgeller@wayne.edu. *Application contact:* Dr. Sharon Lean, Graduate Director, E-mail: gradpolisci@wayne.edu.
Website: http://clas.wayne.edu/politicalscience/

Wayne State University, College of Liberal Arts and Sciences, Department of Sociology, Detroit, MI 48202. Offers applied sociology and urban studies (MA); sociology (MA, PhD). *Faculty:* 11 full-time (7 women). *Students:* 28 full-time (18 women), 6 part-time (5 women); includes 11 minority (10 Black or African American, non-Hispanic/Latino; 1 Two or more races, non-Hispanic/Latino), 5 international. Average age 39. 29 applicants, 31% accepted, 3 enrolled. In 2014, 7 master's, 9 doctorates awarded. *Degree requirements:* For master's, thesis optional, oral exam and public defense of thesis/essay; for doctorate, thesis/dissertation. *Entrance requirements:* For master's, GRE General Test, minimum GPA of 3.3 in upper-division courses; substantial background in sociology, social science research methods, sociological theory, and basic statistics; three letters of reference (at least 2 from college/university faculty); writing sample; statement of interest; for doctorate, GRE General Test, minimum GPA of 3.5 in master's work; three letters of reference (at least 2 from college/university faculty); statement of interest; sample of written work. Additional exam requirements/recommendations for international students: Required—TOEFL (minimum score 550 paper-based; 79 iBT), TWE (minimum score 5.5), Michigan English Language Assessment Battery (minimum score 85); Recommended—IELTS (minimum score 6.5). *Application deadline:* For fall admission, 1/15 for domestic and international students. Application fee: $0. Electronic applications accepted. *Expenses:* Tuition, state resident: full-time $10,294; part-time $571.90 per credit hour. Tuition, nonresident: full-time $29,730; part-time $1238.75 per credit hour. *Required fees:* $1365; $43.50 per credit hour. $291.10 per semester. Tuition and fees vary according to course load and program. *Financial support:* In 2014–15, 21 students received support, including 4 fellowships with tuition reimbursements available (averaging $15,073 per year), 8 teaching assistantships with tuition reimbursements available (averaging $16,838 per year); research assistantships with tuition reimbursements available, scholarships/grants, health care benefits, and unspecified assistantships also available. Financial award application deadline: 3/31; financial award applicants required to submit FAFSA. *Faculty research:* Medical sociology, inequality, urban labor. *Unit head:* Dr. Janet Hankin, Chair and Professor, 313-577-8131, E-mail: janet.hankin@wayne.edu. *Application contact:* Dr. Khari Brown, Director of Graduate Studies, 313-577-0146, Fax: 313-577-2735, E-mail: kharib@wayne.edu.
Website: http://clas.wayne.edu/Sociology/

Wright State University, School of Graduate Studies, College of Liberal Arts, Department of Urban Affairs and Geography, Dayton, OH 45435. Offers public administration (MPA). *Accreditation:* NASPAA. *Degree requirements:* For master's, thesis optional. *Entrance requirements:* For master's, interview, minimum GPA of 2.7. Additional exam requirements/recommendations for international students: Required—TOEFL. *Faculty research:* Strategic planning, economic development, housing and public management.

UNIVERSITY OF DELAWARE
School of Public Policy and Administration

 For more information, visit http://petersons.to/delawarepublicadministration

Programs of Study

The School of Public Policy and Administration offers six graduate degree programs: a Master of Public Administration (M.P.A.), a Master of Arts (M.A.) in urban affairs and public policy, a Ph.D. in urban affairs and public policy, a Master of Science in Disaster Science and Management, and a Ph.D. in Disaster Science and Management.

The M.P.A. is a 36-credit, two-year professional degree program that prepares students for leadership positions in public affairs. It is the preferred professional degree for anyone whose ambition is a career in public or nonprofit management. The program boasts a strong, collaborative, faculty-student research environment and has been accredited by the Network of Schools of Public Policy, Affairs, and Administration (NASPAA) since 1982. Areas of specialization include nonprofit and community leadership, public policy and management, emergency management, or a student-designed area (with faculty approval).

The M.A. in urban affairs and public policy is a 36-credit program that typically involves four semesters of full-time study. It offers students a strong foundation in public policy theory and analysis with a strong focus on solving a variety of societal problems. The program is particularly strong in providing students with many opportunities to apply their new theoretical knowledge and analytical skills to real-world issues. This is done through the careful selection of elective courses, participation in a policy analysis studio, or writing a thesis. Most importantly, this application of skills occurs in the close collaboration with faculty and professional staff in conducting research and public service projects that have clear policy impact. These projects tend to be in the areas of disaster science and management, health policy and services, historic preservation, housing and community development, media and public policy, nonprofits and philanthropy, and urban and regional planning. The program also has a vibrant international component with study trips, organized and led by the faculty and professional staff, to various places in Europe, Asia, Latin America, and Africa.

The Ph.D. is an interdisciplinary, research-oriented degree that focuses on analysis of the critical policy challenges of our times. The program prepares scholars to create usable knowledge that can inform decision-making and improve the quality of life in communities at all scales, from cities to nations. The doctoral program prepares scholars to approach these multifaceted challenges from creative vantage points, reflecting diverse, international perspectives that transcend disciplinary views and embody the highest research standards. A concern for the global policy challenges and opportunities of an urbanizing world cuts across all research. Students work alongside faculty and researchers to create new knowledge and develop innovative approaches to expand the possibilities for community enhancement and policy improvement.

The School offers a nationally recognized internship program that places students in paid professional positions in international, national, state, and local government. All students in the School are eligible; the internship is a requirement for preservice M.P.A. students.

The M.S. and Ph.D. program in disaster science and management covers the theories, research methodologies, and policies informing efforts focused on emergency preparedness, mitigation, management and response. The M.S. degree requires 30 credits (non-thesis requires 24 credits). The Ph.D. degree requires 42 credits of graduate-level course work beyond the master's degree and 9 credits of dissertation.

Research Facilities

The School is centrally located in its own building, with its own classrooms and student offices. One of the most distinguishing characteristics of the School of Public Policy and Administration is the integration of theory and practice through applied research projects with the affiliated research and public service centers. Some full-time students are awarded research assistantships on projects in these centers.

The Center for Applied Demography and Survey Research provides demographic and survey data and information on important public issues to researchers and policy makers at all levels (http://www.cadsr.udel.edu). The Center for Community Research and Service helps public, nonprofit, and private organizations in Delaware to design, implement, and evaluate policies and programs that address the needs of low- and moderate-income families and communities related to economic development, housing, and social services. The center also focuses on issues that are vital to the physical and emotional well-being of the world's population. These questions concern the delivery and financing of health care and the outcomes of health care provided (http://www.udel.edu/CCRS). The Center for Historic Architecture and Design focuses on shaping historic preservation planning and policy, reconstructing historic landscapes, documenting threatened historic properties, and advocating for the preservation of historic resources (http://www.udel.edu/CHAD). The Institute for Public Administration links the resources of the University of Delaware (UD) with the management and policy information needs of public and nonprofit organizations (http://www.ipa.udel.edu).

Financial Aid

The School has competitive financial aid programs, including fellowships, research assistantships, and scholarships. Aid is awarded on merit and is limited by the various restrictions established by the sources of aid. Stipends for 2015–16 are $17,500 for the full academic year. Additional special assistantships, fellowships, and internships are available to students through the University Graduate Scholar's Program, for both newly admitted and graduate students currently enrolled. Awards are competitive and are based on many criteria, including challenging social, economic, educational, cultural, or other life circumstances; academic achievements; first generation graduate student status; and/or need as determined by federal income guidelines (FAFSA). Funds are also available through the Delaware Legislative Fellows Program.

Cost of Study

Graduate students will be billed by the credit. The 2015–16 rate is $1,674 per credit. Fully-matriculated students are automatically assessed nonrefundable charges of $454 for the health services fee, $238 for student-sponsored activities, and a $100 recreational fee.

Living and Housing Costs

The University provides some graduate apartments, and there is plenty of off-campus housing in the surrounding community in many price ranges. For more information, students should contact the Housing Assignment Services Office (302-831-2491; http://www.udel.edu/has).

Student Group

The School has 48 students in the M.P.A. program, 27 in the M.A. and 40 in the Ph.D. Urban Affairs and Public Policy program, and 11 in the M.S. and 14 in the Ph.D. Disaster Science and Management program.

Student Outcomes

Graduates find career positions in government and nonprofit organizations and occasionally in the private sector with consulting firms. With UD's proximity to Washington, D.C.; Philadelphia; and New York, many graduates pursue positions in nearby metropolitan areas, as well as positions in state and local government in the region and in the nation. Several recent graduates have been successful in the highly competitive federal Presidential Management Fellowship Program.

Location

Located midway between Philadelphia and Baltimore, the main campus of the University of Delaware is in Newark, conveniently near New York City; Washington, D.C.; and the seashore. A community of 30,000, with a vibrant Main Street of coffeehouses, restaurants, and small shops, Newark is about 14 miles from Wilmington, Delaware's largest city.

The University

The University is a comprehensive land-, sea-, space-, and urban-grant institution of higher education with an enrollment of approximately 3,765 graduate students in 2015–16. The University offers 124 programs leading to a master's degree and fifty-nine programs leading to a doctoral degree.

University of Delaware

In 2015, the University awarded 231 doctoral degrees and 732 master's degrees.

Applying

SPPA welcomes informal inquiries. Students seeking priority consideration for financial aid or admission to any of the graduate programs should apply by January 15. For the master's programs, candidates must have an undergraduate GPA above 3.0 (on a 4.0 scale). Admission to the Ph.D. program requires a master's degree with at least a 3.5 GPA. A GRE score in the 69th or higher percentile is normally expected; competitive scores for admission are 160 for the verbal section and 155 for the quantitative section. Complete applications contain three letters of recommendation, a personal statement of academic and career objectives (for the Ph.D., include a statement of the applicant's research interests), and academic transcripts. For nonnative speakers of English, a demonstrated proficiency in English is required, with a TOEFL score of at least 105.

Correspondence and Information

School of Public Policy and Administration Admissions
University of Delaware
Newark, Delaware 19716-7310
Phone: 302-831-1687
Fax: 302-831-3296
E-mail: sppa@udel.edu
Website: http://www.sppa.udel.edu

THE FACULTY AND THEIR RESEARCH

At the core of the School of Public Policy and Administration are the dedicated faculty members, who are challenging teachers, seasoned researchers, and experienced practitioners. With interdisciplinary backgrounds as skilled executives, managers, and community leaders, they bring practical experience to the classroom and successfully blend a solid academic base with stimulating practical experience.

Maria P. Aristigueta, Charles P. Messick Professor in Public Administration; Associate Director, School of Public Policy and Administration; and Senior Policy Fellow, Institute for Public Administration; D.P.A., USC, 1997. Administrative behavior, performance management, policy analysis, strategic management.

Nina P. David, Assistant Professor; Ph.D., Michigan, 2008. Land use planning and policy, regional planning and cooperation, growth management, architecture and urban design.

Robert B. Denhardt, Visiting Scholar; Ph.D., Kentucky, 1968. Public sector management, strategic planning and public productivity.

Edward J. Freel, Instructor and Policy Scientist, Institute for Public Administration; M.Ed., Delaware, 1975. Civic education, learning initiatives, public administration.

Raheemah Jabbar-Bey, Assistant Professor and Assistant Policy Specialist, Center for Community Research and Service; M.A., New Hampshire, 1996. Community and economic development planning, organizational capacity building of nonprofits, urban policy analysis.

Eric D. Jacobson, Associate Professor and Policy Scientist, Institute for Public Administration; M.P.A., Delaware, 1981. Public economics, health policy, employee compensation and benefits, tourism development and research, analytical methods.

Janet B. Johnson, Associate Professor, Department of Political Science and International Relations; Ph.D., Cornell, 1978. Subnational politics, environmental policy, research methods, public policy analysis.

Jonathan Justice, Professor; Ph.D., Rutgers, 2003. Public financial management, nongovernmental public administration, urban policy and administration.

Gerald Kauffman, Assistant Professor and Project Director, Water Resources Agency; Ph.D., Delaware. Watershed policy, planning, and management; water resources government and finance; water resources engineering; hydrology and hydraulics.

Jerome R. Lewis, Associate Professor; Director, Institute for Public Administration; and Interim Director, Master of Public Administration Program; Ph.D., NYU, 1968. Public administration, personnel management, urban planning, political leadership.

John G. McNutt, Professor; Ph.D., Tennessee, 1991. Technology, nonprofit management, advocacy and government relations, community organization and planning.

Anthony E. Middlebrooks, Associate Professor; Ph.D., Wisconsin, 1999. Leadership formation and development, creativity and leadership, service and social justice, research methods.

James L. Morrison, Professor; Ed.D., Temple, 1971. Telecommunications and consumer policy, consumer environmental issues, consumer protection

Kathleen M. Murphy, Instructor and Coordinator, Conflict Resolution Program; M.P.A., Delaware. Conflict resolution, mediation, and organizational and leadership development.

Steven W. Peuquet, Associate Professor and Director, Center for Community Research and Service; Ph.D., Pennsylvania, 1996. Strategic planning, housing, homelessness, electronic community networks, public policy analysis and evaluation.

Edward C. Ratledge, Associate Professor and Director, Center for Applied Demography and Survey Research; M.A., Delaware, 1972. Management information systems, econometrics, criminal justice systems.

Daniel Rich, Professor and Director, Urban Affairs and Public Policy Ph.D. Program; Ph.D., MIT, 1972. Public policy and public management.

Breck Robinson, Associate Professor and Director, Public Policy Undergraduate Program; Ph.D., Tennessee, 1994. Financial institutions, public policy, real estate finance.

Andrea Sarzynski, Assistant Professor; Ph.D., George Washington, 2006. Urbanization and environmental change; environmental policy and politics; urban and regional planning; science and policymaking.

Rebecca Sheppard, Assistant Professor and Interim Director, Center of Historic Architecture and Design; Ph.D., Delaware, 2009. Historic preservation planning, history of rural landscapes and the built environment, landscape preservation.

Karen F. Stein, Associate Professor and Director, Organizational and Community Leadership Undergraduate Program; Ph.D., Delaware, 1984. Domestic elder abuse and neglect, leadership studies, consumer and family economic policy analysis.

Leland Ware, Louis L. Redding Chair for the Study of Law and Public Policy and Interim Director, School of Public Policy and Administration; J.D., Boston College, 1973. Employment discrimination law, civil rights law, civil procedure.

Harvey White, Professor of Practice; Ph.D., North Carolina at Chapel Hill, 1985. Human talent development and management, international development and management, social equity and environmental justice, health policy.

Danilo Yanich, Associate Professor; Director, Urban Affairs and Public Policy Master's Program; and Associate Policy Scientist, Center for Community Research and Service; Ph.D., Delaware, 1980. Criminal justice policy, media and public policy, international comparative governance.

Section 26
Social Sciences

This section contains a directory of institutions offering graduate work in social sciences. Additional information about programs listed in the directory may be obtained by writing directly to the dean of a graduate school or chair of a department at the address given in the directory.

For programs offering related work, see also in this book *Area and Cultural Studies, Communication and Media, Criminology and Forensics, Economics, Geography, Family and Consumer Sciences, Political Science and* *International Affairs, Psychology and Counseling,* and *Sociology, Anthropology, and Archaeology.*

CONTENTS

Social Sciences

California Institute of Technology, Division of the Humanities and Social Sciences, Social Science Program, Pasadena, CA 91125-0001. Offers MS, PhD. *Faculty:* 30 full-time (4 women). *Students:* 36 full-time (8 women); includes 1 minority (Asian, non-Hispanic/Latino), 28 international. Average age 27. 254 applicants, 10% accepted, 10 enrolled. In 2014, 8 master's, 1 doctorate awarded. Terminal master's awarded for partial completion of doctoral program. *Degree requirements:* For doctorate, thesis/dissertation. *Entrance requirements:* For doctorate, GRE General Test. Additional exam requirements/recommendations for international students: Required—TOEFL (minimum score 90 paper-based); Recommended—TWE. *Application deadline:* For fall admission, 12/15 for domestic and international students. Application fee: $100. Electronic applications accepted. *Financial support:* In 2014–15, 34 students received support, including 17 fellowships with tuition reimbursements available (averaging $30,000 per year), 4 research assistantships with tuition reimbursements available (averaging $30,000 per year), 13 teaching assistantships with tuition reimbursements available (averaging $30,000 per year); Federal Work-Study, institutionally sponsored loans, and scholarships/grants also available. *Faculty research:* Theoretical and applied microeconomics, experimental social science, political science, quantitative history, behavioral economics and neuroscience. *Unit head:* Dr. Jean Laurent Rosenthal, Chair, 626-395-4082, E-mail: jlr@hss.caltech.edu. *Application contact:* Laurel Auchampaugh, Secretary, 626-395-4206, Fax: 626-405-9841, E-mail: gradsec@hss.caltech.edu. Website: http://www.hss.caltech.edu/content/graduate-studies

California State University, Chico, Office of Graduate Studies, College of Behavioral and Social Sciences, Social Science Program, Chico, CA 95929-0722. Offers social science (MA); social science education (MA). *Students:* 7 full-time (5 women), 9 part-time (8 women); includes 3 minority (all Hispanic/Latino). Average age 38. 3 applicants, 67% accepted, 2 enrolled. In 2014, 2 master's awarded. *Degree requirements:* For master's, thesis or project. *Entrance requirements:* For master's, GRE General Test or MAT, two letters of recommendation, statement of purpose. Additional exam requirements/recommendations for international students: Required—TOEFL (minimum score 550 paper-based; 80 iBT), IELTS (minimum score 6.5), PTE (minimum score 59). *Application deadline:* For fall admission, 3/1 priority date for domestic students, 3/1 for international students; for spring admission, 9/15 priority date for domestic students, 9/15 for international students. Application fee: $55. Electronic applications accepted. *Expenses:* Tuition, state resident: full-time $7002. Tuition, nonresident: full-time $18,162. *Required fees:* $1530. Tuition and fees vary according to program. *Financial support:* Fellowships, teaching assistantships, career-related internships or fieldwork, institutionally sponsored loans, traineeships, and unspecified assistantships available. Financial award application deadline: 3/1; financial award applicants required to submit FAFSA. *Unit head:* Dr. Eddie Vela, Dean, 530-895-6171, Fax: 530-898-5986, E-mail: bss@csuchico.edu. *Application contact:* Judy L. Rice, Graduate Admissions Counselor, 530-898-5416, Fax: 530-898-3342, E-mail: jlrice@csuchico.edu. Website: http://www.csuchico.edu/sosc

California State University, San Bernardino, Graduate Studies, College of Social and Behavioral Sciences, Program in Social Sciences, San Bernardino, CA 92407-2397. Offers MA. *Students:* 4 full-time (2 women), 31 part-time (10 women); includes 19 minority (5 Black or African American, non-Hispanic/Latino; 11 Hispanic/Latino; 3 Two or more races, non-Hispanic/Latino), 1 international. Average age 27. 28 applicants, 64% accepted, 14 enrolled. In 2014, 7 master's awarded. *Entrance requirements:* Additional exam requirements/recommendations for international students: Required—TOEFL. *Application deadline:* For fall admission, 7/17 for domestic students. Application fee: $55. *Expenses:* Tuition, state resident: full-time $6738; part-time $1302 per term. Tuition, nonresident: full-time $17,898; part-time $248 per unit. *Required fees:* $365 per quarter. Tuition and fees vary according to degree level and program. *Financial support:* Fellowships, research assistantships, teaching assistantships, and institutionally sponsored loans available. Financial award application deadline: 5/1. *Unit head:* Dr. Cherstyn Lyon, Coordinator, 909-537-3836, E-mail: clyon@csusb.edu. *Application contact:* Dr. Jeffrey Thompson, Dean of Graduate Studies, 909-537-5058, E-mail: jthompso@csusb.edu.

California University of Pennsylvania, School of Graduate Studies and Research, College of Liberal Arts, Department of Justice, Law and Society, California, PA 15419-1394. Offers social science - criminal justice (MA). Part-time and evening/weekend programs available. *Degree requirements:* For master's, comprehensive exam, thesis optional. *Entrance requirements:* For master's, MAT, minimum GPA of 3.0. Additional exam requirements/recommendations for international students: Required—TOEFL (minimum score 550 paper-based; 80 iBT). Electronic applications accepted. *Expenses:* Tuition, state resident: full-time $10,896; part-time $454 per credit. Tuition, nonresident: full-time $16,344; part-time $681 per credit. *Required fees:* $2425. *Faculty research:* Ethics and law, ethics in police practice, law and morality, police policy, St. Thomas Aquinas and crime.

Campbellsville University, College of Arts and Sciences, Campbellsville, KY 42718-2799. Offers social science (MA). Part-time programs available. *Students:* 2 full-time (both women), 1 (woman) part-time, 1 international. Average age 35. In 2014, 5 master's awarded. *Degree requirements:* For master's, comprehensive exam. *Entrance requirements:* For master's, GRE General Test, LSAT, minimum GPA of 2.9. Additional exam requirements/recommendations for international students: Recommended—TOEFL. *Application deadline:* Applications are processed on a rolling basis. Application fee: $25. Electronic applications accepted. *Financial support:* In 2014–15, 9 students received support. Institutionally sponsored loans and unspecified assistantships available. Financial award application deadline: 6/1; financial award applicants required to submit FAFSA. *Unit head:* Dr. Mike Page, Dean, 270-789-5394. *Application contact:* Monica Bamwine, Assistant Director of Admissions, 270-789-5221, Fax: 270-789-5071, E-mail: mkbamwine@campbellsville.edu. Website: http://www.campbellsville.edu/

Carnegie Mellon University, Dietrich College of Humanities and Social Sciences, Department of Social and Decision Sciences, Pittsburgh, PA 15213-3891. Offers behavioral decision research (PhD); social and decision science (PhD); strategy, entrepreneurship, and technological change (PhD). Terminal master's awarded for partial completion of doctoral program. *Degree requirements:* For doctorate, comprehensive exam, thesis/dissertation, research paper. *Entrance requirements:* For doctorate, GRE General Test. Additional exam requirements/recommendations for international students: Required—TOEFL. Electronic applications accepted. *Faculty research:* Organization theory, political science, sociology, technology studies.

The Citadel, The Military College of South Carolina, Citadel Graduate College, Department of Political Science, Charleston, SC 29409. Offers social science (MA). Part-time and evening/weekend programs available. *Entrance requirements:* For master's, GRE (minimum combined score of 290 verbal and quantitative), MAT (minimum raw score of 396). Additional exam requirements/recommendations for international students: Required—TOEFL (minimum score 550 paper-based). Electronic applications accepted.

Clemson University, Graduate School, Program in International Family and Community Studies, Clemson, SC 29634. Offers PhD. *Faculty:* 5 full-time (3 women), 5 part-time/adjunct (3 women). *Students:* 12 full-time (11 women), 22 part-time (18 women); includes 5 minority (1 Black or African American, non-Hispanic/Latino; 3 Asian, non-Hispanic/Latino; 1 Hispanic/Latino), 15 international. Average age 36. In 2014, 1 doctorate awarded. *Degree requirements:* For doctorate, thesis/dissertation. *Entrance requirements:* For doctorate, GRE General Test. Additional exam requirements/recommendations for international students: Required—TOEFL. *Application deadline:* Applications are processed on a rolling basis. Application fee: $70 ($80 for international students). Electronic applications accepted. *Expenses:* Expenses: Contact institution. *Financial support:* In 2014–15, 9 students received support, including 9 research assistantships with partial tuition reimbursements available (averaging $21,444 per year); fellowships with full and partial tuition reimbursements available, teaching assistantships, career-related internships or fieldwork, institutionally sponsored loans, scholarships/grants, health care benefits, and unspecified assistantships also available. Support available to part-time students. *Total annual research expenditures:* $728,285. *Unit head:* Dr. Mark Small, Director, 864-656-6286, E-mail: msmall@clemson.edu. *Application contact:* Information Contact, 864-656-3195, E-mail: gradapp@clemson.edu. Website: http://www.grad.clemson.edu/programs/Family-Community-Studies/

Columbia University, Graduate School of Arts and Sciences, New York, NY 10027. Offers African-American studies (MA); American studies (MA); anthropology (MA, PhD); art history and archaeology (MA, PhD); astronomy (PhD); biological sciences (PhD); biotechnology (MA); chemical physics (PhD); chemistry (PhD); classical studies (MA, PhD); classics (MA, PhD); climate and society (MA); earth and environmental sciences (PhD); East Asia: regional studies (MA); East Asian languages and cultures (MA, PhD); ecology, evolution and environmental biology (MA), including conservation biology; ecology, evolution, and environmental biology (PhD), including ecology and evolutionary biology, evolutionary primatology; economics (PhD); English and comparative literature (MA, PhD); French and Romance philology (MA, PhD); Germanic languages (MA, PhD); global French studies (MA); Hispanic cultural studies (MA); history (PhD); history and literature (MA); human rights studies (MA); Islamic studies (MA); Italian (MA, PhD); Japanese pedagogy (MA); Jewish studies (MA); Latin America and the Caribbean: regional studies (MA); Latin American and Iberian cultures (PhD); mathematics (MA, PhD), including finance (MA); medieval and Renaissance studies (MA); Middle Eastern, South Asian, and African studies (MA, PhD); modern art: critical and curatorial studies (MA); modern European studies (MA); museum anthropology (MA); music (DMA, PhD); oral history (MA); philosophical foundations of physics (MA); philosophy (MA, PhD); physics (PhD); political science (MA, PhD); psychology (PhD); quantitative methods in the social sciences (MA); religion (MA, PhD); Russia, Eurasia and East Europe: regional studies (MA); Russian translation (MA); Slavic cultures (MA); Slavic languages (MA, PhD); sociology (MA, PhD); South Asian studies (MA); statistics (MA, PhD); theatre (PhD); JD/PhD; MA/MS; MD/PhD; MPA/MA. Dual-degree programs require admission to both Graduate School of Arts and Sciences and another Columbia school. Part-time and evening/weekend programs available. Terminal master's awarded for partial completion of doctoral program. *Degree requirements:* For master's, thesis (for some programs); for doctorate, comprehensive exam, thesis/dissertation. *Entrance requirements:* For master's and doctorate, GRE General Test, GRE Subject Test (for some programs). Electronic applications accepted. *Faculty research:* Humanities, natural sciences, social sciences.

Eastern Michigan University, Graduate School, College of Arts and Sciences, Department of History and Philosophy, Programs in Social Sciences, Ypsilanti, MI 48197. Offers MA, MLS, Graduate Certificate. Part-time and evening/weekend programs available. Postbaccalaureate distance learning degree programs offered (minimal on-campus study). *Students:* 2 full-time (both women), 6 part-time (3 women); includes 3 minority (2 Black or African American, non-Hispanic/Latino; 1 Hispanic/Latino). Average age 39. 4 applicants, 100% accepted, 3 enrolled. In 2014, 1 master's awarded. *Degree requirements:* For master's, thesis optional. *Entrance requirements:* Additional exam requirements/recommendations for international students: Required—TOEFL. *Application deadline:* Applications are processed on a rolling basis. Application fee: $45. *Financial support:* Fellowships, research assistantships with full tuition reimbursements, teaching assistantships with full tuition reimbursements, career-related internships or fieldwork, Federal Work-Study, institutionally sponsored loans, scholarships/grants, tuition waivers (partial), and unspecified assistantships available. Support available to part-time students. Financial award applicants required to submit FAFSA. *Application contact:* Dr. Ronald Delph, Director, 734-487-1018, Fax: 734-487-6835, E-mail: rdelph@emich.edu.

Edinboro University of Pennsylvania, Department of History, Anthropology and World Languages, Edinboro, PA 16444. Offers social sciences (MA), including anthropology, history. Part-time and evening/weekend programs available. *Degree requirements:* For master's, thesis or alternative, competency exam. *Entrance requirements:* For master's, GRE or MAT, minimum QPA of 2.5. Electronic applications accepted.

Florida Agricultural and Mechanical University, Division of Graduate Studies, Research, and Continuing Education, College of Social Sciences, Arts and Humanities, Department of History and Political Science, Program in Applied Social Science, Tallahassee, FL 32307-3200. Offers criminal justice (MASS); history (MASS); political science (MASS); public administration (MASS). Part-time programs available. *Degree requirements:* For master's, thesis optional. *Entrance requirements:* For master's, GRE General Test, minimum GPA of 3.0. *Faculty research:* Southern history, black history, election trends, Presidential history.

George Mason University, Krasnow Institute for Advanced Study, Fairfax, VA 22030. Offers computational social science (PhD). *Faculty:* 24 full-time (7 women), 5 part-time/adjunct (0 women). *Students:* 19 full-time (4 women), 30 part-time (6 women); includes 6 minority (2 Black or African American, non-Hispanic/Latino; 4 Asian, non-Hispanic/Latino), 10 international. Average age 37. 29 applicants, 52% accepted, 12 enrolled. In 2014, 5 doctorates, 5 other advanced degrees awarded. *Entrance requirements:* For doctorate, GRE, expanded goals statement, bachelor's degree in relevant field with minimum GPA of 3.25, 2 copies of official transcripts, 3 letters of recommendation; for Advanced Certificate, undergraduate degree with minimum GPA of 3.0, 2 copies of official transcripts, resume, expanded goals statement. Additional exam requirements/recommendations for international students: Required—TOEFL (minimum score 570 paper-based; 80 iBT), IELTS (minimum score 6.5). Application fee: $65 ($80 for international students). *Expenses:* Tuition, state resident: full-time $9794; part-time

$408 per credit hour. Tuition, nonresident: full-time $26,978; part-time $1124 per credit hour. *Required fees:* $2820; $118 per credit hour. Tuition and fees vary according to course load and program. *Financial support:* In 2014–15, 11 students received support, including 10 research assistantships with full and partial tuition reimbursements available (averaging $20,097 per year), 1 teaching assistantship with full and partial tuition reimbursement available (averaging $3,000 per year); career-related internships or fieldwork, Federal Work-Study, scholarships/grants, unspecified assistantships, and health care benefits (for full-time research or teaching assistantship recipients) also available. Financial award application deadline: 3/1; financial award applicants required to submit FAFSA. *Faculty research:* Molecular neuroscience, computational social science, social complexity, neuroeconomics, neural dynamics. *Total annual research expenditures:* $4.9 million. *Unit head:* Kenneth DeJong, Interim Director, 703-993-4398, Fax: 703-993-4325, E-mail: kdejong@gmu.edu. *Application contact:* Karen Underwood, Assistant Director, Graduate Programs, 703-993-9298, Fax: 703-993-9290, E-mail: kunderwo@gmu.edu.
Website: http://krasnow.gmu.edu/

Graduate Theological Union, Graduate Programs, Berkeley, CA 94709-1212. Offers art and religion (MA, PhD, Th D); biblical languages (MA); biblical studies (MA); Biblical studies (PhD, Th D); Buddhist studies (MA); Christian spirituality (MA, PhD, Th D); cultural and historical studies of religions (MA, PhD, Th D); ethics and social theory (PhD, Th D); history (MA, PhD, Th D); homiletics (MA, PhD, Th D); interdisciplinary studies (PhD, Th D); Jewish studies (MA, PhD, Th D, Certificate); liturgical studies (MA, PhD, Th D); Near Eastern religions (PhD, Th D); Orthodox Christian studies (MA); religion and psychology (MA, PhD, Th D); religion and society/ethics and social theory (MA); systematic and philosophical theology (MA, PhD, Th D). PhD programs in Jewish studies and Near Eastern religions offered jointly with University of California, Berkeley. *Accreditation:* ATS. Terminal master's awarded for partial completion of doctoral program. *Degree requirements:* For master's, one foreign language, thesis; for doctorate, one foreign language, comprehensive exam, thesis/dissertation. *Entrance requirements:* For master's, GRE General Test; for doctorate, GRE General Test, MA or M Div. Additional exam requirements/recommendations for international students: Required—TOEFL. Electronic applications accepted.

Harrison Middleton University, Graduate Program, Tempe, AZ 85282. Offers education (MA, Ed D); humanities (MA); imaginative literature (MA); interdisciplinary studies (DA); jurisprudence (MA); natural science (MA); philosophy and religion (MA); social science (MA). Part-time and evening/weekend programs available. Postbaccalaureate distance learning degree programs offered (no on-campus study). *Degree requirements:* For master's and doctorate, capstone project. *Entrance requirements:* For master's, interview; for doctorate, 2 academic letters of reference, interview, essay. Additional exam requirements/recommendations for international students: Required—TOEFL (minimum score 550 paper-based; 80 iBT). Electronic applications accepted. *Faculty research:* Japanese animation, educational leadership, war art, John Muir's wilderness.

Hollins University, Graduate Programs, Program in Liberal Studies, Roanoke, VA 24020. Offers humanities (MALS); interdisciplinary studies (MALS); leadership (MALS); liberal studies (CAS); social science (MALS); visual and performing arts (MALS). Part-time and evening/weekend programs available. *Students:* 3 full-time (all women), 37 part-time (32 women); includes 6 minority (4 Black or African American, non-Hispanic/Latino; 1 Hispanic/Latino; 1 Two or more races, non-Hispanic/Latino). Average age 44. 13 applicants, 100% accepted, 9 enrolled. In 2014, 15 master's awarded. *Degree requirements:* For master's, thesis. *Entrance requirements:* For master's, letters of recommendation, interview. Additional exam requirements/recommendations for international students: Required—TOEFL (minimum score 550 paper-based; 79 iBT). *Application deadline:* For fall admission, 7/1 priority date for domestic and international students; for spring admission, 12/10 priority date for domestic and international students. Applications are processed on a rolling basis. Application fee: $40. Electronic applications accepted. *Financial support:* In 2014–15, 7 students received support, including 7 fellowships (averaging $1,000 per year); scholarships/grants also available. Support available to part-time students. Financial award application deadline: 7/15; financial award applicants required to submit FAFSA. *Faculty research:* Diversity, gender and women's studies, political science, leadership. *Unit head:* Dr. Joe Leedom, Director, 540-362-6326, Fax: 540-362-6288, E-mail: jleedom@hollins.edu. *Application contact:* Cathy S. Koon, Manager of Graduate Services, 540-362-6326, Fax: 540-362-6288, E-mail: ckoon@hollins.edu.
Website: http://www.hollins.edu/

Humboldt State University, Academic Programs, College of Arts, Humanities, and Social Sciences, Program in Environment and Community, Arcata, CA 95521-8299. Offers MA. *Students:* 20 full-time (12 women), 6 part-time (4 women); includes 6 minority (1 American Indian or Alaska Native, non-Hispanic/Latino; 1 Asian, non-Hispanic/Latino; 3 Hispanic/Latino; 1 Two or more races, non-Hispanic/Latino). Average age 31. 27 applicants, 74% accepted, 12 enrolled. In 2014, 3 master's awarded. *Degree requirements:* For master's, thesis or alternative, qualifying exam. *Entrance requirements:* For master's, minimum GPA of 2.5, 3 letters of recommendation. Additional exam requirements/recommendations for international students; Required—TOEFL (minimum score 500 paper-based). *Application deadline:* For fall admission, 3/1 for domestic students, 3/15 for international students. Applications are processed on a rolling basis. Application fee: $55. *Expenses:* Tuition, state resident: full-time $6738; part-time $3906 per year. Tuition, nonresident: full-time $13,434; part-time $6138 per year. *Required fees:* $1690; $1266 per year. Tuition and fees vary according to program. *Financial support:* Application deadline: 3/1; applicants required to submit FAFSA. *Faculty research:* Geography, political science, ethnic studies, anthropology, economics. *Unit head:* Dr. Noah Zerbe, Graduate Coordinator, 707-826-4494, Fax: 707-826-4496, E-mail: noah.zerbe@humboldt.edu. *Application contact:* Dr. Mark Baker, Coordinator, 717-826-3907, Fax: 707-826-4496, E-mail: j.mark.baker@humboldt.edu.
Website: http://www.humboldt.edu/envcomm/

Indiana University Bloomington, Maurer School of Law, Bloomington, IN 47405-7000. Offers comparative law (MCL); juridical science (SJD); law (LL M, JD); law and social sciences (PhD); legal studies (Certificate); JD/MA; JD/MBA; JD/MLS; JD/MPA; JD/MS; JD/MSES. PhD offered through University Graduate School. *Accreditation:* ABA. *Faculty:* 72 full-time (28 women), 14 part-time/adjunct (4 women). *Students:* 640 full-time (293 women), 46 part-time (22 women); includes 128 minority (41 Black or African American, non-Hispanic/Latino; 2 American Indian or Alaska Native, non-Hispanic/Latino; 30 Asian, non-Hispanic/Latino; 47 Hispanic/Latino; 8 Two or more races, non-Hispanic/Latino), 131 international. Average age 26. 659 applicants, 55% accepted, 179 enrolled. In 2014, 68 master's, 224 doctorates, 1 other advanced degree awarded. *Degree requirements:* For master's, thesis or practicum; for doctorate, thesis/dissertation (for some programs), research seminar (for JD). *Entrance requirements:* For master's, LSAT, 3 letters of recommendation, law degree or license to practice; for doctorate, LSAT. Additional exam requirements/recommendations for international students: Required—TOEFL (minimum score 560 paper-based; 80 iBT). *Application deadline:* For fall admission, 3/1 priority date for domestic and international students. Applications are processed on a rolling basis. Application fee: $55 ($65 for international students). Electronic applications accepted. *Financial support:* In 2014–15, 301

students received support. Fellowships, research assistantships, teaching assistantships, career-related internships or fieldwork, Federal Work-Study, institutionally sponsored loans, scholarships/grants, health care benefits, and unspecified assistantships available. Financial award application deadline: 3/1; financial award applicants required to submit FAFSA. *Faculty research:* Environmental risk assessment and policy analysis, information privacy and security, judicial independence, accountability, ethics. *Total annual research expenditures:* $1.4 million. *Unit head:* Hannah Buxbaum, Interim Dean, 812-855-8886, E-mail: hbuxbaum@indiana.edu. *Application contact:* Will Schaad, Director of Graduate Admissions, 812-856-7217, E-mail: wschaad@indiana.edu.
Website: http://www.law.indiana.edu/

Indiana University–Purdue University Indianapolis, School of Public Health, Indianapolis, IN 46202. Offers biostatistics (MPH); environmental health science (MPH); epidemiology (MPH, PhD); health administration (MHA); health policy and management (MPH, PhD); social and behavioral sciences (MPH). *Accreditation:* CEPH. *Students:* 149 full-time (98 women), 153 part-time (98 women); includes 70 minority (40 Black or African American, non-Hispanic/Latino; 19 Asian, non-Hispanic/Latino; 7 Hispanic/Latino; 1 Native Hawaiian or other Pacific Islander, non-Hispanic/Latino; 3 Two or more races, non-Hispanic/Latino), 11 international. Average age 30. 342 applicants, 47% accepted, 97 enrolled. In 2014, 96 master's awarded. Application fee: $55 ($65 for international students). *Expenses:* Expenses: Contact institution. *Financial support:* Fellowships, research assistantships, and teaching assistantships available. *Unit head:* Dr. Paul Halverson, Dean, 317-274-4242. *Application contact:* Shawne Mathis, Student Services Coordinator, 317-278-0337, E-mail: snmathis@iupui.edu.
Website: http://www.pbhealth.iupui.edu/

Johns Hopkins University, Bloomberg School of Public Health, Department of Health, Behavior and Society, Baltimore, MD 21218-2699. Offers genetic counseling (Sc M); health education and health communication (MSPH); social and behavioral sciences (Dr PH, PhD); social factors in health (MHS). *Degree requirements:* For master's, comprehensive exam (for some programs), thesis (for some programs); for doctorate, comprehensive exam, thesis/dissertation. *Entrance requirements:* For master's, GRE, curriculum vitae, 3 letters of recommendation; for doctorate, GRE, transcripts, curriculum vitae, 3 recommendation letters. Additional exam requirements/recommendations for international students: Required—TOEFL (minimum score 600 paper-based; 100 iBT). Electronic applications accepted. *Faculty research:* Social determinants of health and structural and community-level inventions to improve health, communication and health education, behavioral and social aspects of genetic counseling.

Massachusetts Institute of Technology, School of Humanities, Arts, and Social Sciences, Program in Science, Technology, and Society, Cambridge, MA 02139. Offers history, anthropology, and science, technology and society (PhD). *Faculty:* 11 full-time (6 women). *Students:* 31 full-time (23 women); includes 7 minority (1 Black or African American, non-Hispanic/Latino; 2 American Indian or Alaska Native, non-Hispanic/Latino; 3 Asian, non-Hispanic/Latino; 1 Hispanic/Latino), 7 international. Average age 31. 145 applicants, 7% accepted, 3 enrolled. In 2014, 6 doctorates awarded. *Degree requirements:* For doctorate, comprehensive exam, thesis/dissertation. *Entrance requirements:* For doctorate, GRE General Test. Additional exam requirements/recommendations for international students: Required—TOEFL (minimum score 577 paper-based; 90 iBT), IELTS (minimum score 7). *Application deadline:* For fall admission, 12/15 for domestic and international students. Application fee: $75. Electronic applications accepted. *Expenses: Tuition:* Full-time $44,720; part-time $699 per unit. *Required fees:* $296. *Financial support:* In 2014–15, 29 students received support, including 19 fellowships (averaging $32,800 per year), 2 research assistantships (averaging $35,800 per year), 7 teaching assistantships (averaging $36,600 per year); Federal Work-Study, institutionally sponsored loans, scholarships/grants, health care benefits, and unspecified assistantships also available. Financial award application deadline: 4/15; financial award applicants required to submit FAFSA. *Faculty research:* History of science; history of technology; sociology of science and technology; anthropology of science and technology; science, technology, and society. *Total annual research expenditures:* $64,000. *Unit head:* Prof. David Kaiser, Program Director, 617-253-4062, Fax: 617-258-8118, E-mail: stsprogram@mit.edu. *Application contact:* Academic Administrator, 617-253-9759, Fax: 617-258-8118, E-mail: hasts@mit.edu.
Website: http://web.mit.edu/sts/

Mississippi College, Graduate School, College of Arts and Sciences, School of Humanities and Social Sciences, Department of History, Political Science, Administration of Justice, and Paralegal Studies, Clinton, MS 39058. Offers administration of justice (MSS); history (M Ed, MA, MSS); paralegal studies (Certificate); political science (MSS); social sciences (M Ed, MSS). Part-time programs available. *Degree requirements:* For master's, one foreign language, comprehensive exam, thesis (for some programs). *Entrance requirements:* For master's, GRE or NTE, minimum GPA of 2.5. Additional exam requirements/recommendations for international students: Recommended—TOEFL, IELTS. Electronic applications accepted.

Montclair State University, The Graduate School, College of Education and Human Services, MAT Program in Teaching, Montclair, NJ 07043-1624. Offers art (MAT); biology (MAT); chemistry (MAT); earth science (MAT); English (MAT); French (MAT); health and physical education (MAT); health education (MAT); mathematics (MAT); music (MAT); physical education (MAT); physical science (MAT); social studies (MAT); Spanish (MAT); teacher of English as a second language (MAT). *Students:* 254 full-time (176 women), 205 part-time (167 women); includes 102 minority (50 Black or African American, non-Hispanic/Latino; 1 American Indian or Alaska Native, non-Hispanic/Latino; 17 Asian, non-Hispanic/Latino; 26 Hispanic/Latino; 8 Two or more races, non-Hispanic/Latino), 2 international. Average age 29. 181 applicants, 72% accepted, 120 enrolled. In 2014, 200 master's awarded. *Degree requirements:* For master's, comprehensive exam, thesis or alternative. *Entrance requirements:* For master's, GRE General Test, interview, 2 letters of recommendation. Additional exam requirements/recommendations for international students: Required—TOEFL (minimum score 83 iBT), IELTS (minimum score 6.5). *Application deadline:* Applications are processed on a rolling basis. Application fee: $60. Electronic applications accepted. *Expenses:* Tuition, state resident: full-time $9960; part-time $553.35 per credit. Tuition, nonresident: full-time $15,074; part-time $837.43 per credit. *Required fees:* $1595; $88.63 per credit. Tuition and fees vary according to degree level and program. *Financial support:* Federal Work-Study, scholarships/grants, and unspecified assistantships available. Support available to part-time students. Financial award application deadline: 3/1; financial award applicants required to submit FAFSA. *Unit head:* Dr. David Schwarzer, Chairperson, 973-655-5187. *Application contact:* Amy Aiello, Executive Director of The Graduate School, 973-655-5147, Fax: 973-655-7869, E-mail: graduate.school@montclair.edu.

The New School, The New School for Social Research, New York, NY 10003. Offers M Phil, MA, MS, DS Sc, PhD. Part-time and evening/weekend programs available. Terminal master's awarded for partial completion of doctoral program. *Degree requirements:* For master's, variable foreign language requirement, exam or thesis; for doctorate, variable foreign language requirement, comprehensive exam, thesis/

dissertation, qualifying exam. *Entrance requirements:* For master's, GRE General Test; for doctorate, GRE General Test, MA. Additional exam requirements/recommendations for international students: Required—TOEFL (minimum score 600 paper-based; 100 iBT). Electronic applications accepted. *Expenses:* Contact institution. *Faculty research:* Civil society and democracy, international movements of refugees, minority use of health services, memory, morality and genetics.

New York University, Global Institute of Public Health, New York, NY 10003. Offers biological basis of public health (PhD); community and international health (MPH); global health leadership (MPH); health systems and health services research (PhD); population and community health (PhD); public health nutrition (MPH); social and behavioral sciences (MPH); socio-behavioral health (PhD). Part-time programs available. Postbaccalaureate distance learning degree programs offered (no on-campus study). *Faculty:* 26 full-time (20 women), 104 part-time/adjunct (53 women). *Students:* 161 full-time (136 women), 70 part-time (54 women); includes 74 minority (24 Black or African American, non-Hispanic/Latino; 1 American Indian or Alaska Native, non-Hispanic/Latino; 27 Asian, non-Hispanic/Latino; 11 Hispanic/Latino; 4 Native Hawaiian or other Pacific Islander, non-Hispanic/Latino; 7 Two or more races, non-Hispanic/Latino), 39 international. Average age 29. 802 applicants, 70% accepted, 97 enrolled. In 2014, 1 master's awarded. *Degree requirements:* For master's, thesis (for some programs); for doctorate, thesis/dissertation. *Entrance requirements:* For master's and doctorate, GRE. Additional exam requirements/recommendations for international students: Required—TOEFL. *Application deadline:* For fall admission, 2/1 for domestic and international students. Applications are processed on a rolling basis. Electronic applications accepted. *Financial support:* Federal Work-Study and scholarships/grants available. *Unit head:* Dr. Cheryl G. Healton, Director, 212-992-6741. *Application contact:* New York University Information, 212-998-1212.
Website: http://giph.nyu.edu/

North Dakota State University, College of Graduate and Interdisciplinary Studies, College of Arts, Humanities and Social Sciences, Department of Sociology, Anthropology, and Emergency Management, Fargo, ND 58108. Offers community development (MA, MS); emergency management (MS, PhD); social science (MA, MS); sociology (MS). Part-time programs available. *Degree requirements:* For master's, thesis; for doctorate, comprehensive exam, thesis/dissertation. *Entrance requirements:* For master's, GRE (for emergency management), course work in sociology, minimum GPA of 3.2; for doctorate, GRE, minimum GPA of 3.2. Additional exam requirements/recommendations for international students: Required—TOEFL. Electronic applications accepted. *Faculty research:* Medical sociology, demography, ethnology, archaeology.

The Ohio State University, Graduate School, College of Food, Agricultural, and Environmental Sciences, School of Environment and Natural Resources, Columbus, OH 43210. Offers ecological restoration (MS, PhD); ecosystem science (MS, PhD); environment and natural resources (MENR); environmental social sciences (MS, PhD); fisheries and wildlife science (MS, PhD); forest science (MS, PhD); rural sociology (MS, PhD); soil science (MS, PhD). *Faculty:* 35. *Students:* 82 full-time (51 women), 9 part-time (4 women); includes 13 minority (2 Black or African American, non-Hispanic/Latino; 1 Asian, non-Hispanic/Latino; 8 Hispanic/Latino; 2 Two or more races, non-Hispanic/Latino), 19 international. Average age 28. In 2014, 21 master's, 6 doctorates awarded. *Degree requirements:* For master's, thesis; for doctorate, thesis/dissertation. *Entrance requirements:* For master's and doctorate, GRE. Additional exam requirements/recommendations for international students: Required—TOEFL (minimum score 550 paper-based; 79 iBT), Michigan English Language Assessment Battery (minimum score 82); Recommended—IELTS (minimum score 7). *Application deadline:* For fall admission, 1/1 priority date for domestic students, 12/15 priority date for international students; for spring admission, 11/15 for domestic students, 9/15 for international students. Applications are processed on a rolling basis. Application fee: $60 ($70 for international students). Electronic applications accepted. *Financial support:* Fellowships with tuition reimbursements, research assistantships with tuition reimbursements, teaching assistantships with tuition reimbursements, health care benefits, and unspecified assistantships available. *Unit head:* Dr. Jeff S. Sharp, Director, 614-292-9410, E-mail: sharp.123@osu.edu. *Application contact:* Graduate and Professional Admissions, 614-292-9444, Fax: 614-292-3895, E-mail: gpadmissions@osu.edu.
Website: http://senr.osu.edu/

Ohio University, Graduate College, College of Arts and Sciences, Program in Social Sciences, Athens, OH 45701-2979. Offers MSS. Postbaccalaureate distance learning degree programs offered (no on-campus study). *Degree requirements:* For master's, oral exam. *Entrance requirements:* For master's, minimum GPA of 2.75. Additional exam requirements/recommendations for international students: Required—TOEFL (minimum score 600 paper-based). Electronic applications accepted.

Queens College of the City University of New York, Division of Graduate Studies, Social Science Division, Program in Social Sciences, Flushing, NY 11367-1597. Offers MASS. Part-time and evening/weekend programs available. *Degree requirements:* For master's, thesis. *Entrance requirements:* For master's, minimum GPA of 3.0. Additional exam requirements/recommendations for international students: Required—TOEFL.

St. Edward's University, New College, Program in Liberal Arts, Austin, TX 78704. Offers global issues (MLA); humanities (MLA); liberal arts (Certificate); social justice (MLA); social sciences (MLA). Part-time and evening/weekend programs available. *Students:* 3 full-time (2 women), 49 part-time (36 women); includes 18 minority (2 Black or African American, non-Hispanic/Latino; 15 Hispanic/Latino; 1 Two or more races, non-Hispanic/Latino). Average age 35. 34 applicants, 68% accepted, 17 enrolled. In 2014, 23 master's awarded. *Degree requirements:* For master's, minimum of 24 resident hours. *Entrance requirements:* For master's, minimum GPA of 2.75 in last 60 hours of course work, interview. Additional exam requirements/recommendations for international students: Required—TOEFL (minimum score 79 iBT) or IELTS (minimum score 6). *Application deadline:* For fall admission, 6/1 priority date for domestic and international students; for spring admission, 10/1 priority date for domestic and international students; for summer admission, 3/1 priority date for domestic and international students. Applications are processed on a rolling basis. Application fee: $50. Electronic applications accepted. *Expenses: Tuition:* Full-time $22,448; part-time $1246 per credit hour. *Required fees:* $50 per trimester. Full-time tuition and fees vary according to course load and program. *Unit head:* Dr. H. Ramsey Fowler, Director, 512-448-8648, Fax: 512-448-8492, E-mail: ramseyf@stewards.edu. *Application contact:* Office of Admission, 512-448-8500, Fax: 512-464-8877, E-mail: seu.admit@stedwards.edu.
Website: http://www.stedwards.edu

Southern University and Agricultural and Mechanical College, Graduate School, College of Arts and Humanities, Department of History, Baton Rouge, LA 70813. Offers social sciences (MA). Part-time programs available. *Degree requirements:* For master's, thesis. *Entrance requirements:* For master's, GRE General Test. Additional exam requirements/recommendations for international students: Required—TOEFL (minimum score 525 paper-based).

Stony Brook University, State University of New York, School of Professional Development, Stony Brook, NY 11794. Offers biology (MAT); chemistry (MAT); coaching (Graduate Certificate); earth science (MAT); educational computing (Graduate Certificate); educational leadership (Advanced Certificate); English (MAT); environmental management (Graduate Certificate); French (MAT); German (MAT); higher education administration (MA, Certificate); human resource management (MS, Graduate Certificate); industrial management (Graduate Certificate); information systems management (Graduate Certificate); Italian (MAT); liberal studies (MA); mathematics (MAT); operations research (Graduate Certificate); physics (MAT); school district business leadership (Advanced Certificate); social science and the professions (MPS), including environmental management; social studies (MAT); Spanish (MAT). Part-time and evening/weekend programs available. Postbaccalaureate distance learning degree programs offered. *Faculty:* 100 part-time/adjunct (42 women). *Students:* 216 full-time (119 women), 905 part-time (624 women); includes 224 minority (63 Black or African American, non-Hispanic/Latino; 1 American Indian or Alaska Native, non-Hispanic/Latino; 33 Asian, non-Hispanic/Latino; 119 Hispanic/Latino; 1 Native Hawaiian or other Pacific Islander, non-Hispanic/Latino; 7 Two or more races, non-Hispanic/Latino), 7 international. Average age 28. 422 applicants, 88% accepted, 299 enrolled. In 2014, 362 master's, 146 other advanced degrees awarded. *Degree requirements:* For master's, one foreign language, thesis or alternative. *Application deadline:* For fall admission, 1/15 for domestic students; for spring admission, 10/1 for domestic students. Applications are processed on a rolling basis. Application fee: $100. *Expenses:* Tuition, state resident: full-time $10,370; part-time $432 per credit. Tuition, nonresident: full-time $20,190; part-time $841 per credit. *Required fees:* $1431. *Financial support:* Fellowships, research assistantships, teaching assistantships, and career-related internships or fieldwork available. Support available to part-time students. *Unit head:* Dr. Charles Taber, Vice Provost for Graduate and Professional Education, 631-632-7050, Fax: 631-632-9046, E-mail: charles.taber@stonybrook.edu. *Application contact:* 631-632-7050 Ext. 1, E-mail: spd@stonybrook.edu.
Website: http://www.stonybrook.edu/spd/

Syracuse University, Maxwell School of Citizenship and Public Affairs, Program in Social Sciences, Syracuse, NY 13244. Offers MS Sc, PhD. Part-time and evening/weekend programs available. Postbaccalaureate distance learning degree programs offered. *Students:* 14 full-time (9 women), 41 part-time (25 women); includes 10 minority (2 Black or African American, non-Hispanic/Latino; 1 American Indian or Alaska Native, non-Hispanic/Latino; 3 Asian, non-Hispanic/Latino; 3 Hispanic/Latino; 1 Two or more races, non-Hispanic/Latino), 8 international. Average age 41. 17 applicants, 53% accepted, 3 enrolled. In 2014, 4 master's, 5 doctorates awarded. *Degree requirements:* For doctorate, comprehensive exam, thesis/dissertation. *Entrance requirements:* For doctorate, GRE General Test. Additional exam requirements/recommendations for international students: Required—TOEFL (minimum score 100 iBT). *Application deadline:* For fall admission, 3/15 priority date for domestic and international students. Application fee: $75. Electronic applications accepted. *Expenses: Tuition:* Part-time $1341 per credit. *Financial support:* Fellowships with full tuition reimbursements, research assistantships with full and partial tuition reimbursements, and teaching assistantships with full and partial tuition reimbursements available. Financial award application deadline: 1/1. *Unit head:* Dr. Vernon Greene, Chair, 315-443-2275, Fax: 315-443-1463, E-mail: vgreene@maxwell.syr.edu. *Application contact:* M. Tammy Salisbury, Grad Contact, 315-443-2275, E-mail: mtsalisb@maxwell.syr.edu.
Website: http://www.maxwell.syr.edu/

Texas A&M International University, Office of Graduate Studies and Research, College of Arts and Sciences, Department of Public Affairs and Social Research, Laredo, TX 78041-1900. Offers criminal justice (MS); history and political thought (MA); political science (MA); public administration (MPA). *Degree requirements:* For master's, comprehensive exam (for some programs), thesis (for some programs). *Entrance requirements:* For master's, GRE General Test. Additional exam requirements/recommendations for international students: Required—TOEFL (minimum score 550 paper-based; 79 iBT).

Towson University, Program in Social Science, Towson, MD 21252-0001. Offers MS. Part-time and evening/weekend programs available. *Students:* 4 full-time (2 women), 18 part-time (9 women); includes 7 minority (6 Black or African American, non-Hispanic/Latino; 1 Hispanic/Latino). *Entrance requirements:* For master's, minimum GPA of 3.0, 3 letters of recommendation, statement of intent. *Application deadline:* For fall admission, 10/15 for domestic and international students; for spring admission, 4/15 for domestic and international students. Applications are processed on a rolling basis. Application fee: $45. Electronic applications accepted. *Financial support:* Application deadline: 4/1. *Unit head:* Dr. Michael Korzi, Graduate Program Director, 410-704-5219, E-mail: mkorzi@towson.edu. *Application contact:* Alicia Arkell-Kleis, Information Contact, 410-704-6004, E-mail: grads@towson.edu.
Website: http://www.towson.edu/program/master/socs-ms/

Troy University, Graduate School, College of Arts and Sciences, Program in Social Science, Troy, AL 36082. Offers MS Sc. Part-time and evening/weekend programs available. *Faculty:* 3 full-time (2 women). *Students:* 9 full-time (5 women), 20 part-time (17 women); includes 19 minority (14 Black or African American, non-Hispanic/Latino; 3 Hispanic/Latino; 2 Two or more races, non-Hispanic/Latino). Average age 34. 43 applicants, 93% accepted, 25 enrolled. *Degree requirements:* For master's, comprehensive exam, thesis optional. *Entrance requirements:* For master's, GRE (minimum score of 850 on old exam or 290 on new exam), MAT (minimum score of 385), or GMAT (minimum score of 380), bachelor's degree, minimum undergraduate GPA of 2.5 or 3.0 on last 30 semester hours, letter of recommendation. Additional exam requirements/recommendations for international students: Required—TOEFL (minimum score 523 paper-based; 70 iBT), IELTS (minimum score 6). *Application deadline:* For fall admission, 6/1 for international students; for spring admission, 10/15 for international students. Applications are processed on a rolling basis. Application fee: $50. Electronic applications accepted. *Expenses:* Tuition, state resident: full-time $6570; part-time $365 per credit hour. Tuition, nonresident: full-time $13,140; part-time $730 per credit hour. *Required fees:* $365 per credit hour. *Unit head:* Dr. Annette Allen, Chairman, 334-808-6595, E-mail: aallen40379@troy.edu. *Application contact:* Jessica A. Kimbro, Director of Graduate Admissions, 334-670-3178, E-mail: jacord@troy.edu.

University of California, Merced, Graduate Division, School of Social Sciences, Humanities and Arts, Merced, CA 95343. Offers cognitive and information sciences (MA, PhD); psychology (MA, PhD); social sciences (MA, PhD); world cultures (MA, PhD). *Faculty:* 89 full-time (40 women). *Students:* 114 full-time (79 women), 2 part-time (1 woman); includes 43 minority (3 Black or African American, non-Hispanic/Latino; 1 American Indian or Alaska Native, non-Hispanic/Latino; 10 Asian, non-Hispanic/Latino; 24 Hispanic/Latino; 1 Native Hawaiian or other Pacific Islander, non-Hispanic/Latino; 4 Two or more races, non-Hispanic/Latino), 13 international. Average age 32. 127 applicants, 34% accepted, 22 enrolled. In 2014, 3 master's, 11 doctorates awarded. *Degree requirements:* For master's, variable foreign language requirement, comprehensive exam, thesis; for doctorate, variable foreign language requirement, comprehensive exam, thesis/dissertation. *Entrance requirements:* For master's and doctorate, GRE. Additional exam requirements/recommendations for international students: Required—TOEFL (minimum score 550 paper-based; 68 iBT); Recommended—IELTS. *Application deadline:* For fall admission, 1/15 for domestic and international students. Application fee: $80 ($100 for international students). Electronic applications accepted. *Expenses:* Tuition, state resident: full-time $11,220; part-time

$2805 per semester. *Required fees:* $1940; $970 per semester hour. *Financial support:* In 2014–15, 29 fellowships with full and partial tuition reimbursements (averaging $7,056 per year) were awarded; scholarships/grants also available. *Faculty research:* Psychology, political science, social inequality, interdisciplinary, humanities, cognitive sciences. *Unit head:* Dr. Mark Aldenderfer, Dean, 209-228-7843, Fax: 209-228-4007, E-mail: maldenderfer@ucmerced.edu. *Application contact:* Tsu Ya, Graduate Admissions and Academic Services Manager, 209-228-4521, Fax: 209-228-6906, E-mail: tya@ucmerced.edu.

University of California, Santa Barbara, Graduate Division, College of Letters and Sciences, Division of Mathematics, Life, and Physical Sciences, Department of Psychological and Brain Sciences, Santa Barbara, CA 93106-9660. Offers cognitive science (PhD); psychology (PhD); quantitative methods in the social sciences (PhD); technology and society (PhD). Terminal master's awarded for partial completion of doctoral program. *Degree requirements:* For doctorate, comprehensive exam, thesis/dissertation, teaching assistant training, progress report, papers, mini-convention presentation, 1 quarter of student teaching or teaching assistant class with section lab, continued participation in research and weekly area meetings. *Entrance requirements:* For doctorate, GRE General Test. Additional exam requirements/recommendations for international students: Required—TOEFL (minimum score 550 paper-based; 80 iBT) or IELTS (minimum score 7). Electronic applications accepted. *Faculty research:* Social psychology; developmental and evolutionary psychology; neuroscience and behavior; cognition, perception and cognitive neuroscience.

University of California, Santa Barbara, Graduate Division, College of Letters and Sciences, Division of Social Sciences, Department of Communication, Santa Barbara, CA 93106-4020. Offers cognitive science (PhD); communication (PhD); feminist studies (PhD); language, interaction and social organization (PhD); quantitative methods in the social sciences (PhD); society and technology (PhD); MA/PhD. Terminal master's awarded for partial completion of doctoral program. *Degree requirements:* For doctorate, comprehensive exam, thesis/dissertation. *Entrance requirements:* For doctorate, GRE. Additional exam requirements/recommendations for international students: Required—TOEFL (minimum score 80 iBT), IELTS (minimum score 7). Electronic applications accepted. *Faculty research:* Interpersonal, intercultural, organizational, health, media.

University of California, Santa Cruz, Division of Graduate Studies, Division of Humanities, Program in the History of Consciousness, Santa Cruz, CA 95064. Offers PhD. *Degree requirements:* For doctorate, one foreign language, thesis/dissertation, qualifying exam. *Entrance requirements:* For doctorate, GRE General Test. Additional exam requirements/recommendations for international students: Required—TOEFL (minimum score 550 paper-based; 83 iBT); Recommended—IELTS (minimum score 8). Electronic applications accepted. *Faculty research:* Interdisciplinary humanities and social sciences, political theory, cultural theory, feminist studies, literary theory.

University of Chicago, Division of the Social Sciences, Committee on Social Thought, Chicago, IL 60637. Offers PhD. *Students:* 44 full-time (15 women); includes 4 minority (1 Black or African American, non-Hispanic/Latino; 1 American Indian or Alaska Native, non-Hispanic/Latino; 1 Asian, non-Hispanic/Latino; 1 Hispanic/Latino), 13 international. 110 applicants, 6% accepted, 6 enrolled. In 2014, 3 doctorates awarded. *Degree requirements:* For doctorate, one foreign language, thesis/dissertation, exam. *Entrance requirements:* For doctorate, GRE General Test. Additional exam requirements/recommendations for international students: Required—TOEFL (minimum score 104 iBT), IELTS (minimum score 7). *Application deadline:* For fall admission, 12/15 for domestic and international students. Application fee: $90. Electronic applications accepted. *Expenses: Tuition:* Full-time $46,899. *Required fees:* $347. *Financial support:* In 2014–15, 6 students received support, including 5 fellowships with full tuition reimbursements available (averaging $23,000 per year); career-related internships or fieldwork, Federal Work-Study, institutionally sponsored loans, scholarships/grants, health care benefits, and tuition waivers (full) also available. Financial award application deadline: 12/15. *Unit head:* Prof. Robert Pippin, Chair. *Application contact:* Office of the Dean of Students, 773-702-8415, E-mail: admissions@ssd.uchicago.edu.
Website: http://socialthought.uchicago.edu

University of Chicago, Division of the Social Sciences, Master of Arts Program in the Social Sciences, Chicago, IL 60637. Offers MA. Part-time programs available. *Students:* 137 full-time (68 women); includes 25 minority (7 Black or African American, non-Hispanic/Latino; 2 American Indian or Alaska Native, non-Hispanic/Latino; 8 Asian, non-Hispanic/Latino; 7 Hispanic/Latino; 1 Two or more races, non-Hispanic/Latino), 34 international. 185 applicants, 62% accepted. In 2014, 152 master's awarded. *Degree requirements:* For master's, thesis. *Entrance requirements:* For master's, GRE General Test. Additional exam requirements/recommendations for international students: Required—TOEFL (minimum score 104 iBT), IELTS (minimum score 7). *Application deadline:* For fall admission, 1/5 priority date for domestic and international students. Application fee: $90. Electronic applications accepted. *Expenses: Tuition:* Full-time $46,899. *Required fees:* $347. *Financial support:* In 2014–15, 109 students received support. Federal Work-Study, institutionally sponsored loans, and scholarships/grants available. Financial award application deadline: 1/5. *Unit head:* Prof. Dain Borges, Director, 773-702-8316. *Application contact:* Office of the Dean of Students, 773-702-8415, E-mail: admissions@ssd.uchicago.edu.
Website: http://mapss.uchicago.edu

University of Florida, Graduate School, College of Public Health and Health Professions, Programs in Public Health, Gainesville, FL 32611. Offers biostatistics (MPH); clinical and translational science (PhD); environmental health (MPH); epidemiology (MPH); health management and policy (MPH); public health (MPH, PhD, Certificate); public health practice (MPH); rehabilitation science (PhD); social and behavioral sciences (MPH); DPT/MPH; DVM/MPH; JD/MPH; MD/MPH; Pharm D/MPH. *Accreditation:* CEPH. Postbaccalaureate distance learning degree programs offered. *Students:* 153 full-time (116 women), 69 part-time (44 women); includes 67 minority (27 Black or African American, non-Hispanic/Latino; 1 American Indian or Alaska Native, non-Hispanic/Latino; 25 Asian, non-Hispanic/Latino; 14 Hispanic/Latino), 24 international. 375 applicants, 47% accepted, 71 enrolled. In 2014, 77 master's, 3 doctorates awarded. *Degree requirements:* For master's, internship. *Entrance requirements:* For master's, GRE General Test, minimum GPA of 3.0. Additional exam requirements/recommendations for international students: Required—TOEFL (minimum score 550 paper-based; 80 iBT), IELTS (minimum score 6). *Application deadline:* For fall admission, 7/1 for domestic students, 4/1 for international students. Application fee: $30. *Financial support:* In 2014–15, 5 research assistantships, 10 teaching assistantships were awarded; fellowships also available. Financial award applicants required to submit FAFSA. *Unit head:* Sarah L. McKune, PhD, Program Director, 352-328-0615, Fax: 352-273-6448, E-mail: smckune@ufl.edu. *Application contact:* Telisha Martin, PhD, Associate Director, MPH Program, 352-273-6444, E-mail: martints@ufl.edu.
Website: http://www.mph.ufl.edu/

University of Illinois at Springfield, Graduate Programs, College of Education and Human Services, Program in Human Services, Springfield, IL 62703-5407. Offers alcohol and substance abuse (Graduate Certificate); alcoholism and substance abuse (MA); child and family services (MA); gerontology (MA); social services administration (MA). Part-time and evening/weekend programs available. Postbaccalaureate distance learning degree programs offered (no on-campus study). *Faculty:* 4 full-time (all women), 2 part-time/adjunct (0 women). *Students:* 11 full-time (all women), 69 part-time (60 women); includes 21 minority (17 Black or African American, non-Hispanic/Latino; 1 Asian, non-Hispanic/Latino; 1 Hispanic/Latino; 2 Two or more races, non-Hispanic/Latino). Average age 36. 53 applicants, 30% accepted, 16 enrolled. In 2014, 19 master's, 1 other advanced degree awarded. *Degree requirements:* For master's, internship; project or thesis. *Entrance requirements:* For master's, minimum undergraduate GPA of 3.0, 2 letters of recommendation, statement of intent. Additional exam requirements/recommendations for international students: Required—TOEFL (minimum score 500 paper-based; 61 iBT). Application fee: $60 ($75 for international students). Electronic applications accepted. *Expenses:* Tuition, state resident: full-time $7662; part-time $319.25 per credit hour. Tuition, nonresident: full-time $15,966; part-time $665.25 per credit hour. *Financial support:* In 2014–15, fellowships with full tuition reimbursements (averaging $9,900 per year), research assistantships with full tuition reimbursements (averaging $9,600 per year), teaching assistantships with full tuition reimbursements (averaging $9,600 per year) were awarded; career-related internships or fieldwork, Federal Work-Study, scholarships/grants, health care benefits, and unspecified assistantships also available. Support available to part-time students. Financial award application deadline: 11/15. *Unit head:* Dr. Carolyn Peck, Program Administrator, 217-206-7577, Fax: 217-206-6775, E-mail: peck.carolyn@uis.edu. *Application contact:* Dr. Lynn Pardie, Office of Graduate Studies, 800-252-8533, Fax: 217-206-7623, E-mail: lpard1@uis.edu.
Website: http://www.uis.edu/humanservices

The University of Manchester, School of Social Sciences, Manchester, United Kingdom. Offers ethnographic documentary (M Phil); interdisciplinary study of culture (PhD); philosophy (PhD); politics (PhD); social anthropology (PhD); social anthropology with visual media (PhD); social change (PhD); social statistics (PhD); sociology (PhD); visual anthropology (M Phil).

University of Maryland, Baltimore County, The Graduate School, College of Arts, Humanities and Social Sciences, Doctoral Program in Gerontology at UMB/UMBC, Baltimore, MD 21201. Offers aging policy issues (PhD); epidemiology of aging (PhD); social, cultural, and behavioral sciences (PhD); MA/PhD; MS/PhD. Part-time programs available. *Faculty:* 17 part-time/adjunct (12 women). *Students:* 13 full-time (10 women), 12 part-time (10 women); includes 7 minority (5 Black or African American, non-Hispanic/Latino; 1 Asian, non-Hispanic/Latino; 1 Hispanic/Latino), 2 international. Average age 36. 16 applicants, 31% accepted, 4 enrolled. In 2014, 3 doctorates awarded. *Degree requirements:* For doctorate, comprehensive exam, thesis/dissertation. *Entrance requirements:* For doctorate, GRE General Test. Additional exam requirements/recommendations for international students: Required—TOEFL, TWE. *Application deadline:* For spring admission, 1/15 for domestic and international students. Application fee: $45. Electronic applications accepted. *Expenses:* Tuition, state resident: part-time $557. Tuition, nonresident: part-time $922. *Required fees:* $122 per semester. One-time fee: $200 part-time. *Financial support:* In 2014–15, 12 research assistantships with full tuition reimbursements (averaging $21,750 per year) were awarded; career-related internships or fieldwork, scholarships/grants, traineeships, health care benefits, and unspecified assistantships also available. Financial award application deadline: 2/1; financial award applicants required to submit FAFSA. *Faculty research:* Aging and health policy, behavioral aspects of aging, epidemiology of aging. *Total annual research expenditures:* $52.7 million. *Unit head:* Dr. Leslie Morgan, Co-Director, UMBC Campus, 410-455-2074, Fax: 410-455-1154, E-mail: lmorgan@umbc.edu. *Application contact:* Justine Golden, Academic Coordinator, 410-706-4926, Fax: 410-706-4433, E-mail: jgold002@umaryland.edu.
Website: http://www.gerontologyphd.umaryland.edu

University of Memphis, Graduate School, School of Public Health, Memphis, TN 38152. Offers biostatistics (MPH); environmental health (MPH); epidemiology (MPH); health systems management (MPH); public health (MHA); social and behavioral sciences (MPH). Part-time and evening/weekend programs available. Postbaccalaureate distance learning degree programs offered. *Faculty:* 15 full-time (5 women), 6 part-time/adjunct (1 woman). *Students:* 64 full-time (42 women), 36 part-time (24 women); includes 34 minority (21 Black or African American, non-Hispanic/Latino; 6 Asian, non-Hispanic/Latino; 5 Hispanic/Latino; 2 Two or more races, non-Hispanic/Latino), 15 international. Average age 32. 68 applicants, 94% accepted, 24 enrolled. In 2014, 34 master's awarded. *Degree requirements:* For master's, comprehensive exam, thesis. *Entrance requirements:* For master's, GRE, letters of recommendation. Additional exam requirements/recommendations for international students: Required—TOEFL. *Application deadline:* For fall admission, 4/1 for domestic students; for spring admission, 11/1 for domestic students. Application fee: $35 ($60 for international students). Electronic applications accepted. *Financial support:* In 2014–15, 46 students received support. Research assistantships with full tuition reimbursements available, Federal Work-Study, scholarships/grants, and unspecified assistantships available. Financial award application deadline: 2/15; financial award applicants required to submit FAFSA. *Faculty research:* Health and medical savings accounts, adoption rates, health informatics, Telehealth technologies, biostatistics, environmental health, epidemiology, health systems management, social and behavioral sciences. *Unit head:* Dr. Lisa M. Klesges, Director, 901-678-4637, E-mail: lmklsges@memphis.edu. *Application contact:* Dr. Karen Weddle-West, Information Contact, 901-678-2531, Fax: 901-678-5023, E-mail: gradsch@memphis.edu.
Website: http://www.memphis.edu/sph/

University of Michigan, School of Social Work, Interdisciplinary Program in Social Work and Social Science, Ann Arbor, MI 48109-1106. Offers social work and anthropology (PhD); social work and economics (PhD); social work and political science (PhD); social work and psychology (PhD); social work and sociology (PhD). Programs offered through the Horace H. Rackham School of Graduate Studies. *Faculty:* 57 full-time (33 women), 6 part-time/adjunct (4 women). *Students:* 64 full-time (46 women); includes 24 minority (7 Black or African American, non-Hispanic/Latino; 11 Asian, non-Hispanic/Latino; 6 Hispanic/Latino), 6 international. Average age 32. 108 applicants, 9% accepted, 9 enrolled. In 2014, 11 doctorates awarded. *Degree requirements:* For doctorate, thesis/dissertation, oral defense of dissertation, preliminary exam. *Entrance requirements:* For doctorate, GRE General Test. Additional exam requirements/recommendations for international students: Required—TOEFL. *Application deadline:* For fall admission, 12/1 for domestic and international students. Application fee: $75 ($90 for international students). *Financial support:* In 2014–15, 64 students received support, including 20 fellowships with full tuition reimbursements available (averaging $15,200 per year), 7 research assistantships with full tuition reimbursements available (averaging $18,971 per year), 19 teaching assistantships with full tuition reimbursements available (averaging $18,971 per year); career-related internships or fieldwork, Federal Work-Study, scholarships/grants, traineeships, health care benefits, tuition waivers (full and partial), and unspecified assistantships also available. Financial award application deadline: 12/1; financial award applicants required to submit FAFSA. *Faculty research:* Substance abuse, child welfare, mental health, poverty, aging. *Total annual research expenditures:* $4.1 million. *Unit head:* Dr. Berit Ingersoll-Dayton, Director, 734-763-5768, Fax: 734-615-3192, E-mail: bid@umich.edu. *Application contact:* Graduate Coordinator, 734-647-2554, Fax: 734-615-3192, E-mail: ssw.phd.info@umich.edu.
Website: http://www.ssw.umich.edu/doctoral

Social Sciences

University of Michigan–Flint, College of Arts and Sciences, Program in Social Sciences, Flint, MI 48502-1950. Offers gender studies (MA); global studies (MA); U.S. history and politics (MA). Part-time programs available. *Faculty:* 14 full-time (8 women), 5 part-time/adjunct (3 women). *Students:* 1 (woman) full-time, 20 part-time (13 women); includes 8 minority (6 Black or African American, non-Hispanic/Latino; 1 Hispanic/Latino; 1 Two or more races, non-Hispanic/Latino). Average age 41. 8 applicants, 75% accepted, 3 enrolled. In 2014, 7 master's awarded. *Entrance requirements:* For master's, bachelor's degree from accredited institution, minimum overall GPA of 3.0. Additional exam requirements/recommendations for international students: Required—TOEFL (minimum score 84 iBT), IELTS (minimum score 6.5). *Application deadline:* For fall admission, 8/1 for domestic students, 5/1 for international students; for winter admission, 11/15 for domestic students, 9/1 for international students; for spring admission, 3/15 for domestic students, 1/1 for international students; for summer admission, 5/15 for domestic students. Applications are processed on a rolling basis. Application fee: $55. Electronic applications accepted. *Expenses:* Expenses: Contact institution. *Financial support:* Federal Work-Study, scholarships/grants, and unspecified assistantships available. Support available to part-time students. Financial award application deadline: 3/1; financial award applicants required to submit FAFSA. *Unit head:* Dr. Adam Lutzker, Interim Director, 810-762-3280, Fax: 810-762-3281, E-mail: alutzker@umflint.edu. *Application contact:* Bradley T. Maki, Director of Graduate Admissions, 810-762-3171, Fax: 810-766-6789, E-mail: bmaki@umflint.edu.
Website: http://www.umflint.edu/graduateprograms/social-sciences-ma

The University of North Carolina at Charlotte, College of Liberal Arts and Sciences, Department of Sociology, Charlotte, NC 28223-0001. Offers health research (MA); mathematical sociology and quantitative methods (MA); organizations, occupations, and work (MA); political sociology (MA); race and gender (MA); social psychology (MA); social theory (MA); sociology of education (MA); stratification (MA). Part-time and evening/weekend programs available. *Faculty:* 16 full-time (10 women). *Students:* 11 full-time (5 women), 2 part-time (0 women); includes 5 minority (4 Black or African American, non-Hispanic/Latino; 1 Hispanic/Latino), 1 international. Average age 29. 14 applicants, 71% accepted, 5 enrolled. In 2014, 6 master's awarded. *Degree requirements:* For master's, thesis or comprehensive exam. *Entrance requirements:* For master's, GRE or MAT, minimum GPA of 3.0 in last 2 years, 2.75 overall. Additional exam requirements/recommendations for international students: Required—TOEFL (minimum score 557 paper-based; 83 iBT). *Application deadline:* For fall admission, 4/15 for domestic and international students; for spring admission, 10/1 for domestic and international students. Application fee: $75. Electronic applications accepted. *Expenses:* Tuition, state resident: full-time $4008. Tuition, nonresident: full-time $16,295. *Required fees:* $2755. Tuition and fees vary according to course load and program. *Financial support:* In 2014–15, 10 students received support, including 5 research assistantships (averaging $10,400 per year), 5 teaching assistantships (averaging $9,200 per year); career-related internships or fieldwork, institutionally sponsored loans, scholarships/grants, and unspecified assistantships also available. Support available to part-time students. Financial award application deadline: 4/1; financial award applicants required to submit FAFSA. *Faculty research:* Impact of race on high school course selection; income inequality within the United States and cross-nationally; small group interaction, nonverbal behaviors, identity, emotions, gender, and expectations; mathematical models of social processes. *Total annual research expenditures:* $413,099. *Unit head:* Dr. Lisa Walker, Chair, 704-687-7825, Fax: 704-687-3091, E-mail: lisa.walker@uncc.edu. *Application contact:* Kathy B. Giddings, Director of Graduate Admissions, 704-687-5503, Fax: 704-687-1668, E-mail: gradadm@uncc.edu.
Website: http://sociology.uncc.edu/

University of Northern Iowa, Graduate College, College of Social and Behavioral Sciences, MA Program in Social Science, Cedar Falls, IA 50614. Offers MA. *Students:* 10 part-time (4 women). In 2014, 9 master's awarded. *Entrance requirements:* For master's, minimum GPA of 3.0. Additional exam requirements/recommendations for international students: Required—TOEFL (minimum score 500 paper-based; 61 iBT). Application fee: $50 ($70 for international students). *Expenses:* Tuition, state resident: full-time $7912; part-time $880 per credit. Tuition, nonresident: full-time $17,906; part-time $880 per credit. *Required fees:* $1101; $325.50 per credit. $465.63 per semester. Tuition and fees vary according to course load and program. *Unit head:* Dr. Robert Martin, Department Head, 319-273-2097, Fax: 319-273-2222, E-mail: robert.martin@uni.edu. *Application contact:* Laurie S. Russell, Record Analyst, 319-273-2623, Fax: 319-273-2885, E-mail: laurie.russell@uni.edu.
Website: http://www.uni.edu/continuinged/distance/programs/degrees/social-science-teachers-grades-6-12-ma

University of Regina, Faculty of Graduate Studies and Research, Faculty of Arts, Department of Sociology and Social Studies, Regina, SK S4S 0A2, Canada. Offers social studies (MA); sociology (MA). Part-time programs available. *Faculty:* 10 full-time (5 women), 6 part-time/adjunct (1 woman). *Students:* 13 full-time (5 women), 3 part-time (all women). 19 applicants, 47% accepted. In 2014, 4 master's awarded. *Degree requirements:* For master's, thesis. *Entrance requirements:* Additional exam requirements/recommendations for international students: Required—TOEFL (minimum score 580 paper-based; 80 iBT), IELTS (minimum score 6.5), PTE (minimum score 59). *Application deadline:* Applications are processed on a rolling basis. Application fee: $100. Electronic applications accepted. *Expenses: Tuition, area resident:* Full-time $4900 Canadian dollars; part-time $837.65 Canadian dollars per semester. *International tuition:* $7900 Canadian dollars full-time. *Required fees:* $396 Canadian dollars; $86.90 Canadian dollars per semester. *Financial support:* In 2014–15, 5 teaching assistantships (averaging $2,427 per year) were awarded; fellowships, research assistantships, and scholarships/grants also available. Financial award application deadline: 6/15. *Faculty research:* Social justice, international development, globalization, social policy, political economy. *Unit head:* Dr. John Conway, Department Head, 306-585-4052, Fax: 306-585-4815, E-mail: john.conway@uregina.ca. *Application contact:* Dr. Henry Chow, Graduate Coordinator, 306-585-5604, Fax: 306-585-4815, E-mail: henry.chow@uregina.ca.
Website: http://www.uregina.ca/arts/sociology-social-studies

The University of Texas at Tyler, College of Arts and Sciences, Department of Social Sciences, Tyler, TX 75799-0001. Offers criminal justice (MS); public administration (MPA); sociology (MS). Part-time and evening/weekend programs available. *Degree requirements:* For master's, comprehensive exam, thesis optional. *Entrance requirements:* For master's, GRE General Test, minimum GPA of 3.0. Additional exam requirements/recommendations for international students: Required—TOEFL. *Faculty research:* Urban segregation, minority business, violent crime, gender discrimination.

University of Toronto, School of Graduate Studies, Department of Public Health Sciences, Toronto, ON M5S 2J7, Canada. Offers biostatistics (M Sc, PhD); community health (M Sc); community nutrition (MPH), including nutrition and dietetics; epidemiology (MPH, PhD); family and community medicine (MPH); occupational and environmental health (MPH); social and behavioral health science (PhD); social and behavioral health sciences (MPH), including health promotion. *Accreditation:* CAHME (one or more programs are accredited); CEPH (one or more programs are accredited). Part-time programs available. *Degree requirements:* For master's, thesis (for some programs), practicum; for doctorate, comprehensive exam, thesis/dissertation, oral thesis defense. *Entrance requirements:* For master's, 2 letters of reference, relevant professional/research experience, minimum B average in final year; for doctorate, 2 letters of reference, relevant professional/research experience, minimum B+ average. Additional exam requirements/recommendations for international students: Required—TOEFL (minimum score 580 paper-based; 93 iBT), TWE (minimum score 5). Electronic applications accepted. *Expenses:* Contact institution.

University of Washington, Graduate School, School of Public Health, Department of Health Services, Seattle, WA 98195. Offers clinical research (MS); community-oriented public health practice (MPH); evaluative sciences and statistics (PhD); health behavior and social determinants of health (PhD); health economics (PhD); health informatics and health information management (MHIHIM); health services (MS, PhD); health services administration (EMHA, MHA); health systems and policy (MPH); health systems research (PhD); maternal and child health (MPH); social and behavioral sciences (MPH); JD/MHA; MHA/MBA; MHA/MD; MHA/MPA; MPH/JD; MPH/MD; MPH/MN; MPH/MPA; MPH/MS; MPH/MSD; MPH/MSW; MPH/PhD. Postbaccalaureate distance learning degree programs offered (minimal on-campus study). *Faculty:* 63 full-time (33 women), 62 part-time/adjunct (37 women). *Students:* 124 full-time (100 women), 19 part-time (15 women); includes 48 minority (7 Black or African American, non-Hispanic/Latino; 3 American Indian or Alaska Native, non-Hispanic/Latino; 26 Asian, non-Hispanic/Latino; 11 Hispanic/Latino; 1 Native Hawaiian or other Pacific Islander, non-Hispanic/Latino), 3 international. Average age 30. 292 applicants, 56% accepted, 66 enrolled. In 2014, 56 master's, 3 doctorates awarded. Terminal master's awarded for partial completion of doctoral program. *Degree requirements:* For master's, thesis (for some programs), practicum (MPH); for doctorate, comprehensive exam, thesis/dissertation. *Entrance requirements:* For master's and doctorate, GRE General Test, minimum GPA of 3.0. Additional exam requirements/recommendations for international students: Required—TOEFL (minimum score 580 paper-based; 92 iBT), IELTS (minimum score 7). *Application deadline:* For fall admission, 1/1 for domestic students, 11/1 for international students. Application fee: 85 Albanian leks. Electronic applications accepted. *Expenses:* Expenses: $17,703 state resident tuition and fees, $34,827 non-resident (for MPH); $17,037 state resident tuition and fees, $29,511 non-resident (for MS and PhD). *Financial support:* In 2014–15, 45 students received support, including 12 fellowships with full and partial tuition reimbursements available (averaging $22,000 per year), 9 research assistantships with full and partial tuition reimbursements available (averaging $18,700 per year), 9 teaching assistantships with full and partial tuition reimbursements available (averaging $4,575 per year); institutionally sponsored loans, traineeships, and health care benefits also available. Financial award application deadline: 2/28; financial award applicants required to submit FAFSA. *Faculty research:* Public health practice, health promotion and disease prevention, maternal and child health, organizational behavior and culture, health policy. *Unit head:* Dr. Larry Kessler, Chair, 206-543-2930. *Application contact:* Kitty A. Andert, MPH/MS/PhD Programs Manager, 206-616-2926, Fax: 206-543-3964, E-mail: hservmph@u.washington.edu.
Website: http://depts.washington.edu/hserv/

Wilfrid Laurier University, Faculty of Graduate and Postdoctoral Studies, Faculty of Arts, Cultural Analysis and Social Theory Program, Waterloo, ON N2L 3C5, Canada. Offers body politics (MA); cultural representation and social theory (MA); gender, sexuality and embodiment (MA); globalization, identity and social movements (MA). Part-time programs available. *Entrance requirements:* For master's, honours BA in humanities, social science or interdisciplinary program with social theory, minimum B+ in final year of full-time study. Additional exam requirements/recommendations for international students: Required—TOEFL (minimum score 89 iBT). Electronic applications accepted. *Faculty research:* Globalization; identity and social movements; body politics: gender, sexuality and embodiment; cultural representation and social theory.

Worcester Polytechnic Institute, Graduate Studies and Research, Department of Social Science and Policy Studies, Worcester, MA 01609-2280. Offers interdisciplinary social science (PhD); system dynamics (MS, Graduate Certificate). Part-time and evening/weekend programs available. Postbaccalaureate distance learning degree programs offered (no on-campus study). *Faculty:* 5 full-time (2 women), 2 part-time/adjunct (0 women). *Students:* 2 full-time (1 woman), 13 part-time (2 women); includes 2 minority (1 Black or African American, non-Hispanic/Latino; 1 Hispanic/Latino), 3 international. 8 applicants, 75% accepted, 6 enrolled. In 2014, 2 master's awarded. *Entrance requirements:* For master's and doctorate, GRE General Test, 3 letters of recommendation, statement of purpose. Additional exam requirements/recommendations for international students: Required—TOEFL (minimum score 563 paper-based; 84 iBT), IELTS (minimum score 7). *Application deadline:* For fall admission, 1/1 priority date for domestic students, 1/1 for international students; for spring admission, 10/1 priority date for domestic students, 10/1 for international students. Applications are processed on a rolling basis. Application fee: $70. Electronic applications accepted. *Financial support:* Research assistantships, teaching assistantships, career-related internships or fieldwork, institutionally sponsored loans, scholarships/grants, and unspecified assistantships available. Financial award application deadline: 1/1; financial award applicants required to submit FAFSA. *Unit head:* Dr. James K. Doyle, Head, 508-831-5296, Fax: 508-831-5896, E-mail: doyle@wpi.edu. *Application contact:* Dr. Oleg Pavlov, Graduate Coordinator, 508-831-5296, Fax: 508-831-5896, E-mail: opavlov@wpi.edu.
Website: http://www.wpi.edu/academics/ssps

Worcester Polytechnic Institute, Graduate Studies and Research, Programs in Interdisciplinary Studies, Worcester, MA 01609-2280. Offers bioscience administration (MS); impact engineering (MS); manufacturing engineering management (MS); power systems management (MS); social science (PhD); systems modeling (MS). Part-time and evening/weekend programs available. *Faculty:* 1 part-time/adjunct (0 women). *Students:* 2 full-time (0 women), 74 part-time (15 women); includes 18 minority (3 Black or African American, non-Hispanic/Latino; 7 Asian, non-Hispanic/Latino; 3 Hispanic/Latino; 5 Two or more races, non-Hispanic/Latino), 5 international. 37 applicants, 97% accepted, 29 enrolled. In 2014, 10 master's, 1 doctorate awarded. *Degree requirements:* For master's, thesis; for doctorate, comprehensive exam, thesis/dissertation. *Entrance requirements:* For master's and doctorate, 3 letters of recommendation. Additional exam requirements/recommendations for international students: Required—TOEFL (minimum score 563 paper-based; 84 iBT), IELTS (minimum score 7). *Application deadline:* For fall admission, 1/1 priority date for domestic students, 1/1 for international students; for spring admission, 10/1 priority date for domestic students, 10/1 for international students. Application fee: $70. *Financial support:* Institutionally sponsored loans, scholarships/grants, and unspecified assistantships available. Financial award application deadline: 1/1; financial award applicants required to submit FAFSA. *Unit head:* Dr. Fred J. Looft, Head, 508-831-5231, Fax: 508-831-5491, E-mail: fjlooft@wpi.edu. *Application contact:* Lynne Dougherty, Administrative Assistant, 508-831-5301, Fax: 508-831-5717, E-mail: grad@wpi.edu.

Yale University, School of Medicine, Yale School of Public Health, New Haven, CT 06520. Offers applied biostatistics and epidemiology (APMPH); biostatistics (MPH, MS, PhD), including global health (MPH); chronic disease epidemiology (MPH, PhD), including global health (MPH); environmental health sciences (MPH, PhD), including global health (MPH); epidemiology of microbial diseases (MPH, PhD), including global

health (MPH); global health (APMPH); health management (MPH), including global health; health policy (MPH), including global health; health policy and administration (APMPH, PhD); occupational and environmental medicine (APMPH); preventive medicine (APMPH); social and behavioral sciences (APMPH, MPH), including global health (MPH); JD/MPH; M Div/MPH; MBA/MPH; MD/MPH; MEM/MPH; MFS/MPH; MM Sc/MPH; MPH/MA; MSN/MPH. MS and PhD offered through the Graduate School. *Accreditation:* CEPH. Part-time programs available. Terminal master's awarded for partial completion of doctoral program. *Degree requirements:* For master's, thesis, summer internship; for doctorate, comprehensive exam, thesis/dissertation, residency. *Entrance requirements:* For master's, GMAT, GRE, or MCAT, two years of undergraduate coursework in math and science; for doctorate, GRE General Test. Additional exam requirements/recommendations for international students: Required— TOEFL (minimum score 100 iBT). Electronic applications accepted. *Expenses:* Contact institution. *Faculty research:* Genetic and emerging infections epidemiology, virology, cost/quality, vector biology, quantitative methods, aging, asthma, cancer.

Section 27
Sociology, Anthropology, and Archaeology

This section contains a directory of institutions offering graduate work in sociology, anthropology, and archaeology. Additional information about programs listed in the directory may be obtained by writing directly to the dean of a graduate school or chair of a department at the address given in the directory.

For programs offering related work, see also in this book *Area and Cultural Studies, Art and Art History, History, Humanities, Language and Literature,* and *Psychology and Counseling.*

CONTENTS

Program Directories

Anthropology

The American University in Cairo, School of Humanities and Social Sciences, Department of Sociology, Anthropology, Psychology, and Egyptology, Cairo, Egypt. Offers Egyptology and Coptology (MA); psychology (MA); sociology and anthropology (MA). *Degree requirements:* For master's, one foreign language, thesis. *Entrance requirements:* Additional exam requirements/recommendations for international students: Required—English entrance exam and/or TOEFL. Electronic applications accepted. Tuition and fees vary according to course load and program. *Faculty research:* Development, gender, sociopolitical economic formulations, social science indigenization, Arab world.

American University of Beirut, Graduate Programs, Faculty of Arts and Sciences, Beirut, Lebanon. Offers anthropology (MA); Arab and Middle Eastern history (PhD); Arabic language and literature (MA, PhD); archaeology (MA); biology (MS); cell and molecular biology (PhD); chemistry (MS); clinical psychology (MA); computational sciences (MS); computer science (MS); economics (MA); English language (MA); English literature (MA); environmental policy planning (MS); financial economics (MAFE); geology (MS); history (MA); mathematics (MA, MS); media studies (MA); Middle Eastern studies (MA); physics (MS); political studies (MA); psychology (MA); public administration (MA); sociology (MA); statistics (MA, MS); theoretical physics (PhD); transnational American studies (MA). Part-time programs available. *Faculty:* 107 full-time (32 women), 6 part-time/adjunct (2 women). *Students:* 230 full-time (161 women), 209 part-time (146 women). Average age 26. 261 applicants, 70% accepted, 83 enrolled. In 2014, 68 master's, 2 doctorates awarded. *Degree requirements:* For master's, one foreign language, comprehensive exam, thesis (for some programs); for doctorate, one foreign language, comprehensive exam, thesis/dissertation. *Entrance requirements:* For master's, GRE (for some MA/MS programs), letter of recommendation; for doctorate, GRE, letters of recommendation. Additional exam requirements/recommendations for international students: Required—TOEFL (minimum score 600 paper-based; 97 iBT), IELTS (minimum score 7). *Application deadline:* For fall admission, 4/1 for domestic and international students; for spring admission, 11/1 for domestic and international students. Application fee: $50. Electronic applications accepted. *Expenses: Tuition:* Full-time $15,462; part-time $859 per credit. *Required fees:* $692. Tuition and fees vary according to course load and program. *Financial support:* Research assistantships, career-related internships or fieldwork, institutionally sponsored loans, scholarships/grants, health care benefits, and unspecified assistantships available. Financial award application deadline: 2/4; financial award applicants required to submit FAFSA. *Faculty research:* Determinants of language proficiency among Arab learners of English as a foreign language; opinion mining, information retrieval, runtime verification, high performance computing; solar and fuel cells, self-organizing systems, heterocyclic chemistry, air and water chemistry; complex analysis, harmonic analysis, number theory; social and political psychology, clinical psychology; thin films physics and technology; theory of soft matter; religious and ethnic conflict; sports and politics. *Total annual research expenditures:* $966,000. *Unit head:* Dr. Patrick McGreevy, Dean, 961-1374374 Ext. 3800, Fax: 961-1744461, E-mail: pm07@aub.edu.lb. *Application contact:* Dr. Salim Kanaan, Director, Admissions Office, 961-1350000 Ext. 2590, Fax: 961-1750775, E-mail: sk00@aub.edu.lb.
Website: http://www.aub.edu.lb/fas/

Arizona State University at the Tempe campus, College of Liberal Arts and Sciences, School of Human Evolution and Social Change, Tempe, AZ 85287-2402. Offers anthropology (MA, PhD), including anthropology (PhD), archaeology (PhD), bioarchaeology (PhD), evolutionary (PhD), museum studies (MA), sociocultural (PhD); applied mathematics for the life and social sciences (PhD); environmental social science (PhD), including environmental social science, urbanism; global health (MA, PhD), including complex adaptive systems science (PhD), evolutionary global health sciences (PhD), health and culture (PhD), urbanism (PhD); immigration studies (Graduate Certificate). Terminal master's awarded for partial completion of doctoral program. *Degree requirements:* For master's, thesis or alternative, interactive Program of Study (iPOS) submitted before completing 50 percent of required credit hours; for doctorate, comprehensive exam, thesis/dissertation, interactive Program of Study (iPOS) submitted before completing 50 percent of required credit hours. *Entrance requirements:* For master's and doctorate, GRE, minimum GPA of 3.0 or equivalent in last 2 years of work leading to bachelor's degree. Additional exam requirements/recommendations for international students: Required—TOEFL, IELTS, or PTE. Electronic applications accepted.

Ball State University, Graduate School, College of Sciences and Humanities, Department of Anthropology, Muncie, IN 47306-1099. Offers MA. *Faculty:* 8 full-time (4 women). *Students:* 11 full-time (7 women), 12 part-time (7 women). Average age 27. 15 applicants, 93% accepted, 8 enrolled. In 2014, 10 master's awarded. *Entrance requirements:* For master's, GRE General Test, resume. Application fee: $50. *Financial support:* In 2014–15, 12 students received support, including 9 research assistantships with partial tuition reimbursements available (averaging $7,114 per year). Financial award application deadline: 3/1. *Unit head:* Dr. S. Homes Hogue, Chairman, 765-285-4845, Fax: 765-285-2163, E-mail: sshogue@bsu.edu. *Application contact:* Dr. Robert Morris, Associate Provost for Research and Dean of the Graduate School, 765-285-1300, E-mail: rmorris@bsu.edu.
Website: http://www.bsu.edu/csh/anthro/

Binghamton University, State University of New York, Graduate School, School of Arts and Sciences, Department of Anthropology, Vestal, NY 13850. Offers anthropology (MA, PhD); biomedical anthropology (MS). Part-time programs available. *Faculty:* 16 full-time (7 women), 8 part-time/adjunct (3 women). *Students:* 64 full-time (45 women), 83 part-time (58 women); includes 28 minority (7 Black or African American, non-Hispanic/Latino; 5 American Indian or Alaska Native, non-Hispanic/Latino; 2 Asian, non-Hispanic/Latino; 13 Hispanic/Latino; 1 Native Hawaiian or other Pacific Islander, non-Hispanic/Latino), 23 international. Average age 31. 100 applicants, 60% accepted, 35 enrolled. In 2014, 23 master's, 5 doctorates awarded. Terminal master's awarded for partial completion of doctoral program. *Degree requirements:* For master's, variable foreign language requirement, comprehensive exam (for some programs), thesis (for some programs); for doctorate, variable foreign language requirement, comprehensive exam, thesis/dissertation. *Entrance requirements:* For master's and doctorate, GRE General Test. Additional exam requirements/recommendations for international students: Required—TOEFL (minimum score 550 paper-based; 80 iBT). *Application deadline:* For fall admission, 4/15 priority date for domestic and international students. Applications are processed on a rolling basis. Application fee: $75. Electronic applications accepted. *Expenses:* Tuition, state resident: full-time $7776; part-time $432 per credit. Tuition, nonresident: full-time $15,138; part-time $841 per credit. *Required fees:* $1754; $213 per credit. Tuition and fees vary according to degree level and program. *Financial support:* In 2014–15, 48 students received support, including 1 fellowship with full tuition reimbursement available (averaging $5,000 per year), 1

research assistantship with full tuition reimbursement available (averaging $17,000 per year), 30 teaching assistantships with full tuition reimbursements available (averaging $15,000 per year); career-related internships or fieldwork, Federal Work-Study, institutionally sponsored loans, scholarships/grants, health care benefits, tuition waivers (full and partial), and unspecified assistantships also available. Financial award application deadline: 2/15; financial award applicants required to submit FAFSA. *Unit head:* Dr. Christine Reiber, Chairperson, 607-777-2738, E-mail: creiber@binghamton.edu. *Application contact:* Kishan Zuber, Recruiting and Admissions Coordinator, 607-777-2151, Fax: 607-777-2501, E-mail: kzuber@binghamton.edu.
Website: http://www.binghamton.edu/anthropology/

Biola University, Cook School of Intercultural Studies, La Mirada, CA 90639-0001. Offers anthropology (MA); applied linguistics (MA); intercultural education (PhD); intercultural studies (MA, PhD); linguistics (Certificate); linguistics and Biblical languages (MA); missions (MA); teaching English to speakers of other languages (MA, Certificate). Part-time programs available. *Faculty:* 19. *Students:* 86 full-time (41 women), 119 part-time (58 women); includes 68 minority (7 Black or African American, non-Hispanic/Latino; 1 American Indian or Alaska Native, non-Hispanic/Latino; 42 Asian, non-Hispanic/Latino; 14 Hispanic/Latino; 4 Two or more races, non-Hispanic/Latino), 29 international. In 2014, 29 master's, 16 doctorates awarded. *Entrance requirements:* For master's, minimum undergraduate GPA of 3.0; for doctorate, master's degree or equivalent, 3 years of cross-cultural experience, minimum graduate GPA of 3.3. Additional exam requirements/recommendations for international students: Required—TOEFL. *Application deadline:* For fall admission, 7/1 for domestic students, 6/1 for international students; for spring admission, 12/1 for domestic students; for summer admission, 5/1 for domestic students. Applications are processed on a rolling basis. Application fee: $65. Electronic applications accepted. *Financial support:* Scholarships/grants available. Support available to part-time students. Financial award applicants required to submit FAFSA. *Faculty research:* Linguistics, anthropology, intercultural studies, teaching English to speakers of other languages, missions, missiology. *Unit head:* Dr. Bulus Y. Galadima, Dean, 562-903-4844. *Application contact:* Graduate Admissions Office, 562-903-4752, E-mail: graduate.admissions@biola.edu.
Website: http://cook.biola.edu

Boise State University, College of Social Sciences and Public Affairs, Department of Anthropology, Boise, ID 83725-0399. Offers MA, MAA. *Faculty:* 4 full-time, 3 part-time/adjunct. *Students:* 5 full-time (3 women), 4 part-time (1 woman). 14 applicants, 100% accepted, 6 enrolled. In 2014, 5 master's awarded. *Degree requirements:* For master's, thesis (MA); project (MAA). *Expenses:* Tuition, state resident: part-time $331 per credit hour. Tuition, nonresident: part-time $531 per credit hour. *Financial support:* Scholarships/grants and unspecified assistantships available. *Unit head:* John Ziker, Department Chair, 208-426-2121, E-mail: jziker@boisestate.edu. *Application contact:* Dr. Mark Plew, Graduate Program Coordinator, 208-426-3444, E-mail: mplew@boisestate.edu.
Website: http://sspa.boisestate.edu/anthropology/ma-maa-in-anthropology/

Boston University, Graduate School of Arts and Sciences, Department of Anthropology, Boston, MA 02215. Offers anthropology (PhD); applied anthropology (MA). *Students:* 40 full-time (26 women); includes 1 minority (Black or African American, non-Hispanic/Latino), 11 international. Average age 32. 127 applicants, 7% accepted, 6 enrolled. In 2014, 11 master's awarded. Terminal master's awarded for partial completion of doctoral program. *Degree requirements:* For master's, one foreign language, thesis or alternative; for doctorate, one foreign language, thesis/dissertation. *Entrance requirements:* For master's and doctorate, GRE General Test, 3 letters of recommendation. Additional exam requirements/recommendations for international students: Required—TOEFL (minimum score 550 paper-based; 84 iBT). *Application deadline:* For fall admission, 1/15 for domestic and international students. Application fee: $80. *Expenses: Tuition:* Full-time $45,686; part-time $1428 per credit hour. *Required fees:* $660; $60 per semester. Tuition and fees vary according to program. *Financial support:* In 2014–15, 30 students received support, including 8 fellowships with full tuition reimbursements available (averaging $20,500 per year), 9 teaching assistantships with full tuition reimbursements available (averaging $20,500 per year); Federal Work-Study, scholarships/grants, health care benefits, and unspecified assistantships also available. Support available to part-time students. Financial award application deadline: 1/15. *Unit head:* Matt Cartmill, Chairman, 617-353-2195, Fax: 617-353-2610, E-mail: cartmill@bu.edu. *Application contact:* Martin Wraga, Administrator, 617-353-2196, Fax: 617-353-2610, E-mail: mwraga@bu.edu.
Website: http://www.bu.edu/ANTHROP/

Boston University, School of Medicine, Division of Graduate Medical Sciences, Program in Forensic Anthropology, Boston, MA 02215. Offers MS. *Expenses: Tuition:* Full-time $45,686; part-time $1428 per credit hour. *Required fees:* $660; $60 per semester. Tuition and fees vary according to program. *Financial support:* Applicants required to submit FAFSA. *Unit head:* Dr. Tara L. Moore, Co-Director, 617-638-4054, Fax: 617-638-4922, E-mail: tlmoore@bu.edu. *Application contact:* Patricia Jones, Executive Financial Coordinator, 617-414-2315, E-mail: psterlin@bu.edu.
Website: http://www.bumc.bu.edu/gms/forensicanthro-masters-program/

Boston University, School of Medicine, Division of Graduate Medical Sciences, Program in Medical Anthropology and Cross Cultural Practice, Boston, MA 02215. Offers MA. *Expenses: Tuition:* Full-time $45,686; part-time $1428 per credit hour. *Required fees:* $660; $60 per semester. Tuition and fees vary according to program. *Unit head:* Dr. Linda Barnes, Director, 617-414-4534, Fax: 617-414-5511, E-mail: linda.barnes@bmc.org. *Application contact:* GMS Admissions Office, 617-638-5255, Fax: 617-638-5740, E-mail: natashah@bu.edu.
Website: http://www.bu.edu/bhlp/Education/Masters/index.html

Brandeis University, Graduate School of Arts and Sciences, Department of Anthropology, Waltham, MA 02454. Offers anthropology (MA, PhD); anthropology and women's and gender studies (MA). Part-time programs available. *Faculty:* 9 full-time (5 women), 1 part-time/adjunct (0 women). *Students:* 32 full-time (20 women), 2 part-time (1 woman); includes 6 minority (2 Black or African American, non-Hispanic/Latino; 2 Asian, non-Hispanic/Latino; 1 Hispanic/Latino; 1 Two or more races, non-Hispanic/Latino), 4 international. 38 applicants, 61% accepted, 14 enrolled. In 2014, 6 master's, 8 doctorates awarded. *Degree requirements:* For master's, thesis or alternative; for doctorate, one foreign language, comprehensive exam, thesis/dissertation. *Entrance requirements:* For master's and doctorate, GRE General Test, sample of written work, resume, letters of recommendation. Additional exam requirements/recommendations for international students: Required—TOEFL (minimum score 600 paper-based; 100 iBT), PTE (minimum score 68); Recommended—IELTS (minimum score 7). *Application deadline:* For fall admission, 1/15 for domestic students. Application fee: $75. Electronic

applications accepted. *Financial support:* In 2014–15, 32 students received support, including 8 fellowships with full tuition reimbursements available (averaging $20,800 per year), 24 teaching assistantships with partial tuition reimbursements available (averaging $3,200 per year); Federal Work-Study, scholarships/grants, health care benefits, and tuition waivers (partial) also available. Financial award application deadline: 4/15; financial award applicants required to submit FAFSA. *Faculty research:* Sociocultural anthropology, linguistic anthropology, archaeology, physical anthropology. *Unit head:* Dr. Sarah Lamb, Director of Graduate Studies, 781-736-2210, Fax: 781-736-2232, E-mail: lamb@brandeis.edu. *Application contact:* Laurel Carpenter, Academic Administrator, 781-736-2210, Fax: 781-736-2232, E-mail: lcarpenter@brandeis.edu. Website: http://www.brandeis.edu/gsas

Brigham Young University, Graduate Studies, College of Family, Home, and Social Sciences, Department of Anthropology, Provo, UT 84602. Offers MA. *Faculty:* 10 full-time (1 woman). *Students:* 16 full-time (11 women). Average age 25. 7 applicants, 71% accepted, 1 enrolled. In 2014, 1 master's awarded. *Degree requirements:* For master's, comprehensive exam, thesis. *Entrance requirements:* For master's, GRE General Test, minimum GPA of 3.0 in last 60 hours. Additional exam requirements/recommendations for international students: Required—TOEFL (minimum score 580 paper-based). *Application deadline:* For fall admission, 2/1 for domestic and international students. Application fee: $50. Electronic applications accepted. *Expenses: Tuition:* Full-time $6310; part-time $371 per credit hour. Tuition and fees vary according to program and student's religious affiliation. *Financial support:* In 2014–15, 16 students received support, including 10 research assistantships (averaging $9,000 per year), 5 teaching assistantships (averaging $9,000 per year); fellowships, career-related internships or fieldwork, institutionally sponsored loans, and tuition waivers (partial) also available. Financial award application deadline: 3/1; financial award applicants required to submit FAFSA. *Faculty research:* Archaeology of the Southwest, Near East, and Mesoamerica; Mayan glyphs. *Total annual research expenditures:* $51,800. *Unit head:* Dr. Charles W. Nuckolls, Chair, 801-422-3058, Fax: 801-422-0021, E-mail: charles_nuckolls@byu.edu. *Application contact:* Dr. James R. Allison, Graduate Coordinator, 801-422-3059, Fax: 801-422-0021, E-mail: jallison@byu.edu. Website: http://anthropology.byu.edu/

Brown University, Graduate School, Department of Anthropology, Providence, RI 02912. Offers MA, PhD. *Degree requirements:* For doctorate, one foreign language, thesis/dissertation, preliminary exam.

California State University, Bakersfield, Division of Graduate Studies, School of Social Sciences and Education, Program in Anthropology, Bakersfield, CA 93311. Offers MA. *Degree requirements:* For master's, thesis optional. *Entrance requirements:* For master's, GRE, minimum GPA of 2.5, 3 letters of recommendation. Additional exam requirements/recommendations for international students: Required—TOEFL (minimum score 550 paper-based). *Faculty research:* Human services, social science teaching.

California State University, Chico, Office of Graduate Studies, College of Behavioral and Social Sciences, Department of Anthropology, Chico, CA 95929-0722. Offers anthropology (MA); museum studies (MA). *Faculty:* 3 full-time (2 women), 2 part-time/ adjunct (1 woman). *Students:* 11 full-time (9 women), 17 part-time (12 women); includes 4 minority (all Hispanic/Latino). Average age 26. 65 applicants, 29% accepted, 9 enrolled. In 2014, 7 master's awarded. *Degree requirements:* For master's, comprehensive exam, thesis, oral examination. *Entrance requirements:* For master's, GRE General Test, two letters of recommendation, statement of purpose, curriculum vitae, writing sample. Additional exam requirements/recommendations for international students: Required—TOEFL (minimum score 550 paper-based; 80 iBT), IELTS (minimum score 6.5), PTE (minimum score 59). *Application deadline:* For fall admission, 1/15 for domestic and international students. Application fee: $55. Electronic applications accepted. *Expenses: Tuition:* state resident: full-time $7002. Tuition, nonresident: full-time $18,162. *Required fees:* $1530. Tuition and fees vary according to program. *Financial support:* Fellowships, career-related internships or fieldwork, institutionally sponsored loans, scholarships/grants, and unspecified assistantships available. Financial award application deadline: 3/1; financial award applicants required to submit FAFSA. *Unit head:* Antoinette Martinez, Chair, 530-898-6192, Fax: 530-898-6143, E-mail: anth@csuchico.edu. *Application contact:* Judy L. Rice, Graduate Admissions Coordinator, 530-898-6880, Fax: 530-898-6889, E-mail: jlrice@csuchico.edu. Website: http://www.csuchico.edu/anth/

California State University, East Bay, Office of Academic Programs and Graduate Studies, College of Letters, Arts, and Social Sciences, Department of Anthropology, Geography and Environmental Studies, Hayward, CA 94542-3000. Offers anthropology (MA); geography (MA). Part-time programs available. *Degree requirements:* For master's, variable foreign language requirement, project or thesis. *Entrance requirements:* For master's, minimum GPA of 3.0 in field. Additional exam requirements/ recommendations for international students: Required—TOEFL (minimum score 550 paper-based). *Application deadline:* For fall admission, 6/30 for domestic and international students. Applications are processed on a rolling basis. Application fee: $55. Electronic applications accepted. *Expenses: Tuition:* state resident: full-time $7830; part-time $1302 per credit hour. Tuition, nonresident: full-time $16,368. *Required fees:* $327 per quarter. Tuition and fees vary according to course load and program. *Financial support:* Fellowships, teaching assistantships, career-related internships or fieldwork, Federal Work-Study, institutionally sponsored loans, and scholarships/grants available. Support available to part-time students. Financial award application deadline: 3/2; financial award applicants required to submit FAFSA. *Faculty research:* Sustainability, water resources, GIS, mapping. *Unit head:* Dr. David Larson, Chair, 510-885-3192, E-mail: david.larson@csueastbay.edu. *Application contact:* Prof. David Woo, Graduate Advisor for Geography, 510-885-3160, Fax: 510-885-2353, E-mail: david.woo@csueastbay.edu. Website: http://www20.csueastbay.edu/class/departments/ages/index.html

California State University, Fullerton, Graduate Studies, College of Humanities and Social Sciences, Department of Anthropology, Fullerton, CA 92834-9480. Offers MA. Part-time programs available. *Students:* 9 full-time (6 women), 5 part-time (4 women); includes 4 minority (1 Black or African American, non-Hispanic/Latino; 1 Asian, non-Hispanic/Latino; 2 Hispanic/Latino). Average age 31. 26 applicants, 62% accepted, 13 enrolled. In 2014, 12 master's awarded. *Degree requirements:* For master's, project or thesis. *Entrance requirements:* For master's, minimum GPA of 2.5 in last 60 hours of course work. Application fee: $55. *Financial support:* Career-related internships or fieldwork, Federal Work-Study, institutionally sponsored loans, and scholarships/grants available. Support available to part-time students. Financial award application deadline: 3/1; financial award applicants required to submit FAFSA. *Unit head:* Dr. Mitch Avila, Chair, 657-278-2272. *Application contact:* Admissions/Applications, 657-278-2371.

California State University, Long Beach, Graduate Studies, College of Liberal Arts, Department of Anthropology, Long Beach, CA 90840. Offers anthropology (MA); applied anthropology (MA). Part-time programs available. *Degree requirements:* For master's, one foreign language, comprehensive exam or thesis. Electronic applications accepted. *Faculty research:* Archeology of California, Fiji, and Ireland; cultures of American Indians and Mexico.

California State University, Los Angeles, Graduate Studies, College of Natural and Social Sciences, Department of Anthropology, Los Angeles, CA 90032-8530. Offers MA. Part-time and evening/weekend programs available. *Degree requirements:* For master's, one foreign language, comprehensive exam or thesis. *Entrance requirements:* Additional exam requirements/recommendations for international students: Required— TOEFL (minimum score 500 paper-based). *Expenses:* Tuition, state resident: full-time $6738; part-time $3609 per year. Tuition, nonresident: full-time $15,666; part-time $8073 per year. Tuition and fees vary according to course load, degree level and program. *Faculty research:* Archaeology, folklore, petroglyphs, symbolism, medical anthropology.

California State University, Northridge, Graduate Studies, College of Social and Behavioral Sciences, Department of Anthropology, Northridge, CA 91330. Offers general anthropology (MA); public archaeology (MA). *Students:* 14 full-time (10 women), 27 part-time (18 women); includes 12 minority (1 Asian, non-Hispanic/Latino; 8 Hispanic/ Latino; 3 Two or more races, non-Hispanic/Latino). Average age 32. *Degree requirements:* For master's, thesis or alternative. *Entrance requirements:* For master's, GRE General Test or minimum GPA of 3.0. Additional exam requirements/ recommendations for international students: Required—TOEFL. *Application deadline:* For fall admission, 11/30 for domestic students. Application fee: $55. *Expenses: Required fees:* $12,402. *Financial support:* Career-related internships or fieldwork, Federal Work-Study, and institutionally sponsored loans available. Financial award application deadline: 3/1. *Unit head:* Dr. Cathy Costin, Chair, 818-677-3331. *Application contact:* Dr. Cathy L. Costin, Graduate Adviser, 818-677-3324. Website: http://www.csun.edu/csbs/departments/anthropology/index.html

California State University, Sacramento, Office of Graduate Studies, College of Social Sciences and Interdisciplinary Studies, Department of Anthropology, Sacramento, CA 95819. Offers MA. Part-time programs available. *Degree requirements:* For master's, thesis, departmental qualifying exam, writing proficiency exam. *Entrance requirements:* For master's, GRE, minimum GPA of 3.0 during previous 2 years. Additional exam requirements/recommendations for international students: Required— TOEFL. Electronic applications accepted.

Canisius College, Graduate Division, College of Arts and Sciences, Department of Animal Behavior, Ecology and Conservation, Buffalo, NY 14208-1098. Offers anthrozoology (MS). Applicants accepted in Fall only. Part-time programs available. Postbaccalaureate distance learning degree programs offered (minimal on-campus study). *Faculty:* 4 full-time (2 women), 2 part-time/adjunct (1 woman). *Students:* 18 full-time (17 women), 29 part-time (25 women); includes 6 minority (5 Hispanic/Latino; 1 Two or more races, non-Hispanic/Latino), 2 international. Average age 33. 94 applicants, 32% accepted, 20 enrolled. In 2014, 4 master's awarded. *Entrance requirements:* For master's, official transcript of all college work; bachelor's degree. Additional exam requirements/recommendations for international students: Required— TOEFL (minimum score 550 paper-based, 80 iBT), IELTS (minimum score 6.5), or CAEL (minimum score 70). *Application deadline:* For fall admission, 3/1 for domestic and international students. Applications are processed on a rolling basis. Application fee: $25. Electronic applications accepted. Application fee is waived when completed online. *Financial support:* Scholarships/grants available. Financial award application deadline: 4/30; financial award applicants required to submit FAFSA. *Unit head:* Dr. Michael Noonan, Program Director, 716-888-2770, E-mail: noonan@canisius.edu. *Application contact:* Kathleen B. Davis, Vice President of Enrollment Management, 716-888-2500, Fax: 716-888-3195, E-mail: daviskb@canisius.edu. Website: http://www.canisius.edu/abec/

Carleton University, Faculty of Graduate Studies, Faculty of Arts and Social Sciences, Department of Sociology and Anthropology, Program in Anthropology, Ottawa, ON K1S 5B6, Canada. Offers MA. *Degree requirements:* For master's, comprehensive exam, thesis optional. *Entrance requirements:* For master's, honors degree. Additional exam requirements/recommendations for international students: Required—TOEFL. *Faculty research:* Culture, symbols and mind, anthropology of signs and symbols, Indigenous studies, anthropology of development and underdevelopment.

Case Western Reserve University, Frances Payne Bolton School of Nursing and Department of Anthropology, Nursing/Anthropology Program, Cleveland, OH 44106. Offers MSN/MA. *Application deadline:* For fall admission, 6/1 for domestic and international students; for spring admission, 10/1 for domestic and international students. Applications are processed on a rolling basis. Application fee: $75. *Financial support:* Fellowships, research assistantships, and teaching assistantships available. Financial award application deadline: 6/30; financial award applicants required to submit FAFSA. *Unit head:* Dr. Carol Savrin, Head, 216-368-6304, E-mail: cls18@case.edu. *Application contact:* Donna Hassik, Admissions Coordinator, 216-368-5253, Fax: 216-368-0124, E-mail: dmh7@case.edu. Website: http://fpb.case.edu/MSN/

Case Western Reserve University, School of Graduate Studies, Department of Anthropology, Cleveland, OH 44106. Offers MA, PhD, MD/MA, MD/PhD, MPH/MA, MSN/MA, PhD/MPH. Part-time programs available. *Faculty:* 12 full-time (7 women), 8 part-time/adjunct (3 women). *Students:* 25 full-time (19 women), 2 part-time (1 woman); includes 1 minority (Asian, non-Hispanic/Latino), 5 international. Average age 31. 17 applicants, 41% accepted, 7 enrolled. In 2014, 5 master's, 1 doctorate awarded. Terminal master's awarded for partial completion of doctoral program. *Degree requirements:* For master's, comprehensive exam, thesis optional; for doctorate, one foreign language, thesis/dissertation, language competency if required. *Entrance requirements:* For master's and doctorate, GRE General Test, Statement of purpose; 3 letters of recommendation; official transcripts. Additional exam requirements/ recommendations for international students: Required—TOEFL (minimum score 577 paper-based; 90 iBT), IELTS (minimum score 7). *Application deadline:* For fall admission, 3/1 priority date for domestic students; for spring admission, 11/1 for domestic students. Applications are processed on a rolling basis. Application fee: $50. Electronic applications accepted. *Financial support:* Research assistantships with tuition reimbursements, teaching assistantships with tuition reimbursements, career-related internships or fieldwork, Federal Work-Study, and unspecified assistantships available. Support available to part-time students. Financial award application deadline: 3/1; financial award applicants required to submit CSS PROFILE or FAFSA. *Faculty research:* Medical anthropology, psychological anthropology, cross-cultural aging, physical anthropology, international health. *Unit head:* Lawrence P. Greksa, Chairman, 216-368-2259, Fax: 216-368-5334, E-mail: lawrence.greksa@case.edu. *Application contact:* Kathleen Dowdell, Department Assistant, 216-368-2264, Fax: 216-368-5334, E-mail: kathleen.dowdell@case.edu. Website: http://anthropology.case.edu/

The Catholic University of America, School of Arts and Sciences, Department of Anthropology, Washington, DC 20064. Offers MA. Part-time programs available. *Faculty:* 2 full-time (1 woman), 2 part-time/adjunct (both women). *Students:* 1 (woman) full-time, 2 part-time (both women). Average age 28. 4 applicants, 75% accepted, 1 enrolled. In 2014, 4 master's awarded. *Degree requirements:* For master's, one foreign language, comprehensive exam, thesis or alternative. *Entrance requirements:* For master's, GRE General Test, statement of purpose, official copies of academic transcripts, three letters of recommendation. Additional exam requirements/

recommendations for international students: Required—TOEFL (minimum score 580 paper-based). *Application deadline:* For fall admission, 2/1 priority date for domestic students, 7/15 for international students; for spring admission, 11/15 priority date for domestic students, 10/15 for international students. Applications are processed on a rolling basis. Application fee: $55. Electronic applications accepted. *Expenses: Tuition:* Full-time $40,200; part-time $1600 per credit hour. *Required fees:* $400; $195 per semester. One-time fee: $425. *Financial support:* Fellowships, research assistantships, teaching assistantships, Federal Work-Study, scholarships/grants, tuition waivers (full and partial), and unspecified assistantships available. Financial award application deadline: 2/1; financial award applicants required to submit FAFSA. *Faculty research:* Medical anthropology, ethnopsychology, Latin American studies, ceramic analysis, political anthropology, Middle East studies, Andean archaeology. *Unit head:* Dr. Jon W. Anderson, Chair, 202-319-5080, Fax: 202-319-4782, E-mail: anderson@cua.edu. *Application contact:* Director of Graduate Admissions, 202-319-5057, Fax: 202-319-6533, E-mail: cua-admissions@cua.edu.
Website: http://anthropology.cua.edu/

Central European University, Graduate Studies, Department of Sociology and Social Anthropology, Budapest, Hungary. Offers MA, PhD. *Faculty:* 10 full-time (3 women), 4 part-time/adjunct (1 woman). *Students:* 79 full-time (47 women). Average age 29. 123 applicants, 21% accepted, 22 enrolled. In 2014, 23 master's, 6 doctorates awarded. *Degree requirements:* For master's, one foreign language, thesis; for doctorate, one foreign language, comprehensive exam, thesis/dissertation. *Entrance requirements:* For master's and doctorate, interview. Additional exam requirements/recommendations for international students: Required—TOEFL (minimum score 570 paper-based); Recommended—IELTS (minimum score 6.5). *Application deadline:* For fall admission, 1/24 for domestic and international students. Application fee: $40. Electronic applications accepted. *Expenses: Tuition:* Full-time 12,000 euros. *Required fees:* 200 euros. One-time fee: 500 euros full-time. *Financial support:* In 2014–15, 75 students received support, including 75 fellowships (averaging $6,100 per year); career-related internships or fieldwork, scholarships/grants, health care benefits, and tuition waivers (full and partial) also available. *Faculty research:* Migration studies, postcolonialism, studies of globalization, political and economic sociology, urban studies and sociologies of culture. *Unit head:* Dr. Jacob Rigi, Head of Department, 36 1 327-3000 Ext. 2131, E-mail: sociology@ceu.hu. *Application contact:* Zsuzsanna Jaszberenyi, Admissions Officer, 361-324-3009, Fax: 367-327-3211, E-mail: admissions@ceu.hu.
Website: http://sociology.ceu.hu/

The College of William and Mary, Faculty of Arts and Sciences, Department of Anthropology, Williamsburg, VA 23187-8795. Offers MA, PhD. *Faculty:* 15 full-time (6 women), 2 part-time/adjunct (1 woman). *Students:* 26 full-time (18 women); includes 8 minority (3 Black or African American, non-Hispanic/Latino; 2 Hispanic/Latino; 3 Two or more races, non-Hispanic/Latino), 1 international. Average age 29. 58 applicants, 14% accepted, 5 enrolled. In 2014, 8 master's, 7 doctorates awarded. Terminal master's awarded for partial completion of doctoral program. *Degree requirements:* For master's, thesis, fieldwork; for doctorate, one foreign language, comprehensive exam, thesis/dissertation, fieldwork. *Entrance requirements:* For master's and doctorate, GRE, course work in anthropology or history. Additional exam requirements/recommendations for international students: Required—TOEFL. *Application deadline:* For fall admission, 1/15 for domestic and international students. Application fee: $45. Electronic applications accepted. *Financial support:* In 2014–15, 16 students received support. Research assistantships with full tuition reimbursements available, teaching assistantships with full tuition reimbursements available, career-related internships or fieldwork, institutionally sponsored loans, and scholarships/grants available. Financial award application deadline: 1/15; financial award applicants required to submit FAFSA. *Faculty research:* Historical archaeology, comparative colonialism, biocultural anthropology, African diaspora, historical archaeology of native America. *Total annual research expenditures:* $1.3 million. *Unit head:* Dr. Kathleen J. Bragdon, Chair, 757-221-1067, Fax: 757-221-1066, E-mail: bkbrag@wm.edu. *Application contact:* Dr. Martin D. Gallivan, Director of Graduate Studies, 757-221-3622, Fax: 757-221-1066, E-mail: mdgall@wm.edu.
Website: http://www.wm.edu/anthropology/

Colorado State University, Graduate School, College of Liberal Arts, Department of Anthropology, Fort Collins, CO 80523-1787. Offers MA. Part-time programs available. *Faculty:* 12 full-time (6 women). *Students:* 18 full-time (13 women), 24 part-time (13 women); includes 3 minority (1 Asian, non-Hispanic/Latino; 2 Hispanic/Latino), 2 international. Average age 28. 39 applicants, 38% accepted, 9 enrolled. In 2014, 15 master's awarded. *Degree requirements:* For master's, variable foreign language requirement, comprehensive exam, thesis (for some programs), oral exam. *Entrance requirements:* For master's, GRE General Test, minimum GPA of 3.0, BA/BS, transcripts, statement of purpose, writing sample, 3 letters of recommendation. Additional exam requirements/recommendations for international students: Required—TOEFL (minimum score 550 paper-based; 80 iBT). *Application deadline:* For fall admission, 2/15 priority date for domestic and international students. Applications are processed on a rolling basis. Application fee: $50. Electronic applications accepted. *Expenses:* Tuition, state resident: full-time $9348; part-time $519 per credit. Tuition, nonresident: full-time $22,916; part-time $1273 per credit. *Required fees:* $1584. *Financial support:* In 2014–15, 12 students received support, including 12 teaching assistantships with full tuition reimbursements available (averaging $10,494 per year); research assistantships, career-related internships or fieldwork, Federal Work-Study, scholarships/grants, and unspecified assistantships also available. Financial award application deadline: 3/1; financial award applicants required to submit FAFSA. *Faculty research:* Archaeology, cultural anthropology, biological anthropology, global development, human ecology. *Total annual research expenditures:* $466,751. *Unit head:* Dr. Michelle Glantz, Chair, 970-491-7540, Fax: 970-491-7597, E-mail: mica.glantz@colostate.edu. *Application contact:* Lynn Kwiatkowski, Graduate Contact, 970-491-0280, Fax: 970-491-7597, E-mail: lynn.kwiatkowski@colostate.edu.
Website: http://anthropology.colostate.edu/

Columbia University, Graduate School of Arts and Sciences, New York, NY 10027. Offers African-American studies (MA); American studies (MA); anthropology (MA, PhD); art history and archaeology (MA, PhD); astronomy (PhD); biological sciences (PhD); biotechnology (MA); chemical physics (PhD); chemistry (PhD); classical studies (MA, PhD); classics (MA, PhD); climate and society (MA); earth and environmental sciences (PhD); East Asia: regional studies (MA); East Asian languages and cultures (MA, PhD); ecology, evolution and environmental biology (MA), including conservation biology; ecology, evolution, and environmental biology (PhD), including ecology and evolutionary biology, evolutionary primatology; economics (PhD); English and comparative literature (MA, PhD); French and Romance philology (MA, PhD); Germanic languages (MA, PhD); global French studies (MA); Hispanic cultural studies (MA); history (PhD); history and literature (MA); human rights studies (MA); Islamic studies (MA); Italian (MA, PhD); Japanese pedagogy (MA); Jewish studies (MA); Latin America and the Caribbean: regional studies (MA); Latin American and Iberian cultures (PhD); mathematics (MA, PhD), including finance (MA); medieval and Renaissance studies (MA); Middle Eastern, South Asian, and African studies (MA, PhD); modern art: critical and curatorial studies (MA); modern European studies (MA); museum anthropology (MA); music (DMA, PhD); oral history (MA); philosophical foundations of physics (MA); philosophy (MA, PhD); physics (PhD); political science (MA, PhD); psychology (PhD); quantitative methods in the social sciences (MA); religion (MA, PhD); Russia, Eurasia and East Europe: regional studies (MA); Russian translation (MA); Slavic cultures (MA); Slavic languages (MA, PhD); sociology (MA, PhD); South Asian studies (MA); statistics (MA, PhD); theatre (PhD); JD/PhD; MA/MS; MD/PhD; MPA/MA. Dual-degree programs require admission to both Graduate School of Arts and Sciences and another Columbia school. Part-time and evening/weekend programs available. Terminal master's awarded for partial completion of doctoral program. *Degree requirements:* For master's, thesis (for some programs); for doctorate, comprehensive exam, thesis/dissertation. *Entrance requirements:* For master's and doctorate, GRE General Test, GRE Subject Test (for some programs). Electronic applications accepted. *Faculty research:* Humanities, natural sciences, social sciences.

Concordia University, School of Graduate Studies, Faculty of Arts and Science, Department of Sociology and Anthropology, Montréal, QC H3G 1M8, Canada. Offers social and cultural anthropology (MA); sociology (MA). *Degree requirements:* For master's, comprehensive exam or thesis. *Entrance requirements:* For master's, honors degree in sociology or equivalent. *Faculty research:* Community and ethnic relations, popular culture, regional development in Canada, industrial and social movements, social problems and policies.

Cornell University, Graduate School, Graduate Fields of Arts and Sciences, Field of Anthropology, Ithaca, NY 14853-0001. Offers archaeological anthropology (PhD); biological anthropology (PhD); sociocultural anthropology (PhD). *Degree requirements:* For doctorate, one foreign language, comprehensive exam, thesis/dissertation, teaching experience. *Entrance requirements:* For doctorate, GRE General Test, 3 letters of recommendation, sample of written work. Additional exam requirements/recommendations for international students: Required—TOEFL (minimum score 550 paper-based; 77 iBT). Electronic applications accepted. *Faculty research:* Culture, engaged anthropology, political economy, area studies: Asia, Americas, Europe; interdisciplinary and ethnic studies: Asian-American studies.

Creighton University, Graduate School, College of Arts and Sciences, Program in Medical Anthropology, Omaha, NE 68178-0001. Offers MA. Part-time programs available. Postbaccalaureate distance learning degree programs offered (minimal on-campus study). *Faculty:* 4 full-time (2 women). *Students:* 4 full-time (all women), 12 part-time (7 women); includes 6 minority (2 Black or African American, non-Hispanic/Latino; 2 Asian, non-Hispanic/Latino; 2 Native Hawaiian or other Pacific Islander, non-Hispanic/Latino), 2 international. Average age 31. *Degree requirements:* For master's, thesis optional. *Entrance requirements:* For master's, three recommendations; resume; statement of purpose; writing sample. Additional exam requirements/recommendations for international students: Required—TOEFL. *Application deadline:* For summer admission, 1/15 for domestic and international students. Application fee: $50. Electronic applications accepted. *Expenses: Tuition:* Full-time $14,040; part-time $780 per credit hour. *Required fees:* $153 per semester. Tuition and fees vary according to course load, campus/location, program, reciprocity agreements and student's religious affiliation. *Financial support:* Application deadline: 3/15; applicants required to submit FAFSA. *Unit head:* Dr. Alex Roedlach, Program Director, 402-280-2567, E-mail: alexanderroedlach@creighton.edu. *Application contact:* Lindsay Johnson, Director of Graduate and Adult Recruitment, 402-280-2703, Fax: 402-280-2423, E-mail: gradschool@creighton.edu.

Dalhousie University, Faculty of Arts and Social Science, Department of Sociology and Social Anthropology, Halifax, NS B3H 4R2, Canada. Offers social anthropology (MA, PhD); sociology (MA, PhD). *Entrance requirements:* Additional exam requirements/recommendations for international students: Required—TOEFL, IELTS, CANTEST, CAEL, or Michigan English Language Assessment Battery. Electronic applications accepted. *Faculty research:* Social inequality and social injustice; work, industry, and development (regional and international perspectives); health and illness.

East Carolina University, Graduate School, Thomas Harriot College of Arts and Sciences, Department of Anthropology, Greenville, NC 27858-4353. Offers MA. Part-time programs available. *Degree requirements:* For master's, one foreign language, comprehensive exam, thesis. *Entrance requirements:* For master's, GRE General Test. Additional exam requirements/recommendations for international students: Required—TOEFL. *Expenses:* Tuition, state resident: full-time $4223. Tuition, nonresident: full-time $16,540. *Required fees:* $2184.

Eastern New Mexico University, Graduate School, College of Liberal Arts and Sciences, Department of Anthropology and Applied Archaeology, Portales, NM 88130. Offers anthropology (MA). Part-time programs available. *Degree requirements:* For master's, variable foreign language requirement, comprehensive exam, thesis. *Entrance requirements:* For master's, minimum GPA of 3.0, letters of recommendation, curriculum vitae, writing sample. Additional exam requirements/recommendations for international students: Required—TOEFL (minimum score 550 paper-based; 79 iBT), IELTS (minimum score 6). Electronic applications accepted. *Faculty research:* Paleobotany, remote sensing, conservation archaeology, obsidian hydration.

Edinboro University of Pennsylvania, Department of History, Anthropology and World Languages, Edinboro, PA 16444. Offers social sciences (MA), including anthropology, history. Part-time and evening/weekend programs available. *Degree requirements:* For master's, thesis or alternative, competency exam. *Entrance requirements:* For master's, GRE or MAT, minimum QPA of 2.5. Electronic applications accepted.

Emory University, Laney Graduate School, Department of Anthropology, Atlanta, GA 30322-1100. Offers PhD. *Degree requirements:* For doctorate, thesis/dissertation, qualifying exams. *Entrance requirements:* For doctorate, GRE General Test. Additional exam requirements/recommendations for international students: Required—TOEFL. Electronic applications accepted. *Faculty research:* Primate behavioral ecology, comparative human biology, human growth and development, medical anthropology, globalization, gender and sexuality.

Florida Atlantic University, Dorothy F. Schmidt College of Arts and Letters, Department of Anthropology, Boca Raton, FL 33431-0991. Offers MA. Part-time programs available. *Degree requirements:* For master's, one foreign language, thesis. *Entrance requirements:* For master's, GRE General Test, minimum GPA of 3.0. Additional exam requirements/recommendations for international students: Required—TOEFL (minimum score 500 paper-based; 61 iBT), IELTS (minimum score 6). Electronic applications accepted. *Expenses:* Tuition, state resident: full-time $7396; part-time $369.82 per credit hour. Tuition, nonresident: full-time $19,392; part-time $1024.81 per credit hour. Tuition and fees vary according to course load. *Faculty research:* Archaeological, ethnological, ethnographical, osteological, paleoanthropological, and zoo-archaeological research.

George Mason University, College of Humanities and Social Sciences, Department of Sociology and Anthropology, Fairfax, VA 22030. Offers anthropology (MA); sociology (MA, PhD). *Faculty:* 24 full-time (12 women), 5 part-time/adjunct (2 women). *Students:* 38 full-time (29 women), 56 part-time (35 women); includes 19 minority (8 Black or African American, non-Hispanic/Latino; 1 American Indian or Alaska Native, non-Hispanic/Latino; 2 Asian, non-Hispanic/Latino; 7 Hispanic/Latino; 1 Two or more races, non-Hispanic/Latino), 6 international. Average age 32. 72 applicants, 74% accepted, 23 enrolled. In 2014, 19 master's, 1 doctorate awarded. *Degree requirements:* For master's, thesis; for doctorate, comprehensive exam, thesis/dissertation. *Entrance*

requirements: For master's, official transcript; expanded goals statement; 3 letters of recommendation; writing sample; resume; 3 credits in undergraduate sociology theory, statistics and research methods (for sociology); 3 credits of sociocultural anthropology (for anthropology); for doctorate, GRE General Test, expanded goals statement; 3 letters of recommendation; writing sample; official transcript. Additional exam requirements/recommendations for international students: Required—TOEFL (minimum score 570 paper-based; 80 iBT), IELTS (minimum score 6.5), PTE. Application fee: $65 ($80 for international students). Electronic applications accepted. *Expenses:* Tuition, state resident: full-time $9794; part-time $408 per credit hour. Tuition, nonresident: full-time $26,978; part-time $1124 per credit hour. *Required fees:* $2820; $118 per credit hour. Tuition and fees vary according to course load and program. *Financial support:* In 2014–15, 21 students received support, including 2 fellowships (averaging $10,166 per year), 9 research assistantships with full and partial tuition reimbursements available (averaging $13,941 per year), 12 teaching assistantships with full and partial tuition reimbursements available (averaging $10,555 per year); career-related internships or fieldwork, Federal Work-Study, scholarships/grants, unspecified assistantships, and health care benefits (for full-time research or teaching assistantship recipients) also available. Support available to part-time students. Financial award application deadline: 3/1; financial award applicants required to submit FAFSA. *Faculty research:* Africa, American teenagers, black entrepreneurs, human rights, gambling. *Total annual research expenditures:* $259,232. *Unit head:* Lester Kurtz, Interim Chair, 703-993-1425, Fax: 703-993-1446, E-mail: lkurtz@gmu.edu. *Application contact:* Amy Best, Associate Professor/Graduate Coordinator, 703-993-1426, Fax: 703-993-1446, E-mail: abest@gmu.edu.
Website: http://soan.gmu.edu

The George Washington University, Columbian College of Arts and Sciences, Department of Anthropology, Washington, DC 20052. Offers anthropology (MA, PhD); international development (MA); medical antropology (MA); museum training (MA). Part-time and evening/weekend programs available. *Faculty:* 15 full-time (5 women). *Students:* 38 full-time (29 women), 7 part-time (5 women); includes 6 minority (1 Black or African American, non-Hispanic/Latino; 2 Hispanic/Latino; 3 Two or more races, non-Hispanic/Latino), 6 international. Average age 27. 98 applicants, 39% accepted, 15 enrolled. In 2014, 13 master's, 4 doctorates awarded. *Degree requirements:* For master's, one foreign language, comprehensive exam, thesis or alternative. *Entrance requirements:* For master's, GRE General Test, minimum GPA of 3.0. Additional exam requirements/recommendations for international students: Required—TOEFL (minimum score 550 paper-based; 80 iBT). *Application deadline:* For fall admission, 1/15 priority date for international students; for spring admission, 9/15 priority date for domestic students, 9/1 priority date for international students. Applications are processed on a rolling basis. Application fee: $75. Electronic applications accepted. *Financial support:* In 2014–15, 8 students received support. Fellowships, teaching assistantships, career-related internships or fieldwork, and Federal Work-Study available. Financial award application deadline: 1/15. *Unit head:* Richard Grinker, Chair, 202-994-6984, E-mail: rgrink@email.gwu.edu. *Application contact:* Information Contact, 202-994-6075, E-mail: anth@gwu.edu.
Website: http://anthropology.columbian.gwu.edu/

Georgia State University, College of Arts and Sciences, Department of Anthropology, Atlanta, GA 30302. Offers MA. Part-time programs available. *Faculty:* 9 full-time (6 women). *Students:* 35 full-time (26 women), 13 part-time (9 women); includes 13 minority (5 Black or African American, non-Hispanic/Latino; 4 Hispanic/Latino; 4 Two or more races, non-Hispanic/Latino), 3 international. Average age 31. 24 applicants, 92% accepted, 13 enrolled. In 2014, 5 master's awarded. *Degree requirements:* For master's, one foreign language, comprehensive exam, 33 to 36 credit hours, thesis/practicum defense. *Entrance requirements:* For master's, GRE, statement of purpose, writing sample, official transcripts, two letters of recommendation, curriculum vitae. Additional exam requirements/recommendations for international students: Required—TOEFL (minimum score 550 paper-based; 80 iBT), IELTS (minimum score 6.5). *Application deadline:* For fall admission, 3/15 for domestic and international students; for spring admission, 10/15 for domestic and international students. Applications are processed on a rolling basis. Application fee: $50. Electronic applications accepted. *Expenses:* Tuition, state resident: full-time $6516; part-time $362 per credit hour. Tuition, nonresident: full-time $22,014; part-time $1223 per credit hour. *Required fees:* $2128 per semester. Tuition and fees vary according to course load and program. *Financial support:* In 2014–15, research assistantships with full tuition reimbursements (averaging $4,000 per year) were awarded. Financial award applicants required to submit FAFSA. *Faculty research:* Archaeology, medical anthropology, linguistic anthropology, biological/physical anthropology, cultural anthropology. *Unit head:* Dr. Frank L. Williams, Chair, 404-413-5154, Fax: 404-413-5159, E-mail: frankwilliams@gsu.edu. *Application contact:* Dr. Emanuela Guano, Director of Graduate Studies, 404-413-5152, Fax: 404-413-5159, E-mail: eguano@gsu.edu.
Website: http://www.cas.gsu.edu/anthropology/

The Graduate Center, City University of New York, Graduate Studies, Program in Anthropology, New York, NY 10016-4039. Offers anthropological linguistics (PhD); archaeology (PhD); cultural anthropology (PhD); physical anthropology (PhD). *Degree requirements:* For doctorate, one foreign language, thesis/dissertation. *Entrance requirements:* For doctorate, GRE General Test. Additional exam requirements/recommendations for international students: Required—TOEFL. Electronic applications accepted.

Harvard University, Graduate School of Arts and Sciences, Committee on Middle Eastern Studies, Cambridge, MA 02138. Offers anthropology and Middle Eastern studies (PhD); economics and Middle Eastern studies (PhD); fine arts and Middle Eastern studies (PhD); history and Middle Eastern studies (PhD); regional studies–Middle East (AM). Terminal master's awarded for partial completion of doctoral program. *Degree requirements:* For master's, one foreign language; for doctorate, 2 foreign languages, thesis/dissertation. *Entrance requirements:* For master's, GRE General Test; for doctorate, GRE General Test, 1 year of course work in Middle Eastern regional studies, proficiency in a related language. Additional exam requirements/recommendations for international students: Required—TOEFL.

Harvard University, Graduate School of Arts and Sciences, Department of Anthropology, Cambridge, MA 02138. Offers archaeology (PhD); biological anthropology (PhD); legal anthropology (AM); medical anthropology (AM); social anthropology (AM, PhD); social change and development (AM). Terminal master's awarded for partial completion of doctoral program. *Degree requirements:* For master's, 2 foreign languages, thesis (for some programs); for doctorate, 2 foreign languages, thesis/dissertation, laboratory and/or fieldwork; general, qualifying, or special exams. *Entrance requirements:* For master's and doctorate, GRE General Test. Additional exam requirements/recommendations for international students: Required—TOEFL.

Humboldt State University, Academic Programs, College of Arts, Humanities, and Social Sciences, Department of Anthropology, Arcata, CA 95521-8299. Offers applied anthropology (MA). Part-time programs available. Postbaccalaureate distance learning degree programs offered (minimal on-campus study). *Students:* 12 part-time (9 women); includes 1 minority (American Indian or Alaska Native, non-Hispanic/Latino). Average age 29. 16 applicants, 94% accepted, 12 enrolled. *Degree requirements:* For master's, comprehensive exam, thesis, 180 hours of field placement/internship. *Entrance requirements:* For master's, three letters of recommendation. *Application deadline:* For fall admission, 2/15 priority date for domestic students. Applications are processed on a rolling basis. Application fee: $55. Electronic applications accepted. *Expenses:* Tuition, state resident: full-time $6738; part-time $3906 per year. Tuition, nonresident: full-time $13,434; part-time $6138 per year. *Required fees:* $1690; $1266 per year. Tuition and fees vary according to program. *Financial support:* Applicants required to submit FAFSA. *Unit head:* Dr. Llyn Smith, Chair, 707-826-4441, E-mail: llyn@humboldt.edu. *Application contact:* Cynthia Werner, Administrative Support Coordinator, 707-826-6250, Fax: 707-826-6190, E-mail: apply@humboldt.edu.
Website: http://www2.humboldt.edu/anthropology/

Hunter College of the City University of New York, Graduate School, School of Arts and Sciences, Department of Anthropology, New York, NY 10065-5085. Offers MA. Part-time and evening/weekend programs available. *Faculty:* 3 full-time (0 women), 1 (woman) part-time/adjunct. *Students:* 6 full-time (3 women), 47 part-time (33 women); includes 15 minority (5 Black or African American, non-Hispanic/Latino; 7 Asian, non-Hispanic/Latino; 3 Hispanic/Latino), 2 international. Average age 32. 40 applicants, 58% accepted, 14 enrolled. In 2014, 17 master's awarded. *Degree requirements:* For master's, comprehensive exam, thesis, language or statistics exam. *Entrance requirements:* For master's, GRE General Test, minimum 9 credits of course work in anthropology or a related field. Additional exam requirements/recommendations for international students: Required—TOEFL. *Application deadline:* For fall admission, 4/1 for domestic students, 2/1 for international students; for spring admission, 11/1 for domestic students, 9/1 for international students. *Financial support:* Research assistantships and tuition waivers (full and partial) available. *Faculty research:* Primatology, human ecology, archeology, political anthropology, primate and human evolution. *Unit head:* Gregory A. Johnson, Chair, 212-772-5652, Fax: 212-772-5410, E-mail: gjohnson@hunter.cuny.edu. *Application contact:* William Zlata, Director for Graduate Admissions, 212-772-4482, Fax: 212-650-3336, E-mail: admissions@hunter.cuny.edu.
Website: http://maxweber.hunter.cuny.edu/anthro/

Idaho State University, Office of Graduate Studies, College of Arts and Letters, Department of Anthropology, Pocatello, ID 83209-8005. Offers MA, MS. Part-time programs available. *Degree requirements:* For master's, one foreign language, comprehensive exam, thesis, 4 semesters foreign language, oral defense. *Entrance requirements:* For master's, GRE General Test, GMAT or MAT, minimum GPA of 3.0 in all upper-division classes, 3 letters of recommendation. Additional exam requirements/recommendations for international students: Required—TOEFL (minimum score 550 paper-based; 80 iBT). Electronic applications accepted. *Faculty research:* Native American studies: health care, language/ethnopoetics, prehistory, art, resource environmental management.

Indiana University Bloomington, University Graduate School, College of Arts and Sciences, Department of Anthropology, Bloomington, IN 47405-7000. Offers MA, PhD. *Faculty:* 37 full-time (22 women), 46 part-time/adjunct (21 women). *Students:* 119 full-time (84 women); includes 22 minority (2 Black or African American, non-Hispanic/Latino; 4 American Indian or Alaska Native, non-Hispanic/Latino; 3 Asian, non-Hispanic/Latino; 5 Hispanic/Latino; 8 Two or more races, non-Hispanic/Latino), 17 international. Average age 32. 104 applicants, 15% accepted, 13 enrolled. In 2014, 13 master's, 10 doctorates awarded. Terminal master's awarded for partial completion of doctoral program. *Degree requirements:* For master's, thesis or alternative; for doctorate, one foreign language, comprehensive exam, thesis/dissertation. *Entrance requirements:* For master's and doctorate, GRE General Test, minimum GPA of 3.0. Additional exam requirements/recommendations for international students: Required—TOEFL (minimum score 550 paper-based; 79 iBT). *Application deadline:* For fall admission, 12/1 for domestic and international students. Application fee: $55 ($65 for international students). Electronic applications accepted. *Financial support:* In 2014–15, fellowships with full tuition reimbursements (averaging $15,000 per year), research assistantships with full tuition reimbursements (averaging $15,750 per year), teaching assistantships with full tuition reimbursements (averaging $15,750 per year) were awarded; Federal Work-Study, scholarships/grants, health care benefits, and unspecified assistantships also available. Financial award application deadline: 2/15; financial award applicants required to submit FAFSA. *Faculty research:* Ecologic and economic development, symbolism, arts/dance, paleoarchaeology, bioanthropology. *Total annual research expenditures:* $22.7 million. *Unit head:* Dr. Catherine Tucker, Chair, 812-855-9360, Fax: 812-855-4358, E-mail: tuckerc@indiana.edu. *Application contact:* Debra Wilkerson, Secretary, 812-855-1203, Fax: 812-855-4358, E-mail: dwilkers@indiana.edu.
Website: http://www.indiana.edu/~anthro/index.shtml

Iowa State University of Science and Technology, Department of Anthropology, Ames, IA 50011. Offers MA. *Degree requirements:* For master's, thesis. *Entrance requirements:* For master's, GRE General Test. Additional exam requirements/recommendations for international students: Required—TOEFL (minimum score 550 paper-based; 79 iBT), IELTS (minimum score 6.5). Electronic applications accepted.

Johns Hopkins University, Zanvyl Krieger School of Arts and Sciences, Department of Anthropology, Baltimore, MD 21218-2699. Offers PhD. *Degree requirements:* For doctorate, one foreign language, thesis/dissertation. *Entrance requirements:* For doctorate, GRE General Test. Additional exam requirements/recommendations for international students: Required—TOEFL, IELTS. Electronic applications accepted. *Faculty research:* Social and cultural anthropology of complex societies, gender politics, economic anthropology, religion.

Kent State University, College of Arts and Sciences, Department of Anthropology, Kent, OH 44242-0001. Offers MA. Part-time programs available. *Faculty:* 8 full-time (4 women). *Students:* 13 full-time (5 women), 10 part-time (6 women); includes 2 minority (1 Hispanic/Latino; 1 Two or more races, non-Hispanic/Latino). Average age 28. 32 applicants, 44% accepted, 12 enrolled. In 2014, 5 master's awarded. *Degree requirements:* For master's, thesis. *Entrance requirements:* For master's, GRE General Test, minimum GPA of 3.0, transcript, statement of purpose, 3 letters of recommendation. Additional exam requirements/recommendations for international students: Required—TOEFL (minimum score: paper-based 525, iBT 71), Michigan English Language Assessment Battery (minimum score of 75), IELTS (minimum score of 6.0), PTE Academic (minimum score of 48), or completion of ELS level 112 Intensive Program. *Application deadline:* For fall admission, 2/1 for domestic and international students. Application fee: $45 ($70 for international students). Electronic applications accepted. *Expenses:* Tuition, state resident: full-time $8730; part-time $485 per credit hour. Tuition, nonresident: full-time $14,886; part-time $827 per credit hour. Tuition and fees vary according to campus/location and program. *Financial support:* In 2014–15, 8 students received support. Research assistantships with full tuition reimbursements available, teaching assistantships with full tuition reimbursements available, career-related internships or fieldwork, Federal Work-Study, and unspecified assistantships available. Financial award application deadline: 2/1; financial award applicants required to submit FAFSA. *Unit head:* Dr. Richard S. Meindl, Professor and Chair, 330-672-4363, Fax: 330-672-2999, E-mail: rmeindl@kent.edu. *Application contact:* Dr. Marilyn A. Norconk, Professor and Graduate Coordinator, 330-672-4363, Fax: 330-672-2999, E-mail: mnorconk@kent.edu. Website: http://dept.kent.edu/anthropology/

Anthropology

Louisiana State University and Agricultural & Mechanical College, Graduate School, College of Humanities and Social Sciences, Department of Geography and Anthropology, Baton Rouge, LA 70803. Offers geography (MA, MS); geography and anthropology (PhD). Part-time programs available. *Faculty:* 29 full-time (13 women). *Students:* 72 full-time (37 women), 22 part-time (14 women); includes 6 minority (3 Black or African American, non-Hispanic/Latino; 3 Hispanic/Latino), 28 international. Average age 31. 69 applicants, 75% accepted, 17 enrolled. In 2014, 19 master's, 10 doctorates awarded. Terminal master's awarded for partial completion of doctoral program. *Degree requirements:* For master's, 2 foreign languages, thesis (for some programs); for doctorate, 2 foreign languages, thesis/dissertation. *Entrance requirements:* For master's and doctorate, GRE General Test, minimum GPA of 3.0. Additional exam requirements/recommendations for international students: Required—TOEFL (minimum score 550 paper-based; 79 IBT), IELTS (minimum score 6.5), or PTE (minimum score 59). *Application deadline:* For fall admission, 1/1 priority date for domestic students, 5/15 for international students; for spring admission, 10/15 for domestic and international students; for summer admission, 5/15 for domestic and international students. Applications are processed on a rolling basis. Application fee: $50 ($70 for international students). Electronic applications accepted. *Financial support:* In 2014–15, 73 students received support, including 2 fellowships with full tuition reimbursements available (averaging $23,675 per year), 24 research assistantships with full and partial tuition reimbursements available (averaging $15,302 per year), 31 teaching assistantships with full and partial tuition reimbursements available (averaging $12,842 per year); career-related internships or fieldwork, health care benefits, and unspecified assistantships also available. Financial award application deadline: 3/1; financial award applicants required to submit FAFSA. *Faculty research:* Cultural, coastal, climate, geographic information systems (geography); cultural, linguistics, archaeology (anthropology). *Total annual research expenditures:* $1.2 million. *Unit head:* Dr. Fahui Wang, Chair, 225-578-5942, Fax: 225-578-4420, E-mail: gachair@lsu.edu. *Application contact:* Dr. Robert Tague, Graduate Adviser, 225-578-6094, Fax: 225-578-4420, E-mail: rtague@lsu.edu.
Website: http://www.ga.lsu.edu/

McGill University, Faculty of Graduate and Postdoctoral Studies, Faculty of Arts, Department of Anthropology, Montréal, QC H3A 2T5, Canada. Offers anthropology (MA, PhD); medical anthropology (MA).

McGill University, Faculty of Graduate and Postdoctoral Studies, Faculty of Medicine, Department of Social Studies in Medicine, Montréal, QC H3A 2T5, Canada. Offers medical anthropology (MA, PhD); medical history (MA, PhD); medical sociology (MA, PhD).

McMaster University, School of Graduate Studies, Faculty of Social Sciences, Department of Anthropology, Hamilton, ON L8S 4M2, Canada. Offers MA, PhD. Part-time programs available. *Degree requirements:* For master's, thesis or alternative; for doctorate, one foreign language, comprehensive exam, thesis/dissertation, fieldwork. *Entrance requirements:* Additional exam requirements/recommendations for international students: Required—TOEFL (minimum score 580 paper-based). *Faculty research:* Medical anthropology, contemporary ethnography in an interdisciplinary perspective, archaeological and social theory, linguistics, folklore.

Memorial University of Newfoundland, School of Graduate Studies, Department of Anthropology, St. John's, NL A1C 5S7, Canada. Offers archaeology and physical anthropology (MA, PhD); social and cultural anthropology (MA, PhD). Part-time programs available. *Degree requirements:* For master's, thesis (for some programs); for doctorate, comprehensive exam, thesis/dissertation, oral defense of thesis. *Entrance requirements:* For master's, 2nd class degree in related field. Electronic applications accepted. *Faculty research:* Early European settlements, ethnoarchaeology, economic/political anthropology, land claims and aboriginal rights, marine anthropology.

Michigan State University, The Graduate School, College of Social Science, Department of Anthropology, East Lansing, MI 48824. Offers anthropology (MA, PhD); professional applications in anthropology (MA). Terminal master's awarded for partial completion of doctoral program. *Degree requirements:* For master's, comprehensive exam (for some programs); for doctorate, annual evaluation. *Entrance requirements:* Additional exam requirements/recommendations for international students: Required—TOEFL. Electronic applications accepted.

Minnesota State University Mankato, College of Graduate Studies, College of Social and Behavioral Sciences, Department of Anthropology, Mankato, MN 56001. Offers MS. Part-time programs available. *Students:* 6 full-time (3 women), 20 part-time (9 women). *Degree requirements:* For master's, comprehensive exam. *Entrance requirements:* For master's, minimum undergraduate GPA of 3.0 in last 2 years of course work. Additional exam requirements/recommendations for international students: Required—TOEFL. *Application deadline:* For fall admission, 7/1 priority date for domestic students; for spring admission, 11/1 for domestic students. Applications are processed on a rolling basis. Application fee: $40. Electronic applications accepted. *Financial support:* Unspecified assistantships available. Financial award application deadline: 3/15; financial award applicants required to submit FAFSA. *Unit head:* Dr. Kathleen Blue, Chair, 507-389-6370, Fax: 507-389-6769, E-mail: paul.brown@mnsu.edu. *Application contact:* 507-389-2321, E-mail: grad@mnsu.edu.
Website: http://sbs.mnsu.edu/anthropology/

Mississippi State University, College of Arts and Sciences, Department of Anthropology and Middle Eastern Cultures, Mississippi State, MS 39762. Offers applied anthropology (MA). Part-time programs available. *Faculty:* 10 full-time (3 women). *Students:* 25 full-time (17 women), 25 part-time (13 women); includes 5 minority (2 Black or African American, non-Hispanic/Latino; 2 Hispanic/Latino; 1 Two or more races, non-Hispanic/Latino), 1 international. Average age 28. 27 applicants, 48% accepted, 11 enrolled. In 2014, 2 master's awarded. *Degree requirements:* For master's, thesis. *Entrance requirements:* For master's, GRE, minimum GPA of 3.0 on last 60 hours of undergraduate courses. Additional exam requirements/recommendations for international students: Required—TOEFL (minimum score 477 paper-based; 53 iBT); Recommended—IELTS (minimum score 4.5). *Application deadline:* For fall admission, 4/15 priority date for domestic students, 4/15 for international students; for spring admission, 11/1 priority date for domestic students, 9/1 for international students. Applications are processed on a rolling basis. Application fee: $60. Electronic applications accepted. *Expenses:* Tuition, state resident: full-time $7140; part-time $783 per credit hour. Tuition, nonresident: full-time $18,478; part-time $2043 per credit hour. *Financial support:* In 2014–15, 3 research assistantships with full and partial tuition reimbursements (averaging $9,572 per year), 9 teaching assistantships with full and partial tuition reimbursements (averaging $9,348 per year) were awarded; Federal Work-Study, institutionally sponsored loans, scholarships/grants, and unspecified assistantships also available. Financial award application deadline: 3/15; financial award applicants required to submit FAFSA. *Faculty research:* Archaeology and bioarchaeology, environmental archaeology, cultural archaeology, research projects in Southeastern archaeology and bioarchaeology. *Unit head:* Dr. Michael Galaty, Department Head, 662-325-7525, Fax: 662-325-8690, E-mail: mgalaty@anthro.msstate.edu. *Application contact:* Dr. David Hoffman, Associate Professor/Graduate Coordinator, 662-325-7524, Fax: 662-325-1967, E-mail: dhoffman@anthro.msstate.edu.
Website: http://www.amec.msstate.edu

Missouri State University, Graduate College, College of Humanities and Public Affairs, Department of Sociology and Anthropology, Springfield, MO 65897. Offers applied anthropology (MS). Part-time programs available. *Faculty:* 14 full-time (6 women), 2 part-time/adjunct (0 women). *Students:* 14 full-time (8 women), 7 part-time (2 women). Average age 33. 7 applicants, 86% accepted, 4 enrolled. In 2014, 8 master's awarded. *Degree requirements:* For master's, comprehensive exam, thesis or alternative. *Entrance requirements:* For master's, GRE, minimum GPA of 3.0. Additional exam requirements/recommendations for international students: Required—TOEFL (minimum score 550 paper-based; 79 iBT). *Application deadline:* For fall admission, 7/20 priority date for domestic students, 5/1 for international students; for spring admission, 12/20 priority date for domestic students, 9/1 for international students. Applications are processed on a rolling basis. Application fee: $35 ($50 for international students). Electronic applications accepted. *Expenses:* Tuition, state resident: full-time $2250; part-time $250 per credit hour. Tuition, nonresident: full-time $4509; part-time $501 per credit hour. Tuition and fees vary according to course level, course load and program. *Financial support:* Federal Work-Study, institutionally sponsored loans, scholarships/grants, and unspecified assistantships available. Financial award application deadline: 3/31; financial award applicants required to submit FAFSA. *Faculty research:* Youth delinquency, social inequality, linguistic anthropology, forensic anthropology. *Unit head:* Dr. David Rohall, Department Head, 417-836-5640, Fax: 417-836-6416, E-mail: sociologyanthropology@missouristate.edu. *Application contact:* Misty Stewart, Coordinator of Graduate Recruitment, 417-836-6079, Fax: 417-836-6200, E-mail: mistystewart@missouristate.edu.
Website: http://socantcrim.missouristate.edu

Monmouth University, The Graduate School, Program in Anthropology, West Long Branch, NJ 07764-1898. Offers MA. Part-time and evening/weekend programs available. *Faculty:* 5 full-time (3 women). *Students:* 7 full-time (3 women), 25 part-time (18 women); includes 3 minority (2 Black or African American, non-Hispanic/Latino; 1 Hispanic/Latino). Average age 33. 16 applicants, 100% accepted, 8 enrolled. In 2014, 5 master's awarded. *Degree requirements:* For master's, comprehensive exam (for some programs), thesis (for some programs). *Entrance requirements:* For master's, minimum undergraduate GPA of 3.0, 500-word essay highlighting personal and/or professional goals and objectives for graduate anthropology study, two professional letters of recommendation. Additional exam requirements/recommendations for international students: Required—TOEFL (minimum score 550 paper-based; 7 iBT), IELTS (minimum score 6), TOEFL (minimum score 550 paper-based; 79 iBT), IELTS (minimum score 6), Michigan English Language Assessment Battery (minimum score 77) or Certificate of Advanced English (minimum score B2). *Application deadline:* For fall admission, 7/15 for domestic students, 6/1 for international students; for spring admission, 11/15 for domestic students, 11/1 for international students. Application fee: $50. *Expenses:* Tuition: Full-time $18,072; part-time $1004 per credit. *Required fees:* $157 per semester. *Financial support:* In 2014–15, 29 students received support, including 20 fellowships (averaging $2,025 per year), 5 research assistantships (averaging $9,702 per year). *Faculty research:* Historical archeology, early America, material culture, Native Americans, heritage, diaspora, environmental anthropology, visual anthropology, Latin America. *Unit head:* Dr. Richard Veit, Director, 732-263-5699, E-mail: rveit@monmouth.edu. *Application contact:* Andrea Thompson, Graduate Admission Counselor, 732-571-3452, Fax: 732-263-5123, E-mail: gradadm@monmouth.edu.
Website: http://www.monmouth.edu/academics/schools/humanities/graduate_programs/anthropology/default.asp

New Mexico Highlands University, Graduate Studies, College of Arts and Sciences, Department of Social and Behavioral Sciences, Las Vegas, NM 87701. Offers psychology (MS), including clinical psychology/counseling, general psychology; public affairs (MA), including applied sociology; Southwest studies (MA), including anthropology. Part-time programs available. *Faculty:* 11 full-time (5 women), 3 part-time/adjunct (all women). *Students:* 24 full-time (16 women), 19 part-time (14 women); includes 27 minority (3 Black or African American, non-Hispanic/Latino; 1 American Indian or Alaska Native, non-Hispanic/Latino; 23 Hispanic/Latino), 2 international. Average age 33. 45 applicants, 33% accepted, 15 enrolled. In 2014, 7 master's awarded. *Degree requirements:* For master's, comprehensive exam, thesis or alternative. *Entrance requirements:* For master's, minimum undergraduate GPA of 3.0. Additional exam requirements/recommendations for international students: Required—TOEFL (minimum score 540 paper-based). *Application deadline:* For fall admission, 8/1 priority date for domestic students. Applications are processed on a rolling basis. Application fee: $15. *Financial support:* In 2014–15, 34 teaching assistantships were awarded; career-related internships or fieldwork, Federal Work-Study, institutionally sponsored loans, scholarships/grants, tuition waivers (full and partial), and unspecified assistantships also available. Support available to part-time students. Financial award application deadline: 3/1; financial award applicants required to submit FAFSA. *Faculty research:* Southwest Native American resettlement development, community-level interventions, neurochemistry of personality, comparative criminal justice, social theory and activism. *Unit head:* Dr. Tom Ward, Program Coordinator, 505-454-3196, E-mail: tsward@nmhu.edu. *Application contact:* Diane Trujillo, Administrative Assistant for Graduate Studies, 505-454-3266, Fax: 505-426-2117, E-mail: dtrujillo@nmhu.edu.

New Mexico State University, College of Arts and Sciences, Department of Anthropology, Las Cruces, NM 88003-8001. Offers anthropology (MA); cultural resource management (Graduate Certificate); museum studies (Graduate Certificate). Part-time programs available. *Faculty:* 8 full-time (4 women), 4 part-time/adjunct (2 women). *Students:* 47 full-time (33 women), 31 part-time (22 women); includes 17 minority (1 Black or African American, non-Hispanic/Latino; 1 American Indian or Alaska Native, non-Hispanic/Latino; 13 Hispanic/Latino; 2 Two or more races, non-Hispanic/Latino), 2 international. Average age 32. 44 applicants, 64% accepted, 16 enrolled. In 2014, 17 master's, 6 other advanced degrees awarded. *Degree requirements:* For master's, comprehensive exam (for some programs), thesis optional. *Entrance requirements:* For master's, minimum undergraduate GPA of 3.0. Additional exam requirements/recommendations for international students: Required—TOEFL (minimum score 550 paper-based; 79 iBT), IELTS (minimum score 6.5). *Application deadline:* For fall admission, 2/1 priority date for domestic and international students; for spring admission, 10/1 priority date for domestic and international students. Applications are processed on a rolling basis. Application fee: $40 ($50 for international students). Electronic applications accepted. *Expenses:* Tuition, state resident: full-time $3969; part-time $220.50 per credit hour. Tuition, nonresident: full-time $13,838; part-time $768.80 per credit hour. *Required fees:* $853; $47.40 per credit hour. *Financial support:* In 2014–15, 28 students received support, including 3 fellowships (averaging $3,970 per year), 1 research assistantship (averaging $23,100 per year), 13 teaching assistantships (averaging $8,902 per year); career-related internships or fieldwork, Federal Work-Study, scholarships/grants, traineeships, health care benefits, and unspecified assistantships also available. Support available to part-time students. Financial award application deadline: 3/1. *Faculty research:* Native American culture and society, Latin America and border studies, prehistoric and historic archaeology, medical anthropology, applied anthropology, museum studies. *Total annual research expenditures:* $63,773. *Unit head:* Dr. Rani Alexander, Head, 575-646-2826, Fax: -, E-mail: raalexan@nmsu.edu. *Application contact:* Dr. Lois Stanford, Graduate Advisor, 575-646-6092, E-mail: lstanfor@nmsu.edu. Website: http://anthropology.nmsu.edu

The New School, The New School for Social Research, Department of Anthropology, New York, NY 10003. Offers M Phil, MA, DS Sc, PhD. Part-time and evening/weekend programs available. Terminal master's awarded for partial completion of doctoral program. *Degree requirements:* For master's, comprehensive exam; for doctorate, one foreign language, comprehensive exam, thesis/dissertation, 30 credits, including three proseminars. *Entrance requirements:* For master's, GRE General Test; for doctorate, GRE General Test, MA in anthropology. Additional exam requirements/recommendations for international students: Required—TOEFL (minimum score 600 paper-based; 100 iBT). Electronic applications accepted. *Faculty research:* Critical theory; modern social and cultural systems; race, class, gender.

New York University, Graduate School of Arts and Science, Department of Anthropology, New York, NY 10012-1019. Offers anthropology (MA, PhD), including archaeological anthropology, linguistic anthropology, physical anthropology, sociocultural anthropology; anthropology and French studies (PhD); MA/Advanced Certificate; PhD/Advanced Certificate. Part-time programs available. *Faculty:* 22 full-time, 13 part-time/adjunct. *Students:* 88 full-time (68 women), 7 part-time (5 women); includes 24 minority (2 Black or African American, non-Hispanic/Latino; 1 American Indian or Alaska Native, non-Hispanic/Latino; 8 Asian, non-Hispanic/Latino; 10 Hispanic/Latino; 3 Two or more races, non-Hispanic/Latino), 18 international. Average age 30. 357 applicants, 6% accepted, 15 enrolled. In 2014, 14 master's, 7 doctorates awarded. *Degree requirements:* For master's, thesis; for doctorate, one foreign language, comprehensive exam, thesis/dissertation. *Entrance requirements:* For master's and doctorate, GRE General Test. Additional exam requirements/recommendations for international students: Required—TOEFL. *Application deadline:* For fall admission, 12/18 priority date for domestic students, 12/18 for international students. Application fee: $100. *Financial support:* Fellowships with tuition reimbursements, research assistantships with tuition reimbursements, teaching assistantships with tuition reimbursements, career-related internships or fieldwork, Federal Work-Study, institutionally sponsored loans, scholarships/grants, health care benefits, and unspecified assistantships available. Financial award application deadline: 12/18; financial award applicants required to submit FAFSA. *Faculty research:* Sociocultural anthropology, archaeology, biological anthropology, linguistic anthropology. *Unit head:* Terry Harrison, Chair, 212-998-8550, Fax: 212-995-4014, E-mail: anthropology@nyu.edu. *Application contact:* Tejaswini Ganti, Director of Graduate Studies, 212-998-8550, Fax: 212-995-4014, E-mail: anthropology@nyu.edu.
Website: http://www.nyu.edu/gsas/dept/anthro/

North Carolina State University, Graduate School, College of Humanities and Social Sciences, Department of Sociology and Anthropology, Program in Anthropology, Raleigh, NC 27695. Offers bioarchaeology (MA); cultural anthropology (MA); environmental anthropology (MA).

Northern Arizona University, Graduate College, College of Social and Behavioral Sciences, Department of Anthropology, Flagstaff, AZ 86011. Offers archaeology (MA); cultural anthropology (MA); linguistic anthropology (MA). *Degree requirements:* For master's, thesis (for some programs), internship paper. *Entrance requirements:* For master's, 12 undergraduate hours in anthropology. Additional exam requirements/recommendations for international students: Required—TOEFL (minimum score 550 paper-based; 80 iBT), IELTS (minimum score 7). Electronic applications accepted. *Faculty research:* Economic development, culture change, ethnohistory, archaeology of the Southwest, small town networks and HIV.

Northern Illinois University, Graduate School, College of Liberal Arts and Sciences, Department of Anthropology, De Kalb, IL 60115-2854. Offers MA. Part-time programs available. *Faculty:* 12 full-time (6 women). *Students:* 19 full-time (10 women), 17 part-time (14 women); includes 5 minority (1 Black or African American, non-Hispanic/Latino; 3 Hispanic/Latino; 1 Two or more races, non-Hispanic/Latino). Average age 29. 34 applicants, 74% accepted, 8 enrolled. In 2014, 16 master's awarded. *Degree requirements:* For master's, one foreign language, comprehensive exam, thesis optional. *Entrance requirements:* For master's, GRE General Test, minimum GPA of 2.75, 15 hours of course work in anthropology, course work in statistics. Additional exam requirements/recommendations for international students: Required—TOEFL (minimum score 550 paper-based). *Application deadline:* For fall admission, 6/1 for domestic students, 5/1 for international students; for spring admission, 11/1 for domestic students, 10/1 for international students. Applications are processed on a rolling basis. Application fee: $40. Electronic applications accepted. *Financial support:* In 2014–15, 2 research assistantships with full tuition reimbursements, 14 teaching assistantships with full tuition reimbursements were awarded; fellowships with full tuition reimbursements, career-related internships or fieldwork, Federal Work-Study, scholarships/grants, tuition waivers (full), and unspecified assistantships also available. Support available to part-time students. Financial award applicants required to submit FAFSA. *Faculty research:* Linguistic anthropology of Oceania, Mayan languages, human paleontology, primate evolution, dental anthropology. *Unit head:* Dr. Kendall Thu, Chair, 815-753-0479, Fax: 815-753-7027, E-mail: kthu@niu.edu. *Application contact:* Graduate School Office, 815-753-0395, E-mail: gradsch@niu.edu.
Website: http://www.niu.edu/anthro/

Northwestern University, The Graduate School, Judd A. and Marjorie Weinberg College of Arts and Sciences, Department of Anthropology, Evanston, IL 60208. Offers PhD, JD/PhD. Admissions and degrees offered through The Graduate School. *Degree requirements:* For doctorate, thesis/dissertation. *Entrance requirements:* For doctorate, GRE General Test. Additional exam requirements/recommendations for international students: Required—TOEFL. Electronic applications accepted. *Faculty research:* Archaeology of complex societies, gender, political/urban anthropology, linguistic anthropology, African studies.

The Ohio State University, Graduate School, College of Arts and Sciences, Division of Social and Behavioral Sciences, Department of Anthropology, Columbus, OH 43210. Offers MA, PhD. *Faculty:* 16. *Students:* 52 full-time (35 women), 1 (woman) part-time; includes 9 minority (1 Black or African American, non-Hispanic/Latino; 1 Asian, non-Hispanic/Latino; 6 Hispanic/Latino; 1 Two or more races, non-Hispanic/Latino), 1 international. Average age 29. In 2014, 4 master's awarded. *Degree requirements:* For master's, thesis optional; for doctorate, one foreign language, thesis/dissertation. *Entrance requirements:* For master's and doctorate, GRE General Test, minimum GPA of 3.3 in undergraduate work, 3.5 in all previous graduate work (recommended). Additional exam requirements/recommendations for international students: Required—TOEFL (minimum score 550 paper-based; 79 iBT), Michigan English Language Assessment Battery (minimum score 82); Recommended—IELTS (minimum score 7). *Application deadline:* For fall admission, 11/19 priority date for domestic and international students; for winter admission, 12/1 for domestic students, 11/1 for international students; for spring admission, 3/1 for domestic students, 2/1 for international students. Applications are processed on a rolling basis. Application fee: $60 ($70 for international students). Electronic applications accepted. *Financial support:* Fellowships with tuition reimbursements, research assistantships with tuition reimbursements, teaching assistantships with tuition reimbursements, Federal Work-Study, institutionally sponsored loans, and unspecified assistantships available. Support available to part-time students. *Unit head:* Dr. Clark S. Larsen, Chair, 614-292-4149, Fax: 614-292-4155, E-mail: larsen.53@osu.edu. *Application contact:* Graduate and Professional Admissions, 614-292-9444, Fax: 614-292-3895, E-mail: gpadmissions@osu.edu.
Website: http://anthropology.osu.edu/

Oregon State University, College of Liberal Arts, Program in Applied Anthropology, Corvallis, OR 97331. Offers MA, PhD. *Faculty:* 14 full-time (8 women). *Students:* 43 full-time (31 women), 11 part-time (8 women); includes 16 minority (2 Black or African American, non-Hispanic/Latino; 10 Hispanic/Latino; 4 Two or more races, non-Hispanic/Latino), 2 international. Average age 34. 55 applicants, 35% accepted, 11 enrolled. In 2014, 8 master's awarded. *Degree requirements:* For master's, one foreign language, thesis. *Entrance requirements:* Additional exam requirements/recommendations for international students: Required—TOEFL (minimum score 80 iBT), IELTS (minimum score 6.5). *Application deadline:* For fall admission, 1/15 for domestic and international students. Application fee: $60. *Expenses:* Tuition, state resident: full-time $11,907; part-time $189 per credit hour. Tuition, nonresident: full-time $19,953; part-time $441 per credit hour. *Required fees:* $1472; $449 per term. One-time fee: $350. Tuition and fees vary according to course load and program. *Financial support:* Research assistantships and teaching assistantships available. Financial award application deadline: 1/15. *Faculty research:* Historical anthropology, evolutionary anthropology, medical anthropology, anthropology of food, environmental anthropology. *Unit head:* Dr. Susan M. Shaw, Director of School of Language, Culture and Society. *Application contact:* Dr. Bryan Tilt, Associate Professor, 541-737-3896, E-mail: bryan.tilt@oregonstate.edu.
Website: http://liberalarts.oregonstate.edu/slcs/anthropology

Penn State University Park, Graduate School, College of the Liberal Arts, Department of Anthropology, University Park, PA 16802. Offers MA, PhD. *Unit head:* Dr. Susan Welch, Dean, 814-865-7691, Fax: 814-863-2085, E-mail: swelch@psu.edu. *Application contact:* Lori A. Stania, Director, Graduate Student Services, 814-867-5278, Fax: 814-863-4627, E-mail: gswww@psu.edu.
Website: http://anth.la.psu.edu/

Portland State University, Graduate Studies, College of Liberal Arts and Sciences, Department of Anthropology, Portland, OR 97207-0751. Offers MA. *Faculty:* 8 full-time (6 women), 7 part-time/adjunct (4 women). *Students:* 11 full-time (7 women), 10 part-time (7 women); includes 1 minority (Two or more races, non-Hispanic/Latino), 1 international. Average age 32. 38 applicants, 34% accepted, 9 enrolled. In 2014, 7 master's awarded. *Degree requirements:* For master's, one foreign language, thesis. *Entrance requirements:* For master's, GRE General Test, minimum GPA of 3.25 in upper-division anthropology course work, 3.0 overall; 3 letters of recommendation. Additional exam requirements/recommendations for international students: Required—TOEFL (minimum score 550 paper-based; 80 iBT), IELTS (minimum score 6.5). *Application deadline:* For fall admission, 2/1 for domestic and international students. Application fee: $50. *Expenses:* Tuition, state resident: part-time $222 per credit. Tuition, nonresident: part-time $527 per credit. *Required fees:* $22 per contact hour. $100 per quarter. Tuition and fees vary according to program. *Financial support:* In 2014–15, 2 research assistantships (averaging $9,585 per year), 5 teaching assistantships with full tuition reimbursements (averaging $3,697 per year) were awarded; career-related internships or fieldwork, Federal Work-Study, and unspecified assistantships also available. Support available to part-time students. Financial award application deadline: 3/1; financial award applicants required to submit FAFSA. *Faculty research:* Forensic anthropology, Northwest Coast prehistory, Native Americans, applied anthropology, urban anthropology. *Total annual research expenditures:* $759,913. *Unit head:* Dr. Michele Gamburd, Chair, 503-725-3317, E-mail: gamburdm@pdx.edu. *Application contact:* Connie Cash, Office Coordinator, 503-725-3361, Fax: 503-725-3905, E-mail: cashc@pdx.edu.
Website: http://www.anthropology.pdx.edu/

Portland State University, Graduate Studies, College of Liberal Arts and Sciences, Systems Science Program, Portland, OR 97207-0751. Offers computational intelligence (Certificate); computer modeling and simulation (Certificate); systems science (MS); systems science/anthropology (PhD); systems science/business administration (PhD); systems science/civil engineering (PhD); systems science/economics (PhD); systems science/engineering management (PhD); systems science/general (PhD); systems science/mathematical sciences (PhD); systems science/mechanical engineering (PhD); systems science/psychology (PhD); systems science/sociology (PhD). *Faculty:* 2 full-time (0 women), 1 part-time/adjunct (0 women). *Students:* 6 full-time (2 women), 29 part-time (8 women); includes 6 minority (1 Black or African American, non-Hispanic/Latino; 1 American Indian or Alaska Native, non-Hispanic/Latino; 1 Asian, non-Hispanic/Latino; 3 Hispanic/Latino). Average age 41. 32 applicants, 19% accepted, 6 enrolled. In 2014, 10 master's, 3 doctorates awarded. *Degree requirements:* For master's, comprehensive exam (for some programs), thesis optional; for doctorate, variable foreign language requirement, comprehensive exam (for some programs), thesis/dissertation. *Entrance requirements:* For master's, GRE/GMAT (recommended), minimum GPA of 3.0 undergraduate or graduate work, 2 letters of recommendation, statement of interest; for doctorate, GMAT, GRE General Test, minimum GPA of 3.0 undergraduate, 3.25 graduate; 2 letters of recommendation; statement of interest. Additional exam requirements/recommendations for international students: Required—TOEFL (minimum score 550 paper-based; 80 iBT). *Application deadline:* For fall admission, 1/15 for domestic and international students; for spring admission, 11/1 for domestic students. Application fee: $50. Electronic applications accepted. *Expenses:* Tuition, state resident: part-time $222 per credit. Tuition, nonresident: part-time $527 per credit. *Required fees:* $22 per contact hour. $100 per quarter. Tuition and fees vary according to program. *Financial support:* In 2014–15, 1 research assistantship with full and partial tuition reimbursement (averaging $2,358 per year) was awarded; teaching assistantships with full and partial tuition reimbursements, career-related internships or fieldwork, Federal Work-Study, scholarships/grants, and unspecified assistantships also available. Support available to part-time students. Financial award application deadline: 3/1; financial award applicants required to submit FAFSA. *Faculty research:* Systems theory and methodology, artificial intelligence neural networks, information theory, nonlinear dynamics/chaos, modeling and simulation. *Total annual research expenditures:* $137,833. *Unit head:* Prof. Wayne Wakeland, PhD, Chair, 503-725-4975, E-mail: wakeland@pdx.edu.
Website: http://www.pdx.edu/sysc/

Princeton University, Graduate School, Department of Anthropology, Princeton, NJ 08544-1019. Offers PhD. *Degree requirements:* For doctorate, variable foreign language requirement, thesis/dissertation. *Entrance requirements:* For doctorate, GRE General Test, sample of written work. Additional exam requirements/recommendations for international students: Required—TOEFL (minimum score 600 paper-based). Electronic applications accepted. *Faculty research:* Symbolic anthropology, social theory, gender studies, law and society, political and social anthropology.

Purdue University, Graduate School, College of Liberal Arts, Department of Anthropology, West Lafayette, IN 47907. Offers MS, PhD. Terminal master's awarded for partial completion of doctoral program. *Degree requirements:* For master's, thesis; for doctorate, comprehensive exam, thesis/dissertation. *Entrance requirements:* For master's, GRE General Test, minimum undergraduate GPA of 3.0 or equivalent; for doctorate, GRE General Test, minimum undergraduate GPA of 3.0 or equivalent; master's degree. Additional exam requirements/recommendations for international

students: Required—TOEFL (minimum score 550 paper-based; 77 iBT), TWE. Electronic applications accepted. *Faculty research:* Communiversity survey project, risk, fear, constrained behavior, archaeological services.

Rice University, Graduate Programs, School of Social Sciences, Department of Anthropology, Houston, TX 77251-1892. Offers archaeology (MA, PhD); social-cultural anthropology (MA, PhD). Terminal master's awarded for partial completion of doctoral program. *Degree requirements:* For master's, one foreign language, 3 major papers, dissertation proposal and language exam or thesis; for doctorate, one foreign language, thesis/dissertation. *Entrance requirements:* For master's and doctorate, research proposal. Additional exam requirements/recommendations for international students: Required—TOEFL (minimum score 90 iBT). Electronic applications accepted.

Roosevelt University, Graduate Division, College of Arts and Sciences, Department of Sociology and Anthropology, Chicago, IL 60605. Offers anthropology (MA); sociology (MA). Part-time and evening/weekend programs available. *Degree requirements:* For master's, comprehensive exam, thesis. *Faculty research:* Social theory, urban sociology, gerontology, social organizations.

Rutgers, The State University of New Jersey, New Brunswick, Graduate School-New Brunswick, Program in Anthropology, Piscataway, NJ 08854-8097. Offers MA, PhD. Terminal master's awarded for partial completion of doctoral program. *Degree requirements:* For master's, thesis or alternative; for doctorate, comprehensive exam, thesis/dissertation. *Entrance requirements:* For master's and doctorate, GRE General Test, writing sample. Additional exam requirements/recommendations for international students: Required—TOEFL. Electronic applications accepted. *Faculty research:* Human evolution, lithic technology, behavioral ecology, ethnicity, gender.

San Diego State University, Graduate and Research Affairs, College of Arts and Letters, Department of Anthropology, San Diego, CA 92182. Offers MA. *Degree requirements:* For master's, one foreign language, thesis. *Entrance requirements:* For master's, GRE General Test, 3 letters of recommendation, typed writing sample. Additional exam requirements/recommendations for international students: Required—TOEFL. Electronic applications accepted. *Faculty research:* Meso-American archaeology, cognitive anthropology, ethnomusicology, primate conservation, biomedical anthropology.

San Francisco State University, Division of Graduate Studies, College of Liberal and Creative Arts, Department of Anthropology, San Francisco, CA 94132-1722. Offers archaeology (MA); biological/physical anthropology (MA); social/cultural anthropology (MA); visual anthropology (MA). *Expenses:* Tuition, state resident: full-time $6738. Tuition, nonresident: full-time $17,898; part-time $372 per credit hour. *Required fees:* $498 per semester. *Faculty research:* Immigration, ethnicity, urban anthropology, Californian and Latin American archaeology. *Unit head:* Dr. James Quesada, Chair, 415-338-1633, E-mail: jquesada@sfsu.edu. *Application contact:* Dr. Douglass Bailey, Graduate Coordinator, 415-338-1427, E-mail: dwbailey@sfsu.edu. Website: http://anthropology.sfsu.edu/

San Jose State University, Graduate Studies and Research, College of Social Sciences, Department of Anthropology, San Jose, CA 95192-0001. Offers applied anthropology (MA). *Entrance requirements:* For master's, curriculum vitae or resume, official transcripts, 2 letters of reference.

Simon Fraser University, Office of Graduate Studies, Faculty of Arts and Social Sciences, Department of Sociology and Anthropology, Burnaby, BC V5A 1S6, Canada. Offers anthropology (MA, PhD); sociology (MA, PhD). *Degree requirements:* For master's, thesis; for doctorate, comprehensive exam, thesis/dissertation, cooperative education. *Entrance requirements:* For master's, minimum GPA of 3.0 (on scale of 4.33), or 3.33 based on last 60 credits of undergraduate courses; for doctorate, minimum GPA of 3.5 (on scale of 4.33). Additional exam requirements/recommendations for international students: Recommended—TOEFL (minimum score 580 paper-based; 93 iBT), IELTS (minimum score 7), TWE (minimum score 5). Electronic applications accepted. *Faculty research:* Globalization and development, health, environment and science, knowledge, culture and power, social justice, policy, law and society, women, gender and sexuality.

Sonoma State University, School of Social Sciences, Program in Cultural Resources Management, Rohnert Park, CA 94928. Offers MA. Part-time programs available. *Degree requirements:* For master's, thesis. *Entrance requirements:* For master's, minimum GPA of 3.0. Additional exam requirements/recommendations for international students: Required—TOEFL (minimum score 500 paper-based).

Southern Illinois University Carbondale, Graduate School, College of Liberal Arts, Department of Anthropology, Carbondale, IL 62901-4701. Offers MA, PhD. *Faculty:* 14 full-time (5 women). *Students:* 32 full-time (23 women), 28 part-time (19 women); includes 4 minority (1 Black or African American, non-Hispanic/Latino; 2 Asian, non-Hispanic/Latino; 1 Hispanic/Latino), 11 international. 41 applicants, 37% accepted, 8 enrolled. In 2014, 5 master's, 5 doctorates awarded. *Degree requirements:* For master's, one foreign language, thesis; for doctorate, one foreign language, thesis/dissertation. *Entrance requirements:* For master's, GRE General Test, minimum GPA of 2.7; for doctorate, GRE General Test, minimum GPA of 3.25. Additional exam requirements/recommendations for international students: Required—TOEFL. *Application deadline:* Applications are processed on a rolling basis. Application fee: $50. *Expenses:* Tuition, state resident: full-time $10,176; part-time $1153 per credit. Tuition, nonresident: full-time $20,814; part-time $1744 per credit. *Required fees:* $7092; $394 per credit. $2364 per semester. *Financial support:* In 2014–15, 37 students received support, including 10 fellowships with full tuition reimbursements available, 10 research assistantships with full tuition reimbursements available, 16 teaching assistantships with full tuition reimbursements available; career-related internships or fieldwork, Federal Work-Study, institutionally sponsored loans, scholarships/grants, and tuition waivers (full) also available. Support available to part-time students. Financial award application deadline: 1/15. *Faculty research:* Archaeology, human variability, evolution, cultural ecology, social anthropology. *Unit head:* Dr. John McCall, Chair, 618-536-6651, E-mail: jmccall@siu.edu. *Application contact:* Rebecca Bondi, Graduate Secretary, 618-453-5037, Fax: 618-453-5037, E-mail: bondi@siu.edu. Website: http://anthro.siuc.edu/

Southern Methodist University, Dedman College of Humanities and Sciences, Department of Anthropology, Dallas, TX 75205. Offers anthropology (PhD); medical anthropology (MA). Terminal master's awarded for partial completion of doctoral program. *Degree requirements:* For master's, one foreign language, comprehensive exam, thesis or alternative; for doctorate, one foreign language, comprehensive exam, thesis/dissertation, qualifying exam, defense of dissertation. *Entrance requirements:* For master's and doctorate, GRE General Test, minimum GPA of 3.0. Additional exam requirements/recommendations for international students: Required—TOEFL (minimum score 550 paper-based). *Faculty research:* Health and gender, Paleo-Indians, Mesoamerica, American southwest, migration and ethnicity.

Stanford University, School of Humanities and Sciences, Department of Anthropology, Stanford, CA 94305-9991. Offers archaeology (MA, PhD); culture and society (MS, PhD); ecology and environment (MA, PhD). Terminal master's awarded for partial completion of doctoral program. *Degree requirements:* For master's, thesis; for

doctorate, one foreign language, thesis/dissertation. *Entrance requirements:* For master's and doctorate, GRE General Test. Additional exam requirements/recommendations for international students: Required—TOEFL. Electronic applications accepted. *Expenses: Tuition:* Full-time $44,184; part-time $982 per credit hour. *Required fees:* $191.

Stony Brook University, State University of New York, Graduate School, College of Arts and Sciences, Department of Anthropology, Stony Brook, NY 11794. Offers MA, PhD. *Faculty:* 15 full-time (8 women), 1 part-time/adjunct (0 women). *Students:* 31 full-time (20 women), 2 part-time (0 women); includes 6 minority (1 Black or African American, non-Hispanic/Latino; 3 Hispanic/Latino; 2 Two or more races, non-Hispanic/Latino), 7 international. Average age 30. 45 applicants, 18% accepted, 3 enrolled. In 2014, 3 master's, 8 doctorates awarded. *Degree requirements:* For master's, thesis, fieldwork; for doctorate, one foreign language, thesis/dissertation, fieldwork. *Entrance requirements:* For master's and doctorate, GRE General Test. Additional exam requirements/recommendations for international students: Required—TOEFL. *Application deadline:* For fall admission, 1/15 for domestic students; for spring admission, 10/1 for domestic students. Application fee: $100. *Expenses:* Tuition, state resident: full-time $10,370; part-time $432 per credit. Tuition, nonresident: full-time $20,190; part-time $841 per credit. *Required fees:* $1431. *Financial support:* In 2014–15, 1 fellowship, 1 research assistantship, 19 teaching assistantships were awarded; career-related internships or fieldwork also available. *Faculty research:* Anthropology, primatology, human evolution, archaeology, cultural or social anthropology. *Total annual research expenditures:* $349,611. *Unit head:* Prof. Frederick Grine, Chair, 631-632-7622, E-mail: frederick.grine@stonybrook.edu. *Application contact:* Tara J. Powers, Director, 631-632-7606, Fax: 631-632-9165, E-mail: tara.powers@stonybrook.edu. Website: http://www.sunysb.edu/anthro/

Syracuse University, Maxwell School of Citizenship and Public Affairs, Program in Anthropology, Syracuse, NY 13244. Offers MA, PhD. *Students:* 50 full-time (30 women), 11 part-time (9 women); includes 6 minority (1 Black or African American, non-Hispanic/Latino; 2 Asian, non-Hispanic/Latino; 3 Hispanic/Latino), 13 international. Average age 33. 28 applicants, 46% accepted, 7 enrolled. In 2014, 5 master's, 4 doctorates awarded. *Degree requirements:* For master's, thesis or alternative; for doctorate, one foreign language, comprehensive exam, thesis/dissertation. *Entrance requirements:* For master's and doctorate, GRE General Test. Additional exam requirements/recommendations for international students: Required—TOEFL (minimum score 100 iBT). *Application deadline:* For fall admission, 12/15 priority date for domestic and international students. Application fee: $75. Electronic applications accepted. *Expenses: Tuition:* Part-time $1341 per credit. *Financial support:* Fellowships with full tuition reimbursements, research assistantships with full and partial tuition reimbursements, and teaching assistantships with full and partial tuition reimbursements available. Financial award application deadline: 1/1. *Unit head:* Dr. John Burdick, Chair, 315-443-2200, Fax: 315-443-4860. *Application contact:* Jennette Powell, Recruiting Contact, 315-443-2200, E-mail: jpowell@maxwell.syr.edu. Website: http://www.maxwell.syr.edu/

Teachers College, Columbia University, Graduate Faculty of Education, Department of International and Transcultural Studies, Program in Anthropology and Education, New York, NY 10027-6696. Offers Ed M, MA, Ed D, PhD. *Faculty:* 3 full-time. *Students:* 20 full-time (13 women), 32 part-time (21 women); includes 19 minority (5 Black or African American, non-Hispanic/Latino; 8 Asian, non-Hispanic/Latino; 4 Hispanic/Latino; 2 Two or more races, non-Hispanic/Latino), 9 international. Average age 32. 56 applicants, 75% accepted, 13 enrolled. In 2014, 14 master's, 14 doctorates awarded. *Degree requirements:* For master's, integrative project ; for doctorate, variable foreign language requirement, thesis/dissertation. *Entrance requirements:* For master's and doctorate, GRE General Test. Additional exam requirements/recommendations for international students: Required—TOEFL. *Application deadline:* For fall admission, 1/15 priority date for domestic students. Applications are processed on a rolling basis. Application fee: $65. Electronic applications accepted. *Expenses: Tuition:* Full-time $33,552; part-time $1398 per credit. *Required fees:* $418 per semester. *Financial support:* Career-related internships or fieldwork, Federal Work-Study, institutionally sponsored loans, and tuition waivers (full and partial) available. Support available to part-time students. Financial award application deadline: 2/1; financial award applicants required to submit FAFSA. *Faculty research:* African studies, sociocultural change, education in the developing world, human development in social and cultural contexts, culture and communication theory. *Unit head:* Prof. Herve Varenne, Program Coordinator, 212-678-3190, E-mail: varenne@tc.edu. *Application contact:* Deanna Ghozati, Associate Director of Admission, 212-678-3710, Fax: 212-678-4171, E-mail: tcinfo@tc.edu. Website: http://www.tc.columbia.edu/its/anthro/index.asp?Id-Program+Homenfo-Program+Description

Temple University, College of Liberal Arts, Department of Anthropology, Philadelphia, PA 19122-6096. Offers PhD. Part-time programs available. *Faculty:* 15 full-time (6 women), 2 part-time/adjunct (both women). *Students:* 42 full-time (30 women), 1 part-time (0 women); includes 11 minority (4 Black or African American, non-Hispanic/Latino; 6 Hispanic/Latino; 1 Two or more races, non-Hispanic/Latino), 2 international. 29 applicants, 28% accepted, 6 enrolled. In 2014, 4 doctorates awarded. Terminal master's awarded for partial completion of doctoral program. *Degree requirements:* For doctorate, one foreign language, thesis/dissertation. *Entrance requirements:* For doctorate, GRE General Test, minimum GPA of 3.0; 3 letters of recommendation. Additional exam requirements/recommendations for international students: Required—TOEFL (minimum score 550 paper-based; 79 iBT). *Application deadline:* For fall admission, 1/15 for domestic students, 12/10 for international students. Application fee: $60. Electronic applications accepted. *Expenses:* Tuition, state resident: full-time $14,490; part-time $805 per credit hour. Tuition, nonresident: full-time $19,850; part-time $1103 per credit hour. *Required fees:* $690. Full-time tuition and fees vary according to class time, course load, degree level, campus/location and program. *Financial support:* Fellowships, research assistantships, teaching assistantships, career-related internships or fieldwork, Federal Work-Study, and institutionally sponsored loans available. Financial award application deadline: 1/15; financial award applicants required to submit FAFSA. *Faculty research:* Anthropology of visual communication, political economy of language, historical archaeology, bicultural adaptation. *Unit head:* Dr. Paul Garrett, Director of Graduate Studies, 215-204-7621, Fax: 215-204-1410, E-mail: paul.garrett@temple.edu. *Application contact:* Yvonne Davis, Department Coordinator, 215-204-7775, Fax: 215-204-1410, E-mail: yvonne.davis@temple.edu. Website: http://www.temple.edu/anthro/

Texas A&M University, College of Liberal Arts, Department of Anthropology, College Station, TX 77843. Offers MA, PhD. *Faculty:* 25. *Students:* 58 full-time (33 women), 34 part-time (22 women); includes 13 minority (3 Black or African American, non-Hispanic/Latino; 1 American Indian or Alaska Native, non-Hispanic/Latino; 3 Asian, non-Hispanic/Latino; 3 Hispanic/Latino; 3 Two or more races, non-Hispanic/Latino), 13 international. Average age 32. 5 applicants, 40% accepted, 2 enrolled. In 2014, 11 master's, 7 doctorates awarded. *Degree requirements:* For doctorate, thesis/dissertation. *Entrance requirements:* For master's and doctorate, GRE General Test. Additional exam requirements/recommendations for international students: Required—TOEFL. Application fee: $50 ($90 for international students). *Expenses:* Tuition, state resident:

full-time $4078; part-time $226.55 per credit hour. Tuition, nonresident: full-time $10,594; part-time $577.55 per credit hour. *Required fees:* $2813; $237.70 per credit hour. $278.50 per semester. Tuition and fees vary according to degree level and student level. *Financial support:* In 2014–15, 70 students received support, including 9 fellowships with full and partial tuition reimbursements available (averaging $14,039 per year), 15 research assistantships with full and partial tuition reimbursements available (averaging $6,793 per year), 38 teaching assistantships with full and partial tuition reimbursements available (averaging $7,143 per year); career-related internships or fieldwork, institutionally sponsored loans, scholarships/grants, traineeships, health care benefits, tuition waivers (full and partial), and unspecified assistantships also available. Support available to part-time students. Financial award application deadline: 4/1; financial award applicants required to submit FAFSA. *Faculty research:* Nautical archaeology, archaeological conservation, archaeological palynology, paleoethnobotany, folklore. *Unit head:* Dr. Cynthia Werner, Associate Professor/ Department Head, 979-458-4037, E-mail: werner@tamu.edu. *Application contact:* Marco Valadez, Academic Advisor, 979-845-9333, Fax: 979-845-4070, E-mail: mlvaladez@tamu.edu.
Website: http://anthropology.tamu.edu/html/home.html

Texas State University, The Graduate College, College of Liberal Arts, Program in Anthropology, San Marcos, TX 78666. Offers MA. *Faculty:* 17 full-time (8 women). *Students:* 39 full-time (23 women), 13 part-time (9 women); includes 7 minority (1 Black or African American, non-Hispanic/Latino; 1 Asian, non-Hispanic/Latino; 4 Hispanic/ Latino; 1 Two or more races, non-Hispanic/Latino). Average age 29. 111 applicants, 30% accepted, 16 enrolled. In 2014, 17 master's awarded. *Degree requirements:* For master's, comprehensive exam, thesis. *Entrance requirements:* For master's, GRE (minimum score 300 verbal and quantitative preferred), baccalaureate degree from regionally-accredited university with minimum GPA of 3.0 on last 60 undergraduate semester hours. Additional exam requirements/recommendations for international students: Required—TOEFL (minimum score 550 paper-based; 78 iBT). *Application deadline:* For fall admission, 5/15 for domestic and international students. Applications are processed on a rolling basis. Application fee: $40 ($90 for international students). Electronic applications accepted. *Expenses:* Expenses: $8,834 (tuition and fees combined). *Financial support:* In 2014–15, 38 students received support, including 7 research assistantships (averaging $7,697 per year), 20 teaching assistantships (averaging $6,384 per year); Federal Work-Study, institutionally sponsored loans, scholarships/grants, and unspecified assistantships also available. Support available to part-time students. Financial award application deadline: 4/1; financial award applicants required to submit FAFSA. *Faculty research:* Reu Guatemala, excavation in South Africa, Wilson Pottery Site, El Camino Real Survey, Highland Mesoamerica, herd ranch testing. *Total annual research expenditures:* $864,753. *Unit head:* Dr. Michelle Hamilton, Graduate Advisor, 512-245-8429, E-mail: mh69@txstate.edu. *Application contact:* Dr. Andrea Golato, Dean of Graduate School, 512-245-2581, Fax: 512-245-8365, E-mail: gradcollege@txstate.edu.
Website: http://www.txstate.edu/anthropology/

Texas Tech University, Graduate School, College of Arts and Sciences, Department of Sociology, Anthropology and Social Work, Lubbock, TX 79409-1012. Offers anthropology (MA); social work (MSW); sociology (MA). Part-time programs available. *Faculty:* 25 full-time (14 women), 3 part-time/adjunct (2 women). *Students:* 29 full-time (21 women), 9 part-time (5 women); includes 13 minority (3 Black or African American, non-Hispanic/Latino; 8 Hispanic/Latino; 1 Native Hawaiian or other Pacific Islander, non-Hispanic/Latino; 1 Two or more races, non-Hispanic/Latino), 1 international. Average age 26. 28 applicants, 36% accepted, 8 enrolled. In 2014, 11 master's awarded. *Degree requirements:* For master's, one foreign language, comprehensive exam (for some programs), thesis (for some programs). *Entrance requirements:* For master's, GRE (for MA in anthropology), two letters of recommendation, statement of purpose, writing sample, and curriculum vitae; minimum GPA of 3.0 and coursework in sociology or closely-related fields (for MA in sociology); coursework in anthropology (for MA in anthropology). Additional exam requirements/recommendations for international students: Required—TOEFL (minimum score 550 paper-based; 79 iBT). *Application deadline:* For fall admission, 6/1 priority date for domestic students, 1/15 priority date for international students; for spring admission, 9/1 priority date for domestic students, 6/15 priority date for international students. Applications are processed on a rolling basis. Application fee: $60. Electronic applications accepted. *Expenses:* Tuition, state resident: full-time $6310; part-time $262.92 per credit hour. Tuition, nonresident: full-time $14,998; part-time $624.92 per credit hour. *Required fees:* $2701; $36.50 per credit. $912.50 per semester. Tuition and fees vary according to course load. *Financial support:* In 2014–15, 33 students received support, including 31 fellowships (averaging $5,548 per year), 26 teaching assistantships (averaging $10,942 per year); Federal Work-Study, scholarships/grants, tuition waivers (partial), and unspecified assistantships also available. Financial award application deadline: 4/1; financial award applicants required to submit FAFSA. *Faculty research:* Sociology of criminology/ deviance, population/migration, forensic anthropology, archaeology, social work. *Total annual research expenditures:* $126,995. *Unit head:* Dr. Brett A. Houk, Chair and Associate Professor, 806-834-8107, Fax: 806-742-1088, E-mail: brett.houk@ttu.edu. *Application contact:* Dr. Cristina Bradatan, Associate Professor/Sociology Graduate Program Director, 806-834-1796, E-mail: cristina.bradatan@ttu.edu.
Website: http://www.depts.ttu.edu/sasw/

Trent University, Graduate Studies, Program in Anthropology, Peterborough, ON K9J 7B8, Canada. Offers MA. Part-time programs available. *Degree requirements:* For master's, thesis. *Entrance requirements:* For master's, honors degree. *Faculty research:* Paleoecology, trade and fortification networks, pre-Columbian art.

Tulane University, School of Liberal Arts, Department of Anthropology, New Orleans, LA 70118-5669. Offers MA, PhD. Terminal master's awarded for partial completion of doctoral program. *Degree requirements:* For master's, one foreign language, thesis; for doctorate, 2 foreign languages, thesis/dissertation. *Entrance requirements:* For master's, GRE General Test, minimum B average in undergraduate course work; for doctorate, GRE General Test. Additional exam requirements/recommendations for international students: Required—TOEFL. Electronic applications accepted. *Expenses: Tuition:* Full-time $46,326; part-time $2574 per credit hour. *Required fees:* $1980; $44.50 per credit hour. $550 per term. Tuition and fees vary according to course load and program. *Faculty research:* Linguistics, physical anthropology, sociocultural archaeology, Mesoamerica.

Universidad de las Américas Puebla, Division of Graduate Studies, School of Social Sciences, Program in Anthropology, Puebla, Mexico. Offers anthropology (MA); archaeology (MA). Part-time and evening/weekend programs available. *Degree requirements:* For master's, one foreign language, thesis. *Entrance requirements:* For master's, bachelor's degree in anthropology or equivalent. *Faculty research:* Archaeology, ethnography, and ethnohistory of Mesoamerica.

Université de Montréal, Faculty of Arts and Sciences, Department of Anthropology, Montréal, QC H3C 3J7, Canada. Offers M Sc, PhD. Part-time programs available. *Degree requirements:* For master's, thesis; for doctorate, thesis/dissertation, general exam. Electronic applications accepted. *Faculty research:* Archaeology, ethnolinguistics, ethnology.

Université Laval, Faculty of Social Sciences, Department of Anthropology, Programs in Anthropology, Québec, QC G1K 7P4, Canada. Offers MA, PhD. Terminal master's awarded for partial completion of doctoral program. *Degree requirements:* For master's, thesis; for doctorate, thesis/dissertation. *Entrance requirements:* For master's, knowledge of French, interview; for doctorate, knowledge of French, comprehensive of written English, knowledge of a third language. Electronic applications accepted.

University at Albany, State University of New York, College of Arts and Sciences, Department of Anthropology, Albany, NY 12222-0001. Offers MA, PhD. Terminal master's awarded for partial completion of doctoral program. *Degree requirements:* For master's, comprehensive exam, thesis; for doctorate, 2 foreign languages, thesis/ dissertation, field exams. *Entrance requirements:* For master's and doctorate, GRE. Additional exam requirements/recommendations for international students: Required—TOEFL (minimum score 550 paper-based). Electronic applications accepted. *Faculty research:* Economic and ecological anthropology; language, culture, and cognition; symbolic and interpretive anthropology; human evolution, morphology, demography, and medical anthropology; spatial and settlement archaeology.

University at Buffalo, the State University of New York, Graduate School, College of Arts and Sciences, Department of Anthropology, Buffalo, NY 14260. Offers MA, PhD. *Faculty:* 19 full-time (8 women), 4 part-time/adjunct (2 women). *Students:* 98 full-time (61 women), 3 part-time (all women); includes 11 minority (3 Black or African American, non-Hispanic/Latino; 1 American Indian or Alaska Native, non-Hispanic/Latino; 2 Asian, non-Hispanic/Latino; 5 Hispanic/Latino), 6 international. Average age 30. 62 applicants, 35% accepted, 14 enrolled. In 2014, 17 master's, 7 doctorates awarded. Terminal master's awarded for partial completion of doctoral program. *Degree requirements:* For master's, project; for doctorate, one foreign language, comprehensive exam, thesis/ dissertation, exam. *Entrance requirements:* For master's, GRE General Test, minimum GPA of 3.0; for doctorate, GRE General Test, minimum GPA of 3.2. Additional exam requirements/recommendations for international students: Required—TOEFL (minimum score 600 paper-based; 79 iBT). *Application deadline:* For fall admission, 12/15 priority date for domestic and international students; for winter admission, 5/1 for domestic students, 3/15 for international students. Applications are processed on a rolling basis. Application fee: $75. Electronic applications accepted. *Financial support:* In 2014–15, 7 fellowships with full tuition reimbursements (averaging $19,616 per year), 1 research assistantship with full tuition reimbursement (averaging $13,616 per year), 14 teaching assistantships with full tuition reimbursements (averaging $13,616 per year) were awarded; career-related internships or fieldwork, Federal Work-Study, and institutionally sponsored loans also available. Financial award application deadline: 12/15; financial award applicants required to submit FAFSA. *Faculty research:* Old and New World archaeology, medical anthropology, primatology/human biology, cognition. *Total annual research expenditures:* $800,000. *Unit head:* Dr. Peter Biehl, Chair, 716-645-2414, Fax: 716-645-3808. *Application contact:* Maria Portera, Graduate Coordinator, 716-645-2414, Fax: 716-645-3808, E-mail: mportera@buffalo.edu.
Website: http://www.wings.buffalo.edu/anthropology/

The University of Alabama, Graduate School, College of Arts and Sciences, Department of Anthropology, Tuscaloosa, AL 35487. Offers MA, PhD. *Faculty:* 10 full-time (2 women). *Students:* 32 full-time (23 women), 7 part-time (5 women); includes 5 minority (1 Black or African American, non-Hispanic/Latino; 4 Hispanic/Latino), 1 international. Average age 31. 35 applicants, 57% accepted, 9 enrolled. In 2014, 12 master's, 2 doctorates awarded. *Degree requirements:* For master's, one foreign language, comprehensive exam, thesis optional; for doctorate, one foreign language, comprehensive exam, thesis/dissertation. *Entrance requirements:* For master's, GRE; for doctorate, GRE, MA in anthropology. Additional exam requirements/ recommendations for international students: Required—TOEFL. *Application deadline:* For fall admission, 1/31 for domestic and international students. Application fee: $50 ($60 for international students). Electronic applications accepted. *Expenses:* Tuition, state resident: full-time $9826. Tuition, nonresident: full-time $24,950. *Financial support:* In 2014–15, 25 students received support, including 4 fellowships with full tuition reimbursements available (averaging $15,000 per year), 1 research assistantship with full tuition reimbursement available (averaging $13,500 per year), 21 teaching assistantships with full tuition reimbursements available (averaging $13,500 per year); Federal Work-Study and health care benefits also available. Financial award application deadline: 1/31. *Faculty research:* Medical anthropology, Southeastern archaeology, physical and cultural anthropology. *Unit head:* Dr. Michael D. Murphy, Chair and Professor, 205-348-1953, Fax: 205-348-7937, E-mail: mdmurphy@ua.edu. *Application contact:* Dr. Ian Brown, Professor and Director of Graduate Studies, 205-348-9758, Fax: 205-348-7937, E-mail: ibrown@bama.ua.edu.
Website: http://www.as.ua.edu/ant

The University of Alabama at Birmingham, College of Arts and Sciences, Program in Anthropology, Birmingham, AL 35294. Offers MA. Program offered jointly with The University of Alabama (Tuscaloosa). *Students:* 2 full-time (both women), 5 part-time (3 women); includes 1 minority (Black or African American, non-Hispanic/Latino). Average age 39. *Degree requirements:* For master's, one foreign language, thesis (for some programs). *Entrance requirements:* For master's, GRE General Test. Additional exam requirements/recommendations for international students: Required—TOEFL, TWE. *Application deadline:* For fall admission, 1/31 for domestic students. Electronic applications accepted. *Expenses:* Tuition, state resident: full-time $7090; part-time $370 per credit hour. Tuition, nonresident: full-time $16,072; part-time $869 per credit hour. Full-time tuition and fees vary according to course load and program. *Financial support:* Career-related internships or fieldwork, Federal Work-Study, and institutionally sponsored loans available. *Faculty research:* Ethnicity, medical anthropology, primate conservation, pastoral systems, Southeastern archaeology. *Unit head:* Dr. Loretta Cormier, Program Director, 205-934-6526, Fax: 205-975-8360, E-mail: lcormier@uab.edu. *Application contact:* Susan Noblitt Banks, Director of Graduate School Operations, 205-934-8227, Fax: 205-934-8413, E-mail: gradschool@uab.edu.
Website: http://www.uab.edu/cas/anthropology/graduate-program

University of Alaska Anchorage, College of Arts and Sciences, Department of Anthropology, Anchorage, AK 99508. Offers MA. *Degree requirements:* For master's, comprehensive exam, thesis (for some programs), practicum. *Entrance requirements:* For master's, GRE General Test. Additional exam requirements/recommendations for international students: Required—TOEFL (minimum score 550 paper-based).

University of Alaska Fairbanks, College of Liberal Arts, Department of Anthropology, Fairbanks, AK 99775-7720. Offers MA, PhD. Part-time programs available. *Faculty:* 10 full-time (6 women). *Students:* 23 full-time (17 women), 14 part-time (10 women), 6 international. Average age 33. 28 applicants, 39% accepted, 8 enrolled. In 2014, 3 master's, 2 doctorates awarded. *Degree requirements:* For master's, one foreign language, comprehensive exam, oral defense of project or thesis; for doctorate, one foreign language, comprehensive exam, thesis/dissertation, oral defense of dissertation. *Entrance requirements:* For master's, GRE General Test, bachelor's degree in anthropology with minimum cumulative undergraduate and major GPA of 3.0; for doctorate, GRE General Test, master's degree in anthropology. Additional exam requirements/recommendations for international students: Required—TOEFL (minimum score 550 paper-based; 79 iBT), IELTS (minimum score 6.5). *Application deadline:* For fall admission, 1/15 for domestic and international students; for spring admission, 10/1

for domestic students, 9/1 for international students. Applications are processed on a rolling basis. Application fee: $60. Electronic applications accepted. *Expenses:* Tuition, state resident: full-time $7614; part-time $423 per credit. Tuition, nonresident: full-time $15,552; part-time $864 per credit. Tuition and fees vary according to course level, course load and reciprocity agreements. *Financial support:* In 2014–15, 3 research assistantships with full tuition reimbursements (averaging $6,659 per year), 13 teaching assistantships with full tuition reimbursements (averaging $9,648 per year) were awarded; fellowships with full tuition reimbursements, Federal Work-Study, scholarships/grants, health care benefits, and unspecified assistantships also available. Support available to part-time students. Financial award application deadline: 7/1; financial award applicants required to submit FAFSA. *Faculty research:* Circumpolar archaeology and population biology; rural subsistence; arctic physical, biological and social anthropology; arctic ethnohistory; arctic linguistics. *Total annual research expenditures:* $760,000. *Unit head:* David Koester, Department Chair, 907-474-7288, Fax: 907-474-7453, E-mail: uaf-anthropology@alaska.edu. *Application contact:* Mary Kreta, Director of Admissions, 907-474-7500, Fax: 907-474-7097, E-mail: admissions@uaf.edu.
Website: http://www.uaf.edu/anthro/

University of Alberta, Faculty of Graduate Studies and Research, Department of Anthropology, Edmonton, AB T6G 2E1, Canada. Offers MA, PhD. *Degree requirements:* For master's, thesis; for doctorate, one foreign language, thesis/dissertation. *Entrance requirements:* For master's and doctorate, minimum GPA of 7.0 on a 9.0 scale in last 2 years. Additional exam requirements/recommendations for international students: Required—TOEFL. *Faculty research:* Cultural anthropology of North America, South East Asia; physical anthropology in osteology, forensic primatology; archaeology of North America, South America, Old World/Africa.

The University of Arizona, College of Social and Behavioral Sciences, Department of Anthropology, Tucson, AZ 85721. Offers MA, PhD. Part-time programs available. Terminal master's awarded for partial completion of doctoral program. *Degree requirements:* For master's, thesis or alternative; for doctorate, one foreign language, thesis/dissertation. *Entrance requirements:* For master's and doctorate, GRE General Test, minimum GPA of 3.5, 2 letters of recommendation. Additional exam requirements/recommendations for international students: Required—TOEFL (minimum score 550 paper-based; 79 iBT). Electronic applications accepted. *Faculty research:* Archaeology of pre-Han China, cultural ecology, health and illness-related behavior, interaction of linguistic and social processes, human growth and development under stress.

University of Arkansas, Graduate School, J. William Fulbright College of Arts and Sciences, Department of Anthropology, Fayetteville, AR 72701-1201. Offers MA, PhD. Part-time and evening/weekend programs available. *Degree requirements:* For master's, comprehensive exam. *Entrance requirements:* For master's, GRE General Test, minimum GPA of 3.0; for doctorate, GRE General Test. Electronic applications accepted.

The University of British Columbia, Faculty of Arts, Department of Anthropology, Vancouver, BC V6T1Z1, Canada. Offers MA, PhD. Part-time programs available. *Degree requirements:* For master's, thesis; for doctorate, comprehensive exam, thesis/dissertation. *Entrance requirements:* For master's, BA in anthropology or equivalent with minimum B+ average in upper-level courses; for doctorate, MA in anthropology or equivalent. Additional exam requirements/recommendations for international students: Required—TOEFL (minimum score 600 paper-based; 80 iBT). Electronic applications accepted. *Faculty research:* Cultures of North America, East Asia, Oceania; museum studies; archaeology.

University of Calgary, Faculty of Graduate Studies, Faculty of Arts, Department of Anthropology, Calgary, AB T2N 1N4, Canada. Offers MA, PhD. *Degree requirements:* For master's, thesis; for doctorate, one foreign language, comprehensive exam, thesis/dissertation, candidacy exam. *Entrance requirements:* Additional exam requirements/recommendations for international students: Required—TOEFL. *Faculty research:* Primatology, culture and society, biosocial anthropology, political anthropology, evolutionary theory.

University of California, Berkeley, Graduate Division, College of Letters and Science, Department of Anthropology, Program in Anthropology, Berkeley, CA 94720-1500. Offers PhD. *Degree requirements:* For doctorate, thesis/dissertation. *Entrance requirements:* For doctorate, GRE General Test, minimum GPA of 3.0, 3 letters of recommendation. Additional exam requirements/recommendations for international students: Required—TOEFL.

University of California, Berkeley, Graduate Division, College of Letters and Science, Department of Anthropology, Program in Medical Anthropology, Berkeley, CA 94720-1500. Offers PhD. Program held jointly with University of California, San Francisco. *Degree requirements:* For doctorate, thesis/dissertation. *Entrance requirements:* For doctorate, GRE General Test, minimum GPA of 3.0, 3 letters of recommendation. Additional exam requirements/recommendations for international students: Required—TOEFL.

University of California, Davis, Graduate Studies, Program in Anthropology, Davis, CA 95616. Offers MA, PhD. Terminal master's awarded for partial completion of doctoral program. *Degree requirements:* For master's, one foreign language; for doctorate, one foreign language, thesis/dissertation. *Entrance requirements:* For master's and doctorate, GRE General Test, minimum GPA of 3.0. Additional exam requirements/recommendations for international students: Required—TOEFL (minimum score 550 paper-based). Electronic applications accepted. *Faculty research:* Archaeology, linguistics, biological and sociocultural anthropology.

University of California, Irvine, School of Social Sciences, Department of Anthropology, Irvine, CA 92697. Offers MA, PhD. *Students:* 60 full-time (32 women); includes 13 minority (1 American Indian or Alaska Native, non-Hispanic/Latino; 3 Asian, non-Hispanic/Latino; 7 Hispanic/Latino; 2 Two or more races, non-Hispanic/Latino), 6 international. Average age 30. 103 applicants, 35% accepted, 13 enrolled. In 2014, 8 master's, 4 doctorates awarded. *Degree requirements:* For doctorate, thesis/dissertation. *Entrance requirements:* For master's, GRE, minimum GPA of 3.0; for doctorate, GRE General Test, minimum GPA of 3.0. Additional exam requirements/recommendations for international students: Required—TOEFL (minimum score 550 paper-based). *Application deadline:* For fall admission, 1/15 priority date for domestic and international students. Applications are processed on a rolling basis. Application fee: $90 ($110 for international students). Electronic applications accepted. *Financial support:* Fellowships, research assistantships with full tuition reimbursements, teaching assistantships, institutionally sponsored loans, traineeships, health care benefits, and unspecified assistantships available. Financial award application deadline: 3/1; financial award applicants required to submit FAFSA. *Faculty research:* Cognitive anthropology, sociology of culture, social structure, family and gender. *Unit head:* George Marcus, Chair, 949-824-5345, Fax: 949-824-6046, E-mail: gmarcus@uci.edu. *Application contact:* Tom Boellstorff, Graduate Student Director, 949-824-9944, Fax: 949-824-0646, E-mail: tboellst@uci.edu.
Website: http://www.anthropology.uci.edu/

University of California, Los Angeles, Graduate Division, College of Letters and Science, Department of Anthropology, Los Angeles, CA 90095. Offers MA, PhD. Terminal master's awarded for partial completion of doctoral program. *Degree requirements:* For master's, thesis; for doctorate, thesis/dissertation, oral and written qualifying exams. *Entrance requirements:* For master's and doctorate, GRE General Test, bachelor's degree; minimum undergraduate GPA of 3.0 (or its equivalent if letter grade system not used); writing sample. Additional exam requirements/recommendations for international students: Required—TOEFL. Electronic applications accepted.

University of California, Riverside, Graduate Division, Department of Anthropology, Riverside, CA 92521-0102. Offers MA, MS, PhD. Part-time programs available. Terminal master's awarded for partial completion of doctoral program. *Degree requirements:* For master's, comprehensive exams or thesis; for doctorate, one foreign language, comprehensive exam, thesis/dissertation, qualifying exams. *Entrance requirements:* For master's and doctorate, GRE General Test, sample of written work, minimum GPA of 3.2, 3 letters of recommendation. Additional exam requirements/recommendations for international students: Required—TOEFL (minimum score 550 paper-based; 80 iBT). Electronic applications accepted. *Expenses:* Tuition, state resident: full-time $5399. Tuition, nonresident: full-time $10,433. *Faculty research:* Transnational processes, border communities, political and cultural ecology, Mesoamerican and Western US archaeology, applied anthropology.

University of California, San Diego, Graduate Division, Department of Anthropology, La Jolla, CA 92093. Offers PhD. *Students:* 80 full-time (52 women), 1 part-time (0 women); includes 19 minority (2 American Indian or Alaska Native, non-Hispanic/Latino; 2 Asian, non-Hispanic/Latino; 13 Hispanic/Latino; 2 Native Hawaiian or other Pacific Islander, non-Hispanic/Latino), 12 international. 111 applicants, 24% accepted, 14 enrolled. In 2014, 4 doctorates awarded. *Degree requirements:* For doctorate, comprehensive exam, thesis/dissertation, 1-quarter teaching assistantship. *Entrance requirements:* For doctorate, GRE General Test. Additional exam requirements/recommendations for international students: Required—TOEFL (minimum score 550 paper-based; 80 iBT), IELTS. *Application deadline:* For fall admission, 1/5 for domestic students. Application fee: $90 ($110 for international students). Electronic applications accepted. *Expenses:* Tuition, state resident: full-time $11,220; part-time $5610 per quarter. Tuition, nonresident: full-time $26,322; part-time $13,161 per quarter. *Required fees:* $570 per quarter. Tuition and fees vary according to program. *Financial support:* Fellowships, research assistantships, teaching assistantships, and scholarships/grants available. Financial award applicants required to submit FAFSA. *Faculty research:* Anthropological archaeology, biological anthropology, sociocultural anthropology, psychological anthropology, linguistic anthropology. *Unit head:* Thomas Csordas, Department Chair, 858-534-4145, E-mail: tcsordas@ucsd.edu. *Application contact:* Nikki Gee, Graduate Coordinator, 858-534-0107, E-mail: ngee@ucsd.edu.
Website: http://anthro.ucsd.edu

University of California, San Francisco, Graduate Division, Program in Medical Anthropology, San Francisco, CA 94143. Offers PhD. Program offered jointly with University of California, Berkeley. *Degree requirements:* For doctorate, one foreign language, thesis/dissertation, 3 field statements. *Entrance requirements:* For doctorate, GRE General Test, master's degree in anthropology or a related social or health science. *Faculty research:* Ethnicity, gender, aging, international health, health policy.

University of California, Santa Barbara, Graduate Division, College of Letters and Sciences, Division of Social Sciences, Department of Anthropology, Santa Barbara, CA 93106-2014. Offers archaeology (MA, PhD); integrative anthropological sciences (MA, PhD); sociocultural anthropology (MA, PhD); MA/PhD. Terminal master's awarded for partial completion of doctoral program. *Degree requirements:* For master's, comprehensive exam (for some programs), thesis (for some programs); for doctorate, comprehensive exam (for some programs), thesis/dissertation. *Entrance requirements:* For master's and doctorate, GRE General Test, statement of purpose, personal achievements statement, transcripts, writing sample, curriculum vitae, letters of recommendation. Additional exam requirements/recommendations for international students: Required—TOEFL (minimum score 550 paper-based; 80 iBT), IELTS (minimum score 7). Electronic applications accepted. *Faculty research:* Archaeology, bioarchaeology, biosocial anthropology, evolutionary ecology, evolutionary psychology, sociocultural anthropology.

University of California, Santa Cruz, Division of Graduate Studies, Division of Social Sciences, Department of Anthropology, Santa Cruz, CA 95064. Offers cultural anthropology (PhD). *Degree requirements:* For doctorate, thesis/dissertation, qualifying exam. *Entrance requirements:* For doctorate, GRE General Test. Additional exam requirements/recommendations for international students: Required—TOEFL (minimum score 550 paper-based; 83 iBT); Recommended—IELTS (minimum score 8). Electronic applications accepted. *Faculty research:* Culture and power, women's roles, AIDS, folklore.

University of Central Florida, College of Sciences, Department of Anthropology, Orlando, FL 32816. Offers anthropology (MA); Maya studies (Certificate). *Faculty:* 15 full-time (9 women), 2 part-time/adjunct (1 woman). *Students:* 34 full-time (21 women), 14 part-time (9 women); includes 9 minority (1 Asian, non-Hispanic/Latino; 8 Hispanic/Latino). Average age 30. 44 applicants, 59% accepted, 16 enrolled. In 2014, 15 master's awarded. *Expenses:* Tuition, state resident: part-time $288.16 per credit hour. Tuition, nonresident: part-time $1073.31 per credit hour. *Financial support:* In 2014–15, 28 students received support, including 9 fellowships with partial tuition reimbursements available (averaging $4,800 per year), 3 research assistantships with partial tuition reimbursements available (averaging $4,100 per year), 21 teaching assistantships with full tuition reimbursements available (averaging $6,200 per year). *Unit head:* Dr. Tosha Dupras, Chair, 407-823-2227, Fax: 407-823-3498, E-mail: tosha.dupras@ucf.edu. *Application contact:* Barbara Rodriguez Lamas, Director, Admissions and Student Services, 407-823-2766, Fax: 407-823-6442, E-mail: gradadmissions@ucf.edu.
Website: http://anthropology.cos.ucf.edu/

University of Chicago, Division of the Humanities, Department of Linguistics, Chicago, IL 60637. Offers anthropology and linguistics (PhD); linguistics (PhD). *Students:* 41 full-time (21 women); includes 8 minority (1 American Indian or Alaska Native, non-Hispanic/Latino; 2 Asian, non-Hispanic/Latino; 5 Hispanic/Latino), 12 international. 133 applicants, 21% accepted, 3 enrolled. Terminal master's awarded for partial completion of doctoral program. *Degree requirements:* For doctorate, 2 foreign languages, thesis/dissertation. *Entrance requirements:* For doctorate, GRE General Test. Additional exam requirements/recommendations for international students: Required—TOEFL (minimum score 104 iBT), IELTS (minimum score 7). *Application deadline:* For fall admission, 12/15 for domestic and international students. Application fee: $90. Electronic applications accepted. *Expenses: Tuition:* Full-time $46,899. *Required fees:* $347. *Financial support:* Fellowships with full tuition reimbursements, teaching assistantships with full tuition reimbursements, Federal Work-Study, institutionally sponsored loans, scholarships/grants, and health care benefits available. Financial award application deadline: 12/15; financial award applicants required to submit FAFSA. *Unit head:* Dr. Chris Kennedy, Chair, 773-702-8522. *Application contact:* Braden Grams, Assistant Dean of Students, Admissions and Fellowships, 773-702-1552, Fax: 773-834-9148, E-mail: humanitiesadmissions@uchicago.edu.
Website: http://linguistics.uchicago.edu/

University of Chicago, Division of the Social Sciences, Department of Anthropology, Chicago, IL 60637. Offers PhD. *Students:* 146 full-time (80 women); includes 25 minority (5 Black or African American, non-Hispanic/Latino; 2 American Indian or Alaska Native, non-Hispanic/Latino; 3 Asian, non-Hispanic/Latino; 5 Hispanic/Latino; 10 Two or more races, non-Hispanic/Latino), 48 international. 271 applicants, 10% accepted, 16 enrolled. In 2014, 15 doctorates awarded. *Degree requirements:* For doctorate, one foreign language, thesis/dissertation, exams. *Entrance requirements:* For doctorate, GRE General Test. Additional exam requirements/recommendations for international students: Required—TOEFL (minimum score 104 iB**T**), IELTS (minimum score 7). *Application deadline:* For fall admission, 12/15 for domestic and international students. Application fee: $90. Electronic applications accepted. *Expenses:* Tuition: Full-time $46,899. *Required fees:* $347. *Financial support:* In 2014–15, 16 students received support, including 12 fellowships with full tuition reimbursements available (averaging $23,000 per year); career-related internships or fieldwork, Federal Work-Study, institutionally sponsored loans, scholarships/grants, and health care benefits also available. Financial award application deadline: 12/15. *Unit head:* Prof. Stephan Palmi, Chair. *Application contact:* Office of the Dean of Students, 773-702-8415, E-mail: admissions@ssd.uchicago.edu.
Website: http://anthropology.uchicago.edu

University of Cincinnati, Graduate School, McMicken College of Arts and Sciences, Department of Anthropology, Cincinnati, OH 45221. Offers MA. Part-time programs available. *Degree requirements:* For master's, thesis or alternative. *Entrance requirements:* For master's, GRE General Test. Additional exam requirements/recommendations for international students: Required—TOEFL; Recommended—TWE. Electronic applications accepted. *Faculty research:* Medical anthropology, Mayan prehistory, southwestern U.S. prehistory, skeletal biology and paleoanthropology; immigrants; Mexico.

University of Colorado Boulder, Graduate School, College of Arts and Sciences, Department of Anthropology, Boulder, CO 80309. Offers MA, PhD. *Faculty:* 18 full-time (8 women). *Students:* 35 full-time (22 women), 12 part-time (8 women); includes 5 minority (1 American Indian or Alaska Native, non-Hispanic/Latino; 1 Asian, non-Hispanic/Latino; 3 Hispanic/Latino), 1 international. Average age 31. 59 applicants, 32% accepted, 5 enrolled. In 2014, 10 master's, 4 doctorates awarded. Terminal master's awarded for partial completion of doctoral program. *Degree requirements:* For master's, comprehensive exam, thesis or alternative; for doctorate, one foreign language, thesis/dissertation. *Entrance requirements:* For master's, GRE General Test, minimum undergraduate GPA of 3.0; for doctorate, GRE General Test, minimum undergraduate GPA of 3.0, master's degree in anthropology. *Application deadline:* For fall admission, 1/9 for domestic students, 12/1 for international students. Applications are processed on a rolling basis. Application fee: $50 ($70 for international students). Electronic applications accepted. *Financial support:* In 2014–15, 94 students received support, including 20 fellowships (averaging $3,038 per year), 3 research assistantships with full and partial tuition reimbursements available (averaging $10,433 per year), 33 teaching assistantships with full and partial tuition reimbursements available (averaging $30,386 per year); institutionally sponsored loans, scholarships/grants, health care benefits, and unspecified assistantships also available. Financial award application deadline: 1/15; financial award applicants required to submit FAFSA. *Faculty research:* Anthropology, cultural/social anthropology, archaeology, ethnography, Native Americans. *Total annual research expenditures:* $435,044.
Website: http://www.colorado.edu/anthropology

University of Colorado Denver, College of Liberal Arts and Sciences, Department of Anthropology, Denver, CO 80217. Offers archaeological studies (MA); biological anthropology (MA); medical anthropology (MA); sustainable development and political ecology (MA). Part-time and evening/weekend programs available. *Faculty:* 10 full-time (4 women), 2 part-time/adjunct (1 woman). *Students:* 28 full-time (22 women), 11 part-time (9 women); includes 9 minority (2 Black or African American, non-Hispanic/Latino; 1 Asian, non-Hispanic/Latino; 5 Hispanic/Latino; 1 Two or more races, non-Hispanic/Latino). Average age 30. 50 applicants, 50% accepted, 11 enrolled. In 2014, 17 master's awarded. *Degree requirements:* For master's, comprehensive exam, thesis or alternative, 30-36 credit hours. *Entrance requirements:* For master's, GRE General Test, minimum GPA of 3.0 for all undergraduate studies, transcripts from all undergraduate/ graduate institutions attended, prior training in anthropology, three letters of recommendation, statement of purpose. Additional exam requirements/ recommendations for international students: Required—TOEFL (minimum score 537 paper-based; 75 iBT); Recommended—IELTS (minimum score 6.5). *Application deadline:* For fall admission, 2/15 for domestic students, 1/15 for international students. Application fee: $50 ($75 for international students). Electronic applications accepted. *Financial support:* Fellowships, research assistantships, teaching assistantships, Federal Work-Study, institutionally sponsored loans, scholarships/grants, and traineeships available. Financial award application deadline: 4/1; financial award applicants required to submit FAFSA. *Faculty research:* Applied medical anthropology, primate social behavior, environmental anthropology, Southwestern and Mexican archaeology, human ecology. *Unit head:* Dr. Christopher Beekman, Chair of the Department of Anthropology, 303-556-6040, E-mail: christopher.beekman@ucdenver.edu. *Application contact:* Charles Musiba, Acting Graduate Director, 303-556-6082, Fax: 303-556-8501, E-mail: charles.musiba@ucdenver.edu.
Website: http://www.ucdenver.edu/academics/colleges/CLAS/Departments/ anthropology/Programs/Masters/Pages/Masters.aspx

University of Connecticut, Graduate School, College of Liberal Arts and Sciences, Department of Anthropology, Storrs, CT 06269. Offers MA, PhD. Terminal master's awarded for partial completion of doctoral program. *Degree requirements:* For master's, comprehensive exam; for doctorate, thesis/dissertation. *Entrance requirements:* For master's and doctorate, GRE General Test. Additional exam requirements/ recommendations for international students: Required—TOEFL (minimum score 550 paper-based). Electronic applications accepted.

University of Denver, Division of Arts, Humanities and Social Sciences, Department of Anthropology, Denver, CO 80208. Offers archaeology (MA); cultural anthropology (MA); museum studies (MA). Part-time programs available. *Faculty:* 7 full-time (3 women). *Students:* 1 full-time (0 women), 20 part-time (14 women); includes 5 minority (2 Hispanic/Latino; 3 Two or more races, non-Hispanic/Latino), 1 international. Average age 25. 47 applicants, 49% accepted, 11 enrolled. In 2014, 4 master's awarded. *Degree requirements:* For master's, one foreign language, comprehensive exam, thesis (for some programs), tool, foreign language literacy, or course work. *Entrance requirements:* For master's, GRE General Test, bachelor's degree, transcripts, personal statement, two letters of recommendation. Additional exam requirements/recommendations for international students: Required—TOEFL (minimum score 550 paper-based; 80 iBT). *Application deadline:* For fall admission, 2/4 priority date for domestic and international students. Applications are processed on a rolling basis. Application fee: $65. Electronic applications accepted. *Expenses:* Expenses: $1,199 per credit hour. *Financial support:* In 2014–15, 18 students received support, including 12 teaching assistantships with partial tuition reimbursements available (averaging $5,000 per year); career-related internships or fieldwork, Federal Work-Study, institutionally sponsored loans,

scholarships/grants, and unspecified assistantships also available. Support available to part-time students. Financial award application deadline: 2/15; financial award applicants required to submit FAFSA. *Faculty research:* Human diversity, human rights, historic archaeology, museums and heritage, high-tech field methods. *Unit head:* Dr. Dean J. Saitta, Chair, 303-871-2680, E-mail: dsaitta@du.edu. *Application contact:* Dr. Larry Conyers, Professor/Director of Graduate and Undergraduate Programs, 303-871-2684, E-mail: lconyers@du.edu.
Website: http://www.du.edu/ahss/schools/anthropology/

University of Florida, Graduate School, College of Liberal Arts and Sciences, Department of Anthropology, Gainesville, FL 32611. Offers anthropology (MA, MAT, PhD), including historic preservation (MA, PhD), tropical conservation and development, women's and gender studies (PhD). Part-time programs available. *Faculty:* 18 full-time (6 women), 24 part-time/adjunct (11 women). *Students:* 128 full-time (88 women), 35 part-time (22 women); includes 29 minority (12 Black or African American, non-Hispanic/ Latino; 3 American Indian or Alaska Native, non-Hispanic/Latino; 4 Asian, non-Hispanic/ Latino; 10 Hispanic/Latino), 20 international. 127 applicants, 30% accepted, 21 enrolled. In 2014, 13 master's, 14 doctorates awarded. *Degree requirements:* For master's, thesis optional; for doctorate, comprehensive exam, thesis/dissertation. *Entrance requirements:* For master's and doctorate, GRE General Test, minimum GPA of 3.2. Additional exam requirements/recommendations for international students: Required— TOEFL (minimum score 550 paper-based; 80 iBT), IELTS (minimum score 6). *Application deadline:* For fall admission, 12/15 for domestic students. Application fee: $30. Electronic applications accepted. *Financial support:* In 2014–15, 24 fellowships, 22 research assistantships, 64 teaching assistantships were awarded; career-related internships or fieldwork, Federal Work-Study, institutionally sponsored loans, and unspecified assistantships also available. Support available to part-time students. Financial award applicants required to submit FAFSA. *Faculty research:* Social and cultural anthropology, archaeology, biological anthropology, medical anthropology, linguistic anthropology. *Unit head:* Susan deFrance, PhD, Department Chair and Professor, 352-294-7531, Fax: 352-392-6929, E-mail: sdef@ufl.edu. *Application contact:* Susan Gillespie, Professor and Graduate Coordinator, 352-294-7595, E-mail: sgillesp@ufl.edu.
Website: http://anthro.ufl.edu/

University of Georgia, Franklin College of Arts and Sciences, Department of Anthropology, Athens, GA 30602. Offers anthropology (MA, PhD); archaeological resource management (MS). *Degree requirements:* For master's, one foreign language, thesis; for doctorate, one foreign language, thesis/dissertation. *Entrance requirements:* For master's and doctorate, GRE General Test. Electronic applications accepted.

University of Guelph, Graduate Studies, College of Social and Applied Human Sciences, Department of Sociology and Anthropology, Guelph, ON N1G 2W1, Canada. Offers anthropology (MA); crime and criminal justice policy (MA); sociology (MA, PhD). *Degree requirements:* For master's, thesis or major paper; for doctorate, comprehensive exam, thesis/dissertation. *Entrance requirements:* For master's, minimum B+ average during previous 2 years of course work, honors BA or equivalent; for doctorate, must have an MA in Sociology, must have 80% or higher in graduate level studies. Additional exam requirements/recommendations for international students: Required—TOEFL (minimum score 550 paper-based; 89 iBT) or IELTS (minimum score 6.5). Electronic applications accepted. *Faculty research:* Rural and development sociology; education, employment, and the workplace; race, ethnicity, and native studies; criminology and deviance; social psychology.

University of Hawaii at Manoa, Graduate Division, College of Social Sciences, Department of Anthropology, Honolulu, HI 96822. Offers MA, PhD. Part-time programs available. *Degree requirements:* For master's, thesis optional; for doctorate, comprehensive exam, thesis/dissertation. *Entrance requirements:* For master's and doctorate, GRE General Test. Additional exam requirements/recommendations for international students: Required—TOEFL (minimum score 560 paper-based; 83 iBT), IELTS (minimum score 5). *Faculty research:* Evolution of social complexity, ethnopharmacology, social interaction, faunal analysis, human ecology.

University of Houston, College of Liberal Arts and Social Sciences, Department of Anthropology, Houston, TX 77204. Offers MA. Part-time programs available. *Degree requirements:* For master's, comprehensive exam, thesis. *Entrance requirements:* For master's, GRE General Test (minimum 500 verbal, 500 quantitative), minimum GPA of 3.0 in last 60 undergraduate hours. Additional exam requirements/recommendations for international students: Required—TOEFL (minimum score 550 paper-based; 79 iBT). Electronic applications accepted.

University of Idaho, College of Graduate Studies, College of Letters, Arts and Social Sciences, Department of Sociology and Anthropology, Moscow, ID 83844-1110. Offers anthropology (MA). *Faculty:* 7 full-time, 1 part-time/adjunct. *Students:* 19 full-time, 13 part-time. Average age 32. In 2014, 7 master's awarded. *Degree requirements:* For master's, one foreign language. *Entrance requirements:* For master's, minimum GPA of 2.8. *Application deadline:* For fall admission, 8/1 for domestic students; for spring admission, 12/15 for domestic students. Applications are processed on a rolling basis. Application fee: $60. Electronic applications accepted. *Expenses:* Tuition, state resident: full-time $4784; part-time $280.50 per credit hour. Tuition, nonresident: full-time $18,314; part-time $957.50 per credit hour. *Required fees:* $2000; $58.50 per credit hour. Tuition and fees vary according to program. *Financial support:* Research assistantships and teaching assistantships available. Financial award applicants required to submit FAFSA. *Unit head:* Dr. Mark Warner, Chair, 208-885-6751, E-mail: socanth@uidaho.edu. *Application contact:* Sean Scoggin, Graduate Recruitment Coordinator, 208-885-4001, Fax: 208-885-4406, E-mail: graduateadmissions@uidaho.edu.
Website: http://www.uidaho.edu/class/socanthro

University of Illinois at Chicago, Graduate College, College of Liberal Arts and Sciences, Department of Anthropology, Chicago, IL 60607-7128. Offers anthropology (MA, PhD); environmental and urban geography (MA), including environmental studies, urban geography. Part-time programs available. *Faculty:* 13 full-time (5 women), 5 part-time/adjunct (2 women). *Students:* 46 full-time (24 women), 8 part-time (3 women); includes 11 minority (2 Black or African American, non-Hispanic/Latino; 1 American Indian or Alaska Native, non-Hispanic/Latino; 2 Asian, non-Hispanic/Latino; 5 Hispanic/ Latino; 1 Two or more races, non-Hispanic/Latino), 9 international. Average age 32. 73 applicants, 18% accepted, 6 enrolled. In 2014, 12 master's, 1 doctorate awarded. *Degree requirements:* For doctorate, comprehensive exam. *Entrance requirements:* For master's and doctorate, minimum GPA of 2.75. Additional exam requirements/ recommendations for international students: Required—TOEFL. *Application deadline:* For fall admission, 1/9 for domestic and international students. Applications are processed on a rolling basis. Application fee: $60 ($0 for international students). Electronic applications accepted. *Expenses:* Tuition, state resident: full-time $11,254; part-time $468 per credit hour. Tuition, nonresident: full-time $23,252; part-time $968 per credit hour. *Required fees:* $1217 per term. Part-time tuition and fees vary according to course load, degree level and program. *Financial support:* In 2014–15, 6 students received support. Fellowships with full tuition reimbursements available, research assistantships with full tuition reimbursements available, teaching assistantships with full tuition reimbursements available, career-related internships or fieldwork, Federal Work-

Study, scholarships/grants, traineeships, tuition waivers (full), and unspecified assistantships available. Financial award application deadline: 3/1; financial award applicants required to submit FAFSA. *Faculty research:* Archaeological, physical, and cultural anthropology; environmental and urban geography. *Unit head:* Dr. John Monaghan, Department Head, 312-413-3570, Fax: 312-413-3573, E-mail: monaghan@uic.edu. *Application contact:* Brian S. Bauer, Director of Graduate Studies, 312-413-3731, E-mail: bsb@uic.edu.
Website: http://anthropology.las.uic.edu/

University of Illinois at Urbana–Champaign, Graduate College, College of Liberal Arts and Sciences, Department of Anthropology, Champaign, IL 61820. Offers MA, PhD. *Students:* 60 (43 women). Terminal master's awarded for partial completion of doctoral program. Application fee: $70 ($90 for international students). *Unit head:* Andrew Orta, Head, 217-333-3616, Fax: 217-244-3490, E-mail: aorta@illinois.edu. *Application contact:* Elizabeth M. Spears, Office Support Specialist, 217-244-0296, Fax: 217-244-3490, E-mail: espears@illinois.edu.
Website: http://www.anthro.illinois.edu/

University of Indianapolis, Graduate Programs, College of Arts and Sciences, Department of Anthropology, Indianapolis, IN 46227-3697. Offers MS. *Faculty:* 3 full-time (0 women). *Students:* 12 full-time (10 women), 2 part-time (both women); includes 2 minority (both Two or more races, non-Hispanic/Latino). Average age 25. In 2014, 1 master's awarded. *Entrance requirements:* For master's, GRE General Test (minimum score of 500 on both the verbal and quantitative sections), bachelor's degree with major or minor in anthropology or closely-related field; undergraduate or graduate coursework in anthropology and the natural sciences with minimum C grade (ideally, semester in cultural anthropology, biological anthropology, archeology, statistics, and geology); minimum cumulative undergraduate GPA of 3.2. Additional exam requirements/recommendations for international students: Required—TOEFL (minimum score 550 paper-based; 79 iBT). Application fee: $30. *Unit head:* Dr. Gregory Reinhardt, Chair, 317-788-3440, E-mail: reinhardt@uindy.edu. *Application contact:* Linda Corn, Administrative Assistant, 317-788-3395, E-mail: lcorn@uindy.edu.
Website: http://anthropology.uindy.edu/

The University of Iowa, Graduate College, College of Liberal Arts and Sciences, Department of Anthropology, Iowa City, IA 52242-1316. Offers MA, PhD. *Degree requirements:* For master's, thesis optional, exam; for doctorate, comprehensive exam, thesis/dissertation. *Entrance requirements:* For master's and doctorate, GRE General Test, minimum GPA of 3.0. Additional exam requirements/recommendations for international students: Required—TOEFL (minimum score 550 paper-based; 81 iBT). Electronic applications accepted.

The University of Kansas, Graduate Studies, College of Liberal Arts and Sciences, Department of Anthropology, Lawrence, KS 66045. Offers MA, PhD. *Faculty:* 18 full-time, 2 part-time/adjunct. *Students:* 37 full-time (25 women), 7 part-time (4 women); includes 5 minority (3 Black or African American, non-Hispanic/Latino; 2 Two or more races, non-Hispanic/Latino), 5 international. Average age 32. 34 applicants, 38% accepted, 6 enrolled. In 2014, 9 master's, 5 doctorates awarded. *Degree requirements:* For master's, comprehensive exam (for some programs), thesis; for doctorate, one foreign language, comprehensive exam, thesis/dissertation. *Entrance requirements:* For master's, minimum GPA of 3.2; for doctorate, minimum GPA of 3.5. Additional exam requirements/recommendations for international students: Required—TOEFL. *Application deadline:* For fall admission, 1/5 for domestic and international students. Application fee: $55 ($65 for international students). Electronic applications accepted. *Financial support:* Fellowships with full tuition reimbursements, research assistantships with full and partial tuition reimbursements, teaching assistantships with full and partial tuition reimbursements, career-related internships or fieldwork, institutionally sponsored loans, and unspecified assistantships available. Financial award application deadline: 1/5; financial award applicants required to submit FAFSA. *Faculty research:* Archaeological, biological, cultural, linguistic, and applied anthropology. *Unit head:* Jane W. Gibson, Chair, 785-864-4103, Fax: 785-864-2635, E-mail: jwgc@ku.edu. *Application contact:* Le-Thu Erazmus, Graduate Officer, 785-864-2630, E-mail: lerazmus@ku.edu.
Website: http://anthropology.ku.edu/

University of Kentucky, Graduate School, College of Arts and Sciences, Program in Anthropology, Lexington, KY 40506-0032. Offers MA, PhD. Part-time programs available. *Degree requirements:* For master's, comprehensive exam, thesis optional; for doctorate, one foreign language, comprehensive exam, thesis/dissertation. *Entrance requirements:* For master's, GRE General Test, minimum undergraduate GPA of 2.75; for doctorate, GRE General Test, minimum graduate GPA of 3.0. Additional exam requirements/recommendations for international students: Required—TOEFL (minimum score 550 paper-based). Electronic applications accepted. *Faculty research:* Applied social anthropology, developmental change, medical anthropology, culture history, ethnohistory.

University of Lethbridge, School of Graduate Studies, Lethbridge, AB T1K 3M4, Canada. Offers addictions counseling (M Sc); agricultural biotechnology (M Sc); agricultural studies (M Sc, MA); anthropology (MA); archaeology (M Sc, MA); art (MA, MFA); biochemistry (M Sc); biological sciences (M Sc); biomolecular science (PhD); biosystems and biodiversity (PhD); Canadian studies (MA); chemistry (M Sc); computer science (M Sc); computer science and geographical information science (M Sc); counseling (MC); counseling psychology (M Ed); dramatic arts (MA); earth, space, and physical science (PhD); economics (MA); education (MA); educational leadership (M Ed); English (MA); environmental science (M Sc); evolution and behavior (PhD); exercise science (M Sc); French (MA); French/German (MA); French/Spanish (MA); general education (M Ed); geography (M Sc, MA); German (MA); health sciences (M Sc); individualized multidisciplinary (M Sc, MA); kinesiology (M Sc, MA); management (M Sc), including accounting, finance, general management, human resource management and labor relations, information systems, international management, marketing, policy and strategy; mathematics (M Sc); modern languages (MA); music (M Mus, MA); Native American studies (MA); neuroscience (M Sc, PhD); new media (MA, MFA); nursing (M Sc, MN); philosophy (MA); physics (M Sc); political science (MA); psychology (M Sc, MA); religious studies (MA); sociology (MA); theatre and dramatic arts (MFA); theoretical and computational science (PhD); urban and regional studies (MA); women and gender studies (MA). Part-time and evening/weekend programs available. *Faculty:* 358. *Students:* 445 full-time (243 women), 116 part-time (72 women). Average age 31. 351 applicants, 26% accepted, 87 enrolled. In 2014, 129 master's, 13 doctorates awarded. *Degree requirements:* For master's, thesis (for some programs); for doctorate, comprehensive exam, thesis/dissertation. *Entrance requirements:* For master's, GMAT (for M Sc in management), bachelor's degree in related field, minimum GPA of 3.0 during previous 20 graded semester courses, 2 years' teaching or related experience (M Ed); for doctorate, master's degree, minimum graduate GPA of 3.5. Additional exam requirements/recommendations for international students: Required—TOEFL. Application fee: $100 Canadian dollars. *Financial support:* Fellowships, research assistantships, teaching assistantships, scholarships/grants, health care benefits, and unspecified assistantships available. *Faculty research:* Movement and brain plasticity, gibberellin physiology, photosynthesis, carbon cycling, molecular properties of main-group ring components. *Application contact:* School of Graduate Studies, 403-329-5194, E-mail: sgsinquiries@uleth.ca.
Website: http://www.uleth.ca/graduatestudies/

University of Louisville, Graduate School, College of Arts and Sciences, Department of Anthropology, Louisville, KY 40292-0001. Offers MA. Part-time and evening/weekend programs available. *Students:* 12 full-time (8 women), 7 part-time (3 women); includes 3 minority (1 Native Hawaiian or other Pacific Islander, non-Hispanic/Latino; 2 Two or more races, non-Hispanic/Latino). Average age 27. 14 applicants, 86% accepted, 9 enrolled. In 2014, 3 master's awarded. *Degree requirements:* For master's, thesis or internship. *Entrance requirements:* For master's, GRE (minimum Verbal and Quantitative score of 1100). Additional exam requirements/recommendations for international students: Required—TOEFL (minimum score 550 paper-based; 79 iBT). *Application deadline:* For fall admission, 4/1 for domestic students, 5/1 priority date for international students; for spring admission, 11/1 for domestic students, 11/1 priority date for international students; for summer admission, 4/1 priority date for international students. Applications are processed on a rolling basis. Application fee: $60. Electronic applications accepted. *Expenses:* Tuition, state resident: full-time $11,326; part-time $630 per credit hour. Tuition, nonresident: full-time $23,568; part-time $1311 per credit hour. *Required fees:* $196. Tuition and fees vary according to program and reciprocity agreements. *Financial support:* Teaching assistantships with full tuition reimbursements, career-related internships or fieldwork, and scholarships/grants available. *Faculty research:* Evolutionary anthropology, cultural diaspora studies, archaeology, political economy, violence and the state. *Unit head:* Dr. Lisa Markowitz, Chair, 502-852-2426, Fax: 502-852-4560, E-mail: lisam@louisville.edu. *Application contact:* Libby Leggett, Director, Graduate Admissions, 502-852-3101, Fax: 502-852-6536, E-mail: gradadm@louisville.edu.
Website: http://louisville.edu/anthropology

University of Maine, Graduate School, College of Liberal Arts and Sciences, Department of Anthropology, Orono, ME 04469. Offers anthropology and environmental policy (PhD). *Faculty:* 12 full-time (4 women), 1 part-time/adjunct (0 women). *Students:* 6 full-time (5 women). Average age 28. 33 applicants, 24% accepted, 3 enrolled. *Degree requirements:* For doctorate, comprehensive exam, thesis/dissertation. *Entrance requirements:* For doctorate, GRE General Test. Additional exam requirements/recommendations for international students: Required—TOEFL. *Application deadline:* For fall admission, 1/15 priority date for domestic students. Application fee: $65. *Expenses:* Tuition, state resident: part-time $658 per credit hour. Tuition, nonresident: part-time $1550 per credit hour. *Financial support:* In 2014–15, 5 students received support, including 3 research assistantships (averaging $24,800 per year), 1 teaching assistantship (averaging $14,600 per year). *Faculty research:* Archaeological proxies of past climate, human and climate interactions, environmental policy, human dimensions of natural resource management, environmental risk perception. *Total annual research expenditures:* $1.2 million. *Unit head:* Gregory Zaro, Chair, 207-581-1857, Fax: 207-581-1823, E-mail: gregory.zaro@umit.maine.edu. *Application contact:* Scott G. Delcourt, Assistant Vice President for Graduate Studies and Senior Associate Dean, 207-581-3291, Fax: 207-581-3232, E-mail: graduate@maine.edu.
Website: http://www.umaine.edu/anthropology/

The University of Manchester, School of Arts, Histories and Cultures, Manchester, United Kingdom. Offers anthropology, media and performance (PhD); applied theatre professional (PhD); archaeology (PhD); art history and visual studies (PhD); arts management and cultural policy (PhD); classics and ancient history (PhD); composition (PhD); creative writing (PhD); drama (PhD); economic and social history (PhD); electroacoustic composition (PhD); English and American studies (PhD); history (PhD); humanitarianism and conflict response (PhD); museology (PhD); music (PhD); musicology (PhD); religions and theology (PhD).

The University of Manchester, School of Social Sciences, Manchester, United Kingdom. Offers ethnographic documentary (M Phil); interdisciplinary study of culture (PhD); philosophy (PhD); politics (PhD); social anthropology (PhD); social anthropology with visual media (PhD); social change (PhD); social statistics (PhD); sociology (PhD); visual anthropology (M Phil).

University of Manitoba, Faculty of Graduate Studies, Faculty of Arts, Department of Anthropology, Winnipeg, MB R3T 2N2, Canada. Offers MA, PhD. *Degree requirements:* For master's, thesis or alternative.

University of Maryland, College Park, Academic Affairs, College of Behavioral and Social Sciences, Department of Anthropology, College Park, MD 20742. Offers applied anthropology (MAA). Part-time and evening/weekend programs available. *Degree requirements:* For master's, internship. *Entrance requirements:* For master's, GRE General Test, minimum GPA of 3.0, 3 letters of recommendation. Additional exam requirements/recommendations for international students: Required—TOEFL. Electronic applications accepted. *Faculty research:* Archaeology, human biodiversity, cultural and resource management.

University of Massachusetts Amherst, Graduate School, College of Social and Behavioral Sciences, Department of Anthropology, Amherst, MA 01003. Offers MA, PhD. Part-time programs available. *Faculty:* 28 full-time (15 women). *Students:* 45 full-time (32 women), 24 part-time (16 women); includes 19 minority (5 Black or African American, non-Hispanic/Latino; 4 American Indian or Alaska Native, non-Hispanic/Latino; 4 Hispanic/Latino; 6 Two or more races, non-Hispanic/Latino), 12 international. Average age 34. 117 applicants, 9% accepted, 7 enrolled. In 2014, 4 master's, 5 doctorates awarded. Terminal master's awarded for partial completion of doctoral program. *Degree requirements:* For master's, thesis or alternative; for doctorate, comprehensive exam, thesis/dissertation. *Entrance requirements:* Additional exam requirements/recommendations for international students: Required—TOEFL (minimum score 550 paper-based; 80 iBT), IELTS (minimum score 6.5). *Application deadline:* For fall admission, 1/2 for domestic and international students. Applications are processed on a rolling basis. Application fee: $75. Electronic applications accepted. *Expenses:* Tuition, state resident: full-time $1980; part-time $110 per credit. Tuition, nonresident: full-time $14,644; part-time $414 per credit. *Required fees:* $11,417. One-time fee: $357. *Financial support:* Fellowships with full and partial tuition reimbursements, research assistantships with full and partial tuition reimbursements, teaching assistantships with full and partial tuition reimbursements, career-related internships or fieldwork, Federal Work-Study, scholarships/grants, traineeships, health care benefits, tuition waivers (full and partial), and unspecified assistantships available. Support available to part-time students. Financial award application deadline: 1/2; financial award applicants required to submit FAFSA. *Unit head:* Dr. Elizabeth Krause, Graduate Program Director, 413-545-4101, Fax: 413-545-9494, E-mail: ekrause@anthro.umass.edu. *Application contact:* Lindsay DeSantis, Supervisor of Admissions, 413-545-0722, Fax: 413-577-0010, E-mail: gradadm@grad.umass.edu.
Website: http://www.umass.edu/anthro/

University of Memphis, Graduate School, College of Arts and Sciences, Department of Anthropology, Memphis, TN 38152. Offers medical anthropology (MA); urban anthropology (MA). Part-time programs available. *Faculty:* 6 full-time (5 women), 2 part-time/adjunct (1 woman). *Students:* 16 full-time (13 women), 1 (woman) part-time; includes 1 minority (Black or African American, non-Hispanic/Latino), 1 international. Average age 27. 15 applicants, 80% accepted, 4 enrolled. In 2014, 6 master's awarded.

Degree requirements: For master's, comprehensive exam, practicum. *Entrance requirements:* For master's, GRE General Test, minimum GPA of 3.0, letter of intent, 3 letters of recommendation. *Application deadline:* For fall admission, 11/1 priority date for domestic students; for spring admission, 4/1 priority date for domestic students. Application fee: $35 ($60 for international students). Electronic applications accepted. *Financial support:* In 2014–15, 27 students received support. Fellowships, research assistantships with full tuition reimbursements available, teaching assistantships with full tuition reimbursements available, career-related internships or fieldwork, Federal Work-Study, scholarships/grants, and unspecified assistantships available. Financial award application deadline: 2/15; financial award applicants required to submit FAFSA. *Faculty research:* Community development, medical anthropology, environmental justice, health disparities, cultural identity and heritage. *Unit head:* Dr. Ruthbeth Finerman, Chair, 901-678-3334, Fax: 901-678-2069, E-mail: finerman@memphis.edu. *Application contact:* Dr. Keri Brondo, Coordinator of Graduate Studies, 901-678-2080, Fax: 901-678-2069, E-mail: kbrondo@memphis.edu.
Website: http://www.memphis.edu/anthropology

University of Michigan, Horace H. Rackham School of Graduate Studies, College of Literature, Science, and the Arts, Department of Anthropology, Ann Arbor, MI 48109-1107. Offers archaeological (PhD); biological (PhD); linguistic (PhD); sociocultural (PhD). *Faculty:* 40 full-time (18 women), 6 part-time/adjunct (3 women). *Students:* 99 full-time (59 women); includes 19 minority (1 Black or African American, non-Hispanic/Latino; 1 American Indian or Alaska Native, non-Hispanic/Latino; 6 Asian, non-Hispanic/Latino; 6 Hispanic/Latino; 5 Two or more races, non-Hispanic/Latino), 13 international. Average age 28. 206 applicants, 14% accepted, 15 enrolled. In 2014, 15 doctorates awarded. *Degree requirements:* For doctorate, one foreign language, comprehensive exam, thesis/dissertation, preliminary examination, oral defense of dissertation. *Entrance requirements:* For doctorate, GRE General Test. Additional exam requirements/recommendations for international students: Required—TOEFL (minimum score 560 paper-based; 84 iBT). *Application deadline:* For fall admission, 12/15 for domestic and international students. Application fee: $75 ($90 for international students). Electronic applications accepted. *Financial support:* In 2014–15, 67 students received support, including 47 fellowships with full tuition reimbursements available (averaging $19,350 per year), 4 research assistantships with full tuition reimbursements available (averaging $19,350 per year), 50 teaching assistantships with full tuition reimbursements available (averaging $19,350 per year); institutionally sponsored loans, scholarships/grants, traineeships, health care benefits, tuition waivers (full), and unspecified assistantships also available. Financial award application deadline: 3/1; financial award applicants required to submit FAFSA. *Faculty research:* Sociocultural, linguistic, biological and archaeological anthropology. *Unit head:* Dr. Thomas Fricke, Chair, 734-764-7274, Fax: 734-763-6077. *Application contact:* Katia Kitchen, Graduate Program Assistant, 734-936-7933, Fax: 734-763-6077, E-mail: kitchenk@umich.edu.
Website: http://www.lsa.umich.edu/anthro/

University of Michigan, Horace H. Rackham School of Graduate Studies, College of Literature, Science, and the Arts, Doctoral Program in Anthropology and History, Ann Arbor, MI 48109. Offers PhD. *Degree requirements:* For doctorate, 2 foreign languages, thesis/dissertation, oral defense of dissertation, preliminary exam. *Entrance requirements:* For doctorate, GRE General Test, writing sample. Additional exam requirements/recommendations for international students: Required—TOEFL. Electronic applications accepted. *Faculty research:* Historical anthropology.

University of Michigan, School of Social Work, Interdisciplinary Program in Social Work and Social Science, Ann Arbor, MI 48109-1106. Offers social work and anthropology (PhD); social work and economics (PhD); social work and political science (PhD); social work and psychology (PhD); social work and sociology (PhD). Programs offered through the Horace H. Rackham School of Graduate Studies. *Faculty:* 57 full-time (33 women), 6 part-time/adjunct (4 women). *Students:* 64 full-time (46 women); includes 24 minority (7 Black or African American, non-Hispanic/Latino; 11 Asian, non-Hispanic/Latino; 6 Hispanic/Latino), 6 international. Average age 32. 108 applicants, 9% accepted, 9 enrolled. In 2014, 11 doctorates awarded. *Degree requirements:* For doctorate, thesis/dissertation, oral defense of dissertation, preliminary exam. *Entrance requirements:* For doctorate, GRE General Test. Additional exam requirements/recommendations for international students: Required—TOEFL. *Application deadline:* For fall admission, 12/1 for domestic and international students. Application fee: $75 ($90 for international students). *Financial support:* In 2014–15, 64 students received support, including 20 fellowships with full tuition reimbursements available (averaging $15,200 per year), 7 research assistantships with full tuition reimbursements available (averaging $18,971 per year), 19 teaching assistantships with full tuition reimbursements available (averaging $18,971 per year); career-related internships or fieldwork, Federal Work-Study, scholarships/grants, traineeships, health care benefits, tuition waivers (full and partial), and unspecified assistantships also available. Financial award application deadline: 12/1; financial award applicants required to submit FAFSA. *Faculty research:* Substance abuse, child welfare, mental health, poverty, aging. *Total annual research expenditures:* $4.1 million. *Unit head:* Dr. Berit Ingersoll-Dayton, Director, 734-763-5768, Fax: 734-615-3192, E-mail: bid@umich.edu. *Application contact:* Graduate Coordinator, 734-647-2554, Fax: 734-615-3192, E-mail: ssw.phd.info@umich.edu.
Website: http://www.ssw.umich.edu/doctoral

University of Minnesota, Duluth, Graduate School, College of Liberal Arts, Department of Sociology/Anthropology, Duluth, MN 55812-2496. Offers criminology (MA); liberal studies (MLS). Part-time programs available. *Degree requirements:* For master's, thesis or alternative. *Entrance requirements:* For master's, interview, minimum GPA of 3.0, letters of recommendation. Additional exam requirements/recommendations for international students: Required—TOEFL. *Faculty research:* Nature of knowledge, philosophy of science, ecology, cultural studies, language.

University of Minnesota, Twin Cities Campus, Graduate School, College of Liberal Arts, Department of Anthropology, Minneapolis, MN 55455-0213. Offers MA, PhD. Terminal master's awarded for partial completion of doctoral program. *Degree requirements:* For master's, thesis optional; for doctorate, comprehensive exam, thesis/dissertation. *Entrance requirements:* For master's and doctorate, GRE. Additional exam requirements/recommendations for international students: Recommended—TOEFL. Electronic applications accepted. *Faculty research:* Psychological/psychoanalytic anthropology, gender and feminist anthropology, economic anthropology, medical anthropology, paleoanthropology.

University of Mississippi, Graduate School, College of Liberal Arts, Department of Sociology and Anthropology, University, MS 38677. Offers anthropology (MA); sociology (MA, MSS). *Degree requirements:* For master's, thesis (for some programs). *Entrance requirements:* For master's, GRE General Test, minimum GPA of 3.0. Additional exam requirements/recommendations for international students: Required—TOEFL. Electronic applications accepted.

University of Missouri, Office of Research and Graduate Studies, College of Arts and Science, Department of Anthropology, Columbia, MO 65211. Offers MA, PhD. *Faculty:* 11 full-time (5 women). *Students:* 44 full-time (28 women), 10 part-time (4 women); includes 7 minority (1 Black or African American, non-Hispanic/Latino; 2 Asian, non-Hispanic/Latino; 2 Hispanic/Latino; 2 Two or more races, non-Hispanic/Latino), 3 international. Average age 31. 36 applicants, 36% accepted, 9 enrolled. In 2014, 4 master's, 1 doctorate awarded. *Degree requirements:* For master's, thesis (for some programs); for doctorate, one foreign language, comprehensive exam, thesis/dissertation. *Entrance requirements:* For master's, GRE General Test (minimum score 1000 verbal and quantitative), minimum GPA of 3.25 in last 60 hours and in all anthropology courses; for doctorate, GRE General Test (minimum score 1000 verbal and quantitative), minimum GPA of 3.5 in previous graduate work. Additional exam requirements/recommendations for international students: Required—TOEFL (minimum score 500 paper-based; 61 iBT), IELTS (minimum score 5.5). *Application deadline:* For fall admission, 1/10 priority date for domestic and international students; for winter admission, 10/15 for domestic and international students. Applications are processed on a rolling basis. Application fee: $55 ($75 for international students). Electronic applications accepted. *Financial support:* Fellowships with full tuition reimbursements, research assistantships with full tuition reimbursements, teaching assistantships with full tuition reimbursements, institutionally sponsored loans, scholarships/grants, health care benefits, and unspecified assistantships available. Support available to part-time students. *Faculty research:* Social/cultural anthropology, biological anthropology, archaeology. *Unit head:* Dr. R. Lee Lyman, Department Chair, 573-882-4731, E-mail: lymanr@missouri.edu. *Application contact:* Christine Hudson, Department Administrative Associate, 573-882-4732, E-mail: hudsoncm@missouri.edu.
Website: http://anthropology.missouri.edu/

The University of Montana, Graduate School, College of Humanities and Sciences, Department of Anthropology, Missoula, MT 59812-0002. Offers anthropology (MA, PhD); applied anthropology (PhD); applied medical anthropology (MA); cultural heritage (MA, PhD); forensic anthropology (MA); linguistic anthropology (MA). *Degree requirements:* For master's, thesis (for some programs). *Entrance requirements:* For master's, GRE General Test. Additional exam requirements/recommendations for international students: Required—TOEFL. *Faculty research:* Historical preservation, plateau-plains archaeology and ethnohistory.

University of Nebraska–Lincoln, Graduate College, College of Arts and Sciences, Department of Anthropology and Geography, Program in Anthropology, Lincoln, NE 68588. Offers MA. *Degree requirements:* For master's, thesis optional. *Entrance requirements:* For master's, GRE General Test. Additional exam requirements/recommendations for international students: Required—TOEFL (minimum score 500 paper-based). Electronic applications accepted. *Faculty research:* Cultural, archaeologic, linguistic, and physical anthropology.

University of Nevada, Las Vegas, Graduate College, College of Liberal Arts, Department of Anthropology and Ethnic Studies, Las Vegas, NV 89154-5003. Offers MA, PhD. Part-time programs available. *Faculty:* 11 full-time (3 women). *Students:* 33 full-time (19 women), 15 part-time (13 women); includes 10 minority (1 Black or African American, non-Hispanic/Latino; 1 Asian, non-Hispanic/Latino; 7 Hispanic/Latino; 1 Two or more races, non-Hispanic/Latino), 1 international. Average age 30. 71 applicants, 20% accepted, 9 enrolled. In 2014, 5 master's awarded. *Degree requirements:* For master's, thesis, oral defense of thesis; for doctorate, comprehensive exam, thesis/dissertation, oral defense of dissertation. *Entrance requirements:* For master's and doctorate, GRE General Test. Additional exam requirements/recommendations for international students: Required—TOEFL (minimum score 550 paper-based; 80 iBT), IELTS (minimum score 7). *Application deadline:* For fall admission, 2/1 for domestic students, 5/1 for international students; for spring admission, 10/1 for international students. Application fee: $60 ($95 for international students). Electronic applications accepted. *Financial support:* In 2014–15, 24 students received support, including 1 fellowship with full tuition reimbursement available (averaging $20,000 per year), 13 research assistantships with partial tuition reimbursements available (averaging $12,538 per year), 10 teaching assistantships with partial tuition reimbursements available (averaging $14,300 per year); institutionally sponsored loans, scholarships/grants, health care benefits, and unspecified assistantships also available. Financial award application deadline: 3/1. *Faculty research:* Food and nutrition, adaptive strategies, childhood and parenting, sexuality, gender and identity. *Unit head:* Dr. Barbara Roth, Chair/Professor, 702-895-3646, Fax: 702-895-4823, E-mail: barbara.roth@unlv.edu. *Application contact:* Graduate College Admissions Evaluator, 702-895-3320, Fax: 702-895-4180, E-mail: gradcollege@unlv.edu.
Website: http://anthro.unlv.edu/

University of Nevada, Reno, Graduate School, College of Liberal Arts, Department of Anthropology, Reno, NV 89557. Offers MA, PhD. Terminal master's awarded for partial completion of doctoral program. *Degree requirements:* For master's, thesis; for doctorate, thesis/dissertation. *Entrance requirements:* For master's, GRE, minimum GPA of 2.75; for doctorate, GRE, minimum GPA of 3.0. Additional exam requirements/recommendations for international students: Required—TOEFL (minimum score 500 paper-based; 61 iBT), IELTS (minimum score 6). Electronic applications accepted. *Faculty research:* Ethnology, linguistics, cultural/medical/religious/ethnic relations, ecological anthropology, historical anthropology.

University of New Brunswick Fredericton, School of Graduate Studies, Faculty of Arts, Department of Anthropology, Fredericton, NB E3B 5A3, Canada. Offers MA. Part-time programs available. *Faculty:* 8 full-time (6 women), 2 part-time/adjunct (1 woman). *Students:* 9 full-time (7 women), 2 part-time (1 woman). In 2014, 1 master's awarded. *Degree requirements:* For master's, thesis, proposal. *Entrance requirements:* For master's, minimum GPA of 3.0. Additional exam requirements/recommendations for international students: Required—TOEFL. *Application deadline:* For fall admission, 1/31 for domestic and international students; for winter admission, 1/31 priority date for domestic and international students; for spring admission, 1/31 for domestic and international students. Applications are processed on a rolling basis. Application fee: $50 Canadian dollars. Electronic applications accepted. *Financial support:* Fellowships available. *Faculty research:* Medical anthropology, anthropology of education, community-based fisheries, maritime archaeology, world prehistory, geoarchaeology, zooarchaeology socio-cultural anthropology, bioarchaeology, forensics, globalization, legal anthropology. *Unit head:* Dr. Victoria Gibbon, Director of Graduate Studies, 506-458-7994, Fax: 506-453-5071, E-mail: vgibbon@unb.ca. *Application contact:* Judy Babin, Graduate Secretary, 506-453-4975, Fax: 506-453-5071, E-mail: judy.babin@unb.ca.
Website: http://go.unb.ca/gradprograms

University of New Mexico, Graduate School, College of Arts and Sciences, Program in Anthropology, Albuquerque, NM 87131-2039. Offers archaeology (MA, MS, PhD); ethnology (MA, MS, PhD); evolutionary anthropology (PhD); public archaeology (MA, MS, PhD). *Faculty:* 24 full-time (10 women). *Students:* 90 full-time (53 women), 32 part-time (25 women); includes 30 minority (4 American Indian or Alaska Native, non-Hispanic/Latino; 2 Asian, non-Hispanic/Latino; 19 Hispanic/Latino; 5 Two or more races, non-Hispanic/Latino), 8 international. Average age 32. 101 applicants, 31% accepted, 20 enrolled. In 2014, 18 master's, 14 doctorates awarded. Terminal master's awarded for partial completion of doctoral program. *Degree requirements:* For master's, comprehensive exam (for some programs), thesis or alternative, 1-2 exams; for doctorate, one foreign language, comprehensive exam, thesis/dissertation, exam, proposal, oral defense, skill and/or second language. *Entrance requirements:* For master's and doctorate, GRE General Test, 3 letters of recommendation, letter of

interest, transcripts. Additional exam requirements/recommendations for international students: Required—TOEFL (minimum score 550 paper-based), IELTS (minimum score 7). *Application deadline:* For fall admission, 1/4 for domestic and international students. Application fee: $50. Electronic applications accepted. *Financial support:* In 2014–15, 104 students received support, including 17 fellowships (averaging $9,268 per year), 16 research assistantships with partial tuition reimbursements available (averaging $10,567 per year), 47 teaching assistantships with partial tuition reimbursements available (averaging $8,608 per year); career-related internships or fieldwork, Federal Work-Study, institutionally sponsored loans, scholarships/grants, traineeships, health care benefits, tuition waivers (partial), and unspecified assistantships also available. Support available to part-time students. Financial award application deadline: 3/1; financial award applicants required to submit FAFSA. *Faculty research:* Ethnology, archaeology, evolutionary anthropology, environment, water and land use, gender and social frameworks, Greater Southwest, Latin America, political economy, public anthropology. *Total annual research expenditures:* $1.2 million. *Unit head:* Michael W. Graves, Chair, 505-277-4524, Fax: 505-277-0874, E-mail: mwgraves@unm.edu. *Application contact:* Erika E. Gerety, Program Advisement Coordinator, 505-277-2732, Fax: 505-277-0874, E-mail: erika@unm.edu.
Website: http://www.unm.edu/~anthro/

The University of North Carolina at Chapel Hill, Graduate School, College of Arts and Sciences, Department of Anthropology, Chapel Hill, NC 27599-3115. Offers MA, PhD. Terminal master's awarded for partial completion of doctoral program. *Degree requirements:* For master's, variable foreign language requirement, thesis; for doctorate, variable foreign language requirement, comprehensive exam, thesis/dissertation. *Entrance requirements:* For master's and doctorate, GRE General Test, minimum GPA of 3.0. Additional exam requirements/recommendations for international students: Required—TOEFL. Electronic applications accepted. *Faculty research:* Archeology, ecology and evolution, medical anthropology, social systems, anthropology of meaning.

The University of North Carolina at Charlotte, College of Liberal Arts and Sciences, Department of Anthropology, Charlotte, NC 28223-0001. Offers MA. Part-time programs available. *Faculty:* 11 full-time (8 women), 1 part-time/adjunct (0 women). *Students:* 10 full-time (6 women), 5 part-time (4 women); includes 1 minority (Two or more races, non-Hispanic/Latino). Average age 28. 11 applicants, 55% accepted, 5 enrolled. In 2014, 3 master's awarded. *Degree requirements:* For master's, thesis or alternative, research thesis or applied practicum and project report; oral defense. *Entrance requirements:* For master's, GRE, three letters of recommendation, statement of purpose, minimum undergraduate GPA of 3.0. Additional exam requirements/recommendations for international students: Required—TOEFL (minimum score 557 paper-based; 83 iBT). *Application deadline:* For fall admission, 5/1 for domestic and international students; for spring admission, 11/1 for domestic students. Application fee: $75. Electronic applications accepted. *Expenses:* Tuition, state resident: full-time $4008. Tuition, nonresident: full-time $16,295. *Required fees:* $2755. Tuition and fees vary according to course load and program. *Financial support:* In 2014–15, 9 students received support, including 5 research assistantships (averaging $4,096 per year), 4 teaching assistantships (averaging $7,250 per year); unspecified assistantships also available. Financial award application deadline: 3/15. *Faculty research:* Impact of environment on the social strategies and reproductive careers of Sifaka; molecular anthropology: the application of genetic data; family abuse and women's health; aging cross-culturally; production and circulation of knowledge in material form; the relationship among knowledge, power, policy and practice as they pertain to health and health care; the development of ranked societies in prehistory. *Total annual research expenditures:* $171,987. *Unit head:* Janet E. Levy, Chair, 704-687-5095, E-mail: jelevy@uncc.edu. *Application contact:* Kathy B. Giddings, Director of Graduate Admissions, 704-687-5503, Fax: 704-687-1668, E-mail: gradadm@uncc.edu.
Website: http://anthropology.uncc.edu/

University of North Texas, Robert B. Toulouse School of Graduate Studies, Denton, TX 76203-5459. Offers accounting (MS); applied anthropology (MA, MS); applied behavior analysis (Certificate); applied geography (MA); applied technology and performance improvement (M Ed, MS); art education (MA); art history (MA); art museum education (Certificate); arts leadership (Certificate); audiology (Au D); behavior analysis (MS); behavioral science (PhD); biochemistry and molecular biology (MS); biology (MA, MS); biomedical engineering (MS); business analysis (MS); chemistry (MS); clinical health psychology (PhD); communication studies (MA, MS); computer engineering (MS); computer science (MS); counseling (M Ed, MS), including clinical mental health counseling (MS), college and university counseling, elementary school counseling, secondary school counseling; creative writing (MA); criminal justice (MS); curriculum and instruction (M Ed); decision sciences (MBA); design (MA, MFA), including fashion design (MFA), innovation studies, interior design (MFA); early childhood studies (MS); economics (MS); educational leadership (M Ed, Ed D); educational psychology (MS, PhD), including family studies (MS), gifted and talented (MS), human development (MS), learning and cognition (MS), research, measurement and evaluation (MS); electrical engineering (MS); emergency management (MPA); engineering technology (MS); English (MA); English as a second language (MA); environmental science (MS); finance (MBA, MS); financial management (MPA); French (MA); health services management (MBA); higher education (M Ed, Ed D); history (MA, MS); hospitality management (MS); human resources management (MPA); information science (MS); information systems (PhD); information technologies (MBA); interdisciplinary studies (MA, MS); international studies (MA); international sustainable tourism (MS); jazz studies (MM); journalism (MA, MJ, Graduate Certificate), including interactive and virtual digital communication (Graduate Certificate), narrative journalism (Graduate Certificate), public relations (Graduate Certificate); kinesiology (MS); linguistics (MA); local government management (MPA); logistics (PhD); logistics and supply chain management (MBA); long-term care, senior housing, and aging services (MA); management (PhD); marketing (MBA); mathematics (MA, MS); mechanical and energy engineering (MS, PhD); music (MA), including ethnomusicology, music theory, musicology, performance; music composition (PhD); music education (MM Ed, PhD); nonprofit management (MPA); operations and supply chain management (MBA); performance (MM, DMA); philosophy (MA); political science (MA); professional and technical communication (MA); radio, television and film (MA, MFA); rehabilitation counseling (Certificate); sociology (MA); Spanish (MA); special education (M Ed); speech-language pathology (MA); strategic management (MBA); studio art (MFA); teaching (M Ed); MBA/MS. Part-time and evening/weekend programs available. Postbaccalaureate distance learning degree programs offered. *Faculty:* 651 full-time (215 women), 233 part-time/adjunct (139 women). *Students:* 3,040 full-time (1,598 women), 3,401 part-time (2,097 women); includes 1,740 minority (533 Black or African American, non-Hispanic/Latino; 15 American Indian or Alaska Native, non-Hispanic/Latino; 286 Asian, non-Hispanic/Latino; 746 Hispanic/Latino; 3 Native Hawaiian or other Pacific Islander, non-Hispanic/Latino; 157 Two or more races, non-Hispanic/Latino), 1,145 international. Terminal master's awarded for partial completion of doctoral program. *Degree requirements:* For master's, variable foreign language requirement, comprehensive exam (for some programs), thesis (for some programs); for doctorate, variable foreign language requirement, comprehensive exam (for some programs), thesis/dissertation; for other advanced degree, variable foreign language requirement, comprehensive exam (for some programs). *Entrance requirements:* For master's and doctorate, GRE, GMAT. Additional exam requirements/recommendations for international students: Required—TOEFL (minimum score 550 paper-based; 79 iBT). *Application deadline:* For fall admission, 7/15 for domestic students, 3/15 for international students; for spring admission, 11/15 for domestic students, 9/15 for international students; for summer admission, 5/1 for domestic students. Applications are processed on a rolling basis. Application fee: $60. Electronic applications accepted. *Expenses:* Tuition, state resident: full-time $5450; part-time $3633 per year. Tuition, nonresident: full-time $11,966; part-time $7977 per year. *Required fees:* $1301; $398 per credit hour. $685 per semester. Tuition and fees vary according to program and reciprocity agreements. *Financial support:* Fellowships with partial tuition reimbursements, research assistantships with partial tuition reimbursements, teaching assistantships, career-related internships or fieldwork, Federal Work-Study, institutionally sponsored loans, scholarships/grants, health care benefits, and library assistantships available. Support available to part-time students. Financial award applicants required to submit FAFSA. *Unit head:* Mark Wardell, Dean, 940-565-2383, E-mail: mark.wardell@unt.edu. *Application contact:* Toulouse School of Graduate Studies, 940-565-2383, Fax: 940-565-2141, E-mail: gradsch@unt.edu.
Website: http://tsgs.unt.edu/

University of Oklahoma, College of Arts and Sciences, Department of Anthropology, Norman, OK 73019. Offers anthropology (PhD); applied linguistic anthropology (MA); archaeology (PhD); health and human biology (PhD). *Faculty:* 30 full-time (14 women), 1 part-time/adjunct (0 women). *Students:* 38 full-time (24 women), 27 part-time (10 women); includes 11 minority (2 Black or African American, non-Hispanic/Latino; 6 American Indian or Alaska Native, non-Hispanic/Latino; 2 Hispanic/Latino; 1 Two or more races, non-Hispanic/Latino), 2 international. Average age 31. 40 applicants, 60% accepted, 17 enrolled. In 2014, 7 master's, 4 doctorates awarded. *Degree requirements:* For master's, one foreign language, comprehensive exam (for some programs), thesis; for doctorate, one foreign language, comprehensive exam, thesis/dissertation. *Entrance requirements:* For master's and doctorate, GRE, minimum undergraduate GPA of 3.0, statement of purpose, 2 letters of recommendation, department application. Additional exam requirements/recommendations for international students: Required—TOEFL (minimum score 79 iBT). *Application deadline:* 2/1 for domestic and international students. Application fee: $50 ($100 for international students). Electronic applications accepted. *Expenses:* Tuition, state resident: full-time $4394; part-time $183.10 per credit hour. Tuition, nonresident: full-time $16,970; part-time $707.10 per credit hour. *Required fees:* $2892; $109.95 per credit hour. $126.50 per semester. *Financial support:* In 2014–15, 49 students received support, including 2 fellowships with full tuition reimbursements available (averaging $5,000 per year), 2 research assistantships with partial tuition reimbursements available (averaging $11,000 per year), 17 teaching assistantships with partial tuition reimbursements available (averaging $14,670 per year); career-related internships or fieldwork, Federal Work-Study, scholarships/grants, health care benefits, and unspecified assistantships also available. Financial award application deadline: 6/1; financial award applicants required to submit FAFSA. *Faculty research:* Sociocultural anthropology, North American archeology, linguistic, applied linguistics, health and human biology, Native North America. *Total annual research expenditures:* $560,578. *Unit head:* Dr. Diane Warren, Associate Professor/Academic Chair, 405-325-7609, Fax: 405-325-7386, E-mail: dmwarren@ou.edu. *Application contact:* Dr. Cecil Lewis, Graduate Liaison and Associate Professor, 405-325-3415, Fax: 405-325-7386, E-mail: cmlewis@ou.edu.
Website: http://cas.ou.edu/anthropology

University of Oregon, Graduate School, College of Arts and Sciences, Department of Anthropology, Eugene, OR 97403. Offers MA, MS, PhD. Terminal master's awarded for partial completion of doctoral program. *Degree requirements:* For master's, one foreign language; for doctorate, 2 foreign languages, thesis/dissertation. *Entrance requirements:* For master's and doctorate, GRE General Test. Additional exam requirements/recommendations for international students: Required—TOEFL. *Faculty research:* Prehistory, primatology, cultural anthropology of Native Americans, human evolution, Africa.

University of Ottawa, Faculty of Graduate and Postdoctoral Studies, Faculty of Social Sciences, Department of Sociology and Anthropology, Ottawa, ON K1N 6N5, Canada. Offers MA. *Degree requirements:* For master's, thesis or alternative. *Entrance requirements:* For master's, honors bachelor's degree or equivalent, minimum B average. Electronic applications accepted. *Faculty research:* Inter-ethnic relations, development, political policies.

University of Pennsylvania, School of Arts and Sciences, Graduate Group in Anthropology, Philadelphia, PA 19104. Offers AM, MS, PhD. *Faculty:* 17 full-time (6 women), 10 part-time/adjunct (6 women). *Students:* 56 full-time (33 women), 8 part-time (4 women); includes 10 minority (3 Black or African American, non-Hispanic/Latino; 2 Asian, non-Hispanic/Latino; 2 Hispanic/Latino; 3 Two or more races, non-Hispanic/Latino), 11 international. 194 applicants, 9% accepted, 13 enrolled. In 2014, 1 master's, 7 doctorates awarded. Terminal master's awarded for partial completion of doctoral program. *Degree requirements:* For master's, thesis, final exam; for doctorate, one foreign language, thesis/dissertation, fieldwork, preliminary and final exams. *Entrance requirements:* For doctorate, GRE General Test. Additional exam requirements/recommendations for international students: Required—TOEFL. *Application deadline:* For fall admission, 12/1 priority date for domestic students. Application fee: $70. *Financial support:* Fellowships, teaching assistantships, institutionally sponsored loans, scholarships/grants, traineeships, health care benefits, and unspecified assistantships available. Financial award application deadline: 12/15. *Unit head:* Dr. Ralph M. Rosen, Associate Dean for Graduate Studies, 215-898-7156, Fax: 215-573-8068, E-mail: grad-dean@sas.upenn.edu. *Application contact:* Arts and Sciences Graduate Admissions, 215-573-5816, Fax: 215-573-8068, E-mail: gdasadmis@sas.upenn.edu.
Website: http://www.sas.upenn.edu/graduate-division

University of Pittsburgh, Dietrich School of Arts and Sciences, Department of Anthropology, Pittsburgh, PA 15260. Offers MA, PhD. Part-time programs available. *Faculty:* 19 full-time (6 women), 3 part-time/adjunct (1 woman). *Students:* 69 full-time (41 women); includes 3 minority (1 Black or African American, non-Hispanic/Latino; 1 Hispanic/Latino; 1 Two or more races, non-Hispanic/Latino), 36 international. 105 applicants, 15% accepted, 11 enrolled. In 2014, 4 master's, 9 doctorates awarded. *Degree requirements:* For master's, one foreign language, thesis or alternative; for doctorate, one foreign language, thesis/dissertation. *Entrance requirements:* For master's and doctorate, GRE General Test. Additional exam requirements/recommendations for international students: Required—TOEFL (minimum score 550 paper-based; 90 iBT), IELTS (minimum score 6.5). *Application deadline:* For fall admission, 1/7 priority date for domestic and international students. Applications are processed on a rolling basis. Application fee: $50. Electronic applications accepted. *Expenses:* Tuition, state resident: full-time $20,742; part-time $838 per credit. Tuition, nonresident: full-time $33,960; part-time $1389 per credit. *Required fees:* $800; $205 per term. Tuition and fees vary according to program. *Financial support:* In 2014–15, 62 students received support, including 30 fellowships with full tuition reimbursements available (averaging $21,262 per year), 4 research assistantships with full tuition reimbursements available (averaging $13,980 per year), 26 teaching assistantships with full tuition reimbursements available (averaging $17,800 per year); career-related internships or fieldwork, Federal Work-Study, scholarships/grants, health care benefits,

tuition waivers (full and partial), and unspecified assistantships also available. Support available to part-time students. Financial award application deadline: 1/7. *Faculty research:* Conflict studies; ethnicity, nationalism, and the state; origins of complex societies; Latin American archaeology; human evolutionary biology. *Unit head:* Dr. Bryan K. Hanks, Chair, 412-648-7530, Fax: 412-648-7535, E-mail: bkh5@pitt.edu. *Application contact:* Phyllis J. Deasy, Graduate Coordinator, 412-648-7504, Fax: 412-648-7535, E-mail: pdeasy@pitt.edu.
Website: http://www.anthropology.pitt.edu

University of Regina, Faculty of Graduate Studies and Research, Faculty of Arts, Department of Anthropology, Regina, SK S4S 0A2, Canada. Offers MA. Offered as a special case program. Part-time programs available. *Faculty:* 6 full-time (3 women), 1 part-time/adjunct (0 women). *Students:* 1 full-time (0 women). In 2014, 2 master's awarded. *Degree requirements:* For master's, thesis. *Entrance requirements:* Additional exam requirements/recommendations for international students: Required—TOEFL (minimum score 580 paper-based; 80 iBT), IELTS (minimum score 6.5), PTE (minimum score 59). *Application deadline:* Applications are processed on a rolling basis. Application fee: $100. Electronic applications accepted. *Expenses: Tuition, area resident:* Full-time $4900 Canadian dollars; part-time $837.65 Canadian dollars per semester. *International tuition:* $7900 Canadian dollars full-time. *Required fees:* $396 Canadian dollars; $86.90 Canadian dollars per semester. *Financial support:* Fellowships, research assistantships, teaching assistantships, and scholarships/grants available. Financial award application deadline: 6/15. *Unit head:* Dr. Carlos Londono Sulkin, Department Head, 306-585-5405, Fax: 306-585-4815, E-mail: carlos.londono@uregina.ca. *Application contact:* Dr. Tobias Sperlich, Graduate Coordinator, 306-585-4773, Fax: 306-585-4815, E-mail: tobias.sperlich@uregina.ca.
Website: http://www.uregina.ca/arts/anthropology/

University of Saskatchewan, College of Graduate Studies and Research, College of Arts and Science, Department of Religion and Culture, Saskatoon, SK S7N 5A2, Canada. Offers MA. *Degree requirements:* For master's, thesis. *Entrance requirements:* Additional exam requirements/recommendations for international students: Required—TOEFL (minimum score 80 iBT); Recommended—IELTS (minimum score 6.5). Electronic applications accepted.

University of South Africa, College of Human Sciences, Pretoria, South Africa. Offers adult education (M Ed); African languages (MA, PhD); African politics (MA, PhD); Afrikaans (MA, PhD); ancient history (MA, PhD); ancient Near Eastern studies (MA, PhD); anthropology (MA, PhD); applied linguistics (MA); Arabic (MA, PhD); archaeology (MA); art history (MA); Biblical archaeology (MA); Biblical studies (M Th, D Th, PhD); Christian spirituality (M Th, D Th); church history (M Th, D Th); classical studies (MA, PhD); clinical psychology (MA); communication (MA, PhD); comparative education (M Ed, Ed D); consulting psychology (D Admin, D Com, PhD); curriculum studies (M Ed, Ed D); development studies (M Admin, MA, D Admin, PhD); didactics (M Ed, Ed D); education (M Tech); education management (M Ed, Ed D); educational psychology (M Ed); English (MA); environmental education (M Ed); French (MA, PhD); German (MA, PhD); Greek (MA); guidance and counseling (M Ed); health studies (MA, PhD), including health sciences education (MA), health services management (MA), medical and surgical nursing science (critical care general) (MA), midwifery and neonatal nursing science (MA), trauma and emergency care (MA); history (MA, PhD); history of education (Ed D); inclusive education (M Ed, Ed D); information and communications technology policy and regulation (MA); information science (MA, MIS, PhD); international politics (MA, PhD); Islamic studies (MA, PhD); Italian (MA, PhD); Judaica (MA, PhD); linguistics (MA, PhD); mathematical education (M Ed); mathematics education (MA); missiology (M Th, D Th); modern Hebrew (MA, PhD); musicology (MA, MMus, D Mus, PhD); natural science education (M Ed); New Testament (M Th, D Th); Old Testament (D Th); pastoral therapy (M Th, D Th); philosophy (MA); philosophy of education (M Ed, Ed D); politics (MA, PhD); Portuguese (MA, PhD); practical theology (M Th, D Th); psychology (MA, MS, PhD); psychology of education (M Ed, Ed D); public health (MA); religious studies (MA, D Th, PhD); Romance languages (MA); Russian (MA, PhD); Semitic languages (MA, PhD); social behavior studies in HIV/AIDS (MA); social science (mental health) (MA); social science in development studies (MA); social science in psychology (MA); social science in social work (MA); social science in sociology (MA); social work (MSW, DSW, PhD); socio-education (M Ed, Ed D); sociolinguistics (MA); sociology (MA, PhD); Spanish (MA, PhD); systematic theology (M Th, D Th); TESOL (teaching English to speakers of other languages) (MA); theological ethics (M Th, D Th); theory of literature (MA, PhD); urban ministries (D Th); urban ministry (M Th).

University of South Carolina, The Graduate School, College of Arts and Sciences, Department of Anthropology, Columbia, SC 29208. Offers MA, PhD. Terminal master's awarded for partial completion of doctoral program. *Degree requirements:* For master's, comprehensive exam, thesis; for doctorate, comprehensive exam, thesis/dissertation. *Entrance requirements:* For master's and doctorate, GRE General Test, letters of reference. Additional exam requirements/recommendations for international students: Required—TOEFL. Electronic applications accepted. *Faculty research:* Biocultural anthropology, archaeology, cultural anthropology.

University of Southern Mississippi, Graduate School, College of Arts and Letters, Department of Anthropology and Sociology, Hattiesburg, MS 39406-0001. Offers anthropology (MA). Part-time programs available. *Degree requirements:* For master's, one foreign language, comprehensive exam, thesis (for some programs). *Entrance requirements:* For master's, GRE General Test, minimum GPA of 2.75 in last 2 years, 3.0 in field of study. Additional exam requirements/recommendations for international students: Required—TOEFL, IELTS. *Faculty research:* Archaeology of North America, historic archaeology, bioarchaeology, ethnography of Europe, ethnography of Africa.

University of South Florida, College of Arts and Sciences, Department of Anthropology, Tampa, FL 33620-9951. Offers applied anthropology (MA, PhD), including applied anthropology (PhD), archaeology, biological anthropology, cultural anthropology, medical anthropology; medical anthropology (Graduate Certificate); MA/MPH; PhD/MPH. Part-time programs available. *Faculty:* 18 full-time (10 women). *Students:* 78 full-time (56 women), 52 part-time (35 women); includes 30 minority (8 Black or African American, non-Hispanic/Latino; 2 Asian, non-Hispanic/Latino; 16 Hispanic/Latino; 1 Native Hawaiian or other Pacific Islander, non-Hispanic/Latino; 3 Two or more races, non-Hispanic/Latino), 2 international. Average age 33. 154 applicants, 37% accepted, 34 enrolled. In 2014, 16 master's, 10 doctorates awarded. *Degree requirements:* For master's, one foreign language, comprehensive exam, thesis; for doctorate, one foreign language, comprehensive exam, thesis/dissertation, colloquium presentation. *Entrance requirements:* For master's and doctorate, GRE, minimum GPA of 3.0, 3 letters of recommendation, signed research ethics statement, resume or curriculum vitae; for Graduate Certificate, bachelor's degree with minimum GPA of 3.0. Additional exam requirements/recommendations for international students: Required—TOEFL (minimum score 550 paper-based; 79 iBT) or IELTS (minimum score 6.5). *Application deadline:* For fall admission, 1/15 for domestic students, 1/2 for international students. Application fee: $30. Electronic applications accepted. *Financial support:* In 2014–15, 66 students received support, including 14 research assistantships with tuition reimbursements available (averaging $14,475 per year), 52 teaching assistantships with partial tuition reimbursements available (averaging $12,540 per year); scholarships/grants and tuition waivers (partial) also available. Financial award application deadline: 1/15; financial award applicants required to submit FAFSA. *Faculty research:* Biocultural medical anthropology; archaeology and culture resource management in the Americas; community identity and heritage; urban community issues; verbal and nonverbal communications in media and education; global dynamics of sustainable resource management and economic development; social and cultural constructions of race, ethnicity, and gender. *Total annual research expenditures:* $1.5 million. *Unit head:* Dr. David Himmelgreen, Professor/Department Chairperson, 813-974-2138, Fax: 813-974-2668, E-mail: dhimmelg@usf.edu. *Application contact:* Dr. Heide Castaneda, Assistant Professor and Graduate Director, 813-974-2138, Fax: 813-974-2668, E-mail: hcastaneda@usf.edu.
Website: http://anthropology.usf.edu/graduate/

The University of Tennessee, Graduate School, College of Arts and Sciences, Department of Anthropology, Knoxville, TN 37996. Offers archaeology (MA, PhD); biological anthropology (MA, PhD); cultural anthropology (MA, PhD); zoo-archaeology (MA, PhD). *Degree requirements:* For master's, thesis; for doctorate, one foreign language, thesis/dissertation. *Entrance requirements:* For master's and doctorate, GRE General Test, minimum GPA of 2.7. Additional exam requirements/recommendations for international students: Required—TOEFL. Electronic applications accepted.

The University of Texas at Arlington, Graduate School, College of Liberal Arts, Department of Sociology and Anthropology, Program in Anthropology, Arlington, TX 79019. Offers MA. Part-time and evening/weekend programs available. *Degree requirements:* For master's, comprehensive exam, thesis or alternative. *Entrance requirements:* For master's, GRE General Test, minimum GPA of 3.0, 3 letters of recommendation. Additional exam requirements/recommendations for international students: Required—TOEFL (minimum score 550 paper-based). Electronic applications accepted.

The University of Texas at Austin, Graduate School, College of Liberal Arts, Department of Anthropology, Austin, TX 78712-1111. Offers archaeology (MA, PhD); cultural forms (MA, PhD); linguistic anthropology (MA, PhD); physical anthropology (MA, PhD); social anthropology (MA, PhD). Part-time programs available. Terminal master's awarded for partial completion of doctoral program. *Degree requirements:* For master's, thesis; for doctorate, one foreign language, thesis/dissertation. *Entrance requirements:* For master's and doctorate, GRE General Test. Additional exam requirements/recommendations for international students: Required—TOEFL. Electronic applications accepted.

The University of Texas at El Paso, Graduate School, College of Liberal Arts, Department of Sociology and Anthropology, El Paso, TX 79968-0001. Offers applied anthropology (Certificate); applied social sciences (Certificate); sociology (MA). Part-time and evening/weekend programs available. *Degree requirements:* For master's, thesis. *Entrance requirements:* For master's, GRE General Test, minimum GPA of 3.0. Additional exam requirements/recommendations for international students: Required—TOEFL. Electronic applications accepted. *Faculty research:* U.S.-Mexico border, social inequality, immigration, Chicano culture, Mexico.

The University of Texas at San Antonio, College of Liberal and Fine Arts, Department of Anthropology, San Antonio, TX 78249-0617. Offers MA, PhD. Part-time programs available. *Faculty:* 12 full-time (6 women), 1 part-time/adjunct (0 women). *Students:* 19 full-time (12 women), 47 part-time (33 women); includes 16 minority (1 Asian, non-Hispanic/Latino; 14 Hispanic/Latino; 1 Two or more races, non-Hispanic/Latino), 4 international. Average age 31. 35 applicants, 57% accepted, 16 enrolled. In 2014, 6 master's, 1 doctorate awarded. Terminal master's awarded for partial completion of doctoral program. *Degree requirements:* For master's, comprehensive exam, thesis; for doctorate, comprehensive exam, thesis/dissertation, proficiency in foreign language, statistics, or computer programming. *Entrance requirements:* For master's, GRE General Test, minimum GPA of 3.3 during last 60 hours (preferred), 18 hours in major field, three letters of recommendation, statement of purpose, writing sample; for doctorate, GRE General Test, minimum GPA of 3.3 (preferred), transcripts from all colleges and universities attended, 3 letters of recommendation, statement of purpose, writing sample. Additional exam requirements/recommendations for international students: Required—TOEFL (minimum score 550 paper-based; 79 iBT), IELTS (minimum score 6.5). *Application deadline:* For fall admission, 7/1 for domestic students, 4/1 for international students; for spring admission, 11/1 for domestic students, 9/1 for international students. Application fee: $45 ($80 for international students). Electronic applications accepted. *Expenses:* Expenses: $6,596 full-time resident, $19,994 non-resident. *Financial support:* In 2014–15, 30 students received support, including 3 fellowships (averaging $20,000 per year), 1 research assistantship (averaging $9,600 per year), 14 teaching assistantships (averaging $8,750 per year); scholarships/grants and unspecified assistantships also available. *Faculty research:* Political and cultural ecology, the archaeology of complexity, indigenous and environmental politics, primate and evolutionary ecology, medical anthropology. *Total annual research expenditures:* $186,000. *Unit head:* Dr. Jason Yaeger, Chair and Professor of Anthropology, 210-458-7966, Fax: 210-458-7811, E-mail: jason.yeager@utsa.edu.
Website: http://colfa.utsa.edu/ant/

The University of Texas–Pan American, College of Social and Behavioral Sciences, Department of Psychology and Anthropology, Edinburg, TX 78539. Offers anthropology (MAIS); psychology (MA), including clinical psychology, experimental psychology. Part-time and evening/weekend programs available. *Degree requirements:* For master's, comprehensive exam, thesis optional, internship. *Entrance requirements:* For master's, GRE, letters of recommendation. Additional exam requirements/recommendations for international students: Required—TOEFL. Electronic applications accepted. *Expenses:* Tuition, state resident: full-time $4187; part-time $232.60 per credit hour. Tuition, nonresident: full-time $10,857; part-time $603.16 per credit hour. *Required fees:* $782; $27.50 per credit hour. $143.35 per semester. *Faculty research:* Biofeedback, acculturation, health, stress/trauma, neuropsychological assessment, false memories, children's theory of mind.

University of Toronto, School of Graduate Studies, Faculty of Arts and Science, Department of Anthropology, Toronto, ON M5S 2J7, Canada. Offers M Sc, MA, PhD. Part-time programs available. *Degree requirements:* For master's, research paper; for doctorate, one foreign language, thesis/dissertation, language exam, thesis defense. *Entrance requirements:* For master's, minimum B+ average, 5 full-year anthropology courses, 2 letters of reference, statement of interest; for doctorate, minimum B+ average, master's degree in relevant area, resume, 2 letters of reference, statement of interest. Additional exam requirements/recommendations for international students: Required—TOEFL (minimum score 580 paper-based; 93 iBT), IELTS (minimum score 7), TWE (minimum score 5), Michigan English Language Assessment Battery (minimum score 85), or COPE (minimum score 4). Electronic applications accepted.

The University of Tulsa, Graduate School, Kendall College of Arts and Sciences, Department of Anthropology, Tulsa, OK 74104-3189. Offers MA, PhD, JD/MA. Part-time programs available. *Faculty:* 9 full-time (1 woman), 2 part-time/adjunct (0 women). *Students:* 14 full-time (13 women), 5 part-time (all women); includes 4 minority (1 Black or African American, non-Hispanic/Latino; 1 American Indian or Alaska Native, non-Hispanic/Latino; 2 Two or more races, non-Hispanic/Latino), 2 international. Average age 29. 22 applicants, 64% accepted, 9 enrolled. In 2014, 4 master's awarded. Terminal

master's awarded for partial completion of doctoral program. *Degree requirements:* For master's, thesis (for some programs); for doctorate, comprehensive exam, thesis/dissertation. *Entrance requirements:* For master's, GRE General Test. Additional exam requirements/recommendations for international students: Required—TOEFL (minimum score 577 paper-based; 91 iBT), IELTS (minimum score 6.5). *Application deadline:* Applications are processed on a rolling basis. Application fee: $55. Electronic applications accepted. *Expenses: Tuition:* Full-time $20,160; part-time $1120 per credit hour. *Required fees:* $6 per credit hour. Tuition and fees vary according to course level and course load. *Financial support:* In 2014–15, 14 students received support, including 5 fellowships with full and partial tuition reimbursements available (averaging $1,017 per year), 4 research assistantships with full and partial tuition reimbursements available (averaging $10,489 per year), 8 teaching assistantships with full and partial tuition reimbursements available (averaging $11,899 per year); career-related internships or fieldwork, Federal Work-Study, scholarships/grants, health care benefits, tuition waivers (full and partial), and unspecified assistantships also available. Support available to part-time students. Financial award application deadline: 2/1; financial award applicants required to submit FAFSA. *Faculty research:* Archaeology, paleoanthropology, zooarchaeology, Native American studies. ecological archaeology, lithic analysis, cultural anthropology. *Total annual research expenditures:* $111,129. *Unit head:* Dr. Peter Stromberg, Chairperson, 918-631-2370, Fax: 918-631-2540, E-mail: peter-stromberg@utulsa.edu. *Application contact:* Dr. Thomas Foster, Advisor, 918-631-3082, Fax: 918-631-2540, E-mail: thomas-foster@utulsa.edu.
Website: http://artsandsciences.utulsa.edu/academics/departments-schools/anthropology/

University of Utah, Graduate School, College of Social and Behavioral Science, Department of Anthropology, Salt Lake City, UT 84112. Offers M Phil, MA, MS, PhD. Part-time programs available. *Faculty:* 17 full-time (6 women), 17 part-time/adjunct (13 women). *Students:* 7 full-time (5 women), 34 part-time (18 women); includes 8 minority (2 American Indian or Alaska Native, non-Hispanic/Latino; 1 Asian, non-Hispanic/Latino; 2 Hispanic/Latino; 1 Native Hawaiian or other Pacific Islander, non-Hispanic/Latino; 2 Two or more races, non-Hispanic/Latino), 1 international. Average age 36. 39 applicants, 28% accepted, 11 enrolled. In 2014, 7 master's, 5 doctorates awarded. *Degree requirements:* For master's, variable foreign language requirement, comprehensive exam, thesis optional; for doctorate, variable foreign language requirement, comprehensive exam (for some programs), thesis/dissertation. *Entrance requirements:* For master's, GRE General Test, minimum undergraduate GPA of 3.0; for doctorate, GRE General Test, minimum GPA of 3.0. Additional exam requirements/recommendations for international students: Required—TOEFL (minimum score 500 paper-based). *Application deadline:* For fall admission, 1/15 for domestic and international students. Application fee: $55 ($65 for international students). Electronic applications accepted. *Expenses:* Expenses: $12,000 per semester (for PhD). *Financial support:* In 2014–15, 18 students received support, including 12 fellowships with full tuition reimbursements available, 1 research assistantship with full tuition reimbursement available (averaging $18,000 per year), 16 teaching assistantships with full tuition reimbursements available (averaging $12,500 per year); career-related internships or fieldwork, health care benefits, and unspecified assistantships also available. Financial award application deadline: 11/15. *Faculty research:* Evolutionary ecology, anthropological genetics, hunter-gatherers, North American archaeology. *Total annual research expenditures:* $288,569. *Unit head:* Dr. Leslie Ann Knapp, Chair, 801-581-6251, Fax: 801-581-6252, E-mail: leslie.knapp@anthro.utah.edu. *Application contact:* Linda K. Morgan, Administrative Assistant, 801-581-6251, Fax: 801-581-6252, E-mail: linda.morgan@anthro.utah.edu.
Website: http://www.anthro.utah.edu/

University of Victoria, Faculty of Graduate Studies, Faculty of Social Sciences, Department of Anthropology, Victoria, BC V8W 2Y2, Canada. Offers MA. Part-time programs available. *Degree requirements:* For master's, comprehensive exam (for some programs), thesis (for some programs). *Entrance requirements:* For master's, minimum B+ average in last 2 years of undergraduate course work, writing sample. Additional exam requirements/recommendations for international students: Required—TOEFL (minimum score 575 paper-based), IELTS (minimum score 7).

University of Virginia, College and Graduate School of Arts and Sciences, Department of Anthropology, Charlottesville, VA 22903. Offers MA, PhD. *Faculty:* 22 full-time (11 women), 1 (woman) part-time/adjunct. *Students:* 44 full-time (30 women); includes 8 minority (3 Black or African American, non-Hispanic/Latino; 1 Asian, non-Hispanic/Latino; 2 Hispanic/Latino; 2 Two or more races, non-Hispanic/Latino), 9 international. Average age 31. 75 applicants, 15% accepted, 5 enrolled. In 2014, 5 master's, 7 doctorates awarded. *Degree requirements:* For master's, one foreign language, thesis; for doctorate, 2 foreign languages, thesis/dissertation. *Entrance requirements:* For master's and doctorate, GRE General Test, GRE Subject Test, 3 letters of recommendation. Additional exam requirements/recommendations for international students: Required—TOEFL (minimum score 600 paper-based; 90 iBT), IELTS (minimum score 7). *Application deadline:* For fall admission, 12/15 for domestic and international students. Applications are processed on a rolling basis. Application fee: $60. Electronic applications accepted. *Expenses:* Tuition, state resident: full-time $14,164; part-time $349 per credit hour. Tuition, nonresident: full-time $23,722; part-time $1300 per credit hour. *Required fees:* $2514. *Financial support:* Application deadline: 3/15; applicants required to submit FAFSA. *Unit head:* Susan McKinnon, Chair, 434-924-6822, Fax: 434-924-1350, E-mail: sm@virginia.edu. *Application contact:* Dan Lefkowitz, Director of Graduate Studies, 434-982-3093, Fax: 434-924-6977, E-mail: dl2h@virginia.edu.
Website: http://anthropology.virginia.edu/

University of Washington, Graduate School, College of Arts and Sciences, Department of Anthropology, Seattle, WA 98195. Offers MA, PhD. *Faculty:* 34 full-time (17 women), 15 part-time/adjunct (7 women). *Students:* 52 full-time (33 women), 6 part-time (5 women); includes 13 minority (2 Black or African American, non-Hispanic/Latino; 3 American Indian or Alaska Native, non-Hispanic/Latino; 2 Asian, non-Hispanic/Latino; 5 Hispanic/Latino; 1 Native Hawaiian or other Pacific Islander, non-Hispanic/Latino), 13 international. Average age 32. 64 applicants, 17% accepted, 2 enrolled. In 2014, 7 master's, 7 doctorates awarded. Terminal master's awarded for partial completion of doctoral program. *Degree requirements:* For master's, one foreign language, comprehensive exam (for some programs), thesis optional; for doctorate, one foreign language, comprehensive exam (for some programs), thesis/dissertation (for some programs). *Entrance requirements:* For doctorate, GRE General Test, minimum GPA of 3.6. Additional exam requirements/recommendations for international students: Recommended—TOEFL (minimum score 500 paper-based; 61 iBT), IELTS (minimum score 6). *Application deadline:* For fall admission, 12/15 for domestic and international students. Application fee: $85. Electronic applications accepted. *Financial support:* In 2014–15, 45 students received support, including 10 fellowships with full tuition reimbursements available (averaging $15,000 per year), 13 research assistantships with full tuition reimbursements available (averaging $15,000 per year), 23 teaching assistantships with full tuition reimbursements available (averaging $15,000 per year); Federal Work-Study, institutionally sponsored loans, scholarships/grants, traineeships, health care benefits, and unspecified assistantships also available. Financial award application deadline: 1/15; financial award applicants required to submit FAFSA. *Faculty research:* Sociocultural anthropology, biocultural anthropology, archaeology, environmental anthropology, medical anthropology. *Unit head:* Dr. Janelle S. Taylor, Chair, 206-543-4793, Fax: 206-543-3285, E-mail: jstaylor@u.washington.edu. *Application contact:* Catherine M. Zeigler, Graduate Program Assistant, 206-685-1562, Fax: 206-543-3285, E-mail: gradanth@u.washington.edu.
Website: http://depts.washington.edu/anthweb/

University of Waterloo, Graduate Studies, Faculty of Arts, Department of Anthropology, Waterloo, ON N2L 3G1, Canada. Offers anthropology (MA); public issues (MA). *Entrance requirements:* Additional exam requirements/recommendations for international students: Required—TOEFL. Electronic applications accepted. *Faculty research:* Applied socio-cultural anthropology and archaeology.

The University of Western Ontario, Faculty of Graduate Studies, Social Sciences Division, Department of Anthropology, London, ON N6A 5B8, Canada. Offers MA, PhD. *Degree requirements:* For master's, thesis; for doctorate, thesis/dissertation. *Entrance requirements:* For master's, minimum B average, honors BA. Additional exam requirements/recommendations for international students: Required—TOEFL. Electronic applications accepted. *Faculty research:* Sociocultural anthropology, bioarchaeology, linguistics.

University of West Florida, College of Arts and Sciences: Arts, Division of Anthropology and Archaeology, Pensacola, FL 32514-5750. Offers anthropology (MA); historical archaeology (MA). *Degree requirements:* For master's, internship or thesis. *Entrance requirements:* For master's, GRE, transcripts, minimum GPA of 3.0, 3 letters of recommendation, writing sample, letter of intent describing background, study interests, and professional goals. Additional exam requirements/recommendations for international students: Required—TOEFL (minimum score 550 paper-based).

University of Wisconsin–Madison, Graduate School, College of Letters and Science, Department of Anthropology, Madison, WI 53706-1380. Offers archaeology (PhD); biological anthropology (PhD); cultural anthropology (PhD). Terminal master's awarded for partial completion of doctoral program. *Degree requirements:* For doctorate, thesis/dissertation. *Entrance requirements:* For doctorate, qualifying exam. Electronic applications accepted. *Expenses:* Tuition, state resident: full-time $10,723; part-time $745 per credit. Tuition, nonresident: full-time $24,054; part-time $1578 per credit. *Required fees:* $374 per semester. Tuition and fees vary according to course load, program and reciprocity agreements. *Faculty research:* Archaeology, biological, anthropology, cultural anthropology.

University of Wisconsin–Milwaukee, Graduate School, College of Letters and Sciences, Department of Anthropology, Milwaukee, WI 53201-0413. Offers anthropology (PhD); museum studies (Certificate). *Degree requirements:* For master's, thesis or alternative; for doctorate, one foreign language, thesis/dissertation, departmental qualifying exam. *Entrance requirements:* For master's, GRE; for doctorate, GRE, minimum GPA of 3.0, master's degree. Additional exam requirements/recommendations for international students: Required—TOEFL (minimum score 550 paper-based; 79 iBT), IELTS (minimum score 6.5).

University of Wyoming, College of Arts and Sciences, Department of Anthropology, Laramie, WY 82071. Offers MA, PhD. Part-time programs available. Terminal master's awarded for partial completion of doctoral program. *Degree requirements:* For master's, one foreign language, comprehensive exam, thesis optional; for doctorate, one foreign language, comprehensive exam, thesis/dissertation. *Entrance requirements:* For master's and doctorate, GRE General Test, minimum GPA of 3.0. Electronic applications accepted. *Faculty research:* Paleo-Indian archaeology, osteology, faunal analysis, lithic analysis, hunter-gatherers.

Vanderbilt University, Graduate School, Department of Anthropology, Nashville, TN 37240-1001. Offers MA, PhD. *Faculty:* 13 full-time (4 women). *Students:* 31 full-time (22 women); includes 5 minority (1 American Indian or Alaska Native, non-Hispanic/Latino; 4 Hispanic/Latino), 11 international. Average age 32. 64 applicants, 5% accepted, 2 enrolled. In 2014, 6 master's, 3 doctorates awarded. *Degree requirements:* For master's, comprehensive exam, thesis or alternative; for doctorate, one foreign language, comprehensive exam, thesis/dissertation, general, qualifying, and final exams. *Entrance requirements:* For master's and doctorate, GRE General Test. Additional exam requirements/recommendations for international students: Required—TOEFL (minimum score 570 paper-based; 88 iBT). *Application deadline:* For fall admission, 1/15 for domestic and international students. Application fee: $0. Electronic applications accepted. *Expenses: Tuition:* Full-time $42,768; part-time $1782 per credit hour. *Required fees:* $422. One-time fee: $30 full-time. *Financial support:* Fellowships with full and partial tuition reimbursements, research assistantships with full tuition reimbursements, teaching assistantships with full tuition reimbursements, career-related internships or fieldwork, Federal Work-Study, institutionally sponsored loans, scholarships/grants, and health care benefits available. Financial award application deadline: 1/15; financial award applicants required to submit CSS PROFILE or FAFSA. *Faculty research:* Archaeology, ethnohistory and ethnography, epigraphy, conflict theory, Latin America. *Unit head:* Dr. John Janusek, Director of Graduate Studies, 615-343-6122, Fax: 615-343-0230, E-mail: john.w.janusek@vanderbilt.edu. *Application contact:* Sally Miller, Administrative Assistant, 615-343-6120, Fax: 615-343-0230, E-mail: sally.c.miller@vanderbilt.edu.
Website: http://as.vanderbilt.edu/anthropology/

Washington State University, College of Liberal Arts, Department of Anthropology, Pullman, WA 99164. Offers archaeology (MA, PhD); cultural anthropology (PhD); evolutionary anthropology (MA, PhD). Program applications must be made through the Pullman campus. *Faculty:* 20 full-time (10 women), 1 (woman) part-time/adjunct. *Students:* 59 full-time (33 women), 9 part-time (4 women); includes 8 minority (2 Asian, non-Hispanic/Latino; 4 Hispanic/Latino; 2 Two or more races, non-Hispanic/Latino), 9 international. Average age 30. 85 applicants, 40% accepted, 17 enrolled. In 2014, 10 master's, 3 doctorates awarded. *Degree requirements:* For master's, one foreign language, comprehensive exam (for some programs), thesis; for doctorate, one foreign language, comprehensive exam, thesis/dissertation, written and oral preliminary exam. *Entrance requirements:* For master's and doctorate, GRE General Test, curriculum vitae, statement of intent, official transcripts, 3 letters of recommendation, one or two undergraduate papers (from BA/BS applicants), minimum GPA of 3.0. Additional exam requirements/recommendations for international students: Required—TOEFL (minimum score 550 paper-based), IELTS. *Application deadline:* For fall admission, 1/10 priority date for domestic and international students; for spring admission, 7/1 for domestic and international students. Application fee: $75. Electronic applications accepted. *Expenses:* Tuition, state resident: full-time $11,768. Tuition, nonresident: full-time $25,200. *Required fees:* $960. Tuition and fees vary according to program. *Financial support:* In 2014–15, 67 students received support, including 5 research assistantships with full tuition reimbursements available (averaging $13,706 per year), 5 teaching assistantships with full tuition reimbursements available (averaging $13,952 per year); fellowships, Federal Work-Study, scholarships/grants, health care benefits, and unspecified assistantships also available. Support available to part-time students. Financial award application deadline: 2/15; financial award applicants required to submit FAFSA. *Faculty research:* Quantitative analysis of archaeological data, simulation of aspects of prehistoric behavior, subsistence strategies, language use, inequality and

poverty, gender, pedagogy, Mexico/U.S. border region, childhood, infectious and parasitic diseases, the analysis of mitochondrial DNA (mtDNA) and Y-chromosomal DNA. *Total annual research expenditures:* $673,000. *Unit head:* Dr. Andrew Duff, Chair, 509-335-3441, Fax: 509-335-3999, E-mail: duff@wsu.edu. *Application contact:* Graduate School Admissions, 800-GRADWSU, Fax: 509-335-1949, E-mail: gradsch@wsu.edu.
Website: http://libarts.wsu.edu/anthro/

Washington University in St. Louis, Graduate School of Arts and Sciences, Department of Anthropology, St. Louis, MO 63130-4899. Offers PhD. Terminal master's awarded for partial completion of doctoral program. *Degree requirements:* For doctorate, thesis/dissertation. *Entrance requirements:* For doctorate, GRE General Test. Additional exam requirements/recommendations for international students: Required—TOEFL. Electronic applications accepted. *Faculty research:* Sociocultural anthropology (including medical anthropology), archaeology, physical anthropology (including primate studies, paleontology and human biology).

Wayne State University, College of Liberal Arts and Sciences, Department of Anthropology, Detroit, MI 48202. Offers MA, PhD. Doctoral programs admit for fall only. Part-time programs available. *Students:* 29 full-time (22 women), 20 part-time (12 women); includes 8 minority (3 Black or African American, non-Hispanic/Latino; 4 Hispanic/Latino; 1 Two or more races, non-Hispanic/Latino), 2 international. Average age 34. 37 applicants, 54% accepted, 17 enrolled. In 2014, 11 master's, 3 doctorates awarded. *Degree requirements:* For master's, thesis (for some programs); for doctorate, one foreign language, thesis/dissertation. *Entrance requirements:* For master's, three letters of recommendation, completion of introduction to anthropology, letter of intent, writing sample, minimum undergraduate GPA of 3.2; for doctorate, GRE, three letters of recommendation, completion of introduction to anthropology, letter of intent, writing sample, minimum undergraduate GPA of 3.2. Additional exam requirements/recommendations for international students: Required—TOEFL (minimum score 550 paper-based; 79 iBT), TWE (minimum score 5.5), Michigan English Language Assessment Battery (minimum score 85); Recommended—IELTS (minimum score 6.5). *Application deadline:* For fall admission, 1/10 for domestic and international students; for winter admission, 10/1 for domestic students, 9/10 for international students. Application fee: $0. Electronic applications accepted. *Expenses:* Tuition, state resident: full-time $10,294; part-time $571.90 per credit hour. Tuition, nonresident: full-time $29,730; part-time $1238.75 per credit hour. *Required fees:* $1365; $43.50 per credit hour. $291.10 per semester. Tuition and fees vary according to course load and program. *Financial support:* In 2014–15, 34 students received support, including 3 fellowships with tuition reimbursements available (averaging $17,333 per year), 1 research assistantship (averaging $16,838 per year), 6 teaching assistantships with tuition reimbursements available (averaging $16,986 per year); scholarships/grants, health care benefits, and unspecified assistantships also available. Financial award application deadline: 3/31; financial award applicants required to submit FAFSA. *Faculty research:* Business anthropology and organizational culture, African and African-American religions, medical anthropology, Latin American anthropology and archaeology, urban anthropology and historical archaeology. *Total annual research expenditures:* $142,000.

Unit head: Dr. Thomas Killion, Chair, 313-577-6961, Fax: 313-577-5958, E-mail: thomas.killion@wayne.edu. *Application contact:* Dr. Stephen Chrisomalis, Director of Graduate Studies, 313-577-9922, E-mail: chrisomalis@wayne.edu.
Website: http://clasweb.clas.wayne.edu/anthropology

Western Kentucky University, Graduate Studies, Potter College of Arts and Letters, Department of Folk Studies and Anthropology, Bowling Green, KY 42101. Offers folk studies (MA). *Degree requirements:* For master's, comprehensive exam, thesis optional, written exam. *Entrance requirements:* For master's, GRE General Test, minimum GPA of 3.0. Additional exam requirements/recommendations for international students: Required—TOEFL (minimum score 555 paper-based; 79 iBT). *Faculty research:* Public folklore, folklore and education, vernacular belief, music and culture, historic presentation.

Western Michigan University, Graduate College, College of Arts and Sciences, Department of Anthropology, Kalamazoo, MI 49008. Offers MA. *Degree requirements:* For master's, comprehensive exam, thesis. *Application deadline:* For fall admission, 2/15 for domestic students. *Financial support:* Application deadline: 2/15. *Application contact:* Admissions and Orientation, 269-387-2000, Fax: 269-387-2096.

Western Washington University, Graduate School, College of Humanities and Social Sciences, Department of Anthropology, Bellingham, WA 98225-5996. Offers MA. Part-time programs available. *Degree requirements:* For master's, thesis. *Entrance requirements:* For master's, GRE General Test, minimum GPA of 3.0 in last 60 semester hours or last 90 quarter hours. Additional exam requirements/recommendations for international students: Required—TOEFL (minimum score 567 paper-based). Electronic applications accepted. *Faculty research:* Peoples and culture of the Pacific Rim; prehistory of North America; applied health; community-based action research; globalization and human rights.

Wichita State University, Graduate School, Fairmount College of Liberal Arts and Sciences, Department of Anthropology, Wichita, KS 67260. Offers MA. Part-time programs available. *Entrance requirements:* For master's, minimum GPA of 2.75 in last 60 hours and 3.0 in anthropology. *Unit head:* Dr. Peer H. Moore-Jansen, Chair, 316-978-3195, E-mail: pmojan@wichita.edu. *Application contact:* Jordan Oleson, Admission Coordinator, 316-978-3095, E-mail: jordan.oleson@wichita.edu.
Website: http://www.wichita.edu/anthropology

Yale University, Graduate School of Arts and Sciences, Department of Anthropology, New Haven, CT 06520. Offers M Phil, MA, PhD. *Degree requirements:* For doctorate, thesis/dissertation. *Entrance requirements:* For master's and doctorate, GRE General Test. *Faculty research:* Linguistics, national identity.

York University, Faculty of Graduate Studies, Faculty of Liberal Arts and Professional Studies, Program in Social Anthropology, Toronto, ON M3J 1P3, Canada. Offers MA, PhD. Part-time programs available. *Degree requirements:* For master's, thesis or alternative; for doctorate, comprehensive exam, thesis/dissertation. Electronic applications accepted.

Applied Social Research

California State University, Dominguez Hills, College of Natural and Behavioral Sciences, Program in Sociology, Carson, CA 90747-0001. Offers social research (Certificate); sociology (MA). Part-time and evening/weekend programs available. *Faculty:* 4 full-time (2 women), 2 part-time/adjunct (1 woman). *Students:* 15 full-time (9 women), 20 part-time (17 women); includes 32 minority (13 Black or African American, non-Hispanic/Latino; 1 American Indian or Alaska Native, non-Hispanic/Latino; 1 Asian, non-Hispanic/Latino; 17 Hispanic/Latino). Average age 32. 25 applicants, 60% accepted, 9 enrolled. In 2014, 21 master's awarded. *Degree requirements:* For master's, comprehensive exam, thesis. *Entrance requirements:* For master's and Certificate, minimum GPA of 2.85. *Application deadline:* For fall admission, 6/1 for domestic students. Application fee: $55. *Expenses:* Tuition, state resident: full-time $6738; part-time $3960 per year. Tuition, nonresident: full-time $13,434; part-time $8370 per year. *Required fees:* $623; $623 per year. *Faculty research:* Community studies, social movements, criminology. *Unit head:* Dr. Katy Pinto, Program Coordinator, 310-243-3180, E-mail: kpinto@csudh.edu. *Application contact:* Brandy McLelland, Director of Student Information Services/Registrar, 310-243-3645, E-mail: bmclelland@csudh.edu.
Website: http://www4.csudh.edu/sociology/master/index

Concordia University, School of Theology, Irvine, CA 92612-3299. Offers Christian leadership (MA); research in theology (MA); theology and culture (MA). Part-time and evening/weekend programs available. *Degree requirements:* For master's, project/thesis or vicarage. *Entrance requirements:* For master's, official college transcript(s), statement of intent, 2 references, interview. Additional exam requirements/recommendations for international students: Required—TOEFL. Electronic applications accepted. *Expenses:* Contact institution.

Hunter College of the City University of New York, Graduate School, School of Arts and Sciences, Department of Sociology, Program in Applied Social Research, New York, NY 10065-5085. Offers MS. Part-time and evening/weekend programs available. *Faculty:* 3 full-time (2 women), 1 (woman) part-time/adjunct. *Students:* 4 full-time (2 women), 10 part-time (6 women); includes 6 minority (3 Black or African American, non-Hispanic/Latino; 3 Hispanic/Latino). Average age 32. 17 applicants, 59% accepted, 3 enrolled. In 2014, 9 master's awarded. *Degree requirements:* For master's, internship, research reports. *Entrance requirements:* For master's, GRE General Test or GMAT, 3 credits of course work in statistics, research methods, background in sociology or related social science. Additional exam requirements/recommendations for international students: Required—TOEFL. *Application deadline:* For fall admission, 4/1 for domestic students, 2/1 for international students; for spring admission, 11/1 for domestic students, 9/1 for international students. Applications are processed on a rolling basis. *Financial support:* Fellowships, research assistantships, teaching assistantships, career-related internships or fieldwork, Federal Work-Study, institutionally sponsored loans, scholarships/grants, and tuition waivers (full and partial) available. Support available to part-time students. *Faculty research:* Consumer behavior, new electronic media, voting behavior, policy analysis, sociomedicine. *Unit head:* Dr. Howard Lune, Director, 212-772-5641, E-mail: hlune@hunter.cuny.edu. *Application contact:* Milena Solo, Director of Graduate Admissions, 212-772-4480, E-mail: admission@hunter.cuny.edu.
Website: http://www.hunter.cuny.edu/sociology/graduate

Laurentian University, School of Graduate Studies and Research, Programme in Sociology, Sudbury, ON P3E 2C6, Canada. Offers applied social research (MA). Part-time programs available. *Entrance requirements:* For master's, honors degree in sociology or equivalent. *Faculty research:* Work foundations, managing AIDS organization, tracking laid-off mine workers.

The New School, The New School for Social Research, New York, NY 10003. Offers M Phil, MA, MS, DS Sc, PhD. Part-time and evening/weekend programs available. Terminal master's awarded for partial completion of doctoral program. *Degree requirements:* For master's, variable foreign language requirement, exam or thesis; for doctorate, variable foreign language requirement, comprehensive exam, thesis/dissertation, qualifying exam. *Entrance requirements:* For master's, GRE General Test; for doctorate, GRE General Test, MA. Additional exam requirements/recommendations for international students: Required—TOEFL (minimum score 600 paper-based; 100 iBT). Electronic applications accepted. *Expenses:* Contact institution. *Faculty research:* Civil society and democracy, international movements of refugees, minority use of health services, memory, morality and genetics.

New York University, Steinhardt School of Culture, Education, and Human Development, Department of Humanities and Social Sciences in the Professions, Program in Applied Statistics for Social Science Research, New York, NY 10012-1019. Offers MS. *Students:* 2 full-time (both women), 1 international. Average age 25. 72 applicants, 32% accepted, 2 enrolled. *Entrance requirements:* For master's, GRE, statement of purpose, resume/curriculum vitae, two letters of recommendation, transcripts. Additional exam requirements/recommendations for international students: Required—TOEFL. *Application deadline:* For fall admission, 12/1 priority date for domestic and international students. Electronic applications accepted. *Faculty research:* Causal inference, multi-level models, multivariate analysis, psychometrics, survey research and design. *Unit head:* Dr. Jonathan L. Zimmerman, Chairperson, 212-998-5049, Fax: 212-995-4832. *Application contact:* 212-998-5030, Fax: 212-995-4328, E-mail: steinhardt.gradadmissions@nyu.edu.
Website: http://steinhardt.nyu.edu/humsocsci/applied_statistics/

Portland State University, Graduate Studies, Graduate School of Social Work, Portland, OR 97207-0751. Offers social work (MSW); social work and social research (PhD). *Accreditation:* CSWE (one or more programs are accredited). Part-time programs available. *Faculty:* 32 full-time (23 women), 32 part-time/adjunct (21 women). *Students:* 428 full-time (340 women), 148 part-time (115 women); includes 151 minority (33 Black or African American, non-Hispanic/Latino; 15 American Indian or Alaska Native, non-Hispanic/Latino; 13 Asian, non-Hispanic/Latino; 65 Hispanic/Latino; 25 Two or more races, non-Hispanic/Latino), 4 international. Average age 35. 707 applicants, 41% accepted, 221 enrolled. In 2014, 173 master's, 2 doctorates awarded. *Degree requirements:* For doctorate, comprehensive exam, thesis/dissertation, residency. *Entrance requirements:* For master's, minimum GPA of 3.0 in upper-division course work or 2.75 overall; for doctorate, GRE General Test, 4 references. Additional exam requirements/recommendations for international students: Required—TOEFL (minimum score 550 paper-based; 80 iBT). *Application deadline:* For fall admission, 2/1 for domestic and international students. Application fee: $50. *Expenses:* Tuition, state resident: part-time $222 per credit. Tuition, nonresident: part-time $527 per credit. *Required fees:* $22 per contact hour. $100 per quarter. Tuition and fees vary according to program. *Financial support:* In 2014–15, 2 research assistantships with full and partial tuition reimbursements (averaging $10,375 per year), 9 teaching assistantships with full and partial tuition reimbursements (averaging $11,846 per year) were awarded; career-related internships or fieldwork, Federal Work-Study, scholarships/grants, tuition

waivers (partial), and unspecified assistantships also available. Support available to part-time students. Financial award application deadline: 3/1; financial award applicants required to submit FAFSA. *Faculty research:* Child welfare; child mental health; social welfare policies and services; work, family, and dependent care; adult mental health. *Total annual research expenditures:* $12.6 million. *Unit head:* Dr. Laura B. Nissen, Dean, 503-725-3997, Fax: 503-725-5545, E-mail: nissen@pdx.edu. *Application contact:* Prof. Sarah Bradley, Director of MSW Program, 503-725-8028, Fax: 503-725-5545, E-mail: bradles@pdx.edu.
Website: http://www.ssw.pdx.edu/

University of California, Los Angeles, Graduate Division, School of Public Affairs, Los Angeles, CA 90095. Offers MA, MPP, MSW, PhD, JD/MA, JD/MSW, MA/MA, MBA/MA, MD/PhD. *Accreditation:* CSWE. *Degree requirements:* For doctorate, thesis/dissertation, oral and written qualifying exams. *Entrance requirements:* For master's, minimum GPA of 3.0; for doctorate, minimum undergraduate GPA of 3.0. Additional exam requirements/recommendations for international students: Required—TOEFL. Electronic applications accepted.

Virginia Commonwealth University, Graduate School, College of Humanities and Sciences, Wilder School of Government and Public Affairs, Department of Sociology, Richmond, VA 23284-9005. Offers applied social research (CASR); sociology (MS). *Degree requirements:* For master's, thesis optional. *Entrance requirements:* For master's, GRE General Test. Additional exam requirements/recommendations for international students: Required—TOEFL (minimum score 600 paper-based; 100 iBT); Recommended—IELTS (minimum score 6.5). Electronic applications accepted.

West Virginia University, Eberly College of Arts and Sciences, School of Applied Social Sciences, Division of Sociology and Anthropology, Morgantown, WV 26506. Offers applied social research (MA). Part-time programs available. *Degree requirements:* For master's, thesis or alternative. *Entrance requirements:* For master's, GRE General Test, minimum GPA of 2.75. Additional exam requirements/recommendations for international students: Required—TOEFL. *Faculty research:* Applied sociology, stratification, social/complex organization, research methodology criminology.

Archaeology

American University of Beirut, Graduate Programs, Faculty of Arts and Sciences, Beirut, Lebanon. Offers anthropology (MA); Arab and Middle Eastern history (PhD); Arabic language and literature (MA, PhD); archaeology (MA); biology (MS); cell and molecular biology (PhD); chemistry (MS); clinical psychology (MA); computational sciences (MS); computer science (MS); economics (MA); English language (MA); English literature (MA); environmental policy planning (MS); financial economics (MAFE); geology (MS); history (MA); mathematics (MA, MS); media studies (MA); Middle Eastern studies (MA); physics (MS); political studies (MA); psychology (MA); public administration (MA); sociology (MA); statistics (MA, MS); theoretical physics (PhD); transnational American studies (MA). Part-time programs available. *Faculty:* 107 full-time (32 women), 6 part-time/adjunct (2 women). *Students:* 230 full-time (161 women), 209 part-time (146 women). Average age 26. 261 applicants, 70% accepted, 83 enrolled. In 2014, 68 master's, 2 doctorates awarded. *Degree requirements:* For master's, one foreign language, comprehensive exam, thesis (for some programs); for doctorate, one foreign language, comprehensive exam, thesis/dissertation. *Entrance requirements:* For master's, GRE (for some MA/MS programs), letter of recommendation; for doctorate, GRE, letters of recommendation. Additional exam requirements/recommendations for international students: Required—TOEFL (minimum score 600 paper-based; 97 iBT), IELTS (minimum score 7). *Application deadline:* For fall admission, 4/1 for domestic and international students; for spring admission, 11/1 for domestic and international students. Application fee: $50. Electronic applications accepted. *Expenses: Tuition:* Full-time $15,462; part-time $859 per credit. *Required fees:* $692. Tuition and fees vary according to course load and program. *Financial support:* Research assistantships, career-related internships or fieldwork, institutionally sponsored loans, scholarships/grants, health care benefits, and unspecified assistantships available. Financial award application deadline: 2/4; financial award applicants required to submit FAFSA. *Faculty research:* Determinants of language proficiency among Arab learners of English as a foreign language; opinion mining, information retrieval, runtime verification, high performance computing; solar and fuel cells, self-organizing systems, heterocyclic chemistry, air and water chemistry; complex analysis, harmonic analysis, number theory; social and political psychology, clinical psychology; thin films physics and technology; theory of soft matter; religious and ethnic conflict; sports and politics. *Total annual research expenditures:* $966,000. *Unit head:* Dr. Patrick McGreevy, Dean, 961-1374374 Ext. 3800, Fax: 961-1744461, E-mail: pm07@aub.edu.lb. *Application contact:* Dr. Salim Kanaan, Director, Admissions Office, 961-1350000 Ext. 2590, Fax: 961-1750775, E-mail: sk00@aub.edu.lb.
Website: http://www.aub.edu.lb/fas/

Arizona State University at the Tempe campus, College of Liberal Arts and Sciences, School of Human Evolution and Social Change, Tempe, AZ 85287-2402. Offers anthropology (MA, PhD), including anthropology (PhD), archaeology (PhD), bioarchaeology (PhD), evolutionary (PhD), museum studies (MA), sociocultural (PhD); applied mathematics for the life and social sciences (PhD); environmental social science (PhD), including environmental social science, urbanism; global health (MA, PhD), including complex adaptive systems science (PhD), evolutionary global health sciences (PhD), health and culture (PhD), urbanism (PhD); immigration studies (Graduate Certificate). Terminal master's awarded for partial completion of doctoral program. *Degree requirements:* For master's, thesis or alternative, interactive Program of Study (iPOS) submitted before completing 50 percent of required credit hours; for doctorate, comprehensive exam, thesis/dissertation, interactive Program of Study (iPOS) submitted before completing 50 percent of required credit hours. *Entrance requirements:* For master's and doctorate, GRE, minimum GPA of 3.0 or equivalent in last 2 years of work leading to bachelor's degree. Additional exam requirements/recommendations for international students: Required—TOEFL, IELTS, or PTE. Electronic applications accepted.

Boston University, Graduate School of Arts and Sciences, Department of Archaeology, Boston, MA 02215. Offers MA, PhD. *Students:* 48 full-time (30 women), 1 (woman) part-time; includes 6 minority (1 Black or African American, non-Hispanic/Latino; 1 Asian, non-Hispanic/Latino; 2 Hispanic/Latino; 2 Two or more races, non-Hispanic/Latino), 8 international. Average age 30. 119 applicants, 13% accepted, 8 enrolled. In 2014, 2 master's, 8 doctorates awarded. Terminal master's awarded for partial completion of doctoral program. *Degree requirements:* For master's, one foreign language, comprehensive exam, thesis or alternative; for doctorate, 2 foreign languages, comprehensive exam, thesis/dissertation. *Entrance requirements:* For master's, GRE General Test, 3 letters of recommendation; for doctorate, GRE General Test, scholarly writing sample, 3 letters of recommendation. Additional exam requirements/recommendations for international students: Required—TOEFL (minimum score 550 paper-based; 84 iBT). *Application deadline:* For fall admission, 1/5 for domestic and international students. Application fee: $80. *Expenses: Tuition:* Full-time $45,686; part-time $1428 per credit hour. *Required fees:* $660; $60 per semester. Tuition and fees vary according to program. *Financial support:* In 2014–15, 45 students received support, including 6 fellowships with full tuition reimbursements available (averaging $20,500 per year), 1 research assistantship with full tuition reimbursement available (averaging $20,500 per year), 7 teaching assistantships with full tuition reimbursements available (averaging $20,500 per year); career-related internships or fieldwork, Federal Work-Study, scholarships/grants, health care benefits, and unspecified assistantships also available. Support available to part-time students. Financial award application deadline: 1/5. *Unit head:* James McCann, Chairman, 617-353-2637, Fax: 617-353-6800, E-mail: mccann@bu.edu. *Application contact:* Maria Sousa, Senior Program Coordinator, 617-353-3415, Fax: 617-353-6800, E-mail: mhsousa@bu.edu.
Website: http://www.bu.edu/ARCHAEOLOGY/

Brown University, Graduate School, Department of Egyptology and Ancient Western Asian Studies, Providence, RI 02912. Offers ancient western Asian studies (PhD); Egyptology (PhD); history of the exact sciences in antiquity (PhD). *Degree requirements:* For doctorate, 2 foreign languages, comprehensive exam, thesis/dissertation. *Entrance requirements:* For doctorate, GRE General Test.

Brown University, Graduate School, Joukowsky Institute for Archaeology and the Ancient World, Providence, RI 02912. Offers PhD. *Degree requirements:* For doctorate, thesis/dissertation.

Bryn Mawr College, Graduate School of Arts and Sciences, Department of Classical and Near Eastern Archaeology, Bryn Mawr, PA 19010-2899. Offers MA, PhD. Part-time programs available. *Faculty:* 6 full-time (3 women), 1 (woman) part-time/adjunct. *Students:* 21 full-time (15 women), 2 part-time (0 women); includes 1 minority (Hispanic/Latino), 1 international. Average age 30. 27 applicants, 19% accepted, 4 enrolled. In 2014, 1 doctorate awarded. *Degree requirements:* For master's, 2 foreign languages, thesis; for doctorate, 3 foreign languages, comprehensive exam, thesis/dissertation. *Entrance requirements:* For master's and doctorate, GRE General Test. Additional exam requirements/recommendations for international students: Required—TOEFL (minimum score 600 paper-based). *Application deadline:* For fall admission, 1/3 for domestic and international students. Application fee: $50. *Expenses: Tuition:* Full-time $37,920. *Financial support:* In 2014–15, 15 fellowships with partial tuition reimbursements (averaging $18,100 per year), 2 teaching assistantships with partial tuition reimbursements (averaging $18,500 per year) were awarded; Federal Work-Study and scholarships/grants also available. Support available to part-time students. Financial award application deadline: 1/3. *Unit head:* Maria Dantis, Graduate Program Administrator, 610-526-5074, E-mail: gsas@brynmawr.edu.

California State University, Northridge, Graduate Studies, College of Social and Behavioral Sciences, Department of Anthropology, Northridge, CA 91330. Offers general anthropology (MA); public archaeology (MA). *Students:* 14 full-time (10 women), 27 part-time (18 women); includes 12 minority (1 Asian, non-Hispanic/Latino; 8 Hispanic/Latino; 3 Two or more races, non-Hispanic/Latino). Average age 32. *Degree requirements:* For master's, thesis or alternative. *Entrance requirements:* For master's, GRE General Test or minimum GPA of 3.0. Additional exam requirements/recommendations for international students: Required—TOEFL. *Application deadline:* For fall admission, 11/30 for domestic students. Application fee: $55. *Expenses: Required fees:* $12,402. *Financial support:* Career-related internships or fieldwork, Federal Work-Study, and institutionally sponsored loans available. Financial award application deadline: 3/1. *Unit head:* Dr. Cathy Costin, Chair, 818-677-3331. *Application contact:* Dr. Cathy L. Costin, Graduate Adviser, 818-677-3324.
Website: http://www.csun.edu/csbs/departments/anthropology/index.html

Columbia University, Graduate School of Arts and Sciences, New York, NY 10027. Offers African-American studies (MA); American studies (MA); anthropology (MA, PhD); art history and archaeology (MA, PhD); astronomy (PhD); biological sciences (PhD); biotechnology (MA); chemical physics (PhD); chemistry (PhD); classical studies (MA, PhD); classics (MA, PhD); climate and society (MA); earth and environmental sciences (PhD); East Asia: regional studies (MA); East Asian languages and cultures (MA, PhD); ecology, evolution and environmental biology (MA), including conservation biology; ecology, evolution, and environmental biology (PhD), including ecology and evolutionary biology, evolutionary primatology; economics (PhD); English and comparative literature (MA, PhD); French and Romance philology (MA, PhD); Germanic languages (MA, PhD); global French studies (MA); Hispanic cultural studies (MA); history (PhD); history and literature (MA); human rights studies (MA); Islamic studies (MA); Italian (MA, PhD); Japanese pedagogy (MA); Jewish studies (MA); Latin America and the Caribbean: regional studies (MA); Latin American and Iberian cultures (PhD); mathematics (MA, PhD), including finance (MA); medieval and Renaissance studies (MA); Middle Eastern, South Asian, and African studies (MA, PhD); modern art: critical and curatorial studies (MA); modern European studies (MA); museum anthropology (MA); music (DMA, PhD); oral history (MA); philosophical foundations of physics (MA); philosophy (MA, PhD); physics (PhD); political science (MA, PhD); psychology (PhD); quantitative methods in the social sciences (MA); religion (MA, PhD); Russia, Eurasia and East Europe: regional studies (MA); Russian translation (MA); Slavic cultures (MA); Slavic languages (MA, PhD); sociology (MA, PhD); South Asian studies (MA); statistics (MA, PhD); theatre (PhD); JD/PhD; MA/MS; MD/PhD; MPA/MA. Dual-degree programs require admission to both Graduate School of Arts and Sciences and another Columbia school. Part-time and evening/weekend programs available. Terminal master's awarded for partial completion of doctoral program. *Degree requirements:* For master's, thesis (for some programs); for doctorate, comprehensive exam, thesis/dissertation. *Entrance requirements:* For master's and doctorate, GRE General Test, GRE Subject Test (for some programs). Electronic applications accepted. *Faculty research:* Humanities, natural sciences, social sciences.

Cornell University, Graduate School, Graduate Fields of Arts and Sciences, Field of Archaeology, Ithaca, NY 14853-0001. Offers environmental archaeology (MA); historical archaeology (MA); Latin American archaeology (MA); medieval archaeology (MA); Mediterranean and Near Eastern archaeology (MA); Stone Age archaeology (MA). *Degree requirements:* For master's, one foreign language, thesis. *Entrance*

requirements: For master's, GRE General Test, 3 letters of recommendation, sample of written work. Additional exam requirements/recommendations for international students: Required—TOEFL (minimum score 550 paper-based; 77 iBT). Electronic applications accepted. *Faculty research:* Anatolia, Lydia, Sardis, classical and Hellenistic Greece, science in archaeology, North American Indians, Stone Age Africa, Mayan trade.

Cornell University, Graduate School, Graduate Fields of Arts and Sciences, Field of History of Art, Archaeology and Visual Studies, Ithaca, NY 14853. Offers 19th century art (PhD); African, African American and African diaspora (PhD); American art (PhD); ancient art and archaeology (PhD); Asian American art (PhD); Baroque art (PhD); comparative modernities (PhD); digital art (PhD); East Asian art (PhD); history of photography (PhD); Islamic art (PhD); Latin American art (PhD); medieval art (PhD); modern art (PhD); Renaissance art (PhD); Southeast Asian art (PhD); theory and criticism (PhD); visual studies (PhD). *Degree requirements:* For doctorate, one foreign language, comprehensive exam, thesis/dissertation, general exams in 3 areas. *Entrance requirements:* For doctorate, GRE General Test, sample of written work, 3 letters of recommendation. Additional exam requirements/recommendations for international students: Required—TOEFL (minimum score 550 paper-based; 77 iBT). Electronic applications accepted.

Florida State University, The Graduate School, College of Arts and Sciences, Department of Classics, Tallahassee, FL 32306-1510. Offers ancient history (MA); classical archaeology (MA); classical civilization (MA); classics (MA, PhD), including classical archaeology (PhD), classics (PhD); Greek (MA); Greek and Latin (MA); Latin (MA). Part-time programs available. *Faculty:* 15 full-time (5 women). *Students:* 42 full-time (23 women); includes 2 minority (1 Black or African American, non-Hispanic/Latino; 1 Asian, non-Hispanic/Latino), 2 international. Average age 24. 61 applicants, 51% accepted, 10 enrolled. In 2014, 10 master's, 2 doctorates awarded. Terminal master's awarded for partial completion of doctoral program. *Degree requirements:* For master's, 2 foreign languages, comprehensive exam (for some programs), thesis or alternative; for doctorate, 4 foreign languages, comprehensive exam, thesis/dissertation. *Entrance requirements:* For master's, GRE General Test, minimum GPA of 3.0; for doctorate, GRE General Test, minimum GPA of 3.5. Additional exam requirements/recommendations for international students: Required—TOEFL. *Application deadline:* For fall admission, 1/15 priority date for domestic students, 2/15 for international students. Applications are processed on a rolling basis. Application fee: $30. Electronic applications accepted. *Expenses:* Tuition, state resident: part-time $403.51 per credit hour. Tuition, nonresident: part-time $1004.85 per credit hour. *Required fees:* $75.81 per credit hour. One-time fee: $20 part-time. Tuition and fees vary according to campus/location. *Financial support:* In 2014–15, 42 students received support, including 2 fellowships with full tuition reimbursements available (averaging $18,000 per year), research assistantships with full tuition reimbursements available (averaging $10,000 per year), 33 teaching assistantships with full tuition reimbursements available (averaging $10,000 per year); Federal Work-Study, institutionally sponsored loans, and tuition waivers (full and partial) also available. Support available to part-time students. Financial award application deadline: 1/15; financial award applicants required to submit FAFSA. *Faculty research:* Greek and Latin literature, classical archaeology, mythology, ancient history, religion. *Total annual research expenditures:* $100,000. *Unit head:* Dr. Daniel J. Pullen, Chairman, 850-644-0304, Fax: 850-644-4073, E-mail: dpullen@fsu.edu. *Application contact:* Dr. Allen Romano, Admissions Director, 850-644-0305, Fax: 850-644-4073, E-mail: aromano@fsu.edu.
Website: http://classics.fsu.edu/

Gordon-Conwell Theological Seminary, Graduate and Professional Programs, South Hamilton, MA 01982. Offers Biblical languages (MABL); church history (MACH); counseling (MACO); ministry (D Min); missions/evangelism (MAME); New Testament (MANT); Old Testament (MAOT); religion (MAR); theology (M Div, MATH, Th M, Th D). *Accreditation:* ACIPE; ATS (one or more programs are accredited). Part-time and evening/weekend programs available. *Degree requirements:* For master's, one foreign language, thesis optional; for doctorate, 2 foreign languages, thesis/dissertation. *Entrance requirements:* For master's, minimum GPA of 2.5; for doctorate, minimum GPA of 3.0.

The Graduate Center, City University of New York, Graduate Studies, Program in Anthropology, New York, NY 10016-4039. Offers anthropological linguistics (PhD); archaeology (PhD); cultural anthropology (PhD); physical anthropology (PhD). *Degree requirements:* For doctorate, one foreign language, thesis/dissertation. *Entrance requirements:* For doctorate, GRE General Test. Additional exam requirements/recommendations for international students: Required—TOEFL. Electronic applications accepted.

Harvard University, Graduate School of Arts and Sciences, Department of Anthropology, Cambridge, MA 02138. Offers archaeology (PhD); biological anthropology (PhD); legal anthropology (AM); medical anthropology (AM); social anthropology (AM, PhD); social change and development (AM). Terminal master's awarded for partial completion of doctoral program. *Degree requirements:* For master's, 2 foreign languages, thesis (for some programs); for doctorate, 2 foreign languages, thesis/dissertation, laboratory and/or fieldwork; general, qualifying, or special exams. *Entrance requirements:* For master's and doctorate, GRE General Test. Additional exam requirements/recommendations for international students: Required—TOEFL.

Harvard University, Graduate School of Arts and Sciences, Department of Near Eastern Languages and Civilizations, Cambridge, MA 02138. Offers Akkadian and Sumerian (AM, PhD); Arabic (AM, PhD); Armenian (AM, PhD); biblical history (AM, PhD); Hebrew (AM, PhD); Indo-Muslim culture (AM, PhD); Iranian (AM, PhD); Jewish history and literature (AM, PhD); Persian (AM, PhD); Semitic philology (AM, PhD); Syro-Palestinian archaeology (AM, PhD); Turkish (AM, PhD). *Degree requirements:* For doctorate, variable foreign language requirement, thesis/dissertation, general exams. *Entrance requirements:* For master's, GRE General Test; for doctorate, GRE General Test, proficiency in a Near Eastern language. Additional exam requirements/recommendations for international students: Required—TOEFL.

Harvard University, Graduate School of Arts and Sciences, Department of the Classics, Cambridge, MA 02138. Offers Byzantine Greek (PhD); classical archaeology (PhD); classical philology (PhD); classical philosophy (PhD); medieval Latin (PhD). *Degree requirements:* For doctorate, 4 foreign languages, thesis/dissertation, preliminary and special exams. *Entrance requirements:* For doctorate, GRE General Test. Additional exam requirements/recommendations for international students: Required—TOEFL.

Illinois State University, Graduate School, College of Arts and Sciences, Department of Sociology, Program in Historical Archaeology, Normal, IL 61790-2200. Offers MA, MS.

Indiana University of Pennsylvania, School of Graduate Studies and Research, College of Humanities and Social Sciences, Department of Anthropology, Indiana, PA 15705-1087. Offers applied archaeology (MA). Part-time programs available. *Faculty:* 6 full-time (3 women). *Students:* 17 full-time (12 women), 3 part-time (1 woman); includes 1 minority (Hispanic/Latino). Average age 28. 19 applicants, 68% accepted, 11 enrolled. In 2014, 13 master's awarded. *Degree requirements:* For master's, thesis and/or internship. *Entrance requirements:* For master's, GRE, 2 letters of recommendation.

Additional exam requirements/recommendations for international students: Required—TOEFL (minimum score 540 paper-based). *Application deadline:* Applications are processed on a rolling basis. Application fee: $50. Electronic applications accepted. *Financial support:* In 2014–15, 2 fellowships with partial tuition reimbursements (averaging $1,000 per year), 7 research assistantships with full and partial tuition reimbursements (averaging $3,831 per year) were awarded; Federal Work-Study, scholarships/grants, and unspecified assistantships also available. Financial award application deadline: 4/15; financial award applicants required to submit FAFSA. *Unit head:* Dr. Phillip Neusius, Chair, 724-357-2841, Fax: 724-357-7637, E-mail: phillip.neusius@iup.edu.
Website: http://www.iup.edu/anthropology/

Johns Hopkins University, Zanvyl Krieger School of Arts and Sciences, Department of Near Eastern Studies, Baltimore, MD 21218-2699. Offers archaeology (PhD); Assyriology (PhD); Egyptology (PhD); Hebrew Bible/Northwest Semitics (PhD). *Degree requirements:* For doctorate, 2 foreign languages, comprehensive exam, thesis/dissertation. *Entrance requirements:* For doctorate, GRE. Additional exam requirements/recommendations for international students: Required—TOEFL (minimum score 600 paper-based; 100 iBT); Recommended—IELTS. Electronic applications accepted. *Faculty research:* Egyptology, Assyriology, Hebrew Bible/Northwest Semitic languages, Demotic Egyptian, archaeology.

Massachusetts Institute of Technology, School of Engineering, Department of Materials Science and Engineering, Cambridge, MA 02139. Offers archaeological materials (PhD, Sc D); materials engineering (Mat E); materials science and engineering (SM, PhD, Sc D). *Faculty:* 30 full-time (10 women). *Students:* 199 full-time (47 women); includes 35 minority (2 Black or African American, non-Hispanic/Latino; 23 Asian, non-Hispanic/Latino; 5 Hispanic/Latino; 5 Two or more races, non-Hispanic/Latino), 109 international. Average age 26. 406 applicants, 14% accepted, 34 enrolled. In 2014, 8 master's, 35 doctorates awarded. *Degree requirements:* For master's, thesis; for doctorate, comprehensive exam, thesis/dissertation. *Entrance requirements:* For master's, doctorate, and Mat E, GRE General Test. Additional exam requirements/recommendations for international students: Required—IELTS (minimum score 7). *Application deadline:* For fall admission, 12/15 for domestic and international students. Application fee: $75. Electronic applications accepted. *Expenses:* Tuition: Full-time $44,720; part-time $699 per unit. *Required fees:* $296. *Financial support:* In 2014–15, 178 students received support, including 44 fellowships (averaging $29,400 per year), 134 research assistantships (averaging $33,400 per year), 13 teaching assistantships (averaging $36,400 per year); Federal Work-Study, institutionally sponsored loans, scholarships/grants, traineeships, health care benefits, and unspecified assistantships also available. Financial award application deadline: 4/15; financial award applicants required to submit FAFSA. *Faculty research:* Thermodynamics and kinetics of materials; structure, processing and properties of materials; electronic, structural and biological materials engineering; computational materials science; materials in energy, medicine, nanotechnology and the environment. *Total annual research expenditures:* $26.5 million. *Unit head:* Prof. Christopher Schuh, Department Head, 617-253-3300, Fax: 617-252-1775. *Application contact:* Prof. Christopher Schuh, Department Head, 617-253-3300, Fax: 617-252-1775.
Website: http://dmse.mit.edu/

Memorial University of Newfoundland, School of Graduate Studies, Department of Anthropology, St. John's, NL A1C 5S7, Canada. Offers archaeology and physical anthropology (MA, PhD); social and cultural anthropology (MA, PhD). Part-time programs available. *Degree requirements:* For master's, thesis (for some programs); for doctorate, comprehensive exam, thesis/dissertation, oral defense of thesis. *Entrance requirements:* For master's, 2nd class degree in related field. Electronic applications accepted. *Faculty research:* Early European settlements, ethnoarchaeology, economic/political anthropology, land claims and aboriginal rights, marine anthropology.

Michigan Technological University, Graduate School, College of Sciences and Arts, Department of Social Sciences, Houghton, MI 49931. Offers environmental and energy policy (MS, PhD); industrial archaeology (MS); industrial heritage and archeology (PhD). Part-time programs available. *Faculty:* 29 full-time (12 women), 13 part-time/adjunct (4 women). *Students:* 29 full-time (14 women), 18 part-time (6 women); includes 8 minority (1 Black or African American, non-Hispanic/Latino; 1 American Indian or Alaska Native, non-Hispanic/Latino; 4 Asian, non-Hispanic/Latino; 1 Hispanic/Latino; 1 Two or more races, non-Hispanic/Latino), 10 international. Average age 33. 57 applicants, 32% accepted, 10 enrolled. In 2014, 9 master's awarded. Terminal master's awarded for partial completion of doctoral program. *Degree requirements:* For master's, comprehensive exam (for some programs), thesis (for some programs); for doctorate, comprehensive exam, thesis/dissertation. *Entrance requirements:* For master's and doctorate, GRE, statement of purpose, official transcripts, 3 letters of recommendation, writing sample, resume/curriculum vitae. Additional exam requirements/recommendations for international students: Required—TOEFL (recommended score 100 iBT) or IELTS. *Application deadline:* For fall admission, 2/1 priority date for domestic and international students. Applications are processed on a rolling basis. Electronic applications accepted. *Expenses:* Tuition, state resident: full-time $14,769; part-time $820.50 per credit. Tuition, nonresident: full-time $14,769; part-time $820.50 per credit. *Required fees:* $248; $248 per year. Tuition and fees vary according to course load and program. *Financial support:* In 2014–15, 35 students received support, including 3 fellowships with full and partial tuition reimbursements available (averaging $13,824 per year), 10 research assistantships with full and partial tuition reimbursements available (averaging $13,824 per year), 12 teaching assistantships with full and partial tuition reimbursements available (averaging $13,824 per year); career-related internships or fieldwork, Federal Work-Study, scholarships/grants, health care benefits, unspecified assistantships, and cooperative program also available. Financial award applicants required to submit FAFSA. *Faculty research:* Industrial archeology of early American industry, mining history, environmental and energy policy, land-use policy, environmental decision-making. *Total annual research expenditures:* $746,653. *Unit head:* Dr. Patrick E. Martin, Chair, 906-487-2070, Fax: 906-487-2284, E-mail: pemartin@mtu.edu. *Application contact:* Amy Spahn, Office Assistant, 906-487-2113, Fax: 906-487-2284, E-mail: gradadms@mtu.edu.
Website: http://www.social.mtu.edu/

New York University, Graduate School of Arts and Science, Institute of Fine Arts, Program in Art History and Archaeology, New York, NY 10012-1019. Offers architectural studies (PhD); art history and archaeology (MA, PhD); classical art and archaeology (PhD); curatorial studies (PhD); East and South Asian art (PhD); Near Eastern art and archaeology (PhD); MA/Diploma; PhD/Certificate. Part-time programs available. *Students:* 181 full-time (145 women), 56 part-time (46 women); includes 28 minority (2 Black or African American, non-Hispanic/Latino; 12 Asian, non-Hispanic/Latino; 9 Hispanic/Latino; 5 Two or more races, non-Hispanic/Latino), 37 international. Average age 31. 346 applicants, 43% accepted, 52 enrolled. In 2014, 47 master's, 24 doctorates awarded. Terminal master's awarded for partial completion of doctoral program. *Degree requirements:* For master's, 2 foreign languages, thesis or alternative, 2 qualifying papers; for doctorate, 2 foreign languages, thesis/dissertation. *Entrance requirements:* For master's, GRE General Test; for doctorate, GRE General Test, MA. Additional exam requirements/recommendations for international students: Required—TOEFL.

Archaeology

Application deadline: For fall admission, 12/18 for domestic and international students. Application fee: $100. *Financial support:* Fellowships with tuition reimbursements, research assistantships with tuition reimbursements, teaching assistantships with tuition reimbursements, career-related internships or fieldwork, Federal Work-Study, and institutionally sponsored loans available. Financial award application deadline: 12/18; financial award applicants required to submit FAFSA. *Unit head:* Patricia Rubin, Chair, 212-992-5800, Fax: 212-992-5807, E-mail: ifa.program@nyu.edu. *Application contact:* Alexander Nagel, Director of Graduate Studies, 212-992-5800, Fax: 212-992-5807, E-mail: ifa.program@nyu.edu.
Website: http://www.nyu.edu/gsas/dept/fineart/

Northern Arizona University, Graduate College, College of Social and Behavioral Sciences, Department of Anthropology, Flagstaff, AZ 86011. Offers archaeology (MA); cultural anthropology (MA); linguistic anthropology (MA). *Degree requirements:* For master's, thesis (for some programs), internship paper. *Entrance requirements:* For master's, 12 undergraduate hours in anthropology. Additional exam requirements/recommendations for international students: Required—TOEFL (minimum score 550 paper-based; 80 iBT), IELTS (minimum score 7). Electronic applications accepted. *Faculty research:* Economic development, culture change, ethnohistory, archaeology of the Southwest, small town networks and HIV.

Princeton University, Graduate School, Department of Art and Archaeology, Princeton, NJ 08544-1019. Offers classical art and archaeology (PhD); East Asian art and archaeology (PhD). *Degree requirements:* For doctorate, 2 foreign languages, thesis/dissertation. *Entrance requirements:* For doctorate, GRE General Test. Additional exam requirements/recommendations for international students: Required—TOEFL (minimum score 600 paper-based). Electronic applications accepted.

Rice University, Graduate Programs, School of Social Sciences, Department of Anthropology, Houston, TX 77251-1892. Offers archaeology (MA, PhD); social-cultural anthropology (MA, PhD). Terminal master's awarded for partial completion of doctoral program. *Degree requirements:* For master's, one foreign language, 3 major papers, dissertation proposal and language exam or thesis; for doctorate, one foreign language, thesis/dissertation. *Entrance requirements:* For master's and doctorate, research proposal. Additional exam requirements/recommendations for international students: Required—TOEFL (minimum score 90 iBT). Electronic applications accepted.

St. Cloud State University, School of Graduate Studies, College of Social Sciences, Program in Cultural Resource Management Archeology, St. Cloud, MN 56301-4498. Offers MS. *Entrance requirements:* For master's, GRE General Test, minimum GPA of 2.75. Additional exam requirements/recommendations for international students: Required—Michigan English Language Assessment Battery; Recommended—TOEFL (minimum score 550 paper-based).

San Francisco State University, Division of Graduate Studies, College of Liberal and Creative Arts, Department of Anthropology, San Francisco, CA 94132-1722. Offers archaeology (MA); biological/physical anthropology (MA); social/cultural anthropology (MA); visual anthropology (MA). *Expenses:* Tuition, state resident: full-time $6738. Tuition, nonresident: full-time $17,898; part-time $372 per credit hour. *Required fees:* $498 per semester. *Faculty research:* Immigration, ethnicity, urban anthropology, Californian and Latin American archaeology. *Unit head:* Dr. James Quesada, Chair, 415-338-1633, E-mail: jquesada@sfsu.edu. *Application contact:* Dr. Douglass Bailey, Graduate Coordinator, 415-338-1427, E-mail: dwbailey@sfsu.edu.
Website: http://anthropology.sfsu.edu/

Simon Fraser University, Office of Graduate Studies, Faculty of Environment, Department of Archaeology, Burnaby, BC V5A 1S6, Canada. Offers MA, PhD. *Degree requirements:* For master's, one foreign language, thesis; for doctorate, one foreign language, comprehensive exam, thesis/dissertation. *Entrance requirements:* For master's, minimum GPA of 3.0 (on scale of 4.33), or 3.33 based on last 60 credits of undergraduate courses; for doctorate, minimum GPA of 3.5 (on scale of 4.33). Additional exam requirements/recommendations for international students: Recommended—TOEFL (minimum score 580 paper-based; 93 iBT), IELTS (minimum score 7), TWE (minimum score 5). Electronic applications accepted. *Faculty research:* Archaeometry, cultural resource management, ethnoarchaeology, forensic anthropology, palaeoethnobotany, skeletal biology and zooarchaeology.

Stanford University, School of Humanities and Sciences, Department of Anthropology, Stanford, CA 94305-9991. Offers archaeology (MA, PhD); culture and society (MS, PhD); ecology and environment (MA, PhD). Terminal master's awarded for partial completion of doctoral program. *Degree requirements:* For master's, thesis; for doctorate, one foreign language, thesis/dissertation. *Entrance requirements:* For master's and doctorate, GRE General Test. Additional exam requirements/recommendations for international students: Required—TOEFL. Electronic applications accepted. *Expenses: Tuition:* Full-time $44,184; part-time $982 per credit hour. *Required fees:* $191.

Temple Baptist Seminary, Program in Theology, Chattanooga, TN 37404-3530. Offers biblical languages (M Div); Biblical studies (MABS); Christian education (MACE); English Bible ? language tools (M Div); theology (MM, D Min). Part-time and evening/weekend programs available. Postbaccalaureate distance learning degree programs offered (minimal on-campus study). *Degree requirements:* For doctorate, thesis/dissertation. *Entrance requirements:* For doctorate, minimum GPA of 3.0, M Div.

Trinity International University, Trinity Evangelical Divinity School, Deerfield, IL 60015-1284. Offers Biblical and Near Eastern archaeology and languages (MA); Christian studies (MA, Certificate); Christian thought (MA); church history (MA, Th M); congregational ministry: pastor-teacher (M Div); congregational ministry: team ministry (M Div); counseling ministries (MA); counseling psychology (MA); cross-cultural ministry (M Div); educational studies (PhD); evangelism (MA); history of Christianity in America (MA); intercultural studies (MA, PhD); leadership and ministry management (D Min); military chaplaincy (D Min); ministry (MA); mission and evangelism (Th M); missions and evangelism (D Min); New Testament (MA, Th M); Old Testament (Th M); Old Testament and Semitic languages (MA); pastoral care (M Div); pastoral care and counseling (D Min); pastoral counseling and psychology (Th M); pastoral theology (Th M); philosophy of religion (MA); preaching (D Min); religion (MA); research ministry (M Div); systematic theology (Th M); theological studies (PhD); urban ministry (MA). *Accreditation:* ATS (one or more programs are accredited). Part-time programs available. Postbaccalaureate distance learning degree programs offered (minimal on-campus study). *Degree requirements:* For master's, comprehensive exam, thesis, fieldwork; for doctorate, comprehensive exam (for some programs), thesis/dissertation; for Certificate, comprehensive exam, integrative papers. *Entrance requirements:* For master's, GRE, MAT, minimum cumulative undergraduate GPA of 3.0; for doctorate, GRE, minimum cumulative graduate GPA of 3.2; for Certificate, GRE, MAT, minimum undergraduate GPA of 2.5. Additional exam requirements/recommendations for international students: Required—TOEFL (minimum score 580 paper-based), TWE (minimum score 4). Electronic applications accepted.

Tufts University, Graduate School of Arts and Sciences, Department of Classics, Medford, MA 02155. Offers classical archaeology (MA); classics (MA); classics with teaching licensure (MA). Part-time programs available. *Faculty:* 7 full-time, 4 part-time/adjunct. *Students:* 11 full-time (4 women), 1 (woman) part-time. Average age 26. 38 applicants, 55% accepted, 6 enrolled. In 2014, 6 master's awarded. *Degree requirements:* For master's, 2 foreign languages, comprehensive exam, thesis or alternative. *Entrance requirements:* For master's, GRE General Test, writing sample. Additional exam requirements/recommendations for international students: Required—TOEFL (minimum score 550 paper-based; 80 iBT), IELTS (minimum score 6.5). *Application deadline:* For fall admission, 2/15 for domestic and international students; for spring admission, 10/15 for domestic and international students. Applications are processed on a rolling basis. Application fee: $75. Electronic applications accepted. *Expenses: Tuition:* Full-time $45,590; part-time $1161 per credit hour. *Required fees:* $782. Full-time tuition and fees vary according to degree level, program and student level. Part-time tuition and fees vary according to course load. *Financial support:* Teaching assistantships with full and partial tuition reimbursements, Federal Work-Study, scholarships/grants, tuition waivers (partial), and unspecified assistantships available. Financial award application deadline: 5/15; financial award applicants required to submit FAFSA. *Unit head:* Dr. Vickie Sullivan, Graduate Program Director. *Application contact:* Office of Graduate Admissions, 617-627-3395, E-mail: gradadmissions@tufts.edu.
Website: http://www.ase.tufts.edu/classics/

Universidad de las Américas Puebla, Division of Graduate Studies, School of Social Sciences, Program in Anthropology, Puebla, Mexico. Offers anthropology (MA); archaeology (MA). Part-time and evening/weekend programs available. *Degree requirements:* For master's, one foreign language, thesis. *Entrance requirements:* For master's, bachelor's degree in anthropology or equivalent. *Faculty research:* Archaeology, ethnography, and ethnohistory of Mesoamerica.

Université Laval, Faculty of Letters, Department of History, Programs in Archaeology, Québec, QC G1K 7P4, Canada. Offers MA, PhD. Terminal master's awarded for partial completion of doctoral program. *Degree requirements:* For master's, thesis; for doctorate, comprehensive exam, thesis/dissertation. *Entrance requirements:* For master's and doctorate, English test, knowledge of French. Electronic applications accepted.

University of Alberta, Faculty of Graduate Studies and Research, Department of History and Classics, Edmonton, AB T6G 2E1, Canada. Offers ancient history (PhD); classical archaeology (MA, PhD); classical literature (PhD); classics (MA); history (MA, PhD). Part-time and evening/weekend programs available. *Degree requirements:* For master's, one foreign language, thesis (for some programs); for doctorate, one foreign language, thesis/dissertation. *Entrance requirements:* For master's, minimum B+ average; for doctorate, minimum A- average. Additional exam requirements/recommendations for international students: Required—TOEFL (minimum score 580 paper-based). Electronic applications accepted. *Faculty research:* Western Canada, classical archaeology, Britain, Eastern Europe, East Asia.

The University of British Columbia, Faculty of Arts and Faculty of Graduate Studies, Department of Classical, Near Eastern and Religious Studies, Programmes in Classics, Vancouver, BC V6T 1Z1, Canada. Offers ancient culture, religion, and ethnicity (MA); classical and near eastern archaeology (MA); classics (MA, PhD). Part-time programs available. *Degree requirements:* For master's, 2 foreign languages, thesis or comprehensive exam; for doctorate, 2 foreign languages, comprehensive exam, thesis/dissertation. *Entrance requirements:* For doctorate, MA. Additional exam requirements/recommendations for international students: Required—TOEFL (minimum score 600 paper-based), IELTS (minimum score 7.5). Electronic applications accepted. *Faculty research:* Classical archaeology, ancient historians, late antiquity, ancient prose fiction, epigraphy.

University of Calgary, Faculty of Graduate Studies, Faculty of Arts, Department of Archaeology, Calgary, AB T2N 1N4, Canada. Offers MA. *Degree requirements:* For master's, thesis. *Entrance requirements:* For master's, BA or B Sc in anthropology or archaeology; statement of intent; sample of written work; curriculum vitae. Additional exam requirements/recommendations for international students: Required—TOEFL. Electronic applications accepted. *Faculty research:* Pre-history, ethnoarchaeology, Africa, Latin America, biological anthropology.

University of California, Berkeley, Graduate Division, College of Letters and Science, Department of Classics, Program in Classical Archaeology, Berkeley, CA 94720-1500. Offers MA, PhD. *Degree requirements:* For master's, one foreign language, thesis, exams; for doctorate, 2 foreign languages, thesis/dissertation, qualifying exam. *Entrance requirements:* For master's and doctorate, GRE General Test, minimum GPA of 3.0, 3 letters of recommendation. Additional exam requirements/recommendations for international students: Required—TOEFL (minimum score 570 paper-based), TWE.

University of California, Berkeley, Graduate Division, College of Letters and Science, Group in Ancient History and Mediterranean Archaeology, Berkeley, CA 94720-1500. Offers MA, PhD. *Degree requirements:* For master's, one foreign language, exam or thesis; for doctorate, 2 foreign languages, thesis/dissertation, qualifying exam. *Entrance requirements:* For master's and doctorate, GRE General Test, minimum GPA of 3.0, 3 letters of recommendation. Additional exam requirements/recommendations for international students: Required—TOEFL (minimum score 570 paper-based), TWE.

University of California, Los Angeles, Graduate Division, College of Letters and Science, Interdepartmental Program in Archaeology, Los Angeles, CA 90095. Offers MA, PhD. Terminal master's awarded for partial completion of doctoral program. *Degree requirements:* For master's, one foreign language, comprehensive exam, field experience; for doctorate, 2 foreign languages, thesis/dissertation, oral and written qualifying exams. *Entrance requirements:* For doctorate, GRE General Test, bachelor's degree; minimum undergraduate GPA of 3.0 (or its equivalent if letter grade system not used); writing sample. Additional exam requirements/recommendations for international students: Required—TOEFL. Electronic applications accepted.

University of California, Los Angeles, Graduate Division, College of Letters and Science, Interdepartmental Program in Conservation of Archaeological and Ethnographic Materials, Los Angeles, CA 90095. Offers MA. *Degree requirements:* For master's, one foreign language, thesis, eleven-month internship. *Entrance requirements:* For master's, GRE General Test, bachelor's degree; minimum undergraduate GPA of 3.0 (or its equivalent if letter grade system not used); proficiency in one foreign language; portfolio; writing sample; documented practical experience; interview. Additional exam requirements/recommendations for international students: Required—TOEFL.

University of California, Santa Barbara, Graduate Division, College of Letters and Sciences, Division of Social Sciences, Department of Anthropology, Santa Barbara, CA 93106-2014. Offers archaeology (MA, PhD); integrative anthropological sciences (MA, PhD); sociocultural anthropology (MA, PhD); MA/PhD. Terminal master's awarded for partial completion of doctoral program. *Degree requirements:* For master's, comprehensive exam (for some programs), thesis (for some programs); for doctorate, comprehensive exam (for some programs), thesis/dissertation. *Entrance requirements:* For master's and doctorate, GRE General Test, statement of purpose, personal achievements statement, transcripts, writing sample, curriculum vitae, letters of recommendation. Additional exam requirements/recommendations for international students: Required—TOEFL (minimum score 550 paper-based; 80 iBT), IELTS (minimum score 7). Electronic applications accepted. *Faculty research:* Archaeology,

bioarchaeology, biosocial anthropology, evolutionary ecology, evolutionary psychology, sociocultural anthropology.

University of Chicago, Division of the Humanities, Department of Classics, Chicago, IL 60637. Offers ancient philosophy (PhD); classical archaeology (PhD); classical languages and literatures (PhD). *Students:* 32 full-time (15 women); includes 4 minority (2 Asian, non-Hispanic/Latino; 1 Hispanic/Latino; 1 Two or more races, non-Hispanic/Latino), 3 international. 74 applicants, 31% accepted, 6 enrolled. Terminal master's awarded for partial completion of doctoral program. *Degree requirements:* For doctorate, 2 foreign languages, thesis/dissertation. *Entrance requirements:* For doctorate, GRE General Test. Additional exam requirements/recommendations for international students: Required—TOEFL (minimum score 104 iBT), IELTS (minimum score 7). *Application deadline:* For fall admission, 12/15 for domestic and international students. Application fee: $90. Electronic applications accepted. *Expenses: Tuition:* Full-time $46,899. *Required fees:* $347. *Financial support:* Fellowships with full tuition reimbursements, teaching assistantships, Federal Work-Study, institutionally sponsored loans, scholarships/grants, and health care benefits available. Financial award application deadline: 12/15; financial award applicants required to submit FAFSA. *Unit head:* Dr. Mark Payne, Chair. *Application contact:* Braden Grams, Assistant Dean of Students, Admissions and Fellowships, 773-702-1552, Fax: 773-834-9148, E-mail: humanitiesadmissions@uchicago.edu.
Website: http://classics.uchicago.edu/

University of Colorado Denver, College of Liberal Arts and Sciences, Department of Anthropology, Denver, CO 80217. Offers archaeological studies (MA); biological anthropology (MA); medical anthropology (MA); sustainable development and political ecology (MA). Part-time and evening/weekend programs available. *Faculty:* 10 full-time (4 women), 2 part-time/adjunct (1 woman). *Students:* 28 full-time (22 women), 11 part-time (9 women); includes 9 minority (2 Black or African American, non-Hispanic/Latino; 1 Asian, non-Hispanic/Latino; 5 Hispanic/Latino; 1 Two or more races, non-Hispanic/Latino). Average age 30. 50 applicants, 50% accepted, 11 enrolled. In 2014, 17 master's awarded. *Degree requirements:* For master's, comprehensive exam, thesis or alternative, 30-36 credit hours. *Entrance requirements:* For master's, GRE General Test, minimum GPA of 3.0 for all undergraduate studies, transcripts from all undergraduate/graduate institutions attended, prior training in anthropology, three letters of recommendation, statement of purpose. Additional exam requirements/recommendations for international students: Required—TOEFL (minimum score 537 paper-based; 75 iBT); Recommended—IELTS (minimum score 6.5). *Application deadline:* For fall admission, 2/15 for domestic students, 1/15 for international students. Application fee: $50 ($75 for international students). Electronic applications accepted. *Financial support:* Fellowships, research assistantships, teaching assistantships, Federal Work-Study, institutionally sponsored loans, scholarships/grants, and traineeships available. Financial award application deadline: 4/1; financial award applicants required to submit FAFSA. *Faculty research:* Applied medical anthropology, primate social behavior, environmental anthropology, Southwestern and Mexican archaeology, human ecology. *Unit head:* Dr. Christopher Beekman, Chair of the Department of Anthropology, 303-556-6040, E-mail: christopher.beekman@ucdenver.edu. *Application contact:* Charles Musiba, Acting Graduate Director, 303-556-6082, Fax: 303-556-8501, E-mail: charles.musiba@ucdenver.edu.
Website: http://www.ucdenver.edu/academics/colleges/CLAS/Departments/anthropology/Programs/Masters/Pages/Masters.aspx

University of Denver, Division of Arts, Humanities and Social Sciences, Department of Anthropology, Denver, CO 80208. Offers archaeology (MA); cultural anthropology (MA); museum studies (MA). Part-time programs available. *Faculty:* 7 full-time (3 women). *Students:* 1 full-time (0 women), 20 part-time (14 women); includes 5 minority (2 Hispanic/Latino; 3 Two or more races, non-Hispanic/Latino), 1 international. Average age 25. 47 applicants, 49% accepted, 11 enrolled. In 2014, 4 master's awarded. *Degree requirements:* For master's, one foreign language, comprehensive exam, thesis (for some programs), tool, foreign language literacy, or course work. *Entrance requirements:* For master's, GRE General Test, bachelor's degree, transcripts, personal statement, two letters of recommendation. Additional exam requirements/recommendations for international students: Required—TOEFL (minimum score 550 paper-based; 80 iBT). *Application deadline:* For fall admission, 2/4 priority date for domestic and international students. Applications are processed on a rolling basis. Application fee: $65. Electronic applications accepted. *Expenses:* Expenses: $1,199 per credit hour. *Financial support:* In 2014–15, 18 students received support, including 12 teaching assistantships with partial tuition reimbursements available (averaging $5,000 per year); career-related internships or fieldwork, Federal Work-Study, institutionally sponsored loans, scholarships/grants, and unspecified assistantships also available. Support available to part-time students. Financial award application deadline: 2/15; financial award applicants required to submit FAFSA. *Faculty research:* Human diversity, human rights, historic archaeology, museums and heritage, high-tech field methods. *Unit head:* Dr. Dean J. Saitta, Chair, 303-871-2680, E-mail: dsaitta@du.edu. *Application contact:* Dr. Larry Conyers, Professor/Director of Graduate and Undergraduate Programs, 303-871-2684, E-mail: lconyers@du.edu.
Website: http://www.du.edu/ahss/schools/anthropology/

University of Georgia, Franklin College of Arts and Sciences, Department of Anthropology, Athens, GA 30602. Offers anthropology (MA, PhD); archaeological resource management (MS). *Degree requirements:* For master's, one foreign language, thesis; for doctorate, one foreign language, thesis/dissertation. *Entrance requirements:* For master's and doctorate, GRE General Test. Electronic applications accepted.

University of Lethbridge, School of Graduate Studies, Lethbridge, AB T1K 3M4, Canada. Offers addictions counseling (M Sc); agricultural biotechnology (M Sc); agricultural studies (M Sc, MA); anthropology (MA); archaeology (M Sc, MA); art (MA, MFA); biochemistry (M Sc); biological sciences (M Sc); biomolecular science (PhD); biosystems and biodiversity (PhD); Canadian studies (MA); chemistry (M Sc); computer science (M Sc); computer science and geographical information science (M Sc); counseling (MC); counseling psychology (M Ed); dramatic arts (MA); earth, space, and physical science (PhD); economics (MA); education (MA); educational leadership (M Ed); English (MA); environmental science (M Sc); evolution and behavior (PhD); exercise science (M Sc); French (MA); French/German (MA); French/Spanish (MA); general education (M Ed); geography (M Sc, MA); German (MA); health sciences (M Sc); individualized multidisciplinary (M Sc, MA); kinesiology (M Sc, MA); management (M Sc), including accounting, finance, general management, human resource management and labor relations, information systems, international management, marketing, policy and strategy; mathematics (M Sc); modern languages (MA); music (M Mus, MA); Native American studies (MA); neuroscience (M Sc, PhD); new media (MA, MFA); nursing (M Sc, MN); philosophy (MA); physics (M Sc); political science (MA); psychology (M Sc, MA); religious studies (MA); sociology (MA); theatre and dramatic arts (MFA); theoretical and computational science (PhD); urban and regional studies (MA); women and gender studies (MA). Part-time and evening/weekend programs available. *Faculty:* 358. *Students:* 445 full-time (243 women), 116 part-time (72 women). Average age 31. 351 applicants, 26% accepted, 87 enrolled. In 2014, 129 master's, 13 doctorates awarded. *Degree requirements:* For master's, thesis (for some

programs); for doctorate, comprehensive exam, thesis/dissertation. *Entrance requirements:* For master's, GMAT (for M Sc in management), bachelor's degree in related field, minimum GPA of 3.0 during previous 20 graded semester courses, 2 years' teaching or related experience (M Ed); for doctorate, master's degree, minimum graduate GPA of 3.5. Additional exam requirements/recommendations for international students: Required—TOEFL. Application fee: $100 Canadian dollars. *Financial support:* Fellowships, research assistantships, teaching assistantships, scholarships/grants, health care benefits, and unspecified assistantships available. *Faculty research:* Movement and brain plasticity, gibberellin physiology, photosynthesis, carbon cycling, molecular properties of main-group ring components. *Application contact:* School of Graduate Studies, 403-329-5194, E-mail: sgsinquiries@uleth.ca.
Website: http://www.uleth.ca/graduatestudies/

The University of Manchester, Faculty of Life Sciences, Manchester, United Kingdom. Offers adaptive organismal biology (M Phil, PhD); animal biology (M Phil, PhD); biochemistry (M Phil, PhD); bioinformatics (M Phil, PhD); biomolecular sciences (M Phil, PhD); biotechnology (M Phil, PhD); cell biology (M Phil, PhD); cell matrix research (M Phil, PhD); channels and transporters (M Phil, PhD); developmental biology (M Phil, PhD); Egyptology (M Phil, PhD); environmental biology (M Phil, PhD); evolutionary biology (M Phil, PhD); gene expression (M Phil, PhD); genetics (M Phil, PhD); history of science, technology and medicine (M Phil, PhD); immunology (M Phil, PhD); integrative neurobiology and behavior (M Phil, PhD); membrane trafficking (M Phil, PhD); microbiology (M Phil, PhD); molecular and cellular neuroscience (M Phil, PhD); molecular biology (M Phil, PhD); molecular cancer studies (M Phil, PhD); neuroscience (M Phil, PhD); ophthalmology (M Phil, PhD); optometry (M Phil, PhD); organelle function (M Phil, PhD); pharmacology (M Phil, PhD); physiology (M Phil, PhD); plant sciences (M Phil, PhD); stem cell research (M Phil, PhD); structural biology (M Phil, PhD); systems neuroscience (M Phil, PhD); toxicology (M Phil, PhD).

The University of Manchester, School of Arts, Histories and Cultures, Manchester, United Kingdom. Offers anthropology, media and performance (PhD); applied theatre professional (PhD); archaeology (PhD); art history and visual studies (PhD); arts management and cultural policy (PhD); classics and ancient history (PhD); composition (PhD); creative writing (PhD); drama (PhD); economic and social history (PhD); electroacoustic composition (PhD); English and American studies (PhD); history (PhD); humanitarianism and conflict response (PhD); museology (PhD); music (PhD); musicology (PhD); religions and theology (PhD).

University of Massachusetts Boston, College of Liberal Arts, Program in Historical Archaeology, Boston, MA 02125-3393. Offers MA. Part-time and evening/weekend programs available. *Degree requirements:* For master's, thesis, oral exams, practicum. *Entrance requirements:* For master's, GRE General Test, minimum GPA of 2.75. *Application deadline:* For fall admission, 3/1 for domestic students; for spring admission, 11/1 for domestic students. *Expenses:* Tuition, state resident: full-time $2590; part-time $108 per credit. Tuition, nonresident: full-time $9758; part-time $406.50 per credit. Tuition and fees vary according to course load and program. *Financial support:* Research assistantships with full tuition reimbursements, teaching assistantships, career-related internships or fieldwork, Federal Work-Study, and unspecified assistantships available. Support available to part-time students. Financial award application deadline: 3/1; financial award applicants required to submit FAFSA. *Faculty research:* New World Colonialism, New England archeology, historical and urban archeology, archeological botany, ethnology. *Unit head:* Dr. Stephen Silliman, Associate Director, 617-287-6850, E-mail: stephen.silliman@umb.edu. *Application contact:* Peggy Roldan Patel, Graduate Admissions Coordinator, 617-287-6400, Fax: 617-287-6236, E-mail: bos.gadm@dpc.umassp.edu.

University of Memphis, Graduate School, College of Arts and Sciences, Department of Earth Sciences, Memphis, TN 38152. Offers archaeology (MS); earth sciences (PhD); geographic information systems (Graduate Certificate), including geographic information systems, GIS educator, GIS planning, GIS professional; geography (MA, MS); geology (MS); geophysics (MS); interdisciplinary (MS). Part-time and evening/weekend programs available. *Faculty:* 13 full-time (3 women), 2 part-time/adjunct (0 women). *Students:* 27 full-time (8 women), 26 part-time (7 women); includes 2 minority (1 Black or African American, non-Hispanic/Latino; 1 Asian, non-Hispanic/Latino), 19 international. Average age 32. 36 applicants, 69% accepted, 7 enrolled. In 2014, 7 master's, 5 doctorates awarded. Terminal master's awarded for partial completion of doctoral program. *Degree requirements:* For master's, comprehensive exam, thesis, seminar presentation; for doctorate, thesis/dissertation. *Entrance requirements:* For master's, GRE General Test, 3 letters of recommendation, statement of research interests; for doctorate, GRE General Test, 2 letters of recommendation, resume, personal statement. Additional exam requirements/recommendations for international students: Required—TOEFL (minimum score 550 paper-based). *Application deadline:* For fall admission, 1/31 for domestic students; for spring admission, 11/1 for domestic students. Applications are processed on a rolling basis. Application fee: $35 ($60 for international students). Electronic applications accepted. *Financial support:* In 2014–15, 18 students received support. Fellowships with full tuition reimbursements available, research assistantships with full tuition reimbursements available, teaching assistantships with full tuition reimbursements available, Federal Work-Study, scholarships/grants, and unspecified assistantships available. Financial award application deadline: 2/15; financial award applicants required to submit FAFSA. *Faculty research:* Hazards, active tectonics, geophysics, hydrology and water resources, spatial analysis. *Unit head:* Dr. M. Jerry Bartholomew, Chair, 901-678-4536, Fax: 901-678-4467, E-mail: jbrthlm1@memphis.edu. *Application contact:* Dr. Arlene Hill, Associate Professor and Graduate Program Coordinator, 901-678-4358, Fax: 901-678-2178, E-mail: dlarsen@memphis.edu.
Website: http://www.memphis.edu/des/

University of Memphis, Graduate School, College of Communication and Fine Arts, Department of Art, Memphis, TN 38152. Offers art (Graduate Certificate); art history (MA), including Egyptian art and archaeology, general art history; ceramics (MFA); graphic design (MFA); interior design (MFA); painting (MFA); printmaking/photography (MFA). *Accreditation:* NASAD (one or more programs are accredited). *Faculty:* 19 full-time (7 women), 4 part-time/adjunct (2 women). *Students:* 34 full-time (28 women), 3 part-time (2 women); includes 5 minority (2 Asian, non-Hispanic/Latino; 2 Hispanic/Latino; 1 Two or more races, non-Hispanic/Latino). Average age 30. 24 applicants, 63% accepted, 10 enrolled. In 2014, 14 master's, 14 other advanced degrees awarded. *Degree requirements:* For master's, 2 foreign languages, comprehensive exam, thesis. *Entrance requirements:* For master's, GRE General Test or MAT, portfolio (MFA). *Application deadline:* For fall admission, 8/1 for domestic students; for spring admission, 12/1 for domestic students. Applications are processed on a rolling basis. Application fee: $35 ($60 for international students). *Financial support:* In 2014–15, 38 students received support. Research assistantships with full tuition reimbursements available, teaching assistantships with full tuition reimbursements available, Federal Work-Study, scholarships/grants, and unspecified assistantships available. Financial award application deadline: 2/15; financial award applicants required to submit FAFSA. *Faculty research:* Online collaborative learning, advanced art history studies, electronic publishing/design, studio arts, architectural studies. *Unit head:* Prof. Richard Lou, Chair, 901-678-2216, Fax: 901-678-2735, E-mail: gmyatt@memphis.edu. *Application contact:*

Archaeology

Greely Myat, Graduate Studies Coordinator, 901-678-2650.
Website: http://memphis.edu/art/

University of Michigan, Horace H. Rackham School of Graduate Studies, College of Literature, Science, and the Arts, Department of Anthropology, Ann Arbor, MI 48109-1107. Offers archaeological (PhD); biological (PhD); linguistic (PhD); sociocultural (PhD). *Faculty:* 40 full-time (18 women), 6 part-time/adjunct (3 women). *Students:* 99 full-time (59 women); includes 19 minority (1 Black or African American, non-Hispanic/Latino; 1 American Indian or Alaska Native, non-Hispanic/Latino; 6 Asian, non-Hispanic/Latino; 6 Hispanic/Latino; 5 Two or more races, non-Hispanic/Latino), 13 international. Average age 28. 206 applicants, 14% accepted, 15 enrolled. In 2014, 15 doctorates awarded. *Degree requirements:* For doctorate, one foreign language, comprehensive exam, thesis/dissertation, preliminary examination, oral defense of dissertation. *Entrance requirements:* For doctorate, GRE General Test. Additional exam requirements/recommendations for international students: Required—TOEFL (minimum score 560 paper-based; 84 iBT). *Application deadline:* For fall admission, 12/15 for domestic and international students. Application fee: $75 ($90 for international students). Electronic applications accepted. *Financial support:* In 2014–15, 67 students received support, including 47 fellowships with full tuition reimbursements available (averaging $19,350 per year), 4 research assistantships with full tuition reimbursements available (averaging $19,350 per year), 50 teaching assistantships with full tuition reimbursements available (averaging $19,350 per year); institutionally sponsored loans, scholarships/grants, traineeships, health care benefits, tuition waivers (full), and unspecified assistantships also available. Financial award application deadline: 3/1; financial award applicants required to submit FAFSA. *Faculty research:* Sociocultural, linguistic, biological and archaeological anthropology. *Unit head:* Dr. Thomas Fricke, Chair, 734-764-7274, Fax: 734-763-6077. *Application contact:* Katia Kitchen, Graduate Program Assistant, 734-936-7933, Fax: 734-763-6077, E-mail: kitchenk@umich.edu.
Website: http://www.lsa.umich.edu/anthro/

University of Michigan, Horace H. Rackham School of Graduate Studies, College of Literature, Science, and the Arts, Interdepartmental Program in Classical Art and Archaeology, Ann Arbor, MI 48109. Offers MA, PhD. *Faculty:* 20 full-time (8 women), 1 (woman) part-time/adjunct. *Students:* 23 full-time (15 women), 6 international. 42 applicants, 12% accepted, 3 enrolled. In 2014, 4 doctorates awarded. *Degree requirements:* For doctorate, 4 foreign languages, comprehensive exam, thesis/dissertation, ancient history exam, preliminary exam. *Entrance requirements:* For doctorate, GRE General Test. Additional exam requirements/recommendations for international students: Required—TOEFL (minimum score 560 paper-based; 84 iBT). *Application deadline:* For fall admission, 12/15 for domestic and international students. Application fee: $75 ($90 for international students). Electronic applications accepted. *Financial support:* In 2014–15, 21 students received support, including 9 fellowships with full tuition reimbursements available (averaging $18,234 per year), 1 research assistantship with full tuition reimbursement available (averaging $18,925 per year), 7 teaching assistantships with full tuition reimbursements available (averaging $18,234 per year); career-related internships or fieldwork, health care benefits, and summer research funding (average of $3,500 per student), ad hoc conference travel funding also available. Financial award application deadline: 4/15. *Faculty research:* Greek art and archaeology, Roman art and archaeology, Near Eastern art and archaeology, archaeological theory and methodology. *Unit head:* Prof. Lisa Nevett, Program Director, 734-764-8581, Fax: 734-763-8976, E-mail: lcnevett@umich.edu. *Application contact:* Alexander Zwinak, Graduate Program Coordinator, 734-764-6323, Fax: 734-763-8976, E-mail: ipcaa.office@umich.edu.
Website: http://www.lsa.umich.edu/ipcaa/

University of Minnesota, Twin Cities Campus, Graduate School, College of Liberal Arts, Department of Classical and Near Eastern Studies, Minneapolis, MN 55455-0213. Offers ancient and medieval art and archaeology (MA, PhD); classics (MA, PhD); Greek (MA, PhD); Latin (MA, PhD); religions in antiquity (MA). Part-time programs available. Terminal master's awarded for partial completion of doctoral program. *Degree requirements:* For master's, 2 foreign languages, comprehensive exam, thesis or alternative; for doctorate, variable foreign language requirement, comprehensive exam, thesis/dissertation. *Entrance requirements:* For master's and doctorate, GRE, 3 letters of recommendation, writing sample, copies of transcripts, personal statement. Additional exam requirements/recommendations for international students: Required—TOEFL. Electronic applications accepted. *Faculty research:* Greek and Latin literature, religions in antiquity, ancient Near East.

University of Missouri, Office of Research and Graduate Studies, College of Arts and Science, Department of Art History and Archaeology, Columbia, MO 65211. Offers MA, PhD. *Faculty:* 9 full-time (3 women), 1 (woman) part-time/adjunct. *Students:* 25 full-time (21 women), 4 part-time (all women); includes 1 minority (Hispanic/Latino), 1 international. Average age 30. 34 applicants, 12% accepted, 4 enrolled. In 2014, 1 master's, 2 doctorates awarded. Terminal master's awarded for partial completion of doctoral program. *Degree requirements:* For master's, 2 foreign languages, thesis; for doctorate, 2 foreign languages, thesis/dissertation. *Entrance requirements:* For master's, GRE General Test (minimum score 1000 verbal and quantitative, 4.5 analytical), minimum GPA of 3.0, 3.3 in major field; at least 3 semesters in appropriate foreign language; for doctorate, GRE General Test, minimum GPA of 3.0; MA or equivalent in art history or classical archaeology; master's thesis. Additional exam requirements/recommendations for international students: Required—TOEFL (minimum score 500 paper-based; 61 iBT), IELTS (minimum score 5.5). *Application deadline:* For fall admission, 1/18 priority date for domestic students. Applications are processed on a rolling basis. Application fee: $55 ($75 for international students). Electronic applications accepted. *Financial support:* In 2014–15, 4 fellowships with full tuition reimbursements, 13 research assistantships with full tuition reimbursements, 5 teaching assistantships with full tuition reimbursements were awarded; institutionally sponsored loans, health care benefits, and unspecified assistantships also available. *Faculty research:* Classical Mediterranean archaeology, medieval and Renaissance art, art and architecture of modern Europe and the Americas. *Unit head:* Dr. Susan Langdon, Department Chair, 573-882-6711, E-mail: langdons@missouri.edu. *Application contact:* Linda Garrison, Administrative Associate I, 573-882-2757, E-mail: garrisonl@missouri.edu.
Website: http://aha.missouri.edu/

University of Nebraska–Lincoln, Graduate College, College of Arts and Sciences, Department of Anthropology and Geography, Lincoln, NE 68588. Offers anthropology (MA); geography (MA, PhD); professional archaeology (MA). *Degree requirements:* For master's, thesis optional. *Entrance requirements:* For master's, GRE General Test. Additional exam requirements/recommendations for international students: Required—TOEFL. Electronic applications accepted.

University of New Mexico, Graduate School, College of Arts and Sciences, Program in Anthropology, Albuquerque, NM 87131-2039. Offers archaeology (MA, MS, PhD); ethnology (MA, MS, PhD); evolutionary anthropology (PhD); public archaeology (MA, MS, PhD). *Faculty:* 24 full-time (10 women). *Students:* 90 full-time (53 women), 32 part-time (25 women); includes 30 minority (4 American Indian or Alaska Native, non-Hispanic/Latino; 2 Asian, non-Hispanic/Latino; 19 Hispanic/Latino; 5 Two or more races, non-Hispanic/Latino), 8 international. Average age 32. 101 applicants, 31% accepted, 20 enrolled. In 2014, 18 master's, 14 doctorates awarded. Terminal master's awarded for partial completion of doctoral program. *Degree requirements:* For master's, comprehensive exam (for some programs), thesis or alternative, 1-2 exams; for doctorate, one foreign language, comprehensive exam, thesis/dissertation, exam, proposal, oral defense, skill and/or second language. *Entrance requirements:* For master's and doctorate, GRE General Test, 3 letters of recommendation, letter of interest, transcripts. Additional exam requirements/recommendations for international students: Required—TOEFL (minimum score 550 paper-based), IELTS (minimum score 7). *Application deadline:* For fall admission, 1/4 for domestic and international students. Application fee: $50. Electronic applications accepted. *Financial support:* In 2014–15, 104 students received support, including 17 fellowships (averaging $9,268 per year), 16 research assistantships with partial tuition reimbursements available (averaging $10,567 per year), 47 teaching assistantships with partial tuition reimbursements available (averaging $8,608 per year); career-related internships or fieldwork, Federal Work-Study, institutionally sponsored loans, scholarships/grants, traineeships, health care benefits, tuition waivers (partial), and unspecified assistantships also available. Support available to part-time students. Financial award application deadline: 3/1; financial award applicants required to submit FAFSA. *Faculty research:* Ethnology, archaeology, evolutionary anthropology, environment, water and land use, gender and social frameworks, Greater Southwest, Latin America, political economy, public anthropology. *Total annual research expenditures:* $1.2 million. *Unit head:* Michael W. Graves, Chair, 505-277-4524, Fax: 505-277-0874, E-mail: mwgraves@unm.edu. *Application contact:* Erika E. Gerety, Program Advisement Coordinator, 505-277-2732, Fax: 505-277-0874, E-mail: erika@unm.edu.
Website: http://www.unm.edu/~anthro/

The University of North Carolina at Chapel Hill, Graduate School, College of Arts and Sciences, Department of Classics, Chapel Hill, NC 27599. Offers classical archaeology (MA, PhD); classics (MA, PhD). Terminal master's awarded for partial completion of doctoral program. *Degree requirements:* For master's, one foreign language, comprehensive exam, thesis; for doctorate, 2 foreign languages, comprehensive exam, thesis/dissertation. *Entrance requirements:* For master's and doctorate, GRE General Test, minimum GPA of 3.0. Electronic applications accepted.

University of Oklahoma, College of Arts and Sciences, Department of Anthropology, Norman, OK 73019. Offers anthropology (PhD); applied linguistic anthropology (MA); archaeology (PhD); health and human biology (PhD). *Faculty:* 30 full-time (14 women), 1 part-time/adjunct (0 women). *Students:* 38 full-time (24 women), 27 part-time (10 women); includes 11 minority (2 Black or African American, non-Hispanic/Latino; 6 American Indian or Alaska Native, non-Hispanic/Latino; 2 Hispanic/Latino; 1 Two or more races, non-Hispanic/Latino), 2 international. Average age 31. 40 applicants, 60% accepted, 17 enrolled. In 2014, 7 master's, 4 doctorates awarded. *Degree requirements:* For master's, one foreign language, comprehensive exam (for some programs), thesis; for doctorate, one foreign language, comprehensive exam, thesis/dissertation. *Entrance requirements:* For master's and doctorate, GRE, minimum undergraduate GPA of 3.0, statement of purpose, 2 letters of recommendation, department application. Additional exam requirements/recommendations for international students: Required—TOEFL (minimum score 79 iBT). *Application deadline:* 2/1 for domestic and international students. Application fee: $50 ($100 for international students). Electronic applications accepted. *Expenses:* Tuition, state resident: full-time $4394; part-time $183.10 per credit hour. Tuition, nonresident: full-time $16,970; part-time $707.10 per credit hour. *Required fees:* $2892; $109.95 per credit hour. $126.50 per semester. *Financial support:* In 2014–15, 49 students received support, including 2 fellowships with full tuition reimbursements available (averaging $5,000 per year), 2 research assistantships with partial tuition reimbursements available (averaging $11,000 per year), 17 teaching assistantships with partial tuition reimbursements available (averaging $14,670 per year); career-related internships or fieldwork, Federal Work-Study, scholarships/grants, health care benefits, and unspecified assistantships also available. Financial award application deadline: 6/1; financial award applicants required to submit FAFSA. *Faculty research:* Sociocultural anthropology, North American archeology, linguistic, applied linguistics, health and human biology, Native North America. *Total annual research expenditures:* $560,578. *Unit head:* Dr. Diane Warren, Associate Professor/Academic Chair, 405-325-7609, Fax: 405-325-7386, E-mail: dmwarren@ou.edu. *Application contact:* Dr. Cecil Lewis, Graduate Liaison and Associate Professor, 405-325-3415, Fax: 405-325-7386, E-mail: cmlewis@ou.edu.
Website: http://cas.ou.edu/anthropology

University of Pennsylvania, School of Arts and Sciences, Graduate Group in Art and Archaeology of the Mediterranean World, Philadelphia, PA 19104. Offers AM, PhD. Part-time programs available. *Faculty:* 16 full-time (8 women), 1 (woman) part-time/adjunct. *Students:* 22 full-time (15 women), 2 part-time (1 woman); includes 2 minority (both Two or more races, non-Hispanic/Latino), 3 international. 75 applicants, 8% accepted, 4 enrolled. In 2014, 2 master's, 1 doctorate awarded. Terminal master's awarded for partial completion of doctoral program. *Degree requirements:* For master's, 3 foreign languages, thesis, Greek or Latin exam, German and French or Italian exam; for doctorate, 4 foreign languages, thesis/dissertation, Greek or Latin exam, 2nd ancient language exam, German and French or Italian exam. *Entrance requirements:* For master's and doctorate, GRE General Test, knowledge of Greek or Latin and either French, German, or Italian. Additional exam requirements/recommendations for international students: Required—TOEFL. *Application deadline:* For fall admission, 12/1 priority date for domestic students. Application fee: $70. Electronic applications accepted. *Financial support:* Fellowships, institutionally sponsored loans, scholarships/grants, traineeships, health care benefits, and unspecified assistantships available. Financial award application deadline: 12/15. *Unit head:* Dr. Ralph M. Rosen, Associate Dean for Graduate Studies, 215-898-7156, Fax: 215-573-8068, E-mail: grad-dean@sas.upenn.edu. *Application contact:* Arts and Sciences Graduate Admissions, 215-573-5816, Fax: 215-573-8068, E-mail: gdasadmis@sas.upenn.edu.
Website: http://www.sas.upenn.edu/graduate-division

University of Saskatchewan, College of Graduate Studies and Research, College of Arts and Science, Department of Archaeology, Saskatoon, SK S7N 5A2, Canada. Offers MA, PhD. Part-time programs available. *Degree requirements:* For master's, thesis; for doctorate, comprehensive exam (for some programs), thesis/dissertation. *Entrance requirements:* Additional exam requirements/recommendations for international students: Required—TOEFL (minimum score 80 iBT); Recommended—IELTS (minimum score 6.5).

University of South Africa, College of Human Sciences, Pretoria, South Africa. Offers adult education (M Ed); African languages (MA, PhD); African politics (MA, PhD); Afrikaans (MA, PhD); ancient history (MA, PhD); ancient Near Eastern studies (MA, PhD); anthropology (MA, PhD); applied linguistics (MA); Arabic (MA, PhD); archaeology (MA); art history (MA); Biblical archaeology (MA); Biblical studies (M Th, D Th, PhD); Christian spirituality (M Th, D Th); church history (M Th, D Th); classical studies (MA, PhD); clinical psychology (MA); communication (MA, PhD); comparative education (M Ed, Ed D); consulting psychology (D Admin, D Com, PhD); curriculum studies (M Ed, Ed D); development studies (M Admin, MA, D Admin, PhD); didactics (M Ed, Ed D); education (M Tech); education management (M Ed, Ed D); educational psychology (M Ed); English (MA); environmental education (M Ed); French (MA, PhD); German (MA, PhD); Greek (MA); guidance and counseling (M Ed); health studies (MA, PhD),

including health sciences education (MA), health services management (MA), medical and surgical nursing science (critical care general) (MA), midwifery and neonatal nursing science (MA), trauma and emergency care (MA); history (MA, PhD); history of education (Ed D); inclusive education (M Ed, Ed D); information and communications technology policy and regulation (MA); information science (MA, MIS, PhD); international politics (MA, PhD); Islamic studies (MA, PhD); Italian (MA, PhD); Judaica (MA, PhD); linguistics (MA, PhD); mathematical education (M Ed); mathematics education (MA); missiology (M Th, D Th); modern Hebrew (MA, PhD); musicology (MA, MMus, D Mus, PhD); natural science education (M Ed); New Testament (M Th, D Th); Old Testament (D Th); pastoral therapy (M Th, D Th); philosophy (MA); philosophy of education (M Ed, Ed D); politics (MA, PhD); Portuguese (MA, PhD); practical theology (M Th, D Th); psychology (MA, MS, PhD); psychology of education (M Ed, Ed D); public health (MA); religious studies (MA, D Th, PhD); Romance languages (MA); Russian (MA, PhD); Semitic languages (MA, PhD); social behavior studies in HIV/AIDS (MA); social science (mental health) (MA); social science in development studies (MA); social science in psychology (MA); social science in social work (MA); social science in sociology (MA); social work (MSW, DSW, PhD); socio-education (M Ed, Ed D); sociolinguistics (MA); sociology (MA, PhD); Spanish (MA, PhD); systematic theology (M Th, D Th); TESOL (teaching English to speakers of other languages) (MA); theological ethics (M Th, D Th); theory of literature (MA, PhD); urban ministries (D Th); urban ministry (M Th).

University of South Florida, College of Arts and Sciences, Department of Anthropology, Tampa, FL 33620-9951. Offers applied anthropology (MA, PhD), including applied anthropology (PhD), archaeology, biological anthropology, cultural anthropology, medical anthropology; medical anthropology (Graduate Certificate); MA/MPH; PhD/MPH. Part-time programs available. *Faculty:* 18 full-time (10 women). *Students:* 78 full-time (56 women), 52 part-time (35 women); includes 30 minority (8 Black or African American, non-Hispanic/Latino; 2 Asian, non-Hispanic/Latino; 16 Hispanic/Latino; 1 Native Hawaiian or other Pacific Islander, non-Hispanic/Latino; 3 Two or more races, non-Hispanic/Latino), 2 international. Average age 33. 154 applicants, 37% accepted, 34 enrolled. In 2014, 16 master's, 10 doctorates awarded. *Degree requirements:* For master's, one foreign language, comprehensive exam, thesis; for doctorate, one foreign language, comprehensive exam, thesis/dissertation, colloquium presentation. *Entrance requirements:* For master's and doctorate, GRE, minimum GPA of 3.0, 3 letters of recommendation, signed research ethics statement, resume or curriculum vitae; for Graduate Certificate, bachelor's degree with minimum GPA of 3.0. Additional exam requirements/recommendations for international students: Required—TOEFL (minimum score 550 paper-based; 79 iBT) or IELTS (minimum score 6.5). *Application deadline:* For fall admission, 1/15 for domestic students, 1/2 for international students. Application fee: $30. Electronic applications accepted. *Financial support:* In 2014–15, 66 students received support, including 14 research assistantships with tuition reimbursements available (averaging $14,475 per year), 52 teaching assistantships with partial tuition reimbursements available (averaging $12,540 per year); scholarships/grants and tuition waivers (partial) also available. Financial award application deadline: 1/15; financial award applicants required to submit FAFSA. *Faculty research:* Biocultural medical anthropology; archaeology and culture resource management in the Americas; community identity and heritage; urban community issues; verbal and nonverbal communications in media and education; global dynamics of sustainable resource management and economic development; social and cultural constructions of race, ethnicity, and gender. *Total annual research expenditures:* $1.5 million. *Unit head:* Dr. David Himmelgreen, Professor/Department Chairperson, 813-974-2138, Fax: 813-974-2668, E-mail: dhimmelg@usf.edu. *Application contact:* Dr. Heide Castaneda, Assistant Professor and Graduate Director, 813-974-2138, Fax: 813-974-2668, E-mail: hcastaneda@usf.edu.
Website: http://anthropology.usf.edu/graduate/

The University of Tennessee, Graduate School, College of Arts and Sciences, Department of Anthropology, Knoxville, TN 37996. Offers archaeology (MA, PhD); biological anthropology (MA, PhD); cultural anthropology (MA, PhD); zoo-archaeology (MA, PhD). *Degree requirements:* For master's, thesis; for doctorate, one foreign language, thesis/dissertation. *Entrance requirements:* For master's and doctorate, GRE General Test, minimum GPA of 2.7. Additional exam requirements/recommendations for international students: Required—TOEFL. Electronic applications accepted.

The University of Texas at Austin, Graduate School, College of Liberal Arts, Department of Anthropology, Austin, TX 78712-1111. Offers archaeology (MA, PhD); cultural forms (MA, PhD); linguistic anthropology (MA, PhD); physical anthropology (MA, PhD); social anthropology (MA, PhD). Part-time programs available. Terminal master's awarded for partial completion of doctoral program. *Degree requirements:* For master's, thesis; for doctorate, one foreign language, thesis/dissertation. *Entrance requirements:* For master's and doctorate, GRE General Test. Additional exam requirements/recommendations for international students: Required—TOEFL. Electronic applications accepted.

University of West Florida, College of Arts and Sciences: Arts, Division of Anthropology and Archaeology, Pensacola, FL 32514-5750. Offers anthropology (MA); historical archaeology (MA). *Degree requirements:* For master's, internship or thesis. *Entrance requirements:* For master's, GRE, transcripts, minimum GPA of 3.0, 3 letters of recommendation, writing sample, letter of intent describing background, study interests, and professional goals. Additional exam requirements/recommendations for international students: Required—TOEFL (minimum score 550 paper-based).

University of Wisconsin–Madison, Graduate School, College of Letters and Science, Department of Anthropology, Madison, WI 53706-1380. Offers archaeology (PhD); biological anthropology (PhD); cultural anthropology (PhD). Terminal master's awarded for partial completion of doctoral program. *Degree requirements:* For doctorate, thesis/

dissertation. *Entrance requirements:* For doctorate, qualifying exam. Electronic applications accepted. *Expenses:* Tuition, state resident: full-time $10,723; part-time $745 per credit. Tuition, nonresident: full-time $24,054; part-time $1578 per credit. *Required fees:* $374 per semester. Tuition and fees vary according to course load, program and reciprocity agreements. *Faculty research:* Archaeology, biological, anthropology, cultural anthropology.

Washington State University, College of Liberal Arts, Department of Anthropology, Pullman, WA 99164. Offers archaeology (MA, PhD); cultural anthropology (PhD); evolutionary anthropology (MA, PhD). Program applications must be made through the Pullman campus. *Faculty:* 20 full-time (10 women), 1 (woman) part-time/adjunct. *Students:* 59 full-time (33 women), 9 part-time (4 women); includes 8 minority (2 Asian, non-Hispanic/Latino; 4 Hispanic/Latino; 2 Two or more races, non-Hispanic/Latino), 9 international. Average age 30. 85 applicants, 40% accepted, 17 enrolled. In 2014, 10 master's, 3 doctorates awarded. *Degree requirements:* For master's, one foreign language, comprehensive exam (for some programs), thesis; for doctorate, one foreign language, comprehensive exam, thesis/dissertation, written and oral preliminary exam. *Entrance requirements:* For master's and doctorate, GRE General Test, curriculum vitae, statement of intent, official transcripts, 3 letters of recommendation, one or two undergraduate papers (from BA/BS applicants), minimum GPA of 3.0. Additional exam requirements/recommendations for international students: Required—TOEFL (minimum score 550 paper-based), IELTS. *Application deadline:* For fall admission, 1/10 priority date for domestic and international students; for spring admission, 7/1 for domestic and international students. Application fee: $75. Electronic applications accepted. *Expenses:* Tuition, state resident: full-time $11,768. Tuition, nonresident: full-time $25,200. *Required fees:* $960. Tuition and fees vary according to program. *Financial support:* In 2014–15, 67 students received support, including 5 research assistantships with full tuition reimbursements available (averaging $13,706 per year), 5 teaching assistantships with full tuition reimbursements available (averaging $13,952 per year); fellowships, Federal Work-Study, scholarships/grants, health care benefits, and unspecified assistantships also available. Support available to part-time students. Financial award application deadline: 2/15; financial award applicants required to submit FAFSA. *Faculty research:* Quantitative analysis of archaeological data, simulation of aspects of prehistoric behavior, subsistence strategies, language use, inequality and poverty, gender, pedagogy, Mexico/U.S. border region, childhood, infectious and parasitic diseases, the analysis of mitochondrial DNA (mtDNA) and Y-chromosomal DNA. *Total annual research expenditures:* $673,000. *Unit head:* Dr. Andrew Duff, Chair, 509-335-3441, Fax: 509-335-3999, E-mail: duff@wsu.edu. *Application contact:* Graduate School Admissions, 800-GRADWSU, Fax: 509-335-1949, E-mail: gradsch@wsu.edu.
Website: http://libarts.wsu.edu/anthro/

Washington University in St. Louis, Graduate School of Arts and Sciences, Department of Art History and Archaeology, St. Louis, MO 63130-4899. Offers AM (PhD). *Degree requirements:* For doctorate, 2 foreign languages, comprehensive exam, thesis/dissertation. *Entrance requirements:* For master's and doctorate, GRE General Test, sample of written work. Electronic applications accepted. *Faculty research:* Ancient, medieval, Renaissance, early modern European, modern and contemporary European and American, and Asian art history; classical archaeology.

Wheaton College, Graduate School, Department of Biblical and Theological Studies, Wheaton, IL 60187-5593. Offers Biblical and theological studies (PhD); Biblical archaeology (MA); Biblical exegesis (MA); Biblical studies (MA); general theological studies (MA); historical and systematic theology (MA), including biblical and theological studies; history of Christianity (MA), including Biblical and theological studies. Part-time programs available. *Students:* 64 full-time (13 women), 64 part-time (28 women); includes 10 minority (6 Asian, non-Hispanic/Latino; 3 Hispanic/Latino; 1 Two or more races, non-Hispanic/Latino), 12 international. Average age 33. 159 applicants, 72% accepted, 68 enrolled. In 2014, 48 master's, 9 doctorates awarded. *Degree requirements:* For doctorate, thesis/dissertation. *Entrance requirements:* For master's, GRE General Test. Additional exam requirements/recommendations for international students: Required—TOEFL (minimum score 550 paper-based; 80 iBT), IELTS (minimum score 6.5), TOEFL (minimum score 600 paper-based; 90 iBT) or IELTS (minimum score 7.5) for PhD. *Application deadline:* For fall admission, 1/1 priority date for domestic students, 1/1 for international students; for spring admission, 11/1 for domestic students. Applications are processed on a rolling basis. Application fee: $30. Electronic applications accepted. *Financial support:* Scholarships/grants and unspecified assistantships available. Financial award application deadline: 3/1; financial award applicants required to submit FAFSA. *Unit head:* Dr. Jeffrey Bingham, Associate Dean, 630-752-5905, E-mail: jeffrey.p.greenman@wheaton.edu. *Application contact:* Dusty Di Santo, Director of Graduate Admissions, 630-752-5195, Fax: 630-752-7047, E-mail: graduate.admissions@wheaton.edu.
Website: http://www.wheaton.edu/academics/departments/theology

Yale University, Graduate School of Arts and Sciences, Department of Near Eastern Languages and Civilizations, New Haven, CT 06520. Offers Arabic and Islamic studies (MA, PhD); archaeology of the ancient Near East (MA, PhD); Assyriology (MA, PhD); Egyptology (MA, PhD); Graeco-Arabic studies (MA, PhD); Northwest Semitic, Bible, comparative Semitics (MA, PhD). *Degree requirements:* For doctorate, 2 foreign languages, thesis/dissertation. *Entrance requirements:* For doctorate, GRE General Test.

Yale University, Graduate School of Arts and Sciences, Interdisciplinary Program in Archaeological Studies, New Haven, CT 06520. Offers MA. *Degree requirements:* For master's, thesis. *Entrance requirements:* For master's, GRE General Test.

Biological Anthropology

Duke University, Graduate School, Department of Evolutionary Anthropology, Durham, NC 27708. Offers cellular and molecular biology (PhD); gross anatomy and physical anthropology (PhD), including comparative morphology of human and non-human primates, primate social behavior, vertebrate paleontology; neuroanatomy (PhD). *Degree requirements:* For doctorate, one foreign language, thesis/dissertation. *Entrance requirements:* For doctorate, GRE General Test. Additional exam requirements/recommendations for international students: Required—TOEFL (minimum score 577 paper-based; 90 iBT) or IELTS (minimum score 7). Electronic applications accepted. *Expenses:* Tuition: Full-time $45,760; part-time $2765 per credit. *Required fees:* $978. Full-time tuition and fees vary according to program.

Kent State University, College of Arts and Sciences, School of Biomedical Sciences, Kent, OH 44242-0001. Offers biological anthropology (PhD); cellular and molecular

biology (PhD), including cellular biology and structures, molecular biology and genetics; neurosciences (PhD); pharmacology (MS); physiology (PhD). *Students:* 82 full-time (50 women), 4 part-time (3 women); includes 5 minority (1 Black or African American, non-Hispanic/Latino; 1 Asian, non-Hispanic/Latino; 1 Hispanic/Latino; 2 Two or more races, non-Hispanic/Latino), 33 international. Average age 29. 223 applicants, 13% accepted, 22 enrolled. In 2014, 5 master's, 7 doctorates awarded. Terminal master's awarded for partial completion of doctoral program. *Degree requirements:* For master's, thesis; for doctorate, thesis/dissertation, candidacy exam. *Entrance requirements:* For master's and doctorate, GRE General Test, minimum GPA of 3.0, transcript, goal statement, resume, 3 letters of recommendation. Additional exam requirements/recommendations for international students: Required—TOEFL (minimum score: paper-based 525, iBT 71), Michigan English Language Assessment Battery (minimum score of 75), IELTS

(minimum score of 6.0), PTE Academic (minimum score of 48), or completion of ELS level 112 Intensive Program. *Application deadline:* For fall admission, 1/1 for domestic students. Application fee: $45 ($70 for international students). Electronic applications accepted. *Expenses:* Tuition, state resident: full-time $8730; part-time $485 per credit hour. Tuition, nonresident: full-time $14,886; part-time $827 per credit hour. Tuition and fees vary according to campus/location and program. *Financial support:* In 2014–15, 76 students received support. Research assistantships with full tuition reimbursements available, teaching assistantships, career-related internships or fieldwork, Federal Work-Study, and unspecified assistantships available. Financial award application deadline: 1/1. *Unit head:* Dr. Eric Mintz, Director, 330-672-2263, E-mail: emintz@kent.edu. *Application contact:* 330-672-2263, Fax: 330-672-9391, E-mail: jwearden@kent.edu. Website: http://www.kent.edu/biomedical/

Mercyhurst University, Graduate Studies, Program in Forensic and Biological Anthropology, Erie, PA 16546. Offers MS. *Entrance requirements:* For master's, GRE or MAT, undergraduate degree in related field, interview, resume, essay, three professional references, transcripts. Additional exam requirements/recommendations for international students: Required—TOEFL.

Cultural Anthropology

California Institute of Integral Studies, School of Consciousness and Transformation, San Francisco, CA 94103. Offers anthropology and social change (MA, PhD); creative inquiry/interdisciplinary arts (MFA); East-West psychology (MA, PhD); philosophy and religion (MA, PhD), including Asian and comparative studies, ecology, spirituality, and religion, philosophy, cosmology, and consciousness, women's spirituality; transformative leadership (MA); transformative studies (PhD); writing and consciousness (MFA). Part-time and evening/weekend programs available. Postbaccalaureate distance learning degree programs offered (no on-campus study). *Students:* 385 full-time (256 women), 102 part-time (71 women); includes 124 minority (31 Black or African American, non-Hispanic/Latino; 3 American Indian or Alaska Native, non-Hispanic/Latino; 19 Asian, non-Hispanic/Latino; 39 Hispanic/Latino; 1 Native Hawaiian or other Pacific Islander, non-Hispanic/Latino; 31 Two or more races, non-Hispanic/Latino), 53 international. Average age 43. 196 applicants, 92% accepted, 125 enrolled. In 2014, 75 master's, 41 doctorates awarded. Terminal master's awarded for partial completion of doctoral program. *Degree requirements:* For master's, thesis optional; for doctorate, comprehensive exam, thesis/dissertation, 1 foreign language (for Asian comparative studies). *Entrance requirements:* For master's, minimum GPA of 3.0, letters of recommendation, writing sample; for doctorate, master's degree, minimum GPA of 3.0, letters of recommendation, writing sample. Additional exam requirements/recommendations for international students: Required—TOEFL. *Application deadline:* For fall admission, 2/1 priority date for domestic and international students; for spring admission, 10/15 priority date for domestic and international students. Applications are processed on a rolling basis. Application fee: $65. Electronic applications accepted. *Expenses: Tuition:* Full-time $18,270; part-time $1015 per credit. *Required fees:* $85 per semester hour. *Financial support:* In 2014–15, 445 students received support, including 5 research assistantships (averaging $800 per year), 28 teaching assistantships (averaging $825 per year); career-related internships or fieldwork, Federal Work-Study, and scholarships/grants also available. Support available to part-time students. Financial award application deadline: 4/15; financial award applicants required to submit FAFSA. *Faculty research:* Ecology and sustainability, philosophy and religion, East-West psychology, integrative health, social and cultural anthropology, transformative leadership. *Application contact:* David Townes, Senior Admissions Counselor, 415-575-6152, Fax: 415-575-1268, E-mail: admissions@ciis.edu.
Website: http://www.ciis.edu/

Concordia University, School of Graduate Studies, Faculty of Arts and Science, Department of Sociology and Anthropology, Montréal, QC H3G 1M8, Canada. Offers social and cultural anthropology (MA); sociology (MA). *Degree requirements:* For master's, comprehensive exam or thesis. *Entrance requirements:* For master's, honors degree in sociology or equivalent. *Faculty research:* Community and ethnic relations, popular culture, regional development in Canada, industrial and social movements, social problems and policies.

Cornell University, Graduate School, Graduate Fields of Arts and Sciences, Field of Anthropology, Ithaca, NY 14853-0001. Offers archaeological anthropology (PhD); biological anthropology (PhD); sociocultural anthropology (PhD). *Degree requirements:* For doctorate, one foreign language, comprehensive exam, thesis/dissertation, teaching experience. *Entrance requirements:* For doctorate, GRE General Test, 3 letters of recommendation, sample of written work. Additional exam requirements/recommendations for international students: Required—TOEFL (minimum score 550 paper-based; 77 iBT). Electronic applications accepted. *Faculty research:* Culture, engaged anthropology, political economy, area studies: Asia, Americas, Europe; interdisciplinary and ethnic studies: Asian-American studies.

Duke University, Graduate School, Department of Cultural Anthropology, Durham, NC 27708. Offers physical anthropology (PhD), including comparative morphology of human and non-human primates, primate social behavior; social/cultural anthropology (PhD); JD/AM. *Degree requirements:* For doctorate, one foreign language, thesis/dissertation. *Entrance requirements:* For doctorate, GRE General Test. Additional exam requirements/recommendations for international students: Required—TOEFL (minimum score 577 paper-based; 90 iBT) or IELTS (minimum score 7). *Expenses: Tuition:* Full-time $45,760; part-time $2765 per credit. *Required fees:* $978. Full-time tuition and fees vary according to program.

Eastern University, Program in Theological and Cultural Anthropology, St. Davids, PA 19087-3696. Offers MA. *Students:* 6 full-time (2 women), 1 part-time (0 women); includes 2 minority (1 Black or African American, non-Hispanic/Latino; 1 Hispanic/Latino). Average age 35. 6 applicants, 100% accepted, 5 enrolled. *Entrance requirements:* For master's, minimum GPA of 2.5, previous anthropology courses. Additional exam requirements/recommendations for international students: Required—TOEFL. *Application deadline:* For fall admission, 8/14 for domestic students. Applications are processed on a rolling basis. Application fee: $35. Electronic applications accepted. Application fee is waived when completed online. *Expenses: Tuition:* Full-time $15,600; part-time $650 per credit. *Required fees:* $30; $27.50 per semester. One-time fee: $50. Tuition and fees vary according to course load, degree level and program. *Unit head:* Dr. Eloise Meneses, Director, 610-341-5953, E-mail: emeneses@eastern.edu. *Application contact:* Casey Malone, Director of Enrollment, 610-225-5462, E-mail: cmalone2@eastern.edu.

The Graduate Center, City University of New York, Graduate Studies, Program in Anthropology, New York, NY 10016-4039. Offers anthropological linguistics (PhD); archaeology (PhD); cultural anthropology (PhD); physical anthropology (PhD). *Degree requirements:* For doctorate, one foreign language, thesis/dissertation. *Entrance requirements:* For doctorate, GRE General Test. Additional exam requirements/recommendations for international students: Required—TOEFL. Electronic applications accepted.

Memorial University of Newfoundland, School of Graduate Studies, Department of Anthropology, St. John's, NL A1C 5S7, Canada. Offers archaeology and physical anthropology (MA, PhD); social and cultural anthropology (MA, PhD). Part-time programs available. *Degree requirements:* For master's, thesis (for some programs); for doctorate, comprehensive exam, thesis/dissertation, oral defense of thesis. *Entrance requirements:* For master's, 2nd class degree in related field. Electronic applications accepted. *Faculty research:* Early European settlements, ethnoarchaeology, economic/political anthropology, land claims and aboriginal rights, marine anthropology.

North Carolina State University, Graduate School, College of Humanities and Social Sciences, Department of Sociology and Anthropology, Program in Anthropology, Raleigh, NC 27695. Offers bioarchaeology (MA); cultural anthropology (MA); environmental anthropology (MA).

Northern Arizona University, Graduate College, College of Social and Behavioral Sciences, Department of Anthropology, Flagstaff, AZ 86011. Offers archaeology (MA); cultural anthropology (MA); linguistic anthropology (MA). *Degree requirements:* For master's, thesis (for some programs), internship paper. *Entrance requirements:* For master's, 12 undergraduate hours in anthropology. Additional exam requirements/recommendations for international students: Required—TOEFL (minimum score 550 paper-based; 80 iBT), IELTS (minimum score 7). Electronic applications accepted. *Faculty research:* Economic development, culture change, ethnohistory, archaeology of the Southwest, small town networks and HIV.

Rice University, Graduate Programs, School of Social Sciences, Department of Anthropology, Houston, TX 77251-1892. Offers archaeology (MA, PhD); social-cultural anthropology (MA, PhD). Terminal master's awarded for partial completion of doctoral program. *Degree requirements:* For master's, one foreign language, 3 major papers, dissertation proposal and language exam or thesis; for doctorate, one foreign language, thesis/dissertation. *Entrance requirements:* For master's and doctorate, research proposal. Additional exam requirements/recommendations for international students: Required—TOEFL (minimum score 90 iBT). Electronic applications accepted.

San Francisco State University, Division of Graduate Studies, College of Liberal and Creative Arts, Department of Anthropology, San Francisco, CA 94132-1722. Offers archaeology (MA); biological/physical anthropology (MA); social/cultural anthropology (MA); visual anthropology (MA). *Expenses:* Tuition, state resident: full-time $6738. Tuition, nonresident: full-time $17,898; part-time $372 per credit hour. *Required fees:* $498 per semester. *Faculty research:* Immigration, ethnicity, urban anthropology, Californian and Latin American archaeology. *Unit head:* Dr. James Quesada, Chair, 415-338-1633, E-mail: jquesada@sfsu.edu. *Application contact:* Dr. Douglass Bailey, Graduate Coordinator, 415-338-1427, E-mail: dwbailey@sfsu.edu.
Website: http://anthropology.sfsu.edu/

University of California, Santa Barbara, Graduate Division, College of Letters and Sciences, Division of Social Sciences, Department of Anthropology, Santa Barbara, CA 93106-2014. Offers archaeology (MA, PhD); integrative anthropological sciences (MA, PhD); sociocultural anthropology (MA, PhD); MA/PhD. Terminal master's awarded for partial completion of doctoral program. *Degree requirements:* For master's, comprehensive exam (for some programs), thesis (for some programs); for doctorate, comprehensive exam (for some programs), thesis/dissertation. *Entrance requirements:* For master's and doctorate, GRE General Test, statement of purpose, personal achievements statement, transcripts, writing sample, curriculum vitae, letters of recommendation. Additional exam requirements/recommendations for international students: Required—TOEFL (minimum score 550 paper-based; 80 iBT), IELTS (minimum score 7). Electronic applications accepted. *Faculty research:* Archaeology, bioarchaeology, biosocial anthropology, evolutionary ecology, evolutionary psychology, sociocultural anthropology.

University of California, Santa Cruz, Division of Graduate Studies, Division of Social Sciences, Department of Anthropology, Santa Cruz, CA 95064. Offers cultural anthropology (PhD). *Degree requirements:* For doctorate, thesis/dissertation, qualifying exam. *Entrance requirements:* For doctorate, GRE General Test. Additional exam requirements/recommendations for international students: Required—TOEFL (minimum score 550 paper-based; 83 iBT); Recommended—IELTS (minimum score 8). Electronic applications accepted. *Faculty research:* Culture and power, women's roles, AIDS, folklore.

University of Denver, Division of Arts, Humanities and Social Sciences, Department of Anthropology, Denver, CO 80208. Offers archaeology (MA); cultural anthropology (MA); museum studies (MA). Part-time programs available. *Faculty:* 7 full-time (3 women). *Students:* 1 full-time (0 women), 20 part-time (14 women); includes 5 minority (2 Hispanic/Latino; 3 Two or more races, non-Hispanic/Latino), 1 international. Average age 25. 47 applicants, 49% accepted, 11 enrolled. In 2014, 4 master's awarded. *Degree requirements:* For master's, one foreign language, comprehensive exam, thesis (for some programs), tool, foreign language literacy, or course work. *Entrance requirements:* For master's, GRE General Test, bachelor's degree, transcripts, personal statement, two letters of recommendation. Additional exam requirements/recommendations for international students: Required—TOEFL (minimum score 550 paper-based; 80 iBT). *Application deadline:* For fall admission, 2/4 priority date for domestic and international students. Applications are processed on a rolling basis. Application fee: $65. Electronic applications accepted. *Expenses:* Expenses: $1,199 per credit hour. *Financial support:* In 2014–15, 18 students received support, including 12 teaching assistantships with partial tuition reimbursements available (averaging $5,000 per year); career-related internships or fieldwork, Federal Work-Study, institutionally sponsored loans, scholarships/grants, and unspecified assistantships also available. Support available to part-time students. Financial award application deadline: 2/15; financial award applicants required to submit FAFSA. *Faculty research:* Human diversity, human rights, historic archaeology, museums and heritage, high-tech field methods. *Unit head:* Dr. Dean J. Saitta, Chair, 303-871-2680, E-mail: dsaitta@du.edu. *Application contact:* Dr. Larry Conyers, Professor/Director of Graduate and Undergraduate Programs, 303-871-2684, E-mail: lconyers@du.edu.
Website: http://www.du.edu/ahss/schools/anthropology/

University of Michigan, Horace H. Rackham School of Graduate Studies, College of Literature, Science, and the Arts, Department of Anthropology, Ann Arbor, MI 48109-1107. Offers archaeological (PhD); biological (PhD); linguistic (PhD); sociocultural (PhD). *Faculty:* 40 full-time (18 women), 6 part-time/adjunct (3 women). *Students:* 99 full-time (59 women); includes 19 minority (1 Black or African American, non-Hispanic/Latino; 1 American Indian or Alaska Native, non-Hispanic/Latino; 6 Asian, non-Hispanic/Latino; 6 Hispanic/Latino; 5 Two or more races, non-Hispanic/Latino), 13 international. Average age 28. 206 applicants, 14% accepted, 15 enrolled. In 2014, 15 doctorates awarded. *Degree requirements:* For doctorate, one foreign language, comprehensive exam, thesis/dissertation, preliminary examination, oral defense of dissertation. *Entrance requirements:* For doctorate, GRE General Test. Additional exam requirements/recommendations for international students: Required—TOEFL (minimum score 560 paper-based; 84 iBT). *Application deadline:* For fall admission, 12/15 for domestic and international students. Application fee: $75 ($90 for international students). Electronic applications accepted. *Financial support:* In 2014–15, 67 students received support, including 47 fellowships with full tuition reimbursements available (averaging $19,350 per year), 4 research assistantships with full tuition reimbursements available (averaging $19,350 per year), 50 teaching assistantships with full tuition reimbursements available (averaging $19,350 per year); institutionally sponsored loans, scholarships/grants, traineeships, health care benefits, tuition waivers (full), and unspecified assistantships also available. Financial award application deadline: 3/1; financial award applicants required to submit FAFSA. *Faculty research:* Sociocultural, linguistic, biological and archaeological anthropology. *Unit head:* Dr. Thomas Fricke, Chair, 734-764-7274, Fax: 734-763-6077. *Application contact:* Katia Kitchen, Graduate Program Assistant, 734-936-7933, Fax: 734-763-6077, E-mail: kitchenk@umich.edu.
Website: http://www.lsa.umich.edu/anthro/

University of South Florida, College of Arts and Sciences, Department of Anthropology, Tampa, FL 33620-9951. Offers applied anthropology (MA, PhD), including applied anthropology (PhD), archaeology, biological anthropology, cultural anthropology, medical anthropology; medical anthropology (Graduate Certificate); MA/MPH; PhD/MPH. Part-time programs available. *Faculty:* 18 full-time (10 women). *Students:* 78 full-time (56 women), 52 part-time (35 women); includes 30 minority (8 Black or African American, non-Hispanic/Latino; 2 Asian, non-Hispanic/Latino; 16 Hispanic/Latino; 1 Native Hawaiian or other Pacific Islander, non-Hispanic/Latino; 3 Two or more races, non-Hispanic/Latino), 2 international. Average age 33. 154 applicants, 37% accepted, 34 enrolled. In 2014, 16 master's, 10 doctorates awarded. *Degree requirements:* For master's, one foreign language, comprehensive exam, thesis; for doctorate, one foreign language, comprehensive exam, thesis/dissertation, colloquium presentation. *Entrance requirements:* For master's and doctorate, GRE, minimum GPA of 3.0, 3 letters of recommendation, signed research ethics statement, resume or curriculum vitae; for Graduate Certificate, bachelor's degree with minimum GPA of 3.0. Additional exam requirements/recommendations for international students: Required—TOEFL (minimum score 550 paper-based; 79 iBT) or IELTS (minimum score 6.5). *Application deadline:* For fall admission, 1/15 for domestic students, 1/2 for international students. Application fee: $30. Electronic applications accepted. *Financial support:* In 2014–15, 66 students received support, including 14 research assistantships with tuition reimbursements available (averaging $14,475 per year), 52 teaching assistantships with partial tuition reimbursements available (averaging $12,540 per year); scholarships/grants and tuition waivers (partial) also available. Financial award application deadline: 1/15; financial award applicants required to submit FAFSA. *Faculty research:* Biocultural medical anthropology; archaeology and culture resource management in the Americas; community identity and heritage; urban community issues; verbal and nonverbal communications in media and education; global dynamics of sustainable resource management and economic development; social and cultural constructions of race, ethnicity, and gender. *Total annual research expenditures:* $1.5 million. *Unit head:* Dr. David Himmelgreen, Professor/Department Chairperson, 813-974-2138, Fax: 813-974-2668, E-mail: dhimmelg@usf.edu. *Application contact:* Dr. Heide Castaneda, Assistant Professor and Graduate Director, 813-974-2138, Fax: 813-974-2668, E-mail: hcastaneda@usf.edu.
Website: http://anthropology.usf.edu/graduate/

The University of Tennessee, Graduate School, College of Arts and Sciences, Department of Anthropology, Knoxville, TN 37996. Offers archaeology (MA, PhD); biological anthropology (MA, PhD); cultural anthropology (MA, PhD); zoo-archaeology (MA, PhD). *Degree requirements:* For master's, thesis; for doctorate, one foreign language, thesis/dissertation. *Entrance requirements:* For master's and doctorate, GRE General Test, minimum GPA of 2.7. Additional exam requirements/recommendations for international students: Required—TOEFL. Electronic applications accepted.

University of Wisconsin–Madison, Graduate School, College of Letters and Science, Department of Anthropology, Madison, WI 53706-1380. Offers archaeology (PhD); biological anthropology (PhD); cultural anthropology (PhD). Terminal master's awarded for partial completion of doctoral program. *Degree requirements:* For doctorate, thesis/dissertation. *Entrance requirements:* For doctorate, qualifying exam. Electronic applications accepted. *Expenses:* Tuition, state resident: full-time $10,723; part-time $745 per credit. Tuition, nonresident: full-time $24,054; part-time $1578 per credit. *Required fees:* $374 per semester. Tuition and fees vary according to course load, program and reciprocity agreements. *Faculty research:* Archaeology, biological, anthropology, cultural anthropology.

Washington State University, College of Liberal Arts, Department of Anthropology, Pullman, WA 99164. Offers archaeology (MA, PhD); cultural anthropology (PhD); evolutionary anthropology (MA, PhD). Program applications must be made through the Pullman campus. *Faculty:* 20 full-time (10 women), 1 (woman) part-time/adjunct. *Students:* 59 full-time (33 women), 9 part-time (4 women); includes 8 minority (2 Asian, non-Hispanic/Latino; 4 Hispanic/Latino; 2 Two or more races, non-Hispanic/Latino), 9 international. Average age 30. 85 applicants, 40% accepted, 17 enrolled. In 2014, 10 master's, 3 doctorates awarded. *Degree requirements:* For master's, one foreign language, comprehensive exam (for some programs), thesis; for doctorate, one foreign language, comprehensive exam, thesis/dissertation, written and oral preliminary exam. *Entrance requirements:* For master's and doctorate, GRE General Test, curriculum vitae, statement of intent, official transcripts, 3 letters of recommendation, one or two undergraduate papers (from BA/BS applicants), minimum GPA of 3.0. Additional exam requirements/recommendations for international students: Required—TOEFL (minimum score 550 paper-based), IELTS. *Application deadline:* For fall admission, 1/10 priority date for domestic and international students; for spring admission, 7/1 for domestic and international students. Application fee: $75. Electronic applications accepted. *Expenses:* Tuition, state resident: full-time $11,768. Tuition, nonresident: full-time $25,200. *Required fees:* $960. Tuition and fees vary according to program. *Financial support:* In 2014–15, 67 students received support, including 5 research assistantships with full tuition reimbursements available (averaging $13,706 per year), 5 teaching assistantships with full tuition reimbursements available (averaging $13,952 per year); fellowships, Federal Work-Study, scholarships/grants, health care benefits, and unspecified assistantships also available. Support available to part-time students. Financial award application deadline: 2/15; financial award applicants required to submit FAFSA. *Faculty research:* Quantitative analysis of archaeological data, simulation of aspects of prehistoric behavior, subsistence strategies, language use, inequality and poverty, gender, pedagogy, Mexico/U.S. border region, childhood, infectious and parasitic diseases, the analysis of mitochondrial DNA (mtDNA) and Y-chromosomal DNA. *Total annual research expenditures:* $673,000. *Unit head:* Dr. Andrew Duff, Chair, 509-335-3441, Fax: 509-335-3999, E-mail: duff@wsu.edu. *Application contact:* Graduate School Admissions, 800-GRADWSU, Fax: 509-335-1949, E-mail: gradsch@wsu.edu.
Website: http://libarts.wsu.edu/anthro/

Demography and Population Studies

The American University in Cairo, School of Global Affairs and Public Policy, Center for Migration and Refugee Studies, Cairo, Egypt. Offers forced migration and refugee studies (Diploma); migration and refugee studies (MA). Tuition and fees vary according to course load and program.

Bowling Green State University, Graduate College, College of Arts and Sciences, Department of Sociology, Bowling Green, OH 43403. Offers demography and population studies (MA); social psychology (MA); sociology (PhD). Part-time programs available. *Degree requirements:* For master's, thesis or alternative; for doctorate, comprehensive exam, thesis/dissertation. *Entrance requirements:* For master's and doctorate, GRE General Test. Additional exam requirements/recommendations for international students: Required—TOEFL. Electronic applications accepted. *Faculty research:* Applied demography, criminology and deviance, family studies, population studies, social psychology.

Cornell University, Graduate School, Graduate Fields of Agriculture and Life Sciences, Field of Development Sociology, Ithaca, NY 14853-0001. Offers population and development (MS, PhD); rural and environmental sociology (MS, PhD); state, economy, and society (MS, PhD). *Degree requirements:* For doctorate, comprehensive exam, thesis/dissertation. *Entrance requirements:* For master's and doctorate, GRE General Test, 3 letters of recommendation. Additional exam requirements/recommendations for international students: Required—TOEFL (minimum score 550 paper-based; 77 iBT). Electronic applications accepted. *Faculty research:* Demography (population and development), environmental sociology, international and rural community development, political economy and ecology, sustainable agriculture.

Cornell University, Graduate School, Graduate Fields of Agriculture and Life Sciences, Field of Global Development, Ithaca, NY 14853-0001. Offers development policy (MPS); international agriculture and development (MPS); international development (MPS); international nutrition (MPS); international planning (MPS); international population (MPS); science and technology policy (MPS). *Degree requirements:* For master's, project paper. *Entrance requirements:* For master's, GRE General Test (recommended), 2 years of development experience, 2 letters of recommendation. Additional exam requirements/recommendations for international students: Required—TOEFL (minimum score 550 paper-based; 77 iBT). Electronic applications accepted.

Florida State University, The Graduate School, College of Social Sciences and Public Policy, Center for Demography and Population Health, Tallahassee, FL 32306-2240. Offers demography (MS). Part-time programs available. *Faculty:* 10 full-time (5 women). *Students:* 10 full-time (5 women), 2 part-time (1 woman); includes 3 minority (2 Hispanic/Latino; 1 Two or more races, non-Hispanic/Latino), 1 international. Average age 25. 12 applicants, 92% accepted, 10 enrolled. In 2014, 10 master's awarded. *Degree requirements:* For master's, thesis. *Entrance requirements:* For master's, GRE General Test, minimum upper-division GPA of 3.0. Additional exam requirements/recommendations for international students: Required—TOEFL (minimum score 550 paper-based; 80 iBT). *Application deadline:* For fall admission, 6/1 for domestic and international students. Application fee: $30. Electronic applications accepted. *Expenses:* Tuition, state resident: part-time $403.51 per credit hour. Tuition, nonresident: part-time $1004.85 per credit hour. *Required fees:* $75.81 per credit hour. One-time fee: $20 part-time. Tuition and fees vary according to campus/location. *Financial support:* In 2014–15, 1 fellowship (averaging $4,000 per year) was awarded; career-related internships or fieldwork, Federal Work-Study, institutionally sponsored loans, and tuition waivers (partial) also available. Financial award applicants required to submit FAFSA. *Faculty research:* Aging and life course; families, children, youth; fertility and sexual behavior; mortality, morbidity, and health; mathematical demography. *Unit head:* Dr. Karin L. Brewster, Director, 850-644-7106, Fax: 850-644-8818, E-mail: karin.brewster@fsu.edu. *Application contact:* Barbara G. Rousseau, Program Assistant, 850-644-1762, Fax: 850-644-8818, E-mail: brousseau@fsu.edu.
Website: http://popcenter.fsu.edu

Harvard University, Harvard School of Public Health, Department of Global Health and Population, Boston, MA 02115-6096. Offers SM, SD. Part-time programs available. *Faculty:* 33 full-time (9 women), 24 part-time/adjunct (9 women). *Students:* 49 full-time (28 women), 1 (woman) part-time; includes 13 minority (3 Black or African American, non-Hispanic/Latino; 6 Asian, non-Hispanic/Latino; 3 Hispanic/Latino; 1 Two or more races, non-Hispanic/Latino), 26 international. Average age 27. 239 applicants, 22% accepted, 27 enrolled. In 2014, 23 master's, 8 doctorates awarded. *Degree requirements:* For master's, thesis; for doctorate, thesis/dissertation, qualifying exam. *Entrance requirements:* For master's, GRE, MCAT; for doctorate, GRE. Additional exam requirements/recommendations for international students: Required—TOEFL (minimum score 600 paper-based; 100 iBT); Recommended—IELTS (minimum score 7). *Application deadline:* For fall admission, 12/15 for domestic and international students. Application fee: $120. Electronic applications accepted. *Financial support:* Fellowships, research assistantships, teaching assistantships, Federal Work-Study, scholarships/grants, traineeships, and unspecified assistantships available. Support available to part-time students. Financial award application deadline: 2/15; financial award applicants required to submit FAFSA. *Faculty research:* Health systems, international health policy, economics, population and reproductive health, ecology. *Unit head:* Dr. Wafaie W. Fawzi, Chair, 617-432-2086, Fax: 617-432-2435, E-mail: mina@hsph.harvard.edu. *Application contact:* Vincent W. James, Director of Admissions, 617-432-1031, Fax:

617-432-7080, E-mail: admissions@hsph.harvard.edu.
Website: http://www.hsph.harvard.edu/global-health-and-population/

Johns Hopkins University, Bloomberg School of Public Health, Department of Population, Family and Reproductive Health, Baltimore, MD 21205. Offers child and adolescent health and development (MHS, Dr PH, PhD); demography (MHS); population and health (Dr PH, PhD); reproductive, perinatal and women's health (MHS, Dr PH, PhD). Part-time programs available. *Degree requirements:* For master's, essay, fieldwork; for doctorate, thesis/dissertation, 1-year full-time residency, oral and written exams. *Entrance requirements:* For master's and doctorate, GRE General Test, 3 letters of recommendation, curriculum vitae. Additional exam requirements/recommendations for international students: Required—TOEFL (minimum score 600 paper-based). Electronic applications accepted. *Faculty research:* Child and adolescent health and development, population and health and reproductive, perinatal and women's health.

Miami University, College of Arts and Science, Department of Sociology and Gerontology, Oxford, OH 45056. Offers gerontology (MGS); population and social gerontology (MPSG); social gerontology (PhD). Part-time programs available. *Students:* 40 full-time (31 women), 7 part-time (6 women); includes 3 minority (1 Black or African American, non-Hispanic/Latino; 2 Asian, non-Hispanic/Latino), 15 international. Average age 32. In 2014, 8 master's, 5 doctorates awarded. *Entrance requirements:* For master's, GRE General Test; for doctorate, GRE, bachelor's degree; master's degree (or in process of completing master's degree); written professional statement; curriculum vitae/resume; three letters of recommendation. Additional exam requirements/recommendations for international students: Recommended—TOEFL (minimum score 80 iBT), IELTS (minimum score 6.5), TSE (minimum score 54). *Application deadline:* For fall admission, 2/1 for domestic and international students. Application fee: $50. Electronic applications accepted. *Expenses:* Tuition, state resident: full-time $12,887; part-time $537 per credit hour. Tuition, nonresident: full-time $28,449; part-time $1186 per credit hour. *Required fees:* $530; $24 per credit hour. $30 per quarter. Part-time tuition and fees vary according to course load and program. *Financial support:* Fellowships with full and partial tuition reimbursements, research assistantships with full and partial tuition reimbursements, and teaching assistantships with full and partial tuition reimbursements available. Financial award application deadline: 2/1; financial award applicants required to submit FAFSA. *Unit head:* Dr. Jennifer Kinney, Interim Chair, 513-529-2915, E-mail: kinneyjm@miamioh.edu. *Application contact:* Dr. Scott Brown, Director of Graduate Studies, 513-529-8325, E-mail: sbrow@miamioh.edu.
Website: http://www.MiamiOH.edu/sociology/

New York University, Global Institute of Public Health, New York, NY 10003. Offers biological basis of public health (PhD); community and international health (MPH); global health leadership (MPH); health systems and health services research (PhD); population and community health (PhD); public health nutrition (MPH); social and behavioral sciences (MPH); socio-behavioral health (PhD). Part-time programs available. Postbaccalaureate distance learning degree programs offered (no on-campus study). *Faculty:* 26 full-time (20 women), 104 part-time/adjunct (53 women). *Students:* 161 full-time (136 women), 70 part-time (54 women); includes 74 minority (24 Black or African American, non-Hispanic/Latino; 1 American Indian or Alaska Native, non-Hispanic/Latino; 27 Asian, non-Hispanic/Latino; 11 Hispanic/Latino; 4 Native Hawaiian or other Pacific Islander, non-Hispanic/Latino; 7 Two or more races, non-Hispanic/Latino), 39 international. Average age 29. 802 applicants, 70% accepted, 97 enrolled. In 2014, 1 master's awarded. *Degree requirements:* For master's, thesis (for some programs); for doctorate, thesis/dissertation. *Entrance requirements:* For master's and doctorate, GRE. Additional exam requirements/recommendations for international students: Required—TOEFL. *Application deadline:* For fall admission, 2/1 for domestic and international students. Applications are processed on a rolling basis. Electronic applications accepted. *Financial support:* Federal Work-Study and scholarships/grants available. *Unit head:* Dr. Cheryl G. Healton, Director, 212-992-6741. *Application contact:* New York University Information, 212-998-1212.
Website: http://giph.nyu.edu/

Princeton University, Graduate School, Department of Sociology, Princeton, NJ 08544-1019. Offers sociology (PhD); sociology and demography (PhD). *Degree requirements:* For doctorate, variable foreign language requirement, thesis/dissertation. *Entrance requirements:* For doctorate, GRE General Test, GRE Subject Test (recommended), sample of written work. Additional exam requirements/recommendations for international students: Required—TOEFL (minimum score 600 paper-based). Electronic applications accepted.

Princeton University, Graduate School, Program in Population Studies, Princeton, NJ 08544-1019. Offers demography (PhD, Certificate); economics and demography (PhD); public affairs and demography (PhD); sociology and demography (PhD). *Degree requirements:* For doctorate, thesis/dissertation. *Entrance requirements:* For doctorate, GRE General Test. Additional exam requirements/recommendations for international students: Required—TOEFL (minimum score 600 paper-based). Electronic applications accepted. *Faculty research:* Models, fertility, infant and child mortality, migration.

Université de Montréal, Faculty of Arts and Sciences, Department of Demography, Montréal, QC H3C 3J7, Canada. Offers M Sc, PhD. Terminal master's awarded for partial completion of doctoral program. *Degree requirements:* For master's, one foreign language, thesis; for doctorate, one foreign language, thesis/dissertation, general exam. *Entrance requirements:* For master's, minimum GPA of 2.7. Electronic applications accepted. *Faculty research:* Historical demography, population and development, ethnic and linguistic groups, aging of population, family demography.

Université du Québec, Institut National de la Recherche Scientifique, Graduate Programs, Research Center–Urbanization Culture Society, Montreal, QC H2X 1E3, Canada. Offers demography (M Sc, PhD); research practices and public action (MA, DESS); urban studies (M Sc, PhD). Part-time programs available. *Faculty:* 32 full-time. *Students:* 81 full-time (47 women), 20 part-time (15 women), 11 international. Average age 31. 31 applicants, 84% accepted, 22 enrolled. In 2014, 7 master's, 4 doctorates awarded. *Degree requirements:* For master's, thesis (for some programs); for doctorate, thesis/dissertation. *Entrance requirements:* For master's, appropriate bachelor's degree, proficiency in French; for doctorate, appropriate master's degree, proficiency in French; for DESS, proficiency in French. *Application deadline:* For fall admission, 3/30 for domestic and international students; for winter admission, 11/1 for domestic and international students; for spring admission, 3/1 for domestic and international students. Application fee: $45. Electronic applications accepted. *Financial support:* In 2014–15, fellowships (averaging $16,500 per year) were awarded; research assistantships also available. *Faculty research:* Mobility and migration, cultural policies, knowledge mobilization, spatial analysis of data, social demography. *Unit head:* Claire Poitras, Director, 514-499-4002, E-mail: claire.poitras@ucs.inrs.ca. *Application contact:* Sylvie Richard, Registrar, 418-654-2518, Fax: 418-654-3858, E-mail: sylvie.richard@adm.inrs.ca.
Website: http://www.ucs.inrs.ca

University at Albany, State University of New York, College of Arts and Sciences, Department of Sociology, Albany, NY 12222-0001. Offers demography (Certificate); sociology (MA, PhD); urban policy (Certificate). Terminal master's awarded for partial completion of doctoral program. *Degree requirements:* For master's, thesis; for doctorate, thesis/dissertation, 2 specialization exams, research tool. *Entrance requirements:* For master's and doctorate, GRE General Test. Additional exam requirements/recommendations for international students: Required—TOEFL. Electronic applications accepted. *Faculty research:* Gender and equality, crime and deviance, aging, work and organizations, social demography.

University of Alberta, Faculty of Graduate Studies and Research, Department of Sociology, Edmonton, AB T6G 2E1, Canada. Offers criminal justice (MA); demography (MA, PhD); sociology (MA, PhD). Part-time programs available. *Degree requirements:* For master's, thesis (for some programs); for doctorate, thesis/dissertation. *Faculty research:* Criminology, knowledge and culture, methods and theory, population studies, stratification.

University of California, Berkeley, Graduate Division, College of Letters and Science, Department of Demography, Berkeley, CA 94720-1500. Offers PhD. *Degree requirements:* For doctorate, thesis/dissertation, qualifying exam. *Entrance requirements:* For doctorate, GRE General Test, minimum GPA of 3.0, 3 letters of recommendation.

University of California, Berkeley, Graduate Division, College of Letters and Science, Group in Sociology and Demography, Berkeley, CA 94720-1500. Offers MA, PhD. *Degree requirements:* For doctorate, thesis/dissertation, qualifying exam. *Entrance requirements:* For master's and doctorate, GRE General Test, minimum GPA of 3.0, 3 letters of recommendation. Electronic applications accepted.

University of California, Irvine, School of Social Sciences and School of Social Ecology, Program in Demographic and Social Analysis, Irvine, CA 92697. Offers MA. *Students:* 13 full-time (7 women); includes 6 minority (1 Black or African American, non-Hispanic/Latino; 3 Asian, non-Hispanic/Latino; 1 Hispanic/Latino; 1 Two or more races, non-Hispanic/Latino), 1 international. Average age 28. 28 applicants, 82% accepted, 12 enrolled. In 2014, 14 master's awarded. *Entrance requirements:* For master's, GRE, minimum GPA of 3.0. Additional exam requirements/recommendations for international students: Required—TOEFL (minimum score 550 paper-based). *Application deadline:* For fall admission, 1/15 priority date for domestic and international students. Application fee: $90 ($110 for international students). *Financial support:* Application deadline: 3/1. *Unit head:* Susan Brown, Graduate Director, 949-824-9382, Fax: 949-824-4717, E-mail: skbrown@uci.edu. *Application contact:* John Sommerhauser, Director of Graduate Affairs, 949-824-4074, E-mail: john.sommerhauser@uci.edu.
Website: http://www.demography.uci.edu/

University of Guelph, Ontario Veterinary College and Graduate Studies, Graduate Programs in Veterinary Sciences, Department of Population Medicine, Guelph, ON N1G 2W1, Canada. Offers epidemiology (M Sc, DV Sc, PhD); health management (DV Sc); population medicine and health management (M Sc); swine health management (M Sc); theriogenology (M Sc, DV Sc). *Degree requirements:* For master's, thesis; for doctorate, comprehensive exam, thesis/dissertation. *Entrance requirements:* Additional exam requirements/recommendations for international students: Required—TOEFL.

University of Hawaii at Manoa, John A. Burns School of Medicine, Department of Public Health Sciences and Epidemiology, Global Health and Population Studies Program, Honolulu, HI 96822. Offers Graduate Certificate. Part-time programs available. *Entrance requirements:* For degree, GRE General Test. Additional exam requirements/recommendations for international students: Required—TOEFL (minimum score 550 paper-based; 79 iBT), IELTS (minimum score 5).

University of Pennsylvania, School of Arts and Sciences, Graduate Group in Demography, Philadelphia, PA 19104. Offers AM, PhD. *Faculty:* 37 full-time (17 women), 8 part-time/adjunct (3 women). *Students:* 28 full-time (11 women); includes 6 minority (5 Asian, non-Hispanic/Latino; 1 Hispanic/Latino), 13 international. 42 applicants, 14% accepted, 6 enrolled. In 2014, 5 master's, 4 doctorates awarded. Terminal master's awarded for partial completion of doctoral program. *Degree requirements:* For master's, thesis or alternative; for doctorate, thesis/dissertation. *Entrance requirements:* For master's and doctorate, GRE General Test. Additional exam requirements/recommendations for international students: Required—TOEFL. *Application deadline:* For fall admission, 12/1 priority date for domestic students. Application fee: $70. Electronic applications accepted. *Financial support:* Fellowships, research assistantships, institutionally sponsored loans, scholarships/grants, traineeships, health care benefits, and unspecified assistantships available. Financial award application deadline: 12/15. *Unit head:* Dr. Ralph M. Rosen, Associate Dean for Graduate Studies, 215-898-7156, Fax: 215-573-8068, E-mail: grad-dean@sas.upenn.edu. *Application contact:* Arts and Sciences Graduate Admissions, 215-573-5816, Fax: 215-573-8068, E-mail: gdasadmis@sas.upenn.edu.
Website: http://demog.pop.upenn.edu

University of Puerto Rico, Medical Sciences Campus, Graduate School of Public Health, Department of Social Sciences, Program in Demography, San Juan, PR 00936-5067. Offers MS. Part-time programs available. *Degree requirements:* For master's, thesis. *Entrance requirements:* For master's, GRE, previous course work in algebra and statistics.

The University of Texas at San Antonio, College of Public Policy, Department of Demography, San Antonio, TX 78207. Offers applied demography (PhD). Part-time and evening/weekend programs available. *Faculty:* 5 full-time (2 women). *Students:* 20 full-time (10 women), 15 part-time (9 women); includes 21 minority (4 Black or African American, non-Hispanic/Latino; 3 Asian, non-Hispanic/Latino; 14 Hispanic/Latino), 6 international. Average age 38. 22 applicants, 82% accepted, 14 enrolled. In 2014, 5 doctorates awarded. *Degree requirements:* For doctorate, comprehensive exam, thesis/dissertation, dissertation proposal defense. *Entrance requirements:* For doctorate, GRE, three letters of recommendation, statement of purpose, MA/MS. Additional exam requirements/recommendations for international students: Required—TOEFL (minimum score 550 paper-based; 79 iBT), IELTS (minimum score 6.5). *Application deadline:* For fall admission, 2/1 for domestic students. Application fee: $45 ($80 for international students). Electronic applications accepted. *Expenses:* Tuition, state resident: full-time $4671; part-time $260 per credit hour. Tuition, nonresident: full-time $18,022; part-time $1001 per credit hour. *Financial support:* In 2014–15, 1 fellowship (averaging $5,000 per year), 10 research assistantships (averaging $22,500 per year), 1 teaching assistantship (averaging $5,500 per year) were awarded. *Faculty research:* International migration, health disparities and inequality, food security, poverty, demographic change in communities, demographics of energy use. *Total annual research expenditures:* $50,000. *Unit head:* Dr. Joachim Singelmann, Department Chair, 210-458-3163, Fax: 210-458-3164, E-mail: dem@utsa.edu. *Application contact:* Corey Sparks, Graduate Advisor of Record, 210-458-3166, Fax: 210-458-3164, E-mail: johnelle.sparks@utsa.edu.
Website: http://copp.utsa.edu/demography/

Rural Sociology

Auburn University, Graduate School, Interdepartmental Programs, Graduate Programs in Sociology and Rural Sociology, Auburn University, AL 36849. Offers rural sociology (MS); sociology (MA, MS). Part-time programs available. *Faculty:* 16 full-time (10 women), 3 part-time/adjunct (2 women). *Students:* 9 full-time (4 women), 5 part-time (4 women); includes 5 minority (3 Black or African American, non-Hispanic/Latino; 2 Asian, non-Hispanic/Latino), 3 international. Average age 30. 13 applicants, 77% accepted, 6 enrolled. In 2014, 7 master's awarded. *Degree requirements:* For master's, thesis, computer language (MS), foreign language (MA). *Entrance requirements:* For master's, GRE General Test. *Application deadline:* For fall admission, 7/7 for domestic students; for spring admission, 11/24 for domestic students. Applications are processed on a rolling basis. Application fee: $50 ($60 for international students). *Expenses:* Tuition, state resident: full-time $8586; part-time $477 per credit hour. Tuition, nonresident: full-time $25,758; part-time $1431 per credit hour. *Required fees:* $804 per semester. Tuition and fees vary according to degree level and program. *Financial support:* Research assistantships and teaching assistantships available. Financial award application deadline: 3/15; financial award applicants required to submit FAFSA. *Unit head:* Dr. Allen Furr, Chair, 334-844-5049. *Application contact:* Dr. George Flowers, Dean of the Graduate School, 334-844-4700.

Cornell University, Graduate School, Graduate Fields of Agriculture and Life Sciences, Field of Development Sociology, Ithaca, NY 14853-0001. Offers population and development (MS, PhD); rural and environmental sociology (MS, PhD); state, economy, and society (MS, PhD). *Degree requirements:* For doctorate, comprehensive exam, thesis/dissertation. *Entrance requirements:* For master's and doctorate, GRE General Test, 3 letters of recommendation. Additional exam requirements/recommendations for international students: Required—TOEFL (minimum score 550 paper-based; 77 iBT). Electronic applications accepted. *Faculty research:* Demography (population and development), environmental sociology, international and rural community development, political economy and ecology, sustainable agriculture.

Iowa State University of Science and Technology, Department of Sociology, Ames, IA 50011. Offers rural sociology (MS, PhD); sociology (MS, PhD). *Degree requirements:* For master's, thesis; for doctorate, thesis/dissertation. *Entrance requirements:* For master's and doctorate, GRE General Test. Additional exam requirements/recommendations for international students: Required—TOEFL (minimum score 550 paper-based; 79 iBT), IELTS (minimum score 6.5). Electronic applications accepted.

Iowa State University of Science and Technology, Program in Rural Sociology, Ames, IA 50011. Offers MS, PhD. *Degree requirements:* For master's, thesis; for doctorate, thesis/dissertation. *Entrance requirements:* For master's, GRE General Test; for doctorate, GRE General Test, master's degree. Additional exam requirements/recommendations for international students: Required—TOEFL (minimum score 550 paper-based; 79 iBT), IELTS (minimum score 6.5). Electronic applications accepted.

The Ohio State University, Graduate School, College of Food, Agricultural, and Environmental Sciences, School of Environment and Natural Resources, Program in Rural Sociology, Columbus, OH 43210. Offers MS, PhD. *Unit head:* Linda M. Lobao, Graduate Studies Committee Chair, 614-292-6394, E-mail: lobao.1@osu.edu. Website: http://senr.osu.edu/

Penn State University Park, Graduate School, College of Agricultural Sciences, Department of Agricultural Economics, Sociology, and Education, University Park, PA 16802. Offers agricultural and extension education (M Ed, MS, PhD, Certificate); agricultural, environmental and regional economics (MS, PhD); applied youth, family and community education (M Ed); community and economic development (MPS); rural sociology (MS, PhD). *Unit head:* Dr. Richard T. Roush, Dean, 814-865-2541, Fax: 814-865-3103, E-mail: rtr10@psu.edu. *Application contact:* Lori A. Stania, Director, Graduate Student Services, 814-867-5278, Fax: 814-863-4627, E-mail: gswww@psu.edu. Website: http://aese.psu.edu/

University of Alberta, Faculty of Graduate Studies and Research, Department of Rural Economy, Edmonton, AB T6G 2E1, Canada. Offers agricultural economics (M Ag, M Sc, PhD); forest economics (M Ag, M Sc, PhD); rural sociology (M Ag, M Sc); MBA/M Ag. Part-time programs available. *Degree requirements:* For doctorate, thesis/dissertation. *Entrance requirements:* Additional exam requirements/recommendations for international students: Required—TOEFL. *Faculty research:* Agroforestry, development, extension education, marketing and trade, natural resources and environment, policy, production economics.

University of Missouri, Office of Research and Graduate Studies, College of Agriculture, Food and Natural Resources, Department of Rural Sociology, Columbia, MO 65211. Offers MS, PhD. Part-time programs available. *Faculty:* 4 full-time (2 women), 2 part-time/adjunct (1 woman). *Students:* 21 full-time (16 women), 7 part-time (5 women); includes 2 minority (1 Black or African American, non-Hispanic/Latino; 1 Two or more races, non-Hispanic/Latino), 4 international. Average age 38. 8 applicants, 88% accepted, 7 enrolled. In 2014, 5 master's, 5 doctorates awarded. *Degree requirements:* For doctorate, comprehensive exam, thesis/dissertation. *Entrance requirements:* For master's and doctorate, GRE General Test, minimum GPA of 3.0. Additional exam requirements/recommendations for international students: Required—TOEFL (minimum score 570 paper-based; 89 iBT). *Application deadline:* Applications are processed on a rolling basis. Application fee: $55 ($75 for international students). Electronic applications accepted. *Financial support:* Fellowships with tuition reimbursements, research assistantships with tuition reimbursements, teaching assistantships with tuition reimbursements, institutionally sponsored loans, scholarships/grants, health care benefits, and unspecified assistantships available. Support available to part-time students. *Faculty research:* Rural social organization; social change and development; sociology of agriculture; natural resource management; sociology of consumption, culture and organization; science, technology and society studies; social inequality; survey research; entrepreneurship; state and local public finance; community economics; rural development. *Unit head:* Dr. David O'Brien, Department Chair, 573-882-0392, E-mail: obriendj@missouri.edu. *Application contact:* Carol Swaim, Administrative Assistant, 573-882-7451, E-mail: swaimc@missouri.edu. Website: http://dass.missouri.edu/ruralsoc/grad/

The University of Montana, Graduate School, College of Humanities and Sciences, Department of Sociology, Missoula, MT 59812-0002. Offers criminology (MA); inequality and social justice (MA); rural and environmental change (MA); sociology (MA). *Entrance requirements:* For master's, GRE General Test. Additional exam requirements/recommendations for international students: Required—TOEFL. *Faculty research:* Housing, homelessness, hunger, infant mortality, work safety.

University of Wisconsin–Madison, Graduate School, College of Letters and Science, Department of Sociology, Madison, WI 53706-1380. Offers rural sociology (MS); sociology (MS, PhD). Part-time programs available. Terminal master's awarded for partial completion of doctoral program. *Degree requirements:* For master's, thesis, oral exam; for doctorate, thesis/dissertation, preliminary and final oral exams, 4 seminars. *Entrance requirements:* For master's and doctorate, GRE General Test. Additional exam requirements/recommendations for international students: Required—TOEFL. Electronic applications accepted. *Expenses:* Tuition, state resident: full-time $10,723; part-time $745 per credit. Tuition, nonresident: full-time $24,054; part-time $1578 per credit. *Required fees:* $374 per semester. Tuition and fees vary according to course load, program and reciprocity agreements.

Sociology

Acadia University, Faculty of Arts, Department of Sociology, Wolfville, NS B4P 2R6, Canada. Offers MA. *Degree requirements:* For master's, thesis. *Entrance requirements:* For master's, honors degree, minimum GPA of 3.25. Additional exam requirements/recommendations for international students: Required—TOEFL (minimum score 630 paper-based; 93 iBT), IELTS (minimum score 6.5). *Faculty research:* Atlantic cultures, class analysis, gender and women's studies, religion, symbolism, development studies.

The American University in Cairo, School of Humanities and Social Sciences, Department of Sociology, Anthropology, Psychology, and Egyptology, Cairo, Egypt. Offers Egyptology and Coptology (MA); psychology (MA); sociology and anthropology (MA). *Degree requirements:* For master's, one foreign language, thesis. *Entrance requirements:* Additional exam requirements/recommendations for international students: Required—English entrance exam and/or TOEFL. Electronic applications accepted. Tuition and fees vary according to course load and program. *Faculty research:* Development, gender, sociopolitical economic formulations, social science indigenization, Arab world.

American University of Beirut, Graduate Programs, Faculty of Arts and Sciences, Beirut, Lebanon. Offers anthropology (MA); Arab and Middle Eastern history (PhD); Arabic language and literature (MA, PhD); archaeology (MA); biology (MS); cell and molecular biology (PhD); chemistry (MS); clinical psychology (MA); computational sciences (MS); computer science (MS); economics (MA); English language (MA); English literature (MA); environmental policy planning (MS); financial economics (MAFE); geology (MS); history (MA); mathematics (MA, MS); media studies (MA); Middle Eastern studies (MA); physics (MS); political studies (MA); psychology (MA); public administration (MA); sociology (MA); statistics (MA, MS); theoretical physics (PhD); transnational American studies (MA). Part-time programs available. *Faculty:* 107 full-time (32 women), 6 part-time/adjunct (2 women). *Students:* 230 full-time (161 women), 209 part-time (146 women). Average age 26. 261 applicants, 70% accepted, 83 enrolled. In 2014, 68 master's, 2 doctorates awarded. *Degree requirements:* For master's, one foreign language, comprehensive exam, thesis (for some programs); for doctorate, one foreign language, comprehensive exam, thesis/dissertation. *Entrance requirements:* For master's, GRE (for some MA/MS programs), letter of recommendation; for doctorate, GRE, letters of recommendation. Additional exam requirements/recommendations for international students: Required—TOEFL (minimum score 600 paper-based; 97 iBT), IELTS (minimum score 7). *Application deadline:* For fall admission, 4/1 for domestic and international students; for spring admission, 11/1 for domestic and international students. Application fee: $50. Electronic applications accepted. *Expenses: Tuition:* Full-time $15,462; part-time $859 per credit. *Required fees:* $692. Tuition and fees vary according to course load and program. *Financial support:* Research assistantships, career-related internships or fieldwork, institutionally sponsored loans, scholarships/grants, health care benefits, and unspecified assistantships available. Financial award application deadline: 2/4; financial award applicants required to submit FAFSA. *Faculty research:* Determinants of language proficiency among Arab learners of English as a foreign language; opinion mining, information retrieval, runtime verification, high performance computing; solar and fuel cells, self-organizing systems, heterocyclic chemistry, air and water chemistry; complex analysis, harmonic analysis, number theory; social and political psychology, clinical psychology; thin films physics and technology; theory of soft matter; religious and ethnic conflict; sports and politics. *Total annual research expenditures:* $966,000. *Unit head:* Dr. Patrick McGreevy, Dean, 961-1374374 Ext. 3800, Fax: 961-1744461, E-mail: pm07@aub.edu.lb. *Application contact:* Dr. Salim Kanaan, Director, Admissions Office, 961-1350000 Ext. 2590, Fax: 961-1750775, E-mail: sk00@aub.edu.lb. Website: http://www.aub.edu.lb/fas/

Appalachian State University, Cratis D. Williams Graduate School, Department of Sociology, Boone, NC 28608. Offers gerontology (MA, Graduate Certificate); sociology (Graduate Certificate). Part-time and evening/weekend programs available. Postbaccalaureate distance learning degree programs offered (no on-campus study). *Degree requirements:* For master's, comprehensive exam, thesis or alternative. *Entrance requirements:* For master's, GRE General Test, 3 letters of recommendation. Additional exam requirements/recommendations for international students: Required—TOEFL (minimum score 570 paper-based; 79 iBT), IELTS (minimum score 6.5). Electronic applications accepted. *Faculty research:* Gerontology, demographics, sociology of aging, sociology of crime.

Arizona State University at the Tempe campus, College of Liberal Arts and Sciences, School of Social and Family Dynamics, Tempe, AZ 85287-3701. Offers family and human development (MS, PhD); infant-family practice (MAS); marriage and family therapy (MAS); sociology (MA, PhD). Terminal master's awarded for partial completion of doctoral program. *Degree requirements:* For master's, thesis or alternative, interactive Program of Study (iPOS) submitted before completing 50 percent of required credit

hours; for doctorate, thesis/dissertation, interactive Program of Study (iPOS) submitted before completing 50 percent of required credit hours. *Entrance requirements:* For master's and doctorate, GRE, minimum GPA of 3.0 or equivalent in last 2 years of work leading to bachelor's degree. Additional exam requirements/recommendations for international students: Required—TOEFL, IELTS, or PTE. Electronic applications accepted. *Expenses:* Contact institution.

Arkansas State University, Graduate School, College of Humanities and Social Sciences, Department of Criminology, Sociology, and Geography, State University, AR 72467. Offers criminal justice (MA); sociology (MA); sociology education (SCCT). Part-time programs available. *Faculty:* 9 full-time (5 women). *Students:* 5 full-time (1 woman), 20 part-time (12 women); includes 12 minority (all Black or African American, non-Hispanic/Latino), 2 international. Average age 34. 27 applicants, 52% accepted, 12 enrolled. In 2014, 11 master's, 1 other advanced degree awarded. *Degree requirements:* For master's, one foreign language, comprehensive exam, thesis or alternative; for SCCT, comprehensive exam. *Entrance requirements:* For master's, GRE General Test or MAT, appropriate bachelor's degree, letters of recommendation, official transcripts, immunization records; for SCCT, GRE General Test or MAT, interview, master's degree, official transcript, immunization records. Additional exam requirements/recommendations for international students: Required—TOEFL (minimum score 550 paper-based; 79 iBT), IELTS (minimum score 6), PTE (minimum score 56). *Application deadline:* For fall admission, 5/1 for domestic and international students; for spring admission, 11/1 for domestic and international students. Applications are processed on a rolling basis. Application fee: $30 ($40 for international students). Electronic applications accepted. *Expenses:* Tuition, state resident: full-time $4392; part-time $244 per credit hour. Tuition, nonresident: full-time $8784; part-time $488 per credit hour. *International tuition:* $9484 full-time. *Required fees:* $1134; $63 per credit hour. $25 per term. Tuition and fees vary according to course load and program. *Financial support:* In 2014–15, 4 students received support. Career-related internships or fieldwork, scholarships/grants, and unspecified assistantships available. Financial award application deadline: 7/1; financial award applicants required to submit FAFSA. *Unit head:* Dr. Leslie McCallister, Chair, 870-972-3705, Fax: 870-972-3694, E-mail: lmccallister@astate.edu. *Application contact:* Vickey Ring, Graduate Admissions Coordinator, 870-972-3029, Fax: 870-972-3857, E-mail: vickeyring@astate.edu.
Website: http://www.astate.edu/college/humanities-and-social-sciences/departments/criminology-sociology-and-geography/

Auburn University, Graduate School, Interdepartmental Programs, Graduate Programs in Sociology and Rural Sociology, Auburn University, AL 36849. Offers rural sociology (MS); sociology (MA, MS). Part-time programs available. *Faculty:* 16 full-time (10 women), 3 part-time/adjunct (2 women). *Students:* 9 full-time (4 women), 5 part-time (4 women); includes 5 minority (3 Black or African American, non-Hispanic/Latino; 2 Asian, non-Hispanic/Latino), 3 international. Average age 30. 13 applicants, 77% accepted, 6 enrolled. In 2014, 7 master's awarded. *Degree requirements:* For master's, thesis, computer language (MS), foreign language (MA). *Entrance requirements:* For master's, GRE General Test. *Application deadline:* For fall admission, 7/7 for domestic students; for spring admission, 11/24 for domestic students. Applications are processed on a rolling basis. Application fee: $50 ($60 for international students). *Expenses:* Tuition, state resident: full-time $8586; part-time $477 per credit hour. Tuition, nonresident: full-time $25,758; part-time $1431 per credit hour. *Required fees:* $804 per semester. Tuition and fees vary according to degree level and program. *Financial support:* Research assistantships and teaching assistantships available. Financial award application deadline: 3/15; financial award applicants required to submit FAFSA. *Unit head:* Dr. Allen Furr, Chair, 334-844-5049. *Application contact:* Dr. George Flowers, Dean of the Graduate School, 334-844-4700.

Auburn University at Montgomery, College of Public Policy and Justice, Montgomery, AL 36124-4023. Offers justice and public safety (MS, MSJPS, Certificate), including criminal studies (MSJPS), homeland security (MSJPS), homeland security and emergency management (MS), legal studies (MSJPS), organizational leadership (MSJPS), paralegal (Certificate); liberal arts (MLA); political science and public administration (MIR, MPA, MPS, PhD, Certificate), including international relations (MIR), nonprofit management and leadership (Certificate), political science (MPS), public administration (MPA), public administration and public policy (PhD), public health care administration and policy (Certificate); sociology (MA, MS). Part-time and evening/weekend programs available. *Faculty:* 31 full-time (13 women). *Students:* 24 full-time (15 women), 63 part-time (49 women); includes 20 minority (15 Black or African American, non-Hispanic/Latino; 2 American Indian or Alaska Native, non-Hispanic/Latino; 3 Two or more races, non-Hispanic/Latino), 4 international. Average age 34. 42 applicants, 90% accepted, 15 enrolled. In 2014, 8 master's, 1 other advanced degree awarded. *Degree requirements:* For master's, thesis. *Entrance requirements:* For master's, GRE or MAT. *Application deadline:* Applications are processed on a rolling basis. Electronic applications accepted. *Expenses:* Tuition, state resident: full-time $6264; part-time $348 per credit hour. Tuition, nonresident: full-time $14,094; part-time $783 per credit hour. *Financial support:* In 2014–15, 6 teaching assistantships were awarded; career-related internships or fieldwork and scholarships/grants also available. Support available to part-time students. Financial award application deadline: 3/1; financial award applicants required to submit FAFSA. *Unit head:* Dr. Michael Burger, Dean, 334-244-3380, Fax: 334-244-3740, E-mail: mburger1@aum.edu. *Application contact:* Dr. Eric Sterling, Director of the MLA Program, 334-244-3760, Fax: 334-244-3740, E-mail: esterlin@aum.edu.
Website: http://www.aum.edu/schools/college-of-public-policy-justice

Ball State University, Graduate School, College of Sciences and Humanities, Department of Sociology, Muncie, IN 47306-1099. Offers MA. *Faculty:* 4 full-time (3 women). *Students:* 11 full-time (3 women), 3 part-time (2 women), 1 international. Average age 26. 13 applicants, 77% accepted, 8 enrolled. In 2014, 10 master's awarded. *Entrance requirements:* For master's, GRE General Test. Application fee: $50. *Financial support:* In 2014–15, 12 students received support, including 1 research assistantship with partial tuition reimbursement available (averaging $9,046 per year), 6 teaching assistantships with partial tuition reimbursements available (averaging $8,745 per year); unspecified assistantships also available. Financial award application deadline: 3/1. *Faculty research:* Retention policies for secondary education, community mental health. *Unit head:* Roger Wojtkiewicz, Chairman, 765-285-9040, Fax: 765-285-8980, E-mail: rwojtkie@bsu.edu. *Application contact:* Dr. Rachel Kraus, Director of Graduate Programs, 765-285-0486, Fax: 765-285-8980, E-mail: rmkraus@bsu.edu.
Website: http://www.bsu.edu/csh/sociology/

Baylor University, Graduate School, College of Arts and Sciences, Department of Sociology, Waco, TX 76798-7326. Offers MA, PhD. Terminal master's awarded for partial completion of doctoral program. *Degree requirements:* For master's, thesis; for doctorate, comprehensive exam, thesis/dissertation. *Entrance requirements:* For master's and doctorate, GRE General Test. Additional exam requirements/recommendations for international students: Required—TOEFL. *Faculty research:* Applied sociology/evaluation research, family, community, rural sociology, collective behavior/social movements, demography, racial and ethnic relations, criminology/delinquency, social psychology, religion.

Binghamton University, State University of New York, Graduate School, School of Arts and Sciences, Department of Sociology, Vestal, NY 13850. Offers MA, PhD. *Faculty:* 17 full-time (7 women), 9 part-time/adjunct (2 women). *Students:* 23 full-time (10 women), 47 part-time (19 women); includes 6 minority (2 Black or African American, non-Hispanic/Latino; 1 Asian, non-Hispanic/Latino; 2 Hispanic/Latino; 1 Native Hawaiian or other Pacific Islander, non-Hispanic/Latino), 38 international. Average age 34. 46 applicants, 48% accepted, 7 enrolled. In 2014, 8 master's, 3 doctorates awarded. Terminal master's awarded for partial completion of doctoral program. *Degree requirements:* For doctorate, comprehensive exam, thesis/dissertation. *Entrance requirements:* For master's and doctorate, GRE General Test, writing sample. Additional exam requirements/recommendations for international students: Required—TOEFL (minimum score 550 paper-based; 80 iBT). *Application deadline:* For fall admission, 1/15 priority date for domestic and international students. Applications are processed on a rolling basis. Application fee: $75. Electronic applications accepted. *Expenses:* Tuition, state resident: full-time $7776; part-time $432 per credit. Tuition, nonresident: full-time $15,138; part-time $841 per credit. *Required fees:* $1754; $213 per credit. Tuition and fees vary according to degree level and program. *Financial support:* In 2014–15, 26 students received support, including 1 research assistantship (averaging $13,500 per year), 20 teaching assistantships with full tuition reimbursements available (averaging $15,000 per year); career-related internships or fieldwork, Federal Work-Study, institutionally sponsored loans, scholarships/grants, health care benefits, tuition waivers (full and partial), and unspecified assistantships also available. Financial award application deadline: 2/15; financial award applicants required to submit FAFSA. *Unit head:* Dr. Denis O'Hearn, Chairperson, 607-777-6750, E-mail: dohearn@binghamton.edu. *Application contact:* Kishan Zuber, Recruiting and Admissions Coordinator, 607-777-2151, Fax: 607-777-2501, E-mail: kzuber@binghamton.edu.

Boston College, Graduate School of Arts and Sciences, Department of Sociology, Chestnut Hill, MA 02467-3800. Offers MA, PhD, MBA/MA, MBA/PhD. *Faculty:* 17 full-time. *Students:* 46 full-time (31 women); includes 7 minority (3 Black or African American, non-Hispanic/Latino; 1 Asian, non-Hispanic/Latino; 2 Hispanic/Latino; 1 Two or more races, non-Hispanic/Latino), 10 international. 144 applicants, 35% accepted, 10 enrolled. In 2014, 7 master's, 5 doctorates awarded. Terminal master's awarded for partial completion of doctoral program. *Degree requirements:* For master's, thesis optional; for doctorate, thesis/dissertation. *Entrance requirements:* For master's and doctorate, GRE General Test. Additional exam requirements/recommendations for international students: Required—TOEFL (minimum score 600 paper-based; 100 iBT). *Application deadline:* For fall admission, 1/2 for domestic and international students. Application fee: $75. Electronic applications accepted. *Financial support:* In 2014–15, fellowships with full tuition reimbursements (averaging $20,500 per year), research assistantships with full tuition reimbursements (averaging $20,500 per year), teaching assistantships with full tuition reimbursements (averaging $20,500 per year) were awarded; Federal Work-Study, health care benefits, and unspecified assistantships also available. Support available to part-time students. Financial award application deadline: 3/1; financial award applicants required to submit FAFSA. *Faculty research:* Sociological theory, social economy, social psychology, political sociology, development modernization. *Unit head:* Dr. Juliet Schor, Chairperson, 617-552-4056. *Application contact:* Dr. Sarah Babb, Graduate Program Director, 617-552-2930, E-mail: sarab.babb@bc.edu.
Website: http://www.bc.edu/sociology

Boston University, Graduate School of Arts and Sciences, Department of Sociology, Boston, MA 02215. Offers MA, PhD. *Students:* 34 full-time (24 women), 2 part-time (both women); includes 7 minority (3 Black or African American, non-Hispanic/Latino; 2 Hispanic/Latino; 2 Two or more races, non-Hispanic/Latino), 6 international. Average age 31. 158 applicants, 12% accepted, 7 enrolled. In 2014, 3 doctorates awarded. Terminal master's awarded for partial completion of doctoral program. *Degree requirements:* For master's, one foreign language, comprehensive exam, thesis; for doctorate, one foreign language, comprehensive exam, thesis/dissertation. *Entrance requirements:* For master's, GRE General Test, 3 letters of recommendation, academic writing sample; for doctorate, GRE General Test or MAT, 3 letters of recommendation, academic writing sample. Additional exam requirements/recommendations for international students: Required—TOEFL (minimum score 84 iBT). *Application deadline:* For fall admission, 1/15 for domestic and international students. Application fee: $80. Electronic applications accepted. *Expenses: Tuition:* Full-time $45,686; part-time $1428 per credit hour. *Required fees:* $660; $60 per semester. Tuition and fees vary according to program. *Financial support:* In 2014–15, 35 students received support, including 8 fellowships with full tuition reimbursements available (averaging $20,500 per year), 1 research assistantship with full tuition reimbursement available (averaging $20,500 per year), 6 teaching assistantships with full tuition reimbursements available (averaging $20,500 per year); career-related internships or fieldwork, Federal Work-Study, scholarships/grants, and health care benefits also available. Support available to part-time students. Financial award application deadline: 1/15. *Unit head:* Nazli Kibria, Chairman, 617-358-0634, Fax: 617-353-4837, E-mail: nkibria@bu.edu. *Application contact:* Anna Bakanova, Department Administrator, 617-353-2594, Fax: 617-353-4837, E-mail: bakanova@bu.edu.
Website: http://www.bu.edu/sociology/

Boston University, Graduate School of Arts and Sciences, Interdisciplinary Program in Sociology and Social Work, Boston, MA 02215. Offers PhD. *Students:* 18 full-time (15 women), 4 part-time (all women); includes 5 minority (1 Black or African American, non-Hispanic/Latino; 2 Asian, non-Hispanic/Latino; 2 Hispanic/Latino), 1 international. Average age 37. 40 applicants, 23% accepted, 4 enrolled. *Degree requirements:* For doctorate, one foreign language, comprehensive exam, thesis/dissertation, critical essay. *Entrance requirements:* For doctorate, GRE General Test or MAT, 3 letters of recommendation, professional writing sample. Additional exam requirements/recommendations for international students: Required—TOEFL (minimum score 550 paper-based; 84 iBT). *Application deadline:* For fall admission, 1/15 for domestic and international students. Application fee: $80. Electronic applications accepted. *Expenses: Tuition:* Full-time $45,686; part-time $1428 per credit hour. *Required fees:* $660; $60 per semester. Tuition and fees vary according to program. *Financial support:* In 2014–15, 26 students received support, including 4 fellowships with full tuition reimbursements available (averaging $20,500 per year); career-related internships or fieldwork, Federal Work-Study, scholarships/grants, and health care benefits also available. Support available to part-time students. Financial award application deadline: 1/15. *Faculty research:* Mental health, child welfare, aging, substance abuse. *Unit head:* Ellen DeVoe, Director, 617-353-7885, Fax: 617-353-5612, E-mail: edevoe@bu.edu. *Application contact:* Peg Tamiso, Staff Coordinator, 617-353-9675, Fax: 617-353-5612, E-mail: sswphd@bu.edu.
Website: http://www.bu.edu/ssw/academics/phd/

Bowling Green State University, Graduate College, College of Arts and Sciences, Department of Sociology, Bowling Green, OH 43403. Offers demography and population studies (MA); social psychology (MA); sociology (PhD). Part-time programs available. *Degree requirements:* For master's, thesis or alternative; for doctorate, comprehensive exam, thesis/dissertation. *Entrance requirements:* For master's and doctorate, GRE General Test. Additional exam requirements/recommendations for

international students: Required—TOEFL. Electronic applications accepted. *Faculty research:* Applied demography, criminology and deviance, family studies, population studies, social psychology.

Brandeis University, Graduate School of Arts and Sciences, Department of Sociology, Waltham, MA 02454-9110. Offers Near Eastern and Judaic studies and sociology (PhD); social policy and sociology (PhD); sociology (MA, PhD); sociology and women's and gender studies (MA). Part-time programs available. Terminal master's awarded for partial completion of doctoral program. *Degree requirements:* For master's, thesis, project or exam; for doctorate, comprehensive exam, thesis/dissertation, qualifying exam. *Entrance requirements:* For master's and doctorate, GRE, resume, letters of recommendation, statement of purpose, writing sample, transcript(s). Additional exam requirements/recommendations for international students: Required—TOEFL (minimum score 600 paper-based; 100 iBT), PTE (minimum score 68); Recommended—IELTS (minimum score 7). Electronic applications accepted. *Faculty research:* Social theory and methods; comparative social structures; gender and feminist studies; institutions, culture and religion; sociology of health and illness; politics and social change.

Brigham Young University, Graduate Studies, College of Family, Home, and Social Sciences, Department of Sociology, Provo, UT 84602. Offers MS. *Faculty:* 17 full-time (4 women). *Students:* 17 full-time (7 women); includes 5 minority (2 Black or African American, non-Hispanic/Latino; 2 Asian, non-Hispanic/Latino; 1 Native Hawaiian or other Pacific Islander, non-Hispanic/Latino), 2 international. Average age 30. 13 applicants, 62% accepted, 5 enrolled. In 2014, 10 master's awarded. Terminal master's awarded for partial completion of doctoral program. *Degree requirements:* For master's, thesis. *Entrance requirements:* For master's, GRE General Test, minimum GPA of 3.0 in last 60 hours, writing sample, bachelor's degree in sociology or related field, 3 letters of recommendation, Honor Code commitment. Additional exam requirements/recommendations for international students: Required—TOEFL. *Application deadline:* For fall admission, 1/15 for domestic and international students. Application fee: $50. Electronic applications accepted. *Expenses: Tuition:* Full-time $6310; part-time $371 per credit hour. Tuition and fees vary according to program and student's religious affiliation. *Financial support:* In 2014–15, 13 research assistantships (averaging $15,750 per year) were awarded; institutionally sponsored loans and unspecified assistantships also available. Financial award application deadline: 2/1. *Faculty research:* Demography, race and ethnicity, gender, rural and community, international development, comparative family. *Total annual research expenditures:* $33,500. *Unit head:* Dr. Cardell K. Jacobson, Department Chair, 801-422-2105, Fax: 801-422-0625, E-mail: cardell_jacobson@byu.edu. *Application contact:* Dr. Mikaela J. Dufur, Graduate Coordinator, 801-422-1720, Fax: 801-422-0625, E-mail: mikaela_dufur@byu.edu.
Website: http://sociology.byu.edu/

Brock University, Faculty of Graduate Studies, Faculty of Social Sciences, Program in Critical Sociology, St. Catharines, ON L2S 3A1, Canada. Offers MA.

Brooklyn College of the City University of New York, School of Humanities and Social Sciences, Department of Sociology, Brooklyn, NY 11210-2889. Offers MA, PhD. Part-time and evening/weekend programs available. *Degree requirements:* For master's, comprehensive exam or research essay. *Entrance requirements:* For master's, 12 upper-level credits in sociology, 2 letters of recommendation, essay. Additional exam requirements/recommendations for international students: Required—TOEFL (minimum score 500 paper-based; 61 iBT). Electronic applications accepted. *Faculty research:* Urbanization, religion, family, gender, research methods.

Brown University, Graduate School, Department of Sociology, Providence, RI 02912. Offers MA, PhD. *Degree requirements:* For master's, thesis; for doctorate, thesis/dissertation, oral exam. *Entrance requirements:* For master's and doctorate, GRE General Test.

California State University, Bakersfield, Division of Graduate Studies, School of Social Sciences and Education, Program in Sociology, Bakersfield, CA 93311. Offers MA. *Entrance requirements:* For master's, baccalaureate degree; minimum GPA of 2.5 overall, 3.0 in major. Additional exam requirements/recommendations for international students: Required—TOEFL (minimum score 500 paper-based). Electronic applications accepted.

California State University, Dominguez Hills, College of Natural and Behavioral Sciences, Program in Sociology, Carson, CA 90747-0001. Offers social research (Certificate); sociology (MA). Part-time and evening/weekend programs available. *Faculty:* 4 full-time (2 women), 2 part-time/adjunct (1 woman). *Students:* 15 full-time (9 women), 20 part-time (17 women); includes 32 minority (13 Black or African American, non-Hispanic/Latino; 1 American Indian or Alaska Native, non-Hispanic/Latino; 1 Asian, non-Hispanic/Latino; 17 Hispanic/Latino). Average age 32. 25 applicants, 60% accepted, 9 enrolled. In 2014, 21 master's awarded. *Degree requirements:* For master's, comprehensive exam, thesis. *Entrance requirements:* For master's and Certificate, minimum GPA of 2.85. *Application deadline:* For fall admission, 6/1 for domestic students. Application fee: $55. *Expenses:* Tuition, state resident: full-time $6738; part-time $3960 per year. Tuition, nonresident: full-time $13,434; part-time $8370 per year. *Required fees:* $623; $623 per year. *Faculty research:* Community studies, social movements, criminology. *Unit head:* Dr. Katy Pinto, Program Coordinator, 310-243-3180, E-mail: kpinto@csudh.edu. *Application contact:* Brandy McLelland, Director of Student Information Services/Registrar, 310-243-3645, E-mail: bmclelland@csudh.edu.
Website: http://www4.csudh.edu/sociology/master/index

California State University, Fullerton, Graduate Studies, College of Humanities and Social Sciences, Department of Sociology, Fullerton, CA 92834-9480. Offers MA. Part-time programs available. *Students:* 11 full-time (8 women), 24 part-time (14 women); includes 27 minority (1 Black or African American, non-Hispanic/Latino; 1 American Indian or Alaska Native, non-Hispanic/Latino; 2 Asian, non-Hispanic/Latino; 23 Hispanic/Latino). Average age 29. 30 applicants, 50% accepted, 12 enrolled. In 2014, 12 master's awarded. *Degree requirements:* For master's, thesis. *Entrance requirements:* For master's, minimum GPA of 3.0 in sociology, 2.5 in last 60 units. Application fee: $55. *Financial support:* Career-related internships or fieldwork, Federal Work-Study, institutionally sponsored loans, and scholarships/grants available. Support available to part-time students. Financial award application deadline: 3/1; financial award applicants required to submit FAFSA. *Faculty research:* Gerontology wellness clinic. *Unit head:* Dr. Michael Perez, Chair, 657-278-3022. *Application contact:* Admissions/Applications, 657-278-2371.

California State University, Los Angeles, Graduate Studies, College of Natural and Social Sciences, Department of Sociology, Los Angeles, CA 90032-8530. Offers MA. Part-time and evening/weekend programs available. *Degree requirements:* For master's, comprehensive exam or thesis. *Entrance requirements:* For master's, minimum GPA of 2.5 in last 90 units of course work. Additional exam requirements/recommendations for international students: Required—TOEFL (minimum score 500 paper-based). Electronic applications accepted. *Expenses:* Tuition, state resident: full-time $6738; part-time $3609 per year. Tuition, nonresident: full-time $15,666; part-time $8073 per year. Tuition and fees vary according to course load, degree level and program. *Faculty research:* Criminal and delinquent careers, family and sex, ethnic minorities, demographic trends, human socialization and aging.

California State University, Northridge, Graduate Studies, College of Social and Behavioral Sciences, Department of Sociology, Northridge, CA 91330. Offers MA. *Accreditation:* CSWE. Part-time and evening/weekend programs available. *Students:* 5 full-time (3 women), 20 part-time (13 women); includes 12 minority (3 Black or African American, non-Hispanic/Latino; 2 Asian, non-Hispanic/Latino; 6 Hispanic/Latino; 1 Two or more races, non-Hispanic/Latino), 1 international. Average age 31. *Degree requirements:* For master's, thesis or alternative. *Entrance requirements:* For master's, GRE General Test. Additional exam requirements/recommendations for international students: Required—TOEFL. *Application deadline:* For fall admission, 3/27 for domestic students; for spring admission, 10/17 for domestic students. Application fee: $55. *Expenses: Required fees:* $12,402. *Financial support:* Career-related internships or fieldwork, Federal Work-Study, and institutionally sponsored loans available. Support available to part-time students. Financial award application deadline: 3/1. *Faculty research:* Crime and corrections, relationships between adult children and parents. *Unit head:* Karen Morgaine, Chair, 818-677-3591. *Application contact:* Dr. David Boyns, Graduate Advisor, 818-677-6803.
Website: http://www.csun.edu/csbs/departments/sociology/index.html

California State University, Sacramento, Office of Graduate Studies, College of Social Sciences and Interdisciplinary Studies, Department of Sociology, Sacramento, CA 95819. Offers MA. Part-time programs available. *Degree requirements:* For master's, thesis or project; writing proficiency exam. *Entrance requirements:* For master's, minimum GPA of 3.0 during previous 2 years. Additional exam requirements/recommendations for international students: Required—TOEFL. Electronic applications accepted.

California State University, San Marcos, College of Humanities, Arts, Behavioral and Social Sciences, Program in Sociological Practice, San Marcos, CA 92096-0001. Offers MA. Part-time and evening/weekend programs available. *Students:* 20 full-time (13 women), 16 part-time (12 women); includes 23 minority (2 Black or African American, non-Hispanic/Latino; 2 American Indian or Alaska Native, non-Hispanic/Latino; 1 Asian, non-Hispanic/Latino; 16 Hispanic/Latino; 1 Native Hawaiian or other Pacific Islander, non-Hispanic/Latino; 1 Two or more races, non-Hispanic/Latino). Average age 31. *Degree requirements:* For master's, thesis. *Entrance requirements:* For master's, minimum GPA of 3.0, statement of purpose, writing sample, official transcripts, three letters of recommendation. *Application deadline:* For fall admission, 2/15 for domestic students. Applications are processed on a rolling basis. Application fee: $55. Electronic applications accepted. *Expenses:* Tuition, state resident: full-time $6738. *Required fees:* $1692. Tuition and fees vary according to program. *Financial support:* Research assistantships, teaching assistantships, career-related internships or fieldwork, Federal Work-Study, institutionally sponsored loans, scholarships/grants, traineeships, and unspecified assistantships available. Support available to part-time students. *Faculty research:* Organized crime, juvenile detention, counseling services for minorities, mental-health facilities. *Unit head:* Dr. Marisol Clark-Ibanez, Coordinator, 760-750-4631, E-mail: mibanez@scusm.edu. *Application contact:* Admissions, 760-750-4848, Fax: 760-750-3248, E-mail: apply@csusm.edu.
Website: http://www.csusm.edu/sociology/graduatestudies/

Carleton University, Faculty of Graduate Studies, Faculty of Arts and Social Sciences, Department of Sociology and Anthropology, Program in Sociology, Ottawa, ON K1S 5B6, Canada. Offers MA, PhD. *Degree requirements:* For master's, thesis optional; for doctorate, one foreign language, comprehensive exam, thesis/dissertation. *Entrance requirements:* For master's, honors degree; for doctorate, master's degree. Additional exam requirements/recommendations for international students: Required—TOEFL. *Faculty research:* Canadian society and policy, inequality and mobility, race/ethnic relations, cultural studies, gender studies.

Case Western Reserve University, School of Graduate Studies, Department of Sociology, Cleveland, OH 44106. Offers MA, PhD. *Faculty:* 10 full-time (6 women). *Students:* 30 full-time (20 women), 4 part-time (all women); includes 5 minority (3 Black or African American, non-Hispanic/Latino; 1 Asian, non-Hispanic/Latino; 1 Two or more races, non-Hispanic/Latino), 5 international. Average age 34. 23 applicants, 39% accepted, 5 enrolled. In 2014, 1 master's, 1 doctorate awarded. Terminal master's awarded for partial completion of doctoral program. *Degree requirements:* For master's, comprehensive exam; for doctorate, comprehensive exam, thesis/dissertation. *Entrance requirements:* For master's and doctorate, GRE, writing sample, recommendations, letter of intent. Additional exam requirements/recommendations for international students: Required—TOEFL (minimum score 577 paper-based; 90 iBT); Recommended—IELTS (minimum score 7). *Application deadline:* For fall admission, 2/1 priority date for domestic students. Applications are processed on a rolling basis. Application fee: $50. Electronic applications accepted. *Financial support:* Research assistantships, tuition waivers (full and partial), and student employment available. Financial award application deadline: 1/15; financial award applicants required to submit FAFSA. *Faculty research:* Sociology of aging and the life course, health and medical sociology, research design and methods. *Unit head:* Dr. Dale Dannefer, Chair, 216-368-2700, Fax: 216-368-2676, E-mail: dale.dannefer@case.edu. *Application contact:* Michelle Rizzuto, Department Administrator, 216-368-2214, Fax: 216-368-2676, E-mail: michelle.rizzuto@case.edu.
Website: http://sociology.case.edu/

The Catholic University of America, School of Arts and Sciences, Department of Sociology, Washington, DC 20064. Offers MA. Part-time programs available. *Faculty:* 4 full-time (2 women), 4 part-time/adjunct (0 women). *Students:* 3 full-time (2 women), 1 (woman) part-time; includes 3 minority (1 Black or African American, non-Hispanic/Latino; 2 Hispanic/Latino), 1 international. Average age 25. 5 applicants, 100% accepted, 3 enrolled. In 2014, 5 master's awarded. *Degree requirements:* For master's, comprehensive exam, thesis or alternative. *Entrance requirements:* For master's, GRE General Test, statement of purpose, official copies of academic transcripts, three letters of recommendation. Additional exam requirements/recommendations for international students: Required—TOEFL (minimum score 580 paper-based). *Application deadline:* For fall admission, 7/15 priority date for domestic students, 7/1 for international students; for spring admission, 11/15 priority date for domestic students, 11/1 for international students. Applications are processed on a rolling basis. Application fee: $55. Electronic applications accepted. *Expenses: Tuition:* Full-time $40,200; part-time $1600 per credit hour. *Required fees:* $400; $195 per semester. One-time fee: $425. *Financial support:* Fellowships, research assistantships, teaching assistantships, Federal Work-Study, scholarships/grants, tuition waivers (full and partial), and unspecified assistantships available. Financial award application deadline: 2/1; financial award applicants required to submit FAFSA. *Faculty research:* Social movements, gender structure, political sociology, race and ethnic relations, evaluation methodologies. *Unit head:* Dr. Enrique S. Pumar, Chair, 202-319-5445, Fax: 202-319-4980, E-mail: pumar@cua.edu. *Application contact:* Director of Graduate Admissions, 202-319-5057, Fax: 202-319-6533, E-mail: cua-admissions@cua.edu.
Website: http://sociology.cua.edu/

Central European University, Graduate Studies, Department of Sociology and Social Anthropology, Budapest, Hungary. Offers MA, PhD. *Faculty:* 10 full-time (3 women), 4 part-time/adjunct (1 woman). *Students:* 79 full-time (47 women). Average age 29. 123 applicants, 21% accepted, 22 enrolled. In 2014, 23 master's, 6 doctorates awarded.

Sociology

Degree requirements: For master's, one foreign language, thesis; for doctorate, one foreign language, comprehensive exam, thesis/dissertation. *Entrance requirements:* For master's and doctorate, interview. Additional exam requirements/recommendations for international students: Required—TOEFL (minimum score 570 paper-based); Recommended—IELTS (minimum score 6.5). *Application deadline:* For fall admission, 1/24 for domestic and international students. Application fee: $40. Electronic applications accepted. *Expenses: Tuition:* Full-time 12,000 euros. *Required fees:* 200 euros. One-time fee: 500 euros full-time. *Financial support:* In 2014–15, 75 students received support, including 75 fellowships (averaging $6,100 per year); career-related internships or fieldwork, scholarships/grants, health care benefits, and tuition waivers (full and partial) also available. *Faculty research:* Migration studies, postcolonialism, studies of globalization, political and economic sociology, urban studies and sociologies of culture. *Unit head:* Dr. Jacob Rigi, Head of Department, 36 1 327-3000 Ext. 2131, E-mail: sociology@ceu.hu. *Application contact:* Zsuzsanna Jaszberenyi, Admissions Officer, 361-324-3009, Fax: 367-327-3211, E-mail: admissions@ceu.hu.
Website: http://sociology.ceu.hu/

City College of the City University of New York, Graduate School, College of Liberal Arts and Science, Division of Social Science, Department of Sociology, New York, NY 10031-9198. Offers MA. *Degree requirements:* For master's, one foreign language, comprehensive exam, thesis. *Entrance requirements:* Additional exam requirements/recommendations for international students: Required—TOEFL (minimum score 500 paper-based; 61 iBT). Electronic applications accepted. *Faculty research:* Urban sociology, criminology and deviance, race and ethnicity.

Clark Atlanta University, School of Arts and Sciences, Department of Sociology, Atlanta, GA 30314. Offers MA. Part-time programs available. *Faculty:* 2 full-time (1 woman). *Students:* 2 full-time (1 woman), 1 (woman) part-time; all minorities (all Black or African American, non-Hispanic/Latino). Average age 25. 3 applicants, 100% accepted, 3 enrolled. In 2014, 3 master's awarded. *Degree requirements:* For master's, one foreign language, comprehensive exam, thesis. *Entrance requirements:* For master's, GRE General Test, minimum GPA of 2.5. Additional exam requirements/recommendations for international students: Required—TOEFL (minimum score 500 paper-based; 61 iBT). *Application deadline:* For fall admission, 4/1 for domestic and international students; for spring admission, 11/1 for domestic and international students. Applications are processed on a rolling basis. Application fee: $40 ($55 for international students). Electronic applications accepted. *Expenses: Tuition:* Full-time $14,904; part-time $828 per credit hour. *Required fees:* $746; $373 per semester. *Financial support:* Scholarships/grants and unspecified assistantships available. Financial award application deadline: 4/30; financial award applicants required to submit FAFSA. *Faculty research:* Gerontology, geriatric education. *Unit head:* Dr. Obie Clayton, Chairperson, 404-880-8681, E-mail: oclayton@cau.edu. *Application contact:* Michelle Clark-Davis, Graduate Program Admissions, 404-880-6605, E-mail: cauadmissions@cau.edu.

Clemson University, Graduate School, College of Business and Behavioral Science, Department of Sociology and Anthropology, Clemson, SC 29634. Offers applied sociology (MS). Part-time programs available. *Faculty:* 18 full-time (11 women). *Students:* 6 full-time (4 women), 2 part-time (both women), 3 international. Average age 28. 12 applicants, 67% accepted, 3 enrolled. In 2014, 2 master's awarded. *Degree requirements:* For master's, thesis. *Entrance requirements:* For master's, GRE General Test, minimum GPA of 3.0. Additional exam requirements/recommendations for international students: Required—TOEFL. *Application deadline:* For fall admission, 3/15 priority date for domestic students. Applications are processed on a rolling basis. Application fee: $70 ($80 for international students). Electronic applications accepted. *Expenses:* Expenses: Contact institution. *Financial support:* In 2014–15, 5 students received support, including 5 teaching assistantships with partial tuition reimbursements available (averaging $14,222 per year); fellowships with full and partial tuition reimbursements available, research assistantships with partial tuition reimbursements available, career-related internships or fieldwork, institutionally sponsored loans, scholarships/grants, and unspecified assistantships also available. Support available to part-time students. Financial award application deadline: 3/15; financial award applicants required to submit FAFSA. *Faculty research:* Environmental issues; social inequalities; health and medical development; sociology of food, nutrition, and food security. *Total annual research expenditures:* $83,338. *Unit head:* Dr. Ellen Granburg, Chair, 864-656-3812, E-mail: gramber@clemson.edu. *Application contact:* Dr. Brenda Vander Mey, Graduate Coordinator, 864-656-3821, Fax: 864-656-1252, E-mail: vanmey@clemson.edu.
Website: http://business.clemson.edu/departments/sociology/

Cleveland State University, College of Graduate Studies, College of Liberal Arts and Social Sciences, Department of Sociology, Cleveland, OH 44115. Offers MA. Part-time and evening/weekend programs available. *Faculty:* 4 full-time (2 women), 1 (woman) part-time/adjunct. *Students:* 6 full-time (3 women), 9 part-time (5 women); includes 5 minority (4 Black or African American, non-Hispanic/Latino; 1 Hispanic/Latino). Average age 31. 16 applicants, 75% accepted, 7 enrolled. In 2014, 11 master's awarded. *Entrance requirements:* For master's, minimum GPA of 3.0. Additional exam requirements/recommendations for international students: Required—TOEFL (minimum score 525 paper-based). *Application deadline:* For fall admission, 7/15 priority date for domestic students, 1/15 priority date for international students; for spring admission, 12/1 priority date for domestic students, 9/15 priority date for international students. Applications are processed on a rolling basis. Application fee: $30. Electronic applications accepted. *Expenses:* Expenses: $9,615 full-time, in-state tuition and fees. *Financial support:* In 2014–15, 12 students received support, including 3 research assistantships (averaging $9,000 per year), 4 teaching assistantships (averaging $9,000 per year); scholarships/grants, tuition waivers (full and partial), and unspecified assistantships also available. Support available to part-time students. Financial award application deadline: 7/15. *Faculty research:* Criminology, research methods, theory, symbolic interaction. *Total annual research expenditures:* $45,000. *Unit head:* Dr. Philip Manning, Chair, 216-687-4504, Fax: 216-687-9314, E-mail: p.mannings@csuohio.edu. *Application contact:* Dr. Wendy Regoeczi, Graduate Program Director, 216-687-9349, Fax: 216-687-9314, E-mail: w.regoeczi@csuohio.edu.
Website: http://www.csuohio.edu/sociology/

Colorado State University, Graduate School, College of Liberal Arts, Department of Sociology, Fort Collins, CO 80523-1784. Offers MA, PhD. *Faculty:* 16 full-time (7 women). *Students:* 17 full-time (9 women), 31 part-time (20 women); includes 1 minority (Hispanic/Latino), 6 international. Average age 31. 53 applicants, 26% accepted, 13 enrolled. In 2014, 3 master's, 4 doctorates awarded. *Degree requirements:* For master's, variable foreign language requirement, comprehensive exam (for some programs), thesis (for some programs); for doctorate, variable foreign language requirement, comprehensive exam, thesis/dissertation (for some programs). *Entrance requirements:* For master's, GRE General Test, minimum GPA of 3.0, BA coursework in sociology, letters of recommendation, transcripts, statement of purpose; for doctorate, GRE General Test, minimum GPA of 3.0, BA and MA coursework in sociology, letters of recommendation, transcripts, statement of purpose. Additional exam requirements/recommendations for international students: Required—TOEFL (minimum score 550 paper-based; 80 iBT). *Application deadline:* For fall admission, 1/15 priority date for domestic and international students. Applications are processed on a rolling basis. Application fee: $50. Electronic applications accepted. *Expenses:* Tuition, state resident: full-time $9348; part-time $519 per credit. Tuition, nonresident: full-time $22,916; part-time $1273 per credit. *Required fees:* $1584. *Financial support:* In 2014–15, 24 students received support, including 4 research assistantships (averaging $13,605 per year), 20 teaching assistantships (averaging $14,032 per year); career-related internships or fieldwork, Federal Work-Study, institutionally sponsored loans, scholarships/grants, traineeships, and unspecified assistantships also available. Financial award application deadline: 3/1; financial award applicants required to submit FAFSA. *Faculty research:* Sociology policy analysis, environmental impact, criminology, community development, rural and natural resources. *Total annual research expenditures:* $283,267. *Unit head:* Dr. Michael Carolan, Professor and Chair, 970-491-5797, Fax: 970-491-2191, E-mail: michael.carolan@colostate.edu. *Application contact:* Elizabeth Burkett, Graduate Contact, 970-491-6045, Fax: 970-491-2191, E-mail: elizabeth.burkett@colostate.edu.
Website: http://sociology.colostate.edu/

Columbia University, Graduate School of Arts and Sciences, New York, NY 10027. Offers African-American studies (MA); American studies (MA); anthropology (MA, PhD); art history and archaeology (MA, PhD); astronomy (PhD); biological sciences (PhD); biotechnology (MA); chemical physics (PhD); chemistry (PhD); classical studies (MA, PhD); classics (MA, PhD); climate and society (MA); earth and environmental sciences (PhD); East Asia: regional studies (MA); East Asian languages and cultures (MA, PhD); ecology, evolution and environmental biology (MA), including conservation biology; ecology, evolution, and environmental biology (PhD), including ecology and evolutionary biology, evolutionary primatology; economics (PhD); English and comparative literature (MA, PhD); French and Romance philology (MA, PhD); Germanic languages (MA, PhD); global French studies (MA); Hispanic cultural studies (MA); history (PhD); history and literature (MA); human rights studies (MA); Islamic studies (MA); Italian (MA, PhD); Japanese pedagogy (MA); Jewish studies (MA); Latin America and the Caribbean: regional studies (MA); Latin American and Iberian cultures (PhD); mathematics (MA, PhD), including finance (MA); medieval and Renaissance studies (MA); Middle Eastern, South Asian, and African studies (MA, PhD); modern art: critical and curatorial studies (MA); modern European studies (MA); museum anthropology (MA); music (DMA, PhD); oral history (MA); philosophical foundations of physics (MA); philosophy (MA, PhD); physics (PhD); political science (MA, PhD); psychology (PhD); quantitative methods in the social sciences (MA); religion (MA, PhD); Russia, Eurasia and East Europe: regional studies (MA); Russian translation (MA); Slavic cultures (MA); Slavic languages (MA, PhD); sociology (MA, PhD); South Asian studies (MA); statistics (MA, PhD); theatre (PhD); JD/PhD; MA/MS; MD/PhD; MPA/MA. Dual-degree programs require admission to both Graduate School of Arts and Sciences and another Columbia school. Part-time and evening/weekend programs available. Terminal master's awarded for partial completion of doctoral program. *Degree requirements:* For master's, thesis (for some programs); for doctorate, comprehensive exam, thesis/dissertation. *Entrance requirements:* For master's and doctorate, GRE General Test, GRE Subject Test (for some programs). Electronic applications accepted. *Faculty research:* Humanities, natural sciences, social sciences.

Concordia University, School of Graduate Studies, Faculty of Arts and Science, Department of Sociology and Anthropology, Montréal, QC H3G 1M8, Canada. Offers social and cultural anthropology (MA); sociology (MA). *Degree requirements:* For master's, comprehensive exam or thesis. *Entrance requirements:* For master's, honors degree in sociology or equivalent. *Faculty research:* Community and ethnic relations, popular culture, regional development in Canada, industrial and social movements, social problems and policies.

Cornell University, Graduate School, Graduate Fields of Agriculture and Life Sciences, Field of Development Sociology, Ithaca, NY 14853-0001. Offers population and development (MS, PhD); rural and environmental sociology (MS, PhD); state, economy, and society (MS, PhD). *Degree requirements:* For doctorate, comprehensive exam, thesis/dissertation. *Entrance requirements:* For master's and doctorate, GRE General Test, 3 letters of recommendation. Additional exam requirements/recommendations for international students: Required—TOEFL (minimum score 550 paper-based; 77 iBT). Electronic applications accepted. *Faculty research:* Demography (population and development), environmental sociology, international and rural community development, political economy and ecology, sustainable agriculture.

Cornell University, Graduate School, Graduate Fields of Arts and Sciences, Field of Sociology, Ithaca, NY 14853-0001. Offers economy and society (MA, PhD); gender and life course (MA, PhD); methodology (MA, PhD); organizations (MA, PhD); policy analysis (MA, PhD); political sociology/social movements (MA, PhD); racial and ethnic relations (MA, PhD); social networks (MA, PhD); social psychology (MA, PhD); social stratification (MA, PhD). Terminal master's awarded for partial completion of doctoral program. *Degree requirements:* For master's, thesis; for doctorate, thesis/dissertation, 1 year of teaching experience. *Entrance requirements:* For master's and doctorate, GRE General Test, 2 letters of recommendation, writing sample. Additional exam requirements/recommendations for international students: Required—TOEFL (minimum score 550 paper-based; 77 iBT). Electronic applications accepted. *Faculty research:* Comparative societal analysis, work and family, simulations, social class and mobility, racial segregation and inequality.

Dalhousie University, Faculty of Arts and Social Science, Department of Sociology and Social Anthropology, Halifax, NS B3H 4R2, Canada. Offers social anthropology (MA, PhD); sociology (MA, PhD). *Entrance requirements:* Additional exam requirements/recommendations for international students: Required—TOEFL, IELTS, CANTEST, CAEL, or Michigan English Language Assessment Battery. Electronic applications accepted. *Faculty research:* Social inequality and social injustice; work, industry, and development (regional and international perspectives); health and illness.

DePaul University, College of Liberal Arts and Social Sciences, Chicago, IL 60614. Offers Arabic (MA); Chinese (MA); English (MA); French (MA); German (MA); history (MA); interdisciplinary studies (MA, MS); international public service (MS); international studies (MA); Italian (MA); Japanese (MA); leadership and policy studies (MS); liberal studies (MA); new media studies (MA); nonprofit management (MNM); public administration (MPA); public health (MPH); public service management (MS); social work (MSW); sociology (MA); Spanish (MA); sustainable urban development (MA); women and gender studies (MA); writing and publishing (MA); writing, rhetoric, and discourse (MA); MA/PhD. Part-time and evening/weekend programs available. Postbaccalaureate distance learning degree programs offered (no on-campus study). Terminal master's awarded for partial completion of doctoral program. *Degree requirements:* For master's, variable foreign language requirement, comprehensive exam (for some programs), thesis (for some programs). Electronic applications accepted.

Duke University, Graduate School, Department of Sociology, Durham, NC 27708. Offers AM, PhD. Terminal master's awarded for partial completion of doctoral program. *Degree requirements:* For doctorate, thesis/dissertation. *Entrance requirements:* For master's and doctorate, GRE General Test. Additional exam requirements/recommendations for international students: Required—TOEFL (minimum score 577 paper-based; 90 iBT) or IELTS (minimum score 7). Electronic applications accepted.

Expenses: Tuition: Full-time $45,760; part-time $2765 per credit. *Required fees:* $978. Full-time tuition and fees vary according to program.

East Carolina University, Graduate School, Thomas Harriot College of Arts and Sciences, Department of Sociology, Greenville, NC 27858-4353. Offers MA. Part-time and evening/weekend programs available. *Degree requirements:* For master's, one foreign language, comprehensive exam, thesis. *Entrance requirements:* For master's, GRE General Test. Additional exam requirements/recommendations for international students: Required—TOEFL. *Expenses:* Tuition, state resident: full-time $4223. Tuition, nonresident: full-time $16,540. *Required fees:* $2184.

Eastern Michigan University, Graduate School, College of Arts and Sciences, Department of Sociology, Anthropology and Criminology, Programs in Sociology, Ypsilanti, MI 48197. Offers MA. *Students:* 10 full-time (7 women), 2 part-time (1 woman); includes 2 minority (1 Black or African American, non-Hispanic/Latino; 1 Two or more races, non-Hispanic/Latino). Average age 28. 11 applicants, 73% accepted, 6 enrolled. In 2014, 2 master's awarded. Application fee: $45. *Application contact:* Dr. Rob Orrange, Graduate Coordinator, 734-487-0012, Fax: 734-487-9666, E-mail: rorrange@emich.edu.
Website: http://www.emich.edu/sac/

East Tennessee State University, School of Graduate Studies, College of Arts and Sciences, Department of Sociology and Anthropology, Johnson City, TN 37614. Offers MA. Part-time and evening/weekend programs available. *Faculty:* 10 full-time (4 women). *Students:* 11 full-time (9 women); includes 2 minority (both Two or more races, non-Hispanic/Latino). Average age 32. 18 applicants, 33% accepted, 6 enrolled. In 2014, 11 master's awarded. *Degree requirements:* For master's, comprehensive exam, internship or thesis. *Entrance requirements:* For master's, GRE General Test, minimum GPA of 3.0 in sociology major, three letters of recommendation. Additional exam requirements/recommendations for international students: Required—TOEFL (minimum score 550 paper-based; 79 iBT). *Application deadline:* For fall admission, 6/1 for domestic students, 4/30 for international students; for spring admission, 11/1 for domestic students, 9/30 for international students. Application fee: $35 ($45 for international students). Electronic applications accepted. *Financial support:* In 2014–15, 14 students received support, including 5 research assistantships with full tuition reimbursements available (averaging $6,400 per year), 6 teaching assistantships with full tuition reimbursements available (averaging $6,000 per year); career-related internships or fieldwork, institutionally sponsored loans, scholarships/grants, tuition waivers (full), and unspecified assistantships also available. Financial award application deadline: 7/1; financial award applicants required to submit FAFSA. *Faculty research:* Survey research methodologies, religion, sociology of sport, sociology of emotions, race and gender studies. *Unit head:* Dr. Melissa Schrift, Chair, 423-439-4370, Fax: 423-439-5313, E-mail: schrift@etsu.edu. *Application contact:* Angela Edwards, Graduate Specialist, 423-439-4703, Fax: 423-439-5624, E-mail: edwardag@etsu.edu.
Website: http://www.etsu.edu/cas/sociology/

Emory University, Laney Graduate School, Department of Sociology, Atlanta, GA 30322-1100. Offers PhD. Terminal master's awarded for partial completion of doctoral program. *Degree requirements:* For doctorate, comprehensive exam, thesis/dissertation, 2 preliminary exams, research paper, paper presentation. *Entrance requirements:* For doctorate, GRE General Test, minimum GPA of 3.0. Additional exam requirements/recommendations for international students: Required—TOEFL. Electronic applications accepted. *Faculty research:* Political economy and global analysis, culture, social psychology, criminology, stratification.

Fayetteville State University, Graduate School, Program in Sociology, Fayetteville, NC 28301-4298. Offers MA. Part-time and evening/weekend programs available. *Faculty:* 11 full-time (3 women). *Students:* 2 full-time (both women), 11 part-time (6 women); includes 8 minority (7 Black or African American, non-Hispanic/Latino; 1 Two or more races, non-Hispanic/Latino). Average age 35. 3 applicants, 100% accepted, 3 enrolled. In 2014, 5 master's awarded. *Degree requirements:* For master's, comprehensive exam, internship. *Application deadline:* For fall admission, 4/15 for domestic students; for spring admission, 10/15 for domestic students. Applications are processed on a rolling basis. Application fee: $40. Electronic applications accepted. *Faculty research:* Research methodology, African demography, urban sociology, aging and health, divided social problems, medical sociology, social change. *Unit head:* Dr. Nicole Lucas, Chairperson, 910-672-1122, Fax: 910-672-1378, E-mail: nlucas2@uncfsu.edu. *Application contact:* 910-672-1122, Fax: 910-672-1378, E-mail: nlucas2@uncfsu.edu.

Florida Atlantic University, Dorothy F. Schmidt College of Arts and Letters, Department of Sociology, Boca Raton, FL 33431-0991. Offers MA. Part-time and evening/weekend programs available. *Degree requirements:* For master's, thesis (for some programs). *Entrance requirements:* For master's, GRE General Test, minimum GPA of 3.0. Additional exam requirements/recommendations for international students: Required—TOEFL, IELTS. Electronic applications accepted. *Expenses:* Tuition, state resident: full-time $7396; part-time $369.82 per credit hour. Tuition, nonresident: full-time $19,392; part-time $1024.81 per credit hour. Tuition and fees vary according to course load. *Faculty research:* Gender/race/class, globalization, theory, social control, social movements.

Florida International University, College of Arts and Sciences, Department of Global and Sociocultural Studies, Miami, FL 33199. Offers MA, PhD. Part-time and evening/weekend programs available. *Degree requirements:* For master's, thesis; for doctorate, comprehensive exam, thesis/dissertation. *Entrance requirements:* For master's, GRE General Test, 3 letters of recommendation; minimum undergraduate GPA of 3.25, 3.5 on any previous graduate work; written examples of academic or other relevant professional work; for doctorate, GRE General Test, letter of intent; 3 letters of recommendation; minimum undergraduate GPA of 3.25, 3.5 on any previous graduate work; written examples of academic or other relevant professional work. Additional exam requirements/recommendations for international students: Required—TOEFL (minimum score 550 paper-based; 80 iBT). Electronic applications accepted.

Florida State University, The Graduate School, College of Social Sciences and Public Policy, Department of Sociology, Tallahassee, FL 32306. Offers MA, MS, PhD. *Faculty:* 16 full-time (8 women). *Students:* 50 full-time (31 women), 7 part-time (5 women); includes 12 minority (6 Black or African American, non-Hispanic/Latino; 3 Asian, non-Hispanic/Latino; 3 Hispanic/Latino), 1 international. Average age 28. 58 applicants, 38% accepted, 10 enrolled. In 2014, 8 master's, 7 doctorates awarded. *Degree requirements:* For doctorate, comprehensive exam, thesis/dissertation. *Entrance requirements:* For master's and doctorate, GRE General Test, minimum GPA of 3.0. Additional exam requirements/recommendations for international students: Required—TOEFL (minimum score 550 paper-based; 80 iBT). *Application deadline:* For fall admission, 12/15 priority date for domestic students, 12/15 for international students. Applications are processed on a rolling basis. Application fee: $30. Electronic applications accepted. *Expenses:* Tuition, state resident: part-time $403.51 per credit hour. Tuition, nonresident: part-time $1004.85 per credit hour. *Required fees:* $75.81 per credit hour. One-time fee: $20 part-time. Tuition and fees vary according to campus/location. *Financial support:* In 2014–15, 53 students received support, including 4 fellowships with full tuition reimbursements available (averaging $25,115 per year), 5 research assistantships with full tuition reimbursements available (averaging $21,115 per year), 44 teaching assistantships with full tuition reimbursements available (averaging $21,115 per year); institutionally sponsored loans, scholarships/grants, health care benefits, and unspecified assistantships also available. Financial award application deadline: 12/15; financial award applicants required to submit FAFSA. *Faculty research:* Aging and health, demography, inequality (gender/race and social movements/politics). *Total annual research expenditures:* $428,302. *Unit head:* Dr. Isaac Eberstein, Chair, 850-644-6416, Fax: 850-644-6208, E-mail: ieberstn@fsu.edu. *Application contact:* Jamie Yeargan, Graduate Program Coordinator, 850-644-6506, Fax: 850-644-6208, E-mail: jdyeargan@fsu.edu.
Website: http://coss.fsu.edu/sociology/

George Mason University, College of Humanities and Social Sciences, Department of Sociology and Anthropology, Fairfax, VA 22030. Offers anthropology (MA); sociology (MA, PhD). *Faculty:* 24 full-time (12 women), 5 part-time/adjunct (2 women). *Students:* 38 full-time (29 women), 56 part-time (35 women); includes 19 minority (8 Black or African American, non-Hispanic/Latino; 1 American Indian or Alaska Native, non-Hispanic/Latino; 2 Asian, non-Hispanic/Latino; 7 Hispanic/Latino; 1 Two or more races, non-Hispanic/Latino), 6 international. Average age 32. 72 applicants, 74% accepted, 23 enrolled. In 2014, 19 master's, 1 doctorate awarded. *Degree requirements:* For master's, thesis; for doctorate, comprehensive exam, thesis/dissertation. *Entrance requirements:* For master's, official transcript; expanded goals statement; 3 letters of recommendation; writing sample; resume; 3 credits in undergraduate sociology theory, statistics and research methods (for sociology); 3 credits of sociocultural anthropology (for anthropology); for doctorate, GRE General Test, expanded goals statement; 3 letters of recommendation; writing sample; official transcript. Additional exam requirements/recommendations for international students: Required—TOEFL (minimum score 570 paper-based; 80 iBT), IELTS (minimum score 6.5), PTE. Application fee: $65 ($80 for international students). Electronic applications accepted. *Expenses:* Tuition, state resident: full-time $9794; part-time $408 per credit hour. Tuition, nonresident: full-time $26,978; part-time $1124 per credit hour. *Required fees:* $2820; $118 per credit hour. Tuition and fees vary according to course load and program. *Financial support:* In 2014–15, 21 students received support, including 2 fellowships (averaging $10,166 per year), 9 research assistantships with full and partial tuition reimbursements available (averaging $13,941 per year), 12 teaching assistantships with full and partial tuition reimbursements available (averaging $10,555 per year); career-related internships or fieldwork, Federal Work-Study, scholarships/grants, unspecified assistantships, and health care benefits (for full-time research or teaching assistantship recipients) also available. Support available to part-time students. Financial award application deadline: 3/1; financial award applicants required to submit FAFSA. *Faculty research:* Africa, American teenagers, black entrepreneurs, human rights, gambling. *Total annual research expenditures:* $259,232. *Unit head:* Lester Kurtz, Interim Chair, 703-993-1425, Fax: 703-993-1446, E-mail: lkurtz@gmu.edu. *Application contact:* Amy Best, Associate Professor/Graduate Coordinator, 703-993-1426, Fax: 703-993-1446, E-mail: abest@gmu.edu.
Website: http://soan.gmu.edu

The George Washington University, Columbian College of Arts and Sciences, Department of Sociology, Washington, DC 20052. Offers criminology (MA); sociology (MA). Part-time and evening/weekend programs available. *Faculty:* 13 full-time (6 women). *Students:* 12 full-time (11 women), 9 part-time (8 women); includes 7 minority (4 Black or African American, non-Hispanic/Latino; 3 Asian, non-Hispanic/Latino), 1 international. Average age 26. 46 applicants, 57% accepted, 9 enrolled. In 2014, 11 master's awarded. *Degree requirements:* For master's, comprehensive exam, thesis or alternative. *Entrance requirements:* For master's, GRE General Test, minimum GPA of 3.0. Additional exam requirements/recommendations for international students: Required—TOEFL (minimum score 550 paper-based; 80 iBT). *Application deadline:* For fall admission, 6/1 priority date for domestic students, 1/15 priority date for international students; for spring admission, 11/1 priority date for domestic students, 9/1 priority date for international students. Applications are processed on a rolling basis. Application fee: $75. Electronic applications accepted. *Financial support:* In 2014–15, 7 students received support. Fellowships with full tuition reimbursements available, teaching assistantships with tuition reimbursements available, career-related internships or fieldwork, Federal Work-Study, and tuition waivers available. Financial award application deadline: 1/15. *Unit head:* Dr. Greg Squires, Chair, 202-994-7466, E-mail: squires@gwu.edu. *Application contact:* Information Contact, 202-994-6345, Fax: 202-994-3239, E-mail: soc@gwu.edu.
Website: http://www.gwu.edu/~soc/

Georgia Southern University, Jack N. Averitt College of Graduate Studies, College of Liberal Arts and Social Sciences, Program in Social Science, Statesboro, GA 30460. Offers MA. Part-time and evening/weekend programs available. *Students:* 36 full-time (26 women), 12 part-time (6 women); includes 24 minority (7 Black or African American, non-Hispanic/Latino; 15 Hispanic/Latino; 2 Two or more races, non-Hispanic/Latino), 3 international. Average age 28. 32 applicants, 84% accepted, 17 enrolled. In 2014, 8 master's awarded. *Degree requirements:* For master's, thesis optional. *Entrance requirements:* For master's, GRE General Test. Additional exam requirements/recommendations for international students: Required—TOEFL (minimum score 550 paper-based; 80 iBT), IELTS (minimum score 6). *Application deadline:* For fall admission, 3/1 priority date for domestic and international students; for spring admission, 10/1 priority date for domestic students, 10/1 for international students. Applications are processed on a rolling basis. Application fee: $50. Electronic applications accepted. *Expenses:* Tuition, state resident: full-time $7236; part-time $277 per semester hour. Tuition, nonresident: full-time $27,118; part-time $1105 per semester hour. *Required fees:* $2092. *Financial support:* In 2014–15, 26 students received support, including research assistantships with partial tuition reimbursements available (averaging $7,200 per year), teaching assistantships with partial tuition reimbursements available (averaging $7,200 per year); career-related internships or fieldwork, Federal Work-Study, scholarships/grants, tuition waivers (partial), and unspecified assistantships also available. Support available to part-time students. Financial award application deadline: 4/15; financial award applicants required to submit FAFSA. *Faculty research:* Anthropology, sociology, criminal justice, history, political science. *Total annual research expenditures:* $40,162. *Unit head:* Dr. Peggy Hargis, Department Chair, 912-478-5621, Fax: 912-478-0703, E-mail: har_agga@georgiasouthern.edu.
Website: http://class.georgiasouthern.edu/socianth/

Georgia State University, College of Arts and Sciences, Department of Sociology, Atlanta, GA 30302-3083. Offers MA, PhD, MA/PhD. Part-time and evening/weekend programs available. *Faculty:* 16 full-time (9 women). *Students:* 65 full-time (48 women), 20 part-time (17 women); includes 38 minority (24 Black or African American, non-Hispanic/Latino; 1 American Indian or Alaska Native, non-Hispanic/Latino; 2 Asian, non-Hispanic/Latino; 3 Hispanic/Latino; 8 Two or more races, non-Hispanic/Latino), 4 international. Average age 33. 81 applicants, 48% accepted, 18 enrolled. In 2014, 14 master's, 5 doctorates awarded. Terminal master's awarded for partial completion of doctoral program. *Degree requirements:* For master's, thesis; for doctorate, comprehensive exam, thesis/dissertation. *Entrance requirements:* For master's and doctorate, GRE. Additional exam requirements/recommendations for international students: Required—TOEFL (minimum score 600 paper-based; 100 iBT). *Application*

deadline: For fall admission, 4/15 for domestic students, 2/1 for international students; for spring admission, 4/15 for domestic and international students. Applications are processed on a rolling basis. Application fee: $50. Electronic applications accepted. *Expenses:* Tuition, state resident: full-time $6516; part-time $362 per credit hour. Tuition, nonresident: full-time $22,014; part-time $1223 per credit hour. *Required fees:* $2128 per semester. Tuition and fees vary according to course load and program. *Financial support:* In 2014–15, fellowships with full and partial tuition reimbursements (averaging $5,000 per year), research assistantships with full and partial tuition reimbursements (averaging $17,500 per year), teaching assistantships with full and partial tuition reimbursements (averaging $13,000 per year) were awarded; scholarships/grants and unspecified assistantships also available. Financial award application deadline: 2/1. *Faculty research:* Race and urban studies, gender and sexuality, family, health, life course. *Unit head:* Dr. Donald C. Reitzes, Department Chair, 404-413-6506, Fax: 404-413-6505, E-mail: dreitzes@gsu.edu. *Application contact:* Dr. Leslie Reid, Director of Graduate Studies, 404-413-6521, Fax: 404-413-6505, E-mail: lesleyreid@gsu.edu.
Website: http://cas.gsu.edu/graduate-studies/admissions/

The Graduate Center, City University of New York, Graduate Studies, Program in Sociology, New York, NY 10016-4039. Offers PhD. *Degree requirements:* For doctorate, one foreign language, thesis/dissertation. *Entrance requirements:* For doctorate, GRE General Test, writing sample. Additional exam requirements/recommendations for international students: Required—TOEFL. Electronic applications accepted.

Harvard University, Graduate School of Arts and Sciences, Department of Sociology, Cambridge, MA 02138. Offers PhD. *Degree requirements:* For doctorate, thesis/dissertation, oral exams in 2 subfields. *Entrance requirements:* For doctorate, GRE General Test. Additional exam requirements/recommendations for international students: Required—TOEFL. *Faculty research:* Sociological theory, political theories, quantitative approaches to methodology.

Howard University, Graduate School, Department of Health, Human Performance and Leisure Studies, Washington, DC 20059-0002. Offers exercise physiology (MS); health education (MS); sports studies (MS), including sociology of sports, sports management; urban recreation (MS), including leisure studies. Part-time and evening/weekend programs available. *Degree requirements:* For master's, comprehensive exam, thesis. *Entrance requirements:* For master's, BS in human performance or related field. Additional exam requirements/recommendations for international students: Recommended—TOEFL. Electronic applications accepted. *Faculty research:* Health promotion, cardiovascular hypertension, physical activity, sport and human rights issues.

Howard University, Graduate School, Department of Sociology and Anthropology, Washington, DC 20059-0002. Offers sociology (MA, PhD). Part-time and evening/weekend programs available. *Degree requirements:* For master's, thesis; for doctorate, one foreign language, comprehensive exam, thesis/dissertation, RCR, writing exam. *Entrance requirements:* For master's, GRE General Test, minimum GPA of 3.0; for doctorate, GRE General Test, minimum GPA of 3.5. Additional exam requirements/recommendations for international students: Required—TOEFL. Electronic applications accepted. *Faculty research:* Medical sociology; criminology; race, class and gender; urban sociology.

Humboldt State University, Academic Programs, College of Arts, Humanities, and Social Sciences, Department of Sociology, Arcata, CA 95521-8299. Offers MA. *Students:* 15 full-time (6 women), 5 part-time (3 women); includes 9 minority (1 Black or African American, non-Hispanic/Latino; 3 Asian, non-Hispanic/Latino; 5 Hispanic/Latino), 1 international. Average age 31. 16 applicants, 75% accepted, 10 enrolled. In 2014, 6 master's awarded. *Degree requirements:* For master's, thesis or alternative, qualifying exam. *Entrance requirements:* For master's, minimum GPA of 2.5, 3 letters of recommendation. Additional exam requirements/recommendations for international students: Required—TOEFL (minimum score 500 paper-based). *Application deadline:* For fall admission, 3/15 for domestic students; for spring admission, 12/1 for domestic students. Applications are processed on a rolling basis. Application fee: $55. *Expenses:* Tuition, state resident: full-time $6738; part-time $3906 per year. Tuition, nonresident: full-time $13,434; part-time $6138 per year. *Required fees:* $1690; $1266 per year. Tuition and fees vary according to program. *Financial support:* Application deadline: 3/1; applicants required to submit FAFSA. *Faculty research:* Sociology of women political activists, environmental dispute resolution, prosocial behavior. *Unit head:* Dr. Jennifer Eichstedt, Chair, 707-826-4649, Fax: 707-826-4418, E-mail: jle7001@humboldt.edu. *Application contact:* Dr. Meredith Williams, Coordinator, 707-826-4326, Fax: 707-826-4418, E-mail: mw1167@humboldt.edu.

Hunter College of the City University of New York, Graduate School, School of Arts and Sciences, Department of Sociology, New York, NY 10065-5085. Offers applied social research (MS). *Faculty:* 3 full-time (2 women), 1 (woman) part-time/adjunct. *Students:* 5 full-time (3 women), 11 part-time (7 women); includes 7 minority (3 Black or African American, non-Hispanic/Latino; 1 Asian, non-Hispanic/Latino; 3 Hispanic/Latino). Average age 25. 17 applicants, 59% accepted, 3 enrolled. In 2014, 11 master's awarded. *Degree requirements:* For master's, internship. *Entrance requirements:* For master's, GRE General Test or GMAT, 3 credits of course work in statistics, 2 letters of recommendation. Additional exam requirements/recommendations for international students: Required—TOEFL. *Application deadline:* For fall admission, 4/1 for domestic students, 2/1 for international students; for spring admission, 11/1 for domestic students, 9/1 for international students. *Financial support:* Federal Work-Study and tuition waivers (partial) available. Support available to part-time students. *Unit head:* Dr. Howard Lune, Chairperson, 212-772-5641, Fax: 212-772-5645, E-mail: hlune@hunter.cuny.edu. *Application contact:* Milena Solo, Graduate Admissions Director, 212-772-4480, E-mail: admission@hunter.cuny.edu.
Website: http://maxweber.hunter.cuny.edu/socio/

Idaho State University, Office of Graduate Studies, College of Arts and Letters, Department of Sociology, Pocatello, ID 83209-8114. Offers MA. Part-time programs available. *Degree requirements:* For master's, comprehensive exam, thesis, oral defense of thesis. *Entrance requirements:* For master's, GRE General Test (minimum 40th percentile in one of 3 sections), minimum undergraduate GPA of 3.0, 3 letters of recommendation. Additional exam requirements/recommendations for international students: Required—TOEFL (minimum score 550 paper-based; 80 iBT). Electronic applications accepted. *Faculty research:* Terrorism, social organization, family social work.

Illinois State University, Graduate School, College of Arts and Sciences, Department of Sociology, Normal, IL 61790-2200. Offers historical archaeology (MA, MS); sociology (MA, MS). *Degree requirements:* For master's, thesis. *Entrance requirements:* For master's, GRE General Test, GRE Subject Test, minimum GPA of 2.4 in last 60 hours of course work. *Faculty research:* Japanese Saturday school (Kato).

Indiana University Bloomington, University Graduate School, College of Arts and Sciences, Department of Sociology, Bloomington, IN 47405-7000. Offers MA, PhD. *Faculty:* 18 full-time (9 women). *Students:* 81 full-time (45 women), 2 part-time (both women); includes 18 minority (5 Black or African American, non-Hispanic/Latino; 4 Asian, non-Hispanic/Latino; 8 Hispanic/Latino; 1 Two or more races, non-Hispanic/Latino), 7 international. Average age 29. 127 applicants, 9% accepted, 11 enrolled. In 2014, 9 master's, 8 doctorates awarded. Terminal master's awarded for partial completion of doctoral program. *Degree requirements:* For master's, thesis; for doctorate, comprehensive exam, thesis/dissertation. *Entrance requirements:* For master's and doctorate, GRE General Test. Additional exam requirements/recommendations for international students: Required—TOEFL. *Application deadline:* For fall admission, 1/15 for domestic students, 12/1 for international students. Application fee: $55 ($65 for international students). Electronic applications accepted. *Financial support:* Fellowships with full tuition reimbursements, research assistantships with full tuition reimbursements, teaching assistantships with full tuition reimbursements, scholarships/grants, health care benefits, and unspecified assistantships available. Financial award application deadline: 1/15; financial award applicants required to submit FAFSA. *Faculty research:* Social psychology, political sociology, sociological research methods, stratification/mobility, education. *Unit head:* Prof. Eliza Pavalko, Professor, 812-855-7629, Fax: 812-855-0781, E-mail: epavalko@indiana.edu. *Application contact:* Erin Miller, Information Contact, 812-855-2924, E-mail: elm5@indiana.edu.
Website: http://www.indiana.edu/~soc/

Indiana University of Pennsylvania, School of Graduate Studies and Research, College of Humanities and Social Sciences, Department of Sociology, Program in Sociology, Indiana, PA 15705-1087. Offers MA. Part-time programs available. *Faculty:* 13 full-time (9 women). *Students:* 8 full-time (4 women), 3 part-time (all women); includes 1 minority (Black or African American, non-Hispanic/Latino). Average age 31. 16 applicants, 63% accepted, 5 enrolled. In 2014, 3 master's awarded. *Degree requirements:* For master's, thesis optional. *Entrance requirements:* For master's, GRE, 2 letters of recommendation. Additional exam requirements/recommendations for international students: Required—TOEFL (minimum score 550 paper-based). *Application deadline:* Applications are processed on a rolling basis. Application fee: $50. Electronic applications accepted. *Financial support:* In 2014–15, 1 fellowship with full tuition reimbursement (averaging $1,000 per year), 8 research assistantships with full and partial tuition reimbursements (averaging $4,484 per year) were awarded; career-related internships or fieldwork, Federal Work-Study, scholarships/grants, and unspecified assistantships also available. Financial award application deadline: 4/15; financial award applicants required to submit FAFSA. *Unit head:* Dr. Diane Shinberg, Coordinator, 724-357-4769, E-mail: shinberg@iup.edu.
Website: http://www.iup.edu/grad/sociology/default.aspx

Indiana University–Purdue University Fort Wayne, College of Arts and Sciences, Department of Sociology, Fort Wayne, IN 46805-1499. Offers sociological practice (MA). Part-time programs available. *Faculty:* 11 full-time (3 women). *Students:* 3 part-time (2 women); includes 2 minority (both Black or African American, non-Hispanic/Latino). Average age 34. 2 applicants, 100% accepted, 2 enrolled. In 2014, 2 master's awarded. *Degree requirements:* For master's, thesis optional, practicum. *Entrance requirements:* For master's, minimum GPA of 3.0, 3 letters of recommendation, essay, interview. Additional exam requirements/recommendations for international students: Required—TOEFL (minimum score 550 paper-based; 79 iBT). *Application deadline:* For fall admission, 8/1 for domestic students; for spring admission, 11/1 priority date for domestic students. Applications are processed on a rolling basis. Application fee: $50. *Financial support:* Scholarships/grants and unspecified assistantships available. Support available to part-time students. Financial award application deadline: 3/1; financial award applicants required to submit FAFSA. *Faculty research:* School shootings in the U.S., obesity and social distance. *Total annual research expenditures:* $13,438. *Unit head:* Dr. Peter Iadicola, Chair, 260-481-6663, Fax: 260-481-0474, E-mail: iadicola@ipfw.edu. *Application contact:* Marilyn Morgan, Graduate Secretary, 260-481-6662, Fax: 260-481-0474, E-mail: morganm@ipfw.edu.
Website: http://www.ipfw.edu/sociology

Indiana University–Purdue University Indianapolis, School of Liberal Arts, Department of Sociology, Indianapolis, IN 46202. Offers family/gender studies (MA); medical sociology (MA); work/occupations (MA). *Faculty:* 17 full-time (8 women). *Students:* 9 full-time (7 women), 15 part-time (13 women); includes 3 minority (all Black or African American, non-Hispanic/Latino), 2 international. Average age 30. 16 applicants, 69% accepted, 6 enrolled. In 2014, 10 master's awarded. Application fee: $55 ($65 for international students). *Financial support:* Fellowships and teaching assistantships available. *Unit head:* Dr. Robert W. White, Chair, 317-278-5226, E-mail: rwwhite@iupui.edu. *Application contact:* Dr. Carrie E. Foote, Director of Graduate Studies, 317-274-8454, E-mail: foote@iupui.edu.
Website: http://liberalarts.iupui.edu/sociology/

Iowa State University of Science and Technology, Department of Sociology, Ames, IA 50011. Offers rural sociology (MS, PhD); sociology (MS, PhD). *Degree requirements:* For master's, thesis; for doctorate, thesis/dissertation. *Entrance requirements:* For master's and doctorate, GRE General Test. Additional exam requirements/recommendations for international students: Required—TOEFL (minimum score 550 paper-based; 79 iBT), IELTS (minimum score 6.5). Electronic applications accepted.

Jackson State University, Graduate School, College of Liberal Arts, Department of Sociology, Jackson, MS 39217. Offers criminology and justice services (MA); sociology (MA). Part-time and evening/weekend programs available. *Degree requirements:* For master's, comprehensive exam, thesis or alternative. *Entrance requirements:* For master's, GRE General Test. Additional exam requirements/recommendations for international students: Required—TOEFL (minimum score 520 paper-based; 67 iBT).

Johns Hopkins University, Bloomberg School of Public Health, Department of Health, Behavior and Society, Baltimore, MD 21218-2699. Offers genetic counseling (Sc M); health education and health communication (MSPH); social and behavioral sciences (Dr PH, PhD); social factors in health (MHS). *Degree requirements:* For master's, comprehensive exam (for some programs), thesis (for some programs); for doctorate, comprehensive exam, thesis/dissertation. *Entrance requirements:* For master's, GRE, curriculum vitae, 3 letters of recommendation; for doctorate, GRE, transcripts, curriculum vitae, 3 recommendation letters. Additional exam requirements/recommendations for international students: Required—TOEFL (minimum score 600 paper-based; 100 iBT). Electronic applications accepted. *Faculty research:* Social determinants of health and structural and community-level inventions to improve health, communication and health education, behavioral and social aspects of genetic counseling.

Johns Hopkins University, Zanvyl Krieger School of Arts and Sciences, Department of Sociology, Baltimore, MD 21218-2699. Offers PhD. *Degree requirements:* For doctorate, one foreign language, thesis/dissertation. *Entrance requirements:* For doctorate, GRE General Test. Additional exam requirements/recommendations for international students: Required—TOEFL (minimum score 600 paper-based; 100 iBT), IELTS; Recommended—TWE. Electronic applications accepted. *Faculty research:* Education, immigration, race and gender, world systems, social policy.

Kansas State University, Graduate School, College of Arts and Sciences, Department of Sociology, Anthropology and Social Work, Manhattan, KS 66506. Offers sociology (MA, PhD). Part-time programs available. *Faculty:* 14 full-time (5 women), 1 (woman) part-time/adjunct. *Students:* 31 full-time (18 women), 12 part-time (7 women); includes 8 minority (2 Black or African American, non-Hispanic/Latino; 2 Asian, non-Hispanic/

Latino; 4 Hispanic/Latino), 6 international. Average age 29. 17 applicants, 76% accepted, 9 enrolled. In 2014, 3 master's, 5 doctorates awarded. *Degree requirements:* For master's, thesis or alternative; for doctorate, thesis/dissertation. *Entrance requirements:* For master's, GRE, minimum undergraduate GPA of 3.0; for doctorate, GRE, master's degree in sociology or related field. Additional exam requirements/recommendations for international students: Required—TOEFL (minimum score 550 paper-based), IELTS. *Application deadline:* For fall admission, 1/15 priority date for domestic students, 1/1 priority date for international students; for spring admission, 10/1 priority date for domestic students, 8/1 priority date for international students. Applications are processed on a rolling basis. Application fee: $50 ($75 for international students). Electronic applications accepted. *Financial support:* In 2014–15, 3 research assistantships, 14 teaching assistantships with full tuition reimbursements (averaging $10,600 per year) were awarded; institutionally sponsored loans, scholarships/grants, health care benefits, and unspecified assistantships also available. Support available to part-time students. Financial award application deadline: 1/15; financial award applicants required to submit FAFSA. *Faculty research:* Rural development, gender, criminology, international development/globalization, political sociology/social movements. *Total annual research expenditures:* $300,000. *Unit head:* Dr. Betsy Cauble, Department Head, 785-532-4962, Fax: 785-532-6978, E-mail: bcauble@ksu.edu. *Application contact:* Dr. Laszlo Kulcsar, Graduate Program Director, 785-532-4959, Fax: 785-532-6978, E-mail: kulcsar@ksu.edu.
Website: http://www.k-state.edu/sasw/

Kean University, College of Humanities and Social Sciences, Program in Sociology and Social Justice, Union, NJ 07083. Offers MA. Part-time programs available. *Faculty:* 18 full-time (5 women). *Students:* 4 full-time (all women), 14 part-time (10 women); includes 13 minority (6 Black or African American, non-Hispanic/Latino; 1 American Indian or Alaska Native, non-Hispanic/Latino; 1 Asian, non-Hispanic/Latino; 4 Hispanic/Latino; 1 Two or more races, non-Hispanic/Latino). Average age 31. 5 applicants, 100% accepted, 5 enrolled. In 2014, 6 master's awarded. *Degree requirements:* For master's, comprehensive exam, thesis. *Entrance requirements:* For master's, GRE, minimum cumulative GPA of 3.0, two letters of recommendation, professional resume/curriculum vitae, personal statement, official transcripts from all institutions attended. Additional exam requirements/recommendations for international students: Required—TOEFL (minimum score 550 paper-based; 79 iBT). *Application deadline:* For fall admission, 6/1 for domestic and international students; for spring admission, 12/1 for domestic and international students. Applications are processed on a rolling basis. Application fee: $75 ($150 for international students). Electronic applications accepted. *Expenses:* Tuition, state resident: full-time $12,461; part-time $607 per credit. Tuition, nonresident: full-time $16,889; part-time $744 per credit. *Required fees:* $3141; $143 per credit. Tuition and fees vary according to course load, degree level and program. *Financial support:* In 2014–15, 2 research assistantships with full tuition reimbursements (averaging $3,742 per year) were awarded; scholarships/grants and unspecified assistantships also available. Financial award applicants required to submit FAFSA. *Unit head:* Dr. Julia Nevarez, Program Coordinator, 908-737-4058, E-mail: jnevarez@kean.edu. *Application contact:* Steven Koch, Admissions Counselor, 908-737-7136, Fax: 908-737-7135, E-mail: skoch@kean.edu.
Website: http://grad.kean.edu/masters-programs/sociology-and-social-justice

Kent State University, College of Arts and Sciences, Department of Sociology, Kent, OH 44242-0001. Offers MA, PhD. PhD offered jointly with The University of Akron. Part-time programs available. Postbaccalaureate distance learning degree programs offered. *Faculty:* 30 full-time (16 women). *Students:* 36 full-time (22 women), 10 part-time (6 women); includes 7 minority (4 Black or African American, non-Hispanic/Latino; 1 Asian, non-Hispanic/Latino; 2 Hispanic/Latino). Average age 31. 101 applicants, 55% accepted, 34 enrolled. In 2014, 7 master's, 2 doctorates awarded. Terminal master's awarded for partial completion of doctoral program. *Degree requirements:* For master's, thesis optional; for doctorate, comprehensive exam, thesis/dissertation. *Entrance requirements:* For master's, GRE General Test, minimum GPA of 3.0, transcripts, statement of purpose, resume/curriculum vitae, goal statement, 3 letters of recommendation; for doctorate, GRE General Test, minimum GPA of 3.2, transcripts, personal statement, 3 letters of recommendation. Additional exam requirements/recommendations for international students: Required—TOEFL (minimum score: paper-based 525, iBT 71), Michigan English Language Assessment Battery (minimum score of 75), IELTS (minimum score of 6.0), PTE Academic (minimum score of 48), or completion of ELS level 112 Intensive Program. *Application deadline:* For fall admission, 12/15 for domestic students, 7/12 for international students; for spring admission, 11/29 for domestic and international students. Application fee: $45 ($70 for international students). Electronic applications accepted. *Expenses:* Tuition, state resident: full-time $8730; part-time $485 per credit hour. Tuition, nonresident: full-time $14,886; part-time $827 per credit hour. Tuition and fees vary according to campus/location and program. *Financial support:* Research assistantships with full tuition reimbursements, teaching assistantships with full tuition reimbursements, and Federal Work-Study available. Financial award application deadline: 2/1. *Unit head:* Dr. Richard T. Serpe, Professor and Chair, 330-672-2562, E-mail: rserpe@kent.edu. *Application contact:* Dr. Susan Roxburgh, Professor and Graduate Coordinator, 330-672-2562, E-mail: sroxburg@kent.edu.
Website: http://www.kent.edu/sociology/

Lakehead University, Graduate Studies, Faculty of Social Sciences and Humanities, Department of Sociology, Thunder Bay, ON P7B 5E1, Canada. Offers gerontology (MA); health services and policy research (MA); sociology (MA); women's studies (MA). Part-time and evening/weekend programs available. *Degree requirements:* For master's, research project or thesis. *Entrance requirements:* For master's, minimum B average. Additional exam requirements/recommendations for international students: Required—TOEFL. *Faculty research:* Sociology of medicine, cultural and social change, health human resources, gerontology, women's studies.

Laurentian University, School of Graduate Studies and Research, Programme in Sociology, Sudbury, ON P3E 2C6, Canada. Offers applied social research (MA). Part-time programs available. *Entrance requirements:* For master's, honors degree in sociology or equivalent. *Faculty research:* Work foundations, managing AIDS organization, tracking laid-off mine workers.

Lehigh University, College of Arts and Sciences, Department of Sociology and Anthropology, Bethlehem, PA 18015. Offers sociology (MA). Part-time programs available. *Faculty:* 11 full-time (6 women). *Students:* 15 full-time (11 women), 5 part-time (all women); includes 4 minority (1 Black or African American, non-Hispanic/Latino; 1 Asian, non-Hispanic/Latino; 2 Hispanic/Latino), 3 international. Average age 27. 18 applicants, 72% accepted, 9 enrolled. In 2014, 7 master's awarded. *Degree requirements:* For master's, comprehensive exam, thesis optional. *Entrance requirements:* For master's, GRE General Test. Additional exam requirements/recommendations for international students: Required—TOEFL (minimum score 650 paper-based; 94 iBT). *Application deadline:* For fall admission, 1/15 priority date for domestic and international students. Application fee: $75. Electronic applications accepted. *Expenses:* Expenses: $1,380 per credit. *Financial support:* In 2014–15, 8 students received support, including 3 fellowships with full tuition reimbursements available, 7 teaching assistantships with full tuition reimbursements available; research assistantships with full tuition reimbursements available, career-related internships or fieldwork, Federal Work-Study, institutionally sponsored loans, scholarships/grants, tuition waivers (full and partial), and unspecified assistantships also available. Support available to part-time students. Financial award application deadline: 1/1. *Faculty research:* Juvenile delinquency, parent-child relations, urban sociology, medical sociology, policy studies, globalization. *Total annual research expenditures:* $166,942. *Unit head:* Dr. Nicola Tannenbaum, Chair/Professor, 610-758-3829, Fax: 610-758-6552, E-mail: nt01@lehigh.edu. *Application contact:* Prof. Judith Lasker, Graduate Program Director, 610-758-3811, Fax: 610-758-6552, E-mail: jnl0@lehigh.edu.
Website: http://cas.lehigh.edu/socanthro

Lincoln University, Graduate Studies, Jefferson City, MO 65101. Offers business administration (MBA), including accounting, entrepreneurship, management, public administration and policy; educational leadership (Ed S), including elementary leadership, secondary leadership, superintendency; guidance and counseling (M Ed), including community/agency counseling, elementary school, secondary school; history (MA); school administration and supervision (M Ed), including elementary school administration, secondary school administration, special education administration; school teaching (M Ed), including elementary school teaching, secondary school teaching; sociology (MA); sociology/criminal justice (MA). Part-time and evening/weekend programs available. Postbaccalaureate distance learning degree programs offered (minimal on-campus study). *Students:* 57 full-time (35 women), 83 part-time (50 women); includes 64 minority (47 Black or African American, non-Hispanic/Latino; 1 American Indian or Alaska Native, non-Hispanic/Latino; 14 Asian, non-Hispanic/Latino; 1 Hispanic/Latino; 1 Two or more races, non-Hispanic/Latino), 9 international. Average age 33. 60 applicants, 68% accepted, 31 enrolled. In 2014, 52 master's, 2 other advanced degrees awarded. *Degree requirements:* For master's and Ed S, comprehensive exam, thesis optional. *Entrance requirements:* For master's and Ed S, GRE, MAT or GMAT, minimum GPA of 2.75 in major, 2.5 overall; 3 letters of recommendation; minimum C average in English composition; personal statement of purpose. Additional exam requirements/recommendations for international students: Required—TOEFL (minimum score 500 paper-based; 61 iBT). *Application deadline:* For fall admission, 8/1 priority date for domestic and international students; for spring admission, 12/1 priority date for domestic and international students; for summer admission, 5/1 priority date for domestic and international students. Applications are processed on a rolling basis. Application fee: $30. *Expenses:* Tuition, state resident: full-time $6840; part-time $285 per credit hour. Tuition, nonresident: full-time $12,720; part-time $530 per credit hour. *Required fees:* $737; $737 per year. *Financial support:* In 2014–15, 1 fellowship with tuition reimbursement, 11 research assistantships with tuition reimbursements were awarded; Federal Work-Study and scholarships/grants also available. Support available to part-time students. Financial award application deadline: 3/1; financial award applicants required to submit FAFSA. *Unit head:* Dr. Linda S. Bickel, Dean, 573-681-5247, Fax: 573-681-5106, E-mail: gradschool@lincolnu.edu. *Application contact:* Irasema Steck, Administrative Assistant, 573-681-5247, Fax: 573-681-5106, E-mail: gradschool@lincolnu.edu.
Website: http://www.lincolnu.edu/web/graduate-studies/graduate-studies

Louisiana State University and Agricultural & Mechanical College, Graduate School, College of Humanities and Social Sciences, Department of Sociology, Baton Rouge, LA 70803. Offers MA, PhD. Part-time programs available. *Faculty:* 14 full-time (4 women). *Students:* 45 full-time (20 women), 9 part-time (6 women); includes 17 minority (12 Black or African American, non-Hispanic/Latino; 1 Asian, non-Hispanic/Latino; 4 Hispanic/Latino), 11 international. Average age 31. 45 applicants, 67% accepted, 14 enrolled. In 2014, 4 master's, 2 doctorates awarded. Terminal master's awarded for partial completion of doctoral program. *Degree requirements:* For master's, comprehensive exam, thesis; for doctorate, comprehensive exam, thesis/dissertation. *Entrance requirements:* For master's and doctorate, GRE General Test, minimum GPA of 3.0. Additional exam requirements/recommendations for international students: Required—TOEFL (minimum score 550 paper-based; 79 IBT), IELTS (minimum score 6.5), or PTE (minimum score 59). *Application deadline:* For fall admission, 1/1 priority date for domestic students, 5/15 for international students; for spring admission, 10/15 for domestic and international students; for summer admission, 5/15 for domestic and international students. Applications are processed on a rolling basis. Application fee: $50 ($70 for international students). Electronic applications accepted. *Financial support:* In 2014–15, 41 students received support, including 2 fellowships (averaging $22,440 per year), 4 research assistantships with partial tuition reimbursements available (averaging $16,756 per year), 26 teaching assistantships with partial tuition reimbursements available (averaging $11,362 per year); Federal Work-Study, scholarships/grants, health care benefits, tuition waivers (full and partial), and unspecified assistantships also available. Support available to part-time students. Financial award application deadline: 3/1; financial award applicants required to submit FAFSA. *Faculty research:* Family, stratification, demography, rural sociology, criminology. *Total annual research expenditures:* $346,521. *Unit head:* Dr. Edward Shihadeh, Chair, 225-578-1645, Fax: 225-578-5102, E-mail: edsoc@lsu.edu. *Application contact:* Dr. Yoshimori Kamo, Graduate Adviser, 225-578-5352, Fax: 225-578-5102, E-mail: kamo@lsu.edu.
Website: http://uiswcmsweb.prod.lsu.edu/hss/sociology/

Loyola University Chicago, Graduate School, Department of Sociology, Chicago, IL 60660. Offers MA, PhD. Part-time and evening/weekend programs available. *Faculty:* 14 full-time (6 women), 5 part-time/adjunct (1 woman). *Students:* 47 full-time (26 women), 4 part-time (3 women); includes 18 minority (10 Black or African American, non-Hispanic/Latino; 2 Asian, non-Hispanic/Latino; 5 Hispanic/Latino; 1 Two or more races, non-Hispanic/Latino), 8 international. Average age 33. 82 applicants, 23% accepted, 8 enrolled. In 2014, 5 master's, 8 doctorates awarded. Terminal master's awarded for partial completion of doctoral program. *Degree requirements:* For master's, thesis or alternative; for doctorate, comprehensive exam, thesis/dissertation. *Entrance requirements:* For master's and doctorate, GRE General Test. Additional exam requirements/recommendations for international students: Required—TOEFL. *Application deadline:* For fall and winter admission, 2/1 for domestic and international students. Electronic applications accepted. Application fee is waived when completed online. *Expenses: Tuition:* Full-time $17,370; part-time $965 per credit. *Required fees:* $138 per semester. *Financial support:* In 2014–15, 25 students received support, including 4 fellowships with full tuition reimbursements available (averaging $16,000 per year), 8 research assistantships with full tuition reimbursements available (averaging $16,000 per year), 6 teaching assistantships with full tuition reimbursements available (averaging $16,000 per year); career-related internships or fieldwork, Federal Work-Study, health care benefits, tuition waivers (full), and unspecified assistantships also available. Financial award application deadline: 2/1; financial award applicants required to submit FAFSA. *Faculty research:* Religion, knowledge, culture, urban and social policy, medical. *Total annual research expenditures:* $160,000. *Unit head:* Dr. Rhys Williams, Chair, 773-508-3459, Fax: 773-508-7099, E-mail: rwilliams7s@luc.edu. *Application contact:* Dr. Anne Figert, Graduate Program Director, 773-508-3431, Fax: 773-508-3451, E-mail: afigert@luc.edu.

Marshall University, Academic Affairs Division, College of Liberal Arts, Department of Sociology and Anthropology, Huntington, WV 25755. Offers sociology (MA). *Students:* 8 full-time (4 women), 1 (woman) part-time. Average age 29. In 2014, 4 master's awarded.

Sociology

Degree requirements: For master's, thesis optional. *Entrance requirements:* For master's, GRE. Application fee: $40. *Unit head:* Dr. Marty Loebach, Chair, 304-696-6700, E-mail: sociology@marshall.edu. *Application contact:* Information Contact, Graduate Admissions, 304-746-1900, Fax: 304-746-1902, E-mail: services@marshall.edu.

McGill University, Faculty of Graduate and Postdoctoral Studies, Faculty of Arts, Department of Sociology, Montréal, QC H3A 2T5, Canada. Offers medical sociology (MA); neo-tropical environment (MA); social statistics (MA); sociology (MA, PhD, Diploma).

McGill University, Faculty of Graduate and Postdoctoral Studies, Faculty of Medicine, Department of Social Studies in Medicine, Montréal, QC H3A 2T5, Canada. Offers medical anthropology (MA, PhD); medical history (MA, PhD); medical sociology (MA, PhD).

McMaster University, School of Graduate Studies, Faculty of Social Sciences, Department of Sociology, Hamilton, ON L8S 4M2, Canada. Offers MA, PhD. Part-time programs available. *Degree requirements:* For master's, thesis; for doctorate, comprehensive exam, thesis/dissertation. *Entrance requirements:* For master's and doctorate, minimum B+ average. Additional exam requirements/recommendations for international students: Required—TOEFL (minimum score 580 paper-based). *Faculty research:* Socialization and conversion, ethnic relations, international migration, racism, social implications of the Internet.

Memorial University of Newfoundland, School of Graduate Studies, Department of Sociology, St. John's, NL A1C 5S7, Canada. Offers gender (PhD); maritime sociology (PhD); sociology (M Phil, MA); work and development (PhD). Part-time programs available. *Degree requirements:* For master's, comprehensive exam, thesis optional, program journal (M Phil); for doctorate, one foreign language, comprehensive exam, thesis/dissertation, oral defense of thesis. *Entrance requirements:* For master's, 2nd class degree from university of recognized standing in area of study; for doctorate, MA, M Phil, or equivalent. Electronic applications accepted. *Faculty research:* Work and development, gender, maritime sociology.

Michigan State University, The Graduate School, College of Social Science, Department of Sociology, East Lansing, MI 48824. Offers MA, PhD. Part-time programs available. *Entrance requirements:* Additional exam requirements/recommendations for international students: Required—TOEFL (minimum score 550 paper-based), Michigan State University ELT (minimum score 85), Michigan English Language Assessment Battery (minimum score 83). Electronic applications accepted.

Middle Tennessee State University, College of Graduate Studies, College of Liberal Arts, Department of Sociology and Anthropology, Murfreesboro, TN 37132. Offers sociology (MA). Part-time and evening/weekend programs available. Postbaccalaureate distance learning degree programs offered. *Faculty:* 16 full-time (7 women). *Students:* 6 full-time (5 women), 8 part-time (5 women); includes 6 minority (1 Black or African American, non-Hispanic/Latino; 1 Asian, non-Hispanic/Latino; 3 Hispanic/Latino; 1 Two or more races, non-Hispanic/Latino). 21 applicants, 52% accepted. In 2014, 7 master's awarded. *Degree requirements:* For master's, comprehensive exam, thesis. *Entrance requirements:* For master's, GRE. Additional exam requirements/recommendations for international students: Required—TOEFL (minimum score 525 paper-based; 71 iBT) or IELTS (minimum score 6). *Application deadline:* For fall admission, 6/1 for domestic and international students. Applications are processed on a rolling basis. Application fee: $30. Electronic applications accepted. *Financial support:* In 2014–15, 9 students received support. Tuition waivers available. Support available to part-time students. Financial award application deadline: 4/1; financial award applicants required to submit FAFSA. *Faculty research:* Women's and gender studies, crime and deviance, aging studies, social organizations. *Unit head:* Dr. Jackie Eller, Chair, 615-898-2508, Fax: 615-898-5427, E-mail: jackie.eller@mtsu.edu. *Application contact:* Dr. Michael D. Allen, Vice Provost for Research/Dean, 615-898-2840, Fax: 615-904-8020, E-mail: michael.allen@mtsu.edu.

Minnesota State University Mankato, College of Graduate Studies, College of Social and Behavioral Sciences, Department of Sociology and Corrections, Mankato, MN 56001. Offers sociology (MA); sociology: college teaching (MA); sociology: corrections (MS); sociology: human services planning and administration (MS). Part-time programs available. *Students:* 12 full-time (7 women), 18 part-time (13 women). *Degree requirements:* For master's, comprehensive exam, thesis or alternative. *Entrance requirements:* For master's, minimum GPA of 3.0 during previous 2 years, 3 letters of reference, resume. Additional exam requirements/recommendations for international students: Required—TOEFL. *Application deadline:* For fall admission, 7/1 priority date for domestic students; for spring admission, 11/1 for domestic students. Applications are processed on a rolling basis. Application fee: $40. Electronic applications accepted. *Financial support:* Research assistantships with full tuition reimbursements, teaching assistantships with full tuition reimbursements, career-related internships or fieldwork, Federal Work-Study, institutionally sponsored loans, and unspecified assistantships available. Support available to part-time students. Financial award application deadline: 3/15; financial award applicants required to submit FAFSA. *Faculty research:* Women's suffrage movements. *Unit head:* Dr. Steve Buechler, Chairperson, 507-389-5613. *Application contact:* 507-389-2321, E-mail: grad@mnsu.edu.
Website: http://sbs.mnsu.edu/soccorr/

Mississippi State University, College of Arts and Sciences, Department of Sociology, Mississippi State, MS 39762. Offers MS, PhD. Part-time programs available. *Faculty:* 12 full-time (9 women). *Students:* 23 full-time (14 women), 13 part-time (10 women); includes 10 minority (6 Black or African American, non-Hispanic/Latino; 1 American Indian or Alaska Native, non-Hispanic/Latino; 1 Asian, non-Hispanic/Latino; 2 Hispanic/Latino), 6 international. Average age 30. 35 applicants, 57% accepted, 9 enrolled. In 2014, 6 master's, 4 doctorates awarded. *Degree requirements:* For master's, thesis optional, comprehensive oral or written exam; for doctorate, thesis/dissertation, comprehensive oral and written exam. *Entrance requirements:* For master's, minimum GPA of 3.0 on last two years of undergraduate courses or GRE; academic writing sample in English (student's choice); for doctorate, GRE, academic writing sample in English (student's choice). Additional exam requirements/recommendations for international students: Required—TOEFL (minimum score 477 paper-based; 53 iBT); Recommended—IELTS (minimum score 4.5). *Application deadline:* For fall admission, 4/15 priority date for domestic students, 5/1 for international students; for spring admission, 10/15 priority date for domestic students, 9/1 for international students. Applications are processed on a rolling basis. Application fee: $60. Electronic applications accepted. *Expenses:* Tuition, state resident: full-time $7140; part-time $783 per credit hour. Tuition, nonresident: full-time $18,478; part-time $2043 per credit hour. *Financial support:* In 2014–15, 2 research assistantships (averaging $12,528 per year), 12 teaching assistantships with tuition reimbursements (averaging $12,313 per year) were awarded; Federal Work-Study, institutionally sponsored loans, scholarships/grants, and unspecified assistantships also available. Financial award application deadline: 3/15; financial award applicants required to submit FAFSA. *Faculty research:* Community and regional development, criminology, natural resource development, family sociology, gender. *Total annual research expenditures:* $1.7 million. *Unit head:* Dr. Rick Travis, Interim Department Head, 662-325-2495, Fax: 662-325-4564, E-mail: sociology@soc.msstate.edu. *Application contact:* Dr. Nicole Rader, Graduate Coordinator, 662-325-2495, Fax: 662-325-4564, E-mail: sociology@soc.msstate.edu.
Website: http://www.sociology.msstate.edu/

Morehead State University, Graduate Programs, Caudill College of Arts, Humanities and Social Sciences, Department of Sociology, Social Work and Criminology, Morehead, KY 40351. Offers criminology (MA); general sociology (MA); gerontology (MA); sociology regional analysis (MA); sociology/chemical dependency (MA). Part-time and evening/weekend programs available. *Degree requirements:* For master's, comprehensive exam, thesis (for some programs). *Entrance requirements:* For master's, GRE General Test, minimum GPA of 3.0 in sociology, 2.75 overall; 18 hours of course work in sociology, writing sample. Additional exam requirements/recommendations for international students: Required—TOEFL (minimum score 500 paper-based). Electronic applications accepted. *Faculty research:* Death and dying; aging, drinking, and drugs; economic development; adult children of alcoholics.

Morgan State University, School of Graduate Studies, College of Liberal Arts, Department of Sociology and Anthropology, Baltimore, MD 21251. Offers sociology (MA, MS). Part-time and evening/weekend programs available. *Degree requirements:* For master's, comprehensive exam. *Entrance requirements:* Additional exam requirements/recommendations for international students: Required—TOEFL (minimum score 550 paper-based). *Faculty research:* Domestic violence, homelessness, social movements, marriage and family.

New Mexico Highlands University, Graduate Studies, College of Arts and Sciences, Department of Social and Behavioral Sciences, Las Vegas, NM 87701. Offers psychology (MS), including clinical psychology/counseling, general psychology; public affairs (MA), including applied sociology; Southwest studies (MA), including anthropology. Part-time programs available. *Faculty:* 11 full-time (5 women), 3 part-time/adjunct (all women). *Students:* 24 full-time (16 women), 19 part-time (14 women); includes 27 minority (3 Black or African American, non-Hispanic/Latino; 1 American Indian or Alaska Native, non-Hispanic/Latino; 23 Hispanic/Latino), 2 international. Average age 33. 45 applicants, 33% accepted, 15 enrolled. In 2014, 7 master's awarded. *Degree requirements:* For master's, comprehensive exam, thesis or alternative. *Entrance requirements:* For master's, minimum undergraduate GPA of 3.0. Additional exam requirements/recommendations for international students: Required—TOEFL (minimum score 540 paper-based). *Application deadline:* For fall admission, 8/1 priority date for domestic students. Applications are processed on a rolling basis. Application fee: $15. *Financial support:* In 2014–15, 34 teaching assistantships were awarded; career-related internships or fieldwork, Federal Work-Study, institutionally sponsored loans, scholarships/grants, tuition waivers (full and partial), and unspecified assistantships also available. Support available to part-time students. Financial award application deadline: 3/1; financial award applicants required to submit FAFSA. *Faculty research:* Southwest Native American resettlement development, community-level interventions, neurochemistry of personality, comparative criminal justice, social theory and activism. *Unit head:* Dr. Tom Ward, Program Coordinator, 505-454-3196, E-mail: tsward@nmhu.edu. *Application contact:* Diane Trujillo, Administrative Assistant for Graduate Studies, 505-454-3266, Fax: 505-426-2117, E-mail: dtrujillo@nmhu.edu.

New Mexico State University, College of Arts and Sciences, Department of Sociology, Las Cruces, NM 88003-8001. Offers MA. Part-time programs available. *Faculty:* 8 full-time (6 women), 1 (woman) part-time/adjunct. *Students:* 18 full-time (13 women), 34 part-time (24 women); includes 16 minority (3 Black or African American, non-Hispanic/Latino; 1 American Indian or Alaska Native, non-Hispanic/Latino; 1 Asian, non-Hispanic/Latino; 10 Hispanic/Latino; 1 Native Hawaiian or other Pacific Islander, non-Hispanic/Latino). Average age 34. 41 applicants, 63% accepted, 20 enrolled. In 2014, 15 master's awarded. *Degree requirements:* For master's, comprehensive exam (for some programs), thesis (for some programs). *Entrance requirements:* Additional exam requirements/recommendations for international students: Required—TOEFL (minimum score 550 paper-based; 79 iBT), IELTS (minimum score 6.5). *Application deadline:* For fall admission, 2/15 for domestic and international students. Application fee: $40 ($50 for international students). Electronic applications accepted. *Expenses:* Tuition, state resident: full-time $3969; part-time $220.50 per credit hour. Tuition, nonresident: full-time $13,838; part-time $768.80 per credit hour. *Required fees:* $853; $47.40 per credit hour. *Financial support:* In 2014–15, 12 students received support, including 2 fellowships (averaging $3,970 per year), 7 teaching assistantships (averaging $8,148 per year); career-related internships or fieldwork, Federal Work-Study, scholarships/grants, traineeships, health care benefits, and unspecified assistantships also available. Support available to part-time students. Financial award application deadline: 3/1. *Faculty research:* Environmental sociology, borderland issues, sexualities, race and ethnicity, inequality. *Total annual research expenditures:* $5,928. *Unit head:* Dr. David G. LoConto, Academic Department Head, 575-646-3448, Fax: 575-646-7601, E-mail: dloconto@nmsu.edu. *Application contact:* Dr. Sandra M. Way, Director of Graduate Studies, 575-646-3448, Fax: 575-646-7601, E-mail: sway@nmsu.edu.
Website: http://sociology.nmsu.edu/

The New School, The New School for Social Research, Department of Sociology, New York, NY 10003. Offers sociology (MA, DS Sc, PhD); sociology and historical studies (MA, PhD). Part-time and evening/weekend programs available. Terminal master's awarded for partial completion of doctoral program. *Degree requirements:* For master's, exam; for doctorate, one foreign language, thesis/dissertation, qualifying exam. *Entrance requirements:* For master's, GRE General Test; for doctorate, GRE General Test, MA. Additional exam requirements/recommendations for international students: Required—TOEFL (minimum score 600 paper-based; 100 iBT). Electronic applications accepted. *Faculty research:* Media, culture, urban sociology, democratic transitions, critical theory.

New York University, Graduate School of Arts and Science, Department of Sociology, New York, NY 10012-1019. Offers French studies and sociology (PhD); sociology (MA, PhD); JD/MA. Part-time programs available. *Faculty:* 27 full-time (9 women), 1 part-time/adjunct (0 women). *Students:* 80 full-time (32 women), 8 part-time (5 women); includes 16 minority (4 Black or African American, non-Hispanic/Latino; 4 Asian, non-Hispanic/Latino; 6 Hispanic/Latino; 2 Two or more races, non-Hispanic/Latino), 29 international. Average age 31. 408 applicants, 15% accepted, 22 enrolled. In 2014, 26 master's, 9 doctorates awarded. Terminal master's awarded for partial completion of doctoral program. *Degree requirements:* For master's, thesis or alternative; for doctorate, comprehensive exam, thesis/dissertation. *Entrance requirements:* For master's and doctorate, GRE General Test. Additional exam requirements/recommendations for international students: Required—TOEFL. *Application deadline:* For fall admission, 1/4 priority date for domestic students, 1/4 for international students. Application fee: $100. *Financial support:* Fellowships with tuition reimbursements, research assistantships with tuition reimbursements, teaching assistantships with tuition reimbursements, Federal Work-Study, institutionally sponsored loans, scholarships/grants, health care benefits, and unspecified assistantships available. Financial award application deadline: 1/4; financial award applicants required to submit FAFSA. *Faculty research:* Political sociology and social movements; gender and inequality; deviance, law, and crime; education; stratification and theory. *Unit head:* Guillermina Jasso, Chair, 212-998-8340, Fax: 212-995-4140, E-mail: gsas.sociology.info@nyu.edu. *Application contact:* Paula

England, Director of Graduate Studies, 212-998-8340, Fax: 212-995-4140, E-mail: gsas.sociology.info@nyu.edu. Website: http://www.nyu.edu/gsas/dept/socio/

New York University, Steinhardt School of Culture, Education, and Human Development, Department of Humanities and Social Sciences in the Professions, Program in Sociology of Education, New York, NY 10003. Offers education policy (MA); social and cultural studies of education (MA); sociology of education (PhD). Part-time programs available. *Faculty:* 13 full-time (7 women). *Students:* 32 full-time (26 women), 19 part-time (16 women); includes 12 minority (3 Black or African American, non-Hispanic/Latino; 4 Asian, non-Hispanic/Latino; 5 Hispanic/Latino), 17 international. Average age 26. 96 applicants, 45% accepted, 8 enrolled. In 2014, 24 master's, 2 doctorates awarded. *Degree requirements:* For master's, thesis (for some programs); for doctorate, thesis/dissertation. *Entrance requirements:* For master's, letters of recommendation; for doctorate, GRE General Test, interview. Additional exam requirements/recommendations for international students: Required—TOEFL (minimum score 100 iBT). *Application deadline:* For fall admission, 12/1 priority date for domestic and international students; for spring admission, 10/1 for domestic and international students. Applications are processed on a rolling basis. Application fee: $75. Electronic applications accepted. *Financial support:* Fellowships with full and partial tuition reimbursements, Federal Work-Study, institutionally sponsored loans, scholarships/grants, and tuition waivers (partial) available. Support available to part-time students. Financial award application deadline: 2/1; financial award applicants required to submit FAFSA. *Faculty research:* Legal and institutional environments of schools; social inequality; high school reform and achievement; urban schooling, economics and education, educational policy. *Unit head:* Prof. Lisa Stulberg, Program Director, 212-992-9373, Fax: 212-995-4832, E-mail: lisa.stulberg@nyu.edu. *Application contact:* 212-998-5030, Fax: 212-995-4328, E-mail: steinhardt.gradadmissions@nyu.edu. Website: http://steinhardt.nyu.edu/humsocsci/sociology

North Carolina Central University, College of Behavioral and Social Sciences, Department of Sociology, Durham, NC 27707-3129. Offers MA. Part-time and evening/weekend programs available. *Degree requirements:* For master's, one foreign language, comprehensive exam, thesis. *Entrance requirements:* For master's, GRE, minimum GPA of 3.0 in major, 2.5 overall. Additional exam requirements/recommendations for international students: Required—TOEFL. *Faculty research:* Urban demography, family, statistical methods.

North Carolina State University, Graduate School, College of Humanities and Social Sciences, Department of Sociology and Anthropology, Program in Sociology, Raleigh, NC 27695. Offers M Soc, MS, PhD. Part-time programs available. *Degree requirements:* For master's, practicum (M Soc), thesis (MS); for doctorate, comprehensive exam, thesis/dissertation. *Entrance requirements:* For master's and doctorate, GRE General Test, sample of written work. Electronic applications accepted. *Faculty research:* Inequity: gender, race and class; crime and social control; work and organizations; rural sociology; family and intimate relations.

North Dakota State University, College of Graduate and Interdisciplinary Studies, College of Arts, Humanities and Social Sciences, Department of Sociology, Anthropology, and Emergency Management, Fargo, ND 58108. Offers community development (MA, MS); emergency management (MS, PhD); social science (MA, MS); sociology (MS). Part-time programs available. *Degree requirements:* For master's, thesis; for doctorate, comprehensive exam, thesis/dissertation. *Entrance requirements:* For master's, GRE (for emergency management), course work in sociology, minimum GPA of 3.2; for doctorate, GRE, minimum GPA of 3.2. Additional exam requirements/recommendations for international students: Required—TOEFL. Electronic applications accepted. *Faculty research:* Medical sociology, demography, ethnology, archaeology.

Northeastern University, College of Social Sciences and Humanities, Boston, MA 02115. Offers criminology and criminal justice (MSCJ); criminology and justice policy (PhD); economics (MA, PhD); English (MA, PhD); law and public policy (MS, PhD); political science (MA, PhD); public administration (MPA); public history (MA); security and resilience studies (MS); sociology (MA, PhD); urban and regional policy (MS); world history (MA, PhD). *Degree requirements:* For doctorate, variable foreign language requirement, comprehensive exam, thesis/dissertation. *Entrance requirements:* For master's and doctorate, GRE. Additional exam requirements/recommendations for international students: Required—TOEFL, IELTS. Electronic applications accepted.

Northern Arizona University, Graduate College, College of Social and Behavioral Sciences, Department of Sociology and Social Work, Flagstaff, AZ 86011. Offers applied sociology (MA). Part-time programs available. *Degree requirements:* For master's, thesis or internship. *Entrance requirements:* For master's, minimum GPA of 3.0. Additional exam requirements/recommendations for international students: Required—TOEFL (minimum score 550 paper-based; 80 iBT), IELTS (minimum score 7). Electronic applications accepted. *Faculty research:* Demography, death and dying, criminology, social policy, divorce.

Northern Illinois University, Graduate School, College of Liberal Arts and Sciences, Department of Sociology, De Kalb, IL 60115-2854. Offers MA. Part-time programs available. *Faculty:* 14 full-time (3 women). *Students:* 15 full-time (8 women), 9 part-time (8 women); includes 6 minority (3 Black or African American, non-Hispanic/Latino; 1 Hispanic/Latino; 2 Two or more races, non-Hispanic/Latino), 1 international. Average age 30. 18 applicants, 50% accepted, 8 enrolled. In 2014, 6 master's awarded. *Degree requirements:* For master's, comprehensive exam, thesis optional. *Entrance requirements:* For master's, GRE General Test, minimum GPA of 2.75; course work in social theory, social methods, and statistics. Additional exam requirements/recommendations for international students: Required—TOEFL (minimum score 550 paper-based). *Application deadline:* For fall admission, 6/1 for domestic students, 5/1 for international students; for spring admission, 11/1 for domestic students, 10/1 for international students. Applications are processed on a rolling basis. Application fee: $40. Electronic applications accepted. *Financial support:* In 2014–15, 2 research assistantships with full tuition reimbursements, 18 teaching assistantships with full tuition reimbursements were awarded; fellowships with full tuition reimbursements, career-related internships or fieldwork, Federal Work-Study, scholarships/grants, tuition waivers (full), and unspecified assistantships also available. Support available to part-time students. Financial award applicants required to submit FAFSA. *Faculty research:* Welfare reform, interpersonal disputes, multicultural education, race and ethnicism, social control. *Unit head:* Dr. Kirk Miller, Chair, 815-753-1194, Fax: 815-753-6302, E-mail: kmiller7@niu.edu. *Application contact:* Dr. Keri B. Burchfield, Director, Graduate Studies, 815-753-0302, E-mail: kburchfield@niu.edu. Website: http://www.sociology.niu.edu/

Northwestern University, The Graduate School, Judd A. and Marjorie Weinberg College of Arts and Sciences, Department of Sociology, Evanston, IL 60208. Offers PhD, JD/PhD. Admissions and degrees offered through The Graduate School. *Degree requirements:* For doctorate, thesis/dissertation. *Entrance requirements:* For doctorate, GRE General Test. Additional exam requirements/recommendations for international students: Required—TOEFL. Electronic applications accepted. *Faculty research:* Sociology of culture, social organizations, social inequality, comparative/historical sociology, economic sociology.

Northwestern University, The Graduate School, Kellogg School of Management, Management Programs, Evanston, IL 60208. Offers accounting information and management (MBA, PhD); analytical finance (MBA); business administration (MBA); decision sciences (MBA); entrepreneurship and innovation (MBA); finance (MBA, PhD); health enterprise management (MBA); human resources management (MBA); international business (MBA); management and organizations (MBA, PhD); management and organizations and sociology (PhD); management and strategy (MBA); management studies (MS); managerial analytics (MBA); managerial economics (MBA); managerial economics and strategy (PhD); marketing (MBA, PhD); marketing management (MBA); media management (MBA); operations management (MBA, PhD); real estate (MBA); social enterprise at Kellogg (MBA); JD/MBA. Part-time and evening/weekend programs available. Terminal master's awarded for partial completion of doctoral program. *Degree requirements:* For doctorate, thesis/dissertation, 2 years of coursework, qualifying (field) exam and candidacy, summer research papers and presentations to faculty, proposal defense, final exam/defense. *Entrance requirements:* For master's, GMAT, GRE, interview, 2 letters of recommendation, college transcripts, resume, essays, Kellogg honor code; for doctorate, GMAT, GRE, statement of purpose, transcripts, 2 letters of recommendation, resume, interview. Additional exam requirements/recommendations for international students: Required—TOEFL, IELTS. Electronic applications accepted. *Expenses:* Contact institution. *Faculty research:* Business cycles and international finance, health policy, networks, non-market strategy, consumer psychology.

The Ohio State University, Graduate School, College of Arts and Sciences, Division of Social and Behavioral Sciences, Department of Sociology, Columbus, OH 43210. Offers PhD. *Faculty:* 30. *Students:* 56 full-time (29 women); includes 10 minority (1 Black or African American, non-Hispanic/Latino; 1 American Indian or Alaska Native, non-Hispanic/Latino; 3 Asian, non-Hispanic/Latino; 4 Hispanic/Latino; 1 Two or more races, non-Hispanic/Latino), 6 international. Average age 28. In 2014, 6 doctorates awarded. *Degree requirements:* For doctorate, thesis/dissertation. *Entrance requirements:* For doctorate, GRE General Test. Additional exam requirements/recommendations for international students: Required—TOEFL (minimum score 600 paper-based; 100 iBT); Recommended—IELTS (minimum score 7). *Application deadline:* For fall admission, 12/1 priority date for domestic students, 11/30 priority date for international students; for winter admission, 12/1 for domestic students, 11/1 for international students; for spring admission, 3/1 for domestic students, 2/1 for international students. Applications are processed on a rolling basis. Application fee: $60 ($70 for international students). Electronic applications accepted. *Financial support:* Fellowships with tuition reimbursements, research assistantships with tuition reimbursements, teaching assistantships with tuition reimbursements, Federal Work-Study, and institutionally sponsored loans available. Support available to part-time students. *Unit head:* Dr. Zhenchao Qian, Chair, 614-688-8612, Fax: 614-292-6687, E-mail: qian.26@osu.edu. *Application contact:* Graduate and Professional Admissions, 614-292-9444, Fax: 614-292-3895, E-mail: gpadmissions@osu.edu. Website: http://sociology.osu.edu/

Ohio University, Graduate College, College of Arts and Sciences, Department of Sociology and Anthropology, Athens, OH 45701-2979. Offers sociology (MA). Part-time programs available. *Degree requirements:* For master's, thesis or alternative. *Entrance requirements:* For master's, minimum GPA of 3.0; minimum of 20 hours in sociology including statistics, theory, and research methods. Additional exam requirements/recommendations for international students: Required—TOEFL (minimum score 550 paper-based; 80 iBT) or IELTS (minimum score 6.5). Electronic applications accepted. *Faculty research:* Criminology/deviance, gender studies, inequality, social psychology and rural poverty.

Oklahoma City University, Petree College of Arts and Sciences, Division of Sociology and Justice Studies, Oklahoma City, OK 73106-1402. Offers MA, MS. Part-time and evening/weekend programs available. *Faculty:* 1 full-time (0 women). *Students:* 7 full-time (all women), 13 part-time (11 women); includes 5 minority (2 Black or African American, non-Hispanic/Latino; 1 American Indian or Alaska Native, non-Hispanic/Latino; 2 Hispanic/Latino), 1 international. Average age 32. 16 applicants, 88% accepted, 10 enrolled. In 2014, 9 master's awarded. *Degree requirements:* For master's, thesis or alternative. *Entrance requirements:* For master's, minimum GPA of 3.0, two letters of recommendation. Additional exam requirements/recommendations for international students: Required—TOEFL (minimum score 550 paper-based; 80 iBT). *Application deadline:* Applications are processed on a rolling basis. Application fee: $50. Electronic applications accepted. *Expenses: Tuition:* Part-time $936 per credit hour. *Required fees:* $115 per credit hour. One-time fee: $250. Tuition and fees vary according to course load, degree level, program and student's religious affiliation. *Financial support:* In 2014–15, 4 students received support. Career-related internships or fieldwork, Federal Work-Study, institutionally sponsored loans, scholarships/grants, and tuition waivers available. Support available to part-time students. Financial award application deadline: 6/1; financial award applicants required to submit FAFSA. *Faculty research:* Victims, police, corrections, security, women and crime. *Unit head:* Robert Spinks, Director, 405-208-5368, Fax: 405-208-5447, E-mail: bspinks@okcu.edu. *Application contact:* Matthew Harrington, Director, Graduate Admissions, 800-633-7242, Fax: 405-208-5916, E-mail: gadmissions@okcu.edu. Website: http://www.okcu.edu/petree/soc/

Oklahoma State University, College of Arts and Sciences, Department of Sociology, Stillwater, OK 74078. Offers sociology (MS, PhD). *Faculty:* 16 full-time (8 women), 4 part-time/adjunct (2 women). *Students:* 12 full-time (7 women), 11 part-time (5 women); includes 4 minority (2 Black or African American, non-Hispanic/Latino; 2 Hispanic/Latino), 2 international. Average age 28. 49 applicants, 24% accepted, 9 enrolled. In 2014, 4 master's, 2 doctorates awarded. *Degree requirements:* For master's, thesis; for doctorate, comprehensive exam, thesis/dissertation. *Entrance requirements:* For master's and doctorate, GRE General Test. Additional exam requirements/recommendations for international students: Required—TOEFL (minimum score 550 paper-based; 79 iBT). *Application deadline:* For fall admission, 3/1 priority date for international students; for spring admission, 8/1 priority date for international students. Applications are processed on a rolling basis. Application fee: $40 ($75 for international students). Electronic applications accepted. *Expenses:* Tuition, state resident: full-time $4488; part-time $187 per credit hour. Tuition, nonresident: full-time $18,360; part-time $765 per credit hour. *Required fees:* $2413; $100.55 per credit hour. Tuition and fees vary according to campus/location. *Financial support:* In 2014–15, 4 research assistantships (averaging $21,918 per year), 21 teaching assistantships (averaging $17,850 per year) were awarded; career-related internships or fieldwork, Federal Work-Study, scholarships/grants, health care benefits, tuition waivers (partial), and unspecified assistantships also available. Support available to part-time students. Financial award application deadline: 3/1; financial award applicants required to submit FAFSA. *Faculty research:* Criminology/correction/legal issues; race, ethnicity, and gender in American society; environmental conflict and population problems; international comparative research; social change and social movement in American culture. *Unit head:* Dr. Duane Gill, Department Head, 405-744-6104, Fax: 405-744-5780, E-mail: duane.gill@okstate.edu. *Application contact:* Dr. Andrew Fullerton, Director, Graduate Program, 405-744-8752, Fax: 405-744-5780, E-mail: andrew.fullerton@okstate.edu. Website: http://sociology.okstate.edu

Sociology

Old Dominion University, College of Arts and Letters, Program in Applied Sociology, Norfolk, VA 23529. Offers MA. Part-time and evening/weekend programs available. *Faculty:* 19 full-time (11 women). *Students:* 12 full-time (7 women), 5 part-time (4 women); includes 8 minority (4 Black or African American, non-Hispanic/Latino; 2 Hispanic/Latino; 2 Two or more races, non-Hispanic/Latino). Average age 28. 26 applicants, 65% accepted, 12 enrolled. In 2014, 4 master's awarded. *Degree requirements:* For master's, thesis. *Entrance requirements:* For master's, GRE General Test, minimum GPA of 3.0; 12 credits in criminal justice, sociology, or women's studies. Additional exam requirements/recommendations for international students: Required—TOEFL. *Application deadline:* For fall admission, 3/1 for domestic and international students. Application fee: $50. Electronic applications accepted. *Expenses:* Tuition, state resident: full-time $10,488; part-time $437 per credit. Tuition, nonresident: full-time $26,136; part-time $1089 per credit. *Required fees:* $64 per semester. One-time fee: $50. *Financial support:* In 2014–15, 2 research assistantships (averaging $10,000 per year), 6 teaching assistantships (averaging $10,000 per year) were awarded; career-related internships or fieldwork, scholarships/grants, and unspecified assistantships also available. Financial award application deadline: 2/15; financial award applicants required to submit CSS PROFILE or FAFSA. *Faculty research:* Quantitative methodology, theory, family, gender/class/race, crime. *Total annual research expenditures:* $350,000. *Unit head:* Dr. Ingrid Whitaker, Graduate Program Director, 757-683-3811, Fax: 757-683-5634, E-mail: iwhitake@odu.edu. *Application contact:* Dr. David C. Earnest, Associate Dean, 757-683-6077, Fax: 757-683-5746, E-mail: dearnest@odu.edu.
Website: http://al.odu.edu/sociology/gradprogram/graduatehome.shtml

Oxford Graduate School, Graduate Programs, Dayton, TN 37321-6736. Offers family life education (M Litt); organizational leadership (M Litt); sociological integration of religion and society (D Phil).

Penn State University Park, Graduate School, College of the Liberal Arts, Department of Sociology and Criminology, University Park, PA 16802. Offers criminology (MA, PhD); sociology (MA, PhD). *Unit head:* Dr. Susan Welch, Dean, 814-865-7691, Fax: 814-863-2085, E-mail: swelch@psu.edu. *Application contact:* Lori A. Stania, Director, Graduate Student Services, 814-867-5278, Fax: 814-863-4627, E-mail: gswww@psu.edu.
Website: http://sociology.la.psu.edu/

Portland State University, Graduate Studies, College of Liberal Arts and Sciences, Department of Sociology, Portland, OR 97207-0751. Offers MA, MS, PhD. Part-time programs available. *Faculty:* 14 full-time (7 women), 7 part-time/adjunct (3 women). *Students:* 25 full-time (17 women), 12 part-time (8 women); includes 8 minority (3 Black or African American, non-Hispanic/Latino; 4 Hispanic/Latino; 1 Two or more races, non-Hispanic/Latino), 2 international. Average age 33. 85 applicants, 32% accepted, 19 enrolled. In 2014, 12 master's awarded. *Degree requirements:* For master's, variable foreign language requirement, thesis, written exam; for doctorate, thesis/dissertation. *Entrance requirements:* For master's, GRE General Test, GRE Subject Test, minimum GPA of 3.0 in upper-division course work or 2.75 overall, 3 letters of recommendation. Additional exam requirements/recommendations for international students: Required—TOEFL (minimum score 550 paper-based; 80 iBT), IELTS (minimum score 6.5). *Application deadline:* For fall admission, 1/15 for domestic and international students. Applications are processed on a rolling basis. Application fee: $50. *Expenses:* Tuition, state resident: part-time $222 per credit. Tuition, nonresident: part-time $527 per credit. *Required fees:* $22 per contact hour. $100 per quarter. Tuition and fees vary according to program. *Financial support:* In 2014–15, 18 teaching assistantships with full and partial tuition reimbursements (averaging $6,849 per year) were awarded; fellowships with full tuition reimbursements, research assistantships with full tuition reimbursements, career-related internships or fieldwork, Federal Work-Study, and unspecified assistantships also available. Support available to part-time students. Financial award application deadline: 3/1; financial award applicants required to submit FAFSA. *Faculty research:* Urban sociology, gender and class, development, social change, race/ethnic/minority relations. *Total annual research expenditures:* $513,920. *Unit head:* Matthew Carlson, Chair, 503-725-9554, Fax: 503-725-3957, E-mail: carlsonm@pdx.edu. *Application contact:* Prof. Melissa Thompson, Graduate Comm. Chair, 503-725-3614, E-mail: mthomp@pdx.edu.
Website: http://www.clas.pdx.edu/sociology/

Portland State University, Graduate Studies, College of Liberal Arts and Sciences, Systems Science Program, Portland, OR 97207-0751. Offers computational intelligence (Certificate); computer modeling and simulation (Certificate); systems science (MS); systems science/anthropology (PhD); systems science/business administration (PhD); systems science/civil engineering (PhD); systems science/economics (PhD); systems science/engineering management (PhD); systems science/general (PhD); systems science/mathematical sciences (PhD); systems science/mechanical engineering (PhD); systems science/psychology (PhD); systems science/sociology (PhD). *Faculty:* 2 full-time (0 women), 1 part-time/adjunct (0 women). *Students:* 6 full-time (2 women), 29 part-time (8 women); includes 6 minority (1 Black or African American, non-Hispanic/Latino; 1 American Indian or Alaska Native, non-Hispanic/Latino; 1 Asian, non-Hispanic/Latino; 3 Hispanic/Latino). Average age 41. 32 applicants, 19% accepted, 6 enrolled. In 2014, 10 master's, 3 doctorates awarded. *Degree requirements:* For master's, comprehensive exam (for some programs), thesis optional; for doctorate, variable foreign language requirement, comprehensive exam (for some programs), thesis/dissertation. *Entrance requirements:* For master's, GRE/GMAT (recommended), minimum GPA of 3.0 undergraduate or graduate work, 2 letters of recommendation, statement of interest; for doctorate, GMAT, GRE General Test, minimum GPA of 3.0 undergraduate, 3.25 graduate; 2 letters of recommendation; statement of interest. Additional exam requirements/recommendations for international students: Required—TOEFL (minimum score 550 paper-based; 80 iBT). *Application deadline:* For fall admission, 1/15 for domestic and international students; for spring admission, 11/1 for domestic students. Application fee: $50. Electronic applications accepted. *Expenses:* Tuition, state resident: part-time $222 per credit. Tuition, nonresident: part-time $527 per credit. *Required fees:* $22 per contact hour. $100 per quarter. Tuition and fees vary according to program. *Financial support:* In 2014–15, 1 research assistantship with full and partial tuition reimbursement (averaging $2,358 per year) was awarded; teaching assistantships with full and partial tuition reimbursements, career-related internships or fieldwork, Federal Work-Study, scholarships/grants, and unspecified assistantships also available. Support available to part-time students. Financial award application deadline: 3/1; financial award applicants required to submit FAFSA. *Faculty research:* Systems theory and methodology, artificial intelligence neural networks, information theory, nonlinear dynamics/chaos, modeling and simulation. *Total annual research expenditures:* $137,833. *Unit head:* Prof. Wayne Wakeland, PhD, Chair, 503-725-4975, E-mail: wakeland@pdx.edu.
Website: http://www.pdx.edu/sysc/

Prairie View A&M University, College of Arts and Sciences, Division of Social Work, Behavioral and Political Science, Prairie View, TX 77446-0519. Offers sociology (MA). Part-time and evening/weekend programs available. *Faculty:* 2 full-time (0 women). *Students:* 9 full-time (6 women), 5 part-time (all women); includes 13 minority (11 Black or African American, non-Hispanic/Latino; 1 American Indian or Alaska Native, non-Hispanic/Latino; 1 Hispanic/Latino). Average age 33. 3 applicants, 67% accepted, 2 enrolled. In 2014, 2 master's awarded. *Degree requirements:* For master's, comprehensive exam, thesis optional. *Entrance requirements:* For master's, GRE General Test. Additional exam requirements/recommendations for international students: Required—TOEFL (minimum score 550 paper-based; 79 iBT). *Application deadline:* For fall admission, 7/1 priority date for domestic students, 6/1 priority date for international students; for spring admission, 11/1 priority date for domestic students, 10/1 priority date for international students; for summer admission, 3/1 priority date for domestic students, 2/1 priority date for international students. Applications are processed on a rolling basis. Application fee: $50. *Expenses:* Expenses: $6,686 tuition and fees. *Financial support:* Federal Work-Study and institutionally sponsored loans available. Financial award application deadline: 4/1; financial award applicants required to submit FAFSA. *Faculty research:* Criminology, political sociology, sociology of education, gender, race, African-American mental health, global development-social movements, African-American status attainment. *Unit head:* Dr. Walle Engedayehu, Division Head, 936-261-3200, Fax: 936-261-3229, E-mail: waengedayehu@pvamu.edu. *Application contact:* Pauline Walker, Administrative Assistant II, Research and Graduate Studies, 936-261-3521, Fax: 936-261-3529, E-mail: pmwalker@pvamu.edu.
Website: http://www.pvamu.edu/swbps/

Princeton University, Graduate School, Department of Sociology, Princeton, NJ 08544-1019. Offers sociology (PhD); sociology and demography (PhD). *Degree requirements:* For doctorate, variable foreign language requirement, thesis/dissertation. *Entrance requirements:* For doctorate, GRE General Test, GRE Subject Test (recommended), sample of written work. Additional exam requirements/recommendations for international students: Required—TOEFL (minimum score 600 paper-based). Electronic applications accepted.

Princeton University, Graduate School, Program in Population Studies, Princeton, NJ 08544-1019. Offers demography (PhD, Certificate); economics and demography (PhD); public affairs and demography (PhD); sociology and demography (PhD). *Degree requirements:* For doctorate, thesis/dissertation. *Entrance requirements:* For doctorate, GRE General Test. Additional exam requirements/recommendations for international students: Required—TOEFL (minimum score 600 paper-based). Electronic applications accepted. *Faculty research:* Models, fertility, infant and child mortality, migration.

Purdue University, Graduate School, College of Liberal Arts, Department of Sociology, West Lafayette, IN 47907. Offers MS, PhD. *Degree requirements:* For master's, thesis; for doctorate, comprehensive exam, thesis/dissertation. *Entrance requirements:* For master's, GRE General Test, minimum undergraduate GPA of 3.0 or equivalent; for doctorate, GRE General Test, minimum undergraduate GPA of 3.0 or equivalent; master's degree in sociology with minimum GPA of 3.25 or equivalent. Additional exam requirements/recommendations for international students: Required—TOEFL (minimum score 78 iBT).

Queens College of the City University of New York, Division of Graduate Studies, Social Science Division, Department of Sociology, Flushing, NY 11367-1597. Offers MA. Part-time and evening/weekend programs available. *Degree requirements:* For master's, thesis optional. *Entrance requirements:* For master's, minimum GPA of 3.0. Additional exam requirements/recommendations for international students: Required—TOEFL.

Queen's University at Kingston, School of Graduate Studies, Faculty of Arts and Sciences, Department of Sociology, Kingston, ON K7L 3N6, Canada. Offers communication and Information technology (MA, PhD); feminist sociology (MA, PhD); socio-legal studies (MA, PhD); sociological theory (MA, PhD). Part-time programs available. *Degree requirements:* For master's, thesis; for doctorate, comprehensive exam, thesis/dissertation. *Entrance requirements:* For master's, honors bachelors degree in sociology; for doctorate, honors bachelors degree, masters degree in sociology. Additional exam requirements/recommendations for international students: Required—TOEFL. *Faculty research:* Social change and modernization, social control, deviance and criminology, surveillance.

Rice University, Graduate Programs, School of Social Sciences, Department of Sociology, Houston, TX 77251-1892. Offers PhD.

Roosevelt University, Graduate Division, College of Arts and Sciences, Department of Sociology and Anthropology, Chicago, IL 60605. Offers anthropology (MA); sociology (MA). Part-time and evening/weekend programs available. *Degree requirements:* For master's, comprehensive exam, thesis. *Faculty research:* Social theory, urban sociology, gerontology, social organizations.

Rutgers, The State University of New Jersey, New Brunswick, Graduate School-New Brunswick, Program in Sociology, Piscataway, NJ 08854-8097. Offers MA, PhD. Terminal master's awarded for partial completion of doctoral program. *Degree requirements:* For master's, qualifying paper; for doctorate, thesis/dissertation, qualifying exam, qualifying papers. *Entrance requirements:* For master's, GRE General Test; for doctorate, GRE General Test, sample of written work. Additional exam requirements/recommendations for international students: Required—TOEFL. Electronic applications accepted. *Faculty research:* Comparative-historical, sex and gender, organizations and work, culture and cognition, economics, occupations/professions, religion.

St. John's University, St. John's College of Liberal Arts and Sciences, Department of Sociology and Anthropology, Queens, NY 11439. Offers criminology and justice (MA); sociology (MA). Part-time and evening/weekend programs available. *Students:* 37 full-time (27 women), 14 part-time (10 women); includes 28 minority (12 Black or African American, non-Hispanic/Latino; 4 Asian, non-Hispanic/Latino; 12 Hispanic/Latino), 8 international. Average age 27. 62 applicants, 74% accepted, 18 enrolled. In 2014, 34 master's awarded. *Degree requirements:* For master's, comprehensive exam, thesis optional. *Entrance requirements:* For master's, 18 undergraduate credits in social sciences, minimum GPA of 3.0, bachelor's degree. Additional exam requirements/recommendations for international students: Required—TOEFL (minimum score 600 paper-based; 100 iBT), IELTS (minimum score 7). *Application deadline:* For fall admission, 5/1 priority date for domestic and international students; for spring admission, 11/1 priority date for domestic and international students. Applications are processed on a rolling basis. Application fee: $70. Electronic applications accepted. *Expenses: Tuition:* Full-time $20,610; part-time $1145 per credit. *Required fees:* $170 per semester. *Financial support:* Research assistantships, career-related internships or fieldwork, and scholarships/grants available. Support available to part-time students. Financial award application deadline: 3/1; financial award applicants required to submit FAFSA. *Faculty research:* Community studies and gentrification, global financial crisis, insurance fraud, globalization, immigration and human rights. *Unit head:* Dr. Roberta Villalon, Chair, 718-990-5663, E-mail: villalonr@stjohns.edu. *Application contact:* Robert Medrano, Director of Graduate Admission, 718-990-1601, Fax: 718-990-5686, E-mail: gradhelp@stjohns.edu.

Sam Houston State University, College of Humanities and Social Sciences, Department of Sociology, Huntsville, TX 77341. Offers MA. Part-time and evening/weekend programs available. Postbaccalaureate distance learning degree programs offered (no on-campus study). *Faculty:* 12 full-time (6 women). *Students:* 3 full-time (2 women), 26 part-time (16 women); includes 10 minority (4 Black or African American, non-Hispanic/Latino; 1 American Indian or Alaska Native, non-Hispanic/Latino; 1 Asian, non-Hispanic/Latino; 3 Hispanic/Latino; 1 Two or more races, non-Hispanic/Latino).

Average age 37. 32 applicants, 88% accepted, 20 enrolled. In 2014, 18 master's awarded. *Degree requirements:* For master's, comprehensive exam, thesis optional, professional paper. *Entrance requirements:* For master's, GRE General Test, minimum GPA of 3.0, letter of intent, letters of recommendation. Additional exam requirements/recommendations for international students: Required—TOEFL (minimum score 550 paper-based; 79 iBT), IELTS (minimum score 6.5). *Application deadline:* For fall admission, 8/1 for domestic students, 6/25 for international students; for spring admission, 12/1 for domestic students, 11/12 for international students. Applications are processed on a rolling basis. Application fee: $45 ($75 for international students). Electronic applications accepted. *Expenses:* Tuition, state resident: full-time $2286; part-time $254 per credit hour. Tuition, nonresident: full-time $5544; part-time $616 per credit hour. *Required fees:* $440 per semester. Tuition and fees vary according to course load and campus/location. *Financial support:* In 2014–15, 3 research assistantships (averaging $5,835 per year) were awarded; career-related internships or fieldwork, Federal Work-Study, scholarships/grants, tuition waivers (partial), and unspecified assistantships also available. Support available to part-time students. Financial award application deadline: 3/15; financial award applicants required to submit FAFSA. *Unit head:* Dr. Furjen Deng, Interim Chair, 936-294-1515, Fax: 963-294-3573, E-mail: soc_fjd@shsu.edu. *Application contact:* Dr. Douglas Constance, Interim Director of Graduate Studies, 936-294-1514, Fax: 936-294-3573, E-mail: soc_dhc@shsu.edu. Website: http://www.shsu.edu/academics/sociology/

San Diego State University, Graduate and Research Affairs, College of Arts and Letters, Department of Sociology, San Diego, CA 92182. Offers MA. *Degree requirements:* For master's, thesis. *Entrance requirements:* For master's, GRE General Test, 3 letters of recommendation, writing sample. Additional exam requirements/recommendations for international students: Required—TOEFL. Electronic applications accepted. *Faculty research:* The homeless and mentally ill, medical data relating to the homeless.

San Jose State University, Graduate Studies and Research, College of Social Sciences, Department of Sociology, San Jose, CA 95192-0001. Offers MA. Part-time and evening/weekend programs available. *Degree requirements:* For master's, comprehensive exams or thesis. *Entrance requirements:* For master's, GRE Subject Test, minimum GPA of 3.0. Electronic applications accepted. *Faculty research:* Theory construction, sexuality, sociology of the media, social causes of stress, social change.

Shippensburg University of Pennsylvania, School of Graduate Studies, College of Arts and Sciences, Department of Sociology and Anthropology, Shippensburg, PA 17257-2299. Offers organizational development and leadership (MS), including business, communications, environmental management, higher education structure and policy, historical administration, individual and organizational development, management information systems, public organizations, social structures and organizations. Part-time and evening/weekend programs available. *Faculty:* 4 full-time (all women). *Students:* 11 full-time (4 women), 42 part-time (26 women); includes 11 minority (7 Black or African American, non-Hispanic/Latino; 1 Asian, non-Hispanic/Latino; 2 Hispanic/Latino; 1 Two or more races, non-Hispanic/Latino), 2 international. Average age 30. 53 applicants, 60% accepted, 17 enrolled. In 2014, 21 master's awarded. *Degree requirements:* For master's, capstone experience including internship. *Entrance requirements:* For master's, interview (if GPA less than 2.75), resume, personal goals statement. Additional exam requirements/recommendations for international students: Required—TOEFL (minimum score 580 paper-based); Recommended—IELTS (minimum score 6). *Application deadline:* For fall admission, 4/30 for international students; for spring admission, 9/30 for international students. Applications are processed on a rolling basis. Application fee: $45. Electronic applications accepted. *Expenses: Tuition, area resident:* Part-time $454 per credit. Tuition, state resident: part-time $454 per credit. Tuition, nonresident: part-time $681 per credit. *Required fees:* $133 per credit. *Financial support:* In 2014–15, 15 research assistantships with full tuition reimbursements (averaging $5,000 per year) were awarded; career-related internships or fieldwork, scholarships/grants, unspecified assistantships, and resident hall director and student payroll positions also available. Support available to part-time students. Financial award applicants required to submit FAFSA. *Unit head:* Dr. Barbara Denison, Program Coordinator, 717-477-1735, Fax: 717-477-4011, E-mail: bjdeni@ship.edu. *Application contact:* Jeremy R. Goshorn, Assistant Dean of Graduate Admissions, 717-477-1231, Fax: 717-477-4016, E-mail: jrgoshorn@ship.edu.
Website: http://www.ship.edu/odl/

Simon Fraser University, Office of Graduate Studies, Faculty of Arts and Social Sciences, Department of Sociology and Anthropology, Burnaby, BC V5A 1S6, Canada. Offers anthropology (MA, PhD); sociology (MA, PhD). *Degree requirements:* For master's, thesis; for doctorate, comprehensive exam, thesis/dissertation, cooperative education. *Entrance requirements:* For master's, minimum GPA of 3.0 (on scale of 4.33), or 3.33 based on last 60 credits of undergraduate courses; for doctorate, minimum GPA of 3.5 (on scale of 4.33). Additional exam requirements/recommendations for international students: Recommended—TOEFL (minimum score 580 paper-based; 93 iBT), IELTS (minimum score 7), TWE (minimum score 5). Electronic applications accepted. *Faculty research:* Globalization and development, health, environment and science, knowledge, culture and power, social justice, policy, law and society, women, gender and sexuality.

South Dakota State University, Graduate School, College of Agriculture and Biological Sciences, Department of Sociology and Rural Studies, Brookings, SD 57007. Offers sociology (MS, PhD). Part-time programs available. Postbaccalaureate distance learning degree programs offered. *Degree requirements:* For master's, comprehensive exam (for some programs), thesis, oral and written exams; for doctorate, comprehensive exam, thesis/dissertation, preliminary oral and written exams. *Entrance requirements:* Additional exam requirements/recommendations for international students: Required—TOEFL (minimum score 550 paper-based; 79 iBT). *Faculty research:* Demography, rural families, rural development, Native Americans, rural poverty, sociology of agriculture.

Southeastern Louisiana University, College of Arts, Humanities and Social Sciences, Department of Sociology and Criminal Justice, Hammond, LA 70402. Offers MS. Part-time and evening/weekend programs available. *Faculty:* 11 full-time (3 women). *Students:* 18 full-time (10 women), 12 part-time (7 women); includes 10 minority (6 Black or African American, non-Hispanic/Latino; 1 Asian, non-Hispanic/Latino; 2 Hispanic/Latino; 1 Two or more races, non-Hispanic/Latino). Average age 28. In 2014, 4 master's awarded. *Degree requirements:* For master's, comprehensive exam, thesis (for some programs), internship research (for those who select an internship track). *Entrance requirements:* For master's, GRE General Test (verbal and quantitative), degree in sociology, criminal justice, social work from accredited institution; letter of intent; autobiographical essay; curriculum vitae; two letters of recommendation. Additional exam requirements/recommendations for international students: Required—TOEFL (minimum score 500 paper-based; 61 iBT). *Application deadline:* For fall admission, 7/15 priority date for domestic students, 6/1 priority date for international students; for spring admission, 12/1 priority date for domestic students, 10/1 priority date for international students. Applications are processed on a rolling basis. Application fee: $20 ($30 for international students). Electronic applications accepted. *Financial support:* In 2014–15, 13 research assistantships (averaging $7,826 per year) were awarded; career-related

internships or fieldwork, Federal Work-Study, institutionally sponsored loans, scholarships/grants, and unspecified assistantships also available. Support available to part-time students. Financial award application deadline: 5/1; financial award applicants required to submit FAFSA. *Faculty research:* Criminology, environmental sociology, globalization, race and ethnic relations, stratification. *Unit head:* Dr. Kenneth Bolton, Department Head, 985-549-2110, Fax: 985-549-5961, E-mail: kbolton@selu.edu. *Application contact:* Sandra Meyers, Graduate Admissions Analyst, 985-549-5620, Fax: 985-549-5632, E-mail: admissions@selu.edu.
Website: http://www.selu.edu/acad_research/depts/soc_cj/index.html

Southern Connecticut State University, School of Graduate Studies, School of Arts and Sciences, Department of Sociology, New Haven, CT 06515-1355. Offers MS. Part-time and evening/weekend programs available. *Degree requirements:* For master's, thesis or alternative. *Entrance requirements:* For master's, interview. Electronic applications accepted.

Southern Illinois University Carbondale, Graduate School, College of Liberal Arts, Department of Sociology, Carbondale, IL 62901-4701. Offers MA, PhD. Part-time programs available. *Faculty:* 7 full-time (3 women), 1 (woman) part-time/adjunct. *Students:* 21 full-time (14 women), 4 part-time (3 women); includes 1 minority (Asian, non-Hispanic/Latino), 7 international. Average age 32. 23 applicants, 61% accepted, 5 enrolled. In 2014, 6 master's, 2 doctorates awarded. *Degree requirements:* For master's, thesis; for doctorate, thesis/dissertation. *Entrance requirements:* For master's, minimum GPA of 2.7; for doctorate, minimum GPA of 3.25. Additional exam requirements/recommendations for international students: Required—TOEFL. *Application deadline:* Applications are processed on a rolling basis. Application fee: $50. *Expenses:* Tuition, state resident: full-time $10,176; part-time $1153 per credit. Tuition, nonresident: full-time $20,814; part-time $1744 per credit. *Required fees:* $7092; $394 per credit. $2364 per semester. *Financial support:* In 2014–15, 30 students received support, including 1 fellowship with full tuition reimbursement available, 2 research assistantships with full tuition reimbursements available, 19 teaching assistantships with full tuition reimbursements available; Federal Work-Study, institutionally sponsored loans, and tuition waivers (full) also available. Support available to part-time students. Financial award application deadline: 2/10. *Faculty research:* Deviance, family, social stratification, social change, theory methodology, culture. *Total annual research expenditures:* $10,000. *Unit head:* Dr. Rachel Whaley, Chair, 618-453-2494, Fax: 618-453-3253, E-mail: rwhaley@siu.edu. *Application contact:* Susan Doolin, Office Specialist, 618-453-7613, Fax: 618-453-3253, E-mail: susandoolin@siu.edu.
Website: http://sociology.siuc.edu/

Southern Illinois University Edwardsville, Graduate School, College of Arts and Sciences, Department of Sociology and Criminal Justice Studies, Edwardsville, IL 62026. Offers sociology (MA). Part-time programs available. *Faculty:* 16 full-time (10 women). *Students:* 4 full-time (3 women), 22 part-time (13 women); includes 12 minority (9 Black or African American, non-Hispanic/Latino; 1 Hispanic/Latino; 2 Two or more races, non-Hispanic/Latino). 19 applicants, 84% accepted. In 2014, 3 master's awarded. *Degree requirements:* For master's, thesis (for some programs), internship. *Entrance requirements:* Additional exam requirements/recommendations for international students: Required—TOEFL (minimum score 550 paper-based; 79 iBT), IELTS (minimum score 6.5). *Application deadline:* For fall admission, 7/10 for domestic and international students; for spring admission, 11/15 for domestic and international students; for summer admission, 4/1 for domestic and international students. Application fee: $30. Electronic applications accepted. *Expenses:* Tuition, state resident: full-time $5026. Tuition, nonresident: full-time $12,566. *International tuition:* $25,136 full-time. *Required fees:* $1682. Tuition and fees vary according to course load, campus/location and program. *Financial support:* In 2014–15, 9 students received support, including 7 research assistantships with full tuition reimbursements available, 2 teaching assistantships with full tuition reimbursements available; fellowships with full tuition reimbursements available, institutionally sponsored loans, scholarships/grants, and unspecified assistantships also available. Financial award application deadline: 3/1; financial award applicants required to submit FAFSA. *Unit head:* Dr. Kevin Cannon, Chair, 618-650-3713, E-mail: kcannon@siue.edu. *Application contact:* Melissa K Mace, Assistant Director of Admissions for Graduate and International Recruitment, 618-650-2756, Fax: 618-650-3618, E-mail: mmace@siue.edu.
Website: http://www.siue.edu/artsandsciences/sociology/index.shtml

Stanford University, School of Humanities and Sciences, Department of Sociology, Stanford, CA 94305-9991. Offers PhD. *Degree requirements:* For doctorate, thesis/dissertation, oral exam. *Entrance requirements:* For doctorate, GRE General Test. Additional exam requirements/recommendations for international students: Required—TOEFL. Electronic applications accepted. *Expenses: Tuition:* Full-time $44,184; part-time $982 per credit hour. *Required fees:* $191.

Stony Brook University, State University of New York, Graduate School, College of Arts and Sciences, Department of Sociology, Stony Brook, NY 11794. Offers MA, PhD. *Faculty:* 20 full-time (9 women), 2 part-time/adjunct (both women). *Students:* 54 full-time (34 women), 3 part-time (all women); includes 8 minority (2 Black or African American, non-Hispanic/Latino; 3 Asian, non-Hispanic/Latino; 1 Hispanic/Latino; 2 Two or more races, non-Hispanic/Latino), 21 international. Average age 32. 73 applicants, 37% accepted, 12 enrolled. In 2014, 7 master's, 6 doctorates awarded. *Degree requirements:* For doctorate, thesis/dissertation, comprehensive exam or professional papers, field exam, teaching practicum. *Entrance requirements:* For doctorate, GRE General Test, minimum GPA of 3.0. Additional exam requirements/recommendations for international students: Required—TOEFL. *Application deadline:* For fall admission, 1/15 for domestic students; for spring admission, 10/1 for domestic students. Application fee: $100. *Expenses:* Tuition, state resident: full-time $10,370; part-time $432 per credit. Tuition, nonresident: full-time $20,190; part-time $841 per credit. *Required fees:* $1431. *Financial support:* In 2014–15, 1 research assistantship, 30 teaching assistantships were awarded; fellowships also available. *Faculty research:* Deviant behavior, history of sociology/social thought, marriage and family sociology, political sociology. *Total annual research expenditures:* $36,926. *Unit head:* Dr. John Shandra, Chair, 631-632-7755, Fax: 631-632-8203, E-mail: john.shandra@stonybrook.edu. *Application contact:* Wanda Vega, Coordinator, 631-632-7730, Fax: 631-632-8203, E-mail: wanda.vega@stonybrook.edu.
Website: http://www.sunysb.edu/sociology/

Syracuse University, Maxwell School of Citizenship and Public Affairs, Program in Sociology, Syracuse, NY 13244. Offers PhD. *Students:* 30 full-time (24 women), 8 part-time (6 women); includes 11 minority (5 Black or African American, non-Hispanic/Latino; 2 Asian, non-Hispanic/Latino; 4 Hispanic/Latino), 5 international. Average age 31. 43 applicants, 30% accepted, 6 enrolled. In 2014, 4 doctorates awarded. *Degree requirements:* For doctorate, comprehensive exam, thesis/dissertation. *Entrance requirements:* For doctorate, GRE General Test. Additional exam requirements/recommendations for international students: Required—TOEFL (minimum score 100 iBT). *Application deadline:* For fall admission, 1/10 priority date for domestic and international students. Application fee: $75. Electronic applications accepted. *Expenses: Tuition:* Part-time $1341 per credit. *Financial support:* Fellowships with full tuition reimbursements, research assistantships with full and partial tuition reimbursements, teaching assistantships with full and partial tuition reimbursements, tuition waivers, and

unspecified assistantships available. Financial award application deadline: 1/1. *Faculty research:* Qualitative methods and feminist methods, inequality studies, aging and the life course. *Unit head:* Dr. Andrew London, Graduate Director, 315-443-2347, E-mail: sociology@maxwell.syr.edu. *Application contact:* Janet Coria, Recruiting Contact, 315-443-2347, E-mail: jmcoria@syr.edu.
Website: http://www.maxwell.syr.edu/soc/

Teachers College, Columbia University, Graduate Faculty of Education, Department of Education Policy and Social Analysis, Program in Sociology and Education, New York, NY 10027. Offers Ed M, MA, Ed D, PhD. *Faculty:* 3 full-time, 1 part-time/adjunct. *Students:* 18 full-time (15 women), 50 part-time (41 women); includes 36 minority (12 Black or African American, non-Hispanic/Latino; 7 Asian, non-Hispanic/Latino; 14 Hispanic/Latino; 3 Two or more races, non-Hispanic/Latino), 8 international. Average age 28. 106 applicants, 60% accepted, 25 enrolled. In 2014, 38 master's awarded. *Degree requirements:* For master's, comprehensive exam, exam or essay; for doctorate, thesis/dissertation. *Entrance requirements:* For doctorate, GRE. *Application deadline:* For fall admission, 12/15 for domestic students; for spring admission, 11/1 for domestic students. Application fee: $65. Electronic applications accepted. *Expenses: Tuition:* Full-time $33,552; part-time $1398 per credit. *Required fees:* $418 per semester. *Financial support:* Career-related internships or fieldwork, Federal Work-Study, institutionally sponsored loans, and tuition waivers (full and partial) available. Support available to part-time students. Financial award application deadline: 2/1; financial award applicants required to submit FAFSA. *Faculty research:* Stratification, race and evaluation, desegregation of schools and communities, quantitative research. *Unit head:* Prof. Aaron M. Pallas, Program Coordinator, 212-678-8119, E-mail: pallas@tc.edu. *Application contact:* Melba Remice, Assistant Director of Admission, 212-678-4035, Fax: 212-678-4171, E-mail: ms2545@columbia.edu.
Website: http://www.tc.columbia.edu/epsa/Sociology/index.asp?Id-Homenfo-Welcome

Temple University, College of Liberal Arts, Department of Sociology, Philadelphia, PA 19122-6096. Offers MA, PhD. Part-time and evening/weekend programs available. *Faculty:* 19 full-time (9 women), 1 part-time/adjunct (0 women). *Students:* 41 full-time (28 women), 3 part-time (2 women); includes 8 minority (1 Black or African American, non-Hispanic/Latino; 3 Asian, non-Hispanic/Latino; 2 Hispanic/Latino; 2 Two or more races, non-Hispanic/Latino), 5 international. 58 applicants, 29% accepted, 7 enrolled. In 2014, 6 master's, 3 doctorates awarded. Terminal master's awarded for partial completion of doctoral program. *Degree requirements:* For doctorate, thesis/dissertation. *Entrance requirements:* For master's and doctorate, GRE General Test, minimum GPA of 3.0, 3 letters of recommendation. Additional exam requirements/recommendations for international students: Required—TOEFL (minimum score 600 paper-based; 100 iBT). *Application deadline:* For fall admission, 3/15 for domestic students, 12/15 for international students. Application fee: $60. Electronic applications accepted. *Expenses:* Tuition, state resident: full-time $14,490; part-time $805 per credit hour. Tuition, nonresident: full-time $19,850; part-time $1103 per credit hour. *Required fees:* $690. Full-time tuition and fees vary according to class time, course load, degree level, campus/location and program. *Financial support:* Fellowships with tuition reimbursements, research assistantships with tuition reimbursements, teaching assistantships with tuition reimbursements, career-related internships or fieldwork, Federal Work-Study, institutionally sponsored loans, and scholarships/grants available. Financial award application deadline: 1/15; financial award applicants required to submit FAFSA. *Faculty research:* Urban sociology, gender and sexuality, race and ethnicity, globalization, medical sociology. *Unit head:* Dr. Dustin Kidd, Graduate Director, 215-204-7750, Fax: 215-204-3352, E-mail: dustin.kidd@temple.edu. *Application contact:* Pamela Smallwood, Coordinator, 215-204-7750, Fax: 215-204-3352, E-mail: poppy@temple.edu.
Website: http://www.temple.edu/sociology/

Texas A&M University, College of Liberal Arts, Department of Sociology, College Station, TX 77843. Offers MS, PhD. *Faculty:* 20. *Students:* 63 full-time (41 women), 22 part-time (15 women); includes 51 minority (16 Black or African American, non-Hispanic/Latino; 1 American Indian or Alaska Native, non-Hispanic/Latino; 2 Asian, non-Hispanic/Latino; 31 Hispanic/Latino; 1 Two or more races, non-Hispanic/Latino), 10 international. Average age 32. 46 applicants, 63% accepted, 11 enrolled. In 2014, 8 master's, 8 doctorates awarded. *Degree requirements:* For master's, thesis or alternative; for doctorate, thesis/dissertation. *Entrance requirements:* For master's and doctorate, GRE General Test. Additional exam requirements/recommendations for international students: Required—TOEFL. *Application deadline:* For fall admission, 1/15 priority date for domestic students; for winter admission, 11/1 priority date for domestic students. Applications are processed on a rolling basis. Application fee: $50 ($90 for international students). Electronic applications accepted. *Expenses:* Tuition, state resident: full-time $4078; part-time $226.55 per credit hour. Tuition, nonresident: full-time $10,594; part-time $577.55 per credit hour. *Required fees:* $2813; $237.70 per credit hour. $278.50 per semester. Tuition and fees vary according to degree level and student level. *Financial support:* In 2014–15, 67 students received support, including 13 fellowships with full and partial tuition reimbursements available (averaging $23,446 per year), 40 research assistantships with full and partial tuition reimbursements available (averaging $5,728 per year), 19 teaching assistantships with full and partial tuition reimbursements available (averaging $5,469 per year); career-related internships or fieldwork, institutionally sponsored loans, scholarships/grants, traineeships, health care benefits, tuition waivers (full and partial), and unspecified assistantships also available. Support available to part-time students. Financial award application deadline: 1/15; financial award applicants required to submit FAFSA. *Faculty research:* Crime, deviance, and law; culture; demography and human ecology; political and economic sociology; racial and ethnic relations; social psychology; Latino sociology; gender; Asian studies. *Unit head:* Dr. Jane Sell, Head, 979-845-6120, Fax: 979-862-4057, E-mail: j-sell@tamu.edu. *Application contact:* Dr. Wendy Leo Moore, Graduate Advisor, 979-845-5133, Fax: 979-862-4057, E-mail: wlmoore@tamu.edu.
Website: http://sociology.tamu.edu

Texas A&M University–Kingsville, College of Graduate Studies, College of Arts and Sciences, Department of Psychology and Sociology, Program in Sociology, Kingsville, TX 78363. Offers MA, MS. *Students:* 17 full-time (4 women), 12 part-time (10 women); includes 25 minority (5 Black or African American, non-Hispanic/Latino; 20 Hispanic/Latino). Average age 31. 11 applicants, 82% accepted, 5 enrolled. In 2014, 10 master's awarded. *Degree requirements:* For master's, variable foreign language requirement, comprehensive exam, thesis (for some programs). *Entrance requirements:* For master's, GRE (minimum composite score of 285), MAT, GMAT, minimum GPA of 2.6. Additional exam requirements/recommendations for international students: Required—TOEFL (minimum score 550 paper-based; 79 iBT). *Application deadline:* For fall admission, 8/15 for domestic students, 6/1 for international students; for spring admission, 12/15 for domestic students, 10/1 for international students; for summer admission, 5/15 for domestic students, 4/1 for international students. Applications are processed on a rolling basis. Application fee: $35 ($50 for international students). Electronic applications accepted. *Financial support:* In 2014–15, 5 students received support, including 3 teaching assistantships (averaging $7,530 per year); career-related internships or fieldwork, Federal Work-Study, institutionally sponsored loans, scholarships/grants, health care benefits, tuition waivers (full and partial), and unspecified assistantships also available. Support available to part-time students. Financial award application deadline: 5/1; financial award applicants required to submit FAFSA. *Unit head:* Dr. Richard Miller, Department Chair, 361-593-4181, Fax: 361-593-2707, E-mail: richard.miller@tamuk.edu. *Application contact:* Dr. Lloyd Dempster, Graduate Coordinator, E-mail: lloyd.dempster@tamuk.edu.

Texas Southern University, College of Liberal Arts and Behavioral Sciences, Department of Sociology, Houston, TX 77004-4584. Offers MA. Part-time and evening/weekend programs available. *Degree requirements:* For master's, comprehensive exam, thesis. *Entrance requirements:* For master's, GRE General Test, minimum GPA of 2.5. Additional exam requirements/recommendations for international students: Required—TOEFL. Electronic applications accepted. *Faculty research:* Sociocultural systems, ethnic and regional studies, community sociology.

Texas State University, The Graduate College, College of Liberal Arts, Program in Applied Sociology, San Marcos, TX 78666. Offers MS. Part-time and evening/weekend programs available. *Faculty:* 14 full-time (7 women), 1 part-time/adjunct (0 women). *Students:* 9 full-time (5 women), 4 part-time (2 women); includes 4 minority (1 Black or African American, non-Hispanic/Latino; 3 Hispanic/Latino). Average age 28. 7 applicants, 86% accepted, 4 enrolled. In 2014, 3 master's awarded. *Degree requirements:* For master's, comprehensive exam. *Entrance requirements:* For master's, GRE (preferred), baccalaureate degree from regionally-accredited university with minimum GPA of 3.0 on last 60 undergraduate semester hours. Additional exam requirements/recommendations for international students: Required—TOEFL (minimum score 550 paper-based; 78 iBT). *Application deadline:* For fall admission, 7/15 priority date for domestic students, 6/1 for international students; for spring admission, 10/15 priority date for domestic students, 10/1 for international students; for summer admission, 4/15 for domestic students, 3/15 for international students. Applications are processed on a rolling basis. Application fee: $40 ($90 for international students). Electronic applications accepted. *Expenses:* Expenses: $8,834 (tuition and fees combined). *Financial support:* In 2014–15, 11 students received support, including 1 research assistantship (averaging $10,107 per year), 4 teaching assistantships (averaging $12,308 per year); Federal Work-Study, institutionally sponsored loans, scholarships/grants, health care benefits, and unspecified assistantships also available. Support available to part-time students. Financial award application deadline: 4/1; financial award applicants required to submit FAFSA. *Unit head:* Dr. Patti Giuffre, Graduate Advisor, 512-245-8983, E-mail: pg07@txstate.edu. *Application contact:* Dr. Andrea Golato, Dean of Graduate School, 512-245-2581, Fax: 512-245-8365, E-mail: gradcollege@txstate.edu.
Website: http://www.soci.txstate.edu

Texas State University, The Graduate College, College of Liberal Arts, Program in Sociology, San Marcos, TX 78666. Offers MA. Part-time and evening/weekend programs available. *Faculty:* 14 full-time (7 women), 1 part-time/adjunct (0 women). *Students:* 28 full-time (19 women), 28 part-time (21 women); includes 21 minority (8 Black or African American, non-Hispanic/Latino; 13 Hispanic/Latino), 4 international. Average age 31. 24 applicants, 54% accepted, 11 enrolled. In 2014, 11 master's awarded. *Degree requirements:* For master's, comprehensive exam, thesis optional. *Entrance requirements:* For master's, GRE (preferred), baccalaureate degree from regionally-accredited university with minimum GPA of 3.0 on last 60 undergraduate semester hours. Additional exam requirements/recommendations for international students: Required—TOEFL (minimum score 550 paper-based; 78 iBT). *Application deadline:* For fall admission, 7/15 priority date for domestic students, 6/1 for international students; for spring admission, 10/15 priority date for domestic students, 10/1 for international students; for summer admission, 4/15 for domestic students, 3/15 for international students. Applications are processed on a rolling basis. Application fee: $40 ($90 for international students). Electronic applications accepted. *Expenses:* Expenses: $8,834 (tuition and fees combined). *Financial support:* In 2014–15, 41 students received support, including 3 research assistantships (averaging $11,910 per year), 13 teaching assistantships (averaging $12,515 per year); Federal Work-Study, institutionally sponsored loans, scholarships/grants, health care benefits, and unspecified assistantships also available. Support available to part-time students. Financial award application deadline: 4/1; financial award applicants required to submit FAFSA. *Faculty research:* Harris County protection. *Total annual research expenditures:* $94,537. *Unit head:* Dr. Patti Giuffre, Graduate Advisor, 512-245-8983, Fax: 512-245-2174, E-mail: pg07@txstate.edu. *Application contact:* Dr. Andrea Golato, Dean of Graduate School, 512-245-2581, Fax: 512-245-8365, E-mail: gradcollege@txstate.edu.
Website: http://www.cj.txstate.edu/

Texas Tech University, Graduate School, College of Arts and Sciences, Department of Sociology, Anthropology and Social Work, Lubbock, TX 79409-1012. Offers anthropology (MA); social work (MSW); sociology (MA). Part-time programs available. *Faculty:* 25 full-time (14 women), 3 part-time/adjunct (2 women). *Students:* 29 full-time (21 women), 9 part-time (5 women); includes 13 minority (3 Black or African American, non-Hispanic/Latino; 8 Hispanic/Latino; 1 Native Hawaiian or other Pacific Islander, non-Hispanic/Latino; 1 Two or more races, non-Hispanic/Latino), 1 international. Average age 26. 28 applicants, 36% accepted, 8 enrolled. In 2014, 11 master's awarded. *Degree requirements:* For master's, one foreign language, comprehensive exam (for some programs), thesis (for some programs). *Entrance requirements:* For master's, GRE (for MA in anthropology), two letters of recommendation, statement of purpose, writing sample, and curriculum vitae; minimum GPA of 3.0 and coursework in sociology or closely-related fields (for MA in sociology); coursework in anthropology (for MA in anthropology). Additional exam requirements/recommendations for international students: Required—TOEFL (minimum score 550 paper-based; 79 iBT). *Application deadline:* For fall admission, 6/1 priority date for domestic students, 1/15 priority date for international students; for spring admission, 9/1 priority date for domestic students, 6/15 priority date for international students. Applications are processed on a rolling basis. Application fee: $60. Electronic applications accepted. *Expenses:* Tuition, state resident: full-time $6310; part-time $262.92 per credit hour. Tuition, nonresident: full-time $14,998; part-time $624.92 per credit hour. *Required fees:* $2701; $36.50 per credit. $912.50 per semester. Tuition and fees vary according to course load. *Financial support:* In 2014–15, 33 students received support, including 31 fellowships (averaging $5,548 per year), 26 teaching assistantships (averaging $10,942 per year); Federal Work-Study, scholarships/grants, tuition waivers (partial), and unspecified assistantships also available. Financial award application deadline: 4/1; financial award applicants required to submit FAFSA. *Faculty research:* Sociology of criminology/deviance, population/migration, forensic anthropology, archaeology, social work. *Total annual research expenditures:* $126,995. *Unit head:* Dr. Brett A. Houk, Chair and Associate Professor, 806-834-8107, Fax: 806-742-1088, E-mail: brett.houk@ttu.edu. *Application contact:* Dr. Cristina Bradatan, Associate Professor/Sociology Graduate Program Director, 806-834-1796, E-mail: cristina.bradatan@ttu.edu.
Website: http://www.depts.ttu.edu/sasw/

Texas Woman's University, Graduate School, College of Arts and Sciences, Department of Sociology and Social Work, Denton, TX 76201. Offers sociology (MA, PhD). Evening/weekend programs available. Terminal master's awarded for partial completion of doctoral program. *Degree requirements:* For master's, comprehensive exam, thesis (for some programs); for doctorate, comprehensive exam, thesis/dissertation. *Entrance requirements:* For master's, 2 letters of reference, 2-3 page

statement of interest; for doctorate, GRE General Test, minimum GPA of 3.5 on last 60 undergraduate hours and all graduate coursework, graduate statistics and social sciences research methods, 3 letters of reference, 2-3 page statement of interest. Additional exam requirements/recommendations for international students: Required—TOEFL (minimum score 550 paper-based; 79 iBT). Electronic applications accepted. *Faculty research:* Pre-impact evaluation planning for families of law enforcement, disasters, criminology, immigration, sociological theory, race/ethnicity, culture of breast cancer.

Tulane University, School of Liberal Arts, Department of Sociology, New Orleans, LA 70118-5669. Offers PhD. Terminal master's awarded for partial completion of doctoral program. *Degree requirements:* For doctorate, thesis/dissertation, preliminary exams. *Entrance requirements:* For doctorate, GRE General Test. Additional exam requirements/recommendations for international students: Required—TOEFL. Electronic applications accepted. *Expenses: Tuition:* Full-time $46,326; part-time $2574 per credit hour. *Required fees:* $1980; $44.50 per credit hour. $550 per term. Tuition and fees vary according to course load and program.

Université de Montréal, Faculty of Arts and Sciences, Department of Sociology, Montréal, QC H3C 3J7, Canada. Offers M Sc, PhD. *Degree requirements:* For master's, thesis; for doctorate, thesis/dissertation, general exam. *Entrance requirements:* For master's, minimum GPA of 3.0; for doctorate, minimum GPA of 3.5, proficiency in French. Electronic applications accepted. *Faculty research:* Sociological theory, economy, state and social movements, work, social politics and health.

Université du Québec à Montréal, Graduate Programs, Program in Social Intervention, Montréal, QC H3C 3P8, Canada. Offers MA. Part-time programs available. *Degree requirements:* For master's, thesis. *Entrance requirements:* For master's, appropriate bachelor's degree or equivalent, proficiency in French.

Université du Québec à Montréal, Graduate Programs, Program in Sociology, Montréal, QC H3C 3P8, Canada. Offers MA, PhD. Part-time programs available. *Degree requirements:* For master's, thesis optional; for doctorate, thesis/dissertation. *Entrance requirements:* For master's, appropriate bachelor's degree or equivalent, proficiency in French; for doctorate, appropriate master's degree or equivalent, proficiency in French.

Université Laval, Faculty of Social Sciences, Department of Sociology, Programs in Sociology, Québec, QC G1K 7P4, Canada. Offers MA, PhD. Terminal master's awarded for partial completion of doctoral program. *Degree requirements:* For master's, thesis; for doctorate, comprehensive exam, thesis/dissertation. *Entrance requirements:* For master's, English exam (comprehension of written English), French exam (for some), knowledge of French; for doctorate, English exam (comprehension of written English), French exam may be required, knowledge of French. Electronic applications accepted.

University at Albany, State University of New York, College of Arts and Sciences, Department of Communication, Albany, NY 12222-0001. Offers communication (MA); sociology and communication (PhD). Part-time programs available. *Degree requirements:* For master's, comprehensive exam, thesis or alternative; for doctorate, comprehensive exam, thesis/dissertation. *Entrance requirements:* For master's, minimum GPA of 3.0; for doctorate, GRE, minimum GPA of 3.0. Additional exam requirements/recommendations for international students: Required—TOEFL (minimum score 550 paper-based). Electronic applications accepted. *Faculty research:* Language and social interaction, campaign communication, media agenda-setting, high-speed management, organizational boundary-spanning.

University at Albany, State University of New York, College of Arts and Sciences, Department of Sociology, Albany, NY 12222-0001. Offers demography (Certificate); sociology (MA, PhD); urban policy (Certificate). Terminal master's awarded for partial completion of doctoral program. *Degree requirements:* For master's, thesis; for doctorate, thesis/dissertation, 2 specialization exams, research tool. *Entrance requirements:* For master's and doctorate, GRE General Test. Additional exam requirements/recommendations for international students: Required—TOEFL. Electronic applications accepted. *Faculty research:* Gender and equality, crime and deviance, aging, work and organizations, social demography.

University at Buffalo, the State University of New York, Graduate School, College of Arts and Sciences, Department of Sociology, Buffalo, NY 14260. Offers MA, PhD. Part-time programs available. *Faculty:* 17 full-time (9 women), 3 part-time/adjunct (2 women). *Students:* 51 full-time (31 women), 10 part-time (5 women); includes 18 minority (3 Black or African American, non-Hispanic/Latino; 1 American Indian or Alaska Native, non-Hispanic/Latino; 14 Asian, non-Hispanic/Latino). Average age 30. 59 applicants, 63% accepted, 14 enrolled. In 2014, 3 master's, 3 doctorates awarded. Terminal master's awarded for partial completion of doctoral program. *Degree requirements:* For master's, project or thesis; for doctorate, thesis/dissertation, qualifying paper. *Entrance requirements:* For master's and doctorate, GRE General Test. Additional exam requirements/recommendations for international students: Required—TOEFL (minimum score 550 paper-based; 79 iBT). *Application deadline:* For fall admission, 2/1 priority date for domestic and international students. Applications are processed on a rolling basis. Application fee: $75. Electronic applications accepted. *Financial support:* In 2014–15, 15 students received support, including 6 fellowships with full tuition reimbursements available (averaging $6,333 per year), 15 teaching assistantships with full tuition reimbursements available (averaging $13,880 per year); scholarships/grants, health care benefits, and tuition waivers (full) also available. Financial award application deadline: 1/15; financial award applicants required to submit FAFSA. *Faculty research:* Theory, culture, sociology of law/criminology, urban sociology, family. *Unit head:* Dr. Debra Street, Chair, 716-645-8475, Fax: 716-645-3934, E-mail: dastreet@buffalo.edu. *Application contact:* Dr. Robert Wagmiller, Director of Graduate Studies, 716-645-8479, Fax: 716-645-3934, E-mail: rw26@buffalo.edu.

The University of Akron, Graduate School, Buchtel College of Arts and Sciences, Department of Sociology, Akron, OH 44325. Offers MA, PhD. PhD offered jointly with Kent State University. Part-time programs available. *Faculty:* 13 full-time (6 women), 3 part-time/adjunct (2 women). *Students:* 24 full-time (18 women), 7 part-time (4 women); includes 6 minority (5 Black or African American, non-Hispanic/Latino; 1 Two or more races, non-Hispanic/Latino), 1 international. Average age 31. 23 applicants, 61% accepted, 5 enrolled. In 2014, 2 master's, 5 doctorates awarded. Terminal master's awarded for partial completion of doctoral program. *Degree requirements:* For master's, thesis optional, oral defense of thesis, paper or oral exam; for doctorate, one foreign language, comprehensive exam, thesis/dissertation. *Entrance requirements:* For master's, GRE General Test, minimum GPA of 3.0, three letters of recommendation, writing sample, statement of purpose outlining educational and career objectives; for doctorate, GRE General Test, minimum GPA of 3.5, three letters of recommendation, writing sample, statement of purpose outlining educational and career objectives. Additional exam requirements/recommendations for international students: Required—TOEFL (minimum score 550 paper-based; 79 iBT), IELTS (minimum score 6.5). *Application deadline:* For fall admission, 1/15 priority date for domestic and international students. Application fee: $45 ($70 for international students). Electronic applications accepted. *Expenses:* Tuition, state resident: full-time $7578; part-time $421 per credit hour. Tuition, nonresident: full-time $12,977; part-time $721 per credit hour. *Required fees:* $1388; $35 per credit hour. Tuition and fees vary according to course load. *Financial support:* In 2014–15, 1 research assistantship with full tuition reimbursement, 20 teaching assistantships with full tuition reimbursements were awarded. *Faculty research:* Medical sociology, inequality, social psychology, criminology, mental health. *Total annual research expenditures:* $35,483. *Unit head:* Dr. Matthew Lee, Interim Chair, 330-972-5357, E-mail: mlee2@uakron.edu. *Application contact:* Dr. Stacey Nofziger, Director of Graduate Studies, 330-972-5364, E-mail: sn18@uakron.edu.
Website: http://www.uakron.edu/sociology/

The University of Alabama at Birmingham, College of Arts and Sciences, Program in Medical Sociology, Birmingham, AL 35294. Offers PhD. *Students:* 15 full-time (11 women), 6 part-time (all women); includes 6 minority (2 Black or African American, non-Hispanic/Latino; 1 American Indian or Alaska Native, non-Hispanic/Latino; 2 Asian, non-Hispanic/Latino; 1 Two or more races, non-Hispanic/Latino), 2 international. Average age 35. In 2014, 4 doctorates awarded. *Degree requirements:* For doctorate, comprehensive exam, thesis/dissertation. *Entrance requirements:* For doctorate, GRE, minimum GPA of 3.0, 3.2 on last 60 semester hours of baccalaureate work. Additional exam requirements/recommendations for international students: Required—TOEFL, TWE. *Application deadline:* For fall admission, 3/1 for domestic students; for spring admission, 11/1 for domestic students. Application fee: $45 ($60 for international students). Electronic applications accepted. *Expenses:* Tuition, state resident: full-time $7090; part-time $370 per credit hour. Tuition, nonresident: full-time $16,072; part-time $869 per credit hour. Full-time tuition and fees vary according to course load and program. *Financial support:* Fellowships and research assistantships available. *Unit head:* Dr. Patricia Drentea, Graduate Program Director, 205-934-2562, Fax: 205-975-5614, E-mail: pdrentea@uab.edu. *Application contact:* Susan Noblitt Banks, Director of Graduate School Operations, 205-934-8227, Fax: 205-934-8413, E-mail: gradschool@uab.edu.
Website: http://www.uab.edu/cas/sociology/graduate-programs

The University of Alabama at Birmingham, College of Arts and Sciences, Program in Sociology, Birmingham, AL 35294. Offers MA, PhD. Evening/weekend programs available. *Degree requirements:* For master's, thesis (for some programs); for doctorate, thesis/dissertation. *Entrance requirements:* For master's, GRE General Test. Additional exam requirements/recommendations for international students: Required—TOEFL (minimum score 550 paper-based), TWE. *Application deadline:* For fall admission, 3/1 for domestic students; for spring admission, 11/1 for domestic students; for summer admission, 4/1 for domestic students. Applications are processed on a rolling basis. Application fee: $45 ($60 for international students). Electronic applications accepted. *Expenses:* Tuition, state resident: full-time $7090; part-time $370 per credit hour. Tuition, nonresident: full-time $16,072; part-time $869 per credit hour. Full-time tuition and fees vary according to course load and program. *Financial support:* Fellowships, research assistantships, career-related internships or fieldwork, Federal Work-Study, and institutionally sponsored loans available. Financial award application deadline: 3/1. *Faculty research:* Gerontology, applied sociology, urban sociology. *Unit head:* Dr. Patricia Drentea, Graduate Program Director, 205-934-2562, Fax: 205-975-5614, E-mail: pdrentea@uab.edu. *Application contact:* Susan Noblitt Banks, Director of Student and Academic Services, Graduate Dean's Office, 205-966-5696, Fax: 205-934-8413, E-mail: snoblitt@uab.edu.
Website: http://www.uab.edu/cas/sociology/graduate-programs

University of Alberta, Faculty of Graduate Studies and Research, Department of Sociology, Edmonton, AB T6G 2E1, Canada. Offers criminal justice (MA); demography (MA, PhD); sociology (MA, PhD). Part-time programs available. *Degree requirements:* For master's, thesis (for some programs); for doctorate, thesis/dissertation. *Faculty research:* Criminology, knowledge and culture, methods and theory, population studies, stratification.

The University of Arizona, College of Social and Behavioral Sciences, Department of Sociology, Tucson, AZ 85721. Offers PhD. *Degree requirements:* For doctorate, thesis/dissertation, 2 preliminary exams. *Entrance requirements:* For doctorate, GRE General Test, 3 letters of recommendation, writing samples. Additional exam requirements/recommendations for international students: Required—TOEFL (minimum score 630 paper-based). Electronic applications accepted. *Faculty research:* Organizations, social psychology, social movement, stratification, religion.

University of Arkansas, Graduate School, J. William Fulbright College of Arts and Sciences, Department of Sociology, Fayetteville, AR 72701-1201. Offers MA. Part-time programs available. *Degree requirements:* For master's, thesis. Electronic applications accepted.

The University of British Columbia, Faculty of Arts, Department of Sociology, Vancouver, BC V6T 1Z1, Canada. Offers MA, PhD. *Degree requirements:* For master's, thesis; for doctorate, comprehensive exam, thesis/dissertation. *Entrance requirements:* For master's, BA in sociology or equivalent with minimum B+ average in upper-level courses; for doctorate, master's degree in sociology or equivalent. Additional exam requirements/recommendations for international students: Required—TOEFL (minimum score 600 paper-based). Electronic applications accepted. *Faculty research:* Social and cultural theories and methods; gender, race, class and sexuality; environment economy and development politics; law and social movements.

University of Calgary, Faculty of Graduate Studies, Faculty of Arts, Department of Sociology, Calgary, AB T2N 1N4, Canada. Offers MA, PhD. Terminal master's awarded for partial completion of doctoral program. *Degree requirements:* For master's, thesis, prospectus; for doctorate, comprehensive exam, thesis/dissertation, oral and written candidacy exams, prospectus, qualifying paper. *Entrance requirements:* For master's, minimum GPA of 3.2; for doctorate, minimum GPA of 3.5. Additional exam requirements/recommendations for international students: Required—TOEFL or IELTS. Electronic applications accepted. *Faculty research:* Deviance, gender, medical, religion, ethnicity.

University of California, Berkeley, Graduate Division, College of Letters and Science, Department of Sociology, Berkeley, CA 94720-1500. Offers PhD. *Degree requirements:* For doctorate, thesis/dissertation, qualifying exam. *Entrance requirements:* For doctorate, GRE General Test, minimum GPA of 3.0, sample of academic written work, 3 letters of recommendation. Additional exam requirements/recommendations for international students: Required—TOEFL (minimum score 570 paper-based) or IELTS. Electronic applications accepted. *Faculty research:* Race, gender, political, stratification theory.

University of California, Davis, Graduate Studies, Program in Sociology, Davis, CA 95616. Offers MA, PhD. Terminal master's awarded for partial completion of doctoral program. *Degree requirements:* For master's, written exam; for doctorate, thesis/dissertation, professional paper, qualifying exam. *Entrance requirements:* For master's and doctorate, GRE General Test, minimum GPA of 3.0, writing sample. Additional exam requirements/recommendations for international students: Required—TOEFL (minimum score 550 paper-based). Electronic applications accepted. *Faculty research:* Collective behavior, social movements, comparative sociology, historical sociology, culture development, inequality.

University of California, Irvine, School of Social Sciences, Department of Sociology, Irvine, CA 92697. Offers social networks (PhD); social science (PhD); sociology and social relations (PhD). *Students:* 82 full-time (42 women), 5 part-time (2 women); includes 35 minority (4 Black or African American, non-Hispanic/Latino; 1 American

Indian or Alaska Native, non-Hispanic/Latino; 8 Asian, non-Hispanic/Latino; 19 Hispanic/Latino; 3 Two or more races, non-Hispanic/Latino), 4 international. Average age 30. 151 applicants, 25% accepted, 19 enrolled. In 2014, 13 doctorates awarded. *Degree requirements:* For doctorate, thesis/dissertation. *Entrance requirements:* For doctorate, GRE General Test, minimum GPA of 3.0. *Application deadline:* For fall admission, 1/15 priority date for domestic students, 1/15 for international students. Applications are processed on a rolling basis. Application fee: $90 ($110 for international students). Electronic applications accepted. *Financial support:* Fellowships, research assistantships with full tuition reimbursements, teaching assistantships, institutionally sponsored loans, traineeships, health care benefits, and unspecified assistantships available. Financial award application deadline: 3/1; financial award applicants required to submit FAFSA. *Faculty research:* Cognitive anthropology, sociology of culture, social structure, family and gender. *Unit head:* Prof. Matt Huffman, Chair, 949-824-5341, E-mail: mhuffman@uci.edu. *Application contact:* Ana Hironaka, Graduate Director, 949-824-1311, E-mail: hironaka@uci.edu.
Website: http://www.sociology.uci.edu/

University of California, Los Angeles, Graduate Division, College of Letters and Science, Department of Sociology, Los Angeles, CA 90095. Offers MA, PhD. Terminal master's awarded for partial completion of doctoral program. *Degree requirements:* For master's, thesis or alternative, paper; for doctorate, thesis/dissertation, oral and written qualifying exams. *Entrance requirements:* For doctorate, GRE General Test, bachelor's degree; minimum undergraduate GPA of 3.0 (or its equivalent if letter grade system not used); writing sample. Additional exam requirements/recommendations for international students: Required—TOEFL. Electronic applications accepted.

University of California, Riverside, Graduate Division, Department of Sociology, Riverside, CA 92521-0102. Offers MA, PhD. *Degree requirements:* For doctorate, thesis/dissertation, 1 quarter of teaching experience, professional paper. *Entrance requirements:* For doctorate, GRE General Test, minimum GPA of 3.2. Additional exam requirements/recommendations for international students: Required—TOEFL (minimum score 550 paper-based; 80 iBT). Electronic applications accepted. *Expenses:* Tuition, state resident: full-time $5399. Tuition, nonresident: full-time $10,433. *Faculty research:* Crime/deviance, race/ethnic relations, family/gender, political economy/globalization, theory.

University of California, San Diego, Graduate Division, Department of Sociology, La Jolla, CA 92093. Offers PhD. *Students:* 57 full-time (35 women), 1 (woman) part-time; includes 11 minority (2 Black or African American, non-Hispanic/Latino; 2 American Indian or Alaska Native, non-Hispanic/Latino; 3 Asian, non-Hispanic/Latino; 4 Hispanic/Latino), 6 international. 155 applicants, 18% accepted, 7 enrolled. In 2014, 7 doctorates awarded. *Degree requirements:* For doctorate, comprehensive exam, thesis/dissertation. *Entrance requirements:* For doctorate, GRE General Test, minimum GPA of 3.0. Additional exam requirements/recommendations for international students: Required—TOEFL (minimum score 550 paper-based; 80 iBT), IELTS (minimum score 7). *Application deadline:* For fall admission, 1/15 for domestic students. Application fee: $90 ($110 for international students). Electronic applications accepted. *Expenses:* Tuition, state resident: full-time $11,220; part-time $5610 per quarter. Tuition, nonresident: full-time $26,322; part-time $13,161 per quarter. *Required fees:* $570 per quarter. Tuition and fees vary according to program. *Financial support:* Fellowships, teaching assistantships, scholarships/grants, and readerships available. Financial award applicants required to submit FAFSA. *Faculty research:* Comparative and historical sociology; sociology of culture; sociology of science, technology, and medicine; social inequalities. *Unit head:* Akos Rona-Tas, Chair, 858-534-2779, E-mail: aronatas@ucsd.edu. *Application contact:* Manny dela Paz, Graduate Coordinator, 858-534-4626, E-mail: edelapaz@ucsd.edu.
Website: http://sociology.ucsd.edu/

University of California, San Francisco, Graduate Division, School of Nursing, Department of Social and Behavioral Sciences, San Francisco, CA 94143. Offers sociology (PhD). *Degree requirements:* For doctorate, one foreign language, thesis/dissertation. *Entrance requirements:* For doctorate, GRE General Test, statement of purpose, official transcripts, two letters of recommendation, scholarly writing example, curriculum vitae or resume. Additional exam requirements/recommendations for international students: Required—TOEFL (minimum score 84 iBT). *Faculty research:* Urban social relations; sociology of women's role in healing; sociology of work, occupations, and professions.

University of California, Santa Barbara, Graduate Division, College of Letters and Sciences, Division of Social Sciences, Department of Sociology, Santa Barbara, CA 93106-9430. Offers interdisciplinary emphasis: Black studies (PhD); interdisciplinary emphasis: environment and society (PhD); interdisciplinary emphasis: feminist studies (PhD); interdisciplinary emphasis: global studies (PhD); interdisciplinary emphasis: language, interaction and social organization (PhD); interdisciplinary emphasis: quantitative methods in social science (PhD); interdisciplinary emphasis: technology and society (PhD); sociology (PhD); MA/PhD. Terminal master's awarded for partial completion of doctoral program. *Degree requirements:* For doctorate, comprehensive exam, thesis/dissertation. *Entrance requirements:* For doctorate, GRE General Test. Additional exam requirements/recommendations for international students: Required—TOEFL (minimum score 550 paper-based; 80 iBT), IELTS (minimum score 7). Electronic applications accepted. *Faculty research:* Gender and sexualities, race/ethnicity, social movements, conversation analysis, global sociology.

University of California, Santa Cruz, Division of Graduate Studies, Division of Social Sciences, Department of Sociology, Santa Cruz, CA 95064. Offers PhD. *Degree requirements:* For doctorate, thesis/dissertation, qualifying exam. *Entrance requirements:* For doctorate, GRE General Test. Additional exam requirements/recommendations for international students: Required—TOEFL (minimum score 550 paper-based; 83 iBT); Recommended—IELTS (minimum score 8). Electronic applications accepted. *Faculty research:* Globalization, political economy, and environment; inequality and identity; culture, knowledge, and power.

University of Central Florida, College of Sciences, Department of Sociology, Orlando, FL 32816. Offers sociology (PhD). Part-time and evening/weekend programs available. *Faculty:* 21 full-time (10 women), 4 part-time/adjunct (all women). *Students:* 56 full-time (45 women), 16 part-time (11 women); includes 31 minority (8 Black or African American, non-Hispanic/Latino; 2 American Indian or Alaska Native, non-Hispanic/Latino; 2 Asian, non-Hispanic/Latino; 10 Hispanic/Latino; 7 Native Hawaiian or other Pacific Islander, non-Hispanic/Latino; 2 Two or more races, non-Hispanic/Latino). Average age 31. 48 applicants, 79% accepted, 24 enrolled. In 2014, 12 master's, 8 doctorates awarded. *Degree requirements:* For master's, comprehensive written exam or thesis. *Entrance requirements:* For master's, GRE General Test, minimum GPA of 3.0 in last 60 hours of course work. Additional exam requirements/recommendations for international students: Required—TOEFL. *Application deadline:* For fall admission, 7/15 for domestic students; for spring admission, 12/1 for domestic students. Application fee: $30. Electronic applications accepted. *Expenses:* Tuition, state resident: part-time $288.16 per credit hour. Tuition, nonresident: part-time $1073.31 per credit hour. *Financial support:* In 2014–15, 37 students received support, including 22 fellowships with partial tuition reimbursements available (averaging $3,800 per year), 4 research assistantships with partial tuition reimbursements available (averaging $10,200 per year), 26 teaching assistantships with partial tuition reimbursements available (averaging $10,300 per year); career-related internships or fieldwork, Federal Work-Study, institutionally sponsored loans, tuition waivers (partial), and unspecified assistantships also available. Financial award application deadline: 3/1; financial award applicants required to submit FAFSA. *Faculty research:* Religious subcultures, attitudes toward abortion, population, sport research, stratification. *Unit head:* Dr. Elizabeth Mustaine, Chair, 407-823-6568, E-mail: elizabeth.mustaine@ucf.edu. *Application contact:* Barbara Rodriguez Lamas, Director, Admissions and Student Services, 407-823-2766, Fax: 407-823-6442, E-mail: gradadmissions@ucf.edu.
Website: http://sociology.cos.ucf.edu/

University of Central Missouri, The Graduate School, Warrensburg, MO 64093. Offers accountancy (MA); accounting (MBA); applied mathematics (MS); aviation safety (MA); biology (MS); business administration (MBA); career and technical education leadership (MS); college student personnel administration (MS); communication (MA); computer science (MS); counseling (MS); criminal justice (MS); educational leadership (Ed D); educational technology (MS); elementary and early childhood education (MSE); English (MA); environmental studies (MA); finance (MBA); history (MA); human services/educational technology (Ed S); human services/learning resources (Ed S); human services/professional counseling (Ed S); industrial hygiene (MS); industrial management (MS); information systems (MBA); information technology (MS); kinesiology (MS); library science and information services (MS); literacy education (MSE); marketing (MBA); mathematics (MS); music (MA); occupational safety management (MS); psychology (MS); rural family nursing (MS); school administration (MSE); social gerontology (MS); sociology (MA); special education (MSE); speech language pathology (MS); superintendency (Ed S); teaching (MAT); teaching English as a second language (MA); technology (MS); technology management (PhD); theatre (MA). Part-time programs available. *Faculty:* 314 full-time (137 women), 24 part-time/adjunct (14 women). *Students:* 1,624 full-time (542 women), 1,773 part-time (1,055 women); includes 194 minority (104 Black or African American, non-Hispanic/Latino; 6 American Indian or Alaska Native, non-Hispanic/Latino; 23 Asian, non-Hispanic/Latino; 41 Hispanic/Latino; 3 Native Hawaiian or other Pacific Islander, non-Hispanic/Latino; 17 Two or more races, non-Hispanic/Latino), 1,592 international. Average age 31. 2,800 applicants, 63% accepted, 1223 enrolled. In 2014, 796 master's, 81 other advanced degrees awarded. *Degree requirements:* For master's and Ed S, comprehensive exam (for some programs), thesis (for some programs). *Entrance requirements:* Additional exam requirements/recommendations for international students: Required—TOEFL (minimum score 550 paper-based; 79 iBT). *Application deadline:* For fall admission, 6/1 for domestic students; for spring admission, 10/1 for domestic and international students. Applications are processed on a rolling basis. Application fee: $30 ($75 for international students). Electronic applications accepted. *Expenses:* Tuition, state resident: full-time $6630; part-time $276.25 per credit hour. Tuition, nonresident: full-time $13,260; part-time $552.50 per credit hour. *Required fees:* $29 per credit hour. Tuition and fees vary according to campus/location. *Financial support:* In 2014–15, 118 students received support, including 271 research assistantships with full and partial tuition reimbursements available (averaging $7,500 per year), 109 teaching assistantships with full and partial tuition reimbursements available (averaging $7,500 per year); career-related internships or fieldwork, Federal Work-Study, scholarships/grants, and administrative and laboratory assistantships also available. Support available to part-time students. Financial award application deadline: 3/1; financial award applicants required to submit FAFSA. *Unit head:* Tina Church-Hockett, Director of Graduate School and International Admissions, 660-543-4621, Fax: 660-543-4778, E-mail: church@ucmo.edu. *Application contact:* Brittany Lawrence, Graduate Student Services Coordinator, 660-543-4621, Fax: 660-543-4778, E-mail: gradinfo@ucmo.edu.
Website: http://www.ucmo.edu/graduate/

University of Central Oklahoma, The Jackson College of Graduate Studies, College of Liberal Arts, Department of Sociology, Gerontology, and Substance Abuse Studies, Edmond, OK 73034-5209. Offers gerontology (MA); sociology (MA), including substance abuse studies. Part-time programs available. *Degree requirements:* For master's, variable foreign language requirement, comprehensive exam (for some programs), thesis (for some programs). *Entrance requirements:* For master's, GRE. Additional exam requirements/recommendations for international students: Required—TOEFL (minimum score 550 paper-based; 79 iBT), IELTS (minimum score 6.5). Electronic applications accepted.

University of Chicago, Division of the Social Sciences, Department of Sociology, Chicago, IL 60637. Offers PhD. *Students:* 120 full-time (65 women); includes 31 minority (9 Black or African American, non-Hispanic/Latino; 2 American Indian or Alaska Native, non-Hispanic/Latino; 7 Asian, non-Hispanic/Latino; 8 Hispanic/Latino; 5 Two or more races, non-Hispanic/Latino), 38 international. 212 applicants, 15% accepted, 15 enrolled. In 2014, 10 doctorates awarded. *Degree requirements:* For doctorate, one foreign language, thesis/dissertation, 2 field exams. *Entrance requirements:* For doctorate, GRE General Test. Additional exam requirements/recommendations for international students: Required—TOEFL (minimum score 104 iBT), IELTS (minimum score 7). *Application deadline:* For fall admission, 12/15 for domestic and international students. Application fee: $90. Electronic applications accepted. *Expenses: Tuition:* Full-time $46,899. *Required fees:* $347. *Financial support:* In 2014–15, 14 students received support, including 14 fellowships with full tuition reimbursements available (averaging $23,000 per year); career-related internships or fieldwork, Federal Work-Study, institutionally sponsored loans, scholarships/grants, and health care benefits also available. Financial award application deadline: 12/15. *Unit head:* Prof. Elisabeth S. Clemens, Chair. *Application contact:* Office of the Dean of Students, 773-702-8415, E-mail: admissions@ssd.uchicago.edu.
Website: http://sociology.uchicago.edu

University of Cincinnati, Graduate School, McMicken College of Arts and Sciences, Department of Sociology, Cincinnati, OH 45221. Offers MA, PhD. Part-time programs available. *Degree requirements:* For master's, thesis; for doctorate, thesis/dissertation. *Entrance requirements:* For master's and doctorate, GRE General Test. Additional exam requirements/recommendations for international students: Required—TOEFL. Electronic applications accepted. *Faculty research:* Work and family, race and urban, health and medicine, social psychology.

University of Colorado Boulder, Graduate School, College of Arts and Sciences, Department of Sociology, Boulder, CO 80309. Offers PhD. *Faculty:* 19 full-time (11 women). *Students:* 64 full-time (44 women); includes 14 minority (2 Black or African American, non-Hispanic/Latino; 3 Asian, non-Hispanic/Latino; 5 Hispanic/Latino; 4 Two or more races, non-Hispanic/Latino), 5 international. Average age 31. 128 applicants, 18% accepted, 10 enrolled. In 2014, 6 doctorates awarded. *Degree requirements:* For doctorate, comprehensive exam, thesis/dissertation. *Entrance requirements:* For doctorate, GRE General Test, GRE Subject Test, minimum undergraduate GPA of 2.75. *Application deadline:* For fall admission, 12/1 for domestic and international students. Application fee: $50 ($70 for international students). Electronic applications accepted. *Financial support:* In 2014–15, 172 students received support, including 27 fellowships (averaging $4,422 per year), 10 research assistantships with full and partial tuition reimbursements available (averaging $28,649 per year), 50 teaching assistantships with full and partial tuition reimbursements available (averaging $39,602 per year);

institutionally sponsored loans, scholarships/grants, health care benefits, and unspecified assistantships also available. Financial award application deadline: 1/1; financial award applicants required to submit FAFSA. *Faculty research:* Sociology, minorities and disadvantaged, sociology of sex and gender, criminology, racism/race relations. *Total annual research expenditures:* $2.2 million.
Website: http://SOCSCI.colorado.edu/SOC/

University of Colorado Colorado Springs, College of Letters, Arts and Sciences, Department of Sociology, Colorado Springs, CO 80933-7150. Offers MA. Part-time programs available. *Faculty:* 11 full-time (8 women), 9 part-time/adjunct (6 women). *Students:* 5 full-time (4 women), 38 part-time (23 women); includes 12 minority (5 Black or African American, non-Hispanic/Latino; 2 American Indian or Alaska Native, non-Hispanic/Latino; 2 Asian, non-Hispanic/Latino; 3 Hispanic/Latino). Average age 34. 23 applicants, 91% accepted, 12 enrolled. In 2014, 7 master's awarded. *Degree requirements:* For master's, thesis optional. *Entrance requirements:* For master's, minimum GPA of 3.0 or GRE. Additional exam requirements/recommendations for international students: Recommended—TOEFL (minimum score 550 paper-based; 80 iBT), IELTS (minimum score 6). *Application deadline:* For fall admission, 2/1 priority date for domestic and international students; for spring admission, 12/1 for domestic and international students. Applications are processed on a rolling basis. Application fee: $60 ($100 for international students). *Expenses:* Tuition, state resident: full-time $9900; part-time $1892 per course. Tuition, nonresident: full-time $18,792; part-time $3375 per course. One-time fee: $100. Tuition and fees vary according to course load, program and reciprocity agreements. *Financial support:* In 2014–15, 18 students received support, including 6 teaching assistantships (averaging $1,000 per year); fellowships, career-related internships or fieldwork, Federal Work-Study, and scholarships/grants also available. Support available to part-time students. Financial award application deadline: 3/1; financial award applicants required to submit FAFSA. *Faculty research:* Intersectionality, culture, justice studies and globalization and development. *Unit head:* Dr. Edwardo Portillos, Director of Graduate Studies, 719-255-4143, Fax: 719-255-4450, E-mail: eportill@uccs.edu. *Application contact:* Rosemary Kelbel, Program Assistant, 719-255-4153, Fax: 719-255-4450, E-mail: rkelbel@uccs.edu.
Website: http://www.uccs.edu/~soc/

University of Colorado Denver, College of Liberal Arts and Sciences, Department of Sociology, Denver, CO 80217. Offers MA. Part-time and evening/weekend programs available. *Faculty:* 7 full-time (5 women). *Students:* 9 full-time (8 women), 6 part-time (4 women); includes 4 minority (1 Black or African American, non-Hispanic/Latino; 1 Asian, non-Hispanic/Latino; 2 Hispanic/Latino). Average age 29. 31 applicants, 77% accepted, 11 enrolled. In 2014, 6 master's awarded. *Degree requirements:* For master's, 36 credit hours, project or thesis. *Entrance requirements:* For master's, GRE (recommended), minimum combined GPA of 3.3 for all courses taken at undergraduate or graduate level prior to admission, 3.5 for all sociology courses; writing sample; statement of intent, three letters of recommendation. Additional exam requirements/recommendations for international students: Required—TOEFL (minimum score 537 paper-based; 75 iBT); Recommended—IELTS (minimum score 6.5). *Application deadline:* For fall admission, 3/1 for domestic students, 2/15 for international students. Application fee: $50 ($75 for international students). Electronic applications accepted. *Financial support:* In 2014–15, 6 students received support. Fellowships, research assistantships, teaching assistantships, Federal Work-Study, institutionally sponsored loans, scholarships/grants, and traineeships available. Financial award application deadline: 4/1; financial award applicants required to submit FAFSA. *Faculty research:* Domestic violence, elderly and housing, family demography, immigrants and immigration, social determinants of health behaviors. *Unit head:* Kari Alexander, Sociology Graduate Program Director, 303-315-2137, E-mail: kari.alexander@ucdenver.edu. *Application contact:* Rachel Gallegos, Program Assistant, 303-315-2148, E-mail: rachel.gallegos@ucdenver.edu.
Website: http://www.ucdenver.edu/academics/colleges/CLAS/Departments/sociology/Programs/MasterofArts/Pages/MasterofArts.aspx

University of Colorado Denver, College of Liberal Arts and Sciences, Program in Humanities, Denver, CO 80217. Offers community health science (MSS); humanities (MH); international studies (MSS); philosophy and theory (MH); social justice (MSS); society and the environment (MSS); visual studies (MH); women's and gender studies (MSS). Part-time and evening/weekend programs available. *Faculty:* 1 full-time (0 women), 1 (woman) part-time/adjunct. *Students:* 49 full-time (37 women), 26 part-time (19 women); includes 14 minority (3 Black or African American, non-Hispanic/Latino; 1 American Indian or Alaska Native, non-Hispanic/Latino; 1 Asian, non-Hispanic/Latino; 6 Hispanic/Latino; 3 Two or more races, non-Hispanic/Latino), 1 international. Average age 35. 27 applicants, 63% accepted, 11 enrolled. In 2014, 16 master's awarded. *Degree requirements:* For master's, 36 credit hours, project or thesis. *Entrance requirements:* For master's, writing sample, statement of purpose/letter of intent, three letters of recommendation. Additional exam requirements/recommendations for international students: Required—TOEFL (minimum score 537 paper-based; 75 iBT); Recommended—IELTS (minimum score 6.5). *Application deadline:* For fall admission, 5/15 for domestic students, 5/15 priority date for international students; for spring admission, 10/15 for domestic students, 10/15 priority date for international students; for summer admission, 3/15 for domestic and international students. Application fee: $50 ($75 for international students). Electronic applications accepted. *Financial support:* In 2014–15, 4 students received support. Fellowships, research assistantships, teaching assistantships, Federal Work-Study, institutionally sponsored loans, scholarships/grants, and traineeships available. Financial award application deadline: 4/1; financial award applicants required to submit FAFSA. *Faculty research:* Women and gender in the classical Mediterranean, communication theory and democracy, relationship between psychology and philosophy. *Unit head:* Margaret Woodhull, Director of Humanities, 303-315-3568, E-mail: margaret.woodhull@ucdenver.edu. *Application contact:* Angela Beale, Program Assistant, 303-315-3565, E-mail: angela.beale@ucdenver.edu.
Website: http://www.ucdenver.edu/academics/colleges/CLAS/Programs/HumanitiesSocialSciences/Programs/Pages/MasterofHumanities.aspx

University of Connecticut, Graduate School, College of Liberal Arts and Sciences, Department of Sociology, Storrs, CT 06269. Offers MA, PhD. Terminal master's awarded for partial completion of doctoral program. *Degree requirements:* For master's, comprehensive exam; for doctorate, thesis/dissertation. *Entrance requirements:* For master's and doctorate, GRE General Test. Additional exam requirements/recommendations for international students: Required—TOEFL (minimum score 550 paper-based). Electronic applications accepted.

University of Delaware, College of Arts and Sciences, Department of Sociology and Criminal Justice, Newark, DE 19716. Offers criminology (MA, PhD); sociology (MA, PhD). *Degree requirements:* For master's, thesis; for doctorate, comprehensive exam, thesis/dissertation. *Entrance requirements:* For master's and doctorate, GRE, 3 letters of recommendation. Additional exam requirements/recommendations for international students: Required—TOEFL. Electronic applications accepted. *Faculty research:* Sex and gender, criminology/deviance, theory, methods, collective behavior.

University of Florida, Graduate School, College of Liberal Arts and Sciences, Department of Sociology and Criminology and Law, Gainesville, FL 32611. Offers

criminology, law, and society (MA, PhD); sociology (MA, PhD), including sociology, tropical conservation and development, women's and gender studies (PhD); MA/JD. Part-time programs available. *Faculty:* 19 full-time (9 women), 9 part-time/adjunct (6 women). *Students:* 85 full-time (62 women), 9 part-time (5 women); includes 24 minority (12 Black or African American, non-Hispanic/Latino; 4 Asian, non-Hispanic/Latino; 8 Hispanic/Latino), 22 international. 80 applicants, 34% accepted, 14 enrolled. In 2014, 17 doctorates awarded. Terminal master's awarded for partial completion of doctoral program. *Degree requirements:* For master's, thesis optional; for doctorate, comprehensive exam, thesis/dissertation. *Entrance requirements:* For master's and doctorate, GRE, minimum GPA of 3.0. Additional exam requirements/recommendations for international students: Required—TOEFL (minimum score 550 paper-based; 80 iBT), IELTS (minimum score 6). *Application deadline:* For fall admission, 1/15 for domestic and international students; for spring admission, 6/1 for domestic and international students. Applications are processed on a rolling basis. Application fee: $30. Electronic applications accepted. *Financial support:* In 2014–15, 10 fellowships, 7 research assistantships, 59 teaching assistantships were awarded. Financial award application deadline: 1/15; financial award applicants required to submit FAFSA. *Faculty research:* Law and society, juvenile justice, criminal investigation procedures, deviance, biosocial criminology, environmental sociology, comparative race and ethnic studies, health and aging, families and gender. *Unit head:* Richard Hollinger, PhD, Professor and Chair, 352-392-0265, Fax: 352-392-6568, E-mail: rhollin@ufl.edu. *Application contact:* Barbara Zsembik, PhD, Associate Professor of Sociology/Graduate Coordinator/Associate Chair, 352-294-7190, Fax: 352-392-6568, E-mail: zsembik@soc.ufl.edu.
Website: http://soccrim.clas.ufl.edu/

University of Georgia, Franklin College of Arts and Sciences, Department of Sociology, Athens, GA 30602. Offers MA, PhD. *Degree requirements:* For master's, thesis; for doctorate, thesis/dissertation. *Entrance requirements:* For master's and doctorate, GRE General Test. Additional exam requirements/recommendations for international students: Required—TOEFL. Electronic applications accepted. *Faculty research:* Race, deviance, gender, culture.

University of Guelph, Graduate Studies, College of Social and Applied Human Sciences, Department of Sociology and Anthropology, Guelph, ON N1G 2W1, Canada. Offers anthropology (MA); crime and criminal justice policy (MA); sociology (MA, PhD). *Degree requirements:* For master's, thesis or major paper; for doctorate, comprehensive exam, thesis/dissertation. *Entrance requirements:* For master's, minimum B+ average during previous 2 years of course work, honors BA or equivalent; for doctorate, must have an MA in Sociology, must have 80% or higher in graduate level studies. Additional exam requirements/recommendations for international students: Required—TOEFL (minimum score 550 paper-based; 89 iBT) or IELTS (minimum score 6.5). Electronic applications accepted. *Faculty research:* Rural and development sociology; education, employment, and the workplace; race, ethnicity, and native studies; criminology and deviance; social psychology.

University of Hawaii at Manoa, Graduate Division, College of Social Sciences, Department of Sociology, Honolulu, HI 96822. Offers sociology (MA, PhD). Part-time programs available. *Degree requirements:* For master's, thesis optional; for doctorate, comprehensive exam, thesis/dissertation. *Entrance requirements:* For master's and doctorate, GRE General Test. Additional exam requirements/recommendations for international students: Required—TOEFL (minimum score 500 paper-based; 61 iBT), IELTS (minimum score 5). *Faculty research:* Comparative sociology of Asia; population studies; crime, law, and deviance; health; aging and medical sociology.

University of Houston, College of Liberal Arts and Social Sciences, Department of Sociology, Houston, TX 77204. Offers MA. Part-time programs available. *Degree requirements:* For master's, thesis, 4 core courses, 36 hours. *Entrance requirements:* For master's, GRE (minimum score 1000), minimum GPA of 3.0; letters of recommendation, resume. Additional exam requirements/recommendations for international students: Required—TOEFL (minimum score 550 paper-based; 79 iBT). Electronic applications accepted. *Faculty research:* Immigration, public education, HIV/AIDS.

University of Houston–Clear Lake, School of Human Sciences and Humanities, Programs in Human Sciences, Houston, TX 77058-1002. Offers behavioral sciences (MA), including criminology, cross cultural studies, general psychology, sociology; clinical psychology (MA); criminology (MA); cross cultural studies (MA); family therapy (MA); fitness and human performance (MA); school psychology (MA). *Accreditation:* AAMFT/COAMFTE. Part-time and evening/weekend programs available. Postbaccalaureate distance learning degree programs offered (minimal on-campus study). *Degree requirements:* For master's, thesis or alternative. *Entrance requirements:* For master's, GRE General Test. Additional exam requirements/recommendations for international students: Required—TOEFL (minimum score 550 paper-based). Electronic applications accepted. *Faculty research:* Smoking cessation, adolescent sexuality, white collar crime, serial murder, human factors/human computer interaction.

University of Illinois at Chicago, Graduate College, College of Liberal Arts and Sciences, Department of Sociology, Chicago, IL 60607-7128. Offers MA, PhD. *Faculty:* 12 full-time (9 women), 3 part-time/adjunct (0 women). *Students:* 60 full-time (40 women), 3 part-time (1 woman); includes 20 minority (8 Black or African American, non-Hispanic/Latino; 2 Asian, non-Hispanic/Latino; 8 Hispanic/Latino; 2 Two or more races, non-Hispanic/Latino), 4 international. Average age 30. 76 applicants, 26% accepted, 9 enrolled. In 2014, 3 master's, 2 doctorates awarded. Terminal master's awarded for partial completion of doctoral program. *Degree requirements:* For master's, comprehensive exam, thesis; for doctorate, thesis/dissertation, qualifying exam. *Entrance requirements:* For master's and doctorate, GRE General Test, minimum GPA of 3.0. Additional exam requirements/recommendations for international students: Required—TOEFL. *Application deadline:* For fall admission, 2/15 priority date for domestic students, 2/15 for international students. Applications are processed on a rolling basis. Application fee: $60. Electronic applications accepted. *Expenses:* Tuition, state resident: full-time $11,254; part-time $468 per credit hour. Tuition, nonresident: full-time $23,252; part-time $968 per credit hour. *Required fees:* $1217 per term. Part-time tuition and fees vary according to course load, degree level and program. *Financial support:* In 2014–15, 4 fellowships with full tuition reimbursements were awarded; research assistantships with full tuition reimbursements, teaching assistantships with full tuition reimbursements, career-related internships or fieldwork, Federal Work-Study, scholarships/grants, traineeships, tuition waivers (full), and unspecified assistantships also available. Financial award application deadline: 3/1; financial award applicants required to submit FAFSA. *Faculty research:* Social psychology, social organization, applied sociology, demography and human ecology. *Unit head:* Prof. Barbara Risman, Head, 312-996-3074, E-mail: brisman@uic.edu. *Application contact:* Claire L. Decoteau, Director of Graduate Studies, 312-413-3755, E-mail: decoteau@uic.edu.
Website: http://sociology.las.uic.edu/

University of Illinois at Urbana–Champaign, Graduate College, College of Liberal Arts and Sciences, Department of Sociology, Champaign, IL 61820. Offers MA, PhD. *Students:* 39 (28 women). Application fee: $70 ($90 for international students). *Unit head:* Antoinette Burton, Head, 217-333-1950, Fax: 217-333-5225, E-mail: aburton@illinois.edu. *Application contact:* Shari Day, Office Manager, 217-244-1809,

Fax: 217-333-5225, E-mail: shariday@illinois.edu. Website: http://www.sociology.illinois.edu/

University of Indianapolis, Graduate Programs, College of Arts and Sciences, Department of Social Sciences, Indianapolis, IN 46227-3697. Offers applied sociology (MA). Part-time and evening/weekend programs available. *Faculty:* 5 full-time (1 woman), 1 (woman) part-time/adjunct. *Students:* 7 full-time (2 women), 7 part-time (5 women); includes 2 minority (both Black or African American, non-Hispanic/Latino). Average age 31. In 2014, 9 master's awarded. *Degree requirements:* For master's, thesis optional. *Entrance requirements:* For master's, GRE Subject Test, minimum GPA of 3.0, letter of intent, 3 letters of recommendation. Additional exam requirements/recommendations for international students: Required—TOEFL (minimum score 550 paper-based). *Application deadline:* Applications are processed on a rolling basis. Application fee: $30. Electronic applications accepted. *Financial support:* Federal Work-Study, scholarships/grants, tuition waivers (full and partial), and unspecified assistantships available. Support available to part-time students. Financial award application deadline: 5/1; financial award applicants required to submit FAFSA. *Unit head:* Dr. James Pennell, Chair, 317-788-3535, Fax: 317-788-3480, E-mail: jpennell@uindy.edu. *Application contact:* Linda Corn, Administrative Assistant, 317-788-3395, E-mail: lcorn@uindy.edu.
Website: http://www.uindy.edu/cas/social-sciences

The University of Iowa, Graduate College, College of Liberal Arts and Sciences, Department of Sociology, Iowa City, IA 52242-1316. Offers MA, PhD. *Degree requirements:* For master's, thesis optional, exam; for doctorate, comprehensive exam, thesis/dissertation. *Entrance requirements:* For master's and doctorate, GRE General Test, minimum GPA of 3.0. Additional exam requirements/recommendations for international students: Required—TOEFL (minimum score 600 paper-based; 100 iBT). Electronic applications accepted.

The University of Kansas, Graduate Studies, College of Liberal Arts and Sciences, Department of Sociology, Lawrence, KS 66045. Offers MA, PhD. Part-time programs available. *Faculty:* 19 full-time, 2 part-time/adjunct. *Students:* 40 full-time (22 women), 1 part-time (0 women); includes 2 minority (1 Asian, non-Hispanic/Latino; 1 Two or more races, non-Hispanic/Latino), 4 international. Average age 32. 45 applicants, 47% accepted, 7 enrolled. In 2014, 5 master's, 1 doctorate awarded. *Degree requirements:* For master's, thesis; for doctorate, comprehensive exam, thesis/dissertation. *Entrance requirements:* For master's, GRE General Test, bachelor's degree; minimum GPA of 3.0; 15 credit hours in sociology; 1 course each in sociology theory and sociology statistics; for doctorate, GRE General Test, master's degree in sociology or closely-related field. Additional exam requirements/recommendations for international students: Required—TOEFL (minimum score 550 paper-based; 79 iBT), IELTS (minimum score 6.5). *Application deadline:* For fall admission, 12/15 for domestic students, 12/15 priority date for international students. Applications are processed on a rolling basis. Application fee: $55 ($65 for international students). Electronic applications accepted. *Financial support:* Fellowships with full tuition reimbursements, research assistantships with full tuition reimbursements, teaching assistantships with full and partial tuition reimbursements, scholarships/grants, health care benefits, and unspecified assistantships available. Financial award application deadline: 12/15. *Faculty research:* Gender and sexuality; race and ethnicity; culture; family, life course and aging; political and economic sociology. *Unit head:* David Smith, Chair, 785-864-9417, E-mail: emerald@ku.edu. *Application contact:* Corinne Butler, Graduate Secretary, 785-864-9419, Fax: 785-864-5280, E-mail: cleg@ku.edu.
Website: http://www.sociology.ku.edu/

University of Kentucky, Graduate School, College of Arts and Sciences, Program in Sociology, Lexington, KY 40506-0032. Offers MA, MS, PhD. Part-time programs available. *Degree requirements:* For master's, comprehensive exam, thesis optional; for doctorate, comprehensive exam, thesis/dissertation. *Entrance requirements:* For master's, GRE General Test, minimum undergraduate GPA of 2.75; for doctorate, GRE General Test, minimum graduate GPA of 3.0. Additional exam requirements/recommendations for international students: Required—TOEFL (minimum score 550 paper-based). Electronic applications accepted. *Faculty research:* Work organizations, social inequalities, rural sociology, criminology/deviance, medical sociology.

University of Lethbridge, School of Graduate Studies, Lethbridge, AB T1K 3M4, Canada. Offers addictions counseling (M Sc); agricultural biotechnology (M Sc); agricultural studies (M Sc, MA); anthropology (MA); archaeology (M Sc, MA); art (MA, MFA); biochemistry (M Sc); biological sciences (M Sc); biomolecular science (PhD); biosystems and biodiversity (PhD); Canadian studies (MA); chemistry (M Sc); computer science (M Sc); computer science and geographical information science (M Sc); counseling (MC); counseling psychology (M Ed); dramatic arts (MA); earth, space, and physical science (PhD); economics (MA); education (MA); educational leadership (M Ed); English (MA); environmental science (M Sc); evolution and behavior (PhD); exercise science (M Sc); French (MA); French/German (MA); French/Spanish (MA); general education (M Ed); geography (M Sc, MA); German (MA); health sciences (M Sc); individualized multidisciplinary (M Sc, MA); kinesiology (M Sc, MA); management (M Sc), including accounting, finance, general management, human resource management and labor relations, information systems, international management, marketing, policy and strategy; mathematics (M Sc); modern languages (MA); music (M Mus, MA); Native American studies (MA); neuroscience (M Sc, PhD); new media (MA, MFA); nursing (M Sc, MN); philosophy (MA); physics (M Sc); political science (MA); psychology (M Sc, MA); religious studies (MA); sociology (MA); theatre and dramatic arts (MFA); theoretical and computational science (PhD); urban and regional studies (MA); women and gender studies (MA). Part-time and evening/weekend programs available. *Faculty:* 358. *Students:* 445 full-time (243 women), 116 part-time (72 women). Average age 31. 351 applicants, 26% accepted, 87 enrolled. In 2014, 129 master's, 13 doctorates awarded. *Degree requirements:* For master's, thesis (for some programs); for doctorate, comprehensive exam, thesis/dissertation. *Entrance requirements:* For master's, GMAT (for M Sc in management), bachelor's degree in related field, minimum GPA of 3.0 during previous 20 graded semester courses, 2 years' teaching or related experience (M Ed); for doctorate, master's degree, minimum graduate GPA of 3.5. Additional exam requirements/recommendations for international students: Required—TOEFL. Application fee: $100 Canadian dollars. *Financial support:* Fellowships, research assistantships, teaching assistantships, scholarships/grants, health care benefits, and unspecified assistantships available. *Faculty research:* Movement and brain plasticity, gibberellin physiology, photosynthesis, carbon cycling, molecular properties of main-group ring components. *Application contact:* School of Graduate Studies, 403-329-5194, E-mail: sgsinquiries@uleth.ca.
Website: http://www.uleth.ca/graduatestudies/

University of Louisville, Graduate School, College of Arts and Sciences, Department of Sociology, Louisville, KY 40292. Offers MA, PhD. Part-time and evening/weekend programs available. *Students:* 23 full-time (12 women), 9 part-time (6 women); includes 6 minority (5 Black or African American, non-Hispanic/Latino; 1 Asian, non-Hispanic/Latino). Average age 33. 22 applicants, 73% accepted, 12 enrolled. In 2014, 3 master's, 1 doctorate awarded. *Degree requirements:* For master's, thesis or practicum; for doctorate, comprehensive exam, thesis/dissertation, internship. *Entrance requirements:* For master's and doctorate, GRE General Test. Additional exam requirements/recommendations for international students: Required—TOEFL. *Application deadline:* For fall admission, 6/1 for domestic students, 5/1 priority date for international students; for spring admission, 10/1 for domestic students, 11/1 priority date for international students; for summer admission, 4/1 priority date for international students. Applications are processed on a rolling basis. Application fee: $60. Electronic applications accepted. *Expenses:* Tuition, state resident: full-time $11,326; part-time $630 per credit hour. Tuition, nonresident: full-time $23,568; part-time $1311 per credit hour. *Required fees:* $196. Tuition and fees vary according to program and reciprocity agreements. *Financial support:* Fellowships with full tuition reimbursements and teaching assistantships with full tuition reimbursements available. *Faculty research:* Crime/corrections, gender/sexuality, medicine/health, education, urban. *Unit head:* Dr. Cynthia L. Negrey, Chair, 502-852-8023, Fax: 502-852-0099, E-mail: cynthia.negrey@louisville.edu. *Application contact:* Libby Leggett, Director, Graduate Admissions, 502-852-3101, Fax: 502-852-6536, E-mail: gradadm@louisville.edu.
Website: http://louisville.edu/sociology

The University of Manchester, School of Social Sciences, Manchester, United Kingdom. Offers ethnographic documentary (M Phil); interdisciplinary study of culture (PhD); philosophy (PhD); politics (PhD); social anthropology (PhD); social anthropology with visual media (PhD); social change (PhD); social statistics (PhD); sociology (PhD); visual anthropology (M Phil).

University of Manitoba, Faculty of Graduate Studies, Faculty of Arts, Department of Sociology, Winnipeg, MB R3T 2N2, Canada. Offers MA, PhD. *Degree requirements:* For master's, thesis.

University of Maryland, Baltimore County, The Graduate School, College of Arts, Humanities and Social Sciences, Department of Sociology and Anthropology, Program in Applied Sociology, Baltimore, MD 21250. Offers MA. Part-time and evening/weekend programs available. *Faculty:* 19 full-time (15 women), 2 part-time/adjunct (0 women). *Students:* 16 full-time (11 women), 28 part-time (17 women); includes 19 minority (10 Black or African American, non-Hispanic/Latino; 4 Asian, non-Hispanic/Latino; 4 Hispanic/Latino; 1 Two or more races, non-Hispanic/Latino). Average age 29. 23 applicants, 57% accepted, 9 enrolled. In 2014, 28 master's awarded. *Degree requirements:* For master's, thesis or alternative. *Entrance requirements:* For master's, GRE, minimum GPA of 3.0. Additional exam requirements/recommendations for international students: Required—TOEFL. *Application deadline:* For fall admission, 4/1 priority date for domestic students, 1/1 for international students; for spring admission, 10/15 priority date for domestic students, 5/1 for international students. Applications are processed on a rolling basis. Application fee: $70. Electronic applications accepted. *Expenses:* Tuition, state resident: part-time $557. Tuition, nonresident: part-time $922. *Required fees:* $122 per semester. One-time fee: $200 part-time. *Financial support:* In 2014–15, 13 students received support, including 2 research assistantships with full and partial tuition reimbursements available (averaging $11,768 per year), 9 teaching assistantships with full and partial tuition reimbursements available (averaging $11,768 per year); scholarships/grants, health care benefits, unspecified assistantships, and tuition remission also available. Financial award application deadline: 2/14; financial award applicants required to submit FAFSA. *Faculty research:* Sociology of aging, sociology of health, diversity, gender, and culture. *Unit head:* Dr. John G. Schumacher, Director, 410-455-3184, Fax: 410-455-1154, E-mail: jschuma@umbc.edu. *Application contact:* Angela McNulty, Administrative Assistant II, 410-455-3979, Fax: 410-455-1154, E-mail: amcnulty@umbc.edu.
Website: http://sociology.umbc.edu/graduate/applied_soc.html

University of Maryland, College Park, Academic Affairs, College of Behavioral and Social Sciences, Department of Sociology, College Park, MD 20742. Offers MA, PhD. *Degree requirements:* For master's, thesis; for doctorate, thesis/dissertation, 2 qualifying exams. *Entrance requirements:* For master's, GRE General Test, minimum GPA of 3.0, 3 letters of recommendation; for doctorate, GRE General Test, 3 letters of recommendation. Additional exam requirements/recommendations for international students: Required—TOEFL. Electronic applications accepted. *Faculty research:* Social psychology, sociology of work, sociology of the military, population studies, stratification.

University of Massachusetts Amherst, Graduate School, College of Social and Behavioral Sciences, Department of Sociology, Amherst, MA 01003. Offers MA, PhD. Part-time programs available. *Faculty:* 46 full-time (21 women). *Students:* 63 full-time (41 women), 11 part-time (8 women); includes 26 minority (9 Black or African American, non-Hispanic/Latino; 1 American Indian or Alaska Native, non-Hispanic/Latino; 3 Asian, non-Hispanic/Latino; 10 Hispanic/Latino; 3 Two or more races, non-Hispanic/Latino), 14 international. Average age 31. 173 applicants, 10% accepted, 6 enrolled. In 2014, 7 master's, 3 doctorates awarded. Terminal master's awarded for partial completion of doctoral program. *Degree requirements:* For master's, thesis or alternative; for doctorate, comprehensive exam, thesis/dissertation. *Entrance requirements:* For master's and doctorate, GRE General Test, writing sample, 3 letters of recommendation. Additional exam requirements/recommendations for international students: Required—TOEFL (minimum score 550 paper-based; 80 iBT), IELTS (minimum score 6.5). *Application deadline:* For fall admission, 1/15 for domestic and international students. Applications are processed on a rolling basis. Application fee: $75. Electronic applications accepted. *Expenses:* Tuition, state resident: full-time $1980; part-time $110 per credit. Tuition, nonresident: full-time $14,644; part-time $414 per credit. *Required fees:* $11,417. One-time fee: $357. *Financial support:* Fellowships with full and partial tuition reimbursements, research assistantships with full and partial tuition reimbursements, teaching assistantships with full and partial tuition reimbursements, career-related internships or fieldwork, Federal Work-Study, scholarships/grants, traineeships, health care benefits, tuition waivers (full and partial), and unspecified assistantships available. Support available to part-time students. Financial award application deadline: 1/15; financial award applicants required to submit FAFSA. *Unit head:* Dr. Millicent Thayer, Graduate Program Director, 413-545-4057, Fax: 413-545-3204. *Application contact:* Lindsay DeSantis, Supervisor of Admissions, 413-545-0722, Fax: 413-577-0010, E-mail: gradadm@grad.umass.edu.
Website: http://www.umass.edu/sociol/

University of Massachusetts Boston, College of Liberal Arts, Program in Applied Sociology, Boston, MA 02125-3393. Offers MA. Part-time and evening/weekend programs available. *Degree requirements:* For master's, comprehensive exam, thesis. *Entrance requirements:* For master's, GRE or MAT, minimum GPA of 2.75. *Application deadline:* For fall admission, 3/1 for domestic students; for spring admission, 11/1 for domestic students. *Expenses:* Tuition, state resident: full-time $2590; part-time $108 per credit. Tuition, nonresident: full-time $9758; part-time $406.50 per credit. Tuition and fees vary according to course load and program. *Financial support:* Research assistantships with full tuition reimbursements, teaching assistantships with full tuition reimbursements, career-related internships or fieldwork, Federal Work-Study, and unspecified assistantships available. Support available to part-time students. Financial award application deadline: 3/1; financial award applicants required to submit FAFSA. *Faculty research:* Sociology of education, social deviance and control, women and development, race and ethnic group relations, criminology. *Unit head:* Dr. Russell Schutt, Director, 617-287-6250, E-mail: russell.schutt@umb.edu. *Application contact:* Peggy Roldan Patel, Graduate Admissions Coordinator, 617-287-6400, Fax: 617-287-6236, E-mail: bos.gadm@dpc.umassp.edu.

University of Massachusetts Boston, College of Liberal Arts, Program in Sociology, Boston, MA 02125-3393. Offers PhD. *Expenses:* Tuition, state resident: full-time $2590; part-time $108 per credit. Tuition, nonresident: full-time $9758; part-time $406.50 per credit. Tuition and fees vary according to course load and program. *Financial support:* Teaching assistantships and unspecified assistantships available. *Unit head:* Dr. Reef Youngreen, Director, 617-287-3909, E-mail: reef.youngreen@umb.edu. *Application contact:* Peggy Roldan Patel, Graduate Admissions Coordinator, 617-287-6400, Fax: 617-287-6236, E-mail: bos.gadm@dpc.umassp.edu.
Website: http://www.umb.edu/academics/cla/sociology/graduate_programs/phd_in_sociology

University of Massachusetts Lowell, College of Fine Arts, Humanities and Social Sciences, Program in Regional Economic and Social Development, Lowell, MA 01854. Offers MA, Graduate Certificate. Part-time programs available. *Entrance requirements:* For master's, GRE. Electronic applications accepted.

University of Memphis, Graduate School, College of Arts and Sciences, Department of Sociology, Memphis, TN 38152. Offers MA. Part-time programs available. *Faculty:* 7 full-time (5 women). *Students:* 13 full-time (8 women), 3 part-time (2 women); includes 6 minority (5 Black or African American, non-Hispanic/Latino; 1 Hispanic/Latino), 1 international. Average age 25. 7 applicants, 71% accepted, 1 enrolled. In 2014, 10 master's awarded. *Degree requirements:* For master's, comprehensive exam, thesis (for some programs). *Entrance requirements:* For master's, GRE General Test, 12 undergraduate hours in sociology. Additional exam requirements/recommendations for international students: Required—TOEFL (minimum score 550 paper-based). *Application deadline:* For fall admission, 7/1 for domestic students, 5/1 for international students; for spring admission, 12/1 for domestic students, 9/15 for international students. Applications are processed on a rolling basis. Application fee: $35 ($60 for international students). Electronic applications accepted. *Financial support:* In 2014–15, 12 students received support, including 9 research assistantships with full tuition reimbursements available (averaging $9,600 per year), 1 teaching assistantship with full tuition reimbursement available (averaging $6,000 per year); Federal Work-Study, scholarships/grants, and unspecified assistantships also available. Financial award application deadline: 2/15; financial award applicants required to submit FAFSA. *Faculty research:* Globalization, medical, inequality, religion, urban. *Unit head:* Dr. Martin Levin, Chair, 901-678-2611, Fax: 901-678-2525. *Application contact:* Dr. Larry Petersen, Professor and Graduate Coordinator, 901-678-3341, Fax: 901-678-2525, E-mail: lpetersn@memphis.edu.
Website: http://sociology.memphis.edu

University of Miami, Graduate School, College of Arts and Sciences, Department of Sociology, Coral Gables, FL 33124. Offers MA, PhD. Part-time programs available. Terminal master's awarded for partial completion of doctoral program. *Degree requirements:* For master's, thesis; for doctorate, comprehensive exam, thesis/dissertation. *Entrance requirements:* For master's and doctorate, GRE General Test. Additional exam requirements/recommendations for international students: Required—TOEFL (minimum score 515 paper-based). Electronic applications accepted. *Faculty research:* Crime, violence, mental health, ethnic relations, health.

University of Miami, Graduate School, School of Education and Human Development, Department of Educational and Psychological Studies, Program in Community and Social Change, Coral Gables, FL 33124. Offers MS Ed. Part-time and evening/weekend programs available. *Degree requirements:* For master's, comprehensive exam. *Entrance requirements:* For master's, GRE General Test. Additional exam requirements/recommendations for international students: Required—TOEFL (minimum score 550 paper-based; 80 iBT); Recommended—IELTS (minimum score 6.5). Electronic applications accepted.

University of Miami, Graduate School, School of Education and Human Development, Department of Teaching and Learning, Program in Education and Social Change, Coral Gables, FL 33124. Offers MS Ed. Part-time and evening/weekend programs available. *Degree requirements:* For master's, electronic portfolio. *Entrance requirements:* For master's, GRE General Test. Additional exam requirements/recommendations for international students: Required—TOEFL (minimum score 550 paper-based; 80 iBT); Recommended—IELTS (minimum score 6.5). Electronic applications accepted.

University of Michigan, Horace H. Rackham School of Graduate Studies, College of Literature, Science, and the Arts, Department of Sociology, Ann Arbor, MI 48109. Offers public policy and sociology (PhD); social work and sociology (PhD); sociology (PhD). *Faculty:* 39 full-time (18 women), 9 part-time/adjunct (2 women). *Students:* 93 full-time (59 women); includes 26 minority (6 Black or African American, non-Hispanic/Latino; 5 Asian, non-Hispanic/Latino; 6 Hispanic/Latino; 9 Two or more races, non-Hispanic/Latino), 11 international. Average age 33. 255 applicants, 13% accepted, 14 enrolled. In 2014, 15 doctorates awarded. *Degree requirements:* For doctorate, comprehensive exam, thesis/dissertation, oral defense of dissertation, preliminary exam. *Entrance requirements:* For doctorate, GRE General Test, letters of recommendation, writing sample, academic statement of purpose, personal statement, transcript. Additional exam requirements/recommendations for international students: Required—TOEFL (minimum score 560 paper-based; 84 iBT). *Application deadline:* For fall admission, 12/15 for domestic and international students. Application fee: $75 ($90 for international students). Electronic applications accepted. *Financial support:* In 2014–15, 85 students received support. Health care benefits available. *Faculty research:* Power, history and social change; gender and sexuality; race and ethnicity; economic sociology; social demography. *Total annual research expenditures:* $269,377. *Unit head:* Alford A. Young, Jr., Chair, 734-764-5554, Fax: 734-763-6887, E-mail: ayoun@umich.edu. *Application contact:* Thea Bude, Graduate Program Coordinator, 734-647-4428, Fax: 734-763-6887, E-mail: sociology.graduate.program@umich.edu.
Website: http://www.lsa.umich.edu/soc/

University of Michigan, School of Social Work, Interdisciplinary Program in Social Work and Social Science, Ann Arbor, MI 48109-1106. Offers social work and anthropology (PhD); social work and economics (PhD); social work and political science (PhD); social work and psychology (PhD); social work and sociology (PhD). Programs offered through the Horace H. Rackham School of Graduate Studies. *Faculty:* 57 full-time (33 women), 6 part-time/adjunct (4 women). *Students:* 64 full-time (46 women); includes 24 minority (7 Black or African American, non-Hispanic/Latino; 11 Asian, non-Hispanic/Latino; 6 Hispanic/Latino), 6 international. Average age 32. 108 applicants, 9% accepted, 9 enrolled. In 2014, 11 doctorates awarded. *Degree requirements:* For doctorate, thesis/dissertation, oral defense of dissertation, preliminary exam. *Entrance requirements:* For doctorate, GRE General Test. Additional exam requirements/recommendations for international students: Required—TOEFL. *Application deadline:* For fall admission, 12/1 for domestic and international students. Application fee: $75 ($90 for international students). *Financial support:* In 2014–15, 64 students received support, including 20 fellowships with full tuition reimbursements available (averaging $15,200 per year), 7 research assistantships with full tuition reimbursements available (averaging $18,971 per year), 19 teaching assistantships with full tuition reimbursements available (averaging $18,971 per year); career-related internships or fieldwork, Federal Work-Study, scholarships/grants, traineeships, health care benefits, tuition waivers (full and partial), and unspecified assistantships also available. Financial award application deadline: 12/1; financial award applicants required to submit FAFSA.

Faculty research: Substance abuse, child welfare, mental health, poverty, aging. *Total annual research expenditures:* $4.1 million. *Unit head:* Dr. Berit Ingersoll-Dayton, Director, 734-763-5768, Fax: 734-615-3192, E-mail: bid@umich.edu. *Application contact:* Graduate Coordinator, 734-647-2554, Fax: 734-615-3192, E-mail: ssw.phd.info@umich.edu.
Website: http://www.ssw.umich.edu/doctoral

University of Minnesota, Duluth, Graduate School, College of Liberal Arts, Department of Sociology/Anthropology, Duluth, MN 55812-2496. Offers criminology (MA); liberal studies (MLS). Part-time programs available. *Degree requirements:* For master's, thesis or alternative. *Entrance requirements:* For master's, interview, minimum GPA of 3.0, letters of recommendation. Additional exam requirements/recommendations for international students: Required—TOEFL. *Faculty research:* Nature of knowledge, philosophy of science, ecology, cultural studies, language.

University of Minnesota, Twin Cities Campus, Graduate School, College of Liberal Arts, Department of Sociology, Minneapolis, MN 55455. Offers MA, PhD. Terminal master's awarded for partial completion of doctoral program. *Degree requirements:* For master's, thesis optional; for doctorate, comprehensive exam, thesis/dissertation, preliminary written and oral exam, prospectus hearing, final oral defense and dissertation. *Entrance requirements:* For doctorate, GRE General Test, bachelor's degree, transcripts, minimum GPA of 3.0, personal statement, three letters of recommendation, writing sample. Additional exam requirements/recommendations for international students: Required—TOEFL (minimum score 587 paper-based; 95 iBT). Electronic applications accepted. *Faculty research:* Organizations, work, and markets; inequality: race, class, and gender; law, crime and deviance; family and life course; political sociology and social movements.

University of Mississippi, Graduate School, College of Liberal Arts, Department of Sociology and Anthropology, University, MS 38677. Offers anthropology (MA); sociology (MA, MSS). *Degree requirements:* For master's, thesis (for some programs). *Entrance requirements:* For master's, GRE General Test, minimum GPA of 3.0. Additional exam requirements/recommendations for international students: Required—TOEFL. Electronic applications accepted.

University of Missouri, Office of Research and Graduate Studies, College of Arts and Science, Department of Sociology, Columbia, MO 65211. Offers MA, PhD. *Faculty:* 14 full-time (6 women). *Students:* 41 full-time (19 women), 9 part-time (6 women); includes 13 minority (5 Black or African American, non-Hispanic/Latino; 1 American Indian or Alaska Native, non-Hispanic/Latino; 6 Hispanic/Latino; 1 Two or more races, non-Hispanic/Latino), 5 international. Average age 33. 31 applicants, 45% accepted, 9 enrolled. In 2014, 1 master's, 7 doctorates awarded. *Degree requirements:* For doctorate, one foreign language, comprehensive exam, thesis/dissertation. *Entrance requirements:* For master's and doctorate, GRE General Test, minimum GPA of 3.0; 15 hours of undergraduate sociology with minimum B average, including one course each in sociological theory and basic statistics. Additional exam requirements/recommendations for international students: Required—TOEFL (minimum score 500 paper-based; 61 iBT). *Application deadline:* For fall admission, 1/15 priority date for domestic students. Applications are processed on a rolling basis. Application fee: $55 ($75 for international students). Electronic applications accepted. *Financial support:* Fellowships with full tuition reimbursements, research assistantships with full tuition reimbursements, teaching assistantships with full tuition reimbursements, institutionally sponsored loans, health care benefits, and unspecified assistantships available. *Faculty research:* Culture and identity, political and economic institutions and social movements, social control and deviance, social inequalities. *Unit head:* Dr. Jay Gubrium, Department Chair, 573-882-8331, E-mail: gubriumj@missouri.edu. *Application contact:* Mary Oakes, Administrative Assistant, 573-882-7163, E-mail: oakesm@missouri.edu.
Website: http://sociology.missouri.edu/graduate/requirements.shtml

University of Missouri–Kansas City, College of Arts and Sciences, Department of Sociology, Kansas City, MO 64110-2499. Offers MA. PhD (interdisciplinary) offered through the School of Graduate Studies. Part-time and evening/weekend programs available. *Faculty:* 9 full-time (6 women), 1 (woman) part-time/adjunct. *Students:* 3 full-time (1 woman), 5 part-time (3 women); includes 1 minority (Black or African American, non-Hispanic/Latino). Average age 33. 12 applicants, 33% accepted, 3 enrolled. In 2014, 1 master's awarded. *Degree requirements:* For master's, thesis optional. *Entrance requirements:* For master's, GRE, minimum GPA of 3.0 in major, 2.7 overall. Additional exam requirements/recommendations for international students: Required—TOEFL (minimum score 550 paper-based; 80 iBT). *Application deadline:* For fall admission, 3/1 for domestic and international students; for spring admission, 11/1 for domestic and international students. Applications are processed on a rolling basis. Application fee: $45 ($50 for international students). Electronic applications accepted. *Financial support:* In 2014–15, 4 teaching assistantships with full and partial tuition reimbursements (averaging $12,600 per year) were awarded; research assistantships with full tuition reimbursements, career-related internships or fieldwork, Federal Work-Study, institutionally sponsored loans, and tuition waivers (partial) also available. Support available to part-time students. Financial award application deadline: 3/1; financial award applicants required to submit FAFSA. *Faculty research:* Gerontology, religious movements, urban community and neighborhoods. *Unit head:* Dr. Deborah Smith, Chair, 816-235-2529, Fax: 816-235-1117, E-mail: smithde@umkc.edu. *Application contact:* Tamera Byland, Director of Admissions, 816-235-1111, Fax: 816-235-5544, E-mail: admit@umkc.edu.
Website: http://cas.umkc.edu/soc/

The University of Montana, Graduate School, College of Humanities and Sciences, Department of Sociology, Missoula, MT 59812-0002. Offers criminology (MA); inequality and social justice (MA); rural and environmental change (MA); sociology (MA). *Entrance requirements:* For master's, GRE General Test. Additional exam requirements/recommendations for international students: Required—TOEFL. *Faculty research:* Housing, homelessness, hunger, infant mortality, work safety.

University of Nebraska at Omaha, Graduate Studies, College of Arts and Sciences, Department of Sociology and Anthropology, Omaha, NE 68182. Offers sociology (MA). Part-time programs available. *Faculty:* 12 full-time (7 women). *Students:* 10 full-time (5 women), 25 part-time (18 women); includes 6 minority (3 Black or African American, non-Hispanic/Latino; 3 Hispanic/Latino), 1 international. Average age 31. 17 applicants, 65% accepted, 10 enrolled. In 2014, 5 master's awarded. *Degree requirements:* For master's, comprehensive exam (for some programs), thesis optional. *Entrance requirements:* For master's, 3 letters of recommendation, resume, statement of purpose, writing sample, minimum GPA of 3.0, official transcripts. Additional exam requirements/recommendations for international students: Required—TOEFL, IELTS, PTE. *Application deadline:* For fall admission, 4/15 for domestic and international students; for spring admission, 11/15 for domestic and international students. Applications are processed on a rolling basis. Application fee: $45. Electronic applications accepted. *Financial support:* In 2014–15, 5 students received support, including 2 research assistantships with tuition reimbursements available, 3 teaching assistantships with tuition reimbursements available; Federal Work-Study, institutionally sponsored loans, scholarships/grants, tuition waivers (partial), and unspecified assistantships also available. Support available to part-time students. Financial award application deadline: 3/1; financial award applicants required to submit FAFSA. *Unit head:* Dr. Mary Ann

Powell, Chairperson, 402-554-2341, E-mail: graduate@unomaha.edu. *Application contact:* Dr. Daniel Hawkins, Graduate Program Chair, 402-554-2341, E-mail: graduate@unomaha.edu.

University of Nebraska–Lincoln, Graduate College, College of Arts and Sciences, Department of Sociology, Lincoln, NE 68588. Offers MA, PhD. *Degree requirements:* For master's, thesis optional; for doctorate, comprehensive exam, thesis/dissertation. *Entrance requirements:* For master's and doctorate, GRE General Test, writing sample. Additional exam requirements/recommendations for international students: Required—TOEFL (minimum score 550 paper-based). Electronic applications accepted. *Faculty research:* Family, deviance and social control, ethnic studies, inequality (gender, race, and class).

University of Nevada, Las Vegas, Graduate College, College of Liberal Arts, Department of Sociology, Las Vegas, NV 89154-5003. Offers MA, PhD. Part-time programs available. *Faculty:* 9 full-time (3 women), 1 part-time/adjunct (0 women). *Students:* 34 full-time (15 women), 15 part-time (10 women); includes 9 minority (3 Black or African American, non-Hispanic/Latino; 1 Asian, non-Hispanic/Latino; 5 Hispanic/Latino), 1 international. Average age 36. 22 applicants, 73% accepted, 7 enrolled. In 2014, 3 master's, 1 doctorate awarded. Terminal master's awarded for partial completion of doctoral program. *Degree requirements:* For master's, thesis, oral exams; for doctorate, comprehensive exam, thesis/dissertation, oral exams. *Entrance requirements:* For master's and doctorate, GRE General Test. Additional exam requirements/recommendations for international students: Required—TOEFL (minimum score 550 paper-based), IELTS (minimum score 7). *Application deadline:* For fall admission, 1/31 for domestic students, 5/1 for international students; for spring admission, 10/1 for international students. Application fee: $60 ($95 for international students). Electronic applications accepted. *Financial support:* In 2014–15, 32 students received support, including 2 fellowships (averaging $15,000 per year), 8 research assistantships with partial tuition reimbursements available (averaging $14,515 per year), 22 teaching assistantships with partial tuition reimbursements available (averaging $13,727 per year); institutionally sponsored loans, scholarships/grants, health care benefits, and unspecified assistantships also available. Financial award application deadline: 3/1. *Faculty research:* Urban and community studies, political sociology and social movements, health and environment, culture, social psychology. *Total annual research expenditures:* $136,323. *Unit head:* Dr. Robert Futrell, Chair/Professor, 702-895-0270, Fax: 702-895-4800, E-mail: robert.futrell@unlv.edu. *Application contact:* Graduate College Admissions Evaluator, 702-895-3320, Fax: 702-895-4180, E-mail: gradcollege@unlv.edu.
Website: http://www.unlv.edu/sociology

University of Nevada, Reno, Graduate School, College of Liberal Arts, School of Social Research and Justice Studies, Department of Sociology, Reno, NV 89557. Offers MA. *Degree requirements:* For master's, thesis optional. *Entrance requirements:* For master's, GRE General Test, minimum GPA of 2.75. Additional exam requirements/recommendations for international students: Required—TOEFL (minimum score 500 paper-based; 61 iBT), IELTS (minimum score 6). Electronic applications accepted. *Faculty research:* Statistics, politics and economics, religion and law, industry, theory stratification.

University of New Brunswick Fredericton, School of Graduate Studies, Faculty of Arts, Department of Sociology, Fredericton, NB E3B 5A3, Canada. Offers MA, PhD. Part-time programs available. *Faculty:* 13 full-time (9 women), 13 part-time/adjunct (7 women). *Students:* 20 full-time (12 women), 11 part-time (6 women). In 2014, 1 master's, 3 doctorates awarded. *Degree requirements:* For master's, thesis; for doctorate, comprehensive exam, thesis/dissertation, 6 courses. *Entrance requirements:* For master's, minimum GPA of 3.5; for doctorate, MA in sociology with thesis or equivalent, curriculum vitae, statement of interest about intended research and why UNB was selected. Additional exam requirements/recommendations for international students: Required—TOEFL. *Application deadline:* For fall admission, 3/1 for domestic students; for winter admission, 1/15 priority date for domestic and international students. Applications are processed on a rolling basis. Application fee: $50 Canadian dollars. Electronic applications accepted. *Financial support:* Fellowships, research assistantships, and teaching assistantships with tuition reimbursements available. *Faculty research:* Social policy, media, sociology and cooperative economy, charities and philanthropy, gender health and entrepreneurship, reproductive health and women, international development, criminology, environment, science and technology, family and domestic violence, sociology of health, health policy and social determinants of health, law and social policy. *Unit head:* Dr. Vanda Rideout, Acting Director of Graduate Studies, 506-447-3393, Fax: 506-453-4659, E-mail: vrideout@unb.ca. *Application contact:* Wanda Birch, Acting Graduate Secretary, 506-458-7474, Fax: 506-453-4659, E-mail: wanda.birch@unb.ca.
Website: http://go.unb.ca/gradprograms

University of New Hampshire, Graduate School, College of Liberal Arts, Department of Sociology, Durham, NH 03824. Offers MA, PhD. Part-time programs available. *Faculty:* 12 full-time (4 women). *Students:* 29 full-time (15 women), 8 part-time (all women); includes 7 minority (2 Asian, non-Hispanic/Latino; 5 Hispanic/Latino). Average age 31. 36 applicants, 42% accepted, 7 enrolled. In 2014, 4 master's, 2 doctorates awarded. *Degree requirements:* For master's, thesis; for doctorate, one foreign language, thesis/dissertation. *Entrance requirements:* For master's and doctorate, GRE General Test. Additional exam requirements/recommendations for international students: Required—TOEFL (minimum score 550 paper-based; 80 iBT). *Application deadline:* For fall admission, 4/1 priority date for domestic students, 4/1 for international students; for spring admission, 12/1 for domestic students. Applications are processed on a rolling basis. Application fee: $65. Electronic applications accepted. *Expenses:* Tuition, state resident: full-time $13,500; part-time $750 per credit hour. Tuition, nonresident: full-time $26,460; part-time $1110 per credit hour. *Required fees:* $1788; $447 per semester. *Financial support:* In 2014–15, 20 students received support, including 1 fellowship, 1 research assistantship, 18 teaching assistantships; career-related internships or fieldwork, Federal Work-Study, scholarships/grants, and tuition waivers (full and partial) also available. Support available to part-time students. Financial award application deadline: 2/15. *Faculty research:* Deviance, conflict and control, social psychology, comparative institutional analysis, family. *Unit head:* Dr. Michelle Dillon, Chairperson, 603-862-2500. *Application contact:* Deena Peschke, Administrative Assistant, 603-862-2500, E-mail: sociology.dept@unh.edu.
Website: http://www.cola.unh.edu/sociology/

University of New Mexico, Graduate School, College of Arts and Sciences, Program in Sociology, Albuquerque, NM 87131. Offers MA, PhD. Part-time programs available. *Faculty:* 16 full-time (7 women), 1 part-time/adjunct (0 women). *Students:* 25 full-time (14 women), 15 part-time (10 women); includes 14 minority (1 Black or African American, non-Hispanic/Latino; 12 Hispanic/Latino; 1 Two or more races, non-Hispanic/Latino), 3 international. Average age 33. 41 applicants, 32% accepted, 6 enrolled. In 2014, 4 master's awarded. Terminal master's awarded for partial completion of doctoral program. *Degree requirements:* For master's, thesis; for doctorate, comprehensive exam, thesis/dissertation. *Entrance requirements:* For master's and doctorate, GRE General Test, 2 writing samples, 3 letters of reference, letter of intent. Additional exam requirements/recommendations for international students: Required—TOEFL (minimum score 550 paper-based; 79 iBT), IELTS (minimum score 7). *Application deadline:* For fall admission, 1/15 priority date for domestic and international students; for spring admission, 9/30 for domestic students. Application fee: $50. Electronic applications accepted. *Financial support:* In 2014–15, 25 students received support, including 3 fellowships (averaging $24,000 per year), 25 teaching assistantships with partial tuition reimbursements available (averaging $12,500 per year); research assistantships, institutionally sponsored loans, scholarships/grants, health care benefits, tuition waivers (partial), and unspecified assistantships also available. Support available to part-time students. Financial award application deadline: 1/15; financial award applicants required to submit FAFSA. *Faculty research:* Criminology/crime/law/social control, sociology of health and medicine, social movements, race and ethnicity, comparative sociology, Latin American comparative sociology, political sociology, sociology of science and knowledge, sociology of education. *Total annual research expenditures:* $696,098. *Unit head:* Dr. Richard Santos, Interim Departmental Chair, 505-277-2501, Fax: 505-277-8805, E-mail: santos@unm.edu. *Application contact:* Shannon Kindilien, Academic Advisor, 505-277-2501, Fax: 505-277-8805, E-mail: sadvisor@unm.edu.
Website: http://www.unm.edu/~socdept/

University of New Orleans, Graduate School, College of Liberal Arts, Department of Sociology, New Orleans, LA 70148. Offers MA. Part-time and evening/weekend programs available. *Degree requirements:* For master's, thesis (for some programs). *Entrance requirements:* For master's, GRE General Test. Additional exam requirements/recommendations for international students: Required—TOEFL (minimum score 550 paper-based; 79 iBT), IELTS (minimum score 6.5). Electronic applications accepted. *Faculty research:* Environment and gender.

The University of North Carolina at Chapel Hill, Graduate School, College of Arts and Sciences, Department of Sociology, Chapel Hill, NC 27599. Offers MA, PhD. *Degree requirements:* For master's, comprehensive exam, thesis; for doctorate, comprehensive exam, thesis/dissertation. *Entrance requirements:* For master's and doctorate, GRE General Test, minimum GPA of 3.0. Additional exam requirements/recommendations for international students: Required—TOEFL (minimum score 550 paper-based). Electronic applications accepted. *Faculty research:* Comparative historical, work/organizations, religion, demography, stratification.

The University of North Carolina at Charlotte, College of Liberal Arts and Sciences, Department of Sociology, Charlotte, NC 28223-0001. Offers health research (MA); mathematical sociology and quantitative methods (MA); organizations, occupations, and work (MA); political sociology (MA); race and gender (MA); social psychology (MA); social theory (MA); sociology of education (MA); stratification (MA). Part-time and evening/weekend programs available. *Faculty:* 16 full-time (10 women). *Students:* 11 full-time (5 women), 2 part-time (0 women); includes 5 minority (4 Black or African American, non-Hispanic/Latino; 1 Hispanic/Latino), 1 international. Average age 29. 14 applicants, 71% accepted, 5 enrolled. In 2014, 6 master's awarded. *Degree requirements:* For master's, thesis or comprehensive exam. *Entrance requirements:* For master's, GRE or MAT, minimum GPA of 3.0 in last 2 years, 2.75 overall. Additional exam requirements/recommendations for international students: Required—TOEFL (minimum score 557 paper-based; 83 iBT). *Application deadline:* For fall admission, 4/15 for domestic and international students; for spring admission, 10/1 for domestic and international students. Application fee: $75. Electronic applications accepted. *Expenses:* Tuition, state resident: full-time $4008. Tuition, nonresident: full-time $16,295. *Required fees:* $2755. Tuition and fees vary according to course load and program. *Financial support:* In 2014–15, 10 students received support, including 5 research assistantships (averaging $10,400 per year), 5 teaching assistantships (averaging $9,200 per year); career-related internships or fieldwork, institutionally sponsored loans, scholarships/grants, and unspecified assistantships also available. Support available to part-time students. Financial award application deadline: 4/1; financial award applicants required to submit FAFSA. *Faculty research:* Impact of race on high school course selection; income inequality within the United States and cross-nationally; small group interaction, nonverbal behaviors, identity, emotions, gender, and expectations; mathematical models of social processes. *Total annual research expenditures:* $413,099. *Unit head:* Dr. Lisa Walker, Chair, 704-687-7825, Fax: 704-687-3091, E-mail: lisa.walker@uncc.edu. *Application contact:* Kathy B. Giddings, Director of Graduate Admissions, 704-687-5503, Fax: 704-687-1668, E-mail: gradadm@uncc.edu.
Website: http://sociology.uncc.edu/

The University of North Carolina at Greensboro, Graduate School, College of Arts and Sciences, Department of Sociology, Greensboro, NC 27412-5001. Offers criminology (MA); sociology (MA). Part-time programs available. *Degree requirements:* For master's, comprehensive exam, thesis. *Entrance requirements:* For master's, GRE General Test. Additional exam requirements/recommendations for international students: Required—TOEFL. Electronic applications accepted.

The University of North Carolina Wilmington, College of Arts and Sciences, Department of Sociology and Criminology, Wilmington, NC 28403-3297. Offers MA. *Faculty:* 18 full-time (11 women). *Students:* 15 full-time (9 women), 8 part-time (6 women); includes 4 minority (3 Black or African American, non-Hispanic/Latino; 1 Hispanic/Latino). 26 applicants, 81% accepted, 11 enrolled. In 2014, 10 master's awarded. *Degree requirements:* For master's, comprehensive exam, thesis or internship. *Entrance requirements:* Additional exam requirements/recommendations for international students: Required—TOEFL (minimum score 79 iBT), IELTS. *Application deadline:* For fall admission, 2/15 for domestic students. Application fee: $60. Electronic applications accepted. *Expenses:* Tuition, state resident: full-time $3240. Tuition, nonresident: full-time $9208. *Required fees:* $1967. *Financial support:* Unspecified assistantships available. Financial award applicants required to submit FAFSA. *Unit head:* Dr. Leslie Hossfeld, Chair, 910-962-7849, Fax: 910-962-7385, E-mail: hossfeldl@uncw.edu. *Application contact:* Dr. Christina Lanier, Graduate Coordinator, 910-962-7691, Fax: 910-962-7385, E-mail: lanierc@uncw.edu.
Website: http://www.uncw.edu/socgrad/index.html

University of North Dakota, Graduate School, College of Arts and Sciences, Department of Sociology, Grand Forks, ND 58202. Offers MA. *Degree requirements:* For master's, thesis, final examination. *Entrance requirements:* For master's, minimum GPA of 3.0. Additional exam requirements/recommendations for international students: Required—TOEFL (minimum score 550 paper-based; 79 iBT), IELTS (minimum score 6.5). Electronic applications accepted. *Faculty research:* Criminal justice studies, social psychology, research methods, corrections, social theory.

University of Northern Colorado, Graduate School, College of Humanities and Social Sciences, School of Sociology and Criminal Justice, Greeley, CO 80639. Offers criminal justice (MA); sociology (MA).

University of North Texas, Robert B. Toulouse School of Graduate Studies, Denton, TX 76203-5459. Offers accounting (MS); applied anthropology (MA, MS); applied behavior analysis (Certificate); applied geography (MA); applied technology and performance improvement (M Ed, MS); art education (MA); art history (MA); art museum education (Certificate); arts leadership (Certificate); audiology (Au D); behavior analysis (MS); behavioral science (PhD); biochemistry and molecular biology (MS); biology (MA, MS); biomedical engineering (MS); business analysis (MS); chemistry (MS); clinical health psychology (PhD); communication studies (MA, MS); computer engineering (MS);

computer science (MS); counseling (M Ed, MS), including clinical mental health counseling (MS), college and university counseling, elementary school counseling, secondary school counseling; creative writing (MA); criminal justice (MS); curriculum and instruction (M Ed); decision sciences (MBA); design (MA, MFA), including fashion design (MFA), innovation studies, interior design (MFA); early childhood studies (MS); economics (MS); educational leadership (M Ed, Ed D); educational psychology (MS, PhD), including family studies (MS), gifted and talented (MS), human development (MS), learning and cognition (MS), research, measurement and evaluation (MS); electrical engineering (MS); emergency management (MPA); engineering technology (MS); English (MA); English as a second language (MA); environmental science (MS); finance (MBA, MS); financial management (MPA); French (MA); health services management (MBA); higher education (M Ed, Ed D); history (MA, MS); hospitality management (MS); human resources management (MPA); information science (MS); information systems (PhD); information technologies (MBA); interdisciplinary studies (MA, MS); international studies (MA); international sustainable tourism (MS); jazz studies (MM); journalism (MA, MJ, Graduate Certificate), including interactive and virtual digital communication (Graduate Certificate), narrative journalism (Graduate Certificate), public relations (Graduate Certificate); kinesiology (MS); linguistics (MA); local government management (MPA); logistics (PhD); logistics and supply chain management (MBA); long-term care, senior housing, and aging services (MA); management (PhD); marketing (MBA); mathematics (MA, MS); mechanical and energy engineering (MS, PhD); music (MA), including ethnomusicology, music theory, musicology, performance; music composition (PhD); music education (MM Ed, PhD); nonprofit management (MPA); operations and supply chain management (MBA); performance (MM, DMA); philosophy (MA); political science (MA); professional and technical communication (MA); radio, television and film (MA, MFA); rehabilitation counseling (Certificate); sociology (MA); Spanish (MA); special education (M Ed); speech-language pathology (MA); strategic management (MBA); studio art (MFA); teaching (M Ed); MBA/MS. Part-time and evening/weekend programs available. Postbaccalaureate distance learning degree programs offered. *Faculty:* 651 full-time (215 women), 233 part-time/adjunct (139 women). *Students:* 3,040 full-time (1,598 women), 3,401 part-time (2,097 women); includes 1,740 minority (533 Black or African American, non-Hispanic/Latino; 15 American Indian or Alaska Native, non-Hispanic/Latino; 286 Asian, non-Hispanic/Latino; 746 Hispanic/Latino; 3 Native Hawaiian or other Pacific Islander, non-Hispanic/Latino; 157 Two or more races, non-Hispanic/Latino), 1,145 international. Terminal master's awarded for partial completion of doctoral program. *Degree requirements:* For master's, variable foreign language requirement, comprehensive exam (for some programs), thesis (for some programs); for doctorate, variable foreign language requirement, comprehensive exam (for some programs), thesis/dissertation; for other advanced degree, variable foreign language requirement, comprehensive exam (for some programs). *Entrance requirements:* For master's and doctorate, GRE, GMAT. Additional exam requirements/recommendations for international students: Required—TOEFL (minimum score 550 paper-based; 79 iBT). *Application deadline:* For fall admission, 7/15 for domestic students, 3/15 for international students; for spring admission, 11/15 for domestic students, 9/15 for international students; for summer admission, 5/1 for domestic students. Applications are processed on a rolling basis. Application fee: $60. Electronic applications accepted. *Expenses:* Tuition, state resident: full-time $5450; part-time $3633 per year. Tuition, nonresident: full-time $11,966; part-time $7977 per year. *Required fees:* $1301; $398 per credit hour. $685 per semester. Tuition and fees vary according to program and reciprocity agreements. *Financial support:* Fellowships with partial tuition reimbursements, research assistantships with partial tuition reimbursements, teaching assistantships, career-related internships or fieldwork, Federal Work-Study, institutionally sponsored loans, scholarships/grants, health care benefits, and library assistantships available. Support available to part-time students. Financial award applicants required to submit FAFSA. *Unit head:* Mark Wardell, Dean, 940-565-2383, E-mail: mark.wardell@unt.edu. *Application contact:* Toulouse School of Graduate Studies, 940-565-2383, Fax: 940-565-2141, E-mail: gradsch@unt.edu. Website: http://tsgs.unt.edu/

University of Notre Dame, Graduate School, College of Arts and Letters, Division of Social Science, Department of Sociology, Notre Dame, IN 46556. Offers PhD. *Degree requirements:* For doctorate, thesis/dissertation, 2 area specialty exams. *Entrance requirements:* For doctorate, GRE General Test, GRE Subject Test (strongly recommended). Additional exam requirements/recommendations for international students: Required—TOEFL (minimum score 600 paper-based; 80 iBT). Electronic applications accepted. *Faculty research:* Cultural sociology, development, family, education, historical/comparative sociology.

University of Oklahoma, College of Arts and Sciences, Department of Sociology, Norman, OK 73019. Offers MA, PhD. Part-time programs available. *Faculty:* 13 full-time (9 women), 1 part-time/adjunct (0 women). *Students:* 24 full-time (14 women), 12 part-time (8 women); includes 7 minority (1 Black or African American, non-Hispanic/Latino; 1 American Indian or Alaska Native, non-Hispanic/Latino; 1 Asian, non-Hispanic/Latino; 2 Hispanic/Latino; 1 Native Hawaiian or other Pacific Islander, non-Hispanic/Latino; 1 Two or more races, non-Hispanic/Latino), 1 international. Average age 31. 20 applicants, 70% accepted, 9 enrolled. In 2014, 4 master's, 1 doctorate awarded. Terminal master's awarded for partial completion of doctoral program. *Degree requirements:* For master's, comprehensive exam (for some programs), thesis; for doctorate, comprehensive exam, thesis/dissertation. *Entrance requirements:* For master's and doctorate, GRE. Additional exam requirements/recommendations for international students: Required—TOEFL (minimum score 79 iBT). *Application deadline:* For fall admission, 1/1 for domestic and international students; for spring admission, 11/1 for domestic students, 9/1 for international students. Application fee: $50 ($100 for international students). Electronic applications accepted. *Expenses:* Tuition, state resident: full-time $4394; part-time $183.10 per credit hour. Tuition, nonresident: full-time $16,970; part-time $707.10 per credit hour. *Required fees:* $2892; $109.95 per credit hour. $126.50 per semester. *Financial support:* In 2014–15, 26 students received support, including 8 fellowships with full tuition reimbursements available (averaging $3,500 per year), 1 research assistantship with partial tuition reimbursement available (averaging $13,956 per year), 22 teaching assistantships with partial tuition reimbursements available (averaging $14,921 per year); health care benefits, unspecified assistantships, and summer research fellowships also available. Financial award application deadline: 6/1; financial award applicants required to submit FAFSA. *Faculty research:* Stigma and deviant behavior, incarcerated women and their families, immigrant adaptation, peer influence on pro-social and anti-social behavior, inequality and world systems theory. *Total annual research expenditures:* $50,949. *Unit head:* Dr. Craig St. John, Professor and Department Chair, 405-325-1751, Fax: 405-325-7825, E-mail: cstjohn@ou.edu. *Application contact:* Dr. Trina Hope, Associate Professor and Graduate Director, 405-325-1751, Fax: 405-325-7825, E-mail: thope@ou.edu. Website: http://www.ou.edu/soc

University of Oregon, Graduate School, College of Arts and Sciences, Department of Sociology, Eugene, OR 97403. Offers MA, MS, PhD. Part-time programs available. Terminal master's awarded for partial completion of doctoral program. *Degree requirements:* For doctorate, thesis/dissertation. *Entrance requirements:* For master's and doctorate, GRE General Test, minimum GPA of 3.0. Additional exam requirements/

recommendations for international students: Required—TOEFL. *Faculty research:* Criminology, environment, gender, labor, political economy.

University of Ottawa, Faculty of Graduate and Postdoctoral Studies, Faculty of Social Sciences, Department of Sociology and Anthropology, Ottawa, ON K1N 6N5, Canada. Offers MA. *Degree requirements:* For master's, thesis or alternative. *Entrance requirements:* For master's, honors bachelor's degree or equivalent, minimum B average. Electronic applications accepted. *Faculty research:* Inter-ethnic relations, development, political policies.

University of Pennsylvania, School of Arts and Sciences, Graduate Group in Sociology, Philadelphia, PA 19104. Offers AM, PhD. *Faculty:* 37 full-time (17 women), 8 part-time/adjunct (3 women). *Students:* 49 full-time (34 women), 1 part-time (0 women); includes 16 minority (6 Black or African American, non-Hispanic/Latino; 4 Asian, non-Hispanic/Latino; 6 Hispanic/Latino), 17 international. 218 applicants, 8% accepted, 7 enrolled. In 2014, 5 master's, 7 doctorates awarded. Terminal master's awarded for partial completion of doctoral program. *Degree requirements:* For master's, thesis or alternative; for doctorate, one foreign language, thesis/dissertation. *Entrance requirements:* For master's and doctorate, GRE General Test. Additional exam requirements/recommendations for international students: Required—TOEFL. *Application deadline:* For fall admission, 12/1 priority date for domestic students. Application fee: $70. Electronic applications accepted. *Financial support:* Fellowships, teaching assistantships, institutionally sponsored loans, scholarships/grants, traineeships, health care benefits, and unspecified assistantships available. Financial award application deadline: 12/15. *Unit head:* Dr. Ralph M. Rosen, Associate Dean for Graduate Studies, 215-898-7156, Fax: 215-573-8068, E-mail: graddean@sas.upenn.edu. *Application contact:* Arts and Sciences Graduate Admissions, 215-573-5816, Fax: 215-573-8068, E-mail: gdasadmis@sas.upenn.edu. Website: http://sociology.sas.upenn.edu/graduate_resources

University of Pittsburgh, Dietrich School of Arts and Sciences, Department of Sociology, Pittsburgh, PA 15260. Offers MA, PhD. Part-time programs available. *Faculty:* 16 full-time (9 women), 6 part-time/adjunct (2 women). *Students:* 37 full-time (21 women), 2 part-time (1 woman); includes 8 minority (3 Black or African American, non-Hispanic/Latino; 2 American Indian or Alaska Native, non-Hispanic/Latino; 1 Asian, non-Hispanic/Latino; 2 Hispanic/Latino), 11 international. Average age 28. 73 applicants, 25% accepted, 4 enrolled. In 2014, 1 master's, 2 doctorates awarded. Terminal master's awarded for partial completion of doctoral program. *Degree requirements:* For master's, thesis; for doctorate, comprehensive exam, thesis/dissertation, preliminary exam. *Entrance requirements:* For master's and doctorate, GRE General Test, writing sample. Additional exam requirements/recommendations for international students: Required—TOEFL (minimum score 550 paper-based; 90 iBT). *Application deadline:* For fall admission, 1/15 priority date for domestic and international students. Application fee: $50. Electronic applications accepted. *Expenses:* Tuition, state resident: full-time $20,742; part-time $838 per credit. Tuition, nonresident: full-time $33,960; part-time $1389 per credit. *Required fees:* $800; $205 per term. Tuition and fees vary according to program. *Financial support:* In 2014–15, 26 students received support, including 9 fellowships with full tuition reimbursements available, 3 research assistantships with full tuition reimbursements available, 14 teaching assistantships with full tuition reimbursements available; Federal Work-Study, scholarships/grants, health care benefits, tuition waivers (full and partial), and unspecified assistantships also available. Financial award application deadline: 1/15. *Faculty research:* Collective behavior/social movements, comparative sociology/historical sociology, cultural sociology, political sociology, qualitative methodology, quantitative methodology, sex and gender, social change, theory. *Unit head:* Dr. Suzanne Staggenborg, Chair, 412-648-7584, Fax: 412-648-2799, E-mail: suzstagg@pitt.edu. *Application contact:* Lizzy Stoyle, Graduate Administrator, 412-648-7585, Fax: 412-648-2799, E-mail: ess16@pitt.edu. Website: http://www.sociology.pitt.edu/graduate/

University of Puerto Rico, Río Piedras Campus, College of Social Sciences, Department of Sociology, San Juan, PR 00931-3300. Offers MA. *Degree requirements:* For master's, comprehensive exam, thesis. *Entrance requirements:* For master's, GRE or PAEG, interview, minimum GPA of 3.0, letter of recommendation.

University of Regina, Faculty of Graduate Studies and Research, Faculty of Arts, Department of Sociology and Social Studies, Regina, SK S4S 0A2, Canada. Offers social studies (MA); sociology (MA). Part-time programs available. *Faculty:* 10 full-time (5 women), 6 part-time/adjunct (1 woman). *Students:* 13 full-time (5 women), 3 part-time (all women). 19 applicants, 47% accepted. In 2014, 4 master's awarded. *Degree requirements:* For master's, thesis. *Entrance requirements:* Additional exam requirements/recommendations for international students: Required—TOEFL (minimum score 580 paper-based; 80 iBT), IELTS (minimum score 6.5), PTE (minimum score 59). *Application deadline:* Applications are processed on a rolling basis. Application fee: $100. Electronic applications accepted. *Expenses:* Tuition, area resident: Full-time $4900 Canadian dollars; part-time $837.65 Canadian dollars per semester. *International tuition:* $7900 Canadian dollars full-time. *Required fees:* $396 Canadian dollars; $86.90 Canadian dollars per semester. *Financial support:* In 2014–15, 5 teaching assistantships (averaging $2,427 per year) were awarded; fellowships, research assistantships, and scholarships/grants also available. Financial award application deadline: 6/15. *Faculty research:* Social justice, international development, globalization, social policy, political economy. *Unit head:* Dr. John Conway, Department Head, 306-585-4052, Fax: 306-585-4815, E-mail: john.conway@uregina.ca. *Application contact:* Dr. Henry Chow, Graduate Coordinator, 306-585-5604, Fax: 306-585-4815, E-mail: henry.chow@uregina.ca. Website: http://www.uregina.ca/arts/sociology-social-studies

University of Saskatchewan, College of Graduate Studies and Research, College of Arts and Science, Department of Sociology, Saskatoon, SK S7N 5A2, Canada. Offers MA, PhD. *Degree requirements:* For master's, thesis; for doctorate, comprehensive exam (for some programs), thesis/dissertation. *Entrance requirements:* Additional exam requirements/recommendations for international students: Required—TOEFL (minimum score 80 iBT); Recommended—IELTS (minimum score 6.5). Electronic applications accepted.

University of South Africa, College of Human Sciences, Pretoria, South Africa. Offers adult education (M Ed); African languages (MA, PhD); African politics (MA, PhD); Afrikaans (MA, PhD); ancient history (MA, PhD); ancient Near Eastern studies (MA, PhD); anthropology (MA, PhD); applied linguistics (MA); Arabic (MA, PhD); archaeology (MA); art history (MA); Biblical archaeology (MA); Biblical studies (M Th, D Th, PhD); Christian spirituality (M Th, D Th); church history (M Th, D Th); classical studies (MA, PhD); clinical psychology (MA); communication (MA, PhD); comparative education (M Ed, Ed D); consulting psychology (D Admin, D Com, PhD); curriculum studies (M Ed, Ed D); development studies (M Admin, MA, D Admin, PhD); didactics (M Ed, Ed D); education (M Tech); education management (M Ed, Ed D); educational psychology (M Ed); English (MA); environmental education (M Ed); French (MA, PhD); German (MA, PhD); Greek (MA); guidance and counseling (M Ed); health studies (MA, PhD), including health sciences education (MA), health services management (MA), medical and surgical nursing science (critical care general) (MA), midwifery and neonatal nursing science (MA), trauma and emergency care (MA); history (MA, PhD); history of education

(Ed D); inclusive education (M Ed, Ed D); information and communications technology policy and regulation (MA); information science (MA, MIS, PhD); international politics (MA, PhD); Islamic studies (MA, PhD); Italian (MA, PhD); Judaica (MA, PhD); linguistics (MA, PhD); mathematical education (M Ed); mathematics education (MA); missiology (M Th, D Th); modern Hebrew (MA, PhD); musicology (MA, MMus, D Mus, PhD); natural science education (M Ed); New Testament (M Th, D Th); Old Testament (D Th); pastoral therapy (M Th, D Th); philosophy (MA); philosophy of education (M Ed, Ed D); politics (MA, PhD); Portuguese (MA, PhD); practical theology (M Th, D Th); psychology (MA, MS, PhD); psychology of education (M Ed, Ed D); public health (MA); religious studies (MA, D Th, PhD); Romance languages (MA); Russian (MA, PhD); Semitic languages (MA, PhD); social behavior studies in HIV/AIDS (MA); social science (mental health) (MA); social science in development studies (MA); social science in psychology (MA); social science in social work (MA); social science in sociology (MA); social work (MSW, DSW, PhD); socio-education (M Ed, Ed D); sociolinguistics (MA); sociology (MA, PhD); Spanish (MA, PhD); systematic theology (M Th, D Th); TESOL (teaching English to speakers of other languages) (MA); theological ethics (M Th, D Th); theory of literature (MA, PhD); urban ministries (D Th); urban ministry (M Th).

University of South Carolina, The Graduate School, College of Arts and Sciences, Department of Sociology, Columbia, SC 29208. Offers MA, PhD. Part-time programs available. Terminal master's awarded for partial completion of doctoral program. *Degree requirements:* For master's, thesis; for doctorate, comprehensive exam, thesis/dissertation. *Entrance requirements:* For master's and doctorate, GRE General Test. Additional exam requirements/recommendations for international students: Required—TOEFL (minimum score 570 paper-based; 75 iBT). Electronic applications accepted. *Faculty research:* Social psychology, social inequality.

University of Southern California, Graduate School, Dana and David Dornsife College of Letters, Arts and Sciences, Department of Sociology, Los Angeles, CA 90089. Offers PhD. *Degree requirements:* For doctorate, comprehensive exam, thesis/dissertation. *Entrance requirements:* For doctorate, GRE. Additional exam requirements/recommendations for international students: Required—TOEFL. Electronic applications accepted. *Faculty research:* Family, immigration, gender, culture, race.

University of South Florida, College of Arts and Sciences, Department of Sociology, Tampa, FL 33620-9951. Offers MA, PhD. Part-time programs available. *Faculty:* 13 full-time (9 women). *Students:* 34 full-time (21 women), 5 part-time (3 women); includes 6 minority (1 Black or African American, non-Hispanic/Latino; 2 Asian, non-Hispanic/Latino; 2 Hispanic/Latino; 1 Two or more races, non-Hispanic/Latino), 6 international. Average age 30. 38 applicants, 39% accepted, 11 enrolled. In 2014, 9 master's awarded. *Degree requirements:* For master's, comprehensive exam, thesis; for doctorate, comprehensive exam, thesis/dissertation. *Entrance requirements:* For master's, GRE General Test (minimum preferred scores of 153 verbal and 144 quantitative), minimum GPA of 3.25 in undergraduate coursework, three letters of recommendation, personal statement (1-3 pages), academic writing sample; for doctorate, GRE General Test (minimum preferred scores of 150 verbal and 144 quantitative, 600 verbal and 500 quantitative on old scoring), minimum GPA of 3.5 in graduate work, three letters of recommendation, personal statement, writing sample. Additional exam requirements/recommendations for international students: Required—TOEFL (minimum score 550 paper-based; 79 iBT) or IELTS (minimum score 6.5) for PhD; TOEFL (minimum score 600 paper-based) for MA. *Application deadline:* For fall admission, 2/15 priority date for domestic students, 1/2 priority date for international students; for spring admission, 10/15 for domestic students, 6/1 priority date for international students. Application fee: $30. Electronic applications accepted. *Financial support:* In 2014–15, 21 students received support, including 21 teaching assistantships with tuition reimbursements available (averaging $12,581 per year); unspecified assistantships also available. Financial award application deadline: 3/1. *Faculty research:* Urban development and culture; social inequalities; identities and communities; social problems and social movements; globalization, power, and politics; immigration and migration; community, networks, and wellbeing. *Total annual research expenditures:* $1 million. *Unit head:* Dr. Elizabeth Aranda, Associate Professor and Chairperson, 813-974-7690, Fax: 813-974-6455, E-mail: earanda@usf.edu. *Application contact:* Dr. Margarethe Kusenbach, Associate Professor, 813-974-2595, Fax: 813-974-6455, E-mail: mkusenba@usf.edu.
Website: http://sociology.usf.edu

The University of Tennessee, Graduate School, College of Arts and Sciences, Department of Sociology, Knoxville, TN 37996. Offers criminology (MA, PhD); energy, environment, and resource policy (MA, PhD); political economy (MA, PhD). Part-time programs available. *Degree requirements:* For master's, thesis or alternative; for doctorate, thesis/dissertation. *Entrance requirements:* For master's, GRE General Test, minimum GPA of 3.0; for doctorate, GRE General Test, minimum GPA of 3.5. Additional exam requirements/recommendations for international students: Required—TOEFL. Electronic applications accepted.

The University of Texas at Arlington, Graduate School, College of Liberal Arts, Department of Sociology and Anthropology, Program in Sociology, Arlington, TX 76019. Offers MA. Part-time and evening/weekend programs available. *Degree requirements:* For master's, comprehensive exam, thesis or alternative. *Entrance requirements:* For master's, GRE General Test, 12 hours of undergraduate course work in sociology. Additional exam requirements/recommendations for international students: Required—TOEFL (minimum score 550 paper-based). Electronic applications accepted.

The University of Texas at Austin, Graduate School, College of Liberal Arts, Department of Sociology, Austin, TX 78712-1111. Offers MA, PhD. *Degree requirements:* For master's, thesis; for doctorate, thesis/dissertation. *Entrance requirements:* For master's and doctorate, GRE General Test. Additional exam requirements/recommendations for international students: Required—TOEFL. Electronic applications accepted. *Faculty research:* Criminology, demography, Latin America, health, political sociology.

The University of Texas at Brownsville, Graduate Studies, College of Liberal Arts, Department of Behavioral Sciences, Brownsville, TX 78520-4991. Offers psychology (MA); sociology (MAIS). Part-time and evening/weekend programs available. *Degree requirements:* For master's, comprehensive exam (for some programs), thesis optional, capstone experience. *Entrance requirements:* For master's, GRE General Test, letters of recommendation. Additional exam requirements/recommendations for international students: Required—TOEFL (minimum score 550 paper-based; 77 iBT). Electronic applications accepted.

The University of Texas at Dallas, School of Economic, Political and Policy Sciences, Program in Public Affairs and Sociology, Richardson, TX 75080. Offers applied sociology (MS); public affairs (MPA, PhD). *Accreditation:* NASPAA. Part-time and evening/weekend programs available. *Faculty:* 13 full-time (5 women), 3 part-time/adjunct (0 women). *Students:* 39 full-time (25 women), 64 part-time (40 women); includes 36 minority (15 Black or African American, non-Hispanic/Latino; 3 Asian, non-Hispanic/Latino; 15 Hispanic/Latino; 3 Two or more races, non-Hispanic/Latino), 15 international. Average age 37. 98 applicants, 45% accepted, 20 enrolled. In 2014, 23 master's, 14 doctorates awarded. *Degree requirements:* For master's, internship; for doctorate, thesis/dissertation. *Entrance requirements:* For master's and doctorate, GRE

(minimum combined score of 1000 on verbal and quantitative), minimum GPA of 3.0 in upper-level course work in field. Additional exam requirements/recommendations for international students: Required—TOEFL (minimum score 550 paper-based). *Application deadline:* For fall admission, 7/15 for domestic students, 5/1 priority date for international students; for spring admission, 11/15 for domestic students, 9/1 priority date for international students. Applications are processed on a rolling basis. Application fee: $50 ($100 for international students). Electronic applications accepted. *Expenses:* Tuition, state resident: full-time $11,940; part-time $663 per credit. Tuition, nonresident: full-time $22,282; part-time $1238 per credit. *Financial support:* In 2014–15, 46 students received support, including 9 teaching assistantships with partial tuition reimbursements available (averaging $12,222 per year); research assistantships with partial tuition reimbursements available, career-related internships or fieldwork, Federal Work-Study, institutionally sponsored loans, and scholarships/grants also available. Support available to part-time students. Financial award application deadline: 4/30; financial award applicants required to submit FAFSA. *Faculty research:* Corporate citizenship and urban problem solving, policy analysis, presidential decision-making, hazardous material safety, emergency management. *Unit head:* Dr. Sheryl Skaggs, Program Head, 972-883-4460, Fax: 972-883-2735, E-mail: slskaggs@utdallas.edu. *Application contact:* Dr. Katie Doctor, Graduate Program Administrator, 972-883-4936, Fax: 972-883-2735, E-mail: kdoctor@utdallas.edu.
Website: http://www.utdallas.edu/epps/public-affairs/

The University of Texas at El Paso, Graduate School, College of Liberal Arts, Department of Sociology and Anthropology, El Paso, TX 79968-0001. Offers applied anthropology (Certificate); applied social sciences (Certificate); sociology (MA). Part-time and evening/weekend programs available. *Degree requirements:* For master's, thesis. *Entrance requirements:* For master's, GRE General Test, minimum GPA of 3.0. Additional exam requirements/recommendations for international students: Required—TOEFL. Electronic applications accepted. *Faculty research:* U.S.-Mexico border, social inequality, immigration, Chicano culture, Mexico.

The University of Texas at San Antonio, College of Liberal and Fine Arts, Department of Sociology, San Antonio, TX 78249-0617. Offers MS. Part-time programs available. *Faculty:* 12 full-time (4 women). *Students:* 15 full-time (8 women), 35 part-time (23 women); includes 33 minority (4 Black or African American, non-Hispanic/Latino; 27 Hispanic/Latino; 2 Two or more races, non-Hispanic/Latino), 7 international. Average age 32. 15 applicants, 100% accepted, 12 enrolled. In 2014, 21 master's awarded. *Degree requirements:* For master's, comprehensive exam, internship or thesis. *Entrance requirements:* For master's, GRE (waived if GPA 3.5 or above), BA/BS with 18 credit hours in field of study or other appropriate field of study; official transcripts; statement of purpose; academic writing sample; 3 letters of recommendation; minimum GPA of 3.0. Additional exam requirements/recommendations for international students: Required—TOEFL (minimum score 550 paper-based; 79 iBT), IELTS (minimum score 6.5). *Application deadline:* For fall admission, 7/1 for domestic students, 4/1 for international students; for spring admission, 11/1 for domestic students, 9/1 for international students. Application fee: $45 ($80 for international students). *Expenses:* Expenses: Contact institution. *Financial support:* In 2014–15, 1 fellowship (averaging $2,500 per year), 8 research assistantships (averaging $20,000 per year), 3 teaching assistantships (averaging $2,500 per year) were awarded; career-related internships or fieldwork, scholarships/grants, and unspecified assistantships also available. Financial award application deadline: 4/1; financial award applicants required to submit FAFSA. *Faculty research:* Border studies, Latino studies, race and ethnicity, cultural media, communications studies, family and child development, health and illness, religion. *Total annual research expenditures:* $750,000. *Unit head:* Dr. Xiaohe Xu, Chair, 210-458-4537, Fax: 210-458-4619, E-mail: xiaohe.xu@utsa.edu. *Application contact:* Dr. Terri Earnest, Graduate Advisor of Record, 210-458-6239, Fax: 210-458-6239, E-mail: terri.earnest@utsa.edu.
Website: http://colfa.utsa.edu/Sociology/

The University of Texas at Tyler, College of Arts and Sciences, Department of Social Sciences, Tyler, TX 75799-0001. Offers criminal justice (MS); public administration (MPA); sociology (MS). Part-time and evening/weekend programs available. *Degree requirements:* For master's, comprehensive exam, thesis optional. *Entrance requirements:* For master's, GRE General Test, minimum GPA of 3.0. Additional exam requirements/recommendations for international students: Required—TOEFL. *Faculty research:* Urban segregation, minority business, violent crime, gender discrimination.

The University of Texas–Pan American, College of Social and Behavioral Sciences, Department of Sociology, Edinburg, TX 78539. Offers MS. Part-time programs available. *Degree requirements:* For master's, thesis or journal article. *Entrance requirements:* For master's, minimum GPA of 3.0, BS of BA in sociology or social science. Additional exam requirements/recommendations for international students: Required—TOEFL (minimum score 500 paper-based). *Expenses:* Tuition, state resident: full-time $4187; part-time $232.60 per credit hour. Tuition, nonresident: full-time $10,857; part-time $603.16 per credit hour. *Required fees:* $782; $27.50 per credit hour. $143.35 per semester. *Faculty research:* Border studies, U.S.-Mexico issues, Mexican-American peoples, aging and gerontology.

The University of Toledo, College of Graduate Studies, College of Languages, Literature and Social Sciences, Department of Sociology and Anthropology, Toledo, OH 43606-3390. Offers sociology (MA). Part-time programs available. *Degree requirements:* For master's, thesis or alternative. *Entrance requirements:* For master's, GRE, minimum cumulative point-hour ratio of 2.7 for all previous academic work, three letters of recommendation, statement of purpose, transcripts from all prior institutions attended. Additional exam requirements/recommendations for international students: Required—TOEFL (minimum score 550 paper-based; 80 iBT). Electronic applications accepted. *Faculty research:* Medical and social gerontology, population, social movements, socioeconomic development, corporations and work, race and ethnicity.

University of Toronto, School of Graduate Studies, Faculty of Arts and Science, Department of Sociology, Toronto, ON M5S 2J7, Canada. Offers MA, PhD. Part-time programs available. *Degree requirements:* For doctorate, thesis/dissertation. *Entrance requirements:* For master's, GRE (for applicants from non-Canadian universities, recommended for those from Canadian universities), 5 full-year courses in sociology, basic research and statistical skills; 2 letters of reference; minimum B+ average in each of last two years of post-secondary education; for doctorate, GRE (for applicants from non-Canadian universities; recommended for those from Canadian universities), MA in sociology, minimum A- average, 2 letters of reference, statement of interest. Additional exam requirements/recommendations for international students: Required—TOEFL (minimum score 580 paper-based; 93 iBT), TWE (minimum score 5). Electronic applications accepted.

University of Utah, Graduate School, College of Social and Behavioral Science, Department of Sociology, Salt Lake City, UT 84112-1107. Offers M Stat, MA, MS, PhD. *Faculty:* 15 full-time (9 women), 3 part-time/adjunct (1 woman). *Students:* 25 full-time (17 women), 7 part-time (5 women); includes 4 minority (1 Asian, non-Hispanic/Latino; 3 Hispanic/Latino), 7 international. Average age 32. 25 applicants, 40% accepted, 6 enrolled. In 2014, 4 master's, 3 doctorates awarded. *Degree requirements:* For master's, comprehensive exam (for some programs), thesis; for doctorate, comprehensive exam, thesis/dissertation. *Entrance requirements:* For master's and doctorate, GRE, minimum

undergraduate GPA of 3.0. Additional exam requirements/recommendations for international students: Required—TOEFL (minimum score 550 paper-based). *Application deadline:* For fall admission, 2/1 priority date for domestic and international students. Application fee: $55 ($65 for international students). Electronic applications accepted. *Financial support:* In 2014–15, 2 students received support, including 2 research assistantships with full tuition reimbursements available (averaging $13,500 per year), 23 teaching assistantships with full and partial tuition reimbursements available (averaging $13,500 per year); scholarships/grants, health care benefits, and departmental waivers also available. Financial award application deadline: 2/1; financial award applicants required to submit FAFSA. *Faculty research:* Comparative international sociology, population studies, health disparities, environment, gender. *Total annual research expenditures:* $9,900. *Unit head:* Dr. Kim Korinek, Chair, 801-581-6153, Fax: 801-585-3784, E-mail: kim.korinek@soc.utah.edu. *Application contact:* Dr. Andrew K. Jorgenson, Director of Graduate Studies, 801-581-6153, Fax: 801-585-3784, E-mail: andrew.jorgenson@soc.utah.edu.
Website: http://www.soc.utah.edu/

University of Utah, Graduate School, Interdepartmental Program in Statistics, Salt Lake City, UT 84112-1107. Offers biostatistics (M Stat); econometrics (M Stat); educational psychology (M Stat); mathematics (M Stat); sociology (M Stat). Part-time programs available. *Students:* 61 full-time (34 women), 45 part-time (13 women); includes 18 minority (3 Black or African American, non-Hispanic/Latino; 10 Asian, non-Hispanic/Latino; 3 Hispanic/Latino; 2 Two or more races, non-Hispanic/Latino), 30 international. Average age 32. 50 applicants, 70% accepted, 27 enrolled. In 2014, 18 master's awarded. *Degree requirements:* For master's, comprehensive exam (for some programs), projects. *Entrance requirements:* For master's, GRE General Test (for all but biostatistics); GRE Subject Test (for mathematics), minimum GPA of 3.0; course work in calculus, matrix theory, statistics. Additional exam requirements/recommendations for international students: Required—TOEFL (minimum score 500 paper-based; 61 iBT). *Application deadline:* For fall admission, 7/1 for domestic students, 4/1 for international students. Applications are processed on a rolling basis. Application fee: $55 ($65 for international students). Electronic applications accepted. *Financial support:* In 2014–15, 10 students received support, including 10 research assistantships with full and partial tuition reimbursements available (averaging $1,000 per year); career-related internships or fieldwork, scholarships/grants, and unspecified assistantships also available. *Faculty research:* Biostatistics, sociology, economics, educational psychology, mathematics. *Unit head:* Xiaoming Sheng, Chair, University Statistics Committee, 801-213-3729, E-mail: xiaoming.sheng@utah.edu. *Application contact:* Laura Egbert, Coordinator, 801-585-6853, E-mail: laura.egbert@utah.edu.
Website: http://www.mstat.utah.edu

University of Victoria, Faculty of Graduate Studies, Faculty of Social Sciences, Department of Sociology, Victoria, BC V8W 2Y2, Canada. Offers MA, PhD. PhD by special arrangement. Part-time programs available. *Degree requirements:* For master's, thesis; for doctorate, thesis/dissertation, candidacy exam. *Entrance requirements:* For master's, minimum B+ average. Additional exam requirements/recommendations for international students: Required—TOEFL (minimum score 575 paper-based), IELTS (minimum score 7), TWE (minimum score 4). *Faculty research:* Social and political thought, social justice, health and aging, globalization and social psychology.

University of Virginia, College and Graduate School of Arts and Sciences, Department of Sociology, Charlottesville, VA 22903. Offers MA, PhD. *Faculty:* 18 full-time (8 women), 1 (woman) part-time/adjunct. *Students:* 37 full-time (25 women); includes 9 minority (3 Black or African American, non-Hispanic/Latino; 3 Asian, non-Hispanic/Latino; 2 Hispanic/Latino; 1 Two or more races, non-Hispanic/Latino), 6 international. Average age 30. 70 applicants, 19% accepted, 5 enrolled. In 2014, 3 master's, 4 doctorates awarded. *Degree requirements:* For master's, thesis; for doctorate, comprehensive exam, thesis/dissertation. *Entrance requirements:* For master's and doctorate, GRE General Test, GRE Subject Test, 2 letters of recommendation. Additional exam requirements/recommendations for international students: Required—TOEFL (minimum score 600 paper-based; 90 iBT), IELTS (minimum score 7). *Application deadline:* For fall admission, 1/1 for domestic and international students. Applications are processed on a rolling basis. Application fee: $60. Electronic applications accepted. *Expenses:* Tuition, state resident: full-time $14,164; part-time $349 per credit hour. Tuition, nonresident: full-time $23,722; part-time $1300 per credit hour. *Required fees:* $2514. *Financial support:* Applicants required to submit FAFSA. *Unit head:* Jeffrey Olick, Chair, 434-924-3526, Fax: 434-924-7028, E-mail: sociology@virginia.edu. *Application contact:* Allison Pugh, Director of Graduate Admissions, 434-924-6510, Fax: 434-924-7028, E-mail: apugh@virginia.edu.
Website: http://www.virginia.edu/sociology/

University of Washington, Graduate School, College of Arts and Sciences, Department of Sociology, Seattle, WA 98195. Offers MA, PhD. *Degree requirements:* For master's, thesis; for doctorate, thesis/dissertation. *Entrance requirements:* For master's and doctorate, GRE General Test, minimum GPA of 3.0. Additional exam requirements/recommendations for international students: Required—TOEFL. Electronic applications accepted. *Faculty research:* Demography, criminology, social psychology, race/ethnicity/inequality, family.

University of Waterloo, Graduate Studies, Faculty of Arts, Department of Sociology, Waterloo, ON N2L 3G1, Canada. Offers MA, PhD. Part-time programs available. *Degree requirements:* For master's, thesis (for some programs); for doctorate, one foreign language, thesis/dissertation. *Entrance requirements:* For master's, honors degree, minimum B+ average, resume, writing sample; for doctorate, master's degree, minimum A- average, resumé, writing sample. Additional exam requirements/recommendations for international students: Required—TOEFL, TWE. Electronic applications accepted. *Faculty research:* Theory, methods, stratification deviance, political sociology.

The University of Western Ontario, Faculty of Graduate Studies, Social Sciences Division, Department of Sociology, London, ON N6A 5B8, Canada. Offers MA, PhD. Terminal master's awarded for partial completion of doctoral program. *Degree requirements:* For master's, thesis (for some programs); for doctorate, one foreign language, comprehensive exam, thesis/dissertation. *Entrance requirements:* For master's, minimum B+ average, honors degree; for doctorate, minimum A- average. Additional exam requirements/recommendations for international students: Required—TOEFL. Electronic applications accepted. *Faculty research:* Social demography, class and change, health and aging, theory, methods.

University of West Florida, College of Professional Studies, Department of Health, Leisure, and Exercise Science, Community Health Education Program, Pensacola, FL 32514-5750. Offers aging studies (MS); health promotion and worksite wellness (MS); psychosocial (MS). Part-time and evening/weekend programs available. *Degree requirements:* For master's, thesis or alternative. *Entrance requirements:* For master's, GRE or MAT, official transcripts; minimum GPA of 3.0; letter of intent; three personal references. Additional exam requirements/recommendations for international students: Required—TOEFL (minimum score 550 paper-based).

University of West Georgia, College of Social Sciences, Department of Sociology, Carrollton, GA 30118. Offers MA, Certificate. Part-time and evening/weekend programs available. *Faculty:* 5 full-time (3 women). *Students:* 17 full-time (9 women), 5 part-time (2 women); includes 6 minority (4 Black or African American, non-Hispanic/Latino; 1 Hispanic/Latino; 1 Two or more races, non-Hispanic/Latino), 1 international. Average age 33. 12 applicants, 92% accepted, 7 enrolled. In 2014, 8 master's awarded. *Degree requirements:* For master's, one foreign language, comprehensive exam (for some programs), thesis (for some programs). *Entrance requirements:* For master's, GRE General Test, minimum GPA of 2.5, references, intellectual biography. Additional exam requirements/recommendations for international students: Required—TOEFL (minimum score 523 paper-based; 69 iBT); Recommended—IELTS (minimum score 6). *Application deadline:* For fall admission, 7/31 for domestic students; for spring admission, 11/30 for domestic students. Applications are processed on a rolling basis. Application fee: $40. Electronic applications accepted. *Financial support:* In 2014–15, 2 students received support, including 7 research assistantships with full tuition reimbursements available (averaging $6,000 per year); career-related internships or fieldwork, scholarships/grants, and unspecified assistantships also available. Financial award application deadline: 4/1; financial award applicants required to submit FAFSA. *Faculty research:* Inequality environment, social psychology, political sociology, research methods. *Unit head:* Dr. Paul Luken, Chair, 678-839-6333, Fax: 678-839-6506, E-mail: pluken@westga.edu. *Application contact:* Trish Wells, Graduate Studies Associate, 678-839-5170, Fax: 678-839-5171, E-mail: cclark@westga.edu.
Website: http://www.westga.edu/sociology

University of Windsor, Faculty of Graduate Studies, Faculty of Arts and Social Sciences, Department of Sociology and Anthropology, Windsor, ON N9B 3P4, Canada. Offers criminology (MA); sociology (MA); sociology-social justice (PhD). Part-time programs available. *Degree requirements:* For master's, thesis; for doctorate, comprehensive exam, thesis/dissertation. *Entrance requirements:* For master's, minimum B+ average; for doctorate, writing sample, minimum B+ average. Additional exam requirements/recommendations for international students: Required—TOEFL (minimum score 560 paper-based). Electronic applications accepted. *Faculty research:* Power and social change; criminology/deviance; social psychology; comparative development; race and ethnic relations; family, sex, and gender, social justice.

University of Wisconsin–Madison, Graduate School, College of Letters and Science, Department of Sociology, Madison, WI 53706-1380. Offers rural sociology (MS); sociology (MS, PhD). Part-time programs available. Terminal master's awarded for partial completion of doctoral program. *Degree requirements:* For master's, thesis, oral exam; for doctorate, thesis/dissertation, preliminary and final oral exams, 4 seminars. *Entrance requirements:* For master's and doctorate, GRE General Test. Additional exam requirements/recommendations for international students: Required—TOEFL. Electronic applications accepted. *Expenses:* Tuition, state resident: full-time $10,723; part-time $745 per credit. Tuition, nonresident: full-time $24,054; part-time $1578 per credit. *Required fees:* $374 per semester. Tuition and fees vary according to course load, program and reciprocity agreements.

University of Wisconsin–Milwaukee, Graduate School, College of Letters and Sciences, Department of Sociology, Milwaukee, WI 53201-0413. Offers MA. Part-time programs available. *Degree requirements:* For master's, thesis. *Entrance requirements:* For master's, GRE. Electronic applications accepted.

University of Wyoming, College of Arts and Sciences, Department of Sociology, Laramie, WY 82071. Offers MA. Part-time programs available. *Degree requirements:* For master's, thesis. *Entrance requirements:* For master's, GRE General Test, minimum GPA of 3.0. Additional exam requirements/recommendations for international students: Required—TOEFL (minimum score 525 paper-based). Electronic applications accepted. *Faculty research:* Gender, theory, international studies, law, social inequality.

Utah State University, School of Graduate Studies, College of Humanities, Arts and Social Sciences, Department of Sociology, Logan, UT 84322. Offers MA, MS, MSS, PhD. *Degree requirements:* For master's, thesis; for doctorate, comprehensive exam, thesis/dissertation. *Entrance requirements:* For master's, GRE General Test, minimum GPA of 3.0, recommendation letters; for doctorate, GRE General Test, minimum GPA of 3.0, recommendation letters, transcripts, personal statement, MS degree. Additional exam requirements/recommendations for international students: Required—TOEFL; Recommended—TWE. *Faculty research:* Demography, environmental/natural resource sociology, rural community change, international development, health studies.

Valdosta State University, Department of Sociology, Anthropology, and Criminal Justice, Valdosta, GA 31698. Offers criminal justice (MS); sociology (MS). *Accreditation:* AAMFT/COAMFTE. Part-time and evening/weekend programs available. *Faculty:* 15 full-time (6 women). *Students:* 13 full-time (9 women), 16 part-time (11 women); includes 12 minority (10 Black or African American, non-Hispanic/Latino; 2 Two or more races, non-Hispanic/Latino), 1 international. Average age 23. 9 applicants, 89% accepted, 8 enrolled. In 2014, 10 master's awarded. *Degree requirements:* For master's, thesis or alternative, comprehensive written and/or oral exams. *Entrance requirements:* For master's, GRE General Test or MAT (sociology, marriage and family therapy), minimum GPA of 2.5. Additional exam requirements/recommendations for international students: Required—TOEFL (minimum score 523 paper-based). *Application deadline:* For fall admission, 7/1 for domestic and international students; for spring admission, 11/15 for domestic and international students. Applications are processed on a rolling basis. Application fee: $35. Electronic applications accepted. *Expenses:* Tuition, state resident: part-time $236 per credit hour. Tuition, nonresident: part-time $850 per credit hour. *Required fees:* $1032 per semester. *Financial support:* In 2014–15, 4 students received support, including 5 research assistantships with full tuition reimbursements available (averaging $3,652 per year); career-related internships or fieldwork, institutionally sponsored loans, scholarships/grants, and unspecified assistantships also available. Support available to part-time students. Financial award application deadline: 7/1; financial award applicants required to submit FAFSA. *Unit head:* Dr. Darrell Ross, Head, 229-333-5943, Fax: 229-333-5492. *Application contact:* Michelle Jordan, Admissions Specialist, 229-333-5694, Fax: 229-245-3853, E-mail: sojordan@valdosta.edu.

Vanderbilt University, Graduate School, Department of Sociology, Nashville, TN 37240-1001. Offers MA, PhD. *Faculty:* 21 full-time (7 women), 1 part-time/adjunct (0 women). *Students:* 39 full-time (28 women); includes 11 minority (6 Black or African American, non-Hispanic/Latino; 1 Asian, non-Hispanic/Latino; 3 Hispanic/Latino; 1 Two or more races, non-Hispanic/Latino), 2 international. Average age 28. 138 applicants, 15% accepted, 8 enrolled. In 2014, 9 master's, 5 doctorates awarded. *Degree requirements:* For master's, thesis; for doctorate, comprehensive exam, thesis/dissertation, area, qualifying, and final exams. *Entrance requirements:* For master's and doctorate, GRE General Test. Additional exam requirements/recommendations for international students: Required—TOEFL (minimum score 570 paper-based; 88 iBT). *Application deadline:* For fall admission, 1/15 for domestic and international students. Electronic applications accepted. *Expenses:* Tuition: full-time $42,768; part-time $1782 per credit hour. *Required fees:* $422. One-time fee: $30 full-time. *Financial support:* Fellowships with full tuition reimbursements, research assistantships, teaching assistantships with full tuition reimbursements, Federal Work-Study, institutionally sponsored loans, scholarships/grants, and health care benefits available. Financial award application deadline: 1/15; financial award applicants required to submit CSS PROFILE or FAFSA. *Faculty research:* Criminology; cultural sociology; gender, race, and ethics relations; deviant behavior and social control. *Unit head:* Dr. Mariano Sana,

Director of Graduate Studies, 615-322-4004, Fax: 615-322-7505, E-mail: mariano.sana@vanderbilt.edu. *Application contact:* Linda Willingham, Administrative Assistant, 615-322-7500, Fax: 615-322-7505, E-mail: linda.willingham@vanderbilt.edu.
Website: http://www.vanderbilt.edu/sociology/VDOS_Home.shtml

Virginia Commonwealth University, Graduate School, College of Humanities and Sciences, Wilder School of Government and Public Affairs, Department of Sociology, Richmond, VA 23284-9005. Offers applied social research (CASR); sociology (MS). *Degree requirements:* For master's, thesis optional. *Entrance requirements:* For master's, GRE General Test. Additional exam requirements/recommendations for international students: Required—TOEFL (minimum score 600 paper-based; 100 iBT); Recommended—IELTS (minimum score 6.5). Electronic applications accepted.

Virginia Polytechnic Institute and State University, Graduate School, College of Liberal Arts and Human Sciences, Blacksburg, VA 24061. Offers career and technical education (MS Ed, Ed D, PhD, Ed S); communication (MA); counselor education (MA Ed, Ed D, PhD, Ed S); creative writing (MFA); curriculum and instruction (MA Ed, Ed D, PhD, Ed S); educational leadership and policy studies (MA Ed, Ed D, PhD, Ed S); educational research and evaluation (PhD); English (MA); foreign languages, cultures, and literatures (MA); higher education and student affairs (MA Ed); history (MA); human development (MS, PhD); material culture and public humanities (MA); philosophy (MA); political science (MA); rhetoric and writing (PhD); science and technology studies (MS, PhD); social, political, ethical, and cultural thought (PhD); sociology (MS, PhD); theater arts (MFA). *Faculty:* 421 full-time (216 women), 2 part-time/adjunct (both women). *Students:* 642 full-time (437 women), 537 part-time (344 women); includes 235 minority (132 Black or African American, non-Hispanic/Latino; 2 American Indian or Alaska Native, non-Hispanic/Latino; 27 Asian, non-Hispanic/Latino; 52 Hispanic/Latino; 1 Native Hawaiian or other Pacific Islander, non-Hispanic/Latino; 21 Two or more races, non-Hispanic/Latino), 81 international. Average age 34. 890 applicants, 46% accepted, 303 enrolled. In 2014, 342 master's, 96 doctorates, 33 other advanced degrees awarded. *Degree requirements:* For master's, comprehensive exam (for some programs), thesis (for some programs); for doctorate, comprehensive exam (for some programs), thesis/dissertation (for some programs). *Entrance requirements:* For master's and doctorate, GRE/GMAT (may vary by department). Additional exam requirements/recommendations for international students: Required—TOEFL (minimum score 550 paper-based). *Application deadline:* For fall admission, 8/1 for domestic students, 4/1 for international students; for spring admission, 1/1 for domestic students, 9/1 for international students. Applications are processed on a rolling basis. Application fee: $75. Electronic applications accepted. *Expenses:* Tuition, state resident: full-time $11,656; part-time $647.50 per credit hour. Tuition, nonresident: full-time $23,351; part-time $1297.25 per credit hour. *Required fees:* $2533; $465.75 per semester. Tuition and fees vary according to course load, campus/location and program. *Financial support:* In 2014–15, 19 research assistantships with full tuition reimbursements (averaging $22,141 per year), 231 teaching assistantships with full tuition reimbursements (averaging $19,470 per year) were awarded. Financial award application deadline: 3/1; financial award applicants required to submit FAFSA. *Total annual research expenditures:* $6.5 million. *Unit head:* Elizabeth Spiller, Dean, 540-231-6779, Fax: 540-231-7157, E-mail: espiller@vt.edu. *Application contact:* Melissa Elliott, Executive Assistant, 540-231-6779, Fax: 540-231-7157, E-mail: elliott1@vt.edu.
Website: http://www.clahs.vt.edu/

Washington State University, College of Liberal Arts, Program in Sociology, Pullman, WA 99164. Offers MA, PhD. Program applications must be made through the Pullman campus. Part-time programs available. *Faculty:* 16 full-time (11 women), 1 (woman) part-time/adjunct. *Students:* 35 full-time (17 women), 3 part-time (1 woman); includes 5 minority (1 Black or African American, non-Hispanic/Latino; 3 Hispanic/Latino; 1 Two or more races, non-Hispanic/Latino), 4 international. Average age 29. 50 applicants, 10% accepted, 5 enrolled. In 2014, 7 master's, 3 doctorates awarded. Terminal master's awarded for partial completion of doctoral program. *Degree requirements:* For master's, thesis; for doctorate, comprehensive exam, thesis/dissertation. *Entrance requirements:* For master's, bachelor's degree, minimum GPA of 3.0; for doctorate, MA in sociology, minimum GPA of 3.0. Additional exam requirements/recommendations for international students: Required—TOEFL (minimum score 550 paper-based). *Application deadline:* For fall admission, 1/15 priority date for domestic and international students. Application fee: $75. Electronic applications accepted. *Expenses:* Tuition, state resident: full-time $11,768. Tuition, nonresident: full-time $25,200. *Required fees:* $960. Tuition and fees vary according to program. *Financial support:* In 2014–15, 49 students received support, including 3 research assistantships with full tuition reimbursements available (averaging $11,149 per year), 32 teaching assistantships with full tuition reimbursements available (averaging $13,839 per year); Federal Work-Study, institutionally sponsored loans, scholarships/grants, health care benefits, and unspecified assistantships also available. Support available to part-time students. Financial award application deadline: 4/1; financial award applicants required to submit FAFSA. *Faculty research:* Criminology, environmental sociology, family, gender, social inequality. *Total annual research expenditures:* $113,000. *Unit head:* Dr. Lisa J. McIntyre, Chair, 509-335-4595, Fax: 509-335-6419, E-mail: ljmcint@wsu.edu. *Application contact:* Dr. Jennifer Sherman, Director of Graduate Studies, 509-335-4595, Fax: 509-335-6419, E-mail: schwartj@wsu.edu.
Website: http://libarts.wsu.edu/soc/

Wayne State University, College of Liberal Arts and Sciences, Department of Sociology, Detroit, MI 48202. Offers applied sociology and urban studies (MA); sociology (MA, PhD). *Faculty:* 11 full-time (7 women). *Students:* 28 full-time (18 women), 6 part-time (5 women); includes 11 minority (10 Black or African American, non-Hispanic/Latino; 1 Two or more races, non-Hispanic/Latino), 5 international. Average age 39. 29 applicants, 31% accepted, 3 enrolled. In 2014, 7 master's, 9 doctorates awarded. *Degree requirements:* For master's, thesis optional, oral exam and public defense of thesis/essay; for doctorate, thesis/dissertation. *Entrance requirements:* For master's, GRE General Test, minimum GPA of 3.3 in upper-division courses; substantial background in sociology, social science research methods, sociological theory, and basic statistics; three letters of reference (at least 2 from college/university faculty); writing sample; statement of interest; for doctorate, GRE General Test, minimum GPA of 3.5 in master's work; three letters of reference (at least 2 from college/university faculty); statement of interest; sample of written work. Additional exam requirements/recommendations for international students: Required—TOEFL (minimum score 550 paper-based; 79 iBT), TWE (minimum score 5.5), Michigan English Language Assessment Battery (minimum score 85); Recommended—IELTS (minimum score 6.5). *Application deadline:* For fall admission, 1/15 for domestic and international students. Application fee: $0. Electronic applications accepted. *Expenses:* Tuition, state resident: full-time $10,294; part-time $571.90 per credit hour. Tuition, nonresident: full-time $29,730; part-time $1238.75 per credit hour. *Required fees:* $1365; $43.50 per credit hour. $291.10 per semester. Tuition and fees vary according to course load and program. *Financial support:* In 2014–15, 21 students received support, including 4 fellowships with tuition reimbursements available (averaging $15,073 per year), 8 teaching assistantships with tuition reimbursements available (averaging $16,838 per year); research assistantships with tuition reimbursements available, scholarships/grants, health care benefits, and unspecified assistantships also available. Financial award application deadline: 3/31; financial award applicants required to submit FAFSA. *Faculty research:* Medical sociology, inequality, urban labor. *Unit head:* Dr. Janet Hankin, Chair and Professor, 313-577-8131, E-mail: janet.hankin@wayne.edu. *Application contact:* Dr. Khari Brown, Director of Graduate Studies, 313-577-0146, Fax: 313-577-2735, E-mail: kharib@wayne.edu.
Website: http://clas.wayne.edu/Sociology/

Western Illinois University, School of Graduate Studies, College of Arts and Sciences, Department of Sociology and Anthropology, Macomb, IL 61455-1390. Offers sociology (MA). Part-time programs available. *Students:* 10 full-time (7 women), 4 part-time (2 women); includes 4 minority (all Black or African American, non-Hispanic/Latino), 4 international. Average age 28. 15 applicants, 80% accepted, 5 enrolled. In 2014, 4 master's awarded. *Degree requirements:* For master's, thesis or alternative. *Entrance requirements:* Additional exam requirements/recommendations for international students: Required—TOEFL (minimum score 550 paper-based; 80 iBT). *Application deadline:* Applications are processed on a rolling basis. Application fee: $30. Electronic applications accepted. *Financial support:* In 2014–15, 9 students received support, including 9 teaching assistantships with full tuition reimbursements available (averaging $8,688 per year). Financial award applicants required to submit FAFSA. *Unit head:* Dr. John Wozniak, Chairperson, 309-298-1056. *Application contact:* Dr. Nancy Parsons, Associate Provost and Director of Graduate Studies, 309-298-1806, Fax: 309-298-2345, E-mail: grad-office@wiu.edu.
Website: http://wiu.edu/sociology

Western Kentucky University, Graduate Studies, Potter College of Arts and Letters, Department of Sociology, Bowling Green, KY 42101. Offers criminology (MA); sociology (MA). Postbaccalaureate distance learning degree programs offered. *Degree requirements:* For master's, comprehensive exam, thesis optional, final exam. *Entrance requirements:* For master's, GRE General Test, minimum GPA of 3.0. Additional exam requirements/recommendations for international students: Required—TOEFL (minimum score 555 paper-based; 79 iBT). *Faculty research:* Criminology/delinquency, quantitative and survey research methodology, occupations/professions, sex and gender, demography.

Western Michigan University, Graduate College, College of Arts and Sciences, Department of Sociology, Kalamazoo, MI 49008. Offers MA, PhD. *Degree requirements:* For master's, thesis; for doctorate, one foreign language, thesis/dissertation. *Application deadline:* For fall admission, 2/15 for domestic students. *Financial support:* Application deadline: 2/15. *Application contact:* Admissions and Orientation, 269-387-2000, Fax: 269-387-2096.

West Virginia University, Eberly College of Arts and Sciences, School of Applied Social Sciences, Division of Sociology and Anthropology, Morgantown, WV 26506. Offers applied social research (MA). Part-time programs available. *Degree requirements:* For master's, thesis or alternative. *Entrance requirements:* For master's, GRE General Test, minimum GPA of 2.75. Additional exam requirements/recommendations for international students: Required—TOEFL. *Faculty research:* Applied sociology, stratification, social/complex organization, research methodology criminology.

Wichita State University, Graduate School, Fairmount College of Liberal Arts and Sciences, Department of Sociology, Wichita, KS 67260. Offers MA. Part-time programs available. *Unit head:* Dr. Jodie Hertzog, Chair, 316-978-3280, Fax: 316-978-3281, E-mail: jodie.hertzog@wichita.edu. *Application contact:* Jordan Oleson, Admissions Coordinator, 316-978-3095, Fax: 316-978-3253, E-mail: jordan.oleson@wichita.edu.
Website: http://www.wichita.edu/sociology

Wilfrid Laurier University, Faculty of Graduate and Postdoctoral Studies, Faculty of Arts, Department of Sociology, Waterloo, ON N2L 3C5, Canada. Offers health, family and well-being (MA); internationalization, migration and human rights (MA). *Entrance requirements:* For master's, honours BA with minimum B+ average and major in sociology. Additional exam requirements/recommendations for international students: Required—TOEFL (minimum score 89 iBT). Electronic applications accepted. *Faculty research:* Internationalization, migration and human rights, health, families, and well-being.

William Paterson University of New Jersey, College of Humanities and Social Sciences, Wayne, NJ 07470-8420. Offers applied sociology (MA); clinical and counseling psychology (MA); clinical psychology (Psy.D.); creative and professional writing (MFA); English (MA); history (MA); public policy and international affairs (MA). Part-time and evening/weekend programs available. *Faculty:* 32 full-time (16 women), 3 part-time/adjunct (1 woman). *Students:* 50 full-time (30 women), 114 part-time (88 women); includes 64 minority (7 Black or African American, non-Hispanic/Latino; 1 American Indian or Alaska Native, non-Hispanic/Latino; 4 Asian, non-Hispanic/Latino; 50 Hispanic/Latino; 2 Two or more races, non-Hispanic/Latino), 2 international. Average age 34. 115 applicants, 81% accepted, 65 enrolled. In 2014, 42 master's awarded. Terminal master's awarded for partial completion of doctoral program. *Degree requirements:* For master's, thesis (for some programs), internship (for some programs). *Entrance requirements:* For master's, GRE/MAT, minimum GPA of 3.0; 2 letters of recommendation; writing sample/personal statement. Additional exam requirements/recommendations for international students: Required—TOEFL (minimum score 550 paper-based; 79 iBT), IELTS (minimum score 6). *Application deadline:* For fall admission, 6/1 for domestic students, 3/1 for international students; for spring admission, 11/1 for domestic students, 10/1 for international students. Applications are processed on a rolling basis. Application fee: $50. Electronic applications accepted. *Expenses:* Tuition, state resident: full-time $12,413; part-time $564.21 per credit. Tuition, nonresident: full-time $20,487; part-time $931.21 per credit. *Required fees:* $2107; $95.79 per credit. $478.95 per semester. Tuition and fees vary according to course load and degree level. *Financial support:* Research assistantships with full tuition reimbursements, Federal Work-Study, scholarships/grants, and unspecified assistantships available. Support available to part-time students. Financial award application deadline: 4/1; financial award applicants required to submit FAFSA. *Faculty research:* Sexual violence, history of science in Muslim societies, bioethics, teaching writing for transfer, psychological impact of microagressions on minority communities. *Unit head:* Dr. Kara Rabbitt, Dean, 973-720-2731, Fax: 973-720-2955, E-mail: rabbittk@wpunj.edu. *Application contact:* Tinu Adeniran, Associate Director, Graduate Admissions, 973-720-2764, Fax: 973-720-2035, E-mail: adenirant@wpunj.edu.
Website: http://www.wpunj.edu/cohss

Yale University, Graduate School of Arts and Sciences, Department of Sociology, New Haven, CT 06520. Offers comparative and historical sociology (PhD); cultural sociology and social theory (PhD); social stratification and the life course (PhD). *Degree requirements:* For doctorate, thesis/dissertation. *Entrance requirements:* For doctorate, GRE General Test.

York University, Faculty of Graduate Studies, Faculty of Liberal Arts and Professional Studies, Program in Sociology, Toronto, ON M3J 1P3, Canada. Offers MA, PhD. Part-

time programs available. *Degree requirements:* For master's, thesis or alternative; for doctorate, one foreign language, comprehensive exam, thesis/dissertation, analytical paper. Electronic applications accepted.

York University, Faculty of Graduate Studies, Program in Social and Political Thought, Toronto, ON M3J 1P3, Canada. Offers MA, PhD. Part-time programs available. *Degree requirements:* For master's, one foreign language, thesis or alternative, oral exams; for doctorate, one foreign language, comprehensive exam, thesis/dissertation. Electronic applications accepted.

Survey Methodology

University of Maryland, College Park, Academic Affairs, College of Behavioral and Social Sciences, Joint Program in Survey Methodology, College Park, MD 20742. Offers MS, PhD. Program offered with University of Michigan and Westat. *Degree requirements:* For master's, thesis (for some programs), scholarly paper; for doctorate, thesis/dissertation. *Entrance requirements:* For master's, GRE General Test (recommended), minimum GPA of 3.0, 3 letters of recommendation; for doctorate, GRE General Test, minimum GPA of 3.0, 3 letters of recommendation. Electronic applications accepted.

University of Michigan, Horace H. Rackham School of Graduate Studies, Program in Survey Methodology, Ann Arbor, MI 48104. Offers MS, PhD, Certificate. Part-time programs available. Terminal master's awarded for partial completion of doctoral program. *Degree requirements:* For master's, internships; for doctorate, comprehensive exam, thesis/dissertation. *Entrance requirements:* For master's and doctorate, GRE, 3 letters of recommendation, academic statement of purpose, personal statement, resume or curriculum vitae, academic transcripts; for Certificate, 3 letters of recommendation, academic statement of purpose, personal statement, resume or curriculum vitae, academic transcripts. Additional exam requirements/recommendations for international students: Required—TOEFL (minimum score 560 paper-based; 84 iBT). Electronic applications accepted. *Expenses:* Contact institution. *Faculty research:* Survey methodology, statistics, psychology, sociology, social psychology.

University of Nebraska–Lincoln, Graduate College, Interdepartmental Area of Survey Research and Methodology, Lincoln, NE 68588. Offers MS, PhD. *Degree requirements:* For master's, comprehensive exam. *Entrance requirements:* For master's, GRE General Test or GMAT. Additional exam requirements/recommendations for international students: Required—TOEFL (minimum score 550 paper-based). Electronic applications accepted. *Faculty research:* Survey research and data analysis.

APPENDIXES

Institutional Changes
Since the 2015 Edition

Following is an alphabetical listing of institutions that have recently closed, merged with other institutions, or changed their names or status. In the case of a name change, the former name appears first, followed by the new name.

Adler School of Professional Psychology (Chicago, IL): *name changed to Adler University*

Ambrose University College (Calgary, AB, Canada): *name changed to Ambrose University*

American InterContinental University South Florida (Weston, FL): *closed*

Baptist Bible College of Pennsylvania (Clarks Summit, PA): *name changed to Summit University*

Bay Path College (Longmeadow, MA): *name changed to Bay Path University*

Bethesda University of California (Anaheim, CA): *name changed to Bethesda University*

Blessed John XXIII National Seminary (Weston, MA): *name changed to Pope St. John XXIII National Seminary*

Capitol College (Laurel, MD): *name changed to Capitol Technology University*

Clearwater Christian College (Clearwater, FL): *closed*

Cold Spring Harbor Laboratory, Watson School of Biological Sciences (Cold Spring Harbor, NY): *institution name changed to Cold Spring Harbor Laboratory*

Delaware Valley College (Doylestown, PA): *name changed to Delaware Valley University*

DeVry University (Daly City, CA): *closed*

DeVry University (Elk Grove, CA): *closed*

DeVry University (Miami, FL): *closed*

DeVry University (Tampa, FL): *closed*

DeVry University (Schaumburg, IL): *closed*

DeVry University (Indianapolis, IN): *closed*

DeVry University (St. Louis, MO): *closed*

DeVry University (Portland, OR): *closed*

DeVry University (Pittsburgh, PA): *closed*

DeVry University (Memphis, TN): *closed*

DeVry University (Houston, TX): *closed*

DeVry University (Richardson, TX): *closed*

DeVry University (Bellevue, WA): *closed*

DeVry University (Federal Way, WA): *closed*

DeVry University (Milwaukee, WI): *closed*

DeVry University (Waukesha, WI): *closed*

Harrington College of Design (Chicago, IL): *closed*

Heritage Baptist College and Heritage Theological Seminary (Cambridge, ON, Canada): *name changed to Heritage College and Seminary*

International Baptist College (Chandler, AZ): *name changed to International Baptist College and Seminary*

John Hancock University (Oakbrook Terrace, IL): *name changed to Ellis University*

Jones International University (Centennial, CO): *closed*

Keck Graduate Institute of Applied Life Sciences (Claremont, CA): *now listed as Keck Graduate Institute*

Luther Rice University (Lithonia, GA): *name changed to Luther Rice College & Seminary*

Monterey Institute of International Studies (Monterey, CA): *name changed to Middlebury Institute of International Studies*

Morrison University (Reno, NV): *closed*

Mount St. Mary's College (Los Angeles, CA): *name changed to Mount Saint Mary's University*

New Life Theological Seminary (Charlotte, NC): *name changed to Charlotte Christian College and Theological Seminary*

Northland International University (Dunbar, WI): *merged into Southern Baptist Theological Seminary (Louisville, KY)*

Pacific Lutheran Theological Seminary (Berkeley, CA): *merged into California Lutheran University (Thousand Oaks, CA)*

Ponce School of Medicine & Health Sciences (Ponce, PR): *name changed to Ponce Health Sciences University*

The Richard Stockton College of New Jersey (Galloway, NJ): *name changed to Stockton University*

Sojourner-Douglass College (Baltimore, MD): *closed*

State University of New York Institute of Technology (Utica, NY): *name changed to State University of New York Polytechnic Institute*

Tennessee Temple University (Chattanooga, TN): *merged into Piedmont International University (Winston-Salem, NC)*

Texas State University–San Marcos (San Marcos, TX): *name changed to Texas State University*

Thomas M. Cooley Law School (Lansing, MI): *name changed to Western Michigan University Cooley Law School*

University of Phoenix–Central Massachusetts Campus (Westborough, MA): *closed*

University of Phoenix–Chattanooga Campus (Chattanooga, TN): *name changed to University of Phoenix–Chattanooga Learning Center and no longer profiled as a campus*

University of Phoenix–Cheyenne Campus (Cheyenne, WY): *closed*

University of Phoenix–Cincinnati Campus (West Chester, OH): *closed*

University of Phoenix–Columbus Ohio Campus (Columbus, OH): *closed*

University of Phoenix–Denver Campus (Lone Tree, CO): *name changed to University of Phoenix–Colorado Campus*

University of Phoenix–Eastern Washington Campus (Spokane, WA): *closed*

University of Phoenix–Louisiana Campus (Metairie, LA): *name changed to University of Phoenix–New Orleans Learning Center and no longer profiled as a campus*

University of Phoenix–Madison Campus (Madison, WI): *closed*

University of Phoenix–Minneapolis/St. Louis Park Campus (St. Louis Park, MN): *name changed to University of Phoenix–Minneapolis/St. Paul Campus*

University of Phoenix–Northwest Arkansas Campus (Rogers, AR): *closed*

University of Phoenix–Omaha Campus (Omaha, NE): *closed*

University of Phoenix–Pittsburgh Campus (Pittsburgh, PA): *closed*

University of Phoenix–Southern Colorado Campus (Colorado Springs, CO): *name changed to University of Phoenix–Colorado Springs Downtown Campus*

University of Phoenix–Springfield Campus (Springfield, MO): *closed*

University of Phoenix–Tulsa Campus (Tulsa, OK): *name changed to University of Phoenix–Tulsa Learning Center and no longer profiled as a campus*

University of Phoenix–West Florida Campus (Temple Terrace, FL): *name changed to University of Phoenix–West Florida Learning Center and no longer profiled as a campus*

University of Phoenix–Wichita Campus (Wichita, KS): *closed*

University of South Florida–St. Petersburg Campus (St. Petersburg, FL): *name changed to University of South Florida, St. Petersburg*

Valley Forge Christian College (Phoenixville, PA): *name changed to University of Valley Forge*

Washington State University Spokane (Spokane, WA): *merged into a single entry for Washington State University (Pullman, WA) by request from the institution*

Washington State University Tri-Cities (Richland, WA): *merged into a single entry for Washington State University (Pullman, WA) by request from the institution*

Washington State University Vancouver (Vancouver, WA): *merged into a single entry for Washington State University (Pullman, WA) by request from the institution*

Abbreviations Used in the Guides

The following list includes abbreviations of degree names used in the profiles in the 2016 edition of the guides. Because some degrees (e.g., Doctor of Education) can be abbreviated in more than one way (e.g., D.Ed. or Ed.D.), and because the abbreviations used in the guides reflect the preferences of the individual colleges and universities, the list may include two or more abbreviations for a single degree.

DEGREES

A Mus D	Doctor of Musical Arts
AC	Advanced Certificate
AD	Artist's Diploma
	Doctor of Arts
ADP	Artist's Diploma
Adv C	Advanced Certificate
AGC	Advanced Graduate Certificate
AGSC	Advanced Graduate Specialist Certificate
ALM	Master of Liberal Arts
AM	Master of Arts
AMBA	Accelerated Master of Business Administration
AMRS	Master of Arts in Religious Studies
APC	Advanced Professional Certificate
APMPH	Advanced Professional Master of Public Health
App Sc	Applied Scientist
App Sc D	Doctor of Applied Science
AstE	Astronautical Engineer
ATC	Advanced Training Certificate
Au D	Doctor of Audiology
B Th	Bachelor of Theology
BN	Bachelor of Naturopathy
CAES	Certificate of Advanced Educational Specialization
CAGS	Certificate of Advanced Graduate Studies
CAL	Certificate in Applied Linguistics
CAPS	Certificate of Advanced Professional Studies
CAS	Certificate of Advanced Studies
CASPA	Certificate of Advanced Study in Public Administration
CASR	Certificate in Advanced Social Research
CATS	Certificate of Achievement in Theological Studies
CBHS	Certificate in Basic Health Sciences
CCJA	Certificate in Criminal Justice Administration
CCTS	Certificate in Clinical and Translational Science
CE	Civil Engineer
CEM	Certificate of Environmental Management
CET	Certificate in Educational Technologies
CGS	Certificate of Graduate Studies
Ch E	Chemical Engineer
Clin Sc D	Doctor of Clinical Science
CM	Certificate in Management
CMH	Certificate in Medical Humanities
CMM	Master of Church Ministries
CMS	Certificate in Ministerial Studies
CNM	Certificate in Nonprofit Management
CPASF	Certificate Program for Advanced Study in Finance
CPC	Certificate in Professional Counseling
	Certificate in Publication and Communication
CPH	Certificate in Public Health
CPM	Certificate in Public Management
CPS	Certificate of Professional Studies
CScD	Doctor of Clinical Science
CSD	Certificate in Spiritual Direction
CSS	Certificate of Special Studies
CTS	Certificate of Theological Studies
CURP	Certificate in Urban and Regional Planning
D Admin	Doctor of Administration
D Arch	Doctor of Architecture
D Be	Doctor in Bioethics
D Com	Doctor of Commerce
D Couns	Doctor of Counseling
D Des	Doctorate of Design
D Div	Doctor of Divinity
D Ed	Doctor of Education
D Ed Min	Doctor of Educational Ministry
D Eng	Doctor of Engineering
D Engr	Doctor of Engineering
D Ent	Doctor of Enterprise
D Env	Doctor of Environment
D Law	Doctor of Law
D Litt	Doctor of Letters
D Med Sc	Doctor of Medical Science
D Min	Doctor of Ministry
D Miss	Doctor of Missiology
D Mus	Doctor of Music
D Mus A	Doctor of Musical Arts
D Phil	Doctor of Philosophy
D Prof	Doctor of Professional Studies
D Ps	Doctor of Psychology
D Sc	Doctor of Science
D Sc D	Doctor of Science in Dentistry
D Sc IS	Doctor of Science in Information Systems
D Sc PA	Doctor of Science in Physician Assistant Studies
D Th	Doctor of Theology
D Th P	Doctor of Practical Theology
DA	Doctor of Accounting
	Doctor of Arts
DAH	Doctor of Arts in Humanities
DAOM	Doctorate in Acupuncture and Oriental Medicine
DAT	Doctorate of Athletic Training
	Professional Doctor of Art Therapy
DBA	Doctor of Business Administration
DBH	Doctor of Behavioral Health
DBL	Doctor of Business Leadership
DC	Doctor of Chiropractic
DCC	Doctor of Computer Science
DCD	Doctor of Communications Design
DCL	Doctor of Civil Law
	Doctor of Comparative Law
DCM	Doctor of Church Music
DCN	Doctor of Clinical Nutrition
DCS	Doctor of Computer Science
DDN	Diplôme du Droit Notarial
DDS	Doctor of Dental Surgery
DE	Doctor of Education
	Doctor of Engineering
DED	Doctor of Economic Development
DEIT	Doctor of Educational Innovation and Technology
DEL	Doctor of Executive Leadership
DEM	Doctor of Educational Ministry
DEPD	Diplôme Études Spécialisées
DES	Doctor of Engineering Science
DESS	Diplôme Études Supérieures Spécialisées
DET	Doctor of Educational Technology
DFA	Doctor of Fine Arts
DGP	Diploma in Graduate and Professional Studies
DH Ed	Doctor of Health Education

DH Sc	Doctor of Health Sciences	EDB	Executive Doctorate in Business
DHA	Doctor of Health Administration	EDBA	Executive Doctor of Business Administration
DHCE	Doctor of Health Care Ethics	EDM	Executive Doctorate in Management
DHL	Doctor of Hebrew Letters	EE	Electrical Engineer
DHPE	Doctorate of Health Professionals Education	EJD	Executive Juris Doctor
DHS	Doctor of Health Science	EMBA	Executive Master of Business Administration
DHSc	Doctor of Health Science	EMFA	Executive Master of Forensic Accounting
Dip CS	Diploma in Christian Studies	EMHA	Executive Master of Health Administration
DIT	Doctor of Industrial Technology	EMIB	Executive Master of International Business
	Doctor of Information Technology	EML	Executive Master of Leadership
DJS	Doctor of Jewish Studies	EMPA	Executive Master of Public Administration
DLS	Doctor of Liberal Studies	EMPL	Executive Master in Public Leadership
DM	Doctor of Management	EMS	Executive Master of Science
	Doctor of Music	EMTM	Executive Master of Technology Management
DMA	Doctor of Musical Arts	Eng	Engineer
DMD	Doctor of Dental Medicine	Eng Sc D	Doctor of Engineering Science
DME	Doctor of Manufacturing Management	Engr	Engineer
	Doctor of Music Education	Exec M Tax	Executive Master of Taxation
DMEd	Doctor of Music Education	Exec MAC	Executive Master of Accounting
DMFT	Doctor of Marital and Family Therapy	Exec Ed D	Executive Doctor of Education
DMH	Doctor of Medical Humanities	Exec MBA	Executive Master of Business Administration
DML	Doctor of Modern Languages	Exec MPA	Executive Master of Public Administration
DMP	Doctorate in Medical Physics	Exec MPH	Executive Master of Public Health
DMPNA	Doctor of Management Practice in Nurse Anesthesia	Exec MS	Executive Master of Science
		Executive Fellows MBA	Executive Fellows Master of Business Administration
DN Sc	Doctor of Nursing Science	G Dip	Graduate Diploma
DNAP	Doctor of Nurse Anesthesia Practice	GBC	Graduate Business Certificate
DNP	Doctor of Nursing Practice	GDM	Graduate Diploma in Management
DNP-A	Doctor of Nursing Practice - Anesthesia	GDPA	Graduate Diploma in Public Administration
DNS	Doctor of Nursing Science	GDRE	Graduate Diploma in Religious Education
DO	Doctor of Osteopathy	GEMBA	Global Executive Master of Business Administration
DOT	Doctor of Occupational Therapy		
DPA	Doctor of Public Administration	GMBA	Global Master of Business Administration
DPDS	Doctor of Planning and Development Studies	GP LL M	Global Professional Master of Laws
DPH	Doctor of Public Health	GPD	Graduate Performance Diploma
DPM	Doctor of Plant Medicine	GSS	Graduate Special Certificate for Students in Special Situations
	Doctor of Podiatric Medicine		
DPPD	Doctor of Policy, Planning, and Development	IEMBA	International Executive Master of Business Administration
DPS	Doctor of Professional Studies		
DPT	Doctor of Physical Therapy	IMA	Interdisciplinary Master of Arts
DPTSc	Doctor of Physical Therapy Science	IMBA	International Master of Business Administration
Dr DES	Doctor of Design		
Dr NP	Doctor of Nursing Practice	IMES	International Master's in Environmental Studies
Dr OT	Doctor of Occupational Therapy		
Dr PH	Doctor of Public Health	Ingeniero	Engineer
Dr Sc PT	Doctor of Science in Physical Therapy	JCD	Doctor of Canon Law
DrAP	Doctor of Anesthesia Practice	JCL	Licentiate in Canon Law
DRSc	Doctor of Regulatory Science	JD	Juris Doctor
DS	Doctor of Science	JM	Juris Master
DS Sc	Doctor of Social Science	JSD	Doctor of Juridical Science
DSJS	Doctor of Science in Jewish Studies		Doctor of Jurisprudence
DSL	Doctor of Strategic Leadership		Doctor of the Science of Law
DSS	Doctor of Strategic Security	JSM	Master of the Science of Law
DSW	Doctor of Social Work	L Th	Licenciate in Theology
DTL	Doctor of Talmudic Law	LL B	Bachelor of Laws
	Doctor of Transformational Leadership	LL CM	Master of Comparative Law
DV Sc	Doctor of Veterinary Science	LL D	Doctor of Laws
DVM	Doctor of Veterinary Medicine	LL M	Master of Laws
DWS	Doctor of Worship Studies	LL M in Tax	Master of Laws in Taxation
EAA	Engineer in Aeronautics and Astronautics	LL M CL	Master of Laws in Common Law
EASPh D	Engineering and Applied Science Doctor of Philosophy	M Ac	Master of Accountancy
			Master of Accounting
ECS	Engineer in Computer Science		Master of Acupuncture
Ed D	Doctor of Education	M Ac OM	Master of Acupuncture and Oriental Medicine
Ed DCT	Doctor of Education in College Teaching	M Acc	Master of Accountancy
Ed L D	Doctor of Education Leadership		Master of Accounting
Ed M	Master of Education	M Acct	Master of Accountancy
Ed S	Specialist in Education		Master of Accounting
Ed Sp	Specialist in Education		

M Accy	Master of Accountancy
M Actg	Master of Accounting
M Acy	Master of Accountancy
M Ad	Master of Administration
M Ad Ed	Master of Adult Education
M Adm	Master of Administration
M Adm Mgt	Master of Administrative Management
M Admin	Master of Administration
M ADU	Master of Architectural Design and Urbanism
M Adv	Master of Advertising
M AEST	Master of Applied Environmental Science and Technology
M Ag	Master of Agriculture
M Ag Ed	Master of Agricultural Education
M Agr	Master of Agriculture
M Anesth Ed	Master of Anesthesiology Education
M App Comp Sc	Master of Applied Computer Science
M App St	Master of Applied Statistics
M Appl Stat	Master of Applied Statistics
M Aq	Master of Aquaculture
M Arc	Master of Architecture
M Arch	Master of Architecture
M Arch I	Master of Architecture I
M Arch II	Master of Architecture II
M Arch E	Master of Architectural Engineering
M Arch H	Master of Architectural History
M Bioethics	Master in Bioethics
M Biomath	Master of Biomathematics
M Ch E	Master of Chemical Engineering
M Chem	Master of Chemistry
M Cl D	Master of Clinical Dentistry
M Cl Sc	Master of Clinical Science
M Comp	Master of Computing
M Comp Sc	Master of Computer Science
M Coun	Master of Counseling
M Dent	Master of Dentistry
M Dent Sc	Master of Dental Sciences
M Des	Master of Design
M Des S	Master of Design Studies
M Div	Master of Divinity
M E Sci	Master of Earth Science
M Ec	Master of Economics
M Econ	Master of Economics
M Ed	Master of Education
M Ed T	Master of Education in Teaching
M En	Master of Engineering
M En S	Master of Environmental Sciences
M Eng	Master of Engineering
M Eng Mgt	Master of Engineering Management
M Engr	Master of Engineering
M Ent	Master of Enterprise
M Env	Master of Environment
M Env Des	Master of Environmental Design
M Env E	Master of Environmental Engineering
M Env Sc	Master of Environmental Science
M Fin	Master of Finance
M FSc	Master of Fisheries Science
M Geo E	Master of Geological Engineering
M Geoenv E	Master of Geoenvironmental Engineering
M Geog	Master of Geography
M Hum	Master of Humanities
M IDST	Master's in Interdisciplinary Studies
M Kin	Master of Kinesiology
M Land Arch	Master of Landscape Architecture
M Litt	Master of Letters
M Mat SE	Master of Material Science and Engineering
M Math	Master of Mathematics
M Mech E	Master of Mechanical Engineering
M Med Sc	Master of Medical Science
M Mgmt	Master of Management
M Mgt	Master of Management
M Min	Master of Ministries
M Mtl E	Master of Materials Engineering
M Mu	Master of Music
M Mus	Master of Music
M Mus Ed	Master of Music Education
M Music	Master of Music
M Nat Sci	Master of Natural Science
M Pet E	Master of Petroleum Engineering
M Pharm	Master of Pharmacy
M Phil	Master of Philosophy
M Phil F	Master of Philosophical Foundations
M Pl	Master of Planning
M Plan	Master of Planning
M Pol	Master of Political Science
M Pr Met	Master of Professional Meteorology
M Prob S	Master of Probability and Statistics
M Psych	Master of Psychology
M Pub	Master of Publishing
M Rel	Master of Religion
M Sc	Master of Science
M Sc A	Master of Science (Applied)
M Sc AC	Master of Science in Applied Computing
M Sc AHN	Master of Science in Applied Human Nutrition
M Sc BMC	Master of Science in Biomedical Communications
M Sc CS	Master of Science in Computer Science
M Sc E	Master of Science in Engineering
M Sc Eng	Master of Science in Engineering
M Sc Engr	Master of Science in Engineering
M Sc F	Master of Science in Forestry
M Sc FE	Master of Science in Forest Engineering
M Sc Geogr	Master of Science in Geography
M Sc N	Master of Science in Nursing
M Sc OT	Master of Science in Occupational Therapy
M Sc P	Master of Science in Planning
M Sc Pl	Master of Science in Planning
M Sc PT	Master of Science in Physical Therapy
M Sc T	Master of Science in Teaching
M SEM	Master of Sustainable Environmental Management
M Serv Soc	Master of Social Service
M Soc	Master of Sociology
M Sp Ed	Master of Special Education
M St	Master of Studies
M Stat	Master of Statistics
M Sys E	Master of Systems Engineering
M Sys Sc	Master of Systems Science
M Tax	Master of Taxation
M Tech	Master of Technology
M Th	Master of Theology
M Tox	Master of Toxicology
M Trans E	Master of Transportation Engineering
M U Ed	Master of Urban Education
M Urb	Master of Urban Planning
M Vet Sc	Master of Veterinary Science
MA	Master of Accounting
	Master of Administration
	Master of Arts
MA Comm	Master of Arts in Communication
MA Ed	Master of Arts in Education
MA Ed/HD	Master of Arts in Education and Human Development
MA Ext	Master of Agricultural Extension
MA Min	Master of Arts in Ministry
MA Past St	Master of Arts in Pastoral Studies
MA Ph	Master of Arts in Philosophy

MA Psych	Master of Arts in Psychology
MA Sc	Master of Applied Science
MA Sp	Master of Arts (Spirituality)
MA Th	Master of Arts in Theology
MA-R	Master of Arts (Research)
MAA	Master of Administrative Arts
	Master of Applied Anthropology
	Master of Applied Arts
	Master of Arts in Administration
MAAA	Master of Arts in Arts Administration
MAAAP	Master of Arts Administration and Policy
MAAD	Master of Advanced Architectural Design
MAAE	Master of Arts in Art Education
MAAPPS	Master of Arts in Asia Pacific Policy Studies
MAAS	Master of Arts in Aging and Spirituality
MAASJ	Master of Arts in Applied Social Justice
MAAT	Master of Arts in Applied Theology
	Master of Arts in Art Therapy
MAB	Master of Agribusiness
MABC	Master of Arts in Biblical Counseling
MABE	Master of Arts in Bible Exposition
MABL	Master of Arts in Biblical Languages
MABM	Master of Agribusiness Management
MABS	Master of Arts in Biblical Studies
MABT	Master of Arts in Bible Teaching
MAC	Master of Accountancy
	Master of Accounting
	Master of Arts in Communication
	Master of Arts in Counseling
MACC	Master of Arts in Christian Counseling
	Master of Arts in Clinical Counseling
MACCT	Master of Accounting
MACD	Master of Arts in Christian Doctrine
MACE	Master of Arts in Christian Education
MACH	Master of Arts in Church History
MACI	Master of Arts in Curriculum and Instruction
MACIS	Master of Accounting and Information Systems
MACJ	Master of Arts in Criminal Justice
MACL	Master of Arts in Christian Leadership
	Master of Arts in Community Leadership
MACM	Master of Arts in Christian Ministries
	Master of Arts in Christian Ministry
	Master of Arts in Church Music
	Master of Arts in Counseling Ministries
MACN	Master of Arts in Counseling
MACO	Master of Arts in Counseling
MAcOM	Master of Acupuncture and Oriental Medicine
MACP	Master of Arts in Christian Practice
	Master of Arts in Church Planting
	Master of Arts in Counseling Psychology
MACS	Master of Applied Computer Science
	Master of Arts in Catholic Studies
	Master of Arts in Christian Studies
MACSE	Master of Arts in Christian School Education
MACT	Master of Arts in Communications and Technology
MAD	Master in Educational Institution Administration
	Master of Art and Design
MADR	Master of Arts in Dispute Resolution
MADS	Master of Animal and Dairy Science
	Master of Applied Disability Studies
MAE	Master of Aerospace Engineering
	Master of Agricultural Economics
	Master of Agricultural Education
	Master of Applied Economics
	Master of Architectural Engineering
	Master of Art Education

	Master of Arts in Education
	Master of Arts in English
MAEd	Master of Arts Education
MAEL	Master of Arts in Educational Leadership
MAEM	Master of Arts in Educational Ministries
MAEP	Master of Arts in Economic Policy
	Master of Arts in Educational Psychology
MAES	Master of Arts in Environmental Sciences
MAET	Master of Arts in English Teaching
MAF	Master of Arts in Finance
MAFE	Master of Arts in Financial Economics
MAFLL	Master of Arts in Foreign Language and Literature
MAFM	Master of Accounting and Financial Management
MAFS	Master of Arts in Family Studies
MAG	Master of Applied Geography
MAGS	Master of Arts in Global Service
MAGU	Master of Urban Analysis and Management
MAH	Master of Arts in Humanities
MAHA	Master of Arts in Humanitarian Assistance
MAHCM	Master of Arts in Health Care Mission
MAHG	Master of American History and Government
MAHL	Master of Arts in Hebrew Letters
MAHN	Master of Applied Human Nutrition
MAHR	Master of Applied Historical Research
MAHS	Master of Arts in Human Services
MAHSR	Master in Applied Health Services Research
MAIA	Master of Arts in International Administration
	Master of Arts in International Affairs
MAIDM	Master of Arts in Interior Design and Merchandising
MAIH	Master of Arts in Interdisciplinary Humanities
MAIOP	Master of Applied Industrial/Organizational Psychology
MAIPCR	Master of Arts in International Peace and Conflict Management
MAIS	Master of Arts in Intercultural Studies
	Master of Arts in Interdisciplinary Studies
	Master of Arts in International Studies
MAIT	Master of Administration in Information Technology
MAJ	Master of Arts in Journalism
MAJ Ed	Master of Arts in Jewish Education
MAJCS	Master of Arts in Jewish Communal Service
MAJE	Master of Arts in Jewish Education
MAJPS	Master of Arts in Jewish Professional Studies
MAJS	Master of Arts in Jewish Studies
MAL	Master in Agricultural Leadership
MALA	Master of Arts in Liberal Arts
MALD	Master of Arts in Law and Diplomacy
MALER	Master of Arts in Labor and Employment Relations
MALL	Master of Arts in Language Learning
MALP	Master of Arts in Language Pedagogy
MALS	Master of Arts in Liberal Studies
MAM	Master of Acquisition Management
	Master of Agriculture and Management
	Master of Applied Mathematics
	Master of Arts in Management
	Master of Arts in Ministry
	Master of Arts Management
	Master of Avian Medicine
MAMB	Master of Applied Molecular Biology
MAMC	Master of Arts in Mass Communication
	Master of Arts in Ministry and Culture
	Master of Arts in Ministry for a Multicultural Church
	Master of Arts in Missional Christianity
MAME	Master of Arts in Missions/Evangelism

MAMFC	Master of Arts in Marriage and Family Counseling
MAMFT	Master of Arts in Marriage and Family Therapy
MAMHC	Master of Arts in Mental Health Counseling
MAMS	Master of Applied Mathematical Sciences
	Master of Applied Meditation Studies
	Master of Arts in Ministerial Studies
	Master of Arts in Ministry and Spirituality
MAMT	Master of Arts in Mathematics Teaching
MAN	Master of Applied Nutrition
MANT	Master of Arts in New Testament
MAOL	Master of Arts in Organizational Leadership
MAOM	Master of Acupuncture and Oriental Medicine
MAOT	Master of Arts in Old Testament
MAP	Master of Applied Politics
	Master of Applied Psychology
	Master of Arts in Planning
	Master of Psychology
	Master of Public Administration
MAP Min	Master of Arts in Pastoral Ministry
MAPA	Master of Arts in Public Administration
MAPC	Master of Arts in Pastoral Counseling
MAPE	Master of Arts in Physics Education
	Master of Arts in Political Economy
MAPM	Master of Arts in Pastoral Ministry
	Master of Arts in Pastoral Music
	Master of Arts in Practical Ministry
MAPP	Master of Arts in Public Policy
MAPS	Master of Arts in Pastoral Studies
	Master of Arts in Public Service
MAPT	Master of Practical Theology
MAPW	Master of Arts in Professional Writing
MAR	Master of Arts in Reading
	Master of Arts in Religion
Mar Eng	Marine Engineer
MARC	Master of Arts in Rehabilitation Counseling
MARE	Master of Arts in Religious Education
MARL	Master of Arts in Religious Leadership
MARS	Master of Arts in Religious Studies
MAS	Master of Accounting Science
	Master of Actuarial Science
	Master of Administrative Science
	Master of Advanced Study
	Master of Aeronautical Science
	Master of American Studies
	Master of Animal Science
	Master of Applied Science
	Master of Applied Statistics
	Master of Archival Studies
MASA	Master of Advanced Studies in Architecture
MASD	Master of Arts in Spiritual Direction
MASE	Master of Arts in Special Education
MASF	Master of Arts in Spiritual Formation
MASJ	Master of Arts in Systems of Justice
MASLA	Master of Advanced Studies in Landscape Architecture
MASM	Master of Aging Services Management
	Master of Arts in Specialized Ministries
MASP	Master of Applied Social Psychology
	Master of Arts in School Psychology
MASPAA	Master of Arts in Sports and Athletic Administration
MASS	Master of Applied Social Science
	Master of Arts in Social Science
MAST	Master of Arts in Science Teaching
MAT	Master of Arts in Teaching
	Master of Arts in Theology
	Master of Athletic Training
	Master's in Administration of Telecommunications
Mat E	Materials Engineer
MATCM	Master of Acupuncture and Traditional Chinese Medicine
MATDE	Master of Arts in Theology, Development, and Evangelism
MATDR	Master of Territorial Management and Regional Development
MATE	Master of Arts for the Teaching of English
MATESL	Master of Arts in Teaching English as a Second Language
MATESOL	Master of Arts in Teaching English to Speakers of Other Languages
MATF	Master of Arts in Teaching English as a Foreign Language/Intercultural Studies
MATFL	Master of Arts in Teaching Foreign Language
MATH	Master of Arts in Therapy
MATI	Master of Administration of Information Technology
MATL	Master of Arts in Teacher Leadership
	Master of Arts in Teaching of Languages
	Master of Arts in Transformational Leadership
MATM	Master of Arts in Teaching of Mathematics
MATS	Master of Arts in Theological Studies
	Master of Arts in Transforming Spirituality
MATSL	Master of Arts in Teaching a Second Language
MAUA	Master of Arts in Urban Affairs
MAUD	Master of Arts in Urban Design
MAURP	Master of Arts in Urban and Regional Planning
MAW	Master of Arts in Worship
MAWSHP	Master of Arts in Worship
MAYM	Master of Arts in Youth Ministry
MB	Master of Bioinformatics
MBA	Master of Business Administration
MBA-AM	Master of Business Administration in Aviation Management
MBA-EP	Master of Business Administration–Experienced Professionals
MBAA	Master of Business Administration in Aviation
MBAE	Master of Biological and Agricultural Engineering
	Master of Biosystems and Agricultural Engineering
MBAH	Master of Business Administration in Health
MBAi	Master of Business Administration–International
MBAICT	Master of Business Administration in Information and Communication Technology
MBATM	Master of Business Administration in Technology Management
MBC	Master of Building Construction
MBE	Master of Bilingual Education
	Master of Bioengineering
	Master of Bioethics
	Master of Biomedical Engineering
	Master of Business Economics
	Master of Business Education
MBEE	Master in Biotechnology Enterprise and Entrepreneurship
MBET	Master of Business, Entrepreneurship and Technology
MBID	Master of Biomedical Innovation and Development
MBIOT	Master of Biotechnology
MBiotech	Master of Biotechnology
MBL	Master of Business Law
	Master of Business Leadership
MBLE	Master in Business Logistics Engineering
MBME	Master's in Biomedical Engineering
MBMSE	Master of Business Management and Software Engineering

MBOE	Master of Business Operational Excellence		Master of Clinical Science
MBS	Master of Biblical Studies		Master of Combined Sciences
	Master of Biological Science		Master of Communication Studies
	Master of Biomedical Sciences		Master of Computer Science
	Master of Bioscience		Master of Consumer Science
	Master of Building Science	MCSE	Master of Computer Science and Engineering
	Master of Business and Science	MCSL	Master of Catholic School Leadership
MBST	Master of Biostatistics	MCSM	Master of Construction Science and Management
MBT	Master of Biomedical Technology		
	Master of Biotechnology	MCTM	Master of Clinical Translation Management
	Master of Business Taxation	MCTP	Master of Communication Technology and Policy
MBV	Master of Business for Veterans		
MC	Master of Communication	MCTS	Master of Clinical and Translational Science
	Master of Counseling	MCVS	Master of Cardiovascular Science
	Master of Cybersecurity	MD	Doctor of Medicine
MC Ed	Master of Continuing Education	MDA	Master of Dietetic Administration
MC Sc	Master of Computer Science	MDB	Master of Design-Build
MCA	Master in Collegiate Athletics	MDE	Master of Developmental Economics
	Master of Commercial Aviation		Master of Distance Education
	Master of Criminology (Applied)		Master of the Education of the Deaf
MCAM	Master of Computational and Applied Mathematics	MDH	Master of Dental Hygiene
		MDM	Master of Design Methods
MCC	Master of Computer Science		Master of Digital Media
MCD	Master of Communications Disorders	MDP	Master in Sustainable Development Practice
	Master of Community Development		Master of Development Practice
MCE	Master in Electronic Commerce	MDR	Master of Dispute Resolution
	Master of Christian Education	MDS	Master of Dental Surgery
	Master of Civil Engineering		Master of Design Studies
	Master of Control Engineering		Master of Digital Sciences
MCEM	Master of Construction Engineering Management	ME	Master of Education
			Master of Engineering
MCHE	Master of Chemical Engineering		Master of Entrepreneurship
MCIS	Master of Communication and Information Studies	ME Sc	Master of Engineering Science
		ME-PD	Master of Education–Professional Development
	Master of Computer and Information Science	MEA	Master of Educational Administration
	Master of Computer Information Systems		Master of Engineering Administration
MCIT	Master of Computer and Information Technology	MEAE	Master of Entertainment Arts and Engineering
		MEAP	Master of Environmental Administration and Planning
MCJ	Master of Criminal Justice		
MCL	Master in Communication Leadership	MEB	Master of Energy Business
	Master of Canon Law	MEBD	Master in Environmental Building Design
	Master of Comparative Law	MEBT	Master in Electronic Business Technologies
MCM	Master of Christian Ministry	MEC	Master of Electronic Commerce
	Master of Church Music	Mech E	Mechanical Engineer
	Master of City Management	MED	Master of Education of the Deaf
	Master of Communication Management	MEDS	Master of Environmental Design Studies
	Master of Community Medicine	MEE	Master in Education
	Master of Construction Management		Master of Electrical Engineering
	Master of Contract Management		Master of Energy Engineering
MCMin	Master of Christian Ministry		Master of Environmental Engineering
MCMP	Master of City and Metropolitan Planning	MEEM	Master of Environmental Engineering and Management
MCMS	Master of Clinical Medical Science		
MCN	Master of Clinical Nutrition	MEENE	Master of Engineering in Environmental Engineering
MCOL	Master of Arts in Community and Organizational Leadership		
		MEEP	Master of Environmental and Energy Policy
MCP	Master of City Planning	MEERM	Master of Earth and Environmental Resource Management
	Master of Community Planning		
	Master of Counseling Psychology	MEH	Master in Humanistic Studies
	Master of Cytopathology Practice		Master of Environmental Health
	Master of Science in Quality Systems and Productivity		Master of Environmental Horticulture
		MEHS	Master of Environmental Health and Safety
MCPC	Master of Arts in Chaplaincy and Pastoral Care	MEIM	Master of Entertainment Industry Management
MCPD	Master of Community Planning and Development		Master of Equine Industry Management
		MEL	Master of Educational Leadership
MCR	Master in Clinical Research		Master of English Literature
MCRP	Master of City and Regional Planning	MELP	Master of Environmental Law and Policy
	Master of Community and Regional Planning	MEM	Master of Engineering Management
MCRS	Master of City and Regional Studies		Master of Environmental Management
MCS	Master of Chemical Sciences		Master of Marketing
	Master of Christian Studies		

MEME	Master of Engineering in Manufacturing Engineering	MGE	Master of Geotechnical Engineering
	Master of Engineering in Mechanical Engineering	MGEM	Master of Global Entrepreneurship and Management
MENR	Master of Environment and Natural Resources	MGIS	Master of Geographic Information Science
MENVEGR	Master of Environmental Engineering		Master of Geographic Information Systems
MEP	Master of Engineering Physics	MGM	Master of Global Management
MEPC	Master of Environmental Pollution Control	MGP	Master of Gestion de Projet
MEPD	Master of Environmental Planning and Design	MGPS	Master of Global Policy Studies
MER	Master of Employment Relations	MGREM	Master of Global Real Estate Management
MERE	Master of Entrepreneurial Real Estate	MGS	Master of Gerontological Studies
MERL	Master of Energy Regulation and Law		Master of Global Studies
MES	Master of Education and Science	MGsc	Master of Geoscience
	Master of Engineering Science	MH	Master of Humanities
	Master of Environment and Sustainability	MH Sc	Master of Health Sciences
	Master of Environmental Science	MHA	Master of Health Administration
	Master of Environmental Studies		Master of Healthcare Administration
	Master of Environmental Systems		Master of Hospital Administration
	Master of Special Education		Master of Hospitality Administration
MESM	Master of Environmental Science and Management	MHB	Master of Human Behavior
MET	Master of Educational Technology	MHC	Master of Mental Health Counseling
	Master of Engineering Technology	MHCA	Master of Health Care Administration
	Master of Entertainment Technology	MHCD	Master of Health Care Design
	Master of Environmental Toxicology	MHCI	Master of Human-Computer Interaction
METM	Master of Engineering and Technology Management	MHCL	Master of Health Care Leadership
		MHE	Master of Health Education
MEVE	Master of Environmental Engineering		Master of Human Ecology
MF	Master of Finance	MHE Ed	Master of Home Economics Education
	Master of Forestry	MHEA	Master of Higher Education Administration
MFA	Master of Fine Arts	MHHS	Master of Health and Human Services
MFALP	Master of Food and Agriculture Law and Policy	MHI	Master of Health Informatics
MFAM	Master's of Food Animal Medicine		Master of Healthcare Innovation
MFAS	Master of Fisheries and Aquatic Science	MHIHIM	Master of Health Informatics and Health Information Management
MFAW	Master of Fine Arts in Writing	MHIIM	Master of Health Informatics and Information Management
MFC	Master of Forest Conservation		
MFCS	Master of Family and Consumer Sciences	MHIS	Master of Health Information Systems
MFE	Master of Financial Economics	MHK	Master of Human Kinetics
	Master of Financial Engineering	MHM	Master of Healthcare Management
	Master of Forest Engineering	MHMS	Master of Health Management Systems
MFES	Master of Fire and Emergency Services	MHP	Master of Health Physics
MFG	Master of Functional Genomics		Master of Heritage Preservation
MFHD	Master of Family and Human Development		Master of Historic Preservation
MFM	Master of Financial Management	MHPA	Master of Heath Policy and Administration
	Master of Financial Mathematics	MHPE	Master of Health Professions Education
MFPE	Master of Food Process Engineering	MHR	Master of Human Resources
MFR	Master of Forest Resources	MHRD	Master in Human Resource Development
MFRC	Master of Forest Resources and Conservation	MHRIR	Master of Human Resources and Industrial Relations
MFRE	Master of Food and Resource Economics	MHRLR	Master of Human Resources and Labor Relations
MFS	Master of Food Science		
	Master of Forensic Sciences	MHRM	Master of Human Resources Management
	Master of Forest Science	MHS	Master of Health Science
	Master of Forest Studies		Master of Health Sciences
	Master of French Studies		Master of Health Studies
MFST	Master of Food Safety and Technology		Master of Hispanic Studies
MFT	Master of Family Therapy		Master of Human Services
	Master of Food Technology		Master of Humanistic Studies
MFWB	Master of Fishery and Wildlife Biology	MHSA	Master of Health Services Administration
MFWCB	Master of Fish, Wildlife and Conservation Biology	MHSE	Master of Health Science Education
		MHSM	Master of Health Systems Management
MFWS	Master of Fisheries and Wildlife Sciences	MI	Master of Information
MFYCS	Master of Family, Youth and Community Sciences		Master of Instruction
		MI Arch	Master of Interior Architecture
MG	Master of Genetics	MIA	Master of Interior Architecture
MGA	Master of Global Affairs		Master of International Affairs
	Master of Government Administration	MIAA	Master of International Affairs and Administration
	Master of Governmental Administration		
MGC	Master of Genetic Counseling	MIAM	Master of International Agribusiness Management
MGD	Master of Graphic Design		

MIAPD	Master of Interior Architecture and Product Design		Master of Juridical Studies
MIB	Master of International Business	MK	Master of Kinesiology
MIBA	Master of International Business Administration	MKM	Master of Knowledge Management
		ML	Master of Latin
MICM	Master of International Construction Management	ML Arch	Master of Landscape Architecture
MID	Master of Industrial Design	MLA	Master of Landscape Architecture
	Master of Industrial Distribution		Master of Liberal Arts
	Master of Interior Design	MLAS	Master of Laboratory Animal Science
	Master of International Development		Master of Liberal Arts and Sciences
MIDA	Master of International Development Administration	MLAUD	Master of Landscape Architecture in Urban Development
MIDC	Master of Integrated Design and Construction	MLD	Master of Leadership Development
MIDP	Master of International Development Policy		Master of Leadership Studies
MIE	Master of Industrial Engineering	MLE	Master of Applied Linguistics and Exegesis
MIHTM	Master of International Hospitality and Tourism Management	MLER	Master of Labor and Employment Relations
MIJ	Master of International Journalism	MLI Sc	Master of Library and Information Science
MILR	Master of Industrial and Labor Relations	MLIS	Master of Library and Information Science
MIM	Master in Ministry		Master of Library and Information Studies
	Master of Information Management	MLM	Master of Leadership in Ministry
	Master of International Management	MLPD	Master of Land and Property Development
MIMLAE	Master of International Management for Latin American Executives	MLRHR	Master of Labor Relations and Human Resources
MIMS	Master of Information Management and Systems	MLS	Master of Leadership Studies
			Master of Legal Studies
	Master of Integrated Manufacturing Systems		Master of Liberal Studies
MIP	Master of Infrastructure Planning		Master of Library Science
	Master of Intellectual Property		Master of Life Sciences
	Master of International Policy	MLSCM	Master of Logistics and Supply Chain Management
MIPA	Master of International Public Affairs	MLSP	Master of Law and Social Policy
MIPD	Master of Integrated Product Design	MLT	Master of Language Technologies
MIPM	Master of International Policy Management	MLTCA	Master of Long Term Care Administration
MIPP	Master of International Policy and Practice	MLW	Master of Studies in Law
	Master of International Public Policy	MLWS	Master of Land and Water Systems
MIPS	Master of International Planning Studies	MM	Master of Management
MIR	Master of Industrial Relations		Master of Ministry
	Master of International Relations		Master of Missiology
MIRHR	Master of Industrial Relations and Human Resources		Master of Music
MIS	Master of Imaging Science	MM Ed	Master of Music Education
	Master of Industrial Statistics	MM Sc	Master of Medical Science
	Master of Information Science	MM St	Master of Museum Studies
	Master of Information Systems	MMA	Master of Marine Affairs
	Master of Integrated Science		Master of Media Arts
	Master of Interdisciplinary Studies		Master of Ministry Administration
	Master of International Service		Master of Musical Arts
	Master of International Studies	MMAL	Master of Maritime Administration and Logistics
MISE	Master of Industrial and Systems Engineering	MMAS	Master of Military Art and Science
MISKM	Master of Information Sciences and Knowledge Management	MMB	Master of Microbial Biotechnology
		MMC	Master of Manufacturing Competitiveness
MISM	Master of Information Systems Management		Master of Mass Communications
MISW	Master of Indigenous Social Work		Master of Music Conducting
MIT	Master in Teaching	MMCM	Master of Music in Church Music
	Master of Industrial Technology	MMCSS	Master of Mathematical Computational and Statistical Sciences
	Master of Information Technology	MME	Master of Manufacturing Engineering
	Master of Initial Teaching		Master of Mathematics Education
	Master of International Trade		Master of Mathematics for Educators
	Master of Internet Technology		Master of Mechanical Engineering
MITA	Master of Information Technology Administration		Master of Mining Engineering
			Master of Music Education
MITM	Master of Information Technology and Management	MMF	Master of Mathematical Finance
MJ	Master of Journalism	MMFT	Master of Marriage and Family Therapy
	Master of Jurisprudence	MMH	Master of Management in Hospitality
MJ Ed	Master of Jewish Education		Master of Medical Humanities
MJA	Master of Justice Administration	MMI	Master of Management of Innovation
MJM	Master of Justice Management	MMIS	Master of Management Information Systems
MJS	Master of Judicial Studies	MML	Master of Managerial Logistics
		MMM	Master of Manufacturing Management

Peterson's Graduate Programs in the Humanities, Arts & Social Sciences 2016

	Master of Marine Management		Master of Physician Assistant
	Master of Medical Management		Master of Professional Accountancy
MMP	Master of Management Practice		Master of Professional Accounting
	Master of Marine Policy		Master of Public Administration
	Master of Medical Physics		Master of Public Affairs
	Master of Music Performance	MPAC	Master of Professional Accounting
MMPA	Master of Management and Professional Accounting	MPAID	Master of Public Administration and International Development
MMQM	Master of Manufacturing Quality Management	MPAP	Master of Physician Assistant Practice
MMR	Master of Marketing Research		Master of Public Administration and Policy
MMRM	Master of Marine Resources Management		Master of Public Affairs and Politics
MMS	Master of Management Science	MPAS	Master of Physician Assistant Science
	Master of Management Studies		Master of Physician Assistant Studies
	Master of Manufacturing Systems	MPC	Master of Professional Communication
	Master of Marine Studies		Master of Professional Counseling
	Master of Materials Science	MPD	Master of Product Development
	Master of Mathematical Sciences		Master of Public Diplomacy
	Master of Medical Science	MPDS	Master of Planning and Development Studies
	Master of Medieval Studies	MPE	Master of Physical Education
MMSE	Master of Manufacturing Systems Engineering	MPEM	Master of Project Engineering and Management
MMSM	Master of Music in Sacred Music	MPH	Master of Public Health
MMT	Master in Marketing	MPHE	Master of Public Health Education
	Master of Music Teaching	MPHM	Master in Plant Health Management
	Master of Music Therapy	MPHS	Master of Population Health Sciences
	Master's in Marketing Technology	MPHTM	Master of Public Health and Tropical Medicine
MMus	Master of Music	MPI	Master of Product Innovation
MN	Master of Nursing	MPIA	Master of Public and International Affairs
	Master of Nutrition	MPM	Master of Pastoral Ministry
MN NP	Master of Nursing in Nurse Practitioner		Master of Pest Management
MNA	Master of Nonprofit Administration		Master of Policy Management
	Master of Nurse Anesthesia		Master of Practical Ministries
MNAL	Master of Nonprofit Administration and Leadership		Master of Project Management
MNAS	Master of Natural and Applied Science		Master of Public Management
MNCM	Master of Network and Communications Management	MPNA	Master of Public and Nonprofit Administration
		MPNL	Master of Philanthropy and Nonprofit Leadership
MNE	Master of Nuclear Engineering	MPO	Master of Prosthetics and Orthotics
MNL	Master in International Business for Latin America	MPOD	Master of Positive Organizational Development
MNM	Master of Nonprofit Management	MPP	Master of Public Policy
MNO	Master of Nonprofit Organization	MPPA	Master of Public Policy Administration
MNPL	Master of Not-for-Profit Leadership		Master of Public Policy and Administration
MNpS	Master of Nonprofit Studies	MPPAL	Master of Public Policy, Administration and Law
MNR	Master of Natural Resources	MPPM	Master of Public and Private Management
MNRD	Master of Natural Resources Development		Master of Public Policy and Management
MNRES	Master of Natural Resources and Environmental Studies	MPPPM	Master of Plant Protection and Pest Management
MNRM	Master of Natural Resource Management	MPRTM	Master of Parks, Recreation, and Tourism Management
MNRMG	Master of Natural Resource Management and Geography	MPS	Master of Pastoral Studies
MNRS	Master of Natural Resource Stewardship		Master of Perfusion Science
MNS	Master of Natural Science		Master of Planning Studies
MO	Master of Oceanography		Master of Political Science
MOD	Master of Organizational Development		Master of Preservation Studies
MOGS	Master of Oil and Gas Studies		Master of Prevention Science
MOL	Master of Organizational Leadership		Master of Professional Studies
MOM	Master of Organizational Management		Master of Public Service
	Master of Oriental Medicine	MPSA	Master of Public Service Administration
MOR	Master of Operations Research	MPSG	Master of Population and Social Gerontology
MOT	Master of Occupational Therapy	MPSIA	Master of Political Science and International Affairs
MP	Master of Physiology		
	Master of Planning	MPSL	Master of Public Safety Leadership
MP Ac	Master of Professional Accountancy	MPSRE	Master of Professional Studies in Real Estate
MP Acc	Master of Professional Accountancy	MPT	Master of Pastoral Theology
	Master of Professional Accounting		Master of Physical Therapy
	Master of Public Accounting		Master of Practical Theology
MP Aff	Master of Public Affairs	MPVM	Master of Preventive Veterinary Medicine
MP Th	Master of Pastoral Theology	MPW	Master of Professional Writing
MPA	Master of Performing Arts		Master of Public Works

MQM	Master of Quality Management		Master of Science in Agriculture
MQS	Master of Quality Systems		Master of Science in Analytics
MR	Master of Recreation		Master of Science in Anesthesia
	Master of Retailing		Master of Science in Architecture
MRA	Master in Research Administration		Master of Science in Aviation
MRC	Master of Rehabilitation Counseling		Master of Sports Administration
MRCP	Master of Regional and City Planning		Master of Surgical Assisting
	Master of Regional and Community Planning	MSAA	Master of Science in Astronautics and Aeronautics
MRD	Master of Rural Development		
MRE	Master of Real Estate	MSAAE	Master of Science in Aeronautical and Astronautical Engineering
	Master of Religious Education		
MRED	Master of Real Estate Development	MSABE	Master of Science in Agricultural and Biological Engineering
MREM	Master of Resource and Environmental Management		
		MSAC	Master of Science in Acupuncture
MRLS	Master of Resources Law Studies	MSACC	Master of Science in Accounting
MRM	Master of Resources Management	MSACS	Master of Science in Applied Computer Science
MRP	Master of Regional Planning	MSAE	Master of Science in Aeronautical Engineering
MRRD	Master in Recreation Resource Development		Master of Science in Aerospace Engineering
MRS	Master of Religious Studies		Master of Science in Applied Economics
MRSc	Master of Rehabilitation Science		Master of Science in Applied Engineering
MRTP	Master of Rural and Town Planning		Master of Science in Architectural Engineering
MS	Master of Science	MSAEM	Master of Science in Aerospace Engineering and Mechanics
MS Cmp E	Master of Science in Computer Engineering		
MS Kin	Master of Science in Kinesiology	MSAF	Master of Science in Aviation Finance
MS Acct	Master of Science in Accounting	MSAG	Master of Science in Applied Geosciences
MS Accy	Master of Science in Accountancy	MSAH	Master of Science in Allied Health
MS Aero E	Master of Science in Aerospace Engineering	MSAL	Master of Sport Administration and Leadership
MS Ag	Master of Science in Agriculture	MSAM	Master of Science in Applied Mathematics
MS Arch	Master of Science in Architecture	MSANR	Master of Science in Agriculture and Natural Resources
MS Arch St	Master of Science in Architectural Studies		
MS Bio E	Master of Science in Bioengineering	MSAPM	Master of Security Analysis and Portfolio Management
MS Bm E	Master of Science in Biomedical Engineering		
MS Ch E	Master of Science in Chemical Engineering	MSAS	Master of Science in Applied Statistics
MS Cp E	Master of Science in Computer Engineering		Master of Science in Architectural Studies
MS Eco	Master of Science in Economics	MSAT	Master of Science in Accounting and Taxation
MS Econ	Master of Science in Economics		Master of Science in Advanced Technology
MS Ed	Master of Science in Education		Master of Science in Athletic Training
MS El	Master of Science in Educational Leadership and Administration	MSB	Master of Science in Biotechnology
			Master of Sustainable Business
MS En E	Master of Science in Environmental Engineering	MSBA	Master of Science in Business Administration
			Master of Science in Business Analysis
MS Eng	Master of Science in Engineering	MSBAE	Master of Science in Biological and Agricultural Engineering
MS Engr	Master of Science in Engineering		
MS Env E	Master of Science in Environmental Engineering		Master of Science in Biosystems and Agricultural Engineering
		MSBC	Master of Science in Building Construction
MS Exp Surg	Master of Science in Experimental Surgery		Master of Science in Business Communication
MS Mat E	Master of Science in Materials Engineering	MSBCB	Master's in Bioinformatics and Computational Biology
MS Mat SE	Master of Science in Material Science and Engineering		
		MSBE	Master of Science in Biological Engineering
MS Met E	Master of Science in Metallurgical Engineering		Master of Science in Biomedical Engineering
MS Mgt	Master of Science in Management	MSBENG	Master of Science in Bioengineering
MS Min	Master of Science in Mining	MSBH	Master of Science in Behavioral Health
MS Min E	Master of Science in Mining Engineering	MSBIT	Master of Science in Business Information Technology
MS Mt E	Master of Science in Materials Engineering		
MS Otol	Master of Science in Otolaryngology	MSBM	Master of Sport Business Management
MS Pet E	Master of Science in Petroleum Engineering	MSBME	Master of Science in Biomedical Engineering
MS Sc	Master of Social Science	MSBMS	Master of Science in Basic Medical Science
MS Sp Ed	Master of Science in Special Education	MSBS	Master of Science in Biomedical Sciences
MS Stat	Master of Science in Statistics	MSBTM	Master of Science in Biotechnology and Management
MS Surg	Master of Science in Surgery		
MS Tax	Master of Science in Taxation	MSC	Master of Science in Commerce
MS Tc E	Master of Science in Telecommunications Engineering		Master of Science in Communication
			Master of Science in Computers
MS-R	Master of Science (Research)		Master of Science in Counseling
MSA	Master of School Administration		Master of Science in Criminology
	Master of Science in Accountancy		Master of Strategic Communication
	Master of Science in Accounting	MSCC	Master of Science in Community Counseling
	Master of Science in Administration	MSCD	Master of Science in Communication Disorders
	Master of Science in Aeronautics		Master of Science in Community Development

MSCE	Master of Science in Civil Engineering
	Master of Science in Clinical Epidemiology
	Master of Science in Computer Engineering
	Master of Science in Continuing Education
MSCEE	Master of Science in Civil and Environmental Engineering
MSCF	Master of Science in Computational Finance
MSCH	Master of Science in Chemical Engineering
MSChE	Master of Science in Chemical Engineering
MSCI	Master of Science in Clinical Investigation
MSCIS	Master of Science in Computer and Information Science
	Master of Science in Computer and Information Systems
	Master of Science in Computer Information Science
	Master of Science in Computer Information Systems
MSCIT	Master of Science in Computer Information Technology
MSCJ	Master of Science in Criminal Justice
MSCJA	Master of Science in Criminal Justice Administration
MSCJS	Master of Science in Crime and Justice Studies
MSCLS	Master of Science in Clinical Laboratory Studies
MSCM	Master of Science in Church Management
	Master of Science in Conflict Management
	Master of Science in Construction Management
	Master of Supply Chain Management
MSCNU	Master of Science in Clinical Nutrition
MSCP	Master of Science in Clinical Psychology
	Master of Science in Community Psychology
	Master of Science in Computer Engineering
	Master of Science in Counseling Psychology
MSCPE	Master of Science in Computer Engineering
MSCPharm	Master of Science in Pharmacy
MSCR	Master of Science in Clinical Research
MSCRP	Master of Science in City and Regional Planning
	Master of Science in Community and Regional Planning
MSCS	Master of Science in Clinical Science
	Master of Science in Computer Science
	Master of Science in Cyber Security
MSCSD	Master of Science in Communication Sciences and Disorders
MSCSE	Master of Science in Computer Science and Engineering
MSCTE	Master of Science in Career and Technical Education
MSD	Master of Science in Dentistry
	Master of Science in Design
	Master of Science in Dietetics
MSE	Master of Science Education
	Master of Science in Economics
	Master of Science in Education
	Master of Science in Engineering
	Master of Science in Engineering Management
	Master of Software Engineering
	Master of Special Education
	Master of Structural Engineering
MSECE	Master of Science in Electrical and Computer Engineering
MSED	Master of Sustainable Economic Development
MSEE	Master of Science in Electrical Engineering
	Master of Science in Environmental Engineering
MSEH	Master of Science in Environmental Health
MSEL	Master of Science in Educational Leadership
MSEM	Master of Science in Engineering Management
	Master of Science in Engineering Mechanics

	Master of Science in Environmental Management
MSENE	Master of Science in Environmental Engineering
MSEO	Master of Science in Electro-Optics
MSEP	Master of Science in Economic Policy
MSES	Master of Science in Embedded Software Engineering
	Master of Science in Engineering Science
	Master of Science in Environmental Science
	Master of Science in Environmental Studies
	Master of Science in Exercise Science
MSET	Master of Science in Educational Technology
	Master of Science in Engineering Technology
MSEV	Master of Science in Environmental Engineering
MSF	Master of Science in Finance
	Master of Science in Forestry
	Master of Spiritual Formation
MSFA	Master of Science in Financial Analysis
MSFCS	Master of Science in Family and Consumer Science
MSFE	Master of Science in Financial Engineering
MSFM	Master of Sustainable Forest Management
MSFOR	Master of Science in Forestry
MSFP	Master of Science in Financial Planning
MSFS	Master of Science in Financial Sciences
	Master of Science in Forensic Science
MSFSB	Master of Science in Financial Services and Banking
MSFT	Master of Science in Family Therapy
MSGC	Master of Science in Genetic Counseling
MSH	Master of Science in Health
	Master of Science in Hospice
MSHA	Master of Science in Health Administration
MSHCA	Master of Science in Health Care Administration
MSHCI	Master of Science in Human Computer Interaction
MSHCPM	Master of Science in Health Care Policy and Management
MSHE	Master of Science in Health Education
MSHES	Master of Science in Human Environmental Sciences
MSHFID	Master of Science in Human Factors in Information Design
MSHFS	Master of Science in Human Factors and Systems
MSHI	Master of Science in Health Informatics
MSHP	Master of Science in Health Professions
	Master of Science in Health Promotion
MSHR	Master of Science in Human Resources
MSHRL	Master of Science in Human Resource Leadership
MSHRM	Master of Science in Human Resource Management
MSHROD	Master of Science in Human Resources and Organizational Development
MSHS	Master of Science in Health Science
	Master of Science in Health Services
	Master of Science in Homeland Security
MSI	Master of Science in Information
	Master of Science in Instruction
	Master of System Integration
MSIA	Master of Science in Industrial Administration
	Master of Science in Information Assurance
MSIB	Master of Science in International Business
MSIDM	Master of Science in Interior Design and Merchandising
MSIE	Master of Science in Industrial Engineering
	Master of Science in International Economics

MSIEM	Master of Science in Information Engineering and Management	MSMS	Master of Science in Management Science
MSIID	Master of Science in Information and Instructional Design		Master of Science in Marine Science
			Master of Science in Medical Sciences
MSIM	Master of Science in Information Management	MSMSE	Master of Science in Manufacturing Systems Engineering
	Master of Science in International Management		Master of Science in Material Science and Engineering
MSIMC	Master of Science in Integrated Marketing Communications		Master of Science in Mathematics and Science Education
MSIR	Master of Science in Industrial Relations	MSMT	Master of Science in Management and Technology
MSIS	Master of Science in Information Science		
	Master of Science in Information Studies	MSMus	Master of Sacred Music
	Master of Science in Information Systems	MSN	Master of Science in Nursing
	Master of Science in Interdisciplinary Studies	MSNA	Master of Science in Nurse Anesthesia
MSISE	Master of Science in Infrastructure Systems Engineering	MSNE	Master of Science in Nuclear Engineering
		MSNED	Master of Science in Nurse Education
MSISM	Master of Science in Information Systems Management	MSNM	Master of Science in Nonprofit Management
MSISPM	Master of Science in Information Security Policy and Management	MSNS	Master of Science in Natural Science
			Master of Science in Nutritional Science
MSIST	Master of Science in Information Systems Technology	MSOD	Master of Science in Organization Development
MSIT	Master of Science in Industrial Technology		Master of Science in Organizational Development
	Master of Science in Information Technology	MSOEE	Master of Science in Outdoor and Environmental Education
	Master of Science in Instructional Technology		
MSITM	Master of Science in Information Technology Management	MSOES	Master of Science in Occupational Ergonomics and Safety
MSJ	Master of Science in Journalism	MSOH	Master of Science in Occupational Health
	Master of Science in Jurisprudence	MSOL	Master of Science in Organizational Leadership
MSJC	Master of Social Justice and Criminology	MSOM	Master of Science in Operations Management
MSJE	Master of Science in Jewish Education		Master of Science in Oriental Medicine
MSJFP	Master of Science in Juvenile Forensic Psychology	MSOR	Master of Science in Operations Research
MSJJ	Master of Science in Juvenile Justice	MSOT	Master of Science in Occupational Technology
MSJPS	Master of Science in Justice and Public Safety		Master of Science in Occupational Therapy
MSJS	Master of Science in Jewish Studies	MSP	Master of Science in Pharmacy
MSL	Master of School Leadership		Master of Science in Planning
	Master of Science in Leadership		Master of Speech Pathology
	Master of Science in Limnology	MSPA	Master of Science in Physician Assistant
	Master of Strategic Leadership		Master of Science in Professional Accountancy
	Master of Studies in Law	MSPAS	Master of Science in Physician Assistant Studies
MSLA	Master of Science in Legal Administration	MSPC	Master of Science in Professional Communications
MSLFS	Master of Science in Life Sciences		
MSLP	Master of Speech-Language Pathology	MSPE	Master of Science in Petroleum Engineering
MSLS	Master of Science in Library Science	MSPH	Master of Science in Public Health
MSLSCM	Master of Science in Logistics and Supply Chain Management	MSPHR	Master of Science in Pharmacy
		MSPM	Master of Science in Professional Management
MSLT	Master of Second Language Teaching		Master of Science in Project Management
MSM	Master of Sacred Ministry	MSPNGE	Master of Science in Petroleum and Natural Gas Engineering
	Master of Sacred Music		
	Master of School Mathematics	MSPO	Master of Science in Prosthetics and Orthotics
	Master of Science in Management	MSPPM	Master of Science in Public Policy and Management
	Master of Science in Medicine		
	Master of Science in Organization Management	MSPS	Master of Science in Pharmaceutical Science
	Master of Security Management		Master of Science in Political Science
MSMA	Master of Science in Marketing Analysis		Master of Science in Psychological Services
MSMAE	Master of Science in Materials Engineering	MSPT	Master of Science in Physical Therapy
MSMC	Master of Science in Mass Communications	MSpVM	Master of Specialized Veterinary Medicine
MSME	Master of Science in Mathematics Education	MSR	Master of Science in Radiology
	Master of Science in Mechanical Engineering		Master of Science in Reading
MSMFT	Master of Science in Marriage and Family Therapy	MSRA	Master of Science in Recreation Administration
		MSRE	Master of Science in Real Estate
MSMHC	Master of Science in Mental Health Counseling		Master of Science in Religious Education
MSMIS	Master of Science in Management Information Systems	MSRED	Master of Science in Real Estate Development
			Master of Sustainable Real Estate Development
MSMIT	Master of Science in Management and Information Technology	MSRLS	Master of Science in Recreation and Leisure Studies
MSMLS	Master of Science in Medical Laboratory Science	MSRM	Master of Science in Risk Management
		MSRMP	Master of Science in Radiological Medical Physics
MSMOT	Master of Science in Management of Technology		
		MSRS	Master of Science in Radiological Sciences
MSMP	Master of Science in Medical Physics		Master of Science in Rehabilitation Science

MSS	Master of Security Studies	MTHM	Master of Tourism and Hospitality Management
	Master of Social Science	MTI	Master of Information Technology
	Master of Social Services	MTID	Master of Tangible Interaction Design
	Master of Software Systems	MTL	Master of Talmudic Law
	Master of Sports Science	MTM	Master of Technology Management
	Master of Strategic Studies		Master of Telecommunications Management
	Master's in Statistical Science		Master of the Teaching of Mathematics
MSSA	Master of Science in Social Administration	MTMH	Master of Tropical Medicine and Hygiene
MSSCM	Master of Science in Supply Chain Management	MTMS	Master in Teaching Mathematics and Science
MSSD	Master of Arts in Software Driven Systems Design	MTOM	Master of Traditional Oriental Medicine
		MTPC	Master of Technical and Professional Communication
	Master of Science in Sustainable Design		
MSSE	Master of Science in Software Engineering	MTR	Master of Translational Research
	Master of Science in Special Education	MTS	Master of Theatre Studies
MSSEM	Master of Science in Systems and Engineering Management		Master of Theological Studies
		MTWM	Master of Trust and Wealth Management
MSSI	Master of Science in Security Informatics	MTX	Master of Taxation
	Master of Science in Strategic Intelligence	MUA	Master of Urban Affairs
MSSL	Master of Science in School Leadership	MUCD	Master of Urban and Community Design
	Master of Science in Strategic Leadership	MUD	Master of Urban Design
MSSLP	Master of Science in Speech-Language Pathology	MUDS	Master of Urban Design Studies
		MUEP	Master of Urban and Environmental Planning
MSSM	Master of Science in Sports Medicine	MUP	Master of Urban Planning
MSSP	Master of Science in Social Policy	MUPDD	Master of Urban Planning, Design, and Development
MSSPA	Master of Science in Student Personnel Administration		
		MUPP	Master of Urban Planning and Policy
MSSS	Master of Science in Safety Science	MUPRED	Master of Urban Planning and Real Estate Development
	Master of Science in Systems Science		
MSST	Master of Science in Security Technologies	MURP	Master of Urban and Regional Planning
MSSW	Master of Science in Social Work		Master of Urban and Rural Planning
MSSWE	Master of Science in Software Engineering	MUS	Master of Urban Studies
MST	Master of Science and Technology	MUSA	Master of Urban Spatial Analytics
	Master of Science in Taxation	MVP	Master of Voice Pedagogy
	Master of Science in Teaching	MVPH	Master of Veterinary Public Health
	Master of Science in Technology	MVS	Master of Visual Studies
	Master of Science in Telecommunications	MWC	Master of Wildlife Conservation
	Master of Science Teaching	MWM	Master of Water Management
MSTC	Master of Science in Technical Communication	MWPS	Master of Wood and Paper Science
	Master of Science in Telecommunications	MWR	Master of Water Resources
MSTCM	Master of Science in Traditional Chinese Medicine	MWS	Master of Women's Studies
			Master of Worship Studies
MSTE	Master of Science in Telecommunications Engineering	MWSc	Master of Wildlife Science
		MZS	Master of Zoological Science
	Master of Science in Transportation Engineering	Nav Arch	Naval Architecture
		Naval E	Naval Engineer
MSTL	Master of Science in Teacher Leadership	ND	Doctor of Naturopathic Medicine
MSTM	Master of Science in Technology Management	NE	Nuclear Engineer
	Master of Science in Transfusion Medicine	Nuc E	Nuclear Engineer
MSTOM	Master of Science in Traditional Oriental Medicine	OD	Doctor of Optometry
		OTD	Doctor of Occupational Therapy
MSUASE	Master of Science in Unmanned and Autonomous Systems Engineering	PBME	Professional Master of Biomedical Engineering
		PC	Performer's Certificate
MSUD	Master of Science in Urban Design	PD	Professional Diploma
MSUS	Master of Science in Urban Studies	PGC	Post-Graduate Certificate
MSW	Master of Social Work	PGD	Postgraduate Diploma
MSWE	Master of Software Engineering	Ph L	Licentiate of Philosophy
MSWREE	Master of Science in Water Resources and Environmental Engineering	Pharm D	Doctor of Pharmacy
		PhD	Doctor of Philosophy
MT	Master of Taxation	PhD Otol	Doctor of Philosophy in Otolaryngology
	Master of Teaching	PhD Surg	Doctor of Philosophy in Surgery
	Master of Technology	PhDEE	Doctor of Philosophy in Electrical Engineering
	Master of Textiles	PMBA	Professional Master of Business Administration
MTA	Master of Tax Accounting	PMC	Post Master Certificate
	Master of Teaching Arts	PMD	Post-Master's Diploma
	Master of Tourism Administration	PMS	Professional Master of Science
MTCM	Master of Traditional Chinese Medicine		Professional Master's
MTD	Master of Training and Development	Post-Doctoral MS	Post-Doctoral Master of Science
MTE	Master in Educational Technology	Post-MSN Certificate	Post-Master of Science in Nursing Certificate
MTESOL	Master in Teaching English to Speakers of Other Languages	PPDPT	Postprofessional Doctor of Physical Therapy

Pro-MS	Professional Science Master's	SMACT	Master of Science in Art, Culture and Technology
Professional MA	Professional Master of Arts	SMBT	Master of Science in Building Technology
Professional MBA	Professional Master of Business Administration	SP	Specialist Degree
Professional MS	Professional Master of Science	Sp Ed	Specialist in Education
PSM	Professional Master of Science	Sp LIS	Specialist in Library and Information Science
	Professional Science Master's	SPA	Specialist in Arts
Psy D	Doctor of Psychology	Spec	Specialist's Certificate
Psy M	Master of Psychology	Spec M	Specialist in Music
Psy S	Specialist in Psychology	Spt	Specialist Degree
Psya D	Doctor of Psychoanalysis	SSP	Specialist in School Psychology
S Psy S	Specialist in Psychological Services	STB	Bachelor of Sacred Theology
Sc D	Doctor of Science	STD	Doctor of Sacred Theology
Sc M	Master of Science	STL	Licentiate of Sacred Theology
SCCT	Specialist in Community College Teaching	STM	Master of Sacred Theology
ScDPT	Doctor of Physical Therapy Science	TDPT	Transitional Doctor of Physical Therapy
SD	Doctor of Science	Th D	Doctor of Theology
	Specialist Degree	Th M	Master of Theology
SJD	Doctor of Juridical Sciences	TOTD	Transitional Doctor of Occupational Therapy
SLPD	Doctor of Speech-Language Pathology	VMD	Doctor of Veterinary Medicine
SM	Master of Science	WEMBA	Weekend Executive Master of Business Administration
SM Arch S	Master of Science in Architectural Studies	XMA	Executive Master of Arts

INDEXES

Displays and Close-Ups

Directories and Subject Areas in This Book

Directories and Subject Areas

Following is an alphabetical listing of directories and subject areas. Also listed are cross-references for subject area names not used in the directory structure of the guides, for example, "City and Regional Planning (*see* Urban and Regional Planning)."

Graduate Programs in the Humanities, Arts & Social Sciences

Addictions/Substance Abuse Counseling
Administration (*see* Arts Administration; Public Administration)
African-American Studies
African Languages and Literatures (*see* African Studies)
African Studies
Agribusiness (*see* Agricultural Economics and Agribusiness)
Agricultural Economics and Agribusiness
Alcohol Abuse Counseling (*see* Addictions/Substance Abuse Counseling)
American Indian/Native American Studies
American Studies
Anthropology
Applied Arts and Design—General
Applied Behavior Analysis
Applied Economics
Applied History (*see* Public History)
Applied Psychology
Applied Social Research
Arabic (*see* Near and Middle Eastern Languages)
Arab Studies (*see* Near and Middle Eastern Studies)
Archaeology
Architectural History
Architecture
Archives Administration (*see* Public History)
Area and Cultural Studies (*see* African-American Studies; African Studies; American Indian/Native American Studies; American Studies; Asian-American Studies; Asian Studies; Canadian Studies; Cultural Studies; East European and Russian Studies; Ethnic Studies; Folklore; Gender Studies; Hispanic Studies; Holocaust Studies; Jewish Studies; Latin American Studies; Near and Middle Eastern Studies; Northern Studies; Pacific Area/Pacific Rim Studies; Western European Studies; Women's Studies)
Art/Fine Arts
Art History
Arts Administration
Arts Journalism
Art Therapy
Asian-American Studies
Asian Languages
Asian Studies
Behavioral Sciences (*see* Psychology)
Bible Studies (*see* Religion; Theology)
Biological Anthropology
Black Studies (*see* African-American Studies)
Broadcasting (*see* Communication; Film, Television, and Video Production)
Broadcast Journalism
Building Science
Canadian Studies
Celtic Languages
Ceramics (*see* Art/Fine Arts)
Child and Family Studies
Child Development
Chinese
Chinese Studies (*see* Asian Languages; Asian Studies)
Christian Studies (*see* Missions and Missiology; Religion; Theology)
Cinema (*see* Film, Television, and Video Production)
City and Regional Planning (*see* Urban and Regional Planning)
Classical Languages and Literatures (*see* Classics)
Classics

Clinical Psychology
Clothing and Textiles
Cognitive Psychology (*see* Psychology—General; Cognitive Sciences)
Cognitive Sciences
Communication—General
Community Affairs (*see* Urban and Regional Planning; Urban Studies)
Community Planning (*see* Architecture; Environmental Design; Urban and Regional Planning; Urban Design; Urban Studies)
Community Psychology (*see* Social Psychology)
Comparative and Interdisciplinary Arts
Comparative Literature
Composition (*see* Music)
Computer Art and Design
Conflict Resolution and Mediation/Peace Studies
Consumer Economics
Corporate and Organizational Communication
Corrections (*see* Criminal Justice and Criminology)
Counseling (*see* Counseling Psychology; Pastoral Ministry and Counseling)
Counseling Psychology
Crafts (*see* Art/Fine Arts)
Creative Arts Therapies (*see* Art Therapy; Therapies—Dance, Drama, and Music)
Criminal Justice and Criminology
Cultural Anthropology
Cultural Studies
Dance
Decorative Arts
Demography and Population Studies
Design (*see* Applied Arts and Design; Architecture; Art/Fine Arts; Environmental Design; Graphic Design; Industrial Design; Interior Design; Textile Design; Urban Design)
Developmental Psychology
Diplomacy (*see* International Affairs)
Disability Studies
Drama Therapy (*see* Therapies—Dance, Drama, and Music)
Dramatic Arts (*see* Theater)
Drawing (*see* Art/Fine Arts)
Drug Abuse Counseling (*see* Addictions/Substance Abuse Counseling)
Drug and Alcohol Abuse Counseling (*see* Addictions/Substance Abuse Counseling)
East Asian Studies (*see* Asian Studies)
East European and Russian Studies
Economic Development
Economics
Educational Theater (*see* Theater; Therapies—Dance, Drama, and Music)
Emergency Management
English
Environmental Design
Ethics
Ethnic Studies
Ethnomusicology (*see* Music)
Experimental Psychology
Family and Consumer Sciences—General
Family Studies (*see* Child and Family Studies)
Family Therapy (*see* Child and Family Studies; Clinical Psychology; Counseling Psychology; Marriage and Family Therapy)
Filmmaking (*see* Film, Television, and Video Production)
Film Studies (*see* Film, Television, and Video Production)
Film, Television, and Video Production
Film, Television, and Video Theory and Criticism
Fine Arts (*see* Art/Fine Arts)
Folklore
Foreign Languages (*see* specific language)
Foreign Service (*see* International Affairs; International Development)
Forensic Psychology
Forensic Sciences
Forensics (*see* Speech and Interpersonal Communication)
French
Gender Studies
General Studies (*see* Liberal Studies)

Genetic Counseling
Geographic Information Systems
Geography
German
Gerontology
Graphic Design
Greek (*see* Classics)
Health Communication
Health Psychology
Hebrew (*see* Near and Middle Eastern Languages)
Hebrew Studies (*see* Jewish Studies)
Hispanic and Latin American Languages
Hispanic Studies
Historic Preservation
History
History of Art (*see* Art History)
History of Medicine
History of Science and Technology
Holocaust and Genocide Studies
Home Economics (*see* Family and Consumer Sciences—General)
Homeland Security
Household Economics, Sciences, and Management (*see* Family and Consumer Sciences—General)
Human Development
Humanities
Illustration
Industrial and Labor Relations
Industrial and Organizational Psychology
Industrial Design
Interdisciplinary Studies
Interior Design
International Affairs
International Development
International Economics
International Service (*see* International Affairs; International Development)
International Trade Policy
Internet and Interactive Multimedia
Interpersonal Communication (*see* Speech and Interpersonal Communication)
Interpretation (*see* Translation and Interpretation)
Islamic Studies (*see* Near and Middle Eastern Studies; Religion)
Italian
Japanese
Japanese Studies (*see* Asian Languages; Asian Studies; Japanese)
Jewelry (*see* Art/Fine Arts)
Jewish Studies
Journalism
Judaic Studies (*see* Jewish Studies; Religion)
Labor Relations (*see* Industrial and Labor Relations)
Landscape Architecture
Latin American Studies
Latin (*see* Classics)
Law Enforcement (*see* Criminal Justice and Criminology)
Liberal Studies
Lighting Design
Linguistics
Literature (*see* Classics; Comparative Literature; specific language)
Marriage and Family Therapy
Mass Communication
Media Studies
Medical Illustration
Medieval and Renaissance Studies
Metalsmithing (*see* Art/Fine Arts)
Middle Eastern Studies (*see* Near and Middle Eastern Studies)
Military and Defense Studies
Mineral Economics
Ministry (*see* Pastoral Ministry and Counseling; Theology)
Missions and Missiology
Motion Pictures (*see* Film, Television, and Video Production)
Museum Studies
Music
Musicology (*see* Music)
Music Therapy (*see* Therapies—Dance, Drama, and Music)
National Security

Native American Studies (*see* American Indian/Native American Studies)
Near and Middle Eastern Languages
Near and Middle Eastern Studies
Near Environment (*see* Family and Consumer Sciences)
Northern Studies
Organizational Psychology (*see* Industrial and Organizational Psychology)
Oriental Languages (*see* Asian Languages)
Oriental Studies (*see* Asian Studies)
Pacific Area/Pacific Rim Studies
Painting (*see* Art/Fine Arts)
Pastoral Ministry and Counseling
Philanthropic Studies
Philosophy
Photography
Playwriting (*see* Theater; Writing)
Policy Studies (*see* Public Policy)
Political Science
Population Studies (*see* Demography and Population Studies)
Portuguese
Printmaking (*see* Art/Fine Arts)
Product Design (*see* Industrial Design)
Psychoanalysis and Psychotherapy
Psychology—General
Public Administration
Public Affairs
Public History
Public Policy
Public Speaking (*see* Mass Communication; Rhetoric; Speech and Interpersonal Communication)
Publishing
Regional Planning (*see* Architecture; Urban and Regional Planning; Urban Design; Urban Studies)
Rehabilitation Counseling
Religion
Renaissance Studies (*see* Medieval and Renaissance Studies)
Rhetoric
Romance Languages
Romance Literatures (*see* Romance Languages)
Rural Planning and Studies
Rural Sociology
Russian
Scandinavian Languages
School Psychology
Sculpture (*see* Art/Fine Arts)
Security Administration (*see* Criminal Justice and Criminology)
Slavic Languages
Slavic Studies (*see* East European and Russian Studies; Slavic Languages)
Social Psychology
Social Sciences
Sociology
Southeast Asian Studies (*see* Asian Studies)
Soviet Studies (*see* East European and Russian Studies; Russian)
Spanish
Speech and Interpersonal Communication
Sport Psychology
Studio Art (*see* Art/Fine Arts)
Substance Abuse Counseling (*see* Addictions/Substance Abuse Counseling)
Survey Methodology
Sustainable Development
Technical Communication
Technical Writing
Telecommunications (*see* Film, Television, and Video Production)
Television (*see* Film, Television, and Video Production)
Textile Design
Textiles (*see* Clothing and Textiles; Textile Design)
Thanatology
Theater
Theater Arts (*see* Theater)
Theology
Therapies—Dance, Drama, and Music
Translation and Interpretation
Transpersonal and Humanistic Psychology

Urban and Regional Planning
Urban Design
Urban Planning (*see* Architecture; Urban and Regional Planning;
    Urban Design; Urban Studies)
Urban Studies
Video (*see* Film, Television, and Video Production)
Visual Arts (*see* Applied Arts and Design; Art/Fine Arts; Film,
    Television, and Video Production; Graphic Design; Illustration;
    Photography)
Western European Studies
Women's Studies
World Wide Web (*see* Internet and Interactive Multimedia)
Writing

Graduate Programs in the Biological/Biomedical Sciences & Health-Related Medical Professions

Acupuncture and Oriental Medicine
Acute Care/Critical Care Nursing Administration (*see* Health Services
    Management and Hospital Administration; Nursing and Healthcare
    Administration; Pharmaceutical Administration)
Adult Nursing
Advanced Practice Nursing (*see* Family Nurse Practitioner Studies)
Allied Health—General
Allied Health Professions (*see* Clinical Laboratory Sciences/Medical
    Technology; Clinical Research; Communication Disorders; Dental
    Hygiene; Emergency Medical Services; Occupational Therapy;
    Physical Therapy; Physician Assistant Studies; Rehabilitation
    Sciences)
Allopathic Medicine
Anatomy
Anesthesiologist Assistant Studies
Animal Behavior
Bacteriology
Behavioral Sciences (*see* Biopsychology; Neuroscience; Zoology)
Biochemistry
Bioethics
Biological and Biomedical Sciences—General Biological Chemistry
    (*see* Biochemistry)
Biological Oceanography (*see* Marine Biology)
Biophysics
Biopsychology
Botany
Breeding (*see* Botany; Plant Biology; Genetics)
Cancer Biology/Oncology
Cardiovascular Sciences
Cell Biology
Cellular Physiology (*see* Cell Biology; Physiology)
Child-Care Nursing (*see* Maternal and Child/Neonatal Nursing)
Chiropractic
Clinical Laboratory Sciences/Medical Technology
Clinical Research
Community Health
Community Health Nursing
Computational Biology
Conservation (*see* Conservation Biology; Environmental Biology)
Conservation Biology
Crop Sciences (*see* Botany; Plant Biology)
Cytology (*see* Cell Biology)
Dental and Oral Surgery (*see* Oral and Dental Sciences)
Dental Assistant Studies (*see* Dental Hygiene)
Dental Hygiene
Dental Services (*see* Dental Hygiene)
Dentistry
Developmental Biology Dietetics (*see* Nutrition)
Ecology
Embryology (*see* Developmental Biology)
Emergency Medical Services
Endocrinology (*see* Physiology)
Entomology

Environmental Biology
Environmental and Occupational Health
Epidemiology
Evolutionary Biology
Family Nurse Practitioner Studies
Foods (*see* Nutrition)
Forensic Nursing
Genetics
Genomic Sciences
Gerontological Nursing
Health Physics/Radiological Health
Health Promotion
Health-Related Professions (*see* individual allied health professions)
Health Services Management and Hospital Administration
Health Services Research
Histology (*see* Anatomy; Cell Biology)
HIV/AIDS Nursing
Hospice Nursing
Hospital Administration (*see* Health Services Management and
    Hospital Administration)
Human Genetics
Immunology
Industrial Hygiene
Infectious Diseases
International Health
Laboratory Medicine (*see* Clinical Laboratory Sciences/Medical
    Technology; Immunology; Microbiology; Pathology)
Life Sciences (*see* Biological and Biomedical Sciences)
Marine Biology
Maternal and Child Health
Maternal and Child/Neonatal Nursing
Medical Imaging
Medical Microbiology
Medical Nursing (*see* Medical/Surgical Nursing)
Medical Physics
Medical/Surgical Nursing
Medical Technology (*see* Clinical Laboratory Sciences/Medical
    Technology)
Medical Sciences (*see* Biological and Biomedical Sciences)
Medical Science Training Programs (*see* Biological and Biomedical
    Sciences)
Medicinal and Pharmaceutical Chemistry
Medicinal Chemistry (*see* Medicinal and Pharmaceutical Chemistry)
Medicine (*see* Allopathic Medicine; Naturopathic Medicine;
    Osteopathic Medicine; Podiatric Medicine)
Microbiology
Midwifery (*see* Nurse Midwifery)
Molecular Biology
Molecular Biophysics
Molecular Genetics
Molecular Medicine
Molecular Pathogenesis
Molecular Pathology
Molecular Pharmacology
Molecular Physiology
Molecular Toxicology
Naturopathic Medicine
Neural Sciences (*see* Biopsychology; Neurobiology; Neuroscience)
Neurobiology
Neuroendocrinology (*see* Biopsychology; Neurobiology; Neuroscience;
    Physiology)
Neuropharmacology (*see* Biopsychology; Neurobiology; Neuroscience;
    Pharmacology)
Neurophysiology (*see* Biopsychology; Neurobiology; Neuroscience;
    Physiology)
Neuroscience
Nuclear Medical Technology (*see* Clinical Laboratory Sciences/
    Medical Technology)
Nurse Anesthesia
Nurse Midwifery
Nurse Practitioner Studies (*see* Family Nurse Practitioner Studies)
Nursing Administration (*see* Nursing and Healthcare Administration)
Nursing and Healthcare Administration
Nursing Education
Nursing—General

Nursing Informatics
Nutrition
Occupational Health (*see* Environmental and Occupational Health; Occupational Health Nursing)
Occupational Health Nursing
Occupational Therapy
Oncology (*see* Cancer Biology/Oncology)
Oncology Nursing
Optometry
Oral and Dental Sciences
Oral Biology (*see* Oral and Dental Sciences)
Oral Pathology (*see* Oral and Dental Sciences)
Organismal Biology (*see* Biological and Biomedical Sciences; Zoology)
Oriental Medicine and Acupuncture (*see* Acupuncture and Oriental Medicine)
Orthodontics (*see* Oral and Dental Sciences)
Osteopathic Medicine
Parasitology
Pathobiology
Pathology
Pediatric Nursing
Pedontics (*see* Oral and Dental Sciences)
Perfusion
Pharmaceutical Administration
Pharmaceutical Chemistry (*see* Medicinal and Pharmaceutical Chemistry)
Pharmaceutical Sciences
Pharmacology
Pharmacy
Photobiology of Cells and Organelles (*see* Botany; Cell Biology; Plant Biology)
Physical Therapy
Physician Assistant Studies
Physiological Optics (*see* Vision Sciences)
Podiatric Medicine
Preventive Medicine (*see* Community Health and Public Health)
Physiological Optics (*see* Physiology)
Physiology
Plant Biology
Plant Molecular Biology
Plant Pathology
Plant Physiology
Pomology (*see* Botany; Plant Biology)
Psychiatric Nursing
Public Health—General
Public Health Nursing (*see* Community Health Nursing)
Psychiatric Nursing
Psychobiology (*see* Biopsychology)
Psychopharmacology (*see* Biopsychology; Neuroscience; Pharmacology)
Radiation Biology
Radiological Health (*see* Health Physics/Radiological Health)
Rehabilitation Nursing
Rehabilitation Sciences
Rehabilitation Therapy (*see* Physical Therapy)
Reproductive Biology
School Nursing
Sociobiology (*see* Evolutionary Biology)
Structural Biology
Surgical Nursing (*see* Medical/Surgical Nursing)
Systems Biology
Teratology
Therapeutics
Theoretical Biology (*see* Biological and Biomedical Sciences)
Therapeutics (*see* Pharmaceutical Sciences; Pharmacology; Pharmacy)
Toxicology
Transcultural Nursing
Translational Biology
Tropical Medicine (*see* Parasitology)
Veterinary Medicine
Veterinary Sciences
Virology
Vision Sciences
Wildlife Biology (*see* Zoology)
Women's Health Nursing
Zoology

Graduate Programs in the Physical Sciences, Mathematics, Agricultural Sciences, the Environment & Natural Resources

Acoustics
Agricultural Sciences
Agronomy and Soil Sciences
Analytical Chemistry
Animal Sciences
Applied Mathematics
Applied Physics
Applied Statistics
Aquaculture
Astronomy
Astrophysical Sciences (*see* Astrophysics; Atmospheric Sciences; Meteorology; Planetary and Space Sciences)
Astrophysics
Atmospheric Sciences
Biological Oceanography (*see* Marine Affairs; Marine Sciences; Oceanography)
Biomathematics
Biometry
Biostatistics
Chemical Physics
Chemistry
Computational Sciences
Condensed Matter Physics
Dairy Science (*see* Animal Sciences)
Earth Sciences (*see* Geosciences)
Environmental Management and Policy
Environmental Sciences
Environmental Studies (*see* Environmental Management and Policy)
Experimental Statistics (*see* Statistics)
Fish, Game, and Wildlife Management
Food Science and Technology
Forestry
General Science (*see* specific topics)
Geochemistry
Geodetic Sciences
Geological Engineering (*see* Geology)
Geological Sciences (*see* Geology)
Geology
Geophysical Fluid Dynamics (*see* Geophysics)
Geophysics
Geosciences
Horticulture
Hydrogeology
Hydrology
Inorganic Chemistry
Limnology
Marine Affairs
Marine Geology
Marine Sciences
Marine Studies (*see* Marine Affairs; Marine Geology; Marine Sciences; Oceanography)
Mathematical and Computational Finance
Mathematical Physics
Mathematical Statistics (*see* Applied Statistics; Statistics)
Mathematics
Meteorology
Mineralogy
Natural Resource Management (*see* Environmental Management and Policy; Natural Resources)
Natural Resources
Nuclear Physics (*see* Physics)
Ocean Engineering (*see* Marine Affairs; Marine Geology; Marine Sciences; Oceanography)
Oceanography
Optical Sciences
Optical Technologies (*see* Optical Sciences)
Optics (*see* Applied Physics; Optical Sciences; Physics)
Organic Chemistry

Paleontology
Paper Chemistry (*see* Chemistry)
Photonics
Physical Chemistry
Physics
Planetary and Space Sciences
Plant Sciences
Plasma Physics
Poultry Science (*see* Animal Sciences)
Radiological Physics (*see* Physics)
Range Management (*see* Range Science)
Range Science
Resource Management (*see* Environmental Management and Policy; Natural Resources)
Solid-Earth Sciences (*see* Geosciences)
Space Sciences (*see* Planetary and Space Sciences)
Statistics
Theoretical Chemistry
Theoretical Physics
Viticulture and Enology
Water Resources

Graduate Programs in Engineering & Applied Sciences

Aeronautical Engineering (*see* Aerospace/Aeronautical Engineering)
Aerospace/Aeronautical Engineering
Aerospace Studies (*see* Aerospace/Aeronautical Engineering)
Agricultural Engineering
Applied Mechanics (*see* Mechanics)
Applied Science and Technology
Architectural Engineering
Artificial Intelligence/Robotics
Astronautical Engineering (*see* Aerospace/Aeronautical Engineering)
Automotive Engineering
Aviation
Biochemical Engineering
Bioengineering
Bioinformatics
Biological Engineering (*see* Bioengineering)
Biomedical Engineering
Biosystems Engineering
Biotechnology
Ceramic Engineering (*see* Ceramic Sciences and Engineering)
Ceramic Sciences and Engineering
Ceramics (*see* Ceramic Sciences and Engineering)
Chemical Engineering
Civil Engineering
Computer and Information Systems Security
Computer Engineering
Computer Science
Computing Technology (*see* Computer Science)
Construction Engineering
Construction Management
Database Systems
Electrical Engineering
Electronic Materials
Electronics Engineering (*see* Electrical Engineering)
Energy and Power Engineering
Energy Management and Policy
Engineering and Applied Sciences
Engineering and Public Affairs (*see* Technology and Public Policy)
Engineering and Public Policy (*see* Energy Management and Policy; Technology and Public Policy)
Engineering Design
Engineering Management
Engineering Mechanics (*see* Mechanics)
Engineering Metallurgy (*see* Metallurgical Engineering and Metallurgy)
Engineering Physics
Environmental Design (*see* Environmental Engineering)
Environmental Engineering
Ergonomics and Human Factors

Financial Engineering
Fire Protection Engineering
Food Engineering (*see* Agricultural Engineering)
Game Design and Development
Gas Engineering (*see* Petroleum Engineering)
Geological Engineering
Geophysics Engineering (*see* Geological Engineering)
Geotechnical Engineering
Hazardous Materials Management
Health Informatics
Health Systems (*see* Safety Engineering; Systems Engineering)
Highway Engineering (*see* Transportation and Highway Engineering)
Human-Computer Interaction
Human Factors (*see* Ergonomics and Human Factors)
Hydraulics
Hydrology (*see* Water Resources Engineering)
Industrial Engineering (*see* Industrial/Management Engineering)
Industrial/Management Engineering
Information Science
Internet Engineering
Macromolecular Science (*see* Polymer Science and Engineering)
Management Engineering (*see* Engineering Management; Industrial/Management Engineering)
Management of Technology
Manufacturing Engineering
Marine Engineering (*see* Civil Engineering)
Materials Engineering
Materials Sciences
Mechanical Engineering
Mechanics
Medical Informatics
Metallurgical Engineering and Metallurgy
Metallurgy (*see* Metallurgical Engineering and Metallurgy)
Mineral/Mining Engineering
Modeling and Simulation
Nanotechnology
Nuclear Engineering
Ocean Engineering
Operations Research
Paper and Pulp Engineering
Petroleum Engineering
Pharmaceutical Engineering
Plastics Engineering (*see* Polymer Science and Engineering)
Polymer Science and Engineering
Public Policy (*see* Energy Management and Policy; Technology and Public Policy)
Reliability Engineering
Robotics (*see* Artificial Intelligence/Robotics)
Safety Engineering
Software Engineering
Solid-State Sciences (*see* Materials Sciences)
Structural Engineering
Surveying Science and Engineering
Systems Analysis (*see* Systems Engineering)
Systems Engineering
Systems Science
Technology and Public Policy
Telecommunications
Telecommunications Management
Textile Sciences and Engineering
Textiles (*see* Textile Sciences and Engineering)
Transportation and Highway Engineering
Urban Systems Engineering (*see* Systems Engineering)
Waste Management (*see* Hazardous Materials Management)
Water Resources Engineering

Graduate Programs in Business, Education, Information Studies, Law & Social Work

Accounting

Actuarial Science
Adult Education
Advertising and Public Relations
Agricultural Education
Alcohol Abuse Counseling (*see* Counselor Education)
Archival Management and Studies
Art Education
Athletics Administration (*see* Kinesiology and Movement Studies)
Athletic Training and Sports Medicine
Audiology (*see* Communication Disorders)
Aviation Management
Banking (*see* Finance and Banking)
Business Administration and Management—General
Business Education
Communication Disorders
Community College Education
Computer Education
Continuing Education (*see* Adult Education)
Counseling (*see* Counselor Education)
Counselor Education
Curriculum and Instruction
Developmental Education
Distance Education Development
Drug Abuse Counseling (*see* Counselor Education)
Early Childhood Education
Educational Leadership and Administration
Educational Measurement and Evaluation
Educational Media/Instructional Technology
Educational Policy
Educational Psychology
Education—General
Education of the Blind (*see* Special Education)
Education of the Deaf (*see* Special Education)
Education of the Gifted
Education of the Hearing Impaired (*see* Special Education)
Education of the Learning Disabled (*see* Special Education)
Education of the Mentally Retarded (*see* Special Education)
Education of the Physically Handicapped (*see* Special Education)
Education of Students with Severe/Multiple Disabilities
Education of the Visually Handicapped (*see* Special Education)
Electronic Commerce
Elementary Education
English as a Second Language
English Education
Entertainment Management
Entrepreneurship
Environmental Education
Environmental Law
Exercise and Sports Science
Exercise Physiology (*see* Kinesiology and Movement Studies)
Facilities and Entertainment Management
Finance and Banking
Food Services Management (*see* Hospitality Management)
Foreign Languages Education
Foundations and Philosophy of Education
Guidance and Counseling (*see* Counselor Education)
Health Education
Health Law
Hearing Sciences (*see* Communication Disorders)
Higher Education
Home Economics Education
Hospitality Management
Hotel Management (*see* Travel and Tourism)
Human Resources Development
Human Resources Management
Human Services
Industrial Administration (*see* Industrial and Manufacturing Management)
Industrial and Manufacturing Management
Industrial Education (*see* Vocational and Technical Education)
Information Studies
Instructional Technology (*see* Educational Media/Instructional Technology)
Insurance
Intellectual Property Law
International and Comparative Education

International Business
International Commerce (*see* International Business)
International Economics (*see* International Business)
International Trade (*see* International Business)
Investment and Securities (*see* Business Administration and Management; Finance and Banking; Investment Management)
Investment Management
Junior College Education (*see* Community College Education)
Kinesiology and Movement Studies
Law
Legal and Justice Studies
Leisure Services (*see* Recreation and Park Management)
Leisure Studies
Library Science
Logistics
Management (*see* Business Administration and Management)
Management Information Systems
Management Strategy and Policy
Marketing
Marketing Research
Mathematics Education
Middle School Education
Movement Studies (*see* Kinesiology and Movement Studies)
Multilingual and Multicultural Education
Museum Education
Music Education
Nonprofit Management
Nursery School Education (*see* Early Childhood Education)
Occupational Education (*see* Vocational and Technical Education)
Organizational Behavior
Organizational Management
Parks Administration (*see* Recreation and Park Management)
Personnel (*see* Human Resources Development; Human Resources Management; Organizational Behavior; Organizational Management; Student Affairs)
Philosophy of Education (*see* Foundations and Philosophy of Education)
Physical Education
Project Management
Public Relations (*see* Advertising and Public Relations)
Quality Management
Quantitative Analysis
Reading Education
Real Estate
Recreation and Park Management
Recreation Therapy (*see* Recreation and Park Management)
Religious Education
Remedial Education (*see* Special Education)
Restaurant Administration (*see* Hospitality Management)
Science Education
Secondary Education
Social Sciences Education
Social Studies Education (*see* Social Sciences Education)
Social Work
Special Education
Speech-Language Pathology and Audiology (*see* Communication Disorders)
Sports Management
Sports Medicine (*see* Athletic Training and Sports Medicine)
Sports Psychology and Sociology (*see* Kinesiology and Movement Studies)
Student Affairs
Substance Abuse Counseling (*see* Counselor Education)
Supply Chain Management
Sustainability Management
Systems Management (*see* Management Information Systems)
Taxation
Teacher Education (*see* specific subject areas)
Teaching English as a Second Language (*see* English as a Second Language)
Technical Education (*see* Vocational and Technical Education)
Transportation Management
Travel and Tourism
Urban Education
Vocational and Technical Education
Vocational Counseling (*see* Counselor Education)